If anybody asks you which vermouth you'd like in your dry martini, you could be at the wrong party.

You do want a dry martini and not just plain gin-and-vermouth, don't you?

So all you have to do is remember that the secret of a dry martini is Martini Dry.

If you don't get the right one, you're in the wrong place.

The right one for the dry martini

MARTINI

Photograph by Richard Slade, Camera Press, London

DEBRETT'S

Peerage and Baronetage

WITH HER MAJESTY'S ROYAL WARRANT HOLDERS
1976

Founded in 1769
Renamed Debrett in 1802

COMPRISES INFORMATION CONCERNING
THE ROYAL FAMILY, THE PEERAGE, PRIVY COUNSELLORS,
SCOTTISH LORDS OF SESSION, BARONETS,
AND CHIEFS OF NAMES AND CLANS
IN SCOTLAND

Edited by Patrick Montague-Smith

ARCO PUBLISHING COMPANY, INC.
NEW YORK

Published 1977 by Arco Publishing Company, Inc.
219 Park Avenue South, New York, N.Y. 10003

Library of Congress Catalog Card Number 42–17925

ISBN 0–668–04314–8

Printed in Great Britain

CONTENTS.

ABBREVIATIONS.

A.A., Anti Aircraft, Architectural Association, and Automobile Association.
A.A.A., Amateur Athletic Association.
A.A. & Q.M.G., Assistant Adjutant and Quarter-master-General.
A.A.C.C.A., Associate of Association of Certified Corporate Accountants.
A.A.G., Assistant Adjutant-General.
A.A.I., Associate of Chartered Auctioneers' and Estate Agents' Institute.
A.A.I.M., Associate of Australian Institute of Management.
A.A.M.C. Australian Army Medical Corps.
A.A.S.A., Associate of Australian Society of Accountants.
A. & S. H., Argyll and Sutherland Highlanders.
A/asia., Australasia.
A.B.C M., Associate British College of Music.
A.C., Companion of Order of Australia.
A.C.A., Associate of Institute of Chartered Accountants.
A.C.A.A., Associate of Australian Institute of Cost Accountants.
Acad., Academy.
A.C.C.A., Associate of the Association of Certified Accountants.
A.C.C.S., Associate of Corporation of Secretaries.
A.C.G.I., Associate of City and Guilds of London Institute.
A.C.I.B., Associate of the Corporation of Insurance Brokers.
A.C.I.I., Associate of Chartered Insurance Institution.
A.C.I.S., Associate of Chartered Institute of Secretaries and Administrators.
A.C M.A., Associate of Institute of Cost and Management Accountants.
A.C.T., Australian Capital Territory.
A.C.W.A., Associate of Institute of Cost and Works Accountants.
A.D.C., Aide-de-Camp.
A.D.E.M.E., Assistant Director of Electrical and Mechanical Engineering.
Adj., Adjutant.
Adjt., Adjutant.
Adm., Admiral.
A.D.M.E., Assistant Director of Mechanical Engineering.
Admin., Administrative, Administration.
A.D.M.S., Assistant Director of Medical Services.
A.D.O.S., Assistant Director of Ordnance Services.
A.E., Air Efficiency Award.
A.E.G.I.S., Aid for the Elderly in Government Institutions.
A.E.R., Army Emergency Reserve.
A.E.U., Amalgamated Engineering Union.
A.F.A.I.M., Associate Fellow of Australian Institute of Management.
A.F.C., Air Force Cross.
A.F.G.I., Associate Fellow of Grocers' Institute.
A.F.M., Air Force Medal.
A.F.R.Ae.S., Associate Fellow of Royal Aeronautical Society.
A.-G., Adjutant-General.
A.G.I., Associate Member of Grocers' Institute.
A.I.A.A., Associate Architect Member of Incorporated Association of Architects and Surveyors.
A.I.B., Associate of Institute of Bankers.
A.I.C.E., Associate of Institution of Civil Engineers.
A.I.C.S., Associate of Institute of Chartered Shipbrokers.
A.I.F., Australian Imperial Forces.
A.I.M.M., Associate of Institute of Mining and Metallurgy.
A.Inst.P., Associate of Institute of Physics.
A.I.O.B., Associate of Institute of Building.
A.I.W.S.P., Associate of Institute of Work Study Practitioners.
A.K.C., Associate of King's College, London.
A.L.A.S., Associate of Land Agents Society.
A.M., Albert Medal (now G.M.).
AM, A Member of Order of Australia.
A.M.A., Australian Medical Association.
A.M.B.I.M., Associate Member of the British Institute of Management.
A.M.C.T., Associate of Manchester College of Science and Technology.

A.Met., Associate of Metallurgy (Sheffield University).
A.M.F., Australian Military Forces.
A.M.I.C.E., Associate Member of Institution of Civil Engineers.
A.M.I.E.A., Associate Member of Institute of Engineers, Australia.
A.M.I.E.E., Associate Member of Institution of Electrical Engineers.
A.M I. Ex., Associate Member of Institute of Export.
A.M.I. Gas. E., Associate Member of Institution of Gas Engineers.
A.M.I.Mech.E., Associate Member of Institution of Mechanical Engineers.
A.M.I.Mun.E., Associate Member of Institution of Municipal Engineers.
A.M.Inst.Pet., Associate Member of Institute of Petroleum.
A.M. Inst. W., Associate Member of Institute of Welding.
A.M.I.Nuc.E., Associate Member of Institution of Nuclear Engineers.
A.M.I.P.M., Associate Member of Institute of Personnel Management.
A.M.I.R.S.E., Associate Member of Institution of Railway Signal Engineers.
A.M.I.Struct.E., Associate Member of Institution of Structural Engineers.
A.M.R.I.N.A., Associate Member of Royal Institution of Naval Architects.
A.M.R.T.S., Associate Member Royal Television Society.
A.M.S., Assistant Military Secretary.
A.M.S.E., Associate Member of Society of Engineers.
A.M.T.P.I., Associate of Town Planning Institute.
ante, before
A.N.Z.A.A.S., Australian and New Zealand Association for the Advancement of Science.
A.O. Officer of Order of Australia.
A.O.A., Air Officer in Charge of Administration.
A.O.C., Air Officer Commanding.
A.O.C.-in-C., Air Officer Commander in Chief.
A.P.M., Assistant Provost Marshal.
Apt., Apartment.
A.Q.M.G., Assistant Quartermaster-General.
A.R.A., Associate of Royal Academy.
A.R.Ae.S., Associate of Royal Aeronautical So.
A.R.A.I.A., Associate of Royal Australian Institute of Architects.
A.R.A.M., Associate of Royal Academy of Music.
A.R.C.A., Associate Royal College of Art.
A.R.C.M., Associate of Royal College of Music.
A.R.C.O., Associate of Royal College of Organists.
A.R.C.S., Associate of Royal College of Science.
A.R.C.S.T., Associate of Royal College of Science and Technology (Glasgow).
A.R.C.V.S., Associate of Royal College of Veterinary Surgeons.
A.R.I.B.A., Associate of Royal Institute of British Architects.
A.R.I.C., Associate of Royal Institute of Chemistry.
A.R.I.C.S., Professional Associate of Royal Institution of Chartered Surveyors.
Armd., Armoured.
A.R.R.C., Associate Royal Red Cross.
A.R.S.A., Associate of the Royal Scottish Academy.
A.R.S.M., Associate of Royal School of Mines.
A.R.T.C., Associate of Royal Technical College (Glasgow).
A.R.T.S., Associate of Royal Television Society.
A.S. For., Associate of the Royal Society of Foresters of Great Britain.
A.S.I.A., Associate of Society of Industrial Artists and Designers.
Assist., Assistant.
Asso., Association, Associate.
Assoc.I.C.E., Associate of Institution of Civil Engineers.
Assocn., Association.
A.T.A.F., Allied Tactical Air Force.
A.T.C., Air Training Corps.
A.T.I.I., Associate Member of Institute of Taxation.
A.T.S., Auxiliary Territorial Service.
Aust., Australia.
Austn., Australian.
a.w.s., Graduate of RAF College of Air Warfare.

B., Baron.
b., born.
B.A., Bachelor of Arts.
B.A.C., British Aircraft Corporation.
B.Agr., Bachelor of Agriculture.
B.A.I., Bachelor of Engineering.
B.A.O., Bachelor of Obstetrics.
B.A.O.R., British Army of the Rhine.
Bar., Barrister.
B.Arch., Bachelor of Architecture.
Batn., Battalion.
B.B.C., British Broadcasting Corporation.
B.C., British Columbia.
B.C.E., Bachelor of Civil Engineering.
B.Ch., Bachelor of Surgery.
B.Chir., Bachelor of Surgery.
B.C.L., Bachelor of Civil Law.
B.Com., Bachelor of Commerce.
B.Com.Sc., Bachelor of Commercial Science.
B.D., Bachelor of Divinity.
Bde., Brigade.
B.D.S., Bachelor of Dental Surgery.
B.E., Bachelor of Engineering (Australia).
B.E.A., British European Airways.
B.Ec., Bachelor of Economics (Australia).
B.Econ., Bachelor of Economics.
B.Ed., Bachelor of Education.
B.E.F., British Expeditionary Force.
B.E.M., British Empire Medal.
B.Eng., Bachelor of Engineering.
B.G.S., Brigadier General Staff.
B.L., Bachelor of Law.
B.Litt., Bachelor of Letters.
B.M., Bachelor of Medicine.
B.M.A., British Medical Association.
B.M.E., Bachelor of Mining Engineering.
Bn., Battalion.
B.N.E.C., British National Export Council.
B.O.A.C., British Overseas Airways Corporation.
B. Pharm., Bachelor of Pharmacy.
B.R.C.S., British Red Cross Society.
Brig., Brigadier, Brigade.
B.S., Bachelor of Surgery.
B.Sc., Bachelor of Science.
Bt., Baronet.
Btss., Baronetess.
Bty., Battery.
B.V.Sc., Bachelor of Veterinary Science.
By., Barony.

C., Conservative, *c.*, crowned.
C.A., Member of Institute of Chartered Accountants of Scotland, and County Alderman.
Camb., Cambridge.
Capt., Captain.
Cav., Cavalry.
C.B., Companion of the Bath.
C.B.E., Commander of British Empire.
C.B.I., Confederation of British Industry.
C.C., Companion of Order of Canada and County Councillor.
C.C.R.A., Commander Corps Royal Artillery.
C.D., Canadian Forces Decoration.
C.D.A., College Diploma of Agriculture.
Cdr., Commander.
C.E., Civil Engineer.
C.Eng., Chartered Engineer.
C.E.N.T.O., Central Treaty Organisation.
C.E.O., Chief Education Officer.
C.F.R., Commander of Order of Federal Republic of Nigeria.
c. f. s., Qualified Central Flying School.
C.G.M., Conspicuous Gallantry Medal.
C.G.S., Chief of General Staff.
C.H., Companion of Honour.
Ch., Chief.
Chap., Chaplain.
Chap. St. J., Chaplain of St. John of Jerusalem.
Ch.B., Bachelor of Surgery.
Ch. Ch., Christ Church.
Chm., Chairman.
Ch.M., Master in Surgery.
C.I., Lady of Imperial Order of the Crown of India, and Channel Islands.
C.I.E., Companion of the Indian Empire.
C.I.E.E., Companion of Institution of Electrical Engineers.
C.I. Gas E., Companion of Institution of Gas Engineers.
C.I.G.S., Chief of Imperial General Staff.
C.I.Mar.E., Companion of Institute of Marine Engineers.
C.I.MechE., Companion of Institution of Mechanical Engineers.
C. in C., Commander in Chief.
C.Inst. M.C., Companion Inst. of Measurement and Control.
C.I.O.S., International Committee for Scientific Management.
C.Lit., Companion of Royal Society of Literature.
C.M., Master in Surgery and Member of Order of Canada.

C.M.F., Central Mediterranean Force.
C.M.G., Companion of St. Michael and St. George.
C.M.M., Commander of Order of Military Merit.
C.M.S., Church Missionary Society.
C.N.A.A., Council for National Academic Awards
Co., County, Company.
Col., Colonel.
Coldm. Gds. Coldstream Guards.
Coll., College.
Colls., Collateral Branches.
Com., Commander.
Comd, Commander (Mil.).
Comdg., Commanding.
Comdt., Commandant.
Com.-in-Ch., Commander-in-Chief.
Commn., Commission.
Commr., Commissioner.
Comp. I.E.E., Companion of Institution of Electrical Engineers.
Comp.I.E.R.E., Companion of Institution of Electronic and Radio Engineers.
C.O.N., Commander of Order of the Niger (Nigeria).
Confedn., Confederation.
Cos., Counties, Companies.
C.P.M., Colonial Police Medal for Gallantry and Colonial Police Medal for Meritorious Service.
cr., creation.
C.R.A., Commander Royal Artillery.
C.R.A.C., Commander Royal Armoured Corps.
C.R.A.S.C., Commander Royal Army Service Corps.
C.R.E., Commander Royal Engineers.
C.R.E.M.E., Commander Royal Electrical and Mechanical Engineering.
C.S.C., Conspicuous Service Cross.
C.S.I., Companion of the Star of India.
C.S.I.R.O., Commonwealth Scientific and Industrial Research Organisation.
C.S.O., Chief Signal Officer.
C.St.J., Commander of St. John of Jerusalem.
Cttee., Committee.
C.V., Cross of Valour.
C.V.O., Commander of Royal Victorian Order.

d., died.
D., Duke.
da., dau., daughter.
D.A., Deputy Advocate, and Diploma in Anaesthesia.
D.A. (Dundee), Diploma of Associate, Duncan of Jordanstone College of Art, Dundee.
D.A. (Edin.), Diploma of Associate, Edinburgh College of Art.
D.A.A. & Q.M.G., Deputy Assistant Adjutant and Quartermaster General.
D.A.A.G., Deputy Assistant Adjutant-General.
D.A. & Q.M.G., Deputy Adjutant and Quartermaster-General.
D.A.B.R., Diploma of American Board of Radiology.
D.A.C.G., Deputy Assistant Chaplain-General.
D.A.D.M.S., Deputy Assistant Director of Medical Services.
D.A.D.O.S., Deputy Assistant Director of Ordnance Services.
D.A.D.S.T., Deputy Assistant Director of Supplies and Transport.
D.A.G., Deputy Adjutant-General.
D.A.M.S., Deputy Assistant Military Secretary.
D.A.P.M., Deputy Assistant Provost Marshal.
D.A.Q.M.G., Deputy Assistant Quartermaster-General.
D.Av. Med., Diploma in Aviation Medicine.
D.B.E., Dame Commander of Order of British Empire.
D.C.Ae., Diploma of College of Aeronautics.
D.C.B., Dame Commander of Order of the Bath.
D.C.H., Diploma in Child Health.
D.C.L., Doctor of Civil Law.
D.C.L.I., Duke of Cornwall's Light Infantry.
D.C.M., Distinguished Conduct Medal.
D.C.M.G., Dame Commander of Order of St. Michael and St. George.
D.C.P., Diploma in Clinical Pathology.
D.C.Sc., Doctor of Commercial Science.
D.C.V.O., Dame Commander of Royal Victorian Order.
D.D., Doctor of Divinity.
D.D.E.M.E., Deputy Director of Electrical and Mechanical Engineering.
D.D.M.E., Deputy Director of Mechanical Engineering.
D.D.M.S., Deputy Director of Medical Services.
D.D.O.S., Deputy Director of Ordnance Services.
D.D.S., Doctor of Dental Surgery.
D.D.Sc., Doctor of Dental Science.
D.D.S.T., Deputy Director of Supplies and Transport.
D.E.M.E., Director of Electrical and Mechanical Engineering.

D.Eng., Doctor of Engineering.
Dep., Deputy.
Des.R.C.A., Designer of the Royal College of Art.
D.F.C., Distinguished Flying Cross.
D.F.H., Diploma of Faraday House Engineering College.
D.G.O., Diploma in Gynaecology and Obstetrics.
D.H.L., Doctor of Hebrew Literature.
D.I.C. Diploma of Imperial College of Science.
D.I.H., Diploma in Industrial Health.
Dip.A.D., Diploma in Art and Design.
Dip. Ed., Diploma in Education.
Dipl. INSEAD, Diploma in European Institute of Business Administration (L'Institut Euro-pean d'administration des affaires).
Diplo., Diplomatic.
Dip.T.P., Diploma of Town Planning.
Dir., Director.
Dist., District.
Div., Division.
D.L., Deputy Lieutenant.
D.L.C., Diploma Loughborough College.
D.L.I., Durham Light Infantry.
D.Lit., Doctor of Letters.
D.Litt., Doctor of Letters.
D.L.O., Diploma in Laryngology and Otology.
D.M., Doctor of Medicine.
D.M.E., Director of Mechanical Engineering.
D.Mil.Sc., Doctor of Military Science.
D.M.J., Diploma in Medical Jurisprudence.
D.M.S., Director of Medical Services.
D.Mus., Doctor of Music.
D.Obst.R.C.O.G., Diploma Royal College of Obstetricians and Gynaecologists.
D.O.M.S., Diploma in Ophthalmic Medicine and Surgery.
D.O.S., Director of Ordnance Services.
D.P.A., Diploma in Public Administration.
D.P.H., Diploma in Public Health.
D.Fhil.,Doctor of Philosophy.
D.P.M., Deputy Provost Marshal, Diploma of Psychological Medicine.
D.P.R.M., Diploma in Physical and Rehabilitation Medicine.
D.Q.M.G., Deputy Quartermaster-General.
D.R.A., Director of Royal Artillery.
Dr.Univ., Doctor of University.
D.S.A.O., Diplomatic Service Administration Office
D.S.C.,Distinguished Service Cross.
D.Sc., Doctor of Science.
D.S.I.R., Department of Scientific and Industrial Research.
D.S.M., Distinguished Service Medal.
D.S.O. Companion of Distinguished Service Order.
d.s.p., died without issue.
D.S.T., Director of Supplies and Transport.
D.St.J., Dame of St. John of Jerusalem.
D.T.D., Dekoratie voor Trouwe Dienst (Decora-tion for Devoted Service).
D.Tech., Doctor of Technology.
D.T.M. & H., Diploma in Tropical Medicine and Hygiene.
D.V.S.M., Diploma in Veterinary State Medicine.
D.V.Sc., Doctor of Veterinary Science.

E., Earl.
E.D.,Efficiency Decoration.
ed., educated.
E.D.C., Economic Development Committee.
E.E.C., European Economic Community.
el., eldest.
E.F.T.A., European Free Trade Association.
Eng., Engineering.
E.R.D., Army Emergency Reserve Decoration.
Estab., Establishment.
ext., extinct.
Extraor., Extraordinary.

F.A.A., Fellow of Australian Academy of Science.
F.A.A.H., Fellow of Australian Academy of the Humanities.
F.A.C.C.A., Fellow of Association of Certified and Corporate Accountants.
F.A.C.D, Fellow of American College of Den-tistry.
F.A.C.E., Fellow of Australian College of Educa-tion
F.A.C.M.A., Fellow of Australian College of Medical Administrators.
F.A.C.O G., Fellow American College of Ob-stetricians and Gynaecologists.
F.A.C.P., Fellow of American College of Physi-cians.
F.A.C.S., Fellow of American College of Surgeons
F.A.C.S.T., Fellow of Australian College of Speech Therapists.
F.A.H.A., Fellow of Australian Academy of the Humanities.

F.A.I., Fellow of Chartered Auctioneers and Estate Agents Institute.
F.A.I.A.A., Fellow of American Institute of Aeronautics and Astronautics.
F.A.I.A.S., Fellow of Australian Institute of Agricultural Science.
F.A.I.B., Fellow of Australian Institute of Building.
F.A.I.M., Fellow of Australian Institute of Management.
F.A.N.Y., First Aid Nursing Yeomanry.
F.A.N.Z.C.P., Fellow Australian and New Zealand College of Psychiatrists.
F.A.O., Food and Agricultural Organization.
F.A.P.H.A., Fellow of American Public Health Association.
F.A.P.I., Fellow of Australian Planning Institute
FARELF, Far East Land Forces.
F.A.S.A.,Fellow of Australian Society of Account-ants.
F.B.A., Fellow of British Academy.
F.B.C.S., Fellow of British Computer Society.
F.B.I., Federation of British Industries.
F.B.I.M., Fellow of British Institute of Manage-ment.
F.B.O.A., Fellow of British Optical Association.
F.B.Ps.S., Fellow of British Psychological Society.
F.B.S.,Fellow Building Societies Institute.
F.C.A.,Fellow of Institute of Chartered Account-ants.
F.C.A.A., Fellow of Australasian Institute of Cost Accountants.
F.C.A.N.Z., Fellow of Institute of Chartered Accountants in New Zealand.
F.C.A.S.I., Fellow of Canadian Aeronautics and Space Institute.
F.C.B.A., Fellow of Canadian Bankers Associa-tion.
F.C.C.A., Fellow Association of Certified Account-ants.
F.C.C.P., Fellow of American College of Chest Physicians.
F.C.C.S. Fellow of Corporation of Secretaries.
F.C.G.I., Fellow of City and Guilds of London Institute.
F.C.I.B., Fellow of Corporation of Insurance Brokers.
F.C.I.I., Fellow of Chartered Insurance Institute.
F.C.I.S., Fellow of Chartered Institute of Secre-taries and Administrators.
F.C.I.T., Fellow of Chartered Institute of Trans-port.
F.C.I.V., Fellow of Commonwealth Institute of Valuers (Australia).
F.C.M.A., Fellow of Institute of Cost and Manage-ment Accountants.
F.C.O., Foreign and Commonwealth Office
F.C.O.G., Fellow of College of Gynaecologists.
FCP Fellow of College of Preceptors.
F.C.R.A., Fellow of College of Radiologists of Australia.
F.C.S., Fellow of Chemical Society and Fellow College of Surgeons.
F.D.S., Fellow in Dental Surgery.
F.D.S., R.C.P.S., Fellow in Dental Surgery, Royal College of Physicians and Surgeons (Glasgow).
Fedn., Federation.
F.E.I.S., Fellow of Educational Institute of Scotland.
F.F.A., R.A.C.S., Fellow of Faculty of Anaesthet-ists, Royal Australian College of Surgeons.
F.F.A.,R.C.S., Fellow of Faculty of Anaesthetists, Royal College of Surgeons.
F.F.A., R.C.S.I., Fellow of Faculty of Anaesthet-ists, Royal College of Surgeons in Ireland.
F.F.A. (S.A.), Fellow of Faculty of Anaesthetists, South Africa.
F.F.B., Fellow of Faculty of Building.
F.F.C.M., Fellow of Faculty of Community Medicine.
F.F.D.,R.C.S., Fellow of Faculty of Dentistry, Royal College of Surgeons.
F.F.D.,R.C.S.Ireland, Fellow of Faculty of Dentistry, Royal College of Surgeons, Ireland.
F.F.R., Fellow of Faculty of Radiologists.
F.G.I., Fellow of Grocers' Institute.
F.G.S., Fellow of Geological Society.
F.G.S.M., Fellow of Guildhall School of Music and Drama.
F.H.A., Fellow of Institute of Hospital Adminis-trators.
F.I.A., Fellow of Institute of Actuaries.
F.I.A.L., Fellow of International Institute of Arts and Letters.
F.I.A.M., Fellow of International Academy of Management.
F.I.Arb., Fellow of Institute of Arbitrators.
F.I.A.S., Fellow of Institute of Aeronautical Sciences (U.S.).

F.I.B., Fellow of Institute of Bankers.

F.I.Biol., Fellow of Institute of Biology.

F.I.C.D., Fellow of Institute of Civil Defence.

F.I.C.E., Fellow of Institute of Civil Engineers.

F.I.Ceram., Fellow of Institute of Ceramics.

F.I.C.M., Fellow of Institute of Credit Management.

F.I.C.S., Fellow of Institute of Chartered Shipbrokers.

F.I.E.A., Fellow of Institution of Engineers, Australia.

F.I.E.E., Fellow of Institute of Electrical Engineers.

F.I.E.E.E., Fellow of Institute of Electrical and Electronics Engineers, USA.

F.I.E.I., Fellow of Institution of Engineering Inspection.

F.I.E.R.E., Fellow of Institution of Electronic and Radio Engineers.

F.I.F.S.T., Fellow of Institute of Food Science and Technology.

F.I.H.E., Fellow of Institute of Health Education.

F.I.H.M.. Fellow of Institute of Housing Managers.

F.I.H.V.E., Fellow of Institution of Heating and Ventilating Engineers.

F.I.I.P., Fellow of Institute of Incorporated Photographers.

F.I.L., Fellow of Institute of Linguists.

F.I.M., Fellow of Institution of Metallurgists.

F.I.M.A., Fellow of Institute of Mathematics and its Applications.

F.I.Mech.E., Fellow of Institute of Mechanical Engineers.

F.I.M.I., Fellow of Institute of Motor Industry.

F.I.Min.E., Fellow of Institution of Mining Engineers.

F.I.M.M., Fellow of Institute of Mining and Metallurgy.

F.I.M.T.A., Fellow of Institute of Municipal Treasurers and Accountants.

F.I.Mun.E., Fellow of Institution of Municipal Engineers.

F.Inst.A.M., Fellow of Institute of Administrative Management.

F.Inst.D., Fellow of Institute of Directors.

F.Inst.F., Fellow of Institute of Fuel.

F.Inst.H.E., Fellow of Institute of Highways Engineers.

F.Inst.M., Fellow of Institute of Marketing.

F.Inst.Met., Fellow of Institute of Metals.

F.Inst., Nav. Fellow of Institute of Navigation.

F.Inst.P., Fellow of Institute of Physics and Physical Society.

F.Inst.Pet., Fellow of Institute of Petroleum.

F.Inst.P.S., Fellow of Institute of Purchasing and Supply.

F.Inst.W., Fellow of Institute of Welding.

F.I.O., Fellow of Institute of Ophthalmology.

F.I.O.B., Fellow of Institute of Building.

F.I.P.A., Fellow of Institute of Public Administration.

F.I.Plant.E., Fellow of Institution of Plant Engineers.

F.I.P.M., Fellow of Institute of Personnel Management.

F.I.P.R., Fellow of Institute of Public Relations.

F.I.Prod.E., Fellow of Institution of Production Engineers.

F.I.Q., Fellow of Institute of Quarrying.

F.I.Q.A., Fellow of Institute of Quality Insurance.

F.I.R.E.E.(Aust)., Fellow of Institution of Radio and Electronics Engineers (Australia).

F.I.Struct.E., Fellow of Institution of Structural Engineers.

F.I.W.E., Fellow of Institute of Water Engineers.

F.I.W.M., Fellow of Institution of Works Managers.

F.I.W.S.P., Fellow of Institution of Work Study Practitioners.

F.L.A.S., Fellow of Chartered Land Agents Society.

F.L.C.M., Fellow of London Coll. of Music.

Fl. Lt., Flight Lieutenant.

F.L.S., Fellow of Linnean Society.

F.M.A., Fellow of Museums Association.

F.N.Z.I.E., Fellow of New Zealand Institution of Engineers.

F.N.Z.I.M., Fellow of New Zealand Institute of Management.

F.N.Z.S.A., Fellow of New Zealand Society of Accountants.

F/O., Flying Officer.

F.O.I.C., Flag Officer in Charge.

F.P.A.N.Z., Fellow Public Accountant of New Zealand.

F.Phys.S., Fellow of Physical Society.

F.P.I., Fellow of Plastics Institute.

F P.S., Fellow of Pharmaceutical Society.

F.R.A.C.D.S., Fellow of Royal Australian College of Dental Surgeons.

F.R.A.C.G.P., Fellow of Royal Australian College of General Practitioners.

F.R.A.C.I., Fellow of Royal Australian Chemical Institute.

F.R.A.C.P., Fellow of Royal Australasian College of Physicians.

F.R.A.C.R., Fellow of Royal Australasian College of Radiologists.

F.R.A.C.S., Fellow of Royal Australasian College of Surgeons.

F.R.Ae.S., Fellow of Royal Aeronautical Society.

F.R.Ag.S., Fellow of Royal Agricultural Societies of Great Britain.

F.R.A.I., Fellow of Royal Anthropological Institute.

F.R.A.I.A., Fellow of Royal Australian Institute of Architects.

F.R.A.M., Fellow of Royal Academy of Music.

F.R.A.P.I., Fellow of Royal Australian Planning Institute.

F.R.A.S., Fellow of Royal Astronomical Society.

F.R.A.S.E., Fellow of the Royal Agricultural Society of England.

F.R.C.G.P., Fellow of Royal College of General Practitioners.

F.R.C.M., Fellow of Royal College of Music.

F.R.C.O., Fellow of Royal College of Organists.

F.R.C.O.G., Fellow of Royal College of Obstetricians and Gynaecologists.

F.R.C. Path., Fellow of Royal College of Pathologists.

F.R.C.P.London, F.R.C.P.Ed., and F.R.C.P.I., Fellow of the Royal College of Physicians of London, Edinburgh, and Ireland respectively.

F.R.C.P.A., Fellow of Royal College of Pathologists of Australia.

F.R.C.P. & S., Fellow Royal College of Physicians and Surgeons.

F.R.C.Psych., Fellow Royal College of Psychiatrists.

F.R.C.S.Can., Fellow of Royal College of Surgeons, Canada.

F.R.C.S.England, F.R.C.S.Ed., and F.R.C.S.I., Fellow of Royal College of Surgeons of England, Edinburgh and Ireland respectively.

F.R.C.S.(Glas.), Fellow of Royal College of Surgeons of Glasgow.

F.R.C.V.S., Fellow of Royal College of Veterinary Surgeons.

F.R.Econ.S., Fellow of Royal Economical Society.

F.R.E.S., Fellow of Royal Entomological Society of London.

F.R.F.P.S., Fellow of Royal Faculty of Physicians and Surgeons.

F.R.G.S., Fellow of Royal Geographical Society.

F.R.Hist.S., Fellow of Royal Historical Society.

F.R.H.S., Fellow of Royal Horticultural Society.

F.R.I.A.S., Fellow of Royal Incorporation of Architects in Scotland.

F.R.I.B.A., Fellow of Royal Institute of British Architects.

F.R.I.C., Fellow of Royal Institute of Chemistry.

F.R.I.C.S., Fellow of Royal Institution of Chartered Surveyors.

F.R.I.H., Fellow of Royal Institute of Horticulture (N.Z.).

F.R.I.P.H.H., Fellow of Royal Institute of Public Health and Hygiene.

F.R.M.C.M., Fellow of Royal Manchester College of Music.

FRPS,, Fellow of Royal Photographic Society.

F.R.S., Fellow of Royal Society.

F.R.S.A., Fellow of Royal Society of Arts.

F.R.S.A.M.D., Fellow of Royal Scottish Academy of Music and Drama.

F.R.S.C.M., Fellow of Royal School of Church Music.

F.R.S.E., Fellow of Royal Society of Edinburgh.

F.R.S.G.S., Fellow of Royal Scottish Geographical Society.

F.R.S.H., Fellow of Royal Society for Promotion of Health.

F.R.S.L., Fellow of Royal Society of Literature.

F.R.S.M., Fellow of Royal Society of Medicine.

F.R.S.N.Z., Fellow of Royal Society of New Zealand.

F.R.S.S.A., Fellow of Royal Society of South Africa.

F.R.T.P.I., Fellow Royal Town Planning Institute.

F.R.T.S., Fellow Royal Television Society.

F.R.Z.S. (Scot.), Fellow of Royal Zoological Society of Scotland.

F.S.A., Fellow of Society of Antiquaries.

F.S.A.A., Fellow of Society of Incorporated Accountants and Auditors.

F.S.A.E., Fellow of National Society for Art Education.

F.S.E.. Fellow of Society of Engineers.

F.S.For., Fellow of Society of Foresters of Great Britain.

F.S.I.A., Fellow of Society of Industrial Artists and Designers.
F.S.S., Fellow of Royal Statistical Society.
F.T.C.L., Fellow of Trinity College of Music, London.
F.T.I.A., Fellow of Taxation Institute of Australia.
F.W.A.A.S., Fellow of World Academy of Arts and Sciences.
F.Z.S., Fellow of Zoological Society.

G.A.T.T., General Agreement of Tariffs and Trade.
G.B.E., Knight or Dame Grand Cross of British Empire.
G.C., George Cross.
G.C.B., Knight Grand Cross of the Bath.
G.C.F.R., Grand Commander of Order of Federal Republic of Nigeria.
G.C.I.E., Knigh Grand Commander of Indian Empire.
G.C.M.G., Knight or Dame Grand Cross of St. Michael and St. George.
G.C.O.N., Grand Commander of the Order of Niger (Nigeria).
G.C.S.I., Knight Grand Commander of Star of India.
G.C.St.J., Bailiff or Dame Grand Cross of St. John of Jerusalem.
G.C.V.O., Knight or Dame Grand Cross of Royal Victorian Order.
Gen., General.
G.H.Q., General Headquarters.
G.L.C., Greater London Council.
G.M., George Medal.
G.M.M.G., Grand Master of St. Michael and St. George.
G.O.C., General Officer Commanding.
Gov., Governor.
Govt., Government.
G.P.O., General Post Office.
Gram. Sch., Grammar School.
Gren. Gds., Grenadier Guards.
G.R.S.M., Graduate of Royal School of Music.
G.S.O., General Staff Officer.

h.a., heir apparent.
H.A.A., Heavy Anti Aircraft.
H.A.C., Honourable Artillery Company.
H.C.F., Honorary Chaplain to the Forces.
H.D.D., Higher Dental Diploma.
H.E.I.C.S., Honourable East India Company's Service.
H.G.D.H.. His or Her Grand Ducal Highness.
HGV, Heavy Goods Vehicles.
H.H., His or Her Highness, His Holiness.
H.I.H., His, or Her, Imperial Highness.
H.M., His or Her Majesty.
H.M.S., His or Her Majesty's Ship.
Hon., Honourable, Honorary.
Hon.G.S.M., Honorary Guildhall School of Music.
h.p., heir presumptive.
H.Q., Headquarters.
H.R.H., His or Her Royal Highness.
H.S.H., His or Her Serene Highness.

I.B.A., Independent Broadcasting Authority.
IBERLANT, Iberia Atlantic Area.
I.C.I., Imperial Chemical Industries, Ltd.
I.C.S., Indian Civil Service.
i.d.c., Imperial Defence College.
I.G., Irish Guards.
I.L.E.A., Inner London Education Authority.
I.L.O., International Labour Organization.
I.M.S., Indian Medical Service.
Inc., Incorporated.
Ind., Independent.
Inf., Infantry.
Infra., below.
Inst., Institute.
Instn., Institution.
IPU, Inter-Parliamentary Union.
I.S.C., Indian Staff Corps.
I.S.O., Companion of Imperial Service Order.

J.A.G., Judge Advocate-General.
J.D., Doctor of Jurisprudence.
J.Dip.MA, Joint Diploma in Management Accounting Services.
Jnr., Junior.
J.P., Justice of the Peace.
j.s.s.c., Joint Services Staff College.

K.B., Knight of the Bath (to 1814).
K.B.E., Knight Commander of British Empire.
K.C., King's Counsel.
K.C.B., Knight Commander of the Bath.
K.C.I.E., Knight Commander of Indian Empire.
K.C.M.G., Knight Commander of St. Michael and St. George.

K.C.S.I., Knight Commander of the Star of India
K.C.V.O., Knight Commander of Royal Victorian Order.
K.G., Knight of the Garter.
K.G. St.J., Knight of Grace of St. John of Jerusalem.
K.J.St.J., Knight of Justice of St. John of Jerusalem.
Knt., Knight.
K.O.S.B., King's Own Scottish Borderers.
K.O.Y.L.I., King's Own Yorkshire Light Infantry.
K.P., Knight of St. Patrick.
K.P.F.S.M., King's Police and Fire Service Medal.
K.P.M., King's Police Medal.
K.R.R.C., King's Royal Rifle Corps.
K.S.L.I., King's Shropshire Light Infantry.
K.St.J., Knight of St. John of Jerusalem.
K.T., Knight of the Thistle.

L., Lord, and Lancers.
L., Liberal.
L.A.A., Light Anti Aircraft.
Lab., Labour
L.A.B., Licentiate of the Associated Board (Board being the combined Roy. Coll. of Music and Roy. Acad. of Music).
L A C., Leading Aircraftsman.
L.C.C., London County Council.
L.C.S.T., Licentiate of College of Speech Therapists.
L.D.S., Licentiate of Dental Surgery.
L.G., Life Guards.
L.H.D., Literarum Humaniorum Doctor.
L.I., Light Infantry.
Lib., Liberal.
Lieut., Lieutenant.
Lieut.-Col., Lieutenant-Colonel.
Lit.Hum., Literae Humaniores.
Litt.D., Doctor of Letters.
L.K.Q.C.P., Licentiate of the King and Queen's College of Physicians, Ireland.
LL.B., Bachelor of Laws.
LL.D., Doctor of Laws.
LL.M., Master of Laws.
L.M., Licentiate in Midwifery.
L.M.R.T.P.I., Legal Member Royal Town Planning Institute.
L.M.S.S.A., Licentiate in Medicine and Surgery of the Society of Apothecaries.
Lp., Lordship.
L.R.A.M., Licentiate of Royal Academy of Music.
L.R.C.P., Licentiate of Royal College of Physicians.
L.R.C.P.S., Licentiate of Royal College of Physicians and Surgeons.
L.R.C.S., Licentiate of Royal College of Surgeons.
L.R.F.P.S., Licentiate of Royal Faculty of Physicians and Surgeons, Glasgow.
L.R.I.B.A., Licentiate of Royal Institute of British Architects.
L.S.A., Licentiate of Society of Apothecaries.
L.S.E., London School of Economics.
L.S.I.A., Licentiate of Society of Industrial Artists and Designers.
Lt., Lieutenant.
Lt.-Col., Lieutenant Colonel.
Lt.-Gen., Lieutenant-General.
L.U., Liberal Unionist.
L.V.C.M., Licentiate of the Victoria College of Music.
Ly., Lady.

M., Marquess.
m., married or marriage.
M.A., Master of Arts.
M.A.C.E., Member of Australian College of Education.
M.A.C.R., Member of American College of Radiology.
M.Agr., Master of Agriculture.
M.A.I., Master of Engineering.
M.A.I.M.E., Member of American Institute of Mining and Metallurgical Engineers.
Maj., Major.
Maj.-Gen., Major-General.
M.A.N.Z.C.P., Member Australian and New Zealand College of Psychiatrists.
M.A.O., Master of Obstetric Art.
M.A.S.M.E., Member of American Society of Mechanical Engineers.
M.Aus.I.M.M., Member of Australian Institute of Mining and Metallurgy.
M.B., Bachelor of Medicine and Medal of Bravery.
M.B.A., Master of Business Administration.
M.B.C.S., Member British Computer Society.
M.B.E., Member of Order of British Empire.
M.B.I.M., Member of British Institute of Management.
M.C., Military Cross.
M.C.C., Marylebone Cricket Club.

M.C.E., Master of Civil Engineering.
M.Ch., Master in Surgery.
M.Ch.Orth., Master of Orthopaedic Surgery.
M.C.I.T., Member of Chartered Institute of Transport.
M.C.L., Master in Civil Law.
M.Com., Master of Commerce (Scotland).
M.C.P.A., Member of College of Pathologists of Australia.
M.C.P.S., Member of College of Physicians and Surgeons.
M.C.S.P., Member of Chartered Society of Physiotherapists.
M.D., Doctor of Medicine.
m. diss., marriage dissolved.
M.D.S., Master of Dental Surgery.
M.E., Master of Engineering.
M.E.C., Member of Executive Council.
M.Econ., Master of Economics.
Med., Medical.
M.Ed., Master of Education.
M.E.I.C., Member of Engineering Institute of Canada.
M.E.L.F., Middle East Land Forces.
M.Eng., Master of Engineering.
Met., Metropolitan.
M.F.C.M., Member of Faculty of Community Medicine.
mfg., manufacturing.
M F.H., Master of Foxhounds.
M.G.I., Member of Grocers' Institute.
M.H.A., Member of House of Assembly.
M.H.R., Member of House of Representatives.
M.I.C.E., Member of Institution of Civil Engineers.
M.I.Chem.E., Member of Institution of Chemical Engineers.
M.I.E.A., Member of Institution of Engineers, Australia.
M.I.E.E., Member of Institution of Electrical Engineers.
M.I.E.I., Member of Institution of Engineering Inspection.
M.I.E.India, Member of Institution of Engineers in India.
M.I.E.R.E., Member of Institution of Electronic and Radio Engineers.
M.I.E.S., Member of Institution of Engineers and Shipbuilders in Scotland.
M.I.Ex., Member of Institute of Export.
M.I. Gas. E., Member of Institution of Gas Engineers.
Mil., Military, Militia.
M.I.Mar.E., Member of Institute of Marine Engineers.
M.I.M.C., Member of Institute of Management Consultants.
M.I.Mech.E., Member of Institution of Mechanical Engineers.
M.I.M.I., Member of Institute of Motor Industry.
M.I.Min.E., Member of Institution of Mining Engineers.
M.I.M.M., Member of Institute of Mining and Metallurgy.
M.I.M.T.A., Member of Institute of Municipal Treasurers and Accountants.
M.I.Mun.E., Member of Institution of Municipal Engineers.
Min., Minister or Ministry.
M.I.N., Member of Institute of Navigation.
M.Inst.A.M., Member of Institute of Administrative Management.
M Inst.F., Member of Institution of Fuel.
M.Inst.H.E., Member of Institute of Highway Engineers.
M.Inst.M., Member of Institute of Marketing.
M.Inst.M.C., Member of Institute of Measurement and Control.
M.Inst.Met., Member of Institute of Metals.
M.Inst.Nav., Member of the Institute of Navigation.
M.Inst.Pet., Member of Institute of Petroleum.
M.Inst.P.I., Member of Institute of Patentees and Inventors.
M.Inst.P.S., Member of Institute of Purchasing and Supply.
M.Inst.W., Member of Institute of Welding.
M.I.Nuc.E., Member of Institution of Nuclear Engineers.
M.I.O.B., Member of the Institute of Building.
M.I.P.A., Member of Institute of Public Administration.
M.I.Plant.E., Member of Institution of Plant Engineers.
M.I.P.M., Member of Institute of Personnel Management.
M.I.P.R., Member of Institute of Public Relations.
M.I.Prod.E., Member of Institution of Production Engineers.
M.I.Q., Member of Institute of Quarrying.
M.I.R.S.E., Member of Institution of Railway Signal Engineers.

M.I.S.M. Member of Institue of Supervisory Management.
M.I.Struct.E., Member of Institution of Structural Engineers.
M.I.T.O., Member Institution of Training Officers.
M.I.W.E., Member of Institution of Water Engineers.
M.I.W.M., Member of Institution of Works Managers.
M.I.W.S.P., Member of Institution of Work Study Practitioners.
M.L.A., Member of Legislative Assembly.
M.L.C., Member of Legislative Council.
M.Litt., Master of Letters.
M.M., Military Medal.
M.M.E., Master of Mining Engineering.
M.M.G.I.. Master Member of Grocers' Institute.
M.M.M., Member of Order of Military Merit.
M.M.S.A., Master of Midwifery of Society of Apothecaries.
M.O., Medical Officer.
M.O.D. Ministry of Defence.
M.P., Member of Parliament.
M.P.S., Member of Pharmaceutical Society.
M.R.C.G.P., Member of Royal College of General Practitioners.
M.R.C.P., Member of Royal College of Physicians.
M.R.C.P.A., Member of Royal College of Pathologists of Australia.
M.R.C.P.Ed., Member of Royal College of Physicians, Edinburgh.
M.R.C.P.I., Member of Royal College of Physicians, Ireland.
M.R.C.Psych., Member Royal College of Psychiatry.
M.R.C.S., Member of Royal College of Surgeons.
M.R.C.V.S., Member of Royal College of Veterinary Surgeons.
M.R.I.A.. Member of the Royal Irish Academy.
M.R.I.C.S., Member of Royal Institution of Chartered Surveyors.
M.R.I.N.A., Member of the Royal Institution of Naval Architects.
M.R.S.H., Member of Royal Society for Promotion of Health.
M.R.T.P.I., Member Royal Town Planning Institute.
M.R.T.S., Member Royal Television Society.
M.S., Master of Surgery.
M.S.Aut.E., Member of Society of Automobile Engineers.
M.Sc., Master of Science.
M.S.E., Member of Society of Engineers.
M.S.For., Member of the Society of Foresters of Great Britain.
M.S.I.A., Member of Society of Industrial Artists and Designers.
M.S.I.T., Member Society of Instrument Technology.
M.S.M., Meritorious Service Medal.
M.St.J., Member of St. John of Jerusalem.
Mus.B., Bachelor of Music.
Mus.D., Doctor of Music.
M.V.O., Member of Royal Victorian Order.

N., Nationalist.
N.A.A.F.I., Navy, Army and Air Force Institutes.
N.A.T.O., North Atlantic Treaty Organization.
N.D.A., National Diploma of Agriculture.
N.E.D.C., National Economic Development Council.
N.E.D.O., National Economic Development Office.
N.F.U., National Farmers' Union.
N.L., National Liberal.
N.O.I.C., Naval Officer in Charge.
N.S.P.C.C., National Society for the Prevention of Cruelty to Children.
N.S.W. New South Wales.
NUJ, National Union of Journalists.
NUR, National Union of Railwaymen.
N.U.T., National Union of Teachers.
N.Y., New York.
N.Z.. New Zealand.
N.Z.E.F., New Zealand Exeditdionary Force.

O.B.E., Officer of Order of British Empire.
O.C., Officer Commanding and Officer of Order of Canada.
O.D.A., Overseas Development Administration.
O.E.C.D., Organization for Economic Co-operation and Development.
O.E.E.C., Organization for European Economic Co-operation.
O.M., Member of Order of Merit.
O.M.M., Officer of Order of Military Merit.
O.S.B., Order of St. Benedict.
O.St.J., Officer of St. John of Jerusalem.
O.T.C., Officers' Training Corps.
Oxon., Oxfordshire.

Parl., Parliamentary.
P.C., Privy Counsellor.
Ph.C., Pharmaceutical Chemist.
Ph.D., Doctor of Philosophy.
Plen., Plenipotentiary.
P.M.R.A.F.N.S., Princess Mary's Royal Air Force Nursing Service.
P/O, Pilot Officer.
P.P.S., Parliamentary Private Secretary.
Preb., Prebendary.
Pres., President.
Presb., Presbyterian.
Prin., Principal.
Prof., Professor.
p.s.c., Passed staff college.
Pty., Proprietary.
P.W.D., Public Works Department.

Q.A.I.M.N.S., Queen Alexandra's Imperial Military Nursing Service.
Q.A.L.A.S., Qualified Associate of Land Agents' Society.
Q.A.R.A.N.C., Queen Alexandra's Royal Army Nursing Corps.
Q.A.R.N.N.S., Queen Alexandra's Royal Naval Nursing Service.
Q.C., Queen's Counsel.
Q.F.S.M., Queen's Fire Service Medal.
Q.G.M., Queen's Gallantry Medal.
Q.H.D.S., Queen's Honorary Dental Surgeon.
Q.H.N.S., Queen's Honorary Nursing Sister.
Q.H.P., Queen's Honorary Physician.
Q.H.S., Queen's Honorary Surgeon.
Qld., Queensland.
Q.M.G., Quartermaster-General.
Q.P.M., Queen's Police Medal.
Q.S.M., Queen's Service Medal, NZ.
Q.S.O., Queen's Service Order, NZ.

R., Rector, and Royal (regiments).
R.A..Royal Artillery, Royal Academician.
R.A.A.F., Royal Australian Air Force.
R.A.A.M.C., Royal Australian Army Medical Corps.
R.A.A.S.C., Royal Australian Army Service Corps.
R.A.C., Royal Armoured Corps and Royal Automobile Club.
R.A.Ch.D., Royal Army Chaplain's Dept.
R.A.D.A., Royal Academy of Dramatic Art.
R.A.D.C., Royal Army Dental Corps.
R.A.E.C., Royal Army Educational Corps.
R.A.F., Royal Air Force.
R.A.F.R.O., Reserve of Air Force Officers.
R.A.F.V.R., Royal Air Force Volunteer Reserve.
R.A.M., Member of Royal Academy of Music.
R.A.M.C., Royal Army Medical Corps.
R.A.N., Royal Australian Navy.
R.A.N.R., Royal Australian Naval Reserve.
R.A.N.V.R., Royal Australian Naval Volunteer Reserve.
R.A.O.C., Royal Army Ordnance Corps.
R.A.P.C., Royal Army Pay Corps.
R.A.R.O., Regular Army Reserve of Officers.
R.A.S.C., Royal Army Service Corps.
R.Aux.A.F., Royal Auxiliary Air Force.
R.A.V.C., Royal Army Veterinary Corps.
R.C., Roman Catholic.
R.C.A.F., Royal Canadian Air Force.
r.c.d.s., Royal College of Defence Studies.
R.C.N., Royal Canadian Navy.
R.C.N.C., Royal Corps of Naval Architects.
R.C.S., Royal College of Surgeons.
R.C.T., Royal Corps of Transport.
R.D., Royal Naval Reserve Officer's Decoration.
R.D.C., Rural District Council.
R.D.I., Royal Designer for Industry.
R.E., Royal Engineers.
Regt., Regiment.
R.E.M.E., Royal Electrical and Mechanical Engineers.
Ret., Retired.
Rev., Reverend.
R.F., Royal Fusiliers.
R.F.A., Royal Field Artillery, and Royal Fleet Auxiliary.
R.F.C., Royal Flying Corps.
R.F.N., Registered Fever Nurse.
R.Fus., Royal Fusiliers.
R.G.A., Royal Garrison Artillery.
RGJ, Royal Green Jackets.
R.H.A., Royal Horse Artillery.
R.H.F., Royal Highland Fusiliers.
R.H.G., Royal Horse Guards.
R.H. G/D , The Blues and Royals (Royal Horse Guards and 1st Dragoons).
R.H.R., Royal Highland Regiment.
R.I., Member of Royal Institute of Painters in Water Colour.
R.I.A.C., Royal Irish Automobile Club.
R.I.B.A., Royal Institute of British Architects.

R.I.I.A., Royal Institute of International Affairs.
Rly., Railway.
R.M., Royal Marines
R.M.A., Royal Marine Artillery; Royal Military Academy.
R.M.C., Royal Military College.
R.M.L.I., Royal Marine Light Infantry.
R.M.P., Royal Military Police.
R.M.S., Royal Mail Steamer.
R.N., Royal Navy.
R.N.A.S., Royal Naval Air Service.
R.N.C., Royal Naval College.
R.N.L.I., Royal National Lifeboat Institution.
R.N.R., Royal Naval Reserve.
R.N.T., Registered Nurse Tutor.
R.N.V.R., Royal Naval Volunteer Reserve.
R.N.Z.A.F., Royal New Zealand Air Force.
R.N.Z.A.M.C., Royal New Zealand Army Medical Corps.
R.N.Z.N., Royal New Zealand Navy.
R.O.I., Royal Institute of Oil Painters.
Roy., Royal.
Roy. Signals, Royal Corps of Signals.
R.P., Member of Royal Society of Portrait Painters.
R.R.C., Lady of the Royal Red Cross.
R.R.F., Royal Regiment of Fusiliers.
R.R.W., Royal Regiment of Wales.
R.S.A., Royal Scottish Academician.
R.S.A.C., Royal Scottish Automobile Club.
R.S.F., Royal Scots Fusiliers.
R. Signals., Royal Signals.
R.S.P.C.A., Royal Society for the Prevention of Cruelty to Animals.
R.S.W., Member of Scottish Royal Society of Painters in Water Colours.
Rt., Right.
Rt. Hon., Right Honourable.
R.T.P.I., Royal Town Planning Institute.
R.T.R., Royal Tank Regiment.
R.W.F., Royal Welch Fusiliers.
R.W.S., Member of Royal Society of Painters in Water Colours.

s., succeeded.
S., South.
S.A.S., Special Air Service Regiment.
S.A.S.O., Senior Air Staff Officer.
S.B.St.J., Serving Brother of Order of St. John of Jerusalem.
S.C., Senior Counsel.
S.C., Star of Courage.
Sc.D., Doctor of Science.
S.C.F., Senior Chaplain to the Forces.
Sch., School.
S.C.L.I., Somerset and Cornwall Light Infantry.
S.C.M., State Certified Midwife, and Student Christian Movement.
S.D., Scientiae Doctor (Doctor of Science).
S.E.A.T.O., South East Asia Treaty Organization.
Sec., Secretary.
Ser., Service.
S.G., Scots Guards.
S.G.M., Sea Gallantry Medal.
S.H.A.E.F., Supreme Headquarters Allied Expeditionary Force.
S.H.A.P.E., Supreme Headquarters Allied Powers in Europe.
S J., Society of Jesus.
S.J.D., Scientiae Juridicea Doctor (Doctor of Juridical Science).
S.L.I., Somerset Light Infantry.
S.M., Medal of Service, and Master of Science.
Snr., Senior.
So., Society.
Soc. Society.
Som.L.I., Somerset Light Infantry.
S.P.C.K., Society for Promoting Christian Knowledge
Sqdn., Squadron.
Sqdn.-Ldr., Squadron Leader.
S.R., Supplementary Reserve.
S.R.C., Science Research Council.
S.R.N., State Registered Nurse.
S.S.C., Solicitor, Supreme Court (Scotland).
S.S. St. J., Serving Sister of Order of St. John of Jerusalem.
S.T.S.O., Senior Technical Staff Officer.
Sup., Superintendent and Supplementary.
Supt., Superintendent.
Surg., Surgeon.

T.A., Territorial Army.
T.A. & V.R. Assocn., Territorial Auxiliary and Volunteer Reserve Association.
T. & A.F. Assocn., Territorial and Auxiliary Forces Association.
T. & A. V. R., Territorial & Army Volunteer Reserve.
T.A.R.O., Territorial Army Reserve of Officers
Tas. Tasmania.

T.D., Efficiency (Territorial) Decoration.
T.F., Territorial Force.
Trin., Trinity.
T.U.C., Trades Union Congress.

U., Unionist.
U.D.C., Urban District Council.
U.K., United Kingdom.
U.K.A.E.A., United Kingdom Atomic Energy Authority
U.K.L.F., United Kingdom Land Forces.
U.M.I.S.T., University of Manchester Institute of Science and Technology.
U.N., United Nations
U.N.E.S.C.O., United Nations Educational, Scientific and Cultural Organisation.
U.N.I.C.E.F., United Nations Children's Fund.
U.N.I.D.O., United Nations Industrial Development Organisation.
Univ., University.
U.N.O., United Nations Organization.
U.N.R.R.A., United Nations Relief and Rehabilitation Administration.
U.P.N.I., Unionist Party of N. Ireland.
U.S.P.G., United Society for the Propagation of the Gospel.
U.S.S.R., Union of Soviet Socialist Republics.
U.U.U.C., United Ulster Unionist Coalition.

V., Vicar, Viscount, Volunteer.
V.A., Lady of the Royal Order of Victoria and Albert.
V.A.D., Voluntary Aid Detachment.

V.C., Victoria Cross.
V.D., Volunteer and Colonial Auxiliary Forces Officers' Decorations.
Ven., Venerable.
Vet., Veterinary.
V.M.H., Victoria Medal of Honour (Royal Horticultural Society).
Vol., Volunteer(s).
V.P., Vice-President.
V.R.D., Royal Naval Volunteer Reserve Officer's Decoration.
Vy., Viscountcy.

W.A.A.F., Women's Auxiliary Air Force.
W.A.C.(I), Women's Army Corps, India.
W.E.U., Western European Union.
W.G., Welsh Guards.
W.H.O., World Health Organization.
Wing Cdr., Wing Commander.
W.O.I., Warrant Officer Class 1.
W.O.II., Warrant Officer Class 2.
W.R.A.C., Women's Royal Army Corps.
W.R.A.F., Women's Royal Air Force.
W.R.N.S., Women's Royal Naval Service.
W.R.V.S., Women's Royal Voluntary Service.
W.S., Writer to the Signet.
W.V.S., Women's Voluntary Services.

Yeo., Yeomanry.
Y.M.C.A., Young Men's Christian Association.
Yr., Younger.
Yst., Youngest.
Y.W.C.A., Young Women's Christian Association.

PREFACE.

The Queen's fiftieth birthday

O N April 21st, 1976, the Queen celebrates her fiftieth birthday. She was born at the London house of her maternal grandparents, the Earl and Countess of Strathmore, 17, Bruton Street, almost on the third anniversary of her parents' wedding. At that time she was third in line of succession to the throne. Her father, Prince Albert, Duke of York, was the second son of King George V. It was not then expected that she would one day inherit the throne, for the heir was the popular Prince of Wales.

The Princess was christened Elizabeth Alexandra Mary. the names of her mother, great-grandmother and grandmother, who all became Queens Consort. King George then wrote to Queen Mary: " I have heard from Bertie about the names . . . I quite approve, and will tell him so. He says nothing about Victoria. I hardly think that necessary." (It was then twenty-five years since the death of Queen Victoria, who had wished that all her female descendants would bear her name.) The Queen's christian names have the same initials as her mother, Lady Elizabeth Angela Marguerite Bowes-Lyon, now Queen Elizabeth the Queen Mother.

It is surprising that until the House of Hanover succeeded in 1714 how few of our Sovereigns lived to reach the age of fifty. So far there have only been 24 Sovereigns of England since the Conquest who have achieved that age. Of the Plantagenets, Henry II died when he was fifty-six, Henry III, sixty-six, Edward I, sixty-eight, and Edward III, sixty-four. There was then a long gap, from 1377 until the first Tudor Sovereign, Henry VII, achieved the age of fifty-two. It is popularly supposed that his son, Henry VIII lived to a ripe old age; in fact he died on his birthday at fifty-six. When his daughter, Queen Elizabeth I, became the oldest English Sovereign, she survived until the age of sixty-nine in 1603.

Two monarchs have celebrated their eightieth birthdays, George III, blind and incapacitated under Regency of his son, and his granddaughter Queen Victoria, both of whom lived to be eighty-one. Our oldest Queen Consort was the Queen's grandmother, Queen Mary, who died aged eighty-four on March 24th, 1952, shortly before the Queen's Coronation. One of her last wishes was that this ceremony should not be postponed because of her demise.

The Queen's Silver Jubilee

The United Kingdom and the Commonwealth will celebrate the Queen's Silver Jubilee in 1977, she having succeeded to the throne on February 6th, 1952. Queen Victoria, whose reign was the longest in our history, from 1837 to 1901, had two important Jubilees, the Golden in 1887, and the Diamond, ten years later. When her grandson, King George V, celebrated his Silver Jubilee in May 1935, he was the twelfth ruler to have reigned for twenty-five years. His Accession Day, May 6th, was declared a public holiday, and a Thanksgiving Service was held at St. Paul's Cathedral, London. King George and Queen Mary drove through the cheering crowds of the capital. 80,000 Silver Jubilee Medals were struck, which were designed by Sir William Goscombe John, R.A. The ribbon had a red centre stripe, with two of blue and one of white on each side, each being three-quarters of an inch wide.

Some of the arrangements for the Queen's Silver Jubilee in 1977 have been announced. The Queen has expressed the wish that there should be no undue expenditure involved in the celebrations, particularly by her Government, and local government.

There will be a Thanksgiving Service at St. Paul's on Tuesday, June 7th, preceded by one in Glasgow Cathedral on May 17th. (Edinburgh has the Thistle Day Service in St. Giles Cathedral.) Simultaneously with the meeting of the Commonwealth Heads of Governments, there will be a series of functions in London during June, including a Progress on the Thames on the 9th.

There will be reviews of the Armed Services, including West Germany, and the Police. The Naval Review will take place at Spithead, and an inspection of the Royal Marines at Plymouth. The Queen will make visits to Scotland, Wales, Northern Ireland and the Commonwealth countries of which she is the Sovereign.

On the evening of June 7th the Queen will broadcast a message to the Commonwealth. This day will be a Bank Holiday, and in England, Wales and Northern Ireland the Spring Bank Holiday will be held over until the previous day. The holiday in Scotland will be announced later. The Royal Mint will strike a commemorative Crown Piece, with a face value of 25p.

Succession of the Duke of Gloucester

The Queen's last surviving uncle, Prince Henry, Duke of Gloucester, died on June 10th, 1974, after a long illness, and was succeeded by his younger son, Prince Richard. The elder, Prince William, predeceased him, when he was tragically killed in an air accident in August 1972. The Duke's widow is now styled " Her Royal Highness, Princess Alice, Duchess of Gloucester ". The new Duke has a son, Alexander Patrick Gregers Richard, born on October 24th, 1974, who bears the courtesy title of Earl of Ulster. This is the first time this peerage, created in 1928 with the Dukedom of Gloucester, has been used as a courtesy title, because the young Earl is not Royal under the terms of King George V's Letters Patent of 1917 limiting the size of the Royal Family. It has never been the custom for the heirs of Royal Dukes who are themselves entitled to royal titles and styles to use peerage titles. The young Earl, therefore, is in the same position as his first cousin, the Earl of St. Andrews, son and heir of the Duke of Kent. They both have the surname of Windsor, provided for the descendants of King George V.

The coat of arms of the Duke of Gloucester retains the labels assigned to him when he was Prince Richard of Gloucester. Royal Arms are differenced with labels for various members of the Royal Family. These are normally personal and non-hereditary, but by the Royal Warrant of February 24th, 1975, the Arms granted to the Sovereign's grandchildren have become hereditary to their descendants. This applies also to the Duke of Kent's arms.

The new King of Spain

Don Juan Carlos, the thirty-eight year old grandson of King Alfonso XIII, whose reign terminated in 1931, was sworn in as King of Spain on November 23rd, 1975. Monarchy was restored after this long period since the King was chosen by the Head of State, General Franco, as his successor, despite the fact that the King's father, the Infante Don Carlos, Count of Barcelona, is living. Four days later the new reign formally began with a ceremonial Mass at Los Jeronimos Church, Madrid, at which Cardinal Enrique y Taracon, Archbishop of Madrid, officiated. Among the distinguished guests at this occasion were the Duke of Edinburgh, and the Presidents of France and Germany. By the King's side was his new Queen, Sophie, sister of the exiled King Constantine II of the Hellenes. The King of Spain is a descendant of the British Royal House. His grandmother, the late Queen Victoria Eugenie, better known as Ena of Battenberg, was a granddaughter of Queen Victoria.

During the last fifty years, only two monarchies were established in Europe. In 1928, President Ahmed Zogu became King Zog I of Albania. Then, in 1941, the Duke of Aosta was declared to be King Tomislav I of Croatia by Mussolini, but his reign only lasted for two years. The Greek monarchy has had a chequered career since it came into being in 1863. Twice during this period there were restorations, first in 1935, and then, after the war, in 1946. None of these thrones are now in existence.

Since 1914 two other monarchies were declared in Europe. Prince Wilhelm of Wied, nephew of Carmen Sylva Queen of Roumania, was accepted as Prince of Albania on February 6th 1914, mounting the throne on March 7th, but he was exiled in the following September and went to Roumania where he died in 1945. In Finland, after the Revolution and the defeat of Russia (the Tsar was Grand Duke of Finland), the Finnish Diet by 75 votes to 25 elected as King on 9th October 1918, Prince Friederich Karl of Hesse-Cassel, the Kaiser's brother-in-law. Germany's surrender a month later put an end to this bizarre affair. Like Tomaslav of Croatia, he does not appear to have visited his "kingdom."

Europe now has ten reigning Sovereigns. There are three Queens Regnant, Queen Elizabeth II, and the Queens of the Netherlands and Denmark, and the Kings of the Belgians, Norway, Sweden and Spain. The other rulers are the Grand Duke of Luxembourg, and the Princes of Liechtenstein and Monaco. In addition to the King of Spain, the Queen of Denmark and the Kings of Norway and Sweden are descendants of Queen Victoria. The remainder are related to the Duke of Edinburgh.

Duke has a great-grandson in the direct line of succession

The 7th Duke of Leinster, the premier Duke, Marquess and Earl in the Peerage of Ireland, now has a great-grandson in the direct line of succession. He is Viscount Leinster, born on January 12th, 1974. It is very unusual for four generations to be living at the same time each with a peerage title, and this had not occurred before in the FitzGerald family. It is also unusual for a courtesy title to be identical in name with that of the peer, both being Leinster; but the rank of " Duke " presumably is regarded as being a sufficient means of identification between him and his great-grandson. The only other peerages available are the Baronies of Kildare and Offaly, which would make them identical with the little boy's grandfather and father. The Viscountcy of Leinster was conferred in 1747 on the first Duke, when he was 20th Earl of Kildare, on his marriage to Lady Emilia Lennox, daughter of the 2nd Duke of Richmond, King Charles II's grandson. It is a peerage of Great Britain, and thus enables the Duke to sit in the House of Lords to which he proved his right in 1974, despite having succeeded 54 years ago. Sometimes an invented peerage is used as a courtesy title when there is not an available one, such as Lord Courtenay, son and heir of the Earl of Devon, and Viscount Cole, son and heir of the Earl of Enniskillen.

Vanished Titleholders

When Richard John Bingham, 7th Earl of Lucan, disappeared on the evening of November 7th, 1974, he was not the first titleholder to have vanished. In 1943 Sir Bruce Colin Patrick Campbell of Ardnamurchan, 3rd Baronet, disappeared from his West Kensington boarding house, and has never been traced since. His father, Lieutenant-Colonel Sir John Bruce Stuart Campbell, 2nd Baronet, died during the same year in a Japanese internment camp at Palenbang, Sumatra. His only son, who managed a tin mine in Burma, arrived in London just before the beginning of World War II. A note addressed to his mother said that he was going away. All his bills were paid, and his papers were said to have been in order. He apparently was suffering from sleeping sickness, and may have been a victim of the London blitz. Neither can it be found whether or not he married. One report indicated that he married in Burma, and had a son and two daughters. If this is correct, and Sir Bruce is dead, his son will have succeeded to the baronetcy. Another baronet who was missing for a long period was Sir Peregrine Henniker Heaton, who vanished on the morning of October 5th, 1971. His son found his skeleton in a lumber room at their home on June 23rd, 1974.

Move out of London

During the course of preparation of this edition it has been very noticeable that there has been wholesale movement of those mentioned in Debrett from London to the country. Those who have two addresses have often deleted the London house or flat. These moves are doubtless due to the high cost of living in London. Few seem to have moved to the outer suburbs. The most popular districts are the Home Counties, the West Country, the Cotswolds and East Anglia.

Changes of Addresses

There have been extensive changes of addresses consequent upon the passing of the Local Government Act, 1972, principally due to alteration of county boundaries. Due to the heavy printing costs, it has not been found possible to alter them automatically throughout our pages, but whenever possible addresses have been altered on being informed. This also applies to the addition of a postal code. The reorganisation came into operation in England and Wales on April 1st, 1974.

Certain new English counties were established. These are Tyne and Wear, West Midlands, Merseyside, Greater Manchester, Avon, Cleveland and Humberside. Others have been amalgamated, such as Hereford and Worcester, and Cumbria, which was chiefly formed from the old counties of Cumberland and Westmorland. Some have disappeared. Rutland was transferred to Leicestershire, and Huntingdonshire was swallowed up in Cambridgeshire. The boundary adjustments to such counties as Berkshire, Buckinghamshire, Oxfordshire, Dorset, Hampshire, Lancashire and Cheshire, have resulted in towns such as Bournemouth being transferred from Hampshire to Dorset, and Warrington from Lancashire to Cheshire.

One realises that this is an administrative necessity, but surely in several cases these could have been merely local government changes, leaving the geographical boundaries much as they were in the past, sometimes going back to Anglo-Saxon days. There is also an objection to certain of the new names. Salop is an abbreviation of Shropshire. Hereford and Worcester, without the word " shire ", is pointless, though one should be grateful that " Malvernshire ", at first suggested, was not implemented. Other names lack imagination: West Midlands seems very impersonal. The wholesale changes seem reminiscent of the abolition of certain regiments in the Army, but with far less reason. In that case, when the Army had to be run down, it was obvious that some fine old regiments had either to be disbanded or amalgamated, inevitably tampering with the valuable esprit de corps. A Yorkshireman from Hull will hardly feel the same pride as a " Humbersidean ". Wales has been more fortunate than England. Apart from the splitting up of Glamorganshire into three counties, the new names were taken from old Kingdoms.

The death of Earl Cowley, and dormancy of his peerage

When Debrett was going to press, the 7th Earl Cowley died on December 13th, 1975. As his wife is expecting a child, his peerages become dormant until the birth. If a son, he will be born the 8th Earl Cowley, but if a daughter, the succession passes to the Hon. Garret Graham Wellesley, uncle of the late Earl. There are other examples of posthumous births to widows of peers and baronets. The 8th Earl of Chichester was killed on active service on February 21st, 1944. Two months later, on April 14th, the present Earl was born. Two baronets succeeded at birth, their fathers having previously been killed on active service in World War II. These are Sir Mark Palmer, 5th Baronet, in 1941, and Sir Ranulph Twisleton-Wykeham-Fiennes, 3rd Baronet, in 1944. The British Crown has never been affected by a posthumous birth, but this occurred in Spain. King Alfonso XIII, grandfather of the present King of Spain, was born posthumously on May 17th, 1886, his father the previous King, Alfonso XII, having died on November 25th, 1885, when his widow, Queen Maria Christina of Habsburg, became Regent.

Changes in the contents of DEBRETT

This and subsequent editions of Debrett comprise the Royal Family, Peerage and Baronetage sections only. The Knightage and Companionage sections, which were added to our pages during the last century, appear for the most part in Kelly's Handbook. In future, Debrett will be published at longer intervals than previously. From 1864 Debrett has been issued annually. Our first direct ancestor, the 1769 edition, which was published by John Almon, was called *The New Peerage, or the Present State of the Nobility in England, Scotland and Ireland*. Before the third edition was published in 1784, Almon sold his business to John Debrett, who became both publisher and editor. When Debrett brought out the fifth edition in 1802, he changed the title to *Debrett's Peerage*, which has remained ever since.

P. W. MONTAGUE-SMITH,
Editor.

NEVILLE HOUSE, EDEN STREET, KINGSTON UPON THAMES.

CLUBS REFERRED TO IN THE WORK,

WITH THE ADDRESSES OF THE CLUB HOUSES.

Ladies' Clubs are marked *.

Alpine.—74, South Audley Street, W.1.
American.—95, Piccadilly, W.1.
Argentine.—1, Hamilton Place, W.1.
Army and Navy.—36, Pall Mall, S.W.1.
Arts.—40, Dover Street, W.1.
Arts Theatre—6/7 Great Newport Street, W.C.2.
Athenæum.—107, Pall Mall, S.W.1.
Authors'.—2, Whitehall Court, S.W.1.

Bath.—43, Brook Street, W.1.
Beefsteak.—9, Irving Street, W.C.2.
Boodle's.—28, St. James's Street, S.W.1.
Brooks's.—60, St. James's Street, S.W.1.
Buck's.—18, Clifford Street, W.1.

Caledonian.—9, Halkin St., S.W.1.
Caledonian United Service and Northern.—3, Queensferry St., Edinburgh.
Canning.—1, Hamilton Place, W.1.
Carlton.—69, St. James's Street, S.W.1.
Cavalry and Guards'.—127, Piccadilly, W.1.
Challoner.—59, Pont St., S.W.1.
City Livery.—Sion College, Victoria Embankment, E.C.4.
City of London.—19, Old Broad Street, E.C.2.
City University.—50, Cornhill, E.C.3.
Civil Service.—13, Great Scotland Yard, S.W.1.
Conservative.—72, Waterloo Street, Glasgow, C.2.
Constitutional.—86, St. James's St., S.W.1.
Cowdray.—20, Cavendish Sq., W.1.
Crockford's.—16, Carlton House Terrace, S.W.1.

Devonshire.—50, St. James's Street, S.W.1, and 4 & 5, Arlington Street, S.W.1.
Dublin University.—17, St. Stephen's Green North, Dublin.

East India, Sports and Public Schools.—16, St. James's Square, S.W.1.
Empress.—28, Berkeley Sq., W.1.
English-Speaking Union.—37, Charles St., W.1.
Europe House.—1, Whitehall Place, SW1A 2HA.

Farmers'.—3, Whitehall Court, S.W.1.
Flyfishers'.—3, Whitehall Court, S.W.1.

Garrick.—13, Garrick Street, W.C.2.
Gresham.—15, Abchurch Lane, E.C.4.

Hibernian United Service.—8, St. Stephen's Green North, Dublin.
Highland.—39, High St., Inverness.
Hunts.—17, Upper Grosvenor St., W.1.
Hurlingham.—Ranelagh Gdns. S.W.6.

Irish Turf.—25, Merrion Square, Dublin.

Jockey.—High Street, Newmarket.
Junior Carlton.—At Reform Club.

Kildare Street.—Dublin.

Ladies' Caledonian.—13, Charlotte Square, Edinburgh.
Ladies' V.A.D.—44, Great Cumberland Place, W.1.
Lansdowne.—9, Fitzmaurice Place, Berkeley Sq., W.1.
Leander.—Henley-on-Thames, and Putney, S.W.

Manchester Reform.—81, King Street, Manchester.
Marylebone Cricket Club (MCC).—St. John's Wood, NW8.

National.—30-35, Pall Mall, S.W.1.
National Liberal.—Whitehall Place, S.W.1.
Naval.—38, Hill Street, W.1.
Naval and Military.—94, Piccadilly, W.1.
New.—85, Princes Street, Edinburgh.
Oriental.—Stratford House, Stratford Place, W.1.
Overseas.—Overseas House, Park Place, St. James's Street, S.W.1.
Phyllis Court.—Henley-on-Thames.
Portland.—18B, Charles Street, W.1.
Pratt's.—14, Park Place, St. James's, S.W.1.

Press.—St. Bride's House, Salisbury Square, E.C.4.
Puffin's.—c/o Caledonian Hotel, Prince's St., Edinburgh.

Queen's.—Palliser Road, W. Kensington, W.14.
Queen's.—7, Frederick Street, Edinburgh.
Reform.—104, Pall Mall, S.W.1.
Roehampton.—Roehampton Lane, S.W.15.
Royal Air Force.—128, Piccadilly, W.1.
Royal Air Force Reserve.—14, South Street, W.1.
Royal Air Force Yacht.—Hamble, Southampton.
Royal and Ancient.—St. Andrews.
Royal Automobile.—89, Pall Mall, S.W.1.
Royal Burnham Yacht.—Burnham-on-Crouch.
Royal Channel Islands Yacht.—Jersey.
Royal Cinque Ports Yacht.—Waterloo Cres., Dover.
Royal Commonwealth Society.—18, Northumberland Avenue, W.C.2.
Royal Corinthian Yacht.—Burnham-on-Crouch, Essex.
Royal Dorset Yacht.—6, Charlotte Row, Weymouth.
Royal Irish Automobile.—55, South Mall, Dublin.
Royal Munster Yacht.—Crosshaven, co. Cork.
Royal Naval and Royal Albert Yacht.—Pembroke Road, Portsmouth.
R.N.V.R.—Now the Naval Club.
Royal Ocean Racing.—20, St. James's Place, S.W.1.
Royal Over Seas League.—Over Seas House, Park Place, St. James's, S.W.1.
Royal Scottish Automobile.—11, Blythswood Sq., Glasgow.
Royal Southern Yacht.—Hamble, Southampton.
Royal Thames Yacht.—60, Knightsbridge, S.W.1.
Royal Torbay Yacht.—Torquay.
Royal Ulster Yacht.—Bangor, co. Down.
Royal Victoria Yacht.—St. Thomas Street, Ryde, Isle of Wight.
Royal Western Yacht.—The Hoe, Plymouth.
Royal Yacht Squadron.—Cowes, Isle of Wight.
St. James'.—106, Piccadilly, W.1.
St. James'.—100, Mosley St., Manchester, 2.
St. John House.—50, Eaton Place, S.W.1.
St. Stephen's.—34, Queen Anne's Gate, S.W.1.
Savage.—At National Liberal Club (temporary).
Savile.—69, Brook Street, W.1.
Scottish Conservative.—112, Princes St., Edinburgh.
Scottish Liberal.—109, Princes Street, Edinburgh.
Sesame, Pioneer and Lyceum.—49, Grosvenor Street, W.1.
Ski Club of Great Britain.—118, Eaton Sq., S.W.1.
Special Forces.—8, Herbert Cres., S.W.1.
Stephen's Green.—9, St. Stephen's Green North, Dublin.
Travellers'.—106, Pall Mall, S.W.1.
Turf.—5, Carlton House Terr., S.W.1.
Ulster.—Castle Place, Belfast.
Ulster Reform.—4, Royal Avenue, Belfast.
United Nursing Services.—40, South Street, W.1.
United Service and Royal Aero.—116, Pall Mall, S.W.1.
United Sports.—4, Whitehall Court, S.W.1.
United Oxford and Cambridge University.—1, Suffolk Street, Pall Mall East, S.W.1.
University.—17, St. Stephen's Green North, Dublin.
University Women's.—2, Audley Sq., South Audley St., W.1.
V.A.D.—44, Great Cumberland Place, W.1.
Victoria League.—38, Chesham Place, S.W.1.
West Indian.—4, Whitehall Court, S.W.1.
Western.—147, Buchanan Street, Glasgow.
White's.—37, St. James's Street, S.W.1.
Women's Press.—c/o Arts Theatre Club.
Yorkshire.—17, Museum St., York.

LIFE PEERS AND LAW LORDS

*Law Lords.

Baron Adeane.
Baron Alexander of Potterhill.
Baron Allan of Kilmahew.
Baron Allen of Fallowfield.
Baron Alport.
Baron Annan.
Baron Ardwick.
Baron Armstrong of Sanderstead.
Baron Arwyn.
Baron Ashby.
Baron Ashdown.
Baron Aylestone.
Baron Balerno.
Baron Balniel.
Baron Balogh.
Baron Banks.
Baron Barber.
Baron Beaumont of Whitley.
Baron Beeching.
Baron Bernstein.
Baron Beswick.
Baron Black.
Baron Blake.
Baron Blyton.
Baron Boothby.
Baron Bourne.
Baron Bowden.
Baron Boyd-Carpenter.
Baron Boyle of Handsworth.
Baron Brayley.
Baron Briginshaw.
Baron Brock.
Baron Brockway.
Baron Brooke of Cumnor.
Baron Brown.
Baron Bruce of Donington.
Baron Buckton.
Baron Burntwood.
Baron Butler of Saffron Walden.
Baron Byers.
Baron Caccia.
Baron Campbell of Croy.
Baron Campbell of Eskan.
Baron Caradon.
Baron Casey.
Baron Castle.
Baron Chalfont.
Baron Champion.
Baron Chelmer.
Baron Chelwood.
Baron Clark.
Baron Cole.
Baron Collison.
Baron Cooper of Stockton Heath.
Baron Craigton.
*Baron Cross of Chelsea.
Baron Crowther-Hunt.
Baron Cudlipp.
Baron Darling of Hillsborough.
Baron Davies of Leek.
Baron Davies of Penrhys.
*Baron Denning.
*Baron Devlin.
Baron Diamond.
*Baron Diplock.
Baron Donaldson of Kingsbridge.
Baron Douglass of Cleveland.
Baron Duncan-Sandys.
*Baron Edmund-Davies.
Baron Elworthy.
*Baron Elwyn Jones.
Baron Energlyn.
Baron Evans of Hungershall.
Baron Feather.
Baron Ferrier.
Baron Fisher of Camden.
Baron Fletcher.
Baron Foot.
Baron Franks.
Baron Fraser of Kilmorack.
Baron Fraser of Lonsdale.
*Baron Fraser of Tullybelton.
Baron Fulton.
Baron Gardiner.
Baron Garner.
Baron Geddes of Epsom.
Baron Geoffrey-Lloyd.
Baron George-Brown.
Baron Gibson.
Baron Glenkinglas.
*Baron Goddard.
Baron Goodman.
Baron Gordon-Walker.
Baron Gore-Booth.
Baron Goronwy-Roberts.
Baron Granville of Eye.
Baron Granville-West.

Baron Greene of Harrow Weald.
Baron Greenhill of Harrow.
Baron Greenwood of Rossendale.
Baron Grey of Naunton.
*Baron Guest.
Baron Hailsham of St. Marylebone.
Baron Hale.
Baron Hamnett.
Baron Harmer-Nicholls.
Baron Harris of Greenwich.
Baron Hartwell.
Baron Harvey of Prestbury.
Baron Harvington.
Baron Helsby.
Baron Hewlett.
Baron Heycock.
Baron Hill of Luton.
Baron Hilton of Upton.
Baron Hinton of Bankside.
Baron Hirshfield.
*Baron Hodson.
Baron Holford.
Baron Home of the Hirsel.
Baron Houghton of Sowerby.
Baron Hoy.
Baron Hughes.
Baron Hunt.
Baron Hunt of Fawley.
Baron Jacques.
Baron James of Rusholme.
Baron Janner.
Baron Kahn.
Baron Kaldor.
Baron Kearton.
*Baron Kilbrandon.
Baron Kilmany.
Baron King-Hall.
Baron Kings Norton.
Baron Kissin.
Baron Leatherland.
Baron Lee of Newton.
Baron Lever.
Baron Lindgren.
Baron Llewelyn-Davies.
Baron Lloyd of Hampstead.
Baron Lloyd of Kilgerran.
Baron Lovell-Davis.
Baron Lyons of Brighton.
*Baron MacDermott.
Baron McFadzean.
Baron Mackie of Benshie.
Baron Maclean.
Baron McLeavy.
Baron MacLeod of Fuinary.
Baron Maelor.
Baron Mais.
Baron Marples.
Baron Maybray-King.
Baron Moison.
*Baron Morris of Borth-y-Gest.
Baron Morris of Grasmere.
*Baron Morton of Henryton.
Baron Moyle.
Baron Moyola.
Baron Murray of Newhaven.
Baron Normand.
Baron Nugent of Guildford.
Baron O'Brien of Lothbury.
Baron Olivier.
Baron O'Neill of The Maine.
Baron Orr-Ewing.
Baron Paget of Northampton.
Baron Pannell.
Baron Pargiter.
*Baron Pearce.
*Baron Pearson.
Baron Peddie.
Baron Penney.
Baron Pilkington.
Baron Pitt of Hampstead.
Baron Platt.
Baron Plowden.
Baron Plurenden.
Baron Popplewell.
Baron Porritt.
Baron Pritchard.
Baron Redcliffe-Maud.
Baron Redmayne.
Baron Reigate.
Baron Rhodes.
Baron Rhyl.
Baron Ritchie-Calder.
Baron Robbins.
Baron Robens of Woldingham.
Baron Roberthall.
Baron Rosenheim.
Baron Russell of Killowen.

Baron Ryder of Eaton Hastings.
Baron Sainsbury.
*Baron Salmon.
Baron Seebohm.
Baron Segal.
Baron Shackleton.
Baron Shawcross.
Baron Shinwell.
Baron Simon of Glaisdale.
Baron Slater.
Baron Snow.
Baron Soper.
Baron Stokes.
Baron Stonham.
Baron Stow Hill.
Baron Tanlaw.
Baron Taylor.
Baron Taylor of Mansfield.
Baron Taylor of Gryfe.
Baron Thomas.
Baron Thorneycroft.
Baron Todd.
Baron Tranmire.

Baron Trend.
Baron Trevelyan.
Baron Wade.
Baron Wallace of Campsie.
Baron Wallace of Coslany.
Baron Walston.
Baron Watkins.
Baron Wells-Pestell.
Baron Wheatley.
*Baron Widgery.
Baron Wigg.
Baron Wigoder.
*Baron Wilberforce.
Baron Williamson.
Baron Willis.
Baron Wilson of Langside.
Baron Wilson of Radcliffe.
Baron Winterbottom.
Baron Wolfenden.
Baron Woolley.
Baron Wright of Ashton under Lyne.
Baron Wynne-Jones.
Baron Zuckerman.

LIFE PEERESSES

Baroness Bacon.
Baroness Birk.
Baroness Brooke of Ystradfellte.
Baroness Burton of Coventry.
Baroness Delacourt-Smith of Alteryn.
Baroness Elles.
Baroness Elliot of Harwood.
Baroness Emmet of Amberley.
Baroness Falkender.
Baroness Fisher of Rednal.
Baroness Gaitskell.
Baroness Hornsby-Smith.
Baroness Hylton-Foster.
Baroness Lee of Asheridge.
Baroness Llewelyn-Davies of Hastoe.
Baroness Macleod of Borve.
Baroness Masham of Ilton.
Baroness Northchurch (*Viscountess Davidson*).

Baroness Phillips.
Baroness Pike.
Baroness Robson of Kiddington.
Baroness Seear.
Baroness Serota.
Baroness Sharp.
Baroness Sharples.
Baroness Spencer-Churchill.
Baroness Stedman.
Baroness Stewart of Alvechurch.
Baroness Summerskill.
Baroness Tweedsmuir of Belhevie.
Baroness Vickers.
Baroness Ward of North Tyneside.
Baroness White.
Baroness Wootton of Abinger.
Baroness Young.

HEREDITARY PEERESSES IN THEIR OWN RIGHT

*OF ENGLAND. † OF SCOTLAND. ‡ OF THE UNITED KINGDOM.

*BERKELEY, Baroness.
* BERNERS, Baroness.
†DACRE, Baroness.
*DARCY DE KNAYTH, Baroness.
* DE ROS, Baroness.
*DUDLEY, Baroness.
†DYSART, Countess of.
†ERROLL, Countess of.
*HERRIES OF TERREGLES, Lady.
†KINLOSS, Lady.

†LOUDOUN, Countess of.
*LUCAS OF CRUDWELL AND †DINGWALL, Baroness
*MAR, COUNTESS OF.
†NAIRNE, Lady.
†NEWBURGH, Countess of.
‡PORTAL OF HUNGERFORD, Baroness.
†RUTHVEN OF FREELAND, Lady.
†SEMPILL, Lady.
†SUTHERLAND, Countess of.

PEERS WHO ARE MINORS
AND THE DATES WHEN THEY ARE ELIGIBLE TO SIT IN THE HOUSE OF LORDS.*

CRAVEN, Earl of. Aug. 23rd, 1978.
FAIRFAX OF CAMERON, Lord. Jan. 3rd, 1977.
HARDWICKE, Earl of. Feb. 2nd, 1992.

LONDESBOROUGH, Baron. July 1st 1981.
MILFORD HAVEN, Marquess of. June 5th, 1982.
WOOLTON, Earl of. May 23rd, 1979.

* Legally persons are deemed to obtain their majority, so far as sitting in the House of Lords is concerned on completion of their twenty-first year (i.e. on the day prior to the twenty-first anniversary of their birth)

LIFE PEERAGES GAZETTED AFTER THE PEERAGE SECTION
WENT TO PRESS

Baron Barnetson.
Baron Bradwell.
Baron Brookes.
Baron Carr of Hadley.
Baroness Faithfull.
Baron Gregson.
Baron Jacobson.

Baron Kirkhall.
Baron McCarthy.
Baron Northfield of Telford.
Baron Oram.
Baron Parry.
Baron Schon.
Baron Winstanley.

THE ORDER OF SUCCESSION

1. H.R.H. The Prince of Wales
2. H.R.H. The Prince Andrew
3. H.R.H. The Prince Edward
4. H.R.H. The Princess Anne
5. H.R.H. The Princess Margaret, Countess of Snowdon
6. Viscount Linley
7. Lady Sarah Armstrong-Jones
8. H.R.H. The Duke of Gloucester
9. Earl of Ulster
10. H.R.H. The Duke of Kent
11. Earl of St. Andrews
12. Lord Nicholas Windsor
13. Lady Helen Windsor
14. H.R.H. Prince Michael of Kent
15. H.R.H. Princess Alexandra, the Hon. Mrs. Angus Ogilvy
16. James Robert Bruce Ogilvy
17. Marina Victoria Alexandra Ogilvy
18. The Earl of Harewood
19. Viscount Lascelles
20. Hon. James E. Lascelles
21. Hon. Robert J. H. Lascelles
22. Hon. Gerald D. Lascelles
23. Henry U. Lascelles
24. The Duke of Fife
25. Earl of Macduff

THE QUEEN'S HOUSEHOLD.

BUCKINGHAM PALACE.

Lord Chamberlain	The Lord Maclean, KT, GCVO, KBE.
Lord Steward	The Duke of Northumberland, KG, TD.
Master of the Horse	The Duke of Beaufort, KG, GCVO.
Mistress of the Robes	The Duchess of Grafton, DCVO.
Lords in Waiting	Brigadier the Lord Tryon, GCVO, KCB, DSO (Permanent). Lord Cobbold, KG, GCVO (Permanent). The Earl of Westmorland, KCVO. The Lord Hamilton of Dalzell, MC. The Lord Jacques. The Lords Wells-Pestell. The Lord Winterbottom. The Baroness Stedman, OBE (Baroness in Waiting).
Captain of the Gentlemen at Arms	The Baroness Llewelyn-Davies of Hastoe.
Captain of the Yeomen of the Guard	The Lord Strabolgi.
Treasurer of the Household	Walter Harrison, MP.
Comptroller of the Household	Joseph Harper, MP.
Vice-Chamberlain of the Household	James Hamilton, MP.
Ladies in Waiting	The Marchioness of Abergavenny, CVO. The Countess of Airlie. Hon. Mary Morrison, CVO. Lady Susan Hussey, CVO. Lady Abel Smith, CVO. Mrs. John Dugdale, CVO.

PRIVATE SECRETARY'S OFFICE.

Private Secretary and Keeper of The Queen's Archives	Lt.-Col. the Rt. Hon. Sir Martin Charteris, GCVO, KCB, OBE.
Deputy Private Secretary	Philip Moore, CB, CMG.
Assistant Private Secretary	William Heseltine, CVO.
Chief Clerk	Miss Jean Taylor, CVO.
Press Secretary	Ronald Allison.
Assistant Press Secretaries	Mrs. Michael Wall, CVO. Rodney Moore.
Assistant Keeper of The Queen's Archives	Sir Robert Mackworth-Young, KCVO, FSA.
Defence Services Secretary	Air Vice Marshal Brian Stanbridge, CBE, MVO, AFC.

DEPARTMENT OF THE KEEPER OF THE PRIVY PURSE AND TREASURER TO THE QUEEN.

Keeper of the Privy Purse and Treasurer to The Queen	Major Sir Rennie Maudslay, KCVO, MBE.
Assistant Keeper of the Privy Purse	Major Shane Blewitt.
Deputy Treasurer to The Queen	Russell Wood, MVO, VRD.
Privy Purse, Chief Accountant	Edmund Grove, CVO.
Treasurer's Office, Chief Accountant and Paymaster	Charles Warner, CVO.
Establishment Officer	Peter Wright, MVO.
High Almoner	The Bishop of Rochester (The Rt. Rev. David Say).
Secretary, Royal Almonry	Peter Wright, MVO.

MASTER OF THE HOUSEHOLD'S DEPARTMENT.

Master of the Household	Vice Admiral Sir Peter Ashmore, KCB, MVO, DSC.
Chief Clerk	Gordon Franklin, MVO.

LORD CHAMBERLAIN'S OFFICE.

Comptroller	Lt.-Col. Sir Eric Penn, KCVO, OBE, MC.
Assistant Comptroller	Lt.-Col. John Johnston, MVO, MC.
Secretary	David Buchanan, MVO.
Marshal of the Diplomatic Corps	Major General Lord Michael Fitzalan Howard, KCVO, CB, CBE, MC.
Vice Marshal	Roger du Boulay, CMG, CVO.
Assistant Marshals	Geoffrey Collins. Stanley Martin.
Surveyor of The Queen's Pictures	Sir Oliver Millar, KCVO, FBA, FSA.
Surveyor of The Queen's Works of Art	Geoffrey de Bellaigue, MVO.
Librarian, Royal Library	Sir Robert Mackworth-Young, KCVO, FSA.
Secretary, Central Chancery of the Orders of Knighthood	Major General Peter Gillett, CB, CVO, OBE.

Gentlemen at Arms	
Lieutenant	Colonel Kenneth Savill, DSO.
Clerk of the Cheque and Adjutant	Lt.-Col. Peter Clifton, DSO.
Yeomen of the Guard	
Lieutenant	Lt.-Col. Sir John Hornung, KCVO, OBE, MC.
Clerk of the Cheque and Adjutant	Colonel Hugh Brassey, OBE, MC.
Royal Company of Archers	
Captain General	Colonel the Earl of Stair, CVO, MBE.
Adjutant	Major Sir Hew Hamilton-Dalrymple, Bt, CVO.
Clerk of the Closet	The Rt. Rev. Roger Wilson, KCVO, DD.
Deputy Clerk of the Closet	The Rev. Canon James Mansel, MVO, FSA.
Dean of the Chapels Royal	The Bishop of London (The Rt. Rev. Gerald Ellison).
Sub-Dean of the Chapels Royal	The Rev. Canon James Mansel, MVO, FSA.
Dean of the Chapel Royal in Scotland	The Very Rev. Hugh Douglas, CBE, DD, LLD.
Physician and Head of the Medical Household	Richard Bayliss, MD, FRCP.
Serjeant Surgeon	Hugh Lockhart-Mummery, MD, MChir, FRCS.
Apothecary to The Queen	Nigel Southward, MB, BChir, MRCP.
Windsor Castle	
Constable and Governor	Marshal of the Royal Air Force the Lord Elworthy, GCB, CBE, DSO, MVO, DFC, AFC.
Superintendent	Major William Nash, MBE.
Palace of Holyroodhouse	
Hereditary Keeper	The Duke of Hamilton and Brandon.
Superintendent	Lt.-Col. George Soper, OBE.

CROWN EQUERRY'S DEPARTMENT.

Crown Equerry	Lt.-Col. Sir John Miller, KCVO, DSO, MC.
Equerry	Major Robin Broke.
Superintendent, Royal Mews	Major William Phelps, MBE.

THE DUKE OF EDINBURGH'S HOUSEHOLD.
Buckingham Palace.

Private Secretary	
Treasurer	Lord Rupert Nevill.
Equerry	Major Henry Hugh Smith.
Chief Clerk and Accountant	Leslie Treby, CVO, MBE, BEM.

QUEEN ELIZABETH THE QUEEN MOTHER'S HOUSEHOLD.
Clarence House.

Lord Chamberlain	The Earl of Dalhousie, KT, GBE, MC.
Mistress of the Robes	The Duchess of Abercorn, DCVO.
Private Secretary	Lt.-Col. Sir Martin Gilliat, KCVO, MBE.
Treasurer	Major Sir Ralph Anstruther, Bt., CVO, MC.
Comptroller	Captain Alastair Aird, MVO.
Press Secretary	Major John Griffin, CVO.
Equerry	Captain James Duncan Miller.
Ladies in Waiting	The Dowager Viscountess Hambleden, DCVO. The Lady Grimthorpe. Lady Jean Rankin, DCVO. Hon. Mrs. John Mulholland, DCVO. The Dowager Lady Fermoy, CVO, OBE. Mrs. Patrick Campbell Preston.
Clerk Comptroller	Malcolm Blanch, MVO.

THE PRINCE OF WALES'S HOUSEHOLD.
Buckingham Palace.

Private Secretary	Squadron Leader David Checketts, CVO.

THE PRINCESS ANNE, MRS. MARK PHILLIPS' HOUSEHOLD.
Buckingham Palace.

Private Secretary	Major Benjamin Herman, MVO, RM.
Lady in Waiting	Miss Rowena Brassey, MVO.

THE PRINCESS MARGARET, COUNTESS OF SNOWDON'S HOUSEHOLD.
Kensington Palace.

Treasurer	Major Sir Francis Legh, KCVO.
Private Secretary and Comptroller	Major the Lord Napier and Ettrick.
Lady in Waiting	Hon. Davina Woodhouse.
Personal Secretary	Miss Muriel Murray Brown.

PRINCESS ALICE, DUCHESS OF GLOUCESTER'S HOUSEHOLD.
Kensington Palace.

Private Secretary and Compt	Lt.-Col. Simon Bland, CVO.
Ladies in Waiting	Miss Jean Maxwell-Scott, CVO. Miss Jane Egerton-Warburton (Temporary).

THE DUKE AND DUCHESS OF GLOUCESTER'S HOUSEHOLD.
Kensington Palace.

Private Secretary and Comptroller............... Lt.-Col. Simon Bland, CVO.
Ladies in Waiting .... { Mrs. Michael Wigley.
                                                { Miss Jennifer Thomson.

THE DUKE AND DUCHESS OF KENT'S HOUSEHOLD.
St. James's Palace.

Treasurer .... Sir Philip Hay, KCVO, TD.
Private Secretary .... Lt.-Cdr. Richard Buckley, CVO, RN.
Ladies in Waiting .... { Mrs. Alan Henderson.
                                               { Miss Jane Pugh.

PRINCE MICHAEL OF KENT'S HOUSEHOLD.
Kensington Palace.

Treasurer .... Sir Philip Hay, KCVO, TD.

PRINCESS ALEXANDRA, HON. MRS. ANGUS OGILVY'S HOUSEHOLD.
Kensington Palace.

Lady in Waiting .... Lady Mary Fitzalan-Howard, MVO.
Private Secretary .... Miss Mona Mitchell.

PRINCESS ALICE, COUNTESS OF ATHLONE'S HOUSEHOLD.
Kensington Palace.

Lady in Waiting .... Miss Joan Lascelles.
Secretary .... Miss Mary Goldie, CVO.

HER MAJESTY'S

OFFICERS OF ARMS.

ENGLAND.

COLLEGE OF ARMS, QUEEN VICTORIA STREET, E.C.4.

— ⋘ ⟨⋯⟩ ⋙ —

EARL MARSHAL—His Grace the Duke of Norfolk, CB, CBE, MC.

KINGS OF ARMS.

Garter—Sir Anthony Richard Wagner, KCVO, DLitt, MA, FSA.
Clarenceux—John Riddell Bromhead Walker, Esq., MVO, MC.
Norroy and Ulster (and Secretary to Earl Marshal)—Walter John George Verco, Esq., CVO.

HERALDS.

Windsor—Alexander Colin Cole Esq., BCL, MA, FSA.

Richmond (and Registrar)—John Philip Brooke Brooke-Little, Esq., MVO, MA, FSA.

Somerset—Rodney Onslow Dennys, Esq., MVO, OBE, FSA.

York—Conrad Marshall John Fisher Swan, Esq., PhD, MA, FSA.

Lancaster—Francis Sedley Andrus, Esq., MA.

Chester—Vacant.

PURSUIVANTS.

Portcullis—Michael Maclagan, Esq., MA, FSA.

Rouge Croix—David Hubert Boothby Chesshyre, Esq., MA.

Rouge Dragon — Theobald David Mathew, Esq., BA.

Bluemantle—Peter Llewellyn Gwynn-Jones, Esq., MA.

Norfolk Herald Extraordinary—George Drewry Squibb, Esq., QC, BCL, MA, FSA.

Wales Herald Extraordinary—Maj. Francis Jones, CVO, TD, MA, FSA, DL.

Maltravers Herald Extraordinary—Francis William Steer, Esq., MA, FSA.

Fitzalan Pursuivant Extraordinary—Charles Wilfrid Scott-Giles, Esq., OBE, MA, FSA.

SCOTLAND.

LYON COURT, H.M. NEW REGISTER HOUSE, EDINBURGH.

—⋅∤⋅—

LORD LYON KING OF ARMS—Sir James Monteith Grant, KCVO, MA, LLB, WS, FSA(Scot.)

HERALDS.

Rothesay—Lt.-Col. Harold Andrew Balvaird Lawson, CVO, FSA(Scot.).
Albany—Sir (Rupert) Iain Kay Moncreiffe of that Ilk, Bt., PhD, MA, FSA.
Marchmont—Malcolm Rognvald Innes of Edingight, MA, WS, LLB, FSA(Scot.).

PURSUIVANTS.

Unicorn—John Inglis Drever Pottinger, Esq., MA.
Ormond—Maj. David Maitland Maitland-Titterton, TD, MA, FSA(Scot.).
Carrick—John Alexander Spens, Esq., RD, BA, LLB.
Falkland—Peter de Vere Beauclerk-Dewar, Esq.

A GUIDE TO THE WEARING OF
ORDERS, DECORATIONS, MINIATURES AND MEDALS
WITH DRESS OTHER THAN UNIFORM

[*By courtesy of The Secretary, Central Chancery of Orders of Knighthood,* 1971]

1. Introduction

Members of the various Orders of Chivalry and all persons who have been awarded Decorations and Medals may, should they wish to do so, wear their Insignia on those occasions when the person responsible for a function deems it fitting for Decorations to be worn. This Memorandum gives guidance on the wearing of Orders, Decorations, Miniatures and Medals with Full Evening Dress, Dinner Jacket, Morning Dress, Lounge Suit and Overcoats and supersedes all previous instructions on this subject.

2. Full Evening Dress

(*a*) The occasions when Decorations may be worn can be divided into two categories:

(i) **When The Queen, The Queen Mother or a Member of the Royal Family who is a Royal Highness is present.** The host should ascertain from the Member of the appropriate Household whether it is desired that Decorations should be worn.

(ii) **On all other occasions.** The host should decide whether the nature or importance of the occasion makes it appropriate for Decorations to be worn and then issue instructions on the Invitation Cards.

On occasions when it is desired that Decorations be worn, Invitations should state " Evening Dress—Decorations ".

(*b*) The method of wearing Orders, Decorations and Miniatures when "Decorations " are prescribed is as follows:

(i) **Knights of the Garter and Knights of the Thistle; Knights and Dames Grand Cross, Knights Grand Commanders.**
Broad Riband and Badge of the senior British Order, unless it is more appropriate on certain occasions to wear the Riband and Badge of a junior British or Foreign Order.
Up to four Stars may be worn on the left side of the coat or dress. When wearing more than one Star the precedence of the position of each Star is (looking at the wearer):

Four Stars:	Three Stars:	Two Stars:
1	1	1
2 3	2 3	2
4		

One neck Badge suspended on a ribbon (miniature width) of the Order is worn under the collar and hanging close up below the tie. Miniature Badges of all Orders and Medals are worn on a medal bar. (The Garter, Thistle, Order of Merit, Crown of India, Companion of Honour and Baronet's Badge are not worn in Miniature.) Collars are not worn.

(ii) **Knights and Dames Commanders.** Up to four Stars may be worn on the left side of the coat or dress as in (i) above. One neck Badge suspended on a ribbon (miniature width) of the Order is worn under the collar and hanging close up below the tie. Miniature Badges of all Orders, Decorations and Medals are worn on a medal bar. (The Order of Merit, Crown of India, Companion of Honour and Baronet's Badge are not worn in Miniature). The Ladies' Badge is worn on a bow, below the Miniatures, on the left side.

(iii) **Companions and Commanders.** One neck Badge suspended on a ribbon (miniature width) of the Order is worn under the collar and hanging close up below the tie. Miniature Badges of all Orders, Decorations and Medals are worn on a medal bar. (The Order of Merit and Companion of Honour Badge are not worn in Miniature.) The Badges of a Companion of the Distinguished Service Order or Imperial Service Order are worn in Miniature on a medal bar and not as a neck Badge. The Ladies' Badge is worn on a bow, below the Miniatures, on the left side.

(iv) **Officers and Members.** Miniature Badges are worn on a medal bar.

(v) **Order of Merit, Companion of Honour.** These are neck Badges suspended on a ribbon (miniature width) of the Order worn under the collar and hanging close up below the tie. Only one neck Badge may be worn. Miniature Badges of all other Orders, Decorations and Medals are worn on a medal bar. (The Order of Merit and Companions of Honour Badges are not worn in Miniature.) The Ladies' Badge is worn on a bow, below the Miniatures, on the left side.

(vi) **Baronet.** This Badge is worn as a neck Badge suspended on a ribbon (miniature width) worn under the collar and hanging close up below the tie. Miniature Badges of all other Orders, Decorations and Medals are worn on a medal bar. (The Baronet's Badge is not worn in Miniature.)

(vii) **Knight Bachelor.** This Badge is worn as an Order Star. Alternatively, in smaller dimensions as a neck Badge suspended on a ribbon (miniature width) worn under the collar and hanging close up below the tie. The Badge is also worn in Miniature on a medal bar in the same manner as Miniature Badges of Orders, Decorations and Medals.

(viii) **The Royal Victorian Chain.** This Chain is worn round the neck by men in place of a neck Badge and is adapted for wear by Ladies on a bow of the ribbon of the Order and worn on the left side above Miniatures.

At all times when " Evening Dress—Decorations " is prescribed, those not in possession of Full Evening Dress may wear a Dinner Jacket with Decorations as described in the next paragraph.

3. Dinner Jacket

(*a*) On occasions when it is desired that Dinner Jackets (and not Full Evening Dress) with Decorations are to be worn, Invitations should state " Dinner Jacket—Decorations ".

In addition to Miniatures, only one Star (or the Badge of a Knight Bachelor) and one neck Badge may be worn.

(*b*) The method of wearing Orders, Decorations, Miniatures and Medals with a Dinner Jacket is as follows:

(i) **Knights of the Garter, Knights of the Thistle; Knights Grand Cross, Knights Grand Commanders.** One Star is worn on the left breast. Miniature Badges of all Orders, Decorations and Medals are worn on a medal bar. (The Garter, Thistle, Order of Merit, Crown of India, Companion of Honour and Baronet's Badge are not worn in Miniature.) Neither Collar nor Broad Riband and Badge will be worn.

(ii) **Knights Commanders.** One Star is worn on the left breast and one neck Badge suspended on a ribbon (miniature width) of the Order is worn under the collar and hanging close up below the tie. Miniature Badges of all Orders, Decorations and Medals are worn on a medal bar. (The Order of Merit, Crown of India, Companion of Honour and Baronet's Badge are not worn in Miniature.)

(iii) **Companions and Commanders.** One neck Badge suspended on a ribbon (miniature width) of the Order is worn under the collar and hanging close up below the tie. Miniature Badges of all Orders, Decorations and Medals are worn on a medal bar. (The Order of Merit and Companion of Honour Badge are not worn in Miniature.) The Badges of a Companion of the Distinguished Service Order or Imperial Service Order are worn in Miniature on a medal bar and not as a neck Badge.

(iv) **Officers and Members.** Miniature Badges are worn on a medal bar.

(v) **Order of Merit, Companion of Honour.** These are neck Badges suspended on a ribbon (miniature width) of the Order worn under the collar and hanging close up below the tie. Only one neck Badge may be worn. These Badges are not worn in Miniature.

(vi) **Baronet.** This Badge is worn as a neck Badge suspended on a ribbon (miniature width) worn under the collar and hanging close up below the tie. This Badge is not worn in Miniature.

(vi) **Knight Bachelor**. This Badge is worn as an Order Star. Alternatively, in smaller dimensions as a neck Badge suspended on a ribbon (miniature width) worn under the collar and hanging close up below the tie. The Badge is also worn in Miniature on a medal bar in the same manner as Miniature Badges of Orders, Decorations and Medals.

(viii) **The Royal Victorian Chain.** The Chain may be worn round the neck in place of a neck Badge.

(*c*) **Ladies.** The regulations for the wearing of Orders, Decorations and Medals by Ladies are the same as in paragraph 2 (*b*) (ii) above.

4. Morning Dress

(*a*) The occasions when Orders, Decorations and Medals are worn with Morning Dress are comparatively rare. Such occasions may include special official public functions, religious Services connected with the Orders of Chivalry or Memorial Services. In each case the sponsor of the function or service should indicate whether the wearing of Decorations would be appropriate. When Decorations are prescribed with Morning Dress not more than four Stars, one neck Badge and full size Medals should be worn. If a Star and neck Badge are worn they must be of different Orders.

Even so, on all such occasions the wearing of Insignia will be at the discretion of the holder.

(*b*) The method of wearing Orders, Decorations and Medals, when Decorations with Morning Dress are prescribed, is as follows:

(i) **Knights of the Garter, Knights of the Thistle; Knights and Dames Grand Cross, Knights Grand Commanders.** One Star only is worn on the left breast or, for Ladies, in a corresponding place on the dress. The Broad Riband and Badge is worn. Collars are only worn with Morning Dress if ordered for a special occasion.

(ii) **Knights and Dames Commanders.** One Star only is worn on the left breast or, for Ladies, in a corresponding place on the dress. The neck Badge of a Knight Commander or the corresponding Badge of a Dame Commander may only be worn if belonging to a second Order. If worn with full-size Medals the Ladies' Badge, on a bow, is worn below the medal bar.

(iii) **Companions and Commanders.** One neck Badge suspended on a ribbon (miniature width) of the Order is worn under the collar. The Badge should hang three quarters of an inch below the tie knot in front of the tie. The Ladies' Badge is worn on a bow on the left side. If worn with full-size Medals the Badge is worn below the medal bar.

(iv) **Officers and Members.** The full-size Badge, whether worn singly or mounted on a medal bar, is worn on the left side in the same manner with civilian dress as with uniform. Companions of the Distinguished Service Order or Imperial Service Order wear their Insignia in this manner and not as a neck decoration. The Ladies' Badge, if worn separately, is worn on a bow on the left side of the dress. If worn with other Medals it is normally mounted on a medal bar and worn in the same manner with civilian dress as with uniform.

(v) **Order of Merit, Companion of Honour.** One neck Badge suspended on a ribbon (miniature width) of the Order is worn under the collar. The Badge should hang three quarters of an inch below the tie knot in front of the tie. The Ladies' Badge is worn on a bow on the left side. If worn with full-size Medals the Badge is worn below the medal bar.

(vi) **Baronet.** This Badge is worn as a neck Badge, suspended on a ribbon (miniature width) under the collar. The Badge should hang three quarters of an inch below the tie knot in front of the tie.

(vii) **Knight Bachelor.** This Badge is worn on the left breast as an Order Star. Alternatively, in smaller dimensions as a neck Badge suspended on a ribbon (miniature width) under the collar. The Badge should hang three quarters of an inch below the tie knot in front of the tie.

(viii) **The Royal Victorian Chain.** The Chain may be worn round the neck in place of a neck Badge.

5. Lounge Suit

(*a*) There are some occasions, such as Remembrance Sunday Services or Regimental gatherings, at which those attending are requested to wear Medals with lounge suits. On such occasions it is not customary to wear either Broad Ribands with Badges, Stars or the Royal Victorian Chain. One neck Badge, suspended on a ribbon (miniature width) of the Order, worn under the collar and hanging close up below the tie knot in front of the tie; full-size Insignia mounted on a medal bar and worn on the left side as with uniform. On all such occasions the wearing of Insignia will be at the discretion of the holder.

(*b*) Appropriate strips of Ribbon, unattached to any Insignia, of Orders, Decorations and Medals may be worn on all occasions with all forms of civilian dress at the discretion of the holder. If worn they should be sewn on the coat or dress or on to a medal bar and worn on the left hand side.

6. Overcoats

Full-size Medals may be worn on an overcoat, on the left hand side. No other insignia should be worn.

FOREIGN AND COMMONWEALTH ORDERS.

A

Regulations concerning the Acceptance and Wearing by Persons in the Service of the Crown of Orders, Decorations and Medals conferred by Heads or Governments of Foreign States and by Members of the Commonwealth Overseas of which The Queen is not the Head of State.

(United Kingdom and Dependent Territories)

ORDERS AND DECORATIONS

1.   No person in the service of the Crown may accept and wear the insignia of any Order or decoration without Her Majesty's permission.

2.   Such permission, if granted, will be either
   (a) unrestricted, allowing the insignia to be worn on any occasion; or
   (b) restricted, allowing the insignia to be worn only on particular occasions associated with the country concerned.

The grant of both unrestricted and restricted permission will be conveyed by letter from Her Majesty's Private Secretary.

3.   Full and unrestricted permission is contemplated in the case of Orders conferred:
   (a) for distinguished services in saving or attempting to save life.
   (b) on any officer in the Royal Navy, Army or Royal Air Force, or any United Kingdom official, in recognition of services (a) while lent to a Commonwealth Government or (b) while lent to a foreign Government provided that he is not in receipt of any emoluments from British public funds during the period of the loan.

4.   Restricted permission is particularly contemplated in the case of Orders or decorations conferred in recognition of personal attention to a Head of State, or a member of the Royal Family of a foreign or Commonwealth country, on the occasion of State or official visits by such personages.

5.   Restricted permission will also be given for the wearing of insignia of Orders and decorations conferred:
   (1) on United Kingdom officials in connection with a State visit by Her Majesty The Queen;
   (2) on members of deputations of British regiments to Heads of States;
   (3) on members of Special Missions when The Queen is represented at a Coronation, Wedding, Funeral, or similar occasion; or on any Diplomatic Representative, when specially accredited to represent Her Majesty on such occasions (but not on the members of his Staff).

Permission will *not* be given to:
   (a) the Heads or other members of Her Majesty's Diplomatic or Consular establishments abroad, when leaving, whether on transfer or on final retirement;
   (b) officers of British naval, military or air squadrons or units visiting foreign countries and Member countries of the Commonwealth overseas, except as provided at (2) above.

6. Applications for The Queen's permission, whether full or restricted, will be submitted to Her Majesty by Her Principal Secretary of State for Foreign and Commonwealth Affairs, who however shall be under no obligation to consider them unless, before the bestowal of the Order or decoration, the country concerned has ascertained through the British Diplomatic Representative there or through its Diplomatic Representative at Her Majesty's Court, that having regard to these Regulations the award would not give rise to any objection.

In no case can applications be considered in respect of Orders conferred more than five years previously, or offered in connection with events so long prior to the proposal to award them.

7.   Permission will not be granted for the wearing of the insignia of Orders and decorations conferred otherwise than by the Heads or Governments of States recognised by Her Majesty as such.

MEDALS*

8. Medals with the exceptions specified below, and State decorations not indicating membership of an Order of Chivalry, are subject to the Regulations in the same manner as Orders. If granted, unrestricted permission is given by letter, restricted permission is given by certificate.

9. Medals for saving or attempting to save life whether conferred on behalf of the Head of Government of a foreign or Commonwealth State or by private Life-Saving Societies or Institutions, may be accepted and worn, subject only to the restrictions imposed by the Regulations for the Services concerned.

Applications for Her Majesty's permission to wear other medals conferred by Private Societies or Institutions cannot be entertained.

10. Applications for permission to wear medals gained in warlike operations will not be entertained if the grant of such permission would be at variance with considerations of general policy or public interest.

GENERAL

11. The wives of persons in the service of the Crown are regarded for the purposes of these Regulations as sharing the disabilities of their husbands concerning the acceptance of foreign or Commonwealth awards.

12. Persons employed in the commissioned or salaried service of the Crown on a temporary basis are subject to these Regulations in the same way as those employed on a permanent and pensionable basis.

B

Regulations concerning the Acceptance and Wearing by Persons NOT in the Service of the Crown of Orders, Decorations and Medals conferred by Heads or Governments of Foreign States and by Members of the Commonwealth Overseas of which the Queen is not the Head of State.

(United Kingdom and Dependent Territories)

ORDERS AND DECORATIONS

1. It is the Queen's wish that Her Majesty's subjects should not accept and wear the insignia of any Order or decoration without Her Majesty's permission.

2. Permission, if granted, will allow the insignia to be worn on any occasion, and will be conveyed by letter from Her Majesty's Private Secretary.

3. Permission will not be given:
    (a) when considerations of general policy or public interest must be held to preclude it;
    (b) in respect of Orders relating to services wholly rendered more than five years before the question of eligibility for permission is raised;
    (c) unless authoritative evidence of the award is forthcoming, preferably in the form of a notification through one of the channels prescribed in Rule 4.

4. Applications for The Queen's permission will be submitted to Her Majesty by Her Principal Secretary of State for Foreign and Commonwealth Affairs, who however shall be under no obligation to consider them unless, before the bestowal of the Order, the Government of the foreign or Commonwealth country concerned has ascertained, through the British Diplomatic Representative there or through its Diplomatic Representative at Her Majesty's Court, that having regard to these Regulations the award would not give rise to any objection.

5. Permission will not be granted for the wearing of the insignia of Orders and decorations conferred otherwise than by the Heads or Governments of States recognised by Her Majesty as such.

MEDALS*

6. Medals, with the exceptions specified below, and State decorations not indicating membership of an Order of Chivalry, are subject to the Regulations in the same manner as Orders. No permission is needed for the acceptance of a foreign or Commonwealth medal if it is not designed to be worn.

7. Medals for saving or attempting to save life, whether awarded by the Head or Government of a foreign or Commonwealth State or by private Life-Saving Societies or Institutions, may be accepted and worn without permission; but such medals, if given by private organisations, should be worn on the right breast and not on the left with State awards, and not more than two awards in all should be worn in relation to one act of bravery.

Applications for Her Majesty's permission to wear other medals conferred by Private Societies or Institutions cannot be entertained.

8. Applications for permission to wear foreign or Commonwealth medals gained in warlike operations will not be entertained if the grant of such permission would be at variance with considerations of general policy or public interest.

---

* These Regulations do not relate to awards of campaign or commemorative war medals.

GENERAL

9. The Regulations shall be regarded as applying, in the same way as to British subjects, to British-protected persons who are such by virtue of their connection with a Protectorate or Trust Territory administered under the supervision of Her Majesty's Principal Secretary of State for Foreign and Commonwealth Affairs; they may also be regarded as applying in the same manner to British-protected persons who are such by virtue of their connection with a Protected State administered under the supervision of the said Principal Secretary of State, but Orders, decorations and medals conferred upon such British-protected persons by their Rulers are not regarded as falling within the scope of these Regulations.

Foreign and Commonwealth Office, April 1969.

LIST OF PRINCIPAL COMMONWEALTH
AND FOREIGN ORDERS

Abu Dhabi.
ORDER OF AL NAHAYYAN

Afghanistan.
ORDER OF ALMAR-E-A'LA.
ORDER OF ALMAR-E-A'LI.
ORDER OF SARDAR-E-A'LA.
ORDER OF SARDAR-E-A'LI.
ORDER OF STOR.

Albania.
ORDER OF FREEDOM.
SKANDERBEG ORDER.
ORDER OF THE FLAG.
ORDER OF THE PARTISAN STAR.
ORDER OF THE RED STAR.

Argentina.
ORDER OF LIBERATOR SAN MARTIN.
ORDER OF MAY.

Australia.
ORDER OF AUSTRALIA.

Austria.
ORDER OF MERIT.
DECORATION OF HONOUR FOR SCIENCE
    AND THE ARTS.

Belgium.
ORDER OF LEOPOLD.
ORDER OF THE AFRICAN STAR.
ORDER OF THE LION.
ORDER OF THE CROWN.
ORDER OF LEOPOLD II.

Bolivia.
ORDER OF THE CONDOR OF THE ANDES.

Botswana.
PRESIDENTIAL ORDER OF MERITORIOUS
    SERVICE.
PRESIDENTIAL ORDER OF HONOUR.

Brazil.
ORDER OF THE SOUTHERN CROSS.
NATIONAL ORDER OF MERIT.
ORDER OF RIO BRANCO.
ORDER OF MILITARY MERIT.
ORDER OF NAVAL MERIT.
ORDER OF AERONAUTIC MERIT.

Brunei.
FAMILY ORDER.
ORDER OF PAHLAWAN NEGARA.
ORDER OF THE CROWN.
STIA NEGARA

Bulgaria.
ORDER OF GEORGI DIMITROV.
ORDER OF PEOPLE'S REPUBLIC.
ORDER OF 9TH SEPTEMBER 1944.
ORDER OF PEOPLE'S FREEDOM.
ORDER OF THE RED FLAG.
ORDER OF THE RED FLAG OF LABOUR.
ORDER OF BRAVERY.
PEOPLE'S ORDER OF LABOUR.
ORDER OF CYRIL AND METHODIUS.

Burma.
ORDER OF THUDHAMMA THINGAHA.
ORDER OF PYIDAUNGSU SITHU THINGAHA.

Cambodia.
[See KHMER REPUBLIC

Cameroon Republic.
ORDER OF VALOUR.
ORDER OF MERIT.
ORDER OF CO-OPERATIVE MERIT.

Canada.
ORDER OF CANADA.
ORDER OF MILITARY MERIT.

Central African Republic.
ORDER OF MERIT.

Chile.
ORDER OF MERIT.
ORDER OF BERNARDO O'HIGGINS.

China Peoples Republic.
ORDER OF THE BRILLIANT STAR.
ORDER OF THE PRECIOUS TRIPOD.
ORDER OF NATIONAL GLORY.
ORDER OF BLUE SKY AND WHITE SUN.
ORDER OF LOYALTY AND BRAVERY.
ORDER OF CLOUD AND BANNER.
ORDER OF LOYALTY AND DILIGENCE.
ORDER OF REJUVENATION.
AIR FORCE ORDER OF GREAT UNITY.
AIR FORCE ORDER OF HO-T'U.
AIR FORCE ORDER OF THE ANCIENT
    SYMBOLS.
AIR FORCE ORDER OF CH'LEN YUAN.

Colombia.
ORDER OF BOYACÁ.
ORDER OF SAN CARLOS.
ORDER OF ALMIRANTE PADILLA.
ORDER OF ANTONIO RICAURTE.
ORDER OF GENERAL JOSÉ MARIA CORDOBA.
ORDER OF ANTONIO NARIÑO.
ORDER OF JOSE FERNANDEZ MADRID.
ORDER OF ESTRELLA DE LA POLICIA.
ORDER OF MERITO INDUSTRIAL.

Congo=Brazzaville (People's Republic of the Congo).
ORDER OF CONGOLESE MERIT.

Cuba.
ORDER OF CARLOS MANUEL DE CESPEDES.
ORDER OF CARLOS J. FINLAY.
ORDER OF LANUZA.
ORDER OF JOSE MARIA HEREDIA.
ORDER OF AGRICULTURAL AND INDUSTRIAL
    MERIT.
ORDER OF COMMERCIAL MERIT.
ORDER OF THE RED CROSS.
ORDER OF MILITARY MERIT.
ORDER OF NAVAL MERIT.
ORDER OF POLITICAL MERIT.

Czechoslovakia.
ORDER OF MERIT.
ORDER OF THE WHITE LION FOR VICTORY.
ORDER OF THE WHITE LION.
ORDER OF THE GOLD STAR.
ORDER OF THE REPUBLIC.
ORDER OF SOCIALISM.
ORDER OF LABOUR.

Denmark.
ORDER OF THE ELEPHANT
ORDER OF THE DANNEBROG.

Dominican Republic.
ORDER OF MERIT OF JUAN PABLO DUARTE.
ORDER OF CHRISTOPHER COLUMBUS.
ORDER OF TRUJILLO.

Ecuador.
ORDER OF MERIT.
ORDER OF ABDÓN CALDERÓN.
ORDER OF SAN LORENZO.

Egypt, Arab Republic of.
ORDER OF THE NILE.
ORDER OF THE REPUBLIC.
ORDER OF MERIT.
ORDER OF AL KAMAL.
ORDER OF AGRICULTURE.
ORDER OF SPORTS.
ORDER OF COMMERCE AND INDUSTRY.
ORDER OF SCIENCES AND ARTS.

Ethiopia.
(suspended until further notice)
ORDER OF THE SEAL OF SOLOMON.
ORDER OF THE QUEEN OF SHEBA.
ORDER OF THE TRINITY.
ORDER OF MENELIK II.
ORDER OF THE STAR OF HONOUR.

Finland.
ORDER OF THE CROSS OF LIBERTY.
ORDER OF THE WHITE ROSE.
ORDER OF THE FINNISH LION.

France.
NATIONAL ORDER OF LEGION OF HONOUR.
ORDER OF THE LIBERATION.
NATIONAL ORDER OF MERIT.
ORDER OF ACADEMIC PALMS.
ORDER OF MARITIME MERIT.
ORDER OF AGRICULTURAL MERIT.
ORDER OF ARTS AND LETTERS.

Gabon.
ORDER OF EQUATORIAL STAR.
ORDER OF THE GABONESE MERIT.

Gambia.
ORDER OF THE REPUBLIC.

German Federal Republic.
ORDER OF MERIT.
ORDER OF MERIT FOR SCIENCE AND THE ARTS

Ghana.
ORDER OF THE STAR OF GHANA.
ORDER OF THE VOLTA.

Greece.
ORDER OF THE REDEEMER.
ORDER OF THE PHŒNIX.
ORDER OF BENEVOLENCE.

Guatemala.
ORDER OF THE QUETZAL.
ORDER OF THE REFORMER.
ORDER OF MILITARY MERIT.

Guyana.
ORDER OF EXCELLENCE.
ORDER OF SERVICE.

Haiti.
ORDER OF HONOUR AND OF MERIT.
ORDER OF TOUSSAINT L'OUVERTURE

Holland.
[See NETHERLANDS].

Holy See.
ORDER OF CHRIST.
ORDER OF THE GOLDEN SPUR.
ORDER OF PIUS.
ORDER OF ST. GREGORY THE GREAT
ORDER OF ST. SILVESTER.
ORDER OF THE HOLY SEPULCHRE OF JERUSALEM.

Honduras.
ORDER OF MORAZÁN.

Hungary.
ORDER OF HUNGARIAN PEOPLE'S REPUBLIC
ORDER OF THE RED BANNER.
ORDER OF THE RED BANNER OF LABOUR.
ORDER OF THE RED STAR.
ORDER OF LABOUR.
ORDER OF MERIT.

Iceland.
ORDER OF THE FALCON.

Iran.
ORDER OF THE PAHLAVI.
ORDER OF THE TAJ.
ORDER OF HOMAYOON.
ORDER OF THE KHORSHID (SUN).
ORDER OF THE HAFT PEIKAR.

Italy.
ORDER OF MERIT OF THE REPUBLIC.
MILITARY ORDER OF ITALY.
ORDER OF THE STAR OF ITALIAN SOLIDARITY.
ORDER OF MERIT OF LABOUR.

Ivory Coast.
NATIONAL ORDER OF IVORY COAST.

Jamaica.
ORDER OF NATIONAL HERO.
ORDER OF MERIT.
ORDER OF JAMAICA.
ORDER OF DISTINCTION.

Japan.
SUPREME ORDER OF THE CHRYSANTHEMUM.
ORDER OF THE RISING SUN.
ORDER OF THE PRECIOUS CROWN.
ORDER OF THE SACRED TREASURE.
ORDER OF CULTURE.

Jordan, Kingdom of.
ORDER OF QELADET EL HUSSEIN.
ORDER OF EL NAHDA.
ORDER OF EL KAWKAB.
ORDER OF EL ISTIQLAL.

Kenya.
ORDER OF THE GOLDEN HEARTS.
ORDER OF THE BURNING STAR.

Khmer Republic.
ORDER OF NATIONAL MERIT.
ORDER OF MERIT FOR THE SERVANT OF THE STATE.
ORDER OF THE REPUBLIC.
ORDER OF SAHAMETREI.
ORDER OF SOWATHARA.
ORDER OF MONISARAPHON.
ORDER OF INDUSTRIAL MERIT.
ORDER OF MERIT FOR THE WORKER.

Korea.
GRAND ORDER OF MUGUNGHWA.
ORDER OF MERIT OF NATIONAL FOUNDA-
TION.
ORDER OF MILITARY MERIT.
ORDER OF CIVIL MERIT.
ORDER OF SERVICE MERIT.
ORDER OF DISTINGUISHED DIPLOMATIC
SERVICE MERIT.
ORDERS OF CULTURAL MERIT.
ORDERS OF INDUSTRIAL SERVICE MERIT.

Laos.
ORDER OF THE MILLION ELEPHANTS AND
THE WHITE PARASOL.
ORDER OF THE REIGN.
ORDER OF CIVIL MERIT.
ORDER OF AGRICULTURE.
ORDER OF THE CROWN.

Lebanon.
ORDER OF THE CEDAR.
ORDER OF MERIT.

Liberia.
ORDER OF THE STAR OF AFRICA.
ORDER OF HUMANE AFRICAN REDEMPTION.
ORDER OF KNIGHTHOOD OF PIONEERS OF
THE REPUBLIC.
DISTINGUISHED SERVICE ORDER.

Libya.
ORDER OF COURAGE.
ORDER OF THE REPUBLIC.

Liechtenstein.
ORDER OF MERIT.

Luxembourg.
ORDER OF GOLDEN LION OF HOUSE OF
NASSAU.
ORDER OF ADOLPHUS OF NASSAU.
ORDER OF THE OAK CROWN.
ORDER OF MERIT.

Malagasy.
NATIONAL ORDER OF THE MALAGASY
REPUBLIC.
ORDER OF MERIT.
ORDER OF AGRICULTURAL MERIT.

Malawi.
GRAND ORDER OF THE LION.

Malaysia.
ORDER OF UTAMA KERABAT DI-RAJA
(ROYAL FAMILY).
ORDER OF MAHKOTA NEGARA (THE
CROWN).
ORDER OF PANGKUAN NEGARA (DEFENDER
OF THE REALM).
ORDER OF SETIA MAHKOTA (THE CROWN).

Johore.
ORDER OF DARJAH KARABAT (FAMILY
ORDER).
ORDER OF DARJAH MAHKOTA (THE
CROWN).

Kedah.
ORDER OF MERIT.

Kelantan.
ORDER OF AL-YUNUSI (FAMILY
ORDER).
ORDER OF AL-MOHAMMADI (THE
CROWN).

ORDER OF AL-ISMAILI (THE LIFE OF
THE CROWN).
ORDER OF PAHLAWAN YANG AMAT
GAGAH PERKASA (THE VALOROUS
WARRIOR).

Perak.
ORDER OF DARJAH KERABAT (FAMILY
ORDER).
ORDER OF PADUKA MAHKOTA (THE
CROWN).

Perlis.
ORDER OF THE ROYAL FAMILY.
ORDER OF THE CROWN OF PERLIS.

Sabah.
ORDER OF KINABALU

Sarawak.
ORDER OF THE STAR OF SARAWAK.

Selangor.
ORDER OF DARJAH KERABAT (FAMILY
ORDER).
ORDER OF PADUKA MAHKOTA.

Trengganu.
ORDER OF DARJAH KERABAT (FAMILY
ORDER).
ORDER OF PADUKA MAHKOTA.

Maldives.
ORDER OF GHAZEE.
ORDER OF IZZUDDIN.
ORDER OF SHAHEED ALI.
ORDER OF IBRAHIM.
MILITARY ORDER.

Mauritania.
ORDER OF THE ISLAMIC REPUBLIC.

Mexico.
ORDER OF THE AZTEC EAGLE.

Monaco.
ORDER OF ST. CHARLES.
ORDER OF THE CROWN.
ORDER OF THE GRIMALDIS.
ORDER OF CULTURAL MERIT.

Morocco.
ORDER OF OUISSAM ALOUITE.
ORDER OF RIDA.
ORDER OF MOHAMMADI.

Nepal.
ORDER OF MAHENDRA-MALA.
ORDER OF NEPAL-PRATAPA-BHASKARA.
ORDER OF TRIBHUBAN - PRAJATANTRA
SHREEPADA.
ORDER OF NEPAL-SHREEPADA.
ORDER OF NEPAL-TARA.
ORDER OF OM-RAMA-PATTA.
ORDER OF TRISHAKTI-PATTA.
ORDER OF GORKHA-DAKSHINA-BAHU.

Netherlands.
MILITARY ORDER OF WILLIAM.
ORDER OF THE NETHERLANDS LION.
ORDER OF ORANGE-NASSAU.
ORDER OF THE HOUSE OF ORANGE.
ORDER OF THE CROWN OF THE HOUSE OF
ORANGE.

New Zealand.
QUEEN'S SERVICE ORDER.

Niger.
ORDER OF THE REPUBLIC.

Nigeria.
ORDER OF THE NIGER.
ORDER OF THE FEDERAL REPUBLIC.

Norway.
ORDER OF ST. OLAV.

Oman.

ORDERS OF OMAN.

Pakistan.

ORDER OF PAKISTAN.
ORDER OF SHUJAAT.
ORDER OF IMTIAZ.
ORDER OF QUAID-I-AZAM.
ORDER OF KHIDMAT.

Panama.

ORDER OF VASCO NUÑEZ DE BALBOA.
ORDER OF MANUEL AMADOR GUERRERO.

Paraguay.

NATIONAL ORDER OF MERIT.

Peru.

ORDER OF THE SUN.
ORDER OF AYACHUCO.
ORDER OF MERIT.
ORDER OF AGRICULTURAL MERIT.
ORDER OF HIPÓLITO UNÁNUE.
ORDER OF PALMAS MAGISTERIALES.
ORDER OF DANIEL A. CARRIÓN.
ORDER OF MILITARY MERIT.
ORDER OF THE PERUVIAN CROSS FOR
NAVAL MERIT.
ORDER OF THE PERUVIAN CROSS FOR
AERONAUTICAL MERIT.
ORDER OF THE PERUVIAN CROSS FOR
AGRICULTURAL MERIT.

Philippines.

ORDER OF SIKATUNA.
ORDER OF THE GOLDEN HEART.
LEGION OF HONOUR.

Poland.

ORDER OF THE BUILDERS OF PEOPLE'S
POLAND.
ORDER OF RESTITUTION OF POLAND
(ORDER OF POLONIA RESTITUTA).
ORDER OF MILITARY VALOUR (ORDER OF
VIRTURI MILITARI).
ORDER OF THE GRÜNWALD CROSS.
ORDER OF THE BANNER OF WORK.

Portugal.

ORDER OF THE TOWER AND SWORD.
ORDER OF CHRIST.
ORDER OF AVIZ.
ORDER OF ST. JAMES OF THE SWORD.
ORDER OF PRINCE HENRY THE NAVIGATOR
ORDER OF THE EMPIRE.
ORDER OF PUBLIC INSTRUCTION.
ORDER OF BENEMERENCIA.
ORDER OF AGRICULTURAL AND INDUSTRIAL
MERIT.

Romania.

ORDER OF THE STAR OF THE SOCIALIST
REPUBLIC.
ORDER OF 23RD AUGUST.
ORDER OF TUDOR VLADIMIRESCU.
ORDER OF MOTHERLAND DEFENCE.
ORDER OF SPECIAL SERVICES BROUGHT TO
THE DEFENCE OF SOCIAL AND STATE
SYSTEM.
ORDER OF LABOUR.
ORDER OF SCIENTIFIC MERIT.
ORDER OF CULTURAL MERIT.
ORDER OF MILITARY MERIT.
ORDER OF SERVICES TO THE SOCIALIST
MOTHERLAND.
ORDER OF SPORTING MERIT.

Rwanda.

NATIONAL ORDER.

San Marino.

ORDER OF SAN MARINO.
ORDER OF ST. AGATHA.

Senegal.

NATIONAL ORDER OF SENEGAL.
ORDER OF MERIT.
ORDER OF 20TH OF AUGUST.

Singapore.

ORDER OF TEMASEK.
DISTINGUISHED SERVICE ORDER.

Soviet Union.

ORDER OF LENIN.
ORDER OF OCTOBER REVOLUTION.
ORDER OF VICTORY.
ORDER OF THE RED BANNER.
ORDER OF SUVOROV.
ORDER OF USHAKOV.
ORDER OF KUTUZOV.
ORDER OF NAKHIMOV.
ORDER OF BOGDAN KHMELNITSKY.
ORDER OF ALEXANDER NEVSKY.
ORDER OF THE PATRIOTIC WAR.
ORDER OF THE RED BANNER OF LABOUR.
ORDER OF THE RED STAR.
ORDER OF INSIGNIA OF HONOUR.
ORDER OF GLORY.
ORDER OF THE HEROINE MOTHER.
ORDER OF THE GLORY OF MOTHERHOOD.

Spain.

ORDER OF ISABEL THE CATHOLIC.
ORDER OF CHARLES III.
ORDER OF MILITARY MERIT.
ORDER OF CIVIL MERIT.
ORDER OF ALFONSO X THE SABIO.

Sudan.

ORDER OF HONOUR.
ORDER OF THE REPUBLIC.
ORDER OF THE TWO NILES.
ORDER OF DISTINCTION.
ORDER OF BRAVERY.
ORDER OF MERIT.

Sweden.

ORDER OF THE SERAPHIM.
ORDER OF THE STAR OF THE NORTH.
ORDER OF THE SWORD (*no longer conferred*).
ORDER OF VASA (*no longer conferred*)

Syria.

ORDER OF OMAYYED.
ORDER OF MILITARY HONOUR.
ORDER OF INSTRUCTION.
ORDER OF DEVOTION.

Thailand.

ORDER OF THE RAJAMITRABHORN.
ORDER OF THE ROYAL HOUSE OF CHAKRI.
ORDER OF THE NINE GEMS.
ORDER OF CHULA CHOM KLAO.
ORDER OF RAMA.
ORDER OF THE WHITE ELEPHANT.
ORDER OF THE CROWN OF THAILAND.

Togo.

NATIONAL ORDER OF BENIN.

Trinidad and Tobago.

ORDER OF TRINITY CROSS.

Tunisia.

ORDER OF THE REPUBLIC.
ORDER OF INDEPENDENCE

Union of Soviet Socialist Republics.

[SEE SOVIET UNION]

United States of America.

LEGION OF MERIT.

Venezuela.

ORDER OF THE LIBERATOR.
LEGION OF NATIONAL DEFENCE.
ORDER OF FRANCISCO DE MIRANDA.
ORDER OF MARSHAL SUCRE.
ORDER OF GENERAL RAFAEL URDANETA.
ORDER OF NAVAL MERIT.

Vietnam.

NATIONAL ORDER OF VIETNAM.
ORDER OF KIM KHANH.

Yugoslavia.

ORDER OF THE NATIONAL HERO.
ORDER OF LIBERTY.
ORDER OF THE PARTISAN STAR.
ORDER OF NATIONAL LIBERATION.
ORDER OF SERVICE TO THE NATION.
ORDER OF BROTHERHOOD AND UNITY.
ORDER OF BRAVERY.
ORDER OF LABOUR.

Zaire.

ORDER OF THE LEOPARD.
ORDER OF THE ZAIRE.

Zambia.

ORDER OF DISTINGUISHED SERVICE.

———

Independent Sovereign Order.

SOVEREIGN MILITARY ORDER OF ST. JOHN
OF JERUSALEM, OF RHODES AND OF
MALTA (COMMONLY KNOWN AS KNIGHTS
OF MALTA).

TABLE OF GENERAL PRECEDENCE

PEERS AND PEERESSES (in each Degree) rank among themselves in the following order: those created (1) of England, (2) of Scotland, (3) of Great Britain, (4) of Ireland, and (5) of the United Kingdom and of Ireland created since the Union, according to the dates of their respective patents. BARONETS rank among themselves according to the dates of their respective patents *only*. PRECEDENCE OF LADIES is always derived from the father, or husband, except in the case of a Peeress in her own right.

Official precedence, such as that of the Great Officers of State, confers no corresponding precedence on their wives or daughters. The wives and issue of Archbishops and Bishops at present have no special precedence as such.

A Dowager Peeress, or widow of a Baronet, takes precedence of the wife of the incumbent of the title only while remaining a widow.

The children of a living Peer, or Baronet, have precedence above the children of the previous possessor, or possessors, of the title. If the daughter of a Peer marries a Peer she takes her husband's rank, but if she marry the eldest or younger son of a Peer she ranks either according to her own inherent precedence (*i.e.*, as the daughter of her father), or according to that of her husband (*i.e.*, as the wife of the eldest or younger son of a Duke, Marquess, Earl, etc.), whichever happens to be the higher, no matter what the courtesy title may be.

Foreign Titles of Nobility borne by British subjects afford their holders no precedence in this country.

PRECEDENCE IN ENGLAND
GENTLEMEN

The Duke of Edinburgh.*
  ,,   Heir Apparent.
  ,,   Sovereign's Younger Sons.
  ,,   ,,   Uncle.
  ,,   ,,   Nephew.
Archbishop of Canterbury.
Lord High Chancellor.
Archbishop of York.
Prime Minister.
Lord High Treasurer (when existing).
  ,,   President of the Council.
Speaker of the House of Commons.
Lord Privy Seal.
Ambassadors and High Commissioners.
Lord Great Chamberlain.†

  ,,   High Constable (when existing) ⎫
Earl Marshal.   ⎬ Above all Peers of
Lord Steward of the Household.   ⎪ their own
  ,,   Chamberlain ,,   ,,   ⎭ degree.
Master of the Horse.

Dukes of England.
  ,,   Scotland.
  ,,   Great Britain.
  ,,   Ireland.
  ,,   U.K. and Ireland since the Union.
Eldest Sons of Dukes of the Blood Royal.
Marquesses of England.
  ,,   Scotland.
  ,,   Great Britain.
  ,,   Ireland.
  ,,   U.K. and Ireland since the Union.
Eldest Sons of Dukes.
Earls of England.
  ,,   Scotland.
  ,,   Great Britain.
  ,,   Ireland.
  ,,   U.K. and Ireland since the Union.
Younger Sons of Dukes of the Blood Royal.
Marquesses' Eldest Sons.
Dukes' Younger Sons.
Viscounts of England.
  ,,   Scotland.
  ,,   Great Britain.
  ,,   Ireland.
  ,,   U.K. and Ireland since the Union.
Earls' Eldest Sons.
Marquesses' Younger Sons.
Bishop of London.
Bishop of Durham.
  ,,   Winchester.
Other English Diocesan Bishops according to seniority of consecration.
Suffragan Bishops according to seniority of consecration.

Secretaries of State, if of Baronial rank.
Barons of England.
Lords of Parliament, Scotland.
Barons of Great Britain.
  ,,   Ireland.
  ,,   U.K. and Ireland since the Union, including Life Barons.
Lords Commissioners of the Great Seal (when existing).
Treasurer of the Household.
Comptroller of the Household.
Vice-Chamberlain of the Household.
Secretaries of State, being under Baronial rank.
Viscounts' Eldest Sons.
Earls' Younger Sons.
Barons' Eldest Sons.
Knights of the Garter.
Privy Counsellors.
Chancellor of the Exchequer.
  ,,   ,,   Duchy of Lancaster.
Lord Chief Justice of England.
Master of the Rolls.
President of the Probate, Divorce, and Admiralty Division.
Lord Justices of Appeal according to seniority of appointment.
Judges of the High Court of Justice, according to seniority of appointment.
Viscounts' Younger Sons.
Barons'   ,,   ,,
Sons of Life Peers and Lords of Appeal in Ordinary.
Baronets, according to date of Patent.
*Knights of the Thistle.
  ,,   Grand Cross of the Bath.
  ,,   ,,   Commanders of the Star of India.
  ,,   ,,   Cross of St. Michael and St. George.
  ,,   ,,   Commanders of the Indian Empire.
  ,,   ,,   Cross of Royal Victorian Order.
  ,,   ,,   ,,   the British Empire Order.
  ,,   Commanders of the Bath.
  ,,   ,,   ,,   Star of India.
  ,,   ,,   ,,   St. Michael and St. George.
  ,,   ,,   ,,   Indian Empire.
  ,,   ,,   ,,   Royal Victorian Order.
  ,,   ,,   ,,   the British Empire Order.
  ,,   Bachelor.
Circuit Judges in England and Wales, as follows: (a) Vice-Chancellor of Co. Palatine of Lancaster. (b) Circuit Judges who immediately before Jan. 1st, 1972 held office as Official Referees to Supreme Court. (c) Recorder of London. (d) Recorders of Liverpool and Manchester, according to priority of appointment. (e) Common Serjeant. (f) Additional Judge of Central Criminal Court. (g) Assistant Judge of the Mayor's and City of London Court. County Court judge. (h) Whole time Chm. or whole time Dep. Chm. of courts of quarter session for Gtr. London, Cheshire, Durham, Kent and Lancs, according to priority or order of their respective appointments. (i) Other Circuit Judges according to priority or order of their respective appointments.
Master of Court of Protection.
Companions of the Bath.
  ,,   ,,   the Star of India.
  ,,   ,,   St. Michael and St. George.
  ,,   ,,   the Indian Empire.
Commanders of the Royal Victorian Order.
  ,,   ,,   British Empire Order.
Companions of Distinguished Service Order.
Members of the Royal Victorian Order (4th class).
Officers of the British Empire Order.
Companions of Imperial Service Order.
Eldest Sons of the Younger Sons of Peers.
Eldest Sons of the Baronets.
  ,,   ,,   ,,   Knights of the Garter.
  ,,   ,,   ,,   Knights of the Thistle*
  ,,   ,,   ,,   Knights of the Bath.§
  ,,   ,,   ,,   Knights of the Star of India.§
  ,,   ,,   ,,   Knights of St. Michael and St. George.§
  ,,   ,,   ,,   Knights of the Indian Empire.§
  ,,   ,,   ,,   Royal Victorian Order.§
  ,,   ,,   ,,   British Empire Order.§
  ,,   ,,   ,,   Knights Bachelor.

---

* By Royal Warrant dated 18th September, 1952, it was declared that H.R.H. the Duke of Edinburgh was henceforth to have Precedence next to H.M. the Queen, thus having place before the Heir Apparent.

† When in actual performance of official duty.

§ Eldest sons of Knights Grand Cross take precedence of eldest sons of Knights of the 2nd degree.

* Knights of the Thistle have no relative precedence accorded to them by Statute, but are customarily placed here. In Scotland they follow Knights of the Garter.

Members of the Royal Victorian Order (5th ass).
,, ,, ,, British Empire Order·
Younger Sons of Baronets.
Younger Sons of Knights.
Esquires.
Gentlemen.

* *Lord-Lieutenants and High Sheriffs of Counties have the first places in their own Counties during office, the Lord-Lieutenant taking precedence of the High Sheriff, but neither is assigned any place on the Official Scale of General Precedence. The Lord-Lieutenant has precedence within his jurisdiction over a Mayor, even within his own Borough, when present officially as the representative of the Crown. On all Municipal occasions, however, whether of business or entertainment, the Mayor should preside, or act as host.*

* *Clergy (other than those mentioned above), Naval, Military and Air Force Officers, Members of the Legal and Medical Professions, Graduates of Universities, and Citizens and Burgesses have no precedence assigned to them, either by statute or by any fixed principle.*

LADIES

The Queen.
,, Queen Mother.
,, Sovereign's Daughter.
The Sovereign's Sister.
Wives of the Sovereign's Uncles.
The Sovereign's Niece.
Duchesses of England.
,, Scotland.
,, Great Britain.
,, Ireland.
,, U.K. and Ireland since the Union.
Wives of the Eldest Sons of Dukes of the Blood Royal.
Marchionesses of England.
,, Scotland.
,, Great Britain.
,, Ireland.
, U.K. and Ireland since the Union.
Wives of the Eldest Sons of Dukes.
Daughters of Dukes.
Countesses of England.
,, Scotland.
,, Great Britain.
,, Ireland.
,, U.K. and Ireland since the Union.
Wives of the Younger Sons of Dukes of the Blood Royal.
,, the Eldest Sons of Marquesses.
Daughters of Marquesses.
Wives of the Younger Sons of Dukes.
Viscountesses of England.
,, Scotland.
,, Great Britain.
,, Ireland.
,, U.K. and Ireland since the Union.
Wives of the Eldest Sons of Earls.
Daughters of Earls.
Wives of the Younger Sons of Marquesses.
Baronesses of England.
Ladies of Parliament, Scotland.
Baronesses of Great Britain.
,, Ireland.
,, U.K. and Ireland since the Union, including Life Baronesses and Wives of Life Barons.
Wives of the Eldest Sons of Viscounts.
Daughters of Viscounts.
Wives of the Younger Sons of Earls.
,, ,, Eldest Sons of Barons.
Daughters of Barons.
Wives of Knights of the Garter.
Privy Counsellors (Women)
Wives of the Younger Sons of Viscounts.
,, ,, ,, ,, Barons.

Wives of Sons of Life Peers.
,, Baronets, according to their husband Patents.
,, Knights of the Thistle.
Dames Grand Cross of the Order of the Bath.
,, ,, ,, ,, ,, Order of St. Michael and St. George.
,, ,, ,, ,, ,, Royal Victorian Order.
,, ,, ,, ,, ,, British Empire Order.
Wives of Knights Grand Cross of the Bath.
,, ,, Grand Commanders of the Star of India.
,, ,, Grand Cross of St. Michael and St. George.
,, ,, Grand Commanders of the Indian Empire.
,, ,, Grand Cross of Royal Victorian Order.
,, ,, Grand Cross of British Empire Order.
Dames Commanders of the Order of the Bath.
,, ,, ,, Order of St. Michael and St. George.
,, ,, Royal Victorian Order.
,, ,, British Empire Order.
Wives of Knights Commanders of the Bath.
,, ,, ,, Star of India.
,, ,, ,, St. Michael and St. George.
,, ,, Commanders of the Indian Empire.
,, ,, Commanders of Royal Victorian Order.
,, ,, Commanders of the British Empire Order.
,, ,, Bachelor.
Commanders of the Order of the Bath.
,, ,, Order of St. Michael and St. George.
,, ,, Royal Victorian Order.
,, ,, British Empire Order.
Wives of Companions of the Bath.
,, ,, ,, Star of India.
,, ,, ,, St. Michael and St. George.
,, ,, ,, the Indian Empire.
,, Commanders of Royal Victorian Order.
,, Commanders of the British Empire Order.
,, Companions of the Distinguished Service Order.
Members of the Royal Victorian Order (4th class).
Officer of the British Empire Order.
Wives of Members of the Royal Victorian Order (4th class).
,, Officers of the British Empire Order.
Companions of the Imperial Service Order.
Wives of Companions of Imperial Service Order.
,, the eldest sons of the Younger Sons of Peers.
Daughters of the Younger Sons of Peers.
Wives of the Eldest Sons of Baronets.
Daughters of Baronets.
Wives of the Eldest Sons of Knights of the Garter.
,, ,, ,, ,, Knights.
Daughters of Knights.
Members of the Royal Victorian Order (5th class).
,, ,, British Empire Order.
Wives of Members of Royal Victorian Order (5th class).
,, Members of the British Empire Order.
Wives of the Younger Sons of Baronets.
,, ,, ,, ,, Knights.
,, Esquires.
,, Gentlemen.

* *Wives of the Clergy, Naval, Military and Air Force Officers, Members of the Legal and Medical Professions, Graduates of Universities, and Citizens and Burgesses have no precedence assigned to them, either by statute or by any fixed principle.*

PRECEDENCE IN SCOTLAND.

GENTLEMEN

The Duke of Edinburgh.*
Lord High Commissioner to the General Assembly of the Church of Scotland (during sitting of General Assembly).
Duke of Rothesay (The Prince of Wales).
Sovereign's Younger Sons.
Sovereign's Uncle.
Sovereign's Nephew.
Lords Lieutenant of Counties.†
Lord Provosts of Cities being *ex-officio* Lords Lieutenant of Counties of Cities.†
Sheriffs Principal.†
Lord Chancellor of Great Britain.
Moderator of the General Assembly of Church of Scotland (during office).
The Prime Minister.
Keeper of the Great Seal of Scotland (the Secretary for Scotland) (if a Peer).
Keeper of the Privy Seal of Scotland (if a Peer).
Hereditary High Constable of Scotland.
Hereditary Master of the Household in Scotland.
Dukes (as in English Table).
Eldest Sons of Dukes of Blood Royal.
Marquesses (as in English Table).
Eldest Sons of Dukes.
Earls (as in English Table).
Younger Sons of Dukes of Blood Royal.
Eldest Sons of Marquesses.
Younger Sons of Dukes.
Keeper of the Great Seal (the Secretary for Scotland) (if not a Peer).
Keeper of the Privy Seal (if not a Peer).
Lord Justice-General.
Lord Clerk Register.
Lord Advocate.
Lord Justice-Clerk.
Viscounts (as in English Table).
Eldest Sons of Earls.
Younger Sons of Marquesses.
Barons or Lords of Parliament (Scotland) (as in English Table).
Eldest Sons of Viscounts.
Younger Sons of Earls.
Eldest Sons of Barons or Lords of Parliament.
Knights of the Garter.
Knights of the Thistle.
Privy Counsellors.
Senators of the College of Justice (Lords of Session), including Chairman of Scottish Land Court.
Younger Sons of Viscount.
Younger Sons of Barons or Lords of Parliament.
Baronets.
Knights Grand Cross and Knights Grand Commander of Orders (as in English Table).
Knights Commander of Orders (as in English Table).
Solicitor-General for Scotland.
Lyon King of Arms.
Sheriffs Principal (when not within own county).‡
Knights Bachelor.
Sheriffs
Companions of the Bath.
Thence as in English Table.

Lords-Lieutenants of Counties and of Counties of Cities during their term of office and within the limits of their jurisdiction have precedence before the Sheriffs Principal having concurrent jurisdiction.
‡In Scotland Sheriffs exercise judicial functions.

LADIES

The QUEEN.
The Queen Mother.
Sovereign's Daughter.
Sovereign's Sister.
Wives of Sovereign's Uncles.
Sovereign's Niece.
Duchesses (as in English Table).
Wives of the Eldest Sons of Dukes of Blood Royal.
Marchionesses (as in English Table).
Wives of Eldest Sons of Dukes.
Daughters of Dukes.
Wives of Younger Sons of Dukes of Blood Royal.
Wives of Eldest Sons of Marquesses.
Daughters of Marquesses.
Wives of Younger Sons of Dukes.
Countesses (as in English Table).
Viscountesses (as in English Table).
Wives of Eldest Sons of Earls.
Daughters of Earls.
Wives of Younger Sons of Marquesses.
Baronesses, or Ladies of Parliament (Scotland) (as in English Table).
Wives of Eldest Sons of Viscounts.
Daughters of Viscounts.
Wives of Younger Sons of Earls.
Wives of Eldest Sons of Barons or Lords of Parliament.
Daughters of Barons or Lords of Parliament.
Wives of Knights of the Garter.
Privy Counsellors (Women).
Wives of Younger Sons of Viscounts.
Wives of Younger Sons of Barons.
Wives of Baronets.
Wives of Knights of the Thistle.
Dames Grand Cross of Orders (as in English Table).
Wives of Knights Grand Cross and Knights Grand Commander of Orders (as in English Table).
Dames Commander of Orders (as in English Tables).
Wives of Knights Commander of Orders (as in English Tables).
Wives of Knights Bachelor and Wives of Senators of the College of Justice (Lord of Session) including the wife of the Chairman of the Scottish Land Court.§
Commanders of the Order of the Bath.
Thence as in English Tables.

---

* By Royal Warrant dated 18th September, 1952, it was declared that H.R.H. the Duke of Edinburgh was henceforth to have Precedence next to H.M. the Queen, thus having place before the Lord High Commissioner.
† During term of office, and within their respective Counties, Cities, and Sheriffdoms.

---

§ Taking precedence among themselves according to the dates of their husbands' creation as Knights or appointment as Senators of the College of Justice, respectively.

Members of the Executive and Legislative Councils.—See Honourable in Commonwealth Countries.

Members of Parliament.—According to rank, but adding the initials " MP " after title or name and honours.

Military Officers.—See " Naval, Military, and Air Force Officers."

Minister of the Crown.—If a Privy Counsellor, see that section, otherwise see Member of Parliament or Grade of Peerage. The social form of " Dear Secretary of State," or " Dear Minister " may be used if the matter concerns the Department.

Moderator of the General Assembly of Church of Scotland.—By Order in Council the Moderator has precedence in Scotland and at Court functions immediately after Bishops of the Church of England, and while in office is addressed as " Rt. Rev." Former Moderators, " Very Rev."

Naval, Military, and Air Force Officers.—Professional rank should always precede any titles, *e.g.*, " Adm. (the Right Hon.) the Earl of ———," " Gen. the (Right Hon.) Lord ———," " Air-Marshal Sir ———," but Lieutenants in the Army, and Flying Officers and Pilot Officers in the Air Force are addressed by their social and not their professional rank, *e.g.*, " The Hon. Benjamin ———, Irish Guards," " George ———, Esq., 11th Hussars," or " William ———, Esq., RAF."

Peers and Peeresses by courtesy.—As commoners they are not addressed as " Rt. Hon." or " The " but " Viscount [Brown] " or appropriate title.

Police and Fire Service Medals.—The letters KPM, KPFSM, QPM, QFSM and CPM are now placed after the name. If the Colonial Police Medal were awarded for gallantry the letters CPM are placed before BEM, and if for meritorious service after QFSM (see paragraph 4 at beginning of section).

Prebendary.—As for Canon, but substituting the word Prebendary for Canon.

Prime Minister , The.—See Privy Counsellors. The social form of " Dear (Mr.) Prime Minister " may be used if the matter concerns his office.

Prince.—LETTERS.—*Superscription*, (i) the son of a Sovereign " His Royal Highness The Prince [Andrew] "; (ii) other Princes " His Royal Highness Prince [Michael of Kent] "; (iii) Duke " His Royal Highness The Duke of [Gloucester]." *Commencement*, " Sir." *Conclusion*, " I have the honour to be, Sir, Your Royal Highness's most humble and most obedient servant." PERSONAL ADDRESS, " Your Royal Highness," and henceforward as " Sir." [See also Royal Family.]

Princess. — LETTERS. — *Superscription*, (i) the daughter of a Sovereign " Her Royal Highness The Princess [Anne] "; (ii) other Princesses " Her Royal Highness Princess [Alexandra], the Hon. Mrs. Angus Ogilvy "; (iii) Duchess " Her Royal Highness The Duchess of [Kent]." A Princess Royal is addressed " Her Royal Highness The Princess Royal." *Commencement*, " Madam." *Conclusion*, " I have the honour to be, Madam, Your Royal Highness's most humble and most obedient servant." PERSONAL ADDRESS, " Your Royal Highness," and henceforward as " Ma'am." [See also Royal Family.]

Privy Counsellors, also spelt PRIVY COUNCILLORS. — LETTERS. — *Superscription*, " The Right Hon. ———," but if a peer then as such, followed by the letters " PC," *after* all Orders and Decorations. *Commencement, &c.,* according to the rank of the individual. Privy Counsellors of Northern Ireland, which are no longer created, are entitled to the prefix of Right Hon. and are included in this section. Members of the Privy Council of Canada are entitled to the style of " Hon." for life. *Commencement,* as for Esquire or appropriate rank.

Privy Counsellors, Wives of.—They enjoy no special style or precedence as such.

Provost.—As for Dean, but substituting the word Provost for Dean.

Queen Mother. — LETTERS. — *Superscription,* for formal and state documents, " Her Gracious Majesty Queen Elizabeth The Queen Mother," otherwise " Her Majesty Queen Elizabeth The Queen Mother." *Commencement,* as for the Queen Regnant. *Conclusion,* " I have the honour to remain, Madam, Your Majesty's most humble and obedient servant." PERSONAL ADDRESS, as for the Queen Regnant.

Queen Regnant. — LETTERS. — *Superscriptions,* for formal and state documents, " The Queen's Most Excellent Majesty," otherwise " Her Majesty The Queen," *Commencement,* " Madam," or " May it please your Majesty." *Conclusion,* " I have the honour to remain Madam, Your Majesty's most humble and obedient servant." PERSONAL ADDRESS, " Your Majesty," and henceforth as " Ma'am."

Queen's Counsel. — LETTERS. — *Superscription,* " ——— Esq., QC." In other respects as an Esquire. The letters are used after the name by Circuit Judges, but not by High Court Judges.

Rt. Honourable.—This prefix is borne by Privy Counsellors of Great Britain and Northern Ireland, the Governor General of Canada, the Prime Minister and Chief Justice of Canada *for life;* by Earls, Viscounts and Barons ¦(except peers by courtesy) their wives and widows; and certain Lord Mayors (see Lord Mayors), and Provosts of Edinburgh and Glasgow (see Lord Provosts), and the Chairman of Greater London Council *while in office.*

Royal Dukes.—See " Prince."

Royal Family.—On Dec. 11th, 1917, it was ordained that " The children of any Sovereign of the United Kingdom and the children of the sons of any such Sovereign and the eldest living son of the eldest son of the Prince of Wales, shall have the style, title, or attribute of Royal Highness with their titular dignity of Prince or Princess prefixed to their respective Christian names, or with their other titles of honour; and that the grandchildren of the sons of any such Sovereign in the direct male line (save only the eldest living son of the eldest son of the Prince of Wales) shall have the style and title enjoyed by the children of Dukes." [See also " Queen Regnant," " Queen Mother," " Prince," and " Princess."]

Rural Deans.—No special form of address.

Secretary of State.—See " Minister of the Crown " and " Privy Counsellors."

Sovereign, The.—See " Queen Regnant."

Titles just announced.—See paragraph at commencement of this section.

Trinity House, Elder Brethren of are entitled to be called " Captain, ' with precedence after Naval Captains.

Victoria Cross.—The letters VC take precedence of all other honours and decorations.

Viscount. — LETTERS. — *Superscription,* " The Right Hon. The Viscount ———," or socially " The Viscount ———." In other respects as Baron.

Viscountess. — LETTERS. — *Superscription,* " The Right Hon. The Viscountess ———." or socially, " The Viscountess ———." In other respects as Baroness and Baron's widow. [See also " Viscount's Widow "].

Viscount's Son, and his Wife or Widow *same as Baron's.*

Viscount's Daughter, *same as Baron's.*

Viscount's Widow, *same as Viscountess* if present Viscount is unmarried. For widows where present incumbent of title is married [see " Dowager "]. As to re-marriage, see " Widows."

Wales, Prince of.—See " Prince " and " Royal Family."

Widows.—A Widow who re-marries *loses* any title or precedence she gained by her previous marriage, and is not recognised as having any claim to bear the title of her deceased husband, *e.g.:* at a coronation or other State ceremonial, the widow of a peer would not be summoned as a peeress if she had subsequently married a commoner; and, if having espoused a peer of lesser degree than her former husband, she would only be recognised by the rank acquired by her last marriage. [See also Esquire's Widow.]

PEERAGES THAT HAVE BECOME

EXTINCT, DORMANT, ABEYANT, OR DISCLAIMED

Since 1950. For Extinctions in the years 1900–50 see 1958 and earlier editions.

The family surname appears in *italics* (between parentheses) immediately after the title.
* Peerage of United Kingdom.   † Peerage of Great Britain.   ‡ Peerage of England.
‖ Peerage of Scotland.   § Peerage of Ireland.

HEREDITARY PEERAGES EXTINCT, DORMANT or ABEYANT

* ADAMS, Baron, (*Adams*). Cr. 1949. Ext. 1960.
ALEXANDER OF HILLSBOROUGH, Earl, (*Alexander*). Cr. 1963; also V. Alexander of Hillsborough 1950, and B. Weston-super-Mare, 1963. Ext. 1965.
* ALNESS, Baron, (*Munro*). Cr. 1934. Ext. 1955.
* AMMON, Baron, (*Ammon*). Cr. 1944. Ext. 1960.
* ATHLONE, Earl of, (*Cambridge*). Cr. 1917; also V. Trematon 1917. Ext. 1957.
* BADELEY, Baron, (*Badeley*). Cr. 1949. Ext. 1951.
* BENNETT OF EDGBASTON, Baron, (*Bennett*). Cr. 1953. Ext. 1957.
* BERTIE OF THAME, Viscount, (*Bertie*). Cr. 1918; also B. Bertie of Thame 1915. Ext. 1954.
† BERWICK, Baron, (*Noel-Hill*). Cr. 1784. Ext. 1953.
* BEVERIDGE, Baron, (*Beveridge*). Cr. 1946. Ext. 1963.
* BILSLAND, Baron, (*Bilsland*). Cr. 1950. Ext. 1970.
* BOYD-ORR, Baron, (*Orr*). Cr. 1949. Ext. 1971.
* BRACKEN, Viscount, (*Bracken*). Cr. 1952. Ext. 1958.
* BRAINTREE, Baron, (*Crittall*). Cr. 1948. Ext. 1961.
* BRAND, Baron, (*Brand*). Cr. 1946. Ext. 1963.
* BRUCE OF MELBOURNE, Viscount, (*Bruce*). Cr. 1947. Ext. 1967.
* CAMPION, Baron, (*Campion*). Cr. 1950. Ext. 1958.
* CARISBROOKE, Marquess of, (*Mountbatten*). Cr. 1917; also V. Launceston, E. of Berkhamsted 1917. Ext. 1960.
* CECIL OF CHELWOOD, Viscount, (*Gascoyne-Cecil*). Cr. 1923. Ext. 1958.
* CHARNWOOD, Baron, (*Benson*). Cr. 1911. Ext. 1955.
* CHERWELL, Viscount, (*Lindemann*). Cr. 1956; also B. Cherwell 1941. Ext. 1957.
‡ CHESTERFIELD and †STANHOPE, Earl of, (*Stanhope*). Cr. 1628 and 1718, also ‡B. Stanhope of Shelford 1616. Ext. 1967.
* CHEYLESMORE, Baron, (*Eaton*.) Cr. 1887. Ext. 1974.
* CILCENNIN, Viscount, (*Thomas*). Cr. 1956. Ext. 1960.
§ CLARINA, Baron, (*Massey*). Cr. 1800. Ext. 1952.
§ CLIFDEN, Viscount, (*Agar-Robartes*). Cr. 1781. Also § Baron Clifden 1776, and * Baron Robartes 1869. Ext. 1974.
‡ COBHAM, Baron, (*Alexander*). Cr. 1312–13. Abey. 1951.
* CONESFORD, Baron, (*Strauss*.) Cr. 1955. Ext. 1974.
‖ COOPER OF CULROSS, Baron, (*Cooper*). Cr. 1954. Ext. 1955.
* COURTAULD-THOMSON, Baron, (*Courtauld-Thomson*). Cr. 1944. Ext. 1954.
* COURTHOPE, Baron, (*Courthope*). Cr. 1945. Ext. 1955.
* CROOKSHANK, Viscount, (*Crookshank*). Cr. 1956. Ext. 1961.
* CUNNINGHAM OF HYNDHOPE, Viscount, (*Cunningham*). Cr. 1945. Ext. 1963.
* DORCHESTER, Baron, (*Carleton*). Cr. 1899. Ext. 1963.
* DOUGLAS OF KIRTLESIDE (*Douglas*). Cr. 1948. Ext. 1969.
* DOVERCOURT, Baron, (*Holmes*). Cr. 1954. Ext. 1961.
* DUGAN OF VICTORIA, Baron, (*Dugan*). Cr. 1949. Ext. 1951.
* EGERTON OF TATTON, Baron, (*Egerton*). Cr. 1859. Ext. 1958.
* ELIBANK, Viscount, (*Murray*). Cr. 1911. Ext. 1962.
* ENNISDALE, Baron, (*Lyons*). Cr. 1939. Ext. 1963.
* EVANS, Baron, (*Evans*). Cr. 1957. Ext. 1963.
* EVERSHED, Baron, (*Evershed*). Cr. 1956. Ext. 1966.
‖ FALCONER OF HALKERTON, Lord, (*Keith*). Cr. 1646. Dormant 1966.
* FAIRHAVEN, Baron, (*Broughton*). Cr. 1929. Ext. 1966.
* FARRER, Baron, (*Farrer*). Cr. 1893. Ext. 1964.
* FEVERSHAM, Earl of, (*Duncombe*). Cr. 1868; also V. Helmsley 1868. Ext. 1963.

* FITZ ALAN OF DERWENT, Viscount, (*Fitzalan-Howard*). Cr. 1921. Ext. 1962.
* FLECK, Baron, (*Fleck*). Cr. 1961. Ext. 1968.
* FORSTER OF HARRABY, Baron, (*Forster*). Cr. 1959. Ext. 1972.
FURNIVALL, Baron, (*Dent*). Cr. 1295. Abeyant 1968.
* GLENTANAR, Baron, (*Coats*). Cr. 1916. Ext. 1971.
* GLYN, Baron, (*Glyn*). Cr. 1953. Ext. 1960.
* GREENE, Baron, (*Greene*). Cr. 1941. Ext. 1952.
‡ GREY DE RUTHYN, Baron, (*Butler-Bowdon*). Cr. 1324. Abey. 1963.
§ GUILLAMORE, Viscount, (*O'Grady*). Cr. 1831; also B. O'Grady 1831. Ext. 1955.
* HAILES, Baron, (*Buchan-Hepburn*). Cr. 1957. Ext. 1974.
* HAILEY, Baron, (*Hailey*). Cr. 1936. Ext. 1969.
* HENEAGE, Baron (*Heneage*). Cr. 1896. Ext. 1967.
* HEWART, Viscount, (*Hewart*). Cr. 1940; also B. Hewart 1922. Ext. 1964.
* HEYWORTH, Baron, (*Heyworth*). Cr. 1955. Ext. 1974.
* HOLDEN, Baron, (*Holden*). Cr. 1908. Ext. 1951.
* HORE-BELISHA, Baron, (*Hore-Belisha*). Cr. 1954. Ext. 1957.
* HUDSON, Viscount, (*Hudson*). Cr. 1952. Ext. 1963.
* HUNGARTON, Baron, (*Crawford*). Cr. 1951. Ext. 1966.
* HYNDLEY, Viscount, (*Hindley*). Cr. 1948. Ext. 1963.
* ILKESTON, Baron, (*Foster*). Cr. 1910. Ext. 1952.
* INVERCHAPEL, Baron, (*Kerr Clark Kerr*). Cr. 1946. Ext. 1951.
* INVERCLYDE, Baron, (*Burns*). Cr. 1897. Ext. 1957.
* ISMAY, Baron, (*Ismay*). Cr. 1947. Ext. 1965.
* JACKSON, Baron, (*Jackson*). Cr. 1945. Ext. 1954.
* JOWITT, Earl, (*Jowitt*). Cr. 1951; also B. Jowitt 1945, and V. Jowitt 1947. Ext. 1957.
* §KENMARE, Earl of, (*Browne*). Cr. 1801; also §B. Castlerosse and V. Kenmare 1798, §V. Castlerosse 1801, and *B. Kenmare 1856. Ext. 1952.
* KILMUIR, Earl of, (*Fyfe*). Cr. 1962. Ext. 1967.
* KINTORE, Baron, (*Keith*). Cr. 1838. Ext. 1966.
* LAMBURY, Baron, (*Lord*). Cr. 1962. Ext. 1967.
* LAMINGTON, Baron, (*Cochrane-Baillie*). Cr. 1880. Ext. 1951.
* LAWSON, Baron, (*Lawson*). Cr. 1950. Ext. 1965.
‡ LEEDS, Duke of, (*Osborne*). Cr. 1694; also ‡B. Osborne and ‡V. Latimer, 1673, ‡E. of Danby 1674, ‡M. of Carmarthen 1689. Ext. 1964.
§ LEITRIM, Earl of, (*Clements*). Cr. 1795; also B. Leitrim 1783, V. Leitrim 1793, and *B. Clements 1831. Ext. 1952.
* LLEWELLIN, Baron, (*Llewellin*). Cr. 1945. Ext. 1957.
* MABANE, Baron, (*Mabane*). Cr. 1962. Ext. 1969.
* McCORQUODALE OF NEWTON, Baron. (*McCorquodale*). Cr. 1955. Ext. 1971.
* McENTEE, Baron, (*McEntee*). Cr. 1951. Ext. 1953.
* MAENAN, Baron, (*Taylor*). Cr. 1948. Ext. 1951.
* MAGHERAMORNE, Baron, (*McGarel-Hogg*). Cr. 1887. Ext. 1957.
* MANVERS, Earl, (*Pierrepont*). Cr. 1806; also B. Pierrepont and V. Newark 1796. Ext. 1955.
* MATHERS, Baron, (*Mathers*). Cr. 1952. Ext. 1956.
* MERRIMAN, Baron, (*Merriman*). Cr. 1941. Ext. 1962.
* MONCKTON, Baron, (*Monckton*). Cr. 1887. Ext. 1971.
§ MOUNTMORRES, Viscount, (*de Montmorency*). Cr. 1763. Ext. 1951.
* NORMAN, Baron, (*Norman*). Cr. 1944. Ext. 1950.
* NORMANBROOK, Baron, (*Brook*). Cr. 1963. Ext. 1967.
* NUFFIELD, Viscount, (*Morris*). Cr. 1938; also B. Nuffield 1934. Ext. 1963.

* NUGENT, Baron, (*Nugent*). Cr. 1960. Ext. 1973.
* PERCY OF NEWCASTLE, Baron, (*Percy*). Cr. 1953. Ext. 1958.
* PERRY, Baron, (*Perry*). Cr. 1938. Ext. 1956.
* PETHICK-LAWRENCE, Baron, (*Pethick-Lawrence*). Cr. 1945. Ext. 1961.
* PORTAL OF HUNGERFORD, Viscount, (*Portal*). Cr. 1946. Ext. 1971.
‡ POULETT, Earl, (*Poulett*). Cr. 1706; also ‡ V. Hinton and ‡ Baron Poulett of Hinton St. George (may be Dormant). Ext. 1973.
* QUIBELL, Baron, (*Quibell*). Cr. 1945. Ext. 1962.
* QUICKSWOOD, Baron, (*Gascoyne-Cecil*). Cr. 1941. Ext. 1956.
§ RADSTOCK, Baron, (*Waldegrave*). Cr. 1800. Ext. 1953.
* RAMSDEN, Baron, (*Ramsden*). Cr. 1945. Ext. 1955.
* RANK, Baron, (*Rank*). Cr. 1957. Ext. 1972.
* RHONDDA, Viscount, (*Thomas*). Cr. 1918; also B. Rhondda 1918. Ext. 1958.
* ROBERTS, Countess, (*Roberts*). Cr. 1901; also St. Pierre 1901. Ext. 1955.
* ROBINS, Baron, (*Robins*). Cr. 1958. Ext. 1962.
* ROBINSON, Baron, (*Robinson*). Cr. 1947. Ext. 1952.
* RUFFSIDE, Viscount, (*Brown*). Cr. 1951. Ext. 1958.
* ST. ANDRIES, Baron, (*Fuller-Acland-Hood*). Cr. 1911. Ext. 1971.
* SALTER, Baron, (*Salter*). Cr. 1953. Ext. 1975.
* SCHUSTER, Baron, (*Schuster*). Cr. 1944. Ext. 1956.
* SEATON, Baron, (*Colborne-Vivian*). Cr. 1839. Ext. 1955.
§ SEFTON, Earl of, (*Molyneux*). Cr. 1771; also Viscount Molyneux, and * B. Sefton 1831. Ext. 1972.
* SHERWOOD, Baron, (*Seely*). Cr. 1941. Ext. 1970.
* SIMONDS, Viscount, (*Simonds*). Cr. 1954; also *B. Simonds (Life Baron, Law Lord). 1944, Baron 1952. Ext. 1971.
* STANMORE, Baron, (*Hamilton-Gordon*). Cr. 1893. Ext. 1957.
* STRACHIE, Baron, (*Strachey*). Cr. 1911. Ext. 1973.
† STRANGE, Earl (*Stewart-Murray*). Cr. 1786; also †B. Murray of Stanley 1786 and *B. Glenlyon 1821. Ext. 1957.
* TALBOT DE MALAHIDE, Baron, (*Talbot*). Cr. 1856. Ext. 1973.
* TEMPLEWOOD, Viscount, (*Hoare*). Cr. 1944. Ext. 1959.
* TOVEY, Baron, (*Tovey*). Cr. 1946. Ext. 1971.
* TREDEGAR, Baron, (*Morgan*). Cr. 1859. Ext. 1962.
* TRENT, Baron, (*Boot*). Cr. 1929. Ext. 1956.
* TURNOUR, Baron, (*Turnour*). Cr. 1952. Ext. 1962.
* UVEDALE OF NORTH END, Baron, (*Woodall*). Cr. 1946. Ext. 1974.
* VANSITTART, Baron, (*Vansittart*). Cr. 1941. Ext. 1957.
* WALERAN, Baron, (*Walrond*). Cr. 1905. Ext. 1966.
* WAVELL, Earl, (*Wavell*). Cr. 1947; also V. Wavell 1943, and V. Keren 1947. Ext. 1954.
* WEBB-JOHNSON, Baron, (*Webb-Johnson*). Cr. 1945. Ext. 1958.
* WEEKS, Baron, (*Weeks*). Cr. 1956. Ext. 1960.
‡ WHARTON, Baron, (*Vincent*). Cr. 1544. Abeyant 1974.
* WHITBURGH, Baron, (*Borthwick*). Cr. 1912. Ext. 1967.
* WILLIAMS, Baron, (*Williams*). Cr. 1948. Ext. 1966.
* WILMOT OF SELMESTON, Baron, (*Wilmot*). Cr. 1950. Ext. 1964.
* WINDSOR, Duke of, (*Windsor*). Cr. 1927. Ext. 1972.
* WINSTER, Baron, (*Fletcher*). Cr. 1942. Ext. 1961.

GODDARD, Baron, (*Goddard*). Cr. 1944 (Law Lord), Ext. 1971.
HAIRE OF WHITEABBEY, Baron, (*Haire*). Cr. 1965. Ext. 1966.
HILL OF WIVENHOE, Baron (*Hill*). Cr. 1967. Ext. 1969.
HOBSON, Baron, (*Hobson*). Cr. 1963 (Law Lord). Ext. 1966.
HORSBRUGH, Baroness, (*Horsbrugh*). Cr. 1959. Ext. 1969.
HURD, Baron, (*Hurd*). Cr. 1964. Ext. 1966.
ILFORD, Baron, (*Hutchinson*). Cr. 1962. Ext. 1974.
JACKSON OF BURNLEY, Baron, (*Jackson*). Cr. 1967. Ext. 1970.
JENKINS, Baron, (*Jenkins*). Cr. 1959 (Law Lord). Ext. 1969.
KEITH OF AVONHOLM, Baron, (*Keith*). Cr. 1953. Ext. 1964.
KING-HALL, Baron, (*King-Hall*). Cr. 1966. Ext. 1966.
LINDGREN, Baron, (*Lindgren*). Cr. 1961. Ext. 1971.
MACMILLAN, Baron, (*Macmillan*). Cr. 1930 (Law Lord). Ext. 1952.
MITCHISON, Baron, (*Mitchison*). Cr. 1964. Ext. 1970.
MONSLOW, Baron, (*Monslow*). Cr. 1966. Ext. 1966.
MORRISON OF LAMBETH, Baron, (*Morrison*). Cr. 1959. Ext. 1965.
MORTON OF HENRYTON, Baron, (*Morton*). Cr. 1947 (Law Lord). Ext. 1973.
MOYLE, Baron, (*Moyle*). Cr. 1966. Ext. 1974.
NORMAND, Baron, (*Normand*). Cr. 1947 (Law Lord). Ext. 1962.
OAKSHOTT. Baron (*Oakshott*). Cr. 1959. Ext. 1975.
PARKER OF WADDINGTON, Baron, (*Parker*). Cr. 1958 (Law Lord). Ext. 1972.
PLUMMER, Baron. (*Plummer*). Cr. 1965. Ext. 1972.
PORTER, Baron, (*Porter*). Cr. 1938 (Law Lord). Ext. 1956.
REID, Baron, (*Reid*). Cr. 1948 (Law Lord). Ext. 1975.
ROCHE, Baron, (*Roche*). Cr. 1935 (Law Lord). Ext. 1956.
ROSENHEIM, Baron, (*Rosenheim*). Cr. 1970. Ext. 1972.
ROWLEY, Baron, (*Henderson*). Cr. 1966. Ext. 1968.
ROYLE, Baron, (*Royle*). Cr. 1964. Ext. 1975.
RUNCORN, Baron, (*Vosper*). Cr. 1964. Ext. 1968.
SIEFF, Baron (Sieff). Cr. 1966. Ext. 1972.
SIMEY, Baron, (*Simey*). Cr. 1965. Ext. 1969.
SOMERVELL OF HARROW, Baron (*Somervell*). Cr. 1954 (Law Lord). Ext. 1960.
SORENSEN, Baron, (*Sorensen*). Cr. 1964. Ext. 1971.
STOCKS, Baroness, (*Stocks*). Cr. 1966. Ext. 1975.
STONEHAM, Baron, (Collins). Cr. 1958. Ext. 1971.
STOPFORD OF FALLOWFIELD, Baron, (*Stopford*). Cr. 1958. Ext. 1961.
SWANBOROUGH, Baroness, (*Isaacs*). Cr. 1958. Ext. 1971.
TANGLEY, Baron, (*Herbert*). Cr. 1963. Ext. 1973.
TAYSIDE, Baron ((*Urquhart*). Cr. 1967. Ext. 1975.
TUCKER, Baron, (*Tucker*). Cr. 1950. Ext. 1975.
TWINING, Baron, (*Twining*). Cr. 1958. Ext. 1967.
UPJOHN, Baron, (*Upjohn*). Cr. 1963. (Law Lord), Ext. 1971.
WILLIAMS OF BARNBURGH, Baron, (*Williams*). Cr. 1961. Ext. 1967.
WRIGHT, Baron (*Wright*). Cr. 1932 (Law Lord). Ext. 1964.
WRIGHT OF ASHTON UDDER LYNE, Baron, (*Wright*). Cr. 1968. Ext. 1974.

LIFE PEERAGES EXTINCT

ASQUITH OF BISHOPSTONE, Baron, (*Asquith*). Cr. 1951 (Law Lord). Ext. 1954.
ASQUITH OF YARNBURY, Baroness, (*Bonham Carter*) Cr. 1964. Ext. 1969.
BANNERMAN OF KILDONAN, Baron, (*Bannerman*). Cr. 1967. Ext. 1969.
BLACKETT, Baron, (*Blackett*). Cr. 1969. Ext. 1974.
BOSSOM, Baron, (*Bossom*). Cr. 1960. Ext. 1965.
BOWLES, Baron, (*Bowles*). Cr. 1964. Ext. 1970.
CARRON, Baron, (*Carron*). Cr. 1967. Ext. 1969.
CHUTER-EDE, Baron, (*Chuter-Ede*). Cr. 1965. Ext. 1965.
COHEN, Baron, (*Cohen*). Cr. 1951. Ext. 1973.
COHEN OF BRIGHTON, Baron, (*Cohen*). Cr. 1965. Ext. 1966.
CONSTANTINE, Baron, (*Constantine*). Cr. 1969. Ext. 1971.
COUTANCHE, Baron (*Coutanche*). Cr. 1961. Ext. 1973.
CROWTHER, Baron (*Crowther*). Cr. 1968. Ext. 1972.
DALTON, Baron, (*Dalton*). Cr. 1960. Ext. 1962.
DELACOURT-SMITH, Baron, (*Delacourt-Smith*). Cr. 1967. Ext. 1972.
DONOVAN, Baron, (*Donovan*). Cr. 1963. Ext. 1971.
FISHER OF LAMBETH, Baron, (*Fisher*). Cr. 1961. Ext. 1972.
FISKE, Baron, (*Fiske*). Cr. 1967. Ext. 1975.
FLOREY, Baron, (*Florey*). Cr. 1965. Ext. 1968.
FRANCIS-WILLIAMS, Baron, (*Williams*). Cr. 1962. Ext. 1970.
FRASER OF LODSDALE, Baron, (*Fraser*). Cr. 1958. Ext. 1974.
GARNSWORTHY, Baron, (*Garnsworthy*). Cr. 1967. Ext. 1974.

PEERAGES DISCLAIMED

Under the terms of the Peerage Act, 1963.

* ALTRINCHAM, Barony of, (*Grigg*). Cr. 1945. Disclaimed 1963.
* ARCHIBALD, Barony of, (*Archibald*). Cr. 1949. Disclaimed 1975.
* BEAVERBROOK, Barony of (*Aitken*). Cr. 1917. Disclaimed 1964.
* DURHAM, Earldom of (*Lambton*). Cr. Baron Durham 1828, Viscount Lambton and Earl of Durham 1833. 1828, Viscount Lambton and Earl of Durham 1833. Disclaimed 1970.
* FRASER OF ALLANDER, Barony of, (*Fraser*). Cr. 1964. Disclaimed 1966.
* HAILSHAM, Viscountcy of, (*Hogg*). Cr. Baron Hailsham 1928, and Viscount Hailsham 1929. Disclaimed 1963.
‖ HOME, Earldom of, (*Douglas-Home*). Cr.—‖Lord Home 1473, ‖(or *) Lord Home (or Hume) of Berwick 1604, ‖Earl of Home and Lord Dunglass 1605, and * Baron Douglas 1875. Disclaimed 1963.
§ MONKSWELL, Barony of, (*Collier*). Cr. 1885. Disclaimed 1964.
* REITH, Barony of (*Reith*). Cr. 1940. Disclaimed 1972.
* SANDERSON OF AYOT, Barony of, (*Sanderson*). Cr. 1960. Disclaimed 1971.
‡ SANDWICH, Earldom of, (*Montagu*). Cr.—Baron Montagu, Viscount Hinchinbrooke, and Earl of Sandwich 1660. Disclaimed 1964.
* SILKIN, Barony of (*Silkin*). Cr. 1950. Disclaimed 1972.
† SOUTHAMPTON, Barony of, (*FitzRoy*). Cr. 1780. Disclaimed 1964.
§ STANSGATE, Viscountcy of, (*Benn*). Cr. 1942. Disclaimed 1963.

EXTINCT or DORMANT

Since 1950. For Extinctions in the years 1900-50 see 1958 and earlier editions.

‡ Baronets of England (1611–1707).
|| Baronets of Nova Scotia (or Scotland) (1625–1707).
§ Baronets of Ireland (1619–1800).

† Baronets of Great Britain (1707–1800).
* Baronets of United Kingdom (1801 onwards).

* ALISON.	Cr. 1852.	Ext. 1970.
* ANDERSON.	Cr. 1920.	Ext. 1963.
* AYLWEN.	Cr. 1949.	Ext. 1967.
* BAKER.	Cr. 1802.	Ext. 1959.
* BARBOUR.	Cr. 1943.	Ext. 1951.
* BARLOW, MONTAGUE-.	Cr. 1924.	Ext. 1951.
* BARRATT, LAYLAND-.	Cr. 1908.	Ext. 1968.
* BASS.	Cr. 1882.	Ext. 1952.
* BELL.	Cr. 1909.	Ext. 1955.
* BELL, MORRISON-.	Cr. 1923.	Ext. 1956.
* BENYON.	Cr. 1958.	Ext. 1959.
* BIGGE, SELBY-.	Cr. 1919.	Ext. 1973.
* BILSLAND (Baron Bilsland).	Cr. 1907.	Ext. 1970.
* BLAIR.	Cr. 1945.	Ext. 1962.
† BLAKE.	Cr. 1772.	Ext. 1975.
* BOOT.	Cr. 1916.	Ext. 1956.
‡†BOUGHTON, ROUSE-.	Cr. 1641 and 1791.	Ext. 1963.
‡ BOYNTON.	Cr. 1618.	Ext. 1966.
* BRAITHWAITE.	Cr. 1954.	Ext. 1958.
§ BROWNE (Earl of Kenmare).	Cr. 1622.	Ext. 1952.
* BULLOCK.	Cr. 1954.	Ext. 1966.
‡ BURDETT.	Cr. 1619.	Ext. or Dormant 1951.
|| BURNETT.	Cr. 1626.	Dormant 1959.
* BURNS (Baron Inverclyde).	Cr. 1889.	Ext. 1957.
† BURRARD.	Cr. 1769.	Ext. 1965.
* BUTCHER.	Cr. 1960.	Ext. 1966.
* CAIN.	Cr. 1920.	Ext. 1969.
* CAINE.	Cr. 1937.	Ext. 1971.
* CAIRD.	Cr. 1928.	Ext. 1954.
* CAMERON.	Cr. 1893.	Ext. 1968.
* CAMPBELL.	Cr. 1939.	Ext. 1954.
|| CAMPBELL, HOME-PURVES-HUME-.	Cr. 1665.	Ext. 1960.
* CARGILL.	Cr. 1920.	Ext. 1954.
* CHARLES,	Cr. 1928.	Ext. 1975.
* CHILD.	Cr. 1868.	Ext. 1958.
* CHUBB.	Cr. 1919.	Ext. 1957.
* CHUTE.	Cr. 1952.	Ext. 1963.
* COATS, GLEN-.	Cr. 1894.	Ext. 1954.
* COHEN.	Cr. 1905.	Ext. 1968.
* COLMAN.	Cr. 1952.	Ext. 1966.
* COOPER.	Cr. 1905.	Ext. 1961.
‡ COPE.	Cr. 1611.	Ext. or Dormant 1972.
* COPE.	Cr. 1918.	Ext. 1966.
† CORNEWALL.	Cr. 1764.	Ext. 1962.
* CORNWALL.	Cr. 1918.	Ext. 1962.
* COURTHOPE (Baron Courthope).	Cr. 1925.	Ext. 1955.
* COWAN.	Cr. 1921.	Ext. 1956.
* CRAIK.	Cr. 1926.	Ext. 1955.
* CROSS.	Cr. 1912.	Ext. 1963.
* CROSS.	Cr. 1941.	Ext. 1968.
* CUNNINGHAM (Viscount Cunningham of Hyndhope).	Cr. 1942.	Ext. 1963.
† CURTIS.	Cr. 1794.	Ext. 1954.
* DALRYMPLE.	Cr. 1887.	Ext. 1971.
* DALRYMPLE, ELPHINSTONE-.	Cr. 1828.	Dormant 1956.
|| DALYELL.	Cr. 1685.	Dormant 1935.
* DAVID.	Cr. 1911.	Ext. 1964.
* DAWSON.	Cr. 1929.	Ext. 1974.
* de CAPELL BROOKE.	Cr. 1803.	Ext. 1968.
* DE CRESPIGNY, CHAMPION-.	Cr. 1805.	Ext. 1952.
* DEELEY, MALLABY-.	Cr. 1922.	Ext. 1963.
* DENYS.	Cr. 1813.	Ext. 1960.
‡ DERING.	Cr. 1527.	Ext. 1975.
* DOMVILE, POE-.	Cr. 1912.	Ext. 1959.
† DOUGLAS.	Cr. 1786.	Ext. 1969.
* DUFF.	Cr. 1952.	Ext. 1952.
* DUNCAN.	Cr. 1905.	Ext. 1964.
* DUNCAN.	Cr. 1957.	Ext. 1974.
* DUNDAS.	Cr. 1898.	Ext. 1970.
* DUNN.	Cr. 1917.	Ext. 1971.
* DUNNELL.	Cr. 1922.	Ext. 1960.
* ELLERMAN.	Cr. 1905.	Ext. 1973.
* ELLIS.	Cr. 1932.	Ext. 1956.
* EVANS.	Cr. 1902.	Ext. 1970.
* EVANS, WORTHINGTON-.	Cr. 1916.	Ext. 1971.
* FARRER (Baron Farrer).	Cr. 1883.	Ext. 1964.
* FLANNERY.	Cr. 1904.	Ext. 1959.
* FOSTER.	Cr. 1838.	Ext. 1960.
* FOX.	Cr. 1924.	Ext. 1959.
* FREAKE.	Cr. 1882.	Ext. 1951.
* FRY.	Cr. 1929.	Ext. 1960.
* GAMMANS.	Cr. 1956.	Ext. 1957.
* GLYN (Baron Glyn).	Cr. 1934.	Ext. 1960.
§ GODFREY.	Cr. 1785.	Ext. 1971.
* GOLDNEY.	Cr. 1880.	Ext. 1974.
|| GORDON.	Cr. 1631.	Dormant 1956.
† GRAEME, HAMOND-.	Cr. 1783.	Ext. 1969.
* GREEN.	Cr. 1901.	Ext. 1959.
* GREGORY.	Cr. 1931.	Ext. 1952.
* HAMPSON.	Cr. 1642.	Ext. 1969.
‡ HANSEN.	Cr. 1921.	Ext. 1958.
* HART.	Cr. 1893.	Ext. 1970.
* HAWKEY.	Cr. 1945.	Ext. 1975.
* HAY.	Cr. 1635.	Dormant 1966.
|| HEADLAM.	Cr. 1935.	Ext. 1964.
* HILLS.	Cr. 1939.	Ext. 1955.
* HINDLEY (Viscount Hyndley).	Cr. 1927.	Ext. 1963.
* HOARE (Viscount Templewood).	Cr. 1899.	Ext. 1959.
* HOLDEN.	Cr. 1909.	Ext. 1965.
* HOLLINS.	Cr. 1907.	Ext. 1963.
* HOLT.	Cr. 1916.	Ext. 1968.
* HORNBY.	Cr. 1899.	Ext. 1971.
* HUGHES.	Cr. 1942.	Ext. 1958.
* HUNTER, HUGHES-.	Cr. 1906.	Ext. 1951.
* HUTCHISON.	Cr. 1928.	Ext. 1972.
* JAFFREY.	Cr. 1931.	Ext. 1953.
* JARDINE.	Cr. 1919.	Ext. 1965.
* JARVIS.	Cr. 1922.	Ext. 1965.
* JENNER.	Cr. 1868.	Ext. 1954.
* JOHNSON, WEBB- (Baron Webb-Johnson).	Cr. 1945.	Ext. 1958.
* JONES.	Cr. 1917.	Ext. 1952.
* JONES, PROBYN-.	Cr. 1926.	Ext. 1951.
* JONES, PRYCE-.	Cr. 1918.	Ext. 1963.
* KERR.	Cr. 1957.	Ext. 1974.
† KING, DUCKWORTH-	Cr. 1792.	Ext. 1972.
* LANE.	Cr. 1913.	Ext. 1972.
* LAURIE.	Cr. 1942.	Ext. 1954.
* LAWSON.	Cr. 1831.	Ext. 1959.
* LAWSON.	Cr. 1905.	Ext. 1973.
* LEE.	Cr. 1941.	Ext. 1967.
‡ LEICESTER.	Cr. 1671.	Ext. 1968.
|| LESLIE.	Cr. 1625.	Dormant 1967.

THE SOVEREIGN, ROYAL FAMILY, PEERAGE, BARONETAGE AND OTHER DIGNITIES AND RANKS.

ROYAL CROWN AS HERALDICALLY DEPICTED

THE SOVEREIGN.

THE SOVEREIGN is in honour, dignity, and in power—and the seat and fountain of all three, possessing, according to Camden,

> " Many rights and privileges peculiar to majesty termed by the learned lawyer, *sacra sacrorum*, that is, sacred and individual, or inseparable because they cannot be severed; and the ordinary royal prerogatives, termed the flowers of his crown, in which respect they affirm that the regal material crown is adorned with flowers. Some of these are held by positive or written law, others which, by right of custom, by a silent consent of all men without law, prescription of time has allowed, the king justly enjoys."

The Crown is held under the Act of Settlement (12 and 13 William III, cap. 2), the wording of which, with reference to succession, is:—

> " For default of issue of the said Princess Ann and of His Majesty respectively the crown and regall government of the said kingdoms of England France and Ireland and of the dominions thereunto belonging with the royall state and dignity of the said realms and all honours stiles titles regalties prerogatives powers jurisdictions and authorities to the same belonging and appertaining shall be remain and continue to the said most excellent Princess Sophia [of Hanover] and the heirs of her body being Protestants."

Under the Statute of Westminster, 1931, any alteration in the law touching the Succession to the Throne or the Royal Style and Titles shall require the assent as well of Parliament of all the Dominions as of the Parliament of the United Kingdom.

Among the more clearly defined prerogatives of the British monarch are those of convoking, adjourning, removing, and dissolving Parliament, refusing assent to Bills, without which assent they cannot become law, increasing the number of Peers, declaring war at pleasure, choosing and appointing all commanders and officers by land, sea, and air, and all judges, councillors, officers of state, magistrates, Archbishops, Bishops, and high ecclesiastical dignitaries, bestowing all public honours, and pardoning criminals, besides exercising many other powers, by the advice of the Cabinet Ministers, who, however, alone are responsible, the theory of English law being that the Sovereign cannot commit wrong.

Another theory of our law is that the King (or Queen) never dies—substantially, that the throne is never vacant, the succession of the heir being instantaneous. A meeting of the Privy Council is held immediately after the Demise of the Crown (usually the next day) to give directions for proclaiming the new Sovereign. The proclamation takes place in London at St. James's Palace, at Charing Cross, within the City Boundary at Temple Bar, and at the Royal Exchange, two or three days later. To this first meeting of the Privy Council of the new Reign, the Lord Mayor and Aldermen, etc., of London, although not themselves Privy Councillors, are invited. Since the Reform Act of 1867 Parliament does not dissolve at the Demise of the Crown, and, if at the time adjourned or prorogued, meets immediately, or, if dissolved, the old Parliament must meet at once and may serve for six months. The ceremony of a coronation, although essential, is a solemn recognition and confirmation of the royal descent and consequent right of accession, and is not necessary for the security of the title to the crown.

Before Edward I our Kings began to reign only after their coronations, being styled Duke of Normandy until that time.

Some of the styles of pre-Conquest kings were elaborate, such as King Edgar (957–975) called *Rex Anglorum* and *Basileus Anglorum*, and Edward the Martyr as *Gratia Dei Rex totius Albionis.* For styles since 1066, see " SOVEREIGNS."

It was not until Henry IV adopted the title of " Grace," that prefixes came into use. These prefixes were successively changed to " Excellent Grace," " High and Mighty Prince," and " Highness ", until Henry VIII adopted those of " Majesty " and " Dread Sovereign."

The Sovereign's banner, commonly called the Royal Standard, is the personal flag of the Sovereign, and can only properly be flown over buildings or ships with Her Majesty's permission, which permission is only granted when the Queen is actually present in person, and not when Her Majesty is passing in processions.

THE QUEEN MOTHER.

Takes precedence amongst ladies immediately after the Queen, and has her own Household.

THE HEIR APPARENT TO THE CROWN.

Is next below the Sovereign in all honour and dignity—not as participating or comparing with the latter, who stands alone and supreme, but as enjoying the largest share of the honour which flows from the Crown; though in the present reign HRH the Duke of Edinburgh has ranked next to HM the Queen under the terms of a Royal Warrant dated 18th Sept., 1952.

No person can hold this position save a son of the Sovereign, or, if the former be dead, his direct male descendant.

The Heir Apparent has, since the institution of the title by Edward I (who, in 1301, conferred it on his son, Edward, born at Caernarvon in 1284), usually but not invariably been *created* Prince of Wales. Since 1399, the Earldom of Chester has always been conferred, together with the Principality of Wales. There is no succession to this title, which, at every vacancy, becomes merged in the Crown, and is only renewed by the Sovereign's pleasure. Thus, had George IV died whilst Prince of Wales, his next brother, though heir apparent, would not have become the Prince of Wales without being so created.

PLUME OF THE ELDEST SON OF THE SOVEREIGN.*

The Sovereign's eldest son is Duke of Cornwall (peerage of England) and Duke of Rothesay (peerage of Scotland) from the moment of his birth or the Sovereign's accession, and becomes immediately entitled to the revenues of the Duchy of Cornwall. When there is no Duke of Cornwall, the Duchy is in the custody of, and the revenues are paid to the Crown. The titles of Duke of Cornwall and Duke Rothesay, unlike that of Prince of Wales, do not become merged in the Crown on succession to the Monarchy or at death (unless the Sovereign has no son), but passes at once to the next heir apparent being the eldest living *son* of the Sovereign, to whom it is strictly limited.

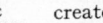

By course of the civil law the heir apparent sits at the right hand of the Sovereign in all solemn assemblies of state and honour; but he has no kingly prerogatives, and acknowledges reverence to his sovereign. He comes of age automatically on becoming Duke of Cornwall however tender his years†. Thus he may take his seat in Parliament at the Sovereign's will.

A statute of Edward III enacts " that to compass or imagine the death of the King's eldest son and heir is *crimen læsæ majestatis* " (high treason).

CORONET OF ELDEST SON OF THE SOVEREIGN.

In 1898 Letters Patent under the Great Seal were granted, declaring that the children of the eldest son of any Prince of Wales shall at all times have the title of " Royal Highness," but by further letters patent December 1917, this privilege was confined to the eldest living son only of the eldest son of the Prince of Wales.

The Prince of Wales was invested at Caernarvon Castle on July 1st, 1969, as the 21st Prince of Wales, and was introduced to the House of Lords on Feb. 11th, 1970.

---

* This plume of feathers, generally spoken of as " The Prince of Wales's feathers," is not in reality such, but is the badge of the Heir Apparent, in whom it is vested whether created Prince of Wales or not.
† Princes (The) Case 1606, 8 Co. Rep. 1a, 13b, and note to Blackstone's Commentaries Vol. 1, 15th ed. p. 242.

MEMBERS OF THE ROYAL FAMILY.
The rank and position of these are defined in the general
" Tables of Precedence."

The Latin *Princeps* signified " the first." Before the reign of Henry VIII the only prince was the Prince of Wales. As a courtesy title the style of Prince and Princess gradually superseded Lord—and Lady—though the latter styles were in use as late as the reign of Charles II for his nieces. In Scotland the style of Prince of Scotland is borne by the eldest son of the Sovereign. The first charter is one granted by Robert III on 10th Dec., 1404, in favour of his son James. Until the Reform Act, 1832, tenancy of 40s. freehold from the Prince of Scotland was a qualification for a vote in Scottish counties.

The Royal Marriages Act prohibits the marriage of personages (descendants of George II) connected with the Blood Royal (except issue of Princesses who have married into Foreign Families) without the sanction of the Sovereign, but this is considerably modified by a conditional proviso, by which a marriage contracted after the age of twenty-five is valid if a year's notice has been given to the Privy Council and both Houses of Parliament, and they have not interfered during that period expressing their disapprobation. Private marriages do not give the rank of the husband to the wife or issue of the marriage, and

| CORONET OF THE YOUNGER SONS, DAUGHTERS, BROTHERS, AND SISTERS OF THE SOVEREIGN. | CORONET OF SONS AND DAUGHTERS OF THE SON AND HEIR APPARENT OF THE SOVEREIGN. | CORONET OF SONS AND DAUGHTERS OF THE SONS OF THE BROTHERS OF THE SOVEREIGN. | CORONET OF SONS AND DAUGHTERS OF THE DAUGHTER OF THE SOVEREIGN. |

although duly consecrated and the issue legitimate, do not confer upon the children any right of succession to hereditary honours.

Up to 1917 the Sovereign's sons, daughters, grandsons and granddaughters (being issue of sons), brothers, sisters, and uncles and aunts (on the Sovereign's side), the children of the eldest son of any Prince of Wales were all styled " Royal Highness." Grandchildren who were issue of daughters were sometimes granted by Royal Warrant the title of " Highness ". Since that date the style of " Royal Highness " has been confined to the issue of any Sovereign and to issue of the sons of any Sovereign. The titles of " Prince " and " Princess " are similarly confined to *all* children of any Sovereign and to the children of the sons of any Sovereign. [See also under Heir Apparent.] The style of " Princess Royal," which is held for life, is customarily granted by declaration to the eldest daughter of the Sovereign after a vacancy has occurred. If, however, a vacancy exists at the time of birth of the first-born daughter of a Reigning Sovereign, she is born " Princess Royal." The first Princess so styled was the eldest daughter of Charles I.

The coronet of the Princes of the Blood Royal is similar to that of the Heir Apparent, but without the arch and orb. All Royal Coronets are chased as jewelled. Princes and Princesses sign with their Christian names only, and not by any Peerage title they may hold.

THE PEERAGE.

LORDS SPIRITUAL.

Lords Spiritual consist of the Archbishops of Canterbury and York and twenty-four Bishops (by rotation, but including always the Bishops of London, Durham, and Winchester). The sixteen Junior Bishops do not have seats in the House of Lords. The Bishop of Sodor and Man is unable to vote in the House of Lords, as he is a legislator in the Isle of Man. It has been the custom to bestow a barony on a retired Archbishop. A bishop on resigning his see ceases to be a peer of Parliament.

The Archbishop of Canterbury is the first peer of England next to the Royal Family, preceding not only all Dukes, but all the great officers of the Crown. The Bishop of London is his provincial Dean, the Bishop of Winchester his Chancellor, and the Bishop of Worcester his Chaplain. " It belongs to him to crown the King "; and the Sovereign and his or her Consort, wherever they may be located, are *speciales domestici parochiani Arch. Cant.* (parishioners of the Lord Archbishop of Canterbury).

The Archbishop of Canterbury is Primate of *all* England, is entitled to the prefix of " Your Grace," and styles himself " By Divine Providence, Lord Archbishop of Canterbury."

The Archbishop of York is the third peer in the United Kingdom, and precedes **all** secular peers, except the Lord High Chancellor. He is " Primate of **England**," and is perpetual chaplain of the Queen Consort. He is entitled to the prefix **of** " Your Grace," styles himself " By Divine Providence, Lord Archbishop **of** York," and possesses within his own province powers nearly equivalent to those exercised by the Archbishop of Canterbury within his. His precedence rests on an Act of Parliament in 31st year of Henry VIII.

An Archbishop's mitre is the same as that of a Bishop.

Diocesan Bishops of England, with the exceptions noted are also peers of the kingdom and of Parliament, and take precedence of the temporal barons.

The Bishops of London, Durham, and Winchester have precedence over all the other bishops who rank according to the seniority of their consecration.

A Diocesan bishop is entitled to the prefix of Lord, and styles himself " Right Reverend Father in God, by Divine Permission, Lord Bishop of——.''

The mitre, placed over the arms of a bishop, is a round cap, pointed and cleft at the top, from which hang two pendants, fringed at the ends, it is surmounted by a fillet of gold, set with precious stones. The mitre of the Bishop of Durham (as nominally Count Palatine of Durham) is represented as issuing out of a ducal crest coronet.

Archbishops and Bishops who are entitled to a seat in the House of Lords possess all the faculties and privileges of Peers of Parliament during the time they hold office.

A bishop impales his arms with those of the See, but he does not bear crest, supporters, or motto.

The wives and children of bishops do not have any precedence as such.

PEERS

The degrees of the Peerage of England, Scotland, Ireland, Great Britain and the United Kingdom are five—viz., *Dukes, Marquesses, Earls, Viscounts,* and *Barons* (including Life Barons).

Scottish peers take precedence of British peers of the same rank created since the Union with Scotland. *Irish peers* created before the Union with Ireland, in like manner, take place of British peers created since. Irish peers of later creation than the Union, rank according to the dates of their patents, among the peers of Great Britain and Ireland. Peers holding only Scottish titles have been enabled to sit in the House of Lords since the passing of The Peerage Act, 1963. By that Act, the enactments relating to the election of Scottish Representative Peers, by which they were elected by their fellow-Peers for one Parliament only, ceased to have effect.

Peers holding only Irish titles are not eligible to sit in the House of Lords Representative Peers were (before establishment of the Irish Free State) elected by their fellow peers for life.

Irish peers are not disqualified from being elected as members in the House of Commons for any constituency in the United Kingdom, and to vote at elections for the House of Commons whether or not they be members of that House.

Peers of England, Scotland, Great Britain, and the United Kingdom are not entitled to sit in the House of Commons.

Since 1958 women have been admitted to the Upper House as Life Peeresses, and also since 1963, hereditary Peeresses of England, Great Britain, the United Kingdom, and Scotland.

Peers may not take their seats in the House of Lords until they are of age. If they then desire to do so they are required to prove their right of succession, after which a writ of summons is issued. Peerage patents are on parchment, and bear no signature, only the Great Seal.

The ceremony of admitting a peer into the House of Lords. He is introduced by two peers of his own degree, who conduct him to the Lord Chancellor. His patent is carried by Garter King of Arms. The new peer presents it together with his writ of summons to the Lord Chancellor, who directs the same to be read. The oaths are administered, the peer takes his seat, and then, rising, he returns to the Chancellor, who congratulates him upon his elevation.

PRIVILEGES OF PEERS

The privileges enjoyed by peers were formerly numerous. Amongst those abolished is the privilege in cases of treason and felony of being tried by their peers only, who gave their verdict simply *upon their honour*, in a court specially fitted up at the expense of the Crown. This was discontinued under the Criminal Justice Act of 1948.

The privileges which continue are:—

Exemption from Jury Service.
Access to the Sovereign.
Immunity from attachment, *i.e.* freedom from arrest in civil cases for a period of 40 days before and after a meeting of Parliament (a privilege shared with Members of Parliament, but it is wider for a Peer, since under Common Law "the person of a Peer is forever sacred and inviolable.")

A peer (but not a peer by courtesy) is entitled to have Supporters granted to be borne with his arms, and to the use of the coronet of his rank.

CLAIMS TO PEERAGES

Claims to dormant or abeyant Peerages or to Peerages whose succession is in dispute, are dealt with by the Committee for Privileges of the House of Lords on petition to the Crown, presented through the Home Secretary, who first refers the accompanying documents to the Attorney-General in order that he may report upon them to the Sovereign and advise in the matter.

These the Attorney-General passes to the Counsel for the Crown in Peerage claims, and he reports to the Attorney-General, who then, to obtain further particulars and elucidate any further details necessary, hears the petitioner and his counsel, after which the Attorney-General himself reports to the Home Secretary. If his report is unfavourable to the petitioner he advises that the petition shall not be referred to the Committee for Privileges. If on the contrary, he considers that the proofs and documents submitted at the hearing made out a *prima facie* case, he advises the House of Lords to refer it to their Committee for Privileges, which goes into the case in detail, the petitioner and any opposing claimant being represented by counsel, while the Crown is represented by the Attorney-General and the counsel for Peerage claims. The Committee for Privileges reports to the Sovereign the conclusions at which it arrives.

The Select Committee on Peerages in Abeyance 1926 made the general recommendations that, in the absence of special circumstances or special reasons to the contrary, no abeyance should be terminated, the first commencement of which occurred more than 100 years before the presentation of the committee, and no petition should be allowed to proceed where the petition represents less than one-third of the entire dignity.

ACCELERATED PROMOTION TO HOUSE OF LORDS

On occasions the eldest son of a peer has been summoned to the House of Lords during his father's lifetime in one of his father's minor titles, and in such cases if he predeceased his father the title and seat passed to his son (if any). The last instance of this practice occurred in 1951 when the eldest son of the 2nd Earl of Ancaster was called to the House of Lords in his father's Barony of Willoughby d'Eresby.

SELECTION OF PEERAGE TITLES

The Sovereign, as the fountain of all honour, can bestow any title She may please, but in practice the following rules are usually observed.

Titles once conferred upon any member of the Royal Family are not again bestowed outside the Royal Circle.

A title once extinct but subsequently revived, is rarely re-created in a lower rank than before, but this rule is not an invariable one.

Every peer below the rank of Earl must be described in his patent as " of——" (somewhere), usually the seat of the recipient, or some place with which he has a connection. Some peers are *created* with a territorial designation as actually *part of the title*, such as *Baron Ritchie of Dundee*, of Welders, Chalfont St. Giles, *Baron Brassey of Apethorpe*, of Apethorpe, and *Baron Ponsonby of Shulbrede*, of Shulbrede. It will be noted that in such cases there is a double territorial designation.

Any semblance of duplication of titles is avoided as far as ever possible.

A surname, if desired, may *always* be adopted as a title, although another dignity of the same style be at the time in existence. In that case the recipients of all such similar (surname) titles of the same rank, except the first (then existing one) to be created, *must* add the territorial designation as an affix to the title by which they are commonly known. For instance, Baron Stanley (creation 1455); Baron Stanley (creation 1832) known as " Lord Stanley of Bickerstaff "; Baron Stanley (creation 1838) as " Lord Stanley of Alderley "; Baron Stanley (creation 1886) as " Lord Stanley of Preston." Again, Baron Curzon (creation 1794), and Baron Curzon (creation 1898) as " Lord Curzon of Kedleston."

In the case of Life Peers the surname is usually adopted.

The name of a county or county town is not as a rule permissible as a peerage title below the rank of earl (although exception may be made in favour of any one particularly eminent either as a statesman or in some other walk of life). Important towns are usually reserved for the higher steps in the peerage.

SIGNATURES

Peers sign by their titles only, as also do the eldest sons of peers bearing as a courtesy title one of their father's minor honours, but a peeress by marriage signs with her Christian name or initial prefixed to the title. A peeress in her own right, however, signs with title only. Archbishops and Bishops sign with their Christian name, followed by province or see (in the cases of diocesan bishops the see is sometimes in Latin).

REMAINDERS TO PEERAGES

A peerage created by patent descends according to the limitation mentioned in the patent of creation, usually to the heir male of the body of the first peer, but special remainders are sometimes granted to others of the family (e.g. to daughters, brothers or sisters, etc., and the heirs male of their bodies).   War leaders such as Nelson, Kitchener, Allenby, Mountbatten and Portal, if there was no male issue to inherit, were given special remainders for the peerages to have an extra chance of survival.

The complicated succession to Baronies, which are held to have been created by a writ of summons to Parliament and the doctrine of abeyance have been discussed in detail in the Complete Peerage, Vol. IV, Appendix H.

In the Peerage of Scotland remainders vary according to the limitation. The destination may be to heirs male whatsoever (i.e. to the senior male heir, despite the extinction of the male line descending from the first peer), heirs male of the body, heirs male of tailzie (entailed estates), heirs whatsoever (i.e. whether male or female), or succession according to a series of named individuals. Some Scottish peerages were granted with " shifting remainders." An example is the Earldom of Selkirk. When a line of Earls became extinct, the next son of the Duke of Hamilton inherited. This occurred in 1885 and again in 1940. Until the Act of Union 1707, Scottish Peerages were capable of being surrendered to the Crown, who re-conferred them with different remainders.

In the Peerage of Ireland succession descends according to the limitation. Though the origin of the more ancient peerages is not always known, it is held that there are now only two which could pass in the female line. These are the Viscountcy of Massereene and the Barony of Loughneagh, created in the 16th century, with remainder, in default of issue male, to the heirs general. Both of these are held by Viscount Massereene and Ferrard.

Legitimated children are included in the Peerage articles, but are not normally in remainder to the peerage concerned, a possible exception being that persons of Scottish domicile may be in remainder to a Peerage of Scotland.

LIFE PEERS AND PEERESSES

Prior to the passing of the Life Peerages Act of 1958 the only Life Peers were the Lords of Appeal in Ordinary and no women sat in the House of Lords. Since then, however, men and women have been appointed peers or peeresses and rank as Barons or Baronesses for life. Each is entitled to a writ of summons to attend, and to sit and vote in the House of Lords.

The Life Barons' wives rank as Baronesses, and are entitled to the prefix of " Lady," while their children, and those of Life Baronesses, are styled " Hon." for life and hold special precedence.

Lords of Appeal in Ordinary hold office during good behaviour, notwithstanding the demise of the Crown, but may be removed from such office, on the address of both Houses of Parliament.

DISCLAIMING OF PEERAGES

The Peerage Act 1963, which received Royal Assent on 31st July, 1963, authorised the disclaimer for life of certain hereditary peerages. The principal provisions are summarized below.

(1) *Disclaimer of certain hereditary Peerages*

A person subsequent to this Act who is already a peer or who succeeds to a peerage of England, Scotland, Great Britain or the United Kingdom may, by an instrument of disclaimer delivered to the Lord Chancellor disclaim that peerage for life.

The instrument for one who succeeds to a peerage shall be delivered within the period of 12 months beginning with the day of succession to the peerage. If the person is under 21 on succession, the period of 12 months begins with the day he attains that age. No instrument shall be delivered in respect of a peerage by one who has applied for a writ of summons to attend the House of Lords.

The period for one who succeeded before the commencement of this Act is 12 months beginning with the commencement of the Act, or if under 21, 12 months beginning with the day he attains that age. An instrument of disclaimer may be delivered notwithstanding that he has applied before commencement of this Act, for a writ of summons to attend the House of Lords.

In either case, in reckoning the period for delivery of the instrument, no account shall be taken of time during which, to the satisfaction of the Lord Chancellor, the person is rendered by infirmity incapable of exercising or determining whether to exercise his rights.

(2) *Disclaimer by M.P.s and Parliamentary Candidates*

The period for a M.P. who succeeds to a peerage is one month beginning with the date of succession. Until that period expires he shall not, by virtue of that peerage, be disqualified from membership of the House of Commons, whether or not he has delivered an instrument of disclaimer, provided he does not sit or vote in the House of Commons whilst exempt from disqualification, or that he has not applied for a writ of summons to attend the House of Lords.

Where a person who succeeds to a peerage has been or is nominated at a Parliamentary election, held in pursuance of a writ issued before his succession, he shall not be disqualified by virtue of that peerage for election to the House of Commons at that election, unless he has applied for a writ of summons to the House of Lords. If he is elected, the above time limit will apply to him as if he had succeeded to the peerage immediately after the declaration of the result of the election.

Where an instrument of disclaimer is delivered by a person to whom this section applies, a copy shall be delivered to the Speaker.

In reckoning the period, no account shall be taken of any time during which (a) proceedings are pending on any parliamentary election petition in which the right to be elected or returned to the House of Commons is in issue, (b) the person is shown to the satisfaction of the Speaker to have any infirmity as in Section 1, (c) Parliament is prorogued, or both Houses are adjourned for more than 4 days. If Parliament is dissolved during the period for delivery of disclaimer, the provisions of this section shall cease to apply to him in respect of the peerage in question.

(3) *Effects of Disclaimer*

The disclaimer of a peerage shall be irrevocable, and shall operate from the date by which the instrument is delivered to divest him, and his wife, of all right and interest to or in the peerage, and all titles, rights, offices, and privileges and precedence attaching thereto, and to relieve him of all obligations and disabilities (including any disqualification in respect of membership of the House of Commons and elections to that House) arising therefrom, but shall not accelerate the succession to that peerage nor affect its devolution on his death.

Where a peerage is disclaimed, no other hereditary peerage shall be conferred, and no writ of acceleration shall be issued in respect of that peerage to the person so entitled on his death.

STYLES AND PRECEDENCE OF THE CHILDREN OF PEERS WHO DISCLAIM THEIR PEERAGES

Statement issued by Garter King of Arms

Paragraph 4(b) of the Report of the Joint Committee on House of Lords Reform recommended that " the wife and descendants of a Peer who surrenders should not use the courtesy titles or enjoy the social precedence derived from such a Peer." The Peerage Act 1963, however, while dealing in terms with the effect of disclaimer on a disclaiming Peer himself and his wife, does not so deal with the effect on his children. This has, therefore, to be inferred and it might be argued on the one hand that the children of a Peer who disclaims are no longer the children of a Peer and so no longer enjoy the style and precedence which they would have enjoyed as such. Or it might be argued on the other hand that the Act does not deprive them of the styles and precedence they have enjoyed prior to their father's disclaimer and they may, therefore, still enjoy these just as the daughters of a peer continue to do so even if their father has died leaving no heir to his peerage."

The Home Office, which is concerned with precedence through the Home Secretary's responsibility for advising the Sovereign on Petitions for special precedence, has so far been unwilling to express a view on the point of law or to deal with the matter by recommending the issue of a Royal Warrant.

It is, therefore, necessary for the Earl Marshal, as the principal authority under The Crown for matters connected with style and precedence, to decide on a policy in the situation as it at present stands.

The Earl Marshal has been advised by Mr. G. D. Squibb, QC, Norfolk Herald Extraordinary, that in his view the children of a disclaiming Peer retain their precedence as the children of a Peer and the same view has been expressed by the Lord Lyon King of Arms.

While, therefore, it is open to any child of a disclaiming Peer to say that he or she no longer wishes to be known by the courtesy title hitherto accorded him or her, in those cases where such children wish still to be accorded their courtesy titles the Earl Marshal and his Officers will so accord them.

PARLIAMENTARY QUALIFICATIONS OF SCOTTISH PEERS, IRISH PEERS, AND PEERESSES IN OWN RIGHT

The holder of a peerage in the peerage of Scotland shall have the same right to receive writs of summons to attend the House of Lords, and to sit and vote in that House, as the holder of a peerage in the peerage of the

United Kingdom; and the enactments relating to the election of Scottish representative peers shall cease to have effect.

The holder of a peerage in the peerage of Ireland shall not by virtue of that peerage be disqualified—

(a) for being or being elected as a member of the House of Commons for any constituency in the United Kingdom, or

(b) for voting at elections for that House whether or not he is a Member of that House.

A woman who is the holder of an hereditary peerage in the peerage of England, Scotland, Great Britain or the United Kingdom shall (whatever the terms of the letters patent or other instrument, if any, creating that peerage) have the same right to receive writs of summons to attend the House of Lords, and to sit and vote in that House, and shall be subject to the same disqualifications in respect of membership of the House of Commons and elections to that House as a man holding that peerage.

DUKE.—This title (from Latin *Dux*, a leader) is the highest in our Peerage. As we have no " princes " outside the blood-royal, so pre-eminent in dignity is the ducal title, that each royal prince, shortly after attaining his majority is usually created a Duke; the titular style of Prince, apart from the Prince of Wales, being one of courtesy. Thus, Prince Henry was created *Duke* of Gloucester.

Since the title Duke signified Sovereign status, *e.g.* William the Conqueror was Duke of Normandy—it was not adopted until 1337, when Edward III conferred the Dukedom of DUKE'S CORONET. Cornwall on his eldest son, the Black Prince. This was followed by Henry Duke of Lancaster in 1351. Both were created, in Parliament by the girding of the sword. Ceremonial attaching to the creation of this dignity was discontinued in 1615, and it now takes place by patent under the Great Seal.

The first subject to receive a dukedom who was not a member of the royal family, nor one nearly connected, was Sir William de la Pole, Marquess of Suffolk, who was created Duke of Suffolk in 1448.

There were no Dukedoms in existence during the reign of Elizabeth I, after the attainder of the Duke of Norfolk 1572, when the whole order according to Judge Blackstone " became utterly extinct." The Ducal order was revived in England by James I in the person of his favourite, George Villiers, Duke of Buckingham.

A Duke is styled *Most Noble* (or less formally *His Grace*), and by the Sovereign in public instruments, *Our right trusty and right entirely beloved cousin,* with the addition of *and counsellor* when a member of the Privy Council.

MARQUESS.—The term *Marchio* was applied in the Norman period to the Earl or Baron guarding the Welsh or Scottish Marches, or border territories. Similarly in Germany the Count or Graf became known as the Markgraf, anglicised to Margrave. By the twelfth century it had lost its territorial significance. It was introduced to England by Richard II, brother-in-law of the Margrave of Brandenburg, the honour being conferred upon Robert de Vere Earl of Oxford, who became Marquess of Dublin in 1385. MARQUESS'S The precedence between Dukes and Earls caused great CORONET. offence to the latter, and the patent was revoked in 1386 in favour of the Dukedom of Ireland. The next recipient did not appreciate the degree. When John Beaufort, Marquess of Dorset, was attainted and the House of Commons appealed to Richard II for its restoration, Beaufort begged the king not to restore this particular title " as the name of Marquess is a strange name in this realm."

The creation to this dignity was formerly attended with nearly the same ceremony as that of a duke.

The style of a marquess is *Most Honourable.* He is formally styled by the Sovereign, *Our right trusty and entirely beloved cousin (and counsellor* when of the Privy Council).

EARL.—Before Canute an ealdorman administered a shire or province for the King. In Latin documents he was styled *Dux* or *Comes,* taking a place between the royal Atheling and the thegn. Under Canute the Danish equivalent of Earl was introduced.

Under the Normans the government of an earl was normally restricted to one county and became hereditary, though losing the functions of the King's representation in the county to the sheriff. An earl was usually invested with the third EARL'S CORONET. penny out of the sheriff's court of the county, of Anglo-Saxon origin.

The dignity was created by the girding on of the sword as a symbol of temporal authority, but this lost some of its significance when in 1328 Roger

Mortimer was created Earl of March, derived neither from a county or a city. The ceremony continued after earls were created by patent, and in the reign of Edward VI a cape of dignity and a golden circlet were added to the ceremony, but in 1615 such ceremonies were discontinued.

Earldoms were originally created in fee, but from the reign of Richard II they were either created for life or in tail male.

An Earl is styled *Right Honourable*, and is formally addressed by the Sovereign as *Our right trusty and entirely beloved cousin (and counsellor* when of the Privy Council.)

VISCOUNT.—This title had its origin in the office of deputy or lieutenant *Vice-Comes)* of a Count, which had become hereditary in the Empire  by the beginning of the tenth century. It was also used as the Sheriff of a county. Henry VI, crowned King of England and France, created John Lord Beaumont in 1440 Viscount Beaumont in England and Viscount Beaumont in France (a title forfeited by the Duke of Alençon in 1415, and vacant on the death of the Duke of Bedford 1435), in order to integrate the titles of the two countries. The peerage title received precedence above all Barons, but it did not become popular until the seventeenth century. Viscounts were always created by patent.

VISCOUNT'S CORONET.

A Viscount's style is *Right Honourable*. He is addressed by the King or Queen as *Our right trusty and well-beloved cousin (and Counsellor* when a Member of the Privy Council).

BARON.—Barons were introduced into England by the Normans, most of whom held that rank in Normandy before the Conquest. Baron meant  literally a man, being the King's tenant in chief, i.e. holding his land directly from him. The burgesses and leading citizens of London were also known collectively as Barons, and this style was allowed them by clerks who wrote the writs of William II and Henry I. The barons of the Cinque Ports are a parallel to the barons of London (see " Norman London " by Sir Frank Stenton, " Social Life in Early England " edited by Geoffrey Barraclough, 1960). In the thirteenth century they were summoned to the Counsel or Parliament, but at first this did not imply that a successor would necessarily also be summoned to subsequent Parliaments. The more important would probably be summoned, but by the reign of Edward III it became usual for successors to receive writs as a matter of course. Thus the Baronage emerged into an hereditary dignity of the Peerage.

BARON'S CORONET.

The first baron created BY PATENT was John Beauchamp de Holt, created Baron Kidderminster, by Richard II in 1387 with remainder to his heirs male, but baronies by writ continued to be created long after this date.

The succession to baronies by writ is not limited to heirs male, but is vested in heirs-general. In the event of the death without male issue of a baron by writ the title will fall into abeyance should he leave two or more daughters, and so will continue until only one daughter or the sole heir of one of the daughters survives. The Crown can, however, at any time terminate the abeyance in favour of any one of the co-heiresses, but it cannot alienate the barony from the respresentatives of the first baron.

When a baron is called to the House of Peers by writ of summons, the writ is in the Sovereign's name.

A baron is styled *Right Honourable* and formally by the Sovereign *Right trusty and well-beloved (and Counsellor* when a Member of the Privy Council).

In Scotland, Sir George Mackenzie, Lord Advocate to Charles II, made it clear that the equivalent of Barons in England are Lords of Parliament in Scotland, as the word " baron " in Scots law relates to Feudal Barons. This claim was immediately and correctly put forward by several Scottish Lords when they received summons as Barons to the House of Lords. Their protests were accepted and they were sent fresh summons as Lords.

LORDS OF SESSION IN SCOTLAND

Are the Senators of the College of Justice in Scotland, and on appointment to the Bench take the judicial title of Lord ————, with the prefix of " Hon.", by which they are known and addressed (though they subscribe by their initials and surname), with the exception of the Lord Justice-General and Lord Justice-Clerk. Both of these are not usually described by the judicial title by which they take their seats but by their official designations, being primarily Officers of State.

By Royal Warrant granted in February 1905, Scottish Lords of Session who have retired are permitted to retain the title of " Honourable Lord," while their wives are also granted the title of " Lady," to be retained after the decease of the husband, but during widowhood only.

Since 1912, a chairman of Scottish Land Court receives a Judicial title, by which he is always known both in office and retirement.   He is treated as a Lord of Session.

BARONETS

The term baronet was first applied to the nobility who lost the right of individual summons to Parliament; and in this sense was used in a statute of Richard II.   It is said that Sir Robert Cotton's discovery of William de la Pole's patent in the 13th year of Edward III, conferring upon him the dignity of a Baronet in return for a sum of money, suggested the revival of the Order.

The hereditary Order of Baronets in England was erected by Letters Patent by King James I on 22nd May, 1611, for the settlement of Ireland. He offered the dignity to 200 gentlemen of good birth, with a clear estate of £1,000 a year, on condition that each one should pay into the King's Exchequer in three equal instalments a sum equivalent to three years' pay to 30 soldiers at 8d. per day per man.   The first instalment was to be paid on the delivery of the patent.   The Baronets form the sixth division of *Nobiles Majores*, following the five degrees of the Peerage.

The *Baronetage of Ireland* was erected on 30th September, 1611; the *Baronetage of Scotland or Nova Scotia* on 28th May, 1625, for the establishment of the plantation of Nova Scotia.   After the union of England and Scotland in 1707 no further Baronets of England or Scotland were created, the style being changed to Baronet of Great Britain.   With the union of Great Britain and Ireland in 1801, all Baronets subsequently created were under the style of the United Kingdom.

The Official Roll of Baronets was first gazetted 23rd February, 1914.   By a further Royal Warrant dated 10th March, 1922, anyone who considers he is entitled to be enrolled therein is at liberty to petition the Crown through the Home Secretary.   Every person succeeding to a Baronetcy must exhibit his proofs of succession to the Secretary of State.   Should the Secretary of State find any difficulty in advising the Crown as to any claim, he refers the matter to the Law Officers for their opinion, and further, may, on consideration of that opinion, direct that the matter be referred to the specially appointed Committee of the Privy Council for examination and advice to the Crown. The Roll is kept at the Home Office by the Registrar of the Baronetage.

The Standing Council of the Baronetage, the office of which is at Kent House, Telegraph Street, EC2, was founded in 1898 to maintain the ancient rights and privileges of the Degree.

A baronet's wife is entitled to the prefix of either " Dame " (followed by christian name) or " Lady " without christian name, but the former style is now only used in legal and formal documents.

A baronet's helmet is depicted as for a knight.

Privileges.—Under the first Letters Patent it was ordained that only two hundred Baronets of England were to exist at any one time.   This limitation was soon withdrawn.   No degree or dignity, etc., was ever to be created which would be superior or equal to the degree and dignity of Baronet.

Under the second Letters Patent it was stated that no person or persons should have or take place between Baronets and the younger sons of Viscounts and Barons.   Privileges included the right of knighthood for Baronets and their eldest sons, and the addition of the Arms of Ulster as a canton or inescutcheon in armorial bearings, argent a sinister hand couped at the wrist and erect gules, known as the Badge of Ulster.   A third Letters Patent, ratified and confirmed the above, and included the precedence of the eldest sons of Baronets before eldest sons of knights whatever the order, and with similar provisions respecting other sons.

BADGE OF ULSTER.

Baronets of Ireland have similar privileges except that in some cases the Baronets of Ireland have used a dexter hand for the Badge of Ulster.

Baronets of Scotland or *Nova Scotia* were to enjoy the same privileges except the Ulster augmentation, and in addition grants of land in Nova Scotia, with plenary baronial rights and jurisdiction, and legislative powers in that plantation, but such grants ceased in 1638.   They were given precedency above lesser Barons in Scotland, the addition of the Arms of Nova Scotia in armorial bearings, power to sit and vote by deputy in the Scottish Parliament when absent from the Kingdom, and the right to wear about the neck the badge of Nova Scotia, suspended by an orange-tawny ribbon.   This consists of an escutcheon argent with a saltire azure thereon, an inescutcheon of the arms of Scotland, with an Imperial Crown above the escutcheon, and encircled with the motto *Fax mentis Honestae Gloria*.   This Badge may be shown suspended by the ribbon below the shield of arms.

BADGE OF NOVA SCOTIA.

Baronets of England and Ireland applied to Charles I for permission to wear a badge.   Although a badge was worn in the 17th century, of which specimens still exist, it was not until 1929 that King George V granted permission to all baronets other than those of Scotland to wear round their necks a Badge. This was composed of the Arms of Ulster, on a silver field, a left hand gules, surmounted by an Imperial Crown, enamelled in proper colours, the whole enclosed by an oval border embossed with scroll work of (4) roses for baronets of England, (2) shamrocks for baronets of Ireland, (3) roses and thistles for baronets of Great Britain, and (4) roses, thistles and shamrocks combined for baronets of UK. The badge to be suspended from an orange riband with a narrow edge of dark blue on both sides, the total breadth to be 1¾ inches, and the breadth of each edge to be ¼ inch. The Badge may be shown suspended by its riband below the shield of arms. Baronets wishing to wear this badge may purchase it at their own expense. Application should be made to the Registrar of the Baronetage or the Standing Council of the Baronetage, if a Member of that body.

BADGE OF BARONETS OF THE UNITED KINGDOM.

Baronets were accorded the courtesy title of Honourable from the erection of the degree, but this fell into disuse at the beginning of the 19th century. Despite petitions, this privilege has not been conceded by the Crown.

George IV revoked the privilege of demanding knighthoods for eldest sons or heirs apparent of Baronets upon attaining their majority, but without prejudicing Letters Patent granted before 19th December, 1827. In 1874, Ludlow Cotter, son of Sir James Lawrence Cotter, 4th baronet of Rockforest, when 21 years of age, received the honour of knighthood. This is the latest instance of the privilege being exercised. Since then few claims have been made and they have all been refused, presumably on the ground that it was unconstitutional for a Sovereign to bind his successors to confer titles in the future on persons unborn.

REMAINDERS TO BARONETCIES

The destination of a baronetcy is in accordance with the limitation mentioned in the patent of creation. Though this is usually to the heirs male of the body of the first baronet, special remainders were sometimes granted (e.g. North of Southwell, 1920, failing heirs male of the body, to the male issue to daughters of the first baronet).

Baronetcies of Nova Scotia, or Scotland, were sometimes created with remainder to heirs male (i.e. the heir male of the first baronet, despite the extinction of his own descendants in the male line) and " heirs male and of tailzie ". There are three existing Scottish baronets with the last remainder, whose descent, together with entail of estates, may pass to the heir general, viz. Dalyell of the Binns, Dunbar of Hempriggs, Hope-Dunbar of Baldoon and Stirling-Maxwell of Pollok.

Legitimated children are included in the Baronetage articles but are not normally in remainder to the baronetcy concerned. A possible exception is that a person of Scottish domicile may be in remainder to a Nova Scotia baronetcy.

KNIGHTS

Knighthood was a medieval institution of chivalry of both a religious and military character. Its birth and growth in Europe is obscure. It was conferred upon sovereigns, princes and others of noble rank, but not on ecclesiastics. The word has an affinity with horsemanship, a Roman knight, *eques*, a horseman, had held rank next below the Senatorial. The name thus indicates its original occupation as a military equestrian, hence the German Reiter and the French Chevalier. In old English *cnight* meant at first a youth or military follower, and later trusted servant.

Knighthood was introduced to England at least as early as the reign of Alfred the Great, who made his grandson, Athelstan, a knight, and gave him a scarlet mantle set with precious stones and a sword with a golden scabbard.

With the arrival of the Normans, knights formed an integral part of the feudal system. In the Conqueror's time there were about 5,000 knights who served as fighting men under the command of the King's Barons. The Barons granted them some of their lands in return for military service when required, *i.e.*, by knight-service, theoretically for periods not exceeding forty days. The knights in turn granted lands to sub-tenants, and by 1100 there was a system of commuting military service by payment of money known as scutage or shield money. Henceforward those in possession of

KNIGHT'S HEL- knights fees did not necessarily take up knighthood. Those MET   eligible received knighthood on coming of age. As a result of

this system, landless knights for service in the field came into existence, from whom evolved the knights bachelor.

In early times a knight was dubbed by his lord, his father or another knight. William Rufus was knighted by Archbishop Lanfranc. Matthew Paris recorded that the Earl of Gloucester invested his brother William with a military girdle, and Gilbert de Clare was knighted by Simon de Montfort. Kings used to send their sons to neighbouring courts to receive the honour of knighthood; thus Henry II sent to David King of Scots, and Malcolm King of Scots to Henry II and Edward I to the King of Castile.

By the reign of Henry III reluctance for taking up knighthood became apparent, and in 1244 that King introduced distraints of knighthood and summons to those who qualified, with a fine for those who declined. Elaborate ceremonial and pageantry were then introduced, accompanied by feasting and jousting to make knighthood more attractive. From those who did not take up knighthood arose the esquire class.

Two main methods of conferring knighthood were used in the Middle Ages. The simpler form used on the battle-field was for the knight elect to kneel before the commander of the army who struck him with the sword on his back and shoulder with words such as " Avancez chevalier au nom de Dieu ". The more elaborate method of knighting for which the dubbing became restricted to the King took place on special occasions. This included presentation of robes, arms and spurs, and was accompanied by vigil and bathing before being dubbed. This later evolved into the Knighthood of the Bath, of whom knights were created at coronations, royal marriages, etc. The first record of these knights is at the coronation of Henry IV, but they were not banded into any Society or Order such as the Garter, founded by Edward III about 1348, until the reign of George I.

Knights Banneret were created from personal distinction in battle rather than on feudal tenure, and were conferred on the field. All the greater nobility were entitled to bear banners, and on the creation of a banneret the points of his pennon were ceremoniously cut by the commander of the army. The last three Knights Banneret are believed to have been conferred by the Protector Somerset after the Battle of Pinkie, 1547, upon Sir Ralph Fane, Sir Francis Bryan and Sir Ralph Sadler.

See Orders of Knighthood for information concerning the various Orders of Chivalry.

The use of prefix " Sir " is not borne by honorary knights of these orders when, as is usually the case, the accolade has not been conferred and no special warrant has been granted permitting use of this appellation. This also applies to clerics of the Established Church, who likewise do not receive the accolade (their wives being entitled to precedence, but not to style of " Lady ").

The Imperial Society of Knights Bachelor has its Registry at 21, Old Buildings, Lincoln's Inn, WC2.

The wife of a knight is entitled to the prefix of either " Dame " (followed by christian name), or " Lady " (without christian name), but the former style is now only used in legal documents.

A knight's helmet is depicted with visor up and without bars. The seventeenth century English rule that the helmet must be full faced may now be disregarded if inconvenient for the design of the crest.

In 1926 a Badge was granted for the use of Knights Bachelor. (See Orders of Knighthood.)

ESQUIRES

Esquire (Latin *scutarius*, shield-bearer) was a personal attendant on a knight, which evolved into an apprentice knight, and later into a lord of a manor. The numbers were swelled by those of the knightly class who did not take up knighthood. By the 14th century an esquire (armiger) practically attained equality with a knight both in function and privileges. With the rise of the use of the term gentleman as a rank, it became increasingly difficult to know where the lower limit should be drawn. Sir John Fearn, in his " Glory of Generositie " 1586, referred to four sorts of esquires; by creation, birth, dignity, and office. He commented that this title " is no less abused and profaned " than that of gentleman, and that " the degree of esquire is through custom tolerated to many other sorts of gentlemen, but they all, or most of them, are . . . in function of some offices of justice or govern-

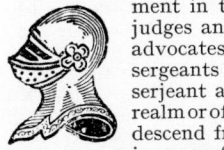

ment in the King's palace, as . . . annexed to the dignities of judges and barons of the benches and courts of justice; to the advocates and procurators of the sovereign; to the degree of sergeants at the coif; to the office of sheriff, escheator, and serjeant at arms; to the eldest born of a baron and peer of the realm or of a knight, besides many others. But that the same should descend from the father to the son, as the state of gentry doth,

ESQUIRE'S HEL- is mere fabulous. For the title of esquire of common right
MET doth appertain to none, except that by creation he receives the same at the sovereign's hand, or else through the bearing of such an office

as a dignity anent to the same, or else by right of birth as in cases aforesaid, and that through custom".

Robert Glover, Somerset Herald, in 1580, drew up a list of those entitled and in 1681 an officer of arms, probably Dugdale, in a similar list, stated that heralds should only allow the title of esquire to · 1, the heir male of the younger son of a nobleman; 2, the heir male of a knight; 3, those by long prescription can show their lineal ancestors so styled; 4, sheriff of a county, a JP or those so styled in the King's commission (who cease to hold the title when the office ceases); 5, certain of the king's servants by reason of the office they bear, such as officers of arms, sergeants at arms, etc.

To these should now be added Royal Academicians (included by George III), Companions, Commanders, Officers and Members of Orders of Knight-hood and Chivalry, Sergeants at law, Queen's Counsel, Deputy Lieutenants and Commissioners of Lieutenancy, Commissioners of the Court of Bank-ruptcy, Masters of the Supreme Court; also persons to whom the Sovereign grants arms with the title of Esquire, persons who are styled Esquires by the Sovereign in their patents, commissions or appointments, and officers of and above the rank of Lieutenant RN, Captain in the Army and Flight Lieutenant.

An esquire's helmet is depicted with visor closed. The seventeenth century English rule that the helmet must be depicted in profile to the dexter may now be disregarded if inconvenient for the design of the crest. In Scotland the visor is garnished with gold.

Scottish Titles.—Scottish law recognizes a number of special titles which fall under the jurisdiction of the Lord Lyon King of Arms, and are recognized by the Crown. Such recognized chiefly styles and territorial designations of chieftains (branch chiefs) and lairds are legally recorded as a part of the surname under Statute 1672, cap. 47. A Scottish feudal baron is allowed the cap of dignity. Supporters are granted to chiefs of clans and ancient fami-lies, and feudal barons older than 1592.

GENTLEMEN

Originally gentleman (latin *gentilis*, Norman-French *gentil* and *gentil-homme*) meant no specific class but included barons, esquires and even franklins (free-tenants), *i.e.*, all who were not ignoble. By the early 15th century it came to have a specific meaning. Sir George Sitwell contended that this arose from an Act of Parliament, 1413 (Statute I, Henry V, cap. 5) that with all writs of action, personal appeals and indictments which involved processes of outlawry, the estate, degree or mystery of the defendant was to be stated. Thus in 1431, as printed in Feudal Aids, land-owners were classed as knights, esquires, gentlemen, yeoman, etc.

When gentlemen became regarded as a distinct order, they were associated with armigers, bearers of coats of arms. As late as the 15th century most of these were not granted in effect by the King, for the greater nobles maintained their own heralds and bestowed arms on their tenants. Sir George Sitwell asserted that heralds " were never authorised by the Crown to make a gentle-man ", but Sir Anthony Wagner, Garter King of Arms (in *Heralds and Heraldry in the Middle Ages*, 1939) points out that there are many refer-ences as early as the reign of Henry VIII to grants containing an ennobling clause. Though a right to arms became decisive evidence of gentility, it is apparent from the records of the High Court of Chivalry that there were those who were non-armigerous who were allowed the status for other reasons, such as military rank held, the fact that the father held a certain office, or that the individual had influential relations. It is also clear that the manner of living had some effect, for yeoman could be more wealthy than a gentleman, though he lived in rougher style. In one family various members were frequently accorded the rank of gentlemen, yeomen and husbandmen. Fearn in 1586 included a student of common law, a groom of the Sovereign's Palace, a churl's son made a priest or canon, those brought up in the service of a Bishop or Baron, governors of cities, etc. Commissioned officers below the rank stated under esquire are given the rank of gentleman. The helmet is as for an esquire, though in Scotland there is a distinction in that a gentleman's helmet is ungarnished. Prior to 1672, Scots gentlemen were allowed shields only.

FOREIGN TITLES

Foreign titles cannot be valued in comparison with British ones, according to their nominal rank. Their devolution is different from and often much wider than the British peerage. Titles of the Holy Roman Empire descend to all male descendants in the male line *ad infinitum*, and certain of those of the old Italian States can be given or left by will at the pleasure of the holder. It was the practice for the Crown, on the advice of the Secretary of State for the Home Department, to grant licences for the use of foreign titles by those domiciled in this country. In 1930 King George V decided that no more licences for the use of foreign titles in this country should be granted. In 1932 a Royal Warrant was issued revoking all licences then in force, with the exception of those issued for the life of the holder and his heir apparent. At that time there were 31 dignities which were allowed under the exception clause.

DEBRETT'S

ALPHABETICAL LIST OF

ROYAL WARRANT HOLDERS.

This list includes the names of individuals and firms holding Warrants of appointment to **H.M. the Queen,** to **H.M. Queen Elizabeth the Queen Mother,** to **H.R.H. the Duke of Edinburgh,** to **H.M. the late King George VI,** to **H.M. the late King George V,** to **H.M. the late Queen Mary,** and to **H.R.H. the late Duke of Windsor,** when **Prince of Wales,** based on the names published in the *London Gazette* dated Jan. 1st, 1975. It is neither official nor necessarily exhaustive, and the body of Warrant Holders is subject to frequent alterations, Warrants being liable to become void by death, retirement, or bankruptcy of the individuals, partners, or directors in whose names they are granted, and also by change of designation of firms.

N.B.—Use of Royal Arms and Insignia for trading purposes is STRICTLY confined to firms HOLDING Royal Warrants of appointment and the words " By Appointment " should be placed underneath. These Warrants, however, do not carry the right to fly the Royal Standard, or to the use of the word " Royal," and by Clause 68 of the Trade Marks Act 1905 any person who without proper Royal authority uses in connection with any trade, business, calling, or profession, the Royal Arms, or any device, emblem, or title, may be restrained by injunction or interdict from continuing so to use the same. At the demise of the Crown, Warrants become void, but in certain circumstances they may be renewed for the new reign. Warrants issued by H.R.H. the late Duke of Windsor, when Prince of Wales, entitle Holders to display the Prince of Wales's Arms and to style themselves "By Appointment " in conjunction with the relevant dates, but not to fly His Royal Highness's Standard, nor to use the word " Royal."

The following marks show to whom the Warrant of Appointment is held:—

¶ To H.M. The Queen.
+ To H.R.H. The Duke of Edinburgh.
○ To Her Majesty Queen Elizabeth The Queen Mother.
△ To The Late King George VI.

* To The Late King George V.
† To The Late Queen Mary.
‡ To The Prince of Wales 1921-1936.

○Ackerman's Chocolates Ltd., Confectioners, 9, Goldhurst ter., Finchley Rd., N.W.6. T N 01-624 2742.

¶Addressograph-Multigraph Ltd., Manufacturers of Office Equipment, Maylands Avenue, Hemel Hempstead, Herts. T N 2251.

△Agnew, Thos., & Sons, Ltd., Fine Art Publishers, 43, Old Bond St., W1X 4BA. T A Resemble, London, W.1; T N 01-629 6176.

¶Airwick, Ltd.

AIRWICK LTD.

Manufacturers of Airwick

Hunting Gate, Wilbury Way

Hitchin, Herts SG4 0TF

By Appointment to H.M. The Queen Manufacturers of Airwick

T.A. Airkemwick, Hitchin, Herts

T.N. Hitchin (0462) 50641

Telex 825016

¶Alden & Blackwell (Eton) Ltd., Booksellers, Eton College, Windsor. T N Windsor 63849.

¶○Allan, James, & Son, Ltd., ¶Boot and Shoe Makers: ○Shoemakers, 123, Princes St., Edinburgh EH2 4AF. T A Shoes, Edinburgh; T N 031-226 6081.

¶Allen & Neale (Chemists), Ltd., Chemists, High St., King's Lynn. T N 0553 2459.

ALLIED BREWERIES (UK) LIMITED

Brewers of Ale and Lager Burton-on-Trent

By Appointment To Her Majesty The Queen Brewers of Ale and Lager

T.N. 0283 45320

T.A. Abuk Burton-on-Trent

¶Alvan Blanch Development Co., Ltd., Suppliers of Grain Driers, Chelworth, Malmesbury, Wilts SN16 9SG. T N Crudwell 333.

○†Amor, Albert, Ltd., ○Suppliers of Fine Porcelain, †Fine Art Dealers, 37, Bury St., St. James's, S.W.1. T N 01-930 2444.

¶+Anderson, William, & Sons, Ltd., Tailors and Kiltmakers, 14 & 16, George St., Edinburgh, EH2 2QD. T N 031-225 6656.

¶Angostura Bitters (Dr. J. G. B. Siegert & Sons), Ltd., Manufacturers of Angostura Aromatic Bitters, Groveland House, 11-12, Bow Churchyard, E.C.1. T A Arutsogna, London, E.C.4 ; T N 01-248 4953.

+**ANSAFONE LTD.,** Manufacturers and Distributors of Telephone Answering Machines, 19, Upper Brook Street, London, W1Y 2HS. T N 01-629 9232; Telex 24946.

¶+Anstee & Co., Ltd., Forage Merchants, 187, Wandsworth High St., SW18 4JE. T N 01-874 1960.

○Aquascutum, Ltd., Makers of Weatherproof Garments, 700, Regent St., W1A 2AQ. T A Aquascutum London, W.1; T N 01-734 6090.

¶Archibald, James L., & Sons, Ltd., Cabinet Makers and Upholsterers, 6-14 & 34, Great Western Rd., Aberdeen, AB9 2LQ. T N 56181.

¶Ardath Tobacco Co., Ltd., Suppliers of Cigarettes, 10, Smith Sq., S.W.1. T A Vectatio, London, S.W.1; T N 01-222 1222.

¶○Arden, Elizabeth, Ltd., Suppliers of Cosmetics, 76, Grosvenor St., W.1. T A Elizarden, London, W1A 2AE; T N 01-629 8211.

¶◯Army & Navy Stores, Limited, Suppliers of Household and Fancy Goods, Victoria St., SWᵢE 6QX. T N 01-834 1234.

¶◯Army & Navy Stores (Bromley) Limited, Suppliers of Household and Fancy Goods, High Street, Bromley, Kent. T N 01-460 9991.

¶Ashwell Scott Ltd.

Ashwell Scott Ltd.
(formerly Ashwell & Nesbit Ltd.)

Mechanical and Electrical Services

By appointment to Her Majesty Queen Elizabeth II Heating Ventilating and Stoker Engineers

62 CLARENDON STREET, NOTTINGHAM NG1 5JH
Telephone: 0602 49761-4

¶◯Asprey & Co. Ltd.

ASPREY & CO. LTD.
Silversmiths and Jewellers

By Appointment to H.M. The Queen Goldsmiths, Silversmiths and Jewellers Asprey & Co. Ltd. London

New Bond Street, London, W1Y 0AR T.A. Culleus, London, W.1; T.N. 01-493 6767 TELEX 25110

By Appointment to H.M. Queen Elizabeth The Queen Mother Jewellers Asprey & Co. Ltd. London

¶Associated Fisheries & Foods Ltd., Fishmongers, Neptune House, 4-28, Varcoe Rd., Bermondsey, S.E.16. T N 01-237 5281.

¶Associated Portland Cement Manufacturers Ltd. (The), Cement Manufacturers, Portland House, Stag Place, London, SWᵢE 5BJ. T N 01-828 3456.

¶Austin-Morris Group—British Leyland (U.K.) Ltd., Manufacturers of Austin Motor Cars, Longbridge Works, Bristol Road South, Birmingham 31. T N 021-475 2101; Telex 33491.

†Autoscan Ltd., Manufacturers of Power Filing Systems, 51, Scrutton St., London EC2A 4PJ. T N 01-739 2877.

△Ayala, Champagne, Purveyors of Champagne, Ay-Champagne, Marne.

¶Aylesbury Mushrooms, Ltd., Purveyors of Mushrooms, Aston Mullins, Ford, Aylesbury. T N 0296 74 444.

†Baily, John, & Son (Poulters), Ltd., Purveyors of Poultry and Game, 116 Mount St., W.1. T N 01-499 1833.

△Baker, J. W. (China & Glass), Ltd., China and Glass Merchants, 136 & 138 Union St., Aberdeen, AB1 1JD. T N 20648.

¶Bamfords, Ltd., Manufacturers of Farm Machinery and Engines, Uttoxeter, Staffs ST14 8JD. Telex 36180; T N 3151.

¶Banbury Buildings Ltd., Manufacturers of Prefabricated Pressed Concrete Garages, P.O. Box 11, Ironstone Works, Banbury. T N 52500.

†BARBOUR, J. & SONS, LTD.,
Manufacturers of Waterproof and Protective Clothing, Beacon Works, Simonside, South Shields NE34 9PD. T N 2251.

¶Barkers & Lee Smith, Ltd., Manufacturers and Suppliers of Animal Feeding Stuffs, Barkers Mills, Lincoln LN5 7HN. T N 0522 27412; Telex 56453.

¶Barron & Shepherd Ltd., Lift Manufacturers, 134, King Street, Hammersmith, London, W6 0QU. T N 01-748 0311; T A Bargram, London, W6.

¶Barrow Hepburn Equipment Ltd., Manufacturers of Royal Maundy Purses, Corunna Works, Stewart's Road, London, SW8 4UZ. T N 01-622 9900.

¶Bartholomew, John, & Son Ltd., Suppliers of ◯Maps, Duncan Street, Edinburgh EH9 1TA. T N 031-667 9341.

¶Bass Production Ltd., Brewers, High St., Burton-on-Trent DE14 1JZ. T N 0283-45301.

†Batsford, B. T., Ltd., Booksellers and Publishers, 4, Fitzhardinge St., W.1. T A Batsfordia, London, W.1; T N 01-486 8484.

¶Baxter, G. G., Ltd., Suppliers of Pork Sausages, 319, Central Markets, Smithfield, EC1A 9AA. T N 01-236 5197.

¶◯Baxter, James, & Son, Purveyors of Potted Shrimps, 1, The Crescent, Morecambe, Lancs. T N 0524 910.

¶◯Baxter, W. A., & Sons, Ltd., ¶Fruit Canners: ◯Purveyors of Scottish Specialities, Fochabers, Scotland IV32 7LD. T A Preserves, Fochabers; T N 393/7.

†Bayntun, George, Bookseller, Manvers St., Bath. T N 0225 66000.

¶B. & E. Boilers, Ltd., Boiler Makers, Easthampstead Road, Bracknell, Berks RG12 1NP. T N 0344-21341; Telex 847520.

¶Beaufort (Air-Sea) Equipment, Ltd., Suppliers of Life-saving Equipment, Beaufort Rd., Birkenhead, Cheshire. T N 051-652 2667.

¶Beecham Products, Suppliers of Lucozade and Schloer, Beecham House, Gt. West Rd., Brentford, Middlesex. T N 01-560 5151.

¶Beeston Boiler Co., Ltd. (The), Manufacturers of Cast Iron Sectional Boilers, Mona St., Beeston, Notts. T A Foundry, Beeston, Notts; T N 0602 254271; Telex 377559.

*Begg, John, Ltd., Scotch Whisky Distillers, Trafalgar House, 75, Hope St., Glasgow, G2 6AN. T A Takapeg; T N 041-221 4518.

+Beken of Cowes, Ltd., Marine Photographers, 16 Birmingham Rd., Cowes, Isle of Wight. T A Beken; T N 2223.

¶Bell Lionel R., Art Photographer, 227 Streatham High Road, London, SW16 6EN. T N 01-769 1458.

¶Belling & Co., Ltd., Manufacturers of Electrical Appliances, Bridge Works, Enfield, Middx. T A Belling; T N 01-804 1212.

¶Bendicks (Mayfair) Ltd., Manufacturers of Chocolates, Moorside Rd., Winnall, Winchester, Hants. T N 63175.

¶Bennett & Fountain Ltd., Suppliers of Electrical Equipment, 182a, High Street, Beckenham, Kent. T N 01-650 7111.

¶Bennett, R. S., & Co., Ltd., Suppliers of Agricultural Machinery and Farm Equipment, Howdale Rd., Downham Market, Norfolk. T N 3245.

¶†Benney, Gerald, Goldsmith and Silversmith, Beenham House, Beenham, Berkshire RG7 5LJ. T N Bradfield 370.

¶Benoist, V., Ltd., Purveyors of Table Delicacies, 78-86, Percy Rd., Hammersmith, London W12 9QD. T A Gourmet, London, W.12; T N 01-743 0161.

△Benson & Clegg, Ltd., Tailors, 34, Bury St., S.W.1. T A Bencle, London, S.W.1; T N 01-930 3625.

¶†Benson & Hedges, Ltd., Tobacconists, 13, Old Bond St., W1X 4QP. T A Hedges, London, W1; T N 01-493 1825.

¶Bentall, E. H., & Co. Ltd., Manufacturers of Agricultural Provender Equipment, Heybridge Works, Maldon, Essex CM9 7NW. T N Maldon (Essex) 54433.

¶Bentley, Joseph, Ltd., Suppliers of Horticultural Chemicals, Barrow-on-Humber, South Humberside DN19 7AQ. T A Bentley, Barrow-on-Humber; T N 0469 30501.

¶Berkel & Parnall, Ltd., Manufacturers of Slicing Machines, Enfield, Middx. T A Berkels, Phone, Enfield; T N 01-804 2001.

¶Berol Ltd., Manufacturers of Venus Pencils, Northway House, High Rd., London, N20 9LP. T N 01-446 3273.

¶Berry Bros. & Rudd, Ltd., Wine and Spirit Merchants, 3, St. James's St., S.W.1. T A Berrinche, London, S.W.1; T N 01-930 1888.

¶Bibby, J., Agriculture, Ltd., Manufacturers of Animal Feeding Stuffs, Richmond House, 1 Rumford Place, Liverpool, L3 9QQ. T A Feeding, Liverpool, L3 9QQ; T N 051-236 6671.

¶Billings & Edmonds, Ltd., Tailors and Outfitters, 22/23 Princes St., Hanover Sq., W1R 8EX. T A Princified, London, W.1; T N 01-629 1266.

¶Binns, Ltd., House Furnishers, 143-149, Princes St., Edinburgh, 2. T N 031-225 2472.

¶○BLACK & EDGINGTON LTD.,

¶Tent & Flag Makers. ○Flag Makers. Queen Elizabeth St., Tower Bridge, London, SE1 2LU. T N 01-407 3734.

△Block, Grey & Block, Limited, Wine Merchants, 26, South Audley St., W.1. T A Blockanko, London, W.1; T N 01-629 4804.

¶BOCM Silcock Ltd., Suppliers of Cattle Foods, Basing View, Basingstoke. T N 29211.

¶Boddy, W. J., & Son Ltd., Manufacturers of Dairy Equipment, 35, St. Giles St., Norwich. T N 20328-9.

¶Bollinger, J., Purveyor of Champagne, Ay-Champagne (Marne).

¶Bond & Lacey Ltd., Bitumen Roofing Contractors, 18, Eaton St., Norwich, Norfolk. T N Norwich 52557.

¶Booth's Distilleries, Ltd., Gin Distillers, 93, Park Lane, London, W1Y 3TA. T N 01-499 8181; T A Booth's Distilleries, London, W.1.; Cables, Membrey, London, W.1.

¶Boots Co. Ltd. (The) Manufacturing Chemists, Nottingham, NG2 3AA. T A Drug, Telex, Nottingham; T N 56111.

¶Boots Farm Sales, Ltd., Suppliers of Horticultural and Agricultural Preparations, Nottingham, NG2 3AA. T A Drug, Telex, Nottingham; T N 56111.

¶Boots The Chemists Ltd., Chemists, Nottingham, NG2 3AA. T A Drug, Telex, Nottingham; T N 56111.

¶Boulton and Paul (Steel Construction) Ltd., Manufacturers of Farm Buildings, Riverside Works, Norwich, Norfolk, NR1 1EB. T N 60133.

△Bovril, Ltd., Suppliers of Bovril, Bovril House, Southbury Rd., Enfield. T A Fluid, Enfield; T N 01-366 1188.

¶BOWATER PACKAGING LTD.,

Manufacturers of Packaging Materials, Portland House, Stag Place, London, SW1E 5DJ. Tel 01-834 9444.

¶Bowker, A. & J., Suppliers of Animal Feeding Stuffs, Boal Quay, King's Lynn. T N 2013 & 3099.

○Brannam, C. H., Ltd., Pottery Makers, Litchdon Pottery, Barnstaple. T A Brannam, Pottery; T N 3035.

¶Brintons, Ltd., Carpet Manufacturers, P.O. Box 16, Exchange St., Kidderminster, DY10 1AG. T N 3444.

+British Equipment Co., Ltd., Suppliers of Office Machinery, 562, Brighton Road, South Croydon, Surrey, CR2 6XL. T N 01-668 7126.

¶BRITISH NOVA WORKS, LTD.

Manufacturers of Floor Maintenance Products and Waxes, 57-61, Lea Road, Southall, Middx., UB2 5QB. T N 01-574 6531; T A Novahouse, Southall.

¶+British Olivetti, Ltd., Manufacturers of Office Equipment, 30, Berkeley Sq., W.1. T A Olitype, London, W.1; T N 01-629 8807.

¶British Sugar Corporation, Ltd., Manufacturers and Refiners of Sugar, Central Offices, P.O. Box 26, Oundle Road, Peterborough PE2 9QU. T N 0733 63171; T A Sugacrop, Peterborough.

¶British Van Heusen Company, Ltd. (The), Shirt Manufacturers, Victoria Street, Taunton, Somerset, TA1 3JD. T N 0823 87941.

¶○†Broadwood, John, & Sons, Ltd., ¶†Pianoforte Manufacturers : ○Pianoforte Tuners, 9, Hanover St., W1R 0HX. T A Broadwoods, London, W.1; T N 01-629 6731, 6732 & 9969.

¶○Bronnley, H., & Co., Ltd., Toilet Soap Makers, 10, Conduit St., London, W.1. T A Bronnley, London; T N 01-629 8711.

¶Brook Bros. & Dean, Ltd., Suppliers of Furnishing Trimming, Anlaby House, Shoreditch High St., E.1. T N 01-739 7983.

○Brooks, W., & Son (Brook-Jones, Ltd.), Purveyors of Fruit and Quick-Frosted Foods, Hatcham Rd., SE15 1TX. T N 01-639 4343; Telex 883301.

¶Brown, David, Tractors, Ltd., Manufacturers of Agricultural Machinery, Meltham, Huddersfield, HD7 3AR. T A Farming, Meltham; T N 0484 850361; Telex 51201.

¶Brown, William & Co. (Ipswich), Ltd., Timber Product Manufacturers, Greyfriars Road, Ipswich, Suffolk, IP1 1UN. T N 0473 56761.

¶Bryant & May, Ltd., Match Manufacturers, Fairfield Rd., Bow, E3 2QE. T N 01-980 4321.

¶Buchanan, James, & Co., Ltd., Scotch Whisky Distillers, Devonshire House, Piccadilly, W1A 1BN. T N 01-499 5381; T A Girple, London, W1X 6BL.

¶+Buckley, Anthony, Ltd., Photographers, 81, Grosvenor St., London, W1X 9DE. T N 01-629 5235.

○Budgen & Co., Ltd., Grocers, 31/32, High St., Ascot, Berks. T N 0990 21131.

¶Bullens Transport Services Ltd., Road Transport Contractors, Elstree Way, Borehamwood, Herts., WD6 1JQ. T N 01-953 1661; Telex 935041.

¶BULMER, H. P., LTD.,

Cider Makers, Ryelands St., Hereford, HR4 0LE. T N 0432 6411; T A Bulmerco Hereford; Telex 35211.

¶◯Burberrys, Ltd.

Burberrys LTD

The Haymarket,
London, S.W.1
Specialists in
Rainwear and Topcoats
01-930 3343

BY APPOINTMENT TO
HER MAJESTY THE QUEEN
WEATHERPROOFERS
BURBERRYS LIMITED
HAYMARKET, LONDON

BY APPOINTMENT TO
H.M QUEEN ELIZABETH
THE QUEEN MOTHER
WEATHERPROOFERS
BURBERRYS LIMITED
HAYMARKET, LONDON

¶Burgess & Co. (Engineers) Ltd., Heating Engineers, Easthampstead Road, Bracknell, Berks., RG12 1NP. T N 0344 21341.

¶Burgess, John, & Son, Ltd., Manufacturers of Pastes & Creamed Horse Radish, Shaftesbury Rd., N18 1SW. T N 01-807 3080; T A Gorgona, Norphone, London, N.18.

¶+Burton Montague, Ltd., Tailors, Hudson Road Mills, Leeds LS9 7DN. T N 36373.

¶Burton Son & Sanders Ltd.

BURTON SON & SANDERS LTD

By Appointment
to H.M. The Queen
Manufacturers
of Fondant

Manufacturers of
Fondant

College Street, Ipswich
IP4 1DE
Tel: 56234 · Telex 98224

¶Bury & Masco Industries, Ltd., Felt & Carpet Manufacturers, P.O. Box 14, Hudcar Mills, Bury, Lancs., BL9 6HD. T N 061-764 2262; T A Progressbury; Telex 669000.

¶Bush, Frank, Ltd., Ironmongers, 196, St Leonards Road, Windsor, Berks. T N Windsor 63837.

¶◯Cadbury Ltd., Cocoa and Chocolate Manufacturers, Bournville, Birmingham. T A Cadbury, Bournville; Telex No. 33-8011; T N 021-458 2000.

◯Caithness Glass Ltd., Glassmaker, Harrow Hill, Wick, Caithness, Scotland. T N 0955 2286.

¶Caldwell Brothers, Printers, 37 George St., Edinburgh 2. T N 031-225 6097.

¶◯Caley's (Cole Brothers Limited), ¶Suppliers of Household and Fancy Goods; ◯Suppliers of Household and Fancy Goods and Millinery, High Street, Windsor, SL4 1LL. T N 95 63241.

¶◯Calman Links (Trading), Ltd., Furriers, 149, Brompton Rd., SW3 1QX. T N 01-581 1927; T A Stylish, London, S.W.3.

¶Calor Gas Ltd., Suppliers of Liquefied Petroleum Gas, Calor House, Windsor Road, Slough, SL1 2EQ. T N Slough 23824.

¶Campbell Brothers (Edinburgh), Ltd., Purveyors of Meat and Poultry, 60, Queen St., Edinburgh. T A Sirloin; T N 031-225 5471.

◯‡Campbell & Co., ◯Tweed Mercers: ‡Suppliers of Highland Tweeds, Highland Tweed House, Beauly, Scotland. T N 239.

¶Campbell, George, & Sons, Suppliers of Fish and Poultry, 18, Stafford St., Edinburgh, EH3 7BE. T N 031-225 7507.

¶Camper & Nicholsons, Ltd.

CAMPER & NICHOLSONS LTD.

By Appointment
to Her Majesty
Queen Elizabeth II
Yacht Builders

William St., Northam,
Southampton SO9 1WG
TEL: Southampton 29461
T.A.: Nicholsons Southampton
Telex: 47669

¶◯**CARAWAGON INTERNATIONAL LTD,**

Carawagon International Ltd

BY APPOINTMENT TO
H.M. THE QUEEN
MANUFACTURERS OF
SPECIALISED TRAILERS

MANUFACTURERS OF
SPECIALISED TRAILERS
THAMES STREET, SUNBURY-ON-THAMES
MIDDLESEX
TELEPHONE: SUNBURY 85205

¶Cargill, D. W. H. (Potatoes), Ltd., Suppliers of Seed Potatoes, Benholm, Montrose, Scotland. T N Benholm 277.

¶Carlsberg Distributors, Limited

CARLSBERG DISTRIBUTORS LIMITED
Carlsberg House
Old Oak Lane, Willesden
London, N.W.10
Tel. No. 01-965 0369

By Appointment to
H.M. THE QUEEN
SUPPLIERS OF LAGER BEER
CARLSBERG DISTRIBUTORS LIMITED

¶Carpenter, J. W., Ltd., Suppliers of Cleaning Stores, Thame Park Industrial Estate, Thame, Oxon. T N Thame 3232.

¶Carpet Manufacturing Co., Ltd. (The), Carpet Manufacturers, New Rd., Kidderminster, Worcs., DY10 1AL. T N 3434.

¶◯Carr's of Carlisle, Ltd., Biscuit Manufacturers, The Biscuit Works, Carlisle. T A Carr, Carlisle, Telex 64174; T N 24431.

¶◯Carrington & Co., Ltd., ¶Silversmith and Jewellers: ◯Jewellers and Silversmiths, 130, Regent St., London, W1R 6HU. T N 01-734 3727.

¶Cartem Engineering, Ltd., Manufacturers of Sack Holders, Hart St., Maidstone, Kent. T N 0622 55409

◯Carters (J. & A.), Ltd., Invalid Furniture Manufacturers, Alfred St., Westbury, Wilts. T N 037-382 2203.

¶◯Carters Tested Seeds Ltd.

CARTERS TESTED SEEDS LTD.

Seedsmen

By Appointment
to
H.M. The Queen
Seedsmen

Upper Dee Mills, Llangollen
Clwyd LL20 8DD
Tel. 0978 860113

¶◯Cartier, Ltd.

CARTIER LTD.

Jewellers and Goldsmiths

175 & 176 New Bond Street,
W1Y 0QA
T.A. Precious, London, W.1;
T.N. 01-493 6962

By Appointment
to H.M. The Queen
Jewellers and
Goldsmiths

¶Cash, J. & J., Ltd., Manufacturers of Woven Name Tapes, Kingfield, Coventry. T N 0203-23001; Telex 31397.

¶Cassie, William C., Pianoforte Tuner, 35, Leslie Rd., Aberdeen.

¶○Castrol Limited, ¶Manufacturers of Motor Lubricants, ○Purveyors of Motor Lubricants, Burmah House, Pipers Way, Swindon, Wilts., SN3 1RE. T A Castrol, Swindon; T N 0793 30151; Telex 449225.

+Central Audio, Ltd., Suppliers of Sound Recording Equipment, 11/13, Charterhouse Buildings, London, EC1M 7AX. T N 01-253 0328.

¶Cerebos, Suppliers of Table Salt and Pepper, Cerebos House, Victoria Rd., Willesden, NW10 6NU. T N 01-965 6565; Telex 24202.

○Chad Valley Co., Ltd. (The), Toymakers, 234-236 Bradford Street, Birmingham, B12 0PP. T A Vallchad; T N 021-773 5331.

¶Chafer, J. W., Ltd., Suppliers of Agricultural Chemicals, Milethorn Lane, Doncaster, Yorkshire. T N 67371 (10 lines).

¶○Champion Sparking Plug Company, Limited

CHAMPION SPARKING PLUG COMPANY LIMITED
Suppliers of Sparking Plugs for the Royal Cars
By appointment to H.M. The Queen Suppliers of Sparking Plugs
By appointment to H.M. Queen Elizabeth The Queen Mother Suppliers of Sparking Plugs
FELTHAM, MIDDLESEX
Tel. : 01-759 6442

¶Chandler, Fredk. J. (Saddler) Ltd., Saddlers, Stonebridge Close, Elcot Lane, Marlborough, Wiltshire. T N Marlborough 2633.

¶CHARBONNEL ET WALKER, LTD.,
Chocolate Manufacturers, 31, Old Bond St., London, W1X 4BT. T N 01-629 4396 & 5149.

○Charles (1820), Ltd., Fishmongers, 46, Elizabeth St., S.W.1. T N 01-730 3321.

¶Charringtons Fuel Oils, Ltd., Suppliers of Fuel Oils, Charringtons House, Bishop's Stortford, Herts., CM23 2EW. T N 55166.

¶Charringtons Solid Fuel, Ltd., Coal Merchants, Charringtons House, Bishop's Stortford, Herts., CM23 2EW. T N 55166.

¶○Chivas Brothers, Ltd., ¶Purveyors of Provisions: ○Provision Merchants, 387-391, Union St., Aberdeen. T A Chivas; T N 53361.

○Chivers & Sons, Ltd., Purveyors of Christmas Puddings, The Orchard Factory, Histon, Cambridge. T A Chivers; T N 0223 58855.

¶CHRISTOPHER & CO., LTD.,
Wine Merchants, 4, Ormond Yard, SW1Y 6JT. T A Orvieto, London, S.W.1; T N 01-930 5557.

¶Chubb Alarms Ltd., Installers of Intruder Alarms, 29, Enfold Street, London, W1H 2AE. T N 01-262 3250.

¶Chubb Fire Security Ltd., Manufacturers of Pyrene Fire Extinguishers, Pyrene House, Sunbury-on-Thames, Middlesex, TW16 5BR. T N 76 85588.

¶Chubb & Son's Lock and Safe Co., Ltd.

CHUBB & SON'S LOCK AND SAFE CO. LTD.
Patent Lock and Safe Makers
14-22 Tottenham Street
Tottenham Court Rd.,W1P 0AA
T.A. Chubb, London, W.1
T.N. 01-637 2377
Telex 261645
By Appointment to H.M. The Queen Patent Lock and Safe Makers

¶Clark, A. A., Ltd., Automobile Engineers, 2, 4 and 6 Frances Rd., Windsor. T N 60131-3.

¶Clarke, W., Saddler, 103, High St., Eton, Bucks. T N Windsor 62824.

¶Classic Restoration & Design Ltd., Architectural Restorers, Station Approach, Gomshall, Surrey.

¶Coca-Cola Southern Bottlers Ltd., Suppliers of Soft Drinks, St John's Rd., Isleworth, Middx. T N 01-568 8787.

¶Cocker, James, & Sons, Suppliers of Roses, Lang Stracht, Aberdeen. T N 33261.

¶Coe, C. & C. (Bircham), Ltd., Haulage Contractors, Lower Farm, Bircham, King's Lynn, Norfolk, PE31 6QT. T N Syderstone 234.

¶Cole & Son (Wallpapers), Ltd., Suppliers of Wallpapers, 18, Mortimer St., W.1. T A Colanson, London, W.1. T N 01-580 1066.

¶○Collingwood of Conduit Street, Ltd., ¶Jewellers and Silversmiths: ○Jewellers, 46 Conduit St., W1R 0HE. T N 01-734 2656.

¶Compton, J., Sons & Webb, Ltd., Uniform Makers, 19, Fitzroy Sq., W1P 5HQ. T N 01-387 9146; Telex 21785; T A Attire London.

○Coombes & Sons (Guildford), Ltd., Suppliers of Motor Cars, Portsmouth Road, Guildford, Surrey. T N 69944.

¶†Cooper, A. C., Ltd., Fine Art Photographers, 9-10, Pollen St., London, W1R 9PH. T N 01-629 7585.

¶Cooper Agricultural Division of The Wellcome Foundation, Ltd., Manufacturers of Animal Health and Hygiene Products, Ravens Lane, Berkhamsted, Herts., HP4 2DY. T N 3333.

¶Cooper, A. C. (Colour), Ltd., Fine Art Photographers, 9-10, Pollen Street, London, W1R 9PH. T N 01-629 7585.

¶Cooper, Frank, Ltd., Marmalade Manufacturers, 114, Old Rd., Headington, Oxford. T N 0092 62484.

¶Cope & Timmins Ltd., Brass Finishers and Spring Makers, Angel Road Works, Edmonton, London, N18 3AY. T N 01-803 6481; T A Tenso, London, N18 3AY.

¶Corney & Barrow, Ltd., Wine Merchants, 109, Old Broad St., EC2N 1AY. T A Brouette, Stock, London, EC2N 1AY; T N 01-638 4761.

¶Cory Bros. (Hospital Contracts Co.), Ltd., Suppliers of Surgical Equipment, 166/168, High Rd., London, N2 9AS. T N 01-349 1081.

¶County Window Cleaning & Steam Carpet Beating Co. (The), Window Cleaners, 49, Waverley Rd., Reading, Berks., RG3 2QB. T N Reading 52326.

△Courvoisier, Ltd., Purveyors of Cognac Brandy, Jarnac-Cognac, France.

¶Cox, Harold, Jeweller, 7, Market St., Windsor. T N 64497 & 67993.

¶CPC (United Kingdom) Ltd., Manufacturers of Corn Oil and Cornflour, Claygate House, Esher, Surrey, KT10 9PN. T N Esher 62181; Telex London 27106.

△Crabtree, J. A., & Co., Ltd., Suppliers of Lighting Switches, Walsall, WS1 2DN; T A Quality; T N 21202.

¶Craig, James W., Manufacturers of Agricultural Machinery, Drumoak, Aberdeenshire. T N Drumoak 240.

¶Crane, Ltd., Suppliers of Heating Materials, 15, Red Lion Court, EC4P 4DH. T A Cranelon, London; Telex 261262/3; T N 01-353 6511.

¶Crawford, William, & Sons, Ltd., Biscuit Manufacturers, 12 Hope St., Edinburgh. T N 031-554 7431.

¶Crendon Concrete Co., Ltd., Suppliers of Reinforced Concrete Buildings, Thame Rd., Long Crendon, Aylesbury, Bucks., HP18 9BB. T N Long Crendon (0844) 208481; Telex 83249.

¶Crompton Parkinson Ltd., Manufacturers of Electric Lamps, 50-52, Marefair, Northampton NN1 1NY. T A 31364, Crompark, Northampton; T N 0604 30201.

¶Cross Paperware Ltd., Manufacturers of Disposable Tableware, P.O. Box 3, Dunstable, Beds., LU6 3HX. T N 0582 62361.

¶○Crosse & Blackwell, Ltd., Purveyors of Preserved Provisions, St. George's House, Croydon, Surrey. T A Unexcelled, Croydon. T N 01-686 3366.

¶Cullen, W. H., Purveyor of Groceries and Provisions, Parsonage House, Station Road, Dorking, Surrey, RH4 1EA. T A Sugar Plum, Dorking; T N Dorking 2291.

¶Cyclax, Ltd.

CYCLAX LTD.

Manufacturers of Cosmetics and Beauty Preparations

17 Old Bond Street
London W1X 4AY

By Appointment to H.M. The Queen
Manufacturers of Beauty Preparations

T.A. Cyclax, London, W.1

T.N. 01-629 4341

○Daimler Cars Division British Leyland (U.K.) Ltd., Motor Car Manufacturers, Sandy Lane, Radford, Coventry. T N Allesley 2121.

¶Daimler Hire, Limited, Motor Car Hirers, 7, Herbrand St., WC1N 1EZ. T A Daimlerdom, London, W.C.1; T N 01-837 2898.

¶Dairy Supply Company—Division of Wincanton Engineering Ltd., Manufacturers of Dairy Appliances, Cumberland Avenue, Park Royal, London, NW10 7RT. T N 01-965 4601.

¶Dale Frank H. Ltd., Suppliers of Farm Buildings and Tubular Equipment, Leominster, Herefordshire, HR6 8EF. T N 2212 (7 lines).

¶Darby (Nursery Stock), Ltd., Suppliers of Soft Fruit Stock, Broad Fen Farm, Methwold Hythe, Thetford, Norfolk.

¶Darby (Sutton) Ltd., Drainage Contractors and Land Reclaimers, The Brook, Sutton, Ely, Cambs. T N Sutton 391.

¶Darville & Son, Ltd., Grocers, Vansittart Estate, Arthur Rd., Windsor. T N 61481-2.

¶○Davidson, W. S., & Sons, Purveyors of Meat and Poultry, Ballater, Scotland.

¶Dawber, Williamson Ltd., Suppliers of Building Materials, Park Rd., Hull. T A Dawber; T N 0482 42234.

*Day & Martin, Boot Polish Manufacturers, Newton Works, Great Dunmow, Essex. T N Great Dunmow 2287 (3 lines).

¶Day, Son & Hewitt, Ltd., Manufacturers of Animal Medicines, Glyn Street, S.E.11. T A Twenty Two, London, S.E.11; T N 01-735 0071.

¶+Day, Son & Hewitt Ltd.

DAY SON & HEWITT LTD.

Kemtheutic House
Grant Street
Bradford BD3 9HF

By Appointment to H.M. The Queen

T.N.
Bradford 22005/7

By Appointment to H.R.H. The Duke of Edinburgh

Manufacturers of Animal Medicines

Grams.: Kemtheutic Bradford

Manufacturers of Veterinary Products

¶Day, Thomas, Motors Ltd., Motor Vehicle Suppliers, 66, Albert Street, Fleet, Hants., GU1 39RN. T N 3303.

¶○Debenham & Freebody, Linen Drapers, 27-37, Wigmore St., W1A 1DW. T A Debenham, London, W.1; T N 01-580 4444.

JOHN DEERE LTD.

Langar

Nottingham NG13 9HT

By Appointment to H.M. The Queen
Suppliers of Agricultural Equipment

T.N. 0949 60491

Telex 37373

†de Faye, F. G., Ltd., Perfumers, David Place, Bath St., St. Helier, Jersey, C.I. T A de Faye, Pharmacist; T N St. Helier 24701.

¶Deimel Fabric Co., Manufacturers of Dr. Deimel Garments, Park Avenue, London, N18 2UH. T N 01-807 2995.

¶Dennison Manufacturing Co., Ltd.

Dennison

Dennison Manufacturing Co., Ltd.

Printers and Paper Converters

By Appointment to H.M. The Queen
Suppliers of Gift Wrapping Material

Colonial Way, Watford, WD2 4JY

T.A. Tagservis, Watford;
T.N. Watford 41244

JOHN DEWAR & SONS LTD.

P.O. Box No. 21
Inveralmond, Perth, Scotland
Telephone: Perth 21231

By Appointment to H.M. The Queen
Scotch Whisky Distillers
John Dewar & Sons Ltd.

Dewar House, Haymarket
London, S.W.1
Telephone: 01-930 4921

△Dickson, Alex., & Sons, Ltd., Nurserymen and Seedsmen, Hawlmark, Newtownards, County Down, N.I. T N 2206; T A Hawlmark, Newtownards.

¶Dictograph Telephones, Ltd.

DICTOGRAPH TELEPHONES LTD

Internal Telephones

197 Knightsbridge

By Appointment to H.M. The Queen
Suppliers of Dictograph Telephones

London SW7 1RL

Tel. 01-589 1471

¶Dilloway, P. W., Ltd., Agricultural Engineers, Hawksworth Industrial Estate, Swindon, Wilts., SN2 1EG. T N Swindon 32303; Telex 449979.

○Dipré, D., & Son, Cutlery Servicers, Knife-grinders and Suppliers of Kitchen Equipment, 10, Ship Tavern Passage, E.C.3. T N 01-626 3800.

†Dixey, C. W., & Son, Ltd., Opticians, 19, Wigmore St., W.1. T N 01-580 1713.

¶DOBBIE & CO., LTD.,
Nurserymen, Melville Nurseries, Lasswade, Midlothian. T N 031-663 1941.

¶Dobbins, J. T., Limited, Suppliers of Household Cleaning Materials, Crown Mill, Charlton Place, Ardwick Green, Manchester, M1 7JS. T A Flagship, Manchester; T N 061-273 2575.

¶Domestic Electric Rentals, Ltd., Suppliers of Television Receivers, Apex House, Twickenham Rd., Feltham, Middx. T N 01-894 5555.

¶Donaldson, Andrew, Ltd., Suppliers of Fish and Ice, 126, Norfolk St., King's Lynn, Norfolk. T N 2241.

¶Dorling & Co. (Epsom), Ltd. Manufrs. of Lapel Badges, Depot Rd., Epsom, Surrey.

¶Dorman Smith Britmac, Ltd., Manufacturers of Electrical Accessories, Atherton Works, Blackpool Rd., Preston PR2 2DQ, Lancs. T N 728271.

+ Douglas (Sales & Service), Ltd., Suppliers of Vespa Scooters & Mopeds, 2, Oak Lane, Fishponds Trading Estate, Bristol, BS5 7XB. T N 654197 & 654882.

¶Doulton Fine China, Ltd., Manufacturers of China, Doulton Fine China Works, Nile Street, Burslem, Stoke-on-Trent, Staffs., ST6 2AJ. T A Fine China, Stoke-on-Trent; T N Stoke-on-Trent 84271.

¶Drake & Fletcher, Ltd., Manufacturers of Agricultural Spraying Machinery, Maidstone, Kent. Telex-Drake 96455; T A Armada; T N 55531 (12 lines).

¶Drew, Clark & Co., Ltd., Manufacturers of Ladders, Lea Bridge Rd., E10 7DW. T N 01-539 2246.

¶Driscoll, Tailors, 21, Ashburnham Gardens, Eastbourne.

¶Dubois Chemicals, Ltd., Suppliers of Dishwashing Compounds and Controls, 371, Horn Lane, London, W3. T N 01-992 5094.

¶Dunhill, Alfred, Ltd., Suppliers of Smokers' Requisites, 30, Duke Street, St. James's, London, S.W.1. T N 01-493 9161.

¶○Dunlop Limited, Manufacturers of Motor Car Tyres, Dunlop House, 25, Ryder St., St. James's, SW1Y 6PX. T N 01-930 6700.

¶DYNATRON RADIO, LTD.,
Manufacturers of Televisions and Radio-gramophones, Ditton Walk, Cambridge CB5 8QD. T N 02205 2781.

¶Dyson & Sons, Ltd., Clockmakers and Silversmiths, 9, Thames St., Windsor. T N 51040-49.

¶Early Charles & Marriott (Witney), Ltd., Manufrs. of Blankets, Witney Mill, Witney, Oxon, OX8 5EB. Telex 83386; T N 3131.

¶Eastern Counties Farmers Ltd., Suppliers of Agricultural Products, P.O. Box No. 34, 86, Princes St., Ipswich, Suffolk. T A Farmers Ipswich; T N Ipswich 56071.

¶+○Ede & Ravenscroft, Ltd., Robe Makers, 93-94, Chancery Lane, WC2 1DU. T N 01-405 0602.

¶Edmondson, R. C., Ltd., Suppliers of Agricultural Machinery, Oak St., Fakenham, Norfolk. T N 2317.

¶Electro-Chemical Research Laboratories, Ltd., Makers of " Mordax " Studs, 3, Ridgeway, Iver, Bucks. T N Iver 651972.

¶○†Electrolux Ltd., ¶Suppliers of Suction Cleaners and Floor Polishers: ○Refrigerator Makers: †Suction Clenaer and Refrigerator Manufacturers, Oakley Road, Luton, LU4 9QQ. T N Luton 53255.

¶Elliott, Thomas, Ltd., Suppliers of Fertilisers and Peat, Hast Hill, Hayes, Bromley, Kent.

*Ellis, Richard, Photographer, Republic Street, Valetta, Malta, G.C. T A Ellis, Kingsway; T N Central 24741.

¶ELLIS & McHARDY LTD.,
Coal Distributors, Leith House, 3, Bedford Road, Aberdeen, AB9 2EW. T N Aberdeen 591601.

¶ELLIS & McHARDY (OILS) LTD.,
Oil Distributors, Leith House, 3, Bedford Road, Aberdeen, AB9 2EW. T N 491601.

¶Ellison Clifford, Picture Restorer, 10, Peterborough Villas, London, S.W.6. T N 01-736 2469.

¶Elsoms Seeds, Ltd., Seedsmen, Pinchbeck Road, Spalding PE11 1QG. T N 0775 5011; Telex 32152.

¶Emile et Cie (London), Ltd.

EMILE et CIE (LONDON) LTD.

Hairdressers

By Appointment to H.M. The Queen Hairdressers

40 Buckingham Palace Road London, S.W.1

T.N. 01-834 5943

¶○EMI Records, Ltd., Manufacturers of Records, Radio, Television and Electrical Household Apparatus, Hayes, Middlesex. T N 01-561 8722.

○EMMETTS STORE,
Curers & Suppliers of Sweet Pickled Hams, Peasenhall, Suffolk. T N Peasenhall 250.

¶En-tout-cas Ltd., Manufacturers of Tennis Courts, Syston, Leicester, LE7 8NP. T N 053-723 3322.

¶Essex Flour & Grain Co., Ltd., Suppliers of Tinned Meats, Vegetables, Fruits and Cereals 385a-385d, Liverpool Rd., N.1. T N 01-607 0236.

¶Esso Petroleum Company, Ltd., Purveyors of Motor Spirit, Victoria St., London, S.W.1. T A Essopet, London, SW1; Telex 24942; T N 01-834 6677; Telex 224942.

¶EXPRESS DAIRY CO. (LONDON), LTD.,
Dairy Suppliers, 430, Victoria Road, South Ruislip, Middx., HA4 0HF. T N 01-845 2345; Telex 934569.

¶Express Lift Co., Ltd. (The), Manufacturers and Suppliers of Passenger Lifts, Abbey Works, Northampton, NN5 5BT; T A Gudelyft Northampton; T N 51221.

¶Facit-Addo, Ltd., Manufacturers of Calculating Machines, Maidstone Road, Rochester, Kent, ME1 3QN. T N 0634 401721.

¶Farman & Son, Reed Thatchers, Station Rd., Salhouse, Norwich. T N Salhouse 294.

¶Farmers & Growers Industries Ltd., Horticultural Sundriesmen, Canterbury Rd., Worthing, Sussex. T N 64411.

¶Farris, Charles, Ltd., Chandlers, Bishopsgate Works, Staines Rd., Hounslow. T A Waxiness, Phone; T N 1161.

¶FERRARI, S., & SONS (SOHO), LTD.,
Suppliers of Kitchen Equipment, 60/66 Wardour St., W1V 3HP. T N 01-437 6515.

D.—C

¶Findlater Mackie Todd & Co., Ltd., Wine and Spirit Merchants, Findlater House, 92, Wigmore St., W1H 0BP. T A Findlater, London, W.1; T N 01-935 9264.

¶○FINDUS LIMITED,
Suppliers of Frozen Foods, St. George's House, Croydon, Surrey, CR9 1NR. T N 01-686 3031.

¶Fine Art Engravers, Ltd., Fine Art Printers, Town End St., Godalming, Surrey. T N 4655.

¶○Firmin & Sons Ltd.

FIRMIN & SONS LTD.
21 Crawford Street
London W1H 1PJ
T.N. 01-486 6141
Telex 21453
T.A. Firmin
London, W.1

By Appointment to H.M. The Queen Button Makers

By Appointment to H.M.Queen Elizabeth The Queen Mother Button Makers

¶Fisher Clark & Co., Ltd., Manufacturers of Baggage Labels, Norfolk Street, Boston, Lincs. T N 5501.

¶FISHER & SONS (FAKENHAM) LTD.,
Building Contractors, Hempton, Fakenham, Norfolk, NR21 7LD. T N 0328 2781.

¶Fisons Ltd.—Fertilizer Division, Makers of Chemical Fertilizers, Harvest House, Felixstowe, Suffolk, IP11 7LP. T A Fisons, Flxstowe; Telex 98273; T N 039-42 4444.

¶Fitch & Son, Ltd., Provision Merchants, 39, Barnham St., SE1 2AA. T N 01-407 4011.

¶FLORIS, J., LTD.,
Perfumers, 89, Jermyn St., SW1Y 6JH. T A Florissima, London, S.W.1; T N 01-930 2885 & 4136.

¶○Floris, The House of, Patissier and Confectioner, 39, Brewer Street, London, W.1. T N 01-437 5155.

△Fodens, Limited, Steam Tractor Manufacturers, Elworth Works, Sandbach, Cheshire, CW11 9HZ. T N 3244 (20 lines); T A Fodenway.

¶+Fonadek International, Ltd., ¶Manufacturers of Television Amplifiers, +Suppliers of Telephone Amplifiers, Vivian Rd., Harborne, Birmingham, 17. T N 021-427 2267.

¶○Forces Help Society and Lord Roberts Workshops (The), ¶Manufacturers of Fancy Goods: ○Furniture Makers, 118-122, Brompton Rd., S.W.3. T A Peaceful, London, S.W.3; T N 01-589 3243.

¶○Ford Motor Company, Ltd., Motor Vehicle Manufacturers, Brentwood, Essex, CM13 3BW. T A Fordmotor, Brentwood; T N Brentwood (0277) 25300; Telex 882121.

¶Forsyth, R. W., Ltd. (Food Hall and Wine Gallery), Suppliers of Provisions, 30, Princes Street, Edinburgh, EH2 2BZ. T N 031-556 3333.

¶○Fortnum & Mason, Ltd.

FORTNUM & MASON LTD.
Piccadilly
London, W1A 1ER
T.A. Fortnum,
London, W.1;
T.N. 01-734 8040
Telex 21160

By Appointment to H.M. The Queen Grocers and Provision Merchants Fortnum & Mason Ltd.

By Appointment to H.M.Queen Elizabeth The Queen Mother Suppliers of Leather and Fancy Goods

¶Foss Electric (U.K.) Limited, Suppliers of Milkmeters, The Chantry, Bishopthorpe, York, YO2 1QF. T N 67944; Telex 57833.

¶○Foster, John, & Co., Ltd., Suppliers of Furnishing Fabrics, 78-79, Long Lane, London, E.C.1. T N 01-606 7674.

¶Fountain & Ansel, Ltd., Suppliers of Animal Feeds, 389, Gosbrook Rd., Lower Caversham, Reading. T N 475933.

¶FOX, FREDERICK, LTD.,
Milliner, 26, Brook Street, London, W1Y 1AE. T N 01-629 5706.

¶Francis, G. C., Heraldic Artist, 2, Walfield Av., Whetstone, N.20. T N 01-445 3655.

¶FRASER, H. S., LTD.,
Furniture Manufacturers, 12-16, Wharf Rd., N1 7SE. T N 01-253 6361.

○Frederick, John, Ltd., Carpet Cleaners, 8, The Ridgeway, Mill Hill, London, N.W.7.

¶FRIGICOLD,
Division of Lonsdale Uniflair, Ltd., Manufacturers of Deep Freeze Packaging, 166, Dukes Rd., W3 0TJ. T N 01-993 1271.

¶○Frodsham, Charles, & Co., Ltd., Clock and Watch Makers, 45, South Audley Street, London, W1Y 5DG. T N 01-493 7449.

¶Gallyon & Sons, Ltd., Gunsmiths, 52, High St., King's Lynn. T N 2322.

¶Galt, James, & Co., Ltd., Manufacturers and Suppliers of Educational Aids, Brookfield Rd., Cheadle, Cheshire, SK8 2PN. T A Vocation; T N Gatley 8511.

†Ganeshi, Lall & Son, Jewellers and Embroiderers, Agra, U.P., India.

¶Gardiner & Co.

GARDINER & CO.
Suppliers of Protective Clothing

154 Tottenham Court Road, London W1P 9LJ
T.N. 01-387 4721 & 8233

By Appointment to H.M. The Queen Suppliers of Protective Clothing

¶Garford, P., Ltd., Suppliers of Fertilizers and Baled Peat, Walpole St. Andrew, Wisbech, Cambs. T N Walpole St. Andrew 282.

¶○Garrard & Co., Ltd., ¶Goldsmiths and Crown Jewellers: ○Jewellers & Silversmiths, 112, Regent St., W1A 2JJ. T N 01-734 7020.

¶○Garrow, Robert, Ltd., Fishmongers, Market Buildings, Aberdeen. T A Garrow, Fishmongers, Aberdeen; T N 20321.

¶Gascoigne, Gush & Dent, Ltd.

GASCOIGNE, GUSH & DENT LTD.
Milking Machine Manufacturers
Berkeley Avenue, Reading
Berkshire RG1 6JW
T.N. 54411
T.A. Gascoignes Reading
Telex 84531

By Appointment to H.M. The Queen Milking Machine Manufacturers

¶Gaunt, J. R., & Son, Ltd., Ribbon Suppliers, 1-8, Bateman Buildings, Soho Square, London, W1A 4AD. T A Fourreau, London, W.1; T N 01-734 0331.

¶Gaybird, Ltd., Suppliers of Stock Game, Great Missenden, Bucks. T N Gt. Missenden 3123.

¶Gaymer, William, & Son, Ltd., Cyder Manufacturers, Attleborough, Norfolk. T A Gaymer's, Attleborough; Telex 97495; T N 452104.

¶○General Trading Company (Mayfair) Ltd., Suppliers of Fancy Goods, 144, Sloane St., SWiX 9BL. T A Equiparta, London, S.W.1; T N 01-730 0411.

¶Gestetner Duplicators, Ltd., Suppliers of Offset and Stencil Duplicating Machines, P.O. Box 23, Gestetner House, 210, Euston Road, London, NW1 2DA. T N 01-387 7021.

¶Gibbons, Stanley, Ltd., Philatelists, 391, Strand, W.C.2. T A Philatelic, London, W.C.2; T N 01-836 8444.

¶Gibbs, J., Ltd., Suppliers of Agricultural Machinery and Implements, Bedfont, Feltham, Middlesex, TW14 8ND. T N Feltham 5071 & 6644.

¶GIDDEN, W. & H., LTD.,
Saddlers, 15d, Clifford Street, New Bond Street, London, W1X 1RF. T N 01-734 2789.

¶+GIEVES & HAWKES, LTD.,
¶Livery and Military Tailors; +Naval Tailors and Outfitters, 1, Savile Row, London, W1X 1AF. T N 01-434 2001.

¶○Gilbert, D., & Son, Suppliers of Racing Colours, 13, High Street, Newmarket, Suffolk. T N 2958.

¶Gilbertson & Page, Ltd., Manufacturers of Dog and Game Foods, Corrys, Roestock Lane, Colney Heath, Herts., AL4 0QW. T N Bowmans Green 22614.

¶Gillman & Spencer, Ltd., Manufacturers and Suppliers of Liquid Supplements, Castle Tower Works, Bilton Road, Bletchley, Bucks. T N 0908 2 2792.

△Girlings Ferro-Concrete Co., Ltd., Suppliers of Ferro-Concrete Work, 729, London Road, Hounslow, Middlesex. T A Girlings; T N 01-570 1158.

¶Glover, Webb & Liversidge, Ltd., Coach Builders, Marlborough Works, 561, Old Kent Rd., S.E.1. T N 01-237 5501.

¶Glyn Protective Clothing, Ltd., Manufacturers of State & Livery Waterproofs, Marshall Works, Ashburton Road, Manchester, M17 1QH.

¶Glynwed, Ltd., Manufacturers of Kitchen and Bathroom Equipment, 28, Brook Street, London, W.1. T N 01-489 8941.

¶○Goddard, J., & Sons, Ltd., ¶Manufacturers of Silver Polishes: ○Suppliers of Dry Clean, Frimley Green, Camberley, Surrey. T N 63456.

¶○†GOODE, THOMAS, & CO. (LONDON), LTD.,
¶○Suppliers of China and Glass: †Purveyors of China and Glass, 17-21, South Audley St., W.1. T A Mnemonics, London, W.1; T N 01-499 2823.

¶○Goodyear, Edward, Florist, 45, Brook St., W.1. T A Afloricayd; T N 01-629 1508.

¶Gordon, Luis, & Sons, Ltd.

LUIS GORDON & SONS, LTD.
9 Upper Belgrave Street, London, S.W.1X 8BD
T.A. Domecq, London, S.W.1
T.N. 01-235 5191
By Appointment to H.M. The Queen Suppliers of Domecq Sherry

¶Gourock Ropework Co., Ltd. (The), Manufacturers of Agricultural Twine, Port Glasgow, PA14 5ND. T A Gourock, Port Glasgow; T N 41261 (7 lines); Telex 77245.

¶Grampian (Paint & Walpaper), Ltd., Suppliers of Paint and Wallpapers, 33-37 Summer Street, Aberdeen, AB9 1NA. T N 0224 27301.

+Grant, Pat, Hairdresser, 11, Crown St., Aberdeen. T N Aberdeen 29321.

¶Gray Chas. & Co. (Stamford) Ltd., Suppliers of Shoeing Iron and Farriers' Equipment, Stamford, Lincs., PE9 2DY. T N Stamford 2468.

¶Gray, J. W., & Son, Ltd., Lightning Conductor Specialists, 17/19, East Place, West Norwood, London, S.E.27. T N 01-670 9281.

¶Gray, James, & Son, Ironmongers & Electricians, Ltd., Suppliers of Cleaning Materials &c. 89, George St., Edinburgh, EH2 3EZ.

¶Grima Andrew, Ltd.

By Appointment to Her Majesty Queen Elizabeth II Jewellers
ANDREW GRIMA LIMITED 80 JERMYN STREET LONDON SW1

○Grosvenor Electrical Co. (Belgravia, London), Ltd., Electrical Contractors, 20, Pimlico Road, SW1W 8LJ. T N 01-730 6138.

¶Hacker Radio, Ltd., Manufacturers of Radio Receivers, Norreys Drive, Cox Green, Maidenhead, Berks., SL6 4BP. T N 22261-5.

○Haggart, P. and J., Ltd., Tartan and Woollen Manufacturers, Woollen Mills, Aberfeldy, Scotland. T A Haggart Mills; T N Aberfeldy 306.

¶Haig, John, & Co., Ltd., Purveyors of Scotch Whisky, Markinch, Fife. T N 758404.

○HALCYON DAYS, LTD.,
Suppliers of Objets D'Art, 14, Brook Street, London, W1Y 1AA. T N 01-499 5784.

¶Hall, Alexander, & Son (Builders), Ltd., Building Contractors, Granitehill Rd., Northfield, Aberdeen, AB9 2AW. T N 0224 40233.

‡Hall Bros., Ltd., Tailors and Hosiers, 119, High St., Oxford. T N 42756.

¶Hall, Leslie, Ltd., Suppliers of Animal Feeding Stuffs, Station Rd., Cottingham, Yorkshire. T N Hull 847428.

+○†Hamblin, Theodore, Ltd., Opticians, 1 Langham Pl., London, W1N 8HS. T N 01-580 4343.

*Hamblin, W. T., & Co., Upholsterers, 432, St. Leonards Rd., Windsor, FL4 3DZ. T N 956 5316.

*Hamer, Edward, & Co., Suppliers of Welsh Mutton, Llanidloes, N. Wales. T N 9.

¶Hamilton & Inches, Ltd.

HAMILTON & INCHES LTD.
Silversmiths and Clock Specialists
87 George Street
Edinburgh EH2 3EY
T.A. Inches; T.N. 031-225 4898
By Appointment to H.M. The Queen Silversmiths and Clock Specialists

¶†Hamleys of Regent Street, Ltd.

 **HAMLEYS**
Toy and Sports
200-202 Regent
Street, W.1

T.A. Pleasingly,
London, W.1:
By Appointment
to H.M. The Queen
Toy and Sports
Merchants
T.N. 01-734 3161
By Appointment
to the late
Queen Mary
Toy and Sports
Merchants

○Hancocks & Co. (Jewellers), Ltd., Goldsmiths and Silversmiths, 1, Burlington Gardens, WIX 2HP. T N 01-493 8904.

△**HANKEY, BANNISTER & CO.,** Wine Merchants, 32, Sackville St., WIX 2DA. T A Saccone, London, W.1; T N 01-734 2061; Telex 23666 Courexpo Ldn.

¶Hardie, R. G., & Co., Bagpipe Makers, 24, Renfrew Street, Glasgow, G2 3BN. T N 041-322 3021.

¶Hardy Amies, Ltd., Dressmakers, 14, Savile Row, WIX 2JN. T A Hardiamies, London, W1; T N 01-734 2436.

¶Hardy Bros., Ltd., Silversmiths, G.12 Gallery Level, The Centre-Point, Sydney, N.S.W.

¶Hardy, T. H., Agricultural Contractor, Cedar Lodge, Austendyke Road, Weston Hills, Moulton, Lincs. T N 225

¶○Hardy Minnis Limited, Mercers of Woollen Cloth, 4, New Burlington St., WIX 2JY. T A Strongbow, London, W1; T N 01-734 1313; Telex No. 262536.

¶Harris, C. & T. (Calne), Ltd., Manufacturers of Bacon, Sausages and Pies, P.O. Box 1, Calne, Wilts, SN11 0JL. T N 0249 812261.

○Harris, D. R., & Co., Ltd., Chemists, 29, St. James's St., S.W.1. T N 01-930 3915.

¶Harris, L. G., & Co., Ltd., Manufacturers of Painting and Decorating Brushes, Stoke Prior Brush Works, Stoke Prior, Worcs. T A Secure, Bromsgrove; T N Bromsgrove 31441.

†Harris, M., & Sons, Dealers in Antique Furniture and Works of Art, 44-52, New Oxford St., WC1A 1ES. T N 01-636 2121.

¶Harris Plating Works, Ltd. (The)

 **THE HARRIS PLATING WORKS LTD.**
Metal Finishing Specialists
18 New Wharf Road, N1 9RS
By Appointment
to H.M. The Queen
Metal Finishing
Specialists
T.A. Arisplatin, London, N.1;
T.N. 01-837 7263

¶+○**HARRISON & SONS,**
Ltd., Printers, Harrison House, Coates Lane, High Wycombe, Bucks. HP13 5EZ. T N High Wycombe (0494) 33321.

¶Harrison & Wilson, Saddlers and Cover Makers, 32, Norfolk St., King's Lynn, Norfolk. T N 2167.

¶+○Harrods, Ltd., +Outfitters

 **HARRODS LTD.**
Suppliers of Provisions, Household Goods, China, Glass and Fancy Goods
Knightsbridge
SW1X 7XL

By Appointment
to H.M. The Queen
Suppliers of
Provisions and
Household Goods
T.A. Harrods, London Telex;
T.N. 01-730 1234;
Telex 24319
By Appointment
to H.M. Queen
Elizabeth The
Queen Mother
Suppliers of
China, Glass and
Fancy Goods

¶Harrold, A. J., & Co., Ltd., Builders and Decorators, 182, Kensington Church St., W.8. T N 01-229 0129 & 6385.

¶○Hartnell, Norman, Ltd., Dressmakers, 26, Bruton St., WIX 8DD. T N 01-629 0992.

¶Harvey, John & Sons, Ltd.

 **JOHN HARVEY & SONS LTD.**
Wine Merchants
12 Denmark Street
Bristol BS99 7JE
By Appointment to
H.M. The Queen
Wine Merchants
Whitchurch (Bristol) 6161

¶Harvey, Matthew & Co., Ltd., Bit Makers, Glebeland Works, Bath Street, Walsall, Staffs. T N 28181.

○†Harvey, Nichols, ○Drapers, †General Drapers, 109-125, Knightsbridge, S.W.1. T A Harveys, London, S.W.1; T N 01-235 5000.

¶Hasler & Company, Ltd., Manufacturers of Horse Nuts, Dunmow, Essex. T N 2271.

¶○+Hatchards, Ltd., Booksellers, 187, Piccadilly, W1V 9DA. T N 01-439 9921.

△Hawes & Curtis, Ltd., Shirt Makers and Hosiers, 2, Burlington Gdns., WIX 1LH. T A Hawecurti, London, WIX 1LH; T N 01-493 3803.

+Hawes & Curtis (Tailors), Ltd., Tailors, 43, Dover St., WIX 1LH. T A Hawecurti, London, W.1; T N 01-493 2200.

¶Hawker, James, & Co., Ltd., Purveyors of "Pedlar" Sloe Gin, Mayflower House, 50, Breton Side, Plymouth. T A Hawker, Plymouth; T N Plymouth 63144/5.

¶Hayters, Ltd., Manufacturers of Agricultural Machinery, Spellbrook, Bishops Stortford, Herts., CM23 4BU. T N 0279 723444; Telex 81241.

¶Haythornthwaite & Sons, Ltd., Manufacturers of Grenfell Cloth, Grenfell House, Rylands St., Burnley, Lancs., BB10 1RQ. T A Grenfell, Burnley; T N 21621.

¶Heal & Son, Ltd., Upholsterers and Suppliers of Bedding, 196, Tottenham Court Rd., W1A 1BJ. T A Heals, London, W.1; T N 01-636 1666.

¶Heering, Peter F., Purveyor of Cherry Heering, Copenhagen.

¶△Heidsieck, Charles, S. A., Purveyor of Champagne, Reims, France.

¶Heinz, H. J., Company Ltd., Purveyors of Heinz Products, Hayes Park, Hayes, Middx., UB4 8AL. T N 01-573 7757.

¶Henderson's, outfitters, Bridge St., Ballater, Aberdeenshire. T N Ballater 432.

¶Hewit, J. & Sons, Ltd., Leather Manufacturers, Kinauld Leather Works, Currie, Edinburgh, EH14 5RS. T N 031-449 2206.

¶○Hicks, Richard (Covent Garden), Ltd., Purveyors of Fruit and Vegetables, 8-10, Dryden St., Covent Garden, W.C.2. T A Hicksfru, London, W.C.2; T N 01-836 6757 & 9133.

¶Hill Construction Co. (Engineers), Ltd.

HILL CONSTRUCTION COMPANY (ENGINEERS) LIMITED
Manufacturers of Steel Buildings
Eastleigh, Southampton, Hants SO5 4ZR
By Appointment to H.M. The Queen Manufacturers and Suppliers of Steel Buildings
Tel.: Eastleigh 4633
Telex 47224
T.A. Hillspan, Soton

¶Hill Thomson & Co., Ltd., Scotch Whisky Distillers, 45, Frederick St., Edinburgh, EH2 1YG. T A Hilltop; T N 031-226 6581.

¶Hill, Wm., & Son and Norman & Beard, Ltd., Organ Builders, Manor Works, 71, High St., Hornsey, N8 7QL; T A Bassoonist, London, N.8; T N 01-340 2271.

○Hillier & Sons, Nurserymen and Seedsmen, Winchester. T N 69245.

+Hodgkinson, T., Ltd., Tiemakers, 112, Jermyn Street, London, S.W.1. T N 01-493 3114.

¶Holder, W., & Son, Picture Restorers, 14a, Caroline Street, London, SW1 8JS. T N 01-730 3607.

+Holland & Holland, Ltd., Rifle Makers, 13, Bruton St., W.1; T A Armourer, London, W.1; T N 01-499 4411.

○Hollings Francis, Ltd., Suppliers of Fancy Goods, IGL House, 177, The Vale, London, W3 7YB. T N 01-749 9131.

¶Hollins, William, & Company, Ltd.

VIYELLA
William Hollins
& *Company Limited*
BY APPOINTMENT TO HER MAJESTY THE QUEEN MANUFACTURERS OF VIYELLA AND CLYDELLA WILLIAM HOLLINS & COMPANY LIMITED VIYELLA HOUSE, SOMERCOTES, DERBY

¶Hooper Struve, & Co., Ltd., Mineral Water Manufrs. 264, Northfield Av., Ealing, London, W.5. T N 01-579 1961.

¶○HOOVER, LIMITED,
¶Manufacturers of Vacuum Cleaners, ○Suppliers of Vacuum Cleaners, Perivale, Greenford, Middx., UB6 8DX. T A Hooswepe, Greenford; T N 01-997 3311; Telex 22675.

△Horlicks, Ltd., Purveyors of Malted Milk, Brentford, Middlesex. T A Beechfoods, Brentford, Middlesex; T N 01-560 5151; Telex 22743.

¶HORNE BROTHERS, LTD., Livery Tailors, Durigo House, King Edward's Rd., London, E9 7SG. T N 01-986 3166.

¶Horrockses Fashions, Ltd., Dressmakers, 107, Worship St., London, EC2A 2BD. T N 01-247 6914.

¶Houseman Hegro, Ltd., Specialists in Water Treatment Services, The Priory, Burnham, Slough, SL1 7LS. T N Burnham 4488.

¶Howard Rotavator Co., Ltd., Manufacturers of Agricultural & Horticultural Equipment, Saxham, Bury St. Edmunds, Suffolk, IP28 6RP. T N 0284 63266; T A Howardsaxham, Bury St. Edmunds; Telex 817321.

¶Humber Manures Ltd., Fertiliser Manufacturers, Stoneferry, Hull. T A Rapid; T N Hull 20458.

¶○HUNTLEY & PALMERS, LTD.,
¶Biscuit Manufacturers; ○Biscuit and Cake Manufacturers, King's Rd., Reading, RG1 3EF. T A Able, Reading; T N Reading 583535.

¶Hurst Gunson Cooper Taber, Ltd., Seedsmen, Witham, Essex, CM8 2DX. T A Hurst Witham; T N Witham 516600; Telex 99142.

¶Hyams & Cockerton, Ltd., Purveyors of Fruits and Vegetables, 10, Southville, London, S.W.8. T N 01-622 4349.

¶Ian Proctor Metal Masts, Ltd., Suppliers of Metal Masts, Duncan Road, Swanwick, Southampton, Hants. T N Locksheath 4146.

¶ICC MACHINES, LTD., Manufacturers of Paper Shredding Machines, Alexandra Rd., Enfield, Middx. T N 01-804 3027.

¶○Idris, Ltd., ¶Manufacturers of Mineral Water and Fruit Beverages: ○Manufacturers of Fruit Beverages: White Hart La., N.17. T N 01-889 4434.

¶Imperial Typewriter Co., Ltd., Typewriter Manufacturers, Imperial House, 133/149, St. Nicholas Circle, Leicester, LE1 4LE. T N Leicester 50481.

¶Incorporated Association for Promoting the General Welfare of the Blind, Suppliers of Stable Mats &c. and Renovators of Mattresses, 8/22, Curtain Rd., London, EC2A 3NQ. T N 01-247 2405.

¶Inglis Green Laundry, Launderers, Slateford, Edinburgh, EH14 2ES. T N 031-443 2361.

¶Jackson, Robert, & Co., Ltd., Grocers, 172, Piccadilly, London, W1V 0LL. T A Succotash, London, W.1; T N 01-493 1033.

¶○Jacob, W. & R., & Co. (Liverpool), Ltd., Biscuit Manufrs., P.O. Box 1, Aintree Biscuit Factory, Liverpool, L9 7BQ. T A Jabisco 9, Liverpool; T N 051-525 3661; Telex, Able, Liverpool 628217.

¶Jaeggi, Leon, & Sons, Ltd., Suppliers of Catering Utensils & Equipment, 232 Tottenham Court Rd., London, W1P 0BL. T N 01-580 1957.

○Jaguar Cars—Division British Leyland (U.K.), Ltd., Motor Car Manufacturers, Browns Lane, Allesley, Coventry, CV5 9DR. T N Allesley 2121.

¶James & Son (Grain Merchants), Ltd., Suppliers of Animal Feeding Stuffs, Olmar Wharf, Malt St., S.E.1. T A Jasbrewgra, London, S.E.1; T N 01-237 2277.

¶Jamieson, William, & Sons, Suppliers of Fruit and Vegetables, 130, Princes St., Edinburgh, 2. T A Superfine, Edinburgh; T N 031-225 3749.

¶○Jarrolds (Sloane St.), Ltd.

 JARROLDS (SLOANE ST.) LTD.
Photograph Frames and Leather Goods
By Appointment to H.M. The Queen Suppliers of Leather Goods
24 Brompton Arcade Knightsbridge
Tel. 01-589 1700 & 2200
By Appointment to H.M. Queen Elizabeth The Queen Mother Suppliers of Leather Goods

+Jekmoth, Ltd., Manufacturers of Garment Bags and Wardrobe Accessories, Jekmoth House, 11-15, Lillie Rd., Fulham, S.W.6. T N 01-385 7838.

¶Jenners Princes St. Edinburgh, Ltd., Suppliers of Furnishing Materials, 47-52, Princes St., Edinburgh. T A Jenners; T N 031-225 2442.

¶○Jeyes' Group, Limited

JEYES GROUP LIMITED

Manufacturers of Hygiene Products

Brunel Way, Thetford
Norfolk

By Appointment to
Her Majesty The Queen
Manufacturers of
Hygiene Products

T.N. Thetford 4567
T.A. Jeyes Thetford
Telex 81401

○Joel, Walter C., Ltd., Clock and Watch Makers, 7, Broadwalk, Crawley, Sussex. T N 22275.

¶John, C., Supplier of Carpets, 70, South Audley St., W.1. T N 01-493 5288.

+Johns & Pegg, Ltd., Military Tailors, 4, Clifford St., W.1. T N 01-734 1713.

¶○Johnson Brothers, Manufacturers of Ceramic Tableware, P.O. Box 10, Hanley, Stoke-on-Trent, Staffs., ST1 3LN. T N Stoke-on-Trent 29581.

¶Johnson, Herbert (Bond Street), Ltd., **Hatters,** 38, New Bond St., W1Y 0BU. T A Browbound, London, W.1; T N 01-629 7177.

¶○Johnson Wax, Ltd., Manufacturers of Wax Polishes, Cleaner and Hygiene Products, Frimley Green, Camberley, Surrey, GU16 5AJ. T N Camberley 63456.

¶Jollye, Leonard F. (Brookmans Park) Ltd., Forage Merchants, 1, Great North Rd., Brookmans Park, Hatfield, Herts., AL9 6LB. T N Potters Bar 57016.

△Jones, Peter, Suppliers of Furnishings, Sloane Sq., London, SW1W 8EL. T N 01-730 3434.

¶○+Jones, Yarrell & Co., Ltd., Newsagents, 227-239, Tooley St., London, SE1 2PA. T A Odmyl, London, S.E.1. T N 01-407 6267.

¶Justerini & Brooks, Ltd., Wine Merchants, 61, St. James's St., London, SW1A 1LZ. T A Justerini, London, S.W.1; T N 01-493 8721.

¶○K Shoes, Ltd., Bootmakers, Netherfield, Kendal, Westmoreland. T N Kendal 24343.

¶+Kagan Textiles, Ltd., Manufacturers & Suppliers of Gannex Products, Gannex Mills, Elland, Yorks. T N 3371-5.

¶○Keen, G. H. & S., Ltd., Furnishers and Upholsterers, Dovecot Rd., Bellfields, High Wycombe, Bucks. T N 24061/2/3.

○Keith Prowse and Company, Ltd., Theatre Ticket Agents, 24, Store Street, London, WC1E 7BA. T N 01-637 3131.

¶Kellogg Company of Great Britain, Ltd., Purveyors of Cereals, Park Rd., Stretford, Manchester. T A Cornflakes, Manchester; T N 061-865 4411.

¶+Kenning Car Mart, Ltd., Motor Car Distributors, St James' House, 105-113, Broadway, Ealing, London, W13 9AJ. T N 01-567 6600.

¶Kent, G. B., & Sons, Ltd., Brush Makers, 24, Old Bond St., W.1. T A Tricho, London, W.1; T N 01-493 1471.

¶Kerner-Greenwood & Co., Manufacturers of Waterproofing Material, St. Ann's Street, King's Lynn. T N 2293.

¶Kidd, Archie, Ltd., Manufacturers of Farm Machinery, Roundway, Devizes, Wilts. T N 0380 2361.

¶Kildew Mothproofing, Ltd., Fur Cleaners and Permanent Mothproofers, 5 & 6, Clipstone St., W.1. T N 01-636 7171.

¶Kilian, H., Ltd., Manufacturers of Horticultural Packaging, Baddow Park, Great Baddow, Chelmsford. T N Chelmsford 72361.

○King Bros. (Fuel Merchants), Ltd., Coal and Coke Merchants, 70, High St., Eton. T N 95 62628.

¶King, John K., & Sons, Ltd., Seedsmen, Coggeshall, Essex. T N Coggeshall 61543; Telex 987264.

¶+Kinloch Anderson, Ltd., Tailors and Kilt Makers, 14-16, George Street, Edinburgh, EH2 2QD. T N 031-225 6656.

+Kiwi Polish Co., Pty., Ltd. (The), Shoe Polish Manufacturers, Brumwill Rd., W5 1DT. T N 01-997 4435.

¶○Kleen-Way (Berkshire) Co., Chimney Sweepers, 8, Brooke Place, Binfield, Berks, RG12 5JU. T N Bracknell 3804.

¶Knapp, Drewett & Sons, Ltd., Printers, 20, Church St., Kingston upon Thames, Surrey, KT1 1RL. T N 01-546 2261.

¶Knight Peter (Beaconsfield), Ltd., Suppliers of Interior Furnishings, 45, London End, Beaconsfield, Bucks., HP9 2HP. T N 04946 5561/4.

¶Knight Peter (Esher), Ltd., Suppliers of Fancy Goods and Lighting, 5, High St., Esher, Surrey, KT10 9QL. T N Esher 64122.

¶○Knowles & Sons (Fruiterers), Ltd., ¶Purveyors of Fruit and Vegetables: ○Fruiterers and Greengrocers, 21, Windmill Brae, Aberdeen, AB1 2HU. T N 52000.

¶Kodak, Ltd., Manufacturers of Photographic Supplies, P.O. Box 66, Kodak House, Station Road, Hemel Hempstead, Herts. T N 61122; Telex 82501.

¶Krug Vins Fins de Champagne.

KRUG

VINS FINS
DE CHAMPAGNE

By Appointment
to H.M. The Queen
Purveyors of
Champagne

Purveyors of Champagne
51—Reims, France

¶Lambert, James, & Sons, Ltd., Suppliers of Building Materials, Snettisham, King's Lynn, Norfolk. T A Lamberts, Snettisham; T N Snettisham 391 (3 lines).

¶Lambourn Ridgeway Transport, Ltd., Horse Transport Contractors, Station Road, Lambourn, Newbury, Berks., RG16 7PH. T N 0488 71710.

¶Langton W. E., Supplier of Milking Machine Components, Collyers Oak Farm, Fillongley, Coventry, CV7 8EJ. T N Fillongley 40342 (STD 0676).

¶Lansing Bagnall Ltd

LANSING BAGNALL LTD.
Kingsclere Road
Basingstoke
Hants
Tel. 0256 3131
Europe's Largest Maker of Electric Lift Trucks

By Appointment to
Her Majesty The Queen
Manufacturers of
Industrial Trucks

¶Lanson Pére et Fils Champagne, Purveyors of Champagne, Reims, France.

¶Latham, James, Ltd., Wood Merchants, Leeside Wharf, Mount Pleasant Hill, Clapton, E.5. T N 01-806 3333; Telex 265670.

¶Launer S. & Co. (London), Ltd., Manufacturers of Handbags, 55, Greek St., London, W.1. T N 01-437 6758

★Lavender & Bateman, Ltd., Roadstone Merchants, Swann Rd., Cambridge. T N 51344-5.

¶Lawrie, R. G., Ltd., Bagpipe Makers, 38, Renfield St., Glasgow, G2 1NB. T A Claymore; T N 041-221 9047.

¶Lea & Perrins, Ltd., Purveyors of Worcestershire Sauce, Midland Rd., Worcester, WR5 1DT. T A Leaper, Worcester; T N 0905 352770.

¶○Leith, G., & Son, Bakers and Confectioners, Church Sq., Ballater, Aberdeenshire. T N 474.

¶○Lever Brothers Ltd,. Soap Makers, 21-23, New Fetter Lane, London, E.C.4. T A Leverbro, London, E.C.4; T N 01-583 9666.

¶Lewis East Ltd., Manufacturers of Stationery, Midland Envelope Mills, Anstey, Leicester, LE7 7DB. Tel Anstey 2128 & 4301.

†Lewis, F. (Publishers), Ltd., Booksellers and Publishers, The Tithe House, 1461, London Rd., Leigh-on-Sea. T N 0702 78163.

¶Lewmar Marine, Ltd., Suppliers of Yacht Fittings and Blocks, Southmoor Lane, Havant, Hants, PO9 1JJ. T N Havant 71841 (STD 0701 2); Cables, Lewmar, Havant; Telex 86342.

¶Leyland Motors Division—British Leyland (U.K.), Ltd., Manufacturers of Leyland Motors, Leyland, Lancs. T N 21400.

○†Liberty & Co., Ltd., Silk Mercers, 210-220, Regent St., W.1. T A Liberty, London, W.1; T N 01-734 1234.

¶○Lidstone, John, Butchers, 12, Lower Belgrave St., Eaton Sq., S.W.1. T N 01-730 9373.

¶○Lilliman & Cox, Ltd., Dry Cleaners, 34, Bruton Place, London, W1X 7AA. T N 01-629 4555.

¶Lillywhites, Ltd., Outfitters, of Piccadilly Circus, S.W.1. T A Lillisports, London, S.W.1; T N 01-930 3181.

¶Lincoln, Bennett & Co., Ltd., Hat Makers, 162, Piccadilly, W.1. T A Linbencoli, London, W1; T N 01-493 9061.

¶Lincolnshire Drainage Co., Ltd., Drainage Contractors, 20a, South Parade, Boston, Lincs. T N 0205 4216.

¶LINER CONCRETE MACHINERY CO., LTD. (THE),

Manufacturers of Concrete Block and Mixing Machinery, 51, Park Rd., Gateshead, NE8 3HR; T A Liner, Gateshead; Telex 53525; T N 0632 772501.

¶Linfield, A. G., Ltd., Suppliers of Horticultural Products, Chesswood Nurseries, Thakeham, Pulborough, Sussex, RH20 3EL. T N West Chiltington 2345/9.

+Linguaphone Institute, Ltd., Publishers of Recorded Language Courses, 207-209, Regent St., W1R 8AU. T N 01-734 1633.

¶Linoleum Manufacturing Company Ltd., Manufacturers of Linoleum, Staines, Middlesex. T A Floorings, Stainesmiddx; T N Staines 51351; Telex 25608.

¶Lister & Co., Ltd., Manufacturers of Furnishing Fabrics, Manningham Mills, Bradford, BD9 4SH. T N 0274 42222.

¶Lister, R. A., & Co., Ltd., Manufacturers of Agricultural Machinery, Dursley, Glos., GL11 4HS. T N Dursley 4141.

¶+Lobb, John, Bootmaker, 9, St. James's St., SW1A 1EF. T N 01-930 3664/5.

+Lock, James, & Co., Ltd., Hatters, 6, St. James's St., S.W.1. T A Lockhatter, London, S.W.1; T N 01-930 8874 & 5849.

¶Lock S., Ltd., Embroiderers, 5, Vereker House, Gresse St., Rathbone Place, W1D 1DF. T N 01-636 9221.

¶London Brick Co., Ltd., Brick Makers, London Brick House, 12, York Gate, Regent's Park, London, NW1 4QL. T N 01-487 4321.

¶London Essence Co., Ltd. (The), Manufacturers of Cleaning Compound, Winsor Terrace, London, E6 4LF. T N 01-476 1488.

¶Longmate, E. C., Ltd., Agricultural Spraying Contractors, Terrington St. John, Wisbech, Cambs; T A Longmate, Terrington St John; T N Terrington St John 491/3.

¶LOWE, F. C., & SON, LTD.,

Dog and Game Food Manufacturers; Regd. Office and Works: Carta Carna Works, Rutland Street, South Shields, Tyne and Wear.

¶Lucas, Joseph, Ltd., Manufacturers of Electrical Equipment, Great King Street, Birmingham, B19 2XF. T N 021-554 5252; Telex 338681.

¶Luxford, Keith (Saddlery), Ltd., Saddlers, Horse Clothiers and Harness Makers, 57-59, High Street, Teddington, Middx. T N 01-977 4964.

+Lyle & Scott, Ltd., Manufacturers of Underwear and Knitwear, Hawick, Scotland. T N 0450 3361.

¶LYONS BAKERY LTD.,

Manufacturers of Cakes, Cadby Hall, London, W14 0PA. T N 01-603 2040.

¶○Lyons, J., & Co., Ltd.

J. LYONS & CO. LTD.
Caterers
Cadby Hall,
W14 0PA
T.A. Kickshaws
Telex 22420
T.N. 01-603 2040

By Appointment
to H.M. The Queen
Caterers

By Appointment
to H.M. Queen
Elizabeth The
Queen Mother
Caterers

¶Mac Fisheries, Ltd., Fishmongers, Ocean House, Bracknell, Berks., RG12 2LZ. T N Bracknell 3111; Telex 848161.

¶○McCALLUM & CRAIGIE, LTD.,

¶Manufacturers of Lan-Air-Cel Blankets, ○Suppliers of Lan-Air-Cel Blankets, Virginia House, 84, Wilson Street, Glasgow, G1 1UB. T N 041-552 4372.

¶McCarthy, D. & F., Ltd., Fruit and Vegetable Merchants, Raynham St., Norwich, Norfolk. T N 0603 29731.

¶Macfarlane, Lang & Co., Ltd., Biscuit Manufacturers, 35 Clydeford Drive, Glasgow, E.2. T N 041-554 4353.

¶Mackay, Hugh & Co., Ltd., Manufacturers of Wilton Carpeting, P.O. Box No. 1, Durham City, DH1 1SH. T N Durham 64444.

△Mackenzie & Moncur, Ltd., Hothouse Builders, Balcarres St., Edinburgh, 10. T A Hothouse, Edinburgh; T N 031-447 2071.

¶McVitie & Price, Ltd., Biscuit Manufacturers, Syon Lane, Isleworth, Middx., TW7 5NN. T N 01-560 3131.

¶Macvitties Guest & Co., Ltd., Bakers and Confectioners and Purveyors, 4, South Charlotte St., Edinburgh, EH2 4AR. T N 031-337 6241.

†Mallett & Son, Ltd., Antique Dealers, 40, New Bond Street, London, W1Y 0BS. T N 01-499 7411; Telex 25692.

¶Manbré & Garton, Limited, Suppliers of Coffee Sugar Crystals, Winslow Rd., Hammersmith, W6 9SG. T A Manbre, London, W.6; T N 01-748 6021.

¶†Manley, J., Gilder and Picture Frame Maker, 27, High St., Eton, Bucks.

¶MANN EGERTON & CO., LTD.,
Automobile Engineers, 5, Prince of Wales Rd., Norwich, Norfolk, NR1 1BB. T A Motors, Norwich; T N 0603 28383.

¶Mappin & Webb, Ltd., Silversmiths, 106, Regent St., W1R 6JH. T N 01-734 5842.

○Marcyle, Madame, Corsetière, Morton Hotel, 1/2, Woburn Place, Russell Square, London, W.C.1. T N 01-278 6234.

¶MARLEY BUILDINGS LTD.,
Building Manufacturers and Constructors, Peasmarsh, Guildford, Surrey, GU3 1LS. T N Guildford 69922.

¶Marley Tile Co., Ltd., Suppliers of Roof & Floor Tiles, Sevenoaks, Kent. T N Sevenoaks 55255; Telex 95231.

¶Marsh & Baxter, Ltd., Suppliers of Ham. P.O. Box No. 6, Hall St., Brierley Hill, West Midlands, DY5 3AH. T N 77121.

○Marshall & Snelgrove, ○Drapers: 334-348, Oxford St., W1A 1EF. T A Marshgrove, London, W.1; T N 01-580 3000.

¶○M. & R. Martini & Rossi, Ltd.

MARTINI & ROSSI LTD.
Suppliers of Martini Vermouth
Martini House
Great West Road
Brentford, Middx.
T.A.
Cocktail Brentford-Hounslow
T.N. 01-560 8351
By Appointment to H.M. The Queen Suppliers of Martini Vermouth
By Appointment to H.M. Queen Elizabeth The Queen Mother Suppliers of Brandy and Martini Vermouth

¶Massey-Ferguson (United Kingdom) Ltd., Manufacturers of Agricultural Machinery, Massey-Ferguson House, 33, Davies St., W1Y 2EA. T A Masferg, London, W.1; T N 01-493 9481.

¶Matthews, Frank P., Ltd., Suppliers of Fruit Trees, Berrington Court, Tenbury Wells, Worcs. T N Tenbury Wells 214.

○Maurice & Robert, Hairdressers, 8, Furloe Place, London, S.W.7. T N 01-589 2184.

¶Maxwell, Henry, & Co., Ltd., Bootmakers, 177, New Bond Street, London, W.1. T N 01-493 1097.

¶May, H. (Ascot), Ltd., Automobile Engineers, Ascot Motor Works, Winkfield Road, Ascot. T N Ascot 20324.

○Mayfair Window Cleaning Co., Ltd., Window Cleaners, 374, Wandsworth Road, London, SW8 4TD. T N 01-720 6447/8.

¶Melroses Ltd., Purveyors of Tea and Coffee, 51-57, Couper St., Leith, Edinburgh, EH6 6HQ. T A Melrose, Edinburgh; T N 031-554 3236.

○Menzies, John, & Co., Ltd., Booksellers, Hanover Buildings, Rose St., Edinburgh, EH2 2YQ. T A Hanover, Edin.; T N 031-225 2491.

¶MERRYWEATHER & SONS LTD.

MERRYWEATHER & SONS LTD.
Greenwich High Road,
London SE10 8LH
Tel. 01-692 7100
By Appointment to H. M. The Queen Fire Engineers
T.A. Merryweather London SE10
Telex 896488

¶Metropolitan Window Cleaning Co., Ltd., Window Cleaners, 33, Endell Street, London, W.C.2.

¶Meyer & Mortimer, Ltd., Military Outfitters, 6, Sackville St., W1X 1DD. T A Meyer Mortimer, London, W.1; T N 01-734 3135.

¶MIDLAND-YORKSHIRE TAR DISTILLERS LTD.,
Suppliers of Creosote, Springfield Chemical Works, Oldbury, Warley, Worcs. T N 021-552 1530.

○Miller Calder J. ,Suppliers of Household Furnishings, Traill St., Thurso, Caithness. T N Thurso 2002.

¶Milton, K. W., Purveyor of Meat and Poultry, Manor Rd., Dersingham, Norfolk. T N 270.

¶†Minear & Munday, Fruiterers and Greengrocers, Victoria Station, S.W.1. T N 01-834 61717 & 2080.

○3M United Kingdom, Ltd., Manufacturers of "Scotchbrite" Scouring Pads, 3M House, Wigmore St., London, W1A 1ET. T A Minnesota, London, W.1; T N 01-486 5522.

¶Minns Bros., Ltd., Builders, Heacham Road, Sedgeford, King's Lynn. T N Snettisham 303.

¶Minton Ltd., China Manufacturers, Stoke-on-Trent. T A Minton; T N Stoke-on-Trent 47771.

¶○Mirman Simone

SIMONE MIRMAN
9 Chesham Place
Belgrave Square
SW1H 8HN
By Appointment to H.M. The Queen Milliner
Telephone 01-235 2656
By Appointment to H.M. Queen Elizabeth The Queen Mother Milliner

¶Mitchell & Muil, Bakers & Confectioners, Northfield Bakery, Granitehill Rd., Aberdeen, AB9 2AX. T N 45221/6.

¶Mobil Oil Co., Ltd.

MOBIL OIL CO. LTD.
Mobil House,
54/60 Victoria Street
London SW1E 6QB
By Appointment to H.M. The Queen Suppliers of Petroleum Fuels and Lubricants
Telephone: 01-828 9777
Telex: 22288

¶Modern Fibre Glass Products Ltd., Manufacturers of Fibreglass Carrying Cases, Castle Works, Court Lane, Hadlow, Tonbridge, Kent. T N Hadlow 495.

¶Moët & Chandon, Purveyors of Champagne, Epernay, France.

¶Moir W., Clock Repairer, 41½, Union St., Aberdeen. T N 22464.

†Moorcroft, W., Ltd., Potters, Burslem, Staffs. T A Moorcroft; T N Stoke-on-Trent 24323.

¶Moreton Nurseries, Suppliers of Nosegays, Moreton House, Churt, Farnham, Surrey. T N Headley Down 2127.

○+Morny, Ltd., Manufacturers of Soap, 17/18, Old Bond St., London, W1X 4AY. T N 01-629 7292.

¶Morris Green Machinery (Sussex), Ltd., Manufacturers of Agricultural Machinery, 69, Victoria Road, Worthing, BN11 1UN. T N 36211.

¶Morton Knight Ltd., Manufacturers of Sportswear, 65, Leonard St., London, EC2A 4QT. T N 01-739 2411.

○**MOWBRAY, A. R., & CO., LTD.,**
Suppliers of Fine Bindings, 28, Margaret Street, London, W1N 7LB. T N 01-580 2812.

¶**MOWLEM, JOHN & CO., LTD.,**
Building Contractors, Westgate House, Ealing Road, Brentford, Middlesex, TW8 0QZ. T N 01-568 9111.

¶○Moyses Stevens Ltd., Florist, Berkeley Square, W1X 5DH. T N 01-629 5211.

¶Mumm, G. H., & Co., Purveyors of Champagne, Reims, France.

*Murchie's Creameries, Ltd., Purveyors of Milk and Cream, Lochrin Place, Edinburgh, EH3 9QU. T A Choice; T N 031-229 4546.

¶Murdins Typewriter Co. Ltd., Suppliers of Office Stationery & Equipment, St. James' Street, King's Lynn. T N 0553 4915.

¶Murkett, Bros., Ltd., Suppliers of Motor Vehicles, St. Mary's Works, Brookside, Huntingdon, Cambs., PE18 6HX. T N Huntingdon 52694.

¶Murphy Chemical Ltd., Suppliers of Agricultural Insecticides, Wheathampstead, St. Albans, Herts., AL4 8QU. T A Alvesco, Wheathampstead, St. Albans; T N 058-283 2001.

○Murray, J. & D., Chemists, Bridge Street, Ballater, Aberdeenshire. T N Ballater 409.

○*‡Musk & Co., ○‡Sausage Manufacturers: *Purveyors of Meat, High St., Newmarket. T A Musk; T N Newmarket 47.

¶**NAIRN FLOORS LTD.,**
Manufacturers of Floor Covering, Kirkcaldy, Scotland KY1 2SB. T N 61111.

¶○Nairobi Coffee & Tea Co., Ltd., Coffee Merchants, Shakespeare Street, Watford, Herts., WD2 5HF. T N Watford 34561.

¶○National Benzole Co., Ltd., Suppliers of Motor Spirit, 110 Euston Road, London, NW1 2DP. T N 01-388 7471.

NCR, Ltd., Suppliers of Accounting Machines, 206, Marylebone Rd., NW1 6LY. T N 01-723 7070.

*National Flooring Co., Ltd., Parquet Flooring Manufacturers: Latymer House, 2, Ravenscourt Rd., Hammersmith, W6 0UX. T A Floorcloth, Hammer, London, W.6; T N 01-748 5225.

¶National Linen Co., Ltd., Suppliers of Linen, 20, Brook Street, London, W.1. T N 01-629 5000.

¶Neaverson, A., & Sons, Ltd., Dog Kennel Manufacturers, Peakirk, Nr. Peterborough, PE6 7NN. T N Peterborough 252225.

¶○Nelson, A., & Co., Ltd., Chemists, 73, Duke St., Grosvenor Sq., London, W1M 6BY. T N 01-629 3118 & 3205.

¶○Nestlé Company, Ltd. (The), ¶Manufacturers of Instant Coffee: ○Manufacturers of Nestlé Products, St. George's House, Croydon, Surrey. T A Nestle Croydon Telex; T N 01-686 3333.

¶Newbeam, Ltd., Suppliers of Canned Foods, 285, Willesden Lane, N.W.2. T N 01-459 5161.

¶Newbery, Henry, & Co., Ltd., Suppliers of Furnishing Trimmings, 80, Mortimer St., W1N 8AU. T N 01-636 5970.

○Newey Goodman, Ltd., Pin Makers and Manufacturers of Hooks and Eyes, Robin Hood La., Birmingham, 28. T A Pins; T N 021-744 6681.

¶Newman, Peter, Picture Restorer & Liner, 1b Hollywood Rd., Fulham Rd., S.W.10. T N 01-352 0968.

¶Nissen, Chas., & Co., Stamp Dealers, 65, Victoria St., SW1H 0HW. T N 01-222 6306.

¶Noilly Prat & Cie., Wine Producers, 165, Rue Paradis, Marseilles, France.

¶**NORFOLK NEWLAY EGG CO., LTD.,**
Suppliers of Eggs, Norwich Airport, Fifer's Lane, Norwich, NR6 6HH. T N Norwich 410741.

¶Norfolk Paints (King's Lynn) Ltd., Suppliers of Wallpaper and Paint, Warehousing Estate, Saddlebow Rd., King's Lynn, Norfolk. T N King's Lynn 4903.

¶Norfolk Reed Thatchers, Ltd., Reed Thatchers, Thatches, Loudwater Lane, Loudwater, Chorleywood, Herts. T N Rickmansworth 72600.

¶North, W. A., & Son, Forage Merchants, West Farm, West St., Bourne, Lincs. T N 2651.

¶**NOTCUTTS NURSERIES LTD.,**
Nurserymen, The Garden Centre, Woodbridge, Suffolk, IP12 4AF. T N Woodbridge 3344.

¶Nuralite Co., Ltd. (The), Suppliers of Roofing Materials, Higham, Rochester, Kent, ME3 7JA. T A Nuralite; T N Shorne (0474 82) 3451; Telex 27387.

¶Nu-Way Heating Plants Ltd.

¶Offord, Gordon J., Coachbuilders, 264, Brompton Rd., London, S.W.3. T N 01-373 3388.

¶O'Hanlon Wm. & Co., Ltd., Suppliers of Window Shade Fabrics, 49 & 51, Dale St., Manchester, M60 1JJ. T N 061-236 3223.

○**OLIVER FORD LTD.,**
Decorators, 59, Grosvenor Street, London, W1X 9DA. T N 01-499 6958.

¶Oliver, Janet, Florist, Prestonfield House, Edinburgh, 9. T N New 3479.

¶Orange Luxury Coaches, Ltd., Coach Hirers, 53-55, Stamford Hill, N16 5TD. T N 01-800 4549 & 4370.

○Osmond & Sons Ltd., Suppliers of Animal Feeding Stuffs, Sheep Dips and Veterinary Medicines, Doughty Rd., Grimsby, South Humberside, DN32 0LW. T N Grimsby 50256.

¶Oxley & Son (Windsor), Ltd., Printers and Stationers, 2-4, Victoria St., Windsor. T A Oxley; T N 69651.

¶○Papworth Industries, ¶Travel Goods Makers: ○Trunk and Cabinet Makers, Papworth Everard, Cambridge, CB3 8RG; T A Pendragon, Cambridge; T N 048-088 345.

¶○Paragon China, Ltd., ¶China Potters: ○Manufacturers of Fine Bone China, Sutherland Rd., Longton, Stoke-on-Trent. T A Paragon, Longton; T N 39266.

¶Paris House, Ltd., Beltmakers, 41, South Molton St., W1Y 2HB. T A Parisous, London, W.1; T N 01-629 5065.

○Parker, Geo., & Sons (Saddlers), Ltd., Saddlers, 12 Upper St. Martin's La., W.C.2. T A Cavesson, London, W.C.2. T N 01-836 1164.

¶Parker Pen Co., Ltd., Manufacturers of Pens, Pencils and Ink, Parker House, 15, Grosvenor Gardens, SW1W 0BL. T A Parkerpen, London, S.W.1; T N 01-834 4641.

¶Patent Steam Carpet Cleaning Co., Ltd. (The), Carpet Cleaners, Furmage Street, London, SW18 4DF. T N 01-874 4333 & 01-253 6121.

¶Patman, C., Clock Repairer, 1d, Arbury Rd., Cambridge. T N 57434.

¶Pattrick & Thompsons, Ltd., Timber Merchants, King's Lynn, Norfolk. T A Thompsons, Phone; T N Kings Lynn 2236.

¶Pauls & Whites Foods Ltd., Manufacturers of Animal Feeding Stuffs, P.O. Box 39, Key St., Ipswich IP4 1BX. T A Paul, Ipswich; T N Ipswich (0473) 56711.

○Paxton & Whitfield, Ltd., Cheesemongers, 93, Jermyn Street, S.W.1. T N 01-930 3380.

¶○Pears, A. & F., Ltd., Soap Manufacturers, Hesketh House, Portman Square, London, W1A 1DY. T N 01-486 1200.

¶○Peck, John, & Co., Ltd., Suppliers of Overalls and Chefs' Clothing, Pexwear Factory, 495, Edge Lane, Liverpool, L13 1AF. T A Washable; T N 051-228 2717.

¶○Peek, Frean & Co., Ltd., Biscuit Manufacturers, Keetons Rd., London, S.W.16. T N 01-237 3570; T A Pickaxe, London.

+Penhaligon's, Ltd.

PENHALIGON'S LTD.

Perfumers

23 Old Bond Street
London W1X 3DA

Tel. 01-493 2961

By Appointment to
H.R.H. The Duke
of Edinburgh
Manufacturers of
Toilet Requisites

△Pennell & Sons, Ltd., Seedsmen and Nurserymen, Princess St., Lincoln, LN5 7QL. T A Pennells; T N 0522 26161.

¶Perkins Engines, Ltd., Manufacturers of Diesel Engines, Peterborough, PE1 5NA. T N 67474; Telex 32132.

△Permutit Co., Ltd. (The), Suppliers of Water Treating Equipment, 632-652, London Road, Isleworth, Middx., TW7 4EZ. T N 01-560 5199; T A Permutit, Hounslow; Telex 24440.

△Perrier-Jouet Champagne, Purveyors of Champagne, Epernay, France.

¶**PETTIFER, THOMAS, & CO., LTD.,**
Manufacturers of Animal Health and Nutrition Products, Eydon House, Midleton Industrial Estate, Guildford, Surrey, GU2 5XW. T N Guildford 34151.

¶**PHILIP & TACEY, LTD.,**
Manufacturers and Designers of Educational Material, North Way, Andover, Hants., SP10 5BA. T N 0264 61171; T A Philotesie, Andover.

+Philips Electrical Ltd., Suppliers of Dictation Machines, Century House, Shaftesbury Avenue, London, WC2H 8AS. T N 01-437 7777.

○†Phillips, S. J., Ltd.

 **S. J. PHILLIPS LTD.**

139 New Bond Street
London W1A 3DL

Antique English and Continental Silver Period Jewels and Objets d'Art
T.A. Euclase,
London W1A 3DL
T.N. 01-629 6261

By Appointment
to H.M. Queen
Elizabeth The
Queen Mother
Antique Dealers

By Appointment
Antique Dealers
to the Late
Queen Mary

○**PHONOTAS CO., LTD.,**
Telephone Cleaners and Sterilizers, 116, College Road, Harrow, Middx., HA1 1HJ. T N 01-863 2377.

¶+Pickfords International, Ltd., Shipping and Forwarding Agents, Regina House, 259, Old Marylebone Road, London, NW1 5RN. T N 01-636 8688; Telex 28832.

¶Pilgrim Payne & Co., Ltd.

PILGRIM PAYNE & CO. LTD.

Park Street Works
Latimer Place
London W10 6QU

Telephone 01-969 3093

By Appointment
to H.M. The Queen
Dyers and Cleaners of
Soft Furnishings and
Carpets

¶Pilkington Brothers Ltd., Manufacturers and Suppliers of Glass, Prescot Rd., St. Helens, Merseyside. T A Pilkington, St. Helens; T N St. Helens 28882.

¶Pink, W., & Sons, Ltd., Grocers and Provision Merchants, Grove Road, Cosham, Portsmouth, PO6 1PZ. T N Cosham 72272.

*Pitt, Charles, & Co., Ltd., Button Makers, 31, Maddox St., W.1. T N Mayfair 1538 & 2305.

¶+○†Plante & Johnson, Ltd., ¶+Silversmiths and Jewellers: ○†Jewellers and Silversmiths, 12, Bury St., St. James's, SW1Y 6AB. T N 01-930 8720.

○**PLAYER, JOHN, & SONS,**
Tobacco Manufacturers, Nottingham, NG7 5PY. T N 0602 77711; Telex 37651.

¶○Plessey Company Limited (The), ¶Suppliers of Car Radios: ○Suppliers of Motor Car Radio Equipment, Ilford, Essex, IG1 4AQ. T A Plessey, Ilford; Telex 23166; T N 01-478 3040.

¶+Poole, E. C., Farrier, 25, Belle Vue Rd., Henley-on-Thames, Oxon. T N 1460.

¶Poole, Henry, & Co. (Savile Row), Ltd., Livery Outfitters, 10-12, Cork St., W.1. T A Eloop, London, W1X 1PD; T N 01-734 5985.

¶Poulton & Nicholson, Ltd., Upholsterers' Warehousemen, 98, Curtain Rd., London, E.C.2. T A Bissacs, London, E.C.2; T N 01-739 6183.

¶Power Petroleum Company, Limited (The), Suppliers of Lubricating Oil, Cecil Chambers, 76, Strand, WC2R 0DX. T N 01-836 1234.

¶P.P. & H., Ltd., Suppliers of Building Materials, P.O. Box 8, 39, Norfolk Street, King's Lynn, Norfolk, PE30 1AS. T N 0553 61711.

¶○Pratt & Leslie Jones Ltd., ¶Suppliers of Fancy Goods: ○Suppliers of China, Glass and Fancy Goods, The Token House, 26, High St., Windsor, SL4 1LH. T N Windsor 63263.

¶Pratt, Thomas & Sons, Ltd., Ecclesiastical Robe Makers, 34-35, Southampton St., Strand, WC2E 7HH. T N 01-836 5718.

¶Prestat, Ltd., Purveyors of Chocolates, 24, South Molton Street, London, W1Y 1HA. T N 01-629 4838.

¶○Prestcold Limited, Manufacturers of Refrigerating Machinery, Station Road, Theale, Reading, RG7 4AF. T N 0734 302222.

¶Price's Patent Candle Co., Ltd., Candlemakers, Belmont Works, Battersea, London, SW11 3RU. T A Luminary, London, SW11 3RU; T N 01-228 2001.

¶Pringle, H. E., Ltd., Forage Merchants, 74 Granby St., Newmarket, Suffolk. T N 2046.

¶○Pringle, John, ¶Motor Engineer: ○Supplier of Motor Spirit, Oil and Accessories, Victoria Garage, Ballater, Scotland. T N 525.

¶○Pringle of Scotland, Ltd., Manufacturers of Knitted Garments, Hawick, Roxburghshire. T N Hawick 3371.

¶○Procter & Gamble, Ltd., ¶Manufacturers of Soap and Detergents: ○Manufacturers of Soaps, Detergents and Shortening, Gosforth, Newcastle upon Tyne, 3. T A Progam, N'Tyne, 3; T N 857141.

¶PROTIM LTD., Manufacturers of Wood Preservatives, Fieldhouse Lane, Marlow, Bucks, SL7 1LS. T N Marlow 6644; Telex 847057.

¶Pugh, Charles H., Ltd., Manufacturers of Motor Mowers, P.O. Box No. 256, Atco Works, Tilton Rd., Birmingham B9 4PR. T N 021-772 2524.

¶†Pugh & Co. (London), Ltd., ¶Coal Merchants: †Coal and Coke Merchants, 28, Churton St., S.W.1. T N 01-834 5282.

¶Pulford, P. W., Builder and Decorator, 21, St. Margaret's Road, Twickenham. T N 01-892 5555.

¶+Purdey, James & Sons, Ltd., ¶Gun and Cartridge Makers: +Gun Makers, Audley House, South Audley St., W1Y 6ED. T A Purdey, London, W.1; T N 01-499 1801.

+Pye Telecommunications, Ltd.

PYE TELECOMMUNICATIONS LTD.
Suppliers of Radiotelephone Equipment
Newmarket Road, Cambridge CB5 8PD
By Appointment to H.R.H. The Duke of Edinburgh Manufacturers of Radio Telephone Equipment
T.A. Pyetelecom;
T.N. Cambridge (Area Code: 0223) 61222

¶PYROTENAX LTD., Manufacturers and Suppliers of Electric Cable, Hedgeley Rd., Hebburn, Tyne and Wear, NE31 1XR. T N 0632 832244; Telex 53573.

¶Quaker Oats Limited, Suppliers of Quaker Products, Southall, Middx. T N 01-574 2388; Telex 934740.

¶Radiomobile, Ltd., Manufacturers of Car Radio Equipment, Goodwood Works, North Circular Rd., N.W.2. T A Mobilerad, London, N.W.2; T N 01-452 0171.

¶Rank Audio Visual, Ltd. (Rank Film Equipment), Manufacturers of Cinematograph Equipment, P.O. Box 70, Great West Rd., Brentford, Middx. T N 01-568 9222.

¶Rank Xerox, Ltd., Manufacturers and Suppliers of Xerographic Copying Equipment and Materials, Rank Xerox House, 338, Euston Rd., N.W.1. T N 01-387 1244.

¶Ransomes Sims & Jefferies, Ltd., Manufacturers of Agricultural and Horticultural Machinery, Ipswich IP3 9QG. T A Ransomes, Ipswich; T N 0473 72222; Telex 98174.

¶Ratsey & Lapthorn, Ltd.

RATSEY & LAPTHORN LTD.
Sailmakers
Medina Loft
Medina Road, Cowes
Isle of Wight PO31 7BY
T.N. 098-382 4051
By Appointment to H.M. The Queen Sail Makers
T.A. Ratsey Sails
Telex 86656

¶RAWLINGS, H. D., LTD., Mineral Water Manufacturers, Winsor Terrace, London, E.6. T N 01-476 1488.

¶○†Rayne, H. & M., Ltd., Shoemakers, 15-16, Old Bond St., London, W.1. T N 01-493 9077.

¶Reckitt & Colman, Food Division, Manufacturers of Mustard and Sauces; Carrow, Norwich, NOR 75A; Telex 97438 Colmans Norwich; T N 0603 60166.

¶Reckitt & Colman, Household Division, Manufacturers of Metal Polish, Shoe Polish & Leather Dressings, Reckitt House, Stoneferry Road, Hull HU8 8DD. T A Reckitts; T N 0482 223141.

¶Reckitt & Colman, Industrial Division, Manufacturers of Hygenol Polishing Preparations; Cressex, High Wycombe, Bucks., HP12 3TL. T N 0494 26131.

¶Reckitt & Colman, Pharmaceutical Division, Manufacturers of Antiseptics; Dansom Lane, Hull. T A Reckitts; T N 0482 26151.

○Rediffusion London, Ltd.

REDIFFUSION LONDON LIMITED
8/12 Camden High Street
London NW1 0JJ
By Appointment to H.M. Queen Elizabeth The Queen Mother Suppliers of Rediffusion
Telephone 01-387 9121
Specialists in T.V. Sales and Rental and T.V. Distribution Systems

¶Redmayne, S., & Sons, Ltd., Tailors, Station Rd., Wigton, Cumberland. T N 09654 2244.

¶REED MEDWAY SACKS, LTD., Suppliers of Domestic Refuse Sacks, Aylesford, Maidstone, Kent, ME20 7PG. T N Maidstone (0622) 77777; Telex 965131.

¶○Reeves, C., & Sons (Staines), Ltd., Purveyors of Meat, 56, High St., Staines. T N 51904-5.

¶Reflectolight (King's Lynn), Ltd., Suppliers of Electrical Installation Materials, Friar Street, King's Lynn. T N King's Lynn 3132 & 3172.

¶Reid, C. J. (Eton), Chemists, 30, High St., Eton. T N Windsor 63819.

¶+Remington Rand, ¶Suppliers of Office Machines and Equipment. See entry under Sperry Remington.

¶Remploy, Ltd., Manufacturers of Knitwear, 415, Edgware Road, London, N.W.2. T N 01-452 8020.

¶○Renshaw, John F., & Co., Ltd., Purveyors of Almond Products, Locks Lane, Mitcham, Surrey, CR4 2XE. T A Jorenco, Mitcham; T N 01-648 3005.

¶Rentokil Ltd., Pest Control and Timber Preservation Services and Products, Felcourt, East Grinstead, Sussex, RH19 2JY. T A Rentokil, East Grinstead; T N East Grinstead 23661.

¶RFD-GQ Ltd., Manufacturers of Inflatable Boats, Godalming, Surrey. T A Airships; T N 4122; Telex 859233.

¶RHM Blue Cross Ltd., Manufacturers of Animal Feeding Stuffs, RHM Centre, 152, Grosvenor Road, SW1V 3JL. T A Millocrat, London, S.W.1. T N 01-821 1444.

¶Rich, Arthur & Partners, Ltd., Suppliers of Leather Preserves and Dressings, 42, Mount Pleasant Drive, Belper, Derbyshire, DE5 1AD. T N 0773 82 2632.

○Riché of Hay Hill, Ltd., Manicurists, 14, Hay Hill, London, W.1.

¶Rickards, Charles (Tours) Limited, Road Transport Contractors, 2, Glenhurst Road, Brentford, TW8 0QR. T N 01-568 0181.

¶○Ridgways, Ltd., ¶Tea Merchants: ○Tea and Coffee Merchants, 290 Old Street, London, EC1V 9DL. T A Ridgways, London, EC1; T N 01-739 8244; Telex Ridgtea London 23443.

¶Rigby, John, & Co. (Gunmakers), Ltd., Rifle and Cartridge Makers, 13, Pall Mall, London, S.W.1. T A Rifling, London; T N 01-734 7611.

¶Rigby & Peller, Corsetières, 12, South Molton St., W1Y 1DF. T N 01-629 6708.

¶Riverside Garage, Automobile and Electrical Engineers, Ballater, Scotland. T N 323.

¶Rivington Carpets, Ltd., Carpet Manufacturers, Blackrod Mill, Horwich, Bolton, Lancs., BL6 5JD. T N Horwich 66711.

¶Roberts' Radio Co., Ltd.

ROBERTS' RADIO CO. LTD.

Radio Manufacturers

Molesey Av., West Molesey, Surrey

By Appointment to H.M. The Queen Radio Manufacturers

T.A. Robrays, East Molesey;

T.N. 01-979 7474

¶Robertson, James, & Sons (P.M.), Ltd., Marmalade Manufacturers, 50, Burnhill Road, Beckenham, Kent, BR3 3LA. T N 01-658 3661.

¶Roederer, Louis, S.A., Champagne, Purveyors of Champagne, Reims, France.

¶Roger & Gallet

By Appointment to H.M. The Queen Manufacturers of Soap

ROGER & GALLET
Successors to
Jean Marie Farina
Manufrs. of Soap

62 Rue du Faubourg Saint Honoré Paris, France

¶Rogers, T., & Co. (Packers), Ltd., Packers and Transporters of Works of Art, 14, Mason's Yard, Duke Street, London, SW1Y 6BY. T N 01-930 4252.

¶Rolls-Royce Motors, Ltd., Motor Car Manufacturers, Crewe, Cheshire, CW1 3PL. T N Crewe (0270) 55155.

+Ronson Products, Ltd., Suppliers of Electric Shavers, Leatherhead, Surrey, KT22 7TF. T N 74444.

¶Rose, L., & Co., Ltd., Suppliers of Lime Juice Cordial, Grosvenor Rd., St. Albans, Herts. T A Esor, St. Albans; T N 56 59242.

¶Ross Optical, Ltd., Manufacturers of Binoculars, Ayling House, King's Rd., Horsham, Sussex. T N 0403 3391.

¶Ross Poultry, Ltd.—Sterling Division, Suppliers of Sykes Live Poultry, Imperial House, 61-65, Rose Lane, Norwich, Norfolk, NR1 1PU.

¶○Rover Triumph Division—British Leyland (U.K.), Ltd., ¶Manufacturers of Rover Motors Cars and Land Rovers: ○Suppliers of Rover Motor Cars and Land rovers, Longbridge Works, Bristol Road South, Birmingham, 31. T N 021-475 2101; Telex 33491.

¶Rowe, Frank, Suppliers of Chrysanthemum Stock, Rylands Nurseries, Wellington, Somerset. T N Wellington 2462.

¶Rowes of Bond Street Ltd., Outfitters, 120, New Bond St., London, W1Y 0BN. T N 01-734 9711.

○Rowntree Mackintosh, Ltd., Makers of Table Jellies, York, YO1 1XY. T A Rowntree, York; T N 0904 53071.

○Royal British Legion Disabled Men's Industries, Ltd., Makers of Leather and Fancy Goods, 70/80, York Way, N.1. T N 01-837 4706.

¶Royal British Legion Poppy Factory Ltd. (The), Royal British Legion Poppy Manufacturers and Suppliers of Rosettes, 20, Petersham Road, Richmond, Surrey, TW10 6UR. T A Remembrance, Richmond (Surrey); T N 01-940 3305.

¶Royal Laundry (Southsea) Ltd., Launderers and Dry Cleaners, 6, Taswell Road, Southsea, Hants., PO5 2RQ. T N Portsmouth (0705) 28408.

¶○Russell, Gordon, Ltd., ¶Manufacturers of Furniture, ○Suppliers of Furniture and Furnishings, Broadway, Worcestershire, WR12 7AD. T N 038-681 3345.

△Ryvita Co., Ltd. (The), Ryvita Manufrs., Old Wareham Rd., Parkstone, Poole, Dorset. T N Parkstone 743090.

¶St. Cuthbert's Co-operative Association, Ltd., Coach Painters, 92, Fountainbridge, Edinburgh, EH3 9QE. T N 031-229 2424.

*Salt & Son, Ltd., Cutlers, 220, Corporation St., Birmingham, 4. T A Saltair; T N 021-236 2235.

+Salter, J., & Son, Suppliers of Polo Sticks, 23, High St., Aldershot, Hants. T N 20692.

¶Sampson, William G., & Son, Farriers, 39, Howard Rd., Newbury, Berks. T N Newbury 43204.

¶Sandeman, Geo. G., Sons & Co., Ltd., Wine Merchants, 37, Albert Embankment, London, SE1 7UA. T N 01-735 7971/5; Telex 267980.

¶Sanderson, Arthur, & Sons, Ltd., Suppliers of Wallpapers, Paints and Fabrics, 52/53, Berners St., London, W1A 2JE. T N 01-636 7800.

¶○Sanderson, William, & Son, Ltd.

WILLIAM SANDERSON & SON LTD.

By Appointment to H.M. The Queen Scotch Whisky Distillers

Scotch Whisky Distillers South Queensferry, West Lothian T.A. Vatsixnine; South Queensferry, Telex Tel: 031-331 1500

¶Sandcliffe Garage, Ltd., Suppliers of Motor Horse Boxes and Automobile Engineers, Nottingham Road, Stapleford, Nottingham. T N Sandiacre 395000.

¶Sanitas Co., Ltd. (The), Manufacturers of Hygiene Products, Sanitas House, Stockwell Green, London, SW9 9JJ. T A Sanitas, London, S.W.9; T N 01-733 7911.

△Sankey, R., & Son, Ltd., Makers of Horticultural Pottery, The Potteries, Bulwell, Nottingham, NG6 8PE. T A Potteries, Bulwell; T N Nottingham 278585-6.

+Saunders, Peter (Easton Grey), Ltd., Makers of Peter Saunders Tweeds, Easton Grey, Malmesbury, Wilts. T N Sherston 345.

¶+○Savory & Moore, Ltd., Chemists, 143, New Bond St., W1Y 0DJ. T N 01-629 4471.

¶○Schweppes, Ltd., Mineral Water Manufacturers, 1-10 Connaught Place, W2 2EX; T A Casch London W2 2EX; T N 01-262 1212.

¶Scoles, R. F. & J., Butchers, Chapel Road, Dersingham, King's Lynn, Norfolk. T N Dersingham 40309.

†Scott. Adie, Ltd., Manufacturers of Scotch Tartan, 14a, Clifford St., W.1. T N 01-629 6331.

○Scott's Fish Shop, Cheesemonger, 3, Bridge St., Kirkwall, Orkney. T N Kirkwall 3170.

¶Scottish Agricultural Industries, Ltd., Manufacturers of Fertilizers, Feeds and Seeds, 25, Ravelston Terrace, Edinburgh, EH4 3ET. T A Scotag, Edinburgh; Telex 72268; T N 031-332 2481.

¶Scottish & Newcastle Breweries, Ltd.

SCOTTISH & NEWCASTLE BREWERIES LIMITED

Brewers

By Appointment to H.M. The Queen Brewers

Edinburgh and Newcastle upon Tyne

¶○Scottish Seed House (The), Seedsmen, South Methven St., Perth. T A Scotseed; T N 23251.

¶Sekers Fabrics, Ltd., Manufacturers of Furnishing Fabrics, 190-192, Sloane St., London, SW1X 9RA; T A Sekersilk, London, S.W.1; T N 01-245 9991; Telex 21387.

○Sergent, Maurice Louis, Hairdresser, c/o Maurice & Robert, 8, Furloe Pl., London, S.W.7. T N 01-589 2184.

¶○**SHARP, EDWARD, & SONS, LTD.,**
¶Confectioners: ○Suppliers of Confectionery and Confectionery Novelties, Trebor Sharps Limited, Kreemy Works, Maidstone, Kent. T A Trebor Sharps, Maidstone; T N Maidstone 57421.

¶Sharpe, Charles, & Co., Ltd., Seedsmen, Sleaford, Lincs. Telex 37189; T N 2002 (6 lines).

¶Sharwood, J. A., & Co., Ltd., Manufacturers of Chutney and Indian Curry Powder, 10, Victoria Road, London, NW10 6NU. T N 01-965 2061.

¶Shaw, Elizabeth, Manufacturers of Confectionery, Cavenham Ho., Colnbrook, Bucks. Tel. Colnbrook 4411.

¶Shepherd's Aerosols, Ltd., Manufacturers of Aerovap, Shernfold Park, Frant, Tunbridge Wells, Kent, TN3 9HH. T N Frant 346.

¶Sheringham & Overman Ltd., Seedsmen, Holt Rd., Fakenham, Norfolk. T N 2295.

¶Shippam, C., Ltd., Manufacturers of Meat and Fish Pastes, East Walls, Chichester. T A Shippam; T N Chichester (0243) 85191 (10 lines).

+Shipton Telstor Ltd., Manufacturers and Distributors of Telephone Answering Machines, Group House, Oval Rd., London, NW1 7DD. T N 01-485 4100.

¶Shirras, Laing & Co., Ltd., Ironmongers, School Hill, Aberdeen. T N Aberdeen 25242 (4 lines).

¶+Simpson (Piccadilly), Ltd., Outfitters, Piccadilly, W1A 2AS. T A Simperos London Telex; T N 01-734 2002.

¶Singer Co. (U.K.) Ltd. (The), Manufacturers of Sewing Machines, 255, High St., Guildford, Surrey, GU1 3DH. T A Singer, Guildford; T N Guildford 71144.

*†‡Skinner, A. E., & Co., *‡Silversmiths: †Jewellers and Silversmiths, 35, Old Bond St., W.1. T N 01-493 5115 & 8909.

¶Sleepeezee, Ltd.

SLEEPEEZEE LTD.

Morden Road, Merton,

London SW19 3XP

T.N. 01-540 9171

By Appointment to H.M. The Queen Bedding Suppliers

Makers of

SLEEPEEZEE

Regd. Products

¶○Slumberland Ltd., Bedding Manufacturers, Sedgley Road East, Tipton, West Midlands, DY4 7RH. T N 021-557 6199.

¶Smedley-HP Foods Ltd., Manufacturers of HP Sauce, Imperial House, Willes Rd., Leamington Spa, Warwickshire. T N 0926-27055; Telex 311205.

¶○Smith, G. & Co., Sporting Outfitters, Bridge St., Ballater. Aberdeenshire. T N 432.

¶○Smith, H. Allen, Ltd., Wine Cooper and Merchant, 7-11, Justice Walk, Old Church St., Chelsea, S.W.3. T N 01-352 4114 & 6516.

¶Smith James (Scotland Nurseries), Ltd.

James Smith (Scotland Nurseries) Ltd.

NURSERYMEN

By Appointment to H.M. The Queen Nurserymen

TANSLEY, MATLOCK, DERBYSHIRE DE4 5GF

T.N. MATLOCK 3036

¶○Smith, Tom, & Co., Ltd., Suppliers of Christmas Crackers, Salhouse Rd., Norwich, NOR 86R, Norfolk. T N Norwich 47204.

¶Smith & Wellstood, Ltd., Manufacturers of Esse Cooking Equipment, Bonnybridge, Stirlingshire. T A Wellstood, Bonnybridge; T N 2171.

¶Smiths Industries, Ltd. (Clock and Watch Division), Manufacturers of Clocks and Watches, No. 1 Site, Wishaw, Lanarkshire, ML2 0RN. T N Wishaw 73461.

¶Smythson, Frank, Ltd., Stationers, 54, New Bond St., W1Y 0DE. T N 01-629 8558.

△**SODASTREAM LTD.,**
Soda-Water Machine Maufacturers, 21 Wainman Rd., Woodston, Peterborough, PE2 0BS. T N Peterborough 231121.

¶Soil Fertility Dunns, Ltd.

	SOIL FERTILITY DUNNS LTD.
By Appointment to H.M. The Queen Seedsmen and Suppliers of Agricultural Fertilisers	Hartham Corsham Wilts SN13 0QA Tel. 0249 712051 Telex 44642

¶Solignum, Ltd., Manufrs. of Wood Preservatives, Thames Rd., Crayford, Kent, DA1 4QJ. T N 29 22322.

¶Southwell, Charles, & Co., Ltd.

	CHARLES SOUTHWELL & CO. LTD.
By Appointment to H.M. The Queen Manufacturers of Confectionery	Manufacturers of Confectionery College Street Ipswich IP4 1DE Telephone 56234 Telex 98224

○†Sparks, John, Ltd.

 JOHN SPARKS LTD.

	JOHN SPARKS LTD. Antiquaries of Chinese Art	
By Appointment to H.M. Queen Elizabeth The Queen Mother Antiquaries of Chinese Art	128 Mount Street, London, W1Y 5HA T.A. Sparkammer London, W1Y 5HA T.N. 01-499 2265 & 1932	By Appointment to her late Majesty Queen Mary Antiquaries of Chinese Art

¶†**SPERRY REMINGTON,**
Suppliers of office machines and equipment, Remington House, 35, Station Road, Wood Green, London, N22 6UT. T N 01-888 1255; Telex 27585.

¶Spillers Farm Feeds Limited, Manufacturers of Animal Feeds, Old Change House, 4-6, Cannon St., EC4M 6XB. T N 01-248 5700.

¶+Spink & Son, Ltd., Medallists, 5-7, King St., St. James's, London, S.W.1. T A Spink, London, S.W.1; T N 01-930 7888.

¶Spode Ltd., Manufacturers of China, Spode Works, Stoke-on-Trent, ST4 1BX. T N 0782 46011; T A Spode, Stoke-on-Trent; Telex 36420.

¶**SPRATT'S PATENT LTD.,**
Suppliers of Dog Foods, Central House, Cambridge Rd., Barking, Essex, IG11 8NL. T N 01-594 7121.

¶○Sproston, W. F., Ltd., ¶Suppliers of Fish: ○Fishmongers, 17-19, Claylands Place, London, SW8 1NL. T N 01-735 3331.

¶Spruce & Wright, Ltd., Forage Merchants, Eastgate Works, Gayton, King's Lynn, Norfolk, PE32 1QF. T N Gayton 357.

¶Sta-Dri (Cabs), Ltd., Manufacturers of Tractor Cabs, Whitefield Rd., Bristol, 5. T N 651204 & 659511.

¶**STANTON HOPE LTD.,**
Suppliers of Forestry Equipment, 422, Westborough Rd., Westcliff-on-Sea, Essex. T N Southend 351281.

¶Staples & Co., Ltd., Manufacturers of Bedsteads & Bedding, Corner of Edgware Rd. & North Circular Rd., Cricklewood, London, N.W.2. T N 01-452 1144.

¶**START-RITE SHOES, LTD.,**
Shoemakers, Norwich, Norfolk, NOR 60A. T A Start-Rite, Norwich; T N 43841.

○†Steiner, ○Chiropodists, †Hairdressers and Perfumers, 66, Grosvenor St., W.1. T N 01-629 5245.

¶Steinway & Sons, Pianoforte Manufacturers, Steinway Hall, 1-2, St. George St., Hanover Sq., W1R 9DG. T A Steinways, London, W.1; T N 01-629 6641.

¶Stenner of Tiverton, Ltd., Manufacturers and Suppliers of Sawmilling Machinery, Lowman Works, Tiverton, Devon, EX16 4JX; T N 3691.

+△Stephens Brothers, Ltd., Hosiers, 16-21, Sackville Street, London, W1A 4EZ. T A Tenova, London, W.1; T N 01-734 2424.

¶Stevens, A. B., Ltd., Florists, Tudor Nurseries, Goff's Oak, Waltham Cross, Herts., EN7 6SH. T N Cuffley 2080.

¶Stevens & Williams, Ltd., Suppliers of Table Glassware, Royal Brierley Crystal Works, North St., Brierley Hill, Staffs., DY5 3SJ. T A Crystal; T N Brierley Hill 77054/5.

¶○Stevenson Brothers (Dundee), Ltd., Launderers, Seaforth Rd., Aberdeen. T N Aberdeen 25375.

¶**STEWART, J. & G., LTD.,**
Suppliers of Scotch Whisky, 9/13, Maritime Street, Leith, Edinburgh, EH6 6SG. T N 031-554 4388; T A Firstblend, Edinburgh.

¶Still, W. M., & Sons, Limited

	W. M. STILL & SONS LIMITED
By Appointment to H.M. The Queen Manufacturers of Kitchen Equipment	Catering Equipment Manufacturers Fellows Road, Hastings East Sussex T.N. 0424 432121 Cables: Stills, Hastings

¶Stoddard, A. F., & Co., Ltd., Carpet Manufacturers, Glenpatrick Works, Elderslie, Johnstone, Renfrewshire, PA5 9UJ. T A Stoddard, Johnstone, Telex; T N Johnstone 21121 (8 lines).

○Stopps, J., & Sons, Ltd., Bakers and Confectioners, 77, Humer Road, Egham, Surrey. T N Egham 2607.

○**STOWELLS OF CHELSEA, LTD.,**
Wine and Spirit Merchants, Great North Road, Hatfield, Herts., AL9 5JY. T N Hatfield 68200.

¶○Strachan, George, Ltd., General Merchants, East Balmoral, Crathie, Aberdeenshire, AB3 5TB. T N Crathie 224.

¶Straker, S., & Sons, Ltd., Printers and Stationers, 49, Fenchurch St., EC3M 3JY. T A Imprintess, London, E.C.3; T N 01-626 8411.

¶Stratstone, Ltd., Motor Car Distributors, 40 Berkeley St., London, W1X 6EN. T N 01-629 4404; T A Strathstone, London.

○Studio Lisa, Ltd., Photographers, Grape St., W.C.2. T N 01-836 4606.

¶Sturgess, Walter E., & Sons, Ltd.

WALTER E. STURGESS & SONS LTD.

115 Aylestone Rd., Leicester LE2 7LP

By Appointment to H.M. The Queen Suppliers of Horse and Carriage Conveyances

Tel.: Leicester (0533) 549191 (4 lines)

¶Sturtevant Welbeck, Ltd., Manufacturers of Vacuum Cleaners, Westgate Road, Moulsecoomb Way, Brighton, BN2 4QB. T N 0273 61666.

¶Supermatic International (U.K.), Ltd., Manufacturers of Heating Appliances, New Park Industrial Estate, Antrim, N. Ireland.

¶○**SUTTON'S SEEDS LTD.,** Seedsmen, The Royal Seed Establishment, Reading. Telex 848215; T N Reading 61151.

¶○†**SWAINE, ADENEY, BRIGG & SONS, LTD.,** ¶Whip and Glove Makers: ○Umbrella Makers: †Glove Makers and Umbrella Manufacturers, 185, Piccadilly, W1V 0HA. T A Swadeneyne, London, W.1; T N 01-734 4277.

¶+Sycamore Laundry & Dry Cleaners (Leman Bros.), Launderers and Dry Cleaners, 4-6, Old Town, London, SW4 0JZ. T N 01-622 3333.

○Symbol Biscuits, Ltd., Biscuit Manufacturers, Devonshire Road, Blackpool, Lancs., FY3 7AN. T N Blackpool 34133.

¶Tanqueray, Gordon & Co., Ltd., Gin Distillers, 260-266, Goswell Rd., EC1V 7EE; T A Gordon, London, E.C.1; T N 01-253 2060.

¶Tate & Lyle, Ltd., Sugar Refiners, 21, Mincing Lane, EC3R 7QY. T A Tatelyle, London, EC3; T N 01-626 6525.

¶Taylor D. & R. Upholsterers, 97A & 107 Norfolk St., King's Lynn, Norfolk.

△Taylor & Henderson, Ltd., Printers and Stationers, 15 & 17, Adelphi, Aberdeen. T N Aberdeen 20844.

¶**TELFER, HENRY, LTD.,** Purveyors of Pork Pies, Moulton Park, Northampton, NN3 1NP. T N 0604 43666.

¶Temple & Crook, Ltd., Suppliers of Brushes and Hardware, 3-5, Kinnerton Street, London, SW1X 8JY. T N 01-235 2166.

¶Thawpit, Ltd., Manufacturers of Thawpit, Chapeltown, Sheffield, S30 4YP. T N 0741-5 3171.

¶Thermos Limited, Manufacturers of Vacuum Vessels, Ongar Rd., Brentwood, Essex, CM15 9AY. T A Thermos, Brentwood, Essex; T N Brentwood 213404-6.

¶Thomas, Ian, Dressmaker, 14, Motcomb St., London, S.W.1. T N 01-235 5342.

○†Thomas, J. Rochelle, Dealer in Works of Art, 1166, Second Av., New York.

○Thomas Window Cleaning, Window Cleaner, 16, Ilex Close, Englefield Green, Surrey. T N Egham 4218.

¶Thompson Cochran Division—Clarke-Chapman, Ltd., Boiler Makers, Lilybank Works, London Road, Glasgow, G31 4SD. T N 041-554 6311.

○Thomson, Donald, Grocer, Main Street, Castletown, Caithness. T N Castletown 231.

¶○Thorn Lighting Ltd., Manufacturers of Electric Lamps, Thorn House, Upper Saint Martin's Lane, London, WC2H 9ED. T N 01-836 2444.

¶○Thresher & Glenny, Ltd., Shirt Makers, Lancaster Pl. (Waterloo Bridge Approach), Strand, WC2E 7EN. T N 01-836 4608.

¶Thwaites & Reed, Ltd., Turret Clockmakers, 8 Castleham Road, Hastings, Sussex. T N 0424 53491.

¶Timber H. G., Ltd., Suppliers of Timber Products, 3, Ways Wharf, 100 Acres, Uxbridge, Middlesex. T N Uxbridge 32233.

†Tomkins, H. J., & Son, Ltd., Upholsterers, 75, Baker St., W.1. T N 01-935 2003.

¶Toye, Kenning & Spencer, Ltd., Suppliers of Gold & Silver Laces, Insignia & Embroidery, Regalia House, 19-21, Great Queen St., WC2B 5BE. T A Ashlar London WC2; T N 01-242 0471 and 01-405 3063.

○Trianco, Ltd., Manufrs. of Domestic Boilers, Stewart House, Brookway, Kingston Road, Leatherhead, Surrey, KT22 7LY. T N Leatherhead 76453.

+Truefitt & Hill (Products) Ltd.

TRUEFITT & HILL (PRODUCTS) LTD.

Gentlemans' Hairdresser Perfumers

By Appointment to H.R.H. The Duke of Edinburgh Hairdressers

23 Old Bond Street, London, W.1.

Tel. 01-493 2961

△Trumper, Geo. F.

GEO. F. TRUMPER

HAIRDRESSER

9 Curzon Street London W1Y 7FL

By Appointment to the late King George VI Hairdresser

Tel. 01-499 1850 & 2932

¶Tuck, Raphael, & Sons, Ltd.

RAPHAEL TUCK & SONS LTD.

Fine Art Publishers

West Parade, Warminster, Wilts. BA12 8NU.

By Appointment to H.M. The Queen Fine Art Publishers

Tel. 098 52 8251

★Turner, Thos., & Co. (Sheffield) Ltd., Clarence St., Sheffield. T A Renrut; T N Sheffield 21391.

¶○Twining, R., & Co., Ltd., Tea and Coffee Merchants, 216, Strand, London, WC2R 1AP. T N 01-353 3511.

¶Twyford Seeds, Ltd., Seedsmen, Adderbury, Banbury, Oxon. T A Twyseed, Adderbury; T N Adderbury 281 (10 lines); Telex 83361.

‡Tyler & Co., Ltd., Grocers and Wine Merchants, Cranleigh, Surrey. T N 300.

¶Tyson, R., Ltd., Makers of Racing Colours, 57, Grafton St., Dublin. T N 777105.

+**UNIROYAL LTD.,**
Manufacturers of Waterproof Footwear, Newbridge, Midlothian. T N 031-333 2700.

¶○United Dairies (London) Ltd.

UNITED DAIRIES (LONDON) LTD.	
Suppliers of Dairy Produce	
Unigate House	
By Appointment to H.M. The Queen Suppliers of Dairy Produce	Western Avenue Acton, W.3 T.N. 01-992 3400	By Appointment to H.M. Queen Elizabeth The Queen Mother Suppliers of Dairy Produce

○Valentines of Dundee, Ltd., Suppliers of Christmas Cards and Calendars, P.O. Box 74, Balgray Place, Dundee, DD1 9NQ. T A Valentine; T N 0382 89291.

¶**VAN DEN BERGHS,**
Manufacturers of Margarine, Sussex House, Civic Way, Burgess Hill, West Sussex, RH15 9AW. T N Haywards Heath 58100.

¶**VAUXHALL MOTORS, LTD.,**
Motor Vehicle Manufacturers, Kimpton Rd., Luton, Beds. T N 21122.

○Vernons Electrical Ltd., Electrical Engineers, 18, High St., Sunningdale, Berks. T N Ascot 20260 & 20377.

¶Vertigan, A. S., Ltd., Haulage Contractors, The Haven, Lynn Rd., Ingoldisthorpe, King's Lynn, Norfolk. T N Dersingham 388.

¶Veuve Clicquot-Ponsardin, B. de Vogüé & Cie., Srs., Purveyors of Champagne, Reims, France.

¶Vincents of Reading, Ltd., Motor Horse Box Makers, 291, Oxford Rd., Reading, RG3 1AT. T A Vincents; T N 54204-8.

*Viners, Ltd., Cutlers and Silversmiths, P.O. Box 13, Broomhall St., Sheffield, S3 7SN. T A Viners, Sheffield; T N 21391/5; Telex 54396.

¶Vitagrass Farms (Holker) Ltd., Manufacturers of Dried Grass Products, Old Park Farm, Cark-in-Cartmel, Grange Over Sands. T N Flookburgh 240.

¶Vitax, Ltd., Manufacturers of Fertilisers and Insecticides, Ormskirk, Lancs. T N Burscough 893311.

¶Vitopan Ltd., Suppliers of Mopping Equipment, 44, Southside, Clapham Common, London, SW4 9BU. T N 01-720 6411.

¶**WADDINGTONS PLAYING CARD CO. LIMITED,**
Manufacturers of Playing Cards, Wakefield Road, Leeds, Yorks, LS10 3TP. T N 0532-712244.

¶Wafcol, Ltd., Suppliers of Dog Foods, 63/65, Higher Hillgate, Stockport, Cheshire. T A Wafcol, Stockport; T N 061-480 9166.

¶Wagg (The Baker), T. R., Ltd., Bakers and Confectioners, Station Rd., Docking, Norfolk. T N Docking 215.

¶Walker Hiram & Sons, Ltd., Suppliers of "Canadian Club" Whisky, 74, Brook St., London, W.1.

¶Walker, J. W., & Sons, Ltd., Organ Builders, Braintree Rd., Ruislip, Middx. T N 01-845 6501.

¶Walker, John, & Sons, Ltd.

	JOHN WALKER & SONS LTD.
	63 St. James's Street London SW1A 1NB
By Appointment to H.M. The Queen Scotch Whisky Distillers	Telephone: 01-493 8155 Telex: 262944

¶○Wall's Meat Company Limited, Suppliers of Sausages and Meat Pies, Wall's House, Old Oak Lane, London, NW10 6DJ. T N 01-965 6543.

¶○Wallace, Cameron & Co., Ltd.

WALLACE, CAMERON & CO. LTD

 ULTRA HOUSE DRAKEMIRE DRIVE GLASGOW G45 9SU Tel. 041-634 6881 (10 lines)

BY APPOINTMENT TO HER MAJESTY THE QUEEN MANUFACTURERS AND SUPPLIERS OF ULTRAPLAST FIRST AID DRESSINGS

By Appointment to Her Majesty Queen Elizabeth The Queen Mother Manufacturers of Ultraplast First Aid Dressings

ULTRAPLAST FIRST AID DRESSINGS

¶+**WALLACE HEATON, LTD.,**
Suppliers of Photographic Equipment, 127, New Bond St., W1A 1AF. T N 01-629 7511.

¶Walpamur Co., Ltd. (The), Manufacturers of Paint, "Crown House," Darwen, Lancs., BB3 0BG. T A Paints, Darwen; T N 74951.

¶○Walpole Brothers (London), Ltd., ¶Linen Drapers: ○Linen Maufacturers, 20, Brook Street, London, W.1. T N 01-629 5000.

¶○Ward, Thomas & Sons, Ltd., ¶Cutlery Manufacturers: ○Manufacturers of Cutlery, Wardonia Works, Countess Rd. and Clough Rd., Sheffield, S.1. T A Wardonia; T N 23217/9.

¶○†Warner & Sons, Limited, Suppliers of Silks and Furnishing Fabrics, Mappin House, Winsley St., W1N 0AS. T N 01-580 1927.

¶○†Wartski Jewellers Ltd.

	WARTSKI JEWELLERS LTD.
	14 Grafton Street
By Appointment to H.M. The Queen Jewellers	London W1X 3LA Telephone 01-493 1141-2-3

¶**WATERER, JOHN, SONS & CRISP, LTD.,**
Garden Contractors and Nursereymen, The Nurseries, Bagshot, Surrey, GU19 5DG. T N Bagshot 72288.

¶Watkins & Watson, Ltd., Organ Blower Manufacturers, Westminster Road, Wareham, Dorset, BH20 4SP. T N 09295 6311.

¶Watney Mann (London & Home Counties), Ltd., Brewers, Watney House, Palace St., SW1E 5BQ. T A Watneys, London, S.W.1; T N 01-834 1266.

¶+○**WEATHERILL, BERNARD, LTD.,**
¶Riding Clothes Outfitters and Livery Tailors: +○Livery Tailors, 33a, Dover St., W1X 3RA. T A Kilmurdie, London. T N 01-629 4283.

¶+Weatherill Bros., Livery Tailors, High St., Windsor, Berks., SL4 1LD. T N Windsor 61830.

¶**WEBB ERNEST A., LTD.,**
Manufacturers of Farm Machinery, Exning, Newmarket, Suffolk, CB8 7HD. T N 063-877 206.

¶○Weetabix, Ltd., Manufacturers of Breakfast Cereals, Station Road, Burton Latimer, Kettering, Northants. T N Burton Latimer 2181.

○Weir, Donald S., Haulage Contractors, West-end Castledown, Thurso, Caithness.

¶West Norfolk Super Lime Co., Ltd., Suppliers and Distributors of Agricultural Lime, Hillington, King's Lynn, Norfolk. T N Hillington 269.

○West, R. & C., Greengrocers and Fruiterers, Station Parade, Sunningdale, Ascot, Berkshire. T N Ascot 20739.

¶Westburn Sugar Refineries, Ltd., Sugar Refiners and Purveyors, Lynedoch St., Greenock. T N Greenock 21241-7; Telex 77522.

¶Whiley, George M., Limited, Suppliers of Gold Leaf, Victoria Road, Ruislip, Middx., HA4 0LG. T N 01-422 0141.

¶**WHITBREAD & CO., LTD.,**
Brewers, Chiswell Street, London, EC1Y 4SD. T N 01-606 4455.

○Whitbread Fremlins, Ltd., Brewers, P.O. Box No. 8, Pale Ale Brewery, Maidstone, Kent. T N 0622 48321.

¶Whitbread Wessex, Ltd., Brewers, 7-10, Admiralty Road, Portsmouth, Hants.

¶**WHITE HORSE DISTILLERS, LTD.,**
Scotch Whisky Distillers, 99, Borron St., Glasgow, G4 9XF. T A Horse; T N 041-332 9900.

¶Whiteheads (Builders' Merchants), Ltd., Suppliers of Building Materials, Whitemyres Avenue, Mastrick, Aberdeen, AB9 2QS. T N 491304.

¶○**WHITWORTHS HOLDINGS, LTD.,**
¶Manufacturers of Dried Fruits: ○Processors and Packers of Food Products, Victoria Mills, London Rd., Wellingborough, Northants., NN8 2DT. T N 76351.

○Wholesale Fittings Co., Ltd. (The), Suppliers of Electrical Equipment, 313-333, Rainham Road South, Dagenham, Essex, RM40 8SX. T N 01-593 8244.

¶Whytock & Reid, Decorators and Furnishers, Sunbury House, Belford Mews, Edinburgh, EH4 3DN. T A Whytock; T N 031-226 4911.

¶Wigg & Plowright—Division of Dalgety-Franklin, Ltd., Suppliers of Agricultural Machines, Cattle Market St., Fakenham, Norfolk. T N 2271.

¶○Wiggins, Arnold, & Sons (Carvers), Ltd., Picture Frame Makers, 30-34, Woodfield Place, Harrow Road, London, W9 2BJ. T N 01-286 9656.

¶Wilder, John (Agricultural) Ltd., Suppliers of Agricultural Machinery, Cattle Market, Reading, RG1 7HJ. T N 53204-6.

¶Wilkin & Sons, Ltd., Jam and Marmalade Manufacturers, Tiptree, Essex, CO5 0RF. T A Preserves, Tiptree; T N Tiptree 815407.

¶+Wilkinson Sword, Ltd.

WILKINSON SWORD LTD.
Sword Cutlers
Sword House
Totteridge Road
High Wycombe, Bucks
T.A. Swordcraft
High Wycombe
Tel. High Wycombe 33300

By Appointment to H.M. Queen Elizabeth II Sword Cutlers

By Appointment to H.R.H. The Duke of Edinburgh Sword Cutlers

¶Williamson, John, & Son, Purveyors of Meat and Poultry, 35, Fountainhall Rd., Aberdeen. T A Williamson, Market; T N Aberdeen 21724.

△†**WILLS & SEGAR, LTD.,**
Florists, 94, Old Brompton Rd., SW7 3RD. T A Flosculo, Wesphone, London, S.W.7; T N 01-589 2454; Telex 919167.

¶Wilson, Andrew, & Sons, Ltd., Catering Equipment Hirers, 39, Spring Gdns., Edinburgh, 8. T N 031-661 2485.

¶Wilson & Son

WILSON & SON
28/30, West Cross Causeway
Edinburgh EH8 9ER
T.N. 031-667 1748

By Appointment to H.M. The Queen Piano and Harpsichord Tuners

¶Wilson, Wm., & Co. (Aberdeen), Ltd., Suppliers of Electrical and Plumbing Materials, 505, Great Western Rd., Aberdeen, AB9 2QF. T A Sanitary, Aberdeen; T N 38641

¶Wilton Royal Carpet Factory, Ltd. (The), Carpet Manufacturers, Wilton, near Salisbury. T N Wilton 2441.

¶Windovers, Ltd., Coachbuilders, The Hyde, Hendon, N.W.9. T A Windovers, London, N.W.9; T N 01-205 4031.

+Winsor & Newton, Ltd., Suppliers of Artists' Materials, Whitefriars Drive, Wealdstone, Harrow, Middx., HA3 5RH. T N 01-427 4343.

¶**WITNEY BLANKET CO., LTD. (THE),**
Bedding Manufacturers, Witney, Oxon., OX8 6BQ. T N 3611.

¶Wolf Electric Tools, Ltd., Suppliers of Electrical Equipment, Pioneer Works, Hanger Lane, London, W5 1DS. T A Wolflede, London, W.5; T N 01-998 2911.

¶Wolfschmidt, Limited, Suppliers of Kummel, 275-281, King St., W6 9LZ. T N 01-748 9876 & 4436.

¶○Wolsey, Ltd., ¶Hosiery Manufacturers: ○Manufacturers of Hosiery and Knitwear, Abbey Meadows, Leicester. T A Wolsey; T N 20871.

¶○Wood, William, & Sons Ltd.

WILLIAM WOOD & SONS LTD.
Bath Road
Taplow
Maidenhead
Berks SL6 0NY
T.A. Gardening
Taplow
Tel.: Burnham
Bucks 4321

By Appointment to H.M. Queen Elizabeth II Garden Contractors and Horticultural Builders

By Appointment to H.M. Queen Elizabeth The Queen Mother Garden Contractors and Horticultural Builders

○Woodard-Yorke, Corsetière, 97, Brookside, Cat Hill, East Barnet, Herts., EN4 8TS. T N 01-449 1239.

*Woodford, Bourne & Co., Ltd., Wine Merchants, 64-65, Patrick St., Cork. T A Woodford; T N 20273-4.

¶○Woodhouse Hume, Ltd., Suppliers of Meat and Poultry, 201, St. John St., London, EC1V 4LX. T N 01-253 5851.

¶Woodrow, J., & Sons, Ltd., Hatters and Trunk Merchants, 27, Higher Hillgate, Stockport, Cheshire, SK1 3EU.

¶Woods Pharmacy, Pharmaceutical Chemists, 50, High Street, Windsor, Berkshire.

¶Worcester Royal Porcelain Co. Ltd. (The), Manufacturers of China & Porcelain, Royal Porcelain Works, Severn St., Worcester. T N Worcester (0905) 23221.

○Worham, Antony, Ltd., Suppliers of Tudor Queen Hams and Tongues, 19, Eastcheap, London, E.C.3. T A Pooshon, London, E.C.3; T N 01-626 6833.

¶Wright, Donald, Saddler, 37, Gordon Street, Huntly, Aberdeenshire. T N Huntly 2782.

¶Wright Rain, Ltd., Manufacturers of Irrigation Equipment, Crowe Arch Rd., Ringwood, Hants., BH24 1PA. T N Ringwood 2251.

¶Wysall Tractor Co. Ltd

¶○Yardley & Co., Ltd., ¶Manufacturers of Soap: ○Perfumers and Manufacturers of Soap, 33, Old Bond Street, London, W1X 4AP. Tel 01-629 9341.

Berkhamsted, Herts.

SWAN HOTEL

Berkhamsted, Herts. Tel. No. Berkhamsted, Herts 71451/2.
6 single rooms, 9 double rooms. Egon Ronay & one star. AA.

Bradford, West Yorks.

Cottage Restaurant

COTTAGE
RESTAURANT

869 THORNTON ROAD, THORNTON, BRADFORD, BD13 3PW. Tel: Bradford 832752

Lunches 12 noon - 2.30 pm · Dinner 7pm - 10.15 pm
Closed all day Tuesday and Saturday lunchtime
* BOOKING ESSENTIAL *

Braithwaite, Keswick, Cumberland.

Ivy House Hotel

IVY HOUSE Hotel

BRAITHWAITE
KESWICK
CUMBERLAND CA12 5SY

Telephone BRAITHWAITE 338

A.A & R.A.C Recommended
American A.A Association

Residential Licence

GENUINE LAKELAND HOUSE PART OF WHICH IS OVER 300 YEARS OLD. BEAMS AND COUNTRY HOUSE ATMOSPHERE.
IN A WORLD OF FRIGHTENING CHANGE AND ABANDONED STANDARDS WE DARE TO BE DISCRIMINATING AND EXCLUSIVE.
ANTIQUES, OIL PAINTINGS, BRASS, COPPER, PLATE AND DECOR TO PLEASE THE AESTHETE.
LOG FIRES, CENTRAL HEATING, ELECTRIC BLANKETS TO COSSET THE PHYSICAL.
FRESHLY COOKED IMPECCABLY SERVED FOOD TO SATISFY THE APPETITE.
UNOBTRUSIVE SERVICE AND ATTENTION TO SOOTHE THE EGO.
ALL CONTRIBUTING TO THE INEFFABLE AMBIENCE SO DEAR TO THE WELL BRED PSYCHE.
AT A TARIFF WHICH EVEN IN THESE INFLATORY DAYS ONE CAN AFFORD.

Bredwardine, Hereford.

THE RED LION HOTEL

Bredwardine, Hereford, HR3 6BU. Tel. Moccas 303.
17th century fully licensed. Residential. Free house. Centrally heated. Rooms with private bathroom. Salmon and Trout fishing on the River Wye; also organised Pheasant and Wild Duck shooting.

Bridge of Allan, Stirlingshire.

Royal Hotel

The Royal Hotel
Bridge of Allan, Stirlingshire.
Telephone 0786 - 83 - 2284

From this Hotel, where Charles Dickens stayed in 1864, you can visit 8 Scottish Counties, 10 Lochs, 6 Castles, 6 Rivers, 10 Golf Courses, a Safari Park, a Bear Park and pass through much of Scotland's lovely scenery, keeping your luggage in the same room.
Situated in the heart of Scotland on the A9 near Motorail termini at Stirling and Perth. Excellent facilities and cuisine.
Write or phone the Manager at Bridge of Allan, Stirlingshire for our brochure.
(Telephone 0786 - 83 - 2284)

Bridport, Dorset.

Eype's Mouth Hotel

THE EYPE'S MOUTH HOTEL

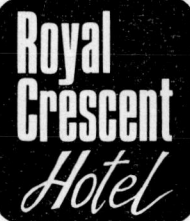

EYPE
BRIDPORT
DORSET DT6 6AL
TELEPHONE:
BRIDPORT 23300

AA. RAC. WCTB. BHR & CA.
FULLY LICENSED FREEHOUSE

4 SINGLE ROOMS. 17 DOUBLE ROOMS (9 WITH PRIVATE BATHROOMS). ALWAYS OPEN. FACING SOUTH. OVERLOOKING SEA AND NATIONAL TRUST LAND. GOOD WINE LIST. SPECIAL DIETS CATERED FOR. CHILDREN AND DOGS WELCOME.

Brighton, Sussex.

Royal Crescent Hotel

Royal Crescent Hotel

MARINE PARADE
BRIGHTON
SUSSEX BN2 1AX
TELEPHONE:
BRIGHTON 66311

12 SINGLE ROOMS
44 DOUBLE ROOMS
6 SUITES

AA & RAC ★★★★

Chelmsford, Essex.

County Hotel, Rainsford Road. Tel Chelmsford 66911.
Comfortable bedrooms. Some with private bath or shower. First class restaurant open to non-residents.

Cornhill on Tweed, Northumberland.

TILLMOUTH PARK HOTEL
RESTAURANT

Cornhill on Tweed. Tel Coldstream 2255.

Coventry, West Midlands.

* make it a grand occasion at the exclusive
Grandstand Restaurant, Coventry

THE EXCELLENT CUISINE, WELL STOCKED CELLARS AND HAPPY AND

EFFICIENT SERVICE WON THE GRANDSTAND AN EGON RONAY AWARD

It's exclusive, intimate, and rated by many as Top Restaurant of the Midlands. Evening & Private parties catered for. Open Monday to Friday from 12 noon - 3p.m For full details write to Maitre d'Hotel, Giovanni, Grandstand Restaurant, Coventry City F. C., King Richard Street, Coventry. Tel: Coventry 25392

Downton, Wiltshire.

The Bull at Downton, Downton, Wiltshire. Tel Downton 20374.

Dublin.

Burlington Hotel, Dublin. Tel 78511.
Sussex Room: 13.30-2.30 pm; 6.30-11 pm. Rooftop Carvery: 12.30-2.30 pm; 8.30 pm-1 am. Annabel's Night Club, Mon/Fri 10 pm-3 am; Sat 9 pm-1 am.

Eastbourne, East Sussex.

CHEZ MAURICE RESTAURANT

(Prop. Messrs H. E. Attewell-Hughes), 118 Seaside Road, Eastbourne. Tel 24894. Eastbourne's original French restaurant. Open seven days for lunch and dinner parties catered for.

Ely, Cambs.

Old Fire Engine House, St. Mary's Street, Ely, Cambs. Tel No Ely (0353) 2582. Restaurant and Gallery.

Exford, Somerset.

CROWN HOTEL

Exford, near Minehead, Somerset. Tel Exford 243.

Glastonbury, Somerset.

George and Pilgrims Hotel and Restaurant, High Street, Glastonbury, Somerset BA6 9DP. Tel Glastonbury (0458) 31146).

Grimsby, South Humberside.

Oaklands Hotel and Country Club, Laceby, Grimsby, Lincs. Tel 0472 72248. Squash, swimming, driving range, dancing, banqueting.

Haslemere, Surrey.

LYTHE HILL HOTEL AND L'AUBERGE DE FRANCE RESTAURANT

Petworth Road. Tel Haslemere 51251. Telex 858402.
Weddings, parties, conferences, historic house. De luxe accommodation. Sports. Weekend rate.

Hope Cove, S. Devon.

LANTERN LODGE HOTEL

Hope Cove, South Devon, TQ7 3HE. Tel. No. Galmpton 280.
Overlooking Fishing Village. Golf, sailing and fishing nearby. Private baths. Licensed. Sauna and solarium. Adults only. No dogs. Egon Ronay, Ashley Courtenay recommended.

Hungerford, Berks.

THE BEAR HOTEL

Hungerford, Berkshire. Tel. No. Hungerford 2512 & 2062.
Type of cuisine : English and Continental. Specialities : Sirloin steak Balmoral. Chicken Devonshire.
Open for Lunch : Noon to 2 p.m. Dinner 7 p.m. to 10 p.m.
Approx. cost per head £3.
Other details : 16th century inn. A.A.**. R.A.C.**. Egon Ronay, B.T.A. recommended.

Hythe, Kent.

Stare Court Hotel, West Parade. Tel 0303 68263.
Family suites with sun lounge, overlooking English Channel, golfing, sailing facilities.

Ipswich, Suffolk.

BELSTEAD BROOK HOTEL

Belstead Road IP2 9HB. Tel 0473 216456/7/8. 24 luxury bedrooms and suites. Gourmet restaurant. 8 acres grounds.

Isle of Mull, Argyll.

Glenforsa Hotel, by Salen, Isle of Mull. See advert

Kettlewell, North Yorkshire.

THE RACE HORSES HOTEL

BD23 5QZ. Tel Kettlewell 233 & 854. A small country hotel in Yorkshire Dales National Park offering peace and quiet, a warm welcome, good food and comfort.

Llangurig, Powys.

THE BLUE BELL INN

Llangurig, near Llanidloes, Powys. Tel No. Llangurig 254.
Other details: Good food guide recommended.
4 miles Wye fishing.

Lockerbie, Dumfriesshire.

DRYFESDALE HOTEL

Lockerbie, Dumfriesshire DG11 2SF. Tel. No. Lockerbie 2427.
Scottish hospitality plus a little style.

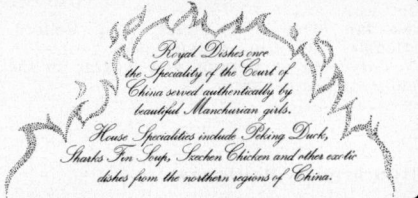
London.

Anarkali Restaurant

CHURCHILL (THE).

Portman Square, London W1H 0AJ. Tel. No. 01-486 5800.
489 double rooms.

GOLDEN CARP RESTAURANT

8a, Mount Street, London, W.1. Tel. No. 01-499 3385.

THE GUINEA GRILL

Prop. R. A. Greig, 30, Bruton Place, London W1X 7AA. Tel. No. 01-629 5613.
The world's finest steaks.

HOSTARIA ROMANA

70 Dean Street, London W.1. Tel. No. 01-734 2869.
Type of cuisine: Italian.
Specialities: Baby lamb Roman style.
Open for lunch: 12 to 3 p.m. Dinner 6 to 11.30 p.m. (last order).
Approx. cost per head: £1·50.
Other details: Typical Roman restaurant with busts of Roman emperors. Sparkling atmosphere.

Kouzina

Manchurian, 42 Baker Street, London W.1. See advert.

Park Tower, Hotel, Lowndes Square, 101 Knightsbridge SW1X 7RN. See advert.

Shafi, 18, Gerrard Street, London, W.1. Tel. No. 01-437 2354.
The Oldest Indian Restaurant in Europe. Established since 1915. Offering exclusive recipes of Mrs. Ishani.

Top of the Tower

Long Melford, Suffolk.

Crown Inn (The), Hall Street, Long Melford, Suffolk. Tel. Long Melford 366. "Purveyors of victuals and lodging to the nobility and gentry."

Milton Ernest, Bedfordshire.

Milton Ernest Hall Hotel

MILTON ERNEST HALL
HOTEL

MILTON ERNEST, BEDFORDSHIRE
TELEPHONE: OAKLEY 4111

The only country house designed by Butterfield;
6 acres of garden on the banks of the Ouse;
garden centre; antiques; Good Food Guide 1975.
Restaurant closed Sun evening & all day Mon.

Mousehole, Cornwall.

THE LOBSTER POT

Mousehole, Cornwall. Tel 0736-73 251. Internationally famous residential hotel and restaurant. Open early February to Mid November.

Perth, Perthshire.

HUNTINGTOWER HOTEL RESTAURANT

Crieff Road, Perth, Perthshire
Telephone: Almondbank 241

Salmon Fishing and Shooting Parties most welcome in this Family Owned Hotel

Timothy's

24 ST. JOHN STREET   **TEL:**
PERTH   **PERTH 26641**

Specialities: Fresh Lobsters, Home cooked Beef & Ham, Smoked Trout & Timothy's own Smorrebrod.   *Lunch 12 - 2.30, Dinner 7 - 10.15*

Pickering, North Yorkshire.

BLACK SWAN HOTEL

Tel 0751-72286. Fully licensed. Residential. Awarded 'Fire Certificate.'

Pillaton, Cornwall.

The Weary Friar

The Weary Friar

A Distinguished 12th Century Hotel

PILLATON, CORNWALL

Telephone St. Dominick 238

For a cosy, intimate atmosphere, dine by candlelight in one of Cornwall's most celebrated old-world inns. English and International Cuisine under owner's personal supervision. Always open for lunches and dinners in the bar and restaurant. Accommodation includes 14 bedrooms all with own bathroom.
The pretty little village of Pillaton lies midway between Saltash and Callington just off the A388 road.
Egon Ronay Recommended   AA RAC**

Port Appin, Argyll.

AIRDS HOTEL

Port Appin, Argyll, PA38 4DF. Tel. Appin 236. 2 single rooms, 18 double rooms.

Rochester, Kent.

The Toastmasters Inn, Church Street, Burham, Rochester, Kent. Tel. No. Medway 61299.

Rugby, Warwickshire.

Andalucia Restaurant, 10, Henry Street, Rugby, Warwickshire. Tel. No. Rugby 6404 & 74274.

Rumbling Bridge, Kinross-shire.

Rumbling Bridge Hotel

RUMBLING BRIDGE HOTEL
RUMBLING BRIDGE, KINROSS-SHIRE KL13 7PX
TELEPHONE: FOSSOWAY 325

A CHARMING OLD COACHING INN SITUATED IN A FAMOUS BEAUTY SPOT. THE HOTEL LACKS NOTHING IN MODERN COMFORT AND IS VERY CONVENIENT FOR GOLF, SHOOTING AND FISHING. FULLY LICENSED AND OPEN ON SUNDAYS. UNDER PERSONAL SUPERVISION.
AA, RAC, RSAC.
OPEN LATE APRIL TO LATE OCTOBER.

St. Albans, Herts.

WATEREND BARN RESTAURANT

Civic Centre AL1 3LE. Tel St. Albans 53477. Restaurant open 9 am to 5.30 pm Monday to Saturday. Specialists in banqueting and functions of all types.

St. Andrew's, Fife.

GRANGE INN

Grange, St. Andrews, Fife. Tel St. Andrews 2670.
First class restaurant, log fires, two bars, golfing facilities, large car park.

Selkirk, Selkirkshire.

Philipburn House Hotel. Tel. Selkirk 20747. Specialist cooking under patron/chef.

Sevenoaks, Kent.

Crossways Hotel, Seal Hollow road, Sevenoaks, Kent. Tel. 54245. Secluded yet central position. Wedding receptions a speciality.

Skegness, Lincs.

The County Hotel

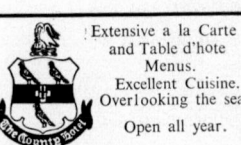

Luxury Leisure Breaks. Holidays. Weekends. Brochure on request.

Extensive a la Carte and Table d'hote Menus. Excellent Cuisine. Overlooking the sea. Open all year.

THE COUNTY HOTEL
SKEGNESS, LINCS PE25 2UB
Phone Skegness 2461

Conferences, Banquets, Receptions and Trade Exhibitions.   Christmas House Party

Stow-on-the-Wold, Gloucs.

WYCK HILL HOUSE

GL54 1HY. Tel. Stow-on-the-Wold 30376. Country house hotel, peaceful in own grounds. Well appointed. Good scenery, food and wine.

South Croydon, Surrey.

SELSDON PARK HOTEL & RESTAURANT

Sanderstead CR2 8YA. Tel 01-657 8811. International hotel with four star rating. Set in 200 acres with golf course, tennis, riding, etc. Colour T.V. in all bedrooms.

Tenbury Wells, Hereford & Worcs.

THE ROYAL OAK HOTEL

Market street. Tel. Tenbury Wells 810417.

Torquay, Devon.

Devonshire Hotel

Devonshire Hotel

PARKHILL ROAD, TORQUAY TQ1 2DY
TEL: TORQUAY (STD 0803) 24850

60 BEDROOMS · LARGE RESTAURANT AND FREE CAR PARK · OPEN ALL YEAR · GARDEN SETTING

AA/RAC ★★★   ASHLEY COURTENAY RECOMMENDED

John Dory Restaurant, 7 Lisburne Square, Torquay, South Devon. Specialising in Seafood and game. Recommended by all leading National Guides.

Fanny's Dining Room

Fanny's Dining Room

Exclusive Licensed Restaurant
55 ABBEY ROAD · TORQUAY

Dinner by Appointment

Table Reservations 28605

Osborne Hotel

THE  OSBORNE HOTEL

AA ★★★★ RAC

MEADFOOT BEACH TORQUAY
SOUTH DEVON TQ1 2LL
TELEPHONE: 0803 22232

EXTENSIVELY MODERNISED. OVER 100 ROOMS
COCKTAIL BAR · TENNIS · HEATED POOL

Windermere, Cumbria.

The Hide-a-Way Hotel

A.A.★   R.S.A.C.   R.A.C.

Lovely English Lakelands

The Hide-a-Way Hotel

PHOENIX WAY, WINDERMERE
CUMBRIA LA23 1DB
TEL: (096 62) 3070

Proprietors: Ron & Joan Stack

Charming Country House Hotel noted for excellent food. Friendly and comfortable. Cheery, well-stocked bar

York, North Yorkshire.

TANGLEWOOD RESTAURANT

Malton Road, York, North Yorkshire YO3 9TW. Tel. No. Flaxton Moor 318. Other details : Luncheon, Dinner, Seafood specialities.
AA ✕✕

OBITUARY

HIS ROYAL HIGHNESS
THE DUKE OF GLOUCESTER.

Died June 10th, 1974.

PEERS AND PEERESSES IN THEIR OWN RIGHT

	Date of Death
ABERDEEN AND TEMAIR, David George Ian Alexander, *CBE, TD*, 4th Marquess of	13. 9.74
AILESBURY, Chandos Sydney Cedric, 7th Marquess of	15. 7.74
ARCHIBALD, George, *CBE*, 1st Baron	27. 2.75
AUDLEY, Rosina Lois Veronica, Baroness	24.10.73
AYLMER, Kenneth Athalmer, 10th Baron	1. 5.75
BELLEW, Edward Henry, *MBE*, 5th Baron	8. 8.75
BIRKENHEAD, Frederick Winston Furneaux, *TD*, 2nd Earl of	10. 6.75
BLACKETT, Patrick Maynard Stuart, *OM, CH, FRS*, (Life) Baron *(ext.)*	13. 7.75
BOLINGBROKE AND ST. JOHN, Vernon Henry, 6th Viscount	1. 5.74
BRABAZON OF TARA, Derek Charles, *CBE*, 2nd Baron	11.12.74
BROOKEBOROUGH, Basil Stanlake, *KG, CBE, MC*, 1st Viscount	18. 8.73
BUCCLEUCH AND QUEENSBERRY, Walter John, *KT, GCVO, TD, PC*, 8th Duke of	4.10.73
BUCKMASTER, Owen Stanley, 2nd Viscount	25.11.75
CASTLEMAINE, John Michael Schomberg Staveley, 7th Baron	31. 7.75
CHEYLESMORE, Francis Ormond Henry, *DSO*, 4th Baron *(ext.)*	21. 4.74
CHURCHILL, Victor Alexander, 2nd Viscount	21.12.73
CLANCARTY, Greville Sidney Rochfort, 7th Earl of	15. 9.75
CLIFDEN, Arthur Victor, *MC*, 8th Viscount *(ext.)*	22.12.74
COLGRAIN, Donald Swinton, *MC*, 2nd Baron	20.10.73
CONESFORD, Henry George, *QC*, 1st Baron *(ext.)*	28. 8.74
CONYNGHAM, Frederick William Burton, 6th Marquess	1. 4.74
COURTOWN, James Montagu Burgoyne, *OBE, TD*, 8th Earl of	23. 7.75
COUTANCHE, Alexander Moncrieff, (Life) Baron *(ext.)*	18.12.73
COWLEY, Richard Francis, 6th Earl	13.12.75
COZENS-HARDY, Herbert Arthur, *OBE*, 4th Baron *(ext.)*	11. 9.75
CRAIGAVON, James, 2nd Viscount	18. 5.74
CRAWFORD AND BALCARRES, David Alexander Robert, *KT, GBE*, 28th Earl of	13.12.75
CROFTON, Edward Blaise, 5th Baron	13. 6.74
DONEGALL, Edward Arthur Donald St. George Hamilton, 6th Marquess of	24. 5.75
DORMER, Charles Walter James, 15th Baron	27. 8.75
DYSART, Wenefryde Agatha, Countess of	2. 6.75
ELPHINSTONE, John Alexander, 17th Lord	15.11.75
FISKE, William Geoffrey, *CBE*, (Life) Baron *(ext.)*	13. 1.75
FRASER OF LONSDALE, (William Jocelyn) Ian, *CH, CBE*, (Life) Baron *(ext.)*	19.12.74
GARNSWORTHY, Charles James, *OBE*, (Life) Baron *(ext.)*	5. 9.74
GEDDES, Ross Campbell, *KBE*, 2nd Baron	2. 2.75
GORT, Standish Robert Gage Prendergast, *MC*, 7th Viscount	21. 5.75
GREENWAY, (Charles) Paul, 3rd Baron	14. 9.75
HADEN-GUEST, Stephen Haden, 2nd Baron	21.12.74
HAILES, Patrick George Thomas, *GBE, CH, PC*, 1st Baron *(ext.)*	5.11.74
HAMPDEN, David Francis, 5th Viscount	4. 9.75
HAMPTON, Humphrey Arthur, *OBE*, 5th Baron	17. 2.74
HARDWICKE, Philip Grantham, 9th Earl of	31.12.74
HEYWORTH, Geoffrey, 1st Baron *(ext.)*	15. 6.74
HILL, Gerald Rowland, 7th Viscount	11. 5.74
HOLFORD, William Graham, (Life) Baron *(ext.)*	17.10.75
HURCOMB, Cyril William, *GCB, KBE*, 1st Baron *(ext.)*	7. 8.75
ILFORD, Geoffrey Clegg, *MC, TD, QC*, (Life) Baron *(ext.)*	20. 8.74
INVERFORTH, Andrew Alexander Morton, 2nd Baron	17.11.75
KILMARNOCK, Gilbert Allan Rowland, *MBE, TD*, 6th Baron	15. 5.75
KINTORE, Ethel Sydney, Countess of	21. 9.74
LYVEDEN, Sydney Munroe Archibald, 5th Baron	19. 9.75
MACCLESFIELD, George Loveden William Henry, 7th Earl of	20. 9.75
MCNAIR, Arnold Duncan, *CBE, QC, LLD*, 1st Baron	22. 5.75
MAR, James Clifton, 30th Earl of	21. 4.75
METHUEN, Paul Ayshford, 4th Baron	7. 1.74
METHUEN, Anthony Paul, 5th Baron	21. 6.75
MINTO, Victor Gilbert Lariston Garnet, 5th Earl of	11. 1.75
MORAY, Archibald John Morton, 19th Earl of	27. 2.74
MORRIS, Michael William, 2nd Baron	11. 3.75
MORTON OF HENRYTON, Fergus Dunlop, *MC, PC*, (Life) Baron *(ext.)*	18. 7.73
MOUNTEVANS, Richard Andvord, 2nd Baron	12.12.74
MOYLE, Arthur, *CBE*, (Life) Baron *(ext.)*	23.12.74
MUNSTER, Geoffrey William Richard Hugh, *KBE, PC*, 5th Earl of	27. 8.75
NORFOLK, Bernard Marmaduke, *KG, GCVO, GBE, TD, PC*, 16th Duke of	31. 1.75
NORTHESK, John Douglas, 12th Earl of	22. 7.75
NUNBURNHOLME, Charles John, 3rd Baron	1. 1.74
OAKSHOTT, Hendrie Dudley, *MBE*, (Life) Baron *(ext.)*	1. 2.75
PLUNKET, Patrick Terence William Span, *CVO*, 7th Baron	28. 5.75
POWIS, Edward Robert Henry, *CBE, TD*, 5th Earl of	15. 1.74
RENWICK, Robert Burnham, *KBE*, 1st Baron	30. 8.73
RITCHIE OF DUNDEE, John Kenneth, *PC*, 3rd Baron	20.10.75
ROBERTSON OF OAKRIDGE, Brian Hubert, *GCB, GBE, KCMG, KCVO, DSO, MC*, 1st Baron	29. 4.74
RODNEY, George Bridges Harley Guest, 8th Baron	18.12.73
ROMNEY, Charles, 6th Earl of	6. 9.75
ROSEBERY, Albert Edward Harry Mayer Archibald, *KT, DSO, MC, PC*, 6th Earl of	30. 5.74
ROTHES, Malcolm George Dyer Edwardes, 20th Earl of	17. 5.75
ROXBURGHE, George Victor Robert John, 9th Duke of	26. 9.74
ROYLE, Charles, (Life) Baron *(ext.)*	30. 9.75
SALTER, (James) Arthur, *GBE, KCB, PC*, 1st Baron *(ext.)*	27. 6.75

Date of Death

SHUTTLEWORTH, Charles Ughtred John, *MC*, 4th Baron	5.10.75
SKELMERSDALE, Lionel, *DSO, MC*, 6th Baron	20. 7.73
SPENCER, Albert Edward John, *TD*, 7th Earl	9. 6.75
SPENS, (William) Patrick, *KBE, PC*, 1st Baron	15.11.73
STOCKS, Mary Danvers (Life) Baroness (*ext.*)	6. 7.75
STRANGE OF KNOKIN, HUNGERFORD AND DE MOLEYNS, Elizabeth Frances, Baroness	12.12.74
TALBOT OF MALAHIDE, Reginald Stanislaus Victor, *MC*, 8th Baron	2. 3.75
TAYSIDE, David Lauchlan, *OBE*, (Life) Baron (*ext.*)	12. 3.75
TOLLEMACHE, John Edward Hamilton, *MC*, 4th Baron	27. 5.75
TORPHICHEN, James Bruce, 14th Lord	12. 7.75
TUCKER, Frederick James, *PC*, (Life) Baron (*ext.*)	17.11.75
UVEDALE OF NORTH END, Ambrose Edgar, *MD, FRCS*, (Life) Baron (*ext.*)	28. 2.74
WEIR, (James) Kenneth, *CBE*, 2nd Viscount	16. 8.75
WHARTON, Elizabeth Dorothy, Baroness (*Abeyant*)	4. 5.74
WRIGHT OF ASHTON UNDER LYNE, Lewis Tatham, *CBE*, (Life) Baron (*ext.*)	15. 9.74

BARONETS

AGNEW, *Sir* Fulque Melville Gerald Noel, 10th Baronet	28. 8.75
AIRD, *Col. Sir* John Renton, *MVO, MC*, 3rd Baronet	20.11.73
HAVELOCK-ALLAN, *Sir* Henry Ralph, 3rd Baronet	4.11.75
BARRAN, *Cdr. Sir* John Leighton, *RNVR*, 3rd Baronet	28.12.74
BERNARD, *Sir* Dallas Gerald Mercer, 1st Baronet	26.11.75
BERNEY, *Sir* Thomas Reedham, *MC*, 10th Baronet	5. 1.75
EVANS-BEVAN, *Sir* David Martyn, 1st Baronet	9. 9.73
SELBY-BIGGE, *Sir* John Amherst, *OBE*, 2nd Baronet (*ext.*)	3.10.73
BLAKE, *Cdr. Sir* Cuthbert Patrick, *DSO, RN*, 6th Baronet (*ext.*)	27. 6.75
BLAKER, *Sir* Reginald, *TD*, 2nd Baronet	3. 1.75
BLAKISTON, *Sir* Arthur Frederick, *MC*, 7th Baronet	31. 1.74
BLUNT, *Sir* Richard David Harvey, 11th Baronet	13. 2.75
BOORD, *Sqdn.-Ldr. Sir* Richard William, 3rd Baronet	12.12.75
BRICKWOOD, *Sir* Rupert Redvers, 2nd Baronet	29. 4.74
BROCKLEBANK, *Maj. Sir* John Montague, *TD*, 5th Baronet	13. 9.74
BROCKLEHURST, *Lt.-Col. Sir* Philip Lee, 2nd Baronet	28. 1.75
LEITH-BUCHANAN, *Sir* George Hector Macdonald, 6th Baronet	1. 8.73
BURBIDGE, *Sir* John Richard Woodman, 4th Baronet	31. 5.74
CHARLES, *Sir* Noel Hughes Havelock, *KCMG, MC*, 3rd Baronet (*ext.*)	8. 9.75
STRICKLAND-CONSTABLE, *Sir* Henry Marmaduke, 10th Baronet	26. 3.75
COUPER, *Sir* Guy, 4th Baronet	30.11.73
COUPER, *Maj. Sir* George Robert Cecil, 5th Baronet	26. 7.75
DAWSON, (*Sir*) Lawrence Saville, 2nd Baronet (*ext.*)	14. 8.74
DERING, *Lt.-Col. Sir* Rupert Anthony Yea, 12th Baronet (*ext.*)	16. 3.75
DODDS, *Sir* (Edward) Charles, *MVO*, 1st Baronet	16.12.73
DU CROS, *Capt. Sir* Philip Harvey, 2nd Baronet	11.10.75
DUNCAN, *Sir* James Alexander Lawson, 1st Baronet (*ext.*)	30. 9.74
DYER, *Sir* Leonard Schroeder Swinnerton, 15th Baronet	10. 6.75
ELPHINSTONE, *Sir* Howard Graham, 4th Baronet	18. 5.75
FERGUSSON, *Sir* James, *LLD*, 8th Baronet	25.10.73
FLOYD, *Lt.-Col. Sir* John Duckett, *TD*, 6th Baronet	1. 4.75
FURNESS, *Sir* Christopher, 2nd Baronet	21. 6.74
GIBSON, *Sir* Ackroyd Herbert, 3rd Baronet	15. 6.75
GOLDNEY, *Sir* Henry Hastings, *MC*, 4th Baronet (*ext.*)	26. 2.74
GORE, *Sir* St. George Ralph, 12th Baronet	13.11.73
GRESLEY, *Sir* Nigel, 12th Baronet	13. 1.74
GREY, *Sir* Robin Edward Dysart, 6th Baronet	2. 6.74
HALL, *Maj. Sir* Julian Henry, 11th Baronet	28. 1.74
HALL, *Col. Sir* Lionel Reid, 12th Baronet	22. 4.75
HANHAM, *Sir* Henry Phelips, 11th Baronet	23.11.73
HARDINGE, *Sir* Robert, 6th Baronet	20. 7.73
HAWKEY, *Sir* Roger Pryce, 2nd Baronet (*ext.*)	11.11.75
HENNIKER HEATON, *Wing-Cdr. Sir* (John Victor) Peregrine, 3rd Baronet	-.12.71
HEWITT, *Maj. Sir* Joseph, 2nd Baronet	1.10.73
HORSFALL, *Sir* (John) Donald, 2nd Baronet	25. 3.75
INGILBY, *Maj. Sir* Joslan William Vivian, 5th Baronet	7. 6.74
INGLIS OF GLENCORSE, *Sir* Maxwell Ian Hector, 9th Baronet	22. 7.74
JOHNSON, *Sir* John Paley, *MBE*, 6th Baronet	14.12.75
KENNEDY, *Sir* James Edward, 5th Baronet	24. 6.74
KERR, *Sir* Hamilton William, 1st Baronet (*ext.*)	26.12.74
KNOWLES, *Sir* Francis Gerald William, *FRS*, 6th Baronet	13. 7.74
LANGRISHE, *Capt. Sir* Terence Hume, 6th Baronet	31.12.73
LAWSON, *Sir* Ralph Henry, 4th Baronet	13. 2.75
LEVER, *Sir* Tresham Joseph Philip, 2nd Baronet	20. 4.75
LOWSON, *Sir* Denys Colquhoun Flowerdew, 1st Baronet	10. 9.75
RAMSAY-FAIRFAX-LUCY, *Maj. Sir* Brian Fulke, 5th Baronet	21. 1.74
McCULLAGH, *Sir* Joseph Crawford, 2nd Baronet (*ext.*)	16. 1.74
MACKENZIE, *Sir* (Lewis) Roderick Kenneth, 9th Baronet	10.12.72
MAPPIN, *Sir* Frank Crossley, 6th Baronet (*ext.*)	25. 1.75
NORIE-MILLER, *Sir* Stanley, 2nd Baronet (*ext.*)	21.12.73
OWEN, *Capt. Sir* John Arthur, 4th Baronet	20. 9.73
PICKTHORN, *Rt. Hon. Sir* Kenneth William Murray, 1st Baronet	12.11.75
PORTER, *Sir* George Swinburne, 3rd Baronet	8. 2.74
RADCLIFFE, *Sir* (Joseph Benedict) Everard Henry, *MC*, 6th Baronet	7. 2.75
REDWOOD, *Sir* Thomas Boverton, 2nd Baronet	11. 4.74
RENWICK, *Sqdn. Ldr. Sir* Eustace Deuchar, 3rd Baronet	3.11.73
RICHARDSON, *Sir* William Wigham, *MBE*, 2nd Baronet	15.11.73
ROBINSON, *Maj. Sir* Frederick Villiers Laud, *MC*, 10th Baronet	19. 3.75
SPEARS, *Maj.-Gen. Sir* Edward Louis, *KBE, CB, MC*, 1st Baronet (*ext.*)	27. 1.74
STUDD, *Sir* Eric, *OBE*, 2nd Baronet	11. 6.75
SYKES, *Sir* (Benjamin) Hugh, 2nd Baronet	22.12.74
VERNER, *Sir* Edward Derrick Wingfield, 6th Baronet (*ext.*)	27. 3.75
VERNEY, *Sir* Harry Calvert Williams, *DSO*, 4th Baronet	23.12.74
WAKEMAN, *Capt. Sir* Offley, *CBE*, 4th Baronet	17. 9.75
WARD, *Cdr. Sir* Melvill Willis, *DSC, RN*, 3rd Baronet (*ext.*)	-. 9.73
WATERLOW, *Sir* Philip Alexander, 4th Baronet	18. 7.73
HUNTINGTON-WHITELEY, *Capt. Sir* (Herbert) Maurice, *RN*, 2nd Baronet	18. 5.75
WILMOT, *Sir* Robert Arthur, 8th Baronet	14.11.74
WILSON, *Sir* John Mitchell Harvey, *KCVO*, 2nd Baronet	6. 2.75
WOOD, *Capt. Sir* John Arthur Haigh, *DSC, MC*, 2nd Baronet (*ext.*)	5. 3.74
WORSLEY, *Sir* William Arthington, 4th Baronet	4.12.73

ORDERS OF KNIGHTHOOD
AND CHIVALRY

CENTRAL CHANCERY OF ORDERS OF KNIGHTHOOD.
St. James's Palace, SW1A 1BG

Secretary—Maj.-Gen. Peter Bernard Gillett, CB, OBE.

On promotion to a higher class of an Order of Chivalry, the recipient should return the insignia of the lower class of that Order to the Central Chancery, unless he or she has been honoured in both the Military and Civil Divisions of the same Order, in which case the insignia of the senior class of both may be retained and worn. The Orders of the Bath and the British Empire have a Military and Civil Division.

Collars are worn by KNIGHTS of the GARTER, THISTLE, and KNIGHTS AND DAMES GRAND CROSS or GRAND COMMANDERS of the various Orders only on "Collar Days" and other special occasions, or when commanded by the Sovereign.

Collar Days are Easter Sunday, Ascension Day, Whit Sunday, Trinity Sunday, New Year's Day, Epiphany, Feb. 6th (Accession Day), St. David, St. Patrick, Lady Day, April 21st (The Queen's Birthday), St. George, St. Philip and St. James, May 29th (Restoration of Royal Family), June 2nd (Coronation Day), June 10th (Duke of Edinburgh's Birthday), St. John the Baptist, St. Peter, Aug. 4th (Queen Elizabeth The Queen Mother's Birthday), St. Michael and All Angels, All Saints, St. Andrew, and Christmas Day, and such other occasions of which due notification is given. Collars are also worn when attending the opening or prorogation of Parliament by the Sovereign, or when taking part in the Ceremony of an introduction of a Peer in the House of Lords, but not after sunset, nor when mounted on Ceremonial Parades, unless directions to that effect are specially given. They are tied on the shoulder by white satin bows $1\frac{1}{2}$ inches wide, the Collar hanging at equal distance back and front.

In the case of possessors of two or more Collars, only one should be worn at a time.

When the Collar (from which the Badge is suspended) is worn, the Riband with its Badge should not be worn, but it may be replaced by the Riband of another Order.

KNIGHTS of the GARTER, THISTLE, and KNIGHTS and DAMES GRAND CROSS of the various Orders are entitled to bear Supporters to their Arms.

Instructions for the Wearing of Orders, Decorations, Miniatures with dress other than uniform will be found in the Preliminary Section. Instructions for wearing them with uniform is as laid down by the Service to which the recipient belongs or belonged. Ladies in uniform conform to the regulations for male holders.

THE MOST NOBLE ORDER OF THE GARTER.

The Order of the Garter, constituted by King Edward III. about August 1348, has, since June 28th, 1831, consisted of the Sovereign and twenty-four Knights Companions, such lineal descendants of King George I., as may have been elected, and of Sovereigns and extra Knights who have been admitted by special statutes. The Prince of Wales is a constituent part of the original institution. The Habit and

Ensigns of the Order are (*i*) A GARTER of dark blue velvet, edged with gold, bearing the motto, *Honi soit qui mal y pense*, in gold letters, with buckle and pendant of gold, richly chased. [It is worn on the left leg, below the knee.] (*ii*) A MANTLE of dark blue velvet lined with white taffeta, with a representation of the Garter encircling the Cross of St. George on an escutcheon argent embroidered on the left shoulder, the Sovereign having the star. (*iii*) A HOOD of crimson velvet. (*iv*) A SURCOAT of crimson velvet, lined with white taffeta. (*v*) A HAT of black velvet, lined with white taffeta, and fastened thereto by a band of diamonds, a plume of white ostrich feathers. (*vi*) A COLLAR of gold (weighing thirty ounces, troy) consisting of twenty-four pieces, each in the form of a Garter surrounding the Tudor Rose, connected by twenty-four knots of chased gold, and pendent thereto (*vii*) the GEORGE, an enamelled figure of St. George on horseback, encountering the dragon. (*viii*) The LESSER GEORGE or BADGE of gold is worn pendent from a four-inch blue ribbon over the left shoulder. (*ix*) The STAR of eight points of silver, in the centre the Cross of St. George gules, encircled with the Garter. At death the Badge and Star are delivered up to Her Majesty by the Knight's male heir, the Collar (with pendant Badge) and Garter being returned to the Central Chancery. The Chapel of St. George, Windsor Castle, is the chapel of the Order.

Insignia of the Order of the Garter.

SOVEREIGN—H.M. The Queen.

LADY OF THE ORDER,—H.M. Queen Elizabeth The Queen Mother,

ROYAL KNIGHTS COMPANIONS: HRH The Duke of Edinburgh.——HRH The Prince of Wales.——EXTRA KNIGHTS COMPANIONS AND LADIES OF THE ORDER: King Leopold III of the Belgians.——Prince Paul of Yugoslavia.——Queen of the Netherlands.——King of Norway.——King of the Belgians.——Emperor of Japan.——Grand Duke of Luxembourg.——KNIGHTS COMPANIONS: Duke of Beaufort.——Viscount Montgomery of Alamein——Earl Mountbatten of Burma.——Duke of Portland.——Earl of Avon.——Duke of Northumberland.——Field Marshal Sir Gerald Templer.——Viscount Cobham.——Viscount Amory.——Viscount De L'Isle.——Baron Casey.——Baron Ashburton.——Baron Cobbold.——Sir Edmund Bacon, Bt.——Sir Cennydd G. Traherne.——Earl Waldegrave.——Earl of Longford.——Baron Butler of Saffron Walden.——Baron Rhodes.——Earl of Drogheda.——Baron Shackleton.——Baron Trevelyan.——Marquess of Abergavenny.

Prelate—The Lord Bishop of Winchester.

Chancellor—Rt. Hon. the Viscount Cobham, KG, GCMG, GCVO, TD.

Register—The Dean of Windsor.

Garter King of Arms—Sir Anthony Richard Wagner, KCVO, DLitt, FSA.

Usher of the Black Rod—Admiral Sir Frank Rodam Twiss, KCB, DSC.

Secretary—Walter John George Verco, Esq., CVO, Norroy and Ulster King of Arms.

D.—D

THE MOST ANCIENT AND MOST NOBLE ORDER OF THE THISTLE.

The date of the foundation of the Order of the Thistle is not known.   When the Order was revived by King James VII and II in 1687 and by Queen Anne in 1703 it was narrated in the Royal Warrants that the Order had been instituted by "Achaius, King of Scots (of glorious memory)".   This is now regarded as legendary.   What seems more probable is that King Achaius

BADGE

STAR

THE COLLAR   AND BADGE.

Insignia of the Order of the Thistle.

instituted the veneration of St. Andrew who became the natural Patron Saint of the Order when in due time it was created. In "Les Souverains du Monde" (1722: Vol. LV: P. 318) James II of Scotland is credited with "reviving" an Order of St. Andrew in 1452 but it is to his eldest son and successor James III (1460-1488) that historical evidence now points as being the true founder of the Most Ancient and Most Noble Order of the Thistle.   The order consists of the Sovereign and sixteen Knights.   Royal Knights and Extra Knights are admitted by special statutes in addition to the number of sixteen. The insignia are (*i*) the STAR, consisting of a St. Andrew's cross of silver embroidery with rays emanating between the points of the cross;   in the centre upon a field of gold, a Thistle of green, heightened with gold, and surrounded by a circle of green, having thereon the motto in letters of gold, *Nemo me impune lacessit*.   [It is worn affixed to the left breast.] (*ii*) The COLLAR of gold consists of thistles intermingled with sprigs of rue, pendant from the centre the St. Andrew of gold enamelled, with the gown green and the surcoat purple, bearing before him the cross enamelled white, and having round the image rays of gold going out from it in the form of a glory.   (*iii*) The MANTLE is of green velvet bound with taffeta and tied with cords and tassels of green and gold;   on the left shoulder is a representation of the Star of the Order.   (*iv*) The BADGE (of gold enamelled) has on one side the image of St. Andrew with the cross before, enamelled as above described or cut in stone, and on the back enamelled a Thistle, gold and green, the flower reddish, with the before-mentioned motto round it, the Thistle on an enamelled green ground. [It is worn attached to a dark green ribbon passing over the left shoulder and resting on the right hip.]   (*v*) The HAT is of black velvet, ornamented with white osprey plumes.   At death the Badge and Star are delivered up to Her Majesty by the Knight's nearest male relative, the Collar (with pendant Badge) being returned to the Central Chancery.   The Chapel of the Order is in St. Giles' Cathedral, Edinburgh, and the Chancery at the Court of the Lord Lyon, HM Register House, Edinburgh.

SOVEREIGN,—H.M. The Queen.

LADY OF THE ORDER,—H.M. Queen Elizabeth The Queen Mother.

ROYAL KNIGHT: HRH The Duke of Edinburgh.——EXTRA KNIGHT: King of Norway.——KNIGHTS: Earl of Haddington.——Earl of Crawford and Balcarres. ——Baron Rowallan.——Lord Home of the Hirsel.——Sir Robert Gordon Menzies.——Sir James Wilson Robertson. ——Earl of Wemyss and March.—— Baron Maclean.——Earl of Dalhousie. ——Gen. Sir Richard Nugent O'Connor. ——Baron Clydesmuir.——Viscount Muirshiel.——Hon. Lord Birsay.——Sir Donald H. Cameron of Lochiel——Baron Ballantrae.

Chancellor—Lord Home of the Hirsel, KT, MP.

Dean—The Very Rev. Prof. John McIntyre, MA, BD, DLitt, DD.

Secretary—Sir James Monteith Grant, KCVO, WS, FSA (Scot.).

Usher of the Green Rod—Lieut.-Col. Sir (John) Reginald Noble Graham of **Larbert**, Bt., **V.C.**, O.B.E.

THE MOST HONOURABLE ORDER OF THE BATH.

From Saxon times the Coronation of King Charles II on great Royal occasions it was customary to confer "a degree of Knighthood" which, from the ceremonies associated with it, became known as the Knighthood of the Bath. Drawing on this ancient tradition, in 1725 King George I created a new military Order and called it the Order of the Bath. The Order was enlarged in 1815 and further extended in 1847, when new statutes regarding appointments were promulgated and the Civil branch established; the statutes were subsequently modified in 1905 and 1912. Under date of July 1925, all former statutes were repealed, and revised and consolidated statutes and ordinances were promulgated; these were further revised in 1930, 1936, 1939, 1969 and 1973. The Order now consists of three classes, each comprising two divisions (military and civil): (*i*) KNIGHTS AND DAMES GRAND CROSS. These Knights and Dames are entitled to receive a grant of supporters to their armorial bearings. (*ii*) KNIGHTS AND DAMES COMMANDERS. Each Knight of the Order is entitled to the distinctive appellation of knighthood. (*iii*) COMPANIONS. The Military division is open to Officers of the Navy, Army, and Air Force, and Naval, Military and Air Forces of the Commonwealth Countries. The Order consists of not more than 115 Knights and Dames Grand Cross (of whom the Great Master is the First and Principal), 328 Knights Commanders and Dames Commanders, and 1,815 Companions exclusive of Honorary Members and any Additional Members that may have been or may be appointed.

The Insignia are (*i*) the COLLAR of gold (weighing thirty ounces troy), composed of nine Imperial Crowns or and eight roses, thistles, and shamrocks, issuing from a gold sceptre, and enamelled in their proper colour, linked together with seventeen knots enamelled argent, and having pendant therefrom the Badge of the Order. (*ii*) The MILITARY KNIGHT AND DAME GRAND CROSS STAR is formed of rays of silver, charged with a Maltese cross or, in the centre whereof on a ground argent three Imperial Crowns, one and two or, the said three Imperial Crowns within a circle gules inscribed with the motto of the Order, *Tria juncta in uno*, in letters of gold, and the said circle encompassed by two branches of laurel proper, issuing from an escrol azure inscribed *Ich dien* in letters of gold. (*iii*) CIVIL KNIGHT AND DAME GRAND CROSS STAR is of rays of silver issuing from a centre and charged with three Imperial Crowns, one and two within a circle gules whereon inscribed the motto of the Order in gold. The Collar and Badge are returned at death to the Central Chancery, but not so the investment Badge and Star. (*iv*) MILITARY KNIGHT AND DAME COMMANDER'S STAR is composed of four rays of silver, between each of which issues a smaller ray, also of silver, and has the same centre as the Knight's Grand Cross, but without a gold Maltese cross thereon. (*v*) CIVIL KNIGHT AND

G.C.B. MILITARY. (STAR)

G.C.B. MILITARY. (COLLAR ∅ BADGE)

K.C.B. MILITARY. (STAR)

K.C.B. MILITARY. (BADGE)

DAME COMMANDER'S STAR is of the same form and size, but without a laurel wreath round the circle containing the motto and the escrol, and without the words *Ich dien* underneath.   [The Crowns in the Stars, which formerly were of

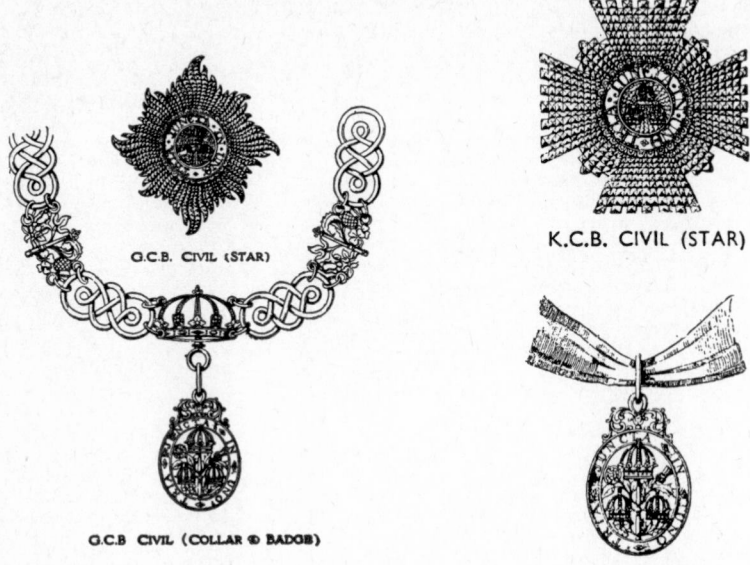

G.C.B. CIVIL (STAR)

K.C.B. CIVIL (STAR)

G.C.B CIVIL (COLLAR & BADGE)

K.C.B. CIVIL. (BADGE)

different designs for the Civil and Military Divisions, are now all of the same pattern.] (*vi*) MILITARY BADGE is a gold Maltese cross of eight points, enamelled argent, edged gold, and terminating with small gold balls having in each of the four angles a lion passant guardant or and in the centre on a ground argent, the rose, thistle, and shamrock, issuing from a sceptre between three Imperial Crowns, all or, within a circle gules, thereon the motto of the Order, *Tria juncta in uno*, in gold letters and encompassed by two branches of laurel proper, issuant from an escrol azure inscribed *Ich dien* in letters of gold.   (*vii*) CIVIL BADGE is of an oval shape, comprised of a rose, thistle, and shamrock, issuing from a sceptre between three Imperial Crowns, the whole pierced and encircled by the motto of the Order, all gold.   The Badge is worn by Knights Grand Cross pendent from a four inch crimson riband, and by Dames Grand Cross pendent from a two and a quarter inch crimson riband passing from the right shoulder obliquely to the left side.   Knights Commanders wear the Badge of a smaller size suspended from the neck by a crimson ribbon of minature width and wear on their left side a Star. Dames Commanders wear the Badge on a Bow except with coats of military pattern, when the Badge is worn in the same manner as a Knight Commander.   The Bow and Star are both worn on the left side.   Gentlemen Com-

C.B. MILITARY. (BADGE)

C.B. CIVIL (BADGE)

panions wear the Badge of a smaller size, on a crimson ribbon of miniature width suspended from the neck.   Lady Companions wear this Badge on a Bow except with a coat of military pattern when the Badge is worn suspended on a ribbon from the neck.   The Badge and Star of a KCB and a DCB and the Badge of a CB are not returned after death, but the Collar and Badge of a GCB should be returned to the Central Chancery of the Orders of Knighthood.   The MANTLE of a Knight and Dame Grand Cross is of crimson satin lined with white taffeta and tied with a cordon of white silk with two tassels of crimson silk and gold attached thereto, on the left side of the mantle below a white silk lace is embroidered a representation of the Star of a Knight Grand Cross.   The HAT is of black velvet, high crowned and with an upright plume of white feathers in the front.   Henry VII's Chapel in Westminster Abbey has been the Chapel of the Order since 1725.

SOVEREIGN,—HM The Queen.

Great Master and First or Principal Knight Grand Cross—HRH The Prince of Wales.

Dean—The Dean of Westminster.

Bath King of Arms—Gen. Sir Richard Wakefield Goodbody, GCB, KBE, DSO.

Secretary and Registrar—Air Marshal Sir Anthony Dunkerton Selway, KCB, DFC.

Genealogist—Conrad Marshall John Fisher Swan, PhD, FSA.

Gentleman Usher of the Scarlet Rod—Rear-Adm. Colin Duncan Madden, CB, CBE, MVO, DSC.

Deputy Secretary—The Secretary of the Central Chancery of the Orders of Knighthood.

THE ORDER OF MERIT.

This is a very exclusive Order (the Ordinary Members of which do not exceed 24 in number), instituted by King Edward VII. on June 23rd, 1902, by letters patent, but carries with it no special title or personal precedence.

The BADGE of the Order consists of a cross of red and blue enamel of eight points, having the words "For Merit" (the motto of the Order) in gold letters within a laurel wreath on a blue enamel centre. The reverse of the badge shows the Royal and Imperial cipher in gold (two silver swords with gold hilts, placed saltirewise between the angles of the cross, being added in the case of members chosen for naval or military distinction) also within a laurel wreath, on a blue enamel centre; and the whole is surmounted by the Imperial Crown enamelled in colour, and suspended by a parti-coloured ribbon of Garter blue and crimson, two inches broad. The Sovereign's insignia, except, of course, for the modifications necessary to distinguish the Royal dignity of the wearer, is similar to the insignia worn by the ordinary members of the Order. The Badge of the Order is always worn round the neck by gentlemen, and may be suspended from Armorial Bearings, is never worn in miniature, and is not returnable at death. Ladies wear the Badge on a Bow on the left side except with coats of military pattern when the Badge is worn in the same manner as by a gentleman. The ceremony of investiture is from time to time conducted by the Sovereign as in the case of any other Order. Members of the Order are entitled to attach a facsimile of its badge and ribbon to their arms, and add the letters O.M. after their names, after G.C.B. The Seal of the Order is a facsimile of the badge, impaled with the Royal Arms, on a white ground, with the legend, "The Seal of the Order of Merit." June 23rd is the anniversary of the Order. The Secretary and Registrar, who wears, as his badge of office, a decoration similar to that worn by the members of the Order, with the addition of two silver pens placed saltirewise between the angles of the cross. The Chancery of the Order is in the Central Chancery of the Orders of Knighthood.

SOVEREIGN,—H.M. The Queen.

Secretary and Registrar—Sir Edward Ford, KCB, KCVO, DL.

Members—HRH The Duke of Edinburgh.——Baron Adrian.——Wilder Penfield.——Sir Macfarlane Burnet.——Graham Sutherland.——Sir Basil Spence.——Henry Moore.——Benjamin Britten.——Dr. Dorothy Hodgkin.——Earl Mountbatten of Burma.——Sir William T. Walton.——Ben Nicholson.——Baron Zuckerman——Malcolm J. MacDonald.——Baron Penney.——Dame C. Veronica Wedgwood.——Sir Isaiah Berlin.——Sir George Edwards.——Sir Alan Hodgkin.——Prof. Paul Dirac.

THE MOST EXALTED ORDER OF THE STAR OF INDIA.

The Order of the Star of India was instituted by Queen Victoria in 1861, and enlarged 1866, 1875, 1876, 1897, 1902, 1911, 1915. 1920. 1927, and 1939, and the dignity of Knight Grand Commander was conferred on Princes or Chiefs of India, or upon British subjects for important and loyal service rendered to the Indian Empire; the second and third classes were for services in the Indian Empire of not less than thirty years in the department of the Sec. of State for India. It consists of the Sovereign, the first class of Knights Grand Commanders, the second class of Knights Commanders, and the third class of Companions. No appointments to this Order have been made since 14th August, 1947.

The Insignia are (*i*) the COLLAR of gold, composed of the lotus flower of India, of palm branches tied together in saltire, of the united red and white rose, and in the centre an Imperial Crown ; all enamelled in their proper colours and linked together by gold chains. (*ii*) The STAR OF A KNIGHT GRAND COMMANDER is composed of rays of gold issuing from a centre, having thereon a star of five points in diamonds resting upon a light blue enamelled circular riband, tied at the ends and inscribed with the motto of the Order, *Heaven's Light our Guide*, also in diamonds. That of a Knight Commander is somewhat different, and is described below. (*iii*) The BADGE, an onyx cameo having Her Majesty Queen Victoria's Royal effigy thereon,

THE COLLAR   AND BADGE.

Insignia of the Order of the Star of India.

set in a perforated and ornamented oval, containing the motto of the Order in diamonds ensigned with a star of five points, composed of silver. (*iv*) The MANTLE of light blue satin lined with white, and fastened with a cordon of white silk with two blue and silver tassels. On the left side a representation of the star of the Order.

The Ribbon of the Order (four inches wide for Knights Grand Commanders) is light blue, having a narrow white stripe towards either edge, and is worn from the right shoulder to the left side. A KNIGHT COMMANDER wears (*a*) around his neck a ribbon two inches in width, of the same colours and pattern as a Knight Grand Commander, and pendent therefrom a badge of a smaller size, (*b*) on his left breast a STAR composed of rays of silver issuing from a gold centre, having thereon a silver star of five points resting upon a light blue enamelled circular ribbon, tied at the ends, inscribed with the motto of the Order in diamonds A Companion wears suspended from the neck a badge of the same form as appointed for a Knight Commander, but of a smaller size pendent to a like ribbon of the breadth of one and a half inches. Only the G.C.S.I. Collar and Badge appendant are returnable at death to the Central Chancery.

Secretary and Registrar—The Secretary of the Central Chancery of the Orders of Knighthood.

THE MOST DISTINGUISHED ORDER OF ST. MICHAEL AND ST. GEORGE.

Ordinary Membership of the Order of St. Michael and St. George, which was instituted in 1818, and enlarged and extended in 1868, 1879, 1887, 1901, 1911, 1915, 1927, 1935, 1937, 1939, 1948, 1953, 1954, 1960, 1965, 1969 and 1974 is conferred on subjects of the Crown of the United Kingdom and certain classes of British protected persons, who may hold, or have held high and confidential offices, or may render or have rendered extraordinary and important services (other than military) within or in relation to any part of the British Dominions or Territories under British Protection or Administration, and in reward for important and loyal services in relation to foreign affairs. The Order consists of not more than one hundred and twenty Knights Grand Cross and Dames Grand Cross (of whom the Grand Master is the First and Principal), three hundred and ninety Knights Commanders and Dame Commanders, and one thousand seven hundred and seventy five Companions, exclusive of Honorary members, and any Additional members that have been or may be appointed. The Knights Grand Cross and Dames Grand Cross are entitled to bear supporters, and to surround their coats of arms with the Collar, circle, and Motto of the Order, and to suspend therefrom the Badge of the Order. The Knights

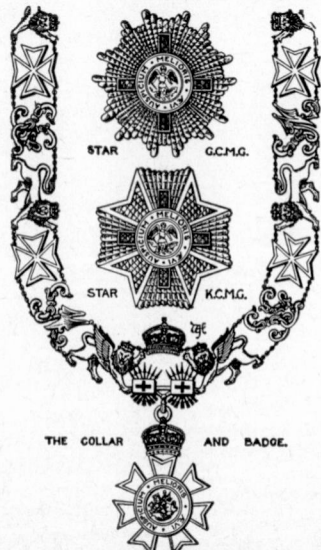

THE COLLAR   AND BADGE.

Insignia of the Order of St. Michael and St. George.

Commanders, Dames Commanders and Companions are permitted to surround their arms with the circle and motto, from which is suspended the ribbon and Badge of the Order. The Insignia are: (i) the STAR of the Knight Grand Cross and Dame Grand Cross which is composed of seven rays of silver having a small ray of gold between each of them, and over all the Cross of St. George gules; in the centre is the representation of the Archangel St. Michael holding in his dexter hand a flaming sword and trampling upon Satan, within a blue circle, inscribed with the motto, Auspicium melioris aevi, in letters of gold. The STAR for Dames being somewhat smaller than that for Knights. (ii) The COLLAR of gold, which is formed alternately of lions of England royally crowned, of Maltese crosses of white enamel, and of the cyphers S.M. and S.G. (also alternately), having in the centre the Imperial Crown over two winged lions, passant guardant, each holding in his fore paw a book and seven arrows; at the opposite end of the Collar are two similar lions, the whole linked together by small gold chains. The Chain for Dames is slightly smaller than that for Knights. (iii) The BADGE, which is a cross of fourteen points enamelled argent, edged gold, having in the centre on one side the Archangel St. Michael holding in his dexter hand a flaming sword and trampling upon Satan, and on the other St. George on horseback and in armour with a spear encountering a dragon, each within a blue circle, on which is inscribed the motto of the Order in letters of gold; the Badge is ensigned by an Imperial Crown, and it is worn by the Knights Grand Cross and Dames Grand Cross (the Badge for Dames to be the same size as that for Knights Commanders) either attached to the Collar or to a four inch Saxon blue ribbon (for Knights Grand Cross) or to a two and one quarter inches ribbon (for Dames Grand Cross) with a scarlet central stripe, from the right shoulder to the left side. (iv) The MANTLE is of Saxon blue satin, lined with scarlet silk, tied with a cardon of blue and scarlet silk and gold, with two tassels of the same colours, and having on the left side an embroidered representation of the Star of the Order. Knight Commanders wear the Badge—one size smaller than the GCMG Badge—suspended on an Order ribbon of miniature width from the neck, and wear on their left side a STAR composed of four rays, thereon a small cross of eight points in saltire argent, surmounted by the Cross of St. George gules, and having the same centre as the Star of the Grand Crosses, while Dames Commanders wear a similar but slightly smaller Badge than Knights Commanders but tied in a bow and worn on the left shoulder, and they wear a slightly smaller Star. Companions wear the Badge or small Cross of the Order—smaller than the KCMG Badge—on an Order ribbon of miniature width, suspended from the neck; a Lady Companion wears the Badge on a bow one and three quarter inches wide and with an additional fitting on a ribbon suspended from the neck. The Chapel of the Order is in St. Paul's Cathedral, London. The Insignia of all classes of this Order are not returned at death, except in the case of the Collar of a Knight or Dame Grand Cross, provided it was awarded after 1948.

SOVEREIGN,—H.M. The Queen.

Grand Master—HRH The Duke of Kent, GCMG, GCVO, ADC.

Prelate—The Rt. Rev. Robert Wilmer Woods, KCVO, MA (Lord Bishop of Worcester).

Chancellor—The Rt. Hon. Viscount De L'Isle, VC, KG, GCMG, GCVO.

Secretary—The Permanent Under-Sec. of State for the Foreign and Commonwealth Office.

Deputy Secretary—The Secretary of the Central Chancery of the Orders of Knighthood.

King of Arms—The Rt. Hon. Sir Morrice James, GCMG, CVO, MBE.

Registrar—The Rt. Hon. Baron Gore-Booth, GCMG, KCVO.

Gentleman Usher of the Blue Rod—Sir Anthony Foster Abell, KCMG.

Dean—The Dean of St. Paul's.

Chancery—Central Chancery of the Orders of Knighthood, St. James's Palace, SW1A 1BG.

THE MOST EMINENT ORDER OF THE INDIAN EMPIRE.

This Order, instituted by H.M. Queen Victoria, Empress of India, Dec. 31st, 1877, and enlarged in 1886, 1887, 1892, 1897, 1902, 1911, 1915, 1920, 1927, and 1939, was conferred for services rendered to the Indian Empire, and consists of the Sovereign, Grand Commanders, Knights Commanders, and Companions. No appointments to this Order have been made since 14th August, 1947.

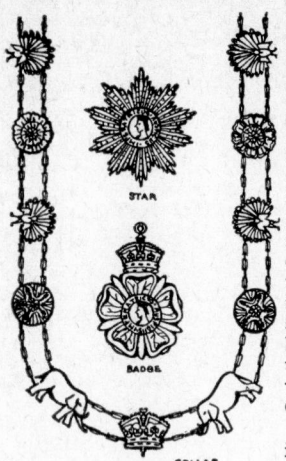

The Insignia are: (*i*) The COLLAR of gold, formed of elephants, lotus flowers, peacocks in their pride, and Indian roses, in the centre the Imperial Crown, the whole linked together with chains; (*ii*) The STAR of the Knight Grand Commander, comprised of five rays of silver, having a smaller ray of gold between each of them, the whole alternately plain and scaled, issuing from a gold centre, having thereon Her Majesty Queen Victoria's Royal Effigy, within a purple circle, inscribed *Imperatricis Auspiciis*, in letters of gold, the circle ensigned by an Imperial Crown, also gold; (*iii*) The BADGE, consisting of a rose enamelled gules, barbed vert, and having in the centre Her Majesty Queen Victoria's Royal Effigy, within a purple circle, inscribed *Imperatricis Auspiciis*, in letters of gold ensigned with an Imperial Crown, also gold; (*iv*) The MANTLE is of purple satin, lined with and fastened by a cordon of white silk, with purple silk and gold tassels attached. On the left side a representation of the Star of the Order.

The ribbon of a KNIGHT GRAND COMMANDER is of Imperial purple and four inches in width. A Knight Commander wears: (*a*) around his neck a riband two inches in width, of the same colour (Imperial purple) and pattern as a Knight Grand Commander, pendent therefrom a badge of smaller size: (*b*) on his left breast a star, similar to that of the first class, but the rays of which are alternately bright and chipped.

Insignia of the Order of the Indian Empire.

Only the G.C.I.E. Collar is returnable at death to the Central Chancery.

A Companion wears suspended from the neck a badge (not returnable at death) of the same form as appointed for a Knight Commander, but of smaller size, pendent to a like ribbon of the breadth of one and a half inches.

Secretary and Registrar—The Secretary of the Central Chancery of the Orders of Knighthood.

THE ROYAL ORDER OF VICTORIA AND ALBERT.

This Order was instituted by H.M. Queen Victoria on February 10th, 1862, to commemorate her happy marriage. Originally it was confined to her daughters and such other Princesses upon whom she might think fit to confer it. The then Crown Princess of Prussia and Princess Alice were considered members from the foundation of the Order and the Queen's other daughters were to become eligible after confirmation.

The Second Class of the Order was established on 10th October, 1864, admitting Ladies who held or had held the Office of Mistress of the Robes, Lady of the Bedchamber or other Office in the Household of the Queen Regnant, or Queen Consort and also upon Ladies not of Royal Rank, nearly connected with the Queen or the Royal Family. The Order was enlarged on 15th March 1880. Ladies previously of the Second Class were transferred to the Third Class. Female descendants and wives of male descendants of the Sovereign, other female members of the Royal House, and Royal and Princely families connected by blood or amity became eligible for the Second Class.

A Third Class was added on 15th November 1865 by which Ladies could be admitted who held or had held the Office of Bedchamber Women or other Office in the Queen's Household, or Ladies of a similar rank. A Fourth Class was added on 15th March 1888.

The insignia consists of an Onyx Cameo, having the Queen's Royal Effigy and also that of the Prince Consort, conjointly thereon in an ornamental Oval set with diamonds, surmounted by an Imperial Crown in precious stones. It is worn on the left shoulder attached to a white moire riband of an inch and a half in width tied in a bow. The insignia is returnable at death.

SOVEREIGN,—HM The Queen.

Second Class.

HRH Princess Alice, Countess of Athlone.

THE IMPERIAL ORDER OF THE CROWN OF INDIA.

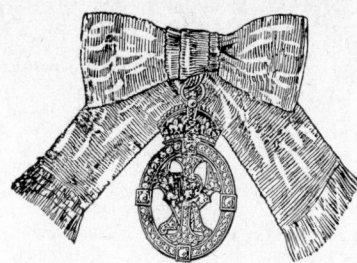

Instituted by Queen Victoria on January 1st, 1878, to commemorate the assumption of the Imperial Title of Empress of India, and revised May 14th, 1927, and March 18th, 1939, this Order consists of the Sovereign, and of such of the Princesses of Her Majesty's Royal House, the wives or other female relatives of Indian Princes, and other Indian ladies, and of the wives or other female relatives of any of the persons who held the office of Viceroy and Governor-General of India, Governors of Madras, Bombay, or Bengal, or of Principal Secretary of State for India, or Commander-in-Chief in India. No appointments to this Order have been made since 14th August 1947.

The Order carries with it no title or precedence, but recipients are permitted to put the initials " C.I." after their names, these being placed immediately before " G.C.V.O." The Badge of the Order consists of the Royal and Imperial Cypher of Queen Victoria, composed of the letters, V, R and I in diamonds, pearls, and turquoises, encircled by a border set with pearls, ensigned with the Imperial Crown jewelled and enamelled in proper colours, and is worn attached to a light blue watered riband, edged white, of an inch and a half in width, tied in a bow, on the left shoulder. The insignia is returnable at death to the Secretary of the Central Chancery of Orders of Knighthood, by whom the Register of the Order is kept.

SOVEREIGN,—HM The Queen.

LADIES OF THE ORDER—HM Queen Elizabeth the Queen Mother.——HRH Princess Alice, Duchess of Gloucester.—— HRH The Princess Margaret, Countess of Snowdon.——The Dowager Countess of Halifax.——HH The Maharani of Travancore.——The Dowager Lady Brabourne. ——The Countess Wavell.

THE ROYAL VICTORIAN ORDER.

This Order, instituted by H.M. Queen Victoria, Empress of India, April 21st, 1896, consists of the Sovereign, a Grand Master, Ordinary Members, and such

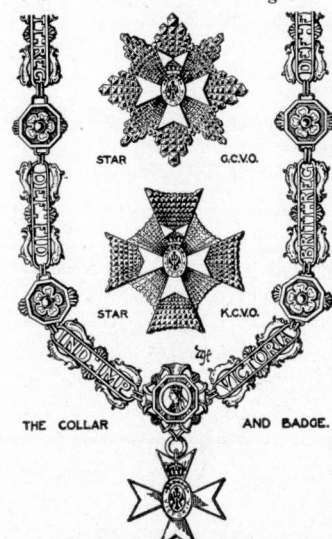

THE COLLAR AND BADGE.

Honorary Members as the Sovereign shall from time to time appoint, the Members being divided into five classes, and designated respectively: (1) Knights and Dames Grand Cross, (2) Knights and Dames Commanders, (3) Commanders. (4) Members of the Fourth Class, and (5) Members of the Fifth Class. Under date of May 29th, 1936, a Warrant was issued consolidating the Statutes of the Order so as to permit of its bestowal upon women.

The persons to be admitted as Ordinary Members of this Order shall be such persons, being male or female subjects of the British Crown, who, having rendered extraordinary, or important, or personal service to the Sovereign, merit Royal favour ; and the Honorary Members of the several classes consist of those Foreign Princes and persons upon whom the Sovereign may think fit to confer the honour of being received into the Order.

The Members of the several grades in the Order are to have place and precedence as follows :—Knights Grand Cross immediately after Knights Grand Commanders of the Order of the Indian Empire, Dames Grand Cross immediately before Dames Grand Cross of the

Royal Victorian Order.

Order of the British Empire, Knights Commanders immediately after Knights Commanders of the Order of the Indian Empire, Dames Commanders immediately before Dames Commander of the Order of the British Empire, men who are Commanders immediately after Companions of the Order of the Indian Empire, women who are Commanders immediately before women who are Commanders of the Order of the British Empire, men who are Members of the Fourth Class immediately after Companions of the Distinguished Service Order, women who are Members of the Fourth Class immediately before women who are Officers of the Order of the British Empire, men who are Members of the Fifth Class immediately after the eldest sons of Knights Bachelors, and women who are Members of the Fifth Class immediately before women who are Members of the Order of the British Empire.

The number of the Members is unlimited, and the anniversary of the Order is the Twentieth day of June every year, being the day of Her late Majesty Queen Victoria's Accession to the Throne of these Realms.

The MANTLE of a Knight or Dame Grand Cross is of dark blue satin, edged with red satin two inches in width, the edging of the collar being half an inch wide, lined with white silk, the mantle being fastened by a cordon of dark blue silk and gold, having two dark blue silk and gold tassels attached thereto ; on the left side of the mantle is embroidered a representation of the Star of a Knight or Dame Grand Cross of the Order. The COLLAR is of gold, composed of octagonal pieces and oblong perforated and ornamental frames alternately, linked together with gold; the said pieces edged and ornamented with gold, each containing upon a blue enamelled ground a gold rose jewelled with a carbuncle, and the said frames are of gold, each containing a portion of the inscription "Victoria . . . Britt. Reg. . . . Def. Fid. . . . Ind. Imp." in letters of white enamel ; in the centre of the collar, within a perforated and ornamental frame of gold, is an octagonal piece, enamelled blue, edged with red, and charged with a white saltire, thereon a gold medallion of Her late Majesty Queen Victoria's effigy, from which hangs the Cross of the Order (detachable).

The BADGE of Knights and Dames Grand Cross consists of a white enamelled Maltese cross of eight points ; on an oval centre of crimson enamel the Royal and Imperial cypher

of Queen Victoria (V.R.I.) in gold, within a blue enamelled circle, thereon the motto of the Order, namely, "Victoria" in letters of gold, the circle being surmounted by an Imperial Crown enamelled in proper colours ; and is worn over the right shoulder, suspended from a dark blue ribbon with a narrow edge either side of three stripes—red, white, and red—of the breadth of three inches in the case of Knights Grand Cross and of two inches and one quarter in the case of Dames Grand Cross, passing from the right shoulder to the left side.

K.C.V.O. and D.C.V.O.
Badge.

The STAR of Knights and Dames Grand Cross consists of a silver chipped star of eight points ; in the centre a representation of the Badge of the First Class of the Order.

The Knights Commanders wear around their necks a ribbon of miniature width of the same colours as that of the Knights Grand Cross, of the breadth of one inch and three-quarters, and pendent therefrom the badge, which is of the same pattern as, but of smaller size than, that of a Knight Grand Cross, whilst the Dames Commanders wear their badges attached to a Riband tied in a bow and worn on the left shoulder. The Star is composed of a Maltese cross in silver, with smaller rays issuing from the centre between the angles of the cross; in the centre the badge of the Order as before described, with the cross in frosted silver instead of white enamel.

Men who are Commanders wear around their necks the like riband and badge as that appointed for the Knights Commanders, and women wear the bow and badge as appointed for Dames Commanders, but neither is entitled to wear the Star.

The Members of the Fourth Class wear a badge of the same form and appearance as that appointed for the Commanders, but of smaller size, pendent from a ribbon of the same colours, of the breadth of an inch and a quarter, attached from the left breast in the case of men and tied in a bow and worn on the left shoulder in the case of women.

The Members of the Fifth Class wear, from the left breast or shoulder, the same riband and badge as that appointed for the Fourth Class, with the exception that the cross is of frosted silver instead of white enamel.

In uniform ladies wear their insignia in the same way as that adopted for male holders.

The Collar is returnable at death or upon receipt of a Collar of an Order of Higher rank, but not the other Insignia.

The Chapel of the Savoy has been the Chapel of the Order since 1938.

["The Royal Victorian Medal" (silver-gilt, silver, or bronze, having on the obverse the Royal effigy, and on the reverse the Royal and Imperial cypher upon an ornamental shield within a wreath of laurel, in base a scroll, thereon the words "Royal Victorian Medal") was also instituted by Queen Victoria. This Medal is worn by men on the left breast of the coat or outer garment pendent to a ribbon of the breadth of one inch and a quarter of the same colour and pattern as that appointed for the members of the Royal Victorian Order, and by women from a ribbon tied in a bow on the left shoulder.]

SOVEREIGN,—HM The Queen.

Grand Master,—HM Queen Elizabeth The Queen Mother.

Chancellor—The Lord Chamberlain.

Secretary—The Keeper of the Privy Purse.

Registrar—The Secretary of the Central Chancery of the Orders of Knighthood.

Chaplain—Rev. Canon Cecil Edwyn Young.

Hon. Genealogist—Walter John George Verco, Esq., CVO.

ROYAL VICTORIAN CHAIN.

King Edward VII. founded in Aug. 1902 the " Royal Victorian Chain," which is only bestowed on special occasions, and, although forming no part of the Royal Victorian Order, may be worn on all occasions when other insignia of British Orders of Chivalry are worn ; it is of a different and much lighter design than the Collar.

HOLDERS OF ROYAL VICTORIAN CHAIN.

HM The Queen.——HM Queen Elizabeth The Queen Mother.——Emperor Haile Sellassie I of Ethiopia.——Prince Paul of Yugoslavia.——King Leopold III of the Belgians.——Shananshah of Iran.——Queen of the Netherlands.——Duke of Beaufort.——King of Norway.—— King of Thailand.——Crown Prince Asfa Wossen of Ethiopia.——King of Jordan.——Zahir Shah of Afghanistan.——Lord Adeane.——Rt. Hon. Roland Michener.——Lord Ramsey of Canterbury.——King of Nepal.

THE MOST EXCELLENT ORDER OF THE BRITISH EMPIRE.

This Order, instituted by H.M. King George V. in June 1917, extended Dec. 1918, and altered March 1919, Dec. 1922, June 1929, Nov. 1933, March 1937, and Oct. 1939, is conferred for important services rendered to the Empire, and is awarded to both men and women. It consists of the Sovereign and five classes:—(I.) Knights Grand Cross and Dames Grand Cross, (II.) Knights Commanders and Dames Commanders, (III.) Commanders, (IV.) Officers, (V.) Members. Foreign persons upon whom the Order is conferred are " Honorary."

Further alterations to the Statutes of the Order were made in September 1959, May 1962, July 1964 and September 1969, limiting the numbers to be admitted to the Order in future, as follows:—

Knights and Dames Grand Cross (not to exceed Military 30, Civil 90), Knights and Dames Commanders (not to exceed Military 248, Civil 622), and Commanders (not to exceed Military 1,720, Civil 6,850),

specifying the numbers of each of these Classes that may be appointed in a given period ;

also Officers (Military not more than 148 in any year, Civil not more than 741 in any year) ;

and Members (Military not more than 261 in any year, Civil not more than 1,209 in any year).

The above-mentioned limitation does not affect those already admitted to the Order prior to December 29th, 1922, who are not to be included within the foregoing numbers allotted to each Class of the Order, nor additional appointments made by special statute in commemoration of special occasions.

Appointments are made on the recommendation of the Minister of Defence, the Secretary of State for Foreign and Commonwealth Affairs, and the appropriate Minister of State for Commonwealth Countries other than the United Kingdom, as regards the Military Division, and the Secretary of State for Foreign and Commonwealth Affairs as regards the Civil Division.

This Order ranks next to and immediately after the Royal Victorian Order; Knights Grand Cross have place and precedency next to and immediately after the Knights Grand Cross of the Royal Victorian Order ; Dames Grand Cross next to and immediately before the wives of Knights Grand Cross of the Bath, and may use the appellation and style of Dame before their Christian or first names ; the Knights Commanders have place and precedency next to and immediately after the Knights Commanders of the Royal Victorian Order ; Dames Commanders next to and immediately before the wives of Knights Commanders of the Bath, and may use the

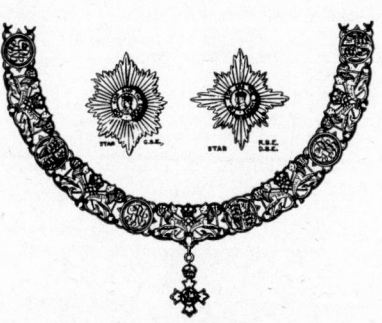

COLLAR OF THE ORDER.

appellation and style of Dame before their Christian or first names ; men who are Commanders have place and precedency next to and immediately after the Members of the Third Class of the Royal Victorian Order and women who are Commanders next to and immediately before the Wives of Companions of the Bath ; men who are Officers have place and precedency next to and immediately after the Members of the Fourth Class of the Royal Victorian Order and women who are Officers next to and immediately before the wives of

Members of the Fourth Class of the Royal Victorian Order; men who are Members have place and precedency next to and immediately after the Members of the Fifth Class of the Royal Victorian Order, and women who are Members next to and immediately before the wives of Members of the Fifth Class of the Royal Victorian Order.

There are both Military and Civil Divisions of this Order; the Insignia for both is the same, but the Ribbon of the Military Division is distinguished by the narrow vertical pearl grey (formerly red) stripe in the centre which varies in width according to Class.

The COLLAR for Knights Grand Cross and Dames Grand Cross is of silver gilt composed of six medallions of the Royal Arms and six medallions of the Royal and Imperial Cypher of King George V alternately linked together with cables thereon the Imperial Crown between two sea-lions, from which hangs the Badge of the First Class of the Order. These Collars are returnable at death or upon receipt of a Collar of an Order of higher rank. The Mantle is of rose pink satin lined with pearl grey silk (originally purple satin lined with white silk) having the Grand Cross Star embroidered on the left side.

The Badge of the First Class of the Order consists of a cross patonce, enamelled pearl, fimbriated or, surmounted by a gold medallion bearing the crowned effigies of King George V. and Queen Mary combined within a circle gules inscribed with the motto, "For God and the Empire," in letters of gold ensigned with the Imperial Crown or, and on the reverse an engraving of the Royal and Imperial Cypher of King George V., the whole suspended from a rose pink riband edged with a pearl grey stripe (originally a purple riband) of the breadth of four inches for Knights Grand Cross, (with the addition, for Military Knights Grand Cross, of a vertical pearl grey stripe in the centre of a width of about one quarter of an inch), and two inches and one quarter for Dames Grand Cross, passing from the right shoulder to the left side, and on the left side of their coats or outer garments a Star (that for Dames being somewhat smaller than that worn by Knights), composed of chipped silver rays of eight points and charged with a medallion as above.

Knights Commanders wear around their necks a riband of miniature width of the same colour and pattern as that of Knights Grand Cross (the pearl grey stripe of Military Knights Commanders being about one sixteenth of an inch in width) and pendent therefrom the badge of the Knights Commanders of the Order, which shall be of similar form and pattern to that appointed for Knights Grand Cross, but of smaller size, and also wear on the left side of their coats or outer garments a chipped silver Star composed of four greater and four lesser points, charged with a medallion as before, while Dames Commanders wear a badge of similar form and pattern as that appointed for Knights Commanders, attached to a riband, also similar to that worn by Knights Commanders, but tied in a bow and worn on the left shoulder, and they wear a like Star.

Commanders in the same manner wear the like riband and badge as that appointed for Knights or Dames Commanders, but are not entitled to wear the Star.

Officers wear a badge of similar form and pattern as that appointed for Commanders, but of a smaller size and of silver gilt, attached to a riband of the same colour and pattern of the breadth of one inch and a half (the vertical pearl grey stripe in the case of the Military Officers to be one sixteenth of an inch in width), attached to the left breast of their coats or outer garments by men, and tied in a bow on the left shoulder by women.

Members wear in like manner the same riband and badge as that appointed to Officers except that it is in silver.

The Insignia of all classes are, on promotion from a lower to a higher class in the same division, to be returned to the Registrar, but not at death except by Officials of the Order.

[There is a Military and Civil medal in connection with the Order which may be awarded to persons not Members of, or eligible for, any of its five classes, who render meritorious service. It is known as the BRITISH EMPIRE MEDAL, and entitles the recipients to place the letters " B.E.M." after their names.]

In 1957 it was decreed that appointments to and promotions in the Order of the British Empire and awards of the British Empire Medal, when granted for gallantry, should be distinguished by the wearing of an Emblem on the riband in crossed oak leaves, and in the announcement by an additional description " for galfantry."

SOVEREIGN—HM The Queen.

Grand Master—HRH The Duke of Edinburgh, KG, KT, OM, GBE.

Prelate—The Lord Bishop of London.

King of Arms—Lt. Gen. Sir George Charles Gordon Lennox, KBE, CB, CVO, DSO.

Registrar—The Secretary of the Central Chancery of the Orders of Knighthood.

Secretary—The Permanent Secretary to the Civil Service Department.

Dean—The Dean of St. Paul's.

Gentleman Usher of the Purple Rod—Sir Robert Ian Bellinger, GBE.

Prelate Emeritus—Rt. Rev. and Rt. Hon. John William Charles Wand, K.C.V.O. D.D.

Genealogist—Walter John George Verco, Esq., CVO.

ORDER OF THE COMPANIONS OF HONOUR.

Instituted on June 4th, 1917, and altered Oct. 15th, 1919, consists of the Sovereign and not more than 65 Members (exclusive of Hon. Members, and certain additional members appointed by special statute in commemoration of special occasions); it may be conferred on persons (women being eligible equally with men) for having done conspicuous national service, and for whom the distinction is deemed the most appropriate form of recognition, constituting as it does an honour dissociated either from acceptance of title or the classification of merit, and carrying with it no title or precedence, but recipients are permitted to put the initials "C.H." after their names, these being placed subsequent to the initials "G.B.E." The Badge of the Order is oval, and consists of a gold medallion with representation of an oak tree and pendant from a branch a shield of the Royal Arms; on the dexter a representation of a knight armed and in armour, mounted on a horse, the whole within a circle inscribed with the motto "In action faithful and in honour clear" in letters of gold ensigned with the Imperial Crown proper. Men suspend it around their necks from a carmine riband 1½ inches wide with a bordure interlaced gold; women wear it attached to a similar riband tied in a bow on the left shoulder. It is never worn in miniature, and is not returnable at death. A representation of the Badge may be suspended from an escutcheon of armorial bearings.

SOVEREIGN,—HM The Queen.

Secretary and Registrar—The Secretary of the Central Chancery of the Orders of Knighthood.

Members of the Order.——Baron Casey.——Prof. Archibald Hill.——Lord David Cecil.——Sir Robert Menzies.——Benjamin Britten.——Baron Butler of Saffron Walden.——Henry Moore.——Sir John L. Kotelwala.——Baron Clark.—— Viscount Boyd of Merton.——Tunku Abdul Rahman.——Selwyn Lloyd.—— Viscount Muirshiel.——Viscount Watkinson.——Sir Keith Holyoake.——Prof. Ivor Richards.——Baron Brooke of Cumnor.——Baron Shinwell.——Graham Greene.——Baroness Summerskill.——Sir Mortimer Wheeler.——Baron Houghton of Sowerby.——Sir Arthur Bryant.—— Rev. Ernest Payne.——Baron Robbins. ——Baron Gordon-Walker.——Sir Adrian Boult.——Michael Stewart.——Sir John McEwen.——Dr. Eric Williams.——Sir Frederick Ashton.——Dame Sybil Thorndike.——Charles Best.——John Gorton. ——Sir Peter Medawar.——William McMahon.——Baron Goodman.——Herbert N. Howells.——John E. C. Piper. ——Sir Robert Mayer.——Baron Duncan-Sandays.——Sir John Ross Marshall. ——Bernard H. Leach.——Baroness Ward of North Tyneside.——Baron Cohen of Birkenhead.——Angela Countess of Limerick.——William Whitelaw. ——Rev. Nathaniel Micklem.——Jack Ashley.——Baron Gardiner.——Max F. Perutz.——Arnold Cantwell Smith.—— Baron Aylestone.——Baron Morris of Borth-y-Gest.——John Diefenbaker.

Honorary Members.—Rene Massigli.—— Lee Kuan Yew.——Dr. Joseph Luns.—— Jean Monnet.

KNIGHTS BACHELOR.

The word Knight is derived from the Saxon Cnyht, which signified a servant or attendant; and Knighthood is the most ancient title of honour known in this country, its origin dating back to Saxon times. The designation Knight Bachelor was in existence as long ago as the reign of King Henry III. Although for many centuries none but the Sovereign, or some person specially designated by him, has been able to create a Knight, originally both ecclesiastical and lay persons could confer the honour. Until 1926 Knights Bachelor had no insignia which they could wear, but in that year H.M. the King issued a Warrant authorising the wearing of a badge on all appropriate occasions. The Imperial Society of Knights Bachelor was founded for the maintenance and consolidation of the Dignity of Knights Bachelor in 1908, and obtained official recognition from the Sovereign in 1912. The Society keeps records of all Knights Bachelor and publishes triennially a Knightage dealing with the Degree, the interests of which its purpose is to maintain. The Knights Bachelor badge, which was approved in 1926, is worn on all appropriate occasions upon the left side of the coat or outer garment of those upon whom the degree of Knight

Bachelor has been conferred. It measures $2\frac{3}{8}$ inches in length and $1\frac{5}{8}$ in width, is described as follows:—

" Upon an oval medallion of vermilion, enclosed by a scroll a cross-hilted sword belted and sheathed, pommel upwards, between two spurs, rowels upwards, the whole set about with the sword belt, all gilt."

In 1974 HM The Queen issued a further warrant authorising the wearing on appropriate occasions of a neck badge, slightly smaller in size, and a miniature.

PATRON—HM The Queen.

Knight Principal—Sir Anthony R. Wagner, K.C.V.O., D.Litt., F.S.A.

Deputy Knight Principal—Sir Gilbert Inglefield, GBE, TD, DL.

Prelate—The Lord Bishop of London.

Hon. Registrar—Sir John Weir Russell.

Hon. Treasurer—Sir John A. G. Howard, FICE.

Clerk—Mrs. E. Reid.

Clerk Consultant—Mrs. Ivor Rodney.

Registry and Library—21 Old Buildings, Lincolns Inn, WC1.

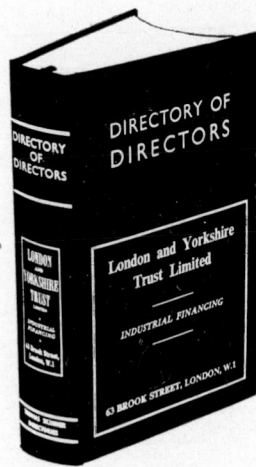
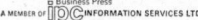

DEBRETT'S
ILLUSTRATED PEERAGE.

THE ROYAL FAMILY.

REIGNING SOVEREIGN.

ELIZABETH II., BY THE GRACE OF GOD, OF THE UNITED KINGDOM OF GREAT BRITAIN, AND NORTHERN IRELAND AND OF HER OTHER REALMS AND TERRITORIES QUEEN, HEAD OF THE COMMONWEALTH, DEFENDER OF THE FAITH*.

Her Majesty ELIZABETH ALEXANDRA MARY, el. dau. of His late Majesty King George VI. and of Lady Elizabeth Angela Marguerite Bowes-Lyon (*H.M. Queen Elizabeth The Queen Mother*) (see page 11), dau. of 14th Earl of Strathmore and Kinghorne ; *b.* April 21st, 1926 : ascended the throne February 6th, 1952, proclaimed Queen February 8th, 1952, and crowned at Westminster Abbey June 2nd, 1953 ; declared in Council April 9th, 1952, that she and her children shall be styled and known as the House and Family of Windsor ; and further Feb. 8th, 1960, that her descendants, other than descendants enjoying the style, title, or attribute of H.R.H. and the titular dignity of Prince or Princess, and female descendants who marry, and their descendants shall bear the name of Mountbatten-Windsor ; Hon. B.Mus., London 1946 ; a F.R.S. 1947 ; Hon. D.C.L., Oxford 1948 ; Hon. LL.D., Edinburgh ; Hon. Mus.D., Wales 1949 ; Hon. LL.D., London 1951 ; Hon. FRCS and FRCOG 1951 ; Lord High Adm. of the United Kingdom, Col.-in-Ch. of Life Guards, Blues and Royals (R. Horse Guards and 1st Dragoons), R. Scots Dragoon Guards (Carabiniers and Greys), 16th/5th Queen's R. Lancers, R. Tank Regt., RE, Grenadier Guards, Coldstream Guards, Scots Guards, Irish Guards, Welsh Guards, R. Welch Fusiliers, Queen's Lancashire Regt., Argyll and Sutherland Highlanders (Princess Louise's), R. Green Jackets, RAOC, Queen's Own Mercian Yeo., Duke of Lancaster's Own Yeo., Corps of R. Canadian Engineers, King's Own Calgary Regt., R. 22e Regt.,

---

Gov.-Gen.'s Foot Guards, Canadian Grenadier Guards, Le Regiment de la Chaudiere, R. New Brunswick Regt., 48th Highlanders of Canada, Argyll and Sutherland Highlanders of Canada (Princess Louise's), R. Canadian Ordnance Corps, Royal Aust. Engineers, Royal Aust. Inf. Corps, R. Aust. Army Ordnance Corps, R. Aust. Army Nursing Corps, R. NZ Engineers, R. NZ Inf. Regt., Malawi Rifles, Capt.-Gen. RA, Hon. Artillery Co., Combined Cadet Force, R. Canadian Artillery, R. Regt. of Aust. Artillery, R. NZ Artillery, R. NZ Armoured Corps, Air-Commodore-in-Chief, R. Aux. AF, RAF Regt., R. Observer Corps, R. Canadian Air Force Aux., Aust. Citizen Air Force, Comdt.-in-Chief, RAF Coll., Cranwell, Hon. Commr., R. Canadian Mounted Police, Master of the Merchant Navy and Fishing Fleets. Head of the Civil Defence Corps, Head of Nat. Hosp. Ser. Reserve; Sovereign of all British Orders of Knighthood, Order of Merit, R. Order of Victoria and Albert, Order of Crown of India, Order of Companions of Honour, Distinguished Ser. Order, Imperial Ser. Order, and Order of Canada, and Sovereign Head of the Order of the Hospital of St. John of Jerusalem§; received Freedom of Drapers' Co., and of Roy. Borough of Windsor 1947, Burgess of Roy. Burgh of Stirling, and Cities of London and Cardiff 1948, and Cities of Edinburgh and Belfast 1949; Patron of R. Coll. of Physicians, Edinburgh, 1963; Order of the Elephant of Denmark 1947, Grand Cordon of Order of El Kemal of Egypt 1948, Grand Cross (or Cordon) of Legion of Honour of France 1948, Order of Ojaswi Rajanya of Nepal 1949, Grand Cross of Order of the Netherlands Lion 1950, Order of the Seraphim of Sweden 1953, Gold Collar of Order of Manuel Amador Guerrero of Panama 1953, Order of Qeladet El-Hussein Ibn Ali of Jordan 1953, Grand Collar of Order of Idris I of Libya 1954, Chain and Collar of Order of the Seal of Solomon of Ethiopia 1954, Grand Cross, with Chain, of Order of St. Olav of Norway 1955, Grand Sash and Cross of the Three Orders of Christ, Aviz and Santiago of Portugal 1955, Grand Order of the Hashimi, with Chain, of Iraq 1956, Chevalier, with Grand Cross and Grand Cordon, of Order of Merit of the Republic of Italy 1958, Special Grand Cross with Star of Order of Merit of Federal Republic of Germany 1958, Grand Cross with diamonds of Order of the Peruvian Sun 1960, Nishan-i-Pakistan 1960, Grand Collar of Order of the Liberator General San Martin of Argentina 1960, Order of Royal House of Chakri of Thailand 1960, Mahendra Chain of Nepal 1961, the Grand Collar of Order of Independence of Tunisia 1961, Collar of Order of the White Rose of Finland 1961, Grand Cross of National Order of Senegal 1961, Grand Cordon of Order of Knighthood of the Pioneers of the Republic of Liberia 1961, Grand Cross of National Order of Ivory Coast 1961, Collar and Grand Cordon of Order of the Chrysanthemum of Japan 1962, Grand Band of Order of the Star of Africa of Liberia 1962, Grand Cross of Order de la Valeur Camerounaise 1963, Grand Cordon of the Order of Leopold of Belgium, 1963, Grand Cross of the Order of the Redeemer of Greece, 1963, Grand Cross, with Chain, of Order of the Falcon of Iceland 1963, the Chain of Honour of the Sudan 1964, Grand Collar of Order of Merit of Chile 1965, Grand Cordon of Australian Order of Merit 1966, Grand Cross of National Order of The Niger 1969, and Order of Al Nahayyan (First Class) 1969, Grand Cross of The Equatorial Star of Gabon, Order of Supreme Sun of Afghanistan 1971, Order of Golden Lion of House of Nassau of Luxembourg 1972, Order of the Great Yugoslav Star 1972, Grand Collar of National Order of Aztec Eagle of Mexico 1973, Star of Indonesia (First Class) 1974, Grand Commander of Order of the Republic of the Gambia 1974, and Collar of the Order of the Nile, of Egypt 1975. The Civil List was fixed by the Civil List Act 1952, and re-enacted by the Civil List Act 1972, which made provision for the Queen's Civil List of £980,000 per annum. The Civil List (Increase of Financial Provision Order 1975) increased the annual sum to £1,400,000, but in other respects the 1972 Act remained unchanged: *m.* Nov. 20th, 1947, HRH The Prince Philip, Duke of Edinburgh, *KG, KT, OM, GBE, PC* [see page 12], and has issue.

Residences,—Buckingham Palace, S.W.1; Windsor Castle, Berkshire; Balmoral Castle, Aberdeenshire; Sandringham, Norfolk.

Crown.—A circle of gold, issuing therefrom four crosses patée and four fleurs-de-lis arranged alternately; from the crosses patée arise two golden arches ornamented with pearls, crossing at the top under a mound also gold, the whole enriched with precious stones. The cap is of crimson velvet, turned up ermine. Royal Arms.†—Quarterly: 1st and 4th, gules, three lions passant guardant in pale or, *England*; 2nd, or, a lion rampant within a double tressure flory counterflory gules, *Scotland*; 3rd, azure, a harp or, stringed argent, *Ireland*, the whole encircled with the Garter. Crests.—*England*, upon the royal helmet the Royal crown proper, thereon statant guardant or, a lion imperially crowned also proper; *Scotland*, on the Crown proper a lion sejant affrontée gules crowned or, holding in the dexter paw a sword, and in the sinister a sceptre erect also proper; *Ireland*, on a wreath or and azure, a tower triple-towered of the first, from the portal a hart springing argent, attired and hoofed gold. Supporters.—*Dexter*, a lion rampant guardant or, crowned as the crest; *sinister*, a unicorn argentarmed, crined, and unguled, or, gorged with a coronet composed of crosses patées and fleurs-de-lis, a chain affixed thereto, passing between the fore-legs, and reflexed over the back, of the last. Badges. —*England*, the red and white rose united, slipped and leaved proper; *Scotland*, a thistle, slipped and leaved proper; *Ireland*, a shamrock leaf slipped vert; also a harp or stringed argent; *United Kingdom*, the Rose of England, the Thistle of Scotland, and the Shamrock of Ireland engrafted on the same stem proper, and an escutcheon charged as the Union Flag (all the foregoing ensigned with the Royal

---

§ As Princess Elizabeth, Her Majesty was appointed a Member of Imperial Order of the Crown of India, a Lady of the Most Noble Order of the Garter, and a Dame Grand Cross of Order of St. John of Jerusalem 1947.

† Scottish usage shows the Royal Arms with the Lion of Scotland in the 1st and 4th quarters, in conformity with the pattern prescribed for the Great Seal of Scotland, and appearing on Scottish official publications and on the tabards of the Scottish Officers of Arms.

Crown); *Wales*, upon a mount vert a dragon passant wings elevated gules, and (Augmented Badge) within a circular riband argent fimbriated or, bearing the motto " Y Ddraig goch Dddyry Cychwyn " in letters vert, and ensigned with a representation of the Crown proper, an escutcheon per fesse argent and vert and thereon the Red Dragon passant; *The Royal House of Windsor*, on a mount vert the Round Tower of Windsor Castle argent mason Sable, flying thereon the Royal Standard, the whole within two branches of oak fructed or and ensigned with the Royal Crown.

The Arms of HRH The Prince Andrew, HRH The Princess Anne, Mrs Mark Phillips, and HRH The Princess Margaret, Countess of Snowdon, are differenced by the following Labels—

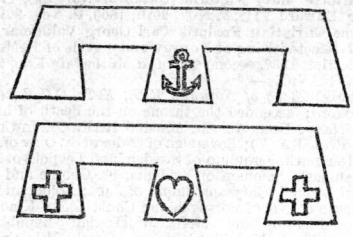

SONS LIVING.

H.R.H. PRINCE CHARLES PHILIP ARTHUR, GEORGE, *KG*, *GCB* (*Prince of Wales*), b. Nov. 14th, 1948. See page 14.

§*H.R.H. Prince* Andrew Albert Christian Edward *b.* Feb. 19th, 1960; ed. at Gordonstoun.

§*H.R.H. Prince* Edward Antony Richard Louis, *b.* March 10th, 1964.

DAUGHTER LIVING†.

H.R.H. *Princess* Anne Elizabeth Alice Louise, *GCVO*, *b.* Aug. 15th, 1950; ed. at Benenden; Col.-in-Ch. 14th/20th King's Hussars, Worcs. and Sherwood Foresters Regt. (29th/45th Foot) and 8th Canadian Hussars (Princess Louise's), Comdt.-in-Ch. WRNS, and Comdt.-in-Ch. Ambulance and Nursing Cadets of St. John Ambulance Bde.; a DStJ; has Grand Gold Cross of Order of Merit of Austria; GCVO 1974: *m.* Nov. 14th, 1973, Capt. Mark Anthony Peter Phillips, CVO, 1st Queen's Dragoon Gds., of Oak Grove House, Sandhurst, Camberley, Surrey.

See page 14.

SISTER LIVING*

H.R.H. *Princess* Margaret Rose (*The Princess Margaret, Countess of Snowdon*), *C.I.*, *G.C.V.O.*, *b.* Aug. 21st, 1930; Hon. D.Mus. London 1957; Hon. LL.D. Camb. 1958; Hon. D.Litt. Keele 1962; Hon. F.R.I.B.A. 1953; Hon. F.R.S.M. 1957, Hon. FRCS, England 1963, and Hon. FRCOG 1966; Hon. Life FZS; a Bencher of Lincoln's Inn and Treasurer 1967; Col.-in-Ch. of R. Highland Fusiliers (Princess Margaret's Own Glasgow and Ayrshire Regt.), 15th/19th King's R. Hussars, Princess Louise Fusiliers, Highland Fusiliers of Canada, QARANC, and WRAAC, and Dep. Col.-in-Ch. of R. Anglian Regt.; Chancellor of Univ. of Keele; Pres. of Dr. Barnardo's, Scottish Children's League of Pity, Victoria League for Commonwealth Friendship, Sunshine Homes and Schs. for Blind Children (R. National Institute for the Blind), R. Ballet, National Soc. for the Prevention of Cruelty to Children, Roy. Scottish Soc. for Prevention of Cruelty to Children, Dockland Settlements, Friends of the Elderly and Gentlefolk's Help, Invalid Children's Aid Assocn. (also Chm. of Council), Sadlers Wells Foundation, English Folk Dance and Song Soc., Horder Centres for Arthritics, of Girl Guides Assocn., and of Chorleywood Coll. for Girls with Little or No Sight; Joint-Pres. of Lowland Bde. Club; Pres. Roy. Agricultural Soc. of England 1966; Patron-in-Ch. of English Harbour Repair Fund; Patron of Light Industry Club, QARANC Assocn., Barristers' Benevolent Assocn., Bristol Roy. Workshops for the Blind, British Sailors' Soc. Guild, Friends of Southwark Cathedral, Friends of St. John's, Mary Hare Gram. Sch. for the Deaf, National Pony Soc., Princess Margaret Rose Hosp., Edinburgh, Services Kinema Corporation, of Roy. Coll. of Nursing and National Council of Nurses of UK, of Princess Margaret Hosp. and Lodge Aux., Toronto, of The Mathilda and Terence Kennedy Inst. of Rheumatology, St. Margaret's Chapel Guild, Edinburgh Castle, Scottish Assocn. of Youth Clubs, Scottish Community Drama Assocn., Suffolk Regimental Assocn., Union of Girls' Schs. for Social Ser., Univ. of London Choir, of W. Indies Olympic Assocn. of Architects' Benevolent Soc., and of Tenovus (Inst. of Cancer Research); Patron (temporary) of Roy. Caledonian Ball since 1956; a CStJ; Grand President of St. John Ambulance Assocn. and Bde.; Life Member of British Legion Women's Section, Hon. Member of Automobile Assocn., Order of the Road, Roy. Automobile Club, of Coventry Cathedral Ten Year Development Plan, and Sealyham Terrier Breeders' Assocn.; Hon. Member and Patron of Grand Antiquity Soc. of Glasgow; a Member of Haberdashers' Co. 1966; received Freedom of City of London 1966; has Grand Cross of Order of Lion of the Netherlands 1948, Order of Brilliant Star of Zanzibar, first class 1956, Grand Cross of Order of Crown of Belgium 1960, Order of the Crown, Lion and Spear of Toro Kingston, Uganda 1965 & Order of Precious Crown of Japan: first class 1971, and Grand Cross (1st class), Order of Merit of Federal Republic of Germany; CI 1947, GCVO 1953: *m.* May 6th, 1960, the 1st Earl of Snowdon, and has issue:—

SON LIVING,—David Albert Charles (*Viscount Linley*), *b.* Nov. 3rd, 1961; ed. at Bedales. DAUGHTER LIVING,—*Lady* Sarah Frances Elizabeth, *b.* May 1st, 1964; ed. at Bedales.

MOTHER LIVING (*Widow of King George VI.*), Her Majesty QUEEN ELIZABETH THE QUEEN MOTHER. See page 11.

See page 11.

WIDOWS LIVING OF SONS OF KING GEORGE V.

See Princess Alice, Duchess of Gloucester, page 15 and Duchess of Windsor, page 17.

page 15 and Duchess of Windsor, page 17.

OTHER LIVING DESCENDANTS OF KING GEORGE V.

Issue of Field-Marshal HRH the late Prince Henry William Frederick Albert, KG, KT, KP, GCB, GCMG, GCVO, PC, 1st Duke of Gloucester, 3rd son of HM the late King George V, *b.* March 31st, 1900, *d.* June 10th, 1974: *m.* Nov. 6th, 1935, Lady Alice Christabel Montagu-Douglas-Scott, GCB, CI, GCVO, GBE (a GCStJ), 3rd da. of 7th Duke of Buccleuch and Queensberry.

See D. Gloucester, page 15.

See D. Gloucester, page 15.

Issue of Air-Commodore H.R.H. the late Prince George Edward Alexander Edmund, K.G., K.T., G.C.M.G., G.C.V.O., P.C., R.A.F., 1st Duke of Kent, 4th son of H.M. the late King George V., *b.* Dec. 20th, 1902, *d.* (on active ser. during European War) Aug. 25th, 1942: *m.* Nov. 29th, 1934, HRH Princess Marina, CI, GCVO, GBE, who *d.* Aug. 27th, 1968, da. of HRH the late Prince Nicholas of Greece, GCB, GCVO:—

See D. Kent, page 16.

See D. Kent, page 16.

Issue of HRH the late Princess (Victoria Alexandra Alice) Mary (*The Princess Royal*), CI, GCVO, CBE, RRC, TD, CD, only da. of HM the late King George V, *b.* April 25th, 1897, *d.* March 28th, 1965; declared Princess Royal Jan. 1st, 1932: *m.* Feb. 28th, 1922, the 6th Earl of Harewood, KG, GCVO, DSO, who *d.* May 24th, 1947:—

See E. Harewood.

See E. Harewood.

§ Under the Civil List Act 1972, provision is made for Her Majesty's younger sons to receive £20,000 per annum at the age of 18 and before marriage, and an additional annual amount of £30,000 after marriage.

† Under the Civil List Act 1972, provision is made for a married daughter of Her Majesty to receive £35,000 per annum.

* Under the Civil List Act 1972, provision is made for Her Royal Highness to receive £35,000 per annum.

OTHER LIVING DESCENDANTS OF KING EDWARD VII.

Grandson of H.R.H. the late Princess Louise Victoria Alexandra Dagmar (*The Princess Royal, Duchess of Fife*), el. da. of King Edward VII., *b.* Feb. 20th, 1867, *d.* Jan. 4th, 1931; declared Princess Royal Nov. 28th, 1905: *m.* July 27th, 1889, the 1st Duke of Fife, KG, KT, GCVO, who *d.* Jan. 29th, 1912:—

Issue of H.H. the late Princess Maud Alexandra Victoria Georgina Bertha (*Countess of Southesk*), *b.* April 3rd, 1893, *d.* Dec. 14th, 1945; granted title of Princess, with style and attribute of "Highness" and precedence immediately after all members of Royal Family enjoying style of "Royal Highness" 1905: *m.* Nov. 12th, 1923, the 11th Earl of Southesk, KCVO.

See D. Fife.

Issue of H.M. the late Maud Charlotte Mary Victoria (*Queen of Norway*), V.A., C.I., G.C.V.O., youngest dau. of King Edward VII., *b.* Nov. 26th, 1869, *d.* Nov. 20th, 1938: *m.* July 22nd, 1896, H.R.H. Prince Christian Frederik Carl Georg Valdemar Axel of Denmark, K.G., G.C.B., G.C.V.O. [elected King of Norway under style of H.M. Haakon VII. Nov. 18th 1905], who *d.* Sept. 21st, 1957, second son of H.M. the late King (Frederik VIII.) of Denmark, K.G., G.C.B., G.C.V.O.:—

Norway
Olav V. [Alexander Edward Christian Frederik] (*King of Norway*), K.G., K.T., G.C.B., G.C.V.O., *b.* July 2nd, 1903; ed. at Balliol Coll., Oxford; ascended the throne on the death of his father, Sept. 21st, 1957; is Hon. Adm. of Roy. Navy, Hon. Air Ch. Marshal RAF, Col.-in-Ch., Green Howards, and Hon. Col. of 100 (E) Medium Regt. RA (V); Sovereign of Order of St. Olav of Norway; has Grand Cross of Orders of Elephant of Denmark, Seraphim of Sweden, and Leopold of Belgium, Grand Cdr. of Orders of Dannebrog of Denmark, Solomon of Ethiopia, St. George and St. Constantine of Greece, Tadj. of Iran, Falcon of Iceland, Chrysanthemum of Japan, Lion and Orange Nassau of Netherlands, Sun of Peru, St. Bento d'Avis of Portugal, and Chula Chom Klao of Thailand with Chain of Yugoslavian Grand Star and Merit of Italian Republic, U.S. Legion of Merit, French Croix de Guerre and Medaille Militaire, Greek Mil. Cross, and Mil. Cross of Netherlands, and Grand Cross, Special Class of Order of Merit of Federal Republic of Germany; received Roy. Victorian Chain 1955; GCVO (Hon.) 1923, GCB (Hon. Mil) 1946, KG 1959, KT 1962: *m.* March 21st, 1929, HRH Princess Märtha Sophie Louise Dagmar Thyra of Sweden, who *d.* April 5th, 1954, da. of HRH the late Duke (Oscar Carl Wilhelm) of Västergötland, GCVO, and has issue living, *Prince Harald, GCVO* (*Crown Prince of Norway*), *b.* Feb. 21st, 1937; ed. at Balliol Coll., Oxford; has Grand Cross of Orders of St. Olav of Norway, Elephant of Denmark, Seraphim of Sweden, Leopold of Belgium, Southern Cross of Brazil, White Rose of Finland, St. George and St. Constantine of Greece, Falcon of Iceland, Merit of Republic of Italy, Merit of Austria, Chula Chom Klao of Thailand, Star of Yugoslavia, and Grand Cross of Order of Merit of Federal Republic of Germany; GCVO (Hon.) 1955: *m.* Aug. 29th, 1968, Sonja, da. of Karl August Haraldsen, and has issue living, *Prince* Haakon Magnus *b.* July 20th, 1973, *Princess* Märtha Louise, *b.* Sept. 22nd, 1971,—*Princess* Ragnhild, Alexandra, *b.* June 9th, 1930: *m.* May 15th, 1953, Erling Sven Lorentzen, and has issue living, Haakon *b.* Aug. 23rd, 1954, Ingeborg *b.* Feb. 27th, 1957, Ragnhild Alexandra *b.* May 8th, 1968,—*Princess* Astrid Maud Ingeborg, *b.* Feb. 12th, 1932; ed. at Lady Margaret Hall, Oxford; Grand Cross of Orders of St. Olav of Norway, and White Rose of Finland: *m.* Jan. 12th, 1961, Johan Martin Ferner, of Vinderen, Oslo, and has issue living, Alexander *b.* March 15th, 1965, Carl Christian, *b.* Oct. 22nd, 1972, Cathrine *b.* July 22nd, 1962, Benedikte *b.* Sept. 27th, 1963, Elizabeth *b.* March 30th, 1969. *Residence,*—Det Kgl. Slott, Oslo, Norway.

OTHER LIVING DESCENDANTS OF QUEEN VICTORIA.

Descendants of *HRH the Duke of Edinburgh* (*Duke of Saxe-Coburg and Gotha*), 2nd son of Queen Victoria.

Grandchildren of H.R.H. the late Princess Marie Alexandra Victoria (*Queen of Roumania*), V.A., C.I., R.R.C. (infra):—

Issue of H.M. the late King Carol II., K.G., G.C.V.O., *b.* Oct. 16th, 1893, *d.* April 4th, 1953; renounced succession to the throne of Roumania Dec. 8th, 1925, subsequently proclaimed King as Carol II, June 8th 1930; left Roumania Sept. 6th, 1940: *m.* 1st, March 10th 1921 (marriage dissolved June 21st, 1928), H.R.H. Princess Hélène, el. dau. of H.M. the late King (Constantine) of the Hellenes (infra); 2ndly, July 3rd, 1947, Elena (granted the style of Princess), (of Vila Marasol, 7, Rua Afonso Henriques, Estoril, Portugal), da. of Nicolas Lupescu:—

Roumania
(By 1st marriage) *King* Mihai (Michael), G.C.V.O., *b.* Oct. 25th, 1921; reigned as King of Roumania (under Regency) July 20th, 1927 to June 8th, 1930; re-ascended the throne on departure of his father, Sept. 6th, 1940: deprived of the throne Dec. 30th, 1947; is Hon. Air Ch. Marshal Roy. Hellenic Air Force; a Ch. Com. of American Legion of Merit; has Grand Cross of Order of the German Eagle, Orders of Victory of Russia, and of Annunciation of Italy, and Legion of Honour; G.C.V.O. (Hon.) 1938: *m.* June 10th, 1948, H.R.H. Princess Anne Antoinette Françoise Charlotte, dau. of H.R.H. the late Prince René Charles Marie Joseph of Bourbon-Parma, and has issue living, *Princess* Margaret, *b.* March 26th, 1949,—*Princess* Helen, *b.* Nov. 15th, 1950,—*Princess* Irina, *b.* Feb. 28th, 1953,—*Princess* Sophie, *b.* Oct. 29th, 1957,—*Princess* Maria, *b.* July 13th, 1964. *Residence,*—106, Route de Suisse, 1290, Versoix-Geneva, Switzerland.

Grandchildren of Adm. of the Fleet H.R.H. the late Prince Alfred Ernest Albert, K.G., K.T., K.P., G.C.B., G.C.S.I., G.C.M.G., G.C.I.E., G.C.V.O., P.C., Duke of Edinburgh (cr. 1866), and Duke of Saxe-Coburg and Gotha, 2nd son of Queen Victoria:—

Issue of H.R.H. the late Princess Marie Alexandra Victoria (*Queen of Roumania*), V.A., C.I., R.R.C., *b.* Oct. 29th, 1875, *d.* July 18th, 1938: *m.* Jan. 11th, 1893, H.M. the King (Ferdinand) of Roumania, K.G., G.C.B., who *d.* July 20th, 1927:—

Prince Nicolas HOHENZOLLERN, *b.* Aug. 18th, 1903; ed. at Eton; was first of the three Regents July 1927 to June 1930; late Gen. of Div. Roumanian Army, Air Marshal Roumanian Air Force; Hon. Lt. in British Navy, a Chevalier of Order of Ferdinand I. of Roumania, and a Bailiff Grand Cross of Sovereign Order of Malta; has Gold Chain of Order of Carol I. of Roumania, Grand Cross of Legion of Honour, and of Orders of Leopold of Belgium, White Eagle of Poland, White Lion of Czechoslovakia, and Redeemer of Greece; deprived of membership of Roy. Family and Roy. rights and privileges April 9th, 1937, and assumed the surname of Brana; assumed by Royal Decree July 10th, 1942, the surname of Hohenzollern, and recognised as H.R.H. Prince of Hohenzollern and his wife as HRH Princess of Hohenzollern: *m.* 1st, Oct. 28th, 1931, Ioana, who *d.* Feb. 19th, 1962, having in 1928 assumed her grandmother's surname of Doletti, da. of Ion-Dumitrescu-Tohani, and formerly wife of Radu Saveanu; 2ndly, June 13th, 1967, Thereza, da. of Jeronymo de Avellar Figueira de Mello. *Residences,*—34, Calle Alfonso XII, Madrid 14, Spain; 65, Avenue de Bethusy, Lausanne, 1012, Switzerland.——*Princess* Ileana, *b.* Jan. 5th, 1909; a religious (Mother Alexandra): *m.* 1st, July 26th, 1931 (m. diss. 1954), HI and RH the Archduke Anton of Austria; 2ndly, June 19th, 1954 (m. diss. 1965), Dr. Stefan Issarescu, and has issue living (by 1st m.) *Archduke* Stefan of (28403, Beech Hill Rd., Farmington, Michigan, USA), *b.* Aug. 15th, 1932: *m.* Aug. 26th, 1954, Jerrine, da. of Charles B. Soper, of Boston, USA, and has issue living, Christopher, *b.* Jan. 26th, 1957, Peter *b.* Feb. 19th, 1959, Anton *b.* Nov. 7th, 1964, Ileana *b.* Jan. 4th, 1958, Constantza *b.* Oct. 2nd, 1960,—*Archduke* Dominic (of Hernstein, Berndorf, Lower Austria), *b.* July 4th, 1937: *m.* June 11th, 1960, Engel, da. of Ernst von Voss, of Houston, Texas, USA, and has issue living, *Archduke* Sandor *b.* Feb. 13th, 1965, *Archduke* Gregor *b.* Nov. 20th, 1965,—*Archduchess* Alexandra, *b.* May 21st, 1935: *m.* Aug. 1962, HRH Duke Eugen Eberhard Albrecht Maria Joseph Joan Rylski Robert Ulrich Philipp Odo Carl Hubert, of Württemberg,—*Archduchess* Maria Magdalena, *b.* Oct. 2nd, 1939: *m.* Aug. 29th, 1959, Baron Hans Ulrich von Holzhausen, of 23, Rennbahnstrasse, Salzburg-Parsch, Austria, and has issue living, *Baron* Johann Friedrich Anton *b.* July 29th, 1960, *Baron* Georg-Ferdinand, *b.* Feb. 16th, 1962, *Baroness* Alexandra Maria *b.* Jan. 22nd, 1963,—*Archduchess* Elizabeth, *b.* Jan. 15th, 1942: *m.* Aug. 3rd, 1964, Friedrich Josef Sandhofer, MD, of Walserberg, nr. Salzburg, Austria, and has issue living, Anton Dominic

Austria

Friedrich *b*. Oct. 26th, 1966, Margareta Elisabeth *b*. Sept. 10th, 1968, Andrea Alexandra *b*. Dec. 13th, 1969, Elisabeth Victoria Magdalena *b*. Nov. 16th, 1971. *Residence*—Monastery of the Transfiguration, Ellwood City, Pa., USA.

Grandson of HRH the late Princess Marie (Queen Marie of Yugoslavia), (infra):—
Issue of HM the late King Peter II of Yugoslavia (reigned 1934-45), *b*. Sept. 6th, 1923, *d*.
Nov. 3rd, 1970: *m*. HRH Princess Alexandra, da. of HM the late King Alexander of the
Hellenes (infra):—
Prince Alexander (*Crown Prince of Yugoslavia*) (Redlands Farm, Kirdford, nr. Billingshurst, Sussex; **Yugoslavia**
Cavalry Club), *b*. July 17th, 1945; Lt. 16th/5th The Queen's R. Lancers: *m*. 1972, Dona Maria
Gloria, da. of Dom Pedro Gastao of Orleans Braganza.

Grandsons of the late H.R.H. Princess Marie Alexandra Victoria (*Queen of
Roumania*), V.A., C.I., R.R.C. (ante) :—
Issue of H.R.H. the late Princess Marie (*Queen Marie of Yugoslavia*), *b*. Jan. 9th, 1900,
d. June 22nd, 1961 : *m*. June 8th, 1922, H.M. the King (Alexander) of Yugoslavia, who
d. (by assassination) Oct. 9th, 1934 :—
Prince Tomislav, *b*. Jan. 19th, 1928; ed. at Oundle, and at Clare Coll., Camb.: *m*. June 6th, 1957
HGDH Princess Margarita Alice Thyra Viktoria Marie Louise Scholastica, da. of HRH the late Margrave (Berthold) of Baden (infra), and has issue living, *Prince* Nikolas, *b*. March 15th, 1958,—*Princes;*
Katarina, *b*. Nov. 28th, 1959. *Residence*,—Redlands Farm, Kirdford, Billingshurst, Sussex.——
Prince Andrej, *b*. June 28th, 1929; ed. at Oundle, and at Clare Coll., Camb. (BA 1950): *m*. 1s;,
Aug. 2nd, 1956 (divorce Feb. 20th, 1962), HH Princess Christina Margarete, da. of HH the late
Prince Christoph Ernst August of Hesse [infra]; 2ndly, Sept. 28th, 1963, HSH Princess Kira Melita
Feodora Marie Viktoria Alexandra, da. of HSH the 6th Prince of Leiningen (infra), and has issu;
living, (by 1st m.) *Prince* Marko, *b*. Feb. 4th, 1960,—*Princess* Marija Tatiana, *b*. July 18th, 1957,—
(by 2nd m.) *Prince* Karl Vladimir, *b*. March 11th, 1964,—*Prince* Dimitri, *b*. April, 1965. *Residence,*—
Place de la Mairie, F-06 St Paul, France, A.M.

Granddaughter of H.R.H. Princess Ileana of Roumania (ante) :—
Issue of H.I. and R.H. the late Archduchess Maria Ileana, *b*. Dec. 18th, 1933, *d*. Jan. 11th,
1959 : *m*. Dec. 7th, 1957, Count Jaroslav Franz Josef Ignazius Maria Kottulinsky, who *d*.
Jan. 11th, 1959 :—
Countess Ileana, *b*. Aug. 25th, 1958.

Grandson of HRH Prince Alfred Ernest Albert, Duke of Edinburgh (ante):—
Issue of H.R.H. the late Princess Victoria Melita (" VICTORIA FEODOROVNA ") (*Grand
Duchess Kirill (Cyril) of Russia*), V.A., C.I., *b*. Nov. 25th, 1876, *d*. Nov. 2nd, 1936:
m. 1st, April 19th, 1894 (marriage dissolved Dec. 21st, 1901), H.R.H. Ernst Ludwig Karl
Albert Wilhelm, then Reigning Grand Duke of Hesse, who *d*. Oct. 9th, 1937 (infra);
2ndly, Oct. 8th, 1905, H.I.H. the Grand Duke Kirill (Cyril) Wladimirovitch of Russia,
who *d*. Oct. 12th, 1938 (first cousin of the late Tsar, Nicholas II.):— **Russia**
(By 2nd marriage) *Grand Duke* Wladimir Kirillovitch, *b*. Aug. 30th, 1917; ed. at London Univ.;
is Head of the House of Romanoff (Imperial House of Russia): *m*. Aug. 13th, 1948, HRH Princess
Leonida, da. of HRH the late Prince George Alexandrovitch Balgration of Mukhrani (Head of former
Royal House of Georgia), and widow of Sumner Moore Kirby, and has issue living, *Grand Duchess*
Marie, *b*. Dec. 23rd, 1953. *Residence*,—Guisando 17, Ciudad Puerta de Hierro, Madrid 35, Spain.

Grandchildren of HRH the late Princess Victoria Melita (*Grand Duchess Kirill of
Russia*), V.A., C.I. (ante) :—
Issue of the late H.I.H. Grand Duchess Marie Kirillovna, *b*. Feb. 2nd, 1907, *d*. Oct. 27th, 1951:
m. Nov. 24th, 1925, H.S.H. the 6th Prince (Friedrich Karl) of Leiningen, who *d*. Aug. 2nd,
1946 :— **Leiningen**
Prince Emich Cyrill Ferdinand Hermann (*7th Prince of Leiningen*), *b*. Oct. 18th, 1926 : *m*. Aug. 10th,
1950, H.H. Duchess Eilika Stephanie Elisabeth Thekla Juliana, dau. of H.R.H. the Hereditary
Grand Duke (Nikolaus Friedrich Wilhelm) of Oldenburg, and has issue living, *Prince* Karl-
Emich Nikolaus Friedrich Hermann, *b*. June 12th, 1952,—*Prince* Andreas, *b*. Nov. 27th, 1955,—
Princess Melita Elisabeth Bathildis Helene Margarita, *b*. June 10th, 1951,—*Princess* Stephanie
Margarita, *b*. Oct. 1st, 1958. *Residence,*—Fürstl. Palais, Amorbach, Bavaria, Germany.——
Prince Karl Vladimir Ernst Heinrich, *b*. Jan. 2nd, 1928: *m*. Feb. 20th, 1957, (m. diss. 4th Dec. 1965),
HRH Princess Marie-Luise, da. of the HM late King Boris III of Bulgaria, and has issue living.
Prince Karl Boris Frank Markwart, *b*. April 17th, 1960,—*Prince* Hermann Friedrich Roland Fer-
nando *b*. April 16th, 1963.——*Prince* Fredrich Wilhelm Berthold, *b*. June 18th, 1938: *m*. July 9th,
1960 (divorce July 4th, 1962), Karin Evelyne Goss. *Residence*,—Fürste Palais Amorbach, Bavaria,
Germany.——*Princess* Kira Melita Feodora Marie Viktoria Alexandra, *b*. July 18th, 1930: *m*. Sept.
28th, 1963, HRH Prince Andrej of Yugoslavia (ante).——*Princess* Margarita Ileana Viktoria, *b*. May
9th, 1932: *m*. Feb. 3rd, 1951, HH Prince Friedrich Wilhelm Ferdinand Josef Maria Manuel Georg
Meinrad Fidelis Benedikt Michael Hubertus of Hohenzollern, and has issue living, *Prince* Karl **Hohenzollern**
Friedrich Emich Meinrad Benedikt Fidelis Maria Michael Gerold, *b*. April 20th, 1952,—*Prince*
Albrecht Johannes Hermann Meinrad Stephan, *b*. Aug. 3rd, 1954,—*Prince* Ferdinand Maria Fidelis
Leopold Meinrad Valentin, *b*. Feb. 14th, 1960. *Residence*,—Landhaus Josefslust, Sigmaringen, Hohen-
zollern, Germany.——*Princess* Mechtilde Alexandra, *b*. Jan. 2nd, 1936: *m*. Nov. 25th, 1961, Karl
Anton Bauscher, of 8600 Bamberg, Georgenstrasse 10/12a, Germany, and has issue living, Ulf Karl
Heinz Stephan Kraft, *b*. Feb. 20th, 1963,—Berthold Alexander Eric, *b*. Oct. 31st, 1958.

Issue of the late H.I.H. Grand Duchess Kira Kirollovna, *b*. May 9th, 1909: *d*. Sept. 8th,
1967: *m*. May 2nd, 1938, H.R.H. Prince Louis Ferdinand Viktor Eduard Adalbert Michael
Hubertus of Prussia (infra):—
(*Prince*) Friedrich Wilhelm (Louis Ferdinand Hubertus Michael Kirill), *b*. Feb. 9th, 1939: *m*. Aug. 22nd **Prussia**
1967, Waltraud, da. of the late Alois Freydag, lawyer, of Plön, Germany and has issue living, (*Prince*)
Philip Kirill Friedrich Wilhelm Moritz Boris Zdenko *b*. April 23rd, 1968.——(*Prince*) (Wilhelm Hein-
rich) Michael (Louis Ferdinand Friedrich Franz Wladimir) (Mozartstrasse 48, 6232 Bad Soden/
Taunus, Germany), *b*. March 22nd, 1940: *m*. Sept. 23rd, 1966, Jutta, da. of Otto Jörn, and has issue
living (*Princess*) Micaela Maria, *b*. March 5th, 1967, (*Princess*) Nataly Alexandra Caroline Jan. 13th,
1970.——(*Prince*) Louis Ferdinand (Oskar Christian), *b*. Aug. 25th, 1944: *m*. May 24th, 1975,
Countess Donata, only da. of Siegfried, 4th Prince of Castel-Rudenhausen.——*Prince* Christian
Sigismund (Louis Ferdinand Killan), *b*. March 14th, 1946.——*Princess* Marie-Cécile (Kira Viktoria
Luise), *b*. May 28th, 1942: *m*. Dec. 3rd, 1965, HH Duke Friedrich August Wilhelm Christian Ernst
of Oldenburg, of 2432, Sievershagen, W. Germany, and has issue living *Duke* Paul Wladimir Nikolaus
Louis Ferdinand Peter Max Karl Emich, *b*. Aug. 16th, 1969,—*Duchess* Rixa Marie Alix Kira Altburg,
b. Sept. 17th, 1970.——*Princess* Kira (Auguste Viktoria Frederike), *b*. June 27th, 1943: *m*. Sept. 11th,
1973, Thomas Frank Liepsener, of 71, Krennerweg 4, Munich, 8.——*Princess* Xenia (Sophie Charlotte
Cecilie), *b*. Dec. 9th, 1949: *m*. Jan. 26th, 1973, Per-Edvard Lithander.

Grandchildren of HRH the late Princess Alexandra Louise Olga Victoria (*Princess
Hohenlohe-Langenburg*) (infra) :—
Issue of H.S.H. the late Prince Gottfried Viktor Hermann Alfred Paul Maximilian (8th
Prince of Hohenlohe-Langenburg), *b*. March 24th, 1897, *d*. May 11th, 1960 : *m*. April 20th,
1931, H.R.H. Princess Margarita (of Langenburg Castle, Württemberg, Germany), dau. of
HRH the late Prince Andrew of Greece, GCVO (infra):— **Hohenlohe-**
Prince Kraft Alexander Ernst Ludwig Georg Emich (*9th Prince of Hohenlohe-Langenburg*), *b*. June 25th, **Langenburg**
1935: *m*. June 5th, 1965, HSH Princess Charlotte Alexandra Maria Clothilde, da. of HSH Prince
Alexander Georg Maria Josef Ignatius of Croy, and has issue living, *Prince* Philipp Gottfried Alex-
ander, *b*. Jan. 20th, 1970,—*Princess* Cécile Marita Dorothea, *b*. Dec. 16th, 1967,—*Princess* Xenia
Margarita Anne, *b*. July 8th, 1972. *Residence*,—Langenburg Castle, Württemberg, Germany.——
Prince Georg Andreas Heinrich (Graf Spee Platz 14, 8, Munich 82, Germany), *b*. Nov. 24th, 1938:

m. Aug. 14th, 1968, HSH Princess Luise Pauline Amelie Vibeke Emma, da. of HSH Prince Georg Ulrich of Schönburg-Waldenburg, and has issue living, *Princess* Katarina Clementine Beatrix, *b.* Nov. 21st, 1972,—*Princess* Tatiana Louise, *b.* Feb. 10th, 1975.——*Prince* Ruprecht Sigismund Philipp Ernst, *b.* April 7th, 1944.——*Prince* Albrecht Wolfgang Christoph (twin), *b.* April 7th, 1944.——*Princess* Beatrix Alice Melita Margarita, *b.* July 10th, 1936.

Issue of HSH the late Princess Marie Melita Leopoldine Victoria Feodora Alexandra Sophie, *b.* Jan. 18th, 1899; *d.* Nov. 8th, 1967: *m.* Feb. 15th, 1916, HH (Wilhelm) Friedrich Christian Günther Albert Adolf Georg, Duke of Schleswig-Holstein-Sonderburg-Glücksburg, **Schleswig-** who *d.* Feb. 10th, 1965:—
Holstein
Prince (Friedrich Ernst) Peter (*Duke of Schleswig-Holstein-Sonderburg-Glucksburg*) (2335, Grünholz Kreis Eckenförde, Germany), *b.* April 30th, 1922: *m.* Oct. 9th, 1947, HSH Princess Marie Alix da .of HSH Prince Stephan of Schaumburg-Lippe, and has issue living, *Prince* Christoph, *b.* Aug 22nd, 1949,—*Prince* Alexander, *b.* July 9th, 1953,—*Princess* Marita, *b.* Sept. 5th, 1948: *m.* May 23rd, 1975, Baron Wilfried von Plotho,—*Princess* Ingeborg, *b.* July 9th, 1956.——*Princess* Marie Alexandra Caroline Mathilde Viktoria Irene, *b.* July 9th, 1927.

Grandchildren of HRH Prince Alfred Ernest Albert, Duke of Edinburgh (ante):—
Issue of H.R.H. the late Princess Alexandra Louise Olga Victoria, *b.* Sept. 1st, 1878, *d.* April 16th, 1942 : *m.* April 20th, 1896, H.S.H. Ernst Wilhelm Friedrich Karl Maximilian, 7th Prince of Hohenlohe-Langenburg, who *d.* Dec. 11th, 1950 :—
Princess Irma Helene, *b.* July 4th, 1902. *Residence,*—Langenburg Castle, Württemberg, Germany.
Issue of H.R.H. the late *Princess* Beatrice Leopoldine Victoria, *VA, b.* April 20th, 1884, **Bourbon-** *d.* July 13th, 1966: *m.* July 15th, 1909, H.R.H. Prince Alfonso Maria of Orleans, Infante of
Orleans Spain, 2nd Duke of Galliera, who *d.* Aug. 6th, 1975:—
Prince Alvaro (Antonio Fernando Carlos Philip) (*Duke of Galliera*) (Via Luigi Capucci 12, Rome 00147, Italy), *b.* April 20th, 1910; ed. at Winchester; is an AFRAeS, and an AMIMechE: *m.* July 10th, 1937 Carla, el da. of the late Senator Leopoldo Gerolamo Parodi-Delfino, and has issue living, *Prince* Alfonso (Ramonal Vuelta de los Perjaros, Santacruz de Tenerife, Canary Islands), *b.* Aug. 23rd, 1941: *m.* Jan. 12th, 1966, Donna Emilia Ferrara-Pignatelli di Strongoli, da. of Vincenzo Prince of Strongoli, and has issue living, *Prince* Alfonso *b.* Jan. 2nd, 1968, *Prince* Alvaro *b.* Oct. 4th, 1969,— *Prince* Alvaro, *b.* March 1st, 1947,—*Princess* Gerarda, *b.* Aug. 25th, 1939 : *m.* July 26th, 1963, Harry Freeman Saint, of 211, Central Park, New York, NY 10024, USA, and has issue living, Marc *b.* March 20th, 1969, Carla *b.* May 22nd, 1967,—*Princess* Beatriz, *b.* April 27th, 1943 : *m.* April 25th, 1964, *Count* Tomaso Farini, and has issue living, *Count* Gerardo *b.* Nov. 23rd, 1967, *Countess* Elena *b.* Oct. 27th, 1969.

Descendants of HRH the Duke of Connaught and Strathearn, 3rd son of Queen Victoria.

Grandchildren of H.R.H. the late Princess Margaret (Victoria Augusta Charlotte Norah) (*Crown Princess of Sweden, Duchess of Skåne*) (infra) :—
Issue of H.R.H. the late Prince Gustaf Adolf (Oscar Fredrik Arthur Edmund) (*Duke of Västerbotten*), G.C.V.O., *b.* April 22nd, 1906, *d.* Jan. 26th, 1947 : *m.* Oct. 20th, 1932, HH Princess Sibylla Calma Marie Alice Bathildis Feodora, who *d.* Nov. 28th, 1972, da. of HRH the late Prince (Leopold) Karl Eduard Georg Albert, Duke of Saxe-Coburg and Gotha (infra):—
Sweden *King* Carl Gustaf XVI (Folke Hubertus) (*King of Sweden*) (Royal Palace, 11130 Stockholm, Sweden; Solliden, Öland, Stenhammar, Södermanland), *b.* April 30th, 1946; *s.* Sept. 15th, 1973; Hon. Adm. RN 1975. Orders of Seraphim of Sweden, Elephant of Denmark, Falcon of Iceland, Saint Olav of Norway, White Rose of Finland, and Chrysanthemum of Japan.——*Princess* Margaretha (Desirée Victoria), *b.* Oct. 31st, 1934; has Order of Seraphim of Sweden: *m.* June 30th, 1964, John Kenneth Ambler (Knt. Cdr. Roy. Vasa Order), of Chippinghurst Manor, Cuddesdon, Oxon., and has issue living, Charles Edward, *b.* July 14th, 1966,—James Patrick, *b.* June 10th, 1969,—Sybilla Louise, *b.* April 14th, 1965.——*Princess* Birgitta (Ingeborg Alice), *b*, Jan. 19th, 1937; has Order of Seraphim of Sweden: *m.* May 30th, 1961, HSH Prince Johann Georg (Carl Leopold Eitel Friedrich Meinrad Maria Hubertus Michael) of Hohenzollern, and has issue living, *Prince* Carl Christian (Friedrich Johannes Maria Meinrad Hubertus Edmund), *b.* April 5th, 1962,—*Prince* Hubertus Gustav-Adolf Veit Georg Meinrad Maria Alexander, *b.* June 10th, 1966,—*Princess* Désirée Margaretha Victoria Louise Sibylla Catharina Maria, *b.* Nov. 27th, 1964. *Residence,*—70, Maxstrasse, Grünwald, Munich, Germany.——*Princess* Désirée (Elisabeth Sibylla), *b.* June 2nd, 1938; has Order of Seraphim of Sweden: *m.* June 5th, 1964, Baron Niclas (Nils August Otto Carl) Silfverschiöld, of Koberg, Sollebrunn, Sweden, and has issue living, *Baron* Carl Otto Edmund, *b.* March 22nd, 1965,—*Baroness* Christina-Louise Ewa Madelaine, *b.* Sept. 29th, 1966,—*Baroness* Hélène Ingeborg Sibylla, *b.* Sept. 20th, 1968.——*Princess* Christina (Louise Helena), *b.* Aug. 3rd, 1943; has Order of Seraphim of Sweden: *m.* June 15th, 1974, Tord Magnuson, of Stockholm, and has issue living, Gustaf, *b.* Aug. 8th, 1975.

Grandchildren of F-M HRH Prince Arthur William Patrick Albert, 1st Duke of Connaught and Strathearn, 3rd son of Queen Victoria:—
Issue of H.R.H. the late Princess Margaret (Victoria Augusta Charlotte Norah) (*Crown Princess of Sweden, Duchess of Skåne*), *b.* Jan. 15th, 1882, *d.* May 1st, 1920 : *m.* June 15th, 1905, H.R.H. the Crown Prince (Oscar Fredrik Willhelm Olaf Gustaf Adolf) of Sweden, Duke of Skåne, GCB, GCVO,—later HM King Gustaf VI Adolf, who *d.* Sept. 15th, 1973:—

Count Sigvard (Oscar Fredrik) BERNADOTTE (of Villagatan 10, Stockholm, O, Sweden), *b.* June 7th, 1907; renounced right of succession March 1934 adopting the surname of Bernadotte; is no longer a member of the Roy. House of Sweden ; *cr.* Count Bernadotte of Wisborg July 2nd, 1951 ; has Order of Star of North of Sweden, and Order of Elephant of Denmark: *m.* 1st, March 8th, 1934 (m. diss. Oct. 14th, 1943), Erika Maria Regina Rosalie, da. of Anton Patzek; 2ndly, Oct. 26th, 1943, Sonia Hélène (m. diss. 1961), da. of the late Robert Alexander Robbert shipowner, of Copenhagen, Denmark; 3rdly, July 30th, 1961, Marianne LINDBERG, da. of Helge Lindberg of Helsingborg, and has issue living, (by 2nd m.) *Count* Michael (Sigvard), *b.* April 21st, 1944.——*Prince* Bertil (Gustaf Oscar Carl Eugen) (*Duke of Halland*), GCB, *b.* Feb. 28th, 1912; Adm. Swedish Navy; was Assist. Naval Attaché to London 1942-45; has Orders of Seraphim of Sweden, and of Elephant of Denmark; GCB (Hon. Civil) 1956. *Residence,*—Villa Solbacken, Djurgardsbrunn, Stockholm, Sweden.——*Count* Carl Johan (Arthur) BERNADOTTE, *b.* Oct. 31st, 1916; renounced right of succession Feb. 22nd, 1946, adopting the name of Bernadotte, and is no longer a member of the Roy. House of Sweden; *cr.* Count Bernadotte of Wisborg July 2nd, 1951: *m.* Feb. 19th, 1946, (Elin) Kerstin (Margareta), da. of Henning Wijkmark, of Stockholm, Dr. of Theology, and previously wife of Axel Johnson.——*Princess* Ingrid (Victoria Sofia Louise Margareta) (*HM Queen Ingrid, Queen Mother of Denmark*), *b.* March 28th, 1910: *m.* May 24th, 1935, HM King **Denmark** Frederik IX of Denmark, KG, GCB, GCVO, who *d.* Jan. 14th, 1972, and has issue living, *Princess* Margrethe (Alexandrine Thorhildur Ingrid) (*HM Queen of Denmark*), *b.* April 16th, 1940; ed. at Girton Coll., Camb.: *m.* June 10th, 1967, Count Henri Marie Jean André de Laborde de Monpezat (*cr.* HRH Prince Henrik of Denmark June 10th, 1967), and has issue living, *Prince* Frederik (André Henrik Christian) (*Crown Prince of Denmark*), *b.* May 26th, 1968, *Prince* Joachim (Holger Waldemar Christian) *b.* June 7th, 1969,—*Princess* Benedikte (Astrid Ingeborg Ingrid), *b.* April 29th, 1944: *m.* Feb. 3rd, 1968, HSH Prince Richard Casimir Karl August, Konstantin (6th) Prince of Sayn-Wittgenstein-Berleburg, and has issue living, *Prince* Gustav (Frederik Philip Richard) *b.* Jan. 12th, 1969, *Princess* Alexandra (Rosemary Ingrid Benedikte), *b.* Nov. 20th, 1970,—*Princess* Anne-Marie (Dagmar Ingrid) (*HM Queen of the Hellenes*), *b.* Aug. 30th, 1946; has Grand Cross of the Redeemer of Greece: *m.* Sept. 18th, 1964, HM King Constantine II of the Hellenes (infra), and has issue living, *Prince* Paul (*Crown Prince of the Hellenes, Duke of Sparta*), *b.* May 20th, 1967, *Prince* Nicolaos, *b.* Oct. 1st, 1969, *Princess* Alexia *b.* July 10th, 1965. *Residences,*—Amalienborg Palace, Copenhagen, Denmark; Fredensborg Palace, Denmark; Graasten Palace, Denmark.

Issue of the late HRH Lady (Victoria Patricia Helena Elizabeth Ramsay, VA, CI, *b.* March 17th, 1886, *d.* Jan. 12th, 1974; who on her marriage renounced by Roy. permission, the style and title of " HRH " and " Princess ", and adopted that of " Lady ", with precedence before Marchionesses of England: *m.* Feb. 27th, 1919, Adm. the Hon. Sir Alexander Robert Maule Ramsay, GCVO, KCB, DSO, who *d.* Oct. 8th, 1972:—

See E. Dalhousie, colls.

Descendants of HRH the Duke of Albany, 4th son of Queen Victoria.

Grandchildren of HRH the late Prince (Leopold) Carl Eduard (Georg Albert), Duke of Saxe-Coburg and Gotha (infra):—

Issue of HRH the late Hereditary Prince (Johann) Leopold Wilhelm Albert Ferdinand Viktor, *b.* Aug. 2nd, 1906, *d.* May 4th, 1972: *m.* 1st, March 14th, 1932 (divorce Feb. 26th, 1962), Baroness Feodora Maria Alma Margarete, da. of Baron Bernhard von der Horst, and formerly wife of Baron Wolf Sigismund Pergler von Perglas; 2ndly, May 3rd, 1962, Maria Theresa Elisabeth (MUELLER), da. of Max Reindl, of Bad Reichenhall:—

Saxe-Coburg and Gotha

(By 1st m.), *Hereditary Prince* Ernst Leopold (Eduard Wilhelm Josias), *b.* Jan. 14th, 1935: *m.* 1st, Feb. 4th, 1961 (divorce May 23rd, 1963), Ingeborg, da. of Richard Henig, of Herrenberg, Württemberg; 2ndly, May 29th, 1963. Gertraude, da. of Hermann Horst Pfeiffer, and has issue living (by 1st m.), *Prince* Hubertus Richard Ernst Eduard, *b.* Dec. 8th, 1961,—(by 2nd m.) *Prince* Ernst Josias, *b.* May 13th, 1965,—*Prince* Carl Eduard, *b.* July 25th, 1966,—*Prince* Ferdinand Christian, *b.* Dec. 13th, 1968,—*Princess* Victoria, *b.* Oct. 7th, 1963.——*Prince* Peter Albert Friedrich Josias, *b.* June 12th, 1939: *m.* May 11th, 1964, Roswitha, da. of Robert Breuer, and has issue living, *Prince* Peter, *b.* Oct. 4th, 1964,—*Prince* Malte, *b.* June 10th, 1966.——*Princess* (Caroline Mathilde Adelheid Sibylla) Marianne (Erika), *b.* April 5th, 1933: *m.* Dec. 5th, 1953, Michael (Adalbert Winifred) Nielsen, of 6601 Rubingen/Saar, Tannenstrasse 8, Germany, and has issue living, Margarete-Brigitte, *b.* Sept. 30th, 1954,—Renaté Christine, *b.* April 1st, 1957.

Grandchildren of HRH the late Prince Leopold George Duncan Albert, 1st Duke of Albany (infra):—

Issue of H.R.H. the late Prince (Leopold) Carl Eduard (Georg Albert), *b.* (posthumous) July 19th, 1884, *d.* March 6th, 1954: *s.* at his birth to the Dukedom of Albany (deprived of British peerages 1919), and to the Dukedom of Saxe-Coburg and Gotha July 30th, 1900 (deprived of this Dukedom Nov. 14th, 1918): *m.* Oct. 11th, 1905, H.H. Princess Victoria Adelheid Hélène Luise Marie Friederike, who *d.* Oct. 3rd, 1970, el. da. of HH the late Friedrich Ferdinand Georg Christian Karl Wilhelm, Duke of Schleswig-Holstein-Sonderburg-Glücksburg:—

Prince Friedrich Josias Carl Eduard Ernst Kyrill Harald, *b.* Nov. 29th, 1918: *m.* 1st, Jan. 25th, 1942 (divorce Sept. 19th, 1946) Countess Viktoria Luise (Friederike Caroline Mathilde), da. of Count Hans Solms Baruth; 2ndly, Feb. 14th, 1948 (m. diss. Sept. 1964), Denyse Henriette, da. of the late Robert Gaston de Muralt, of Berne; 3rdly, Oct. 30th, 1964, Katrin Anna Dorothea, da. of the late Dietrich Carl Bremme, of Berlin, and has issue living, (by 1st m.) *Prince* Andreas Michael Armin, Siegfried Hubertus Friedrich Hans (Weidenstieg 14, 2105 Seevetal 2, Germany), *b.* March 21st 1943: *m.* June 18th, 1971, Carin Dabelstein, and has issue living, *Princess* Stephanie Sibylla *b.* Jan. 31st, 1972,—(by 2nd m.) *Prince* Adrian Vinzenz Edward, *b.* Oct. 18th, 1955,—*Princess* Marie Claudia Sibylla, *b.* May 22nd, 1949: *m.* March 27th, 1971, Gion Schäfer, of Dennigkofenweg 73, 3073, Güemligen, Switzerland, and has issue living, Maria Christina Sibylla, *b.* June 23rd, 1972,—*Princess* Beatrice Charlotte, *b.* July 15th, 1951. *Residences,*—Schloss Greinburg, Grein-on-Danube, Austria; Coburg, Elsässerstrasse 8, Germany.——*Princess* Caroline Mathilde Helene Ludwiga Auguste Beatrice, *b.* June 22nd, 1912: *m.* 1st, Dec. 14th, 1931 (divorce May 2nd, 1938), Count Friedrich Wolfgang zu Castell-Rüdenhausen, who *d.* (presumed killed in action) June 11th, 1940; 2ndly, June 22nd, 1938, Capt. Max Schnirring, German Air Force, who *d.* (killed on active service during 1939-45 War) July 7th, 1944; 3rdly, Dec. 21st, 1948 (marriage annulled Oct. 10th, 1949) Jim Andree, and has issue living, (by 1st m.) *Count* Bertram Friedrich (Nibelungenstrasse 3/16, Vienna I, Austria), *b.* July 12th, 1932: *m.* Oct. 10th, 1964, Countess Felicitas, da. of Count Hanno Herward Maria Josef Leo von Auersperg, and has issue living, *Count* Dominik Dmitriy Johannes Fredrich, *b.* July 20th, 1965, *Count* Michael Alexis Wolfgang Friedrich, *b.* 1967,—*Count* Konradin Friedrich (Vesta, Finland), *b.* Oct. 10th 1933: *m.* July 6th, 1961, Märta, da. of Bjarne Lönegren, of Vesta, Finland, and has issue living, *Count* Carl Eduard (Friedrich Hubertus) *b.* March 15th, 1964, *Countess* Anne Charlotte (Catharina Victoria) *b.* April 7th, 1962,—*Countess* Victoria Adelheid Clementine Louise, *b.* Feb. 26th, 1935: *m.* June 20th, 1960, (John) Miles Huntington-Whiteley [see Huntington-Whiteley, Bt.],—(by 2nd m.) Calma Barbara, *b.* Nov. 18th, 1938: *m*, July 5th, 1961, Richard Berger, and has issue living, Richard, *b.* July 7th, 1962, Victor, *b.* 1963, Samuel Clinton, *b.* May 28th, 1965, Wesley, *b.* May 11th, 1967, David, *b.* Sept. 25th, 1968, Sascha, *b.* Sept. 22nd, 1961,—Dagmar Sibylla, *b.* Nov. 22nd, 1940: *m.* Feb. 26th, 1964, Henry Walz, of Hohensteinstrasse, 11, Memmelsdorf, Bamberg, Germany, and has issue living, Maria *b.* Aug. 14th, 1965, Larissa *b.* Sept. 16th, 1967. *Residence—*

Issue of H.R.H. the late Prince Leopold George Duncan Albert, K.G., K.T., G.C.S.I., G.C.M.G., P.C., 1st Duke of Albany, 4th son of H.M. the late Queen Victoria, *b.* April 7th, 1853, *d.* March 28th, 1884: *m.* April 27th, 1882, H.S.H. Princess Helene Friederike Auguste, V.A., C.I., R.R.C., who *d.* Sept. 1st, 1922, dau. of H.S.H. the late Georg (II.) Viktor, G.C.B., Reigning Prince of Waldeck and Pyrmont:—

Athlone

H.R.H. *Princess* Alice Mary Victoria Augusta Pauline (*Princess Alice, Countess of Athlone*), *V.A., G.C.V.O., G.B.E.,* *b.* Feb. 25th, 1883 ; Hon. D.Litt. London Univ. 1933, Queen's Univ., Kingston, Canada 1943, McGill Univ., Canada 1944, and Birmingham Univ. 1946 ; Hon. LL.D. St. Andrews Univ. 1951; a D.G.St.J., and Comdt.-in-Ch. Women's Transport Ser. (First Aid Nursing Yeo.); Chancellor of Univ. of W. Indies 1950-71; sometime Chm. of Govs. of Roy. Holloway Coll.; received Hon. Freedom of Weavers' Co. 1947, of Vintners' Co. 1956, and of Gold and Silver Wyre Drawers Co. 1965; Grand Cross of Legion of Honour; GBE (Civil) 1937, GCVO 1948: *m.* Feb. 10th, 1904, Maj.-Gen. the 1st Earl of Athlone, KG, GCB, GCMG, GCVO, DSO, PC, who *d.* Jan. 16th, 1957, 3rd son of HH Prince Francis Duke of Teck, GCB, and HRH the late Princess Mary Adelaide Wilhelmina Elizabeth, da. of 1st Duke of Cambridge, son of King George III, and has issue living [see E. Athlone (ext.)]. *Residence,*—Clock House, Kensington Palace, W8.

Descendants of HRH Princess Victoria Adelaide Mary Louise VA, CI, RRC (Princess Royal), German Empress and Queen of Prussia, el. da. of Queen Victoria.

Grandchildren of HIM Wilhelm II, German Emperor (infra):—

Issue of H.I.H. the late Crown Prince Friedrich Wilhelm Victor August Ernst of Prussia, *b.* May 6th, 1882 ; renounced succession to the throne of Germany Dec. 1st, 1918 ; *d.* July 20th, 1951 : *m.* June 6th, 1905, H.H. Duchess Cecilie Auguste Marie, who *d.* May 6th, 1954, dau. of H.R.H. the late Friedrich Franz III, Reigning Grand Duke of Mecklenburg-(Schwerin) :—

Prussia

Prince Louis Ferdinand Viktor Eduard Adalbert Michael Hubertus, *b.* Nov. 9th, 1907 ; Dr. Phil. 1931, formerly Lieut. German Air Force : *m.* May 2nd, 1938, H.I.H. the Grand Duchess Kira Kirillovna, who *d.* Sept. 8th, 1967, da. of H.I.H. the late Grand Duke Kirill (Cyril) Wladimirovitch of Russia (ante) and has issue living [see ante]. *Residences,*—Wuemmehof, Bremen-Borgfeld, Germany; 9, Koenigsallee, Berlin-Grunewald, Germany.——*Princess* Alexandrine Irene, *b.* April 7th, 1915. *Residence,*—5, Ottostrasse, Starnberg, Upper Bavaria, Germany.——*Princess* Cecilie Viktoria Anastasia Zita Thyra Adelheid, *b.* Sept. 5th, 1917, *d.* April 21st, 1975: *m.* June 21st, 1949, Capt. Clyde Kenneth Harris, US Army, who *d.* March 2nd, 1958, and has issue living, Kira Alexandrine Brigid Cecilie Ingrid, *b.* Oct. 20th, 1954. *Residence,*—2410, van Buren St., Amarillo, Texas, USA.

Grandchildren of the late Crown Prince Friedrich Wilhelm Viktor August Ernst of Prussia (ante) :—

Issue of H.R.H. the late Prince Wilhelm Friedrich Franz Joseph Christian Olaf of Prussia.
Lieut. German Inf., *b.* July 4th, 1906 ; renounced his rights as first-born son 1933 ; *d*,
(of wounds received in action during European War) May 26th, 1940 : *m.* June 3rd, 1933.
Dorothea, who *d.* May 7th, 1972, only da. of the late Alexander von Salviati :—
Princess Felicitas Cecilie Alexandrine Helene Dorothea, *b.* June 7th, 1934 : *m.* Sept. 12th, 1958 (m. diss.
May, 1972), Dinnies Friedrich Karl von der Osten, and has issue living, Dinnies Wilhelm Karl
Alexander, *b.* Feb. 15th, 1962,—Hubertus Christoph Joachim Friedrich, *b.* May 5th, 1964,—Fried-
erike Thyra Marion Wilhelmine Dorothea, *b.* July 14th, 1959,—Cecilie Felicitas Katharina Sophie, *b.*
March 12th, 1967. *Residence*,—2055, Wohltcrf, nr. Hamburg, Am Sachsenwald 3, Germany.——
Princess Christa Friederike Alexandrine Viktoria (Flemingstrasse 67, 8 Munchen 81, Germany), *b.*
Oct. 31st, 1936: *m.* March 24th, 1960, Peter Paul Eduard Maria Clemens Maximilian Franz von
Assisi Liebes, who *d.* May 5th, 1967.

Issue of H.R.H. the late Prince Hubertus Karl Wilhelm, of Prussia, *b.* Sept. 30th, 1909, *d.*
April 8th, 1950 : *m.* 1st, Dec. 29th, 1941 (divorce Jan 4th, 1943), Baroness Maria Anna
Sybilla Margarete, dau. of Baron Alexander Wilhelm Bernhard Ernst von Humbolt-
Dachroeden: 2ndly, June 5th, 1943, HSH Princess Magdalena Pauline (647, Büdingen,
Oberhof, Germany), da. of the late HSH Prince Heinrich XXXVI. Reuss:—
(By 2nd marriage) *Princess* Anastasia Victoria Cecilie Hermine, *b.* Feb. 14th, 1944: *m.* Nov. 8th
1965, H.S.H. the Hereditary Prince Aloys Konstantin Karl Eduard Joseph Johann Antonius
Gerhard Georg Benediktus Pius Eusebius Maria of Löwenstein-Wertheim-Rosenberg, of 8764,
Kleinheubach/M, Germany, and has issue living, *Prince* Carl Friedrich Hubertus Georg Eduardo
Paolo Niccolo Franz Alois Igatius Hieronymus Maria, *b.* Sept. 30th, 1966,—*Prince* Hubertus Franz Maxi-
millan Gabriel Louis Franz Constantin Dominik Wunibald Maria, *b.* Dec. 18th, 1968,—*Princess*
Christina Marie, *b.* April 4th, 1974.
Issue of HRH the late Prince Friedrich George Wilhelm Christoph of Prussia, *b.* Dec.
19th, 1911, *d.* (disappeared April 19th and found drowned May 1st), 1966 (naturalised a
British subject 1947, and acquired dual nationality by re-admission as a German subject
1953); assumed by deed poll 1951 the surname of von Preussen: *m.* July 30th, 1945, Lady
Brigid Katharine Rachel Guinness (who *m.* 2ndly, June 3rd, 1967, Maj. Anthony Patrick
Ness, of Patmore Hall, Hadham, Herts., Letterellen, by Aberfeldy, Perths., and 7, Iveagh
House, Ormond Yard, SW1, da. of 2nd Earl of Iveagh:—
Frederick Nicholas VON PREUSSEN (Patmore Hall, Hadham, Herts), *b.* May 3rd, 1946.——William
Andrew VON PREUSSEN, *b.* Nov. 14th, 1947.——Rupert Alexander Friedrich VON PREUSSEN, *b.*
April 28th, 1955.——Victoria Marina Cecilie VON PREUSSEN, *b.* Feb. 22nd, 1952.——Antonia Elizabeth
Brigid Louise VON PREUSSEN (twin), *b.* April 28th, 1955.

Grandchildren of HIM Wilhelm II, German Emperor (infra):—
Issue of H.R.H. the late Prince Adalbert (Berengar Ferdinand Victor) of Prussia, *b.* July
14th, 1884, *d* Sept. 22nd, 1948 : *m.* Aug. 3rd, 1914, H.S.H. Princess Adelheid (Erna
Karoline Marie-Elisabeth), who *d.* April 25th, 1971, dau. of HH the late Prince Friedrich
of Saxe-Meiningen:—
Prince Wilhelm Victor Freund (Ernst Friedrich Georg Adalbert), *b.* Feb. 15th, 1919 ; Capt. German
Army (retired): *m.* July 20th, 1944, Countess Marie-Antoinette (Franziska Ladislaja Josepha Paula
Bernhardine Agnes) recognized as Princess of Prussia, July 20th, 1944), dau. of the late Count Fried-
rich (Heinrich Joseph Maria Gregor Kolumbus) Hoyos, and has issue living, *Prince* Adalbert-Alex-
ander (Friedrich Joachim Christian), *b.* March 4th, 1948,—*Princess* Marie-Louise (Marina Franziska),
b. Sept. 18th, 1945: *m.* May 22nd, 1971, Count Rudolf Maria Emil Franz Friedrich Carl Antonius
Christopherus Hubertus Joseph Wenzel Michael von Schönburg-Glauchau, of Marbella Quinta Maria
Louisa, Costa del Sol, Spain. *Residence*.—59, Feuerbacher-Heide, Stuttgart, W. Germany.——
Princess Victoria Marina, *b.* Sept. 11th, 1917; known as " Countess Victoria-Marina Lingen ": *m.*
Sept. 26th, 1947, Kirby William Patterson, lawyer, and has issue living, Berengar Orin Bernhard
Kirby, *b.* Aug. 21st, 1948,—Marina Adelaide Emily (twin), *b.* Aug. 21st, 1948.—Dohna-Maria,
b. Aug. 7th, 1954: *m.* July 28th, 1974, Stephen Pearl. *Residence*,—Le Tourne-Sol, 122216, North
61st St., Paradise Valley, Arizona, 85254, USA.

Issue of H.R.H. the late Prince August Wilhelm (Heinrich Günther Viktor) of Prussia,
b. Jan. 9th, 1887 ; *d.* March 5th, 1949 : *m.* Oct. 2nd, 1908, H.H. Princess Alexandra
Viktoria (from whom he obtained a divorce March 16th, 1920; she *d.* April 14th, 1957,
having *m.* 2ndly, Jan. 7th, 1922 (marriage dissolved 1933), Capt. Arnold Rümann), dau. of
HH the late Friedrich Ferdinand, Duke of Schleswig-Holstein-Sonderburg-Glücksburg:—
Prince Alexander Ferdinand Albrecht Achilles Wilhelm Joseph Viktor Karl Feodor, *b.* Dec. 26th,
1912 ; is a Merchant: *m.* Dec. 19th, 1938, Irmgard, dau. of the late Major Friedrich Weygand,
German Artillery, and formerly wife of Werner Rosendorff and has issue living, *Prince* Stephan
Alexander Dieter Friedrich (Neckarstrasse 5, 7121, Grossregersheim, Germany) *b.* Sept. 30th, 1939:
m. Feb. 28th, 1964, Heide, da. of Ernst Arthur Julius Schmidt, and has issue living, *Princess* Stephanie Viktoria Luise Irmgard Gertrud, *b.* Sept. 21st 1966. *Residence*,—Am Birnbaum, 35 Wies-
baden-Sonnenberg, 62, Germany.

Issue of H.R.H. the late Prince Oskar Carl Gustav Adolf of Prussia, *b.* July 27th, 1888, *d.*
27th Jan. 1958 : *m.* July 31st, 1914, Countess Ina Marie (cr. Countess of Ruppin. July 27th,
1914, recognised as Princess of Prussia, June 21st, 1920), who *d.* Sept. 17th, 1973, da. of the
late Karl, 3rd Count von Bassewitz-Levetzow:—
Prince Burchard Friedrich Max Werner Georg, *b.* Jan. 8th, 1917; Maj. (ret.) 8th German Inf., a Lawyer,
and Reinsurance Co. Exec.: *m.* Jan. 31st, 1961, Countess Eleonora Vera Alexia Anna Maria,
dau. of Count Leopold Heinrich Karl Friedrich Maria Fugger von Babenhausen, formerly wife of
Robert Bee. *Residence*,—81, Pienzenauerstrasse 1, 8 Munich 81, Bavaria, Germany.——*Prince*
Wilhelm Karl Adalbert Erich Detloff, *b.* Jan. 30th, 1922; 1st Lieut. (ret.) German Army; is a
Merchant, and Com. of Order of St. John: *m.* March 1st, 1952, Armgard Helene Else, dau. of Fried-
rich von Veltheim, and has issue living, *Prince* Wilhelm Karl Oskar Friedrich, *b.* Aug. 26th, 1955,—
Prince Oskar Michael Hans Carl, *b.* May 6th, 1959,—*Princess* Donata Victoria Ina Maria Ottonia, *b.*
Dec. 24th, 1952. *Residence*,—21, Einbeckerstrasse, Holzminden 345, Germany.——*Princess* Herze-
leide Ina Marie Sophie Charlotte Else, *b.* Dec. 25th, 1918: *m.* Aug. 16th, 1938, HSH Prince Karl Peter
Franz Andreas Biron von Curland, and has issue living, *Prince* Ernst Johann Karl Oskar Franz
Eitel Friedrich Peter Burchard (Underbiberger-strasse 10, Munich 83, Germany), *b.* Aug. 6th, 1940:
m. Aug. 15th, 1967, Countess Elisabeth Victoria Raimonda, da. of Count Ludwig Joseph Albert
Franz Heinrich Dieter von Ysenburg,—*Prince* Michael Karl August Wilhelm (Rabenkopfstrasse
27, Munich 90, Germany), *b.* Jan. 20th, 1944: *m.* July 2nd, 1969, Kristin, da. of Joachim Leo Jürgen
Karl Martin von Oertzen, and has issue living, *Princé* Alexander *b.* Sept. 18th, 1972, *Princess* Veronika
b. Jan. 23rd, 1970,—*Princess* Viktoria Benigna Ina Marie Cecilie Friederike Luise Helene, *b.* July 2nd,
1939: *m.* May 6th, 1968, Baron Johann (John) Robert von Twickel, of Defreggerstrasse 7, Munich 90,
Germany, and has issue living [see Throckmorton, Bt.]. *Residence*,—6, Flemingstrasse, Munich, 81,
Bavaria, Germany.

Grandchildren of the late Prince Joachim Franz Humbert of Prussia, 6th son of
HIM Wilhelm II, Emperor of Germany (infra):—
Issue of HRH the late Prince (Karl) Franz Josef (Wilhelm Friedrich Eduard Paul), *b.* Dec.
15th, 1916, *d.* Jan. 22nd, 1975: *m.* Oct 1st, 1940 (divorce Sept. 5th, 1946), HSH Princess
Henriette Hermine Wanda Ida Luise, yr. da. of HSH the late Prince Johann Georg of
Schönaich-Carolath; 2ndly, Nov. 9th, 1946 (divorce 1959), Luise Dora, who *d.* April
23rd, 1961, da. of Max Emil Theodor Hartmann, of Hamburg and formerly wife of Fritz
Simon; 3rdly, 1959, Donna Eva Maria Herrera-Valdeavellano, da. of Don Norberto
Herrara, of Lima:—
(By 1st m.) *Prince* Franz Wilhelm (Viktor Christof Stefan) (Rennbahn-Swasse 44, Frankfurt on Main-
Niederrad, 6), *b.* Sept. 3rd, 1943.——Prince (Franz) Friedrich (Christian) *b.* Oct. 17th, 1944.——(By

3rd m.) *Princess* Alexandra (Maria Augusta Juana Consuelo Eva), *b.* April 29th, 1960.——*Princess* Desirée (Anastasia Marie Benedicta), *b.* July 13th, 1961.

Grandchildren of HIM the late Victoria Adelaide Mary Louise VA, CI, RRC (*The Princess Royal*), German Empress and Queen of Prussia, el. da. of Queen Victoria:—

Issue of the late H.I.M. Friedrich Wilhelm Viktor Albert (Kaiser Wilhelm II.), *b.* Jan. 27th, 1859 ; *d.* June 4th, 1941 ; *s.* his father as Kaiser Wilhelm II., German Emperor and King of Prussia 1888 ; abdicated Nov. 28th, 1918 : *m.* 1st, Feb. 27th, 1881, H.H. Princess Auguste Viktoria Friederike Luise Feodora Jenny, who *d.* April 11th. 1921, el. dau. of HH the late Friedrich, Duke of Schleswig-Holstein-Sonderburg-Augustenburg; 2ndly, Nov. 5th, 1922, H.S.H. Princess Hermine, who *d.* Aug. 7th, 1947, dau. of H.S.H. the late Reigning Prince Heinrich XXII. Reuss, and widow of H.S.H. Prince Johann Georg of Schönaich-Carolath :—

Princess Victoria Louise Adelheid Mathilde Charlotte, *b.* Sept. 13th, 1892 ; has Grand Cross of Order of St. Olga and St. Sophia of Greece (of Stresemannstrasse 5, Brunswick, Germany); *m.* May 24th, 1913, H.R.H. Ernst August Christian George, Duke of Brunswick-Lüneburg, who *d.* Jan. 30th, 1953, and has issue living, *Prince* Ernst August George Wilhelm Christian Ludwig Franz Joseph Nikolaus (*Duke of Brunswick and Luneberg, and Prince of Hanover*) (Calenberg, 3211, Schulenburg, a.dg Leine, Hanover, and Königinvilla, Gmunden, Upper Austria), *b.* March 18th, 1914; ed. at Univ. Coll., Oxford; LLD Göttingen; Head of Houses of Brunswick, and Hanover; has Grand Cross of Orders of St. George, Guelph, and Ernst August of Hanover, and of Order of Redeemer of Greece, and Orders of Henry the Lion of Brunswick, of Black Eagle of Prussia, of St. Hubert of Bavaria, and of Elephant of Denmark: *m.* Sept. 4th, 1951, H.H. Princess Ortrud Bertha Adelheid Hedwig, dau. of H.H. the late Prince Albert Christian Adolf Karl Eugen of Schleswig-Holstein-Sonderburg-Glücksburg, and has issue living, *Prince* Ernst August Albert Paul Otto Rupprecht Oskar Berthold Friedrich-Ferdinand Christian-Ludwig *b.* Feb. 26th, 1954, *Prince* Ludwig Rudolf Georg Wilhelm Philipp Friedrich Wohlrath Maximilian *b.* Nov. 21st, 1955, *Prince* Heinrich Julius Christian Otto Friedrich Franz Anton Günther *b.* April 29th, 1961, *Princess* Marie Victoria Louise Hertha Friederike *b.* Nov. 26th, 1952, *Princess* Olga Sophie Charlotte Anna *b.* Feb. 17th, 1958, *Princess* Alexandra Irene Margaritha Elisabeth Bathildis *b.* Feb. 18th, 1959,— *Prince* Georg Wilhelm (Ernest August Friedrich Axel) (of Neuhaus, Schliersee, Bavaria, Germany), *b.* March 25th, 1915; ed. at Marlborough, and at Vienna and Göttingen Univ.; LLD 1948; LLD Göttingen; late Maj. 10th Cavalry Regt.; has Grand Cross of Orders of St. George, Guelph, and Ernst August of Hanover, and of Redeemer of Greece: *m.* April 23rd, 1946, H.R.H. Princess Sophie, da. of HRH the late Prince Andrew of Greece, GCVO (infra), and widow of HH Prince Christoph Ernst August of Hesse (infra), and has issue living, *Prince* Welf (Ernst August Andreas Philip George Wilhelm Ludwig Berthold) *b.* Jan. 25th, 1947: *m.* May, 1969, Wilbke, da. of Harry van Gunsteren, and has issue living, *Princess* Tania, *b.* July 24th, 1970, *Prince* George (Paul Christian) *b.* Dec. 9th 1949, *Princess* Friederike-Elizabeth *b.* Oct. 15th, 1954,—*Prince* Christian Oskar Ernst August Wilhelm Viktor George Heinrich, *b.* Sept. 1st, 1919; late Capt. German Army, has Grand Cross of Orders of St. George, Guelph, and Ernst August of Hanover, and of Redeemer of Greece: *m.* Nov. 23rd 1963, Mireille, da. of Armand Dutry, and has issue living, *Princess* Caroline-Luise Mireille Irene Sophie, *b.* May 3rd, 1965,—*Prince* Welf-Heinrich Ernst August Georg Christian Berthold Friedrich Wilhelm Louis Ferdinand (of 22, Neuwiesenstrasse, Frankfurt on Main, Niederrad, Germany) *b.* March 11th, 1923, ed. at Munich, at Vienna and at Göttingen Univ. (LLD 1953); has Grand Cross of Orders of St. George, Guelph, and Ernst August of Hanover, and of Redeemer of Greece: *m.* Sept. 21st, 1960, HSH Princess (Sophie) Alexandra Cecilie Anna Maria Friederike Benigna Dorothea, da. of HSH Otto Friedrich, 7th Prince of Ysenburg and Büdingen,—*Princess* Friederika Luise Thyra Victoria Margarete Sophie Olga Cécilie Isabella Christa (*HM Queen Frederika, Queen Mother of Greece*), *b.* April 18th, 1917; has Grand Cross of Orders of Redeemer and of St. Olga and St. Sophia of Greece: *m.* Jan. 9th, 1938, H.M. King Paul of the Hellenes, who *d.* March 6th, 1964 (infra), and has issue living, *King* Constantine II *b.* June 2nd, 1940; reigned as King of the Hellenes March 6th, 1964 to June 1st, 1973 is Sovereign of Orders of Redeemer, of St. George and St. Constantine, of George I and of Phoenix of Greece, has Grand Cross of Elephant of Denmark, St. Olav of Norway, of House of Orange of the Netherlands, and the Grand Cordons of Legion of Honour of France and of King Idris I of Libya and Order of Merit of Republic of Italy; is Grand Officer of St. Charles of Monaco and Cdr. of Legion of Merit of USA, Grand Cdr. of Order of Dannebrog of Denmark, Collar of Order of the Nile of United Arab Republic, of Aztec Eagle of Mexico, and of Roy. Order of Chakri of Thailand, and Grand Cross of the Roy. Order of Leopold of Belgium, of Seraphim of Sweden, of Ah Nadha of Jordan, and Order of the Republic of Senegal: *m.* Sept. 18th, 1964, HRH Princess Anne-Marie (Dagmar Ingrid), da. of HM King Frederik IX of Denmark (ante),—*Princess* Sophie (*Queen of Spain*), *b.* Nov. 2nd, 1938 : *m.* May 14th, 1962, HM King Juan Carlos Alfonso Victor Maria of Spain (infra), and has issue living, *Infante:* Felipe Juan Pablo Alfonso Todos Los Santos, *b.* Jan. 30th, 1968, *Infanta* Elena Maria Isabel Dominica *b.* Dec. 20th, 1963, *Infanta* Christina Frederica Victoria *b.* June 13th, 1965,—*Princess* Irene *b.* May 11th, 1942; has Grand Cross of Roy. Order of St. Olga and St. Sophia of Greece.

Issue of H.R.H. the late Grand Adm. Prince (Albert Wilhelm) Heinrich of Prussia, *b.* Aug. 14th, 1862, *d.* April 20th, 1929 : *m.* May 24th, 1888, H.G.D.H. Princess Irene Marie Luise Anna, who *d.* Nov. 11th, 1953, dau. of H.R.H. the late Ludwig IV., Reigning Grand Duke of Hesse, KG, and HRH Princess Alice Maud Mary VA, 2nd da. of HM Queen Victoria:—

Prince (Wilhelm Viktor Karl August Heinrich) Sigismund, *b.* Nov. 27th, 1896 ; is a Plantation Owner : *m.* July 11th, 1919. H.H. Princess Charlotte Agnes, dau. of HH the late Ernst II., formerly Reigning Duke of Saxe-Altenburg, and has issue living, *Prince* Alfred Friedrich Ernst Heinrich Konrad, *b.* Aug. 17th, 1924,—*Princess* Barbara Irene Adelheid Viktoria Elisabeth Bathildis, *b.* Aug. 2nd, 1920 : *m.* July 11th, 1954, H.R.H. Duke Christian Ludwig Ernst August Maximilian Johann Albrecht Adolf Friedrich, Duke of Mecklenburg, of 2331 Hemmelmark uber Eckernforde, Schleswig-Holstein, and has issue living, *Duchess* Donata *b.* March 11th, 1956, *Duchess* Edwina *b.* Sept. 25th, 1960. *Residence,*—Finca San Miguel, Barranca, Costa Rica.

Grandchildren of H.R.H. the late Princess Sophie Dorothea Ulrika Alice, V.A. (*Queen of the Hellenes*) (infra):—

Issue of H.M. the late King Alexander of the Hellenes. *b.* Aug. 1st, 1893, *d.* Oct. 25th, 1920: *m.* Nov. 4th, 1919 (recognized by Roy. Decree Sept. 10th, 1922), Aspasia, who *d.* Aug. 1972, da. of Col. Petros Manos:—

Princess Alexandra (*H.M. Queen Alexandra of Yugoslavia*), *b.* (*posthumous*) March 25th, 1921 ; has Grand Cross of Order of Star of Karadjordje of Yugoslavia, and Orders of White Eagle and Crown of Yugoslavia: *m.* March 20th, 1944, HM King Peter II of Yugoslavia, who *d.* Nov. 3rd, 1970 (ante). *Residence,*—Venice, Italy.

Issue of H.M. the late King Paul of the Hellenes, KG, GCVO, *b.* Dec. 14th, 1901, *d.* March 6th, 1964: *m.* Jan. 9th, 1938, H.R.H. Princess Friederika Luise Thyra Victoria Margarete Sophie Olga Cécilie Isabella Christa, only dau. of H.R.H. the late Prince Ernst August Christian Georg, Duke of Brunswick (ante).

Issue of HRH Princess Irene, *b.* Feb. 13th, 1904, *d.* April 14th, 1974: *m.* July 2nd, 1939, Adm. HRH Prince Aimone Roberto Margherito Mario Giuseppe Torino, Duke of Aosta, who *d.* Jan. 29th, 1948:—

Amadeo Umberto Constantine George Paul Maria Helen Firenze (*Duke of Aosta*), *b.* Sept. 27th, 1943: *m.* July 22nd, 1964, HRH *Princess* Claude Marie Agnes Catharine of France, da. of HRH Prince Henri Robert Ferdinand Marie Louis Philippe of Bourbon-Orleans, Count of Paris, and has issue living, *Prince* Aimone Umberto Emanuele Luigi Amadeo Elena Maria Fiorenzo, *b.* Oct. 15th, 1967,— *Princess* Bianca Irene Olga Elena Isabella Fiorenza Maria, *b.* April 2nd, 1966,—*Princess* Mafalda Giovanna Jolanda Shams Maria, *b.* Sept. 20th, 1969.

Brunswick-Hanover

Greece

Prussia

Greece

Savoy-Aosta

Grandchildren of H.I.M. the late Victoria Adelaide Mary Louisa, VA, CI, RRC
(*The Princess Royal*), German Empress and Queen of Prussia (ante):—

Issue of H.R.H. the late Princess Sophie Dorothea Ulrika Alice, V.A., *b.* June 14th, 1870,
d. Jan. 13th, 1932 : *m.* Oct. 27th, 1889, H.M. King Constantine of the Hellenes, who
d. Jan. 11th, 1923 (abdicated for himself and his el. son June 11th, 1917, resumed the
Crown Dec. 19th, 1920, and again abdicated Sept. 28th, 1922) :—

Princess Hélène (*H.M. Queen Helen, Queen Mother of Roumania*), *b.* May 3rd, 1896; has Grand Cross
of Orders of Carol of Roumania and of St. Olga and St. Sophia of Greece: *m.* March 10th, 1921
(marriage dissolved June 21st, 1928), H.M. King Carol II of Roumania, K.G. GCVO (ante), who
d. April 4th, 1955, having ceased to reign Sept. 6th, 1940. *Residence,*—Villa Sparta, San Domenico
di Fiesole, Florence, Italy.——*Lady* Katherine, *b.* May 4th, 1913; granted by Roy. Warrant the
rank of a Duke's daughter Aug. 25th, 1947; has Grand Cross of Order of St. Olga and St. Sophia
of Greece: *m.* April 21st, 1947, Maj. Richard Campbell Andrew Brandram, MC, RA, and has issue
living, Richard Paul George Andrew, *b.* April 1st, 1948: *m.* Feb. 12th, 1975, Jennifer D., da. of
Lt.-Col. Robert Steele, of St. Leonard's Grange, Beaulieu, Hants. *Residence,*—Croft Cottage,
Marlow, Bucks.

Issue of H.R.H. the late Princess Margarethe Beatrice Feodora of Prussia, *b.* April 22nd, 1872,
d. Jan. 22nd, 1954: *m.* Jan. 25th, 1893, HRH Friedrich Karl Ludwig Konstantin, Landgrave of Hesse, who *d.* May 28th, 1940:—

Hesse

Prince Philipp (*Landgrave of Hesse*), *b.* Nov. 6th, 1896: *m.* Sept. 23rd, 1925, HRH Princess Mafalda
Maria Elisabetta Anna Romana, who *d.* (in Buchenwald Concentration Camp) Aug. 27th, 1944, second
da. of HM the late King Victor Emmanuel III of Italy, and has issue living, *Prince* Moritz Friedrich
Karl Emanuel Humbert (of 2321 Panker Castle, East Holstein, Germany), *b.* Aug. 6th, 1926; adopted as
heir by his kinsman the late Louis, Prince of Hesse and the Rhine, who *d.* May 30th, 1968: *m.* June 3rd,
1964 (m. diss. Oct. 16th, 1974), HSH *Princess* Tatjana Luise Therese Elsa, da. of HSH the late
Prince Gustav Albrecht (5th Prince) of Sayn-Wittgenstein-Berleburg, and has issue living, *Prince*
Heinrich Donatus Philipp Umberto *b.* Oct. 17th, 1966, *Prince* Philipp Robin, *b.* Sept. 17th, 1970,
Princess Mafalda Margaretha *b.* July 6th, 1965, *Princess* Elena Elisabeth Madeleine *b.* Nov. 8th,
1967,—*Prince* Heinrich Wilhelm Konstantin Viktor Franz (of Villa Polissena, Via di San Filippo
Martire, 6, Rome, Italy), *b.* Oct. 30th, 1927,—*Prince* Otto Adolf (Via del Casone 29, 50124, Florence),
b. June 2nd, 1937: *m.* April 5th, 1965 (m. diss. Feb. 3rd, 1969), Angela Mathilde Agathe, da. of Maj.-
Gen. Wilhelm Konrad Rodrigo Bernd von Doering,—*Princess* Elisabeth Margarethe Elena Johanna
Maria Yolanda Polyxena, *b.* Oct. 8th, 1940: *m.* Feb. 26th, 1962, Count Friedrich Carl Eduard
Wilhelm Hans Franz Eusebius Michael Hubert Maria von Oppersdorff, of Fasanenstr. 24, 6078,
Neu-Isenburg, Gravenbruch, Germany, and has issue living, *Count* Friedrich Carl Philipp Wilhelm
Hans Moritz Maria *b.* Dec. 1st, 1962, *Count* Alexander Wolfgang Johannes Georg Victor Emanuel
Maria *b.* Aug. 3rd, 1965. *Residence,* Schloss Friedrichshof, 6242 Kronberg, Germany.——*Prince*
Wolfgang Moritz, *b.* (twin) Nov. 6th, 1896: *m.* 1st, Sept. 17th, 1924, HGDH Princess Marie Alex-
andra, who *d.* (killed in an Air Raid) Jan. 29th, 1944, only da. of HGDH the late Prince Maximilian
Alexander Friedrich Wilhelm of Baden; 2ndly, Sept. 7th, 1948, Ottilie, da. of Ludwig Möller.
Residence,—Schloss Friedrichshof, 6242 Kronberg, Germany.

Grandchildren of H.R.H. the late Princess Margarethe Beatrice Feodora of Hesse
(ante) :—

Issue of H.H. the late Prince Christoph Ernst August of Hesse, *b.* (twin), May 14th, 1901,
d. Oct. 7th, 1943 : *m.* Dec. 15th, 1930, H.R.H Princess Sophie [who *m.* 2ndly, April 23rd,
1946, HRH Prince Georg Wilhelm (Ernst August Friedrich Axel) of Hanover (ante)], da.
of HRH the late Prince Andrew of Greece, GCVO (infra):—

Prince Karl Adolph Andreas, (Denningerstrasse 102, 8 Munich 81, Germany) *b.* March 26th, 1937: *m.*
18th April, 1966, Countess Yvonne Margit Valerie, da. of Count Béla Szapáry de Muraszombath, and
has issue living, *Prince* Christoph, *b.* June 18th, 1969,—*Princess* Irina Verena, *b.* April 1st, 1971.
——*Prince* Rainer Christoph Friedrich (Breitensteinstrasse 1, 8166, Neuhaus, Germany), *b.* Nov.
18th, 1939.——*Princess* Christina Margarete, *b.* Jan. 10th, 1933: *m.* 1st, Aug. 2nd, 1956 (divorce
Feb. 20th, 1962), HRH Prince Andrej of Yugoslavia [ante); 2ndly, Dec. 3rd, 1962 (divorce May 31st,
1968), Robert Floris van Eyck, and has issue living (by 1st m.) (ante) (by 2nd m.) Mark Nicholas,
b. Feb. 16th, 1966, Helen Sophia, *b.* Oct. 25th, 1963——*Princess* Dorothea Karin Charlotte, *b.* July
24th, 1934: *m.* April 1st, 1959, HSH Prince Friedrich Karl Hugo Maximilian Maria Cyrillus Felix
Hubertus zu Windisch-Graetz, and has issue living, *Princess* Marina Margherita Sophia Leontina
Christina *b.* Dec. 3rd, 1960.—*Princess* Clarissa Elisabetha Fiore, *b.* Aug. 6th, 1966. *Residence,*—
Ca'Lupo, 22040, Alserio, Provincia di Como, Italy.——*Princess* Clarissa Alice. (Clarisse de Hesse)
b. (posthumous) Feb. 6th, 1944: *m.* July 20th, 1971, Claude Jean Derrien.

Descendants of HRH Princess Alice (Grand Duchess of Hesse and the Rhine), 2nd da. of Queen Victoria.

Descendants of the late George Louis Victor Henry Serge, GCVO, 2nd Marquess of
Milford Haven, el. son of the late Victoria Alberta Elizabeth Mathilde Marie, VA,
Marchioness of Milford Haven (infra), el. da. of HRH the late Princess Alice
[see M. Milford Haven].

Grandson of HRH the late Princess Alice (ante):—

Mountbatten

Issue of the late Victoria Alberta Elizabeth Mathilde Marie (*Marchioness of Milford Haven*),
V.A., *b.* April 5th, 1863 ; discontinued title of Princess June 1917 ; *d.* Sept. 24th, 1950 :
m. April 30th, 1884, Adm. of the Fleet the 1st Marquess of Milford Haven, G.C.B., G.C.V.O.,
K.C.M.G., who *d.* Sept. 11th, 1921 :—

Rt. Hon. Lord Louis Francis Albert Victor Nicholas, *KG, GCB, OM, GCSI GCIE, GCVO, DSO, PC,
FRS* (*Earl Mountbatten of Burma*) [see that title].

Grandchildren of the late Victoria Alberta Elizabeth Mathilde Marie, VA (*Marchioness of Milford Haven*) (ante):—

Issue of HRH the late Princess (Victoria) Alice Elizabeth Julia Marie, RRC, *b.* Feb. 25th
1885, *d.* Dec. 5th, 1969: *m.* 1903, HRH Prince Andrew of Greece, GCVO, who *d.* Dec. 3rd,
1944:—

HRH Prince Philip, *KG, KT, OM, GBE, PC* (*Duke of Edinburgh*), *b.* June 10th, 1921; cr. *Duke of
Edinburgh* 1947 [see page 12].——*Princess* Margarita, *b.* April 18th, 1905: *m.* April 20th, 1931, HSH
Gottfried Viktor Hermann Alfred Paul Maximilian, 8th Prince of Hohenlohe-Langenburg, who *d.*
May 11th, 1960 (ante).——*Princess* Sophie, *b.* June 26th, 1914: *m.* 1st, Dec. 15th, 1950, HRH
Prince Christoph Ernst August of Hesse, who *d.* Oct. 7th, 1943 (ante); 2ndly, April 24th, 1946, HRH
Prince Georg Wilhelm (Ernst August Friedrich Wilhelm Axel) of Hanover (ante).

Grandchildren of HRH the late Princess (Victoria) Alice Elizabeth Julia Marie, RRC
(*Princess Andrew of Greece*), (ante):—

Issue of HRH the late Princess Théodora of Greece, *b.* May 30th, 1906, *d.* Oct 16th, 1969:
m. Aug. 17th, 1931, HRH Prince Berthold Friedrich Wilhelm Ernst August Heinrich Karl
(*Margrave of Baden*), who *d.* Oct. 27th, 1963:—

Baden

Prince Maximilian Andrew Friedrich Gustav Ernst August Bernhard (*Margrave of Baden*) (Schloss
Salem, D7777, Salem, Baden, Germany), *b.* July 3rd, 1933: ed. at Gordonstoun: *m.* Sept. 29th, 1966,
HI and RH the Archduchess Valerie Isabelle Marie Anna Alfonsa Desideria Brigitte Sophia Thomasia
Huberta Josepha Ignatia, da. of HI and RH the late Archduke Hubert Salvator Rainer Maria Joseph
Ignatius of Austria, and has issue living, *Hereditary Prince* Bernhard Max Friedrich August Louis
Kraft *b.* May 27th, 1970,—*Prince* Leopold Max Christian Ludwig Clemens Hubert, *b.* Oct. 1st, 1971,
—*Princess* Marie-Louise (Elisabeth Mathilde Theodora Cecilie Sarah Charlotte), *b.* July 3rd, 1969,
——*Prince* Ludwig Wilhelm Georg Ernst Christoph (Schloss, D-6931, Zwingenberg, N., Germany),
b. March 16th, 1937: *m.* Sept. 21st, 1967, HSH Princess Marianne Henriette Eleonore Gobertina,

da. of HSH Prince Karl Alain Maria Gobertus von Auersperg-Breunner.——*Princess* Margarita Alice Thyra Viktoria Marie Louise Scholastica, *b.* July 14th, 1932: *m.* June 6th, 1957, HRH Prince Tomislav of Yugoslavia (ante).

Descendants of HRH Princess Beatrice, 5th da. of Queen Victoria.

Grandchildren of HRH the late Princess Beatrice Mary Victoria Feodore (*Princess Beatrice*), VA, CI, GCVO, GBE, RRC, 5th da. of Queen Victoria:—
Issue of the late Alexander Albert Mountbatten, G.C.B., G.C.V.O., 1st Marquess of Carisbrooke, *b.* Nov. 23rd, 1886, *d.* Feb. 23rd, 1960 : *m.* July 19th, 1917, Lady Irene Frances Adza Denison, *G.B.E.*, who *d.* July 16th, 1956, dau. of 2nd Earl of Londesborough :—

See M. Carisbrooke (ext.).

Grandsons of HRH the late Princess Victoria Eugenie Julia Ena (*HM Queen Victoria Eugenie of Spain*) (infra):—
Issue of the late Infante Jaime Luitpoldo Isabelino Enrique Alejandro Alberto Alfonso Victor Acacio Pedro Pablo Maria (*Duke of Segovia*), *b.* June 23rd, 1908; renounced the right of succession June 11th, 1933; *d.* March 20th, 1975: *m.* 1st, March 4th, 1935 (m. diss. in Roumania, May 6th, 1947), Eamnuela Vittoria Jeanne Josephine Piere Marie de Dampierre, da. of the late Vicomte Roger (Richard Charles Henri Etienne), 2nd Duke of San Lorenzo; 2ndly, Aug. 3rd, 1949 (in Austria), Charlotte Auguste Luise, da. of Otto Tiedemann, of Königsberg, E. Prussia:—
(By 1st m.) *Don* Alfonso Jaime (*Duke of Cadiz*), *b.* April 20th, 1936; Spanish Ambassador to Sweden 1970-72: *m.* March 8th, 1972, Maria de Carmen Esperanza Alejandra de la Santissima Trinidad y de Todos los Santos Martinez Bordiu y Franco, da. of Christobal Martinez Bordiu Marques de Villaverde, and has issue living, *Don* Francisco Alfonso Jaime Christobal Victor José Gonza lez Cecilio, *b.* Nov. 22nd, 1972,—*Don* Luis Alfonso, *b.* April 25th, 1974.——*Don.* Gonzalo Victor, *b.* June 5th, 1937. **Spain**

Issue of HRH the late Princess Victoria Eugenie Julia Ena* (*HM Queen Victoria Eugenie of Spain*) VA, da. of HRH the late Prince Henry Maurice of Battenberg, KG, *b.* Oct. 24th, 1887, *d.* April 15th, 1969: *m.* May 31st, 1906, HM King Alfonso XIII of Spain, KG, GCVO, who *d.* Feb. 28th, 1941 (having reigned May 17th, 1886, to April 14th, 1931, when he left Spain):—
Infante Juan Carlos Teresa Silverio Alfonso (*Count of Barcelona*) (of Villa Giralda, Estoril, Portugal) *b.* June 20th, 1913; was a Midshipman in British RN 1933-35; appointed Hon. Lieut. 1936; is Sovereign of Order of Golden Fleece of Spain: *m.* Oct. 12th, 1935, HRH Princess Marie Mercedes Christine Genara Isabelle Louise Caroline Victoria, da. of HRH the late Prince Charles Marie François d'Assise Pasqual Ferdinand Antoine de Padoue François de Paule Alphonse André Avelino Tancred de Bourbon-Siciles, Infante of Spain, and has issue living, *King* Juan Carlos Alfonso Victor Maria (*King of Spain*), (Palacio Zarzuela, Madrid, Spain), *b.* Jan. 5th, 1938; *s.* as King of Spain Nov. 23rd, 1975: *m.* May 14th, 1962, HRH Princess Sophie, da. of the late HM King Paul of the Hellenes (ante), —*Infanta* Maria del Pilar Alfonsa Juana Victoria Luisa Ignacia (*Duchess of Badajoz*), *b.* July 30th, 1936: *m.* May 5th, 1967, Don Luis Gomez-Acebo y Duque de Estrada, Visconde de la Torre, and has issue living Juan Filiberto Nicolas *b.* Dec. 6th, 1969, Bruno Alexander, *b.* June 15th, 1971, Beltran Luis Ataulfo *b.* May 20th, 1973, Ferdinando Umberto *b.* Sept. 13th, 1974, (Fatima) Simonetta *b.* Oct. 29th, 1968,—*Infanta* Margarita Marie de la Victoria Esperanza Jacoba Felicidad, *b.* March 6th, 1939: *m.* Oct. 12th, 1972, Dr. Carlos Zurita y Delgado, of Madrid, and has issue living, Alfonso Juan Carlos *b.* Aug. 9th, 1973, Maria Sofia Emilia Carmen *b.* Sept. 1975.——*Infanta* Beatriz Isabel Frederica Alfonsa Eugenia Christina Maria Teresa Bienvenida Ladislaa, *b.* June 22nd, 1909: *m.* Jan. 14th, 1935, Alessandro Torlonia, Prince of Civitella Cesi, of Palazzo Torlonia, 78 Via Bocca di Leone, Rome, Italy, and has issue living, *Don* Marco Alfonso, *b.* July 2nd, 1937: *m.* 1st, Sept. 15th, 1960, Orsetta, da. of Don Adolfo Caraccioli dei Principé di Castagneto; 2ndly, 19—, Philippa McDonald, and has issue living, (by 1st m.), Giovanni *b.* April 18th, 1962,—*Don* Marino Riccardo Francesco Maria Giuseppe *b.* Dec. 13th, 1939,—*Donna* Sandra Vittoria *b.* Feb. 14th, 1936: !*m.* June 20th, 1958, Clemente Lequio di Assaba, who *d.* 1971, and has issue living, Alessandro Vittorio Eugenio Enrico *b.* July 17th, 1960, Desideria Beatrice Elsye Francesca *b.* Sept. 19th, 1962,—*Donna* Olympia *b.* Jan. 27th, 1943: *m.* June 26th, 1965, Paul Annik Weiller, Le Noviciat, 1 Rue le l'Ermitage, Versailles, S. et O., France, and has issue living, Paul Alexander *b.* Feb. 12th, 1975, Aliki Beatrice Victoria *b.* March 23rd, 1967, Sibilla Sandra *b.* June 12th, 1968.——*Infanta* Maria Christina Teresa Alejandra Guadelupo Concepcion Idlefonsa Victoria Eugenia *b.* Dec. 12th, 1911: *m.* June 10th, 1940, Count Enrico Eugenio Francesco Antonio Marone, who *d.* Oct. 23rd, 1968, and has issue living, Vittoria Alfonsa Alberta Pilar Enrica Paola, *b.* March 5th, 1941: *m.* Jan. 12th, 1961, José Carlos Alvarez de Toledo y Gross, and has issue living, Francisco de Borja *b.* March 27th, 1964, Marco Alfonso *b.* Jan. 31st, 1965, Victoria Eugenia *b.* Oct. 8th, 1961,—Giovanna Paola Gabriella, *b.* Jan. 31st, 1943,—Maria Teresa Beatrice, *b.* Jan. 4th, 1945: *m.* April 22nd, 1967, José Ruiz de Arana, Marques Brenes, and has issue living,—Anna Alessandra *b.* Dec. 31st, 1948: *m.* June 21st, 1969, Gian Carlo Stavro Santorosa, and has issue living, Astrid Cristina Antonia *b.* April 24th, 1972.

PREDECESSORS.—See " Sovereigns of England since the Conquest," page 18.

PREDECESSORS.—See " Sovereigns of England since the Conquest," page 18.

HER MAJESTY QUEEN ELIZABETH THE QUEEN MOTHER.†

Her Majesty ELIZABETH ANGELA MARGUERITE, *Lady of Order of the Garter, Lady of Order of the Thistle, C.I., G.C.V.O., G.B.E.* (*Queen Elizabeth The Queen Mother*), dau. of 14th Earl of Strathmore; *b.* Aug. 4th, 1900; Hon. LL.D., Queen's Univ., Belfast 1924, St. Andrews 1929, Glasgow 1932, Edinburgh 1937, Cape Town 1947, Camb. 1948, Manchester 1951, Leeds and Columbia Univ., N.Y. 1954, Melbourne and Liverpool 1958, Auckland 1966, Halifax (Nova Scotia) and Dundee 1967; Hon. DCl, Oxford 1931; Hon.D.Litt. London 1937 and W. Indies 1965; Hon.Litt.D. Keele 1965; Hon.D.Mus., Sheffield 1966; Hon. FRCOG 1949; Hon. FRCS England 1950; Hon. FRCP Edinburgh 1953; FRCP 1962; Bencher Middle Temple 1944 (Treasurer 1949); FRS; Col.-in-Ch. 1st The Queen's Dragoon Guards, The

---

* Granted style of " Royal Highness " April 3rd, 1900.
† Under the Civil List Act 1972, provision is made for Her Majesty to receive £95,000 per annum.

Queen's Own Hussars, 9th/12th Roy. Lancers (Prince of Wales's), King's Regt., R. Anglian Regt., Light Inf., The Black Watch (R. Highland Regt.), The RAMC; Hon. Col. R. Yeo, The London Scottish (The Gordon Highlanders) (TA), and Univ. of London Contingent Officers' Training Corps.; Col.-in-Ch. The Black Watch (R. Highland Regt.) of Canada, The Toronto Scottish Regt. RCAMC and RAAMC; Comdt.-in-Ch. WRNS, WRAC, RAF Central Flying Sch., and WRAF, Air Ch. Comdt.; WRAAF; Comdt.-in-Ch. Nursing Corps and Divs., St. John Ambulance Bde.; Hon. Freeman of Grocers' Co., Merchant Taylors' Co., Shipwrights' Co., Musician Co., and Barbers' Co.; Hon. Member of Lloyds; Pres. of British Red Cross Soc. 1937-52, since when Dept. Pres.; a GCStJ; has Grand Cross of Legion of Honour, and of Orders of the Lion of the Netherlands, of the Crown of Roumania, of St. Olga and St. Sophia of Greece, of St. Sava of Serbia, of Lernor Ala of Afghanistan, of Sun of Peru, of Independence of Republic of Tunisia, and of Ojaswi Rajanya of Nepal; has French Red Cross Medal and Norwegian War Cross; received Freedom of City of Glasgow 1927, of Burghs of Stirling and Dunfermline 1928, of City of Perth 1935, of City of Edinburgh 1936, of Burgh of Inverness and of City of London 1953, of City of Dundee and of Borough of King's Lynn 1954, of Burghs of Forfar, Musselburgh, and Wick 1956, of City of Aberdeen 1959, and of City of St. Albans 1961; Pres. of Roy. Highland and Agricultural Soc. 1963-64; awarded gold Albert Medal of Roy. Soc. of Arts 1952; appointed Grand Master of Roy. Victorian Order 1937; Pres. of Univ. Coll. of Rhodesia and Nyasaland 1957-70; elected Chancellor of London Univ. 1955, and first Chancellor of Dundee Univ. 1967; received Roy. Victorian Chain 1937; GBE (Civil) 1927, CI 1931, Lady of Order of the Garter 1936, GCVO and Lady of Order of the Thistle 1937: *m.* April 26, 1923, HM King George VI, who *d.* Feb. 6th, 1952.

Arms,—The Royal Arms, impaling quarterly 1st and 4th the arms of Bowes-Lyon; i.e. 1st and 4th argent, a lion rampant azure, armed and langued gules, within a double tressure flory-counterflory of the second, *Lyon*; 2nd and 3rd ermine, three bows, strings palewise proper, *Bowes.* **Supporters,**—*Dexter,* that of the Sovereign; *sinister,* a lion per fesse or and gules, being one of the supporters of the Earl of Strathmore and Kinghorne.

Residences,—Clarence House, S.W.1 Royal Lodge, Windsor Great Park, Berks; Castle of Mey, Caithness.

DUKE OF EDINBURGH.

*‡His Royal Highness The Prince PHILIP, *KG, KT, OM, GBE, PC,* 1st Duke, only son of H.R.H. the late Prince Andrew of Greece and Denmark *GCVO,* by HRH the late Princess (Victoria) Alice Elizabeth Julia Marie, *R.R.C.,* dau. of 1st Marquess of Milford Haven; *b.* June 10th, 1921; ed. at Cheam Sch., at Salem, Baden, at Gordonstoun, and at Roy. Naval Coll., Dartmouth; 1939-45 War, with Mediterranean Fleet, in Home Waters, and with British Pacific Fleet in SE Asia and the Pacific [despatches, Greek War Cross, 1939-45, Atlantic, Africa, Burma (with Pacific rosette), and Italy Stars, War medal 1939-45 (with oak leaf) and French Croix de Guerre (with Palm)]; Hon. LLD Wales 1949, London 1951, Edinburgh and Camb. 1952, Karachi 1959, Malta 1964, and California 1966; Hon. DCL Durham 1951, and Oxford 1964; Hon. DSc Delhi 1959, Reading 1960, Salford (Lancs.) and Southampton 1967; Hon. Degree in Engineering, Lima 1962; Hon. FRCP London 1952; Hon. FRCSE, and Hon. FRCS England; Hon. Fellow Univ. Coll., Oxford 1963; a Personal ADC to HM King George VI 1948; Adm. of the Fleet, Field Marshal, Marshal of the RAF, Adm. of the Fleet RAN, Field Marshal Aust. Mil. Forces, Marshal of the RAAF, Adm. of the Fleet R. NZ Navy, Capt. Gen., R. Marines, Col.-in-Ch., Queen's R. Irish Hussars, Duke of Edinburgh's R. Regt. (Berks. and Wilts.), Queen's Own Highlanders (Seaforth and Camerons), REME, Army Cadet Force, R. Canadian Regt., Seaforth Highlanders of Canada, Cameron Highlanders of Ottawa, Queen's Own Cameron Highlanders of Canada, R. Canadian Army Cadets, R. Aust. Electrical and Mechanical Engineers, Aust. Cadet Corps, Corps of R. NZ Electrical and Mechanical Engineers, Col. of Grenadier Guards, Hon. Col. Edinburgh and Heriot-Watt Univs. Officers' Training Corps, Trinidad and Tobago Regt., Adm., Sea Cadet Corps, R. Canadian Sea Cadets, Air Commodore-

* Under the Civil List Act 1972, provision is made for His Royal Highness to receive £65,000 per annum.

‡ By warrant dated Sept. 18th, 1952, the Duke was granted precedence next to H.M. the Queen except where otherwise provided by Act of Parliament.

in-Chief Air Training Corps, R. Canadian Air Cadets. Comdt.-in.Chr. and Extra Master, Merchant Navy; a Member of Council of Duchy of Cornwall since 1952, Ranger of Windsor Great Park since 1952, and Lord High Steward of Plymouth since 1960; Chancellor of Univs. of Wales since 1948, Edinburgh since 1952 and Salford 1967-71; Visitor of Upper Canada Coll. since 1955, Manchester Coll. of Science and Technology since 1957, and Churchill Coll., Camb. since 1959; Life Gov. of King's Coll., London since 1954, Master of the Bench of Inner Temple since 1954; Elder Brother of Trin. House since 1952 (Master since 1969) and Hon. Brother of Hull Trin. House since 1953; Roy. Gov. of Charterhouse since 1953; Pres. in Ch. of British Racing Drivers' Club since 1952 and Pres. of British Amateur Athletic Board since 1952, Commonwealth Games Fedn. since 1955, British Sportsman's Club since 1958, Central Council of Physical Recreation since 1951, City and Guilds of London Inst. since 1951, Council for Nat. Academic Awards 1964-75, English-Speaking Union of the Commonwealth since 1952, Guinea Pig Club since 1960, Guards' Polo Club since 1955, Roy. Agric. Society of the Commonwealth since 1958, Roy. Coll. of Gen. Practitioners 1972-73, Roy. Commn. for Exhibition of 1851 since 1965, Roy. Household Cricket Club since 1953, Roy. Merchant Navy Sch. since 1952, Roy. Mint Advisory Cttee. on design of seals, coins and medals since 1952, Roy. Society of Arts since 1952, World Wild Life Fund, British Nat. Appeal since 1961, Council of Engineering Insts. 1965-75, Council of Trustees of Air Centre 1968-73, Maritime Trust 1969-79, Nat. Council of Social Ser. 1970-73, Zoological Soc. of London 1960-77, Inst. of Work Study Practitioners 1972-77, and Wild Fowl Trust 1972-77; Vice-Pres. Soc. of the Friends of St. George's and the Descendants of Knights of the Garter since 1948; FRS 1951; Permanent Fellow of Inst. of Petroleum since 1963; Hon. Fellow of Roy. Soc. of Canada since 1957, Australian Acad. of Science since 1961, and Roy. Zoological Soc. of Scotland since 1963; Trustee of Nat. Maritime Museum, Greenwich since 1948, and Roy. Agric. Soc. of England since 1957; Patron and first Hon. Fellow of Ghana Acad. of Sciences (Hon. Pres. 1959-61) since 1961; Patron of Inst. of Navigation and Lord's Taverners (Pres. of Council 1962-63, since when Twelfth Man), of Charities Aid Foundation, and Instn. of Chemical Engineers; Patron and Trustee of The Duke of Edinburgh's Award; Chm. of the Duke of Edinburgh's Cttee. for The Queen's Awards to Industry since 1965; a Liveryman and Assist. of Shipwrights' Co. (Prime Warden 1954, Permanent Master since 1965), a Freeman and Liveryman of Fishmongers' Co. (Prime Warden 1961, 4th Warden 1962-63), a Freeman and Liveryman of Mercers' Co., Adm. of the Master Mariners' Co., Grand Master of Guild of Air Pilots and Air Navigators, a Guild Brother of Glasgow, of Craft Rank Qua Hammermen, Trades House of Glasgow, Adm. and Commodore of Roy. Yacht Squadron 1961-68; Adm. of House of Lords Yacht Club, of Roy. Motor Yacht Club, of RN Sailing Assocn., of Roy. Southern Yacht Club, of Bar Yacht Club, of Roy. Dart Yacht Club, of Roy. Gibraltar Yacht Club, of Roy. Yacht Club of Victoria, Australia, and of Great Navy of State of Nebraska, USA; received Freedom of City of London, Greenwich and City of Edinburgh 1948, City of Belfast 1949, City of Cardiff 1952, City of Glasgow 1955, City of Melbourne 1956, City of Dar-es-Salaam 1961, City of Nairobi 1963, and cities of Guadalajara and Acapulco, Mexico, and Bridgetown, Barbados 1964 and City of Los Angeles and Hon. Citizen of Chicago 1966; Grand Cross Order of Redeemer of Greece 19—, Order of Phoenix of Greece 19—, Grand Cross Order of George I (with swords) of Greece 19—, Order of St. George and St. Constantine (with swords) of Greece (4th Class) 19—, Knight of Order of the Elephant of Denmark 1947, Grand Cross of Order of St. Charles of Monaco 1951, of Order of St. Olav of Norway 1952, and of Manuel Amador Guerrero of Panama 1953, Order of the Seraphim of Sweden, and Chain of Most Exalted Order of the Queen of Sheba of Ethiopia 1954, Grand Cross of Order of the Tower and the Sword (Civil) of Portugal 1955, of Order of King Faisal I of Iraq 1956, and of the Legion of Honour of France 1957, Knight Grand Cross of Order of Merit of the Italian Republic, Grand Cross of Order of the Lion of the Netherlands, and of Order of Merit of Federal German Republic (1st Class) 1958, Order of Ojaswai Rajanya of Nepal 1960, Knight Grand Band of Star of Africa, of Liberia 1961, Grand Cross of Order of San Martin of Argentina, of Order of the Condor of Bolivia, and of National Order of Southern Cross of Brazil, Chain of Chilean Order of Merit, Grand Cross Extraordinary of Order of Boyacá of Colombia, Grand Cross of National Order of Merit of Ecuador, National Order of Merit of Paraguay, and Great Cross of Order of the Sun with Brilliants, of Peru, 1962; Grand Cordon of Order of Leopold of Belgium and Order of the Brilliant Star of Zanzibar (1st Class) 1963, and Decoration of Republic of Sudan (1st class) and Grand Cross of Order of the Icelandic Falcon 1963, and Collar of the Aztec Eagle of Mexico 1964, Decoration of Honour for Services to Republic of Austria, Grand Cordon 1966, Order of White Rose of Finland 1969, Order of Superior Sun of Afghanistan 1971, Grand Cordon of Supreme Order of Chrysanthemum of Japan 1971, Most Esteemed Family Order of Brunei 1972, Chevalier Grand Cross Order of Golden Lion of Luxembourg 1972, a Member of Distinguished Order of Izzuddin, of Republic of Maldives 1972, Hon. Member of Darjah Utama Temasek of Singapore 1972, Grand Cross Yugoslav Star of Yugoslavia

1972, Collar of Order of Prince Henry the Navigator of Portugal 1973, Grand
Cordon of National Order of the Leopard (Mil.) of Zaire 1973, Grand Collar of
National Order of Infante Dom Henrique of Portugal 1973; King George VI
Coronation Medal (1937), and Queen Elizabeth II Coronation Medal (1953);
appointed Grand Master and First or Principal Knt. of Order of British Empire
1953; *cr.* KG, *Baron Greenwich*, of Greenwich co. London, *Earl of Merioneth*,
and *Duke of Edinburgh* (peerage of United Kingdom) 1947, KT 1952, GBE
(Mil) 1953, and OM 1968: naturalized a British subject and adopted the surname of Mountbatten Feb. 28th, 1947; granted title, style and attribute of
Royal Highness 1947; introduced to PC 1951, and to PC Canada 1957;
granted style and titular dignity of a Prince of UK 1957; **m.* Nov. 20th, 1947,
HM Queen Elizabeth II, and has issue.

    Arms,—Quarterly; 1st, or, semee of hearts gules, three lions passant in pale azure ducally crowned
of the first; 2nd, azure, a cross argent; 3rd, argent, two pallets sable; 4th, argent, upon a rock proper
a castle triple towered sable, masoned argent, windows, port, turret caps, and vanes gules. Crest,
—A plume of five ostrich feathers alternately sable and argent issuant from a ducal coronet
or. Supporters,—Dexter, a representation of Heracles girt about the loins with a lion skin,
crowned with a chaplet of oak leaves and holding in the dexter hand a club proper; sinister, a
lion queue fourchee ducally crowned or and gorged with a naval coronet azure. Coronet,—A
coronet composed of crosses-patée and fleur-de-lis alternately or.

    Residences,—Buckingham Palace, S.W.1; Windsor Castle, Berkshire; Balmoral Castle, Aberdeen-
shire; Sandringham, Norfolk.

PRINCE OF WALES.

§*His Royal Highness Prince*
CHARLES PHILIP ARTHUR
GEORGE, *KG, GCB, Prince of
Wales and Earl of Chester,
Duke of Cornwall and Rothesay,
Earl of Carrick, and Baron of
Renfrew, Lord of the Isle and
Great Steward of Scotland,* el.
son of HM Queen Elizabeth II;
b. Nov. 14th, 1948; ed. at
Cheam Sch., at Gordonstoun,
at Geelong Gram. Sch., Trin.
Coll., Camb. (MA), and Univ.
Coll. of Wales, Aberystwyth;
Bar. Gray's Inn 1974, Hon.
Bencher 1975; Personal ADC
to HM since 1973; Lt. RN
since 1973; Col.-in-Ch. R.
Regt. of Wales (24th/41st
Foot) since 1969; Col. Welsh
Gds. since 1974; Fl. Lt.
RAF since 1971; Pres. Soc. of
St. George's and Descendants
of KGs since 1975; Commo-
dore of R. Thames Yacht
Club; represented HM at
Memorial Ser. for PM of
Aust. 1967, at Independence Celebrations in Fiji 1970, at Requiem Mass for
Gen. Charles de Gaulle 1970, at Bahamas Independence Celebrations 1973, and
at Coronation of King of Nepal 1975; Pres. of Welsh Environment Foundation
since 1971; Chm. of Admin. Council of King George's Jubilee Trusts (for
Youth) since 1974; High Steward of Roy. Borough of Windsor and Maiden-
head since 1974; Coronation Medal 1953; Grand Cross of White Rose of
Finland 1969; Grand Cordon of Supreme Order of Chrysanthemum of Japan
1971; Grand Cross of The House of Orange of the Netherlands 1972; Grand
Cross of Order of Oak Crown of Luxembourg 1972; Knt. Order of Elephant of
Denmark 1974 and Grand Cross of Order of Ojasvi Rajanya of Nepal 1975;
cr. Prince of Wales and Earl of Chester July 26th, 1958 (invested July 1st,
1969); KG 1958 (invested and installed 1968), GCB and Great Master of Order
of the Bath 1975; received Freedom of City of Cardiff 1969, of Roy. Borough
of New Windsor 1970, of City of London 1971, and of Chester 1973; Liveryman of Fishmongers' Co.; a Freeman of Drapers' Co.

    * It was declared by Letters Patent of Oct. 22nd, 1948, that the children of this marriage shall
enjoy the style of "H.R.H." and the titular dignity of Prince or Princess.
    § Since attaining his majority in 1969, the Prince of Wales receives one-half of the annual net
revenues of the Duchy of Cornwall. The other half is voluntarily surrendered to the Exchequer.

Arms.—The Royal Arms, differenced by a label of three points argent, and in the centre an escutcheon of the arms of the Principality of Wales, viz., Quarterly or and gules, four lions passant guardant counterchanged, ensigned by the coronet of His degree. **Crest.**—Royal crest, differenced with a label of three points argent, but with the coronets those of the Heir Apparent. **Supporters.**—Same as the Royal Arms differenced by a label of three points argent, the *dexter* crowned with the Heir Apparent coronet, and the *sinister* gorged with a coronet of fleur-de-lis and crosses-pattée, a chain affixed thereto passing between the fore-legs and reflexed over the back, or. **Badges,**—*Dexter*, a plume of three ostrich feathers argent, enfiled by a coronet, composed of fleur-de-lis, and crosses-pattée or alternately with motto *Ich Dien*; *sinister*, a representation of the Badge of Wales, namely on a mount vert, a dragon passant gules, differenced as in the Crest with a label of three points argent. *Personal Flag in Wales*, Quarterly or and gules, four lions passant guardant counterchanged, over all an inescutcheon vert charged with the coronet of the Prince of Wales.

DUKE OF GLOUCESTER.

His Royal Highness Prince RICHARD ALEXANDER WALTER GEORGE, *GCVO*; 2nd Duke; *b.* Aug. 26th, 1944; *s.* 1974; ed. at Eton, and Magdalene Coll., Camb. (MA, Dip. of Arch.); RIBA; KStJ; a partner of Hunt Thompson Assos.; Comdt.-in-Ch. Ambulance Corps. and DIVS., St. John Ambulance Bde. and Pres. Inst. of Advanced Motorists since 1971; Queen's Trustee of British Museum since 1973; Col.-in-Ch. The Gloucestershire Regt. since 1975; Grand Prior, Order of St. John of Jerusalem since 1975; Vice-Pres. of British Leprosy Relief Assocn.; Liveryman of Vintners' Co. & Hon. Freeman of Grocers' Co.; Hon. Freeman and Liveryman of Goldsmiths' Co.; has Grand Cross Order of St. Olav of Norway; GCVO 1974: *m.* July 8th, 1972, Birgitte Eva, DStJ; (Pres. of London Region WRVS, of Roy. Alexander and Albert Sch., and of Cambridge House), da. of Asger Preben Wissing Henriksen, lawyer, of Odense, Denmark (by his 1st wife, Vivian, da. of the late Waldemar Oswald Van Deurs, whose name she assumed), and has issue.

Arms,—The Royal Arms, differenced by a label of five points argent, the centre and two outer charged with a lion passant guardant, and the two inner with a cross gules. **Crest,**—On a coronet composed of four crosses-patée alternated with four strawberry leaves, a lion statant guardant or, crowned with the like coronet, and differenced with the label as in the Arms. **Supporters,**—The Royal Supporters, differenced with the like coronet and label. (By Royal Warrant dated Feb. 24th, 1975, the Arms which were assigned to a grandchild of a Sovereign became hereditary.)
Residences,—Kensington Palace, W8; Barnwell Manor, Peterborough. *Clubs,*—Bath, Cavalry, Buck's, Royal Ulster Yacht.

SON LIVING.
ALEXANDER PATRICK GREGERS RICHARD (*Earl of Ulster*), *b.* Oct. 24th, 1974.

WIDOW LIVING OF FIRST DUKE.*

Lady Alice Christabel Montagu-Douglas-Scott, *GCB, CI, GCVO, GBE* (*HRH Princess Alice, Duchess of Gloucester*), (1, Kensington Palace, W8; Barnwell Manor, Peterborough), 3rd da. of 7th Duke of Buccleuch and Queensberry; *b.* Dec. 25th, 1900; ed. at St. James's Sch., W. Malvern and in Paris; Air Marshal WRAF, Col.-in-Ch. KOSB, R. Hussars and RCT, Dep. Col.-in-Ch. R. Anglian Regt., and a Member of Council British Red Cross Soc.; Dep. Comdt.-in-Ch. of Nursing Corps and DIVS. since 1937; GCStJ; received Freedom of City of Edinburgh 1937, Gloucester 1939, and Belfast 1952; GBE (Civil) and CI 1937, GCVO 1948, GCB (Civil) 1975: *m.* Nov. 6th, 1935, HRH Prince Henry William Frederick Albert, KG, KT, KP, GCB, GCMG, GCVO, PC, 1st Duke of Gloucester, who *d.* June 10th, 1974, 3rd son of HM King George V.

Residences,—Kensington Palace, W8; Barnwell Manor, Peterborough.

PREDECESSOR.—[1] *HRH Prince* Henry William Frederick Albert, *KG, KT, KP, GCB, GCMG, GCVO, PC*, 3rd son of his late Majesty King George V; *b.* March 31st, 1900; Field Marshal, and Marshal of RAF; Gov.-Gen. and C-in-C, Commonwealth of Australia 1944-47; received Roy Victorian Chain 1932; cr. *Baron Culloden, Earl of Ulster,* and *Duke of Gloucester* (peerage of UK) 1928: *m.* Nov. 6th, 1935, Lady Alice Christabel Montagu-Douglas-Scott, GCB, CI, GCVO, GBE, 3rd da. of 7th Duke of Buccleuch, *d.* June 10th, 1974; *s.* by his yr. son [2] RICHARD ALEXANDER WALTER GEORGE, 2nd Duke, and present peer; also Earl of Ulster, and Baron Culloden, and has issue.

---

* Under the Civil List Act 1972, provision is made for Her Royal Highness Prin cess Alice, Duchess of Gloucester, to receive in widowhood £20,000 per annum.

DUKE OF KENT.

His Royal Highness Prince
EDWARD GEORGE NICHOLAS PAUL
PATRICK, *GCMG, GCVO*, 2nd Duke;
b. Oct. 9th, 1935; *s.* 1942; ed. at
Eton, in Switzerland, and at RMA,
Sandhurst; Hon. DCL Durham
1961; Lt. Col. R. Scots Dragoon
Gds. (Carabiniers and Greys); Col.
in-Ch. R. Regt. of Fusiliers; Col.
Scots Gds. since 1974; acted as
Special Representative of HM the
Queen at Independence Celebra-
tions in Sierra Leone 1961, Uganda
1962, the Gambia 1965, and Guyana
and Barbados 1966, and at Corona-
tion of King of Tonga 1967; per-
sonal ADC to HM since 1966; GSO
II E. Command 1966-68, and a Coy.
Instructor, RMA, Sandhurst 1968-
70, and in command C Sqdn. R.
Scots Greys 1970-71; Grand Master
of United Grand Lodge of Free-
masons of England and Grand
Master of Order of St. Michael and
St. George since 1967; Pres. of Wellington Coll., since 1969, of Commonwealth
War Graves Comm. since 1970, and of Scout Assocn. since 1975; Hon. Free-
man of Clothworkers Co., Freeman & Mercers' Co., and Hon. Liveryman of
Salters' Co.; received Hon. Freedom of City of Georgetown, Guyana, 1966;
has Orders of St. George and St. Constantine of Greece (1st Class), of Tri
Shakti Patta of Nepal (1st Class), Grand Band of Order of The Star of Africa,
of Liberia, and Grand Cross of Order of Al-Nahda of Jordan; GCVO 1960,
GCMG 1967: *m.* June 8th, 1961, Katharine Lucy Mary, only da. of the late
Sir William Arthington Worsley, 4th Bt., and has issue.

Arms.—The Royal Arms, differenced by a label of five points argent, the points charged with
an anchor azure and a cross gules alternately. *Crest,*—On a coronet of four crosses
patée alternated with four strawberry leaves, a lion statant guardant or, crowned with the like
coronet, and differenced with a label as in the Arms. *Supporters.*—The Royal Supporters, differenced
with the like coronet and label. (By Royal Warrant dated Feb. 24th, 1975, the Arms which were
assigned to a grandchild of a Sovereign became hereditary.)

Residences,—York House, SW2; Anmer Hall, Kings Lynn, Norfolk.

SONS LIVING.

GEORGE PHILIP NICHOLAS (*Earl of St. Andrews*), *b.* June 26th, 1962; ed. at Eton.
Lord Nicholas Charles Edward Jonathan *Windsor, b.* July 25th, 1970.

DAUGHTER LIVING.

Lady Helen Marina Lucy *Windsor, b.* April 28th, 1964.

BROTHER LIVING.

H.R.H. *Prince* Michael George Charles Franklin,
b. July 4th, 1942; ed. at Eton, and at R.M.A.
Sandhurst; Capt. R. Hussars (PWO);
Foreign Attaché, Liaison Div., Min. of
Defence 1969-71.
Residence,—Kensington Palace, W8.

SISTER LIVING.

HRH *Princess* Alexandra Helen Elizabeth
Olga Christabel (*Princess Alexandra, the
Hon. Mrs. Angus Ogilvy*), *GCVO, b.* Dec.
25th, 1936: Hon. LL.D Brisbane Univ.,
Australia 1959, Hong Kong 1961, and
Mauritius 1974; Chancellor of Lancaster
Univ. 1964 and of Univ. of Mauritius 1974,
Hon. Fellow of Roy. Faculty of Physicians and Surgs., Glasgow 1960, known as Roy. Coll. since
1962, and in Faculty of Anaesthetists, Roy. Coll. of Surgs. of England since 1967, and of Roy. Coll.
of Obstetricians and Gynaecologists since 1969; Col.-in-Ch. 17th/21st Lancers since 1969, and
Queen's Own Rifles of Canada since 1960; Dep. Col.-in-Ch. the LI since 1969, Dep. Hon. Col. of
Roy. Yeo. TAVR since 1975; Air Ch. Comdt. of Princess Mary's RAF Nursing Ser. since 1966,
Hon. Comdt. General Roy. Hong Kong Police Force, and Roy. Hong Kong Aux. Police Force since
1969, and Hon. Comdt. of Women's R. Aust. Naval Ser. since 1969; acted as Special Representative
of HM the Queen at Independence Celebrations in Nigeria 1960, and at 150th Anniversary Celebrations of founding of Modern Singapore 1969; Patron of QARNNS; Pres. Roy Commonwealth
Soc. for the Blind, Children's Country Holidays Fund, Queen Alexandra's House Assocn., Star
and Garter Home for Disabled Sailors, Soldiers and Airmen, Alexandra Day, British Sch. at Rome,
and Roy. Humane Soc., Vice-Pres. British Red Cross Soc. and Grand Pres. of Roy. Life Saving
Soc.; GCVO 1960: *m.* April 24th, 1963, the Hon. Angus James Bruce Ogilvy, 2nd son of 12th Earl
of Airlie, and has issue living, James Robert Bruce, *b.* Feb. 29th, 1964,—Marina Victoria Alexandra,
b. July 31st, 1966. *Residence,*—Thatched House Lodge, Richmond Park, Surrey.

PREDECESSOR.—[1] *H.R.H. Prince* GEORGE EDWARD ALEXANDER EDMUND, *K.G., K.T.,
G.C.M.G., G.C.V.O., P.C.*, 4th son of His late Majesty King George V. ; *b.* Dec. 20th, 1902 ; Rear-
Adm., Maj.-Gen. in the Army, and Air Commodore R.A.F., received Roy. Victorian Chain 1936 ; cr.
Baron Downpatrick, Earl of St. Andrews, and Duke of Kent (peerage of United Kingdom) 1934 : *m.*

Nov. 29th, 1934, HRH Princess Marina, *CI*, *GCVO*, *GBE*, who *d.* Aug. 27th, 1968, youngest da. of HRH the late Prince Nicholas of Greece, *GCB*, *GCVO*; *d.* (killed on active ser. during European War) Aug. 25th, 1942; *s.* by his el. son [2] EDWARD GEORGE NICHOLAS PAUL PATRICK, 2nd Duke and present peer; also Earl of St. Andrews and Baron Downpatrick.

DUKEDOM OF WINDSOR (Windsor) [Extinct 1972.]

WIDOW LIVING OF FIRST AND LAST DUKE.

Mrs. WALLIS WARFIELD (formerly Simpson), (*Her Grace the Duchess of Windsor*), (4, Route du Champ D'Entrainement, Bois de Boulogne, Paris XVI), da. of the late Teakle Wallis Warfield, of Baltimore, Maryland, USA: *m.* June 3rd, 1937, His Royal Highness Prince Edward Albert Christian George Andrew Patrick David, KG, KT, KP, GCB, GCSI, GCMG, GCIE, GCVO, GBE, ISO, MC, 1st Duke of Windsor, who *d.* May 28th, 1972, when the title became ext.

SOVEREIGNS

SINCE THE NORMAN CONQUEST.

WILLIAM I., surnamed "The Conqueror"; styled *Willielmus Rex Anglorum*; b. 1028; obtained the crown by conquest Oct. 14th, 1066; c. Dec. 25th, 1066: m. 1053, Maud, or Matilda, who d. 1083, dau. of Baldwin V., Count of Flanders; d. at Hermentrude, near Rouen Sept. 9th, 1087; bur. at Caen; s. by his 2nd son,

WILLIAM II., surnamed "Rufus"; styled *Dei Gratiâ Rex Anglorum*; b. about 1056; c. Sept. 26th, 1087; accidentally killed in the New Forest, Aug. 2nd, 1100; bur. in St. Swithin's, Winchester; s. by his brother,

HENRY I., surnamed "Beauclerc"; styled the same as William II.; b. 1070; c. Aug. 5th, 1100: m. 1st, Nov. 11th, 1100, Matilda, who d. 1118, dau. of Malcolm III., Caenmor, King of Scots; 2ndly, Feb. 2nd, 1121, Adeliza (who m. 2ndly William de Albini), dau. of Godfrey, Duke of Louvaine and Count of Brabant; d. at St. Denis, in Normandy, Dec. 1st, 1135; bur. in Reading Abbey; s. by his nephew,

STEPHEN, third son of Stephen, Count of Blois and Chartres, and Adela, 4th dau. of William I.; styled *Rex Anglorum Dux Normannorum*; b. 1096; c. Dec. 26th, 1135: m. 11—, Matilda, who d. 1151, dau. and heir of Eustace, Count of Boulogne; d. at Dover Oct. 25th, 1154; bur. in Faversham Abbey; s. by his cousin,

HENRY II., el. son of Geoffrey Plantagenet, Count of Anjou, and Matilda [or Maud], dau. of Henry I.; styled *Rex Angliæ, Dux Normanniæ et Aquitaniæ et Comes Andegaviæ*; b. 1133; c. Dec. 19th, 1154: m. 1151, Eleanor, who d. 1202, the divorced wife of Louis VII. of France, and dau. and a co.-heiress of William V., Duke of Aquitaine; d. at Chinon, near Tours, July 6th, 1189; bur. at Fontevraud in Anjou; s. by his el. surviving son,

RICHARD I., surnamed "Cœur de Lion"; styled the same as Henry II.; b. Sept. 8th, 1157; c. Sept. 3rd, 1189: m. 1191, Berengaria, dau. of Sancho IV., King of Navarre; d.s.p. at Chalus, France, April 6th, 1199; bur. at Fontevraud; s. by his brother,

JOHN, surnamed "Lackland"; styled *Rex Angliæ, Dominus Hiberniæ, Dux Normanniæ, et Dux Aquitaniæ*; b. Dec. 24th, 1166; c. May 27th, 1199: m. 1st, 1189, Isabella [whom he divorced upon the plea of consanguinity], dau. and co-heiress of William, Earl of Gloucester; 2ndly, 1200, Isabella [who d. 1246, having m. 2ndly Hugh le Brun, Lord of Lusignan and Valence in Poitou], dau. and co-heiress of Aymer Taillefer, Count of Angoulême; d. at Newark Castle, Oct. 19th, 1216; bur. in Worcester Cathedral; s. by his el. son,

HENRY III.; styled during the greater part of his reign the same as his father, and during the latter portion *Rex Angliæ, Dominus Hiberniæ et Dux Aquitaniæ*; b. Oct. 10th, 1206; c. Oct. 28th, 1216: m. 1236, Eleanor, who d. 1291, dau. and co.-heiress of Raymond Berengar, Count of Provence; d. at Westminster, Nov. 16th, 1272; bur. in Westminster Abbey; s. by his el. surviving son,

EDWARD I.; styled the same as Henry III.; b. June 17th, 1239; c. Aug. 19th, 1274: m. 1st, 1254, Eleanor, who d. 1290, dau. of Ferdinand III., King of Castile; 2ndly, 1299, Margaret, who d. 1317, dau. of Philip II. of France; d. at Burgh-on-the-Sands July 7th, 1307; bur. in Westminster Abbey; s. by his el. son,

EDWARD II., surnamed "of Carnarvon"; styled the same as Henry III.: b. April 25th, 1284; c. Feb. 23rd, 1308: m. Jan. 28th, 1308, Isabella who d. 1358, dau. of Philip IV. of France; deposed by Parliament Jan. 7th, 1327; murdered at Berkeley Castle Sept. 21st, 1327; bur. at Gloucester; s. by his son,

EDWARD III.; styled the same as Henry III. until 1339 and afterwards *Rex Angliæ et Franciæ et Dominus Hiberniæ*; b. Nov. 13th, 1312; proclaimed King Jan. 25th, 1327; c. Feb. 1st, 1328: m. Jan. 24th, 1329, Philippa, who d. Aug. 15th, 1369, dau. of William, Count of Holland and Hainault; d. at Shene, Surrey, June 21st, 1377; bur. in Westminster Abbey; s. by his grandson,

RICHARD II., 2nd son of Edward the "Black Prince"; styled the same as Edward III.; b. Jan. 6th, 1367; c. July 16th, 1377: m. 1st, Jan. 22nd, 1383, Anne, who d. 1395, dau. of Emperor Charles IV. of Bohemia; 2ndly, Oct. 31st, 1396, Isabel [who m. 2ndly, Charles the poet Duke of Orleans], 2nd dau. of Charles VI. of France; deposed Sept. 30th, 1399; murdered in Pontefract Castle Feb. 14th, 1400; bur. in Westminster Abbey; s. by his cousin,

HENRY IV., el. son of John of Gaunt, Duke of Lancaster, K.G., who was 4th son of Edward III.; styled the same as Edward III.; b. 1367; c. Oct. 13th, 1399: m. 1st, 1380, Lady Mary de Bohun, who d. July 4th, 1394, dau. and co.-heiress of Humphrey, Earl of Hereford; 2ndly, 1403, Joan, who d. June 10th, 1437, dau. of Charles II., King of Navarre, and widow of John de Montfort, Duke of Brittany; d. in the Jerusalem Chamber, Westminster, March 20th, 1413; bur. at Canterbury; s. by his son,

HENRY V.; styled the same as Edward III. until 1420, and afterwards *Rex Angliæ, Hæres et Regens Franciæ, et Dominus Hiberniæ*; b. Aug. 9th, 1387; c. April 9th, 1413: m. June 3rd, 1420, Katherine [who m. 2ndly Owen Tudor], yst. dau. of Charles VI, King of France; d. at Vincennes, in France, Aug. 31st, 1422; bur. in Westminster Abbey; s. by his son,

HENRY VI.; styled *Rex Angliæ et Franciæ et Dominus Hiberniæ*; b. Dec. 6th; 1421, c. Nov. 6th, 1429, and also c. King of France in Notre Dame, Paris, Dec. 17th, 1431, m. April 22nd, 1445, Margaret of Anjou, who d. 1482, dau. of René, titular King of Sicily, Naples and Jerusalem; deposed Mar. 4th, 1461; recovered his crown Oct. 9th, 1470; deposed secondly May 21st, 1471, and d. in the Tower of London a few days after, it is supposed by violence; bur. at Windsor; s. by his kinsman,

EDWARD IV., Duke of York, el. son of Richard, Duke of York, the "Protector of England," who was great-great-grandson of Lionel, Duke of Clarence, 3rd son of Edward III.; styled the same as Henry VI.; b. April 28th, 1442; proclaimed March 4th and c. June 29th, 1461: m. May 1st, 1464, Elizabeth, who d. June 1492, dau. of Sir Richard Woodville, Earl Rivers and widow of Sir John Grey of Groby; d. at Westminster, April 9th, 1483; bur. at Windsor; s. by his son,

EDWARD V.; styled the same as HENRY VI.; b. Nov. 2nd, 1470; proclaimed King on the death of his father but was never crowned; was imprisoned in the Tower of London, where he and his only brother, the Duke of York, were murdered on June 22nd, 1483, at the instigation, it is said, of their uncle, the Duke of Gloucester, who had usurped the throne under the title of

RICHARD III.; styled the same as Henry VI.; b. Oct. 2nd, 1452; c. July 6th, 1483: m. July 12th, 1472, Lady Anne Nevill, who d. March 16th, 1485, dau. of Richard Nevill, Earl of Warwick, and widow of Edward, Prince of Wales, son of Henry VI; killed at Bosworth Field Aug. 22nd, 1485, where his forces were defeated by Henry Tudor Earl of Richmond, grandson of Queen Katherine [see Henry V.] by her 2nd marriage with Owen Tudor, and great-great-grandson of John of Gaunt, Duke of Lancaster, 4th son of Edward III.; bur. in Grey Friars Abbey, Leicester; s. by his rival, Henry, Earl of Richmond (ante) who ascended as

HENRY VII.; styled the same as Henry VI.; *b.* Jan. 28th, 1457; proclaimed on the field of Bosworth Aug. 22nd, 1485; *c.* Oct. 30th, 1485: *m.* Jan. 18th, 1486, the Lady Elizabeth (Plantagenet), who *d.* Feb. 11th, 1503, el. dau. and heiress of Edward IV.; *d.* at Richmond April 21st, 1509; *bur.* in Westminster Abbey; *s.* by his 2nd son,

HENRY VIII.; styled 1521–42 *King of England and France, Defender of the Faith, Lord of Ireland, and of the Church of England on Earth Supreme Head,* and in 1542 and afterwards, *King of England France and Ireland, Defender of the Faith, and of the Church of England and also of Ireland in Earth the Supreme Head;* was the first English sovereign who bore the title of *Majesty; b.* Jan. 28th, 1491; *c.* June 24th, 1509: *m.* 1st, June 11th, 1509, Princess Katharine, who *d.* Jan. 6th, 1536, dau. of Ferdinand V., King of Aragon, and widow of his el. brother, Prince Arthur, Prince of Wales; this marriage was annulled May 23rd, 1533, when he avowed his marriage (which had taken place on Jan. 25th, 1533, and was confirmed judicially May 28th, 1533) with Anne Boleyn (cr. Marchioness of Pembroke Sept. 1st, 1532), dau. of Thomas, Earl of Wiltshire and Ormonde; on May 15th, 1536, the Queen and her brother Viscount Rochford were arraigned at the Tower and condemned to death, and on the 17th the marriage was declared invalid; on the 19th of the same month they were executed; on the following day, May 20th, the King *m.* 3rdly, Jane, who *d.* Oct. 14th, 1537, dau. of Sir John Seymour, Knt. Banneret; on Jan. 6th, 1539, the King *m.* 4thly, Princess Anne, dau. of John, Duke of Cleves, and in July of the same year he divorced her; she *d.* July 15th, 1557; the King *m.* 5thly, Aug. 8th, 1540, Katharine, dau. of Lord Edmund Howard, who was 3rd son of the 2nd Duke of Norfolk; this lady was attainted, and on Feb. 13th, 1542, was beheaded on Tower Hill; the King *m.* 6thly, July 12th, 1543, Katherine, dau. of Sir Thomas Parr, and widow of the Hon. Sir Edward Burgh and of John Nevill, 3rd Lord Latymer [this Queen survived the King and *d.* Sept. 5th, 1548, having in May, 1547, remarried Thomas, Lord Seymour of Sudeley, K.G., Lord High Adm., uncle of Edward VI., and brother of Queen Jane Seymour]; the King *d.* at Whitehall Jan. 28th, 1547; *bur.* at Windsor; *s.* by his only son (by his marriage with Jane Seymour),

EDWARD VI.; styled the same as Henry VIII.: *b.* Oct. 12th, 1537; *c.* Feb. 25th, 1547; *d.s.p.* at Greenwich July 6th, 1553; *bur.* in Westminster Abbey: *s.* by his half-sister (the only dau. of Queen Katharine of Aragon),

MARY I.; styled the same as Henry VIII. until her marriage, when she and her husband were styled *Philip and Mary, by the Grace of God, King and Queen of England and France, Naples, Jerusalem, and Ireland, Defenders of the Faith, Princes of Spain and Sicily, Archdukes of Austria, Dukes of Milan, Burgundy and Brabant; b.* Feb. 8th, 1516; *c.* Oct. 1st, 1553: *m.* July 25th, 1554, Philip II., King of Spain; *d.s.p.* Nov. 17th, 1558; *bur.* in Westminster Abbey; *s.* by her half-sister (the only dau. of Queen Anne Boleyn),

ELIZABETH I.; styled *Queen of England, France and Ireland, Defender of the Faith; b.* Sept. 7th, 1533; *c.* Jan. 15th, 1559; *d.* at Richmond, unmarried, Mar. 24th, 1603; *bur.* in Westminster Abbey; *s.* by her kinsman, only son of Mary Queen of Scots and Henry Stuart, Lord Darnley, and great-grandson of Margaret, el. dau. of Henry VII.,

JAMES I., who in 1567 had *s.* as King James VI. of Scotland [see "SOVEREIGNS OF SCOTLAND"]; styled *King of England, Scotland, France and Ireland, Defender of the Faith; b.* June 19th, 1566; crowned King of England, July 25th, 1603: *m.* Aug. 20th, 1589, Princess Anne, who *d.* Mar. 2nd, 1619, dau. of Frederick II., King of Denmark; *d.* at Theobalds, Herts, Mar. 27th, 1625; *bur.* in Westminster Abbey; *s.* by his 2nd and el. surviving son,

CHARLES I.; styled the same as James I.; *b.* Nov. 19th, 1600; *c.* Feb. 2nd, 1626: *m.* May 11th, 1625, Princess Henrietta Maria, who *d.* 1669, dau. of Henry IV., King of France; on Jan. 27th, 1649, the King was found guilty of high treason by a "High Court of Justice" appointed by Parliament, and being condemned to death, was beheaded at Whitehall on the 30th of that month; *bur.* in St. George's Chapel, Windsor.

After the execution of King Charles, there was an interregnum entitled the "COMMONWEALTH." A Republic was established, and continued until Dec. 16th, 1653, when Oliver Cromwell was [declared *Lord Protector:* he *d.* Sept. 3rd, 1658, and was *s.* in the Protectorate by his son Richard, who held the office until April 1659, when a Republic was re-established. This form of government continued until May 8th, 1660, when

CHARLES II., el. surviving son of Charles I., was proclaimed by the same style as James I, his reign having legally commenced on the death of his father; *b.* May 29th, 1630; *c.* King of Scotland Jan. 1st, 1651, and King of England, April 23rd, 1661: *m.* May 21st, 1662, Princess Katharine of Braganza, Infanta of Portugal, who *d.* Nov. 30th, 1705, dau. of John IV., King of Portugal; *d.* at Whitehall, Feb. 6th, 1685; *bur.* in Westminster Abbey *s.* by his brother,

JAMES II.; styled the same as James I.; *b.* Oct. 14th, 1633; *c.* April 23rd, 1685: *m.* 1st, Nov. 24th, 1659, Lady Anne Hyde, who *d.* March 31st, 1671, el. dau. of 1st Earl of Clarendon, Lord Chancellor; 2ndly, Sept. 30th, 1673, Princess Mary Beatrice Eleanora d'Este, who *d.* May 8th, 1718, dau. of Alphonso III., Duke of Modena; declared by Act of Parliament 1689 to have abdicated Dec. 11th, 1688; *d.* at St. Germain Sept. 16th, 1701; *bur.* there: *s.* by his dau. Mary and her husband William Prince of Orange (son of Mary, Princess Royal, dau. of Charles I.), who ascend the throne jointly as

WILLIAM III. AND MARY II.; styled *King and Queen of England, Scotland, France and Ireland, Defenders of the Faith;* proclaimed Feb. 13th, 1689; crowned together April 11th, 1689; the Queen was *b.* April 30th, 1662: *m.* Nov. 4th, 1677, William, Prince of Orange [infra]; *d.* at Kensington Dec. 28th, 1694; *bur.* in Westminster Abbey. The King was *b.* Nov. 14th, 1650: *m.* Nov. 4th, 1677, Princess Mary [ante], dau. of James II., *d.* Mar. 8th, 1702; *bur.* in Westminster Abbey; *s.* by the sister of Queen Mary II.,

ANNE; styled *Queen of Great Britain, France and Ireland, Defender of the Faith; b.* Feb. 6th, 1665; *c.* April 23rd, 1702: *m.* July 28th, 1683, Prince George, who *d.* Oct. 28th, 1708, son of Frederick III., King of Denmark; *d.* at Kensington Aug. 1st, 1714, leaving no surviving issue; *bur.* in Westminster Abbey; *s.* in accordance with the Act of Settlement of 1701 by her kinsman, el. son of Ernest, Elector of Hanover, by the Princess Sophia, granddau. of James I., who ascended the throne as

GEORGE I.; styled *King of Great Britain, France and Ireland, Duke of Brunswick-Lüneburg, Elector of Hanover, Defender of the Faith; b.* May 28th, 1660; *s.* his father as Duke of Brunswick-Lüneburg and Elector of Hanover Jan. 23rd, 1698; *c.* Oct. 20th, 1714: *m.* Nov. 21st, 1682, Princess Sophia Dorothea, who *d.* Nov. 13th, 1726 (having been divorced, according to Hanoverian Law, Dec. 28th, 1694), dau. of George William, Duke of Brunswick and Zelle; *d.* at Osnabrück June 11th, 1727; *bur.* at Hanover (re-buried at Herrenhausen 1957); *s.* by his son,

GEORGE II.; styled the same as George I.; *b.* Oct. 30th, 1683; *c.* Oct. 11th, 1727: *m.* Aug. 22nd [old style], 1705, Princess Wilhelmina Charlotte Caroline, who *d.* Nov. 20th, 1737, dau. of John Frederick, Margrave of Brandenburg-Anspach; *d.* at Kensington Oct. 25th, 1760; *bur.* in Westminster Abbey; *s.* by his grandson,

GEORGE III., el. son of Frederick, Prince of Wales; styled the same as George I. until Jan. 1st, 1801, and afterwards *By the Grace of God, of the United Kingdom of Great Britain and Ireland King, Defender of the Faith* (also *Elector of Hanover* until Aug. 12th, 1814, when that Country was recognized by the Allied Powers as a Kingdom, and he became *King of Hanover*) *b.* June 4th, 1738; *c.* Sept. 22nd, 1761:

m. Sept. 8th, 1761, Princess Charlotte Sophia, who *d.* Nov. 17th, 1818, dau. of Charles Louis Frederick, Duke of Mecklenburg-Strelitz; *d.* at Windsor Jan. 29th, 1820; *bur.* in St. George's Chapel, Windsor; *s.* by his son,

GEORGE IV.; styled the same as

George III.; *b.* Aug. 12th, 1762; was *Regent of the United Kingdom* from Feb. 5th, 1811, until his accession to the throne; *c.* July 19th, 1821: *m.* April 8th, 1795, his cousin Princess Caroline Amelia Elizabeth, who *d.* Aug. 7th, 1821, 2nd dau. of Charles William Ferdinand, Reigning Duke of Brunswick-Wolfenbuttel; *d.* June 26th, 1830; *bur.* at Windsor; *s.* by his brother,

WILLIAM IV.; styled the same as

George III.; *b.* Aug. 21st, 1765; *c.* Sept. 8th, 1831: *m.* July 11th, 1818, Princess Adelaide Louisa Theresa Caroline Amelia, who *d.* Dec. 2nd, 1849, el. dau. of George, Reigning Duke of Saxe-Meiningen; *d.* June 20th, 1837; *bur.* at Windsor; *s.* as Queen of the United Kingdom by his niece, Alexandrina Victoria, only child of H.R.H. Edward, Duke of Kent and Strathearn, 4th son of George III., and as King of Hanover (under the Salic Law) by his next surviving brother, Ernest Augustus, Duke of Cumberland and Teviotdale. Alexandrina Victoria ascended the throne as

VICTORIA; styled the same as George

III. until Jan. 1st, 1877, afterwards *By the Grace of God, of the United Kingdom of Great Britain and Ireland, Queen, Defender of the Faith, Empress of India*; *b.* May 24th, 1819; *c.* June 28th, 1838; proclaimed Empress of India Jan. 1st, 1877: *m.* Feb. 10th, 1840, H.R.H. Prince Francis Albert Augustus Charles Emmanuel, Duke of Saxony, Prince of Saxe-Coburg and Gotha (Prince Consort) [*cr.* His Royal Highness, Feb. 7th, 1840, and Prince Consort, June 25th, 1857], who *d.* Dec. 14th, 1861, second son of Ernest Frederick Anthony Charles Louis, Reigning Duke of Saxe-Coburg and Gotha; *d.* at Osborne Jan. 22nd, 1901; *bur.* at Frogmore; *s.* by her el. son,

EDWARD VII.; styled the same

as Queen Victoria, until Aug. 17th, 1901, afterwards *By the Grace of God, of the United*

Kingdom of Great Britain and Ireland, and of the British Dominions beyond the Seas, King, Defender of the Faith, Emperor of India; *b.* Nov. 9th, 1841; *c.* Aug. 9th, 1902: *m.* March 10th, 1863, Princess Alexandra Caroline Mary Charlotte Louisa Julia of Denmark, who *d.* Nov. 20th, 1925, el. dau. of the late Christian IX. King of Denmark; *d.* at Buckingham Palace, May 6th, 1910; *bur.* at Windsor; *s.* by his second but only surviving son,

GEORGE V; styled the same as

King Edward VII., until May 13th, 1927, afterwards *By the Grace of God, of Great Britain, Ireland and the British Dominions beyond the Seas, King, Defender of the Faith, Emperor of India*; *b.* June 3rd, 1865; *c.* June 22nd, 1911; assumed by Roy. Proclamation on July 17th, 1917, the name of Windsor for his House and family: *m.* July 6th, 1893, H.S.H. Princess Victoria Mary Augusta Louisa Olga Pauline Claudine Agnes, who *d.* March 24th, 1953, only da. of H.H. the late Duke (Francis Paul Charles Louis Alexander) of Teck; *d.* at Sandringham, Jan. 20th, 1936; *bur.* at Windsor; *s.* by his el. son,

EDWARD VIII.; styled the same as

King George V.; *b.* June 23rd, 1894; abdicated Dec. 11th, 1936, when he also renounced the Throne for his descendants; never crowned: *m.* June 3rd, 1937, Mrs. (Bessie) Wallis Warfield (formerly Simpson), da. of the late Teakle Wallis Warfield, of Baltimore USA; *d.* May 28th 1972; *bur.* at Frogmore, Windsor, *s.* by his brother,

GEORGE VI.; styled the same as

King George V. until June 22nd, 1948, when by Roy. Proclamation he discontinued the style of Emperor of India; *b.* Dec. 14th, 1895; *c.* May 12th, 1937: *m.* April 26th, 1923, Lady Elizabeth Angela Marguerite Bowes-Lyon, dau. of 14th Earl of Strathmore and Kinghorne; *d.* at Sandringham, Feb. 6th, 1952; *bur.* at Windsor; *s.* by his el. dau.,

ELIZABETH II.; styled the same as

King George VI until March 26th, 1953, and afterwards *By the Grace of God, of the United Kingdom of Great Britain, and Northern Ireland and of her other Realms and Territories Queen, Head of the Commonwealth, Defender of the Faith.*

THE PEERAGE.

The scope of EACH ARTICLE IN THE PEERAGE is designed to include information concerning every *living* male descended in the male line from the first Peer and of all *living* females being issue of males so descended. Legitimated children are included, but are not normally in remainder, except for the Peerage of Scotland.

DECEASED FEMALE COLLATERALS and their issue are not generally included.

ISSUE, where both parents are mentioned in the work, will be found under the father's name.

CHRISTIAN NAMES OF THE HEIR apparent or heir presumptive are given in capital letters.

CREATIONS :—
E. = England (prior to May 1st, 1707).
S. = Scotland (prior to May 1st, 1707).
I. = Ireland.
G.B. = Great Britain (May 1st, 1707 to Dec. 31st, 1800).
U.K. = United Kingdom (since Jan. 1st, 1801).

ABERCONWAY, BARON. (McLaren.) [Baron U.K. 1911, Bt. U.K. 1902.]

I am a son of the Church

CHARLES MELVILLE MCLAREN, 3rd Baron, and 3rd Baronet ; *b.* April 16th, 1913 ; *s.* 1953 ; ed. at Eton, and at New Coll., Oxford (B.A.) ; Bar. Middle Temple 1937 ; late R.A. ; Chm. of John Brown & Co. Ltd., of Sheepbridge Engineering Ltd., and English China Clays Ltd. ; a Dir. of Westland Aircraft Ltd., and Nat. Westminster Bank ; a Vice-Chm. of Sun, Alliance & London Insurance Co. Ltd. ; High Sheriff for Denbighshire 1950 ; Pres. of Roy. Horticultural Soc. since 1961 : *m.* 1st, 1941 (m. diss. 1949), Deirdre, da. of John Knewstub ; 2ndly, 1949, Ann Lindsay (BULLARD), only da. of Mrs. Alexander Lindsay Aymer, of New York City, U.S.A., and has issue living by 1st and 2nd marriages.

Arms,—Or, two chevronelles inverted gules between two shepherds' crooks in chief and in base a castle triple towered and with flags flying sable. Crest,—A representation of the Virgin Mary with the dexter arm uplifted vested azure, holding in the sinister arm the child Jesus. Supporters,—On either side a wyvern argent, wings erect gules, each supporting a banner or charged with a horse-shoe sable.

Seat,—Bodnant, Tal-y-Cafn, Denbighshire. *Town Residence,*—25, Egerton Terrace, S.W.3.

SONS LIVING. (*By 1st marriage.*)
Hon. HENRY CHARLES, *b.* May 26th, 1948 ; ed. at Eton.

(*By 2nd marriage*)
Hon. Michael Duncan, *b.* 1958 ; ed. at Eton.

DAUGHTERS LIVING. (*By 1st marriage.*)
Hon. Julia Harriet, *b.* 1942.
Hon. Caroline Mary, *b.* 1944.

BROTHER LIVING.
Hon. Christopher Melville (31, Upper Addison Gdns., W14 8AJ), *b.* 1934 ; ed. at Eton, and King's Coll., Camb. ; Bar. Inner Temple 1961.

SISTERS LIVING.
Hon. Elizabeth Mary, *b.* 1911 : *m.* 1938, Maj. Kenneth Ralph Malcolm Carlisle, Rifle Brigade, and has issue living, Kenneth Melville, *b.* 1941,—Christabel Mary (*Lady Watson*), *b.* 1939 : *m.* 1965, Sir James Andrew Watson, 5th Bt. (cr. 1866),—Katharine Jane (twin), *b.* 1941 : *m.* 1970, Victor Michael Newell,—Barbara Ann, *b.* 1951. *Residence,*—7, Laurie House, 16, Airlie Gdns., W8 7AW.
Hon. Anne Laura Dorinthea, *b.* 1927 ; ed. at Lady Margaret Hall, Oxford (Scholar, D.Phil. 1952) : *m.* 1952 (marriage dissolved 1959), Donald Michie, D.Phil., and has issue living, Jonathan Mark, *b.* 1957,—Susan Fiona Dorinthea, *b.* 1955,—Caroline Ruth, *b.* 1959. *Residence,*—9, Steele's Rd., NW3.

WIDOW LIVING OF SON OF SECOND BARON.
Lady Rose Mary Primrose Paget, dau. of 6th Marquess of Anglesey : *m.* 1940, Squadron Leader the Hon. John Francis McLaren, R.A.F. (retired), who *d.* 1953, and has issue living [see colls., infra]. *Residences,*—24, Coulson St., SW3 ; Old Bodnod ,Eglwysbach, Colwyn Bay, Denbighshire.

COLLATERAL BRANCHES LIVING.
Issue of the late Squadron Leader the Hon. John Francis McLaren, RAF, 2nd son of 2nd Baron, *b.* 1919, *d.* 1953: *m.* 1940, Lady Rose Mary Primrose Paget (ante) da. of 6th Marquess of Anglesey:—
Victoria Mary Caroline, *b.* 1945: *m.* 1966, Jonathan Jeremy Kirwan Taylor, of 42, Addison Rd., W14, yst. son of Sir Charles Stuart Taylor, TD, and has issue living, Arabella Lucy Kirwan, *b.* 1969,—Lucinda Sophia Kirwan, *b.* 1972.———Harriet Diana Christabel, *b.* 1949: *m.* 1972, Hugh John Reay Geddes of 12, Camden Sq., NW1, and Nantyreglwys, Llanboidy, Dyfed [see B. Geddes].

Issue of the late Hon. Francis Walter Stafford McLaren, M.P., 2nd Lieut. Roy. Flying Corps, younger son of 1st Baron, b. 1886, d. (killed in action during 1914-18 War) 1917: m. 1911, Dame Barbara, GBE [who d. 1973, having m. 2ndly, 1922, the 1st Baron Freyberg, who d. 1963, da. of the late Col. Sir Herbert Jekyll, KCMG, of Munstead House, Godalming:—

Martin, b. 1914; ed. at Eton (King's Scholar), at New Coll., Oxford (MA), and at Harvard Univ., USA; Bar. Middle Temple 1948; 1939-45 War as Maj. Gren. Guards and a GSO; MP for NW Div. of Bristol (C) 1959-66, and 1970-74; Asst. Govt. Whip 1961-63, and a Lord Commr. of the Treasury 1963-64; PPS to Sec. of State for Foreign and Commonwealth Affairs 1970-74; a Dir. of English China Clays, Ltd., and Archway Unit Trust Managers, Ltd.: m. 1943, Nancy, da. of the late Gordon Ralston, and has issue living, Richard Francis, b. 1946; ed. at Eton, and Oxford Univ.—Patrick Andrew, b. 1963. Residences,—The Old Rectory, Inkpen, Newbury; 30, Smith Sq., SW1.——Guy Lewis Ian, b. 1915; ed. at Eton, and at Univ. Coll., Oxford (BA); late Maj. Coldstream Guards; a Dir. of Clive Lester Ltd., and Trans. Ocean Sers. Ltd.: m. 1946, Maryse, da. of the late Alfred Jubin, of Lausanne, Switzerland, and has issue living, Michael, b. 1947,—Mary Caroline, b. 1951: m. 1971, Nicholas John Durlacher, of 44, Eaton Pl., SW1. Residence,—Pierrefleurs, Vineuil St. Firmin, Oise, France.

PREDECESSORS.—[1] Rt. Hon. CHARLES BENJAMIN BRIGHT McLaren, K.C., 3rd son of the late Duncan McLaren (sometime M.P. for Edinburgh), of Newington House, Edinburgh; b. 1850; M.P. for Stafford (L) 1880-86, and for W., or Bosworth, Div. of Leicestershire 1892-1910; cr. a Baronet 1902, P.C. 1908, and Baron Aberconway, of Bodnant, co. Denbigh (peerage of United Kingdom) 1911: m. 1877, Laura, C.B.E., who d. 1933, dau. of the late Henry Davis Pochin, of Bodnant, Denbighshire; d. 1934; s. by his el. son [2] HENRY DUNCAN, C.B.E., 2nd Baron; b. 1879; was Parliamentary Private Sec. to Pres. of Board of Trade (Rt. Hon. D. Lloyd George, M.P.) 1906-08, and Parliamentary Private Sec. to Chancellor of the Exchequer (Rt. Hon. D. Lloyd George, M.P.) 1908-10; Pres. of Roy. Horticultural Society 1931-53; sat as M.P. for Staffordshire, W. Div. (L) 1906-10, for Leicestershire, W., or Bosworth, Div. 1910-18, and Bosworth Div. 1918-22: m. 1910, Christabel Mary Melville, who d. 1974, da. of the late Sir Melville Leslie Macnaghten, CB [Macnaghten, Bt., colls.]; d. 1953; s. by his el. son [3] CHARLES MELVILLE, 3rd Baron and present peer.

ABERCORN, DUKE OF. (Hamilton.)

[Duke I. 1868, Bt. I. 1660.]

SOLA·NOBILITAS·VIRTUS

Virtue is the only nobility.

JAMES EDWARD HAMILTON, 4th Duke, and 14th Baronet; b. Feb. 29th, 1904; s. 1953; ed. at Eton; Capt. Grenadier Guards; Hon. Col. 5th Bn. Roy. Inniskilling Fusiliers (T.A.) since 1963; a Senator of N. Ireland 1949-62; Lord-Lieut. for co. Tyrone since 1950 (High Sheriff 1946), Co. Councillor for Tyrone since 1946, Chm. of Trustees, Ulster Museum since 1962, and Chancellor of New Univ. of Ulster since 1970; Pres. of Roy. U.K. Beneficient Assocn., of N.I. Council of YMCAs, of N.I. Branch "Not Forgotten Assocn.", of RNLI and Nat. Playing Fields Assocn., of Army Cadet Force Assocn., and of Western Assocn. T.A. & V.R. Assocn. NI; Vice-Pres. of Roy. British Legion NI Area; Pres., Roy. Forestry Soc. 1964-66: m. 1928, Lady Mary Kathleen Crichton, DCVO, sister of 5th Earl Erne, and has issue.

Arms,—Quarterly: 1st and 4th gules, three cinque foils pierced ermine, Hamilton; 2nd and 3rd argent, an ancient ship or lymphad, with one mast, the sails furled and oars out sable, Arran. [Also claims,—over all an escutcheon azure, charged with three fleurs-de-lis or, surmounted by a French ducal coronet, Chatelherault.] Crest,—Out of a ducal coronet or, an oak tree proper, fructed and penetrated through the stem transversely by a frame-saw proper, frame gold, the blade inscribed with the word "Through." Supporters.—Two antelopes argent, horned, unguled, ducally gorged, hoofed, and the chains reflexed over their backs or.
Seat,—Barons Court, Omagh, co. Tyrone. Club,—Turf.

SONS LIVING.

JAMES (Marquess of Hamilton) (7, Upper Belgrave St., SW1; Turf and Ulster Clubs; and RAC), b. July 4th, 1934; ed. at Eton, and Roy. Agric. Coll., Cirencester; late 2nd Lt. Gren. Guards; MP for Fermanagh and S. Tyrone (UU) 1964-70: m. 1966, Alexandra Anastasia, el. da. of Lt.-Col. Harold Pedro Joseph Phillips, FRGS, Coldstream Guards [see Wernher, Bt., ext.], and has issue:—
SON LIVING,—James Harold Charles (Viscount Strabane), b. Aug. 19th, 1969.
DAUGHTER LIVING,—Lady Sophia Alexandra, b. 1973.
Lord Claud Anthony, b. 1939; ed. at Eton; 2nd Lieut. Irish Guards.

DAUGHTER LIVING.

Lady Moyra Kathleen, C.V.O., b. 1930; a Maid of Honour to H.M. the Queen at Coronation 1953; appointed Lady-in-Waiting (temporary) to H.R.H. Princess Alexandra of Kent 1954-64, a Lady-in-Waiting 1964-66 and an Extra Lady-in-Waiting 1966-69; CVO 1963: m. 1966, Cdr. Peter Colin Drummond Campbell, MVO, RN, of Hollybrook House, Randalstown, co. Antrim, son of Maj.-Gen. Sir (Alexander) Douglas Campbell, KBE, CB, DSO, MC, and has issue living, Rory Gerald Peter, b. 1967,—Michael James Douglas, b. 1970.

SISTERS LIVING.

Lady Mary Cecilia Rhodesia, b. 1896: m. 1st, 1917, Capt. Robert Orlando Rodolph Kenyon-Slaney, Grenadier Guards, who d. 1965, having obtained a divorce 1930 [see B. Kenyon, colls.]; 2ndly, 1930, Sir John Little Gilmour, 2nd Bt. Residence,—Carolside, Earlston, Berwickshire.

Lady Katharine, D.C.V.O., b. 1900; was a Woman of the Bedchamber to H.M. Queen Mary 1927-30, an Extra Woman of the Bedchamber 1930-53, and a Woman of the Bedchamber to H.M. Queen Elizabeth the Queen Mother 1937-60, since when an Extra Woman of the Bedchamber: O.V.O. 1939, D.O.V.O. 1961: m. 1930, as his second wife, Lieut.-Col. Sir Reginald Henry Seymour, K.C.V.O., who d. 1938 [see M. Hertford, colls.]. Residence,—Strettington House, Chichester, Sussex.

UNCLE LIVING. *(Son of 2nd Duke.)*

Lord Claud Nigel, *G.C.V.O., C.M.G., D.S.O., b.* 1889; ed. at Wellington Coll.; is Capt. Grenadier Guards (Reserve of Officers); has been Dep. Master of the Household; sometime an Equerry-in-Ordinary to H.R.H. the Prince of Wales, whom he accompanied during Australian Tour 1920; appointed an Extra Equerry to H.M. 1922, and an Equerry-in-Ord. 1924; was Comptroller, Treasurer, and Extra Equerry to H.M. Queen Mary 1936-53, since when an Extra Equerry to H.M. the Queen; European War 1914-18 as an Extra A.D.C. on Staff (despatches, D.S.O., M.V.O., French Croix de Guerre, Order of Crown of Italy). European War 1939-42; D.S.O. 1914, M.V.O. (4th class) 1916, C.M.G. 1920, C.V.O. 1933, K.C.V.O. 1937, G.C.V.O. 1949: *m.* 1933, Mrs. Violet Ruby Newall, dau. of James Ashton, of London. *Residence,*—8, Russell Court, St. James's, S.W.1.

WIDOW LIVING OF SON OF THIRD DUKE.

Genesta Mary (c/o Lloyds Bank, 39, Old Bond St., W1), da. of the late Cuthbert Heath, of Anstie Grange, Holmwood, Surrey: *m.* 1946, Lord Claud David Hamilton, who *d.* 1968.

COLLATERAL BRANCHES LIVING.

Issue of the late Col. the Rt. Hon. Lord Claud John Hamilton, 2nd son of 1st Duke, *b.* 1843, *d.* 1925: *m.* 1878, Carolina, who *d.* 1911, dau. of the late Edward Sacheverell Chandos-Pole, of Radbourne Hall, Derby [E. Harrington]:—

Ida, *b.* 1883: *m.* 1909, Hugh Duncombe Flower [Pauncefort-Duncombe, Bt.], from whom she obtained a divorce 1932, and has issue living, Peter Hugh (of 20, Blomfield Road, W.9. *Club,*— Guards'); *b.* 1910; ed. at Harrow; Lieut.-Col. (retired) late Coldstream Guards; was Assist. Mil. Attaché, Greece 1956-7, and France 1957-9: *m.* 1937, Lydia Josephine, younger dau. of Major Geoffrey Edward Huth [Pigott-Brown, Bt.], and has issue living, Charles Hugh *b.* 1941; ed. at Harrow, Venetia *b.* 1939: *m.* 1964, Andrew Hugh Smith, of The Manor, Grendon Underwood, Aylesbury. *Residence,*—Vivenda Bunga, Birre-Cascais, Portugal.

Granddaughter of the late Rt. Hon. Lord George Francis Hamilton, G.C.S.I., 3rd son of 1st Duke:—
Issue of the late Ronald James Hamilton, O.B.E., *b.* 1872, *d.* 1958: *m.* 1915, Florence Marguerite (the actress, "Sarah Brooke"), who *d.* 1959, only dau. of the late Major J. Hanna:—

Maud Sarah, *b.* 1917: *m.* 1939 (Count) Manfred Maria Edmund Ralph Beckett Czernin, D.S.O., M.C., D.F.C., Squadron Leader R.A.F., who *d.* 1962, and from whom she obtained a divorce 1947 [B. Grimthorpe], and has issue living, Manfred Nicholas, *b.* 1942: *m.* 1970, Danielle Alligier, and has issue.—Carolyn Lucile, *b.* 1941: *m.* 1966, Charles Norman George Peploe, and has issue. *Residence,*— 1, Egerton Gdns., SW3.

Issue of the late Capt. Lord Ernest William Hamilton, 7th son of 1st Duke, *b.* 1858, *d.* 1939: *m.* 1891, Pamela Louisa Augusta Ambrose, who *d.* 1931, dau. of the late Capt. Frederic Augustus Campbell [Campbell, Bt., cr. 1815. colls.]:—
Mary Brenda (The Garden House, Arrow, Alcester, Warwickshire), *b.* 1897: *m.* 1922, Lt.-Col. Prince Alphonse de Chimay, TD, formerly Scots Guards, who *d.* 1973, and has issue living, *Countess* Pamela Therese Louise (*Marchioness of Hertford*), *b.* 1932: *m.* 1956, the 8th Marquess of Hertford.——Jean Barbara (39, Eaton Sq., SW1), *b.* 1898: *m.* 1921 (*m. diss.* 1944), Sir John William Buchanan-Jardine, 3rd Bt., who *d.* 1969.

(Not in remainder to the Dukedom).
Grandchildren of the late Rt. Hon. Lord Claud Hamilton, M.P., brother of 1st Duke:—
Issue of the late Col. Douglas James PROBY, *b.* 1856, *d.* 1931 (assumed by Roy. licence 1904, the surname of Proby, in lieu of his patronymic): *m.* 1882, Lady Margaret Frances Hely-Hutchinson, who *d.* 1937, dau. of 4th Earl of Donoughmore:—
Sir Richard George, *M.C., b.* 1888; cr. a *Baronet* 1952 [see " BARONETAGE "].——Jocelyn Campbell Patrick, *b.* 1900; ed. at Eton, and at Magdalen Coll., Oxford (B.Litt., M.A.); Bar. Inner Temple 1923; sometime History Lecturer at Toronto Univ.: *m.* 1st, 1930, Elisabeth Angélique, who *d.* 1962, da. of the late W. A. H. Kerr, of Toronto; 2ndly, 1969, Baroness Katherine de Robeck. *Residence,*—Ballyraine House, Arklow, **co.** Wicklow.——Betty Alice Adeline (*Lady Lowry-Corry*), *b.* 1889: *m.* 1920, Lt.-Col. Sir Henry Charles Lowry-Corry, MC, who *d.* 1973, [see E. Belmore, colls.]. *Residence,*—Edwardstone Hall, near Boxford, Suffolk.

Descendants of the late John Hamilton (son of the late John Hamilton, son of the late William Hamilton, brother of 6th Earl of Abercorn), who was cr. a *Baronet* 1776:—
See Hamilton, Bt., cr. 1776.

PREDECESSORS.—[1] CLAUD Hamilton, *b.* 1543, 4th son of James, 1st Duke of Chatelherault in kingdom of France, and 2nd Earl of Arran, in peerage of Scotland, was cr. *Lord Paisley* 1578; *d.* 1621; his son JAMES, cr. *Lord Abercorn* (peerage of Scotland) 1603, and *Earl of Abercorn,* and *Lord Paisley, Hamilton, Mountcastell, and Kilpatrick* (peerage of Scotland) 1606; *d.* March 1617, leaving with other issue [2] JAMES, 2nd Earl, and CLAUD, cr. *Baron of Strabane* (peerage of Ireland) 1634, an honour that had been conferred in 1617 upon the 2nd Earl who, however, petitioned King Charles I. to transfer the dignity to his next brother; JAMES was *s.* by his 3rd son [3] GEORGE, 3rd Earl, who *d.* unmarried, when the earldom devolved upon [4] CLAUD, P.C., 4th Earl, who had previously *s.* as 4th Baron Strabane; in 1691 he was outlawed and the estates and Barony of Strabane were forfeited; he was *s.* in the Earldom by his brother [5] CHARLES, 5th Earl, who obtained a reversal of the attainder and restoration of the estates; *d.s.p.* 1701, when the honours devolved upon [6] JAMES, 6th Earl, grandson of the Hon. Sir George Hamilton (cr. a *Baronet* 1660), 4th son of 1st Earl; cr. *Baron Mountcastle* and *Viscount Strabane* (peerage of Ireland) 1701; *d.* 1734; *s.* by his el. son [7] JAMES, P.C., F.R.S., 7th Earl; *d.* 1744; *s.* by his el. son [8] JAMES, 8th Earl, cr. *Viscount Hamilton* (peerage of Great Britain) 1785, with remainder to the son of his next brother John; *d.* unmarried 1789: *s.* by his nephew [9] JOHN JAMES, K.G., 9th Earl, cr. *Marquess of Abercorn* (peerage of Great Britain) 1790; *d.* 1818; *s.* by his grandson [10] JAMES K.G., P.C., D.C.L., LL.D., 2nd Marquess; *b.* 1811; was Groom of the Stole to the late Prince Consort 1846-59, Viceroy of Ireland 1866-8 and 1874-6. Envoy Extraor. upon a special mission to King of Italy 1878, Lord-Lieut. of Donegal, Grand Master of Masonic Order in Ireland, Lieut.-Gen. of Royal Co. of Archers, and Chancellor of Royal Univ. of Ireland; in 1864 established his claim to the French Dukedom of Chatelherault (cr. 1548), and assumed the title of *Duke of Chatelherault,* which had been abeyant since 1651, and his right was not contested before the French tribunals, but Napoleon III. granted a new creation of the same title to the 12th Duke of Hamilton; cr. *Marquess of Hamilton* and *Duke of Abercorn* (peerage of Ireland) 1868: *m.* 1832, Lady Louisa Jane Russell, *V.A.,* who *d.* 1905, dau. of 6th Duke of Bedford; *d.* Oct. 31st, 1885: *s.* by his son [11] JAMES, *K.G., P.C., C.B.,* 2nd Duke; *b.* 1838; a Lord of the Bedchamber to the Prince of Wales 1866-86, Groom of the Stole 1886-1910, and Lieut. of co. Donegal; M.P. for co. Donegal (*C*) 1860-80; acted as High Constable of Ireland at Coronation of King George V. 1911: *m.* 1869, Lady Mary Anna Curzon, who *d.* 1929, dau. of 1st Earl Howe; *d.* 1913; *s.* by his el. son [12] JAMES ALBERT EDWARD, K.G., K.P., 3rd Duke; *b.* 1869; was M.P. for Londonderry City (*C*) 1900-13, Treasurer of the Household 1903-5, and first Gov. of N. Ireland 1922-45; appointed a P.C. (Great Britain) 1945, and (N. Ireland) 1946; bore Canopy at Coronation of King George VI: *m.* 1894, Lady Rosalind Cecilia Caroline Bingham, *D.B.E., LL.D.,* who *d.* 1958, dau. of 4th Earl of Lucan; *d.* 1953: *s.* by his el. son [13] JAMES EDWARD, 4th Duke and present peer; also Marquess of Hamilton, Viscount Strabane, Baron of Strabane, Baron of Mountcastle, Marquess of Abercorn, Earl of Abercorn, Viscount Hamilton, Lord Paisley, Lord Abercorn, and Lord Paisley, Hamilton, Mountcastell, and Kilpatrick.

ABERDARE, BARON. (Bruce.) [Baron U.K. 1873.]

FUIMUS

OFNER·NA·OFNE·ANGAU

MORYS GEORGE LYNDHURST BRUCE, *PC*, 4th Baron; *b.* June 16th, 1919; *s.* 1957; ed. at Winchester, and at New Coll., Oxford; late Major Welsh Guards, a GCStJ, and a DL of Glamorgan; Min. of State, Health and Social Security 1970-74; PC 1974: *m.* 1946, Maud Helen Sarah, only da. of Sir John Lindsay Dashwood, 10th Bt. (cr. 1707), and has issue.

Arms.—Or, a saltire gules, on a chief of the last a martlet of the field. Crest.—A cubit arm in armour in bend, the hand holding a sceptre in bend sinister proper. Supporters.—*Dexter*, a lion argent collared or, pendant therefrom an escutcheon of the arms of *Knight*, viz., paly of six argent and azure, on a canton of the last a spur rowel downwards leathered or; *sinister*, a lion azure, collared or, pendant therefrom an escutcheon charged with the arms.
Residence,—1, St. Peter's Sq., W6 9AE.
Clubs,—Lansdowne, M.C.C.

SONS LIVING.

Hon. ALASTAIR JOHN LYNDHURST, *b.* May 2nd, 1947: *m.* 1971, Elizabeth Mary Culbert, da. of John Foulkes, and has issue living, Hector Morys Napier, *b.* 1974.
Hon. James Henry Morys, *b.* 1948.
Hon. Henry Adam Francis, *b.* 1962.
Hon. Charles Benjamin, *b.* 1965.

BROTHER LIVING.

Hon. Nigel Henry Clarence (Maitland Lodge, Duddingston Village, Edinburgh 15; Lansdowne Club), *b.* 1921; ed. at Winchester, and at New Coll., Oxford; late Capt. Welsh Guards: *m.* 1964, Catherine Marion, da. of the late Thomas Wolfe.

SISTERS LIVING.

Hon. Rosalind Louise Balfour, *b.* 1923; was in WRNS: *m.* 1956, Benjamin Coote Heywood, and has issue living, Annabel Jane Louise, *b.* 1958,—Olivia Sarah Rosalind, *b.* 1961. *Residence*,—1, Elm Park Rd., SW3.
Hon. Gwyneth Margaret, *b.* 1928: *m.* 1952, Robert McCheyne Andrew, of Hams Barton, Chudleigh, nr. Exeter, and has issue living, Robert Hugh Clarence, *b.* 1954,—Caroline Margaret, *b.* 1956,—Jennifer Anne Louise, *b.* 1960.

UNCLE LIVING. (Son of 2nd Baron.)

Hon. Victor Austin, *b.* 1897; ed. at Wye Agricultural Coll.; European War 1914-18 in The Buffs, Army Ser. Corps, and R.M.: *m.* 1st, 1926 (marriage dissolved 1941), Mildred Mary, dau. of the late Lawrence Joseph Petre [see B. Petre, colls.]; 2ndly, 1941, Margaret Charlotte, dau. of E. A. Beechey, of the Old Vicarage, Hilgay, near Downham Market, Norfolk, and has issue living, (by 2nd m.) Colin Michael Lyndhurst, *b.* 1944,—Margaret Jill, *b.* 1943: *m.* 1970, Thomas Richardson Hope, of 12, Moorland Close, Westone, Northampton, and has issue living, Louise Margaret, *b.* 1971,— Karen Anne, *b.* 1972,—Wendy Elizabeth, *b.* 1948: *m.* 1966, Richard Keith Grimmond, of White Clovers, Wood Street Green, Guildford, and has issue living, Michael Richard, *b.* 1971, Nicola Jane *b.* 1966, Caroline Anne, *b.* 1967. *Residence*,—Little Inholms, Wood Street Green, Guildford, Surrey'

AUNTS LIVING. (Daughters of 2nd Baron.)

Hon. Dame Eva Isabel Marian (*Eva, Countess of Rosebery*), *DBE*, *b.* 1892: Hon LLD Edinburgh 1957; is a JP for Bucks, and a Chevalier of Legion of Honour; DBE (Civil) 1955: *m.* 1st, 1911, the 3rd Baron Belper, who *d.* 1956, and from whom she had obtained a divorce in 1922; 2ndly, 1924, as his second wife, the 6th Earl of Rosebery, who *d.* 1974. *Residences*,—Mentmore, Leighton Buzzard; Cleveland House, Newmarket.
Hon. Constance Pamela Alice, *O.B.E.* (*Pamela, Baroness Digby*), *b.* 1895; Co. Comdt. Dorset A.T.S. 1938-39, and Ch. Com. A.T.S. 1939-46; a JP for Dorset; a Co. Councillor for Dorset 1943-46 and 1952-57, since when a Co. Alderman; Pres of Dorset Branch, British Red Cross Soc. 1964-72, since when Hon. Vice-Pres.; has Red Cross Badge of Honour; OBE (Mil) 1944: *m.* 1919 the 11th Baron Digby, who *d.* 1964. *Residence*,—Cerne Abbey, Dorchester, Dorset.

WIDOW LIVING OF SON OF SECOND BARON.

Cynthia Juliet Grant Duff (Coates Castle, Fittleworth, Pulborough, Sussex) (a D. St. J.), da. of the late Julian Grant Duff Ainslie (who assumed the surname of Grant Duff [V. Molesworth, colls.] : *m.* 1923, the Hon. John Hamilton Bruce, C.B.E., who *d.* 1964, and has issue living [see colls. infra].

WIDOW LIVING OF THIRD BARON.

GRIZELDA HARRIET VIOLET FINETTA GEORGIANA (*Grizelda, Baroness Aberdare*), dau. of the late Dudley Francis Amelius Hervey, C.M.G. [see M. Bristol, colls.] : *m.* (Sept.) 1957, as his second wife, the 3rd Baron, who *d.* (Oct.) 1957. *Club*.—Lansdowne.

COLLATERAL BRANCHES LIVING.

Issue living of the late Hon. John Hamilton Bruce, C.B.E., 3rd son of 2nd Baron, *b.* 1889, *d.* 1964: *m.* 1923, Cynthia Juliet Grant Duff (ante), da. of the late Julian Grant Duff Ainslie (who assumed the surname of Grant Duff) [V. Molesworth, colls.]:—

David Hamilton Grant Duff (Coates Castle, Fittleworth, Pulborough, Sussex), *b.* 1933; ed. at Winchester, and New Coll., Oxford; late Coldstream Guards: *m.* 1960 (m. diss. 1965), Diana Rosemary, da. of Douglas Sinclair Miller.——Daphne Juliet; (Coates Castle, Fittleworth, Pulborough), *b.* 1928: *m.* 1953, Baron Carlo Giuseppe Ando, and has issue living, Alexander Francis Carlo *b.* 1955,— Roderick David Clarence, *b.* 1960.

Issue of the late Hon. William Napier Bruce, C.H., C.B., LL.D., 2nd son of 1st Baron, *b.* 1858, *d.* 1936: *m.* 1882, Emily, who *d.* 1937, dau. of the late Gen. Sir William Montagu Scott MacMurdo, G.C.B.:—

William Fox, *D.S.O., M.C., T.D., b.* 1883 ; ed. at New Coll., Oxford ; Lieut.-Col. and Brevet Col. (retired) Roy. Signals (T.A.) ; European War 1914-18 (despatches thrice, M.C., D.S.O., prisoner), European War 1940-42 ; sometime Dep. Ch. Inspector of Fisheries, Min. of Agriculture and

Fisheries; has Roy. Humane So.'s medal; D.S.O. 1918: *m.* 1921, Sibyl, who *d.* 1954, dau. of the late Major Alfred Owen Lyon, and widow of Major Francis Maxwell Chenevix Trench, R.A. [B. Ashtown, colls.]. *Residence,*—Shelley's Barn, Piltdown, Sussex. *Clubs,*—Brooks's, Anglo-Belgian.

PREDECESSORS.—[1] HENRY AUSTIN Bruce, *G.C.B., P.C., D.C.L.,* 2nd son of the late John Bruce Pryce, of Duffryn, Glamorgan; *b.* 1815; M.P. for Merthyr Tydvil (*L*) 1852-68, and Renfrewshire 1869-73; was Under-Sec. for Home Depart. 1862-4, Vice-Pres. Education Board 1864-6, Second Church Estates Commr. 1865-6, Sec. of State for Home Depart. 1868-73, and Lord Pres. of Council 1873-4; cr. *Baron Aberdare,* of Duffryn, co. Glamorgan (peerage of United Kingdom) 1873: *m.* 1st, 1846, Annabella, who *d.* 1852, dau. of the late Richard Beadon, of Clifton; 2ndly, 1854, Norah Crema Blanche, who *d.* 1897, dau. of the late Gen. Sir William Francis Patrick Napier, K.C.B.; *d.* 1895; *s.* by his el. son [2] HENRY CAMPBELL, 2nd Baron, *b.* 1851; Vice-Lieut. for Glamorgan: *m.* 1880, Constance Mary, who *d.* 1932, only dau. of the late Hamilton Beckett; *d.* 1929; *s.* by his son [3] CLARENCE NAPIER, *G.B.E.,* 3rd Baron; *b.* 1885; Hon. LL.D. Wales 1953; Bar. Inner Temple 1911; Hon. Col. 282nd (Welsh) Regt. R.A. (T.A.) 1930-52; Chm. of National Fitness Council 1937-9, and Pres. of National Children's Playground Asso. 1942-52; Prior of Priory for Wales of Order of St. John of Jerusalem, and Chm. of National Asso. of Boys' Clubs, and of Queen's Institute of Dist. Nursing: *m.* 1st, 1912, Margaret Bethune, who *d.* 1950, dau. of Adam Black; 2ndly, 1957, Grizelda Harriet Violet Finetta Georgiana, dau. of the late Dudley Francis Amelius Hervey, C.M.G.; *d.* 1957; *s.* by his el. son [4] MORYS GEORGE LYNDHURST, 4th Baron and present peer.

ABERDEEN AND TEMAIR, MARQUESS OF. (Gordon.) [Marquess U.K. 1916 Earl S. 1682, Bt. S. 1642.]

Let fortune follow.

ARCHIBALD VICTOR DUDLEY GORDON, 5th Marquess, 11th Earl, and 13th Baronet; *b.* July 9th, 1913; *s.* 1974; ed. at Harrow.

Arms,—Azure, three boars' heads couped or armed proper and langued gules within a double tressure flowered and counter-flowered interchangeably with thistles, roses, and fleurs-de-lys of the second. **Crest,**—Two arms holding a bow and arrow straight upwards in a shooting posture and at full draught all proper. **Supporters,**—*Dexter,* an Earl, and *sinister,* a Doctor of Laws, both habited in their robes proper.

Residence,—The Grange, Haughley, Stowmarket, Suffolk.

BROTHER LIVING.

Lord ALASTAIR NINIAN JOHN (Quick's Green, nr. Pangbourne, Berks.; Arts, and Puffins Clubs, MCC), *b.* July 20th, 1920; ed. at Harrow; a Member of Queen's Body Guard for Scotland (Roy. Co. of Archers) and of British Section, Assocn. Internationale des Critiques d'Art; 1939-45 War, as Capt. Scots Guards: *m.* 1950, Anne, da. of Lt.-Col. Gerald Barry, MC [see Barry, Bt., colls.], and has issue living, Alexander George, *b.* 1955,—Emma Cecile, *b.* 1953,—Sophia Catherine, *b.* 1960.

SISTER LIVING.

Lady Jessamine Cecile Marjorie, *b.* 1910: *m.* 1937, (Stanley George) Michael St. John Harmsworth, of Thrumster House, Caithness, and has issue living, Andrew Vyvyan Michael Istvan St. John, *b.* 1939; late Capt. 1st Queen's Own Highlanders: *m.* 1967, Sarah Katherine Susan, el. da. of Col. W. I. Moberly, of Blackford, Yeovil, Somerset, and has issue living, Alasdair William Michael Gordon *b.* 1971, Laura Jessamine *b.* 1969,—Peter Michael Patrick John, *b.* 1952,—Marigold Ishbel Geraldine Mary Jessamine, *b.* 1940: *m.* 1963 (Victor) Francis Pym of 18, The Peth, Durham, and has issue living, Alexander Michael Francis *b.* 1970, John Andrew Dudley *b.* 1971,—Caroline Sophia, *b.* 1946, Angela Mary Cecile, *b.* 1949: *m.* 1970, Donald Sinclair, of Thrumster, and has issue living, Fiona Gwendolen Isobel *b.* 1970,—Islay Jane Winifred, *b.* 1951.

WIDOWS LIVING OF THIRD AND FOURTH MARQUESSES.

MARGARET GLADYS, *ARRC, JP (Margaret, Marchioness of Aberdeen),* (Sycamore Cottage, Forest Row, Sussex), da. of the late Lt.-Col. Reginald George Munn, CMG: *m.* 1949, as his 2nd wife, the 3rd Marquess, who *d.* 1972.

BEATRICE MARY JUNE, *MBE (Marchioness of Aberdeen and Temair)* (Haddo House, Aberdeen); MBE (Civil) 1971; da. of the late Arthur Paul Boissier, of Moretons, Harrow-on-the-Hill: *m.* 1939, the 4th Marquess, who *d.* 1974.

COLLATERAL BRANCHES LIVING.

(In remainder to Earldom of Aberdeen.)
Grandchildren of the late Gen. the Hon. Sir Alexander Hamilton Gordon, KCB, 2nd son of 4th Earl:—
Issue of the late Lt.-Gen. Sir Alexander Hamilton-Gordon, KCB, *b.* 1859, *d.* 1939: *m.* 1888, Isabel, who *d.* 1947, da. of Maj.-Gen. George Newmarch, formerly RE:—
Alan Herschel, *b.* 1898; ed. at Winchester; formerly Lieut. R.F.A.; entered Diplo. Ser. 1921; H.M.'s Consul at Porto Alegre, Brazil, 1948-56; sometime Major and a G.S.O. (Joint Intelligence Staff) War Cabinet Office: *m.* 1933, Deenya Kovachevska, of Sofia, Bulgaria. *Address,*—Caixa Postal 499, Porto Alegre, Brazil.——Eileen Muriel, *b.* 1889: *m.* 1st, 1912, Capt. Peter Benson Maxwell, E. Yorkshire Regt., who *d.* (wounds in action) 1914; 2ndly, 1919, Claude Pemberton Wilkinson Lloyd, late Lt. Indian Army Reserve, and Indian Educational Ser., who *d.* 1966, and has issue living, (by 1st marriage) Joan (7, Shawfield St., SW3), *b.* 1913: *m.* 1936, Air Commodore John Newall Tomes, CBE, and has issue living, Ian Naxwell, *MC,* (c/o Lloyds Bank, 6, Pall Mall, SW1) *b.* 1940; Maj. R. Regt. of Fusiliers: *m.* 1968, Verena Meyer, and has issue living, Sacha Christopher *b.* 1969, Kieran Malcolm *b.* 1973,—Simon Christopher *b.* 1944,—(by 2nd m.) Sheila Rosemary, *b.* 1922: *m.* 1950, Alan Chapman-Lloyd Browne, FIMechE, MICE, of 41, Beauchamp Av., Leamington Spa, and has issue living, Christopher St. John Lloyd, *b.* 1950. *Residence,* 7, Vincent Court, Denmark Av., Wimbledon, SW19.

Granddaughter of the late Rev. the Hon. Douglas Hamilton Gordon, 3rd son of 4th Earl:—
Issue of the late Douglas George Hamilton-Gordon, O.B.E., J.P., *b.* 1852, *d.* 1938: *m.* 1st, 1877, Edith Anne, who *d.* 1929, dau. of the late Rev. Walter Trevelyan Bullock, of Faulkbourn Hall, Witham, Essex; 2ndly, 1929, Annie Amelia, who *d.* 1965, da. of the late W. J. Arkcoll:—
Edmée Veronica (23B, Malcolm Rd., SW19), *b.* 1900.

Descendants of the late William Gordon (2nd son of the late Hon. Alexander Gordon, 4th son of 2nd Earl), who *s.* his maternal uncle, Sir James Duff, 1st Bt., 1815, and assumed the additional surname of Duff.
See Duff-Gordon, Bt.

PREDECESSORS.—[1] *Sir* GEORGE Gordon, of Haddo, 3rd *Baronet* of Nova Scotia (cr.
1642), successively a Senator of the College of Justice, Pres. of Court of Session, and Lord
High Chancellor of Scotland, was cr. *Lord Haddo, Methlic, Tarves, and Kellie, Viscount Formartine,* and *Earl of Aberdeen* (peerage of Scotland) 1682; *d.* 1720: *s.* by his only surviving son
[2] WILLIAM, 2nd Earl, a Representative Peer for Scotland; *d.* 1745; *s.* by his el. son [3]
GEORGE, 3rd Earl, a Representative Peer for Scotland; *d.* 1801; *s.* by his grandson [4] GEORGE,
K.G., K.T., P.C., F.R.S., 4th Earl, el. son of George, Lord Haddo; *b.* 1784; was Lord-Lieut.
of Aberdeenshire, and a distinguished statesman who filled various high diplomatic and
ministerial offices, and was First Lord of the Treasury and Prime Minister 1852-5; cr.
Viscount Gordon (peerage of United Kingdom) 1814; assumed by Roy. licence 1818, the
additional surname, arms, and supporters of Hamilton; *d.* 1860; *s.* by his el. son [5] GEORGE
JOHN JAMES, 5th Earl, *b.* 1816; *m.* 1840, Mary, who *d.* 1900, dau. of the late George Baillie,
and sister of 10th Earl of Haddington; *d.* 1864; *s.* by his el. son [6] GEORGE, 6th Earl, *b.*
1841; having pursued a life of romantic adventure was accidentally drowned on Jan. 27,
1870, off the coast of America when serving on board the "Hera"; *s.* by his brother [7] *Rt. Hon.*
JOHN CAMPBELL, K.T., G.C.M.G., G.C.V.O., 7th Earl, *b.* 1847; Lord-Lieut. of Aberdeenshire
1880-1934, Lord High Commr. to General Assembly of Church of Scotland 1881-5, and again
1915, Lord Lieut. of Ireland, Jan. to July 1886; Gov.-Gen. of Canada 1893-8, and again Lord-
Lieut. of Ireland 1905-15; cr. *Earl of Haddo,* in co. of Aberdeen, and *Marquess of Aberdeen and
Temair,* in co. of Aberdeen, in co. of Meath, and in co. of Argyll (peerage of United Kingdom)
1916: *m.* 1877, the Hon. Ishbel Maria Marjoribanks, G.B.E., LL.D., who *d.* 1939, dau. of 1st
Baron Tweedmouth; *d.* 1934; *s.* by his el. son [8] GEORGE *OBE,* 2nd Marquess, *b.* 1879; Lord
Lieut. of Aberdeenshire 1934-59: *m.* 1st, 1906, Mary Florence, who *d.* 1937, da. of the late Joseph
Clixby, of Ownby Cliff, Lincs., and widow of Edward Shepherd Cockayne, of Sheffield; 2ndly,
1940, Sheila, who *d.* 1949, da. of the late Lt.-Col. John Foster Forbes, JP, DL, of Rothiemay Castle,
Banffshire, and widow of Capt. James William Guy Innes, CBE, DL, JP, RN [Innes, Bt. colls.];
d. 1965; *s.* by his brother [9] DUDLEY GLADSTONE, DSO, 3rd Marquess, *b.* 1883; Lt.-Col. Comdg.
8th/10th and 5th Bns. Gordon Highlanders: *m.* 1st, 1907, Cecile Elizabeth, who *d.* 1948, da. of the
late George James Drummond [E. Perth, colls.]; 2ndly, 1949, Margaret Gladys, ARRC, JP, only
da. of the late Lt.-Col. Reginald George Munn, OMG; *d.* 1972; *s.* by his el. son [10] DAVID GEORGE
IAN ALEXANDER, *CBE, TD,* 4th Marquess, *b.* 1908; Lord-Lieut. for Aberdeenshire 1973-74: *m.* 1939,
Beatrice Mary June, MBE, da. of the late Arthur Paul Boissier, of Moretons, Harrow-on-the-Hill;
d. 1974; *s.* by his brother [11] ARCHIBALD VICTOR DUDLEY, 5th Marquess and present peer; also
Earl of Aberdeen, Earl of Haddo, Viscount Formartine, Viscount Gordon, and Lord Haddo, Methlic,
Tarves, and Kellie.

ABERGAVENNY, MARQUESS OF. (Nevill.) [Marquess U.K. 1876.]

Form no mean wish.

JOHN HENRY GUY NEVILL, *KG,
OBE,* 5th Marquess; *b.* Nov. 8th, 1914;
s. 1954; ed. at Eton and at Trin.
Coll., Camb.; Lt.-Col. late Life Guards;
1939-45 War in France (despatches),
N-W Europe (OBE); Hon. Col. Kent
and Co. of London Yeo. 1948-62; a
JP and DL for Sussex (Vice Lieut.
1970-74; Lord-Lieut. of E. Sussex
since 1974; KStJ); a Dir. of Lloyds
Bank (Chm. SE Reg. Board), and
other Directorships; Member E. Sussex
Co. Council 1947-54 (Alderman 1954-
62); a Member of Nat. Hunt Cttee.
since 1942 (Sen. Steward 1955 and 63);
Pres. British Horse Soc. 1970-71; a
Trustee of Ascot Authority since 1952;
HM's Representative at Ascot since
1972; OBE (Mil.) 1945, KG 1974: *m.*
1938, Mary Patricia, CVO, da. of Maj.
John Fenwick Harrison, JP [B.
Burnham], and has issue.

Arms,—Gules, a saltire argent, charged
with a rose of the field. **Crest,**—Out of a ducal
coronet or, a bull's head proper, charged with
a rose gules. **Supporters**—On either side a bull
argent, pied sable, armed, unguled, collared, and
chained or, the latter terminating in a staple.
Badges,—*Dexter,* a rose gules, barbed and seeded
proper; *sinister,* a portcullis or.

Seat,—Eridge Park, Tunbridge Wells. *Town Residence,*—19, Lowndes Square. SW1. *Clubs,*—
Turf, White's.

DAUGHTERS LIVING.

Lady Anne Patricia, *b.* 1938: *m.* 1971, Martin F. Whiteley, of Dalmar House, Culworth, Oxon.
Lady Vivienne Margaret, *b.* 1941: *m.* 1962, Alan Lillingston, of Mount Coote, Kilmallock, co. Limerick
    and has issue living, Luke, *b.* 1963,—Andrew Harry, *b.* 1972,—Georgina Patricia, *b.* 1965,—Sophie
    Susan, *b.* 1967.
Lady Rose, *b.* 1950.

BROTHER LIVING.

Lord RUPERT CHARLES MONTACUTE, *b.* Jan. 29th, 1923; ed. at Eton; Capt. late Life Guards; is a
DL Sussex (High Sheriff 1952-53); Chm. of British Olympics Assocn. 1966; Treasurer to HRH
The Duke of Edinburgh since 1970: *m.* 1944, Lady Anne Camilla Eveline Wallop, da. of 9th Earl
of Portsmouth, and has issue living, Guy Rupert Gerard, *b.* 1945; ed. at Eton; was a Page of
Honour to HM 1958-61,—Christopher George Charles, *b.* 1955; ed. at Harrow,—Angela Isabel Mary,
b. 1948,—Henrietta Emily Charlotte, *b.* 1964. *Residences,*—Horsted Pl., Uckfield, Sussex; 20A,
Stanhope Gdns., SW7.

SISTER LIVING.

Lady Angela Isabel Nellie (*Countess of Cottenham*), *b.* 1910: *m.* 1st, 1930 (marriage annulled on her petition 1933), Major Sir Mark Vane Milbank, K.C.V.O., M.C., 4th baronet; 2ndly, 1933, the 7th Earl of Cottenham, who *d.* 1968. *Residence,*—The Hollies, Eridge Green, Tunbridge Wells.

COLLATERAL BRANCHES LIVING.
(*In remainder to Earldom and Barony of Abergavenny, and Viscountcy of Nevill only.*)

Grandson of the late Percy Llewelyn Nevill (infra):—
Issue of the late Michael George Ralph Nevill, Lieut. Scots Guards, *b.* 1917, *d.* (killed in action) 1943: *m.* 1940, Maureen Ethné David, JP (who *m.* 2ndly, 1947, John Valentine Balfour, DSO, of Walnut Tree Farm, Birling, Maidstone, Kent [Price, Bt., colls.]), da. of the late Capt. (Arthur) Tahu (Gravenor) Rhodes, MVO [B Plunket]:—
David Michael Ralph (Birling Place, Birling, Maidstone, Kent), *b.* 1941; ed. at Bryanston: *m.* 1972, Katherine Mary, da. of Rossmore Derrick Westenra, of Halswell, Christchurch, NZ, and has issue living, Guy Michael Rossmore, *b.* 1973.——Michael George Rathmore (posthumous), *b.* 1943; ed. at Eton.

Granddaughters of the Hon. Ralph Pelham Nevill, 2nd son of 4th Earl:—
Issue of the late Percy Llewelyn Nevill, *b.* 1877, *d.* 1927: *m.* 1905, Marjorie, who *d.* 1945, dau. of the late Lord George Montacute Nevill:—
Joan Helen, *b.* 1906: *m.* 1st, 1935, Charles Austen Field-Marsham, Lieut. Life Guards, who *d.* (on active ser. during European War) 1941 [see E. Romney, colls.]; 2ndly, 1950, as his second wife, Major Robert Edward Field-Marsham, The Bays [see E. Romney, colls.]. *Residence,*—Tophill Farm, Langton Green, Kent.——Sylvia Eleanor, *b.* 1907.——Rosemary (*Rosemary, Lady Brooke*), *b.* 1912: *m.* 1945 (marriage dissolved 1963), Major Sir John Weston Brooke, 3rd Bt. (cr. 1919).—— Cicely Rose, *b.* 1915: *m.* 1947, Peter Richard Nickols, and has issue living, Richard Henry, *b.* 1948,—Charles Michael Ralph, *b.* 1951,—Rose Mary (twin), *b.* 1951. *Residence,*—Byards Lodge, Knaresborough, Yorks.

PREDECESSORS.—[1] *Sir* RALPH Nevill, *K.G.*, 6th son of 1st Earl of Westmorland, and 4th Baron Nevill, of Raby (cr. 1294) (titles forfeited 13th Elizabeth), a confidant of Edward IV., was summoned to the English Parliament as *Baron Bergavenny* 1450-72 ; *d.* 1476 ; *s.* by his son [2] *Sir* GEORGE, K.B., 2nd Baron; was knighted at the battle of Tewkesbury ; he *d.* 1492, and was *s.* by his el. son [3] *Sir* GEORGE, K.G., K.B., 3rd Baron; was companion in arms of Henry VIII. in his French wars, and held high and important commands; *d.* 1536; *s.* by his el. son [4] HENRY, 4th Baron ; was committed to ward for striking the Earl of Oxford in the chamber of presence, but received special pardon within a month : was one of the peers who sat in judgment upon Mary Queen of Scots ; *d.* 1586; at his decease the Barony was unsuccessfully claimed by his dau. Mary, wife of Sir Thomas Fane, who however, was subsequently granted the Barony of Le Despencer (cr. by writ 1264); to which she was a co-heir ; *s.* by his cousin [5] EDWARD, 5th Baron, el. son of Sir Edward Nevill, 2nd son of 2nd Baron ; *d.* 1589 ; *s.* by his el. son [6] EDWARD, 6th Baron ; unsuccessfully claimed the Earldom of Westmorland; *d.* 1622 ; *s.* by his el. son [7] HENRY, 7th Baron ; *d.* 1641 ; *s.* by his el. son [8] JOHN, 8th Baron; *d.* 1660 ; *s.* by his brother [9] GEORGE, 9th Baron ; *d.* 1666 ; *s.* by his only son [10] GEORGE, 10th Baron, *d.s.p.* 1694, when the barony reverted to his kinsman [11] GEORGE, 11th Baron, el. son of Sir Christopher Nevill, 2nd son of 6th Baron; *d.* 1720 ; *s.* by his el. son [12] GEORGE, 12th Baron ; *d.s.p.* 1723 ; *s.* by his brother [13] EDWARD, 13th Baron ; *d.* 1724 ; *s.* by his cousin [14] WILLIAM, 14th Baron, brother of 11th Baron; the first to be styled *Lord Abergavenny* (in lieu of Bergavenny); *d.* 1745 ; *s.* by his el. son [15] GEORGE, 15th Baron ; cr. *Viscount Nevill* and *Earl of Abergavenny* (peerage of Great Britain) 1784 ; *d.* 1785 ; *s.* by his son [16] HENRY, *K.T.*, 2nd Earl ; *d.* 1843 ; *s.* by his son [17] *Rev.* JOHN, 3rd Earl ; *d.* 1845 ; *s.* by his brother [18] *Rev.* WILLIAM, 4th Earl, *b.* 1792 : *m.* 1824, Caroline, who *d.* 1873, dau. of Ralph Leeke, of Longford Hall, Salop ; *d.* Aug. 17th, 1868 ; *s.* by his el. son [19] WILLIAM, K.G., 5th Earl, *b.* 1826 ; Lord-Lieut. of Sussex 1892-1905 ; cr. *Earl of Lewes* and *Marquess of Abergavenny* (peerage of United Kingdom) 1876 : *m.* 1848, Caroline, who *d.* 1892, sister of 1st Baron Derwent; *d.* 1915 ; *s.* by his el. son [20] REGINALD WILLIAM BRANSBY, 2nd Marquess, *b.* 1853 ; *d.* 1927 ; *s.* by his brother [21] HENRY GILBERT RALPH, 3rd Marquess, *b.* 1854 : *m.* 1st, 1876, Violet, who *d.* 1880, dau. of the late Lieut.-Col. Henry Dorrien Streatfeild, of Chidingstone Park, Kent ; 2ndly, 1886, Maud Augusta, who *d.* 1927, dau. of the late William Beckett, M.P. [B. Grimthorpe]; 3rdly, 1928, Mary Frances, who *d.* 1954, dau. of the late Hon. Ralph Pelham Nevill, and widow of 3rd Viscount Hardinge; *d.* 1938 ; *s.* by his nephew [22] GUY TEMPLE MONTACUTE Larnach-Nevill (el. son of the late Lord George Montacute Nevill, 3rd son of 1st Marquess), 4th Marquess ; *b.* 1883 ; Capt. Scots Guards ; assumed by deed poll 1919 the additional surname of Larnach for himself and his wife only : *m.* 1909, Isabel Nellie, who *d.* 1953, only child of the late James Walker Larnach: *d.* 1954 ; *s.* by his el. son [23] JOHN HENRY GUY, 5th Marquess and present peer ; also Earl of Abergavenny, Earl of Lewes, Viscount Nevill, and Baron Abergavenny (formerly Bergavenny).

ABERTAY, BARONY OF. (Barrie.) [Extinct 1940.]
DAUGHTERS LIVING OF FIRST BARON.

Hon. June Coupar, *b.* 1928: *m.* 1952, Col. Alan Norman Breitmeyer, late Grenadier Guards, and has issue living, Timothy Hugh, *b.* 1959,—Patricia Anne, *b.* 1954. *Residences,*—20, Chancellor House, Hyde Park Gate, SW7; Bartlow Park, Bartlow, Cambs.

Hon. Rosemary Coupar, *b.* 1931: *m.* 1952, John Stuart Maitland, and has issue living, John Andrew Charles, *b.* 1954,—Robin Neil, *b.* 1958,—Angus Kenneth, *b.* 1963,—Fiona Romaire, *b.* 1961. *Residence,*—Alkerton Grange, Eastington, nr. Stonehouse, Glos.

Hon. Caroline Barbara Coupar, *b.* 1933 : *m.* 1955, Capt. John Neil Buchanan-Baillie-Hamilton, The Black Watch (retired) [see E. Haddington, colls.]. *Residence,*—Cambusmore, Callander, Perthshire.

WIDOW LIVING OF FIRST BARON.

ETHEL (*Baroness Abertay*), da. of the late Sir James Thomson Broom: *m.* 1926, the 1st Baron, who *d.* 1940, when the title became ext. *Residence,*—Mansefield, Callander, Perthshire.

Abingdon, Earl of, see Earl of Lindsey and Abingdon.

ABINGER, BARON. (Scarlett.) [Baron U.K. 1835.]

He stands by his own strength.

JAMES RICHARD SCARLETT, 8th Baron; *b.* Sept. 28th, 1914; *s.* 1943; ed. at Eton, and at Magdalene Coll., Camb. (BA); Lt.-Col. late RA; a DL of Essex 1968; CStJ: *m.* 1957, Isla Carolyn, only da. of the late Vice-Adm. James William Rivett-Carnac, CB, CBE, DSC [see Rivett-Carnac, Bt.], and has issue.

Arms.—Checky or and gules, a lion rampant ermine; on a canton azure, a castle, triple towered argent. **Crest.**—A Tuscan column, checky, or and gules, supported on either side by a lion's jamb ermines, erased gules. **Supporters.**—On either side an angel vested argent, tunic azure, wings or; in the exterior hand of each a sword in bend proper, pommel and hilt or.

Residences,—40, Draycott Place, Chelsea, S.W.3; Clees Hall, Bures, Suffolk. *Clubs,*—Carlton, Royal Automobile.

SONS LIVING.
Hon. JAMES HARRY, *b.* May 28th, 1959.
Hon. Peter Richard, *b.* 1961.

BROTHER LIVING.
Hon. John Leopold Campbell, *CBE, b.* 1916; ed. at Eton, and at Magdalene Coll., Camb. (BA 1938); formerly Major RA; an Esquire of Order of St. John of Jerusalem; *cr.* CBE (Civil) 1973: *m.* 1947, Bridget, da. of the late H. B. Crook, of 102, Stafford Court, W8, and has issue living, Hugh Lawrence, *b.* 1953,—Felix James, *b.* 1958,—Sarah Elizabeth, *b.* 1954. *Residence,*—Sadlers, Cousley Wood, Wadhurst, Sussex.

PREDECESSORS.—[1] *Sir* JAMES Scarlett, *P.C., K.B., D.C.L.*; called to the Bar 1791; sat successively as M.P. for Cockermouth, Peterborough, and Norwich, and was sometime Attorney-Gen.; appointed Lord Chief Baron of the Exchequer 1834, and *cr. Baron Abinger,* of Abinger, co. Surrey (peerage of United Kingdom) 1835; *d.* 1844; *s.* by his el. son [2] ROBERT CAMPBELL, 2nd Baron, *b.* 1794; was a Barrister-at-Law: *m.* 1824, Sarah, who *d.* 1878, dau. of the late George Smith, Chief Justice of the Mauritius; *d.* June 24, 1861; *s.* by his el. son [3] WILLIAM FREDERICK, *C.B.,* 3rd Baron, *b.* 1826; Lieut.-Gen. in the Army: *m.* 1863, Helen, who *d.* 1915, dau. of Commodore George Allan Magruder, of the U.S. Navy; *d.* 1892; *s.* by his son [4] JAMES YORKE MACGREGOR, 4th Baron, *b.* 1871; *d.* 1903; *s.* by his cousin [5] SHELLEY LEOPOLD LAURENCE (son of the late Lieut.-Col. Leopold James Yorke Campbell Scarlett, son of the late Hon. Peter Campbell Scarlett, *C.B.* (3rd son of 1st Baron), 5th Baron, *b.* 1872; Hon. Com. Roy. Naval Vol. Reserve; served during European War 1915-16: *m.* 1899, Lila Lucy Catherine Mary, who *d.* 1941 (having *m.* 3rdly, 1921, Jean de Belot), dau. of the late Rt. Hon. Sir William Arthur White, *P.C., G.C.B., G.C.M.G.,* British Ambassador at Constantinople, and widow of Kammerherr Carl E. de Geijer, Swedish Diplo. Ser.; *d.* 1917; *s.* by his brother [6] ROBERT BROOKE CAMPBELL, 6th Baron: *m.* 1917, Jean Marguerite (Madame de Serignac), who *d.* 1954, dau. of the late Edouard Japy, and widow of M. Steinheil, of Paris; *d.* 1927; *s.* by his brother [7] HUGH RICHARD, *D.S.O.,* 7th Baron, *b.* 1878; Lieut.-Col. R.A. (retired): S. Africa 1900-1902; European War 1914-18 (D.S.O.): *m.* 1913, Marjorie Ursula, who *d.* 1965, dau. of John MacPhillamy, of Blair Athol, Bathurst, N.S. Wales; *d.* 1943; *s.* by his el. son [8] JAMES RICHARD, 8th Baron and present peer.

Aboyne, Earl of,   son of Marquess of Huntly.

ACTON, BARON. (Lyon-Dalberg-Acton.) [Baron U.K. 1869, Bt. E. 1644.]

Deo adjurante.
God assisting.

Residence,—Ca-na Rosalinda, Pollensa, Mallorca.

JOHN EMERICH HENRY LYON-DALBERG-ACTON, *C.M.G., M.B.E., T.D.,* 3rd Baron, and 10th Baronet; *b.* Dec.15th,1907; *s.* 1924; ed. at Downside, and at Trin. Coll., Camb.; a Patrician of Naples, and Maj. R.A. (T.A.); patron of one living (but, being a Roman Catholic, cannot present); M.B.E. (Mil.) 1945, C.M.G. 1963: *m.* 1931, the Hon. Daphne Strutt, dau. of 4th Baron Rayleigh, and has issue.

Arms.—Quarterly: 1st and 4th gules semée of cross-crosslets fitchée or, two lions passant in pale argent, *Acton*; 2nd quarterly, 1st and 4th azure, six fleurs-de-lis, three, two, and one argent, a chief dancettée of the last, 2nd and 3rd or, a cross patonce gules, over all an escutcheon of the first, thereon a tower argent, a chief dancettée of the last, *Dalberg*; 3rd azure, a lion passant or between three plates each charged with a griffin's head erased sable, *Lyon*. **Crest.**—In front of a lion's head erased argent two hurts, *Lyon*. **Supporters.**—On either side a lion guardant proper, gorged with a chain or, and charged with a cross patonce gules.

SONS LIVING.

Hon. RICHARD GERALD (95, Ebury St., SW1), *b.* July 30th, 1941, ed. at Trin. Coll., Oxford; a Dir. of Coutts & Co.: *m.* 1st, 1965, Hilary Juliet Sarah, who *d.* 1973, da. of Dr. L. O. C. Cookson, of Perth, W. Australia; 2ndly, 1974, Judith Garfield, da. of R. S. Garfield Todd, of Hokonu Ranch, P.O. Dadaya, Rhodesia, formerly P.M. of S. Rhodesia and has issue living (by 1st m.) John Charles Ferdinand Harold, *b.* 1966.

Rev. Hon. John Charles (Westminster Diocesan Seminary, 28, Beaufort St., SW3), *b.* 1943; ed. at Gregorian Univ., Rome; Prof. of Dogmatic Theology, Westminster Diocesan Seminary.

Hon. Robert Peter (Wellground, Wormsley Estate, Stokenchurch, High Wycombe, Bucks.), *b.* 1946: *m.* 1974, Michele, da. of Henri Laigle, of 61, Rue du Commerce, 92, Colombe, France.

Hon. Edward David Joseph (6, Westmeadow Close, Willingham, Cambs.); *b.* 1949; ed. at York Univ.: *m.* 1972, Stella Marie, da. of Henry Conroy, of 8, Stirling Rd., Bolton, and has issue living, Helen, *b.* 1974.

Hon. Peter Hedley (c/o Tirling Place, Chelmsford, Essex); *b.* 1950; ed. at Cirencester Agric. Coll.

DAUGHTERS LIVING.

Hon. Pelline Margot, *b.* 1932 : *m.* 1953, Laszlo de Marffy von Versegh, and has issue living, Denis, *b.* 1954,—Miklos, *b.* 1956,—Joseph, *b.* 1957,—Paul, *b.* 1958,—Robert, *b.* 1962,—Stephen, *b.* 1965,— Gabriella, *b.* 1960. *Residence,*—Ealing Farm, P.O. Box 29, Umvukwes, Rhodesia.

Hon. Catherine, *b.* 1939: *m.* 1960, the Hon. Joseph Mervyn Corbett [see B. Rowallan]. *Residence,*—Chittlegrove, Rendcomb, near Cirencester, Glos.

Hon. Jill Mary Joan, *b.* 1947: *m.* 1970, Nicholas Lampert, of 26, Lonsdale Rd., Harborne, Birmingham, 17 [see V. Ridley, colls.].

Hon. Mary Anne, *b.* 1951: *m.* 1972, Timothy John Sheehy, of 27, Baalbec Rd., N5, and has issue living, Jane Elizabeth, *b.* 1973,—Clare Ann, *b.* 1975.

Hon. Jane, *b.* 1954.

SISTERS LIVING.

Hon. Marie Immaculée Antoinette, *b.* 1905 ; is a Dame of Honour and Devotion of Sovereign Order of Malta; has Cross Pro Ecclesia et Pontifice: *m.* 1933, John Douglas Woodruff, CBE, of Marcham Priory, Abingdon, Berks.

Hon. (Dorothy Elizabeth Anne) Pelline, *b.* 1906: *m.* 1928, Edward Eyre, who *d.* 1962, and has issue living, Edward (Park Farm, Upper Lambourn, Newbury, Berks.), *b.* 1929; Bar. Inner Temple 1957: *m.* 1969, Ethel Mary, da. of Cdr. Charles H. Drage, R.N. (ret.), of 38, Sheffield Terr., W8, and widow of Roderick Andrew Joseph Fraser [see L. Lovat, colls.], and has issue living, Robert Edward John *b.* 1971, Mathilda Elizabeth Mary Pelline *b.* 1970, Virginia Margaret Dorothy *b.* 1974,—James Ainsworth Campden Gabriel (21, Melbury Rd., W14), *b.* 1930; Lt.-Col. RHG/D: *m.* 1967, Monica Ruth Esther, da. of the late Michael Joseph Smyth, FRCS, MCh, of London, and has issue living, James Patrick *b.* 1969, Annabelle Catherine *b.* 1970,—John Michael Simon William (125, Main St., Easthampton, Long Island, NY, USA), *b.* 1935: *m.* 1960, Susan, da. of Cdr. Maxwell Cole, US Navy, and has issue living, Maxwell John *b.* 1961, Christopher Maxwell *b.* 1963, Giles Stephen *b.* 1966, Julian Patrick *b.* 1970,—Peter Gervase Joseph, *b.* 1940,—Patrick Giles Andrew (twin), *b.* 1940,— Dorothy Elizabeth Mary Pelline, *b.* 1938: *m.* 1972, Charles Gilbert Remmick, of 400, East 56 St., New York, NY 10022, USA,—Caroline Elisa Margaret, *b.* 1945. *Residence,*—Peartree Cottage, Orchard La., East Hendred, Berks.

Hon. Helen Mary Grace (602 Park West, W1)," *b.* 1910: *m.* 1933 (m. diss. 1958), Prince Guglielmo Camillo Carlo Rospigliosi [see Cs. Newburgh, colls.]

Hon. Joan Henrica Josepha Mary Clare, *b.* 1915. *Residence,*—1, Churchgate, Southport.

Hon. Margaret Mary Teresa (602, Park West, W1), *b.* 1919.

Hon. Ædgyth Bertha Milburg Mary Antonia Frances, *b.* 1920 : *m.* 1949, John Alexander Callinicos, and has issue living, Alexander Theodore, *b.* 1950,—Anastiasus John, *b.* 1957. *Residence,*—Villa Ithaki, Twentydales Road, Hatfield, Salisbury, Rhodesia.

COLLATERAL BRANCHES LIVING. (*Male line of which is in remainder to Baronetcy only*)

Granddaughter of the late Vice-Adm. William Acton (Italian Navy), son of the late Commodore Charles Acton (infra):—
    Issue of the late Henry Acton, *b.* 1858, *d.* 1928: *m.* 1892, Elly, who *d.* 1960, dau. of Prince Cléon Rizo Rangabè:—
Dorothy (of 243, Goldstone Cres., Hove, 4), *b.* 1893: *m.* 1921, Prince Raoul Bibica Rosetti, who *d.* 1967, formerly Greek Ambassador to Canada, and has issue living, Roxane Bibica-Rosetti, *b.* 1932: *m.* 1956, Prince John Lobanov-Rostovsky, of Swallowdale, 67, Woodruff Av., Hove, 4, and has issue living, Paul *b.* 1956, Dimitry *b.* 1962, Helena *b.* 1964.

Grandsons of the late Vice-Adm. Ferdinando Acton, son of the late Commodore Charles Acton, el. son of the late Lt.-Gen. Joseph Edward Acton, brother of 6th baronet:—
    Issue of the late Adm. Baron Alfredo Acton (Hon. K.C.B.: cr. a Baron in Kingdom of Italy 1925), *b.* 1867, *d.* 1934: *m.* 1907, Livia, who *d.* 1963 (a Dame of Honour and Devotion of the Sovereign Order of Malta, and Dame Grand Cross of Constantinian Order of St. George; Cross Pro Ecclesia et Pontifice), dau. of Giuseppe Giudice Caracciolo, 9th Prince of Villa and Cellamare, of Naples:—
Baron Ferdinando Amedeo Maria, *LL.D.* (*Prince of Leporano*), *b.* 1908 ; a Patrician of Naples, a 1st class Grandee of Spain, 12th Prince of Leporano, and a Knt. of Sovereign Order of Malta, and Bailiff, Knt. Grand Cross, and Great Inquisitor of Constantinian Order of St. George; formerly in 1st Italian Grenadiers: *m.* 1946, Emilia (a Dame of Justice of Constantinian Order of St. George), only da. of the late Count Gioacchino del Balzo di Presenzano, and has issue living, Giovanni Alfredo Maria, *b.* 1948; a Patrician of Naples, and a Knight of Justice of Constantinian Order of St. George,— Maria Eleonora Carlotta, *b.* 1949; a Dame of Justice, Constantinian Order of St. George: *m.* 1972, Pier Luigi Taccone di Sitizano, a Patrician of Tropea, a Knt. of Justice, Constantinian Order of St. George, of Palazzo Cellences, Naples, and Pizzo di Calabria. *Residences,*—Palazzo Cellamare a Chiaja, Naples, Italy; 58, Via Panama, Rome, Italy; La Chiusa, nr. Cittanova di Calabria, Italy; Cannavá, nr. Gioia Tauro, Italy.——*Baron* Francesco Eduardo Maria, *b.* 1910 ; a Patrician of Naples Capt. Italian Navy, and a Knight of Sovereign Order of Malta, and of Constantinian Order of St George; cr. a Baron of Kingdom of Italy 1940: *m.* 1941, Marida (Dame, of Justice of Constantinian Order of St. George), only dau. of Baron Ameglio. *Residence,*—Palazzo Cellamare a Chiaja, Naples, Italy.

Grandchildren of the late Capt. Richard George Acton, only son of the late Maj. Henry Acton, son of the late Capt. Henry Acton, 2nd son of the late Lt.-Gen. Joseph Edward Acton (ante):—
    Issue of the late Paul Reginald Acton, *b.* 1886, *d.* 1951: *m.* (Feb.) 1907, Bertha Helen (Vera Cruz Rd., RFD No. 1, Center Valley, Pa. 18034, USA), da. of Jules Le Duc. of Stone County, Missouri, USA:—
Richard Le Duc (P.O. Box 1794, Costa Mesa, Cal. 92626, USA), *b.* 1913: *m.* 1933, Alberta Althea, da. of Francis Joseph Budwiser, of Dubuque, Iowa, USA, and has issue living, Dennis Richard (20641, Tiller Circle, Huntington Beach, Cal. 92646, USA), *b.* 1938: *m.* 1961, Susan Caroline, da. of Hartvige Rudolph Miklethun, of Minneapolis, Minnesota, USA, and has issue living, Christopher Michael

b. 1962, Paul Reginald *b.* 1968, Julia Ann *b.* 1964,—Paul Reginald, *b.* 1943.——Pauline Laura (Vera Cruz Rd., RFD No. 1, Center Valley, Pa. 18034, USA), *b.* 1907: *m.* 1929, Charles Henry Heiney, who *d.* 1950.

PREDECESSORS.—[1] *Sir* EDWARD Acton, of Aldenham Hall (10th in lineal descent from William de Acton Burnel, temp. Edward III.), cr. a *Baronet*, for his fidelity to Charles I. 1644; *d.* 1659; *s.* by his el. son [2] *Sir* WALTER, *M.P.*; *d.* 1665; *s.* by his el. son [3] *Sir* EDWARD, *M.P.*; *d.* 1716; *s.* by his el. son [4] *Sir* WHITMORE; *d.* 1731; *s.* by his son [5] *Sir* RICHARD; *d.* 1791; *s.* by his kinsman [6] *Sir* JOHN FRANCIS EDWARD, great-grandson of Walter, 2nd son of 2nd Bt.; was successively Com.-in-Ch. of the land and Sea forces in Naples, and Neapolitan Prime Minister; *d.* 1811; *s.* by his son [7] *Sir* FERDINAND RICHARD EDWARD, *b.* 1801; assumed by Roy. licence in 1833 the additional surname of Dalberg: *m.* 1832, Marie Louise Pellina (who *m.* 2ndly, 1840, the 2nd Earl Granville, and *d.* 1860), only child and heir of Emeric Joseph, Duke of Dalberg; *d.* 1837; *s.* by his son [8] *Sir* JOHN EMERICH EDWARD, K.C.V.O., *b.* 1834; M.P. for Carlow (*L*) 1859-65 and for Bridgnorth 1865-6; a Lord-in-Waiting to H.M. Queen Victoria 1892-5; Regius Professor of Modern History in Camb. Univ. 1895-1902; cr. *Baron Acton* (peerage of United Kingdom) 1869: *m.* 1865, Countess Marie, who *d.* 1923, el. dau. of Count Arco-Valley, of Munich; *d.* 1902; *s.* by his son [9] RICHARD MAXIMILIAN, K.C.V.O., 2nd Baron, *b.* 1870; a Lord-in-Waiting to King Edward VII. 1905-10, and to King George V. 1910-15, and Envoy Extraor. and Min. Plen. to Finland 1919-20; assumed by Roy. licence the additional surname and arms of Lyon 1919: *m.* 1904, Dorothy, who *d.* 1923, only child of the late Thomas Henry Lyon, J.P., D.l., of Appleton Hall, Cheshire, and Rutland Lodge, Rutland Gardens, S.W.; *d.* 1924; *s.* by his son [10] JOHN EMERICH HENRY, 3rd Baron, and present peer,

ADDINGTON, BARON.　(Hubbard.)　[Baron U.K. 1887.]

JAMES HUBBARD, 5th Baron; *b.* Nov. 3rd, 1930; *s.* 1971; ed. at Eastbourne Coll.; patron of one living: *m.* 1961, Alexandra Patricia, yr. da. of the late Norman Ford Millar, and has issue.

Arms.—Vert, a chevron engrailed, plain cotised argent, between three eagles' heads erased of the second, each gorged with a collar fleurettée gules. **Crest.**—In front of a fasces fessewise proper an eagle's head as in the arms. **Supporters.**—On either side an eagle argent, wings addorsed, gorged with a collar fleurettée gules, and pendent therefrom an escutcheon ermine charged with a rose gules.

Residence,—

Seeking things above.

SONS LIVING.

Hon. DOMINIC BRYCE, *b.* Aug. 24th, 1963.
Hon. Michael Walter Leslie, *b.* 1965.

DAUGHTERS LIVING.

Hon. Frances Linden, *b.* 1962.
Hon. Sally Anne, *b.* 1966.

BROTHER LIVING.

Peter (Folly Farm, Bramfield, Halesworth, Suffolk), *b.* 1932; ed. at Eastbourne Coll.

HALF-SISTER LIVING.

Nicolette, *b.* 1926: *m.* 1953, Richard Joseph Pike, of Hillbrow Cottage, Terrace Rd., Binfield, Berks., and has issue living, James Eben, *b.* 1955,—William Joseph Fitzgerald, *b.* 1960.

MOTHER LIVING.

Betty Riversdale (Wink's Isle, Darsham, Suffolk), da. of the late Horace West, Clerk to House of Commons: *m.* 1930, as his 3rd wife, Lt.-Col. John Francis Hubbard, OBE, who *d.* 1953.

COLLATERAL BRANCHES LIVING.

Grandchildren of the late Hon. Arthur Gellibrand Hubbard (infra):—
Issue of the late Capt. Gerald Napier Hubbard *b.* 1882, *d.* 1939: *m.* (Jan.) 1908, Bertha Caroline, who *d.* 1969, da. of the late Rev. Edward Southwell Garnier, R. of Quidenham, Attleborough:—

Ralph Arthur, *b.* (Oct.) 1908; ed. at Eton: *m.* 1st, 1940, the Hon. Marian Woodruff (ROYDS) (who obtained a divorce 1954), dau. of 1st Baron Ashfield; 2ndly, 1954, Elizabeth Gertrude (WOODWARD), younger dau. of the late Stephen Cozens, of Mackney Manor, Wallingford, Berks., and widow of Capt. Michael Norton-Griffiths, R.E. [see Norton-Griffiths Bt., colls.], and has issue living, (by 1st marriage) Rosemary Jane, *b.* 1942: *m.* 1962, Andrew Peter Harold Parsons, Scots Guards, of The Rectory Cottage, East Worldham, Alton, Hants., and has issue living, James Alastair Thomas *b.* 1964, Edward Charles William *b.* 1968, Annabel Jane *b.* 1969,—Angela Mary, *b.* 1945: *m.* 1st, 1965, (Luke Edward) Timothy Hue Williams; 2ndly, 1972, Peter Anthony Charles Mordaunt, of Sparrows Farm, Debden Green, Saffron Walden, Essex [see Mordaunt, Bt.]. *Residence,*—1, Shorecroft, Aldwick, Bognor Regis.——Thomas Edward (Le Cottage, Route St. Jacques, Auribeau-sur-Siagne 06, France), *b.* 1911; ed. at Eton; Sqdn.-Ldr. (ret.) Aux.AF; 1939-45 War (despatches): *m.* 1939, Bridget, da. of the late Charles Churchill Branch, OBE, and has issue living, Gerald Thomas Guy, *b.* 1947,—Charles Benjamin, *b.* 1950,—Harriet Anne, *b.* 1943.——Derek, *b.* 1920; ed. at Eton; 1939-45 War as Capt. Sussex Yeo.: *m.* 1951, Joanne, da. of the late Donald Maclean, and has issue living, Rowan, *b.* 1954,—Joanne Candida, *b.* 1957. *Residence,*—Vine Cottage, Effingham, Surrey.——Susan d'Esterre, *b.* 1914: *m.* 1st, 1936, Edward Ernest Harrison, from whom she obtained a divorce 1951; 2ndly, 1952, Capt. Herbert John Tindal Carter, late Roy. Horse Guards, and has issue living, (by 1st m.) Martin Edward (51/3, Suncroft St., SE11), *b.* 1937: *m.* 1955, Reziya Ahmad,—(by 2nd m.) Carolyn Rachel, *b.* 1955. *Residence,*—Whiteacres, Gedney, Lincs.

Issue of the late Hon. Arthur Gellibrand Hubbard, 4th son of 1st Baron, *b.* 1848, *d.* 1896: *m.* 1881, Amy d'Esterre, who *d.* 1930, dau. of the late Charles Hugh Huntly, C.M.G., formerly Civil Commr. and Resident Magistrate of Albany Cape Colony:—

Kathleen d'Esterre (Coombe House, Grants Hill, Uckfield, Sussex), *b.* 1886: *m.* 1911, the Rev. Charles Hamilton Mylne, V. of East Meon, who *d.* 1941, and has issue living, Boris Hamilton, *MBE* (3, Oxford Rd. North, Chiswick, W4), *b.* 1912; Major (ret.) Probyn's Horse, Indian Army: Mohmand Operations 1935, Waziristan 1937-38, Assam and Burma 1942-4 (MBE); MBE (Mil) 1945,—Jean d'Esterre, *b.* 1914: *m.* 1947, Nigel Henry Howard, of 49 Burton Court, Chelsea, SW3 and has issue living, Audrey d'Esterre *b.* 1948, Catherine Rosalind *b.* 1950.——Noël Agnes (Coombe House, Grants Hill, Uckfield, Sussex), *b.* 1891: *m.* 1919, Walter Francis Glencairn Campbell, late Senior Commr., British E. Africa, who *d.* 1935, and has issue living, Cloe Anne, *b.* 1932: *m.* 1964, Ronald Alastair Carr, of Renby Grange, Boars Head, Crowborough, Sussex, and has issue living, Claudia Noël *b.* 1965, Suzanna *b.* 1966.

Grandchildren of the late Hon. Evelyn Hubbard, 5th son of 1st Baron:—

Issue of the late Eric Wyndham Hubbard, *b.* 1885, *d.* 1946 : *m.* 1918, Sylvia (now of Maycotts, Matfield, Tonbridge, Kent), dau. of Herbert Picton Morris, of 61, Pont Street, S.W.:—

Evelyn Raymond WHEATLEY-HUBBARD (of Boyton, near Warminster, Wiltshire), *b.* 1921; ed. at Eton; European War 1940-45 with Coldstream Guards; assumed by deed poll 1949 the additional surname of Wheatley before his patronymic: *m.* 1949, Ann Christobel, only child of the late Col. C. J. H. Wheatley, of Berkswell Hall, Coventry, and has issue living, Thomas Henry, *b.* 1952,—Caroline Sophia, *b.* 1950.——Jasper Picton, *b.* 1923; ed. at Eton, and at Ch. Ch., Oxford: *m.* 1951, Ethne Mary, only da. of the late Henry Charles Frederick Pelham-Clinton [see D. Newcastle, colls.], and has issue living, John Louis Pelham, *b.* 1954,—Charlotte Anne, *b.* 1952,—Rose Mary, *b.* 1957. *Residence,*—Lewes Heath, Horsmonden, Kent.——Virginia, *b.* 1919.

PREDECESSORS.—[1] JOHN GELLIBRAND Hubbard, P.C., son of the late John Hubbard, of Stratford Grove, Essex, *b.* 1805; sat as M.P. for Buckingham (*C*) 1859-68, and for City of London 1874-87; cr. *Baron Addington*, of Addington, Bucks (peerage of United Kingdom) 1887: *m.* 1837, the Hon. Maria Margaret, who *d.* 1896. dau. of 9th Baron Napier; *d* 1889; *s.* by his el. son [2] EGERTON, 2nd Baron ; *b.* 1842; partner in firms of John Hubbard and Co., Russian Merchants, of London, and Egerton Hubbard and Co., of Petrograd; M.P. for Buckingham (*C*) 1874-80, and for N., or Buckingham, Div. of Buckinghamshire 1886-9 : *m.* 1880, Mary Adelaide, who *d.* 1933. dau. of Sir Wyndham Spencer Portal, 1st Bt.: *d.* 1915: *s.* by his el. son [3] JOHN GELLIBRAND, OBE, 3rd Baron; *b.* 1883; British Custodian of Enemy Property in China 1923-28; *d.* 1966; *s.* by his brother [4] RAYMOND EGERTON, 4th Baron; *b.* 1884; *d.* 1971; *s.* by his kinsman [5] JAMES (el. son of Lt.-Col. John Francis Hubbard, OBE, el. son of the Hon. Cecil John Hubbard, 3rd son of 1st Baron), 5th Baron and present peer.

ADDISON, VISCOUNT. (Addison.) [Viscount U.K. 1945.]

To serve is to live

CHRISTOPHER ADDISON, 2nd Viscount; *b.* Dec. 8th, 1904; *s.* 1951; ed. at Univ. Coll. Sch., and at Newton Coll., Newton Abbot; 1939-45 War as Maj. R.A. and S. Staffordshire Regt.; a Member of London Stock Exchange (ret. 1969); Past Chmn. of S.W. Metropolitan Regional Hosp. Board, past Pres. of Inst. of Motor Industry, and a Co. Dir.: *m.* 1928, Brigit Helen Christine, da. of Ernest Edwin George Williams, Bar.-at-law, of Wimbledon, S.W., and has issue.

Arms,—Per chevron vert and or, in chief a snake embowed head debruised between two garbs of the last and in base an anchor sable. **Crest,**—In front of two keys in saltire, wards upwards, a sword point downwards or. **Supporters,**—On either side a Lincolnshire red bull proper, the headstall also proper charged with a sun in splendour or.

Residence,—The Mount, Uffculme, Devon.

DAUGHTERS LIVING.

Hon. Jacqueline Faith, *b.* 1944: *m.* 1966, Jeremy Warren Payne, of 11, Canaan La, EH10.
Hon. Christine Gray, *b.* 1946: *m.* 1966, Terry Frederick Tidborough.

BROTHER LIVING.

Hon. MICHAEL, *b.* April 12th, 1914; ed. at Hele's Sch., Exeter, and at Balliol Coll., Oxford; formerly Flying Officer R.A.F. Vol. Reserve: *m.* 1936, Kathleen, dau. of the Rt. Rev. and Rt. Hon. Bishop John William Charles Wand, K.C.V.O., D.D., formerly 110th Bishop of London, and has issue living, William Matthew Wand (Kingerby Hall, Market Rasen, Lincs.), *b.* 1945: *m.* 1970, Joanna Mary, el. da. of J. I. C. Dickinson, of Blyborough Grange, Gainsborough, and has issue living, Paul Wand *b.* 1973, Sarah Louise *b.* 1971,—Eleanor Brigit, *b.* 1938: *m.* 1972, Michael Girling,—Caroline Ruth, *b.* 1942: *m.* 1965, John Hollis Wearing, of Nelson, NZ, and has issue living, Patrick John *b.* 1969, Jacalyn Ruth *b.* 1966. *Residence,*—Maplehurst Cottage, Maplehurst, Horsham.

SISTER LIVING.

Hon. Isobel Gray, *b.* 1907: *m.* 1932, Nicholas Cheshire, and has issue living, Paul, *b.* 1941.—Susan, *b.* 1933: *m.* 19—, Peter Howell,—Isobel, *b.* 1936: *m.* 1957, Lt. David William Ingham Brooke, RN [*see* Hewett, Bt.]. *Residence,*—Clacks Cottage, Ballinger, Great Missenden, Bucks.

WIDOW LIVING OF FIRST VISCOUNT.

BEATRICE DOROTHY (*Dorothy, Viscountess Addison*), dau. of the late F. Percy Low, of Thames View House, Staines, Middlesex : *m.* 1937, as his second wife. the 1st Viscount, who *d.* 1951. *Residence,*—6, Edgecote House, Amersham Hill, High Wycombe, Bucks.

PREDECESSOR.—[1] *Rt. Hon.* Christopher Addison, K.G., P.C., M.D., F.R.C.S., son of the late Robert Addison, of Hogsthorpe, Lincolnshire ; *b.* 1869; appointed Hunterian Professor and Examiner in Anatomy in Camb. and London Univs. 1901, Parliamentary Sec. to Board of Education 1914, Sec. to Min. of Munitions 1915, Min. of Munitions in National Ministry 1916, Min. of Reconstruction

1917, Pres. of Local Govt. Board 1919, first Min. of Health 1919 (with seat in the Cabinet from 1919), Min. without Portfolio (with a seat in the Cabinet) April 1921 (resigned in July 1921), Parliamentary Sec. to Min. of Agriculture 1929, Min. of Agriculture and Fisheries 1930 (resigned 1931), and Sec. of State for Dominion Affairs (afterwards Commonwealth Relations) and Leader of House of Lords 1945; was Lord Privy Seal 1947-51 (also Paymaster-Gen. 1948-49) and Lord Pres. of the Council March to Oct. 1951 ; elected Leader of Labour Party in House of Lords 1940 ; Chm. of Med. Research Council 1948-51 ; author of "Politics from Within," etc., and numerous medical works ; sat as M.P. for Hoxton Div. of Shoreditch (L.) 1910-18, for Shoreditch 1918-22, and for Swindon Div. of Wilts 1929-31 and 1934-35 ; cr. *Baron Addison*, of Stallingborough, co. Lincoln (peerage of United Kingdom) 1937, and *Viscount Addison*, of Stallingborough, co. Lincoln (peerage of United Kingdom) 1945 : *m*. 1st, 1902, Isobel, who *d*. 1934, dau. of the late Archibald Gray ; 2ndly, 1937, Beatrice Dorothy, dau. of the late F. Percy Low, of Thames View House, Staines, Middlesex ; *d*. 1951 ; *s*. by his son [2] CHRISTOPHER, 2nd Viscount and present peer.

ADEANE, BARON.   (Adeane.)   [Life Baron 1972.)

Fruitful by the sword and the pen.

MICHAEL EDWARD ADEANE, *GCB, GCVO, PC,* son of the late Capt. Henry Robert Augustus Adeane, Coldm. Gds. [By. Stamfordham], *b*. Sept. 30th, 1910; ed. at Eton, and Magdalene Coll., Camb. (MA Hon. Fellow since 1972); Lt.-Col. Coldm. Gds. (Reserve of Officers); a Page of Honour to HM King George V 1923-27; ADC to Gov.-Gen. of Canada 1934-36; Assist. Private Sec. to HM King George VI 1937-52, and to HM Queen Elizabeth II 1952-53, and Private Sec. to HM and Keeper of the Queen's Archives 1953-72, since when Chm. of Roy. Commn. on Historical Monuments (England), and a Member of British Library Board; a Gov. of Wellington Coll., and a Dir. of Phoenix Assurance Co., Ltd., Banque Belge Ltd., and Roy. Bank of Canada; 1939-45 War as Maj. Coldm. Gds. (wounded, despatches); *cr.* MVO (4th class) 1946, CB (Civil) 1947, KCVO 1951, PC 1953, KCB (Civil) 1955, GCVO 1962, GCB (Civil) 1968, Roy. Victorian Chain 1972, and *Baron Adeane,* of Stamfordham, co. Northumberland (Life Baron) 1972: *m*. 1939, Helen, da. of the late Richard Chetwynd-Stapylton [see V. Chetwynd, colls.], and has issue.

Arms,—Vert, within two chevronels between three griffins' heads erased, as many estoiles or. **Crest,**—Between two wings vert, each charged with a sword erect proper, pommelled and hilted or, a griffin's head also vert, beaked gules, and gorged with a collar gold. **Supporters,**—*Dexter*, a scribe proper, over his shoulders a chain or, holding in the exterior hand a pen; *sinister*, a man at arms proper.

Residence,—22, Chelsea Sq., SW1.   *Clubs,*—Beefsteak, Brooks's, Pratt's.

SON LIVING.
Hon. George Edward (Albany, Piccadilly, W1), *b*. 1939; ed. at Eton and Magdalene Coll., Camb. (BA); Bar. Middle Temple 1962; a Page of Honour to HM 1954-56.

ADRIAN, BARON.   (Adrian.)   [Baron U.K. 1955.]

EDGAR DOUGLAS ADRIAN, *O.M., M.D.*, 1st Baron, son of the late Alfred Douglas Adrian, C.B., K.C. ; *b*. Nov. 30th, 1889 ; ed. at Westminster, and at Trin. Coll., Camb. (B.A. 1911, M.B. 1915, M.A. and M.D. 1919) ; M.R.C.P. London 1916, F.R.C.P. 1924 ; Hon. D.Sc. Philadelphia 1931, Oxford and Harvard 1936, Lyons 1946, London and Manchester 1947, Durham and John Hopkins 1950, Belfast 1952, Wales 1953, New York, Sheffield and Hull 1955, Paris 1957, Leicester, and Allahabad 1958, Rockefeller 1959, and Strathclyde 1965; Hon. LLD McGill 1934, St. Andrews 1938, Glasgow 1951, Brazil 1956, Liverpool and Dalhousie 1958, and Edinburgh 1959; Hon. M.D. Brussels and Louvain 1949, Montreal 1953, Bologna and Freiburg 1957, and Cracow 1964; a FRS (Pres. 1951), and a Chevalier of Legion of Honour; Pres. of Roy. Soc. of Medicine 1960-62; Master of Trin. Coll., Camb. 1951-65; Chancellor of Leicester Univ. 1957-71, and of Camb. Univ. since 1968 (Vice-Chancellor 1957-59); Nobel prize 1932 Copley medal 1946, gold Albert medal of Roy. So. of Arts 1953, and Harben medal of Roy. Inst. of Public Health and Hygiene 1955; 1914-18 War as Capt. RAMC; cr. OM 1942, and *Baron Adrian,* of Cambridge, co. Cambridge (peerage of UK) 1955; *m*. 1923, Hester Agnes, DBE, BEM, who *d*. 1966, da. of the late Hume Chancellor Pinsent, and has issue.

Arms,—Vert, three estoiles argent, on a chief of the last a lion passant sable. **Crest,**—The astronomical sign of mercury or, between two roses gules, barbed and seeded proper. **Supporters,**—On either side a lion sable semee of pentacles or. **Motto,**—Non temere credere.
Residence,—Trinity College, Cambridge.   *Club,*—Athenæum.

SON LIVING.

Hon. RICHARD HUME, (3 Adams Rd., Cambridge; Savile Club) *b.* Oct. 16th, 1927; *ed.* at Westminster, and at Trin. Coll., Camb.; a Fellow of Churchill Coll., Camb.: *m.* 1967, Lucy el. da. of Alban Douglas Rendall Caroe, of 15, Campden Hill Sq., W.8.

DAUGHTERS LIVING.

Hon. Anne Pinsent, *b.* 1924 : *m.* 1945, Richard Darwin Keynes, and has issue living, Adrian Maynard, *b.* 1946,—Randal Hume, *b.* 1948,—Roger John ,*b.* 1951,—Simon Douglas, *b.* 1952. *Residence,—*3, Herschel Road, Cambridge.

Hon. Jennet Parker, *b.* 1927: *m.* 1953, Peter Watson Campbell, and has issue living, Sally Anne, *b.* 1958,—Emma Jane, *b.* 1960. *Residence,—*16, Stonehill Road, SW14.

AILESBURY, MARQUESS OF. (Brudenell-Bruce.) [Marquess U.K. 1821, Bt. E. 1611.]

MICHAEL SYDNEY CEDRIC BRUDENELL-BRUCE, 8th Marquess and 14th Baronet; *b.* March 31st, 1926; *s.* 1974; *ed.* at Eton; late Lt. RHG (Reserve); 30th Hereditary Warden of Savernake Forest; a Member of London Stock Exchange: *m.* 1st, 1952, Edwina Sylvia, from whom he obtained a divorce 1961, da. of Lt.-Col. Sir (Ernest) Edward de Winton Wills, 4th Bt. (cr. 1904); 2ndly, 1963 (m. diss. 1974), Juliet Adrienne Lethbridge, da. of the late Hilary Lethbridge Kingsford; 3rdly, 1974, Caroline Elizabeth, da. of Cdr. Owen Francis MacTier Wethered, RN (ret.), and formerly wife of Simon Romilly, and has issue by 1st and 2nd *m.*

Arms,—Quarterly: 1st and 4th or, a saltire and chief gules; on a canton argent, a lion rampant azure, *Bruce*; 2nd and 3rd argent, a chevron gules, btween three caps of maintenance, their fronts turned towards the sinister, *Brudenell.* **Crests,—**1st, a lion statant, tail extended azure; 2nd, a seahorse naiant proper. **Supporters,—**Two savages proper wreathed about the temples and loins vert, each holding in his exterior hand a lance, thereon a banner of the arms of Bruce.

*Residence,—*Cadley House, Savernake Forest, Marlborough, Wilts.

SON LIVING (*By 1st m.*)

DAVID MICHAEL JAMES (*Earl of Cardigan*), *b.* Nov. 12th, 1952; *ed.* at Eton.

DAUGHTERS LIVING (*By 1st m.*)

Lady Sylvia Davina, *b.* 1954.
Lady Carina Doune, *b.* 1956.

(*By 2nd m.*)

Lady Louise, *b.* 1964.
Lady Kathryn Juliet, *b.* 1965.

BROTHER LIVING.

Lord Chandos Gerald Piers (Cortijo de la Plata, Zahara de los Atunes, Cadiz, Spain), *b.* 1929; *ed.* at Harrow: *m.* 1st, 1951 (m. diss. 1957), Annie, only da. of Henry Angelé, of Yamaa-el-Mokra, Tangier; 2ndly, 1958, Nelida Garcia Otero, da. of Mariano Garcia Villalba, of Madrid, Spain, and has issue living (by 2nd m.), Tamara Angela, *b.* 1966,—Sandra Teresa, *b.* 1969.

HALF-BROTHER LIVING.

Lord Charles Adam, *b.* 1951; *ed.* at Eton; Lt. R. Hussars.

AUNTS LIVING (*Daughters of 6th Marquess*)

Lady Ursula Daphne, *b.* 1905 : *m.* 1944, Alec Thomas Taylor, and has issue living, Peter Alec, *b.* 1945,—Martin Chandos, *b.* 1952. *Residence,—*2, Howard Rd., Newbury, Berks.
Lady Rosemary Enid, *b.* 1907. *Residence,—*The Kennels, Savernake, Marlborough, Wilts.

WIDOW LIVING OF SEVENTH MARQUESS

JEAN FRANCES MARGARET (*Jean, Marchioness of Ailesbury*) (Bel au Vent, St. Lawrence, Jersey), da. of the late John Addison Wilson, of Bodicote, Banbury, Oxon., and widow of Sqdn.-Ldr. Richard Williamson, MBE, RAFVR: *m.* 1950, as his 3rd wife, the 7th Marquess, who *d.* 1974.

COLLATERAL BRANCHES LIVING.

Grandchildren of the late Lord Robert Thomas Brudenell-Bruce (*infra*):—

Issue of the late George Lionel Thomas BRUDENELL, *b.* 1880, *d.* 1962, who assumed by Roy. licence 1917, the surname and arms of Brudenell only: *m.* 1923, Mary Julia, who *d.* 1972, da. of Stephen Schilizzi [Ralli Bt.]:—

Edmund Crispin Stephen James George, *b.* 1928: *m.* 1955, the Hon. Marian Cynthia Manningham-Buller, el. da. of 1st Viscount Dilhorne, and has issue living, Robert Edmund, *b.* 1956; *ed.* at Stanbridge Earls Sch.,—Thomas Mervyn (twin), *b.* 1956; *ed.* at Eton,—Anna Maria *b.* 1960. *Seat,—*Deene Park, Corby, Northants. *Residence,—*18, Laxford House, Ebury St., SW1.

Issue of the late Col. Robert Hanbury Brudenell-Bruce, D.S.O., Norfolk Regt., *b.* 1881, *d.* 1955 : *m.* 1st, 1913, Olive Vere, who *d.* 1920, dau. of Charles H. Richardson, formerly of Cedar Hurst, co. Down: 2ndly, 1922, Judith Iris (now of Hill Farm, Hartley Wintney, Hants), dau. of the late Major Bertram William Arnold Keppel [see E. Albemarle, colls.]:—

(By 2nd m.) Chandos Robert Henry (Trainers House, Moulton Paddocks, Newmarket), *b.* 1923: *m.* 1949 Dana Moira Angela, da. of Stanhope Joel, of Perots Island, Bermuda, and has issue living, Andrew Robert Joel, *b.* 1951: *m.* 1974, Sophie Inch, and has issue living, Alice *b.* 1974,—Joanna Dana, *b.* 1954, *m.* 1975, Charles FitzRoy [see By. Southampton],—Sara Vivien, *b.* 1960.——(By 1st m.) Daphne Helen Anne (*Hon. Mrs. Robert F. H. Preston*) *b.* 1915: *m.* 1st, 1934, Lieut.-Cdr. Reginald Hughes-Onslow, RN, who *d.* 1947, having obtained a divorce 1946 [see E. Onslow, colls.]; 2ndly, 1946 (m. diss. 1967), Maj. John Edward Mountague Bradish-Ellames; 3rdly, 1970, the Hon. Robert Francis Hubert Preston of Bosworth House, Arthingworth, Market Harborough, Leics. [see V. Gormanston] and has issue (by 1st m.) [see E. Onslow, colls.],—(by 2nd m.) Elizabeth Laura, *b.* 1947: *m.* 1971, John Harvey, of 1, Miles Rd., Clifton, Bristol.

Issue of the late John Charles Brudenell-Bruce, M.B.E., *b.* 1885, *d.* 1960 : *m.* 1st, 1913, (marriage dissolved 1925). Else, dau. of Capt. C. F. Dreschel, of Copenhagen ; 2ndly, 1928, Sigrid (Little Denmark, Tortola, British Virgin Islands, W. Indies), da. of Anders Ammentorp, of Copenhagen:—

David John, *b.* 1927.——Simon Robert (Tomarata, RD4, Wellsford, NZ), *b.* 1928: *m.* 1964, Christine Muriel Heald, of Pokeno, and has issue living, Peter Gregory, *b.* 1965,—Barbara Ann, *b.* 1967,—Penelope Jane, *b.* 1970.——Barbara Karen (twin), *b.* 1928: *m.* 1953, Charles Zeese.——Diana Mary, *b.* 1936.——Arabella Anne, *b.* 1940: *m.* 1st, 1962 (m. diss. 1969), Jack Ball, of Puerto Rico; 2ndly, 1972, Morgan J. Gatten, of Detroit, Michigan, USA, and has issue living (by 1st m.) Robert J. *b.* 1968,—Lesley Anne, *b.* 1963.—Beth Sigrid, *b.* 1965,—(by 2nd m.) Michael J., *b.* 1972.

Grandchildren of the late John Charles Brudenell-Bruce, MBE (ante):—
Issue of the late Marc Hadrian Brudenell-Bruce, *b.* 1930, *d.* 1965: *m.* 1st, 1953 (m. diss. 1957); 2ndly, 1957, Rayna Ellen Howell:—
(By 2nd marriage) Marc Raymond Christopher, *b.* 1962.——Karen Suzanne *b.* 1958.
Issue of the late Lord Robert Thomas Brudenell-Bruce, 4th son of 3rd Marquess, *b.* 1845, *d.* 1912: *m.* 1878, Emma, who *d.* 1921, dau. of the late Capel Hanbury Leigh, of Pontypool Park, Monmouth:—
Frances Edith Agnes, *b.* 1883: *m.* 1907, Col. Herbert Anderton Foster, T.D., who *d.* 1930, and has issue living, Herbert Frederick Brudenell, *T.D.* (Park House, Drumoak, Aberdeenshire), *b.* 1908; ed. at Radley, and at Peterhouse, Camb.; a JP for Aberdeenshire; an OStJ; 1939-45 War as Maj. Scottish Horse (despatches): *m.* 1945, Christine Leonard, da. of Sir Archibald Leonard Lucas Lucas-Tooth, 2nd Bt., cr. 1906 (ext.), and has issue living, John Leonard William, *b.* 1948, Francis Derick, *b.* 1953, Madeline Rosa Edith, *b.* 1946: *m.* 1967, Clive Lyon of 10, Blomfield Rd., W9 (and has issue living, Charles Henry *b.* 1971),—William Robert Brudenell (Lexham Hall, King's Lynn, Norfolk and Gannochy, Angus), *b.* 1911; ed. at Wellington Coll., and at Corpus Christi Coll., Oxford (MA); FRSA, late Capt. 6th Bn. Black Watch: *m.* 1942, Jean Leslie, da. of Leslie Urquhart, of Brasted Place, Kent, and has issue living, Neil, *b.* 1943, Richard Francis (29, Bedford Gdns., W8), *b.* 1945: *m.* 1970, the Hon. Sarah Rachel Jane Kay-Shuttleworth, da. of 4th Baron Shuttleworth (and has issue living, Henrietta Victoria *b.* 1973), Charles, *b.* 1955, Melanie, *b.* 1948. *Residence,*—Moulton Priory, Newmarket, Suffolk.

PREDECESSORS.—[1] CHARLES Bruce, 4th Earl of Elgin, 3rd Earl of Ailesbury, and 6th Lord Kinloss ; was the last male descendant of that branch of the Bruce family which settled in England circa 1603.　He selected as his heir his nephew, the Hon. Thomas Brudenell, 4th son of 3rd Earl of Cardigan by Elizabeth Bruce ; cr. *Baron Bruce,* of Tottenham (peerage of Great Britain) 1746, with remainder to the Hon. Thomas Brudenell (ante) ; *d.* 1747 without surviving male issue, when the Earldom of Ailesbury became ext., the Earldom of Elgin reverted to the 9th Earl of Kincardine, the Lordship of Kinloss became abeyant, and the Barony of Bruce devolved upon his nephew (ante) [2] THOMAS, 2nd Baron ; inherited also the Wardenship of Savernake Forest in Wilts (an ancient office which became hereditary in the Esturmy family (1066-1427), passed thence into the Seymour family [see D. Somerset]) and so in 1676 to the Bruces; he assumed the additional name and arms of Bruce ; cr. *Earl of Ailesbury* (peerage of Great Britain) 1776 ; *d.* 1814 ; *s.* by his son [3] CHARLES, *K.T.,* 2nd Earl ; cr. *Viscount Savernake, Earl Bruce,* and *Marquess of Ailesbury* (peerage of United Kingdom) 1821 : *m.* 1st, 1793, the Hon. Henrietta Maria Hill, who *d.* 1831, dau. of 1st Baron Berwick ; 2ndly, 1833, Maria Elizabeth, who *d.* 1893, dau. of the Hon. Charles Tollemache ; *d.* 1856 ; *s.* by his el. son [4] GEORGE WILLIAM FREDERICK, *K.G.,* 2nd Marquess, *b.* 1804 ; summoned to House of Lords in his father's Barony of Bruce 1839 ; was Lord-Lieut. of Wilts and Master of the Horse 1868-74; *s.* his kinsman, the 7th Earl of Cardigan, 1868 [see infra *₊*] : *m.* 1837, Lady Mary Caroline Herbert, who *d.* 1892, dau. of 11th Earl of Pembroke; *d.* Jan. 6, 1878 ; *s.* by his brother [5] ERNEST AUGUSTUS CHARLES, *P.C,* 3rd Marquess ; was Lord-Lieut. of Berks, M.P. for Marlborough (C) 1832-78, and Vice-Chamberlain to H.M. 1841-6, and 1852-8 : *m.* 1834, the Hon. Louisa Elizabeth Horsley-Beresford, who *d.* 1891, dau. of 2nd Baron Decies ; *d.* 1886 ; *s.* by his grandson [6] GEORGE WILLIAM THOMAS (son of George John Brudenell-Bruce, who *d.* 1868, el. son of 3rd Marquess), 4th Marquess, *b.* 1863 : *m.* 1884, Dorothy Julia, who *d.* 1917, dau. of Thomas Haseley, of Brighton; *d.* 1894; *s.* by his uncle [7] HENRY AUGUSTUS, 5th Marquess; *b.* 1842 ; M.P. for N.-W., or Chippenham, Div. of Wiltshire (C) 1886-92: *m.* 1870, Georgiana Sophia Maria, who *d.* 1902, dau. of G. H. Pinckney, formerly of Tawstock Court, Barnstaple : *d.* 1911 : *s.* by his son [8] GEORGE WILLIAM JAMES CHANDOS, *D.S.O., T.D.,* 6th Marquess ; *b.* 1873 ; late 3rd Batn. Argyll and Sutherland Highlanders, Roy. Wilts. Yeo., Middlesex Yeo., Wilts. Regt., R.A.S.C. and R.F.A. (T.A.) ; S. Africa 1899-1900 with Army Transports as D.A.A.G. (D.S.O.), European War 1915-19 with Guards Div. Train : *m.* 1st, 1903, Caroline Sydney Anne, who *d.* 1941, dau. of the late John Madden ; 2ndly, 1945, Mabel Irene, who *d.* 1954, dau. of the late John Samuel Lindsay, of Wrexham ; 3rdly, 1955, Alice Maude Emily, who *d.* 1960, dau. of the late Capt. John Forbes Pinhey, and widow of (i) Col. John Henry Arthur Boyce, (ii) Col. Francis Byrne Johnson, and (iii) Col. Rowland Money ; *d.* 1961 ; *s.* by his son [9] CHANDOS SYDNEY CEDRIC, 7th Marquess; *b.* 1904: *m.* 1st, 1924, Joan Houlton, who *d.* 1937, da. of Stephen Salter, of Pondwell, Ryde, I. of Wight; 2ndly, 1944 (m. diss. 1948) Joyce Frances, da. of Charles Warwick-Evans, and formerly wife of Peter Quennell; 3rdly, 1950, Jean Frances Margaret, da. of the late John Addison Wilson, of Bodlicote, Oxon., and widow of Sqdn.-Ldr. Richard Williamson, MBE, RAF; *d.* 1974; *s.* by his el. son [10] MICHAEL SYDNEY CEDRIC, 8th Marquess and present peer; also Earl of Cardigan, Earl Bruce, Viscount Savernake, Baron Brudenell, and Baron Bruce.

₊ [1] *Sir* THOMAS Brudenell, a zealous supporter of the royal cause during the Civil War, suffered long imprisonment in the Tower; cr. a *Baronet* 1611, *Baron Brudenell* (peerage of England) 1628, and *Earl of Cardigan* (peerage of England) 1661 ; *d.* 1663 ; *s.* by his el. son [2] ROBERT, 2nd Earl ; *d.* 1703 : *s.* by his grandson [3] GEORGE, 3rd Earl ; Master of the Buckhounds to Queen Anne; *d.* 1732; *s.* by his el. son [4] GEORGE, *K.G.,* 4th Earl; Gov. to the Prince of Wales and Prince Frederick; cr. *Marquess of Monthermer* and *Duke of Montagu* (peerage of Great Britain) 1776, and *Baron Montagu,* of Boughton (peerage of Great Britain) 1786, with remainder to his grandson Henry James, 2nd son of 3rd Duke of Buccleuch ; *d.* 1790 without surviving male issue, when the Marquessate and Dukedom became extinct, the Barony passed to his grandson (ante), and the Earldom devolved upon his brother [5] JAMES, 5th Earl ; *d.s.p.* 1811 ; *s.* by his nephew [6] ROBERT, 6th Earl, son of the Hon. Robert, 3rd son of 3rd Earl; *d.* 1837; *s.* by his son [7] JAMES THOMAS, *K.C.B.,* a Lieut.-Gen. in the Army and Col. 11th Hussars; served with distinction in the Crimea; *d.s.p.* 1868; *s.* by his cousin [8] GEORGE WILLIAM FREDERICK, 2nd Marquess of Ailesbury [see ante].

AILSA, MARQUESS OF. (Kennedy.) [Marquess U.K. 1831.]

ARCHIBALD DAVID KENNEDY, *OBE,* 7th Marquess; *b.* Dec. 3rd, 1925; *s.* 1957; formerly Lieut. Scots Guards; Lt.-Col. R.S.F. (TA); a DL of Ayrshire; OBE (Mil) 1968: *m.* 1954, Mary, da. of the late John Burn, of Amble, Northumberland, and has issue.

Arms,—Argent, a chevron gules, between three cross crosslets fitchée sable, the whole within a double tressure flory counterflory of the second. *Crest,*—A dolphin naiant, proper. *Supporters,*—Two swans, wings inverted proper, beaked and membered gules.

Residence,—Cassillis House, Maybole, Ayrshire. *Club,*—New (Edinburgh).

Consider the end.

SONS LIVING.
ARCHIBALD ANGUS CHARLES (*Earl of Cassillis*), *b.* Sept. 13th, 1956.
Lord David Thomas, *b.* 1958.

DAUGHTER LIVING.
Lady Elizabeth Helen, *b.* 1955.

AUNT LIVING. (*Daughter of 3rd Marquess.*)
Lady Marjory, *b.* 1898: *m.* 1921, Sir Laurence Pierce Brooke Merriam, MC, JP, DL, who *d.* 1966, and
has issue living, Peter Hugh Kennedy (of Holton Lodge, Holton St. Mary, Colchester), *b.* 1922; ed. at
Eton and at Univ. Coll., Oxford; 1939-45 War as Lt. and temp. Capt. Coldstream Guards:
m. 1949, Helen Mary Frances, el. da. of the late Francis Errington Scott, of Hatfield
Heath, Bishop's Stortford, and has issue living, Charles Kennedy Scott *b.* 1949, Richard
Henry Faber *b.* 1957, Aline Frances *b.* 1951, Susanna Helen *b.* 1954,—Michael Kennedy (Stowell
House, nr. Sherborne, Dorset), *b.* 1925; ed. at Eton; 1939-45 War as Sub-Lieut. RNVR: *m.* 1947,
Anne Teresa, only dau. of the late Lieut.-Col. Philip Moss Elvery, DSO, MC, RAMC, of Bunny Creek,
New Milton, Hants, and has issue living, Andrew William Kennedy *b.* 1948, Teresa Anne *b.* 1954.
Residence,—Loom House, Dedham, Colchester.

WIDOW LIVING OF SON OF THIRD MARQUESS.
Katharine Louisa Clare (27, The Abbey, Romsey, Hants.), da. of Francis Henry Atherton, of Pathfield,
Shalford, Guildford: *m.* 1925, Lord Hugh Kennedy, MC, who *d.* 1970, and has issue living [see colls.
infra.].

COLLATERAL BRANCHES LIVING.
Issue of the late Lt.-Col. Lord Hugh Kennedy, MC, yst. son of 3rd Marquess, *b.* 1895,
d. 1970: *m.* 1925, Katharine Louisa Clare (ante), da. of Francis Henry Atherton,
of Pathfield, Shalford, Guildford:—
Nigel, *b.* 1926; ed. at Radley.

Grandchildren of the late John Gilbert Kennedy, el son of the late Lord Gilbert
Kennedy, 5th son of the late Earl of Cassillis, son of 1st Marquess:—
Issue of the late Capt. Nigel Augustus Kennedy, *b.* 1886, *d.* 1957 : *m.* 1st, 1917 (marriage
dissolved 1944), Gertrude Vera, dau. of the late Brig.-Gen. Lionel Godolphin Brooke, C.B.
[see V. Brookeborough, colls.]; 2ndly, 1946, Dorothy Mary, who *d.* 19—, widow of Lieut.-Col.
R. C. Cooper, Canadian Inf. :—
(By 1st marriage) Ian Michael Godfrey, *b.* 1921; European War 1941 as Pilot Officer R.A.F. (invalided:
m. 1960, Josephine Helen, da. of John Leslie Price, of Warham Court, Breinton, Hereford, and
has issue living, Angus Michael David, *b.* 1962,—Virginia Anne Nicola, *b.* 1964. *Residence,*—The
Camp Farm, Caynham, nr. Ludlow, Salop.——Lonia Hersey Joy, *b.* 1924: *m.* 1944 (*m.* diss. 1966).
Donald MacLean, late Lt. RCN, and has issue living, John Kennedy, *b.* 1946,—Alan Michael,
b. 1948,—Brian William, *b.* 1950. *Residence,*—3269, W. 32nd Av., Vancouver, 8, British Columbia,

Grandchildren of the late Capt. William Henry Kennedy-Erskine, son of the late
Hon. John Kennedy-Erskine, 2nd son of 12th Earl of Cassillis (afterwards 1st
Marquess):—
Issue of the late Augustus John William Henry Kennedy-Erskine, *b.* 1866, *d.* 1908: *m.*
1896, Alice Marjorie Cunningham, who *d.* 1947, dau. of the late Rev. A. L. R. Foote,
D.D., of Rosehill, Brechin :—
Augustus John, *b.* 1900.——Millicent Alison Augusta, *b.* 1899: *m.* 1943, as this third wife, Lt.-Col.
Thomas Maitland Lovett, who *d.* 1946. *Residence,*—Bromley House, Montrose, Angus.

Granddaughters of the late Sir John Gordon Kennedy, KCMG, el. son of the late
John Kennedy (infra):—
Issue of the late Capt. Aubrey Leo Kennedy, MC, *b.* 1885, *d.* 1965: *m.* 1921, Sylvia Dorothy,
who *d.* 1968, da. of the late Arthur Herbert Meysey-Thompson [see Meysey-
Thompson, Bt., colls.]:—
Elizabeth Dorothy (4, Gordon Place, W8), *b.* 1922: *m.* 1st, 1945, Charles Russell Scarr, from whom
she obtained a divorce 1958; 2ndly, 1960 her cousin, Jeremy John Le Mesurier [see Meysey-
Thompson, Bt., colls.], and has issue living, (by 1st marriage) Aubrey Mark Kennedy, *b.* 1949,—
Caroline Sarah, *b.* 1951.——Horatia Clare, *b.* 1926: *m.* 1969, Brian Huleatt Heddy, HM Dip. Ser.,
of 38, Thurloe Sq., SW7.——Diana Helen Majorie, *b.* 1929.

(*In remainder to Earldom of Cassillis*)
Grandchildren of Edward Briggs Kennedy, 3rd son of John Kennedy (infra):—
Issue of the late Capt. Edward Coverley Kennedy, R.N.; *b.* 1879, *d.* (on active service
during 1939-45 War) 1939: *m.* 1918, Rosalind Margaret Innes (The Sunbury Homes,
Thames St., Sunbury-on-Thames, Middx.), da. of Sir Ludovic James Grant, 11th Bt.:—
Ludovic Henry Coverley, *b.* 1919 ; ed. at Eton, and at Oxford Univ. ; is a Television Broadcaster,
Writer, and Lecturer; European War 1939-45 as Lieut. R.N.V.R.: *m.* 1950, Moira Shearer, dau.
of the late Harold Charles King, and has issue living, Alastair Charles Coverley, *b.* 1963,—Ailsa
Margaret, *b.* 1952,—Rachel Katherine, *b.* 1956,—Fiona Jane, *b.* 1961. *Residence,*—The Old Manse,
Makerstoun, by Kelso, Roxburghshire.——Morar Margaret, *b.* 1926: *m.* 1st, 1948, John Hamish Orr-
Ewing, from whom she obtained a divorce 1954; 2ndly, 1954, Royce T. C. Ryton, of 64, Kingfisher
Drive, Ham, Richmond, Surrey, and has issue living, (by 1st m.) Roderick Coverley Hugh, *b.* 1951,—
(by 2nd m.) Charlotte Susan, *b.* 1955.——Katherine, *b.* 1927: *m.* 1947, Ion Melville Calvocoressi,
MBE, MC, late Maj. Scots Guards, and has issue living, James Melville Ion, *b.* 1948 : *m.* 1971, Richenda
Victoria Hanson, el. da. of Peter Blandy, of 46, Jubilee Place, SW3, and has issue living, Matthew
James, *b.* 1973,—Richard Edward Ion, *b.* 1951,—Andrew Matthew Ion, *b.* 1953,—Iona Rosalind,
b. 1957. *Residence,*—Court Lodge, Westerham, Kent.

Grandchildren of the late John Kennedy, only son of the late Hon. Robert Kennedy,
3rd son of 11th Earl of Cassillis:—
Issue of the late Gilbert George Kennedy, *b.* 1844, *d.* 1908: *m.* 1874, Alice, who *d.* 1943,
dau. of the late Edward Lyon, of Johnson Hall, Eccleshall :—
John de Navarre, OBE, QC, *b.* 1888; Bar BC 1918; Ont. 1921, a KC 1948; Co. Court Judge, co.
Peterborough, Ontario, 1952-63; Editor of *Chitty's Law Journal* since 1963; Dir.-Gen. of Legal
Branch, Dept. of Munitions and Supply, Ottawa 1940-44; a Member of Canadian Soc. of Painters in
Water Colour; author of " The History of the Department of Munitions and Supply ", and " Aids to
Jury Charges—Criminal ", and of three novels: OBE (Civil) 1946: *m.* 1st, 1914, Elsie Margaret, who
d. 1969, da. of the late Edwin Charles Pinks, of Lindsell, Essex; 2ndly, 1970, Marjorie Helen Troop,
da. of the late Albert Morton, of Dudley, Worcs., and has issue living (by 1st m.), Anne Macomb,
b. 1930: *m.* 1953, Frank Edward Dudas, of 146, Collier Street, Toronto, Ontario, Canada, and has
issue living, Edward Tibor *b.* 1959, Linda Julianna Kennedy *b.* 1956, Yone Anne Pinks *b.* 1962.
Residence,—707, Weller St., Peterborough, Ont., K9H 4X2, Canada. *Clubs,*—Arts & Letters
(Toronto), Royal Canadian Yacht (Toronto), and Toronto:

PREDECESSORS.—[1] *Sir* GILBERT Kennedy, *K.B.*, cr. *Lord Kennedy* (peerage of Scotland)
1452: was one of the six Regents of the Kingdom during the minority of James III.; *s.* by his
son [2] JOHN, 2nd Lord; *d.* 1508; *s.* by his son [3] DAVID, *P.C.*, 3rd Lord; cr. *Earl of Cassilis*
1502; killed at battle of Flodden 1513; *s.* by his son [4] GILBERT, 2nd Earl; assassinated 1527
by Sir Hugh Campbell, of Loudon, Sheriff of Ayr, and a supporter of the Angus faction, from

whom he had unsuccessfully attempted to rescue James V. the previouseary; *s.* by his son
[5] GILBERT, 3rd Earl, Lord High Treasurer of Scotland; *d.* 1558; *s.* by his son [6] GILBERT,
4th Earl; *d.* 1576; *s.* by his son [7] GILBERT, 5th Earl, Lord Treasurer of Scotland; *d.*1615;
s. by his nephew [8] JOHN, 6th Earl; *s.* by his son [9] JOHN, 7th Earl; *d.* 1701; *s.* by his
grandson [10] JOHN, 8th Earl; *d.s.p.*, 1759, and in 1762 was by a resolution of House of Lords
s. by his kinsman [11] *Sir* THOMAS Kennedy, 4th Bt. (cr. 1682), of Culzean, 9th Earl; *d.*
unmarried 1775; *s.* by his brother [12] DAVID, 10th Earl; *d.s.p.* 1792, when the Baronetcy
became ext., and the peerage titles descended to the great-great-great-grandson of the Hon.
Thomas, 2nd son of 3rd Earl [13] ARCHIBALD, 11th Earl, Capt. R.N.; *d.* 1794; *s.* by his son
[14] ARCHIBALD, *K.T.*, *F.R.S.*, 12th Earl; cr. *Baron Ailsa* (peerage of United Kingdom) 1806,
and *Marquess of Ailsa* (peerage of United Kingdom) 1831; *d.* 1846; *s.* by his grandson [15]
ARCHIBALD, *K.T.*, 2nd Marquess, *b.* 1816; Lord-Lieut. of Ayrshire: *m.* 1846, Julia, who *d.* 1899,
dau. of Sir Richard Mounteney Jephson, 1st Bt.; *d.* 1870; *s.* by his son [16] ARCHIBALD, 3rd
Marquess, *b.* 1847; Lord-Lieut. of Ayrshire: *m.* 1st, 1871, the Hon. Evelyn Stuart, who *d.* 1888,
3rd dau. of 12th Baron Blantyre; 2ndly, 1891, Isabella, who *d.* 1945, dau. of the late Hugh
M'Master, of Kausani, N.-W. Provinces, India; *d.* 1938; *s.* by his son [17] ARCHIBALD, 4th
Marquess, *b.* 1872: *m.* 1903, Frances Emily, who *d.* 1949, dau. of Sir Mark John MacTaggart-Stewart,
1st Bt.; *d.* 1943; *s.* by his brother [18] CHARLES, 5th Marquess, *b.* 1875; Capt. Ayrshire Yeo., and
Lieut. 3rd Batn., Roy. Scots Fusiliers: *m.* 1st, 1925, Constance Barbara, who *d.* 1931, dau. of the
late Edward Clark of Avishays, Chard, and widow of Adm. Sir John Kennedy Erskine Baird,
K.C.B.; 2ndly, 1933, Helen Ethel, *M.B.E.*, who *d.* 1959, only dau. of the late James McDouall, J.P.,
D.L., of Logan, and widow of Major Richard John Cuninghame, M.C., of Hensol, Kirkcudbrightshire,
d. 1956; *s.* by his brother [19] ANGUS, 6th Marquess; *b.* 1882; formerly Capt. R.A.F.: *m.* 1922;
(Gertrude) Millicent, who *d.* 1957, dau. of Gervas Weir Cooper, of Wordwell Hall, Bury St. Edmunds;
d. 1957; *s.* by his son [20] ARCHIBALD DAVID, 7th Marquess and present peer; also Earl of Cassillis,
Lord Kennedy, and Baron Ailsa.

AILWYN, BARON. (Fellowes.) [Baron U.K. 1921.]

Patience and perseverance with
magnanimity.

ERIC WILLIAM EDWARD FELLOWES
C.B.E., 3rd Baron; *b.* Nov. 24th, 1887;
s. 1936; ed. at Stubbington Sch. and
HMS *Britannia*; Capt. (ret.) RN; a JP
and DL of Suffolk; Dep. Chm. of Comttees
and Dep. Speaker of House of Lords
1957-72; 1914-19 War in North Sea,
European War 1939-44; a Member of
Parliamentary Mission to China 1942;
Pres. of China Asso. 1943-8; has Order of
Brilliant Star of China; CBE (Civil)
1962: *m.* 1935, Cecil Lorna, da. of
the late Col. Hugh Gurney Barclay,
M.V.O., of Colney Hall, Norwich [B.
Magheramorne], and widow of Brigadier
Malise Graham, D.S.O. [Graham, Bt.,
cr. 1662, colls.].

    Arms,—Azure, a fesse dancettée ermine between
three lions' heads erased or, murally crowned argent,
a crescent for difference. Crest,—A lion's head as in
the arms, charged with a fesse dancettée ermine.
Supporters,—On either side a lynx argent, spotted
sable, ducally gorged and chained or, pendant from
the coronet an escutcheon ermine charged with a ram's eye proper.
Residence,—Sweffling Grange, Saxmundham, Suffolk. *Clubs*,—United Service, Travellers'.

BROTHER LIVING.

Hon. CAROL ARTHUR, *T.D.*, *b.* Nov. 23rd, 1896; is a J.P. for Herts. and Middlesex; sometime Lieut.
Roy. Norfolk Regt.; was Agent to Earl of Strafford 1930-52, and Assist. Sec., Roy. Agricultural Soc.
1952-9; European War 1939-45 as Major 33rd (St. Pancras) Anti-Aircraft Batn. R.E. (T.A.) and on
Staff of Anti-Aircraft Command; Mesopotamia 1917-18: *m.* 1936, Caroline (CUDEMORE), dau. of the
late Maynard Cowan, of Victoria, British Columbia. *Residence*,—The Cottage, Gissing, Diss,
Norfolk.

WIDOW LIVING OF SON OF FIRST BARON.

Audrey Janet (The Flat, Old Brewery House, Malmesbury, Wilts.), da. of the late Col. Lionel Richard
Cavendish Boyle [see E. Cork, colls.]: *m.* 1st, 1916, Major Hedworth George Ailwyn Fellowes, MC,
who *d.* (killed in action during 1914-18 War) 1917; 2ndly, 1922, Wilfrid Valentine Denison.

PREDECESSORS.—[1] AILWYN EDWARD Fellowes, *K.C.V.O.*, *K.B.E.*, *P.C.*, 2nd son of 1st
Baron de Ramsey; *b.* 1855; was Vice-Chamberlain of Queen Victoria's Household July 1895 to
Nov. 1900, a Junior Lord of the Treasury Nov. 1900 to March 1905, Pres. of Board of Agriculture
(with a seat in the Cabinet) March to Dec. 1905, and a Dep. Director-Gen. of Food Production
and Chm. of Agriculture Wages Board 1917-19; M.P. for Huntingdonshire, N., or Ramsey, Div.
(C) Aug. 1887 to Jan. 1906: cr. *Baron Ailwyn*, of Honingham, co. Norfolk (peerage of United
Kingdom) 1921: *m.* 1886, the Hon. Agatha Eleanor Augusta Jolliffe, who *d.* 1938, only dau.
of 2nd Baron Hylton; *d.* 1924: *s.* by his son [2] RONALD TOWNSHEND, 2nd Baron: *b.* 1886; Lieut.-
Col. (ret. Rifle Brig.); 1914-18 War (MC, DSO): *m.* 1916, Mildred, who *d.* 1974, el. da. of the late
Lorraine King, of Calcutta, and Tayport, Fife; *d.* 1936; *s.* by his brother [3] ERIC WILLIAM EDWARD,
3rd Baron and present peer.

AIREDALE, BARON. (Kitson.) [Baron U.K. 1907, Bt. U.K. 1886.]

PALMAM QUI MERUIT FERAT

Let him who merits bear the palm.

OLIVER JAMES VANDELEUR KITSON, 4th Baron and 4th Baronet ; *b.* April 22nd, 1915 ; *s.* 1958 ; ed. at Eton, and at Trin. Coll., Camb. ; Bar. Inner Temple 1939 ; is Major Green Howards ; assumed by deed poll 1935, the additional forename of Vandeleur ; appointed Dep. Chm. of Committees, House of Lords 1961, and Dep. Speaker 1962.

Arms.—Or, on a pale azure, a pike hauriant of the first, on a chief of the second an annulet between two mill-rinds or. Crest.—Issuant from a fence of paling proper, a demi-unicorn argent, collared azure. Supporters.—On either side an owl argent, gorged with a plain collar gules, pendent therefrom a shield of the arms.

Residence,—Ufford Hall, Stamford, Lincolnshire.

SISTER LIVING.

Hon. Verona Vandeleur, *MBE, TD, b.* 1920; Maj. W.R.A.C. (T.A.); MBE (Mil.) 1960. *Residence,*—Pasture House, North Luffenham, Oakham, Rutland.

DAUGHTERS LIVING OF SECOND BARON.

Hon. Marguerite Emily (Alandale Nursing Home, 8, Rectory Rd., Burnham-on-Sea, Somerset), *b.* 1891: *m.* 1920, the Rev. Halstead Latham Connor, V. of Benhall, and R. of Sternfield, who *d.* 1959.

Hon. Florence Evelyn, *b.* 1893: *m.* 1st, 1919, Harold Oscar Nevett, MC, who *d.* 1940, Bar.-at-law and Solicitor, formerly Lt. RFA ; 2nd, 1967, Capt. Francis Joseph McGovern, MC, The Green Howards (ret.), of Cushlough, Leslie Manor, Camperdown, Victoria, Australia, and has issue living, (by 1st m.) George Chester (69, Gould St., Long Island, Frankston, Vic., Aust. 3199), *b.* 1925: *m.* 1951, Margaret Ann Norris, and has issue living, Peter Michael Chester *b.* 1958, Matthew Dougal *b.* 1961, Jonathan Montague *b.* 1965, Christian Marcus Vandeleur *b.* 1971, Amanda Jane *b.* 1954, Megan Veronica *b.* 1956, Evelyn Mitzi *b.* 1959, Melanie Margaret-Ann *b.* 1967, Emma Michelle *b.* 1968,—James Guy Kitson (701, Toorak Rd., Kooyong, Vic., Aust. 3144), *b.* 1931: *m.* 1956, Joanna Prentice, who *d.* 1974, and has issue living, Melissa *b.* 1961, Genevieve *b.* 1965,—Jane (Lower Church Hall, St. George's Sq., SW1), *b.* 1926, MusB, Melbourne, and LRAM,—Doris Evelyn, *b.* 1922: *m.* 1945, John Reed Johnston (Aramuta, 2, Boundary Rd., Mount Eliza, Vic., Aust.), and has issue living, Evelyn Jane *b.* 1946; ed. at Monash Univ., Aust. (BA); Dip. Ed: *m.* 1971, Glenn Richard Hildebrant, of Wardner, BC, Canada, Katherine Newton *b.* 1948: *m.* 1967, Lambert Christopher Van Kalken, of Balmoral, Vic., Aust., Serena Doris *b.* 1957, Helen Mary *b.* 1959,—Elizabeth Anne, *b.* 1927: *m.* 1950; Colin Gardner Valentine Browne (c/o B. F. Brown, Box 130, Panguna, Bougainville, New Guinea, and has issue living, Colin Peter *b.* 1953, James Robert Hugh *b.* 1960, Sarah Anne *b.* 1951, Elizabeth Mary (twin) *b.* 1951, Janet Victoria *b.* 1955, Venetia Kitson *b.* 1957.

Hon. Doris Claire, *b.* 1894: *m.* 1918 (marriage dissolved 1947), John McNaughton, M.C who *d.* 1959, and has issue living, Catherine Jill, *b.* 1925: *m.* 1956, Lt.-Cdr. Peter Ashley Miller, RN (ret.), of Reedham Old Hall, Norfolk, and has issue living, Mark *b.* 1962, Bridget *b.* 1957, Catherine *b.* 1959. *Address,*—c/o Midland Bank, City Sq., Leeds, 1.

Hon. Thelma Eirene, *b.* 1902: *m.* 1923, Noel Gordon Harris, M.D., B.S., M.R.C.S., F.R.C.P., D.P.M., who *d.* 1963, son of Sir (Charles) Alexander Harris, K.C.M.G., C.B., C.V.O., and has issue living, James Gordon Shute (The Cottage, Ford, Wiveliscombe, Taunton), *b.* 1933,—Joyce Estelle, *b.* 1924, ARIBA: *m.* 1953, Edward Fyfe Griffith, MRCS, LRCP, of 77, Talbot Rd., N6 4QX,—Leslie Beryl, *b.* 1926: *m.* 1951, Michael Yate Johnson, MA, of Greensyke, Cumdivock, Dalston, Carlisle, and has issue living, Martin Charles Yate *b.* 1958, Sally Yate *b.* 1956, Jennifer Anne *b.* 1957,—Jean Constance, *b.* 1931: *m.* 1952, James T. Arnot, of 9, Willified Way, NW11, and has issue living, Keith James *b.* 1955, Jacqueline Margaret *b.* 1953. *Residence,*—The Cottage, Ford, Wiveliscombe, Taunton.

Hon. Angela Estelle, *b.* 1905: *m.* 1927, George Herbert Goff, who *d.* 1957, and has issue living, George Stephen, *b.* 1928,—Jennifer Florence, *b.* 1932: *m.* 1st, 1954 (m. diss. 1965), Donald Iain Macaulay, 2nd, 1967, Brian Malcolm Richardson, and has issue living, (by 1st m.) Donald George Stuart *b.* 1956, Angela Elisabeth Louise *b.* 1958. *Residence,*—The Old Forge, Brompton Ralph, Taunton, Somerset.

COLLATERAL BRANCH LIVING.

Issue of the late Hon. Edward Christian Kitson, 3rd son of 1st Baron, *b.* 1873, *d* 1922: *m.* 1903, Mary Katharine (who *d.*1944, having *m.* 2ndly, 1926, Walter John Burt, Bar.-at-law, who *d.* 1931), el. dau. of Samuel Hirst, formerley of 3, The Crescent, Scarborough :—

Christine Annabel (Bury Gate House, Pulborough, Sussex), *b.* 1908: *m.* 1932, Cyril Alfred Roberts CBE, Bar.-at-law, and has issue living, Francis Kitson (Parma, Oakhill Rd., Sevenoaks, Kent) *b.* 1935: *m.* 1962, Joan Lena Lorna Dawes, and has issue living, Guy Francis Cyril *b.* 1963, Philip Maurice Dawes, *b.* 1966, Cressida Lorna Joan *b.* 1971,—David Christopher, *b.* 1944,—Geoffrey Michael, *b.* 1947,—Penelope Christine Mary, *b.* 1937: *m.* 1961, Lt.-Col. Thomas Anthony Boam, OBE, Scots Gds., of The Old Thatch, Finchampstead, Berks., and has issue living, Thomas Edward *b.* 1964, Caroline Christine *b.* 1962, Katharine Penelope *b.* 1968.

PREDECESSORS.—[1] JAMES Kitson, *P.C.*, son of the late James Kitson, J.P., of Elmet Hall, Leeds ; *b.* 1835 ; first Lord Mayor of Leeds 1896-7 ; M.P. for Yorkshire, W. Riding, S. Part, Colne Valley Div. 1892-1907 ; cr. a *Baronet* 1886, and *Baron Airedale*, of Gledhow, W. Riding of co. of York (peerage of United Kingdom) 1907: *m.* 1st, 1860, Emily, who *d.* 1873, dau. of Joseph Cliff ; 2ndly, 1881, Mary Laura, who *d.* 1939, only dau. of the late Edward Fisher Smith, of The Priory, Dudley; *d.* 1911: *s.* by his son [2] ALBERT ERNEST, 2nd Baron ; *b.* 1863 ; an Iron and Steel Manufacturer, a Director of London City and Midland Bank, Ltd., and a Member of Lloyds: *m.* 1890, Florence, who *d.* 1942, dau. of the late Edward Schunck; *d.* 1944: *s.* by his half-brother [3] ROLAND DUDLEY, *D.S.O., M.C.,* 3rd Baron ; *b.* 1882 ; High Sheriff of co. London 1928 ; late Capt. Prince of Wales's Own (W. Yorkshire Regt.) ; European War 1914-18 (M.C., D.S.O.): *m.* 1st 1913, Sheila Grace, who *d.* 1935, dau. of the late Frank E. Vandeleur, of 52, Evelyn Gardens, SW ; 2ndly, 1937, Dorothy Christabel, who *d.* 1970, da. of the late Rev. Canon Raymond Percy Pelly [Pelly, Bt., colls.] and widow of Hugh Mortimer Rowland; *d.* 1958; *s.* by his son [4] OLIVER JAMES VANDELEUR, 4th Baron and present peer.

AIRLIE, EARL OF. (Ogilvy.) [Earl S. 1639.]

To the end.

DAVID GEORGE COKE PATRICK OGILVY, 13th Earl, *b.* May 17th, 1926; *s.* 1968; ed. at Eton; Capt. Scots Guards (Reserve); DL of Angus; ADC to C-in-C, 2nd Bn. Germany 1945, and High Commr. Austria 1947-48; Chmn., Ashdown Investment Trust Ltd., J. Henry Schroder Wagg & Co., and Westpool Investment Trust Ltd., a Dir. of General Accident Fire & Life Assurance Corpn., Scottish & Newcastle Brewers Ltd., and other cos.; Tres. of The Scout Assocn.; 1939-45 War; Malaya 1948-50; *m.* 1952, Virginia Fortune, da. of John Barry Ryan, of Moorland Farm, Newport, Rhode Island, and has issue.

Arms,—Argent, a lion passant guardant gules crowned with an imperial crown and collared with an open one proper. Crest,—A lady from the waist upwards affrontée azure holding a portcullis gules. Supporters,—Two bulls sable, armed and unguled vert, and gorged with a garland of flowers.

Seats,—Cortachy Castle, and Airlie Castle, Kirriemuir, Angus. *Residence,*—13 St. Leonards' Terr., SW3.

SONS LIVING.
DAVID JOHN (*Lord Ogilvy*), *b.* March 9th, 1958; appointed a Page of Honour to HM 1971.
Hon. Bruce Patrick Mark, *b.* 1959.
Hon. Patrick Alexander, *b.* 1971.

DAUGHTERS LIVING
Lady Doune Mabell, *b.* 1953.
Lady Jane Fortune Margaret, *b.* 1955.
Lady Elizabeth Clementina, *b.* 1965.

BROTHERS LIVING
Hon. Angus James Bruce, *b.* 1928; ed. at Eton, and at Oxford Univ.; is Capt. Scots Guards (Reserve); Grand Officer of Order of the Lion of Finland, and of Order of the Oak Crown of Luxembourg: *m.* 1963, H.R.H. Princess Alexandra Helen Elizabeth Olga Christabel, G.C.V.O., dau. of H.R.H. the 1st Duke of Kent [see " ROYAL FAMILY "], and has issue living, James Robert Bruce, *b.* 1964, Marina Victoria Alexandra, *b.* 1966. *Residence,*—Thatched House Lodge, Richmond Park, Surrey.
Hon. James Donald Diarmid, *b.* 1934; ed. at Eton; Lieut. Scots Guards (Reserve); a Partner, Rowe & Pitman; a Page of Honour to HM 1947-51: *m.* 1959, Magda June, da. of Robert Ducas [see B. Mowbray, colls.], and has issue living, Shamus Diarmid, *b.* 1966,—Diarmid James Ducas, *b.* 1970,— Laura Jane, *b.* 1960,—Emma Louise, *b.* 1962. *Residence,*—Canal House, 23, Blomfield Rd., Little Venice, W9.

SISTERS LIVING
Lady Victoria Jean Marjorie Mabell (*Baroness Lloyd*), *b.* 1918: *m.* 1942, the 2nd Baron Lloyd. *Residence,*—Clouds Hill, Offley, Hitchin, Herts.
Lady Margaret Helen Isla Marion, *b.* 1920; formerly in W.R.N.S.: *m.* 1946, Capt. Iain Mark Tennant, D.L., Scots Guards [see B. Glenconner, colls.]. *Residence,*—Innes House, Elgin, Morayshire.
Lady Griselda Davina Roberta, *b.* 1924: *m.* 1948 (m. diss. 1967), Maj. Peter Edward Gerald Balfour, Scots Guards [E. Balfour], and has issue living, Hew Edward Ogilvy, *b.* 1952,—Fergus George, *b.* 1953: *m.* 1975, Gail Lesley, el. da. of John Williams, of Broomlands, Lorton, Cockermouth,—Bridget Georgina (twin), *b.* 1952.

UNCLE LIVING. (*Son of 11th Earl.*)
Hon. Bruce Arthur Ashley, *M.V.O., M.C., b.* 1895 : ed. at Wellington Coll., and at R.M.C.; Capt. 12th Lancers Reserve of Officers; European War 1914-18 with 12th Lancers, and as Capt. Irish Guards (wounded, M.C.); was an Equerry-in-Ord. to H.R.H. the Prince of Wales 1921-30; M.V.O. (5th class) 1922: *m.* 1931, Primrose, who *d.* 1961, dau. of R. W. O'Brien, of Bank of Ireland House, Drogheda. *Address,*—Danny, Hurstpierpoint, Sussex.

WIDOW LIVING OF TWELFTH EARL.
Lady ALEXANDRA MARIA BRIDGET COKE (*Dowager Countess of Airlie*), (Airlie Castle, Kirriemuir, Angus), da. of 3rd Earl of Leicester: *m.* 1917, the 12th Earl, who *d.* 1968.

COLLATERAL BRANCHES LIVING.
Issue of the late Hon. Lyulph Gilchrist Stanley Ogilvy, DSO, 2nd son of 10th Earl, *b.* 1861; *d.* 1947: *m.* 1902, Edith Gertrude Boothroyd, who *d.* 1908, of Waterdale, Loveland, Colorado, U.S.A.:—
Jack David Angus, *b.* 1903: *m.* 1940, Dorothy Stanley, of Boulder, Colorado, U.S.A. *Residence,*— 1525, 9th Street, Boulder, Colorado, U.S.A.

Granddaughter of the late Col. the Hon. Donald Ogilvy, brother of 10th Earl:—
Issue of the late Walter Ogilvy, *b.* 1822, *d.* 1894: *m.* 1879, Ellen, who *d.* 1896, dau. of Alexander Smith:—
Dorothea Sophia Bessie, *b.* 1889. *Residence,*—

PREDECESSORS.—[1] *Sir* JAMES Ogilvy, *K.B.*; Ambassador from Scotland to Denmark 1491, was in that year cr. *Lord Ogilvy of Airlie* (peerage of Scotland); *d.* 1504; *s.* by his el. son [2] JOHN, 2nd Lord; he was *s.* by his el. son [3] JAMES, 3rd Lord; *s.* by his el. son [4] JAMES, 4th Lord, an Extraor. Lord of Session; *d.* 1554; *s.* by his grandson [5] JAMES, 5th Lord; *d.* 1606; *s.* by his son [6] JAMES, 6th Lord; *d.* 1617; *s.* by his son [7] JAMES, 7th Lord, a zealous partisan of Charles I.; cr. *Lord Ogilvy of Alyth and Lintrathen,* and *Earl of Airlie* (peerage of Scotland) 1639; *s.* by his el. son [8] JAMES, *P.C.,* 2nd Earl; being taken prisoner at the battle of Philiphaugh 1644, he was sentenced to death by the Parliament at St. Andrew's, Nov. 26, 1645, but escaped in his sister's clothes the night before his intended execution; pardoned by

Act of Parliament 1649, and at the Restoration was sworn of the Privy Council; *s.* by his son [9] DAVID, 3rd Earl; *d.* 1717; his el. son [10] JAMES, 4th Earl, assisted in the Earl of Mar's rising 1715, was attainted by Act of Parliament during his father's life, and afterwards pardoned; *d.* 1731; *s.* by his brother [11] JOHN, 5th Earl; *d.* 1761; *s.* by his son [12] DAVID, 6th Earl; he joined the Chevalier at Edinburgh 1745 at the head of 600 men, and was attainted by Act of Parliament; after the battle of Culloden he escaped to France where he commanded a Regiment of Foot, and attained the rank of Lt.-Gen.; in 1778 he received a pardon under the Great Seal; *d.* 1803; *s.* by his son [13] DAVID, 7th Earl; *d.* unmarried; *s.* by his uncle [14] WALTER, 8th Earl; *d.* 1819; *s.* by his el. son [15] DAVID, 9th Earl, who had his honours confirmed by Act of Parliament 1826; was Lord-Lieut. of Forfarshire and a Scottish Representative Peer; *d.* 1849; *s.* by his son [16] DAVID GRAHAM DRUMMOND, *KT*, 10th Earl, *b.* 1826; a Representative Peer for Scotland, and Lord High Commr. to Church of Scotland 1872-3: *m.* 1851, the Hon. Henrietta Blanche Stanley, who *d.* 1921, da. of 2nd Baron Stanley of Alderley; *d.* Sept. 25th, 1881; *s.* by his el. son [17] DAVID STANLEY WILLIAM, 11th Earl; *b.* 1856: *m.* 1886, Lady Mabell Frances Elizabeth Gore, *GCVO*, *OBE*, who *d.* 1956, da. of 5th Earl of Arran; *d.* (killed during S. African War) 1900; *s.* by his son [18] DAVID LYULPH GORE WOLSELEY, *KT*, *GCVO*, *MC*, 12th Earl; *b.* 1893; C ol. Scots Guards; Repres. Peer for Scotland 1922-63; Lord-in-Waiting to HM 1926-29; Lord Chamberlain to HM Queen Elizabeth the Queen Mother 1937-65: *m.* 1917, Lady Alexandra Marie Bridget Coke, da. of 3rd Earl of Leicester; *d.* 1968; *s.* by his el. son [19] DAVID GEORGE COKE PATRICK, 13th Earl and present peer; also Lord Ogilvy of Airlie, and Lord Ogilvy of Alyth and Lintrathen.

Aithrie, Viscount, grandson of Marquess of Linlithgow.

ALANBROOKE, VISCOUNT. (Brooke.) [Viscount U.K. 1946.]

ALAN VICTOR HAROLD BROOKE, 3rd Viscount; *b.* Nov. 24th, 1932; *s.* 1972; ed. at Harrow; Capt. (ret.) RA.

Arms,—Or, a cross engrailed per pale gules and sable, in the first quarter a crescent of the second. Crest,—A brock, proper. Supporters,—On either side an officer of the Royal Horse Artillery in full dress proper supporting with the exterior hand an escutcheon azure charged with seven barrulets wavy argent surmounted by a salmon rising gules.
Residence,—Ferney Close, Hartley Wintney, Hants.

Glory the end.

HALF-SISTER LIVING
Hon. Rosemary, *b.* 1918: *m.* 1945, Capt. Ronald Alastair Macdonald, RA, of Bottom Farm, Berkhamsted, Herts., and has issue living, Alastair Alan Graham, *b.* 1947,—Ian Ronald, *b.* 1952,—Janey Rosemary, *b.* 1949.

PREDECESSORS.—[1] *Field Marshal Sir* ALAN FRANCIS Brooke, *KG*, *GCB*, *OM*, *GCVO*, *DSO*, 6th son of Sir Victor Alexander Brooke, 3rd Bt. (cr. 1822) [see V. Brookeborough]; *b.* 1883; late R.A.; Inspector of R.A. 1935-6, Dir. of Mil. Training War Office 1936-7, G.O.C., Mobile Div. 1937-8, C.-in-C., A.A. Command (T.A.) 1938-9, G.O.C.-in-C., S. Command 1939, G.O.C. 2nd Corps 1939-40. C.-in-C. Home Forces 1940-41, C.I.G.S. 1941-6; Col. Comdt. R.A. 1939-57, R.H.A. 1940-57, and Hon.Artillery Co. 1946-54, Master Gunner, St. James's Park 1946-56, and Constable of Tower of London 1950-55; Lord High Constable of England at Coronation of H.M. Queen Elizabeth II: *m.* 1st, 1914, Jane Mary, who *d.* 1925. dau. of the late Col. John Mervyn, Carleton Richardson; 2ndly, 1929, Benita Blanche, who *d.* 1968, dau. of Sir Harold Pelly, 3rd Bt., and widow of Sir Thomas Evan Keith Lees, 2nd Bt. (cr. 1897); *d.* 1963; *s.* by his el. son [2] THOMAS, 2nd Viscount; *b.* 1920; *d.* 1972; *s.* by his half-brother [3] ALAN VICTOR HAROLD, 3rd Viscount and present peer.

ALBEMARLE, EARL OF. (Keppel.) [Earl E. 1696.]

WALTER EGERTON GEORGE LUCIAN KEPPEL, *M.C.*, 9th Earl; *b.* Feb. 28th, 1882; *s.* 1942; ed. at Eton; an Alderman for Norfolk, a Member of Church Assembly, a KStJ; formerly Pres. of Norfolk St. John Ambulance Brig.; late Major Scots Guards (Reserve), and Lt.-Col. and Brevet Col. Comdg. (Norfolk and Suffolk Yeo.) RFA (TA); Lt.-Col. Comdg. Prince of Wales's Own Civil Ser. Rifles 1920-22; 1914-18 War as Lt.-Cdr. RN Div. (Antwerp), and formed Machine Gun Co., 3rd Guards Brig. (despatches twice, MC); ADC to Gov.-Gens. of Canada 1904-05 and India 1907-08, and to Gov. of Orange River Colony 1907-08; Grand Cross of Order of Orange Nassau of the Netherlands; elected Pres. of Anglo-Netherlands So. 1942, and Vice-Pres. of Riverboards Asso. 1953; Vice-Lt. for Norfolk 1942-44; Pres. of Tatton Park Gardens Soc.: *m.* 1st, 1909, Lady Judith Sydney Myee Carrington, who *d.* 1928, da. of 1st Marquess of Lincolnshire (ext.); 2ndly, 1931, *Dame* Diana Cicely, *DBE*, *DLitt*, *DCL*, *LLD*, da. of the late Maj. John A. Grove, and has issue by 1st and 2nd marriages.

Do not yield to misfortunes.

Arms,—Gules, three escallops argent. Crest,—Out of a ducal coronet or, a swan's head and neck argent. Supporters,—Two lions ducally crowned or.
Residence,—Beacon Hill, Woodbridge, Suffolk.

GRANDCHILDREN LIVING

Issue of the late Derek William Charles (*Viscount Bury*), *b.* 1911, *d.* 1968: *m.* 1st, 1940 (*m.* diss. 1958), Lady Mairi Elizabeth Vane-Tempest-Stewart, JP, da. of the 7th Marquess of Londonderry; 2ndly, 1964, Marina (ARIBA; A.A. Dip), (Piazza di Bellosquaedo 10, Florence 50124, Italy), da. of the late Lt.-Cdr. Count Serge Orloff-Davidoff, RNVR [see B. Howard de Walden and Seaford]:—

(By 2nd *m.*) RUFUS ARNOLD ALEXIS (*Viscount Bury*), *b.* July 16th, 1965.——(by 1st *m.*) *Hon.* Elizabeth Mairi, *b.* 1941: *m.* 1962, Alastair Michael Hyde Villiers [D. Roxburghe], and has issue living, Charles Alastair Hyde, *b.* 1963,—Charlotte Mairi, *b.* 1965.——*Hon.* Rose Deirdre Margaret (50, Onslow Gdns., SW7), *b.* 1943: *m.* 1975, Peter Lathrop Lauritzen, of Palazzo Contarini delle Figure, San Marco 3327, Venice, Italy.

SON LIVING. (*By 1st marriage.*)

Hon. Walter Arnold Crispian, *D.S.C., R.N.*, *b.* 1914; European War 1939-45 as Lieut.-Com. and Observer with Fleet Air Arm (D.S.C.): *m.* 1941, Aline Lucy, dau. of the late Brig.-Gen. John Harington, C.B. C.M.G., D.S.O. [see Harington, Bt., colls.], and has issue living, Crispian Walter John, *b.* 1948,—Colin Rupert Harington, *b.* 1951,—Judith Cynthia Aline, *b.* 1942: *m.* 1964, Desmond Leon Corcoran, of 76, Palace Gardens Terr., W8, and has issue living, Alexander Martin Desmond *b.* 1968, Sibylla Monacella *b.* 1966, Aline Rose *b.* 1972. *Residence,*—Barton House, Meonstoke, Hants.

DAUGHTERS LIVING. (*By 1st marriage.*)

Lady Cecilia Elizabeth, *b.* 1910: *m.* 1934, David McKenna, CBE, late Lt.-Col. RE, son of the late Rt. Hon. Reginald McKenna, and has issue living, Myce Miranda, *b.* 1935: *m.* 1958, John Francis Hyde Villiers [see E. Clarendon, colls.],—Pamela Primrose, *b.* 1937: *m.* 1961, Christopher James Folke Arnander [see E. Crawford],—Sophia Mary, *b.* 1944: *m.* 1965 (m. diss. 1971), John Boyd Wilson. *Residences,*—Rosteague, Portscatho, Truro, Cornwall; 81, Onslow Sq., SW7.

Lady Cynthia Rosalie, *b.* 1918: *m.* 1944, Professor Michael Moissey Postan, Fellow of Peterhouse, Cambridge, and has issue living, Basil David, *b.* 1946: *m.* 1968, Maria, da. of Samuel Carr, of Paultons Sq., SW3,—Alexander Henry Keppel, *b.* 1948. *Residences,*—2, Sylvester Rd., Cambridge; Penrallt Goch, Festiniog, Merionethshire.

(*By 2nd marriage.*)

Lady Anne-Louise Mary, *b.* 1932: *m.* 1954, Maj. Sir Hew Fleetwood Hamilton-Dalrymple, CVO, 10th Bt. *Residence,*—Leuchie, North Berwick, East Lothian.

WIDOW LIVING OF SON OF EIGHTH EARL.

Mildred (1A, Swan Court, Southsea Rd., Datchet, Bucks.), da. of the late William Stanley Rodber, of Richmond, Yorks., and widow of Allan Stanley Carter, Flying Officer, RAF: *m.* 1952, as his 3rd wife, the Hon. Arnold Joost William Keppel, who *d.* 1964.

SISTER LIVING

Lady Elizabeth Mary Gertrude, *A.R.R.C.*, *b.* 1890; served as a V.A.D. Nurse in France 1915-19 (despatches, A.R.R.C., 1915 star, two medals): *m.* 1923, as his second wife. Gen. Sir Torquhil George Matheson, KCB, CMG, 5th Bt., who *d.* 1963. *Residence,*—Cedar House, Woodbridge, Suffolk.

COLLATERAL BRANCHES LIVING.

Issue of the late Lieut.-Col. the Hon. Sir Derek William George Keppel, G.C.V.O., K.C.B., C.M.G., C.I.E., V.D., 2nd son of 7th Earl, *b.* 1863, *d.* 1944: *m.* 1898, the Hon. Bridget Louisa Harbord, who *d.* 1951, dau. of 5th Baron Suffield:—

Victoria Winifred (Ley Corner, East Lane, Everton, Hants.), *b.* 1905.

Issue of the late Lieut.-Col. the Hon. George Keppel, M.V.O., 3rd son of 7th Earl, *b.* 1865, *d.* 1947: *m.* 1891, Alice Frederica, who *d.* 1947, dau. of Adm. Sir William Edmonstone, 4th Bt.:—

Sonia Rosemary, *OBE*, *b.* 1900; is a DStJ; OBE (Civil) 1959: *m.* 1920, the Hon. Roland Calvert Cubitt (from whom she obtained a divorce 1947), later 3rd Baron Ashcombe, who *d.* 1962. *Residence* —Hall Place, West Meon, Hants.

Grandchildren of the late Adm. of the Fleet the Hon. Sir Henry Keppel, G.C.B., O.M., D.C.L., 7th son of 4th Earl:—

Issue of the late Adm. Sir Colin Richard Keppel, G.C.V.O., K.C.I.E. C.B., D.S.O., *b.* 1862, *d.* 1947 : *m.* 1889, Henrietta, who *d.* 1957 [sometime Lady-in-Waiting to H.R.H. the Duchess of Edinburgh (Duchess of Saxe-Coburg and Gotha)], dau. of Major-Gen. Richard Blundell-Hollinshead-Blundell :—

Marie Henrietta Margaret (*Countess of Romney*), *b.* 1891: *m.* 1918, the 6th Earl of Romney, Lieut.-Col.(retired) Coldstream Guards. *Residence,*—Gayton Hall, King's Lynn.——Melita Agnes Mary (58, Richmond Court, 200, Sloane St., SW1X 9QU), *b.* 1892: *m.* 1920, Maurice Robert Hely-Hutchinson, MC, who *d.* 1961 [see E. Donoughmore, colls.].

Grandson of the late Rev. Ellice Keppel, 3rd son of the late Rev. the Hon. Thomas Robert Keppel (infra):—

Issue of the late Rev. Derek Harold Ellice Keppel, B.D., *b.* 1875, *d.* 1963: *m.* 1908, Dora, who *d.* 1957, el. dau. of the late Rev. Arthur Herbert Knott, V. of St. Peter's, Dulwich Common, S.E.:—

Rev. Oswald Francis Arnold (28, Culliford Rd., Dorchester), *b.* 1910; ed. at King's Coll., London (Asso. 1934); R. of Woodsford, Dorset 1942-66.

Granddaughter of the late Rev. the Hon. Thomas Robert Keppel, 8th son of 4th Earl:—

Issue of the late Capt. Henry Keppel, *b.* 1848, *d.* 1938: *m.* 1874, Alicia Menella, who *d.* 1892, dau. of Sir Robert John Harvey, 1st Bt.:—

Augusta Vera, *b.* 1883: *m.* 1912, Alfred Morland Jee, who *d.* 1932, and has issue living, Edward Henry MORLAND-JEE, *TD* (Elm Tree Farm, Stockton on the Forest, York), *b.* 1913; Lt.-Col. (ret.); CEng., MIMechE; Prin. Professional Eng. Civil Ser. REME; assumed by deed poll 1953 the additional surname of Morland; 1939-45 War (despatches), Korea 1950-52: *m.* 1st, 1939, Barbara Joan Stafford, of Scawthorpe House, Doncaster, from whom he obtained a divorce 1952; 2ndly, 1954, Elizabeth Eleanor Carter, formerly Lt. QARANC, and has issue living, (by 2nd m.) Elizabeth Ann *b.* 1956,—Marion Elizabeth, *b.* 1914: *m.* 1940, David Duncan Malease Attwell of The Little Nook, Dale Rd., Walton-on-Thames, Surrey,—Evelyn Alicia Vera, *b.* 1915; formerly LAW; WAAF, H.M. Civil Ser. since 1947. *Residence,*—29, Highfield Drive, Ewell, Epsom, Surrey.

Grandchildren of the late Lieut.-Col. William Henry Augustus Keppel, son of the late Rev. William Arnold Walpole Keppel (infra) :—

Issue of the late Major Bertram William Arnold Keppel, *b.* 1876, *d.* 1949: *m.* 1898, the Hon. Alice Evelyn Agatha Hanbury-Tracy, who *d.* 1955, dau. of 4th Baron Sudeley:—

William Bertram Arnold Joost, *M.B.E.*, *b.* 1909; Wing-Com. Auxiliary Air Force; Colonial Civil Ser. (Nigeria) 1946-61; M.B.E. (Civil) 1953: *m.* 1962, Nancy Ethel Reeves. *Address,*—P.O. Box 60, Umhlanga Rocks, Durban, Natal.——Judith Iris, *b.* 1900: *m.* 1922, Col. Robert Hanbury Brudenell-

Bruce, DSO, late Norfolk Regt., who *d.* 1955 [see M. Ailesbury, colls.]. *Residence,*—Hill Farm, Hartley Wintney, Hants.

Granddaughters of the late Col. Edward George Keppel, M.V.O., son of the late Rev. William Arnold Walpole Keppel, son of the late Right Rev. the Hon. Frederick Keppel, D.D., Bishop of Exeter, 4th son of 2nd Earl (ante) :—
Issue of the late Lieut.-Col. Arnold Ramsay Keppel, *b.* 1879, *d.* 1930: *m.* 1922, Launa Margaret (*Dowager Lady Pease*) [who *m.* 2ndly, 1961, Sir Richard Arthur Pease, 2nd Bt. (cr. 1920)], who *d.* 1969, da. of Hughes Martin, formerly of Tullaghreine, co. Cork:—
June Cecilia, *b.* 1924: *m.* 1946, Capt. Edward Percy Canning Loyd, Coldstream Guards [B. Brabourne], of 10, Cadogan Sq., SW1, and has issue living, David William Arnold, *b.* 1949,—Caroline Evelyn, *b.* 1947.——Bridget Anne (*Lord Mrs. Martin Fitzalan Howard*), *b.* 1925: *m.* 1948, Capt. the Lord Martin Fitzalan Howard, late Gen. Gds., of Brockfield Hall, York [see D. Norfolk].——Lavinia Mary (*Hon. Mrs. Richard B. Beaumont*) (58, South Audley St., W1), *b.* 1928: *m.* 1971, the Hon. Richard Blackett Beaumont [see V. Allendale].

PREDECESSORS.—[1] ARNOLD JOOST Van Keppel, *K.G.*, a Member of the Nobles in Holland, accompanied the Prince of Orange in his expedition 1688, and on the establishment of the Prince on the throne of England was cr. *Baron Ashford, Viscount Bury,* and *Earl of Albemarle* (peerage of England) 1696; *d.* 1718; *s.* by his son [2] WILLIAM ANNE, *K.G.*, 2nd Earl, a distinguished Gen. and sometime Ambassador at the Court of Versailles; *d.* 1754; *s.* by his el. son [3] GEORGE, *K.G.*, 3rd Earl, a Lt.-Gen. in the Army; *d.* 1772; *s.* by his son [4] WILLIAM CHARLES, 4th Earl; *b.* 1772: *m.* 1792, the Hon. Elizabeth Southwell, who *d.* 1817, dau. of 17th Baron Clifford; 2ndly, 1822, Charlotte Susannah, who *d.* 1862, dau. of Sir Henry Hunloke, Bt.; *d.* 1849; *s.* by his el. son [5] AUGUSTUS FREDERICK, 5th Earl: *d.s.p.* 1851 *s.* by his brother [6] GEORGE THOMAS, 6th Earl, *b.* 1799: served at Battle of Waterloo; M.P. for E. Norfolk 1832-5, and for Lymington (L) 1847-50: *m.* 1831, Susan, who *d.* 1885, dau. of Sir Coutts Trotter, 1st Bt.; *d.* 1891; *s.* by his el. son [7] WILLIAM COUTTS, *K.C.M.G.*, *P.C.*, 7th Earl, *b.* 1832; M.P. for Norwich (L) 1857-9, for Wick 1860-65, and for Berwick 1868-74; Treasurer of Queen Victoria's Household 1859 and Under-Sec. of State for War 1878-80 and 1885-6; a Vol. A.D.C. to Queen Victoria; called to House of Lords during his father's lifetime as Baron Ashford 1876: *m.* 1855, Sophia, who *d.* 1917, dau. of the Hon. Sir Allan Napier Macnab, 1st Bt. (*ext.*), Prime Min. of Canada; *d.* 1894; *s.* by his el. son [8] ARNOLD ALLAN CECIL, *G.C.V.O., C.B., V.D., T.D.,* 8th Earl, *b.* 1858; Col. in the Army; Vice-Lieut. for Norfolk: S. Africa 1900 (despatches, medal with four clasps, C.B.) ; an A.D.C. to H.M. King Edward VII. 1903-10 and King George V. 1910-25, and a Lord-in-Waiting to H.M. Nov. 1922-4; M.P. for Birkenhead (C) 1892-94: *m.* 1881, Lady Gertrude Lucia Egerton, who *d.* 1943, only child of 1st Earl Egerton of Tatton; *d.* 1942; *s.* by his el. son [9] WALTER EGERTON GEORGE LUCIAN, 9th Earl and present peer: also Viscount Bury, and Baron Ashford.

ALDENHAM, AND HUNSDON OF HUNSDON, BARON. (Gibbs.) [Baron U.K. 1896 and 1923.]

ANTONY DURANT GIBBS, 5th Baron Aldenham and 3rd Baron Hunsdon of Hunsdon, *b.* May 18th, 1922; *s.* 1969; ed. at Eton, and Ch. Ch., Oxford; a Dir. of Antony Gibbs Holdings Ltd., merchants and bankers; 1939-45 war as Lt. RNVR: *m.* 1947, Mary Elizabeth, only da. of the late Walter Parkyns Tyser, and has issue.

Tenacious of purpose.

Arms,—Argent, three battle-axes erect within a bordure nebuly sable. *Crest,*—In front of a rock a dexter arm embowed in armour, the hand gauntleted proper, bearing a battle-axe in bend sinister sable. *Supporters,*—On either side a man habited in buff leather jerkin, gloves, and boots, armed with a three-barred helmet, long gorget, and sword, all proper, and holding in the exterior hand a battle-axe over the shoulder sable.
Residence,—Stanstead Lodge, Stanstead Abbotts, Herts.

SONS LIVING.
Hon. VICARY TYSER, *b.* June 9th, 1948; ed. at Eton.
Hon. George Henry Paul (Essex Cottage Farm, Anstey, Buntingford, Herts.), *b.* 1950: *m.* 1973, Janet Elizabeth, da. of Harold Leonard Scott, and has issue living, Piers Antony Scott, *b.* 1973.

DAUGHTER LIVING.
Hon. Antonia Mary, *b.* 1958.

UNCLES LIVING (Sons of 1st Baron Hunsdon of Hunsdon).
Hon. Sir Geoffrey Cokayne, *KCMG.*, *b.* 1901; ed. at Eton, and at Ch. Ch., Oxford; Hon DCL Oxford; Assist. Sec., Min. of Economic Warfare 1943-5; Chm. of Managing Trustees of Nuffield Foundation, and of National Corporation for the care of the Aged; Chm. of Advisory Council, Export Credits Guarantee Depart. 1948-62; elected Master of Grocers' Co. 1938; appointed Chm. of Imperial Relations Trust 1952; CMG 1945, KCMG 1955: *m.* 1926, Helen Margaret, *CBE* (formerly Ch. Commr. for Overseas Territories of Girl Guides Asso.), da. of the late Charles Frederick Henry Leslie, of Epcombs, Hertford, and has issue living, David Charles Leslie (48, Millswyn St., S. Yarra, Melbourne, Aust.), *b.* 1927; ed. at Eton, and Ch. Ch., Oxford; a Dir. of Antony Gibbs & Sons, Ltd., and other cos.: *m.* 1965, Charmian Fleur, only da. of Dalzell Pulteney Mein, of Toolang, Coleraine, Vic., Aust., and has issue living, Hugo Dalzell *b.* 1967, Justin Geoffrey *b.* 1969, Emma Victoria *b.* 1966, Arabella Sarah *b.* 1970,—Stephen Cokayne (Dougarie, Isle of Arran), *b.* 1929; ed. at Eton; late 2nd Lt. KRRC: *m.* 1972, Lavinia Winifred, da. of Sir Edmund Castell Bacon, Bt., KG, KBE, TD, and has issue living, James Edward Geoffrey *b.* 1975, Emily Anna Maria *b.* 1973,— Julian Herbert, *b.* 1932; ed. at Eton,—Roger Geoffrey, *b.* 1934; ed. at Eton,—Christopher Henry, *b.* 1938,—Elizabeth Helen (twin), *b.* 1938: *m.* 1963, Valentine Patrick Fleming of Stonewall Park, Chiddingstone Heath, Edenbridge, Kent [see Borthwick, Bt., colls.]. *Residence,*—The Manor House, Clifton Hampden, Abingdon-on-Thames. [He. *d.* July 6th, 1975.]
Rt. Hon. Sir Humphrey Vicary, *GCVO, KCMG, OBE, b.* 1902; ed. at Eton, and at Trin. Coll., Camb.; Hon. LLD Birmingham; Hon. DCL E. Anglia; a Farmer; Gov. of S. Rhodesia (now Rhodesia)

1959-69; a K.St.J.; OBE (Civil) 1959, KCMG 1960, KCVO 1965, GCVO 1969, PC 1969: *m.* 1934, Dame Molly Peel, *DBE* (C.St.J.), da. of the late J. Peel Nelson, of Bulawayo, and has issue living, Jeremy Herbert (103, Lansdowne Rd., W11), *b.* 1935: *m.* 1958, Alison Douglas, da. of Col. D. M. Martin, of Dunchattan, Troon, Ayrshire, and has issue living, Elizabeth Belinda *b.* 1959, Barbara Anne Camilla *b.* 1961, Lucinda Jane *b.* 1965, Arabella Sophie *b.* 1967,—Nigel Henry Vicary, *b.* 1937, *m.* 1967, Barbara, da. of Canon Edward George Paterson, and has issue living, Paul Humphrey Paterson *b.* 1968, Douglas Robert Nigel *b.* 1972, Mairi Rosalind Diana *b.* 1970,—Timothy Durant, *b.* 1938,—Kenneth Richard (41, Sackville Cres., Ashford, Kent) *b.* 1941: *m.* 1966, Mary Elizabeth Frances, da. of Francis Beamish, and has issue living, Vicary James *b.* 1973, Sara Jane *b.* 1970,— Simon Humphrey (Brunswick Cottage, Church St., Kelvedon, Essex), *b.* 1947: *m.* 1974, Philippa Mary Brand. *Address,*—Private Bag 5583W, Bulawayo, Rhodesia. *Clubs,*—Athenaeum, Salisbury, Bulawayo, Ruwa Country.

AUNTS LIVING   (*Daughters of 1st Baron Hunsdon of Hunsdon*).
Hon. Winifred Marian (*Hon. Lady Ponsonby*), *b.* 1886: *m.* 1912, Col. Sir Charles Edward Ponsonby TD, 1st Bt. *Residences,*—Woodleys, Woodstock, Oxon; 6, Eresby House, Rutland Gate, SW7.
Hon. Rosalind Mary, *b.* 1898.

WIDOW LIVING OF SON OF FOURTH BARON ALDENHAM.

Jean Frances (*Hon. Mrs. Andrew C. V. Elphinstone*), *C.V.O.*, dau. of the late Capt. Angus Valdimar Hambro, M.P.; appointed a Lady-in-Waiting to H.M. when Princess Elizabeth 1945, and an Extra Woman of the Bedchamber to H.M. 1953 ; C.V.O. 1953 : *m.* 1st, 1942, Capt. the Hon. Vicary Paul Gibbs, Grenadier Guards, who *d.* (killed in action in Holland) 1944 ; 2ndly, 1946, the Rev. the Hon. Andrew Charles Victor Elphinstone, who *d.* 1975 [see L. Elphinstone], and has issue living (by 1st m.) [see colls. infra] (by 2nd m.) [see L. Elphinstone, colls.]. *Residence,*—Maryland, Worplesdon, Surrey.

WIDOW LIVING OF FOURTH BARON ALDENHAM

BEATRIX ELINOR (*Dowager Baroness Aldenham*) (The Old Rectory, Hundson, Ware, Herts.), da. of the late Herbert Woodfield Paul [Mackworth, Bt., colls.], and widow of Algernon Hyde Villiers [see E. Clarendon]: *m.* 1919, the 4th and 2nd Baron, who *d.* 1969.

COLLATERAL BRANCHES LIVING.

Issue of the late Capt. the Hon. Vicary Paul Gibbs, Grenadier Guards, el. son of 4th Baron Aldenham, *b.* 1921: *d.* (killed in action in Holland) 1944 : *m.* 1942, Jean Frances (*Hon. Mrs. Andrew C. V. Elphinstone*). *C.V.O.* (ante ; who *m.* 2ndly, 1946, the Rev. the Hon. Andrew Charles Victor Elphinstone, who *d.* 1975 [see L. Elphinstone]), da. of the late Capt. Angus Valdimar Hambro, MP:—
Jennifer Susan, *b.* 1944: *m.* 1974, Lt.-Cdr. Michael Charles Gordon-Lennox, RN, [see D. Richmond and Lennox colls.)   .

(*Male line in remainder to the Barony of Aldenham only.*)

Issue of the late Ven. the Hon. Kenneth Francis Gibbs, D.D., 5th son of 1st Baron Aldenham, *b.* 1856, *d.* 1935 : *m.* 1894, Mabel Alice, who *d.* 1953, dau. of Charles Edward Barnett [R. Ormathwaite] :—
Raymond Kenneth (The Manor House, Yatton Keynell, nr. Chippenham, Wilts., SN14 7EL), *b.* 1901; ed. at Winchester, and at Ch. Ch., Oxford; Lieut.-Col. Herts Regt. (TA): *m.* 1941, Kathleen, da. of the late Rev. W. H. Carnegie, Canon and Sub-Dean of Westminster Abbey.——Bernard Vicary, *TD*, *b.* 1905; ed. at Winchester; 1939-45 War as Major Anti-Aircraft Regt., RA (TA). *Residence,*— Blacknest Lodge, Brimpton Common, nr. Reading.——Andrew Antony, *MBE*, *TD*, *b.* 1914; ed. at Winchester, and at Ch. Ch., Oxford (BA 1937, MA 1946); Major Herts Regt. (TA Reserve), and a Dir. of Barclays Bank; 1939-45 War (despatches, MBE); MBE (Mil.), 1945: *m.* 1947, Elizabeth Joan, dau. of Major Eric Charles Montagu Flint, DSO, and widow of Capt. Peter George William Savile Foljambe, Herts Regt. [see E. Liverpool], and has issue living, John Kenneth Andrew, *b.* 1948: ed. at Winchester,—Alan Francis, *b.* 1953; ed. at Winchester, and Ch. Ch., Oxford. *Residence,*—Kilvington Hall, Thirsk, Yorks. *Clubs,*—Travellers', Pratt's, Yorkshire (York).——Dorothea Louisa (*Dorothea, Lady Goodenough*), *b.* 1897: *m.* 1924, Sir William Macnamara Goodenough, 1st Bt., who *d.* 1951. *Residence,*—Filkins Hall, Lechlade, Glos.——*Dame* Anstice Rosa, *DCVO*, *CBE* (twin), *b.* 1905; Ch. Commr., British Commonwealth Girl Guides Asso. 1956-66; a Member of Cttee. of World Asso. of Girl Guides and Girl Scouts 1952-60, and Vice-Chm. 1957-60; CBE, (Civil) 1960, DCVO 1971. *Residence,*—Blacknest Lodge, Brimpton Common, nr. Reading.

Granddaughter of the late Hon. Henry Lloyd Gibbs (infra):—
Issue of the late Maurice Antony Crutchley Gibbs, *b.* 1888, *d.* 1974: *m.* 1st, 1912 (m. diss. 1924), Elma, who *d.* 1973, da. of Sir William Gordon Gordon-Cumming, 4th Bt.; 2ndly, 1933, Margaret Falkiner, who *d.* 1964, only da. of the late Daniel Grant McBean, of Fairley Grange, NSW, and formerly wife of Reginald Francis Egerton, RN:—
(By 1st m.) Daphne Marion, *b.* 1912: *m.* 1934, Percy Kirwan Agar, of La Haute, Dominica, and has issue living, Antony Edward, *b.* 1936 (La Haute, Dominica), *b.* 1936: *m.* 1967, Madeleine Carmel, da. of the late Stephen Morrison, of Nova Scotia, and has issue living, Stephen Kirwan *b.* 1968,—Elizabeth Anne *b.* 1938: *m.* 1958, Mark Varvill, of The White House, Abinger Common, nr. Dorking, Surrey, and has issue living, Richard Antony *b.* 1961, Katherine Mary *b.* 1963.

Issue of the late Hon. Henry Lloyd Gibbs, youngest son of 1st Baron Aldenham *b.* 1861, *d.* 1907: *m.* 1887, Alice Mary, who *d.* 1942, youngest dau. of the late Gen. Charles Crutchley, of Sunninghill Park, Ascot :—
Helen Bridget (*Lady Orr Ewing*), *MBE*, *b.* 1896; MBE (Civil) 1948: *m.* 1917, Sir Ian Leslie Orr Ewing, MP, who *d.* 1958 [see Orr Ewing, Bt., colls.]. *Residence,*—Adcombe Edge, Corfe, Taunton, Somerset.

PREDECESSORS.—[1] HENRY HUCKS Gibbs, *F.S.A.*, son of the late George Henry Gibbs, of Aldenham House, Herts, *b.* 1819 ; senior partner in the firm of Antony Gibbs and Sons, bankers and merchants, of 15, Bishopsgate Street Within, E.C.; a Director of the Bank of England 1853-1901 (Gov. 1875-7); M.P. for City of London (*C*) 1891-2 ; cr. *Baron Aldenham*, of Aldenham, co. Hertford (peerage of United Kingdom) 1896 : *m.* 1845, Louisa Anne, who *d.* 1897, dau. of William Adams, LL.D., formerly of Thorpe, Chertsey, Surrey; *d.* 1907 : *s.* by his el. son [2] ALBAN GEORGE HENRY, 2nd Baron, *b.* 1846; M.P. for City of London (*C*) 1892-1906: *m.* 1873, Bridget who *d.* 1896, dau. of the late Rt. Hon. Alexander James Beresford Beresford Hope, P.C., of Bedgebury Park, Kent ; *d.* 1936; *s.* by his only son [3] GERALD HENRY BERESFORD, 3rd Baron, *b.* 1879, a partner in the firm of Antony Gibbs & Sons, merchants and bankers, of 22, Bishopsgate, E.C. : *m.* 1905, Lillie Caroline, who *d.* 1950, el. dau. of the late Rev. William Thomas Houldsworth, of 44, Lennox Gardens, S.W.; *d.* 1939; *s.* by his cousin [4] WALTER DURANT, 4th Baron, 2nd Baron Hunsdon of Hunsdon [see infra *⁎⁎*], b. 1888; Chm. of Antony Gibbs & Sons, 1939-65, and Westminster Bank 1950-61; *m.* 1919, Beatrix Elinor, da. of the late Herbert Woodfield Paul [Mackworth, Bt., colls.], and widow of Algernon Hyde Villiers [E. Clarendon]: *d.* 1969; *s.* by his yr. son [5] ANTONY DURANT, 5th Baron and present peer; also 3rd Baron Hunsdon of Hunsdon.

⁎⁎ [1] *Hon.* HERBERT COKAYNE Gibbs, 4th son of 1st Baron Aldenham, *b.* 1854; a partner in the firm of Antony Gibbs & Sons, bankers and merchants, of 22, Bishopsgate, E.C. ; High Sheriff of Herts 1913 ; cr. *Baron Hunsdon of Hunsdon*, of Briggens, co. Hertford (peerage of United Kingdom) 1923 : *m.* 1885, Anna Maria, who *d.* 1938, dau. of the late Richard Durant, of High Canons, Herts, and Sharpham, Devon ; *d.* 1935; *s.* by his el. son [2] WALTER DURANT, 2nd Baron, who *s.* as 4th Baron Aldenham 1939 (ante).

ALDINGTON, BARON. (Low.) [Baron U.K. 1962.]

Hope

TOBY (AUSTIN RICHARD WILLIAM) Low, K.C.M.G., C.B.E., D.S.O., T.D., P.C., 1st Baron, son of the late Col. Stuart Low, D.S.O. [B. Atkin]; b. May 25th, 1914; ed. at Winchester, and at New Coll., Oxford (B.A. 1936); Bar. Middle Temple 1939; Chm. of National and Grindlays Bank Ltd., 23, Fenchurch St., EC3, Brandt, Ltd., Port of London Authority, Sun Alliance and London Insurance Ltd., Nat. Nuclear Corpn., Inst. of Neurology, and of Gen. Advisory Council of BBC, Dep. Chm. General Electric Co., Ltd., a Dir. of Lloyds Bank Ltd., and First Nat. City Corpn.; Brig. late The Rangers, KRRC (TA); Parl. Sec. to Min. of Supply 1951-54, Min. of State, Board of Trade 1954-57, and Dep. Chm. of Conservative Party Organization 1959-63; 1939-45 War in Middle East and Italy (despatches, DSO, MBE, CBE, French Croix de Guerre, Com. of American Legion of Merit); MP for N. Div. of Blackpool (C) 1945-62; cr. DSO 1941, MBE (Mil) 1944, CBE (Mil) 1945, PC 1954, KCMG 1957, and Baron Aldington, of Bispham, in Co. Borough of Blackpool (peerage of UK) 1962: m. Felicité Anne Araminta (BOWMAN), da. of the late Sir Harold Alfred MacMichael, GCMG, DSO, and has issue.

Arms,—Gules a pale ermine on a chief argent masoned sable three saffrons stalked and leafed proper. Crest,—Out of the embattlements of a tower or a cubit arm proper, the hand grasping a hurt. Supporters,—Dexter, a stag proper; sinister a black Labrador dog proper; pendant from the neck of each by its own chains a portcullis or.

Residence,—Knoll Farm, Aldington, Kent; Club,—Carlton.

SON LIVING.

Hon. CHARLES HAROLD STUART, b. June 22nd, 1948; ed. at Winchester, and New Coll., Oxford.

DAUGHTERS LIVING.

Hon. Priscilla Jane Stephanie, b. 1949; ed. at Cranborne Chase Sch., and Westfield Coll., London Univ.
Hon. Lucy Ann Anthea, b. 1956; ed. at Cranborne Chase Sch.

Alexander, Viscount, son of Earl of Caledon.

ALEXANDER OF HILLSBOROUGH, EARLDOM OF. (Alexander.) [Extinct 1965.]

DAUGHTER LIVING OF FIRST EARL

Lady Beatrix Dora, b. 1909; ed. at London Univ. (B.Sc. Econ. 1932); a JP of Middlesex: m. 1936, William Bernard Evison, BCom, and has issue living, Alexander Bernard, b. 1948: m. 1969, Joan Susan Hepworth, and has issue living, Deborah Claire b. 1974,—Jennifer Anne, b. 1940; ed. at King's Coll., London (BSc and AKO 1962): m. 1963, Fl. Lt. Barry Charles Hunt, BSc, RAF, of 66, Longfields, Swaffham, Norfolk, PE37 7RJ, and has issue living, Geoffrey Alexander Waters b. 1964. Toby Barry b. 1966, Simon Charles b. 1968, Christopher Bernard b. 1970. Residence,—Cranleigh, 101, Old Park Av., Enfield, Middx.

ALEXANDER OF POTTERHILL, BARON. (Alexander.) [Life Baron 1974.]

WILLIAM PICKEN ALEXANDER, son of the late Thomas Alexander, of Paisley; b. Dec. 13th, 1905; ed. at Paisley Gram. Sch., and Glasgow Univ. (MA, BSc, MEd, PhD); FBPsS; FCP; a Dir. of Education, Walthamstow 1934–35, Margate 1935-39, and Sheffield 1939-44; Gen. Sec. of Assocn. of Education Cttees. of England and Wales since 1944; Joint Sec. to Management Panels of Burnham and Allied Cttees. 1944-73; cr. Knt. 1960, and Baron Alexander of Potterhill, of Paisley, co. Renfrew (Life Baron) 1974: m. 1949, Joan Mary, da. of Robert Baxter Williamson, of Sheffield, and has issue.

Residence,—Woodhey, Pembroke Rd., Moor Park, Herts., HA6 2HP. Club,—National Liberal.

SONS LIVING.

Hon. Robert William Paul, b. 1950.
Hon. Thomas Bruce, b. 1951.

ALEXANDER OF TUNIS, EARL. (Alexander.) [Earl U.K. 1952.]

By land, by sea, by the stars

SHANE WILLIAM DESMOND ALEXANDER, 2nd Earl; *b.* June 30th, 1935; *s.* 1969; ed. at Harrow and Ashbury Coll., Ottawa; Lt. Irish Guards (Reserve); Liveryman Mercers' Co.; a Lord-in-Waiting to HM Jan. to March 1974: *m.* 1971, Hilary, only da. of John van Geest, of Molecey Hill House, Market Deeping, Lincs.

Arms,—Per pale argent and sable, a chevron, and in base a crescent, all counterchanged; on a canton azure a harp or, stringed argent. Crest,—An arm, in armour, embowed proper holding a sword of the last hilt and pommel or. Supporters,—Dexter, a piper of the Irish Guards holding under the interior arm a bagpipe; *sinister*, a sepoy of the 3rd/2nd Punjabi Regiment supporting with the exterior hand a rifle proper, each charged on the shoulder with an escutcheon barry nebuly of six argent and azure.

Residence—Alconbury House-Alconbury, Hants.

BROTHER LIVING.

Hon. BRIAN JAMES, *b.* July 31st 1939; ed. at Harrow; Lieut. Irish Guards (Reserve).

SISTER LIVING.

Lady Rose Maureen, *b.* 1932: *m.* 1956, Lt.-Col. Humphrey Crossman, R.A., and has issue living, David Lindisfarne Alexander, *b.* (Nov.) 1956,—Emma Margaret, *b.* 1959. *Residence,*—Cheswick House, Berwick-on-Tweed, Northumberland.

WIDOW LIVING OF FIRST EARL.

Lady MARGARET DIANA BINGHAM, *GBE, JP* (*Dowager Countess Alexander of Tunis*), (Winkfield Lodge, Windsor Forest, Berks.); JP and DL for Berks.; GBE (Civil) 1954; da. of 5th Earl of Lucan; *m.* 1931, The 1st Earl, who *d.* 1969.

PREDECESSOR.—[1] F. M. *Sir* HAROLD RUPERT LEOFRIC GEORGE ALEXANDER, *KG, GCB, OM, GCMG, CSI, DSO, MC, PC,* 3rd son of 4th Earl of Caledon; *b.* 1891; C-in-C British Forces in Burma 1942 and Middle East 1942-43, Dep. C-in-C N. Africa 1943, C-in-C 18th Army Group, N. Africa 1943, C-in-C Allied Forces in Italy 1943-44 and Supreme Allied Comd. Med. 1944-45, Gov.-Gen. of Canada 1946-52, and Min. of Defence 1952-54; Col. Irish Guards 1947-69; *m.* 1931, Lady Margaret Diana Bingham, OBE, JP, da. of 5th Earl of Lucan; *d.* 1969; *s.* by his eld. son [2] SHANE WILLIAM DESMOND, 2nd Earl and present peer.

ALINGTON, BARONY OF. (Sturt.) [Extinct 1940.]

DAUGHTER LIVING OF THIRD BARON.

Hon. Mary Anna Sibell Elizabeth, *b.* 1929: *m.* 1949, George Gosselin Marten, M.V.O., D.S.C., late Lieut.-Com. R.N., son of the late Vice-Adm. Sir Francis Arthur Marten, K.B.E., C.B., C.M.G., CVO, and has issue living, Napier Anthony Stuart *b.* 1959; a Page of Honour to HM 1973-75,—Victoria Mary, *b.* 1950,—Charlotte Diana, *b.* 1952: *m.* 1975, Oswald Alexander Mosley [see Mosley, Bt.],—Geogina Elizabeth, *b.* 1953: *m.* 1973, Presley Francis Norton, of Salinas, Ecuador,—Amabel Catherine, *b.* 1954,—Sophia Harriet, *b.* 1962. *Residence,*—Crichel, Wimborne, Dorset.

ALLAN OF KILMAHEW, BARON. (Allan.) [Life Baron 1973.]

ROBERT ALEXANDER ALLAN, *DSO, OBE,* yr. son of the late Claud A. Allan, JP, of Kilmahew Castle, Cardross, Dunbartonshire; *b.* July 11th, 1914; ed. at Harrow, Clare Coll., Camb., and Yale Univ., USA; 1939-45 War as Cdr. RNVR (OBE, DSO, despatches five times, Cdr. Legion of Honour, French Croix de Guerre, Officer Legion of Merit of USA); Dep. Ch. of Naval Information, Washington 1945-46; Pres. Scottish Jnr. Unionists 1948-51; MP for S. Paddington (*C*) 1951-66; Assist. Whip 1953-55, PPS to PM 1955-58, Parl. and Financial Sec., Admiralty 1958-59, Parl. Under-Sec. of State, FO 1959-60, a Treasurer, Conservative and Unionist Party Organization 1960-65, Chm. Conservative Central Board of Finance 1961-66; Chm. Longman Penguin Group of Cos. since 1972; Dep. Chm. Pearson Longman, a Dir. Bank of Scotland, and other cos.; a Gov. of Harrow Sch. since 1968, and of BBC since 1971; *cr.* OBE (Mil.) 1942, DSO 1944, and *Baron Allan of Kilmahew,* of Cardross, co. Dunbarton (Life Baron) 1973: *m.* 1947, Maureen, da. of the late Harold Stuart-Clark, of Singapore, and has issue.

Arms,—not exemplified at time of going to press.

Residence,—5, Campden House Terr., W8; Royal Yacht Squadron.

SON LIVING.

Hon. Alexander Claud Stuart, *b.* 1951.

DAUGHTER LIVING.

Hon. Jane Maureen (Copse Hill Farm, Lower Froyle, Alton, Hants.), *b.* 1952.

ALLEN OF FALLOWFIELD, BARON. (Allen.) [Life Baron 1974.]

ALFRED WALTER HENRY ALLEN, *CBE*, son of Walter Charles Allen, of Colston Rd., Bristol; *b.* July 7th, 1914; ed. at E. Bristol Central Sch.; a Member of Govt. Cttee. of Inquiry Statutory Smallholdings 1963-67, Gen. Sec. of Union of Shop Distribution and Allied Workers since 1962, a Crown Estate Commr. since 1965: a Member of Gen. Council TUC (Economic, and Production Cttees.), of Central Training Council, and of NEDC, and a Dir. of Industrial Training Sers.; Chm. of TUC 1973-74; 1939-45 War as Sgt. RAF, in France and Germany; cr. CBE (Civil) 1967, and *Baron Allen of Fallowfield,* of Fallowfield in Greater Manchester (Life Baron) 1974: *m.* 1940, Ruby Millicent, da. of Albert Hounsell, and has issue.

Residence,—83, Manley Rd., Sale, Cheshire.

SON LIVING.

Hon. Lionel Paul, *b.* 1943.

DAUGHTER LIVING.

Hon. Judith Felicity, *b.* 1946: *m.* 1973, Graham Tonge, of 38, Raven Rd., Timperley, Cheshire.

ALLEN OF HURTWOOD, BARONY OF. (Allen.) [Extinct 1939.]

DAUGHTER LIVING OF FIRST BARON.

Hon. Joan Colette (Polly) Clifford, *b.* 1922. *Residence,*—10, Selwood Terr., SW7.

WIDOW LIVING OF FIRST BARON.

MAJORY (*Baroness Allen of Hurtwood*), dau. of George Gill: *m.* 1921, the 1st Baron, who *d.* 1939, when the title became ext. *Residence,*—10, Selwood Terr., SW7.

ALLENBY, VISCOUNT. (Allenby.) [Viscount U.K. 1919.]

With faith and labour.

DUDLEY JAFFRAY HYNMAN ALLENBY 2nd Viscount; *b.* Jan. 8th, 1903; *s.* 1936; ed. at Eton; Lieut.-Col. (retired) 11th Hussars; European War 1939-40 : *m.* 1st, 1930, Gertrude Mary Lethbridge (who obtained a divorce 1949), dau. of Edward Champneys, of Otterpool Manor, Sellindge, Kent; 2ndly, 1949, Mrs. Daisy Neame (C.St.J.), da. of the late Charles Francis Hancox, and has issue by 1st marriage.

Arms,—Per bend argent and gules, in the sinister three crescents, two and one of the second, and in the dexter, three horses' heads erased, one and two, of the first, all within a bordure azure. Crest,— Issuant out of a crescent gules, a demi-lion proper. Supporters,—*Dexter,* a horse reguardant or; *sinister,* a camel reguardant argent.

Residence,—Parsonage Farm, Westwell, Ashford, Kent. *Club,*—Cavalry.

SON LIVING. (*By 1st marriage.*)

Hon. MICHAEL JAFFRAY HYNMAN, *b.* April 20th, 1931; ed. at Eton; Lt.-Col. R. Hussars; appointed CO R. Yeo. 1974: *m.* 1965, Sara Margaret, only da. of Lt.-Col. Peter Milner Wiggin [see Wiggin, Bt., colls.], and has issue living, Henry Jaffray Hynman, *b.* July 29th, 1968. *Residence,*—Newnham Lodge, Newnham, Basingstoke, Hants. *Club,*—Cavalry.

BROTHER LIVING.

(*Raised to the rank of a Viscount's son* 1939.)

Hon. Claude William Hynman, *b.* 1912; ed. at Stowe; late Lt.-Col. 11th Hussars (Reserve); European War 1939-40 : *m.* 1st, 1939, Sheila Patsy (who obtained a divorce 1948), dau. of G. P. Price, of Beechfield, Petworth; 2ndly, 1951, Barbara Marion, dau. of John Hall, of Felpham, Sussex. *Residence,*—29, Hovedene, Cromwell Rd., Hove. *Club,*—Cavalry.

PREDECESSOR.—[1] *Field-Marshal Sir* EDMUND HENRY HYNMAN Allenby, *G.C.B., G.C.M.G., G.C.V.O.,* son of the late Hynman Allenby, of Felixstowe House, Felixstowe; *b.* 1861; Bechuanaland Expedition 1884-5, Zululand 1888, S. Africa 1899-1902, in command of a column (despatches, Brevets Lieut.-Col. and Col., C.B.), European War 1914-19, Comdg. Cav. Corps, and subsequently 5th Army Corps, 3rd Army, and Egyptian Expeditionary Force (despatches, K.C.B., Promoted Gen. and Field-Marshal, Grand Cordons of the Nile, White Eagle of Serbia, Redeemer of Greece, Crown of Roumania, Wen Hu of China, Rising Sun of Japan (with flowers of Paulownia), El Nahda of the Hedjaz, and Michael the Brave of Roumania, Grand Officer of Legion of Honour, and Orders of Leopold of Belgium and Savoy of Italy, G.C.M.G., American D.S.M., G.C.B., French and Belgian Croix de Guerre, thanked by Parliament, cr. Viscount, granted £50,000); High Commr. in Egypt 1919-25 [Arabic title—*Mandub es sami* (Very High Delegate)]; received Grand Cordon of the Order of Mohamet Ali 1925, 1st class of Order of Al Rafidain of Iraq 1933, and Grand Cross (Mil.) of Order of Leopold of

Belgium 1935; Capt. of Deal Castle 1925-7; elected Lord Rector of Edinburgh Univ. 1935; cr.
Viscount Allenby, of Megiddo, and of Felixstowe. co. Suffolk (peerage of United Kingdom) 1919,
with remainder, in default of male issue, to his brother, Capt. Frederick Claude Hynman
Allenby, C.B.E., R.N., and his male issue: *m.* 1896, Adelaide Mabel, who *d.* 1942, dau. of the
late Horace Edward Chapman, of Donhead House, Salisbury; *d.* 1936; *s.* by his nephew [2]
DUDLEY JAFFRAY HYNMAN (son of the late Capt. Frederick Claude Hynman Allenby, C.B.E.,
R.N. [ante]), 2nd Viscount and present peer.

ALLENDALE, VISCOUNT. (Beaumont.) [Viscount U.K. 1911.]

Trust, but see whom you trust.

WENTWORTH HUBERT CHARLES BEAU-
MONT, 3rd Viscount; *b.* Sept. 1922;
s. 1956; ed. at Eton; Flight-Lieut.
R.A.F. Vol. Reserve, Hon. Air Commodore 3508 (co. of Northumberland)
Fighter Control Unit, Pres. of Northumberland and Durham Asso. of Building
Sos., a D.L. for Northumberland,
and an O.St.J.; Steward of Jockey Club
1963-65; A.D.C. to Viceroy of India
1946; 1939-42 War (wounded, prisoner):
m. 1948, the Hon. Sarah Field Ismay,
da. of 1st Baron Ismay, and has issue.

Arms,—Gules, a lion rampant or, armed and
langued azure, between eight crescents in orle of the
second. Crest,—A bull's head erased quarterly
argent and gules, charged with a mullet sable.
Supporters,—*Dexter*, a lion argent, semée of crescents
gules; *sinister*, a bull quarterly argent and gules, the
horns of the first tipped or.

Residences,—Bywell Hall, Stocksfield-on-Tyne,
Northumberland; Allenheads Hall, Allenheads,
Northumberland.

SONS LIVING.

Hon. WENTWORTH PETER ISMAY, *b.* Nov. 14th, 1948; ed. at Harrow: *m.* 1975, Theresa Mary,
2nd da. of Francis Ambrose More O'Ferrall [see Mather-Jackson, Bt.].
Hon. Mark Henry, *b.* 1950; ed. at Eton.
Hon. Charles Richard, *b.* 1954.

BROTHERS LIVING.

Hon. Richard Blackett (of 58, S. Audley St., W1), *b.* 1926; ed. at Eton; late Sub-Lt. RNVR: *m.* 1971,
Lavinia Mary, yst. da. of the late Lt.-Col. Arnold Ramsay Keppel [see E. Albemarle, colls.].
Hon. Edward Nicholas Canning, *b.* 1929; ed. at Eton; Capt. (retired) Life Guards: *m.* 1953, Jane
Caroline Falconer, dau. of Alexander Lewis Paget Falconer Wallace, J.P., of Candacraig, Strathdon,
Aberdeen, and has issue living, Thomas Wentworth, *b.* 1962,—Henry Alexander Nicholas, *b.* 1966.
Residence,—Royal Enclosure Lodge, Ascot, Berks.
Hon. Matthew Henry (Flat 9, 50, Cornwall Gdns., SW7), *b.* 1933; ed. at Bradfield: *m.* 1st, 1959 (*m.*
diss. 1972), Anne C. Margaret, el. da. of Gerard Hamilton, of 35, Thurloe Sq., SW7; 2ndly, 1973,
Belinda Jane Elizabeth, el. da. of the late Harold David Cuthbert, of Beaufront Castle, Hexham,
Northumberland [see Milnes Coates Bt.], and has issue living (by 1st m.), Justin George Gerald, *b.*
1960,—Charlotte Catherine Lucinda, *b.* 1962.

SISTER LIVING.

Hon. Ela Hilda Aline (*Countess of Carlisle*), *b.* 1925; an OStJ.: *m.* 1945, the 12th Earl of Carlisle.
Residence,—Naworth Castle, Brampton, Cumberland.

UNCLE LIVING. (*Son of 1st Viscount.*)

Hon. Ralph Edward Blackett, *CBE*, *TD*, *b.* 1901; ed. at Eton, and Ch. Ch., Oxford (MA); Lt.-Col.
636th (Roy. Welch) Light Anti-Aircraft Regt., RA (TA), and a JP for Montgomeryshire (High
Sheriff 1957, Vice-Lt. 1962-74); a DL for Powys; PPS to Postmaster-Gen. 1935-39, and to Sec. of
State for War 1942-45, Chm., Montgomeryshire co. Agriculturla Exec. Ctte. 1948-69, a Development
Commr. 1952-69; a Member of Council on Tribunals 1958-70, of Welsh Economic Council 1965-68, and
of Welsh Council 1968-71; a Member of Management Cttee. of Council for Small Industries in Rural
Areas (Chm. of Welsh Ctte.); 1939-45 War; MP for Central Div. of Portsmouth (*U*) 1931-45; CBE
(Civil) 1967: *m.* 1926, Helena Mary Christine, who *d.* 1962, da. of Brig.-Gen. John Cecil Wray,
CB, CMG, MVO, and has issue living, John Ralph (Plas Llwyngwern, Pantperthog, Machynlleth,
Powys), *b.* 1927; ed. at Ch. Ch., Oxford (MA); a JP for Powys: a Member of Federal Assembly
of Rhodesia and Nyasaland 1962-63: *m.* 1951, Audrey, yr. da. of the late E. T. Hickling, of York, and
has issue living, Ralph Wentworth Christopher *b.* 1952, Nigel Canning Vane *b.* 1954, Andrew John
Blackett *b.* 1956, Hugh Edward Stewart *b.* 1959, Peter John Tempest, *b.* 1964, Louise Christine
Winsmore (twin) *b.* 1956,—David Christopher (of Poolspringe, Much Birch, Herefordshire), *b.* 1929:
m. 1954, Mrs. Marion Edith Davison, da. of the late H. J. Mallard, of 14, Stanbury Rd., Victoria Park,
Bristol, and has issue living, Timothy David *b.* 1955, Sally Aline Christine *b.* 1956,—Diana, *b.* 1934:
m. 1954, Cdr. Brian Robert Outhwaite, RN, of Roseberry House, Westbourne, Emsworth, Hants.,
and has issue living, Mark Robert Canning *b.* 1957, James Edward *b.* 1961, Charles Cedric *b.* 1965.
Residence,—Bron-y-Wennol, Pantperthog, Machynlleth, Powys.

AUNT LIVING. (*Daughter of 1st Viscount.*)

Hon. Agatha Violet (*Hon. Lady Perowne*), *b.* 1903; is an O.St.J.: *m.* 1933, Sir John Victor Thomas
Woolrych Tait Perowne, KCMG, who *d.* 1951, and has issue living, John Florian Canning (The Old
Vicarage, Leavenheath, Colchester), *b.* 1942; ed. at Eton, and Corpus Christi Coll., Camb. (MA);
Solicitor 1968: *m.* 1968, Elizabeth Mary, da. of the Rev. Shirley Beckett Freeman, of 22, Pettitts La.,
Dry Drayton, Cambs. *Residence*,—11, Montagu Sq., W1H 1RB.

WIDOW LIVING OF SECOND VISCOUNT.

VIOLET LUCY EMILY (*Dowager Viscountess Allendale*), da. of the late Sir Charles Hilton Seely, 2nd Bt.:
m. 1921, the 2nd Viscount, who *d.* 1956. *Residence*,—21, Cadogan Sq., SW1.

COLLATERAL BRANCH LIVING. (*In remainder to the Barony only.*)

Grandson of the late Hon. Hubert George Beaumont, 3rd son of 1st Baron:—
Issue of the late Major Michael Wentworth Beaumont, T.D., *b.* 1903, *d.* 1958: *m.* 1st, 1924, the
Hon. Faith Muriel Pease, who *d.* 1935, dau. of 1st Baron Gainford; 2ndly, 1935, Doreen
Christian (Harristown House, Brannockstown, co. Kildare), da. of Sir Herbert William
Goff Davis-Goff, 2nd Bt.:—
(By 1st marriage) *Rev.* Timothy Wentworth, *b.* 1928; *cr.* Baron Beaumont of Whitley (Life Peer)
Nov. 1967 [see that title].

PREDECESSORS.—[1] WENTWORTH BLACKETT Beaumont, son of the late Thomas Wentworth Beaumont; *b.* 1829; M.P. for S. Northumberland (*L*) July 1852 to Nov. 1885, and for Tyneside Div. of Northumberland July 1886 to July 1892; cr. *Baron Allendale,* of Allendale and Hexham, co. Northumberland (peerage of United Kingdom) 1906: *m.* 1st, 1856, Lady Margaret Anne, who *d.* 1888, dau. of 1st Marquess of Clanricarde; 2ndly, 1891, Edith Althea, who *d.* 1927, dau. of the late Maj.-Gen. Henry Meade Hamilton, C.B., and widow of Maj.-Gen. Sir George Pomeroy Pomeroy-Colley, K.C.S.I., C.B., C.M.G.; *d.* 1907; *s.* by his el. son [2] WENTWORTH CANNING BLACKETT, 2nd Baron, 1st Viscount, *b.* 1860; Vice-Chamberlain to H.M.'s Household Dec. 1905 to Feb. 1907, Capt. of the Yeomen of the Guard 1907-11, and a Lord-in-Waiting to H.M. 1911-16; sat as M.P. for Hexham Div. of Northumberland (*L*) 1895-1907; cr. *Viscount Allendale,* of Allendale and Hexham, Northumberland (peerage of United Kingdom), 1911; *m.* 1889, Lady Alexandrina Louisa Maud Vane-Tempest, who *d.* 1945, dau. of 5th Marquess of Londonderry; *d.* 1923; *s.* by his el. son [3] WENTWORTH HENRY CANNING, *K.G., C.B., C.B.E., M.C.,* 2nd Viscount; *b.* 1890; Lieut.-Col. and Brevet Col. Northumberland Yeo., and Lord Lieut. for Northumberland; a Lord-in-Waiting to H.M. 1931-2, 1937-51, and 1952-4, and a Permanent Lord-in-Waiting 1954-6: *m.* 1921, Violet Lucy Emily, dau. of Sir Charles Hilton Seely, 2nd Bt. *d.* 1956; *s.* by his el. son [4] WENTWORTH HUBERT CHARLES, 3rd Viscount, and present peer; also Baron Allendale.

ALLERTON, BARON. (Jackson.) [Baron U.K. 1902.]

GEORGE WILLIAM LAWIES JACKSON, 3rd Baron; *b.* July 23rd, 1903; *s.* 1925; ed. at Eton; Squadron-Leader (retired) Auxiliary Air Force; formerly Lieut. Coldstream Guards Reserve: *m.* 1st, 1926, Joyce (who *d.* 1953, having obtained a divorce 1934), dau. of the late J. R. Hatfield, of Thorp Arch Hall, Yorkshire; 2ndly, 1934, Hope Aline (from whom he obtained a divorce 1947), dau. of the late Allan Havelock-Allan [see Havelock Allan, Bt., colls.]; 3rdly, 1947, Anne Lorina, dau. of the late James F. Montagu, of Skippetts, Basingstoke, and has issue by 1st and 3rd marriages.

Try.

Arms,—Party per chevron gules and or, in chief two suns in splendour of the last, and in base three annulets, one and two interlaced of the first. Crest,—A horse or, holding in the mouth an ear of wheat slipped vert, resting. Supporters,—On either side a horse sable, collared vair the dexter fore leg on three annulets as in the arms and charged on the shoulders with three annulets as in the arms.

Seat,—Loddington Hall, Lleicestershire. *Clubs,*—White's, Turf, Pratt's.

SON LIVING. *(By 1st marriage.)*

Hon. EDWARD LAWIES, *b.* March 23rd, 1928; ed. at Eton; Capt. (retired) Roy. Horse Guards: *m.* 1st, 1953 (m. diss. 1971), Sally Moore, only dau. of the late Ian M. Hezlett, of Cranbourne Corner, Ascot, Berks.; 2ndly, 1971, Susannah Albinia, da. of (Alfred) Drewett Chaytor [see Chaytor, Bt., colls.], and has issue Lawies, *b.* 1954: *m.* 1974, J. Nicholas H. Purvis (c/o Cramond House, Pirbright, Woking, Surrey),—Lavinia Jane Lawies, *b.* 1957. *Residence,* —Dunesslin, by Dunscore, Dumfriesshire. *Club,*—White's.

DAUGHTER LIVING. *(By 3rd marriage.)*

Hon. Melinda Catherine, *b.* 1953.

COLLATERAL BRANCH LIVING.

Granddaughter of the late Rt. Hon. Sir (Francis) Stanley Jackson, G.C.S.I., G.C.I.E., 2nd son of 1st Baron:—
Issue of the late Maj. Henry Stanley Lawies Jackson, *b.* 1903, *d.* 1963: *m.* 1927, Grace Diana, who *d.* 1974, da. of Arthur Philip Beddard, MD:—
Frances Harriet Philippa (80, Melton Court, SW7), *b.* 1947.

PREDECESSORS—[1] WILLIAM LAWIES Jackson, *P.C.,* son of the late William Jackson, of Leeds, *b.* 1840; Financial Sec. to Treasury Jan. 1886 and July 1886 to Nov. 1891, Ch. Sec. for Ireland Nov. 1891 to Aug. 1892; M.P. for Leeds (*C*) 1880-85, and for Leeds, N. Div., Nov. 1885 to June 1902; cr. a P.C. 1890, and *Baron Allerton,* of Chapel Allerton, W. Riding of Yorks (peerage of United Kingdom) 1902: *m.* 1860, Grace, who *d.* 1901, dau. of George Tempest; *d.* 1917; *s.* by his el. son [2] GEORGE HERBERT, 2nd Baron, *b.* 1867: *m.* 1899, Katharine Louisa, who *d.* 1956, dau. of the late William Wickham Wickham, of Chestnut Grove, Boston Spa, Yorkshire; *d.* 1925; *s* by his son [3] GEORGE WILLIAM LAWIES, 3rd Baron and present peer.

ALNESS, BARONY OF. (Munro.) [Extinct 1955.]

WIDOW LIVING OF FIRST BARON.

OLGA MARIE (*Baroness Alness*), dau. of the late J. G. Grumler, of Dinard, France: *m.* 1921, as his second wife, the 1st Baron, who *d.* 1955, when the title became ext. *Residence,*—7, Milner Rd., Bournemouth.

ALPORT, BARON. (Alport.) [Life Baron 1961.]

CUTHBERT JAMES McCALL ALPORT
T.D., P.C., son of the late Professor
Arthur Cecil Alport; *b.* March 22nd, 1912;
ed. at Haileybury, and at Pembroke Coll.,
Camb. (MA); Bar. Middle Temple 1944;
a DL for Essex; Assistant PMG 1955-7,
Under-Sec. of State, Common-
wealth Relations Office 1957-9, Min. of
State, Commonwealth Relations Office
1959-61, and British High Commr. in
Federation of Rhodesia and Nyasaland
1961-63; a Repres. at Council of Europe
1964; Special Repres. to Rhodesia 1967;
High Steward of Colchester 1967;
Master of Skinners' Co. 1969; a Dep.
Speaker 1971; Pro-Chancellor City
Univ., London 1972; 1939-45 War;
Hon. Lt.-Col.; MP for Colchester (*C*)
1950-61; PC 1960, and *Baron Alport*,
of Colchester, co. Essex (Life Baron)
1961: *m.* 1945, Rachel Cecilia, da. of
Lt.-Col. Ralph Charles Bingham, CVO, DSO, Coldstream Guards (ret.) [see
E. Lucan colls.], and has issue.

Arms,—Barry wavy argent and azure, on a bend or a Tudor Rose argent on gules between two
oyster shells gules. **Crest,**—a demi lion or gorged with a mural crown gules, within a Norman arch
proper. **Supporters,**—*Dexter*, a representation of a Roman centurion supporting a vexillum of the
XXth Legion proper ; *sinister*, a representation of an Ancient Briton proper.
Residence,—The Cross House, Layer de la Haye, Colchester. *Clubs,*—Farmers', Pratt's.

SON LIVING.
Hon. Arthur Edward Bingham, *b.* 1954.

DAUGHTERS LIVING.
Hon. Cecilia Alexandra Rose, *b.* 1946: *m.* 1969, the Rev. Geoffrey Wilfrid Francis Lang, of Willian
Rectory, nr. Letchworth, Herts. SG6 2AA, and has issue.

Hon. Lavender Lilias Carole, *b.* 1950: *m.* 1974, Ian Colin Taylor, MBE, of Hill Cottage, Manor Rd.
Kenilworth, Warwicks.

Altamont, Earl of, son of Marquess of Sligo.

Althorp, Viscount, son of Earl Spencer.

ALTRINCHAM, BARONY OF. (Grigg.) [Baron U.K. 1945, disclaimed 1963.]

To serve and to save

JOHN EDWARD POYNDER GRIGG,
b. April 15, 1924; *s.* as 2nd
Baron Dec. 1st, 1955; disclaimed
his Peerage for life July 31st,
1963 ; a Journalist; Editor of
National and English Review
1954-60; 1943-45 War as Lieut.
Grenadier Guards: *m.* 1958,
(Marian) Patricia, dau. of H. E.
Campbell, of 79, Somerton Rd.,
Belfast.

Arms.—Sable, three owls argent, a
chief azure, issuant from the base thereof a
sun in splendour or. **Crest.**—A grenade
sable fired proper, between two roses argent
barbed and seeded also proper. **Supporters,**
(borne by Barons Altrincham),—On either
side a lion gules gorged with a chain collar
pendent therefrom a portcullis or, and
supporting a date palm fructed proper.

Residence,—32, Dartmouth Row,
S.E.10. *Club,*—Beefsteak.

BROTHER LIVING.
Hon. ANTHONY ULICK DAVID
DUNDAS, *b.* Jan. 12th, 1934 ; ed. at Eton
and New Coll., Oxford; late 2nd Lieut.
Grenadier Guards: *m.* 1965, Eliane d.
Cassagne de Beaufort, da. of the Marquis
de Miramon, of 4, Hanover Terr., NW1,
and has issue living, Edward Sebastian,
b. 1965,—Steven Thomas, *b.* 1969,—Anne
Casilda, *b.* 1967. *Residence* —31, Ladbroke
Grove, W11.

SISTER LIVING.
Hon. Annabel Désirée, *b.* 1931.

WIDOW LIVING OF FIRST BARON.
Hon. JOAN ALICE KATHERINE DICKSON-POYNDER (*Baroness Altrincham*), dau. of 1st Baron Islington:
m. 1923, the 1st Baron, who *d.* 1955. *Residence,*—Tormarton Court, Badminton, Glos.

PREDECESSOR.—[1] *Rt. Hon. Sir* EDWARD WILLIAM MACLEAY GRIGG, *K.C.M.G., K.C.V.O., D.S.O., M.C., P.C.,* son of the late Henry Bidewell Grigg, C.I.E., I.C.S.; *b.* 1879; was Mil. Sec. to H.R.H. Prince of Wales during visits to Canada 1919 and Australia and New Zealand 1920, Private Sec. to Prime Min. (Rt. Hon. D. Lloyd George) 1921-2, Gov. and Com.-in-Ch., Kenya 1925-30, Parliamentary Sec. to Min. of Information 1939-40, Financial Sec. to War Office April to May, 1940, Joint Under-Sec. of State for War 1940-2, and Min. Resident in Middle East 1944-5; M.P. for Oldham (*NL*) 1922-5, and for Altrincham Div. of Cheshire (*C*) 1933-45; *cr. Baron Altrincham,* of Tormarton, co. Gloucester (peerage of U.K.) 1945: *m.* 1923, the Hon. Joan Alice Katherine Dickson-Poynder, dau. of 1st Baron Islington; *d.* 1955; *s.* by his el. son [2] JOHN EDWARD POYNDER, 2nd Baron, until he disclaimed his Peerage 1963.

ALVERSTONE, VISCOUNTCY OF. (Webster.) [Extinct 1915.]
WIDOW LIVING OF SON OF FIRST BARON.
Gwladys Marie de Grasse, dau. of Sir Francis Henry Evans, K.C.M.G., M.P., 1st Bt. (cr. 1902, ext, is a Dame of Grace of Order of St. John of Jerusalem; has Order of League of Mercy: *m* 1st, 1898, the Hon. Arthur Harold Webster, who *d.* 1902; 2ndly, 1905, Capt. Iain Ramsay, J.P. Argyll and Sutherland Highlanders, who *d.* 1959. *Address,*—c/o Messrs. Child & Co., 1, Fleet St. EC4.

ALVINGHAM, BARON. (Yerburgh.) [Baron U.K. 1929.]
[Name pronounced "**Yarborough.**"]

ROBERT GUY EARDLEY YERBURGH, *OBE*, 2nd Baron; *b.* Dec. 16th, 1926; *s.* 1955; ed. at Eton; Col. late Coldm. Gds.; OBE (Mil.) 1972: *m.* 1952, Beryl Elliott, dau. of the late W. D. Williams, of Hindhead, Surrey, and has issue.

Arms,—Per pale argent and azure, on a chevron between three chaplets of roses counterchanged. *Crest,*—A falcon close, belled or, preying on a mallard proper. *Supporters,*—On either side a falcon, wings expanded, belled or, gorged with a chaplet of roses azure.
Residence,—Bix Hall, Henley-on-Thames. *Club,*—Guards'.

SON LIVING.
Hon. ROBERT RICHARD GUY, *b.* Dec. 10th, 1956.
DAUGHTER LIVING.
Hon. Susannah Elizabeth, *b.* 1953.
SISTERS LIVING.
Hon. Dorothy Joan, *b.* 1913: *m.* 1934, Lieut-Col. William Aspinall Turner, late The Queen's Bays, and has issue living, Adrian Vernon Aspinall, *b.* 1946,—Caroline Sarah, *b.* 1943: *m.* 1965, Robin Gilman Arculus, of Willow Tree House, Knowl Hill, Reading, and has issue living, James Edward Gilman *b.* 1970, Henry William *b.* 1974, Sophie Louise *b.* 1972. *Residence,*—Old Rectory Farm, Cheselbourne, Dorchester.
Hon. Marjorie Elizabeth, *b.* 1916: *m.* 1st, 1938 (at Alexandria, Egypt), Abdul Hamid Mustafa Risk, 2ndly, 1952, Leon Setchim, and has issue living, (by 2nd marriage) Richard Victor, *b.* 1954,—(by 1st marriage) Diana, *b.* 1940. *Residence,*—134, Lynton Rd., W3.

WIDOW LIVING OF FIRST BARON.
MAUD LYTTON GREY (BRIGHT) (*Dowager Baroness Alvingham*) (33, Eresby House, Rutland Gate, SW7), da. of the late Charles Morgan, of Fairlight, Sussex: *m.* 1936, as his second wife, the 1st Baron, who *d.* 1955.

PREDECESSOR.—[1] ROBERT DANIEL THWAITES Yerburgh, son of the late Robert Armstrong Yerburgh, J.P., D.L. (27 years M.P. for Chester), of Caythorpe Court, Lincolnshire (the Royal approval of a Peerage to whom had been signified in 1916, but died before the patent was issued); *b.* 1899; sat as M.P. for S. Div. of Dorset (*C*) 1922-9; *cr. Baron Alvingham,* of Woodfold, co. Lancaster (peerage of United Kingdom) 1929: *m.* 1st, 1911 his cousin Dorothea Gertrude, who *d.* 1927, dau. of the late John Eardley Yerburgh, of Wavendon Lodge, Bucks; 2ndly, 1936, Maud Lytton Grey (BRIGHT), dau. of the late Charles Morgan, of Fairlight, Sussex; *d.* 1955; *s.* by his son [2] ROBERT GUY EARDLEY, 2nd Baron and present peer.

AMHERST, EARL. (Amherst.) [Earl U.K. 1826.]

By constancy and valour.

JEFFERY JOHN ARCHER AMHERST, *M.C.*, 5th Earl; *b.* Dec. 13th, 1896; *s.* 1927; ed. at Eton, and at R.M.C.; Major (retired) Coldstream Guards and Hon. Wing-Com. R.A.F.; is a Manager of British European Airways; has been Director of Associated Cos. of British European Airways Corporation since 1946; on staff of *New York Morning World* 1923-9; Commercial Air Pilot and Gen. Manager Air Line Co. 1929-39; Assist. Air Adviser to British Railways 1945-6; European War 1914-18 in France and Belgium (twice wounded, despatches, M.C., 1914-15 star, two medals), European War 1940-45 in Middle East (despatches).

Arms,—Gules, three tilting spears erect or, points argent. *Crest,*—On a mount vert three tilting spears, points upwards, one in pale and two in saltire as in the arms, entwined by a wreath of laurel, proper. *Supporters,*—*Dexter,* a Canadian Indian of copper colour, his exterior arm embowed holding an axe erect, proper, rings in his nose and ears, and bracelets on his arms and wrists argent, over his shoulder two buff belts in saltire, suspended from one his powder horn on his right side, and from the other his scalping knife on his left, before him a short apron azure, tied round the waist with a belt gules, fimbriated or, on the legs blue gaiters, seamed gold, his ankles fettered together and the chain, affixed to the bracelet on his exterior wrist, proper; *sinister*, a similar Indian, holding in his exterior hand a tomahawk, the lower end resting on his hip, and on the upper end a scalp proper.

Clubs,—Guards', Travellers'.

SISTERS LIVING.

Lady Joan Gertrude Elizabeth AMHERST, *b.* 1899 : has resumed the surname of Amherst : *m.* 1931 (marriage dissolved 1947), John Stebbing, formerly Major Oxfordshire and Bucks L.I. *Residence,*— Flat 9, 74, Elm Park Gardens, S.W.10.

Lady Mary Evelyn, *b.* 1902: *m.* 1932, Charles Casamaijor Loftus Gaussen, and has issue living, Timothy Humphreys Loftus, *b.* 1933,—David Casamaijor, *b.* 1935,—Hugh Nicholas, *b.* 1938. *Residence,*—Gringegalgona, Victoria, Australia.

PREDECESSORS.—[1] *Field-Marshal Sir* JEFFERY Amherst, *K.B.*; Com. in Ch. of British Army in North America 1758-64, and of H.M. King George III.'s Land Forces in Great Britain 1788 : cr. *Baron Amherst* (peerage of Great Britain) 1788, with remainder to his nephew, William Pitt Amherst; *d.* 1797; *s.* by his nephew [2] WILLIAM PITT, 2nd Baron, *b.* 1773; was successively Ambassador to China and Gov.-Gen. of India ; cr. *Viscount Holmesdale* and *Earl Amherst* (peerage of United Kingdom) 1826 ; *d.* Mar. 13th, 1857; *s.* by his son [3] WILLIAM PITT, 2nd Earl ; *b.* 1805: *m.* 1834, Gertrude, dau. of the late Right Rev. the Hon. Hugh Percy, D.D., Bishop of Carlisle [D. Northumberland, colls.]; *d.* March 26th, 1886; *s.* by his son [4] WILLIAM ARCHER, 3rd Earl, *b.* 1836; M.P. for W. Kent (C) 1859-68, and for Mid Kent 1868-80 ; called to House of Lords in his father's Barony of Amherst 1880: *m.* 1st, 1862, Lady Julia Maria Cornwallis, who *d.* 1883, dau. of 5th and last Earl Cornwallis ; 2ndly, 1889, Alice Dalton, who *d.* 1933, dau. of Edmund Probyn, and widow of 5th Earl of Lisburne (she *m.* 3rdly, 1914, H.S.H. Prince Jean Sapieha-Kodenski) ; *d.* 1910 ; *s.* by his brother [5] HUGH, 4th Earl, *b.* 1856 : *m.* 1896, Eleanor Clementina, who *d.* 1960, dau. of 1st Baron St. Levan ; *d.* 1927 ; *s.* by his son [6] JEFFERY JOHN ARCHER, 5th Earl and present peer ; also Viscount Holmesdale, and Baron Amherst.

AMHERST OF HACKNEY, BARON. (Cecil.) [Baron U.K. 1892.]

One heart, one way.

WILLIAM ALEXANDER EVERING CECIL, *C.B.E.*, 3rd Baron; *b.* May 31st, 1912; *s.* 1919; ed. at Eton, and at Trin. Coll., Camb. (B.A. 1933); Major (ret.) Roy. Horse Guards and a C.St.J.; 1939-45 War; C.B.E. (Civil) 1963: *m.* 1939, Margaret Eirene Clifton, dau. of the late Brig.-Gen. Howard Clifton Brown, M.P. [see Brown Bt., cr. 1863, colls.], and has issue.

Arms,—Quarterly: 1st and 4th, barry of ten argent and azure, six escutcheons, three, two, and one sable, each charged with a lion rampant argent, a mullet for difference, *Cecil*; 2nd and 3rd, gules, three tilting spears, two and one or, headed argent, *Amherst* [also quartering Daniel, Tyssen, Auchmuty, Evering, Wayland, Sidnor, Morris, Earde, Babisford, and Leach]. *Crest,*— On a chapeau gules, turned up with ermine, a garb or, supported by two lions rampant, the dexter argent, the sinister azure. *Supporters,*— Two herons proper, collared or.

Residences,—Shroner Wood, Martyr Worthy, Winchester; 29, Eaton Mews South, SW1.

SONS LIVING.

Hon. WILLIAM HUGH AMHERST (63, Park Gate Rd., SW11), *b.* Dec. 28th, 1940; ed. at Eton: *m.* 1965, Elizabeth, da. of Hugh H. Merriman, of Hazel Hall, Peaslake, Surrey, and has issue living, Hugh William Amherst, *b.* 1968,—Aurelia Margaret Amherst, *b.* 1966.

Hon. Anthony Henry Amherst (69, Park Walk, SW10), *b.* 1947; ed. at Eton: *m.* 1st, 1969 (m. diss. 1974), Fenella Jane, da. of David George Crichton, MVO [see E. Erne, colls.]; 2ndly, 1974, Jane Elizabeth Holbrook, of 4, Sloane Court East, SW3.

DAUGHTER LIVING.

Hon. Angela Margaret Amherst, *b.* 1955.

WIDOW LIVING OF BROTHER OF THIRD BARON.

Elizabeth Rohays Mary (*Lady Boyd-Rochfort*), only da. of the late Maj.-Gen. Sir James Lauderdale Gilbert Burnett of Leys, 13th Bt. (cr. 1626), CB, CMG, DSO: *m.* 1st, 1938, the Hon. Henry Kerr Auchmuty Cecil, Lt. Gordon Highlanders and Army Air Corps, who *d.* (killed in action) 1942 ; 2ndly, 1944, Capt. Sir Cecil Boyd-Rochfort, KCVO, and has issue living (by 1st m.) [see colls., infra]. *Residence,*—Kilnahard Castle, Ballyheelan, co. Cavan.

WIDOWS LIVING OF SONS OF MARY ROTHES MARGARET, BARONESS AMHERST OF HACKNEY.

Vera, 2nd dau. of Hedworth Trelawny Barclay : *m.* 1912, the Hon. Thomas James Amherst Cecil, who *d.* 1955, and has issue living [see colls., infra].

Cornelia, dau. of the late George W. Vanderbilt, of U.S.A. : *m.* 1924, the Hon. John Francis Amherst Cecil, who *d.* 1954, and has issue living [see colls., infra]. *Residence,*—

Hon. Yvonne Cornwallis, dau. of 1st Baron Cornwallis: *m.* 1923, Com. the Hon. Henry Mitford Amherst Cecil, OBE, RN, who *d.* 1962, and has issue living [see colls., infra]. *Residence,*—Green-oaks, Bishop's Waltham, Hants.

COLLATERAL BRANCHES LIVING.

Issue of the late Hon. Henry Kerr Auchmuty Cecil, Lieut. Gordon Highlanders and Army Air Corps, brother of 3rd Baron, *b.* 1914, *d.* (killed in action) 1942: *m.* 1938, Elizabeth Rohays Mary (*Lady Boyd-Rochfort*) [(ante), who *m.* 2ndly, 1944, Capt. Sir Cecil Boyd-Rochfort, KCVO], only da. of Maj.-Gen. Sir James Lauderdale Gilbert Burnett, 13th Bt. (cr. 1626), CB, CMG, DSO:—

John Strongbow Amherst (88, Warwick Gdns., W14), *b.* 1939; ed. at Eton; Lt. Scots Guards (Reserve): *m.* 1966, Elizabeth Clare, da. of C. Michael Hughes, of Penton Manor, Andover, and has issue living, Richard Strongbow Amherst *b.* 1973,—Miranda Elizabeth Rohays *b.* 1974.——James Comyn

Amherst BURNETT OF LEYS (House of Crathes, Banchory, Kincardineshire), *b.* 1941; ed. at Eton; recognized in the surname of Burnett of Leys by decree of Lyon Court 1966: *m.* 1971, Fiona Mercedes da. of Lt.-Col. Harold Pedro Joseph Phillips [see Wernher, Bt. ext.], and has issue living, Alexander *b.* 1973.——Henry Richard Amherst (posthumous) (Beech House, Cheveley, Newmarket), *b.* 1943; ed. at Canford: *m.* 1966, Julia, da. of C. F. N. Murless, of Warren Place, Newmarket, and has issue living, Arthur Noel Amherst, *b.* 1973,—Katrina Henrietta Amherst, *b.* 1971.——David Henry Amherst (posthumous) (twin) (51, Hasker St., SW3), *b.* 1943; ed. at Canford: *m.* 1966 (m. diss. 1972), the Hon. Fiona Elizabeth Cameron Corbett, da. of 2nd Baron Rowallan; 2ndly, 1973, Vanessa Josephine Bronislawna, da. of the late J. R. Gallica, and has issue living (by 1st m.), Rupert Lawrence Amherst, *b.* 1967,—Benjamin David Amherst, *b.* 1968.

Issue of the late Hon. Thomas James Amherst Cecil, 2nd son of Mary Rothes Margaret, Baroness Amherst, *b.* 1887, *d.* 1955 : *m.* 1912, Vera (ante), 2nd dau. of Hedworth Trelawny Barclay :—

Barclay James Amherst, *b.* 1913 ; late Lieut. Australian Forces : *m.* 1941 (marriage dissolved 1950), Suzanne, dau. of Frederick Dennett, of Melbourne, Australia, and has issue living, Timothy Dennett Amherst, *b.* 1942,—Jonathan Peter Hedworth, *b.* 1944. *Residence,*—Belmont Lodge, Belmont Rd., Maidenhead.

Issue of the late Hon. John Francis Amherst Cecil, 3rd son of Mary Rothes Margaret, Baroness Amherst of Hackney, *b.* 1890, *d.* 1954 : *m.* 1924, Cornelia (ante), dau. of the late George W. Vanderbilt, of U.S.A. :—

George Henry Vanderbilt, *b.* 1925: *m.* 1955, Nancy, dau. of C. D. Owen, of Biltmore, North Carolina, U.S.A., and has issue living, John Francis Amherst Vanderbilt, *b.* 1956,—Christopher Henry Amherst, *b.* 1965,—Edith Ann, *b.* 1957,—Catherine Amherst, *b.* 1959,—Margaret Elizabeth, *b.* 1961,—Louisa Owen, (twin), *b.* 1965. *Residence,*—Biltmore Estate, Biltmore, North Carolina, U.S.A.——William Amherst Vanderbilt (Biltmore Estate, Biltmore, N. Carolina, USA), *b.* 1928: *m.* 1957, Mary Lee, da. of the late John J. Ryan, of New York, and has issue living, William Amherst Vanderbilt, *b.* 1958.

Issue of the late Hon. Henry Mitford Amherst Cecil, OBE, RN, 4th son of Mary Rothes Margaret, Baroness Amherst of Hackney *b.* 1893, *d.* 1962: *m.* 1923, the Hon. Yvonne Cornwallis (ante), da. of 1st Baron Cornwallis:—

Oswald Nigel Amherst (c/o C. Hoare & Co., 37, Fleet St., EC4), *b.* 1925; ed. at RNC Dartmouth; Capt. RN; OStJ; Naval ADC to HM 1975; 1939-45 War: *m.* 1961, Annette, da. of the late Maj. Robert Edward Barclay, TD, and has issue living, Robert Barclay Amherst, *b.* 1965.——Rachel Mary, b. 1924: *m.* 1954, Brig. Mortimer Cecil Lanyon, MBE, MC, of Woodman's Farm House, W. Meon, Hants., and has issue living, Robert Henry Mortimer, *b.* 1962,—Charlotte Yvonne, *b.* 1955,— Victoria Clare, *b.* 1956.——Alison Yvonne, *b.* 1931: *m.* 1961, John Alfred Leavett-Shenley, of The Holt, Upham, Hants., and has issue living, Christopher John, *b.* 1963,—Mark Henry, *b.* 1967,— Katherine Yvonne, *b.* 1965.

PREDECESSORS.—[1] WILLIAM AMHERST Tyssen-Amherst, son of the late William George Tyssen Tyssen-Amhurst, of Didlington, Norfolk; *b.* 1885 ; assumed by Roy. licence the surnames of Tyssen-Amherst in lieu of Tyssen-Amhurst 1877 ; M.P. for W. Norfolk (C) 1880-85, and for S.-W. Div. of Norfolk 1885-92 ; cr. *Baron Amherst of Hackney*, in co. London (peerage of United Kingdom) 1892, with remainder, in default of issue male. to his el. dau. and her issue male: *m.* 1856, Margaret Susan, who *d.* 1919, only child and heiress of the late Adm. Robert Mitford, of Mitford, Northumberland, and Hunmanby Hall, York ; *d.* 1909, when the Barony devolved upon his el. dau. [2] MARY ROTHES MARGARET, *b.* 1857: *m.* 1885, Lord William Cecil, C.V.O., who *d.* 1943, 3rd son of 3rd Marquess of Exeter ; *d.* 1919 ; *s.* by her grandson [3] WILLIAM ALEXANDER EVERING (el. son of her el. son. the late Capt. the Hon. William Amherst Cecil, M.C., who *d.* (killed in action) 1914, having *m.* in 1910, Gladys (granted style and title of Baroness Amherst of Hackney 1920), da. of Col. Henry Charles Baggallay), 3rd Baron and present peer.

AMMON, BARONY OF. (Ammon.) [Extinct 1960.]

DAUGHTERS LIVING OF FIRST BARON.

Hon. Ada Mary, *MBE, b.* 1900; MBE (Civil 1960). *Residence,*—2, The Oaks, Paddockhall Rd., Haywards Heath, Sussex.

Hon. May Joyce, *b.* 1910. *Residence,*—7, Oakfield Gardens, Dulwich Wood Avenue, S.E.19.

AMORY, VISCOUNT. (Heathcoat-Amory.) [Viscount 1960, Bt. U.K. 1874.]

By love not violence

DERICK HEATHCOAT-AMORY, *KG, GCMG, TD, PC,* 1st Viscount, and 4th Baronet, 2nd son of Sir Ian Murray Heathcoat-Amory, CBE, 2nd Bt.; *b.* Dec. 26th, 1899; *s.* to Baronetcy 1972; ed. at Eton, and Ch. Ch., Oxford; Hon. LLD Exeter, and McGill; Hon. DCL Oxford; DL for Devon; Min. of Pensions 1951-53, Min. of State, Board of Trade 1953-54, Min. of Agriculture and Fisheries 1954-58 (also Min. of Food 1954-58), Chancellor of the Exchequer 1958-60, British High Commr. in Canada 1961-63; Gov. of Hudson's Bay Co. 1965-70; Chancellor of Exeter Univ. since 1971; 1939-45 War as Lt.-Col. Gen. Staff; MP for Tiverton (C) 1945-60; cr. PC 1953, *Viscount Amory,* of Tiverton, co. Devon (peerage of UK) 1960, GCMG 1961, and KG 1968.

Arms,—Quarterly : 1st and 4th argent, two bars gules ; on a bend engrailed with plain cottises sable, two annulets of the field, *Amory* ; 2nd and 3rd, vert, three piles, one reversed in base between the others issuant from the chief, each charged with a pomme, thereon a cross of the second, *Heathcoat.* Crests,—1st, the battlements of a tower or, therefrom issuant a talbot's head azure charged with two annulets fessewise, and interlaced gold, *Amory* ; 2nd, upon a mount vert, between two roses springing from the same gules, stalked and leaved proper, a pomme charged with a cross or, *Heathcoat.* Supporters.—On either side a weaver bird proper legged and purfled or, the dexter gorged with a chain pendant therefrom a portcullis, the sinister gorged with a cord pendant therefrom a purse or.

Residence,—150, Marsham Court, Westminster, S.W.1. *Clubs,*—Brooks's, Carlton.

BROTHERS LIVING.

WILLIAM, *DSO* (Calverleigh Court, Tiverton, Devon; Craig Lodge, Glendaruel, Argyll), *b.* Aug. 19th, 1901; *h.p.* to *Baronetcy only*; ed. at Eton; Lt.-Col. KRRC; a Member of H.M. Bodyguard of Hon. Corps of Gentlemen-at-Arms 1952-56; 1939-45 War in Middle East, Italy, and France (DSO); DSO 1943: *m.* 1933, Margaret Isabella Dorothy Evelyn, da. of Col. Sir Arthur Havelock James Doyle, 4th Bt., and has issue living, Ian, *b.* 1942: *m.* 1972, Frances Louise, da. of Jocelyn Francis Brian Pomeroy [see V. Harberton, colls.],—Charles, *b.* 1945,—Diana Chrystal, *b.* 1938: *m.* 1962, Peter Sichel, of Chateau d'Angludet, Cantanac, Gironde, France, and has issue living, Allan Gordon *b.* 1962, James William *b.* 1963, Charles Edward (twin) *b.* 1963, Benjamin Pierre *b.* 1966, David Mark *b.* 1968,—Catherine (twin), *b.* 1945: *m.* 1967, Michael Godfrey Melvin Groves (Calverleigh Court, Tiverton Devon), and has issue living, Alistair Michael William *b.* 1968, Henry Grenville Havelock *b.* 1971.

Roderick, *MC* (Oswaldkirk Hall, York), *b.* 1907; ed. at Eton; Brig. late Royals; High Sheriff of Yorks. 1971-72; 1939-45 War in Middle East, Italy and France (MC): *m.* 1947, Sonia Myrtle, da. of the late Commodore Edward Conyngham Denison, MVO, RN [see B. Londesborough, colls.], and widow of Maj. Edgar Fitzgerald Heathcoat-Amory, R. Devon Yeo. [see infra], and has issue living, David Philip, *b.* 1949,—Bridget Alexandra, *b.* 1952.

WIDOW LIVING OF SECOND BARONET.

Joyce (*Lady Heathcoat-Amory*) (Knigtshayes Court, Tiverton; Glenfernate Lodge, Blairgowrie, Perthshire), only da. of Newton Wethered, of Brook Corner, Brook, Surrey: *m.* 1937, Capt. Sir John Heathcoat-Amory, 3rd Bt., who *d.* 1972.

COLLATERAL BRANCHES LIVING.
(Male line in remainder to Baronetcy only).
Grandchildren of the late Lieut.-Col. Harry William Ludovic Heathcoat Heathcoat-Amory (infra):—
Issue of the late Richard Frank Heathcoat-Amory, *b.* 1903 *d.* 1957: *m.* 1938, the Hon. Margaret Irene Graenor Scott-Ellis (Hele Manor, Dulverton, Som.; 88, Cadogan Place, SW1, da. of 8th Baron Howard de Walden:—

Ian Mark, *b.* 1941; ed. at Eton, and at Ch. Ch., Oxford.——Evelyn Helen, *b.* 1939: *m.* 1960, Martin Wakefield Jacomb, and has issue living, Matthew Barnabas Wakefield, *b.* 1963,—Thomas Richard *b.* 1964,—Emma Félise, *b.* 1961. *Residence*, 45, Canonbury Sq., N.1.——Rachel Belinda, *b.* 1946: *m.* 1973, Christopher Joseph Ryan, of 208, Broomwood Rd., SW11.

Issue of the late Lieut.-Col. Harry William Ludovic Heathcoat Heathcoat-Amory, 3rd son of 1st baronet, *b.* 1870; *d.* 1945: *m.* 1st, 1898, Evelyn Mary, who *d.* 1929, da. of the late Edward James Stanley [E. Derby, colls.]; 2ndly, 1931, Marjorie Una, who *d.* 1973, da. of the Rev. Edgar Astley Milne, R. of Compton Valence, Dorset, and widow of E. P. Gundry, of Chilfrome, Dorchester:—
(By 1st marriage) Mary Millicent, *b.* 1907: *m.* 1930, Capt. Adam Trevor Smail, 11th Hussars, and has issue living, Simon Trevor, *b.* 1934; ed at Eton; late Capt. 11th Hussars: *m.* 1960, Margaret, da. of the late Maj. the Hon. Arthur Bernard John Grenfell [see B. Grenfell, colls.], and has issue living, Lucy Jane *b.* 1962. *Residence*, Rock, Exebridge, Dulverton, Som.

Grandchildren of the late Major Ludovic Heathcoat-Amory, 5th son of 1st baronet:—
Issue of the late Major Edgar Fitzgerald Heathcoat-Amory, Roy. Devon Yeo., *b.* 1917, *d.* (killed in action in Normandy) 1944: *m.* 1940, Sonia Myrtle [who *m.* 2ndly, 1947, Brigadier Roderick Heathcoat-Amory, MC, The Royals (ante)], only da. of Commodore Edward Conyngham Denison, MVO, RN [see B. Londesborough, colls.]:—
Michael FitzGerald (Chevithorne Barton, Tiverton, Devon), *b.* 1941; ed. at Eton, and Ch. Ch., Oxford: *m.* 1965 (m. diss. 1970), Harriet Mary Sheila, da. of the late Lt.-Gen. Sir Archibald Edward Nye, GSCI, GCMG, GCIE, KCB, KBE, MC [see E. Ranfurly, colls.], and has issue living, Edward Fitzgerald, *b.* 1967.——Amanda Mary (posthumous) (*Viscountess Garmoyle*) (Queen Hoo Hall, Tewin, Herts.), *b.* 1944: *m.* 1964, Simon Dallas, Viscount Garmoyle, el. son of 5th Earl Cairns.

PREDECESSORS [1] JOHN HEATHCOAT Heathcoat-Amory, only son of Samuel Amory, Solicitor, of The Priory, Homerton, and Portland Place, London, by Anne, da. and co-heir of John Heathcoat, MP, of Bolham, Devon; *b.* 1810: partner, J. Heathcoat Amory & Co., Lace Manufacturers; MP for Tiverton (*Lib.*) 1868-85; assumed by Roy. Licence the additional surname and arms of Heath-coat, and cr. a *Baronet* 1874: *m.* 1863, Henrietta Mary, who *d.* 1923, only da. of William Unwin, *d.* 1914; *s.* by his el. son [2] *Sir* IAN MURRAY HEATHCOAT, CBE, *b.* 1865; High Sheriff of Devon, 1924: *m.* 1893, Alexandra Georgina, OBE, who *d.* 1942, el. da. of Vice-Adm. Henry George Seymour; CB [M. Hertford, colls.]; *d.* 1931; *s.* by his el. son [3] *Sir* JOHN, 3rd Bt.; High Sheriff of Devon 1942; Chm. of John Heathcoat & Co.; *d.* 1972; *s.* by his brother [4] DERICK, *KG, GCMG, TD, PC*, 1st Viscount and present peer.

AMPTHILL, BARON. (Russell.) [Baron U.K. 1881.]

GEOFFREY DENIS ERSKINE RUSSELL, 4th Baron; *b.* Oct. 15th, 1921; *s.* 1973; ed. at Stowe; 1939-45 War as Capt. Irish Gds.; he petitioned HM the Queen for a Writ of Summons as Baron Ampthill on the death of the 3rd Baron, which has not been granted at the time of going to press: *m.* 1st, 1946 (m. diss. 1971), Susan Mary, da. of the late Hon. Charles John Frederic Winn [see B. St. Oswald, colls.]; 2ndly, 1972, Elisabeth Anne Marie, da. of the late Claude Henri Mallon, of Paris, and has issue by 1st m.

Arms.—Argent, a lion rampant gules, on a chief sable three escal ops argent, a mullet or for difference. **Crest.**—A goat statant, armed and unguled or, charged on the body with a mullet sable for difference. **Supporters.**—*Dexter*, a lion gules, ducally gorged and charged on the shoulder with a mullet or; *sinister*, an heraldic antelope gules, armed, crined and tufted or, ducally gorged, and charged on the shoulder with a mullet also or.

CHE·SARA·SARA

What will be, will be.

Residence,—24 Egerton Terr., SW3. *Club*,—Guards'.

SONS LIVING. *(By 1st marriage.)*
Hon. DAVID WHITNEY ERSKINE, *b.* May 27th, 1947; ed. at Stowe.
Hon. Anthony John Mark, *b.* 1952; ed. at Stowe.

DAUGHTER LIVING *(By 1st marriage.)*
Hon. Vanessa Mary Linda, *b.* 1960.

HALF BROTHER LIVING.
Hon. John Hugo Trenchard (6, Springfield Rd., NW8), *b.* 1950; ed. at Eton.

HALF SISTER LIVING.
Hon. Georgiana Adeline Villiers (6, Springfield Rd., NW8), *b.* 1953.

UNCLES LIVING *(Sons of 2nd Baron).*
Hon. Sir Guy Herbrand Edward, *G.B.E., K.C.B., D.S.O., b.* 1898; Adm. (retired); Dardanelles 1915 (despatches), European War 1939-44 (despatches, G.B.E., D.S.O.); became Com. Naval Staff Coll. 1932, Flag Officer Comdg. 2nd Cruiser Squadron 1947, and Adm. Comdg. Reserves 1949; was Com.-in-Ch., Far East 1951-53, Second Sea Lord of the Admiralty and Ch. of Naval Personnel 1953-5, and Comdt. Imperial Defence Coll. 1956-8; First and Principal Naval A.D.C. to H.M. 1954-58, and Chm., National Assocn. of Boys' Clubs 1958-63, of Council of Missions to Seamen since 1960, of Radley Coll. Council 1964-69, and of Exec. Cttee. of Gordon Boys' Sch. 1965-69; OBE (Mil) 1943, DSO 1944, CB (Mil) 1948, KCB (Mil) 1951, GBE (Mil) 1953: *m.* 1939, the Hon. (Helen) Elizabeth Blades, da. of 1st Baron Ebbisham and has issue living, James Rowland (Broome Cottage Betchworth, Surrey), *b.* 1940; ed. at Radley, and at Clare Coll., Camb. (MA, MB, BChir, D.Obst.RCOG); Surg.-Lt. RN: *m.* 1965, Glenys Pearl, da. of H. G. Lofting, of Nairobi, and has issue living, Robert James *b.* 1966, Katherine May *b.* 1968, Elizabeth Sarah *b.* 1970, Mary Glenys *b.* 1973,—Oliver Henry (Sudbrook Lodge Ham Common, Richmond, Surrey), *b.* 1942; ed. at Radley, and at Magdalene Coll., Camb.; a Page of Honour to HM 1957-59: *m.* 1967, Clare Nancy, da. of Maj. Sir Ewan George Macpherson-Grant, 6th Bt., and has issue living, Guy Ewan *b.* 1968, Edward Oliver *b.* 1970, Lucy Clare Nancy *b.* 1972,—Margaret Elizabeth, *b.* 1945. *Residence,*—The Old Vicarage, Shamley Green, Guildford, Surrey. *Club,*—United Service.

Hon. Edward Wriothesley Curzon, *O.B.E., b.* 1901 ; ed. at Eton, and at Trin. Coll., Camb. (B.A. 1922), formerly Managing Editor of *Morning Post* ; sometime Wing-Com. R.A.F. Vol. Reserve; O.B.E (Mil.) 1946 : *m.* 1941, Barbara, dau. of the late Baron Korff, of Russia, and has issue living, Diana, *b.* 1943.—Margaret Angela, *b.* 1946. *Residences,*—2601, Foxhall Road, Washington, D.C., U.S.A.; Pony's Point, Iona, C.B.1, Nova Scotia, Canada. *Clubs,*—Metropolitan (Washington, D.C.), Chevy Chase.

Hon. Leopold Oliver, *C.B.E., T.D., b.* 1907 ; ed. at Eton ; is Hon. Brigadier late Bedfordshire and Herts Regt. (T.A.) ; was Director of British Institute of Management 1947-56 ; has been Director-Gen. of Cement and Concrete Asso., since 1958 ; OBE (Mil) 1944, CBE (Civil) 1970: *m.* 1935 (m. diss. 1954), Rosemary, da. of the late Capt. Charles John Wintour, RN. *Residences,*—Kettlebaston, nr. Bildeston, Suffolk; 17, Onslow Sq., SW7. *Clubs,*—Brooks's, Buck's, Beefsteak, Pratt's.

AUNT LIVING *(Daughter of 2nd Baron).*
Hon. Phyllis Margaret, *O.B.E., b.* 1909; an O.St.J.; a temporary Lady-in-Waiting to H.R.H. The Princess Royal 1963-65; 1939-45 War with British Red Cross So. (despatches, OBE); OBE (Civil) 1946: *m.* 1940 (marriage annulled on her petition 1942), Capt. William George Preston Thorold, who *d.* 1943 [Thorold, Bt., colls.]. *Residence,*—55, Ebury Mews, SW1.

MOTHER LIVING.
Christabel Hulme (Lisduff, Craughwell, co. Galway), da. of the late Lt.-Col. John Hart, of Broadhurst, Heathfield, Sussex [Erskine Bt., colls.]: *m.* 1918 (m. diss. 1937), the 3rd Baron, who *d.* 1973.

WIDOW LIVING OF THIRD BARON.
ADELINE MARY CONSTANCE *(Adeline, Baroness Ampthill)* (6, Springfield Rd., NW8), el. da. of the Rev. Canon Henry Evelyn Hone, late V. of Godalming: *m.* 1948, as his 3rd wife, the 3rd Baron, who *d.* 1973.

COLLATERAL BRANCHES LIVING.

Issue of the late Hon. Sir Odo William Theophilus Villiers Russell, KCMG, KOVO, CB, 2nd son of 1st Baron, *b.* 1870, *d.* 1951: *m.* 1910, Countess Marie Louise Ernestine, who *d.* 1966, da. of Count Rudolf Karl Caspar von Rex:—
Cosmo Rex Ivor (Parapet House, Lenham, Kent), *b.* 1911; ed. at Eton, and at Trin. Coll., Oxford; Public Relations Consultant Dep. Dir. of Information, Council of Europe 1949-56, and Head, Political Studies Div., Secretariat-General of Council of Europe, 1956-63; a Public Relations Consultant 1963-71, since when a Reviser and Translator, European Commn.; Maj. Queen's Westminsters, KRRC (TA); sometime a Councillor of New Windsor, and a Co. Councillor of Berks.; Council of Europe Commemoration Medal; 1939-45 War (despatches, American Bronze Star Medal, Officer of Order of Orange Nassau of the Netherlands with swords): *m.* 1941, Agnes Mary, da. of the late Rev. Canon Richard Edward Parsons [see E. Rosse, colls.], and has issue living, Nicholas Odo Richard Desmond, *b.* 1946; ed. at Strasbourg, Brickwall Sch., Northiam, and Munich Univ.; translator, European Integration Dept., FCO 1972,—John Drummond Athelstan (Waterloo House, Pye Corner, Ulcombe, Kent), *b.* 1948; ed. at Strasbourg, and Brickwall Sch., Northiam; Lt. IG Reserve; European Marketing Exec. 1974: *m.* 1968, Toril, da. of the late Finn Tennfjord, of Norway, and has issue living, Maikki Natacha *b.* 1969, Natacha Ann *b.* 1971, Tatiana Agnes *b.* 1973,—Cecilia Hester Marie Louise Constance, *b.* 1942: *m.* 1965, Peter Robert Nutting, of 31, Pembroke Rd., W8 [see Nutting, Bt., colls.],—Jennifer Rose Ann, *b.* 1945: *m.* 1966, Julian Goldsmid, of Ricks, Rotherwick, Hook, Hants., and has issue living, Tara Alexandra *b.* 1970,—Theodosia Mary, *b.* 1952,—Katharine Agnes, *b.* 1955.——Alaric Charles William, *b.* 1912; ed. at Eton; a Member of the London Stock Exchange, and Maj. Queen's Westminsters KRRC (TA): *m.* 1940, Iris Charmian, da. of Noel Van Raaite [see Graham, Bt., colls., cr. 1783], and has issue living, Michael Noel, *b.* 1941,—Amanda Charmian, *b.* 1946: *m.* 1966, Martyn A. Hedley of 18, Halsey St., SW3. *Residence,*—20, Mulberry Walk, Chelsea, SW3. *Clubs,*—Buck's, Pratt's.——David Hastings Gerald, *b.* 1915; late Lt. RNVR: *m.* 1940, Hester Clere, da. of the late Rev. Canon Richard Parsons [see E. Rosse, colls.], and has issue living, Wriothesley David Xavier, *b.* 1941; ed. at Eton and Trin. Coll., Dublin,—Rupert Edward Odo (88, Cambridge St., SW1; Ski Club of Gt. Britain), *b.* 1944; ed. at Selwyn House Sch., Montreal, and Rannoch Sch., Perths.; Solicitor 1973; a Member of Law Soc. *Residence,*—88, Cambridge St., SW1.

Issue of the late Lt.-Col. the Hon. Victor Alexander Frederick Villiers Russell, CBE, son of 1st Baron, *b.* 1874, *d.* 1965: *m.* 1905, Annora Margaret Bromley, who *d.* 1949, da. of the late George Edward Martin, of Ham Court, Upton-on-Severn:—
Rosemary, *b.* 1907: *m.* 1935, Lt.-Col. William Douglas Gosling, MBE, TD, RA (TA), of Thrimley House, Farnham, Bishops Stortford [M. Lothian], and has issue living, Petronella Margaret, *b.* 1936: *m.* 1965, Charles William Humphreys, of The Folly, Farnham Green, Bishops Stortford, and has issue living, Christopher Charles *b.* 1968, Thomas William *b.* 1972, Lucinda Ferelith *b.* 1966, Susannah Rosemary *b.* 1970,—Lucy Annora, *b.* 1938,—Gwendolin Frances, *b.* 1946: *m.* 1972, Thomas O. H. Lyons, of 115, Knatchbull Rd., SE5.——Angela Irene, *b.* 1912: *m.* 1938, Robert Alexander Bennet Gosling, of Mutton Hall, Wetherden, Stowmarket, Suffolk [M. Lothian], and has issue living, Alexander Bennet (The Old Manor House, Linton, Cambridge), *b.* 1940: *m.* 1963, Mary,

yr. da. of Duncan Macrae, of 22, The Little Boltons, SW10, and has issue living, Henrietta Mary,
b. 1966, Louisa Katherine b. 1968,—Andrew Edward, b. 1944: m. 1966, Rosemary Ailsa, el. da. of
Col.John Lyon Corbett Winder, OBE, MC, of Vaynor Park, Berriew, Welshpool, and has issue living,
Amanda Sophia Jane b. 1968, Catherine Angela Rose b. 1970,—Robert Anthony (Pulham Cottage,
Wetherden, Stowmarket, Suffolk), b. 1948: m. 1969, Clarissa Beatrice, yr. da. of Maj. John Whit-
combe, of 7, Astell St., SW3 [see E. Halifax, colls.], and has issue living, Richard Bennet b. 1972,
Charlotte Arabella Ida b. 1974,—Annabel Victoria, b. 1942: m. 1965, Nathaniel Charles Sebag-
Montefiore, and has issue living, Matthew Oliver b. 1971,—Victoria Alice b. 1969.

Issue of the late Brig.-Gen. the Hon. Alexander Victor Frederick Villiers Russell
(twin), CMG, MVO, 4th son of 1st Baron, b. 1874, d. 1965: m. 1909, Marjorie
Gladys, who d. 1949, da. of the late Claude Hume Campbell Guinness:—
William Rodney Villiers, MC (Pointers South, Cobham, Surrey), b. 1914; ed. at Wellington, Lt.-Col.
(ret.) Rifle Bde.; 1939-45 War in Burma (MC): m. 1950, Diana Marigold, da. of Arthur Trafford,
of Paignton, and has issue living, Rupert Alick Villiers, b. 1951,—Sarah Caroline Villiers, b. 1956.——
Stephen Alexander Villiers (Godford Land, Honiton, S. Devon), b. 1916; ed. at Wellington: Capt.
Black Watch; 1939-45 War (prisoner): m. 1945, Alisa Mary Pilcher, and has issue living, John
Alick Stephen Villiers, b. 1946,—Camilla Mary Louise, b. 1949,—Lucy Marjorie Eileen, b. 1954.

PREDECESSORS.—[1] Lord Odo William Leopold Russell, G.C.B., G.C.M.G., P.C.,
brother of 9th Duke of Bedford, b. 1829; the eminent diplomatist; was Sec. at Constantinople
Washington, and Florence, and afterwards for twelve years H.M.'s Representative at Rome ;
went on Special Mission to Versailles during Franco-Prussian War 1870 ; joint Plenipotentiary
(with Earl of Beaconsfield and Marquess of Salisbury) at Berlin Congress 1878; was
Ambassador to the Court of Germany 1871-84; cr. Baron Ampthill, of Ampthill, co. Bedford
(peerage of United Kingdom) 1881: m. 1868, Lady Emily Theresa Villiers, who d. 1927, dau.
of 4th Earl of Clarendon; d. 1884; s. by his son [2] Oliver Arthur Villiers, G.C.S.I.,
G.C.I.E., 2nd Baron, b. 1869; was Gov. of Madras 1899-1906 (Viceroy and Gov.-Gen. of India ad
interim 1904); European War 1914-19 (despatches thrice, Brevet Col.): m. 1894, Lady Margaret Lygon, C.I., G.C.V.O., G.B.E., who d. 1957, dau. of 6th Earl Beauchamp; d. 1935; s. by his
el. son [3] JOHN HUGO, CBE, 3rd Baron, b. 1896; Cdr. RN: m. 1st, 1918 (m. diss. 1937), da. of Lt.-Col.
John Hart, of Broadhurst, Heathfield, Sussex [Erskine, Bt., colls.]; 2ndly, 1937, Sibell Faithfull,
who d. 1947, da. of Thomas Wilkinson Lumley; 3rdly, 1948, Adeline Mary Constance, el. da. of the
Rev. Canon Henry Evelyn Hone, V. of Godalming; d. 1973; s. by his el. son [4] GEOFFREY DENIS
ERSKINE, 4th Baron and present peer.

AMULREE, BARON. (Mackenzie.) [Baron U.K. 1929.]

BASIL WILLIAM SHOLTO MACKENZIE, M.D.,
2nd Baron, b. July 25th, 1900; s. 1942; ed. at
Lancing, and at Gonville and Caius Coll.,
Camb. (B.A. 1922, M.A. 1925, M.B. and
B.Ch. 1927, M.D. 1936); M.R.C.S. England
and L.R.C.P. London 1925, M.R.C.P. London
1928, F.R.C.P. London 1946; appointed Ch.
Liberal Whip in House of Lords 1955.

Arms,—Azure, a stag's head caboshed or, on a chief
ermine a rose gules, barbed and seeded proper, between
two millrinds of the second. Crest,—A dexter cubit
arm charged with a thistle leaved and slipped and grasping
in the hand a sword point upwards proper, pommel and
hilt or. Supporters,—On either side an eagle reguardant
proper collared or, that on the dexter holding in the beak
a sprig of mountain ash fructed proper, and that on the
sinister a sprig of myrtle also fructed proper.

Residence,—18, Egerton Terrace, S.W.3.

SISTER LIVING.
Hon. Angela Lilian, b. 1905: m. 1931, Patrick James
Eggar. Residence,—The Manor House, Ditcheat ,Somer-
set.

PREDECESSOR—[1] Rt. Hon. Sir WILLIAM WARRENDER Mackenzie, G.B.E., K.C., son of the late
Robert Mackenzie; b. 1860; was Pres. of Industrial Court 1919-26, Chm. British Industrial Mission to
U.S.A. and Canada 1926-7, and of Roy. Commn. on Liquor Laws 1929-31, and Sec. of State for
Air Oct. 1930 to Aug. 1931, and (in National Govt.) Aug. to Nov. 1931; Chm. of Roy. Commn. on
Newfoundland 1933; Chm. of Council of Roy. So. of Arts 1937-9: cr. Baron Amulree, of Strath-
braan, co. Perth (peerage of United Kingdom) 1929: m. 1897, Lilian, who d. 1916, el. dau. of the
late W. H. Bradbury; d. 1942: s. by his only son [2] BASIL WILLIAM SHOLTO, 2nd Baron, and
present peer.

AMWELL, BARON. (Montague.) [Baron U.K. 1947.]

FREDERICK NORMAN MONTAGUE, 2nd Baron, b. Nov. 6th, 1912; s. 1966;
an ARAeS: m. 1939, Kathleen Elizabeth, da. of Arthur Percival Fountain,
and has issue.
Residence,—34, Halliford Rd., Sunbury on Thames, Middlesex.

ON LIVING.
Hon. KEITH NORMAN (57, Bridgewater Rd., Berkhamsted, Herts.), b. April 1st, 1943; ed. at Ealing
Gram. Sch. and Nottingham Univ. (BSc); C.Eng., MICE, AMInst HE, FGS: m. 1970, Mary, only
da. of Frank Palfreyman, of Potters Bar, Herts.

DAUGHTER LIVING.
Hon. Sheila Elizabeth, b. 1949.

SISTERS LIVING.
Hon. Constance, b. 1915 : m. 1938, Albert Henry Cecil Slade, and has issue living, David, b. 1943,—
Lesley, b. 1946,—Stephanie, b. 1956. Residence,—27, Howitt Road, N.W.3.
Hon. Betty, b. 1920: m. 1941, John Forbes Dudley, and has issue living, Lysbeth, b. 1947. Residence,
—Step Aside, Upper Hayesden, Tonbridge, Kent.

PREDECESSOR.—[1] FREDERICK Montague, CBE, son of John Montague, of Clerkenwell, E.C.,
b. 1876; Under-Sec. of State for Air 1929-31, Parl. Sec. Min. of Transport 1940-41, and Min. of
Aircraft Production 1941-42; M.P. for W. Islington (Lab.) 1923-31, and 1935-47; cr. Baron
Amwell, of Islington, co. London (peerage of UK) 1947: m. 1911, Constance, who d. 1964, da. of
James Craig, of Runcorn; d. 1966; s. by his only son [2] FREDERICK NORMAN, 2nd Baron and
present peer.

ANCASTER, EARL OF. (Heathcote-Drummond-Willoughby.) [Earl U.K.
1892, Baron E. 1313, Bt. G.B. 1733.]

[Name pronounced "Hethcut-Drummond-Willowby."]

Loyalty binds me.

GILBERT JAMES HEATHCOTE-DRUM-
MOND-WILLOUGHBY, *KCVO, TD*, 3rd
Earl, 26th Baron Willoughby de
Eresby, 4th Baron Aveland, and 8th
Baronet; *b.* Dec. 8th, 1907; *s.* 1951;
ed. at Eton and at Magdalene Coll.,
Camb. (BA 1929, MA 1954); is Maj.
RA (TA); on resignation of his father,
1950, became Joint Hereditary Lord
Great Chamberlain (acting for reign of
King George VI); European War 1939-
45 (despatches); a J.P. for Parts of
Kesteven, Lord-Lieut. for Lincolnshire,
and a K.St.J.; has been an Alderman
for Kesteven Co. Council since 1954;
bore St. Edward's Staff at Coronation
of Queen Elizabeth II; sat as M.P. for
Rutland and Stamford Div. of Parts of
Kesteven and Rutland (*C*) Nov. 1933
to Feb. 1950; called to House of Lords
in his father's Barony of Willoughby
de Eresby Jan. 1951; KCVO 1971: *m.* 1933, the Hon. (Nancy) Phyllis Louise
Astor, who *d.* 1975, da. of 2nd Viscount Astor, and has issue.

Arms,—Quarterly: 1st and 4th or, fretty azure, *Willoughby*; 2nd or, three bars wavy gules,
Drummond; 3rd ermine, three pomeys, each charged with a cross or, *Heathcote*. Crests,—
1st, a Saracen's head affronté, couped at the shoulders proper, ducally crowned or, *Willoughby*; 2nd, on a
ducal coronet or, a sleuth hound argent, collared and leashed gules, *Drummond*; 3rd, on a mural crown
azure, a pomey as in the arms, between two wings displayed ermine, *Heathcote*. Supporters,—(for
Barony of Willoughby de Eresby)—*Dexter*, a grey friar habited proper, holding in his exterior hand a
crutch and rosary or; *sinister*, a wild man wreathed round the temples and loins with oak
proper.

Seats—Grimsthorpe, Bourne, Lincolnshire; Drummond Castle, Crieff, Perthshire.

DAUGHTER LIVING (*h.p.* to *Barony of Willoughby de Eresby*).
Lady NANCY JANE MARIE, *b.* Dec. 1st, 1934. *Residence,*—Grimsthorpe, Bourne, Lincs.

SISTERS LIVING.
Lady Catherine Mary Clementina. *b.* 1906: *m.* 1st, 1935 (marriage dissolved 1948), John St. Maur
Ramsden, who *d.* 1948, el. son of Sir John Frencheville Ramsden, 6th Bt. [see Pennington-Ramsden,
Bt.]; 2ndly, 1948, Charles Wedderburn Hume. *Residence,*—Hunting Ridge Farm, Charlottesville,
Virginia, U.S.A.
Lady Priscilla, *b.* 1909: *m.* 1939, Col. Sir John Renton Aird, 3rd Bt., MVO, MC, late Gren. Gds., who *d.*
1973. *Residence,*—Forest Lodge, The Great Park, Windsor.

WIDOW LIVING OF SON OF FIRST EARL.
Pamela May, dau. of the late Brig.-Gen. Sir Walter Charteris Ross, K.B.E., C.B., C.M.G., of
Cromarty: *m.* 1st, 1913, Lieut.-Com. the Hon. Peter Robert Heathcote-Drummond-Willoughby,
who *d.* (killed in action) 1914; 2ndly, 1917, Capt. William Duncan Phipps, CVO, RN, who *d.* 1967.

COLLATERAL BRANCHES LIVING.
(*In remainder to Barony of Willoughby de Eresby only.*)
Granddaughter of the late Brig.-Gen. the Hon. Charles Strathavon Heathcote-
Drummond-Willoughby, CB, CMG (infra):—
Issue of the late Charles Peregrine Heathcote-Drummond-Willoughby, *b.* 1905, *d.* 1965: *m.*
1939, Anne Eveline (1311, Beach Av., Vancouver 5, BC, Canada), da. of the late James
Fitzsimmons:—
Anne Leucen, *b.* 1949.

Issue of the late Brig.-Gen. the Hon. Charles Strathavon Heathcote-Drummond-Willoughby
C.B. C.M.G., 2nd son of 1st Earl, *b.* 1870, *d.* 1949: *m.* 1903, Lady Muriel Agnes Stuart
Erskine, who *d.* 1967, da. of 14th Earl of Buchan:—
Rosalie (*Baroness Nugent*) (21, Chelsea Sq., SW3), *b.* 1908: *m.* 1935, the 1st Baron Nugent, who *d.*
1973, when the title became ext.

Issue of the late Lady Margaret Mary Heathcote-Drummond-Willoughby, 2nd da. of 1st
Earl, *b.* 1866, *d.* 1957: *m.* 1902, Gideon Macpherson Rutherford, Bar.-at-law, who *d.*
1907:—
Margaret Evelyn, *b.* 1903: *m.* 1930, Lieut.-Com. Reginald Arthur Forbes, R.N. (retired), from whom
she obtained a divorce 1944 [see Stuart-Forbes, Bt.]. *Residence,*— Cottage Farm, Lovedean Lane,
Horndean, Hants.——Christine Jane, *b.* 1906: *m.* 1934, Group Capt. W. H. Poole, A.F.C., M.M.,
RAF, who *d.* 1971. *Residence,*—4, Leicester Close, Northfield End, Henley-on-Thames.

Issue of the late Lady Cecilie Heathcote-Drummond-Willoughby, 4th da. of 1st Earl, *b.*
1874, *d.* 1960: *m.* 1896, Major Thomas Clarence Edward Goff, J.P., D.L., Roy. Scots,
who *d.* 1949 [E. Munster, colls.]:—
Elizabeth Moyra, *b.* 1897. *Residences,*—46, Pont St., SW1; The Courts, Holt, Wilts.

Issue of the late Lady Mary Adelaide Heathcote-Drummond-Willoughby, yst. da. of 1st
Earl, *b.* 1878, *d.* 1960: *m.* 1903, the 14th Earl of Dalhousie, who *d.* 1928:—
See E. Dalhousie.

(*In remainder to Baronetcy only.*)
Grandchildren of Robert Heathcote (*b.* 1843), only son of George Augustus Frederick
Heathcote, el. son of Robert Heathcote, 3rd son of 3rd baronet:—
Issue of the late Lt.-Col. Robert Evelyn Manners Heathcote, DSO, *b.* 1884, *d.* 1970: *m.* 1st,
1912, Edith Millicent (who obtained a divorce 1922), da. of the late William Walton, of
Horsley Priory, Nailsworth, Glos.; 2ndly, 1922, Nesta (Manton Hall, Oakham; Lob-
thorpe, Lincs.), da. of the late Evan Hanbury, of Braunston Manor, Oakham:—
(By 1st m.) (GILBERT) SIMON, CBE (Manton Hall, Oakham; Upton Dean, Upton, nr. Andover; Army and
Navy Club), *b.* Sept. 21st, 1913; *h.p.* to *Baronetcy*; ed. at Eton; Brig. (ret.) RA; CRA 50th Div.
1960-62, Ch. of Staff, Middle East, Command 1962-64, and Brig. RA, Scottish Command 1964-66:
1939-45 War in N-W Europe; MBE (Mil) 1945, CBE (Mil) 1964: *m.* 1939, Patricia Margaret, da. of
Brig. James Travers Leslie, MC, and has issue living, Mark Simon Robert, *b.* 1941; ed. at Eton, and
Magdalene Coll., Camb.,—Joanna, *b.* 1947.——Evelyn Suzanne Valhalla, *b.* 1917: *m.* 1st, 1938 (m. dis.

1952), Henry Lester Louis Morriss, who *d.* 1963; 2ndly, 1952, Robert John Colling, of Hodcott House, W. Ilsley, Newbury, and has issue living, (by 1st m.), Hugo Henry, *b.* 1939,—Amanda Mary, *b.* 1942.——(by 2nd m.) Diana Nesta (Belton House, Uppingham, Rutland), *b.* 1923: *m.* 1953, Michael James Mellows, BA, who *d.* 1974, and has issue living, Anna Caroline *b.* 1954,—Julia Dominica, *b.* 1956,—Antonia Philippa, *b.* 1960.

> **Grandchildren of the late Rev. Thomas Heathcote, 2nd son of the late Robert Heathcote, 3rd son of 3rd baronet (ante):—**
> Issue of the late Frank Augustus George Heathcote, *b.* 1871, *d.* 1939: *m.* 1902, Enid Muriel, who *d.* 1944, youngest dau. of Bennet Rothes Langton, of Langton Hall, Spilsby, Lincolnshire:—

Dorothy Enid, *b.* 1903 : *m.* 1931, James Hanley, novelist, and has issue living, Liam Powys, *b.* 1933. *Residence,*—51, Lissenden Mansions, Highgate Rd., NW5.

> Issue of the late William Lionel Heathcote, *b.* 1874, *d.* 1961: *m.* 1919, Alice Mabel, who *d.* 1972, dau. of the late Rev. John Dand Todd, R. of Newton Folkingham:—

Gilbert Michael, *b.* 1924 : *m.* 1953, Dorothy, da. of H. W. Pratchett, and has issue living, Jane Michele, *b.* 1954,—Amanda Joy, *b.* 1959. *Residence,*—Janda Cote, 8, Armand Close, Nascot Wood, Watford, Herts.

> **Grandsons of the late John Moyer Heathcote, el. son of the late John Heathcote, M.P. (*b.* 1834), son of the late John Moyer Heathcote, grandson of 2nd baronet:—**
> Issue of the late Arthur Ridley Heathcote, *b.* 1877 ; *d.* 1951: *m.* 1909, Margaret Georgina, who *d.* 1944, only surviving dau. of the late Horace Broke, of Gladwyns, Essex:—

John Horace Broke, *b.* 1910 ; ed. at Eton, and at Trin. Coll., Camb. (B.A. 1932): *m.* 1949, Dorelle Geraldine, da. of the late Lt.-Col. Gerald Dominic Rice, DSO, of Fermoy, co Cork, and has issue living, Miranda Lydia, *b.* 1950,—Venetia Catherine, *b.* 1951. *Residence,*—Conington House, Peterborough.——Norman Richard, *b.* 1914; ed. at Eton, and at Trin. Coll., Camb.: *m.* 1946, Margaret Enid, da. of Alan Keith Burnett, of Durban, S. Africa, and has issue living, Richard John, *b.* 1951,—Katherine Louise, *b.* 1952,—Diana Elizabeth (twin), *b.* 1952. *Address,*—c/o Rhodesia House, 429, Strand, WC2.

PREDECESSORS.—[1] ROBERT Willoughby, having been actively engaged in the French any Scottish wars of Edward I., was summoned to Parliament of England as a Baron 1313; *s.* bp his son [2] JOHN, 2nd Baron ; was one of the principal commanders at the battle of Crécy; summoned to Parliament 1332-49; *s.* by his son [3] JOHN, 3rd Baron ; served at Poictiers; *d.* 1373; *s.* by his son [4] ROBERT, 4th Baron ; *d.* 1390; *s.* by his son [5] WILLIAM, 5th Baron ; was a Peer of Parliament when Richard II. made a formal resignation in 1399; *s.* by his son [6] ROBERT, K.G., 6th Baron ; an eminent military commander, *temp.* Henry VI.; cr. *Baron Willoughby of Monblay and Beaumesquil* and *Earl of Vendome and Beaumont,* in France, which titles expired at his death in 1452; *s.* in Barony of Willoughby de Eresby by his dau. [7] JOAN, wife of Sir Richard Welles, Knt., who in right of his wife was summoned to Parliament as 7th Baron Willoughby de Eresby 1455-66; his lordship was only son of Leo, 6th Baron Welles (cr. 1299), who was killed at the battle of Towton Field 1461, and at his decease his estates and honours were attainted ; in 1468 the attainders were reversed and he became 7th Baron Welles ; having become through his son involved in the vibrating fortunes of the red and white roses he was treacherously beheaded by the order of King Edward IV. 1469; *s.* by his son [8] ROBERT, 8th Baron, who having heard of the king's treachery attacked the royal army, but being defeated was taken prisoner and immediately beheaded ; *s.* in both baronies by his sister [9] JOANE, wife of Richard Hastings, who was summoned to Parliament as Baron Welles 1482-3 ; he *d.* 1503 when his Barony of Welles became extinct ; the Baroness *d.* 1506 when the old Barony of Welles became abeyant and still remains so, while the Barony of Willoughby de Eresby passed to [10] WILLIAM Willoughby, 10th Baron, lineal descendant of Sir Thomas Willoughby, 2nd son of 5th Baron ; *d.* 1525; *s.* by his dau. [11] KATHERINE : *m.* 1st, Charles Brandon, K.G., 1st Duke of Suffolk, and 2ndly, Richard Bertie; *d.* 1580; *s.* by her son by her 2nd marriage [12] PEREGRINE Bertie, 12th Baron ; summoned to Parliament 1581; *d.* 1601; *s.* by his son [13] ROBERT, K.G., 13th Baron ; established (through his mother, sister and heiress of 17th Earl of Oxford) his right to be hereditary Lord Great Chamberlain of England ; cr. *Earl of Lindsey* (peerage of England) 1626; *s.* by his son [14] MONTAGU, K.G., 2nd Earl ; *d.* 1666; *s.* by his son [15] ROBERT, 3rd Earl ; *d.* 1701; *s.* by his son [16] ROBERT, 4th Earl; summoned to Parliament as Baron Willoughby de Eresby in his father's lifetime; cr. *Marquess of Lindsey* (peerage of Great Britain) 1706, and *Duke of Ancaster and Kesteven* (peerage of Great Britain) 1715; *d.* 1723; *s.* by his son [17] PEREGRINE, 2nd Duke; *d.* 1742 ; *s.* by his son [18] PEREGRINE, 3rd Duke; *d.* 1778; *s.* by his son [19] ROBERT, 4th Duke; *d.* unmarried 1779, when the dukedom and all honours except the Barony of Willoughby de Eresby passed to his uncle Brownlow (see E. Lindsey), and the Barony of Willoughby fell into abeyance between his grace's sisters, Priscilla, wife of 1st Baron Gwydyr, and Georgiana, wife of 1st Marquess of Cholmondeley, each of whom became Joint Hereditary Great Chamberlain ; in 1780 the abeyance was terminated in favour of the former [20] PRISCILLA BARBARA ELIZABETH : *m.* 1779, Sir Peter Burrell, Bt., who in 1796 was cr. Baron Gwydyr ; she *d.* 1828; *s.* by her son [21] PETER ROBERT, 21st Baron, who in 1820 had *s.* his father as 2nd Baron Gwydyr; assumed in 1807 by sign manual the additional surname of Drummond : *d.* 1865; *s.* by his son [22] ALBERIC, 22nd Baron ; was Joint Hereditary Great Chamberlain of England ; *d.* unmarried 1870, when the Barony of Gwydyr devolved upon his cousin Peter Robert Burrell, and the Barony of Willoughby de Eresby fell into abeyance between his sisters, Clementina, wife of 1st Baron Aveland, and Charlotte, wife of 2nd Baron Carrington each of whom became entitled to a moiety of the office of Joint Hereditary Great Chamberlain ; in 1871 the abeyance was terminated in favour of [23] CLEMENTINA ELIZABETH, *b.* 1809 ; assumed in 1870 by Roy. licence the additional surname and arms of Drummond, and in 1872, the additional and principal surname of Willoughby: *m.* 1827, the 1st Baron Aveland ; *d.* 1888; *s.* by her el. son [24] GILBERT HENRY, 2nd Baron Aveland (infra), 24th Baron Willoughby de Eresby ; *b.* 1830; in 1872, assumed by Roy. licence the additional surnames of Willoughby and Drummond; MP for Boston (*L*) 1852-56, and for Rutland 1956-67; cr. *Earl of Ancaster,* in co. Lincoln (peerage of United Kingdom) 1892: *m.* 1863, Lady Evelyn Elizabeth Gordon, who *d.* 1921, 2nd dau. of 10th Marquess of Huntly; *d.* 1910 ; *s.* by his son [7] GILBERT, G.C.V.O., T.D., 2nd Earl *b.* 1867 ; Parliamentary Sec. to Min. of Agriculture and Fisheries 1921-4. (also Dep. Min. therefor from Oct. 1921), Lord-Lieut. of Rutland 1921-51 ; Joint Hereditary Lord Great Chamberlain (acting for reign of King George VI) 1936-50 ; sat as M.P. (*C*) for Lincolnshire, S. Lindsey or Horncastle Div. 1894-1910 : *m.* 1905, Eloise, *O.B.E., J.P.,* who *d.* 1953, el. dau. of the late W. L. Breese, of New York, U.S.A. ; *d.* 1951 ; *s.* by his el. son [8] GILBERT JAMES, 3rd Earl and present peer; also Baron Willoughby de Eresby, and Baron Aveland.

⁎⁎[1] *Sir* GILBERT Heathcote, *K.B., M.P.* in four Parliaments, Lord Mayor of London 1711, and one of the originators of the Bank of England ; cr. a Baronet 1733; *d.* 1733; *s.* by his son [2] *Sir* JOHN, 2nd Bt.; was M.P. for Grantham 1715-22, and for Bodmin 1733-4; *d.* 1759; *s.* by his son [3] *Sir* GILBERT, 3rd Bt., M.P. for Shaftesbury ; *d.* 1785; *s.* by his son [4] *Sir* GILBERT, 4th Bt.; was M.P. for Lincolnshire 1796-1802 and 1806, and for Rutland (*L*) 1812-41 ; *d.* 1851 ; *s.* by his son [5] *Sir* GILBERT JOHN, 5th Bt., *b.* Jan. 16, 1795; sat as M.P. for Boston (*L*) 1820-31. Lincolnshire South 1832-41 and Rutland 1841-6; was Lord-Lieut. of Lincolnshire : cr. *Baron Aveland* (peerage of United Kingdom) 1856 : *m.* 1827, the Hon. Clementina Elizabeth, in her own right Baroness Willoughby de Eresby, dau. of 19th Baron Willoughby de Eresby; *d.* 1867; *s.* by his son [6] GILBERT HENRY, 2nd Baron, who *s.* as 24th Baron Willoughby de Eresby (ante) 1888.

Ancram, Earl of, son of Marquess of Lothian.

Andover, Viscount, son of Earl of Suffolk and Berkshire.

ANGLESEY, MARQUESS OF. (Paget.) [Marquess U.K. 1815, Bt. I. 1730, Earl G.B. 1714, Baron E. 1552.]

By its opposite.

GEORGE CHARLES HENRY VICTOR PAGET, 7th Marquess, and 10th Baronet; *b.* Oct. 8th, 1922; *s.* 1947; ed. at Eton; Major Roy. Horse Guards, Commodore of Roy. Welsh Yacht Club, Freeman of City of London, FSA, Hon. FRIBA, FRSL, a DL for Anglesey; Pres. of National Museum of Wales, 1962-68; a Member of Historic Buildings Council for Wales, of Redundant Churches Fund, an Hon. Fellow, Roy. Cambrian Acad., and Pres., Friends of Friendless Churches, patron of four livings, and Lord of the Manor of Burton-on-Trent: *m.* 1948, Elizabeth Shirley Vaughan, dau. of the late Charles Morgan, LL.D., and has issue.

ᵆrms,—Sable, on a cross engrailed between four eagles displayed argent, five lions passant guardant, of the field. Crest,—A demi heraldic tiger sable, maned, tufted, and ducally gorged argent. Supporters—Two heraldic tigers sable, maned, tufted, and ducally gorged argent.

Seat,—Plas Newydd, Llanfair P.G., Isle of Anglesey.
Town Residence,—29, Wellington Sq., SW3.

PER IL SUO CONTRARIO

SONS LIVING.
CHARLES ALEXANDER VAUGHAN (*Earl of Uxbridge*), *b.* Nov. 13th, 1950; ed. at Eton, and Exeter Coll., Oxford.
Lord Rupert Edward Llewellyn, *b.* 1957; ed. at Westminster.

DAUGHTERS LIVING.
Lady Henrietta Charlotte Eiluned, *b.* 1949.
Lady Elizabeth Sophia Rhiannon, *b.* 1954.
Lady Amelia Myfanwy Polly, *b.* 1963.

SISTERS LIVING.
Lady (Alexandra Mary) Caroline Cecilia, *b.* 1913 : *m.* 1949, Sir (Charles) Michael Robert Vivian Duff, 3rd Bt. *Residence,*—Vaynol, near Bangor, Caernarvonshire.
Lady Elizabeth Hester Mary, *b.* 1916; was a Train Bearer to the Queen at Coronation of King George VI.; readmitted to British Nationality 1940 : *m.* 1939, as his second wife, Raimund von Hofmannsthal, who *d.* 1974, and has issue living, Octavian Charles Hugo, *b.* 1946,—Sarah Arabella Marjorie, *b.* 1942: *m.* 1964, Piers von Westenholz, from whom she obtained a divorce 1969. *Residence,*—15, Connaught Sq., W.2.
Lady Mary Patricia Beatrice Rose, *b.* 1918. *Residence,*—Orchard Lea, Churchill, Somerset.
Lady Rose Mary Primrose, *b.* 1919 : *m.* 1940, the Hon. John Francis McLaren, Squadron-Leader RAF (ret.), who *d.* 1953 [see B. Aberconway]. *Residences,*—24, Coulson St., SW3; Old Bodnod, Eglwysbach, Colwyn Bay, Denbighshire.
Lady Katharine Mary Veronica (twin), *b.* 1922: *m.* 1st, 1941 (m. diss. 1948), Lt.-Col. Jocelyn Eustace Gurney, DSO, MC, Welsh Gds., who *d.* 1973, son of the late Sir Eustace Gurney; 2ndly, 1949, Charles Farrell, MC, late Major Scots Gds., and HM Foreign Ser., and has issue living (by 1st m.) Judith Marjorie Katherine, *b.* 1942: *m.* 1964, James Bowen, of The Red House, Mountain Bower, N. Wraxall, nr. Chippenham, Wilts.,—(by 2nd *m.*) Gerald Charles William, *b.* 1956,—Louisa Caroline Mary, *b.* 1949: *m.* 1970, Robin James Lane-Fox,—Diana Eileen Mary, *b.* 1958,—Marjorie Elizabeth Mary, *b.* 1962. *Residence,*—Pyrton Manor, Watlington, Oxon.

WIDOW LIVING OF BROTHER OF SIXTH MARQUESS
Mavis, dau. of William Crockford, and widow of Major Herbert Dawson, M.C.: *m.* 1935, as his third wife, Capt. Lord Victor William Paget, MC, who *d.* 1952. *Residence,*—54, Blandford St., W.1.

COLLATERAL BRANCHES LIVING.
Issue of the late Capt. Lord Victor William Paget, M.C., brother of 6th Marquess, *b.* 1889, *d.* 1952: *m.* 1st, 1913, Olive Mary (the actress, "Miss Olive May") (who *d.* 1947, having obtained a divorce 1921), dau. of George Meatyard ; 2ndly, 1922, the Hon. Bridget (who *d.* 1975, having obtained a divorce 1932), da. of 1st Baron Colebrooke (ext.); 3rdly, 1935, Mavis (ante), da. of William Crockford, and widow of Maj. Herbert Dawson, MC:—
(By 1st m.) Henry Alexander Reginald (12, Alley Nine, St. Lucia St., Naxxar, Malta, GC), *b.* 1914: *m.* 1938, Sonia, da. of the late Count Paul Chatoulenco, and has issue living, Tessa Ann, *b.* 1947, ——— Peggy Hester Pauline, *b.* 1913: *m.* 1st, 1935, Nigel Arthur St. George Gibbes, Lieut. 8th. Hussars, who *d.* (of wounds received in action) 1942; 2ndly, 1944 (marriage dissolved 19—), Major Peter Barrow, MC, RA; 3rdly, 19—, Ian Coward, of 131, Hope St., Mosta, Malta GC, and has issue living, (by 2nd m.) a son, *b.* 1946.——(By 2nd m.) Nicholas David, *b.* 1924: *m.* 1st, 1952 (m. diss. 1956), Heather Betty (BEVIS), da. of the late Charles Smetham; 2ndly, 1956, Moya Lillian (HAYIM), who *d.* 1962, da. of Capt. William John Enright, OBE, RD, RNR; 3rdly, 1962, Ellen Bridget O'Neill, who *d.* 1963, and has issue living (by 3rd m.), John David *b.* 1962,—Jane Bridget, *b.* 1963.——Ann, *b.* 1923.

Grandchildren of the late Gen. the Rt. Hon. Sir Arthur Henry Fitzroy Paget,
GCB, KCVO, el. son of the late Gen. Lord Alfred Henry Paget, CB (infra):—
Issue of the late Capt. Arthur Wyndham Louis Paget, MC, *b.* 1888, *d.* 1966: *m.* 1928,
Rosemary Victoria, who *d.* 1970, da. of the late Brig.-Gen. Noel Armar Lowry-Corry, DSO
[E. Belmore, colls.]:—
David Arthur Fitroy, *b.* 1929.——Rosalind Louise (East Kennett Manor, Marlborough), *b.* 1931: *m.*
1958, Dr. Clive Bremner Cameron.

Grandchildren of the late Gen. Lord Alfred Henry Paget, C.B., 5th son of 1st
Marquess:—
Issue of the late Adm. Sir Alfred Wyndham Paget, K.C.B., K.C.M.G., D.S.O., *b.* 1852,
d. 1918: *m.* 1906, Viti, who *d.* 1918, el. dau. of the Rt. Hon. Sir William MacGregor
G.C.M.G., C.B., M.D., LL.D., D.Sc.:—
Honor Cecilia, *b.* 1907: *m.* 1st, 1928, Com. Vivian Russell Salvin Bowlby, R.N. (retired), who obtained
a divorce 1930; 2ndly, 1936 (marriage dissolved 1946), Ralph Gledhill; 3rdly 1952, Count François
Hurault de Vibraye. *Residence,*—
Issue of the late Sir Almeric Hugh Paget, G.B.E., who was cr. *Baron Queenborough* 1918 [see
that title].
[*In remainder to Earldom of Uxbridge and Barony of Paget of Beaudesert only.*]

Grandchildren of the late Howard Francis Paget (infra):—
Issue of the late Francis Edward Howard Paget, *b.* 1886, *d.* 1945: *m.* 1st, 1909, Anna Maria
(who *d.* 1965, having obtained a divorce 1918), da. of the late George Richard Dyott;
2ndly, 1922, Jane Florence, who *d.* 1970, da. of the late Capt. C. F. Lang:—
(By 1st m.) Edward Francis Howard (Capel Llanlluan Farm, Gorslas, Llanelly), *b.* 1910; 1939-45 War
as Capt. Grenadier Guards: *m.* 1948, Bridget, from whom he obtained a divorce 1972, dau. of the
late Charles H. Ellis, of Willington House, near Maidstone, and has issue living, Caroline Charlotte,
b. 1950; BSc: *m.* 1974, Hensel Peters, of Jamestown, St. Helena, and has issue living, Howard
b. 1974.——Elizabeth Beatrice Howard (3, Ash Lawn, Benenden, Kent), *b.* 1913: *m.* 1938, Maj.
Charles Rochfort-Boyd, RA (ret.), from whom she obtained a divorce 1968.
Issue of the late Salisbury Howard Paget, *b.* 1889, *d.* 1940 : *m.* 1915, Florence, dau. of A. J.
McMahon :—
John Henry Howard, *b.* 1925 : *m.* 19—, Grace, dau. of E. Tunnicliffe, of Austrey, Warwickshire, and
has issue living, Deborah Anne, *b.* 1952. *Residence,*—

Granddaughters of the late Rev. Francis Edward Paget (infra):—
Issue of the late Howard Francis Paget, *b.* 1858, *d.* 1935 : *m.* 1884, Alice Catharine, who *d.*
1934, dau. of the late Rev. John Thomas Jeffcock, R. of St. Peter's, Wolverhampton, and
Preb. of Lichfield:—
Alice Katharine Howard, *b.* 1898: *m.* 1924, Capt. Roderick Cecil Williams, who *d.* 1966, and has issue
living, Roderic Greville David, *b.* 1927; Cdr. RN: *m.* 1950, Susan Margaret Edward, and has issue
living, Nigel David Blackstone *b.* 1952, Timothy Nicholas Edward *b.* 1954,—Michael Montague, *b.*
1930,—Patricia Jane (twin), *b.* 1930: *m.* 1955, Maj. Michael Aston (ret.), Intelligence Corps, of 2,
Manor Rd., Salisbury, Wilts., and has issue living, Roderic Charles Mark, *b.* 1956, Salisbury Edward
Henry, *b.* 1959. *Residence,*—Shute Lane, Iwerne Minster, Blandford, Dorset.——Charlotte Gabrielle Howard, *b.* 1900: *m.* 1929, J. Harold Hodgetts, who *d.* 1965, and has issue living, Harold
Patrick (of The Model Farm, Elford, Tamworth, Staffs.), *b.* 1933: *m.* 1956, Mary Watts, and has issue
living, George Harold *b.* 1958, Charles *b.* 1960, Edward *b.* 1962,—Mary Undine *b.* 1932: *m.* 1958, John
Keith Sykes, Bar.-at-law, of 50, Knowles Hill Rd., Newton Abbot, S. Devon, and has issue living,
Adam Keith *b.* 1964, Abigail Charlotte *b.* 1960, Gabrielle Anne *b.* 1961, Emma Frances *b.* 1963,
Rebecca Marguerite (twin) *b.* 1964. *Residence,*—52, Knowles Hill Rd., Newton Abbot, Devon,
TQ12 2PR.

Grandchildren of the late Rev. Edward Heneage Paget, son of the late Gen. the
Hon. Sir Edward Paget, GCB, 4th son of 1st Earl of Uxbridge:—
Issue of the late Hugh Arthur Paget, *b.* 1862, *d.* 1924 : *m.* 1902, Catherine Honoria, who *d.*
1943, dau. of the late Capt. Arthur Watson de Capell Brooke [B. Brooke of Oakley] :—
Clarence Arthur Edward (Green Farm House, Langmere, Diss, Norfolk; 85, Langford Court, Abbey
Rd., NW8), *b.* 1909; ed. at Eton; 1939-45 War as Capt. RA attached Intelligence Corps: *m.* 1942,
Cynthia Mary, da. of the late H. Hutchings, of Langton Cottage, Stoodleigh, Devon, and has issue
living, Hugh Charles Edward, *b.* 1946; ed. at Eton and Merton Coll., Oxford,—Caroline Hermione,
b. 1942: *m.* 1966, Dr. Theodore Bennett Robbins, of North Pomfret, Vermont, 05053, USA,—
Frances Catherine, *b.* 1947,—Selina Mary, *b.* 1950.

Issue of the late Eric Morton Paget, *b.* 1867, *d.* 1929 : *m.* 1904, Georgina Byng, who *d.*
1916, dau. of the late Herbert Byng Paget, of Darley House, Darley Dale, Derbyshire:—
Celia Mary (twin), *b.* 1916 : *m.* 1st, 1942, Charles Cecil Patrick Kirwan from whom she obtained a
divorce, 1946; 2ndly, 1954, Arthur John Goodman, who *d.* 1964, and has issue living, (by 2nd m.),
Mark, *b.* 1957,—Ariane, *b.* 1955. *Residence,*—9, Latham Rd., Cambridge, CB2 2EG.

Grandchildren of the late Leopold Cecil Paget, 2nd son of the late Berkeley Paget
(infra):—
Issue of the late Edward Catesby Paget, *b.* 1903, *d.* 1963: *m.* 1940, Mrs. Sibyl Gladys Rodney
Bingley (who *m.* 3rdly, 1963, Col. Thomas Cromwell Williamson, DSO), da. of the late
Col. Charles Edward Duff, CB:—
Anthony Berkeley, *b.* 1946.——Diana Jenefer, *b.* 1943.

Grandchildren of the late Berkeley Paget, el. son of the late Capt. Catesby Paget,
2nd son of the late Hon. Berkeley Thomas Paget (infra):—
Issue of the late Algernon Berkeley Paget, *b.* 1877, *d.* 1928 : *m.* (Jan.) 1909, Elizabeth
Anne Henniker, who *d.* 1925, dau. of Sir John Henniker Heaton, 1st Bt. :—
Victor Berkeley, *b.* 1911 ; European War 1939-45 as Capt. R.A. *Address,*—c/o National Provincial
Bank, Fawley, Southampton.——Rose, *b.* 1909 : *m.* 1933, Eric Stafford Nuttall, and has issue
living, Michael John Berkeley, *b.* 1936,—Edward James Stafford, *b.* 1938,—Elizabeth Mary, *b.*
1946. *Residence,*—Flat 25, Westley Close, Winchester.

Grandson of the late Col. Leopold Grimston Paget, 3rd son of the late Hon. Berkeley
Thomas Paget, 6th son of 1st Earl of Uxbridge:—
Issue of the late Com. Claude Paget, R.N., *b.* 1851, *d.* 1917: *m.* 1880, Theodosia, who *d.*
1920, dau. of the late John Henry Parnell [B. Congleton, colls.] :—
Cyril Nevil, *V.D.*, *b.* 1891 ; Bar. Gray's Inn 1912 ; was Chm., Public Ser. Commn., Burma 1945-7, and
Chm., Public Ser. Commn., Ceylon 1947-50 ; European War 1914-18 as Capt. London Regt. (severely
wounded), Afghan War 1919 (medal with clasp), European War 1943-5 as Lieut.-Col. Indian Army :
m. 1928, Eveleen Mary, dau. of the late Barnaby Lanktree, of Cork, and has issue living, Richard
Berkeley (Heath Corner, Hollybank Rd., Hook Heath, Woking, GU22 0JN), *b.* 1928: *m.* 1965, Nicola,

da. of Archibald Baird-Murray, of Old Park, Warninglid, Sussex, and has issue living, Henrietta
Elizabeth *b.* 1966, Annabelle Mary *b.* 1968, Charlotte Patricia *b.* 1971,—Mary Patricia, *b.* 1931:
m. 1969, Lawrence Butterfield, TD, FRIBA, of Shepherds Wood, Sheffield Park, Sussex,—Caroline
Eve Mary, *b.* 1935: *m.* 1956, Anthony Aljoe, of 46, Middleway, NW11, and has issue living, Mark
Coade *b.* 1959.   *Residence,*—Corners, The Way, Angmering-on-Sea, Sussex.

Grandson of the late Rev. Cecil George Paget (infra):—
Issue of the late Bernard Leopold Paget, *b.* 1892; *d.* 1974: *m.* 1935, Violet Gwendoline, da.
of the late Lennox Robertson, FRIBA, of 14, Chargot Rd., Llandaff:—
Michael Robertson (207, Aldwick Rd., Bognor Regis), *b.* 1936; ed. at King's Sch., Bruton; Composer
and teacher; late Cpl. Greenjackets Bde.; Cyprus 1956-59: *m.* 1960, Mrs. Betty May Hobden, and
has issue living, Gerardine Carol-Louise *b.* 1961,—Sarah Catherine *b.* 1963.

Grandchildren of the late Col. Leopold Grimston Paget (ante):—
**Issue of the late Rev. Cecil George Paget, *b.* 1853, *d.* 1929 : *m.* 1887, Innes Elisabeth, who
d. 1944, dau. of the late C. B. Skinner, of The Chantry, Ipswich :—**
Felix Barnaby (28, Homefield, Shortwood Green, Nailsworth, Glos.), *b.* 1904: *m.* 1st, 1932, Marjorie
Thérèse, who *d.* 1962, da. of the late Lt.-Col. Charles Seaver-Smith, RAMC (ret.); 2ndly, 1964,
Dora Josephine Adams Clark, MRCS, LRCP, and has issue living (by 1st m.), Susan Jane Seaver,
b. 1933; is a Dental Surg.: *m.* 1957, J. Keith Wood, MSc, PhD, AMIEE, of 147, Prescot Rd., Aughton,
Ormskirk, Lancs., and has issue living, Jonathan Piers Martin *b.* 1962, Carolyn Jane *b.* 1965, Elizabeth
Anne *b.* 1967,—Carolyn Elizabeth, *b.* 1935: *m.* 1962, Arthur James Sanderson, ACII, of 35, St.
Peter's Rd., Pedmore, nr. Stourbridge, Worcs., and has issue living, Helen Louise *b.* 1965, Wendy
Elizabeth *b.* 1967, Clare Marjorie *b.* 1970.——Averil Mary, *b.* 1887: *m.* 1921, Ronald John Barcham
Leney, who *d.* 1965, and has issue living, Robin Christopher Paget, *b.* 1927,—Anne Frances (24,
Christchurch Rd., Winchester), *b.* 1922.   *Residence,*—24, Christchurch Rd., Winchester, Hants.——
Cecily Innes, *b.* 1902.   *Residence,*—Beevor Cottage, 6, Abbey St., Cerne Abbas, Dorchester, Dorset.

**Issue of the late Lieut.-Col. Arthur Leopold Paget, *b.* 1856, *d.* 1906 : *m.* 1885, Ina Blanche
Georgie, who *d.* 1910, dau. of the late Rt. Hon. Lord Otho Augustus Fitzgerald, M.P.
[D. Leinster, colls.] :—**
Cynthia Geraldine Ursula, *b.* 1888 : *m.* 1921, Nicholas Henry Lambert, who *d.* 1943, and has
issue living, Desmond Ambrose (of Dysertmore, New Ross, co. Wexford), *b.* 1923; is Major Irish
Guards: *m.* 1957, Olive Eustace, youngest dau. of H. Eustace Duckett, of Castlemore, Tullow
co. Carlow.   *Residence,*—Carraigeven, New Ross, co. Wexford.

**Issue of the late Mark John Paget, *b.* 1864, *d.* 1938 : *m.* 1898, Frances Carr, who *d.* 1941,
dau. of the late Capt. Carr Stuart Glyn [Glyn, Bt., cr. 1800, colls.]:—**
John Francis. *b.* 1903 ; ed. at Rugby : *m.* 1932, Ann Millicent, dau. of Peter Arthur Blundell, formerly
of Ridgelands, Cooparoo, Brisbane, Aust., and has issue living, Peter Jeremy Valentine (Glebe House,
Debden, Saffron Walden; RNVR Club), *b.* 1933; ed. at Malvern; Lt.-Cdr. RNR and Master Mariner:
m. 1963, Helene Boye Hansen, of Ormoy, Stavanger, Norway, and has issue living, Mark Sebastian
Boye *b.* 1967, Charles John *b.* 1974, Caroline Elizabeth Astrid *b.* 1964,—Sarah Ann Victoria, *b.* 1945:
m. 1968, James Lewis, of 101, High St., Marshfield, Chippenham, and has issue living, Brett *b.* 1970,
Kim *b.* 1973,—Jane Melanie, *b.* 1947: *m.* 1967, Maj. Richard Seymour Corkran, Gren. Gds., of The
Old Thatch, Hellingly, Hailsham, Sussex and has issue living, Claire Melanie *b.* 1973.   *Residence,*—
The Old Post, Stokenchurch, Bucks.——Evelyn May Selina, *b.* 1900: *m.* 1926 (m. diss. 1930), Lt.-Col.
Osmund John Francis Fooks, formerly 14/20th King's Hussars, and has issue living, Maurice Osmund
John, *b.* 1927; 14th/20th King's Hussars (Reserve): *m.* 1951, Leonore Margaret Celia Hastings, da.
of Frank Robert Jowitt Whitwell [see L. Belhaven, colls.].   *Address,*—

Granddaughter of the late Lieut.-Col. Arthur Leopold Paget (ante) :—
Issue of the late Oswald Leopold Paget, Durham L.I., *b.* 1893, *d.* 1955 : *m.* 1931, Barbara
Mackintosh, who *d.* 1968, da. of Arthur Forman Balfour Paul, MC, FRIBA, of Peffermill,
Craigmillar:—
Susan Blanche, *b.* 1933: *m.* 1956, Capt. William Mitchell Miller, MVO, late Grenadier Guards, of
Craighill, Kinellan Rd., Edinburgh, 12, and has issue living, Richard Neville, *b.* 1964,—Anna
Caroline, *b.* 1959,—Victoria Jane, *b.* 1961.

[In remainder to Baronetcy only.]

Grandchildren of the late Col. Edward Richard Bayly, grandson of the late Rev.
Edward Bayly, R. of Killurin, son of the late Lambert Bayly, 3rd son of 1st Bt.:—
Issue of the late Major Edward Archibald Theodore Bayly, D.S.O., *b.* 1877, *d.* 1959 : *m.* 1921,
Ileene Caroline Ethel Otway, who *d.* 1960, dau. of the late Major Arthur A. H. Inglefield,
of Old Church House, Beckington, Bath :—
Edward Archibald Richard (Ballyarthur, Arklow, co. Wicklow), *b.* 1922; ed. at St. Columba's
Coll., Trin. Coll., Dublin, and Trin. Coll., Oxford: *m.* 1964, Rosemarie Evelyn Gisela Steins, only
da. of the late Paul Heinrich Johann Minkley, of Frankfurt-on-Main, and has issue living, Edward
Alexander Christian Lambart *b.* 1967,—Selina Ileene Suzanne Rosemarie, *b.* 1965.——Adelaide
Elizabeth Mary, *b.* 1923: *m.* 1955, Patrick Mullen, 76, Landscape Park, Churchtown, co. Dublin,
and has issue living, Anthony Patrick Theodore, *b.* 1956,—Annabelle Sandra, *b.* 1957.——Rosabelle
Ileene Zahra, *b.* 1931: *m.* 1957, Wing-Cdr. Donald Brian Robinson, R.A.F., c/o District Bank,
3, Water St., Liverpool, 2, and has issue living, Colan Denis, *b.* 1958,—Timothy Rupert, *b.* 1965,—
Judith Sarah, *b.* 1962.

PREDECESSORS.—[1] *Sir* WILLIAM Paget, *K.G., P.C.,* was summoned to Parliament of England
as *Lord Paget de Beaudesert* 1552 ; *d.* 1563 ; *s.* by his el. son [2] *Sir* HENRY, *K.B.,* 2nd Baron,
d. 1568 ; *s.* by his brother [3] THOMAS, 3rd Baron, who was attainted by Parliament and his
property confiscated ; *d.* 1589 ; *s.* by his only son [4] WILLIAM, 4th Baron, who was restored to
his rank and honours by Parliament ; *d.* 1629 ; *s.* by his el. son [5] WILLIAM, 5th Baron, Lord-
Lieut. of Bucks ; *d.* 1678 ; *s.* by his son [6] WILLIAM, 6th Baron, Ambassador to the Sublime
Porte ; *d.* 1713 ; *s.* by his son [7] HENRY, 7th Baron, cr. *Baron Burton* 1712, and *Earl of Uxbridge*
(peerage of Great Britain) 1714 ; *d.* 1743 ; *s.* by his grandson [8] HENRY, 2nd Earl; *d.* unmarried
1769, when the Barony of Burton and Earldom of Uxbridge became extinct, and the Barony of
Paget devolved upon the son of Caroline, Lady Bayly, wife of Sir Nicholas Bayly, 2nd Bt., and
dau. of Brig.-Gen. Thomas Paget, son of Henry, 2nd son of 5th Baron [9] HENRY, 9th Baron,
assumed the surname and arms of Paget only ; cr. *Earl of Uxbridge* (peerage of Great Britain,
1784   *d.* 1812 ; *s.* by his son [10] *Field-Marshal* HENRY WILLIAM, *K.G., G.C.B., G.C.H.,* 2nd
Earl, a distinguished Cavalry officer in the Peninsular war, who at the head of the United British,
Hanoverian and Belgian Horse, rendered exceptionally substantial aid at the battle of Waterloo,
where he lost a leg ; was Col. of Royal Horse Guards, Lord-Lieut. of cos. Anglesey and Stafford,
twice Lord-Lieut. of Ireland, and Master-Gen. of Ordnance, &c. ; cr. *Marquess of Anglesey* (peerage
of United Kingdom) 1815 ; *d.* 1854 ; *s.* by his el. son [11] HENRY, *P.C.,* 2nd Marquess, *b.* 1797 ;
a Col. in the Army and Lord-Lieut of Anglesey; summoned to House of Lords 1832 in his father's
barony of Paget : *m.* 1st, 1819, Eleanora, who *d.* 1828, dau. of John Campbell, of Shawfield ; 2ndly,
Henrietta Maria, who *d.* 1844, dau. of the Rt. Hon. Sir Charles Bagot, G.C.B. ; 3rdly, 1860, Ellen
Jane, who *d.* 1874, dau. of George Burnand ; *d.* 1869 ; *s.* by his el. son [12] HENRY WILLIAM GEORGE,
3rd Marquess ; *d.s.p.* 1880 ; *s.* by his half-brother [13] HENRY, 4th Marquess, *b.* 1835 ; *m.* 1st,
1858, Elizabeth, who *d.* 1873, dau. of Joseph Norman ; 2ndly, 1874, Blanche Mary, who *d.* 1877,
dau. of Curwen Boyd, of Merton Hall, co. Wigton ; 3rdly, 1880, Mary Livingstone, who *d.* 1931,
dau. of J. P. King, of Sandhills, Georgia, U.S.A., and widow of the Hon. Henry Wodehouse ; *d.*

1898; *s.* by his son [14] HENRY CYRIL, 5th Marquess, *b.* 1875: *m.* 1898, Lilian Florence Maud (who *d.* 1962, having *m.* 2ndly, 1909, Capt. John Francis Grey Gilliat), dau. of Sir George Chetwynd, 4th Bt.; *d.* 1905; *s.* by his cousin [15] CHARLES HENRY ALEXANDER, *G.C.V.O.* (son of the late Lord Alexander Victor Paget, 3rd son of 2nd Marquess), 6th Marquess, *b.* 1885; Lord-Lieut. of Anglesey; Lord Chamberlain to H.M. Queen Mary 1922-47: *m.* 1912, Lady Victoria Marjorie Harriet Manners, who *d.* 1946, dau. of 8th Duke of Rutland; *d.* 1947; *s.* by his only son [16] GEORGE CHARLES HENRY VICTOR, 7th Marquess and present peer also Earl of Uxbridge and Lord Paget of Beaudesert.

ANNALY, BARON. (White.) [Baron U.K. 1863.]

My strength and valour.

LUKE ROBERT WHITE, 5th Baron; *b.* March 15th, 1927; *s.* 1970; ed. at Eton, and Trin. Coll., Camb.; F/O RAF 1944-48; RAuxAF 1948-53; a Liveryman of Haberdashers' Co., and a partner, W. Greenwell & Co., Members of London Stock Exchange: *m.* 1st, 1953, Lady Marye Isabel Pepys (who *d.* 1958, having obtained a divorce 1957), da. of 7th Earl of Cottenham; 2ndly, 1960, (m. diss. 1967), Jennifer Margaret, da. of Rupert Sausmarez Carey, OBE, of East Hoe Manor, Hambledon, Hants., and has issue by 1st and 2nd m.

Arms.—Argent, on a chevron engrailed gules, between three roses of the last, a cross crosslet or. Crest,—A cubit arm, proper, charged with a chevron engrailed gules, thereon a cross crosslet or; in the hand three roses gules, slipped proper. Supporters,—*Dexter,* a horse argent, caparisoned with the trappings of 14th regiment of Light Dragoons, proper; *sinister,* an Irish wolf-hound proper, gorged with an antique crown, and chained or.

Residence,—Welches, Bentley, Hants. *Clubs,*—Turf, Beefsteak, Pratt's, RAF, MCC.

SON LIVING (*By 1st m.*).
Hon. LUKE RICHARD, *b.* June 29th, 1954; ed. at Eton; 2nd Lt. R. Hussars.

DAUGHTERS LIVING (*By 2nd m.*).
Hon. Doone Patricia, *b.* 1961.
Hon. Caroline Davina, *b.* 1963.

SISTER LIVING.
Hon. Elizabeth Patricia, *b.* 1923; European War 1942-5 in W.A.A.F.: *m.* 1945, Lieut.-Com. James Osborne King, D.S.C., R.N.V.R., and has issue living, James, *b.* 1952,—Elizabeth Lavinia Sara, *b.* 1946: *m.* 1969, David Hugh Montgomery,—Patricia Rose, *b.* 1947: *m.* 1970, Antony Douglas G. North. *Residence,*—Rademon, Crossgar, co. Down.

AUNTS LIVING (*Daughters of 3rd Baron*).
Hon. Lilah Charlotte Sarah, *b.* 1889: *m.* 1911, Col. John George Lowther, C.B.E., D.S.O., M.C., T.D. [see Lowther Bt., cr. 1824]. *Residences,*—Guilsborough Court, Northampton; 2, Wesley Street, W.1.
Hon. Lucia Emily Margaret (*Dowager Viscountess Galway*), *b.* 1890; was a Maid of Honour to Queen Alexandra 1919-22: *m.* 1922, the 8th Viscount Galway, who *d.* 1943. *Residence,*—Serlby Hall, Bawtry, Doncaster, Yorkshire.

COLLATERAL BRANCH LIVING.
Issue of the late Major the Hon. Charles James White, 3rd son of 2nd Baron, *b.* 1860, *d.* 1930: *m.* 1901, Evelyn, who *d.* 1946, dau. of the late F. B. Bulkeley, Johnson:—
Margaret Lucia (*Margaret Lady Blois*), *b.* 1902: *m.* 1948, as his second wife, Capt. Sir Gervase Ralph Edmund Blois, MC, 10th Bt., who *d.* 1968. *Residence,*—The Vicarage, Ballyhooly, co. Cork.

PREDECESSORS.—[1] HENRY, son of the late Luke White, M.P. for Leitrim, *b.* 1790; Lord-Lieut. of co. Longford, and M.P. for Dublin (*L*) 1823-32, and for co. Longford 1837-47 and 1857-63; *cr. Baron Annaly* (peerage of United Kingdom) 1863: *m.* 1828, Ellen, who *d.* 1868, dau. of William S. Dempster, of Skibo Castle, Sutherlandshire; *d.* 1873; *s.* by his el. son [2] LUKE, *K.P.*, 2nd Baron, *b.* 1829; sat as M.P. for Longford (*L*) 1861-2, and f or Kidderminster 1862-6; was Lord-Lieut. of co. Longford 1873-4: *m.* 1853, Emily, who *d.* 1915, dau. of James Stuart; *d.* 1888; *s.* by his el. son [3] LUKE, *G.C.V.O.*, 3rd Baron, *b.* 1857; a Lord of the Bedchamber to Prince of Wales 1908-10, and Permanent Lord-in-Waiting to King George V. 1910-21: *m.* 1884, the Hon. Lilah Georgiana Augusta Constance Agar-Ellis, who *d.* 1944, dau. of 3rd Viscount Clifden; *d.* 1922; *s.* by his son [4] LUKE HENRY, *MC*, 4th Baron, *b.* 1885; Maj. 11th Hussars: *m.* 1919, Lady Lavinia Emily Spencer, who *d.* 1955, da. of 6th Earl Spencer; *d.* 1970; *s.* by his son [5] LUKE ROBERT, 5th Baron and present peer.

ANNAN, BARON. (Annan.) [Life Baron 1965]

NOEL GILROY ANNAN, OBE, son of the late James Gilroy Annan, of Bryanston Court, W1; *b.* Dec. 25th, 1916; ed. at Stowe, and at King's Coll., Camb. (Fellow 1944-56, Provost 1956-66); a Member of Academic Planning Board of Univ. of E. Anglia, and Chm. of Academic Planning Board of Univ. of Essex; Senior Fellow of Eton Coll. 1956-66; a Gov. of Stowe Sch. 1945-66, and of Queen Mary Coll., London 1956-60; Univ. Lecturer in Politics since 1948, a Trustee of Churchill Coll., Camb. since 1958, and of British Museum since 1963; Provost of Univ. Coll., London since 1966; 1939-45 War as Lt.-Col. with Mil. Intelligence in War Cabinet Office in London, and in France and Germany; Cdr. of Roy. Order of King George I of the Hellenes; *cr.* OBE (Mil.) 1946, *Baron Annan,* of Royal Burgh of Annan, co. Dumfries (Life Peerage) 1965: *m.* 1950, Gabriele, da. of Louis Ferdinand Ullstein, of Berlin, and has issue.

Address,—University College, London, Gower St., WC1E 6BT.

DAUGHTERS LIVING.
Hon. Amanda Lucy, *b.* 1952.
Hon. Juliet Louise, *b.* 1955.

ANNESLEY, EARL. (Annesley.) [Earl I. 1789.]

ROBERT ANNESLEY, 9th Earl; *b.* Feb.
20th, 1900; *s.* 1957; Civil Servant (ret.);
European War 1914-18 with R.N., European War 1939-44 in France and W. Africa
with Roy. Corps of Signals: *m.* 1922,
Nora, youngest dau. of Walter Harrison,
of Sapperton, near Cirencester, Gloucestershire, and has issue.

Arms.—Paly of six argent and azure, a bend
gules. **Crest.**—A Moor's head, couped at the shoulders, in profile, proper, wreathed round the temples
argent and azure. **Supporters**—*Dexter*, a Roman
soldier in armour or, tunic azure, helm of the first,
thereon three feathers argent and azure, resting
his right hand on an antique shield or buckler
proper; *sinister*, a Moorish prince in armour or,
wreathed round the temples argent and azure, a
quiver of arrows pendant from a belt over his
left shoulder, and his left hand resting on a bow
proper.
Residence,—67, Vegal Crescent, Englefield Green,
Surrey.

From the love of valour.

SONS LIVING.
PATRICK (*Viscount Glerawly*), *b.* Aug. 12th, 1924;
ed. at Strode's Gram. Sch., Egham; late R.N.: *m.* 1947, Catherine, only dau. of John Burgess,
of Edinburgh, and has issue :—

DAUGHTERS LIVING,—*Hon.* Jane Margaret, *b.* 1948: *m.* 1966, Vernon Hugh Gamester
of Baroda, 18, St. Paul's Rd., Staines, and has issue living
Carl Vernon *b.* 1970,—Colette Louise *b.* 1967,—Juliet Dawn
b. 1969.
Hon. Nora Kathleen, *b.* 1950.
Hon. Patricia Catherine, *b.* 1952.
Hon. Frances Elizabeth, *b* 1957.
Residence,—35, Spring Rise, Egham, Surrey.
Hon. Philip Harrison, *b.* 1927 ; ed. at Strode's Gram. Sch., Egham ; late R.E.M.E. : *m.* 1951, Florence
Eileen, only dau. of the late John Arthur Johnston, of Gillingham, Kent. *Residence,*—48, Shackle-
ton Rd., Tilgate, Crawley, Sussex.
Hon. Michael Robert, *b.* 1933; ed. at Strode's Gram. Sch., Egham; Warrant Officer RAF; Asso.
Member Soc. of Licenced Aircraft Eng. and Technologists: *m.* 1956, Audrey Mary, only da. of
Ernest Goodwright, of Dartford, Kent, and has issue living, Michael Stephen, *b.* 1957,—Robert
Francis, *b.* 1962,—Sheila Marie, *b.* 1961. *Residence,*—Valentia, Brize-Norton, Oxon.

SISTER LIVING. (*Raised to the rank of an Earl's daughter* 1964.)
Lady Elizabeth, *b.* 1906: *m.* 1926, Eric Carwardine Francis, F.S.A., and has issue living, Katharine
Annesley, *b.* 1930: *m.* 1955, John Alexander Henderson, late 14th/20th King's Hussars, of Wicks
Manor, Tolleshunt Major, Essex, and has issue living, Fergus Alexander *b.* 1956, Emma Annesley
b. 1958,—Julie Carwardine, *b.* 1938: *m.* 1958, Robert Whitford. *Residence,*—Long Meadow, West
Monckton, nr. Taunton.

DAUGHTERS LIVING OF FIFTH EARL.
Lady Clare (Dalemead, 10/12, Riverdale Gdns., Twickenham, Middx.), *b.* 1893.
Lady Constance Mary, *b.* 1895: *m.* 1915, William Miles Malleson, who *d.* 1969, and from whom she
obtained a divorce 1923. *Residence,*—Lavenham, Suffolk.

WIDOW LIVING OF EIGHTH EARL.
JOSEPHINE MARY (*Josephine, Countess Annesley*), dau. of the late Philip Brandell, of New York City,
U.S.A., and widow of Capt. George Seymour Repton, Irish Guards; during 1939-45 War was
Founder and National Chm. of American Friends of Britain: *m.* 1945, as his second wife, the 8th
Earl, who *d.* 1957. *Residences,*—785, Fifth Av., New York City 22, USA; Palais St. James, Monte
Carlo, Monaco. *Clubs,* Metropolitan (New York); Guards' Boat (Maidenhead).

COLLATERAL BRANCHES LIVING.
Granddaughter of the late Maj.-Gen. William Richard Annesley, el. son of James
Annesley, el. son of Robert Annesley, el. son of 2nd Earl:—
Issue (by 2nd marriage) of the late Capt. Arthur James Patrick Annesley, *b.* 1869, *d.*
1934: *m.* 1st, 1899. Florence Lillie (from whom he obtained a divorce 1914), dau. of
the late Frederick Burcher; 2ndly, 1915, Winifred Mabel, who *d.* 1971, dau. of the late
Vincent Cornelius Garman, MD, formerly of Heigham Hall, Norwich, and widow of R. W.
Martin, of Victoria, British Columbia:—
Sheila Isabel Ina, *b.* 1921: *m.* 1st, 1942, Wing-Com. George Harcus Sheehan, R.A.F., who *d.*
(killed in action during European War) 1942 ; 2ndly, 1944, Major Eric Weston Tory, T.D.,
Dorsetshire Regt., and has issue living, (by 2nd marriage) Patrick James Weston, *b.* 1945,—Robert
Michael Annesley, *b.* 1946: *m.* 1970, Faith Charlotte Grant,—Charles Peter Hamilton, *b.* 1952,—
Frances Shelagh, *b.* 1950: *m.* 1974, Michael Duncan McNeil, son of Sir Hector McNeil, OBE, of
Bramber, St. George's Hill, Weybridge, Surrey. *Residence,*—Perrysfield Farm, Oxted, Surrey.

Granddaughters of the late Francis Charles Annesley, son of the late James
Annesley (ante):—
Issue of the late Lieut.-Col. James Howard Adolphus Annesley, C.M.G., D.S.O., *b.* 1868,
d. 1919: *m.* 1900, Helene Marie, who *d.* 1949, dau. of the late Charles Edward Johnston,
formerly of 23, Queen's Gate Terrace, S.W.:—
Patricia Moyra (*Lady Perkins*), *b.* 1904 : *m.* 1st, 1926, Air Commodore Sir (Henry) Nigel St. Valery
Norman, C.B.E., 2nd Bt., who *d.* (on active ser. during European War) 1943 ; 2ndly, 1944, Sir
Walter Robert Dempster Perkins, MP. *Residence,*—The Manor House, Downton, Wilts.—Sheila
Cecilia Louise (2, Moot Lane, Downton, Salisbury, Wilts., SP5 3JP), *b.* 1905: *m.* 1934, Lt.-Col.
Christopher John Burlison, OBE, TD, RA, who *d.* 1958, and has issue living, John James, *b.* 1940,—
Celia Margaret, *b.* 1936: *m.* 1961, Maj. Edward Martin Shewell Turner, RA.——Dorothy Maud
(17, Culford Mansions, Culford Gdns., SW3), *b.* 1906.

Grandchildren of the late Richard Grove Annesley, el. son of the late Lt.-Gen. the
Hon. Arthur Grove Annesley, 3rd son of 2nd Earl:—
Issue of the late Richard Arthur Grove Annesley, *b.* 1879, *d.* 1966: *m.* 1907, Hilda Margaret,
who *d.* 1961, da. of the Rt. Hon. Sir Francis Edmund Workman-Macnaghten, 3rd Bt.:—

Richard Francis Michael Grove (Eidelweiss, Pennington, S. Coast, Natal), *b.* 1908: *m.* 1st, 1931, Elizabeth (from whom he obtained a divorce 1939), da. of J. Anderson, of Edinburgh; 2ndly, 1939, Elise de Beere, of Cape Province, S. Africa, and has issue living, (by 1st marriage) Diana Elisabeth Doreen, *b.* 1932: *m.* 1954, Robin Keitley Duff, of The British Consulate, Box 10101, Johannesburg and Duffs Drift, Box 67419, Bryanston, Transvaal, and has issue living, Hugh Robert Keitley *b.* 1958, Margaret Keitley *b.* 19—,— (by 2nd m.) Richard Daniel Fergus Robert Grove (22, Northlyn, Somtsen Rd., N. Beach, Durban, Natal), *b.* 1940; sales representative for Burroughs Wellcome (Pty.) Ltd. in Natal: *m.* 1966, Marina Soares, of Salsibury, Rhodesia, and has issue living, Michael Richard Edward Grove *b.* 1970, Robert Patrick Sean *b.* 1971,—Rozanne Mary, *b.* 1942: *m.* 1967, David Worsley (Manager, c/o Checkers Departmental Store, High St., Grahamstown, Cape, S. Africa), and has issue living, Nicolette *b.* 19—.——Diana Patricia (twin), *b.* 1911: *m.* 1932, (William) Martin Hill, CMG, former Asst. Sec. Gen. UN, of 260, Snowden La., Princeton, New Jersey, U.SA, and has issue living, Colin Patrick Annesley Martin (13, Ladbroke Grove, W11), *b.* 1941: *m.* 1966, Margaret Lydia Faith, da. of the late Maj. Charles Robert Purdon Coote [see Coote, Bt., colls.], and has issue living, Sebastian Martin Coote *b.* 1967, Brendan Colin Charles *b.* 1970.

Grandsons of the late Richard Arthur Grove Annesley (ante):—
Issue of the late Edmund Patrick Grove Annesley, OBE; *b.* 1911; *d.* 1975: *m.* 1939, Ruth (Annes Grove, Castletownroche, co. Cork), da. of the late A. N. Rushforth, of Bouley Bay, Jersey:—
Arthur Noël Grove (46, Grove Lane, SE5), *b.* 1941; ed. at Harrow, and Worcester Coll., Oxford; a Dir. of Christie: *m.* 1968, Caroline Susan Aurea, da. of T. H. W. Lumley, of 5, Robert Close, W9, and has issue living, Marcus Robert Grove *b.* 1972.——James Alexander Grove, *b.* 1974.——Francis Patrick Grove (24, Versailles Rd., SE20), *b.* 1943; ed. at Harrow, and Univ. Coll., Oxford: *m.* 1968, Jane Frances, da. of E. J. N. Holder, of Squire's Hill, Tilford, Surrey, and has issue living, Melanie Jane Ruth *b.* 1969.——Cressida Mary Siobhan *b.* 1971.

Granddaughters of the late Henry Robert Grove Annesley, 5th son of the late Lieut.-Gen. the Hon. Arthur Grove Annesley (ante):—
Issue of the late Arthur Geoffrey Grove Annesley, *b.* 1867, *d.* 1954: *m.* 1898, Mary Edith, who *d.* 1972, dau. of the late William J. Roe, of Landscape, Celbridge, co. Kildare:—
Stella Edith, *b.* 1899.——Phyllis Kathleen Rhona, *b.* 1907: *m.* 1934, Brigadier Averell John Daniell, OBE, DSO, Col. Comdt. RA, and has issue living, Patrick John, *b.* 1939; Maj. RA,—Michael Hugh, *b.* 1946,—Susan Mary, *b.* 1937: *m.* 1973, Guy Vivian Fennell Robinson, of 16, Old Court House, Old Court Place, W8. *Residence,*—Oak Lodge, Hythe, Kent.

Grandchildren of the late George Wolfe West, son of Georgiana Grove Annesley (who *m.* 1840, George White West, Bar.-at-Law, who *d.* 1869), da. of Lt.-Gen. the Hon. Arthur Grove-Annesley (ante):—
Issue of the late Laurie Annesley, *b.* 1884, *d.* 1950 : *m.* 1911, Ralph Osmond Williams, M.D., B.S., who *d.* 1942:—
Thomas West, *b.* 1918 ; is a Grazier : *m.* 1940, Alison, dau. of the late C. John Barnard, of Bathurst, N.S. Wales, and has issue living, Thomas Hugh Annesley, *b.* 1942,—Victoria Annesley, *b.* 1945. *Residence,*—Chatsworth, R.M.B. 111, Binda, N.S.Wales.——Valerie Gwynne, *b.* 1915 : *m.* 1937, Geoffrey Patrick Shepherd, grazier, and has issue living, Michael Anthony, *b.* 1940,—Wendy Anne, *b.* 1938,—Megan Patricia, *b.* 1944—Valerie Jill Annesley, *b.* 1945,—Penelope Lee, *b.* 1948,—Christine Annesley, *b.* 1950,—Josephine Annesley, *b.* 1955. *Residence,*—Bannister, R.M.B. 743, Goulburn. N.S. Wales.——Margaret O'Hara, *b.* 1926 : *m.* 1948, Neville Edward Burkitt, grazier, and has issue living, Guy Neville, *b.* 1951,—Anthony Neville, *b.* 1958,—David William, *b.* 1959,—Patricia Annesley, *b.* 1953. *Residence,*—Spring Ponds, Bungonia, via Goulburn, N.S. Wales.

Grandchildren of the late Lt.-Col. Robert Michael Smith Annesley, 4th son of Capt. the Hon. Francis Charles Annesley, RN, 4th son of 2nd Earl:—
Issue of the late Col. Arthur Stephen Robert Annesley, C.M.G., *b.* 1869, *d.* 1939 : *m.* 1895 Kate Talbot, who *d.* 1939, dau. of Gen. W. Howey :—
Vera Kathleen. *b.* 1897 : *m.* 1921, Com. Wilfrid Edmund Warner, D.S.C., R.N., who *d.* 1951, and has issue living, Elizabeth Vivienne Annesley, *b.* 1921: *m.* 1st, 1941, Loyzeleur Campbell Smith, who *d.* 1949; 2ndly, 1952, Harold Basil Toller Foy, of Broxmead, Ewehurst Lane, Speldhurst, Kent, and has issue living, (by 1st marriage), Heather Jane *b.* 1944: *m.* 1964, Roger Norman Alwen of Glebeland, Rectory Lane, Brasted, Kent (and has issue living, Mark James *b.* 1967, Kate Annesley *b.* 1969). *Residence,*—Flat 20, Rochdale Gdns., Sevenoaks.

Issue of the late Eve Edwardes Annesley, *b.* 1877, *d.* 1956 : *m.* 1902, Freeman Archibald Grant Haynes, who *d.* 1915 :—
Annesley Freeman (11, Heathcroft, Hampstead Way, NW11), *b.* 1909: *m.* 1939, Iris, da. of George Saward, and has issue living, Michael Annesley, *b.* 1944,—Annette Patricia, *b.* 1953.——Faith Freeman, *b.* 1910: *m.* 1939, Humphrey Byron Dolphin, MC, TD, and has issue living, Timothy John, *b.* 1950,—Clare Frances, *b.* 1947: *m.* 1972, Stephen Richard Jakeman,—Valentia Margot, *b.* 1949. *Residence,*—Vine Cottage, Chacombe, Banbury, Oxon.

Grandson of the late Capt. William Henry Annesley, RN, 5th son of 2nd Earl:—
Issue of the late Capt. William Robert Ewart Annesley, Roy, Berks. Regt., *b.* 1872, *d.* 1917: *m.* 1906, Eleanor Mary, who *d.* 1969, da. of the late Surg.-Maj. William Ferguson, Army Med. Dept.:—
William Alan Cecil, *b.* 1907; Maj. (ret.) R.A.S.C.: *m.* 1935, Dorothy (VAUGHAN), who *d.* 1971, da. of the late Frank Yewdall, ICS, and has issue living, David Robert Ewart (45, Canfield Gdns., NW6), *b.* 1936; is Flying Officer RAF: *m.* 1960, Patricia, da. of V. I. Jones, of London, and has issue living, Benjamin *b.* 1961,—William Gerald, *b.* 1937,—Simon Richard, *b.* 1939: *m.* 1961, Janine, da. of the late Ramand Vautir, of France, and has issue living, Emanuel *b.* 1961,—Sarah Elizabeth, *b.* 1943: *m.* 1962, Henry William Peter Thompson, and has issue living, Howard Luke *b.* 1964, Paul David *b.* 1966. *Address,*—c/o Lloyds Bank, 6, Pall Mall, SW1.

PREDECESSORS.—[1] WILLIAM, 6th son of Francis Annesley, 4th son of 1st Viscount Valentia, was cr. *Baron Annesley,* of Castlewellan, co. Down (peerage of Ireland) 1758, and *Viscount Glerawly,* of co. Fermanagh (peerage of Ireland, 1766; *d.* 1770; *s.* by his el. son [2] FRANCIS CHARLES, 2nd Viscount; cr. *Earl Annesley,* of Castlewellan, co. Down (peerage of Ireland) 1789; *d.* 1802; under a special remainder was *s.* by his brother [3] RICHARD, 2nd Earl; *d.* 1824; *s.* by his son [4] WILLIAM RICHARD, 3rd Earl, *b.* 1772: *m.* 1st, 1803, Lady Isabella St. Lawrance, who *d.* 1827, dau. of 2nd Earl of Howth (marriage dissolved 1821) ; 2ndly, 1828, Priscilla Cecilia, dau. of Hugh Moore, of Eglantine, co. Down; *d.* 1838; *s.* by his el. son [5] WILLIAM RICHARD, 4th Earl, RN for Great Grimsby (C) 1852-7, and sometime a Representative Peer; *d.s.p.* 1874: *s.* by his brother [6] HUGH, 5th Earl, *b.* 1831; a Representative Peer ; Lieut.-Col. Scots Guards; M.P. for co. Cavan (C) 1851-4: *m.* 1st, 1877, Mabel Wilhelmina Frances, who *d.* 1891, dau. of Col. William Thomas Markham ; 2ndly, 1892, Priscilla Cecilia, who *d.* 1941, dau. of the late William Armitage Moore, of Arnmore, co. Cavan ; *d.* 1908 ; *s.* by his son [7] FRANCIS, 6th Earl, *b.* 1884 ; was a Sub-Lieut. Roy. Naval Reserve : *m.* 1909, Evelyn Hester (Harrison), who *d.* 1947, dau. of Alfred Edward Miller Mundy, of Shipley Hall, Derby ; *d.* (killed in action during European War) while serving in Roy. Flying Corps 1914 ; *s.* by his cousin [8] WALTER BERESFORD (son of the late Hon. William Octavius Beresford Annesley, 6th son of 3rd Earl), 7th Earl, *b.* 1861: *m.* 1st, 1893, Maud Fleming, who *d.* 1923] dau. of Haynes Bingham Higginson, of Glebe House, Walmer, Kent; 2ndly, 1924, Mabel Frances Aganoor, who *d.* 1931, el. dau. of the late John Burnet; *d.* 1934 ; *s.* by his son [9]

BERESFORD CECIL BINGHAM, 8th Earl; *b.* 1894; sometime Lieut. Roy. Fusiliers: *m.* 1st, 1921, Edith Constance (who *d.* 1950, having obtained a divorce 1941), dau. of Major Alexander Albemarle Rawlinson, formerly of 4, Aldford Street, Park Lane, W.1; 2ndly, 1945, Mrs. Josephine Mary Repton; *d.* 1957; *s.* by his kinsman [10] Robert (son of the late Arthur Albert O'Donel Valentia Annesley, grandson of the late James Annesley, son of the late Hon. Robert Annesley, 2nd son of 2nd Earl), 9th Earl and present peer; also Viscount Glerawly, and Baron Annesley of Castlewellan.

ANTRIM, EARL OF. (McDonnell.) [Earl I. 1785.]

RANDAL JOHN SOMERLED McDONNELL, KBE, 8th Earl of 2nd creation [see Predecessors]; *b.* May 22nd, 1911; *s.* 1932; ed. at Eton, and at Ch. Ch., Oxford; Hon. D.Litt., New Univ., Ulster; Capt. (ret.) RNVR, and a JP for Antrim; is Chm., National Trust; Chm. TA and AF Assocn. for co. Antrim 1948-52; Hon. Attaché, HM Legation, Teheran 1932; was a Clerk in House of Lords 1933-35; appointed Hon. Col. 429th Coast Regt. R.A. (TA) 1953, and Vice-Lieut. of co. Antrim 1955; commanded Ulster Div. of RNVR 1954-57; Prime Warden of Fishmongers' Co. 1965-66; 1939-45 War; KBE (Civil) 1970: *m.* 1934, Angela Christina, da. of Col. Sir (Tatton Benvenuto) Mark Sykes, 6th Bt. cr. 1783), and has issue.

Always ready.

Arms,—Quarterly, 1st and 4th grand quarters, quarterly 1st or, a lion rampant gules; 2nd, or a dexter arm, issuant from the sinister fesse point, out of a cloud, proper, in the hand a cross crosslet fitchée, erect azure; 3rd argent, a ship, with sails furled sable; 4th per fesse azure and vert, a dolphin naiant in fesse proper, *McDonnell*; 2nd and 3rd grand quarters, quarterly, 1st and 4th, azure, a sun in splendour or, 2nd, gules on a chevron argent three mullets of the field, 3rd, sable on a chevron between three unicorns' heads, argent, as many mullets of the field, *Kerr*. **Crests,**—Firs, A dexter arm embowed in fesse, coupled at the shoulder, vested or, cuffs argent, holding in the hand a cross crosslet fitchée erect azure *McDonnell*; 2nd, a sun in splendour or, *Kerr*. **Supporters**—*Dexter* a wild man wreathed about the temple and loins with ivy, all proper; *sinister*, a falcon, wings inverted, proper, beaked, membered and belled or.

Seat,—Glenarm Castle, Glenarm co. Antrim. *Town Residence,*—14, Moore St., SW3. *Clubs,*—Brooks's, Beefsteak.

SONS LIVING.

ALEXANDER RANDAL MARK (*Viscount Dunluce*) (5, Templar St., SE5), *b.* Feb. 3rd, 1935; ed. at Downside, and at Ch. Ch., Oxford: *m.* 1963 (m. diss. 1974), Sarah Elizabeth Anne, 2nd da. of St. John Bernard Vyvyan Harmsworth [see Boothby, Bt. colls.], and has issue living:—
    SON LIVING, Hon. Randal Alexander St. John, *b.* July 2nd, 1967.
    DAUGHTERS LIVING, Hon. Flora Mary, *b.* 1963. Hon. Alice Angela Jane, *b.* 1964.
Hon. Hector John (3, Love Walk, SE5), *b.* 1947: *m.* 1969, Catherine Elizabeth, da. of Ronald Chapman, of Buttermilk Hall, Brill, Bucks., and has issue living, Colquitto Angus, *b.* 1972,—Hannah, *b.* 1971.

DAUGHTER LIVING.

Lady Christina Alice, *b.* 1938: *m.* 1963, Joseph Andrew Christopher Hoare, of 34, Seymour Walk, SW10, son of the late Sir Reginald Hervey Hoare, KCMG [D. Portland, colls.], and has issue living, Charles William Reginald, *b.* 1966,—Jane Alice Patience, *b.* 1963,—Lucy Mary Christina, *b.* 1968.

BROTHER LIVING.

Hon. James Angus Grey, *b.* 1917; ed. at Eton; is 2nd Lieut. 7th Batn. Roy. Norfolk Regt. (T.A.); European War 1939-40 (prisoner): *m.* 1939, Jeanne Irene, dau. of the late Col. Stanley Leonard Barry, C.M.G., C.B.E.. D.S.O. [see Barry Bt., colls.], and has issue living, Sorley James, *b.* 1940,—Louisa, *b.* 1946. *Residence,*—36, Farley Court, Melbury Rd., W14.

SISTERS LIVING.

Lady Rose Gwendolen Louisa, *DCVO*, *b.* 1909; a Woman of the Bedchamber of HM 1952-73, since when an Extra Woman of The Bedchamber; CVO 1964, DCVO 1972: *m.* 1933, Francis Anthony Baring, who *d.* (killed in action) 1940 [see B. Revelstoke, colls.]. *Residence,*—43 Pembroke Sq., W.8. Lady Jean Meriel. *b.* 1914: *m.* 1939, the Hon. William Speke Philipps [see B. Milford]. *Residence,*—Slebech Park, Haverfordwest, Pembrokeshire.

PREDECESSORS.—[1] Sir RANDAL MACSORLEY MacDonnell, *K.B.*; cr. *Viscount Dunluce* (peerage of Ireland) 1618 and *Earl of Antrim* (peerage of Ireland) 1620; *d.* 1636, *s.* by his el, son [2] RANDAL, 2nd Earl, cr. *Marquess of Antrim* (peerage of Ireland) 1644; *d.s.p.* 1682. when the Marquessate became extinct, and the inferior dignities devolved upon his brother [3] ALEXANDER, *P.C.*, 3rd Earl, M.P. for Wigan in several Parliaments; his titles were twice attainted and twice restored; *d.* 1699; *s.* by his son [4] RANDAL, 4th Earl; *d.* 1721; *s.* by his only son [5] ALEXANDER, 5th Earl; *d.* 1775; *s.* by his son [6] RANDAL WILLIAM, 6th Earl; cr. *Viscount Dunluce* and *Earl of Antrim* (peerage of Ireland) 1785 with remainder to his daughters primogeniturely and their male issue, and *Marquess of Antrim* (peerage of Ireland) 1789; *d.* (without male issue) 1791, when the Viscountcy of Dunluce (cr. 1618), the Earldom of Antrim (cr. 1620), and the Marquessate of Antrim (cr. 1644) became extinct, while the Viscountcy of Dunluce and Earldom of Antrim (cr. 1785) devolved upon his dau. [7] ANNE CATHERINE, 1st Countess of 2nd creation; *d.* 1834; *s.* by her sister [8] CHARLOTTE, 2nd Countess of 2nd creation, wife of Adm. Lord Mark Robert Kerr [M. Lothian]; *d.* 1835; *s.* by her son [9] HUGH SEYMOUR, 4th Earl of 2nd creation; assumed in 1836 the surname of McDonnell by Roy. licence; *d.* 1855; *s.* by his brother [10] MARK, 5th Earl of 2nd creation; *b.* 1814; *m.* 1849, Jane Emma Harriet, dau. of Major Macan, of Carriff, co. Armagh; *d.* Dec. 19th, 1869; *s.* by his el. son [11] WILLIAM RANDAL, 6th Earl, *b.* 1851; *m.* 1875. Louisa Jane, *V A.*, who *d.* 1949, 3rd dau. of the late Gen. the Hon. Charles Grey; *d.* 1918; *s.* by his el son [12] RANDAL MARK KERR, 7th Earl, *b.* 1878: *m.* 1904, Margaret Isabel, who *d.* 1974, da. of the late Rt. Hon. John Gilbert Talbot, DCI [E. Shrewsbury, colls.]; *d.* 1932; *s.* by his son [13] RANDAL JOHN SOMERLED, 8th Earl of 2nd creation and present peer; also Viscount Dunluce.

Apsley, Lord, son of Earl Bathurst.

ARBUTHNOTT, VISCOUNT OF. (Arbuthnott.) [Viscount S. 1641.]

Praise be to God.

JOHN CAMPBELL ARBUTHNOTT, *DSC*, 16th Viscount; *b.* Oct. 26th, 1924; *s.* 1966; ed. at Fettes, and Gonville and Caius Coll., Camb. (MA); FRICS; JP of Kincardineshire; Far East and Pacific 1944-45 with Fleet Air Arm (DSC): *m.* 1949, Mary Elizabeth Darley, el. da. of the late Cdr. Christopher B. Oxley, DSC, RN, and has issue.

 Arms,—Azure, a crescent between three mullets argent. Crest,—A peacock's head, couped at the neck, proper. Supporters,—Two wyverns, wings elevated, tails nowed vert, and vomiting flames proper.

Seat,—Arbuthnott House, by Laurencekirk, Kincardineshire.

SON LIVING.

Hon. JOHN KEITH OXLEY (*Master of Arbuthnott*), *b.* July 18th, 1950; ed. at Fettes, and North Scotland Coll. of Agric., Aberdeen (Higher Nat. Diploma): m. 1974, Jill Mary, el. da. of Capt. Colin Farquharson, of Whitehouse, Alford, Aberdeenshire, and has issue living, Clare Anne, *b.* 1974.

DAUGHTER LIVING.
Hon. Susanna Mary, *b.* 1954; ed. at Overstone, Northants.

BROTHERS LIVING.
Hon. William David, *MBE*, *b.* 1927; ed. at Fettes; Col. late Black Watch; Korea 1952-3, Kenya, 1953-55, N. Ireland 1974 (despatches); *MBE* (Mil) 1964: m. 1955, Sonja Mary, da. of Col. Charles Newbigging Thomson, CBE, DSO, TD, of The Garden House, Panmure, Carnoustie, Angus, and has issue living, Charles Robert, *b.* 1956,—Georgina, *b.* 1964,—Elizabeth Christian, *b.* 1967. *Address,*— c/o Bank of Scotland, 31, High St., Montrose, Angus.
Hon. Hugh Sinclair (c/o Bank of Scotland, 79, High St., Montrose, Angus), *b.* 1929; ed. at Fettes, at Gonville and Caius Coll., Camb. (BA 1952), and at Edinburgh Univ. (LLB 1954); late Lt. 4th/5th Batn. Black Watch; is with Shell International Petroleum Co., London: m. 1963, Anne Rosamond, only da. of C. B. Terdre, of Appledore, Cherry Walk, High Salvington, Worthing, and has issue living, Hugh James Hamilton, *b.* 1967,—Katherine Anne, *b.* 1970.

SISTER LIVING.
Hon. Christian Keith, *b.* 1933; ed. at Edinburgh Univ. (MA 1954): m. 1954, Cdr. Peter John Bing, OBE, CEng, FIMechE, FCIS, RN, of 30, Queen St., Helensburgh, Dunbartonshire, and has issue living, Alan Charles, *b.* 1956,—Robert Adrian, *b.* 1958,—Andrew John Collingwood, *b.* 1960,—Sarah Lucy *b.* 1969.

AUNTS LIVING.
Margaret Ogilvy, *b.* 1892 : m. 1915, Lieut.-Col. Hastings Roy Harington, Indian Army (retired), who *d.* 1942, and has issue living, Timothy, *b.* 1926,—Pamela, *b.* 1919 : m. 1955, as his third wife, Brigadier Ronald Montague Montague-Jones, C.B.E., and has issue living, Roy Ronald *b.* 1958. *Residence,*—10, Battlemead, Swanage, Dorset.
Susannah Mary, *b.* 1901 : m. 1925, Col. Adrian Kelso Hamilton, D.S.O., M.C., late Black Watch, who *d.* 1960, and has issue living, Bruce Meade, *MBE* (Glencarse House, Glencarse, Perthshire), *b.* 1926; Col. Black Watch; MBE (Mil) 1965: m. 1953, Mary Elizabeth Walter,—Isabel Mary, *b.* 1929: m. 1951, Col. Ian Ranald Critchley, OBE, late The Black Watch, of Lindores, Muthill, Perthshire, and has issue living, Rowland Bruce Ranald *b.* 1953, Adrian Hugh *b.* 1962, Anna Mary *b.* 1951, Julia Clare *b.* 1956. *Residence,*—Peelers, Muthill, Perthshire.

DAUGHTER LIVING OF THIRTEENTH VISCOUNT
Hon. Norah Gertrude, *b.* 1885. *Residence,*—Cairnhill, Forfar, co. Angus.

WIDOWS LIVING OF FOURTEENTH AND FIFTEENTH VISCOUNTS.
DOROTHY (*Dorothy, Viscountess of Arbuthnott*), O.B.E., youngest dau. of the late Adm. Charles Lister Oxley, of The Hall, Ripon, Yorkshire ; O.B.E. (Civil) 1951 : m. 1914, the 14th Viscount, who *d.* 1960. *Residence,*—Balhall Lodge, Menmuir, Angus.
URSULA (*Dowager Viscountess of Arbuthnott* (Dower House, Arbuthnott, by Laurencekirk, Kincardineshire), da. of the late Sir William Collingwood, KBE: m. 1924, the 15th Viscount, who *d.* 1966.

COLLATERAL BRANCHES LIVING.
Grandchildren of the late Hugh Corsar Arbuthnott (*infra*):—
Issue of the late Lt.-Col. Hugh Arbuthnott, *b.* 1896, *d.* 1961: m. 1923, Jess Agnes (35, Loch Drive, Helensburgh, Dunbartonshire), da. of Robert Henderson:—
Hugh John, *b.* 1924; ed. at Sedbergh, and at Camb. Univ. (B.A. honours 1950, M.A. 1955); late Capt. R.E.; European War 1945 (wounded, despatches): m. 1954, Dorothy Ferguson, only da. of Sir William Lang Denholm, TD, of Glenmill, Kilmacolm, Renfrewshire, and has issue living, Carolyn Ann, *b.* 1955,—Sarah Jean, *b.* 1957,—Susan Mary, *b.* 1962,—Christine Elizabeth, *b.* 1966. *Residence,*—Ardmoy, Rhu, Dunbartonshire.——Mary, *b.* 1926; BSc honours 1946: m. 1949, Col. Laurence MacLellan Young, MBE, MC, late RE, of Tan-yr-Ywen Cottage, Llanddulas, Abergele. Denbighshire LL22 8ND, and has issue living, Alice Mary, *b.* 1951: m. 1972, Peter James, Summerhayes,—Christina Jess, *b.* 1954.——Marianne Jean Elspeth, *b.* 1937: m. 1967, William Richard Woods Ballard, of Oliver's Cottage, Capel St. Mary, Ipswich [see V. Molesworth, colls.].

Grandchildren of the late Lt.-Col. the Hon. Hugh Arbuthnott, 3rd son of 8th Viscount:—
Issue of the late Hugh Corsar Arbuthnott, *b.* 1860, *d.* 1915: m. 1886, Marianne, *J.P.*, who *d.* 1943, dau. of the late Archibald Gibson:—
Archibald, *M.B.E.*, *E.D.*, *b.* 1898; ed. at Cheltenham Coll.; Lieut. (retired) R.E., Major Malay States Vols., and a Chartered Accountant; European War 1917-18 in France (wounded), Malaya 1941-45; MBE (Mil) 1946: m. 1931, Barbara Joan, da. of J. H. Worters, of the White, House, Chipstead, and has issue living, John (Halfacre, 86, Wheathampstead Rd., Harpenden, Herts.) *b.* 1933; ed. at Sedbergh, and at Camb. Univ. (BA honours 1955): m. 1956, Ann, yr. da. of the late Arthur Garton, of Gwynn House, Lower Sloane St., SW1, and has issue living, Ian *b.* 1958. David *b.* 1961, Fiona *b.* 1957, Jane *b.* 1966,—Robert, *b.* 1936; ed. at Sedbergh, and at Emmanuel Coll., Camb. (MA); with British Council: m. 1962, Robina, el. da. of Mrs. S. M. Axford, of Benacre, Plummers Plain, Horsham, and has issue living, Robert Keith *b.* 1968, Alison Mary *b.* 1963, Catherine Anne *b.* 1965. *Residence,*—Kingfishers Reach, Tidmarsh, Berks.——Robert, *MBE*,

TD (Ardmoy, Rhu, Dunbartonshire), *b.* 1900; ed. at Cheltenham Coll.; late Maj. REME (TA); Lord Lieut. Dunbartonshire, since 1968: NW Europe 1944-45; MBE (Mil) 1945.

Grandchildren of the late Hon. David Arbuthnott, C.S.I., 4th son of 8th Viscount:—
Issue (by 1st marriage) of the late Lindsay George Arbuthnott, *b.* 1853, *d.* 1927 : *m.* 1st, 1907, Gertrude Forbes, who *d.* 1924, dau. of Clifford E. F. Nash, Bar.-at-Law ; 2ndly, 1924, Gertrude Amy, who *d.* 1940, dau. of the late John Gaskoin :—
Bernard David Ogilvy, *b.* 1908.——Margaret Wedderburn, *b.* 1913 : *m.* 1939, Lieut.-Col. Hew Angus Christopher Blair-Imrie,D.S.O.,M.C.,Black Watch, who *d.*(killed in action in Normandy) 1944, and has issue living, Dorothy Margaret, *b.* 1940: *m.* 1966, Charles Evan Bruce-Gardyne, of Middleton, Arbroath, Angus, and has issue living, Evan David, *b.* 1967, Hew Alan Charles, *b.* 1971, Diana Dorothy, *b.* 1969. *Residence*,—The Lodge, Edzell, Angus.
Issue of the late Donald Stuart Arbuthnott, C.E., *b.* 1860, *d.* 1918: *m.* 1892, Annie Elizabeth, who *d.* 1944, dau. of James Brand, formerly of 10, Marchmont Terrace, Glasgow :—
James Gordon (Swifts, Beckley, Rye, Sussex), *b.* 1894; Cdr. (ret.) RN: *m.* 1931 Margaret Georgiana, da. of J. W. Hyde, and has issue living, John Hyde (Road End House, Beckley, Rye), *b.* 1932; late Lt. RN: *m.* 1955, Patience Sarah, da. of Charles Wainman, of Balure, Bembridge, Isle of Wight, and has issue living, Anthony St. John Gordon *b.* 1956, Nicholas Charles *b.* 1958,—Hugh James, (c/o FCO, King Charles St., SW1), *b.* 1936; ed. at Ampleforth, and New Coll., Oxford: *m.* 1964, Vanessa Rose, only da. of Edward Dyer, and has issue living, Dominic Hugh *b.* 1965, Justin Edward James *b.* 1967, Giles Sebastian *b.* 1970,—Georgina Mary, *b.* 1940: *m.* 1966, William Robert Sparling, of Campagne Friqouret, 83, Villecroze, France,—Elisabeth Grace, *b.* 1945: *m.* 1967, Rupert Arthur Rees Evans, Bar.-at-Law, of 16, Chepstow Villas, W11, and has issue living, Marcus James Julius *b.* 1972.——John St. Clair, *b.* 1898; ed. at Downside: *m.* 1st, 1932, Constance Clare, who *d.* 1964, da. of Frank Fairlie, of Baldorny, Nairn; 2ndly, 1967, Catherine Wellborn Morgan, of Aiken, S. Carolina, USA.——Hugh Forbes, *b.* 1906; ed. at Wadham Coll., Oxford (MA) is a Knight of Honour and Devotion of Sovereign Order of Malta: *m.* 1937, Janet Elizabeth, da. of Vice-Adm. Herbert John Temple Marshall, of Gayton Hall, Ross, Herefordshire, and has issue living, Robert Marshall, *b.* 1938,—James Frances, *b.* 1940; Maj. Black Watch: *m.* 1974, the Hon. Louisa Nina Hughes-Young, yst. da. of the 1st Baron St. Helens,—Simon David, *b.* 1942: *m.* 1970, Suzanne Ruth, el. da. of Allen Mainwaring Parker, of Osmonds, Droitwich, and has issue living, Thomas, *b.* 1974,— Lucy Margaret, *b.* 1972,—Charles Philip, *b.* 1946,—Hugh Andrew, *b.* 1958,—Nicholas Octavius, *b.* 1952,— Margaret Mary (*Hon. Mrs. Hugh D. Donovan*), *b.* 1943: *m.* 1968, the Hon. Hugh Desmond Donovan of Flat 1, Fulham Park House, Fulham Rd., SW6, el. son of Baron Donovan (Life Peer), who *d.* 1971,— Janet Felicity, *b.* 1950. *Residence*,—Winterfold House, Chaddesley, Corbett, Worcs.——*Rev. Canon* Edmund Stephen (Clergy House, Santos Rd., SW18), *b.* 1909; ed. at Wimbledon Coll., and at Camb. Univ. (MA); Canon of St. George's Cathedral, Southwark (RC) since 1956.——Anne, *b.* 1897: *m.* 1930, John Cyril Taylor Rains, MA, BCL, Bar.-at-law, of 52, Shakespeare Rd., Worthing.——Eliza Mary, *b.* 1900.——Mary Frances Clementina, *b.* 1904: *m.* 1930, Phillip Adrian Flood, MRCS, LRCP, and has issue living, Tomothy Adrian, *b.* 1931,—David Gybrian, *b.* 1933,—John Charles Arbuthnott, *b.* 1947,—Mary Ann Therese, *b.* 1935,—Philippa Mary, *b.* 1937: *m.* 1960, Clive Beck, of 2, Parkside Gdns., Wimbledon, SW19, and has issue living, David Clive *b.* 1962, Andrew Philip *b.* 1964, Simon Charles *b.* 1965, Nicola Anne *b.* 1961, Emma Louise *b.* 1967, Sarah Antonia *b.* 1971. *Residence*,— Cintra, 27, St. Mary's Rd., Wimbledon, SW19.

PREDECESSORS.—[1] *Sir* ROBERT Arbuthnott, was cr. *Lord Inverbervie* and *Viscount of Arbuthnott*, with remainder to his heirs male (peerage of Scotland) 1641; *d.* 1655; *s.* by his el. son [2] ROBERT, 2nd Viscount; *d.* 1682, *s.* by his el. son [3] ROBERT, 3rd Viscount; *d.* 1694; *s.* by his el. son [4] ROBERT, 4th Viscount; *d.s.p.* 1710; *s.* by his brother [5] JOHN, 5th Viscount; *d.s.p.* 1756; *s.* by his kinsman [6] JOHN, 6th Viscount, son of Hon. John Arbuthnott, 2nd son of 2nd Viscount; *d.* 1791; *s.* by his el. son [7] JOHN, 7th Viscount; *d.* 1800; *s.* by his el. son [8] JOHN, 8th Viscount, *b.* 1778; was Lord Lieut. of Kincardineshire: *m.* 1805, Margaret, who *d.* 1870, da. of the Hon. Walter Ogilvy [E. Airlie]; *d.* Jan. 10, 1860; *s.* by his el. son [9] JOHN, 9th Viscount, *b.* 1806: *m.* 1837, Lady Jean Graham Drummond Ogilvy, da. of 8th Earl of Airlie; *d.* 1891; *s.* by his el. son [10] JOHN, 10th Viscount, *b.* 1843: *m.* 1871, Anna Harriet, who *d.* 1892, da. of the late Edmund Allen: *d.* 1895; *s.* by his brother [11] DAVID, 11th Viscount, *b.* 1845; *d.* 1914; *s.* by his brother [12] WILLIAM, 12th Viscount, *b.* 1849; *d.* 1917; *s.* by his cousin [13] WALTER CHARLES WARNER (son of the late Capt. the Hon. Walter Arbuthnott, 2nd sen of 8th Viscount), 13th Viscount, *b.* 1847: *m.* 1878, Emma Marion, who *d.* 1930, dau. of the late Rev. John Hall Parlby, J.P., of Manadon, near Plymouth ; *d.* 1920 ; *s.* by his el. son [14] JOHN OGILVY, 14th Viscount ; *b.* 1882 ; H.M. Lieut. for Kincardineshire 1926-60 ; Convenor of Kincardineshire Co. Council 1933 ; a Representative Peer for Scotland 1944-55 : *m.* 1914, Dorothy, O.B.E., youngest dau. of the late Adm. Charles Lister Oxley, of The Hall, Ripon, Yorkshire; *d.* 1960; *s.* by his kinsman [15], ROBERT KEITH, CB, OBE, DSO, MC (son of John Campbell Arbuthnott, CIE, el. son of the late Lt.-Col. the Hon. Hugh Arbuthnott, 3rd son of 8th Viscount) 15th Viscount; *b.* 1897; Maj.-Gen. late Black Watch (Col. 1960-64); Lord Lt. of Kincardineshire 1960-66: *m.* 1924, Ursula, da. of the late Sir William Collingwood, KBE; *d.* 1966; *s.* by his el. son [16] JOHN CAMPBELL, DSC, 16th Viscount and present peer; also Lord Inverbervie.

ARCHIBALD, BARON. (Archibald.) [Baron U.K. 1949, disclaimed 1975.]

GEORGE CHRISTOPHER ARCHIBALD; *b.* Dec. 30th, 1926; *s.* as 2nd Baron Archibald Feb. 25th, 1975; disclaimed his peerage for life March 7th, 1975; ed. at King's Coll., Camb. (MA), and London Sch. of Economics (BSc Econ); late Capt. RAEC; formerly Prof. of Economics, Univ. of Essex, Lecturer in Economics, Otago Univ., NZ, and London Sch. of Economics, and Leon Fellow, London Univ.; Prof. of Economics, BC Univ.: *m.* 1st, 1951 (m. diss. 1964) Liliana Leah, only da. of Dr. Noah Barou; 2ndly, 1971, Daphne May Vincent, da. of George Henry Henham.

Address,—c/o Department of Economics, University of British Columbia, Vancouver, 8, BC Canada.

WIDOW LIVING OF FIRST BARON.
CATHERINE EDITH MARY (*Baroness Archibald*), (3, Martlett Lodge, Oak Hill Park, Frognal, NW3), da. of the late Rt. Hon. Andrew Bonar Law, MP, and formerly wife of Kent Colwell: *m.* 1961, as his 2nd wife, the 1st Baron, who *d.* 1975.
PREDECESSOR.—[1] GEORGE Archibald, *CBE*, son of George W. Archibald, of Glasgow; *b.* 1898; Controller Min. of Information 1944-45; Chm. of Fedn. of British Film Makers 1957-66; Dep. Pres. of Film Production of Gt. Britain 1966-68; cr. *Baron Archibald*, of Woodside, City of Glasgow (peerage of UK) 1949: *m.* 1st, 1926, Dorothy Howard, who *d.* 1960, da. of George Henry Edwards, of Liverpool; 2ndly, 1961, Catherine Edith Mary, da. of the late Rt. Hon. Andrew Bonar Law, MP, and formerly wife of Kent Colwell; *d.* 1975; *s.* by his son [2] GEORGE CHRISTOPHER, 2nd Baron until he disclaimed his peerage.

Ardee, Lord, son of Earl of Meath.

ARDWICK, BARON. (Beavan.) [Life Baron 1970.]

Prepared in all things

JOHN COWBURN BEAVAN, son of the late Silas Beavan; *b.* April 19th, 1910; ed. at Manchester Gram. Sch.; News Editor, *Manchester Evening News,* Manchester 1936-40, Assist. Editor, Londoner's Diary, *Evening Standard,* and leader writer 1940-42, News Editor and Ch. Sub *Observer* 1942-43, Editor, *Manchester Evening News* 1943-46, Dir. *Manchester Guardian* and *Evening News* Ltd. 1943-55, London Editor, *Manchester Guardian* 1946-55; Assist. Dir. Nuffield Foundation 1955-60; Editor *Daily Herald* 1960-62; Political Adviser to *Daily Mirror* Group 1962; a Member of European Parliament, Strasbourg since 1975; *cr. Baron Ardwick,* of Barnes, London Borough of Richmond upon Thames (Life Baron) 1970: *m.* 1934, Gladys, da. of the late William Jones.

Arms.—Or a dragon passant between two roses gules, barbed and seeded proper, in chief and in base on a pile reversed gules, an owl argent. **Crest,**—A cock criant standing upon a hand mirror proper, the frame and handle or. **Supporters,**—On either side a representation of an angel holding in the superior hand a shepherd's crook proper.

Address,—10, Chester Close, Queen's Ride, SW13.   *Clubs,*—Garrick, Press.

ARGYLL, DUKE OF. (Campbell.) [Duke S. 1701 and U.K. 1892, Bt. (N.S.) 1627.]

Forget not.

IAN CAMPBELL, 12th Duke, and 14th Baronet; *b.* Aug. 28th, 1937; *s.* 1973; ed. at Le Rosey, Trin. Coll., Glenalmond, and McGill Univ., Canada; late Capt. Argyll and Sutherland Highlanders; Hereditary Master of H.M.'s Household in Scotland, Keeper of The Great Seal of Scotland, Keeper of Dunoon, Carrick, Dunstaffnage and Tarbert Castles, Adm. of the Western Isles, and Hereditary Sheriff of Argyll: *m.* 1964, Iona Mary, only da. of Capt. Sir Ivar Iain Colquhoun of Luss, 8th Bt., and has issue.

Arms,—Quarterly: 1st and 4th gyronny of eight or and sable, *Campbell;* 2nd and 3rd argent a lymphad or ancient galley, sails furled, flags and pennants flying gules, and oars in action sable, *Lorne;* behind the shield are placed saltirewise a baton gules powdered with thistles or, ensigned with an Imperial crown proper thereon the Crest of Scotland (*Hereditary Great Master of Household in Scotland*), and a sword proper, pommel and hilt or (*High Justiciar of Scotland*). **Crest,**—A boar's head fessewise, erased or, armed argent, langued gules. **Supporters,**—Two lions guardant gules.

Seat,—Inverary Castle, Argyll.

SON LIVING.

TORQUHIL IAN (*Marquess of Lorne*), *b.* May 29th, 1968.

DAUGHTER LIVING.

Lady Louise Iona, *b.* 1972.

BROTHER LIVING.

Lord Colin Ivar, *b.* 1946: *m.* 1974, Georgia Ariana, da. of Michael Ziadie, of Kingston, Jamaica.

HALF-SISTER LIVING.

Lady Jeanne Louise, *b.* 1928: *m.* 1st, 1962 (m. diss. 1963), Norman Mailer; 2ndly, 1963, John Sergeant Cram. of Foot Point Plantation, Bluffton, S. Carolina, USA; 315 E 72nd St., New York 10021, and Hopewell House, Irish Town, Jamaica, and has issue living (by 1st m.), Kate, *b.* 1962,—(by 2nd m.) Ousi Charlotte Campbell Sergeant, *b.* 1967.

WIDOW LIVING OF ELEVENTH DUKE.

MATHILDA COSTER (*Dowager Duchess of Argyll*), (c/o Coutts & Co., 10, Mount St., W1Y 6DP), da. of Stanley Mortimer, of Lichfield, Conn., USA, and formerly wife of Prof. Clemens Heller, of Paris: *m.* 1963, as his 4th wife, the 11th Duke, who *d.* 1973.

COLLATERAL BRANCHES LIVING.

(*All in male line in remainder to Dukedom, Earldom and other titles in the Peerage of Scotland.*)

    Grandson of Archibald Argyll Lochnell Campbell, 13th of Lochnell, el. son of Rev. Colin Campbell, 4th son of Archibald Campbell, 11th of Lochnell, 8th in descent from John (Gorm) Campbell, 2nd son of 3rd Earl:—

Issue of the late Alexander Andrew Lochnell Campbell, 15th of Lochnell, *b.* 1881, *d.* 1950: *m.* 1920, Marjorie Irene, who *d.* 1960, yr. da. of the late Alexander Campbell, of Eastbourne and Shanghai:—

Alexander (Alasdair) Duncan Lochnell (The Great House, Little Sodbury, nr. Chipping Sodbury, Glos.) *b.* 1921; ed. at Radley; 16th of Lochnell; 1939-45 War with London Scottish Regt.: *m.* 1958

Rosemary Georgiana, only da. of Cdr. Hugh Hope-Grant Begbie, RN, and has issue living, Alexander Hugh Edward, *b.* 1961,—Iain Charles Lochnell, *b.* 1962,—Caroline Irene Lochnell, *b.* 1965

Granddaughters of the late Brig.-Surg. Alexander Dugald Campbell, MD, IMS, son of the late Rear-Adm. Donald Campbell, 5th of Achanduin, and 3rd of Barbreck, gt.-grandson of Archibald Campbell, 1st of Achanduin, 3rd son of Colin Campbell, 5th of Lochnell, 4th in descent from John (Gorm) Campbell (ante):—
Issue of the late Col. James Donald Campbell, DSO, 10th of Achanduin and 8th of Barbreck, *b.* 1884, *d.* 1974: *m.* 1911, Hazel, who *d.* 1950, da. of the late Col. Benjamin W. Marlow, CSI, CIE:—
Margaret Mary (87, Bedford Gdns., W8 7EQ), *b.* 1915.——Elizabeth Jean, *b.* 1920.

Granddaughter of the late James Campbell, 10th of Jura, 5th in descent from Duncan Campbell, 1st of Jura, 3rd son of Sir Alexander Campbell, 3rd of Lochnell grandson of John (Gorm) Campbell (ante):—
Issue of the late Colin Campbell, 11th of Jura, *b.* 1851, *d.* 1933: *m.* 1876, Frances Monteath, who *d.* 1925, da. of Charles Sidey:—
Mary Ruby Irene (Flat 5, 155, Sloane St., SW1), *b.* 1894.

Granddaughter of the late Colin Campbell, 11th of Jura (ante):—
Issue of the late Capt. James Archibald Campbell, *b.* 1879, *k.* in action 1915: *m.* 1914, Dorothy Rosalinda Frances, who *d.* 1973, da. of Sir Robert James Black, 1st Bt. (cr. 1922):—

Celia Elizabeth Lochnell, *b.* 1915 (posthumous): *m.* 1939, Anthony Lambert Mackesay Cullin, of Highstones, Yopps Green, Plaxtol, Kent, and has issue living, Judith Mackesay, *b.* 1940: *m.* 1966, Rodney Charles Crouch, of 33, Serpentine Rd., Sevenoaks, Kent, and has issue living, Andrew Charles Mackesay, *b.* 1966, James Charles Campbell *b.* 1968, Charlotte Louise Montague *b.* 1970, Fiona Victoria Byrom *b.* 1971,—Elizabeth Anne (twin), *b.* 1940: *m.* 1963, Frederick Charles Raven, of The Knoll, Ightham, Kent and has issue living, Julian Charles Campbell, *b.* 1965, Alexander Charles Montgomery *b.* 1967, Rupert Charles Henry *b.* 1970.

Grandchildren of the late Lt.-Col. Colin George Pelham Campbell, 6th of Stonefield, 8th in descent from Archibald Campbell, 4th son of Archibald Campbell, 2nd of Lochnell, son of John (Gorm) Campbell (ante):—
Issue of the late Lt.-Col. Geordie Osmond Lorne Mackie-Campbell, MC, DL; *b.* 1896, *d.* 1956: *m.* 1921, Jessie Isobel, who *d.* 1971, da. of Sir Peter Jeffrey Mackie, 1st and last Bt. (cr. 1920):—

Peter Lorne (Stonefield, Tarbert, Argyll; Army and Navy Club), *b.* 1925; ed. at Eton, and Magdalene Coll., Camb.; JP of Argyll; Capt. (ret.) Rifle Bde.; 1939-45 War with RAF and Rifle Bde.: *m.* 1954, Ann Gillian, da. of Ian Pountney Coats, DL, and has issue living, George Logan, *b.* 1956,—Ileene, *b.* 1958.——Colena Ileene, *b.* 1922: *m.* 1946, Iain Arthur Campbell (Arduiane, Oban, Argyll), son of the late Brig. Sir Bruce Atta Campbell, KCB, CBE, TD, and has issue living, Nigel Bruce, *b.* 1948,—Sheila Jean, *b.* 1950.——Patricia Isobel, *b.* 1923: *m.* 1946, Niall Campbell Macdiarmid (Stibbington Hall, Wansford-in-England, nr. Peterborough), son of the late Sir Allan Macdiarmid, and has issue living, Fiona Jane, *b.* 1949: *m.* 1969, Roger Montague Prichard, son of Sir Montague Illtyd Prichard, CBE, MC, and has issue living, Duncan Montague *b.* 1973, Cara Mae *b.* 1971,—Glenda Ileene, *b.* 1954.

Issue of the late Sir Nigel Leslie Campbell, yr. brother of the late Lt.-Col. Colin George Pelham Campbell, 6th of Stonefield (ante), *b.* 1878, *d.* 1948: *m.* 1905, Harriette, da. of Judge Leslie W. Russell of New York:—

Lesley, *b.* 1908: *m.* 1944 (m. diss. 1963), Edmund Seyd.——Margaret, *b.* 1911: *m.* 1st, 1931, Alan Fitzroy Campbell of Airds, RN, who *d.* 1956; 2ndly, 1961, Leslie Lloyd Williams, of 48, John St., Wollahra, NSW, 2025.——Alison (*Lady Whitley*) (Little Salterns, Bucklers Hard, Beaulieu, Hants.), *b.* 1913: *m.* 1st, 1936, John Howard Russell, who *d.* 1951; 2ndly, 1967, Air Marshal Sir John René Whitley, KBE, CB, DSO, AFC.

Descendants of Sir John (Ian) Campbell, 3rd son of 2nd Earl:—
Campbells of Cawdor [see E. Cawdor], Ardchattan, Aros, and Clunes, and their cadets.
Descendants of Donald Campbell, 4th son of 2nd Earl:—
Campbells of Keithock, and their cadets.
Descendants of Thomas Campbell, 2nd son of 1st Earl:—
Campbells of Lundy, and their cadets.
Descendants of Colin Campbell, 1st son (by 2nd m.) of 1st Lord Campbell:—
Campbells of Glenorchy [see E. Breadalbane] and their cadets, including Campbell of Aberuchill Bt. (cr. 1668).
Descendants of Colin Campbell, 2nd son (by 2nd m.) of 1st Lord Campbell:—
Campbells of Auchinbreck [see Campbell Bt. cr. 1628], Glencardel, Glensaddel, Kilduskland, Kilmorie Wester Kames, Kilberry, Dana, and their cadets.
Descendants of Neil Campbell, 4th son (by 2nd m.) of 1st Lord Campbell:—
Campbells of Ormidale, Ellengreig, and their cadets.

PREDECESSORS.—[1] *Sir* DUNCAN Campbell, of Lochow, assumed the designation of Argyll, and was cr. *Lord Campbell* (peerage of Scotland) 1445; *d.* 1453; *s.* by his grandson [2] COLIN, 2nd Lord, Lord High Chancellor of Scotland, cr. *Earl of Argyll* (peerage of Scotland) 1457, and *Lord Lorne* 1470; *d.* 1493; *s.* by his son [3] ARCHIBALD, 2nd Earl, killed at Flodden 1513; *s.* by his son [4] COLIN, 3rd Earl, Hereditary High Sheriff of Argyllshire and Justice Gen. of Scotland; *d.* 1533; *s.* by his son [5] ARCHIBALD, 4th Earl, the first important personage in Scotland who embraced the Protestant religion; *d.* 1558; *s.* by his el. son [6] ARCHIBALD, 5th Earl, he espoused the cause of Queen Mary, and commanded H.M.'s Forces at battle of Langside 1568; was subsequently Lord High Chancellor of Scotland; *d.* 1575; *s.* by his half-brother [7] *Sir* COLIN, P.C., 6th Earl, Lord High Chancellor of Scotland; *d.* 1584; *s.* by his son [8] ARCHIBALD, 7th Earl, a distinguished military officer; *d.* 1638; *s.* by his el. son [9] ARCHIBALD, 8th Earl, cr. *Marquess of Argyll* (peerage of Scotland) 1641; was the first Commr. from Scotland to the Parliament of England, and at the Coronation at Scone placed the crown upon Charles II.'s head; subsequently recognised Cromwell as Protector; upon the restoration of monarchy the Marquess repaired to London, but H.M. refused to see him and ordered his committal to the Tower; on May 25th, 1661, he was tried for high treason and condemned to death, and on May 27th, he was beheaded at Edinburgh; *s.* by his el. son [10] ARCHIBALD, 9th Earl, who was restored to the Earldom; for refusing to subscribe to the Test Act was found guilty of high treason and condemned to death; he escaped, but was subsequently taken in an abortive attempt to invade Scotland, *temp.* James II., and was beheaded Jan. 30th, 1685; *s.* by his el. son [11] ARCHIBALD, 10th Earl, in whom the *Baronetcy*, cr. (N.S.) 1627, of Lundy (conferred upon Colin Campbell, grandson of 6th Earl of Argyll, with remainder to heirs male whatsoever), became vested in 1696 after the death of the 2nd Bt.; cr. in 1701 *Lord Inverary, Mull, Morvern, and Tiry, Viscount Lochow and Glenilla, Earl of Campbell and Cowal, Marquess of Kintyre and Lorne,* and *Duke of Argyll* (peerage of Scotland), with remainder to heirs male whomsoever; *d.* 1703; *s.* by his el. son [12] JOHN, 2nd Duke, a Field Marshal in the Army, and a celebrated military commander; cr. *Baron Chatham* and *Earl of Greenwich*, Kent (peerage of England) 1707, and *Duke of Greenwich* (peerage of Great Britain) 1719; *d.* 1743 without male issue when the peerages of 1707 and 1719 became ext.; *s.* in Scottish titles by his brother [13] ARCHIBALD, 3rd Duke who in 1706 had been cr. *Lord Oronsay, Dunoon and Arase, Viscount Ilay,* and *Earl of*

Ilay (peerage of Scotland), which honours became extinct at his death 1761; *s.* by his cousin [14] JOHN, 4th Duke, son of the Hon. John Campbell, M.P., 2nd son of 9th Earl; *d.* 1770, *s.* by his el. son [15] JOHN, 5th Duke, cr. *Baron Sundridge* (peerage of Great Britain) 1766, whose wife was cr. *Baroness Hamilton* (peerage of Great Britain) 1776; *d.* 1806; *s.* by his el. son [16] GEORGE WILLIAM, 6th Duke, who in 1790 had *s.* to his mother's Barony of Hamilton; *d.* 1839; *s.* by his brother [17] JOHN DOUGLAS EDWARD HENRY, 7th Duke, *b.* 1777: *m.* 1st, 1802, Elizabeth, who *d.* 1818, dau. of W. Campbell, of Fairfield; 2ndly, 1820, Joan, who *d.* 1828, dau. of John Glassel, of Long Niddry; 3rdly, 1831, Anne Colquhoun, dau. of John Cunninghame; *d.* April 26th, 1847; *s.* by his son [18] GEORGE DOUGLAS, K.G., P.C., K.T., 8th Duke; *b.* 1823; Lord Privy Seal 1853-5, 1859-66, and 1880-81; Postmaster-Gen. 1855-8, and Sec. of State for India 1868-74; Lord-Lieut. of Argyllshire; cr. *Duke of Argyll* (peerage of United Kingdom) 1892: *m.* 1st, 1844, Lady Elizabeth Georgina, Sutherland-Leveson-Gower, who *d.* 1878, el. dau. of 2nd Duke of Sutherland, K.G.; 2ndly, 1881, Amelia Maria, who *d.* 1894, dau. of the late Right Rev. Thomas Legh Claughton, D.D., (formerly Bishop of St. Albans), of Danbury Palace, Essex, and widow of Col. the Hon, Augustus Henry Archibald Anson, V.C. [see E. Lichfield]; 3rdly, 1895, Ina Erskine, *V.A.*, who *d.* 1925, dau. of the late Archibald McNeil, of Colonsay; *d.* 1900; *s.* by his el. son [19] JOHN DOUGLAS SUTHERLAND, K.T., G.C.M.G., G.C.V.O., P.C., 9th Duke; *b.* 1845; M.P. for Argyllshire (*L*) 1868-78 and for Manchester, S. Div. (*LU*) 1895-1900; Private Sec. to his father at India Office 1868-71, Gov.-Gen. of Canada and Com.-in-Ch. of Prince Edward Island 1878-83, and Gov. and Constable of Windsor Castle 1892-1914; was Gov. of Knights of Windsor, Lord-Lieut. of Argyllshire, Hereditary Master of H.M.'s Household in Scotland, Adm. of the Western Isles, Chancellor of Order of St. Michael and St. George, Keeper of the Great Seal of Scotland, and Keeper of Dunoon, Carrick, and Dunstaffnage Castles: *m.* March 21st, 1871, H.R.H. the Princess Louise Caroline Alberta, *V.A.*, *C.I.*, *G.C.V.O.*, *G.B.E.*, *R.R.C.*, who *d.* 1939, 4th dan. of H.M. the late Queen Victoria; *d.* 1914; *s.* by his nephew [20] NIALL DIARMID (only son of the late Lord Archibald Campbell, 2nd son of 8th Duke), 10th Duke: *b.* 1872; was Lord-Lieut. of Argyll shire; *d.* 1949; *s.* by his kinsman [21] IAN DOUGLAS, *TD* (only son of the late Douglas Walter Campbell, son of the late Lord Walter Campbell, 3rd son of 8th Duke), 11th Duke; *b.* 1903: *m.* 1st, 1927 (m. diss. 1934) the Hon. Janet Gladys Aitken, da. of 1st Baron Beaverbrook; 2ndly, 1935 (m. diss. 1951), Louise, who *d.* 1970, da. of the late Henry Clews, of The Chateau of La Napoule, Alpes Maritimes, France, and formerly wife of the late Hon. Andrew Nicholas Armstrong Vanneck, MC [B. Huntingfield]; 3rdly, 1951 (m. diss. 1963), Margaret, da. of the late George Hay Whigham, and formerly wife of Charles Sweeny; 4thly, 1963, Mathilda Coster, da. of Stanley Mortimer, of Lichfield, Conn., USA, and formerly wife of Prof. Clemens Heller, of Paris; *d.* 1973; *s.* by his son [22] IAN, 12th Duke and present peer; also Marquess of Kintyre and Lorne, Earl of Argyll, Earl of Campbell and Cowal, Viscount Lochow and Glenilla, Lord Campbell, Lord Lorne, Lord Inveraray, Mull, Morvern and Tiry, Baron Sundridge, and Baron Hamilton.

ARMSTRONG, BARON. (Watson-Armstrong.) [Baron U.K. 1903.]

WILLIAM HENRY CECIL JOHN ROBIN WATSON-ARMSTRONG, 3rd Baron; *b.* March 6th, 1919; *s.* 1972; ed. at Eton, and Trin. Coll., Camb.; Underwriting Member of Lloyd's; N-W Europe 1944-45 as Capt. Scots Gds. (wounded): *m.* 1927, Maria-Teresa, da. of the late Gen. Fabrizio Enea Chiodelli-Manzoni, and formerly wife of Baron Jean Marie Christain Colette Alphonse Jules du Four.

Arms,—Quarterly: 1st and 4th gules, in fesse a tilting spear or, headed argent, between two dexter arms embowed in armour, couped at the shoulder fesseways proper, the hand extended also proper, *Armstrong*; 2nd and 3rd argent, a fesse raguly gules between two crosses-bottony in chief and martlet in base gules, *Watson*. **Crests,**—1st, a dexter arm embowed in armour couped at the shoulder, and encircled at the elbow by a wreath of oak, the hand grasping all proper, *Armstrong*; 2nd, in front of an arm embowed in armour proper garnished or, holding a palm branch vert, a martlet between two crosses-bottony gules, *Watson*. **Supporters,**—On either side a figure habited as a smith holding with the exterior hand a hammer resting on the shoulder all proper. **Badge,**—A balista.

Strong in arms.

Seats,—Cragside, Rothbury, Morpeth, Northumberland; Bamburgh Castle, Northumberland. *Residence,*—237, Knightsbridge, SW7. *Clubs*—St. James', Beefsteak.

WIDOW LIVING OF SECOND BARON.

ZAIDA CÉCILE (*Zaida, Baroness Armstrong*), (Flat 1, 9, Cheyne Row, SW3), da. of the late Cecil James Drummond Wolff, of Caplanne Billère, Pau, France: *m.* 1917, the 2nd Baron, who *d.* 1972.

PREDECESSORS [1] WILLIAM HENRY ARMSTRONG FITZ-PATRICK Watson-Armstrong, only son of the late John William Watson, of Adderstone Hall, Belford, Northumberland, and 65, Eccleston Square, S.W.; *b* 1863; some ime a Director of the well-known Elswick works and of N.-E. Railway Co.; assumed by Roy. licence 1889 the additional surname and arms of Armstrong; cr. *Baron Armstrong* of Bamburgh and Cragside, co. Northumberland (peerage of United Kingdom) 1903: *m.* 1st, 1889, Winifreda, who *d.* 1914, el. dau. of the late Gen. Sir John Miller Adye, G.C.B.; 2ndly, 1916, Beatrice Elizabeth, who *d.* 1934, dau. of the late Jonathan Cowx, of Tudhoe; 3rdly, 1935, Kathleen, who *d.* 1970, da. of the late Rev. C. T. England; *d.* 1941; *s.* by his only son [2] WILLIAM JOHN MONTAGU, 2nd Baron, *b.* 1892; 1914-18 War, as Capt. Northumberland Fus. (severely wounded): *m.* 1917, Zaida Cécile, da. of the late Cecil James Drummond Wolff, of Caplanne, Billère, Pau, France, BP; *d.* 1972; *s.* by his only son [3] WILLIAM HENRY CECIL JOHN ROBIN, 3rd Baron and present peer.

ARMSTRONG OF SANDERSTEAD, BARON. (Armstrong.) [Life Baron 1975.]

WILLIAM ARMSTRONG, *GCB, MVO, PC,* son of William Armstrong, of Stirling; *b.* March 3rd, 1915; ed. at Bec. Sch., London, and Exeter Coll., Oxford (MA; Hon. Fellow 1963); Visiting Fellow of Nuffield Coll., Oxford 1964-72; Hon DCL Oxford; Assist. Prin. Board of Education 1938, and Assist. Private Sec. to Pres. of Board of Education 1940; Private Sec. to Sec. of War Cabinet 1943-46. Prin. Private Sec. to Chancellor of Exchequer 1949-53, Under-Sec. Overseas and Home Finance Div. HM Treasury 1953-58, Third Sec. Home Finance Div. 1958-62, Joint Permanent Sec. to Treasury 1962-68, and Permanent Sec. to Civil Ser. Dept. and Head of Civil Ser. 1968-74; a Dir. of Midland Bank (Dep. Chm. since 1974), Pres. Manpower Soc. 1970-73, Chm. Coll. Council, Mansfield Coll., Oxford, and a Member Governing Council Oxford Centre for Management Studies since 1970, and Manchester Business Sch. 1970-74; Trustee of Wellcome Trust since 1974; Hon. Liveryman of Salters' Co.; cr. MVO (4th class) 1945, CB (Civil) 1957, KCB (Civil) 1963, GCB (Civil) 1968, PC 1973, and *Baron Armstrong of Sanderstead,* of City of Westminster (Life Baron) 1975: *m.* 1942, Gwendoline Enid, da. of John Bennett, of Putney, SW15, and has issue.

Arms,—Not exemplified at time of going to press.

Address,—c/o Midland Bank, 27/32, Poultry, EC2P 2BX.

SON LIVING.
Hon. Peter William (19, Rosebery Gdns., Ealing, W13), *b.* 1943: *m.* 1967, Kathleen Frances Widdicombe.

DAUGHTER LIVING.
Hon. Janet Elizabeth, *b.* 1947: *m.* 1968, Malcolm Turnbull, of Kirkleven, Manor Close, Stokesley, Middlesbrough, Yorks.

ARRAN, EARL OF. (Gore.) Sits as BARON SUDLEY (U.K. 1884).
[Earl I. 1762, Bt. I. 1662.]

IN·HOC·SIGNO·VINCES

Under this sign thou shalt conquer.

ARTHUR KATTENDYKE STRANGE DAVID ARCHIBALD GORE, 8th Earl, and 10th Baronet; *b.* July 5th, 1910; *s.* 1958; ed. at Eton, and Balliol Coll., Oxon; Attaché, British Legation, Berne 1940-41, and British Embassy, Lisbon 1941-42, in Min. of Information 1942-45 (Dir. of Overseas Gen. Div. 1945), and in Central Office of Information 1945-49 (Dir. of Secretariat); a Dir. of *Daily Mail,* and General Trust Chm. of Children's Country Holidays Fund, and Hon. Treasurer of Moorfields Eye Hospital: *m.* 1937, Fiona Bryde, el. da. of Sir Iain Colquhoun, 7th Bt., KT, DSO, and has issue.
Arms,—Gules, a fesse between three cross crosslets fitchée or. Crest,—A wolf rampant argent collared gules. Supporters,—Two horses argent.
Residence,—Pimlico House, Hemel Hempstead, Herts. *Clubs,*—Turf, Beefsteak.

SON LIVING.
ARTHUR (DESMOND) COLQUHOUN, (*Viscount Sudley*), *b.* July 14th, 1938; Vice-Chm. of Children's Country Holiday Fund: *m.* 1974, Eleanor, el. da. of Bernard van Cutsem [see E. Fortescue], and has issue living, Laura Melissa, *b.* 1975.

COLLATERAL BRANCHES LIVING.
Grandchildren of the late Sir Francis Charles Gore, KCB (infra):—
Issue of the late Charles Henry Gore, O.B.E., *b.* 1881, *d.* 1941: *m.* 1st, 1911, Marguerite, who *d.* 1918, dau. of Walter Langley; 2ndly, 1920, the Hon. Violet Kathleen Annesley, who *d.* 1963, da. of 11th Viscount Valentia:—
(By 2nd m.) Paul Annesley, *CMG, CVO* (1, Burkitt Rd., Woodbridge, Suffolk), *b.* 1921; Capt. late 16th/5th Lancers; Colonial Admin. Ser. 1948-65; cr. CVO 1962, CMG 1964: *m.* 1946, Gillian Mary, da. of the late Capt. T. Allen-Stevens, and has issue living, Charles Alexander, *b.* 1947: *m.* 1970 (*m.*

diss. 1973), Penelope, yr. da. of R. C. Caunce, of Maidenhead,—William Henry, b. 1950,—Nicholas David, b. 1952.——Ursula Mary, b. 1922: m. 1947, Com. Edward Graham Ducat-Hamersley, RN, of Paddock House, Pyrton, Watlington, Oxon., and has issue living, Penelope Tara, b. 1948,— Priscilla Rosemary, b. 1951, Felicity, b. 1954,—Joanna, b. 1957.——Rosemary Kathleen, b. 1924; formerly in WRNS: m. 1945, A. E. Mabin, Lt. Roy. NZNVR, and has issue living, Richard Peter b. 1965, Susan Kathleen, b. 1946,—Caroline Ruth, b. 1947,—Helen Rosemary, b. 1950,—Victoria Jane, b. 1953. Residence,—80, Cleveland Terr., Nelson, NZ.

Grandson of the late Hon. Charles Alexander Gore, brother of 4th Earl:—
Issue of the late Sir Francis Charles Gore, K.C.B., b. 1846, d. 1940: m. 1879, Constance Mary, who d. 1925, dau. of the late Lieut.-Gen. Robert Bruce [Corbet, Bt., colls.], brother of 1st Baron Aberdare :—
John Francis, CVO, TD, b. 1885; ed. at Radley, and at Trin. Coll., Oxford (MA); Bar. Inner Temple 1909; late Capt. Bedfordshire Yeo.; a JP of Sussex 1932-58; an Author and Journalist; 1914-19 War (despatches); CVO 1941: m. 1926, Lady Janet Helena Campbell, da. of 4th Earl Cawdor, and has issue living, Charles John (35, Morton Hall Rd., Edinburgh, EH9), b. 1932: m. 1961, Jean, yr. da. of the late Col. Charles Ian Fraser, CBE, TD, of Reelig, Kirkhill, Inverness-shire, and has issue living, Ian Simon Francis, b. 1965, John, b. 1971, Helena Mary, b. 1962,—Moyra, b. 1927,—Mary Elizabeth (Lady Cave), b. 1929: m. 1957, Sir Charles Edward Coleridge Cave, 4th Bt. Residence,— Littlehay, Burley, nr. Ringwood, Hants.

Grandchildren of the late Spencer William Gore, 2nd son of Hon. Charles Alexander Gore (ante):—
Issue of the late George Pym Gore, b. 1875, d. 1959: m. 1914, Alexandra Leila, who d. 1970, da. of the late Rev. Canon Frederick Alfred John Hervey, CBO [M. Bristol, colls.], and widow of Lt. Sir Walter Clervaux Chaytor, RN, 5th Bt.:—
Victoria Maud Lavinia Mary, b. 1915 : m. 1944, Ian Alexander Kennedy, 16th/5th Lancers, from whom she obtained a divorce 1955, and has issue living, Lavinia Susan, b. 1948. Residence,— High Row, Gainford, Darlington, co. Durham.
Issue of the late Spencer Frederick Gore, b. 1878, d. 1914 : m. 1912, Mary Joanna, who d. 1968, da. of Capt. John Kerr:—
Frederick John Pym b. 1913; ed. at Lancing Coll., and at Trin. Coll., Oxford; ARA; a Trustee of Imperial War Museum since 1967; 1940-45 War as Maj. RA: m. 1st 1945, (m. diss. 19—) Lili Reneé, da. of L. Gaber; 2ndly 19—, Constance Irene, da. of W. H. Smith, of Brentford, Middx. and has issue living, (by 1st m.) Georgiana Sarah, b. 1950,—(by 2nd m.) Charles David, b. 1954,—Geraldine Lucy, b. 1957.——Margaret Elizabeth, b. 1912: m. 1940, Samuel Richard Cowie, and has issue living, Christopher Frederick, b. 1941,—John Richard, b. 1944.—Martin George Charles, b. 1956,— Frances Mary, b. 1947. Residence,—Dorrington Cottage, Meopham, Kent.

Granddaughters of the late Ven. John Ribton Gore, son of the late Very Rev. the Hon. George Gore, LL.D., Dean of Killala, 3rd son of 2nd Earl :—
Issue (by 2nd marriage) of the late Arthur Saunders Gore, b. 1848, d. 1901: m. 1st, 1878, Frances Elizabeth, who d. 1879, dau. of the late William Fraser, of Madras; 2ndly, 1881, Elizabeth, who d. 1950 : dau. of the late James Baldwin, of Mount Pleasant, co. Cork :—
Mabel (Jill), b. 1891: m. 1959, Chambré Baldwin, who d. 1969. Residence,—86, Harlaxton Drive, Lenton Sands, Nottingham.
Issue of the late Lieut.-Col. Ribton Gore, b. 1852, d. 1924: m. 1881, Ada Sophia, who d. 1944 (having m. 2ndly, 1930, Lieut.-Col. Alan Mackenzie-Penderel (retired), who d. 1940), dau. of the late Robert Dendy, J.P., of The Warren. Chichester :—
Ada Mary Frances, b. 1882: m. 1919, Capt. Robert John Mackessack, MD, ChB, formerly RAMC, who d. 1970, and has issue living, John Ribton Gore, b. 1921; ed. at Edinburgh Univ. (MB, ChB): m. 1955, Nicolette, da. of the late Henry Freston, of Oakleigh, Alderley Edge, Ches.,—Evelyn Mary, b. 1924: m. 1954, Maj. Robert Henry Brydges Oatts, KOSB (School of Infantry, Warminster, Wilts.), and has issue living, Andrew Robert Brydges b. 1955, Jeremy Roderick Henry b. 1958, Victoria Mary b. 1960.

Grandchildren of the late Arthur Saunders Gore (ante):—
Issue of the late Arthur Henry Baldwin Gore, b. 1883, d. 1953: m. 1913, Jane Browne (919, North Sunset, W. Covina, Calif., USA):—
Arthur Francis, MD (376, W. Badillo, Covina, Calif., USA), b. 1914: m. 1939, Helen Claire Mullen, of Omaha, Nebraska, USA, and has issue living, James Arthur, b. 1950,—Judith Ann, b. 1940: m. 1964, Fernando Joseph Ramirez, of 8719, La Roca, Fountain Valley, Calif., USA, and has issue living, Jane Ellen b. 1965, Ann Marie b. 1969,—Nancy Jane, b. 1942,—Margaret Francis, b. 1946,—Pamela, Elizabeth, b. 1948: m. 1969, Paul Everett Adkins, and has issue living, Jennifer Claire b. 1975,— Jill Marie, b. 1957,—Martha Jane, b. 1959,—John Douglas, b. 1916: m. 1946, Evelyn Mae (Lyn) Wagner, of Los Angeles, Calif., USA, and has issue living, John Douglas b. 1947,—Theresa Ann, b. 1951,—Margaret Jane, b. 1957. Residence,—11510, Kibbee, Whittier, 90604, Calif., USA.
Issue of the late John Ribton Gore, b. 1886, d. 1939: m. 1912, Valentine Curran (213, Jefferson St., Bakersfield, Calif. 93305, USA):—
Patricia Ellard, b. 1914: m. 1st, 1934, Clayton Dougherty, who d. 1935; 2ndly, 1937, Edward Newell Steele, of 2155, Fairway Drive, San Leandro, Calif. 94577, USA, and has issue living, (by 2nd m.) John Stanley (2744, Sheffield Place, Castro Valley, Calif. 94546, USA), b. 1939: m. 1st, 1960, Donna McColly; 2ndly, 1970, Terry Lee Sanborn, and has issue living, (by 1st m.) Timothy Edward, b. 1961, Todd William b. 1970,—Valerie Ann, b. 1941: m. 1961, Thomas Arthur Benge, of 1806, Diamond Ave., S. Pasadena, Calif. 91030, USA.

Grandchildren of the late Major James Arthur Charles Gore, son of the late Gen. the Hon. Sir Charles Gore, K.H., G.C.B., 6th son of 2nd Earl :—
Issue of the late Col. Edward John Mounsey Gore, b. 1863 ; d. 1949 : m. 1899, the Hon. Emilia Herbert Fullerton Napier, who d. 1932, dau. of 1st Baron Napier of Magdala:—
Humphry Gerard Napier, b. 1916 ; ed. at Sherborne ; Major (retired) late Roy. Ulster Rifles : m. 1948, Leslie Marshal Peabody, of New York, U.S.A., and has issue living, Mark Staveley, b. 1952,— Brendon Bostwick, b. 1955,—Timothy Francis, b. 1957. Residence,—The Red Cottage, South Park, Sevenoaks, Kent.——Irene Frances Cecilia, b. 1908 : m. 1947, William James Curtis, of Wheelwrights, Stoney Stratton, Evercreech, Somerset.
Issue of the late William Stuart Gore, b. 1868, d. 1946 : m. 1894, Emly Winn, who d. 1956 :—
William James Stuart, b. 1894: m. 19—, Lilliam May, dau. of James Knight.——Erroll Napier (5, Barrie Cres., Stockton, NSW 2295), b. 1897: m. 1926, Alma Maude, da. of William Edward Kessell, and has issue living, William Erroll (1, Newcastle St., Stockton, NSW), b. 1926: m. 1951, Joan Hetherington, and has issue living, Arran William b. 1965, Jennifer Louise b. 1957, Susan Michelle b. 1959, Alyson Maree b. 1961, Catherine Anne b. 1968,—Stuart Maxwell, b. 1929,—Ian Winn Bazelgette, b. 1932; Maj., Australian Staff Corps: m. 1961, Evelyne Phyllis, da. of the late Maj. Charles William Sayers, of Melbourne, and has issue living, Robert Ian Charles b. 1966, Belinda Jane b. 1967,—Laurence James, b. 1935,—Pamela Mary, b. 1939: m. 1961, Graham Richard Westwood, and has issue living, Nicholas Ian Richard b. 1964, Jo-Anne Louise b. 1963.——Vere Hunt, b. 1899.—— Gwendoline Arran, b. 1908: m. 1931, Michael Ernest Seymour [see Culme-Seymour, Bt., colls.]. Residence,—14, Thomas St., Northmead, NSW.

Granddaughter of the late Richard Frederick John Gore (infra):—
Issue of the late Edward Gore, b. 1880, d. 1935 : m. 1913, Constance May Campbell, who d. 1958, dau. of George William Campbell Wilson :—
Isabelle Ada Louie Langton, b. 1915 : m. 1944, Lloyd Blaine Reck, late U.S.A. Med. Corps, and has issue living, Juanita Ann, b. 1949. Residence,—

Grandchildren of the late Capt. John Gore, son of the late Hon. Richard Gore, 2nd son of 1st Earl :—
Issue of the late Richard Frederick John Gore, *b.* 1836, *d.* 1914 : *m.* 1874, Susan Jane, who *d.* 1937, dau. of the late William Stephenson, of Meaford, Canada, and widow of Frederick Featherstonhaugh, of Wicklow :—
Frederick John, *b.* 1879; late Lt. Australian Reserve of Officers; European War 1914-19: *m.* 1918, Constance Victoria, dau. of William Somerville Paul.——Arthur Charles, *b.* 1884 ; is a Stock and Station Agent.——Mary Eileen, *b.* 1887: *m.* 1911, Ernest Noel Mills. *Residence,—*

Granddaughters of the late William John Gore, son of the late Capt. Ralph Gore, RN, 2nd son of the late Hon. Paul Gore, 3rd son of 1st Earl:—
Issue of the late Charles Arthur Gore, *b.* 1845, *d.* 1926: *m.* 1st, 1883, Mary Goacher, who *d.* 1894; 2ndly, 1907, Constance Gertrude; she *m.* 3rdly, 1928, John James Sayers, who *d.* 1955), da. of John Burch, of 148, Ebury Street, SW1, and widow of Henry William Willis:—
Cecilia Mary, *b.* 1884 : *m.* 1908, Albert Reynolds. *Resides in* Australia.——(By 2nd marriage) Constance Joyce Gwendolen, *b.* 1911 ; is a S.R.N. : *m.* 1937, Ernest Killingback, B.Sc., A.R.C.S., who *d.* 1939, and has issue living, Peter Gore (11A, Leckhampton Rd., Woodlands Estate, Loughborough) *b.* 1939; ed. at King Edward VI Gram. Sch., Aston, London Sch. of Pharmacy (B. Pharm.), and Manchester Univ. (MSc): *m.* 1968, Janet Mary Reason, BSc. *Residence,—*5, Orchard Cres., Enfield, Middx.

(In Remainder to Baronetcy only.)
Descendants of the late John Ralph ORMSBY-GORE (fourth in descent from the late William Gore, M.P., 3rd son of 1st Baronet), who was cr. *Baron Harlech* 1876 [see that title].

PREDECESSORS.—[1] *Sir* ARTHUR Gore, second son of Sir Paul Gore (who was cr. a Baronet of Ireland 1621); cr. a *Baronet* of Ireland 1662; *s.* by his grandson [2] ARTHUR, 2nd Bt. ; *M.P.* for co. Longford; *d.* 1741; *s.* by his el. son [3] ARTHUR, 3rd Bt. ; cr. *Baron Saunders* and *Viscount Sudley* (peerage of Ireland) 1758, and *Earl of the Arran Islands* (peerage of Ireland) 1762; *d.* 1773; *s.* by his el. son [4] ARTHUR SAUNDERS, K.P., 2nd Earl; *d.* 1809; *s.* by his el. son [5] ARTHUR SAUNDERS, 3rd Earl; *d.* 1837; *s.* by his nephew [6] PHILIP YORKE, K.P., 4th Earl, *b.* 1801: *m.* 1838, Elizabeth Marianne, who *d.* 1899, dau. of the late Gen. Sir William Francis Patrick Napier, K.C.B.; *d.* June 25th, 1884; *s.* by his son [7] ARTHUR SAUNDERS WILLIAM CHARLES FOX, K.P., 5th Earl; *b.* 1839; cr. *Baron Sudley*, of Castle Gore, co. Mayo (peerage of United Kingdom), 1884 : *m.* 1st, 1865, the Hon. Edith Jocelyn, who *d.* 1871, dau. of Robert, Viscount Jocelyn, M.P., and sister of 4th Earl of Roden ; 2ndly, 1889, Winifred Ellen, who *d.* 1921, dau. of the late John Reilly, and widow of the Hon. John Montagu Stopford, *d.* 1901 ; *s.* by his son [8] ARTHUR JOCELYN CHARLES, K.P., P.C., 6th Earl ; *b.* 1868 : Brevet Major, Roy. Horse Guards ; was H.M. Lieut. and Custos Rotulorum for co. Donegal 1917-20 and a K.G.St.J. : *m.* 1st, 1902, Mathilde Jacqueline Marie Beauclerk (a D.G.St.J.), who *d.* 1927, only dau. of Baron Huyssen van Kattendyke, of Kattendyke, Zeeland, Netherlands; 2ndly, 1929, Lilian Constance, who *d.* 1961, dau. of the late John Quick, of Crossdeep Place, Twickenham, and widow of Frank Browne, of Pyecroft Place, Chertsey ; *d.* (Dec. 19th) 1958 ; *s.* by his el. son [9] ARTHUR PAUL JOHN CHARLES JAMES, *b.* 1903 ; A.D.C. to Gov.-Gen. of S. Africa 1931 ; *d.* (Dec. 28th) 1958 ; *s.* by his brother, [10] ARTHUR STRANGE KATTENDYKE DAVID ARCHIBALD, 8th Earl and present peer ; also Viscount Sudley, Baron Saunders, and Baron Sudley.

ARUNDELL OF WARDOUR, BARONY. (Arundell.) [Extinct 1944.]

DAUGHTERS LIVING OF FIFTEENTH BARON.
Hon. Blanche Mary (10, Haldane Rd., SW6; Casa Blanca, Nerja, Malaga, Spain), *b.* 1908: *m.* 1935, (m. diss. 1954) Ninian John Frederick Hanbury-Tracy, who *d.* 1971 [see B. Sudeley, colls.].

Hon. Mary Isabella, *b.* 1913: *m.* 1935 (m. diss. 1955), Air Commodore Thomas Patrick Feltrim Fagan, RAF, and has issue living, Patrick Feltrim, *MBE* (The Coach House, Fairmile Lea, Cobham, Surrey) *b.* 1935; MBE (Mil.) 1966; Lt.-Col. RE: *m.* 1967, Veronica, da. of J. J. Lorant, and widow of Capt. C. J. C. Thompson, RE, and has issue living, Daragh Patrick Feltrim *b.* 1969, Rory Michael Feltrim *b.* 1972,—Michael John, *b.* 1940,—Deirdre Mairi, *b.* 1937. *Address,—*c/o Midland Bank, Shaftesbury, Dorset.

ARWYN, BARON. (Arwyn.) [Life Baron 1964.]

ARWYN RANDALL ARWYN, son of the Rev. William Davies, of Glais, Glamorgan; *b.* April 17th, 1897; assumed surname of Arwyn in lieu of Davies by deed poll 1964; ed. at Ystalyfera Gram. Sch., and at Swansea Tech. Coll.; Past Pres., Cornish Inst. of Mining Engineers, a Member of Mineral Development Cttee. 1946-49, Chartered Mining Eng. and Consultant, a Dir. of Cos., Dep. Chm. of Bath and Portland Group Ltd.; Chm. of Atkinson Electrical & Engineering Co. Ltd., and of Webb Electronics (Bath) Ltd.; a Member of China Clay Council 1950-71, and of North Atlantic Assembly (Mil. Scientific & Tech. Cttees.) 1968-74; 1914-18 War with Glamorgan Yeo. and R.W.F. Machine Gun Corps, and RAF; 1939-45 War; Specialist Ser. Research Development and use of explosives; *cr. Baron Arwyn*, of Glais, co. Glamorgan (Life Baron) 1964: *m.* 1st, 1929 (m. diss. 1945), Norah Gwynne, da. of Ernest Watkins, of Mumbles, Swansea; 2ndly, 1946, Beatrix Emily Bassett, da. of Capt. F. H. Organ, of St. Austell, Cornwall, and has issue by 1st and 2nd marriages.

Arms,—Per chevron vert and or, on a chevron between in dexter chief a pick proper and a sword in saltire argent hilt and pomel or, in sinister chief a like sword and pick in saltire, and in base a three masted ship in full sail sable a cross formy gules between two open books chevronwise proper. Crest,— On the battlements of three turrets instant from the battlements of a tower gules a ram about to charge sable armed, imguled and villene or. Supporters,—Dexter, a Cornish chough proper; sinister, a dragon gules both with wings addressed.
Residences,—Ormonde, Lostwithiel, Cornwall; Ewart, Ashley Rd., Bathford, Somerset. Clubs,— Reform, RAC, Royal Cornwall Yacht, House of Lords Yacht, Flushing Sailing.

SON LIVING. *(By 2nd marriage.)*
Hon. Arwyn Hugh Davies, *b.* 1949; Bar. Grays Inn 1972.

DAUGHTERS LIVING. (*By 1st marriage.*)

Hon. Mary Gwynne, *b.* 1932: *m.* 1954, Geoffrey James Webb, of 107, Shakespeare Av., Bath, and has issue.

Hon. Elisabeth Jocelyn, *b.* 1938: *m.* 1962, John Robb Macnab, of 186, Sedlescombe Rd. North, St. Leonards-on-Sea, and has issue.

ASHBOURNE, BARON. (Gibson.) [Baron U.K. 1885.]

Open, oh, ye heavenly gates.

EDWARD RUSSEL GIBSON, *C.B., D.S.O.,* 3rd Baron; *b.* June 1st, 1901; *s.* 1942; ed. at R.N. Coll., Dartmouth, and Gonville and Caius Coll., Camb.; Vice-Adm. (ret.); a JP for Devon; on Naval Staff at Admiralty 1945-47; Commanded HMS *Mauritius* 1947-48, UK Naval Representative on Mil. Staff Cttee. UN 1948-50, and Flag Officer, Gibraltar and Adm. Sup. of H.M. Dockyard, Gibraltar 1950-52; an OStJ; 1914-18 War in *HMS Superb, Dreadnought,* and *Monarch*; 1939-45 War, on Staff of Adm. Sir Max Kennedy Horton, KCB, DSO 1940-42, Sen. Naval Officer (Landing) in Sicily assault 1943, commanded HMS *Ariadne,* and 3rd Submarine Flotilla (DSO, American Legion of Merit); DSO 1943, CB (Mil) 1950: *m.* 1929, Reta Frances Manning, el. da. of E. M. Hazeland, of Hong Kong, and has issue.

Arms,—Ermine, three keys fesswise in pale azure, and in chief as many trefoils slipped vert. Crest,—A pelican in her piety on a bank of reeds proper. Supporters,—*Dexter,* a female figure representing Mercy standing upon a fasces proper, habited argent, charged on the breast with a trefoil slipped vert, and resting her right hand on a sword point downwards proper, pommel or; *sinister,* a like figure representing Justice habited, charged and standing as the dexter, holding in her right hand a balance and in the left a sword erect proper.

Residence,—56, Chiltley Way, Midhurst Rd., Liphook, Hants. *Club,*—United Service and Royal Aero.

SON LIVING.

Hon. EDWARD BARRY GREYNVILLE (107, Sussex Rd., Petersfield, Hants.; United Service and Royal Aero Club), *b.* Jan. 28th, 1933; ed. at Rugby; Lt.-Cdr. RN (ret); stockbroker: *m.* 1967, Yvonne Georgina, da. of the late Maj. Gordon William Ham, and has issue living, Edward Charles D'Olier, *b.* 1967,—William Rodney Colles, *b.* 1970.

DAUGHTER LIVING.

Hon. Oonagh Elizabeth, *b.* 1935: *m.* 1963, John William Jeffrey, of Upway, Grosvenor Rd., Godalming, Surrey, and has issue living, Edward Paul John, *b.* 1966,—Katharine Helen, *b.* 1964.

BROTHER LIVING. (*Raised to the rank of a Baron's son* 1943.)

Hon. William David, *OBE, TD* (Buckley Cottage, Batson, Salcombe, Devon), *b.* 1914; ed. at Sherborne, and at Trin. Coll., Camb. (MA); 1939-45 War in Sicily and Italy as Lt.-Col. Intelligence Corps and in Austria as Lt. Col. Gen. Staff (despatches twice, OBE); OBE (Mil.) 1944: *m.* 1947, Sabine, da. of Dr. E. Landsberg, of Cape Town, S. Africa, and has issue living, Celia Mary, *b.* 1948,—Monica Anne, *b.* 1951,—Philippa Constance, *b.* 1953.

SISTERS LIVING. (*Raised to the rank of a Baron's daughters* 1943.)

Hon. Erica Alba, *b.* 1903 : *m.* 1929, Patrick Hope Rutland, and has issue living, Jeremy Charles, *b.* 1930,—Jonathan Patrick, *b.* 1935. *Residence,*—Flat 3, 4, Linden Park Rd., Tunbridge Wells.

Hon. Kathleen Mary, *b.* 1908: *m.* 1930, James Hamilton Russell, and has issue living, Michael Anthony Hamilton, *b.* 1932,—Timothy Patrick Hamilton, *b.* 1934,—David Patrick Roland, *b.* 1938,—Robin James, *b.* 1947,—Jill Mary, *b.* 1935,—Diana Elizabeth (twin), *b.* 1938. *Residences,*—Rushmere, Denbigh Rd., Cape Town, S. Africa; De Mond, Hermanus, Cape Town, S. Africa.

COLLATERAL BRANCH LIVING.

Issue (by 2nd marriage) of the late Hon. (Ernest) Victor Gibson, youngest son of 1st Baron, *b.* 1875, *d.* 1922: *m.* 1st, 1905, Mary Wood Salisbury, who *d.* 1905, dau. of Joseph L. R. Wood, of New York ; 2ndly, 1909, Caroline, who *d.* 1952, dau. of Frederic de Billier, of New York :—

John Frederic, *DSC, b.* 1919; is Lt. RNVR; 1939-45 War (DSC): *m.* 1st, 1941 (m. diss. 1946), Margaret A. Booth; 2ndly, 1947, Lorna M. Pickering, and has issue living, (by 1st m.) Victor Russell, *b.* 1943,—(by 2nd m.) Simon John, *b.* 1952.——Amelie Sheila, *b.* 1916: *m.* 1940, (Ralph) Neville Salvesen, and has issue living, Neil Theodore Ralph, *b.* 1944,—Keith Neville, *b.* 1951,—Amélie Camilla, *b.* 1941. *Residence,*—Capel Lodge, Beare Green, Surrey.

PREDECESSORS.—[1] Rt. *Hon.* EDWARD Gibson, *LL.D.,* son of the late William Gibson, J.P., of Merrion Square, Dublin ; *b.* 1837 ; Attorney-Gen. for Ireland 1877-80, and Lord Chancellor of Ireland with a seat in the Cabinet 1885 to Jan. 1886, July 1886 to Aug. 1892, and June 1895 to Dec. 1905 (many times acted as a Lord Justice of Ireland during absence of Lord-Lieut.) ; M.P. for Dublin Univ. (C) 1875-85; cr. *Baron Ashbourne,* of Ashbourne, co. Meath (peerage of United Kingdom) 1885: *m.* 1868, Frances Maria Adelaide, who *d.* 1926, dau. of the late Henry Cope Colles ; *d.* 1913 ; *s.* by his el. son [2] WILLIAM, 2nd Baron ; *b.* 1868: *m.* 1896, Marianne, who *d.* 1953, dau. of M. de Monbrison, of Avenue de Jena, Paris ; *d.* 1942 ; *s.* by his nephew [3] EDWARD RUSSELL (el. son of the late Hon. Edward Graves Mayne Gibson, 3rd son of 1st Baron), 3rd Baron and present peer.

ASHBROOK, VISCOUNT. (Flower.) [Viscount I. 1751.]

DESMOND LLOWARCH EDWARD FLOWER, *M.B.E.*, 10th Viscount; *b.* July 9th, 1905 ; *s.* 1936; ed. at Eton, and at Balliol Coll., Oxford (BA); a DL for Cheshire (JP 1946-67, Vice-Lieut. 1961-67) and a Member of Council of Duchy of Lancaster; formerly a Chartered Accountant; Chm. of Country Gentleman's Assocn. 1955-62; 1939-45 War as Maj. RA (TA); MBE (Mil) 1945: *m.* 1934, Elizabeth, el. da. of the late Capt. John Egerton-Warburton [see Grey-Egerton, Bt., colls.], and has issue.

Arms.—Quarterly: 1st and 4th argent, two chevronels between three ravens, each having an ermine spot in its beak, sable, and between the chevronels, three pellets ; 2nd and 3rd gules, three towers argent. Crest,— A raven, having an ermine spot in its beak. Supporters.— Two tigers reguardant proper, ducally collared and chained or.

A mind conscious of rectitude.

Residence,—Arley Hall, Northwich, Cheshire. *Club,*—Brooks's.

SONS LIVING.

Hon. MICHAEL LLOWARCH WARBURTON, *b.* Dec. 9th, 1935 ; ed. at Eton, and at Worcester Coll., Oxford (MA); 2nd Lt. Gren. Guards 1955; Solicitor 1963: *m.* 1971, Zoë Mary, yst. da. of the late Francis H. A. Engleheart, of The Priory, Stoke-by-Nayland, Suffolk, and has issue living, Roland Francis Warburton, *b.* 1975,—Eleanor Filumena *b.* 1973. *Residence,*—13, Paultons Sq., SW3 5AP.

Hon. Anthony John Warburton, *b.* 1938; ed. at Eton: *m.* 1970, Bridget Karen, yr. da. of J. Duncan, and has issue living, Alexandra Jane, *b.* 1972.

DAUGHTER LIVING.

Hon. Jane Mary Elizabeth, *b.* 1943; ed. at Lady Margaret Hall, Oxford (BA), and London Sch. of Econ. and Political Science (MSc): *m.* 1967, Charles Francis Foster, of 18, Stanley Gdns., W11, and has issue living, Rupert Rowland, *b.* 1970,—Antonia Elizabeth, *b.* 1969.

COLLATERAL BRANCH LIVING.

Issue of the late Hon. Reginald Henry Flower, younger son of 8th Viscount, *b.* 1871, *d.* 1938 : *m.* 1901, Katherine Ella (Kate), who *d.* 1957, dau. of Col. Cuming, formerly of Crovar, co. Cavan :—

Mollie Francis, *b.* 1902 : *m.* 1st, 1929, J. Peacey, from whom she obtained a divorce 1945 ; 2ndly, 1947, Maj. Wilfrid Allen, of Riverside, Allenby Rd., RR3, Duncan BC, Canada.——Honor Florence, *b.* 1904: *m.* 1923, Terence Dampier Dyson, and has issue living, Peter Spencer Dampier (of RR3, Kelowna, British Columbia), *b.* 1926: *m.* 1952, Margaret Helen Stevens, of Rutland, British Columbia, and has issue living, Steven Dampier *b.* 1962, Helen Honor *b.* 1953: *m.* 1971, Delbert Wayne Radomske (RR3, Kelowna, BC) (and has issue living, Jarret Delbert *b.* 1974, Virginia Lea *b.* 1971), Katherine Mary *b.* 1955, Virginia Ann *b.* 1957;—Terence Alexander, *b.* 1942,—Pamela Florence, *b.* 1924,— Virginia Nina, *b.* 1925: *m.* 1946, Arthur Orsi, of 2409, Thacker Drive, Westbank, BC, and has issue living, Kim Arthur *b.* 1959, Judith Anne *b.* 1947: *m.* 1966, Henry Grant Maddock, of 2414, Taylor Cres., Kelowna, BC, Canada, (and has issue living, Brett Andrew *b.* 1972, Jacqueline Lee *b.* 1968). *Address,*—RR3, Kelowna, BC.

PREDECESSORS.—[1] WILLIAM Flower, *M.P.* for co. Kilkenny; cr. *Baron Castle Durrow* (peerage of Ireland) 1733; *d.* 1746; *s.* by his son [2] HENRY, 2nd Baron; cr. *Viscount Ashbrook* (peerage of Ireland) 1751; *d.* 1752; *s.* by his son [3] WILLIAM, 2nd Viscount; *d.* 1780; *s.* by his el. son [4] WILLIAM, 3rd Viscount; *d.* 1802; *s.* by his brother [5] HENRY JEFFREY, 4th Viscount; *d.* 1847; *s.* by his son [6] HENRY JEFFREY, 5th Viscount, *b.* 1806: *m.* 1828, Frances, who *d.* 1886, dau. of Sir John Robinson, 1st Bt.; *d.* 1871: *s.* by his el. son [7] HENRY JEFFREY, 6th Viscount; *d.* 1882; *s.* by his brother [8] WILLIAM SPENCER, 7th Viscount. *b.* 1830: *m.* 1861, Augusta Madeline Henriette, who *d.* 1906, dau. of the late George Marton, of Capernwray Hall, Lancaster; *d.* 1906; *s.* by his brother [9] ROBERT THOMAS, 8th Viscount, *b.* 1836 : *m.* 1866, Gertrude Sophia, who *d.* 1911, dau. of the late Rev. Sewell Hamilton, of Bath ; *d.* 1919 : *s.* by his el. son [10] LLOWARCH ROBERT, 9th Viscount, *b.* 1870: *m.* 1899, Gladys Lucille, who *d.* 1968, dau. of the late Gen. Sir George Wentworth Alexander Higginson, G.C.B., G.C.V.O.; *d.* 1936 ; *s.* by his son [11] DESMOND LLOWARCH EDWARD, 10th Viscount and present peer ; also Baron Castle Durrow.

ASHBURTON, BARON. (Baring.) [Baron U.K. 1835.]

ALEXANDER FRANCIS ST. VINCENT BARING, *KG, KCVO*, 6th Baron; *b.* April 7th, 1898; *s.* 1938; ed. at Eton and RMC; late Lt. R. Scots Greys and Group Capt. AAF; Lord Lieut. of Hants. and I. of Wight 1960-73; Receiver-Gen. to Duchy of Cornwall 1961-73, and High Steward of Winchester since 1967; Co. Councillor Hants. 1945, Co. Alderman 1955-74, JP for Hants since 1951, and a DL since 1973; Chm. Hants. Police Authority since 1967 (Chm. Hants. & I. of Wight Police Authority 1961-67); Pres. Hants. and I. of Wight T & AF Assocn. 1960-67 and E. Wessex TA & VR Assocn. 1968-70; Treasurer King Edward VII Hosp. Fund for London 1955-64; Trustee St. Cross Hosp., Winchester since 1961, and Chantrey Bequest since 1963; Man. Dir. Baring Bros. & Co. Ltd. 1928-62; a KStJ ; France and Belgium 1918 (two medals)

Fortitude under difficulties.

KCVO 1961, KG 1969: *m.* 1924, the Hon. Doris Mary Thérèse Harcourt, da. of 1st Viscount Harcourt, and has issue.

Arms.—Azure, a fesse or, in chief a bear's head proper, muzzled and ringed, of the Second, differenced by a cross formy fitchy azure. **Crest,**—A mullet erminois, between two wings, argent. **Supporters,**—On either side a bear proper, muzzled, collared, and chained, or, charged on the shoulder with a cross patée fitchée of the last.
Residence,—Itchen Stoke House, Alresford, Hants. *Clubs,*—Turf, Hampshire (Winchester).

SONS LIVING.

Hon. JOHN FRANCIS HARCOURT, *b.* Nov. 2nd, 1928 ; ed. at Eton, and at Trin. Coll., Oxford (MA); Chm. of Baring Brothers & Co., Ltd., a Dir. of Outwich Ltd., Johannesburg, of Pye Holdings Ltd., of Royal Insurance Co. Ltd., of Trafford Park Estates, Ltd., Chm. of Outwich Investment Trust Ltd.; Receiver-Gen. Duchy of Cornwall; a Rhodes Trustee since 1970: *m.* 1955, the Hon. Susan Mary Renwick, el. da. of 1st Baron Renwick, and has issue living, Mark Francis Robert, *b.* 1958,—Alexander Nicholas John, *b.* 1964,—Lucinda Mary Louisa, *b.* 1956,—Rose Theresa, *b.* 1961. *Residence,*—Stratton Park, Micheldever, nr. Winchester. *Club,*—Pratt's.
Hon. Robin Alexander, *b.* 1931 ; ed. at Eton ; late Sub-Lieut. R.N.V.R. : *m.* 1960, Ann Caroline Thalia, el. dau. of Major Edward Fitzhardinge Peyton Gage [see V. Gage, colls.], and has issue living, Francesca Rhiannon, *b.* 1963.

SISTERS LIVING.

Hon. Aurea Vera, *b.* 1891 : *m.* 1917, Major Charles James Balfour, who *d.* 1939 [E. Antrim].
Residence,—Newton Don, Kelso, Berwickshire.
Hon. Angela Mildred, *b.* 1893. *Residence,* -Itchen Stoke Manor, Alresford, Hants.

COLLATERAL BRANCHES LIVING.

Issue of the late Capt. the Hon. Frederick Arthur Baring, 2nd son of 4th Baron, *b.* 1867, *d.* 1961 : *m.* 1890, Laura Louise, who *d.* 1951, da. of F. Hobson :—
Evelyn Claire, *b.* 1891. *Residence,*—Chilton Cottage, Chilton Candover, Alresford, Hants.

Grandchildren of the late Lieut.-Col. the Hon. Guy Victor Baring, M.P. (infra):—
Issue of the late Simon Alexander Vivian Baring, *b.* 1905, *d.* 1962: *m.* 1st, 1935 (marriage dissolved 1946), Jeanne, dau. of Felix Salmond, of London and New York; 2ndly, 1946, Pamela Rachel (CAMERON), da. of the late Sir Mark Beresford Russell Grant-Sturgis, KCB [E. Wharncliffe]:—
(By 1st m.) Julian Guy Alexander (Manor Farm, Bradley, Basingstoke, Hants.), *b.* 1935: *m.* 1971, Isla, da. of the late Frank Samuel Tait, of Toorak, Vic., Aust., and has issue living, Justin Frank Alexander, *b.* 1971,—Rebecca Alexandra Rose, *b.* 1973.——(by 2nd m.) Francis Esmond, *b.* 1948.—— Camilla Jane, *b.* 1952.
Issue of the late Lt.-Col. the Hon. Guy Victor Baring, MP, Coldstream Guards, 4th son of 4th Baron, *b.* 1873, *d.* (killed in action) 1916: *m.* 1903, Olive, who *d.* 1964, da. of Hugh Colin Smith, of Mount Clare, Roehampton, SW:—
Amyas Evelyn Giles (Montana Cottage, West End, Southampton), *b.* 1910; ed. at Gresham's Sch., Holt, and at Magdalene Coll., Camb.: m. 1st, 1935, Mrs. Mona Husband, da. of Lt.-Col. W. B. Mullins, of Ambersham House, Midhurst, Sussex; 2ndly, 1949, Peggy Michell (REEVES), da. of Surg. Vice-Adm. Sir Arthur Gaskell, KCB, OBE, FRCS, and has issue living, (by 1st m.) Claire Leonora (27, Egerton Terr., SW3), *b.* 1936: *m.* 1956 (m. diss. 1974), the Hon. Peter Alastair Ward [see E. Dudley].
——Aubrey George Adeane, *DFC, b.* 1912; is Sqd. Ldr. RAF VR; 1939-44 War (DFC): *m.* 1952, Marina, el. da. of Basil Bessel, of 22, Farley Court, W14, and formerly wife of Sir Charles Richard Andrew Oakeley, 6th Bt., and has issue living, Alexander Esmond, *b.* 1953,—Adrian Hugh Vasili, *b.* 1962,—Louise Olivia, *b.* 1955. *Residence,*—Lake House, Avington, Winchester, Hants.——
Olivia Constance Leonora, *b.* 1908: *m.* 1941, Maj. Cecil Henry Feilden, Coldstream Gds. (Supplementary Reserve) [see V. Hampden, colls.]. *Residence,*—Bramdean House, Alresford, Hants.

Grandchildren of the late Lt.-Col. the Hon. Guy Victor Baring, M.P., ante):—
Issue of the late Lt.-Col. Esmond Charles Baring, O.B.E., *b.* 1914, *d.* 1963: *m.* 1st, 1936 (marriage dissolved 1951), Zalia, da. of the late Sir Harold Edward Snagge, K.B.E. [B. Avebury, colls.]; 2ndly, 1960, Judith (RADWAY), (Hopetoun House, S. Queensferry, W. Lothian) (who m. 3rdly, 1965, the 3rd Marquess of Linlithgow) da. of the late Stanley Mathew Lawson, of Cincinnati, U.S.A.:—
(By 1st m.) Oliver Alexnader Guy (Horsington Grange, Templecombe, Som.), *b.* 1944: *m.* 1967, Veronica, da. of the late Capt. Ian Alexander Henderson [see B. Faringdon, colls.], and has issue living, Rupert Esmond Ian, *b.* 1968,—Emma Rose, *b.* 1970.——Guy Esmond (Warragandra, Toggannoggera, via Braidwood, NSW), *b.* 1945: *m.* 1967, Raina, da. of David Campbell, of Palerang, Bungendore, NSW, and has issue living, Ben, *b.* 1970,—Ned, *b.* 1975,—Samantha, *b.* 1969.—— Caroline Venetia, *b.* 1937: *m.* 1957, Henry Giles Francis Lascelles, of Hillwatering Farm, Langham, Bury St. Edmunds [see E. Harewood, colls.].——Patricia, *b.* 1938: *m.* 1965, Maj. Henry Claude Lyon Garnett, OBE, of 98, Eaton Terr., SW1.
Issue of the late Hon. Caryl Digby Baring, youngest son of 4th Baron, *b.* 1880, *d.* 1956: *m.* 1907, Ivy, who *d.* 1971, da. of the late Humphrey Brooke Firman (formerly 16th Lancers), JP, of Stone Court, St. Leonards-on-Sea:—
Denzil, *b.* 1909; ed. at Eton; late Capt. Royal Corps of Signals. *Residence,*—8, Oakley House, 103, Sloane St., SW1.——Leonora Jacqueline, *b.* 1912.

PREDECESSORS.—[1] The *Right Hon.* ALEXANDER Baring, *P.C., D.C.L.,* 2nd son of Sir Francis Baring, 1st Baronet [B. Northbrook], and cousin of Richard Dunning, 2nd Baron Ashburton (cr. 1782, extinct 1823); cr. *Baron Ashburton* (peerage of United Kingdom) 1835, was sometime Pres. of Board of Trade and Master of the Mint; *d.* 1848: *s.* by his el. son [2] WILLIAM BINGHAM, *P.C.,* 2nd Baron ; was Sec. of Board of Control 1841-5. Paymaster of the Forces and Treasurer of the Navy 1845-6, and seventeen years M.P. for various constituencies: *d.* 1864 ; *s.* by his brother [3] FRANCIS, 3rd Baron, *b.* May 24, 1800; sat as M.P. for Thetford (L) 1832-41 and 1848-57 : *m.* 1832, Claire Hortense, who *d.* 1882, dau. of the Duke of Bassano, Minister of Napoleon I.: *d.* Sept. 6, 1868; *s.* by his son [4] ALEXANDER HUGH, 4th Baron: *b.* 1835: sat as M.P. for Thetford (LC) 1857-67 : *m.* 1864, the Hon. Leonora Caroline, who *d.* 1930, dau. of 9th Baron Digby : *d.* 1889 ; *s.* by his el. son [5] FRANCIS DENZIL EDWARD, 5th Baron : *b.* 1866 *m.* 1st, 1889, the Hon. Mabel Edith Hood. who *d.* 1904, dau. of 4th Viscount Hood ; 2ndly, 1906, Frances, who *d.* 1959, dau. of J. O. Donnelly, of New York ; *d.* 1938 ; *s.* by his only son [6] ALEXANDER FRANCIS ST. VINCENT, 6th Baron and present peer.

ASHBY, BARON. (Ashby.) [Life Baron 1973.]

ERIC ASHBY, *FRS,* son of Herbert Charles Ashby, of Bromley, Kent; *b.* Aug. 24th, 1904; ed. at City of London Sch., Imperial Coll. of Science, London Univ. (MA, DSc; Hon. Fellow 1955), and Chicago Univ.; Hon. ScD Dublin; Hon. DSc Nat. Univ. of Ireland, Nigeria and Chicago; Hon. LLD St. Andrews, Aberdeen, Belfast, Rand, Wales, London, Columbia, Bath, Michigan, Yale,

W. Aust., Manchester, and Windsor; Hon. DLitt W. Ontario, and Sydney; Hon. DCL E. Anglia; FRS; OStJ; Prof. of Botany Sydney Univ. 1938-49, and Manchester Univ. 1947-50; Pres. and Vice-Chancellor of Queen's Univ., Belfast 1950-59, and Chancellor since 1971; Vice-Chancellor Camb. Univ. 1967-69; Master of Clare Coll., Camb. since 1959; a Trustee of British Museum since 1968; Chm. Roy. Commn. on Environmental Pollution 1970-73; *cr.* Knt. 1956 and *Baron Ashby*, of Brandon, co. Suffolk (Life Baron) 1973: *m.* 1931, Elizabeth Helen Margaret, da. of Francis Farries, of Castle Douglas, Kirkcudbrightshire, and has issue.

Residences,—Master's Lodge, Clare College, Cambridge; Norman Cottage, Brandon, Suffolk.
Club,—United Oxford and Cambridge University.

SONS LIVING.

Hon. Michael Farries (51, Maids Causeway, Cambridge), *b.* 1935; ed. at Campbell Coll., Belfast, and Queen's Coll., Camb. (BA, PhD); Prof. of Engineering, Univ. of Camb.: *m.* 1962, Maureen, da. of S. James Stewart, of White House, Montgomery, Powys.

Hon. Peter (60, Mann Av., Toronto, Canada), *b.* 1937; ed. at Queen's Univ., Belfast (MB, BCh, MD); Assist. Prof., Univ. of Toronto: *m.* 1967, Moya, da. of Rear-Adm. Maurice Henry Adams, of Canberra, Rock, Cornwall.

ASHCOMBE, BARON. (Cubitt.) [Baron U.K. 1892.]

HENRY EDWARD CUBITT, 4th Baron, *b.* March 31st, 1924; *s.* 1962; ed. at Eton; 1939-45 War with RAF: *m.* 1st, 1955 (m. dis. 1968), Ghislaine (ALEXANDER), only da. of Cornelius Willem Dresselhuys, of Long Island, New York, USA; 2ndly, 1973, the Hon. Virginia Carington, yr. da. of the 6th Baron Carrington.

Arms,—Checky or and gules, on a pile argent issuing from the chief, a lion's head erased sable. *Crest.*—A column proper, in front two scimitars in saltire argent, pommel and hilt or. *Supporters.*—*Dexter*, a stonemason proper, habited in brown coat and hat, apron argent, in his right hand a mallet sable; *sinister*, a carpenter proper, habited in brown vest, apron argent, in his left hand a pair of compasses or.

Happy is the prudent man.

Residence,—Denbies, Dorking, Surrey. *Clubs,*—White's, St. James'.

SISTER LIVING.

Hon. Rosalind Maud, *b.* 1921: *m.* 1946, Major Bruce Shand, M.C., late 12th Roy. Lancers, and has issue living, Mark Roland, *b.* 1951,—Camilla Rosemary, *b.* 1947: *m.* 1973, Maj. Andrew Henry Parker-Bowles, Blues and Roys [see E. Macclesfield, colls.],—Sonia Annabel, *b.* 1949: *m.* 1972, Simon John Elliot, son of the late Air Ch. Marshal Sir William Elliot, GCVO, KCB, KBE, DFC. *Residence,*—The Laines, Plumpton, Sussex.

UNCLE LIVING. (Son of 2nd Baron.)

Hon. (Charles) Guy, *CBE, DSO, TD* (High Barn, Effingham, Leatherhead, Surrey; Cavalry Club), *b.* 1903; ed. at Eton, and RMC; late Lt. 1st The R. Dragoons, and Hon. Col. Surrey Yeo. (98th Field Regt.) RA (TA); a Co. Councillor, Surrey 1955-67, an Alderman 1965, a DL 1956, and High Sheriff 1955-56; a Dir. Cubitt Estates 1927-70; a partner, Cubitt West 1929-72; Chm. E. H. Cummins & Co. 1930-71; Chm. British Horse Soc. 1947-57 (Pres. 1952), The Pony Club 1945-70 (Life Pres.), and Combined Training Cttee. 1967-73; a Member of British Equestrian Fedn. since 1972; 1939-45 War as Lt.-Col. Surrey Yeo. in France, Middle East and Italy (despatches); DSO 1943, CBE (Civil) 1973: *m.* 1927, Rosamond Mary Edith, da. of Capt. Sir Montague Aubrey Rowley Cholmeley, 4th Bt., and has issue living, Hugh Guy (of Chapel House, West Humble, Dorking, Surrey), *b.* 1928: *m.* 1958, Linda Ishbel, yst. da. of the late Hon. Angus Dudley Campbell, OBE [see B. Colgrain, colls.], and has issue living, Jonathan Guy *b.* 1962, Joanna Mary *b.* 1960, Victoria Jane *b.* 1964,—Sylvia Rosemary, *b.* 1930: *m.* 1951, Maj. Ronald James Grant Dallas, 3rd Hussars, of Glebe House, Shipton Moyne, Tetbury, Glos. ,and has issue living, Nigel Alexander *b.* 1962, Caroline Rosamund *b.* 1952, Jennifer Mary *b.* 1954,—Celia Mary (*Hon. Mrs. Patrick T. Conolly-Carew*), *b.* 1939: *m.* 1962, Capt. the Hon Patrick Thomas Conolly-Carew, el. son of 6th Baron Carew.

MOTHER LIVING.

Sonia Rosemary, *O.B.E.*, dau. of Lieut.-Col. the late Hon. George Keppel, M.V.O.[see E. Albemarle, colls.]; a D.St.J.; OBE (Civil) 1959; *m.* 1920, as his 1st wife, the Hon. Roland Calvert Cubitt (later 3rd Baron Ashcombe), from whom she obtained a divorce 1947. *Residence,*—Hall Place, W. Meon, Hants.

COLLATERAL BRANCHES LIVING.

Issue of the late Hon. Jeremy John Cubitt, younger son of 3rd Baron, *b.* 1927, *d.* 1958: *m.* 1952, Diana Edith (who obtained a divorce 1957; she *m.* 2ndly, 1957, Capt. Nigel Arthur Tunnicliffe [see B. Mowbray, colls.]), el. da. of Com. Peter Du Cane, OBE, RN (ret.) [see Pole, Bt., cr. 1628]:—
Sarah Victoria, *b.* 1953.

Issue of the late Maj. the Hon. Archibald Edward Cubitt, 5th son of 2nd Baron, *b.* 1901, *d.* 1972: *m.* 1st, 1926, Lady Irene Helen Pratt (from whom he obtained a divorce 1933), da. of 4th Marquess Camden; 2ndly, 1934, Sibell Margaret (from whom he obtained a divorce 1949), da. of Ronald Collet Norman [Collet, Bt., ext.]:—

(By 1st m.) ALICK JOHN ARCHIBALD (Chetwode Manor, Buckingham), *b.* Aug. 10th, 1927; late Capt. R. Dragoons: *m.* 1st, 1956, Priscilla Rosemary, who *d.* 1957, el. da. of Thomas Cecil Gouldsmith [Laurie, Bt., colls]; 2ndly, 1961, Jennifer Faith, da. of the late Lt.-Gen. William Henry Ewart Gott, OB, OBE, DSO, MC, and has issue living, (by 1st m.) Amanda Jane, *b.* 1966.——(by 2nd m.) Mark Robin (Annagh, Coolbawn, Nenagh, co. Tipperary), *b.* 1936: ed. at Gordonstoun: *m.* 1962, Juliet Perpetua, da. of Edward Corbet Woodall, OBE [Crawley-Boevey, Bt., colls.], and has issue living, Mark Edward, *b.* 1964,—David Antony, *b.* 1966,—Hugo John, *b.* 1967.——Priscilla Margaret (*Countess of Harrington*) (Greenmount, Patrickswell, c. Limerick), *b.* 1941: *m.* 1964, as his 3rd wife, the 11th Earl of Harrington.

PREDECESSORS.—[1] GEORGE Cubitt, *P.C.*, son of the late Thomas Cubitt, of Denbies, Surrey, *b.* 1828: sat as M.P. for W. Surrey (*C*) 1360-85, and for Mid, or Epsom, Div. of Surrey Dec. 1885 to June 1892; *cr.* P.C. 1880, and *Baron Ashcombe*, of Dorking, co. Surrey, and Bodiam Castle, Sussex (peerage of United Kingdom) 1892: *m.* 1853, Laura, who *d.* 1904, dau. of the late Rev. James Joyce, V. of Dorking; *d.* 1917; *s.* by his son [2] HENRY, *CB, TD*, 2nd Baron; *b.* 1867; sometime Lt.-Col. and Hon. Col. Comdg. Surrey Yeo.; Lord-Lt. of Surrey 1905-39; MP for Surrey S-E or Reigate Div. (*C*) 1892-1906: *m.* 1890, Maud Marianne, who *d.* 1945, da. of the late Col. Archibald Motteaux Calvert, of Ockley Court, Dorking; *d.* 1947; *s.* by his 4th but. el. surviving son [3] ROLAND

CALVERT, 3rd Baron, b. 1899: m. 1st, 1920, Sonia Rosemary, OBE (who obtained a divorce 1947), da. of the late Lt.-Col. the late Hon. George Keppel, MVO [E. Albemarle, colls.]; 2ndly, 1948 Idina Joan (MILLS), who d. 1954, da. of the late Col. Robert Edward Myddelton, TD, DL, JP, of Chirk Castle, Denbighshire; 3rdly, 1959, Jean, who d. 1973, da. of the late Charles Tuller Garland, of Moreton Hall, Warwickshire, and formerly wife of Sir Robert George Maxwell Throckmorton, 11th Bt.; d. 1962; s. by his el. son [4] HENRY EDWARD, 4th Baron and present peer.

ASHDOWN, BARON.   (Silverstone.)   [Life Baron 1974.]

ARNOLD SILVERSTONE, yr. son of the late Henry Silverstone; b. Sept. 28th, 1911; ed. at Llanelly County Intermediate Sch., and Univ. Coll., Swansea; 1939-45 War as Maj.; Bar. Middle Temple 1953; a Co. Dir.; a Member of Repres. Council of Family Welfare Assocn. 1961-65, and a Member of Roy. Homeopathic Hosp. Management Cttee. 1964-65; Joint Treasurer Greater London Area of Conservative and Unionist Assocn. 1963-74; Joint Treasurer Conservative Party since 1974; Freeman of City of London, a Member of Court, Needlemakers' Co., a Gov. of Queen Charlotte's and Chelsea Hosps., a Member of Cttee. of Management, Inst. of Obstetrics and Gynaecology; cr. Knt. 1964, and Baron Ashdown, of Chelwood, co. E. Sussex (Life Baron) 1974: m. 1937, Lillian Nell, CBE (Civil 1971), da. of Ralph King.

Residences,—Gale, Chelwood Gate, Haywards Heath, Sussex; Flat 14, 45, Lowndes Sq., SW1. Clubs,—Carlton, Junior Carlton.

ASHFIELD, BARONY OF.   (Stanley.)   [Extinct 1948.]
DAUGHTERS LIVING OF FIRST BARON.

Hon. Marian Woodruff (Ann Cottage, Kilmeston, Alresford, Hants.), b. 1906: m. 1st, 1927, James Hart Rutland, from whom she obtained a divorce 1934; 2ndly, 1934, James Henry Royds [E. Perth, colls.], from whom she obtained a divorce 1940; 3rdly, 1940, Ralph Arthur Hubbard [see B. Addington, colls.], from whom she obtained a divorce 1954; 4thly, 1964, Edward James Barford, MC (infra), from whom she obtained a divorce 1971, and has issue living, (by 1st marriage) David John Stanley, b. 1930: m. 1953 (m. diss. 1958), Shirley Follett, da. of Lt.-Col. Frank Follett Holt, of Danbury, Essex, and has issue living, Davina Jane b. 1954,—(by 2nd marriage) Julia Elizabeth b. 1935,—(by 3rd marriage) [see B. Addington, colls.].

Hon. Grace Lowrey, b. 1907: m. 1st, 1928, Edward James Barford, M.C. (ante), who obtained a divorce 1940; 2ndly, 1940, as his third wife, Capt. Herbert John Buckmaster, late R. Horse Guards (Special Reserve), who d. 1966, and has issue living, (by 1st m.) Olive Julian Stanley (Pibworth House, Aldworth, Berks.), b. 1933: m. 1961, Helen Gay Woodroffe, da. of the Hon. Mr. Justice (Sir Peter Harry Batson Woodroffe) Foster, MBE, TD, and has issue living, James Edward Clive b. 1972, Emma Jane b. 1962, Amanda Helen b. 1964, Charlotte Gay b. 1967,—Edwina Patricia Lowrey, b. 1930: m. 1956, Rudolph Eugene Burger, of 2, Pembroke Gdns., W8, and has issue living, Rudolph Edward b. 1958, Alexander Stanley b. 1963, Eugenie Grace b. 1959,—Caroline Juliette Helen (twin), b. 1933: m. 1962, Robin St. Clair Hardy, 75, Eaton Terr., SW1, and has issue living, Justin St. Clair b. 1964, Arabella Lucy b. 1967. Residence,—Eresby House, Rutland Gate, SW7.

ASHTON OF HYDE, BARON.   (Ashton.)   [Baron U.K. 1911.]

With faith and valour.

THOMAS HENRY RAYMOND ASHTON, 2nd Baron ; b. Oct. 2nd, 1901 ; s. 1933 ; ed. at Eton, and at New Coll., Oxford (B.A. 1924, M.A. 1934) ; sometime Major Roy. Gloucestershire Hussars (T.A.) ; is a J.P. and a D.L. for Gloucestershire : m. 1925, Marjorie Nell, J.P., dau. of the late Hon. Marshall Jones Brooks [see B. Crawshaw, colls.], and has issue.

Arms,—Sable, on a pile between two crescents in base argent, a mullet pierced of the first. Crest,—On a mount vert, a mower proper, vested paly argent and sable, in the act of whetting his scythe also proper. Supporters,—Dexter, a mower proper, vested paly argent and sable, holding in the exterior hand a scythe also proper ; sinister, a boar argent semée of mullets sable pierced.

Residence,—Broadwell Hill, Moreton-in-Marsh, Gloucestershire. Club,—Boodle's.

SON LIVING.

Hon. THOMAS JOHN, T.D., b. Nov. 19th, 1926 ; ed. at Eton, and at New Coll., Oxford (B.A. 1950, M.A. 1955) ; formerly Lieut. 11th Hussars, and Maj. R. Gloucestershire Hussars (T.A.); a JP of Oxon.: m. 1957, Pauline Nell, el. da. of Lt.-Col. Robert Henry Langton Brackenbury, OBE, of Yerdley House, Long Compton, Shipston on Stour, and has issue living, Thomas Henry, b. 1958,—John Edward, b. 1966,—Charlotte Trewlove, b. 196 , —Katharine Judith, b. 1962. Residence,—Ashton Grange, nr. Chester. Club,—Boodle's.

SISTERS LIVING.

Hon. Marion Evelyn. b. 1890 : m. 1913, Major Robert Wood, who d. 1940, formerly Roy. Warwickshire Regt. Residence,—44, Victoria St., Toronto, Canada.

Hon. Margaret Joan, b. 1893 : m. 1925, Hugh Whistler, J.P., who d. 1943, formerly Indian Police, and has issue living, Ralfe Ashton (The Old Rectory, Sandhurst, Hawkhurst, Kent), b. 1930; ed. at Eton, and Selwyn Coll., Camb. (MA): m. 1953, Jane, da. of I. A. McCarthy, of Montreal, Canada, and has issue living, Brian Hugh b. 1954, Nicholas McCarthy b. 1955, John Daniel Ralfe b. 1964, Clare Evelyn Joan b. 1958, Lucy Julia b. 1960,—Benedicta (Flat 6, 8, The Paragon, Blackheath, SE3), b. 1927; ed. at Sherborne Sch. for Girls and at Newnham Coll., Camb. (BA 1949, MA 1952). Residence,—Caldbec House, Battle, Sussex.

PREDECESSOR.—[1] THOMAS GAIR Ashton, son of the late Thomas Ashton, J.P., D.L., of Hyde, Cheshire; b. 1855; M.P. for Hyde Div. of Cheshire (L) 1885-6, and for S., or Luton, Div. of Bedfordshire 1895-1911; cr. Baron Ashton of Hyde, co. Chester (peerage of United Kingdom) 1911; m. 1886, Eva Margaret, who d. 1938, dau. of the late John Henry James, of Kingswood, Watford, Herts: d. 1933; s. by his younger son [2] THOMAS HENRY RAYMOND, 2nd Baron and present peer.

ASHTOWN, BARON. (Trench.) [Baron I. 1800.]

DUDLEY OLIVER TRENCH, *OBE*, 5th Baron; *b.* July 11th, 1901; *s.* 1966; ed. at Wellington Coll.; Lt.Col. (ret.) KRRC; an Assist. Ch. Constable, War Dept. Constabulary 1947-64; OBE (Civil) 1961: *m.* 1st, 1932, Ellen Nancy, who *d.* 1949, da. of the late William Garton, of Brixedone, Bursledon, Hants.; 2ndly, 1955, Sheelah Adrienne Sarah, who *d.* 1963, yr. da. of the late Brig.-Gen. Lewis Frederic Green-Wilkinson, CMG, DSO; 3rdly, 1966, Frances Natalie, widow of Maj. James De Sales La Terrière, and has issue by 1st marriage.

Arms.—Argent, a lion passant gules, between three fleurs-de-lis, azure, on a chief of the last a sun in splendour or. Crest.—A dexter arm embowed in armour, the hand grasping a scimitar, all proper. Supporters.—Dexter, a lion gules, semée-de-lis, and ducally crowned or; sinister, a stag proper, attired, unguled, ducally collared and lined or. Second Motto—Dieu pour la Tranche, qui contre ("God for the Trench, whoever may oppose!").

Fortune is the companion of virtue.

Residence,—Woodlawn, King's Somborne, Stockbridge, Hants. Club,—English-Speaking Union.

DAUGHTERS LIVING. (By 1st marriage.)

Hon. Anne Rosemary, *b.* 1936: *m.* 1st, 1958, Capt. Timothy Patrick Arnold Gosselin, Scots Guards, who *d.* 1961 [E. Midleton, colls.]; 2ndly, 1962, Lt.-Col. Greville W. Tufnell, Gren. Gds. (The Old Rectory, North Cerney, nr. Cirencester, Glos.), and has issue living, (by 1st m.) Nicola Jane, *b.* 1960,— (by 2nd m.) Caroline Elizabeth, *b.* 1963,—Belinda Sheelah Anne, *b.* 1964,—Georgina Frances, *b.* 1966.

Hon. Jacqueline Noël, *b.* 1940: *m.* 1966, Alastair Gordon Eadie, of Bourne Orchard, Brickendon, Herts., and has issue living, James Alastair, *b.* 1967,—Christopher John, *b.* 1969,—Edward Charles Eadie, *b.* 1972.

WIDOW LIVING OF FOURTH BARON.

OONAH ANNE (*Oonah Baroness Ashtown*), (Brooklands, Ballysheedy, co. Limerick), el. da. of the late Brig.-Gen. Lewis Frederic Green-Wilkinson, CMG, DSO: *m.* 1950, as his 2nd wife, the 4th Baron, who *d.* 1966.

COLLATERAL BRANCHES LIVING. (In remainder to Barony.)

Grandchildren of the late Hon. William Cosby Trench, brother of 3rd Baron :—

Issue of the late Walter Frederick Oliver Trench, *b.* 1899, *d.* 1960; *m.* 1st, 1921, Norah Maude, who *d.* 1958, da. of the Ven. John Richard Hedges Becher, Archdeacon of Ross; 2ndly, 1960, Marion Gwendolyn (Castle Oliver, Killmallock, co. Limerick), da. of Robert Young, of Woolley, Yorks.:—

(By 1st marriage) Olga Ann Oliver, *b.* 1922: *m.* 1948, William Hugh Hindley (P.O. Box 15017, Nairobi, Kenya), and has issue living, Michael Edward Oliver, *b.* 1951,—Douglas William John, *b.* 1963,—Sheila Rachel, *b.* 1949.——Norah Susan Oliver, *b.* 1936: *m.* 1957, Walter Stuart Gash, MBE, of Rocklea, Mitchell Rd., Walliston, W. Aust., 6076, and has issue living, Maureen Susan, *b.* 1959,—Sheila Ann, *b.* 1960.

Issue of the late Algernon Oliver Trench, *b.* 1900, *d.* 1954: *m.* 1928, Muriel Dorothy, who *d.* 1954, el. dau. of the late Frank Thorne, of Weston-super-Mare :—

CHRISTOPHER OLIVER, *b.* March 23rd, 1931.

Grandchildren of the late Capt. the Hon. Cosby Godolphin Trench, 2nd son of 2nd Baron:—

Issue of the late Capt. Charles Sadleir Musgrave Trench, *b.* 1874, *d.* 1958 : *m.* 1914, Helen Cowley, who *d.* 1937, dau. of the late Robert Lidwell Brown, of Clonboy, O'Brien's Bridge, co. Clare :—

Cosby Patrick Musgrave, *b.* 1915 ; ed. at Eton, and at Trin. Coll., Dublin : *m.* 1956, Julia Violetta May, dau. of the late Frank Porch, and widow of Frank Whiting. Residence,—Sopwell Hall, Cloughjordan, co. Tipperary.

Issue of the late Clive Newcombe Trench, *b.* 1884, *d.* 1964: *m.* 1910, Kathleen (Queen's Mead, Odiham, Hants.), da. of the late Maj. Ivar MacIvor:—

Nigel Clive Cosby, *CMG* (British Embassy, Lisbon, Portugal; Bath Club), *b.* 1916; ed. at Eton, and at Corpus Christi Coll., Camb.; 1939-45 War as Maj. KRRC; entered HM Foreign Ser. (now Dip. Ser.) 1946; Ambassador to Korea 1969-71, and to Portuguese Republic since 1974; CMG 1966: *m.* 1939, Marcelle Catherine, yst. da. of Johan Jacob Clotterbooke Patyn van Kloetinge, and has issue living, Roderick Nigel Godolphin (May Cottage, Fletching St., Mayfield, Sussex), *b.* 1944; ed. at Eton, and Stanford Univ., USA; *m.* 1st, 1967, Janet, who *d.* 1971, da. of Harold Hamilton-Faulkner, of Redwood City, Cal., USA; 2ndly, 1973, Susan Barbara, da. of L. F. Day, FRCS, DLO, of Cooden, Sussex, and formerly wife of Michael R. J. Wright, and has issue living (by 1st m.), Timothy Roderick Hamilton *b.* 1968.——Lois Eileen, *b.* 1910: is a JP for Nairnshire: *m.* 1937, Capt. Charles Algernon Mackintosh-Walker, MBE, of Geddes, Nairn, and has issue living, Charles James, *b.* 1939,—Serena Mary, *b.* 1946.

Grandchildren of the late Charles Steuart Trench, 2nd son of the late Henry Trench (*b.* 1806), 4th son of the late Very Rev. Thomas Trench, Dean of Kildare, 3rd son of Frederick Trench, and brother of 1st Baron:—

Issue of the late Henry Marryat Trench, *b.* 1876, *d.* 1948: *m.* 1904, Juliet Benham, who *d.* 1946, el. dau. of the late William Seaman, of Staten Island, New York, U.S.A.:—

Edith Katharine, *b.* 1905: *m.* 1930, Albert Irwin Dorr, who *d.* 1947. Residence,—11, Jackson Avenue, Mystic, Connecticut, U.S.A.

Issue of the late Thomas Perceval Trench, *b.* 1880, *d.* 1924: *m.* 1921, Phyllis Clare Hume, who *d.* 1968, da. of the late Arthur Hume-Spry, BomCS:—

Thomas Perceval Hume, *b.* 1924 (posthumous); ed. at Rossall. Residence,—Trenchacres, Ballybrittas, Port Laoise, co. Leix.

Granddaughters of the late John Townsend Trench, son of William Steuart Trench, 5th son of the late Very Rev. Thomas Trench (ante):—

Issue of the late Rev. George Frederick Trench, *b.* 1881; *d.* 1966: *m.* 1919, Muriel Leonore, da. of the late Leslie S. Robertson, MICE:—

Leonore Elisita, *b.* 1920; ed. at Girton Coll., Camb. (BA): *m.* 1945, Henry Denis Whitwell Powell, FRCS, MB, ChB, of Ravensmere, Cryers Hill, High Wycombe, and has issue living, John Denis Trench, *b.* 1951,—Margaret Leonore, *b.* 1945: *m.* 1968, Frank William Taylor, and has issue living, Michael John *b.* 1970, Peter Hugh *b.* 1972,—Janet Elisita, *b.* 1949: *m.* 1972, Derek Peacock,—Clare Louise, *b.* 1954.——Bridget Wray, *b.* 1928; a Member of Assocn. of Occupational Therapists, and Canadian Occupational Therapy Assocn.: *m.* 1959, Robin Blakeway Dickens, of 3091, 1st Av., Prince George, BC, Canada, and has issue living, Mark Lester, *b.* 1961,—Lynn Catherine, *b.* 1963.

Granddaughter of the late Rev. Frederic Fitz-William Trench, son of the late William Trench, 4th son of Frederick Trench, and brother of 1st Baron:—
Issue of the late Rev. William Robert Trench, *b.* 1838, *d.* 1913: *m.* 1877, Edith Anne Hamilton, who *d.* 1892, dau. of the late Charles Langton, D.L., of Barkhill, Liverpool:—
Mary Ellinor, *b.* 1883: *m.* 1907, Capt. Francis Standfield Symons, who *d.* 1941. *Residence,—*

Granddaughter of the late Louis Trench, yst. son of the late Frederic Fitz-William Trench (ante):—
Issue of the late Geoffrey FitzLouis Trench, *b.* 1885, *d.* 1971: *m.* 1927, Olive Muriel (Church View, Sparkford, Yeovil, Somerset), da. of George Constance:—
Joanna Mary, *b.* 1937: *m.* 1959, Timothy Francis Cox, of Priors Mesne, Aylburton, Lydney, Glos., and has issue living, Dermot Francis, *b.* 1963,—Miranda Josephine, *b.* 1961.

Granddaughter of the late Col. Frederic Charles TRENCH-GASCOIGNE, son of the late Charles Trench, 4th brother of 1st Baron:—
Issue of the late Col. Frederic Richard Thomas TRENCH-GASCOIGNE, D.S.O., *b.* 1851, *d.* 1937: *m.* 1892, Laura Gwendolen Douglas, *C.B.E.*, who *d.* 1949, dau. of the late Capt. Sir Douglas Galton, K.C.B.:—
Cynthia Mary (*Cynthia, Baroness Sandys*), *b.* 1898: *m.* 1924, the 6th Baron Sandys, who *d.* 1961. *Residence,—*Himbleton Manor, Droitwich, Worcs.

Grandchildren of the late Most Rev. and Rt. Hon. Richard Chenevix Trench PC, DD, Archbishop of Dublin 1864-84, 2nd son of the late Richard Trench (all of whose descendants in the male line assumed in 1873 the name and arms of Chenevix), 5th brother of 1st Baron:—
Issue of the late Maj.-Gen. Frederic Chenevix Trench, C.M.G. (20th Hussars), *b.* 1837, *d.* 1894: *m.* 1873, Mary Frederica Blanche, who *d.* 1924, dau. of the late Capt. Charles Blood Mulville, formerly 3rd Dragoon Guards:—
Frances Melesina, *b.* 1887. *Residence,—*55, Chesterfield House, Chesterfield Gardens, W.1.

Grandchildren of the late Col. Charles Chenevix Trench, 3rd son of the late Most Rev. and Rt. Hon. Richard Chenevix Trench, PC, DD, (ante):—
Issue of the late Lieut.-Col. Sir Richard Henry Chenevix Trench, C.I.E., O.B.E., Indian Army, *b.* 1876, *d.* 1954: *m.* 1913, Evelyn May, dau. of the late Capt. Harry Evelyn Stracy Pocklington, 15th Hussars :—
Charles Pocklington, *MC* (Lisnamoe House, Ballymackey, Nenagh, co. Tipperary), *b.* 1914; ed. at Winchester, and at Oxford Univ.; Maj. (ret) late Indian Army; author of "The Royal Malady" and other works; 1939-45 War in Italy (MC): *m.* 1st, 1946, Patricia Jane, who *d.* 1963, da. of Maj. G. F. Gretton, of 62, Melton Court, SW7; 2ndly, 1954, Mary Elizabeth, da. of Lt.-Col. George Kirkbride, of Mullion, Cornwall, and has issue living, (by 1st marriage), Richard Hugh Roger, *b.*1949,—Charlotte Ann, *b.* 1946,—Priscilla Jane, *b.* 1947,—(by 2nd marriage), Lucy, *b.* 1956,—Georgia, *b.* 1959.——Evelyn Jane Chenevix, *b.* 1917: *m.* 1950, Richard Christian Allhusen, and has issue living, Christian Henry, *b.* 1956,—Richard Frederick, *b.* 1960,—Elizabeth Mary, *b.* 1952,—Rosalind Jane, *b.* 1954. *Residences,—*Bradenham Hall, Thetford, Norfolk; 61, Eaton House, Upper Grosvenor St., W1.

Grandchildren of the late Charles Godfrey Chenevix Trench, CIE (infra):—
Issue of the late Christopher John CHENEVIX-TRENCH, MBE, *b.* 1911, *d.* 1971: *m.* 1936, Mary Elizabeth Catherine (Cobblestones, Sheepstor, Yelverton, Devon), el. da. of the late G. H. Allen, of Branksome, Poole:—
Timothy Christopher John, *b.* 1938; ed. at King's Sch., Canterbury, and Corpus Christi Coll., Oxford: *m.* 1961 (m. diss. 1973), Penelope Mary Travers, el. da. of G. C. Walton, of Maidensgrove, Henley-on-Thames, and has issue living, Katherine Rae, *b.* 1964,—Alison Mary, *b.* 1965,—Phillida Clare, *b.* 1969.——John Richard (Mowden Hall School, Newton, Stockfield, Northumberland), *b.* 1948: *m.* 1970, Pauline, da. of James Stephen Alexander, of 2, Seawood Place, Grange Over Sands, Cambria.——Elizabeth Mary, *b.* 1941: *m.* 1964, Anthony Savile Stephen Rowe, of Penmoor, Meavy Lane, Yelverton, Devon, and has issue living, Jonathan Stephen, *b.* 1969,—James Benedict, *b.* 1970,—Antonia Jane, *b.* 1967.

Grandchildren of the late Col. Charles Chenevix Trench (infra):—
Issue of the late Charles Godfrey Chenevix Trench, C.I.E., *b.* 1877, *d.* 1964: *m.* 1910, Margaret May (Pudding Lane, Kelling, Holt, Norfolk), el. da. of John Holmes Blakesley, C.E.:—
Richard Blakesley CHENEVIX-TRENCH (21, Church Rd., Davenport Green, Wilmslow, Ches.), *b.* 1912; ed. at Shrewsbury; Lt.-Cdr. (ret.) RN; 1939-45 War (despatches): *m.* 1939, Nancy Carey, only da. of James Munro, of Shanghai, and has issue living, Fenella Anne, *b.* 1943: *m.* 1969, Richard Law Townsend, 1271, Cumnock Cres., Oakville, Ontario, and has issue living, Simon Andrew *b.* 1974.——Godfrey Maxwell CHENEVIX-TRENCH, *DSC, RN, b.* 1917; ed. at Shrewsbury; Cdr. and employed by Port of London Authority; 1939-45 War (DSC and Bar): *m.* 1945, Nancy Louise, da. of the Rev. A. Clarkson Birch, of Cloughton, Scarborough, and has issue living, Juliet, *b.* 1947,—Frances, *b.* 1949.——Anthony CHENEVIX-TRENCH (Fettes College, Comely Bank, Edinburgh, 4; Public Schs., and Vincent's (Oxford) Clubs), *b.* 1919; ed. at Shrewsbury, and at Ch. Ch., Oxford (MA); Asst. Master at Shrewsbury 1948-51, Classical Tutor, Ch. Ch., Oxford 1951-52, Housemaster, Shrewsbury 1952-55, Headmaster of Bradfield 1955-63, and of Eton 1963-70; Headmaster of Fettes Coll. since 1971; 1939-45 War as Capt. RA (prisoner): *m.* 1953, Elizabeth Chalmers, da. of Capt. Sir Stewart Dykes Spicer, RN, 3rd Bt., and has issue living, Richard Thomas Chalmers, *b.* 1958,—Jonathan Charles Stewart, *b.* 1961,—Josephine Dykes, *b.* 1954,—Laura Lefroy (twin), *b.* 1954.
Issue of the late Col. Lawrence Chenevix Trench, C.M.G., D.S.O., *b.* 1883, *d.* 1958 : *m.* 1908, Winifred Ross, who *d.* 1969, da. of Edward H. Tootal:—
Katherine Anne, *b.* 1912: *m.* 1st, 1932, Lt.-Col. George William Frederic Leicester, Cheshire Regt. who *d.* 1944 [see Leicester, Bt., colls.], 2ndly, 1945, Lt.-Col. A. Frankland, who *d.* 1969, and has issue living, (by 1st marriage) [see Leicester, Bt., colls.],—(by 2nd marriage) Philip, *b.* 1946; ed. at Tonbridge,—John, *b.* 1949; ed. at King's Sch., Canterbury,—Sarah, *b.* 1947: *m.* 1969, Dr. Peter Morris, of Ware, Herts. *Residence,—*The Gables, Hopton Cangeford, Ludlow, Salop.
Issue of the late Brig. Ralph Chenevix-Trench, CB, OBE, MC, *b.* 1885, *d.* 1974: *m.* 1916, Meriel Edith (Little Westport, Wareham, Dorset), da. of the late Rev. Dr. Jelf, Master of Charterhouse:—
John Gordon (Windmill Farm, Coleshill, Amersham, Bucks.), *b.* 1920; late Capt. R. Signals: *m.* 1944, Ann Patricia, da. of Norman Moore, of 34, Jubilee Place, SW3, and has issue living, Maxwell John, *b.* 1952,—Jessica, *b.* 1949: *m.* 1970, Jonathan Yardley, and has issue living, Thomas James *b.* 1974.——Susan Meriel, *b.* 1925: *m.* 1950, Oscar Patrick Wood, of Christ Church, Oxford, and has issue living, Charles William Chenevix, *b.* 1955,—Silas James London, *b.* 1965,—Lucy Melesina, *b.* 1956.

Issue of the late Alfred Saward Chenevix Trench, M.C., *b.* 1887, *d.* 1963: *m.* 1st, 1920, Helne Winifred, who *d.* 1945, da. of George Fowler; 2ndly, 1949, Sylvia Mary Crawford (Flat 25, Douglas Court, 109, Wilderness Rd., Earley, nr. Reading, Berks.), da. of the late Francis Crawford Caffin:—

(By 1st marriage) Dudley Alfred Chenevix (Meadow View, Vines Cross Rd., Horam, E. Sussex). *b.* 1928; ed. at Bradfield Coll.; late Lieut. R.A.: *m.* 1955, Isobel Margaret Logie, dau. of William Low McDonald, of Port Elizabeth, S. Africa, and has issue living, Jennifer Elizabeth Chenevix, *b.* 1957,—Helen Winifred Chenevix, *b.* 1959.——Gillian Chenevix, *b.* 1920: *m.* 1947, Major James Thomas Benedictus Notley, D.S.O., late Duke of Cornwall's L.I., of Redcote, 48, Port Hill Gdns., Shrewsbury, and has issue living, Christopher John Marwood *b.* 1949; Lt. 1st Bn. LI,—Helen Ann Hamilton *b.* 1950: *m.* 1971, Timothy Rowland Hunt.

Grandchildren of the late Rev. Herbert Francis Chenevix Trench (infra):—
Issue of the late Col. Arthur Henry Chenevix Trench, CIE, *b.* 1884, *d.* 1968: *m.* 1913, Dorothy Pauline, who *d.* 1950, da. of the late Allan Gibson Steel, KC, Recorder of Oldham:—

Reginald Allan (Ryefield, Sandhurst, Camberley, Surrey), *b.* 1920; Maj. RE (ret.): *m.* 1957, Sophie Sybella Strathern, da. of Air Ch.-Marshal Sir Douglas Claude Strathern Evill, GBE, KCB, DSC, AFC, RAF (ret.) [see Kleinwort, Bt.], and has issue living, Ivo Richard, *b.* 1959,—Angus, *b.* 1960, Katharine, *b.* 1964,—Jessica Sophie, *b.* 1966.——Margaret Georgina, *b.* 1915, formerly in FANY: *m* 1944, Patrick Millington Synge, late Maj. Intelligence Corps, of Byworth Edge, Petworth, Sussex, and has issue living, Arthur Hugh Millington, *b.* 1951,—Robert Patrick, *b.* 1957.——Dorothy Anne, *b.* 1916; formerly WRNS: *m.* 1942, Roderick Peter Garratt Wilson, of Three Chimneys, Fittleworth, Pulborough, Sussex, son of Sir Roderick (Roy) Wilson, and has issue living, Nicholas Allan Roy, *b.* 1945; BA, Oxon; Bar. Inner Temple 1967,—Francesca Dorothy, *b.* 1952; BA Camb.

Issue of the late Maj. Charles Reginald Chenevix Trench, *b.* 1888, *d.* (killed in action during European War) 1918: *m.* 1915, Clare Cecily (now of Farthings, Friston, Sussex), da. of the late Henry Blunt Howard, of Bark Hart, Orpington, Kent:—

Isabel Clare, *b.* 1915; Dip. Social Studies, London: *m.* 1939, (Clarence) John Molyneux Fletcher MA, FSA, of Bekynton House, Sutton Courtenay, Abingdon, Berks., and has issue living, Anthony John, *b.* 1941; MA, Oxon: *m.* 1967, Tresna Russell, BA, and has issue living, Crispin Hilary Trench *b.* 1970, Dickon Anthony Railton *b.* 1972,—Martin Chenevix, *b.* 1942: *m.* 1972, Diana Cantillon, and has issue living, Alison Chenevix *b.* 1973,—Joanna Delle, *b.* 1946,—Hilary Clare, *b.* 1951.

Issue of the late Herbert Chenevix Trench, *b.* 1892, *d.* 1971: *m.* 1922, Marjorie, who *d.* 1962, da. of R. C. Bell, of Melbourne:—
Frances Robina Chenevix, *b.* 1925: *m.* 1953, R. Raymond Lockyer, ARIBA, and has issue living, Sarah Frances Chenevix, *b.* 1954,—Victoria Robina Chenevix, *b.* 1957.——Valerie Hester Chenevix, *b.* 1929; BA (honours) 1952: *m.* 1959, David McKie Kerslake, OBE, PhD, DSc, MB, BS, of Lime Tree Cottage, Yateley, Camberley, Surrey, and has issue living, Michael John Chenevix, *b.* 1962,—Caroline Julia Chenevix, *b.* 1961.

Grandchildren of the late Philip Charles Chenevix Trench, 3rd son of the late Richard Trench, 6th son of Frederick Trench, and brother of 1st Baron.
Issue of the late Philip Francis Chenevix Trench, *b.* 1849, *d.* 1911: *m.* 1882, Frances Angel, who *d.* 1947, dau. of the late Robert Reeves, of 5, Fitzwilliam Place, Dublin:—

Robert Denis, *b.* 1899; ed. at Winchester; Capt. King's Royal Rifle Corps; European War 1918 in France (two medals), European War 1939-43 in Far East (prisoner). *Residence,*—7, Eaton Terrace, S.W.1. *Club,*—Naval and Military.——Muriel Emily, *b.* 1882. *Residence* —7, Eaton Terr., SW1.——Oonah Frances, *b.* 1895. *Residence,*—7. Eaton Terr., SW1.

Grandchildren of the late Richard Bayley Chenevix Trench, yst. son of the late Philip Charles Chenevix Trench (ante):—
Issue of the late Capt. Hugo Chenevix Trench, *b.* 1890, *d.* 1965: *m.* 1920, Emma Margaret Florence, who *d.* 1948, having obtained a divorce 1933, da. of Sir Robert McAlpine, 1st Bt.:—
Brian Robert David (13, Holland Park, W.11), *b.* 1927: *m.* 1st, 1956 (*m.* diss. 19—), Bridget, da. of K. R. J. Saxon, of Boscombe, Hants.; 2ndly, 1963, Elspeth Charlesworth, yr. da. of T. D. Ross, of Stamford.

Issue of the late Ivor Chenevix Trench, *b.* 1892, *d.* 1960 : *m.* 1918, Doris Mary, who *d.* 1951, dau. of the late John Francis Gaskell of Cambus O'May, Aberdeenshire :—
Diana Doris, *b.* 1920 : *m.* 1st, 1943 (divorce 1947), Capt. Brodie Knight, Welsh Guards ; 2ndly, 1947, Gilbert Younghusband, late Capt. Roy. Horse Guards. *Address,*—

Issue of the late Lionel Chenevix Trench, *b.* 1901, *d.* 1930: *m.* 1925, Doris Maud (of Ratton Barn, Willingdon, nr. Eastbourne) (who *m.* 2ndly, 1933, George Sweeting, who *d.* 1956), el. da. of the late Charles D. Turrall, of Downes, Torrington, N. Devon:—
Keith Everard George (Blyth Cottage, Blyth Lane, Wivenhoe, nr. Colchester), *b.* 1926; ed. at Stowe; 1939-45 War as Sub-Lt. RNVR: *m.* 1952 (m. diss. 1972), Bridget, da. of the late Lt.-Col. K. R. O'Brien, MC, late Roy. Ulster Rifles, and has issue living, Guy Charles, *b.* 1955,—Rupert George, *b.* 1957.

Granddaughters of the late Wilbraham FitzJohn Trench (infra) :—
Issue of the late Patrick Mackenzie FitzJohn Trench, *b.* 1905, *d.* 1948 : *m.* 1st, 1926, Frances Cautley (who obtained a divorce 1930), dau. of the late Cecil Cautley Baker ; 2ndly, 1930, Eveleen, who *d.* 1945, da. of John Hayden; 3rdly, 1947, Winifred Frances (1, Fountain Rd., Pontymoile, Pontypool, Gwent), da. of the late Arthur Edward Stidolph:—

(By 2nd marriage) Patricia Anne, *b.* 1930 : *m.* 1954, Pierre Edouard Marie Ghislain Verstraete, and has issue living, Philippe, *b.* 1957,—Jacques Michel, *b.* 1962,—Catherine, *b.* 1955,—Brigide, *b.* 1956,—Anne, *b.* 1960. *Residence,*—19, Chemin des Pinsons, Lausanne, Switzerland.——Eveleen Mary, *b.* 1932: *m.* 1952, Thomas William Lane (269, Glengrove Av. W., Toronto 305, Canada), and has issue living, William, *b.* 1955,—Patricia, *b.* 1954.

Grandchildren of the late John Alfred Trench, son of the late Rev. Frederic Fitz-John Trench, son of the late John Trench, 6th brother of 1st Baron:—
Issue of the late Wilbraham FitzJohn Trench, *b.* 1873, *d.* 1939 : *m.* 1903, Mary Alicia, who *d.* 1930, el. dau. of the late Edward Cross, formerly Lieut. R.A., of Hollywood, Portishead, Somerset:—

Chalmers Edward FitzJohn, *b.* 1909 : *m.* 1940, Beatrice Esther, dau. of the late Charles St. George Orpen, of Lisheens, Carrickmines, co. Dublin, and has issue living, Fiachra Terence Wilbraham (37, Cowley Rd., SW14), *b.* 1941; M.Mus. Cincinnati: *m.* 1965, Micaela Fredericka, da. of the late Edgar H. Maus, of Hamilton, Ohio, USA, and has issue living, Michael Chalmers Wilbraham, *b.* 1966,—Brian Arthur Wilbraham, *b.* 1945,—Patrick Chalmers Wilbraham, *b.* 1955,—Beatrice Mary Wilbraham, *b.* 1948: *m.* 1968, Sydney Douglas Saunders, of R1113, 2000, Jasmine Cres., Ottawa, Canada. *Residence,*—Killrian, Slane, Navan, co. Meath.——Sheela Wilbraham Fitzjohn, *b.* 1907: *m.* 1st, 1929, Diarmid Coffey, who *d.* 1964: 2ndly, 1971, Erwin Strunz, of Carrick-free, Glencormac, Kilmacanogue, co. Wicklow, and has issue living (by 1st m.), Donal Manus George (Glendarragh Hill, Newtownmountkennedy, co. Wicklow), *b.* 1935: *m.* 1959, Patricia Ann, da. of Daniel Taylor, of Glasgow, and has issue living, Aedan Diarmid Cailean, *b.* 1961, Fiona Ann Champagne *b.* 1962,—Saive Frances Mary, *b.* 1930,—Helen Dairine, *b.* 1933.

Granddaughters of the late William Wallace Trench, son of the late Rev. Frederic FitzJohn Trench (ante):—
Issue of the late Claud Llewellyn (Pomeroy) Trench, *b.* 1881, *d.* 1945 : *m.* 1911, Annie Elizabeth, who *d.* 1972, el. da. of the late William Charles Davis, of Cheltenham:—
Muriel Ellen (Wilmurand, Church Rd., Lelant, St. Ives, Cornwall), *b.* 1915; SRN: *m.* 1st, 1939, George Edward Bonner, RASC, who *d.* (killed in action) 1940; 2ndly, 1948, William Leslie Walter Davison, who *d.* 1974, and has issue living, (by 2nd m.) Andrea Elaine, *b.* 1951: *m.* 1973, James Andrew Rouncefield, BSc, of 16, Byron House, Chapel Close, Chapel Hill, Crayford, Kent.——Eileen Elizabeth, *b.* 1917: *m.* 1937, Cecil H. F. Knight, and has issue living, Bernard Cecil Frank, *b.* 1939; Coldstream Guards: *m.* 1965, Jacqueline Ann, da. of William John Rudkin, of 94, Heacham Drive, Leicester, and has issue living, Paul *b.* 19—,—Elizabeth Ann, *b.* 1937: *m.* 1956, John David Heighton, of The Birches, 11A, Willow Park Drive, Wigston, Leicester, and has issue living, David Peter, *b.* 1957, Brian John *b.* 1958, Suzanne Elizabeth *b.* 1961,—Catherine Beryl, *b.* 1945: *m.* 1968, Patrick James Roddy, of 37, Rainsborough Gdns., Market Harborough, and has issue living, Christopher James *b.* 1970, Paula Louise *b.* 1972,—Hazel Mary, *b.* 1949. *Residence*,—51, Oadby Rd., Wigston Magna, Leicester.——Jean Olive, *b.* 1922; is a Registered Sick Children's Nurse: *m.* 1944, Denis S. W. Foreman, RASC. *Residence*,—61, Roehampton Drive, Wigston Fields, Leicester.

Grandchildren of the late George Frederic Trench, son of the late Rev. Frederic FitzJohn Trench (ante):—
Issue of the late Col. Ernest Frederic Crosbie Trench, CBE, TD, *b.* 1869, *d.* 1960: *m.* 1895, Netta Wilbraham, who *d.* 1950, dau. of the late Herbert Wilbraham Taylor, of Hadley Bourne, Herts :—
Dermot George Crosbie, *b.* 1904 ; ed. at Charterhouse, and at Trin. Coll., Camb. (B.A. 1924) : *m.* 1938, Nancy Muriel (O'NEIL), dau. of the late Dr. S. A. Smith, of Sydney, N.S. Wales, and has issue living, Anthony Crosbie, *b.* 1941,—Patricia Ann, *b.* 1944. *Residence*,—El Mirador MG-CA197 Javea, Alicante, Spain——Brian Morley Crosbie (Kyson House, Woodbridge, Suffolk) *b.* 1908,' ed. at Charterhouse, and at New Coll., Oxford (MA); admitted a Solicitor 1933: *m.* 1938, Harriet; Milward, da. of the late John Lyons Agnew, of Ontario, and has issue living, Jonathan Agnew (10t· Earlham Rd., Norwich), *b.* 1939: *m.* 1969, Sarah, da. of Don C. Williams, of Kansas Ci ty, USA and has issue living, Mary Olivia, *b.* 1972,—Amanda Milward, *b.* 1941: *m.* 1961, Jonathan Radice' of 184, Kensington Park, Rd., W11, and has issue living, James Heneage *b.* 1961, Daniel Brett *b.* 1967.——Noreen Charlotte (*Lady Holmes*), *b.* 1899: *m.* 1922, Sir Stephen Lewis Holmes, KCMG. MC, and has issue living, Michael Trench, *b.* 1923; ed. at Eton, and at Ch. Ch., Oxford (MA), admitted a Solicitor 1950; formerly Lt. RNVR: *m.* 1968, Thelma, da. of the late J. H. A. Magor, and has issue living, Charlotte Clemency Magor *b.* 1971,—Richard Tilt (of 1, Baronsmead Rd., SW13); *b.* 1924; ed. at Charterhouse, and at Ch. Ch., Oxford; formerly Fl.-Lt. RAF Vol. Res.; is a Chartered Architect: *m.* 1954, Susan, da. of the late C. H. B. Chatteris, and has issue living, Jasper Stephen *b.* 1962, Prudence Mary *b.* 1956, Miranda Jane *b.* 1959,—Jennifer Prudence Trench *b.* 1929: *m.* 1953, Cholmondeley Darvall, Bar.-at-Law, of Sydney, Aust., and has issue living, Cholmondeley *b.* 1957, Cassandra Holmes *b.* 1964. *Residence*,—Pinyons, Sandhurst, Hawkhurst, Kent.

Grandson of the late Col. Ernest Frederic Crosbie Trench, CBE, TD (ante):—
Issue of the late Peter Crosbie Trench, *b.* 1912, *d.* 1969: *m.* 1st, 1941 (m. diss. 1946), Nan Dorice Hunter; 2ndly, 1947, Joy Seymour (62, Manor Drive, Wembley Park, Middx.), da. of the late H. Shave, of Calcutta:—
By 2nd m.) Colin Crosbie, *b.* 1949.

Grandsons of the late George Frederic Trench (ante):—
Issue of the late William Launcelot Crosbie Trench, C.I.E., *b.* 1881, *d.* 1949 : *m.* 1st, 1910, Mar garet Zephanie, who *d.* 1934, dau. of the Rev. W. P. Huddleston; 2ndly, 1935, Eileen Beatrice Cecil, dau. of H. C. Marsh :—
By 1st m.) George Shan Crosbie (of 116, Streetly Lane, Four Oaks, Sutton Coldfield Warwickshire), *b.* 1913; ed. at Stowe; Lt.-Col. (ret.) late RA; 1939-45 War in Middle East (despatches, prisoner): *m.* 1945, Myrtle Sheila, dau. of H. Jerrett, of Meols, Cheshire, and has issue living, Barney George Crosbie. *b.* 1947,—Margaret Felicity, *b.* 1953.——*Sir* David Clive Crosbie, *GCMG, MC* (Barwood, The Milldown, Blandford Forum, Dorset), *b.* 1915; ed. at Tonbridge Sch., and at Jesus Coll., Camb. (MA); High Commr. for W. Pacific Territories 1961-64, and Gov. of Hong Kong 1964-71; K.St.J.; S.-W. Pacific 1942-45 as Lt.-Col. Solomon Islands Defence Force (MC, American Legion of Merit); CMG 1960, KCMG, 1962, GCMG 1969: *m.* 1944, Margaret, da. of the late Jay D. Gould, of New York, USA, and has issue living, Katherine Elizabeth, *b.* 1956.

Granddaughters of Col. Ernest Frederic Crosbie Trench, C.B.E., T.D. (ante):—
Issue of the late Flight-Lieut. Desmond Ernest Crosbie Trench, *b.* 1911, *d.* (killed in action 1941): *m.* 1937, Dorothy (who *m.* 2ndly, 1953, Major William Spencer), da. of the late Major H. C. Shewell, RGA:—
Josephine Crosbie, *b.* 1938: *m.* 1965, David McCowan, and has issue living, Jonathan David, *b.* 1965,— Deborah Kate, *b.* 1967.——Kerry Deborah (posthumous), *b.* 1941: *m.* 1965, Michael Honnor, of Broomhill, Harford, Ivybridge, Devon.

Grandchildren of the late Frederic Herbert Trench (infra):—
Issue of the late Waldo Trench FOX, M.C., *b.* 1892, *d.* 1954, having assumed by deel poll 1934 the name of Waldo Trench Fox in lieu of Wallace Talbot Trench : *m.* 1933, Janet Mary Kennedy (Penjerrick. Falmouth), dau. of MacIvor Bassett. of Lelant, Cornwall :—
Robert Trench (Cheriton House, Alresford), *b.* 1937: *m.* 1962, Lindsay Garrett, da. of Sir Donald Forsyth Anderson, of The Manor, Notgrove, Glos., and has issue living, Barclay Trench, *b.* 1971— Caspar Lloyd, *b.* 1972,—Fenella Garrett, *b.* 1964,—Tamara Forsyth, *b.* 1967.——Jill Trench, *b.* 1935: *m.* 1st, 1955, Lieut. Rodney Frances Power Carne, RN, who *d.* 1959; 2ndly, 1961, Capt. Donald Barns Morison, RN, and has issue living, (by 1st marriage) Rupert Barclay Power, *b.* 1958,— Nicola Trench, *b.* 1957,—(by 2nd marriage) Barnaby Daniel Barns, *b.* 1964,—Candida Trench, *b.* 1963. *Residence*,—The White House, Cokes Lane, Chalfont St. Giles, Bucks.——Rachel Trench, *b.* 1943: *m.* 1965, Raymond Joseph Morin, of 52, Bellevue Av., Haverhill, Mass., USA.

Issue of the late Desmond Patrick Trench, *b.* 1893, *d.* 1967: *m.* 1st, 1916, Elfrida Mary Eliott, who *d.* 1942, da. of the Rev. Daniel Eliott Young (formerly V. of St. Mary's, Penzance); 2ndly, 1947, Hilda Olive (Little Chenhall, Mawnan, Falmouth), da. of A. A. J. Akhurst, of Lyncrest, Southbourne, Hants.:—
(By 1st m.) Anthony Barclay (25, Elizabeth St., Thornhill, Toronto), *b.* 1919; AMIEE (England); Consulting Eng., Ontario; 1939-45 War, as Fl.-Lt. RAFVR (prisoner): *m.* 1940, Sheila Mary, da. of Lawrence Lois Keith, of Hastings, Sussex, and has issue living, Simon Patrick, *b.* 1946.—— Heather Mavis, *b.* 1925: *m.* 1948, Robin Krohn Pooley, Headmaster of Dane Court School, Pyrford, Woking, and has issue living, Peter John, *b.* 1950.

Granddaughter of the late William Wallace Trench (ante):—
Issue of the late Frederic Herbert Trench, *b.* 1865, *d.* 1923 : *m.* 1891, Lilian Isabel, who *d.* 1961, dau. of Robert Fox, of Penjerrick, Falmouth :—
Avice Blanaid (16, Boslowick Court, Falmouth, Cornwall) *b.* 1898: *m.* 1933 (m. diss. 1938) John Hanbury Martin.

Granddaughters of the late John Trench, 6th brother of 1st Baron:—
Issue of the late James Currie Trench, *b.* 1848 ; *d.* 1936 : *m.* 1883, Annie Gertrude, who *d.* 1944, el. dau. of the late John Haughton, of Ardreigh, Athy, co. Kildare:—
Aileen Agnes (Our Lady's Manor, Bulloch Castle, Dalkey, co. Dublin), *b.* 1891: *m.* 1936, Louis W. E. Evans, who *d.* 1952.——Amy Feodora, *b.* 1896: *m.* 1922, James Alfred Stuart Watt, and has issue living, Lionel Robert (3, Ystrad Buildings, Trethomas, Newport, Mon.), *b.* 1924: *m.* 1959, Elizabeth Maureen Buckley. *Residence*,—36 Castlewood Park, Rathmines, Dublin, 6.

PREDECESSORS.—[1] FREDERIC Trench, M.P. for Portarlington in the Irish Parliament, **was** cr. Baron Ashtown (peerage of Ireland) 1800, with remainder to the heirs of his deceased father; d. 1840 ; s. by his nephew [2] FREDERIC MASON, 2nd Baron, b. 1804 : m. 1st, Harriet, who d. 1845, dau. of Thomas Phillips Cosby, of Stradbally Hall, Queen's co. ; 2ndly, 1852, Elizabeth, who d. 1893, dau. and co-heir of Richard Oliver Gascoigne, of Parlington, Yorkshire ; d. 1880 ; s. by his grandson [3] FREDERIC OLIVER (son of the late Hon. Frederic Sydney Charles Trench el. son of 2nd Baron), 3rd Baron, b. 1868 ; was a Representative Peer for Ireland 1908-15 : m. 1894, Violet Grace, who d. 1945. youngest dau. of Col. Robert Ushworth Godolphin Cosby, of Stradbally Hall, Queen's co.; d. 1946; s. by his el. surviving son [4] ROBERT POWER, 4th Baron, b. 1897: m. 1st, 1926, Geraldine Ida (who d. 1940, and from whom he obtained a divorce 1938), da. of Sir Henry Foley Grey, 7th Bt.; 2ndly, 1950, Oonah Anne, el. da. of the late Brig.-Gen. Lewis Frederic Green-Wilkinson, CMG, DSO; d. 1966; s. by his brother [5] Dudley Oliver, OBE, 5th Baron and present peer.

ASKWITH, BARONY OF. (Askwith.) [Extinct 1942.]

DAUGHTER LIVING OF FIRST BARON.

Hon. Betty Ellen, b. 1909 : m. 1950, Keith Miller Jones. Residence,—8, Egerton Terrace, S.W.3.

Asquith, Viscount, son of Earl of Oxford and Asquith.

ASQUITH OF BISHOPSTONE, BARON. (Asquith.) [Extinct 1954.]

SONS LIVING OF LIFE PEER.

Hon. Luke, b. 1919; ed. at Winchester; 1939-45 War in N. Africa, and Italy as GOC III and Liaison Officer 8th Army; a Dir. of Holt Products Ltd., and other cos.: m. 1954, (Ethel) Meriel, da. of Maurice O. Evans, of Arrow Lawn, Eardisland, Herefordshire, and has issue living, Lucy, b. 1962,— Anne, b. 1965. Residence,—9, Milborne Grove, SW10.
Hon. Paul (26, Laxford House, Cundy St., SW1; Hawkwell House, Pembury, Kent), b. 1927; ed. at Eton: m. 1st, 1953 (m. diss. 1963), Helena Mary, da. of the Hon. Geoffrey John Orlando Bridgeman, MC, MB, FRCS, LRCP [see V. Bridgeman, colls.; 2ndly, 1963, Caroline Anne, yr. da. of Sir John Gawen Carew Pole, DSO, TD, 12th Bt. (cr. 1628), and has issue living, (by 1st m.) Jonathan Paul, b. 1956,—(Mary) Clare, b. 1954,—(by 2nd m.) Rupert, b. 1965,—Emily Anne, b. 1964.

DAUGHTERS LIVING OF LIFE PEER.

Hon. Jane, b. 1922. Residence,—9, Milborne Grove, S.W.10.
Hon. Frances Rose (Hon. Lady Stephenson), b. 1925: m. 1951, the Rt. Hon. Lord Justice (Sir John Frederick Eustace) Stephenson [E. Shrewsbury, colls.], and has issue living, David Guy, b. 1954,— Daniel Paul, b. 1960,—Mary, b. 1952: m. 1972, Philippe G. Wines,—Laura Jane, b. 1958. Residence —30, Drayton Gdns., SW10.

ASQUITH OF YARNBURY, BARONY OF. (Bonham Carter.) [Extinct 1969.]

SONS LIVING OF LIFE BARONESS.

Hon. Mark Raymond (49, Victoria Rd., W8), b. 1922; late Capt. Gren. Gds.; Chm. of Race Relations Board 1966-71, since when Chm. of Community Relations Commn.; 1939-45 War (despatches, prisoner, escaped); MP for Torrington Div. of Devon (L.) 1958-59: m. 1955, Leslie, da. of the late Condé Nast, of New York, USA, and formerly wife of the 2nd Baron St. Just, and has issue.
Hon. Raymond Henry (7, West Heath Av., NW11), b. 1929; Lt. Irish Gds.: m. 1958, Elena, da. of the late Don Eduardo Propper de Callejon, and has issue.

DAUGHTERS LIVING OF LIFE BARONESS.

Hon. Helen Laura Cressida (Pinchards, Stockton, Warminster, Wilts.), b. 1917: m. 1939, Jasper Alexander Maurice Ridley, Lt. KRRC, who d. (on active service in Italy) 1943 [see V. Ridley, colls.].
Hon. Laura Miranda, b. 1918 m. 1938, the Rt. Hon. Joseph Grimond, PC, TD, MP, of The Old Manse, of Firth, Grimbister, Orkney, and 71, Kew Green, Richmond, Surrey, and has issue.

ASTOR, VISCOUNT. (Astor.) [Viscount U.K. 1917.]

To the stars.

WILLIAM WALDORF ASTOR, 4th Viscount; b. Dec. 27th, 1951; s. 1966; ed. at Eton.

Arms.—Or, a falcon resting on a dexter hand couped at the wrist, proper and gauntleted gules in chief two fleurs-de-lys of the last. Crest.—From a mount vert falcon rising proper, ensigned by three mullets gold, Supporters,—Dexter, a North American Indian; sinister, a North American fur trapper; each habited, accoutred, and holding in the exterior hand a rifle, all proper.
Residences,—Ginge Manor, Wantage, Berks.; 28, Markham Sq., SW3.

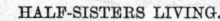

HALF-SISTERS LIVING.

Hon. Emily Mary, b. 1956.
Hon. Janet Elizabeth, b. 1961.
Hon. Pauline Marian, b. 1964.

UNCLES LIVING. (Sons of 2nd Viscount.)

Hon. (FRANCIS) DAVID LANGHORNE, b. March 5th, 1912; ed. at Eton, and at Balliol Coll., Oxford; late Capt. RM; Editor of The Observer since 1948; 1939-45 War (Croix de Guerre): m. 1st, 1945 (m. diss. 1951), Melanie, da. of Philip Hauser, of Berne, Switzerland; 2ndly, 1952, Bridget Aphra, da. of Maj. Cyril Wreford, of Yew Tree House, Goosey, Faringdon, Berks., and has issue living, (by 1st m.) Frances Christine Langhorne, b. 1947: m. 1970, Dr. Miles Frankel, of En Cotachau, 1111, Lussy-sur-Morges, Vaud, Switzerland,—(by 2nd m.), Richard David Langhorne, b. 1955,—Thomas Robert Langhorne, b. 1962,—Alice Margaret Frances, b. 1953: m. 1972, Lawrence Woodward,—Lucy Aphra Nancy, b. 1958,—Nancy Bridget Elizabeth, b. 1960. Residences,—9, Cavendish Av., NW8 9JD; Manor House, Sutton Courtenay, Berks.
Hon. Michael Langhorne, b. 1916; ed. at Eton, and New Coll., Oxford; Capt. RA (TA); MP for E. Surrey (C) 1945-51; author of " Tribal Feeling " 1963: m. 1st, 1942 (m. diss. 1961), Barbara Mary Cclonsay, da. of the late Capt. Ronald Frank Rous McNeill; 2ndly, 1961 (m. diss. 1968), (Patricia David) Pandora (JONES), da. of the late Hon. Sir Bede Edmund Hugh Clifford [see B. Clifford of Chudleigh, colls.]; 3rdly, 1970, Judy, da. of Paul Innes, and has issue living, (by 1st m.) David Waldorf (Bruern Grange, Milton-under-Wychwood, Oxon.), b. 1943: m. 1968, Clare Pamela, da. of Cdr. Michael Beauchamp St. John, DSC, RN [see B. St. John of Bletso, colls.], and has issue living, Henry Waldorf b. 1969, Thomas David b. 1972, Joanna Colonsay Clare b. 1970,—James Colonsay Langhorne (13, Dawson Place, W2 4TH), b. 1945: m. 1972, Jane M. S., da. of Charles de Chazal, of Lumpers, Farway, Colyton, Devon,—Kathleen Nancy Jane, b. 1949,—Georgina Mary (Hon. Mrs.

Anthony Ramsay), *b.* 1952: *m.* 1973, the Hon. Anthony Ramsay [see E. Dalhousie],—(by 3rd m.), Polly Michael, *b.* 1971. *Residence,*—Bruern, Churchill, Oxon.

Hon. John Jacob, *MBE*, *b.* 1918; ed. at Eton, and at New Coll., Oxford; Maj. Life Gds., and DL for Cambs.; Chm., Agric. Research Council since 1968; N-W Europe 1944-45 (MBE, Legion of Honour, French Croix de Guerre); MP for Sutton Div. of Plymouth (*C*) 1951-59; MBE (Mil) 1945: *m.* 1944 (m. diss. 1971), Ana Inez, da. of Senor Dr. Don Miguel Carcano, KBE, late Argentine Ambassador in London, and has issue living, Michael Ramon Langhorne, *b.* 1946,—Stella, *b.* 1949: *m.* 1974, Martin Wilkinson. *Residence,*—Hatley Park, Hatley St. George, Sandy, Beds.

MOTHER LIVING.

Hon. Sarah Katharine Elinor Norton (23, Scarsdale Villas, W8), da. of 6th Baron Grantley: *m.* 1st, 1945 (m. diss. 1953), the 3rd Viscount, who *d.* 1966; 2ndly, 1953, Maj. Thomas Michael Baring, Derbyshire Yeo., from whom she obtained a divorce 1965 [see B. Northbrook, colls.].

WIDOW LIVING OF THIRD VISCOUNT.

JANET BRONWEN ALUN, (*Viscountess Astor*) (Tuesley Manor, Tuesley, Godalming, Surrey), da. of the late His Honour Sir (John) Alun Pugh: *m.* 1960, as his 3rd wife, the 3rd Viscount, who *d.* 1966.

COLLATERAL BRANCH LIVING.

Issue of the late Hon. John Jacob Astor, 2nd son of 1st Viscount, who was cr. *Baron Astor of Hever* 1956 [see that title.]

PREDECESSORS.—[1] WILLIAM WALDORF Astor, only son of John Jacob Astor, of New York : *b.* 1848 ; United States Min. to Italy 1882-5 ; naturalised 1899 ; cr. *Baron Astor*, of Hever Castle, co. Kent (peerage of United Kingdom) 1916, and *Viscount Astor*, of Hever Castle, co. Kent (peerage of United Kingdom) 1917 : *m.* 1878, Mary Dahlgren, who *d.* 1894, dau. of James W. Paul, of Philadelphia ; *d.* 1919 ; *s.* by his el. son [2] WALDORF, 2nd Viscount, *b.* 1879 ; Chm. of Directors of *The Observer*, and High Steward of Maidenhead ; European War 1914-17 as temporary Major and Inspector of Q.M.G. Sers. (despatches) ; Parliamentary Private Sec. to Prime Min. 1917-18, Parliamentary Sec. to Min. of Food 1918, and to Local Govt. Board Jan. to June 1919 (also Chm. National Health Insurance Joint Committee Feb. to June 1919), and first Parliamentary Sec. to Min. of Health 1919-21 ; appointed Hon. Col. Devon and Cornwall, Heavy Brig. R.A. (T.A.) 1933 ; Chm. of Roy. Institute of International Affairs 1939-49, and of League of Nations Committee on Nutrition 1936-37 ; Lord Mayor of Plymouth 1939-44 : M.P. for Plymouth (*C*) 1910-18, and for Sutton Div. thereof 1918-19: *m.* 1906, Nancy Witcher, *C.H.*, *D.Litt.*, who *d.* 1964, da. of the late Col. Chiswell Dabney Langhorne, of Mirador, Greenwood, Virginia, U.S.A., and formerly wife of Robert Gould Shaw; *d.* 1952; *s.* by his el. son [3] WILLIAM WALDORF, 3rd Viscount; *b.* 1907; P.P.S. to First Lord of the Admiralty 1936-37, and to Home Sec. 1937-39; MP for E. Fulham (*C.*) 1935-45, and for Wycombe 1951-52: *m.* 1st, 1945 (m. diss. 1953), the Hon. Sarah Katharine Elinor Norton, da. of 6th Baron Grantley; 2ndly, 1955 (m. diss. 1960), Philippa Victoria, da. of Lt.-Col. Henry Philip Hunloke [D. Devonshire]; 3rdly, 1960, Janet Bronwen Alun, da. of His Honour Sir (John) Alun Pugh; *d.* 1966; *s.* by his only son [4] WILLIAM WALDORF, 4th Viscount, and present peer; also Baron Astor.

ASTOR OF HEVER, BARON. (Astor.) [Baron U.K. 1956.]

GAVIN ASTOR, 2nd Baron, *b.* June 1st, 1918; *s.* 1971; ed. at Eton, and New Coll., Oxford; Chm. of Times Publishing Co. 1959-66, and Co.-Chief Proprietor of *The Times* 1962-66; Life Pres. of Times Newspapers, Ltd. since 1967, a Dir. of Alliance Assurance Co., Ltd.; Pres. of Council Commonwealth Press Union since 1972 (Chm. 1959-72), Chm. of Council of Roy. Commonwealth Soc. since 1972, and Lord-Lieut. of Kent since 1972; High Sheriff of Sussex 1955-56; Seneschal of Canterbury Cathedral since 1973; 1939-45 War as Capt. Life Guards: *m.* 1945, Lady Irene Violet Freesia Janet Augusta Haig, da. of 1st Earl Haig, and has issue.

Arms,—Argent eight barrulets sable over all resting on a dexter hand couped at the wrist proper gauntleted gules a falcon also gules in chief two fleurs de lys of the last. **Crest,**—Rising from a mount vert a falcon proper ensigned by three mullets or. **Supporters,**—*Dexter*, the figure of Aesculapius, and *sinister*, that of Mercury, both proper.

To the stars.

Residences,—Hever Castle, Edenbridge, Kent; 11, Lyall St., SW1; Tillypronie, Tarland, Aberdeenshire. *Clubs,*—White's, Bath, Hurlingham.

SONS LIVING.

Hon. JOHN JACOB (Cobham Cottage, Hever, Kent; White's and Turf Clubs), *b.* June 16th, 1946; ed. at Eton; Life Gds. 1965-70: *m.* 1970, Fiona Diana Lennox, da. of Capt. Roger Edward Lennox Harvey, of Parliament Piece, Ramsbury, Wilts. [see Mainwaring, Bt., ext.], and has issue living, Camilla Fiona, *b.* 1974.

Hon. Philip Douglas Paul, *b.* 1959.

DAUGHTERS LIVING.

Hon. Bridget Mary, *b.* 1948.
Hon. Elizabeth Louise, *b.* 1951.
Hon. Sarah Violet, *b.* 1953: *m.* 1975, the Hon. George Edward Lopes [see B. Roborough].

BROTHERS LIVING.

Hon. Hugh Waldorf, *b.* 1920; ed. at Eton, and at New Coll., Oxford ; Dep. Chm. of Times Publishing Co. Ltd. 1959-66, a Dir. of Hutchinsons Ltd., Hambro's Ltd., Phoenix Assurance Co. Ltd., Winterbottom Trust Ltd. and Olympia Ltd. (Dep. Chm. 1971-73); Dep Chm. of Middlesex Hosp. 1962-64; a Member of Fishmongers' Co. (Warden 1974) and a JP for Berks.; High Sheriff of Berks. 1963-64; a Gov. of Bradfield Coll., and Greshams Sch., a Trustee of Trust House Forte Ltd. (Chm. of Council of Trustees since 1971); 1939-45 War as Lt.-Col. Intelligence Corps: *m.* 1950, Emily Lucy, da. of Sir Alexander Davenport Kinloch, 12th Bt., and has issue living, Robert Hugh, *b.* 1958,—James Alexander Waldorf, *b.* 1965,—Virginia Lucy, *b.* 1951,—Rachel Mary, *b.* 1955,—Jean Violet, *b.* 1961. *Residences,*—Folly Farm, Sulhamstead, Berks.; 14, Culross St., W1. *Clubs,*—Brooks's, Buck's, and Royal Yacht Squadron.

Hon. John, *b.* 1923; ed. at Eton; a Co. Councillor for Berks since 1953, and an Alderman and Chm. Berks Education Cttee. since 1960; MP for Newbury Div. of Berks (*C*) 1964-74; 1939-45 War as Flight-Lt. RAFVR: *m.* 1950, Diana Kathleen, da. of the late George Henry Drummond [see E. Perth, colls.], and has issue living, John Richard, b. 1953,—George David, b. 1958,—Elizabeth Kathleen b. 1951. Residence,—Kirby House, Inkpen, nr. Newbury, Berks. Club,—Buck's, and Royal Yacht Squadron.

PREDECESSOR.—[1] Hon. JOHN JACOB Astor, 2nd son of 1st Viscount Astor, b. 1886; Ch. Proprietor of The Times Newspaper 1922-66, Chm. of Middx. Hosp. 1938-62, and of Middx. Hosp. Med. Sch. 1945-62; MP for Dover (U) 1922-45; cr. Baron Astor of Hever, of Hever Castle, Kent (peerage of (UK) 1956: m. 1916, Lady Violet Mary Elliot, who d. 1965, da. of 4th Earl of Minto and widow of Maj. Lord Charles George Francis Mercer-Nairne, OVO [M. Lansdowne]; d. 1971; s. by his el. son [2] GAVIN, 2nd Baron and present peer.

ATHLONE, EARLDOM OF. (Cambridge.) [Extinct 1957]

WIDOW LIVING OF FIRST EARL.

H.R.H. Princess ALICE MARY VICTORIA AUGUSTA PAULINE (H.R.H. Princess Alice, Countess of Athlone), V.A., G.C.V.O., G.B.E., dau. of H.R.H. the late Prince Leopold George Duncan Albert, K.G., K.T., G.C.S.I., G.C.M.G., P.C., 1st Duke of Albany [see ROYAL FAMILY]: m. 1904, the 1st Earl, (brother of HM Queen Mary), who d. 1957, when the title became ext. Residence,—Clock House, Kensington Palace, W8.

DAUGHTER LIVING OF FIRST EARL.

Lady May Helen Emma (Lady May Abel Smith), b. Jan. 23rd, 1906; is a C.St.J.: m. Oct. 24th, 1931, Col. Sir Henry Abel Smith, K.C.M.G., K.C.V.O., D.S.O., late Roy. Horse Guards [D. Somerset, colls.], and has issue living, Richard Francis Abel (Blidworth Dale, Linby, Notts.), b. 1933; ed. at Eton; late Capt. Roy. Horse Guards: m. 1960, Marcia, da. of Maj.-Gen. Sir Douglas Anthony Kendrew, KCMG, CB, CBE, DSO, and has issue living, Katharine, b. 1961,—Anne Mary Sibylla, b. 1932: m. 1957, David Ian Liddell-Grainger [see E. Lindsey],—Elizabeth Alice, b. 1936: m. 1965 (m. diss. 1974), Peter Ronald Wise. Residence,—Barton Lodge, Winkfield, Windsor.

ATHOLL, DUKE OF. (Murray.) [Duke S. 1703.]

GEORGE IAIN MURRAY, 10th Duke b. June 19th, 1931; ed. at Eton, and at Ch. Ch., Oxford; s. 1957; a Representative Peer for Scotland 1958-63.

Arms,—Quarterly: 1st, paly of six or and sable, Atholl : 2nd, or a fess checky azure and argent, Stewart : 3rd, argent, on a bend azure three stags' heads cabossed or, Stanley : 4th, gules, three legs in armour proper, garnished and spurred or, flexed and conjoined in triangle at the upper part of the thigh, Ensigns of Isle of Man : over all an inescutcheon en surtout azure three mullets argent, within a double tressure flory, ensigned of a Marquess's coronet : Chiefship of the name of Murray and Marquessate of Tullibardine. Crests,—1st, a mermaid holding in her dexter hand a mirror, and in her sinister a comb, all proper, Murray ; 2nd, a demi-savage proper, wreathed about the temples and waist with laurel, his arms extended, and holding in the right hand a dagger, in the left a key, all proper, Atholl; 3rd, a peacock's head and neck proper, accompanied on either side by two arms from the elbow proper, and vested in maunches azure doubled argent. Supporters,—Dexter, a savage proper, wreathed about the temples and loins with juniper, his feet in fetters, the chain held in his right hand proper; sinister, a lion rampant gules, armed and langued azure, gorged with a plain collar of the last charged with three mullets argent.

Seat,—Blair Castle, Blair Atholl, Perthshire. Residence,—31, Marlborough Hill, NW8. Clubs,— Turf, White's and Puffin's.

MOTHER LIVING.

Hon. Angela Pearson, dau. of 2nd Viscount Cowdray : m. 1st, 1930, Lieut.-Col. George Anthony Murray, O.B.E., R.A., who d. (killed in action in Italy) 1945; 2ndly, 1950, Lieut.-Col. Robert Modan Campbell-Preston, OBE, MC. Residences,—Ardchattan Priory, Connel, Argyll; 31, Marlborough Hill, N.W.8.

COLLATERAL BRANCHES LIVING.

Grandchildren of the late Rev. George Edward Murray, el. son of the late Rt. Rev. George Murray, D.D., Bishop of Rochester, 2nd son of the late Rt. Rev. Lord George Murray, D.D., Bishop of St. David's, 2nd son of 3rd Duke :—

Issue of the late Col. Arthur Mordaunt Murray, O.B., M.V.O., b. 1852, d. 1920: m. 1st, 1895, Isabel, who d. 1896, dau. of Richard Laurence Pemberton, formerly of Hawthorn Tower, Seaham Harbour, Durham; 2ndly, 1898, Mabel, who d. 1964, el. da. of Frederick Francis Nicolson, formerly of Seaforth, Lancs.—

(By 2nd marriage) ARTHUR STEWART PAKINGTON (Hazelwood Hall, Friston, Saxmundham; Suffolk; Club,—Guards'), b. Sept. 9th 1899; ed. at Eton; Brig. (ret.) late Grenadier Guards, 1939-45 War: m. 1961, Winifreda Irene, da. of Edmund Henry Bevan.—Godfrey Pemberton, DSO, b. 1901; ed. at Radley; Lt.-Col. (ret.) Seaforth Highlanders: Superintending Queen's Messengers 1957-67; 1939-45 War (DSO); DSO 1945: m. 1934, Mary Isabel, da. of J. Brownlee, of Middlesbrough, and has issue living, Susan Elizabeth, b. 1935: m. 1959, David Hill, of 95, Clarendon Rd., W11, and has issue living, Simon Sebastian b. 1961, David Alexander b. 1964, Tobias Hunter b. 1967,—Mary Jennifer, b. 1939: m. 1964, James Vickers. of 45, Beever Rd., Ashford, Kent, and has issue living, Sandra b. 1965. Residence,—10, Gloucester Walk, W8.——Olive Penelope, MBE (Lady Norton), b. 1908; MBE (Civil) 1968: m. 1, 1928 (m. diss. 1942), Charles Russell Wood; m. 2, 1948, Sir (Walter) Charles Norton, MBE, MC, Solicitor, who d. 1974, and has issue living, (by 1st m) Peter, b. 1930. Residences.—23, Hans Place, SW1; Little Granthams, Chiddingfold, Surrey.

Peter, b. 1930. Residences,—23, Hans Place, SW1; Little Granthams, Chiddingfold, Surrey.

Grandchildren of the late Rev. Douglas Stuart Murray, 3rd son of the Rev. George Edward Murray (ante):—

Issue of the late Col. Walter Murray, O.B.E., M.C., R.E., b. 1882, d. 1945 m 911, Evelyn, dau. of William E. Adie, of The Rowans, Buxton, Derbyshire :—

Donald Stuart (of 8, Pages Lane, Bexhill-on-Sea, Sussex), b. 1917; is Major R.A.: m. 1948, Margaret Ann, dau. of Ernest Simmons, of The Glebe House, Boughton Aluph, Ashford, Kent, and has issue living, Elizabeth Anne, *b.* 1949,—Jean Margaret, *b.* 1951.——Jean Pamela, *b.* 1920: *m.* 1947, Col. James Andrew Fraser, MC, of Guisachan, by Beauly, Inverness-shire, and has issue living, Simon John, *b.* 1950,—Donald James, *b.* 1951,—Jean Catherine, *b.* 1954.

Issue of the late Major George Murray, *b.* 1884, *d.* (on active ser. during European War) 1940: *m.* 1928, Joan (Thorndrift, Box 168, Louis Trichardt, N. Transvaal), da. of the late William Eastwood, of Buffelspoort, Mara, N. Transvaal :—
John, *b.* 1929 : *m.* 1956, Margaret Yvonne, only dau. of Ronald Leonard Leach, of Louis Trichardt, N. Transvaal, and has issue living, Bruce George Ronald, *b.* 1960,—Craig John, *b.* 1963,—Jennifer, *b.* 1958. *Address,*—P.O. Box 722, Germiston, Transvaal, S. Africa.

    Granddaughter of the late Robert Hay Murray, 3rd son of the late Rt. Rev. George Murray, D.D., Bishop of Rochester (ante):—
Issue of the late Robert Evelyn Hay Murray, *b.* 1851, *d.* 1910: *m.* 1879, Frances Charlotte, who *d.* 1917, da. of the late Rev. E. Jacson, of Thruxton, Hereford:—
Rhona Evelyn Hay, *b.* 1888: *m.* 1915, Capt. Claude Spence Macnab, Queen's Own Cameron Highlanders (Reserve), and has issue living, Rhonette Alison (33, Drayton Gdns., SW10), *b.* 1917: *m.* 1940, Evelyn Helby Gardiner, who *d.* 1952, and has issue living, Robert Evelyn Napier *b.* 1941, Penelope-Anne *b.* 1945,—Jacqueline Frances, *b.* 1919: *m.* 1954, David Brown, of The Old School, Nesscliffe, Shrewsbury, and has issue living, Anthony Malcolm *b.* 1957, Caroline Susan *b.* 1955, Jennifer Anne *b.* 1960. *Residence,*—Duncton Cottage, Duncton, nr. Petworth, Sussex.

    Grandchildren of the late Sir Herbert Harley Murray, K.C.B., 4th son of the late Rt. Rev. George Murray, D.D., Bishop of Rochester (ante) :—
Issue of the late Major Stewart Lygon Murray, *b.* 1863, *d.* 1930 : *m.* 1895, Harriet Sophia, who *d.* 1948, dau. of the late Col. John Clark Kennedy, C.B. [E. Brownlow, colls.] :—
Elsie Dorothea Isabel, *b.* 1897: *m.* 1931, John Stewart Heber, and has issue living, James William (Park Cottage, Pipehouse Lane, Freshford, Bath), *b.* 1938; MB, BS, DA, D(Obst.) RCOG: *m.* 1960, Margaret Leslie Cooper, and has issue living, Andrew *b.* 1963, Jeremy *b.* 1966,—Janet Elizabeth, *b.* 1934: *m.* 1956, Robert Bruce Holgate Butler, and has issue living, Susan *b.* 1958, Anne *b.* 1960 , Jennifer *b.* 1963. *Residence,*—The Haven, Chesham Rd., Berkhamsted.——Christian Charlotte (The Flat, Hangerfield, Witley, Surrey), *b.* 1904: *m.* 1937, Ronald Peers Williams, who *d.* 1968, and has issue living, Richard Murray, *b.* 1947,—Jennifer Mary, *b.* 1940: *m.* 1965, Colin Willmott, of 43, Princess Rd., NW1, and has issue living, Giles Benedict Paddington *b.* 1967, Victoria *b.* 1965,— Susan *b.* 1942,—Penelope Ann, *b.* 1944.——Joan Margaret Vere, *b.* 1909: *m.* 1933, Henry Robert Stewart, of 66, Mount Ephraim, Tunbridge Wells, and has issue living, Richard John (Larachmhor, Birnam, Perthshire), *b.* 1936: *m.* 1958, Morag McLellan Stewart, and has issue living, Robert Murray *b.* 1959, Roderick Iain *b.* 1960, Alisdair James *b.* 1961, Careen Ann *b.* 1962,—Geoffrey Edward (Box 19, Ioco, BC, Canada), *b.* 1938: *m.* 1965, Valerie Louise Twells.

    Granddaughter of the late Gerald Otway Hay Murray (infra):—
Issue of the late Herbert Frederick Murray, *b.* 1906, *d.* 1971: *m.* 1942, Doris Mary Rowsel (Grove Cottage, Stoke St. Mary, nr. Taunton):—
Kathleen Elizabeth (c/o Grove Cottage, Stoke St. Mary, nr. Taunton), *b.* 1943: *m.* 1969, Richard John May, Capt. 2nd Bn. LI, and has issue living, Amanda Jane, *b.* 1969,—Emma Louise May, *b.* 1972.

    Grandchildren of the late Sir Herbert Harley Murray, KCB (ante):—
Issue of the late Gerald Otway Hay Murray, *b.* 1868, *d.* 1951 : *m.* 1905, Charlotte, who *d.* 1944, youngest dau. of Dudley George Cary-Elwes, formerly of Conway, Florida, U.S.A. :—
Douglas Gerald, *b.* 1907; formerly in RAF: *m.* 1940, Brenda, yr. da. of Earle R. Waight, and has issue living, Julian Charles, *b.* 1946. *Residence,*—Jolly Woodman, Chancery Lane, Beckenham, Kent.——
Stewart Hay, *b.* 1909: *m.* 1939, Freda Woodland, and has issue living, John Stewart (30, Salisbury Rd., Redland, Bristol, BS6 7AP), *b.* 1940: *m.* 1970, Alison, da. of Humphrey Trembath, of Reigate, and has issue living, Charles Humphrey Stewart *b.* 9171, Jennifer Mary Ellen *b.* 1974,—Peter Gerald Stewart (74, Bishops Rd., SW6), *b.* 1944: *m.* 1967, Jane, da. of Alexander Wood, of Epsom, and has issue living, Rupert Hay *b.* 1969, William Alexander *b.* 1972,—Geoffrey Charles Stewart, *b.* 1948. *Residence,*—29, High St., Lacock, Wilts.——Arthur Frank (29 High St., Lacock, Wilts.), *b.* 1911: *m.* 1937, Ruby Joyce Hooper, and has issue living, Ann Jennifer, *b.* 1939: *m.* 1959, Neil Jarman, of 19, Buchanan Av., Bournemouth,—Peter Gerald Stewart (74, Bishops Rd., SW6), *b.* 1944: *m.* 1967, Jane, da. of Alexander Wood, of Epsom, and has issue living, Rupert Hay *b.* 1969, William Alexander *b.* 1972,—Geoffrey Charles Stewart, *b.* 1948.——Arthur Frank, *b.* 1911: *m.* 1937, Ruby Joyce Hooper, and has issue living, Ann Jennifer, *b.* 1939: *m.* 1959, Neil Jarman, and has issue living, Ian *b.* 1960, Frances Ann *b.* 1962, Rebecca *b.* 1965. *Residence,*—Fivehead, nr. Taunton, Somerset.——Keith Robert, *b.* 1912: formerly in RE: *m.* 1941, Ellen Woodland, and has issue living, Andrew Keith, *b.* 1946,—Joan Ursula, *b.* 1945.——Kathleen Margaret Augusta, *b.* 1916. *Residence,* Grove Cottage, Stoke St. Mary, nr. Taunton, Somerset.

    Grandchildren of the late Caroline Sophia Smith, dau. of the late Rt. Rev. George Murray, D.D., Bishop of Rochester (ante) :—
Issue of the late Eleanor Smith, who *d.* 1937 : *m.* 1884, John Frederick Clerk, who *d.* 1931 :—
See Clerk, Bt., colls
Issue of the late Constance Smith, who *d.* 1928 : *m.* 1883, Major Charles Herring-Cooper R.A., who *d.* 1890 :—
John Gustavus, *b.* 1889 ; Lieut.-Col. late Roy. Leicestershire Regt. ; European War 1914-15 and 1918 (wounded). *Residence,*—3, Berkeley Sq., Rondebosch, Cape Town, S. Africa. *Club,*—Army and Navy.

    Grandchildren of the late Rev. Frederick Auriol MURRAY-GOURLAY (who assumed additional surname of Gourlay), el. son of the late Rev. Frederick William Murray, youngest son of the Rt. Rev. George Murray, D.D. Bishop of Rochester (ante) :—
Issue of the late (George) Ronald Auriol MURRAY-GOURLAY, *b.* 1900, *d.* 1961 : *m.* 1926, Phyllis (Peverill Point, Swanage, Dorset), da. of the late Walter Langford Rowley, of Edgbaston, and Birlingham Grange, Worcs.:—
Brian Austin Walter MURRAY-GOURLAY (Bugle Inn, Twyford, Hants.), *b.* 1927; late RN: *m.* 1st, 1953 (m. diss. 1962), Margaret, yr. da. of William Bryant, of Elmsleigh, Cribbs Causeway, Glos.; 2ndly, 1973, Patricia Mary, yr. da. of Daniel Eric Fewtrell, of Dudley, Worcs., and formerly wife of Charles Desmond Small, and has issue living (by 1st m.), Hugh William Auriol, *b.* 1960.——Auriol Mary, *b.* 1933: *m.* 1957, Capt. Frederick Ernest Herring, R. Norfolk Regt., of Ballard Cottage, Studland, Dorset, and has issue living, Jonathan James Aruiol, *b.* 1959,—Christopher John Murray, *b.* 1962.

    Grandchildren of the late Rev. Frederick William Murray (ante) :—
Issue of the late Rev. Charles Hay Murray, *b.* 1869, *d.* 1923 : *m.* 1906, Mabel, who *d.* 1953, dau. of the late S. C. Umfreville, of Ingress Abbey, Greenhithe, Kent :—
Sir (Francis) Ralph (Hay), *KCMG, CB* (The Old Rectory, Stoke Hammond, Bletchley, Bucks), *b.* 1908; British Ambassador to Greece 1962-67, since when a Gov. of BBC; CMG 1950, CB (Civil) 1957, KCMG 1962: *m.* 1935, Countess Mauricette Vladimira Marie, only child of the late Count Bernhard Kuenburg, of Payerbach, Austria, and has issue living, Ingram Bernard Hay (23, Dunton Rd. Stewkley, Leighton Buzzard, Beds.), *b.* 1937: *m.* 1963, Juliet Anne Thackeray, da. of the late Capt. J. M. T. Ritchie, and has issue living, Alistair James *b.* 1968, Xenia Margaret Thackeray *b.* 1966, Francesca Helen Ann *b.* 1970,—Nicholas Julyan Edward, *b.* 1939,—Simon Anthony, *b.* 1948,— Georgina Teresa, *b.* 1942: *m.* 1965, Roy Ashworth, of 29, Calton Av., Dulwich Village, SE21, and has issue living, Simon *b.* 1966, Jessica *b.* 1968.——Stephen Umfreville Hay, *b.* 1912; Actor; formerly

Capt.: *m.* 1937, Joan, da. of John Joseph Moy Butterfield, and has issue living, Amanda, *b.* 1942.——Anna Kathleen, *b.* 1907. *Residence,*—Goldmartin, Rattlesden, Bury St. Edmunds.

Issue of the late Rev. Maurice William Murray, *b.* 1870, *d.* 1943 *m.* 1909, Eva Margaret, who *d.* 1958, dau. of Charles Hubback Watson, formerly of Stone Castle, Greenhithe, Kent:—

Kathleen Joan, *b.* 1911: *m.* 1958, Alfred E. Roberts, of 86, Prince Albert Rd., N.W.8, and Church Cottage, Hardham, Pulborough, Sussex.——Margaret Elizabeth, *b.* 1915: *m.* 1943, Cecil McCullagh, of The Old Bank House, Chulmleigh, N. Devon.——Ursula Mary, *b.* 1919: *m.* 1941, Alan A. White, late Major Border Regt., of Reddaways Cottage, Alleyn Lane, Cookham Deane, Berks., and has issue living, Christopher Douglas, *b.* 1943,—David Ian (twin) (49a, Granville Place, Finchley, N12), *b.* 1943: *m.* 19—, Margaret Ann Griffith, and has issue living, Jonathan Alan *b.* 1974.

Grandsons of the late Col. Charles Edward Gostling Murray, yr. son of the late Rev. Edward Murray, 4th son of the late Rt. Rev. Lord George Murray (ante):—
Issue of the late Capt. Rupert Auriol Conant Murray, Seaforth Highlanders, *b.* 1882, *d.* (of wounds received in action during 1914-18 War) 1915: *m.* 1913, Ivy Maud (who *d.* 1946, having *m.* 2ndly, 1918, Brig. Hector Robert Hume Greenfield, OBE, late Argyll and Sutherland Highlanders), da. of Sir Henry Edward Dering, 10th Bt.:—
Anthony Ian Rupert, *OBE, b.* 1914; ed. at Eton; Col. (ret.) Seaforth Highlanders; 1939-45 War, MBE (Mil) 1944, OBE (Mil) 1957: *m.* 1944, Alexandra Elizabeth, only da. of the late Lt.-Col. (Douglas William) Alexander Dalziel Mackenzie, CVO, DSO, of Farr, Inverness-shire, and has issue living, John Rupert, *b.* 1945,—Ian James, *b.* 1947; Capt. Queen's Own Highlanders,—Andrew Edward, *b.* 1950. *Residence,*—Farr Mains, Inverness, IV1 2XB.

Issue of the late Stracey Montagu Atholl Murray, *b.* 1888, *d.* 1970: *m.* 1926, Irene Margaretta (White Inch, Littlestone-on-Sea, New Romney, Kent), yr. da. of Capt. William W. Waring:—
Edward William Atholl (14, Postwood Green, Hertford Heath, Herts.), *b.* 1927: *m.* 1st, 1959, Anne Oakeley, who *d.* 1972, da. of the late Maj. Loraine Macgregor Kerr, MC [Oakley, Bt.]; 2ndly, 1974, Elizabeth Dawn, da. of the late H. D. Harman, and has issue living, (by 1st m.) James Henry Atholl, *b.* 1960,—Charlotte Melloney Loraine, *b.* 1964.——Fane Robert Conant (Park House Farm, Cotherstone, Barnard Castle, co. Durham), *b.* 1929: *m.* 1962, Margaret Carsina, da. of Lt.-Col. Leslie George Gray-Cheape, of Carse Gray, Forfar, Angus, and has issue living, Rupert Charles, *b.* 1963,—Emma Jane, *b.* 1965.

Grandchildren of the late George Delmé-Murray, 3rd son of Vice-Adm. James Arthur Murray, only son of the late William Murray, 3rd son of 3rd Duke:—
Issue of the late Major George Arthur Delmé Murray, D.S.O., *b.* 1879, *d.* 1944: *m.* 1906, Dorothea Emily Anne, who *d.* 1938, dau. of the late T. Alexander Webb, of Waynwern, Monmouthshire:—
George Philip Alexander, *DSO, MBE, b.* 1921; Lt.-Col. KSLI; formerly Major Indian Army; Burma 1943-45 (wounded, DSO); DSO 1945, MBE (Mil) 1966; *m.* 1951, Alison Elizabeth, yr. da. of Col. William John Beddows, M.C., T.D., J.P., D.L., of Ackleton House, near Wolverhampton, and has issue living, Caroline Alison, *b.* 1953,—Rosemary Janet, *b.* 1956. *Address,*—c/o State Bank of India, 25, Old Broad St., EC——Corin Georgina Florence, *b.* 1919: *m.* 1947, William R. Wilson.

Granddaughters of the late Rev. Richard Paget Murray (infra):—
Issue of the late Capt. Henry James Stewart Murray, R.E., *b.* 1874, *d.* 1942: *m.* 1919, Maude Amelia (who *m.* 2ndly, 1947, Thomas Rosser Dummer, of Cape Town, S. Africa), youngest dau. of George Jonathan Mills, of Norwich :—
Margaret Dorothea, *b.* 1926: *m.* 1946, Stanley Alastair Miller, and has issue living, Pamela Ann, *b.* 1950,—Sheila Frances, *b.* 1951,—Wendy Margaret, *b.* 1954. *Residence,*—Valley House, Simonstown, Cape Province, S. Africa.

Issue of the Rev. Athole Evelyn Murray, *b.* 1881, *d.* 1962: *m.* 1917, Ellen Emily, who *d.* 1960, dau. of Henry Frederic Tiarks:—
Anne (1, Sherrington, Warminster), *b.* 1920, BMusDurham: *m.* 1954, John Edward Page, who *d.* 1964, and has issue living, Edward John Atholl, *b.* 1956,—Henry Stewart Murray (twin), *b.* 1956,—Thomas Patrick Murray, *b.* 1960,—Susan Margaret, *b.* 1955: *m.* 1974, Julian Marc Piers Bryant, of Flat 2, Nethermoor, Hillside, S. Brent, Devon.

Granddaughter of the late Col. Henry Murray, RA, son of the late Lt.-Col. Richard Murray, son of the late Lord Henry Murray, 4th son of 3rd Duke:—
Issue of the late Rev. Richard Paget Murray, *b.* 1842, *d.* 1908 : *m.* 1st, 1868, Emily Blanche who *d.* 1877, dau. of the late Gen. James Webber-Smith, C.B. ; 2ndly, 1880, Ada Constance, who *d.* 1943, dau. of Henry Richard Woodhouse :—
(By 2nd m.) Violet Constance (c/o The Rev. Mother, St. Mary's Convent, Holmhurst, St. Leonards-on-Sea, Sussex), *b.* 1885; is an Oxford Mission Sister of the Epiphany.

Grandson of the late Lieut.-Col. Henry Murray, son of the late Col. Henry Murray R.A. (ante):—
Issue of the late Major Henry Francis Farquharson Murray, Black Watch, *b.* 1881, *d.* (killed in action during European War) 1917: *m.* 1915, Madeline Elizabeth, who *d.* 1966, da. of the late Arthur H. Giles, formerly of The Court, Churchill, Somerset:—
Ian Henry, *M.C., b.* 1916; ed. at Wellington; Lt.-Col. and Hon. Col. late Roy. Highland Fusiliers; 1939-45 War (wounded, M.C.): *m.* 1940, Eleanor Fownes, dau. of the late Rev. Geoffrey Lionel Porcher, formerly R. of Weston-super-Mare, and has issue living, Alison Fownes, *b.* 1941: *m.* 1970, Oliver William Wilkins, of 29, Eversley Rd., Surbiton,—Jacqueline Dorothea, *b.* 1942. *Residence,*—15, Montague Rd., Richmond, Surrey.

Granddaughters of the late Col. Henry Murray, RA (ante):—
Issue of the late Charles Nathaniel Murray, *b.* 1855, *d.* 1922: *m.* 1885, Annie Isabel, who *d.* 1966, da. of the late W. C. Wright, of Alma Cottage, Cambridge, New Zealand:—
Athole Alma Emily Clare, *b.* 1887: *m.* 1910, John Nicholas Quick, and has issue living, Dudley John Athole, *b.* 1921,—Glory Isabel, *b.* 1911: *m.* 1938, Major Thomas Henry Bevan, DSO, NZF, of 1, Hoheria Rd., Onehunga, Auckland, NZ, and has issue living, Isabel Jeanette *b.* 1939: *m.* 1958, Noel Gordon Thomson, of Waiheke I., Auckland, NZ, (and has issue living, Michael Rex *b.* 1959, David Jeffrey *b.* 1967, Kathryn Mary *b.* 1961, Linda Joanne *b.* 1963), Cynthia Ann *b.* 1945: *m.* 1967, Peter Todd, (and has issue living, Dominic Xan *b.* 1971), Jennifer Mary *b.* 1950,—Heather Murray, *b.* 1919: *m.* 1939, Francis Phillip Richardson, and has issue living, Lindsay Stuart *b.* 1944. *Residence,*—14, Peet Av., Epsom, Auckland, NZ.——Kathleen Stewart, *b.* 1892: *m.* 1913, Joseph Willford Sanderson, and has issue living, Aroha Kathleen Stewart, *b.* 19—,—Margaret Gwen, *b.* 19—. *Residence,*—.

Grandchildren of the late Rev. Arthur Silver Murray (infra):—
Issue of the late Arthur Evelyn Francis Murray, *b.* 1888, *d.* 1972: *m.* 1927, Louise Isabelle (Oliviershoek, Bergville, Natal), da. of Lt.-Col. Addis Delacombe, DSO, of Shrewton Manor, nr. Salisbury:—
James, *b.* 1941; ed. at Stellenbosch Univ. (BSc Agric).——Jean Evelyn Louise (White Lodge, Startley, Chippenham, Wilts.), *b.* 1932; ed. at Stellenbosch Univ. (BA): *m.* 1959, Maj. Jonathan Beresford Oliphant, 7th Duke of Edinburgh's Own Gurkha Rifles (ret.), and has issue living, Angus Laurence, *b.* 1966,—Catriona Jane, *b.* 1960,—Janet Elizabeth, *b.* 1963.

Grandsons of the late Col. Henry Murray, R.A (ante):—

Issue of the late Rev. Arthur Silver Murray, *b.* 1858, *d.* 1932 : *m.* 1887, Rose Evelyn, who *d.* 19—, da. of Henry Richard Woodhouse (ante):—

Kenneth Andrew Silver, *b.* 1904.——Douglas Vivian (Paradeisou Odos 10, Nea Kifissia, Athens, Greece), *b.* 1905; ed. at Westminster, and at Gonville and Caius Coll., Camb.; former Headmaster of Great Sanders Sch., Sedlescombe, Sussex: *m.* 1st, 1932 (m. diss. 1958), Isabel Mary Farquhar, da. of Dr. Andrew Grierson Fausset-Farquhar, of Bridgeton House, St. Cyrus, Kincardineshire; 2ndly, 1958, Beryl Violet, da. of Lt.-Col. Wybergh, of Heath Brow, Ewshot, Farnham, Surrey, and has issue living, (by 2nd m.) Hamish Douglas, *b.* 1959,—Andrew Vivian, *b.* 1961,—Anne Beryl Charlotte de la Trémouille, *b.* 1963.

Grandchildren of the late Hugh Percy Murray-Aynsley, son of John Murray-Aynsley, son of the Very Rev. Lord Charles Murray-Aynsley, 5th son of 3rd Duke:—

Issue of the late Charles Percy Murray-Aynsley, *b.* 1862, *d.* 1936 : *m.* 1st, 1911, Ina Winifred who *d.* 1917, dau. of the late H. H. Prins, M.D. ; 2ndly, 1921, Gladys, who *d.* 1959, dau. of the late Francis Turnor :—

(By 2nd marriage) Francis Percy, *b.* 1924 : *m.* 1950, Diana Gray, dau. of W. Gray Young, of Lowry Bay, Wellington, New Zealand, and has issue living, Charles William Percy, *b.* 1955,—Susan Jane, *b.* 1951,—Bridget Anne, *b.* 1952. *Residence,*—Wi Waka, Eketahuna, New Zealand.——(By 1st marriage) Elizabeth, *b.* 1912: *m.* 1935, John Duncan Simpson, and has issue living, Charles William *b.* 1936,—Duncan Murray *b.* 1938: *m.* 1961, Judith Margaret Mary, dau. of H. Simmons, of Hawkes Bay, New Zealand, and has issue living, Michael Paul *b.* 1961, Toby Duncan *b.* 1963,—Patricia Mary, *b.* 1940. *Residence,*—Dalvey, Turakina, New Zealand.——(By 2nd marriage) Mary Beatrice. *b.* 1923: *m.* 1948, John Alfred Loring Tansley, of 40, Thurso St., Invercargill, NZ, and has issue living, Sara Lorraine, *b.* 1949: *m.* 1968, Grant Alistair Marshall, of 10, Domain Cres., Muriwai Beach, Auckland, NZ, and has issue living, Noah John *b.* 1973,—Philippa Ann, *b.* 1952: *m.* 1972, Ian James McKenzie, of 89, Buccleugh St., Dunedin, NZ, and has issue living, Kerith Jayne *b.* 1974,—Pamela Winnifred, *b.* 1961.

(In special remainder to Dukedom).

Descendants of Lord Charles Murray (2nd son of 1st Marquess), who was cr. Earl of Dunmore [see that title.]

PREDECESSORS—[1] Sir JOHN MURRAY, *P.C.*, 12th feudal Baron of Tullibardine, was cr. *Lord Murray of Tullibardine* (peerage ot Scotland) 1604, and *Earl of Tullibardine* (peerage of Scotland) 1606 ; *d.* 1609 ; *s.* by his el. son [2] WILLIAM, 2nd Earl; appointed Hereditary Sheriff of Perthshire 1600 for rescuing the King at Perth from the attempt of the Earl of Gowrie ; he *m.* Lady Dorothea Stewart, dau. of John, 5th and last Earl of Atholl, Charles I. having on petition agreed to revive the Earldom of Atholl on the issue of the Countess of Tullibardine, the Earl by consent of the crown resigned his dignities to his brother Patrick (see *°₀°* infra) ; *d.* 1626 ; *s.* by his son [3] JOHN, cr. *Earl of Atholl* (peerage of Scotland) 1629 ; *d.* 1642 ; *s.* by his son [4] JOHN, *K.T.*, 2nd Earl, who on the death of his cousin James in 1670 became 5th Earl of Tullibardine ; cr. *Marquess of Atholl, Earl of Tullibardine, Viscount of Balquhidder, and Lord Murray, Balveny, and Gask* (peerage of Scotland with remainder to heirs male of his body) 1676 ; *d.* 1703 ; *s.* by his el. son [5] JOHN, *K.T.*, 2nd Marquess ; cr. (in his father's lifetime) *Earl of Tullibardine, Viscount Glenalmond, and Lord Murray* (peerage of Scotland for life) 1696, *Lord Murray, Balvenie and Gask, Viscount of Balwhidder, Glenalmond, and Glenlyon, Earl of Strathtay and Strathardle, Marquess of Tullibardine, and Duke of Atholl* (peerage of Scotland) 1703, with special remainder failing heir's male of his body to those of his father ; his el. surviving son having joined the Earl of Mar 1715, was charged with high treason, and attainted by Parliament ; *d.* 1724 ; *s.* by his 2nd son [6] JAMES, *K.T.*, 2nd Duke, upon whom the family honours were settled by Act of Parliament ; on the death of the 10th Earl of Derby, he *s.* through his grandmother to the *Barony of Strange* (peerage of England, cr. 1628), and the Sovereignty of the Isle of Man ; *d.* 1764, when the Barony of Strange and the Sovereignty of the Isle of Man devolved upon his dau. Charlotte, and the Scotch honours reverted to his nephew (el. son of Lord George Murray, 5th son of the 1st Duke) [7] JOHN, *K.T.*, 3rd Duke, who *m.* his cousin Charlotte, Baroness Strange (ante) ; the Duke and Duchess disposed of their Sovereignty in the Isle of Man to the British Govt. for £70,000 ; *d.* 1774 ; *s.* by his el. son [8] JOHN, *K.T.*, 4th Duke, cr. *Baron Murray of Stanley* and *Earl Strange* (peerage of Great Britain) 1786, and *s.* to English Barony of Strange 1805 ; he disposed of his remaining property and privileges in the Isle of Man to the crown for £409,000 ; *d.* 1830 ; *s.* by his son [9] JOHN, 5th Duke ; *d.* 1846 ; *s.* by his nephew (el. son of James, 1st *Baron Glenlyon* (peerage of United Kingdom, cr. 1821), 2nd son of 4th Duke) [10] GEORGE AUGUSTUS FREDERICK JOHN, *K.T.*, 6th Duke, *b.* 1814 ; *s.* his father as 2nd *Baron Glenlyon* 1837 : *m.* 1839, Anne, *V.A.*, who *d.* 1897, dau. of the late Henry Home Drummond, of Blair Drummond, Perth ; *d.* 1864 ; *s.* by his son [11] JOHN JAMES HUGH HENRY, *K.T.*, 7th Duke, *b.* 1840 ; in 1865 inherited *Barony of Percy* (cr. by writ 1722, peerage of Great Britain) and registered at Lyon Court his assumption of the sur-name of Stewart before his patronymic ; was Lord-Lieut. of Perthshire 1878-1917 ; in 1893 reverted to the original form of spelling the title ("Atholl " instead of "Athole ") : *m.* 1863, Louisa, who *d.* 1902, el. dau. of Sir Thomas Moncrieffe ; 7th Bt. ; *d.* 1917 ; *s.* by his el. son [12] JOHN GEORGE, *K.T., G.C.V.O., C.B.. D.S.O., T.D.,, P.C.*, 8th Duke, *b.* 1871 ; Lord-Lieut. of Perthshire ; appointed Lord High Commr. to Gen. Assembly of Ch. of Scotland 1918, 1919, and 1920 ; was Lord Chamberlain of the Household 1921-2 ; Nile Expedition 1898 (D.S.O.), South Africa 1899-1902, in command of two Regts. of Scottish Horse (which he raised) with rank of Lieut.-Col., European War 1914-19 in Gallipoli and Egypt, with Regts. of Scottish Horse (which he raised), and Comdg. a Scottish Horse Brig., and subsequently 8th and 10th Cyclist Brigs. (O.B.) ; an A.D.C. to H.M. 1920-31 ; sat as M.P. for Perthshire, W. Div. (C) 1910-17 : *m.* 1899, Katharine Marjory, *D.B.E., LL.D., D.C.L.*, who *d.* 1960, dau. of Sir James Henry Ramsay, 10th Bt., of Banff ; *d.* 1942 ; *s.* by his brother [13] JAMES THOMAS, 9th Duke ; *b.* 1879 ; formerly Major Queen's Own Cameron Highlanders ; *d.* 1957, when the Barony of Strange (peerage of England cr. 1628) fell into abeyance [see B. Strange]; the Barony of Percy, cr. by writ 1722 (peerage of Great Britain) passed to the Duke of Northumberland, and the Earldom of Strange (peerage of Great Britain) 1786, and the Baronies of Murray of Stanley (peerage of Great Britain) 1786, and of Glenlyon (peerage of UK), 1821, became ext.; *s.* in his other peerages by his kinsman [14] GEORGE IAIN, 10th Duke (son of the late Lt.-Col. George Anthony Murray, OBE, RA, son of the late Sir (George) Evelyn Pemberton Murray, KCB, grandson of the late Rev. George Edward Murray, grandson of the Rt. Rev. Lord George Murray, DD, 2nd son of 3rd Duke), 10th Duke and present peer; also Mar-quess of Atholl, Marquess of Tullibardine, Earl of Atholl, Earl of Tullibardine, Earl of Strathtay and Strathardle, Viscount of Balwhidder, Glenalmond and Glenlyon, Lord Murray, Balvenie and Gask, and Lord Murray of Tullibardine.

°₀°[1] *Hon.* PATRICK Murray was cr. *Earl of Tullibardine* and *Lord Murray of Gask* (Peerage of Scotland) 1628, with remainder to his heirs male whatsoever, presumably with original precedence of 1606 and 1604 respectively, in consequence of resignation of that Earldom and Lordship by his brother, 2nd Earl of Tullibardine; *b.* 15—: *m.* Elizabeth, who *d.* before 1656, dau. and co-heir of John Dent, of London, and widow of Francis Vere; *d.* 1644; *s.* by his son [2] JAMES, 4th Earl of Tullibardine, *b.* 1617: *m.* 1st, 1643, Lady Lilias Drummond, dau. of 2nd Earl of Perth; 2ndly, 1664, Lady Anne Murray, dau. of 1st Earl of Atholl (ante); 3rdly, 1667, Lilias (who *m.* 2ndly, 16—, James Drummond, 4th Earl of Perth), dau. of Sir James Drummond of Machany; *d.* 1670; *s.* by his kinsman [3] JOHN Murray, 2nd Earl of Atholl (ante).

DAUGHTER LIVING OF FIRST BARON.

Hon. Alice Hamilton. *b.* 1895: *m.* 1925, Bernard Marsham Hallward, D.S.O., and has issue living, Hugh Graham, *b.* 1926: *m.* 1955, Martha, da. of P. S. Fisher, and has issue living, Graham Fisher *b.* 1956, John Atholstan *b.* 1961, Margaret Alice *b.* 1957, Faith Hamilton *b.* 1959, Annabel *b.* 1963,— John Marsham (3150, Trafalgar Av., Montreal, Quebec, H37 1H7), *b.* 1929: *m.* 1956, Clare, da. of the late Sir Everard Charles Lindley Meynell, OBE, MC [see E. Halifax, colls.], and has issue living, Peter Marsham *b.* 1968, Christopher Graham *b.* 1973, Jennifer Rose *b.* 1963, Julia Anne *b.* 1965, Mary Clare *b.* 1966, Katherine Rosemary *b.* 1972. *Residence,*—1227, W. Sherbrooke St., Montreal, 25, Canada.

ATKIN, BARONY OF. (Atkin,) [Extinct 1944.]

SON LIVING OF LIFE PEER.

Hon. William Robert, *b.* 1901: *m.* 1st, 1929, Constance Emilia Bourchier, who *d.* 1930; 2ndly, 1935 Mary McMurtrie, and has issue. *Residence,*—Willow Wood, Thorney Green, Stowupland, Suffolk

DAUGHTERS LIVING OF LIFE PEER.

Hon. Margaret Lucy: *m.* 1920, Lieut.-Com. Richard Henry Kennard Hope, R.N., who *d.* 1962, and has issue. *Residence,*—The Thatched Cottage, East Harting, Petersfield, Hants.
Hon. Nancy : *m.* 1st, 1924, John Douglas Trustram Eve, from whom she obtained a divorce 1933; 2ndly, 1933, Harold Brash Thomas Morison, and has issue. *Residence,*—2, Ensor Mews, SW7.
Hon. Elizabeth ; Bar. Gray's Inn 1955: *m.* 1st, 1932, John Kennedy Cockburn Millar, Bar.-at-Law, who *d.* 1952; 2ndly, 1960, His Honour Judge Denis Hicks Robson, QC. *Residences,*—Glendalough, Caragh Lake, co. Kerry; 59, Campden Street, W8.

ATTLEE, EARL. (Attlee.) [Earl U.K. 1955.]

Labour conquers all.

MARTIN RICHARD ATTLEE 2nd Earl; *b.* Aug. 10th 1927; *s.* 1967; ed. at Millfield Coll., and Southampton Univ.; late Merchant Navy; Assist. Public Relations Officer, S. Region, British Rail since 1970: *m.* 1955, Anne Barbara, el. da. of the late James Henderson, CBE, of Bath, and has issue.

Arms,—Azure, on a chevron or, between three hearts of the last winged argent, as many lions rampant sable. Crest,—On a mount vert two lions rampant addorsed or. Supporters,—On either side a Welsh terrier sejant proper.

Residence,—125, Hendon Lane, N3 3PR.

SON LIVING.

JOHN RICHARD (*Viscount Prestwood*), *b.* Oct. 3rd, 1956.

DAUGHTER LIVING.

Lady Jane Elizabeth, *b.* 1959.

SISTERS LIVING.

Janet Helen, *b.* 1923; does not use courtesy title: *m.* 1947, Harold William Shipton (820, Woodside Drive, Iowa City, Iowa, USA), and has issue living, Ann Helen, *b.* 1948: *m.* 1969, Charles William Nandell.
Lady Felicity Ann, *b.* 1925: *m.* 1955, John Keith Harwood, and has issue living, Richard James Attlee, *b.* 1963,—Penelope Ann, *b.* 1956,—Joanna Patricia, *b.* 1958,—Sally Alexandra, *b.* 1960. *Residence,* —Meadway, 47, Penn Rd., Beaconsfield, Bucks.
Lady Alison Elizabeth, *b.* 1930 : *m.* 1952, Richard Lionel Lance Davis, and has issue living, Jennifer Alison, *b.* 1953,—Tessa Meriel, *b.* 1955,—Belinda Jane, *b.* 1957. *Residence,*—Westcott, Beacon Rise, Sevenoaks.

PREDECESSOR.—[1] *Rt. Hon.* CLEMENT RICHARD Attlee, KG, OM, CH, PC, 4th son of Henry Attlee, Solicitor, of Westcott, Putney, SW; *b.* 1883; MP for Limehouse (*Lab.*) 1922-50, and W. Walthamstow 1950-55; Leader of Labour Party 1935-55, Dep. Prime Min. 1943-45, Prime Min. 1945-51, and Leader of Opposition 1951-55; *cr.* Earl Attlee, and Viscount Prestwood, of Walthamstow, co. Essex (peerage of UK) 1955: *m.* 1922, Violet Helen, who *d.* 1964; yst. da. of Henry Edward Millar, of Heathdown, Hampstead, NW; *d.* 1967; *s.* by his only son [2] MARTIN RICHARD 2nd Earl, and present peer; also Viscount Prestwood.

AUCKLAND, BARON. (Eden.) [Baron I. 1789 and G.B. 1793.]

IAN GEORGE EDEN, 9th Baron; *b.* June 23rd, 1926; *s.* 1957; *m.* 1954, Dorothy Margaret, dau. of H. J. Manser, of Beechwood, Friday Street, Eastbourne, and has issue.

Arms,—Gules, on a chevron argent, between three garbs or, banded vert, as many escallops sable. **Crest.**— A dexter arm embowed in armour proper, the hand grasping a garb or, the upper part of the arm encircled by an annulet gules. **Supporters,**—*Dexter,* a horse guardant argent, charged on the breast with a fleur-de-lis or; *sinister,* a horse argent, charged on the breast with a tower or.
Residence,—Tudor Rose House, 30, Links Rd., Ashtead, Surrey. *Clubs,*—Constitutional, City Livery, Epsom.

SON LIVING
Hon. ROBERT IAN BURNARD, *b.* July 25th, 1962.

DAUGHTERS LIVING.
Hon. Margaret Fiona, *b.* 1955.
Hon. Rachel Andrey, *b.* 1959.

BROTHER LIVING.
If there be but prudence.

Hon. Ronald John, *b.* 1931: *m.* 1957, Rosemary Dorothy Marion, dau. of Sir John (Frederick) Ellenborough Crowder, M.P., J.P. [see B. Petre, colls.], and has issue living, Henry Vane, *b.* 1958,—Edward John, *b.* 1959. *Residence,*—Cromlix, Dunblane, Perthshire.

AUNT LIVING. (*Raised to the rank of a Baron's daughter* 1942.)
Hon. Ivy Maude, *b.* 1899: *m.* 1927, John Dawson, of 3, Copse Hill, Robbery Bottom Lane, Welwyn, Herts.

DAUGHTERS LIVING OF SEVENTH BARON.
Hon. Joan Edith, *b.* 1920; JP of Essex: *m.* 1st, 1941, the Rev. Alfred Lisinea Pond, V. of Potten End and Nettleden, who *d.* 1947; 2ndly, 1948, the Rev. Arthur Harrington Franklin, MBE, TD, and has issue living, (by 1st m.) Rosemary Jane, *b.* 1942: *m.* 1966, John Edward Rendall, of 39, Park Rd., Teddington, Middx., and has issue living, Amelia Jane *b.* 1969, Sophie Charlotte *b.* 1971,—Sarah Joan, *b.* 1945: *m.* 1972, David Alexander Platts, of 22, Palace Mansions, W14,—(by 2nd m.) Elizabeth, *b.* 1949: *m.* 1970, Michael Peter Withycombe Lance (Flat 11, Doctors Residences, Hull Royal Infirmary, Hull),—Caroline, *b.* 1952. *Residence,*—Hea Corner, Mill Rd., Felsted, Dunmow, Essex.
Hon. Elizabeth, *b.* 1928: *m.* 1954, Maj. Frederic Edward Isdale (Robin) Mason, late 1st R. Anglian Regt., and has issue living, Timothy Robin, *b.* 1957,—Edward Geoffrey, *b.* 1961,—Catherine Elizabeth, *b.* 1955. *Residence,*—Reed Hall, Holbrook, nr. Ipswich.

DAUGHTER LIVING OF SIXTH BARON.
Hon. Susan Constance, *b.* 1918 : *m.* 1st, 1942 (marriage dissolved 1956), Jose Diaz de Rivera; 2ndly, 1957, Guillermo Pakenham Bridges, H.M.'s Hon. Vice-Consul at Rio Grande, Argentina, and has issue living, (by 1st marriage) Jose Diaz, *b.* 1944. *Residence,*—Estancia Viamonte, Rio Grande, Tierra del Fuego, Argentina.

COLLATERAL BRANCHES LIVING.
Granddaughters of the late Hon. Robert Henley Shaw Eden, 4th son of 3rd Baron:—
Issue of the late Robert Hildyard Henley Eden, *b.* 1863, *d.* 1932: *m.* 1887, Baroness Maud Effie Mary, who *d.* 1957, dau. of the late Baron Otto von Guttenberg, of Steinenhausen, Bavaria:—
Dulcibella (Crossways, Sway, Hants), *b.* 1891: *m.* 1st, 1914, Llewellyn Arthur Hugh-Jones, OBE, who *d.* 1970, having obtained a divorce 1924; 2ndly, 1924, Eustace Gurney Pelly, who *d.* 1954 [Pelly, Bt. colls.], and has issue living, (by 1st m.) Brenda Mary (White Cottage, Stradishall, Newmarket, Suffolk), *b.* 1916: *m.* 1st, 1941, Fl. Lt. Derek L. Rawnsley, RAFVR, who *d.* (killed in action) 1943; 2ndly, 1949 (*m.* diss. 1952), Geoffrey Keighley, OBE, who *d.* 1966, and has issue living, (by 2nd m.) Jonathan Eden, *b.* 1950 (58, Park St., W1); ed. at Eton, and Trinity Coll., Camb.,—Margaret Claire (Tresco Abbey, Isles of Scilly), *b.* 1920: *m.* 1st, 1939, Philip Dalton Worthington, MBE, who *d.* 1964; 2ndly, 1967, Lt.-Cdr. Thomas Dorrien Smith, JP, RN (ret.), who *d.* 1973, and has issue living, (by 1st m.) Richard Philip (King's Farm House, Stratfield Saye, Berks.), *b.* 1941: *m.* 1967, Sara, da. of Capt. Michael Anthony Callender, [E. Coventry colls.] (and has issue living, Simon Philip *b.* 1970, Camilla Mary *b.* 1969, Selina Mary *b.* 1972), Margaret Joan *b.* 1943: *m.* 1968, Johnny Pierre Nicolas Mengers, of 6, Pembroke Gdns. Close, W8 (and has issue living, Jason Eden *b.* 1970, Jake Curtis *b.* 1972), Rosemary Claire *b.* 1950.——Phyllis Eleanor *b.* 1893: *m.* 1916, Maj. Robert Henry Evans, MBE, JP, Shropshire Yeo., who *d.* 1960, and has issue living, Richard, *MC* (The Mead House, Eyton, Leominster) *b.* 1920; Lt.-Col. (ret.) KSLI; a JP of Herefords.; 1939-45 War (MC): *m.* 1965, Marian Elizabeth Magee Cuff, and has issue living, Richard Jonathan *b.* 1966,— Ann, *b.* 1918: *m.* 1948, Maj. Robert Leycester Otter-Barry, MC, King's Shropshire LI (ret.), of The Old Rectory, Bagendon, Cirencester, Glos. [Cs. Dysart, colls.], and has issue living, Janetta Beryl *b.* 1953, Eleanor Ann Louise *b.* 1956,—Kathleen, *b.* 1921: *m.* 1947, Col. Guy Mytton Thornycroft, KSLI (ret.) of The Mount, Cressage, Shrewsbury, and has issue living, David Charles *b.* 1949, Mark Robert *b.* 1950. *Residence,*—The Mead House, Eyton, Leominster.

Grandsons of the late William Annesley Eden (infra):—
Issue of the late Edward Hildyard Eden, *b.* 1898 *d.* 1968: *m.* 1942, Annie Sylvester:—
Ernest John (Box 59, Sangudo, Alberta, Canada), *b.* 1943: *m.* 1967, Allison Carolynne Wilde, and has issue living, Buckey John, *b.* 1974,—Heidi Anne, *b.* 1969.——William Edward (RRI Sundre, Alberta, Canada), *b.* 1945: *m.* 1967, Maureen T. O'Hagan, and has issue living, Joseph Edward, *b.* 1970.

Grandchildren of the late Hon. Robert Henley Shaw Eden (ante):—
Issue of the late William Annesley Eden, M.R.C.S., L.R.C.P., *b.* 1868, *d.* 1939: *m.* 1895, Mabel Louisa Homfray, who *d.* 1951, dau. of the late Sir Robert Pinsent, D.C.L., a Puisne Judge of the Supreme Court of Newfoundland :—
George Henley, *TD* (17, Clarence Rd., Wallington, Surrey), *b.* 1904; Maj. RA: *m.* 1st, 1928, Avril Edith, who *d.* 1966, having obtained a divorce 1949, da. of the late R. O. Simmons; 2ndly, 1951 (*m.* diss. 1974) Doreen Rosamund Averil Tobeason; 3rdly, 1974, Stella Frances, da. of the late W. H. Duplock, and has issue living, (by 1st m.) Annesley Kathleen, *b.* 1928: *m.* 1949, David George Warre Yeats Brown, of 151, Oakwood Court, W14, and has issue living, Richard Andrew *b.* 1955, Caroline *b.* 1950, Sarah Kate *b.* 1961,—Avril Jane, *b.* 1930: *m.* 1957, Peter Milne Horley (P.O. Box 65425, Benmore, Sandton, Transvaal), and has issue living, Rupert *b.* 1958,—Sally Mabel Henley, *b.* 1932: *m.* 1964, Johann Leusink, and has issue living, Andrew Hamilton Henley *b.* 1968.—— Frederick Reeve (Bridge House, Raaus Rd., Amersham, Bucks.), *b.* 1908: *m.* 1953, Beatrice Helena, da. of the late Montague Smith, and has issue living, Sarah Ursula, *b.* 1954.——Ursula, *b.* 1896; Subaltern (ret.) ATS; 1914-18 War with Queen Mary's Aux. Army Corps (despatches, two medals), 1939-45 War as Junior Com. ATS. *Address,*—c/o National Westminster Bank, West Malling, Kent.

Issue of the late Alice Mary Eden, *b*. 1866, *d*. 1931 : *m*. 1889, the Rev. Harold Smith, formerly
R. of Himley, who *d*. 1938 :—
Muriel Jessie, *b*. 1893 : *m*. 1917, James Arthur Higgs-Walker (M.A. Oxon), formerly Head Master of
Sevenoaks Sch., and has issue living, Bridget Jean, *b*. 1918 : *m*. 1939, Michael Hedley Harmer,
FRCS, of Perrot Wood, Graffham, Petworth, Sussex, and has issue living, William Russell *b*. 1943; ed.
at Marlborough: *m*. 1970, Sarah Emily Harben, da. of Hector Valentine, of 86, Iverna Court, W8
(and has issue living, Douglas Russell Eden *b*. 1973, Arabell Louise Eden *b*. 1972), Juliet Linda
b. 1941: *m*. 1967 (m. diss. 1973) William Squire. *Residence,*—Long Barn, Chelwood Gate, Sussex.
——Audrey Helen, *b*. 1896: *m*. 1919, Col. William Collis Spackman, FRCSE, FRCOG, late IMS.
Residence,—Rickstones, E. Grinstead, Sussex.——Sybil Mildred (Thor's Cottage, Beacon Drive,
W. Kirby, Ches.), *b*. 1902: *m*. 1923, Alexander Caryl Ziegler, who *d*. 1964, and has issue living,
Josephine Earnshaw, *b*. 1924: *m*. 1947, Raymond Ewart Whiston of 46, Moorshead Mansions,
Moorshead Rd., W9, and has issue living, Richard Paul, *b*. 1950: *m*. 1973, Helen, only da. of
F. Willmott, of Axbridge, Somerset, Anthony David *b*. 1952, Nigel Peter, *b*. 1956.

PREDECESSORS.—[1] *Rt. Hon.* WILLIAM Eden, *P.C.*, 3rd son of Sir Robert Eden, 3rd Bt.;
b. 1744; was Ch. Sec. for Ireland, and Ambassador to Versailles, Madrid, &c.: *m*. 1776,
Eleanor, who *d*. 1818, dau. of the Rt. Hon. Sir Gilbert Elliot, P.C., 3rd Bt.; cr. *Baron Auckland*
(peerage of Ireland) 1789, and *Baron Auckland* (peerage of Great Britain) 1793; *d*. 1814; *s*. by
his el. son [2] GEORGE, *G.C.B.*, 2nd Baron; *b*. 1784; Gov.-Gen. of India 1836-41; cr. *Baron
Eden* and *Earl of Auckland* (peerage of United Kingdom) 1839; *d.s.p.* 1849, when the earldom
became extinct; *s*. in peerages of 1789 and 1793 by his brother [3] the *Rt. Rev.* ROBERT
JOHN, 3rd Baron, *b*. 1799; was Lord Bishop of Sodor and Man 1847-54, and of Bath and
Wells 1854-69 : *m*. 1825, Mary, who *d*. 1872, el. dau. of Francis Edward Hurt, of Alderwasley,
co. Derby; *d*. 1870; *s*. by his el. son [4] WILLIAM GEORGE, 4th Baron, *b*. 1829; in Diplo. Ser.
1847-61 : *m*. 1st, 1857, Lucy Walbanke, who *d*. 1870, dau. of John Walbanke Childers, of Cantley,
Yorkshire; 2ndly, 1872, Lady Mabel Emily Finch-Hatton, who *d*. 1872, dau. of 11th Earl of
Winchilsea; 3rdly, 1875, Edith, who *d*. 1931, dau. of Sir William Eden, 6th Bt. ; *s*. by his el.
son [5] WILLIAM MORTON, 5th Baron, *b*. 1859: *m*. 1891, Sybil Constance, who *d*. 1955, el. dau.
of the late George Morland Hutton, O.B., *d*. 1917; *s*. by his only surviving son [6] FREDERICK
COLVIN GEORGE, 6th Baron; *b*. 1895; Flight-Lieut. R.A.F. Vol. Reserve: *m*. 1st, 1917, Susan
Livingstone (who obtained a divorce in U.S.A. 1925), only dau. of Augustus Griffin Hartridge,
of Jacksonville, Florida, U.S.A.; 2ndly, 1939, Constance Caroline, who *d*. 1946, dau. of Benno
Hart, of San Francisco, California, U.S.A.; *d*. (result of enemy action during European War)
1941; *s*. by his cousin [7] GEOFFREY MORTON, *M.B.E.* (son of the late Hon. George Eden 3rd
son of 4th Baron), 7th Baron; *b*. 1891; Capt. R.A.S.C. (retired); European War 1914-18
(despatches twice, M.B.E.), European War 1939-41: *m*. 1919, Dorothy Ida, who *d*. 1964, dau. of the
Rev. Francis Clyde Harvey, V. of Hailsham, and Preb. of Chichester; *d*. 1955; *s*. by his brother
[8] TERENCE, *M.C.*, 8th Baron; *b*. 1892; Major Roy. Armoured Corps (T.A.); European War
1914-18 as Capt. Machine Gun Corps (despatches, M.C. with Bar): European War 1939-41: *m*.
1925, Evelyn Vane (DRUMMOND OF CROMLIX), who *d*. 1971, da. of the late Col. Arthur William Henry
Hay-Drummond; *d*. 1957; *s*. by his el. son [9] IAN GEORGE, 9th Baron and present peer.

AUDLEY, BARON. (Souter.) [Baron E. 1312-13.]

RICHARD MICHAEL THOMAS SOUTER, 25th
Baron, *b*. May 31st, 1914; *s*. 1973; ed. at
Uppingham; Lt. RA: *m*. 1941, Lily Pauline,
da. of Dallas Louis Eskell, and has issue.

Arms,—not exemplified at time of going to press.

Residence,—Friendly Green, Cowden, Edenbridge,
Kent.

———

DAUGHTERS LIVING (*Co-heiresses presumptive.*)
Hon. PATRICIA ANN, *b*. Aug. 10th, 1946: *m*. 1969, Carey
Leigh Mackinnon, and has issue living, Angus Carey,
b. 1974.
Hon. JENNIFER MICHELLE, *b*. May 23rd, 1948.
Hon. AMANDA ELIZABETH, *b*. May 5th, 1958.

SISTER LIVING.
Charlotte Pamela, *b*. 1916: *m*. 1954, William Francis
Harvey, of 2, St. Aubyn's Park, Tiverton, Devon, and has
issue living, John Richard, *b*. 1959,—Katharine Mary,
b. 1955,—Amelia Anne, *b*. 1957.

STEP-MOTHER LIVING OF ROSINA LOIS VERONICA, BARONESS AUDLEY
Lillie Kathleen, dau. of the late George Ross, of co. Monaghan : *m*. 1st, 1923, as his second wife,
Thomas Touchet Tuchet-Jesson, who *d*. 1939, having assumed by deed poll 1937 the additional
surname of Tuchet; 2ndly, 1941, George Wynter Gray, who *d*. 1945.

WIDOW LIVING OF TWENTY-THIRD BARON.

Hon. SARAH MILLICENT HERMIONE (*Sarah, Baroness Audley*) (c/o Fladgate & Co., 8, Waterloo Place-
Pall Mall, SW1); actress, poet and author; da. of the late Rt. Hon. Sir Winston Leonard Spencer
Churchill, KG, OM, CH, TD [see D. Marlborough, colls. and Bs. Spencer-Churchill], widow of Antony
Roger Beauchamp, and formerly wife of the late Vic Oliver: *m*. as his 2nd wife, the 23rd Baron,
who *d*. 1963.

PREDECESSORS..—[1] NICHOLAS Audley, or Aldithley, of Heleigh, Staffordshire; *b*. 1298;
summoned to Parliament by writ as *Baron Audley* 1312-13 : *m*. 1312, Joan, only child of 1st Baron
Martin, and widow of 6th Earl of Lincoln (cr. circa 1147); *d*. 1316; *s*. by his son [2] JAMES,
2nd Baron; *b*. 1313: *m*. 1st, 13—, Joan, dau. of 1st Earl of March; 2ndly, 13—, Isabel, dau.
of 5th Baron Strange of Knokin; *d*. 1386; *s*. by his son [3] NICHOLAS, 3rd Baron; *b*. 13—: *m*.
13—, Elizabeth, who *d*. 1400, dau. of 1st Baron Beaumont; *d*. 1391, when the Barony fell into
abeyance between his sisters; this abeyance was terminated in 1405 in favour of his great-nephew
[4] JOHN Tuchet (son of John Tuchet, son of Sir John Tuchet, by Joan, dau. of 2nd Baron), 4th
Baron; *b*. 1371: *m*. 13—, Isabel, dau. of ——; *d*. 1408; *s*. by his son [5] JAMES, 5th Baron;
b. 1398: *m*. 1st, 14—, Margaret, dau. of 7th Baron de Ros; 2ndly, 14—, Eleanor, natural dau. of
Thomas, Earl of Kent; *d*. 1459; *s*. by his son [6] JOHN, *P.C.*, 6th Baron; *b*. 14—; sometime
Lord Treasurer: *m*. 14—, Anne, who *d*. 1498, dau. of Sir Thomas Echingham, and widow of John
Rogers, of Bryanston, Dorset; *d*. 1490; *s*. by his son [7] JAMES, *K.B.*, 7th Baron; *b*. 1463: *m*.
1st, 14—, Margaret, dau. of Sir Richard Dayrell; 2ndly, 14—, Joan, who *d*. 1532, dau. of Fulk,
Lord Fitz-Warine ; joined Cornish insurrection and was beheaded 1497, when the title became
forfeited; *s*. by his son [8] JOHN, 8th Baron; *b*. 1483; secured restoration of the title 1512 :

m. 15—, Mary, da. of John Griffin, of Braybrooke, Northants; *d. c.* 1557; *s.* by his son [9] GEORGE, 9th Baron; *b.* 15—: *m.* 1st, 15—, Elizabeth, da. of Sir Brian Tuke; 2ndly, 1560, Joan Platt; *d.* 1560; *s.* by his son [10] HENRY, 10th Baron; *b.* 15—: *m.* 15—, Elizabeth, dau. of Sir William Sneyd, of Bradwell, Staffordshire; *d.* 1563; *s.* by his son [11] George, 11th Baron; *b.* 1551; sometime Gov. of Utrecht, Netherlands, and of Kells, co. Meath; cr. *Baron Audley,* of Orier, co. Armagh, and *Earl of Castlehaven,* co. Cork (peerage of Ireland) 1616: *m.* 1st, 15—, Lucy, only dau. of Sir James Mervyn; 2ndly, 1611, Elizabeth (who *m.* 2ndly, 1619, Sir Piers Crosby), dau. of Sir Andrew Noel; *d.* 1617; *s.* by his son [12] MERVYN, 2nd Earl; *b.* 1593: *m.* 1st, 1619, Elizabeth, dau. of Benedict Barnham, of London; 2ndly, 1624, Anne, who *d.* 1647, dau. of 5th Earl of Derby, and widow of 5th Baron Chandos of Sudeley; convicted of felony and beheaded 1631, when the English Barony became forfeited; *s.* (in the Irish Earldom and Barony) by his son [13] JAMES, 3rd Earl; *b.* 16— ; cr. *Baron Audley* of Hely [with precedence of the former Barony (cr. 1312-13)] 1633, subsequently confirmed by Act of Parliament 1678: *m.* 1st, 16—, Elizabeth, who *d.* 1679, dau. of 5th Baron Chandos of Sudeley ; 2ndly, 1679, Elizabeth, dau. of ———; *d.* 1684 ; *s.* by his brother [14] MERVIN, 4th Earl; *b.* 16—: *m.* 16—, Mary, dau. of Sir Francis Fortescue, and widow of 10th Earl of Shrewsbury; *d.* 1686; *s.* by his son [15] JAMES, 5th Earl; *b.* 16—: *m.* 16—, Anne, who *d.* 1733, dau. of Richard Pelson, of St. George's-in-the-Fields, Middlesex; *d.* 1700: *s.* by his son [16] JAMES, 6th Earl; *b.* 16—: *m.* 1722, Elizabeth, who *d.* 1743, dau. of 4th Baron Arundell of Wardour; *d.* 1740; *s.* by his son [17] JAMES, 7th Earl; *b.* 1723; *d.* 1769; *s.* by his brother [18] JOHN, 8th Earl; *b.* 17—: *m.* 17—, Susanna, who *d.* 1789, dau. of Henry Drax, of Ellerton Abbey, Yorkshire, and widow of William Oracraft; *d.* 1777, when the Earldom of Castlehaven, and the Barony of Audley of Orier, became extinct, and the Barony of Audley of Hely devolved upon his kinsman [19] GEORGE (son of Philip Thicknesse, by Elizabeth, dau. of 5th Earl), 19th Baron; *b.* 1758; assumed by Roy. licence 1783, the additional surname of Tuchet after that of Thicknesse: *m.* 1st, 1781, Elizabeth, who *d.* 1785, dau. of Sir John Hussey Delaval, 1st Bt.; 2ndly, 1792, Augusta Henrietta Catherina, who *d.* 1844, youngest dau. of the Rev. André Boisdaune, and widow of Col. Moorhouse; *d.* 1818; *s.* by his son [20] GEORGE JOHN, 20th Baron; *b.* 1783: *m.* 1816, Anne Jane, who *d.* 1855, dau. of Vice-Adm. Sir Ross Donelly, K.C.B.; *d.* 1837; *s.* by his son [21] GEORGE EDWARD, 21st Baron; *b.* 1817: *m.* 1st, 1857, Emily, who *d.* 1860, dau. of Sir Thomas Livingstone Mitchell; 2ndly, 1868, Margaret Anne, who *d.* 1888, widow of James William Smith; *d.* 1872, when the Barony fell into abeyance between his two daughters, on the death of the younger of whom in 1937, the title devolved upon the el. [22] MARY; *b.* 1858; *d.* 1942; *s.* by her kinsman [23] THOMAS PERCY HENRY TOUCHET *Tuchet-Jesson, MBE,* son of the late Thomas Touchet Tuchet-Jesson, son of the late Thomas Jesson, by Charlotte Anna, dau. of the late Hon. John Nicholas Thicknesse-Tuchet, son of 20th Baron), *b.* 1913; Maj. Worcestershire Regt.; assumed by deed poll 1937, the additional surname of Tuchet: *m.* 1st, 1952 (marriage dissolved 1958), June Isabel (DE TRAFFORD), M.B.E., dau. of Lt.-Col. Reginald Chaplin; 2ndly, 1962, Sarah Millicent Hermione (BEAUCHAMP), dau. of the Rt. Hon. Sir Winston Leonard Spencer-Churchill, K.G., O.M., C.H., T.D., M.P.[D. Marlborough, colls.]; *d.* 1963; *s.* by his sister, [24] ROSINA LOIS VERONICA, *b.* 1911; assumed by deed poll 1937 the additional surname of Tuchet: *m.* 1943, John Archibald Joseph Macnamee; *d.* 1973; *s.* by her cousin [25] RICHARD MICHAEL THOMAS *Souter* [son if the late Sir Charles Alexander Souter, KCIE, CSI, and his wife the late Charlotte Dorothy Jesson, aunt of 23rd Baron], 25th Baron, and present peer.

AUSTIN, BARONY OF, (Austin.) [Extinct 1941.]

DAUGHTERS LIVING OF FIRST BARON.

Hon. Irene, *b.* 1891: *m.* 1918, Col. Arthur Cyril Roy Waite, M.C., Australian Reserve of Officers. *Residence,*—Fernhill Park, Windsor Forest, Berks.
Hon. Zita Eline, *b.* 1902: *m.* 1928, (m. diss. 1948) Charles Powel, Lambert, and has issue living, Austin Gerald (Sadlers Wood, Chattis Hill, Stockbridge, Hants.), *b.* 1934: *m.* 1960, Elizabeth Jane, yr. da. of Douglas B. Lowman, of Colsons, Braishfield, Romsey, Hants., and has issue living, Tessa Elaine *b.* 1966, Amanda Jane *b.* 1968. *Residence,*—Wigley Manor, Ower, Hants.

AVEBURY, BARON. (Lubbock.) [Baron U.K. 1900, Bt. U.K. 1806.]

ERIC REGINALD LUBBOCK, 4th Baron, and 7th Baronet; *b.* Sept. 29th, 1928; *s.* 1971; ed. at Upper Canada Coll., Harrow and Balliol Coll., Oxford (BA); Lt. Welsh Gds.; MP for Orpington (*L*) 1962-70, and Liberal Ch. Whip 1963-70: *m.* 1953, Kina-Maria, da. of Count Joseph Henry O'Kelly de Gallagh, and has issue.

The author makes the value.

Arms,—Argent, on a mount vert a stork close ermine, on a chief gules three estoiles of the field. Crest.—A stork, wings elevated ermine, supporting an antique shield azure, bordered or, charged with a lion rampant-guardant argent. Supporters,—Two storks, wings elevated ermine, each gorged with a chain or, and pendent therefrom an escutcheon gules charged with an estoile argent.
Residence,—Combe House, Sundridge, Kent.

SONS LIVING.

Hon. LYULPH AMBROSE JONATHAN, *b.* June 15th, 1954.
Hon. Maurice Patrick Guy, *b.* 1955.

DAUGHTER LIVING.

Hon. Victoria Sarah Maria, *b.* 1959.

SISTER LIVING.

Alice Olivia Maureen, *b.* 1926: *m.* 1951, William Geoffrey Keighley, MLC, (Erowari, Wallendbeen, NSW, 2588), and has issue living, Francis Stephen, *b.* 1953,—John William, *b.* 1959,—Pamela Jane, *b.* 1956,—Josephine, *b.* 1961.

DAUGHTER LIVING OF THIRD BARON.

Hon. Emma Rachel, *b.* 1952.

SISTER LIVING OF THIRD BARON. (*Raised to the rank of a Baron's daughter* 1931).

Hon. (Ursula) Moyra, *b.* 1917: *m.* 1938 (marriage dissolved 1949), Dorian Williams. *Residence,*—Leyland Farm, Gawcott, Buckingham.

WIDOW LIVING OF SON OF FIRST BARON.

Hon. Dorothy Charlotte (*Dorothy, Baroness Wardington*), da. of 1st Baron Forster: *m.* 1st, 1914, Capt. the Hon. Harold Fox Pitt Lubbock, Grenadier Guards, who *d.* (killed in action during European War) 1918: 2ndly, 1923, the 1st Baron Wardington, who *d.* 1950, and has issue living (by 1st marriage) [see ante],—(by 2nd marriage) [see B. Wardington]. *Residence*—Lepe House, Exbury, Southampton.

MOTHER LIVING.

Hon. Mary Katharine Adelaide Stanley, da. of 5th Baron Stanley of Alderley: *m.* 1926, the Hon. Maurice Fox Pitt Lubbock, who *d.* 1957. *Residence,*—High Elms, Clock House, Downe, Orpington, Kent.

WIDOW LIVING OF THIRD BARON.

BETTY GAY (*Betty, Baroness Avebury*), da. of the late William Oscar Ingham, and formerly wife of —————— Goode: *m.* 1955, as his 3rd wife, the 3rd Baron, who *d.* 1971.

COLLATERAL BRANCHES LIVING.

(*In remainder to Baronetcy only*).

Grandchildren of the late Henry James Lubbock, second son of 3rd baronet :—
Issue of the late Major Geoffrey Lubbock, *b.* 1873, *d.* 1932: *m.* 1907, Marguerite Agaranthe, who *d.* 1943, dau. of the late Col. Charles Miles, of Burtonhill, Malmesbury, and widow of Sir Charles Tennant, 1st Bt. [B. Glenconner]:—
Peter Geoffrey, *b.* 1909 ; ed. at Eton. *Residence,*—37, Chapel Street, Belgrave Square, S.W.1.—— David Miles, *b.* 1911; ed. at Eton; 1939-45 War as Lt. RNVR (prisoner): *m.* 1939, the Hon. Helen Anne Boyd Orr, da. of 1st Baron Boyd Orr (ext.), and has issue living., Geoffrey Orr, *b.* 1946,—John Nicholas Andrew, *b.* 1948,—Kenneth Miles Boyd, *b.* 1950,—Ann Patricia, *b.* 1941: *m.* 1972, John Daniel Gooch, VRD, of The Schoolhouse, Oathlaw, Forfar, Angus [see Gooch, Bt., colls., cr. 1866]. *Residence,*—Farnell, Brechin, Angus.

Issue of the late Capt. Rupert Egerton Lubbock, R.N., *b.* 1886, *d.* (on active ser. during European War) 1943: *m.* 1912, Vera Isabel, who *d.* 1962, dau. of G. R. Wingrove, of Shanghai:—
Rupert James, *b.* 1916 ; is Capt. 5th Batn. Leicestershire Regt. (T.A.); European War 1939-45 (prisoner): *m.* 1954, Jeanette Patricia, only dau. of A. van Beugen Bik, of Broughton, Esher, Surrey, and has issue living, Rupert Guy Anthony, *b.* 1956,—David Alexander, *b.* 1958,—Fiona Jeanette Ariane, *b.* 1960. *Residence,*—Mannings Hill, Cranleigh, Surrey.——Christopher William Stuart, *b.* 1920 ; ed. at Charterhouse, and at Brasenose Coll., Oxford ; European War 1939-45 as Lieut. R.N.V.R. : *m.* 1947, Hazel Gordon Chapman, and has issue living, Rupert James Gordon, *b.* 1948,—Victoria Margaret, *b.* 1950. *Residence,*—New Barn House, Great Horkesley, Essex.——Nancy Diana Mary, *OBE* (*Lady Shuckburgh*), *b.* 1914; Pres. Warwicks Branch BRCS; OBE (Civil) 1970: *m.* 1937, as his second wife, Sir Charles Gerald Stewkley Shuckburgh, 12th Bt. *Residence,*—Shuckburgh, nr. Daventry.

Grandchildren of the late Hugh Nevile Lubbock (infra) :—
Issue of the late Ralph Hugh Lubbock, M.C., *b.* 1891, *d.* 1961 : *m.* 1st, 1914, Adelaide Margaret Constance (who *d.* 1940, having obtained a divorce 1922), da. of the late Samuel Hynman Montgomerie [E. Eglinton] ; 2ndly, 1923, Louise, dau. of James Charles Vogel, of Durban :—
(By 2nd m.) John Ralph (Guards' Club), *b.* 1926; ed. at Malvern; 1939-45 War as Lt. Coldm. Gds.: *m.* 1st, 1950 Patricia Helen Winifred (from whom he obtained a divorce 1957), da. of the late Brig.- Gen. the Hon. Roger Brand, CMG, DSO [see V. Hampden, colls.]; 2ndly, 1957 (m. diss. 1961), Jane Marjorie, da. of Major Evelyn Ronald Moncrieff Fryer, MC, Grenadier Guards [see E. Peel, colls.]; 3rdly, 1963 (m. diss. 1966), Helene Frances, da. of the late Maj. Ferguson Thomson; 4thly, 1967, Anne Elizabeth, da. of the late Frank Colville Pearce, and has issue living, (by 1st m.) Hugh Roger, *b.* 1951,—(by 2nd m.) Thomas, *b.* 1957,—(by 4th m.) Stephen Henry Ralph, *b.* 1970,— Elizabeth Serena, *b.* 1967.——(By 1st m.) Ursula Egidia, *b.* 1919: *m.* 1941, Peter Bellamy, of West End Cottage, Eythorne, nr. Dover, and has issue living, Geraldine Anne, *b.* 1943: *m.* 1964, Michael Wyant, of Littlebourne, Canterbury, Kent.

Grandchildren of the late Sir Nevile Lubbock, KCMG, 3rd son of 3rd baronet:—
Issue of the late Hugh Nevile Lubbock, *b.* 1865, *d.* 1938 : *m.* 1st, 1890, Margaret Agnes (who obtained a divorce 1934), dau. of the late Henry F. Tiarks, of Foxbury, Chislehurst ; 2ndly, 1934, Lilian, who *d.* 1937, widow of Alexander M. Somerville, of China :—
Mark Hugh, *b.* 1898 ; ed. at Eton ; European War 1918-19 as 2nd Lieut. Labour Corps : *m.* 1930, Beatrice Isabel, da. of Edgar Howe. *Residence,*—The Garden Flat, 67, Redcliffe Gdns., SW10.—— Mary Harriet Margaret, *b.* 1903: *m.* 1928, Paul Schoeffler, and has issue living, Peter Walter Paul (Woodmuir, 10, Clifton Rd., Chesham Bois, Amersham, Bucks.), *b.* 1931; ed. at Radley Coll.; in RNVR: *m.* 1955, Patricia, da. of Louis Hofmens, and has issue living, Paul Geoffrey *b.* 1958, Andrea Mary *b.* 1964. *Residence,*—Hoffburg Palace, Vienna 1, Austria.

Issue of the late Arthur Nevile Lubbock, *b.* 1869, *d.* 1939 : *m.* 1895, Alice Ellen, who *d.* 1944, dau. of Henry F. Tiarks, of Foxbury, Chislehurst :—
Ivo Arthur, *b.* 1908; ed. at Eton.——Gilian (*Gilian, Viscountess Chelmsford*), *b.* 1906: *m.* 1927, the 2nd Viscount Chelmsford, who *d.* 1970. *Residence,*—Hazelbridge Court, Chiddingfold, Surrey.

Issue of the late Reginald Nevile Lubbock, *b.* 1876, *d.* 1942 : *m.* 1907, Lilian Stephenson, who *d.* 1942, dau. of William Stephenson Swift, formerly of Westfields, Retford, Notts :—
Ruth Elizabeth Stephenson, *b.* 1907: *m.* 1931, Thomas Marshall Bell, M.B., B.Ch., M.R.C.S., L.R.C.P., of Greenwood, 5a, Stourwood Av., Bournemouth, and has issue living, Michael Nevile Marshall (23, Bowhayes Lane, Bothenhampton, Bridport, Dorset), *b.* 1933; ed. at Charterhouse, and Christ's Coll., Camb. (MA); Solicitor 1964: *m.* 1964, Joyce Violet, da. of the late Eustace Graham Long, of London, and has issue living, Francis Graham Thomas *b.* 1965, Harry Adrian John *b.* 1971, Lucy Anne Caroline *b.* 1969,—Robin John Marshall (3, The Avenue, Burton on Stather, Scunthorpe), *b.* 1935; ed. at Charterhouse, and Christ's Coll., Camb. (MA, MB, B.Ch.); DCH, DRCOG, MRCPE.

Grandchildren of the late Frederic Lubbock (infra) :—
Issue of the late Brig.-Gen. Guy Lubbock, C.M.G., D.S.O., *b* 1870, *d.* 1956 : *m.* 1912, Lettice Isabella (Monks Way, Westerham, Kent), da. of Robert Harvey Mason, of Necton Hall, Swaffham:—
Joseph Guy, *b.* 1915 ; ed. at Eton, and at Trin. Coll., Camb. (B.A. 1937) ; late Capt. R.E. (T.A.) : *m.* 1941, Ruth Cecilia, dau. of Major Quintin Edward Gurney, of Bawdeswell Hall, Norfolk, and has issue living, Jennifer, *b.* 1942: *m.* 1966, the Marchese Ciaralli-Parenzi, of Low Farm, Keswick, Norwich, and has issue living, Elena *b.* 1967, Andrea *b.* 1969,—Catherine, *b.* 1944: *m.* 1968, Stuart Jennings, MB, BS, and has issue living, Mark *b.* 1970, Samuel *b.* 1971,—Lucinda, *b.* 1948: *m.* 1974, Thomas Henry Carew, [see B. Carew]. *Residence,*—High Elms, Waldringfield, Suffolk.

Issue of the late Cecil Lubbock, *b.* 1872, *d.* 1956 : *m.* 1898, Edith, who *d.* 1960, 4th dau. of the late Ven. Charles Wellington Furse, Archdeacon of Westminster, of 1, Abbey Garden, Great College Street, S.W.1 and Halsdon House, N. Devon :—
Michael Ronald, *MBE* (Apt. 606, 21, Dale Av., Toronto, Ontario, Canada), *b.* 1906; ed. at Eton, and at Trin. Coll., Oxford; Lt.-Col. and temporary Col. R. Corps of Signals (TA); Gold Cross of Order of King George I of the Hellenes; 1939-45 War in Middle East (despatches thrice, MBE); MBE (Mil.) 1943: *m.* 1st, 1929 (m. diss. 1956), Diana Beatrice, da. of the late Henry Ernest Crawley [Crawley-Boevey, Bt., colls.]; 2ndly, 1957, Inga Olga, da. of the late Eugene Ivan de Rudez, of Zagreb, Jugoslavia, widow of Col. Geoffrey Moule, and has issue living, (by 1st m.) Jeremy Michael (Flat 2, 12, Elsworthy Rd., NW3), *b.* 1931: *m.* 1st, 1956 (m. diss. 1959), Jill Caroline, da. of the late Eric Nicholls; 2ndly, 1963, Shelagh Mary, da. of Richard Lang, MB, of Kenilworth, Cape, and has issue living, (by 1st m.) Justin Roger *b.* (Dec.) 1956, (by 2nd m.) Lindsay Brigid *b.* 1965,—John David Peter, *b.* 1945,—Judith Caroline Gurney, *b.* 1934: *m.* 1956, Martin Marriott, of Trevelyan, Haileybury, Herts., and has issue living, Charles John Phillip *b.* 1964, Virginia Elizabeth *b.* 1958,

Rebecca Jane b. 1960,—Jessica Rose, b. 1937: m. 1961, Flt.-Lt. David Brook, RAF, and has issue living, William b. 1965, Julie Nicola b. 1961,—Joanna, b. 1941: m. 1965, Michael Coleridge Seligman, and has issue living, Simon Michael Hugo b. 1966, Kate Sophia b. 1968,—(by 2nd m.) Inga Cecilia, b. 1957.——Cynthia Margaret (Fieldside, Blewbury, Didcot, Berks.), b. 1899: m. 1921, Alexander Henry Melvill Wedderburn, OBE, who d. 1968 [see Oglivy-Wedderburn, Bt., colls.].——Joan Catherine (of 12A, St. Olaves Court, St. Petersburgh Place, W2) b. 1903: m. 1925 (m. diss. 1952), the 2nd Baron Cunliffe, who d. 1963.——Margaret Hester, b. 1910: m. 1932, William Rathbone, of Greenbank, Mill Lane, Dyer's Hill, Charlbury, Oxon., OX7 3QG.——Viola, b. 1912: m. 1939, Lt.-Col. Charles Arthur Chadwyck-Healey, RA [see Chadwyck-Healey, Bt.]. Residence,—Old Middleton, Westmeston, Hassocks, Sussex.

Issue of the late Samuel Gurney Lubbock, b. 1873, d. 1958: m. 1915, Irene Scharrer, who d. 1971.
Ian Gurney, b. 1917; ed. at Eton: m. 1st, 1938 (marriage dissolved 1943), Lys de la Tour Dunlap; 2ndly, 19—, Gunvor Callisen.——Rachel Gurney, b. 1920: m. 1945 (marriage (voidable) annulled 1950), Denys Gravenor Rhodes [B. Plunket]. Residence,—17, Paulton's House, Paulton's Sq., SW3.

Issue of the late Frederic Lubbock, 6th son of 3rd baronet, b. 1844, d. 1927: m. 1869, Catherine, who d. 1934, only dau. of the late John Gurney, of Earlham Hall, Norfolk:—
Roy, b. 1892; ed. at Eton, and at King's Coll., Camb. (BA 1914, MA and Fellow of Peterhouse 1919): m. 1919, Yvonne Vernham, and has issue living, Jocelyn Roy (of Via del Pellegrino 75, Rome, Italy). b. 1920; ed. at Eton and at Peterhouse, Camb. (BA 1941, MA 1945, Mus.B. 1946): m. 1948, Frances Georgette Coningsby (WHITELEY), da. of the late Capt. George Ashmead-Bartlett, and has issue living, Annina Nicolette Mary b. 1949,—Hubert Timothy (1, Keswick Close, Cringleford, Norwich), b. 1923; ed. at Eton, and at Peterhouse, Camb. (BA 1944, MA 1948): m. 1958, Barbara Ann Caruth, and has issue living, Catherine Fiona b. 1960, Lucinda Anne b. 1964. Residence,—Riding Oaks, Hildenborough, Kent.——Sir Alan (of Adhurst St. Mary, Petersfield, Hants.: Oxford and Cambridge University, and Leander Clubs), b. 1897; ed. at Eton, and at King's Coll., Camb. (BA 19—, MA 1922, Fellow 1923-28); a F.S.A.; formerly Maj. R.A. and Assist. Mil. Attaché, Madrid; a JP and DL for Hants (High Sheriff 1949); Chm., Hants. Co. Council 1955-67 and of Council, Southampton Univ. 1957-69; 1914-18 War; as Lt. RGA; 1939-45 War as Maj. RA; Knt. 1963: m. 1918, Helen Mary, only child of the late John Bonham-Carter, of Adhurst St. Mary, Petersfield, and has issue living, Roger John, DSC (Weatherall Lodge, Well Rd., NW3. Club,—Beefsteak), b. 1922; ed. at Eton, and at King's Coll., Camb. (MA): m. 1955, Moyra (SUTHERLAND), da. of John Newton Mappin Fraser, and has issue living, Guy John b. 1957, Paul Nigel b. 1960,—Martin (of Brown's Copse, Heyshott, Midhurst, Sussex), b. 1925; ed. at Eton, and at King's Coll., Camb.; is Lieut. RNVR; European War 1943-5: m. 1957, Elizabeth (LLOYD), da. of Roland Marshal, of W. Kirby, Yorks., and has issue living, Toby b. 1959, Robin Alan b. 1961.

Issue of the late Edgar Lubbock, LL.B., 8th son of 3rd baronet, b. 1847, d. 1907: m. 1886, Amy Myddelton (Baroness Kesteven), who d. 1941 (having m. 2ndly, 1914, the 2nd Baron Kesteven, who d. 1915), dau. of Christopher Gilbert Peacock, of Greatford Hall, Stamford:—
Nancy Induna Frances Caroline (Hon. Mrs. James K. E. Howard), b. 1897: m. 1925, the Hon. James Knyvett Estcourt Howard, who d. 1964, [see E. Suffolk]. Residence,—The Red House, Tydehams, Newbury, Berks.——Marigold Rosemary Joyce LONDESBOROUGH, b. 1903; formerly Senior Comdt. ATS; assumed by deed poll 1952 the surname of Londesborough: m. 1935, the 4th Earl of Londesborough, who d. 1937 [see B. Londesborough]; 2ndly, 1948 (marriage dissolved 1952), Zygmunt de Lubicz-Bakanowski, formerly Capt. 18th Lancers, Polish Army. Residence,—

PREDECESSORS.—[1] JOHN Lubbock, son of the Rev. William Lubbock, R. of Lammas, Norfolk; an opulent banker of the City of London; cr. a Baronet 1806: m. 1771, Elizabeth Christiana, da. of Frederick Commerell, of Hanwell; d.s.p. 1816; s. by his nephew [2] JOHN WILLIAM, 2nd Bt., b. 1774; an eminent banker: m. 1799, Mary, da. of James Entwhistle, of Rusholme, Manchester; d. 1840; s. by his son [3] JOHN WILLIAM, 3rd Bt.; b. 1803; a banker, a distinguished scientific author, and Vice-Pres. of Roy. So.: m. 1833, Harriet, dau. of Lieut.-Col. George Hotham, of York; d. 1865; s. by his son [4] JOHN, P.C., D.C.L., LL.D., 4th Bt.; d. 1834; cr. Baron Avebury, of Avebury, Wilts (peerage of United Kingdom) 1900; was head of London banking firm of Robarts, Lubbock, and Co., of 15, Lombard Street, E.C. (now amalgamated with Coutts and Co.), Pres. of So. of Antiquaries, of Roy. Microscopical So., of Royal So., of Central Asso. of Bankers, and of London Chamber of Commerce; sat as M.P. for Maidstone (L) 1870-80, when he was defeated, and for the Univ. of London 1880-1900: m. 1st, 1856, Ellen Frances, who d. 1879, da. of the late Rev. Peter Horden, of Chorlton-cum-Hardy; 2ndly, 1884, Alice Augusta Laurentia, who d. 1947, da. of the late Maj.-Gen. Augustus Henry Kane Fox-Pitt-Rivers; d. 1913; s. by his el. son [5] JOHN BIRK-BECK, 2nd Baron, b. 1858; a Director of Coutts and Co., and of National Provincial and Union Bank of England; d. 1929; s. by his nephew [6] JOHN (son of the late Capt. the Hon. Harold Fox Pitt Lubbock (4th son of 1st Baron), who d. killed in action 1918), 3rd Baron, b. 1915: m. 1st, 1938 (m. diss. 1945), Cicely Kathleen, da. of the late Dr. N. A. K. Sparrow; 2ndly, 1946 (m. diss. 1951), Diana Mary Margaret Westcott, da. of the late Capt. Edward Westcott King, RA; 3rdly, 1955, Betty Gay, da. of the late William Oscar Ingham, and formerly wife of ———— Goode; d. 1971; s. by his cousin [7] ERIC REGINALD (only son of the late Hon. Maurice Fox Pitt Lubbock, yst. son of 1st Baron), 4th Baron and present peer.

AVON, EARL OF. (Eden.) [Earl U.K. 1961.]

If there be but prudence.

SI·SIT·PRUDENTIA

(ROBERT) ANTHONY EDEN, KG, MC, PC, 1st Earl, son of Sir William Eden, 7th Bt. of 1st and 5th of 2nd creation; b. June 12th, 1897; ed. at Eton, and at Ch. Ch., Oxford (BA 1922, Student 1941); Hon. DCL Oxford and Durham; Hon. LLD, Bristol, Birmingham, Camb., Leeds, Sheffield, Belfast, Toronto, California, McGill, Columbia and Denver; Hon. Fellow Trin. Hall, Camb.; Hon. Bencher Middle Temple 1952; 1914-18 War with KRRC and as Bde. Maj. Gen. Staff (MC); Maj. The Rangers, KRRC (TA) 1939; Hon. Col. Queen's Westminsters, KRRC 1952-60, and Queen's R. Rifles 1960-62; a Gov. of Roy. Shakespeare Theatre, Stratford-on-Avon (Pres. 1958-66); a Trustee of Shakespeare's Birthplace, and of Historic

Churches Preservation Trust, an Hon. Freeman of Fishmongers' and Salters' Cos., an Elder Brother of Trinity House, Hon. Life Patron of Young Conservative Organization and a JP for co. Durham; Pres. of Anglo-Ethiopian Soc. since 1966, and Patron of Hereford Herd Book Soc. since 1968; PPS to Under-Sec. of State for Home Affairs 1925-26, and to Sec. of State for Foreign Affairs 1926-29; appointed Under-Sec. of State for Foreign Affairs (in National Govt.) Sept. 1931, Lord Privy Seal Jan. 1934, a Trustee of National Gallery 1935-49, and Min. without Portfolio for League of Nations Affairs June 1935; Sec. of State for Foreign Affairs Dec. 1935 to Feb. 1938, Sec. of State for Dominion Affairs Sept. 1939 to May 1940, Sec. of State for War May to Dec. 1940, again Sec. of State for Foreign Affairs Dec. 1940 to July 1945 (Leader of House of Commons Nov. 1942 to July 1945), and Oct. 1951 to April 1955, Chm., Organisation for European Economic Co-operation 1952-4, and Prime Min. and First Lord of the Treasury April 1955 to Jan. 1957; Chancellor of Birmingham Univ. 1945-73; became Pres. of Young Conservative and Unionist Organisation 1954, and a Joint Pres. of United and Cecil Club 1957; received Freedom of Durham 1945, of Leamington, Warwick, Belfast and Athens 1947, and of Perth 1956; attended Imperial Press Conference in Australia 1925; M.P. for Warwick and Leamington 1923 to 1957; PC 1934, KG 1954, and *Viscount Eden*, of Roy. Leamington Spa, co. Warwick and *Earl of Avon* (peerage of U.K.) 1961: *m.* 1st, 1923, Beatrice Helen (who *d.* 1957, and from whom he had obtained a divorce 1950, dau. of the Hon. Sir (William) Gervase Beckett, 1st Bt.; 2ndly, 1952, Clarissa, only dau. of the late Major John Strange Spencer-Churchill, D.S.O. [see D. Marlborough, colls.], and has issue by 1st marriage.

Arms,—Gules, on a chevron argent between three garbs or, banded vert, as many escallops sable. Crest,—A dexter arm, embowed in armour, couped at the shoulder proper and grasping a garb fessewise as in the arms, banded vert. Supporters,—*Dexter*, a leopard guardan or, resting the sinister hind paw on a garb of the last, banded vert, and *sinister*, a like leopard resting the dexter hind paw on a similar garb.

Residence,—Manor House, Alvediston, Salisbury, Wilts. *Clubs,*—Buck's, Carlton.

SON LIVING. *(By 1st marriage.)*

NICHOLAS (*Viscount Eden*), OBE, TD (17, Sumner Place, SW7), *b.* Oct. 3rd, 1930; ed. at Eton; 2nd Lt. KRRC 1950-51, ADC to Gov.-Gen. of Canada 1952-53; DL of Greater London; Capt. Queen Victoria Rifles (TA) 1953-61, Maj. Queen's R. Rifles (TA) 1961-65, and Lt.-Col. 1965-70; Hon. Col. ACF Greater London (NE Sector) 1970; Col. (TAVR) 1972-75 (Col. RARO since 1945); OBE (Mil) 1970.

AVONMORE, VISCOUNTCY OF. (Yelverton.) [Dormant 1910.]

This peerage has been dormant since the death of the 6th Viscount in 1910. The senior male descendant in the male line of the Hon. Augustus Yelverton, 3rd son of 2nd Viscount, presumably is heir to the title.]

COLLATERAL BRANCHES LIVING.

Grandchildren of the late Foster Goring Yelverton (infra):—

Issue of the late Barry Augustus Yelverton, *b.* 1895, *d.* 1960: *m.* 1921, Margaret Ethel, who *d.* 1970, da. of John Thomas Green, of Christchurch, NZ:—

Barry Goring, *b.* 1923 ; European War 1944-5 with New Zealand Forces : *m.* 1950, Frances Winifred, dau. of William Francis Battersby, of Glasgow Terrace, Feilding, New Zealand, and has issue living, Ian Foster, *b.* 1950,—Avon Barry, *b.* 1954. *Address*, c/o Bank of New Zealand, Woodville, NZ.——Michael Curran, *b.* 1928: *m.* 1949, Marjory Ruth, da. of Arthur William Hall, of Gisborne, NZ, and has issue living, Kevin Barry, *b.* 1949,—Mark Amour, *b.* 1961,—Sharon Anne, *b.* 1950. *Address,*—c/o Bank of NZ, Pio Pio, NZ.

Issue of the late Hermann Stratton Yelverton, *b.* 1896, *d.* 1973: *m.* 1923, Janetta Ferguson, who *d.* 1963, da. of John McEwen, of Palmerston North, NZ:—

Stratton Barton (Mokoia Rd., Ngongotaha, NZ), *b.* 1926: *m.* 1962, Jill Marion, da. of the late Colin Fergus Tennent-Brown, and has issue living, John Stratton, *b.* 1962,—Andrew Colin, *b.* 1964,— Bruce Avonmore, *b.* 1966,—Sally Janetta, *b.* 1969.——June Avonmore, *b.* 1924: *m.* 1944, Charles Herbert Dudley Scantlebury, of 3, Bretton Terr., Hillcrest, Hamilton, NZ, and has issue living, Dudley Addison, *b.* 1945,—Gavin Stratton, *b.* 1946: *m.* 1971, Vivienne Mary, da. of Wilfred John Westbury, of Adelaide, S. Aust.,—Gerald Avonmore, *b.* 1955,—Mark Jonathan, *b.* 1958,—Rosamund Karen Jane, *b.* 1948: *m.* 1973, Lester Thur Banfield,—Jennifer Marie, *b.* 1956.——Matel, *b.* 1928: *m.* 1951, Raymond William Watson, of 23, Manurere Av., Takapuna, NZ, and has issue living, Christopher Raymond, *b.* 1952,—Nicholas Stratton, *b.* 1956,—Nigel Alexander, *b.* 1963.

Grandsons of the late Augustus Barrymore Yelverton, son of the late Hon. Augustus Yelverton, 3rd son of 2nd Viscount :—

Issue of the late Foster Goring Yelverton, *b.* 1867, *d.* 1952 : *m.* 1895, Annie Caroline, who *d.* 1947, dau. of Alfred Mason, of Featherston, New Zealand :—

Macey Goring, *b.* 1898; 1914-18 War with RNVR: *m.* 1922, Pauline, da. of Jarrett Owen Allen, of Nottingham, and has issue living, Enid, *b.* 1929: *m.* 1952, Arthur Joseph Byrne, of 7, Knightwood Av., Lyndhurst, Hants., and has issue living, Stephen Martin, *b.* 1953, Carol Patricia *b.* 1954, Vanessa Elaine *b.* 1963. *Address,*—

Issue of the late Longworth Ridge Yelverton, *b.* 1876, *d.* 1936 : *m.* 1900, Beatrice, who *d.* 1953, dau. of Thomas Lawry, of Featherston, New Zealand .—

William Henry, *b.* 1903 : *m.* 1st, 1934, Doris Elizabeth Rose, who *d.* 1953, dau. of James Miller, of Dannevirke, New Zealand ; 2ndly, 1954, Gwendolen Hilda Carter (from whom he obtained a divorce 1960), dau. of William Edward Jones, of Southampton ; 3rdly, 1960, Zoe May, dau. of Samuel Burnett, of Wairoa, NZ. *Residence,*—Te Awa Av., Napier, NZ.

AYLESFORD, EARL OF. (Finch-Knightley.) [Earl G.B. 1714.]

CHARLES IAN FINCH-KNIGHTLEY, 11th Earl; *b.* Nov. 2nd, 1918; *s.* 1958; ed. at Oundle; Capt. Black Watch, a JP for Warwickshire (Vice-Lieut. 1964-74); Lord Lieut. of W. Midlands since 1974; Warwickshire Co. Commr. for Boy Scouts Assocn. 1949-74, since when Patron; an OStJ; a Member of Advisory Cttee. World Wild Life Fund since 1970; 1939-45 War (wounded): *m.* 1946, Margaret Rosemary, only da. of the late Maj. Austin Arnold Tyer, MVO, TD, of Tunstall, Wadhurst, and has issue.

To live with will unfettered.

Arms,—Argent, a chevron between three griffins passant sable. Crest,—A griffin passant sable. Supporters,—*Dexter*, a griffin sable, ducally gorged or; *sinister*, a lion or, ducally gorged azure.

Seats,—Packington Hall, Coventry; Diddington Hall, Coventry.

SON LIVING.

CHARLES HENEAGE (*Lord Guernsey*) (Rookwood, Packington Park, Meriden, nr. Coventry, Warwicks.), *b.* Mar. 27th, 1947; ed. at Oundle, and Trin. Coll., Camb.: *m.* 1971, Penelope Anstice, da. of Kenneth A. G. Crawley, of London, and has issue.
DAUGHTERS LIVING,—*Hon.* Rachel Louise, *b.* 1974,—*Hon.* Kate Pamela (twin), *b.* 1974.

DAUGHTERS LIVING.

Lady Sarah Elizabeth Jane, *b.* 1950: *m.* 1974, Angus Nigel Garnet Maclean.
Lady Clare Charlotte Rosemary *b.* 1959.

BROTHER LIVING.

Hon. Anthony Heneage, *b.* 1920; ed. at Oundle; Lt. and temp. Capt. Black Watch; a JP of Huntingdon; Middle East 1940-44 (despatches): *m.* 1948, Susan Mary, da. of Maj.-Gen. Geoffrey Woodroffe Palmer, C.B., C.B.E., and has issue living, Minette Jane, *b.* 1950,—Joanna Elizabeth, *b.* 1954. *Residence*,—Broomleigh, Huntingdon Road, Brampton, Hunts.

WIDOWS LIVING OF NINTH AND TENTH EARLS.

PAMELA ELIZABETH (DUGDALE) (*Pamela, Countess of Aylesford*), dau. of the late Col. the Hon. John Charles Coventry [see E. Coventry, colls.]: *m.* 1940, the 9th Earl, who *d.* (killed in action during European War) 1940. *Residence*,—105, Dorset House, Gloucester Place, N.W.1.
AILEEN JANE CHARTRES (*Aileen, Countess of Aylesford*), dau. of the late William McCormac Boyle: *m.* 1918, the 10th Earl, who *d.* 1958. *Residence*,—Guernsey Flat, Packington Hall, Coventry.

COLLATERAL BRANCHES LIVING.

Grandson of the late Charles Wynne-Finch, M.P., son of the late Charles Wynne Griffith-Wynne, son of the Hon. Charles Finch, 2nd son of 3rd Earl:—
Issue of the late Lieut.-Col. Charles Arthur Wynne Finch, *b.* 1841, *d.* 1903 : *m.* 1889, Maud Emily, who *d.* 1945, dau. of the late Lieut.-Col. the Hon. Richard Charteris [E. Wemyss, colls.] :—
John Charles, *CBE, MC, b.* 1891; ed. at Eton; Col. late Coldstream Guards; Lord-Lieut. of Denbighshire 1951-66; a KStJ; 1914-18 War (wounded, despatches, MC); CBE (Civil) 1956: *m.* 1914, Alice Mary Sybil, who *d.* 1970, da. of the late Rt. Rev. the Hon. Edward Carr Glyn, DD [B. Wolverton, colls.], and has issue living, Charles Edward Ifan (Cefnamwlch, Tudweiliog, Pwllheli, Caerns.), *b.* 1929; late Capt. Coldstream Guards; Sheriff of Denbighshire: *m.* 1967, Rosemary Dorothea, da. of Lt.-Col. Clive Grantham Austin, RHA, JP, DL [see E. Scarbrough], and has issue living, David Heneage *b.* 1970, Mary Davina *b.* 1968, a da. *b.* 1971.—Elizabeth Jane Mfyanwy, *b.* 1918: *m.* 1948, Alexander Dougal Malcolm, of Phillips's House, Much Marcle, Ledbury, and has issue, James Ronald *b.* 1951, Janet Mary *b.* 1949, Elizabeth Anne *b.* 1960,—Olwen Mary (The Bantam House, White Roding, Dunmow, Essex, CM6 1RJ), *b.* 1924: *m.* 1944 (m. diss. 1969), Roger Wake [see Wake, Bt.]. *Residence*,—Voelas, Bettws-y-Coed, Caernarvonshire.

Granddaughter of the late Edward Heneage Wynne-Finch, son of the late Charles Wynne-Finch, M.P. (ante) :—
Issue of the late Arthur Wynne-Finch, *b.* 1878, *d.* 1936 : *m.* 1926, Florence (now of Back End, Stokesley, Yorkshire), dau. of the late Very Rev. Charles Thomas Ovenden, Dean of St. Patrick's, Dublin :—
Anne, *b.* 1927: *m.* 1954 (m. diss. 1968), John Vavasour Earle, MB, BCh, and has issue living, Belinda Diana, *b.* 1957,—Jenny Ruth, *b.* 1959,—Polly Joan, *b.* 1961. *Residence*, Beech House, Carlton-in-Cleveland, Stokesley, Middlesbrough, Yorks.

PREDECESSORS—[1] *Rt. Hon.* HENEAGE Finch, *P.C.*, 2nd son of the 1st Earl of Nottingham and brother of 6th Earl of Winchilsea ; was Solicitor-Gen. 1678-86, when he was removed by James II., and M.P. for Oxford Univ. 1678-9, and for Guildford 1685; cr. *Baron Guernsey* (peerage of Great Britain) 1702, and *Earl of Aylesford* (peerage of Great Britain) 1714; *d.* 1719 ; *s.* by his el. son [2] HENEAGE, 2nd Earl ; *d.* 1757 ; *s.* bv his son [3] HENEAGE, 3rd Earl, *LL.D.* ; M.P. for Leicestershire 1732-41, and for Maidstone 1754 ; *d.* 1777 ; *s.* by his el. son [4] HENEAGE, 4th Earl, Lord Steward of the Household ; *d.* 1812 ; *s.* by his el. son [5] HENEAGE, 5th Earl ; *d.* 1859 ; *s.* by his el. son [6] HENEAGE, 6th Earl, *b.* Dec. 24, 1824; was M.P. for Warwickshire South 1849-57 : *m.* 1846, Jane Wightwick, who *d.* 1911, da. of John W. Knightley, of The Bury, Leamington Spa ; *d.* Jan. 10, 1871 ; *s.* by his el. son [7] HENEAGE, 7th Earl ; *b.* 1849: *m.* 1871, Edith, who *d.* 1897, dau. of the late Lieut.-Col. Peers Williams, M.P., of Temple House, Great Marlow ; *d.* 1885 ; *s.* by his brother [8] CHARLES WIGHTWICK, 8th Earl ; established his claim to the Earldom and Barony July 1885 ; *b.* 1851: *m.* 1st, 1873, the Hon. Georgina Agnes, who *d.* 1874, el. dau. of 3rd Baron Bagot ; 2ndly, 1879, Ella Victoria, who *d.* 1939, dau. of the late John Ross, of Benena, and widow of Capt. J. H. Linton, of Hemingford Abbots, Hunts : *d.* 1924 ; *s.* by his grandson [9] HENEAGE MICHAEL CHARLES (son of the late Capt. Heneage Greville, Lord Guernsey, Irish Guards (el. son of 8th Earl) (who *d.* killed in action during European War 1914), 9th Earl, *b.* 1908; Capt. R.A. (T.A.): *m.* 1940, Pamela Elizabeth (DUGDALE), dau. of the late Col. the Hon. John Charles Coventry ; *d.* (killed in action during European War) 1940; *s.* by his uncle [10] CHARLES DANIEL FINCH-KNIGHTLEY (2nd son of 8th Earl), 10th Earl ; *b.* 1886; assumed the additional surname of Knightley 1912 ; late Capt. Rifle Brig. (Prince Consort's Own): *m.* 1918, Aileen Jane Chartres, dau. of the late William McCormac Boyle ; *d.* 1958 ; *s.* by his el. son [11] CHARLES IAN, 11th Earl and present peer ; also Baron Guernsey.

AYLESTONE, BARON. (Bowden.) [Life Baron 1967.]

HERBERT WILLIAM BOWDEN, *CH, CBE, PC,* son of Herbert Henwood Bowden, of Cardiff; *b.* Jan. 20th, 1905; ed. at Canton High Sch., Cardiff; Member of Leicester City Council 1938-45, PPS to Postmaster-Gen. 1947-49, a

Lord Commr. of the Treasury 1950-51, Dep. Ch. Opposition Whip 1951-55, Ch. Opposition Whip 1955-64, Lord Pres. of Council and Leader of the House, 1964-66, Sec. of State for Commonwealth Affairs 1966-67; Chm. of IBA (formerly ITA) 1967-75; MP for S. Leicester (*Lab.*) 1945-50, and for SW Leicester 1950-67: 1939-45 War with RAF; *cr.* CBE (Civil) 1953, PC 1962, *Baron Aylestone* of Aylestone, City of Leicester (Life Baron) 1967, and CH 1975: *m.* 1928, Louisa Grace, da. of William Brown of Cardiff, and has issue.

Address,—c/o House of Lords, SW1.

DAUGHTER LIVING.

Hon. Brenda Dolores, *b.* 1929: *m.* 1951, John Leonard Billingham, of 67, Kingsmead Av., Worcester Park, Surrey, and has issue.

AYLMER, BARON. (Aylmer.) [Baron I. 1718, Bt. I. 1662.]

BASIL UDOLPHUS AYLMER, 11TH Baron, and 14TH Baronet; *b.* May 20TH, 1886; *s.* 1974; 1914-18 War with Canadian Forces: *m.* 1ST, 1916,, Bessie Irving ARRC, who *d.* 1956, da. of The late Joseph Watson, of Westward Park, Cumberland; 2ndly, 1960, Helen Cooper, da. of The late Thomas Hogg, of Toronto, Canada, and widow of Frederick Gordon Risebrough.

Arms.—Argent, a cross sable, between four Cornish choughs proper. **Crest.**—Out of a ducal coronet or a Cornish chough rising proper. **Supporters.**—Two marines vested with fur caps, brown jackets and blue breeches, their waists girt with bunting and dressed at all points like complete sailors, the *dexter* holding in his exterior hand a forestaff, and the *sinister* a deep-sea line, the plummet pendent, all proper.

Address,—R.R.3, Nelson, BC, Canada.

WIDOW LIVING OF NINTH BARON.

GERTRUDE EMMA (*Gertrude, Baroness Aylmer*), (2351-37th Av. W., Vancouver 13, BC, Canada), da. of the late Colin Black, CE, of Vic., BC, Canada: *m.* 1928, the 9th Baron, who *d.* 1970.

COLLATERAL BRANCHES LIVING.

Granddaughter of the late Hon. Henry Aylmer, brother of 7th Baron :—
Issue of the late John Athalmer Aylmer, *b.* 1847, *d.* 1934 : *m.* 1883, Mary Christine, who *d.* 1957, dau. of His Honour the late Judge Pringle, of The Elms, Cornwall, Ontario :—
Mary Dorothy, *b.* 1888: *m.* 1919, Eric G. McDougall, who *d.* 1943.——Muriel Esmée: *m.* 1921, George Meredith Morrison, who *d.* 1967, and has issue living, John Alexander Aylmer, *b.* 1924,—Beverley Ann, *b.* 1925.

Grandson of the late Henry Lovell Aylmer, son of the late Maj.-Gen. Henry Aylmer, (infra) :—
Issue of the late Arthur Lovell Aylmer, *b.* 1873, *d.* 1961 : *m.* 1st, 1900, Georgina Henrietta Emmeline (Ghetta), who *d.* 1936, dau. of the late Lieut.-Col. J. F. Sweeny ; 2ndly, 1937, Charlotte G., who *d.* 1968, da. of George Cornell Yates, of Oil Springs, Ontario, Canada:—
(By 1st m.) HUGH YATES, *b.* Feb. 5th, 1907; formerly 2nd Lt. 5th (British Columbia) Coast Brig., Canadian Artillery : *m.* 1939, Althea, el. dau. of the late Lieut.-Col. John Talbot, Indian Army, and has issue living, Ann Kathleen, *b.* 1941: *m.* 1972, Gregor Byron Miller, of 1874, Ventura Way, Victoria, BC, Canada, and has issue living, Jonathan Brown Aylmer *b.* 1975. *Residence,*—601-1159, Beach Drive, Victoria BC, V85 2N2, Canada.

Grandchildren of the late Maj.-Gen. Henry Aylmer, grandson of the Rev. the Hon. John Aylmer, 4th son of 2nd Baron :—
Issue of the late Col. Frederick Arthur Aylmer, *b.* 1849, *d.* 1918 : *m.* 1890, Constance Isabella, who *d.* 1923, dau. of the late Charles William Grenfell, M.P. [E. Harewood, colls.] :—
Henry Gerald (Flat 7, 23, Sloane Gdns., SW1), *b.* 1896; ed. at Cheltenham Coll.; Maj. (ret.) Essex Regt.; 1914-18 War, with R. Dublin Fus. in France and Belgium: *m.* 1927, Nancy, da. of the late Drake Hollick, of The Old House, Sheering, Harlow, Essex, and has issue living, John Henry (46, Rosaville Rd., SW6, Hurlingham Club), *b.* 1936; ed. at Radley; Member of London Stock Exchange: *m.* 1st, 1959 (m. diss. 1970), Venetia Mary, da. of Ian Henderson, of Pond House, Crawley, Hants.; 2ndly, 1971, Mrs. Margaret Gillian Elliot, da. of John Musker, and has issue living, (by 1st m.), Miranda Jane *b.* 1962, Juliet Rose *b.* 1965,—Constance Bridget, *b.* 1928: *m.* 1951, Geoffrey Ralph Merton, MC, of Radlett Place, Avenue Rd., NW8, son of Sir Thomas Ralph Merton,—Rachel Moyra (*Lady Pauncefort-Duncombe*), *b.* 1930: *m.* 1951, Maj. Sir Philip Digby Pauncefort-Duncombe, Gren. Gds. (ret.), 4th Bt.——Rose Caroline Georgiana (43, Cadogan Place, SW1), *b.* 1893: *m.* 1918, Henry Francis Lascelles, late Lt. Welsh Gds., who *d.* 1937 [see E. Harewood, colls.].

Grandsons of the late Col. Frederick Arthur Aylmer (ante) :—
Issue of the late Christopher Aylmer, *b.* 1890, *d.* 1955 : *m.* 1st, 1922, Marjorie Marianne Ellison (who obtained a divorce 1927), dau. of Percival Ellison Barber, of Sheffield, and widow of Reginald Barber; 2ndly, 1931, Margaret, who *d.* 1974, da. of Robert Brotherton, of Antwerp, Belgium:—
(By 1st marriage) Michael Anthony, *b.* 1923 ; ed. at Trin. Hall, Camb. (Exhibitioner, B.A. 1944, LL.B. 1945, M.A. 1948) ; admitted Solicitor 1948 : *m.* 1950, Countess Maddalena Sofia Maria Gabriella Cecilia Stefania Francesca, da. of the late Count Arbeno Attems [By. Pirbright], and has issue living, Anthony Julian, *b.* 1951; ed. at Westminster Sch., and Trin. Hall, Camb. (BA),—Giola Francesca, *b.* 1953. *Residence,*—42, Brampton Grove, NW4.

Issue of the late Capt. Edward Arthur Aylmer, RN, *b.* 1892, *d.* 1974: *m.* 1925, Gwladys Phoebe, who *d.* 1968, da. of the late David Evans, of Brecon:—
Gerald Edward (48, Marygate, York, YO1 5DD), *b.* 1926; ed. at Winchester, and Balliol Coll., Oxford (BA); 1939-45 War with RN; Prof. of History, Univ. of York: *m.* 1955, Ursula Adelaide, only da. of the late Maj. Brian George Michael Frederick Nixon.

Issue of the late Lieut.-Col. Claud Aylmer, R.A., b. 1900, d. 1952 : m. 1928, Margaret Victoria (Outspan, Shipton Gorge, Bridport, Dorset) (who m. 2ndly, 1954, Com. John Rudolf Perronet Thompson, R.N., who d. 1965), da. of the late Frank Hemming, of Franklyns, Great Waltham, Chelmsford:—
Richard Grenfell (Barnstone, Hog End, Bloxham, Banbury, Oxon.), b. 1932; ed. at Wellington Coll., and at London Univ. (B.A. 1952); Capt. (ret.) R.A.: m. 1964, Marelyn Joyce, only da. of Sir James Miller, GBE, and has issue living, Christopher James, b. 1966,—Kenneth Malcolm, b. 1970.

PREDECESSORS—[1] MATTHEW Aylmer, 2nd son of Sir Christopher Aylmer, 1st Bt. (cr. 1662); was M.P. for Portsmouth 1695-8, and for Dover 1698-1718, Gov. of Deal Castle 1710, Com.-in-Ch. of the Fleet 1709, Master of Greenwich Hospital, and Rear-Adm. of Great Britain, &c. ; cr. *Lord Aylmer, Baron of Balrath* (peerage of Ireland) 1718 ; d. 1720; s. by his son [2] HENRY, 2nd Baron ; d. 1754; s. by his son [3] HENRY, 3rd Baron, Capt. R.N. ; d. 1766; s. by his son [4] HENRY, 4th Baron, who s. his kinsman as 7th Bt. 1780; d. 1785; s. by his son [5] MATTHEW, G.C.B., 5th Baron ; a Gen. in the Army and Col. 18th Foot; assumed 1825 by Roy. licence the additional surname of Whitworth ; was Gov. Gen. of Canada 1830-35 ; d.s.p. 1850; s. by his brother [6] FREDERICK WILLIAM, K.C.B., 6th Baron ; was an Adm. ; d. Mar. 5th, 1858; s. by his cousin [7] UDOLPHUS (el. son of Capt. John Athalmer Aylmer, R.N., grandson of the Rev. the Hon. John Aylmer, 4th son of 2nd Baron), 7th Baron ; b. 1814: m. 1841, Mary Eliza, who d. 1881, dau. of Edward Journeaux, of Melbourne, Canada; d. 1901 ; s. by his el. son [8] MATTHEW, 8th Baron ; b. 1842 ; Maj.-Gen. ; sometime A.-G. and Inspector-Gen. Canadian Forces; m. 1875, Amy Gertrude, who d. 1935, dau. of the late Hon. John Young, of Montreal; d. 1923; s. by his el. son [9] JOHN FREDERICK WHITWORTH, 9th Baron; b. 1880: m. 1928, Gertrude Emma, da. of the late Colin Black, CE, of Vic., BC; d. 1970; s. by his brother [10] KENNETH ATHALMER, 10th Baron; b. 1883: m. 1924, Eleanor Katharine, who d. 1970, da. of the late John Francis Rogers, of Swanington, Norfolk; d. 1974; s. by his brother [11] BASIL UDOLPHUS, 11th Baron and present peer.

BACON, BARONESS.   (Bacon.)   [Life Baroness 1970.]

ALICE MARTHA BACON, *CBE, PC,* da. of the late Benjamin Bacon, of Normanton, Yorks.; ed. at Elementary Schs., Normanton, and Normanton Girls' High Sch.; formerly a School Teacher; a Member of Nat. Exec. Cttee. of Labour Party 1941-70, Chm. of Labour Party 1950-51, Min. of State, Home Office 1964-67, and a Min. of State, Dept. of Education and Science 1967-70; MP for NE Leeds (*Lab.*) 1945-55, and for SE Leeds 1955-70; cr. CBE (Civil) 1953, PC 1966, and *Baroness Bacon,* of City of Leeds, and of Normanton in W. Riding of co. York. (Life Baroness) 1970.
Residence,—53, Snydale Rd., Normanton, Yorks.

BADEN-POWELL, BARON.   (Baden-Powell.)   [Baron U.K. 1929, Bt. U.K. 1922.]
[Name and title pronounced "Bayden Poell"]

ROBERT CRAUSE BADEN-POWELL, 3rd Baron, and 3rd Baronet; b. Oct. 15th, 1936; s. 1962; ed. at Bryanston; RN 1955-57; Ch. Scouts Commr. Scout Assocn.: m. 1963, Patience Hélène Mary, da. of Maj. Douglas Myers Batty, of Melsetter, Rhodesia.

Arms,—Quarterly: 1st and 4th, per fesse or and argent, a lion rampant guardant gules between two tilting spears erect proper, *Powell*; 2nd and 3rd, argent, a lion rampant proper, on the head a crown vallary or between four crosses patée gules and as many fleur-de-lis azure alternately, *Baden.* Crests,— 1st, a lion passant or, in the paw, a broken tilting spear in bend proper, pendent therefrom by a riband gules and escutcheon resting on a wreath sable, charged with a pheorn, or,
Powell; 2nd, out of a crown vallary or a demi-lion rampant gules, charged on the shoulder with a cross patée argent, and supporting with the paws a sword erect proper, pommel and hilt gold, *Baden.* Supporters,—*Dexter,* an officer of 13th/18th Hussars in full dress, his sword drawn over his shoulder proper; *sinister,* a boy scout holding a staff also proper.
Residence,—Chapel Farm, Ripley, Surrey.

BROTHER LIVING.
Hon. DAVID MICHAEL (18, Kalang Rd., Camberwell, Mel., Vic. 3124, Aust.), b. Dec. 11th, 1940; ed. at Pierreport House; a Member of Mercers' Co., and a Freeman of City of London: m. 1966, Joan Phillips, da. of Horace William Berryman, of Camberwell, Melbourne, Australia, and has issue living, David Robert, b. Jan. 6th, 1971,—Alexander Peter, b. 1973.

SISTER LIVING.
Hon. Wendy Dorothy Lilian (Turnstones, Old Bursledon, Southampton, 303 8DJ), b. 1944.

AUNTS LIVING. (*Daughters of 1st Baron.*)
Hon. Heather Grace, b. 1915 : m. 1940, Wing Com. John Hall King, R.A.F., and has issue living, Timothy John, b. 1946; ed. at Charterhouse: m. 1971, Marion, da. of Herbert Ingram, of Beds., and widow of Christopher Parrott. *Residence,*—Swerbrook Farm, Wigginton, Banbury, Oxon.
Hon. Betty St. Clair, b. 1917: m. 1936, Gervas Charles Robert Clay, late Dir., Rhodes-Livingstone Museum, Livingstone, Zambia, and has issue living, Robin Baden, b. 1939; ed. at Michaelhouse and at Loughborough Coll.: m. 1971, Susan, el. da. of the Rev. Charles Patrick de Candole, of Witchampton Rectory, Dorset, and has issue living, Toby b. 1973,—Nigel Gerard Arden, b. 1943; ed. at Peterhouse, and at Rhodesia Univ.: m. 1969, Elaine, da. of A. Hughes, of Bournemouth, and has issue living, Gerard b. 1970, Olivia b. 1973,—Crispin David Powell, b. 1944; ed. at Peterhouse,

and St. David's Coll., Lampeter, Univ. of Wales: *m.* 1973, Ortrud Wiese, of Windhoek, S-W Africa, and has issue living, Eric *b.* 1974,—Gillian Ella St. Clair, *b.* 1937: *m.* 1968, William Leigh Strudwick Clay and has issue living, Rawley *b.* 1971, Daphne *b.* 1970. *Residence,*—Ford Lodge, Wiveliscombe, Taunton, Som.

WIDOWS LIVING OF FIRST AND SECOND BARONS.

OLAVE ST. CLAIR, *G.B.E.* (*Olave, Baroness Baden-Powell*), dau. of the late Harold Soames, of Parkstone, Dorset ; has Orders of White Rose of Finland, of Phoenix of Greece, of Honour and Merit of Haiti, of Bernado O'Higgins of Chile, of Sun of Peru, of Vasco Nunez de Balboa of Panama, of the Cedar of Lebanon, of Sacred Treasure of Japan, and of Order of the Oak Leaf Crown of Luxembourg; GBE (Civil) 1932: *m.* 1912, the 1st Baron, who *d.* 1941. *Residence,*—Hampton Court Palace, East Molesey, Surrey.
CARINE CRAUSE (*Carine, Baroness Baden-Powell*) (Turnstones, Old Bursledon, Hants.), da. of the late Clement Hamilton Crause Boardman, of Johannesburg: *m.* (Jan.) 1936, the 2nd Baron, who *d.* 1962.

PREDECESSORS—The Powell family were resident in Suffolk until David Powell (*d.* 1784) became a merchant in London. He *m.* 1723, Susanna, dau. and heir of Edward Thistlethwaite, Registrar to the Bishop of Salisbury, by Susanna, dau. of Andrew Baden, of Salisbury. [1] *Lieut.-Gen. Sir* ROBERT STEPHENSON SMYTH Baden-Powell, *O.M.*, *G.C.M.G.*, *G.C.V.O.*, *K.C.B.*, 5th son of the late Rev. Professor Baden Powell (Savilian Professor of Geometry to Oxford Univ.), *b.* 1857; Lt.-Gen. late 13th Hussars; Afghanistan 1880-81, Zululand 1888, Ashanti Expedition 1895-96, in command of Native Contingent, which he raised, Matabeleland 1896, S. Africa 1898-1900, raising Rhodesian Frontier Force, then Comdg. troops defending Mafeking during memorable siege of that place; founded Boy Scouts Organization 1908, and Girl Guides Organization 1910; became Ch. Scout of the World 1920; cr. a *Baronet* 1922, and *Baron Baden-Powell*, of Gilwell, Essex (peerage of United Kingdom) 1929: *m.* 1912, Olave St. Clair, *GBE*, da. of the late Harold Soames, of Parkstone, Dorset; *d.* 1941; *s.* by his only son [2] ARTHUR ROBERT PETER, 2nd Baron, *b.* 1913; in British S. Africa Police 1934-37, and Native Affairs Dept., S. Rhodesia 1937-45: *m.* 1936, Carine, da. of the late Clement Hamilton Crause Boardman, of Johannesburg; *d.* 1962; *s.* by his el. son [3] ROBERT CRAUSE, 3rd Baron and present peer.

BAGOT, BARON. (Bagot.) [Baron G.B. 1780, Bt. E. 1627.]

REGINALD WALTER BAGOT, 8th Baron, and 13th Baronet; *b.* Aug. 24th, 1897; *s.* 1973; ed. at Wellington Coll.; Maj. (ret.) RM: *m.* 1st, 1922, Winifred Gwyneth Bowen, from whom he obtained a divorce 1934; 2ndly, 1934, Millicent Brenda, only da. of the late Henry White Bowden, of Mobwell House, Gt. Missenden, Bucks.

𝕬rms,—Ermine, two chevronels azure. 𝕮rest,—Out of a ducal coronet of five leaves or, a goat's head argent, armed gold. 𝕾upporters— Two goats argent, armed and bearded or.

Residence,—Milchester House, Eastbourne, Sussex.

HALF-BROTHER LIVING.
HENEAGE CHARLES, *b.* June 11th, 1914; ed. at Harrow; late Major Indian Army: *m.* 1939, Muriel Patricia, da. of the late Maxwell James Moore Boyle, of Tullyvin House, co. Cavan, and Lareen House, co. Leitrim, and has issue living, Charles Hugh Shaun, *b.* 1944,—Caroline Patricia, *b.* 1942: *m.* 1962, Hugh Alexander James Cameron-Rose, of Tradsfield House, St. Martins, Oswestry, and has issue living, Hugh Charles *b.* 1962, Georgina Louise Stella *b.* 1968. *Residence,*—Hillcott, Bitterley, Ludlow, Shropshire.

ANTIQUUM OBTINENS

Possessing antiquity.

STEP-MOTHER LIVING.
Alice Lorina, dau. of the late Thomas Farr, of Chittelhambolt Manor, Devon : *m.* 1909, as his second wife, Charles Frederick Heneage Bagot, who *d.* 1939. *Residence,*—Hillcot, Bitterley, Ludlow, Shropshire.

WIDOWS LIVING OF SIXTH AND SEVENTH BARONS.
NANCY CONSTANCE BAGOT, da. of the late F. A. Spicer, of Sydney; resumed the surname of Bagot by deed poll 1971: *m.* 1st, 1940, as his second wife, the 6th Baron, who *d.* 1961; 2ndly, 1965 (m. diss. 1972), George Kenneth Whitehead. *Residence,*—Blithfield Hall, Rugeley, Stafford.
MARY FRANCES (*Mary, Baroness Bagot*), (7, Pembroke Place, W8), da. of the late Lt.-Col. George Frederick Hibbert, late 7th Fus., and widow of Lt.-Col. (Albert) Claude Hewitt, late R. Fus.: *m.* 1972, as his 2nd wife, the 7th Baron, who *d.* 1973.

COLLATERAL BRANCHES LIVING.
Granddaughter of the late Col. Charles Bagot, el. son of the late Rt. Hon. Sir Charles Bagot, GCB, 2nd son of the 1st Baron:—
Issue of the late Lieut.-Col. Josceline FitzRoy Bagot (of Levens), M.P., who was nominated a *Baronet* Jan. 1913, but *d.* March 1913, before the patent passed the Great Seal :—
Mary (*Lady Jones*) *b.* 1889: *m.* 1910, Sir Vincent Strickland Jones, KBE, who *d.* 1967, and has issue living, Desmond Vincent VINCENT-JONES, *DSC* (High End House, Broomfield Park, Sunningdale, Berks.), *b.* 1912; Capt. RN (ret.); 1939-45 War (DSC and Bar); assumed by deed poll 1944 the additional surname of Vincent: *m.* 1944, Jacqueline, da. of Col. Arthur John Henry Sloggett, DSOI Rifle Brig., and has issue living, Anne Jacqueline *b.* 1945: *m.* 1968, Christopher Nicholas Copeman, el. son of Vice-Adm. Sir Nicholas Alfred Copeman, KBE, CB, DSO, Averil Theresa *b.* 1952,—Barbara Vincent VINCENT-JONES, *b.* 1914; late WRNS; assumed by deed poll 1944 the additional surname of Vincent. *Residence,*—Brae House, Melvill La., Willingdon, Eastbourne.

Granddaughter of the late Col. Alexander Bagot, son of the late Rt. Hon. Sir
Charles Bagot, G.C.B. (ante):—
Issue (by 2nd marriage) of the late Charles FitzRoy Alexander Hallifax Bagot,
b. 1853, *d*. 1901: *m*. 1st, 1881, Emily Maynard Palmer (who *d*. 1901, and from whom he
had obtained a divorce 1890), dau. of the late Col. Charles Oldfield; 2ndly, 1891,
Beatrice Laura, who *d*. 1922, dau. of Chevalier L. Desanges, and widow of Gen. John
Studholme Brownrigg, C.B.:—
Alexandra, *b*. 1894: *m*. 1924, Gerald Vivian Palmer, late Lieut. Queen's Bays. *Residence*,—

Grandchildren of the late Rev. Frederic Bagot, D.C.L., 8th son of the late Rt.
Rev. the Hon. Richard Bagot, D.D., Bishop of Bath and Wells, 3rd son of
1st Baron:—
Issue of the late Cecil Villiers Bagot, *b*. 1865, *d*. 1940: *m*. 1903, Ethel, who *d*. 1944,
younger dau. of the late Jesse Garratt, of Wateringbury, Kent:—
Charles Frederic Villiers, *O.B.E.*, *b*. 1912 ; ed. at Radley ; Lieut.-Col. R.A. (retired), late Essex Regt. ;
appointed a Queen's Messenger 1961 ; N.-W. Europe 1944-45 (despatches) ; O.B.E. (Mil.) 1955 :
m. 1st, 1939, Lucy Violet Kathleen de la Cloche, who *d*. 1972, da. of the late Harold Marriott, of 60,
Great Cumberland Place, W1; 2ndly, 1975, Anne Elizabeth Dyke Drapple, of Docking, Norfolk, and
has issue living (by 1st m.), Richard Charles Villiers, *b*. 1941,—Julian William D'Arcy, *b*. 1943,—
Harriet Anne Elizabeth, *b*. 1951,—Patricia Mary, *b*. 1953. *Residence*,—Sandford House, Avening,
Tetbury, Gloucestershire. *Club*,—Army and Navy.——Millicent Jessie Eleanor, *CBE*, *b*. 1907; ed.
at Lady Margaret Hall, Oxford (MA); attached to Min. of Defence; MBE (Civil) 1949; CBE (Civil)
1967. *Residence*,—25, Rusholme Rd., Putney, SW15.

(*In remainder to Baronetcy only*.)
Grandsons of the late Rev. John Greville Chester (infra):—
Issue of the late Major Anthony James Bagot Chester, M.C., *b*. 1892, *d*. 1952: *m*. 1924, Gladys
Mabel, who *d*. 1974, el. da. of the late Rev. Frederick Charles Stamer [Stamer, Bt., colls.]:—
John Greville Bagot, *MC*, *b*. 1925; Maj. (ret.) Coldstream Guards; 1944-45 War (MC). *Residence*,—
The Old Rectory, North Crawley, Newport Pagnell, Bucks.

Issue of the late Henry Montague Bagot Chester, *b*. 1896, *d*. 1969: *m*. 1924, Alyce Amy
Maude Tranchell, who *d*. 1934.
Greville Derrick Bagot, *b*. 1925.——Hugh Malcolm, *b*. 1929.

Granddaughters of the late Lt.-Col. Charles Montague Chester, son of the late
Rev. William Chester, son of the late Charles Bagot Chester (infra):—
Issue of the late Rev. John Greville Chester, *b*. 1852, *d*. 1923: *m*. 1883, Amy, who *d*. 1915,
dau. of Arthur Hughes:—
Dorothy Mary: *m*. 1st, 1915, Maj. Robert Francis Ruck Keene, RFA, who *d*. 1918; 2ndly, 1922,
Herbert St. John Durnford, who *d*. 1951, and has issue living, (by 1st m.) John Robert, *MBE*, *TD*
(Chenies Cottage, Copperkins Grove, Chesham Bois, Amersham, Bucks.), *b*. 1917; ed. at Eton, and at
Trin. Coll., Camb.; late Major Oxford and Bucks LI (TA); 1939-45 War (MBE); MBE (Mil) 1946:
m. 1951, Beryl Mary Manistre, and has issue living, Robert John *b*. 1952, Edmund Arthur *b*. 1955,—
(by 2nd m.) Mary St. John, *b*. 1924. *Residence*,—9, Woodstock Close, Oxford,——Kathleen Agnes.

Grandchildren of the late John St. Leger, el. son of Lt.-Gen. John Chester,
4th son of Charles Bagot-Chester, 2nd son of 5th baronet:—
Issue of the late Maj. Arthur John Bonfoy ST. LEGER, *b*. 1859; *d*. 1939: *m*. 1896, Hilda,
Geraldine, who *d*. 1961, dau. of the late Lieut.-Col. Sir Gerard Smith, K.C.M.G.:—
Brenda Mary, *b*. 1897: *m*. 1918, Achille Sabbe, who *d*. 1962, having assumed by Roy. licence 1940,
the surname of St. Leger in lieu of his patronymic, and has issue living, Julian (of 20, Princedale Rd.,
Holland Park, W11), *b*. 1927; ARIBA: *m*. 1st, 1950, (m. diss. 1955) Patricia, da. of Brig. Sir Eric
Alexander Ogilvy Hutchison, 2nd Bt. (cr. 1923; ext.); 2ndly, 1972, Michiko, da. of Yasuo Fujimoto,
of Grand Forks, BC, Canada, and has issue living (by 1st m.), Harriet Claire *b*. 1951, (by 2nd m.)
Anthony Jasper Genji *b*. 1974. *Residence*,—Little Honington, Matching Green, Essex.——Vera,
b. 1900: *m*. 1964, Ian Alexander Beith, of Flat 91, 6 Hall Rd., NW8.
Issue of the late Reginald Warham Antony ST. LEGER, *b*. 1868, *d*. 19—: *m*. 1888, Amy
Eva, who *d*. 1942, da. of the late George Sloan, of Dumfries:—
Gaspard Douglas Anthony, *b*. 1890.——Geoffrey Bayard, *b*. 1892.——Roderic Craufurd, *b*. 1894.——
Victor Robert, *b*. 1896.——Evangeline, *b*. 1900.

Granddaughter of the late Col. Heneage Charles BAGOT-CHESTER, yr. son of Lt.-Gen.
John Chester [ante]:—
Issue of the late Capt. Hugh Augustus BAGOT-CHESTER, *b*. 1876, *d*. 1938: *m*. 1st, 1895,
Margaret Kathleen Julia, who *d*. 1951, having obtained a divorce 1908, only dau. of the late
Col. R. E. Oakes, B.S.C.; 2ndly, 1913, Clotilde Mary Hamilton, who *d*. 1964, dau. of the
late Hon. Arthur Henry Browne [B. Kilmaine, colls.]:—
(By 2nd m.) Peggy Mary Clotilde (16, Swan Court, Flood St., Chelsea, SW3), *b*. 1914: *m*. 1st, 1937,
Wallace Stuart Finlayson; 2ndly, 1947 (m. diss. 1954), Edward Ralph Harley, CBE.

PREDECESSORS.—[1] Sir HERVEY Bagot, Sheriff of Staffordshire 1626, a staunch loyalist;
cr. a Bt. 1627 ; *d*. 1660 ; *s*. by his el. son [2] Sir EDWARD, 2nd Bt., M.P. for Stafford in the
Restoration Parliament ; *d*. 1673 ; *s*. by his son [3] Sir EDWARD, 3rd Bt., M.P. for Staffordshire
in seven Parliaments ; *d*. 1704 ; *s*. by his son [4] Sir EDWARD, 4th Bt., M.P. for co. Stafford;
d. 1712 ; *s*. by his son [5] Sir WALTER WAGSTAFFE, LL.D., 5th Bt., successively M.P. for
Newcastle-under-Lyme, Staffordshire, and Oxford Univ.; *d*. 1768 ; *s*. by his el. son [6] Sir WILLIAM,
6th Bt., M.P. for co. Stafford 1754-80 ; cr. Baron Bagot (peerage of Great Britain) 1780 ; *d*. 1798 ;
s. by his el. son [7] WILLIAM, LL.D., 2nd Baron ; distinguished for scientific attainments : *m*.
1st, 1799, the Hon. Emily FitzRoy, who *d*. 1800, dau. of 1st Baron Southampton ; 2ndly, 1807,
Lady Louisa Legge—who *d*. 1816—dau. of 3rd Earl of Dartmouth, *d*. 1856 ; *s*. by his el. son
[8] WILLIAM, 3rd Baron ; sat as M.P. for Denbighshire (C) 1835-52 : *m*. 1851, Hon. Lucia Caroline
Elizabeth Agar-Ellis, el. dau. of 1st Baron Dover, and sister of 3rd Viscount Clifden ; *d*. 1887 ;
s. by his el. son [9] WILLIAM, 4th Baron, *b*. 1857 ; a Gentleman Usher of Privy Chamber to
H.M. Queen Victoria 1885-7, and a Lord-in-Waiting to H.M. Queen Victoria 1896-1901 : *m*.
1903, Lilian Marie, who *d*. 1958, dau. of the late Henry May, of Maryland, U.S.A.; *d*. 1932 ; *s*. by his
cousin [10] GERALD WILLIAM (son of the late Vice-Adm. Henry Bagot, son of 3rd son of 1st
Baron), 5th Baron, *b* 1866 ; *d*. 1946 ; *s*. by his cousin [11] CARYL ERNEST (son of the late Rev.
Lewis Richard Charles Bagot, son of the late Rev. Charles Walter Bagot, 4th son of the late
Rt. Rev. the Hon. Richard Bagot, D.D., Bishop of Bath and Wells, 3rd son of 1st Baron), 6th
Baron ; *b*. 1877 ; formerly Lieut. Irish Guards ; European War 1914-19 : *m*. 1st, 1911, Margaret
who *d*. 1937, dau. of J. McMenemy ; 2ndly, 1940, Nancy Constance, dau. of the late F. A. Spicer
of Sydney, NSW; *d*. 1961; *s*. by his cousin [12] HARRY ERIC (son of the late Charles Frederick
Heneage Bagot, 4th son of the late Rev. Charles Walter Bagot [ante]) 7th Baron; *b*. 1894: *m*. 1st,
1951, Kathleen Elizabeth Saddler, who *d*. 1972, widow of Noel Murray Puckle, of Melbourne, Aust.;
2ndly, 1972, Mary Frances, da. of the late Lt.-Col. George Frederick Hibbert, late 7th Fus., and widow
of Lt.-Col. (Albert) Claude Hewitt, late R. Fus.; *d*. 1973; *s*. by his brother [13] REGINALD WALTER,
8th Baron and present peer.

BAILLIEU, BARON. (Baillieu.) [Baron U.K. 1953.]

JAMES WILLIAM LATHAM BAILLIEU,
3rd Baron; *b.* Nov. 16th, 1950; ed. at
Radley; *s.* 1973: *m.* 1974, Cornelia
Masters, da. of W. Ladd, of London.

Arms,—Sable on a pile between two eagles'
heads erased or, three escutcheons gules, each
charged with a fleur-de-lis of the second. *Crest,*
—Upon a billet fessewise azure, charged with three
plates, a martlet sable, holding in the beak a fleur-
de-lis as in the Arms. *Supporters,—Dexter,* a
yellow Labrador dog; *sinister,* a Kangaroo, both
proper.

Residence,—44, Hawkesburn Rd., S. Yarra,
Vic. 3141, Aust.

SANS CHANGER.

Without changing.

BROTHER LIVING.
Hon. DAVID CLIVE LATHAM, *b.* Nov. 2nd, 1952;
ed. at Seaford, and Radley.

UNCLES LIVING (Sons of 1st Baron.)
Hon. Robert Latham, *MBE, TD, b.* 1917; ed. at Winchester, and at Magdalen Coll., Oxford (MA);
Solicitor 1954; Man. Dir. of Dawnay Day & Co. Ltd., a Dir. of Dawnay Day Gp. Ltd., C. H. Goldrei,
Foucard and Son Ltd., and View Forth Investment Trust Ltd.; 1939-45 War as Major Middx. Yeo.
(despatches, MBE); MBE (Mil) 1945: *m.* 1949, Delphine Mary, yr. da. of the late Edgar Hastings
Dowler [see Reynolds, Bt.], and has issue living, Simon, *b.* 1951,—Anthony Robert *b.* 1956,—Mary
Clare, *b.* 1950: *m.* 1974, James Neil Percival Cranston—Celia Maria, *b.* 1953. *Residence,*—Flat 2,
Rutland Gate House, 43/44, Rutland Gate, SW7.

Hon. Edward Latham, *b.* 1919, ed. at Winchester, and at Brasenose Coll., Oxford (B.A. 1942, M.A.
1947); a Member of London Stock Exchange, and a Dir. of Rio-Tinto Zinc Corpn. Ltd., Embankment Trust Ltd., and ANZ Banking Group; 1939-45 War as Capt. RA and RHA (invalided): *m.*
1942, Betty Anne Jardine, da. of the late Henry Leslie Jardine Taylor, of Crofton Lodge, Sunningdale, Berks., and has issue living, Christopher Latham, *b.* 1949,—Philip Latham, *b.* 1958,—Annette
Leslie, *b.* 1955. *Residence,*—Tangle Copse, West Drive, Sunningdale, Berks.

AUNT LIVING (Daughter of 1st Baron.)
Hon. Yvette Latham, *b.* 1922: *m.* 1946, Robert Ruttan Wilson, of Durford Knoll, Upper Durforde
Wood, Petersfield, Hants. [see Bs. Berners, colls.].

MOTHER LIVING.
Anne Bayliss, el. da. of Leslie William Page, of Southport, Qld., Aust.: *m.* 1st, 1945, (m. diss. 1961),
the Hon. William Latham Baillieu, later 2nd Baron Baillieu, who *d.* 1973; 2ndly, 1964, (Harry)
Anthony Rupert Dodd, of Covenanter, Cattle St., Nutley, Sussex.

WIDOW LIVING OF SECOND BARON.
DELIA MURIEL (*Delia, Baroness Baillieu*), da. of   , and formerly wife of
Champion: *m.* 1962, as his 2nd wife, the 2nd Baron, who *d.* 1973.

PREDECESSORS.—[1] *Sir* CLIVE LATHAM Baillieu, KBE, CMG, son of the late Hon. William Lawrence
Baillieu, of Melbourne, Australia; *b.* 1889; Dir.-Gen. British Purchasing Commn., Washington
1941-42; Head of British Raw Materials Mission, Washington, and British Repres. on Combined
Raw Materials Board 1942-43, Pres. of FBI 1945-47, Chm. of Dunlop Rubber Co 1949-57, and Pres.
1957-67; cr *Baron Baillieu,* of Sefton Commonwealth of Australia and of Parkwood, Co. Surrey
(peerage of UK) 1953: *m.* 1915, Ruby Florence Evelyn, who *d.* 1962, da. of William Clark, of
Windlesham Moor, Surrey; *d.* 1967; *s.* by his el. son [2] WILLIAM LATHAM, 2nd Baron; *b.* 1915:
m. 1st 1945 (m. diss. 1961), Anne Bayliss, el. da. of Leslie William Page, of Southport, Qld.; 2ndly
1962, Delia Muriel, da. of   , and formerly wife of   Champion; *d.* 1973; *s*
by his el. son [3] JAMES WILLIAM LATHAM, 3rd Baron and present peer.

Balcarres, Earl of, see Earl of Crawford and Balcarres.

BALDWIN OF BEWDLEY, EARL. (Baldwin.) [Earl U.K. 1937.]

(ARTHUR) WINDHAM BALDWIN, 3rd
Earl; *b.* March 22nd, 1904; *s.* 1958;
ed. at Eton, and at Trin. Coll., Camb.;
1939-45 War in RAF: *m.* 1936, Elspeth,
da. of the late C. A. Tomes, of New York,
and has issue.

Arms,—Argent, on a saltire sable a quatrefoil or.
Crest,—A cockatrice sejant, wings addorsed argent,
combed, wattled, and beaked or, gorged with a crown
vallary, lined and reflexed over the back gold and
charged on the shoulder with a rose gules, barbed and
seeded proper. *Supporters,*—On either side a white
owl proper, that on the sinister holding in the beak a
sprig of broom also proper.
Residence,—Bushey House, Apperley, Gloucester.
Club,—Reform.

*With the help of my God I leap over
the wall.*

SON LIVING.
EDWARD ALFRED ALEXANDER (*Viscount Corve-
dale*), (Jacaranda Cottage, Water End, Hemel
Hempstead, Herts.), *b.* Jan. 3rd, 1938; ed. at Eton,
and at Trin. Coll., Camb.: *m.* 1970, Sarah Mac-
Murray, el. da. of Evan James, of Upwood Park,
Abingdon, Berks., and has issue.
SON LIVING.—*Hon.* Benedict Alex-
ander Stanley, *b.* Dec. 28th, 1973.

SISTERS LIVING.
Lady Diana Lucy, *b.* 1895: *m.* 1st, 1919, Capt. Richard
Gordon Munro, M.C., late 4th Dragoon Guards

(CMG 1946, KCMG 1947); who *d*. 1967, and from whom she obtained a divorce 1934; 2ndly, 1934, George Durant Kemp-Welch, Grenadier Guards, who *d*. (killed by enemy action) 1944, and has issue living, (by 1st marriage) Colin Gordon, *MC*, *b*. 1920; late Capt. Roy. Armoured Corps; Italy 1943-45 (MO). *Residence*,—Dunhampton Cottage, nr. Stourport-on-Severn.

Lady Leonora Stanley, *b*. 1896 : *m*. 1922, Capt. the Hon. Sir Arthur Jared Palmer Howard, K.B.E., CVO, who *d*. 1971 [see B. Strathcona and Mount Royal]. *Residences*,—Wappingthorn, Steyning, Sussex; 6, Chesterfield Street, W1.

Lady (Pamela) Margaret, *b*. 1897 : *m*. 1919, Capt. Sir (Herbert) Maurice Huntington-Whiteley, 2nd Bt., RN, who *d*. 1975. *Residence*,—8, Crown Lea Av., Barnards Green, Malvern, WR14 2DP.

Lady Esther Louisa (Betty), *b*. 1902. *Residence*,—Spinney Corner, W. Chiltington, Sussex.

PREDECESSORS.—[1] *Rt. Hon. Sir* STANLEY Baldwin, *K.G.*, son of the late Alfred Baldwin (M.P. for W., or Bewdley, Div. of Worcestershire), of Wilden House, Stourport ; *b*. 1867 ; a Junior Lord of the Treasury Jan. to June 1917 ; Joint Financial Sec. to the Treasury June 1917 **to April 1921, Pres. of Board of Trade April 1921 to Oct. 1922, Chancellor of the Exchequer Oct. 1922 to Aug. 1923, Leader of the Conservative Party May 1923 to May 1937, Prime Min. and First Lord of the Treasury May 1923 to Jan. 1924, again Prime Min. and First Lord of the Treasury Nov. 1924 to June 1929, Lord Pres. of the Council Aug. 1931 to June 1935 (also Lord Privy Seal Sept. 1932 to Jan. 1934), and again Prime Min. and First Lord of the Treasury June 1935 to May 1937;** acted as a Counsellor of State during H.M. King George V.'s absence abroad 1925, and during H.M.'s illness 1928-9; cr. *Viscount Corvedale*, of Corvedale, co. Salop, and *Earl Baldwin of Bewdley* (peerage of United Kingdom) 1937: *m*. 1892, Lucy, *G.B.E.* (a D.G.St.J.), who *d*. 1945, el. dau. of the late Edward Lucas J. Ridsdale, of Rottingdean, Sussex; *d*. 1947; *s*. by his son [2] OLIVER RIDSDALE, 2nd Earl; *b*. 1899; an Author and Journalist; sometime Parliamentary Private Sec. to Sec. of State for War; was Gov. and Com.-in-Ch. of Leeward Islands 1948-50; sat as M.P. for Dudley (*Lab.*) 1929-31, and for Paisley 1945-47, *d*. 1958 ; *s*. by his brother [3] (ARTHUR) WINDHAM, 3rd Earl, and present peer.

BALERNO, BARON. (Buchanan-Smith.) [Life Baron 1963.]

ALICK DRUMMOND BUCHANAN-SMITH, *C.B.E.*, *T.D.*, son of the late Very Rev. Sir George Adam Smith, D.D.; *b*. Oct. 9th, 1898; ed. at Glasgow Acad., Trin. Coll., Glenalmond, Aberdeen Univ. (MA, BSc), and Iowa, USA; DSc Edinburgh, and Heriot-Watt; Brig. (ret.) late Gordon Highlanders (TA), Dep. Chm. Unionist Party in Scotland 1960-63; a JP and DL; Hon. Col. 5/6 Bn. Gordon Highlanders 1958-61; 1914-18 War in France and Belgium (two medals); assumed the additional surname of Buchanan; *cr*. O.B.E. (Mil.) 1939, C.B.E. (Mil.) 1945, Knt. 1956, and *Baron Balerno*, of Currie, co. Midlothian [Life Baron] 1963: *m*. 1926, Mary Kathleen, who *d*. 1947, dau. of the late Capt. George Smith, of Pittodrie, Aberdeenshire, and has issue.

Arms,—Vert, a saltire between a bough pot or, charged with three salmon fishes in fret proper, and containing as many lilies of the garden, the dexter in bud, the centre full blown, and the sinister half blown also proper in chief, a cross-crosslet in each flank, and a lion rampant in base holding in his dexter paw an Imperial crown or. **Crest**.—A skylark rising proper. **Supporters**,—*Dexter*, a bull or, horned as those of Ayrshire bulls, gules, unguled of the last, and gorged of a collar of ivy proper; *sinister*, a boar or, armed vert langued, crined and unguled gules.

Residence,—House of Cockburn, Balerno, Midlothian. *Clubs*,—Caledonian, Royal Automobile, New (Edinburgh), Royal Northern (Aberdeen).

SONS LIVING.

Rev. the Hon. George Adam (Glencorse House, Fettes College, Edinburgh, 4), *b*. 1929; ed. at Edinburgh Univ. (MA), and at Union Theological Seminary, New York (BD): *m*. 1961, Margaret McIntosh Bowden, and has issue.

Hon. Alick Laidlaw, *M.P.* (of House of Cockburn, Balerno, Midlothian; Caledonian, and New (Edinburgh) Clubs), *b*. 1932; ed. at Edinburgh Acad., at Trin. Coll., Glenalmond, and at Pembroke Coll., Camb. (MA); Capt. Gordon Highlanders (TA); Under-Sec., Scottish Office 1970-74; MP for N. Angus and Mearns (*C*) since 1964: *m*. 1956, Janet, da. of the late Thomas Lawrie, CBE, and has issue.

Rev. the Hon. Robert Dunlop (Eriska, Ledaig, Connel, Argyll; New (Edinburgh) Club), *b*. 1936; ed. at Edinburgh Acad., at Trin. Coll., Glenalmond, at Pembroke Coll., Camb. (BA), at New Coll., Edinburgh, and at Princeton Theological Seminary, New Jersey (ThM); Min. of Christ's Church, Dunollie, Oban, 1962-66; Chap. to 8th Bn. Argyll and Sutherland Highlanders 1963, and of 3rd Bn. Argyll and Sutherland Highlanders, and of 51st Highland Volunteers 1967-68; Chap. of St. Andrew's Univ. 1966-73, and Preacher to USA for British Council of Churches 1968: *m*. 1966, Sheena Mary, da. of the late Alexander W. Edwards, and has issue.

Hon. Jock Gordon (Pitcaple Farm, RR2, Hespeler, Ont. N3C 2V4, Canada; Royal Northern (Aberdeen) and Caledonian Clubs), *b*. 1940; ed. at Trin. Coll., Glenalmond, at Aberdeen Univ., and at Iowa State Univ., USA, PhD, Oklahoma; Lt. Gordon Highlanders; TA (Reserve); Assist. Prof. Univ. of Guelph: *m*. 1964, Virginia Lee, el. da. of John S. Maxson, of Dallas, Texas.

DAUGHTER LIVING.

Hon. Mary Drummond, *b.* 1927; ed. at St. Denis, and at Edinburgh Univ. (M.A. 1949): *m.* 1953, Col. Charles Herbert Kenneth Corsar, TD, JP, of Mauricewood House, Penicuik, Midlothian; Frostineb, Blackshiels, Midlothian, and Burg, Torloisk, Isle of Mull, and has issue.

BALFOUR, EARL OF. (Balfour.) [Earl U.K. 1922.]

Virtue strives towards heaven.

GERALD ARTHUR JAMES BALFOUR, 4th Earl; *b.* Dec. 23rd, 1925; *s.* 1968; ed. at Eton; Master Mariner; Co. Councillor and a JP for E. Lothian; 1939-45 War in Merchant Navy: *m.* 1956, Mrs. Natasha Georgina Lousada, da. of the late Capt. George Anton.

Arms (as recorded at Lyon Office),—Argent, on a chevron engrailed between three mullets sable as many otters' heads erased of the field. **Crest,**—A palm tree proper. **Supporters,**—Two otters proper, collared or.

Residence,—Whittingehame Tower, Haddington, East Lothian.

SISTERS LIVING.

Lady Evelyn Jean Blanche, *b.* 1929 : *m.* 1948, Michael William Brander, late 10th Hussars, and has issue living, Andrew Michael, *b.* 1949,— Kathleen Jean, *b.* 1950,—Evelyn Ann, *b.* 1952.— *Residence,*—Whittingehame Mains, Haddington, East Lothian.

Lady Alison Emily, *b.* 1934: *m.* 1963, Thomas Kremer, MA, of 25, St. James's Gdns., W11, and has issue living, David Lytton, *b.* 1964,—Amanda Lili, *b.* 1966,—Kim Madeleine, *b.* 1969.

AUNTS LIVING. (*Daughters of 2nd Earl*)

Lady Eleanor, *b.* 1890: *m.* 1917, the Hon. Galbraith Lowry Egerton Cole, who *d.* 1929 [see E. Enniskillen]. *Residence,*—Kekopey, P.O. Box 127, Gilgil, Kenya.

Lady Mary Edith, *b.* 1894. *Residence,*—10 New Winton, Tranent, E. Lothian.

Lady Evelyn Barbara, *b.* 1898; ed. at Reading Univ.; a Consultant, The Soil Assocn. *Residence,*— 4, Rattla Corner, Theberton, Leiston, Suffolk.

Lady Kathleen Constance Blanche (Woodhall Cottage, Pencaitland, E. Lothian), *b.* 1912; ed. at Newnham Coll., Camb. (BA 1934, MA 1949): *m.* 1933, Richard Charles Oldfield, who *d.* 1972, and has issue living, Frances Elizabeth, *b.* 1935; BSc, PhD: *m.* 1963, Roderick Whitfield, MA, PhD, of 164, Duke's Av., Muswell Hill, N10, and has issue living, Aldus Francis *b.* 1970, Martha Ming *b.* 1965, Tanya Thisbe *b.* 1967,—Margaret Cayley, *b.* 1939; ed. at Bristol Univ., MA: *m.* 1960, Agbo Folarin, of Ife University, Nigeria, and has issue living, Oliver Abiola Raschid *b.* 1973, Evelyn Adeola *b.* 1970.

WIDOW LIVING OF THIRD EARL.

JEAN LILY (*Dowager Countess of Balfour*), (West Roundel, Broxmouth Park, Dunbar), da. of the late Rev. John James Cooke-Yarborough [see Cooke, Bt., colls.]: *m.* 1925, the 3rd Earl, who *d.* 1968.

COLLATERAL BRANCH LIVING. (*In special remainder.*)

Issue of the late Lt.-Col. Francis Cecil Campbell Balfour, CIE, CVO, CBE, MC, el. son of Col. Eustace James Anthony Balfour, yst. brother of 1st Earl, *b.* 1884, *d.* 1965: *m.* 1920, the Hon. Phyllis Evelyn Goschen (Old Peans, Robertsbridge, Sussex), da. of 2nd Viscount Goschen:—

EUSTACE ARTHUR GOSCHEN (8, Avenue des Pages, 78110, Le Vesinet, France), *b.* May 26th, 1921; ed. at Eton; 1939-45 War as Capt. Scots Guards in N. Africa and Italy (wounded); with Mather & Platt, Ltd. (France): *m.* 1946 (m. diss. 1971), Anne, da. of the late Maj. Victor Yule, and has issue living, Roderick Francis Arthur, *b.* 1948; ed. at Eton: *m.* 1971, Lady Tessa Mary Isabel Fitzalan Howard, el. da. of the 17th Duke of Norfolk, and has issue living, Willa Anne *b.* 1973,—Charles George Yule, *b.* 1951; ed. at Eton: *m.* 1971, Mrs. Paula Susan Cuene-Grandidier, da. of the late John Maurice Davis, MBE, of Church Lane House, Bovingdon, Herts.

PREDECESSORS.—[1] *Sir* ARTHUR JAMES Balfour, K.G., O.M., P.C., LL.D., D.C.L., D.Ph., F.R.S., el. son of the late James Maitland Balfour, of Whittingehame, by Lady Blanche Mary Harriett Cecil, who *d.* 1872, second dau. of 2nd Marquess of Salisbury: *b.* 1848; was employed on Special Mission of Lords Beaconsfield and Salisbury to Berlin 1878, Assist. Private Sec. to Sec. of State for Foreign Affairs (Marquess of Salisbury) 1878-80, Pres. of Local Govt. Board June 1885 to Jan. 1886, Sec. for Scotland July 1886 to March 1887 (with a Seat in the Cabinet from Nov. 1886), Ch. Sec. for Ireland March 1887 to Oct. 1891, First Lord of the Treasury and Leader of the House of Commons Oct. 1891 to Aug. 1892, Leader of the Opposition 1892-5, again First Lord of the Treasury and Leader of the House of Commons 1895-1900 and 1900-1902, Prime Min., First Lord of the Treasury, and Leader of the House of Commons 1902-5 (also Lord Privy Seal 1902-3), Leader of the Opposition 1905-11, First Lord of the Admiralty May 1915 to Dec. 1916 (also a Member of Cabinet War Council), Sec. of State for Foreign Affairs in National Min. 1916-19, Lord Pres. of the Council 1919-22 and 1925-9, and Pres. British Acad. 1921-8; appointed a Member of Munitions of War Committee 1915, a British Representative at Peace Conference 1919, and British Delegate to Washington Conference 1921; Chm. Med. Research Council 1924-9; M.P. for Hertford (*C*) 1874-85, for E. Div. of Manchester 1885-1906, and for City of London Feb. 1906 to April 1922; went as Head of Special Mission to U.S.A. 1917; a British Representative on League of Nations up to 1923: cr. *Earl of Balfour,* and *Viscount Traprain,* of Whittingehame, co. Haddington (peerage of United Kingdom) 1922, with special remainder in default of heirs male of his body, to (1) his brother, the *Rt. Hon.* Gerald William Balfour, and the heirs male of his body; (2) to his nephew, Francis Cecil Campbell Balfour, and the heirs male of his body: and (3) to his nephew, Oswald Herbert Campbell Balfour, and the heirs male of his body; *d.* 1930: *s.* under the special remainder by his brother [2] GERALD WILLIAM, P.C., 2nd Earl: *b.* 1853; was Ch. Sec. for Ireland 1895-1900, and Pres. of Board of Trade 1900-1905; M.P. for Central Division of Leeds (*C*) 1885-1906: *m.* 1887, Lady Elizabeth Edith Bulwer-Lytton, who *d.* 1942, dau. of 1st Earl of Lytton; *d.* 1945: *s.* by his son [3] ROBERT ARTHUR LYTTON 3rd Earl; *b.* 1902; Chm. Scottish Div. NCB 1946-51: *m.* 1925, Jean Lily, da. of the late

Rev. John James Cooke-Yarborough [Cooke, Bt., colls.]; *d.* 1968 ; *s.* by his son [4] GERALD ARTHUR JAMES, 4th Earl and present peer; also Viscount Traprain.

BALFOUR OF BURLEIGH, LORD. (Bruce.) [Lord S. 1607.]

Every land is the home   We have
of a brave man.   been.

ROBERT BRUCE, 8th (de facto) and 12th (but for the attainder) Lord; *b.* Jan. 6th, 1927; *s.* 1967; ed. at Westminster; CEng; FIEE; Treas. The Roy. Scottish Corpn. since 1967; a Dir. of Bank of Scotland since 1968, and The Scottish Investment Trust Ltd., Edinburgh since 1970; Chm. of Scottish Arts Council, and Viking Oil Ltd. since 1971; Commnr. Forestry Commn. 1971-74; Foreman and Supt. The English Electric Co. Ltd., Stafford & Liverpool 1952-57, Gen. Manager The English Electric Co. India, Ltd. 1957-64, of English Electric Netherton Works 1964-66, and of D. Napier and Son, Ltd. 1967-68: *m.* 1971, Jennifer, da. of the late E. S. Manasseh, and formerly wife of John Brittain Catlin, and has issue.

Arms,—Quarterly: 1st and 4th argent, on a chevron sable, an otter's head erased of the field, *Balfour*; 2nd and 3rd or, a saltire and chief gules, the latter charged with a mullet argent, *Bruce*. Crests,—1st, upon a rock a mermaid, holding in the dexter hand an otter's head, erased at the neck, and in the sinister hand a swan's head also erased, all proper; 2nd, a dexter arm in fesse, embowed, in armour, couped at the shoulder, the hand holding a sceptre in bend sinister, or. Supporters,—*Dexter*, an otter proper; *sinister*, a swan also proper. *Residence,*—Brucefield, Clackmannan.

DAUGHTER LIVING.
Hon. VICTORIA, b. April 5th, 1973.

BROTHER LIVING.
Hon. George John Done (6, Pembroke Walk, W8; Athenaeum), *b.* 1930; ed. at Westminster; Hon. Sec. of Roy. Soc. of Portrait Painters.

SISTERS LIVING.
Hon. Laetitia Mary, *b.* 1920; MB, ChB St. Andrews 1946; is a JP for Northumberland: *m.* 1955, Dr. Ian Metcalfe Telfer, and has issue living, John Bruce, *b.* 1956,—George Metcalfe, *b.* 1961,—Mary Daubeny, *b.* 1958. *Residence,*—Wallbottle Hall, Newcastle upon Tyne, NE15 8JD.
Hon. Katherine Gordon BRUCE (25, Kew Green, Kew, Richmond, Surrey), *b.* 1922; reverted by deed poll 1975 to the surname of Bruce: *m.* 1946, Thomas Riviere Bland, MC, from whom she obtained a divorce 1961, and has issue living, Charles Riviere, *b.* 1949.—Susanna Katherine, *b.* 1947,—Louise Margaret, *b.* 1953.
Hon. Jean, *b.* 1924; formerly in WRNS: *m.* 1949 (m. diss. 1971), John Shirley Ward, and has issue living, John Shirley, *b.* 1961,—Lætitia, *b.* 1951,—Reavis Mary, *b.* 1955. *Residence,*—1115, Buena Vista, S. Pasadena, 2, California 91105, USA.
Hon. Margaret, *b.* 1934: *m.* 1967, David Graham Worthy, of 33, Sloane Gdns., SW1, and Keepers Cottage, Hare Warren Hollow, Merrow Downs, Guildford, and has issue living, Henry Jonathan David Bruce, *b.* 1971.

WIDOW LIVING OF SEVENTH LORD.
VIOLET DOROTHY EVELYN, *MBE* (*Dorothy Lady Balfour of Burleigh*) (Hartshaw, Clackmannan; 14, Parkside, SW1), da. of the late Richard Henry Done, of Tarporley, Cheshire; MBE (Civil) 1920: *m.* 1919, the 7th Lord, who *d.* 1967.

COLLATERAL BRANCHES LIVING.
Descendants of the Hon. Mary Bruce, *OBE*, el. da. of 6th Lord, who *m.* Sir John Augustus Hope, 16th Bt. (cr. 1628):—
See Hope, Bt. (cr. 1628).

Grandson of the late Maj. Francis Walter Balfour, el. son of the late Francis Balfour, great-grandson of the late Lt.-Col. the Hon. John Balfour, 2nd son of 3rd Lord:—
Issue of the late Francis Balfour, *b.* 1867, *d.* 1926: *m.* 1903, Katharine Morgan, dau. of Harry Chubb, formerly of Burlingham, Chislehurst:—
Francis Keir, *b.* 1905; ed. at Eton, and at Clare Coll., Camb.: *m.* 1932, Katharine Augusta, da. of Sir George Alexander Dolby, of Silwood Park, Sunninghill, Berks. *Residence,*—Dirnanean, Blairgowrie, Perthshire.

Grandchildren of the late Francis Balfour (ante):—
Issue of the late Patrick Small Keir Balfour; *b.* 1910; *d.* 1967: *m.* 1936, Lila Camilla Spicer:—
Robert William Keir, *b.* 1942: *m.* 1964, Evelyn Mary Douglas, and has issue living, Michael Patrick Keir, *b.* 1965.——Frances Norah, *b.* 1941: *m.* 1965, Hugh Manning Tregarthen.——Sheila Katharine, *b.* 1946.

PREDECESSORS.—[1] *Sir* MICHAEL Balfour, *K.B.*, *P.C.*, Ambassador to the Duke of Tuscany and Lorraine, was cr. *Lord Balfour of Burleigh* (peerage of Scotland) 1607 ; *d.* 1619 ; *s.* by his only dau. [2] MARGARET, who *m.* Robert Arnot, who assumed the name of Balfour, and sat as Lord Balfour of Burleigh in the Scottish Parliament, of which he was President 1640-1 ; she *d.* 1663 ; *s.* by son [3] JOHN, 3rd Lord ; *d.* about 1696 ; *s.* by his son [4] ROBERT, 4th Lord ; *d.* 1713 ; *s.* by his son [5] ROBERT, 5th Lord, who previously to the death of his father had in 1709 been condemned to death for murder, but escaped from prison by exchanging clothes with his sister; he subsequently engaged in the rebellion of 1715, and in 1716 was attainted by Act of Parliament ; *d.s.p.* 1757 ; *s.* (but for the attainder) by his sister [6] MARGARET, *b.* 16— *d.* 1769 ; *s.* by her nephew [7] ROBERT (son of the Hon. Mary Balfour, who *m.* 1714, Brig.-Gen. Alexander Bruce of Kennet), *b.* 1718 ; a Judge of Court of Session with title of *Lord Kennet* 1764 : *m.* 1754, Helen, who *d.* 1786, dau. of George Abercromby of Tullibody ; *d.* 1785 ; *s.* by his son [8] ALEXANDER, *b.* 1755 : *m.* 1793, Hugh, who *d.* 1851, dau. of Hugh Blackburn, of Glasgow ; *d.* 1808 ; *s.* by his son [9] ROBERT, who claimed the lordship before the Committee for Privileges, House of Lords, but *d.* before a decision was made : *b.* 1794 : *m.* 1st, 1825, Anne, who *d.* 1846, dau. of William Murray, of Touchadam ; 2ndly, 1848, Jane Dalrymple Hamilton, who *d.* 19—, dau. of Sir James Fergusson of Kilkerran, 4th Bt. ; *d.* 1864 ; *s.* by his son [10] ALEXANDER HUGH, *K.T.*, *G.C.M.G.*, *G.C.V.O.*, *P.C.*, 6th Lord, whose peerage was allowed by House of Lords 1868, the attainder of 1715 having been reversed by Act of Parliament 1869 ; *b.* 1849 ; a Lord-in-Waiting to H.M. Queen Victoria 1887-88, Parliamentary Sec. to Board of Trade 1888-92. Sec. for Scotland with a seat in the Cabinet 1895-1903, and Lord Warden of the Stannaries and Rider and Master Forester of Dartmoor 1908-21 ; Capt. Roy. Co. of Archers (H.M. Body Guard for Scotland) : *m.* 1876, Lady Katherine Eliza Gordon, who *d.* 1931, dau. of 5th Earl of Aberdeen ; *d.* 1921 ; *s.* by his son [11] GEORGE JOHN GORDON, 7th Lord, *b.* 1883; Pres. of Inst. of Bankers 1948-49; Chm. of Kensington Housing Trust 1926-49, of Medical Research Council 1936-48, of Cttee, of London Clearing Bankers 1950-52, and of Lloyds Bank 1946-54; a Representative Peer for Scotland 1922-63: *m.* 1919, Violet Dorothy Evelyn, MBE, da. of the late Richard Henry Done, of Tarporley, Cheshire, *d.* 1967; *s.* by his el. son [12] ROBERT, 8th Lord and present peer.

BALFOUR OF INCHRYE, BARON. (Balfour.) [Baron U.K. 1945.]
God be with me.

HAROLD HARINGTON BALFOUR, *M.C.*, *P.C.*, 1st Baron, son of Col. Nigel Harington Balfour, O.B.E., of Belton, Camberley, Surrey ; *b.* Nov. 1st, 1897; ed. at Chilverton Elms, and at R.N. Coll., Osborne ; European War 1914-19 with 60th Rifles, R.F.C., and R.A.F. (M.C. and Bar, 1914-15 star, two medals); was Parliamentary Under-Sec. of State for Air 1938-44, and Min. Resident in W. Africa 1944-45; is a Freeman of City of London ; unsuccessfully contested Stratford Div. of W. Ham (*C*) Oct. 1924 ; sat as M.P. for Isle of Thanet Div. of Kent May 1929 to June 1945 ; cr. P.C. 1941, and *Baron Balfour of Inchrye*, of Shefford, co. Berks (peerage of United Kingdom) 1945: *m.* 1st, 1921, Diana Blanche (who obtained a divorce 1946), dau. of Sir Robert Grenville Harvey, 2nd Bt. [cr. 1868 (ext.)] ; 2ndly, 1947, Mary Ainslie, dau. of the late Baron Albert Profumo, K.C., and has issue by 1st and 2nd marriages.

Arms,—Argent, on a chevron indented sable between in chief a rose gules and in base a saltire couped azure, an otter's head erased of the first, a bordure engrailed of the third. *Crest,*—A dexter hand grasping an olive branch, all proper. *Supporters,*—*Dexter,* an otter per fess or and azure; *sinister,* a peregrine falcon proper, bells argent, jesses sable.

Residences,—End House, St. Mary Abbots Place, W.8; Tressady, Rogart, Sutherland. *Clubs,*—Carlton, Pratt's.

SON LIVING. (*By 1st marriage.*)

Hon. IAN, *b.* Dec. 21st, 1924 ; ed. at Eton, and at Magdalen Coll., Oxford ; European War 1942-5 with R.N.: *m.* 1953, Josephine Maria Jane, dau. of Morogh Wyndham Percy Bernard [see E. Bandon, colls.], and has issue living, Roxane, *b.* 1955. *Residence,*—10, Limerston St., SW10.

DAUGHTER LIVING. (*By 2nd marriage.*)

Hon. Mary Ann, *b.* 1949: *m.* 1974, the Hon. Martin Dewman Sutherland-Janson [see Cs. Sutherland] .

Balgonie, Lord, son of Earl of Leven and Melville.

BALLANTRAE, BARON. (Fergusson.) [Life Baron 1972.]
Sweeter out of difficulties

BERNARD EDWARD FERGUSSON, *KT*, *GCMG, GCVO, DSO, OBE,* 3rd son of the late Gen. Sir Charles Fergusson of Kilkerran, GCB, GCMG, DSO, MVO, LLD, 7th Bt.; *b.* May 6th, 1911; ed. at Eton; Hon.D.Litt St. Andrews, Hon. DCL Canterbury; Hon. Dr. Waikato; Hon. LLD Strathclyde, and Dundee; KStJ; Brig. (ret.) late The Black Watch; Col. The Black Watch since 1969; Gov.-Gen. of NZ 1962-67; Chm. of British Council since 1972; Chancellor of St. Andrews Univ. since 1973; Lord High Commr. to Gen. Assembly of Church of Scotland 1973-74, Middle East 1940-42, Burma 1943-44 (DSO); *cr.* DSO 1943, OBE (Mil.) 1950, GCMG 1962, GCVO 1963, *Baron Ballantrae,* of Auchairne, co. Ayr, and of Bay of Islands, NZ. (Life Baron) 1972, and KT 1974: *m.* 1950, Laura Margaret, da. of the late Lt.-Col. Arthur Morton Grenfell, DSO, TD [V. Cobham, colls.], and has issue.

Arms,—Quarterly: 1st grand quarter, azure, a buckle argent between three boars' heads couped or, armed and langued gules, *Fergusson;* 2nd grand quarter, counterquartered, 1st and 4th, argent, an eagle displayed sable, beaked and membered gules, *Ramsay;* 2nd and 3rd, gules, a chevron betwixt three fleur-de-lys or, *Broun of Colston;* 3rd grand quarter, counter-quartered, 1st and 4th, or, a lion rampant couped at all joints gules, within a double tressure flory counter-flory azure, *Maitland;* 2nd and 3rd, argent a shakefork sable, *Cuninghame of Glencairn;* 4th grand quarter, or, on a saltire azure nine lozenges of the first, on a bordure of the second eight mullets and as many boars' heads erased, alternated argent, *Dalrymple of New Hailes.* *Crest*—A bee on a thistle proper. *Supporters,*— *Dexter* a soldier of the 42nd Highlanders, The Black Watch (Royal Highland Regiment), attired in the full dress uniform of that Regiment, including sporran and feather bonnet as worn in the early XXth century; *Sinister*, a Maori Chieftain attired about the waist in a horowai (or mat) argent, embellished with strings sable, and over his left shoulder another horowai or, also embellished with strings sable, and embroidered sable and gules, two huia feathers in his hair, his face tattooed, a kuru (greenstone pendant) suspended from his dexter ear, his sinister hand grasping the shaft, and his dexter hand the tuft, of a taiaha (spear) held in bend sinister, point downwards proper.

Residence,—Auchairne, Ballantrae, Ayrshire. *Clubs*,—White's, New.

SON LIVING.
Hon. George Duncan, *b*. 1955; ed. at Eton.

BALNIEL, BARON. (Lindsay.) [Life Baron 1974.]
See E. Crawford and Balcarres.

BALOGH, BARON. (Balogh.) [Life Baron 1968.]

THOMAS BALOGH, son of the late Emil Balogh, of Budapest, and Holland Park, W11; *b*. Nov. 2nd, 1905; ed. at the Gymnasium of Budapest Univ., and Budapest, Berlin and Harvard Univs.; a Fellow of Balliol Coll., Oxford since 1945, and Reader in Economics, Oxford since 1960; Economic Adviser to the Cabinet 1964-67, and Consultant to the Prime Min. 1968; Economic Adviser to UN Agencies and to Foreign Govs. since 1954; Min. of State for Energy since 1974; *cr. Baron Balogh*, of Hampstead, in Greater London (Life Baron) 1968: *m*. 1st, 1945 (*m*. diss. 1970), Penelope, who *d*. 1975, da. of the Rev. Henry Bernard Tower, and widow of Oliver Gatty; 2ndly, 1970, Catherine Storr, MRCS, LRCP, and has issue by 1st m.

Residences,—Old Bank House, Hampstead High St., NW3; The Cottage, Greenfields, Watlington, Oxon.; Fongives, Campagne, Dordogne, France. *Clubs*,—Reform, Little French.

SONS LIVING. (*By 1st m*.).
Hon. Stephen Bernard, *b*. 1946; ed. at Westminster and Balliol Coll, Oxford.
Hon. Christopher Thomas, *b*. 1948; ed. at Westminster and King's Coll., Camb.

DAUGHTER LIVING. (*By 1st m*.).
Hon. Penelope Kathryn Teresa, *b*. 1957.

BANBURY OF SOUTHAM, BARON. (Banbury.) [Baron U.K. 1924, Bt. U.K] 1902.]

CHARLES WILLIAM BANBURY, 2nd Baron and 2nd Baronet; *b*. (*posthumous*) May 18th, 1915; *s*. 1936; ed. at Stowe; late Capt. 12th Lancers; a Member of Glos. Co. Council, and Conservator of R. Thames; 1939-45 War (despatches); a DL of Glos.: *m*. 1945 (m. diss. 1958), Hilda Ruth, da. of the late A. H. R. Carr, of Malone, Belfast, and has issue.

Arms,—Ermine, a cross patée between five mullets of six points each within an annulet, three in chief and two in base, all gules. **Crest**,—A demi-antelope proper, supporting between its feet a cross patée as in the arms and charged on the shoulder with a garb gules. **Supporters**,—On either side a collie dog proper, each charged on the shoulder with a cross patée gules.

Residence,—Daglingworth Place, Cirencester, Gloucestershire. *Club*,—Bath.

SON LIVING.
Hon. CHARLES WILLIAM, *b*. July 29th, 1953.
DAUGHTERS LIVING.
Hon. Carolyn, *b*. 1947.
Hon. Anna Josephine, *b*. 1950.

SISTER LIVING. (*Raised to the rank of a Baron's daughter* 1938.)
Hon. Mary Heritage, *b*. 1914: *m*. 1st, 1941, Siegfried Buchmayr; 2ndly, 1964, Richard D. Greenogh of 120, East 79 St., New York NY 10026 USA, and has issue living, (by 1st marriage) Siegfried Beale, *b*. 1942,—Norbert Gant (triplet), *b*. 1942,—Charles Rupert (triplet), *b*. 1942.

PREDECESSOR.—[1] *Rt. Hon*. FREDERICK GEORGE Banbury, *P.C*., el. son of the late Frederick Banbury, of Shirley House, Surrey: *b*. 1850; M.P. for Peckham Div. of Camberwell (*C*.) 1892-1906, and for City of London 1906-1924; *cr. Baron Banbury of Southam*, of Southam, co.

Warwick (peerage of United Kingdom) 1924 : *m.* 1873, Elizabeth Rosa, who *d.* 1930, dau. and co-heiress of the late Thomas Barbot Beale, of Brettenham Park, Suffolk ; *d.* 1936 ; *s.* by his grandson [2] CHARLES WILLIAM (son of the late Capt. Charles William Banbury, Coldstream Guards (only son of 1st Baron), who *d.* (killed in action during European War) 1914, 2nd Baron and present peer.

BANDON, EARL OF. (Bernard.) [Earl I. 1800.]

VIRTUS PROBATA FLOREBIT

Proved virtue will flourish.

PERCY RONALD GARDNER BERNARD, *G.B.E., C.B., C.V.O., D.S.O.,* 5th Earl ; *b.* Aug. 30th, 1904 ; *s.* 1924 ; ed. at Wellington Coll. ; Air Ch. Marshal R.A.F. (ret.) ; was Air Officer Comdg. 224th Group R.A.F. 1944-45 ; commanded Roy. Observer Corps 1945-48 ; Air Officer Comdg. No. 2 Group R.A.F. 1950-51, and No. 11 Group 1951-3, Assist. Ch. of Air Staff (Training) 1953-6, Com.-in-Ch. of 2nd Tactical Air Force, Com. of 2nd Allied Tactical Air Force 1955-7, Com.-in-Ch., Far East Air Force 1957-60; and appointed Com. of Allied Air Forces, Central Europe 1961-63; European War 1939-45 in S.-E. Asia and Burma as acting Air Vice-Marshal (despatches thrice, D.S.O., C.B., American D.F.C. and Bronze star); cr. D.S.O. 1940, C.B. (Mil.) 1945, C.V.O. 1953, K.B.E. (Mil.) 1957, G.B.E. (Mil.) 1960: *m.* 1st, 1933 (marriage dissolved 1946), (Maybel) Elizabeth, da. of Raymond Playfair, of Nairobi, Kenya; 2ndly, 1946, Mrs. Lois White, da. of Francis Russell, of Victoria, Australia, and has issue by 1st marriage.

Arms,—Argent, on a bend azure three escallops of the field. **Crest.**—A demi-lion argent holding a snake proper. **Supporters,**—*Dexter,* a stag argent, attired, unguled, ducally collared and chained or; *sinister,* a unicorn argent armed unguled crined tufted and ducally collared and chained or.

Seat,—Castle Bernard, Bandon, co. Cork.

DAUGHTERS LIVING. (By 1st marriage.)

Lady Jennifer Jane, *b.* 1935.
Lady Frances Elizabeth, *b.* 1943: *m.* 1967, Paul Mark Carter, of 2, Briar Walk, SW15, and has issue living, Emma Margaret, *b.* 1969,—Annabelle Petrea, *b.* 1971.

BROTHER LIVING. (Raised to the rank of an Earl's son 1925.)

Hon. CHARLES BRODRICK AMYAS, *C.B.E.* (twin), *b.* Aug. 30th, 1904; ed. at Wellington Coll.; late Maj. 1st Bn. Oxfordshire and Bucks LI; Chm. of E. Suffolk Co. Council 1967; 1939-41 War (despatches); CBE (Civil) 1962: *m.* 1937, the Hon. Ursula Margaret Vivian, who *d.* 1963, da. of 3rd Baron Swansea. *Residence,*—By the Crossways, Kelsale, Saxmundham, Suffolk.

SISTER LIVING. (Raised to the rank of an Earl's daughter 1925.)

Lady Cynthia Lettice Margaret, *b.* 1905 : *m.* 1st, 1925 (marriage dissolved 1936), Lieut.-Col. Francis Christian Darby Tothill, Rifle Brig. ; 2ndly, 1947, Air Commodore Lionel Guy Stanhope Payne, CBE, MC, AFC, who *d.* 1965, and has issue living, (by 1st marriage) Betsann, *b.* 1927: *m.* 1947, Capt. Matthew Page Page Wood, Coldstream Guards [see Page-Wood, Bt.]. *Residence,*—Palazana San Petro de Alcantara, Malaga, Spain.

COLLATERAL BRANCH LIVING.

Grandson of the late Rt. Rev. the Hon. Charles Brodrick Bernard, DD, Lord Bishop of Tuam, son of 2nd Earl:—

Issue of the late Percy Brodrick Bernard, *b.* 1844. *d.* 1912: *m.* 1st, 1872, Isabel Emma Beatrice, who *d.* 1876, dau. of the late John Newton Lane, of King's Bromley, Lichfield ; 2ndly, 1880, Mary Lissey, who *d.* 1898, dau. of the late Denis Kirwan, of Castle Hacket, co. Galway ; 3rdly, 1900, Eva, who *d.* 1950 (having *m.* 2ndly, 1919, the Hon. Charles Hedley Strutt, who *d.* 1926 [B. Rayleigh]), dau. of the late Henry Hoare, of Staplehurst, Kent:—

(By 3rd marriage) Morogh Wyndham Percy, *b.* 1902 ; ed. at Wellington Coll. : *m.* 1929, the Hon. Diana Pearl Dundas, dau. of 7th Viscount Melville, and has issue living, Josephine Maria Jane (*Hon. Mrs. Ian Balfour*), *b.* 1934 : *m.* 1953, the Hon. Ian Balfour, only son of the 1st Baron Balfour of Inchrye. *Residence,*—8, Bloomfield Terrace, SW1.

PREDECESSORS.—[1] FRANCIS Bernard, son of the late James Bernard ; *b.* 1755 ; M.P. for Bandon Bridge ; cr. *Baron Bandon* (peerage of Ireland) 1793, *Viscount Bandon* (peerage of Ireland) 1795, and *Viscount Bernard and Earl of Bandon* (peerage of Ireland) 1800 : *m.* 1784, Lady Catherine Henrietta Boyle, who *d.* 1815, only dau. of 2nd Earl of Shannon ; *d.* 1830 ; *s.* by his el. son [2] JAMES, 2nd Earl ; *b.* 1785 ; sometime M.P. for co. Cork, Lord-Lieut. of Cork, and a Representative Peer : *m.* 1809, Mary Susan, who *d.* 1870, dau. of the late Hon and Most Rev. Charles Brodrick, Lord Archbishop of Cashel [V. Midleton] ; *d.* 1856 ; *s.* by his el. son [3] FRANCIS, 3rd Earl, *b.* 1810 ; was M.P. for Bandon 1842-56, Lord-Lieut. of co. Cork; and a Representative Peer: *m.* 1832, Catherine Mary, who *d.* 1873, dau. of Thomas Whitmore of Apley, Salop ; *d.* 1877 ; *s.* by his son [4] JAMES FRANCIS, *K.P.,* 4th Earl, *b.* 1850 ; High Sheriff of Co. and City of Cork 1875 : *m.* 1876, the Hon. Georgina Dorothea Harriet Evans-Freke, *C.B.E.,* who *d.* 1942, dau. of 7th Baron Carbery ; *d.* 1924 ; *s.* by his cousin [5] PERCY RONALD GARDNER (el. son of the late Lieut.-Col. Ronald Percy Hamilton Bernard, great-grandson of 2nd Earl), 5th Earl and present peer ; also Viscount Bernard, Viscount Bandon and Baron Bandon.

BANGOR, VISCOUNT.   (Ward.)   [Viscount I. 1781.]

Salvation beneath the Cross.

EDWARD HENRY HAROLD WARD, 7th
Viscount, b. Nov. 5th, 1905 ; s. 1950 ;
ed. at Harrow and at R.M.A.; is a
Broadcaster : m. 1st, 1933, Elizabeth
(who obtained a divorce 1937), dau. of
Thomas Balfour, J.P., of Wrockwar-
dine Hall, Wellington, Salop: 2ndly,
1937, May Kathleen, who d. 1969, da.
of W. Middleton, of Shanghai; 3rdly,
1947, Leila Mary (who d. 1959, and
from whom he had obtained a divorce
1951), da. of David Rimington Heaton,
DSO, of Brookfield, Crownhill, S.
Devon; 4thly, 1951, Marjorie Alice
(SIMPSON), da. of the late Peter Banks,
of St. Leonards-on-Sea, and has issue
by 3rd and 4th marriages.

Arms,—Quarterly : 1st and 4th azure, a cross
patonce or, Ward; 2nd and 3rd gules, three
cinquefoils ermine, on a chief of the second a
man's heart of the first, Hamilton. Crest,—A
man's head couped at the shoulders affrontée
proper, wreathed about the temples or and
azure, and adorned with three ostrich feathers. Supporters,—Dexter, a Knight in complete armour
proper, charged on the breast with a cross moline gules, behind him a flowing crimson robe, a cross
moline argent on its sinister side.   On the helmet a plume of feathers of the last, his dexter hand resting
on a drawn sword point downwards proper, pommel and hilt or ; sinister, a Turkish prince vested in
robes of blue and gold, white stockings, yellow sandals, gold sash and fringe round the waist, behind
him a loose brown robe of fur, on the head a white turban with black feathers, and his hands in
fetters proper.
Residence,—105, Devonshire Mews South, W1.

SONS LIVING. (By 3rd marriage.)
Hon. WILLIAM MAXWELL DAVID, b. Aug. 9th, 1948; ed. at St. Edward's Sch., Oxford.
(By 4th marriage.)
Hon. Edward Nicholas, b. 1953.
DAUGHTER LIVING. (By 4th marriage.)
Hon. Sarah, b. 1951.
SISTERS LIVING.
Hon. Mary Helen Kathleen, b. 1909: m. 1934, Peter Mansfield Weatherby, and has issue living, Simon
    Maxwell (The Old Rectory, Sutton-under-Brailes, Banbury, Oxon.), b. 1938: m. 1964, Caroline Anne,
    yr. da. of the late Lt.-Col. Conolly Rober. McCausland, MO, DL, JP [see E. Mount Edgcumbe], and
    has issue living, Maxwell Peter, b. 1965, Richard Conolly b. 1970, Rebecca Margaret b. 1966,—Juliet
    Mary b. 1935: m. 1963, Florin Virgil Cucos, of 41, Bromfelde Rd., SW4, and has issue living, Peter
    Constantin b. 1964, Stefan Crosby b. 1968, Mihail Roman b. 1972, Maria Emma b. 1964. Residence,—
    Forest Hill Cottage, Chute Forest, Andover, Hants.
Hon. Helen Elizabeth, b. 1912.   Residence,—7, Sydney Street, Chelsea, S.W.3.
Hon. Margaret Bertha Meriel, b. 1914: m. 1st, 1938, Major Desmond Charles Forde. Coldstream
    Guards, who obtained a divorce 1947: 2ndly, 1947 (m. diss. 1962) Gavin Robert Sligh; 3rdly,
    1969, Maj. Dennis Eric Smith, of Much More, E. Garston, Berks., and has issue living, (by 1st marriage)
    Patrick Mathew Desmond (Seaforde, co. Down), b. 1940: m. 1965, Lady Anthea Geraldine Lowry-
    Corry, da. of 7th Earl of Belmore, and has issue living, Mathew Galbraith b. 1967, Charles Patrick
    b. 1972, Emily Louise b. 1966,—Sylvia Helena, b. 1938.

COLLATERAL BRANCHES LIVING.
Issue of the late Lieut.-Gen. the Hon. Bernard Matthew Ward, C.B., 4th son of
3rd Viscount, b. 1831, d. 1918: m. 1st, 1865, Emily Maria, who d. 1868, dau. of
J. La Touche, J.P., D.L., of Harristown, co. Kildare ; 2ndly, 1873, Laura, who
d. 1928, el. dau. of Maj.-Gen. Evan Maberly, C.B.:—
(By 2nd m.) Constance Katharine (Roman River, Layer de la Haye, Colchester, Essex), b. 1891:
    m. 1926, Paul André Pilette, who d. 1972.

Grandchildren of the late Lieut.-Gen. the Hon. Bernard Matthew Ward, C.B.
(ante) :—
Issue of the late Capt. Herbert Bernard Ward, b. 1876, d. 1957 : m. 1918, Evelyn Annie,
who d. 1925, dau. of the Rt. Hon. Sir Daniel Dixon, P.C., M.P., 1st Bt. :—
Diana, b. (Dec.) 1918; 1940-45 War with St. John Ambulance Brig. and WRNS: m. 1967, W. R. M.
    Gemmill, of Johannesburg.   Residence,—12, Radnor Walk, SW3.

Issue of the late Maxwell William Bernard Ward, b. 1889, d. 1960: m. 1st, 1919, Ruth
    Elizabeth (who obtained a divorce 1931), only dau. of the late John Flasby
    Lawrance Whittingdale, O.B.E., M.D., of Sherborne, Dorset, and Thornton-in-
    Lonsdale, Yorkshire ; 2ndly, 1934, Josephine, youngest dau. of the Rev. Hugh
    Robert Coulthard, Hon. Canon of Truro, and V. of Breage, Cornwall, and widow
    of Guy Nelson Brown :—
(By 1st m.) Bernard Maxwell, MVO (Rockalls Hall, Polstead, Colchester, Essex; Cavalry, Garrick
    and New Clubs), b. 1921; ed. at Sherborne; Maj. (ret.) RHA; 1939-45 War with Duke of Lancaster
    Yeo., and Roy. Bucks Yeo.; MVO (4th class) 1952: m. 1948, Sunniva, who d. 1962, el. da. of Maj. Sir
    Basil Hamilton Hebden Neven-Spence, and has issue living, Maxwell Colin Bernard, b. 1949.——John
    Maxwell b. 1922; ed. at Sherborne; MROS England, and LRCP London 1945: m. 1948, Evelyn
    Millicent, da. of J. P. Usher, and has issue living, Peter Evan, b. 1949,—Michael John, b. 1951,—
    Nicholas Crosbie, b. 1956,—Philippa Jane, b. 1957.   Address,—PO Box 72, Que Que, Rhodesia.

Grandsons of the late Edward Crosbie Ward, son of the late Maj.-Gen. Sir Edward
Wolstenholme Ward, K.C.M.G. (infra) :—
Issue of the late Major John Crosbie Ward, S. Wales Borderers, b. 1911, d. 1952 : m. 1935,
    Margaret Llewellyn (Flat E, Linley Hall, Broseley, Salop), da. of the late Rev. Llewellyn
    Christopher Watson Bullock, of Gt. Wigborough, Colchester:—
Christopher John Robert Crosbie (c/o Glyn Mills Co., Kirkland House, Whitehall, SW1), b. 1937;
    ed. at Wellington Coll.; Maj. Bde. of Gurkhas.——David Edward Crosbie, b. 1941; ed. at Wellington
    Coll.

Granddaughter of the late Maj.-Gen. Sir Edward Wolstenholme Ward, K.C.M.G.,
son of the late Hon. John Petty Ward, B.C.S., brother of 3rd Viscount :—
Issue of the late Lieut.-Col. Guy Bernard Campbell Ward, D.S.O., b. 1875, d. 1933 : m.
    1904, Beatrice Constance Charlotte, who d. 1959, dau. of the late Hon. Charles Lennox
    Butler [B. Dunboyne, colls.] :—

Constance Isabel (37, Cromwell Grove, W6), *b.* 1905: *m.* 1932, Charles Lawrence Mackness, Lieut. The Buffs, who *d.* (killed in action) 1943, and has issue living, Caroline Anne, *b.* 1940: *m.* 1968, John Sullivan, of 37, Cromwell Grove, W6, and has issue living, Mercedes *b.* 1969.

Grandchildren of the late Sir William Erskine Ward, K.C.S.I., son of the late Hon. John Petty Ward, B.C.S. (ante):—

Issue of the late John Petty Ward, *b.* **1871,** *d.* **1956 :** *m.* **1906, Rose Gladys May, who** *d.* **1937, dau. of the Rev. Richard Marsh Marsh-Dunn, V. of St. Nicholas'. Shaldon, Devon :—**
Sir Richard Erskine, *KCB*, *DSO*, *MC*, (c/o Williams & Glyn's Bank, Ltd., Kirkland House, Whitehall, SW1) *b.* 1917; ed. at Marlborough; Gen. late RTC; Vice-Adj-Gen. 1968-70, and Cdr. British Forces, Hong Kong 1970-73; Ch. of Personnel and Logistics MOD, and Repres. Col. Cdr. RTR since 1974; Col. Comdt., RTR since 1970; 1939-45 War in Middle East (despatches twice MC, DSO and Bar); Korea 1952-53 (despatches); Belgian Croix de Guerre with Palm; Chevalier of Order of Leopold II of Belgium with Palm; DSO and Bar 1943, CB (Mil) 1969, KCB (Mil) 1971: *m.* 1947, Stella Elizabeth, da. of the late Brig. Philip Neville Ellis, RA, of Rhyllech, nr. Pwellheli, Caernarvon, and has issue living, Anthony Richard Bangor, *b.* 1960,—Jeremy Neville, *b.* 1961,—Léonie, *b.* 1949,—Stephanie Rachel, *b.* 1952.——Myrtle Josephine, *b.* 1907: *m.* 1st, 1929 (m. diss. 1972), Donald Stuart Denholm Fraser; 2ndly, 1972, Theodore Aldred Raymond, of Dale Cottage, Great Langdale, Westmorland, and has issue living, (by 1st m.), June, *b.* 1930: *m.* 1963, Allen Hans Cull, of 5, Combemartin Rd., Southfields, SW18, and has issue living, Zoë Gail, *b.* 1970,—Sally, *b.* 1936: *m.* 1971, Clive Freshwater, of The Hall, Kincraig, Inverness-shire, and has issue living, Duncan *b.* 1971,—Joanna, *b.* 1950.

Issue of the late Noel Edward Ward, *b.* **1872,** *d.* **1944:** *m.* **1st, 1898, Jessie Mabel Wood, who** *d.* **1968, da. of James B. Wood, of Woodbine Tea Estate, Assam; 2ndly, 1922, Muriel, da. of Edward Dalton, of Leeds, Yorkshire:—**
(By 1st m.) James Palmer (Silver Stream, Ballywaltrim, Bray, co. Wicklow), *b.* 1902: *m.* 1931, Yvonne Lockington, da. of Cedric Lockington Flood, of Dublin, and has issue living, Michael James (20, Cluny Grove, Killiney, co. Dublin), *b.* 1934; ed. at Aldenham: *m.* 1959, Jocelyn Mary, da. of Arthur George Kelly, of Athlone, and has issue living, Jeremy Charles Arthur James *b.* 1960, Alexandra Rowena *b.* 1963,—Patrick Erskine, *b.* 1937; ed. at Nautical Coll., Pangbourne: *m.* 1962, Eldrith Janet, da. of John Bararis Delbridge, of Bulawayo, and has issue living, Richard Bangor *b.* 1967, Julia *b.* 1963, Jannette *b.* 1964.——Jack Lionel (Merrydown, Yew Tree Lane, Rotherfield. Sussex), *b.* 1910; ed. at Bradfield: *m.* 1939, Beatrice Mary Caroline, da. of George Austin Wareham, of King's Langley, and has issue living, Edward Nicholas *b.* 1945; ed. at Winchester, and Trin. Coll., Camb.: *m.* 1973, Felicity Lilian Beatrice, da. of John Richard Gibbs, of Bromley, and has issue living, Lucy Beatrice Alice, *b.* 1974,—Gillian Elizabeth *b.* 1939.——(By 2nd m.) Noel Erskine, *b.* 1925; ed. at Marlborough; a Co. Dir.: *m.* 1948, June Margaret, da. of Albert Ellerton-Long, of Gravesend, and has issue living, Jonathan Philip, *b.* 1951; ed. at St. Edmund's Sch.,—Graeme David, *b.* 1953; RN.

Issue of the late Lancelot Bangor Ward, *b.* **1883,** *d.* **1954:** *m.* **1910, Agnes Frances Jean, who** *d.* **1959, dau. of the Rev. Richard Marsh Marsh-Dunn (ante) :—**
Margaret Jean, *b.* 1920: *m.* 1945, Walter Ralph Melford, US Army, of 5, Ravine Drive, Hastings-on-Hudson, NY, USA, and has issue living, Anthony George Bangor, *b.* 1947: *m.* 1974, Mary Elizabeth Niedringhaus, of St. Louis, Mo., USA,—Michael Ralph, *b.* 1950: *m.* 1974, Doborah Hayes, of Massapequa Park, New York,—Greta Jean, *b.* 1947: *m.* 1973, Dr. Reed Kindermann, of Chatham, New Jersey.——Pamela Erskine (twin), *b.* 1920: *m.* 1946, James Routledge, and has issue living, David Patrick, *b.* 1952,—Martin John, *b.* 1954. *Residence,*—Tavycot, 56, Salisbury Av., Cheam, Surrey.

Granddaughter of the late Crosbie Ward, 3rd son of the late Rev. the Hon. Henry Ward, brother of 3rd Viscount:—

Issue of the late Edward William Townsend Ward, *b.* **1861,** *d.* **1921** : *m.* **1895, Florence who** *d.* **1946, dau. of the late Alexander Morten, of 21, Hogarth Road, Earl's Court S.W., and widow of Ogle Peck, of Toronto, Canada :—**
Margaret Flora, *b.* 1899.

Grandchildren of the late John Hamilton Ward, 4th son of the late Rev. the Hon. Henry Ward (ante):—

Issue of the late Edward Robert Ward, *b.* **1859,** *d.* **1941:** *m.* **1901, Edith Georgina, who** *d.* **1948, dau. of Albert George Sheriff :—**
Albert Edward Hamilton, *b.* 1902: *m.* 1932, Violet Kate, da. of John Henderson Jones, and has issue living, John Albert (4, Rectory Court, Lewknor, Oxon.), *b.* 1933: *m.* 1956, Judith Mary, da. of Richard R. Lamdin, and has issue living, Stuart John *b.* 1964, Fiona Marion *b.* 1959.——Robert Hamilton, *b.* 1906. *Residence,*—Woodside, Warren Rd., Banstead, Surrey.——John Hamilton (Tredole, Prussia Cove, Rosudgeon, Penzance, Cornwall), *b.* 1907: *m.* 1939, Peggy Elizabeth Louise, da. of William Allen Hazeldine, and has issue living, Edward Hamilton (14, Millbank Demesne Rd., Wallington, Surrey), *b.* 1944: *m.* 1971, Jean Audrey, da. of Alfred Hudson,—Roger Hamilton (42, Redruth House, Grange Rd., Sutton, Surrey), *b.* 1947.——Marcia Hamilton, *b.* 1904; BA (Honours), London. *Residence,*—Woodside, Warren Rd., Banstead, Surrey.

Issue of the late Arabella Crosbie Ward, *b.* **1876,** *d.* **1960** : *m.* **1902, the Rev. Horace Rollo Meyer, Hon. Canon of St. Albans, who** *d.* **1953 :—**
Horace Noel Denys, *b.* 1903 ; ed. at Haileybury : *m.* 1st, 1933 (marriage dissolved 1942), Phyllis Rosemary, dau. of the late Arthur Wild, I.C.S. (ret.), of Fairfield, Upper Basildon; 2ndly, 1943, Bridget Mary, dau. of the late F. H. Ellis, of 5, South Road, The Park, Nottingham, and has issue living, (by 2nd m.) Anthony Rollo, *b.* 1947: *m.* 1974, Joan, da. of L. M. Rolls,—David Francis (twin), *b.* 1947,—Alice Favell Margaret, *b.* 1944: *m.* 1968, Graham Thomas Kenyon, of Pix Hall, Hawkhurst, Kent, and has issue living, Peter Thomas *b.* 1974, Emily Favella *b.* 1970, Belinda Alice *b.* 1971. *Residence,*—16, Ravens Croft, Eastbourne, Sussex.——Rollo John Oliver, *OBE* (Little Scotland Farm, Panborough, Wedmore, Somerset), *b.* 1905; ed. at Haileybury, and at Pembroke Coll., Camb. (MA); founder and formerly Headmaster of Millfield Sch.; formerly Fl.-Lt. RAFVR; OBE (Civil) 1967: *m.* 1931, Joyce Evelyn, da. of Richard Symons, and has issue living, Jillian Rollo Dawn, *b.* 1932: *m.* 1958, Albert Prestwich, MB, BS, of Hunters Lodge, St. Andrew's Lane, Titchmarsh, nr. Kettering, Northants, and has issue living, Oliver David Warren *b.* 1962, Matthew Paul Alexander *b.* 1965, Isobel Valerie Ward *b.* 1960,—Jacqueline Valerie Fay, *b.* 1933: *m.* 1955, Capt. Reginald Nicholas Mander, of Rowan House, 68, Pierrefondes Av., Farnborough, Hants., and has issue living, Brian Anthony *b.* 1956, Julian Nicholas *b.* 1960, Suzanne Jillian *b.* 1957.——Derek Leycester Rutherford, *b.* 1913; ed. at Haileybury; is an AMIEE: *m.* 1st, 1939 (m. diss. 1951), Alison Moya (Jane), da. of Lt.-Col. J. A. Garton; 2ndly, 1953, Valerie Helen Gove, *BSc*, and has issue living, (by 1st m.) Denys James Rollo, *b.* 1943. *Residence,*—East House, Nempnett Thrubwell, Chew Stoke, Bristol.——Constance Evelyn (*Hon. Mrs. Bertie Ponsonby*), *b.* 1907: *m.* 1933, the Hon. Bertie Brabazon Ponsonby, who *d.* 1967 [see E. Bessborough]. *Residence,*—44 Hallmores, St. Catharine's Rd., Broxbourne, Herts.

Grandchildren of the late Rev. the Hon. Henry Ward (ante):—

Issue of the late Thomas Lawrence Frederick Ward, *b.* **1837,** *d.* **1926:** *m.* **1871, Elizabeth Mary, who** *d.* **1927, dau. of David Green, formerly of Nelson, New Zealand :—**
Mary Clifford, *b.* 1880: *m.* 1907, William Richard Stanley Hickson, who *d.* 1930, and has issue living, Lawrence Stanley, *b.* 1910,—Mary Clifford, *b.* 1912: *m.* 1945, Gerald Frodsham Watkinson, of 98, Donald St., Karori, Wellington, NZ, and has issue living, Gerald Clifford *b.* 1951, Edward Paul *b.* 1955, Jan Elizabeth *b.* 1949,—Alison May, *b.* 1918: *m.* 1945, Samuel Whaler Burkitt, of 3, Minimbah Rd., Northbridge 2063, Sailor Bay, Sydney, Australia, and has issue living, Janice Anne *b.* 1947. *Residence,*—97, Webb St., Wellington, NZ.

Granddaughter of the late Francis Michael Ward (infra):—
Issue of the late Basil Edward Ward, *b.* 1886, *d.* 1953: *m.* 1912, Hazel C. Smith, who *d.* 1948:—
Caroline Anne (624, San Miguel Av., Berkeley, Cal., USA), *b.* 1914: *m.* 1st, 1939, Robert Frederick McKean, who *d.* 1966; 2ndly, 1967, Darrell Wiltse Walker, and has issue living (by 1st m.), Robert Basil, *b.* 1943,—Barbara Anne, *b.* 1940,—Patricia Ann, *b.* 1951.

Granddaughter of the late Rev. the Hon. Henry Ward (ante):—
Issue of the late Francis Michael Ward, *b.* 1847, *d.* 1903: *m.* 1875, **Anne Jane, who** *d.* 1934, dau. of the late James Clarke, of Felmingham, Norfolk:—
Muriel May, *b.* 1876: *m.* 1906, William Somerville Clarke, and has issue living, Francis Woodchurch, *b.* 1907,—Philip, *b.* 1910,—Robert, *b.* 1914,—Harriet Fay, *b.* 1908.

Granddaughters of the late Thomas Lawrence Frederick Ward (ante):—
Issue of the late Frederic Valentine Ward, *b.* 1878, *d.* 1960 : *m.* 1908, Florence Grace, who *d.* 1961, dau. of James Dalziel, of Auckland, New Zealand :—
Kathleen Florence Mary, *b.* 1909.——Doreen Mabel Valerie, *b.* 1915. *Residence,*—

Grandchildren of the late Lieut.-Col. Bernard Edward Ward, son of the late Rev. Bernard John Ward, 3rd son of the late Col. the Rt. Hon. Robert Ward, 3rd son of 1st Viscount:—
Issue of the late Capt. Bernard John Hamilton Ward, O.B.E., R.N., *b.* 1875, *d.* 1938 : *m.* 1908, Annie Lilias (of Thames Cottage, Wallingford, Berks.), dau. of the late Ralph Dalyell, C.B. [E. Warwick, colls.] :—
Bernard Ralph Henry, *O.B.E.* (of Trotts Close, Trotts Lane, Westerham, Kent), *b.* 1911; Lt.-Cdr. R.N. (ret.); entered Executive Class, Home Civil Ser. 1957; O.B.E. (Mil.) 1946: *m.* 1st, 1943 (marriage dissolved 1951), Tamara Estya Jasvoin; 2ndly, 1955, Marian Violet, who *d.* 1958, dau. of the late Capt. Percy William Rimington, O.B.E., R.N.; 3rdly, 1961, Daphne Thalia, dau. of John Lumsden, M.B.E., Vice-Consul, Casablanca, and has issue living, (by 3rd marriage) Nicholas Ralph Dalyell, *b.* 1964,—Annie Christabel, *b.* 1965.——Barbara Mary (*Lady Hedges*), *b.* 1910: *m.* 1st, 1940, Lt.-Cdr. Richard Scobell Palairet, R.N., who *d.* 1953; 2ndly, 1957, Sir John Francis Hedges, CBE, of St. Nicholas, High St., Wallingford, Berks.

Grandson of the late Adm. Thomas Le Hunte Ward, CB, son of the late Rev. Bernard John Ward (ante):—
Issue of the late Capt. John Richard Le Hunte Ward, O.B.E., R.N., *b.* 1870, *d.* 1953 : *m.* 1905, Violet Ella Mary, who *d.* 1962, dau. of the late Lieut.-Col. Bernard Edward Ward [V. Bangor] :—
Edward Le Hunte, *b.* 1906 ; Lieut.-Col. (retired) late Roy. Norfolk Regt. ; European War 1939-45 : *m.* 1946, Mary Flora, dau. of the late Capt. William Balfour Macdonald, D.S.O., R.N. *Residence,*—Brackencombe House, Ashburton, S. Devon.

Grandson of the late Capt. John Richard Le Hunte Ward, O.B.E., R.N. (ante):—
Issue of the late Maj. Michael Bernard John Ward, *b.* 1910, *d.* 1963: *m.* 1944, Marjory, who *d.* 1966, widow of Capt. A. T. R. Symonds, Queen's Regt.:—
John Michael Barrie, *b.* 1945; ed. at Wellington.

Grandchildren of the late Lt. Robert Frederick Ward, RN, only son of the late Vice-Adm. James Hamilton Ward, 5th son of the late Col. the Rt. Hon. Robert Ward (ante):—
Issue of the late Maj. Hamilton Frederick Ward, *b.* 1880, *d.* 1971: *m.* 1913, Violet Enid Jane who *d.* 1972, da. of the late Sir Henry Conway Belfield, KCMG:—
John Frederick, *b.* 1923; Capt. late Irish Guards; 1939-45 War: *m.* 1950, Pamela Swinton, da. of Lt.-Col. G. A. Swinton Home, of Soy, Kenya, and has issue living, Edward, *b.* 1958,—Sarah, *b.* 1953. ——Sheila Marie Jane, *b.* 1914: *m.* 1939, Alexander Frederick Reynard, of 41, Marais St., Pretoria, S. Africa, and has issue living, Edward Anthony, *b.* 1945: *m.* 1969, Margaret Marian, da. of Thomas Allan Fairbairn, of Standalane, Peebles, and has issue living, Iain Michael *b.* 1971,—John William, *b.* 1947,—Monica Mary, *b.* 1942.

Granddaughter of the late William Robert Ward, 6th son of the late Col. the Rt. Hon. Robert Ward (ante):—
Issue of the late Lieut.-Col. Edward Ward, M.B.E., *b.* 1852, *d.* 1929; *m.* 1900, Harriette Caroline Adeline (Etta), who *d.* 1937, dau. of the late John Steuart Maconchy.
Charlotte Hazel, *b.* 1900. *Residence,*—Collonbeg, Bryansford, Newcastle, co. Down.

PREDECESSORS.—[1] BERNARD Ward, M.P. for co. Down 1749-70 ; cr. *Baron Bangor* (peerage of Ireland) 1770, and *Viscount Bangor* (peerage of Ireland) 1781 ; *d.* 1781, and was *s.* by his el. son [2] NICHOLAS, 2nd Viscount; *d.s.p.* 1827 ; *s.* by his nephew (el. son of the Hon. Edward Ward, 2nd son of 1st Viscount) [3] EDWARD SOUTHWELL, 3rd Viscount: *m.* 1826, Harriet Margaret, who *d.* 1880, dau. of 6th Baron Farnham ; *d.* 1837 ; *s.* by his el. son [4] EDWARD, 4th Viscount, a Representative Peer ; *d.s.p.* 1881 ; *s.* by his brother [5] HENRY WILLIAM CROSBIE, 5th Viscount, *b.* 1828 ; a Representative Peer: *m.* 1st, 1854, Mary, who *d.* 1869, dau. of the late Rev. Henry King, of Ballylin, King's co. ; 2ndly, 1874, Elizabeth, who *d.* 1919, dau. of the late Major Hugh Eccles, of Cronroe, co. Wicklow ; *d.* 1911 ; *s.* by his son [6] MAXWELL RICHARD CROSBIE, P.C., *O.B.E.*, 6th Viscount, *b.* 1868 ; a Representative Peer for Ireland ; sometime Parliamentary Private Sec. to Prime Min. of N. Ireland ; was a Member of Senate, N. Ireland 1921-50, and Speaker 1930-50: *m.* (Jan.) 1905, Agnes Elizabeth, who *d.* 1972, da. of the late Dacre Mervyn Archdall Hamilton, *d.* 1950; *s.* by his son [7] EDWARD HENRY HAROLD, 7th Viscount and present peer; also Baron Bangor.

BANKS, BARON. (Banks.) [Life Baron 1974.]

DESMOND ANDERSON HARVIE BANKS, *CBE,* son of James Harvie Banks, OBE; *b.* Oct. 23rd, 1918; ed. at Univ. Coll. Sch., Hampstead, NW3; Insurance Broker; Chm. Liberal Party Exec. 1961-63 and 1969-70, and Pres. Liberal Party 1968-69; 1939-45 War as Maj. RA in Middle East, Persia, Iraq and Italy; cr. CBE (Civil) 1972, and *Baron Banks,* of Kenton, Greater London (Life Baron) 1974: *m.* 1948, Barbara, da. of Richard Taylor Wells, and has issue.

Residence,—58, The Ridgeway, Kenton, Harrow, Middx. *Club,*—National Liberal.

SONS LIVING.

Hon. Alistair Richard Harvie, *b.* 1950.
Hon. Graham Thornton Harvie, *b.* 1953.

BANNERMAN OF KILDONAN, BARONY OF. (Bannerman.) [Extinct 1969.]

SONS LIVING OF LIFE BARON.

Hon. John Walter MacDonald, *b.* 1932; MA (Hons.)Glas.; BA (Hons.) Camb.; PhD Camb.
Hon. Calum Ruairi Mundell, *b.* 1936; BA Camb.

DAUGHTERS LIVING OF LIFE BARON.

Hon. Janet Ray, *b.* 1934; LOST: *m.* 1957, Lt.-Col. Iain Michie, RAMC, of Tigh an Eas, Oban, Argyll.
Hon. Elizabeth Mary (The Braes, Uplawmoor, Renfrewshire), *b.* 1938: *m.* 1st, 1960 (m. diss. 1971),
  D. S. Munro; 2ndly, 1972, Iain Buchanan Anderson.

WIDOW LIVING OF LIFE BARON.

RAY (*Baroness Bannerman of Kildonan*) (The Old Manse, Balmaha, Stirlingshire), da. of the late
  Walter Mundell, of Swordale, Evanton, Ross-shire: *m.* 1931, Baron Bannerman of Kildonan (Life
  Peer), who *d.* 1969.

BARBER, BARON. (Barber.) [Life Baron 1974.]

ANTHONY PERRINOTT LYSBERG BARBER, *TD*, *PC*, son of the late John
Barber, CBE; *b.* July 4th, 1920; ed. at Retford Sch., and Oriel Coll., Oxford
(MA, LLB, Hon. Fellow 1971); 1939-45 War as Lt. RA and pilot RAF (prisoner,
despatches); Bar. Inner Temple 1948; PPS to Under-Sec. of State for Air
1952-54, Govt. Whip 1953-57, Lord Commr. of Treasury 1957-58, PPS to PM
1958-59, Economic Sec. to Treasury 1959-62, and Financial Sec. to same
1962-63, and Min. of Health 1963-64; Chancellor of the Duchy of Lancaster
June to July 1970, and Chancellor of the Exchequer 1970-74; Chm. of Standard
and Chartered Banking Gp. since 1974; cr. PC 1963, and *Baron Barber*, of
Wentbridge, W. Yorks. 1974: *m.* 1950, Jean Patricia, da. of Milton Asquith,
of Wentbridge, W. Yorks., and has issue.

Residences,—Wentbridge, Pontefract, W. Yorks.; 15, Montpelier Sq., SW7. *Club,*—Carlton.

DAUGHTERS LIVING.

Hon. Louise Patricia Lysberg, *b.* 1951.
Hon. Josephine Julia Asquith, *b.* 1952.

BARNARD, BARON. (Vane.) [Baron E. 1698.]

HARRY JOHN NEVILLE VANE, *T.D.*, 11th
Baron; *b.* Sept. 21st, 1923; *s.* 1964; ed.
at Eton; patron of ten livings; K.St.J.; a
JP of co Durham; Lord Lieut. since 1970;
Lt.-Col. comdg. Northumberland Hussars
1964-66; a Co. Councillor for Durham
1952-61; Pres. North of England TAVR
Assocn. since 1974; 1939-45 War as F/O
RAFVR: *m.* 1952, Lady Davina Mary Cecil,
el. da. of 6th Marquess of Exeter, and has
issue.

Arms,—Azure, three sinister gauntlets or. **Crest,**—A
dexter hand in armour couped at the wrist grasping a
sword in bend all proper, pommel and hilt or. **Supporters,**—
Dexter, a griffin argent, gorged with a collar azure
thereon three sinister gauntlets or as in the arms; *sinister*, an antelope or, gorged with a collar
azure, thereon three martlets or.

Seat,—Raby Castle, Staindrop, Darlington, co. Durham, DL2 3HF. *Residence,*—Selaby, Gainford, Darlington, co. Durham, DL2 3HF. *Club,*—Brooks's.

SON LIVING.

Hon. HENRY FRANCIS CECIL, *b.* March 11th, 1959.

DAUGHTERS LIVING.

Hon. Carolyn Mary, *b.* 1954.
Hon. Elizabeth Anne, *b.* 1956.
Hon. Sophia Rosalind, *b.* 1962.
Hon. Louise Cicely, *b.* 1968.

BROTHER LIVING.

Hon. Gerald Raby, *b.* 1926; ed. at Eton, and at Trin. Coll., Camb.; late DLI; a Member of Newbury
  Dist. Council. *Residence,*—20, Midgham Green, Reading, Berks., RG7 5TT.

SISTER LIVING.

Hon. Rosemary Myra, *b.* 1921; a Member of Barnard Castle RDO (Chm. 1972-73); Chm. Durham Co.
  Fedn. of Women's Insts.: *m.* 1948, Angus Josslyn Gore-Booth [see Gore-Booth, Bt.] from whom who
  obtained a divorce 1954. *Residence,*—The White House, Gainford, Darlington, DL2 3DN.

WIDOW LIVING OF TENTH BARON.

SYLVIA MARY (*Dowager Baroness Barnard*) (The White House, Gainford, Darlington), da. of Herbert
  Straker, formerly of Hartforth Grange, Richmond, Yorks.; late Ch. Comdr. A.T.S.: *m.* 1920,
  the 10th Baron, who *d.* 1964.

COLLATERAL BRANCH LIVING.

  Issue of the late Col. the Hon. William Lyonel Vane (*raised to the rank of a
    Baron's son* 1892), brother of 9th Baron, *b.* 1859; *d.* 1920: *m.* 1904, Lady
    Katharine Louisa Pakenham, who *d.* 1954, dau. of 4th Earl of Longford :—

William Morgan FLETCHER-VANE, *T.D.* (*Baron Inglewood*), *b.* 1909; *cr.* Baron 1964 [see that title].
——Katharine Selina (Broomfield Bank, Moniaive, Thornhill, Dumfriesshire), *b.* 1906: *m.* 1932,
Hugh Bullock Hall, who *d.* 1949, and has issue living, Alexander Bullock (of Craiglearan, Moniaive,
Thornhill, Dumfriesshire), *b.* 1934: *m.* 1964, Rosalind Mary, only child of Cdr. Robert Brian Halliwell, DSO, RN, of Twomerkland, Dumfriesshire, and has issue living, Robert Hugh Bullock *b.*
1965, Richard Alexander Bullock *b.* 1971, Rosemary Joan Katharine *b.* 1967,—David Bullock
(Church Farm, Langrish, Petersfield, Hants.), *b.* 1936: *m.* 1st, 1961 (m. diss. 1971), Susan Stephanie,
yr. da. of Samuel William Prittle Perry-Aldworth, of Littlestone-on-Sea, Kent; 2ndly, 1971, Ellen,
da. of Leonard Turner, of Florida, USA, and has issue living, (by 1st m.) Katrina Favell *b.* 1968, (by
2nd m.) Mark Bullock *b.* 1973,—Elizabeth Katharine Favell, *b.* 1938.——Margaret Cicely, *b.* 1910.

PREDECESSORS.—[1] *Rt. Hon.* CHRISTOPHER Vane, 7th and only surviving son of Sir Henry
Vane, the younger, who was beheaded for treason 1662; *cr. Baron Barnard,* of Barnard Castle,
in the County Palatine of Durham (peerage of England) 1698; *d* 1723; *s.* by his son [2]
GILBERT, 2nd Baron; *d.* 1753; *s.* by his son [3] HENRY, 3rd Baron; successively M.P. for
Launceston, St. Mawes, Ripon, and co. Durham, Paymaster in Ireland, a Lord of the
Treasury, and Lord-Lieut. and Vice-Adm. of Durham; *cr. Viscount Barnard* and *Earl of
Darlington* (peerage of Great Britain) 1754; *d.* 1758; *s.* by his son [4] HENRY, 2nd Earl,
M.P. for Downton and for co. Durham; Lord-Lieut. and Vice-Adm. of Durham, Master
of the Jewel Office, and Gov. of Carlisle; *d.* 1792; *s.* by his son [5] WILLIAM HARRY, K.G.,
3rd Earl, *b.* 1766; Lord-Lieut. and Vice-Adm. of Durham; M.P. for Totnes 1788-90 and for
Winchelsea 1790-92; *cr. Marquess of Cleveland* (peerage of United Kingdom) 1827 and *Baron
Raby* and *Duke of Cleveland* (peerage of United Kingdom) 1833: *m.* 1st, 1787, Lady Katharine
Margaret Powlett, dau. and co-heir of Harry, 6th and last Duke of Bolton; *d.* 1842; *s.* by
his el. son [6] HENRY, K.G., 2nd Duke; a Lieut. Gen. in the Army; M.P. 1812-42; *d.s.p.*
1864; *s.* by his brother [7] WILLIAM JOHN FREDERICK, 3rd Duke; assumed the surname of
Powlett by Roy. licence 1813, and resumed his patronymic, Vane, by Roy. licence 1864;
M.P. 1812-31 and 1846-57; *d.* 1864: *s.* by his brother [8] HARRY GEORGE, K.G., 4th Duke, *b.*
1803; M.P. for S. Durham (*L*) 1841-59, and for Hastings 1859-64; assumed in 1864 the name
and arms of Powlett in lieu of Vane: *m.* 1854, Catherine Lucy Wilhelmine, who *d.* 1901, dau.
of 4th Earl Stanhope, and widow of Lord Dalmeny, el. son of 4th Earl of Rosebery; *d.* 1891,
when all his honours became extinct with the exception of the Barony of Barnard, which
devolved upon [9] HENRY DE VERE (son of Sir Henry Morgan Vane, a descendant of the 2nd
Baron), who was adjudged 9th Baron by Cttee. for Privileges, House of Lords, 1892; *b.* 1854:
m. 1881, Lady Catherine Sarah Cecil, who *d.* 1918, da. of 3rd Marquess of Exeter; *d.* 1918; *s.* by his
son [10] CHRISTOPHER WILLIAM, *CMG, OBE, MC, TD,* 10th Baron, *b.* 1888, Lt.-Col. and Brevet-
Col. 6th DLI; Lord-Lieut. of co. Durham 1958-64: *m.* 1920, Sylvia Mary, da. of Herbert Straker
late of Hartforth Grange, Richmond, Yorks.; *d.* 1964; *s.* by his el. son [11] HARRY JOHN NEVILLE,
11th Baron and present peer.

BARNBY, BARON.— (Willey.) [Baron U.K. 1922.]

Tenacious of purpose.

FRANCIS VERNON WILLEY, *C.M.G.,
C.B.E., M.V.O., T.D.,* 2nd Baron;
b. Sept. 29th, 1884 ; *s.* 1929 ; ed. at
Eton, and at Magdalen Coll., Ox-
ford (MA); Hon Dr (Tech.) Brad-
ford; Brevet Col. (ret.) TA, and
Lord of the Manors of Blyth and
Barnby Moor; formerly Lieut.-Col.
Comdg. Notts Yeo. (Sherwood
Rangers); Controller of Wool Sup-
plies, Min. of Munitions Supply
1916-20, Assist. Director RAOC
1918, and a Member of Govt.
Surplus Property Disposals Board
1919-22, and of Overseas Trade
Development Council 1937; Chm.
Gen. Purposes Committee British
Commonwealth Union 1923, Pres.
of Federation of British Industries
1925-6, and a Member of Central
Electricity Board 1927-46, and of
Oversea Settlement Board 1937;
Pres. of Textile Inst. 1961-62;
Past Master of Woolmen's Co.; formerly a Dir. of Lloyds Bank Ltd., and
of Commercial Union Assurance Co. Ltd.; Egypt and Gallipoli 1915-16; a
Chevalier of Legion of Honour; MP for S. Div. of Bradford (*Co.U*) 1918-22;
CMG and MVO 1918, CBE (Mil.) 1919: *m.* 1940, Banning, da. of William
Drayton Grange, of Brook House, Bryn Mawr, Pennsylvania, USA.

Arms.—Per pale or and gules, three chevronels countercharged, over all a pale ermine charged
with three martlets sable. **Crest.**—In front of a reindeer's head erased proper, two crosses patée
gules. **Supporters.**—On either side a reindeer proper, charged on the shoulder with a rose gules.

Residences,—35, Grosvenor Sq., W1; Hillthorpe, Ashtead, Surrey. *Office,*—2, Caxton St., SW1.
Clubs,—Carlton, St. Stephen's, Bath, Cavalry, Hurlingham.

SISTER LIVING.

Hon. Florence Evelyne, *b.* 1882 : *m.* 1914, Major Duncan Elidor Campbell, D.S.O., who *d.* 1930
[see E. Cawdor, colls.]. *Residence,*—Poulton House, Cirencester, Gloucestershire.

PREDECESSOR.—[1] FRANCIS Willey, son of the late John Willey, of Moor House, Bradford,
Yorkshire, *b.* 1841 ; Chm. of Francis Willey and Co. (Limited), wool merchants, of Bradford;
cr. Baron Barnby, of Blyth, co. Nottingham (peerage of United Kingdom) 1922 : *m.* 1880,
Florence, who *d.* 1933, dau. of the late Frederick Chinnock, of Portland Place, W., and
Dinorbin Court, Hants; *d.* 1929 ; *s.* by his son [2] FRANCIS VERNON, 2nd Baron and
present peer.

BARRINGTON, VISCOUNT. (Barrington.) Sits as BARON SHUTE. (U.K. 1880.) [Viscount I. 1720.]

Honour before splendour.

PATRICK WILLIAM DAINES BARRINGTON, 11th Viscount; *b.* Oct. 29th, 1908; *s.* 1960; ed. at Eton, and at Magdalen Coll., Oxford (B.A. 1930); Bar. Inner Temple 1940; late 2nd Lieut. R.A.; formerly Hon. Attaché, H.M.'s Embassy in Berlin; sometime in Foreign Office.

Arms,—Argent, three chevronels gules, a label of three points azure. Crest.—A hermit's bust in profile vested, and having on the head a cowl paly of six argent and gules. Supporters.—Two griffins, wings elevated or, each gorged with a label of three points azure.

Residence,—

SISTER LIVING.

Priscilla Mary, *b.* 1907.

UNCLE LIVING. (*Son of 9th Viscount.*)

Hon. RUPERT EDWARD SELBORNE, *D.S.O.*, *b.* Dec. 10th, 1877; ed. at Charterhouse; Hon. Maj. in the Army; late Maj. Yeo., and Lieut.-Col. Comdg. a Batn. Roy. Highlanders; S. Africa 1900-01, with 11th Batn. Imperial Yeo., European War 1914-18 (despatches thrice, D.S.O., wounded); served in S. African Constabulary 1901-7; sometime Organizing Sec. to Village Clubs Assocn.; DSO 1918: *m.* 1903, Mary Georgina, who *d.* 1971, da. of Lt.-Col. George Arthur Ferguson [V. Bridport], and has issue living, Eric Rupert Walter (of Hayne, Corfe, Taunton), *b.* 1904; Lt. RA: *m.* 1st 1929, Hester Maude Vere, OBE (from whom he obtained a divorce 1938), dau. of the Rev. Guy Ronald Campbell [see E. Cawdor, colls.]; 2ndly, 1941, Mabel Susannah, da. of the late C. W. Taylor, of Westoe, South Shields.

COLLATERAL BRANCH LIVING.

Granddaughter of the late Hon. Percy Evelyn Barrington, youngest son of 9th Viscount:—

Issue of the late Miguel O'Brien Shute Barrington, *b.* 1909, *d.* 1937: *m.* 1935, Yvonne Guary-Dommergues, who *d.* 1948, dau. of Madame Nebel, of Paris:—

Michaelle Susan (posthumous), *b.* 1937; BA Oxford.

PREDECESSORS.—[1] JOHN Shute, Barrister of the Inner Temple, and Commr. of Customs 1708-11, having inherited by will the estate of John Wildman of Becket, Berks, subsequently succeeded by settlement to the estates of Francis Barrington, of Tofts, Essex, whose surname he assumed 1717 by Roy. licence; sat as M.P. for Berwick 1714-22, when he was expelled from the House in consequence of being connected with the Harbourg lottery; cr. *Baron Barrington* and *Viscount Barrington* (peerage of Ireland) 1720; *d.* 1734; *s.* by his el. son [2] WILLIAM WILDMAN, 2nd Viscount; held numerous high appointments 1754-78, including the offices of Sec. at War, Chancellor of the Exchequer, &c.; *d.* 1793; *s.* by his nephew [3] WILLIAM WILDMAN, 3rd Viscount, son of Maj.-Gen. the Hon. John Barrington, 2nd son of 1st Viscount; *d.s.p.* 1801; *s.* by his brother [4] RICHARD, 4th Viscount; *d.s.p.* 1813; *s.* by his brother [5] *Rev.* GEORGE, 5th Viscount, Prebendary of Durham, and Rector of Sedgefield; *d.* 1829; *s.* by his el. son [6] WILLIAM KEPPEL, 6th Viscount; was M.P. for Berkshire (*C*) 1837-57; *m.* 1823, the Hon. Jane Elizabeth Liddell, who *d.* 1883, dau. of 1st Baron Ravensworth; *d.* 1867; *s.* by his el. son [7] GEORGE WILLIAM, *P.C.*, 7th Viscount; sat as M.P. for Eye (*C*) 1866-80; was Vice-Chamberlain of H.M.'s Household 1874-80, and Capt. of Corps of Gentlemen at Arms 1885-6; cr. *Baron Shute*, of Beckett (peerage of United Kingdom), 1880, with remainder to his brother Percy: *m.* 1846, Isabel Elizabeth, who *d.* 1898, only child of the late John Morritt, of Rokeby, Barnard Castle: *d.* Nov. 6th, 1886; *s.* by his brother [8] PERCY, 8th Viscount; *b.* 1825: *m.* 1845, Louisa, who *d.* 1884, only dau. of Tully Higgins, Esq.; *d.* 1901; *s.* by his son [9] WALTER BULKELEY, 9th Viscount; *b.* 1848: *m.* 1st, 1870, Mary Isabella, who *d.* 1903, dau. of the late Rev. Richard Bogue, V. of Denbury, Devon; 2ndly, 1905, Charlotte Mary Leicester, who *d.* 1935, dau. of the late Major George Montagu Stopford, R.E., and widow of John Arden Birch; *d.* 1933; *s.* by his el. son [10] WILLIAM REGINALD SHUTE, 10th Viscount; *b.* 1873; Capt. and Hon. Major Oxford and Bucks L.I.; *d.* 1960; *s.* by his nephew [11] PATRICK WILLIAM DAINES (son of the late Hon. (Walter) Bernard Louis Barrington, 2nd son of 9th Viscount), 11th Viscount and present peer; also Baron Barrington, and Baron Shute.

BASING, BARON (Sclater Booth.) [Baron U.K. 1887.]

[Name pronounced "**Slater-Booth.**"]

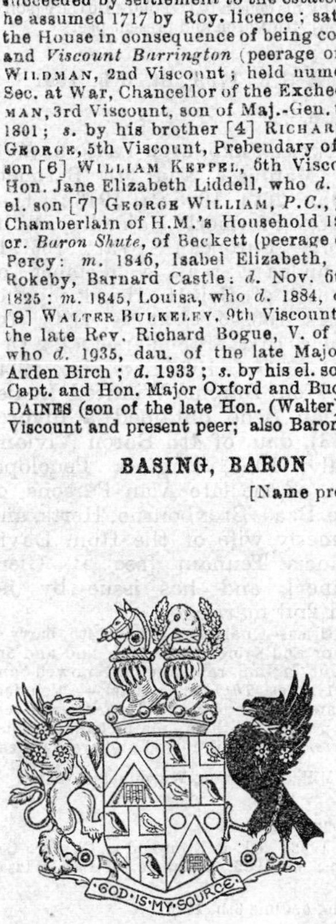

GEORGE LUTLEY SCLATER-BOOTH, 4th Baron; *b.* Dec. 7th, 1903; *s.* 1969; ed. at Winchester: *m.* 1st, 1938 (m. diss. 1944) Jeanette, who *d.* 1957, da. of the late Neil Bruce MacKelvie, of New York; 2ndly, 1951, Cynthia, da. of the late Charles W. Hardy, of Salt Lake City, Utah, and widow of Carl H. Beal, of Los Angeles, and has issue by 1st m.

Arms,—Quarterly; 1st and 4th, gules a chevron, between in chief two bezants, and in base a portcullis chained or, *Booth*; 2nd and 3rd, argent a cross gules between two penguins proper in the first and fourth quarters and two martlets azure in the second and third quarters, *Sclater.* Crests,—*Dexter,* a horse's head erased proper, bridled and reined or, charged with a roundel argent, thereon a boar's head erect and erased sable, *Booth; sinister,* Between two sprigs of oak proper, fructed or, a woodcock's head erased proper, gorged with a collar argent, charged with a saltire azure, *Sclater.* Supporters,—*Dexter,* a winged lion queue fourchee; *sinister,* an eagle sable; each gorged with a saltire azure affixed to the collar a chain reflexed over the back argent, the wings charged on the covert and secondary feathers with three cogwheels in chevron or.

Address,—PO Box 301, Pebble Beach, Cal., USA.

SON LIVING.

Hon. NEIL LUTLEY (112, East 74th St., New York, N.Y. 10021, USA) (*Clubs*, Harvard, Meadow Brook), *b.* Jan. 16th, 1939; ed. at Eton, and Harvard Univ. (BA): *m.* 1967, Patricia Ann, da. of the late George Bryan Whitfield, of 598, Prospect St., New Haven, Conn., USA, and has issue living, Stuart Whitfield, *b.* Dec. 18th, 1969,—Andrew Limbrey, *b.* 1973.

DAUGHTERS LIVING OF THIRD BARON.

Hon. Diana Penelope Florence *b.* 1925: *m.* 1946, James Tennant Bailward, and has issue living, Christopher John, *b.* 1949,—Clare Penelope, *b.* 1947. *Residence,*—Causeway House, Radipole, near Weymouth, Dorset.
Hon. Barbara Amy, *b.* 1926: *m.* 1961, Peter Michell Luttman-Johnson, and has issue living, William Michell, *b.* 1963,—Anne Elizabeth, *b.* 1962,—Catherine Mary, *b.* 1966. *Residence,*—Redhill House, Petworth, Sussex.
Hon. Gabrielle Mary, *b.* 1929: *m.* 1953, Com. Martin Parnell Seth-Smith, R.N., and has issue living Nicholas John, *b.* 1961,—Imogen Gabrielle, *b.* 1963. *Residence,*—The Triangle, Wildhern, Andover.

DAUGHTERS LIVING OF SECOND BARON.

Hon. Joan Penelope, *b.* 1892: *m.* 1919, Capt. Roger Grenville Peek, 9th Lancers, who *d.* 1921 [see Peek, Bt., colls.]. *Residence,*—Flete House, Ermington, Ivybridge, S. Devon.
Hon. Lydia Joyce, *b.* 1898: *m.* 1921, Capt. Anthony Harley Mark Bell, MC, 3rd Hussars, who *d.* 1964, and has issue living, Mark Robert Anthony (Jenny Green Cottage, Trinity Rd., Bentworth, Alton, Hants.), *b.* 1924: *m.* 1962, Rosemary, da. of Lt.-Col. Gibson Bishop, MC, New Zealand Forces, and has issue living, Harley Mark Gibson *b.* 1963, Anthony Mark David *b.* 1965,—David Harley Mark (of Little Heath, Mortimer West End, Reading), *b.* 1929: *m.* 1959, Gillian, da. of Group Capt. Freke William Wiseman-Clarke, CBE, RAF, and has issue living, William Mark *b.* 1967, Susan Mary, *b.* 1961, Caroline Margaret *b.* 1963,—Rosemary, *b.* 1921: *m.* 1946, Capt. Michael Hall, R. Scots Greys, of The Bridge, Kilternan, co. Dublin, and has issue living, Robert Michael Anthony *b.* 1954, Rozanne Penelope *b.* 1947, Veronica Rosemary *b.* 1950. *Residence,*—

COLLATERAL BRANCH LIVING.

Issue of the late Brig.-Gen. the Hon. Walter Dashwood Sclater-Booth, C.B., C.M.G., D.S.O., late RA, yst. son of 1st Baron, *b.* 1869, *d.* 1953: *m.* 1913, Frances Mary, who *d.* 1949, da. of the late Rowland Burdon, of Castle Eden, co. Durham [Slade, Bt., colls.]:—
Eleanor Mary, *b.* 1914. *Residence,*—Sherborne Cottage, Upton Grey, Basingstoke, Hants.——Nora Frances, *b.* 1916.

PREDECESSORS.—[1] GEORGE Sclater, *P.C.*, el. son of the late William Lutley Sclater, of Hoddington House, Hants; *b.* 1826; assumed by Roy. licence 1856 the additional surname of Booth; M.P. for N. Hants (*C*) 1857-85, and for Hants, N., or Basingstoke, Div. 1885-7; Parliamentary Sec. to Poor Law Board 1867-8, Financial Sec. to Treasury 1868, and Pres. of Local Govt. Board 1874-80; cr. *Baron Basing* (peerage of United Kingdom) 1887: *m.* 1857, Lydia Caroline, who *d.* 1881, dau. of the late Major George Birch, of Clare Park, Hants; *d.* 1894; *s.* by his el. son [2] GEORGE LIMBREY, *C.B*, *b.* 1860: Lieut.-Col. and Brevet.-Col. 1st (Roy.) Dragoons, and Brig.-Gen.: *m.* 1889, Mary, who *d.* 1904, dau. of the late John Hargreaves, of Maiden Erlegh Berks, and Whalley Abbey, Lancashire: *d.* 1919; *s.* by his only son [3] JOHN LIMBREY ROBERT, *TD*, 3rd Baron, *b.* 1890: *m.* 1924, Mary Alice Erle, who *d.* 1970, da. of the late Lt.-Col. Richard Erle Benson, E. Yorks. Regt.; *d.* 1969, *s.* by his cousin [4] GEORGE LUTLEY [son of the Hon. Charles Lutley Sclater-Booth, 2nd son of 1st Baron], 4th Baron and present peer.

BATH, MARQUESS OF. (Thynne.) [Marquess G.B. 1789, Bt. G.B. 1641.]

[Name pronounced "Thin."]

I have good reason.

HENRY FREDERICK THYNNE, *E.D.*, 6th Marquess, and 9th Baronet; *b.* Jan. 26th, 1905; *s.* 1946: ed. at Harrow; formerly Major Roy. Wilts Yeo.; European War 1939-44 (wounded); was a member of Council of H.R.H. the Prince of Wales 1933-6; sat as M.P. for Frome Div. of Somerset (*C*) Oct. 1931 to Oct. 1935: *m.* 1st, 1926, the Hon. Daphne Winifred Louise Vivian (who obtained a divorce 1953), dau. of 4th Baron Vivian; 2ndly, 1953, Virginia Penelope, dau. of the late Alan Parsons, of The Baas, Broxbourne, Herts, and formerly wife of the Hon. David Francis Tennant [see B. Glenconner], and has issue by 1st and 2nd marriages.

Arms.—Quarterly: 1st and 4th, barry of ten or and sable, *Botteville*; 2nd and 3rd argent, a lion rampant tail nowed and erect gules, *Thynne*. Crest.—A reindeer statant or. Supporters.—*Dexter*, a reindeer or, gorged with a plain collar sable: *sinister*, a lion tail nowed and erect gules.

Seat,—Longleat, Warminster, Wilts. *Residence,*—Job's Mill, Crockerton, Warminster, Wilts.

SONS LIVING. (By 1st marriage.)

ALEXANDER GEORGE (*Viscount Weymouth*), *b.* May 6th, 1932; ed. at Eton and at Ch. Ch., Oxford; formerly Lieut. Life Guards, and Roy. Wilts. Yeo.: *m.* 1969, Anna, da. of Laszlo Izsak Gyarmathy, of Los Angeles, Cal. USA, and has issue:—
SON LIVING,—*Hon.* Ceawlin Henry Laszlo, *b.* June 6th, 1974.

DAUGHTER LIVING,—*Hon.* Lenka Abigail, *b.* 1969.
Residence,—Longleat, Warminster, Wilts.

Lord Christopher John (51, Edith Grove, SW10), *b.* 1934; ed. at Eton; late 2nd Lt. Life Guards: *m.* 1968, Antonia Mary, da. of Maj. Sir Anthony Frederick Mark Palmer, 5th Bt., cr. 1886.

Lord Valentine Charles (Woodwards, Horningsham, Warminster, Wilts.), *b.* 1937; ed. at Eton; late 2nd Lieut. Life Guards: *m.* 1st, 1961 (m. diss. 1971), Veronica Ann, only da. of Col. G. E. Jackson, of Stratford, NZ; 2ndly, 1971, Susanne Caroline, da. of Edgar Harold Alder, of Primrose Farm, Little Wilbraham, Cambs., and formerly wife of Christopher Hodgson Moore, and has issue living (by 1st m.), Lucien, *b.* 1965,—Xenia, *b.* 1962.

DAUGHTERS LIVING. (*By 1st marriage.*)

Lady Caroline Jane, *b.* 1928 : *m.* 1950, David Robert Somerset [see D. Beaufort colls.].   *Residence,—* 90, Eaton Terrace, S.W.1.

(*By 2nd marriage.*)

Lady Silvy Cerne, *b.* 1958.

SISTERS LIVING.

Lady (Alice) Kathleen Violet, *b.* 1891: *m.* 1919, Lieut.-Col. the Hon. Oliver Hugh Stanley, D.S.O., RHA, who *d.* 1952 [see B. Stanley of Alderley].   *Residence,—*East Woodlands Vicarage, Frome, Somerset.

Lady Emma Marjory, *O.B.E.*, *b.* 1893 ; formerly Regional Administrator, S. Region, Women's Vol. Sers.; O.B.E. (Civil) 1943 : *m.* 1921, the 6th Marquess of Northampton, from whom she obtained a divorce 1942.   *Residence,—*The Curatage, Horningsham, Warminster, Wilts.

COLLATERAL BRANCHES LIVING.

Grandchildren of the late Rt. Hon. Lord Henry Frederick Thynne, 2nd son of 3rd Marquess :—

Issue of the late Col. Ulric Oliver Thynne, C.M.G., C.V.O., D.S.O., T.D., *b.* 1871, *d.* 1957: *m.* 1st, 1899, Marjory, who *d.* 1950, dau. of Edward Wormald ; 2ndly, 1951, Elspeth Stiven, who *d.* 1955, dau. of the late David Tullis of Rutherglen, and widow of 1st Baron Invernairn :—

(By 1st marriage), Oliver St. Maur, *T.D.*, *b.* 1901 ; ed. at Eton, and at New Coll., Oxford (B.A. 1923), late Major Roy. Wiltshire Yeo. and Lieut.-Col. Gen. Staff ; European War 1939-45 in Iraq, Syria; Persia, Egypt, and France (despatches): *m.* 1936, Mary Wroughton (DILL), dau. of Herbert Francis Morris, and has issue living, Sheridan Ulric (Flint House, Whitchurch, nr. Reading), *b.* 1939; ed. at Eton; late Lt. Roy. Wilts. Yeo.: *m.* 1964, Eve, da. of Lt.-Cdr. G. J. Cardew, RN, of Beech-wood, Upper Basildon, Berks., and has issue living, Louise Sarah *b.* 1965, Marika Helen *b.* 1973, Tamara Jane *b.* 1974.   *Residence,—*Panters, South Stoke, Oxon.——Brian Sheridan, *CBE, AFC, b.* 1907; ed. at Eton; Group Capt. (ret.) AAF, and a JP for Sussex; 1939-45 War (despatches, AFC, OBE); CBE (Mil) 1946: *m.* 1st, 1940 (m. diss. 1948), Naomi (BOURN), only da. of C. E. Waters, of Sydney; 2ndly, 1952, Maria Fernanda Herrero, da. of the Marqués de Aledo, of Madrid, Spain and has issue living, (by 1st m.) Harriet Anne *b.* 1941,—(by 2nd m.) Ulrica Maria Teresa, *b.* 1954,—Jane Georgiana, *b.* 1955.   *Residence,—*Westlands, W. Grinstead, Horsham.——Ulrica Marjory, *b.* 1911: *m.* 1936 (m. diss. 1961), Maj. George Anthony Murray Smith, late Roy. Horse Guards [B. Belper]. *Residence,—*Gaddesby, Leicestershire.

Grandson of the late Francis John Thynne, 2nd son of the Rev. Lord John Thynne, DD, 3rd son of 2nd Marquess:—

Issue of the late Capt. George Augustus Carteret Thynne, late Roy. N. Devon Yeo., *b.* 1869, *d.* 1945 : *m.* 1915, the Hon. Gladys Isabel Annette Adderley, who *d.* 1960, dau. of 2nd Baron Norton :—

John Grenville, *b.* 1917 ; ed. at Stowe ; late Major Roy. Horse Guards ; European War 1939-45 in Iraq, Syria, Persia, Egypt, Italy, Holland, and Germany : *m.* 1946, Baroness Marianne Madeleine, dau. of the late Baron H. R. de Jenner, of Château de Landshut, Berne, and has issue living, Bevil Grenville de Jenner, *b.* 1947; ed. at Stowe: *m.* 1970, Gertrude Dagnie, da. of Arvid G. Ekman, of Skansen, Lodöse, Sweden, and has issue living, Christopher John Grenville *b.* 1972,—Richard George Grenville, *b.* 1950,—Joanna Sybil Marcia, *b.* 1949.

Grandchildren of the late Rev. Canon Arthur Christopher Thynne, 3rd son of the Rev. Lord John Thynne (ante):—

Issue of the late Capt. Hugh Edward Granville Thynne, R.E., *b.* 1881, *d.* 1952 : *m.* 1907, Marguerite, who *d.* 1964, dau. of W. Hearne:—

Christopher William Granville, *b.* 1910 ; ed. at Leys; 1939-45 War, 2/8 Field Artillery, AIF in Middle East and Pacific: *m.* 1954, Emmeline, widow of Leon le Fevre, of Paris, France.   *Residence,—* Rocheqaie, Quai Pasteur, 37, Chinon, France I. et L.——Marguerite Isabel Gwenllian Granville, *b.* 1908: *m.* 1930, Clifford Charles Gulliver, and has issue living, Michael Charles Granville, *b.* 1933,— Anthony Frances Granville, *b.* 1943,—Timothy Edward Granville, *b.* 1945,—Ann Marguerite Granville, *b.* 1936.   *Residence,—*Penquite, Landrake, Cornwall.——Grace Marian Granville, *b.* 1913: *m.* 1934, Kenneth Taylor Thomson, and has issue living, Peter Granville *b.* 1936,—Jeremy Clayton *b.* 1938,—Robert Hugh *b.* 1942.   *Residence,—*The Old Hall, Burton Leonard, Harrogate, Yorks.

Granddaughters of the late Rev. Lord John Thynne, D.D. (ante) :—

Issue of the late Maj.-Gen. Sir Reginald Thomas Thynne, K.C.B., *b.* 1843, *d.* 1926: *m.* 1890, Louise, who *d.* 1933, dau. of Douglas Du Bois and widow of Major William Ewing :—

Katharine Angela (*Lady Baddeley*), *M.B.E.*, *b.* 1893 ; in War Office during European War 1914-19 (M.B.E.); M.B.E. (Civil) 1920: *m.* 1933, Sir Vincent Wilberforce Baddeley K.C.B., who *d.* 1961. *Residence,—*77, Melton Court, SW7.

PREDECESSORS.—[1] *Sir* HENRY FREDERICK Thynne, cr. a *Baronet* 1641 ; *s.* by his el. son [2] *Sir* THOMAS, *P.C.*, 2nd Bt. ; Pres. of Board of Trade 1702-7 ; sometime M.P. for Oxford University and Tamworth ; inherited Longleat after the murder of his kinsman, and was cr. *Baron Thynne of Warminster* and *Viscount Weymouth* (peerage of G.B.) 1682, with remainder to his brother Henry Frederick; *d.* 1714; *s.* by his grand-nephew, grandson of Henry Frederick, (ante) [3] THOMAS, 2nd Viscount; Ranger of Hyde and St. James's Parks; *d.* 1751; *s.* by his son [4] THOMAS, *K.G.*, 3rd Viscount : was Lord of the Bedchamber 1760-63, Master of the Horse to Queen Charlotte 1765, Lord-Lieut. of Ireland 1765, Sec. of State for Northern Depart. 1768, and Groom of the Stole 1782-96 ; cr. *Marquess of Bath* (peerage of Great Britain) 1789 ; *d.* 1796 ; *s.* by his el. son [5] THOMAS, *K.G.*, 2nd Marquess, Lord-Lieut. of co. Somerset ; *d.* 1837 ; *s.* by his son [6] HENRY FREDERICK, 3rd Marquess, *b.* 1797 ; Capt. R.N.: *m.* 1830. the Hon. Harriet, dau. of 1st Baron Ashburton ; *d.* 1837 ; *s.* by his el. son [7] JOHN ALEXANDER. 4th Marquess, *b.* 1831 ; Lord-Lieut. of Wilts: *m.* 1861, the Hon. Frances Isabella Catherine Vesey, who *d.* 1915, el. dau. of 3rd Viscount de Vesci ; *d.* 1896 ; *s.* by his el. son [8] THOMAS HENRY, *K.G., C.B., T.D., P.C.*, 5th Marquess, *b.* 1862 ; Lord-Lieut. for Somerset ; Under-Sec. of State for India 1905 ; Chm. of Wilts County Council 1906-46, and Master of the Horse 1922-4 ; M.P. for Frome Div. of Somerset (C) 1886-92 and 1895-6 : *m.* 1890, Violet Caroline, who *d.* 1928, dau. of Sir Charles Mordaunt, 10th Bt.; *d.* 1946 : *s.* by his son [9] HENRY FREDERICK, 6th Marquess and present peer ; also Viscount Weymouth, and Baron Thynne of Warminster.

BATH and WELLS, LORD BISHOP OF. (Bickersteth.)

Rt. Rev. JOHN MONIER BICKERSTETH, yr. son of the Rev. Canon Edward Monier Bickersteth; *b.* Sept. 6th, 1921; ed. at Rugby, Ch. Ch. Oxford (MA) and Wells Theological Coll.; Capt. Buffs and RA in Normandy and India 1941-46; V. St. John, Hurst Green, Oxted 1954-62, and St. Stephen Chatham 1962-70; consecrated Bishop of Warrington (Suffragan for Diocese of Liverpool) 1970; translated as 75th Bishop of Bath and Wells 1975: *m.* 1955, Rosemary, da. of the late Edward Cleveland-Stevens, of Gaines, Oxted.

Patron of one hundred and forty-one livings, the Prebends and Canonries in his Cathedral, and the Archdeaconries of Bath, Wells, and Taunton.

This See was established by King Edward the Elder, in 909.

Episcopal Signature—John Bath: et Well:

ARMS OF THE SEE,—Azure: a saltire per saltire, quarterly quartered, or and argent.

Residence,—The Palace, Wells, Somerset, BA5 2UJ.

BATHURST, EARL. (Bathurst.) [Earl G.B. 1772.]

TIEN·TA·FOY·

Keep thy faith.

HENRY ALLEN JOHN BATHURST, 8th Earl; *b.* May 1st, 1927; *s.* 1943; ed. at Ridley Coll., Canada, at Eton, and at Ch. Ch. Oxford; Capt. Roy. Gloucestershire Hussars (T.A. Reserve), and a D.L. for Gloucestershire; formerly Lieut. 10th Roy. Hussars; appointed Gov. of Hospital of St. Lawrence, Cirencester 1944, and of Roy. Agricultural Coll. 1948, and Chancellor of Primrose League 1959; a Lord-in-Waiting to H.M. 1957-61, and Joint Parl. Under-Sec. of State, Home Office 1961-2; a Member of Councils, Country Landowners' Assocn., and Timber Growers Orgn.; Vice-Pres. of Roy. Forestry Soc. 1974: *m.* 1959, Judith Mary, only da. of A. C. Nelson, of Fosse Corner, Cirencester, and has issue.

Arms.—Sable, two bars ermine, in chief three crosses patée, or. *Crest.*—A dexter arm embowed, armed in mail, the hand, proper, grasping a spiked club or. *Supporters,*—Two stags, argent, each gorged with a collar gemellé ermine.

Seat,—Cirencester Park, Cirencester, Glos., GL7 2BT. *Clubs,*—Turf, White's.

SONS LIVING.
ALLEN CHRISTOPHER BERTRAM (*Lord Apsley*), *b.* March 11th, 1961.
Hon. Alexander Edward Seymour, *b.* 1965.

DAUGHTER LIVING.
Lady Henrietta Mary Lilias, *b.* 1962.

BROTHER LIVING.
Hon. George Bertram, *b.* 1929, ed. at Eton, and at Trin. Coll., Oxford (BA); late Capt. R. Wiltshire Yeo.; late Lt. 10th Hussars: *m.* 1973, Susan, da. of Malcolm Messer, of Manor Farm House, Tarlton, Glos. *Club,*—Cavalry.

COLLATERAL BRANCH LIVING.

Grandsons of the late Lt.-Col. the Hon. (Allen) Benjamin Bathurst, 3rd son of 6th Earl.
Issue of the late Group Capt. Peter Bathurst, *b.* 1903, *d.* 1970: *m.* 1927, Lady Elizabeth Ann (Tolzey Cottage, Queen Charlton, nr. Bristol), da. of the late Capt. the Hon. Chandos Graham Temple-Gore-Langton [see E. Temple of Stowe]:—
David Benjamin (6, Crouchmans Cl., SE26. *Clubs,*—Army and Navy, MCC, *b.* 1936; ed. at Eton; Capt. RN: *m.* 1959, Sarah Christian Pandora, yst. da. of the late Maj. (Basil Arthur) John Peto [see Peto, Bt. (cr. 1927), colls.], and has issue living, Benjamin John, *b.* 1964,—Alice Patricia, *b.* 1962,—Anna Christian, *b.* 1968,—Lucilla Ruby, *b.* 1970.——Timothy Seymour (59, Spencer Park, SW18), *b.* 1939; ed. at Eton; late 2nd Lt. Rifle Bde.; a Dir. of Arthur Tooth & Sons Ltd.: *m.* 1st, 1960, (*m.* diss. 1973) Elizabeth Mary, da. of Philip Michael Armitage; 2ndly, 1973, Mrs. Charlotte Anne Belloc-Lowndes, da. of the late Richard Formby, of Firwood, Formby, Lancs., and has issue living (by 1st *m.*), Jonathan Chandos Seymour, *b.* 1965,—Joanna Mary, *b.* 1963,—Elizabeth Sarah, *b.* 1968.

PREDECESSORS.—*Sir* Benjamin Bathurst, M.P., Gov. of the H.E.I.C. 1688-9, Treasurer of the Household to Princess Anne, and on her accession Cofferer of the Household, had with other issue [1] ALLEN, P.C.; sat as M.P. for Cirencester 1705-11; cr. *Baron Bathurst* (peerage of Great Britain) 1711, and *Earl Bathurst* (peerage of Great Britain) 1772; *d.* 1775: *s.* by his el. son [2] HENRY, P.C., who in 1771 had been appointed Lord High Chancellor and cr. 1771

Baron Apsley (peerage of Great Britain): sat as M.P. for Cirencester 1735-54; was sometime a Justice of the Common Pleas and Lord Pres. of the Council; *d.* 1794; *s.* by his son [3] HENRY, K.G., P.C., 3rd Earl; was Pres. of Board of Trade 1807-12, Sec. of War and Colonies 1812-27. and Pres. of the Council 1828-30; *d.* 1834; *s.* by his el. son [4] HENRY GEORGE, 4th Earl; was M.P. for Cirencester 1812-34, and a Commr. of India Board 1812-18; *d.s.p.* 1866; *s.* by his brother [5] WILLIAM, 5th Earl; was Clerk of the Privy Council 1827-60; *d.s.p.* 1878; *s.* by his nephew [6] ALLEN ALEXANDER (son of Lt.-Col. the Hon. Seymour Thomas Bathurst, 3rd son of 3rd Earl), 6th Earl, *b.* 1832; M.P. for Cirencester (*C*) 1857-78; *m.* 1st, 1862, the Hon. Meriel Leicester Warren, who *d.* 1872, dau. of 2nd Baron de Tabley; 2ndly, 1874, Evelyn, who *d.* 1927, dau. of George James Barnard Hankey, of Fetcham Park, Leatherhead; *d.* 1892; *s.* by his el. son [7] SEYMOUR HENRY, C.M.G., T.D., 7th Earl, *b.* 1864; Hon. Col. Gloucestershire Regt.: *m.* 1893, the Hon. Lilias Margaret Frances Borthwick, who *d.* 1965, da. of 1st Baron Glenesk (ext.); *d.* 1943; *s.* by his grandson [8] HENRY ALLEN JOHN (son of the late Lt.-Col. Allen Algernon Bathurst, DSO, MC, TD, MP, Lord Apsley, who *d.* (killed on active ser.) 1942, el. son of 7th Earl), 8th Earl and present peer; also Baron Bathurst, and Baron Apsley.

BAYFORD, BARONY OF. (Sanders.) [Extinct 1940.]
DAUGHTER LIVING OF FIRST BARON
Hon. Vera Elizabeth, *OBE*, *b.* 1902; JP for Devon; OBE (Civil) 1955: *m.* 1933, Maj.-Gen. the Hon. Theobald Patrick Probyn Butler, DSO, who *d.* 1970 [see B. Dunboyne]. *Residence,*—Kentisbeare House, Cullompton, Devon.

Bayham, Viscount, grandson of Marquess Camden.

BEARSTED, VISCOUNT. (Samuel.) [Viscount U.K. 1925, Bt. U.K. 1903.]

MARCUS RICHARD SAMUEL, *T.D.*, 3rd Viscount, and 3rd Baronet; *b.* June 1st, 1909; *s.* 1948; ed. at Eton, and at New Coll., Oxford; late Major Warwickshire Yeo. (T.A.); is a D.L. for Warwickshire; European War 1939-45 in Middle East (wounded): *m.* 1st, 1947 (m. diss. 1966), Elizabeth Heather, el. da. of G. Firmston-Williams, of 252, Old Brompton Rd., SW5; 2ndly, 1968, Mrs. Jean Agnew Somerville, da. of R. A. Wallace, of 10, Eton Terr., Edinburgh, and has issue by 1st m.

Arms,—Gules, on a chevron between two lions' heads erased in chief and in base a naval crown or, a heart gules. Crest,—A dexter arm embowed proper, grasping a battle-axe argent, the head charged with two triangles interlaced sable. Supporters,—Dexter, a horse argent; sinister, a dragon gules; each charged on the shoulder with a heart or.

Deeds, not words.

Seats,—Upton House, near Banbury; *Residence,*—1, Eaton Close, S.W.1. *Clubs,*—White's, Cavalry.

DAUGHTER LIVING. (By 1st m.)
Hon. Felicity Ann, *b.* 1948.

BROTHERS LIVING.
Hon. PETER MONTEFIORE, *M.C.*, *T.D.*, *b.* Dec. 9th, 1911; ed. at Eton, and at New Coll., Oxford; Major Warwickshire Yeo. (T.A.): European War 1939-45 in Middle East (despatches, M.C.): *m.* 1st, 1939 (m. diss. 1942), Deirdre du Barry; 2ndly, 1946, the Hon. Elizabeth Adelaide Cohen, da. of the late Baron Cohen (Life Baron), and widow of Capt. Arthur John Pearce-Serocold, Welsh Gds. (Supplementary Res.) [B. Sheffield], and has issue living, (by 2nd m.) Nicholas Alan, *b.* 1950: *m.* 1975, Caroline Jane, da. of Dr. David Sacks,—Michael John, *b.* 1952,—Sarah Virginia, *b.* 1947: *m.* 1969, Duncan John Lloyd Fitzwilliams. *Residences,*—12, Rutland Court, SW7 1BN; Farley Hall, Farley Hill, nr. Reading, RG7 1UL; Phones, Newtonmore, Inverness-shire, PH20 1BE. *Club,*—White's.

Hon. Anthony Gerald, *b.* 1917; ed. at Eton, and at New College, Oxford; European War 1939-45 as Lt. and acting Capt. Intelligence Corps: *m.* 1st, 1946, Mary Eve (m. diss. 1961), da. of the late John Comyn Higgins, CIE, of Alford, Lincs., 2ndly, 1962, (m. diss. 1966) Jenifer, da. of Major Kenneth Alfred Bridge Puckle, R.M. (ret.) of Farnham; 3rdly, 1966, Mercy Haystead, and has issue living, (by 1st marriage) Eve, *b.* 1948,—Daphne Lavinia, *b.* 1951. *Residences,*—Heywood, Cobham, Surrey; 29, St. Leonard's Terr., SW1; Arndilly House, Craigellachie, Banffshire. *Club,*—White's.

PREDECESSORS.
—[1] *Sir* MARCUS Samuel, 2nd son of the late Marcus Samuel, of 18, Upper Bedford Place, W.; *b.* 1853; was a Shipowner and Merchant; Lord Mayor of London 1902-3 (Sheriff 1894-5); Founder (many years Chm.) of Shell Transport and Trading Co. (Limited); cr. a *Baronet* 1903, Baron *Bearsted*, of Maidstone, co. Kent (peerage of United Kingdom, 1921, and *Viscount Bearsted*, of Maidstone, co. Kent (peerage of United Kingdom) 1925: *m.* 1881, Fanny Elizabeth, who *d.* Jan. 16th, 1927, only dau. of the late Benjamin Benjamin; *d.* Jan. 17th, 1927; *s.* by his son [2] WALTER HORACE, *M.C.*, 2nd Viscount; *b.* 1882; was a Trustee of National Gallery 1936-43 (Chm. 1942-3), and again 1947-8, and of the Tate Gallery 1938-42: *m.* 1908, Dorothea Montefiore, who *d.* 1949, dau. of the late Edward Montefiore Micholls, Bar.-at-Law, of 11, Queen's Gate, S.E.; *d.* 1948; *s.* by his son [3] MARCUS RICHARD, 3rd Viscount and present peer; also Baron Bearsted.

BEATTY, EARL. (Beatty.) [Earl U.K. 1919.]

DAVID BEATTY, 3rd Earl; *b.* Nov. 21st, 1946; *s.* 1972; ed. at Eton: *m.* 1971, Ann, yr. da. of A. Please, of Wokingham, Berks.

Ᾱrms,—Azure, a beehive beset with nine bees volant or a chief argent charged with the Cross of St. George gules., Crest,—A demi-lion gules holding in the dexter paw a crescent or. Supporters,—*Dexter*, a Sailor of the Royal Navy; *sinister*, a Soldier of the Royal Marines, both proper. *Residence,*—11, Edwardes Sq., W.8.

NON · VI
SED
ARTE

Not by force but by art.

HALF-BROTHER LIVING.
Hon. NICHOLAS DUNCAN, *b.* April 1st, 1961.

HALF-SISTERS LIVING.
Lady Diana Adrienne, *b.* 1952.
Lady Miranda Katharine, *b.* 1963.

MOTHER LIVING.
Dorothy Rita (Longbranch, Millwood, Virginia, U.S.A.), da. of the late Michael James Furey, of New Orleans, and widow of Sgt. Edward Bragg, RAF: *m.* 1946, as his 2nd wife (m. diss. 1950), the 2nd Earl, who *d.* 1972.

WIDOW LIVING OF SECOND EARL.
DIANE, da. of John Rutherford Blundell, of Havant, Hants., and adopted da. of Capt. Duncan Kirk: *m.* 1st, 1959, as his 4th wife, the 2nd Earl, who *d.* 1972; 2ndly, 1973, John Grenfell Nutting, of 56, Hans Place, SW1, and Chears Orchard, Fawley, Oxon., el. son of the Rt. Hon. Sir (Harold) Anthony Nutting, 3rd Bt.

PREDECESSORS.—[1] *Adm. of the Fleet Sir* DAVID Beatty, *GCB, OM, GCVO, DSO, PC,* 2nd son of the late David Longfield Beatty, of Borodale, Enniscorthy; *b.* 1871; Dongola Expedition, 1896 (despatches D.S.O.), Nile Expedition 1897 and 1898 (despatches twice, 4th class Order of Medjidie, promoted Com.), China 1900 (despatches, wounded, promoted Capt.), European War 1914-19, Comdg. Battle Cruiser Squadron and Naval Forces in Heligoland Bight and Dogger Bank actions, and Battle Cruiser Fleet at battle of Jutland, and finally as Com.-in-Ch. of Grand Fleet (despatches, K.C.V.O., G.C.B., Grand Cross of Order of Redeemer of Greece, Grand Officer Legion of Honour, G.C.V.O., Mil. Order of Savoy, Grand Cordon of Japanese Order of the Rising Sun (with Paulowina), Croix de Guerre, Orders of Leopold of Belgium and Star of Roumania, Grand Cordon (preciously brilliant) of Excellent Crop (China) Adm. of the Fleet, thanked by Parliament, cr. Earl, granted £100,000); was First Sea Lord of the Admiralty 1919-27; had 4th class of Russian Order of St. George; elected Lord Rector of Edinburgh Univ. 1917; cr. *Earl Beatty, Viscount Borodale,* of Wexford, co. Wexford, and *Baron Beatty,* of the North Sea, and of Brooksby, co. Leicester (peerage of United Kingdom) 1919: *m.* 1901, Ethel, who *d.* 1932, dau. of Marshall Field. senr.. of Chicago, U.S.A.; *d.* 1936: *s.* by his son [2] DAVID FIELD *DSC,* 2nd Earl; *b.* 1905; Lt.-Cdr. RN (ret); PPS to Parl. and Financial Sec. of the Admiralty 1931-36, and Joint Under-Sec. of State for Air 1945; MP for Peckham (*c*) 1931-36: *m.* 1st, 1937 (m. diss. 1945), Dorothy Sands, who *d.* 1966, da. of Thomas Sarsfield Kent Power, of Va. and formerly wife of the late Harry Ester Reynolds Hall; 2ndly, 1946 (m. diss. 1950), Dorothy Rita, da. of the late Michael James Furey of New Orleans, and widow of Sgt. Edward Bragg, RAF; 3rdly, 1951 (m. diss. 1958), Adelle, da. of M. Dillingham of Oklahoma City, USA, and formerly wife of William V. O'Connor; 4thly, 1959, Diane (who m. 2ndly, 1973, John Grenfell Nutting, el. son of the Rt. Hon. Sir (Harold) Anthony Nutting, 3rd Bt.), da. of John Rutherford Blundell, of Havant, Hants., and adopted da. of Capt. Duncan Kirk; *d.* 1972; *s.* by his el. son [3] DAVID, 3rd Earl and present peer; also Viscount Borodale, and Baron Beatty.

BEAUCHAMP, EARL. (Lygon.) [Earl U.K. 1815.]
[Title Pronounced "Beecham." Name Pronounced "Liggon."]

WILLIAM LYGON, 8th Earl; *b.* July 3rd 1903; *s.* 1938; ed. at Eton, and at Magdalen Coll., Oxford; is a J.P. and D.L. for Worcestershire and an O. St. J.; was an Assist. Liberal Whip in National Govt. (unpaid) 1929-31, Parliamentary Private Sec. (unpaid) to the late Lord Hore-Belisha, when Parliamentary Sec. to Board of Trade, Financial Sec. to the Treasury, Min. of Transport, and Sec. of State for War 1937-38, and a Co. Councillor for Worcestershire 1940-52; Pres. of Three Counties Show 1964; 1939-45 War as Capt. R.A.O.C.; M.P. for E. Div. of Norfolk (*L*) 1929-38: *m.* 1936, Else, *MBE* (a DStJ, Grand Cdr., Order of Dannebrog of Denmark), da. of the late Viggo Schiwe, and widow of Dornon-

The lot is fallen unto me in a fair ground.

ville de la Cour, of Copenhagen.

Ᾱrms,—Argent, two lions passant in pale tails fourchée gules. Crest,—A Saracen's head affrontée couped at the shoulders, proper. Supporters,—*Dexter*, a bear proper, plain collared, muzzled, and chained or; from the collar pendant a shield of the arms of *Beauchamp of Powyke,* viz gules, a fesse between six martlets or; *sinister*, a swan argent wings inverted gules, gorged with a ducal coronet or, therefrom a line reflexed over the back azure, and pendant from the coronet a shield charged as the dexter.

Seat,—Madresfield Court, Malvern. *Town Residence,*—The Stables, 8, Halkin Place, S.W.1. *Club,*—St. James'.

SISTERS LIVING.

Lady Sibell, *b.* 1907 : *m.* 1939, Flight-Lieut. Michael Richard Bernard Rowley, who *d.* 1952, Auxiliary Air Force [Corbet, Bt.]. *Residence,*—Payne's Place, Bushley, Tewkesbury, Gloucestershire.

Lady Mary LYGON, *b.* 1910; resumed the surname of Lygon 1956: *m.* 1939 (m. diss. 1956) H.H. Prince Vsevolode Joannovitch of Russia, who *d.* 1973. *Residence,*—19, The Boltons, SW10.
Lady Dorothy, *b.* 1912 ; late Section Officer W.A.A.F. *Address,*—c/o Messrs C. Hoare & Co., 37, Fleet Street, E.C.4.

WIDOW LIVING OF SON OF SEVENTH EARL
Patricia Janet (Pyndar House, Hanley Castle, Worcester), da. of the late Rev. T. K. Norman: *m.* 1939, the Hon. Richard Edward Lygon, who *d.* 1970, and has issue living [see colls. infra].

COLLATERAL BRANCHES LIVING.
Issue of the late Hon. Richard Edward Lygon, yr. son of 7th Earl, *b.* 1916, *d.* 1970: *m.* 1939, Patricia Janet (ante), da. of the late Rev. T. K. Norman:—

Lettice Patricia Mary, *b.* 1940.——Rosalind Elizabeth, *b.* 1946: *m.* 1967, Gerald John Ward, of Chilton Park Farm, Hungerford, Berks. [see E. Dudley, colls.].

Issue of the late Lt.-Col. the Hon. Robert Lygon, MVO, MC, Gren. Guards, 3rd son of 6th Earl, *b.* 1879, *d.* 1952: *m.* 1903, Cecil Albinia, who *d.* 1956, da. of the late Sir George Gough Arbuthnot [Arbuthnot, Bt., colls.]:—

REGINALD ARTHUR, *b.* July 28th, 1904; ed. at Eton, and at New Coll., Oxford: *m.* 1930, Agnes Mary Louise, who *d.* 1969, da. of the late Rev. George Fancourt Bell, V. of Riverhead, Sevenoaks, and Hon. Canon of Rochester, and has issue living, Margaret Annora Mary, *b.* 1931: *m.* 1955, Michael Richard West de Wend Fenton of Ebberston Hall, Yorks. [E. Buchan, colls.], and has issue living Jonathan Lygon West *b.* 1958, Mathew Mark Ross *b.* 1960, Rosalie Marye Margaret *b.* 1957, Clarissa Emily *b.* 1962,—Anne Juliet, *b.* 1937,—Eleanor Barbara Muriel, *b.* 1938: *m.* 1st, 1960 (m. diss. 1965), William James Cavendish-Bentinck, who *d.* 1966 [D. Portland, colls.]; 2ndly, 1966, Robert Gore Langrishe, of 9, York Mansions, Prince of Wales Drive, SW11 [see Langrishe, Bt.]. *Residence,*— River House, 3, Chelsea Embankment, SW3.

PREDECESSORS.—[1] WILLIAM Lygon, el. son of the late Reginald Lygon (who had assumed that surname by Act of Parliament, in lieu of his patronymic of Pyndar on becoming heir to the Madresfield Estates through his mother, Margaret Lygon); *b.* 1747; sat as M.P. for Worcestershire 1776-1806; cr. *Baron Beauchamp of Powyke* (peerage of United Kingdom) 1806, and *Viscount Elmley* and *Earl Beauchamp* (peerage of United Kingdom) 1815 : *m.* 1780, Catherine, who *d.* 1844, dau. of James Denn; *d.* 1816 ; *s.* by his el. son [2] WILLIAM, 2nd Earl; M.P. for Worcestershire 1806-16; *d.s.p.* 1823; *s.* by his brother [3] JOHN, 3rd Earl ; assumed for himself by Roy. licence the surname of Pindar only: *m.* 1st, 1814, Lady Charlotte Scott, who *d.* 1846, only dau. of 1st Earl of Clonmell; 2ndly, 1850, the Hon. Catherine Otway, who *d.* 1875, dau. of Baroness Braye, and widow of Henry Murray ; *d.* 1853 ; *s.* by his brother, [4] HENRY BEAUCHAMP, 4th Earl, *b.* 1785; was Gen. in the Army, Col. 2nd Life Guards, and sometime M.P. for West Worcestershire : *m.* 1824, Lady Susan Caroline Eliot, who *d.* 1835, dau. of 2nd Earl of St. Germans; *d.* 1863; *s.* by his el. son [5] HENRY, 5th Earl; was Capt. 1st Life Guards, and M.P. for West Worcestershire 1853-63; *d.s.p.* 1866; *s.* by his brother [6] FREDERICK, P.C., 6th Earl, *b.* 1830 ; Lord-Lieut. of Worcestershire ; M.P. for Tewkesbury (C) 1857-63, and for W. Worcestershire 1863-6 ; Lord of Admiralty 1859, Lord Steward of H.M.'s Household 1874-80, and Paymaster-Gen. 1885-6 and 1886-7 : *m.* 1st, 1868, Lady Mary Catherine Stanhope, who *d.* 1876, dau. of 5th Earl Stanhope; 2ndly, 1878, Lady Emily Annora Charlotte Pierrepont, who *d.* 1935, dau. of 3rd Earl Manvers ; *d.* 1891 ; *s.* by his el. son [7] WILLIAM, K.G., P.C., K.C.M.G., T.D., 7th Earl, *b.* 1872; was Gov. and Com.-in-Ch. of N.S. Wales 1899-1901, Capt. of H.M.'s Corps of Gentlemen-at-Arms 1906-7, Lord Steward of the Household 1907-10, Lord Pres. of the Council 1910, First Commr. of Works 1910-14, Lord Warden of the Cinque Ports 1913-34, again Lord Pres. of the Council 1914-15, and Leader of Liberal Party in House of Lords 1924-31: *m.* 1902, Lady Lettice Mary Elizabeth Grosvenor, who *d.* 1936, dau. of the late Earl Grosvenor, el. son of 1st Duke of Westminster; *d.* 1938 ; *s.* by his el. son [8] WILLIAM, 8th Earl and present peer : also Viscount Elmley, and Baron Beauchamp of Powyke.

BEAUFORT, DUKE OF. (Somerset.) [Duke E. 1682.]

MUTARE VEL TIMERE SPERNO

I scorn to change or to fear.

HENRY HUGH ARTHUR FITZROY SOMERSET, *K.G., G.C.V.O., P.C.,* 10th Duke ; *b.* April 4th, 1900 ; *s.* 1924 ; ed. at Eton ; is Hereditary Keeper of Raglan Castle, Lord-Lieut. of Bristol and Gloucestershire, a KStJ. Dep. Hon. Col. A & C Sqdns'. Wessex Yeo, RAC, TAVR since 1972, and late Capt. Roy. Horse Guards; has Grand Cross of Order of Leopold of Belgium, of Legion of Honour, of Orders of Faithful Service of Roumania, of St. Olav of Norway, of Dannebrog of Denmark, of North Star of Sweden, of Menelek II of Ethiopia, of Christ of Portugal, and of House of Orange of the Netherlands; a Grand Officer of Orders of Orange Nassau of the Netherlands, and of Al Rafidain of Iraq; appointed High Steward of Bristol and Gloucester 1925, Master of the Horse to H.M. 1936, Freeman of City of Gloucester 1945, High Steward of Tewkesbury 1948, and Chancellor of Bristol Univ. 1966-70; Hon. LLD Bristol; Pres. of Marylebone Cricket Club 1952-53; GCVO 1930, PC 1936, KG 1937; received Roy. Victorian Chain 1953: *m.* 1923, Lady (Victoria Constance) Mary Cambridge, da. of 1st Marquess of Cambridge.

Arms.—Quarterly, 1st and 4th azure, three fleurs-de-lis or, *France* ; 2nd and 3rd gules, three lions passant guardant in pale or, *England ;* all within a bordure compony argent and azure. Crest.—A portcullis or, nailed azure, chains gold. Supporters.—*Dexter,* a panther argent, flames issuing from his mouth and ears proper, plain collared and chained or, and semée of torteaux, hurts and pommes alternately ; *sinister,* a wyvern, wings endorsed vert, in the mouth a sinister hand, couped at the wrist gules.
Seat,—Badminton House, Gloucestershire.

COLLATERAL BRANCHES LIVING.

(Co-heirs presumptive to Baronies of Botetourt and Herbert cr. 1461 only)

Granddaughters of the late Lady Blanche Linnie Somerset (infra):—

Issue of the late Lady Rosemary Alexandra Eliot, *b.* 1919, *d.* 1963: *m.* 1st, 1939, Capt. Edward Christian Frederick Nutting, RHG, who *d.* (on active ser.) 1943, 2nd son of the late Sir Harold Stansmore Nutting, 2nd Bt.; 2ndly, 1945 (m. annulled 1949), Lt.-Cdr. David Frederick Hew Dunn, RN; 3rdly, 1949, Col. Ralph Alexander Rubens, Sherwood Foresters:—

(By 1st m.) DAVINA ROSEMARY ENID NUTTING, *b.* 1940; resumed by deed poll 1969 her maiden surname of Nutting: *m.* 1960 (*m.* diss. 1969), as his 2nd wife, John Martin Brentall Cope, and has issue living [see Nutting, Bt., colls.].——(by 3rd m.) ALEXANDRA LOUISE (27, Gertrude St., SW10), *b.* 1951.

Issue of the late Lady Blanche Linnie Somerset, da. of 9th Duke, *b.* 1897, *d.* 1968: *m.* 1st, 1918, the 6th Earl of St. Germans, who *d.* 1922; 2ndly, 1924, Capt. George Francis Valentine Scott Douglas, who *d.* 1930 [Douglas Bt., cr. 1786, ext.]:—

(By 1st m.) LADY CATHLEEN BLANCHE LILY, *b.* 1921: *m.* 1st, 1946, Capt. John Seyfried, RHG, who obtained a divorce 1956; 2ndly, 1957, Havelock Henry Trevor Hudson, and has issue by 1st and 2nd *m.* [see E. St. Germans].

(Male line in remainder to Dukedom and other peerages)

Grandchildren of the late Henry Charles Somers Augustus Somerset, OBE, only son of the Rt. Hon. Lord Henry Richard Charles Somerset, 2nd son of 8th Duke:—

Issue of the late Capt. Henry Robert Somers Fitzroy de Vere Somerset, DSO, *b.* 1898, *d.* 1965: *m.* 1922, Bettine Violet (The Round House, Netton, Salisbury), da. of the late Maj. Charles Edward Malcolm [see Malcolm, Bt., colls.]:—

DAVID ROBERT (90, Eaton Terr., SW1. *Club*,—White's), *b.* Feb. 23rd, 1928; ed. at Eton; late Lt. Coldstream Guards; *h.p.* to Dukedom and all other peerages except Baronies of Botetourt and Herbert, cr. 1461: *m.* 1950, Lady Caroline Jane Thynne, da. of 6th Marquess of Bath, and has issue living, Henry John Fitzroy, *b.* 1952,—Edward Alexander, *b.* 1958,—John Robert, *b.* 1964,—Anne Mary, *b.* 1955.——(Elizabeth) Anne, *b.* 1929: *m.* 1953, Maj. David Alwyn Carne Rasch, Grenadier Guards [see Rasch, Bt.].

Grandchildren of the late Henry Plantagenet Somerset (infra):—

Issue of the late Capt. Charles William Henry Rollo Somerset, M.C., *b.* 1895, *d.* 1936: *m.* 1925, Glory Kathleen (now of 162, Prince Edward Parade, Redcliffe, Queensland), dau. of Frederick Albert Turner, of Glenbardi, Toogoolawah, Queensland:—

Arthur Henry, *b.* 1926; S.-W. Pacific 1944-5 with Roy. Australian Navy: *m.* 1950, Dorothy Joan, only dau. of William Harrison, of Brisbane, Queensland, and has issue living, Arthur Rollo Henry Plantagenet, *b.* 1953,—John William Plantagenet, *b.* 1965,—Andrea Helen, *b.* 1957. *Residence,*— 31, Rangeview St., Aspley, Brisbane, Queensland.——Patricia Honor, *b.* 1928: *m.* 1953, Norman David Thomas Butler, and has issue living, Luke Norman, *b.* 1954, Robert David, *b.* 1957,—Glory Patricia, *b.* 1962. *Residence,*—Bowman Rd., Caloundra, Queensland.——Barbara Joan, *b.* 1933.

Grandchildren of the late Col. Charles Henry Somerset, C.B., el. son of the late Lieut.-Gen. Sir Henry Somerset, K.C.B., K.H., el. son of the late Gen. Lord Charles Henry Somerset, M.P., 2nd son of 5th Duke:—

Issue of the late Com. William Henry Somerset, R.N., *b.* 1849, *d.* 1922: *m.* 1892, Kate Eliza Bramley, who *d.* 1909, el. dau. of the late Capt. Edwin George Mainwaring, 91st Highlanders:—

Nina Evelyn Mary (c/o 455, Charminster Rd., Bournemouth), *b.* 1893.

Issue of the late Henry Plantagenet Somerset, *b.* 1852, *d.* 1936: *m.* 1879, Katherine Rose who *d.* 1935, dau. of David Cannon M'Connel, of Cressbrook, Queensland:—

Hereward Henry Plantagenet (Durong, Tingoora, Queensland), *b.* 1900: *m.* 1923, Jean Castle, da. of Frederick Albert Turner, of Glenbardi, Toogoolawah, Queensland, and has issue living, Edward Plantagenet (Banhinia Park, Wandoan, Queensland), *b.* 1924; European 1942-44 War with RAAF: *m.* 1952, Elsie Joy, only dau. of Stanley Morrow, of Lismore, N.S. Wales, and has issue living, Richard John Plantagenet *b.* 1960, Pru-Ellen *b.* 1956,—David Plantagenet (of Peek-a-Do, Taroom, Queensland), *b.* 1926 : *m.* 1953, Margaret Pamela, dau. of David Victor Staines, of Jandowae, Queensland, and has issue living, Jennifer Margaret *b.* 1954, Kerri Jane *b.* 1957, Erica Jan *b.* 1959,—Robert Plantagenet (Caboonbah, Proston, Queensland), *b.* 1930: *m.* 1952, Leslie Rawdons. only da. of Rawdon Briggs, of Swindon, Mount Perry, Queensland, and has issue living, Robert Plantagenet *b.* 1959, Leslie Ann *b.* 1953, Katherine Nina *b.* 1957, Victoria Joyce *b.* 1967, Jane Elizabeth *b.* 1968,—William Plantagenet, *b.* 1934; late RAN: *m.* 1961, Marion Helene, da. of M. Blackman, of Brisbane, and has issue living, Mark William Plantagenet *b.* 1965, Steven Plantagenet *b.* 1968, Christene Helene *b.* 1963,—Charles Plantagenet, *b.* 1944,—Susan Somerset, *b.* 1945: *m.* 1969, Heath Hill Hassall, of Derbarby, Mundubbera 4626, Qld., and has issue living, Rem Hill *b.* 1970, Martine Dione *b.* 1974.——Gwendolin Frances, *b.* 1888.——Doris Henrietta, *b.* 1893: *m.* 1917, Aldred Richard Waite, and has issue living, Aldred Charles Derek, *b.* 1920; 1939-45 War with Austn. Imperial Force,—Rollo Beaufort (c/o Cunningham Laboratory, St. Lucia, Brisbane), *b.* 1931; with CSIRO: *m.* 1964, Jennifer Ann, da. of L. G. Johnson, of Birkdale, Qld., late of Newbury, Be ks., and has issue living Philipa Joan *b.* 1967,—Lo'a Katharine, *b.* 1925: *m.* 1949. Richard James Alexander Anderson, of Tinton Biarra, Esk, Qld., and has issue living, David Dunlop *b.* 1955, Hans *b.* 1957, Alexandra Jane *b.* 1950, Karn *b.* 1953, Peta *b.* 1961. *Residence,*—3rd Av., Mayes Estate, Calaundra, Qld.——Ealhswith Anne Matilda (5, Holland Rd., Holland Park 4121, Qld., Aust.), *b.* 1897: *m.* 1921, Percival Dent Ridgeway Drane, who *d.* 1962, and has issue living, Roland Dent (of 50, Hawkwood St., Mount Gravatt, Qld.), *b.* 1931: *m.* 1958, Judith Mary Saunders, and has issue living, Donald Andrew *b.* 19—, Colin Samuel *b.* 1964, Louise Mary *b.* 1959,—Neil Dent (of 34, Hale St., Margate, Queensland) *b.* 1938,—Lima Rose, *b.* 1922: *m.* 1946, James Peter Wilson, of 23, Forbes St., Turner, Canberra Aust., and has issue living, Brian James *b.* 1947, Noel Peter *b.* 1950, Rosanne Mary *b.* 1948: *m.* 1967, David Bell, of 22, Inlander Cres., Flynn, Canberra, ACT (and has issue living, Darryn David *b.* 1972, Leanne Peta *b.* 1970),—Moira Anne Somerset, *b.* 1925: *m.* 1st, 1949, George Wallington Michael, who *d.* 1961; 2ndly, 1969 Alexander Evans Thomson, of Gira Gira, Linville, Qld., Aust., and has issue living (by 1st m.) George Jason *b.* 1950, Murry Percival *b.* 1953, Douglas Henry *b.* 1957, Maureen Jeanette *b.* 1951,—Claudia, *b.* 1929: *m.* 1955, Stanley Askey Sharpe, and has issue living, Sue Claudia *b.* 1956, Heather Anne *b.* 1959. *Residence,*—20, Ricardo St., Kelvin Grove, Qld.

Grandchildren of the late Brig.-Gen. Charles Wyndham Somerset, CB, CMG, MVO. yr. son of the late Col. Henry George Edward Somerset, 2nd son of the late Lt.-Gen. Sir Henry Somerset, KCB, KH, (ante):—

Issue of the late Major Alan Fitz Roy Somerset, *b.* 1902, *d.* 1940: *m.* 1927, Nell Lauder, who *d.* 1951, dau. of the late Harold E. Pyman :—

Robin Fitzroy (16, Kingsgate St., Winchester), *b.* 1930; ed. at Eton; late Capt. Rifle Bde.——Barbara Carol (9, Queens Gate Pl., SW7), *b.* 1933.

Grandchildren of the late Fitz Roy Maclean Henry Somerset, 3rd son of the late Lt.-Gen. Sir Henry Somerset, KCB, KH (ante):—

Issue of the late Fitz Roy Henry Somerset, *b.* 1881, *d.* 1946 : *m.* 1902, Martha Johanna (now of 32a, Connolly Place, Beaconsfield, Cape Province, S. Africa), dau. of Philip Watermeyer, of Hanover, S. Africa :—

Raglan Henry, *b.* 1903; is a Boilermaker, Daggafontein Mines: *m.* 1928, Hendrica Alida Van der Burg, of Bloemfontein, S. Africa, and has issue living, Eugene, *b.* 1929 : *m.* 1951, Valerie Rene Stewart, of Benoni, S. Africa, and has issue living, Sharon *b.* 1952, Geraldine *b.* 1954,—John Fitzroy, *b.* 1933,—Eunice, *b.* 1931.——Philip Arthur, *b.* 1905. *Residence,*—32A, Connolly Place, Beaconsfield, Cape Province, S. Africa.——Harry Edward, *b.* 1914 : *m.* 1939, Muriel Elizabeth Watkins, and has issue living, Ronald Arthur, *b.* 1940,—Beryl Louise, *b.* 1946.——Lilian Blanche, *b.* 1906 : *m.* 1st, 1933, Richard Flagg, who *d.* 1940 ; 2ndly, 1949, Thomas Grieve, and has issue living, (by 1st marriage) John Richard, *b.* 1937,—Marjorie, *b.* 1935. *Residence,*—Floreat, 8, Paschendale Road, Delville, Germiston, S. Africa.——Winifred Mary, *b.* 1925 : *m.* 1948, Derrick Egerton Moult. and has issue living, Adrian Thomas, *b.* 1951,—Kathleen Dawn, *b.* 1949.

Granddaughter of the late Maj. Henry Calthorpe Somerset (infra):—
Issue of the late Henry George FitzRoy Somerset, *b.* 1885, *d.* 1958 : *m.* 1913, Honore, *d.* 19—, dau. of J. Olive, of Ravenswood, Queensland :—
Margot, *b.* 1916: *m.* 1943, Donald Campbell, 39, Shellcove Rd., Neutral Bay, Sydney, NS Wales, and has issue living, Bruce Ronald, *b.* 1946,—Anne-Marie, *b.* 1944.

Granddaughter of the late Rev. Villiers Henry Plantagenet Somerset, 3rd son of Gen. Lord Charles Henry Somerset, M.P. (ante) :—
Issue of the late John Henry William Somerset, *b.* 1848, *d.* 1928 : *m.* 1st, 1889, Mary de Chair, who *d.* 1892, dau. of the late Rev. William Charles Denshire, of Thetford House, Lincolnshire; 2ndly, 1893, Isabel Maud, dau. of Frederick Courtney, formerly of Larkhall Rise, Clapham, S.W. :—
(By 2nd marriage) Isabel Maud Mary de Chair, *b.* 1894. *Residence,*—

Granddaughter of the Rev. Henry Plantagenet Somerset, son of the Rev. Villers Plantagenet Somerset (ante):—
Issue of the late Capt. Noel Henry Plantagenet Somerset, *b.* 1885, *d.* 1921 : *m.* 1915, Helen Barbara, who *d.* 1952, dau. of the late Joseph Arderne Ormerod, M.D., F.R.C.P., of Greenhill, Upham, Hants, and 25, Upper Wimpole Street, W. :—
Mary Arderne Frances, *b.* 1920.

Grandchildren of the late Vere Francis John Somerset, son of the late Col. Poulett George Henry Somerset, C.B., M.P., son of the late Gen. Lord Charles Henry Somerset, M.P. (ante):—
Issue of the late William Francis Somerset, *b.* 1876, *d.* 1942: *m.* 1st, 1899, Laura Helen, who *d.* 1926, dau. of W. H. Thoms, of Port Sydney, Muskoka, Ontario, Canada; 2ndly, 1927, Ann Margaret Vibert, who *d.* 1955, dau. of C. V. Lawrence, of Allensville, Ontario, Canada :—
(By 1st m.) Lionel Francis (Ladell Heights, Port Sydney, Muskoka, Ont., Canada), *b.* 1903: *m.* 1937, Wanda Gertrude, da. of Arthur W. Clarke, of Port Sydney, Ontario, and has issue living, Lionel Vere, *b.* 1938: *m.* 1970, Janet Mary, da. of Maj. David Colin Heggie, GM, of Brampton, Ontario,— Cyril Henry, *b.* 1940: *m.* 1963 (m. diss. 1972), Bonnie Erin, da. of Lloyd W. Wood, of Port Sydney, and has issue living, Robin Marie *b.* 1964,—William John, *b.* 1944.——Helen Louisa (Port Sydney, Muskoka, Ont., Canada), *b.* 1902.——Jessie Catherine, *b.* 1907: *m.* 1944, Brodie Kay, of Port Sydney, Muskoka, Ont., Canada, and has issue living, William Douglas, *b.* 1949.——Lenora Mary, *b.* 1909: *m.* 1936, George Simmens, who *d.* 1973, and has issue living, Donald Wayne, *b.* 1938: *m.* 1970, Elaine Mary, da. of Robert Bailey, of Cartier, Ont., and has issue living, David Robert *b.* 1974,— Norma Helen, *b.* 1944. *Residence,*—129, Whitney Av., North Bay, Ont., Canada.

Issue of the late Charles Somerset, *b.* 1878, *d.* 1941: *m.* 1913, Doris Amy (16, Allenby Rd., Dalkeith, W. Aust.), da. of Edward George Cronin:—
Henry Charles Fitzroy (16, Allenby Rd., Dalkeith, W. Aust.), *b.* 1919: *m.* 1946, Patricia Barr, da. of the late Rudolph George Barr Goyder, and has issue living, Charles Nigel Fitzroy, *b.* 1953,—Virginia Fitzroy, *b.* 1947,—Suzette Fitzroy, *b.* 1950,—Mary Ursula Fitzroy, *b.* 1958,—Georgina Patricia Fitzroy, *b.* 1963.——Claud Edward Ralph, *b.* 1925.——Mary Poulett, *b.* 1916.——Diana, *b.* 1918.—— Susette, *b.* 1920. *Residence,*—Ferndale, Balingup, W. Australia.

Issue of the late Hugh Somerset, *b.* 1879, *d.* 1953: *m.* 1911, Elizabeth Jane, who *d.* 1963, da. of the late William Verran, of Herodsfoot, Cornwall:—
Annette Joan (Argyll House, Camelford, Cornwall), *b.* 1915.
Issue of the late Vere Edward Somerset, M.R.C.S., L.R.C.P., *b.* 1884, *d.* 1961: *m.* 1910, Gladys Mildred, da. of Richard Baker, of Dolton, Devon:—
Vere Murielle Cecily Idina, *b.* 1912: *m.* 1st, 1934, Fl.-Lt. Dudley Dudley Scorgie, RAF; 2ndly, 1959, Capt. Alan Abraham, late RASC, and has issue living (by 1st m.), Vera Roderick, *b.* 1938,—Annette Idina, *b.* 1939: *m.* 1966, Alan Peter Crow, of Cherrington Manor, Newport, Salop.

Grandson of the late Col. Poulett George Henry Somerset, C.B., M.P. (ante):—
Issue (by 3rd marriage) of the late Capt. Henry Charles FitzRoy Somerset, *b.* 1860, *d.* 1925 : *m.* 1st, 1889, Amy, who *d.* 1889, dau. of Henry Cox, formerly of 8, Falkner Square, Liverpool, 2ndly, 1894, Barbara, who *d.* 1894, widow of James Alfred Cochran, of North Wakool Station, Riverina, Australia; 3rdly, 1897, Isabella Goodsir, who *d.* 1941, dau. of the late John Mowat, J.P., of Glasgow, and widow of John Anthony Inglis, shipbuilder, of Glasgow, and Inchalloch, Dunbartonshire:—
Charles Alexander, *b.* 1901 ; ed. at Radley ; late temporary Capt. R.A., and in Directorate of Selection of Personnel, War Office : *m.* 1st, 1926, Audrey Vernon, who *d.* 1935, dau. of G. W. L. Thompson, of Olton, Warwickshire ; 2ndly, 1955, Winifred May, dau. of J. A. Helyar, of Windyridge, East Coker, Somerset, and has issue living, (by 1st marriage) Audrey Barbara, *b.* 1929. *Residence,*— Hawkesgrove, Grinstead, Salisbury.

Granddaughter of the late Charles Bruce Henry Somerset, 3rd Buffs, son of the late Col. Henry Charles Capel Somerset, son of the late Rev. Lord William George Henry Somerset, 6th son of 5th Duke :—
Issue of the late Sybil Mary Blanche Somerset, *d.* 1932 : *m.* 1901, Major George Frederick Molineux-Montgomerie, Grenadier Guards, who *d.* (killed in action during European War) 1915 :—
Rosemary Heartsease Beare, *b.* 1908 : *m.* 1st, 1937, Norman Miller ; 2ndly, 1941, Capt. Reginald Dilworth Howard, R.N. (retired), who *d.* 1949 ; 3rdly, 1953, Thomas James [see B. Northbourne, colls.]. *Residence,*—Handen Farm, Aldington, near Ashford, Kent.

Grandchildren of the late FitzRoy William Henry Somerset, son of the late Col. Henry Charles Capel Somerset (ante):—
Issue of the late Henry Charles FitzRoy Somerset, *b.* 1870, *d.* 1940 : *m.* 1920, Winifred Marion, dau. of the late George Bartram, of London, N. :—
Francis Charles, *b.* 1921 : *m.* 1945, Sheila Marion, dau. of Aldred Davis, of Yass, N.S. Wales, and has issue living, Susan, *b.* 1952. *Residence,*—

Issue of the late Raglan Somerset, *b.* 1872, *d.* 1940 : *m.* 1900, Madeleine Blanche, dau. of
George Nowland, of Quirindi, N.S. Wales:—

Fitzroy Raglan (81, Anthony St., Ascot, Brisbane 4007, Qld.) *b.* 1901: *m.* 1924, Alma Lauderdale, da. of
Henry Lauderdale Maitland, of Melbourne, Aust., and has issue living, Raglan Fitzroy, *DM*, *b.* 1925:
m. 19—, Lenore Miller, of Brisbane, and has issue living, Stephen *b.* 1956.——Lola Alice, *b.* 1905: *m.*
1929, Noel Lauderdale Maitland, Lochiel, Toorak Rd., Hamilton, Brisbane, Qld., and has issue living,
Diana Lauderdale, *b.* 1931: *m.* 1952, Carl Lindsay Cilento, MB, BS, of Brisbane, Qld., son of Sir
Raphael West Cilento, MD, and has issue living, Peter Carl *b.* 1953, Richard West *b.* 1961, Miranda
b. 1955, Joanne *b.* 1957, Belinda (twin) *b.* 1957, Madeline *b.* 1966.——Blanche Helen, *b.* 1911: *m.* 1st,
1934, Kenneth Peter Robertson; 2ndly, 1958, James Richard Lambert Hyne, and has issue living,
(by 1st m.) Peter Kenneth, *b.* 1936,—Susan Blanche, *b.* 1938: *m.* 1957, Capt. Warren John Murray,
of Woomera, S. Aust., and has issue living, Kenneth Peter *b.* 1958, Niell Julian *b.* 1960. *Residence,*—
Ilfracombe, 335, Lennox St., Maryborough, Qld.

Granddaughter of the late Raglan Turberville Henry Somerset (infra):—
Issue of the late Raglan Horatio Edwyn Henry Somerset, Q.C., *b.* 1885, *d.* 1956 : *m.* 1915,
Adelaide Millicent Blanche Gwendolen, who *d.* 1958, only dau. of the late Arthur William
FitzRoy Somerset (infra):—

Anna Millicent Horatia FitzRoy, *b.* 1929: *m.* 1950, William John Francis Tribe, and has issue living,
William John Raglan Horatio, *b.* 1955,—Raglan Horatio Andrew Harold, *b.* 1961,—Mary Anna
Kathleen Horatia, *b.* 1958. *Residence,*—Hill House, Raglan, Monmouthshire.

Grandchildren of the late Rev. William Somerset, son of the late Rev. Lord
William George Henry Somerset, 6th son of 5th Duke :—
Issue of the late Raglan Turberville Henry Somerset, *b.* 1859, *d.* 1938: *m.* 1884, Elizabeth
Horatia Anne, who *d.* 1929, dau. of the late Rev. Horatio Nelson Nelson-Ward, R. of
Radstock, Bath :—

Lily Horatia Ethel Georgina, *b.* 1888 ; author of "The Somerset Sequence": *m.* 1913, Lieut.-Col.
Hugh Norcott Durant, formerly Roy. Irish Rifles, who *d.* 1948. *Residence,*—2, High St., Raglan,
Mon.

Issue of the late Charles Edward Henry Somerset, *b.* 1862, *d.* 1939: *m.* 1908, Edith
who *d.* 1932, dau. of Lionel Alexander Weatherly, M.D., of Winsley House, Stourwood
Bournemouth :—

William Raglan Henry Guy, *b.* 1912: *m.* 1st, 1932 (*m.* diss. 1950), Edna Margaret, da. of Ernald Dry-
brough Smith, MD, FRCS, of Hastings; 2ndly, 1955, Evelyn, da. of William Lee, of Bradford, and
has issue living, (by 1st m.) William Michael John Charles (82, Bourne Cres., Kings Heath, Northampton), *b.* 1934: *m.* 1967, Pearl Langley, and has issue living, John Reginald *b.* 1970,—Margaret Dry-
brough (c/o Lloyds Bank, Wareham, Dorset), *b.* 1933: *m.* 1951, Herbert Paul Liquorish, RHG (Head
Keepers Lodge, Wake Arms, Epping, Essex), and has issue living, Susan Carlotta Anne Somerset *b.*
1953, Deri Jane Somerset *b.* 1957, Cherillyn Mary Somerset *b.* 1959, Karin Melinda Somerset *b.*
1963,—(by 2nd m.) Nicholas Anthony, *b.* 1956,—Stephanie Lynn, *b.* 1960,—Amanda Jayne *b.* 1961.
——Herbert Michael John Charles, *b.* 1920. *Residence,*—Ashbrook Hall, Hollington, St. Leonards-
on-Sea.——Charlotte Georgina Rose Mary, *b.* 1909; ed. at Oxford Univ. (BA 1932): *m.* 1933, Jules
Omer Malfroy, LLM, and has issue living, Jules Michel Charles Somerset, *b.* 1939; MA Camb.: *m.*
1967, Moira Gore, and has issue living, Emma Charlotte Mary Somerset *b.* 1968,—Deborah Mary
Somerset, *b.* 1934; MA Camb.,—Louise Georgiana Somerset, *b.* 1942; BSc St. Andrews Univ.: *m.*
1965, Richard Kent Percival, BSc, of 8081, Schöngeising, Am Oberfeld 9, W. Germany, and has issue
living, Charlotte Georgiana *b.* 1972. *Residence,*—The Bridge House, Great
Shelford, Cambridgeshire.——Anne Blanche Edwina Alma, *b.* 1918.

Grandchildren of the late Arthur William FitzRoy Somerset, son of the late Col.
FitzRoy Molyneux Henry Somerset, R.E., son of the late Rev. Lord William
George Henry Somerset (ante) :—
Issue of the late Arthur Plantagenet Francis Cecil Somerset, *b.* 1889. *d.* 1957: *m.* 1916,
Mary Frances Elizabeth (25, Ashfield Park, Martock, Somerset), el. da. of the late Felton
George Randolph [Nepean, Bt., colls.]:—

John FitzRoy Pechell, *b.* 1923 ; ed. at Wellington Coll., and at London Univ. (B.Sc. 1949): is a
qualified Asso. of Chartered Land Agents So., and an A.R.I.C.S. ; European War 1942-45 with
King's Roy. Rifle Corps (wounded) : *m.* 1952, Daphne Marigold, younger dau. of the late Col.
Clement Topham, O.B.E.. M.C., and has issue living, Clement Charles FitzRoy, *b.* 1956,—Annabel
Mary, *b.* 1953,—Philippa Margaret, *b.* 1965. *Residence,*—Holt Farm House, Clapham, nr. Worthing,
Sussex.——Cecily Mary Adelaide, *b.* 1919: *m.* 1946, Maj. Laurence James Howe-Ely, 60th Rifles,
and has issue living, Christopher Laurence Somerset *b.* 1946,—Michael FitzRoy, *b.* 1950,—Anne
Diana Mary, *b.* 1948. *Residence,*—7, Chelmscote Mansions, Baines Av., Salisbury, Rhodesia,
——Diana Millicent, *b.* 1921: *m.* 1943, Cdr. Geoffrey Inderwick Palmer, R.N., and has issue living.
Juliet Elizabeth *b.* 1945: *m.* 1967, Lt.-Col. Simon Christie Cooper, Life Gds., of West End House,
Donhead St. Andrew, Shaftesbury, and has issue living, Jonathan Francis Christie *b.* 1969, Venetia
Elizabeth Somerset *b.* 1971,—Anthea Somerset, *b.* 1947,—Catherine Annabella Inderwick, *b.* 1952.
Residence,—The Treasurer's House, Martock, Somerset.

Grandchildren of the late Rev. Boscawen Thomas George Henry Somerset, son of
the late Rev. Lord William George Henry Somerset (ante) :—
Issue of the late William Horace Boscawen Somerset, *b.* 1880, *d.* 1946 : *m.* 1921, Ruble
Drummond-Nairne (Thackit Eaves, Highclere, Newbury), da. of the late William Redston
Warner:—

FitzRoy Douglas Boscawen (Thackit Eaves, Highclere, Newbury), *b.* 1923; ed. at Marlborough, and
at Exeter Coll., Oxford (BA 1949, MA 1957); formerly Lt. King's Shropshire LI; in Colonial
Administrative Ser., Nigeria 1950-57, and Assist. Adviser, Aden Protectorate 1957-68; 1939-45
War (wounded): *m.* 1962, Sheila Jean, da. of Dr. D J. B. Wilson, of High Wycombe, Bucks, and
has issue living, Douglas William Boscawen, *b.* 1965,—Eirene Helen Giffard *b.* 1963.——Helen Jane
Boscawen, *b.* 1925; ed. at Oxford Univ. (MA 1950): *m.* 1950, Henry Ensor Fosset Lock, of Deer
Leap House, Moreton, Dorchester, Dorset, and has issue living, Edward Henry Somerset, *b.* 1953,—
Charles John Somerset, *b.* 1955,—Richard Michael Somerset, *b.* 1959,—Amanda Mary Somerset,
b. 1966.

Descendants of the late Field-Marshal Lord FitzRoy James Henry Somerset,
G.C.B. (8th son of 5th Duke), who was cr. *Baron Raglan* 1852 [see that title].

PREDECESSORS.—[1] *Sir* CHARLES Somerset, *K.G.*, natural son of Henry Beaufort, 3rd Duke
of Somerset, who was 3rd in descent from John of Gaunt and Catherine Swynford ; Sir Charles
was summoned to Parliament in right of his wife, as *Lord Herbert* (peerage of England, cr.
1461); cr. *Baron Herbert of Raglan*, Chepstow and Gower (peerage of England) 1506, and *Earl
of Worcester* (peerage of England) 1513 ; appointed Lord Chamberlain for life; *d.* 1526 ; s. by
his el. son [2] HENRY, 2nd Earl ; *d.* 1549 ; s. by his el. son [3] WILLIAM, *K.G.*, 3rd Earl ; *d.*
1589; s. by his son [4] EDWARD, *K.G.*, 4th Earl; was Master of the Horse 1601-15; his 3rd
son, cr. *Viscount Somerset*, was Master of the Horse to Queen Anne, consort of James I , the
Earl *d.* 1628; s by his el. son [5] HENRY, 5th Earl; a devoted royalist; garrisoned Raglan
Castle, and at his own expense held it for nearly four years against the Parliamentary forces;
cr. *Marquess of Worcester* (peerage of England) 1642; *d.* 1646; s. by his el. son [6] EDWARD,

2nd Marquess; a zealous partisan of Charles I., who addressed him as *Earl of Glamorgan* before he *s.* as Marquess; *d.* 1667; *s.* by his son [7] HENRY, KG, PC, 3rd Marquess; Lord Pres. of Wales; cr. *Duke of Beaufort* (peerage of England) 1682: on the accession of William and Mary he refused to take the oath of allegiance and afterwards lived in retirement; *d.* 1699; *s.* by his grandson [8] HENRY, K.G., 2nd Duke; *d.* 1714; *s.* by his el. son [9] HENRY, K.G., 3rd Duke; *d.* 1746; *s.* by his brother [10] CHARLES NOEL, 4th Duke: *m.* Elizabeth, sister of 4th Baron Botetourt [see *⁎* infra]; *d.* 1756; *s.* by his son [11] HENRY, K.G., 5th Duke; was Master of the Horse to Queen Charlotte 1768-80; *s.* as *Baron Botetourt* [see *⁎* infra]; *d.* 1803; *s.* by his el. son [12] HENRY CHARLES, K.G., 6th Duke, Lord-Lieut. of cos. Gloucester, Monmouth, and Brecon; *d.* 1835; *s.* by his el. son [13] HENRY, K.G., 7th Duke; *b.* 1792; served with distinction in Peninsula War: *m.* 1st, 1814, Georgiana Frederica, who *d.* 1821, dau. of the Hon. Henry FitzRoy [B. Southampton]; 2ndly, 1822, Emily Frances, dau. of Culling Charles Smith; *d.* 1853; *s.* by his son [14] HENRY CHARLES FITZROY, K.G., P.C., 8th Duke, *b.* 1824; Lord-Lieut. of Monmouthshire; M.P. for E. Gloucestershire (*C*) 1842-56; was Master of the Horse 1858-9 and 1866-8: *m.* 1845, Lady Georgiana Charlotte Curzon, el. dau. of 1st Earl Howe, G.C.H.; *d.* 1899; *s.* by his el. son [15] HENRY ADELBERT WELLINGTON FITZROY, 9th Duke, *b.* 1847; High Steward of Gloucester and Bristol; bore Curtana at Coronation of King George V. 1911 : *m.* 1895, Louise Emily, who *d.* 1945, dau. of the late William Henry Harford, JP, DL, of Oldtown, Tockington, and widow of Baron Carlo de Tuyll; *d.* 1924; *s.* by his only son [16] HENRY HUGH ARTHUR FITZROY, 10th Duke and present peer; also Marquess of Worcester, Earl of Worcester, Baron Herbert of Raglan, Chepstow and Gower, Lord Herbert, and Baron Botetourt.

⁂ [1] JOHN de Botetourt, an eminent military commander, took a leading part in the Scottish Wars of Edward I.; was entrusted with the government of the strongest castles, the command of the Fleet, and other duties of the highest importance; summoned to Parliament of England as *Baron Botetourt* 1305-24; *d.* 1324; *s.* by his grandson [2] JOHN, 2nd Baron; was constantly engaged in the French Wars of Edward III.; summoned to Parliament 1342-85; his son John predeceased him, leaving one dau. Joyce (infra); the Baron *d.* 1385, leaving three surviving daus.; *s.* by his grand-dau. [3] JOYCE (ante), wife of Sir Hugh Burnell, Knt.; *d.* 1406, when the barony became abeyant between her three aunts (ante), and the abeyance continued until 1764, when it was terminated in favour of [4] NORBORNE Berkeley, 4th Baron, as the descendant of Katherine (youngest dau. of 2nd Baron) by her marriage with Maurice de Berkeley, of Stoke Gifford, co. Gloucester; the Baron *d.s.p.* 1776, when the barony again became abeyant and continued so until 1803, when the abeyance was terminated in favour of his nephew [5] HENRY, 5th Duke of Beaufort (ante), son of Elizabeth, only sister and sole heiress of 4th Baron.

BEAUMONT OF WHITLEY,' BARON. (Beaumont.) [Life Baron 1967.]

I can do no other.

Rev. TIMOTHY WENTWORTH BEAUMONT, son of the late Maj. Michael Wentworth Beaumont, TD [see V. Allendale, colls.], *b.* Nov. 22nd, 1928; ed. at Eton, Gordonstoun, and Ch. Ch., Oxford (MA); V. of Ch. Ch. Kowloon, Hong Kong 1957-59; Proprietor of *Prism* 1960-65 and *New Christian*, 1965-70, Chm. of Studio-Vista Ltd. 1963-68, Hon. Treasurer of Liberal Party 1962-63, Head of Liberal Party Organisation 1965-66, Chm. of Liberal Party 1967-68, and Pres. 1969-70; Liberal Spokesman of Education since 1971; Chm. of Inst. for Research into Mental Retardation 1972-74; Proprietor and Editor of *New Outlook* 1972-74; Pres. British Fedn. of Film Socs. since 1974; cr. *Baron Beaumont of Whitley,* of Child's Hill, Greater London (Life Baron) 1967: *m.* 1955, Mary Rose, da. of Lt.-Col. Charles Edward Wauchope, MC, of Sandhill House, Rogate, Sussex, and has issue.

Arms,—Gules, a lion rampant or, armed and langued azure, between eights crescents in orle of the second. **Crest,**—A bull's head erased quarterly argent and gules, charged with a mullet sable. **Supporters,**—*Dexter*, a phoenix; *sinister*, a pelican vulning herself proper.

Residence,—59, West Heath Rd., NW3. *Clubs,*—Beefsteak, National Liberal.

SONS LIVING.

Hon. Hubert Wentworth, *b.* 1956.
Hon. Alaric Charles Blackett, *b.* 1958.

DAUGHTERS LIVING.

Hon. Atalanta Armstrong, *b.* 1961.
Hon. Ariadne Grace, *b.* 1963.

BEAVERBROOK, BARONY OF. (Aitken.) (Baron U.K. 1917, disclaimed 1964, Bt. U.K. 1916.)

Sir MAX (JOHN WILLIAM MAXWELL) AITKEN, *DSO, DFC,* 2nd *Baronet; b.* Feb. 15th, 1910; *s.* as 2nd Baron Beaverbrook June 9th, 1964; disclaimed his peerage for life June 12th, 1964; ed. at Westminster and at Pembroke Coll., Camb.; Group Capt. Auxiliary Air Force; 1939-45 War (despatches, DFC, DSO, Czechoslovakian Mil. Cross); M.P. for Holborn (*C*) 1945-50: *m.* 1st, 1939, Cynthia H. G. (marriage dissolved 1944), da. of Col. Hugh Glencairn Monteith, D.S.O., O.B.E.; 2ndly, 1946, Ursula Jane (LINDSAY) (marriage dissolved 1950), da. of the late Maj. Robert Orlando Rudolph Kenyon-Slaney [see B. Kenyon, colls.]; 3rdly, 1951, Violet, da. of the late Sir Humphrey Edmund de Trafford, MC, 4th Bt., and has issue by 2nd and 3rd marriages.

Arms.--Argent, two barrulets wavy azure between in chief two maple leaves slipped and in base a thistle eradicated gules, a border sable charged with eight besants. *Crest,*--Upon a drum proper a cock gules, wattled, armed and legged or. *Supporters,*--(borne by Barons Beaverbrook). On either side a beaver reguardant holding in the mouth a fish proper.

Residence,--The Garden House, Cherkley, Leatherhead, Surrey. *Clubs,*--White's, Bucks' and Royal Yacht Squadron.

Things for me, not I for things.

SON LIVING. (*By 3rd marriage.*)

Hon. MAXWELL WILLIAM HUMPHREY, *b.* Dec. 29th, 1951: *m.* 1974, Susan Angela More, el. da. of Francis Ambrose More O'Ferrall [see Mather-Jackson, Bt.]

DAUGHTERS LIVING. (*By 2nd marriage.*)

Hon. Kirsty Jane, *b.* 1947: *m.* 1966, Jonathan Derek Morley,
Hon. Lynda Mary Kathleen, *b.* 1948: *m.* 1969, Nicholas Saxton.

(*By 3rd marriage.*)

Hon. Laura, *b.* 1953.

SISTER LIVING.

Hon. Janet Gladys, *b.* 1908: *m.* 1st, 1927, Ian Douglas Campbell (from whom she obtained a divorce 1934) later 11th Duke of Argyll, who *d.* 1973; 2ndly, 1935, the Hon. (William) Drogo Sturges Montagu, F/O Aux. Air Force, who *d.* (on active ser. during 1939-45 War) 1940 [see E. Sandwich]; 3rdly, 1942, Maj. Thomas Edward Dealtry Kidd, MBE, Roy. Canadian Artillery, and has issue living (by 1st m.) [see D. Argyll],—(by 2nd m.) [see E. Sandwich],—(by 3rd m.) John Edward Aitken (Old House, Ewhurst Green, Surrey), *b.* 1944: *m.* 1973, Wendy Madeline, da. of Sir John Rowland Hodge, MBE, 2nd Bt., and formerly wife of Michael Dennis Whiting,—Jane *b.* 1943: *m.* 1972, Graham Morison Vere Nicoll [see Madden, Bt.]. *Residence,*—Slythehurst, Ewhurst, Surrey.

WIDOW LIVING OF SON OF FIRST BARON.

(Marie) Patricia, da. of Michael Maguire, of Melbourne, Australia: *m.* 1st, 1942, as his second wife, Capt. the Hon. Peter Rudyard Aitken, Roy. Fusiliers, who *d.* 1947; 2ndly, 1948, Richard David Rafe Lycett Green, who *d.* 1969. having obtained a divorce 1956 [see Green, Bt., *cr.* 1886, colls.], and has issue living, by 1st marriage [see colls., infra]. *Residence,*—

WIDOW LIVING OF FIRST BARON.

MARCIA ANASTASIA (*Baroness Beaverbrook*), (of Saint Andrews, New Brunswick, Canada), da. of John Christoforides, of Leyswood, Groombridge, Sussex, and widow of Sir James Hamet Dunn, Q.C., 1st Bt. (cr. 1921); Hon. LL.D. Dalhousie; Chancellor of Dalhousie Univ. since 1968: *m.* 1963, as his 2nd wife, the 1st Baron, who *d.* 1964.

COLLATERAL BRANCH LIVING.

Issue of the late Capt. the Hon. Peter Rudyard Aitken, Roy. Fusiliers, 2nd son of 1st Baron, *b.* 1912, *d.* 1947: *m.* 1st, 1934, Janet Ruth Murrene (who obtained a divorce 1939), da. of Prof. Murray Macneill, of Dalhousie Univ., Halifax, Nova Scotia; 2ndly, 1942, (Marie) Patricia (ante); who *m.* 2ndly, 1948, Richard David Rafe Lycett Green, who obtained a divorce 1956 [see Green, Bt., *cr.* 1886, colls.], da. of Michael Maguire, of Melbourne, Australia:—
(By 2nd marriage) Timothy Maxwell, *b.* 1944; ed. at Repton.——Peter Michael, *b.* 1946; ed. at Malvern.——(By 1st marriage) Caroline Anne Christine, *b.* 1935: *m.* 1957, Conyers Collingwood Massy Baker, Lt., RCNR, of 28, Whitney Av., Toronto 5, Ontario, and has issue living, William Hugh Massy, *b.* 1958,—Philip Massy, *b.* 1960,—Jonathan Piers Massy, *b.* 1967.

PREDECESSOR [1] (WILLIAM) MAXWELL Aitken, *C.D., P.C.,* son of Rev. William Cuthbert Aitken Presbyterian Min. of Newcastle, New Brunswick, Canada; *b.* 1879; M.P. for Ashton-under-Lyne (*C*) 1910-16, with Canadian Expeditionary Force 1915, and Canadian Govt. Representative at Front 1916, Chancellor of Duchy of Lancaster, and Min. of Information 1918; formerly proprietor of *Daily Express, Sunday Express* (which he founded 1920), and *Evening Standard;* Min. of Aircraft Production 1940, Min. of State and Min. of Supply 1941, a Member of War Cabinet 1940-42, Lord Privy Seal 1943-45; *cr.* a *Baronet* 1916, and *Baron Beaverbrook,* of Beaverbrook, Prov. on New Brunswick, Canada, and of Cherkley, co. Surrey (peerage of U.K.) 1917: *m.* 1st, 1906, Gladys, who *d.* 1927, da. of Brig.-Gen. Charles William Drury, C.B., of Halifax, Nova Scotia; 2ndly, 1963, Marcia Anastasia, da. of John Christoforides, of Leyswood, Groombridge, Sussex, and widow of Sir James Hamet Dunn, Q.C., 1st Bt. (cr. 1921); *d.* 1964; *s.* by his el. son [2] JOHN WILLIAM MAXWELL, 2nd Baron, until he disclaimed his peerage, and 2nd Baronet.

Bective, Earl of, son of Marquess of Headfort.

BEDFORD, DUKE OF. (Russell.) [Duke E. 1694.]

What will be, will be.

JOHN ROBERT RUSSELL, 13th Duke; b. May 24th, 1917 ; s. 1953 ; European War 1939-40 in Coldstream Guards (invalided) : m. 1st, 1939, Clare Gwendolen (HOLLWAY), who d. 1945, dau. of John Bridgman ; 2ndly, 1947, the Hon. Lydia Yarde-Buller (who obtained a divorce 1960), dau. of 3rd Baron Churston and widow of Capt. Ian Archibald de Hoghton Lyle, Black Watch, el. son of Sir Archibald Moir Park Lyle, 2nd Bt., M.C. ; 3rdly, 1960, Madame Nicole Milinaire, dau. of Paul Schneider, of Paris, and has issue by 1st and 2nd marriages.

Arms,—Argent, a lion rampant gules ; on a chief sable, three escallops of the first. Crest.— A goat statant argent, armed and unguled or. Supporters.—Dexter, a lion rampant gules, gorged with a collar argent, charged with three escallops sable ; sinister, a goat argent, armed, unguled and bearded or.

Residences,—8, Quai d'Orléans, 75004, Paris, France; Arlington House, Piccadilly, W1.

SONS LIVING. *(By 1s tm.)*
HENRY ROBIN IAN (*Marquess of Tavistock*), b. Jan. 21st, 1940; ed. at La Rosey and Harvard Univ.: m. 1961, Henrietta Joan, only da. of Henry Frederic Tiarks, of 11, Hyde Park Gardens, W2, and has issue:—

SONS LIVING,—ANDREW IAN HENRY (*Lord Howland*), b. March 30th, 1962.
Lord Robin Loel Hastings, b. 1963.
Lord James Edward Herbrand, b. 1975.

Seat,—Woburn Abbey, Bedfordshire, *London Residence,*—3, Clarendon Place, W2. *Clubs,*— Buck's, Jockey, White's.
Lord Rudolph, b. 1944 ; ed. at Gordonstoun.

(By 2nd marriage.)
Lord Francis Hastings (Munster House, Roland Way, SW7), b. 1950 ; ed. at Eton: m. 1971, Mrs. Faith Diane Carrington, da. of the late Dr. S. I. M. Ibrahim, of Singapore.

BROTHER LIVING.
Lord Hugh Hastings, b. 1923 ; ed. at Christ's Coll., Camb.; is an Asso. Member of Roy. Institute of Chartered Surveyors: m. 1957, Rosemary, yr. da. of Keith Freeling Markby, of Treworder, Blisland, Bodmin, Cornwall, and has issue living, Mark Hugh, b. 1960,—Karen Diana, b. 1961. *Residence,*— Bathampton House, Wylye, Wilts.

SISTER LIVING.
Lady Daphne Crommelin, b. 1920. *Residence,*—Oak Cottage, Beckley, Rye, Sussex.

COLLATERAL BRANCHES LIVING.

Grandchildren of the late Lord Arthur John Edward Russell, next brother of 9th Duke:—
Issue of the late Harold John Hastings Russell, b. 1868, d. 1926: m. 1896, Lady Victoria Alberta Leveson-Gower, who d. 1953, dau. of 2nd Earl Granville:—
Anthony Arthur, b. 1904 ; ed. at Eton, and at Balliol Coll., Oxford : m. 1947, Alicia Charlotte, dau. of the late Seton Eustace, of Stoodwell, Merrow, Surrey, and has issue living, Francis Anthony, b. 1948,— Hugo Eustace Arthur, b. 1951,—Julia Alicia, b. 1950,—Victoria Evelyn Elizabeth, b. 1953. *Residence,*—The Ridgeway, Shere, Guildford.——Elizabeth Frances, b. 1899 : m. 1925, Richard George Hubert Plunket Greene, from whom she obtained a divorce 1943 [Parry, Bt.]. *Residence,*—59, Park Walk, SW10.——Rachel Georgiana, b. 1903: m. 1929, Hugh Noel Blakiston, and has issue living, Rachel Castalia (31, Edith Grove, SW10), b. 1930: m. 1951 (m. diss. 1968), James Gordon Akers Campbell, and has issue living, Julian James Noel b. 1953 : m. 1971, Saundra Hale, Marcus George Akers b. 1954, Benedict Robert Gordon b. 1958, Cosmo Thomas Aretas b. 1960,— Caroline Georgiana, b. 1933: m. 1970, Adam Russell Hunter, of 1, Dancer Rd., SW6. *Residence,*— 6, Markham Sq., SW3.
Issue of the late Maj. Gilbert Byng Alwyne Russell, b. 1875, d. 1942: m. 1917, Maud (North End House, Mottisfont, Romsey, Hants.), da. of the late Paul Nelke:—

Martin Basil Paul, b. 1918; ed. at Eton, and at King's Coll., Camb. (MA); with KRRC 1939-40; Assist. Private Sec. to Rt. Hon. Duff Cooper (later Viscount Norwich), when Min. of Information 1940-41, and to Brendan Bracken (later Viscount Bracken) 1941, and Private Sec. to Rt. Hon. Duff Cooper when Chancellor of Duchy of Lancaster, on Mission to Far East 1941-42; with H.Q. Ceylon Army Command 1942-43 and H.Q. Allied Land Forces, S.E. Asia, Kandy and Singapore 1943-46; author of "The Art of George Keyt", 1949; with British S. Africa Co. 1954-61, Minerals Separation 1961-63 and Ionian Bank 1964-66; founded M. B. P. Russell & Co. Ltd., 1967; a Member of Council of Roy. Soc. for India, Pakistan and Ceylon: m. 1954, Anne Swinton (has Croix de Guerre), da. of the late Brig. Stanlake Swinton Lee, OBE, DSO, and has issue living, Julian Hugh, b. 1955,— Stephen Raymond (twin), b. 1955,—Laura Diana, b. 1959,—Emily Esther, b. 1962. *Residence,*— 62, Eaton Place, SW1. *Clubs,*—White's, Brooks's, Buck's, Travellers' (Paris).

Issue of the late Rt. Hon. Lord Odo William Russell, G.C.B., G.C.M.G. (younger brother of 9th Duke), who was cr. *Baron Ampthill* 1881 [see that title].
Descendants of the late Lord John Russell (3rd son of 6th Duke), who was cr. *Earl Russell* 1861 [see that title].
Grandchildren of the late Rev. Henry Charles Russell, son of the late Lieut.-Col. Lord Charles James Fox Russell, 6th son of 6th Duke :—
Issue of the late Maj.-Gen. Sir Thomas Wentworth Russell, K.B.E., C.M.G. (2nd son, and a co-heir to Baronies of Beauchamp and Mordaunt), b. 1879, d. 1954 : m. 1911, Evelyn Dorothea Temple, *MBE*, who d. 1968, da. of the late Francis Moore:—
Sir John Wriothesley, *GCVO, CMG*, b. 1914; ed. at Eton, and at Trin. Coll., Camb. (MA); appointed Third Sec., Foreign Office 1937 and Moscow 1939, Second Sec., Washington 1942, and First Sec., Warsaw 1945, FO 1948 (1st Dir.-Gen. Brussels Treaty Permanent Organization), and Rome 1950, Director-Gen. of British Information Sers., New York 1953, Counsellor, Teheran 1956, Head of News Dept., FO 1959, Ambassador to Ethiopia 1962-66, to Brazil 1966-69, and to Spain 1966-74; Coronation Medal (1953); CMG 1958, KCVO 1965, GCVO 1968: m. 1945, Aliki, da. of George Diplarakos, of Athens, and has issue living, Alexander Charles Thomas Wriothesley, b. 1950,— Georgina Alexandra, b. 1947. *Residences,*—The Vine Farm, Northbourne, Kent; 80, Chester Sq.,

SW1. *Clubs,*—White's, Beefsteak, Garrick.——Camilla Georgiana, *b.* 1912: *m.* 1936, Christopher Hugh Sykes [see Sykes, Bt., cr. 1783]. *Residence,*—Swyre House, Swyre, Dorchester.

Grandchildren of the late Lord Alexander George Russell, G.C.B., 10th son of 6th Duke:—

Issue of the late Major Leonard George Russell, *b.* 1858; *d.* 1946: *m.* 1890, Agnes Harriet, who *d.* 1934, el. dau. of the late Rev. Godfrey Bolles Lee, Warden of Winchester Coll.:—

Violet Agnes Mary (Fairmont, Kings Worthy, Winchester), *b.* 1891.——Eileen Worsley, *b.* 1906: *m.* 1935, Jocelyn Walter Hoare, of Pyotts Burh, Old Basing, Basingstoke, and has issue living, Janet Eileen, *b.* 1936: *m.* 1957, Robert Francis Norman Duke, FROS, of The Old Manor, Pillerton Hersey, Warwick, only son of Sir (Robert) Norman Duke, KBE, CB, DSO, MC, and has issue living, Diana Mary *b.* 1958, Jacqueline Frances *b.* 1961, Rosalind Jean *b.* 1965,—Elizabeth Jocelyn, *b.* 1938: *m.* 1964, Kenneth James Ross Johnston, of Hill Place, Linton, Maidstone, and has issue living, Fiona Susan *b.* 1965, Coralie Dawn *b.* 1966, Katrina Anne *b.* 1971, Bryony Ruth *b.* 1972,—Alison Mary, *b.* 1942: *m.* 1974, Maj. Richard Michael Arnold Hudson, RA, and has issue living, Joanna Margaret *b.* 1974.

Descendants of the late Com. John Russell, R.N. [el. son of the late Lord William Russell (infra)], who *m.* 1822, Sophia, *Baroness de Clifford* (in her own right) [see that title].

Grandson of the late George Russell, son of the late William Russell (infra):—

Issue of the late George William Henry Russell, *b.* 1864, *d.* 1908: *m.* 1893, Mabel Mary, who *d.* 1942, el. dau. of W. H. Walker, of Ceylon:—

Odo George Henry, *b.* 1899; ed. at Wellington Coll.; Major (retired) Black Watch (Roy. Highland Regt.): European War 1939-45 (wounded, prisoner): *m.* 1927, Lisalie Maude, dau. of the late Marcus Beresford Armstrong, J.P., D.L. [V. Hawarden, colls.]. *Residence,*—Broadmead Manor, Folkestone.

Granddaughter of the late William Russell, son of the late Lord William Russell, brother of 5th and 6th Dukes:—

Issue of the late Reginald Russell, *b.* 1839, *d.* 1897: *m.* 1881, Nina, dau. of the late Capt. McGeachy Alleyne, 7th Dragoons:—

Muriel Elsie Augusta, *b.* 1884: *m.* 19—, — Greenfield, who *d.* 1930. *Residence,*—

PREDECESSORS.—[1] JOHN Russell, *K.G.,* one of the most accomplished gentlemen of his time, attended the Archduke Philip of Austria (who had been stranded on the coast near Weymouth) to the Court of Henry VII. in 1506, where he was appointed a Gentleman of the Privy Chamber; accompanied Henry VIII. in his French Wars, and having held various high appointments, was cr. *Baron Russell* (peerage of England) 1539, and in 1540 obtained a grant of the site of Tavistock Abbey and of the extensive possessions belonging thereto; in 1550, *temp.* Edward VI., he received a grant of the Monastery of Woburn and was cr. *Earl of Bedford* (peerage of England); was Lord Privy Seal to Queen Mary, and went as Ambassador to Spain to conduct H.M.'s royal consort, Philip II., into England; *d.* 1555; *s.* by his son [2] FRANCIS, *K.G.,* P.C., 2nd Earl, a nobleman of great eminence, *temp.* Elizabeth I; *d.* 1585; *s.* by his grandson [3] EDWARD, 3rd Earl; *d. s. p.* 1627; *s.* by his cousin, son of Sir William, cr. *Baron Russell of Thornhaugh* (peerage of England) 1603, [4] FRANCIS, 4th Earl, who had previously *s.* as 2nd Baron Russell; *d.* 1641; *s.* by his son [5] WILLIAM, *K.G.,* 5th Earl, cr. *Marquess of Tavistock* and *Duke of Bedford* (peerage of England) 1694; his el. son, William, the celebrated Lord Russell, was executed July 21, 1683, for high treason, as a participator in the Rye-House conspiracy; he *d.* 1700, and the attainder upon Lord Russell having been annulled, he was *s.* by his grandson [6] WRIOTHESLEY, *K.G.,* 2nd Duke; summoned to Parliament as *Baron Howland* (peerage of England) 1695; *d.* 1711; *s.* by his son [7] WRIOTHESLEY, 3rd Duke; *d. s. p.* 1732; *s.* by his brother [8] JOHN, *K.G.,* 4th Duke; successively Lord-Lieut. of Ireland and Ambassador to France: *d.* 1771; *s.* by his grandson [9] FRANCIS, 5th Duke; *d.* unmarried 1802; *s.* by his brother [10] JOHN, *K.G.,* 6th Duke; *d.* 1839; *s.* by his son [11] FRANCIS, *K.G.,* 7th Duke; summoned to Parliament in his father's Barony of Howland 1833; *d.* 1861; *s.* by his son [12] WILLIAM, 8th Duke: *d. s. p.* 1872; *s.* by his cousin [13] FRANCIS CHARLES HASTINGS, *K.G.,* 9th Duke (el. son of Maj.-Gen. Lord George William, G.C.B., 2nd son of 6th Duke, by Elizabeth Anne, dau. of the Hon. John Theophilus Rawdon, brother of 1st Marquess of Hastings), *b.* 1819; M.P. for Bedfordshire (L) 1847-72 Lord-Lieut. of Hunts: *m.* 1844, Lady Elizabeth Sackville-West, *V.A.,* who *d.* 1897, el. dau. of 6th Earl De La Warr; *d.* 1891; *s.* by his el. son [14] GEORGE WILLIAM FRANCIS SACKVILLE, 10th Duke, *b.* 1852; M.P. for Bedfordshire (L) 1875-85 : *m.* 1876, Lady Adeline Marie Somers-Cocks, G.B.E., who *d.* 1920, dau. of 3rd Earl Somers (*ext.*); *d.* 1893: *s.* by his brother [15] HERBRAND ARTHUR, *K.G., K.B.E.,* 11th Duke; *b.* 1858; was Lord-Lieut. of Middlesex 1898-1926: *m.* 1888, *Dame* Mary Du Caurroy *D.B.E., R.R.C.,* who *d.* 1937, dau. of the Ven. W. H. Tribe, formerly Archdeacon of Lahore; *d.* 1940; *s.* by his son [16] HASTINGS WILLIAM SACKVILLE, 12th Duke; *b.* 1888; formerly Lieut. 10th Batn. Duke of Cambridge's Own (Middlesex) Regt. : *m.* 1914, Louisa Crommelin Roberta Jowitt, who *d.* 1960, dau. of the late Robert Jowitt Whitwell, of Thornbury Lodge, 70, Banbury Road, Oxford; *d.* 1953; *s.* by his el. son [17] JOHN ROBERT, 13th Duke and present peer; also Marquess of Tavistock, Earl of Bedford, Baron Russell, and Baron Howland.

BEECHING, BARON. (Beeching.) [Life Baron 1965.]

RICHARD BEECHING, son of Hubert J. Beeching, of Maidstone; *b.* April 21st, 1913; ed. at Maidstone Gram. Sch., and at Imperial Coll. of Science and Technology (ARCS, BSc, DIC, PhD London, Fellow of Imperial Coll.); CIMechE, FBIM, FInstP, FCIT; Hon. LLD London; Hon. DSc Nat. Univ. of Ireland; Armaments Design Dept., Min. of Supply 1943-46, and Dep. Ch. Engineer of Armaments Design 1946-48; joined ICI 1948; a Dir. 1957-61 and 1965; Vice-Pres. ICI of Canada 1953-55, and Chm. of Metals Div. 1955-57; a Member of Special Advisory Group on British Transport Commission 1960, and of National Economic Development Council 1962-64; Chm. of British Transport Commn. 1961-62, of British Railways Board 1962-65, and of Roy. Commn. on the Admin. of Justice through Assizes and Quarter Sessions 1966-69; a

STRAIGHT-DOWN-THE-MIDDLE

Dep. Chm. of ICI 1966-68; First Pres. Inst. of Work Study Practitioners 1967-72; Pres. R. Soc. for Prevention of Accidents 1968-73; a Member of Top Salaries Review Body since 1971; Chm. of Redland Ltd., of Furness Withy & Co. Ltd., and of Economic Insurance Co. Ltd.; a Dir. of Lloyds Bank; *cr. Baron Beeching,* of E. Grinstead, co. Sussex (Life Peerage) 1965: *m.* 1938, Ella Margaret da. of William J. Tiley, of Maidstone.

Arms,—Gules, on a bend double cotised or, three beech leaves vert, a chief ermine. **Crest,**—A cubit arm, erect vested sable, cuffed argent, the hand proper supporting a sword sheathed point upwards gules, hilt, pomel, quillons and chape or, and grasping two arrows in saltire, points upward, or, all between two branches of beech proper. **Supporters,**—On either side a lion, that to the dexter gules, the sinister or, each charged on the shoulder with an annulet enclosing two bars wavy counterchanged and resting the interior hind paw on a rock proper.

Residence,—Little Manor, Lewes Rd., East Grinstead, Sussex.

BELHAVEN and STENTON, LORD. (Hamilton.) [Lord S. 1647.]

ROBERT ANTHONY CARMICHAEL HAMILTON, 13th Lord ; *b.* Feb. 27th, 1927; *s.* 1961; ed. at Eton: *m.* 1st, 1952, (m. diss. 1972), Elizabeth Ann, da. of the late Col. Arthur Henry Moseley, DSO, of Hastings Rd., Warrawee, NSW; 2ndly, 1973, Rosemary, da. of the late Sir Herbert Geraint Williams, 1st Bt., MP (cr. 1953), and formerly wife of Sir Ian (John) Auld Mactaggart, 3rd Bt., and has issue by 1st m.

Arms,—Quarterly, 1st and 4th, gules, a mullet argent between three cinquefoils ermine *Hamilton of Udston*; 2nd and 3rd gules, a man's heart proper, shadowed or, between three cinquefoils ermine, all within a bordure argent *Hamilton of Raploch.* **Crest,**—A horse's head couped argent, bridled gules. **Supporters,**—Two horses argent, bridled gules.

Residence,—Tighcargaman, Port Ellen, Isle of Islay, Argyll.

SON LIVING (*By 1st m.*)

Hon. FREDERICK CARMICHAEL ARTHUR (*Master of Belhaven*), *b.* Sept. 27th, 1953; ed. at Eton.

DAUGHTER LIVING (*By 1st m.*)

Hon. Julia Elizabeth Heather, *b.* 1956.

AUNTS LIVING. (*Daughters of 11th Lord.*)

Hon. Margaret de Hauteville UDNY-HAMILTON, *b.* 1939: *m.* 1964, C. Keith W. Schellenberg, of Udny Castle, Aberdeenshire, and has issue living, Nicholas Udny, *b.* 1966,—Amy Julia Udny, *b.* 1971,—Rose Camilla Joan Udny, *b.* 1973.

Hon. Victoria Edith UDNY-HAMILTON, *b.* 1941.

DAUGHTER LIVING OF NINTH LORD.

Hon. Georgina Violet, *b.* 1889: *m.* 1st, 1913, James Cowie Simpson, Lieut. R.E., who *d.* (killed in action during European War) 1916 [Watson, Bt., cr. 1895] ; 2ndly, 1921, Squadron-Leader Alfred George Horsley-Carr, O.B.E., R.A.F., who *d.* 1926, and has issue living, (by 2nd marriage) Estelle Winifred Hamilton, *b.* 1922. *Address,*—

WIDOW LIVING OF SON OF TENTH LORD.

Lady Grizel Winifred Louisa, dau. of 12th Earl of Dundonald: *m.* 1904, Lieut.-Col. the Hon. Ralph Gerald Alexander Hamilton, R.F.A., Master of Belhaven, who *d.* (killed in action during European War) 1918 (despatches twice, 1914 star, Croix de Guerre with palm). *Residence,*—Stowlangtoft Hall, Bury St. Edmunds.

MOTHER LIVING.

Heather Mildred Carmichael, dau. of Lieut.-Col. Richard Carmichael Bell, D.S.O., O.B.E., late Central India Horse : *m.* 1st, 1926, the Hon. Robert Alexander Benjamin Hamilton, Master of Belhaven (afterwards 12th Baron Belhaven and Stenton), from whom she obtained a divorce for desertion in the Scottish Courts 1941 ; 2ndly, 1944, Major Basil William Seager, C.M.G., O.B.E. *Residence,*—16, Broadwater Down, Tunbridge Wells.

WIDOW LIVING OF TWELFTH LORD.

CYRILLA MARY, da. of the late Raymund Louis Binns: *m.* 1st, 1942, as his second wife, the 12th Lord, who *d.* 1961; 2ndly, 1969, Dennis Beaumont Vale, OBE, of Brenta Lodge, Monkmead Lane, Pulborough, Sussex.

COLLATERAL BRANCHES LIVING.

Issue of the late Hon. Leonore Agnes Watson Nisbet Hamilton, da. of 9th Lord, *b.* 1878, *d.* 1946: *m.* 1903, Capt. Robert Borras Whiteside, RASC, who *d.* (on active ser.) 1915:—

Rev. Leslie William Hamilton, *b.* 1908 ; is R. of St. Edmund the King, City of London ; sometime Chap. R.N.V.R. : *m.* 1943, Julia, dau. of the late Col. Bruce-Kingsmill, of Airth, and has issue living, Christopher Hamilton, *b.* 1945. *Residence,*—Gabriel Hill, Pilgrims Way, Kemsing, Kent.—— Georgina Penelope Hamilton, *b.* 1905: *m.* 1928, Frank Robert Jowitt Whitwell, Capt. late Scots Guards, and has issue living, Leonore Margaret Celia Hastings, *b.* 1929: *m.* 1951, Maurice Osmund John Fooks, 14th/20th King's Hussars (Reserve). *Residence,*—Barrington House, Haywards Heath, Sussex.

Grandchildren of the late Hon. Mrs. Leonore Agnes Watson Whiteside (ante):—

Issue of the late Borras Noel Hamilton Whiteside, *b.* 1903, *d.* 1948: *m.* 1935, Dorothy Mai (3, Rowan Terr., Brook Green, W6) [who *m.* 2ndly, 1960 (m. diss. 1971), Cdr. Nigel Loftus Henry Fane, RNR, who *d.* 1973 [see E. Westmorland, colls.], but resumed the name of Whiteside by deed poll 1969], only da. of the late John Farrington, Resident at Rotumah, Pacific:—

Diana Elizabeth, *b.* 1942: *m.* 1964, John Newton Davies, of Sharps Bridge House, Piltdown, Sussex.

Issue of the late Cecil Trevor Hamilton Whiteside, MC, MRCS, *b.* 1909, *d.* 1965: *m.* 1941, Charlotte (Lanescott, Par, Cornwall), da. of the late Rev. John Lesley Parker, V. of Lanteglos, Fowey, and widow of Lt.-Col. Almeric Arthur William Spencer [see V. Churchill, colls.]:—

Hugh Cecil Hamilton, *b.* 1944: *m.* 1971, Ruth Marian Eastwood.

Granddaughter of the late Capt. Henry George Hamilton, uncle of 10th Lord:—
Issue of the late Adm. Sir Frederick Tower Hamilton, G.C.V.O., K.C.B., *b.* 1856, *d.* 1917:
  m. 1889, Maria Walpole, who *d.* 1952, dau. of the late Adm. of the Fleet the Hon. Sir
  Henry Keppel, G.C.B., O.M. [E. Albemarle, colls.] :—
Jean, *b.* 1899. *Residence,*—39, Lennox Gardens, SW1.

Grandchildren of the late Arthur Richard Hamilton, uncle of 10th Lord:—
Issue of the late Arthur Richard Hamilton, *b.* 1872, *d.* 1930 : *m.* 1906, Mabel, who *d.*
  1918 dau. of John Harrower, of Baldur, Manitoba :—
Gladys Dorothy, *b.* 1908: *m.* 1928, Walter Jorgeson.

Issue of the late Charles Augustus Hamilton, *b.* 1874, *d.* 1960: *m.* 1906, Alice May, da. of
  Benjamin Thorn, of Souris, Manitoba:—
Frederick William, *MC* (1481, Wellington Cres., Winnipeg, 9, Canada), *b.* 1910; 1939-45 War as
  Capt. Roy. Canadian Engineers (MC): *m.* 1945, Alice Elizabeth, who *d.* 1969, da. of George A.
  Stevenson, of Morris, Manitoba, and has issue living, Mary Ellen, *b.* 1947: *m.* 1969, D. K. Trueman,
  of Winnipeg, Canada,—Catherine Alice, *b.* 1949.——Richard Terrick (Baldur, Manitoba), *b.* 1912:
  m. 1933, Muriel, da. of John Mcleod, of Belmont, Manitoba, and has issue living, Betty Lorraine,
  b. 1934,—Margaret Rose, *b.* 1935,—Gertrude Joan, *b.* 1937,—Elaine Joyce *b.* 1938.——Rose Aileen,
  b. 1908: *m.* 1st, 1954, George W. Easter, who *d.* 1958; 2ndly 1964, the Rt. Rev. William Henry
  Howes Crump, Bishop of Saskatchewan, of Pine Thorpe, Whitby, Canada.

Granddaughters of the late Ven. Anthony Hamilton (infra) :—
Issue of the late Clement Edward Hamilton, *b.* 1854, *d.* 1923 : *m.* 1898, Fanny, who *d.* 1955,
  dau. of James Winch, J.P., of Rochester :—
Ethel Isabel Roby, *b.* 1900.——Eleanor Clara Roby, *b.* 1902.——Marjorie Francis Roby, *b.* 1907.
Residence,—Belhaven, 13, Neil St., Frankston, Vic. 3199, Aust.

Grandchildren of the late Terrick Alfred Hamilton (infra):—
Issue of the late Terrick Elyston Scott Hamilton, *b.* 1881, *d.* 19—: *m.* 19—, Agnes, who
  d. 1944, da. of W. Lynch:—
Anthony Elyston John (Edward St., Tambo, Barcoo River, Qld., Aust.), *b.* 1905: *m.* 1928, Helen
  Margaret Doherty, and has issue living, Patrick Hamilton, *b.* 1928: *m.* 1952, Dulcie Emily Hafie,
  and has issue living, Patrick William *b.* 1954, Anthony John *b.* 1955, Terrick Danial *b.* 1957, Dale
  Thomas *b.* 1959,—Elyston William *b.* 1936: *m.* 1960, Norma Merion Ilott,—Reginald John, *b.* 1940,—
  Margaret, *b.* 1930: *m.* 1952, Brian George Denny, who *d.* 1959, and has issue living, Annette Margaret
  b. 1953, Denise *b.* 1958,—Marjorie Jean, *b.* 1935: *m.* 1954, Donald Allan McKnights,—Helen Margaret,
  b. 1938: *m.* 1957, Russell McQuie,—Rita Grace, *b.* 1941.——Vernon Harvey (Albert St., Tambo,
  Barcoo River, Qld.), *b.* 1914: *m.* 1943, Gloria Volk, and has issue living, Ian Vernon, *b.* 1944,—Joy
  Agnes, *b.* 1947: *m.* 1967, Geoffrey Francis O'Neill, and has issue living, Lindsay Francis Louis *b.* 1968
  ——John Edward (Arthur St., Tambo, Barcoo River, Qld.), *b.* 1917: *m.* 1937, Olive Russell, and
  has issue living, Peter John, *b.* 1939: *m.* 1960, Joan Adele Kuhn, and has issue living, Geoffrey *b.*
  1962,—Alan, *b.* 1952,—Margaret, *b.* 1938: *m.* 1st, 1957 (m. diss. 1969), Colin Miller; 2ndly, 1970,
  William John Dolgner, of 104, Wren St., Longreach, Qld., and has issue living (by 1st m.) Kimberley
  Mark *b.* 1957, Rodney John *b.* 1961, Kara Lea *b.* 1964, (by 2nd m.) Jason Ashley *b.* 1970,—Mary
  Rose, *b.* 1948: *m.* 1964, W. Eckel, and has issue living, William John *b.* 1965.——William Robert
  (Edward St., Tambo, Barcoo River, Qld.), *b.* 19—: *m.* 19—, Jean Higgins, and has issue living, Diane,
  b. 19—,—Marie, *b.* 19—,—Lynda, *b.* 19—,—Mary, *b.* 19—.——Julia Agnes, *b.* 1908 : *m.* 1938,
  John Edward Whitman, of Hamilton, Rundle-Jardine Sts., Wandal, Rockhampton, Qld., and has
  issue living, Barry John (Kenigan St., N. Rockhampton, Qld.), *b.* 1944: *m.* 1969, Margaret Collins,
  and has issue living, Joanne Maree *b.* 1970,—Michael John (Heulihan St., N. Rockhampton, Qld.),
  b. 1948: *m.* 1970, Lynette Wallace,—Paulanne Mary, *b.* 1939: *m.* 1961, Edward John Kelly, of 49,
  Blenheim St., Cherside West, Brisbane, Qld., and has issue living, Chris James *b.* 1965, Kim Edward
  b. 1967, Lee Michael *b.* 1969,—Julie Anne, *b.* 1941: *m.* 19—, Philip J. Walsh, of 4, Shar St., Toowoomba, Qld., and has issue living, Anthony John *b.* 1965, Justin Phillip *b.* 1966, John Edward *b.*
  1969.——Mary Alice, *b.* 1911: *m.* 1939, Thorwald Harold Widt, of 22, Boowgala Rd., Florida Gdns.,
  Gold Coast, Qld., and has issue living, Peter Anthony, *b.* 1945: *m.* 1967, Diane McCallum, and has
  issue living, Stephen Anthony, *b.* 19—, — Helen Margaret, *b.* 1940.——Eileen Marjorie, *b.* 1925:
  m. 1947, Roland Mervyn Smith, and has issue living, Terrick Elyston Scott, *b.* 1953,—Linda Ngaio,
  b. 1949,—Ruth Bronwen, *b.* 1954.

Grandson of the late Edward William Terrick Hamilton, son of the late Ven. An-
    thony Hamilton (*b.* 1778), Archdeacon of Taunton, great-uncle of 10th Lord:—
Issue of the late Terrick Alfred Hamilton, *b.* 1851, *d.* 1925: *m.* 1878, Alice, da. of John
  Scott, of Newcastle, N.S. Wales:—
John Helenus, *b.* 1888.

Grandchildren of the late Terrick Alfred Hamilton (ante):—
Issue of the late Charles Hamilton, *b.* 1885, *d.* 1961: *m.* 1911, Olivia Abbott Palmer:—
Charles Clive *b.* 1919: *m.* 19—, Nellie Olive Watson, and has issue living, Noel Peter, *b.* 1953,—
  Judith Helen, *b.* 1945,—Lexie Mae, *b.* 1949.——Olivia Jessie, *b.* 1913: *m.* 19—, Edmund Rockett,
  and has issue living, James Edward, *b.* 1947.——Margaret Jean, *b.* 1915: *m.* 1st, Ernest Henry
  Bellingham; 2ndly, 1965, William Edward McCulloch, and has issue living (by 1st m.) Alan Ward
  (4, Murray St., Campbelltown 2560, NSW), *b.* 1941: *m.* 1966, Lynette Fawcett.——Kepple Osborne,
  b. 1917: *m.* 19—, Dudley Halliwell Milton, and has issue living, Raymond Charles, *b.* 1945.

Granddaughters of the late Edward William Terrick Hamilton (ante):—
Issue of the late Charles Gipps Hamilton, *b.* 1857, *d.* 1955 : *m.* 1892, Anna Gertrude Mont-
  gomerie. who *d.* 1937, dau. of Hugh Morris Lang :—
Margaret Graham, MBE (of Flat B, 45, Sloane St., S.W.1), *b.* 1895: MBE (Civil) 1946.——Winifred
  Anna (Greenhaugh Hall, Tarset, Hexham), *b.* 1905: *m.* 1926, James Seymour Spencer, who *d.*
  1967, and has issue living, Antony James, *b.* 1927,—Simon Charles, *b.* 1929.

Issue of the late Harvie Cavendish Hamilton, *b.* 1861, *d.* 1917: *m.* 1890, Edith, who *d.*
  1917, dau. of David Moore, of Melbourne, Australia:—
Sybil Edith (Lyncroft, Flinders, Vic., Aust.), *b.* 1899.

PREDECESSORS.—[1] John Hamilton, of Broomhill (son of James Hamilton, of
Broomhill, cr. a Bt. of Nova Scotia 1635), was cr. *Lord Belhaven and Stenton,* of co. Haddington
(peerage of Scotland) 1647. In 1675 he surrendered his Lordship to the crown, and received a new
patent with remainder to John Hamilton, of Pressmannan, husband of his granddau. Margaret, and
in failure of that line to his heirs male whatsoever ; *d.* 1679 ; *s.* by his son-in-law [2] John, 2nd Lord,
a Lord of the Treasury 1704, and a zealous opponent of the Union ; was imprisoned in the Tower of
London as an ally of the Chevalier St. George ; *d.* 1708 ; *s.* by his son [3] John, 3rd Lord, a Representative Peer ; having been appointed Gov. of Barbados, was drowned in his passage out 1721 ;
s. by his son [4] John, 4th Lord ; *d.s.p.* 1764 ; *s.* by his brother [5] James, 5th Lord ; *d.s.p.* 1777,
when the title was incorrectly assumed by Capt. William Hamilton (descended from John Hamilton
of Coltness, el. great-uncle of 2nd Lord), who voted at the election of Scottish Peers in 1790 ; it was
resolved by the Committee for Privileges 1793 that his vote was not good, and the title in 1790 was
determined in favour of [6—7] William, 7th Lord, son of Robert Hamilton, of Wishaw, (great-great
grandson of William Hamilton, 2nd great-uncle of 2nd Lord) who was *de jure* 6th Lord, William *d.*
1814 ; *s.* by his son [8] Robert Montgomery, *K.T.,* 8th Lord ; Lord-Lieutenant of Lanarkshire ; cr. *Baron Hamilton,* of Wishaw (peerage of United Kingdom) 1831 ; *d.s.p.* 1868, when
the barony of Hamilton became extinct, and the Lordship of Belhaven and Stenton became dormant,
and remained so until 1875, when the House of Lords adjudged it to [9] James, 9th Lord (son of the

late Archibald Hamilton, Surgeon 92nd Regt.), b. 1822 : m. 1877, Georgina, who d. 1940, dau. of
Sir John Watson, Bt., of Earnock and Neilsland, Lanarkshire ; d. 1893, when the Lordship was
claimed by [10] ALEXANDER CHARLES (son of the late William John Hamilton, M.P., a descendant
of the late William Hamilton [ante], through whom the 9th Lord was descended), b. 1840 ; was
served heir to his kinsman, voted at the election of Scottish Representative Peers, matriculated
Arms at the Lyon Office as 10th Lord, and was elected a Representative Peer for Scotland in the
House of Lords : m. 1880, Georgina Katharine, who d. 1932, dau. of the late Legh Richmond ;
d. 1920 ; s. by his nephew [11] ROBERT EDWARD ARCHIBALD, C.I.E. (son of the late Archibald
William Hamilton, R.N., younger brother of 10th Lord), 11th Lord, b. 1871 ; Lieut.-Col. (retired)
4th Gurkhas (Indian Army) ; was Representative Peer for Scotland 1922-45 ; assumed the additional
surname of Udny 1934 : m. 1st, 1898, Kathleen Gonville, who d. 1935, dau. of Sir Benjamin Parnell
Bromhead, C.B., 4th Bt.; 2ndly, 1938, Sheila de Hauteville, who d. 1962, only dau. of Capt. Algernon
George Pearson, D.S.O., late Roy. Berkshire Regt.: d. 1950; s. by his son [12] ROBERT ALEXANDER
BENJAMIN, 12th Lord ; b. 1903 ; Hon. Lieut.-Col., Roy. Scots Fusiliers, an author, and an authority
on S.-W. Arabia ; was Political Officer Aden Protectorate 1934-9 : m. 1st, 1926, Heather Mildred
Carmichael (who obtained a divorce for desertion in the Scottish Courts 1941), dau. of Lieut.-Col.
Richard Carmichael Bell, D.S.O., O.B.E., late Central India Horse ; 2ndly, 1942, Cyrilla Mary
who m. 2ndly, 1969, Dennis Beaumont Vale, OBE), da. of the late Raymund Louis Binns; d. 1961;
s. by his only son [13] ROBERT ANTHONY CARMICHAEL, 13th Lord and present peer.

BELLEW, BARON. (Bellew.) [Baron I. 1848, Bt I. 1688.]

All from above.

EDWARD HENRY BELLEW, M.B.E., 5th
Baron and 11th Baronet ; b. Feb. 6th, 1889 ;
s. 1935 ; ed. at Oratory Sch., and at Trin.
Hall, Camb. ; European War 1914-19 as
Capt. R.F.C. : M.B.E. (Mil.) 1919 : m. 1912,
Barbara Helen Mary, who d. 1967, da.
of the late Sir Henry Farnham Burke,
KCVO, CB, Garter Principal King of
Arms. [The 5th Baron d. Aug. 8th, 1975.]
Arms,—Sable, fretty or. Crest,—An arm
embowed, in armour, holding a sword proper.
Supporters—Dexter, a leopard or, gorged with a
mural crown azure; sinister, a wolf azure, gorged
with a ducal coronet or.
Seat,—Barmeath Castle, Dunleer, co. Louth.

BROTHER LIVING. (Raised to the rank
of a Baron's son 1935.)
Hon. BRYAN BERTRAM, M.C., b. June 11th, 1890 ;
formerly Lieut. Cav. Special Reserve; 1914-18 War
(MC): m. 1918, Jeanie Ellen Agnes, who d. 1973,
dau. of the late James O. Jameson, and has issue
living, James Bryan, b. 1920; late Capt. Irish
Guards: m. 1942, Mary Elizabeth, da. of the
Rev. Edward Eustace Hill, and has issue living,
Bryan Edward b. 1943; Maj. Irish Guards: m.
1968, Rosemary Sarah, da. of Maj. R. K. B
Hitchcock, of East House, Long Crendon, Bucks
(and has issue living, Patrick Edward b. 1969,
Anthony Richard Brooke b. 1972), Christopher
James b. 1954, Angela Mary b. 1944: m. 1964, Capt. Simon Hugh Walford, 17/21 Lancers, of Sum-
merstown House, Trim, co. Meath (and has issue living, Jeanie Anne b. 1966, Caroline Sarah b. 1968).
Residence,—Barmeath Castle, Dunleer, co. Louth.

HALF-BROTHERS LIVING. (Raised to the rank of a Baron's sons 1935.)
Hon. Sir George Rothe, K.C.B., K.C.V.O., F.S.A., b. 1899 ; ed. at Wellington Coll., and at Ch. Ch.
Oxford ; was Portcullis Pursuivant of Arms 1922-26, Somerset Herald 1926-51, Registrar of Coll.
of Arms 1935-51, and Garter Principal King of Arms, Genealogist of Order of the Bath, and Hon.
Genealogist to Order of St. John of Jerusalem 1951-61 ; late Squadron-Leader R.A.F. Vol. Reserve ;
a KStJ; Knight Principal of Imperial So. of Knights Bachelor 1957-61, and Sec. of Order of
the Garter 1961-74; 1939-45 War (despatches); MVO (4th class) 1935, OVO and Knt. 1950, KCVO
1953, KCB (Civil) 1961: m. 1935, Ursula Kennard, da. of Anders Eric Knös Cull, of Warfield House,
Berks., and has issue living, Richard George (Thameside, Teddington, Middx.), b. 1936; late 2nd Lt.
Irish Guards, and an OStJ: m. 1965, Shona (KNOWLES), only da. of the late Col. John Edward
Mercer Ewart Clark Leask, MBE, and has issue living, Henry Edward Courtenay b. 1973, Serena
Leonie Georgia b. 1969. Residence,—The Grange, Farnham, Surrey.
Hon. Patrick Herbert (Litchfield, Conn., USA), b. 1905; ed. at Trin. Coll., Camb.; formerly Lieut.
RNVR: m. 1st, 1936, the Hon. Catherine Moya de la Poer Beresford (who d. 1967, having obtained
a divorce in USA 1946), da. of 5th Baron Decies; 2ndly, 1954, Helen Carol, da. of the late Walter
Clinton Louchheim, of New York, and has issue living (by 1st m.), John Jeremy, b. 1937.

SISTERS LIVING. (Raised to the rank of a Baron's daughters 1935.)
Hon. Guendaline Ada (of The Old Rectory, Hinton Waldrist, nr. Faringdon, Berks.), b. 1891: m.
1916, Hugh Lloyd Thomas, C.M.G., C.V.O., who d. 1938 [Hobhouse, Bt.], and has issue living,
David Courtney William (Lidwells House, Goudhurst, Kent; Army and Navy Club), b. 1922; ed.
at Eton, and Ch. Ch., Oxford; late Capt. Irish Guards: m. 1950, Nighean, only child of the late
Col. Alastair Norman Fraser, DSO, and has issue living, Gavin Hugh b. 1966, Davina b. 1951, Sandra
b. 1952, Nicola b. 1955,—Pamela (The Dower House, Holker Hall, Cark-in-Cartmel, Cumbria), b.
1918: m. 1937, Capt. Richard Edward Osborne Cavendish, JP, DL, who d. 1972 [see D. Devonshire,
colls.],—Anne, b. 1923: m. 1st, 1943 (m. diss. 1956), Lt.-Col. Christian de Lisle, 11th Hussars, only
son of Gen. Sir (Henry) de Beauvoir de Lisle, KCB, KCMG, DSO; 2ndly, 1956, Capt. Ian Weston
Smith, late Scots Guards, of Overbury Court, Alton, Hants., and has issue living, (by 1st m.) David
b. 1945, Vanessa b. 1947, (by 2nd m.) Richard b. 1958, Dominic b. 1962.
Hon. Ada Kate (Rathmore Park, Tullow, co. Carlow), b. 1893: m. 1st, 1917, Charles Barry Domvile,
who d. 1936: 2ndly, 1937, Lieut.-Col. the Hon. Herbrand Charles Alexander, DSO, who d. 1965 [see
E. Caledon], and has issue living, (by 1st m.) Denys Barry Herbert (of Brook House, Sutton Courtenay, Berks.), b. 1921; ed. at Eton, and at Trin. Coll., Oxford; Capt. Life Guards, and Maj. Inns of
Court Regt. issue living, Rowland Barry John b. 1960, Katherine Lake b. 1959, Rosamond Lucy
b. 1965.

COLLATERAL BRANCHES LIVING.
(In remainder to Baronetcy only.)
Sir Edward Bellew, 6th Bt., had eight brothers, Mathew, John, William,
Patrick, Michael, Richard, Robert and Francis. Some of these married, and
their male descendants, if any, are in remainder to the Baronetcy.

PREDECESSORS.—[1] Sir PATRICK Bellew, son of Sir John Bellew, Knt., M.P. for co. Louth
1639; cr. a Baronet 1688; d. 1716; s. by his son [2] JOHN, 2nd Bt.; d. 1734; s. by his son

[3] EDWARD, 3rd Bt.; *d.* 1741; *s.* by his el. son [4] JOHN, 4th Bt.; *d.* 1750; *s.* by his brother [5] PATRICK, 5th Bt.; *d.* 1795; *s.* by his son [6] EDWARD, 6th Bt.; *d.* 1827; was *s.* by his son [7] the *Rt. Hon. Sir* PATRICK, *P.C.*, 7th Bt.; *b.* 1798; cr. *Baron Bellew* (peerage of Ireland) 1848, was Lord-Lieut. of co. Louth: *m.* 1829, Anna Femina, dau. of Don José Maria de Mendoza y Rios; *d.* 1866; *s.* by his son [8] EDWARD JOSEPH, 2nd Baron, *b.* 1830: *m.* 1853, Augusta Mary, who *d.* 1904, dau. of Col. George Bryan, of Jenkinstown, Kilkenny; *d.* 1895, without having established his right to vote at the Elections of Irish Representative Peers; *s.* by his el. son [9] CHARLES BERTRAM, 3rd Baron, *b.* 1855: *m.* 1883, Mildred Mary Josephine, who *d.* 1934, dau. of Sir Humphrey De Trafford, 2nd Bt., *d.* 1911; *s.* by his brother [10] GEORGE LEOPOLD Bryan, 4th Baron, *b.* 1857; a Representative Peer for Ireland; sometime Major 10th Hussars and Yorkshire Regt. (T.F.); Afghan War 1878-9, Nile Expedition 1884-5, S. Africa 1900, European War 1914-18; assumed by Roy. licence 1881 the surname of Bryan in lieu of his patronymic: *m.* 1927, Elaine Carlisle, who *d.* 1973, dau. of the late John B. Leach, of Queenstown, S. Africa, and widow of Herbert Lloyd-Dodd, of Johannesburg, Transvaal, *d.* 1935; *s.* by his nephew [11] EDWARD HENRY (son of the late Hon. Richard Eustace Bellew, 4th son of 2nd Baron), 5th Baron and present peer.

BELMORE, EARL. (Lowry-Corry.) [Earl I. 1797.]

Virtue flourishes for ever.

JOHN ARMAR LOWRY-CORRY, 8th Earl; *b.* Sept. 4th, 1951; *s.* 1960.

Arms,—Quarterly: 1st grand quarter quarterly, 1st and 4th gules, a saltire argent, in chief a rose of the last, *Corry*; 2nd and 3rd sable, a cup argent, with a garland between two laurel branches issuing therefrom vert, *Lowry*; 2nd grand quarter gules, a saltire argent, in chief a rose or; 3rd grand quarter argent, on a bend azure, three buckles or, *Leslie*; 4th grand quarter or, a lion rampant gules, over all a bend sable, *Abernethy*. Crests,— 1st, a cock proper; 2nd, a garland of laurel, between two branches of the same, all proper. Supporters.—Two tiger cats, guardant proper, ducally collared and chained or.

Residence,—Castle Coole, Enniskillen, co. Fermanagh.

SISTERS LIVING.

Lady Anthea Geraldine, *b.* 1942: *m.* 1965, Patrick Mathew Desmond Forde, of Seaforde, co. Down [see V. Bangor].

Lady Sarah Lillian (Aspen, Colorado, USA), *b.* 1945.

AUNT LIVING. (*Raised to the rank of an Earl's daughter,* 1951.)

Lady Doreen Stella, *b.* 1916; formerly 2nd Officer WRNS: *m.* 1948, the Rev. John Gwinnett, MC, Chap. to the Forces, and has issue living, Adrian John (33, Cavendish Av., N.), *b.* 1949; ed. at Sherborne: *m.* 1971, Jane Elliot Allen, and has issue living, Giles Marcus *b.* 1974. *Address,*—The Parsonage, Brafield on The Green, Northampton.

DAUGHTER LIVING OF FOURTH EARL.

Lady Margaret (Castle Coole, Enniskillen, co. Fermanagh), *b.* 1883.

WIDOW LIVING OF SEVENTH EARL.

GLORIA ANTHEA (c/o Army and Navy Club, Pall Mall, SW1), da. of the late Herbert Bryant Harker, of Melbourne, Aust.: *m.* 1st, 1939, the 7th Earl, who *d.* 1960; 2ndly, 1963, Col. Robert James Thompson Irwin, MC, R. Inniskilling Fusiliers.

COLLATERAL BRANCHES LIVING.

Grandchildren of the late Col. the Hon. Henry William Lowry-Corry (*infra*):— Issue of the late Lt.-Col. Sir Henry Charles Lowry-Corry, MC, *b.* 1887, *d.* 1973: *m.* 1920, Betty Alice Adeline (Edwardstone Hall, Boxford, Suffolk), da. of the late Col. Douglas James Proby [see D. Abercorn, colls.]:—

FREDERICK HENRY (15, Smith St., Chelsea, SW3), *b.* Dec. 23rd, 1926; ed. at Eton; Lt. RN ret.; 1939-45 War: *m.* 1949, the Hon. Rosemary Diana Lavinia Plumer, da. of 2nd Viscount Plumer, and has issue living, Charles Frederick Armar, *b.* 1951,—James Leopold Vincent, *b.* 1955.——*Rev.* Armar Douglas (The Vicarage, Oakham), *b.* 1929; ed. at Eton; V. of Oakham since 1968.——Elizabeth Margaret, *b.* 1921.——Edith (*Lady Carver*), *b.* 1923: *m.* 1947, FM Sir (Richard) Michael Power Carver, GCB, CBE, DSO, MC, and has issue living, Andrew Richard, *b.* 1950: *m.* 1973, Anne Rosamunde, da. of Brian Stewart, of The Broich, Crieff, Perthshire,—John Antony, *b.* 1961,— Susanna Mary, *b.* 1948,—Alice Elizabeth, *b.* 1954.

Issue of the late Col. the Hon. Henry William Lowry-Corry, 4th son of 3rd Earl, *b.* 1845, *d.* 1927: *m.* 1876, the Hon. Blanche Edith Wood who *d.* 1921, dau. of 1st Viscount Halifax:—

Emily Mary (*Dowager Lady Rycroft*), *b.* 1882: *m.* 1911, Maj. Sir Richard Nelson Rycroft, 5th Bt., who *d.* 1925. *Residence,*—The Vicarage, Hewish, Weston-super-Mare.——Alice Frances Louisa, *b.* 1885. *Residence,*—Hedingham Castle, Halstead, Essex.

Grandchildren of the late Armar Henry Lowry-Corry, son of Rt. Hon. Henry Thomas Lowry-Corry, M.P., 1st Lord of the Admiralty, 2nd son of 2nd Earl:— Issue of the late Brig.-Gen. Noel Armar Lowry-Corry, D.S.O., *b.* 1867, *d.* 1935: *m.* 1st, 1895, Rosalind Gertrude, who *d.* 1903, dau. of Lieut.-Col. Robert Hamilton Lloyd-Anstruther [Anstruther, Bt., colls.]; 2ndly, 1904, the Hon. Clare O'Brien, who *d.* 1950, dau. of 14th Baron Inchiquin:—

(By 2nd marriage) Montagu William, *b.* 1907; ed. at Harrow; Bar. Inner Temple 1933; formerly Capt. Grenadier Guards; a Member of LCC 1958-65 and Westminster City Council 1964-68 (Dep. Chm. 1964-65); 1939-45 War (wounded): *m.* 1st, 1929, the Hon. Mary Constance (who obtained a divorce 1938), da. of 2nd Baron Biddulph; 2ndly, 1969, Jean Trefusis, da. of the late Hon. Arthur Owen Crichton [see E. Erne, colls.], and widow of Lt.-Col. Eion James Henry Merry, MC, and has issue living (by 1st m.), Josephine Clare, *b*. 1931: *m*. 1957, HSH Prince Rupert Ludwig Ferdinand zu Löwenstein-Wertheim-Freudenberg [By. Pirbright], of 11, Holland Villas Rd., W14, and has issue living, *Prince* Rudolf Amadeus *b*. 1957, *Prince* Konrad Friedrich Ferdinand Johannes Ottokar Sylvester *b*. 1958, *Princess* Maria Theodora Marjorie *b*. 1966. *Residences*,—Clover Farm, Shalden, Alton, Hants.; 11, Holland Villas Rd., W14. *Clubs*,—White's, Beefsteak, and Royal Yacht Squadron.——(By 2nd m.) Patricia, *b*. 1905. *Residence*,—41, Ennismore Gdns., SW7.

Issue of the late Reginald Charles Lowry-Corry, *b*. 1875, *d*. 1945 : *m*. 1912, Dorothy Cecilia who *d*. 1936, dau. of the late Capt. Gerald Cecil Stewart Paget, and widow of Capt. Christopher Egerton Balfour, D.S.O. [M. Anglesey, colls.]:—
Faythe, *b*. 1913 : *m*. 1st, 1933 (marriage dissolved 1942), Bernard Clifford Lee-Hutson ; 2ndly, 1951, Gerald Rawson Coldstream, and has issue living, (by 1st marriage) Peter Clifford John, *b*. 1936.
——Nina Arlette, *b*. 1915. *Residence*,—

PREDECESSORS.—Galbraith Lowry, M.P. for co. Tyrone; assumed in 1764 the additional surname of Corry ; *d*. 1769, having had with other issue [1] ARMAR, M.P. for co. Tyrone, cr. *Baron Belmore* 1781, *Viscount Belmore* 1789, and *Earl Belmore* (peerage of Ireland) 1797; *d*. 1802; *s*. by his son [2] SOMERSET, 2nd Earl; was Custos Rotulorum of co. Tyrone; sometime M.P. for co. Tyrone, Gov. of Jamaica and a Representative Peer for Ireland; *d*. 1841; *s*. by his son [3] ARMAR, 3rd Earl, *b*. 1801; was M.P. for co. Fermanagh: *m*. 1834, Emily Louise, who *d*. 1904, dau. of William Shepherd, of Bradbourne, Kent; *d*. Dec. 17th, 1845; was *s*. by his son [4] SOMERSET RICHARD, G.C.M.G., P.C., M.R.I.A., 4th Earl; *b*. 1835 ; for fifty-six years a Representative Peer ; Under-Sec. of State for Home Depart. 1866-7, Gov. of N.S. Wales 1867-72, and one of the Lords Justices of Ireland during the absence of Lord-Lieut. in 1885, 1890, 1891, 1895, 1896, 1897 and 1898; Lieut. for co. Tyrone 1892-1913 : *m*. 1861, Anne Elizabeth Honoria, who *d*. 1919, second dau. of the late Capt. John Neilson Gladstone, R.N., M.P.; *d*. 1913 ; *s*. by his el. son [5] ARMAR, 5th Earl; *b*. 1870; Bar. Inner Temple 1897; High Sheriff of co. Fermanagh 1895, and of co. Tyrone 1901; *d*. 1948; *s*. by his brother [6] CECIL, 6th Earl; *b*. 1873,; was High Sheriff of co. Tyrone 1916, and of co. Fermanagh 1922, and Chm. of Fermanagh Co. Council 1943; *d*. 1949; *s*. by his cousin [7] GALBRAITH ARMAR (son of the late Major Adrian Lowry-Corry, 5th son of the late Adm. the Hon. Armar Lowry-Corry, 2nd son of 3rd Earl), 7th Earl; *b*. 1913; Major Roy. Inniskilling Fusiliers, and a D.L. and J.P. for co. Fermanagh : *m*. 1939, Gloria Anthea, dau. of the late Herbert Bryant Harker, of Melbourne, Australia ; *d*. 1960 ; *s*. by his only son [8] JOHN ARMAR, 8th Earl and present peer ; also Viscount Belmore, and Baron Belmore.

BELPER, BARON. (Strutt.) [Baron U.K. 1856.]

PROPOSITI TENAX

Firm of purpose.

(ALEXANDER) RONALD GEORGE STRUTT, 4th Baron, *b*. April 23rd, 1912 ; *s*. 1956 ; is Major Coldstream Guards, and patron of two livings ; European War 1939-44 (wounded): *m*. 1940, Zara Sophie Kathleen Mary (from whom he obtained a divorce 1949), dau. of Sir Harry Stapleton Mainwaring, 5th Bt. (ext.), and has issue.

Arms.—Per pale sable and azure, two chevronels engrailed, between three cross crosslets fitchée or. **Crest.**—In front of rays of the sun proper, a cubit arm erect, vested, bendy of six or and sable, cuffed argent, in the hand a roll of paper proper. **Supporters.**—On either side a leopard proper, gorged with a collar gemellé azure, therefrom pendant an escutcheon also azure, charged with a cross crosslet fitchée or.

Seat,—Kingston Hall, Nottingham.

SON LIVING.

Hon. RICHARD HENRY (Slaughter Farm, Bourton-on-the-Water, Glos.), *b*. Oct. 24th, 1941; ed. at Harrow: *m*. 1966, Jennifer Vivian, da. of the late Capt. Peter Winser, and has issue living, Michael Henry, *b*. 1969,—Henrietta Lavinia, *b*. 1970.

HALF-BROTHERS LIVING.

Hon. Peter Algernon, *M.C.*, *b*. 1924 ; ed. at Eton ; is a Director of Tollemache & Cobbold Breweries, Ltd., and of Eastern Counties Building So. ; European War 1943-45 as Lieut. Coldstream Guards (MC): *m*. (Jan.) 1953, Gay Margaret, da. of Sir (Frank Guy) Clavering Fison, of Crepping Hall, Stutton, Suffolk, and has issue living, Henry Clavering Tollemache, *b*. (Dec.) 1953,—Martin Andrew, *b*. 1958,—Jane Mariota, *b*. 1956,—Elisabeth, *b*. 1963. *Residence*,—Stutton Hall, Ipswich.

Hon. (Desmond) Rupert, *b*. 1926; ed. at Eton; formerly Capt. Coldstream Guards: *m*. 1st, 1951, (m. diss. 1961), Jean Felicity, da. of the late Hon. Francis Walter Erskine [see E. Mar and Kellie, colls.]; 2ndly, 1964, Lucy Gwendolen, only da. of Maj. James William Stirling Home Drummond Moray, late Scots Guards, of Abercairny, Crieff, Perthshire [see D. Buccleuch, colls.], and has issue living, (by 1st m.) Jeremy Bevil, *b*. 1954,—Christopher Charles, *b*. 1955,—(by 2nd m.) Dominick James, *b*. 1966,—James Edward, *b*. 1969. *Residence*,—Rockleys, Goldhanger, Essex. *Clubs*,—Boodle's, Guards'.

SISTER LIVING.

Hon. Lavinia Mary, *CBE* (*Lavinia, Duchess of Norfolk*), *b*. 1916; bore the Queen's Canopy at Coronation of King George VI; Lord Lieut. of W. Sussex since 1975; CBE (Civil) 1971: *m*. 1937, the 16th Duke of Norfolk, who *d*. 1975. *Residence*,—Arundel Park, Sussex.

AUNTS LIVING. (*Daughters of 2nd Baron.*)

Hon. Margaret, *b*. 1886. *Residence*,—Waterbridge, Watton-at-Stone, Herts.

Hon. Muriel, *b*. 1890; formerly Senior Com. A.T.S.: *m*. 1916, Major Frank Haultain Hornsby, late RFA, who *d*. 1935, and has issue living, Pamela Margaret (of Courtwood, Nayland, Suffolk), *b.* 1918; formerly Subaltern ATS: *m.* 1945, Maj. Edward Charles Mann, DSO, MC, 12th Lancers, who *d.* 1959 [see Mann, Bt.]. *Residence,*—Courtwood, Nayland, Suffolk.

WIDOW LIVING OF SON OF THIRD BARON

Arielle, (Catnip Corner, Bellevue Av., Newport, Rhode Island, USA), da. of Jos ph Washington Fraser, of Newport, Rhode Island, USA: *m.* 1st, 1939, the Hon. Michael Strutt, P/O, RCAF, who *d.* (killed on active ser.) 1942; 2ndly, 1947 (m. diss. 1967), Eric Eweson.

MOTHER LIVING.

Hon. Dame Eva Isabel Marian Bruce (*Eva, Countess of Rosebery*), *DBE,* da. of 2nd Baron Aberdare; Hon. LLD Edinburgh; a JP for Bucks., and a Chevalier of Legion of Honour: DBE (Civil), 1955; *m.* 1st, 1911, the 3rd Baron Belper, who *d.* 1956, and from whom she had obtained a divorce 1922; 2ndly, 1924, as his second wife, the 6th Earl of Rosebery, who *d.* 1974. *Residences,*—Mentmore, Leighton Buzzard; Cleveland House, Newmarket, Suffolk.

WIDOW LIVING OF THIRD BARON.

ANGELA MARIOTA, dau. of the late Hon. Douglas Alfred Tollemache [see B. Tollemache colls.]: *m.* 1st 1923, as his second wife, the 3rd Baron, who *d.* 1956; 2ndly, 1958, the Rev. (Harry) Norman Tollemache (formerly Wrigley). *Residence,*—Bentley House, Ipswich.

PREDECESSORS.—[1] EDWARD Strutt, *P.C.*, *F.R.S.*, *LL.D.*, son of William Strutt, of St. Helen's House, Derby; *b.* 1801; sat as M.P. (*L*) for Derby 1830-48, for Arundel 1851-2, and for Nottingham 1852-6; was Chancellor of Duchy of Lancaster 1852-4, and Lord-Lieut. of Nottinghamshire 1864-80; cr. *Baron Belper* (peerage of United Kingdom) 1856: *m.* 1837, Amelia Harriet, dau. of the late Right Rev. William Otter, D.D., Lord Bishop of Chichester; *d.* June 30th, 1880, and was *s.* by his son [2] HENRY, *P.C.*, 2nd Baron; *b.* 1840; M.P. for Derbyshire East (*L*), 1868-74, and for Berwick-on-Tweed in 1880; was Capt. of H.M.'s Corps of Gentlemen-at-Arms 1895-1906: *m.* 1874, Lady Margaret Coke, who *d.* 1922, dau. of 2nd Earl of Leicester; *d.* 1914; *s.* by his only son [3] ALGERNON HENRY, 3rd Baron; *b.* 1883; Capt. Household Cav. and Major Reserve of Officers: *m.* 1st, 1911, the Hon. Dame Eva Isabel Marian Bruce, *D.B.E.*, *J.P.* (who obtained a divorce, 1922), dau. of 2nd Baron Aberdare; 2ndly, 1923, Angela Mariota, who *m.* 2ndly, 1958, Rev (Harry) Norman Tollemache (formerly Wrigley), da of the late Hon Douglas Alfred Tollemache; *d* 1956; *s* by his el son [4] (ALEXANDER) RONALD GEORGE, 4th Baron and present peer.

BELSTEAD, BARON. (Ganzoni.) [Baron U.K. 1938, Bt. U.K. 1929.]

FIDELITAS · VINCIT

Fidelity overcomes.

JOHN JULIAN GANZONI, 2nd Baron and 2nd Baronet; *b.* Sept. 30th, 1932; *s.* 1958; ed. at Eton, and at Ch. Ch., Oxford; a JP of Ipswich; a Parl. Under-Sec. of State, Depart. of Education and Science 1970-73, and Parl. Under Sec. of State for N. Ireland 1973-74; Chm. of Governing Bodies Assocn. since 1974.

Arms,—Per fesse azure and argent a gentian plant, flowered and eradicated proper, between in chief a mullet and an increscent both or. **Crest,**—A demi-lion or supporting a gentian plant as in the arms. **Supporters,**—On either side a seahorse proper, gorged with a collar pendent therefrom a portcullis chained or.

Residence,—The Old Rectory, Gt. Bealings, Woodbridge, Suffolk. *Clubs,*—Bath, Ipswich and Suffolk (Ipswich), All England Lawn Tennis, MCC.

SISTER LIVING.

Hon. Mary Jill, *b.* 1931.

PREDECESSOR—[1] (FRANCIS) JOHN CHILDS Ganzoni, only son of the late Julius Charles Ganzoni, of Prince's Gardens, S.W.7; *b.* 1882; was Parliamentary Private Sec. to Postmaster Gen. 1924-9, temporary Chm. of Committees, House of Commons 1932-34, and Chm. of Private Bills Committee, House of Lords 1940-58; sat as MP for Ipswich (*C*) 1914-23, and 1924-37; cr. a *Baronet* (UK, of Ipswich) 1929, and *Baron Belstead,* of Ipswich, Suffolk (peerage of UK) 1938: *m.* 1930, Gwendolen Gertrude, who *d.* 1962, el. da. of the late Arthur Turner, of Ipswich; *d.* 1948; *s.* by his only son [2] JOHN JULIAN, 2nd Baron and present peer.

BERKELEY, BARONESS. (Foley Berkeley.) [Baron E. 1421.]

MARY LALLE FOLEY BERKELEY (*Baroness Berkeley*); *b.* Oct. 9th, 1905; *s.* (on termination of abeyance) 1967; assumed by deed poll 1951 the additional surname of Berkeley.

Arms.—Not exemplified at time of going to press.

Residence,—Pickade Cottage, Great Kimble, Aylesbury, Bucks.

SISTER LIVING (*h.p. to Barony*).

Hon. CYNTHIA ELLA, *b.* Jan. 31st, 1909: *m.* 1937, Brig. Ernest Adolphus Leopold Gueterbock, late RE, and has issue living, Anthony Fitzhardinge, *b.* 1939; ed. at Eton and Trin. Coll., Camb.: *m.* 1965, Diana Christine, el. da. of Eric William John Townsend, MRCS, LRCP, and has issue living, Thomas Fitzhardinge *b.* Jan. 5th, 1969, Robert William *b.* 1970. *Residence,*—The Plough, Terrick, Aylesbury, Bucks.

COLLATERAL BRANCHES LIVING.

Grandchildren of the late Adm. Frederick Augustus Maxse, yr. son of Lady Caroline FitzHardinge Berkeley (who *m.* 1829, James Maxsi), 2nd da. of 5th Earl of Berkeley:—

Issue of the late Gen. Sir (Frederick) Ivor Maxse, K.C.B., C.V.O., D.S.O., *b.* 1862, *d.* 1958 : *m.* 1899, the Hon. Mary Caroline Wyndham, who *d.* 1944, dau. of 2nd Baron Leconfield :—

John Herbert, *b.* 1901; ed. at Eton; Major (retired) Col Istream Guar ls; late A.D.C. to Maj.-Gen . Comdg. W iziristan Dist.: *m.* 1931, Dorinda Mary, *J.P.*, dau. of William Hobart Houghton Thorne, a Judge of Mixed Courts of First Instance, Egypt, and has issue living, Anthony John (Pelham Place, Alton, Hants.), *b.* 1932; ed. at Eton; late Capt. Coldstream Gds., ARICS; ADC to Gov. of Cyprus 1959-60: *m.* 1961, Susan Jane, da. of the late F. J. Emson, MC, and has issue living John James Ivor, *b.* 1968, Georgina Anne *b.* 1962, Sarah Charlotte *b.* 1964,—Martin Frederick William (Catercross, Fittleworth, Pulborough, Sussex; (*Club,*—Guards'), *b.* 1935; ed. at Eton; Maj. Coldstream Guards: *m.* 1959, Penelope Ann, da. of Maj. Charles Chichester [see Fowke, Bt.], and has issue living, Charles John Chichester *b.* 1962, Edward William *b.* 1969, Clare Caroline *b.* 1960,—Christopher James Ivor (King's Paddock, Meonstoke, Southampton; *Club,*—Royal Automobile) *b.* 1942; ed. at Eton. *Residence,*—Catercross, Fittleworth, Pulborough, Sussex.——Violet Constance, *b.* 1905; 1939-45 as Jun. Com. ATS. *Residence,*—Hatchetts, West Burton, Pulborough, Sussex.

Grandchildren of the late Ella Henrietta Maxse (who *d.* 1916, having *m.* 1862, as his second wife, Lieut.-Gen. the Hon. Edward Thomas Gage, C.B., who *d.* 1889), dau. of Lady Caroline Fitz Hardinge Berkeley (who *m.* 1829, James Maxse), 2nd dau. of 5th Earl of Berkeley :—
See V. Gage, colls.

Grandchildren of the late Capt. Sydney Augustus Berkeley Capel, son of Lady Emily Elizabeth Fitz Hardinge Capel, 3rd da. of 5th Earl of Berkeley:—
Issue of the late Winifred Laura, *b.* 1875, *d.* 1927 : *m.* 1905, Dr. Ernest Faber Fookes, who *d.* 1948:—
Sydney Faber, *LLB* (22, Kahikatea St., Inglewood, NZ), *b.* 1906: is a Bar. and Solicitor: *m.* 1939, Lorna Kathleen Joblin, and has issue living, Timothy Faber (c/o Bell, Gully & Co., Wellington, NZ), *b.* 1940: *m.* 1972, Sandra Jane Field,—Sally Faber, *b.* 1941: *m.* 1965, Barrie Miles Owen, of 409, Otumoetai Rd., Taurangan, NZ, and has issue living, Simon John *b.* 1972, Angela Jane *b.* 1967, Philippa Ann *b.* 1969.——Kenneth Faber, *b.* 1907; *m.* 1936, Constance Joyce Christian Boden, and has issue living, Patrick Faber, *b.* 1937,—Alister Faber, *b.* 1941,—Russel Faber, *b.* 1947,—Jennifer Faber, *b.* 1942. *Residence,*—19, Paynter's Avenue, Fitzroy, New Plymouth, New Zealand. ——Ernestine Emily Faber, *b.* 1912: *m.* 1940, Stuart Alexander Black, and has issue living, Anna Catherine, *b.* 1946. *Residence,*—598, Devon Street East, New Plymouth, NZ.

Issue of the late Maude Harold Capel, *b.* 1885, *d.* 1962: *m.* 1907, Leslie Adams Nolan, who *d.* 1945:—
David (PO Box 76, New Plymouth, NZ), *b.* 1912: *m.* 1940, Elsa Isabel Mooney, and has issue living, Robert Leslie (352, Philip Av., Frenchville, North Rockhampton, Qld. 4701, Aust.), *b.* 1941: *m.* 1967, Maureen Anne Heffernan, and has issue living, Brent Robert *b.* 1972, Kim Kathleen *b.* 1974,—Susanne Margaret, *b.* 1944: *m.* 1970, David Thomas Thorp, of Sentry Hill, Lepperton, Taranaki, NZ,—Elizabeth Mary, *b.* 1945: *m.* 1969, Charles Miles Brown,—Catherine Ruth, *b.* 1947: *m.* 1971, Ian James Robinson, Egmont Village, Taranaki, NZ.——Nina Leslie, *b.* 1908: *m.* 1935, John Dixon Law (11, Mangorei Rd., New Plymouth, NZ), and has issue living, Barry (c/o Australia and NZ Bank, Wellington, NZ), *b.* 1936: *m.* 1961, Faith Georgina Gordon Glassford, and has issue living, Michael Barry *b.* 1963, Stephanie Jane *b.* 1968,—John Berkeley (28, Taimui St., New Plymouth, NZ), *b.* 1941: *m.* 1970, Janet Elizabeth Slater, and has issue living, Richard Berkeley *b.* 1973,—Janet Capel, *b.* 1947: *m.* 1969, Bryan Alexander Cleland, of 11, Longview Drive, New Plymouth, NZ, and has issue living, Scott Law *b.* 1971, Sarah Jane Capel *b.* 1974.

Descendants of the late Hon. Thomas Berkeley, 4th son of 6th Baron Berkeley :—

Grandchildren of Robert Valentine Berkeley (infra):—
Issue of the late Capt. Robert George Wilmot Berkeley, *b.* 1898, *d.* 1969: *m.* 1927, the Hon. Myrtle Emmeline Theresa Dormer, da. of 14th Baron Dormer:—
Robert John Grantley, *TD*, (Berkeley Castle, Glos.; Spetchley, Worcs.), *b.* 1931; ed. at Oratory Sch. and Magdalen Coll., Oxford; Maj. Queen's Own Warwicks. and Worcs. Yeo.; late Lt. 10th Roy. Hussars; a JP of Glos.; High Sheriff of Worcs. 1967; Joint Master of Berkeley Foxhounds: *m.* 1967, Georgina Bridget, el. da. of the late Maj Andrew Charles Stirling Home Drummond Moray, of Easter Ross, Comrie, Perthshire, and has issue living, Robert Charles, *b.* 1968,—Henry John Mowbray, *b.* 1969.——Rosalind Magdalen Ellen, *b.* 1928; is a nun.——Juliet Elizabeth Mary, *b.* 1930.

Granddaughter of the late Robert Berkeley (*b.* 1823), el. son of the late Robert Berkeley (*b.* 1794), 10th in descent from the late Hon. Thomas Berkeley (ante) :—
Issue of the late Robert Valentine Berkeley, *b.* 1853, *d.* 1940: *m.* 1891, Rose, who *d.* 1922, dau. of the late Frederick Willmott, of Warley Place, Great Warley, Essex :—
Margaret Elizabeth, *b.* 1902; is a nun. *Residence,*—Spetchley, Worcester.

Grandsons of the late Maj. Henry William Berkeley, 3rd son of Robert Berkeley (*b.* 1794):—

Issue of the late Lieut.-Col. Christopher Robert Berkeley, C.M.G.. D.S.O., O.B.E., late Welch Regt., *b.* 1877, *d.* 1959 : *m.* 1919, Nest (of 5, Forsyte House, Chelsea Manor Street, S.W.3), dau. of the late Col. Sir Joseph Alfred Bradney, C.B.:—
Maurice (Rectory Farm, Rectory Lane, Sevenoaks, Kent; RAO), *b.* 1921; ed. at Beaumont; Lt.-Col. RA (ret.): *m.* 1950, Sylvia Mary Close, da. of the late M. B. Tennant-Maudsley, and has issue living, Hugh Christopher, *b.* 1952; ed. at Stonyhurst,—John Henry, *b.* 1956; ed. at Worth,—Michael Frederick, *b.* 1958; ed. at Worth.——Basil Robert, *b.* 1925; ed. at Beaumont, late Capt. Irish Gds.: *m.* 1953, Gillian Rosamond Wellesley, yst. da. of the late Dr. R. H. Spencer, of Alcester, and has issue living, Giles Robert, *b.* 1959,—Roger Maurice, *b.* 1961. *Residence,*—Highmoor House, Mayfield, Sussex. *Club,*—Guards'.

Grandchildren of the late Lt.-Col. Christopher Robert Berkeley, C.M.G., D.S.O., O.B.E. (ante):—

Issue of the late Capt. Edward Henry Berkeley, *b.* 1923, *d.* 1962: *m.* 1951, Joyce Louise (who. *m.* 2ndly, 1965, Charles Michael Philips) da. of the late D. C. Duncan, of Valparaiso, Chile:—
Grantley William Andrew, *b.* 1954; ed. at Stonyhurst.——Wulstan Hubert, *b.* 1956; ed. at Stonyhurst. ——Thurstan Timothy Edward, *b.* 1961.——Fiona Maria Louise (twin), *b.* 1956.

PREDECESSORS.—[1] THOMAS de Berkeley, 6th Feudal Lord, was summoned to Parliament as a Baron 1295-1321: *d.* 1321; *s.* by his son [2] MAURICE, 2nd Baron by writ; summoned to Parliament of England as *Lord Berkeley*; having joined Thomas Plantagenet, Earl of Lancaster, he was imprisoned in Wallingford Castle, where he *d.* 1326; *s.* by his son [3] THOMAS, 3rd Baron; summoned to Parliament 1329-60: was sometime Custodian of Edward II, and after the murder of that King was arraigned as a participator in the deed and honourably acquitted; *d.* 1361; *s.* by his son [4] MAURICE, 4th Baron: summoned to Parliament 1342; was wounded at Poitiers; *s.* by his son [5] THOMAS, 5th Baron; *d.* 1417; *s.* by his nephew [6] JAMES, 6th Baron; summoned to Parliament by writ as *Baron Berkeley* 1421-61, *d.* 1463; *s.* by his el. son [7] WILLIAM, 7th Baron; cr. *Viscount Berkeley* 1481, *Earl of Nottingham* 1483, and *Marquess of Berkeley* (peerage of England) 1489; the castle, lands, and lordships composing the Barony of Berkeley he settled upon Henry VII and his heirs male, failing which to descend to his own rightful heirs, a circumstance that had its origin in his next brother having married the da. of a Bristol Alderman; *d.* 1491, when his own honours became extinct and his brother [8] MAURICE *de jure* 8th Baron was in consequence of the settlement referred to, deprived of the Barony; *d.* 1506; *s.* by his son [9] *Sir* MAURICE *de jure* 9th Baron; *d.* 1526; *s.* by his brother [10] *Sir* THOMAS *de jure* 10th Baron; *d.* 1533; *s.* by his son

[11] THOMAS 11th Baron; summoned to Parliament 1534; *d.* 1534; *s.* by his son [12] HENRY,
12th Baron, to whom the Barony and lands of Berkeley descended on the death of Edward VI, the
last heir male of Henry VII; *d.* 1613; *s.* by his grandson [13] *Sir* GEORGE, 13th Baron; *d.*
1658; *s.* by his son [14] GEORGE, 14th Baron; cr. *Viscount Dursley* and *Earl of Berkeley* (peerage
of England) 1679; *d.* 1693; [15-19] the Barony of Berkeley remained merged in the Earldom
until the death of the 6th Earl de jure in 1882, when the Earldom devolved upon his kinsman,
George Lennox Rawdon Berkeley, and the Barony upon his niece [20] LOUISA MARY Milman
(only da. of the late Hon. Craven Fitzhardinge Berkeley, 3rd son of 5th Earl of Berkeley), to whom
the title was confirmed by Roy. Warrant 1893; *b.* 1840; *m.* 1872, Maj.-Gen. Gustavus Hamilton
Lockwood Milman, RA, who *d.* 1915; *d.* 1899; *s.* by her da. [21] EVA MARY FITZ-HARDINGE, *b.*
1875: *m.* 1903, Col. Frank Wigram Foley, CBE, DSO; R. Berks. Regt., who *d.* 1949; *d.* 1964,
when the Barony fell into abeyance between her two daughters, the Hon. Mary Lalle Foley Berkeley
and the Hon. Mrs. Cynthia Ella Gueterbock, and so continued until 1967, when the abeyance was
terminated in favour of the elder [22] MARY LALLE, present peeress.

Berkshire, Earl of,   see Earl of Suffolk and Berkshire.

BERNERS, BARONESS.   (Williams.)   [Baron E. 1455.]

VERA RUBY WILLIAMS (*Baroness
Berners*) ; *b.* Dec. 25th, 1901 ; *s.*
1950 : *m.* 1927, Harold Williams,
J.P., and has issue.

Arms.—Gules, three lapwings or. *Supporters,*—*Dexter,* a falcon rising, wings inverted argent, belled and jessed or ; *sinister,* a
greyhound proper, gorged with a collar gules,
studded or.

Residence,—Ashwellthorpe,   Charlton
Lane, Cheltenham, Glos.

DAUGHTERS LIVING.
(*Co-heiresses to the Barony.*)

Hon. PAMELA VIVIEN, *b.* Sept. 30th, 1929 :
m. 1952, Michael Joseph Sperry Kirkham,
and has issue living, Rupert William Tyrwhitt, *b.* 1953,—Robin Raymond Tyrwhitt,
b. 1958,—Caroline Rosemary Tyrwhitt, *b.*
1956.   *Residence,*—Parwich Lees, Derbyshire.

Hon. ROSEMARY TYRWHITT, *b.* July 20th, 1931: *m.* 1959, Kelvin Alexander Pollock, and has
issue living, Simon Kelvin Tyrwhitt, *b.* 1962,—Alastair Michael Tannahill, *b.* 1964. *Residence,*—
Malt House, Hollingbourne, Kent.

COLLATERAL BRANCHES LIVING.

Grandsons of the late Hon. Sibyl Grace Wheeler (infra):—
Issue of the late Wing-Com. Vashon James Wheeler, M.C., D.F.C., *b.* 1898. *d.* (killed in
action during 1939-45 War) 1944: *m.* 1930, Josephine Hermione (The Coach House,
Nevern, Newport, Pembs.), da. of Maj. John Charles Spencer-Phillips, DSO, of Ridley
House, Kingswear, Devon:—
John Vashon Tyrwhitt, *b.* 1931 ; ed. at Eton, and at Trin. Coll., Camb. (B.A. 1953, M.A. 1960) : *m.*
1957, Geraldine Noel, younger dau. of W. Noel Jones, of Little Gables, Glasllwch Lane, Newport,
Monmouthshire, and has issue living, James Vashon, *b.* 1960,—Nicholas Charles Tyrwhit, *b.* 1965,—
Justin Alexander Noel, *b.* 1970,—Susan Verity, *b.* 1958. *Residence,*—Bitterley Court, Ludlow, Salop.
——Peter James, *b.* 1933: *m.* 1960, Eileen Mary, only da. of A. E. Larcombe, of Brierley, Livesey
Rd., Ludlow, and has issue living, Gavin Vashon *b.* 1972,—Karen Wanda Grace *b.* 1970,—Amanda
Hermione (twin), *b.* 1972. *Residence,*—Llwyngoras, Velindre, nr. Crymmych, Pembs.

Issue of the late Hon. Sibyl Grace Tyrwhitt, dau. of Emma Harriet, Baroness
Berners, *b.* 1866, *d.* 1962: *m.* 1895, James Volant Wheeler, who *d.* 1939:—
Hugh Volant, *D.S.C., R.N.* (of Calgary, P.O. Box 27, Salisbury, S. Rhodesia), *b.* 1901; European
War 1939-44 as Lieut.-Com. (D.S.C. and Bar): *m.* 1st, 1938, Pauline, dau. of Maj. — Johnstone;
2ndly, 1947, Diana Joan, dau. of Maj. Albert Herbert MacIlwaine, D.S.O., M.C., of Larkhill, Mar-
andellas, S. Rhodesia, and has issue living, (by 2nd marriage) David Hugh, *b.* 1949.——Gilbert
Ty rwhitt, *DSO* (2, Withyholt Park, Charlton Kings, Cheltenham), *b.* 1902; ed. at Wellington Coll.;
Col. Indian Cav. (ret.); D.S.O. 1945: *m.* 1932, Beryl Audrey, dau. of H. J. Landon, of New England
Hill, W. Chobham, and has issue living, Audrey Julia, *b.* 1933: *m.* 1960, Capt. William G. McO.
Burn, RN, of Pentland House, Middle Hill, Englefield Green, Surrey, and has issue living, Peter
William *b.* 1960, Hugh Tyrwhitt *b.* 1965, Jenifer Julia *b.* 1962,—Jacqueline Mary, *b.* 1935: *m.* 1960,
Don H. Oslon, of 30, Forest St., Lexington, Mass., USA, and has issue living, Sven Tyrwhitt *b.* 1967,
Sonja Landon *b.* 1964.——Allen Henry, *CBE* (of Whistley Bridge Field, Twyford, Berks.; RAF and
Roy. Aero Clubs), *b.* 1903; ed. at Eton, and at Trin. Coll., Camb. (BA 1924, MA 1929); Air Com-
modore RAF (ret.); an Aviation Consultant, a Trustee of Shuttleworth Trust, and a FRAeS;
1939-45 War (OBE, Netherlands DFC); OBE (Mil.) 1945, CBE (Mil.) 1955); *m.* 1st, 1934, Ruth
Margaret, da. of George Ballard, of the Lowe, Stockton, Worcester; 2ndly, 1949, Barbara Aanes
da. of Basil Alfred Slade, of Whistley Bridge House, Twyford, Berks., and has issue living, (by 1ft
marriage) Ardyn Margaret, *b.* 1937,—Meris Ann, *b.* 1939.——Grace Mary, *b.* 1896.——Dorothy
Sibyl, *b.* 1897: *m.* 1922, E. Brande Don, of Guild House, Denmark Rd., Gloucester, and has issue
living, Volant Geoffrey Vincent *b.* 1930.

Granddaughter of the late John Bracebridge Wilson, el. son of the Rev. Edward
Wilson, el. son of the Rev. George Wilson, brother of 9th and 10t h Barons:—
Issue of the late Oriana Mary Bracebridge Wilson, *b.* 1864, *d.* 1956 : *m.* 1894, Lieut.-Col,
Albert Finchett Garrard, V.D., Australian Forces, who *d.* 1947 :—
Edith May Bracebridge, *b.* 1895: *m.* 1926, Harold Bruce Adair, Lieut. Australian Army Med. Corps,
and has issue living, John Bracebridge Garrard (21, Collins St., Werribee, Vic., Aust.), *b.* 1933:
m. 1954, Joy Isabel Balcombe, and has issue living, Robyn Maree *b.* 1957, Tracey Anne *b.* 1960,
Kerri Frances (twin) *b.* 1960, Helen Therese *b.* 1965,—Helen Becher Bracebridge, *b.* 1930. *Residence,*
—Atherstone, 1625, Sturt St., Ballarat, Victoria, Aust.

Grandsons of the late Frederick Wilson, 10th son of the Rev. George Wilson (ante):—
Issue of the late Henry Fletcher Wilson, *b.* 1852, *d.* 1929: *m.* 1890, Eugenie, who *d.* 1959, da. of
Stephen Jauchler, of New Orleans, La., USA:—

Knyvet McDonald (241, Celeste Av., River Ridge, La., USA 70123), *b.* 1909: *m.* 1937, Ethel, da. of James W. McKnight, of St. Louis, Mo., USA, and has issue living, Knyvet Robert (1810, Taylor St., Kenner, La., USA), *b.* 1942: *m.* 1967, Alice Ann, da. of John Alexander Neely, of Anderson, SC, USA, and has issue living, Michael Patrick *b.* 1969, Christine Suzanne *b.* 1970,—Barbara Ethel, *b.* 1938: *m.* 1965, Robert Wayne Raley, of 804, Downing Dr., Richardson, Texas, and has issue living, Kevin Wayne *b.* 1967, Craig Wade *b.* 1968, Kathleen Elaine *b.* 1971.——Maude Alice, *b.* 1899: *m.* 1929, Hugh Francis Hart, of 2809, Law St., New Orelans, La., USA 70117, and has issue living, Gerard Hugh (610, Fos St., Harvey, La., USA), *b.* 1930: *m.* 1951, Lela, da. of Wallace Chaisson, of Harvey, La., USA, and has issue living, Gerard Maurice *b.* 1953, Stephen Francis *b.* 1955, David Sidney *b.* 1959, Susan Louise *b.* 1957, Cindy Ann *b.* 1965,—Maurice Henry (4616, Dreyfous Av., Metairie, La., USA), *b.* 1932: *m.* 1956, Audrey, da. of Leonce Gaudet, of Paincourtville, La., USA, and has issue living, Brian David *b.* 1959, Keith Michael *b.* 1965, Jo Ann *b.* 1957.

Issue of the late Archdale McDonald Wilson, *b.* 1860, *d.* 1944: *m.* 1889, Elizabeth, who *d.* 1942, dau. of Adam Cook, of Hamilton, Ontario:—

Arthur Knyvet, *MC* (136, Bay St., Apt. 902, Hamilton, Ont., Canada, L8P 3H5), *b.* 1895; Major 3rd Reserve Batn. Roy. Hamilton LI, Canadian Mil.; 1914-18 War in France and Belgium (MC, two medals): *m.* 1923, Dorothy Enid, da. of the late Lt.-Col. Walter W. Stewart, and has issue living, John Knyvet (339, Camelot Court, Burlington, Ont., Canada, L7L 2G2), *b.* 1933: *m.* 1956, Marian Culham, and has issue living, David Knyvet *b.* 1961, Peter John *b.* 1964,—Nancy Margaret, *b.* 1928: *m.* 1953, William Arnold Parker, of 867, Montgomery Drive, Ancaster, Ont., Canada, and has issue living, Jeffrey Stewart *b.* 1955, Gregory Wilson *b.* 1957.——Roland Frederick, *QC, LLB, b.* 1901; a Member of the legal firm of Day, Wilson, Campbell & Martin, of Toronto: *m.* 1934, Adelaide Bernice Sill, da. of Dr. W. T. Langrill, of Hamilton, Ont., Canada, and has issue living, Donald Langrill (284, Inglewood Drive, Toronto 7, Canada) *b.* 1935; a Member of Roy. Arch. Inst. of Canada, and MArch, Harvard: *m.* 1960, Judie Jean Arnold, dau. of R. F. Chisholm, of Toronto, and has issue living, Robert Frederick *b.* 1962, Wendy Jean *b.* 1964,—Stephen Roland, *b.* 1941,—Frances Elizabeth, *b.* 1939. *Residence,*—120, Rosedale Drive, Toronto, Canada.

Grandsons of the late Archdale McDonald Wilson (ante):—
Issue of the late Marion Alice Wilson, *b.* 1893, *d.* 1974: *m.* 1920, Lt.-Col. Harold Brownlee Stuart, MBE, ED, RCE, who *d.* 1946:—

Ronald Samuel (26, Stratheden Rd., Toronto, Ont., M4N 1E4, Canada), *b.* 1927; BA 1950; MBA 1951; FCIS; formerly Lt. RCN (Reserve): *m.* 1954, Marjorie Irene, only da. of Albert Parker Willis, of Mount Royal, Quebec, and has issue living, William Hugh Knyvet, *b.* 1966.

Issue of the late Archdale McDonald Wilson, *b.* 1899, *d.* 1960: *m.* 1930, Norah Elizabeth (of 11, Summit Av., Sault Ste. Marie, Ont.), and has issue living:—

Walter Archdale (158, Adie St., Sudbury, Ont.), *b.* 1936: *m.* 1963, Freda Dian, da. of the late Wallace Frederick Bond Roberts, of Toronto.——William Martin Connell (91, King St. West, Bolton, Ont., Canada), *b.* 1942: *m.* 1968, Sandra May, da. of Elwood C. Bobzien, of 5995, Lincoln Court, Newfane, New York.

Grandson of the late Alice (who *m.* 1871, Charles J. S. Naftel), *b.* 1845, *d.* 1940, da. of the late Frederick Wilson (ante):—
Issue of the late Frederick John Naftel, *b.* 1871, *d.* 1943: *m.* 1900, Caroline Mabel, who *d.* 195-, da. of R. J. Drummond:—

Frederick Robb Knyvett (RR2, Roslen, Ontario, Canada), *b.* 1903: Cdr. RCN (ret.); *b.* 1903: *m.* 1933, Ruth Short, and has issue living, William, *b.* 1940,—Dorothy Carolyn Drummond, *b.* 1936: *m.* 1964, M. E. Heggens.

Grandchildren of the late Knyvett Eustace Naftel (infra):—
Issue of the late Charles Knyvett Naftel, *b.* 1910, *d.* 1969: *m.* 1937, Elizabeth, da. of Cuthbert Burt:—

Paul *b.* 1939; ed. at Western Univ., London, Ont. (MSc): *m.* 1967, Lillian Armbruster, of Prince Albert. ——Judith, *b.* 1943: *m.* 1965, David Mackintosh, CAF, and has issue living, Todd, *b.* 1968,—Brian, *b.* 1972.

Grandchildren of the late Alice Naftel (ante):—
Issue of the late Knyvett Eustace Naftel, *b.* 1881, *d.* 1951: *m.* 1907, Marion Grace, who *d.* 1966, da. of Andrew Crawford:—

James Eustace (19, St. Vincent St., Goderich, Ont., Canada), *b.* 1913: *m.* 1938, Pearl, da. of Thomas Sandy and has issue living, Sandy James, *b.* 1939,—Kathryn, *b.* 1943: *m.* 1967, James Lachlan Carson.——Leslie Roland (92, Wellington St. West, Barrie, Ont., Canada), *b.* 1917; ed. at Wayne State Univ., Detroit (BSc); Fl. Lt. (ret.) RCAF; 1939-45 War (despatches, King's Commendation): *m.* 1942, Anna Kathleen, da. of William A. Logan, and has issue living, Logan, *b.* 1943 ——Marion Alice Grace, *b.* 1908: *m.* 1930, Joseph L. Kulp, who *d.* 1965, and has issue living, Joan Grace, *b.* 1932: *m.* 1952, Earl Roth, of 455, Wilshire Drive, Bloomfield Hills, Mich. 48013, USA, and has issue living, Lawrence Knyvett *b.* 1953, Earl Lee *b.* 1956, Leslie Ann *b.* 1958.

Grandsons of the late Horace Alling Wilson, son of the late John Coombe Wilson, 12th son of the Rev. George Wilson (ante):—
Issue of the late Arthur Alling Wilson, *b.* 1881, *d.* 1934: *m.* 1st, 1908, Lucie Nenon, who *d.* 1924, el. da. of R. A. Ruttan, of Port Arthur, Ontario; 2ndly, 1926, Caroline Argyll (who *m.* 2ndly, 1938, Julian Parks Hartley, of 351, East Main St., Grass Valley, Calif., USA), da. of John Roberts Allen, of Kentucky and New York City, USA:—

(By 1st m.) Arthur John (PO Box 43, Baldwin, Michigan 49304, USA), *b.* 1909: *m.* 1951, Ardis Irene, da. of Ira Price Jones, of Chicago, USA.——Robert Ruttan (Durford Knoll, Upper Durford Wood, Petersfield), *b.* 1913: *m.* 1946, the Hon. Yvette Latham Baillieu, only da. of 1st Baron Baillieu, and has issue living, Nenon Baillieu, *b.* 1948,—Elizabeth Ruttan, *b.* 1950,—Merilyn Yvette, *b.* 1953,—Deborah Baillieu, *b.* 1955.——(By 2nd m.) Clarke Knyvet (1460, El Rey St., Salt Lake City, Utah, 84108, USA) *b.* 1929: *m.* 1954, Sydney Ann Richardson, of Tacoma, Wash., USA, and has issue living, Robert Carroll, *b.* 1962,—Loree Ann, *b.* 1957,—Caroline Allen, *b.* 1959.

Granddaughters of the late Rev. Herbert Wilson (ante):—
Issue of the late Major Archdale Irby Wilson, *b.* 1859, *d.* 1915 : *m.* 1887, Marye, who *d.* 1951 (having *m.* 2ndly, 1925, Arthur Maynard Talbot, Bar.-at-law, who *d.* 1955), dau. of the late William Hill, of Southampton :—

Margaret Isabelle Knyvet, *b.* 1888. *Address,*—c/o Lloyds Bank, 79, Brompton Road, S.W.3.

Issue of the late Brereton Knyvet Wilson, *b.* 1868, *d.* 1939 : *m.* 1890, Gertrude Brenda, who *d.* 1950, dau. of James Christie, of Manor House, Framingham Pigot :—

Dorothy Beatrice Knyvet (Remenham Cottage, Remenham, Henley-on-Thames), *b.* 1893: *m.* 1917, Lt.-Col. Henry Marshall, Roy. Lincolnshire Regt., who *d.* 1952, and has issue living, Patricia Robena Knyvet, *b.* 1918: *m.* 1942, Maj. David Young, MC, RA (ret.), of Remenham Cottage, Remenham, Henley-on-Thames, and has issue living, Julian David Knyvet *b.* 1946, Anthony Charles Mayne *b.* 1948: Lt. RN, Simon John, *MC, b.* 1950, R. Green Jackets,—Leslie Philippa Knyvet (13, Church St., Boughton Monchelsea, Maidstone), *b.* 1926; Maj. (ret.) QARANC.——Audrey Brenda Knyvet, *b.* 1894: *m.* 1st, 1917, Maj.-Gen. Horatio Pettus Mackintosh Berney-Ficklin, CB, MC, late Highland LI, who *d.* 1961, having obtained a divorce, 1935; 2ndly, 1935, Maj. John Robert Cowan-Douglas, DSO, MC, who *d.* 1970. *Residence,*—Yetholm, Kelso, Roxburghshire.

Granddaughter of the late Rev. Herbert Wilson, yst. son of the late Rev. George Wilson (ante):—
Issue of the late Roland Henry Bourchier Wilson, *b.* 1861, *d.* 1945: *m.* 1891, Lucy, who *d.* 1903, da. of the late N. Edwards, MLC, New Zealand:—

Lucy Amyot (Fair Fields, Langton Green, Eye, Suffolk), *b.* 1897: *m.* 1932, Roland Mann, who *d.* 1959.

PREDECESSORS.—[1] *Sir* John Bourchier, *K.G.*, 4th son of *Sir* William Bourchier, Count of Eu, was summoned to the Parliament of England as John Bourchier *de Berners* 1455-72 : *m.* 14—, Margery, who *d.* 1475, dau. of Sir Richard Berners, and widow of John Ferreby ; *s.* by his grandson [2] JOHN, 2nd Baron (son of Sir Humphrey Bourchier), *b.* 14— ; summoned to Parliament 1495-1529 : *m.* 14—, Lady Katharine Howard, who *d.* 1536, dau. of 1st Duke of Norfolk ; *d.* 1533 ; *s.* by his only surviving dau. [3] JANE, *de jure* Baroness Berners, *b.* 15— ; did not assume the title : *m.* 15—, Edmund Knyvet, of Ashwellthorpe, who *d.* 1539 ; *d.* 1561 ; *s.* by her grandson [4] *Sir* THOMAS *de jure* 4th Baron (son of John Knyvett), *b.* 1539 ; obtained 1616 a certificate from the Commrs. for the Office of Earl Marshal of his right to the Barony, but *d.* before obtaining the King's confirmation : *m.* 15—, Muriel, who *d.* 1616, dau. of Sir Thomas Parry, Treasurer of the Household ; *d.* 1618 ; *s.* by his grandson [5] THOMAS, *de jure* 5th Baron (son of Sir Thomas Knyvett), *b.* 1596 : *m.* 1620, Katherine, who *d.* 1658, dau. of 3rd Baron Burgh ; *d.* 1658 ; *s.* by his el. son [6] *Sir* JOHN, *K.B.*, *de jure* 6th Baron ; *b.* 16— : *m.* 1655, Mary, who *d.* 1713, el. dau. of Sir Thomas Bedingfield ; *d.* 1673 ; *s.* by his el. son [7] THOMAS, *de jure* 7th Baron, *b.* 1656 ; M.P. for Dunwich 1685-7, and for Eye 1689-90 ; *d.* unm. 1693, when the barony fell into abeyance between his sisters, Elizabeth, wife of Thomas Glenham, and Katharine, wife of John Harris, and so continued until 1711, when on the death without issue of Capt. Thomas Glenham, only child of Elizabeth Glenham, the barony devolved on [8] KATHARINE, Baroness Berners ; *b.* 1658 ; her title was confirmed by resolution of House of Lords 1920 : *m.* 1st, 1685, John Harris, who *d.* 1686 ; 2ndly, 1696, Richard Bokenham, who *d.* 1721: *d.* 1743, when the Barony again fell into abeyance between the heirs of (i) Elizabeth Knyvett (wife of Henry Wilson, of Ashwellthorpe), and (ii) Lucy Knyvett (wife of Thomas Holt, and 2ndly, of John Field), granddaughters of John Knyvett, younger brother of *de jure* 6th Baron, and remained so until 1832, when the abeyance was terminated in favour of [9] ROBERT Wilson, 9th Baron, grandson of Elizabeth Knyvett (ante) ; *b.* 1761, *d.* unm. 1838 ; *s.* by his brother [10] *Rev.* HENRY, 10th Baron, *b.* 1762 ; summoned to Parliament by writ dated April 23rd, 1838 : *m.* 1788, Elizabeth, who *d.* 1845, dau. of Thomas Sumpter ; *d.* 1851 ; *s.* by his son [11] HENRY WILLIAM, 11th Baron, *b.* 1797 : *m.* 1st, 1823, Mary Letitia, dau. and co-heir of Col. George Orump, of Alexton Hall ; 2ndly, 1857, the Hon. Henrietta Charlotte Cholmondeley, who *d.* 1874, dau. of 1st Baron Delamere ; *d.s.p.* June 27th, 1871 ; *s.* by his niece [12] EMMA HARRIET, Baroness Berners, dau. of the late Rev. the Hon. Robert Wilson, R. of Ashwellthorpe, by Harriet, widow of John Sheppard, of Campsey Ash, and dau. and co-heir of Col. George Crump (ante), *b.* 1835 : *m.* 1853, Sir Henry Thomas Tyrwhitt, 3rd Bt., who *d.* 1894 ; *d.* 1917 ; *s.* by her el. son [13] *Sir* RAYMOND ROBERT TYRWHITT-WILSON, 13th Baron, *b.* 1885 ; assumed the additional surname of Wilson and the arms of Wilson only by Roy. licence 1892, and had *s.* as 4th Bt. in 1894 ; *d.* 1918 ; *s.* by his nephew [14] GERALD HUGH, 14th Baron (son of the late Capt. the Hon. Hugh Tyrwhitt, C.V.O., C.S.I., R.N., 3rd son of the late Emma Harriet Baroness Berners), *b.* 1883 ; assumed by Roy. licence 1919 the additional surname of Wilson and the arms of Wilson quarterly with those of Tyrwhitt ; *d.* 1950, when the Baronetcy became ext., and he was *s.* in the Barony by his kinswoman [15] VERA RUBY, Baroness Berners (dau. of the late Major the Hon. Rupert Tyrwhitt, 5th son of Emma Harriet, Baroness Berners), present peeress.

BERNSTEIN, BARON.   (Bernstein.)   [Life Baron 1969.]

SIDNEY LEWIS BERNSTEIN, son of Alexander Bernstein; *b.* Jan. 30th, 1899; Hon. LLD, Manchester; a Founder of Film Soc. 1924, and Saturday morning matinées for children 1927; Films Adviser, Min. of Information 1940-45; Liaison, British Embassy, Washington 1942, Ch. of Film Section, Allied Forces HQ N. Africa 1942-43, and of Film Section SHAEF 1943-45; Lecturer on Film and Internat. Affairs, New York Univ. 1946, and Yale 1947; Chm. of Granada Television, Ltd. 1965-71; Chm. of Granada Group Ltd., Granada Theatres, Ltd., Granada Publishing Ltd., and Granada TV Rental Ltd.; *cr. Baron Bernstein*, of Leigh, co. Kent (Life Baron) 1969: *m.* 1954, Sandra, da. of Charles Malone, of Toronto, and has issue.

Arms,—Quarterly sable and argent a spade between a decrescent and a sun all counterchanged. Crest,—A bear's head erased sable, collared company argent and sable, rimmed or. Supporters,— *Dexter,* A bear, and *sinister,* a fighting bull sable, each gorged of a torse argent and sable. Badge,—a roundel quarterly sable and argent fimbriated vert and charged with a spade.

Address,—36, Golden Sq., W1. *Club,*—Garrick.

BESSBOROUGH, EARL OF.   (Ponsonby.)   [Earl I. 1739, and U.K. 1937.]

[Name and Title Pronounced "Punsonby."]

For the king, the law, and the people.

FREDERICK EDWARD NEUFLIZE PONSONBY, 10th Earl; *b.* March 29th, 1913; *s.* 1956; ed. at Eton, and at Trin. Coll., Camb. (M.A.), Capt. 98th (Surrey and Sussex Yeo.) Field Brig. R.A. (T.A. Reserve); on Staff of High Commn. for Refugees 1936-39, 2nd Sec. British Embassy, Paris, 1944-48, and 1st Sec. 1948-49, with Robert Benson, Lonsdale & Co. Ltd., Merchant bankers 1950-56, and a Dir. ATV, Ltd. 1955-63, Chm. of (International) Atlantic Cttee. 1952-55, Pres. European-Atlantic Group 1954-62; Parl. Sec. for Science 1963-64, and Joint Parl. Under-Sec. of State for Education and Science 1964; Dep. Chm. of Metrication Board 1969-70; Min. of State, Min. of Tech., 1970; Member of European Parl., Strasbourg since 1975; Pres. of Chichester Festival Theatre Trust, of British Drama League and of Men of the Trees; an author of plays and other publications, a

Member of The Roy. Instn., a FRGS, an OStJ, and a Chevalier of Legion of Honour; 1939-45 War in France, W. Africa, and N. Africa, and as ADC to GOC, 1st Canadian Corps: *m.* 1948, Mary, da. of Charles A. Munn, of New York and Paris, and has issue.

Ᾱrms,—Gules, a chevron between three combs argent. Crest,—Out of a ducal coronet azure, three arrows, points downwards, one in pale and two in saltire, entwined at the intersection by a snake proper. Supporters.—Two lions reguardant proper

Seat,—Stansted Park, Rowlands Castle, Hants. *Residence,*—4, Westminster Gdns., SW1. *Clubs,*—Turf, Garrick, Carlton.

DAUGHTER LIVING.
Lady Charlotte Mary Roberte Paul, *b.* 1949: *m.* 1974, Yanni Petsopoulos.

SISTER LIVING.
Lady Moyra Blanche Madeleine, *OBE, b.* 1918; State Enrolled Nurse 1946; Chm., Hospitality Cttee., Victoria League 1956-62, and Vice-Chm., Central Council Victoria League 1961-65; Dep., Supt.-in-Ch., St. John Ambulance Bde. 1964-70, since when Supt.-in-Ch.; a DStJ; OBE (Civil) 1962: *m.* 1945, as his 2nd wife, Sir Denis John Wolko Browne, KCVO, FRCS, who *d.* 1967, and has issue living, Desmond John Michael, *b.* 1947: *m.* 1973, Jennifer M., da. of Frank Welmore, of Brierfield, Lancs.,—Rosemary Anne Roberte, *b.* 1950: *m.* 1974, Count Franco Aleramo Lanza. *Residence,* —16, Wilton St., SW1.

AUNT LIVING. (*Daughter of 8th Earl.*)
Lady Gweneth Frida, *b.* 1888; is a J.P. for Kent; has Order of League of Mercy: *m.* 1st, 1913, the Hon. Windham Baring, who *d.* 1922 [see E. Cromer]; 2ndly, 1926, Col. Ralph Henry Voltelin Cavendish, CBE, MVO, DL, who *d.* 1968 [D. Devonshire, colls.]. *Residence,*— Yaldham Manor, Kemsing, Kent.

WIDOWS LIVING OF SONS OF EIGHTH EARL.
Rita Narcissa, el. dau. of the late Lieut.-Col. Mountifort John Courtenay Longfield, of Castle Mary, Cloyne, co. Cork: *m.* 1st, 1911, Major the Hon. Cyril Myles Brabazon Ponsonby, M.V.O., who *d.* (killed in action) 1915; 2ndly, 1918, Neville Alfred Cyril Flower, who *d.* 1931 [Pauncefort-Duncombe, Bt.], and has issue living (by 1st marriage) [see colls., infra]. *Residence,*—Castle Mary, Cloyne, co. Cork.

Constance Evelyn (*Hon. Mrs. Bertie B. Ponsonby*), (44, Hallmores, St. Catharines Rd., Broxbourne, Herts.), da. of the late Rev. Horace Rollo Meyer, Hon. Canon of St. Albans [V. Bangor, colls.]: *m.* 1933, the Hon. Bertie Brabazon Ponsonby, who *d.* 1967.

WIDOW LIVING OF NINTH EARL.
ROBERTE (*Dowager Countess of Bessborough*), only da. of Baron de Neuflize, of Paris; a G.C.St.J.; a JP of Sussex 1943-56; Co. Pres. of St. John Ambulance Bde., Sussex 1940-60, and Pres. of Council of Soc. for Overseas Settlement of British Women 1937-64; a Member of CRO Migration Board 1953-65, and of Ch. of England Council for Commonwealth migration 1956-69; Chm. of Roy. Sch. of Needlework 1957-68; a Chevalier Legion of Honour: *m.* 1912, the 9th Earl, who *d.* 1956. *Residence,* —55, Onslow Sq., SW7 3LR.

COLLATERAL BRANCHES LIVING. (*Not in remainder to United Kingdom Earldom.*
Issue of the late Major the Hon. Cyril Myles Brabazon Ponsonby, M.V.O., Grenadier Guards, 2nd son of 8th Earl, *b.* 1881, *d.* (killed in action) 1915: *m.* 1911, Rita Narcissa [(ante): she *m.* 2ndly, 1918, Neville Alfred Cyril Flower, who *d.* 1931], el. dau. of the late Lieut.-Col. Mountifort John Courtenay Longfield, of 20, Pont Street, S.W., and Castle Mary, Cloyne, co. Cork :—
ARTHUR MOUNTIFORT LONGFIELD, *b.* Dec. 11th, 1912; ed. at Harrow, and at Trin. Coll., Camb. (B.A. 19—); European War 1939-45 as Capt. Welsh Guards: *m.* 1st, 1939, Patricia, who *d.* 1952, dau. of Col. Fitzhugh Lee Minnigerode, of Virginia, U.S.A.; 2ndly, 1956 (marriage dissolved 1963), Anne-Marie (GALITZINE), dau. of the late Lieut.-Gen. Sir Rudolf Carl Slatin, Pasha (Baron von Slatin), G.C.V.O., K.C.M.G., C.B.; 3rdly, 1963, Madeleine Lola Margaret, dau. of Maj.-Gen. Laurence Douglas Grand, C.B., C.I.E., C.B.E., and has issue living, (by 1st marriage) Myles Fitzhugh Longfield (58, Cumberland St., SW1), *b.* 1941: *m.* 1972, Alison, da. of William Storey, and has issue living, Frederick Arthur William, *b.* 1974,—Sarah, *b.* 1943,—(by 3rd m.) Matthew Douglas Longfield, *b.* 1965,—Charles Arthur Longfield, *b.* 1967. *Residence,*—Castle Mary, Cloyne, co. Cork.
Issue of the late Hon. Arthur Cornwallis Ponsonby, 4th son of 7th Earl, *b.* 1856, *d.* 1918: *m.* 1892, Kathleen Evelyn, who *d.* 1944, dau. of the late Henry Sillery :—
Judith Cornwallis (6, Culford Gdns., Chelsea, SW3), *b.* 1912.

Grandchildren of the late Robert Charles Ponsonby, 3rd son of the Rt. Hon. Sir Spencer Cecil Brabazon Ponsonby-Fane, GCB, ISO (infra):—
Issue of the late Sir George Arthur Ponsonby, KCVO, *b.* 1878, *d.* 1969: *m.* 1st, 1906, Julia Winifred Maitland (Sheila), who *d.* 1918, da. of the late Phineas A. R. Oldfield; 2ndly, 1921, Elisa (Flat 8, 34, Sloane Court West, SW3), (Lady-in-Waiting to the late Queen Maud of Norway), da. of the late Capt. Hendrick Andreas Broch, of Oslo:—
(By 1st m.) Robert Martin Dominic (2, Gordon House, Sunningdale, Berks.), *b.* 1911; Lt.-Cdr. (ret.); 1939-45 War (despatches): *m.* 1st, 1941 (m. diss. 1962), Dorothy Edith Jane (CUTHBERT), da. of the late John Henry Hervey Vincent Lane [B. Kensington]; 2ndly, 1962, Jane Frances, da. of the late Thomas Hood Henderson Walker, LLD, JP, of Tigh-na-Muira, Monifieth, Angus, and widow of (i) Capt. William Morris, and (ii) Maj. George Reginald Benson, and has issue living, (by 1st m.), Hermione, *b.* 1945.——Rosamond Mary, *b.* 1906: *m.* 1930, Oliver Peter Haig, T.D., of Beechwood, Strathtay, Perthshire, and has issue living, Anthony Oliver, *b.* 1932,—Iona Sheila, *b.* 1941.——(By 2nd m.), Maud Elisabeth, *b.* 1922: *m.* 1957, Lt.-Cdr. William Hutton-Attenborough, RN (32, Maidenhead Rd., Stratford-upon-Avon), and has issue living, George William, *b.* 1958,—John Frederick, *b.* 1960.——Victoria, *b.* 1926: *m.* 1947, Capt. Rupert Mahaffy, late Irish Guards, of 11, Cadogan St., SW3 [V. Dillon], and has issue living, Henrietta Clare Elisabeth, *b.* 1949,—Sarah Georgiana, *b.* 1952, —Kate Alexandra Mary, *b.* 1959,—Susanna Victoria, *b.* 1963.

Grandchildren of the late Rt. Hon. Sir Spencer Cecil Brabazon Ponsonby-Fane, GCB, ISO, 6th son 4th Earl:—
Issue of the late Sydney Alexander PONSONBY, *b.* 1863, *d.* 1940: *m.* 1893, the Hon. Audrey Catherine St. Aubyn, who *d.* 1936, dau. of 1st Baron St. Levan :—
Eleanor Elizabeth Anne, *b.* 1899. *Address,*—c/o Child & Co., 1, Fleet Street, EC4.
Issue of the late Hugh Spencer Ponsonby, *b.* 1865, *d.* 1934: *m.* 1894, Anitha Magdalene, who *d.* 1938, dau. of Hermann Lorenz Feuerheerd :—
David Brabazon, *b.* 1901.

Grandchildren of the late Gen. the Rt. Hon. Sir Henry Frederick Ponsonby, G.C.B., son of Maj.-Gen. the Hon. Sir Frederick Cavendish Ponsonby, G.C.M.G., K.C.B., K.C.H., 2nd son of 3rd Earl :—
Issue of the late Rt. Hon. Sir Frederick Edward Grey Ponsonby, G.C.B., G.C.V.O., who was cr. *Baron Sysonby* 1935 [see that title].
Issue of the late Arthur Augustus William Harry, who was cr. *Baron Ponsonby of Shulbrede* 1930 [see that title].

Descendants of the late Hon. William Francis Spencer Ponsonby (3rd son of 3rd Earl), who was cr. *Baron de Mauley* 1838 [see that title].

Grandchildren of the late Chambré Brabazon Ponsonby, son of the late Chambré
Brabazon Ponsonby-Barker, grandson of 1st Viscount :—
Issue of the late Thomas Brabazon Ponsonby, *b.* 1878. *d.* 1946 : *m.* 1909, Frances May
(now of 46, Nutley Park, Ballsbridge, Dublin), dau. of the late Major George
Paynter, of Eaton Grange, Grantham, and 21, Belgrave Sq, S.W. :—
Chambré Brabazon (Low Port, Linlithgow, W. Lothian), *b.* 1911; Lt.-Col. (ret.) 10th Hussars;
Comptroller to Gov.-Gen. of Australia 1936-37: *m.* 1st, 1941, Merelina, only da. of the late Lt.-Col.
James Tindal Ives Bosanquet; 2ndly, 1954, Diana Wray Hurt, of Reigate, Surrey, and has issue
living, (by 1st m.) Merelina Karin, *b.* 1946,—(by 2nd m), Richard Brabazon, *b.* 1955,—Miles
Chambré, *b.* 1957.——George Thomas, *MC*, *b.* 1913; Maj. (ret.) 17th/21st Lancers; 1939-45 War
in N. Africa and Italy (severely wounded, MC and Bar): *m.* 1948, Elizabeth Penelope Melville,
da. of Capt. Walter Douglas Melville Wills CBE and has issue living, Thomas Charles George
b. 1950,—Henry Brabazon, *b.* 1952,—Peter Douglas, *b.* 1955. *Residence,*—Kilcooley Abbey,
Thurles, co. Tipperary.——Henry Jeffrey, *b.* 1930: *m.* 1960, Rosemary Jane, da. of Ernest Sydney
Wells, of Buxted, Sussex, and has issue living, Julian Henry, *b.* 1963,—Jane Frances, *b.* 1965,
Rosanna, *b.* 1966. *Residence,*—Grove, Fethard, co. Tipperary.——Noreen de Vere, *b.* 1917: *m.*
1939, Brig. Henry Lawrence Savill Young, DSO, late Irish Gds. [see Young, Bt., cr. 1769, colls.].
Residence,—Hoddenscombe Lodge, Holford, Bridgwater, Somerset.
Issue of the late Brigadier Henry Chambre Ponsonby, D.S.O., M.C., late King's Roy. Rifle
Corps, *b.* 1883, *d.* 1953 : *m.* 1923, Beatrice Maud Cecil, who *d.* 1961, dau. of Sir William
Henry Levinge, 9th Bt. :—
Eileen Dorothy, *b.* 1925. *Residence,*—Ansty Water Farm, Ansty, Salisbury, Wilts.

PREDECESSORS.—[1] WILLIAM Ponsonby, *P.C.*, *M.P.* for co. Kilkenny, *temp.* Anne and
George I., was cr. *Baron Bessborough* 1721, and *Viscount Duncannon* 1722, (peerage of
Ireland) ; *d.* 1724 ; *s.* by his el. son [2] BRABAZON, 2nd Viscount; M.P. for co. Kildare 1704
and for Newtown 1713-15 ; cr. *Earl of Bessborough* 1739 (peerage of Ireland), and *Baron
Ponsonby of Sysonby* 1749 (peerage of Great Britain) ; *d.* 1758 ; *s.* by his el. son [3] WILLIAM,
P.C., 2nd Earl, successively M.P. for Kilkenny, Derby, Saltash and Harwich, a Lord of the
Treasury and Joint Postmaster-Gen.; *d.* 1793 ; *s.* by his son [4] FREDERICK, 3rd Earl, M.P. for
Knaresborough, and a Lord of the Admiralty ; *d.* 1844 ; *s.* by his son [5] JOHN WILLIAM, 4th
Earl, *b.* 1781, sometime Lord-Lieut. of Ireland and Ch. Commr. of Woods and Forests: *m.* 1805,
Lady Maria Fane, dau. of 10th Earl of Westmorland, K.G.; *s.* cr. *Baron Duncannon* (peerage of
Great Britain) 1834 ; *d.* 1847; *s.* by his el. son [6] JOHN GEORGE BRABAZON, 5th Earl ; was Lord
Lieut. of co. Carlow, Master of H.M.'s Staghounds, and Lord Steward of the Household ; *d.*
1880 ; *s.* by his brother [7] FREDERICK GEORGE BRABAZON, 6th Earl, *b.* 1815 ; *d.s.p.* 1895 ; *s.* by
his brother [8] *Rev.* WALTER WILLIAM BRABAZON, 7th Earl, *b.* 1821 ; R. of Stutton, Ipswich
1884-94 : *m.* 1850, Lady Louisa Susan Cornwallis Eliot, who *d.* 1911, dau. of 3rd Earl of St.
Germans, G.C.B. ; *d.* 1906 ; *s.* by his son [9] EDWARD, *K.P.*, *C.B.*, *C.V.O.*, 8th Earl, *b.* 1851 ;
Sec. to Speaker of House of Commons 1884-95: *m.* 1875, Blanche Vere, *C.B.E.*, who *d.* 1919,
youngest dau. of Sir Josiah John Guest, 1st Bt. ; *d.* 1920 ; *s.* by his el. son [10] VERE BRABAZON,
G.C.M.G., *P.C.*, 9th Earl; *b.* 1880 ; Gov.-Gen. and Com.-in-Ch., Dominion of Canada 1931-5 ;
sat as M.P. for Cheltenham (*C*) Jan.-Nov. 1910, for Dover 1913-18, and for Dover Div. of Kent
(*Co.U.*)1918-20 ; *cr. Earl of Bessborough* (peerage of United Kingdom) 1937 : *m.* 1912, Roberte, *J.P.*
(a D.G. St. J.), only dau. of Baron de Neuflize, of Paris ; *d.* 1956 ; *s.* by his el. son [11] FREDERICK
EDWARD NEUFLIZE, 10th Earl and present peer; also Earl of Bessborough (cr. U.K. 1937), Viscount
Duncannon, Baron Duncannon, Baron Bessborough, and Baron Ponsonby of Sysonby.

BESWICK, BARON. (Beswick.)   [Life Baron 1964.]]

FRANK BESWICK, *PC*, son of Jesse Beswick, of Hucknall, Notts.; *b.* 1912; a
JP of co. London; Govt. Observer, Bikini Atomic Tests 1946, PPS to
Parl. Under-Sec. of State for Air 1946-49, Parl. Sec. to Min. of Civil Aviation
1950-51, Dir. Air Schools Ltd., and Derby Aviation Ltd. 1953-57, Chm. of
Labour Party Civil Aviation Group 1951-59, and of Co-operative Party Parl.
Group 1955-59, and a Lord-in-Waiting to HM 1964-65; Under-Sec. of State
Commonwealth Office 1965-67, and Capt. of HM Body Guard of Hon. Corps of
Gentlemen-at-Arms and Ch. Govt. Whip, House of Lords 1967-70; Ch.
Opposition Whip, House of Lords 1970-74, since when Min. of State Depart. of
Industry, and Dep. Leader House of Lords; Special Advisor to Chm. of BAC
1970-74; Vice-Pres. of British Airline Pilots Assocn.; MP for Uxbridge
Div. of Middlesex (Lab.) 1945-59; 1939-45 War as Flight-Lt. RAF; *cr.*
Baron Beswick, of Hucknall, co. Nottingham (Life Baron) 1964, and PC 1968:
m. 1936, Dora, da. of Edward Plumb, of Kettering, and has issue.
Residence,—28, Skeena Hill, SW18.

SON LIVING.
Hon. Frank Jesse, *b.* 1949; ed. at Latymer Upper Sch.

DAUGHTER LIVING.
Hon. Patricia, *b.* 1939: *m.* 1961, Anthony Woodbridge Atkinson, of 13, The Drive, Bexley, Kent.

BETHELL, BARON. (Bethell.)   [Baron U.K. 1922, Bt. U.K. 1911.]

NICHOLAS WILLIAM BETHELL, 4th Baron,
and 4th Baronet; *b.* July 19th, 1938; *s.*
1967; ed. at Harrow, and Pembroke Coll.,
Camb.; a Lord-in-Waiting to HM 1970-71;
Member of European Parl., Strasbourg since
1975: *m.* 1964 (m. diss. 1971), Cecilia Mary
Lothian, el. da. of Prof. Alexander Mackie
Honeyman, of Cowan's Rigg, St. Andrews, and
has issue.

Arms,—Or, a chevron azure charged with an estoile
of the first, in chief two boars' heads couped of the second.
Crest,—Upon a rock proper a boar's head couped azure.
Supporters.—*Dexter,* a wolf proper charged on the shoulder
with an estoile or; *sinister,* a wolf proper charged with
a portcullis or.

I will keep faith.

Residence —73, Sussex Sq., W2.

SONS LIVING.
Hon. JAMES NICHOLAS, b. Oct. 1st, 1967.
Hon. William Alexander, b. 1969.

SISTER LIVING.
Sally Ann, b. 1943: m. 1965, Anthony Francis Wigram, of 7, Gloucester Sq., W2, and has issue living, Maximilian John Lionel, b. (March) 1966,—Camilla Ann, b. (Dec.) 1966,—Lucy Olga (twin), b. (Dec.) 1966.

DAUGHTERS LIVING OF SECOND BARON.
Hon. Jennifer Mary, b. 1930 : m. 1954, Edward Peter Moncrieff Brown, and has issue living, Alistair Peter, b. 1955,—Craig Edward, b. 1957,—James David, b. 1959,—David Francis, b. 1960. Residence,—Tullecombe, Rogate, Petersfield, Hants.
Hon. Patricia Catherine, b. 1933: m. 1956, Michael William Nesbitt, D.F.C., and has issue living, William Patrick, b. 1963,—Anna Catherine, b. 1957,—Caroline Mary, b. 1959. Residence,—Catteshall Rough, Munstead, nr. Godalming, Surrey.

AUNTS LIVING. (Daughters of 1st Baron.)
Hon. Dorothy Frances, b. 1897 : m. 1930, Lt.-Col. Ian Ferguson Macalpine, from whom she obtained a divorce 1957, and re-married 1966. Residence,—17, Grosvenor Sq., W1.
Hon. Grace, b. 1898: m. 1st, 1927 (m. diss. 1956), Frederick Joseph Parsons, who d. 1966; 2ndly, 1958 (m. diss. 1963), Henry Seton Middleditch, and has issue living, (by 1st marriage) Frank Joseph Timothy, b. 1928: m. 1957, Elizabeth (WRAGG), da. of Gerald Wilkes, of Constantina, S. Africa,—Sarah Penelope Ann, b. 1934: m. 1957, Philip Macgregor Rue. Residence,—

MOTHER LIVING.
Ann Margaret Frances, only da. of the late Lt.-Col. Robert George Barlow, of The Holt, Ledbury, Herefordshire: m. 1st, 1937 (m. diss. 1946), the late Hon. William Gladstone Bethell, who d. 1964, 3rd son of 1st Baron; 2ndly, 1946, John Rupert Dupree, who d. 1965; 3rdly, 1965, Roger Thornycroft, DSC, of Home Farm, Bembridge, I. of Wight.

PREDECESSORS.—[1] JOHN HENRY BETHELL, son of the late George Bethell, of South Woodford, Essex; b. 1861: a Director of Barclays Bank. Ltd.; sat as M.P. for S. or Romford Div. of Essex (L) 1906-18, and for N. Div. of East Ham 1918-22; cr. a Baronet (UK of Park House) 1911, and Baron Bethell, of Romford, co. Essex (peerage of UK) 1922: m. 1895, Florence, who d. 1957, da. of James Woolley Wyles; d. 1945, s. by his el. surviving son [2] JOHN RAYMOND, 2nd Baron; b. 1902: m. 1st, 1927 (m. diss. 1948), Veronica Eileen, da. of the late Hon. Sir James Daniel Connolly; 2ndly, 1948, Joan, who d. 1966,da. of the late Brig.-Gen. Norman William Webber, CMG, DSO, and widow of Lt.-Cdr. H. N. Reid, RN; d. 1965, s. by his only son [3] GUY ANTHONY JOHN, 3rd Baron; b. 1928; d. 1967; s. by his cousin [4] NICHOLAS WILLIAM (only son of the late Hon. William Gladstone Bethell, 3rd son of 1st Baron), 4th Baron, and present peer.

BICESTER, BARON. (Smith.) [Baron U.K. 1938.]

ANGUS EDWARD VIVIAN SMITH, 3rd Baron; b. Feb. 20th, 1932; s. 1968; ed. at Eton.

Arms,—Or, a chevron cottised sable, between three demi-griffins couped of the last, the two in chief respecting each other. Crest,—An elephant's head erased or, charged on the neck with three fleurs de lis, one and two azure. Supporters,—On either side a griffin sable charged on the shoulder with a horse-shoe inverted or.

BROTHER LIVING.
HUGH CHARLES VIVIAN, b. Nov. 8th, 1934; ed. at Eton, and Worcester Coll., Oxford; late 2nd Lt. RAC.

DAUGHTERS LIVING OF SECOND BARON.
Hon. Gillian Mary Randal, b. 1924 : m. 1946, John Ernest Harley Collins, M.B.H., DSO, and has issue living, John Randal Timothy, b. 1951: m. 1974, Catherine Anastazia, da. of Christopher Petherick, of 83, Addison Rd., W14. [see E. Radnor].—Sarah Elizabeth, b. 1948: m. 1968, Denzil R. O. How, and has issue living, Nicola Jane Audrey b. 1970. Residence,—Tusmore Park, Bicester, Oxon.

TENAX·IN·FIDE

Steadfast in the faith.

Hon. Jane Beatrix Randal, b. 1928 : m. 1949, John Richard Daniel Green, and has issue living, John James Randal, b. 1953,—Elizabeth Jane, b. 1950,—Amanda Carol, b. 1957. Residence,—38, Chelsea Park Gardens, S.W.3.

UNCLE LIVING. (Son of 1st Baron.)
Hon. Hugh Adeane Vivian, M.B.E., b. 1910; ed. at Eton, and at Ch. Ch., Oxford; European War 1939-45 as Major Irish Guards (despatches, M.B.E.); M.B.E. (Mil.) 1945 : m. 1933, Lady Helen Dorothy Primrose, dau. of 6th Earl of Rosebery, and has issue living, George Harry Vivian, b. 1934: m. 1st, 1962, June Rose Jager, da. of Basil William Foster-Towne, of S. Africa; 2ndly, 1967, Susan, da. of Frank Goodfellow, of Johannesburg, and has issue living, (by 1st m.) Charles James Vivian b. 1963,—Elizabeth Vivian, b. 1939: m. 1960, Alexander James Macdonald-Buchanan [see By. Woolavington]. Residence,—Souldern Manor, Bicester, Oxon.

AUNTS LIVING. (Daughters of 1st Baron.)
Hon. Mary Constance Vivian (Baroness Rennell), b. 1901 : m. 1928, the 2nd Baron Rennell. Residence, —The Rodd, near Presteigne, Herefordshire.
Hon. Joyce Sybil Vivian, b. 1905 : m. 1926, Maj.-Gen. Gerald Lloyd Verney, D.S.O., M.V.O., late Irish Guards, who d. 1957 [see Verney, Bt., cr. 1818, colls.]. Residence,—Lower Town Farm House, Clifton Hampden, near Abingdon, Berks.
Hon. Honor Mildred Vivian, OBE, b. 1908; ed. at London (BSc, BS, MD), and Oxford (MA) Univs.; MRCS England and LRCP London 1940; MRCP 1954, FRCP 1965; OBE (Civil) 1962. Residence, —Croft Lodge, Yarpole, Leominster, Herefords.

WIDOW LIVING OF SON OF FIRST BARON.
Mabel, Mus. Bac., dau. of the late A. W. R. Lovering: m. 1948, as his second wife the Hon. Stephen Edward Vivian Smith, who d. 1952. Residence,—Long Shaw, East Chiltington, nr. Lewes, Sussex.

MOTHER LIVING.
Elenor Anderson (Resides in USA), da. of Edward Shepherd Hewitt, of New York City: m. 1929 (m. diss. 1947), the late Lt.-Col. Hon. Stephen Edward Vivian Smith, late Coldstream Guards, who d. 1952, 2nd son of 1st Baron.

PREDECESSORS.—[1] VIVIAN HUGH Smith, son of the late Hugh Colin Smith; b. 1867; Chm. of
Morgan Grenfell, Ltd., and an Hon. Freeman of Oxfordshire; was Lord-Lieut. of Oxfordshire
1934-54; cr. *Baron Bicester*, of Tusmore, co. Oxford (peerage of United Kingdom) 1938: *m.* 1897,
Lady Sybil Mary McDonnell, who *d.* 1959, dau. of 6th Earl of Antrim; *d.* 1956; *s.* by his el. son [2]
RANDAL HUGH VIVIAN, 2nd Baron; *b.* 1898; High Sheriff of Oxon. 1945: *m.* 1922, the Hon.
Dorothea Gwenllian James, who *d.* 1974, da. of 3rd Baron Northbourne; *d.* 1968; *s.* by his nephew
[3] ANGUS EDWARD VIVIAN (2nd son of the late Lt.-Col. Hon. Stephen Edward Vivian Smith, 2nd
son of 1st Baron), 3rd Baron, and present peer.

BIDDULPH, BARON. (Biddulph.) [Baron U.K. 1903.]

Let us aim at loftier things.

ROBERT MICHAEL CHRISTIAN BIDDULPH,
4th Baron; *b.* Jan. 6th, 1931; *s.* 1972; ed.
at Canford; late Lt. 16/5th Queen's R.
Lancers: *m.* 1958, Lady Mary Helena
Maitland, da. of the late Ivor Colin James,
Viscount Maitland, son of 15th Earl of
Lauderdale, and has issue.

Arms,—Vert, an eagle displayed argent, armed and
langued gules, a canton of the second. Crest,—A wolf
salient argent, charged on the shoulder with a trefoil
slipped gules. Supporters,—On either side a wolf
argent, semée of trefoils slipped gules.

Residence,—Makerstoun, Kelso, Roxburghshire. *Club*,
—Cavalry.

SONS LIVING.

Hon. ANTHONY NICHOLAS COLIN. *b.* April 8th, 1959.
Hon. William Ian Robert, *b.* 1963.

DAUGHTER LIVING.

Hon. Fiona Mary, *b.* 1961.

BROTHER LIVING.

Hon. Edward Sidney, *b.* 1934; ed. at Eton; Lt. (ret.) R. Horse Guards. *Residence*,—Under Down,
Ledbury, Herefords. *Club*,—White's.

SISTERS LIVING.

Hon. Marjorie Amy, *b.* 1927: *m.* 1947, Thomas Ian Michael Walker-Munro, who *d.* 1965 [see Munro,
Bt., cr. 1825, colls.]. *Residence*,—Hurdcott House, Barford St. Martin, by Salisbury, Wilts.
Hon. Susan Louise, *b.* 1929.

AUNTS LIVING. (*Daughters of 2nd Baron*)

Hon. Adelaide Mary, *b.* 1901: *m.* 1929, Henry Vincent Yorke, who *d.* 1974 [see E. Hardwicke, colls.]
Residence,—30, Wilton Place, SW1.
Hon. Mary Constance, *b.* 1906: *m.* 1929, Montagu William Lowry-Corry, Lieut. Grenadier Guards
Reserve, from whom she obtained a divorce 1938 [see E. Belmore, colls.]. *Residence*,—39, Bury
Walk, S.W.3.

WIDOW LIVING OF THIRD BARON.

Lady AMY LOUISE AGAR (*Amy Baroness Biddulph*), (Under Down, Ledbury, Herefordshire), da. of
4th Earl of Normanton: *m.* 1925, The 3rd Baron, who *d.* 1972.

COLLATERAL BRANCH LIVING.

Issue of the late Hon. Claud William Biddulph, *b.* 1871, *d.* 1954: *m.* 1906, Margaret, who *d.*
1970, da. of the late Alfred John Howard [E. Carlisle, colls.]:—
Anthony, *T.D.*, *b.* 1910; ed. at Eton; is Major Roy. Gloucestershire Hussars (T.A.): *m.* 1938, Mary
Dearman, da. of Maj. Sir John Dearman Birchall, MP, and has issue living, Simon (The Laines,
Rodmarton, Cirencester), *b.* 1942; ed. at Eton: *m.* 1970, Christina, da. of George McCorquodale
[see B. Luke], and has issue living, John Simon *b.* 1971, Anthony George, *b.* 1973,—Anthony Jasper,
b. 1946; ed. at Eton,—Clarissa Mary, *b.* 1939: *m.* 1962, James Richard Ferard, Tredean, Devawden
Green, Chepstow, Gwent, and has issue living, Richard Anthony *b.* 1963, Charles Edward *b.* 1970,
Susan Mary *b.* 1965. *Residence*,—Rodmarton Manor, Cirencester.——Marjory Mary (*Lady Findlay*),
b. 1915: *m.* 1st, 1938 (m. diss. 1962), as his 2nd wife, Maj. Philip Wilfred Cripps, son of Maj. Sir
Frederick William Beresford Cripps, DSO; 2ndly, 1964, as his 2nd wife, Lt.-Col. Sir Roland Lewis
Findlay, 3rd Bt., and has issue living, (by 1st m.) John Philip, *b.* 1940; ed. at Eton,—Diana Josephine,
b. 1953.

PREDECESSORS—[1] MICHAEL Biddulph, son of the late Robert Biddulph, M.P., of
Ledbury; *b.* 1834; a partner in London banking firm of Cocks, Biddulph and Co.; M.P. for
Herefordshire (L) July 1865 to Nov. 1885, and S, or Ross, Div. of Herefordshire (LU) 1885-1900;
cr. *Baron Biddulph*, of Ledbury, co. Hereford (peerage of United Kingdom) 1903: *m.* 1st, 1864,
Adelaide Georgiana, who *d.* 1872, dau. of the late Gen. the Rt. Hon. Jonathan Peel, M.P.;
2ndly, 1877, Lady Elizabeth Philippa, *V.A.*, who *d.* 1916, widow of Henry John Adeane, M.P.,
and dau. of 4th Earl of Hardwicke; *d.* 1923; *s.* by his el. son [2] JOHN MICHAEL GORDON,
2nd Baron, *b.* 1869: *m.* 1896, Marjorie Caroline Susan, who *d.* 1961, dau. of the late Col. William
Mure; *d.* 1949; *s.* by his el. son [3] MICHAEL WILLIAM JOHN, 3rd Baron, *b.* 1898: *m.* 1925, Lady
Amy Louise Agar, da. of 4th Earl of Normanton; *d.* 1972; *s.* by his el. son [4] ROBERT MICHAEL
CHRISTIAN, 4th Baron and present peer.

BILSLAND, BARON. (Bilsland.) [Extinct 1970.]

WIDOW LIVING OF 1ST BARON.

AMY (*Baroness Bilsland*), da. of the late David Colville, of Jerviston House, Motherwell: *m.* 1922, the
2nd Baron, who *d.* 1970.

Bingham, Baron, title of Earl of Lucan on Roll of H. L.

Bingham, Lord, son of Earl of Lucan.

BINGLEY, BARONY OF. (Lane Fox.) [Extinct 1947.]

DAUGHTERS LIVING OF FIRST BARON.

Hon. Marcia Agnes Mary, *b.* 1904: *m.* 1929, Lieut.-Col. Francis Gordon Ward Jackson, Roy. Horse Guards, who assumed by deed poll 1937 names of Francis Lane Fox in lieu of his patronymic, and has issue living, George Francis (Bramham Park, Wetherby, Yorks.), *b.* 1931, Major Roy. Horse Guards: *m.* 1962, Victoria, only da. of the late Major C. E. R. Duff, 8th King's R. Irish Hussars, and has issue living, George Charles Nicholas *b.* 1963, James Richard *b.* 1966,—Richard Sackville (of 17, Princedale Rd., W11), *b.* 1933: *m.* 1960, the Hon. Janet Hamilton, da. of 3rd Baron Hamilton of Dalzell, and has issue living, Andrew Ward Jackson *b.* 1969, Harriot *b.* 1966,—Marcia Elizabeth, *b.* 1940: *m.* 1963, Antony Charles Wakeham, of Wothersome Grange, Bramham, Wetherby, Yorks., and has issue living, William Francis Charles *b.* 1966, Richard Thomas Hugh *b.* 1968, Charlotte Elizabeth *b.* 1971. *Residence,*—The Little House, Bramham Park, Wetherby, Yorks.

Hon. Mary Kathleen (*Viscountess Bridgeman*), *b.* 1905; is a J.P.: *m.* 1930, the 2nd Viscount Bridgeman. *Residence,*—Leigh Manor, Minsterley, Shropshire.

Hon. Dorothy Mary, *O.B.E.* (*Hon. Lady Parkinson*), *b.* 1909; O.B.E. (Civil) 1953: *m.* 1937, Sir Kenneth Wade Parkinson, and has issue living, Jane, *b.* 1939: *m.* 1970, Simon Egerton Scrope, of 6, Blomfield Rd., W9 IAH [see D. Sutherland]. *Residence,*—Aketon Close, Follifoot, Harrogate.

Hon. Margaret, *b.* 1913; a Lady in Waiting to HRH the late Princess Royal 1964-65: *m.* 1st, 1939, Maj. Charles William Christopher Packe, Roy. Fusiliers, who *d.* (killed in action in Normandy) 1944; 2ndly, 1951 James Edward Hunter, who *d.* 1957; 3rdly, 1969, Brig. Kenneth Hargreaves, CBE, TD, of Castle Garth, Wetherby, Yorks., and has issue living, (by 1st m.) Rosemary Margaret *b.* 1941: *m.* 1967, John Alexander Richard Grove, of 63, Broxash Rd., SW11,—Jane Elizabeth Mary, *b.* 1944: *m.* 1966, Ian Reginald Edward Gow, of The Dog House, Hankham, Pevensey, Sussex.

Binning, Lord, son of Earl of Haddington.

BIRDWOOD, BARON. (Birdwood.) [Baron U.K. 1938, Bt. U.K. 1919.]

MARK WILLIAM OGILVIE BIRDWOOD, 3rd Baron and 3rd Baronet; *b.* Nov. 23rd, 1938; *s.* 1962; ed. at Radley, and at Trin. Coll., Camb. (BA 1962); late 2nd Lt. RHG: *m.* 1963, Judith Helen, el. da. of Reginald Gordon Seymour Roberts, of Newton Aycliffe, co. Durham, and has issue.

Arms,—Azure, five martlets, two, two and one within an inescutcheon voided a representation of the Southern Cross, all argent. Crest,—Out of a mural crown gules, a martlet argent between two branches of laurel proper. Supporters,—*Dexter*, a Sergeant of the XIIth (Prince of Wales's Royal) Lancers, mounted on a bay horse; *sinister*, a Sikh Daffadar of the XIth (Prince of Wales's Own) Bengal Lancers mounted on a chestnut horse both habited and accoutred proper.

Residence,—7, Bloomfield Terr., S.W.1.

Calm in action.

DAUGHTER LIVING.

Hon. Sophie Frederika, *b.* 1964.

SISTER LIVING.

Hon. Sonia Gina Ogilvie, *b.* 1933: *m.* 1956, Geoffrey Thynne Valentine Archer, and has issue living, David Birdwood, *b.* 1959,—Sarah-Jane Birdwood, *b.* 1957. *Residence,*—41, Stubbs Rd., Hong Kong.

AUNTS LIVING. (*Daughters of 1st Baron.*)

Hon. Constance Jean Gonville, *b.* 1895: *m.* 1919, Frank Colin Craig, sometime R.A.F., and has issue living, Robert Colin Birdwood (Boranaig, Thirlmere, NSW), *b.* 1920; ed. at Guildford Sch., Perth, W. Australia; is Maj. Australian Army; formerly Capt. Probyn's Horse, Indian Army: *m.* 1952, Judith Mary McCovey, and has issue living, Amanda Anderson Birdwood *b.* 1954, Fiona Jane Birdwood *b.* 1957, Victoria Mary Birdwood *b.* 1959,—Judith Mary Birdwood, *b.* 1923,—Janette Elfred, *b.* 1928: *m.* 1965, Jeremy Carlos-Clarke. *Residence,*—Mount St., Perth, W. Australia.

Hon. Judith Horatia Maud, *b.* 1910: *m.* 1st, 1939 (m. diss. 1947), Roger William Colville Wallis, who *d.* 1959; 2ndly, 1947, Budolph Putnam Messel, who *d.* 1958. *Residence,*—1, Broad Lane, Halingfield, Cambridge.

MOTHER LIVING.

(Elizabeth) Vere Drummond, *CVO*, da. of Lt.-Col. Sir George Drummond Ogilvie, KCIE, CSI, Indian Political Ser.; MVO (5th class) 1958, CVO 1972: *m.* 1931 (m. diss. 1954), the 2nd Baron, who *d.* 1962. *Residence,*—12, Royal Avenue, Chelsea, SW3.

WIDOW LIVING OF SECOND BARON.

JOAN POLLOCK (*Dowager Baroness Birdwood*), (100, Philbeach Gdns., SW5), da. of Christopher Norman Graham: *m.* 1954, as his second wife, the 2nd Baron, who *d.* 1962.

PREDECESSORS.—[1] *F.-M. Sir* WILLIAM RIDDELL Birdwood, *G.C.B., G.C.S.I., G.C.M.G., G.C.V.O., C.I.E., D.S.O., D.C.L., LL.D.,* el. surviving son of the late Herbert Mills Birdwood, C.S.I., LL.D., J.P., I.C.S.; *b.* 1865; Field-Marshal; Hazara Expedition 1891 (medal with clasp), Isaza Expedition 1892, Tirah Expedition 1897-8 (despatches, medal with three clasps), S. Africa 1899-1902, as Staff Officer, Brig. Maj. Mounted Brig. (Natal) and D.A.A.G., and Mil. Sec. to Com.-in-Ch. (Gen. Lord Kitchener) (severely wounded, despatches five times, Queen's medal with six clasps. King's medal with two clasps, Brevets Major and Lieut.-Col.), Mohmand Expedition 1908, as Ch. of Staff, present at action of Kargha (despatches, medal with clasp, D.S.O.), European War 1914-18 with Mediterranean Expeditionary Force, first Comdg. Australian and New Zealand Army Corps, then Com.-in-Ch. Mediterranean Expeditionary Force, and Comdg. Dardanelles Army during Evacuation, and subsequently Comdg. Australian and New Zealand troops and 5th Army in France (wounded, despatches many times, K.C.M.G., Lieut.-Gen., K.C.B., Grand Cordon of Legion of

Honour, French Croix de Guerre with Palm, Belgian Order de la Couronne and Croix de Guerre, D.S.M. of U.S.A.. Order of the Nile, Order of Aviz and of Christ and Grand Cordon of Tower and Sword of Portugal, 1st class of Orders of Rising Sun of Japan and Timsa of Persia, Order of Star of Nepal, G.C.M.G., thanked by Parliament, cr. Baronet, granted £10,000); was Q.M.G., India May to Nov. 1912, Sec. to Govt. of India, Army Depart., and a Member of Legislative Council of Gov.-Gen. of India 1912-14, Gen. Officer Comdg. Australian Imperial Forces 1915-20, A.D.C. to King Edward VII. 1906-10 and to King George V. 1910-11, an A.D.C. Gen. to H.M. 1917-22, and Gen. Officer Comdg.-in-Ch., N. Army, India 1920-24; acted as Com.-in-Ch. in India 1924, Com.-in-Ch. in India 1925-30, and Master of Peterhouse, Camb. 1931-8; cr. a *Baronet* (UK, of Anzac and Totnes) 1919, and *Baron Birdwood*, of Anzac, and of Totnes, co. Devon (peerage of UK) 1938: *m*. 1894, Janetta Hope Gonville, *CI*, who *d*. 1947, el. da. of Col. Sir Benjamin Parnell Bromhead, 4th Bt., CB; *d*. 1951; *s*. by his son [2] CHRISTOPHER BROMHEAD, *MVO*, 2nd Baron; *b*. 1899; Lt.-Col. Probyn's Horse, Indian Army, a Commentator, Lecturer, and Author on International Affairs : *m*. 1st, 1931 (marriage dissolved 1954) (Elizabeth) Vere Drummond, C.V.O., dau. of Lieut.-Col. Sir George Drummond Ogilvie, K.C.I.E., C.S.I. ; 2ndly, 1954, Joan Pollock, dau. of Christopher Norman Graham ; *d*. 1962 ; *s*. by his son [3] MARK WILLIAM OGILVIE, 3rd Baron and present peer.

BIRK, BARONESS. (Birk.) [Life Baroness 1967.]

ALMA LILLIAN BIRK, da. of the late Barnett Wilson, of London; ed. at South Hampstead High Sch., and London Sch. of Economics (BSc Econ Hons); a JP since 1952; a Member of Fabian Soc. since 1946, and of Finchley Borough Council 1950-53, Sec. of Fabian Soc. Research Cttee. on Marriage and Divorce 1951-52, and a Member of Hendon Group Hosp. Manage- ment Cttee. 1951-59; Chm. of Health Education Council 1969-72; a Member of Howard League for Penal Reform since 1948; Asso. Editor of *Nova* 1965-69; a Member of Youth Ser. Development Council 1967-71, Vice-Pres. of H. G. Wells Soc. since 1967, and Stamford Hill Asso. Clubs 1967-70, Vice-Pres. of Council for Children's Welfare, and a Member of Panel of Pregnancy Advisory Ser. since 1968, and of Redbridge Jewish Youth Centre since 1970; Vice-Pres. of Divorce Law Reform Union since 1969; a Member of Advisory Council of Birth Control Campaign; a Member of Hon. Cttee. of Albany Trust; a Gov. of London Sch. of Econ. since 1971; a Baroness-in-Waiting to HM March to Oct. 1974, since when Under-Sec. of State, Dept. of the Environment; *cr. Baroness Birk*, of Regent's Park, in Greater London (Life Baroness) 1967: *m*. 1939, Ellis Samuel Birk, and has issue.

Residence,—13, Hanover Terr., Regent's Park, NW1 4RJ.

SON LIVING.
Hon. David Barry Wilson (5, Fairfax Place, NW6), *b*. 1943; ed. at Clifton Coll., Jesus Coll., Camb., and Hull and London Univs.: *m*. 1969, Kate, da. of Joseph Green, of London, NW8.

DAUGHTER LIVING.
Hon. Angela Felicity, *b*. 1947; ed. at Camden Sch. for Girls and London Univ.: *m*. 1970, Richard Camber, of 3, Hopping La., Canonbury, N1.

BIRKENHEAD, EARL OF. (Smith.) [Earl U.K. 1922, Bt. U.K. 1918.]

FREDERICK WILLIAM ROBIN SMITH, 3rd Earl, and 3rd Baronet; *b*. April 17th, 1936; *s*. 1975; ed. at Eton and Ch. Ch., Oxford.

Arms,—Ermine, on a pale gules between four crosses-crosslet of the second a like cross or. Crest,—A cubit arm couped fessewise vested gules, cuffed argent, the hand proper grasping a sword erect of the second, pommelled and hilted or. Supporters,—*Dexter*, a gryphon or, wings per fesse or and sable; *sinister*, a lion azure, charged on the shoulder with a crozier or.

Residences,—Charlton, Banbury; 48, Arthur Rd., SW19. *Clubs,*—Buck's, White's, St. James'.

Smith of my own fortune.

SISTER LIVING.
Lady Juliet Margaret, *b*. 1941; a Lady-in-Waiting to HRH The Princess Margaret, Countess of Snowdon 1965-71, since when an Extra Lady-in-Waiting: *m*. 1970, John Richard Townsend, of 12, Chelsea Park Gdns., SW3, and has issue living, Eleanor Mary, *b*. 1971,—Alice Jane, *b*. 1974.

AUNT LIVING. *(Daughter of 1st Earl.)*
Lady Pamela Margaret Elizabeth (*Baroness Hartwell*), *b*. 1914: *m*. 1936, Baron Hartwell (Life Peer). *Residences,*—Oving House, Whit- church, nr. Aylesbury; 18, Cowley St., SW1.

WIDOW LIVING OF SECOND EARL.
Hon. Sheila Berry (*Countess of Birkenhead*) (Charlton, Banbury; 24, Wilton St., SW1), da. of 1st Viscount Camrose: *m*. 1935, the 2nd Earl, who *d*. 1975.

PREDECESSORS.—[1] *Rt. Hon. Sir* FREDERICK EDWIN SMITH, *GCSI, PC, KC,* son of the late Frederick Smith(Bar.-at-Law of Middle Temple) ; *b.* 1872; Solicitor-Gen. May to Nov. 1915, Attorney-Gen. (with a seat in the Cabinet) Nov. 1915 to Dec. 1916, again Attorney-Gen. (in National Min.) Dec. 1916 to Jan. 1919, Lord High Chancellor (with a seat in the Cabinet) Jan. 1919 to Oct. 1922, and Sec. of State for India Nov. 1924 to Oct. 1928 ; M.P. for Walton Div. of Liverpool (*C*) Jan. 1906 to Nov. 1918, and for W. Derby Div. thereof Dec. 1918 to Jan. 1919 ; cr. a *Baronet* (UK, of Charlton) 1918, *Baron Birkenhead,* of Birkenhead, co. Chester (peerage of UK) 1919, *Viscount Birkenhead,* of Birkenhead, co. Chester (peerage of UK) 1921, and *Viscount Furneaux,* of Charlton, co. Northampton, and *Earl of Birkenhead* (peerage of UK) 1922: *m.* 1901, Margaret Eleanor, who *d.* 1968, 2nd da. of the late Rev. H. Furneaux, Fellow of Corpus Christi Coll., Oxford; *d.* 1930; *s.* by his only son [2] FREDERICK WINSTON FURNEAUX, TD, 2nd Earl, *b.* 1907; PPS to Sec. of State for Foreign Affairs (Viscount Halifax) 1938-39, a Lord-in-Waiting to HM King George VI 1938-40 and 1951-52, and to the Queen 1952-55; Maj. 53rd (Oxfordshire Yeo.) Anti-Tank Regt. RA (TA) (attached British Mil. Mission to Yugoslav Partisans 1944-45); High Steward of HM Manor of the Savoy 1942-75; historian and biographer: *m.* 1935, the Hon. Sheila Berry, da. of 1st Viscount Camrose; *d.* 1975; *s.* by his only son [3] FREDERICK WILLIAM ROBIN, 3rd Earl, and present peer; also Viscount Birkenhead, Viscount Furneaux, and Baron Birkenhead.

BIRKETT, BARON. (Birkett.) [Baron U.K. 1958.]

The Law is my light

MICHAEL BIRKETT, 2nd Baron ; *b.* Oct. 22nd, 1929 ; *s.* 1962 ; ed. at Stowe, and at Trin. Coll., Camb.; Film Producer: *m.* 1960, Mrs. Junia Crawford, who *d.* 1973, da. of Harold Elliott.

Arms,—Gules three full bottomed wigs argent. Crest,—Between two wings gules a Viking ship proper charged on the sail with a raven close sable. Supporters,—*Dexter,* a lion or semee of roses gules ; *sinister,* a wolf sable semee of mullets gold.
Address,—c/o House of Lords, SW1.

SISTER LIVING.

Hon. Linnea, *b.* 1923 : *m.* 1949, Gavin Cliff Hodges, and has issue living, Marcus Birkett Adam, *b.* 1959,—Victoria Françoise, *b.* 1951,—Gabrielle, *b.* 1953,—Charmian Sophie, *b.* 1957. *Residence,*—Leasowe House, Sibford Gower, Banbury, Oxon.

PREDECESSOR.—[1] WILLIAM NORMAN Birkett, *P.C.,* son of the late Thomas Birkett, of Ulverston, Lancashire ; *b.* 1883 ; sat as M.P. for E. Div. of Nottingham (*L*) 1923-24, and 1929-31 ; Judge of High Court of Justice (King's Bench Div.) 1941-50, and a Lord Justice of Appeal 1950-57 ; cr. *Baron Birkett,* of Ulverston, co. Palatine of Lancaster (peerage of U.K.) 1958 : *m.* 1920, Ruth, who *d.* 1969, dau. of Emil Nilsson ; *d.* 1962 ; *s.* by his son [2] MICHAEL, 2nd Baron and present peer.

BIRMINGHAM, LORD BISHOP OF. (Brown.)

Rt. Rev. LAURENCE AMBROSE BROWN, son of Frederick John Brown; *b.* Nov. 1st, 1907; ed. at Luton Gram. Sch., and Queen's Coll., Camb. (MA), and Cuddesdon Theological Coll., Oxford; Curate, St. John the Divine, Kennington 1932-35, Curate in charge, St. Peter, Luton, Beds. 1935-40, V. of Hatfield Hyde, Welwyn Garden City 1940-46, Sec. of Southwark Diocesan Reorganisation Cttee. 1946-60, Sec. S. London Church Fund and Southwark Diocesan Board of Finance 1952-60; Canon Residentiary, Southwark 1950-60, Archdeacon of Lewisham 1955-60, Vice-Provost of Southwark Cathedral 1956-60; Suffragan Bishop of Warrington 1960-69; appointed 5th Lord Bishop of Birmingham 1969; Chm. of Advisory Council for Church Ministry 1966-71: *m.* 1935, Florence Blanche, da. of W. G. Marshall, of Luton, Beds.

Patron of sixty-one livings, and part Patron of others, and Patron of the Archdeaconries of Birmingham and Aston, and of twenty-four Hon. Canonries.

This See was founded by Act of Parliament 1904.

Episcopal Signature,—" Laurence Birmingham."

ARMS OF THE SEE,—Per pale indented or and gules, five roundels, two, two, and one, and in chief two crosses patée all counterchanged.

Residence,—Bishop's Croft, Harborne, Birmingham, B17 0BG.

BLACK, BARON. (Black.) [Life Baron 1968].

WILLIAM RUSHTON BLACK, son of James William Black, of Barrow in Furness; *b.* Jan. 12th, 1893; ed. at Barrow Secondary Sch., and Barrow Tech. Sch.; a JP of Middlesex 1950-58; Chm. of National Research Development Corpn. 1957-69, and of Leyland Motor Corpn., Ltd. 1963-67; Chm. of Park Royal Vehicles, Ltd. since 1960, Managing Dir. of Asso. Commercial Vehicles since 1954, and a Dir. of British Rail Hovercraft, and RAC Travel Sers. Ltd.; *cr.* Knt. 1958, and *Baron Black,* of Barrow in Furness, co. Palatine of Lancaster (Life Baron) 1968: *m.* 1916, Margaret Patricia, da. of James Dallas, of Dundee, and has issue.

Arms,—Gules two wheels in fess a four-bladed propellor in base and on a chief or a rose gules barbed and seeded between two bees volant proper. **Crest,**—On a chapean gules turned up ermine a sedan chair or. **Supporters,**—*Dexter,* A basset hound; *Sinister,* a rhesus monkey, both proper. *Residence,*—Birchwood Grange, Ruxley Cres., Claygate, Surrey.

DAUGHTER LIVING.
Hon. Patricia Margaret, *b.* 1919: *m.* 1942, Leslie John Smyth, of Rushtons, Longdown, Guildford, and has issue.

BLACKBURN, LORD BISHOP OF. (Martineau.)

Rt. Rev. ROBERT ARNOLD SCHURHOFF MARTINEAU, son of the late Prof. C. E. Martineau, MA, M.Com, FCA; *b.* Aug. 22nd, 1913; ed. at King Edward's Sch., Birmingham, Trin. Hall, Camb. (MA), and Westcott House, Camb.; Curate of Melksham 1938-41; Chap. RAFVR 1941-46; V. of Ovenden, Halifax 1946-52, and Allerton, Liverpool 1952-66; Hon. Canon of Liverpool 1961; Rural Dean of Childwall 1964; Proctor in Convocation 1964; consecrated Bishop of Huntingdon (Suffragan for Diocese of Ely) 1966, and translated 5th Bishop of Blackburn 1972: *m.* 1941, Elinor Gertrude, da. of the late Rev. Keinion Ap-Thomas.

Patron of sixty-five livings, the Archdeaconries of Lancaster and Blackburn, and eighteen Hon. Canonries.

This See was founded by Act of Parliament Nov. 1926.

Episcopal Signature,—" Robert Blackburn."

ARMS OF THE SEE,—Per fesse gules and or, two keys in saltire wards downwards argent in chief and a **rose** also gules barbed and seeded proper in base. *Residence,*—Bishop's House, Clayton-le-Dale, Blackburn.

BLACKETT, BARONY. (Blackett.) [Extinct 1974.]

SON LIVING OF LIFE BARON.
Hon. Nicolas Maynard (32, Woodstock Rd., Carshalton, Surrey), *b.* 1928; ed. at Bristol Univ. (BSc, PhD): *m.* 1951, Patricia, da. of Henry William Tankins.

DAUGHTER LIVING OF LIFE BARON.
Hon. Giovanna, *b.* 1926: *m.* 1950, Kenneth Bloor, of 9, Queens Rd., West Didsbury, Manchester 20.

WIDOW LIVING OF LIFE BARON.
COSTANZA (*Baroness Blackett*), (806, Nelson House, Dolphin Sq., SW1), da. of the late Eugenio Bayon: *m.* 1924, the 1st Baron, who *d.* 1974, when the title became ext.

BLACKFORD, BARON. (Mason.) [Baron U.K. 1935, Bt. U.K. 1918.]

KEITH ALEXANDER HENRY MASON, *DFC*, 3rd Baron and 3rd Baronet; *b.* Feb. 3rd, 1923; *s.* 1972; ed. at Eton; Bar. Middle Temple 1947; formerly Wing-Cdr. RAFVR; 1939-45 War in N. Africa and N-W Europe (DFC): *m.* 1957, (*m.* diss. 1971), Sarah, da. of Sir (William) Shirley Worthington Worthington-Evans, 2nd Bt. (ext.), and has issue.

Arms,—Or three spur rowels azure on a chief of the last, a plate charged with a fleur-de-lis between two like plates each charged with a cross couped all gules. **Crest,**—A stag's head erased azure attired and charged on the neck with three cross-crosslets in fesse or. **Supporters,**—On either side a stag proper, charged on the shoulder with a patriarchal cross gules.

Deeds not words.

Clubs,—White's and Portland.

Residence,—48, Hyde Park Gate, SW7;

SON LIVING.

Hon. WILLIAM KEITH, *b.* March 27th, 1962.

DAUGHTER LIVING.

Hon. Elizabeth-Anne, *b.* 1965.

PREDECESSORS,—[1] WILLIAM JAMES PEAKE Mason, son of the late George Holt Mason, of Castleton, Tunbridge Wells; *b.* 1862; Lord of the Manors of Compton Pauncefoot and Blackford; High Sheriff of Somerset 1928; cr. a *Baronet* 1918, and *Baron Blackford*, of Compton Pauncefoot, co. Somerset (peerage of United Kingdom) 1935: *m.* 1885, Edith, who *d.* 1958, dau. of the late Alexander Murray Affleck, of Dumfries; *d.* 1947; *s.* by his son [2] GLYN KEITH MURRAY, *CBE, DSO*, 2nd Baron, *b.* 1887; MP for Croydon N. (*C*) 1922-40: *m.* 1918, Grace Ellinor, who *d.* 1972, da. of Nimrod Keen; *d.* 1972, *s.* by his son [3] KEITH ALEXANDER HENRY, *DFC*, 3rd Baron and present peer.

BLAKE, BARON. (Blake.) [Life Baron 1971.]

ROBERT NORMAN WILLIAM BLAKE, *FBA*, son of William Joseph Blake, of Brundall, Norfolk; *b.* Dec. 23rd, 1916; ed. at King Edward VI Sch., Norwich, and Magdalen Coll., Oxford (MA); 1939-45 War as Capt., RA; N. Africa 1942, POW Italy 1942-44, escaped 1944, despatches 1944; a JP of Oxford; a Member of Oxford City Council 1957-64; Lecturer in Politics Ch. Ch. Oxford 1946-47, Student and Tutor in Politics Ch. Ch. 1947-68; Censor 1950-55, Senior Proctor 1959-60; Ford's Lecturer in English History 1967-68; Provost of the Queen's Coll., Oxford since 1968; author of " The Private Papers of Douglas Haig " 1952, " The Unknown Prime Minister (Life of Andrew Bonar Law) " 1955, " Disraeli " 1966, " The Conservative Party from Peel to Churchhill " 1970; *cr. Baron Blake*, of Braydeston, co. Norfolk (Life Baron) 1971: *m.* 1953, Patricia Mary, el. da. of Thomas Richard Waters, of Great Plumstead, Norfolk, and has issue.

Residences,—Provost's Lodgings, Queen's College, Oxford; Riverview House, Brundall, Norfolk. *Clubs,*—Brooks's, Beefsteak and United Oxford and Cambridge University.

DAUGHTERS LIVING.

Hon. Deborah Cicelie, *b.* 1955.
Hon. Letitia Lindley, *b.* 1960.
Hon. Victoria Mary, *b.* 1963.

BLAKENHAM, VISCOUNT. (Hare.) [Viscount U.K. 1963.]

JOHN HUGH HARE, *O.B.E.*, *P.C.*, 1st Viscount, 3rd son of 4th Earl of Listowel; *b.* Jan. 22nd, 1911; ed. at Eton; an Alderman of London County Council 1937-52, Chm. of London Municipal Soc. 1947-52, Vice-Chm. of Conservative Party 1952-55, Min. of State for Colonial Affairs 1955-56, Sec. of State for War 1956-58, Min. of Agriculture, Fisheries and Food 1958-60, Min. of Labour 1960-63, and Chancellor of Duchy of Lancaster 1963-64; Dep. Leader of House of Lords 1963-64, and Chm. of Conservative Party Organisation 1963-65; Chm. of Toynbee Hall since 1966; Treas. Roy.

I hate whatever is profane.

Horticultural Soc. since 1970; DL of Suffolk since 1968; VMH 1974; Chm. of Gov. Peabody Donation Fund since 1967; Lt.-Col. 55th (Suffolk and Norfolk) Anti-Tank Regt., RA (TA); 1939-45 War in N. Africa and Italy (despatches, MBE, OBE, Officers of American Legion of Merit); MP for Woodbridge Div. of E. Suffolk (C) 1945-50, and for Sudbury and Woodbridge Div. of E. Suffolk 1905-63; cr. MBE (Mil.) 1943, OBE (Mil.) 1945, PC 1955, and Viscount Blakenham, of Little Blakenham, co. Suffolk [peerage of UK] 1963: m. 1934, the Hon. Beryl Nancy Pearson, da. of 2nd Viscount Cowdray, and has issue.

Arms,—Gules, two bars and a chief indented or. Crest,—A demi-lion rampant argent, ducally gorged or. Supporters,—Dexter, a dragon ermine armed and langued gules; Sinister, a Guernsey cow proper.

Residences,—10, Holland Park, W11 3TH; Cottage Farm, Little Blakenham, nr. Ipswich.

SON LIVING.

Hon. MICHAEL JOHN, b. Jan. 25th, 1938; ed. at Eton, and at Harvard Coll., U.S.A. (B.A. 1961); late 2nd Lt. Life Guards: m. 1965, Marcia Persephone, da. of Maj. the Hon. Alan Victor Hare, MC [see E. Listowel].

DAUGHTERS LIVING.

Hon. Mary Anne, b. 1936: m. 1964, Timothy Mark Sergison-Brooke [see V. Brookeborough, colls.
Hon. Joanna Freda, b. 1942: m. 1967, Stephen Breyer, of 9, Maynard Pl., Cambridge, Mass., USA.

Blandford, Marquess of, son of Duke of Marlborough.

BLEDISLOE, VISCOUNT. (Bathurst.) [Viscount U.K. 1935.]

Hold to thy faith.

BENJAMIN LUDLOW BATHURST, Q.C., 2nd Viscount; b. Oct. 2nd, 1899; s. 1958; ed. at Eton, and at Magdalen Coll., Oxford; Bar. Inner Temple 1927, a Q.C. 1952, and a Bencher Lincoln's Inn 1956; is Lord of the Manors of Lydney, Purton and Aylburton; European War 1918-19, European War 1939-45: m. 1933, Joan, only dau. of the late Otto Krishaber, and has issue.

Arms,—Sable, two bars ermine, in chief three cross-patée or. Crest,—A dexter arm in mail embowed, the hand proper grasping a club with spikes or. Supporters,—On either side a bull guardant, ringed and a line therefrom reflexed over the back or.

Seat,—Lydney Park, Gloucestershire. London Address,—14, Mulberry Walk, S.W.3. Chambers,— 4, Stone Buildings, Lincoln's Inn, W.C.2. Clubs,— Garrick, Alpine, Portland, Leander.

SONS LIVING.

Hon. CHRISTOPHER HILEY LUDLOW (of 4, Essex Villas, W8, and 2, Crown Office Row, Temple, EC4; Garrick Club), b. June 24th, 1934; ed. at Eton, and at Trin. Coll., Oxford; Bar. Gray's Inn 1959; late Lt. 11th Hussars: m. 1962, Elizabeth Mary, da. of Sir Edward Walter Thompson, of Gatacre Park, Bridgnorth, Salop. [E. Coventry, colls.], and has issue living, Rupert Edward Ludlow, b. 1964,—Otto Benjamin Charles, b. 1971,—Matilda Blanche, b. 1967.
Hon. David Charles Lopes (South Lodge, East Heath Rd., NW3; Boodle's and Garrick Clubs), b. 1937; ed. at Eton, and at Magdalen Coll., Oxford; Lt. 12th Lancers; a Dir. of Christie, Manson & Woods; m. 1967, Mary Cornelia, da. of Andrew Kirkwood, of Culter Allers, Biggar, Lanarkshire, and has issue living, Arabella Rose, b. 1969,—Lucy Celeste, b. 1974.

SISTER LIVING.

Hon. Ursula Mary, b. 1900: m. 1929 (marriage dissolved 1942), Horace Field Parshall, and has issue living, John Field, b. 1932; ed. at Eton: m. 1958, Mary Elizabeth, da. of W. R. Whitney, Residence,—The Cottage, Tylers Green, Penn, Bucks.

PREDECESSOR.—[1] CHARLES Bathurst, G.C.M.G., K.B.E., P.C., son of the late Charles Bathurst of Lydney Park, Gloucestershire ; b. 1867 ; Bar. Inner Temple 1892 ; was Parliamentary Sec., Min. of Food 1916-17, Chm. of Central Chamber of Agriculture 1915, Director of Sugar Distribution 1918-19, Parliamentary Sec. to Min. of Agriculture 1924-28, Gov.-Gen. and Com.-in-Ch. of New Zealand 1930-35, and Pro-Chancellor of Bristol Univ. 1934-47 ; cr. Viscount Bledisloe, of Lydney, co. Gloucester (peerage of United Kingdom) 1935 : *m.* 1st, 1898, the Hon. Bertha Susan Lopes, who *d.* 1936, dau. of 1st Baron Ludlow ; 2ndly, 1928, the Hon. Alina Kate Elaine (a D.G.St.J.), who *d.* 1956, dau. of 1st Baron Glentawe, and widow of Thomas Cooper-Smith; *d.* 1958 ; *s.* by his el. son [2] BEN-JAMIN LUDLOW, 2nd Viscount and present peer.

BLYTH, BARON. (Blyth.) [Baron U.K. 1907, Bt. U.K. 1895.]
[Name and Title pronounced "Bly."]

I hope for better things.

IAN AUDLEY JAMES BLYTH, 3rd Baron and 3rd Baronet; *b.* Oct 28th 1905; *s.* 1943: *m.* 1928, Edna Myrtle, dau. of Ernest Lewis, of Wellington, New Zealand, and has issue.
Arms.—Azure, on a mount vert a bull statant argent, ringed and chained or, one chief arched of the fourth, a stag's head erased proper between two annulets gules. Crest.—In front of a stag's head erased, gorged with a wreath of vine leaves proper, three roses argent. Supporters.—Two stags proper, semée of annulets or, each gorged with a wreath of vine leaves, fructed proper. *Residence,*—Rockfield House, Athenry, co. Galway.

SONS LIVING.
Hon. ANTHONY AUDLEY RUPERT (c/o The Bank of Ireland, Kill O'The Grange, co. Dublin), *b.* June 3rd, 1931: *m.* 1st, 1954 (m. diss. 1962), Elizabeth Dorothea, da. of Robert T. Sparrow, of Vancouver, Canada; 2ndly, 1963, Oonagh Elizabeth Ann, yr. da. of the late William Henry Conway, of Dundrum, Dublin, and has issue living (by 1st m.), Riley Audley John, *b.* 1955,—Marcia Edna Dorothea, *b.* 1956,—(by 2nd m.) James Audley Ian, *b.* 1970,—Lucinda Audley Jane, *b.* 1966.
Hon. Adrian Ulrick Christopher David, *b.* 1944.

DAUGHTERS LIVING.
Hon. Tanya Ormonde Audley, *b.* 1929.
Hon. Barbara Edna Patricia, *b.* 1936.
Hon. Anne Shelagh Jennifer (twin), *b.* 1936.

PREDECESSORS.—[1] JAMES Blyth, elder son of the late James Blyth, of Chelmsford, Essex, by Caroline, dau. of the late Henry Gilbey [Gilbey, Bt.], of Bishop's Stortford, Herts ; *b.* 1841 ; was a Director of W. and A. Gilbey, wine merchants, of The Pantheon, Oxford Street, W., and Vice-Pres. Roy. So. of Arts ; deeply interested in agriculture and farming, and a recognized authority on vine culture and commerce connected therewith ; cr. a *Baronet* (UK, of Blythwood) 1895, and *Baron Blyth,* of Blythwood, Stansted Mountfitchet, co. Essex (peerage of UK) 1907: *m.* 1865, Eliza, who *d.* 1894, dau. of William Mooney, of Clontarf, co. Dublin ; *d.* 1925 : *s.* by his el. son [2] HERBERT WILLIAM, 2nd Baron; *b.* 1868: *m.* 1927, Sylvia Mary (COLE), who *d.* 1974, da. of the late Edwin E. Dennis; *d.* 1943; *s.* by his nephew [3] IAN AUDLEY JAMES (son of the late Hon. JAMES Audley Blyth, 2nd son of 1st Baron), 3rd Baron and present peer.

BLYTON, BARON. (Blyton.) [Life Baron 1964.]

WILLIAM REID BLYTON, son of the late Charles H. Blyton, of S. Shields; *b.* May 2nd, 1899; ed. at Holy Trin. and Dean Rd. Elementary Schs., S. Shields; a Member of Durham Miners Exec. Cttee. 1930-31, 1933-34, and 1942-43, a co. Councillor of S. Shields 1935-45, Sec. of Harton Miners Lodge 1942-45 (Chm. 1928-42), Chm. of S. Shields Education Cttee. 1943, and of S. Shields Electrical Cttee. 1937-40, P.P.S. to Min. of Civil Aviation 1947-49, and Chm. of Parl. Fuel and Power Cttee., Labour Party 1957-64; 1914-18 War, as Able Seaman H.M. Submarines; M.P. for Houghton-le-Spring Div. of co. Durham (*Lab.*) 1945-64; *cr. Baron Blyton,* of South Shields, co. Durham (Life Baron) 1964: *m.* 1919, Jane Brown, da. of the late Edward Ord, of S. Shields, and has issue.

Residence,—139, Brockley Av., S. Shields, co. Durham.

DAUGHTERS LIVING.
Hon. Jane (84, Nevison Av., S. Shields), *b.* 1920: *m.* 1943, John Johansen, who *d.* 1955, and has issue.
Hon. Marion Rose, *b.* 1926: *m.* 1948, John Plank, of 36, Gerald St., S. Shields, and has issue.
Hon. Rita, *b.* 1930: *m.* 1954, — Scott, of 67, Australia Grove, S. Shields, and has issue.

BOLINGBROKE and ST. JOHN, VISCOUNT. (St. John.) [Viscount G.B. 1712,
Bt. E. 1611.]

[Name and Title pronounced "**Bullingbrook and Sinjun.**"]

Neither to seek nor to despise honours.

KENNETH OLIVER MUSGRAVE ST.
JOHN, 7th Viscount, and 11th
Baronet; *b.* March 22nd, 1927; *s.*
1974; ed. at Eton; patron of one
living; a Fellow of Aust. Inst. of
Travel; Pres. of Travel Agents
Assocn. of NZ 1966-68; Dir. of
World Assocn. of Travel Agencies
since 1968, and Chm. of Australian
Council of Tour Wholesalers since
1972: *m.* 1st, 1953, (m. diss. 1972),
Patricia Mary, da. of B. J. McKenna,
of Christchurch, NZ; 2ndly, 1972,
Jainey Anne, da. of the late Alex-
ander Duncan McRae, of Timaru,
NZ, and has issue by 1st and 2nd m.

Arms,—Argent, on a chief gules two mullets
or. **Crest.**—On a mount vert, a falcon rising
or, ducally gorged gules. **Supporters.**—*Dexter,*
a falcon, wings displayed, or, ducally gorged
gules; *sinister,* an eagle, wings displayed, or,
charged on the breast with the hames, an
ancient badge of the family of *Tregoze.* [This
badge resembles an antique shield rimmed gold,
the field per pale argent and gules, and charged
with a crescent sable, thereon a label of three
points or.]

Addresses,—PO Box 3711, Sydney, NSW; Peel Forest, S. Canterbury, NZ. *Clubs,*—Bath;
(London), Christchurch (Christchurch, NZ).

SONS LIVING. (*By 1st m.*)
Hon. HENRY FITZROY, *b.* May 18th, 1957.

(*By 2nd m.*)
Hon. Oliver John, *b.* 1972.
Hon. Nicholas Alexander, *b.* 1974.

BROTHER LIVING.
Henry Ferdinand Musgrave (The Oast House, Titness Park, Sunninghill, Berks.), *b.* 1928; ed. at Eton;
late Lt. LG: *m.* 1956, Patricia Margaret Mary, da. of Edward Ryan, of Exeter, Devon, and has issue
living, Olivier Geoffrey, *b.* 1958.

SISTER LIVING.
Antonia Josephine (c/o Midland Bank, 799, Fulham Rd., SW6), *b.* 1933: *m.* 1st, 1955, (m. diss. 1966),
Henry Wilson; 2ndly, 1967, Peter Johnson, and has issue living (by 2nd m.), Melanie Joanne, *b.* 1967.

Grandchildren of the late Maj. John Henry St. John, 2nd son of the Hon. Ferdinand
St. John (infra):—
Issue of the late Henry Warren St. John, *b.* 1860, *d.* 1931 : *m.* 1916, Justina Margaret, dau.
of the late Duncan Mackenzie, of Hill View, East Grinstead :—
Margaret Irene, *b.* 1917: *m.* 1939, Gerald Francis William Matthews (from whom she obtained
a divorce 1947), and has issue living, Texicia, *b.* 1940,—Peggy, *b.* 1941. *Residence,*—Ibstock,
Rowplatt Lane, Felbridge, near East Grinstead.

Issue of the late Walter Cecil Hompesch St. John, *b.* 1867, *d.* 1955 : *m.* 1908, Salome Rod-
rigues, who *d.* 1930 :—
Walter Warren, *b.* 1921: *m.* 1949, Lida Goicoechea, and has issue living, Henry William, *b.* 1951,
Alice, *b.* 1950. *Residence,*—Calle Madero, 755, Buenos Aires, Argentina.——Lila Ramona
del Rosario, *b.* 1910: *m.* 1935, Dr. Ernesto Christensen, and has issue living, Eduardo
Ernesto, *b.* 1936; Advocate,—Lilian Margarita, *b.* 1943: *m.* 1935, Rodolfo Diedrich, of Cerro Azul,
Misiones, Argentina, and has issue living, Rodolpho *b.* 1967, Constanza *b.* 1966. *Residence,*—166,
Calle Entre Rios, Santiago del Estero, Argentina.——Fanny del Valle, *b.* 1912; has Medal of Merit,
Red Cross of Argentina: *m.* 1938, Dr. Ramon Bernardo Juarez, and has issue living, Hugo Ramon
(of 487, Calle 9 de Julio, Province de Santiago del Estero, Argentina), *b.* 1939: *m.* 1959, Maria
Cristina Rodriguez, and has issue living, Hugo Walter *b.* (Dec.) 1959, Gustavo Alejandro *b.* 1963,
Monica Alicia *b.* 1961,—Enrique José, *b.* 1944: *m.* 1969, Maria Virginia Espindola Araoz, of Cale
Buenos Aires 282, Province de Santiago de Estero, Argentina,—Fanny Celina, *b.* 1940: *m.* 1965,
Roberto Varela Vasquez, and has issue living, Roberto Enrique *b.* 1968, Sebastian Ernesto *b.* 1971,
Gabriela Celina *b.* 1966. *Residence,*—282, Calle Buenos Aires, Province de Santiago del Estero,
Argentina.——Margarita del Carmen, *b.* 1913: *m.* 1941, Luis Frederico Quade, and has issue living,
Josefa Margarita, *b.* 1943: *m.* 1954, José Alberto Renée Cisneros, of Calle Motu Botello, 848, Cata-
marca, Argentina, and has issue living, José Maria *b.* 1966, Luis Edward *b.* 1967, Marcela Inez
b. 1968,—Luisa Celina, *b.* 1949. *Residence,*—Calle Buenos Aires 57, Ciudad de Frias, Province de
Santiago del Estero, Argentina.——Rose Pastora, *b.* 1916: *m.* 1940, Ubaldo Garcia, and has issue
living, Guillermo Ubaldo, *b.* 1946,—Graciela Salomé, *b.* 1941,—Maria Rosa del Carmen, *b.* 1942,—
Teresa Pastora, *b.* 1945. *Residence,*—Calle Buenos Aires 57, Ciudad de Frais, Province Santiago del
Estero, Argentina.

Issue of the late Edward Archibald St. John, *b.* 1876, *d.* 1949 : *m.* 1922, Clare Esmeralda Magno, of 813, Calle Martinez, Capital, Buenos Aires, Argentina :—
Zeline Mabel Alice, *b.* 1923.——Gloria Alida, *b.* 1924: *m.* 19—, Prof. Cesar Guerresi, and has issue living, a son, *b.* 19—.

Grandchildren of the late Hon. Ferdinand St. John, 2nd son of 3rd Viscount :—
Issue of the late Sir Frederick Robert St. John, K.C.M.G., *b.* (twin) 1831, *d.* 1923 : *m.* 1882, Isabella Annie, who *d.* 1943, dau. of the late Capt. the Hon. James Terence Fitz-maurice [see E. Orkney, colls.] :—
Frederick Oliver, *DSO, MC* (Journeys End, East Looe, Cornwall), *b.* 1886; *h.p.* to Earldom of Orkney; Lt.-Col. R. Signals (ret.); late R. Scots; France 1914-15, Mesopotamia 1915-19, Cmdg. a Unit (MC, DSO); DSO 1917: *m.* 1st, 1923, Dotie (from whom he obtained a divorce 1929), da. of Sydney Bernard Burney, CBE; 2ndly, 1931, Elizabeth, da. of E. H. Pierce, of Peachland, BC, and has issue living, (by 2nd m.) Oliver Peter (200, Dromore Av., Winnipeg 9, Manitoba, Canada), *b.* 1938, BA, MSc (Econ.); Associate Prof. Political Science Univ. of Manitoba: *m.* 1963, Mary Juliet, da. of W. G. Scott-Brown, of 61, Harley St., W1, and has issue living, Oliver Robert *b.* 1969, Juliet Elizabeth *b.* 1964, Nicola Jane *b.* 1966, Lucy Margaret *b.* 1972.——Dorothea Emily Olga (*Lady Lowther*), *b.* 1884: *m.* 1906, Sir Henry Crofton Lowther, GCVO, KCMG, who *d.* 1939, and has issue living, Oliver Peter (Brookside, Wineham, Sussex), *b.* 1910: *m.* 1937, Jean, da. of C. J. Inder, of NZ, and has issue living, James Brabazon *b.* 1939,—Esmée Katalin, *b.* 1913: *m.* 1936, Com. John Harry Boughton, RN of Commons Farm, Fersfield, Diss, Norfolk, and has issue living, Jeremy John Lowther *b.* 1944, Priscilla Dorothy *b.* 1937, Jacqueline Esmée *b.* 1951. *Residence,*—

Granddaughter of the late Sir Frederick Robert St. John, K.C.M.G. (ante) :—
Issue of the late Terence Alexander DE ST. JOHN, *b.* 1896, *d.* 1951 (having assumed by deed poll (enrolled at College of Arms) 1933, the surname of de St. John in lieu of his patro-nymic) : *m.* 1st, 1923, Simone Suzanne Marie Anne (from whom he obtained a divorce 1932), only dau. of Jean Baptiste Guthmann, of Paris; 2ndly, 1944, Winifred Giles, of 5, Chichester Close, Saltdean, Sussex :—
(By 1st marriage) Rosemary Anne, *b.* 1927.

Granddaughters of the late Major George Frederick Berkeley St. John, son of the late Gen. the Hon. Frederick St. John, 2nd son of 2nd Viscount :—
Issue of the late Henry Augustus Bolingbroke St. John, *b.* 1847, *d.* 1921 : *m.* 18—, Anna, dau. of the late Major — Henderson, H.E.I.C.S. :—
Mary Constance, *b.* 1889. *Residence,*—1171, Newport Avenue, Victoria, British Columbia.—— Margaret, *b.* 1896: *m.* 1928, Gordon Sweet. *Residence,*—

Grandchildren of the late Alexander Storey St. John (infra):—
Issue of the late Alexander Bolingbroke St. John, *b.* 1910, *d.* 1968: *m.* 1937, Gladys Spencer (Charter Cottage, 157, Middle St., Deal):—
Stewart Bolingbroke, *b.* 1942.——Janet Eleanor, *b.* 1938: *m.* 1962, Michael Stanley Hall, of 7, Rowan Shaw, Tonbridge, Kent.

Granddaughter of the late Frederick Charles St. John, son of the late Charles William George St. John, son of the late Gen. the Hon. Frederick St. John (ante):—
Issue of the late Alexander Storey St. John, *b.* 1867, *d.* 1923 : *m.* 1906, Mabel Eleanor who *d.* 1928, third dau. of the late Inspector-Gen. Sir Henry Frederick Norbury K.C.B., M.D., F.R.C.S., R.N., of St. Margarets, Eltham, Kent :—
Stella Swithina Legge, *b.* 1907. *Address,*—Kingsway Hall, WC2.

Grandchildren of the late Adm. Henry Craven St. John, son of the late Charles William George St. John, son of the late Gen. the Hon. Frederick St. John (ante):—
Issue of the late Montagu Rodney St. John, *b.* 1861, *d.* 1944 : *m.* 1898, Theodora Mary Land, who *d.* 1958, dau. of the late Dr. H. N. L. James, Army Med. Depart.:—
Henrietta Doreen, *b.* 1900 : *m.* 1928, Lieut.-Col. Douglas Graham Moncrieff Wright, M.C., late Cameronians (Scottish Rifles) (who was officially recognized by decree of the Lord Lyon King of Arms 1946 in the name of Moncrieff of Kinmonth) and has issue living, John Graham, yr. of Kinmonth (Loyal Lodge, Sutherland; Presses House, Nunton, Salisbury, Wilts.; Army and Navy, Kandahar, and Shikar Clubs), *b.* 1929; ed. at Eton; Lt.-Col. The Black Watch, and a Member of Queen's Body Guard for Scotland (Roy. Co. of Archers); Korea 1952-53 (despatches), Kenya 1953 (medal and clasp); Aden 1962-63, and Singapore 1966-68: *m.* 1966, Susan Mary, yr. da. of Rupert Claude Martin, MA, JP, of Quantocks, Burnham-on-Sea, and has issue living, Andrew Graham *b.* 1969, Mary Rose *b.* 1971,—Charles St. John Graham (Kinmonth, Rhynd, nr. Perth), *b.* 1931; ed. at Eton; Capt. Scots Guards (ret.): *m.* 1957, Joanna Dava, da. of the late Maj. (Basil Arthur) John Peto, King's Dragoon Guards [see Peto, Bt., cr. 1927, colls.], and has issue living, Alexander Charles Graham *b.* 1967, Charlotte Henrietta *b.* 1959, Miranda Caroline *b.* 1961, Rosanna Claire *b.* 1965,—Dora Heather Graham, *b.* 1938: *m.* 1961, Donald John Harper Gow, of Pitscandly, Forfar, Angus, and has issue living, Alastair John Moncrieff *b.* 1963, Jeremy Douglas Moncrieff *b.* 1965, Colin Rodney Moncrieff *b.* 1968. *Residences,*—Elcho Park, Rhynd, nr. Perth; Kinloch, Tongue, by Lairg, Sutherland.

Issue of the late Vice-Adm. Francis Gerald St. John, C.B., M.V.O., *b.* 1869, *d.* 1947: *m.* 1st, 1898, Winifred Jessie, who *d.* 1898, dau. of George Haward Trollope; 2ndly 1902, Emily Frances Louise, who *d.* 1969, el. da. of the late Allan Turner, of Bombay:—
(By 2nd marriage) Stratford Allan Gerald, *R.N.*, *b.* 1911; became Capt. 1956; European War 1939-44, operations off Norway and Sicily (despatches twice): *m.* 1942, Honor Madeleine, dau. of Philip Smiles, of Belfast.——Betty Allane, *b.* 1905.——Peggy Katharine Mary (Hillview Cottage, Carpenters Hill, St. Helens, I. of Wight), *b.* 1908: *m.* 1939, Maj. Leslie Fairfax d'Arch Smith, from whom she obtained a divorce 1948, and has issue living, Nicola Lesley, *b.* 1940: *m.* 1962, Charles Quentin James, of The Lodge, 1, Kirkby Rd., Desford, Leicester, and has issue living, Andrew Thurstan Trewartha *b.* 1965, Simon Charles Trewartha *b.* 1969, Emma Charlotte *b.* 1963, Sophie Louise *b.* 1971.

PREDECESSORS.—OLIVER St. John (a descendant of Oliver St. John, second son of Sir Oliver St. John of Bletso [see B. St. John of Bletso]), who obtained considerable renown in the wars of Elizabeth and James, in Ireland, was cr. *Viscount Grandison* 1620, in peerage of Ireland (with remainder to the issue of his niece Barbara, wife of Sir Edward Villiers), and *Baron Tregoze* (peerage of England) 1626; *d. s. p.*, when the Barony became ext. and the Viscountcy (now merged in the Earldom of Jersey) descended to William, son of Barbara (ante). His nephew [1] JOHN, brother of Barbara (ante), a zealous royalist, had three sons slain in fighting under the royal standard; cr. a *Baronet* 1611; s. by his grandson [2] *Sir* JOHN, 2nd Bt., *d.s.p.* 1656 ; s. by his uncle [3] *Sir* WALTER, 3rd Bt., M.P. for co. Wilts; *d.* 1708; s. by his son [4] *Sir* Henry, 4th Bt. ; cr. *Baron St. John of Battersea* and *Viscount, St. John* (peerage of Great Britain) 1716, with remainder to his 2nd and 3rd sons, his el. son Henry, a famous statesman and writer, having in 1712 been cr. *Baron St. John*, of Lydiard Tregoze, and *Viscount Bolingbroke* (peerage of Great Britain), with remainder to his father and his father's issue; in 1714 Viscount Bolingbroke was attainted, but in 1723 he was restored in blood, and in 1725 his estates were restored without his honours; Viscount St.

John *d.* 1742, and was *s.* by his 2nd son [5] JOHN, 2nd Viscount St. John; *d.* 1748; *s.* by his son [6] FREDERICK, 3rd Viscount St. John, who in 1751, on the demise of his uncle Henry without issue, *s.* to the Barony of St. John of Lydiard Tregoze and the Viscountcy of Bolingbroke; *d.* 1787; *s.* by his son [7] GEORGE RICHARD, 3rd Viscount Bolingbroke; *d.* 1824; *s.* by his son [8] HENRY, 4th Viscount Bolingbroke, *b.* 1786: *m.* 1812, Maria, dau. of Sir Henry Paulet St. John Mildmay, 3rd Bt.; *d.* 1851; *s.* by his son [9] HENRY MILDMAY, 5th Viscount Bolingbroke, *b.* 1820: *m.* 1893, Mary Emily Elizabeth, who *d.* 1940, dau. of Robert Howard: *d.* 1899; *s.* by his son [10] VERNON HENRY, 6th Viscount Bolingbroke and St John *b.* 1896 (claim admitted by Cttee. for Privileges of House of Lords 1922, and writ of summons issued April 1926): *m.* 1950 (m. annulled 1952), Valenzina, da. of the late Frederick William Frohawk, of Sutton, Surrey; *d.* 1974; *s.* by his kinsman [11] KENNETH OLIVER MUSGRAVE (el. son by 2nd m. of Capt. Geoffrey Robert St. John, MC, el. son of Henry Percy St. John, el. son of the Rev. Maurice William Ferdinand St. John, DD, el. son of the Hon. Ferdin and St. John, 2nd son of 3rd Viscount), 7th Viscount and present peer; also Baron St. John of Lydiard Tregoze, and Baron St. John of Battersea.

BOLTON, BARON. (Orde-Powlett.) [Baron G.B. 1797.]

,[Name pronounced "Ord-Pawlett."]

Love loyalty.

RICHARD WILLIAM ALGAR ORDE-POWLETT, 7th Baron; *b.* July 11th, 1929; *s.* 1963; ed. at Eton, and at Trin. Coll., Camb. (B.A. 1951); a J.P. for N. Riding of Yorks.; Chm., Yorks. branch, Roy. Forestry Soc. 1963-64; a Dir. of Yorkshire General Life, Chm. of Waterers Group, and Yorks. Soc. of Agric.: *m.* 1951, the Hon. Christine Helena Weld-Forester, da. of the 7th Baron Forester, and has issue.

Arms,—Sable: three swords in pile, points downwards argent, pommels and hilts or, on a canton argent, an escutcheon sable, charged with a salmon hauriant proper. Crest,—A falcon rising or, ducally gorged azure, charged on the breast with an estoile gules, and holding in the beak a salmon proper. Supporters,—Dexter, a hind proper, ducally gorged or, and charged on the shoulder with a white rose; *sinister*, a Cornish chough proper, also charged on the shoulder with a white rose proper.

Seat,—Bolton Hall, Leyburn, Yorkshire.
Clubs,—Turf, Flyfishers', Central African Deep Sea Fishers'.

SONS LIVING.

Hon. HARRY ALGAR NIGEL, *b.* Feb. 14th, 1954; ed. at Eton.
Hon. Michael Brooke, *b.* 1959.

DAUGHTER LIVING.

Hon. Rosemary Victoria, *b.* 1952: *m.* 1974, John Richard Bentley North.

BROTHER LIVING.

Hon. Patrick Christopher (Crabtree Lodge, Hezely Heath, Hartley Wintney, Hants.), *b.* 1931; ed. at Eton, and at Jesus Coll., Camb. (MA), ARICS; Forestry Adviser, and Council-Member, Assocn. Professional Foresters; Financial Adviser in Assocn. with First Investors Financial Sers. Ltd.: *m.* 1962, Elizabeth Jane, da. of A. S. Kent, of The Thatched House, Worlington, Bury St. Edmunds, and has issue living, Rosamund Jane, *b.* 1964,—Heather Victoria, *b.* 1966.

AUNT LIVING. (*Daughter of 5th Baron.*)

Hon. Elaine Letitia Algitha, *b.* 1895 : *m.* 1922, the Rt. Rev. Bishop Percy Mark Herbert, K.C.V.O. DD, who *d.* 1968 [see E. Powis, colls.]. *Residence,*—Smithy House, Chirbury, Powys.

PREDECESSORS.—[1] *Rt. Hon.* THOMAS Orde, son of the late John Orde, D.L., of Morpeth: *m.*, 1778, Jean Mary Powlett, natural dau. of Charles, 5th Duke of Bolton [see M. Winchester], and having *s.* to his estates, assumed in 1795 by sign manual the additional surname of Powlett; cr. *Baron Bolton* (peerage of Great Britain) 1797; *d.* 1807; *s.* by his el. son [2] WILLIAM, 2nd Baron: *m.* 1810, the Hon. Maria, who *d.* 1863, dau. of 1st Baron Dorchester; *d.* 1850; *s.* by his nephew [3] WILLIAM HENRY, 3rd Baron (son of the late Hon. Thomas Orde-Powlett, 2nd son of 1st Baron), *b.* 1818: *m.* 1844, Letitia, who *d.* 1882, dau. of Col. Crawfurd, of Newfield, Ayrshire; *d.* 1895; *s.* by his el. son [4] WILLIAM THOMAS, 4th Baron, *b.* 1845: *m.* 1868, Lady Algitha Frederica Mary Lumley, who *d.* 1919, el. dau. of 9th Earl of Scarbrough; *d.* 1922; *s.* by his son [5] WILLIAM GEORGE ALGAR, 5th Baron: *b.* 1869; Lord-Lieut. for N. Riding of Yorkshire: M.P. for Yorkshire, N. Riding, Richmond Div. (C) 1910-18: *m.* 1893, the Hon. Elizabeth Mary Gibson, who *d.* 1943, dau. of 1st Baron Ashbourne, *d.* 1944; *s.* by his son [6] NIGEL AMYAS, 6th Baron; *b.* 1900: *m.* 1928, Victoria Mary Mary, who *d.* 1933, dau. of Henry Montagu Villiers, M.V.O. [E. Clarendon, colls.]; *d.* 1963; *s.* by his el. son, [7] RICHARD WILLIAM ALGAR, 7th Baron and present peer.

Booth, see Baron Gore-Booth.

BOOTHBY, BARON. (Boothby.) [Life Baron 1958.]

The death of Christ is to me the death of death.

ROBERT JOHN GRAHAM BOOTHBY, *K.B.E.*, son of the late Sir Robert Tuite Boothby, K.B.E., of Beechwood, Murrayfield, Midlothian ; *b.* Feb. 12th, 1900 ; ed. at Eton, and at Magdalen Coll., Oxford (B.A. 1921, M.A. 1959) ; elected Rector of St. Andrews Univ. 1958 (Hon. LL.D. 1959) ; is an Officer of Legion of Honour, and Pres. of Anglo-Israel Assoc. ; was Parliamentary Sec. to Min. of Food 1940-41, and British delegate to Consultative Assembly, Council of Europe 1949-57; a Freeman of Peterhead, Fraserburgh, Turriff, and Rosehearty ; appointed Radner Lecturer Columbia Univ., New York, 1960; Chm., Roy. Philharmonic Orchestra 1961-63; MP for E. Div. of Aberdeenshire and Kincardineshire (*C*) 1924-55, and for E. Div. of Aberdeenshire 1955-58; *cr.* KBE (Civil) 1953, and *Baron Boothby*, of Buchan and Rattray Head, co. Aberdeen (Life Baron) 1958: *m.* 1st, 1935 (m. diss. 1937), Diana, da. of the late Col. the Rt. Hon. Lord Richard Frederick Cavendish, CB, CMG [see D. Devonshire, colls.]; 2ndly, 1967, Wanda, da. of Giuseppe Sanna, of Sardinia.

Arms,—Argent, four beech-leaves vert alternately with as many saltires couped azure, a dexter canton (occluding the saltire in dexter chief) sable, charged with a lion's gamb erased erect or. **Crest,**—A lion's gamb erased erect or, armed azure. **Supporters,**—*Dexter*, a farmer proper habited in a fore and aft Buchan cap and tweed jacket, all Brunatre, knickerbockers of the same and gaiters proper, supporting within his exterior arm the blade of a binder-harvester ; *sinister*, a fisherman habited in a sou' wester proper and a jersey azure, blue serge trousers and gum-boots proper, and over his sinister shoulder a fishing net also proper.

Residence,—1, Eaton Sq., S.W.1.   *Club,*—White's.

Boringdon, Viscount, son of Earl of Morley.

BORTHWICK, LORDSHIP OF. (Borthwick.) [Lord S. 1452.] [Dormant 1910.]

COLLATERAL BRANCHES LIVING.

Descendants of the Hon. John Borthwick of Crookston, 2nd son of 1st Lord :—

Grandson of the late William Henry Borthwick of Borthwick, 15th of Crookston (whose el. brother *d.s.p.*, and whose father, the late John Borthwick of Borthwick, 13th of Crookston, repurchased Borthwick Castle 1812 to which, had it not been alienated, he would have *s.* under a settlement of 1538) 12th in descent from the Hon. John Borthwick:—

Issue of the late Henry Borthwick of Borthwick, 16th of Crookston, *b.* 1868, *d.* 1937: *m.* 1902, Melena Florence (Dame of Crookston, Heriot, Midlothian), da. of the late Capt. James Pringle of Torwoodlee:—

John Henry Stuart, *TD, b.* 1905; claims to be heir male and *de jure* 24th Lord; Maj. RA (TA), and a DL and JP of Midlothian; with Allied Mil. Govt. Staff 1944: *m.* 1938, Margaret Frances, da. of Alexander Campbell Cormack, and has issue living, John Hugh (The Neuk, nr. Gilston, by Heriot, Midlothian) *b.* 1940: *m.* 1974, Adelaide, only da. of Archy Birkmyre, of Overdale, Crieff, Perthshire [see Birkmyre, Bt.],—James Henry Alexander (twin), *b.* 1940: *m.* 1972, Elspeth, da. of Lt.-Col. A. D. MacConachie, of Aviemore, and has issue living, Malcolm Henry, *b.* 1973. *Residence,*—Crookston, Heriot, Midlothian.   *Club,*—New (Edinburgh).

Granddaughters of the late William Henry Borthwick of Borthwick, 15th of Crookston, 2nd son of the late John Borthwick of Borthwick, 13th of Crookston (ante):—

Issue of the late Capt. Alfred Edward Borthwick of Burnhouse, LL.D., *b.* 1871, *d.* 1955: *m.* 1907, Mary Simcoe Violet, who *d.* 1967, da. of the late Capt. James Pringle of Torwoodlee:—

Ann Violet: *m.* 1936, Alexander Charles Stephen, DSc, FRSE, who *d.* 1966, and has issue living, Jean Violet, *b.* 19—: *m.* 1970, Kenneth J. G. Morley. *Residence,*—17, Cammo Cres., Barnton, Edinburgh, 4.——Grizel Rebecca: *m.* 1939, James Alexander Barclay, MD, of 302 Quinton Rd., Birmingham, and has issue living, Alfred Donald Walker (30, Church Hill, Belbroughton, Worcs.), *b.* 1941: *m.* 1970, Mary Taylor Mackie, and has issue living, Claire Elizabeth *b.* 1972,—Bruce James Walker, *b.* 1944.——Marjorie Elspeth. *Residence,*—14, Napier Rd., Edinburgh, EH10 5AY.

Grandson of the late Lt.-Col. Alexander Borthwick, MVO, 3rd son of John Borthwick of Borthwick, 13th of Crookston (ante):—

Issue of the late Capt. Arthur Sandilands Borthwick, *b.* 1879, *d.* 1968: *m.* 1910, Vera Janet (Mons Egitna, Mougins, A.M., France), da. of William Bethel Hervey:—

Richard Quentin (6, Onslow Sq., SW7.   *Club*,—Bath), *b*. 1911; ed. at Camb. Univ.:   *m*. 1942, Vivien, from whom he obtained a divorce 1955, da. of Arthur Henry de Kantzow.

Granddaughters of the late Francis Borthwick, youngest son of John Borthwick of Borthwick, 13th of Crookston (ante):—
Issue of the late Francis John Gordon Borthwick, W.S., *b*. 1871, *d*. 1948 :   *m*. 1912, Eugenie Helen Franklyn, dau. of Edmund Stow Thompson :—
Mary Alice (*Hon. Mrs. Douglas D. E. Vivian*) (Monastery Garden, Edington, Westbury, Wilts.): *m*. 1943, Lt.-Com. the Hon. Douglas David Edward Vivian, RN, DSO [see B. Vivian], who *d*. 1973.
——Margaret Eugenie: *m*. 1944, Maj. Ian Rupert Farquhar, Gren. Gds. [see Farquhar, Bt., colls.].
Residences,—Hamlyns, Chudleigh, S. Devon; 48, Paultons Sq., SW3.

BORWICK, BARON.   (Borwick.)   [Baron U.K. 1922, Bt. U.K. 1916.]

JAMES HUGH MYLES BORWICK, *M.C.*, 4th Baron, and 4th Baronet ;   *b*. Dec. 12th, 1917 ; *s*. 1961 ;   ed. at Eton ;   is Major (retired) Highland L.I. ;   European War   1939-45 (M.C.) :   *m*. 1954, Hyllarie Adalia Mary, dau. of the late Lieut.-Col. William Hamilton Hall Johnston, D.S.O., M.C., D.L., of Bryn-y-Groes, Bala, N. Wales, and has issue.

Arms.—Argent, three escarbuncles fesseways sable between three bears' heads erased of the last, muzzled or. **Crest.**—Upon a mount proper, in front of a staff raguly erect azure, a stag browsing or, attired sable. **Supporters,**—On either side a bear sable, muzzled and charged on the shoulder with an escarbuncle or.

Residence,—Keeping, Beaulieu, Hants.   *Clubs*,—Caledonian, Royal Ocean Racing.

DAUGHTERS LIVING.
Hon. Angela Jane, *b*. 1955.
Hon. Mary-Anne, *b*. 1957.
Hon. Diana, *b*. 1959.
Hon. Amanda Gwyneth Rosemary, *b*. 1965.

It passes.

HALF-BROTHERS LIVING.
Hon. GEORGE SANDBACH (18, Kinnerton St., SW1; Garrick and Bath Clubs), *b*. Oct. 18th, 1922; ed. at Eton.
Hon. Robin Sandbach, *b*. 1927: ed. at Eton; late Lt. The L.G.: *m*. 1950, Patricia Garnett, only da. of Sir (Robert) Edwin McAlpine [see McAlpine, Bt.], and has issue living, Geoffrey Robert James, *b*. 1955; ed. at Eton,—Richard David, *b*. 1960; ed. at Eton,—Judith Patricia, *b*. 1952: *m*. 1971, Padriac Desmond Curry-Towneley-O'Hagan, of 13, Arlington Av., N1. [see B. O'Hagan]. *Residence*,—Casa de Rohan, Zebbug, Malta, GC.   *Clubs*,—Cavalry, Casino Maltese (Valletta).

SISTERS LIVING.
Hon. Katherine Hilda, *b*. 1914: *m*. 1938, Ashton Jack Ulyate, of 1, Caefron Av., Westville, nr. Durban, Natal, and has issue living, Stanley Ian Robert Borwick (Wankie Safari Lodge, Dett, Rhodesia), *b*. 1939: *m*. 1973, Margaret Mary Anne Morling, and has issue living, William Robert *b*. 1973,—Raymond Grant, *b*. 1955,—Sandra Irene Borwick, *b*. 1945: *m*. 1972, Peter Leslie Berry, of 59, Cleland Rd., Scottsville, Pietermaritzburg, Natal, and has issue living, Cynthia Jacqueline *b*. 1972.
Hon. Phyllis Dorothy, *b*. 1916: *m*. 1963, John A'Court Bergne, of 16, Woodlane, Falmouth, Cornwall,

PREDECESSORS.—[1] ROBERT HUDSON Borwick, last surviving son of the late George Borwick, of Morven, Torquay; *b*. 1845; was a Director of George Borwick & Sons, Ltd., and a J.P. for co. London ; cr. a *Baronet* 1916, and *Baron Borwick*, of Hawkshead, co. Lancaster (peerage of United Kingdom) 1923: *m*. 1872, Caroline Smith, who *d*. 1936, dau. of the late Richard Daniel Johnston, of Kurnool, Madras; *d*. 1936; *s*. by his el. son [2] GEORGE, 2nd Baron, *b*. 1880: *m*. 1st, 1908, Mary Mason (who obtained a divorce 1913), dau. of Lewis Cruger Hassell, of New York ; 2ndly, 1918, Dorothea Gertrude (from whom he obtained a divorce 1938), dau. of the late Charles Gray, of Anerley, S.E.; *d*. 1941; *s*. by his brother [3] ROBERT GEOFFREY, 3rd Baron ; *b*. 1886 ; formerly Lieut. 20th Hussars ; European War 1914-18 as Capt. Hertfordshire Regt. and Lt. RFA: *m*. 1st, 1913, Irene Phyllis (who *d*. 1969, and from whom he obtained a divorce 1920), dau. of the late Thomas Main Patterson, of Littlebourne House, Canterbury ; 2ndly, 1920, Margaret Elizabeth, who *d*. 1969, da. of the late Gilbert Robertson Sandbach, of Stone-Leigh, Rossett; *d*. 1961; *s*. by his el. son JAMES HUGH MYLES, 4th Baron and present peer.

BOSSOM, BARONY OF.   (Bossom.)   [Extinct 1965.]

SON LIVING OF LIFE BARON.
Hon. SIR CLIVE BOSSOM, *MP*, 2nd Bt., who *s*. to baronetcy (cr. 1953), 1965.
[see Bossom, Bt.].

BOSTON, BARON. (Irby.) [Baron G.B. 1761, Bt. E 1704.]

Honour is the reward of fidelity.

GERALD HOWARD BOTELER IRBY, *MBE*, 9th Baron, and 10th Baronet; *b.* Aug. 29th, 1897; *s.* 1972; 1914-18 War as Lt. KRRC (MBE); 1939-45 War as Maj. RASC; MBE (Mil) 1918: *m.* 1st, 1926 (m. diss. 1931), Katherine Gertrude, da. of Capt. C. M. H. Edwards, late RASC; 2ndly, 1936, Erica, da. of T. H. Hill, and has issue by 1st and 2nd m.

Arms,—Argent, fretty sable, on a canton gules, a chaplet or. Crest.—A Saracen's head in profile proper, wreathed round the temples argent and sable. Supporters—Two antelopes gules, each gorged with a chaplet or.

Residence,—Flat 11, Gunters Mead, Copsem Lane, Esher, Surrey.

SON LIVING. (*By 2nd m.*)

Hon. TIMOTHY GEORGE FRANK BOTELER (33, Cloncurry St., SW6), *b.* March 27th, 1939: *m.* 1967, Rhonda Anne, da. of R. A. Bate, of Balgowlah, NSW, and has issue living, George William Eustace Boteler, *b.* 1971,—Jonathan Charles, *b.* 1975,—Rebecca Frances Anne, *b.* 1970.

DAUGHTER LIVING (*By 1st m.*)

Hon. Anne Pauline, *b.* 1927.

BROTHER LIVING.

Anthony Paul, *TD*, (7, South Bolton Gdns., SW5 0DH), *b.* 1908; ed. at Eton, and Trin. Coll., Camb. (BA); Bar. Lincoln's Inn 1932; formerly Sen. Assist. Parl. Counsel; 1939-45 War as Maj. Rifle Bde.: *m.* 1st, 1934, Countess Mary Apponyi, who *d.* 1952, el. da. of the late Count Anton Apponyi; 2ndly, 1957, Mrs. Beryl Harrison, da. of the late Harold Mayman, of Bramsgore, Hants., and has issue living, (by 1st m.) Paul Anthony (30, Cadogan Sq., SW1), *b.* 1935; ed. at Eton; late 2nd Lt. KRRC,—George Anthony Peter, *b.* 1942; ed. at Eton; Maj. R. Green Jackets,—Charles Leonard Anthony (17, Lilyville Rd., SW6), *b.* 1945; ed. at Eton: *m.* 1971, Sarah Jane, da. of David Sutherland.

DAUGHTERS LIVING OF SEVENTH BARON.

Hon. Rachel Elizabeth Cicely, *b.* 1914: *m.* 1940, Lt. Darsie Rawlins, RNVR, and has issue living, Adrian Drake, *b.* 1942,—Anthony Irby, *b.* 1944,—Diana Caroline Zoë, *b.* 1949,—Christina Elizabeth, *b.* 1955. *Residence,*—Red Tiles, Kingswood Avenue, Penn, Bucks.

Hon. Isobel Caroline, *b.* 1917: *m.* 1st, 1946, Major Vernon Owain Roberts, The Buffs, from whom she obtained a divorce 1950; 2ndly, 1950, Edward Horatio Sales, and has issue living, (by 2nd m.) Christian Caroline, *b.* 1950,—Alexandra Josephine, *b.* 1952. *Residence,*—53, Stanhope Gardens, SW7.

Hon. Christian Florance, *b.* 1921: *m.* 1947, Etienne Humblet, who *d.* 1971. *Address,*—Apart. 3/A Windsor, 33, Koningslaan, 8390, Knokke-Heist, Belgium.

WIDOW LIVING OF SEVENTH BARON.

IRENE FRANCES (*Irene, Baroness Boston*), dau. of the late Francis Holt, of Ewell, Surrey, and widow of Harry Mills: *m.* 1954, as his second wife, the 7th Baron, who *d.* 1958. *Residence,*—155, Oakwood Court, W.14.

COLLATERAL BRANCHES LIVING.

Grandchildren of the late Edward de Crespigny Irby, el. son of the late Edward Irby (infra):—

Issue of the late Francis Edward Irby, *b.* 1877, *d.* 1960: *m.* 1925, Katie Lorna (Towri, 99, Hare St., Casino, 2470, NSW), da. of the late W. Tibbits, of Gilgandra, NSW:—

Edith Elizabeth (16, Pappenbarra Parade, Port Macquarie, NSW), *b.* 1927: *m.* 1953, Richard E. Wratten, who *d.* 1969, and has issue living, Nigel Richard Irby, *b.* 1955.——Eunice Lorna (c/o Towri, 99, Hare St., Casino 2470, NSW), *b.* 1928: *m.* 1954, Thomas Henry Hocking, who *d.* 1972, and has issue living, Gregory Francis, *b.* 1955,—Gwendolyn Jean, *b.* 1963.——Isla Frances, *b.* 1930: *m.* 1954, Wilfred Charles Tibbits, JP, of The Lodge, Studio Park, Sunny Corner, via Bathurst, NSW.

Issue of the late Paul Anthony Irby, *b.* 1882: *d.* 1968: *m.* 1914, Mabel, who *d.* 1960, da. of Mrs. Olive, of Casino, Sydney, NSW:—

Paul Anthony (2, Ray St., Bray Park, Murwillumbah, NSW), *b.* 1916; New Guinea and Solomon Islands 1944-45 with AIF: *m.* 1948, Dorothy Mary, da. of R. H. Hogg, of Wahroonga, Cecil Plains, Qld., and has issue living, Paul Anthony Richard, *b.* 1949,—Ross James, *b.* 1959,—Judith Jessie, *b.* 1951.——Gordon Edward (Mooball, NSW), *b.* 1922; formerly AIF: *m.* 1950, Beryl Margaret Mills, and has issue living, Leonard Edward, *b.* 1951,—Kenneth Francis, *b.* 1954,—Stephen Victor, *b.* 1960,—Robyn Joyce, *b.* 1953,—Sharon Lea, *b.* 1966.——John Charles (Mooball, NSW), *b.* 1928: *m.* 1952, Orene Ethel, da. of R. Scott, of Burringbar, NSW, and has issue living, Douglas John, *b.* 1953,—Michael Anthony, *b.* 1961,—Delmoy Orene, *b.* 1955,—Janelle May, *b.* 1957,—Elsie Moree, *b.* 1959,—Shirley Ellen, *b.* 1963.——Florence Mabel, *b.* 1919; a JP: *m.* 1946, Dalley Leslie Griffin, JP, of 15, Napier Cres., N. Ryde, 2113, NSW, and has issue living, David Leslie Paul, *b.* 1947,—Brian Arthur Charles, *b.* 1948; Aust. Forces, Vietnam; a JP: *m.* 1972, Cheryl Trescott, BA, DipEd.,—Elizabeth, Ann, *b.* 1951; SRN.——Nancy, *b.* 1926: *m.* 1946, Nervyn James Carthy, of Myponga, via Adelaide, S. Aust., and has issue living, Terry James, *b.* 1947,—Peter, *b.* 1950; Aust. Forces, Vietnam,—Graeme, *b.* 1956,—Anne, *b.* 1953.

Issue of the late Llewellyn George Irby, *b.* 1883, *d.* 1964: *m.* 1914, Mary Louisa, el. da. of the late Rev. R. W. Stockdale, of Grafton, NSW:—

Kenneth Allan (1, Gibbons St., Wynnard, Tasmania), *b.* 1920; 1939-45 War in Middle East and S. Pacific with RAAF: *m.* 1948, Mary Rushton, da. of the Rev. E. E. Johnson, R. of Carrick, Tas., and has issue living, Philip Anthony Kenelm, *b.* 1951,—Judith Mary, *b.* 1949.——Mary Edith (Rosemary) *b.* 1915: *m.* 1943, George Philip MacDonell, of Hedsor Park, Goulburn, NSW.—— Elspeth Douglas, *b.* 1917, late Sister in Australian Army Nursing Ser.: *m.* 1948, the Rev. Frederick Searle Ingoldsby, ThL, DipRE, of 38, Breakwater Rd., East Geelong, Vic. 3219, Aust., and has issue living, James Douglas, *b.* 1949,—David Llewellyn, *b.* 1954,—Marilyn Margaret, *b.* 1950,—Pamela Jean, *b.* 1952,—Janet Elspeth Irby, *b.* 1959.

Issue of the late Arthur Algernon Irby, *b.* 1890, *d.* 1967: *m.* 1927, Mary Isabel Marsden:—

John, *b.* 1929: *m.* 1949, Peggy May White, who *d.* 1968.——Brian Keith (3, Banyeena Place, Belrose 2085, Sydney, NSW), *b.* 1931: *m.* 1952, June Eve Hutton, and has issue living, Peter Brian Edward, *b.* 1956,—Donna-Elizabeth, *b.* 1953.

Grandsons of the late Edward Irby, 4th son of the late Rev. the Hon. Paul Anthony
Irby, 5th son of 2nd Baron:—
   Issue of the late Charles Augustus Irby, *b.* 1861, *d.* 1941: *m.* 1888, Eva Georgiana,
   dau. of Richard Roberts, of Sydney, N.S. Wales:—
Beverley Keith, *b.* 1899: *m.* 1942, Kathleen Pilley, of Mudgee. *Residence,*—7, Alfred St., Campsie,
NSW.——Richard Wilfred, *b.* 1901: *m.* 1939, Margery McMillan, of Bathurst, Aust., and has issue
living, Jenny Eva, *b.* 1942: *m.* 1964, Raymond Thomas Connell, of 27, Hope St., Penrith, NSW.——
Roland Frank, *b.* 1906: *m.* 1938, Mary Brown. *Residence,*—Kar-Mar, Wallacia, NSW.

Grandson of the late Rev. the Hon. Paul Anthony Irby, 5th son of 2nd Baron:—
   Issue of the late Rev. George Powell Irby, *b.* 1838, *d.* 1910: *m.* 1869, Emma Sarah
   Bransby, who *d.* 1930, dau. of the late John Lewis Aubert, of Nunsbury, Herts:—
Lewis Michael Aubert, *b.* 1882; ed. at Lancing Coll., and at Hertford Coll., Oxford (B.A. 1908);
European War 1916-18 as Lt. RAOC: *m.* 1914, Isabel Kate, who *d.* 1972, da. of the late G. M.
Thornton, and has issue living, Audrey Cynthia Yvette, *b.* 1915: *m.* 1955, Christopher Lucian
Chamberlin, TD, of Withybed Cottage, Butleigh Wotton, Glastonbury,—Beryl Diana Noel, *b.* 1919:
m. 1951, Henry John Bunting, of Exeter Villa, Cranham Rd., Cheltenham, and has issue living,
George Irby *b.* 1952: *m.* 1974, Julia Angela Davey, James Walter Irby *b.* 1954, Edward Irby *b.* 1959,
Richard Irby *b.* 1962. *Residence,*—Sandown Lawn, Albert Rd., Cheltenham.

PREDECESSORS.—[1] EDWARD Irby, son of the late Anthony Irby ; M.P. for Boston; cr. a
   Baronet 1704; *d.* 1718; *s.* by his son [2] *Sir* WILLIAM, *M.P.*, 2nd Bt., Lord Chamberlain 1761;
   cr. Baron Boston (peerage of Great Britain) 1761 ; *d.* 1775; *s.* by his son [3] FREDERICK,
   D.C.L., 2nd Baron, for fifty years a Lord of the Bedchamber to George III.; *d.* 1825 ; *s.* by
   his son [4] GEORGE, 3rd Baron ; *b.* 1777 ; *d.* 1856 ; *s.* by his son [5] GEORGE IVES, 4th
   Baron ; *b.* 1802 ; *d.* 1869 : *m.* 1st, 1830, Fanny Elizabeth, who *d.* 1860, dau. of W. R. Hopkins-
   Northey ; 2ndly, 1861, the Hon. Caroline Amelia, who *d.* 1927, dau. of 3rd Baron de Saumarez ;
   d. 1869; *s.* by his son [6] FLORANCE GEORGE HENRY, 5th Baron; *b.* 1837: *m.* 1859, the Hon.
   Augusta Caroline, who *d.* 1929, dau. of 3rd Baron de Saumarez: *d.* 1877; *s.* by his son [7]
   GEORGE FLORANCE, 6th Baron; *b.* 1860; a Lord-in-Waiting to H.M. Queen Victoria 1885-6;
   m. 1890, Cecilia Constance, who *d.* 1938, dau. of the late Hon. Augustus Anthony Frederick
   Irby ; *d.* 1941; *s.* by his nephew [8] GREVILLE NORTHEY (son of the late Hon. Cecil Saumarez
   Irby, 2nd son of 5th Baron); *b.* 1889; Hon. Capt. (retired) Oxford and Bucks L.I. ; sometime
   Principal in Colonial Office: *m.* 1st, 1913, Constance Beryl, who *d.* 1969, da. of the late William
   Richard Lester, of Alderley, Llandudno; 2ndly, 1954, Irene Frances, da. of the late Francis Holt, of
   Ewell, Surrey, and widow of Harry Mills; *d.* 1958; *s.* by his brother [9] CECIL EUSTACE, *MC*, 8th
   Baron, *b.* 1897, *d.* 1972; *s.* by his kinsman [10] GERALD HOWARD BOTELER, *MBE* (el. son of Lt.-Col.
   Leonard Paul Irby, OBE, son of Lt.-Col. Leonard Howard Loyd Irby, son of Rear-Adm. the Hon.
   Frederick Paul Irby, CB, 2nd son of 2nd Baron), 9th Baron, and present peer.

BOURNE, BARON. (Bourne.) [Life Baron 1964.]

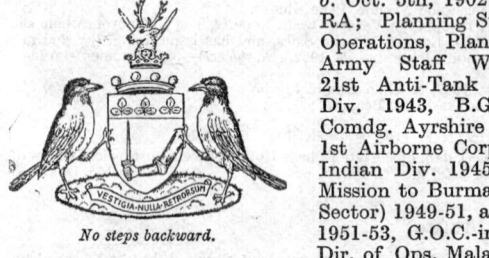

No steps backward.

GEOFFREY KEMP BOURNE, *GCB, KBE,
CMG*, son of the late Col. Walter Kemp
Bourne, OBE, of Kettlethorns, Sway, Hants.;
b. Oct. 5th, 1902; ed. at Rugby; Gen. late
RA; Planning Staff, London 1939-41, Brig.
Operations, Plans and Intelligence British
Army Staff Washington 1942, Comdg.
21st Anti-Tank Regt., Guards Armoured
Div. 1943, B.G.S., S.-E. Asia 1943-44,
Comdg. Ayrshire Yeo. in Italy 1944, B.G.S.
1st Airborne Corps. 1945, C.R.A., GOC 5th
Indian Div. 1945-46, Head of British Sers.
Mission to Burma 1948, GOC Berlin (British
Sector) 1949-51, and 16th Airborne Div. (TA)
1951-53, G.O.C.-in-C. E. Command 1953-54,
Dir. of Ops. Malaya 1954-56, C.-in-C. MELF
1957, and Comdt. Imperial Defence Coll.
1958-59; Col. Comdt. RA 1954-67; Hon. Col.
10th Bn. Parachute Regt. TA 1960-65; Chm. National Building Agency 1967;
Officer of American Legion of Merit. American Silver Star; *cr.* OBE (Mil) 1942,
CBE (Mil) 1947, CB (Mil) 1949, CMG 1952, KBE (Mil) 1954, KCB (Mil) 1957,
GCB (Mil) 1960, and *Baron Bourne,* of Atherstone, co. Warwick (Life Baron)
1964: *m.* 1928, Agnes Evelyn, da. of the late Sir (William) Ernest Thompson,
and has issue.

Arms—Azure issuant from the sinister flank a dexter arm embowed in armour the hand grasping
a sword erect proper hilt and pomel or on a chief argent three strawberry leaves proper. Crest—Out
of a coronet or in front of two swords in saltire as in the arms a stag's head proper. Supporters—On
either side a magpie proper.

Residence,—Drove House, Cranborne, Dorset.   *Club,*—Army and Navy.

SON LIVING.
Hon. Michael Kemp (Chrishall Grange, Heydon, Royston, Herts.), *b.* 1937: *m.* 1963, Penelope Jane, da.
of Capt. H. W. Blyth, of Melgund Glen, Minto, Hawick, Roxburghshire, and has issue.

DAUGHTER LIVING.
Hon. Elizabeth Anne, (c/o Barclays Bank, High St., Salisbury, Wilts.), *b.* 1931: *m.* 1952, Ian McKay
Robertson, Maj. Gordon Highlanders, and has issue.

BOWDEN, BARON. (Bowden.) [Life Baron, 1963.]

BERTRAM VIVIAN BOWDEN, son of B. C. Bowden, of Chesterfield; *b.* Jan.
18th, 1910, ed. at Chesterfield Gram. Sch., at Emmanuel Coll., Camb. (M.A.,
PhD), and at Univ. of Amsterdam; FIEE, and MSc Tech; Physics
Master, Liverpool Collegiate Sch. 1935-37, Ch. Physics Master, Oundle
Sch. 1937-40, Radar Research in England 1940-43, and in U.S.A. 1943-46,
Sir Robert Watson Watt and Partners 1947-50, and Ferranti Ltd., Manchester
(Digital Computers) 1950-53; Prin., Manchester Coll. of Science and Tech-
nology and Dean of the Faculty of Technology, Manchester Univ. 1953-64;
Chm. of Electronics Research Council, Min. of Aviation 1960-64, Pres. of The

Science Master's Assocn. 1962; and Min. of State, Department of Education and Science 1964-65; Prin. of Univ. of Manchester Inst. of Science and Technology since 1966; author of " Faster than Thought ", and " The Development of Manchester College of Science and Technology ", and a contributor to *The New Scientist* and other journals; *cr. Baron Bowden,* of Chesterfield, co. Derby [Life Baron] 1963: *m.* 1st, 1939 (m. diss. 1954), Marjorie Browne, who *d.* 1956; 2ndly, 1967, Mary, who *d.* 1971, da. of the late Bernard Whitman Maltby, of Ilkeston; 3rdly, 1974, Phyllis, da. of Stanley Ernest Myson, and widow of John Henry Lewis James, and has issue by 1st m.

Residence,—Pine Croft, Stanhope Rd., Bowdon, Ches.

SON LIVING. (*By 1st m.*)

Hon. Robin, *b.* 1945; ed. at Old Swinford Hosp. Sch., and at Loughborough Coll. of Advanced Technology.

DAUGHTERS LIVING. (*By 1st m.*)

Hon. Mary, *b.* 1940; teacher of deaf children: *m.* 1964, Dr. Roger George Davey (Box 582, 95, Oakland Av., Hudson Heights, J0P 1JO, Quebec, Canada), and has issue.

Hon. Virginia, *b.* 1943; ed. at E. Anglian Girls' Sch., and at Reading and Manchester Univs.: *m.* 1967, David Ian Murray, of 61, Woburn Drive, Hale, Cheshire, and has issue.

BOWLES, BARONY OF. (Bowles.) [Extinct 1970.]

WIDOW LIVING OF LIFE BARON.

KATHLEEN AMY (*Baroness Bowles*), (88, St. James's St., SW1A 1PW); BA Manchester Univ.; el. da. of the late Edward Hugh Musgrove, and widow of Air Commodore Edward Donald McLulich Hopkins: *m.* 1950, Baron Bowles (Life Peer), who *d.* 1970.

BOYD-CARPENTER, BARON. (Boyd-Carpenter.) [Life Baron 1972.]

JOHN ARCHIBALD BOYD-CARPENTER, *PC,* only son of the late Maj. Sir Archibald Boyd-Carpenter, MP, River House, Walton-on-Thames; *b.* June 2nd, 1908; ed. at Stowe and Balliol Coll., Oxford (BA), Diploma Econ.; Pres. of Oxford Union 1930; Bar. Middle Temple 1934; Financial Sec., Treasury 1951-54, Min. of Transport and Civil Aviation 1954-55, Min. of Pensions and Nat. Insurance 1955-62, Ch. Sec., Treasury and Paymaster Gen. 1962-64, and Chm. Public Accounts Cttee. 1964-70; Chm. Orion Insurance Co. 1968-72, and CLRP Investment Trust 1969-72, and formerly a Dir. of other cos.; appointed High Steward of Roy. Borough of Kingston upon Thames 1972; a DL of Greater London 1973; 1939-45 War served Scots Gds., Maj. 1943); MP for Kingston upon Thames (*C*) 1945-72; Chm. of Civil Aviation Authority since 1972; *cr.* PC Aviation Authority since 1972; *cr.* PC 1954, and *Baron Boyd-Carpenter,* of Crux Easton, co. Southampton (Life Baron) 1972: *m.* 1937, Margaret Mary, da. of the late Lt.-Col. George Leslie Hall, OBE, RE (ret.) [E. Coventry, colls.], and has issue.

Arms,—Not exemplified at time of going to press.

Residences,—12, Eaton Terr, SW1; Crux Easton House, Crux Easton, Highclere, Hants. *Clubs,*—Carlton, Farmers'.

SON LIVING.

Hon. Thomas Patrick John, *MBE,* (Sun Hill Farm, Chieveley, Newbury, Berks.), *b.* 1938; Lt.-Col. Scots Gds.; MBE (Mil) 1973: *m.* 1972, Mary Jean, da. of John Elwes Duffield, BM, BCh, of The Tithe House, Church St., Marcham, Berks, and has issue.

DAUGHTERS LIVING.

Hon. Anne Mary, *b.* 1942.

Hon. Sarah Elizabeth Mary, *b.* 1946: *m.* 1968, the Hon. Douglas Martin Hogg, of 11, Mallord St. SW3 [see B. Hailsham of St. Marylebone].

BOYD OF MERTON, VISCOUNT. (Lennox-Boyd.) [Viscount U.K. 1960.]

ALAN TINDAL LENNOX-BOYD, C.H., P.C., 1st Viscount, son of Alan Walter Lennox-Boyd; b. Nov. 18th, 1904; ed. at Sherborne, and at Ch. Ch., Oxford; was Parliamentary Sec. to Min. of Labour 1938-39, to Min. of Home Security 1939, to Min. of Food 1939-40, and to Min. of Aircraft Production 1943-45, Min. of State for Colonial Affairs 1951-2, Min. of Transport and Civil Aviation 1952-4, and Sec. of State for the Colonies 1954-9; European War 1940-43 as Lieut. R.N.V.R.; sat as M.P. for Mid. Div. of Bedfordshire (C) Oct. 1931 to July 1960; cr. P.C. 1951, and Viscount Boyd of Merton, of Merton-in-Penninghame, co. Wigtown (peerage of United Kingdom) 1960: m. 1938, Lady Patricia Florence Susan Guinness, dau. of 2nd Earl of Iveagh, and has issue.

Arms,—Azure a fess chequy argent and gules, between an abbatical mitre simplex of the second filleted of the third in chief, and in base a rose of the second, seeded vert and barbed of the third Crest,—A dexter hand erect in pale, having two fingers turned in and the rest pointing upwards proper the wrist habited in a close sleeve azure, with cuff chequy argent and gules. Supporters,—Two squirrels proper, having collars chequy argent and gules.

Residences,—6, Iveagh House, Ormond Yard, St. James's, SW1; Ince Castle, Saltash, Cornwall. Clubs,—Carlton, Pratt's, Buck's, RNVR., and Royal Yacht Squadron.

SONS LIVING.

Hon. SIMON DONALD RUPERT NEVILLE, b. Dec. 7th, 1939; ed. at Eton, and at Ch. Ch., Oxford: m. 1962, Alice Mary, dau. of the late Maj. Mersey George Dallas Clive [see E. Longford], and has issue living, Benjamin Alan, b. 1964,—Edward George, b. 1968,—Charlotte Mary, b. 1963,—Philippa Patricia, b. 1970. Residences,—4, Eaton Close, SW1; Wivelscombe, Saltash, Cornwall.
Hon. Christopher Alan, b. 1941; ed. at Eton, and Ch. Ch., Oxford.
Hon. Mark Alexander (11, Cavendish Av., NW8), b. 1943; ed. at Eton, and Ch. Ch., Oxford; Bar. Inner Temple 1968: m. 1974, Mrs. Arabella Lacloche, only da. of Piero Parisi, of Rome.

BOYD-ORR, BARONY OF (Orr.) [Extinct 1971.]

DAUGHTERS LIVING OF FIRST BARON.

Hon. Elizabeth Joan Boyd, b. 1916 : m. 1944, Lieut.-Col. Kenneth Alfred John Barton, and has issue living, Robert John Orr, b. 1944,—Kenneth Callum Orr, b. 1949,—Elizabeth Jill Orr, b. 1947. Residence,—Brathinch, Brechin, Angus.
Hon. Helen Anne Boyd, b. 1919: m. 1939, David Miles Lubbock [see B. Avebury, colls.]. Residence,—Farnell, Brechin, Angus.

WIDOW LIVING OF FIRST BARON.

ELIZABETH, (Baroness Boyd-Orr), (Newton of Stracathro, Brechin, Angus), da. of the late John Callum, of West Kilbride: m. 1915, the 1st Baron, who d. 1971, when the title became ext.

Boyle, Viscount, son of Earl of Shannon.

BOYLE OF HANDSWORTH, BARON, (Boyle.) [Life Baron 1970, Bt. UK 1904]

EDWARD CHARLES GURNEY BOYLE, PC. Life Baron, and 3rd Baronet; b. Aug. 31st, 1923; s. to Baronetcy 1945; ed. at Eton, and Ch. Ch. Oxford (Scholar); Hon. LLD Leeds, Southampton, Bath, and Sussex; Hon DSc Aston; PPS to Under-Sec. of State for Air 1951-52, to Parl. Sec. to Min. of Defence 1952-54, and to Min. of Supply 1954-55, Econ. Sec. to the Treasury 1955-56, Parl. Sec. to Min. of Educ. 1957-59, Financial Sec. to the Treas. 1959-62, and Min. of Educ. 1962-64, and Min. of State for Educ. and Science April to Oct. 1964; MP for Handsworth Div. of Birmingham (C) 1950-70; Vice-Chancellor of Leeds Univ., a Trustee of British Museum since 1970, and Chm. Top Salaries Review Body since 1971; a Representative on High Council of European Univ. Inst. at Florence 1973; cr. PC 1962, and Baron Boyle of Handsworth, of Salehurst, co. Sussex (Life Baron) 1970.

Arms—Per bend raguly gules and argent, two staves raguly in bend counterchanged. Crest,— In front of a lion's head couped argent, a staff fessewise gules. Supporters,—Dexter, an owl proper; Sinister, a lion argent.
Residence,—The Vice-Chancellor's Lodge, Grosvenor Rd., Leeds, 6.
Clubs,—Carlton, Pratt's.

In remainder to Baronetcy only.

BROTHER LIVING.

RICHARD GURNEY (Kemps Cottage, Hare St., nr. Buntingford, Herts.), *b.* May 14th, 1930: *m.* 1961, Elizabeth Ann, yr. da. of Norman Dennes, of Middle Green, Poulshot, Devizes.

SISTER LIVING.

Ann Constance Beatrice, *b.* 1926: *m.* 1948, Jack Brunner Gold [Brunner, Bt.], of 234, Kew Rd., Richmond, Surrey.

PREDECESSORS.—[1] EDWARD Boyle, *MP, KC,* son of Edward O'Boyle, CE, of London, *b.* 1848; a Dir. of London and India Docks and Imperial Life Office; MP for Taunton (C) 1906-9; cr. a Baronet 1904; *d.* 1909; *s.* by his only son [2] ELWARD, 2nd Bt., *b.* 1878; High Sheriff of Sussex 1927; *d.* 1945; *s.* by his el. son [3] EDWARD CHARLES GURNEY, *PC,* 3rd Bt.; cr. *Baron Boyle of Handsworth,* of Salehurst, co. Sussex (Life Baron) 1970.

Boyle of Marston, Baron, title of Earl of Cork and Orrery on Roll of H. L.

BOYNE, VISCOUNT. (Hamilton-Russell.) Sits as BARON BRANCEPETH.
(U.K. 1866)   [Viscount I. 1717.]

NEC TIMEO NEC SPERNO

I neither fear nor despise.

GUSTAVUS MICHAEL GEORGE HAMILTON-RUSSELL, 10th Viscount; *b.* Dec. 10th, 1931 ; *s.* 1942 ; ed. at Eton ; Lieut. (ret.) Grenadier Guards, a JP and DL for Salop: *m.* 1956, Rosemary Anne, dau. of Sir Denis Frederick Bankes Stucley, 5th Bt., and has issue.

Arms,—Quarterly: 1st and 4th argent, between two chevronels a cinquefoil, the whole between three cross crosslets fitchée sable, *Russell;* 2nd and 3rd gules, three cinquefoils pierced ermine, *Hamilton.* Crests,—1st, a goat passant argent, collared gemelle, and charged on the body with an escallop sable, *Russell;* 2nd, out of a ducal crown or, an oak tree fructed proper, and penetrated transversely in the main stem by a frame-saw proper, the frame gold, above the motto, "Through," *Hamilton.* Supporters,—Two mermaids proper, hair dishevelled or, each holding in the exterior hand a mirror, of the last.

Seat,—Burwarton, Bridgnorth, Salop. *Club,* —Turf.

SON LIVING.

Hon. GUSTAVUS MICHAEL STUCLEY, *b.* May 27th, 1965.

DAUGHTERS LIVING.

Hon. Caroline Veronica, *b.* 1957.
Hon. Sara Emma, *b.* 1959.
Hon. Lucy Jane, *b.* 1961.

UNCLE LIVING. *(Son of 9th Viscount.)*

Hon. Richard Gustavus, *DSO, b.* 1909; ed. at Eton; Brig. late 17th/21st Lancers; a Member of HM's Bodyguard of Hon. Corps of Gentlemen-at-Arms since 1956; High Sheriff of Yorks. 1968, and a DL since 1973; 1939-45 War in N. Africa and Italy (DSO and Bar); DSO 1943 (Bar 1944): *m.* 1939, the Hon. Pamela Penelope Cayzer, da. of 1st Baron Rotherwick, and has issue living, Brian Gustavus (c/o C. Hoare & Co., 37, Fleet St., EC4), *b.* 1940; ed. at Eton; Maj. 17th/21st Lancers: *m.* 1967, Lea, only da. of Col. Noel Wild, of Shelley Court, Tite St., Chelsea, and has issue living, Henry William Gustavus *b.* 1969,—Richard Desmond (Old Lordship Farmhouse, Much Hadham, Herts.), *b.* 1943; ed. at Eton; late 2nd Lt. 17th/21st Lancers: *m.* 1965, Prudence Sophia, da. of the late Maj. R. P. Pockney, of The Old Barn, Bishopthorpe, York, and has issue living, Charles Richard *b.* 1965, Emma Sophia *b.* 1968, Katharine Roseanna *b.* 1972,—Veronica Anne, *b.* 1949: *m.* 1971, Nicholas Michael Houssemayne Jones, of 6, Cheyne Row, SW3 5HL. *Residences,*—Smeaton Manor, Northallerton, Yorks.; 42, Cranmer Court, Sloane Av., SW3.

AUNT LIVING. *(Daughter of 9th Viscount.)*

Hon. Rosemary Katharine *(Lady Forbes), b.* 1921: *m.* 1942, the 23rd Lord Forbes. *Residences,*— Balforbes, Alford, Aberdeenshire; Castle Forbes, Alford, Aberdeenshire.

WIDOW LIVING OF NINTH VISCOUNT.

MARGARET SELINA *(Dowager Viscountess Boyne), C.B.E., LL.D.,* dau. of 5th Earl of Harewood; Hon. LL.D. Leeds 1951 ; is a D.G.St.J., a J.P., and an Alderman of Salop Co. Council; C.B.E. (Civil) 1920; *m.* 1906, the 9th Viscount, who *d.* 1942. *Residence,*—Dower House, Burwarton, nr. Bridgnorth.

COLLATERAL BRANCHES LIVING.

Issue of the late Major the Hon. John Hamilton-Russell, MC, 3rd son of 9th Viscount, *b.* 1911, *d.* (on active ser. during 1939-45 War) 1943: *m.* 1937, Lady Diana Legge [who *d.* 1970, having *m.* 2ndly, 1946, Lt.-Col. A. L. Matthews], da. of 7th Earl of Dartmouth:—

James Gustavus (c/o C. Hoare & Co., 37, Fleet St., EC4), *b.* 1938; ed. at Eton; Maj. Household Cavalry: *m.* 1965, Alison, da. of Dr. Sydney Haydn Heard, MBE, of Albecq, Guernsey, and has issue living, Mark John Gustavus *b.* 1969, Edward Haydn James (twin) *b.* 1969, Julia Mary *b.* 1967.

Issue of the late Hon. Claud Eustace Hamilton-Russell, 4th son of 8th Viscount, *b.* 1871, *d.* 1948: *m.* 1899, Maria Lindsay, who *d.* 1963, el. dau. of Sir Lindsay Wood, 1st Bt. (ext.):—

Edric Claud, *b.* 1904: ed. at Eton, and Trin. Coll., Camb. (BA); Mining Engineer (ret.): *m.* 1932, Helen Rosa, dau. of the late William Humble, of Skellow Grange, Doncaster, and has issue living, Ann Katharine, *b.* 1933: *m.* 1953, Lt.-Col. William Frank Philip Currie, Queen's R. Irish Hussars and has issue living, Richard William *b.* 1955, Joanna *b.* 1959. *Residence,*—Shildon Grange, Corbridge, Northumberland.——Jean Katharine, *b.* 1907: *m.* 1931, Lt.-Col. Arthur Heywood Lonsdale, CBE, MC, Grenadier Guards [B. Hamilton of Dalzell], and has issue living, John Henry (Tittenley, Market Drayton, Salop), *b.* 1935: *m.* 1966 (m. diss. 1973), Amalia Clare, da. of Maj. F. John Yates, of The Wood, Codsall Wood, Wolverhampton,—Timothy Claud (The Old Laundry, Shavington, Market Drayton, Salop), *b.* 1937: *m.* 1964, Jennifer Elizabeth, only da. of William Beck, of Tabley Grange, Knutsford, Ches., and has issue living, William Pemberton *b.* 1970, Nichola Caroline *b.* 1966. *Residence,*—Shavington Grange, Market Drayton, Salop.

Issue of the late Major the Hon. Arthur Hamilton-Russell, 5th son of 8th Viscount, *b.* 1872, *d.* 1951: *m.* 1905, Marion Lilias, who *d.* 1934, dau. of the late Henry Harris, of Steventon, Whitchurch, Hants:—

David Henry Gustavus, b. 1911 : m. 1950, Pauline Albinia, dau. of the late George Penkivil Slade, K.C., of St. Michaels, Painswick, Gloucestershire, and has issue living, Marion Albinia, b. 1952, —Georgiana Mary, b. 1955,—Annette Katharine, b. 1958,—Margaret Louisa, b. 1960. *Residences,—* 7, Morland Close, Hampstead Way, NW11; Yew Tree Cottage, Little Gaddesden, Berkhamsted, Herts.

Issue of the late Hon. Eustace Scott Hamilton-Russell, O.B.E., 6th son of 8th Viscount, b. 1878, d. 1962: m. 1906, Olive Mary, who d. 1951, dau. of Col. Francis Alexander Wolryche-Whitmore, formerly 3rd Batn. Shropshire L.I., of Dudmaston, Bridgnorth, Salop:—
Rachel Katharine (*Lady Labouchere*), b. 1908: m. 1st, 1930, Malcolm Findanus MacGregor, from whom she obtained a divorce 1940 [see MacGregor of MacGregor, Bt., colls.]; 2ndly, 1943, Sir George Peter Labouchere, GBE, KCMG, of Dudmaston, Bridgnorth, Salop.

Grandchildren of the late Henry Augustus Hamilton-Cox (infra):—
Issue of the late William Hamilton-Cox, b. 1884, d. 19—: m. 1910, Caroline, da. of the late William Colling:—
Walter (2209, 2nd St., Peru, Illinois, USA), b. 1915; a Horologist: m. 1938, Lola, da. of Clarence Bradley, and has issue living, Carolyn Jane, b. 1940,—Linda Jean, b. 1947.——Louise Rose, b. 1917: m. 1942, Clinton Charlton King, Horologist, of 2523, 7th St., Peru, Illinois, USA, and has issue living, James Hamilton, b. 1944.

Granddaughter of the late William John Hamilton-Cox, son of the late Henry Hamilton-Cox, son of the late Joshua Hamilton, 2nd son of the late Hon. Henry Hamilton, M.P., 3rd son of 1st Viscount :—
Issue of the late Henry Augustus Hamilton-Cox, b. 1841, d. 1890: m. 1878, Rose, Josephine, who d. 1922, dau. of Johann Hofmarksrichter :—
Teresa Rebecca, b. 1880: m. 1906, Arthur Stanley Bayne, Dr. of Dental Surgery, who d. 1951, and has issue living, Paula Teresa, b. 1907: m. 1928, Maj. Floyd Albert Spencer, PhD, US Army, and Author, and has issue living, Philip Gordon Hamilton Spencer b. 1929,—Beulah Margaret, b. 1917: m. 1940, Richard Carleton Clay, and has issue living, Richard Bayne b. 1941, Curtis Arthur b. 1948, Robert Bruce b. 1949. *Residence,—*

Grandchildren of the late Sackville Berkeley Hamilton, el. son of Sackville Deane Hamilton, grandson of the Rt. Hon. Sackville Hamilton, 3rd son of the Hon. Henry Hamilton, MP (ante):—
Issue of the late Col. Sackville William Sackville Hamilton, D.S.O., M.B.E., b. 1882, d. 1956: m. 1920, Margaret Dowell (of 4, Pagoda Avenue, Richmond, Surrey), dau. of S. C. Hester, of Laleham, Isle of Thanet :—
James Berkeley Sackville (Acklam Grange, Acklam, Malton, Yorks.), b. 1923; ed. at King's Coll., Camb. (MA); Lt.-Col. RE (ret.): m. 1947, Mary Grizel, da. of the late Col. Cecil Alexander Boyle, CIE, DSO [see E. Glasgow, colls.], and has issue living, Charles Patrick Sackville, b. 1949,—Andrew James Sackville, b. 1951,—Nigel Ruaraidh Sackville, b. 1953,—Patricia Margaret Sackville, b. 1956. ——Anne Margaret Sackville, b. 1925; MA Camb.: m. 1950, David MacEwen, and has issue living, Diana Cushla, b. 1951,—Helen Margaret, b. 1953,—Penelope Anne Georgina, b. 1965. *Residence,—*North Leigh Lodge, Colehill, Wimborne, Dorset.

Issue of the late Maj. Charles Sackville Hamilton, b. 1885, d. 1971: m. 1918, Averina Jane (Reena), who d. 1973, da. of Richardson Oliver of Kil-na-Mulla, Buttevant, co. Cork:—
Averina Rachel Grace Sackville, b. 1923: m. 1951, Colin Oliver Hargreave, of The Willows, Lytham, Lans., and has issue living, Jeremy David Hamilton, b. 1955.——Patricia May Sackville, b. 1924; ARCA: m. 1948, Lt. Derek Richard Spooner, RN, of The Manor House, Martin, Fordingbridge, Hants., and has issue living, Richard Hamilton, b. 1952.——Jane Rosemary Eleanor, b. 1955.

PREDECESSORS.—[1] Gustavus Hamilton, *P.C.*, son of the Hon. Sir Frederick Hamilton K.B., youngest son of 1st Lord Paisley [D. Abercorn], a distinguished military commander and M.P. for co. Donegal 1703, was cr. *Baron Hamilton,* of Stackallan 1715, and *Viscount Boyne* 1717 (peerage of Ireland); d. 1723; s. by his grandson [2] Gustavus, *P.C.*, 2nd Viscount; sat as M.P. for Newport, I. of W., 1735; d. unmarried 1746; s. by his cousin [3] Frederick, 3rd Viscount; d. s. p. 1772; s. by his brother [4] Richard, 4th Viscount; d. 1789; s. by his son [5] Gustavus, 5th Viscount; d. 1826: s. by his son [6] Gustavus, 6th Viscount; d. 1855; s. by his son [7] Gustavus Frederick, 7th Viscount, b. 1797; assumed by Roy. licence the additional surname of Russell, and was cr. *Baron Brancepeth* (peerage of United Kingdom) 1866: m. 1828, Emma Maria, dau. of Matthew Russell, M.P., of Brancepeth Castle; d. 1870; s. by his son [8] Gustavus Russell, 8th Viscount, b. 1830: m. 1858, Lady Katherine Frances Scott, who d. 1903, dau. of 2nd Earl of Eldon; d. 1907; s. by his son [9] Gustavus William, 9th Viscount, b. 1864: m. 1906, Lady Margaret Selina Lascelles, C.B.E., dau. of 5th Earl of Harewood; d. 1942; s. by his grandson [10] Gustavus Michael George (son of the late Hon. Gustavus Lascelles Hamilton-Russell, Lieut. Grenadier Guards (el. son of 9th Viscount), who d. (killed in action during European War) 1940), 10th Viscount and present peer; also Baron Hamilton of Stackallan, and Baron Brancepeth.

BRABAZON OF TARA, BARON. (Moore-Brabazon.) [Baron U.K. 1942.]

My life is vowed

Ivon Anthony Moore-Brabazon, 3rd Baron, b. Dec. 20th, 1946; s. 1974; ed. at Harrow; an Underwriting Member of London Stock Exchange.

Arms,—Quarterly; 1st and 4th gules on a bend or three martlets sable, *Brabazon;* 2nd and 3rd azure on a chief per pale argent and or three mullets gules, *Moore.* *Crests,*—1st a falcon rising, belled or, *Brabazon;* 2nd issuant from a coronet composed of eight mullets set upon a rim or a Moor's head and shoulders proper wreathed about the temples argent and azure, *Moore.* *Supporters,*—On either side a gull volant over water supporting the shield with its beak all proper.
Residences,—24, Sloane Gdns., SW1; The Watch House, Bembridge, Isle of Wight. *Clubs,*—White's, City of London.

WIDOW LIVING OF FIRST BARON.

HILDA MARY (*Hilda, Baroness Brabazon of Tara*) (of Ridgemount Cottage, Sunningdale, Berks.), da. of Charles Henry Krabbé, of Buenos Aires: *m.* 1906, the 1st Baron, who *d.* 1964.

WIDOW LIVING OF SECOND BARON.

HENRIETTA MARY (*Baroness Brabazon of Tara*), (The Watch House, Bembridge, Isle of Wight), da. of the late Sir (Alfred) Rowland Clegg, and widow of Ivor Krabbe: *m.* 1939, the 2nd Baron, who *d.* 1974.

PREDECESSORS.—[1] JOHN THEODORE CUTHBERT Moore-Brabazon, *GBE, MC, PC,* son of Col. Arthur Henry Moore-Brabazon, of Tara Hall, co. Meath; *b.* 1884; pioneer in aviation; made first flight by any Briton in Great Britain 1909; received first pilot's certificate issued by Roy. Aero Club; P.P.S. to Sec. of State for Air 1919-21, Parl. Sec., Min of Transport 1923-27, Min. of Transport 1940-41, and Min. of Aircraft Production 1941-42; M.P. for Chatham Div. of Rochester (*U*) 1918-29, and for Wallasey 1931-42; cr. *Baron Brabazon of Tara,* of Sandwich, co. Kent (peerage of U.K.) 1942: *m.* 1906, Hilda Mary, da. of Charles Henry Krabbé, of Buenos Aires; *d.* 1964, *s.* by his el. son [2] DEREK CHARLES, *CBE,* 2nd Baron, *b.* 1910; Member of London Stock Exchange; Chm. S. Kensington Conservative Assocn. 1952-54, and Pres. Kensington Conservative Assocn. 1966-74: *m.* 1939, Henrietta Mary, da. of the late Sir (Alfred) Rowland Clegg, and widow of Ivor Krabbe; *d.* 1974; *s.* by his only son [3] IVON ANTHONY, 3rd Baron and present peer.

BRABOURNE, BARON. (Knatchbull.) [Baron U.K. 1880, Bt. E. 1641.]

[Title pronounced "Braybn."]

My glory is in the cross

JOHN ULICK KNATCHBULL, 7th Baron, and 16th Baronet ; *b.* Nov. 9th, 1924 ; *s.* 1943 ; ed. at Eton and at Oxford Univ. ; a Film and Television Producer; formerly Capt. Coldstream Guards; 1939-45 War in S.-E. Asia (wounded): *m.* 1946, Lady Patricia Edwina Victoria Mountbatten, el. da. of 1st Earl Mountbatten of Burma, and has issue.

Arms,—Quarterly: 1st and 4th argent, on a mount vert, two boars' erect, respecting each other sable, their forelegs resting against an oak tree proper, *Hugessen*; 2nd and 3rd azure, three cross crosslets fitchée between two bendlets or, *Knatchbull.* **Crests,**—1st, an oak tree proper, between two wings elevated, pinions azure, feathered or, *Hugessen*; 2nd, on a chapeau azure, turned up ermine, an ounce statant argent, spotted sable, *Knatchbull.* **Supporters**— On either side a leopard argent pelletty, gorged with an oak wreath vert, fructed gold, and holding in the mouth a cross crosslet fitchée or.

Residences,—Newhouse, Mersham, Ashford, Kent; 39 Montpelier Walk, S.W.7.

SONS LIVING.

Hon. NORTON LOUIS PHILIP, *b.* Oct. 8th, 1947; ed. at Gordonstoun, and Univ. of Kent.

Hon. Michael John Ulick, *b.* 1950; ed. at Gordonstoun, and Reading Univ.

Hon. Philip Wyndham Ashley, *b.* 1961.
Hon. Nicholas Timothy Charles, *b.* 1964.
Hon. Timothy Nicholas Sean, (twin), *b.* 1964.

DAUGHTERS LIVING.

Hon. Joanna Edwina Doreen, *b.* 1955.
Hon. Amanda Patricia Victoria, *b.* 1957.

GREAT-UNCLE LIVING. (*Son of 1st Baron.*)

Hon. Adrian Norton KNATCHBULL-HUGESSEN. Q.C., *b.* 1891; ed. at Eton, and at McGill Univ., Montreal; Bar. Quebec 1914, and a K.C. 1931; LL.D. 1961; European War 1916-18 in France and Belgium (two medals); a Member of Senate of Canada 1937-67: *m.* 1922, Margaret Cecilia Ross, da. of George Herrick Duggan, of 3,636, McTavish St., Montreal, and has issue living, Andrew John, *b.* 1926: *m.* 1952, Jane Frances, da. of Douglas Gilfillan Currie, of Montreal, Canada, and has issue living, Brian Andrew *b.* 1954, John *b.* 1958, Wendy Jane (twin) *b.* 1954, Martha *b.* 1960, —James Cornelius (17, Forden Av., Montreal), *b.* 1933; ed. at Balliol Coll., Oxford, and at McGill Univ., Montreal; Bar. Quebec 1958; Puisne Judge of Superior Court and Court of Queen's Bench, Quebec since 1972: *m.* 1958, Mary Rosamond, da. of R. Ewart *b.* 1965, Ross Adrian *b.* 1969, Kathleen Jill *b.* 1960, Alicia Mary *b.* 1962,—Mary Cecelia, *b.* 1929: *m.* 1955, Stephen John Keynes, of 16, Canonbury Park South, N1, yr. son of Sir Geoffrey Langdon Keynes, and has issue living, Gregory Robert Edward *b.* 1956, Toby William *b.* 1959, Zachary Edmund *b.* 1962, Elizabeth Harriet *b.* 1957, Martha Paganel *b.* 1961. *Residence,*—4306, Montrose Av., Westmount, Montreal 6, Canada. *Clubs,*— University (Montreal), Rideau (Ottawa).

WIDOW LIVING OF FIFTH BARON.

DOREEN GERALDINE, *C.I.* (*Dowager Baroness Brabourne*), dau. of the 6th Marquess of Sligo; is a D.St.J.; was Dep. Vice-Chm. of Overseas League 1953-6 : O.I. 1937 : *m.* 1919, the 5th Baron, who *d.* 1939. *Residence,*—64, Kingston House North, Knightsbridge, SW7.

COLLATERAL BRANCHES LIVING.

Grandchildren of the Hon. Adrian Norton KNATCHBULL-HUGESSEN, Q.C., (ante),
3rd son of 1st Baron, *b.* 1891 : *m.* 1922, Margaret Cecilia Ross, dau. of George
Herrick Duggan, of 3636, McTavish Street, Montreal, Canada :—

Issue of the late Edward Herrick KNATCHBULL-HUGESSEN, *b.* 1923, *d.* 1955 : *m.* 1947, Mary
Louise, who *d.* 1969, da. of Walter Asahel Newton, of Montreal:—

Kenneth Norton, *b.* 1949: *m.* 1969, Karen, da. of Olaf Wolff, of Montreal, and has issue living, Arlo
Edward, *b.* 1970.——Kathleen Mary, *b.* 1950.——Patricia Margaret, *b.* 1952.

(*In remainder to Baronetcy only.*)

Granddaughters of the late Rev. Reginald Bridges Knatchbull-Hugessen (infra):—

Issue of the late Major Everard Knatchbull-Hugessen ; *b.* 1871 ; *d.* 1946 : *m.* 1908, Grace
Marshall, who *d.* 1937, dau. of James Arthur Hindmarsh, of Ayr:—

Mary, O.B.E. (of Quabrook, Coleman's Hatch, Sussex), *b.* 1909; formerly Regional Woman Fire
Officer, Headquarters, National Fire Ser.; a Serving Sister of Order of St. John of Jerusalem;
O.B.E. (Civil) 1946: *m.* 1932, William Pateïson Keith, M.V.O., who *d.* 1963.——Pleasance Anne,
b. 1920: *m.* 1948, John Stuart Comery, M.C , of Home Farm, Upper Hayesden, Tonbridge, Kent,
and has issue living, William Knatchbull, *b.* 1952,—Patricia Mary, *b.* 1950.

Issue of the late Sir Hughe Montgomery Knatchbull-Hugessen, KCMG, *b.* 1886, *d.* 1971:
m. 1912, Mary (4, South Close, The Precincts, Canterbury), da. of Brig.-Gen. Sir Robert
Gordon Gilmour, 1st Bt., CVO, CB, DSO, cr. 1926:—
Alethea (Flat 3, 107, Ladbroke Rd., W11), *b.* 1918.

Issue of the late Rev. Reginald Bridges KNATCHBULL-HUGESSEN. 7th son of 9th
baronet, *b.* 1831, *d.* 1911: *m.* 1st, 1866, Maria, who *d.* 1880, 2nd dau. of the late
Rev. Tatton Brockman, M.A. ; 2ndly, 1885, Rachel Mary, who *d.* 1929, dau.
of Adm. Sir Alexander Leslie Montgomery, 3rd Bt.:—

Rachel Joyse, *b.* 1893: *m.* 1917, the Ven. Hugh Henry Molesworth Bevan, Archdeacon Emeritus of
Ludlow, and Preb. of Hereford, who *d.* 1970 [V. Molesworth], and has issue living, Roger Hugh
(Parsonage Farm, Croscombe, Wells), *b.* 1918; ed. at Shrewsbury, and at Queen's Coll., Oxford (MA);
MusB, Dublin; Dir. of Music, Downside Sch.; European War 1939-45 as Capt. R.A.: *m.* 1943,
Cecilia Mary Margaret, da. of Francis Baldock, and has issue living, John Francis Xavier *b.* 1946:
m. 1974, Jennifer Mary, da. of the Rev. L. M. Wheeler, of Reading, Berks., David Hugh Benedict *b.*
1951, Anthony Roger *b.* 1953. Rupert Stephen Jude *b.* 1955, Joseph Henry Christopher *b.* 1957,
Jeremy Martin Eugene *b.* 1958, Daniel Richard Edward *b.* 1963, Benjamin Dunstan, *b.* 1969, Mary,
b. 1948: *m.* 1971, Robert Michael Fysh, Bar. at Law, of 59, Leverton St., NW5, Gwen *b.* 1949: *m.*
1970, Timothy James Williamson, BChir, of 8, Shelley Rd., Bath, Rachel *b.* 1952, Cicely *b.* 1956,
Stella *b.* 1959, Helen *b.* 1961,—Maurice Guy Smalman (45, Court Way, Twickenham, Middx.),
b. 1921; ed. at Shrewsbury, and at Magdalen Coll., Oxford; 1939-45 War: *m.* 1948, Anne Christine
Mary Josephine, da. of Maj. C. Alderson, Colonial Ser., and has issue living, Jessica Josephine
Rosemary *b.* 1951,—Christopher Henry Knatchbull (c/o Corvedale, Croscombe, Wells), *b.* 1933; ed.
at Shrewsbury, and at St. John's Coll., Camb. (MA); PhD Nottingham: *m.* 1960, Elinor, da. of
Dr. F. C. V. Brightman, and has issue living, Sarah Caroline *b.* 1961. *Residence,*—Corvedale,
Croscombe, Wells.

Grandchildren of the late Lieut.-Gen. Reginald Edward Knatchbull, 7th son of
8th baronet :—

Issue of the late Brig.-Gen. George Wyndham Chichester Knatchbull, C.M.G., *b.* 1862, *d.*
1943 : *m.* 1900, Constance, who *d.* 1913, dau. of Alexander Marsden, M.D., F.R.C.S.E. :—

Wyndham Marsden (Cuilnagriene, Jubilee Lane, Boundstone, Farnham, Surrey), *b.* 1901; ed. at Marl-
borough; Lt.-Col. (ret.) Queen's Own Roy. W. Kent Regt.: *m.* 1934, Eileen Mary, el. da. of the late
Lt.-Col. William Chapman Croly, DSO, RAMC and has issue living, Patrick Wyndham (Murlough,
Cultra Av., Cultra, co. Down), *b.* 1936; Lt. Cdr. RNR: *m.* 1966, Mary, da. of L. F. Kelly, of Tile
Hatch, Bishops Down Park Rd., Tunbridge Wells, and has issue living, Simon Marsden *b.* 1967,
Andrew Wyndham *b.* 1969, Felicity Jane *b.* 1972,—Michael Walter (1, Greenview Park, Upper
Malone, Belfast, 9) (twin), *b.* 1936: *m.* 1959, Rhona Dorothy, da. of the late John Sinclair Gunning,
of Holywood, co. Down, and has issue living, Richard Edward Walter *b.* 1971, Fiona Bridgid *b.*
1962, Lucy Rhona *b.* 1964, Gillian Mary *b.* 1966.—Bridget Eileen Mary (10A, Chaucer Rd., Cambridge),
b. 1943: *m.* 1964, James Seymour Emerson, from whom she obtained a divorce 1971. [see Keane, Bt.]

Issue of the late Rev. Henry Dalrymple Knatchbull, *b.* 1864, *d.* 1932: *m.* 1902, Cecilia
Maud, who *d.* 1947, youngest dau. of the late Samuel Woodhouse, J.P., D.L., of Norley
Hall, Cheshire :—
Mary, *b.* 1903. *Residence,*—The Cottage, Southfield, Minchinhampton, Glos. GL6 9DY.——Ursula,
b. 1906. *Residence,*—Keyhold Cottage, Bussage, Stroud, Gloucestershire.

Issue of the late Owen Edward Knatchbull, *b.* 1868, *d.* 1946 : *m.* 1892, Amy Elizabeth,
dau. of Edward Bingley Wright :—
Reginald Edward, *b.* 1893; late Capt. Indian Army Reserve of Officers.——Daphne Mary Knatchbull, *b.* 1902. *Residence,*—

Granddaughters of the late Wadham Knatchbull, 2nd son of the late Rev. Wadham
Knatchbull, LLD, 3rd son of 4th Bt.:—

Issue of the late Edward Wadham Knatchbull, *b.* 1863, *d.* 1937 : *m.* 1894, Gertrude Louise,
who *d.* 1958, dau. of the late Rev. Thomas Sellwood Stephens, R. of St. Erme, Cornwall :—

Dorothea Wyndham, *b.* 1897: *m.* 1927, Wing-Cdr. Richard Maelor Thomas, RAF, who *d.* 1966, and
has issue living, Pamela Trevelyan, *b.* 1930,—Diana Margaret, *b.* 1933. *Residence,*—The Manor
House, Winsley, Bradford-on-Avon, Wilts.——Beatrice Wadham, *b.* 1898.

Grandchildren of the late Lt.-Col. Francis Knatchbull, 3rd son of the Rev. Wadham
Knatchbull, LLD (ante):—

Issue of the late Maj. Wyndham Persse Knatchbull, *b.* 1873, *d.* 1967: *m.* 1911, Sybil Mathilde,
who *d.* 1957, da. of the late Ulick Burke [Burke, Bt., colls.]:—

Charles Norton (Batch Farm, Kilmersdon, Bath), *b.* 1918; ed. at Sherborne; 1940-45 War with
RN (Submarine Ser.): *m.* 1940, Jacqueline Nora, da. of Henry P. Veall, of Netley. Hants.,
and has issue living, Henry Norton (10, Stalbridge Rd., Poole, Dorset), *b.* 1942,—Richard Wyndham
(Brown's Cottage, Kilmersdon, nr. Bath), *b.* 1947 : *m.* 1970, Susan Ann, only da. of Arthur Candy, of
Mells, Som., and has issue living, Paul Wyndham *b.* 1973.——Angela Alice, *b.* 1912: *m.* 1948, Reginald
Cyril Neville Owbridge, of 59, Stockens Green, Knebworth, Herts., and has issue living, Anthony
Wyndham, *b.* 1949: *m.* 1972, Barbara Jean, only da. of Lawrence Lacy, of Chesham, Bucks.——
Zara Eleanor, *b.* 1920; 1939-45 War with ATS: *m.* 1st, 1942, John Mackay, from whom she obtained a
divorce 1953; 2ndly, 1953, Christopher Jocelyn Lapage, of 54, Bridgedown, Bridge, Canterbury,
and has issue living, (by 2nd m.) Fiona Anne, *b.* 1954.

Granddaughter of the late Col. Norton Knatchbull, 4th son of the late Rev. Wadham
Knatchbull, LLD, (ante):—

Issue of the late Lieut-Col. Reginald Norton Knatchbull, D.S.O., Leicestershire Regt.
b. 1872, *d.* (on active ser. in Mesopotamia) 1917 : *m.* 1906, Winifred, who *d.* 1910,
dau. of the late William Felton Peel, of Hawley Hall, Blackwater, Hants, and The
Bungalow, Fleming, Alexandria:—

Ida Winifred, b. 1907 : m. 1930, Walter Francis George Kingsbury [E. Bradford, colls.], and has issue living, Richard Norton Orlando, b. 1932,—Hugh Wyndham Evelyn KNATCHBULL-KINGSBURY, b. 1936; has assumed by deed poll 1958 the surname of Knatchbull before his patronymic: m. 1968, Emily Sofia Thorburn, of Gothenburg, Sweden. Residence,—Quinta da Fonte dos Cedros, Cintra, Portugal.

PREDECESSORS.—[1] Rt. Hon. EDWARD HUGESSEN Knatchbull, PC, 6th son of the Rt. Hon. Sir Edward Knatchbull, MP, 9th Bt.; b. 1829; assumed by Roy. licence the additional surname of Hugessen 1849; MP for Sandwich (L) 1857-80; was a Lord of the Treasury 1859-66, Under-Sec. of State for Home Depart. 1866, and 1868-71, and Under Sec. for Colonies 1871-4; cr. Baron Brabourne, of Brabourne, co. Kent (peerage of United Kingdom) 1880: m. 1st, 1852, Anna Maria Elizabeth, who d. 1889, da. of the late Rev. Marcus R. Southwell, of St. Stephen's Herts.; 2ndly, 1890, Ethel Mary, who d. 1929, da. of Col. Sir George Gustavus Walker, KCB, of Crawfordton, Dumfriesshire, d. 1893: s. by his el. son [2] EDWARD, 2nd Baron, b. 1857; MP for Rochester (L) 1889-92; m. 1880; the Hon Amy Virginia Beaumont, who d. 1949, da. of 1st Baron Allendale: d. 1909; s. by his son, [3] WYNDHAM WENTWORTH, 3rd Baron; b. 1885; Lt. Grenadier Guards; d. (killed in action during European War) 1915; s. by his uncle [4] CECIL MARCUS, 4th Baron; b. 1863; s. in 1917 his cousin as 13th Baronet of Mersham Hatch (cr. 1641): m. 1893, Helena Regina Frederica, who d. 1919, da. of the late Hermann von Flesch-Brunningen, Imperial Councillor of Vienna; d. 1933: s. by his only son [5] MICHAEL HERBERT RUDOLF, GCSI, GCIE, MC, 5th Baron; b. 1895: assumed by deed poll 1919, the surname of Knatchbull only; was MP for Ashford Div. of Kent (C) 1931-3, and Gov. of Bombay 1933-7, and of Bengal 1937-9 (acted as Viceroy of India, June-Sept. 1938): m. 1919, Lady Doreen Geraldine Browne, CI, da. of 6th Marquess of Sligo: d. 1939; s. by his son [6] NORTON CECIL MICHAEL, 6th Baron: b. 1922; Lt. Grenadier Guards; d. (killed on active ser. during European War) 1943; s. by his brother [7] JOHN ULICK, 7th Baron and present peer.

BRADBURY, BARON. (Bradbury.) [Baron U.K. 1925.]

Justice, equity, and good faith.

JOHN BRADBURY, 2nd Baron ; b. Jan. 7th, 1914 ; s. 1950; ed. at Westminster, and at Brasenose Coll. Oxford : m. 1st, 1939, Joan, dau. of W. D. Knight, of Darley, Addlestone, Surrey ; 2ndly, 1946, Gwerfyl, dau. of the late E. Stanton Roberts, of Gellifor, Ruthin, Denbighshire, and has issue by 1st and 2nd marriages.

Arms,—Sable, a chevron ermine, between in chief two buckles and in base a fleur-de-lis argent Crest,—In front of two ostrich feathers in saltire argent, a boar's head erect proper. Supporters,— Dexter, a raven ; sinister, a dove ; both proper.

Residence,—Sunridge, Downsway, Merrow, Guildford, Surrey. Club,—United University.

SON LIVING. (By 1st m.)
Hon. JOHN (3, Ashchurch Park Villas, Hammersmith, W12), b. March 17th, 1940; ed. at Gresham's Sch., Holt, and Bristol Univ.: m. 196g, Susan, da. of the late W. Liddiard of East Shefford, Berks., and has issue living, John, b. 1973.

DAUGHTERS LIVING. (By 1st m.)

Hon. Elizabeth Joan (twin), b. 1940: m. 1965, Warren Hansen, of 5538, Crestwood Drive, Kansas City, Missouri, USA 64110, and has issue living, Karl Geoffrey, b. 1971,—Christine Joan, b. 1967.

(By 2nd m.)
Hon. Anne, b. 1947: m. 1970, Alastair James Ker-Lindsay, of 30, Porchester Terr., W2, and has issue living, James, b. 1972,—Mark, b. 1973.

BROTHER LIVING.

Hon. Paul, b. 1915 ; ed. at Westminster, and at Brasenose Coll., Oxford: m. 1940, Margaret Amy, da. of the late J. W. Stammers, of Purley, Surrey, and has issue living, Richard (Milcote House, Long Wood Drive, Jordans, Beaconsfield, Bucks.), b. 1941: m. 1966, Elizabeth Mary Auchinleck, da. of Douglas C. L. Love, of 3, Glenmore House, Richmond, Surrey, and has issue living, Clare b. 1967, Jane (twin) b. 1967, Philippa b. 1972,—James (Barnford, Holy Cross, Clent, Worcs.), b. 1945: m. 1967, Patricia Mary, da. of Hedley A. Funnell, of Grey's Mead, Thame, Oxon, and has issue living, Anthony James b. 1969, Jonathan Paul b. 1971, Charlotte Ann b. 1973,—David (93, Campbell Rd., Florence Park, Oxford), b. 1950: m. 1973, Janet Ann Salier, da. of David H. Davidson, of Battramsley Cottage, Boldre, Lymington, Hants.). Residence,—Chelvey Batch, Brockley, Bristol, Avon.

SISTER LIVING.

Hon. Margaret, b. 1911: m. 1937 (marriage dissolved 1950) Stanley George Hooker, C.B.E., D.Ph., and has issue living, Jane Margaret (Lady Barran), b. 1940: m. 1965, Sir John Napoleon Ruthven Barran, 4th Bt. Residence,—The Old Forge, Winchelsea.

PREDECESSOR.—[1] Sir John Swanwick Bradbury, G.C.B., son of the late John Bradbury, of Winsford, Cheshire; b. 1872: Under Treasurer of Natal 1904-5, Private Sec. to Chancellor of Exchequer (Rt. Hon. Herbert H. Asquith, M.P.) 1905-8, Principal Clerk in the Treasury and First Treasury Officer of Accounts 1908-11, Joint Permanent Sec. to the Treasury, 1913-19, Principal British Delegate to Reparation Commn. (Paris) 1919-25, Chm. of International Relief Credits Committee 1920, of National Food Council 1925-9, and of Bankers' Clearing House Committee and British Bankers' Asso. 1929-30 and 1935-6 ; cr. Baron Bradbury, of Winsford, co. Chester (peerage of United Kingdom) 1925 : m. 1911, Hilda Maude, who d. 1949, 2nd dau. of William Arthur Kirby, of Goldhurst Terrace, Hampstead, N.W.; d. 1950 ; s. by his son [2] JOHN, 2nd Baron and present peer.

BRADFORD, EARL OF. (Bridgeman.)   [Earl U.K. 1815, Bt. E. 1660.]

Neither rashly nor timidly.

GERALD MICHAEL ORLANDO BRIDGE-
MAN, *T.D.*, 6th Earl, and 11th Baronet;
b. Sept. 29th, 1911 ; *s.* 1957 ; ed. at
Harrow, and at Trin. Coll., Camb.
(MA); Capt. Shropshire Yeo. (TA)
(ret.), a JP for Salop; a Vice-Lieut.
1970-74; patron of five livings;
a Crown Estate Commr. 1956-67;
Pres. of Country Landowners' Assoc.
1955-7, and of Timber Growers Organization 1962-64, and Chm. of Forestry
Cttee. of Great Britain 1964-66;
received Freedom of Shrewsbury 1957;
1939-45 War (despatches): *m.* 1946,
Mary Willoughby, da. of the late
Lt.-Col. Thomas Hassard Montgomery,
DSO, of Cadogan House, Shrewsbury,
and has issue.

Arms,—Sable, ten plates, four, three, two,
and one; on a chief argent, a lion passant
ermine. Crest,—A demi-lion rampant argent,
holding in the paws a wreath of laurel proper.
Supporters,—Two leopards guardant gules
pelletée.
Seat—Weston Park, Shifnal, Salop. *Town
Residence,*—61D, Eaton Sq., SW1.   *Clubs,*—Turf,
Farmers', MCC, Ski Club of Gt. Britain.

SONS LIVING.
RICHARD THOMAS ORLANDO (*Viscount New-
port*), *b.* Oct. 3rd, 1947; ed. at Harrow, and
Trin. Coll., Camb.
Hon. Charles Gerald Orlando, *b.* 1954; ed. at
Harrow.
DAUGHTERS LIVING.
Lady Serena Mary, *b.* 1949.
Lady Caroline Louise, *b.* 1952: *m.* 1974, Brian Martin Garnell.

SISTER LIVING.
Lady Anne Pamela (*Lady Anne Cowdray*), *b.* 1913: *m.* 1939, the 3rd Viscount Cowdray, who obtained
a divorce 1950. *Residences,*—Broadleas, Devizes, Wilts; 97b, Drayton Gdns., SW10.

WIDOW LIVING OF SON OF FOURTH EARL.
Joan (50, Lennox Gdns., SW1), da. of the late Hon. Bernard Constable-Maxwell [see L. Herries of
Terregles, colls.]: *m.* 1930, Col. the Hon. Henry George Orlando Bridgeman, DSO, MC, who *d.* 1972,
and has issue [see colls. infra].

COLLATERAL BRANCHES LIVING.
Issue of the late Col. the Hon. Henry George Orlando Bridgeman, DSO, MC, yst. son
of 4th Earl, *b.* 1882, *d.* 1972: *m.* 1930, Joan (ante), da. of the late Hon. Bernard
Constable-Maxwell [see L. Herries of Terregles, colls.]:—
Peter Orlando Ronald (Fallodon Hall, Embleton, Alnwick, Northumberland), *b.* 1933 ; Lt.-Col. R.
Northumberland Fus. (TA): *m.* 1967, Sarahjane, da. of Patrick Corbett, of Silverlands, Boar's
Head, Crowborough, and has issue living, Mark George Orlando, *b.* 1968,—Emma Virginia, *b.* 1969,—
Davina Sacha, *b.* 1972.——John Henry Orlando (Boreland House, Lockerbie, Dumfriesshire), *b.*
1938: *m.* 1970, Susan Gay, da. of A. Leonard Hill, of Boreland of Dryfe, Lockerbie, Dumfriesshire,
and has issue living, Camilla Jane, *b.* 1971,—Alexandra Mary, *b.* 1973.——Mary Helena, *b.* 1932:
m. 1960, William Simon Rodolph Kenyon-Slaney [see B. Kenyon, colls.].——Alice Christina, *b.*
1936: *m.* 1967, Bruce McKenzie (Knowle, Cranleigh, Surrey, and P.O. Box 30135, Nairobi, Kenya);
Min. of Agric., Kenya, Kim Alexander, *b.* 1969,—James Malcolm, *b.* 1971.
Issue (by 1st marriage) of the late Brig.-Gen. the Hon. Francis Charles Bridgeman,
son of 3rd Earl, *b.* 1846, *d.* 1917 : *m.* 1st, 1883, Gertrude Cecilia, who *d.* 1911,
dau. of George Hanbury, of Blythewood, Maidenhead ; 2ndly, 1913, Agnes
Florence, who *d.* 1947, dau. of the late Richard Holt Briscoe :—
Selina Adine KAY-SHUTTLEWORTH, *b.* 1886, assumed by deed poll 1920 the additional surname of
Shuttleworth, and resumed by deed poll 1935 the surname of Kay-Shuttleworth in lieu of that of
Shuttleworth-King: *m.* 1st, 1913, Capt. the Hon. Lawrence Ughtred Kay-Shuttleworth, Bar.-at-law,
RFA, who *d.* (killed in action during 1914-18 War) 1917, el. son of 1st Baron Shuttleworth; 2ndly,
1920, as his second wife, Maj.-Gen. William Birchall Macaulay King, CMG, DSO, who *d.* 1950, and
has issue living (by 1st m.) [see B. Shuttleworth]. *Residence,*—House of the Sons of God, Clareville
Grove, SW7.
Grandchildren of the late Brig.-Gen. the Hon. Francis Charles Bridgeman
(ante):—
Issue of the late Reginald Francis Orlando Bridgeman, CMG, MVO, *b.* 1884, *d.* 1968: *m.* 1923,
Olwen Elizabeth (Waxwell Farm Cottage, Pinner, Middx.), da. of Maurice Jones, MPS:—
Henry Clive Orlando, *b.* 1946.——Victoria Mary, *b.* 1926: 1939-45 War with WRNS.——Olwen
Valery, *b.* 1928: BA London: *m.* 1962, Anthony Mark Barrington Golding, MB, B.Chir., of 12,
Clifton Hill, NW8, and Keepers Cottage, Byworth, Petworth, Sussex, and has issue living, Richard
Mark Orlando, *b.* 1965,—Rosemary Victoria Anne, *b.* 1963,—Catherine Elizabeth Marian, *b.* 1967,—
Charlotte Valery Patricia, *b.* 1970.
Issue of the late Com. Francis Paul Orlando Bridgeman, R.N., *b.* 1888, *d.* 1930 : *m.*
1922, Alice (now of Dowdeswell Manor, Andoversford, Gloucestershire), dau. of Herman
Greverus Kleinwort, of 45, Belgrave Square, S.W.1 :—
Gerald William Paul Orlando, *b.* 1929: *m.* 1965, Mrs. Rosemarie Ingrams, da. of Willis Tomlinson.
Residences,—Dowdeswell Manor, Andoversford, Glos.; 43, Cheval Place, SW7; 51, Mixnam's Lane,
Chertsey, Surrey.——Jeannine Patricia, *b.* 1923: *m.* 1st, 1951 (m. diss. 1955), Alan Forde Scott, late
Tanganyika Admin. Ser.; 2ndly, 1969, Rear Adm. Josef Czeslaw Bartosik, CB, DSC, of 33, Cheval
Pl., SW7.——Marigold Helen, *b.* 1925. *Residences,*—Dowdeswell Manor, Andoversford, Glos.; 43,
Cheval Pl. SW7.
Grandson of the late Charles George Orlando Bridgeman, yr. son of the Rev. the
Hon. George Thomas Orlando Bridgeman, 2nd son of 2nd Earl:—
Issue of the late Maj. Roger Orlando Bridgeman, *b.* 1889, *d.* 1975: *m.* 1929, Marjorie Susan
(The Lodge, Beaminster, Dorset), da. of the late Lt.-Gen. the Hon. Sir (Alan) Richard
Montagu-Stuart-Wortley, KCB, KCMG, DSO [see E. Wharncliffe, colls.]:—

Richard Lynedoch Orlando (123, Castelnau, SW13; Boodle's and Queen's Clubs, and MCC), b. 1931; ed. at Harrow; late 1st Bn. Rifle Bde. and 1st Bn. Liverpool Scottish (TA): m. 1965, Romayne Georgette Ord., only da. of Ingram Ord Capper, of The Mill, Polstead, Suffolk, and has issue living, Leopold Orlando, b. 1968,—Constantine Orlando, b. 1970,—Celestine Victoria, b. 1966.

Grandsons of the late Rev. the Hon. John Robert Orlando Bridgeman, 3rd son of 2nd Earl :—
Issue of the late Rt. Hon. William Clive Bridgeman, who was cr. Viscount Bridgeman 1929 [see that title].

PREDECESSORS.—[1] Sir ORLANDO Bridgeman, successively Lord Chief Baron of Exchequer, Lord Chief Justice of Common Pleas, and Lord Keeper of Great Seal; cr. a Baronet 1660; d. 1674; s. by his son [2] Sir JOHN, 2nd Bt.; d. 1710; s. by his son [3] Sir JOHN, 3rd Bt.; d. 1747; s. by his son [4] Sir ORLANDO, 4th Bt., M.P. for Shrewsbury, who m. Lady Ann Newport, dau. of Richard, 2nd Earl of Bradford (title extinct 1762, on death of 4th Earl); d. 1764; s. by his son [5] Sir HENRY, 5th Bt., cr. Baron Bradford (peerage of Great Britain) 1794; d. 1800; s. by his son [6] ORLANDO, 2nd Baron, cr. Viscount Newport and Earl of Bradford (peerage of United Kingdom) 1815; d. 1825; s. by his son [7], George Augustus Frederick Henry, 2nd Earl, b. 1789: m. 1st, 1818, Georgina Elizabeth, who d. 1842, dau. of Sir Thomas Moncreiffe, 5th Bt.; 2ndly, 1849, Helen, who d. 1869, dau. of Æneas Mackay, of Scotston, and widow of Sir David Moncreiffe, 6th Bt.; d. 1865; s. by his son [8] ORLANDO GEORGE CHARLES, P.C., 3rd Earl, b. 1819; sometime Lord-Lieut. of Salop; M.P. for S. Shropshire (C) 1842-65; Vice-Chamberlain of H.M. Queen Victoria's Household 1852 and 1858-9, Lord Chamberlain 1866-8, and Master of the Horse 1874-80 and 1885-6 : m. 1844, the Hon. Selina Louisa Forester, who d. 1894, dau. of 1st Baron Forester; d. 1898; s. by his el. son [9] GEORGE CECIL ORLANDO, 4th Earl, b. 1845; Lieut. 1st Life Guards 1864-7, and Capt. Shropshire Yeo. 1867; M.P. for N. Shropshire (C) 1867-85: m. 1869, Lady Ida Frances Annabella Lumley, who d. 1936, 2nd dau. of 9th Earl of Scarbrough; d. 1915; s. by his el. son [10] ORLANDO, 5th Earl; b. 1873; was Assist. Private Sec. to Sec. of State for Foreign Affairs (Marquess of Salisbury) 1898-1900, and to Prime Min. (Marquess of Salisbury) 1902, Private Sec. to Prime Min.(Rt. Hon. A. J. Balfour, M.P.) 1902-5, and a Lord-in-Waiting to H.M. 1919-24: m. 1904, the Hon. Margaret Cecilia Bruce, who d. 1949, el. dau. of 2nd Baron Aberdare ; d. 1957; s. by his only son [11] GERALD MICHAEL ORLANDO, 6th Earl and present peer; also Viscount Newport, and Baron Bradford.

BRADFORD, LORD BISHOP OF. (Hook.)

Rt. Rev. ROSS SYDNEY HOOK, MC, only son of the late Sydney Frank Hook; b. Feb. 19th, 1917; ed. at Christ's Hosp., Peterhouse, Camb. (MA), and Ridley Hall, Camb.; Assist. Curate, Milton, Hants. 1941-43; Chap. RNVR (RM Commandos) 1943-46; Chap. Ridley Hall, Camb. 1946-48, R. Chorlton-cum-Hardy, Manchester 1948-52, R. and Rural Dean, Chelsea, 1952-61; Chap. Chelsea Hosp. for Women, 1954-61, and St. Luke's Hosp., Chelsea 1957-61; Canon of Rochester and Precentor, 1961-65; Exam. Chap. to Bishop of Rochester 1961-65, and to Bishop of Lincoln 1966-72; Preb. of Brampton (Lincoln Cathedral) 1966-72; Dean of Stamford 1971-72; consecrated Bishop of Grantham (Suffragan for Diocese of Lincoln) 1965; translated 5th Bishop of Bradford 1972: m. 1948, Ruth Leslie, da. of the late Rev. Herman Masterman Biddell.
Patron of forty-five livings, the Archdeaconries, and eighteen Hon. Canonries.
This See was Founded in 1919.

Episcopal Signature " Ross Bradford."

ARMS OF THE SEE,—Azure, two keys in saltire or, in chief a woolpack proper, corded of the second.
Residence,—Bishopscroft, Ashwell Road, Heaton, Bradford, 9.

BRAIN, BARON. (Brain.) [Baron U.K. 1962, Bt. U.K. 1954.]
I am, therefore I think.

CHRISTOPHER LANGDON BRAIN, 2nd Baron and 2nd Baronet; b. Aug. 30th, 1926; s. 1966; ed. at Leighton Park Sch., and New Coll., Oxford (MA): m. 1953, Susan Mary, da. of George Philip Morris, and has issue.

Arms,—Per pale or and argent, three cats' heads erased gules. Crest,—A falcon sable armed and belled or, supporting with the dexter claw a representation of the silver staff of office of the President of the Royal College of Physicians of London proper. Supporters,—Dexter, a lion statant guardant or, gorged with a coronet composed of fleurs-de-lys argent, set upon a rim gobony silver and azure, holding in the interior paw a pomegranate slipped proper; sinister, a griffin gold beaked gules, gorged with a like coronet, holding in the interior claw a poppy slipped also proper.

The mind the star of the brain.

Residence,—New House, Park Lane, Langham, Colchester, Essex.

DAUGHTERS LIVING.
Hon. Nicola Dorothy, b. 1955.
Hon. Fiona Janice, b. 1958.
Hon. Naomi Melicent, b. 1960.

BROTHER LIVING.
Hon. MICHAEL COTTRELL, *b.* Aug. 6th, 1928; ed. at Leighton Park Sch., and Oxford Univ. (MA, BCh. DM); FRCP London; FRCP Canada; late Capt. RAMC: *m.* 1960, Dr. the Hon. Elizabeth Ann Herbert, el. da. of the late Baron Tangley (Life Peer), and has issue living, Thomas Russell, *b.* 1965,—Hilary Catherine, *b.* 1961,—Philippa Harriet, *b.* 1963. *Residence,*—889, Park Av. W., Burlington, Ont., Canada.

SISTER LIVING.
Hon. Janet Stella, *b.* 1931: *m.* 1954, Leonard John Henry Arthur, MB, BCh, MRCP, of Royal Oak Cottage, Church Broughton, Derby [*see* Arthur, Bt., colls.].

WIDOW LIVING OF FIRST BARON.
STELLA (*Stella, Baroness Brain*) (9, Fairways, Broom Rd., Teddington, Middlesex), da. of the late Reginald Langdon Langdon-Down, MB, BCh, of Teddington, Middlesex: *m.* 1920, the 1st Baron, who *d.* 1966.

PREDECESSOR.—[1] (WALTER) RUSSELL BRAIN, son of Walter John Brain, of Reading; *b.* 1895; DM, FRCP, FRCPI, FRCPE; Pres. of Roy. Coll. of Physicians 1950-57, and of British Assocn. 1963-64; cr. a *Baronet* (UK, of Reading) 1954, *Baron Brain,* of Eynsham, co. Oxford (peerage of UK) 1962: *m.* 1920, Stella, da. of Reginald Langdon Langdon-Down, MB, BCh; *d.* 1966; *s.* by his el. son [2] CHRISTOPHER LANGDON, 2nd Baron, and present peer.

BRAINTREE, BARONY OF.   (Crittall.)   [Extinct 1961.]
DAUGHTERS LIVING OF FIRST BARON.
Hon. Valentine Ellen MacDermott, *b.* 1918: *m.* 1939, Karl Stewart Richardson, and has issue living, Peter Valentine, *b.* 1942,—Jeremy Stewart, *b.* 1946. *Residence,*—Hungry Hall, Witham, Essex.
Hon. Jane Olive, *b.* 1921: *m.* 1947, Thomas Anthony Inglis Hall, and has issue living, Barnaby Inglis, *b.* 1948,—Thomas Valentine Inglis, *b.* 1949,—Sophia Charlotte. *b.* 1954. *Residence,*—6, Windsor Terrace, Clifton, Bristol.
Hon. Mary Frances, *b.* 1922: *m.* 1950, Germano Facetti, and has issue living, Lucia Olivia Josephine, *b.* 1954. *Residence,*—51, Gloucester Avenue. N.W.1.

Brancepeth, Baron,   title of Viscount Boyne on Roll of H. L.

BRAND, BARONY OF. (Brand.)   [Extinct 1963.]
DAUGHTERS LIVING OF FIRST BARON.
Hon. Virginia (*Hon. Lady Ford*), *b.* 1918: *m.* 1st, 1939, John Metcalfe Polk, who *d.* 1948: 2ndly 1949, Sir Edward William Spencer Ford, KCB, KCVO [E. Shrewsbury, colls.], and has issue living, (by 1st m.) John Robert, *b.* 1942: *m.* 1969, Benedetta Maryons, da. of David Grose, of 49, Elystan St., SW3,—Robert Brand, *b.* 1944,—(by 2nd m.) Richard George, *b.* 1951; Page of Honour to HM 1964-66,—David Lionel, *b.* 1952. *Residence,*—Eydon Hall, Eydon, Daventry, Northants.
Hon. Dinah, *b.* 1920: *m.* 1st, 1943, Lyttleton Fox: 2ndly, 1953, Christopher Charles Cyprian Bridge, and has issue living, (by 1st m.) James Lyttleton, *b.* 1945: *m.* 1970, Valérie Mariane, da. of Alain Lalonde, of 15, Rue de l'Universite, Paris VIII,—Phyllis Langhorne, *b.* 1944,—(by 2nd m.) Charles Robert, *b.* 1956,—Joanna, *b.* 1954. *Residence,*—The Old Vicarage, Firle, Sussex.

Brandon, Duke of,   see Duke of Hamilton and Brandon.

BRASSEY OF APETHORPE, BARON (Brassey.) [Baron U.K. 1938, Bt. U.K. 1922.]

ARDUIS · SÆPE · METU · NUNQUAM
H N E.

Often in difficulties, never in fear.

DAVID HENRY BRASSEY, 3rd
Baron, and 3rd Baronet; b.
Sept. 16th, 1932; s. 1967; ed.
at Stowe; Maj. (ret.) Gren. Gds.;
a JP and a DL of Northants.; m.
1958, Myrna Elizabeth, who d.
1974, only da. of Lt.-Col. John
Baskervyle-Glegg, of 9, The
Gateways, Chelsea, SW3, and
has issue.

Arms,—Quarterly; 1st, per fesse
indented sable and argent, in the first
quarter a mallard of the second; 2nd,
gules, in chief three mullets argent, and in
base a dexter hand apaumée couped at
the wrist of the last; 3rd, sable, a chevron
between three bulls' heads cabossed
argent; 4th, argent, on a chevron gules,
three trefoils slipped of the field. Crest,
—A mallard proper. Supporters,—On
either side a mallard holding in the beak
an ear of wheat slipped and leaved proper.

Residence,—The Manor House, Apethorpe, Peterborough.

SON LIVING.
Hon. EDWARD, b. March 9th, 1964.
BROTHER LIVING.
Hon. Thomas Ian (Manor Close, Oving, Aylesbury), b. 1934; ed. at Stowe; formerly Lt. Gren. Guards:
m. 1960, Valerie Christine, da. of Alan David Finlason, and has issue living, Thomas Hugh, b. 1971,—
Miranda, b. 1963,—Louise, b. 1964,—Davina Christine, b. 1969.

UNCLE LIVING. (Son of 1st Baron.)
Hon. Peter Esmé (Close House, Barnack, Stamford), b. 1907; ed. at Eton, and at Magdalene Coll.,
Camb.; Bar. Inner Temple 1930; is Lt.-Col. Northants Yeo., Lord Lieut. of Cambs. 1975; 1939-45
War as Lt.-Col. (wounded): m. 1944, Lady Romayne Elizabeth Algitha Cecil, ARRC, da. of 5th
Marquess of Exeter, and has issue living, Henry Charles, b. 1947: m. 1972, Linda, da. of Geoffrey
Pinnock, of Fern Cottage, Ripley, Surrey, and has issue living, Thomas b. 1974,—Richard Edwin,
b. 1949: m. 1971, Tania, da. of Norman William Duckworth, and has issue living, Pikka (da.) b. 1973,
Rowena Jane, MVO, b. 1945; appointed a Lady-in-Waiting to HRH Princess Anne 1970, MVO
(4th Class) 1974.

WIDOW LIVING OF SON OF FIRST BARON.
Hon. Victoria Ivy Louise Spencer (Worton, Devizes, Wilts.), da. of 1st Viscount Churchill: m. 1920,
Capt. the Hon. Cecil Henry Brassey, who d. 1949.

WIDOW LIVING OF SECOND BARON.
BARBARA (Barbara, Baroness Brassey of Apethorpe) (Bridge House, Blatherwyke, Peterborough),
da. of the late Leonard Jorgensen and formerly wife of Lt.-Col. Herbert Campbell Westmorland:
m. 1963, as his second wife, the 2nd Baron, who d. 1967.

PREDECESSORS.—[1] (HENRY) LEONARD (CAMPBELL) Brassey, son of the late Henry Arthur
Brassey (formerly M.P. for Sandwich), of Preston Hall, Kent; b. 1870; Major W. Kent Yeo.;
Sheriff of Northants 1907; sat as M.P. for N. Div. of Northampton 1910-18, and for Peterborough
Div. thereof 1918-29; cr. a Baronet 1922, and Baron Brassey of Apethorpe, of Apethorpe, co.
Northampton (peerage of United Kingdom) 1938: m. 1894, Lady Violet Mary Gordon-Lennox,
who d. 1946, dau. of 7th Duke of Richmond and Gordon: d. 1958; s. by his 5th son [2] BERNARD
THOMAS, MC, TD, 2nd Baron, b. 1905: m. 1st, 1931, Crystal Gloria, who d. 1962, da. of the late
Lt.-Col. Francis William George Gore [E. Sondes]; 2ndly, 1963, Mrs. Barbara Westmorland, da. of
the late Leonard Jorgenson; d. 1967; s. by his el. son [3] DAVID HENRY, 3rd Baron, and present peer.

BRAYBROOKE, BARON. (Neville.) [Baron G.B. 1788.]

NE VILE VELIS

Incline to nothing base.

HENRY SEYMOUR NEVILLE, 9th Baron;
b. Feb. 5th, 1897; s. 1943; ed. at Shrewsbury, and at Magdalene Coll., Camb.
(Hon. M.A. 1948); is an Hereditary
Visitor of Magdalene Coll., Camb., a D.L.
and J.P. for Essex, and patron of three
livings; European War 1915-19 as
Flight-Com. R.N.A.S. and Capt. R.A.F.:
m. 1st, 1930, Muriel Evelyn, who d.
1962, dau. of the late William Charles
Manning, and widow of Euan C. Cartwright; 2ndly, 1963, Angela Mary,
da. of the late W. H. Hollis, and
widow of John Ree, and has issue by
1st marriage.

Arms,—Quarterly: 1st and 4th gules, on a saltire
argent, a rose of the field, barbed and seeded
proper; 2nd and 3rd or, fretty gules; on a canton
of the first a lymphad sable. Crest,—A bull statant
argent, collared and chained or. Supporters—Two
lions reguardant argent, maned sable, and gorged
with wreaths of olive proper.

Residence,—Mutlow Hall, Wendens Ambo,
Saffron Walden, Essex.

SON LIVING. (By 1st marriage.)
Hon. ROBIN HENRY CHARLES, b. Jan. 29th, 1932 ; ed. at Eton, and at Magdalene Coll., Camb.,
m. 1st, 1955 (m. diss. 1974), Robin Helen, only da. of the late T. A. Brockhoff, of Rose Bay, Sydney,
NSW; 2ndly, 1974, Linda, da. of Arthur Norman, of Saffron Walden, Essex, and has issue living,
(by 1st m.) Amanda Muriel Mary, b. 1962,—Caroline Emma, b. 1963,—Henrietta Jane, b. 1965,—
Victoria, b. 1970,—Arabella (twin), b. 1970. Residence,—Abbey House, Audley End, Saffron
Walden, Essex.

BROTHER LIVING. (Raised to the rank of a Baron's son 1944.)
Hon. Grey Aldworth, b. 1900 ; Com. (retired) R.N. ; European War 1917-19 (two medals), European
War 1939-45 (three medals) : m. 1930, Margaret Emily Cortlandt, dau. of the late Rev. Henry
Cortlandt Stokes, of Elmdene, Sandown, Isle of Wight. Residence,—Kingsdown, King's Road, St.
Peter Port, Guernsey.

SISTER LIVING. (Raised to the rank of a Baron's daughter 1944.)
Hon. Audrey, b. 1895. Residence,—Rose Cottage, Church Oakley, Basingstoke, Hants.

DAUGHTER LIVING OF SEVENTH BARON.
Hon. Catherine Dorothy, b. 1922 : m. 1954, Gordon Alexander Egerton Ruck, and has issue living,
Louise Dorothy Catherine, b. 1959. Residence,—Croft House, Stansted Mountfitchet, Essex.

COLLATERAL BRANCHES LIVING.

Grandson of the late Ralph Neville-Grenville, M.P., son of the late Very
Rev. the Hon. George Neville-Grenville, 3rd son of 2nd Baron :—
Issue of the late Claud NEVILLE, b. 1858, d. 1944 : m. 1897, Frances Cromwell, who d. 1959,
dau. of Col. Sir William Adolphus Frankland, 9th Bt. :—
Edward, b. 1904 ; Com. (retired) R.N. ; is a J.P. for Somerset ; was Naval Attaché to British
Embassies at The Hague and Brussels 1947-49 ; European War 1939-45 : m. 1960, Mrs. Gabrielle
Helen Naomi Vandy, dau. of the late Ellis Taylor Collins, of Chislehurst, Kent. Residence,—The
Abbey, Charlton Adam, Somerton, Somerset. Club,—United Service.

Grandchildren of the late Adm. Sir George Neville, KCB, CVO (infra):—
Issue of the late Com. Ralph NEVILLE, b. 1887, d. 1958: m. 1918, the Hon. Letice Cary
(who d. 1963, having m. 2ndly, 1937, as his second wife, Major Philip John Sherwin
Pearson-Gregory, M.C.), dau. of 12th Viscount Falkland :—
Richard (75, Holland Park, W.11.; Guards' and St. James' Clubs), b. 1922 : m. 1960, Pauline, only da.
of James Annett Fisher, MA, JP, and formerly wife of Michael Forrester.

Issue of the late Brigadier Alfred Geoffrey Neville, O.B.E., M.C., late R.A., b. 1891, d. 1955:
m. 1922, Philippa (Summerhaugh Cottage, St. Mary Bourne, Andover, Hants), da. of the
late Vice-Adm. Sir George Price Webley Hope, KCB, KCMG [see M. Linlithgow, colls.]:—
Caroline Philippa (Lady Newman), b. 1935 : m. 1960, Sir Gerard Robert Henry Sigismund Newman,
3rd Bt. Residences,—Burloes, Royston, Herts.; 27, Bloomfield Ter., SW1.

Grandson of the late Adm. Sir George NEVILLE, K.C.B., C.V.O., b. 1850, d. 1923: m. 1886,
Fairlie Florence, who d. 1960, dau. of the late D. Lloyd Jones, of Llandovery, Carmarthenshire, and Victoria, Australia :—
Philip Lloyd, CVO, RN, b. 1888; became Capt. 1936; ret. 1937; 1914-19 War (three medals, 4th
Class Order of the Nile of Egypt); 1939-45 War; a Gentleman Usher to HM King George VI 1937-
52, and to HM Queen Elizabeth II 1953-66, since when an Extra Gentleman Usher; CVO 1954: m.
1942, Eleanor, who d. 1972, da. of Duncan Fellowes, of Toronto, Canada, and has issue living, George,
b. 1943,—John b. 1944. Residence,—Henstridge, Templecombe, Somerset. Club.—United Service.

Granddaughter of the late Louis Neville, 4th son of the late Ralph Neville Grenville, MP
(ante):—
Issue of the late Bertram Neville, b. 1880, d. 1950: m. 1919, Gertrude May Thompson, of
The Lilacs, Wedmore, Somerset:—
Beryl Edith, b. 1925: m. 1954, Derek George Rands, and has issue living, Margaret Elizabeth, b. 1957,—
Pauline Jane, b. 1961. Residence,—51, Wychwood Av., Luton, Bedfordshire.

PREDECESSORS.—[1] Field-Marshal Sir John Griffin-Whitwell (heir-general of 3rd and last
Baron Griffin of Braybrooke) was summoned to Parliament 1784 as 4th Baron Howard de
Walden, and in 1788 was cr. Baron Braybrooke (peerage of Great Britain), with remainder
to Richard Neville-Aldworth, of Billingbere; d. 1797, when the Barony of Howard de
Walden fell into abeyance and the Barony of Braybrooke devolved upon [2] RICHARD Aldworth-
Neville, 2nd Baron; b. 1750; was Lord Lieut. and Vice-Adm. of Essex, Provost-Marshal of
Jamaica, &c.; assumed by Roy. licence 1798 the additional and principal surname of Griffin:
m. 1780, Catherine, who d. 1796, dau. of the Rt. Hon. George Grenville, P.C.; d. 1825;
s. by his son [3] RICHARD Neville, LL.D., 3rd Baron, b. 1783; editor of the "Diary of Samuel
Pepys": m. 1819, Lady Jane, who d. 1856, dau. of 2nd Marquess Cornwallis; d. 1858: s. by
his son [4] RICHARD CORNWALLIS, 4th Baron; d. 1861; s. by his brother [5] CHARLES CORN-
WALLIS, 5th Baron, b. 1823: m. 1849, the Hon. Florence Priscilla Alicia Maude, who d.
1914, 3rd dau. of 3rd Viscount Hawarden; d. 1902; s. by his brother [6] Rev. LATIMER, 6th
Baron, b. 1827 ; Master of Magdalene Coll., Camb. : m. 1853, Lucy Frances, who d. 1918, el. dau.
of John Le Marchant ; d. 1904 : s. by his el. son [7] HENRY, 7th Baron; b. 1855 : m. 1st, Emelie
Pauline, who d. 1912, dau. of the late Antoine Gonin, of Château de Condemine, Mâcon ; 2ndly,
1917, Dorothy Edith, who d. 1973, yst. da. of the late Sir George Lawson, KCB; d. 1941; s. by his
el. son [8] RICHARD HENRY CORNWALLIS, 8th Baron; b. 1918 ; Lieut. Grenadier Guards; d.
(killed in action during European War) 1943 ; s. by his cousin [9] HENRY SEYMOUR (son of
the late Rev. the Hon. Grey Neville, 2nd son of 6th Baron), 9th Baron and present peer.

BRAYE, BARON. (Verney-Cave.) [Baron E. 1529.]

Beware. One alone.

Beware.

THOMAS ADRIAN VERNEY-CAVE, 7th Baron;
b. July 26th, 1902 ; s. 1952 ; ed. at Eton ;
Major (retired) 13th/18th Hussars, formerly
Flying Officer R.A.F.; served on Personal
Staff of H.R.H. The Prince of the Netherlands 1945-46; a JP and a DL for Leicestershire, and heir-gen. of the Earls Verney of
Claydon (ext. 1791); 1939-45 War; has
Order of Orange Nassau of the Netherlands with Swords: m. 1934, Dorothea, da.
of the late Daniel C. Donoghue, of Philadelphia, USA, and has issue.

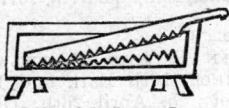

Badge of the Barons Braye.

Arms,—Quarterly, 1st and 4th azure, fretty argent *Cave*; 2nd and 3rd azure, on a cross argent five mullet gules, *Verney*. **Crests,**—1st, a greyhound courant sable collared and belled argent, holding in its mouth a scroll inscribed with the motto "Gardez;" *Cave*, 2nd, a demiphœnix in flames, looking at the rays of the sun proper *Verney*. **Supporters,**—Two lions guardant or, winged vaire. *Badge,*—A hemp-breaker.
Seat,—Stanford Hall, Lutterworth, Leics., LE17 GOH.

DAUGHTER LIVING.
Hon. PENELOPE MARY, *b.* Sept. 29th, 1941.

BROTHER LIVING.
Hon. Ambrose Jordan, *b.* 1906 ; ed. at Ampleforth Coll.; formerly Flight-Lieut. R.A.F. Vol. Reserve *Residence*,—The Cottage, Lodge Park, Aldsworth, Gloucestershire.

SISTER LIVING.
Hon. Lucy Agnes Vera, *b.* 1905 ; formerly a Ferry Pilot Air Transport Auxilliary: *m.* 1935, Capt. Lucien Leslie Falkiner, Oxford and Bucks L.I., who *d.* (killed in action during European War) 1940 [Falkiner, Bt.]. *Residence.*—The Cottage, Lodge Park, Aldsworth, Gloucestershire.

COLLATERAL BRANCHES LIVING.
Issue of the late Hon. Cecily Violet, el. dau. of 5th Baron, *b.* 1876, *d.* 1950: *m.* 1903, Maj. Kurt de Gratzy, of Merano, Italy:—
Vera Cecilia, *b.* 1906: *m.* 1929, Claude Henry Browne, of Dawn Hill, Wentworth, Surrey, and has issue living, Linda Kathleen, *b.* 1930: *m.* 1965, Cdr. Christopher Henry Fothergill, RN, of Otway House, Chobham, Surrey, and has issue living, Nicholas Henry *b.* 1965, Alexander Edmund Verney *b.* 1967,—Theresa Beatrice, *b.* 1934.

Issue of the late Hon. Vera Angela, dau. of 5th Baron, *b.* 1881, *d.* 1952 : *m.* 1905, Major Charles Hillary Wild, J.P., late Roy. W. Kent Regt., who *d.* 1954 :—
Charles Edric Verney, *b.* 1906; ed. at Ampleforth; late Capt. Green Howards. *Residence.*—Moors Lodge, Hook Norton, Oxon. *Clubs,*—United Service, Flyfishers'.

PREDECESSORS.—[1] Sir Edmund Braye, Knt., of Eaton Braye, co. Bedford, nephew of Sir Reginald Braye, K.G., Prime Min. to Henry VII., was summoned to Parliament as a *Baron* of England 1529; *d.* 1539; *s.* by his son [2] JOHN, 2nd Baron, summoned to Parliament 1545-55; was Master of the Ordnance to Queen Mary; *d.* without issue 1557, when the Barony became abeyant, and remained so until 1839, when it was terminated in favour of [3] SARAH, only dau. of Sir Thomas Cave, 6th Bt., of Stanford Hall, co. Leicester, and wife of Henry Otway, she being the descendant of Elizabeth, 2nd dau. of the 1st Baron, and wife of Sir Ralph Verney, Knt., of Claydon; she resumed in 1819 by Roy. licence the additional surname of Cave, and *d.* 1862. leaving four daus., among whom the title again remained abeyant until May 13th, 1879, when it passed to the last survivor of them [4] HENRIETTA : *m.* 1844, Edgell Wyatt-Edgell, who *d.* 1888, 2nd son of the late Edgell Wyatt-Edgell, of Milton Place, Egham, Surrey; *d.* Nov. 14th, 1879; *s.* by her son [5] ALFRED THOMAS TOWNSHEND, 5th Baron; *b.* 1849 ; assumed in 1880 by Roy. licence the surnames of Verney-Cave in lieu of Wyatt-Edgell: *m.* 1873, Harriet Cecilia, who *d.* 1935, dau. of the late William Gerard Walmesley, of Westwood House, Wigan; *d.* 1928 ; *s.* by his son [6] ADRIAN VERNEY, 6th Baron; *b.* 1874 ; Lieut.-Com. R.N.V.R.: *m.* 1900, Ethel Mary, who *d.* 1955, dau. of the late Capt. Edward Bouverie Pusey, R.N. ; *d.* 1952 ; *s.* by his son [7] THOMAS ADRIAN, 7th Baron and present peer.

BRAYLEY, BARON. (Brayley.) [Life Baron 1973.]

(JOHN) DESMOND BRAYLEY, *MC,* son of Frederick Brayley; *b.* Jan. 29th, 1917; FICA; Chm. Canning Town Glass Works Ltd., Dale Brown & Co. Ltd., Phoenix Glass Co. Ltd., and Towmaster Transport Ltd., a Dir. The Gen. and Eng. Industries Gp. of Cos., Patron Roy. Masonic Hosp., Vice-Patron Roy. Masonic Sch., and Chm. Finance & Gen. Purposes Cttee., and a Member of Board of Management RA Assocn.; Under-Sec. of State Min. of Defence (Army) Feb. to Oct. 1974; a JP of Middx. Area, Greater London, and a DL of Greater London; Hon. Col. Comdt. RA 1970-75, 1939-45 War as Capt. Parachute Regt. (MC, despatches); cr. Knt. 1970, and *Baron Brayley,* of City of Cardiff, and co. Glamorgan (Life Baron) 1973: *m.* 1945 (m. diss. 1960), Queenie E. S. Bee, and has issue.

Arms,—Not available at time of going to Press.

Residence,—82, Arlington House, St. James's, SW1. *Club,*—Eccentric.

DAUGHTERS LIVING.
Hon. Avril Gay *b.* 19—: *m.* 19—.
Hon. Tessa Ann *b.* 19—: *m.* 19—.

BREADALBANE AND HOLLAND, EARL OF. (Campbell.) [Earl S. 1677. Bt. S. 1625.]

[Name pronounced "Bredawlben."]

JOHN ROMER BORELAND CAMPBELL, 10th Earl, and 14th Baronet; *b.* April 28th, 1919; *s.* 1959; ed. at Eton; formerly Lieut. Black Watch; European War 1939-42 (despatches, invalided): *m.* 1949, Coralie, dau. of Charles Archer.

Arms,—Quarterly: 1st and 4th gyronny of eight or and sable, *Campbell*; 2nd argent, a lymphad with sails unfurled and oars in action sable, *Lorn*; 3rd or, a fesse checky azure and argent, *Stewart of Lorn.* **Crest,**—A boar's head erased proper. **Supporters,**—Two stags proper, attired and unguled or.

Residence,—29, Mackeson Rd., Hampstead, NW3.

AUNT LIVING. *(Raised to the rank of an Earl's daughter 1924.)*

Lady Mary Gwynnedd, *MM, b.* 1893; MM 1918: *m.* 1925, Lt.-Com. Reginald Victor Barton, RN, who *d.* 1967 [E. Peel, colls.], and has issue living, Shelagh Hope, *b.* 1926. *Residence,*—Stone Cottage, Gellifor, Ruthin, N. Wales.

WIDOW LIVING OF NINTH EARL.

ARMORER ROMER (*Armorer, Countess of Breadalbane*), dau. of Romer Williams, D.L., J.P., of Newnham Hall, Daventry, and widow of Capt. Eric Nicholson, 12th Roy. Lancers; *m.* 1918, the 9th Earl, who *d.* 1959. *Residence,*—Invereil Coach House, Dirleton, E. Lothian.

COLLATERAL BRANCHES.

Descendants, if any, of George Andrew Campbell, 2nd son of John Campbell of Boreland, great-uncle of 6th Earl, *b.* 1791, *d.* 1852: *m.* 1830, Margaret, who *d.* 1884, da. of Col. James Campbell, having had issue, John Breadalbane Campbell, of Florida, *b.* 1839, *d.* 1918: *m.* 1873, Katherine McDonald.

Descendants, if any, of the late Colin Campbell, Surg. 39th Regt., el. son of Capt. Robert Campbell, great-great-uncle of 6th Earl, *d.* in Guadeloupe 1794.

Descendants, if any, of William Campbell (*d.* before 30th Aug., 1784) (4th son of Robert Campbell of Glenfalloch, great-great-great-uncle of 6th Earl), whose son Archibald, Sgt. Middlesex Militia, had a son, Colin.

Descendants, if any, of Duncan Campbell, yst. son of Robert Campbell of Glenfalloch (ante), of whom Colin Campbell went to America, and James Campbell was bookbinder to the Queen.

PREDECESSORS—[1] *Sir* DUNCAN Campbell, Knt. (7th Laird of Glenorchy); was cr. a *Baronet* 1625; *d.* 1631; was *s.* by his son [2] *Sir* COLIN, 2nd Bt.; he *d.* without issue 1640; *s.* by his brother [3] *Sir* ROBERT, 3rd Bt., M.P. for Argyllshire 1639-47: *d.* 1657; *s.* by his son [4] *Sir* JOHN, 4th Bt.; *d.* 1686; *s.* by his son [5] *Sir* JOHN, P.C.; this gentleman being principal creditor of George, 6th Earl of Caithness, received from that nobleman an assignment of his Earldom, his whole estate, his heritable jurisdictions and titles of honour, and the right to assume the surname and arms of Sinclair; in return he became responsible for the Earl's debts, upwards of 1,000,000 marks, and after his lordship's death in 1676, he obtained in 1677 a patent creating him *Earl of Caithness*; however, in 1681, the Privy Council found that George Sinclair of Keiss, was heir male of the last Earl, and in consequence John Campbell relinquished his Earldom of Caithness, and in the same year was cr. *Lord Glenorchy, Benederaloch, Ormelie and Weick, Viscount of Tay and Paintland,* and *Earl of Breadalbane and Holland* (peerage of Scotland) with precedency of 1677, and with remainder to (i) whichever of his sons (by his 1st marriage) he should designate in writing, (ii) to the heirs male of his body, and (iii) to his heirs whatsoever; *d.* 1716; *s.* by his 2nd son, whom in 1684 he had designated as heir, viz.:—[6] JOHN, 2nd Earl; was Lord-Lieut. of Perthshire, and a Representative Peer; he *d.* 1752, and was *s.* by his son [7] JOHN, K.B., 3rd Earl; was M.P. for many years, and successively Master of the Horse to Princess Royal, Ambassador to Copenhagen and St. Petersburg, a Lord of the Admiralty, Master of the Jewel Offices, a Representative Peer and Keeper of the Privy Seal in Scotland; *d.* without surviving issue 1782, when the male line of the 1st peer failed and the titles devolved upon the great-grandson of Colin, 3rd son of 3rd Bt. [8] JOHN, 4th Earl; Maj.-Gen. in the Army and a Representative Peer; cr. *Baron Breadalbane, Earl of Ormelie* and *Marquess of Breadalbane* (peerage of United Kingdom) 1806; *d.* 1834; *s.* by his son [9] JOHN, K.T., 2nd Marquess, Lord-Lieut. of Argyllshire; *d.* 1862, when the English honours became extinct and the Scottish peerage devolved upon the great-grandson of William, 5th son of 3rd Bt. [10] JOHN ALEXANDER GAVIN, 6th Earl; *b.* 1824: *m.* 1850, Mary Theresa, dau. of J. F. Edwards; *d.* 1871; *s.* by his son [11] GAVIN, K.G., P.C., 7th Earl; *b.* 1851; cr. *Baron Breadalbane,* of Kenmore, co. Perth (peerage of United Kingdom) 1873, and *Earl of Ormelie,* co. Caithness, and *Marquess of Breadalbane* (in peerage of United Kingdom) 1885; a Lord-in-Waiting to Queen Victoria 1873-4, Treasurer of Queen Victoria's Household 1880 85, Lord Steward of Queen Victoria's House, hold 1892-5, Lord High Commr. to Gen. Assembly of Church of Scotland 1893, 1894, and 1895, and Lord Keeper of Privy Seal of Scotland 1907-22: *m.* 1872, Lady Alma Imogen Carlotta Leonora, who *d.* 1932, dau. of 4th Duke of Montrose; *d.* 1922, when the English honours became ext., and the Scottish peerages devolved upon his nephew [12] IAIN EDWARD HERBERT (son of the late Capt. the Hon. Ivan Campbell, 2nd son of 6th Earl), 8th Earl, *b.* 1885; *d.* 1923; *s.* by his kinsman [13] CHARLES WILLIAM, M.C. (son of the late Maj.-Gen. Charles William Campbell of Boreland; a descendant of 5th son of 3rd Bt.), 9th Earl; *b.* 1889; a Representative Peer, Major R.H.A., a Member of Queen's Body Guard for Scotland (Roy. Co. of Archers), and a Member of H.M. Hon. Corps of Gentlemen-at-Arms; sometime Lieut.-Col. Comdg. 8th Batn., Argyll and Sutherland Highlanders (T.A.): *m.* 1918, Armorer Romer, dau. of Romer Williams, D.L., J.P., of Newnham Hall, Daventry, and widow of Capt. Eric Nicholson, 12th Roy. Lancers; *d.* 1959; *s.* by his only son [14] JOHN ROMER BORELAND, 10th Earl and present peer; also Viscount of Tay and Paintland, and Lord Glenorchy, Benederaloch, Ormelie and Weick.

Brecknock, Earl of, son of Marquess Camden.

BRECON, BARON. (Lewis.) [Baron U.K. 1958.]

As well as I can.

DAVID VIVIAN PENROSE LEWIS, *P.C.*, 1st Baron, son of the late Alfred William Lewis, of Craiglas, Talybont-on-Usk; *b.* Aug. 14th, 1905; ed. at Monmouth Sch.; a J.P. for Brecknockshire; formerly a Proprietor of Quarries; Hon. Col. 638th (Brecknockshire and Monmouthshire) Light AA Regt. RA (TA) 1959-63, Gov. of Christ Coll., Brecon, and of Monmouth Schs., Pres. Newport Athletic Club; Chm. of Conservative Party in Wales and Monmouthshire 1956-58; Pres., Brecon and Radnor Young Conservatives 1950-60 and Vice-Pres. Wales and Monmouthshire Area Young Conservatives 1958-59; Patron, Brecon and Radnor Young Conservatives since 1960; a Member of European Parl. since 1973; Chm. of Welsh Nat. Water Development Authority since 1974; Chm. of A.B. Electronic Components, Abercynon, a Dir. of Powell Duffryn Ltd., and of Aberthaw & British Channel Portland Cement Co. Ltd., and a Trustee of Municipal & Mutual Insurance Co. Ltd.; Min. of State of Welsh Affairs 1957-64; cr. *Baron Brecon*, of Llanfeigan, co. Brecknock (peerage of UK) 1958, PC 1960: *m.* 1933, Mabel Helen, CBE (High Sheriff of Breconshire 1971-72), 2nd da. of the late John McColville, of Abergavenny, and has issue.

Arms,—Per fess argent and vert per chevron counterchanged in chief two dexter gauntlets sable garnished or and in base a mantle of estate purpure lined ermine corded and tasselled or. Crest,—Out of a coronet composed of four leeks set upon a rim or a rock proper standing thereon a swan wings elevated and addorsed proper, mantled vert doubled argent. Supporters,—On either side a dragon gules gorged with a mural crown therefrom a line reflexed over the back or.

Residence,—Greenhill, Cross Oak, Powys, LD3 7UJ. *Clubs,* Carlton, Cardiff and County, MCC.

DAUGHTERS LIVING.

Hon. Rosalind Helen Penrose, *b.* 1938: *m.* 1963, Arthur Leolin Price, QC, of 32, Hampstead Grove, NW3, and has issue living, Evan David Lewis, *b.* 1967,—Thomas Leolin Alfred, *b.* 1971,—Mary Ceridwen, *b.* 1964,—Sophie Katharine, *b.* 1966.
Hon. Janet Mary Penrose, *b.* 1944; ed. at Cheltenham Ladies' Coll.: *m.* 1969, Christopher John Foss, of 3, Sterling St., Montpelier Sq., SW7, and has issue living, Penrose Margaret Helen, *b.* 1970,—Charlotte Sophia Louise, *b.* 1975.

BRENTFORD, VISCOUNT. (Joynson-Hicks.) [Viscount U.K. 1929, Bt. U.K. 1919.]

Virtue is the safest helmet.

LANCELOT WILLIAM JOYNSON-HICKS, 3rd Viscount, 3rd Baronet of Holmbury and 1st Baronet of Newick; *b.* April 10th, 1902; *s.* to the Viscountcy and Baronetcy (of Holmbury) 1958; ed. at Winchester, and at Trin. Coll., Oxford (B.A. 1923, M.A. 1926); admitted a Solicitor 1926; was Parliamentary Sec. Min. of Fuel and Power Nov. 1951 to Dec. 1955; European War 1939-45 as acting Lieut.-Com. RNVR; Senior Partner in the legal firm of Joynson-Hicks & Co. 1938-66; Chm. of Automobile Asso. 1957-74; MP for Chichester Div. of W. Sussex (*C*) May 1942 to June 1958; cr. a *Baronet* (of Newick) 1956: *m.* 1931, Phyllis, only dau. of the late Major Herbert Allfrey, of Newnton House, Tetbury, Gloucestershire, and has issue.

Arms,—Gules, on a fesse wavy between three fleurs-de-lis or, a portcullis sable, all within a bordure of the second. Crest,—A stag's head proper gorged with a collar or, thereon five roses gules, and charged on the neck with a fleur-de-lis gold. Supporters,—On either side a stag proper gorged with a collar or, thereon five roses gules and charged on the neck with a fleur-de-lis gold.

Residence,—Newick Park, Sussex.

Hon. CRISPIN WILLIAM (25, Argyll Rd., W8), *b.* April 7th, 1933; ed. at Eton, and at New Coll., Oxford; Solicitor 1960; a partner in the legal firm of Joynson-Hicks & Co.; late Lt. 9th Lancers: *m.* 1964, Gillian Evelyn, el. da. of Gerald Edward Schluter, OBE, of Nairobi, Kenya, and has issue living, Paul William, *b.* 1971,—Emma Rosalie, *b.* 1966,—Rowena Phyllis, *b.* 1967.

WIDOW LIVING OF SECOND VISCOUNT.

Grace Esther (*Grace, Viscountess Brentford*), (216, Cradock Heights, Cradock Av., Rosebank, Johannesburg, S. Africa), dau. of the late A. E. A. Tothill, of Cape Town, and widow of D. S. T. McNellan, of Johannesburg, S. Africa: *m.* 1955, as his 2nd wife, the 2nd Viscount, who *d.* 1958.

PREDECESSORS.—[1] WILLIAM Joynson-Hicks, P.C., son of the late Henry Hicks, of Plaistow Hall, Kent; b. 1865; founder of legal firm of Joynson-Hicks & Co., solicitors; Parliamentary Sec. (Overseas Trade Depart.) to Board of Trade Oct. 1922 to March 1923, Postmaster-Gen. (also Paymaster-Gen.) March to May 1923, Financial Sec. to the Treasury (with a seat in the Cabinet), May to Sept. 1923, Min. of Health Sept. 1923 to Jan. 1924, and Sec. of State for Home Depart. Nov. 1924 to June 1929; M.P. for N.-W. Div. of Manchester (C) April 1908 to Jan. 1910, for Brentford Div. of Middlesex March 1911 to Nov. 1918, and for Twickenham Div. thereof Dec. 1918 to May 1929; cr. a Baronet 1919, and Viscount Brentford, of Newick, Sussex (peerage of United Kingdom) 1929: m. 1895, Grace Lynn, who d. 1952, dau. of Richard Hampson Joynson, J.P. (whose surname he assumed), formerly of Chasefield, Bowdon, Cheshire; d. 1932; s. by his son [2] RICHARD CECIL, 2nd Viscount, b. 1896; sometime on Staff of Gov. of Jamaica: m. 1st, 1920, Evelyn Mary Rothery, who d. 1954, only dau. of the late John F. McNellan, of Dollar, Clackmannanshire; 2ndly, 1955, Grace Esther, dau. of the late A. E. A. Tothill, of Cape Town, and widow of D. S. T. McNellan, of Johannesburg, S. Africa; d. 1958; s. by his brother [3] LANCELOT WILLIAM, 3rd Viscount and present peer.

BRIDGEMAN, VISCOUNT. (Bridgeman.) [Viscount U.K. 1929.]

ROBERT CLIVE BRIDGEMAN, K.B.E., C.B., D.S.O., M.C., 2nd Viscount; b. April 1st, 1896; s. 1935; ed. at Eton; Col. late Rifle Brig. (Prince Consort's Own), Hon. Maj.-Gen.; Hon. Col. 4th Batn. King's Shropshire LI (TA) 1949-59; Lord-Lieut. for co. Salop 1951-69, and Alderman of Salop Co. Council 1951-74; Brig. Major 7th Inf. Brig. 1932-34, and GSO War Office 1935-37; 1915-18 War (wounded, MC), 1939-45 War (despatches, DSO, CB); Private Sec. to his father when Parliamentary Sec. to Min. of Labour 1918; Director-Gen. Home Guard 1941-44, and DAG 1944-45; a KStJ; DSO 1940, CB (Mil) 1944, KBE (Civil) 1954: m. 1930, the Hon. Mary Kathleen Lane-Fox, JP, da. of 1st Baron Bingley (ext.), and has issue.

Neither rashly nor timidly.

Arms,—Sable, ten plates, four, three, two, and one, on a chief argent, a lion passant ermines. A Crest,—demi-lion rampant argent, holding in the paws a wreath of laurel proper. Supporters,—On either side a leopard guardant gules pelletée, charged on the shoulder with a portcullis or.

Seat,—Leigh Manor, Minsterley, Shropshire.　Clubs,—Beefsteak, Naval and Military.

DAUGHTERS LIVING.

Hon. Anne Caroline Mary, b. 1932: m. 1955, the Rev. Nicolas David Stacey, and has issue living, David Robert, b. 1958,—Caroline Jill, b. 1956,—Mary Elizabeth, b. 1961. Residence,—Bartholomew House, Selling, Faversham, Kent.

Hon. Susan Elizabeth, b. 1935; was Lady-in-Waiting to Lady May Abel Smith, wife of H.E. the Gov. of Queensland 1958-60: m. 1962, David Kenneth Dudley Foster, and has issue living, Robert Peter Dudley, b. 1966,—Edward Kenneth Clive, b. 1967,—Simon David Thomas, b. 1969. Residence,—Beech House, Shifnal, Salop.

Hon. Mary Selina, b. 1940: m. 1962, Jeremy David Bagot Bayliss, of Sheepbridge Court, Swallowfield, Reading, and has issue living, Jonathan Andrew Bagot, b. 1964,—Richard Charles, b. 1965,—Patrick Thomas Clive, b. 1968.

BROTHER LIVING.

Hon. Sir Maurice Richard, K.B.E., b. 1904; ed. at Eton, and at Trin. Coll., Camb.; was Petroleum Adviser, Min. of Economic Warfare 1939-40, and Principal Assist. Sec. Min. of Fuel and Power, 1944-46; is a KStJ; CBE (Civil) 1946, KBE (Civil) 1964: m. 1933, Diana Mary Erica, da. of the late Humphrey Minto Wilson, of 9, South Audley St., W.1, and has issue living, Erica Jane, b. 1934: m. 1960, Jeremiah Le Roy Harman, QC, of 22, Stafford Terr., W8, and Great Shefford House, Great Shefford, Newbury, Berks., son of the Rt. Hon. Sir Charles Eustace Harman, and has issue living, Charles Richard Le Roy b. 1963, Toby John b. 1967, Sarah Jane b. 1962,—Teresa Anne, b. 1937: m. 1960, Peter Baring, of 13, Chalcot Cres., NW1, and Inglewood Lodge, Kintbury, Berks. [see B. Revelstoke, colls.],—Elizabeth Caroline, b. 1944: m. 1971, Martin Dru Drury, of 3, Victoria Rise, SW4, and has issue, Matthew Orlando Dru b. 1972, Augusta Daisy Elizabeth b. 1974,—Rachel Diana, b. 1947: m. 1972, Philip Benjamin Hay of 3, Amner Rd., SW11, and has issue living, Thomas Alexander b. 1974. Residences,—The Glebe House, Selham, Petworth, Sussex; 10, Kylestrome House, Ebury St., SW1. Club,—White's.

COLLATERAL BRANCH LIVING.

Issue of the late Hon. Geoffrey John Orlando Bridgeman, MC, MB, FRCS, LRCP, 2nd son of 1st Viscount, b. 1898, d. 1974: m. 1929, Mary Meriel Gertrude, who d. 1974, da. of the late Rt. Hon. Sir George John Talbot [E. Shrewsbury, colls.]:—

ROBIN JOHN ORLANDO (51, Sloane Gdns., SW1; Watley House, Sparsholt, Hants); b. Dec. 5th, 1930; ed. at Eton; Lt. R. Green Jackets (RARO): OA 1958: m. 1966, Victoria Harriet Lucy, da. of Ralph Meredyth Turton, of Kildale Hall, Whitby [see V. Chetwynd, colls.], and has issue living, William Orlando Caspar, b. 1968,—Luke Robinson Orlando, b. 1971,—Esmond Francis Ralph Orlando, b. 1974.——Helena Mary, b. 1932: m. 1st, 1953 (m. diss. 1963), the Hon. Paul Asquith [see By. Asquith of Bishopstone]; 2ndly, 1963, James Francis Leslie Bayley, of Wassall House, Rolvenden Layne, Rolvenden, Cranbrook, Kent, and has issue living (by 1st m.) [see By. Asquith of Bishopstone), (by 2nd m.) Thomas Francis, b. 1966,—Rachel Helena, b. 1964.——Daphne, b. 1940: m. 1965, William Howard Clive Montgomery, and has issue living, Hugh Geoffrey Clive, b. 1966,—Rose Evelyn, b. 1968,—Frances Mary, b. 1970,—Flora Anne Selina, b. 1974.

PREDECESSOR.—[1] Rt. Hon. WILLIAM CLIVE Bridgeman, P.C., son of the late Rev. the Hon. John Robert Orlando Bridgeman, 3rd son of 2nd Earl of Bradford; b. 1864; Chm. of British Broadcasting Corporation, and of Govs. of Shrewsbury Sch., a Fellow of Eton Coll., and an Elder Brother of Trinity House; Assist. Private Sec. to Sec. of State for Colonies 1889-92, Private Sec. to Chancellor of Exchequer 1895-9, Junior Lord of the Treasury 1915-16, Assist. Director, War Trade Depart. 1916, Parliamentary Sec. to Min. of Labour 1916-18, and to Board of Trade 1919-20, Sec. of Mines Aug. 1920 to Oct. 1922, Sec. of State for Home Depart. Oct. 1922 to Jan, 1924, and First Lord of the Admiralty Nov. 1924 to June 1929; M.P. for Salop, W. or Oswestry Div. (C) 1906-29: cr. Viscount Bridgeman of Leigh, co. Salop (peerage of United Kingdom; 1929: m. 1895, Dame Caroline Beatrix, D.B.E., who d. 1961, dau. of the late Hon. Cecil Thomas Parker [E. Macclesfield, colls.]; d. 1935; s. by his son [2] ROBERT CLIVE, 2nd Viscount and present peer.

BRIDGES, BARON. (Bridges.) [Baron U.K. 1957.]

To act without speaking.
Address,—c/o FCO, SW1

THOMAS EDWARD BRIDGES, CMG, 2nd Baron; b. Nov. 27th, 1927; s. 1969; ed. at Eton, and New Coll., Oxford; HM Diplo. Ser. since 1951; seconded as Private Sec. for Overseas Affairs to Prime Min. 1972-74; CMG 1975: m. 1953, Rachel Mary, yst. da. of Sir Henry Nöel Bunbury, KCB, and has issue.

Arms,—Argent a cross sable charged with a wreath of laurel fructed of the field a chief chequy also sable and of the first. Crest,—A man's head and shoulders couped proper wreathed about the temples argent the ribands gules, vested paly of six sable and argent. Supporters,—On either side a swan wings elevated and addorsed proper gorged with a collar chequy sable and argent.

SONS LIVING.
Hon. MARK THOMAS, b. July 25th, 1954; ed. at Eton.
Hon. Nicholas Edward, b. 1956.

DAUGHTER LIVING.
Hon. Harriet Elizabeth, b. 1958.

BROTHER LIVING.
Hon. Robert Oliver (12, Hillside, SW19), b. 1930; ed. at Eton, and at Magdalen Coll., Oxford; an ARIBA: m. 1963, Rosamund Theresa, yr. da. of the late Roger C. V. de Wesselow and has issue living, John Edward, b. 1968,—James George Robert, b. 1970.

SISTERS LIVING.
Hon. Shirley Frances, b. 1924: m. 1957, Hilary Topham Corke, and has issue living, William Edward Orlando, b. 1961,—Emma Lucy, b. 1958,—Cicely Catharine, b. 1960.—Georgiana Phoebe ,b. 1963. Residence,—Eversheds, Abinger Hammer, Surrey.
Hon. Margaret Evelyn, b. 1932: m. 1st, 1954 (m. diss. 1969), Trevor Henry Aston; 2ndly, 1971, Paul William Jex Buxton, of Castle House, Ongar, Essex [see Buxton, Bt., colls.].

WIDOW LIVING OF FIRST BARON.
Hon. KATHARINE DIANTHE FARRER (Katharine, Baroness Bridges), (Goodman's Furze, Headley, Surrey), d a. of 2nd Baron Farrer: m. 1922, the 1st Baron, who d. 1969.

PREDECESSOR.—[1] Rt. Hon. Sir EDWARD ETTINGDENE BRIDGES, KG, GCB, GCVO, MC, PC, FRS, son of the late Robert Seymour Bridges, OM (Poet Laureate, of Chilswell, Oxford; b. 1892;; Sec. to the Cabinet 1938-46; Permanent Sec. to HM Treasury and Head of Civil Ser. 1945-56 Chm. of British Council 1954-67; cr. Baron Bridges, of Headley, co. Surrey, and of St. Nicholas at Wade, co. Kent (peerage of UK) 1957: m. 1922, the Hon. Katharine Dianthe Farrer, da. of 2nd Baron Farrer; d. 1969; s. by his son [2] THOMAS EDWARD, 2nd Baron and present peer.

BRIDPORT, VISCOUNT. (Hood.) [Viscount U.K. 1868.]

ALEXANDER NELSON HOOD, 4th Viscount; b. March 17th, 1948; s. 1969; ed. at Eton, and the Sorbonne; 7th Duke of Bronte in Sicily (cr. 1799): m. 1972, Linda Jacqueline, da. of Lt.-Col. Vincent Rudolph Paravicini, of Nutley Manor, Basingstoke, and has issue.

Arms,—Quarterly: 1st and 4th azure, a fret argent; on a chief or three crescents sable, Hood; 2nd and 3rd, or, a cross patonce sable, a bend gules surmounted of another engrailed of the field charged with three bombs fired proper, on a chief undulated argent, waves of the sea from which a palm tree issuant between a disabled ship on the dexter, and a battery in ruins on the sinister all proper, over all a fess wavy azure, thereon inscribed the word "Trafalgar" or, Nelson. Crest,—A Cornish chough proper, the dexter foot resting on the fluke of an anchor in bend sinister or. Supporters,—Dexter, a figure of Neptune, crowned with an Eastern crown or a green robe flowing round his loins, holding a trident in the left hand, and resting the right on an anchor, also or; sinister, a sea lion argent, the back fin and top of the tail gules, resting the sinister paw on an anchor or.

Residence,—Castello di Maniace, 95030, Maniace di Bronte, Provincia di Catania, Sicily. Club,—Brooks's.

SON LIVING.
Hon. PEREGRINE ALEXANDER NELSON, b. Aug. 30th, 1974.
WIDOW LIVING OF THIRD VISCOUNT.
SHEILA JEANNE AGATHA (Sheila, Viscountess Bridport), (Castello di Maniace, 95030, Maniace di Bronte, Provincia di Catania, Sicily), only da. of the late Johan Hendrik van Meurs, and widow of Wing-Cdr. J. H. Little, DFC, Aux.AF: m. 1946, the 3rd Viscount, who d. 1969.

COLLATERAL BRANCH LIVING. (In remainder to Barony only.)
Descendants of Alexander Hood (uncle of 1st Baron), Sir (Alexander) William Fuller-Acland-Hood, 5th hand 6th Bt.

PREDECESSORS.—[1] Adm. Sir ALEXANDER HOOD, MP (yr. brother of 1st Viscount Hood) a celebrated naval commander, was cr. Baron Bridport (peerage of Ireland) 1794 with remainder to his great-nephew, the Hon. Samuel Hood, 2nd son of 2nd Viscount Hood, and in failure thereof to the heirs male of his uncle, Alexander Hood, Baron Bridport, of Cricket St. Thomas, Somerset (peerage of Great Britain) 1796, and Viscount Bridport, of Cricket St. Thomas (peerage of U.K.)

1800; *d.* without issue 1814, when the English honours expired, and the Irish peerage devolved upon his great-nephew (ante) [2] SAMUEL, 2nd Baron, *b.* 1788: *m.* 1810, Lady Charlotte Mary Nelson, Duchess of Bronte, who *d.* 1873, only surviving child and heiress of 1st Earl Nelson; *d.* 1868; *s.* by his son [3] *Gen.* ALEXANDER NELSON, *GCB,* 1st Viscount, *b.* 1814; cr. *Viscount Bridport* (peerage of United Kingdom) 1868; Groom-in-Waiting to H.M. Queen Victoria 1841-58, Clerk Marshal to the late Prince Consort 1853-61, an Equerry to H.M. Queen Victoria 1858-84, a Lord-in-Waiting to H.M. Queen Victoria 1884-1901, and an Extra Equerry to H.M. Queen Victoria 1884-1901; was an Hon. Equerry to H.M. King Edward VII: *m.* 1838, Lady Mary Penelope Hill, who *d.* 1884, da. of 3rd Marquess of Downshire; *d.* 1904; *s.* by his son [4] Col. ARTHUR WELLING-TON ALEXANDER NELSON, *C.B.,* 2nd Viscount, *b.* 1839; M.P. for W. Somerset (*C*) 1868-80: *m.* 1872, Lady Maria Georgiana Julia Fox-Strangways, who *d.* 1922, sister of 5th Earl of Ilchester; *d.* 1924; *s.* by his grandson [5] ROWLAND ARTHUR HERBERT NELSON (only son of the late Lieut. the Hon. Maurice Henry Nelson Hood, Roy. Naval Div., who *d.* (killed in action) 1915, 2nd son of 2nd Viscount), 3rd Viscount, *b.* 1911; Lord-in-Waiting to HM 1939-40: *m.* 1st, 1934 (m. diss. 1945), Pamela Aline Mary, only da. of the late Charles J. Baker; 2ndly, 1946, Sheila Jeanne Agatha, only da. of Johan Hendrik van Meurs, and widow of Wing-Cdr. J. H. Little, DFC, Aux.AF; *d.* 1969; *s.* by his son [6] ALEXANDER NELSON, 4th Viscount and present peer; also Baron Bridport.

BRIGINSHAW, BARON. (Briginshaw.) [Life Baron, 1974.]

RICHARD WILLIAM BRIGINSHAW, son of   Briginshaw; *b.* 19—;
ed. at Stuart Sch., London; Hon. LLD New Brunswick; 1939-45 War; Gen. Sec., Nat. Soc. of Operative Printers, Graphical and Media Personnel since 1951; a Member of Gen. Council of TUC since 1965, and of Joint Cttee. on Manpower since 1965: a Gov. of Dulwich Coll.; cr. *Baron Briginshaw* of Southwark, Greater London (Life Baron) 1974: *m.* 19—,
Address,—13/16, Borough Rd., SE1.

BRISTOL, LORD BISHOP OF. [Tinsley.]

Right Rev. ERNEST JOHN TINSLEY, *BD,* son of the late Ernest William Tinsley, of Sedgefield, co. Durham; *b.* March 22nd, 1919; ed. at Stockton-on-Tees Sec. Sch. for Boys, St. John's Coll., Durham (MA, BD, Fellow 1942-44) and Westcott House Theo. Coll., Camb.; Lecturer in Theology, Univ. Coll., Hull 1946-54, Snr. Lecturer 1954-61, and Head 1961-62; Lecturer of St. Mary, Lowgate, Hull 1955-62, Examining Chap. to Archbishop of York 1957-63 and to Bishop of Sheffield 1963-75; Prof. of Theology Leeds Univ. 1962-75, and Hon. Canon of Ripon 1966-75; consecrated 53rd Bishop of Bristol 1976: *m.* 1947, Marjorie, da. of Joseph Ernest Dixon.

Patron of ninety-eight livings, of six with joint patronage, and of the Archdeaconries of Bristol and Swindon.

The See of Bristol is one of the six Bishoprics created by Henry VIII in 1541; and was united with the See of Gloucester from 1836-97.

𝔈𝔭𝔦𝔰𝔠𝔬𝔭𝔞𝔩 𝔖𝔦𝔤𝔫𝔞𝔱𝔲𝔯𝔢,—"John Bristol."

ARMS OF THE SEE,—Sable, three ducal coronets in pale or.
Residence,—Bishop's House, Clifton Hill, Bristol, BS8 1BW.

BRISTOL, MARQUESS OF. (Hervey.) [Marquess U.K. 1826.]
[Name pronounced "Harvy."]

I shall never forget.

VICTOR FREDERICK COCHRANE HERVEY, 6th Marquess, *b.* Oct. 6th, 1915; *s.* 1960; ed. at Eton, and RMC; Hereditary High Steward of the Liberty of St. Edmund, patron of thirty livings, Chm. of Estate Associates, Ltd., Ickworth Forestry Contractors, Ltd., The Marquis of Bristol & Co., V.L.C. Associates, Ltd., Sleaford Investments Ltd., Eastern Caravan Parks Ltd., Bristol Publishing Co., Dominica Paradise, Ltd., The Bristol Powersport Co., British Internat. Airways Ltd., The Atlantis Project Cyprus, and other cos.; Gov. Dir. Cyprus Enterprises Co., Ickworth (Bahamas) Aust. Ltd., Dominica Paradise Ltd., Emerald Hillsides Estates, Dominica, and other cos.; a Council Member of Nat. Yacht Harbour Assocn., and a Member of W. India Cttee., and of European Atlantic Group; Owner of Ickworth Stud: *m.* 1st, 1949 (m. diss. 1959), Pauline Mary, da. of the late Herbert Coxon Bolton; 2ndly, 1960 (m. diss. 1972), Lady Anne Juliet Dorothea Maud Wentworth Fitzwilliam, only child of the 8th Earl Fitzwilliam; 3rdly, 1974, Yvonne Marie, only da. of Anthony Sutton, of Woodstock, The Glen, Farnborough Park, Kent and has issue by 1st and 2nd marriages.

Arms,—Gules, on a bend argent, three trefoils slipped vert. Crest,—An ounce passant sable, spotted, ducally collared, and chain reflexed over the back or, holding in the dexter paw a trefoil slipped vert. Supporters,—Two ounces sable, bezantée, ducally collared, and chain reflexed over the back or.

Seat,—Ickworth, Bury St. Edmunds, Suffolk.
Residence,—15, Chapel Street, Belgrave Square, S.W.1.
Clubs,—United Hunts, Hurlingham, Eccentric, East Hill (Nassau), House of Lords Yacht. Clermont.

SONS LIVING. (By 1st marriage.)
FREDERICK WILLIAM JOHN AUGUSTUS (Earl Jermyn), b. Sept. 15th, 1954; ed. at Harrow.
(By 2nd marriage.)
Lord Frederick William Charles Nicholas Wentworth, b. 1961.

DAUGHTER LIVING OF FOURTH MARQUESS.
Lady Phyllis, b. 1899; formerly Junior Com. A.T.S.: m. 1921, Capt. John Duncan George MacRae, Seaforth Highlanders, who d. 1966, and has issue living, John Duncan Hervey (of Eilean Donan Castle, Ross-shire, and Nairnside House, by Inverness), b. 1925: m. 1950, Marigold Elizabeth, da. of the late G. H. Tritton, and has issue living, Miranda Mary b. 1951: m. 1974 ,Baron Rudolf Willem van Lynden, Mairi Jean b. 1952: m. 1974, Gregory Bibo, of Melbourne, Aust., Rosalind Claire b. 1955, Valerie Anne b. 1960, Georgina b. 1963,—Merelina Mary Phyllis, b. 1922,—Jean Margaret (Countess of Northesk), b. 1927: m. 1949, the 13th Earl of Northesk of Fair Oak, Rogate, Petersfield. (Residences,—19, Coleherne Mews, SW10; Hatchery House, Barrow, Bury St.Edmunds.

COLLATERAL BRANCHES LIVING.

Grandchildren of the late Sir George William Hervey, K.C.B., e:. son of the la't Lord William Hervey, C.B., 3rd son of 1st Marquess:—
Issue of the late Gerald Edward William Hervey, b. 1881, d. 1934: m. 1914, Elizabeth Margaret (Lily), dau. of S. J. du Toit, of 62, Noord Street, Johannesburg, S. Africa:—
Alexander George, b. 1920; European War 1939-45 (prisoner). Residence,—78, Second Avenue, Melville, Johannesburg, S. Africa.——Hazel Lilly, b. 1915: m. 1937, William Christian Bouwer, who d. 1944, and has issue living, Kenneth William, b. 1940. Residence,—
Issue of the late Claude Arthur Hervey, b. 1891, d. 1927: m. 1920, Edith Kathleen, who d. 1972, da. of the late Humphry B. Lamb. of Penn, Staffordshire:—
Cecilia Dora, b. 1923: m. 1945, John Quay, and has issue living, Jacqueline Teresa, b. 1950. Residence,—48, Garden Wood Rd., East Grinstead, Sussex, RH19 1NL.

Grandchildren of the late Francis Arthur Hervey, son of the late Lord William Hervey, C.B. (ante):—
Issue of the late Alec Francis Hervey, b. 1885. d. 1949: m. 1st, 1912, Winifred Victoria (who d. 1963, having obtained a divorce 1924), dau. of the late Frederick George Cosens, of 7, Observatory Gdns., W, and Bacton, Norfolk; 2ndly, 1925, Edyth Cecilia (LOCK-INGTON) (Trecynon, Grange Rd., Uckfield, Sussex), da. of John Charles Cowan:—
(By 1st m.) Ronald Frederick William, b, 1919: m., 1st, 1943 (m. diss. 1948), Constance Mary, da. of the late J. D. Bunce, and widow of Alexander Zatonski, Flying Officer RAF; 2ndly, 1958, Jeanne Patricia, da. of the late Rev. A. W. Dowse, and has issue living, (by 2nd marriage) Timothy Hugh, b. 1960,—Jennifer Charlotte, b. 1962. Address,—c/o Westminster Bank, 1, Kensington High St., W.8.——Patricia Leila, b. 1914: m. 1940, Capt. Martin Edward Scobell Boissier, D.S.O., R.N., who d. 1964. Residence,—4, Salter's Acres, Weeke, Winchester.

Granddaughter of the late Rt. Rev. Lord Arthur Charles Hervey, DD, Lord Bishop of Bath and Wells, 4th son of 1st Marquess:—
Issue of the late George Henry William Hervey, b. 1843, d. 1933: m. 1st, 1876, Emma, who d. 1877, dau. of the late William Arkwright, of Sutton Scarsdale, Derby 2ndly, 1879, Mary, who d. 1900, dau. of the late William Wells Cole:—
(By 2nd marriage) Evelyn Victoria, b. 1887: m. 1915, Edward Bertram Parker, who d. 1926, formerly Assist. Paymaster R.N., and has issue living, Robin, b. 1918,—Thelma, b. 1916,—Pamela (1490, Sacramento St., Apt. 4D, San Francisco, Cal., 94109, USA), b. 1921: m. 1955, Charles E. Reid-Selth, DSM, who d. 1962. Residence.—Coolinge, Smoke Lane, Reigate.

Granddaughter of the late Douglas George Hervey (infra):—
Issue of the late Edward George Hervey, b. 1917, d. 1959: m. 1956, Sheila Mary Howard (Lady Sebright), who m. 2ndly, 1965, Sir Hugo Giles Edmund Sebright, 14th Bt., da. of Walter Howard Rocke, of Salisbury, Rhodesia:—
Elizabeth Lepel Howard b, 1957.

Grandchildren of the late George Henry William Hervey (ante):—
Issue of the late Douglas George Hervey, b. 1880, d. 1965: m. 1913, Ida Constance, who d. 1972, da. of the late Rev. Edward Clowes, of Colworth, Bexhill-on-Sea:—
Constance Valentine, b. 1920: m. 1951, D. C. Lamsdale, of the Duke of Edinburgh, Nightingale Lane, Wanstead, E11, and has issue living, Judith, b. 1952,——Susan Sarah, b. 1956.——Margery, b. 1922: m. 1947, Arthur Thomas Hingle, of 14320, Tanglewood Drive, Dallas, Texas 75234, USA, and has issue living, Michael, b. 1949,—Peter John Benedict, b. 1956,—Jane, b. 1948,—Gillian, b. 1951,—Veronica Anne, b. 1954,—Margaret Mary Bridget, b. 1959.
Issue of the late Gerald Arthur Hervey, Lieut. (T.F.) R.G.A., b. 1881, d. (killed in action during European War) 1917: m. 1912, Dorothy, who d. 1949, dau. of the late Alfred Symes, of Tendring, Essex:—
Anthony Gerald, b. 1915; ed. at Marlborough, and at Pembroke Coll., Camb.: m. 1948, Aileen Margaret, dau. of Dr. L. R. Pickett, of 167, Cooden Sea Road, Cooden, Sussex, and has issue living, Gerald Edward, b. 1949,—Christopher Symes, b. 1952. Residence,—38, Westbury Road, North-wood, Middx.——Elizabeth Mary (6, Bucklehaven, Sandy Lane Rd., Charlton Kings, Cheltenham), b. 1913: m. 1948, John Charles Jones, MBE, who d. 1969.

Grandchildren of the late Rev. Lord Charles Amelius Hervey, D.D., 5th son of 1st Marquess:—
Issue of the late Dudley Francis Amelius Hervey, C.M.G., b. 1849, d. 1911: m. 1894, Griselda Mary Theophila, who d. 1929, dau. of Col. Sir Edward FitzGerald Campbell, 2nd Bt. (cr. 1815):—
Griselda Harriet Violet Finetta Georgiana (Griselda, Baroness Aberdare), b. 1901: m. (Sept.) 1957, as his second wife, the 3rd Baron Aberdare, who d. (Oct.) 1957. Club,—Lansdowne.
Issue of the late William George Edward Hervey, b. 1850, d. 1913: m. 1886, Eva Florence, who d 1942, dau. of the late Henry West, Q.C., Judge of County Court, of Loughlingstown :—
Osyth Christina Frederica, b. 1897: m. 1918, Maj. Frank Pilkington Scott, late RAF, who d. 1974, and has issue living, Rae Hervey, MB, ChB, b. 1922: m. 1946, Thomas Straton, MB, ChB, of The Paddocks, Market Place, Fordingbridge, Hants, and has issue living, David b. 1949: m. 1972, Elizabeth Turner, Peter b. 1956, Nicola b. 1951: m. 1971, David Simon Crump (and has issue living, Diana b. 1972, Philippa b. 1973,—Pauline Hervey (Flight Deck, Above Town, Dartmouth, Devon), b. 1924: m.

1948 (m. diss. 1971), Maj. Raymond Charles Crossley Dodd, MC, TD, RA, and has issue living, Andrew Hervey Crossley b. 1951, James Scott Crossley b. 1953; Sub-Lt. RN: m. 1974, Nichola Ann Anstey,—Veronica Hervey, b. 1930: m. 1951, Maj. William Wemyss Ker, RE, of Kittisford Barton, Wellington, Somerset, and has issue living, Alan Wemyss b. 1955, Sheila Hilary b. 1956. Residence,—Rest Harrow, 75, Above Town, Dartmouth, Devon, TQ6 9RH.

Descendants of the late Frederick Anne Hervey-Bathurst, next brother of the late Felton Elwell Hervey-Bathurst (el. son of the late Felton Lionel Hervey, son of the late Hon. Felton Hervey, 8th son of 1st Earl of Bristol), who was cr. a Baronet 1818, and whom he s. (under special remainder) 1819 :—

See Hervey-Bathurst, Bt.

PREDECESSORS.—[1] JOHN Hervey, of Ickworth, Suffolk, MP for Bury St. Edmunds 1690-1 and 1695-1703, was cr. Baron Hervey of Ickworth (peerage of England) 1703, and Earl of Bristol (peerage of GB) 1714: m. 1st, 1688, Isabella, who d. 1693, da. and heir of Sir Robert Carr, 3rd Bt.; 2ndly, 1695, Elizabeth, who d. 1741, da. and co-heir of Sir Thomas Felton, 4th Bt., by Lady Elizabeth Howard, da. and co-heir of 3rd Earl of Suffolk, and 3rd Lord Howard de Walden; his el. son by 2nd m., John, who had been summoned to Parl. as Lord Hervey 1733, d. 1743, leaving, by his wife Mary Lepel, issue of whom three sons succeeded to the title; the Earl d. 1751; s. by his grandson [2] GEORGE WILLIAM, 2nd Earl; Ambassador to Spain 1758-61; Lord Lt. of Ireland 1766-67; d. unm. 1775; s. by his brother [3] AUGUSTUS JOHN, 3rd Earl, Vice-Adm. of the Blue, and a Lord of the Admiralty in 1799; d. s.p. 1779; s. by his brother [4] Rt. Rev. FREDERICK AUGUSTUS, 4th Earl, b. 1730; Bishop of Derry, who by descent from his grandmother s. de jure to the Barony of Howard de Walden, which title was in 1806 confirmed upon his great-grandson, the 2nd Baron Seaford; the Bishop m. 1752, Elizabeth, who d. 1800, sister and heir of Sir Charles Davers, 5th Bt. (and gt.-grandda. of 2nd Baron Jermyn); d. 1803; s. by his el. surv. son [5] FREDERICK WILLIAM, 5th Earl; cr. Earl Jermyn and Marquess of Bristol (peerage of UK) 1820; m. 1798, Elizabeth Albana, who d. 1844, da. of 1st Baron Templetown; d. 1859; s. by his son [6] FREDERICK WILLIAM, 2nd Marquess, b. 1880; MP for Bury St. Edmunds 1826-59; Treasurer of Roy. Household 1841-46: m. 1830, Lady Katharine Isabella Manners, who d. 1848, da. of 5th Duke of Rutland; d. 1864; s. by his son [7] FREDERICK WILLIAM JOHN, 3rd Marquess, b. 1834; MP for W. Suffolk (C) 1859-64, and Lord-Lt. of Suffolk 1886-1907: m. 1862, Geraldine Georgina Mary, who d. 1927, da. of Gen. the Hon. George Anson; d. 1907; s. by his nephew [8] FREDERICK WILLIAM FANE, MVO (son of Lord Augustus Henry Charles Hervey, MP, 2nd son of 2nd Marquess), 4th Marquess, b. 1863; Rear-Adm.; MP for Bury St. Edmunds (C) 1906-07: m. 1896, Alice Frances Theodora, who d. 1957, da. of George Edward Wythes, of Copt Hall, Epping; d. 1951; s. by his brother [9] HERBERT ARTHUR ROBERT, 5th Marquess, b. 1870; Min. and Consul-Gen. to Colombia 1919-23, and Min. to Peru and Equador 1923-29: m. 1st, 1914, Lady Jean Alice Elaine Cochrane (who d. 1955, having obtained a divorce 1933), da. of 12th Earl of Dundonald; 2ndly, 1952, Dora Frances Emblin, who d. 1953, widow of Don Pedro de Zulueta; d. 1960; s by his only son [10] VICTOR FREDERICK COCHRANE, 6th Marquess and present peer; also Earl of Bristol, Earl Jermyn, and Baron Hervey of Ickworth.

BROADBRIDGE, BARON. (Broadbridge.) [Baron U.K. 1945, Bt. U.K. 1937.]

PETER HEWETT BROADBRIDGE, 3rd Baron and 3rd Baronet ; b. Aug. 19th, 1938; s. 1972; ed. at Hurstpierpoint, and St. Catherine's Coll., Oxford (MA, BSc): m. 1967, Mary, only da. of W. O. Busch, of An Der Brücke, Dittershausen, Kassel, Germany, and has issue.

Arms,—Gules, in chief two pens in saltire or and in base over water a stone bridge of a single span embattled proper. Crest,—A dolphin hauriant argent between two gilly-flowers gules slipped and leaved vert. Supporters,—On either side a dolphin proper charged with a sword erect gules.

Residence,—31, Ockenden Rd., Islington, N1.

DAUGHTERS LIVING.

Hon. Jemima Louise, b. 1970.
Hon. Sophie Mary, b. 1972.

By industry and perseverance.

UNCLES LIVING. (Sons of 1st Baron)

Hon. RALPH GEORGE CAMERON, b. Nov. 20th, 1901; ed., at Shoreham Gram. Sch.; LDSRCS England 1924; is a Dental Surg.: m. 1925, Emma Rose Hancock, da. of Henry Van der Weyden, and has issue living, Enid Rose, b. 1926: m. 1948, Alexander Rolland. and has issue living, Andrew b. 1949, Martin b. 1951, Nigel b. 1955,—June, b. 1927,—Anita, b, 1928: m. 1949, Dennis Robert Hutchins, and has issue living, Anthony David b. 1953, Lucy Jane, b. 1955. Residence,—Old School House, Church Walk, Sturminster Newton, Dorset.

Hon. Hugh Trevor (19, Hanover Close, Sturminster Newton, Dorset), b. 1903; ed. at Shoreham Gram. Sch.: m. 1927, Anne Marjorie, da. of J. Locke Elfick, and has issue living, Martin Hugh (The Old Candle House, Mill Lane, North Cave, E. Yorks.), b. 1929: m. 1st, 1954, Norma, da. of the late Maj. Herbert Sheffield, MC; 2ndly, 1968, Elizabeth, da. of J. E. Trotman,—Jill, b. 1932: m. 1954, John Damment, RAF (c/o Lloyds Bank, 6, Pall Mall, SW1Y 5NH), and has issue living, Stephen b. 1957, Helen b. 1956, Deborah b. 1958, Louise b. 1959, Susan b. 1962.

Hon. Howard Eustace (12, Texel, Alexandra Rd., Pietermaritzburg, Natal), b. 1904: m. 1935, Margaret Ada Marion, da. of Capt. H. H. Witherington, and has issue living, Sally Kathleen, b. 1937: m. 1966, Peter Jeremy Chadwick Horne, and has issue living, Lance Chadwick b. 1969, Timothy George Chadwick b. 1971.

Hon. Rupert Guy, b. 1906; Ethiopia and N. Africa 1941-45: m. 1948, Margaret Anne, dau. of the late George S. Cumming, of Bloemfontein, S. Africa, and has issue living, Beverley (a dau.), b. 1949. Residence,—199, Kingsway, Warner Beach, Natal, S. Africa.

PREDECESSORS,—[1] Sir GEORGE Broadbridge, KCVO, son of the late Henry Broadbridge, of Brighton: b. 1869: an Alderman (Candlewick Ward) for City of London (Sheriff 1933-34), Lord Mayor of London 1936-37; sat as MP for City of London (C) 1938-45; cr. a Baronet (UK, of Wargrave Place) 1937, and Baron Broadbridge, of Brighton, co. Sussex (peerage of United Kingdom) 1945: m. 1st 1895, Fanny Kathleen, who d. 1928, da. of the late Richard Brigden, of Brighton; 2ndly, 1929, Clara Maud, who d. 1949, da. of the late John Swornsbourne, of Bognor Regis, Sussex; d. 1952; s. by his el. son [2] ERIC WILBERFORCE, 2nd Baron, b. 1895: m. 1924, Mabel Daisy, who d. 1966, da. of Arthur Edward Clarke; d. 1972; s. by his only son [3] PETER HEWETT, 3rd Baron and present peer.

Brocas, Viscount, son of Earl Jellicoe.

BROCK, BARON. (Brock.) [Life Baron 1965.]

By work rather than theory.

RUSSELL CLAUDE BROCK, son of Herbert Brock, of London; *b*. Oct. 24th, 1903; ed. at Christ's Hosp.; Hon LLD Leeds; MB (hon) and MS London; FRCP; FRCS England; Hon. FACS; Hon. FRACS; Hon. MD Camb., Hamburg and Munich; Surg. at Guy's and Brompton Hosps, since 1936, and a Member of Council of Roy. Coll. of Surgs. since 1949 (Vice-Pres. 1956-63, and Pres. 1963-66); *cr*. Knt. 1954, and *Baron Brock*, of Wimbledon, London Borough of Merton (Life Peerage) 1965: *m*. 1926, Germaine Louise, da. of Louis Ladeveze, of Paris, and has issue.

Arms,—Per chevron sable and argent, in chief two brocks passant or, and in base a human heart ensigned with a mitre sans lappets azure. Crest,—A brock passant or resting the dexter forepaw on a human heart. Supporters,—*Dexter*, a Siberian tiger statant guardant proper; *Sinister*, a lion guardant gules holding in the dexter paw a brock proper.
Residences.—2, Harley St., London W1; The Old Rectory House, Church Rd., Wimbledon, SW19. *Club.*—Athenæum.

DAUGHTERS LIVING.

Hon. Angela Mary, *b*. 1929; ed. at Malvern Girls' Coll., and at Somerville Coll., Oxford (BA, BM, BCh): *m*. 1954, Colin Thomson Howe, 5, Woodhyrst Gdns., Firs Rd., Kenley, Surrey, and has issue.
Hon. Mary Rose, *b*. 1933; ed. at Wycombe Abbey Sch.: *m*. 1959, Keith Vanstone, of 80, Church Rd., SW19, and has issue.
Hon. Margaret Louise, *b*. 1936; ed. at Malvern Girls' Coll.: *m*. 1962 (John Alexander) Simon Cary Mayhew, of Ballards Wood, Rosemary Lane, Ticehurst, Sussex [see V. Falkland].

BROCKET, BARON. (Nall-Cain.) [Baron U.K. 1933, Bt. U.K. 1921.]

The cat stroked is meek.

CHARLES RONALD GEORGE NALL-CAIN, 3rd Baron, and 3rd Baronet; *b*. Feb. 12th, 1952; *s*. 1967; ed. at Eton.
Arms,—Quarterly: 1st and 4th argent, three salmon haurient gules, in chief an oak tree eradicated proper, *Cain*; 2nd and 3rd per chevron barry of six gules and or and of the first, in chief two stags' heads caboshed proper and in base a lion rampant guardant of the second, *Nall*. Crest,—1st, a cat salient guardant erminois holding between the paws a dexter hand couped gules, *Cain*; 2nd, within a leather garter buckled gules a bee or, *Nall*. Supporters,—Two cats guardant erminois.
Residence.—Brocket Hall, Welwyn, Herts.

BROTHERS LIVING.
(Raised to the rank of a Baron's sons 1969.)
Hon. RICHARD PHILIP CHRISTOPHER, *b*. April 5th, 1953; ed. at Eton.
Hon. David Michael Anthony, *b*. 1955; ed. at Harrow.

UNCLE LIVING. *(Son of 2nd Baron.)*
Hon. David Lawrence Robert (Carton, Maynooth, co. Kildare; Cavalry Club), *b*. 1930; ed. at Eton, and at Magdalene Coll., Camb. (BA 1953, MA 1957), late 2nd Lt. 12th Roy. Lancers: *m*. 1958, the Hon. Katherine Elizabeth Palmer, da. of the late William Matthew, Viscount Wolmer [see E. Selbourne], and has issue living, James Alexander, *b*. 1961,—Caroline Davina, *b*. 1959,—Annabel Priscilla Angela, *b*. 1963.

AUNT LIVING. *(Daughter of 2nd Baron.)*
Hon. Elizabeth Angela Veronica Rose, *b*. 1938: *m*. 1st, 1958 (m. diss. 1969), the 6th Marquess of Headfort; 2ndly, 1970, William Murless Knight, of Horsley Hall, Eccleshall, Stafford, and has issue living (by 1st m.) [see M. Headfort], (by 2nd m.), Peregrine Robert Christian Murless, *b*. 1971.

MOTHER LIVING.
Elizabeth Mary, da. of R. J. Stallard, of Tresayes, Fauvic, Grouville, Jersey: *m*. 1st, 1950, the Hon. Ronald Charles Manus Nall-Cain, who *d*. 1961; 2ndly, 1964, Colin John Richard Trotter, of Mells Park, Frome, Somerset.

PREDECESSORS.—The family of O'Cahan was settled in Northern Ireland from the earliest times, owning a large territory there called O'Cahan's country. The O'Cahans, who trace their descent from Niall of the Nine Hostages, King of Ulster in the 5th century (also ancestor of the O'Neills) were Lords of the Route and Princes of Limavady. They owned the fishing rights in the three rivers, Bann, Foyle, and Roe prior to the Plantation of Ulster, hence the three salmon in the Cain Arms, while the wild cat now used as a crest and supporters in the Arms is reputed to have been used on the shield of The O'Cahan in 850. Manus Cathan an Duin, Prince of Limavady, was killed in the Battle of Down in 1260. Sir Donall O'Cahan of Limavady was knighted in 1607. His grandson, Eanagh, was deprived of his lands on the Plantation of Ulster and settled in co. Galway in 1631, Joseph O'Cahan, great-grandson of Eanagh, *d*. in Ballybane, co. Galway in 1756. and his 2nd son, William, *m*. Catherine O'Malley, and was the father of James O'Cahan, *b*. (in the parish of St. Nicholas, Galway) 1787. James changed his name to Cain, joined the 88th Regiment of Foot (later the Connaught Rangers), and fought in the Peninsular War. He *m*. Mary, dau. of Alexander Deane of Cork, and sister of Sir Thomas Deane, the well-known Architect and Lord Mayor of Cork. Their son, Robert Cain, *b*. on Spike Island, Cork, 1826, emigrated to England in 1844: *m*. 1848, Ann, dau. of James Newall, of Lowton. He founded the firm of Robert Cain & Sons, and had with other issue a 3rd son, William Ernest, *b*. 1864, cr. 1st Baronet of Wargrave, and a 4th [1] CHARLES ALEXANDER, *b*. 1866; Chm. of Walker Cain, Ltd., a JP and DL for Herts (High Sheriff 1925), Pres. of Hitchin Dist. of League of Mercy, and a K.G.St.J.; assumed additional surname of Nall; *cr.* a *Baronet* 1921, and *Baron Brocket*, of Brocket Hall, co. Hertford (peerage of United Kingdom) 1933 : *m.* 1st, 1888, Florence, who *d.* 1927, youngest dau. of the late William Nall, of Kegworth, Derbyshire ; 2ndly, 1928, Anne Page, *J.P.*, who *d.* 1949, dau. of the late Richard Benyon Croft, J.P., D.L., of Fanhams Hall, Ware ; *d.* 1934 ; *s.* by his son [2] ARTHUR RONALD NALL, 2nd Baron, *b.* 1904; a JP for Herts.; MP for Wavertree Div. of Liverpool (*C*) 1931-34: *m.* 1927, Angela Beatrix, who *d* 1975. yr. da. of the late Rev. Preb. William Geoffrey Pennyman, of Ormesby Hall, Yorks. [Walker, Bt., cr. 1868], *d.* 1967; *s.* by his grandson [3] CHARLES RONALD GEORGE (el. son of the late the Hon. Ronald Charles Manus Nall-Cain, el. son of 2nd Baron) 3rd Baron, and present peer.

BROCKWAY, BARON. (Brockway.) [Life Baron 1964]

(ARCHIBALD) FENNER BROCKWAY, son of the late Rev. W. G. Brockway, of Calcutta; *b.* Nov. 1st, 1888; ed. at Eltham Coll.; Sec. to ILP 1923, Chm. 1931-33, Gen. Sec. 1928 and 1933-39, and Political Sec. 1939-46, and a Member of International Cttee. of Movement for United Socialist Europe 1947-48; first Chm. of Congress of Peoples against Imperialism 1948-54, and Pres. of Asian and Overseas Socialist Fellowship 1959-66, of Movement for Colonial Freedom 1954-67, of British Council for Peace in Vietnam 1965-68, and of Peace in Nigeria Cttee., 1968-70; MP for Leyton, E. Div. of Essex (*Lab.*) 1929-31, and for Eton and Slough (*Lab.*) 1950-64; *cr. Baron Brockway*, of Eton and Slough, co. Buckinghamshire (Life Baron) 1964: *m.* 1st, 1914, Lilla (m. diss. 1946), da. of the late Rev. W. Harvey-Smith, of Long Sutton; 2ndly, 1946, Edith Violet, da. of the late Archibald Herbert King, of Catford, SE6, and has issue by 1st and 2nd m.

Residence,—67, Southway, Totteridge, N20 8DE.

SON LIVING. (*By 2nd marriage.*)
Hon. Christopher Fenner, *b.* 1946.

DAUGHTERS LIVING. (*By 1st marriage.*)
Hon. Joan Vera, *b.* 1921: *m.* 1944, Capt. Everett Samuel Pover, of 27, Avenue Rise, Bushey, Herts., and has issue.
Hon. Olive Fenna, *b.* 1924: *m.* 1944, Cecil Outrim, of Pass Christian, Hosey Hill, Westerham, Kent, and has issue.

Brooke, Lord, son of Earl Brooke and of Warwick. (See Warwick.)

Brooke and of Warwick, Earl. (See Warwick.)

BROOKE OF CUMNOR, BARON. (Brooke.) [Life Baron 1966.]

HENRY BROOKE, *CH, PC*, son of the late L. Leslie Brooke; *b.* April 9th, 1903; ed. at Marlborough, and Balliol Coll., Oxford (MA); Councillor of Borough of Hampstead 1936-53, and Alderman 1953-57, a Co. Councillor for London 1945-55 (Leader of Conservative Party 1945-52), Financial Sec. to the Treasury 1954-57, Min. of Housing and Local Govt., and Min. for Welsh Affairs 1957-61, Ch. Sec. to Treasury and Paymaster-Gen. 1961-62, and Home Sec. 1962-64; MP for W. Lewisham (*C*) 1938-45, and Hampstead 1950-66; *cr.* PC 1955, CH, 1964 and *Baron Brooke of Cumnor*, of Cumnor, Royal Co. of Berks. (Life Baron) 1966: *m.* 1933, Barbara Muriel (*Baroness Brooke of Ystradfellte*), DBE, yst. da. of the late Rev. Canon Alfred Augustus Mathews, and has issue.

Residence,—The Glebe House, Mildenhall, Marlborough, Wilts.

SONS LIVING.
Hon. Peter Leonard (2, Holly Terr., Highgate West Hill, N6), *b.* 1934: *m.* 1964, Joan, da of the late Frederick George Smith, of São Paulo, Brazil, and has issue.
Hon. Henry (39, Downshire Hill, NW3), *b.* 1936: *m.* 1966, Bridget Mary, da. of W. G. Kalaugher, of Appledene, Marlborough, and has issue.

DAUGHTERS LIVING.
Hon. Honor Leslie, *b.* 1941: *m.* 1966, Dr. Thomas Nigel Miller, of Laurel Hill, Repton, Derby, and has issue.
Hon. Margaret Hilary Diana, *b.* 1944: *m.* 1971, James Douglas Pulfer, of 24, rue St. Georges, Apt. 102, Ste. Anne de Bellevue, PQ, Canada, and has issue.

BROOKE OF YSTRADFELLTE, BARONESS. (Brooke.) [Life Baroness 1964.]

BARBARA MURIEL BROOKE, *DBE*, da. of the late Rev. Canon Alfred Augustus Mathews, of Llanwern, Gwent; *b.* Jan. 14th, 1908; ed. at Queen Anne's Sch., Caversham, and at Glos. Training Coll. of Domestic Science; a Member of Hampstead Borough Council 1948-65, and Vice-Chm. of Conservative Party Organization 1954-64; a Member of N.-W. Metropolitan Regional Hosp. Board 1955-66; Chm of Governing Body of Godolphin and Latymer Sch. since 1960, and of Exec. Cttee. of Queen's Inst. of Dist. Nursing 1961-71; a Member of Management Cttee., King Edward's Hosp. Fund for London 1967-70; Hon. Fellow of Westfield Coll.; *cr.* DBE (Civil) 1960, and *Baroness Brooke of Ystradfellte*, of Ystradfellte, co. Brecknock (Life Baroness) 1964: *m.* 1933, Baron Brooke of Cumnor, Life Peer, and has issue [see that title].

Residence,—The Glebe House, Mildenhall, Marlborough, Wilts. *Club,*—University Women's.

BROOKEBOROUGH, VISCOUNT. (Brooke.) **Viscount U.K. 1952. Bt. U.K. 1822.]**

GLORIA FINIS

Glory is the end.

JOHN WARDEN BROOKE, *PC*, 2nd Viscount, and 6th Baronet; *b.* Nov. 9th, 1922; *s.* 1973; ed. at Eton; late Capt. 10th Hussars; MP for Lisnaskea (*U*) NI 1968-72; Ch. Whip and Min. of State for Finance NI 1971-72; cr. Member of NI Assembly (*UPNI*) 1973-74, and of N. Ireland Convention since 1975; Chm., Co. Council, co. Fermanagh; High Sheriff 1955; 1939-45 War (wounded); cr. PC (NI) 1972: *m.* 1949, Rosemary Hilda, da. of the late Lt.-Col. Arthur O'Neil Cubitt Chichester, OBE, MC [see M. Donegall, colls.], and has issue.

Arms,—Or, a cross engrailed per pale gules and sable, a crescent for difference. Crest,—A brock, or badger, passant argent. Supporters,—*Dexter*, a dolphin sable; *sinister*, a lion double queued gules langued azure.

Seat,—Colebrooke, co. Fermanagh. *Residence,*—Ashbrooke, Brookeborough, co. Fermanagh.

SONS LIVING.

Hon. ALAN HENRY, *b.* June 30th, 1952; ed. at Harrow, and Millfield.
Hon. Christopher Arthur, *b.* 1954; ed. at Gordonstoun.

DAUGHTERS LIVING.

Hon. Rosalind Juliana, *b.* 1950: *m.* 1973, Maj. Nigel Cowie.
Hon. Melinda Charlotte, *b.* 1958.
Hon. Susanna Cynthia, *b.* 1962.

AUNT LIVING.

Sheelah (*Hon. Lady Mulholland*), *b.* 1895: *m.* 1914, the Rt. Hon. Sir Henry George Hill Mulholland, 1st Bt., who *d.* 1971, (2nd son of 2nd Baron Dunleath). *Residence,*—Ballyscullion Park, Bellaghy, co. Derry.

WIDOW LIVING OF FIRST VISCOUNT.

SARAH EILEEN BELL (*Eileen, Viscountess Brookeborough*), Carnbeg, Spa, Ballynahinch, co. Down), da. of Henry Healey, of Belfast, and widow of Cecil Armstrong Calvert, FRCS: *m.* 1971, as his 2nd wife, the 1st Viscount, who *d.* 1973.

COLLATERAL BRANCHES LIVING. (*In remainder to Baronetcy only*).

Issue of the late Sir Alan Francis Brooke, K.G., G.C.B., O.M., G.C.V.O., D.S.O., 6th son of 3rd baronet, who was cr. *Viscount Alanbrooke* 1946 [see that title].

Grandson of the late Capt. Sir Harry Vesey Brooke, K.B.E. (infra):—
Issue of the late Col. Arthur Brooke, Indian Army, *b.* 1886, *d.* 1952: *m.* 1913, Aimée Isabella Brooman, da. of the late Richard Charles Brooman White, of Arddarroch, Dunbartonshire, and 11, Cambridge Square, W [E. Orkney]:—
Basil Arthur, *MC* (Mulberry, Wisborough Green, Billingshurst, Sussex), *b.* 1917; ed. at Trin. Coll., Glanalmond; Maj. late 15th/19th Hussars; formerly Lt. Gordon Highlanders; 1939-45 War (prisoner, MC): *m.* 1st, 1946, Mora Allison, da. of the late Col. James Alexander Stewart Balmain, of Alford House, Somerset; 2ndly, 1968, Mrs. Jane Samuel, and has issue living (by 1st m.), Patricia Alison, *b.* 1946,—Sheelah Anne, *b.* 1949,—Diana Eva, *b.* 1951.

Issue of the late Capt. Sir Harry Vesey Brooke, K.B.E., 2nd son of 2nd baronet, *b.* 1845, *d.* 1921: *m.* 1879, Patricia, who *d.* 1951, only child of the late James Gregory Moir-Byres, J.P., of Tonley and Fairley, Aberdeenshire:—
(Alice) Irene, *b.* 1897: *m.* 1926, Lt.-Col. Richard Gilbert Lees, MBE, late Gordon Highlanders. *Residence,*—Corrennie, Torphins, Aberdeenshire.

Grandchildren of Arthur Basil Brooke, 3rd son of 2nd baronet:—
Issue of the late Lt.-Gen. Sir Bertram Norman SERGISON-BROOKE, KCB, KCVO, CMG, DSO, *b.* 1880, *d.* 1967: *m.* 1st, 1915, Prudence Ida Evelyn, who *d.* 1918, da. of the late Capt. Charles Warden Sergison, of Cuckfield Park, Sussex [B. Sudeley]; 2ndly, 1923, Hilda, who *d.* 1954, da. of Mark Fenwick, of Abbotswood, Stow-on-the-Wold:—
(By 1st m.) Patience Ann (*Lady Windley*), *b.* 1916: *m.* 1939, Sir Edward Henry Windley, KCMG, KCVO, who *d.* 1972, and has issue living, Edward John Sergison, *b.* 1944,—Davina (*Countess of Portarlington*), *b.* 1940: *m.* 1961, the 7th Earl of Portarlington,—Fiona Prudence, *b.* 1943: *m.* 1965, Capt. Michael G. L. Whiteley, of Little Weald, Bampton, Oxon.——(by 2nd m.) Timothy Mark (3, Addison Cres., W14), *b.* 1924; ed. at Eton; 1939-45 War with Grenadier Guards: *m.* 1964, the Hon. Mary Anne Hare, el. da. of 1st Viscount Blakenham, and has issue living, Nicholas Mark, *b.* 1966,—Kate Constantia, *b.* 1968.

Grandson of the late Brig.-Gen. Henry Francis Brooke, el. son of the late George Augustus Frederick Brooke, 8th son of 1st baronet:—
Issue of the late Major George Cecil Brooke, *b.* 1870, *d.* (killed in action at Gallipoli) 1915: *m.* 1912, Barbara (now of Hampton Court Palace, Middlesex), only child of the late Capt. W. H. Allen, of Dhuariele Castle, co. Cork:—
Henry John Allen, *MBE, DSC, RN, b.* 1913; ed. at Wellington Coll.; is Com.; acting Capt. and Senior Officer Reserve Ships, Portsmouth 1960-61; MOD (Navy Dept.) isnce 1963; 1939-45 War with Arctic Convoys and in Pacific (despatches, DSC); MBE (Civil) 1974: *m.* 1946, Lesley Mary, second da. of the late Capt. Eric Noble, of Harpsden Court, Henley-on-Thames, and has issue, Michael Henry Hastings (Army and Navy Club), *b.* 1948; ed. at Pangbourne; Capt. RE: *m.* 1971, Philippa Wendy, da. of Brig. Rupert Crowdy, OBE, and has issue living, Simon Mark Hastings *b.* 1974,—George John (East India Sports and Public Schools Club), *b.* 1952; ed. at Wellington Coll., St. Peter's Coll. Oxford (BATheo), St. John's Coll., Camb., and Claremont Graduate Sch., Cal., USA,—Sarah Lesley, *b.* 1949: *m.* 1973, John Nigel Pointing,—Mary Barbara, *b.* 1954. *Residence,*—Benbow, Bosham, Sussex. *Clubs,*—Army and Navy, Civil Service; Royal Yacht Squadron.

Grandchildren of the late George Augustus Frederick Brooke (ante):—
Issue of the late Brig.-Gen. Lionel Godolphin Brooke, O.B., *b.* 1849, *d.* 1931: *m.* 1st, 1881, Emma, who *d.* 1882, dau. of Lord John Henry Taylour [M. Headfort]; 2ndly, 1895, Gertrude Isabella, who *d.* 1930, dau. of Col. Henry Hills Goodeve (formerly R.A.), of Tower, near Tenby, S. Wales:—

By 2nd m.) Ruth Isa Patricia, b. 1896.——Gertrude Vera, b. 1899: m. 1st, 1917 (m. diss. 1944) Nigel Augustus Kennedy, late Capt. Argyll and Sutherland Highlanders, who d. 1957 [see M. Ailsa, colls.]; 2ndly, 1944, Sidney Vanden Bergh.——Amy Dorothy, b. 1901. *Residence,—*

Grandsons of the late Rt. Hon. Frank (Francis) Theophilus Brooke, yst. son of George Angustus Frederick Brooke (ante):—
Issue of the late Lt.-Col. George Frank Brooke, DSO: m. 1907, Theodora Olivia, who d. 1967, da. of the late Richard Meredith Jackson, of Natal:—
Frank Hastings, CB, CBE, DSO (Club,—Army and Navy), b. 1909; Maj.-Gen. (ret.), late Welch Regt., late Gen. Staff, British Sers. Mission, Burma, and Com. 1st Malay Inf. Brig.; Com. 1st Malay Inf. Bde. 1953-54, and GOC, Fedn. of Malaya Army 1956-59; Col. The Welch Regt. 1965-69; Commr. R. Hosp. Chelsea since 1969; 1939-45 War (DSO, American Bronze Star); DSO 1945, CBE (Mil) 1954, CB (Mil) 1958: m. 1st, 1935, Helen Edith Mary, who d. 1973, da. of the late Maj. R. Berkeley; 2ndly, 1974, Mrs. S. N. Carson, and has issue living (by 1st m.) George Hugo Hastings (White Ladies, Hazeley Bottom, Hartley Wintney, Hants., RG27 8LU), b. 1936; Capt. (ret.) late RTR: m. 1962, Sarah, yr. da. of the late Robert Blackburn, of Bowcliffe Hall, Boston Spa and has issue living, Andrew Robert Hastings b. 1969, Belinda Jane b. 1965,—Nigel Francis b. 1937.—
Oliver George, CBE, DSO (The Manor House, Gt. Cheverell, Devizes, Wilts. Club,—Army and Navy), b. 1911; Brig. (ret.) late Welch Regt.; Col. Comdt., Somaliland Scouts 1959-60; Middle East, Sicily and Italy 1939-45 (MBE, DSO); MBE (Mil) 1944, DSO 1945, CBE (Mil) 1958: m. 1961, Gillian Leonora (NUTTING), da. of Edward Jolliffe Strutt [see B. Rayleigh, colls.].

PREDECESSORS—[1] HENRY Brooke, son of Francis Brooke, of Whibrooke, Ireland, and Hannah, dau. of Henry Prittie, and sister of 1st Lord Dunally; b. 1770; cr. a Baronet 1822: m. 1792, Harriet, dau. of the Hon. John Butler, 4th son of 1st Viscount Lanesborough: d. 1834; s. by his son [2] Sir ARTHUR BRINSLEY, 2nd Bt.; b. 1797; M.P. for Fermanagh (C.) 1840-54: m. 1841, the Hon. Julia Henrietta Anson, who d. 1886, dau. of Gen. Sir George Anson, G.C.B.; d. 1854; s. by his son [3] Sir VICTOR ALEXANDER, 3rd Bt.; b. 1843; m. 1864, Alice Sophia, who d. 1920, dau. of Sir Alan Edward Bellingham, 3rd Bt.; d. 1891; s. by his son [4] Sir ARTHUR DOUGLAS, 4th Bt.; b. 1865; a J.P. and D.L. for Fermanagh: m. 1887, Gertrude Isabella, who d. 1918, dau. of Stanlake Batson; d. 1907; s. by his son [5] Sir BASIL STANLAKE, 5th Bt., KG, CBE, MC, b. 1888; Member of Senate NI 1921-29, MP for Lisnaskea (U) N.I. 1929-68; Min. of Commerce and Production 1941-45 and PM 1943-63; cr. Viscount Brookeborough, of Colebrooke, co. Fermanagh (peerage of UK 1952): m. 1st, 1919, Dame Cynthia Mary, DBE, who d. 1970, da. of the late Capt. Charles Warden Sergison [B. Sudeley]; 2ndly, 1971, Sarah Eileen Bell, da. of Henry Healey, of Belfast, and widow of Cecil Armstrong Calvert, FRCS; d. 1973; s. by his only son [6] JOHN WARDEN, PC, 2nd Viscount and present peer.

BROUGHAM and VAUX, BARON. (Brougham.) [Baron U.K. 1860.]

[Title and name pronounced "**Broom**."]

MICHAEL JOHN BROUGHAM, 5th Baron; b. Aug. 2nd, 1938; s. 1967; ed. at Millfield: m. 1st, 1963 (m. diss. 1967), Olivia Susan, only da. of Rear-Adm. Gordon Thomas Seccombe Gray, DSC, of Hollies, Stedham, Mid-hurst; 2ndly, 1969, Catherine Jill, el. da. of William Gulliver, and has issue by 1st and 2nd m.

ᗩrms,—Gules, a chevron between three lucies hauriant argent. Crest,—A dexter arm in armour embowed proper the hand holding a lucy fesse-wise argent, and charged on the elbow with a rose gules. Supporters,—Dexter, a lion vert, armed and langued gules, gorged with a Vaux collar checky or and of the second; sinister, a stag argent, attired and unguled or, holding in the mouth a rose gules, barbed and seeded vert.

*Residence,—*28, Westmoreland Place, SW1. *Club,—*Turf.

For the king, the law, and the people.

SON LIVING (By 2nd m.)
Hon. CHARLES WILLIAM, b. Nov. 9th, 1971.

DAUGHTER LIVING (By 1st m.)
Hon. Henrietta Louise, b. 1965.

BROTHER LIVING.
Hon. David Peter (11, Margaretta Terr., SW3), b. 1940; ed. at Sedbergh: m. 1969, Moussie Christina Margareta Hallström, da. of Sven Hörnblad, of Stockholm, Sweden, and has issue living, Henry Peter, b. 1971.

UNCLE LIVING.
Anthony Charles, b. 1915; ed. at Oundle; 2nd Lt. S. Lancs. Regt.: m. 1st, 1940 (m. diss. 1961), Sonya, who d. 1970, da. of the late Ivan Salzman; 2ndly, 1961, Doreen Margaret (WARREN), da. of the late Roland Billington, and has issue living, (by 1st m.) Christopher Anthony Henry (28, Valley Av., N12) b. 1941: m. 1967, Ann Elizabeth, el. da. of Cecil Goldridge, of 72, Savernake Rd., NW3, and has issue living, Benjamin Paul b. 1972, Guy Christopher b. 1975,—Adrian Charles, b. 1945. Residence,—Redwalls, 9, Moreton End Lane, Harpenden, Herts.

AUNT LIVING.
Eileen Cynthia Millicent Eva, b. 1912. m. 1940, Col. Francis Thomas Davies, Grenadier Guards son of Gen. Sir Francis John Davies, K.C.B., K.C.M.G., K.C.V.O., and has issue living Hugh Francis John, b. 1941,—Charles Henry Thomas, b. 1947,—Lavinia Diana, b. 1948. Residence,—4, Chester St., S.W.1.

WIDOW LIVING OF SON OF THIRD BARON.
———, Baroness Hengelmüller, dau. of Baron von Hengervar, sometime Austro-Hungarian Ambassador to U.S.A.: m. 1923, as his second wife, Capt. the Hon. Henry Brougham (infra), who d. 1927. Residence,—

MOTHER LIVING.
Jean (Holanducia, Marbella, Spain), da. of the late Brig.-Gen. Gilbert Burrell Spencer Follett, DSO, MVO [E. Dunmore], b. 1915: m. 1st, 1935, as his 2nd wife, the 4th Baron, who d. 1967, and from whom she obtained a divorce 1942; 2ndly, 1946, Felix Alouis Caspar Guépin, who d. 1966.

WIDOW LIVING OF FOURTH BARON.
EDITH ELLALINE (HART-DAVIS) (*Edith, Baroness Brougham and Vaux*), da. of Leonard Teichman: *m.* 1942, as his 3rd wife, the 4th Baron, who *d.* 1967.

COLLATERAL BRANCH LIVING.

Grandchildren of the late Hon. Wilfrid Brougham, 2nd son of 2nd Baron:—
Issue of the late Wilfrid Francis Brougham, *b.* 1864, *d.* 1938: *m.* 1889, Mathilda
Carolina, who *d.* 1928, dau. of the late Alexander Donald Macgregor, of Melrose,
Guernsey :—
Francis St. John Macgregor, *b.* 1890.——Mary Monica Amita: *m.* 1925, Frederick George
Metcalf. *Residence,—*
PREDECESSORS.—[1] *Rt. Hon.* HENRY Brougham, P.C., an eminent statesman, orator
philosopher and writer ; Attorney-Gen. for Queen Caroline 1820 ; successively M.P. for Camelford, Winchilsea, Knaresborough and Yorkshire, and Lord High Chancellor 1830-4; cr. *Baron
Brougham and Vaux* 1830, and *Baron Brougham and Vaux* (peerage of United Kingdom) 1860,
with remainder to his brother; *d.* 1868; *s.* by his brother [2] WILLIAM, 2nd Baron, *b.* 1795;
sat as M.P. for Southwark 1835-40 : *m.* 1834, Emily Frances, who *d.* 1884, dau. of Sir Charles
William Taylor, 1st Bt. ; *d.* Jan. 3rd, 1886; *s.* by his son [3] HENRY CHARLES, K.C.V.O.,
3rd Baron, *b.* 1836 ; a Clerk in House of Lords 1857-70 : *m.* 1882, Adora Frances Olga, who *d.*
1925, dau. of Peter Wells, of Forest Farm, Windsor Forest, and widow of Sir Richard
Courtenay Musgrave, M.P., 11th Bt. : *d.* 1927; *s.* by his grandson [4] VICTOR HENRY PETER
(son of the late Capt. the Hon. Henry Brougham, son of 3rd Baron), 4th Baron, *b.* 1909: *m.* 1st,
1931, Violet Valerie (who obtained a divorce 1934), da. of the late Lt.-Col. the Hon. Edward Gerald
Fleming French, DSO [E. Ypres]; 2ndly, 1935, Jean, (who obtained a divorce 1942), da. of the late
Brig.-Gen. Gibert Burrell Spencer Follett, DSO, MVO [E. Dunmore]; 3rdly, 1942, Mrs. Edith Ellaline
Hart-Davis, da. of Leonard Teichman; *d.* 1967; *s.* by his el. son [5] Michael John, 5th Baron, and
present peer.

BROUGHSHANE, BARON. (Davison.) [Baron U.K. 1945.]

PATRICK OWEN ALEXANDER DAVISON, 2nd Baron ; *b.* June 18th, 1903 ;
s. 1953 ; ed. at Winchester, and at
Magdalen Coll., Oxford ; Bar. Inner
Temple 1926; 1939-42 War with Irish
Gds.; Assist. Sec. (Mil.), War Cabinet
1942-5; has American Legion of
Merit: *m.* 1929, Bettine, da. of the
late Sir Arthur Edward Ian Montague
Russell, 6th Bt. (cr. 1812), and has
issue.

Arms—Gules a stag trippant and in chief a
celestial crown and a fleur de lys or.   **Crest**,—
Upon a billet fessewise, a stag's head between two
wings or.   **Supporters**,—On either side a stag or,
gorged with a chain gules, and pendant therefrom
torteau the dexter charged with a portcullis and
the sinister with a grenade fired or.

Strength consists in action.

Residence,—21, Eaton Sq., S.W.1.   *Clubs,*—White's, Garrick.

SON LIVING.
Hon. ALEXANDER, *b.* Jan. 11th, 1936: *m.* 1961 (m. diss. 1966), Teresa Clare, only da. of James
Bramwell [see Smith-Marriott, Bt., colls.]; 2ndly, 1970, Cecilia Ann, da. of J. W. Ingrams, of Furlong,
Patching, Sussex, and has issue living, (by 1st m.) Emma Bettine, *b.* 1962,—Harriett Laura, *b.* 1964—,
(by 2nd m.) Arundell, *b.* 1972.

BROTHER LIVING.
Hon. (William) Kensington, D.S.O., D.F.C. (of 3, Godfrey St., S.W.3. *Club,*—Garrick), *b.* 1914; ed. at
Shrewsbury, and at Magdalen Coll., Oxford; Bar. Inner Temple 1939; formerly Wing-Com. R.A.F.
Vol. Reserve; European War 1939-45 (D.F.C., D.S.O.); D.S.O. 1945.

SISTERS LIVING.
Hon. Joyce Margaret, *b.* 1900: *m.* 1922, Humphrey Bowstead Wilson, O.B.E., M.B., and has issue
living, Michael, *b.* 1923,—Diana June, *b.* 1926.   *Residence,* Fyfield Close, Fyfield, Abingdon, Berks.
Hon. Sheila Beatrice, *b.* 1907: *m.* 1936, Group Capt. George Edward Gordon-Duff, CBE, who *d.*
1966, and has issue living, Roderick, *b.* 1940: *m.* 1965, Patricia Anne, da. of Bruce Watson,
of Fishing Cottage, Littleton Panell, Wilts.   *Residence,*—10, Jameson St., W8.

PREDECESSOR.—[1] WILLIAM HENRY DAVISON, K.B.E., youngest son of the late Richard Davison,
of Beechfield, Ballymena, co. Antrim ; *b.* 1872 ; an Alderman of Roy. Borough of Kensington
(Mayor 1913-19), a F.S.A., Vice-Pres. Roy. So. of Arts, a Gov. of Foundling Hospital, a Freeman
of City of London, a Member of Clothworkers' Co. (Master 1941-42), and Pres. Kensington
Chamber of Commerce; during European War 1914-19 raised and equipped 22nd Batn. Roy.
Fusiliers and assisted in raising 2 Territorial Batns.; Chm. of Metropolitan National Union of
Conservative Assocns. 1928-30; sat as MP for Kensington, S. Div. (C) 1918-45; cr. *Baron Broughshane*, of Kensington, co. London (peerage of United Kingdom) 1945: *m.* 1st, 1898, Beatrice Mary
(who *d.* 1971, having obtained a divorce 1929), da. of the late Sir Owen Roberts, DCL, LLD, FSA,
DL; 2ndly, 1929, Louisa Mary Constance, who *d.* 1971, da. of the late Maj. Charles Frederick Marriott [B. Stafford, colls.], *d.* 1953; *s.* by his son [2] PATRICK OWEN ALEXANDER, 2nd Baron, and
present peer.

BROWN, BARON. (Brown.) [Life Baron 1964.]

WILFRED BANKS DUNCAN BROWN, *MBE, PC,* son of the late Peter Brown,
of Greenock; *b.* Nov. 29th, 1908; ed. at Rossall; Min. of State, Board of
Trade 1965-70; *cr.* MBE (Civil) 1943, *Baron Brown,* of Machrihanish, co.
Argyll (Life Baron) 1964, and PC 1970: *m.* 1st, 1935, Barbara, who *d.* 1937,
da. of Cuyler Findlay; 2ndly, 1939, Marjorie Hershell, da. of J. H. Skinner,
of Ealing, W., and has issue by 2nd m.

Residence,—Flat 13, 23, Prince Albert Rd., NW1.   *Club,*—Reform.

SONS LIVING.   (*By 2nd marriage.*)
Hon. Richard Banks Duncan, *b.* 1942; ed. at Bryanston and Brunel Univ.: *m.* 1968, Gillian Mary, da. of
John Kennedy Cater, of Crowthorne, Berks., and has issue.
Hon. Michael Colin Duncan, *b.* 1944; ed. at Bryanston: *m.* 1970, Fenella, da. of Peter Barnard, of
White House, Rose Hill, Dorking.
Hon. Angus John Duncan, *b.* 1951: *m.* 1974, Polonca, da. of Janez Baloh, of Ljubljana, Yugoslavia.

Brown, see Baron George-Brown.

BROWNLOW, BARON.   (Cust.) [Baron G.B. 1776, Bt. E. 1677.]

To be rather than to seem

PEREGRINE FRANCIS ADELBERT CUST, 6th
Baron, and 9th Baronet; *b.* April 27th, 1899;
s. 1927; ed. at Eton, and at RMC; late Lt.
and Adj. Grenadier Guards; a JP and a DL of
Lincolnshire, and patron of ten livings;
sometime ADC to Gen. Officer Comdg.
London Dist.; 1918 War, 1939-45 War as
Sqdn.-Ldr. RAF Vol. Reserve; attached
Bomber Command, Air Min. (Plans), and
American Air Force; Mayor of Grantham
1934-35; was a Lord-in-Waiting (personal)
to HM July to Dec. 1936, and Lord-Lieut.,
and Custos Rotulorum of Lincolnshire
1936-50; appointed Parliamentary Private
Sec. to Min. of Aircraft Production 1940: *m.* 1st, 1927, Katherine Hariot,
who *d.* 1952, da. of Brig.-Gen. Sir David Alexander Kinloch, CB, MVO, 11th
Bt. (cr. 1686); 2ndly, 1954, Dorothy (SANDS), who *d.* 1966, da. of T. S. Power,
of Virginia, USA, and formerly wife of 2nd Earl Beatty; 3rdly, 1969, Leila
Joan, da. of the late Maj. Philip Guy Reynolds, DSO, formerly wife of the late
John Dane Player, and widow of 2nd Baron Manton, and has issue by 1st m.

Arms,—Ermine, on a chevron sable, three fountains proper.   Crest,—A lion's head erased
sable, gorged with a collar paly wavy of six, argent and azure.   Supporters,—Two lions reguardant argent, each gorged with a collar paly wavy of six argent and azure.

Residences,—Belton House, Grantham; 2, Belgrave Mews West, SW1; Devotion Cottage, Corinth
PO, Grenada, W. Indies.   *Clubs*,—White's, Travellers (Paris).

SON LIVING.   (*By 1st marriage.*)
Hon. EDWARD JOHN PEREGRINE (146, New King's Rd., SW6; The Mill, Manthorpe, Grantham;
Clubs, White's, Garrick), *b.* March 25th, 1936; ed. at Eton; late Gren. Guards: *m.* 1964, Shirlie,
2nd da. of the late John Yeomans, of Manor Farm, Hill Croome, Upton-on-Severn, Worcs., and has
issue living, Peregrine Edward Quintin, *b.* July 9th, 1971.

DAUGHTER LIVING.   (*By 1st marriage.*)
Hon. Caroline Elizabeth Maud (68, Scarsdale Villas, W8 6PP), *b.* 1928: *m.* 1954 (m. diss. 1973), John
Arthur Partridge, and has issue living, Frank David Peregrine, *b.* 1955,—Claude Edward, *b.* 1962,—
Sophia Josephine, *b.* 1969.

SISTER LIVING.
Hon. Sarah Marie Adelaïde (of The Wooden House, Manton, Oakham), *b.* 1906: *m.* 1930, Edward
Jan Hoos, who *d.* 1962, and has issue living, Peter Hendrik Peregrine (Flat 1, 34, St. Marks Rd.,
St. Helier, Jersey, and 23, Rue Claude Ydrone, Lectoure, Gers, France), *b.* 1937: *m.* 1968, Caroline
Fleur, da. of the late Col. Henry Monckton Vatcher, MC, of Valeran, St. Brelade's, Jersey, and
widow of 11th Duke of Leeds,—Henrietta Sarah Angenis, *b.* 1933: *m.* 1955, David Ralph Davies-
Cooke, of Aspland House, Wicken, Ely, and 25, Barkston Gdns., SW5 [see Cooke, Bt., colls.].

COLLATERAL BRANCHES LIVING.

Grandchildren of the late Sir Lionel Henry Cust, KCVO, LittD, son of the late Sir
Reginald John Cust, son of the late Rev. the Hon. Henry Cockayne Cust, 2nd
son of 1st Baron:—
Issue of the late Col. Sir Lionel George Archer Cust, CBE, *b.* 1896, *d.* 1962: *m.* 1925, Mar-
garet Violet Louisa, who *m.* 2ndly, 1975, the 5th Viscount Templetown, rel. da. of the late
Lt.-Col. Henry Arthur Clowes, 1st Life Gds. [B. Hatherton, colls.]:—
Christopher Ivo Henry, *b.* 1930.——Elizabeth Jemina Mary, *b.* 1926: *m.* 1947, Jack Musson Benn
(P.O. Box 270, Somerset West, Cape Prov., S. Africa), and has issue living, Anthony Christopher,
b. 1948,—Michael Robert, *b.* 1950,—Elizabeth Philippa, *b.* 1952: *m.* 1970, Istvan Benedek de
Ujfalussy, of 2, 6th Av., Parkhurst, Johannesburg, and has issue living, Catherine *b.* 1970, *b.* Louisa
1972.——Margaret Sybil, *b.* 1928: *m.* 1950, Paul Oliver Ziegler, of Windwhistle, Hightown, Ringwood, Hants., and has issue living, Adam Charles (Foulford Farm, Foulford Bottom, Ringwood,
Hants.), *b.* 1952: *m.* 1974, Christine Margaret Codling, of Ibsley, Hants.,—William James Archer,
b. 1956.

Grandchildren of the late Rev. William Arthur Purey-Cust (infra):—
Issue of the late Brig. Richard Brownlow Purey-Cust, CBE, DSO, MC, *b.* 1888, *d.* 1958: *m.*
1928, Gertrude Patricia Zoë (Pinchbeck Cottage, Donhead St. Mary, Shaftesbury, Dorset),
only da. of the late Francis Julian Laurence Birch:—
John Richard, *b.* 1934; ed. at Eton and Edinburgh Univ. (BSc).——Veronica Caroline, *b.* 1937: *m.*
1969, Hermann Portmann, of Harewood Rd., Nanaimo, BC, Canada.

Granddaughters of the late Very Rev. Arthur Perceval PUREY-CUST, DD, son of
the late Hon. William Cust, 4th son of 1st Baron:—
Issue of the late Rev. William Arthur PUREY-CUST, *b.* 1855, *d.* 1938: *m.* 1882, Lucy Caroline,
who *d.* 1916, da. of the late Lt.-Gen. Sir William Jervois, GCMG, CB:—
Honoria Katharine, *b.* 1892.   *Residence*,—37, Lauderdale Drive, Petersham, Richmond, Surrey.

Issue of the late Adm. Sir Herbert Edward PUREY-CUST, KBE, CB, *b.* 1857; *d.* 1938: *m*
1895, Alice Ella, who *d.* 1949, da. of the late George Stuart Hepburn, of Smeaton, Victoria
Australia:—
Marjorie (c/o Barclays Bank, 19, Fleet St., EC4), *b.* 1905.

PREDECESSORS.—[1] RICHARD CUST, *MP* for co. Lincoln 1635; cr. a Baronet 1677; *d.* 1700;
s. by his grandson [2] *Sir* RICHARD, 2nd Bt.; *d.* 1734; *s.* by his son [3] *Sir* JOHN, *PC*, *MP*, 3rd
Bt., was Speaker of House of Commons 1761-70; inherited the estates of his uncle Viscount
Tyrconnel (*ext.*); *d.* 1770; *s.* by his son [4] *Sir* BROWNLOW, 4th Bt.; cr. *Baron Brownlow* (peerage
of United Kingdom) 1776; *d.* 1807; *s.* by his son [5] JOHN, 2nd Baron, *b.* 1779; cr. *Viscount Alford*
and *Earl Brownlow* (peerage of United Kingdom) 1815; was Lord Lt. of co. Lincoln; his el. son

John Hume, Viscount Alford, MP, who *m*. Lady Marian Margaret Compton, da. of 2nd Marquess of Northampton, assumed by Roy. licence the surname of Egerton, and pre-deceased him 1851; *d*. 1853; *s*. by his grandson [6] JOHN WILLIAM SPENCER, 2nd Earl; assumed by Roy. licence 1853 the surname of Egerton, and in 1863 the additional surname of Cust; *d*. 1867; *s*. by his brother [7] ADELBERT WELLINGTON BROWNLOW, *GCVO, PC*, 3rd Earl; *b*. 1844; Lord-Lt. of Lincolnshire 1867-1921, Parliamentary Sec. to Local Govt. Board 1885-86, Paymaster-Gen. 1887-89, and Under-Sec. of State for War 1889-92: *m*. 1868, Lady Adelaide Talbot, who *d*. 1917, 3rd da. of 18th Earl of Shrewsbury; *d*. 1921, when the Earldom became ext., and the Barony devolved upon his kins-man [8] ADELBERT SALUSBURY COCKAYNE (second son of the late Capt. Henry Francis Cockayne Cust, MP, grandson of 1st Baron), 5th Baron; *b*. 1867: *m*. 1895, Maud, who *d*. 1936, da. of the late Capt. S. Buckle, RE; *d*. 1927; *s*. by his son [9] PEREGRINE FRANCIS ABELBERT, 6th Baron and present peer.

Bruce, Lord, son of Earl of Elgin.

BRUCE OF DONNINGTON, BARON. (Bruce.) [Life Baron 1974.]

DONALD WILLIAM TREVOR BRUCE, son of the late William Trevor Bruce, of Norbury, Surrey: *b*. Oct. 3rd, 1912; ed. at Donnington Gram. Sch., Lincs; FCA; economist; 1939-45 War as Maj. with R. Signals (despatches); MP for N. Portsmouth (*Lab*.) 1945-50; PPS to Min. of Health 1945-50; a Member of Min. of Health delegation to Sweden and Denmark 1946, and of House of Commons Select Cttee. on Public Accounts 1948-50; a Member of European Parl. since 1975; cr. *Baron Bruce of Donington*, of Rickmansworth, Herts. (Life Baron) 1974: *m*. 1939, Joan Letitia, da. of Hamilton Claude Butcher, of Maida Vale, W9, and has issue.

Residence,—Pinecroft, Heronsgate, Rickmansworth, Herts. *Club*,—Reform.

SON LIVING.

Hon. Michael Gordon, *b*. 1952.

DAUGHTERS LIVING.

Hon. Ann, *b*. 1942.
Hon. Mary Trevor, *b*. 1945: *m*. 1968, Shuhada Hilmy, of 19, Longfellow Drive, Newport Pagnall, Bucks.

BRUNTISFIELD, BARON. (Warrender.) [Baron U.K. 1942, Bt. G.B. 1715.]

Industry promotes.

VICTOR ALEXANDER GEORGE ANTHONY WARRENDER, *M.C.*, 1st Baron, and 8th Baronet; *b*. June 23rd, 1899; *s*. to the Baronetcy 1917, and was cr. *Baron Bruntisfield*, of Boroughmuir, City of Edinburgh (peerage of United Kingdom) 1942; ed. at Eton; 2nd Lieut. (retired) Grenadier Guards; European War 1917-18 (M.C., Orders of St. Stanis-las and St. Anne of Russia with swords, Order of Star of Roumania); was Private Sec. to Sir Robert S. Horne, G.B.E., K.C., M.P. 1920-22, and Chm. Young Conserva-tives' Union 1929-30; appointed Parliamentary Private Sec. (unpaid) to Parliamentary Under-Sec. of State for India Nov. 1924, an Assist. Conservative Whip Jan. 1928, a Junior Lord of the Trea-sury (in National Govt.) Nov. 1931, Vice-Chamberlain of the Household Sept. 1932, Comptroller of H.M.'s Household May 1935, Parliamentary and Financial Sec. to the Admiralty June 1935, and Financial Sec. to War Department and a Member of Army Council Nov. 1935; Parliamentary Sec. to Admiralty April 1940 to July 1945; sat as M.P. for Kesteven and Rutland, Grantham Div. (*C*) Dec. 1923 to Feb. 1942: *m*. 1st, 1920 (marriage dissolved 1946), Dorothy Etta, who *d*. 1975, da. of the late Col. Richard Hamilton Rawson, MP [E. Lichfield]; 2ndly, 1948, Tania, da. of Dr. M. Kolin, of St. Jacob, Dubrovnik, Yogoslavia, and has issue by 1st and 2nd marriages.

Arms,—Quarterly: 1st and 4th, argent, on a bend wavy, between six roses gules, three plates, *Warrender*; 2nd, or, a lion rampant gules, couped in all joints of the field, within a double tressure flory counter flory azure, *Maitland*; 3rd grand quarter, counter-quartered 1st quarter 1st and 4th vert, a lion rampant argent; 2nd and 3rd argent, three papingoes vert, beaked and membered gules, *Hume*; 2nd quarter gyronny of eight gules and ermine, *Campbell of Cessnock*; third quarter azure, on a fesse between three mascles argent, as many cinquefoils of the first, *Purves of Purves*; 4th quarter, 1st and 4th gules, three piles engrailed argent, *Polwarth of that ilk*; 2nd and 3rd argent, a cross engrailed azure, *Sinclair of Hermiston*, on surtout of the grand quarter an inescutcheon argent charged with an orange imperially crowned and slipped all proper. Crest,—A hare sejant proper. Supporters,—Two lions reguardant argent.

Residence,—Chalet les Pommiers, 3780 Gstaad, Switzerland. *Clubs*,—Turf and Royal Yacht Squadron.

SONS LIVING. (By 1st marriage.)

Hon. JOHN ROBERT, *OBE, MC, TD*, *b*. Feb. 7th, 1921; ed. at Eton; Col. RARO, a Member of Queen's Body Guard for Scotland (Roy. Co. of Archers), and a DL for Somerset; late Capt. 2nd Dragoons, R. Scots Greys; ADC to Gov. of Madras 1946-48, and Comdg. N. Som. Yeo. 44th; Roy Tank Regt. 1957-62 (OBE); 1939-45 War in Middle East, Italy, and NW Europe (MC); Knt. of Sovereign Mil. Order of Malta; OBE (Mil) 1963: *m*. 1948, Ann Moireen, da. of Lt.-Col. Sir Walter Fendall Campbell, KCIE, and has issue living, Michael John Victor, *b*. 1949; ed. at Downside, RMA, and Durham Univ (BA); Lt. Irish Guards,—Jonathan James, *b*. 1954; ed. at Downside,—Julian

Mary, *b.* 1950: *m.* 1974, Francis Alexander Moreton Akers-Douglas [see V. Chilston, colls.].—Sarah Jane, *b.* 1952: *m.* 1971, Anthony David Bune. *Residences,*—Whitelaws, Garvald, Haddington, E. Lothian; 97, Cadogan Gdns., SW3. *Clubs,*—Cavalry, New (Edinburgh).

Hon. Simon George, *D.S.C.*, *b.* 1922; ed. at Eton, is a Co. Director and Insurance Broker, and an Asso. of Insurance Brokers (London), of Roy. Aeronautical So. and of British Interplanetary Soc.; Consul for Uruguay in State of Victoria; late Lt. R.N.V.R.; 1939-45 War (DSC): *m.* 1950, Pamela, da. of Sir Norman Myer, of Toorak, Victoria, Australia, and has issue living, Alexander Victor Simon, *b.* 1955,—Simon Hamilton Angus Norman, *b.* 1962,—Edwina, *b.* 1952, Alicia Gizelle, *b.* 1953. *Clubs,*—Bath, Turf, Royal Aero, RNVR, Melbourne.

Hon. Robin Hugh (Widcombe Manor, Bath; White's, City of London, and Portland Clubs), *b.* 1927; ed. at Eton, and at Trin. Coll., Oxford: *m.* 1951, Gillian Elizabeth, da. of Leonard Lewis Rossiter [see Oppenheimer, Bt.], and has issue living, Hugh Mark, *b.* 1968,—Carolyn Robin, *b.* 1953,—Annabel Rose, *b.* 1956. *Residence,*—46, Brompton Sq., SW3.

(*By 2nd marriage.*)

Hon. Anthony Michael, *b.* 1950; ed. at Eton, and Ch. Ch., Oxford.

DAUGHTER LIVING. (*By 2nd marriage.*)

Hon. Victoria Isabella Anne, *b.* 1952.

SISTER LIVING.

Violet Helen Marie, *b.* 1896: *m.* 1921, Major Alexander Ruthven Pym, Irish Guards, who *d.* 1971 [E. Leven and Melville, colls.], and has issue living, Victor Francis, *b.* 1924: formerly Sub-Lieut. R.N.V.R.,—Martin Hugh, *b.* 1927; formerly Lieut. Irish Guards. *Residence,*—Wakeley House, Charing, Kent.

PREDECESSORS—[1] GEORGE Warrender, son of the late George Warrender; a Merchant and M.P. for Edinburgh 1715-21 ; cr. a *Baronet* 1715 : *m.* 1st, 16—, Margaret Lawrie, of Edinburgh; 2ndly, Grizel, dau. of Hugh Blair, of Edinburgh ; *d.* 1721 ; *s.* by his el. son [2] JOHN, 2nd Bt.: *m.* 1720, Henrietta, dau. of the late Sir Patrick Johnston, M.P., sometime Lord Provost of Edinburgh; *d.* 1772 ; *s.* by his only surviving son [3] PATRICK, 3rd Bt. ; *b.* 1731 ; Lieut.-Col. 11th Dragoons; M.P. for Haddington Burghs 1768-74, and King's Remembrancer of Court of Exchequer 1771-91 : *m.* 1780, Miss H. Blair, who *d.* 1838 ; *s.* by his el. son [4] *Rt. Hon.* GEORGE, *P.C.*, 4th Bt. ; *b.* 1782 ; M.P. for Haddington Burghs 1807-12, for Truro 1812-18, for Sandwich 1818-26, for Westbury 1826-30, and for Honiton 1830-32 ; a Lord of the Admiralty 1812-22, and a Commr. of Board of Control 1822-8 : *m.* 1810, the Hon. Anne Evelyn Boscawen, who *d.* 1871, dau. of 3rd Viscount Falmouth ; *d.* 1849 ; *s.* by his brother [5] JOHN, 5th Bt. ; *b.* 1786 ; Capt. in the Army : *m.* 1st, 1823, Lady Julian Jane Maitland, who *d.* 1827, dau. of 8th Earl of Lauderdale ; 2ndly, 1831, the Hon. Frances Henrietta, who *d.* 1852, dau. of 1st Baron Alvanley ; *d.* 1867 ; *s.* by his only son [6] GEORGE, 6th Bt. ; *b.* 1825 ; sometime Capt. Coldstream Guards : *m.* 1854, Helen, who *d.* 1875, dau. of Sir Hugh Purves-Hume-Campbell, 7th Bt. ; *d.* 1901 ; *s.* by his el. surviving son [7] GEORGE JOHN SCOTT, *K.C.B.*, *K.C.V.O.*, 7th Bt. ; *b.* 1860 ; Vice-Adm. : *m.* 1894, Lady Ethel Maud Ashley-Cooper, who *d.* 1945, dau. of 8th Earl of Shaftesbury ; *d.* 1917 ; *s.* by his el. son [8] VICTOR ALEXANDER GEORGE ANTHONY 8th Bt., and present peer.

BUCCLEUCH and QUEENSBERRY, DUKE OF. (Montagu-Douglas-Scott.)
[Duke S. 1663, Duke S. 1684.]

[Title pronounced "Buckcloo."]

I love.

WALTER FRANCIS JOHN MONTAGU-DOUGLAS-SCOTT, *VRD*, 9th Duke of Buccleuch, and 11th of Queensberry; *b.* Sept. 28th, 1923; *s.* 1973; ed. at Eton, and Ch. Ch., Oxford; Lt.-Cdr. RNR; Lt. Queen's Body Guard for Scotland (Roy. Co. of Archers); Lord-Lieut. of Roxburghshire since 1974, and of Selkirk since 1975; PPS to Sec. of State for Scotland 1962-64; Pres. of Roy. Highland and Agric. Soc. 1969-70; MP for N. Div. of Edinburgh (*C*) 1960-73; 1939-45 War: *m.* 1953, Jane, only da. of John McNeill, QC, of Drumavuie, Appin, Argyllshire, and has issue.

Arms,—Quarterly: 1st grand quarter, the arms of King Charles II. debruised by a baton sinister argent; 2nd grand quarter, or, on a bend azure, a mullet of six points between two crescents of the field, *Scott*; 3rd grand quarter, quarterly, 1st and 4th argent, a human heart gules, crowned with an imperial crown or; and on a chief azure, three mullets of the field, *Douglas*; 2nd and 3rd azure, a bend between six cross-crosslets fitchée or, *Mar*; the whole (of this grand quarter) within a bordure or, charged with the double tressure of Scotland gules; 4th grand quarter, quarterly, 1st, argent, three fusils in fess gules, a bordure sable, *Montagu*; 2nd, or, an eagle displayed vert, beaked and membered gules, *Monthermer*; 3rd, sable, a lion rampant argent, on a canton of the last a cross gules, *Churchill*; 4th, argent, a chevron gules between three morions azure, *Brudenell*. **Crest.**—A stag trippant proper, attired and unguled or. **Supporters.**—Two female figures, habited from the waist downwards, in blue kirtles gathered up at the knees, the arms and bosoms uncovered; around the shoulders flowing mantles vert, suspended by the exterior hand; girdles and sandals gules, and their heads adorned with a plume of three ostrich feathers argent.

Seats,—Bowhill, Selkirk; Boughton House, Kettering; Drumlanrig Castle, Thornhill, Dumfriesshire. *Residences,*—Eildon Hall, Melrose, Roxburghshire; 46, Bedford Gdns., W8.

SONS LIVING.

RICHARD WALTER JOHN (*Earl of Dalkeith*), *b.* Feb. 14th, 1954; ed. at Eton; a Page of Honour to HM Queen Elizabeth The Queen Mother 1967-69.

Lord William Henry John, *b.* 1957.

Lord Damian Tonquil Francis Charles, *b.* 1969.

DAUGHTER LIVING.

Lady Charlotte-Anne, *b.* 1966.

SISTERS LIVING.
Lady Elizabeth Diana (*Duchess of Northumberland*), *b*. 1922; 1939-45 War in WRNS: *m*. 1946, the 10th Duke of Northumberland. *Residences*,—Alnwick Castle, Northumberland; Syon House, Brentford. *Lady* Caroline Margaret, *b*. 1927: *m*. 1951, the Rt. Hon. Ian Hedworth John Little Gilmour, MP. el. son of Sir John Little Gilmour, 2nd Bt. *Residences*,—The Ferry House, Old Isleworth, Middx.; Thwaite House, Aldborough, Norwich.

UNCLE LIVING   (*Son of 7th Duke*).
Lord George Francis John, *b*. 1911 ; ed. at Eton and at Ch. Ch., Oxford ; is Brevet-Col. (T.A. Reserve of Officers), a Member of Queen's Body Guard for Scotland (Roy. Co. of Archers); formerly Maj. 10th Hussars, 23rd Hussars, and Lt.-Col., Northants Yeo.; 1939-45 War in France, Belgium, Holland and Germany (despatches): *m*. 1938, Mary Wina Mannin (Molly), only da. of Lt.-Col. H. O. Bishop, of Harewood, Andover, Hants, and has issue living, David Henry George, *b*. 1945: *m*. 1967. Laura Jane, da. of St. John Bernard Vyvyan Harmsworth, of Horsted Keynes, Sussex [see Boothby, Bt., colls.], and has issue living, Lucy Rose *b*. 1969, Harriet Mary *b*. 1972,—Georgina Mary (*Baroness O'Neill*), *b*. 1940: *m*. 1963, the 4th Baron O'Neill (Shane's Castle, Antrim),—Charmian Rachel, *b*. 1942: *m*. 1964, Archibald Hugh Stirling, yr. of Keir [see Stirling-Maxwell, Bt.]. *Residence*,—The Old Almshouse, Weekley, Kettering, Northants. *Club*,—Cavalry.

AUNTS LIVING (*Daughters of 7th Duke*).
Lady Margaret Ida, *b*. 1893: *m*. 1926, Adm. Sir Geoffrey Alan Brooke Hawkins, KBE, CB, MVO, DSC, and has issue living, James Walter, *b*. 1933,—Alice Anne, *CVO*, *b*. 1928; Assist. Press Sec. to HM since 1958; CVO 1972,—Renira Margaret Ida *b*. 1930: *m*. 1953, Alistair Allan Horne (Membury House, Ramsbury, Wilts.), son of the late Sir (James) Allan Horne [E. Kinnoull, colls.], and has issue living, Camilla Margaret *b*. 1954, Alexandra Julia *b*. 1957,—Vanessa Renira *b*. 1961. *Residence*—, Grafton Underwood, Kettering, Northants.

Lady Sybil Anne (of 8, Cumberland Mansions, George St., W.1), *b*. 1899: *m*. 1919, Charles Bathurst Hele Phipps, Lt. 1st Life Guards (Reserve), who *d*. 1960, and has issue living, (Charles) Nicholas (Chalcot Stables, Westbury, Wilts), *b*. 1925: *m*. 1966, Christian Fiona, da. of Colin Hercules Mackenzie, CMG, of Kyle House, Kyleakin, Skye [see E. Clanwilliam, colls.], and has issue living, Charles Mackenzie *b*. 1967, Alice *b*. 1969,—Clare Margaret, *b*. 1920: *m*. 1950, Maj. David George Hadow, MC, and has issue living, Susan Margaret *b*. 1952, Rosemary Una (twin) *b*. 1952,—Eileen Sybil, *b*. 1922; was a Lady-in-Waiting to HRH the Duchess of Gloucester 1944-47; 1939-45 War as Junior Com., ATS: *m*. 1948, Philip Kingsmill Parbury, DSO, MC, of Dunmore, NSW, and has issue living, Charles Adam Phipps *b*. 1954, Philip Piers Hueford *b*. 1957, Anabel Elizabeth Kingsmill *b*. 1950,—Diana, *b*. 1927: *m*. 1959, John de Normann (Ashwell House, Ashwell Baldock, Herts.), son of Sir Eric (Norman) de Normann, KBE, CB, and has issue living, John Roderick Charles *b*. 1959, Anthony Leigh *b*. 1961.

Lady Alice Christabel, *GCB, CI, GCVO, GBE* (*HRH Princess Alice the Duchess of Gloucester*), *b*. 1901; a GCStJ, Air Marshal WRAF, Col.-in-Ch. of KOSB and R. Hussars, Dep. Col.-in-Ch. R. Anglian Regt., and a Member of Council of British Red Cross So.; received Freedom of City of Edinburgh 1937, of Gloucester 1939, and of Belfast 1952; GBE (Civil) and CI 1937, GCVO 1948, GCB (Civil) 1975: *m*. Nov. 6th, 1935, HRH Prince Henry William Frederick Albert, KG, KT, KP, GCB, GCMG, GCVO, PC, Duke of Gloucester, who *d*. June 10th, 1974, 3rd son of HM King George V [see "ROYAL FAMILY"]. *Residences*,—1, Kensington Palace, W8; Barnwell Manor, Peterborough.

Lady Mary Theresa (*Lady Mary Burghley*), *b*. 1904 ; is a C.St.J. : *m*. 1929, Lord Burghley, K.C.M.G.— now 6th Marquess of Exeter—(from whom she obtained a divorce 1946). *Residence*,—21, Hyde Park Gardens Mews, W.2.

Lady Angela Christine Rose, *b*. 1906: *m*. 1936, Vice-Adm. Sir Peter Dawnay, K.C.V.O., C.B., D.S.C. [see V. Downe, colls.]. *Residence*,—Hattingley House, Medstead, near Alton, Hants.

WIDOW LIVING OF SON OF SEVENTH DUKE
Lady Rachel Douglas-Home, da. of 13th Earl of Home [see B. Home of the Hirsel]: *m*. 1937, Lord William Walter Montagu-Douglas-Scott, who *d*. 1958, and has issue living [see colls., infra.]. *Residence*,—Beechwood, Melrose.

WIDOW LIVING OF EIGHTH DUKE.
VREDA ESTHER MARY (*Mary, Duchess of Buccleuch*) (Bowhill, Selkirk; Boughton House, Kettering; Drumlanrig Castle, Thornhill, Dumfries-shire), da. of the late Maj. William Frank Lascelles, [see E. Harewood, colls.]: *m*. 1921, the 8th Duke, who *d*. 1973.

COLLATERAL BRANCHES LIVING.
Issue of the late Lord William Walter Montagu-Douglas-Scott, M.C., 2nd son of 7th Duke, *b*. 1896, *d*. 1958: *m*. 1937, Lady Rachel Douglas-Home (ante), da. of 13th Earl of Home [see B. Home of the Hirsel]:—

Walter William, *b*. 1946.——Margaret Elizabeth, *b*. 1938.——Frances Henrietta (*Baroness Cranworth*), *b*. 1940: *m*. 1968, the 3rd Baron Cranworth.——Rosemary Alice (twin), *b*. 1940.——Jean Louise, *b*. 1943: *m*. 1968, George Christopher Cadafael Tapps-Gervis-Meyrick, son of Lt.-Col. Sir George David Elliott Tapps-Gervis-Meyrick, 6th Bt.

Issue of the late Lieut.-Col. Lord George William Montagu-Douglas-Scott, O.B.E., 3rd son of 6th Duke, *b*. 1866, *d*. 1947: *m*. 1903, Lady Elizabeth Emily Manners, who *d*. 1924, dau. of 7th Duke of Rutland :—

John Henry, *M.C.*, *b*. 1911; ed. at Eton; Lieut.-Col. (ret.) 9th Lancers, a Member of Queen's Body Guard for Scotland (Roy. Co. of Archers), and a J.P. and D.L. for Roxburghshire; European War 1939-45 (wounded, M.C.): *m*. 1954, Anne Peace Arabella (WARRE), dau. of the late Capt. Angus Alexander Mackintosh, Roy. Horse Gds. [D. Devonshire], and has issue living, James George, *b*. 1959,—Elizabeth Arabella, *b*. 1956. *Residence*,—Kirklands, Ancrum.——Claud Everard Walter, *M.C.*, *b*. 1915; ed. at Eton, and at Ch. Ch., Oxford; formerly Lieut.-Col. Lothians and Border Yeo. (T.A.); is a Member of the Queen's Body Guard for Scotland (Roy. Co. of Archers); European War 1939-45 in N. Africa and Italy (M.C.): *m*. 1941, Margaret Francis, dau. of the late Brig.-Gen. Lewis Francis Philips, CB, CMG, DSO, OBE [E. Ducie, colls.], and has issue living, Thomas Walter. *b*. 1943: *m*. 1973, Marion Miranda, da. of the Hon. Claud Stephen Phillimore [see B. Phillimore],—Katharine Margaret, *b*. 1946: *m*. 1975, Robert Vere Spencer Bernard [see D. Marlborough, colls.]. *Residence*,—Bourton Hill House, Moreton-in-Marsh, Glos.——Phyllis Anne, *b*. 1904: *m*. 1924, the 4th Baron Delamere, from whom she obtained a divorce 1944. *Residence*,—26, Holland Park Road, W14.——Jeanetta Ruth (Arnbank, Abercairny, Crieff, Perthshire) *b*. 1906: *m*. 1937, Maj. James William Stirling Home Drummond, Moray, Scots Gds., who *d*. 1968, and has issue living, William George (Abercairny, Crieff, Perthshire), *b*. 1940; ed. at Eton: *m*. 1969, Angela Jane, da. of the late Lt. Cdr. Michael John Baring, RN [see B. Northbrook, colls.], and has issue living, a da. *b*. 1971,— John Robert, *b*. 1943; ed. at Eton; Capt. Scots Gds.: *m*. 1971, Meriel Frances, dau. of P. D. M. Stirling-Aird,—David Maurice, *b*. 1945; ed. at Eton; Lt. Scots Gds.,—Lucy Gwendolen (*Hon. Mrs. D. Rupert*

Strutt), *b.* 1939: *m.* 1964, as his 2nd wife, Capt. the Hon. (Desmond) Rupert Strutt, 4th son of 3rd Baron Belpher.——Marjorie Katharine (twin), *b.* 1906: *m.* 1st, 1935, Maj. Thomas Archibald Hackett Pain, Irish Gds., who *d.* (killed in action) 1940; 2ndly, 1943, Adma Bell, who *d.* 1966, and has issue living (by 2nd m.) Charles James, *b.* 1944,—Louisa, *b.* 1947.

Grandchildren of the late Lt.-Col. Lord Herbert Andrew Montagu-Douglas-Scott, CMG, DSO:—

Issue of the late Brig. (Claud) Andrew Montagu-Douglas-Scott, DSO, *b.* 1906, *d.* 1971; *m.* 1st, 1929, Lady Victoria Doris Rachel Haig (who obtained a divorce 1951), da. of 1st Earl Haig; 2ndly, 1951, Zalia (Tumble Cottage, Runcton, Chichester, Sussex), yst. (twin) da. of the late Sir Harold Edward Snagge, KBE, [B. Avebury, colls.], and formerly wife of the late Lt.-Col. Esmond Charles Baring, OBE [B. Ashburton]:—

(By 1st m.) Douglas Andrew (Whitcombe, Overbury, Tewkesbury, Glos.), *b.* 1930; late Capt. IG: *m.* 1954, Bridget Elizabeth, da. of the late Air Vice-Marshal Sir Robert Allingham George, KCVO, KBE, CB, MC.——Henrietta, *b.* 1934: *m.* 1962, Maj. Arthur John Stewart Griffin, CVO, of Bartons Cottage, Bushy Park, Teddington, Middx., and has issue living, Andrew Michael Stewart, *b.* 1963,— Phillip Anthony Stewart, *b.* 1965.——(by 2nd m.) Nicholas Herbert, *b.* 1954.

Issue of the late Lt.-Col. Lord Herbert Andrew Montagu-Douglas-Scott, CMG, DSO, 5th son of 6th Duke, *b.* 1872, *d.* 1944: *m.* 1905, Marie Josephine, who *d.* 1965, da. of the late James Edwards, of Dovercourt, Essex:—

Marian Louisa (*Lady Elmhirst*) *b.* 1908: *m.* 1st, 1927, Col. Andrew Henry Ferguson, late Life Guards, who *d.* 1966 [see V. Hampden, colls.]; 2ndly, 1968, Air Marshal Sir Thomas Walker Elmhirst, KBE, CB, AFC. *Residence*,—The Cottage, Dummer, Basingstoke, Hants.——Patricia Katharine (*Countess of Dundee*), *b.* 1910: 1st, 1931, Lt.-Col. Walter Douglas Faulkner, MC, Irish Guards, who *d.* (killed in action) (May) 1940; 2ndly (Sept.) 1940, Lt.-Col. (the Hon.) David Scrymgeour Wedderburn, DSO, Scots Guards, who *d.* (of wounds received in action) 1944 [see E. Dundee]; 3rdly, 1946, the 11th Earl of Dundee, and has issue living, (by 1st m.) David James (or David Rose, Longworth, Abingdon, Oxon.), *b.* 1932; Maj. late IG: *m.* 1958, Victoria Mary Rose, el. da. of Robert James Buxton, MB, BChir, MRCS, LRCP, DOMS [see Buxton, Bt., colls.], and has issue living, John Douglas *b.* 1959, Thomas Patrick *b.* 1965, Matthew James *b.* 1968, Robert David *b.* 1970, Katharine Rose *b.* 1960,—Hermione Patricia (*Lady Moncreiffe of that Ilk*) *b.* 1937: *m.* 1966, as his 2nd wife, Sir Rupert Iain Kay Moncreiffe of that Ilk, 11th Bt.—(by 2nd and 3rd m.) [see E. Dundee]. *Residence*, —Birkhill, Cupar, Fife.

Issue of the late Lieut.-Col. Lord Francis George Montagu-Scott, K.C.M.G., D.S.O., youngest son of 6th Duke, *b.* 1879, *d.* 1952 : *m.* 1915, Lady Eileen Nina Evelyn Sibell Elliot, who *d.* 1938, dau. of 4th Earl of Minto :—

Pamela Violet, *b.* 1916. *Residence*,—Deloraine, Rongai, Kenya.——Moyra Eileen, *b.* 1919; 1939-45 War with ATS (FANY) (despatches): *m.* 1st, 1942, Maj. Hugo Douglas Tweedie, Scots Gds., who *d.* (killed in action in NW Europe) 1945; 2ndly, 1947, Col. David de Crespigny Smiley, MVO, OBE, MC, of Benihome, Beniarbeig, Alicante, Spain [see Smiley, Bt.], and has issue living (by 1st m.), Gavin Hugo, *b.* 1944; MA (Oxon); Maj. The Blues & Royals: *m.* 1974, Philippa Mary, da. of Maj. Michael Andrews, of Quarry House, Shepton Mallet, Som.,—Anna Bridget Eileen, *b.* 1942; MCSP: *m.* 1971, Peter Robert McFerran, and has issue living, Lucinda *b.* 1972,—(by 2nd m.) [see Smiley, Bt.]. *Residence*,—Tara, el Trencall, Javea, Alicante, Spain.

Issue of the late Lord Henry John Douglas-Scott-Montagu, 2nd son of the 5th Duke of Buccleuch, who was cr. *Baron Montagu of Beaulieu* 1885 [see that title].

Issue of the late Adm. Lord Charles Thomas Montagu-Douglas-Scott, G.C.B., 4th son of 5th Duke, *b.* 1839, *d.* 1911 : *m.* 1883, Ada Mary, who *d.* 1943, dau. of Charles Ryan, of Derriweit Heights, Macedon, Victoria :—

Sir David John, *KCMG, OBE, b.* 1887; ed. at Eton; formerly Dep. Under-Sec. of State, Foreign Office; ret. 1947; Hon. Maj. late Roy. Scots (Lothian Regt.); 1914-18 War (wounded, despatches, Legion of Honour, OBE); OBE (Mil) 1919, CMG 1935, KCMG 1941: *m.* 1st, 1918, Dorothy Charlotte, who *d.* 1965, da. of the late Capt. Cecil George Assheton Drummond [E. Perth, colls.]; 2ndly, 1970, Valerie, da. of the late Cdr. Steriker Finnis, RN. *Residence*,—Boughton House, Kettering. *Club*,— Travellers'.

PREDECESSORS.—[1] *Sir* WALTER Scott, Knt., a powerful chieftain, and a military commander of renown in the Netherlands under the Prince of Orange, was in 1606 cr. *Lord Scott of Buccleuch* (peerage of Scotland); *d.* 1611; *s.* by his son [2] WALTER, 2nd Lord : cr. *Lord Scott of Whitchester and Eskdaill* and *Earl of Buccleuch* (peerage of Scotland) 1619, with remainder to his heirs whatsoever; *d.* 1633; *s.* by his only son [3] FRANCIS, 2nd Earl; *d.* 1651; *s.* by his dau. [4] MARY, when 11 years of age she *m.* Walter Scott (then 14 years old) afterwards Earl of Tarras for life; *d.* withoutissue; *s.* by her sister [5] ANNE: *m.* 1st, 1663, James, K.G., Duke of Monmouth, who assumed on his marriage the surname of Scott; in 1663 he and his wife were cr. *Lord and Lady Scott of Whitchester and Eskdaill, Earl and Countess of Dalkeith,* and *Duke and Duchess of Buccleuch* (peerage of Scotland), with remainder to the heirs male whatsoever descending from the Duke's body; the Duke was executed July 15, 1685, when all his honours were forfeited, but the honours vested in the Duchess were not attainted; her Grace *m.* 2ndly, Charles, 3rd Baron Cornwallis, by whom she had issue; *d.* 1732; *s.* by her grandson [6] FRANCIS, K.T., 2nd Duke, son of James, Earl of Dalkeith, a Representative Peer; in 1743, was restored by Act of Parliament to the English honours of his grandfather, and became *Earl of Doncaster* and *Baron Scott of Tynedale* (peerage of England, cr. 1663); *d.* 1751; *s.* by his grandson [7] HENRY, K.G., K.T., 3rd Duke; by the death, in 1810, of the 4th Duke of Queensberry, he became, under a special designation (granted in 1706), *Lord Douglas of Kinmont, Middlebie and Dornoch, Viscount of Nith, Thorthorwald and Ross, Earl of Drumlanrig and Sanquhar, Marquess of Dumfriesshire,* and *Duke of Queensberry* (peerage of Scotland); *d.* 1812; *s.* by his son [8] CHARLES WILLIAM, K.T., 4th Duke of Buccleuch and 6th Duke of Queensberry; called up in his father's Barony of Tyndale 1807: *d.* 1819; *s.* by his son [9] WALTER FRANCIS, K.G., P.C., D.C.L., LL.D., F.R.S., 5th Duke of Buccleuch and 7th Duke of Queensberry ; *b.* 1806; was Lord Privy Seal 1842-6, President of the Council 1846, Lord-Lieut. of Midlothian and Roxburghshire, and Chancellor of Glasgow Univ.: *m.* 1829, Lady Charlotte Anne Thynne, *V.A* , who *d.* 1895, 3rd dau. of 2nd Marquess of Bath ; *d.* April 16th, 1884; *s.* by his son [10] WILLIAM HENRY WALTER, K.G., K.T., P.C., 6th Duke of Buccleuch and 8th Duke of Queensberry, *b.* 1831 ; M.P. for Edinburghshire (C) 1853-68 and 1874-80; Lord-Lieut. of co. Dumfries 1858-1914; *m.* 1859, Lady Louisa Jane Hamilton, V.A., who *d.* 1912, dau. of 1st Duke of Abercorn. K.G. ; *d.* 1914 ; *s.* by his el. son [11] JOHN CHARLES, K.T., G.C.V.O., 7th Duke of Buccleuch, and 9th Duke of Queensberry ; *b.* 1864 ; M.P. for Roxburghshire (U) 1895-1906 ; Lord Lieut. of co. Dumfries: *m.* 1893, Lady Margaret Alice Bridgeman, who *d.* 1954, dau. of 4th Earl of Bradford; *d.* 1935; *s.* by his el. son [12] WALTER JOHN, KT, GCVO, TD, PC, 8th Duke of Buccleuch, and 10th Duke of Queensberry, *b.* 1894; Lord Steward of the Household 1937-40, Lord Clerk Register of Scotland, and Keeper of the Signet 1956-73, Capt.-Gen. Queen's Body Guard for Scotland (Roy. Co. of Archers), and Gold Stick for Scotland 1962-73, Chancellor of Order of Thistle 1966-73, MP for Roxburghshire and Selkirkshire (C) 1923-35, and Lord Lt. of Roxburghshire 1932-73: *m.* 1921, (Vreda Esther) Mary, da. of the late Maj. William Frank Lascelles [E. Harewood, colls.]; *d.* 1973; *s.* by his son [13] WALTER FRANCIS JOHN, VRD, 9th Duke of Buccleuch,'and 11th Duke of Queensberry, present peer; also Marquess of Dumfriesshire, Earl of Drumlanrig and Sanquhar, Earl of Buccleuch, Earl of Doncaster, Earl of Dalkeith, Viscount Nith, Thorthorwald and Ross, Lord Douglas of Kinmont, Middlebie and Dornoch, Lord Scott of Buccleuch, Lord Scott of Whitchester and Eskdaill, and Baron Scott of Tynedale.

BUCHAN, EARL OF. (Erskine.) [Earl S. 1469.]

DONALD CARDROSS FLOWER ERSKINE, 16th Earl ; *b*. June 3rd, 1899 ; *s*. as 7th Baron Erskine 1957, and as 16th Earl of Buchan 1960 ; ed. at Charterhouse ; Lieut.-Col. (retired) 9th Lancers : *m*. 1927, Christina, dau. of the late Hugh Woolner, and adopted dau. of the late Lloyd Harry Baxendale, J.P., of Greenham Lodge, Newbury, Berks, and has issue.

Arms,—Quarterly of four : 1st azure, a barrulet en crancelin of four strawberry leaves between three garbs or. *Buchan* ; 2nd argent, a pale sable, in dexter canton a rose gules, barbed and seeded vert. *Erskine* ; 3rd or, a lymphad sable, sails furled and oars in action and at the masthead a beacon all proper, surmounted of a fess chequy azure and argent charged with a mullet of the second, *Stewart of Buchan* ; 4th argent, a lion passant guardant gules, crowned with an imperial and gorged with an open crown or, a label of three points of the second, the centre point charged with a crescent of the third, *Ogilvie of Auchterhouse*, on an inescutcheon en surtout gules,an eagle displayed or, armed and members azure, looking towards the sun in his splendour in dexter chief for lordship of *Cardross*. Crest.—A dexter arm issuant from the wreath attired in a manche gules doubled ermine, the hand proper and grasping a club or. Supporters—Two ostriches proper, armed, beaked and membered or.

Residence,—The Manor, Bourton on the Water, Gloucestershire.

SON LIVING
MALCOLM HARRY (*Lord Cardross*), *b*. July 4th, 1930 ; ed. at Eton: *m*. 1957, Hilary Diana Cecil, dau. of the late Sir Ivan McLannahan Power, 2nd Bt., and has issue:—
SONS LIVING,—*Hon.* Henry Thomas Alexander, *b*. May 31st, 1960.
Hon. Montagu John, *b*. 1966.
DAUGHTERS LIVING,—*Hon.* Seraphina Mary, *b*. 1961.
Hon. Arabella Fleur, *b*. 1969.
Residence,—24, The Little Boltons, SW10.

DAUGHTERS LIVING.
Lady Sarah Louisa, *b*. 1931: *m*. 1957 (m. diss. 1972), Major Norman Neill-Fraser, and has issue living, James Montagu Nicholas, *b*. 1959. *Residence,*—Willow Cottage, South Hay, Kingsley, Bordon, Hants.
Lady Caroline Flower, *b*. 1935: *m*. 1963, John Robin William Lingard, of Burnt Oak House, East Bergholt, Suffolk, and has issue living, Christina Helen, *b*. 1964,—Victoria Margaret, *b*. 1966.

BROTHER LIVING.
Hon. (Richard) Alastair, *b*. 1901 ; ed. at Charterhouse : *m*. 1933, Patricia, dau. of the late Major Paul FitzGerald Norbury, D.S.O., formerly of The Lench House. Stratford-on-Avon, and has issue living, Duncan Fitzgerald (Achnamara House, Connel, Argyll), *b*. 1936: *m*. 1964, Jillian Lavinia Mary, da. of Brig. Vincent Alexander Prideaux Budge, CBE, MVO, and has issue living, Rory Alistair *b*. 1972, Alexander Fitzgerald (quadruplet) *b*. 1972, Charlotte Annabel (quadruplet) *b*. 1972. *Residence,*—Cheesecombe Farm, Hawley, Liss, Hants.

SISTER LIVING.
Hon. Victoria Esme (34, Bryanston Sq., W1), *b*. 1897: *m*. 1932, Air Commodore Harry Aitken Hewat, CBE, RAF, who *d*. 1970.

COLLATERAL BRANCHES LIVING.
Issue (by 2nd marriage) of the late Capt. the Hon. Albany Mar Stuart Erskine, 2nd son of 13th Earl, *b*. 1852, *d*. 1933: *m*. 1st, 1878, Alice Ellen, who *d*. 1902 (having obtained a divorce 1900), dau. of the late Alfred Keyser, of Cross Oak, Berkhamsted ; 2ndly, 1909, Elizabeth Kate, who. *d*. 1965, da. of George Samuel Craddock, of Melbourne, Australia:—
Rose Agnes Jessie Stuart (The Golliwogs, Windmill Rd., Mortimer, Berks.), *b*. 1910.——Gladys Evelyn Stuart, *b*. 1916: *m*. 1949, Johannes Adelbert Hopmann, of The Golliwogs, Windmill Rd., Mortimer, Berks.

Descendants of the late Hon. Sir Thomas Erskine, K.T. (3rd son of 10th Earl of Buchan, and 5th Lord Cardross), who was cr. *Baron Erskine* 1806.
Issue (by 2nd marriage) of the late Hon. David Erskine, 3rd son of 2nd Baron Erskine, *b*.1816, *d*. 1903 ; *m*. 1st, 1839, Annie Maria, who *d*. 1860, dau. of the late Josiah Spode, of Tasmania: 2ndly, 1870, Florence, who *d*. 1927, dau. of Capt. Charles J. Harford, formerly of 12th Lancers :—
Sevilla Florence, *b*. 1875 : *m*. 1908, George Glass Hooper, C.E., who *d*. 1932, and has issue living, George Erskine Glass, *b*. 1911; ed. at Harrow; 1939-45 War as Capt. Wiltshire Regt.: *m*. 1st, 1935 (m. diss. 19—), Dorothea Parnell; 2nd, 1950, Shirley, da. of George Bentinck, MC, and has issue living, (by 1st marriage) Sevilla *b*. 1937, (by 2nd marriage) Graham Charles *b*. 1951,—Mary Erskine, *b*. 1909,—Sevilla Janey Glass (*Lady Lindsay*) (of Ardchyline, St. Catherine's, Argyll), *b*. 1911: *m*. 1937 (m. diss. 1962), Sir William O'Brien Lindsay, KBE, and has issue living, Robert Erskine *b*. 1948, Vanessa *b*. 1939: *m*. 1964, William David Prosser, Advocate, of 7, Randolph Cres., Edinburgh (and has issue living, Joanna Mary *b*. 1965, Sarah Dallas *b*. 1966, Shira *b*. 1945: *m*. 1969, Duncan Adam Gordon, of Clutha, Ardoch, Cardross, Dunbartonshire. *Residence,*—Wykes Court, Bridport, Dorset.

Grandchildren of the late Rev. Thomas Erskine, son of the Rt. Hon. Thomas Erskine, 3rd son of 1st Baron Erskine :—
Issue of the late Col. Henry Adeane Erskine, C.B., C.M.G., C.B.E., V.D., T.D., *b*. 1857, *d*. 1953 : *m*. 1891, Florence Eliza Palmer, who *d*. 1943, dau. of the late Ven. Frank Robert Chapman, formerly Archdeacon of Sudbury and Canon of Ely :—
Christian Mary (Little Bisterne, Burley, Ringwood, Hants.), *b*. 1894.——Griselda Beatrice (High Lea, Verwood, Dorset), *b*. 1900: *m*. 1921, the Rev. Canon George David Archer, who *d*. 1971, and has issue living, Henry David, *DFC*, *b*. 1922; is Wing-Cdr. RAF; 1939-45 War (DFC): *m*. 1957, Valda Mildred, da. of John Smart, of Wimbledon Park, SW, and has issue living, John David *b*. 1958, Matthew George *b*. 1962, Margaret Elizabeth *b*. 1959, Charlotte Christian *b*. 1961,—Richard George (Park Corner, Old Hollow, Worth, Sussex), *b*. 1925: *m*. 1956, Elizabeth Rosemary, da. of the late Kingsley Dykes, OBE, MC, of Ottinge Court, Kent, and has issue living, Caroline Griselda Erskine, *b*. 1959, Elizabeth Georgiana *b*. 1964,—Elizabeth Margaret Griselda, *b*. 1923: *m*. 1946, Lt.-Col. Robert Kerr Montgomery, MC, RE (ret.), of 27, Barton Rd., W14, and has issue living, Robert Michael *b*. 1947, David Richard *b*. 1949,—Alethea Mary, *b*. 1926: *m*. 1947, Com. C. P. Evensen,

DSC, RNVR, of Sherwoods, Staplehay, Trull, Taunton, Som., and has issue living, James Peter *b.* 1951, Patricia Christian *b.* 1948: *m.* 1974, Alan Tucker, of Taunton, Som., Susan Alethea *b.* 1950: *m.* 1974, Donald Francis Heather Bent, of 7, Parkland Court, Addison Rd., W14, Fiona Mary *b.* 1952: *m.* 1972, David Perratt, of Heatherbank, Trull, Taunton, Som. (and has issue living, Diana Karen *b.* 1974),—Mary Pamela, *b.* 1929: *m.* 1951, Capt. Richard Ewen Hartley, RN, of 3, Newton Rd., Canford Cliffs, Poole, Dorset, and has issue living, Christopher Richard *b.* 1952, Michael Peter *b.* 1956, Helen Mary *b.* 1955,—Helen Christian, *b.* 1935: *m.* 1970, Alastair Nigel Courtney Bruce, of Cobweb Cottage, Netton, Salisbury.

Issue of the late Thomas Edward Erskine, *b.* 1859, *d.* 1916: *m.* 1888, Amy Gertrude, who *d.* 1939, da. of Lt.-Gen. Robert Bruce [Corbet, Bt., colls.]:—
John Steuart (PO Box 234, Wolfville, Nova Scotia), *b.* 1900; ed. at Acadia Univ. (BA), and McGill Univ. (MA): *m.* 1928, Rachel, da. of the late Lt.-Col. Arthur Wilmot Rickman, and has issue living, David Steuart (71, Green Bush Rd., Willowvale 443, Ont., Canada), *b.* 1929; ed. at Acadia Univ (BSc 1948), and at Toronto Univ. (MA 1952): *m.* 1957, Elizabeth Fyodorovna, da. of the late Fyodor Ivanovitch Kramarev, and has issue living, John David *b.* 1958, Maria *b.* 1960,—Anthony John (1215, Agincourt Rd., Ottawa, Ont., Canada, K2C 2H8), *b.* 1931; ed. at Acadia (BSc 1952), Queen's (MA 1955, PhD 1957), and British Columbia (MA 1960) Univs.: *m.* 1955, Janet Madeline Clarke, of Canning, Nova Scotia, and has issue living, Thomas Edward *b.* 1957, Rachel Julia Andrée *b.* 1958, Sally Eileen *b.* 1961,—Roger Thomas, (Carron Point, RR1, Bathurst, New Brunswick) *b.* 1933; ed. at Acadia Univ. (BSc), at Nova Scotia Tech. Coll. (BEng), and at Queen's Univ. (MSc): *m.* 1956, Florence Elizabeth Taylor, of Windsor, Nova Scotia, and has issue living, Gerald Conrad *b.* 1957, Neil Steuart *b.* 1960, Joseph Christian *b.* 1962, Jane Elizabeth *b.* 1966.——Marjory Rachel Helen, *b.* 1889; is a nun.——Diana Isobel, *b.* 1892: *m.* 1920, Sir Hugo Meynell FitzHerbert, 6th Bt., who *d.* 1934, and from whom she obtained a divorce 1930. *Residence,*—Puesta del Sol. Marbella, Province de Malaga, Spain.——Violet Amy (*Lady Seymour*), *b.* 1894: *m.* 1917, Sir Horace James Seymour, GCMG, CVO [see M. Hertford, colls.]. *Residence,*—Bratton House, Westbury, Wilts.

Issue of the late Edward John Erskine, *b.* 1864, *d.* 1917: *m.* 1888, Gertrude, who *d.* 19— da. of H. Harding, of Sydney, NSW:—
Steuart Edward (1550, Lawson Av., W. Vancouver, BC, Canada), *b.* 1902: *m.* 1930, Marjory Luxton Clendening, and has issue living, John Steuart (9448, Olympia Fields Drive, San Ramon, Cal., 94583, USA), *b.* 1937: *m.* 1967, Sharyl Tomes, of Omaha, Nebraska, and has issue living, Karen *b.* 1968,—Patricia Louise (Le Petit Dixcart, Sark, Channel Isles) *b.* 1934.——Sybil Gertrude, *b.* 1892: *m.* 1919, Capt. John Joseph Power, OBE, who *d.* 1959, and has issue living, Peter John Geoffrey (of 2325, Nelson Av., West Vancouver, British Columbia) *b.* 1921; 1939-45 War in Merchant Ser.: *m.* 1953, Patricia Irene, da. of Com. C. H. Hudson, and has issue living, Christopher James *b.* 1956, David John Charles *b.* 1958,—Christopher John (51, Manor Way, Beckenham, Kent), *b.* 1929: *m.* 1956, Ann Elizabeth, da. of R. Woolard, of Sydenham Hill, SE21, and has issue living, Bridget Madeleine *b.* 1957, Kate Elizabeth *b.* 1960, Wendy Ann *b.* 1962,—Mary Sybil, *b.* 1925: *m.* 1949, Basil George Crismas Wood, late Capt. Roy. Armoured Corps, of 63, Stradella Rd., Herne Hill, SE24, and has issue living, Jonathan Crismas *b.* 1953, Simon Edward *b.* 1961, Jennifer Ann *b.* 1950, Sarah Jane *b.* 1957. *Residence,*—205, Clive Rd., W. Dulwich, SE21.——Ona Maud, *b.* 1894: *m.* 1924, John Eynon Wood. *Residence,*—205, Clive Rd., W. Dulwich, SE21.

Grandchildren of the late Capt. Sir (Henry) David Erskine, KCVO, son of the late James Erskine, el. son of David Erskine, 3rd in descent from the Hon. John Erskine, 3rd son of 2nd Lord Cardross:—
Issue of the late Brig.-Gen. James Francis Erskine, CB, CMG, MVO, *b.* 1862, *d.* 1936: *m.* 1896, Margaret Beatrix, who *d.* 1952, da. of the late Henry Lambton, of Redfield, Winslow:—
Christian, *b.* 1901: *m.* 1926, Capt. Hugh Salvin Bowlby, RN, and has issue living, Angela Margaret, *b.* 1932,—Daphne Christian, *b.* 1934: *m.* 1961, Richard James Lea Watson, of Stocks, Castle Hedingham, Halstead, Essex, and has issue living, Malcolm Edward *b.* 1966, Fiona Catherine *b.* 1969. *Residence,*—The Hermitage, Kelso, Roxburghshire.

Issue of the late Alan David Erskine, OBE, *b.* 1872, *d.* 1947: *m.* 1897, Enid, who *d.* 1931, da. of the late Lachlan M. Rate, of Milton Court, Dorking:—
Patience Lina, *b.* 1901. *Residence,*—Strawberry Hill, Aldington, Ashford, Kent.

Issue of the late Col. Sir Arthur (Edward) Erskine, GCVO, DSO, *b.* 1881, *d.* 1963: *m.* 1921, Rosemary Freda, who *d.* 1970, da. of the late Brig.-Gen. Edward William David Baird, CBE:—
Donald Seymour [of Cleish House, Cleish, Kinross-shire. *Club,*—New (Edinburgh)], *b.* 1925; ed. at Wellington; FRICS; a DL of Kinross-shire, and a Member of Queen's Body Guard for Scotland (Roy. Co. of Archers); 1939-45 War as Capt. RA: *m.* 1953, Catharine Annandale, only da. of the late Kenneth McLelland, of Wester Housebyres, Melrose, Roxburghshire, and has issue living, James Malcolm Kenneth, *b.* 1957,—Caroline Janet, *b.* 1954,—Fiona Catharine, *b.* 1956,—Julia Rosemary, *b.* 1962,—Joanna Christian, *b.* 1968.——Angus Bruce (1, Farrow Drive, Corpach, Fort William Inverness-shire), *b.* 1928; Cdr. RN: *m.* 1961, Alison Gillian, yr. da. of the late Dr. Comyn Duthie, of Welkom, Orange Free State, S. Africa, and has issue living, Alexander David, *b.* 1964,—Keith Malcolm, *b.* 1967.

Grandchildren of the late Maj.-Gen. George Elphinstone Erskine, el. son of Capt. George Keith Erskine, 4th son of David Erskine (ante):—
Issue of the late Gen. Sir George Watkin Eben James Erskine, GCB, KBE, DSO, *b.* 1899, *d.* 1965: *m.* 1930, Ruby, who *d.* 1974, da. of Sir Evelyn Andros de la Rue, 2nd Bt.:—
Philip Niel (Ida's Valley Homestead, PO Box 132, Stellenbosch, Cape S. Africa), 1933; Maj. Scots Gds.; Equerry to HRH the Duke of Gloucester 1962-64: *m.* 1960, Alice Fiona, da. of the late Maj. Edward Copleston Radliffe, late 9th Lancers, of Lyndhurst House, Somerset West, Cape, S. Africa, and has issue living, Rupert Alexander, *b.* 1961,—George Edward, *b.* 1966,—Lucy Rose, *b.* 1962.——Robert Keith (Clifton Wood, Newbridge, Midlothian), *b.* 1936: *m.* 1964, Susan Morag, da. of the late Sir Archibald Charles Edmonstone, 6th Bt., and has issue living, Hamish Robert Coll Charles, *b.* 1967,—Alexander William Ian Marshall, *b.* 1970,—Iona Mary, *b.* 1965.——Elizabeth Polly, *b.* 1945: *m.* 1967, Paul L. H. Bristol, of Claverham Manor, Berwick, Polegate, Sussex, and has issue living, Pollyanna, *b.* 1969,—Sophy Louisa, *b.* 1972.

PREDECESSORS.—Buchan was one of the seven original Mormaerships (or Earldoms) of Scotland. In 1469 [1] *Sir* JAMES STEWART, 2nd son of Sir James Stewart of Lorn (" the Black Knight of Lorn "), by Joan, widow of James I. of Scotland, was cr. *Earl of Buchan* and *Lord Auchterhouse;* High Chamberlain of Scotland and Ambassador to France: *m.* (before) 1466, Margaret, da. of Sir Alexander Ogilvy, of Auchterhouse; *s.* by his son [2] ALEXANDER, 2nd Earl; *d.* 1505; *s.* by his son [3] JOHN, 3rd Earl; *s.* by his granddaughter [4] CHRISTIAN: *m.* Robert Douglas, of Lochleven, who in right of his wife became Earl of Buchan; *s.* by his son [5] JAMES, 5th Earl; *d.* 1601; *s.* by his da. [6] MARY: *m.* James Erskine, 2nd son of John, KG, 2nd Earl of Mar, who thereupon assumed the Earldom of Buchan; his wife resigned the dignity, and in 1617 she and her husband were cr. by royal charter *Earl and Countess of Buchan* (peerage of Scotland), with remainder to the heirs-male of the marriage, whom failing, to the legitimate and nearest heirs-male and assignees of the Earl; in 1625 they had a further charter with similar limitation of the Earldom; in 1633 the precedency of the Earldom was established by Act of Parliament as 1469; the Countess *d.* 1628, and the Earl 1640; *s.* (under the charters of 1617 and 1625) by his son [7] JAMES, 7th Earl; *d.* 1664; *s.* by his son [8] WILLIAM, 8th Earl; *d.* unmarried 1695; *s.* by the heir male of 6th Earl [9] DAVID, PC, 9th Earl, and 4th Lord Cardross [see infra *****], described in the Rolls of Parliament as 4th Earl of Buchan; right to this Earldom acknowledged by Parliament 1698; was a Representative Peer and Lord-Lieut. of cos. Stirling and Clackmannan; *d.* 1745; *s.* by his son [10] HENRY DAVID, 10th Earl; *d.* 1767; *s.* by his son [11] DAVID STEWART, 11th Earl; *d.* 1829; *s.* by his nephew [12] HENRY DAVID, 12th Earl; was *m.* three times, 1st, 1809, to Elizabeth Cole, who *d.* 1828, da. of Maj.-Gen. Sir Charles Shipley: he *d.* 1857, and was *s.* by his 2nd son by 1st marriage [13] DAVID STUART, 13th Earl, *b.* 1815: *m.* 1st, 1849, Agnes Graham, who *d.* 1875, da. of James Smith, of Craigend Castle, Stirlingshire; 2ndly, 1876, Maria, da. of William James, and widow of Jervoise Collas, of St. Martin's House, Jersey; *d.* 1898; *s.* by his el. son [14] SHIPLEY GORDON STUART, 14th Earl, *b.* 1850: *m.* 1876, Rosalie Louisa, who *d.* 1943, da. of the late Capt. Jules Alexandre Sartorius, of Hopsford Hall, Coventry; *d.* 1934; *s.* by his only son [15] RONALD DOUGLAS STUART MAR, 15th Earl; *b.* 1878; formerly Lieut. Argyll and Sutherland Highlanders, Scots Gds. and E. Riding Yeo.; S. Africa 1900-1902, European War 1915-17 in Egypt, Salonika and Palestine as Lieut. RASC; *d.* 1960; *s.* by his kinsman [16] DONALD CARDROSS FLOWER, 7th Baron Erskine [see infra†], 16th Earl and present peer; also Lord Cardross, Lord Auchterhouse and Baron Erskine.

⁎ [1] JOHN, 2nd Earl of Mar, was cr. *Lord Cardross* (peerage of Scotland) 1610, and acquired the right to assign the Lordship to whomsoever he might select, which privilege he exercised by Charter 1617 in favour of Henry, his 2nd son by his 2nd marriage; *d.* 1634; *s.* by his grandson [2] DAVID, 2nd Lord; *d.* 1671; *s.* by his son [3] HENRY, PC, 3rd Lord; suffered from religious persecution and was heavily fined and imprisoned; established a colony in Carolina, USA; was Gov. of the Mint; *d.* 1693; *s.* by his son [4] DAVID, 4th Lord, afterwards 9th Earl of Buchan (ante).

†—[1] The *Hon.* THOMAS ERSKINE, KT, 3rd son of 10th Earl of Buchan, having served both in Army and Navy was called to the English Bar and became a distinguished Advocate; Attorney-Gen. to H‡RH the Prince of Wales 1783, Chancellor of Duchy of Cornwall 1802, and Lord High Chancellor 1806; cr. *Baron Erskine*, of Restormel Castle, co. Cornwall (peerage of United Kingdom) 1806: *m.* 1st, 1770, Frances, who *d.* 1805, da. of David Moore, MP; 2ndly, 18—, Sarah Buck; *d.* 1823; *s.* by his son [2] DAVID MONTAGU, 2nd Baron, *b.* 1777: *m.* 1st, 1799, Frances, who *d.* (March) 1843, da. of Gen. John Cadwalader, of Philadelphia, USA; 2ndly (July), 1843, Ann Bond, who *d.* 1851, da. of the late John Travis; 3rdly, 1852, Anna, who *d.* 1886 (having *m.* 3rdly, 1856, the Ven. J. Sandford, BD, Archdeacon of Coventry), widow of Thomas Calderwood Durham, of Largo; *d.* 1855; *s.* by his el. son [3] THOMAS AMERICUS, 3rd Baron, *b.* 1802: *m.* 1830, Louisa, who *d.* 1867, da. of G. Newnham, of New Timber Place, Sussex, and widow of Thomas Legh, of Adlington; *d.* 1877; *s.* by his brother [4] JOHN CADWALLADER, 4th Baron; *b.* 1805; served in BCS 1826-53: *m.* 1st, 1829, Margaret, who *d.* 1862, da. of John Martyn, of co. Tyrone; 2ndly, 1865, Mary Louisa, who *d.* 1889 (having *m.* 2ndly, 1886, Philip Henry Egerton), da. of Col. Alexander Campbell, CB, KH, of Blackburn House, Ayrshire; *d.* Mar. 28, 1882; *s.* by his son [5] WILLIAM MACNAGHTEN, 5th Baron, *b.* 1841: *m.* 1864, Caroline Alice Martha, who *d.* 1922, da. of the late William Grimble; *d.* 1913; *s.* by his son [6] MONTAGU, 6th Baron; *b.*, 1865; formerly Lieut.-Com. RNVR: *m.* 1895, Florence, who *d.* 1936, 4th da. of Edgar Flower, JP, formerly of Middlehill Park, Broadway, Worcestershire, and The Hill, Stratford-on-Avon; *d.* 1957; *s.* by his el. son [7] DONALD CARDROSS FLOWER, 7th Baron and afterwards 16th Earl of Buchan (ante).

Buckhurst, Lord, son of Earl De La Warr.

BUCKINGHAMSHIRE, EARL OF. (Hobart-Hampden)
[Earl G.B. 1746, Bt. E. 1611.]

VERE FREDERICK CECIL HOBART-HAMPDEN, 9th Earl and 13th Baronet; *b.* May 17th, 1901; *s.* 1963; ed. in Switzerland, and at St. Lawrence Coll., Ramsgate; 1939-45 War with RAAF: *m.* 1972, Margot Macrae, da. of John Storey Rodger, of NSW, Aust., and widow of F. C. Bruce Hittman, MD, of Sydney, Aust.

Arms,—Quarterly: 1st and 4th argent, a saltire gules, between four eagles displayed azure, *Hampden:* 2nd and 3rd sable, an estoile of six rays or, between two flaunches ermine, *Hobart.* **Crests,**—1st, a talbot statant ermine, collared and line reflexed thereto, tied in a knot over the back gules, *Hampden;* 2nd, a bull statant per pale sable and gules, bezantée, in the nose a ring or, *Hobart.* **Supporters,**—*Dexter,* a buck; *sinister,* a talbot, both reguardant proper, each gorged with a radiant collar, and a line reflexed over the back or. **Second Motto,**—Vestigia nulla retrorsum (*No steps backward*).

Address,—c/o Barclays Bank, 160, Piccadilly, W1.

The giver makes precious.

DAUGHTER LIVING OF SEVENTH EARL
Lady Sidney Mary Catherine Anne, *MBE, b.* 1900; was a MLC, Kenya Colony 1938-42; 1939-45 War in E. Africa and Middle East as Maj. E. Africa Women's Territorial Ser. (despatches); MBE (Mil) 1941: *m.* 1924, Capt. Thomas Innis Farrar, MC, who *d.* 1934, formerly Devonshire Regt., and has issue living, Thomas Ewan (of Kamara, Mau Summit, Kenya), *b.* 1927: *m.* 1955, Judith Ann, da. of Kenneth Horne, of Coombe Corner, South Park Hill Road, South Croydon, Surrey. *Residence,*—Mau Summit, Kenya.

SISTER LIVING
Lucy Sybil (c/o Centennial Manor, Bancroft, Ont., Canada), *b.* 1898: *m.* 1923, William Terence Webb McCarthy, MM, who *d.* (killed in action in Italy) 1944, and has issue living, Patrick Duniam (Bancroft, Ont., Canada), *b.* 1924; MD 1952: *m.* 1952, Patricia, da. of Archibald J. Stewart, of Toronto, Canada,—Christopher Frank Renwick, *b.* 1926: *m.* 1953, Ola Roma Bretzlaff, of Ladysmith, Quebec, —Elizabeth Sybil Ai-mei, *b.* 1928.

COLLATERAL BRANCHES LIVING
Granddaughter of the late Hon. George Augustus Hobart-Hampden, 5th son of 6th Earl:—
Issue of the late Awdry George Hobart-Hampden, *b.* 1858, *d.* 1937: *m.* 1893, Elsie Angel Heath, who *d.* 1958, da. of Col. Duncan George Pitcher, formerly Indian Army:—
Alison Elizabeth, *b.* 1899: *m.* 1922, Lieut.-Com. Michael Robert Cross, RNVR [B. Phillimore], who *d.* 1969, and has issue living, Phyllida Anne, *b.* 1923: *m.* 1944, Thomas Worrall Kent, of Apt. 1803, Cabot House, King's Rd., Sidney, Nova Scotia, and has issue living, Duncan Miles Stephen *b.* 1948, Oliver Robert Thomas *b.* 1950, Andrew John Francis *b.* 1953,—Nicolette Elizabeth, *b.* 1930: *m.* 1955, George Buchan McIntosh, of 6975, Adera St., Vancouver, BC, and has issue living, James Cameron *b.* 1965, Fiona Alison *b.* 1959, Georgia Margaret *b.* 1968. *Residence,*—Suggetts, Fullers Rd., Aston Tirrold, Didcot, Berks.

Grandchildren of the late Ernest Miles Hobart-Hampden, CMG, 6th son of the late
Hon. George Augustus Hobart-Hampden (ante):—
Issue of the late Cyril Langel Hobart-Hampden, b. 1902, d. 1972: m. 1936, Margaret Mon-
crieff Hilborne (19, Fairlea Cres., Northam, Bideford, Devon), only da. of the late George
Hilborne Jolliffe, formerly of Frocester, Govinna, Ceylon:—
GEORGE MILES (c/o Royal Bank of Scotland, Charing Cross West Branch, 9, Clifton Place, Glasgow,
C3 7LD), b. Dec. 15th, 1944; ed. at Clifton Coll., Exeter Univ. (BA), and London Univ. (MA): m.
1968, Susan Jennifer, only da. of R. W. Adams, of Halesowen, Worcs.——Helen Moncrieff, b.
1937: m. 1962, Hughes Motteux, c/o Standard Bank, P.O. Box 37, Nelspruit, E. Transvaal) and has
issue living, Thierry (son), b. 1968,—Jean Paul, b. 1973,—Nicole, b. 1970.

Descendants of Sir Robert Henry Hobart, KCVO, CB, cr. a Baronet 1914, el. son
of the Very Rev. the Hon. Henry Lewis Hobart, 4th son of 3rd Earl:—
See Hobart, Bt.

Granddaughter of Very Rev. the Hon. Henry Lewis Hobart (ante):—
Issue of the late Col. George Bertie Benjamin Hobart, b. 1838, d. 1907: m. 1889, Rose
Armatrude Frances, who d. 1927, having assumed by deed poll 1912, the surname of
Grimston in addition to and after that of Hobart), dau. and heiress of the late Col.
Marmaduke J. Grimston, of Grimston Garth, Yorkshire:—
Armatrude Bertie Sophia Effie (Lady Waechter de Grimston), b. 1890 ; is a J.P. ; assumed by deed
poll 1928, the additional name of de Grimston: m. 1912, as his second wife, Sir Max Leonard
Waechter, who d. 1924.   Residences,—All Hallows Cottage, Goodmanham, Market Weighton, Yorks;
St. Oswald's Close, Sleights, W. Whitby, Yorks.

Grandchildren of the late Charles Hobart (infra), el. son of Lt.-Col. Charles Robert
Hobart, 2nd son of the Rev. Henry Charles Hobart, only son of the Hon. Henry
Hobart, yst. son of 1st Earl:—
Issue of the late Charles Guy Reginald Vivian Beauchamp Hobart, b. 1881, d. 1944 : m.
1905, Maria Anna (now of Central Road, Nunawading, Victoria, Australia), dau. of the
late Thomas Frederick Hammond, of N.S. Wales :—
Guy Verna, b. 1906: m. 1934, Louise Gertrude Menzies.——John Bertram, b. 1911: m. 1944, June
Mary Barnes, and has issue living, Roger John, b. 1956,—Hilary Rosamond, b. 1958.   Residence,—
1, Milfay Av., Kew, Vic., Aust.——Wallace Elliott, MB, BS, b. 1922: m. 1st, 1946 (m. diss. 1956),
Joyce Stella Hussey; 2ndly, 1957, Halina Zofia Bobinska, MB, ChB, and has issue living, (by 2nd m.)
Mark Michael, b. 1958,—Pauline Ann, b. 1960.   Residence,—70, McIntyre Rd., Sunshine, Vic.,
Aust.——Phyllis Marion, b. 1920.   Residence,—

Grandchildren of the late Lt.-Col. George Hobart, 2nd son of Lt.-Col. Charles
Robert Hobart (ante):—
Issue of the late Irene Hobart, b. 1878, d. 1960: m. 1901, the Rev. Canon George Henry
Round-Turner, who d. 1951:—
Charles Douglas (154, Southgate St., Bury St. Edmunds), b. 1902; Capt. (ret.), N. Borneo Armed
Constabulary: m. 1929, Barbara Maxwell, da. of Lieut.-Col. H. S. Bond, formerly Comdg. N. Borneo
Armed Constabulary, and has issue living, David Henry, b. 1929: m. 1954, Betty, da. of Robert
Evans, of Sabatia, Kenya, and has issue living, Michael Charles b. 1955, Andrew Henry Douglas
b. 1961, Susan Mary, b. 1956,—John Lewis (The Commons, Rishworth, Yorks.), b. 1934; Cdr. RN :
m. 1960, Irene, da. of H. C. Gregory, of Littleborough, Lancs., and has issue living, Charles William,
b. 1970,—Amanda Jane, b. 1963.——John Bardolph (of 8th St., Harvey, W. Aust.) b. 1908. ——
Michael (48, Cedar Walk, Waltham Abbey, Essex), b. 1917; is Capt. Suffolk Regt.: m. 1941, Margaret
Cynthia, da. of the late H. W. Nelson, and has issue living, Mark Charles Nelson (101, Manor Rd.,
Chigwell, Essex), b. 1947: m. 1971, Pamela Jean, da. of R. Chalcroft,—Geoffrey Paul Michael (528,
Limes Av., Chigwell, Essex), b. 1948: m. 1st, 1970 (m. diss. 1974), Annette Theodora, da. of D. L.
Maugey; 2ndly, 1974, Catherine Theresa Mullins, and has issue living (by 1st m.), Julie Ann b. 1942,—
Joy Veronica Margaret, b. 1953: m. 1973, Dietmar Erich Helmut Beyer, of Stephanstrasse 7, 63,
Giessen, W. Germany, and has issue living, Michael Helmut b. 1974.——Irene Heather Mary, b.
1919.

Issue of the late Rev. William Henry Hobart, b. 1855, d. 1918: m. 1881, Margaret
Emily, who d. 1940, dau. of the late Gen. Edward Dayot Watson, of 2, Portland Place,
Bath :—
Mary Dorothea, b. 1888.   Residence,—89, Bedford Gdns., W8.——Margaret Adelaide, b. 1890.   Resi-
dence,—Cherrycroft, Compton, Winchester.——Ruth Awdry (of 26, Sutton Rd., Bournemouth),
b. 1894: m. 1923, George Edwin Oxenham, who d. 1963, and has issue living, David George Henry
(1015, South Goldenwest Ave., Arcadia, Cal., USA), b. 1925: m. 1956, Sharalee, da. of the late Frank
Chandler, of Battle Creek, Nebrasks, USA, and has issue living, Gabrielle Ruth b. 1963,—Anthony
Sydenham Charles (Rose Cottage, Feock, Truro, Cornwall), b. 1928: m. 1st, 1949 (m. diss. 1971),
Diana Margaret, da. of Alfred Willey, of Canterbury; 2ndly, 1971, Juliet Hulme, and has issue living
(by 1st m.), Mark David b. 1953, Adele Margaret b. 1951, Madeleine Ruth b. 1957, (by 2nd m.)
James Anthony b. 1973, Annabel Jane (twin) b. 1973.

Grandsons of the late Rev. William Henry Hobart (ante) :—
Issue of the late Rev. Charles Hampden Hobart, b. 1886, d. 1961 : m. 1924, Alice, who d.
1960, dau. of Samuel Plumbly, of 80, Vale Avenue, Findon Valley, Worthing :—
John Hampden (Orchard Cottage, The Green, Upton, Southwell, Notts.), b. 1925; Maj. (ret.) late 5th
Roy. Inniskilling Dragoon Gds.: m. 1961, Maureen, da. of Alfred Clowes, of 85, Cavour St., Stoke-on-
Trent, and has issue living, Andrew Hampden, b. 1962,—Jeremy Charles, b. 1963.——Christopher
Beauchamp (Prins Clausstraat, 29, s'Gravenzande, Netherlands), b. 1927: m. 1st, 1953 (m. diss.
1970), Margaret, da. of Gilbert Reed, of Lingfield, Surrey; 2ndly, 1970, Joanna Margaret, da. of
Rear Adm. Anthony Davies, CB, OVO, of Barn House, Aldbourne, Marlborough, Wilts., and has
issue living (by 1st m.), Richard Hampden, b. 1960,—Simon Vere, b. 1964,—(by 2nd m.) Edward
Beauchamp, b. 1971,—Robert Anthony, b. 1973.

PREDECESSORS.—[1] Sir HENRY Hobart, successively M.P. for Norwich and Yarmouth, and
Lord Chief Justice of the Common Pleas; was cr. a Baronet 1611; d. 1625; s. by his son [2] Sir
JOHN, M.P., 2nd Bt.; d. 1647; s. by his nephew [3] Sir JOHN, M.P., 3rd Bt.; s. by his el. son (by
his 1st marriage with Mary, dau. of the patriot John Hampden) [4] Sir HENRY, M.P., 4th Bt.;
Equerry to King William III. at the battle of the Boyne 1690; killed in a duel by Oliver le Neve,
1698; s. by his son [5] Sir JOHN, 5th Bt.; cr. Baron Hobart of Blickling (peerage of Great Britain)
1728, and Earl of Buckinghamshire (peerage of Great Britain) 1746; d. 1756; s. by his son [6] JOHN,
2nd Earl; was Ambassador to Court of Russia 1762, and Viceroy of Ireland 1777; d. 1793; s. by
his brother [7] GEORGE, 3rd Earl; d. 1804; s. by his son [8] ROBERT, P.C., 4th Earl; was successively
M.P. for Bramber, Sussex, and Armagh, Gov. of Madras, Ch. Sec. for Ireland, Sec. of State for
War, and Sec. of State for the Colonies, &c.; summoned to Parliament as Baron Hobart 1797;
d. 1816; s. by his nephew [9] GEORGE ROBERT, 5th Earl (son of the Hon. George Vere Hobart by
Jane, dau. of Horace Cataneo, Esq.); sat as M.P. for St. Michael 1812-3; assumed by Roy. licence
in 1824 the surname of Hampden in lieu of Hobart; d. 1849; s. by his brother [10] Rev. AUGUSTUS
EDWARD, 6th Earl; b. 1793; assumed by Roy. licence 1878 the additional surname of Hampden,
m. 1st, 1816, Mary, who d. 1825, dau. of John Williams, King's Sergeant; 2ndly, 1826, Maria Isabella:
who d. 1873, dau. of the Rev. Godfrey Egremont; d. 1885; s. by his grandson [11] SIDNEY CARR,
O.B.E. (son of Frederic John, Lord Hobart, 2nd son of 6th Earl, by Catherine Annesley, dau. of the
Right Rev. Thomas Carr, D.D., formerly Bishop of Bombay), 7th Earl, b. 1860; a Lord-in-Waiting
to Queen Victoria 1895; assumed, by Roy. licence 1903, the additional surnames of Mercer-Henderson for himself and issue: m. 1888, Georgina Wilhelmina (authorised by Roy. licence 1903, to use
the surnames of Mercer-Henderson only and to subscribe herself by the surnames and title " Lady
Henderson, Buckinghamshire "), who d. 1937, dau. of the late Hon. Hew Adam Dalrymple Haldane-
Duncan-Mercer-Henderson; d. 1930; s. by his son [12] JOHN HAMPDEN, 8th Earl, b. 1906; Dep.

Chm. of Cttees. House of Lords 1952-4, and Dep. Speaker House of Lords 1954-63; assumed by Roy. licence 1938 the surname of Mercer-Henderson only in lieu of Hobart-Hampden-Mercer-Henderson; *d.* 1963; *s.* by his kinsman [13] VERE FREDERICK CECIL Hobart-Hampden (2nd son of the late Arthur Ernest Hobart-Hampden, 2nd son of the late Capt the Hon. Charles Edward Hobart-Hampden, 4th son of 6th Earl), 9th Earl and present peer; also Baron Hobart.

BUCKLAND, BARONY OF. (Berry.) [Extinct 1928.]

DAUGHTERS LIVING OF FIRST BARON

Hon. (Mary) Lorraine, *b.* 1911: *m.* 1st, 1934, Lt.-Col. Gwyn William Morgan-Jones, Life Guard) [Nelson, Bt.], who *d.* 1964; 2ndly, 1965, Capt. Arthur Smith-Bingham, of Milbourne Manor, Malmesbury, Wilts., and has issue living, (by 1st m.) David Gwyn (29, Bradbourne St., SW6), *b.* 1937; Capt. Life Guards: *m.* 1st, 1965 (m. diss. 1969), Jennifer, da. of Maj. M. Hammond Maude; 2ndly, 1970, Carolyn, da. of Maj. The Count Kenneth Diacre de Liancourt,—Rhyddian James, *b.* 1944: *m.* 1974, Mrs. Patricia Kuederli, da. of Richard Bird, of Braywick, Berks.,—Elizabeth Mary, *b.* 1950.
Hon. Dorothy Margaret, *b.* 1914: *m.* 1939, Col. Dennis Douglas Pilkington Smyly, DSO, JP, DL, 16th/5th Queen's Roy. Lancers, and has issue living, David Henry (Stanton Fields, Broadway, Worcs.), *b.* 1941: *m.* 1963, Patricia Kathleen Evetts, da. of Maj. Neville Ewart Hyde Chance [see B. Ismay], and has issue living, Giles Richard Ismay *b.* 1966, Susannah Louise *b.* 1964,—Richard Mark, *b.* 1943; Capt. 16th/5th Queen's R. Lancers,—Robert Dennis (Sunderland Hall, Galashiels, Selkirkshire), *b.* 1945: *m.* 1968 (Charmian) Miranda, da. of Sir Robert Henry Muir Mackenzie, 6th Bt., and has issue living, Henry Richard *b.* 1972, Henrietta Miranda *b.* 1970,—Susan Jane, *b.* 1950: *m.* 1973, Rhett Lewis Webb, of Qld., Aust. *Residence,*—Hill House, Hartpury, Glos.
Hon. (Joan) Sybil, *b.* 1919: *m.* 1942, Col. Michael Colvin Watson, OBE, MC, R. Wilts. Yeo. [E. Verulam, colls.], and has issue living, Rupert Michael Colvin, *b.* 1949: *m.* 1973, Emma Caroline, da. of John Miller-Stirling,—Caroline Susan, *b.* 1946: *m.* 1968, Maj. Robert Shaun Longsdon, 17th/21st Lancers, and has issue living, Robert James *b.* 1971, Rupert Michael Shaun *b.* 1972,—Virginia Sybil, *b.* 1951. *Residence,*—Eastington House, Cirencester, Glos.
Hon. Cecily Eveline, *b.* 1921: *m.* 1st, 1940, Maj. Patrick Magor Leatham, MC, 10th Roy. Hussars, who *d.* 1951; 2ndly, 1952, Lt.-Col. Richard Ian Griffith Taylor, DSO, MC, JP, DL [Waldie, Griffith, Bt., ext.], and has issue living, (by 1st m.) Simon Patrick (Hayes House, Corbridge, Northumberland; Cavalry Club), *b.* 1944: *m.* 1967, Lady Victoria Diana Cecil, da. of 6th Marquess of Exeter, and has issue living, Richard David *b.* 1971, Miranda Rosemary *b.* 1969,—Philip William (Burleigh Hall, Brunscombe, Glos.), *b.* 1946: *m.* 1971, the Hon. Rowena Margaret Hawke, da. of 9th Baron Hawke, and has issue living, Patrick Hawke, *b.* 1974,—Jonathan Grant, *b.* 1948: *m.* 1973, Lizanne, da. of John Seabrook, of New York City,—(by 2nd m.) Penelope Josephine *b.* 1953: *m.* 1974, Robert John Elkington,—Charlotte Sybil, *b.* 1956. *Residence,*—Chipchase Castle, Wark-on-Tyne, Northumberland.

BUCKMASTER, VISCOUNT. (Buckmaster.) [Viscount U.K. 1933.]

MARTIN STANLEY BUCKMASTER, 3rd Viscount; *b.* April 11th, 1921; *s.* 1974; ed. at Stowe; FRGS; entered FO 1946, First Sec. (Information), British Embassy, Benghazi 1958-62, and Tripoli, 1962-63, First Sec. (Political) Bahrain 1963-67, FO 1967-69; First Sec. and British High Commr., Kampala 1969-71, British Embassy; Beirut 1971-73, since when FCO; Capt. R. Sussex R. in Middle East during 1939-45 War.

𝕬rms,—Or, semée of fleurs-de-lis azure, a lion rampant of the last, on a chief of the second a portcullis of the first. 𝕮rest,—A demi-lion azure, holding in the dexter paw a fleur-de-lis and charged on the shoulder with a portcullis, both or. 𝕾upporters,—On either side a bulk proper, each gorged with a chain pendant therefrom a portcullis or.

Address,—c/o FCO (Records Section, Personnel Department), King Charles St., SW1.

Residences,—8, Redcliffe Sq., SW10 9J2; Furzefield House, Wineham, Henfield, Sussex. *Club,*—Travellers'.

Equanimitas, magnanimitas.
Equanimity, magnanimity.

BROTHER LIVING

Hon. COLIN JOHN (of Ryece Hall, Brettenham, Ipswich), *b.* April 17th, 1923; ed. at Winchester; late Fl. Lt. RAF: *m.* 1946, May, only da. of Charles Henry Gibbon, of The Lodge, Great Bentley, Essex, and has issue living, Adrian Charles, *b.* 1949,—Simon John, *b.* 1956,—Michael Anthony, *b.* 1959,—Ann Susan, *b.* 1950,—Sarah Janet. *b.* 1952.

MOTHER LIVING.

Joan (9, Cadogan Mansions, Sloane Sq., SW1), da. of the late George Angustus Garry Simpson MRCS of 89, Lancaster Gate, W: *m.* 1916 (m. diss. 1944) the 2nd Viscount, who *d.* 1974.

WIDOW LIVING OF SECOND VISCOUNT.

DIANA CONSTANCE (*Viscountess Buckmaster*) (Furzefield House, Wineham, Henfield, Sussex), da. of Maj. Kenneth Arthur Seth-Smith, and formerly wife of Charles Stewart McDonnell Vane-Tempest [see M. Londonderry, colls.]: *m.* 1961, as his 2nd wife, the 2nd Viscount, who *d.* 1974.

PREDECESSORS.—[1] *Rt. Hon. Sir* STANLEY OWEN Buckmaster, GCVO, PC, son of the late John Charles Buckmaster, of Ashleigh, Hampton Wick; *b.* 1861; sat as MP for Camb. Borough (L) 1906-10, and for Keighley Div. of N. Part of W. Riding of Yorkshire 1911-15; was Solicitor-Gen. Oct. 1913 to May 1915, and Lord High Chancellor of England May 1915 to Dec. 1916; cr. *Baron Buckmaster,* of Cheddington, Buckinghamshire (peerage of United Kingdom) 1915 and *Viscount Buckmaster,* of Cheddington, Buckinghamshire (peerage of United Kingdom) 1933: *m.* 1889, Edith Augusta, who *d.* 1935, da. of S. R. Lewin, of Widford, Herts: *d.* 1934: *s.* by his son [2] OWEN STANLEY, 2nd Viscount, *b.* 1890; Bar. at law and an underwriting member of Lloyds; Member of Cttee., London Stock Exchange 1938-42: *m.* 1st, 1916 (m. diss. 1944), Joan, da. of George Angustus Gary Simpson, MRCS; 2ndly, 1961, Diana Constance (VANE-TEMPEST), da. of Maj. Kenneth Arthur Seth-Smith; *d.* 1974; *s.* by his el. son [3] OWEN STANLEY, 3rd Viscount and present peer: also Baron Buckmaster.

BUCKTON, BARON.   (Storey.)   [Life Baron 1966, Bt.U.K. 1960.]

SAMUEL STOREY, *Life Baron* and *1st Baronet*, el. son of the late Frederick George Storey, JP; *b*. Jan. 18th, 1896; ed. at Haileybury, and at Trin. Coll., Camb. (MA); Bar. Inner Temple 1919; PPS to Parl. Sec. to Min. of Health 1939-42, a Member of Chm's Panel, House of Commons 1957-64, Dep. Chm. of Ways and Means 1964-65 and Chm. 1965-66; MP for Sunderland (*C*) 1931-45, and for Stretford 1950-66; *cr*, a *Baronet* (UK, of Settrington) 1960, and *Baron Buckton*, of Settrington, in East Riding, co. York (Life Baron) 1966: *m*. 1929, Elisabeth, JP, who *d*. 1951, da. of Brig.-Gen. Wilfrid James Woodcock, DSO, and has issue.

Arms—Per fesse argent and sable a pale counterchanged three storks also sable. Crest—In front of an escallop or a stork's head erased sable gorged with a mural crown gold. Supporters—On either side a stork sable, in the beak an escallop or.

Residence,—Settrington House, Settrington, Malton, N. Yorks., YO17 8ND.   *Club,*—Carlton.

SON LIVING.   (*In remainder to Baronetcy only*)
Hon. RICHARD (Greystone House, Settrington, Malton, Yorks; 7, Douro Place, W8); *b*. Jan. 23rd, 1937; ed. at Winchester, and Trin. Coll., Camb. (BA, LL.B); Bar. Inner Temple 1962; *h.a.* to Baronetcy: *m*. 1961, Virginia Anne, da. of the late Sir Kenelm Henry Ernest Cayley, 10th Bt., and has issue living, Kenelm, *b*. 1963,—Elisabeth, *b*. 1964,—Melissa, *b*. 1968.

DAUGHTER LIVING.
Hon. Jacquetta, *b*. 1930: *m*. 1956, Francis Cator, of The Old House, Ranworth, Norfolk, and 9, Halkin Place, SW1, and has issue living, Charles Francis, *b*. 1959,—Mark, *b*. 1960,—Harry, *b*. 1964,—Elisabeth Anne, *b*. 1957.

BURDEN, BARON.   (Burden.)   [Baron U.K. 1950.]

PHILIP WILLIAM BURDEN, 2nd Baron; *b*. June 21st, 1916; *s*. 1970; ed. Raines Foundation Sch.: *m*. 1951, Audrey Elsworth, da. of Maj. Wilfred Elsworth Sykes, of Kirk Ella, Hull, and has issue.

Residence,—North Down House Farm, Churchinford, Taunton, Som.

SONS LIVING.
Hon. ANDREW PHILIP, *b*. July 20th, 1959.
Hon. Fraser William Elsworth, *b*. 1964.
Hon. Ian Stuart, *b*. 1967.

DAUGHTERS LIVING.
Hon. Carol Mary, *b*. 1952.
Hon. Corynne Lesley, *b*. 1955.
Hon. Adrienne Gail, *b*. 1957.

WIDOW LIVING OF FIRST BARON.
AUGUSTA (*Augusta, Baroness Burden*), (North Down House Farm, Churchinford, Taunton, Som), da. of David Sime, of Aberdeen: *m*. 1910, the 1st Baron, who *d*. 1970.

PREDECESSOR.—[1] THOMAS WILLIAM Burden, *CBE*, son of Thomas Burden, of Mile End, E.; *b*. 1885; 2nd Church Estates Commr. 1945-50, a Member of House of Laity of Church Assembly 1947-50 and a Lord in Waiting to HM 1950-51; MP for Park Div. of Sheffield (*Lab.*) 1942-50; *cr*. Baron Burden, of Hazlebarrow, co. Derby (peerage of UK) 1950: *m*. 1910, Augusta, da. of David Sime, of Aberdeen; *d*. 1970; *s*. by his only son [2] PHILIP WILLIAM, 2nd Baron and present peer.

Burford, Earl of,   **son of Duke of St. Albans.**

BURGH, BARON.   (Leith.)   [E. 1529.]

[Title pronounced "Borough."]

ALEXANDER PETER WILLOUGHBY LEITH, 7th Baron ; *b*. March 20th, 1935 ; *s*. 1959 ; ed. at Harrow, and at Magdalene Coll., Camb. ; formerly in R.A.F. : *m*. 1957, Anita Lorna, dau. of Frederick C. Eldridge, of Gillingham, Kent, and has issue.

Arms,—Quarterly, 1st and 4th or, a cross-crosslet fitchée sable between three crescents in chief and as many fusils in base barwise gules, all within a bordure azure, *Leith* ; 2nd azure, three fleur-de-lis ermine, *Burgh* ; 3rd, quarterly, 1st and 4th or, a lion rampant azure, armed and langued gules, *Percy* ; 2nd and 3rd semée of six or and sable, *Strabolgi*. Crest,—1st, a cross-crosslet fitchée sable, *Leith* ; 2nd, a falcon argent, beaked, legged and ducally gorged or, *Burgh*. Supporters,—On either side a stag azure charged with three fleur-de-lis ermine in pale.

Residence,—174, Chesterton Rd., Cambridge.

SONS LIVING.
Hon. ALEXANDER GREGORY DISNEY, *b*. March 16th, 1958.
Hon. Patrick Simon Vincent, *b*. 1964.

DAUGHTER LIVING.
Hon. Rebecca Moraigh Eveleigh, *b*. 1959.

HALF-BROTHER LIVING.

Hon. John Barnabas (72, Puxton Drive, Wolverley Park, Kidderminster), *b.* 1947; ed. at Wellington, and Exeter Univ.: *m.* 1970, Erica Jane, da. of David M. Lewis, of Winchester, and has issue living, Alexander David Kalimat, *b.* 1973.

AUNTS LIVING. (*Daughters of 5th Baron.*)

Hon. Eveleigh Julia, *b.* 1904. *Residence,*—Sexton's, Speen, Newbury, Berks.
Hon. Mildred Katherine, *b.* 1894. *Residence,*—Barn Cottage, Crowlink, Friston, Eastbourne.

WIDOW LIVING OF SON OF FIFTH BARON.

Mona (Glenkindie, Aberdeenshire), da. of the late C. R. Simpson: *m.* 1938, Capt. the Hon. John Disney Leith, who *d.* 1968.

MOTHER LIVING.

Elizabeth Rose, dau. of the late Arthur Rose Vincent, O.B.E. : *m.* 1934, the 6th Baron, who *d.* 1959, having obtained a divorce 1943. *Residence,*—

WIDOW LIVING OF SIXTH BARON.

JOYCE WATTS, dau. of W. Wilson Wilson, of 10, Curzon Road, Hoylake, Cheshire : *m.* 1st, 1947, as his second wife, the 6th Baron, who *d.* 1959; 2ndly, 1960, Rupert Walter Westmacott. *Residence,*—Beag Farm, Llandissilio, Clynderwen, Pembrokeshire.

PREDECESSORS.—[1] THOMAS Burgh, *de jure* 5th Baron Strabolgi, son of Sir Edward Burgh, M.P. for co. Lincoln (who is held to have succeeded to the Barony of Strabolgi as 4th Baron in 1496); summoned to Parliament as Lord Burgh, of Gainsborough, co. Lincoln 1529 : *m.* 1st, 1496, Agnes, dau. of Sir William Tyrwhitt ; 2ndly, 15—, Alice, dau. of William London, and widow (i) of Sir Thomas Bedingfeld, and (ii) of Edmund Rokewood ; *d.* 1550 ; *s.* by his el. surviving son [2] WILLIAM, 2nd Baron Burgh, and *de jure* 6th Baron Strabolgi ; summoned to Parliament as Lord Burgh 1551-80 : *m.* 15—, Catherine, dau. of Edward, Earl of Lincoln ; *d.* 1584 ; *s.* by his el. surviving son [3] THOMAS, K.G., 3rd Baron Burgh, and *de jure* 7th Baron Strabolgi ; summoned to Parliament as Lord Burgh 1584-97 ; Ambassador to Scotland 1593, and Lord Dep. of Ireland 1597 : *m.* 15—, Frances, dau. of John Vaughan, of Sutton-on-Derwent, and his dau. Elizabeth *m.* George Brooke [see B. Cobham]; *d.* 1597 ; *s.* by his el. surviving son [4] ROBERT, 4th Baron Burgh, and *de jure* 8th Baron Strabolgi; *d.s.p.* (about) 1600, when the Baronies fell into abeyance between his four sisters, among whose descendants they so remained until the abeyances were determined in 1916, the Barony of Burgh being called out of abeyance in favour of [5] ALEXANDER HENRY Leith, 5th Baron (son of the late Gen. Robert William Disney Leith, C.B., by Mary Charlotte Julia, who *d.* 1926, dau. of Sir Henry Percy Gordon, 2nd Bt., F.R.S., cr. 1818 (*ext.*), by Lady Mary Agnes Blanche, dau. of 3rd Earl of Ashburnham), *b.* 1866 : also established his claim before Committee for Privileges of House of Lords as senior co-heir to the Baronies of Burgh and Cobham 1912, and to the Barony of Strabolgi 1914, and in 1916 the abeyance in the Barony of Burgh was determined in his favour : *m.* 1st, 1893, Mildred Catherine, who *d.* 1894, el. da. of the late Gen. Stuart Nicholson, CB: 2ndly, 1902, Phyllis, who *d.* 1972, da. of Col. Mark Goldie, RE; *d.* 1926: *s.* by his son [6] ALEXANDER LEIGH HENRY, 6th Baron; *b.* 1906: Lieut. Black Watch : *m.* 1st, 1934, Elizabeth Rose, from whom he obtained a divorce 1943, dau. of the late Arthur Rose Vincent, O.B.E. : 2ndly, 1947, Joyce Watts, dau. of W. Wilson Wilson, of 10, Curzon Road, Hoylake, Cheshire ; *d.* 1959 ; *s.* by his el. son [7] ALEXANDER PETER WILLOUGHBY 7th Baron and present peer.

BURGHCLERE, BARONY OF. (Gardner.) [Extinct 1921.]

DAUGHTERS LIVING OF FIRST BARON.

Hon. Mary Sidney Katherine Almina, *b.* 1896: *m.* 1st, 1914, the Hon. Geoffrey Hope-Morley (who obtained a divorce 1928),—now 2nd Baron Hollenden ; 2ndly, (Jan.) 1929, Capt. Alan Hugh Hillgarth, C.M.G., O.B.E., R.N. (retired), from whom she obtained a divorce 1947, and has issue living (by 1st marriage) [see B. Hollenden],—(by 2nd marriage) Jocelyn Nigel Herbert Gardner Alan Aubrey (330, Waverley St., Belmont, Mass., USA), *b.* (Sept.) 1929; PhD: *m.* 1966, Nina, widow of Richard Foster. *Residence,*—Son Torrella de Santa Maria, Isla de Mallorca, Spain.
Hon. Evelyn Florence Margaret Winifred, *b.* 1903: *m.* 1st, 1928, Evelyn Arthur St. John Waugh, who obtained a divorce 1930 ; 2ndly, 1930, John Edward Nourse Heygate (now 4th Bt.), from whom she obtained a divorce 1936; 3rdly, 1937, Ronald Nightingdale, and has issue living, (by 3rd m.) William Benedict Herbert (40, Broomhouse Rd., SW6): *b.* 1939, *m.* 1964, Anne, da. of Bryan O. Redmon, of Bernardsville, N.J., U.S.A., and has issue living, Auberon Christopher Redmon Herbert, *b.* 19—; Elizabeth Magdalen Margaret *b.* 1969,—Virginia Margaret Ann, *b.* 1943. *Residence,*—Orchard Cottage, Ticehurst, Wadhurst, Sussex.

Burghersh, Lord, son of Earl of Westmorland.

Burlington, Earl of, grandson of Duke of Devonshire.

BURNHAM, BARON. (Lawson.) [Baron U.K. 1903, Bt. U.K. 1892.]

WILLIAM EDWARD HARRY LAWSON; 5th Baron and 5th Baronet; *b.* Oct. 22nd, 1920; *s.* 1963; ed. at Eton; Lt.-Col. (ret.) Scots Guards; Comdg. 1st Bn. 1959-62; JP of Bucks; 1939-45 War in France, Middle East, N. Africa and Italy; Malaya 1950-51 (despatches): *m.* 1942, Anne, da. of the late Maj. George Gerald Petherick [see E. Radnor], and has issue.

Arms.—Quarterly: 1st and 4th azure, three bars geme, argent, over all a winged morion or; 2nd and 3rd gules, a saltire double parted and fretted or between in fesse two rams' heads, couped in fesse argent. **Crests.**—1st, in, front of a terrestrial globe proper a winged morion or; 2nd a ram argent holding in the mouth a trefoil slipped vert and resting the dexter fore leg on a quatrefoil or. **Supporters.** —*Dexter,* the figure of Clio, the Muse of history proper; *sinister,* the figure of Hermes vested argent, mantled azure; on the head a winged morion, on his heels wings, and in his exterior hand a caduceus or.

OF · OLD · I HOLD

Residence,—Hall Barn, Beaconsfield, Bucks.

DAUGHTERS LIVING.

Hon. Jenefer Anne, *b.* 1949.
Hon. Harriet Mary, *b.* 1954.
Hon. Sarah Jane, *b.* 1955.

BROTHER LIVING.

Hon. HUGH JOHN FREDERICK (Woodlands Farm, Beaconsfield, Bucks; Turf, and Garrick Clubs), *b.* Aug. 15th, 1931; ed. at Eton, and at Balliol Coll., Oxford; Lt. Scots Guards (Reserve): *m.* 1955, Hilary M., da. of Alan Hunter, of Huntingtowerfield House, Almondbank, Perthshire, and has issue living, Harry Frederick Alan, *b.* 1968,—Ann Charlotte, *b.* 1960,—Emma Lucia, *b.* 1961.

SISTER LIVING.

Hon. Lucia Edith, *b.* 1922; European War 1939-45 in France and Germany as Co. Sergeant-Major ATS (despatches): *m.* 1st, 1946, the Hon. Roger David Marquis—2nd Earl of Woolton (who *d.* 1969, having obtained a divorce 1953); 2ndly, 1966, John Whitehead, of 25, Hyde Park St., W2.

WIDOW LIVING OF FOURTH BARON.

MARIE ENID (*Enid, Baroness Burnham*), *CBE* (Wycombe End House, Beaconsfield, Bucks.), da. of Hugh Scott Robson, of London and Buenos Aires; CBE (Civil) 1957: *m.* 1920, the 4th Baron, who *d.* 1963.

PREDECESSORS.—[1] *Sir* EDWARD Levy-Lawson, *K.C.V.O.*, son of the late Joseph Moses Levy, J.P., one of the principal founders of the Cheap Press in London ; *b.* 1833 ; was principal proprietor of the *Daily Telegraph* ; assumed by Roy. licence 1875 the surname of Lawson in addition to and after that of Levy ; cr. a *Baronet* 1892, and *Baron Burnham*, of Hall Barn, Beaconsfield, Buckinghamshire (peerage of United Kingdom) 1903 : *m.* 1862, Harriette Georgiana, who *d.* 1897, dau. of the late Benjamin N. Webster, of Pen-y-craig, co. Denbigh ; *d.* 1916 ; *s.* by his el. son [2] HARRY LAWSON WEBSTER, *G.C.M.G.*, *C.H.*, 2nd Baron, *b.* 1862 ; sometime Principal Proprietor of the *Daily Telegraph*, and Chm. of Newspaper Proprietors' Asso. ; Pres. of Institute of Journalists 1910, and a Member of Indian Statutory Commn. 1927-30 ; cr. *Viscount Burnham*, of Hall Barn, co. Buckingham (peerage of United Kingdom) 1919 : *m.* 1884, Olive, who *d.* 1939, dau. of Gen. Sir Henry Percival de Bathe, 4th Bt. ; *d.* 1933, when the Viscountcy became ext. and the Barony and Baronetcy passed to his brother [3] WILLIAM ARNOLD WEBSTER, *D.S.O.*, 3rd Baron, *b.* 1864 ; Capt. Scots Guards and Lieut.-Col. and Brevet Col. Bucks Yeo. ; S. Africa 1900-1901 (D.S.O.) : *m.* 1887, Sybil Mary (from whom he obtained a divorce 1912), dau. of the late Lieut.-Gen. Sir Frederick Marshall, K.C.M.G. : *d.* 1943 ; *s.* by his son [4] EDWARD FREDERICK, *C.B.*, *D.S.O.*, *M.C.*, *T.D.*, 4th Baron, *b.* 1890 ; Maj.-Gen. T.A. ; O.R.A. 48th (S. Midland Div.) T.A. 1938-41, and G.O.C. Yorkshire Div. 1941-2, and Dir. of Public Relations War Office and Senior Mil. Adviser, Min. of Information 1942-5: *m.* 1920, Marie Enid, O.B.E., dau. of Hugh, Scott Robson, of London, and Buenos Aires; *d.* 1963; *s.* by his el. son [5] WILLIAM EDWARD HARRY, 5th Baron and present peer.

BURNTWOOD, BARON. (Snow.) [Life Baron 1970.]

JULIAN WARD SNOW, son of the late Henry Martin Snow, CVO, of Eltham, Kent; *b.* Feb. 24th, 1910; ed. at Haileybury; with Dunlop Rubber Co. 1928-37, and John Lewis & Co. Ltd., 1938-39, 1939-45 War as Capt. RA; MP for Portsmouth Central (*Lab.*) 1945-50, and for Lichfield and Tamworth, Staffs. 1950-70; Vice-Chamberlain to Roy. Household 1945-46, a Lord Commr. of HM Treasury and a Govt. Whip 1946-50; Parl. Sec. Min. of Aviation 1966-67, and Min. of Health 1967-68, and Parl. Under-Sec. of State Dept. of Health and Social Security 1968-69; Vice-Pres. British-Japanese Parl. Group; *cr. Baron Burntwood,* of Burntwood, co. Stafford (Life Baron) 1970: *m.* 1948, Flavia Ria Joan, yr. da. of the late Sir Ralph Barrett Macnaughten Blois, 9th Bt., and has issue.

Residences,—Flat 2, 37, Chester Way, SE11; The Thatched Cottage, Walberswick, Southwold, Suffolk.

DAUGHTER LIVING.

Hon. Harriet Louise Julia, *b.* 1950.

BURTON, BARON. (Baillie.) [Baron U.K. 1897.]

What is brighter than the stars?

MICHAEL EVAN VICTOR BAILLIE, 3rd Baron; *b.* June 27th, 1924; *s.* 1962; ed. at Eton; late Lieut. Scots Guards; a J.P. of Inverness: *m.* 1948, Elizabeth Ursula Forster, dau. of Capt. Anthony F. Wise, of 89, Winchester Court, W.8, and has issue.

Seats,—Dochfour, Inverness; The Gables, Rangemore, Burton-on-Trent. *Clubs,*—Guards', Brooks's, New (Edinburgh) and Highland (Inverness).

Arms—Quarterly, 1st and 4th azure, nine stars, three, three, two and one argent, within a border engrailed or, charged with six cinquefoils of the field, *Baillie*; 2nd and 3rd, gules on a chevron cottised argent between three plates each charged with a fleur-de-lys azure, a demi lion couped of the first, *Bass.* **Crest**— A boar's head couped argent, armed or, langued gules. **Supporters**—On either side a lion reguardant sable each charged on the shoulder with a plate thereon a fleur-de-lys azure and resting the inner hind leg on a stag's head caboshed proper.

SONS LIVING.

Hon. EVAN MICHAEL RONALD, *b.* March 19th, 1949; ed. at Harrow: *m.* 1970, Lucinda, el. da. of Robert Law, of Turnpike House, Withersfield, Haverhill, Suffolk, CB9 7RU.
Hon. Alexander James, *b.* 1963.

DAUGHTERS LIVING.

Hon. Elizabeth Victoria, *b.* 1950: *m.* 1970, the Hon. Angus Grenfell Maclay, of Westruther Mains, Gordon, Berwickshire [see B. Maclay].
Hon. Philippa Ursula Maud, *b.* 1951.
Hon. Georgina Frances, *b.* 1955.
Hon. Fiona Mary, *b.* 1957.

BROTHER LIVING.
(Raised to the rank of a Baron's son 1964.)

Hon. Peter Charles, *b.* 1927; late Maj. The Life Guards; a JP of Hants: *m.* 1955, Jennifer Priscilla, da. of Com. Harold Reginald Newgass, GC, of Stafford House, W. Stafford, Dorset, and has issue living, Catriona Margaret, *b.* 1956,—Elizabeth Mary Eilidh, *b.* 1959,—Susan Jennifer, *b.* 1960,— Rachel Emma, *b.* 1963. *Residences,*—Wootton Hall, New Milton, Hants.; Avon House, 22, Avonmore Rd., W14. *Club,*—Cavalry.

SISTER LIVING.
(Raised to the rank of a Baron's daughter 1964.)

Hon. Judith Evelyn Maud, *b.* 1925; formerly in A.T.S.: *m.* 1949, Lieut.-Col. Angus Cameron, M.C., Scots Guards, and has issue living, Angus Iain, *b.* 1952,—Hester Caroline, *b.* 1950. *Residence,*— Aldourie Castle, Inverness.

WIDOW LIVING OF SON OF NELLIE LISA, BARONESS BURTON.
Rosemary (Aline, by Stornaway, Isle of Lewis), da. of the late Brig-Gen. Sir Joseph Frederick Laycock, KCMG, DSO [E. Listowel, colls.]: *m.* 1927, the Hon. Arthur Malcolm Augustus Baillie, who *d.* 1963, and has issue [see colls., infra].

COLLATERAL BRANCH LIVING.

Grandson of the late Nellie Lisa, Baroness Burton:—
Issue of the late Maj. the Hon. Arthur Malcolm Augustus Baillie, *b.* 1896, *d.* 1963: *m.* 1927, Rosemary (ante), dau. of the late Brig.-Gen. Sir Joseph Frederick Laycock, K.C.M.G., D.S.O. [E. Listowel, colls.]:—

Ian Bruce (Congham Lodge, Hillington, King's Lynn, Norfolk, PE31 6BZ; White's, Cavalry and Pratt's Clubs), *b.* 1928; Col. (ret.); Lt.-Col. Comdg. Household Cav. and Silver Stick-in-Waiting 1969-72: *m.* 1962, June Marion Cloudesley, da. of Arthur Cloudesley Smith, FRCS, and widow of (Arthur) Henry Bellingham [see Bellingham, Bt., colls.], and has issue living, Katherine Victoria Harriet, *b.* 1962,—Sarah Rosemary Caroline, *b.* 1964.

PREDECESSORS.—[1] *Sir* MICHAEL ARTHUR BASS, *K.C.V.O.,* el. son of the late Michael Thomas Bass, M.P. for Derby 1848-83 ; *b.* 1837 ; a Director of Bass, Ratcliff, Gretton and Co. (Limited), of Burton-on-Trent; M.P. for Stafford (*L*) 1865-8, for E. Staffordshire 1868-85, and for Burton Div. of Staffordshire 1885-6; cr. a *Baronet* 1882, *Baron Burton,* of Rangemore and Burton-on-Trent, co. Stafford (peerage of United Kingdom) 1886, and *Baron Burton,* of Burton-on-Trent, and of Rangemore, co. Stafford (peerage of United Kingdom) 1897, with special remainder, in default of issue male, to his dau. and her male issue : *m.* 1869, Harriet Georgina, who *d.* 1931, dau. of the late E. Thornewill, of Dove Cliff, co. Stafford; *d.* 1909; when the Barony (cr. 1886) became *ext.,* the baronetcy passed to his nephew, William Arthur Hamar Bass, and the Barony (cr. 1897) devolved under the special remainder upon his dau. [2] NELLIE LISA, *b.* 1873: *m.* 1st, 1894, Col. James Evan Bruce Baillie, M.V.O., R.H.A., (T.F.), who *d.* 1931; 2ndly, 1932, Major William Eugene Melles, who *d.* 1953; *d.* 1962; *s.* by her grandson [3] MICHAEL EVAN VICTOR (son of the late Brigadier the Hon. George Evan Michael BAILLIE, M.C., T.D.), 3rd Baron and present peer.

BURTON OF COVENTRY, BARONESS. (Burton.) [Life Baroness 1962.]

ELAINE FRANCES BURTON, dau. of the late Leslie Aubrey Burton, of Haddon Villa, Skipton Rd., Harrogate; *b.* March 2nd, 1904; ed. at Leeds Girls' Modern Sch., and at City of Leeds Training Coll.; Teacher, Leeds 1924-35, a Member of S. Wales Council of Social Welfare 1935-7, and of National Fitness Council 1938-9; M.P. (*Lab.*) for S. Div. of Coventry 1950-9, when she was defeated; cr. *Baroness Burton of Coventry,* of Coventry, co. Warwick (Life Baroness) 1962.

Residence,—47, Molyneux St., W.1.

Bury. Viscount, grandson of Earl of Albemarle.

BUTE, MARQUESS OF. (Crichton-Stuart.) [Marquess G.B. 1796, Bt. S. 1627.]
[Name pronounced " Cryton-Stuart."]

He flourishes in an honourable ancestry.

JOHN CRICHTON-STUART, 6th Marquess, and 11th Baronet ; *b.* Feb. 27th, 1933 ; *s.* 1956 ; ed. at Ampleforth, and at Trin. Coll., Camb. ; is Lieut. Scots Guards (Reserve), Hereditary Sheriff and Coroner of co. Bute, Hereditary Keeper of Rothesay Castle, and patron of nine livings (but being a Roman Catholic cannot present), a JP ; Lord-Lieut. for Bute since 1967 : *m.* 1955, Beatrice Nicola Grace, only da. of the late Lt.-Cdr. Wolstan Beaumont Charles Weld-Forester, RN (ret.) [see B. Forester, colls.], and has issue.

Arms.—Quarterly: 1st and 4th or, a fesse checky azure and argent, within a double tressure flory counterflory gules, and in dexter chief of the first quarter a canton of Nova Scotia, *Stuart* : 2nd and 3rd argent, a lion rampant azure, armed and langued gules, *Crichton*; behind the shield are placed in saltire a key or, having within its handle a fesse checky azure and argent, and a rod gules surmounted of a tower argent masoned sable, conically capped loopholes and port gules (*Insignia of Office of Heritable Keeper*) a coronet. *Crests,* —1st, a dragon vert, crowned with an open crown of four strawberry leaves langued or, *Crichton*; 2nd, a demi-lion rampant gules, armed and langued azure *Stuart*; 3rd, argent and azure, a wyvern proper, holding in the mouth a sinister hand couped gules (*for the Lordship and Fief of Cardiff*). *Supporters,*—*Dexter,* a stag proper, attired or, gorged with an Earl's coronet also proper, having therefrom a chain reflexed over the back gules; *sinister,* a horse argent, bridled gules.

Seats,—Mount Stuart, Rothesay, Isle of Bute; Dumfries House, Cumnock, Ayrshire. *Clubs,*— Turf, White's, Cardiff and County, New (Edinburgh), Puffins (Edinburgh).

SONS LIVING.
JOHN COLUM (*Earl of Dumfries*), *b.* April 26th, 1958.
Lord Anthony, *b.* 1961.

DAUGHTERS LIVING.
Lady Sophia Anne, *b.* 1956.
Lady Eileen Caroline, *b.* 1957.

BROTHERS LIVING.
Lord David Ogden (twin), (Mill House, Crosshill, Maybole, Ayrshire; Cavalry and St. James' Clubs), *b.* 1933; ed. at Ampleforth: *m.* 1972, Helen, da. of William Kerr McColl, and has issue living, Kenneth Edward David, *b.* 1975,—Elizabeth Rose, *b.* 1973.
Lord James Charles, *b.* 1935; ed. at Ampleforth, and at Trin. Coll., Camb.; is Lieut. Scots Gds. (Reserve): *m.* 1st, 1959 (m. diss. 1968), Sarah Frances, only da. of Lt.-Col. A. E. Croker Poole, of 19, Launceston Place, W8; 2ndly, 1970, Anna Rose, da. of the late Maj. H. Bramwell, of The White House, Mallow, co. Cork, and has issue living, (by 2nd m.), William Henry, *b.* 1971,—(by 2nd m.) Hugh Bertram, *b.* 1973.   *Residence,*—115, Woodsford Sq., Addison Rd., W14.   *Club,*—Turf.

SISTER LIVING.
Lady Caroline Moira Fiona, *b.* 1941: *m.* 1959, Capt. Michael Lowsley-Williams, 16th/5th Lancers, Guadacorte, Estacion de San Roque, Cadiz, Spain [Makins, Bt.], and has issue living, Patrick David Edward, *b.* 1960,—Mark Ogden Francis, *b.* 1961,—Paul John Fermin, *b.* 1964,—Michael Charles Javier, *b.* 1967.

UNCLE LIVING.   (*Son of 4th Marquess.*)
Lord Robert, *b.* 1909; ed. at Downside, and at Trin. Coll., Camb. (BA 1933); Capt. (ret.) Scots Gds.; is a KSJ; Lord-Lieut. of co. of Bute 1958-63: *m.* 1934, Lady Janet Egidia Montgomerie, da. of 16th Earl of Eglinton and Winton, and has issue living, Ninian, *b.* 1935,—Henry Colum (Cheshunts, Boxted, Essex), *b.* 1938: *m.* 1963, Patricia Margaret, da. of Brig. Hugh Ronald Norman, of St. Clere, Kemsing, Kent, and has issue living, Alexander Colum *b.* 1967, Camilla *b.* 1964, Serena *b.* 1965, Teresa Clare *b.* 1971.   *Residence,*—Holmhill, Thornhill, Dumfries-shire, DC3 4AB.

AUNTS LIVING.   (*Daughters of 4th Marquess.*)
Lady MARY STUART-WALKER, *b.* 1906; retained the surname of Stuart before that of Walker by deed poll 1933: *m.* 1933, Edward Alan Walker, 1st Sec. Diplo. Ser. (ret.), and has issue living, Ione Mary Stuart (Vallehermoso 32, Madrid 15), *b.* 1934: *m.* 1955, Baron Christian von Oppenheim, who *d.* 1967, and has issue living, Edward Harold *b.* 1958, Corinna Pimpinella *b.* 1956, Flora Monica *b.* 1960, Maria Gabriella *b.* 1963,—Helia Immaculata Stuart, *b.* 1935: *m.* 1957, Frederick Villeneuve Nicolle, MChir, FRCS, and has issue living, Hugo Arthur Villeneuve *b.* 1963, Miranda Camilla *b.* 1958, Edwina Mary *b.* 1961.   *Residences,*—The Manor, Kington Langley, Chippenham, Wilts.; San Bernardo, 107, Madrid 8, Spain.
Lady Jean (*Lady Jean Bertie*) *b.* 1908; is a Dame of Honour and Devotion of Sovereign Mil. Order of Malta: *m.* 1928, Lt.-Cdr. the Hon. James Willoughby Bertie, RN, who *d.* 1966, [see E. Lindsey and Abingdon.].   *Residence,*—Casa de Piro, Attard, Malta, GC.

WIDOWS LIVING OF SONS OF FOURTH MARQUESS.
Selina (Locharthur, Beeswing by Dumfries), da. of Frederick Gerth van Wijk, late Min. Plen. for the Netherlands in Paris: *m.* 1939, Capt. Lord Rhidian Crichton-Stuart, RA, who *d.* 1969, and has issue [see colls. infra].
Ursula Sybil (CLIFTON) (The Old Place of Mochrum, Port William, Wigtownshire), da. of the late Sir Edward Hussey Packe, KBE [By. Colebrooke]: *m.* 1940, Lord David Stuart, who *d.* 1970, having discontinued the surname of Crichton by decree of Lord Lyon 1934, and has issue living, [see colls. infra].

WIDOW LIVING OF FIFTH MARQUESS.
Lady EILEEN BEATRICE FORBES (*Dowager Marchioness of Bute*), da. of 8th Earl of Granard: *m.* 1932, the 5th Marquess, who *d.* 1956.   *Residence,*—Dumfries House, Cumnock, Ayrshire.

COLLATERAL BRANCHES LIVING.

Issue of the late Lord David STUART, 3rd son of 4th Marquess, *b.* 1911; discontinued use of surname of Crichton by decree of Lord Lyon 1934: *m.* 1940, Ursula Sybil CLIFTON (ante), da. of the late Sir Edward Hussey Packe, KBE [By. Colebrooke.]:—
Flora, *b.* 1941.

Issue of the late Lord Patrick Crichton-Stuart, 4th son of 4th Marquess, *b.* 1913, *d.* 1956: *m.* 1st, 1937, Jane, who *d.* 1944, da. of Capt. von Bahr, of Stockholm, Sweden; 2ndly, 1947, Linda Irene, who *d.* 1974, only da. of William Evans, of St. Mellons, Monmouth:—
(By 1st marriage) Charles Patrick Colum Henry (16, Douglas Court, West End Lane, NW6), *b.* 1939, late RAF; Flying Instructor, London Sch. of Flying, Elstree, and Racing Driver: *m.* 1967, Shirley Ann Field.——Angela Mary Monica, *b.* 1942: *m.* 1963, Simon Mark Pilkington, of Flatfield House, Symington, by Kilmarnock, Ayrshire [see B. Faringdon, colls.].

Issue of the late Capt. Lord Rhidian Crichton-Stuart, RA, yst. son of 4th Marquess, *b.* 1917, *d.* 1969: *m.* 1939, Selina (ante), da. of Frederick Gerth van Wijk, late Min. Plen. for the Netherlands in Paris:—
Frederick John Patrick (Hillside, Kirtlewater, Gretna, Dumfries-shire), *b.* 1940; a Knt. of Sovereign Order of Malta: *m.* 1964, Elizabeth Jane Douglas, el. da. of Ernest J. Whitson, and has issue living, Rhidian Colum, *b.* 1967,—Edward Neil James, *TD*, *b.* 1974,—Ione Jane, *b.* 1965,—Amanda Mary, *b.* 1968,—Alexandra, *b.* 1972.——Jerome Niall Anthony, *b.* 1948; Capt. Scots Gds.; a Knt. Sovereign Mil. Order of Malta: *m.* 1971, Susan, el. da. of Patrick Dwyer-Joyce, of Errislannan, Sandycove, co. Dublin, and has issue living, Rhidian Charles Patrick, *b.* 1974.——Mary Margot Patricia, *b.* 1942: *m.* 1962, Edward Henry Lovell, of 17, Foxmore Rd., SW11, and has issue living, Peter Henry James, *b.* 1965,—Nicola Mary, *b.* 1963,—Henrietta, *b.* 1971.

Issue of the late Lieut.-Col. Lord Ninian Edward Crichton-Stuart, MP, Welch Regt., 2nd son of 3rd Marquess, *b.* 1883, *d.* (killed in action) 1915: *m.* 1906, the Hon. Ismay Lucretia Mary Preston, who *d.* 1975: she *m.* 2ndly, 1917, Capt. Archibald Henry Maule Ramsay, Coldm. Gds., who *d.* 1955 [E. Dalhousie, colls.], only da. of 14th Viscount Gormanston:—
Michael Duncan David Crichton STUART, *MC*, *b.* 1915; ed. at Eton, and at Ch. Ch., Oxford; Maj. (ret.) Scots Gds., Hereditary Keeper of Falkland Palace, a Member of Queen's Body Guard for Scotland (Roy. Co. of Archers), a JP and DL for Fife, Knight of Sovereign Order of Malta, and an OStJ; Middle East and Italy 1939-43 (MC): *m.* 1941, Barbara, only da. of the late Lieut.-Col. Sir (George) Stewart Symes, GBE, KCMG, DSO, and has issue living, Ninian John, *b.* 1957,—Elspeth Ann, *b.* 1954.   *Residence,*—Falkland Palace, Fife.——Ismay Catharine, *b.* 1909: *m.* 1st, 1930, Viscount Tiverton (from whom she obtained a divorce 1936)—now 3rd Earl of Halsbury; 2ndly, 1937, Donald Ross, yr. son of the late Brig.-Gen. Sir Walter Charteris Ross of Cromarty, KBE, CB, CMG, and has issue living (by 1st m.) [see E. Halsbury],—(by 2nd m.), Ismay Victoria, *b.* 1944.   *Residence,*—Dorranmhor House, Crinan, Lochgilphead, Argyll.——Claudia Miriam Joanna, *b.* 1913: *m.* 19—, Peter Vigne, of 15, Saville Row, Sydney, NSW.

Grandson of the late Lieut.-Col. James Frederick Dudley Crichton-Stuart, son of the late Patrick James Herbert Crichton-Stuart, MP, 2nd son of John, Lord Mountstuart, el. son of 1st Marquess:—
Issue of the late Patrick James Crichton-Stuart, *b.* 1868, *d.* 1935: *m.* 1st, 1894, Sophia Matilda (Cecil), who *d.* 1895, da. of the late John Kirk, JP, DL, of Annevale, co. Armagh; 2ndly, 1904, Helen Katherine, who *d.* 1948, da. of the late Hon. J. C. Phillippo, MD, of Jamaica, and widow of the Hon. Arthur James Dudley Stuart St. Aubyn [B. St. Levan]:—

(By 2nd m.) Patrick Dudley, *b.* 1909; ed. at Downside and at Balliol Coll., Oxford (BA); Maj. Intelligence Corps (Reserve); a Knt. of Sovereign Order of Malta; 1939-45 War: *m.* 1948, Sheila Mary, da. of Lt.-Col. J. D. K. Restler, of 1, Sloane Gdns., SW1, and has issue living, Patrick James, *b.* 1954; 2nd Lt. Scots Gds.,—Caroline Mary Katherine, *b.* 1949. *Residences,*—Langton House, Alresford, Hants; 1, Sloane Gdns., SW1. *Club,*—Travellers.

Granddaughter of the late Herbert Crichton-Stuart, son of the late Patrick James Herbert Crichton-Stuart, MP (ante):—
Issue of the late James Fortescue Crichton-Stuart, *b.* 1864, *d.* 1932: *m.* 1894, Lilian Louisa, who *d.* 1950, da. of the late Thomas Holdsworth Newman [Newman, Bt., cr. 1836, colls.]:—
Joan Evelyn, *b.* 1895: *m.* 1922, Richard John Vereker Astell, late 2nd Sec. Diplo. Ser., who *d.* 1969 [V. Gort]. *Residence,*—Woodbury Hall, Sandy, Bedfordshire.

Grandchildren of the late Lt.-Col. Henry John Richard Villiers-Stuart, el. son of Capt. William Villiers-Stuart, MP, 2nd son of Lord Henry Stuart, 5th son of 1st Marquess:—
Issue of the late Major Charles Herbert Villiers-Stuart, *b.* 1874, *d.* (killed in action) 1915: *m.* 1913, Joan Lascelles, who *d.* 1950, da. of Robert Shepley Shepley, of Torkington, Cheshire:—
Charles Henry, *b. (posthumous)* 1915; ed. at Eton, and at Wye Agricultural College.; 1939-45 War with Oxford and Bucks LI, and as Capt. Roy. Indian Army Ser. Corps. *Residence;*—Brummell Court, Hanley Swan, Worcester, WR8 0DN.
Issue of the late Col. John Patrick Villiers-Stuart, CB, DSO, OBE, *b.* 1879, *d.* 1958: *m.* 1st, 1914, Phyllis Mary, who *d.* 1933, da. of the late James Read; 2ndly, 1933, Eileen Nora (The Beeches, Catsfield, Battle, Sussex), da. of the late Col. Alexander John Maunsell MacLaughlin, CIE, of Derryheen, Hook Heath, Woking:—
(By 1st m.) John Michael (Trinity Cottage, Kings Walden, Hitchin, Herts.), *b.* 1927; Maj. Queen's Own Highlanders (ret.): *m.* 1960, Bridget Mary, da. of Lt.-Col. Patrick Grant, of Knockie, Whitebridge, Inverness-shire, and has issue living, Michael Patrick, *b.* 1961,—Marianne, *b.* 1963.——Stella, *b.* 1918; formerly Assist. Section Officer, WAAF: *m.* 1st, 1941, Squadron-Leader Donald Maitland Wellings, DFC, RAF, who *d.* (killed in action during 1939-45 War) 1944; 2ndly, 1949, Lt.-Col. Anthony Hamilton Gerald Barton, MC, late RA, of Orchard Hill, Swan Barn Rd., Haslemere, Surrey, and has issue living, (by 1st m.) Donald James, *b.* 1942,—(by 2nd m.) Patrick Anthony Richard, *b.* 1956,—Julia Penelope Susan, *b.* 1950.

Granddaughter of the late Henry Stuart, son of the late Rear-Adm. Lord George Stuart, CB, 7th son of 1st Marquess:—
Issue of the late Capt. Dudley Charles Stuart, RN, *b.* 1844, *d.* 1906: *m.* 1875, Amy Clara, who *d.* 1943, da. of the late Col. Charles Harrison Page, of Dulwich House, Cardiff:—
Heather Sybil (57, Corbière Av., Parkstone, Dorset), *b.* 1900: *m.* 1930, Alfred Mutlow Grosvenor Herd, who *d.* 1970, and has issue living, Brenda Amy Grosvenor, *b.* 1932: *m.* 1969, Christopher Patrick Cavendish Pelly, of 57, Corbière Av., Parkstone, Dorset, [see Pelly, Bt., colls.].

Granddaughters of the late John Windsor Stuart, son of the late Henry Stuart (ante):—
Issue of the late Capt. Henry Campbell Stuart, The Black Watch, *b.* 1874, *d.* 1953: *m.* 1904, Eileene Barbara (now of Hill of Burns, Creetown, Kirkcudbright), da. of Major H. G. Fenton Newall, of Hare Hill, Lancashire:—
Margaret Windsor, *b.* 1908: *m.* 1934, George Thomas Balfour-Kinnear, Fl. Lt. RAF, who *d.* 1945, and has issue living, George Henry Charles (Bank Cottage, Ide Hill, Kent; 16, Bourne St., SW1), *b.* 1935; ed. at Trin. Coll., Glenalmond; Capt. R. Scots Fus. (TA) (ret.): *m.* 1st, 1958 (m. diss. 1970), Angela Rodney, da. of Col. R. A. G. Bingley, of Pegglesworth, Andoversford, Glos.; 2ndly, 1973, Mrs. Jennifer Nora Parry, da. of Dr. Paul Hosein Faridany, and has issue living (by 1st m.), Caroline Rodney *b.* 1963, Annabel *b.* 1965 (by 2nd m.) James Edward Stuart *b.* 1974. *Residence,*—Hill of Burns, Creetown, Kirkcudbright.——Flora Emily Windsor, *b.* 1910: *m.* 1932, Group Capt. Cyril Henry William Boldero, RAF, and has issue living, Ann Barbara Stuart, *b.* 1933,—Helen Cecilia Stuart, *b.* 1936. *Residence,*—High Doon, Newton Stewart, Wigtownshire.

Grandchildren of the late Com. Dudley Charles Stuart, RN (ante):—
Issue of the late Com. Evelyn Charles Henry Stuart, RN (ret.), *b.* 1875, *d.* 1945: *m.* 1906, Anna Knutzen Grane, who *d.* 1944:—
Dudley Evelyn, *b.* 1907.——Amy Ingeborg Sybil Eda, *b.* 1911.
Issue of the late Henry Stuart, *b.* 1886, *d.* 1936: *m.* 1919, Jane Elizabeth Henderson, of 8, Harlaw Terrace, Aberdeen:—
Muriel Mary Henderson, *b.* 1926: *m.* 1946, Federico Santi, and has issue living, Stuart Michael, *b.* 1947. *Residence,*—
Issue of the late Eric Hoy Stuart, *b.* 1890, *d.* 1950: *m.* 1918, Dorothie Primrose, (who m 2ndly, 1958, as his third wife, the Hon. Michael Scott, OBE, who *d.* 1959 [see E. Eldon], and 3rdly, 1969, Surg. Vice-Adm. Sir Clarence Edward Greeson, KBE, CB, of 14, Denton Rd., Eastbourne), da. of Maj. C. Murray-Stewart:—
Patricia Elizabeth *b.* 1923: *m.* 1st, 1946 (m. diss. 1950), Thomas Daniel, and 2ndly, 1972, Philip Baxendale, of Dolphin Cottage, Alderney, and has issue (by 1st m.), Timothy Hugh, *b.* 1946.
Descendants of the late Rt. Hon. James Archibald STUART-WORTLEY (son of the Hon. James Archibald Stuart, 2nd son of 3rd Earl of Bute), who was cr. *Baron Wharncliffe* 1820 [see E. Wharncliffe].

Granddaughters of the late Charles Pole Stuart, son of the late William Stuart (infra):—
Issue of the late Robert Alexander Stuart, *b.* 1862, *d.* 1899: *m.* 1897, Edith Margaret Nina, (who *m.* 2ndly, 1924, Major Ernest Dawson, formerly Indian Army, who *d.* 1949), da. of the late Rev. H. E. Stoker:—
Enid Frances Anne, *b.* 1898. *Residence,*—The Old Rectory, Minchinhampton, near Stroud, Gloucestershire.
Issue of the late Major Reginald Pole Stuart, *b.* 1863, *d.* 1934: *m.* 1895, Hester Elizabeth Stuart, who *d.* 1939, da. of the late Gerhard Myburgh, Consul-Gen. for the Netherlands for S. Africa:—
Kathleen Anne Pole, *b.* 1899: *m.* 1926, Group Capt. Frederick Robert Wynne, MBE, RAF, and has issue living, Frederick Owen Stuart (Hall Farm, Sutton Cheney, Nuneaton), *b.* 1933; Capt. RE: *m.* 1955, Susan Sheila Bushell, and has issue living, Owen Christopher Robert *b.* 1959,—Lucy Elizabeth Anne, *b.* 1930: *m.* 1961, Alan Turner, architect, of 62, Northchurch Rd., N1,—Althea Kathleen, *b.* 1936: *m.* 1960, Philip Harold Dresman, of The Cottage, St. Mary Bourne, Andover, Hants., and has issue living, Philip Barnabas John *b.* 1966, Ruth Kathleen Beatrice, *b.* 1961, Rebecca *b.* 1962. *Residence,*—Lynwood, 142, Aldershot Rd., Church Crookham, Hants.—— Rosalind Esme Pole, *PhD, b.* 1900; ed. at London Univ. (BA 1924, PhD 1927); is a JP. *Residence,*—Leonis, 4, The Bayle, Folkestone.

Granddaughters of the late Col. William Stuart, son of the late William Stuart, son of the late Most Rev. the Hon. William Stuart (Lord Archbishop of Armagh), 5th son of 3rd Earl of Bute:—
Issue of the late Henry Esme Stuart, *b.* 1865, *d.* 1905: *m.* 1899, Emily, who *d.* 1927 (having *m.* 2ndly, 1911, Leonard Just), da. of James Cornwell:—

Margaret Esme Sylvia, *b.* 1902: *m.* 1928, James Douglas Lyle.——Winifred Hilda Muriel (twin), *b.* 1902: *m.* 192–, Laurence Des Jardins.——Dorothea Frances Irma, *b.* 1904: *m.* 1930, Clifford Frank Butcher, and has issue living, Anthony Frank Stuart, *b.* 1935,—Pamela May Irma, *b.* 1932. *Residence,*—

Granddaughters of the late John Crichton Stuart M'Douall (*b.* 1818), el. son of Rev. William M'Douall (*b.* 1775), son of the late John M'Douall, brother of 6th Earl of Dumfries:—
Issue of the late Patrick James Crichton M'Douall, *b.* 1848, *d.* 1943: *m.* 1883, Laura May, who *d.* 1941, el. dau. of Charles Swanston, of Victoria, Australia:—
May, *b.* 1892. *Residence,*—52, Fiddens Wharf Rd., Killara, NSW.——Gwendolen, *b.* 1894: *m.* 1951 John Mountfort Adnam, of 2, Elouera Rd., Avalon Beach, NSW 2107.——Elizabeth, *b.* 1899. *Residence,*—52, Fiddens Wharf Rd., Killara, NSW.

Grandchildren of the late John Crichton Stuart McDouall, O.B.E. (infra):—
Issue of the late Capt. John Crichton Stuart McDouall, Roy. Signals, *b.* 1920, *d.* 1951: *m.* 1945, Dorothy Anne (who *m.* 2ndly, 1954, Major J. H. A. Bryden, R.A., c/o Lloyds Bank, 6, Pall Mall, S.W.1), dau. of the late Rev. C. A. H. Going, of Shrewsbury:—
John Crichton Stuart, *b.* 1950.——Philip Lewis (twin), *b.* 1950.——Patricia Anne, *b.* 1945: *m.* 1971, James Downing, of 25, Gleneagles Av., Glenrothes, Fife, and has issue living, Frederick James, *b.* 1972.——Elizabeth Jean, *b.* 1947: *m.* 1971, Jean Labaye, and has issue living, Jean Simon, *b.* 1972.

Grandchildren of the late Willoughby Crichton McDouall (infra):—
Issue of the late John Crichton Stuart McDouall, O.B.E., *b.* 1878; *d.* 1942: *m.* 1914, Marguerite Lavinia, who *d.* 1950, dau. of Frank Garrett, of Highgate, N.:—
Lewis Willoughby, *b.* 1924: *m.* 1964, Madeline, da. of George Hall. *Address,*—c/o Lloyds Bank, Sutton, Surrey.——Mary Crichton, *b.* 1917: *m.* 1950, Charles Grenville Parsons, DSC, and has issue living, Susan Mary, *b.* 1952,—Jane Elizabeth, *b.* 1955. *Residence,*—Hillside, 62, Brattle Wood, Sevenoaks, Kent.——Marguerite Lavinia, *b.* 1922: *m.* 1941, Capt. Ian Sibbald McCormick, MB, who *d.* 1967, and has issue living, John Sibbald, *b.* 1944,—Jennifer Anne, *b.* 1943,—Marguerite Lavina, *b.* 1948.

Issue of the late Rev. Crichton Willoughby McDouall, *b.* 1881, *d.* 1966: *m.* 1st, 1911 Florence Charlotte, who *d.* 1923, da. of the late William Bampfield Cogan, of Clifton, Bristol; 2ndly, 1935, Jessie Kentish (4, The Lane, Suummersdale, Chichester), da. of the late George Rudolf Cole, of Sheffield:—
(By 1st m.) John Crichton, *CMG* (The Old School, Souldern, Oxon.), *b.* 1912; ed. at Monkton Combe; MA Camb.; Ch. Social Welfare Officer, Malaya 1952-57, and Sec. for Chinese Affairs, Hong Kong 1957-67: 1939-45 War, Lt. Hong Kong RNVR; CMG 1966: *m.* 1946, Kathleen Glover, da. of the late A. B. Moir, and has issue living, Brian John, *b.* 1952,—Anne Glover, *b.* 1948: *m.* David Thomas Douglas James, and has issue living, Simon Alan *b.* 1969, Annabel Louise *b.* 1971,—Heather Crichton, *b.* 1949.——Kenneth Willoughby (2, King Edward's Close, Ascot, Berks.), *b.* 1914, ed. at Monkton Combe; MA Camb.; CMS Sudan 1951-63: *m.* 1958, Edith Joan Sears, and has issue living, Rhoda Mary, *b.* 1959.——(by 2nd m.) David Christopher (Logan, Pine Tree Close, Highland Park, Wimborne Minster, Dorset), *b.* 1936; ed. at Radley, and Jesus Coll., Camb. (MA): *m.* 1969, Veronica Mary, da. of H. Earl Heighway, of Hagley, Worcs., and has issue living, Sara Frances, *b.* 1972,—Fiona Mary, *b.* 1974.

Grandson of John Crichton Stuart McDouall (*b.* 1818) (ante):—
Issue of the late Willoughby Crichton McDouall, *b.* 1852, *d.* 1914: *m.* 1875, Mary Edith Emily, who *d.* 1943, dau. of P. H. M'Ardell, of Melbourne, Victoria:—
Philip Hastings, *b.* 1884; Bachelor of Engineering, NZ Univ.: *m.* 1917, Ivy Harrie, da. of Henry Charles Sanders, formerly Public Works Dept., India, and has issue living, Philip John, *b.* 1924: *m.* 1950, Hazel Rosemary Bowring, and has issue living, Andrew Crichton *b.* 1951, Janet Mary *b.* 1953, Ellen Margaret Rosemary *b.* 1963.——Margaret Heather (Rua Garcia de Orta, 70, Lisbon, Portugal), *b.* 1920: *m.* 1946, Leonardo Rey Colaco de Castro Freire who *d.* 1970, and has issue living, Martin Anthony *b.* 1952, George Leonard *b.* 1956, Alexander Anthony *b.* 1959, Philippa Maria *b.* 1949: *m.* 1972, Joao Manuel Bliebernicht Rocheta, Catherine Maria *b.* 1954,—Mabel Frances Harrie, *b.* 1926. *Residence,*—The Cottage, 49, Ide Lane, Alphington, Devon.

Grandchildren of the late Willoughby Crichton McDouall (ante):—
Issue of the late Eric Oldfield McDouall, *b.* 1886, *d.* 1918: *m.* 1913, Elizabeth Carpenter, who *d.* 1954, dau. of Richard Morrish, of Lincoln, Canterbury, New Zealand:—
Ella Barbara, *b.* 1914: *m.* 1937, the Rev. Henry Jackson Eaton (St. Peter's Church, Upper Riccarton, Christchurch, NZ) and has issue living, Michael McDouall (22, Scotston Av., Christchurch, NZ), *b.* 1937; ed. at Univ. of NZ (Diplo. in Fine Arts); FRSA: *m.* 1962, Lynne Eleanor, da. of Lester Heyward, and has issue living, Jonathan Heyward McDouall *b.* 1964, Benjamin Herriot McDouall *b.* 1967, Penelope Jane *b.* 1962, Sarah Lynne *b.* 1969,—Derek Lionel, *b.* 1941: *m.* 1964, Alice Janice, da. of George Maslin, and has issue living, Simeon Michael *b.* 1968, Stephen Daniel *b.* 1969.——Kathleen Oldfield, *b.* 1916: *m.* 1947, Capt. William John Enright, OBE, RD, RNR, and has issue living, John Oldfield, *b.* 1950,—Shirley Elizabeth, *b.* 1952. *Residence,*—103, Tomes Rd., Christchurch, NZ.

Issue of the late Gerald William McDouall, *b.* 1887, *d.* 1969: *m.* 1920, Dora Olive (113, Hamilton Av., Fendalton, Christchurch, NZ), da. of Arthur Alexander McKinnon, of Oamaru, NZ:—
Eric Willoughby (22, Greendale Rd., Glen Hills, Leicester), *b.* 1921: *m.* 1944, Marion Maud, da. of J. Holder, of Tetbury, Glous, and has issue living Maurice Willoughby (11, Napier Cres., Catisfield, Fareham, Hants.), *b.* 1945; RN: *m.* 1967, Bernice Towers, da. of Lindon Towers Cunliffe, of Fareham, and has issue living, Fiona Bernice *b.* 1968, Rebecca Jane *b.* 1972,—Geraldine Ann, *b.* 1950.——Gerald Ian Crichton (11, St. Leonards St., St. Johns Hill, Wanganui, NZ), *b.* 1929: *m.* 1963, Shirley Maureen, da. of the late Thomas Sanson, of Wanganui, and has issue living, Gerald Andrew, *b.* 1964.—Hamish Crichton, *b.* 1968,—Rachael Deborah, *b.* 1963.——Patricia Ellen, *b.* 1923: *m.* 1947, Wing-Cdr. George Stuart Alexander Stevenson, DFC, RNZAF (ret.), and has issue living, Hugh William, *b.* 1951,—Jeremy Stuart, *b.* 1956,—Helen Patricia, *b.* 1953.——Alison Crichton, *b.* 1926: *m.* 1957, Philip John Poulett Wells, of St. Mary's Rd., Stratford-on-Avon, and has issue living, Philip David Crichton *b.* 1961,—Diana Jane, *b.* 1958,—Elizabeth Joanna, *b.* 1966.

Issue of the late Alan Edward Crichton McDouall, *b.* 1895, *d.* 1962: *m.* 1922, Doris Anne (25, Severn St., Oamaru, New Zealand), da. of Joseph Preston of Oamaru:—
Stuart Preston, *b.* 1922: *m.* 1951, Winifred Edith Jones, and has issue living, Philip Stuart, *b.* 1955,—Patricia Mary, *b.* 1952,—Judith Anne, *b.* 1954,—Heather, *b.* 1959.——Willoughby Alan (PO Box 114, Kurow, N. Otago, NZ), *b.* 1935: *m.* 1963, Pamela Anne Rudduck, and has issue living, John Alan Crichton *b.* 1971, Fiona Mary *b.* 1969, Joanna Louise *b.* 1974.——Doris Mary, *b.* 1924: *m.* 1947, Ernest Benjamin Lyons, of 69, Wilson St., Geraldine, NZ, and has issue living, Alan Mark, *b.* 1950,—John McDouall, *b.* 1952,—David Wayne, *b.* 1954,—Anthony Bruce, *b.* 1956,—Kenneth Brett, *b.* 1957,—Susan Mary, *b.* 1948: *m.* 1972, Graeme Norris Sherwood, of Palmerston N, NZ,—Josephine Anne, *b.* 1926.——Ellen Coverdale, *b.* 1928: *m.* 1952, James Bruce Anderson, of Geraldine, NZ, and has issue living, Duncan Bruce, *b.* 1955,—Ian James, *b.* 1959,—Helen Mary, *b.* 1954,—Barbara Ellen, *b.* 1958, Susan Grace, *b.* 1960.

Granddaughters of the late John Crichton Stuart McDouall (ante):—
Issue of the late Herbert Crichton M'Douall, M.R.C.S., L.R.C.P., D.P.H., *b.* 1860, *d.* 1947: *m.* 1899, Hester Maria Corry, who *d.* 1942, dau. of the late C. S. Hartigan, of Blackheath S.E.:—

Edith Isabella Stewart (of Yalgatta, Nimmitabel, N.S. Wales), *b.* 1900: *m.* 1926, Lindsay Fraser Single, and has issue living, Mark McDouall (of Yalgatta, Nimmitabel, N.S. Wales), *b.* 1930: *m.* 1963, Jean Margaret, da. of J. M. Vicars, of Lindfield, Sydney,——Marion Elizabeth McDouall, *b.* 1928: *m.* 1st, 1950, Douglas Lascelles Ryrie, who *d.* 1959; 2ndly, 1966, Peter Cowper, of Coo ltah, Narromine, NSW, and 180, Queen St., Woollahra, NSW, and has issue living, (by 1st m.) Mark Douglas *b.* 1957.——Barbara Crichton, *b.* 1902: *m.* 1930, J. Jeffereys Ralph, and has issue living, Richard Nethersole, *b.* 1937: *m.* 1965, Pamela, da. of J. J. Dunphy, of Duaringa, Queensland. *Residence,*—43, Hilltop Cres., Mollymook, NSW.——Penelope Crichton, *b.* 1903. *Residence,*—Balgreggan, 34, Fox Valley Rd., Wahroonga, NSW.——Janet Hester Crichton (Balgreggan, 34, Fox Valley Rd., Wahroonga, NSW), *b.* 1905: *m.* 1954, Frederick Tooth, MRCS, LRCP, who *d.* 1969.——Margaret Ellen Crichton, *b.* 1907: *m.* 1st, 1938, Harry G. Doyle, a planter in New Guinea, who *d.* 1942; 2ndly, 1951, William Stanley Leslie, Headmaster of Barker Coll., Hornsby, NSW, who *d.* 1957. *Residence,*—Balgreggan, 34, Fox Valley Rd., Wahroonga, NSW.——Mary Crichton Stuart, *b.* 1909: *m.* 1938, Alexander Bain, Master Mariner, of 38, Cook Rd., Lindfield, NSW, 2070, and has issue living, Roderick Alexander Crichton, *b.* 1940,—John Herbert Crichton (28, Stapylton St., Holder, ACT), *b.* 1944: BSc (New England): *m.* 1969, Peta Jane, da. of F. W. Holdsworth, of Somerton Park, Adelaide, S. Aust., and has issue living, Scott James *b.* 1971.

Grandchildren of the late Rev. William Sutherland M'Douall, 2nd son of the Rev. William M'Douall (*b.* 1775) (ante):—
Issue of the late Claud Hay M'Douall, *b.* 1864, *d.* 1905: *m.* 1904, Alice May, who *d.* 1955, dau. of George Redding:—
Joan Alma, *b.* 1905: *m.* 1931, Brian Miller, of Charnwood, Little Kingshill, Gt. Missenden, Bucks., and has issue living, Ian Claud (110, Stanway Rd., Shirley, Solihull, W. Midlands, B90 3JG), *b.* 1932: *m.* 1955, Violet Grace Waters, and has issue living, Nicola Anne, *b.* 1960,—Peter Gerald (59, Waima Cres., Titirangi, Auckland, NZ), *b.* 1934: *m.* 1955, Patricia Ann Collins, and has issue living, Rogan Edward Oliver *b.* 1966, Cameron Peter *b.* 1970, Carolyn Jane *b.* 1959, Philippa Jane *b.* 1961.
Issue of the late Kenneth Gilbert M'Douall, *b.* 1867, *d.* 1939: *m.* 1904, Evelyn Caroline Locke, who *d.* 1948, dau. of the late Ferdinand Marshall Huth:—
Ferdinand Huth, *b.* 1905: *m.* 1931, Lilian Hall, da. of the late W. J. Saville, and has issue living, Kenneth Hugh (2, West St., Denbury, Newton Abbot, S. Devon TQ12 6DP), *b.* 1935: *m.* 1964, Jean, da. of W. L. Crouch, and has issue living, Duncan Hugh *b.* 1969, Justin Ian *b.* 1972,—Sidney Morris (15, Dorset St., Richmond, Nelson, NZ), *b.* 1944: *m.* 1974, Virginia Helen, el. da. of M. N. Charters, of Rangiona, NZ,—Evelyn Susan (Spring Cottage, 99, Greys Rd., Henley-on-Thames), *b.* 1937: *m.* 1962 (m. diss. 1968), Stuart Wallace MacGregor, and has issue living, Fiona Judith *b.* 1964, Alison Catherine *b.* 1966. *Residence,*—Valeska, Gringer Hill, Maidenhead, Berks.——Penelope, *b.* 1909. *Residence,*—86B, Bouverie Road West, Folkestone.

Grandchildren of the late Alan Patrick M'Douall (infra):—
Issue of the late Patrick Sutherland M'Douall, *b.* 1904, *d.* 1950: *m.* 1941, Esther Mary (who *m.* 2ndly 1952, George Black, of 3, Front Street, Cassop, Ferryhill, co. Durham), dau. of the late Jack William Albutt, of Newcastle:—
Alan Sutherland (65, Princess Av., Finchley, N3), *b.* 1946: *m.* 1970, Jennifer Ann Lingard, da. of Kenneth John Jarvis, and has issue living, Alec Douglas Sutherland, *b.* 1971,—Morwenna Jane, *b.* 1973.——Joy Mary, *b.* 1942: *m.* 1963, John Wilson, of The Bungalow, Knight Bios, Cambridge Rd., Fen Stanton, Hunts., and has issue living, Anthony John, *b.* 1966,—Ian Patrick, *b.* 1969.

Grandchildren of the late Rev. William Sutherland M'Douall (ante):—
Issue of the late Alan Patrick M'Douall, *b.* 1872, *d.* 1947: *m.* 1902, Frances Ethel, who *d.* 1968, da. of the late Edward Reeves, of Wellington, NZ:—
Alan Reeves, *b.* 1906: *m.* 1930, Helma Hornfelt, of Saskatchewan, and has issue living, Katherine McDouall, *b.* 1931; adopted the surname of McDouall 1961: *m.* 1st, 1947 (marriage dissolved 1961), Raymond Frederick Flood; 2ndly, 1962, Royden Gilbert Young, of 956, Quadling Av., Coquitlam, New Westminster, BC, Canada, and has issue living, (by 2nd m.) Robert James *b.* 1967, Douglas Alan *b.* 1968,—Audrey Ethel. *b.* 1933: *m.* 1955, Ronald O'Day, and has issue living, Frederick Alan *b.* 1956, Ronald Patrick *b.* 1957, Kathryn Rosanne *b.* 1958, Lorraine Janet *b.* 1959. *Residence,*—956, Quadling Av., Coquitlam, New Westminster, BC, Canada.——Barbara (of 3, Hickman's Close, Lindfield, Sussex), *b.* 1905.——Mary Grace (of 3, Hickman's Close, Lindfield, Sussex), *b.* 1908.

Grandchildren of the late Rawdon M'Douall, son of the late Rev. William M'Douall (*b.* 1775) (ante):—
Issue of the late Rawdon George Herbert M'Douall, *b.* 1852, *d.* 1919: *m.* 1906, Mary Somerville Townshend, who *d.* 1968:—
Rawdon Townshend, *b.* 1907: *m.* 1933, Elizabeth, dau. of the late A. Cameron, of Glencoe, Narrabri, NSW, and has issue living, David Rawdon (Dunbeacon, Upper Horton, NSW), *b.* 1937: *m.* 1962, Margaret Joan, da. of Keith McDonald, of Strathallan, Warialda, NSW, and has issue living, Rawdon Angus *b.* 1963, Ian Alexander *b.* 1968, Helen Anette *b.* 1964. *Residence,*—Doorah, Upper Horton, via Barraba, NSW.——Lucy Kathrine Shawford, *b.* 1913: *m.* 1946, Thomas Clark Capel, of The Oaks, Narrabri, NSW, and has issue living, Donald Gilbert, *b.* 1949——Katherine Shawford, *b.* 1950,—Nancy, *b.* 19——, Patricia Hastings, *b.* 1916: *m.* 1954, Eric Limburg, of Windi, Bingara, NSW, and has issue living, Richard Eric *b.* 1955,—David Patrick Rawdon, *b.* 1957,—Elizabeth May, *b.* 1960.——Margaret Somerville, *b.* 1918: *m.* 1951, Jack Lattimore, of 21, Trelawney St., Thornleigh, Sydney, NSW, and has issue living, Andrew Stuart, *b.* 1958,—Mary-Ann Elizabeth *b.* 1954,—Margaret Louise, *b.* 1960.

Grandchildren of the late William Edward M'Douall (infra):—
Issue of the late Daniel Crichton Stuart M'Douall *b.* 1905, *d.* 1961: *m.* 1930, Jean (4, Bowen St., Narrabri, NSW), da. of P. A. McAlister, of Narrabri, NSW:—
Peter Crichton Stuart, *b.* 1933: *m.* 1959, Kay Margaret, yr. da. of Kenneth Field Clemson, of Wyndella, Collarenebri, NSW, and has issue living, Sandra Anne, *b.* 1961,—Vicki Jane, *b.* 1963,—Angela Susan, *b.* 1967. *Residence,* Bald Hill, Narrabri, NSW.——Judith, *b.* 1931: *m.* 1954, Allan Richard McMaster, of Blairmore, Bellata, NSW, and has issue living, Stuart Allan, *b.* 1955,—Margaret Jean *b.* 1957,—Cathryn Mary, *b.* 1960.

Grandchildren of the late Rawdon M'Douall (ante):—
Issue of the late William Edward M'Douall, *b.* 1865, *d.* 1936: *m.* 1904, May Edna, who *d.* 1961, dau. of Robert Scholes:—
Hastings Uchrid, *b.* 1907: *m.* 1938, Nancy May, da. of Ernest Capel, of Burren Junction, N.S. Wales, and has issue living, Richard Hastings, *b.* 1940: *m.* 1966, Susan Anne Etheridge, and has issue living, Stuart John *b.* 1966, Graham Richard *b.* 1968,—Donald Hastings, *b.* 1946,—Pamela Hastings (twin) *b.* 1940: *m.* 1963, Roderick Warren Scotton, MB, BS, of Grafton, NSW, and has issue living, Richard Stuart *b.* 1966, Peter Roderick *b.* 1969, Sandra Louise *b.* 1965. *Residence,*—Lowana, Upper Horton, via Barraba, NS Wales.——Robert William, *b.* 1909: *m.* 1934, Nancy Spencer, and has issue living, William Robert, *b.* 1939,—Arthur Frank, *b.* 1942,—Phillipa May, *b.* 1937. *Residence,*—Eungai, Upper Horton, via Barraba, NS Wales——Noel Edward, *b.* 1911: *m.* 1942, Amy Patricia Hawke, and has issue living, Malcolm Noel (14, Upper Cliff Rd., Northwood, NSW), *b.* 1943: *m.* 1968, Louise, da. of the late R. A. Pedlingham, of Pymble, NSW, and has issue living, Matthew Richard Stuart *b.* 1970,—Jullian May, *b.* 1946: *m.* 1967, Michael Thomas Mahony, of Peri, Caroda, NSW, and has issue living, Camilla, *b.* 1972. *Residence,*—Peri, Carolda, NSW.——Harold Stuart (Ulumbarella, Upper Horton, Via Barraba, NSW 2347) *b.* 1920; Fl.-Lt. (ret.) RAAF: *m.* 1st, 1947, Doris Marion, who *d.* 1970, da. of Maj. W. Squires; 2ndly, 1974, Gloria Geraldine, da. of the late

Capt. W. G. F. Leadbeater, MN, and has issue living, by 1st m. Garry Stuart, b. 1949: m. 1971, Linda Anne, da. of Richard Littlejohn, of The Meadows, Harden, NSW,—Michael William, b. 1953,—Diane Marion, b. 1950: m. 1971, Peter Russell Jones, and has issue living, Heulwen b. 1973.——Edna May, b. 1918: m. 1941, John Murray Bowman, of Tarpoly, Upper Manilla, NSW 2346, and has issue living, Roger Murray, b. 1943: m. 1973, Sara Wilkin Smith, and has issue living, Katherine Sara b. 1974,— Graham Edward, b. 1945: m. 1972, Nanette Mary Mahony, and has issue living, Luke Edward b. 1974,—Christopher George, b. 1953,—Julie May, b. 1950.

Issue of the late Frederick Crichton McDouall, b. 1871, d. 1932: m. 1908, Florence Ethel Jackson, who d. 1961:—

John Stuart Crichton, E.M., b. 1908; European War 1939-45 as Lieut. Australian Imperial Force: m. 1935, Patricia Mitchell Moore. Residence,—6/40, Raglan St., Mosman, NSW 2088.——Joan Shawford, b. 1910: m. 1936, Noel Peter Dawson, Maj. AIF, of 45, Congewoi Rd., Mosman 2088, NSW, and has issue living, Susanne Jane, b. 1943: m. 1970, Anthony Keith Wadey, Lt. RANR, of 44, Ben Boyd Rd., Neutral Bay, NSW.——Gwendolen Melville, b. 1918: m. 1936, Frederick Neville Griffiths, and has issue living, Frederick Ronald Neville, b. 1936,—Richard John Neville, b. 1941,— Hugh Douglas, b. 1951,—Elizabeth Joan, b. 1943. Residence,—Rose Hill, Gurley, NSW.

PREDECESSORS—[1] Sir James Stuart of Ardmaleish, Bute, 7th in descent from John Stuart, "The Black Stewart," natural son of Robert II, sided with Charles I; in 1640 his estates were sequestrated, but he was Commr. for Bute 1643-8 and attended sittings in Parliament; dispossessed of custody of Rothesay Castle by Cromwell; cr. a Baronet of Nova Scotia 1627; m. Grizel, da. of Sir Dugall Campbell of Auchinbreck, 1st Bt.: d. 1662; s. by his son [2] Sir DUGAL, 2nd Bt.: m. 1658, Elizabeth, dau. of John Ruthven, of Dunglass; d. 1670; s. by his son [3] Sir JAMES, P.C.; a Commr. to treat for a Union between Scotland and England; cr. Earl of Bute, Viscount Kingarth, Lord Mount Stuart, Cumrae, and Inchmarnock (peerage of Scotland) 1703, with remainder to heirs male whatsoever: m. 1st, 1680, Agnes, dau. of Sir George MacKenzie of Rosehaugh; 2ndly, Christian, dau. of William Dundas of Kincavel; d. 1710; s. by his son [4] JAMES, 2nd Earl; Representative Peer 1715-23; Lord of the Bedchamber 1721-3: m. 1711, Lady Anne Campbell (who d. 1736, having m. 2ndly, 1731, Alexander Fraser of Strichen), dau. of 1st Duke of Argyll; d. 1723; s. by his son [5] JOHN, K.G., 3rd Earl; b. 1713; Representative Peer 1737-41, and 1761-80; First Lord of the Treasury 1762-3: m. 1736, Mary [cr. Baroness Mount Stuart of Wortley, Co. York (peerage of Great Britain) 1761, with remainder to heirs male by her then marriage], who d. 1794, dau. of Edward Wortley-Montagu; d. 1792; s. by his son [6] JOHN, 4th Earl, who in 1776 had been cr. Baron Cardiff, of Cardiff Castle (peerage of Great Britain), and in 1796 was cr. Marquess of Bute, Earl of Windsor and Viscount Mountjoy, of Isle of Wight, with remainder to heirs male of his body: m. 1st, 1766, Charlotte Jane Windsor, who d. 1800, dau. and heir of 2nd Viscount Windsor of Black-castle, and Baron Mountjoy, of Isle of Wight (through whom the estates of the Earls of Pembroke passed to the house of Bute); 2ndly, 1800, Frances, who d. 1832, dau. of Thomas Coutts, banker; d. 1814; s. by his grandson [7] JOHN, K.T., (son of John, Viscount Mount Stuart by his wife Penelope, dau. and heir of 6th Earl of Dumfries), 2nd Marquess; b. 1793; s. his maternal grandfather as 7th Earl of Dumfries (see infra*₊*); assumed in 1805 by Roy. licence the additional surname of Crichton before Stuart: m. 1st, 1818, Maria, who d. 1841, el. dau. of 3rd Earl of Guildford; 2ndly, 1845, Sophia, who d. 1859, dau. of 1st Marquess of Hastings; d. 1848; s. by his only son [8] JOHN PATRICK, K.T., LL.D., 3rd Marquess; b. 1847; Lord-Lieut. of Buteshire: m. 1872, the Hon. Gwendolene Mary Anne Fitzalan-Howard, who d. 1932, el. dau. of 1st Baron Howard of Glossop; d. 1900; s. by his el. son [9] JOHN, K.T., 4th Marquess; b. 1881: m. 1905, Dame Augusta Mary Monica, D.B.E., who d. 1947, dau. of Sir (Alan) Henry Bellingham, 4th Bt.; d. 1947; s. by his son [10] JOHN, 5th Marquess; b. 1907; Vice-Lieut. for co. Bute 1948-56: m. 1932, Lady Eileen Beatrice Forbes, dau. of 8th Earl of Granard; d. 1956; s. by his el. son [11] JOHN, 6th Marquess and present peer; also Earl of Windsor, Earl of Dumfries, Earl of Bute, Viscount Mountjoy, Viscount Kingarth, Viscount of Air, Baron Mount Stuart of Wortley, Baron Cardiff, Lord Crichton, and Lord Mount Stuart, Cumrae and Inchmarnock.

₊[1] Sir ROBERT CRICHTON, of Sanquhar, co. Dumfries, probably descended from a younger son of Alexander Crichton of Crichton, co. Edinburgh 1296; cr. Lord Crichton of Sanquhar (peerage of Scotland) 1488: m. 1st, Margaret Hay; 2ndly c. 1457, Christian, da. of Sir John Erskine of Kinnoull, and widow of John Crichton; d. 1494-95; s. by his grandson [2] ROBERT (son of Robert Crichton by Marion Stewart, dau. of 1st Earl of Lennox), 2nd Lord; m. c. 1491, Marion Maxwell; d. 1513; s. by his son [3] ROBERT, 3rd Lord: m. Elizabeth, (who m. 2ndly Herbert Maxwell), dau. of Cuthbert Murray of Cockpool; d. 1516-20; s. by his son [4] ROBERT, 4th Lord: m. c. 1534, Elizabeth (who m. 3rdly the 4th Earl of Glencairn), dau. and heir of John Campbell of W. Loudoun, and widow of William Wallace of Craigie; d. a minor c. 1535; s. by his brother [5] WILLIAM, 5th Lord: m. c. 1540, Elizabeth, dau. of 3rd Lord Fleming; d. (stabbed by Robert, Master of Sempill) 1550; s. by his son [6] ROBERT, 6th Lord: m. Margaret, dau. of John Cunningham of Caprington, and widow of Gilbert Kennedy; d. 1561; s. by his brother [7] EDWARD, 7th Lord: m. 1561, Margaret (who m. 2ndly, 1571, 5th Earl of Menteith), da. of Sir James Douglas of Drumlanrig; d. 1569; s. by his son [8] ROBERT, 8th Lord; b. c. 1568: m. 1608, Anne (who d. 1675, having m. 2ndly, 1615, 6th Earl of Thomond), da. of Sir George Fermor, of Easton Neston, Northants; having connived at the murder of a fencing master John Turner, who had deprived him of the sight of an eye, he was hanged in Great Palace Yard, Westminster, 1612; s. by his kinsman [9] WILLIAM, (son of William, 5th son of 5th Lord) 9th Lord; cr. Viscount of Air and Lord of Sanquhar (peerage of Scotland) 1622, and Earl of Dumfries, Viscount of Air, and Lord Crichton of Sanquhar and Cumnock (peerage of Scotland) 1633, this creation with remainder to heirs male bearing the name and arms of Crichton: m. 1st Eupheme, dau. of James Seton of Touch, and widow of Patrick Hamilton; 2ndly, Ursula, dau. of Stephen Barnham, and widow of Sir Robert Swift; d. 1642-3; s. by his son [10] WILLIAM, P.C. (Scotland), 2nd Earl; resigned his honours to the Crown 1690, and obtained a new grant with same precedence, and with remainder to his grandson, then the four daughters of his deceased son Charles, Lord Crichton, failing whom to the latter's nearest heirs: m. 1618, Penelope, dau. of Sir Robert Swift, and sister of 1st Viscount Carling-ford; d. 1691; s. by his grandson [11] WILLIAM (son of Charles, Lord Crichton, by Sarah, dau. of 1st Viscount Stair), 3rd Earl; d. young 1694; s. by his sister [12] PENELOPE: m. 1698, the Hon. William Dalrymple, 2nd son of 1st Earl of Stair; d. 1742; s. by her son [13] WILLIAM Dalrymple-Crichton, KT (who also s. as 4th Earl of Stair 1760: m. 1st, 1731, Lady Anne Gordon, who d. 1755, da. of 2nd Earl of Aberdeen; 2ndly, 1762, Anne, da. of William Duff, of Crombie Advocate); d. 1768; s. in Earldom of Dumfries by his nephew [14] PATRICK MacDouall Crichton (el. son of Elizabeth Dalrymple-Crichton, who m. John MacDouall of Freugh): b. 1726, Capt. 3rd Foot Guards; Representative Peer 1790-1803: m. 1771, Margaret, who d. 1799, da. of Ronald Craufurd of Restalrig; d. 1803; s. by his grandson [15] JOHN, 2nd Marquess of Bute (ante) (son of Elizabeth Penelope, who m. 1792, John Stuart, Viscount Mount Stuart, el. son of 1st Marquess of Bute).

BUTLER OF SAFFRON WALDEN, BARON. (Butler.) [Life Baron 1965.]

RICHARD AUSTEN BUTLER, *KG, CH, PC*s son of the late Sir Montagu Sherard Dawe, Butler, KCSI, CB, CIE, CVO, CBE; *b.* Dec. 9th, 1902; ed. at Marlborough, and at Pembroke Coll., Camb. (MA); Fellow of Corpus Christi 1925-29; Hon. LLD Camb., Nottingham, Bristol, Sheffield, St. Andrews, Glasgow, Reading, Durham, Calgary and Liverpool; Hon. DCL Oxford; Hon. Dr. Essex, and Leeds; a FRGS and FRSL, a DL of Essex, a Freeman of Saffron Walden, and Pres. of National Assocn. for Mental Health; Under-Sec. of State for India 1932-37, Parl. Sec. to Min. of Labour 1937-38, Under-Sec. of State for Foreign Affairs 1938-41, Pres. of Board of Education 1941-44, Min. of Education 1944-45, and Min. of Labour and National Ser. May to July 1945, Chancellor of the Exchequer 1951-55, Lord Privy Seal 1955-59, Leader of House of Commons 1957-61, Chm. of Conservative Party 1959-61, Home Secretary 1957-62, First Sec. of State 1962-63, Min. responsible for Central African Federation 1961-63, and Sec. of State for Foreign Affairs 1963-64; Rector of Glasgow Univ. 1956-59; High Steward of Cambridge 1958-65; Chancellor of Sheffield Univ. since 1960, and Essex Univ. since 1962, and Master of Trin. Coll., Camb. since 1965; MP for Saffron Walden Div. of Essex (U) 1929-65; *cr.* PC 1939, CH 1954, *Baron Butler of Saffron Walden,* of Halstead, co. Essex (Life Baron) 1965, and KG 1971: *m.* 1st, 1926, Sydney Elizabeth, who *d.* 1954, da. of the late Samuel Courtauld, of 12, North Audley St., W1; 2ndly, 1959, Mollie, da. of the late Frank Douglas Montgomerie, of Castle Hedingham, Essex [see L. Napier and Ettrick, colls.], and widow of Augustine Courtauld, and has issue by 1st marriage.

Arms,—Gules, on a chevron cottised between three covered cups, all or, a cross couped azure. **Crest,**—A falcon rising, belled and jessed, the dexter leg resting on a covered cup, all or. **Supporters,**—*Dexter,* a falcon belled or; *sinister,* an eagle proper; each standing on a book or.

Residences,—Trinity College, Cambridge; Flat 142, Whitehall Court, SW1. *Clubs,*—Carlton Beefsteak, Farmers'.

SONS LIVING. (*By 1st marriage.*)

Hon. Richard Clive (Penny Pot, Halstead, Essex), *b.* 1929; ed. at Eton, and at Pembroke Coll., Camb. (MA); late 2nd Lt. R. Horse Guards; High Sheriff of Essex 1969-70; a Farmer; a DL of Essex, Dep.-Pres. NFU since 1971 (Vice-Pres. 1970); Managing Dir. of Butler's Peas, Ltd., and Essex Peas, Ltd., and a Liveryman of Skinners' Co.: *m.* 1952, Susan Anne Maud, only da. of Maj. Patrick Bruce Walker, MBE, late RA, of Barry's Close, Long Crendon, Bucks. [see Walker, Bt., *cr.* 1868], and has issue living, Richard Michael, *b.* 1956,—Christopher Patrick (twin), *b.* 1956,—Antonia Mary, *b.* 1954.

Hon. Adam Courtauld, *MP* (The Old Rectory, Lighthorne, nr. Warwick), *b.* 1931; ed. at Eton, and at Pembroke Coll., Camb. (BA); late 2nd Lt. KRRC; ADC to Gov.-Gen. of Canada 1954-55: a Dir. of Kayser Bondor Ltd., and a Liveryman of Goldsmiths' Co.; an Assist. Govt. Whip since 1974; MP for Bosworth (C) since 1970: *m.* 1955, Felicity Sybil, only da. of Guy Kemyel Molesworth-St. Aubyn, of Larks Hill, Braughing, Ware, Herts. [see Molesworth-St. Aubyn, Bt.], and has issue living, Samuel Montagu Guy, *b.* 1957,—Edward Adam, *b.* 1962,—Alexandra Katharine, *b.* 1959.

Hon. (Samuel) James (11, St. Albans Grove, W8), *b.* 1936; ed. at Eton, and at Pembroke Coll., Camb.; late 2nd Lt. Roy. Horse Gds.: *m.* 1960, Lucilla Blanche, yr. da. of the late Algernon Malcolm Borthwick, MC, TD, of Wethersfield Place, Braintree, Essex [see Borthwick, Bt., colls.], and has issue living, Malcolm James, *b.* 1964,—George Victor, *b.* 1969,—Sydney Louise, *b.* 1962,—Fleur Josephine, *b.* 1967,—Lucilla Katherine Joan, *b.* 1973,—Emily Rebecca (twin), *b.* 1973.

DAUGHTER LIVING. (*By 1st marriage.*)

Hon. Sarah Theresa Mary, *b.* 1944: *m.* 1969, Anthony John Willis Price, and has issue living, Jack Jerome, *b.* 1972,—Edward Mulligan, *b.* 1973.

BUXTON, EARLDOM OF. [Extinct 1934.]

DAUGHTER LIVING OF FIRST EARL. (*By 2nd marriage.*)

Lady Alethea Constance Dorothy Sydney, *b.* 1910: *m.* 1934, the Ven. Peter Charles Eliot, M.B.E. TD, late Lt.-Col. RA (TA), of 12, College Green, Worcester [see E. St. Germans, colls.].

Buxton, see Baron Noel-Buxton.

BYERS, BARON. (Byers.) [Life Baron 1964.]

(CHARLES) FRANK BYERS, *OBE, PC,* son of the late Charles Cecil Byers, of The Logs, Lancing, Sussex; *b.* July 24th, 1915; ed. at Westminster, and at Ch. Ch., Oxford (MA); MP for N. Div. of Dorset (*Lib.*) 1945-50, Lib. Ch. Whip 1946-50, and Executive Dir. of Rio Tinto Co. Ltd., 1951-63, and of

Rio Tinto-Zinc Corporation Ltd. 1962-73; Chm. of Co. Pensions Information Centre since 1973; Liberal Leader in House of Lords since 1967; 1939-45 War as Lt.-Col. RA in Middle East, Italy, and NW Europe (GSO1 8th Army, and 21st Army Group, OBE, despatches thrice); *cr.* OBE (Mil) 1944, *Baron Byers,* of Lingfield, co. Surrey (Life Baron) 1964, and PC 1972: *m.* 1939, Joan Elizabeth, da. of the late William Oliver, and has issue.

Residence,—Hunters Hill, Blindley Heath, Lingfield, Surrey. *Club,*—Reform.

SON LIVING.
Hon. Charles William, *b.* 1949; ed. at Westminster, and Ch. Ch., Oxford.

DAUGHTERS LIVING.
Hon. Elizabeth Frances, *b.* 1941: *m.* 1961, Charles Alasdair Ronald Malcolm, of Achadh Nan Sgiath, Duror of Appin, Argyll, and has issue.
Hon. Ann Luise, *b.* 1946.
Hon. Sara Margaret, *b.* 1952.

BYRON, BARON. (Byron.) [Baron E. 1643.]

RUPERT FREDERICK GEORGE BYRON, 11th Baron ; *b.* Aug. 13th, 1903; *s.* 1949 ; a Farmer and Grazier; 1939-45 War as Lt. RANVR: *m.* 1931, Pauline Augusta, da. of the late T. J. Cornwall, of Wagin, W. Australia, and has issue.

Arms, — Argent, three bendlets enhanced gules. **Crest,**—A mermaid proper. **Supporters,**— Two horses of a brown bay colour unguled or.
Residence,—16, Barnsley Rd., Mt. Claremont, W. Australia.

DAUGHTER LIVING.
Hon. Isobel Ann, *b.* 1932 : *m.* 1951, Robert Reford Corr, and has issue living, John Byron Reford, *b.* 1953,—Anthony Byron Reford, *b.* 1956,— Helen Jane, *b.* 1961. *Residence,*—60, Mayfair St., Mount Claremont, W. Australia.

SISTER LIVING.
Daphne Mary, *b.* 1909: *m.* 1930, Leo Forbes O'Connor, who *d.* 1958, and has issue living, Michael Villiers Forbes, *b.* 1933,—Diana Mary Angela Forbes, *b.* 1931 : *m.* 1952, John Michael Poland [see B. Stafford, colls.]. *Residence,*—The White Cottage, Headley Road, Liphook, Hants.

Trust Byron.

COLLATERAL BRANCHES LIVING.

Grandchildren of the late Maj.-Gen. John Byron, son of the late Rev. John Byron, son of the late Rear-Adm. Richard Byron, C.B., el. son of the late Rev. the Hon. Richard Byron, 3rd son of 4th Baron :—
Issue of the late Col. Richard Byron, D.S.O., *b.* 1870, *d.* 1939: *m.* 1896, Mabel Mackenzie, who *d.* 1962, dau. of Charles Albert Winter, J.P., formerly of 33, Hyde Park Sq., W.:—
RICHARD GEOFFREY GORDON, *D.S.O., b.* Nov. 3rd, 1899 ; ed. at Eton ; Lieut.-Col. 4th/7th Roy. Dragoon Guards ; European War 1939-45 in France (D.S.O.) ; D.S.O. 1944: *m.* 1st, 1926, Margaret Mary, dau. of F. G. Steuart, of Fyfhyde, Winchester, Hants ; 2ndly, 1946, Dorigen, only child of P. Kennedy Esdaile, and has issue living, (by 2nd marriage) Richard Noel, *b.* 1948,—Robert James, *b.* 1950. *Residence,*—Langford Hall, Maldon, Essex.——Sheila Margaret, *b.* 1903: *m.* 1st. 1923, James Roy Notter Garton, who *d.* 1939, formerly Capt. King's Roy. Rifle Corps, and from whom she obtained a divorce 1929 ; 2ndly, 1929, Edward William Standish, of Marwell Hall, Win-chester, who *d.* 1933 ; 3rdly, 1935, George Munro Kerr, who *d.* 1970, and has issue living, (by 2nd m.) Edward Anthony Byron, *b.* 1931,—Susan Felicity, *b.* 1929. *Residence,*—9, Rutland Court, Knights-bridge, SW1.

Grandson of the late Henry James Byron (dramatist and actor), grandson of the Rev. Henry Byron, 3rd son of Rev. the Hon. Richard Byron (ante):—
Issue of the late George Frederick Byron, *b.* 1862, *d.* 1939 : *m.* 1892, Mary Clarissa, who *d.* 1936, dau. of the late Rev. John Maurice Gillington, of Yarmouth, Isle of Wight :—
Charles, *b.* 1897 ; Wing-Com. (retired) R.A.F.: *m.* 1929, Joyce Evelyn, dau. of Thomas Godwin Chance, of Cambridge. *Residence,*—

PREDECESSORS.—[1] *Sir* JOHN Byron, K.B., M.P. for Nottingham, a faithful adherent of Charles I., Gov. to H.R.H. the Duke of York, and F. M. Gen. of the Forces in Worcester, Salop Chester, and N. Wales; was cr. *Baron Byron,* of Rochdale, co. Lancaster (peerage of England) 643, with remainder to his brothers Richard, William, Thomas, Robert, Gilbert, and Philip ; *d.s.p.* 1652; *s.* by his brother [2] RICHARD, *K.B.,* 2nd Baron, Gov. of Appleby Castle, West-morland, and of Newark ; *d.* 1679 ; *s.* by his son [3] WILLIAM, 3rd Baron ; *d.* 1695; *s.* by his son [4] WILLIAM, 4th Baron, gentleman of the Bedchamber to George, Prince of Denmark; *d.* 1736; *s.* by his son [5] WILLIAM, 5th Baron: having killed William Chaworth, Esq., in a duel, Jan. 26, 1765, was arraigned before his peers and found guilty of manslaughter, but claiming the benefit of the statute of Edward VI., was discharged by simply paying the fees ; *d.* without surviving issue 1798; *s.* by his great-nephew [6] GEORGE GORDON, 6th Baron, grandson of the Hon. John, 2nd son of 4th Baron; celebrated as a poet; *d.* 1824, without male issue; *s.* by his cousin [7] GEORGE ANSON, 7th Baron, an Adm. and an Extra Lord-in-Waiting to H.M. Queen Victoria; *d.* 1868; *s.* by his son [8] GEORGE ANSON, 8th Baron: *m.* 1843, Lucy Elizabeth Jane, who *d.* 1912, dau. of the late Rev. William Westcomb, R. of Langford ; *d.s.p.* 1870; *s.* by his nephew [9] GEORGE FREDERICK WILLIAM, 9th Baron, *b.* 1855. *m.* 1901, *Dame* Fanny Lucy, *D.B.E.,* who *d.* 1936, dau. of the late Thomas Radmall, of St. Margarets, Twickenham [Brinckman, Bt.], and formerly wife of Lieut.-Col. Theodore Francis Brinckman (afterwards 3rd Bt.) (she *m.* 3rdly, 1924, Sir Robert Paterson Houston, 1st Bt., who *d.* 1926); *d.* 1917; *s.* by his brother [10] *Rev.* FREDERICK ERNEST CHARLES (son of the Hon. Frederick Byron, 2nd son of 7th Baron), 10th Baron, *b.* 1861; sometime V. of Thrumpton and R. of Barton-in-Fabis: *m.* 1921, Lady Anna Ismay Ethel, who *d.* 1966, dau. of the late Lord Charles Edward Fitzroy [D. Grafton]; *d.* 1949; *s.* by his kinsman [11] RUPERT FREDERICK GEORGE (son of the late Col. Wilfrid Byron, son of the Rev. the Hon. William Byron, 4th son of 7th Baron), 11th Baron and present peer.

CACCIA, BARON. (Caccia.) [Life Baron 1965.]

[Pronounced "Catch-a".]

HAROLD ANTHONY CACCIA, *GCMG, GCVO*, son of the late Anthony (Mario Felix) Caccia, CB, MVO; *b.* Dec. 21st, 1905; ed. at Eton, and at Trin Coll., Oxford (Hon. Fellow 1965); Laming Travelling Fellowship, Queen's Coll., Oxford 1928; Hon. Fellow Queen's Coll., Oxford 1974; Min. (local rank) Athens 1945, Assist. Under-Sec. of State, Foreign Office 1946, Dep. Under-Sec. of State 1949, Min. to Austria 1949-51, British High Commr. 1950 and Ambassador 1951-53, again Dep. Under-Sec. of State, Foreign Office 1954-56, Ambassador to USA 1956-61, and Permanent Under-Sec. of State, Foreign Office 1961-65, since when Provost of Eton Coll.; Pres. of MCC 1973-74; a GCStJ and Lord Prior of Order of St. John; *cr.* CMG 1945, KCMG 1950, KCVO 1957, GCMG 1959, GCVO 1961 and *Baron Caccia,* of Abernant, co. Brecknock (Life Baron) 1965: *m.* 1932, Anne Catherine, da. of Sir George Lewis Barstow, KCB [B. Trevethin and Oaksey], and has issue.

Arms.—Per bend barry of six gules and argent, and or in base a lion's gamb erased of the first. **Crest.**—An eagle wings elevated sable gorged with a collar paly argent and gules, resting the dexter claw on a roundel argent charged with a fleur de lys gules. **Supporters.**—On either side a lion gules supporting between the fore paws a staff at the head a fleur de lys or.

Residences,—The Provost's Lodge, Eton College, Windsor, Berks.; 1, Chester Pl., Regent's Park, NW1; Abernant, Builth Wells, Breconshire.

SON LIVING.

Hon. David Anthony Lawrence (c/o C. Hoare & Co., 37, Fleet St., EC4P 4DQ), *b.* 1936; ed. at Eton and Trin. Coll., Oxford, *m.* 1962, Angela Margaret, da. of E. J. Reid, of Johannesburg, and has issue.

DAUGHTERS LIVING.

Hon. Clarissa Sabina, *b.* 1939: *m.* 1959, David Eugene Henry Pryce-Jones, 1, Phillimore Lodge Phillimore Terr., W8, and has issue.
Hon. Antonia Catherine, *b.* 1947: *m.* 1970, (m. diss. 1974), Barton Midwood.

CADMAN, BARON. (Cadman.) [Baron U.K. 1937.]

Always ready.

JOHN ANTHONY CADMAN, 3rd Baron; *b.* July 3rd, 1938; *s.* 1966; ed. at Harrow, Selwyn Coll., Camb., and at Roy. Agricultural Coll., Cirencester.

Arms,—Azure, three fleur-de-lys in pale between four pellets indented argent. **Crest.**—A stork's head holding in the beak a sprig of columbine proper. **Supporters,**—*Dexter* a stork, and *Sinister* a peacock argent beaked gules, each gorged with a collar azure charged with a fleur-de-lys also argent.

Residence,—Eakley Manor Farm, Stoke Goldington, Newport Pagnell, Bucks.

BROTHER LIVING.

Hon. JAMES RUPERT, *b.* June 9th, 1944; ed. at Harrow.

UNCLE LIVING. (Son of 1st Baron.

Hon. Arthur Denys, *b.* 1911; ed. at Harrow, and at Harvard Univ.: *m.* 1933, Cary, dau. of Burke Baker, of Texas, U.S.A., and has issue living, John Denys (Rua Amado Nervo 49, Alto da Boa Vista, Rio de Janeiro), *b.* 1941: ed. at Princeton Univ. (BSE), and Univ. of Cal. (MS, PhD): *m.* 1964, Judith Ann, da. of Warren Whittaker, of Miami, and has issue living, Cynthia *b.* 1965, Cary Anne *b.* 1968,—David Baker (1115, Fifth Av., New York City, USA), *b.* 1948,—Anne *b.* 1935: *m.* 1957, John Edward McCrea Lawrence, of 98 Ruskin, Ottawa, Canada, and has issue living, Edward Burke *b.* 1959, John Cadman *b.* 1960, Denys McCrea *b.* 1962, Cary Edwina *b.* 1964,—Mary Betty *b.* 1937: *m.* 1958, Robert Alexander Calvin, of 464, Oriole Parkway, Toronto, Canada, and has issue living, Robert Denys *b.* 1960, John Collamer *b.* 1962, Isobel Anne *b.* 1965,—Cary (92, Orchard St., Sommerville, Mass. 02144, USA), *b.* 1945; BA, Chatham Coll., Pittsburgh, USA. *Residence,*—1115, Fifth Av., New York, NY 19028.

AUNTS LIVING. (*Daughters of 1st Baron.*)

Hon. Marguerite Betty (Gorsedown, Birling Gap, Eastbourne), *b.* 1913: *m.* 1940, the Rev. John Joseph Tatum, who *d.* 1966, and has issue living, Michael Jon, *b.* 1941: *m.* 1963, Marcia Spencer, of Eastbourne, and has issue living, Nicholas Benjamin *b.* 1969, Sarah Louise *b.* 1965,—Denys John, *b.* 1948,—Frances Jane, *b.* 1943; BSc London: *m.* 1968, Jon David Levine.

Hon. Sybil Mary (Rhagatt Hall, Corwen, Merionethshire), *b.* 1916: *m.* 1st, 1938, Maj.-Gen. William Pat Arthur Bradshaw, CB, DSO, late Scots Guards, who *d.* 1966; 2ndly, 1968, James Simon Cadman, and has issue living (by 1st m.) Christopher Patrick Cadman (4, Douai Grove, Hampton, Middx.), *b.* 1941; ed. at Eton, and St. Andrews Univ. (BSc): *m.* 1973, Susan Elizabeth, da. of D. W. Vasey, of Downways, Old Bosham, Sussex.—Francis John Cadman, *b.* 1946; ed. at Pangbourne Nautical Coll.; Lt. RN,—Caroline *b.* 1939: *m.* 1959, Francis Rokeby Black, of The Old Vicarage, Wing, Bucks., and has issue living, James Pat Rokeby *b.* 1963, Alexander William Francis *b.* 1967, Lucinda Rosalie *b.* 1960,—Rosalie Annette *b.* 1944: *m.* 1965, David Bernard Butler Adams, of The Old Vicarage, Rickling, Saffron Walden, and has issue living, William David *b.* 1974, Sophie Anne *b.* 1966, Amanda Jane *b.* 1968, Fiona *b.* 1972.

WIDOW LIVING OF SECOND BARON.

MARJORIE ELIZABETH (*Baroness Cadman*) (Overlands, 157, Church Rd., Combe Down, Bath), da. of Byron William Bunnis: *m.* 1936, the 2nd Baron, who *d.* 1966.

PREDECESSORS—[1] JOHN CADMAN, *G.C.M.G., D.Sc., F.R.S.*, son of the late James Cope Cadman, M.I.C.E., of Newcastle-under-Lyme; *b.* 1877; a Mining Engineer and Petroleum Technologist; cr. *Baron Cadman*, of Silverdale, co. Stafford (peerage of United Kingdom) 1937: *m.* 1907, Lilian Julia, who *d.* 1963, dau. of the late John Harragin, of Trinidad; *d.* 1941; *s.* by his son [2] JOHN BASIL COPE, 2nd Baron; *b.* 1909: *m.* 1936, Marjorie Elizabeth, da. of Byron William Bunnis; *d.* 1966; *s.* by his son [3] JOHN ANTHONY, 3rd Baron, and present peer.

CADOGAN, EARL. (Cadogan.) [Earl G.B. 1800.]

[Title pronounced "Caduggan."]

WILLIAM GERALD CHARLES CADOGAN, *M.C.*, 7th Earl; *b.* Feb. 13th, 1914; *s.* 1933; ed. at Eton; late Capt. Coldm. Gds. (Reserve), and Lt.-Col. R. Wilts. Yeo. (TA); patron of three livings, and a DL; Mayor of Chelsea 1964; a Member of Chelsea Borough Council 1954-59; 1939-45 War in Middle East and Italy (MC): *m.* 1st, 1936, the Hon. Primrose Lilian Yarde-Buller (who *d.* 1970, and from whom he obtained a divorce 1959), da. of 3rd Baron Churston; 2ndly, 1961, Cecilia, da. of Maj. Henry K. Hamilton-Wedderburn, and has issue by 1st m.

Arms.—Quarterly: 1st and 4th gules, a lion rampant reguardant or, *Cadogan*; 2nd and 3rd argent, three boars' heads couped sable. **Crest.**—Out of a ducal coronet or, a dragon's head vert. **Supporters,**—*Dexter,* a lion reguardant or, gorged with a collar gemeflory counterflory gules; *sinister,* an eagle wings elevated sable, beaked, membered, and navally crowned or, gorged with a riband argent, fimbriated gules, pendent therefrom a representation of the cross of Imperial Austrian military order of Maria Theresa.

QUI INVIDET MINOR EST

He who envies is the inferior.

Residences,—Snaigow, Murthly, Perthshire; 28, Cadogan Square, S.W.1. *Club,*—White's.

SON LIVING (*By 1st marriage.*)

CHARLES GERALD JOHN (*Viscount Chelsea*) (51, Chelsea Sq., SW3; White's Club), *b.* March 24th, 1937; ed. at Eton: *m.* 1963, Lady Philippa Dorothy Bluett Wallop, dau. of 9th Earl of Portsmouth, and has issue:—

SONS LIVING,—*Hon.* Edward Charles, *b.* May 10th, 1966.
Hon. William John, *b.* 1973.
DAUGHTER LIVING,—*Hon.* Anna-Karina, *b.* 1964.

DAUGHTERS LIVING. (*By 1st marriage.*)

Lady Sarah Primrose Beatrix, *b.* 1938: *m.* 1958, the Hon. James Hugh Cecil, of 6, Manresa Rd., S.W.3, el. son of 2nd Baron Rockley.

Lady Daphne Magdalen, *b.* 1939: *m.* 1961, David Malcolm Graham Bailey, of The Kieve, Devenish Rd., Sunningdale, Berks., and has issue living, Alexander Graham, *b.* 1962,—Kevin David, *b.* 1964, Leonie Daphne, *b.* 1965.

Lady Caroline Ann, *b.* 1946: *m.* 1965, Euan Woodroffe Foster, of 57, Cadogan Sq., SW1, and has issue living, Guy Peter Woodroffe, *b.* 1968,—Hugo Woodroffe, *b.* 1971.

SISTERS LIVING.

Lady Beatrix Lilian Ethel, *b.* 1912: *m.* 1st, 1931, Henry Péregrine Rennie Hoare [M. Bristol], who obtained a divorce 1941; 2ndly, 1942, Col. Edward Leighton Fanshawe, el. son of the late Lieut.-Gen. Sir Edward Arthur Fanshawe, KCB, and has issue living, (by 1st m.) Henry

Cadogan (Gasper Mill, Stourton, Warminster, Wilts.), *b.* 1931: *m.* 1959, Pamela Saxon, dau. of Col. G. F. Bunbury,—Melanie Beatrix, *b.* 1937: *m.* 1963, Charles Henry Petre [see B. Petre, colls.],— (by 2nd marriage) Ann Erika, *b.* 1943,—Clodagh Frances, *b.* 1945. *Residence,*—Rossie, Fleet, Hants.

Lady Alexandra Mary, *b.* 1920: *m.* 1st, 1940, Maj. Robert Gilliam Buchanan, King's Own Scottish Borderers, who obtained a divorce 1949; 2ndly, 1951, Norman Hutchison Smith, c/o Iranian Oil Consortium, P.O. Box 1065, Teheran, Iran, and has issue living, (by 2nd marriage) Adam Gerald Norman, *b.* 1959,—Alexandra Josephine, *b.* 1952,—Andrula Mary, *b.* 1944.

ISSUE LIVING OF ELDEST SON OF FIFTH EARL.

Issue of the late Henry Arthur (*Viscount Chelsea*), el. son of 5th Earl, *b.* 1868, *d.* 1908: *m.* 1892, the Hon. Mildred Cecilia Harriet Sturt, who *d.* 1942, dau. of 1st Baron Alington (ext.):—

Hon. Victoria Laura, *OBE, TD, b.* 1901; formerly Controller ATS; acted as Lady-in-Waiting to HM Queen Elizabeth the Queen Mother when Duchess of York during tour in New Zealand and Australia 1927 (OBE); OBE (Civil) 1927: *m.* 1922, John Little Gilmour (afterwards 2nd Bt.), from whom she obtained a divorce 1929. *Residence,*—Dacres, Bentworth, Hants.

WIDOW LIVING OF SON OF FIFTH EARL.

Lady Theodosia Acheson (2, Westminster Gdns., SW1), da. of 4th Earl of Gosford: *m.* 1912, the Rt. Hon. Sir Alexander George Montagu Cadogan, OM, GCMG, KCB, who *d.* 1968, and has issue [see colls., infra].

COLLATERAL BRANCHES LIVING.

Issue of the late Rt. Hon. Sir Alexander George Montagu Cadogan, OM, GCMG, KCB, yst. son of 5th Earl, *b.* 1884, *d.* 1968: *m.* 1912, Lady Theodosia Acheson (ante), da. of 4th Earl of Gosford:—

Ambrose Alec Patrick George (8 Wilton Road, Reading, Berks.), *b.* 1914 : *m.* 1955 (m. diss. 1971), Mrs. Pamela Maud Hope-Johnstone, da. of the late Lt.-Col. John Murray Cobbold, Scots Guards [see D. Devonshire].——Patricia, *b.* 1916: *m.* 1939, Lt.-Col. Gerald Edward Coke, OBE, Scots Guards (ret.) [see E. Leicester, colls.].——Cynthia (*Lady Goschen*), *b.* 1918; formerly Co. Assist. ATS: *m.* 1946, Maj. Sir Edward Christian Goschen, 3rd Bt., DSO.——Gillian Moyra, *b.* 1922: *m.* 1948, Maj. Patrick Henry Douglas Crichton, Berks. Yeo. (TA), [see E. Erne, colls.].

Issue of the late John Cecil Cadogan, *b.* 1883, *d.* 1970: *m.* 1911, Ella, who *d.* 1971, da. of the late Gustav Kraft, of Gothenburg, Sweden:—

Erik (Wasperton Hill, Barford, Warwick), *b.* 1913; a JP for Warwicks.: *m.* 1939, Caroline, da. of Count Wachtmeister, of Malmö, and has issue living, Charles John, *b.* 1954.——Caroline Monica (*Hon. Mrs. Peter H. Lewis*), *b.* 1942: *m.* 1974, Maj. the Hon. Peter Herbert Lewis (see B. Merthyr),— Patricia Elisabeth, *b.* 1945.

Grandchildren of the late John Cecil Cadogan (ante):—
Issue of the late Peter Cadogan, *b.* 1918, *d.* 1962: *m.* 1st, Joan (m. diss. 1955), da. of the late Adm. F. A. F. Banbury; 2ndly, 1955, Pamela Mary, da. of the late Alexander Henry Burman, OBE:—
(By 1st m.) Gerald (c/o University of Cincinnati, Ohio, USA), *b.* 1942: *m.* 1968, Lucy Dodd, da. of Walter Ramberg, of Wash., DC, and has issue living, Leo, *b.* 1975.——Sarah, *b.* 1944: *m.* (1st) 1966 (m. diss. 1970), Geoffrey Hugh Kenion; 2ndly, 1973, Robert Andrew Burns, of 6, Quickswood, NW3, and has issue living (by 1st m.) Ella Jane, *b.* 1968.

Granddaughter of Com. Francis Charles Cadogan, RN (infra):—
Issue of the late Capt. Christopher Michael Cadogan, Roy. Berks. Regt., *b.* 1917, *d.* (drowned on active ser. during 1939-45 War) 1941: *m.* 1940, Stella Irena (*Lady Wallinger*) (who *m.* 2ndly, 1943, David Rhys Ellias, from whom she obtained a divorce 1955, and 3rdly, 1958, Sir Geoffrey Arnold Wallinger, KCMG), da. of Konrad Zilliacus, MP:—
Catharine, *b.* 1941.

Granddaughter of the late Hon. Charles George Henry Cadogan (ante):—
Issue of the late Cdr. Francis Charles Cadogan, RN, *b.* 1885, *d.* 1970: *m.* 1913, Ruth Evelyn, who *d.* 1962, da. of the late Sir (Edward) Stafford Howard, KCB [D. Norfolk, colls.], and widow of Gardner Sebastian Bazley [Bazley, Bt.]:—
Henriette Alice, *CVO* (*Lady Abel Smith*), *b.* 1914; a JP; appointed a Lady-in-Waiting to HM The Queen when HRH Princess Elizabeth 1949, a Woman of the Bedchamber to HM The Queen 1952, an Extra Woman of the Bedchamber 1953-73, since when again Woman of the Bedchamber, CVO 1964: *m.* 1st, 1939, Maj. Sir Anthony Frederick Mark Palmer, 4th Bt. (cr. 1886), RA, who *d.* (killed in action) 1941; 2ndly, 1953, Brig. Sir Alexander Abel Smith, TD, JP [D. Somerset, colls.], of The Old Rectory, Quenington, Glos., and 63, Cadogan Gdns., SW3, and has issue living, (by 1st m.) [see Palmer, Bt., cr. 1886], (by 2nd m.) Christopher Abel, *b.* 1954,—Juliet Sarah, *b.* 1955.

PREDECESSORS.—[1] *Gen. the Rt. Hon. Sir* William Cadogan, *K.T., P.C.,* successively M.P. for Woodstock, Ambassador to Brussels, Master of the Robes, Ambassador to the States Gen., Master-Gen. of the Ordnance and Com.-in-Ch. of H.M.'s Forces, was cr. *Baron Cadogan,* of Reading, co. Berks (peerage of Great Britain) 1716, and *Baron Cadogan,* of Oakley, co. Bucks. with remainder to his brother Charles, and *Viscount Caversham* and *Earl Cadogan* (peerage of Great Britain) 1718 ; *d.* 1726, without male issue, when the Barony of Cadogan of Reading 1716, and the Earldom and Viscountcy of 1718 became ext.; *s.* in Barony of Cadogan of Oakley by his brother [2] Charles, 2nd Baron ; was a Gen. of Horse, M.P. and Gov. of Sheerness, &c.; *d.* 1776; *s.* by his son [3] Charles Sloane, 3rd Baron; was M.P. for Cambridge 1749-76, and Master of the Mint, &c.; cr. *Viscount Chelsea* and *Earl Cadogan* (peerage of Great Britain) 1800; *d.* 1807; *s.* by his son [4] Charles Henry Sloane, 2nd Earl; *d.* 1832; *s.* by his half-brother [5] George, *C.B.,* 3rd Earl, a distinguished Adm., who in 1831 had been cr. *Baron Oakley,* of Caversham, co. Oxford (peerage of United Kingdom); *d.* 1864; *s.* by his son [6] Henry Charles, *P.C.,* 4th Earl, *b.* 1812; was M.P. for Reading 1841-7 and for Dover 1852-7, and Capt. of Yeomen of the Guard 1866-68: *m.* 1836, his cousin, Mary Sarah, who *d.* 1873, da. of the late Rev. the Hon. Gerald Valerian Wellesley, D.D. [E. Cowley]; *d.* June 8, 1873; *s.* by his son [7] George Henry, *K.G., P.C.,* 5th Earl, *b.* 1840 ; M.P. for Bath (*C*) 1873; Under-Sec. for War 1875-8, and for the Colonies 1878-80, Lord Privy Seal 1886-92, and Lord-Lieut. of Ireland with a Seat in the Cabinet 1895-1902; held Canopy at Coronation of King George V. 1911: *m.* 1st, 1865, Lady Beatrix Jane Craven *V.A.,* who *d.* 1907, dau. of 2nd Earl of Craven: 2ndly, 1911, Countess Adele Palagi, who *d.* 1960, dau. of Lippo Neri, Count Palagi, a Florentine Patrician; *d.* 1915, *s.* by his third but el. surviving son [8] Gerald Oakley, *C.B.E.,* 6th Earl, *b.* 1869 ; sometime Lt. 1st Life Gds., and Capt. 3rd Batn. Suffolk Regt.: *m.* 1911, Lilian Eleanor Marie, who *d.* 1973, da. of George Stewart Coxon, formerly of Craigleith, Cheltenham ; *d.* 1933, *s.* by his only son [9] William Gerald Charles, 7th Earl and present peer; also Viscount Chelsea, Baron Cadogan of Oakley, and Baron Oakley.

CAIRNS, EARL. (Cairns.) [Earl U.K. 1878.]

I flourish.

DAVID CHARLES CAIRNS, GCVO, CB, 5th Earl; b. July 3rd, 1909; s. 1946; Rear Adm. (ret.); Pres. of Naval Coll., Greenwich 1958-61; Marshal of Diplomatic Corps 1961-71; Prime Warden of Fishmongers' Co. 1972-73; Pres. of Navy League since 1967; an Extra Equerry to HM since 1972; 1939-45 War (despatches); CB (Mil.) 1960, KCVO 1969, GCVO 1972: m. 1936, Barbara Jeanne Harrison, yst. da. of the late Sydney H. Burgess, of Heathfield, Bowdon, Cheshire, and has issue.

Arms,—Gules, three martlets argent within a bordure of the second, charged with three trefoils slipped vert. Crest,—A martlet argent, charged on the breast with a trefoil slipped vert. Supporters—On either side a hawk, wings expanded proper, collared belled and chained or, holding in its beak a trefoil slipped vert.
Residences,—Clopton Hall, Woodbridge, Suffolk.

SONS LIVING.

SIMON DALLAS (*Viscount Garmoyle*) (Queen Hoo Hall, Tewin, Herts.), b. May 27th, 1939; ed. at Eton, and at Camb. Univ.: m. 1964, Amanda Mary, only da. of the late Maj. Edgar Fitzgerald Heathcoat-Amory [see V. Amory, colls.], and has issue:—

SONS LIVING—*Hon.* Hugh Sebastian, b. March 26th, 1965.
Hon. David Patrick, b. 1967.
Hon. Alistair Benedict, b. 1969.

Hon. Hugh Andrew David (21, Ovington Gdns., SW3), b. 1942; ed. at Wellington Coll., and at Dublin Univ.: m. 1966, Elizabeth, da. of Lt.-Col. F. C. L. Bell, of Cross Glades, Chiddingfold, Surrey, and has issue living, Bertram Wilfred Arthur b. 1972,—Katherine Frances, b. 1974.

DAUGHTER LIVING.

Lady Elisabeth Olive, b. 1944: m. 1965, Capt. Martin Ralph Lowe, 9th/12th R. Lancers (ret.), of Castle End, Ross-on-Wye, and has issue living, Alexander Charles, b. 1970.

SISTERS LIVING.

Lady Hester Margaret (of The Old Mill House, Bradford Abbas, Sherborne),b.1895; Vice-Chm. of Conservative Party Organization, and Pres. of National Soc. of Conservative and Unionist Women Organizers 1939-43: m. 1917, Capt. the Rt. Hon. Robert Croft Bourne, M.P., who d. 1938 [Croft, Bt., cr. 1818], and has issue living, Robert Morice Antony (Manor House, Beaminster, Dorset), b. 1918; ed. at Eton, and at New Coll., Oxford (B.A. 1945, M.A. 1945); is an Assist. Master at Eton; Hon. Lieut.-Col. T.A. (retired); European War 1939-40 (prisoner): m. 1949, Margaret Rose, dau. of the late Hon. George William Lyttelton [see V. Cobham, colls.], and has issue living, Robert Humphrey Lyttelton b. 1954, George Julian b. 1960, Harriet Madeline b. 1950, Charlotte Elizabeth b. 1952, Lucy Jane b. 1956, Emily Hester b. 1963,—John Wilfrid, b. 1922; ed. at Eton, and in New Coll., Oxford; Bar. Middle Temple 1948; late Capt. Rifle Brig.; is in Lord Chancellor's Office: m. 1958, Elizabeth Juliet, da. of the late Romney Fox, of Trewardreva, Constantine, Falmouth, and has issue living, Robert William b. 1959, Antony John b. 1960,—Sheila Désirée (*Lady Bolitho*), (Tresidder, Buryan, Penzance, Cornwall), b. 1920, a J.P. of Cornwall: m. 1950, as his second wife, Lt.-Col. Sir Edward Hoblyn Warren Bolitho, KBE, CB, DSO, MC, who d. 1969, and has issue living, John Geoffrey b. 1958, Catherine Mary b. 1951, Hester Veronica b. 1954, Iris Norah b. 1956.
Lady Ursula Helen, b. 1899: m. 1921, Maj. John Roland Abbey, late Rifle Bde., who d. 1969, and has issue living, Juliet Hermione (Whitwick Manor, Yarkhill, Ledbury, Herefordshire), b. 1925: m. 1948, (m. diss. 1968), Lt.-Cdr. John Somerville Kendal Oram, RN (ret.), and has issue living, Miranda b. 1962,—Gloria Jean, b. 1936. *Residence,*—Mansby, Fittleworth, Sussex.
Lady Sheila Mary, b. 1905: m. 1930, Maj. Charles Ivor Patrick Holroyd, late Rifle Bde. and has issue living, Charles John (Providence Cottage, Chute Cadley, Andover), b. 1933; Maj. R. Green Jackets: m. 1969, Amanda Jane, da. of Col. Sir Richard Hamilton Glyn, OBE, TD, MP, 9th Bt., and has issue living, Charles Wilfrid b. 1970, Joanna Mary Ursula b. 1972,—Richard Norton, b. 1946,—Alice Elizabeth, b. 1936,—Serena Jane, b. 1939,—Susan Virginia, b. 1943. *Residence,*—Dunstan Lodge, Letcombe Regis, Wantage, Berks.

WIDOW LIVING OF SON OF FOURTH EARL.

Barbara Elisabeth (*Lady Hogg*), younger dau. of the late Capt. Arden Franklyn, of New Place, Shedfield, Hants.: m. 1st, 1936, Brigadier Viscount Garmoyle, D.S.O., late Rifle Brig., who d. (killed in action during European War) 1942; 2ndly, 1948, Sir John Nicholson Hogg, T.D., of The Red House, Shedfield, Southampton, and 11, Melton Court S.W.7 [see Hogg, Bt., colls.].

COLLATERAL BRANCH LIVING.

Issue of the late Hon. Douglas Halyburton Cairns, 5th son of 1st Earl, b. 1867, d. 1936: m. 1908, Lady Constance Anne Montagu-Douglas-Scott, who d. 1970, da. of 6th Duke of Buccleuch:—

Hugh William, M.C., b. 1911; Lieut.-Col late Cameron Highlanders; European War 1939-45 (wounded, M C.): m. 1939, Diana Soames, and has issue living, Peter Granville, b. 1940,—Francis John Hugh, b. 1942,—Celia Helen, b. 1944: m. 1968, David William Barclay, of Higham, Bury St. Edmunds. *Residence,*—Whitelee, St. Boswells, Roxburghshire.——Helen Christina (*Hon. Mrs. Andrew C. Campbell*), b. 1909: m. 1935, Maj. the Hon. Andrew Charles Campbell, formerly Cameron Highlanders [see E. Cawdor]. *Residence,*—Chapelhead, Avoch, Ross-shire.

PREDECESSORS.—[1] *Rt. Hon. Sir* HUGH MACCALMONT CAIRNS, *D.C.L., LL.D.*, 2nd son of the late William Cairns, of Cultra, co. Down; b. 1819; sat as M.P. for Belfast (C) 1852-66; was Solicitor, Gen. 1858-59, Attorney-Gen. 1866, a Lord Justice of Appeal 1866-68, and Lord High Chancellor 1868 and 1874-80; cr. *Baron Cairns*, of Garmoyle, co. Antrim (peerage of United Kingdom) 1867, and *Viscount Garmoyle* and *Earl Cairns* (peerage of United Kingdom) 1878: m. 1856, Mary Harriet, who d. 1919, dau. of the late John McNeile, of Parkmount, co. Antrim; d. 1885; s. by his son [2] ARTHUR WILLIAM, 2nd Earl, b. 1861: m. 1887, Olivia Elizabeth, O.B E., who d. 1951 (having m. 2ndly, 1899, Major Roger Cyril Hans Sloane Stanley, who d. 1944), dau. of the late Alexander Augustus Berens, of

Castlemead, Windsor; *d.* 1890; *s.* by his brother [3] HERBERT JOHN, 3rd Earl; *b.* 1863; *d.* 1905; *s.* by his brother [4] WILFRID DALLAS, *C.M.G.*, 4th Earl; *b.* 1865; sometime Capt. Rifle Brig. and Lieut.-Col. Comdg. London Rifle Brig.; S. Africa 1902, European War 1914-19 (C.M.G.): *m.* 1894, Olive, who *d.* 1952, dau. of the late J. P. Cobbold, M.P., of The Cliffe, Ipswich; *d.* 1946; *s.* by his son [5] DAVID CHARLES, 5th Earl and present peer; also Viscount Garmoyle, and Baron Cairns.

CAITHNESS, EARL OF. (Sinclair.) [Earl S. 1455, Bt. S. 1631.]

MALCOLM IAN SINCLAIR, 20th Earl and 15th Baronet; *b.* Nov. 3rd, 1948; *s.* 1965; ed. at Marlborough, and Roy. Agric. Coll., Cirencester; ARICS: *m.* 1975, Diana Caroline, da. of Maj. Richard Lovel Coke, DSO, MC [see E. Leicester, colls.]

Arms,—Quarterly; 1st azure, a lymphad at anchor or, flagged gules sails furled argent oars erect in saltire, within a double tressure flory of the second, *Earldom of Orkney;* 2nd and 3rd or, a lion rampant gules armed and langued azure, *Sparr-Nithsdale;* 4th azure, a three-masted ship or, flagged gules under sail argent, *Earldom of Caithness;* over all dividing the quarters a cross engrailed and countercharged argent and sable, *Sinclair.* Crest,—A cock proper armed and beaked or. Supporters,—Two griffins gules wings elevated, armed beaked and winged or.

Seat,—Girnigoe Castle, Caithness. *Residence,* —Hampton Court Palace, E. Molesey, Surrey.

HALF-SISTERS LIVING.

Lady Jean Elizabeth, *b.* 1936: *m.* 1961, David Peere Williams-Freeman, of Glendean Trout Hatcheries, Nottingham Rd., Natal, and has issue living, Andrew Frederick Peere, *b.* 1962,—Juliet Margaret, *b.* 1964,—Teresa Jean, *b.* 1966,—Kim Jannette (twin), *b.* 1966.

Lady Margaret Nicola, *b.* 1937: *m.* 1959, Capt. David Colin Kirkwood Brown, late Gordon Highlanders, of 38, Settrington Rd., SW6, and has issue living, Nicola Jane Kirkwood, *b.* 1960,—Olivia Grizel Kirkwood, *b.* 1962.

Lady Fiona Catharine, *b.* 1941: *m.* 1969, Capt. Michael Stephen Whitfield, R. Scots Dragoon Gds. [see Renshaw, Bt.].

SISTER LIVING.

Lady Bridget Sarah, *b.* 1947.

AUNTS LIVING. (Raised to the rank of an Earl's daughters 1943.

Lady (Margaret) Alison, *b.* 1910. *Residence,*—Wych Elm Kennington, Oxford.
Lady (Euphemia) Meredith, *b.* 1915. *Residence,*—King John's Thorn, Hethel, Norwich.

DAUGHTERS LIVING OF EIGHTEENTH EARL.

Lady Lucy BUCHAN, *b.* 1902 : *m.* 1928, Sir Thomas Innes of Learney, G.C.V.O., LL.D., F.S.A. (Scot.) who *d.* 1971, [see Innes, Bt., cr. 1628, colls.]. *Residence,*—The Laigh Riggs, Torphins, Aberdeen shire.

Lady Augusta Lilian BUCHAN, *M.B.E.*, *b.* 1910; formerly Food Advice Organizer, W. of Scotland Div., Min. of Food ; M.B.E. (Civil) 1943. *Residence,*—8, Eton Terrace, Edinburgh.

WIDOW LIVING OF NINETEENTH EARL.

(MADELEINE) GABRIELLE (*Gabrielle, Countess of Caithness*) (Hampton Court Palace, E. Molesey, Surrey). da. of Herman Edward de Pury, and widow of Capt. George Wareing Drewry Ormerod, RA : *m.* 1946, as his 2nd wife, the 19th Earl, who *d.* 1965.

COLLATERAL BRANCH LIVING.

Descendants of the late James Sinclair (grandson of the late Alexander Sinclair, youngest son of the Hon. George Sinclair. 3rd son of 4th Earl). who was cr. a Baronet 1704, of whom *Sir* JOHN ROLLO NORMAN BLAIR SINCLAIR, 9th Bt., is *h.p.* to the Earldom.

PREDECESSORS.—*Sir* William Sinclair, of Roslin, sat in the Scottish Parliament at Scone 1283-4; his great-grandson, *Sir* Henry Sinclair, was admitted to be Earl of Orkney in 1379, by Hakon VIth King of Norway, and his grandson [1] WILLIAM, 3rd Earl of Orkney, and Lord High Chancellor of Scotland, was cr. *Earl of Caithness* (peerage of Scotland) 1455, and styled Earl of Orkney and Caithness; James III. having acquired the islands of Orkney in marriage with Margaret of Denmark, the Earl surrendered to the king the Earldom of Orkney in 1471 ; passing over his el. son (ancestor of the Lords Sinclair), was *s.* by his 2nd son [2] WILLIAM 2nd Earl, slain at Flodden 1513 ; *s.* by his son [3] JOHN, 3rd Earl; killed 1529 in attempting to take possession of the Orkneys, to which he asserted a right; *s.* by his grandson [4] GEORGE, 4th Earl, who resigned his Earldom to James V., who in 1545 granted a charter thereof to John, the Earl's heir-apparent, with remainder to his heirs male and assigns, whom failing to his father's heirs male whatever; *d.* 1582; *s.* by his grandson [5] GEORGE, 5th Earl; resigned Earldom and obtained a novodamus 1592 with remainder to his el. son William (subsequently known as *Lord Berriedale*) and his heirs male and assigns whatsoever; in 1606 received charter of lands forming Barony of Berriedale; *d.* 1643; *s.* by his great-grandson [6] GEORGE, 6th Earl; being heavily indebted to Sir John Campbell, 5th Bt., of Glenorchy, he assigned his estates and " Earldom of Caithness" (as held under a charter of apprizing) to that gentleman; *d.* 1676, and Sir John Campbell (ante) was cr Earl of Caithness 1677, which honour he resigned 1681 (see E. Breadalbane), the apprizing and assignation carrying only the land of the Earldom, whilst the honours then passed to the rightful heir [7] GEORGE, 7th Earl, son of Francis (of Northfield), 2nd son of 5th Earl; *d.s.p.* 1698; *s.* by his kinsman [8] JOHN, 8th Earl, lineal descendant of 4th Earl; *d.* 1706; *s.* by his son [9] ALEXANDER, 9th Earl; *d.* 1765; *s.* by his kinsman [10] WILLIAM, 10th Earl, heir male of Sir John, grandson of 4th Earl; *d.* 1779; *s.* by his son [11] JOHN, 11th Earl; *d.* 1789; *s.* by his kinsman [12] Sir JAMES Sinclair (7th Bt., cr. 1631, of Canisbay), 12th Earl, heir male of George, of Mey, youngest son of 4th Earl; Lord-Lieut. of Caithness, a Representative Peer, and Postmaster-Gen. of Scotland; *d.* 1823; *s.* by his son [13] ALEXANDER, 13th Earl; Lord-Lieut. of Caithness; *d.* 1855; *s.* by his son [14] JAMES, *F.R.S.,* 14th Earl, *b.* 1821; Lord-Lieut. and Vice-Adm. of Caithness, and Lord-in-Waiting to H.M. Queen Victoria 1856 and 1859-66; cr. *Baron Barrogill* (peerage of United Kingdom) 1866: *m.* 1st, 1847, Louisa Georgiana, who *d.* 1870, dau. of Sir George Richard Philips, Bt.; 2ndly, 1872, Marie, who *d.* 1895 (having been cr. in her own right Duchess de Pomár by Pope Leo XIII. in 1879), dau. of Don Antonio José de Mariategui, of Santa Catalina Macuriges, and widow of Gen. the Count de Pomár; *d.* 1881; *s.* by his son [15] GEORGE PHILIPS ALEXANDER, 15th Earl, *b.* 1858; Lord-Lieut. of Caithness; *d.* 1889, the title remaining dormant until 1890, when the nearest heir male of the 15th Earl was adjudged to be [16] JAMES AUGUSTUS (son of Lt.-Col. John Sutherland Sinclair, R.A., a descendant of Robert Sinclair, of Durran, younger son of Sir James Sinclair, 1st Bt., of Mey), 16th Earl, *b.* 1827: *m.* 1855, Janet, dau. of Roderick Macleod, M.D., of London; *d.* 1891; *s.* by his el. son [17] JOHN SUTHERLAND, 17th Earl, *b.* 1857; *d.* 1914; *s.* by his brother [18] NORMAN MACLEOD, *C.B.E.,* 18th Earl, *b.* 1862; admitted a Solicitor 1887; a Representative Peer for Scotland 1918-29; Lieut.-Col. late Gordon Highlanders [T.A.); assumed 1911, the surname and arms of Buchan in lieu of his patronymic: *m.* 1893, Lilian, who *d.* 1933, dau. of the late Higford Higford, of 23, Eaton Place, SW; *d.* 1947; *s.* by his nephew [19] JAMES RODERICK, *CVO, CBE, DSO* (son of the late Rev. the Hon. Charles Augustus Sinclair, 3rd son of 16th Earl), 19th Earl *b.* 1906; a Representative Peer for Scotland 1950-63; Brig. and Col. Gordon Highlanders; Comdg. Ceylon Army 1949-52: *m.* 1st, 1933, Grizel Margaret, who *d.* 1943, da. of Sir George Miller-Cunningham, KBE, CB; 2ndly, 1946, Madeleine Gabrielle, da. of Herman Edward de Pury, and widow of Capt. George Wareing Drewry Ormerod, RA; *d.* 1965; *s.* by his only son [20] MALCOLM IAN, 20th Earl and present peer; also Lord Berriedale.

CALDECOTE, VISCOUNT. (Inskip.) [Viscount U.K. 1939.]

ROBERT ANDREW INSKIP, *D.S.C.,* 2nd Viscount; *b.* Oct. 8th, 1917; *s.* 1947; ed. at Eton (Fellow), and at King's Coll., Camb. (MA, Fellow 1948-55); MRINA, a FIMechE, a FIEE, Pres. of Dean Close Sch., a Gov. of St. Lawrence Coll.; 1939-45 War as Lt.-Cdr. RNVR; a Member of House of Laity, Church Assembly 1949-55, and of UK delegation to UN Assembly 1952; Vice-Pres. of Eurospace 1961-68, Pres. of Soc. of British Aerospace Cos. 1965-66, of AICMA 1966-68, and of Parl. and Scientific Cttee. 1966-69; Exec. Dir. of English Electric Co. 1955-69, and of British Aircraft Corpn. 1960-66; Chm. of EDC for Movements of Exports 1965-71, and of Export Council for Europe 1970-71; Exec. Dir. Delta Metal Co. since 1969, Dir. Consolidated Goldfields, Ltd. since 1969, and of Lloyds Bank since 1974, a Member of Review Board for Govt. Contracts since 1969 (Chm. 1972), and Chm. of Council since 1972: *m.* 1942, Jean Hamilla, da. of the late Rear-Adm. Hugh Dundas Hamilton, of Limes Haddenham, Bucks., and has issue.

Arms,—Per chevron azure and argent in chief two crosses pattée or and in base an eagle displayed of the first. Crest,—Upon the battlements of a tower a grouse's leg erased proper. Supporters,—*Dexter,* a talbot; *sinister,* a pegasus proper; each charged on the shoulder with a garb or.

Residence,—Orchard Cottage, South Harting, Petersfield, Hants. *Clubs,*—Pratt's, Royal Ocean Racing, Boodle's, Royal Yacht Squadron.

SON LIVING.

Hon. PIERS JAMES HAMPDEN, *b.* May 20th, 1947; ed. at Eton: *m.* 1970, Susan Bridget, da. of the late W. P. Mellen, of Hill Farm, Gt. Sampford, Essex.

DAUGHTERS LIVING.

Hon. Serena Helen Christian, *b.* 1943: *m.* 1965, John Andrew Brodie Armit, of 98, St. Paul's Rd., N1, and has issue living, Jerome Nathan, *b.* 1971,—Vashti Imogen, *b.* 1969.

Hon. Antonia Jane Hamilla, *b.* 1952: *m.* 1972, Piers Rowlandson, and has issue living, Titus, *b.* 1973.

PREDECESSOR.—[1] *Rt. Hon.* Sir THOMAS WALKER HOBART Inskip, *C.B.E.,* son of the late James Inskip, of Clifton Park House, Bristol; *b.* 1876; was Chancellor of Diocese of Truro 1920-22, Solicitor-Gen. Oct. 1922 to Jan. 1924 and Nov. 1924 to March 1928, Attorney-Gen. March 1928 to June 1929, Solicitor-Gen. in National Govt. Sept. 1931 to Jan. 1932, again Attorney-Gen. Jan. 1932 to March 1936, Min. for Co-ordination of Defence March 1936 to Jan. 1939, Sec. of State for Dominion Affairs Jan. to Sept. 1939, Lord High Chancellor Sept. 1939 to May 1940, again Sec. of State for Dominion Affairs May to Oct. 1940, and Lord Ch. Justice of England 1940-46; M.P. for Central Div. of Bristol 1918-29 and for Fareham Div. of Hampshire 1931-9; cr. *Viscount Caldecote,* of Bristol, co. Gloucester (peerage of United Kingdom) 1939: *m.* 1914, Lady Augusta Helen Elizabeth, who *d.* 1967, da. of 7th Earl of Glasgow, and widow of Charles Lindsay Orr-Ewing, MP; *d.* 1947; *s.* by his son [2] ROBERT ANDREW, 2nd Viscount and present peer.

Calder, see Baron Ritchie-Calder.

CALEDON, EARL OF. (Alexander.) [Earl I. 1800.]

By sea and by land.

Denis James Alexander, 6th Earl; b. Nov. 10th, 1920; s. 1968; Maj. Irish Gds. and Ulster Defence Regt.: m. 1st, 1943 (m. diss. 1948), Ghislaine, only da. of Cornelius Dresselhuys, of Long Island, USA; 2ndly, 1952, Baroness Anne, who d. 1963, da. of the late Baron Nicolai de Graevenitz; 3rdly, 1964, Marie Elisabeth, da. of the late Maj. Richard Burton Allen, and formerly wife of Maj. the Hon. Ian Maxwell Erskine, and has issue by 1st and 2nd m.

Arms,—Per pale argent and sable, a chevron, and in base a crescent counterchanged; on a canton azure, a harp or, stringed argent. Crest,—A dexter arm embowed in armour, the hand holding a sword proper. Supporters,—Dexter, a mermaid with a mirror in her right hand proper; sinister, an elephant argent.

Seat,—Caledon Castle, co. Tyrone.

SON LIVING. (By 2nd m.)
NICHOLAS JAMES (Viscount Alexander), b. May 6th, 1955.

DAUGHTERS LIVING. (By 1st m.)
Lady Tana Marie, b. 1945: m. 1973, Paul Everard Justus Focke.
(By 2nd m.)
Lady Elizabeth Jane, b. 1962.

WIDOW LIVING OF SON OF FOURTH EARL.
Hon. Ada Kate (Rathmore Park, Tullow, co. Carlow), da. of the late Hon. Richard Eustace Bellew and widow of Charles Barry Domvile [see B. Bellew]: m. 1937, as his 2nd wife, Lt.-Col. the Hon. Herbrand Charles Alexander, DSO, who d. 1965.

MOTHER LIVING
(Millicent) Valla, (The Dairy, Calsdon Castle, co. Tyrone), da. of Sir Henry Bayly Meredyth, 5th Bt. (ext.): m. 1st, 1919, Lt.-Col. the Hon. Herbrand Charles Alexander, DSO, who d. 1965, having obtained a divorce 1927; 2ndly, 1927, Richard Allan; 3rd, 1939 (m. diss. 1946), Lt.-Col. Guy Andrew Heinckey Buxton, who d. 1948.

COLLATERAL BRANCHES LIVING.
Issue of the late Harold Rupert Leofric George Alexander (Earl Alexander of Tunis), KG, GCB, OM, GCMG, CSI, DSO, MC, P.C. 3rd son of 4th Earl, b. 1891, d. 1969 [see that title.]

Issue of the late Col. the Hon. William Sigismund Patrick Alexander, DSO, yst. son of 4th Earl, b. 1895, d. 1972: m. 1934, Jane Hermione, who d. 1967, da. of the late Cdr. Bernard Buxton, DSO, [Buxton, Bt., colls.]:—
Allistair Patrick Lindsay (2665, Laguna St., San Francisco, Cal. 94123, USA), b. 1935; ed. at Eton; late Lt. I.G.: m. 1961, Evenlyn, da. of Massimimo Forte, of 28, Via San Sebastiano, Rome, and has issue living, Simone Eugenia, b. 1962.——Desmond Charles Bernard, b. 1938; ed. at Eton, Univ. of British Columbia (B. Com.), and Lancaster Univ. (MA).——Annabella Elizabeth Hero (Gobions House Farm, Mowsley, Rugby), b. 1943.

Granddaughter of the late Col. the Hon. Walter Philip Alexander, 2nd son of 3rd Earl :—
Issue of the late Capt. Philip Sylvester Alexander, 8th Hussars, b. 1883, d. 1953: m. 1926, Violet (now of Kilmorna, Lismore, co. Waterford), dau. of the late H. Hendrick Aylmer, of Kerdiffstown, co. Kildare :—
Patricia Margaret (Lady Gray), b. 1929: m. 1959, the 22nd Lord Gray. Residence,—Airds Bay House, Taynuilt, Argyll.

Grandchildren of Lt.-Col. the Hon. Charles Alexander (infra):—
Issue of the late Capt. Conn Alexander, b. 1883, d. 1970: m. 1st, 1906, Gladys Constance, who d. 1944, da. of the late Thomas Wrigley Grimshaw, CB; 2ndly, 1944, Doris Minnie (19, Normandy Lane, E. Preston, Sussex), da. of the late Robert Pacey, of Hove:—
(By 1st m.) James Conn (Salisbury, Rhodesia), b. 1907: m. 1939, Beatrice Mary, da. of the late George Herbert Stringer, of 41, Lexden Rd., Colchester, Essex.——Mona (Ayesha Castle, Killiney, co. Dublin), b. 1909: m. 1939, Col. Richard Michael Aylmer, who d. 1975, and has issue living, Justin Michael, b. 1940; ed. at Wellington,—Dennis Fenton, b. 1942; ed. at Wellington.——Marjorie (The Manor House, Rathlin I., co. Antrim), b. 1912: m. 1931, Brig. Richard Francis O'Donnell Gage, OBE, MC, who d. 1973, and has issue living, Ezekiel Conn, b. 1933; ed. at Wellington; Maj. RA,—Patrick Richard, b. 1938; ed. at Wellington; Lt.-Cdr. RN.

Issue of the late Lieut.-Col. the Hon. Charles Alexander, 3rd son of 3rd Earl, b. 1854; d. 1909: m. 1880, Catherine, who d. 1946, dau. of Charles Stayner, of Halifax, Nova Scotia :—
Cethlyn Sarah Mohred (RR1, Hopewell, Pictou Co., Nova Scotia), b. 1901: m. 1925, Cdr. Bredin Delap, RN (ret.), who d. 1970, and has issue living, Etain Evelyn Catherine, b. 1926: m. 1951, Robert E. Thompson, and has issue living, Robert Bredin b. 1953, Jana Joy b. 1964,—Eirene Macha, b. 1938: m. 1961, Elmer M. Mackay (MP, Nova Scotia), and has issue living, Peter Gordon b. 1965, Andrew Bredin b. 1971, Cethlyn Laura b. 1963, Mary Louise b. 1968.

PREDECESSORS.—[1] James Alexander (of whose family the Alexanders of Milford, co. Carlow, are the senior branch), having filled several important offices in India, was cr. Baron Caledon, of Caledon, co. Tyrone (peerage of Ireland) 1790, Viscount Caledon (peerage of Ireland) 1797, and Earl of Caledon (peerage of Ireland) 1800; d. 1802; s. by his son [2] Du Pre, KP, 2nd Earl; first Gov. of Cape of Good Hope; a Representative Peer; d. 1839; s. by his son [3] James Du Pre, 3rd Earl, b. 1812; a Representative Peer, Capt. Coldstream Gds., and Col. of Tyrone Militia: m. 1845, Lady Jane Frederica Harriot Mary Grimston, VA, who d. 1888, 4th da. of 1st Earl of Veralam; d. 1855; s. by his son [4] James, KP, 4th Earl, b. 1846; a Representative Peer for Ireland: m. 1884, Lady Elizabeth Toler, who d. 1939, da. of 3rd Earl of Norbury; d. 1898; s. by his el. son [5] Erik James Desmond, 5th Earl; b. 1885, d. 1968; s. by his nephew [6] Denis James (son of Lt.-Col. the Hon. Herbrand Charles Alexander, DSO, who d. 1965), 6th Earl and present peer; also Viscount Caledon, and Baron Caledon.

Calne and Calstone, Viscount, grandson of Marquess of Lansdowne.

CALTHORPE, BARON. (Gough-Calthorpe.) [Baron G.B. 1796, Bt. G.B. 1728.]

[Title pronounced "**Callthorpe**," name pronounced "**Goff-Callthorpe.**"]

PETER WALDO SOMERSET GOUGH-CALTHORPE, 10th Baron, and 11th Baronet; *b.* July 13th, 1927; *s.* 1945; ed. at Stowe; formerly Lieut. Welsh Guards: *m.* 1956 (m. diss. 1971), Saranne Francis, only da. of J. H. Alexander, of co. Dublin.

Arms,—Quarterly: 1st and 4th checky, or and azure a fesse ermine, *Calthorpe;* 2nd and 3rd gules, on a fesse argent, between three boars' heads couped or, a lion passant azure, *Gough.* **Crests,**—1st, a boar's head couped at the neck azure, *Calthorpe;* 2nd, a boar's head couped argent, pierced through the cheek with a broken spear, *Gough.* **Supporters,**—Two wild men, wreathed about the temples and loins with oak, and each holding in his exterior hand a club erect or.

Address,—c/o MV Fantôme de Mer, Guernsey.

The same way by different steps.

MOTHER LIVING.
(Rose Mary) Dorothy, da. of the late Leveson William Vernon-Harcourt [see B. Vernon, colls.]: *m.* 1st, 1922, the Hon. Frederick Somerset Gough-Calthorpe, who *d.* 1935; 2ndly, 1949, Lt.-Col. Guy Alexander Ingram Dury, MC, late Grenadier Guards. *Residence,*—Siggswood, Waldron, E. Sussex.

PREDECESSORS.—[1] *Sir* Henry Gough, M.P. for Totnes 1732, and for Bramber; cr. a *Baronet* 1728; *d.* 1774; *s.* by his son [2] *Sir* Henry, 2nd Bt.; in 1788 inherited the Elvetham estates of his uncle, Sir Henry Calthorpe, K.B., and assumed by Roy. licence the additional sur-name of Calthorpe; sat as M.P. for Bramber 1774-90; cr. *Baron Calthorpe,* of Calthorpe, co. Norfolk (peerage of Great Britain) 1796; *d.* 1798; *s.* by his el. son [3] CHARLES, 2nd Baron, *d.* 1807; *s.* by his brother [4] GEORGE, 3rd Baron; *d.* 1851; *s.* by his brother [5] FREDERICK, 4th Baron; *b.* 1790; assumed for himself in 1845 the name of Gough only: *m.* 1823, Lady Charlotte Sophia Somerset, who *d.* 1865, el. dau. of 6th Duke of Beaufort; *d.* 1868; *s.* by his el. son [6] FREDERICK HENRY WILLIAM, 5th Baron, *b.* 1826; M.P for E. Worcester-shire (*L*) 1859-68; *d.* unm. 1893; *s.* by his brother [7] AUGUSTUS CHOLMONDELEY, 6th Baron, *b.* 1829: *m.* 1869, Maud Augusta Louisa, who *d.* 1925. youngest dau. of the late Col. the Hon. Octavius Duncombe: *d.* 1910: *s.* by his brother [8] SOMERSET JOHN, K.C.B., 7th Baron, *b.* 1831; Lieut.-Gen. in the Army: *m.* 1862, Eliza Maria, who *d.* 1919, only child of Capt. Frederick Chamier, R.N., and widow of Capt. Frederick Crewe; *d.* 1912; *s.* by his el. son [9] SOMERSET FREDERICK, 8th Baron; *b.* 1862: *m.* 1891, Mary, who *d.* 1940, dau. of the late Ogden Hoffman Burrows, of Newport, Rhode Island, U.S.A.; *d.* 1940; *s.* by his grandson [10] RONALD ARTHUR SOMERSET (son of the late Hon. Frederick Somerset Gough-Calthorpe, only son of 8th Baron), 9th Baron, *b.* 1924; Flying Officer R.A.F.; *d.* (on active ser.) 1945; *s.* by his brother [11] PETER WALDO SOMERSET, 10th Baron and present peer.

CALVERLEY, BARON. (Muff.) [Baron U.K. 1945.]

CHARLES RODNEY MUFF, 3rd Baron *b.* Oct. 2nd, 1946; *s.* 1971; ed. at Moravian Fulneck Sch. for Boys, Fulneck, Pudsey: *m.* 1972, Barbara Ann, da. of Jonathan Brown.

Arms,—Azure, within two barrulets wavy argent between in chief a rose of the second barbed and seeded proper, and in base a fleece or, three ducal coronets of the last. **Crest,**—In front of two miners' picks in saltire a miner's safety lamp all proper. **Supporters,**—On either side a calf proper.

Residence,—10, Briarwood Grove, Wibsey, Bradford, 6.

BROTHER LIVING.
Hon. PETER RAYMOND, *b.* Aug. 12th, 1953.

WIDOW LIVING OF SECOND BARON.
MARY (*Mary Baroness Calverley*), da. of Arthur Farrar, of Halifax: *m.* 1940 the 2nd Baron, who *d.* 1971.

Labour conquers all.

PREDECESSORS.—[1] GEORGE Muff, son of the late George Muff, miner, of Bradford; *b.* 1877; sat as M.P. for E. Div. of Kingston-upon-Hull (*Lab.*) 1929-31, and 1935-45; cr. *Baron Calverley,* of City of Bradford, W. Riding of Yorkshire (peerage of United Kingdom) 1945: *m.* 1909, Ellen Eliza, who *d.* 1965, el. da. of the late Charles W. Orford, of Bath: *d.* 1955: *s.* by his only son [2] GEORGE RAYMOND ORFORD, 2nd Baron *b.* 1914: *m.* 1940, Mary, da. of Arthur Farrar, of Halifax; *d.* 1971; *s.* by his el. son [3] CHARLES RODNEY, 3rd Baron and present peer.

CAMBRIDGE, MARQUESS OF. (Cambridge.) [Marquess U.K. 1917.]

GEORGE FRANCIS HUGH CAMBRIDGE, *G.C.V.O.*, 2nd Marquess; *b.* Oct. 11th, 1895: *s.* 1927; ed. at Eton, and at Magdalen Coll., Oxford; Roy. Trustee of British Museum 1947-73; Lt. 1st Life Gds. Reserve Regt. 1916-19, Lt. Shropshire Yeo. 1921, Capt. 16th Bn. London Regt. 1929-32, and Capt. RASC (TA) 1939; an ADC on Personal Staff 1918-19; KCVO 1927, GCVO 1935: *m.* 1923, Dorothy Isabel Westenra, da. of the late Capt. the Hon. Osmond William Toone Westenra Hastings [see E. Huntingdon, colls.], and has issue.

Fidens et fidelis.
Trusting and faithful.

Arms,—Quarterly-quartered, 1st grand quarter, 1 and 4 England, 2 Scotland, 3 Ireland, in chief a label of three points argent, the centre point charged with a cross of St. George gules, and each of the other points with two hearts in pale also gules: upon an escutcheon of pretence the arms of *Hanover*, gules, two lions passant guardant in pale or, impaling or semée of hearts gules a lion rampant azure, on a point in point gules a horse courant; 2nd and 3rd grand quarters, party per pale, on the dexter side three stags attires fesseways in pale the points of each attire to the sinister sable, on the sinister side three lions passant in pale sable, langued gules, the dexter forepaws of the last, over all an inescutcheon of the arms of the *Duchy of Teck*, paly bendy sable and or. Crest,—A dog's head paly bendy sinister sable and argent. Supporters,—*Dexter*, a lion sable, the paws flayed to the shoulder gules; *sinister*, a stag proper.

Residence,—The Old House, Little Abington, Cambridgeshire.

DAUGHTER LIVING.

Lady Mary Ilona Margaret, *b.* 1924: *m.* 1950, Peter Whitley, only son of Sir Norman Henry Pownall Whitley, M.C., and has issue living, Charles Francis Peter, *b.* 1961,—Sarah Elizabeth, *b.* 1954. *Residence*,—Penharbour, Hurstpierpoint, Sussex.

SISTER LIVING.

Lady (Victoria Constance) Mary (*Duchess of Beaufort*), *b.* 1897; is a C.St.J.: *m.* 1923, the 10th Duke of Beaufort. *Residence*,—Badminton, Gloucestershire.

PREDECESSOR.—[1] ADOLPHUS CHARLES ALEXANDER ALBERT EDWARD GEORGE PHILIP LOUIS LADISLAUS Cambridge, *G.C.B.*, *G.C.V.O.*, *C.M.G.*, son of H.H. the late Francis Paul Charles Louis Alexander, Duke of Teck, G.C.B., G.C.V.O., by H.R.H. the late Princess Mary Adelaide Wilhelmina Elizabeth, *CI*, *RRC*, da. of 1st Duke of Cambridge, son of King George III; *b.* 1868; Lt.-Col. (ret.), sometime Comdg. 1st Life Guards; a Personal ADC to HM; appointed Constable and Gov. of Windsor Castle 1914; S. Africa 1899-1900, 1914-18 War Comdg. a Regt. of Household Cav. and as Mil. Sec. Gen. Headquarters, with rank of Brig.-Gen.; Mil. Attaché at Vienna 1904-09; granted style of "Highness" June 1911 (use discontinued by Roy. Warrant, at H.M.'s request, July 1917); assumed by Roy. Warrant July 1917 the surname of Cambridge; cr. *Viscount Northallerton*, in the co. of York, *Earl of Eltham*, and *Marquess of Cambridge* (peerage of United Kingdom) July 17th, 1917: *m.* 1894, Lady Margaret Grosvenor, who *d.* 1929, dau. of 1st Duke of Westminster; *d.* 1927; *s.* by his el. son [2] GEORGE FRANCIS HUGH, 2nd Marquess and present peer; also Earl of Eltham, and Viscount Northallerton.

CAMDEN, MARQUESS. (Pratt.) [Marquess U.K. 1812.]

JOHN CHARLES HENRY PRATT, 5th Marquess; *b.* April 12th, 1899; *s.* 1943; ed. at Eton; Major Reserve of Officers late Scots Guards, Hon. Col. 516th Light Anti-Aircraft Regt. R.A., a D.L. and a J.P. for Kent, a Younger Brother of Trin. House, a Member of Fedn. Internationale des Automobiles, Patron of Coll. of Automobile and Aeronautical Training, Chelsea, Joint Patron of Roy. Tunbridge Wells Civic Assocn., Pres. of Tonbridge Area of League of Mercy, of Tunbridge Wells Area of So. for the Prevention of Cruelty to Animals, of Tunbridge Wells Amateur Dramatic and Operatic So., and of Asso. of Men of Kent and Kentish Men, Pres. of Tunbridge Wells Branch, and a Vice-Pres. and Member of Committee of Management of Roy. National Life-boat Institution, a Member of Council of S.-E. Cos. Agricul-

The judgment of my peers, or the law of the land.

tural So. (Pres. 1948), Pres. of St. Pancras Almshouses, Vice-Pres. of Marine Motoring Asso., of Tonbridge Fat Stock Show Asso., and of Lamberhurst Gdns. Asso., a Fellow of Institute of Directors, a Director of Roy. Automobile Club

Buildings Co., Ltd., of Roy. Automobile Golf and Country Club, Ltd., Roy. Automobile Travel Ser. Ltd., and of Bayard Cars, Ltd., of Great Portland Street, W.1., Chm. of Segrave Trophy Awarding Committee and Butlin Trophy for World's Unlimited Water Speed Record, and a Member of Roy. Agricultural So. of England, and of Council of Boy Scouts Asso. for Kent ; late Pres. of Boys' Convalescent Home, Hawkenbury, Tunbridge Wells ; an A.D.C. to Gen. Officer Comdg. London Dist. 1920-24 ; European War 1939-45 Comdg. 45th Battery (which he raised), 16th Light Anti-Aircraft Regt., R.A. and with Scots Guards ; a Gold Staff Officer at Coronation of King George VI.: *m.* 1st, 1920, Marjorie Minna, DBE, who obtained a divorce 1941, only child of the late Col. Atherton Edward Jenkins, of Wherwell Priory, Andover; 2ndly, 1942, Averil (HALLETT), el. da. of the late Col. Henry Sidney John Streatfeild, DSO [E. Lichfield], and has issue by 1st and 2nd marriages.

Arms,—Quarterly : 1st and 4th sable, on a fesse between three elephants' heads erased argent as many mullets of the field, *Pratt ;* 2nd and 3rd sable, a chevron between three spears' heads argent, the points embrued, *Jeffreys.* Crests,—1st, an elephant's head erased argent ; 2nd, a dragon's head erased vert, holding in the mouth a sinister hand couped at the wrist gules, and about the neck a gold chain, and pendant therefrom a portcullis or. Supporters.—*Dexter,* a griffin sable ; beak and claws gules, gorged with a plain collar argent, charged with three mullets sable: *sinister,* a lion or, collared as the dexter.

Seat,—Bayham Abbey, Lamberhurst, Kent. *Town Residence,*—42, Belgrave Mews South, SW1. *Clubs,*—Turf, Royal Yacht Squadron (Vice-Commodore 1954-65, Guards', St. Jame's, Pratt's, Royal Automobile (Steward of Appeal and Senior Vice-Chm., 1949-52), Royal Aero, RAF Yacht, Royal Artillery Yacht, Household Brigade Yacht, Royal Motor Yacht (Rear-Adm.), House of Lords Yacht (Vice-Commodore), Royal Naval Sailing Assocn. (Hon. Member).

SONS LIVING. (*By 1st marriage.*)

DAVID GEORGE EDWARD HENRY (*Earl of Brecknock*), *b.* Aug. 13th, 1930 ; ed. at Eton ; late 2nd Lt. Scots Guards: *m.* 1961, Virginia Ann, only da. of the late Francis Harry Hume Finlaison, of Arklow Cottage, Windsor, Berks., and has issue:—

SONS LIVING,—James William John (*Viscount Bayham*), *b.* Dec. 11th, 1965.
Hon. Jonathan Bruce Charles, *b.* 1970.

DAUGHTER LIVING,—*Lady* Samantha Caroline, *b.* 1964.
Residence,—Lodsworth House, Lodsworth, Petworth, Sussex.

(*By 2nd marriage.*)
Lord Michael John Henry, *b.* 1946 ; ed. at Eton, and Balliol Coll., Oxford.

DAUGHTER LIVING. (*By 1st marriage.*)

Lady Mary Clementine, *b.* 1921; is a C.St.J.: *m.* 1st, 1940, Flight-Lieut. the Hon. (Herbert) Oswald Berry, who *d.* 1952 [see V. Kemsley]; 2ndly, 1953, (Shafto) Gerald Strachan Pawle. *Residence,*— Trehiven House, Madron, Penzance, Cornwall.

BROTHER LIVING.

Lord Roderic Arthur Nevill, *b.* 1915; ed. at Eton, and at Trin. Coll., Camb. (BA); Maj. late Life Guards and Chm. of Roderic Pratt Underwriting Agencies Ltd., a Dir. of Tennant Budd & Roderic Pratt Ltd., and Tennant Roderic Pratt (L & P) Ltd.; an underwriting member of Lloyds; 1939-45 War in Middle East, Italy, and Germany (wounded): *m.* 1945, Ursula Eva, el. da. of Capt. the Hon. Valentine Maurice Wyndham-Quin, RN [see E. Dunraven], and has issue living, Adrian John Charles, *b.* 1952,—Zara Elizabeth, *b.* 1955. *Residence,*—Saxonbury House, Frant, Tunbridge Wells. *Clubs,*—Buck's, Turf.

SISTERS LIVING.

Lady Irene Helen, *b.* 1906: *m.* 1st, 1926, the Hon. Archibald Edward Cubitt, who *d.* 1972, having obtained a divorce 1933 [see B. Ashcombe, colls.]; 2ndly, 1933, James Cameron Clark, of New Jersey, USA, who obtained a divorce (in USA) 1937; 3rdly, 1937, Charles Claud Jervis Crawfurd [Pigot, Bt.], and has issue living, (by 1st m.) [see B. Ashcombe], (by 3rd m.) Peter Roderic, Jervis *b.* 1938: *m.* 1964, Judith Marian, el. da. of E. W. Weatherby of Croughton Lodge, Brackley, and has issue living, John Roderic *b.* 1965.

Lady Fiona (*Fiona, Countess of Normanton*), *b.* 1911: *m.* 1st, 1931, Maj. Sir (John) Gerard Henry Fleetwood Fuller. 2nd Bt., Life Guards (retired), from whom she obtained a divorce 1944; 2ndly, 1944, the 5th Earl of Normanton, who *d.* 1967. *Residence,*—North End Park, Harbridge, Ringwood, Hants.

COLLATERAL BRANCH LIVING.

Issue of the late Lieut.-Col. Lord Charles Robert Pratt, 3rd son of 2nd Marquess, *b.* 1847, *d.* 1905: *m.* 1881, Florence Maria, who *d.* 1930, dau. of Major G. R. Stevenson, formerly of 7th Dragoon Guards:—

Ven. Ronald Arthur Frederick (twin), *b.* 1886; ed. at Tonbridge Sch., and at Gonville and Caius Coll., Camb. (BA 1909, MA 1913); late Chap. of Kent and Canterbury Hospital, Canterbury; formerly Archdeacon of Belize, British Honduras, and V. of St. Barnabas, Derby; sometime a temporary Chap. RN: *m.* 1925, Margaret, da. of George Elam, MD, formerly of 41, Wickham Rd., Beckenham, Kent. *Residence,*—173, Old Dover Rd., Canterbury.

PREDECESSORS.—[1] Sir CHARLES Pratt, Knt., MP for Downton, an eminent lawyer, was successively Attorney-Gen. and Ch. Justice of the Common Pleas; cr. *Baron Camden*, of Camden Place, co. Kent (peerage of Great Britain), 1765; appointed Lord High Chancellor 1766, and Lord Pres. of the Council 1784; cr. *Viscount Bayham* and *Earl Camden* (peerage of Great Britain) 1786; *d.* 1794; *s.* by his son [2] JOHN JEFFREYS, KG, 2nd Earl; successively MP, a Lord of the Treasury, a Lord of the Admiralty, Viceroy of Ireland, and Chancellor of Univ. of Camb.; cr. *Earl of Brecknock* and *Marquess Camden* (peerage of United Kingdom) 1812; *d.* 1840; *s.* by his son [3] GEORGE CHARLES, KG, 2nd Marquess; summoned to House of Lords 1835 as Baron Camden; *d.* 1866; *s.* by his son [4] JOHN CHARLES, 3rd Marquess; *b.* 1840; MP for Brecon 1866: *m.* 1866, Lady Clementine Augusta Spencer-Churchill, who *d.* 1886, da. of 6th Duke of Marlborough; *d.* 1872; *s.* by his son [5] JOHN CHARLES, *GCVO, TD,* 4th Marquess, *b.* 1872; late Major W. Kent Yeo. and Hon. Col. 58th (Kent) Brig. RA (TA); Lord-Lieut. for Kent 1905-43: *m.* 1898, Lady Joan Marion Nevill, *CBE,* who *d.* 1952, da. of 3rd Marquess of Abergavenny; *d.* 1943; *s.* by his son [6] JOHN CHARLES HENRY, 5th Marquess and present peer; also Earl Camden, Earl of Brecknock, Viscount Bayham, and Baron Camden.

CAMOYS, BARON. (Stonor.) [Baron E. 1383.]

(RALPH ROBERT WATTS) SHERMAN STONOR, 6th Baron; *b.* July 5th, 1913; *s.* 1968; Maj. (ret.) Oxford and Bucks. LI (TA); a DL for Oxon, and a patron of one living (but being a Roman Catholic cannot present) *m.* 1938, Mary Jeanne, da. of the late Capt. Herbert Marmaduke Joseph Stourton, OBE [see B. Mowbray, colls.], and has issue.

Arms,—Azure, two bars dancettée or, a chief argent **Crest,**—A falcon standing on a rock and regarding a projection of that rock argent, all semee of hurts, bezants, torteaux and pommeis, the rock tufted with grass vert and the falcon holding in his beak a ruby proper. **Supporters.**—*Dexter,* a lion rampant or; *sinister* a lion rampant sable.

Seat,—Stonor Park, Henley-on-Thames, Oxon.

SONS LIVING

Hon. RALPH THOMAS CAMPION GEORGE SHERMAN (Alston Court, Nayland, Suffolk), *b.* April 16th, 1940; ed. at Eton, and Balliol Coll., Oxford: *m.* 1966, Elisabeth Mary Hyde, da. of the late Sir William Stephen Hyde Parker, Bt. [see Parker, Bt., cr. 1681], and has issue living, Ralph William Robert Thomas *b.* 1974,—Alina Mary, *b.* 1967,—Emily Mary Julia, *b.* 1969,—Sophia Ulla, *b.* 1971.
Hon. John Edmund Robert (Oscott Coll., Sutton Coldfield, Warwicks.), *b.* 1946; ed. at Beaumont.

DAUGHTERS LIVING.

Hon. Julia Maria Cristina Mildred STONOR SAUNDERS (The Coach House, 70a, Grove Park Terr., W4). *b.* 1939; ed. at St. Mary's Convent, Ascot; assumed additional surname of Stonor 1972: *m.* 1963. Donald Robin Slomnicki Saunders, and has issue living, Alexander William Joseph Stonor, *b.* 1964,— Frances Hélène Jeanne Stonor, *b.* 1966.
Hon. Georgina Mary Hope (Flat 24, Elm Park Gdns., SW10) *b.* 1941; ed. at St. Mary's Convent, Ascot, and Reading Inst. of Tech.
Hon. Harriet Pauline Sophia, *b.* 1943: *m.* 1965, Jonathan Julian Cotterell, of 3, Clarendon Close, Hyde Park, W2, and has issue living, Edmund Julian Francis, *b.* 1967,—Rupert Sherman John, *b.* 1969,—Alice Ellinor Mary, *b.* 1966.

SISTERS LIVING.

Hon. (Pamela Sophia) Nadine, *b.* 1917: *m.* 1941. Lieut.-Col. Charles Donald Leslie Pepys, King's Own Yorkshire L.I. [see E. Cottenham, colls.]. *Residence,*—Brightling Place, Robertsbridge, Sussex.
Hon. (Mildred Sophia) Noreen, *b.* 1922: *m.* 1941, John R. Drexel, and has issue living, John Nicholas, *b.* 1945: *m.* 1969, Pamela, da. of Bernardo Rionda Braga,—Pamela Sandra Noreen, *b.* 1942: *m.* 1966, Bradford Hastings Walker, of 3412, Washington St., San Francisco, Cal. 94118, and has issue living, Andrew *b.* 1968, James Drexel *b.* 1971, Noreen Elizabeth Mildred, *b.* 1961. *Residence,*—Stonor Lodge, Bellevue Av., Newport, Rhode Island, USA.

COLLATERAL BRANCHES LIVING.

Issue of the late Major the Hon. Edward Maurice Stonor. 2nd son of 4th Baron, *b.* 1885, *d.* 1931: *m.* 1st, 1909, Bertha (from whom he obtained a divorce 1921), dau. of the late John Oliver; 2ndly, 1925, Florence Hilda, who *d.* 1965, dau. of the late Thomas W. Rothschild, of Pretoria:—

(By 1st marriage) Betty Joyce, *b.* 1910: *m.* 1938, Benjamin Rudolph Bonas, who *d.* 1965, and has issue living, Benjamin Reginald Francis Stonor (16 Hereford Sq., SW7), *b.* 1940: *m.* 1967, Jacqueline de Brabant, and has issue living, Charles Benjamin *b.* 1969, Oliver Henry *b.* 1971. *Residence,*— 5, Norfolk Rd., NW8 6HE.

Granddaughters of the late Charles Joseph Stonor (infra):—
Issue of the late Capt. Edmund Charles Joseph Stonor, *b.* 1866, *d.* 1929: *m.* 1896, Mary Louisa, who *d.* 1943, dau. of the late Thomas William Charles Riddell [E. Fingall]:—
Winefride Mary Angela (Vale Royal Hotel, Tunbridge Wells, Kent), *b.* 1897.

Issue of the late Oswald Francis Gerald Stonor, C.M.G., *b.* 1872: *d.* 1940: *m.* 1906, Florence Mary Josephine, who *d.* 1956, dau. of the late Edward Talbot Wolseley [Wolseley, Bt., cr. 1628, colls.]:—
Evelyn Mary, *b.* 1911: *m.* 1935, Com. Denis Hugh Bryan Barrett, D.S.C., R.N. [B. Kensington], and has issue living, Michael Patrick Denis, *b.* 1937: *m.* 1951, Kytia Buchs,—Bryan Nicholas, *b.* 1940: Lt. RN: *m.* 1964, Sally Lois, da. of Arthur Maxwell Hankin, CMG, and has issue living, Claire Fiona *b.* 1966, Georgina Mary *b.* 1968. *Residence,*—The Castle Cottage, Lockeridge, Marlborough.

Granddaughters of the late Oswald Francis Gerald Stonor, C.M.G. (ante):—
Issue of the late Joan Florence Mary Stonor, *b.* 1907, *d.* 1956: *m.* 1st, 1927 (marriage dissolved 1948), John Colburn Bennett, C.M.G., C.B.E.; 2ndly, 1948, John Keith Macara [see Macara, Bt.]:—
(By 1st marriage) Jill Mary, *b.* 1929: *m.* 1954, David Noel Templer Scott, and has issue living, John Andrew Templer, *b.* 1960,—Virginia Jane, *b.* 1957. *Residence,*—15, Gloucester Mews West, W.2.
——Veronica Anne, *b.* 1942: *m.* 1964, Michael Edward Rudman, of 2, Bramshill Gdns., NW5, and has issue living, Amanda Joan, *b.* 1967,—Katherine Rose, *b.* 1970.

Grandchildren of the late Charles Joseph Stonor, only son of Charles Henry Stonor, brother of 3rd Baron:—
Issue of the late Charles Henry Joseph Stonor, *b.* 1874, *d.* 1930: *m.* 1912, Hylda, who *d.* 1968, dau. of Henry Lloyd-Carter, formerly of Bryn Seiont, Caernarvon:—
Henry Anthony (Chemor Estate, Jerantut, PO Pahang, Malaysia), *b.* 1926; ed. at Downside, and at Shrewsbury; late Lt. R. Welch Fusiliers.——Beatrice Maude, *b.* 1913: *m.* 1949, Ralph Aldersey, who *d.* 1971, and has issue living, William Ralph *b.* 1950. *Residence*—Aldersey Hall, Cheshire.—— Pamela Mary, *b.* 1915: Senior Welfare Officer, Brit. Red Cross So. (despatches).——Sheila Mary, *b.* 1916: *m.* 1946, Brig. Ernest James Cholmeley Harrison, OBE, Roy. Signals, son of the late Sir Charlton Scott Cholmeley Harrison, CIE, and has issue living, James Hugh Cholmeley, *b.* 1947,— Robert Mark Cholmeley, *b.* 1950,—Sally Ann Monamie, *b.* 1951. *Residence,*—Foxglade, Shinfield, nr. Reading.——Stella Frances Ursula, *b.* 1922.——Ann, *b.* 1929: *m.* 1955, Peter B. Sawdy of Leweston, West St., Mayfield, Sussex, and has issue living, Caroline Ann, *b.* 1957,—Susan Angela Lumley, *b.* 1962.

Issue of the late Francis Cyril Stonor, *b.* 1880, *d.* 1955: *m.* 1909, Juliana Tindal, who *d.* 1963, dau. of Lieut.-Col. Bernard Tindal Bosanquet, formerly of Claysmore, Enfield:—
Bernard Francis. *b.* 1909 : *m.* 19—, Elsie Graham, and has issue living, Mortimer, *b.* 1941,—Anne.*b.* 1935,—Juliana, *b.* 1937,—Virginia, *b.* 1946. *Residence,*—Bramley, Margaret River. W. Australia.
——Charles Robert, *b.* 1912. *Residence,*—Brooklands (North), Sarisbury Green, Hants.

PREDECESSORS.—[1] *Sir* THOMAS de Camoys, *K.G.*, an eminent warrior, commanded the left wing of the English army at Agincourt 1415; summoned to Parliament as a Baron of England 1383-1421 ; *d.* 1421 ; *s.* by his grandson [2] HUGH, 2nd Baron; *d.* 1426, when the title went into abeyance between his sisters Margaret and Alianora, and it remained abeyant until 1889, when it was terminated in favour of the descendant of Margaret [3] THOMAS Stonor, 3rd Baron; sat as M.P. for Oxford 1832-3; was a Lord-in-Waiting to H.M. Queen Victoria 1846-52, 1853-8, 1859 66, and 1868-74; *d.* Jan. 18, 1881, and was *s.* by his grandson [4] FRANCIS ROBERT, 4th Baron (son of the late Hon. Francis Stonor, 2nd son of 3rd Baron ; *b.*1856; Lord-in-Waiting to H.M. Queen Victoria 1886 and 1892-5 : *m.* 1881, Jessie Philippa, who *d.* 1928, second dau. of the late Robert Russell Carew, of Carpenders. Herts : *d.* 1897: *s.* by his el. son [5] RALPH FRANCIS JULIAN, 5th Baron; *b.* 1884: *m.* 1911, Mildred, who *d.* 1961, da. of the late William Watts Sherman, of New York; *d.* 1968; *s.* by his only son [6] (RALPH ROBERT WATTS) SHERMAN, 6th Baron, and present peer.

Campbell, Baron see Baron Stratheden and Campbell.

CAMPBELL OF CROY, BARON (Campbell.) [Life Baron 1974.]

GORDON THOMAS CALTHROP CAMPBELL, *MC, PC,* son of the late Maj.-Gen James Alexander Campbell, DSO; *b.* June 8th, 1921; ed. at Wellington; Maj. (ret.) RA; 1939-45 War in NW Europe, OC 320 Field Bty., 15th (Scottish) Div. 1942-45 (MC and Bar, wounded); Diplo. Ser. 1946-57; UK Mission at UN New York 1949-52; Private Sec. to Sec. of Cabinet 1954-56, First Sec., Vienna 1956-57, Govt. Whip 1961-63, Under-Sec. of State for Scotland 1963-65, and Sec. of State for Scotland 1970-74; MP for Moray and Nairn *(C)* 1959-74; cr. PC 1970, and *Baron Campbell of Croy,* of Croy, co. Nairn (Life Baron) 1974: *m.* 1949, Nicola Elizabeth Gina, da. of the late Capt. Geoffrey Spencer Madan [see Noble, Bt., cr. 1902], and has issue.
Residence,—Holme Rose, Cawdor, Nairn. *Club,*—Brooks's.

SONS LIVING.
Hon. Colin Ian Calthrop, *b.* 1950.
Hon. Alastair James Calthrop, *b.* 1952.
DAUGHTER LIVING.
Hon. Christina Marjorie, *b.* 1953.

CAMPBELL OF ESKAN, BARON. (Campbell.) (Life Baron 1966.)

JOCK (JOHN MIDDLETON) CAMPBELL, son of the late Colin Algernon Campbell, of Colgrain, Dunbartonshire, and Underriver House, Sevenoaks [see Barrington, Bt., colls.]; *b.* Aug. 8th, 1912; ed. at Eton, and Exeter Coll., Oxford; Chm. of Milton Keynes Development Corpn., Commonwealth Sugar Exporters Assocn., and Statesman & Nation Publishing Co., Pres. of W. India Cttee. since 1957 and of Booker, McConnell, Ltd. since 1967 (Chm. 1952-67); a Dir. Commonwealth Development Corpn., a Member of Council of Overseas Development Inst., and of Community Relations Commn., a Trustee of Runnymede Trust; cr. Knt. 1957, and *Baron Campbell of Eskan,* of Camis Eskan, co. Dunbarton (Life Baron) 1966: *m.* 1st, 1938 (m. diss. 1948) Barbara Noel, da. of the late Leslie Arden Roffey; 2ndly, 1948, Phyllis Jacqueline Gilmour (Taylor), da. of the late Henry Boyd, CBE, and has issue by 1st m.

Arms,—Gyronny of eight pieces or and sable, and in chief a mullet counterchanged of the field, all within a bordure embattled vert, charged with eight buckles of the first. **Crest,**—A boar's head, erect and erased or. **Supporters,**—Two jaguars proper, gorged of chaplets of bog-myrtle also proper.
Residences.—Crocker End House. Nettlebed, Oxon; 15, Eaton Sq., SW1.
Clubs,—Garrick, Beefsteak, West Indian, MCC, All England Lawn Tennis.

SONS LIVING. *(By 1st marriage.)*
Hon. John Charles Middleton, *b.* 1940; ed. at Eton: *m.* 1965, Patricia Ann, el. da. of the late Tom Webster, and has issue.
Hon. Peter Mark Middleton, *b.* 1946; ed. at Eton.

DAUGHTERS LIVING. *(By 1st marriage.)*
Hon. Rosalind Leonora Middleton, *b.* 1942.
Hon. Agneta Joanna Middleton, *b.* 1944: *m.* 1966, Jonathan Geoffrey William Agnew, of 6, Brompton Sq., SW3 [see Agnew, Bt., colls., cr. 1895].
Lord Campbell of Eskan is descended from Colin Campbell, 2nd of Colgrain. 1st Baron Colgrain was el. son of George William Campbell, yr. brother of Colin Campbell.

Campden, Viscount, son of Earl of Gainsborough.

CAMPION BARONY OF. (Campion.) [Extinct 1958.]

WIDOW LIVING OF FIRST BARON.

HILDA MARY (*Baroness Campion*), dau. of the late W. A. Spafford : *m.* 1920, the 1st Baron, who *d.* 1958, when the title became ext. *Residence*,—Little Bowes, Abinger Hammer, Surrey.

CAMROSE, VISCOUNT. (Berry.) [Viscount U.K. 1941, Bt. U.K. 1921.]

Live with courage.

(JOHN) SEYMOUR BERRY, *T.D.*, 2nd Viscount and 2nd Baronet; *b.* July 12th, 1909; *s.* 1954; ed. at Eton, and at Ch. Ch., Oxford; Dep. Chm. of the *Daily Telegraph and Morning Post*; a Younger Brother of Trinity House; late Maj. City of London Yeo., RA (TA); 1939-45 War in N. Africa and Italy (despatches); MP for Hitchin Div. of Herts. (*C*) 1941-45.

Arms,—Argent, three bars gules, over all a pile, ermine. *Crest*,—A griffin sejant reguardant sable, collared or. *Supporters*,—On either side a wolf proper gorged with a collar or, pendent therefrom an escutcheon sable, charged with two pens in saltire argent.

Seat,—Hackwood Park, near Basingstoke, Hants. *Clubs*,—White's, Buck's, Beefsteak, Royal Yacht Squadron, MCC.

BROTHERS LIVING.

Hon. (WILLIAM) MICHAEL, *MBE, TD* (*Baron Hartwell*), *b.* May 18th, 1911; *cr.* Baron Hartwell (Life Peerage) 1968 [see that title].

Hon. Julian, *O.B.E., b.* 1920; ed. at Eton; Lieut.-Col. Comdg. Roy. Horse Guards 1958-60 and Col. Comdg. Household Cav. and Silver Stick in Waiting 1960-64; a JP and a DL of Hampshire; 1939-45 War in Middle East and Italy, Cyprus 1959 (OBE); has American Bronze Star Medal; OBE (Mil.) 1959: *m.* 1946, Denise, da. of Maj. J. Leslie Rowan-Thomson, and has issue living, Simon Ewert, *b.* 1955,—Caroline Denise, *b.* 1948: *m.* 1969, Jeremy James Wagg, of Fordel, Glenfarg, Perthshire [Horlick, Bt.], and has issue living, Julian James *b.* 1972, Katharine Denise *b.* 1974. *Residence*,—The Old Rectory, Tunworth, nr. Basingstoke, Hants. *Clubs*,—White's, Jockey and Royal Yacht Squadron.

SISTERS LIVING.

Hon. Mary Cecilia, *b.* 1906 : *m.* 1930, Major Ronald Guthrie McNair Scott, and has issue living Thomas Michael (Highfields House, Augerez, St. Peter, Jersey), *b.* 1935: *m.* 1959, Susannah, da. of Frederick Leslie Hodges, and has issue living, Simon Guthrie McNair *b.* 1960, Sarah *b.* 1966,— Nigel Guthrie, *b.* 1945: *m.* 1968, Anna Margaret, only da. of W. R. Colquhoun, of Cecily Hill House, Cirencester, and has issue living, Robert William *b.* 1970, Alistair Nigel *b.* 1972,—Gillian Mary, *b.* 1931: *m.* 1951, Charles Ivor Mervyn Williams, MC, and has issue living, Oliver Mervyn *b.* 1953, Richard Charles *b*, 1955, Thomas Morgan *b.* 1959, Lucinda Mary *b.* 1956,—Alison Linda, *b.* 1936: *m.* 1963, Lawrence Kelly, of 44, Ladbroke Grove, W11, yr. son of the late Sir David Victor Kelly, GCMG, MC, and has issue living, Nicolas Tara *b.* 1967, Rosanna Mary *b.* 1964, Rachel Sophia, *b.* 1965,—Valerie Susan *b.* 1939: *m.* 1964, Thomas Frank Dermot Pakenham, el. son of 7th Earl of Longford. *Residence*,—Huish House, Old Basing, nr. Basingstoke, Hants.

Hon. Sheila (*Countess of Birkenhead*), *b.* 1913; was a Lady-in-Waiting (temporary) to H.R.H. the Duchess of Kent 1949-53; author of "Against Oblivion" 1943, "Peace in Piccadilly" 1958, "Illustrious Friends" 1965: *m.* 1935, the 2nd Earl of Birkenhead, who *d.* 1975. *Residences*,— Charlton, Banbury; 24, Wilton St., SW1.

Hon. Molly Patricia (*Hon. Lady Cotterell*), *b.* 1915 : *m.* 1st, 1936, Capt. Roger Charles George Chetwode, who *d.* 1940, only son of 1st Baron Chetwode; 2ndly, 1942, the 1st Baron Sherwood, from whom she obtained a divorce 1948; 3rdly, 1958, as his second wife, Sir Richard Charles Geers Cotterell, CBE, TD, 5th Bt. *Residence*,—Garnons, Hereford.

Hon. Diana Phyllis, *b.* 1924 : *m.* 1948, William Perine Macauley, and has issue living, William Francis *b.* 1953,—Mark Justin, *b.* 1956,—Rupert Timothy, *b.* 1962,—Isabel Tara Mary, *b.* 1949: *m.* 1972, Desmond Gilroy, and has issue living, Casper Alexander, *b.* 1973,—Virginia Margaret Diana, *b.* 1950: *m.* 1974, the Hon. Alastair James Harold Hoyer Millar [see B. Inchyra],—Mary Rosalind (twin), *b.* 1953. *Residence*,—Ballyward House, Blessington, co. Wicklow.

WIDOW LIVING OF SON OF FIRST VISCOUNT.

Jenifer Susan, dau. of William Arthur Fearnley-Whittingstall, T.D., Q.C., of The Old Manor House, Melbourn, Cambs.: *m.* 1st, 1955, the Hon. Rodney Mathias Berry, T.D., who *d.* 1963; 2ndly, 1964, Henry Lambert Middleton, of Bur ey Grange, Burley, nr. Ringwood, Hants., and 11, Clareville Court, Clareville Grove, SW7 [see Middleton, Bt., colls.].

PREDECESSOR.—[1] WILLIAM EWERT BERRY, 2nd son of the late Alderman John Mathias Berry, J.P. of Gwaelodygarth, Merthyr Tydfil ; *b.* 1879 ; a journalist and Newspaper Proprietor, Editor-in-Ch. of *Daily Telegraph* and *Morning Post*, and Chm. of Amalgamated Press, Ltd.; founder of Advertising World 1901. Editor-in-Ch *Sunday Times* 1915-36, Chm. of Financial Times Ltd. 1919-45, and of Allied Newspapers Ltd. 1924-35: cr. a Baronet 1921, *Baron Camrose*, of Long Cross, Surrey (peerage of United Kingdom) 1929, and *Viscount Camrose*, of Hackwood Park, co. Southampton 1941: *m.* 1905, Mary Agnes, who *d.* 1962. el. dau. of the late Thomas Corns, of 2, Bolton St. Piccadilly, W.1; *d.* 1954; *s.* by his el. son [2] (JOHN) SEYMOUR, 2nd Viscount and present peer; also Baron Camrose.

CANTERBURY, LORD ARCHBISHOP OF. (Coggan.)

Most Rev. and Rt. Hon. (FREDERICK) DONALD COGGAN, *PC, DD,* son of the late Cornish Arthur Coggan, of London; *b.* Oct. 9th, 1909; ed. at Merchant Taylors' Sch., at St. John's Coll., Camb. (MA), and at Wycliffe Hall, Oxford; BD Toronto 1941; DD Lambeth 1957; Hon DD Toronto, Leeds, Cambridge, Hull, Aberdeen, Tokyo, Saskatoon, Huron, and Manchester; HHD Westminster Choir Coll., Princeton, NJ, Hon. DLitt Lancaster 1967, STD New York, Hon. LLD Liverpool; Assist. Lecturer in Semitic Languages and Literature, Manchester Univ. 1931-34, Curate of St. Mary's, Islington N. 1934-37, Professor of New Testament, Wycliffe Coll., Toronto 1937-44, Principal of London Coll. of Divinity 1944-56, and Examining Chap. to Bishop of Lincoln 1946-56, to Bishop of Manchester 1951-56, to Bishop of Southwark 1954-56, and to Bishop of Chester 1955-56; select Preacher of Oxford Univ. 1961; consecrated 3rd Bishop of Bradford 1956, enthroned 93rd Archbishop of York, Primate of England and Metropolitan 1961, and translated 101st Archbishop of Canterbury, Primate of All England and Metropolitan 1974; enthroned 1975; Sub-Prelate of Order of St. John 1960, and Prelate 1967; Pro-Chancellor of York Univ. 1962-74, and Hull Univ. 1968-74; and Chm. of Coll. of Preachers; author of " The Ministry of the Word " 1945, " The Glory of God " 1950, " Stewards of Grace " 1958, " Five Makers of the New Testament " 1962, " Christian Priorities " 1963, " The Prayers of the New Testament " 1967, " Sinews of Faith " 1969, and " Word and World " 1971; PC 1961: *m.* 1935, Jean Braithwaite, da. of Dr. W. Loudon Strain.

Patron of one hundred and seventy-seven livings, the Archdeaconries of Canterbury and Maidstone (each endowed with a Canonry), the Archdeaconry of Croydon, and the six Cathedral Preacherships.

The Province comprises twenty-nine Sees. It was founded by Augustine, the 1st Bishop under Ethelbert, King of Kent, 597.

ARMS OF THE SEE,—Azure, an Archiepiscopal cross in pale or, surmounted by a Pall proper, charged with four crosses patée fitchée sable.

Archiepiscopal Signature,—" Donald Cantuar ":

Residences,—Lambeth Palace, S.E.1 ; Old Palace, Canterbury.

CARADON, BARON. (Foot.) [Life Baron 1964.]

HUGH MACKINTOSH FOOT, *GCMG, KCVO, OBE, PC,* son of the late Rt. Hon. Isaac Foot; *b.* Oct. 8th, 1907; ed. at Leighton Park Sch., Reading, and at St. John's Coll., Camb. (BA); K.St.J.; Admin. Officer, Palestine Govt. 1929-39, Assist. British Resident, Transjordan, 1939-42, in British Mil. Admin. 1943, Colonial Sec., Cyprus 1943-45 and Jamaica 1945-47, Ch. Sec., Nigeria 1947-50, Capt.-Gen. and Gov.-in-Ch. Jamaica 1950-57, Gov. of Cyprus 1957-60, Permanent UK, UN Representative on Trustee Council of UN, and Special Adviser and Ambassador in UK Mission to UN 1961-62, Consultant to Special Fund of UN 1963-64 and Min. of State for Foreign Affairs, and Permanent UK

! or Law and Liberty.

Representative at UN 1964-70; *cr.* OBE (Civil) 1939, CMG, 1946, KCMG 1951, KCVO 1953, GCMG 1957, *Baron Caradon,* of St. Cleer, co. Cornwall (Life Baron) 1964, and PC 1968: *m.* 1937 (Florence) Sylvia (CStJ), da. of Arthur Tod, and has issue.

Arms,—Or, on a chevron engrailed sable between three lions' gambs erect and erased gules, three wheels or. Crest,—Perching on a tower sable, supported by two lions' gambs erect gules, a Cornish chough proper. Supporters,—On either side an African lion proper, charged on the shoulder with the head of a trident or, within a wreath of two olive branches leaved and the stems crossed in saltire argent, the whole on a compartment of rock, in the middle thereof a pit proper.

Residence,—Trematon Castle, Saltash, Cornwall.

Clubs,—Travellers', West Indian.

SONS LIVING.

Hon. Paul Mackintosh (14, Canfield Gdns., NW6), *b.* 1937; ed. at Univ. Coll., Oxford; is a Journalist: *m.* 1962 (m. diss. 1970), Monica, da. of Dr. Robert P. Beckinsale, of Oxford, and has issue.

Hon. Oliver Isaac, *b.* 1947; ed. at Leighton Park Sch., Cirencester Agric. Coll., and Goddard Coll., Vermont, USA.

Hon. Benjamin Arthur, *b.* 1949.

DAUGHTER LIVING.

Hon. Sarah Dingle, *b.* 1939: *m.* 1961, Maj. Timothy Nicholas Percival Winter Burbury, The Blues & Royals (HQ London District, Horse Guards, Whitehall, SW1), and has issue.

CARBERY, BARON. (Evans-Freke.) [Baron I. 1715, Bt. I. 1768.]

PETER RALFE HARRINGTON EVANS-FREKE, 11th Baron, and 7th Baronet; *b.* March 20th, 1920; *s.* 1970; ed. at Downside; MICE; a Member of London Stock Exchange 1955-67; 1939-45 War as Capt. RE in India and Burma: *m.* 1941, Joyzelle Mary, only da. of the late Herbert Binnie, of Sydney, NSW, and has issue.

Liberty.

Arms,—Quarterly: 1st and 4th sable, two bars, and in chief three mullets or, *Freke*; 2nd and 3rd argent, three boars' heads couped sable, *Evans*. **Crests.**—1st, a bull's, head couped at the back sable, collared and chained or, *Freke*; 2nd, a demi-lion rampant reguardant or, holding in the paws a boar's head sable, *Evans*. **Supporters.**—Two lions reguardant or, ducally crowned azure.

Residence,—Dormans Cross, Lingfield, Surrey.

SONS LIVING.

Hon. MICHAEL PETER (Lye House, Pertenhall, Beds.), *b.* Oct. 11th, 1942; ed. at Downside, Ch. Ch. Oxford (MA), and Univ. of Strathclyde (MBA): *m.* 1967, Claudia Janet Elizabeth, only da. of Capt Percy Lionel Cecil Gurney, of Little Chart, Penshurst, and has issue living, Dominic Ralfe Cecil *b.* 1969,—Richenda Clare, *b.* 1971,—Isabel Lucy, *b.* 1973.

Hon. John Anthony (North Lodge, Castle Hill, nr. Barnstaple, N. Devon), *b.* 1949; ed. at Downside, and Roy. Agric. Coll., Cirencester; ARICS: *m.* 1972, Veronica Jane, yst. da. of Maj. Eric Williams, of House of Lynturk, Alford, Aberdeenshire.

Hon. Stephan Ralfe, *b.* 1952; ed. at Downside, and Trin. Coll., Camb.

DAUGHTERS LIVING.

Hon. Maura Clare, *b.* 1946: *m.* 1966, Richard Henry William Fanshawe, of 12, Kensington Place, W8 [see E. Lindsey and Abingdon].

Hon. Angela Mary, *b.* 1954: *m.* 1975, Martin David Tomlins of Red Lodge, Braydon, Wilts.

HALF SISTER LIVING.

Anne Mary Elizabeth, *b.* 1933: *m.* 1957, Ross Young, of North Frith Farm, Hadlow, Kent, and has issue living, Paul Ralfe, *b.* 1958,—Clare Elizabeth, *b.* 1960,—Diana Mary, *b.* 1967.

DAUGHTERS LIVING OF TENTH BARON.

Hon. Fabienne José, *b.* 1916: *m.* 1st, 1936, (m. diss. 1946), Com. John Dudley Dowse-Finnemor, RN, who *d.* 1971, having assumed by Roy. licence 1938, the additional surname and arms of Finnemor; 2ndly, 1947, Philip Claridge, of Cloonagh, Monkstown, co. Cork.

Hon. Virginia Sistare Juanita Carberry, *b.* 1925. *Address,*—Anchorage, PO Box 96094, Likoni, via Mombasa, Kenya.

WIDOW LIVING OF SON OF NINTH BARON.

Dorothy May (15, Queen Elizabeth Close, Palace Plain, Norwich), da. of H. G. Surrey: *m.* 1941, as his 3rd wife, Maj. the Hon. Ralfe Evans-Freke, MBE, who *d.* 1969 [see colls. infra].

MOTHER LIVING.

Vera Mary (Flat 3, Hamilton Mansions, Fourth Av., Hove), da. of the late C. Harrington Moore: *m.* 1919, Maj. the Hon. Ralfe Evans-Freke, MBE, who *d.* 1969, and from whom she obtained a divorce 1929.

WIDOW LIVING OF TENTH BARON.

JUNE WEIR MOSLEY (*June Baroness Carbery*) (Saxondale, Johannesburg, S. Africa): *m.* 1930, as his 3rd wife, the 10th Baron, who *d.* 1970.

COLLATERAL BRANCHES LIVING.

Issue of the late Lieut.-Col. the Hon. Percy Cecil Evans-Freke, 2nd son of 8th Baron, *b.* 1871, *d.* (killed in action) 1915 : *m.* 1895, Eva, whc *d.* 1942, dau. of the late Charles Kirwan, of Dalgan Park, co. Mayo:—

Maida Cecil, *b.* 1897: *m.* 1927, Capt. Edmund Michael Gordon Loeventhorpe Boyle, R.N. (ret.) [see E. Cork, colls.]. *Residence,*—Queen's Lodge, St. Cross Rd., Winchester, Hants.

(*Male line in special remainder to the Barony.*)

Grandchildren of the late Eyre Frederick Fitz-George Evans (infra):—

Issue of the late Savage Corry Evans, *b.* 1878, *d.* 1968: *m.* 1st, 1902, (m. diss. 1920), da. of H. Healey, of Naseby, NZ; 2ndly, 1927, Alicia Madeleine Isabel Gifford, da. of the late Charles Gifford Moore, of Oamaru, NZ; 3rdly, 19—, Lilian Fair (20, Phrosso Rd., W. Worthing):—

(By 1st m.) Trevor George Corry, OBE, TD (Old Dairy House, Mudford, Yeovil), *b.* 1910; ed. abroad and R. Agric. Coll., Cirencester; a JP; formerly Ch. Agent to Duke of Norfolk; 1939-45 War as Lt.-Col. R. Sussex Regt. (OBE (Mil.) 1946: *m.* 1937, Sara Gwendolyn, da. of R. C. Drummond, of Nasterton, NZ, and has issue living, Michael George Corry, *b.* 1938,—Stephen Telford Eyre (Brackenhill, by Kilmaurs, Ayrshire), *b.* 1939; ed. at Rugby, and Roy. Agric. Coll., Cirencester: *m.* 1970, Susan Biron, da. of Michael Pallister Young, of Bishopsbourne, Kent,—Patrick Heugh Robert Eyre (Little Orchard, Kitt Hill, Shaftesbury, Dorset), *b.* 1944: *m.* 1970, Jennifer Robin, da. of the late Capt. Brian Granville White, RM, of Chaldon, Surrey.——Nina Corry, *b.* 1903: *m.* 1st, 1934, Walter Briggs, who *d.* 1938; 2ndly, 1949, Robert Workman, of Mertown Hall, Holywood, co. Down.——Kathleen Ann, *b.* 1906.——Sylvia Elizabeth, *b.* 1907.

Issue of the late Percy Evans, *b.* 1871, *d.* 1959 : *m.* 1916, Ethel Margaret, who *d.* 1951, dau. of T. Dickson, formerly of Wanganui, New Zealand :—

Jean Charlotte, *b.* 1917: *m.* 1960, Robert Gibson Bauld, of 8, Parsons St., St. John's Hill, Wanganui, NZ.——Margaret Lees, *b.* 1925: *m.* 1947, Clifford Roy Dewe. *Residence,*—12, Aorangi St., Fielding, NZ.

Grandchildren of the late Major George Thomas Evans, son of the late Eyre Evans (infra):—

Issue of the late Eyre Frederick Fitz-George Evans, *b.* 1842, *d.* 1919: *m.* 1st, 1868, Charlotte, who *d.* 1882, dau. of James Lees, of Taranaki, N.Z., and formerly of Clarkesfield, Oldham, Lancashire; 2ndly, 1888, Mary, dau. of William Alderson, of Cheltenham :—

(By 1st marriage) Rev. Eric, *b.* 1882; 1917-18 War with New Zealand Expeditionary Forces as Chap. to the Forces (medal): *m.* 1910, Dora Handforth, and has issue living, Rev. Philip Eyre, *b.* 1910: *m.* 1935, Florence Anne, da. of Richard U. Reaves, of Melbourne, and has issue living, Rodger Eyre *b.* 1937, Wendy Gillian *b.* 1940,—Llewellyn Handforth, *b.* 1913: *m.* 1st, 1940, Ivy Edith, who *d.* 1949, da. of William Elliot, of Melbourne; 2ndly, 1951, Una Jessie, da. of the late Charles A. Drew of Melbourne, and has issue living, (by 1st marriage) Peter Handforth *b.* 1941, Corry Margret, *b.* 1942, Jean Rebecca *b.* 1949,— Raymond Austin (of 26, Chapman Av., Beecroft, NWS), *b.* 1915: *m.* 1958, Lucy Margaret Blomfield, and has issue living, Bruce Raymond Blomfield *b.* 1962, Kathryn Margaret *b.* 1959,—Denison Anthony (of 1, Gardiner Rd., Hawthorn, Melbourne, Australia), *b.* 1925: *m.* 1962, Janette Relleen Peacocke, of Hove, Sussex, and has issue living, Charles Anthony

b. 1963,—Rhoda Caroline, *b.* 1916. *Residence,*—6, Beech St., Camberwell, Melbourne, Australia.
——Eva, *b.* 1880: *m.* 1920, Clarence James, who *d.* 1936, and has issue living, Kenneth Evans (of
94, Chemiston Av., Dunedin, NZ), *b.* 1921: *m.* 1943, Frances Mary, da. of James Gordon Graham,
of Ranfurly, Otago, NZ, and has issue living, Kenneth Gordon *b.* 1944, Keith Graham *b.* 1946,
Susan Mary *b.* 1949. *Residence,*—44, Wansbeck St., Oamaru, Otago, NZ.

Grandchildren of the late Eyre Frederick Fitz-George Evans (ante):—
Issue of the late Thomas Charles Evans, *b.* 1890, *d.* 1960: *m.* 1st, 1919, Elsa Phyllis Heckler,
  of Masterton, New Zealand, who *d.* 1924 ; 2ndly, 1925, Elsie Edith Smith, of 32, Seddon
  Crescent, Marewa, Napier, Hawke's Bay, New Zealand :—
(By 2nd marriage) Ashley Ogilvie (of 8, Williams St., Marewa, Napier, Hawkes Bay, New Zealand),
  b. 1926: *m.* 1950, Ruth Martin Napier, of Hawkes Bay, New Zealand, and has issue living, Neil
  Martin, *b.* 1951,—Robert Denis, *b.* 1954,—Philip Leslie, *b.* 1958, Allan Ashley, *b.* 1960,—Bruce
  Raymond, *b.* 1962.——Lees Ogilvie, *b.* 1932: *m.* 1954, Rae Irene Anne Croudis, and has issue living,
  Laurence Thomas, *b.* 1958,—Suzanne Mary, *b.* 1955,—Cynthia Anne, *b.* 1957,—Kathleen Pauline,
  b. 1962.——Olwyn Ogilvie, *b.* 1927: *m.* 1952, Eion John Davies, and has issue living, Garth Raynsley,
  b. 1953,—Mark Thomas, *b.* 1955,—Tracey Elizabeth, *b.* 1958. *Residence,*—Napier Rd., Havelock
  North, Hawke's Bay, New Zealand.——José Ogilvie, *b.* 1929.——Fabienne Ogilvie (twin), *b.* 1932:
  m. 1953, Neale Thomas Grenfell, of 23, Sharlick St., Avondale, Wainoni, Christchurch, New Zealand,
  and has issue living, Peter Andrew *b.* 1954, Frank James *b.* 1956.

Grandchildren of the late Capt. Thomas Williams Evans, son of the late Eeyr
  Evans, grandson of the late Thomas Evans, M.P., 3rd brother of 1st Baron:—
Issue of the late Stewart Eyre Evans, *b.* 1852, *d.* 19— : *m.* 1877, Harriette, who *d.* 1882, dau. of
  the late James McKenny :—
John Stewart Moncreiffe, *b.* 1881. *Resides in* New Zealand.——Emily Helen McKenny, *b.* 1879.

Grandson of the late Capt. George William Wallace D'Arcy Evans (infra):—
Issue of the late Cdr. Hardress Waller Eyre D'Arcy Evans, RN, *b.* 1898, *d.* 1962: *m.* 1934,
  Mary Frideswide Leslie (7, Glyn Idris, Moore Rd., Durban, Natal), da. of the late W. W.
  Jessop Sharpe:—
John Hardress Waller (15, Jan Smuts Av., Northdene, Queensburgh, Natal), *b.* 1938: *m.* 1965, Janet
  Barbara, da. of Francis Spence Ware, and has issue living, Andrew Hardress Eyre, *b.* 1966,—Stephan
  Elystan Waller, *b.* 1973,—Jennifer Francis, *b.* 1968.——Wendy Nina Mary, *b.* 1940: *m.* 1970, M. B.
  Fowkes, of Riverside, Lismore Av., Tokai, Cape Province, and has issue living, Jeremy Michael
  Matthew, *b.* 1973,—Sarah Isobel Mary, *b.* 1970.

Granddaughter of John D'Arcy Evans, 2nd son of James D'Arcy-Evans, 2nd son of
  Rev. Thomas Waller Evans, LLD, 2nd son of Thomas Evans, MP (ante:—)
Issue of the late Capt. George William Wallace D'Arcy Evans, *b.* 1860, *d.* 1906: *m.* 1889
  Harriette Marian Gledstanes (who *d.* 1960, and from whom he obtained a divorce 1902),
  el. da. of the late Capt. George Gledstanes Richards, of Macmine Castle, co. Wexford:—
Marian Sylvia Lucretia, *b.* 1896: *m.* 19—, S. Wilson. *Resides in* Canada.

Grandchildren of the late Eyre Waller D'Arcy-Evans (infra):—
Issue of the late Eyre Henry D'Arcy-Evans, *b.* 1892, *d.* 1957: *m.* 1923, Mary Eleanor, who *d.*
  1959, da. of John Garmony, of Killylea, co. Armagh:—
Trevor Wallace (101, The Promenade, Mt. Pleasant, W. Aust. 6153), *b.* 1926: *m.* 1952, Shirley June
  Lovatt, and has issue living, Andrew Thomas, *b.* 1956,—Clive Hugh, *b.* 1958,—Alan William, *b.* 1959,
  —Christopher Michael, *b.* 1962.——Ethne Elizabeth, *b.* 1931: *m.* 1964, Ronald James Manton (Unit
  6, Overton Gdns., Cottesloe, W. Aust. 6011).——Joy, *b.* 1924: *m.* 1949, Dr. Eric Brian Jeffcoat
  Smith, of 4, Kinnane Pl., Attadale, W. Aust. 6156, and has issue living, Nicola, *b.* 1953,—Deirdre,
  b. 1953,—Vanessa, *b.* 1960.

Issue of the late John Wallace D'Arcy-Evans, *b.* 1894: *m.* 19—, Nancy Ann Fairfield (57,
  Osborne Rd., E. Fremantle, W. Aust. 6160:—
John (Melbourne), *b.* 19—: *m.* 19—, —, and has issue living, a son, *b.* 19—,— a da., *b.* 19—,—.——
  Eyre James (139, Moreing Rd., Attadale, W. Aust. 6156), *b.* 19—: *m.* 19—, —, and has issue living, a
  son, *b.* 19—,— a son, *b.* 19—,— a da., *b.* 19—.——Trevor Hugh, *b.* 19—: *m.* 19—, —, and has issue
  living, a son, *b.* 19—, — a son, *b.* 19—.

Issue of the late George William D'Arcy-Evans, *b.* 1898, *d.* 1967: *m.* 1923, Flora Eleanor, da.
  of Thorpe Edwards:—
Peter (16, Brinsley Rd., Camberwell, Vic., Australia), *b.* 1924: *m.* 1953, Isabel Blair, and has issue
  living, Paul William, *b.* 1955,—John, *b.* 1959,—Ian, *b.* 1961,—Clare Louise, *b.* 1966.——John
  Eyre (Fircones, Raans Rd., Amersham, Bucks.), *b.* 1932: *m.* 1959, Susan Kathleen, da. of Henry
  Gerard de Visme Gipps, and has issue living, Guy William, *b.* 1961,—Richard Henry, *b.* 1962,—
  Patrick John, *b.* 1965,—Jane, *b.* 1968,—Kate, *b.* 1971.

Issue of the late Elystan Cecil D'Arcy-Evans, *b.* 1906, *d.* 1960: *m.* 1953, Rosemonde Lovell
  Pryor Rainbird (31, Georges Rd., Lesmurdie 6076, W. Aust.):—
Donald Hugh, *b.* 1955.——Ainslie Jean, *b.* 1957.

Granddaughters of the late John D'Arcy-Evans (ante):—
Issue of the late Eyre Waller D'Arcy-Evans, *b.* 1864, *d.* 1926: *m.* 1890, Elizabeth McKenna,
  who *d.* 1937:—
Marian Sylvia (81, Hamersley Rd., Subiaco, W. Aust. 6008), *b.* 1900: *m.* 1927, Frederick Laird Woodward Morison, Civil Eng., who *d.* 1972, and has issue living, Ian George, *b.* 1928; BSc, PhD: *m.* 1955,
  Susette May, da. of Dr. D. R. Gawler, and has issue living, Ian Andrew *b.* 1956, John Laird *b.* 1959,
  Michael Leonard *b.* 1962, Deborah Anne *b.* 1958,—Robin Frederick, *b.* 1929; LLB; Col. Aust. Army:
  m. 1951, Bernadette Patricia Raleigh, and has issue living, Anthony John *b.* 1959, Michael Robin
  b. 1964, Ann Maree *b.* 1953, Suzette Jane *b.* 1955.——Sylvia Elizabeth, *b.* 1905: *m.* 1945, Mervyn Leo
  Connick, Eng. (Sevenacres, M/S 236, Maryborough, Qld. 4650).

PREDECESSORS.—George Evans, Bar.-at-law, a zealous promoter of the Revolution of
1688, was after the accession of William III. sworn of the Privy Council, and returned as M.P.
for Charleville, co. Cork, and subsequently declined a peerage offered by George I., an honour
however, that was accepted by his son [1] GEORGE, *M.P.,* cr. *Baron Carbery,* of Carbery, co.
Cork (peerage of Ireland) 1715, with remainder to the male issue of his father; *d.* 1749; *s.* by
his son [2] GEORGE, *M.P.,* 2nd Baron; *d.* 1759; *s.* by his son [3] GEORGE, 3rd Baron; *d.* 1783;
s. by his son [4] GEORGE, 4th Baron, M.P. for Rutland; *d.s.p.* 1804: *s.* by his uncle [5] JOHN,
5th Baron (2nd son of 2nd Baron); *d.* 1807, without surviving male issue; *s.* by his kinsman
[6] *Sir* JOHN Evans-Freke, 6th Baron (whose father, grandson of the 1st Baron, had been cr. a
Baronet (l.) 1768, and assumed the additional surname of Freke); was a Representative Peer;
d.s.p. 1845; *s.* by his nephew [7] GEORGE PATRICK, 7th Baron (son of Percy Evans-Freke, 3rd
son of 1st Bt.), by Dorothea, dau. of the Rev. Christopher Harvey, D.D., of Kyle, co.
Wexford, *b.* 1807: *m.* 1852, Harriet Maria Catherine, who *d.* 1884, dau. of Lieut.-Gen. Edward
William Shuldham, H.E.I.C., of Dunmanway, co. Cork; *d.* 1889; *s.* by his brother [8]
WILLIAM CHARLES, 8th Baron, *b.* 1812; a Representative Peer for Ireland: *m.* 1st, 1840, Lady
Sophia Sherard, who *d.* 1851, dau. of 5th Earl of Harborough (*ext.*), and widow of Sir Thomas
Whichcote, 6th Bt.; 2ndly, 1866, Lady Victoria Cecil, who *d.* 1932, dau. of 2nd Marquess
of Exeter: *d.* 1894; *s.* by his el. son [9] ALGERNON WILLIAM GEORGE, 9th Baron, *b.* 1868;
m. 1890, Mary, who *d.* 1949, dau. of the late Henry J. Toulmin, of The Prè, St. Albans;
d. 1898; *s.* by his son [10] JOHN, 10th Baron, *b.* 1892: assumed name of John Evans Carbery by
deed poll in Nairobi 1920: *m.* 1st, 1913 (m. diss. 1919) José, da. of Evelyn James Metcalfe; 2ndly,
1922, Maia Ivy, who *d.* 1928, da. of Alfred Anderson, of Nairobi; 3rdly, 1930, June Weir Mosley;
d. 1970; *s.* by his nephew [11] PETER RALFE HARRINGTON, 11th Baron and present peer.

Cardigan, Earl of, son of Marquess of Ailesbury.

Cardross, Lord, son of Earl of Buchan.

CAREW, BARON. (Conolly-Carew.) [Baron I. 1834, and U.K. 1838.]

To wonder at nothing.

WILLIAM FRANCIS CONOLLY-CAREW, *CBE*, 6th Baron; *b.* April 23rd, 1905; *s.* 1927; ed. at Wellington Coll.; Major (ret.) Duke of Cornwall's L.I., a Trustee of Irish Sailors and Soldiers Land Trust, and a C.St.J.; ADC to Gov. and Com.-in-Ch. of Bermuda 1931-36; National Chm. of British Legion 1963-66; 1939-45 War (wounded); assumed by deed poll 1938, the additional surname of Conolly; *cr.* CBE (Civil) 1966: *m.* 1937, Lady Sylvia Gwendoline Eva Maitland (C.St.J.), da. of 15th Earl of Lauderdale, and has issue.

Arms.—Or, three lions passant in pale sable. *Crest.*—An heraldic antelope passant sable, horned and tufted or. *Supporters*—Two heraldic antelopes gules, horned and tufted or.

Residence,—Mount Armstrong, Donadea, co. Kildare.

Clubs,—Army and Navy, Kildare Street.

SONS LIVING.

Hon. PATRICK THOMAS, *b.* March 6th, 1938; ed. at Harrow; late Capt. Roy. Horse Guards; *m.* 1962, Celia Mary, younger dau. of Col. the Hon Charles Guy Cubitt, *CBE, DSO, TD, DL* [see B. Ashcombe], and has issue living, William Patrick, *b.* 1973,—Virginia Mary, *b.* 1965,—Nicola Rosamond, *b.* 1966,—Camilla Sylvia, *b.* 1969. *Residence,*—Donadea House, Naas, co. Kildare. *Club,*—Cavalry.

Hon. Gerald Edward Ian MAITLAND-CAREW (Thirlestone Castle, Lauder, Berwickshire), *b.* 1941; Capt. (ret.) 15th/19th Hussars; assumed by deed poll 1971 the surname of Maitland-Carew: *m.* 1972, Rosalind Averil, da. of Lt.-Col. Neil Hanning Reed Speke, MC.

DAUGHTERS LIVING.

Hon. Diana Sylvia, *b.* 1940.

Hon. Sarah Catherine, *b.* 1944: *m.* 1966, Ian Arthur Cluny Macpherson of 6, Parkgate Close, Kingston Hill, Surrey, KT2 7LO, and has issue living, John Gavin, *b.* 1967,—Caroline Emma Louisa, *b.* 1969, —Katharine Heather Elizabeth, *b.* 1974.

BROTHERS LIVING.

Hon. Gavin George CAREW, *MBE, TD* (Gellillyndu, Llanio, Tregaron, Dyfed), *b.* 1906; ed. at Clifton; late Maj. Co. London Yeo.; 1939-45 War in W. Desert, Italy, Belgium, and Germany (despatches, MBE, Officer of American Legion of Merit); MBE (Mil) 1945: *m.* 1932, Aileen Hilda Frances, who *d.* 1974, da. of the late Ean Francis Cecil [M. Exeter, colls.], and has issue living, Anne Hilda Catherine, *b.* 1933: *m.* 1953, John Dix, of Gellillyndu, Llanio, Tregaron, Dyfed.

Hon. Peter Cuthbert CAREW, *b.* 1908 ; Lieut.-Com. (retired) R.N. : *m.* 1937, Barbara, dau. of the late Henry Wolley Leigh-Bennett [Price, Bt., cr. 1815, colls.], and has issue living, David Edward, *b.* 1942,—Thomas Henry, *b.* 1947: *m.* 1974, Lucinda, yst. da. of Joseph Guy Lubbock, of High Elms, Waldringfield, Suffolk, [see B. Avebury, colls.],—Susan Catherine, *b.* 1944: *m.* 1971, William David Madel, MP. *Residence,*—Croft House, Great Bealings, Woodbridge, Suffolk.

PREDECESSORS.—[1] ROBERT SHAPLAND Carew, Lord-Lieut. of co. Wexford ; *cr. Baron Carew* (peerage of Ireland) 1834, and *Baron Carew,* of Castle Boro, co. Wexford (peerage of United Kingdom) 1838; *d.* 1856; *s.* by his son [2] ROBERT SHAPLAND, *K.P.*; *b.* 1818; Lord Lieut. of co. Wexford, and M.P. for Waterford (L) 1840-7: *m.* 1844, Emily Anne, dau. of Sir George Richard Philips, *M.P.*, 2nd Bt.: *d.* 1881: *s.* by his son [3] ROBERT SHAPLAND GEORGE JULIAN, 3rd Baron; *b.* 1860: *m.* 1888, Julia Mary, who *d.* 1922, dau. of the late Albert Arthur; Erin Lethbridge [Lethbridge, Bt., colls.]; *d.* 1923; *s.* by his brother [4] GEORGE PATRICK JOHN, 4th Baron; *b.* 1863: *m.* 1888, Maud Beatrice, who *d.* 1955, dau. of the late John Ramsay; *d.* 1926 ; *s.* by his cousin [5] GERALD SHAPLAND (son of the late Hon. Shapland Francis Carew, son of 1st Baron), 5th Baron; *b.* 1860: *m.* 1904, Catherine, only dau. of the late Thomas Conolly, M.P., of Castletown, co. Kildare; *d* 1927 *s.* by his el. son [6] WILLIAM FRANCIS, 6th Baron and present peer.

CARISBROOKE, MARQUESSATE OF. (Mountbatten.) [Extinct 1960.]

DAUGHTER LIVING OF FIRST MARQUESS.

Lady Iris Victoria Beatrice Grace MOUNTBATTEN BRYAN, *b.* Jan. 13th, 1920; was a Train Bearer to the Queen at Coronation of King George VI.; resumed the surname of Mountbatten in lieu of O'Malley by deed poll 1949 : *m.* 1st, Feb. 15th. 1941 (marriage dissolved 1946), Major Hamilton Joseph Keyes O'Malley, Irish Guards; 2ndly, May 5th, 1957 (m. diss. 1957), Michael Kelly Bryan; 3rdly, Dec. 11th, 1965, William Kemp, and has issue living, (by 2nd marriage) Robin Alexander *b.* Dec. 20th, 1957. *Residence,*—Toronto, Canada.

Carleton, Baron, title of Earl of Shannon on Roll of H.L.

CARLISLE, EARL OF. (Howard.) [Earl E. 1661.]

CHARLES JAMES RUTHVEN HOWARD, M.C., 12th Earl; b. Feb. 21st, 1923; s. 1963; ed. at Eton; h.a. to Lordship of Ruthven of Freeland; a FLAS; a Forestry Commr. since 1967; 1939-45 War as Lt. Rifle Bde. (severely wounded, MC): m. 1945, the Hon. Ela Hilda Aline Beaumont, only da. of 2nd Viscount Allendale, and has issue.

Arms.—Quarterly of six: 1st gules, a bend between six cross crosslets fitchée argent, on the bend an escutcheon or, charged with a demi-lion, pierced through the mouth with an arrow, within a double tressure flory counterflory, all gules, and above the escutcheon a mullet sable, for difference, Howard; 2nd gules, three lions passant guardant or, and a label of three points argent, Thomas of Brotherton, son of Edward I.; 3rd checky, or and azure, Warren, Earl Warren and Surrey; 4th gules, a lion rampant argent; Mowbray, Duke of Norfolk; 5th gules, three escallops argent, Dacre; 6th barry of eight argent and azure, three chaplets of roses proper, Greystock. Crest,—On a chapeau gules, turned up ermine, a lion statant guardant, with the tail extended or, ducally gorged argent. Supporters,— Dexter, a lion argent, charged with a mullet sable or difference; sinister a bull gules, armed unguled, ducally gorged and lined or.

I am willing, but not able

Seat,—Naworth Castle, Brampton, Cumberland.

SONS LIVING.
GEORGE WILLIAM BEAUMONT (Viscount Morpeth), b. Feb. 15th, 1949; ed. at Eton, and Balliol Coll., Oxford; Capt. 9th/10th R. Lancers.
Hon. Philip Charles Wentworth, b. 1963.

DAUGHTERS LIVING.
Lady Jane Annabelle, b. 1947: m. 1968, John David Vaughan Seth-Smith, of 34, Epirus Rd., SW6, and has issue living, Gemma Bridget Annabel, b. 1972.
Lady Emma Bridget, b. 1952: m. 1974, John Langton-Lockton.

SISTER LIVING.
Lady Carolyn Bridget Dacre (The Old Tannery, Temple Sowerby, Penrith), b. 1919; 1939-45 War as Subaltern ATS.

HALF-SISTER LIVING.
Lady Susan Ankaret, b. 1948: m. 1967, Charles James Buchanan-Jardine, of 5, Campden Grove, W8 [see Buchanan-Jardine, Bt.].

MOTHER LIVING.
Bridget Helen (Dowager Viscountess Monckton of Brenchley), CBE (113, Eaton Sq., SW1), da. of 9th Lord Ruthven of Freeland: s. as Lady Ruthven of Freeland 1956: m. 1st, 1918 (m. diss. 1947), the 11th Earl of Carlisle; 2ndly, 1947, as his second wife, the 1st Viscount Monckton of Brenchley, who d. 1965.

WIDOW LIVING OF ELEVENTH EARL.
ESME MARY SHRUBB (Esme, Countess of Carlisle) (17, Sheffield Terr., W8), da. of Charles Edward Iredell: m. 1947, as his second wife, the 11th Earl, who d. 1963.

COLLATERAL BRANCHES LIVING.
Issue of the late Hon. Oliver Howard, 4th son of 9th Earl, b. 1875, d. 1908 : m. 1900, Muriel Mary Temple, M.B.E., who d. 1952 (having m. 2ndly, 1909, the 5th Earl of Clanwilliam), dau. of Russell Stephenson :—
Hubert Arthur George, b. 1901; ed. at Eton, and Ch. Ch., Oxford (MA): m. 1930, Moira, da. of the late Rev. John Arthur Victor Magee, V. of St. Mark's, Hamilton Terr., W. [Wilson, Bt., cr. 1874], and has issue living, David Charles Hubert (Hilltop Farm, Awbridge, nr. Romsey, Hants.), b. 1940; ed. at Eton: m. 1962 (m. diss. 1969), Pamela Mary, da. of Frederick Thomas Rose, of Kenilworth, and has issue living, Susan Mary b. 1963, Rosalind Emma b. 1966,—Lavinia Moira, b. 1944: m. 1963, Christopher Thomas Bernard Turville-Constable Maxwell, of Harfield Farm, Chilcombe, Winchester, Hants. [see L. Herries of Terregles, colls.]. Residence,—Merrets, Andrew Lane, Ropley, Hants.

Issue of the late Hon. Geoffrey William Algernon Howard, 5th son of 9th Earl b. 1877, d. 1935 : m. 1915, the Hon. Ethel Christian, who d. 1932, dau. of 3rd Baron Methuen :—
George Anthony Geoffrey, b. 1920; ed. at Eton, and at Balliol Coll., Oxford; 1939-45 War in Burma as Maj. The Green Howards (wounded): m. 1949, Lady Cecilia Blanche Genevieve Fitz Roy, who d. 1974, da. of 8th Duke of Grafton, and has issue living, Henry Francis Geoffrey, b. 1950,— Nicholas Paul Geoffrey, b. 1952,—Simon Bartholomew Geoffrey, b. 1956,—Anthony Michael Geoffrey, b. 1958. Residences,—Castle Howard, York; 18, Ennismore Mews, SW7.——Rosemary Christian, b. 1916. Residence,—Coneysthorpe, York.——Katharine Cecilia Gabriel, b. 1930: m. 1953, Stephen Nicholas Spens, son of Sir Will Spens, CBE. Residence,—Chanting Hill, Stoneyfields, Farnham, Surrey.

Issue of the late Hon. Michael Francis Stafford Howard, 6th son of 9th Earl, b. 1880, d. (killed in action during European War) 1917 : m. 1911, Nora Elizabeth. who d. 1961, dau. of the late Col. William Hensman, R.A.M.C. :—
Geraldine Mary (twin), M.B., B.S., b. 1917 : m. 1st, 1943 (marriage annulled on his petition 1944), Frederick Hume Jackson, RA; 2ndly, 1944, Hugh Reginald Jolly, MD, FRCP, DCH, formerly Capt. RAMC, and has issue living, (by 2nd m.) Christopher John Howard, b. 1944,—Paul Howard, b. 1951,—Caryl Ann Howard, b. 1947, assumed the additional christian name of Howard 1963, Residence,—The Garden House, Warren Park, Kingston Hill, Surrey.

Grandchildren of the late Col. Frederick Compton Howard, 3rd son of the late Frederick John Howard, son of the late Hon. Frederick Howard, 3rd son of 5th Earl:—
Issue of the late Richard Fitzroy Howard, b. 1879, d. 1962: m. 1914, Elsie Anne, who d. 1936, el. dau. of the late Robert Clarkson, of Scarborough:—
Richard Frederick Robert, (PO Himeville, Natal; Club,—Royal Natal Yacht), b. 1916: 1939-45 War as Capt. Green Howards (wounded): m. 1946, Jean McBride Taylor, and has issue living, Jane Anne McBride, b. 1951: m. 1969, Andrew Hugh Ross MacLennan (P. Bag Manzengwenya, PO Hluhluwe, Zululand), and has issue living, Morag Jean b. 1970.——George William, b. 1924; is an AMIMechE: m. 1952, Barbara Enid, da. of Reginald Edgar Everett, of Mill Hill, NW7, and has issue living, Katherine Margaret, b. 1954,—Lesley Jane, b. 1957,—Sarah Barbara, b. 1960. Residence,—109, Southella Way, Kirkella, E. Yorks.——Bertha Frances Grace (73, Silkham Rd., Oxted, Surrey), b. 1914: m.

1943 (m. diss. 1960), Douglas Haley, and has issue living, Ian Richard (33, Lowfield Lane, Newark, Notts.), *b.* 1944: *m.* 1965, Elizabeth Rose O'Reilly, of co. Cavan, and has issue living, Damien Michael Douglas *b.* 1974, Siobhan Geraldine *b.* 1972,—Helen Veronica, *b.* 1946: *m.* 1974, Brian S. Liddell, of 5, Orchard Close, Henley-on-Thames, Oxon.——Kathleen Victoria, *b.* 1918: *m.* 1941, John Alan Lake, and has issue living, Ann Cecilia Mary, *b.* 1942,—Susan Margaret, *b.* 1949. *Residence,*—19, St. James St., Scarborough, Yorks.——Elsie Anne, *b.* 1927: *m.* 1951, William Byass Temple, and has issue living, Janet, *b.* 1954,—Wendy, *b.* 1956,—Diane, *b.* 1962. *Residence,*—Oak Wood, 19, Throxemby Lane, Newby, Scarborough, Yorks.

Issue of the late George Frederick Howard, *b.* 1894, *d.* 1957: *m.* 1919, Jane Anne Scott, who *d.* 1961, dau. of John Young Myrtle, of Edinburgh:—
Margaret Anne Myrtle, *M.B., Ch.B., D.P.H., b.* 1921: formerly Capt. R.A.M.C.: *m.* 1946, Ralph Kenyon Hardy, and has issue living, Christopher Nigel, *b.* 1947,—Peter Ralph Howard, *b.* 1953. *Residence,*—28, Embercourt Rd., Thames Ditton, Surrey.

Grandchildren of the late Alfred John Howard, 4th son of the late Frederick John Howard (ante):—
Issue of the late Capt. William Gilbert Howard, O.B.E., R.N., *b.* 1877, *d.* 1960 : *m.* 1912. the Hon. Agnes Caroline Sophia Parnell, *JP,* who *d.* 1968, da. of 4th Baron Congleton:—
Frederick Henry, *D.S.O., M.C., b.* 1915 ; Lieut.-Col. (retired) 3rd Hussars ; Palestine 1936 (M.C.); European War 1939-45 in N. Africa, and N.-W. Europe (Bar to M.C., D.S.O.) ; D.S.O. 1946 : *m.* 1st, 1941, Estelle Georgette (from whom he obtained a divorce 1946), dau. of Capt. Sharp, of Londjani, Kenya ; 2ndly, 1952, the Hon. Jean Margaret Parnell, dau. of 6th Baron Congleton, and has issue living, (by 2 nd m.) Henry James, *b.* 1956,—John Dugald, *b.* 1958,—Rose, *b.* 1953. *Residence,*—Isle of Gometra, by Mull, Argyll. *Clubs,*—United Service, New (Edinburgh), Royal Highland Yacht.——John William (Appletree Cottage, Staplecross, Robertsbridge, Sussex; Alpine and Royal and Ancient Clubs, MCC), *b.* 1917; MA Camb.; Colonial Admin. Ser., Kenya, 1939-63; 1939-45 War in Abyssinia and Madagascar as Capt. 5th King's African Rifles (despatches twice): *m.* 1949, Elizabeth Bligh, yst. da. of Capt. Robert Francis Veasey, RN [E. Darnley, colls.], and has issue living, Jonathan Arthur Francis, *b.* 1955; ed. at Eton,—Sarah Elizabeth Anne, *b.* 1951: *m.* 1973, Robert James Rogers,—Eva Jane Agnes, *b.* 1953.——Mark Alfred, *b.* 1919; is a Grazier; N. Africa and Greece 1939-45 as Lt. Austn. Forces (prisoner): *m.* 1950, Judith Ruth, da. of F. E. Selwyn Scott, MBE, JP, of Scotsburn, Victoria, Aust., and has issue living, Michael Gilbert, *b.* 1950,— William Mark, *b.* 1959,—Margaret Jean, *b.* 1952. *Residence,*—Stonegate, Dunkeld, Vic., Aust. *Club,* —Naval and Military (Melbourne).——Margaret (twin), *b.* 1919; formerly Subaltern ATS: *m.* 1945, Brig. Christopher Charles Lloyd Browne, OBE, late RA, who *d.* 1972, and has issue living, Elizabeth, *b.* 1947,—Felicity, *b.* 1958.——Carolyn, *b.* 1958. *Residence,*—Dean House, W. Dean, Salisbury, Wilts.——Agnes, *b.* 1921: formerly Leading Wren WRNS: *m.* 1945, Maj. John Singleton Hattersley, RE (ret.), and has issue living, Charles William, *b.* 1949,—Margaret Sarah, *b.* 1950,—Victoria Vera, *b.* 1955,—Helen Jean, *b.* 1961. *Residence,*—The Hyde Farm, Little Yeldham, Essex.

Issue of the late Vice-Adm. Ronald Howard, *b.* 1878, *d.* 1959: *m.* (Jan.) 1913, Ruth Evelyn, who *d.* 1968, da. of the late William Coryton [Parker Bt., cr. 1884, colls.]:—
Michael William, *MC* (The Kennels, Sampford Spiney, Devon), *b.* 1917; Maj. (ret.) Devonshire Regt.; 1939-45 War in Italy and N.-W. Europe (MC and Bar): *m.* 1949, Gillian Hester, da. of Sir John Frederick Shelley, 10th Bt. (cr. 1611).——Roger Alexander, *TD* (of Old Barn, Churt, Farnham, Surrey), *b.* 1919; Maj. (ret.) R.A.O.C.: *m.* 1944, Jean, dau. of the late Vice-Adm.A. H., Alington, and has issue living, Alexandra Nancy, *b.* 1946: *m.* 1971, Christopher Skidmore Taylor, of 48, King Henry's Rd., Primrose Hill, NW3, and has issue living, Emily *b.* 1973,—Miranda Jane *b.* 1948: *m.* 1973, Petar Djedovic, of 18, Primrose Court, 159, Hydethorpe Rd., SW12, and Petrovac Na Moru, Montenegro,—Elvina Lucy *b.* 1949: *m.* 1974, Peter Siddon, of 31, Abbotsbury Rd., Holland Park, W14 8EH.——Millicent, *b.* (Dec.) 1913: *m.* 1937, Col. Charles Richard Spencer, OBE, 12th Roy. Lancers, of Elfordtown, Yelverton, S. Devon, and has issue living, Edward Charles, *b.* 1946,— Elizabeth Janet *b.* 1938.

Grandsons of the late Gerald Richard Howard (infra):—
Issue of the late Bertram Marcus Howard, *b.* 1890, *d.* 1970: *m.* 1924, Phyllis Maude (Coronation Villa, Mousehole, Penzance, Cornwall), da. of Robert James Lamb, of Surbiton, Surrey:—
Michael Cavendish (White Gates, 27, Souberie Av., Broadway, Letchworth, Herts.), *b.* 1926; ed. at King's Coll., Taunton; ARIC; W. Africa 1944-45 with REME: *m.* 1956, Muriel, widow of W. T. Mullings, BSc, MD.——Richard Cavendish (Patterdale, 14, Cold Bath Rd., Harrogate, N. Yorks), *b.* 1936; ed. at King's Coll., Taunton: *m.* 1959, Diana Mary, da. of Frank B. Wharton, of Lichfield, Staffs., and has issue living, Dale Robin Cavendish, *b.* 1960,—Timothy Richard Cavendish, *b.* 1962,— James David Cavendish, *b.* 1968,—Angela Claire, *b.* 1961.

Grandchildren of the late Frederick John Howard (ante) :—
Issue of the late Gerald Richard Howard, *b.* 1853, *d.* 1945 : *m.* 1886, Ada, who *d.* 1937, dau. of the late Charles Curtis :—
Alfred. *b.* 1887; Staff Sergeant (ret.) Roy. Canadian Mounted Police: *m.* 1922, Merle Ethel, da. of the late James McEwen, of Ontario.——Joan Edith Barbara (Manor Farm Cottage, Fairford, Glos.), *b.* 1898; Polish Grand Cross of Merit: *m.* 1922, Bertram Eric Edmonds, who *d.* 1965, and has issue living, Richard Edward Howard (Micklefield Hall, Rickmansworth, Herts. *Club,*—Alpine), *b.* 1925; ed. at Wellington Coll., and at Oriel Coll., Oxford; formerly Lt. Airborne Artillery: *m.* 1958, Sarah Anne, da. of Hugh Humphrey Merriman, DSO, MC TD, and has issue living, Charles Hugh Howard *b.* 1960, Anna Louise *b.* 1959, Harriet Holden *b.* 1963,—Ann Gyllian Howard, *b.*, 1928: *m.* 1949, Philip Moore, formerly Capt. RA, of 59, Drax Av., Wimbledon, SW20, and has issue living, Richard Philip Julian *b.* 1957, Elizabeth Gyllian *b.* 1951: *m.* 1971, Capt. Roger Christopher Bolter, RCT, (and has issue living, Nicholas Christopher Alwyn *b.* 1972, Miranda Gyllian *b.* 1973), Susannah Joan *b.* 1961,—Mary St. Joan Howard (Mallam Waters, Fairford, Glos., GL7 4DT), *b.* 1930: *m.* 1st, 1951, James Ewing Kennaway, who *d.* 1968; 2ndly, 1972, Brian C. Kennaway Cummins, and has issue living, (by 1st m.) Guy Charles *b.* 1957, David Bell *b.* 1959, Emma Elizabeth *b.* 1953, Victoria Jane *b.* 1955.——Blanche Esther Muriel (Chesterfield House, Feckenham, Worcs.), *b.* 1904: *m.* 1928, Angelo Victor John de Rin (known in Italy as The Noble Angelo de Rin de Capodistria), who *d.* 1944, and has issue living, Diana Maria, *b.* 1930: *m.* 1955, Hilary George Gosling, of Chesterfield House, Feckenham, Worcs., and has issue living, Oliver *b.* 1958, Jane Dorothy Blanche *b.* 1956, Rosemary Jean *b.* 1961, Veronica *b.* 1963,—Victoria, *b.* 1931: *m.* 1959, David Lynn Pratt, PhD, AMICE, of 6, Tite St., Chelsea, SW3, and Fox Lodge, Guildford, Surrey, and has issue living, Jonathan de Rin, *b.* 1960, James Lynn *b.* 1963.

Grandson of the late Very Rev. the Hon. Henry Edward John Howard, DD, Dean of Lichfield, 4th son of 5th Earl:—
Issue of the late Capt. John Henry Howard, *b.* 1827, *d.* 1925 : *m.* 1874, Eliza, who *d.* 1929. dau. of the late Rev. J. Salt, of Standon Rectory, Stafford :—
Edmund John, *b.* 1891; ed. at Wellington Coll.; 1914-18 War with RA. *Residence,*—Butts Hill, Challock, Ashford, Kent.

Grandchildren of the late Capt. John Henry Howard (ante) :—
Issue of the late Cdr. Robert John Howard, RN, *b.* 1878, *d.* 1965: *m.* 1918, Violet Mary, who *d.* 1930, da. of the late Thurstan Collins, of Newton Ferrers, Cornwall:—
John Thurstan Collins, *MC* (College Green Farm, East Pennard, Shepton Mallet, Som.), *b.* 1919; ed. at Eton; Lt.-Col. SCLI: *m.* 1949, Margaret, only da. of Col. Edyvean, of Mawgan, Cornwall.

Issue of the late Com. Charles Wilbraham John Howard, R.N., *b.* 1880, *d.* 1959 : *m.* 1909, Dorothy Ida Leigh, who *d.* 1968, da. of Sir Thomas Leigh Hare, 1st Bt., MVO (cr. 1905):—

Geoffrey Charles (Somerford House, Little Somerford, Chippenham), b. 1910; Maj. (ret.) Black Watch; 1939-45 War: m. 1939, Katharine, da. of the late Adm. Sir Eric John Arthur Fullerton, KCB, DSO [B. Fisher].——Susan Elizabeth, b. 1913. Residence,—Wall, Broadwindsor, Dorset.

Issue of the late Algitha Fanny Howard, who d. 1940: m. 1909, Brig.-Gen. Charles Græme Higgins, C.M.G., D.S.O., D.L., who d. 1961 :—

Fergus Howard Græme, b. 1914; is Lieut.-Col. 1st Greenjackets; European War 1939-45 in Abyssinia and N.-W. Europe (twice wounded): m. 1950, Anne, only dau. of Lieut.-Col. E. T. McDougal, MC, late Scots Guards, and has issue living, Annabel Cynthia, b. 1958. Residence,— Badbury Hill, Faringdon, Berks.——Anne, b. 1919: m. 1938, Maj. Hugh Edward Montgomery, Oxford and Bucks. LI, who d. 1969, and has issue living, William Howard Clive, b. 1940,—David Hugh, b. 1942. Residence,—Grey Abbey, co. Down.

Granddaughter of the late Rev. Henry Frederick Howard (infra):—
Issue of the late Major Bernard Henry Howard, b. 1879, d. (killed in action during European War) 1916: m. 1909, Margaret Ellen Edith McLean (Frithville, 106, Park Rd., Teddington, Middx.), da. of the late Lieut.-Col. Donat Edmund McMahon:—

Marjorie Isabella, b. 1910: m. 1st, 1938, Lieut.-Com. Robert Lampard, R.N., who d. (killed in action during European War) 1941; 2ndly, 1945, Lieut.-Com. Roger Hoyle, R.N., and has issue living, (by 2nd marriage) Hugo Charles John, b. 1949,—Angela Felicity, b. 1947. Residences,— Swandown, Axford, Marlborough, Wilts.

Granddaughters of the late Very Rev. the Hon. Henry Edward John Howard, D.D. (ante):—
Issue of the late Rev. Henry Frederick Howard, b. 1844, d. 1938: m. 1878, Eliza Mima, who d. 1938, dau. of the late Rev. John Spearman Wasey (formerly V. of Compton Parva), of Priors Court, Newbury :—

Evelyn Frances, b. 1884: m. 1912, Anthony Dod, who d. 1960, and has issue living, Philip William (of Middle Farm, Chieveley, Newbury, Berks.), b. 1914; formerly F/O RAFVR: m. 1st 1940 (m. diss. 1967), Adèle Margaret, da. of the late Harry Vivash, of Holmbush, Findon, Worthing; 2ndly, 1968, Marion Ada Harding, and has issue living, (by 1st m.) Peter Philip, b. 1946: m. 1968, Astrid Irene Clark, Robert Vivash William b. 1950, Patricia Marilyn b. 1943: m. 1964, Raymond George Brind, of 39, The Faulklands, Baydon Rd., Lambourn (and has issue living, Philip Raymond b. 1965, Richard Timothy b. 1967) (by 2nd m.) Simon James b. 1970—Michael Henry Anthony (Bank Top, Grindleford, Derbyshire), b. 1915, formerly Capt. RE; 1939-45 War with Central Mediterranean Force and in N.-W. Europe: m. 1938, Isabel Joyce, da. of the late Laurence Hebron Goundry, of Trecoun, Scunthorpe, and has issue living, Richard Michael b. 1945: m. 1974, Jacqueline Page, da. of Harry Thompson, of Redcar, Yorks., Robin Anthony b. 1947: m. 1971, Janet, da. of Ralph Beesley, of Grange Hill, Withybrook, Warwicks., Rosemary Sandra b. 1940: m. 1959, Frederick Roy Windsor Clarke, of Nevis, W. Indies (and has issue living, Shaun Frederick Lawrence b. 1960, Nicole Sandra b. 1961),—Barbara Margaret b. 1913; formerly Junior Com. ATS. Residence,—Edgehill, Trebor Av., Farnham, Surrey,—Maud Agnes Mima, b. 1887.——Henrietta Dorothea, b. 1892. Residence,—46, Lynch Rd., Farnham, Surrey.

PREDECESSORS.—[1] CHARLES Howard, P.C., great-grandson of Lord William Howard 3rd son of 4th Duke of Norfolk; cr. Viscount of Morpeth by Oliver Cromwell 1658, and Baron Dacre of Gillesland, Viscount Howard of Morpeth, and Earl of Carlisle 1661; was subsequently Ambassador to the Czar of Muscovy and Gov. of Jamaica; d. 1686; s. by his son [2] EDWARD, 2nd Earl; d. 1692; s. by his son [3] CHARLES, 3rd Earl; was First Lord of the Treasury, Constable of the Tower, and Gov. of Windsor Castle; d. 1738; s. by his son [4] HENRY, K.G.; d. 1758; s. by his son [5] FREDERICK, K.G., K.T.; Viceroy of Ireland 1780-2; d. 1825, s. by his son [6] GEORGE, K.G., 6th Earl; b. 1773; was Lord-Lieut. of E. Riding of York; m. 1801, Lady Georgiana Dorothy Cavendish, dau. of 5th Duke of Devonshire; d. 1848; s. by his el. son [7] GEORGE WILLIAM FREDERICK, K.G., P.C.; was Ch. Sec. for Ireland 1835-41, Ch. Commr. of Woods and Forests 1846-50, Chancellor of Duchy of Lancaster 1850-2, and Lord-Lieut. of Ireland 1855-8 and 1859-64; d. unmarried 1864; s. by his brother [8] WILLIAM GEORGE, 8th Earl, b. 1808; R. of Londesborough 1832-77; d. unmarried 1889; s. by his nephew [9] GEORGE JAMES (son of the late Hon. Charles Wentworth George Howard, M.P., 4th son of 6th Earl), 9th Earl; b. 1843; M.P. for E. Cumberland (L) 1879-80, when he was defeated, and 1881-5: m. 1864, the Hon. Rosalind Frances, who d. 1921, dau. of 2nd Baron Stanley of Alderley; d. 1911: s. by his son [10] CHARLES JAMES STANLEY, 10th Earl; b. 1867; sat as M.P. for Birmingham, S. Div. (LU) 1904-11: m. 1894, Rhoda Ankaret, who d. 1957, dau. of Col. Paget W. L'Estrange, formerly RA; d. 1912; s. by his only son [11] GEORGE JOSSLYN L'ESTRANGE, 11th Earl, b. 1895; Chm. of U.K. Commercial Corporation, Ankara, 1941-3: m. 1st, 1918 (marriage dissolved 1947), dau. of 9th Lord Ruthven of Freeland; 2ndly, 1947, Esme Mary Shruble, dau. of Charles Edward Iredell; d. 1963; s. by his only son [12] CHARLES JAMES RUTHVEN, 12th Earl and present peer; also Viscount Howard of Morpeth, and Baron Dacre of Gillesland.

CARLISLE, LORD BISHOP OF. (Halsey.)

Rt. Rev. HENRY DAVID HALSEY, son of George Halsey, MBE; b. Jan. 27th, 1919; ed. at King's Coll., London (BA), and Wells Theo. Coll.; Curate Petersfield 1942-45, Chap. RNVR 1946-47, Curate, St. Andrew Plymouth 1947-50, V. of Netheravon, and R. of Fittleton 1950-53, V. of St. Stephen, Chatham 1953-62, Chap. Bromley Hosp. 1962-68, Rural Dean of Bromley 1966-68, and Bishop Suffragan of Tonbridge 1968-72; translated 64th Bishop of Carlisle 1972: m. 1947, Rachel Margaret Neil, da. of the Rev. Neil Campbell Smith.

Patron of sixty-three livings, the Archdeaconries of Carlisle, Westmorland and Furness, and W. Cumberland, and the Canonries in his Cathedral.
This See was established by Henry I. in 1133, soon after the foundation of the Cathedral by William Rufus.
Episcopal Signature—David Carliol:
ARMS OF THE SEE,—Argent, on a cross sable, a mitre with labels or.
Residence,—Rose Castle, Dalston, Carlisle, Cumbria.

Carlow, Viscount, son of Earl of Portarlington.

CARNARVON, EARL OF. (Herbert.) [Earl G.B. 1793.]

One I will serve.

HENRY GEORGE ALFRED MARIUS VICTOR FRANCIS HERBERT, 6th Earl; *b.* Nov. 7th, 1898; *s.* 1923; ed. at Eton, and at R.M.C.; is Lieut.-Col. 7th (Queen's Own) Hussars; European War 1916-19 in Mesopotamia: *m.* 1st, 1922, Catherine (who obtained a divorce 1936), dau. of the late Jacob Wendell, of New York; 2ndly, 1939, Ottilie (JAMES) (who obtained a divorce 1947), dau. of Eugene Losch, of Vienna, and has issue by 1st marriage.

Arms,—Per pale azure and gules, three lions rampant argent, a crescent for difference. Crest,— A wyvern, wings elevated, vert, in the mouth a sinister human hand couped at the wrist gules. Supporters,—*Dexter*, a panther argent, incensed proper, spotted with hurts and torteaux alternately; *sinister*, a lion argent; both ducally gorged per pale azure and gules, with chain reflexed over the back or, and charged on the shoulder with an ermine spot sable.

Seat,—Highclere Castle, Newbury. *Club*,— White's.

SON LIVING. (*By 1st marriage.*)

HENRY GEORGE REGINALD MOLYNEUX (*Lord Porchester*), *b.* Jan. 19th, 1924; ed. at Eton; late Lieut. Roy. Horse Guards; Hon. Col. 115th (Hampshire Fortress) Engineer Regt. (TA) 1963; appointed Racing Manager to HM 1970: *m.* 1956, Jean Margaret, da. of the Hon. Oliver Malcolm Wallop [see E. Portsmouth], and has issue:—
ONS LIVING,—*Hon.* George Reginald Oliver Molyneux, *b.* Nov. 10th, 1956; a Page of Honour to HM 1969-73.
Hon. Henry Malcolm, *b.* 1959.
DAUGHTER LIVING,—*Hon.* Carolyn Penelope, *b.* 1962.
Residence,—Milford Lake House, Newbury, Berks. *Club*,—White's.

DAUGHTER LIVING. (*By 1st marriage.*)

Lady (Anne) Penelope Marian, *b.* 1925: *m.* 1945, Gerrit van der Woude, Grenadier Guards, and has issue living, Michael Gerrit, *b.* 1946,—David Anthony, *b.* 1947,—Penelope Catherine Mary, *b.* 1952. *Residence*,—Herondon, Eastry, Sandwich, Kent.

SISTER LIVING.

Lady Evelyn Leonora Almina, *b.* 1901: *m.* 1923, Sir Brograve Campbell Beauchamp, 2nd Bt. (cr. 1911). *Residence*,—19, Kingston House, Princes Gate, S.W.7.

WIDOW LIVING OF SON OF FOURTH EARL.

Mary Elizabeth, dau. of J. E. Willard, formerly Ambassador for U.S.A. at Madrid: *m.* 1921, the Hon. Mervyn Robert Howard Molyneux Herbert, who *d.* 1929, and has issue living [see colls., infra]. *Residence*,—25, Eaton Sq., SW1.

COLLATERAL BRANCHES LIVING.

Issue of the late Lieut.-Col. the Hon. Aubrey Nigel Henry Molyneux Herbert, M.P., 2nd son of 4th Earl, *b.* 1880, *d.* 1923: *m.* 1910, the Hon. Mary Gertrude Vesey, who *d.* 1970, da. of 4th Viscount De Vesci:—
Gabriel Mary Hermione, *b.* 1911: *m.* 1943, Maj. Alexander Dru, Intelligence Corps, and has issue living, Auberon Alexander Bernard, *b.* 1951,—Angela Mary Domenica, *b.* 1943,—Mary Sophia *b.* 1945,— Laura Jane Veronica *b.* 1946. *Residence*,—Bickham Manor, Timberscombe, nr. Minehead.— Anne Brigit Domenica, *b.* 1914: *m.* 1935, Capt. Allister Edward Grant, late 9th Lancers, who *d.* 1947, and has issue living,—Robert John David, *b.* 1942: *m.* 1970, Harriet Reeve, and has issue living, —Mary Christina, *b.* 1937: *m.* 1962, Michael Melotte, and has issue living,—Anne Evelyn Elizabeth, *b.* 1938: *m.* 1958, Ian Fraser, and has issue living.

Issue of the late Hon. Mervyn Robert Howard Molyneux Herbert, 3rd son of 4th Earl, *b.* 1882, *d.* 1929: *m.* 1921, Mary Elizabeth (ante), dau. of J. E. Willard, formerly Ambassador for U.S.A. at Madrid :—
Edward Alan Mervyn Henry Molyneux, *b.* 1926; ed. at Eton; ARIBA; Bar. Middle Temple 1952; late Capt. Coldstream Guards: *m.* 1966, Bridget Anne, da. of Maj. Hugh Washington Hibbert [E. Inchcape], and has issue living, Alan Mervyn Edward Hugh, *b.* 1971,—Mary Patricia *b.* 1967,— Elizabeth Anne, *b.* 1968,—Penelope Serena *b.* 1969. *Residences*,—Tetton House, Taunton; 37, Morpeth Mansions, SW1. *Club*,—St. James.——Mary Elizabeth Catherine Gwendolen, *b.* 1922: *m.* 1st, 1946, Radu Tilea (from whom she obtained a divorce 1957); 2ndly, 1970, Count Denys Halka Ledochowsky, and has issue living (by 1st m.), Mary Catherine Ileana Camilla, *b.* 1950,—Elizabeth Helen Rodica *b.* 1953: *m.* 1973, John Harrap, of 31, Childs Place, SW5. *Residence*,—3, Sheridan Court, 63, Barkston Gdns., SW5.——Margaret Anne Antonia, *b.* 1923: *m.* 1954, Timothy Walter Horn, and has issue living, Nicholas Charles D'Arcy, *b.* 1962,—Magdalen Sarah, *b.* 1955,—Mary Virginia Louise, *b.* 1957,—Harriet Ann Serena, *b.* 1958. *Residences*,—Donhead Hall, Shaftesbury, Dorset; 37, Evelyn Mansions, SW1.

PREDECESSORS.—Maj.-Gen. the Hon. William Herbert, 5th son of 8th Earl of Pembroke M.P. for Wilton 1734-37 ; *d.* 1756, leaving with other issue [1] HENRY ; cr. *Baron Porchester*, of High Clere, co. Southampton (peerage of Great Britain), 1780, and *Earl of Carnarvon* (peerage of Great Britain) 1793; was Master of the Horse 1806; *d.* 1811; *s.* by his son [2] HENRY GEORGE, 2nd Earl, *d.* 1833 ; *s.* by his son [3] HENRY JOHN GEORGE, 3rd Earl; *b.* 1800; *m.* 1830, Henrietta Anna, who *d.* 1876, dau. of Lord Henry Thomas Molyneux-Howard [D. Norfolk]; *d.* 1849 ; *s.* by his son [4] HENRY HOWARD MOLYNEUX, P.C., 4th Earl. *b.* 1831: Under Sec. of State for Colonies 1857-9, Sec. of State thereof 1866-7 and 1874-8, and Lord-Lieut. of Ireland 1885-6: *m.* 1st, 1861, Lady Evelyn Stanhope, dau. of 6th Earl of Chesterfield; 2ndly, 1878, Elizabeth Catharine, who *d.* 1928, el. dau. of the late Henry Howard; *d.* 1890; *s.* by his el. son [5] GEORGE EDWARD STANHOPE MOLYNEUX, 5th Earl, *b.* 1866: *m.* 1895, Almina Victoria Maria Alexandra, who *d.* 1969, (having m. 2ndly, 1923, Lt.-Col. Ian Onslow Dennistoun, MVO, who *d.* 1938), da. of the late Frederick Charles Wombwell; *d.* 1923; *s.* by his son [6] HENRY GEORGE ALFRED VICTOR FRANCIS, 6th Earl and present peer; also Baron Porchester.

CARNOCK, BARON. (Nicolson.) [Baron U.K. 1916, Bt. N.S. 1637.]

Nothing to stand against

ERSKINE ARTHUR NICOLSON, *D.S.O.*, 3rd Baron and 13th Baronet ; *b.* March 26th, 1884 ; *s.* 1952 ; Capt. R.N. (retired) ; European War 1914-19 (Legion of Honour, Russian Order of St. Anne, promoted, D.S.O.) ; is a J.P.; D.S.O. 1919 : *m.* 1919, the Hon. Katharine Frederica Albertha Lopes, who *d.* 1968, da. of 1st Baron Roborough, and has issue.

Arms,—Or, a lion's head between three falcons' heads erased gules, within a bordure azure. Crest, —A lion's head erased gules. Supporters,—Two falcons reguardant proper.

Residence,—Burrator House, Sheepstor, Yelverton, S. Devon.

SON LIVING.

Hon. DAVID HENRY ARTHUR, *b.* July 10th, 1920 ; ed. at Winchester, and at Balliol Coll., Oxford; admitted a Solicitor 1949 ; European War 1940-45 as Major Roy. Devon Yeo., Artillery and Staff. *Residences,*—90, Whitehall Court, SW1; Ermewood House, Harford, Ivybridge, Devon. *Clubs,*—Travellers', Beefsteak.

SISTER LIVING.

Hon. Clementina Gwendolen Catharine (*Baroness St. Levan*), *b.* 1896; is a JP: *m.* 1916, the 3rd Baron St. Levan. *Residence,*—Avallon, Green Lane, Marazion, Cornwall.

COLLATERAL BRANCH LIVING.

Issue of the late the Hon. Sir Harold George Nicolson, KCVO, CMG, yst. son of 1st Baron, *b.* 1886, *d.* 1968; *m.* 1913, the Hon. Victoria Mary Sackville-West, CH, who *d.* 1962, da. of the 3rd Baron Sackville:—

(Lionel) Benedict, *CBE*, *MVO* (45B, Holland Park, W11; Brooks's and Beefsteak Clubs), *b.* 1914; ed. at Eton, and Balliol Coll., Oxford; Dep. Surveyor of the King's Pictures 1939-47, since when Editor of the *Burlington Magazine*; 1939-45 War as Capt. Intelligence Corps; MVO (4th class) 1947, CBE (Civil) 1971: *m.* 1955 (m. diss. 1962), Luisa, da. of Prof. Giacomo Vertova, of Florence, and has issue living, Vanessa Pepita Giovanna, *b.* 1956.——Nigel, *MBE* (Sissinghurst Castle, Kent), *b.* 1917; ed. at Eton, and Balliol Coll., Oxford; 1939-45 War as Capt. Grenadier Guards (despatches, MBE); MP for E. and Christchurch Div. of Bournemouth (*C*) 1952-59; MBE (Mil.) 1945: *m.* 1953 (m. diss. 1970), Philippa Janet, da. of Sir (Eustace) Gervais Tennyson-d'Eyncourt, 2nd Bt., and has issue living, Adam, *b.* 1957,—Juliet, *b.* 1954,—Rebecca, *b.* 1963.

PREDECESSORS.—[1] THOMAS Nicolson of Carnock, was cr. a *Baronet* of Nova Scotia, with remainder to heirs-male whatsoever 1636, *d.* 1646; *s.* by his son [2] THOMAS, 2nd Bt., *d.* 1664; *s.* by his son [3] THOMAS, 3rd Bt., *b.* 1647; *d.* 1670; *s.* by his son [4] THOMAS, 4th Bt., *b.* 1669 ; *s.* as 4th Lord Napier of Merchistoun 1683 ; *d.* 1686 when the Peerage devolved upon his maternal aunt, and the Baronetcy passed to his cousin and heir-male [5] THOMAS, 5th Bt., son and heir or Sir John Nicolson of Tillicoultry ; *d.* 1699 ; *s.* by his son [6] GEORGE, 6th Bt. : *m.* Charlott; Halkett; *d.* 1771 ; *s.* by his son [7] WALTER PHILIP, 7th Bt.: *m.* Helen Carpenter; *d.* 1786 ; *s.* by his brother [8] DAVID, 8th Bt. ; *d.* 1808; *s.* by his cousin and heir-male [9] WILLIAM, 9th Bt. (only son of George Nicolson of Tarviston), *b.* 1758; Maj.-Gen. in the Army: *m.* 1804, Mary Russell ; *d.* 1820 ; *s.* by his son [10] FREDERICK WILLIAM ERSKINE, 10th Bt. ; Adm., and sometime Chm. of Thames Conservancy Board : *m.* 1st, 1847, Clementina Maria Marion, dau. of James Loch, of Drylaw ; 2ndly, 1855, Augusta Sarah, dau. of Robert Cullington, and widow of Capt. Hay ; 3rdly, 1867, Anne, dau. of R. Crosse ; *d.* 1899 ; *s.* by his son [11] ARTHUR, *G.C.B.*, *G.C.M.G.*, *G.C.V.O.*, *K.C.I.E.*, *P.C.*, 11th Bt., *b.* 1849 ; was Assist. Private Sec. to Earl Granville at Foreign Office 1872-4 ; on Staff of Earl of Dufferin in Egypt 1882, acting Chargé d'Affaires at Athens 1882-5, Sec. of Legation at Teheran, and Acting Chargé d'Affaires in Persia 1885-8, Consul-Gen. for Hungary 1888-93, Sec. of Embassy at Constantinople 1893-4, and Agent and Consul-Gen. in Bulgaria 1894-5, Envoy Extraor. and Min. Plen. at Tangier and Consul-Gen. in Morocco 1895-1904, Ambassador Extraor. and Plen. to Spain 1904-5, and at St. Petersburg 1906-10, and Permanent Under-Sec. of State for Foreign Affairs 1910-16; British Representative at Algeciras Conference 1905-6 ; cr. *Baron Carnock*, of Carnock co. Stirling (peerage of United Kingdom) 1916 : *m.* 1882, Mary Catherine, who *d.* 1951, dau. of the late Archibald Rowan Hamilton of Killyleagh Castle, co. Down ; *d.* 1928 ; *s.* by his el. son [2] FREDERICK ARCHIBALD, *M.C.*, 2nd Baron ; *b.* 1883 ; Bar. Inner Temple 1924 ; Major 15th King's Hussars ; sometime A.D.C. to Viceroy of India ; *d.* 1952 ; *s.* by his brother [3] ERSKINE ARTHUR, 3rd Baron, and present peer.

CARNWATH, EARLDOM OF. (Dalzell.) [Extinct or Dormant 1941.]

DAUGHTER LIVING OF THIRTEENTH EARL.

Lady Muriel Marjorie, *b.* 1903 : *m.* 1927, Lieut.-Col. John Norton Dalzell, Indian Army, who *d.* 1957 (only son of James Taylor, of Lisnamallard, co. Tyrone), when they assumed by Roy. licence the surname and arms of Dalzell in lieu of that of Taylor, and has issue living, John Victor Robert, *b.* 1929. *Residence,*—Sand House, Wedmore, Somerset.

Carpenter, see Baron Boyd-Carpenter.

CARRICK, EARL OF. (Butler.) Sits as **BARON BUTLER OF MOUNT JULIET.** (U.K. 1912). [Earl I. 1748.]

Be steadfast.

BRIAN STUART THEOBALD SOMERSET CAHER BUTLER, 9th Earl; *b.* Aug. 17th, 1931 ; *s.* 1957 ; ed. at Downside ; Man. Dir. Ralli Internat. Ltd., Chm. Ralli Brothers & Coney Ltd., a Member of Council of Cotton Research Corpn., British Cotton Growing Assocn., and a Dir. of Reynolds & Gibson (Cotton) Ltd., The Bacup Warehousing Co. Ltd., Liverpool Uganda Co. Ltd., Maclaine Wasson Ltd., and Naumann Gepp & Co. Ltd.: *m.* 1951, (Mary) Belinda, da. of Maj. David Constable-Maxwell, TD [see L. Herries of Terregles, colls.], and has issue.

Arms,—Or, a chief indented azure, a crescent for difference. Crest,—Out of a ducal coronet or, a plume of ostrich feathers, and issuant therefrom a demi-falcon rising all argent. Supporters,—*Dexter*, a falcon, wings inverted argent, beaked, membered and belled, or ; *sinister*, a male griffin argent, beaked, membered, armed, collared and chained, or ; on each supporter a crescent for difference.

Residence,—Wonersh House, nr. Guildford, Surrey.

SON LIVING.
DAVID JAMES THEOBALD SOMERSET (*Viscount Ikerrin*), *b.* Jan. 9th, 1953; ed. at Downside: *m.* 1975, Philippa, yr. da. of Wing Cdr. L. V. Craxton, RAF (ret.), of Mills Meadow, Wonersh Park.

DAUGHTER LIVING.
Lady Juliana Mary Philomena, *b.* 1960.

UNCLES LIVING. (*Sons of 7th Earl.*)
Hon. Guy Somerset Lionel (Red Acres, Wivelsfield Green, Sussex), *b.* 1905; ed. at Tonbridge; late Lt. Indian Army (Reserve), Maj. Roy. Canadian Dragoons (Canadian Army Reserve); Managing Dir. of Guy Butler & Co. Ltd.: *m.* 1st 1939, Patricia Anne (TENNANT), da. of the late William Dunne; 2ndly, 1961, Mrs. Janet Frances Parker, da. of the late Alexander Gordon Preston, and has issue living, (by 1st m.) Rupert Lionel Somerset (c/o Midland Bank, 154, Upper St., N1), *b.* 1940; Fl.-Lt., RAF: *m.* 1968, Jenifer Mary, da. of Norman Rush, of High Wood, Henley, Haslemere, Surrey, and has issue living, Piers Somerset Patrick *b.* 1970, Eli Somerset James *b.* 1971, Matthew Somerset Guy *b.* 1972,—Dermot Somerset Launcelot, *b.* 1941.
Hon. Godfrey Claud Somerset Pierce (of 106, Divinity Rd., Oxford), *b.* 1907; ed. at Stowe Sch.; late Pilot Officer R.A.F. Vol. Reserve.

AUNT LIVING. (*Daughter of 7th Earl.*)
Lady (Irene) June Beatrice, *M.B.E., b.* 1901: is an O.St.J., and Sup. of St. John Ambulance Brig., Overseas, Burma ; M.B.E. (Civil) 1943 : *m.* 1st, 1923, John Sills Charlton, from whom she obtained a divorce 1934 ; 2ndly, 1934, Col. Anthony Gordon Hobson (retired), Indian Army, and has issue living, (by 1st marriage) Michael Tobias Peter (of 83, Rosetta Road, Durban, S. Africa), *b.* 1925; formerly Capt. Indian Army : *m.* 1953, Marie Margarite Celine Eda, dau. of René Feuilherade, and has issue living, John Sills Somerset Anthony *b.* 1957, Marie Dominique Alexa *b.* 1953. *Address,* —Quinta de Sao Bento, Sintra, Portugal.

WIDOWS LIVING OF SONS OF SEVENTH EARL.
Barbara, da. of M. S. Jacomb-Hood: *m.* 1928, the Hon. (Horace) Somerset Edmond Butler, CIE, who *d.* 1962, and has issue living [see colls., infra].
Dorothea (11, Rushfield, Sawbridgeworth, Herts.), yst. da. of T. W. Bennett: *m.* 1957, as his 2nd wife Maj. the Hon. Pierce Alan Somerset David Butler, TD, who *d.* 1964 [see colls., infra].

WIDOW LIVING OF EIGHTH EARL.
RUTH (*Ruth, Countess of Carrick*) (Box 1190, Pinehurst, N. Carolina 28374, USA), da. of Francis T. M. McEnery, of Chicago, Ill., USA: *m.* 1954, as his 3rd wife, the 8th Earl of Carrick, who *d.* 1957.

COLLATERAL BRANCHES LIVING.
Issue of the late Hon. (Horace) Somerset Edmond Butler, C.I.E., 2nd son of 7th Earl, *b.* 1903; *d.* 1962: *m.* 1928, Barbara (ante), dau. of M. S. Jacomb-Hood:—
Georgina Carolin Eve, *b.* 1931: *m.* 1st, 1954, David Goldberg; 2ndly, 1961, Renato Fratini; 3rdly, 1969, James Allan Short (actor Jimmy Logan), of The Cottage, 44, Grove End Rd., NW8.

Issue of the late Maj. the Hon. Pierce Alan Somerset David Butler, T.D., 5th son of the 7th Earl, *b.* 1909, *d.* 1964: *m.* 1st, 1933 (marriage dissolved 1957), Leri, el. da. of Dr. G. Llywelyn-Jones, of Bryn Glas, Llangefni, Anglesey ; 2ndly, 1957, Dorothea (ante), yst. da. of T. W. Bennett.
(By 1st m.) David Llywelyn Somerset (Brook Farm, Wethersfield, Braintree, Essex), *b.* 1937: *m.* 1966, Anne, da. of A. S. Haigh, of White Roding, Essex, and has issue living, Michael Somerset, *b.* 1969,— Hilary Mary, *b.* 1971.——Helen Sarah Ann, (c/o Harris, Colley & Collins, Ltd., 68, New London Rd., Chelmsford, Essex), *b.* 1936: *m.* 1957, Anthony Thomas Colley.

Grandsons of the late Rev. Pierce Armar Butler (infra) :—
Issue of the late Rev. Pierce Rollo Butler, *b.* 1885, *d.* 1950 : *m.* 1911, Ethel Florence, who *d.* 1943, dau. of the Rev. Thomas Legge Symes :—
Theobald Rollo Pierce, *B.E.M.* (15, Eastwood Rd., S. Woodford, E.18), *b.* 1913; late Detective, Sergeant Metropolitan Police Force: *m.* 1st, 1940 (marriage dissolved 1963), Christine Helen, da. of Gilbert William Harding; 2ndly, 1964, Gwendoline Mary Emily, da. of Frederick George Jennings- and has issue living, (by 1st marriage) Jeremy Somerset Pierce, *b.* 1944,—Charlotte Veronica Pierce, *b.* 1942.——Kenelm Somerset Priaulx, *b.* 1917; late Lt.-Col. Falkland Islands Defence Force, and Admin. Officer, S. Georgia; formerly Capt. Roy. Corps of Signals (TA): *m.* 1954, Janet Cooper, da. of James Gilmour. *Residence,*—

Granddaughters of the late Rev. Pierce Rollo Butler (ante):—
Issue of the late James Armar Cory Butler, *b.* 1916, *d.* 1973: *m.* 1944, Marjorie Wells, (140, Broom Rd., Teddington, Middx.):—
Sandra Leigh, *b.* 1945.——Melanie Ann, *b.* 1949.

Grandchildren of the late Rev. Pierce Butler, son of the late Lieut.-Gen. Hon. Henry Edward Butler, 2nd son of 2nd Earl :—

Issue of the late Rev. Pierce Armar Butler, *b.* 1863, *d.* 1924 : *m.* 1885, Emily, who *d.* 1933, dau. of Capt. W. J. Russwurm, W. India Regt. :—

Hubert Blennerhassett, *b.* 1887 ; sometime Capt. Dorset Regt. and Major R.E.: *m.* 1919, Sophie Marie, dau. of Jules Castravelli, of Bacos, Alexandria, Egypt, and has issue living, Marjorye Marie, *b.* 1921 : *m.* 1944, Major Peter Quentin Logan, S. Staffordshire Regt., of Batchelors Tyning, Heytesbury, Warminster, Wilts., and has issue living, Michael Roderic Quentin *b.* 1947: *m.* 1971, Gillian, da. of Cdr. J. McC. Rutherford, RN, of Henley-on-Thames,—Noreen May, *b.* 1923: *m.* 1944, Col. Frank Hilary Bristowe, RM, and has issue living, Rosamund Gillian *b.* 1947, June Hilary *b.* 1949, Nicola Catherine Diana *b.* 1960.   *Residence*,—Dolphins, Archery Sq., Walmer, Deal, Kent.——Norah Veronica Pierce, *b.* 1904.   *Residence*,—1, Angel Lane, Woodbridge, Suffolk.

PREDECESSORS.—[1] Sir PIERCE Butler, Knt.; Lt.-Gen. of the Irish Army under Lord Mountgarret, was cr. *Viscount Ikerrin* (peerage of Ireland) 1629; *s.* by his son [2] PIERCE, 2nd Viscount; *s.* by his son [3] JAMES, 3rd Viscount; *d.* 1688; *s.* by his son [4] PIERCE, 4th Viscount; *d.* 1710; *s,* by his son [5] JAMES, 5th Viscount; *d.* a minor 1712; *s.* by his uncle [6] THOMAS, 6th Viscount, Chaplain-Gen. to Army in Flanders under James, Duke of Ormonde; *d.* 1719; *s.* by his son [7] JAMES, 7th Viscount; *d.* 1721: *s.* by his brother [8] SOMERSET HAMILTON, 8th Viscount; cr. *Earl of Carrick* (peerage of Ireland) 1748; *d.* 1774; *s.* by his son [9] HENRY THOMAS, 2nd Earl; *d.* 1813; *s.* by his son [10] SOMERSET RICHARD, 3rd Earl; *b,* 1779: *m.* 1st, 1811, Anne, who *d.* 1829, dau. of Owen Wynne, of Haslewood, co. Sligo ; 2ndly, 1833, Lucy, who *d.* 1884, dau. of the late Arthur French, of French Park; *d.* 1838, *s.* by his el. son [11] HENRY THOMAS, 4th Earl; *d.* a minor 1846; *s.* by his brother [12] SOMERSET ARTHUR, 5th Earl, *b.* 1835 ; *d.* 1901; *s.* by his cousin [13] CHARLES HENRY SOMERSET (son of the late Capt. Charles George Butler, 86th Regt., grandson of 2nd Earl), 6th Earl, *b.* 1851 ; present during repulse of an incursion of Fenians into Canada 1870: *m.* 1st, 1873, Kathleen Emily Hamilton, who *d.* 1888, dau. of Lieut.-Col. Albert Ernest Ross, 5th Fusiliers : 2ndly, 1896, Emily Codrington, who *d.* 1915, dau. of the late Mark Jones ; *d.* 1909 ; *s.* by his son [14] CHARLES ERNEST ALFRED FRENCH SOMERSET, O.B.E., 7th Earl, *b.* 1873 ; Comptroller of the Household to Lord-Lieut. of Ireland 1913-15; cr. *Baron Butler of Mount Juliet*, co. Kilkenny (peerage of United Kingdom) 1912: *m.* 1898, Ellen Rosamond Mary, who *d.* 1946, dau. of the late Lieut.-Col. Henry Gore Lindsay, *d.* 1931; *s.* by his son [15] THEOBALD WALTER SOMERSET HENRY, 8th Earl ; *b.* 1903 ; European War 1939-44 as acting Com. R.N.V.R., British Naval Liaison Officer in USA and Senior RN Officer: *m.* 1st, 1930, Marion Caher (EDWARDS), (who *d.* 1973, having obtained a divorce 1938), da. of Daniel C. Donoghue of Philadelphia, USA; 2nd, 1938, Margaret (DRUM), who *d.* (July) 1954, da. of Charles B. Power, of Helena, Montana, USA; 3rdly, Oct 1954, Ruth, da. of Francis T. M. McEnery, Chicago, Ill., USA), *d.* 1957; *s.* by his only son [16] BRIAN STUART THEOBALD SOMERSET CAHER, 9th Earl and present peer; also Viscount Ikerrin, and Baron Butler, of Mount Juliet.

CARRINGTON, BARON. (Carington.) [I. 1796, G.B. 1797.]

Persevering and faithful.

PETER ALEXANDER RUPERT CARINGTON, K.C.M.G., M.C., P.C., 6th Baron ; *b.* June 6th, 1919; *s.* 1938; ed. at Eton; Maj. (ret.) Grenadier Guards; Fellow of Eton 1966; Parl. Sec. Min. of Agriculture and Fisheries 1951-54, Parl. Sec. to Min. of Defence 1954-56, High Commr. for UK in Australia 1956-59, First Lord of the Admiralty 1959-63, Min. without Portfolio, and Leader of House of Lords 1963-64, Leader of the Opposition of House of Lords 1964-70, and since 1974; Sec. of State for Defence 1970-74, and Sec. of State Depart. of Energy Jan. to Feb. 1974; Min. of Aviation Supply 1971; Chm. of Conservative Party 1972-74; a Dir. of Amalgamated Metal Corpn., Ltd., 1965-70, of Hambros Bank 1967-70, Barclays Bank 1967-70, and since 1974, Cadbury Schweppes, Ltd. 1968-70, and since 1974, Intercontinental Banking Sers., Ltd. 1968-70; Joint Dep. Chm. of Aust. & NZ Bank 1965-67, Chm. 1967-69; a Dir. of Rio Tinto-Zinc Corpn. since 1974; 1939-45 War (MC); KCMG 1958, PC 1959: *m.* 1942, Iona, da. of Lt.-Col. Sir Francis Kennedy McClean, AFC, and has issue.

Arms,—Or, a chevron cottised, between three demi-griffins, the two in chief respectant sable. **Crest**,—An elephant's head erased or, eared gules, charged on the neck with three fleurs-de-lis, two and one azure. **Supporters**,—Two griffins' wings elevated sable, the *dexter* charged with three fleurs-de-lis palewise or, the *sinister* with three trefoils slipped palewise of the last.

Seat,—The Manor House, Bledlow, near Aylesbury, Bucks. *Town Residence*,—32A, Ovington Square, S.W.3.   *Clubs*,—Beefsteak, Turf, Carlton.

SON LIVING.

Hon. RUPERT FRANCIS JOHN, *b.* Dec. 2nd, 1948; ed. at Eton and Bristol Univ.

DAUGHTERS LIVING.

Hon. Alexandra, *b.* 1943: *m.* 1965, Maj. Peter N. de Bunsen, Coldm. Gds. (ret.), of Holbrook Lodge, Ipswich, and has issue living, Charles Rupert, *b.* 1970,—Peter James, *b.* 1973,—Victoria, *b.* 1968.
Hon. Virginia (*Baronness Ashcombe*), *b.* 1946: *m.* 1973, the 4th Baron Ashcombe.

SISTER LIVING.

Hon. Elizabeth, *b.* 1917 : *m.* 1943, William Lionel Dove, M.B., Ch.B., M.R.C.S., L.R.C.P., and has issue living, Anthony Edward, *b.* 1946,—John Andrew, *b.* 1951.   *Residence*,—Elm House, Childwall, Liverpool, 16.

PREDECESSORS.—[1] ROBERT Smith, *M.P.* for Nottingham 1779-96; cr. *Baron Carrington*, of Bulcot Lodge (peerage of Ireland) 1796, and *Baron Carrington*, of Upton, Notts (peerage of Great Britain) 1797; *d.* 1838; *s.* by his son [2] ROBERT JOHN, 2nd Baron; *b.* 1796; M.P. for Wendover 1818-20, Buckinghamshire 1820-30, and High Wycombe 1831-8; Lord-Lieut. of Bucks; assumed the surname of Carington in lieu of Smith by Roy. licence 1839 : *m.* 1st, 1822, the Hon. Elizabeth Katherine, who *d.* 1832, dau. of 1st Baron Forester; 2ndly, 1840, the Hon.

Augusta Annabella Drummond-Willoughby, who *d.* 1879, da. of 21st Baron Willoughby D'Eresby; *d.* 1868; *s.* by his son [3] CHARLES ROBERT, 3rd Baron; *b.* 1843; Joint Hereditary Lord Great Chamberlain (appointed to act for Reign of King George V.); sat as M.P. for Wycombe (*L*) 1865-8; surname of Carington confirmed by Roy. licence 1880; subsequently granted Roy. licence 1896 to assume the surnames of Wynn-Carrington; was Gov. and Com.-in-Ch. of New South Wales 1885-90, Lord Chamberlain to Queen Victoria's Household 1892-5, Pres. of Board of Agriculture Dec. 1905 to Oct. 1911, and Lord Privy Seal Oct. 1911 to Feb. 1912; bore St. Edward's Staff at Coronation of King Edward VII.; cr. *Viscount Wendover*, of Chepping Wycombe, Bucks, *Earl Carrington* (peerage of United Kingdom) 1895, and *Marquess of Lincolnshire* (peerage of United Kingdom) 1912: *m.* 1878, the Hon. Cecilia Margaret Harbord, el. dau. of 5th Baron Suffield; *d.* 1928, when the Marquessate of Lincolnshire, the Earldom of Carrington, and the Viscountcy of Wendover became ext. (his only son, Albert Edward Samuel Charles Robert, *Viscount Wendover*, *b.* 1895; Lieut. Roy. Horse Guards, having *d.* of wounds in action during European War 1915), while the two Baronies of Carrington devolved upon his brother [4] RUPERT CLEMENT GEORGE Carington, *C.V.O.*, *D.S.O.*, 4th Baron, *b.* 1852; M.P. for Buckinghamshire (*L*) 1880-85; surname of Carington confirmed by Roy. licence 1880; *m.* 1891, Edith, who *d.* 1908, dau. of John S. Horsfall, of Widglewa, N.S. Wales; *d.* 1929; *s.* by his son [5] RUPERT VICTOR JOHN, 5th Baron, *b.* 1891: *m.* 1916, the Hon. Sybil Marion Colville, who *d.* 1946, dau. of 2nd Viscount Colville of Culross; *d.* 1938; *s.* by his son [6] PETER ALEXANDER RUPERT, 6th Baron, and present peer.

CARRON, BARONY OF. (Carron). [Extinct 1969.]

DAUGHTERS LIVING OF LIFE BARON.

Hon. Hilary Mary, *b.* 1933: *m.* 1959, John Simon Weidemann, of 48a, Brockley Rise, Forest Hill, SE23, and has issue.

Hon. Patricia Ann, *b.* 1945.

WIDOW LIVING OF LIFE BARON.

MARY EMMA (*Baroness Carron*) (174, Grierson Rd., SE23), da. of John McGuire, of Hull: *m.* 1931, Baron Carron (Life Peer), who *d.* 1969.

CARSON, BARONY OF. (Carson.) [Extinct 1935.]

SON LIVING OF LIFE PEER. (*By 2nd marriage.*)

Hon. Edward, *b.* 1920; ed. at Eton, and at Trin. Hall, Camb.; is Lieut. Life Guards, European War 1939-45 in Syria, Italy. and Germany; sat as M.P. for Isle of Thanet Div. of Kent (*C*) July 1945 to Feb. 1953: *m.* 1943, Heather, dau. of Frank Arthur Sclater, O.B.E., M.C., of Milford, Surrey, and has issue. *Residence,*—Cleve Court, Minster-in-Thanet.

CASEY, BARON. (Casey.) [Life Baron 1960.]

Strength and Unity.

RICHARD GARDINER CASEY, KG, GCMG, CH, DSO, MC, PC, son of the late Richard Gardiner Casey, of Melbourne, Australia; *b.* Aug. 29th, 1890; ed. at Melbourne Church of England Gram. Sch., at Melbourne Univ., and at Trin. Coll., Camb. (B.A. 1913); formerly Major Australian Forces, and Liaison Officer between Australian Commonwealth Govt. and Foreign and Dominions Offices; European War 1914-18, in Egypt, Gallipoli, and France (despatches, D.S.O., M.C.); was a Member of House of Representatives, Commonwealth of Australia 1931-40, Assist. Treasurer, 1933-5, Treasurer 1935-9, Min. for Development 1937-40 (also Min. for Supply 1939-40), Australian Min. to U.S.A. 1940-42, Min. of State for United Kingdom in Middle East (Member of War Cabinet) 1942-3, Gov. of Bengal 1944-6, Min. for National Development and for Works, and Housing, Australia 1949-51, and Min. for External Affairs 1951-60 (also Min. in charge of Commonwealth Scientific and Industrial Research Organisation 1949-60); Gov.-Gen. of Commonwealth of Australia 1965-69; a K.St.J.; cr. DSO 1918, PC 1939, CH 1944, *Baron Casey*, of Berwick, Victoria, Australia, and of City of Westminster (Life Baron) 1960, GCMG 1965, and KG 1969: *m.* 1926, Ethel Marian (Maie), da. of the late Maj.-Gen. Sir Charles Snodgrass Ryan, KBE, CB, CMG, MB, and has issue.

Arms,—Chevron sable and azure, in chief a cogwheel and sun in splendour or, in base above four barrulets wavy a representation of the constellation of the Southern Cross argent. **Crest,**—A sea gull wings expanded proper. **Supporters,**—*Dexter* an Australian worker of European stock, habited in a white shirt and khaki trousers, *sinister*, an Asian worker habited in a white coat and dhoti, all proper. *Residences,*—Edrington, Berwick, Vic., Aust.; 159, Gipps St., East Melbourne, Aust. *Clubs,*—Melbourne, Athenaeum, Union and Oxford and Cambridge University.

SON LIVING.

Hon. (Richard Charles) Donn (141, Newmarket Rd., Cambridge), *b.* 1931.

DAUGHTER LIVING.

Hon. Jane Alice, *b.* 1928: *m.* 1955, Murray Macgowen, of 17, Eastbourne Rd., Darling Point ,NSW 2027.

Cassillis, Earl of,   Son of Marquess of Ailsa.

CASTLE, BARON.   (Castle.)   [Life Baron 1974.]

EDWARD CYRIL CASTLE, son of Frederick Richard Castle, of Cadmore End, Bucks.; *b.* May 5th, 1907; ed. at Abingdon Sch., and Portsmouth Gram. Sch.; journalist; Assist. Editor *Daily Mirror* 1942-44, Assist. Editor *Picture Post* 1944-50, and Editor 1950-51; Alderman GLC 1964-70, and Islington since 1971; a Member of European Parl. since 1975; *cr. Baron Castle*, of Islington, in Greater London (Life Baron) 1974; *m.* 1944, the Rt. Hon. Barbara Anne Castle, MP [see Privy Council], da. of Frank Betts.

Residences,—Flat G, 19, John Spencer Sq., N1; Hell Corner Farm, Ibstone, High Wycombe, Bucks.

CASTLEMAINE, BARON.   (Handcock.)   [Baron I. 1812.]

ROLAND THOMAS JOHN HANDCOCK, 8th Baron; *b.* April 22nd, 1943; *s.* 1973; Capt. Army Air Corps: *m.* 1969, Pauline Anne, el. da. of John Taylor Bainbridge, of The Moat House, Rede Hall Rd., Burstow, Horley, Surrey.

Arms,—Ermine, on a chief sable, a dexter hand between two cocks argent, armed, crested, and jelloped gules. Crest.– a demi-lion rampant azure, holding a lozenge argent, charged with a cock gules. Supporters,– Dexter, a lion guardant azure; sinister, a cock, proper.

Residence,—4, Crossways, Crondall Rd., Crookham Village, Hants.

VIGILATE ET ORATE
Watch and pray.

SISTERS LIVING.

Hon. Eileen Esther, *b.* 1931: *m.* 1959, F/O Terence Frank Adams, RAF (c/o National Westminster Bank, 851, Gleadless Rd., Sheffield 12), and has issue living, Patrick Joseph John, *b.* 1960,—Niall Michael, *b.* 1968,—Siobhan Mary, *b.* 1962.
Hon. Edith Deirdre, *b.* 1936: *m.* 1957, Keith Moss, BEM, and has issue living, Julian Duncan, *b.* 1962.

AUNT LIVING.

Leonie Caroline Esther, *b.* 1905: *m.* 1931, as his 2nd wife, Thomas MacGregor Greer, DL, who *d.* 1941. *Residences,*—Tullylagan Manor, Cookstown, co. Tyrone; Blackwood, Helen's Bay, co. Down.

DAUGHTER LIVING OF SIXTH BARON.

Hon. Violet Louisa, *b.* 1895: *m.* 1919 (m. diss. 1931), Maj. Charles Moorhouse Duncan, MC, formerly RFA, who *d.* 1939, and has issue living, Hazel Patricia, *b.* 1920: *m.* 1944, Vivian Roger Bishop, of Sheepcote, Clifford, Herefordshire, and has issue living, Valerie *b.* 1945, Diana *b.* 1947, Joanna *b.* 1953,—Pamela Jean, *b.* 1927. *Address,*—The Prince of Wales Hotel, Athlone, co. Westmeath.

DAUGHTER LIVING OF FIFTH BARON.

Hon. Evelyn Constance (*Hon. Lady Gairdner*), *b.* 1897: *m.* 1925, Lieut.-Gen. Sir Charles Henry Gairdner GBE, KCMG, KCVO, CB, late 10th Hussars. *Residence,*—24, The Esplanade, Peppermint Grove, W. Australia.

WIDOW LIVING OF SEVENTH BARON.

REBECCA ELLEN (*Rebecca, Baroness Castlemaine*), only da. of William T. Soady, RN: *m.* 1930, the 7th Baron, who *d.* 1973.

COLLATERAL BRANCHES LIVING.

Grandchildren of the late Hon. Robert John Handcock, 2nd son of 3rd Baron :—
Issue of the late Richard Henry Handcock, *b.* 1858, *d.* 1891: *m.* 1886, Katharine Eleonora, who *d.* 1936, dau. of the late Ven. Arthur Palmer, Archdeacon of Toronto :—
Dorothy Madeline, *b.* 1888.——Florence Guy (posthumous), *b.* 1892: *m.* 1924, Reginald John Foort, from whom she obtained a divorce 1941, and has issue living, Ann Elizabeth, *b.* 1926,—Iris Eve, *b.* 1927,—Barbara Jane, *b.* 1935. *Residence—*

Grandchildren of the late Henry Handcock (infra):—
Issue of the late Richard Henry Algernon Handcock, *b.* 1895; *d.* 1974: *m.* 1943, Catherine, who *d.* 1971, da. of the late Emmanuel Breham, of Pont de l'Arche, France, and widow of John Morgan Keeley Knight, Lt. RFC:—
Clifford Marcel (Rancher, Beaconsfield Rd., Farnham Royal, Bucks.), *b.* 1925; late CQMS, KOSB; 1939-45 War with 1st Airborne Div.: *m.* 1944, Joyce Morton, and has issue living, Linda, b. 1945.——Claude Desmond Richard (Kilindini, School Lane, Gt. Barford, Beds.), *b.* 1928; WO1, REME: *m.* 1948, Enid Perry, and has issue living, Andre Patrick James, *b.* 1950,—Peter Michael Roland, *b.* 1951,—Teresa Catherine Rose, *b.* 1954.——Sheila Annette Kathleen, *b.* 1927: *m.* 19—, Brinley Aurelius, of 42, Humber Way, Langley, Bucks., and has issue living, Geoffrey, *b.* 1955,—Heather, *b.* 1947.——Heather, *b.* 1939: *m.* 1961, Robert Henry Harvey, of 12, Clanfield Cres., Tilehurst, Reading, and has issue living, Sandra, *b.* 1963.

Issue of the late Henry Handcock, *b.* 1869, *d.* 1917: *m.* 1892, Charlotte, who *d.* 1922, dau. of the late Richard Cole:—
CLIFFORD FREDERICK, *b.* Oct. 3rd, 1896: *m.* 1928, Margaret, who *d.* 1954, da. of the late Capt. Philip Nicholls, of Penzance.——Terence Robin (53, Kidbrooke Park Rd., Blackheath, SE3), *b.* 1902: *m.* 1933, Eva Mary, da. of Charles Taylor, and has issue living, Michael Robin (The Annexe, 6, Pond Rd., Blackheath, SE3), *b.* 1934: *m.* 1961, Jean Anne, only da. of J. T. Smoker, and has issue living,

Jenny Samantha b. 1969.——Desmond Fitz-Gerald, b. 1903: m. 19—.——Patrick Francis Denys, (Blue Waters, St. Agnes, Cornwall), b. 1913: m. 1st, 1933, Kathleen Joan, who d. 1972, da. of Frederick Lyle; 2ndly, 1972, Hilary Maybelle, widow of Sqd.-Ldr. D. W. Willis, RAF, and has issue living (by 1st m.), Patrick Michael, b. 1934.

Grandson of the late Rev. John Harward Jessop Handcock, son of the late Rev. John Gustavus Handcock, 4th son of 2nd Baron :—
Issue of the late Harward Devereux Handcock, b. 1874, d. 1944 : m. 1907, Eleanor Winifred, who d. 1966, da. of the late Henry John Potts, of Glan-yr-afon, Mold, Flintshire, and Ollerton, Cheshire:—
John Harward (Anderida, Brook Green, Cuckfield, Sussex), b. 1924: m. 1949, Brenda Tenrill, da. of Donald Stewart Alexander Simpson, and has issue living, Jeremy John, b. 1953,—Timothy Charles, b. 1964,—Fiona Elizabeth Jane, b. 1956.

Grandchildren of the late Robert Harris Temple Handcock, only son of Edward Stanley Handcock, yst. son of the late Lt.-Col. the Hon. Robert French Handcock, 8th son of 2nd Baron.
Issue of the late Cdr. William Stanley Handcock, R.N., b. 1908, d. 1964: m. 1933, Joan Mary (of Whitedale, Hambledon, Hants), dau. of the late Sir Ralph Molyneux Combe:—
Timothy Stannus, b. 1938.——Deirdre Elizabeth, b. 1935: m. 1960, Capt. Colin Prinsep James, M.C. late Rifle Bde., of Cotleigh House, Honiton, Devon, and has issue living, Emma Louise b. 1962,—Belinda Anne Nonie, b. 1964.——Luleen Annette, b. 1946.

PREDECESSORS.—[1] WILLIAM Handcock, Constable and Gov. of Athlone; cr. Baron Castle-maine, of Moydrum, co. Westmeath (peerage of Ireland) 1812, with remainder to his brother and Viscount Castlemaine (peerage of Ireland) 1822; d. 1839, when the Viscountcy became extinct; s. in Barony by his brother [2] RICHARD, 2nd Baron; d. 1840; s. by his son [3] RICHARD, 3rd Baron: b. 1791; a Representative Peer: m. 1822, Margaret, dau. of Michael Harris, of Dublin; d. 1869; s. by his son [4] RICHARD, 4th Baron, b. 1826; a Representa-tive Peer, and Lord-Lieut. of co. Westmeath: m. 1857, the Hon. Louisa Matilda, who d. 1892, dau. of 2nd Baron Harris: d. 1892; s. by his el. son [5] ALBERT EDWARD, 5th Baron; b. 1863; a Representative Peer: m. 1895, Annie Evelyn, who d. 1955, dau. of the late Col. Thomas Joseph Barrington; d. 1937; s. by his brother [6] ROBERT ARTHUR, 6th Baron; b. 1864; a D.L. for co. Westmeath; European War 1914-19 as Lieut. R.A.S.C.: m. 1894, Ethel Violet, who d. 1934, dau. of the late Col. Sir Edmond Bainbridge, K.C.B., of Sheringham, Norfolk; d. 1954; s. by his kinsman [7] JOHN MICHAEL SCHOMBERG STAVELEY (only son of the late Robert John Handcock, 2nd son of the late Hon. Robert John Handcock, 2nd son of 3rd Baron), 7th Baron, b. 1904: m. 1930, Rebecca Ellen, only da. of William T. Soady, RN; d. 1973; s. by his son [8] ROLAND THOMAS JOHN, 8th Baron and present peer.

CASTLE STEWART, EARL. (Stuart.) [Earl I. 1800, Bt. S. 1628.]

ARTHUR PATRICK AVONDALE STUART, 8th Earl and 15th Baronet; b. Aug. 18th, 1928 ; s. 1961 ; ed. at Eton, and at Trin. Coll., Camb. (B.A. 1950) ; late Lieut. Scots Guards ; is a Farmer : m. 1952, Edna, dau. of William Edward Fowler, of Harborne, Birmingham, and has issue.

Arms.—Quarterly of four: 1st the Royal arms of Scotland; 2nd or, a fesse checky azure and argent, and in chief a label of three points gules, Stuart ; 3rd argent, a saltire between four roses gules, barbed and seeded proper, Lennox ; 4th or, a lion rampant gules, Macduff ; the whole within a bordure com-pony argent and azure. Crest.—An unicorn's head couped at the neck argent, armed, crined, and tufted or. Supporters.—Two wyverns, their tails nowed or, armed proper and langued gules.
Seat,—Stuart Hall, Stewartstown, co. Tyrone. Residence,—Stone House, East Pen-nard, near Shepton Mallet, Somerset.

SON LIVING.
ANDREW RICHARD CHARLES (Viscount Stuart), (8, Southport Av., Redhills, Exeter, EX4 1RA), b. Oct. 7th, 1953; ed. at Mill-field: m. 1973, Annie Yvette, da. of Robert le Poulain, of 65, Av. de Marville, St. Malo, France.

DAUGHTER LIVING.
Lady Bridget Ann, b. 1957.

BROTHER LIVING.
Hon. Simon Walter Erskine (16, Neville Drive, N2), b. 1930; ed. at Eton, and at Trin. Coll., Camb. (BA 1953, MA 1957); late 2nd Lt. Scots Gds.; an Assist. Master at Haberdashers' Aske's Sch.: m. 1973, Deborah Jane, da. of Michael Mounsey, of Stablegartin, Padbury, Buckingham, and has issue living, Thomas Harry Erskine, b. 1974.

WIDOW LIVING OF SEVENTH EARL.
ELEANOR MAY (Eleanor, Countess Castle Stewart), da. of Solomon R. Guggenheim, of New York, USA: m. 1920, the 7th Earl, who d. 1961. Residence,—Old Lodge, Nutley, Sussex.

COLLATERAL BRANCHES LIVING.

Grandsons of the late Rev. the Hon. Andrew Godfrey Stuart, 4th son of 2nd Earl :—
Issue of the late Richard Wingfield Stuart, b. 1843, d. 1914: m. 1st, 1869, Jeannie Miriam, who d. 1889, dau. of John Macdermott, of Gayfield, Sydney; 2ndly, 1891, Isabel Clare, who d. 1953, el. dau. of Charles Lee, M.L.A. of N.S. Wales for Tenterfield :—

(By 2nd marriage) John William Wingfield, b. 1901 ; is a Civil Engineer, Irrigation Depart., Sydney:
m. 1930, Dorothy Eleanor, dau. of T. Baker Insoll, of Hamilton, New Zealand, and has issue living,
Mary Rose Dorothy Wingfield, b. 1931: m. 1954, the Rev. Leonard Russell Goggs, of St. Andrew's
Rectory, 41, Church Terr., Walkerville, S. Australia, and has issue living Stephen John b. 1962:
Brenda Margaret b. 1955, Catherine Mary b. 1956, Ursula Anne b. 1958, Sarah Louise b. 1963.
Residence,—115, Fullers Rd., Chatswood, Sydney, N.S. Wales.——Godfrey Richard Wingfield, b.
1905.   Residence,– 115, Fullers Rd., Chatswood, Sydney, N.S. Wales.

Grandchildren of Andrew Thomas Stuart, el. son of the Hon. Andrew Godfrey
Stuart, 2nd son of 1st Earl:—
Issue of the late George Joseph Stuart, b. 1842, d. 1921 : m. 1875, Elizabeth Sarah,
who d. 1877, dau. of Abraham Rheuben, of Tasmania:—
Arthur Burleigh, b. 1876. Residence,—

Grandchildren of the late Robert Walter Stuart, 3rd son of Andrew Thomas Stuart
(ante):—
Issue of the late Walter Burleigh Stuart, b. 1875, d. 1912 : m. 1901, Helen Gertrude (who d.
1956, having m. 2ndly, 1913, John Martin Muir, of Sorell, Tasmania, who d. 1943), dau. of
Edward Mace, of Burnie, Tasmania :—
Burleigh Athol, b. 1904 : m. 1927, Winifred May, dau. of the late Ernest Kerrison, of Beaconsfield,
Tasmania, and has issue living, Ernest Martin, b. 1935: m. 1965, June Rosalyn, da. of Stanley
Bastian, of Como, W. Aust., and has issue living, Conway Athol b. 1968, Kym Robina b. 1967,—
Claire Leila, b. 1928: m. 1951, Reginald Edward Johnston, of 19, Rialannah Rd., Mount Nelson,
Hobart, Tasmania, and has issue living, Kent Reginald b. 1952, Vivienne Claire b. 1955, Celia Anne
b. 1963, Dianne Ruth b. 1965,—Winifred Ellen, b. 1929: m. 1950, John Robert Sinclair Mackey, of
Lileah, N.-W. Coast, Tasmania, and has issue living, Andrew John Sinclair b. 1956, Denise Claire,
b. 1952: m. 1972, Robert John Wells (c/o ANZ Banking Group, Emmett St., Smithton, Tasmania),—
Alma Elaine, b. 1931: m. 1955, James Maxwell Carter, of 71, Corinth St., Howrah, Hobart, Tas-
mania, and has issue living, Stuart James b. 1958, Michael Jackson b. 1960, Lee Andrea b. 1956.
Residence,—75, Montagu St., New Town, Hobart, Tasmania.——Sylvia Annie, b. 1902.   Residence,—

Grandson of the late Andrew Thomas Stuart (ante):—
Issue of the late Audley Mervyn Stuart, b. 1860, d. 1942 : m. 1892, Alice Anne Rogers, of
Hobart, Tasmania, who d. 1897 :—
Audley Andrew Mervyn, b. 1897: m. 1934, Beryl Elizabeth, dau. of Edward Alfred Irwin, of Hobart,
Tasmania, and has issue living, Elizabeth Anne Castle b. 1937,—Helen Christine Castle, b. 1939,—
Margaret Lyndsay Castle, b. 1942.   Residence,—71, Colville Street, Battery Point, Hobart, Tasmania.

Grandson of the late Maj. Burleigh William Henry Fitz-Gibbon Stuart, 4th son of
the Hon. Andrew Godfrey Stuart (ante):—
Issue of the late Major Godfrey Richard Conyngham Stuart, C.B., E. Lancashire Regt., b.
1866, d. 1955 : m. 1899, Alice Mabel, who d. 1936, youngest dau. of the late John Acheson
Smyth, of Ardmore, co. Londonderry :—
Godfrey Walter Burleigh (of 13, Woodlands Grove, Isleworth, Middlesex), b. 1901: Lt.-Col. (ret.)
late E. Lancs. Regt.: m. 1933, Christine Valerie, dau. of Col. Stephen Simpson, T.D., D.L., of
Bowerswood, nr. Garstang, Lancashire, and has issue living, Jane Christine, b. 1934,—Wendy
Mary, b. 1935.

Grandchildren of the late Maj. Godfrey Richard Conyngham Stuart, CB, (ante):—
Issue of the late Lt.-Col. Robin Charles Burleigh Stuart, b. 1907, d. 1970: m. 1939, Evelyn
Alice, (Glenroy, Gadshill Rd., Charlton Kings, Glos.), da. of Harry Freegard, of Charlton
Kings, Glos.:—
Douglas Charles Burleigh (14, Cherrywood Court, Bundoora, Melbourne, Vic., Aust.), b. 1940; ed. at
Cheltenham, and Nautical Coll., Pangbourne; with Air Traffic Control, Melbourne: m. 1962, Pamela,
da. of Gordon Sivyer, of Wembley, W. Aust., and has issue living, Andrew John Burleigh, b. 1967,—
Joanna Mary, b. 1965.——Rosemary Ann, b. 1945: m. 19—, Michael John Ridlington [see E
Ilchester, colls.]

Grandsons of the late Maj. Burleigh William Henry Fitz-Gibbon Stuart (ante):—
Issue of the late Brig.-Gen. Burleigh Francis Brownlow Stuart, CB, CMG, b. 1868, d. 1952:
m. 1916, Evelyn Margaret, JP, who d. 1970, da. of Lt.-Col. Sir Edward Henry St. Lawrence
Clarke, 4th Bt., CMG, DSO (cr. 1804, ext.);—
John William Brownlow, MBE, MC (Corner Cottage, Radford, Inkberrow, Worcs.), b. 1917; ed. at
Rugby; Col. Worcestershire Regt. (ret.); OC 1st Bn. 1959-61; Palestine 1939 (MC), Sudan and
Eritrea 1940-41, W. Desert and Egypt 1941-45 (despatches), Italy 1944-45 (MBE), Kenya 1956-57
(Africa Gen. Ser. Medal with clasp); MBE (Mil.) 1945: m. 1954, Anthea Joan, el. da. of the late
Ashley Ernest Herman, OBE, FRCS, of Shipton Hill, Hambledon, Godalming.——Burleigh Edward
St. Lawrence, b. 1920; ed. at Rugby, and at Oxford Univ. (MA); Colonial Forest Ser. 1952-63; on
staff of Colonial Forestry Bureau, Oxford; formerly Capt. Worcestershire Regt.; N.-W. Frontier of
India 1940, Burma 1944-45: m. 1952, Joan Elizabeth, da. of Col. Matthew George Platts, CIE,
OBE, MC, and has issue living, Edward John Burleigh, b. 1953,—Elizabeth Helen, b. 1955,—Cather-
ine Frances, b. 1958. Residence,—Hunter's Close, Ickford, Aylesbury.

PREDECESSORS.—[1] ANDREW Stuart, cr. Lord Avondale (peerage of Scotland) 1459, was afterwards Chancellor of Scotland ; d. 1488 ; s. by his nephew [2] ALEXANDER, 2nd Lord ; one of the
Lords Auditors ; d. 1489 ; s. by his son [3] ANDREW, 3rd Lord ; fell at Flodden 1513 ; s. by his son
[4] ANDREW, 4th Lord ; exchanged his Lordship with Sir James Hamilton for that of Ochiltree, and
by Act of Parliament 1542 was ordained to be styled Lord Stuart of Ochiltrie ; d. 1548 ; s. by his
son [5] ANDREW, 2nd Lord Stuart of Ochiltrie ; d. 1592 ; s. by his grandson [6] ANDREW, 3rd
Lord Stuart of Ochiltrie, a Lord of the Bedchamber to James I. of England ; resigned his title to
his cousin, Sir James Stuart with the consent of the Crown, and was himself cr. Baron Castle Stuart
(peerage of Ireland) 1619, and received from the King considerable estates in co. Tyrone ; d. 1628;
s. by his son [7] Sir ANDREW, 2nd Baron, who in 1628 had been cr. a Baronet (Nova Scotia) ; d. 1639;
s. by his son [8] ANDREW, 3rd Baron ; d. 1650 ; s. by his brother [9] JOSIAS, 4th Baron ; d.s.p. 1652.
s. by his uncle [10] JOHN, 5th Baron ; d. unmarried 1678, when the Peerage and Baronetcy became
dormant, and remained so until 1774, when they were successfully claimed by [11] ANDREW THOMAS,
9th Baron, the descendant in the 4th generation of Col. the Hon. Robert, 3rd son of 1st Baron ; cr.
Viscount Castle Stuart (peerage of Ireland) 1793, and Earl Castle Stewart (peerage of Ireland) 1800;
d. 1809 ; s. by his son [12] ROBERT, 2nd Earl ; d. 1854 ; s. by his el. son [13] EDWARD, 3rd Earl ;
d. 1857 ; s. by his brother [14] CHARLES KNOX, 4th Earl ; b. 1810: m. 1835, Charlotte Raffles
Drury, dau. of the late Quintin Thompson ; d. 1874 ; s. by his son [15] HENRY JAMES, 5th
Earl, b. 1837 ; assumed in 1867, by Roy. licence, the additional surname of Richardson : m. 1866,
Augusta le Vicomte Massy Richardson, who d. 1908, widow of Major Hugh Massy (85th Foot),
youngest dau. and heiress of the late Major Richardson-Brady, of Drum Manor, co. Tyrone ; d.
1914 ; s. by his cousin [16] ANDREW JOHN (2nd son of the late Rev. the Hon. Andrew Godfrey
Stuart, 4th son of 2nd Earl), 6th Earl ; b. 1840 ; in M.C.S. : m. 1876, Emma Georgiana, dau. of Maj.-
Gen. Arthur Stevens ; d. 1921 ; s. by his son [17] ARTHUR, M.C., 7th Earl ; b. 1889 ; Bar. Inner

Temple 1943 ; European War 1914-18 as Major Machine Gun Corps and a G.S.O. (M.C.) ; sat as M.P. for Harborough Div. of Leicestershire (U.) 1929-33 : m. 1920, Eleanor May, dau. of Solomon R. Guggenheim, of New York, USA; d. 1961; s. by his son [18] ARTHUR PATRICK AVONDALE, 8th Earl and present peer; also Viscount Castle Stuart, and Baron Castle Stuart.

CATHCART, EARL. (Cathcart.) [Lord S. about 1452, Earl U.K. 1814.]

ALAN CATHCART, CB, DSO, MC, 6th Earl; b. Aug. 22nd, 1919; s. 1927; ed. at Eton, and at Magdalene Coll., Camb.; Maj.-Gen.; Lt. Col. Comdg. Scots Gds. 1960-62, Col. AQ Scottish Command 1962-63, Imperial Defence Coll. 1964, Commander 152nd Highland Inf. Bde. (TA) 1965-66, Brig. Operations Div. SHAPE 1967-69, GOC Yorks Dist. 1969-70, and GOC Berlin (British Sector) 1970-73; ret. 1973; Brig. Queen's Body Guard for Scotland (R. Co. of Archers); NW Europe 1944-45 (despatches, MC, DSO); DSO 1945; CB (Mil) 1973: m. 1946, Rosemary Clare Marie Gabrielle, da. of the late Air-Commodore Sir Henry Percy Smyth-Osbourne, CMG, CBE, and has issue.

Arms,—Azure, three cross crosslets fitchée issuing out of as many crescents argent. **Crest,**—A dexter hand couped above the wrist and erect proper, grasping a crescent argent as in the arms. **Supporters,**—Two parrots wings inverted proper.

Residences,—Auchindoune, Cawdor, Nairn; 14, Eaton Mews South, SW1. *Clubs,*—Brooks's, Guards, Royal Yacht Squadron.

I·HOPE·TO·SPEED

SON LIVING.
CHARLES ALAN ANDREW (*Lord Greenock*), b. Nov. 30th, 1952; ed. at Eton.

DAUGHTERS LIVING.
Lady Louisa, b. 1948.
Lady Charlotte Mary, b. 1951: m. 1972, Capt. Anthony C. McCallum, 1st The Queen's Dragoon Gds., and has issue living, Sophia, b. 1975.

MOTHER LIVING.
Vera Estelle (*Dowager Lady Hodge*), dau. of the late John Fraser, of Cape Town, and widow of Capt. de Grey Warter, 4th Dragoon Guards: m. 2ndly, 1919, the 5th Earl, who d. 1927, having obtained a divorce 1922 ; 3rdly, 1930, as his second wife, Sir Rowland Frederic William Hodge, 1st Bt., who d. 1950. *Residence,*—50, Lennox Gdns., SW1.

COLLATERAL BRANCHES LIVING.

Grandchildren of the late Maj. Frederick Adrian Cathcart, el. son of the Hon. Augustus Murray Cathcart (infra):—
Issue of the late Maj. Alan Reginald Cathcart, b. 1908, d. 1967: m. 1934, Daphne Victoria Catherine (Ardendee, Kirkcudbright), da. of the late Maj.-Gen. John Archibald Henry Pollock, CB [see Montague-Pollock, Bt., colls.]:—
Charles Alan (Ardendee, Kirkcudbright), b. 1940: m. 1973, Carol Ann, yr. da. of the late A. E. Jenner, and has issue living, Daniel Edward, b. 1974.——Julia Mary, b. 1936: m. 1959, Angus George Millar, WS, of 94, Murrayfield Gdns., Edinburgh, and has issue living, James George, b. 1961,—Charles Angus, b. 1963,—Roderick Alan, b. 1967.

Issue of the late Lt.-Col. Charles Frederick Cathcart, DSO, b. 1912, d. 1971: m. 1st, 1939 (m. diss. 1954), Pamela Violet, da. of the late Lt.-Col. Patrick Douglas Stirling, OBE, MC, JP, of Kippendavie, Kippenross, Dunblane, Perths.; 2ndly, 1955, Pamela Vera (12, Cornwall Mews South, SW7), da. of the late Maj. Harry Sebastian Garrard, of Welton Pl., Daventry, and widow of Maj. Sir Arthur Ralph Wilmot, 7th Bt.:—
By 1st m.) Clovannis Jane, b. 1942: m. 1961, Maj. Colin Berowald Innes, Black Watch [see Innes, Bt. (cr. 1628) colls.].——Miranda Jane (twin), b. 1942.——Sarah Camilla, b. 1946.

Granddaughter of the Hon. Augustus Murray Cathcart yr. son of 2nd Earl:—
Issue of the late Capt. Augustus Ernest Cathcart, King's Roy. Rifle Corps, b. 1875, d. (killed in action during European War) 1914 : m. 1913, Hilda Renée, who d. 1958, dau. of the late Major William Frederick Lee, of Grove Hall, Knottingley:—
Eva Renée, OBE, b. 1914; late Junior Com. ATS; is a JP for N. Riding of Yorkshire; OBE (Civil) 1971. *Residence,*—Warwick House, Aiskew, Bedale, Yorkshire.

PREDECESSORS.—[1] Sir ALAN Cathcart, Knt., Warden of the West Marches and Master of Artillery, cr. *Lord Cathcart* (peerage of Scotland) 1447 ; d. 1499 ; s. by his grandson [2] JOHN, 2nd Lord ; d. 1535 ; s. by his grandson [3] ALAN, 3rd Lord ; killed at battle of Pinkie 1547; s. by his son [4] ALAN, 4th Lord ; d. 1618 ; s. by his grandson [5] ALAN, 5th Lord ; d. 1628; s. by his son [6] ALAN, 6th Lord ; s. by his son [7] ALAN, 7th Lord ; d. 1732; s. by his son [9] CHARLES, 8th Lord, a Representative Peer and a Lord of the Bedchamber to George II; appointed Com. in Ch. of the British Forces in America 1740, but d. in the passage out ; s. by his son [9] CHARLES, K.T., P.C., 9th Lord, a Representative Peer, Lieut.-Gen. in the Army, First Lord of Police, Ambassador to Russia, &c.; d. 1776; s. by his son [10] WILLIAM SCHAW 10th Lord, a Representative Peer, a Gen. in the army, and sometime Ambassador to St. Petersburg ; cr. *Baron Greenock,* of Greenock, co. Renfrew and *Viscount Cathcart,* of Cathart, co. Renfrew (peerage of United Kingdom) 1807, and *Earl Cathcart* (peerage of United Kingdom) 1814; d. 1843; s. by his son [11] CHARLES MURRAY, G.C.B., 2nd Earl; b. 1783; a Gen. in the Army, and Gov.-Gen. and Com.-in-Ch. in British N. America, &c.; m. 1818, Henrietta dau. of Thomas Mather; d. 1859; s. by his son [12] ALAN FREDERICK, 3rd Earl; b. 1828; Chm. of N. Riding Quarter Sessions 1858-68 : m. 1850, Elizabeth Mary, who d. 1902, el. dau. and co-heiress of Sir Samuel Crompton, Bt. (ext.); d. 1905; s. by his son [13] ALAN, 4th Earl, b. 1856; d. 1911; s. by his brother [14] GEORGE, 5th Earl, b. 1862 : m. 1919, Vera Estelle (from whom he obtained a divorce 1922, and who m. 3rdly, 1930, Sir Rowland Frederic William Hodge, 1st Bt.) dau. of the late John Fraser, of Cape Town, and widow of Capt. de Grey Warter, 4th Dragoon Guards; d. 1927; s. by his son [15] ALAN, 6th Earl and present peer; also Viscount Cathcart, Lord Cathcart, and Baron Greenock.

CATTO, BARON. (Catto.) [Baron U.K. 1936, Bt. U.K. 1921].

STEPHEN GORDON CATTO, 2nd Baron,
and 2nd Baronet ; b. Jan. 14th, 1923 ;
s. 1959; ed. at Eton, and Trin. Coll.,
Camb.; formerly Flt. Lt. RAF VR; a
Member of Advisory Council of Export
Credits Guarantee Dept. 1959-65; a
part-time Member of London Transport
Board 1962-68; Chm. of Morgan Gren-
fell & Co., Ltd., of Yule, Catto & Co.,
Ltd., and of Aust. Mutual Provident
Soc. (UK Branch); a Dir. of Gen.
Electric Co. Ltd., News International
Ltd., Aust. United Corpn. Ltd. (Mel-
bourne) and of other cos.; a Member of
London Advisory Cttee. of Hongkong &
Shanghai Banking Corpn.: m. 1st, 1948
(m. diss. 1965), Josephine Innes, el. da.
of George Herbert Packer, of Alexandria,
Egypt; 2ndly, 1966, Margaret, da. of
James Stuart Forrest, of Dilston, Tas-
mania, and has issue, by 1st and 2nd
marriages.

Arms,—Or, on a chevron between three lymphads sable as many boars' heads couped of the field.
Crest,—A wild cat sejant proper, resting the dexter paw on a garb or.   Supporters,—On either side
a tiger proper, charged on the shoulder with an ivy leaf or.
Residences,—41, William Mews, Westminster, SW1X 9HQ; House of Schivas, Ythanbank, Aberdeenshire.

SONS LIVING. (By 1st marriage.)
Hon. INNES GORDON, b. Aug. 7th, 1950.
Hon. Alexander Gordon, b. 1952; ed. at Westminster.
(By 2nd marriage.)
Hon. James Stuart Gordon, b. 1966.
DAUGHTERS LIVING. (By 1st marriage.)
Hon. Christian Victoria Gordon, b. 1955.
Hon. Ariane Madeleine Gordon, b. 1960.
(By 2nd marriage.)
Hon. Georgina Lucinda Gordon, b. 1969.
SISTERS LIVING.
Hon. Isabel Ida Gordon, OBE (61, Cadogan Gdns., SW3), b. 1912; a Gov. of PNEU Schs.; World Pres.,
YWCA 1955-63; Pres. of YWCA of Gt. Britain 1966-72; OBE (Civil) 1952.
Hon. Ruth Gordon, b. 1919; formerly in W.A.A.F.: m. 1947, Francis Ernest Herman Bennett, C.B.E.,
son of the late Sir Ernest Nathaniel Bennett, M.P., and has issue living, David Francis, b.
1948,—Adam Gordon Greverus, b. 1954,—Olivia Gay, b. 1950. Residence,—42, Netherhall Gdns.,
Hampstead, N.W.3.
WIDOW LIVING OF FIRST BARON.
GLADYS FORBES (Gladys, Lady Catto), dau. of Stephen Gordon, of Elgin : m. 1910, the 1st Baron,
who d. 1959. Residence,—Holmdale, Holmbury St. Mary, Surrey.

PREDECESSOR.—[1] Rt. Hon. Sir THOMAS SIVEWRIGHT CATTO, C.B.E., son of William Catto, of
Peterhead, Aberdeenshire ; b. 1879 ; E. India Merchant and Banker, and Managing Director of
Morgan Grenfell & Co., Ltd., of London, of Yule, Catto & Co., Ltd., of London, and of Andrew Yule &
Co., of Calcutta ; was Gov. of Bank of England 1944-9 ; cr. a Baronet 1921, and Baron Catto, of
Cairncatto, co. Aberdeen (peerage of U.K.) 1936 : m. 1910, Gladys Forbes, dau. of Stephen Gordon,
of Elgin ; d. 1959 ; s. by his son [2] STEPHEN GORDON, 2nd Baron and present peer.

CAVAN, EARL OF. (Lambart.) [Earl I. 1647.]

Prepared on every side.

MICHAEL EDWARD OLIVER LAMBART,
T.D., 12th Earl ; b. Oct. 29th, 1911 ; s.
1950; ed. at Radley; Lt.-Col. (ret.)
Shropshire Yeo. (Comdg. 1955-58); Hon.
Col., C Sqdn., Queen's Own Mercian Yeo.
TAVR since 1974; DL for Salop; 1939-45
War (despatches): m. 1947, Essex Lucy,
da. of the late Henry Arthur Cholmondeley [see B. Delamere, colls.], and
has issue.
Arms,—Gules, three gillieflowers pierced argent.
Crest.—On a mount vert a centaur argent drawing
a bow or. Supporters,—Two knights in complete
armour sable, garnished or, with an under habit
gules, fringed of the second, the beaver up, and on
the helmet seven plumes alternately of the third
and argent.
Residence,—Waters Upton Manor, Wellington,
Salop.

DAUGHTERS LIVING.
Lady Sarah Audrey, b. 1948: m. 1968, Capt. Alistair
Charles Sinclair, 17th/21st Lancers, of 72, Gowan
Av., SW6, and has issue living, Harry Charles
Lambart, b. 1972,—Rupert Alistair Grenville, b.
1973.
Lady Katherine Lucy, b. 1955.
SISTERS LIVING.
Lady Mary Veronica, b. 1908: m. 1934, Col. Edward
Henry Cadogan, C.B.E., late Roy. Welch Fusiliers,

of Shallows House, Boldre, Lymington, Hants., and has issue living, Henry Michael Edward (Braces Quay, Beaulieu, Hants.), *b.* 1935; ed. at Winchester; Maj. R. Welch Fusiliers: *m.* 1966, Daphne Jane Richards, da. of the late H. Ashley Mason, and has issue living, Edward Ashley David *b.* 1970, Camilla Mary *b.* 1968,—Alexander John, *b.* 1937; ed. at Radley; a Dir. of Taylor Mills, Ltd.: *m.* 1973, Christine Margaret, only da. of Edward Winstanley, of 49, Fairacres, Roehampton Lane, SW15, and has issue living, Charles Alexander Henry *b.* 1974,—Oliver Roger, *b.* 1946; ed. at Radley; late 2nd Lt. R. Welch Fusiliers.

Lady Daphne Olive (75, Nun St., St. Davids, Dyfed), *b.* 1909: *m.* 1944, Maj. Kenneth Gordon Grierson, E. Surrey Regt. (ret.), and has issue living, William, *b.* 1947; with BBC: *m.* 1972, Barbara Edwina, da. of Edwin Locke, of Haywards Heath, Sussex.

DAUGHTERS LIVING OF TENTH EARL. (*By 2nd marriage.*)

Lady Elizabeth Mary (Bishopstone House, Salisbury), *b.* 1924: *m.* 1949, Mark Frederic Kerr Longman, who *d.* 1972, and has issue living, Caroline Elizabeth, *b.* 1951,—Jane, *b.* 1955,—Emma, *b.* 1959.
Lady Joanna, *b.* 1929: *m.* 1955, Maj. Michael Godwin Plantagenet Stourton, Grenadier Guards (ret.), of The Old Rectory, Great Rollright, Chipping Norton, Oxon. [see B. Mowbray].

GRANDDAUGHTER LIVING OF NINTH EARL.

Issue of the late Capt. the Hon. Lionel John Olive Lambart, D.S.O., R.N., 2nd son of 9th Earl, *b.* 1873, *d.* (killed in action during European War) 1940: *m.* 1906, Adelaide Douglas, who *d.* 1972, yr. da. of the late Capt. Arthur Randolph Randolph, 15th Hussars, of Eastcourt, Wilts:—

Lady Edith Sybil, *b.* 1918: raised to rank of an Earl's daughter 1947: *m.* 1940, Ivan Cottam Foxwell, Maj. Roy. Norfolk Regt. (Reserve), and has issue living, Zia, *b.* 1940: *m.* 1968, David Joseph Kruger, of 26, Ranelagh House, Elystan Pl., SW3, and has issue living, Patrick Gene *b.* 1972,—Atalanta Edith, *b.* 1956: *m.* 1973, Prince Stefano Massimo, and has issue living, Zaffiro *b.* 1974. *Residences,*—Home Farm, Sherston, Wilts.; 45, Chester Sq., SW1.

WIDOW LIVING OF TENTH EARL.

(HESTER) JOAN BYNG, *D.B.E.* (*Joan, Countess of Cavan*), dau. of 5th Earl of Strafford, and widow of Capt. the Hon. Andrew Edward Mulholland [see B. Dunleath]: was Lady-in-Waiting to H.R.H. Princess Mary 1918-22, and to H.M. Queen Elizabeth, the Queen Mother (when Duchess of York) during tour of Australia and New Zealand 1927; an Extra Lady-in-Waiting to H.R.H. the Princess Royal 1932-66, DBE (Civil) 1927: *m.* 1922, as his second wife, the 10th Earl, who *d.* 1946. *Residence,*—39, Knightsbridge Court, Sloane St., SW1.

COLLATERAL BRANCHES LIVING.

Granddaughters of the late Hon. Octavius Henry Lambart, 5th son of 8th Earl:—
Issue of the late Howard Frederick John Lambart, *b.* 1880, *d.* 1946: *m.* 1st, 1908, Helen Marianne, who *d.* 1932, dau. of the late Samuel Shelley Wallbridge, LL.B.; 2ndly, 1938, May, dau. of the late Hon. Robert Bickerdike, of Montreal, Canada:—
(By 1st marriage) Helen Hyacinthe, *b.* 1908 ; ed. at McGill Univ., Montreal (B.A. 1930). *Address.*—RRI, Grenville, Province of Quebec, Canada.——Evelyn Mary, *b.* 1914. *Residence,*—Mudgett Rd., RR No. 4, Sutton, Quebec, J0E 2K0, Canada.

Granddaughter of the late Maj. Frederick Richard Henry Lambart, 2nd son of the late Cdr. the Hon. Oliver William Matthew Lambart, RN, 6th son of 7th Earl:—
Issue of the late Capt. Richard Frederick Lacon Lambart, *b.* 1875, *d.* 1924: *m.* 1st, 1899, Enid (who *d.* 1963, having obtained a divorce 1909), dau. of Spencer Brunton; 2ndly, 1913, Faith Bevan (who obtained a divorce 19—); 3rdly, 1922, Kitty Gibbens (she *m.* 2ndly 1924, Herbert Alfred Rich):—
(Kathleen) Joy Lydia Lacon, *b.* 1923.
Issue, if any, of the late Capt. Harry Godfrey Randolph Lambart (3rd son of the late Maj. Frederick Richard Henry Lambart (ante), *b.* 1876: *m.* 1st, 1901, Ruby, dau. of M. J. Kerchoff, of Cape Town; 2ndly, 19—.

Grandchildren of the late Maj. Charles Edward Kilcoursie Lambart [yst. son of the late Maj. Frederick Richard Henry Lambart (ante)], *b.* 1877, *d.* (killed in action) 1916: *m.* 1st, 18— (marriage dissolved 19—), Isabel Dora, who *d.* 1936, dau. of the late Edward Jeffrey, of Boar's Hill House, Berks; 2ndly, 1901, Florence Marion, who *d.* 1961, dau. of Frederick Mancesseh Brandon:—
Issue of the late Frederick Cavan Lambart, *b.* 1902, *d.* 1963: *m.* 1st, 1924 (marriage dissolved 1942), Adelaide Constance, dau. of Ottywell Butler; 2ndly, 1942 (marriage dissolved 1948), Audrey May, dau. of the late Albert Charles Dunham; 3rdly, 1958, Kathleen Elizabeth (c/o Barclays Bank, 27, Regent St., S.W.1), el. dau. of Edward James Henry Darvill, of Port Vale House, Hertford:—
(By 2nd m.) Roger Cavan (of 34, Woodleigh Gdns., SW16), *b.* 1944; presumed *h.p.*——(By 1st m.) Olive, *b.* 1925: *m.* 1950, Ernest Ephraim Corrett, of Montrose, 25, Roedean Cres., Roehampton, SW15, and has issue living, Paul *b.* 1952,—Graham, *b.* 1954.——(By 3rd m.) Elizabeth, *b.* 1959.

Grandson of the late Arthur Oliver Lambart (infra):—
Issue of the late Ford Augustus Oliver Lambart, *b.* 1880, *d.* 1940: *m.* 1908, Daisy Elizabeth Margaret, el. dau. of A. Reid Nicholson, of Edinburgh.
Arthur Oliver Reid, *b.* 1909.

Grandchildren of the late Com. the Hon. Oliver William Matthew Lambart, R.N. (ante):—
Issue of the late Arthur Oliver Lambart, *b.* 1854, *d.* 1903: *m.* 1879, Annie Louisa, who *d.* 1918, dau. of the late Augustus Hillier, of the Ordnance Depart.:—
Alice Mary Helen, *b.* 1888.——Blanche Mary, *b.* 1893: *m.* (Jan.) 1919, Samuel Alexander Vintcent Melvill, who *d.* 1963, and has issue living, Jack Vintcent (of Melwyn, 19, Menin Av., Newlands, Cape Town, S. Africa), *b.* 1921: *m.* 1959, Shirley, younger dau. of the late L. A. Wyndham, of Fresnaye, Sea Point, Cape Town, and has issue living, David Leonard Vintcent *b.* 1960, Eric Wyndham *b.* 1961, Robert John *b.* 1964, Catherine Joy *b.* 1967.——May Hensleigh, *b.* 1899: *m.* 1927, Stephen Peter Meintjes, ret. bank manager, of 7, Gayleigh, Acton Rd., Rondebosch, Cape Province, S. Africa, and has issue living, John Lambart (8, Gayleigh, Acton Rd., Rondebosch, S. Africa), *b.* 1928: *m.* 1st, 1955 (m. diss. 1963), Jean Paton, da. of J. W. Davidson, of Pinelands, Cape Province, S. Africa; 2ndly, 1973, Denise Wynn, da. of F. W. Short, of E. London, C.P., S. Africa, and has issue living (by 1st m.), Peter James, *b.* 1958,—Muriel Edgar, *b.* 1931: *m.* 1955, Sidney Charles Housdon, of 32, Forest Drive, Pinelands, Cape Province, S. Africa, and has issue living, Michael Charles *b.* 1963, Jennifer May *b.* 1961, Carolyn Janet *b.* 1969,—Elizabeth Ann, *b.* 1938: *m.* 1960, Edward James Wyndham Quin, of Bishops Glen, Orange Free State, S. Africa, and has issue living, Michael John Wyndham *b.* 1965, Ann Sharon Wyndham *b.* 1961, Margaret Lynn Wyndham *b.* 1962.

Issue of the late Brig.-Gen. Edgar Alan Lambart, C.B., *b.* 1857, *d.* 1930: *m.* 1st, 1884, Hannah Geraldine, who *d.* 1887, dau. of the late Capt. James Stirling Crawfurd Stirling-Stuart [Stirling-Maxwell, Bt., colls.]; 2ndly, 1891, Mary Louisa, who *d.* 1948, dau. of Sir James Robert Walker, 2nd Bt., of Sand Hutton, York:—

(By 2nd m.) Julian Harold Legge, *b.* 1893; ed. at Eton; 1914-18 War as Capt. RFA (Croix de Guerre): *m.* 1948, Margaret, only child of the late Rev. Canon William Evans, R. of Narberth, and widow of Sir (Henry) Walford Davies, KCVO, OBE, MusD, DMus. *Residence,*—67, Goat St., St. Davids, Haverfordwest, Dyfed.

Issue of the late Alfred Charlemagne Lambart, *b.* 1861, *d.* 1943: *m.* 1st, 1897, Constance (who *d.* 1948, having obtained a divorce 1914), el. dau. of the late Capt. Edmund Lyons Green, R.N.; 2ndly, 1920, Anne (who *d.* 1943, having obtained a divorce 1926, dau. of the late Rev. Andrew Holmes Belcher, of Fasque, Kincardineshire, and widow of 5th Earl of Mexborough :—
(By 1st marriage) Lydia Abigail Mary, *b.* 1901 : *m.* 1925, Ivan Estridge, and has issue living, Christopher Robert Ivan (Rose Hill, Brook Lane, Alderley Edge, Cheshire), *b.* 1926: *m.* 1952, Patricia, el. da. of John Archibald. *Residence,*—14, Devonshire Drive, Alderley Edge, Cheshire.
    Issue of the late Lieut.-Col. (Gustavus) Francis William Lambart, C.V.O. [el. son of the late Gustavus William Lambart (infra)], who was cr. a *Baronet* 1911:—
See Lambart, Bt.

Grandchildren of the late Gustavus William Lambart, 5th in descent from the Hon. Oliver Lambart, MP, 2nd son of 1st Earl:—
Issue of the late Cyril Henry Edward Lambart, *b.* 1866, *d.* 1955: *m.* 1900, Ethel Caroline Annie, who *d.* 1960, da. of Albert Thomas Ward, of Newton Hall, Rosebery Topping, Yorks.:—
Charles Albert George (27, Richmond St., Chelmer, Brisbane 4068, Qld.), *b.* 1901.——Cyril Alwyn Lawrence (19, Birt Av., Surfers' Paradise, Qld.), *b.* 1910: *m.* 1940, Claire Gilmore, and has issue living, Charles Dennis, *b.* 1943: *m.* 1967, Mary Bambrick, and has issue living, Sally Ann *b.* 1970, Juliette *b.* 1972,—Richard Gilmore, *b.* 1947,—Robin Francis, *b.* 1953,—Jacqueline Anne, *b.* 1945. ——George Desmond Richard (27, Richmond St., Chelmer, Brisbane, Qld.), *b.* 1912.

Grandchildren of the late Cyril Henry Edward Lambart (ante):—
Issue of the late Terence Edward William Lambart, *b.* 1903, *d.* 1965: *m.* 1946, Valma Johnson, who *m.* 2ndly, 1973, Philip John Richardson, of Coomero Gorge Drive, Tamborine Mountain, Qld.:—
Cavan, *b.* 1957.——Diana, *b.* 1948: *m.* 1968, Peter Athol McLauchlan, of 8, Ware St., Mooroora, Brisbane, Qld., and has issue living, Fraser Burnett *b.* 1968,—Ashley Lambart, *b.* 1970,—Burnett Hunter, *b.* 1972.——Vivienne, *b.* 1950; ed. at Qld. Univ. (BA, DipEd).——Rosalind, *b.* 1952: *m.* 1973, Michael Angus Robinson, of Wollongong, NSW.

PREDECESSORS.—[1] *Sir* OLIVER Lambart, *P.C.*, Knt., Gov. of Connaught 1601, and M.P. for co. Cavan 1613, &c.; cr. *Lord Lambart, Baron of Cavan* (peerage of Ireland) 1617; *d.* 1618; *s.* by his son [2] CHARLES, *P.C.*, 2nd Baron, M.P. for Bossiney, Cornwall, 1625-7, and Com.-in-Ch. of Forces in City of Dublin 1642, &c.; cr. *Viscount Kilcoursie* and *Earl of Cavan* (peerage of Ireland) 1647; *d.* 1660; *s.* by his son [3] RICHARD, 2nd Earl; *s.* by his son [4] CHARLES, 3rd Earl; *d.* 1702; *s.* by his son [5] RICHARD, 4th Earl; *d.* 1741; *s.* by his son [6] FORD, 5th Earl; *d.* 1772; *s.* by his cousin [7] RICHARD, 6th Earl, son of the Hon. Henry Lambart, 3rd son of 3rd Earl; *d.* 1778; *s.* by his son [8] RICHARD FORD WILLIAM, 7th Earl; a Gen. in the Army; commanded a Div. under Sir Ralph Abercrombie in Egypt 1800; *d.* 1837; *s.* by his grandson [9] FREDERICK JOHN WILLIAM, 8th Earl, son of George Frederick Augustus, Viscount Kilcoursie, by Sarah, dau. of J. P. Coppin, of Cowley, Oxfordshire, *b.* 1815: *m.* 1838, the Hon. Caroline Augusta, who *d.* 1892, dau. of 1st Baron Hatherton; *d.* 1887; *s.* by his el. son [10] FREDERICK EDWARD GOULD, *K.P.*, *P.C.*, 9th Earl, *b.* 1839; Vice-Chamberlain of the Household 1886; served throughout siege of Sebastopol 1854; present at bombardment of Canton 1856, and with "forlorn hope" at attack of Peiho Forts 1858; M.P. for S. Div. of Somersetshire (L) 1885-92 : *m.* 1863, Mary Sneade, who *d.* 1905, only child of the late Rev. John Olive; *d.* 1900; *s.* by his el. son [11] FREDERIC RUDOLPH, *K.P.*, *G.C.B.*, *G.C.M.G.*, *G.C.V.O.*, *G.B.E.*, 10th Earl, *b.* 1865; Field-Marshal; sometime Lieut. of Tower of London; Ch. of Imperial Gen. Staff 1922-6 ; Capt. of Hon. Corps of Gentlemen-at-Arms 1929-31; S. Africa 1899-1902 (despatches), European War 1914-19 in France and Comdg. British Troops in Italy (despatches seven times, C.B., K.C.B., G.C.M.G., Orders of St. Maurice and St. Lazarus of Italy, Crown of Belgium and W en Hu of China, Legion of Honour, Mil. Order of Savoy, French and Italian Croix de Guerre): *m.* 1st, 1893, Caroline Inez, who *d.* 1920, dau. of the late George Baden Crawley; 2ndly, 1922, Lady Hester Joan Byng, *D.B.E.*, dau. of 5th Earl of Strafford, and widow of Capt. the Hon. Andrew Edward Somerset Mulholland; *d.* 1946; *s.* by his brother [12] HORACE EDWARD SAMUEL SNEADE, 11th Earl; *b.* 1878; Archdeacon Emeritus of Salop, Preb. Emeritus and Provost of Denstone; sometime V. of St. Mary-the-Virgin, Shrewsbury : *m.* 1907, Audrey Kathleen, who *d.* 1942, dau. of the late Alfred Basil Loder; *d.* 1950; *s.* by his son [13] MICHAEL EDWARD OLIVER, 12th Earl and present peer; also Viscount Kilcoursie, and Lord Lambart, Baron of Cavan.

CAWDOR, EARL. (Campbell.)   [Earl U.K. 1827.]

HUGH JOHN VAUGHAN CAMPBELL, 6th Earl, and 24th Thane of Cawdor; *b.* Sept. 6th, 1932; *s.* 1970; ed. at Eton, and Magdalen Coll., Oxford; FRICS; High Sheriff of Carmarthenshire 1964: *m.* 1957, Cathryn, da. of Maj.-Gen. Sir (William) Robert Norris Hinde, KBE, CB, DSO, and has issue.

Arms,—Quarterly of four: 1st or, a stag's head cabossed sable attired gules, *Calder*; 2nd gyronny of eight, or and sable, *Campbell*; 3rd argent, a lymphad or ancient galley sable, *also Campbell*, 4th per fesse azure and gules, a cross or, *Lort*. Crest,—A swan proper, crowned or. Supporters,—*Dexter*, a lion guardant gules; *sinister*, a stag proper.

Seat,—Cawdor Castle, Nairn. *Residence,*—Golden Grove House, Broad Oak, Carmarthenshire.

SONS LIVING.
COLIN ROBERT VAUGHAN (*Viscount Emlyn*), *b.* June 30th, 1962.
Hon. Frederick William, *b.* 1965.

DAUGHTERS LIVING.

Lady Emma Clare, *b.* 1958.
Lady Elizabeth, *b.* 1959.
Lady Laura Jane, *b.* 1966.

BROTHER LIVING.

Hon. James Alexander (Tretire Mill, St. Owen's Cross, Hereford), *b.* 1942 ; ed. at Eton; ARCA: *m.* 1964, Brigid, da. of the late Capt. Patrick Owen Lyons, and has issue living, Slaine Catherine, *b.* 1966,—Cara Jenny, *b.* 1968.

SISTER LIVING.

Lady Caroline Mairi, *b.* 1930 : *m.* 1953, Baron Bernard Henry Hubert Friesen, of the Park House, Stackpole, Pembroke, and has issue living, Alexander Christian Edward, *b.* 1961,—Hero Arabella Mairi Elizabeth, *b.* 1963.

UNCLE LIVING.   (*Son of* 4*th Earl.*)

Hon. Andrew Charles, *b.* 1907; ed. at Eton, and at Ch. Ch., Oxford (B.A. 1929, M.A. 1933); formerly Major Cameron Highlanders: *m.* 1935, Helen Christina, dau. of the late Hon. Douglas Halyburton Cairns [see E. Cairns, colls.]. *Residence,*—Chapelhead, Avoch, Ross-shire.

AUNTS LIVING.   (*Daughters of* 4*th Earl.*)

Lady Janet Helena, *b.* 1899 : *m.* 1926, Capt. John Francis Gore, C.V.O. [see E. Arran, colls.] *Residence,*—Littlehay, Burley, near Ringwood, Hants.
Lady Mary Agatha. *b.* 1905 : *m.* 1931, Brigadier Henry Claude Warrington Eastman, D.S.O., MVO, late RA, and has issue living, David William (Wern Uchaf, Halfway Bridge, Bangor, Caerns.), *b.* 1937: *m.* 1969, Antonia Catherine, da. of Anthony Dorman, of Mill House, Netherbury, Bridport, Dorset,—Sylvia, *b.* 1935. *Residence,*—Leigh House, Newtown, Newbury, Berks.

WIDOW LIVING OF SON OF THIRD EARL.

Marjorie Edith, dau. of Horace George Devas: *m.* 1914, as his second wife, Lieut.-Col. the Hon. Ralph Alexander Campbell, O.B.E., who *d.* 1945. *Residence,*—Manor House, Padworth, Reading.

MOTHER LIVING.

Wilma Mairi (c/o Lloyds Bank, 46, Victoria St., SW1), el. da. of the late Vincent C. Vickers, of 38, Prince's Gate, SW7: *m.* 1929, the 5th Earl, from whom she obtained a divorce 1961.

WIDOW LIVING OF FIFTH EARL.

ELIZABETH (*Elizabeth, Countess Cawdor*), (Constabulary Garden, Nairn), da. of J. Topham Richardson, JP, of Harps Oak, Merstham, Surrey, and widow of Maj. Sir Alexander Penrose Gordon-Cumming, MC, 5th Bt.: *m.* 1961, as his 2nd wife, the 5th Earl, who *d.* 1970.

COLLATERAL BRANCHES LIVING.

Issue of the late Rev. the Hon. Nigel Campbell, 2nd son of 3rd Earl, *b.* 1873, *d.* 1951: *m.* 1902, Violet, who *d.* 1940, el. dau. of the late Charles Wyndham Rodolph Kerr [M. Lothian, colls.] :—
Olivia (*Hon. Mrs. Roger N. Frankland*), *b.* 1905 : *m.* 1st, 1934, Arthur Edmund Leveson, who obtained a divorce 1943 ; 2ndly, 1943, Major S. J. R. Bucknell, Irish Guards, who *b.* (killed in action during European War) 1943 ; 3rdly, 1947, as his second wife, the Hon. Roger Nathaniel Frankland [see B. Zouch]. *Residence,*—39, Cadogan Sq., SW1.——Jean Edith, *b.* 1911. *Residence,*—Flat 18, Queen's Court, St. John's Rd., Newbury, Berks., RG14 7PX.

Issue of the late Lieut.-Col. the Hon. Ralph Alexander Campbell, O.B.E., 3rd son of 3rd Earl, *b.* 1877, *d.* 1945 : *m.* 1st, 1906, Marjorie Theophila, who *d.* 1911, dau. of Sir John Arthur Fowler, 2nd Bt. ; 2ndly, 1914, Marjorie Edith (ante), dau. of Horace George Devas :—
(By 2nd marriage) David Archibald, *OBE*, *TD*, *b.* 1915; ed. at Eton, and at Trin. Hall, Camb.; is Lt.-Col. and Brevet Col. late Berks Yeo.; OBE (Mil) 1954. *Residence,*—Englefield Estate House, Theale, Berks.——Angus Mervyn, *TD*, *b.* 1918; ed. at Eton; late Maj. Surrey Yeo.; 1939-45 War (despatches) : *m.* 1950, Rosemary Madeline Hamilton, only da. of Hugh Alastair Hamilton Fraser [D. Somerset, colls.], and has issue living, Ian Angus Ralph, *b.* 1951; ed. at Bradfield,—James Malcolm, *b.* 1955; ed. at Eton,—Catherine Rosemary, *b.* 1964. *Residence,*—Wasing Lodge, Aldermaston, Berks.——Rosemary Edith, *b.* 1921.

Issue of the late Hon. Elidor Ronald Campbell, 4th son of 3rd Earl, *b.* 1881, *d.* 1957 : *m.* 1913, Violet, who *d.* 1975, da. of Octavius Edward Bulwer-Marsh, of Bryngwyn Manor, Raglan, Monmouthshire:—
Elidor Diarmid Calder (of Sandford House, Kingsclere, Newbury, Berks.), *b.* 1916; Maj. (ret.) R.A.: *m.* 1947, Liliana, da. of Maj. Anthony Zarich.——Fiona Mary, *b.* 1925.

Grandchildren of the late Capt. the Hon. Ronald George Elidor Campbell, 2nd son of 2nd Earl :—
Issue of the late Rev. Guy Ronald Campbell, *b.* 1874, *d.* 1950 : *m.* 1901, the Hon. Vere Annesley (now of Nadder Cottage, Donhead, Shaftesbury), el. da. of 11th Viscount Valentia:—
Colin Arthur Ronald, *b.* 1910.——Hester Maud Vere, *CBE* (of Nadder Cottage, Donhead, Shaftesbury), *b.* 1903; MBE (Civil) 1947, CBE (Civil), 1963: *m.* 1929, Eric Rupert Walter Barrington, who obtained a divorce 1938 [see V. Barrington].

Issue of the late Brig.-Gen. John Vaughan Campbell, V.C., C.M.G., D.S.O., *b.* 1876, *d.* 1944: *m.* 1st, 1904, Amy Dorothy, who *d.* 1927, el. dau. of the late John Penn, M.P. for Lewisham ; 2ndly, 1937, Margaret Emily Robina, dau. of Dr. A. Tennyson-Smith, of Rodborough Grange, Bournemouth :—
(By 1st marriage) Diana Marion, *b.* 1909 : *m.* 19—, and has issue living. *Residence,*—

Issue of the late Lieut.-Col. Robert Campbell, D.S.O., *b.* 1878, *d.* 1945 : *m.* 1926, Mary Emelda (of 3, Salisbury Rd., Hove, Sussex), da. of the late William Robert Wood:—
Robin John Ronald, *b.* 1927; ed. at Eton ; Maj. (ret.) Queen's Own Highlanders ; Malaya 1951 (despatches): *m.* 1954, Alison Barbara Rose, dau. of the late Major Horace Cave-Browne [see Cave-Browne-Cave, Bt., colls.], and has issue living, Ian Robert, *b.* 1956,—James Farquhar Robin *b.* 1958. *Address,*—c/o Lloyds Bank, High St., Uckfield, Sussex.——Alan, *b.* 1929; ed. at Eton ; Maj. Queen's Own Highlanders (formerly Cameronians); Malaya 1952 (despatches): *m.* 1963, Sylvia, da. of Richard Hermon, and has issue living, Alexander, *b.* 1964,—James, *b.* 1967,—Andrew, *b.* 1969,—Nicholas, *b.* 1971—Theresa Ann, *b.* 1965. *Address,*—c/o Williams & Glyns Bank (Holts), 22, Whitehall, SW1.

Grandson of the late Capt. the Hon. Alexander Francis Henry Campbell, 3rd son of 2nd Earl :—
Issue of the late Major Duncan Elidor Campbell, D.S.O., *b.* 1880, *d.* 1930 : *m.* 1914, the Hon. Florence Evelyne Willey (now of Poulton House, Cirencester, Gloucestershire), dau. of 1st Baron Barnby :—
Ian Robert, *CBE*, *AFC*, *b.* 1920; ed. at Eton; Air Vice-Marshal RAF; Ch. of Staff, No. 18 Gp. RAF since 1973; 1939-45 War in Middle East and Italy (prisoner); CBE (Mil) 1964: *m.* 1953, Beryl Evelyn, da. of the late Brig. Thomas Kennedy Newbigging, MC, and has issue living, Alister Neil, *b.* 1955. *Residence,*—Poulton House, Cirencester, Glos. *Clubs,*—Boodle's, RAF.

Granddaughter of the late Rev. the Hon. Archibald George Campbell, 2nd son of
1st Earl:—
Issue of the late Donald Campbell, *b.* 1860, *d.* 1923 : *m.* 1888, Edith Mary, who *d.*
1931, dau. of Henry Smith Wright [B. Denman]:—
d velyn Hope, *b.* 1894 : *m.* 1935, Arthur William Glenton Lennard, who *d.* 1943. *Residence,*—Apple
Tree Cottage, Bridge Street, Sidmouth, S. Devon, EX10 0RU.

PREDECESSORS.—Pryse Campbell, M.P. (a descendant of Sir John Campbell, 3rd son of 2nd
Earl of Argyll), had with other issue [1] JOHN, *M.P.* for Nairnshire 1777-80 and for Cardigan
1780-96 ; cr. *Baron Cawdor* (peerage of Great Britain) 1796 ; *d.* 1821 ; *s.* by his son [2] JOHN
FREDERICK, F.R.S., D.D., 2nd Baron ; *b.* 1790 ; cr. *Viscount Emlyn* and *Earl
Cawdor* (peerage of United Kingdom) 1827 : *m.* 1816, Lady Elizabeth Thynne, dau. of 2nd
Marquess of Bath ; *d.* 1860 ; *s.* by his son [3] JOHN FREDERICK VAUGHAN, 2nd Earl, *b.* 1817,
M.P. for Pembrokeshire (*LC*) 1841-59 ; Lord-Lieut. of Carmarthenshire : *m.* 1842, Sarah Mary,
who *d.* 1881, dau. of the late Gen. the Hon. Henry Frederick Compton Cavendish ; *d.* 1898 ;
s. by his el. son [4] FREDERICK ARCHIBALD VAUGHAN, P.C., 3rd Earl, *b.* 1847 ; Chm. of Great
Western Railway 1895-1905, and Lord-Lieut. of Pembroke 1896-1911 ; M.P. for Carmarthenshire
(*C*) 1874-85 ; First Lord of the Admiralty 1905 : *m.* 1868, Edith Georgina, who *d.* 1926, el. dau. of
the late Christopher Turnor, of Stoke Rochford ; *d.* 1911 ; *s.* by his el. son [5] HUGH FREDERICK
VAUGHAN, 4th Earl, *b.* 1870 : *m.* 1898, Joan Emily Mary, who *d.* 1945, dau. of John Charles
Thynne [see M. Bath, colls.]; *d.* 1914 ; *s.* by his el. son [5] JOHN DUNCAN VAUGHAN, *TD, FSA*, 5th
Earl, *b.* 1900 : *m.* 1st, 1929, Wilma Mairi (who obtained a divorce 1961), el. da. of the late Vincent C.
Vickers, of 38, Prince's Gate, SW7 ; 2ndly, 1961, Elizabeth, da. of J. Topham Richardson, JP, o
Harps Oak, Merstham, Surrey, and widow of Maj. Sir Alexander Penrose Gordon-Cumming, MC, 5th
Bt.; *d.* 1970 ; *s.* by his el. son [6] HUGH JOHN VAUGHAN, 6th Earl and present peer ; also Viscount
Emlyn, and Baron Cawdor.

CAWLEY, BARON. (Cawley.)   [Baron U.K. 1918, Bt. U.K. 1906.]

I desire, I believe, I have.

FREDERICK LEE CAWLEY, 3rd
Baron and 3rd Baronet ; *b.* July
27th, 1913 ; ed. at Eton, and
at New Coll., Oxford (B.A. 1935,
M.A. 1942) ; Bar. Lincoln's Inn
1938 ; Capt. RA ; Dep. Chm. of
Cttees., House of Lords 1958-67 ;
1939-44 War (wounded) : *m.* 1944,
Rosemary Joan, dau. of Reginald
Edward Marsden [see V. Dillon],
and has issue.

Arms,—Sable, three swans' heads erased
argent, guttée de poix, a chief arched or,
thereon a rose gules, barbed and seeded
proper, between two garbs azure. Crest,—
Upon a mount vert, a swan's head erased
argent between six bullrushes stalked and
leaved, three on either side, or. Supporters
—On either side a swan, wings surgeant
tergiant argent, guttée de poix, each standing
upon a garb fessewise or.

Seat,—Berrington Hall, Leominster.
Residence,—Bircher Hall, Leominster, Herefordshire, OAX HR6.

SONS LIVING.

Hon. JOHN FRANCIS (Castle Grounds, Ashton, Leominster, Herefordshire), *b.* Sept. 28th, 1946 ;
ed. at Eton.
Hon. William Frederick, *b.* 1947 ; ed. at Eton, and New Coll., Oxford.
Hon. Richard Kenneth, *b.* 1949 ; ed. at Eton, and Durham Univ.

Hon. Justin Robert, *b.* 1953 ; ed. at Milton Abbey Sch.
Hon. Charles Michael, *b.* 1955 ; ed. at Milton Abbey Sch.
Hon. Mark Andrew, *b.* 1957 ; ed. at Eton.

DAUGHTER LIVING.

Hon. Vanessa Mary, *b.* 1951, *m.* 1971, John Anthony Marston, of 25, Stoke Grove, Bristol, 9.

BROTHER LIVING.

Hon. Stephen Robert, *b.* 1915 ; ed. at Eton, and at New Coll., Oxford (B.A. 1937, B.Sc. 1938, M.A.,
1946) ; European War 1940-2 with Roy. Signals ; unsuccessfully contested High Peak Div. of
Derbyshire (*L*) May 1955 : *m.* 1952, Iris Edrica, dau. of Reginald Edward Marsden [see V. Dillon],
and has issue living, Robin Alexander, *b.* 1954,—James Edward, *b.* 1956,—Martin Harold, *b.* 1959,—
Foland Diana, *b.* 1957. *Residence,*—The Old House, Englefield Green, Egham, Surrey.

WIDOW LIVING OF SECOND BARON.

VIVIENNE (*Vivienne*, Baroness *Cawley*), dau. of Harold Lee, of Broughton Park, Manchester : *m.* 1912,
the 2nd Baron, who *d.* 1954. *Residence,*—Berrington Hall, Leominster.

PREDECESSORS.—[1] *Rt. Hon.* FREDERICK Cawley, P.C., son of the late Thomas Cawley, of
Priestland, Cheshire ; *b.* 1850 ; Chancellor of the Duchy of Lancaster in National Min. 1916-18 ;
M.P. for Prestwich Div. of Lancashire (S.E.) (*L*) 1895-1918 ; cr. a *Baronet* 1906, and *Baron
Cawley*, of Prestwich, co. Palatine of Lancaster (peerage of United Kingdom) 1918 : *m.* 1876,
Elizabeth, who *d.* 1930, dau. of John Smith, of Kynsal Lodge, Audlem ; *d.* 1937 ; *s.* by his
son [2] ROBERT HUGH, 2nd Baron, *b.* 1877 ; S. Africa 1900-01 : *m.* 1912, Vivienne, dau. of Harold
Lee, of Broughton Park, Manchester ; *d.* 1954 ; *s.* by his son [3] FREDERICK LEE, 3rd Baron and
present peer.

CHALFONT, BARON, (Gwynne Jones.) [Life Baron 1964.]

(ALUN) ARTHUR GWYNNE JONES, OBE, MC, PC, son of Arthur Gwynne Jones, of Cwmbran, Newport, Mon.; b. Dec. 5th, 1919; ed. at W. Monmouth Sch.; Brevet Lt.-Col. (ret.) S. Wales Borderers (Regular Army Officer 1940-61); Defence and Mil. correspondent, The Times 1961-64; Min. of State, Foreign Office 1964-70, and British Permanent Representative to WEU 1969. 70; 1939-45 War in Burma (MC); cr, OBE (Mil) 1961, PC 1964, and Baron Chalfont, of Llantarnam, co. Monmouth (Life Baron) 1964: m. 1948, Mona, MB, ChB, da. of Harry Douglas Mitchell, of Grimsby.

Arms yield to the toga.

Arms,—Gules a sword point downwards proper pommel and hilt or within an orle of two branches of olive fructed gold. **Crest,**—A dragon sejant gules supporting a column sable charged with nine bars argent, the capital also argent. **Supporters,** Dexter, a private of the Grenadier Company, 24th Foot (South Wales Borderers) in the uniform of circa 1751, supporting with the exterior hand a bamboo cane leaved proper; sinister, a herald vested in a tabard of the arms proper and holding in the exterior hand a sprig of olive fructed or.
Residence,—65, Ashley Gdns., SW1P 1QG. Clubs,—Garrick, City Livery, MCC.

CHAMPION, BARON. (Champion.) [Life Baron 1962.]

ARTHUR JOSEPH CHAMPION, PC, son of the late William Champion, of Glastonbury; b. July 26th, 1897; ed. at St. John's Elementary Sch., Glastonbury; Hon. ARCVS; JP of Glamorgan; a Railwayman; PPS to Min. of Food 1949-50, and to Sec. of State for War 1950-51, Joint Parliamentary Sec. to Min. of Agriculture and Fisheries 1951, a Dir. of British Sugar Corporation 1960-64 and again since 1967 and Min. without Portfolio 1964-67; Dep. Speaker and Dep. Chm. of Cttees., House of Lords since 1967; 1914-18 War, as 2nd Lt. Roy. Welsh Fusiliers; MP for S. Derbys. (Lab.) 1945-50, and for S.-E. Derbys. 1950-59; cr. Baron Champion, of Pontypridd, co. Glamorgan (Life Baron) 1962, and PC 1967: m. 1930, Mary Emma, da. of William Williams, and has issue.

Residence,—22, Lanelay Terrace, Pontypridd, Glamorgan.

DAUGHTER LIVING.

Hon. Barbara, b. 1931: m. 1957, Trevor Chubb. Residence,—10, Salisbury Rd., Redland, Bristol, BF6 7AW.

CHANDOS, VISCOUNT. (Lyttelton.) [Viscount U.K. 1954.]

ANTONY ALFRED LYTTELTON, 2nd Viscount; b. Oct. 23rd, 1920; s. 1972; ed. at Eton, and Trin. Coll., Camb. (MA); 1939-45 War, Mediterranean (despatches): m. 1949, Caroline Mary, da. of the Rt. Hon. Sir Alan Frederick Lascelles, GCVO, KCB, CMG, MC [see E. Harewood, colls.], and has issue.

Arms,—Argent, a chevron between three escallops sable a cross moline for difference. **Crest,**—A Moor's head in profile couped at the shoulders proper, wreathed round the temples argent and sable. **Supporters**—On either side a merman proper holding in the outer hand a trident pendant from a rope around the inner shoulder an escutcheon or charged with a pile gules.

Do what must be done, come what may.

Residence,—The Vine, Sherborne St. John, Basingstoke, Hants.

SONS LIVING.

Hon. THOMAS ORLANDO, b. Feb. 12th, 1953; ed. at Eton, and Worcester Coll., Oxford.
Hon. Matthew Peregrine Antony, b. 1956; ed. at Eton.

DAUGHTERS LIVING.

Hon. Laura Katharine, b. 1950; ed. at Cranborne Chase Sch., and St. Anne's Coll., Oxford (BA).
Hon. Deborah Clare, b. 1963.

BROTHER LIVING.

Hon. Nicolas Adrian Oliver, b. 1937; ed. at Eton: m. 1960, Margaret, dau. of Harold Hobson, and has issue living, Francis Sebastian Jasper, b. 1967,—Celia Melissa Francesca, b. 1960. Residence,—30, Paulton's Sq., SW3.

SISTER LIVING.

Hon. Rosemary (Viscountess Chaplin), b. 1922: m. 1951, as his second wife, the 3rd Viscount Chaplin. Residence,—Wadstray House, Blackawton, Totnes, S. Devon.

WIDOW LIVING OF FIRST VISCOUNT.

Lady MOIRA GODOLPHIN OSBORNE (Dowager Viscountess Chandos, known as Lady Moira Lyttelton), (Flat 4, Harrowby Court, Harrowby St., W1), da. of the 10th Duke of Leeds: m. 1920, the 1st Viscount, who d. 1972.

PREDECESSOR.—[1] *Rt. Hon.* OLIVER LYTTELTON, *KG, DSO, MC, PC,* son of the late Rt. Hon. Alfred Lyttelton, KC, MP, 8th son of 4th Baron Lyttelton [V. Cobham], *b.* 1893; Pres. of Board of Trade 1940-41 and 1945, Min. of State Cairo, and Member of War Cabinet 1941, Min. of Production 1942-45, and Sec. of State for Colonies, of Aldershot, co. Southampton (peerage of UK) 1954: *m.* 1920, Lady Moira Godolphin Osborne, da. of 10th Duke of Leeds; *d.* 1972; *s.* by his son [2] ANTONY ALFRED, 2nd Viscount and present peer.

CHAPLIN, VISCOUNT. (Chaplin.) [Viscount U.K. 1916.]

ANTHONY FRESKYN CHARLES HAMBY CHAPLIN, 3rd Viscount ; *b.* Dec. 14th, 1906 ; *s.* 1949; ed. at Radley; 1939-45 War as Fl. Lt. RAF; appointed Hon. Sec. of Zoological So. of London 1952: *m.* 1st, 1933, (m. diss. 1950), Alvilde, da. of Lt.-Gen. Sir (George) Tom Molesworth Bridges, KCB, KCMG, DSO; 2ndly, 1951, the Hon. Rosemary Lyttelton, da. of 1st Viscount Chandos, and has issue by 1st and 2nd marriages.

Arms,—Ermine, on a chief indented vert three griffins' heads erased or. Crest,—A griffin's head erased or, gorged with a mural crown vert. Supporters,— *Dexter,* upon a garb fessewise proper, banded gules, a hawk wings endorsed and inverted argent, beaked, membered, and the inside of the wings or, suspended from the neck by a riband sable an escutcheon of the arms of *Sutherland, i.e.* gules, three mullets or within a bordure of the last charged with a double tressure flory counter-flory of the field ; *sinister,* a chestnut-coloured racehorse in a white headstall, banded rose colour, pendant therefrom a blue lead all proper.

Residence,—Wadstray House, Blackawton, Totnes, S. Devon.

Rest in heaven.

DAUGHTERS LIVING. (By 1st marriage.)

Hon. Oenone Clarissa, *b.* 1934 : *m.* 1958, Michael Charles Deane Luke, son of Sir Harry Charles Luke, KCMG, and has issue living, Igor Charles de Zander, *b.* 1965,—Chloe Oleanda Alvilde, *b.* 1959,— (Enone Jemima, *b.* 1960,—Cressida Eugénie, *b.* 1961. *Residence,*—22, Eaton Sq., SW1.

(*By 2nd marriage.*)

Hon. Miranda Amadea, *b.* 1956.
Hon. Christina Susanna, *b.* 1958.

WIDOW LIVING OF SON OF SECOND VISCOUNT.

Angela Marjory (of Flat 4, 34, Ennismore Gdns., SW7 1AE), da. of the late Hon. Claud Lambton [see E. Durham, colls.]: *m.* 1961, as his second wife, the Hon. Niall Greville Chaplin, who *d.* 1963.

PREDECESSORS.—[1] *Rt. Hon.* HENRY Chaplin, *P.C.,* son of the late Rev. Henry Chaplin ; *b.* 1841 ; Chancellor of Duchy of Lancaster 1885-6, 1st Pres. of Board of Agriculture, with a seat in the Cabinet 1889-92, and Pres. of Local Govt. Board June 1895 to Nov. 1900 ; M.P. for Mid Lincolnshire (C) 1868-85, for N. Kesteven, or Sleaford, Div. of Lincolnshire 1885-1906, and for N.-E., or Wimbledon, Div. of Surrey 1907-16 ; cr. *Viscount Chaplin,* of St. Oswald's, Blankney, co. Lincoln (peerage of United Kingdom) 1916 : *m.* 1876, Lady Florence Leveson-Gower, who *d.* 1881, da. of 3rd Duke of Sutherland; *d.* 1923: *s.* by his son [2] ERIC, 2nd Viscount, *b.* 1877; Vice-Lieut, for co. Sutherland: *m.* 1905, the Hon. Gwladys Alice Gertrude Wilson, who *d.* 1971, da. of 1st Baron Nunburnholme; *d.* 1949; *s.* by his son [3] ANTHONY FRESKYN CHARLES HAMBY, 3rd Viscount and present peer.

CHARLEMONT, VISCOUNT. (Caulfeild.) [Viscount I. 1665.]

[Title pronounced "Shar-le-mont."]

RICHARD WILLIAM ST. GEORGE CAULFEILD, 12th Viscount; *b.* March 13th, 1887; *s.* 1971; formerly in Civil Ser. Federated Malay States: *m.* 1914, Dorothy Laura, who *d.* 1961, da. of the late Frank Giles, formerly ICS, and has issue.

Arms,—Quarterly, 1st and 4th, barry of ten argent and gules, on a canton of the second a lion passant guardant or, *Caulfeild;* 2nd and 3rd, or, a chevron checky argent and azure between three martlets sable, *Houston.* Crest,—A dragon's head erased gules, gorged with a bar gemelle argent. Supporters,—Two dragons gules, wings elevated, each gorged with a bar gemelle argent.

Residence,—Lane End Orchard, Elmstead, Colchester, Essex.

DEO DUCE FERRO COMITANTE

God my leader, the sword my companion.

DAUGHTERS LIVING.

Hon. Dorothy Frances Lucy St. George, *b.* 1915: *m.* 1945, Robert Hender Trowbridge, late Fl.-Lt. RAAF, of White Lodge, Alresford, Colchester, and has issue living, Mark, *b.* 1947,—Keith, *b.* 1950.

Hon. Alicia St. George, *b.* 1918: *m.* 1939, Gp. Capt. Gordon Hackworth Stuart, MD, RAF, of 3, Lovel Hill, Windsor Forest, Berks., and has issue living, Colin, *b.* 1940.

DAUGHTERS LIVING OF ELEVENTH VISCOUNT.

Hon. Constance Ada, *b.* 1918: *m.* 1943, Henry Edward Pearce, of 254, Mooroondu Rd., Thorneside, Qld. 4518, Aust., and has issue living, Edward Charles (44, Dawson Rd., Ormiston Heights, Qld. 4163), *b.* 1943: *m.* 1967, Beverley Ellen Cooper, and has issue living, Sandra Ellen *b.* 1970,—Donald John, *b.* 1947: *m.* 1971, Rosa Janina Zvirblis, and has issue living, Scott Ramon *b.* 1975,—Pamela Ann, 1946: *m.* 1966, Hendrik Wouter Veenstra, of Ayr, Qld.,—Janet May, *b.* 1950,—Wendy Roslyn, *b.* 1958.

Hon. Janie St. George, *b.* 1921: *m.* 1942, David Dominic Moore, of 30, Maxwell St., Turramurra, Sydney, NSW, and has issue living, Colleen Janie, *b.* 1944: *m.* 1967, Alan Charles Watts, and has issue living, Tracey Colleen *b.* 1968, Kellie Mary Jane *b.* 1972,—Margaret Louise, *b.* 1947: *m.* 1972, Keith Douglas Brodie, of Sao Paulo, Brazil.

DAUGHTERS LIVING OF NINTH VISCOUNT.

Hon. Shelah St. George, *b.* 1914: *m.* 1946 John Arnold Hawkes, B. Com., A.C.A., late Professor Natal Univ. Coll., Durban, and has issue living, Richard John *b.* 1947. *Residence,*—Roxborough, 17, Somerset Rd., Ferring-by-Sea, Sussex.

Hon. Patricia St. George, *b.* 1920; 1939-45 War as 3rd Officer WRNS. *Residence,*—14, Craigmore Tower, Guildford Rd., Woking, Surrey.

COLLATERAL BRANCHES LIVING.

Granddaughter of the late Francis John Rothe Toby St. George Caulfeild, ISO, MICE, 6th son of Rt. Rev. Charles Caulfeild, DD, Bishop of Nassau, el. son of the late Rev. Hans Caulfeild (*d.* 1854), son of the late Rev. Charles Caulfeild, 3rd son of the late Rev. the Hon. Charles Caulfeild, 5th son of 2nd Viscount:—
Issue of the late Major Harry Frowd St. George Caulfeild, *b.* 1881, *d.* 1961: *m.* 1914, Geraldine Marguerite, who *d.* 1922, dau. of Lieut.-Col. Charles Purvis Boyd :—
Geraldine St. George, *b.* 1918: *m.* 1st, 1947, Maj. Peter Lawry Matthews, TD, RASC, who *d.* 1970; 2ndly, 1975, Hugh Alan Mason, of West Cottage, Prinsted, Emsworth, Hants., and has issue living, (by 1st m.) Toby St. George, *b.* 1950,—Helen Bronté, *b.* 1953.

Grandsons of the late Rev. Hans Caulfeild (*b.* 1833), el. son of the Rev. Wilberforce Caulfeild, 4th son of the late Rev. Hans Caulfeild (*d.* 1854) (ante):—
Issue of the late Charles Hans Caulfeild, *b.* 1869, *d.* 1950: *m.* 1898, Ethel Jessie, who *d.* 1973, da. of the late D. G. R. Mann:—
CHARLES WILBERFORCE, *b.* March 10th, 1899 (RR2, Cumberland Ont., Canada); late Civil Ser. (Canada): *m.* 1930, Dorothy Jessie, da. of the late A. A. Johnston, of Ottawa.——Eric St. George (43, Smithwood Drive, Islington, Ontario M9B 4S1), *b.* 1900; late Auditor Metropolitan Life Insurance Co. (Canada): *m.* 1933, Edith Evelyn, da. of F. W. Day, of Ottawa, and has issue living, John Day (39, Rossburn Drive, Etobicoke, Ont., Canada), *b.* 1934: *m.* 1st, 1964, Judith Ann, who *d.* 1971, da. of James E. Dodd, of Islington, Ont.; 2ndly, 1972, Janet Evelyn, da. of Orville R. Nancekivell, of Salford, Ont., and has issue living (by 1st m.), John Dodd *b.* 1966, Janis Ann *b.* 1968,—Edith Jane, *b.* 1941: *m.* 1963, Edward John Cobeau, of 46, Johnstone Blvd., Walkerton, Ont., and has issue living, Robert John *b.* 1967, Stephen *b.* 1971, Susan Jane *b.* 1968.——*Ven.* Arthur Edward Lampay (23, Seaside Drive, St. Andrews, New Brunswick, EO9 2XO), *b.* 1906; BA; DD; is R. of Trin. Church, Saint John, New Brunswick; Chap. Roy. Canadian Air Force 1941-51: *m.* 1940, Emilie Kathleen Irene, da. of the Rev. E. F. Salmon, DD, of Philadelphia, USA, and has issue living, David Arthur (2352, Haddington Cres., Ottawa, K1H 8J4, Canada), *b.* 1942; M.Arch; MRAI Civil Ser. (Canada): *m.* 1965, Diane, BSc, da. of the late E. P. Du Vernet, of Ottawa, and has issue living, Sean David *b.* 1966, Derek Arthur *b.* 1969,—Charles Patrick (Kingston, Ont.), *b.* 1946; BEng: *m.* 1968, Marjorie Agnes Reid, of Saint John, New Brunswick.

Grandson of the late Hans James Caulfeild (infra):—
Issue of the late Capt. Alfred Hans Waring Caulfeild, M.B., *b.* 1870, *d.* 1940: *m.* 1st, 1917, Mary Harris, who obtained a divorce 1934, dau. of Sir Evan Davies Jones, 1st Bt., and widow of Major Malcolm Nixon Harman, D.S.O.; 2ndly, 1934, Adèle Edith, dau. of the late Melfort Boulton, of Toronto :—
(By 1st marriage) Evan Michael St. George, *b.* 1918; ed. at Toronto Univ. (B.A. 1948); Chartered Accountant, Ontario; 1939-45 War with British Army and Canadian Forces: *m.* 1948, Shirley Joyce, dau. of Harry Scutt Burt, of Richmond Hill, Ontario, Canada. and has issue living, Toby Michael Hans, *b.* 1949; BA Toronto. *Residence,*—2, Clearside Place, Markland Woods, Etobicoke, Ont., Canada.

Grandchildren of the late Hans Caulfeild, M.D., 6th son of the Rev. Hans Caulfeild (*d.* 1854) (ante):—
Issue of the late Hans James Caulfeild, *b.* 1849, *d.* 1928: *m.* 1st, 1872, Jennie Elizabeth, who *d.* 1901, dau. of Samuel Brasher ; 2ndly, 1904, Ida Mary, who *d.* 1908, dau. of William Rowntree, of Toronto, Canada; 3rdly, 1909, Mary Louise Burkart, who *d.* 1963:—
(By 3rd marriage) (James) Gordon, *b.* 1917: *m.* 1943, Olive (Irene), dau. of Thomas Henry Bradley, of Goderich, Ont., Canada, and has issue living, Roddy Terence, MD, *b.* 1946: *m.* 1969, Patricia Ann Rogers, and has issue living, Stephen Michael *b.* 1972,—Caroline Diane, *b.* 1948: *m.* 1969, Peter Stanley Wardell, of 63, Rustic Cres., Orangeville, Ont., Canada.

Grandchildren of the late Edwin James Stuart Widdrington Caulfeild (infra):—
Issue of the late Edwin Vivian Stuart Caulfeild, *b.* 1874, *d.* 1958 : *m.* 1903, Edith Helen (of Vesenaz, Geneva, Switzerland), dau. of Claude L. Ferneley, formerly of Loughborough :—
Stewart Frederick Barry, *b.* 1907.——Leonore Alicia, *b.* 1906.

Granddaughter of the late Com. Edwin Toby Caulfeild, R.N., el. son of the late Wade Toby Caulfeild (infra) :—
Issue of the late Edwin James Stuart Widdrington Caulfeild, *b.* 1848, *d.* 1914: *m.* 1872, Florence Elizabeth Middleton, who *d.* 1925, dau. of Col. John Frederick Sales Clarke, late Scots Greys :—
Florence Madeline Lenore : *m.* 1915, Leslie Sloane Palmer. *Residence,*—

Grandchildren of the late Francis William Caulfeild, yr. son of the late Rev. Edward Warren Caulfeild, yr. son of the late Wade Toby Caulfeild, el. son of Col. William Toby, 2nd son of the Hon. Toby Caulfeild, 3rd son of 1st Viscount:—
Issue of the late Vice-Adm. Francis Wade Caulfeild, O.B.E., *b.* 1872, *d.* 1947: *m.* 1898, Katharine Anne, who *d.* 1940, dau. of J. C. Hawkshaw, formerly of Hollycombe, Sussex.
Wade Toby (of Hookland, Midhurst, Sussex), *b.* 1902; ed. at Eton, and at New Coll., Oxford: *m.* 1935, Philippa Mary, dau. of Capt. H. C. R. Brocklebank, of Charlton House, Shaftesbury, Dorset, and has issue living, James Alexander Toby, *b.* 1937,—Charlotte Antonia, *b.* 1939.——Cicely, *b.* 1899: *m.* 1921, Henry Vernon Flower Barran, who *d.* 1943 [see Barran, Bt., colls.]. *Residence,*—Madehurst Lodge, Arundel, Sussex.——Ann Katharine (The Cottage, Heyshott Green, Midhurst, Sussex), *b.* 1907; A.R.C.M.

Grandchildren of the late Col. Robert Caulfeild, 2nd son of Lt.-Col. John Caulfeild,
el. son of Col. William Caulfeild (d. 1831), el. son of Ven. John Caulfeild, 2nd
son of Col. William Caulfeild (ante):—
Issue of the late Brig.-Gen. Francis William John Caulfeild, C.B.E., b. 1859, d. 1938 : m.
1897, Alys, who d. 1950, dau. of James Hornidge Finnemor, formerly of Ounavarra, Gorey,
Ireland :—
Robert, O.B.E., b. 1907 ; ed. at Bromsgrove ; is Col. King's Own Scottish Borderers, and Manager,
White Hunters (Africa) Ltd., of Nairobi ; cr. O.B.E. (Mil.) 1952. Address,—P.O. Box 12450,
Nairobi, Kenya.——Joan, b. 1903 : m. 1926, Capt. Ludovic Ernest Porter, R.N., and has issue
living, Simon Hugh Ludovic, b. 1934; ed. at Eton,—Jeremy Michael, b. 1937; ed. at Eton; Cdr.
RN. Residence,—Warrenhurst, Old Farnham Lane, Farnham.

Issue of the late Col. Gordon Napier Caulfeild, D.S.O., b. 1862, d. 1922: m. 1902, Mildred,
who d. 1963, youngest dau. of Philip O'Reilly, D.L., of Colamber, Westmeath:—
Judith Mary, b. 1907 : m. 1938, Robert FitzRichard Barry, and has issue living, Gordon, b. 1938,—
Robert, b. 1943,—Jennifer, b. 1941. Residence,—75, Highfield Park, Dundrum Rd., Dublin, 14.——
Irene Mildred, b. 1909; a Nun.

Issue of the late Brig.-Gen. Charles Trevor Caulfeild, C.M.G., b. 1863, d. 1947 : m. 1903
Kathleen Mary, who d. 1946, dau. of the late Rt. Hon. Sir John Edge, of 123, Oakwood
Court, Kensington. W. :—
Norah Frances (c/o Lloyds Bank, Berkeley Sq., W1), b. 1904.

Issue of the late Lieut.-Col. St. George Robert Sanderson Caulfeild, b. 1868, d. 1916 :
m. 1902, Winifred Mary, who d. 1963, dau. of Reginald W. Butterworth, J.P., formerly
of 21, St. James's Sq., Bath:—
Arthur James (of 31, Paardestraat, Sittard, Limburg, Netherlands), b. 1906; ed. at Cheltenham
Coll.; Lieut.-Col. R.A. (ret.): m. 1947, Marie Antoinette Tholen, of Sittard, Netherlands.

Granddaughter of the late Brig.-Gen. Charles Trevor Caulfeild, CMG (ante):—
Issue of the late John Trevor Caulfeild, b. 1908, d. 1968: m. 1948, Elisabeth Allie Madeleine,
who d. 1968, da. of the late Gerald de Mestral of Berne and Mont sur Rolle, Switzerland:—
Catherine Norah (1824, Caux, Switzerland), b. 1949.

Granddaughter of the late Lt.-Col. John Caulfeild (ante):—
Issue of the late Col. Robert Caulfeild, b. 1829, d. 1905: m. 1857, Caroline Harriet, who
d. 1918, dau. of William Magill, of Lyttelton, co. Westmeath :—
Hilda Louisa Hamilton : m. 1920, Lieut.-Col. Ambrose Boxwell, C.I.E., who d. 1959. Residence,—
Coologe, Carickmines, co. Dublin.

Grandson of the late Brig.-Gen. James Edward Wilmot Smyth Caulfeild, CMG
(infra):—
Issue of the late Col. St. George Frederick Gordon Caulfeild, RM, b. 1881, d. 1973: m. 1917,
Eila Rosslyn, who d. 1973, da. of Reginald John, of Colombo:—
Toby St. George, CBE (Garton, Loxwood, Sussex), b. 1919; ed. at Wellington Coll., Brig. late RA;
Instructor Staff Coll. 1955-57, and OC, 7th Parachute Regt., RHA 1960-62; UK Nat. Mil. Repres.
SHAPE since 1971; France 1939-40, S-E Asia 1942-45, Korea 1952, Malaya 1958-59; MBE (Mil.)
1952, CBE (Mil.) 1974: m. 1st, 1942, Mary (from whom he obtained a divorce 1951), da. of the late
Sir William Lindsay Murphy, KCMG; 2ndly, 1959, Agnes Sheila, da. of Edward Buckmaster Robin-
son, of Tankerton, Kent, and has issue living, (by 1st m.) Toby St. George (Rougham, Chantry,
Bury St. Edmunds), b. 1943: m. 1967, Gillian, da. of C. M. Rhead, and has issue living, Patrick
William St. George b. 1968,—Grania Mary, b. 1947: m. 1970, Richard Hugh Cavendish [see D.
Devonshire, colls.].

Grandchildren of the late Rev. William Caulfeild, only son of Commodore Thomas
Gordon Caulfeild, 2nd son of the Ven. John Caulfeild (ante):—
Issue of the late Brig.-Gen. James Edward Wilmot Smyth Caulfeild, C.M.G., b. 1850, d.
1925 : m. 1876, Sophia Morley, who d. 1932, dau. of the late William Alexander
Parker, formerly Ch. Justice of British Honduras:—
Wilmot Smyth, MC, b. 1887; ed. at Bradfield Coll.: Lt.-Col. RA (ret.) late E. Surrey Regt.;
1914-18 War with Leinster Regt. (despatches twice, MC, 1914 star, Croix de Guerre), 1939-45 War
with RA (Defence medal, War medal 1939-45): m. 1st, 1923, Meredith De Lisle, who d. 1924, da.
of the late Reginald John, of Mereworth Lawn, Wrotham; 2ndly, 1928, Shellah, da. of the late
John J. Bevan, of Dublin, and has issue living, (by 1st m.) Pamela Ann De Lisle, b. 1924; a JP
of Salop: m. 1st, 1944, Maj. Philip Hugh Godsal, 52nd LI; 2ndly, 1970, Capt. Walter Edward
Browning Godsal, RN, of Edbrooke, Winsford, Somerset, and has issue living, (by 1st m.) Philip Caulfeild b. 1945, David Hugh b. 1947, Rupert Charles b. 1952, Caroline Mary b. 1950, Meredith Jane b. 1956,
—(by 2nd m.) Eileen Ruth Morley, b. 1929: m. 1952, Henry Edward Percy [see D. Northumberland,
colls.], Barbara Joan Shellah, b. 1932: m. 1969, Preston Caradoc Hardinge Mostyn Prichard, of 44,
Earls Court Sq., SW5 [see V. Hardinge, colls.]. Residence,—The Mill House, Horstead, Norwich.
——Ruth (of Edithmead, nr. Burnham-on-Sea, Som.), b. 1889: m. 1912, the Rev. Benjamin
Hayward Fisher, who d. 1962, and has issue living, Stella Margaret, b. 1916,—Ruth Mary, b. 1918,
m. 1963, John Walter Rocke Swayne, MC, TD, of The Lighthouse, Burnham-on-Sea, Som.——
Stella Evelyn, ARRC (of Lee Britten, Milvil Rd., Lee-on-Solent, Hants), b. 1890; 1914-18 War
(ARRC).

Grandchildren of the late Capt. George Blake Caulfeild, yr. son of the late George
Caulfeild, 4th son of Lt.-Gen. James Caulfeild, C.B., yst. son of the Ven. John
Caulfeild (ante):—
Issue of the late Leslie Alexander Caulfeild, b. 1902, d. (result of enemy action) 1940: m.
1930, Jennie Ida (who obtained a divorce 1936), dau. of the late Charles Deering Manson:—
A son, b. 193-.

Issue of the late William Henry Caulfeild, b. 1911, d. (on active ser. in Burma) 1943: m. 1935,
Lorna (Flat 9, 26, Sussex Sq., Brighton, BN2 5AB), da. of the late Cuthbert Wilkinson, of
The Clock House, Nether Stowey, Som.:—
Anne Marie, b. 1941: m. 1965, Rupert Alan Travis, of 35, Gunter Grove, SW10, and has issue living, a
da., b. 1972.

PREDECESSORS.—[1] Rt. Hon. Sir Toby Caulfeild, P.C.. a distinguished soldier, M.P. for
Armagh 1613, Master of the Ordnance 1614, &c., was cr. Lord Caulfeild, Baron of Charlemont
(peerage of Ireland) 1620, with remainder to his nephew Sir William Caulfeild, Knt.; d.
unmarried 1627 ; s. by his nephew [2] Sir William, 2nd Baron : Master Gen. of the Ordnance
1627-34; d. 1640; s. by his son [3] Toby, 3rd Baron; when Governor of Charlemont, during
the Rebellion of 1641, he was surprised and taken prisoner and subsequently shot by the
order of Sir Phelim O'Neile; d. unmarried; s. by his brother [4] Robert, 4th Baron;
d. 1642, from an over-dose of opium; s. by his brother [5] William, 5th Baron; apprehended
Sir Phelim O'Neile, and had him executed for the murder of his brother the 3rd Baron ; cr.
Viscount Charlemont (peerage of Ireland) 1665; d. 1671; s. by his son [6] William, 2nd
Viscount ; zealously opposed the cause of James II., by whose parliament he was attainted,

but King William, after the rebellion was quelled, gave him a regt. offoot and made him Gov. of cos. Tyrone and Armagh, &c.; *d.* 1726; *s.* by his son [7] JAMES, 3rd Viscount, M.P. for Charlemont 1727 ; *d.* 1734 ; *s.* by his son [8] JAMES, *K.P.,* 4th Viscount; cr. *Earl of Charlemont* (peerage of Ireland) 1763 ; was Com. in Ch. of Vol. Army in Ireland 1779 ; *d.* 1799; *s.* by his son [9] FRANCIS WILLIAM, *K.P.,* 2nd Earl, *b.* 1775; a Representative Peer ; cr. *Baron Charlemont* (peerage of United Kingdom) 1837, with remainder to his brother: *m.* 1802, Anne, dau. and co-heir of William Bermingham, of Ross Hill, co. Galway ; *d.* 1863 ; *s.* by his nephew [10] JAMES MOLYNEUX, *K.P.,* 3rd Earl (son of the Hon. Henry, 2nd son of 1st Earl), *b.* 1820 ; Lord-Lieut. of co. Tyrone ; M.P. for Armagh co. (*L*) 1847-67 : *m.* 1st, 1856, the Hon. Elizabeth Jane Somerville, who *d.* 1882, dau. of 1st Baron Athlumney; 2ndly, 1883, Anna Lucy, who *d.* 1925, dau. of the Rev. Charles James Lambart; *d.* 1892, when the Earldom (1763) and the Barony (1837) became extinct, and the Peerages of 1620 and 1665 devolved upon his cousin [11] JAMES ALFRED, *C.B.* (son of Edward Houston Caulfeild, great-grandson of the Rev. the Hon. Charles Caulfeild, 5th son of 2nd Viscount), 7th Viscount, *b.* 1830 ; Capt. Coldstream Guards ; served in Crimean War 1854-6 ; Comptroller of Household to successive Viceroys of Ireland 1868-95; Usher of Black Rod to Order of St. Patrick : *m.* 1858, the Hon. Annette Handcock, who *d.* 1888, dau. of 3rd Baron Castlemaine ; *d.* 1913 ; *s.* by his nephew [12] JAMES EDWARD, *P.C.* (son of the late Hon. Marcus Piers Francis Caulfeild, brother of 7th Viscount), 8th Viscount, *b.* 1880 ; Vice-Lieut. for co. Tyrone 1923-39 ; a Member of Senate of N. Ireland 1925-37, and Min. of Education and Leader of the Senate 1926-37 : *m.* 1st, 1914, Evelyn, who *d.* (result of enemy action) Oct. 1940, and from whom he had obtained a divorce April 1940 ; 2ndly, 1940, Hildegarde, who *d.* 1969, da. of Rodolphe Slock-Cottell, of Malstapel, Buysselede, Belgium ; *d.* 1949; *s.* by his kinsman [13] CHARLES EDWARD ST. GEORGE (only son of the late Hans St. George Caulfeild, 2nd son of the late Rt. Rev. Charles Caulfeild, DD, Bishop of Nassau, el. son of the Rev. Hans Caulfeild, grandson of the Rev. the Hon. Charles Caulfeild, 5th son of 2nd Viscount), 9th Viscount: *m.* 1911, Mabel, el. da. of James Hawthorn; *d.* 1964; *s.* by his kinsman [14] ROBERT TOBY ST. GEORGE [2nd son of the late Henry St. George Caulfeild, 1st son of the late James Caulfeild, 2nd son of the late Rev. Hans Caulfeild (ante)], 10th Viscount; *b.* 1881; *d.* 1967; *s.* by his brother [15], CHARLES ST. GEORGE, 11th Viscount, *b.* 1884: *m.* 1915, Lydia Clara, who *d.* 1973, da. of Charles James Kingston, of Aramac; *d.* 1971;*s.* by his brother [16], RICHARD WILLIAM ST. GEORGE, 12th Viscount and present peer; also Lord Caulfeild, Baron of Charlemont.

CHARLEVILLE, EARLDOM OF. (Bury.) [Extinct 1875]

COLLATERAL BRANCH LIVING.

Grandchildren of the late Lady Beaujolois Eleanora Catherine Bury (who *m.* 1853, Hastings Dent), da. of 2nd Earl:—

Issue of the late Alfred Robert Tighe Dent, *b.* 1861, *d.* 1922: *m.* 1887, Ida M., da. of Napoleon Richards, of Minneapolis, USA:—

Alfred Charles, *b.* 1889: *m.* 1913, Marion Tucker, and has issue living, Stephen Tucker (La Canada, Cal., USA), *b.* 1917: *m.* 1947, Clo O'Neal,—Peter Campbell (831, Ford St., Burbank, Cal. 91505, USA), *b.* 1925: *m.* 1953, Constance Gillespie, and has issue living, Elena Marie, *b.* 1955.——Ardo Ronald Beaujolois, *b.* 1894.——Audrey Hope, *b.* 1902: *m.* 1926, William John Burke, of 1136, S. Hudson Av., Los Angeles, Cal. 90019, USA, and has issue living, Robert John (Glendale, Cal. USA), *b.* 1932: *m.* 1st, 1953, Sarone Birdsell; 2ndly, 1963, Virginia Sue Parker, and has issue living, (by 1st m.) Kevin Patrick *b.* 1958, Kim Lorayne *b.* 1957: *m.* 1975, Rory Strahan, of Tujunga, Calif.,—Beaujolois Joan, *b.* 1927: *m.* 1963, Michael Joseph Phillips, of Bellevue, Washington, USA, and has issue living, Michele Ann, *b.* 1964, Madeleine Louise, *b.* 1965,—Connaught Marie, *b.* 1929: *m.* 1960, Earl Robert Lieberg, of Los Angeles, Cal. USA, and has issue living, Scott Robert *b.* 1970, Laura Marie, *b.* 1961, Robin Diane, *b.* 1965.

CHARNWOOD, BARONY OF. (Benson.) [Extinct 1955.]

WIDOW LIVING OF SECOND BARON.

BERYL JOAN (*Baroness Charnwood*), dau. of the late Percy Cuthbert Quilter [see Quilter, Bt. colls.]: *m.* 1933, the 2nd Baron, who *d.* 1955 when the title became ext. *Residence,*—Court Lodge Farm, East Brabourne, Kent.

DAUGHTER LIVING OF FIRST BARON.

Hon. Antonia Mary Roby (*Viscountess Radcliffe*), *b.* 1903: *m.* 1st, 1929 (marriage dissolved 1939), Maj. John Tennant, TD, late RA, who *d.* 1967 [see B. Glenconner, colls.]; 2ndly, 1939, 1st Viscount Radcliffe. *Residences,*—5, Campden Hill Gate, Duchess of Bedford Walk, W.8; Hampton Lucy House, Warwick.

Castlereagh, Viscount, son of Marquess of Londonderry.

CHATFIELD, BARON. (Chatfield.) [Baron U.K. 1937.]

ERNLE DAVID LEWIS CHATFIELD, 2nd Baron; *b.* Jan. 2nd, 1917; *s.* 1967; ed. at Trin. Coll., Camb.; late Hon. Lt. RNVR; an ADC to Gov. Gen. of Canada 1940-45: *m.* 1969, (Felicia Mary) Elizabeth, da. of the late Dr. John Roderick Bulman, of Hereford.

𝕬rms,—Or, a griffin segreant sable, on a chief purpure an anchor between two escallops of the first. 𝕮rest,—An heraldic antelope's head erased, argent, gorged with a naval crown or. 𝕾upporters, —*Dexter,* an Admiralty Messenger holding in the exterior hand his staff; *sinister,* a Seaman Gunner of the Royal Navy resting the exterior hand on a shell all proper.

Address,—P.O. Box 98, Williamstown, Ont., Canada.

SISTER LIVING.

Hon. (Mary) Katharine Medina, *OBE, b.* 1911; with Women's Vol. Sers. 1939-46; OBE (Civil) 1946: *m.* 1947, Henry George Austen De L'Etang Herbert Duckworth, RA, son of the late Sir

For our altars and our hearths.

George Herbert Duckworth, CB, FSA [E. Carnarvon], and has issue living, Sarah Margaret Katharine *b.* 1951: *m.* 1974, Hector William Munro [see Munro, Bt., cr. 1634],—Harriet Angela Victoria (twin), *b.* 1951. *Residence,*—Dalingridge Place, Sharpthorne, Sussex.

WIDOW LIVING OF FIRST BARON.

LILLIAN EMMA (*Lillian, Baroness Chatfield*) (The Small House, Farnham Common, Bucks.); a C.St.J.; da. of the late Maj. George L. Matthews, TF: *m.* 1909, the 1st Baron, who *d.* 1967.

PREDECESSOR,—[1] *Adm. of the Fleet Sir* (ALFRED) ERNLE MONTACUTE Chatfield, *GCB, OM, KCMG, CVO, PC,* son of the late Adm. Alfred John Chatfield, CB; *b.* 1873; Present at actions of Heligoland Bight 1914, Dogger Bank 1915, and Jutland 1916, as Flag Capt. *HMS Lion,* Third Sea Lord and Controller of Navy 1925-28, C.-in-C. Atlantic Fleet 1929-30, and Med. Fleet 1930-32, First Sea Lord 1933-38, and Min. for Co-ordination of Defence 1939-40; *cr. Baron Chatfield,* of Ditchling, co. Sussex (peerage of UK) 1937: *m.* 1909, Lillian Emma (C.St.J.), da. of the late Maj. George L. Matthews, TF; *d.* 1967; *s.* by his son [2] ERNLE DAVID LEWIS, 2nd Baron and present peer.

Chaworth, Baron, title of Earl of Meath on Roll of H.L.

CHELMER, BARON. (Edwards) [Life Baron 1963]

ERIC CYRIL BOYD EDWARDS, *M.C., T.D.,* son of Col. Cyril Ernest Edwards, D.S.O., M.C., T.D., D.L., of Bullwood Hall, Hockley, Essex; *b.* Oct. 9th, 1914; ed. at Felsted Sch., and at London Univ. (LL.B.1937); Solicitor 1937; a Gen. Commr. of Taxes; Chm. of Home Counties N. Area of Conservative Party 1950-53, and Vice-Chm. 1954 and 1955, Chm. of National Union of Conservative Assocns. 1956-65 and Pres. 1966-67, Chm. of National Union Exec. Cttee. 1957-63; a Treasurer of Conservative Party 1965; late Lt.-Col. Essex Yeo.; 1939-45 War (MC); *cr.* Knt. 1954, and *Baron Chelmer,* of Margaretting, co. Essex (Life Baron) 1963: *m.* 1939, Enid, da. of Frank William Harvey, and has issue.

Arms,—Sable a lion rampant or on a chief or two martlets sable. **Crest,**—In front of a sun rising or a bull's head and neck gules armed or. **Supporters,**—*Dexter,* a lion rampant proper; *Sinister,* a peacock in his pride proper.

Residence,—Peacocks, Margaretting, Essex. *Clubs,*—Carlton, Royal Ocean Racing, Royal Burnham Yacht.

SON LIVING.

Hon. Robin Ernest (1, Landisdale, Cherry Garden Lane, Danbury, Essex), *b.* 1940: *m.* 1967, Carol Mayes, and has issue living.

CHELMSFORD, LORD BISHOP OF. (Trillo.)

Rt. Rev. ALBERT JOHN TRILLO, son of the late Albert Chowns Trillo; *b.* July 4th, 1915; ed. at Quintin Sch., and King's Coll., Univ. of London (BD, MTh); Fellow of King's Coll., London 1959; Curate Ch. Ch. Fulham 1938-41, and St. Gabriel's, Cricklewood (in charge of St. Michael's) 1941-45; Sec. SCM in Schs. 1945-50; R. of Friern Barnet, and Lecturer in New Testament Greek, King's Coll., London 1950-55; Prin. Bishops' Coll., Cheshunt 1955-63; Examining Chap. to Bishop of St. Edmundsbury and Ipswich 1955-63 and to Bishop of St. Albans 1963-71; Hon. Canon of St. Albans 1958-63, and Canon Residentiary 1963-65; Proctor-in-Convocation for Dean and Chapter of St. Albans 1963-64; Proctor-in-Convocation for the Clergy 1965-71; consecrated Bishop of Bedford (Suffragan for Diocese of St. Albans) 1963-68, translated Bishop of Hertford (Suffragan for Diocese of St. Albans) 1968-71; and 6th Lord Bishop of Chelmsford 1971: *m.* 1942, Patricia Eva, da. of the Rev. Canon Gilbert Hemming Williams, DD.

Patron of two hundred and seventy-four livings, twenty-four Canonries, three Residentiary Canonries, and the Archdeaconries of West Ham, Colchester, and Southend.
This See was founded 1914.

Episcopal Signature,—John Chelmsford.

ARMS OF THE SEE,—Or, on a saltire gules, a pastoral staff of the first and a sword argent pomel and hilt also of the first.
Palace,—Bishopscourt, Chelmsford, Essex, CM2 6BJ.

CHELMSFORD, VISCOUNT. (Thesiger.) [Baron U.K. 1858, Viscount U.K. 1921.

Hope and fortune.

FREDERIC JAN THESIGER, 3rd Viscount; *b.* March 7th, 1931; *s.* 1970; late Lt. Inns of Court Regt.: *m.* 1958, Clare Rendle, da. of Dr. George Rendle Rolston, of Bambers, Haslemere, Surrey, and has issue.

Arms,—Gules, a griffin segreant or, within an orle of roses argent, barbed and seeded proper. Crest,—A cornucopia fessewise, the horn or, the fruit proper, thereon a dove holding in the beak a sprig of laurel also proper. Supporters,—On either side a griffin or, winged vaire.

Residence,—26, Ormonde Gate, SW3.

SON LIVING.
Hon. FREDERIC CORIN PIERS, *b.* March 6th, 1962.

DAUGHTER LIVING.
Hon. Tiffany Gay, *b.* 1968.

SISTERS LIVING.
Hon. Dawn Loraine, *b.* 1934.
Hon. Philippa Merryn, *b.* 1939.

AUNT LIVING. (*Daughter of 1st Viscount.*)
Hon. Bridget Mary, *b.* 1900: *m.* 1st, 1919, Major Richard Hasell Sheepshanks, D.S.O., M.V.O., who *d.* 1951, and who had obtained a divorce 1937; 2ndly, 1938, Nello Beccari, who *d.* 1957, and has issue living, (by 1st m.) Robin John (The Rookery, Eyke, Woodbridge, Suffolk), *b.* 1925; ed. at Eton; late Capt. King's Dragoon Guards: *m.* 1951, Lilias Mulgrave, only da. of Sir Humphrey Brunel Noble, MBE, MC, 4th Bt., and has issue living, David Richard *b.* 1952, Richard John *b.* 1955, Andrew Charles *b.* 1960, Christopher James *b.* 1964. *Residence,*—Villa Beccari, Bandino, Florence, Italy.
Hon. Margaret St. Clair Sydney, *b.* 1911: *m.* 1934, John Monck, who assumed by deed poll 1938 the names of John Monck in lieu of those of John Monk Goldman [E. Peel], and has issue living, Robert, *b.* 1938: *m.* 1962, Barbara, da. of A. Lloyd, of Liverpool,—Charles, *b.* 1945: *m.* 1974, Charlotte, yst. da. of John Moritz Makower, MBE, MC, of Holmwood, Binfield Heath, Oxon. *Residence,* —Aldern Bridge House, Newbury, Berks.

WIDOW LIVING OF SECOND VISCOUNT.
GILIAN (*Gilian, Viscountess Chelmsford*) (Hazelbridge Court, Chiddingfold, Surrey), da. of the late Arthur Nevile Lubbock [see B. Avebury, colls.]: *m.* 1927, the 2nd Viscount, who *d.* 1970.

COLLATERAL BRANCHES LIVING. (*In remainder to Barony only.*)
Issue of the late Hon. Percy Mansfield Thesiger, M.B.E., 2nd son of 2nd Baron, *b.* 1869, *d.* 1959 : *m.* 1900, Katharine Frances, who *d.* 1958, dau. of the late Alexander Falconer Wallace, of Candacraig, Strathdon, Aberdeenshire :—
Donald Adrian Wallace, *b.* 1901; ed. at Winchester, and at Peterhouse, Camb. : *m.* 1927, Frances Nina, who *d.* 1968, da. of the late Brig.-Gen. Sylvester Bertram Grimston, CMG, and has issue living, Nina Frances, *b.* 1928,—Rua Susan, *b.* 1930: *m.* 1961, Lt.-Col. Michael Alistair Lowry, MC, of The White House, Middle Coombe, Shaftesbury, Dorset, and has issue living, Robert Michael *b.* 1967, Susan Jane *b.* 1964, Patricia Gillian *b.* 1965,—Zara Jane, *b.* 1933: *m.* 1969, Arthur Mark Farrar, of The Brick House, Finchingfield, Essex, and E12, Sloane Av. Mansions, SW3, and has issue living, Frances *b.* 1971. *Residences,*—Boytons, Hempstead, Saffron Walden, Essex; Tornashean, Strathdon, Aberdeenshire; 29, Sloane Av., Chelsea, SW.

Issue of the late Capt. the Hon. Wilfred Gilbert Thesiger, DSO, 3rd son of 2nd Baron, *b.* 1871, *d.* 1920: *m.* 1909, Kathleen, CBE, who *d.* 1973, having *m.* 2ndly, 1931, as his 2nd wife, Reginald Basil Astley, who *d.* 1942 (B. Hastings, colls.)], da. of the late Thomas Mercer Cliffe Vigors, of Burgage, co. Carlow [B. Castlemaine, colls.]:—
Wilfred Patrick, *CBE, DSO* (15, Shelley Court, Tite St., SW3; Brooks's, Travellers, Pratt's Clubs), *b.* 1910; ed. at Eton, and at Magdalen Coll., Oxford (MA); Hon. DLit. Leic.; author of " Arabian Sands ", and " The Marsh Arabs "; Sudan Civil Ser. 1935-44; 1939-45 War in Abyssinia as Bimbashi Sudan Defence Force, and in Middle East as Maj. with Special Air Ser. (despatches, DSO); attached to HRH the Duke of Gloucester's Mission to Ethiopia 1930 (Star of Ethiopia 3rd class); Founder's gold medal of Roy. Geographical Soc., Roy. Central Asian Soc.'s Lawrence of Arabia Medal, Livingstone Gold Medal of Roy. Scottish Geographical Soc., Roy. Soc. of Literature Award, and Roy. Asian Soc. Burton Gold Medal; DSO 1941, CBE (Civil) 1968.——Brian Peirson DOUGHTY-WYLIE, *MC, b.* 1911; ed. at Eton, and at New Coll., Oxford; Col. (ret.) late R. Welch Fusiliers; Probation Officer for Flintshire 1959-65; 1939-45 War (MC); Suez Operations 1956 as Col. Intelligence; assumed by deed poll 1933 the surname of Doughty-Wylie in lieu of his patronymic: *m.* 1937, Diana, only child of the late Maj. Vere de Hoghton [see de Hoghton, Bt., colls.], and has issue living, Daphne Susan, *b.* 1940: *m.* 1961, Capt. Jonathan Reeves, R. Welch Fusiliers, and has issue

living, Thomas Somerville Thesiger *b.* 1969, Emma de Hoghton *b.* 1963, Katherine Rebecca *b.* 1966,—
Philippa Vere Thesiger (c/o Childs & Co., 1, Fleet St., EC4), *b.* 1942: *m.* 1964, Capt. John Lewarne
Harvey, SCLI, and has issue living, Rupert Lewarne *b.* 1965, James Thesiger *b.* 1969, Pippa Vere
Karenza *b.* 1971.   *Residence,*—Pen-y-Graig, Tremeirchion, St. Asaph, Denbighshire.   *Club,*—United
Hunts.——Roderic Miles Doughty (22, Bedford Gdns., W8: Brooks's Club), *b.* 1915; ed. at Eton, and
at Ch. Ch., Oxford (BA 1938); 1939-45 War as Capt. Welsh Gds., and Parachute Regt. (twice
wounded): *m.* 1st, 1940 (m. diss. 1946), Mary Rose, who *d.* 1962, da. of the Hon. Guy Lawrence
Charteris [E. Wemyss and March]; 2ndly, 1946, Ursula Joan, da. of Aymer William Whitworth
[M. Bristol, colls.], and has issue living, (by 2nd m.) Simon Dermot, *b.* 1950: *m.* 1973, Concepción,
da. of Pérez Chávez, of Coyuca de Catalan, Mexico,—Sarah Elizabeth, *b.* 1947: *m.* 1974, Christopher
S. Wintle.

Issue of the late Lieut.-Col. Hon. Eric Richard Thesiger, D.S.O., youngest son of
2nd Baron, *b.* 1874, *d.* 1961 : *m.* 1st, 1904, Pearl Marie, who *d.* 1922, dau. of the
late John Coupland, of 16, Connaught Square, W.; 2ndly, 1929, Sydney Hilda,
who *d.* 1930, dau. of Arthur Hutton Croft, of Aldborough Hall, Yorkshire, and
widow of Major George Philip du Plat Taylor, O.B.E., Grenadier Guards ; 3rdly,
1953, Mrs. Mary Anderson, who *d.* 1954:—

(By 1st m.) Osric Wilfrid, *b.* 1905; formerly acting Capt. Indian Army: *m.* 1934, Cecily, da. of the late
F. Vandertaelen, and has issue living, Michael Eric (Ridgecrest, Church Rd., Earlswood Common,
Redhill, Surrey), *b.* 1936; ed. at Downside: *m.* 1964, Patricia Low, da. of G. Waddington, and has
issue living, Edward Osric *b.* 1967, Antony Martin *b.* 1968, Justin Michael *b.* 1970, Robert Cedric
(twin) *b.* 1970, Georgina Mary *b.* 1965.   *Residence,*—18, Gloucester Walk, W8.——Cedric Paul
(Lower Heathfield, Sandle Heath, Fordingbridge, Hants), *b.* 1915; ed. at Eton; BA (Architecture)
1938: *m.* 1942, Barbara Cecilia, da. of the late Maj. H. C. D. Jarrett, Indian Army, and has issue
living, Peter Hubert (3636, Glenview Court, N. Vancouver, BC), *b.* 1943: *m.* 1969, Jill Patricia, da,
of E. J. Worthy, Lt. Cdr. RCN (ret.),—Richard Paul (602, East Coast Rd., Brown's Bay, Auckland.
NZ), *b.* 1945: *m.* 1971, Susan, da. of J. Sydes, and has issue living, Robin Bruce *b.* 1973,—John Bede,
b. 1947.——Désirée, *b.* 1908; " Mother Mary Peter ".   *Residence,*—Assumption Convent, Sidmouth.

Grandchildren of Lt.-Gen. the Hon. Charles Wemyss Thesiger, 2nd son of
1st Baron:—
Issue of the late Maj.-Gen. George Handcock Thesiger, C.B., C.M.G., Rifle Brig. (Prince
Consort's Own), *b.* 1868, *d.* (killed in action) 1915 : *m.* 1902, Frances, who *d.* 1950, dau. of
the late Maj.-Gen Fitzroy Fremantle, C.B. [Campbell, Bt., cr. 1815]:—

Hon. Sir Gerald Alfred, *M.B.E.,* *b.* 1902 ; ed. at Gresham's Sch., and at Magdalen Coll., Oxford (B.A.
1925, M.A. 1929); Bar. Inner Temple 1926, a K.C. 1948, and a Bencher 1956 ; appointed a Judge
of High Court of Justice (Queen's Bench Div.) 1958; Dep. Chm., Boundary Commn. for England
1962; 1939-45 War as Maj. in Office of Judge Advocate-Gen. (M.B.E.); a Member of Fulham
Borough Council 1934-7, and of Chelsea Borough Council 1937-8 (Mayor 1944-6, Alderman 1945,
Freeman 1963); Chm. of Govs., United Westminster Schs. 1947-58; Recorder of Rye 1937-42, of
Hastings 1943-57, and of Southend 1957-58; Chm. of W. Kent Quarter Sessions 1947-58; M.B.E.
(Mil) 1946: *m.* 1932, Marjorie Eileen, who *d.* 1972, da. of the late Raymond Guille, of Long Island,
NY, and has issue living, Oonah Caroline, *b.* 1936: *m.* 1957, Vincent Vine, of 34, Maling Rd., Canter-
bury, Victoria 3126, Australia, and has issue living, Peter Gerald *b.* 1958, Juliet Mary *b.* 1960, Anita
Oonah *b.* 1962,—Juliet Elizabeth, *b.* 1943: *m.* 1966, Roderick Carl Warwick Neville, of The Oast
House, Glaziers Forge Farm, Dallington, Sussex, and has issue living, Tom *b.* 1968, Nicola Ingalisa
b. 1967.   *Residence,*—44, Chelsea Park Gdns., SW3.   *Club,*—Hurlingham.——Oonah Pamela,
b. 1905: *m.* 1928, John McLean Buckley, Solicitor, who *d.* 1972, and has issue living, Thomas George
McLean (Tithe Barn, Newnham, Hook, Hants.), *b.* 1932; ed. at Eton, and Magdalen Coll., Oxford;
Solicitor 1958: *m.* 1963, Valeria Frances, da. of Edgar Donald Reid Shearer, and has issue living,
William Donald McLean *b.* 1965, Edward John McLean *b.* 1967, Thomas Fitzpatrick McLean *b.*
1971,—Guy James McLean (75, Lansdowne Rd., W11), *b.* 1936; ed. at Eton, and at Magdalen Coll.,
Oxford; solicitor 1963: *m.* 1968, Elena Rose, da. of Hamish Deans, of Auchenflower, Darfield,
Canterbury, NZ, and has issue living, Virginia Rose *b.* 1969, Elizabeth Oonah *b.* 1972.   *Residence,*—
46, Chelsea Park Gdns., SW3.

Grandchildren of the late Hon. Sir Edward Peirson Thesiger, KCB, yst. son of
1st Baron:—
Issue of the late His Honour Arthur Lionel Bruce Thesiger, *b.* 1872, *d.* 1968: *m.* 1902, Florita
Maria Engracia, OBE, who *d.* 1966, da. of the late Edward J. Knight, of Tregroes, Pencoed,
Glam.:—

Richard Edward Knight, *OBE* (Orchard Cottage, Stoke Trister, Wincanton, Som.), *b.* 1912; ed. at
Winchester, and at Magdalen Coll., Oxford; Bar. Inner Temple 1936; 1939-45 War as Lt.-Col. Devonshire Regt.; on Staff of Allied Commn. for Austria (Legal Div.) 1944-46, and Assist. Solicitor, Lord
Chancellor's Office 1946-74; OBE (Civil) 1953: *m.* 1st, 1934, Carolin Sophie (from whom he obtained a
divorce 1947), da. of the late Norman M. Grant, of New York; 2ndly, 1947, Eileen Alice, only da. of
the late John Still, and has issue living, (by 1st m.) David Arthur Grant (5, Southborough Rd.,
Surbiton, Surrey), *b,* 1934; ed. at Winchester, and at Trin. Hall, Camb.; solicitor 1965: *m.* 1963,
Margaret Evelyn, da. of A. E. Thomas, and has issue living, Amanda Caroline Thomas *b.* 1964,
Clare Margaret *b.* 1966,—(by 2nd m.) John Still, *b.* 1948; ed. at Winchester, and Magdalen Coll.,
Oxford (BA),—Anne Alice Florita, *b.* 1951; ed. at Bristol Univ. (BA): *m.* 1974, Paul Towner, of 9,
Windsor Av., St. Johns, Worcester,—Frances Georgina, *b.* 1956.——Patience Elizabeth Florita, *TD*
(Eleven Plus, Hungershall Park, Tunbridge Wells), *b.* 1908; a Borough Councillor; Mayor of Roy.
Tunbridge Wells 1969-70; late Jun. Com. ATS.

PREDECESSORS.—[1] *Rt. Hon. Sir* FREDERIC Thesiger, *K.B., D.C.L., F.R.S.; b.* 1794; served as
a Midshipman, R.N., at battle of Copenhagen 1807; called to the bar at Gray's Inn 1818;
became a K.C. 1834; was Solicitor-Gen 1844-5, Attorney-Gen. 1845-6 and 1852, M.P. for Woodstock (C) 1840-4, for Abingdon 1844-52, and for Stamford 1852-8, and Lord High Chancellor
1858-9 and 1866-8; cr. *Baron Chelmsford,* of Chelmsford, co. Essex (peerage of United
Kingdom) 1858 : *m.* 1822, Anna Maria, dau. of William Tinling, of Southampton; *d.* 1878;
s. by his son [2] FREDERIC AUGUSTUS, *G.C.B., G.C.V.O.,* 2nd Baron; *b.* 1827 ; a Gen. in the
Army, and Col. 2nd Life Guards; served in Crimea, during Indian Mutiny, and in Abyssinia ;
commanded forces during Kaffir and Zulu Campaigns; an A.D.C. to H.M Queen Victoria 1868-77,
and Lieut. of Tower of London 1884-9: *m.* 1867, Adria Fanny, who *d.* 1926, dau. of the late
Maj.-Gen. Heath, Bombay Army; *d.* 1905; *s.* by his son [3] *Rt. Hon.* FREDERIC JOHN NAPIER,
G.C.S.I., G.C.M.G., G.C.I.E., G.B.E., 3rd Baron; *b.* 1868; Gov. of Queensland 1905-9, and of
N.S. Wales 1909-13, Viceroy of India 1916-21, and First Lord of the Admiralty Jan. to Nov.
1924; a K.J.St.J.; cr. *Viscount Chelmsford,* of Chelmsford, co. Essex (peerage of United
Kingdom) 1921 : *m.* 1894, the Hon. Frances Charlotte Guest, *C.I., G.B.E.,* who *d.* 1957, dau. of 1st
Baron Wimborne; *d.* 1933; *s.* by his son [4] ANDREW CHARLES GERALD, 2nd Viscount; *b.* 1903:
m. 1927, Gilian, da. of the late Arthur Nevile Lubbock [B. Avebury, colls.]; *d.* 1970; *s.* by his son [5]
FREDERIC JAN, 3rd Viscount, and present peer; also Baron Chelmsford.

Chelsea, Viscount, son of Earl Cadogan.

CHELWOOD, BARON. (Beamish.) [Life Baron 1974.]

TUFTON VICTOR HAMILTON BEAMISH, *MC*, son of the late Rear-Adm. Tufton Percy Hamilton Beamish, CB; *b.* Jan. 27th, 1917; ed. at Stowe Sch., and RMC; Maj. late R. Northumberland Fus.; Hon. Col. Sussex TA Artillery Regt. 1951-57; Palestine 1938-39, 1939-45 War in France, Singapore, Burma, N. Africa and Italy (twice wounded, despatches, MC); psc 1945; MP for Lewes (*C*) 1945-74; Joint Vice-Chm. of 1922 Cttee. 1958-74 (Joint Hon. Sec. 1947-50), Chm. of Conservative Foreign Affairs Cttee. 1960-64 (Joint Hon. Sec. 1946-53), and Hon. Sec. of Defence Cttee. 1952-53; a Member of C. of E. Council on Inter-Church Relations 1949-61; Chm. of Special Cttee. Council of Europe which watches interests of non-member countries 1951-53, Vice-Chm. of British Gp. of Inter-Parl. Union 1951-54, and a Member of Exec. Cttee. 1955-59; a Member of Pensions and Nat. Insurance Central Advisory Cttee. 1959-74; Chm. of Conservative Gp. for Europe 1970-73; a Member of Exec. and Gen. Purposes Cttee. British Council European Movement, and of Monnet Action Cttee.; Pres. of Roy. Soc. for the Protection of Birds 1966-70, and Sussex Trust for Nature Conservation since 1971; a DL for Sussex, a Gov. of Stowe Sch., Hon. Freeman of Lewes, and FRSA; author of " Must Night Fall?" 1950, " Battle Royal " 1965, and " Half Marx " 1970; cr. Knt. 1960, and *Baron Chelwood,* of Lewes, co. of E. Sussex (Life Baron) 1974: *m.* 1st, 1950 (m. diss. 1973), Janet McMillan, who *d.* 1975, yr. da. of Andrew Stevenson, of New York, USA; 2ndly, 1975, Maria Pia, da. of Baron Ernest von Roretz, of Schloss Breiteneich, Vei Horn, Austria, and formerly wife of Alan McHenry, and has issue by 1st m.

𝔄rms,—not exemplified at time of going to press.

Residence,—Chelworth House, Chelwood Gate, Haywards Heath, Sussex. *Clubs,*—Brooks's, White's, MCC.

DAUGHTERS LIVING (By 1*st m.*)

Hon. Claudia Hamilton, *b.* 1952.
Hon. Andrea Tufton, *b.* 1955.

CHESHAM, BARON. (Cavendish.) [Baron U.K. 1858.]

Secure by caution.

JOHN CHARLES COMPTON CAVENDISH, *PC,* 5th Baron; *b.* June 18th, 1916; *s.* 1952; ed. at Eton; is Capt. RA (TA), and Patron of two livings; appointed a Lord in Waiting to H.M. 1955; Joint Parl. Sec., Min. of Transport 1959-64; Chm. Internat. Road Fedn. since 1973; Exec. Vice-Chm. RAC 1966-70, and Vice-Pres. British Road Fedn. since 1972 (Pres. 1966-72); Pres. of Gun Trades Assocn. 1969, and of Fellowship of Motor Industry 1969-71; Pres. Inst. of Road Transport Engineers 1971, and British Parking Assocn. 1972; Hon. Member of Inst. of Highway Engineers; PC 1964: *m.* 1937, Mary Edmunds, da. of the late David Gregory Marshall, MBE, of White Hill, Cambridge, and has issue.

𝔄rms,—Sable three stags' heads cabossed argent. 𝔠rest,—A snake, nowed proper. Supporters, —*Dexter,* a buck proper, gorged with a chaplet of roses argent and azure; *sinister,* a greyhound argent gorged with a plain collar gules, thereon three buckles or.

Residence,—South Hall, Preston Candover, Basingstoke, Hants.

SONS LIVING.

Hon. NICHOLAS CHARLES (132, Fletcher St., Woollahra, Sydney, NSW 2025), *b.* Nov. 7th, 1941; ed. at Eton; ACA: *m.* 1st, 1965, Susan Donne, from whom he obtained a divorce 1969, da. of Frederick Guy Beauchamp, MD, MRCS [see By. North]; 2ndly, 1973, Suzanne Adrienne, el. da. of the late Alan Gray Byrne, of Sydney, and has issue living (by 2nd m), Charles Gray Compton, *b.* Nov. 1st, 1974.
Hon. John Charles Gregory, *b.* 1952; ed. at Eton, and Jesus Coll., Camb.

DAUGHTERS LIVING.

Hon. Joanna Mary, b. 1938: m. 1960, Peter Henry Mabille Price, and hast issue living, Nicholas Henry Maurice, b. 1971,—Caroline Mary, b. 1967. Residence,—The Mill House, Itchen Abbas, Winchester.
Hon. Georgina Mary, b. 1944: m. 1967, (Michael) Wynne Tufnell, of Riverhill Farm, Binsted, Alton, Hants, and has issue living, Christopher Wynne, b. 1969,—Michael Greville, b. 1971.

MOTHER LIVING.

Margot, dau. of the late John Layton Mills, of Tansor Court, Oundle: m. 1st 1915, the 4th Baron, who d. 1952, and from whom she had obtained a divorce 1937; 2ndly, 1941, Francis Lorne, FRIBA, who d. 1964. Residence,—8, Maxwell Rd., Mount Pleasant, Salisbury, Rhodesia.

COLLATERAL BRANCH LIVING.

Grandchildren of the late Brig.-Gen. the Hon. William Edwin Cavendish, M.V.O. 3rd of 2nd Baron:—
Issue of the late Capt. Evan George Charles Cavendish, O.B.E., R.N.V.R., b. 1891, d. 1955: m. 1923, Esmé Frances Sylvia IRBY, who d. 1959, dau. of the late Hon. Gilbert Neville Smyth [B. Boston, colls.]:—
Greville Adrian (Hopetown, Abaco, Bahamas), b, 1925; Lt.-Cdr. RN (ret.): m. 1st, 1952 (m. diss. 1974), Hazel Colleen Elizabeth, only da. of J. H. May, of Jersey, and has issue living, Rupert Edward Greville, b. 1955,—Piers Antony Charles, b. 1956,—Kiloran Arabella, b. 1959: 2ndly, 1974, Gillian, da. of L. G. Webb, of W. Hagley, Worcs.——Susan, b. 1924: m. 1st, 1951, David Murray Martin, from whom she obtained a divorce 1955; 2ndly, 1955, Leslie Gordon Graham, and has issue living, (by 1st m.) Trudy Carol, b. 1952,—Amanda Jane, b. 1954,—(by 2nd m.) Sarah Frances, b. 1956. Residence,—

PREDECESSORS.—[1] Hon. CHARLES COMPTON CAVENDISH, 4th son of 1st Earl of Burlington [see D. Devonshire], M.P. for E. Sussex (L) 1832-41, for Youghal 1841-47, and for Buckinghamshire 1847-57; cr. Baron Chesham (peerage of United Kingdom) 1858; d. 1863; s. by his son [2] WILLIAM GEORGE, 2nd Baron, b. 1815; M.P. for Peterborough (L) 1847, and for Buckinghamshire 1857-63: m. 1849, Henrietta Frances, who d. 1884, dau. of the late Right Hon. William Saunders Sebright Lascelles [E. Harewood]; d. June 26th, 1882; s. by his son [3] CHARLES COMPTON WILLIAM, 3rd Baron, K.C.B., P.C., b. 1850; Master of the Buckhounds 1900-1901, and a Lord of the Bedchamber to H.R.H. the Prince of Wales 1901-7: m. 1877, Lady Beatrice Constance Grosvenor, R.R.C., who d. 1911, 2nd dau. of 1st Duke of Westminster; d. 1907; s. by his son [4] JOHN COMPTON, M.C., 4th Baron; b. 1894; Capt. 10th Hussars and Squadron Leader R.A.F. Vol. Reserve: m. 1st, 1915, Margot (who obtained a divorce 1937), dau. of the late John Layton Mills, of Tansor Court, Oundle; 2ndly, 1938, Marion Caher (EDWARDS), who d. 1973, da. of Daniel C. Donoghue, of Philadelphia, USA, and formerly wife of 8th Earl of Carrick; d. 1952; s. by his only son [5] JOHN CHARLES COMPTON, 5th Baron, and present peer.

CHESTER, LORD BISHOP OF. (Whitsey)

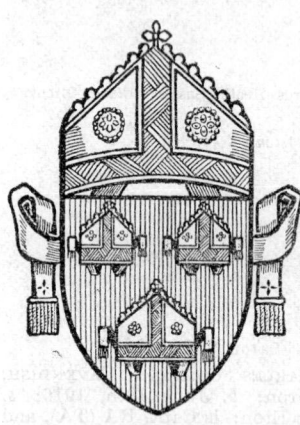

Rt. Rev. HUBERT VICTOR WHITSEY, son of Samuel Whitsey, of Blackburn, Lancs.; b. Nov. 21st, 1916; ed. at Queen Elizabeth's Gram. Sch., Blackburn, Tech. Coll., Blackburn, St. Edmund Hall, Oxon (MA), and Westcott House, Camb.; 1939-45 War with RA (TA), (Lt.-Col. 1945); V., Farington, Lancs. 1952-55, St. Thomas, Halliwell, Bolton 1955-60 (Assist. Rural Dean, Bolton 1957-60), All Saints and Martyrs, Langley, Manchester 1960-68, and Downham, Lancs. 1968-71; Hon. Canon Manchester Cathedral 1963, Canon Emeritus 1968; consecrated Bishop of Hertford (Suffragan for Diocese of St. Albans) 1971, and translated 38th Bishop of Chester 1973: m. 1950, Jean Margaret, da. of Silas Theodore Bellinger, of Burnley.

Patron of one hundred and fourteen livings; the Canonries of his Cathedral, the Archdeaconries of Chester and Macclesfield, and the Chancellorship of the Diocese.

This See, anciently part of the diocese of Lichfield, was erected into a distinct Bishopric by Henry VIII. in 1541, and the abbey-church of St. Werburgh became its Cathedral.

Episcopal Signature—" Victor Cestr : "

ARMS OF THE SEE,—Gules, three mitres with labels or two and one.
Address.—Bishop's House, Chester.

CHESTERFIELD AND STANHOPE, EARLDOM OF. (Scudamore-Stanhope.)
[Extinct 1967.]

DAUGHTER LIVING OF TWELFTH EARL OF CHESTERFIELD.
Lady Evelyn Patricia Mary, b. 1917: m. 1st, 1938 (marriage dissolved 1947), Lieut.-Com. Ian Mc-Donald, Roy. Australian Navy; 2ndly, 1947, as his third wife, John Harford Stanhope Lucas-Scudamore, D.L., and has issue living, (by 2nd marriage) John Edward Stanhope, b. 1951,—Charlotte Mary Frances, b. 1949. Residence,—Kentchurch Court, Hereford.

SISTER LIVING OF TWELFTH EARL OF CHESTERFIELD.
(Raised to the rank of an Earl's daughter 1938.)
Lady Enid Doreen Grace (c/o Barclays Bank, 36, Curzon St., W1), b. 1899: m. 1926, as his second wife, Major Alexander Browne, and has issue living, Angus Aidan Evelyn Vivian, b. 1929: m. 1963, Darea Joan, da. of Francis A. G. Blackwood, and has issue living, Aidan Charles b. 1966, Julia Harriett b. 1968.

COLLATERAL BRANCHES LIVING.

Decandants of Sir John Stanhope of Elvaston, Derbys., half-brother of 1st Earl of Chesterfield [see E. Harrington].

CHETWODE, BARON.   (Chetwode.)   [Baron U.K. 1945, Bt. E. 1700.]

CORONA MEA CHRISTUS

Christ is my crown.

PHILIP CHETWODE, 2nd Baron and 8th
Baronet ; *b.* March 26th, 1937 ; *s.* 1950 ; ed.
at Eton; Capt. (ret.) RHG: *m.* 1967, Susan
Janet, el. da. of the late Capt. Voltelin James
Howard Van der Byl, DSC, RN (ret.),
and formerly wife of Alwyn Richard Dudley
Smith, and has issue.

Arms,—Quarterly argent and gules, four crosses patée
counterchanged. Crest,—Out of a ducal coronet or, a
demi-lion rampant gules. Supporters,—*Dexter*, a Crusader
in chain armour and surcoat resting the exterior hand
proper on a shield of the arms of Chetwode; *sinister*, an
Officer of the 19th Royal Hussars resting his exterior hand
on the hilt of his sword proper.

Residence,—Crowood House, nr. Ramsbury, Wilts.

SONS LIVING.
Hon. ROGER, *b.* May 29th, 1968.
Hon. Alexander, *b.* 1969.
DAUGHTER LIVING.
Hon. Miranda, *b.* 1974.

BROTHER LIVING.
(*Raised to the rank of a Baron's son* 1951.)
Hon. Christopher Roger (Hockley House, Cheriton,
Alresford, Hants.), *b.* 1940; ed. at Eton: *m.* 1961, the Hon.
Philippa Mary Imogen Brand, da. of the 5th Viscount
Hampden, and has issue living, Michael Walhouse David,
b. 1962,—Richard Christopher *b.* 1964,—Charles Philip.
b. 1967,—William Robin, *b.* 1973,—James Nicholas,
b. 1975.

AUNT LIVING. (*Daughter of 1st Baron.*)
Hon. Penelope Valentine Hester (*Hon. Lady Betjeman*), *b.* 1910: *m.* 1933, Sir John Betjeman, CBE,
and has issue living, Paul, *b.* 1937; late 2nd Lieut. 15/19th Hussars,—Candida Rose, *b.* 1942: *m.* 1963,
Rupert William Lycett Green [see Green, Bt., cr. 1886, colls.]. *Residence,*—The New House,
Cusop, Hay-on-Wye, Herefordshire.

MOTHER LIVING.
Hon. Molly Patricia Berry (*Hon. Lady Cotterell*), da. of 1st Viscount Camrose: *m.* 1st, 1936, Capt. Roger
Charles George Chetwode, who *d.* 1940 ; 2ndly, 1942, the 1st Baron Sherwood, from whom she
obtained a divorce 1948; 3rdly, 1958, as his second wife, Sir Richard Charles Geers Cotterell,
CBE, TD, 5th Bt. *Residence,*—Garnons, Hereford.

COLLATERAL BRANCHES LIVING. (*In remainder to Baronetcy only.*)

Grandchildren of the late Adm. Sir George Knightley Chetwode, K.C.B., C.B.E.
(infra):—
Issue of the late Paymaster-Lieut. John Chetwode, R.N.R., *b.* 1909, *d.* (killed in action
during European War) 1941 : *m.* 1934, Joan Muriel (who *d.* 1951, having *m.* 2ndly, 1947,
Capt. Joseph Anthony Collings, M.B.E., late N. Somerset Yeo., who *d.* 1954), dau. of
Lieut.-Col. Frederick George Glyn Bailey [E. Inchcape] :—
John Simon Knightley, *b.* 1935 ; ed. at Eton, and at Ch. Ch., Oxford ; is Lieut. Roy. Wiltshire Yeo.
(Prince of Wales Own) late Derbyshire Yeo. and 12th Roy. Lancers and Student-at-law, Inner
Temple.——Janet Amanda Alice, *b.* 1937; ed. at Westonbirt, and at St. Clare's Coll., Oxford.

Issue of the late Adm. Sir George Knightley Chetwode, K.C.B., C.B.E., *b.* 1877, *d.* 1957 ;
m. 1st, 1908, Alice, who *d.* 1937, dau. of the late Major Vaughan Hanning Vaughan-Lee,
M.P. for W. Div. of Somersetshire ; 2ndly, 1939, Elizabeth (DAWSON), (c/o Westminster
Bank, Ilminster, Somerset), dau. of Frederick Taylor, of Jericho, Queensland :—
(By 1st marriage) George David, *M.B.E.*, *b.* 1914 ; Major Coldstream Guards ; sometime A.D.C.
to Gov. of Bombay ; European War 1939-45 in N. Africa and Italy (wounded, M.B.E.) ; M.B.E.
(Mil.) 1944: *m.* 1946, Lady Willa Elliot, da. of 5th Earl of Minto, and has issue living, Joshua
Leriston Knightley, *b.* 1967,—Davina Marion (28, Holmead Rd., SW6), *b.* 1947: *m.* 1968 (m. diss.
1975), W. John N. Moore, and has issue living, Lucy, *b.* 1970,—Sarah Alice, *b.* 1948: *m.* 1969, Andrew
Donald Cox,—Emma Bridget, *b.* 1950: *m.* 1971, Simon Keswick,—Willa Mary Gabriel, *b.* 1954,—
Georgina Caroline, *b.* 1955. *Residence,* —The Mantles, Blyth, Worksop, Notts.

PREDECESSORS.—[1] JOHN Chetwode, el. son of the late Philip Chetwode, of Oakley, Staffs,
b. 1666 ; cr. a *Baronet* 1700: *m.* 1st, 1695, Mary, who *d.* 1702, dau. of the late Sir Jonathan Raymond, of Barton Court, Berks ; 2ndly, 17—, Catherine, who *d.* 1717, dau. of the late John Tayleur,
of Rodington, Shropshire ; *d.* 1733 ; *s.* by his son [2] Sir PHILIP TOUCHET, 2nd Bt. ; *b.* 1700 : *m.*
1727, Elizabeth, who *d.* 1745, only dau. of the late George Venables, of Agdon, Cheshire ; *d.* 1764;
s. by his el. son [3] Sir JOHN, 3rd Bt. : *b.* 1732 : *m.* 1756, Dorothy, who *d.* 1769, dau. of the late Tobias
Bretland, of Thorncliffe, Cheshire ; *d.* 1779 ; *s.* by his only surviving son [4] Sir JOHN, 4th Bt. ; *b.*
1764 : *m.* 1st, Lady Elizabeth Grey, who *d.* 1826, dau. of 5th Earl of Stamford and 1st Earl of
Warrington ; 2ndly, 1827, Elizabeth, who *d.* 18—(having *m.* 2ndly, 1848, Andrew Kennedy Hutchinson, of Chester Square, Pimlico, S.W.) ; *d.* 1845 ; *s.* by his el. son [5] Sir JOHN, 5th Bt. ; *b.* 1788 ;
assumed by Roy. licence 1826 the additional surnames of Newdigate-Ludford : *m.* 1st, 1821,
Elizabeth Juliana, who *d.* 1859, el. dau. of the late John Newdigate-Ludford, of Ansley Hall, Warwickshire ; 2ndly, 1861, Arabella Phyllis, only child of the late Samuel Denton, and widow of
James Reade, of Lower Berkeley Street, W. ; *d.* 1873 ; *s.* by his nephew [6] Sir GEORGE (2nd son of
the late Rev. George Chetwode, 2nd son of 4th Bt.), 6th Bt. ; *b.* 1823 ; Lieut.-Col. 8th Hussars:
m. 1868, Alice Jane, who *d.* 1919, dau. of the late Michael Thomas Bass, M.P., of Rangemore, Staffs,
d. 1905 ; *s.* by his el. son [7] Sir PHILIP WALHOUSE, *G.C.B.*, *O.M.*, *G.C.S.I.*, *K.C.M.G.*, *D.S.O.*, 7th
Bt. ; *b.* 1869 ; became Field-Marshal 1933 ; Chin Hills Expedition 1892-3, S. Africa 1899-1902 (despatches thrice, D.S.O.), European War 1914-18 in France Comdg. 5th Cav. Brig. (original) and 2nd
Cav. Div., in Sinai Comdg. Desert Corps, and in Palestine and Syria Comdg. 20th Army Corps which
captured Jerusalem (wounded, despatches eight times, C.B., promoted Maj.-Gen. and Lieut.-Gen.
K.C.M.G., K.C.B.) ; Assist. Mil. Sec., Aldershot 1906-8 ; commanded London Mounted Brig.,
Territorial Force 1912-14 : appointed Mil. Sec. to Sec. of State for War, and Sec. of Selection Board
1919, Dep. Ch. of Imperial Gen. Staff and a Member of Army Council 1920, A.G. to the Forces 1922,
Gen. Officer Comdg.-in-Ch., Aldershot Command 1923, Col. Roy. Scots Greys (2nd Dragoons) 1925,
A.D.C.-Gen. to H.M. 1927, Ch. of Gen. Staff in India 1928, Col. 8th King George's Own Light Cav.
(Indian Army) 1932, and Hon. Col. 2nd/10th Dragoons, Canadian Mil. 1935 ; Com.-in-Ch. in India
and a M.E.C. 1930-35 ; Constable of Tower of London 1943-8 ; Col. 15th/19th King's Roy. Hussars
1944-7 ; received Grand Cross of Orders of St. Olav of Norway, and of George I. of Greece, and Order
of Brilliant Star of China with Grand Cordon ; a Knight Grand Cross of Order of Orange-Nassau
of the Netherlands ; cr. *Baron Chetwode*, of Chetwode, co. Buckingham (peerage of United Kingdom)
1945 : *m.* 1899, Alice Hester Camilla, who *d.* 1946, dau. of the late Col. the Hon. Richard Southwell
George Stapleton-Cotton; *d.* 1950 ; *s.* by his grandson [8] PHILIP (son of the late Capt. Roger Charles
George Chetwode, son of 1st Baron), 8th Baronet and present peer.

CHETWYND, VISCOUNT. (Chetwynd.) [Viscount I. 1717.]

Probity is true honour.

ADAM RICHARD JOHN CASSON CHET-
WYND, 10th Viscount; *b.* Feb. 2nd, 1935;
s. 1965; ed. at Eton; Lt. Queen's Own
Cameron Highlanders: *m.* 1966 (m. diss.
in Rhodesia 1974), Celia Grace, da. of Cdr.
Alexander Robert Ramsay, DSC, RNVR
[see Ramsay, Bt., colls., cr. 1806], and has
issue.

    Arms,—Azure, a chevron between three mullets
or. *Crest,*—A goat's head erased argent, horns gold.
Supporters,—Two unicorns argent, gorged with chaplets of roses gules, and having a chain of the same
reflexed over their backs.
    Residence,—Ty'n-y-Coed, Arthog, Gwynedd.

SONS LIVING.
Hon. ADAM DOUGLAS, *b.* Feb. 26th, 1969.
Hon. Robert Duncan (twin), *b.* 1969.

DAUGHTER LIVING.
Hon. Emma Grace, *b.* 1967.

SISTERS LIVING.
Hon. Philippa Mary Agnes Joan, *b.* 1930: *m.* 1959, Major
    John Anthony Hawtrey Luard, Coldstream Guards,
    of Ford House, Eversley, Basingstoke, and has issue
    living, David Andrew John, *b.* 1961,—Sophia Mary, *b.*
    1960.
Hon. Julian Isabella Joan, *b.* 1932: *m.* 1960, Maj. Philip
    David Miles, of Hinton Hall, Lea Cross, Shrewsbury,
    Salop [see Greenwell, Bt.].

HALF-SISTERS LIVING.
Hon. Catherine Sophia Marianne, *b.* 1956.   *Hon.* Frances Diana Dorothea, *b.* 1959.

AUNT LIVING. (*Daughter of 8th Viscount.*)
Hon. (Mary Diana) Eve, *b.* 1908.   *Residence,*—6, Hulton Drive, Emberton, Olney, Bucks.

WIDOW LIVING OF SON OF EIGHTH VISCOUNT.
Margaret Agnes (3, Cadogan Sq., SW1), da. of the late Maj.-Gen. Hugh Clement Sutton, CB, CMG
[see Sutton, Bt., colls.]: *m.* 1937, the Hon. John Julian Chetwynd, 2nd son of 8th Viscount, who
d. 1966, and has issue living [see colls., infra].

MOTHER LIVING.
JOAN GILBERT (*Joan, Viscountess Chetwynd*) (Ty'n-y-Coed, Arthog, Gwynedd, LL39 2LR), da. of the
late Herbert Alexander Casson, CSI, and formerly wife of Victor Alexander Charles Findlay; OStJ;
1939-45 War as Sqdn. Officer, WAAF: *m.* 1928 (m. diss. 1951), the 9th Viscount, who *d.* 1965.

WIDOW LIVING OF NINTH VISCOUNT.
DOROTHEA MARIANNE DUNCAN-JOHNSTONE, *MBE* (*Dorothea, Viscountess Chetwynd*) (Polesdon House,
Stype, Hungerford, Berks.); MBE (Civil) 1974: *m.* 1952, as his 2nd wife, the 9th Viscount, who *d.*
1965.

COLLATERAL BRANCHES LIVING.

    Granddaughters of the late Capt. the Hon. Henry Weyland Chetwynd, R.N., 3rd
    son of 6th Viscount:—
    Issue of the late Henry Goulburn Willoughby Chetwynd, A.M.I.C.E., el. brother of
    8th Viscount, *b.* 1858, *d.* 1909: *m.* 1893, Eva Constance Elizabeth Fanny, who *d.* 1936,
    dau. of the late Augustus Berney [Berney, Bt., colls.]:—
Sylvia Evelyn, *b.* 1902: *m.* 1931, Anthony Makower, and has issue living, Peter (of 2, Lillian Rd.,
Barnes, SW13), *b.* 1932; ed. at Trin. Coll., Camb. (MA); FRIBA; MRTPI: *m.* 1960, Katharine, da. of
Jack Howarthe Paul Chadburn, MBE, and has issue living, Andrew *b.* 1961, Timothy *b.* 1965, Mary
b. 1963,—Michael Stanley (Gogar House, Blairlogie, by Stirling), *b.* 1936: *m.* 1960, Selina Elizabeth,
da. of the late Henry Vernon Flower Barran [see Barran, Bt., colls.], and has issue living, Sophia
Galiena *b.* 1962, Janet Elizabeth Agnes *b.* 1964, Margaret Eleanor *b.* 1966,—*Rev.* Malory (Ridley Hall,
Cambridge), *b.* 1938; ed. at Dublin Univ. (BA), and St. John Coll., Oxford (MA, DPhil): *m.* 1967,
Mary Nöel, da. of R. E. Stokes, and has issue living, Philip *b.* 1969, Caroline *b.* 1968, Sandra *b.* 1972,—
Anne, *b.* 1934: *m.* 1955,—Christopher O'Connell Fitz-Simon, of 8, Richmond Hill, Monkstown, co.
Dublin, and has issue living, Adrian Christopher *b.* 1967, Vanessa Una *b.* 1965. *Residence,*—15,
Addison Cres., W14.——Enid Elizabeth, *b.* 1907: *m.* 1933, the Rev. Eric Campbell Douglas, and
has issue living, David Campbell Justyn, *b.* 1939,—Penelope Stopford, *b.* 1934. *Residence,*—The
Pightle, Barnham Broom, Norwich, NOR. 35X.

    Issue of the late Hon. John Julian Chetwynd, 2nd son of 8th Viscount, *b.* 1906,
    d. 1966: *m.* 1937, Margaret Agnes (ante), da. of the late Maj.-Gen. Hugh Clement
    Sutton, CB, CMG [see Sutton, Bt., colls.]:—
Richard Walter (3, Larpent Av., SW15), *b.* 1938; ed. at Eton: *m.* 1964, Judith Mary, only da. of
Capt. Selwyn Victor Jephson, RN, of the Red House, Hambledon, Hants., and has issue living,
Mark Richard, *b.* 1972,—Katharine Margaret, *b.* 1965,—Sarah Alexandra, *b.* 1967.——John Hugh
(3, Cadogan Sq., SW1), *b.* 1942; ed. at Stowe: *m.* 1st, 1966 (m. diss. 1971), Denyse Jacqueline, da. of
Col. H. de Frisching, of Berne; 2ndly, 1973, Caroline, el. da. of John Fitzwilliams, and has issue
living (by 1st m.), Hugh Nigel, *b.* 1967,—Philip Mark, *b.* 1969.

    Issue of the late Capt. the Hon. Louis Wentworth Pakington Chetwynd, R.N.
    brother of 8th Viscount, *b.* 1866, *d.* 1914: *m.* 1903, Augusta, who *d.* 1955, dau. of
    the late E. R. Robinson, of 23, Washington Square, New York:—
Wentworth Randolph, *MBE* (Goetre Hall, Trapp, Llandilo, Carmarthenshire), *b.* 1903; ed. at Eton,
and at New Coll., Oxford; Maj. (ret.) Gren. Guards; MBE (Mil) 1954: *m.* 1st, 1931 (m. diss. 1964),
Bridget, da. of Col. Theobald Alfred Walsh, DSO; 2ndly, 1964, Mary, da. of Francis Rosser, and has
issue living, (by 1st m.) Rupert Milo Talbot (Waterloo House, Egmond Chetwynd, Salop), *b.* 1934:
m. 1st 1956 (m. diss. 1970), Antonia, da. of the late Denis Clark, DFC; 2ndly, 1970, Luciana Maria
Arrighi, el. da. of the late Count Ernest Arrighi, and has issue living, (by 1st m.) Rupert Jonathan
Richard *b.* 1957, Dominic Jeremy *b.* 1959, Crispin *b.* 1961, Alexander *b.* 1964, Persephone Catherine
b. 1965, (by 2nd m.) Aaron St. George Francesco Arrighi *b.* 1971,—Tom Wentworth Guy (12, Mornington Terr., NW1), *b.* 1938; is 2nd Lt. RAC: *m.* 1959, Helène, da. of Baron Pierre de Bosmelet, and has
issue living, Yoland *b.* 1960, Natasha *b.* 1961, Bridget *b.* 1966.——Victoria Edith Joan *b.* 1912:
m. 1933 (m. diss. 1945), Sir (Archibald) Laurence Patrick Kirwan, KCMG, TD, and has issue living,
Anne Jennifer, *b.* 1933: *m.* 1964, Antony Martin Preston, of 13, Crondace Rd., SW6. *Residence,*—
Bell Meadow, Bury Gate, nr. Pulborough, Sussex.

Grandchildren of the late Henry Edward Chetwynd-Stapylton, el. son of the late
Maj. Henry Richard Chetwynd-Stapylton, el. son of the late Maj.-Gen. the
Hon. Granville Anson Chetwynd-Stapylton, 2nd son of 4th Viscount:—
Issue of the late Henry Goulburn Chetwynd-Stapylton, *b.* 1852, *d.* 1926 *m* 1886, **Mary,**
who *d.* 1951, dau. of the late Charles Watkin Williams-Wynn [Williams-Wynn, Bt.,
colls.]:—
Annora Esther, *b.* 1889 : *m.* 1921, Arthur Edward Osmaston, Conservator Indian Forest Ser. (retired),
and has issue living, Henry Arthur (Regil Farm, Winford, Bristol), *b.* 1922; ed. at Eton, and at
Worcester Coll., Oxford (MA, BSc, DPhil); Colonial Forest Ser., Uganda (ret.); 1939-45
War as Maj. REME: *m.* 1948, Ellinor Mary Anna Laetitia Wingate, da. of the late Wing-Cdr.
Archibald Graham Weir, RAF, of Pensbury House, Shaftesbury, Dorset, and has issue living,
John Arthur Nigel *b.* 1957, Amiel Mary Ellinor *b.* 1951, Janet Elizabeth Anna *b.* 1953, Charlotte
Esther Chetwynd *b.* 1959,—Miles Francis (of The White Cottage, Sendmarsh, Ripley, Surrey),
b. 1925; ed. at Radley, and at Worcester Coll., Oxford (BA 1949, MA 1950): *m.* 1956, Margaret
Helena, da. of the Rev. Canon George Elwes Allen Whitworth, of Trin. Coll., Camb., and has issue
living, Francis Andrew *b.* 1961, John Miles *b.* 1963, Mary Clare *b.* 1957, Elizabeth Anne *b.* 1959.
Residence,—Cossins House, Downside, Cobham, Surrey, KT11 3LZ.

Grandchildren of the late Miles Chetwynd-Stapylton, yr. son of the late Henry
Edward Chetwynd-Stapylton (ante):—
Issue of the late Philip Miles Chetwynd-Stapylton, *b.* 1889, *d.* 1965: *m.* 1920, Esmé (Buryfield
House, Odiham, Hants.), da. of the late W. G. Eveleigh:—
Henry Philip, 8, Semaphore Rd., Guildford, Surrey), *b.* 1921; ed. at Radley; late Capt. Indian Army;
B.Arch. 1952; an ARIBA; 1939-45 War: *m.* 1962, Elizabeth Bentinck, yst. da. of the late E. E.
Chambers, of Ringwood, Hants., and has issue living, Henry Edward, *b.* 1966,—Diana Rachel,
b. 1970.——Esmé Elizabeth, *b.* 1927: *m.* 1954, Col. Robert Edward Waight, OBE, late LI, and has
issue living, Richard Edward Charles, *b.* 1960,—Deborah Anne, *b.* 1957.

Grandchildren of the late Lieut.-Gen. Granville George Chetwynd-Stapylton, 2nd
son of the late Major Henry Richard Chetwynd-Stapylton (ante):—
Issue of the late Major Granville Joseph Chetwynd-Stapylton, *b.* 1871, *d.* (killed in
action) 1914 : *m.* 1906, Elizabeth Grace, who *d.* 1930, dau. of the late Christopher
Lethbridge, of 19, Chester Square, S.W.:—
Granville Richard (Ragleth House, Little Stretton, Salop.), *b.* 1909; ed. at Charterhouse; Lieut.-Col.
(retired) Somerset LI: *m.* 1934, Emma, yst. da. of the late Col. W. A. Young, and has issue living,
Richard Granville Hugh (Murrell, Murrell Green, Hartley Wintney, Hants) *b.* 1939; ed. at Charterhouse; Maj. LI: *m.* 1968, Janet Mary Agnes, da. of Cdr. Alastair Shand Cumming, RN, and has
issue living, Margot Emma *b.* 1969, Polly Rose *b.* 1971,—Sarah Elizabeth, *b.* 1936: *m.* 1962, Lt.-Col.
I. Guy Mathews (ret.), SCLI, Trecilla House, Llangarron, Ross-on-Wye, and has issue living, Nicola,
b. 1963, Amanda, *b.* 1965.——Christopher George, *b.* 1913; Lt.-Col. RA: *m* 1952, Bridget (WILSON),
yr. da. of H. S. Dixon-Spain, of Little Massingham, Norfolk, and has issue living, Elizabeth Alice,
b. 1954. *Residence,*—Roanoke, Feock, Truro, Cornwall.——Barbara Mary Elizabeth, *b.* 1907: *m.*
1934, Ronald Anthony Birch, and has issue living, George Anthony, *b.* 1935,—William, *b.* 1938,—
John Montagu, *b.* 1941.

Issue of the late Col. Bryan Henry Chetwynd-Stapylton, C.B.E., *b.* 1873, *d.* 1958 : *m.* 1905,
Dorothy Constance, who *d.* 1942, dau. of the late Chambré Brabazon Ponsonby [B.
Bessborough, colls.]:—
Edward Henry, *b.* 1912; ed. at Eton; Major (retired) Cheshire Regt.: *m.* 1957, Priscilla, dau. of
Maj. Robert Gerald Wright, of Tunstall Grange, Richmond, Yorkshire, and has issue living, Miles
Edward, *b.* 1958; ed. at Bradfield. *Residence,*—Ewelands House, Felixkirk, Thirsk, N. Yorks.
Club,—Army and Navy.——Mary Blanche, *b.* 1910: *m.* 1936, Ralph Mereith Turton, and has issue
living, Cecilia Mary, *b.* 1936: *m.* 1959, John H. V. Sutcliffe, of Chapelgarth, Gt. Broughton, Middles-
brough, and has issue living, Andrew Harold Wentworth *b.* 1960, John Ralph Beaumont *b.* 1964,
Mark David Chetwynd *b.* 1967, Henrietta Cecilia *b.* 1961,—Lavinia Rose, *b.* 1939: *m.* 1964, John
Simon Horsburgh-Porter, of Bowers Croft, Magpie Lane, Amersham, Bucks. [see Horsburgh-Porter,
Bt.],—Victoria Harriet Lucy, *b.* 1942; ed. at Trin. Coll., Dublin (MA)· *m.* 1966, Robin John Orlando
Bridgeman, of 51, Sloane Gdns., SW1 [see V. Bridgeman, colls.],—Sylvia Dorothy, *b.* 1947. *Residence,*
—Kildale Hall, Whitby, Yorks.

Grandchildren of the late Edward Chetwynd-Stapylton (infra):—
Issue of the late Richard Chetwynd-Stapylton, *b.* 1880, *d.* 1945 : *m.* 1915, Vera Helen, who
d. 1959, dau. of the late Andrew Coventry Maitland-Makgill-Crichton [E. Lauderdale,
colls.]:—
Edward Mark, *b.* 1919; ed. at Winchester, and at Magdalene Coll., Camb.; formerly Maj. KRRC;
1939-45 War in Middle East attached E. Africa Reconnaissance Regt. (despatches): *m.* 1946, Anne
Phillida (formerly WRNS), da. of Sir Alfred Edward Pease, 2nd Bt. (cr. 1882), and has issue living,
Judy Anne, *b.* 1948,—Phillida Helen, *b.* 1949,—Joanna Elizabeth *b.* 1951. *Residence,*—12, Kennington Palace Court, Sancroft St., SE11.——Helen (*Baroness Adeane*) (22, Chelsea Sq., W1), *b.*
1916: *m.* 1939, Baron Adeane, GCB, GCVO——Vera Rosemary (82, North End House, Fitz James
Av., W14), *b.* 1924: *m.* 1946 (m. diss. 1970), Maj. Derek Leslie Lloyd, MC, 5th Fusiliers (ret.), and has
issue living, Julian Richard Leslie, *b.* 1947; ed. at Eton: *m.* 1972, the Hon. Victoria Mary Ormsby—
Gore, da. of 5th Baron Harlech, and has issue living, Poppy *b.* 1972, a da. *b.* 1974—Carolyn Rosemary,
b. 1948, Athea Victoria, *b.* 1950.

Grandchildren of the Rev. Canon William Chetwynd-Stapylton, 3rd son of the
late Maj. Henry Richard Chetwynd-Stapylton (ante):—
Issue of the late Edward Chetwynd-Stapylton *b.* 1855, *d.* 1938 : *m.* 1st, 1879, Beatrice
Mary, who *d.* 1923, dau. of the late Henry Cowie, of Calcutta; 2ndly, 1924, Elizabeth
Gordon, who *d.* 1940, dau. of the late Capt. Robert W. Ker, R.N.R., and widow of Major
Cavaliere Scipione Giordano, of Turin :—
By 1st marriage) William Eric (of Bowling Green Cottage, Windlesham, Surrey), *b.* 1895; sometime
Capt. London Regt.: *m.* 1st, 1924, Vivienne, who *d.* 1961, dau. of Harry Spurling, formerly of
Upton Park, Slough; 2ndly, 1962, Audrey Margaret, dau. of Percival Hardy, formerly of London,
and widow of Ian T. B. Cash, and has issue living, (by 1st marriage) Violet Mary, *b.* 1926; late
W.R.N.S.: *m.* 1955, Richard Nevill Vaughan Fairbank, T.D., late Capt. Hon. Artillery Co., of
Coopers Green, Windlesham, Surrey, and has issue living, David Richard Stapylton *b.* 1956, Anthony
William Vaughan *b.* 1963, Victoria Mary Nevill *b.* 1959.——Dorothy, *b.* 1883: *m.* 1st, 1909, Lt.-Cdr.
Walter John Fletcher, RN, who *d.* 1917 [E. Courtown, colls.]; 2ndly, 1919, William Miskin, of
Bodsham Lodge, Elmsted, Ashford, Kent, and has issue living, (by 1st marriage) Wyndham John
Stapylton, *MC, TD.*(Bodsham Lodge, Bodsham, Ashford, Kent), *b.* 1910; ed. at Lancing, Maj. RA 1934-
45 War (despatches, MC): *m.* 1st, 1934, Betty O'Brien Horsford; 2ndly, 1959, Elizabeth Villiers, and
has issue living, (by 1st m.) Rodney Stapylton *b.* 1935; ed. at Wellington: *m.* 1964, Nicola Jane
Bannister (and has issue living, Timothy Wyndham *b.* 19568, Louise Alison *b.* 1966), Sally Stapylton
b. 1939: *m.* 1962, Lt.-Cdr. Neil Oswell Macleay. RN (and has issue living, Rory Daniel Oswell *b.* 1969,
Catherine *b.* 1963, Alexandra *b.* 1964, Fiona *b.* 1966), Jennifer Stapylton *b.* 1941: *m.* 1st, 1964,
Capt. Daniel Jacot De Boinod, Coldstream Guards, who *d.* 1964; 2ndly, 1967, Capt. Nicholas Mylne,
10th Hussars (and has issue living (by 2nd m.) Patrick Mark Daniel *b.* 1970, Lucinda Catherine
Lara *b.* 1968, Sophie Caroline *b.* 1973),—Marion Stapylton (Bodsham Lodge, Bodsham, nr. Ashford,
Kent), *b.* 1914: *m.* 1937, Humphrey Pares, TD, of Studfall, Lympne, Kent, and has issue living,
Penelope Iris *b.* 1939, Susan Caroline *b.* 1941, Teresa Judith *b.* 1946, Frances Campbell *b.* 1948.
——Grace Mary (Bracken Close, Sandy Lane, Milford, Surrey), *b.* 1887: *m.* 1911, Edgar Reginald
Godson, who *d.* 1963, and has issue living, Clement Patrick Chetwynd, (Milford Heath House,

D.—9

Milford, Godalming, Surrey), b. 1913; ed at Charterhouse: m. 1941, Dorothy Frances, da. of the late Dr. G. F. Graham, and has issue living, Mark Chetwynd b. 1943; ed. at Charterhouse: m. 1970, Lois Caroline Duncan Millar, Antony Graham b. 1946; ed. at Bradfield Coll.: m. 1971, Catriona Madeline Liddell, Richard Hugh, b. 1947; ed. at Bradfield Coll.

Grandaughters of the late Granville Chetwynd-Stapylton, yst. son of the late Rev. Canon William Chetwynd-Stapylton (ante):—
Issue of the late Col. Granville Brian Chetwynd-Stapylton, CB, OBE, TD, b. 1887, d. 1964: m. 1922, Catherine (3, Gresham House, Ditton Close, Watts Rd., Thames Ditton), da. of the late Herbert Lyne, of Newport, Mon.:—
Lucy, b. 1923: m. 1945, Paul Anthony Robinson, Fl.-Lt. late RAFVR, of 11, Portsmouth Av., Thames Ditton, Surrey, and has issue living, Nigel Anthony, b. 1946,—Jennifer Chetwynd, b. 1949.——
Bridget (Lawn Cottage, Old Rectory Gardens, Park Lane, Abbots Worthy, Winchester SO21 1DW), b. 1924: m. 1948, Dennis Worsley Wilks, MB, BS, who d. 1969, and has issue living, David Michael Worsley (27, Castletown Rd., W14 9HF), b. 1949; MB, BS: m. 1972, Patricia Dorothea Joyce, da. of Charles Anthony Philip Hackforth, DSO,—John Richard Stapylton, b. 1955,—Nicholas Paul, b. 1960.——Mary Elizabeth, b. 1926: m. 1949, Grahame Archer Nicholls, BSc, of 12A Lillington Av., Leamington Spa, and has issue living, Granville Richard, b. 1952,—David Chetwynd, b. 1957,— Janet Archer, b. 1950.

PREDECESSORS.—[1] WALTER Chetwynd, son of the late John Chetwynd; M.P. for boroughs of Stafford and Lichfield 1703-35, and sometime Ambassador at Turin and Master of the Stag hounds; cr. *Baron of Rathdown*, co. Dublin, and *Viscount Chetwynd*, of Bearhaven, co Kerry (peerage of Ireland) 1717, with remainder to the issue male of his father; d. 1735; s. by his brother [2] JOHN, 2nd Viscount; Ambassador to Madrid 1717; d. 1767; s. by his brother [3] WILLIAM RICHARD, 3rd Viscount; Resident at Republic of Genoa 1708-12, M.P. 1714, Commr. of the Admiralty 1717-27, and Master of the Mint 1727; d. 1770; s. by his son [4] WILLIAM, 4th Viscount, b. 1721: m. 1751; d. 1791; s. by his son [5] RICHARD, 5th Viscount: d. 1821; s. by his son [6] RICHARD WALTER, 6th Viscount, b. 1800: m. 1st, 1822, Mary, who d. 1857, dau. of Robert Moss; 2ndly, 1861, Mary, who d. 1901, dau. of the late John Hussey; d. Dec. 6th, 1879; s. by his son [7] RICHARD WALTER, 7th Viscount, b. 1823 : m. 1858, Harriet Johanna, who d. 1898, dau. of the late Walter Campbell; d. 1911; s. by his nephew [8] GODFREY JOHN BOYLE, C.H. (2nd son of the late Capt. the Hon. Henry Weyland Chetwynd, R.N., 3rd son of 6th Viscount), 8th Viscount, b. 1863; was Managing Director of National Shell Filling Factory at Chilwell, Notts 1915-19: m. 1st, 1893, Baroness Hilda von Alvensleben (from whom he obtained a divorce), dau. of Baron George von Alvensleben-Rusteberg; 2ndly, 1904, the Hon. Mary Eden, who d. 1925, dau. of 4th Baron Auckland; d. 1936; s. by his son [9] ADAM DUNCAN, TD, 9th Viscount b. 1904; a FSA, and Lt.-Col. RA: m. 1st, 1928, Joan Gilbert (FINDLAY), from whom he obtained a divorce 1951, only child of the late Herbert Alexander Casson, OSI; 2ndly, 1952, Dorothea Marianne, da. of Lt.-Col. Angus, Colin Duncan-Johnstone, MBE, ED; d. 1965; s. by his only son [10] ADAM RICHARD JOHN CASSON, 10th Viscount and present peer; also Baron Rathdown.

Chewton, Viscount, son of Earl Waldegrave.

CHEYLESMORE, BARONY OF. (Eaton.) [Extinct 1974.]

COLLATERAL BRANCH LIVING.
Issue of the late Hon. Herbert Edward Eaton, 2nd son of 3rd Baron, b. 1895, d. 1962: m. 1st, 1921, Sheila Marguerite (Ashton Case) (who d. 1967, having obtained a div. 1944), da. of Alan Dunbleton, of British Columbia; 2ndly, 1944, Barrie Kinghorn (WILLIAMS), who d. 1972, da. of Walter Grey, of Edinburgh:—
By 1st marriage) Elizabeth Valerie (Bernstrasse 1, 3122, Kehrsatz, Switzerland), b. 1922: m. 1949, Edward John Kynaston Cross, and has issue living, Richard Anthony Kynaston, b. 1951.

CHICHESTER, EARL OF. (Pelham.) [Earl U.K. 1801, Bt. E. 1611.]

JOHN NICHOLAS PELHAM, 9th Earl and 14th Baronet; b. (posthumous) April 14th, 1944; s. 1944.

Arms,—Quarterly : 1st and 4th azure, three pelicans vulning themselves argent ; 2nd and 3rd gules, two pieces of belts with buckles, erect in pale, the buckles upwards argent. Crest.—A peacock in pride argent. Badge,—The buckle of a belt or. Supporters,—*Dexter*, a horse of a mouse dun colour; and *sinister*, a bear proper, each collared with a belt, buckle and pendant or.
Residence,—Little Durnford Manor, Salisbury.

SISTER LIVING.
Lady Georgiana Joceleyn, b. 1942.

WIDOW LIVING OF SON OF FIFTH EARL.
Barbara Clare, da. of the late Col. J. E. D. Taunton, late DQMG, Australian Mil. Forces: m. 1928, as his second wife, the Hon. Anthony Ashley Ivo Pelham, who d. 1951. *Residence*,—Halland Clyst St. Mary, Exeter.

The love of my country prevails.

WIDOW LIVING OF EIGHTH EARL.
URSULA, da. of the late Walter de Pannwitz, of de Hartekamp, Bennebroek, Holland: m. 1st, 1940, the 8th Earl, who d. (on active ser.) 1944; 2ndly, 1957 (m. diss. 1971), Ralph Gunning Henderson. *Residences*,—Estancia La Catalina, Fiego de Alvear, FCGSM, Argentina; Uriburu 694, Beccar, FCGBM, Buenos Aires, Argentina.

COLLATERAL BRANCHES LIVING.

Grandchildren of the Hon. Henry George Godolphin Pelham (infra):—
Issue of the late Maj. Anthony George Pelham, *b.* 1911, *d.* 1969: *m.* 1938, Ann-Margret (55,
Egerton Cres., SW3), da. of the late Axel Bergengren, of Borås, Sweden:—
RICHARD ANTHONY HENRY, *b.* Aug. 1st, 1952; ed. at Eton.——Ella Christine, *b.* 1940: *m.* 1961,
John Raymond Perring, of 21 Somerset Rd., Wimbledon, S.W.19, el. son of Sir Ralph Edgar Perring,
1st Bt.——Judith Henrietta, *b.* 1943: *m.* 1968, Christopher John Chetwood, of The White House,
Odiham, Hants.

Issue of the late Hon. Henry George Godolphin Pelham, 2nd son of 5th Earl, *b.*
1875, *d.* 1949: *m.* 1st, 1906. Agnes Lee, who *d.* 1930, dau. of the late T. J.
Ollerhead, of Hillbury, Minehead, Somerset; 2ndly, 1938, Dorothy Mary, who *d.*
1972, da. of the late George Bridger Shiffner [Shiffner, Bt., colls.]:—
By 1st m.) Joan Ursula, *b.* 1907; is a JP for Surrey: *m.* 1929, John Edward Sealy, who
d. 1968, and has issue living, Nicholas John Elliot (Timber Hill, Chobham, Surrey), *b.* 1938; ed. at
Eton; la..e Capt. Rifle Bde.: *m.* 1971, the Hon. Lavinia Caroline Piercy, twin da. of the 2nd Baron
Piercy,—Agnes Coral Pelham, *b.* 1932: *m.* 1954, James Gilbert Curwen, of Chobham House, W.
Chobham, Surrey, and has issue living, Henry James Gospatric *b.* 1957, Simon Charles Edward
b. 1959, Philip Mark Ivo *b.* 1963, Rachel Helen Vanessa *b.* 1962,—Ann Pelham, *b.* 1934: *m.* 1957,
Fereydoun Ala, MB, ChB, MRCPE, FRCP, and has issue living, a son *b.* 1957, a son *b.* 1960, a son
b. 1967. *Residence,*—Timber Hill, Chobham, Surrey.——Beryl Northup, *b.* 1908: *m.* 1940, Lawrence
Swan, late Sqdn.-Ldr. RAFVR, of Elm House, Gibbs Acre, Pirbright, Woking, Surrey.

Grandchildren of the late Hon. Thomas Henry William Pelham, C.B., 3rd son of
3rd Earl:—
Issue of the late Rev. Walter Henry Pelham, *b.* 1886, *d.* 1949: *m.* 1914, Ruth Mary, who *d.*
1950, dau. of the late Claude Leatham:—
Rev. Thomas Bertram, *b.* 1915; ed. at Charterhouse (Whitchurch Rectory, Reading, RG8 JDF); R. of
Whitchurch on Thames, Oxon.; 1939-45 War as Capt. R. Indian Army Ser. Corps.: *m.* 1948, Gudrun
Elizabeth, da. of the late Rev. U. A. V. Almgren, of Goteborg, Sweden, and has issue living Philip
Henry *b.* 1949,—David Almgren, *b.* 1950,—Peter Thomas, *b.* 1952: *m.* 1974, Linda Margaret, da. of
Capt. P. H. Phillips, of Newlyn, Cornwall,—Erik John Christopher *b.* 1954,—James Richard,
b. 1955,—Astrid Louisa (twin), *b.* 1955,—Susan Margaret, *b.* 1959.——Robert Henry, *b.* 1919; ed. at
Canford; 1939-45 War as Capt. RA: *m.* 1951, Anne Farebrother Dalziel, da. of Capt. Geoffrey Dalziel
Mayer, of Abinger, Surrey, and has issue living, Michael Henry, *b.* 1953,—Sarah Mary, *b.* 1955.
Residence,—Tresco House, Ogbourne St. Andrew, Marlborough, Wilts.——Patricia Mary, *b.* 1917:
m. 1st, 1937 (m. diss. 1949), Lt.-Col. Charles Reginald Clayton Albrecht, OBE; 2ndly, 1949, Harold
Holtby, MB, BS, who *d.* 1961, and has issue living, (by 1st m.) Nicholas Charles Pelham, *b.* 1938:
m. 1964, Francoise, da. of Théophile Henri Buchet, of Talmont, Vendée, France, and has issue living,
Marc Henry Pelham *b.* 1965,—Perenna Jane Pelham, *b.* 1941: *m.* 1969, Duncan Charles Pennock,
of The Old Bank House, Llan Ffestiniog, Merioneth, and has issue living, Catherine Patricia Pelham
b. 1970. *Residence,*—Elm Cottage, Holbrook, Ipswich.

Granddaughter of the late Rt. Rev. the Hon. John Thomas Pelham, D.D., sometime
Bishop of Norwich, 4th son of 2nd Earl :—
Issue of the late Henry Francis Pelham, Pres. of Trin. Coll., Oxford, *b.* 1846, *d.* 1907:
m. 1873, Laura Priscilla, who *d.* 1918, dau. of Sir Edward North Buxton, 2nd Bt. :—
Laura Grace, *b.* 1888: *m.* 1915, Lieut.-Col. David Francis Bickmore, D.S.O., Norfolk Regt., and
attached Gordon Highlanders, who *d.* (killed in action) 1918 [Dundas, Bt., cr. 1821], and has issue
living, John David Pelham (55, Ladbroke Rd., W11), *b.* 1917; ed. at Harrow, and at New Coll.,
Oxford; Dir. Experimental Cartography Unit, Natural Environment Research Council, a Member of
Queen's Body Guard for Scotland (R. Co. of Archers); 1939-45 War as Maj. RE: *m.* 1st 1939 (m. diss.
1971) Anne Denise, da. of the late Sir Eustace Gurney; 2ndly, 1971, Mary Alison, da. of Sydney
Herbert Shaw, CMG, OBE, and has issue living (by 1st m.), Peter John *b.* 1944, David Anthony
b. 1952, Elizabeth Anne *b.* 1946: *m.* 1969, Robin Anthony Guy Henry Courage (and has issue living,
Archibald *b.* 1970, Miles *b.* 1973, Cara *b.* 1975), Catherine Jane *b.* 1949, (by 2nd m.) Francis Giles
b. 1975. *Residence,*—13, Winchester Rd., Oxford.

Grandchildren of the late Sir (Edward) Henry Pelham, K.C.B., *b.* 1876, *d.* 1949 : *m.* 1905, the Hon.
Irene Lubbock, who *d.* 1961, dau. of 1st Baron Avebury :—
Eric Thomas, *b.* 1915; ed. at Harrow, and at Balliol Coll., Oxford ; Major Welsh Guards : *m.* 1940,
Barbara Hilda, who *d.* 1969, yst. da. of the late Henry Fordham, and has issue living, Henry Thomas,
b. 1943,—Richard John, *b.* 1945,—Charles Herbert, *b.* 1947,—William Robert, *b.* 1950. *Residence,*
—The Old Rectory, Spaldwick, Huntingdon——Alice Catherine, *b.* 1911 : *m.* 1933, Patrick Robert
Sandars, OBE, of Court Acre, Crondall, Farnham, Surrey, and has issue living, Patrick George
Henry, *b.* 1935; ed. at Wellington and Balliol Coll., Oxford (MA, DPhil.): *m.* 1959, Patricia Barbara,
da. of E. J. Hall, of Oxford,—Anthony Thomas, *b.* 1937.——Irene Joan, *b.* 1912: *m.* 1961, Brig.
Maurice Leslie Hayne, CBE, who *d.* 1971. *Residence,*—Oak Beams, Church Lane, Gaydon, War-
wickshire.——Susan, *b.* 1918: *m.* 1940, Air Vice-Marshal Cresswell Montagu Clementi, CB, CBE, of 8
Chiswick Staithe, W4 3TP, only son of the late Sir Cecil Clementi, GCMG, and has issue living,
Christopher Pelham, *b.* 1943; ed. at Bradfield—David Cecil, *b.* 1949: ed. at Winchester, Lincoln Col.,
Oxford, and Harvard Business Sch.: *m.* 1972, Sarah Louise, da. of Dr. A. B. Cowley, of E. Molesey,
Surrey,—Nancy, *b.* 1946: *m.* 1972, Peter Lambert Tribe.

PREDECESSORS.—[1] THOMAS Pelham, *M.P.* for Sussex 1586, and Sheriff of Surrey and
Sussex 1589; cr. a *Baronet* 1611; *d.* 1624; *s.* by his son [2] Sir THOMAS, 2nd Bt., M.P. for
Sussex; *d.* 1654; *s.* by his son [3] Sir JOHN, 3rd Bt., M.P. for Sussex in five parliaments; *d.*
1703; *s.* by his son [4] Sir THOMAS, 4th Bt., M.P. for many years; cr. *Lord Pelham, Baron
of Pelham,* of Laughton, co. Sussex (peerage of Great Britain); *d.* 1712; *s.* by his son [5]
THOMAS, *K.G.,* 2nd Baron, cr. *Viscount Houghton and Earl of Clare,* co. Suffolk (peerage of
Great Britain) 1714, with remainder to his brother Henry; Marquess of Clare and Duke of
Newcastle (peerage of Great Britain) 1715, with similar limitation ; Duke of Newcastle-under-
Lyme (peerage of Great Britain) 1756, with remainder to Henry, 9th Earl of Lincoln, who had
m. Catherine, dau. of his brother Henry (ante) ; and *Baron Pelham of Stanmer* (peerage of Great
Britain) 1762, with remainder to his cousin Thomas, grandson of Henry, 3rd son of 3rd
Bt. ; *d.* without male issue 1768, when the peerages of 1712, 1714, 1715 became extinct,
the dukedom of 1756 passed to the Earl of Lincoln, and the peerage of 1762 devolved
upon his kinsman [6] THOMAS, P.C., 2nd Baron Pelham; was successively M.P. for Sussex,
Commr. of Trade and Plantations, a Lord of the Admiralty, and Comptroller of the Household ;
cr. *Earl of Chichester* 1801; *d.* 1805; *s.* by his son [7] THOMAS, 2nd Earl; *b.* 1756; M.P. for
Sussex 1790-90; was successively Sec. to Lord-Lieut. of Ireland, and Sec. of State for Home
Depart., Chancellor of Duchy of Lancaster, and Postmaster Gen.; called to House of Lords
in his father's barony 1801: *m.* 1801, Mary Henrietta Juliana, who *d.* 1862, dau. of 5th Duke of
Leeds; *d.* 1826; *s.* by his son [8] HENRY THOMAS, 3rd Earl; *b.* 1804; was Lord-Lieut. of
Sussex : *m.* 1828, Lady Mary Brudenell, who *d.* 1867, dau. of 6th Earl of Cardigan; *d.* March
1886 ; *s.* by his son [9] WALTER JOHN, 4th Earl ; *b.* 1838 ; M.P. for Lewes (L) 1865-74 : *m.*
1861, Elizabeth Mary, who *d.* 1911, dau. of the late Hon. Sir John Duncan Bligh, K.C.B. ; *d.*
1902 ; *s.* by his brother [10] *Rev.* FRANCIS GODOLPHIN, 5th Earl ; *b.* 1844: *m.* 1870, the Hon. Alice
Catt Glyn, who *d.* 1934, dau. of 1st Baron Wolverton : *d.* 1905 ; *s.* by his son [11] JOCELYN
BRUDENELL, *O.B.E.,* 6th Earl, *b.* 1871 ; a Public Works Loan Commr. 1904-26 : *m.* 1898, Ruth,

dau. of the late Francis William Buxton; *d.* Nov. 14th, 1926; *s.* by his el. son [12] FRANCIS GODOLPHIN HENRY, 7th Earl, *b.* 1905; *d.* Nov. 22, 1926; *s.* by his brother [13] JOHN BUXTON, 8th Earl, *b.* 1912; Capt. Scots Guards: *m.* 1940, Ursula, dau. of the late Walter de Pannwitz, of Hautekamp, Bennebroek, Holland; *d.* (killed on active ser. during European War) 1944; *s.* by his son [14] JOHN NICHOLAS, 9th Earl nd present peer; also Baron Pelham of Stanmer.

CHICHESTER, LORD BISHOP OF. (Kemp.)

Rt. Rev. ERIC WALDRAM KEMP, *DD*, son of Tom Kemp; *b.* April 27th, 1915; ed. at Brigg Gram. Sch., Lincs., Exeter Coll., Oxford (MA), and St. Stephen's House, Oxford; DD Oxford 1961; Librarian of Pusey House, Oxford 1941-46, Fellow and Chap. of Exeter Coll., Oxford 1946-69 and Dean of Worcester 1969-74; consecrated 99th Bishop of Chichester 1974: *m.* 1953, Leslie Patricia, da. of Kenneth Escott Kirk.

Patron of ninety-six livings, and of nine alternately, the three Archdeaconries of Chichester, Hastings, and Lewes, and the Prebends in his Cathedral (including the three Residentiaries).

This Bishopric was founded in the Isle of Selsey, in 680, by Wilfrid, 2nd Archbishop of York. Stigand, 23rd Prelate, removed the seat of the Bishopric to Chichester in 1071.

Episcopal Signature,—"Eric Cicestr:"

ARMS OF THE SEE,—Azure, Our Blessed Lord in judgment seated on His throne, His right hand up-raised or, His left hand holding an open book proper, and out of His mouth a two-edged sword, point to the sinister gules.

Palace,—Chichester, Sussex.   *Club,*—National Liberal.

CHILSTON, VISCOUNT. (Akers-Douglas.) [Viscount U.K. 1911.]

ERIC ALEXANDER AKERS-DOUGLAS, 3rd Viscount; *b.* Dec. 17th, 1910; *s.* 1947; ed. at Eton, and at Trin. Coll., Oxford; is Flight-Lieut. R.A.F. Vol. Reserve and patron of one living: *m.* 1955, Marion, who *d.* 1970, dau. of the late Capt. Charles William Howard, R.E.

Arms,—Quarterly: 1st and 4th argent, a man's heart gules, ensigned with an imperial crown and pierced by an arrow fessewise, the pheon to the dexter, proper; on a chief azure, three mullets of the field, *Douglas*; 2nd and 3rd, gules, three escallops or within a bordure argent, charged with eight acorns proper, *Akers*. **Crests**, —1st, an arm in armour embowed proper, garnished or, the gauntlet grasping a dagger also proper, *Douglas*; 2nd, an arm in armour embowed proper, garnished or, the gauntlet grasping a pennon barry of four azure and argent, *Akers*. **Supporters,**—Dexter, a horse argent, supporting a banner azure charged with three mullets also argent; *sinister*, a like horse supporting a similar banner ermine, charged with a man's heart gules, ensigned with an imperial crown, and pierced by an arrow fessewise, the pheon to the dexter, proper.

Wisdom and Truth.

Seats,—Chilston Park, Maidstone;   Craigs, near Dumfries.   *Club,*—Brooks's.

COLLATERAL BRANCHES LIVING.

Grandchildren of the late Lieut.-Col. the Hon. George Alexander Akers-Douglas, Roy. Fusiliers (infra):—

Issue of the late Capt. Ian Stanley Akers-Douglas, Berks Yeo., *b.* (Nov.) 1909, *d.* 1952: *m.* 1st, 1933, Joan Holroyd (from whom he obtained a divorce 1943), only child of Major Charles B. Toms, of 109, Oakwood Court, Kensington, W.14; 2ndly, 1945, Phyllis Rosemary (The Old Rectory, Upper Stondon, Henlow, Beds.) (who *m.* 2ndly, 1965, John Anthony Cobham Shaw [see By. Cobham), da. of the late Arthur David Clere Parsons [see E. Rosse, colls.]:—

(By 2nd m.) ALASTAIR GEORGE (Crofton Lodge, Lathingdon, Chelmsford, Essex), *b.* Sept. 1946: *m.* 1971, Juliet A., da. of Lt.-Col. Nigel Lovett, of The Old Rectory, Inwardleigh, Okehampton, Devon, and has issue living, Oliver Ian, *b.* 1973.——(By 1st m.) Jennifer, *b.* 1938: *m.* 1958, George David Henry Wiggin [see Wiggin, Bt., colls.].   *Residence,*—Newtown House, Newbury, Berks.——

(By 2nd m.) Diana, *b.* 1948: *m.* 1968, Simon Harrap, of Perryland, Bentley, Farnham, Hants.

Issue of the late Lt.-Col. the Hon. George Alexander Akers-Douglas, Roy. Fusiliers, 2nd son of 1st Viscount, *b.* 1878, *d.* 1955: *m.* (Jan.) 1909, Doris, who *d.* 1971, da. of Stanley Christopherson, formerly of Bramley, Surrey:—

Anthony George (Roe Downs, Medstead, Alton, Hants.) *b.* 1914; ed at Eton, Maj. (ret.) 13th/18th R.H.: *m.* 1941, Dorothy Louise, da. of the late Brig.-Gen. Moreton Foley Gage, DSO [see V. Gage, colls.], and has issue living, Adrian Anthony, *b.* 1943,—Francis Alexander Moreton, *b.* 1948: *m.* 1974, Julian Mary, da. of the Hon. John Warrender [see B. Bruntisfield],—Laura Dorothy, *b.* 1957.

PREDECESSORS.—[1] ARETAS Akers-Douglas, *G.B.E.*, *P.C.*, son of the late Rev. Aretas Akers, of Malling Abbey, Kent; *b.* 1851; Patronage Sec. to the Treasury June 1885 to Jan. 1886, July 1889 to Aug. 1892, and June to July 1895, First Commr of Works, with a seat in the Cabinet July 1895 to Aug. 1902, and Sec. of State for Home Depart. Aug. 1902 to Dec. 1905; assumed in 1875, by Roy. licence, the additional surname of Douglas; M.P. for E. Kent (*C*) 1880-85, and for St. Augustine's Div. of Kent 1885-1911; cr. *Baron Douglas of Baads*, co. Midlothian, and *Viscount Chilston*, of Boughton Malherbe, co. Kent (peerage of United Kingdom) 1911; *m.* 1875, Adeline, who *d.* 1929, dau. of Horatio Austen Smith, of Hayes Court, Kent; *d.* 1926; *s.* by his el. son [2] ARETAS, *G.C.M.G.*, *P.C.*, 2nd Viscount, *b.* 1876; was Envoy Extraor. and Min. Plen. at Vienna 1921-8, and at Budapest 1928-33, and Ambassador at Moscow 1933-8: *m.* 1903, Amy, who *d.* 1962, dau. of J. R. Jennings Bramley, R.H.A.; *d.* 1947; *s.* by his 2nd son [3] ERIC ALEXANDER, 3rd Viscount and present peer; also Baron Douglas of Baads.

CHOLMONDELEY, MARQUESS OF. (Cholmondeley.) [Marquess U.K. 1815.]

[Name and Title pronounced "**Chumley.**"]

GEORGE HUGH CHOLMONDELEY, *MC*, 6th Marquess; *b.* April 24th, 1919; *s.* 1968; ed. at Eton, and Camb. Univ.; late Maj. Grenadier Guards; a DL of Cheshire; Joint Hereditary Lord Great Chamberlain of England (acting for reign of Queen Elizabeth II since 1966); 1939-45 War in Middle East, Italy, France, Germany, with 1st R. Dragoons (MC): *m.* 1947, Lavina, da. of the late Lt.-Col. John Leslie, DSO, MC, of Brancaster, Norfolk, and has issue.

Arms,—Gules, in chief two esquires' helmets argent, and in base a garb or. **Crest,—**A demi-griffin segreant sable, beaked, winged, and membered or, holding between the claws a helmet as in the arms. **Supporters,—**Dexter, a griffin sable, beaked, winged, and membered or, langued gules; sinister, a wolf or, collared vaire, armed and langued gules.

Virtue is the safest helmet.

Seat,—Cholmondeley Castle, Malpas, Cheshire. *Clubs,*—Turf, Cavalry, Guards'.

SON LIVING.
DAVID GEORGE PHILIP (*Earl of Rocksavage*), *b.* June 27th, 1960; appointed a Page of Honour to H.M. the Queen 1974.

DAUGHTERS LIVING.
Lady Rose Aline, *b.* 1948.
Lady Margot Lavinia, *b.* 1950.
Lady Caroline Mary, *b.* 1952.

BROTHER LIVING.
Lord (George) John, *b.* 1920; ed. at Eton, and at Magdalene Coll., Camb.; Lieut. (**A**) R.N.V.R, (retired): *m.* 1957, Cristina, only dau. of the late Giorgio Solari, and has issue living, Charles George, *b.* 1959.—Joanna Antonia, *b.* 1958. *Residence,*—22, Hyde Park Gardens, W.2. *Clubs,*—Bath, Buck's, Turf, Pratt's, City of London.

SISTER LIVING.
Lady Aline Caroline, *b.* 1916. *Residence,*—Flat 5, 6, Strathearn Place, W2.

WIDOW LIVING OF FIFTH MARQUESS.
SYBIL RACHEL BETTY CÉCILE, *CBE* (*Dowager Marchioness of Cholmondeley*) (12, Kensington Palace Gdns., W8; Houghton Hall, King's Lynn), da. of Sir Edward Albert Sassoon, 2nd Bt. (cr. 1890) ext.; 1914-18 War as Assist. Prin. WRNS; 1939-45 War as Sup. WRNS; CBE (Mil.) 1946: *m.* 1913, the 5th Marquess, who *d.* 1968.

COLLATERAL BRANCH LIVING.
Issue of the late Lord George Hugo CHOLMONDELEY, *O.B.E.*, *M.C.*, son of 4th Marquess, *b.* 1887, *d.* 1958: *m.* 1st, 1911, Clara Elizabeth, who *d.* 1925 (having obtained a divorce 1921), dau. of Charles Henry Taylor, of Washington, U.S.A. and formerly wife of Major John Alexander Stirling, D.S.O., M.C.; 2ndly, 1921 (m. diss. 1948), Ina Marjorie Gwendoline (LOWTHER), *OBE* (who *d.* 1969, having obtained a divorce 1948), da. of the late Rev. Canon Raymond Percy Pelly [Pelly, Bt., colls.]; 3rdly, 1948, Diana, who *d.* 1965, da. of the late Hon. Rupert Evelyn Beckett [B. Grimthorpe, colls.], and widow of Albany Kennet Charlesworth, M.C. [Laurie, Bt.]:—
By 1st marriage) Irene, *b.* 1913: *m.* 1947, Stanislaw Falkowski, M.D., late Major R.A.M.C., who assumed 19—, the names of Stephen Falkland, and has issue living, Priscilla Susan, *b.* 1948. *Residence,*—Magny, par Ferney-Voltaire, Ain (OI), France.

PREDECESSORS.—Robert Cholmondeley; cr. a *Baronet* 1611, *Viscount Cholmondeley, of Kells* (peerage of Ireland) 1628, *Baron Cholmondeley*, of Wiche Malbank (peerage of England) 1645 and *Earl of Leinster* (peerage of England) 1646; *d. s. p.* 1659, when the honours became extinct and his estates passed to his nephew [1] ROBERT Cholmondeley; cr. *Viscount Cholmondeley, of Kells*, 1661; *d.* 1681; *s.* by his son [2] HUGH, 2nd Viscount: cr. *Baron Cholmondeley*, of Namptwich (peerage of England) 1689, with remainder to his brother George, and *Viscount Malpas* and *Earl of Cholmondeley* (peerage of Great Britain) 1706, with similar remainder: *d.* unmarried 1724; *s.* by his brother [3] GEORGE, 2nd Earl, who had previously been cr. *Baron Newborough*, of Newborough, co. Wexford (peerage of Ireland) 1715, and *Baron Newburgh* in the Isle of Anglesey (peerage of Great Britain) 1716; a distinguished military officer; commanded Horse Guards at battle of the Boyne; *d.* 1733; *s.* by his son [4] GEORGE, *K.B.*, *P.C.*, 3rd Earl; M.P. for East Looe 1724 and Windsor 1727; successively Master of the Robes; Chancellor of Duchy of Lancaster, Keeper of Privy Seal, Paymaster Gen., and Treasurer of War for Ireland; *d.* 1770; *s.* by his grandson [5] GEORGE JAMES, *K.G.*, 4th Earl; *b.* 1749; was Lord Steward of the Household; cr. *Earl of Rocksavage* and *Marquess of Cholmondeley* (peerage of United Kingdom) 1815; *d.* 1827; *s.* by his son [6] GEORGE HORATIO, *P.C.*, 2nd

Marquess; b. 1792; summoned to House of Lords in his father's Barony of Newborough 1821; s. his mother as Joint Hereditary Great Chamberlain of England 1838; d. s. p. 1870; s. by his brother [7] WILLIAM HENRY HUGH, 3rd Marquess; b. 1800; sat as M.P., for Castle Rising 1822-32, and for S. Hampshire (C) 1852-57; d. 1884; s. by his grandson [8] GEORGE HENRY HUGH (son of the late Charles George Cholmondeley, by Susan Caroline, who d. 1891, da. of Sir George Dashwood, 4th Bt.), PC, 4th Marquess, b. 1858; Joint Hereditary Lord Great Chamberlain (acted for reign of King Edward VII): m. 1879, Winifred Ida, OBE, who d. 1938, da. of the late Col. Sir Robert Nigel Fitzhardinge Kingscote, KCB, of Kingscote, Wotton-under-Edge [E. Howe]; d. 1923; s. by his son [9] GEORGE HORATIO CHARLES, GCVO, 5th Marquess b. 1883; Joint Hereditary Lord Great Chamberlain (acted for reign of King Edward VII, and for reign of Queen Elizabeth II 1952-66): m. 1913, Sybil Rachel Betty Cécile, CBE, da. of Sir Edward Albert Sassoon, 2nd Bt. (cr. 1890) ext.; d. 1968; s. by his son [10] GEORGE HUGH, 6th Marquess, and present peer; also Earl of Rocksavage, Earl of Cholmondeley, Viscount Malpas, Baron Cholmondeley, Baron Newborough, and Baron Newburgh.

CHORLEY, BARON.　(Chorley.)　[Baron U.K. 1945.]

PROPOSITI TENAX

Tenacious of purpose.

ROBERT SAMUEL THEODORE CHORLEY, Q.C., 1st Baron, son of Richard Fisher Chorley, of Kendal; b. May 29th, 1895; ed. at Kendal Sch., and at Queen's Coll., Oxford (B.A. 1916, M.A. 1922); Bar. Inner Temple 1920, and a Q.C. 1961; was a Junior Clerk in Foreign Office 1916-17, in Min. of Labour 1917-19, Professor of Commercial Law, Univ. of London 1930-49, a Principal, Home Office 1940-41, Assist. Sec., Min. of Home Security 1941-2, Dep. Regional Commr. for Civil Defence (N.-W. Region) 1942-4, a Member of Committee on National Parks 1945, and of Roy. Commn. on Justices of the Peace 1946, Chm. of Committee on Salaries of Higher Civil Servants 1948, and a Lord-in-Waiting to HM 1946-50; Pres. of Institute for Study and Treatment of Delinquency 1956-72; Pres. of Commons and Footpaths Preservation So., Vice-Pres. of Council for Protection of Rural England, and of Friends of the Lake District, ex-Pres. of Asso. of Univ. Teachers, and a JP for Westmorland (Chm. of Quarter Sessions 1945-68); 1918 War with Cheshire Regt., and RASC; cr. Baron Chorley, of Kendal, co. Westmorland (peerage of United Kingdom) 1945: m. 1925, Katharine Campbell, only da. of Edward Hopkinson, DSc, of Alderley Edge, Cheshire, and has issue.

Arms,—Per chevron argent and vert, in chief two blue-bottles proper and in base a fountain. Crest,—In front of two torches in saltire or and inflamed, a teazle stalked and leaved proper. Supporters,—On either side a buzzard proper.

Residence,—The Rookery, Stanmore, Middlesex.　Club,—Alpine.

SONS LIVING.

Hon. ROGER RICHARD EDWARD (69, Bedford Gdns., W8; Alpine Club), b. Aug. 14th, 1930; ed. at Stowe, and at Gonville and Caius Coll., Camb.: m. 1964, Ann, yr. da. of A. S. Debenham, of Ingatestone, Essex, and has issue living, Nicholas Rupert Debenham, b. 1966,—Christopher Robert Hopkinson, b. 1968.

Hon. Geoffrey Patrick Hopkinson, b. 1933; ed. at Stowe, and at New Coll., Oxford: m. 1955 (m. diss. 1972), Daria Antonia Maria, da. of the Marquis de Merindof, of 34, Gordon Place, W8, and Villa Roussalka, San Remo, Italy and has issue living, Alexandra Maria, b. 1956,—Elizabeth Henrietta Marianne, b. 1961. Residence,—40, Castelnau Mansions, SW13.

DAUGHTER LIVING.

Hon. Gillian Theodore Marianne, b. 1929; ed. at Liverpool Coll. for Girls, and at St. Anne's Coll., Oxford: m. 1965, F. Godfrey Goodwin, of 29, Chalcot Sq., NW1, and has issue living, Robert Theodore Chorley, b. 1969.

CHURCHILL, VISCOUNT.　(Spencer.)　[Viscount U.K. 1902.]

God defend the right.

VICTOR GEORGE SPENCER, 3rd Viscount; b. (posthumous) July 31st, 1934; s. 1973; ed. at Eton, and New Coll., Oxford (MA); Lt. Scots Gds., 1953-55.

Arms.—Quarterly argent and gules, in the 2nd and 3rd quarters a frette or, over all on a bend sable, three escallops of the first. Crest,—Out of a ducal crest coronet or, a griffin's head, between two wings expanded argent, gorged with a bar gemelle gules. Supporters—Dexter, a griffin wings elevated per fesse argent and or, gorged with a collar or, charged with three escallops sable, line reflexed over the back also or; sinister, a wyvern wings elevated gules, gorged with a collar or, charged with three escallops sable.

Residence,—6, Cumberland Mansions, George St., W1.

HALF-SISTER LIVING

Hon. Victoria Ivy Louise, *b.* 1897 : *m.* 1920, Capt. the Hon. Cecil Henry Brassey, formerly 1st Life Guards, who *d.* 1949, el. son of 1st Baron Brassey of Apethorpe. *Residence,*—Worton, Devizes, Wilts.

SISTER LIVING

Hon. Sarah Faith Georgina, *b.* 1931: *m.* 1951, Richard John Palmer, JP, and has issue living, David Charles, *b.* 1955,—James Nicholas, *b.* 1963,—Christopher Richard, *b.* 1967,—Caroline Mary, *b.* 1952. *Residence,*—Queen Anne's Mead, Swallowfield, Berks.

COLLATERAL BRANCHES LIVING. (*In remainder to Barony only.*)

Granddaughter of the late Col. John Winston Thomas MUNRO-SPENCER, who assumed the additional surname of Munro 1911, son of the late Lieut.-Col. the Hon. George Augustus Spencer, 2nd son of 1st Baron :—
Issue of the late Capt. Almeric Stuart John Spencer, *b.* 1885, *d.* 1960 : *m.* 1912, Phyllis Margaret (who *d.* 1971, having obtained a divorce 1928), da. of the late Charles Richard Rivers, of 20, Palmeira Square, Hove, and Orrell, Lancashire:—
Synolda Joan Margaret (Phoenix House, Hinton St. George, Crewkerne, Somerset), *b.* 1914: *m.* 1949, Capt. Cecil Campbell Hardy, DSO, RN, who *d.* 1963, and has issue living, Charles Rupert Almeric, *b.* 1951; ed. at Wellington and Magdalene Coll., Camb.,—Theodora Margaret, *b.* 1953.

Grandsons of the late Lieut.-Col. Augustus Campbell Spencer (infra):—
Issue of the late Col. Richard Augustus Spencer, D.S.O., O.B.E., *b.* 1888, *d.* 1956: *m.* 1925, Maud Evelyn (of Flat 16, Melton Court, S.W.3), dau. of the late Lieut.-Col. Henry Lushington Ramsay [see E. Dalhousie, colls.]:—
RICHARD HARRY RAMSAY (12, Neville Terr., SW7), *b.* Oct. 11th, 1926; h.p. to Barony of Churchill; late Lt. Coldm. Gds.; ARIBA: *m.* 1958, Antoinette Rose-Marie, dau of Godefroy de Charriere, of Preverenges, Lausanne, Switzerland, and has issue living, Michael Richard de Charriere, *b.* 1960,—David Anthony, *b.* 1970.——Charles Geoffrey Campbell (of Stokke Common, Marlborough, Wilts.; Guards' Club), *b.* 1928; late Lt. Coldstream Guards; served in Malaya 1948-50, and Kenya 1954-56: *m.* 1964, Cherry Elizabeth, da. of William Carlyle Clarke.

Grandsons of the late Gen. the Hon. Sir Augustus Almeric Spencer, G.C.B., 3rd son of 1st Baron :—
Issue of the late Lieut.-Col. Augustus Campbell Spencer, *b.* 1851, *d.* 1912: *m.* 1886, Hilda, who *d.* 1952, dau. of the late Alexander William Thorold Grant-Thorold, of Cosgrove Hall, Northants :—
Edward Almeric, *O.B.E., b.* 1892 ; ed. at Wellington Coll.; Lieut.-Col. late R.A. ; European War 1914 in France and Belgium (wounded, 1914 star, two medals), N.-W. Europe 1944-5 (despatches, O.B.E.); Coronation medal (1937); OBE (Mil) 1945: *m.* 1918, Elsie Winifred, who *d.* 1969, da. of the late Arthur Macan, DL, of Drumcashel, co. Louth, and has issue living, Guinevere Elsie (The Old Rectory, Buriton, Petersfield, Hants), *b.* 1920: *m.* 1945, Charles Arthur Wellesley Williamson, MC, TD, late Major Sherwood Foresters, and has issue living, Richard Almeric Spencer *b.* 1949; ed. at Winchester: *m.* 1970, June, da. of Wilfrid Mansfield, Michael Anthony Wellesley *b.* 1952,—Francis Charles Fitzroy *b.* 1959, Patrick Alexander Campbell *b.* 1960, Sarah Lavinia *b.* 1946. *Residence,*—1, The Square, Prinsted, Emsworth, Hants. *Club,*—United Service.

Grandchildren of the late Brig.-Gen. John Almeric Walter Spencer, CMG, DSO, son of the late Capt. William Francis Spencer, son of the late Rev. the Hon. William Henry Spencer, 4th son of 1st Baron:—
Issue of the late John Lawrence Spencer, *b.* 1917, *d.* 1967: *m.* 1943, Jane Lilian (Chyllas, Sedbergh, Yorks.), da. of the late Col. Granville Duff, MC, of Heydon, Norfolk:—
John William James, *b.* 1957.——Caroline Mary, *b.* 1948.

Granddaughter of the late Col. Almeric George Spencer, son of the late Rev. the Hon. William Henry Spencer (ante):—
Issue (by 2nd marriage) of the late Lieut.-Col. Almeric Arthur William Spencer, *b.* 1874, *d.* 1934: *m.* 1st, 1907, Sybil (from whom he obtained a divorce 1927), dau. of Frederick William Lawson, formerly of Oaklands, Adel, Leeds; 2ndly, 1930, Charlotte (who *m.* 2ndly, 1941, Cecil Trevor Hamilton Whiteside, MC, MRCS, who *d.* 1965 [see B. Belhaven, colls.]), da. of the late Rev. John Lesley Parker, V. of Lanteglos, Fowey:—
Ann Frances SPENCER (Lanescott, Par, Cornwall), *b.* 1931; has resumed her maiden name of Spencer: *m.* 1957 (m. annulled 1963), the Rev. Leslie Vandernoll Wright.

Grandchildren of the late Charles Francis Henry Spencer, el. son of the late Rev. the Hon. Charles Frederick Octavius Spencer, 9th son of 1st Baron:—
Issue of the late Col. Francis Elmhirst Spencer, DSO, MC, *b.* 1881, *d.* 1972: *m.* 1916, Augusta (Vera), who *d.* 1956, da. of the late Col. Arthur Tracey, formerly RGA:—
Francis Tracey (882, Island Rd., Victoria, BC., V8S 2T9, Canada), *b.* 1917: ed. at Blundell's Sch.; Capt. (ret.) York and Lancaster Regt.: *m.* 1962, Diana, el. da. of Dennis Haines, of Wattisfield Croft, Suffolk, and has issue living, Philip Henry, *b.* 1966.——Joan Elizabeth, *b.* 1921; late QARNNS (Reserve): *m.* 1949, Surg.-Cdr. Geoffrey Norman Shell, RN (ret.), of Gomorin, Court Woods, Newton Ferrers, Plymouth, and has issue living, Peter Geoffrey, *b.* 1951; ed. at Haileybury,—David Spencer, *b.* 1954; ed. at Milton Abbey.

Granddaughter of Major Henry Montagu Spencer, 2nd son of the late Rev. the Hon. Charles Frederick Octavius Spencer (ante):—
Issue of the late Henry Beresford Spencer, Lieut. Tank Corps, *b.* 1881, *d.* (killed in action during European War) 1918 : *m.* 1908, Dorothy Acton, who *d.* 1950, dau of the late Rev. Frederick Farrer of Bravfield, Bucks:—
Audrey Joan, *b.* 1911 : *m.* 1939, Major John Alexander Sneyd Hawkins, R.A., and has issue living, David John, *b.* 1940,—Timothy Spencer, *b.* 1943,—Denzil, *b.* 1946. *Residence,*—Taw Leat, Sticklepath, Okehampton, Devon.

PREDECESSORS.—[1] *Lord* FRANCIS ALMERIC Spencer, *D.C.L.,* 2nd son of 4th Duke of Marlborough; *b.* 1779 ; cr. *Baron Churchill,* of Wychwood, co. Oxford (peerage of United Kingdom) 1815: *d.* 1845; *s.* by his son [2] FRANCIS GEORGE, *D.C.L.,* 2nd Baron; *b.* 1802; *m.* 1849, Lady Jane Conyngham, *V.A.,* who *d.* 1900, dau. of 2nd Marquess Conyngham ; *d.* Nov. 24th, 1886; *s.* by his son [3] VICTOR ALBERT FRANCIS CHARLES, *G.C.V.O.,* 3rd Baron, *b.* 1864: was a Page of Honour to Queen Victoria 1876-81, and a Lord-in-Waiting to Queen Victoria 1889-92, and 1895-1901, and to King Edward VII. 1901-5 ; Chm. of Great Western Railway Co., and of British Overseas Bank ; Master of the Buckhounds 1900, Lord Chamberlain 1902, and Master of the Robes at Coronation of King George V. 1911 ; K.C.V.O. 1900, G.C.V.O. 1902; cr. *Viscount Churchill,* of Rolleston, co. Leicester (peerage of United Kingdom) 1902 : *m.* 1st, 1887, Lady Verena Maud, *V.A.* who *d.* 1938 (from whom he had obtained a divorce for desertion in the Scottish Courts 1927), da. of 3rd Earl of Lonsdale; 2ndly, 1927, Christine McRae, who *d.* 1972, having *m.* 2ndly, 1937 (m. diss. (Reno) 1938), Lt.-Col. Ralph Heyward Isham, CBE, who *d.* 1955, and 3rdly, 1939, Sir Lancelot Oliphant, KCMG, CB, who *d.* 1965, da. of William Sinclair; *d.* 1934; *s.* by his son [4] VICTOR ALEXANDER, 2nd Viscount, *b.* 1890; FRAS: *m.* 1st, 1916, Kathleen, who *d.* 1943, da. of the late Hon. Robert Beaven, formerly Premier of Victoria, BC, Canada, and widow of Capt. Stanley Venn Ellis, RN; 1949, Joan, who *d.* 1947, da. of the late Joseph Baron Black; *d.* 1973; *s.* by his half-brother [5] VICTOR GEORGE, 3rd Viscount and present peer; also Baron Churchill.

CHURSTON, BARON. (Yarde-Buller.) [Baron U.K. 1858, Bt. G.B. 1790.]

AQVILA NON CAPIT·MUSCAS

The eagle does not catch flies.

Residence,—Woodcote, St. Andrews, Guernsey.

RICHARD FRANCIS ROGER YARDE-BULLER, *V.R.D.*, 4th Baron and 6th Baronet; *b.* Feb. 12th, 1910; *s.* 1930; Lieut.-Com. R.N.V.R.; is patron of two livings; bore one of the Golden Spurs at Coronations of King George VI. and Queen Elizabeth II : *m.* 1st, 1933, Elizabeth Mary (who *d.* 1951,and from whom he had obtained a divorce 1943), dau. of Lieut.-Col. William Baring Du Pre, J.P., D.L., of Wilton Park, Beaconsfield. Bucks; 2ndly, 1949, Sandra, da. of Percy Needham, and formerly wife of (i) Claud Harold Bertram Arthur Griffiths and (ii) Jack Dunfee and has issue by 1st marriage.

Arms,—Quarterly: 1st and 4th sable, on a cross argent quarterly, pierced of the field, four eagles displayed of the first, *Buller;* 2nd and 3rd argent, a chevron gules, between three water-bougets sable,*Yarde.* *Crest,*—A Saracen's head couped, proper. *Supporters,*—*Dexter,* an ostrich proper, in the beak a horse-shoe or; *sinister,* an eagle sable.

SON LIVING. (By 1st marriage.)

Hon. JOHN FRANCIS (Yowlestone House, Puddington, Tiverton, S. Devon; *b.* Dec. 29th, 1934; ed. at Eton; late 2nd Lt. RHG: *m.* 1973, Alexandra Joana, only da. of Anthony Contomichalos, of 23, Eaton Place, SW1, and has issue living, Benjamin Francis Anthony, *b.* 1974. Buck's and White's Clubs).

DAUGHTER LIVING. (By 1st marriage.)

Hon. Nicole, *b.* 1936: *m.* 1st, 1958 (marriage dissolved 1962), Richard Wilfred Beavoir Berens; 2ndly, 1963, Michael Russell, of The Chantry House, Wilton, Salisbury, and has issue living, (by 1st marriage) Thomas Richard, *b.* 1960,—Jessica Primrose, *b.* 1959,—(by 2nd marriage), Francis, ꞋꞋ. 1966,—Alexander, *b.* 1969,—Lorna, *b.* 1963.

ꞋꞋSISTERS LIVING.

Hon. Joan Barbara, *b.* 1908 : *m.* 1st, 1927, Wing-Com. Thomas Loel Evelyn Bulkeley Guinness, O.B.E., Auxiliary Air Force (Reserve), who obtained a divorce 1936 ; 2ndly, 1936 (divorce 1949), Aly Khan, who *d.* 1960, son of HH the late Rt. Hon. the Aga Khan, GCSI, GCIE, GCVO, and has issue living, (by 2nd m.) *HH Prince* Karim (*HH the Aga Khan*) (1, Rue des Ursins, Paris IV), *b.* 1936; ed. at Le Rosey, and at Harvard Univ.; *s.* his grandfather as 4th Aga Khan 1957; is spiritual leader and Imam of Ismaili Muslims all over the world; received personal title of Highness 1957: *m.* 1969, Sarah Frances, only da. of Lt.-Col. A. E. Croker Poole, of 95, Eaton Sq., SW1, and formerly wife of Lord James Charles Crichton-Stuart [see M. Bute], and has issue living, *Prince* Rahim *b.* 1971, *Princess* Zahra *b.* 1970,—*Prince* Amyn, *b.* 1937. *Residence,*—8, Hobart Place, SW1.

Hon. Denise Margaret *b.* 1916: *m.* 1941 (m. diss. 1954), as his second wife, the 5th Baron Ebury, who *d.* 1957. *Residence,*—Barton's Lodge, Eversholt, Bletchley, Bucks.

Hon. Lydia, *b.* 1917 : *m.* 1st, 1938, Capt. Ian Archibald de Hoghton Lyle, Black Watch, who *d.* (killed in action during European War) 1942, el. son of Sir Archibald Moir Park Lyle, 2nd Bt., M.C.; 2ndly, 1947, the 13th Duke of Bedford, from whom she obtained a divorce 1960. *Residence,*—Little Ribsden, Windlesham, Bagshot, Surrey.

ꞋWIDOW LIVING OF SON OF THIRD BARON.

Gwendolen, dau. of the late Rev. Charles Roots, of Heathfield, Sussex: *m.* 1939, the Hon. John Reginald Henry Yarde-Buller, who *d.* 1962, and has issue living [see colls., infra]. *Residence,* Le Vallon, Mont Félard, Jersey.

COLLATERAL BRANCHES LIVING.

Issue of the late Hon. John Reginald Henry Yarde-Buller, 2nd son of 3rd Baron, *b.* 1915, *d.* 1962: *m.* 1939, Gwendolen (ante), dau. of the late Rev. Charles Roots, of Heathfield, Sussex:—
Roger Charles John, *b.* 1942.——Anthony Reginald Lawrence, *b.* 1946.

Issue of the late Hon. Geoffrey Yarde-Buller, brother of 2nd Baron, *b.* 1861, *d.* 1952: *m.* 1892, Olegaria Venancia, dau. of Don Florencio Alvarez, formerly of Estancias, San Justo Feliceano, Entre Rios, Argentina:—
John, *b.* 1893.——Geoffry (of Monte Caseros, Argentina), *b.* 1894: *m.* 1919, Hortensia, who *d.* 1957, dau. of Leon Naboulet, of Parana, Argentina, and has issue living, Norberto (of Las Heras 1601, Buenos Aires), *b.* 1922: *m.* 1946, Yolanda, dau. of Carlos Devillier, of Florida, Argentina, and has issue living, Daniel *b.* 1954, Norberto *b.* 1959, Rita, *b.* 19 —, Susana *b.* 19 —,—Eduardo (Calles Mármol y Pringles C18 Dto. 9, Lomas del Mirador San Junto, Pcia. de Buenos Aires, Argentina), *b.* 1926: *m.* 1953, Isabel Ester, da. of Francisco Hinojosa, of Buenos Aires, and has issue living, Liliana Beatriz *b.* 1955,—Lilian, *b.* 1920: *m.* 19 —, Oswaldo Alizeri, and has issue living, Estela *b.* 1945, Diana *b.* 1947,—Delia, *b.* 1932: *m.* 1949, Don Rafael M. Parravicini Piaggio, of 843, Avenue Uruguay, Montevideo, Uruguay, and has issue living, Octavio *b.* 1950, Rafael *b.* 1952, Denisse Oriental *b.* 1959,—Dorys, *b.* 19 —,—Estella, *b.* 19 —.——Edmund, *b.* 1897.——Henry, *b.* 1899.——Manuel, *b.* 1901.——Albert (of Urquiza, y Albardi, Cuajari (Entre Rios), Argentina), *b.* 1903: *m.* 1942, Ella Cristina, da. of Dugaldo Farquharson.——Olga, *b.* 1896.——Agnes, *b.* 1903.——Charlotte, *b.* 1906.

(In remainder to Baronetcy only.)

Descendants of Sir Edward Manningham-Buller (who assumed the additional surname and arms of Manningham) 3rd son of 2nd Bt. [see V. Dilhorne].

PREDECESSORS.—[1] *Sir* FRANCIS Buller, *K.B.*, *K.C.*, a very eminent lawyer and a Justice of the Common Pleas; cr. a *Baronet* 1790; *d.* 1800; *s.* by his son [2] *Sir* FRANCIS, 2nd Bt., M.P. for Totnes; assumed the additional and final surname of Yarde by Roy. licence 1800; *d.* 1833; *s.* by his son [3] JOHN, *D.C.L.*, 3rd Bt.: M.P. for S. Devon (*C*) 1835-58; assumed the surname of Yarde-Buller by Roy. licence 1860; cr. *Baron Churston*, of Churston Ferrers, and Lupton, Devon (peerage of United Kingdom) 1858; *d.* 1871; *s.* by his grandson [4] JOHN, 2nd Baron, son of the Hon. John, el. son of 1st Baron, by Charlotte, dau. of Edward Sacheverell Chandos-Pole, of Radborne, co. Derby, *b.* 1846: *m.* 1872, the Hon. Barbara, who *d.* 1924, dau. of the late Adm. Sir Hastings Reginald Yelverton, G.C.B., and of the late Barbara (in her own right) Baroness Grey de Ruthyn, widow of 2nd Marquess of Hastings; *d.* 1910; *s.* by his son [5] JOHN REGINALD LOPES, *M.V.O.*, *O.B.E.*, 3rd Baron; *b.* 1873; an A.D.C. to Viceroy of India (Baron Curzon of Kedleston) 1902-3, and A.D.C. to Inspector-Gen. of the Forces (F.-M. H.R.H. the Duke of Connaught) 1904-6; sometime Inspector of Q.M.G. Sers.: *m.* 1907, Jessie (who *d.* 1960, and from whom he had obtained a divorce 1928), only dau. of the late Alfred Smither, *d.* 1930; *s.* by his son [6] RICHARD FRANCIS ROGER, 4th Baron and present peer.

CITRINE, BARON. (Citrine.) [Baron U.K. 1946.]

Strive for right.

WALTER MCLENNAN CITRINE, *G.B.E.*, *P.C.*, 1st Baron, son of Alfred Citrine, of Wallasey; *b.* Aug. 22nd, 1887; Hon. LL.D. Manchester 1955; was Assist. Gen. Sec. of Electrical Trades Union 1920-23, Assist. Sec. of Trades Union Congress 1924-5, and Gen. Sec. 1926-46, a Member of National Coal Board and Chm. of Miners' Welfare Commn. 1946-7, and of Central Electricity Authority 1947-57, and Pres. of Electrical Development Asso. 1948-52, and of Electrical Research Asso. 1950-2, and again 1956-7; is a Companion of Institution of Electrical Engineers, and a Member of Directing Committee (Pres. 1955), of Union Internationale des Producteurs et Distributeurs d'Energie Electrique; Pres. of International Federation of Trade Unions 1928-45, a Member of Govt. Economic Advisory Council 1930-33, of Roy. Commn. to W. Indies 1938-9, of Cinematograph Films Council, 1938-48, and of Executive Committee of Red Cross and St. John War Organization 1939-46, a Trustee of Imperial Relations Trust 1937-49, and Nuffield Trust for the Forces of the Crown 1939-46, Visiting Fellow, Nuffield Coll. 1939-47, and a Member of Consultative Council to Treasury 1940-46; Chm. of Committee on Regional Boards (Munitions Production) 1942; Pres. of World Federation of Trade Unions 1945-6; author of "British Trade Unions", "Men and Work", "Two Careers", and other publications; cr. KBE (Civil) 1935, PC 1940, *Baron Citrine*, of Wembley, co. Middlesex (peerage of U.K.) 1946, and GBE (Civil) 1958: *m.* 1913, Doris Helen, who *d.* 1973, da. of Edgar Slade, and has issue. 🔳🔳🔳

Arms,— Argent, on waves of the sea in base, an ancient three-masted ship in full sail proper, on a chief gules a Saxon crown between two seaxes points downwards or, the dexter in bend, the sinister in bend sinister. *Crest,*—A cubit arm habited azure cuffed argent, the hand grasping a citrine proper. *Supporters,*—*Dexter,* an alsatian wolfhound proper, on the shoulder a terrestial globe or, charged with a human heart; *sinister,* a lion proper, on the shoulder a torteau charged with a spade and a pickaxe in saltire and a pen-nib in pale or.

Residence,—Gorse Cottage, Berry Head, Brixham, S. Devon.

SONS LIVING.

Hon. NORMAN ARTHUR, *LL.B.*, *b.* Sept. 27th, 1914; ed. at Univ. Coll. Sch.; LL.B. London 1938; admitted a Solicitor 1937; is author of legal textbooks and other works; was Legal Adviser to Trades Union Congress 1946-51; European War 1940-45 as Lieut. R.N.V.R.: *m.* 1939, Kathleen Alice, dau. of the late George Chilvers, of Saxmundham, Suffolk, and has issue living, Patricia Deirdre Angela *b.* 1939. *Residence,*— Gorse Cottage, Berry Head, Brixham, S. Devon.

Hon. Ronald Eric, *M.R.C.S.*, *L.R.C.P.*, *b.* 1919; ed. at Univ. Coll. Sch., and at Univ. Coll., London: *m.* 1945, Mary, dau. of Reginald Williams, of Wembley, Middlesex. *Residence,*—Paihia, Bay of Islands, North Island, New Zealand.

CLANCARTY, EARL OF. (Le Poer Trench.) Sits as VISCOUNT (U.K. 1823).
[Earl I. 1803.]

GREVILLE SIDNEY ROCHFORT LE POER TRENCH, 7th Earl, and Marquis of Heusden in The Netherlands; *b.* Dec. 10th, 1902; *s.* 1971; ed. at RNCS Osborne and Dartmouth: *m.* 1926, Beatrice Georgiana, yst. da. of the late Capt. James Gordon Miller, of Thurlow Hall, Suffolk. [The 7th Earl *d.* Sept. 18th, 1975].

Arms.—Quarterly: 1st and 4th argent, a lion passant gules, between three fleurs-de-lis azure, on a chief azure, a sun in splendour, *Trench;* 2nd and 3rd argent, a chief indented sable, *Le Poer.* Over all an escutcheon or, ensigned with the coronet of a Marquis of the Netherlands and charged with a wheel of six spokes gules. Crests.—1st, a dexter arm embowed in armour, the hand grasping a scimitar proper; 2nd, a lion rampant or, imperially crowned, holding in the dexter fore paw a naked sword argent, pommel and hilt gold, and in the sinister a sheaf of arrows also or; 3rd, a stag's head cabossed argent, attired or, and between the attires a crucifix. Supporters.—*Dexter*, a lion gules, semée of fleurs-de-lis or; *sinister*, a stag guardant proper, attired or, between the attires a crucifix, and supporting with the sinister fore paw a lance resting bendwise over the shoulder proper, and thereon a banner of the arms of Le Poer.

By counsel and prudence.

Residence,—Rivey House, Buckland, Faringdon, Berks.

DAUGHTERS LIVING OF SIXTH EARL.

Lady Maureen Isabel, *b.* 1923 : *m.* 1949, Christopher Colin Cooper, and has issue living, Simon Richard Colon, *b.* 1956,—Claudia, *b.* 1952. *Residence,*—El Madvonal, San Pedro de Alcantara, Malaga, Spain.

Lady Patricia Ann, *b.* 1928: *m.* 1946, Eugene Szpiganowicz, who *d.* 1965. *Residence,*—Flat 9, Eyol House, D'Oyly Carte Island, Weybridge, Surrey.

Lady Caragh Seymour, *b.* 1933: *m.* 1st, 1953 (m. diss. 1961), Lt.-Cdr. John Anthony Lake, RN; 2ndly, 1961, Capt. Arthur Jay Oken, USAF; 3rdly, 1966, Capt. Donald Van Horn Lee, USAF; 4thly, 19—; 5thly, 19—, Jefferson, of 218, Pershing Av., San Antonio, Texas, 78209, USA, and has issue living (by 1st m.) Henry John Challoner, *b.* 1955,—Catherine Challoner, *b.* 1957,—Jean Challoner, *b.* 1959.

HALF-BROTHER LIVING.

Hon. WILLIAM FRANCIS BRINSLEY (38, Chesterfield House, Chesterfield Gdns., W1Y 5TD), *b.* Sept. 18th, 1911; ed. at Nautical Coll., Pangbourne: *m.* 1st, 1940, Diana Joan (from whom he obtained a divorce 1974), da. of Sir William Robert Younger, 2nd Bt.; 2ndly, 1961, Mrs. Wilma Dorothy Belknap (from whom he obtained a divorce 1969), da. of S. R. Vermilyea; 3rdly, 1974, Mrs. Mildred Alleyn Spong, who *d.* 1975, da. of R. Bensusan.

WIDOW LIVING OF SIXTH EARL.

CORA MARIE EDITH (*Cora, Countess of Clancarty*) (Croft Cottage, Wheathampstead, Herts), da. of the late H. H. Spooner, of Thornton Hall, Surrey; *m.* 1919, as his 2nd wife, the 6th Earl, who *d.* 1971.

COLLATERAL BRANCHES LIVING.
Issue of the late Hon. Power Edward Ford Le Poer Trench, yst. son of 5th Earl, *b.* 1917, *d.* 1975: *m.* 19—, Jocelyn Louise Courtenay, who *d.* 1963:—
Nicholas Power Richard (97, Gresham Rd., Staines, Middlesex), *b.* 1952.——Caroline Mary Jessica, *b.* 1954.

Granddaughter of the late Adm. the Hon. William Le Poer Trench, 3rd son of 1st Earl:—
Issue of the late Frederick Netterville Le Poer Trench, *b.* 1844, *d.* 1893: *m.* 1878, Sarah Frances, who *d.* 1913, dau. of the late Very Rev. John Fiennes Twisleton Crampton, R. of Aughrim:—
Eileen May (c/o Fitzpatrick House, 13, Chesterton Hall Cres., Cambridge), *b.* 1883: *m.* 1910, the Rev. Allan Gairdner Wyon, who *d.* 1962, and has issue living, Venetia Madeline Le Poer, *b.* 1922: *m.* 1948, Philip Charles Watson, FRCS, of 19, Sibsey Rd., Boston, Lincs., and has issue living, Allan Philip *b.* 1949, Nicholas Andrew *b.* 1952, Mark Benjamin, *b.* 1957, Georgina Clare *b.* 1955, Zoë Elizabeth *b.* 1964.

Granddaughter of the late Charles Edward Le Poer Trench (*b.* 1838), son of the late Rev. John le Poer Trench, son of the late Adm. the Hon. William Le Poer Trench (ante):—
Issue of the late Charles Edward Le Poer Trench, *b.* 1877, *d.* 1935: *m.* 1909, Evelyn Agnes, who *d.* 1967, da. of the late H. J. Salmon, of St. Ives, Cornwall:—
Laura Joan, *b.* 1912: *m.* 1932, Lt.-Col. Charles Smith, RTR, of Green Willows, Timsway, Staines, Middx., and has issue living, Michael Charles, *b.* 1934,—Robert Sherwin, *b.* 1938.

PREDECESSORS.—[1] WILLIAM POWER KEATING Trench, *M.P.* for Galway 1768-97; cr. *Baron Kilconnel,* of Garbally, co. Galway (peerage of Ireland) 1793, *Viscount Dunlo* (peerage of Ireland) 1801, and *Earl of Clancarty* (peerage of Ireland) 1803: *d.* 1805; *s.* by his son [2] RICHARD, G.C.B., 2nd Earl; cr. *Baron Trench* (peerage of United Kingdom) 1815, and *Viscount Clancarty* (peerage of United Kingdom) 1823 ; appointed Ambassador to the Hague 1813; cr. *Marquis of Heusden,* in the Kingdom of the Netherlands 1818, and in 1824 received the royal permission to bear the title in this country; *d.* 1837; *s.* by his son [3] WILLIAM THOMAS, 3rd Earl; *b.* 1803: *m.* 1832, Lady Sarah Juliana Butler, dau. of 3rd Earl of Carrick; *d.* 1872; *s.* by his son [4] RICHARD SOMERSET, 4th Earl, *b.* 1834: *m.* 1866, Lady Adeliza Georgiana Hervey, who *d.* 1911, dau. of 2nd Marquess of Bristol; *d.* 1891; *s.* by his el. son [5] WILLIAM

FREDERICK, 5th Earl, *b.* 1868 : *m.* 1st, 1889, Isabel Maude Penrice, who *d.* 1906, dau. of John George Bilton, of Charlton, Kent; 2ndly, 1908, Mary Gwatkin, who *d.* 1974, dau. of the late W. F. Rosslewin Ellis, Bar.-at-Law, of Fulford, Yorkshire; *d.* 1929: *s.* by his son [6] RICHARD FREDERICK JOHN DONOUGH, 6th Earl, *b.* 1891: *m.* 1st, 1915, Edith Constance, (who *d.* 1950, and from whom he obtained a divorce 1918), da. of Maj. Alexander Albemarle Rawlinson; 2ndly, 1919, Cora Marie Edith, da. of the late H. H. Spooner, of Thornton Hall, Surrey; *d.* 1971; *s.* by his brother [7] Greville Sydney Rochfort, 7th Earl and present peer; also Viscount Dunlo, Viscount Clancarty, Baron Kilconnel, and Baron Trench.

CLANMORRIS, BARON. (Bingham.) [Baron I. 1800.]

JOHN MICHAEL WARD BINGHAM, 7th Baron ; *b.* Nov. 3rd, 1908 ; *s.* 1960 ; ed. at Cheltenham ; is a novelist "John Bingham " ; author of " My Name is Michael Sibley," " Five Roundabouts to Heaven," " The Third Skin," and other books : *m.* 1934, Madeleine Mary, dau. of the late Clement Ebel, of Copyhold Place, Cuckfield, Sussex, and has issue.

Arms.—Azure, a bend cottised between six crosses-patée or. **Crest.**—On a mount a falcon rising all proper. **Supporters.**—Two lions azure.

Residence,—24, Abingdon Villas, W.8.

SPES MEA CHRISTUS

Christ is my hope.

SON LIVING.
Hon. SIMON JOHN WARD (28, Norfolk Mansions, Prince of Wales Drive, SW11), *b.* Oct. 25th, 1937; ed. at Downside, and at Queen's Coll., Camb.: *m.* 1971, Gizella Maria, da. of Zandor Zverko, of Budapest, and has issue living, Lucy Katherine Grizella, *b.* 1974.

DAUGHTER LIVING.
Hon. Charlotte Mary Thérèse, *b.* 1942 ; ed. at The Priory, Haywards Heath, and the Sorbonne, Paris: *m.* 1964, Terence Joseph Brady, of 111, East Sheen Av., SW14, and has issue living, Matthew Joseph Mulligan, *b.* 1972,—Candida Marie Thérèse, *b.* 1965.

WIDOWS LIVING OF SONS OF FIFTH BARON.
Dorothea Minnie, dau. of the late J. A. Sinclair, Bar.-at-law, of Lahore: *m.* 1912, the Hon. Hugh Terence de Burgh Bingham, who *d.* 1957, and has issue living [see colls., infra]. Barbara Melville (Hilldrop House, Newcastle, Natal), yst. da. of the late Col. Charles Henry Joubert de la Terte, IMS: *m.* 1921, Capt. the Hon. George Roderick Bentinck Bingham, who *d.* 1972.

COLLATERAL BRANCHES LIVING.
Issue of the late Lieut.-Col. the Hon. (John) Denis Yelverton Bingham, D.S.O., 2nd son of 5th Baron, *b.* 1880, *d.* 1940: *m.* 1926, Vera, who *d.* 1972, da. of the late Major Norman Darbyshire, of Sefton Park, Liverpool:—
Elizabeth Rosemary, *b.* 1927: *m.* 1949, Maxwell John Denham, of Lock Farm, Tixall, Stafford, and has issue living, John Alistair Campbell, *b.* 1955,—Iain Maxwell, *b.* 1957.——(Mary) Mavourneen Denise, *b.* 1931: *m.* 1951, Albert Schiff, and has issue living, Robert John Denis, *b.* 1958,—Miranda Caroline, *b.* 1952. *Residence,*—Broomlands, Langton Green, nr. Tunbridge Wells, Kent.

Issue of the late Hon. Edward Barry Stewart Bingham, V.C., O.B.E., 3rd son of 5th Baron, *b.* 1881, *d.* 1939 : *m.* 1915, Vera (who obtained a divorce 1937), dau. of Edward Temple Patterson, formerly of 10, Culford Gardens, S.W.:—
John Temple, *b.* 1923 : *m.* 1949, Joan Muriel Bowen, who *d.* 1955.——Lavinia Mary. *b.* 1921 : *m.* 1946, Simon Campbell [V. Hawarden, colls.], and has issue living, Luke Bingham, *b.* 1948,—Julian Simon, *b.* 1949,—Roderick Barry, *b.* 1951,—Nicholas Edward Angus, *b.* 1956,—Thomas Neil *b.* 1961. *Residence,*—Barn Close, Shankill, co. Dublin.

Issue of the late Hon. Hugh Terence de Burgh Bingham, 4th son of 5th Baron, *b.* 1885, *d.* 1957: *m.* 1912, Dorothea Minnie (ante), dau. of the late J. A. Sinclair, Bar.-at-law, of Lahore:—
John Peter Derrick, *b.* 1913 ; ed. at Cheltenham Coll. : *m.* 1st, 1939, Mary Machen (who obtained a divorce 1954), el. dau. of the late Robert Morehead Rose, of Sydney, N.S. Wales ; 2ndly, 1954, Jean, el. dau. of the late Robert Harold Hogarth, of Waverley, Tasmania. and has issue living, (by 1st m.) Robert Michael Terence, *b.* 1941,—Angela Rose, *b.* 1944: *m.* 1969, Anthony William Steyn, MB, BS, of Sydney, NSW. *Residence,*—Foxford, Helen Street, Launceston, Tasmania.——Elizabeth Maude, *b.* 1922: *m.* 1944, Jelle Roel Hogeveen Veenbaas, and has issue living, Peter Hans, *b.* 1946. *Residence,*—Erwarton Hall Farm, near Ipswich, Suffolk.

Grandchildren of the Hon. Hugh Terence de Burgh Bingham (ante):—
Issue of the late Capt. Hugh Denis Sinclair Bingham, Roy. Inniskilling Fusiliers ; *b.* 1914, *d.* 1946: *m.* 1939, Margaret Douglas BINGHAM (Home Farm, Ingleden Park, Tenterden, Kent) (she *m.* 2ndly, 1948 (m. diss. 1953), George Lennox Barrow, and resumed surname of Bingham by deed poll 1951), da. of the late Maj. Robert Stevenson, DL, of Aloha, Dungannon, co. Tyrone:—
Robert Derek de Burgh (25, Gorst Rd., SW11 6JB), *b.* 1942: *m.* 1969, Victoria Mary, yr. da. of P. A. Pennant-Rea, of Laurel Tree Cottage, Guiting Power, Glo., and has issue living Alexandra Louise Clare, *b.* 1974.——Jane Victoria Clare, *b.* 1941: *m.* 1966, Bela Peter de Danyi, of 185, Hammersmith Grove, W6 0NP, and has issue living, Imre Patrick Béla, *b.* 1973,—Katherine Emma Margaret, *b.* 1967,—Sophie Jane Clare, *b.* 1968.

PREDECESSORS.—[1] JOHN Bingham, son of the late Henry Bingham, of Newbrook, co. Mayo ; *b.* 1762 ; cr. *Baron Clanmorris*, of Newbrook, co. Mayo (peerage of Ireland), 1800 ; *d.* 1821 ; *s.* by his son [2] CHARLES BARRY, 2nd Baron; *d.s.p.* 1829 ; *s.* by his brother [3] DENIS ARTHUR, 3rd Baron ; *d.* 1847: *m.* 1825, Maria Helena, who *d.* 1899, dau. of Robert Persse, of Roxborough ; *s.* by his son [4] JOHN CHARLES ROBERT, 4th Baron; *b.* 1826: *m.* 1849, Sarah Selina, who *d.* 1907, dau. of Burton Persse, of Moyode Castle, co. Galway; *d.* 1876: *s.* by his son [5] JOHN GEORGE BARRY, 5th Baron ; *b.* 1852: *m.* 1878, (Maude) Matilda Catherine, who *d.* 1941, only child and heiress of the late Robert Edward

Ward, of Bangor Castle, co. Down: *d.* 1916; *s.* by his son [6] ARTHUR MAURICE ROBERT. 6th Baron; *b,* 1879; Capt. Lancers: *m.* 1907, Leila, who *d.* 1969, da. of the late Gordon Cloete, JP, of Rosebank, Cape Town, S. Africa; *d.* 1960; *s.* by his son [7] JOHN MICHAEL WARD, 7th Baron and present peer.

This family descends from the Binghams of Melcombe Bingham, Dorset. Sir George, 3rd son of Robert Bingham of Melcombe (*d.* 1561), was father of Sir Henry Bingham, 1st baronet, ancestor of the Earls of Lucan, and of John Bingham of Foxford, co. Mayo, ancestor of Barons Clanmorris.

CLANWILLIAM, EARL OF. (Meade.) Sits as BARON (U.K. 1828).
[Earl I. 1776, Bt. I. 1703.]

Always ready.

JOHN CHARLES EDMUND CARSON MEADE, 6th Earl, and 9th Baronet; *b.* June 6th, 1914; *s.* 1953; ed. at Eton; Major (retired) Coldstream Guards; is H.M. Lieut. of co. Down, and an O.St.J.; European War 1939-45 in Middle East (despatches twice): *m.* 1948, Catherine, youngest dau. of the late A. T. Loyd, of Lockinge, Wantage, Berks, and has issue.

Arms,—Quarterly, 1st and 4th gules a chevron ermine between three trefoils slipped argent, *Meade*; 2nd and 3rd quarterly, 1st and 4th azure, three peewits argent, *Magill*, 2nd and 3rd per chevron argent and vert, three stags trippant proper, *Hawkins*. Crest,—An eagle with two heads displayed sable, armed or. Supporters—*Dexter*, an eagle close sable; *sinister*, a falcon close proper, both plain collared and chained or.

Residence,—Montalto, Ballynahinch, co. Down.

DAUGHTERS LIVING.

Lady Selina Catherine, *b.* 1950: *m.* 1972, Nicholas George Lawrence Timpson. [see Houstoun-Boswall, Bt.]
Lady Mary Jane, *b.* 1952.
Lady Julia Elizabeth, *b.* 1953
Lady Laura Louise, *b.* 1957.
Lady Katharine Anne, *b.* 1959.
Lady Sophia Hester, *b.* 1963.

SISTER LIVING.

Lady Elizabeth Louise Margaret, *b.* 1911: *m.* 1933, Lt.-Col. Charle Rankin Scott, KRRC, who *d.* 1965, and has issue living, Edward John Rankin, *b.* 1939,—William Nigel Charles, *b.* 1941. *Residence,*—Culkerton, Tetbury, Gloucestershire.

GRANDDAUGHTER LIVING OF FOURTH EARL.

Issue of the late Richard Charles, Lord Gillford, el. son of 4th Earl, *b.* 1868, *d.* 1905 : *m.* 1895, Lady Mary Elizabeth Margaret Douglas-Home, who *d.* 1951, el. dau. of 12th Earl of Home :—
Hon. Theodosia Beatrix Catherine Mary, *b.* 1898 : *m.* 1961, Angus Julian Drummond [see E. Perth, colls.]. *Residence,*—62, Ashley Gardens, S.W.1.

WIDOW LIVING OF SON OF FOURTH EARL.

Margaret Isabel Frances (*Hon. Lady Meade-Fetherstonhaugh*) (Clive Lodge, Albury, Surrey), da. of the late Rt. Rev. the Hon. Edward Carr Glyn, DD [see B. Wolverton, colls.]: *m.* 1911, Adm the Hon. Sir Herbert Meade-Fetherstonhaugh, GCVO, CB, DSO, who *d.* 1964 and has issue living· see colls., infra].

COLLATERAL BRANCHES LIVING.

Granddaughters of Adm. the Hon. Sir Herbert MEADE-FETHERSTONHAUGH, G.C.V.O., C.B., D.S.O. (infra):—
Issue of the late Richard James MEADE-FETHERSTONHAUGH, *b.* 1913, *d.* 1958 : *m.* 1948, Jean Phyllis (17, Argyll Rd., W8, and Uppark, Petersfield), da. of the late Maj. Basil Falkner:—
Harriet Sarah, *b.* 1949: *m.* 1969, John de Bianchi Cossart, of 6 Darlan Rd., SW6 5BT, and has issue living, Charles Richard, *b.* 1972,—Henrietta-Maria *b.* 1974.——Emma Mary, *b.* 1951.——Sophia Theresa, *b.* 1954.

Issue of the late Adm. the Hon. Sir Herbert MEADE-FETHERSTONHAUGH, GCVO C.B., D.S.O. (who assumed by Roy. licence 1932 the surname of Fetherstonhaugh after Meade, and the arms quarterly), 3rd son of 4th Earl *b.* 1876, *d.* 1964: *m.* 1911, Margaret Isabel Frances (*Hon. Lady Meade-Fetherstonhaugh*) (ante), da. of the late Rt. Rev. the Hon. Edward Carr Glyn, DD [see B. Wolverton, colls.]:—
JOHN HERBERT *MEADE* (11. Milner St., SW3; Turf Club), *b.* Sept. 27th, 1919: *m.* 1956, Maxine, only da. of J. Hayden Scott, and has issue living, Patrick James, *b.* 1960,– Rowena Katherine, *b.* 1957,—Tania Frances *b.* 1963.——Anne Margaret (*Baroness Rockley*), *b.* 1912: *m.* 1933, the 2nd Baron Rockley.——Jean Mary, *b.* 1917: *m.* 1943, Brig. Michael James Babington-Smith, CBE, son of the late Sir Henry Babington Smith, GBE, CH, KCB, CSI [E. Elgin], and has issue living, Alan, *b.* 1946,—Louisa, *b.* 1944: *m.* 1967, Maj. James Richard Macfarlane, Coldstream Guards, of Red Hatch, Cricket Hill, Yateley, Hants., and has issue living, Edward Michael Richard *b.* 1969, David Peter *b.* 1970,—Susan Mary, *b.* 1950.

Grandchildren of the late Sir Robert Henry Meade, GC B, 2nd son of 3rd Earl:—
Issue of the late Charles Francis Meade, *b.* 1881, *d.* 1975: *m.* 1913, Lady Eileen Hilda Brodrick, who *d.* 1970, da. of 1st Earl of Midleton:—

Simon Robert Jasper (Pen-y-lan, Meifod, Montgomeryshire), b. 1928: m. 1957, Lady Sophia Catherine Gathorne-Hardy, da. of 4th Earl of Cranbrook, and has issue living, Jasper, b. 1962,—Benjamin, b. 1963, —Camilla, b. 1958,—Rachel b. 1965.——Evelyn Clodagh, b. 1916: m. 1940, Hercules Mackenzie, CMG, of Kyle House, Kyleakin, I. of Skye, only son of the late Maj.-Gen. Sir Colin John Mackenzie, KCB, and has issue living, Christian Fiona, b. 1941: m. 1966, (Charles) Nicholas Phipps, of Chalcot Stables, Westbury, Wilts. [see D. Buccleuch].——Flavia Mary (*Baroness Ebbisham*) (The Old Rectory, Bletchingley, Surrey), b. 1920: m. 1949, the 2nd Baron Ebbisham.

Granddaughters of the late Francis Henry Meade, CBE, only son of the late Rev. the Hon. Sidney Meade, 3rd son of 3rd Earl:—
Issue of the late Lt.-Col. Robert Sidney Stuart, b. 1901, d. 1971: m. 1st, 1930, Veronica Augusta, who d. 1968, da. of Lt.-Col. Herbert Vere Wilbraham; 2ndly, 1970, Baroness Maria Elisabeth Johanna Rosalia Ottilia (The Hangingshaw, Selkirk), da. of the late Baron August Hermann Georg Victor Ramberg, Capt. Imperial Austrian Navy, and widow of Count Ferdinand Zdenko Karl Emmerick Maria von Thun und Hohenstein:—
(By 1st m.) Daphne Theresa, b. 1936.——Jane Cecilia, b. 1940: m. 1967, Maj. David Henry George Corsellis, RE, 8, Horburg Mews, W11, and has issue living, Nicholas Robert Alexander, b. 1968,— James Henry Merrick, b. 1970.

Grandsons of the late Capt. John Meade, son of the late Lieut.-Gen. the Hon. Robert Meade, 2nd son of 1st Earl:—
Issue of the late Capt. John Percy Meade, b. 1847, d. 1919: m. 1894, Helena Frances, who d. 1946, dau. of Sir John Allen Johnson-Walsh, 4th Bt.:—
John Windham (Earsham Lodge, Bungay, Suffolk; Army and Navy, and Royal London Yacht Clubs), b. 1894; ed. at Eton; Maj. (ret.) Oxfordshire and Bucks LI; is a JP for co. Down; was Permanent Pres. Field Gen. Courts Martial to 30th and 12th Corps, to Hanover Dist., and to British Troops in Berlin 1943-48; 1914-19 War in France, Mesopotamia, and N. Russia (twice wounded), 1939-45 War in NW Europe: m. 1932, Grace Dorothea, JP, da. of the late Sir Cecil Fane De Salis, KCB, and has issue living, John Michael (84, Forest Rd., Kew, Richmond, Surrey), b. 1935; ed. at Stowe: m. 1967, Princess Valentine, da. of the late Prince Nicholas Galitzine, and has issue living, Nicholas b. 1969, Catherine b. 1968, Tatiana (twin) b. 1968, Elizabeth Meade b. 1971,—Francis Windham (Earsham Lodge, Bungay, Suffolk), b. 1941 ; ed. at Stowe, and at London Univ. (BSc 1962),—Theodosia Frances, b. 1932.

Granddaughter of the late Maj. Richard Raphael Meade, son of the late Lt.-Gen. the Hon. John Meade, 3rd son of 1st Earl:—
Issue of the late Richard John Edward Meade, O.B.E., b. 1870, d. 1957 : m. 1894, Helen Venetia Digby, who d. 1944, dau. of the Rev. George Digby Newbolt:—
Patricia Helen Isabel (Saxlingham Hall Nursing Home, Norwich, NOR 63W), b. 1899.

PREDECESSORS.—[1] Sir JOHN Meade, K.B.; M.P. successively for Dublin Univ. and co. Tipperary, and Attorney-Gen. to James, Duke of York; cr. a *Baronet* of Ireland 1703; d. 1711; s. by his son [2] Sir PIERCE, 2nd Bt.; d. s. p.; s. by his brother [3] Sir RICHARD, 3rd Bt.; d. 1744; s. by his son [4] Sir JOHN, 4th Bt.; cr. *Baron Gilford* and *Viscount Clanwilliam* (peerage of Ireland) 1766, and *Earl of Clanwilliam* (peerage of Ireland) 1776; d. 1800; s. by his son [5] RICHARD, 2nd Earl; d. 1805; s. by his son [6] RICHARD, G.C.H., 3rd Earl; b. 1795; Under-Sec. for Foreign Affairs 1822, and Ambassador at Berlin 1823-8; cr. *Baron Clanwilliam*, of Clanwilliam, co. Tipperary (peerage of United Kingdom) 1828: m. 1830, Lady Elizabeth Herbert, who d. 1858, dau. of 11th Earl of Pembroke; d. 1879; s. by his son [7] RICHARD JAMES, G.C.B., K.C.M.G., 4th Earl; b. 1832; an Adm. of the Fleet; a Naval A.D.C. to H.M. Queen Victoria 1872-6, and a Lord of the Admiralty 1874-80: m. 1867, Elizabeth Henrietta, who d. 1925, el. dau. of the late Sir Arthur Edward Kennedy; d. 1907; s. by his second son [8] ARTHUR VESEY, M.C., 5th Earl, b. 1873; was Capt. and Adj. Roy. Horse Guards, and Assist. Provost Marshal; S. Africa 1900-02, European War 1914-18 (M.C.): m. 1909, Muriel Mary Temple, M.B.E., dau. of Russell Stephenson and widow of the Hon. Oliver Howard [E. Carlisle]; d. 1953; s. by his only son [9] JOHN CHARLES EDMUND CARSON, 6th Earl and present peer; also Viscount Clanwilliam, Baron Clanwilliam, and Baron Gilford.

CLARENDON, EARL OF. (Villiers.) [Earl G.B. 1776.]

[Name pronounced "Villers."]

GEORGE FREDERICK LAURENCE HYDE VILLIERS, 7th Earl; b. Feb. 2nd, 1933; s. 1955; ed. at Eton; Page of Honour to HM 1948-49; Lt. RHG (AER): m. 1974, Jane Diana, da. of Edward William Dawson, of Idmiston, Salisbury, Wilts.

Arms,—Argent, a cross gules, charged with five escallops or. Crest,—A lion rampant argent ducally crowned or. Supporters,—Two eagles, wings expanded and inverted sable, beaked, membered, and ducally crowned or, and charged on the breast with a plain cross argent.

Residence,—8, Chelsea Sq., SW3 6LF.

The cross, the test of faith.

SISTER LIVING.

(*Raised to the rank of an Earl's daughter* 1956.)
Lady Rosemary Verena Edith (posthumous), b. 1935 : m. 1959, Richard Hugh Jordan Steel, el. son of Sir Christopher Eden Steel, G.C.M.G., M.V.O. [Buxton, Bt., colls.], and has issue living, James Thomas Jordan, b. 1960,—Oliver George Nigel, b. 1962,—Arabella Rosemary Louise, b. 1966. *Residence,*—Glebe House, Notgrove, Cheltenham, Glos.

UNCLE LIVING. (*Son of 6th Earl.*)

Hon. (WILLIAM) NICHOLAS SOMERS LAURENCE HYDE, b. July 17th, 1916 ; ed. at Eton, and at New Coll., Oxford ; is Major Grenadier Guards (Supplementary Reserve), a J.P. for Hants, and an O.St.J. : m. 1939, Mary Cecilia Georgina, dau. of Major the Hon. Edric Alfred Cecil Weld-Forester, OVO [see B. Forester], and has issue living, Caroline Jane (The Garden Flat, 122, Cambridge St., SW1), b. 1940: m. 1964 (m. diss. 1974), J. Kenneth Havard,—Nerena Anne Hyde, b. 1941: m. 1966, Timothy Congreve Stephenson, of Loughgall, co. Armagh [see V. Hawarden, colls.].— Elizabeth Georgina Gail, b. 1952. *Residence,*—Firs Farm, Milbourne, Malmesbury, Wilts.

COLLATERAL BRANCHES LIVING.

Issue of the late Rt. Hon. Sir Francis Hyde Villiers, G.C.M.G., G.C.V.O., C.B., 4th son of 4th Earl, b. 1852, d. 1925 : m. 1876, Virginia Katharine, who d. 1937, dau. of Eric Carrington Smith, of Ashfold, Handcross, Sussex:—

Marjory Mildred, *b.* 1890: *m.* 1919, Ivan Edward Snell, MC, Bar.-at-Law, and a Metropolitan Police Magistrate, and formerly Capt. Black Watch (Roy. Highlanders), who *d.* 1958, and has issue living, Francis, *b.* 1923: *m.* 1968, Maureen Francesca Braithwaite Bell, and has issue living, Ivan Edward *b.* 1969, Christopher Malcolm *b.* 1971,—Julianna, *b.* 1920: *m.* 1945, Ralph Walford Selby, CMG, Diplo. Ser., son of Sir Walford Harmood Montague Selby, KCMG, CB, OVO, of Mengeham House Lodge, Hayling Island, and has issue living, Mary Virginia *b.* 1947, Pamela Marjory Dorothy *b.* 1949, Cynthia Elizabeth Mildred *b.* 1953. *Residence,*—Mengeham House, Hayling Island.

Grandchildren of the late Rt. Hon. Sir Francis Hyde Villiers, G.C.M.G., G.C.V.O., C.B. (ante):—
Issue of the late Eric Hyde Villiers, DSO, Capt. Highland L.I., *b.* 1881, *d.* 1964: *m.* 1928, Joan Ankaret (Ulcombe Place, Maidstone), da. of the late John Edward Talbot [see E. Shrewsbury, colls.]:—
Henry Hyde (Ulcombe Place, nr. Maidstone, Kent; Boodle's Club), *b.* 1931; ed. at Wellington: *m.* 1959 Mary Elizabeth Cavan, da. of Robert Hugh Swan Corbett, of Yalding, Kent, and has issue living Charles James Hyde, *b.* 1967,—Robert Henry Hyde, *b.* 1969,—Charlotte Amelia, *b.* 1961,—Henrietta Barbara, *b.* 1962.——James Michael Hyde (Deep Cut Place, Camberley, Surrey), *b.* 1933; ed. at Wellington: *m.* 1966, Patricia, da. of William Donovan, of Fern House, Pembroke.——John Francis Hyde (52, Montpelier Rd., Brighton; Ormos Fellou, Gavrion, Andros, Greece; St. James' Club), *b.* 1936; ed. at Winchester, and at King's Coll., Camb. (MA, PhD): *m.* 1958 (Myee) Miranda, el. da. of Lt.-Col. David McKenna, OBE [see E. Albemarle], and has issue living, Daniel James Hyde, *b.* 1960,— Cecilia Ankaret, *b.* 1962,—Antonia Aniela, *b.* 1965,—Susanna Sophia (twin), *b.* 1965.

Issue of the late Algernon Hyde Villiers, Lieut. Yeo., attached Machine Gun Corps, *b.* 1886, *d.* (killed in action during 1914-18 War) 1917: *m.* 1911, Beatrix Elinor (*Dowager Baroness Aldenham and Hunsdon of Hunsdon*): [she *m.* 2ndly, 1919, the 4th Baron Aldenham and Hunsdon of Hunsdon, who *d.* 1969], da. of the late Herbert Woodfield Paul, of Cherry Orchard, Forest Row, Sussex [Mackworth, Bt., colls.]:—
Sir Charles English Hyde, *MC* (of Blacknest House, Sunninghill, Berks), *b.* 1912; ed. at Eton, and at New Coll., Oxford; Lt.-Col. Gren. Gds. (SR); Grand Officer of Order of Leopold II of Belgium); 1939-45 War, MC; Knt. 1975: *m.* 1st, 1938, Pamela Constance, who *d.* 1943, dau. of the late Maj. John Flower, 60th Rifles; 2ndly, 1946, Marie José, dau. of Comte Henri de la Barre d'Erquelinnes, and has issue living (by 1st m.), Nicholas Hyde, *b.* 1939; is Lt. Grenadier Guards (Army Emergency Reserve),— (by 2nd m.) Diana Mary, *b.* 1947.—Anne Hyde, *b.* 1950: *m.* 1973, Paul Nuttall Kesterton.——Mary Theresa (*Lady Wilkinson*), *b.* 1917; formerly in WRNS: *m.* 1945, Lt.-Col. Sir Peter Allix Wilkinson, KCMG, DSO, OBE, Ambassador to Austria, and has issue living, Virginia Caroline, *b.* 1947,—Alexandra, *b.* 1953.

Grandson of Col. Ernest Villiers, el. son of the Hon. Edward Ernest Villers, 4th brother of 3rd Earl:—
Issue of the late Edward Ernest Villiers, *b.* 1867, *d.* 1942: *m.* 1891, Florence, who *d.* 1956, dau. of the late Francis Ricardo, of The Friary, Old Windsor:—
Algernon Edward, *b.* 1892; ed. at Eton, and at Univ. Coll., Oxford (BA and MA 1918); MIEE; 1914-18 War as Capt. KRRC: *m.* 1924, Annie Augusta Merewether, dau. of the late G. L. Massy, of Berridge, Sunningdale, and has issue living, George Edward, *TD* (73, Carlton Hill, NW8; Boodle's Club), *b.* 1931; ed. at Wellington Coll., and at Brasenose Coll., Oxford (MA); late Maj. Berks. and Westminster Dragoons (TA); late Lt. RHA: *m.* 1962, Anne Virginia, el. da. of the late C. R. F. Threlfall, of Warstone House, Bewdley, and has issue living, Edward Richard *b.* 1963, Henry Raymond, *b.* 1965, Theresa Anne *b.* 1968,—Elizabeth Anne, *b.* 1925, —Barbara Jane, *b.* 1927. *Residence,*—The New House, Broomfield Park, Sunningdale, Berks. *Club,*—Royal Thames Yacht.

Grandchildren of the late Rev. Henry Montagu Villiers (infra):—
Issue of the late Henry Montagu Villiers, M.V.O., *b.* 1863, *d.* 1948 : *m.* 1896, Carmen, who *d.* 1953, dau of the late Dr. Lührsen, Envoy Extraor. and Min. Plen. for German Empire in Colombia, S. America :—
George Dumba, *R.N.*, *b.* 1900 : is Com. (Emergency List); European War 1916-18, European War 1939-45 : *m.* 1926, Anne Hilda Whellens, dau. of the late James Barton Hall, of Longframlington, Northumberland, and has issue living, Simon William George (Lower Coxs Street Farm House, Detling, Kent. *Club,*—Naval and Military), *b.* 1927; Maj. (ret.) RA, attached to Malay Regt., Malaya 1958 (despatches, Order of Ali Manghu Negra): *m.* 1956, Patricia de Lacey, and has issue living, Clive Mathew George *b.* 1957, Virginia Anne *b.* 1959, Moira Lillian *b.* 1963,—Janet Mary, (The Cottage, Aldersey Rd., Guildford), *b.* 1929; Snr. Mistress of Middle Sch., Tormead Sch. for Girls, Guildford. *Residence,*—Vane House, Warren Rise, New Malden, Surrey.——Margaret Adelaide Rhoda, *b.* 1913: *m.* 1936, Rupert Huber, and has issue living, Anita, *b.* 1939.——Renate Krexentia, *b.* 1941. *Residence,*—Villa Hubertus, Kossen, Tyrol, Austria.——Margaret Anne Theresa (twin), *b.* 1913: *m.* 1944, Ronald Basil Strickland. *Resides in* Australia.

Grandson of the late Henry Montagu Villiers, M.V.O. (ante):—
Issue of the late Edmund Rollo Stanley Villiers, *b.* 1909, *d.* 1960 : *m.* 1st, 1934 (marriage dissolved 1957), Margit Cleland, dau. of the late Robert Rogerson, of Marchmount, Dumfries ; 2ndly, 1957, Christine Joan (of 13, Lowndes Square, S.W.1), dau. of the late Com. W. O. H. Lambert, R.N., of The Toll, Buxted, Sussex :—
(By 1st m.) Charles Russell (Wargrave Lodge, Wargrave-on-Thames, Berkshire), *b.* 1938; ed. at Cheltenham, and at Corpus Christi Coll., Camb. (BA), MB, BChir, DMRD; FFR: *m.* 1971, Barbara Clare, 3rd da. of Fredwin R. McMaster, of Nottinghill, Belfast.

Grandchildren of the late Rev. Henry Montagu Villiers (infra):—
Issue of the late John Russell Villiers, *b.* 1866, *d.* 1958: *m.* 1893, Grace Elizabeth, who *d.* 1962, dau. of the late Maj.-Gen. William Earle, C.B., C.S.I. [Earle, Bt., colls.]:—
Arthur Henry, *M.C.*, *b.* 1894 ; ed. at Radley ; formerly 2nd Lieut. King's Roy. Rifle Corps ; European 1915-19 (MC): *m.* 1919, Vera Adeline, da. of Charles Howe, of Durban, Natal, and has issue living, Peter William (13, Welbeck Rd., Harrow, Middlesex, HA2 0RN), *b.* 1922; ed. at Lancing Coll.; late Lt. KRRC; Film Dir.: *m.* 1st, 1945, June (from whom he obtained a divorce 1958), only child of W. Friedhoff; 2ndly, 1959, Alice, da. of A. J. Startup, and has issue living, (by 1st m.) Roger Peter *b.* 1946,—Geoffrey Richard (292, Valparaiso Av., Atherton, Cal., USA), *b.* 1924; ed. at Lancing Coll.; 1939-45 War as Sub-Lt. RNVR: *m.* 1948, Janet Myra, da. of Dr. Leonard W. Trott, of Adelaide, S. Aust., and has issue living, Mary Jane *b.* 1954, Lisa Kathleen *b.* 1959,—Christopher Nigel, *b.* 1929; ed. at Lancing Coll.: *m.* 1953, Brenda Margaret, yr. da. of D. R. Penny, of Ferring, Sussex, and has issue living, Nigel Richard *b.* 1956, Gillian Grace *b.* 1958. *Residence,*—117, Clarence Gate Gdns., Baker St., NW1.——John Michael, *b.* 1899: *m.* 1st, 1947, May, who *d.* 1966, da. of the late John Horwood, of Headington, Oxford; 2ndly, 1969, Elizabeth, da. of William Coxon. *Residence.*—212, New Rd., Booker, High Wycombe, Bucks.

Grandchildren of the late John Russell Villiers (ante):—
Issue of the late Brig. Richard Montagu Villiers, DSO, *b.* 1905, *d.* 1973: *m.* 1932, Nancy (Nutwood, Strathpeffer, Ross-shire), el. da. of the late Lt.-Gen. Sir Charles Alexander Campbell Godwin, KCB, CMG, DSO:—
Timothy Charles (c/o Lloyds Bank, 6, Pall Mall, SW1 Y5N) *b.* 1943; ed. at Eton, and RMA; Capt. 15th/19th KRH: *m.* 1971, Maureen, da. of the late Ven. R. G. H. McCahearty, and has issue living, Louise, *b.* 1973.——Judith Annette, *b* 1935: *m.* 1960, Maj. Rupert H. G. McCarthy, 15th/19th

KRH, and has issue living, William Rupert, *b.* 1963,—Sarah Victoria, *b.* 1961, Meriel Anne, *b.* 1966.——Victoria Belinda, *b.* 1938: *m.* 1963, Robert Quentin Yeatman, of Winder Farm, Bethersden, Kent, and has issue living, Catherine Victoria, *b.* 1964,—Lucy Belinda, *b.* 1966,—Rosanna Charlotte, *b.* 1973.——Carol Elspeth, *b.* 1944: *m.* 1965, Gerald Charles Mordaunt, of Hovell's Farm, Pattiswick, Coggeshall, Essex [see Mordaunt, Bt., colls.].

Grandsons of Sir Thomas Lister Villiers, 3rd son of the Rev. Henry Montagu Villiers (infra):—
Issue of the late Com. Thomas Hyde Villiers, RN, *b.* 1902, *d.* 1955: *m.* 1925, Eleanor, who *d.* 1958, da. of the late Francis Edgar Croft [Croft, Bt., cr. 1818, colls.]:—
Nicholas Lister (Grange Orchards, Clopton, Woodbridge, Suffolk, IP13 6QR), *b.* 1926; ed. at Eton; late Lieut. RN: *m.* 1954, Betty Midelton, 2nd da. of Sidney Ralph Midelton Barlow, of Wayside, Chalfont St. Giles, Bucks. and has issue living, Derek Midelton Lister, *b.* 1958.—Caroline Patricia, *b.* 1960.——Stephen Hyde (Cranes Farm House, Mill End Green, Gt Easton, Dunmow, Essex), *b.* 1931; ed. at Eton: *m.* 1958, Elizabeth Jill, da. of John Stewart Jeffrey Chapple, of Clayton, Hadham Road, Bishop's Stortford, Herts., and has issue living, Harry Hyde, *b.* 1959,—Timothy Stewart, *b.* 1960,—Hugo James, *b.* 1962.

Granddaughters of the late Rev. Henry Montagu Villiers (infra):—
Issue of the late Godfrey Robert Randall Villiers, *b.* 1877, *d.* 1925: *m.* 1967, Sylvia, who *d.* 1926, da. of the late Dr. James Moore Bennett, formerly of Princes Road, Liverpool:—
Sylvia Betty. *b.* 1915: *m.* 1934, Stavros Sirakos, and has issue living, Denise Catherine, *b.* 1935: *m.* 1961, Philippe Moulierac, of Michelet de Lattre, B2, Marseilles, France, and has issue living, Christopher *b.* 1964, Pascale *b.* 1967. *Residence,*—15 ter, Rue Meyerbeer, Nice, France, A.M.

Issue of the late Maj. Paul Frederick Villiers, DSO, *b.* 1884, *d.* 1968: *m.* 1912, Evelyn, who *d.* 1973, da. of the late Edward Webb:—
Pauline Mary Lethbridge, *b.* 1914: *m.* 1936, Dennis Estyn Dunnill, MB, BS, MRCS, LRCP, DA, of 12, South Cliff, Bexhill-on-Sea, and has issue living, Richard Paul Hyde, *b.* 1945: *m.* 1971, Rosamund Strange,—Veronica Mary, *b.* 1937: *m.* 1963 (m. diss. 1973), Timothy Mawdsley Welch, and has issue living, Andrew Ronald Mawdsley, *b.* 1968,—Nicola Mary, *b.* 1966,—Angela Evelyn, *b.* 1939: *m.* 1966, William Raymond Barker, of Fairfield, 10, South Close, Tranmere Park, Guiseley, Yorks., and has issue living, Christopher Paul Howard *b.* 1967, Caroline Susan *b.* 1969.

Grandchildren of the late Rev. Henry Montagu Villiers (infra):—
Issue of the late Capt. Gerald Berkeley Villiers, OBE, RN, *b.* 1885, *d.* 1959: *m.* 1918, Rachel Joan (11, Chelsea Close, Manor Rd., Bexhill-on-Sea; Royal Aero Club), da. of the late Rev. Henry Vernon Heber Percy [see D. Northumberland, colls.]:—
Anthony Henry Heber, *b.* 1921; Capt. late Grenadier Guards; 1939-45 War: *m.* 1948, Rosemary Elizabeth, da. of the late Maj. (William) Bertram Bell, 12th Lancers [By. Barrymore], and has issue living, Anthony James Valentine, *b.* 1949,—Charles Henry, *b.* 1954,—Rosemary Henrietta Dorothy, *b.* 1950: *m.* 1973, Peregrine Banbury,—Emma Helen, *b.* 1963. *Residence,*—The Old Priory, N. Woodchester, Stroud, Glos. *Club,*—Guards',

Grandson of the late Rt. Rev. the Hon. Henry Montagu Villiers, DD, Bishop of Durham, brother of 4th Earl:—
Issue of the late Rev. Henry Montagu Villiers, *b.* 1837, *d.* 1908: *m.* 1st, 1861, Lady Victoria Russell, who *d.* 1880, dau. of 1st Earl Russell; 2ndly, 1883, Charlotte Louisa Emily, who *d.* 1947, dau. of the late Hon. Frederick William Cadogan [E. Cadogan, colls.]:—
(By 2nd m.) Oliver George Graham, *DSO*, *b.* 1886; ed. at Harrow; Maj. (ret.) RAF; in Directorate of Civil Aviation 1919-39, Dir. of Special Intelligence Branch, Min. of Home Security 1939-48, and in Min. of Defence 1948-51; 1914-18 War with RNVR and RAF (despatches, DSO, Legion of Honour, Croix de Guerre); DSO 1918: *m.* 1918, Aleen Judith, da. of the late Rev. Henry Vernon Heber-Percy [see D. Northumberland, colls.], and has issue living, Judith Rosemary, *b.* 1919: *m.* 1949, Peter George Locke-Wheaton, of Brickfields, E. Keal, Spilsby, Lincs., and has issue living, Henry George *b.* 1950: *m.* 1973, Cynthia Jane Bagley, John Antony Charles *b.* 1952, Philip James *b.* 1955, Richard Oliver *b.* 1957, Henrietta Mary-Anne *b.* 1951: *m.* 1970, Richard Peter Noble, of Belon, Hagworthingham, Lincs., Caroline Elizabeth Susan-Ann *b.* 1953, Sarah Louise *b.* 1974. *Residence,*—53, Brockhill Rd., Hythe, Kent.

Grandchildren of Maj. Oliver George Graham Villiers, D.S.O. (ante):—
Issue of the late Wing-Com. David Hugh Villiers, D.F.C., *b.* 1921, *d.* 1962: *m.* 1st, 1942, Patricia (from whom he obtained a divorce 1948), only child of the late Richard Payne; 2ndly, 1954, Elizabeth Barbara, 8, Glebe Place, SW3 (assumed by deed poll 1949 the surname of Prideaux in lieu of her patronymic), da. of the late Horace Leonard Hobbins:—
(By 1st marriage) Robin Julian (25, Pierrepoint, 19 Ross Rd., SE23), *b.* 1945: *m.* 1974, Birgitte, da. of Peter Stafford.——(by 2nd marriage) Christopher Francis, *b.* 1958.——Jonathan Paul, *b.* 1961.—— Catherine Judith, *b.* 1955.

Grandchildren of the late Capt. Frederick Ernest Villiers, yr. son of the Rt. Rev. the Hon. Henry Montagu Villiers, DD, (ante):—
Issue of the late Major George Frederick Montagu Villiers, *b.* 1870, *d.* 1934: *m.* 1908, Mary Seton, who *d.* 1949, el. dau. of Thomas Jackson, of Coats, N.B. [Baird, Bt., cr. 1897].
Jean Baird, *b.* 1909. *Residence,*—Courthill, Rosemarkie, Ross-shire.

Issue of the late Lieut.-Col. Charles Walter Villiers, C.B.E., D.S.O., *b.* 1873, *d.* 1938: *m.* 1903, Lady Kathleen Mary Cole, who *d.* 1956, dau. of 4th Earl of Enniskillen :—
Francis Berkeley Hyde, *O.B.E.*, *b.* 1906; ed. at Eton; is Lieut. Col. R.A.O.C.; N.-W. Europe 1944-5 (O.B.E.); O.B.E. (Mil.) 1945: *m.* 1938, Rose Marie von Passavant, and has issue living, Nicholas, *b.* 1939. *Residence.*—Stone House, Stone, near Kidderminster, Worcestershire.——Florence Angela (*Angela Baroness Teviot*), *b.* 1904: *m.* 1930, as his second wife, the 1st Baron Teviot, who *d.* 1968. *Residence,*—Timber Ash House, Chaddleworth, Newbury.

Issue of the late Reginald Hyde Villiers, D.S.O., *b.* 1876, *d.* 1953: *m.* 1906, Florence Marianne, who *d.* 1937, dau. of Dr. George Stockwell, formerly of Dunedin, New Zealand :—
Frederick Montagu Hyde, *b.* 1907; late Major Ceylon L.I.: *m.* 1st, 1936 (marriage dissolved 1947), Maisie Marguerite Hunt; 2ndly, 1948, Ann Sybella (*Countess* VON SCHIMMELMANN), dau. of the Rev. N. Chetwode Ram, of Petersfield, Hants, and has issue living (by 1st m.) Judith Marianne, *b.* 1937.——George Pelham, *b.* 1909: *m.* 1st, 1937 (m. diss. 1945), Gladys Mildred Moehr; 2ndly, 1945, Ursula Alison Paterson, who *d.* 1957, da. of John Hodgson, of Kotapala, Ceylon, and has issue living, Ursula Georgette Victoria Maria, *b.* 19—.——Lyspeth Desirée (La Vida, Cuesta del Salon, Nerja-Malaga, Spain), *b.* 1911: *m.* 1st, 1931 (m. diss. 1944), Fl.-Lt. James Bryan Robertson, RAF; 2ndly, 1944, as his second wife, Cdr. Leonard Evelyn Romaine Govett, RNVR, who *d.* (killed on active ser.) 1945; 3rdly, 1949, Richard Vernon Lea, and has issue living (by 1st m.) Elizabeth Rayne, *b.* 1933: *m.* 1957, Cdr. Frederick Anthony Collins, Warfleet Boathouse, Darmouth, S. Devon, and has issue living, Elizabeth Alexandra Kim, *b.* 1958, Evelyn Patricia Jaye *b.* 1960, Katherine Marianne Emma *b.* 1965, —Evelyn Clodagh, *b.* 1935: *m.* 1956, Maj. Hugh Champion de Crespigny, 15/19th King's R. Hussars, and has issue living, Shaunagh Rose Romaine *b.* 1957, Fleur Heulin *b.* 1962.

Issue of the late Evelyn Charles Arthur Villiers, *b.* 1884, *d.* 1968: *m.* 1907, Dorothy Katherine (22, Park Cres., Brighton), da. of the late Col. George Howard Moore-Lane, CMG [B. Kingsale, colls.]:—

Robert Alexander, *CBE* (Robinsgreen, Warnham, Sussex, and 33, Ennismore Gdns., SW7; Army and Navy Club), *b.* 1908; Capt. RN; 1939-45 War (despatches), Korea 1951-52 as Ch. of Staff to Flag Officer, Comdg. Commonwealth Naval Forces; CBE (Mil.) 1952: *m.* 1st, 1933, Leila Alexandra, who *d.* 1938, da. of Lt.-Col. W. A. V. Findlater, of Tenterden, Kent; 2ndly, 1939 (m. dis·. 1958), Elizabeth Mary, da. of Maj.-Gen. Arthur Leslie Irvine Friend, CB, CBE, MC; 3rdly, 1960, Irene Mary, da. of W. Ellis-Jones, of W. Kirby, Cheshire, and has issue living (by 1st m.) Diana Susan, *b.* 1935: *m.* 1963, Ian Buchanan Watt, CMG, of Rosewood House, Thames Ditton, Surrey, and has issue living, James Alexander Macdonald *b.* 1965, Robert John Alexander *b.* 1969, Harriet Leila Elizabeth *b.* 1970—(by 2nd m.) Michael Alexander, *b.* 1941; ed. at Eton,—Charles Nigel (twin) (8, Sutherland St., SW1), *b.* 1941; ed. at Winchester, and New Coll., Oxford: *m.* 1970; Sally Priscilla, da. of the late Capt. D. H. Magnay, RN, and has issue living, Caroline Harriet *b.* 1974,—Sarah Jane Amanda, *b.* 1956——Kenneth Charles Howard, *b.* 1912; 1939-45 War as Lt.-Cdr. RN.——Marjorie Frances (Sanctuary, Copers Cope Rd., Beckenham, Kent), *b.* 1909: *m.* 1932, Henry Samuel Malortie Hoare, and has issue living, Charles Antony Richard, *b.* (Jan.) 1934; ed. at King's Sch., Canterbury, and Merton Coll., Oxford (MA); Prof., Queen's Coll., Belfast,—Arthur Howard Malortie, *b.* (Dec.) 1934; ed at King's Sch., Canterbury, and Trin. Coll., Oxford (MA, PhD),—Henry Ronald John, *b.* 1936; ed. at King's Sch., Canterbury, and St. John's Coll., Camb. (BA, MSc),—Dorothy Ann Katherine, *b.* 1945; ed. at St. Hugh's Coll., Oxford (MA)—Janet Frances Mary, *b.* 1948; ed at St. Aidan's Coll., Durham (BA).

PREDECESSORS.—[1] *Rt. Hon.* THOMAS Villiers, 2nd son of 2nd Earl of Jersey; successively Ambassador to Dresden, Poland, and Vienna, a Lord of the Admiralty, Joint Postmaster-Gen-Chancellor of the Duchy of Lancaster, and Ambassador to Berlin; cr. *Baron Hyde*, of Hindon, Wilts (peerage of Great Britain) 1756, with remainder to the heirs male of his body by his then wife (Charlotte), dau. of 3rd Earl of Essex by Jane Hyde, dau. of 4th Earl of Clarendon (cr. 1661), and in default to his said wife and the heirs male of her body, *Earl of Clarendon* (peerage of Great Britain) 1776, and a Baron of the Kingdom of Prussia 1782, which honour he received the Roy. licence to enjoy; *d.* 1786; *s.* by his son [2] THOMAS, 2nd Earl; *d.* unmarried 1824; *s.* by his brother [3] JOHN CHARLES, 3rd Earl; *d.* 1838; *s.* by his nephew [4] GEORGE WILLIAM FREDERICK, *K.G., G.C.B., D.C.L.,* 4th Earl, el. son of the Hon. George, 3rd son of 1st Earl; *b.* 1800; was First Commr. of Excise 1824-33, Ambassador at Madrid 1833-9, Lord Privy Seal 1840-41, Pres. of Board of Trade 1846-7, Viceroy of Ireland 1847-52, Sec. for Foreign Affairs 1853-8 and 1868-70, and Chancellor of Duchy of Lancaster 1864-5: *m.* 1839, Lady Katherine Grimston, dau. of 1st Earl of Verulam, and widow of John Barham; *d.* June 27, 1870; *s.* by his el. surviving son [5] EDWARD HYDE, *G.C.B., G.C.V.O.,* 5th Earl, *b.* 1846; M.P. for Brecon (*L*) 1869-70; a Lord-in-Waiting to Queen Victoria 1895-1901, and Lord Chamberlain of the Household to King Edward VII 1901-5 and Lord-Lieut. for Herts 1902-14: *m.* 1st, 1876, Lady Caroline Elizabeth Agar, who *d.* 1894, dau. of 3rd Earl of Normanton; 2ndly, 1908, Emma Mary Augusta, who *d.* 1935, dau. of the late Lieut.-Gen. George Cliffe Hatch, C.S.I., and widow of the Hon. Edward Roden Bourke [E. Mayo]; *d.* 1914; *s.* by his el. son [6] GEORGE HERBERT HYDE, *K.G., G.C.M.G., G.C.V.O., P.C.,* 6th Earl; *b.* 1877; Lord-in-Waiting to H.M. 1921-2, Ch. Govt. Whip in House of Lords, and Capt. of H.M. Corps. of Gentlemen-at Arms 1922-4 and 1924-5, Parliamentary Under-Sec. of State for Dominion Affairs 1925-7, Chm. British Broadcasting Corporation 1927-30, Gov.-Gen. and Com.-in-Ch., Union of S. Africa 1931-7, Lord Chamberlain of the Household and Chancellor of Roy. Victorian Order 1938-52, Chancellor of Order of St. Michael and St. George 1942-55, and a permanent Lord-in-Waiting to H.M. 1952-5: *m.* 1905, Adeline Verena Ishbel, *LL.D., J.P.,* who *d.* 1963, dau. of the late Herbert Haldane Somers-Cocks, and sister of 6th Baron Somers: *d.* 1955; *s.* by his grandson [7] GEORGE FREDERICK LAURENCE HYDE [son of the late George Herbert Arthur Edward Hyde, Lord Hyde (who *m*. 1932, the Hon. Marion Feodorovna Louise Glyn, DCVO, who *d.* 1970, da. of 4th Baron Wolverton), el son of 6th Earl], 7th Earl and present peer; also Baron Hyde.

CLARINA, BARONY OF. (Massey.) [Extinct 1952.]

DAUGHTER LIVING OF SIXTH BARON.

Hon. (Erin) Moira, *b.* 1909: *m.* 1939, Maj. Peter Roddam Holderness-Roddam, who *d.* 1970, and has issue living, Robert Christian Clarina, *b.* 1943. *Residence.*—Roddam Hall, Wooperton, Alnwick, Northumberland.

DAUGHTERS LIVING OF FIFTH BARON.

Hon. Sophia Isabelle ("Zoe") BUTLER-MASSEY, *b.* 1888: *m.* 1910, Capt. the Hon. Eric Brand Butler-Henderson, who *d.* 1953 [see B. Faringdon]. *Residence.*—Faccombe Manor, Andover. *Club,*—Farmers'.

CLARK, BARON, (Clark.) [Life Baron 1969.]

KENNETH MCKENZIE CLARK, *CH, KCB*, son of Kenneth McKenzie Clark, of Sudbourne Hall, Suffolk, and Ardnamurchan, Argyllshire; *b.* July 13th, 1903; ed. at Winchester, and Trin. Coll., Oxford (MA, Hon. Fellow); Fellow of Magdalen Coll., Oxford 1933-37; Hon. LLD Glasgow, and Liverpool; Hon. DLitt. Columbia, Oxford, London, Camb., York, and New York; Hon. FRIBA; a Member of Advisory Council of Victoria and Albert Museum; Keeper of Dept. of Fine Art, Ashmolean Museum, Oxford 1931-33, Dir. of Nat. Gallery 1933-46, Surveyor of the King's Pictures 1934-44, Slade Prof. of Fine Art, Oxford 1946-58 and 1961-62, Chm. of Arts Council of Gt. Britain 1953-60, and Chm. of ITA 1954-57; Chancellor of York Univ. since 1969; FBA; Cdr. of Legion of Honour of France, of Order of Merit of Italy, of Order of Finnish Lion, and Grand Cross of Order of Merit (2nd class) of Australia, and Gold Medal of New York Univ.; *cr.* KCB (Civil) 1938, CH 1959, and *Baron Clark*, of Saltwood, co. Kent, (Life Baron) 1969: *m.* 1927, Elizabeth Winifred, da. of Robert Macgregor Martin, and has issue.

Residence,—The Garden House, Castle Rd., Saltwood, nr. Hythe, Kent. *Clubs,*—St James's, Garrick.

SONS LIVING.

Hon. Alan Kenneth McKenzie, *MP* (Saltwood Castle, Kent), *b.* 1928; ed. at Eton, and Ch. Ch., Oxford; Bar. Inner Temple 1955; Gov. St. Thomas Hosp.; Mil-Historian, MP of Plymouth, Sutton (*C*) since Feb. 1974; *m.* 1958, Caroline Jane, da. of Col. Leslie Brindley Bream Beuttler, and has issue [see E Seafield, colls.].

Hon. Colin MacArthur (40, Cheyne Place, SW3), *b.* 1932; ed. at Eton, and Ch. Ch., Oxford: *m.* 1st, 1961 (m. diss. 1969), Violette Verdy; 2ndly, 1971, Mrs. Faith Shuckburgh.

DAUGHTER LIVING.

Hon. Colette Elizabeth Dickson (twin), *b.* 1932; ed. at Cheltenham Coll., and Lady Margaret Hall, Oxford (BA).

CLIFDEN, VISCOUNTCY OF. (Agar-Robartes.) [Extinct 1974.]

DAUGHTER LIVING OF EIGHTH VISCOUNT.

Hon. Rachel Mary, *b.* 1922: *m.* 1941, Capt. Cromwell Felix Justin Lloyd-Davies, DSO, DSC, RN, of Oakwood, Cannon Hill, Bray, Berks., and has issue living, Ann, *b.* 1942: *m.* 1964, Colin Victor Kenneth Williams of Highclere, Wentworth, Surrey, and has issue living, Andrew Nicholas Victor *b.* 1967, Simon Justin Colin *b.* 1972, Zara Alison *b.* 1970.

WIDOW LIVING OF EIGHTH VISCOUNT.

MARGARET (*Viscountess Clifden*) (La Vielle Demure, Beaumont, Jersey), da. of Ray Carter, of St. Louis, USA, formerly wife of John Harvey Thursky, and widow of John Eaton Monins: *m.* 1948, as his 2nd wife, the 8th Viscount, who *d.* 1974, when the title became ext.

CLIFFORD OF CHUDLEIGH, BARON. (Clifford.) [Baron E. 1672.]

Always ready.

LEWIS HUGH CLIFFORD, *OBE*, 13th Baron *b.* April 13th, 1916; *s.* 1964; ed. at Hertford Coll., Oxford (BA); Col. (late) Devonshire Regt.; Hon. Col. Devon Territorials (R. Devon Yeo/1st Rifle Vol.) T & AVR 1968-71, and Dep. Hon. Col. Wessex Yeo. RAC, TAVR 1971-72, since when Hon. Col. D Sqdn. Wessex Yeo. RAC, TAVR; a DL of Devon; ADC to HM 1964-69; 1939-45 War (prisoner, escaped 1943); OBE (Mil) 1962: *m.* 1945, the Hon. Katharine Fisher, da. of 2nd Baron Fisher, and has issue.

Arms,—Checky or and azure, a fesse gules. Crest,— Out of a ducal coronet or, a demi-wyvern gules. Supporters,—Two wyverns purpure.

Seat,—Ugbrooke Park, Chudleigh, S. Devon.

SONS LIVING.

Hon. THOMAS HUGH, *b.* March 17th, 1948; ed. at Downside; Capt. Coldm. Gds.
Hon. Rollo Hugh, *b.* 1954; ed. at Downside.

DAUGHTERS LIVING.

Hon. Cecilia Alice, *b.* 1945: *m.* 1968, Nicholas Breakspear Kirby, Lt. RN, of Langtrees, Landford, Salisbury, Wilts., and has issue living, Samantha Mary, *b.* 1969,—Christina Mary Anna, *b.* 1971.
Hon. Sarah Amy, *b.* 1956.

SISTERS LIVING.

Hon. Mary, *b.* 1919: *m.* 1943, Major Jack Philip Albert Galvin Clifford Wolff, MBE, and has issue living, Rosamund Elizabeth, *b.* 1944: *m.* 1966, John David Arnold Wallinger, of 7, Paultons Sq., SW3, son of Sir Geoffrey Arnold Wallinger, GBE, KCMG,—Antoinette Mary, *b.* 1946: *m.* 1970, David B. Parkes, of 12, Lyall St., SW1. *Residence,*—Barkham Manor, Barkham, Wokingham, Berks.
Hon. Rosamund Ann (*Baroness Fisher*), (Kilverstone Hall, Thetford; Marklye, Rushlake Green, Heathfield, Sussex); *b.* 1924: *m.* 1st, 1946 (m. diss. 1965), Geoffrey Forrester Fairbairn; 2ndly, 1970, the 3rd Baron Fisher, and has issue living (by 1st m.), James Clifford, *b.* 1950,—Charles Marcus Clifford, *b.* 1955,—Katrina Elizabeth, *b.* 1947.

DAUGHTER LIVING OF ELEVENTH BARON.

Hon. Agnes Mary, *b.* 1918: *m.* 1944, Robert Weatherhead Stallybrass, and has issue living, Hugh Greville, *b.* 1948: *m.* 1969, Carey, da. of L. R. Pullen, of Worthing,—Helen Hope, *b.* 1945,—Emma Catherine, *b.* 1951. *Residence,*—The Old Laundry, Oakhill, nr. Bath.

WIDOW LIVING OF SON OF TENTH BARON.

Alice Devin (*Hon.* Lady Clifford), (c/o Queen Anne's Farm, Jacob's Well, nr. Guildford); a CSJ ; da. of John Murton Gundry, of Cleveland, Ohio, USA: *m.* 1925, Capt. the Hon. Sir Bede Edmund Hugh Clifford, GCMG, CB, MVO, who *d.* 1969, and has issue living [see colls. infra].

WIDOW LIVING OF TWELFTH BARON.

MARY ELIZABETH (*Elizabeth, Baroness Clifford of Chudleigh*), (El Reposo, San Roque, Spain), da. of the late Rt. Hon. Sir Adrian Knox, KCMG, KC, LLB, sometime Ch. Justice of Australia: *m.* 1934, as his 2nd wife, the 12th Baron, who *d.* 1964.

COLLATERAL BRANCHES LIVING.

Issue of the late Capt. the Hon. Sir Bede Edmund Hugh Clifford, GCMG, CB, MVO, yst. son of 10th Baron, *b.* 1890, *d.* 1969: *m.* 1925, Alice Devin (ante), da. of John Murton Gundry, of Cleveland, Ohio, USA:—

Anne Frances May (*Viscountess Norwich*), (24, Blomfield Rd., W9), *b.* 1929: *m.* 1952, the 2nd Viscount Norwich.——(Patricia David) Pandora (Queen Anne's Farm, Jacob's Well, nr. Guildford), *b.* 1930: *m.* 1st, 1948 (m. diss. 1960), Timothy Angus Jones, son of Sir (George) Roderick Jones, KBE; 2ndly, 1961 (m. diss. 1968), the Hon. Michael Langhorne Astor [see V. Astor], and has issue living (by 1st m.) Alexander Roderick, *b.* 1955,—Annabel Lucy Veronica, *b.* 1948: *m.* 1969, Reginald Adrian Berkeley Sheffield [see Sheffield, Bt.].——Alice Devin Atalanta, *b.* 1932: *m.* 1st, 1955, Richard Fairey, who *d.* 1960, son of Sir (Charles) Richard Fairey, MBE; 2ndly, 1963, Wing-Cdr. Timothy

Ashmead Vigors, DFC; 3rdly, 1972, Michael Henry Dennis Madden, of Titching Farm, Jacobstow, Cornwall, and has issue living (by 1st m.) Leanda Alice Devin Joan, b. 1957,—(by 2nd m.), Thomas Ashmead Merton, b. 1969,—(by 3rd. m.) Henry George Bede, b, 1973.

Granddaughter of the late Maj.-Gen. the Hon. Sir Henry Hugh Clifford, V.C., K.C.M.G., C.B., 3rd son of 7th Baron :—
Issue of the late Sir Hugh Charles Clifford, G.C.M.G., G.B.E., b. 1866, d. 1941: m. 1st, 1896, Minna, who d. 1907, dau. of the late Gilbert à Beckett ; 2ndly, 1910, Elizabeth Lydia Rosabelle, C.B.E., who d. 1945, dau. of the late Edward William Bonham (sometime H.M.'s Consul at Calais), and widow of Henry Philip Ducarel de la Pasture, of Llandogo Priory, Monmouthshire :—
(By 1st marriage) Mary Agnes Philippa (Lady Holmes), b. 1898 : m. 1920, Maj.-Gen. Sir Noel Galway Holmes, K.B.E., C.B., M.C., late E. Yorkshire Regt., and has issue living, Hugh Clifford (Dennington, The Ridgeway, Woking), b. 1924: m. 1953, Gloria Joan Mary, only da. of the late Sir Harold Ernest Georges West, and has issue living, Robert Hugh b. 1955, Mark David b. 1958, Loretta Anne b. 1954, Michèle Therese b. 1956,—Bettine Mary (of Thatches, Hinksey Hill, Oxford), b, 1921: m. 1949, Capt. Peter G. F. Sutton, MC, Roy. Welch Fusiliers, who d. (killed in action in Malaya) 1958, and has issue living, Paul Anthony b. 1950, Piers Hugh b. 1953, Térèse Mary b. 1951. Residence,— Rockwood, Branksome Wood Rd., Fleet, Hants.

Descendants of the late Sir Charles Clifford (el. son of the late George Lambert Clifford, 5th son of the late Hon. Thomas Clifford, 2nd son of 3rd Baron), who was cr. a Baronet 1887 :—
See Clifford, Bt., cr. 1887.

PREDECESSORS.—[1] Rt. Hon. THOMAS Clifford, P.C.; M.P. for Totnes, Comptroller of the Household 1666, Treasurer of the Household 1668, and Principal Sec. of State and Lord High Treasurer 1672 ; cr. Baron Clifford of Chudleigh, co. Devon, 1672; d. 1673; s. by his son [2] HUGH, 2nd Baron; d. 1739; s. by his son [3] HUGH, 3rd Baron; d. 1732; s. by his son [4] HUGH, 4th Baron ; d. 1783; s. by his el. son [5] HUGH EDWARD HENRY, 5th Baron; d.s.p. 1793 ; s. by his brother [6] CHARLES, 6th Baron: m. the Hon. Eleanor Mary (a Countess of the Holy Roman Empire), dau. of 8th Baron Arundell of Wardour; d. 1831; s. by his son [7] HUGH CHARLES, 7th Baron, and in right of his mother, a Count of the Holy Roman Empire ; d. 1858 ; s. by his son [8] CHARLES HUGH, 8th Baron, b. 1819: m. 1845, the Hon. Agnes Catherine Louisa, who d. 1880, dau. of 11th Baron Petre ; d. 1880 ; s. by his son [9] LEWIS HENRY HUGH, 9th Baron, b. 1851: m. 1890, Mabel Anne, who d. 1921, dau. of Col. John Towneley, of Towneley, Lancashire; d. 1916; s. by his brother [10] WILLIAM HUGH, 10th Baron, b. 1858: m. 1st, 1886, Catherine Mary, who d. (March) 1943, dau. of R. Basset; 2ndly, (May) 1943, Grace Muriel, who d. 1963, dau. of the late W. St. Clair Munro, of Glasgow; d. (July) 1943; s. by his el. son [11] CHARLES OSWALD HUGH, 11th Baron; b. 1887; Lieut. 5th Batn. Devon Regt. (T.A.) and Sub-Lieut. R.N.V.R.: m. 1st. 1917, Dorothy, who d. 1918, dau. of the late Alfred Joseph Hornyold; 2ndly, 1940, Clare Mary, who d. 1975, da. of the late Capt. Jasper Graham Mayne, CBE, and widow of Charles Struthers White Ogilvie; d. 1962; s. by his brother, [12] LEWIS JOSEPH HUGH 12th Baron; b. 1889: m. 1st, 1914, Amy, who. d. 1926, el. da. of John A. Webster, MD; 2ndly, 1934, Mary Elizabeth, da. of the late Rt. Hon. Sir Adrian Knox; d. 1964; s. by his only son [13] LEWIS HUGH, 13th Baron and present peer.

Clifton of Leighton Bromswold, Baron, title of Earl of Darnley on Roll of House of Lords.

CLINTON, BARON. (Fane Trefusis.) [Baron E. 1299.]

GERARD NEVILE MARK FANE TREFUSIS, 22nd Baron; b. Oct. 7th, 1934; s. (on termination of abeyance) 1965; assumed by deed poll 1958 the surname of Trefusis after his patronymic: m. 1959, Nicola Harriette, da. of the late Maj. Charles Robert Purdon Coote [see Coote, Bt. colls.], and has issue.

Arms,—Argent semy of cross crosslets fitchy sable in a chief azure two mullets or pierced gules, Clinton, charged with a inescutcheon quarterly, 1st, argent, on a fess azure three dexter gauntlets appaumy or, Fane, 2nd, argent, a chevron between three spindles sable, Trefusis, 3rd, azure, three boars' heads couped argent, muzzled gules, a cross crosslet argent, for distinction, Forbes of Pitsligo, 4th, or, a bend gules, surmounted by a fess checky azure and argent, in chief a crescent azure, a canton ermine for difference, Stuart. Crest,—A bull's head erased sable armed, and about the neck an ancient crown attached thereto a line or, in the mouth a rose gules barbed seeded slipped and leafed proper. Supporters,—On either side a greyhound argent collared with line reflexed over the back gules, in the mouth a gauntlet as in the arms, Clinton.

Residence,—Heanton Satchville, Okehampton, Devon.

SON LIVING.
Hon. CHARLES PATRICK ROLLE, b. March 21st, 1962.

DAUGHTERS LIVING.
Hon. Caroline Harriet, b. 1960.
Hon. Henrietta Jane, b. 1964.

SISTERS LIVING.
Carol, b. 1937: m. 1959, Hugo Peter Charles Bevan, of Kingsbridge Farm, Steeple Claydon, Bucks., and has issue living, Rupert Charles, b. 1965,—Georgina Lucy, b. 1963,—Charlotte Adèle, b. 1967,— Sophy Alexandra, b. 1968.
Fiona, b. 1939: m. 1962, Sylvanus John Connolly, of Estate House, Heytesbury, Wilts., and has issue living, Daniel Charles, b. 1970,—Nicola Jane, b. 1964,—Alice Louise, b. 1965,—Claudia Gay, b. 1969.

UNCLE LIVING.
John Henry Mark FANE, MBE (25, Wooburn Manor Park, Wooburn Green, Bucks), b. 1917; is Capt. Green Howards; 1939-45 War (prisoner, escaped, MBE); MBE (Mil.) 1944: m. 1st, 1939 (m. diss. 1954), Catherine Adelaide Anne, only child of the late Gabriel Noel Dyer [Legard, Bt., colls.]; 2ndly, 1954 (m. diss. 1962), Eleanor Sybil Ruth Archdeacon; 3rdly, 1964, Elizabeth, da. of Kenneth W. Cowell, of Les Mouriaux, Alderney, and has issue living, (by 2nd marriage) Simon John Nevile, b. 1954,—Robert Trefusis, b. 1958,—Harriet Jane, b. 1956,—Briony Ann, b. 1957.

AUNTS LIVING.

Anne Charmian FANE, *b.* 1916; resumed the surname of Fane 19—: *m.* 1st, 1937 (m. diss. 1949), Maj. Robert Henry Arthur Rivers-Bulkeley, Scots Guards [see E. Wemyss, colls.]; 2ndly, 1949, Peter Richard Hampton, MC, and has issue living, (by 1st m.) [see E. Wemyss, colls.].
Etheldreda Flavia, *b.* 1922.

MOTHER LIVING.

Gladys Mabel (West Monkton House, Taunton), da. of the late Rt. Hon. Sir Gerard Augustus Lowther, GCMG, CB, 1st Bt. (cr. 1914, ext.): *m.* 1st, 1933, Capt. Charles Nevile Fane, who *d.* (killed in action) 1940; 2ndly, 1942, Lt.-Col. James Hayton Greenhill Black, late Argyll and Sutherland Highlanders, who *d.* 1966.

COLLATERAL BRANCHES LIVING.

Issue of the late Hon. Fenella Hepburn-Stuart-Forbes-Trefusis, yr. da. of 21st Baron, *b.* 1889, *d.* 1966: *m.* 1914, the Hon. John Herbert Bowes-Lyon, who *d.* 1930 [see E. Strathmore].

Grandchildren of the late Maj. the Hon. Henry Walter Hepburn-Stuart-Forbes-Trefusis, Sco,s Gds, 2nd son of 20th Baron:—
Issue of the late Henry Trefusis, late Lt. Cdr. RNVR, who relinquished the surnames of Hepburn-Stuart-Forbes by statutory declaration 1939, *b.* 1908, *d.* 1975: *m.* 1940, Sheila Margaret (Trefusis, Falmouth), da. of Herman Bryan, of Lanthwaite, Eaton Hill, Norwich:
Nicholas John TREFUSIS (Trefusis, Falmouth); *b.* 1943; Lieut. RN: *m.* 1973, Servane, yst. da. of Louis Mélénec, of Brest, and Landévenneg,—Thomasine Mary, *b.* 1942: *m.* 1970, Philip Henry Faudel Heycock, of 47, Cloudesley Rd., N1 0EL, and has issue living, Thomas Henry Trefusis, *b.* 1971,— Eleanor Rachel, *b.* 1974.——Morwenna Jane, *b.* 1945.——Ann Kerensa, *b.* 1949.

Issue of the late Hon. Robert Henry Hepburn-Stuart-Forbes-Trefusis, yst. son of 20th Baron, *b.* 1888, *d.* 1958: *m.* 1914, Lady Dorothy Marguerite Elizabeth, OBE, who *d.* 1956, da. of the late Col. Edward William Herbert, CB [E. Powis]—
Helen Beatrice Margaret, *b.* 1917: *m.* 1936, Maj. Simon Whitbread, KRRC, of The Mallowry, Riseley, Bedford [see E. Mayo, colls.].

Issue of the late Hon. Evelyn Mary Hepburn-Stuart-Forbes-Trefusis, 5th da. of 20th Baron, *b.* 1883, *d.* 1963: *m.* 1911, Col. Harry Stuart Ravenhill, CMG, who *d.* 1930:—
Alec Trefusis (of 139, Peppard Rd., Caversham, Berks), *b.* 1914.

Issue of the late Hon. Harriet Margaret Hepburn-Stuart-Forbes-Trefusis, yst. da. of 20th Baron, *b.* 1891, *d.* 1975: *m.* 1914, Lt.-Col. Eustace Widdrington Morrison-Bell, who *d.* 1947.
See Morrison-Bell, Bt., cols., cr. 1905.

Grandchildren of the late Col. the Hon. Walter Rodolph Trefusis, CB, 3rd son of 19th Baron:—
Issue of the late Margaret Harriet Trefusis, *b.* 1885, *d.* 1966: *m.* 1911, Lt.-Col. Edgar Hugh Brassey, MVO, who *d.* 1946.
Hugh Trefusis, OBE, MC (Manor Farm, Little Somerford, Chippenham, Wilts.), *b.* 1915; ed. at Eton; Lt.-Col. and Brevet Col., late comdg. R. Wilts Yeo; late Maj. R. Scots Greys; a JP for Wilts; High Sheriff of Wilts 1959, and Vice-Lieut. 1969; Exon. of Queen's Bodyguard of Yeomen of the Guard since 1969; 1939-45 War (MC, Croix de Guerre); OBE (Mil) 1959: *m.* 1939, Joyce Patricia, da. of Capt. Maurice John Kingscote [B. Gifford], and has issue living, Antony Hugh Owen, *b.* 1945,— Kim Maurice, *b.* 1955,—Jane Margaret, *b.* 1946.—Sarah Patricia *b.* 1949.——Marjorie Eva, *b.* 1911: *m.* 1933, Hugh Myddleton Peacock, TD, DL, of The Ferry, Milton, Peterborough, and has issue living, Michael Hugh, *b.* 1946: *m.* 1974, Caroline Mary, yst. da. of Maj. Robert Hoare, of Hambleton Hall, Oakham,—Idina Caroline, *b.* 1933: *m.* 1957, Col. James William Gordon Pirie, 60th Rifles, of 38, Kew Green, Richmond, Surrey, and has issue living, James Hugh Pirie *b.* 1959, Amanda Caroline *b.* 1962,—Susan Margaret, *b.* 1938: *m.* 1964, Michael Andrieus Jones, of 955, W. Santa Inez, Hillsborough, Cal., USA, and has issue living Philip Andrieus *b.* 1966, Idina Maria *b.* 1968.

Issue of the late Col. the Hon. John Schomberg TREFUSIS, C.M.G., 4th son of 19th Baron, *b.* 1852, *d.* 1932: *m.* 1883, Eva Louisa Bontein, who *d.* 1949, dau. of the late James Bontein, Groom of the Privy Chamber, and H.M.'s Clerk of the Robes [Shelley, Bt., colls., cr. 1611]:—
Elizabeth Katharine Mary, *b.* 1887: *m.* 1907, Capt. Garth Neville Walford, V.C., R.H.A., who *d.* (killed in action) 1915, and has issue living, Naomi, *b.* 1908,—Phyllida, *b.* 1915: *m.* 1944, Kenneth Ellis, who *d.* 1972. *Residence,*—Gapperies, W. Porlock, Minehead, Som.

Granddaughter of the late Capt. the Hon. George Walpole Rolle Trefusis, R.N., 3rd son of 17th Baron:—
Issue of the late Rt. Rev. Robert Edward Trefusis, Bishop of Crediton (Suffragan for Diocese of Exeter), D.D., *b.* 1843, *d.* 1930: *m.* 1874, Emma Mary, who *d.* 1927, dau. of the late Owen Wethered, of Remnantz, Great Marlow :—
Hilda, *b.* 1891. *Residence,*—18, Windmill Lane, Northam, Bideford, N. Devon.

Grandson of the Rt. Rev. Robert Edward Trefusis, D.D. (Bishop of Crediton) (ante) :—
Issue of the late Major George Rodolph Trefusis (el. son), *b.* 1875, *d.* 1927: *m.* 1911, Elsis Jane, who *d.* 1946, da. of the late James Start Harrison of Sydney, NSW:—
Robert John Rodolph, *b.* 1914; formerly Maj. Scots Guards; CEng, MICE and FIMechE; HM's Foreign Ser. 1946-54: *m.* 1955, Shirley Adeline Scott, da. of the late Charles Scott Barton, of Sullington, Sussex, and has issue living, Charles Rodolph, *b.* 1961,—Rosemary Jane, *b.* 1959. *Residence,*— 44, Halsey St., SW3 2PT. *Club,*—Carlton.

PREDECESSORS.—[1] JOHN de Clinton, summoned to Parliament of England 1299; his grandson [2] JOHN, 2nd Baron, summoned to Parliament 1332-5; *s.* by his son [3] *Sir* JOHN, Knt., 3rd Baron, summoned to Parliament 1357-97; *d.* 1397; *s.* by his grandson [4] WILLIAM, 4th Baron; *d.* 1432; *s.* by his son [5] JOHN, 5th Baron; a staunch Yorkist, was attainted 1461, and subsequently restored; *d.* 1464: *s.* by his son [6] JOHN, 6th Baron; *d.* 1488; *s.* by his son [7] JOHN, 7th Baron; *d.* 1514; *s.* by his son [8] THOMAS, 8th Baron; *d.* 1517; *s.* by his son [9] EDWARD, K.G., P.C., 9th Baron, Lord High Adm.; cr. *Earl of Lincoln* (peerage of England) 1572; *d.* 1585; *s.* by his son [10] HENRY, K.B., 2nd Earl; *d.* 1616; *s.* by his son [11] THOMAS, 3rd Earl; *d.* 1618; *s.* by his son [12] THEOPHILUS, K.B., 4th Earl; *d.* 1667; *s.* by his grandson [13] EDWARD, 5th Earl; *d.s.p.* 1692, when the Earldom devolved upon his cousin [see D. Newcastle], and the barony became abeyant between the issue of his aunts; in 1721 the abeyance was terminated in favour of [14] HUGH Fortescue, 14th Baron; cr. *Baron Fortescue,* of Castlehill, co. Devon, with limitation to his half-brother Matthew, and *Earl of Clinton* (peerage of Great Britain) 1746, *d.s.p.* 1751, when the Earldom of Clinton became extinct, the Barony of Fortescue passed to his half-brother [see E. Fortescue], and the Barony of Clinton devolved upon his cousin [15] MARGARET, wife of 2nd Earl of Orford, and wife of the Hon. Sewallis Shirley [E. Ferrers]; *d.* 1781; *s.* by her son [16] GEORGE, 3rd *Earl of Orford* and 16th Baron Clinton; *d.s.p.* 1791, when the Earldom passed to his nephew, and in 1794 the Barony of Clinton was successfully claimed by his cousin [17] ROBERT GEORGE WILLIAM Trefusis, 17th Baron, the descendant of Lady Arabella Rolle, 2nd dau. of 4th Earl of Lincoln; *d.* 1797; *s.* by his el. son [18] ROBERT COTTON ST. JOHN, 18th Baron; a Lord of the Bedchamber to George III.; *d.* 1832; *s.* by his brother [19] CHARLES RODOLPH, 19th Baron, *b.* 1791; *m.* 1831, Lady Elizabeth Georgiana Kerr, who *d.* 1871, dau. of 6th Marquess of Lothian; *d.* 1866; *s.* by his son [20]

CHARLES HENRY ROLLE, 20th Baron, *b.* 1834; sat as M.P. for N. Devon (*LC*) 1857-66; Under Sec. of State for India 1867-8, a Charity Commr. 1874-80, and Lord-Lieut. of Devonshire 1887-1904; assumed by Roy. licence 1867, the additional surnames of Hepburn-Stuart-Forbes: *m.* 1st, 1858, Harriet Williamina, who *d.* 1869, dau. and heiress of Sir John Stuart Forbes, 8th Bt.; 2ndly, 1875, Margaret, who *d.* 1930, dau. of Sir John Walrond Walrond, 1st Bt.: *d.* 1904: *s.* by his son [21] CHARLES JOHN ROBERT, *G.C.V.O., P.C.*, 21st Baron; *b.* 1863; High Steward of Barnstaple; was Joint Parliamentary Sec. to Board of Agriculture and Fisheries 1918, a Member of Council of Duchy of Cornwall (1911-33) and Keeper of the Privy Seal (1913-33) of H.R.H. the Prince of Wales, and Lord Warden of the Stannaries 1921-33; Chm. of Forestry Institute 1924-9, and of Forestry Commn. 1927-9: *m.* 1886, Lady Jane Grey McDonnell (a C.St.J.), who *d.* 1953, da. of 5th Earl of Antrim; *d.* 1957, when the Barony fell into abeyance between his two daughters, the Hon. Harriet, who *m.* Maj. Henry Nevile Fane, and *d.* 1958, and the Hon. Fenella, who *d.* 1966, having *m.* the Hon. John Herbert Bowes-Lyon, and so continued until 1965, when the abeyance was terminated in favour of the senior co-heir [22] GERARD NEVILE MARK (only son of the late Capt. Charles Nevile Fane, el. son of the late Hon. Harriet Fane), 22nd Baron and present peer.

CLITHEROE, BARON. (Assheton.) [Baron U.K. 1955, Bt. U.K. 1945.]

I am neither proud nor afraid.

RALPH ASSHETON, *P.C.*, 1st Baron, and 2nd Baronet; *b.* Feb. 24th, 1901; *s.* to the Baronetcy (Sept.) 1955; ed. at Eton (Oppidan Scholar), and at Ch. Ch. Oxford (MA); Bar. Inner Temple 1925; Lord of the Manor of Downham, and other manors; High Steward of Westminster since 1962; Lord-Lt. of co. Lancaster since 1971; Member of Council of Duchy of Lancaster, JP of Lancs., FSA; a Dir. of Tanganyika Concessions, Ltd., and other Cos.; formerly Chm. of Borax (Holdings), Ltd. and The Mercantile Investment Trust, Ltd., 1956-71, Dep. Chm. Nat. Westminster Bank, Ltd. Nat. Provincial Bank, Ltd., and Tube Investments, Ltd. a Dir. of Coutts & Co., Rio Tinto-Zinc Corpn., John Brown & Co., LNER Co., and other Cos.; Member of London Stock Exchange 1927-39, and of Church Assembly 1930-50, PPS to Rt. Hon. W. Ormsby Gore (when 1st Commr. of Works and Sec. of State for Colonies) 1936-38, Parliamentary Sec. to Min. of Labour Sept. 1939 to Feb. 1942, and Min. of Supply Feb. 1942 to Dec. 1942, Financial Sec. to Treasury Dec. 1942 to Oct. 1944, and Chm. of Conservative and Unionist Party Organization Oct. 1944 to July 1946; a Member of Roy. Commn. to W. Indies 1938-39; Chm. of Public Accounts Cttee. 1948-50, and of Select Cttee. on Nationalised Industries 1951-53; MP Rushcliffe Div. of Notts (*C*) 1934-35, for City of London 1945-50 and for W. Div. of Blackburn 1950-55; cr. P.C. 1944, and *Baron Clitheroe*, of Downham, co. Lancaster (peerage of United Kingdom) (June) 1955: *m.* 1924, the Hon. Sylvia Benita Frances Hotham, da. of 6th Baron Hotham, and has issue.

Arms,—Argent a mullet sable pierced of the field. **Crest,**—On a cap of maintenance, a mower, vested and capped quarterly, argent and sable, sleeves and stockings counter changed, holding a scythe azure, handled or, the point of the blade towards the dexter. **Supporters,**—*Dexter,* a Labrador dog sable; *sinister,* a bull argent armed or.

Residences,—Downham Hall, near Clitheroe, Lancashire; 17, Chelsea Park Gardens, S.W.3. *Clubs,*—Carlton, City of London, Royal Automobile.

SONS LIVING.

Hon. RALPH JOHN, *b.* Nov. 3rd, 1929; ed. at Eton (Oppidan Scholar), and at Ch. Ch., Oxford (Scholar, MA); Lord of the Honour of Clitheroe and Hundred of Blackburn, a Dir. of Rio Tinto Zinc Corpn. Ltd., and Borax Holdings Ltd., and a Liveryman of Skinners' Co.; late 2nd Lt. Life Guards: *m.* 1961, Juliet, da. of Lt.-Col. Christopher Lionel Hanbury, MBE, TD, of Juniper Hill, Burnham, Bucks, and has issue living, Ralph Christopher, *b.* 1962,—John Hotham, *b.* 1964,—Elizabeth Jane, *b.* 1968. *Residence,*—Burners Cottage, Wexham, Stoke Poges, Bucks. *Clubs,*—Carlton, Royal Automobile.

Hon. Nicholas, *b.* 1934; ed. at Ch. Ch., Oxford (MA); Member of London Stock Exchange (Member of Council 1969), partner in the firm of Montagu, Loebl, Stanley & Co., Stockbrokers, a Dir. of Nat. Mutual Life Assocn. of Australasia, and a Liveryman of Vintners' Co.; formerly 2nd Lieut. Life Guards, and Lieut. Inns of Court Regt.: *m.* 1960, Jacqueline Jill, dau. of Marshal of the RAF Sir Arthur Travers Harris, GCB, OBE, AFC, 1st Bt., and has issue living, Thomas, *b.* 1963,—Caroline, *b.* 1961,—Mary Thérèse, *b.* 1967. *Residence,*—5, Astell St., SW3. *Clubs,*—Carlton, City of London.

DAUGHTER LIVING.

Hon. Bridget *[Hon. Lady Worsley],* *b.* 1926; late WRNS: *m.* 1955, Sir (William) Marcus John Worsley, 5th Bt. *Residences,*—Hovingham Hall, York; 25, Flood St., SW3.

SISTERS LIVING.

Mary Monica, b. 1903 ; is a J.P. for Lancashire : m. 1940, Capt. Charles Peter Fleetwood Fleetwood-Hesketh, T.D., D.L., Duke of Lancaster's Own Yeo., and has issue living, Everilda Dorothea, b. 1941. Residences,—The Manor House, Hale, near Liverpool ; 57, Great Ormond Street, W.C.1.

Eleanor, C.B.E., b. 1907 ; was Vice-Chm. of the Yorkshire Provincial Area of National Union of Conservative and Unionist Assos. 1952-5 ; C.B.E. (Civil) 1956 : m. 1926, Major John Edward Evelyn Yorke, J.P., and has issue living, David John (of Hall Foot, Clitheroe, Lancs.), b. 1927; ed. at Eton, and at Trin. Coll., Camb. (MA); late The Life Guards; a JP of Lancs.: m. 1957, Susan Alexandra, da. of Lt.-Col. Scrope Arthur Francis Sutherland Egerton, Highland LI (ret.) [see D. Sutherland, colls.], and has issue living, John Alexander b. 1959, Charles Scrope Edward b. 1965, Sophia Caroline Annabel b. 1961,—Felicity Anne, b. 1931: m. 1955, James Patrick Ashley Cooper, son of Sir Patrick Ashley Cooper, of Hexton Manor, Hitchin, Herts., and has issue living, Patrick John Ashley b. 1957, Edward James Ashley b. 1966, Katharine Mary b. 1956, Felicity b. 1961. Residence,—Halton Pl., Hellifield, Skipton, Yorks.

PREDECESSOR.—[1] Ralph Cockayne Assheton, son of the late Ralph Assheton, M.P., of Downham Hall, Clitheroe, Lancashire, and Cuerdale, Lancashire; b. 1860; High Sheriff of Lancashire 1919; was a Co. Councillor for Lancashire 1892-1902, and a Co. Alderman 1902-49; cr. a Baronet 1945 : m. 1898, Mildred Estelle Sybella, C.B.E., J.P., who d. 1949, dau. and co-heiress of John Henry Master, J.P., of Montrose House, Petersham, Surrey; d. (Sept.) 1955 ; s. by his only son [2] RALPH, 2nd Bt. and present peer.

CLONBROCK, BARONY OF. (Dillon.) [Extinct 1926.]

SISTER LIVING OF FIFTH BARON.

Hon. Ethel Louisa, b. 1880. Residence,—Clonbrock, Ahascragh, co. Galway.

CLONMELL, EARLDOM OF. (Scott.) [Extinct 1935.]

DAUGHTER LIVING OF SEVENTH EARL.

Lady Sheila Mary (162, Rivermead Court, Ranelagh Gdns., SW6), b. 1906: m. 1st, 1926, Major Mansel Halkett Jackson, DSO, MC, Indian Cav., who obtained a divorce 1930; 2ndly 1931 (m. diss. 1947), Sir Osmond Otho Durlacher [Hanson, Bt., cr. 1887], and has issue living, (by 1st m.) Michael Rupert, b. 1926; ed. at Gordonstoun,—by 2nd m.) Timothy Esmond (68, Courtfield Gdns., SW5), b. 1931: m. 1958 (dir. 1968), Joanna June, da. of Bertram Hutchinson Osmaston, and has issue living, Susan Emma b. 1962,—Richard Frederic (59, Victoria Rd., W8), b. 1933; ed. at Radley: m. 1964, Wendy Raphael, and has issue living, Noel b. 1965, Natasha b. 1967, Samantha b. 1971,—Elizabeth Mary, b. 1938: m. 1965, Sergio Berlinquer, c/o Italian Embassy, 14, Three King's Yard, W1, and has issue living, Francesca Moira b. 1968, Maria Sheila b. 1971.

CLWYD, BARON. (Roberts.) [Baron U.K. 1919, Bt. U.K. 1908.]
[Title pronounced "Cloo-id."]

(JOHN) TREVOR ROBERTS, 2nd Baron and 2nd Baronet ; b. Nov. 28th, 1900 ; s. 1955 ; ed. at Trin. Coll., Camb. (B.A. 1922) ; Bar. Gray's Inn 1930 ; is a J.P. for co. London ; was Assist. Sec. of Commns., Lord Chancellor's Depart., of House of Lord 1949-61 : m. 1932, Joan de Bois, dau. of the late Charles R. Murray, of Woodbank, Partickhill, Glasgow, and has issue.

Arms,—Per fesse azure and argent, a lion rampant between three ostrich feathers all counterchanged. Crest,—A lion rampant per fesse argent and azure, holding in its paws an ostrich feather. Supporters,—Dexter, a dragon proper, collared or ; sinister, a sable bear, also collared or.

Residences,—15, Aubrey Rd., Kensington, W8; Trimmings, Gracious St., Selborne, Hants.

SON LIVING.

Hon. JOHN ANTHONY (24, Salisbury Av., Cheam, Sutton, Surrey, SM1 2DJ), b. Jan. 2nd, 1935; ed. at Harrow, and at Trin. Coll., Camb.: Bar. Gray's Inn 1970: m. 1969, Geraldine, yr. da. of C. E. Cannons, of Sanderstead and has issue living, John Murray, b. Aug. 27th, 1971,—Jeremy Trevor, b. 1973.

DAUGHTER LIVING.

Hon. Alison de Bois, b. 1939: m. 1st, 1965 (m. diss. 1972), George Stricevic; 2ndly, 1972, Anthony H. Brown, of 9, Royal Terr., Glasgow, G3 7NT, and has issue living (by 1st m.) Milorad, b. 1967,—(by 2nd m.) Barnaby Joseph, b. 1973.

BROTHER LIVING.

Hon. (William Herbert) Mervyn, b. 1906; ed. at Trin. Coll., Camb. (BA); ARCM; LMusTCL; ALCM: m. 1947, Eileen Margaret, da. of the late A. T. Easom, of Hillside, Abergele, and has issue living, Catherine Angela, b. 1950. Residence,—Arunlea, 41, Worthing Road, Horsham, Sussex.

WIDOW LIVING OF SON OF FIRST BARON.

Aileen Mary, dau. of the late Charles Edward Burrow, of Sale, Cheshire: m. 1936, the Hon. David Stowell Roberts, who d. 1956, and has issue living [see infra]. Residence,—Box Cottage, Box, Stroud, Glos.

COLLATERAL BRANCH LIVING.
Issue of the late Hon. David Stowell Roberts, 2nd son of 1st Baron, b. 1900, d.
1956: m. 1936, Aileen Mary (ante), dau. of the late Charles Edward Burrow, of
Sale, Cheshire:—
Hugh Martin (3, Poplar Close, Roxton, Bedford), b. 1941; ed. at Christ's Hosp. Sch., and Merton Coll.,
Oxford; Dep. Headmaster, Sandy Comprehensive Sch., Beds.: m. 1966, Diana, da. of Denis C.
Cochran, of Cape Town, and has issue living, Thomas Owen, b. 1973.—Sarah Megan b. 1971.——
Peter Gareth, b. 1947; ed. at Christ's Hosp. Sch., and Univ. of E. Anglia.——Fenella, b. 1940: m.
1968, Peter Rosenwald, of 28, Paulton's Sq., SW3, and has issue living, David Joseph, b. 1972,—
Celia Janet, b. 1974.

PREDECESSOR.—[1] JOHN HERBERT Roberts, el. son. of the late John Roberts (sometime M.P.
for Flint Dist.) of Bryngwenallt, Abergele, N. Wales; b. 1863; Chm. of Welsh Liberal Parliamentary
Party 1912-18 (formerly Sec.); M.P. for W. Div. of Denbighshire (L) 1892-1918; cr. a Baronet 1908,
and Baron Clwyd, of Abergele, Co. Denbigh (peerage of United Kingdom) 1919: m. 1893, Hannah
Rushton, who d. 1951, dau. of the late William Sproston Caine, M.P., of 33, North Side, Clapham
Common, S.W.; d. 1955: s. by his el. son [2] (JOHN) TREVOR, 2nd Baron and present peer

CLYDESMUIR, BARON.   (Colville.)   [Baron U.K. 1948.]

I cannot forget.

RONALD JOHN BILSLAND COLVILLE,
KT, CB, MBE, TD, 2nd Baron; b.
May 21st, 1917; s. 1954; ed. at Char-
terhouse, and at Trin. Coll., Camb.
(BA); Hon. LLD Strathclyde; Hon.
DSc Heriot-Watt; Hon. Col. R. Scots
and Cameronians Territorials TA &
VR 1967-72; Brig. of Queen's Body
Guard for Scotland (R. Co. of Archers),
Pres. of Council and Pres. of Lowlands
of Scotland TA & VR Assocns.; Pres. of
Scottish Branch Nat. Playing Fields
Asscn., Gov. Bank of Scotland, a
Dir. of Scotbits Securities Ltd., of
Scottish Provident Instn., of Scottish
Western Investment Co., and of
Barclays Bank; Chm. of North Sea
Assets Ltd.; a Dir. of British Steel
Corpn. Strip Mills Div., 1970-73; a
Dir. of Caledonian Offshore Co. Ltd.,
Chm. of Exec. Cttee., Scottish Council
(Development and Industry) since
1966, and of Scottish Exports Cttee.
since 1970; Lord High Commr. to
Gen. Assembly of Church of Scotland 1971 and 1972; Lord Lieut. for Lanark-
shire since 1963; 1939-45 War (despatches); MBE (Mil) 1944, CB (Civil)
1965, KT 1972: m. 1946, Joan Marguerita, da. of Lt.-Col. Ernest Brabazon
Booth, DSO, MD, and has issue.

Arms,—Argent, a cross moline sable, on a chief of the last a thistle slipped proper between two
bulls' heads also argent. Crest,—A hind's head erased proper. Supporters,—A roebuck and a doe,
both proper.

Residence,—Langlees House, Biggar, Lanarkshire. Clubs,—Caledonian, New (Edinburgh),
Western (Glasgow).

SONS LIVING.
Hon. DAVID RONALD, b. April 8th, 1949.
Hon. Andrew John, b. 1953.

DAUGHTERS LIVING.
Hon. Diana Mary, b. 1947: m. 1973, Christopher I. C. Munro.
Hon. Elizabeth Anne. b. 1956.

SISTERS LIVING.
Hon. Mary Helen, b. 1922: m. 1949, Capt. North Edward Frederick Dalrymple-Hamilton, C.V.O.
MBE, DSC, RN, of Lovestone House, Girvan, Ayrshire [see E. Stair, colls.].
Hon. Rosemary Anne Heather, b. 1927: m. 1954, Philip Arthur Whitcombe, of Green Cross Farm,
Churt, Farnham, Surrey, and has issue living, Robert John, b. 1955,—Susan Anne Clare, b. 1957.

PREDECESSOR.—[1] Rt. Hon. Sir DAVID JOHN Colville, G.C.I.E., T.D., P.C., son of the late John
Colville, M.P., J.P., of Cleland House, Lanarkshire; b. 1894; was Parliamentary Private Sec. to
Under-Sec. of State for Scotland Sept. to Nov. 1931, Parliamentary Sec. to Depart. of Overseas
Trade 1931-5. Under-Sec. of State for Scotland 1935-36, Financial Sec. to the Treasury 1936-8,
Sec. of State for Scotland 1938-40 and Gov. of Bombay 1943-48 (acted as Viceroy and Gov.-Gen.
of India on four occasions); a Gov. of British Broadcasting Corporation 1950-4 and National Gov.
for Scotland 1952-4; sat as M.P. for N. Div. of Midlothian and Peeblesshire (U) 1929-43; cr. Baron
Clydesmuir, of Braidwood, co. Lanark (peerage of United Kingdom) 1948: m. 1915, Agnes Anne,
CI, who d. 1970, da. of Sir William Bilsland, 1st Bt., LLD; d. 1954; s. by his only son [2] RONALD
JOHN BILSLAND, 2nd Baron and present peer.

COBBOLD, BARON. (Cobbold.) [Baron U.K. 1960.]

CAMERON FROMANTEEL COBBOLD, KG, GCVO, PC, 1st Baron, son of the late Lieut.-Col. Clement John Fromanteel Cobbold; b. Sept. 14th, 1904; ed. at Eton (Fellow 1951-67), and at King's Coll., Camb.; Hon. DSc(Econ) London; Hon. LLD Mc-Gill; a Lt. for City of London; DL for Herts.; High Sheriff for Co. of London 1946-47, and Gov. of Bank of England 1949-61; a Dir. of Hudson's Bay Co. 1962-75 and of British Petroleum Co., Ltd. 1962-74, and of Guardian Royal Exchange 1968-74; a Member of Advisory Board of Chemical Bank New York Trust Co. 1966-75; Chm. of Middx. Hosp., and of Med. Sch. Council 1963-74; Lord Chamberlain of the Household 1963-71, since when a Lord-in-Waiting to HM; Pres. of British Heart Foundation since 1969; Steward of the Courts, Eton Coll., since 1973; cr. PC 1959, Baron Cobbold, of Knebworth, co. Hertford (peerage of UK) 1960, GCVO 1963, and KG 1970: m. 1930, Lady (Margaret) Hermione (Millicent) Lytton, da. of 2nd Earl of Lytton, and has issue.

Arms,—Sable a chevron or between in chief two bezants and in base a lion passant guardant gold on a chief dancetty of the last two ducal coronets azure. **Crest,**—A lion statant guardant argent crowned with a ducal coronet azure supporting with the dexter paw an escutcheon vert thereon three escutcheons also argent each having a bordure engrailed or. **Supporters,**—On either side a yellow labrador dog proper each resting the interior hind foot on a battering ram fessewise the head inward also proper headed and garnished azure.

Residence,—Lake House, Knebworth, Herts. *Club*—White's.

SONS LIVING.

Hon. DAVID ANTONY FROMANTEEL *LYTTON COBBOLD*, b. 1937; assumed by deed poll 1960 the additional surname of Lytton before his patronymic: m. 1961, Christine Elizabeth, dau. of Sir Dennis Frederick Bankes Stucley, 5th Bt., and has issue living, Henry Fromanteel, b. 1962. —Peter Guy Fromanteel, b. 1964,—Richard Stucley Fromanteel, b. 1968,—Rosina Kim, b. 1971. *Residence,*—Knebworth House, Knebworth, Herts.

Hon. Rowland John Fromanteel (PO Box 402, St. Johns, Antigua), b. 1944: m. 1969, Sophia Augusta, da. of B. N. White-Spunner, of Lansdowne, Nenagh, co. Tipperary, and has issue living, Patrick Alexander Fromanteel, b. 1974,—Lorna Bridget, b. 1971.

DAUGHTER LIVING.

Hon. Susan Victoria, b. 1933: m. 1957, Squadron Leader Christopher Charles Blount, M.V.O., R.A.F., and has issue living, James Hubert Rowland, b. 1958,—Oliver Charles, b. 1959,—Catherine Victoria Jane, b. 1962,—Pamela Jane, b. 1965. *Residence.*—Manor Farm, Barkway, Herts.

COBHAM, BARONY OF. (Alexander.) [Baron E. 1312-13.] [Abeyant 1951.]

ROBERT DISNEY LEITH ALEXANDER, 13th Baron (16th but for the attainder), in whose favour the abeyance was determined in 1933 ; d. 1951.

SISTERS LIVING OF THIRTEENTH BARON.
(Raised to the rank of a Baron's daughters 1917.)

Hon. Mary Isabel, b. 1882 : m. 1st, 1916, Capt. John Leslie Morton Shaw, Duke of Wellington's (W. Riding Regt.), who d. 1925 ; 2ndly, 1927, John Bazley Bazley-White, M.C., who d. (on active service during European War) 1940 [E. Rothes], and has issue living, (by 1st marriage) John Anthony Cobham, MC (The Old Rectory, Upper Stondon, Henlow, Beds.), b. 1917; ed. at Eton; 1939-45 War as Maj. RA (MC and Bar): m. 1st, 1945, Rhondda, who d. 1964, da. of the late Brig.-Gen. Charles Herbert Rankin, CB, CMG, DSO [see Rankin, Bt., cr. 1898, colls.]; 2ndly, 1965, Phyllis Rosemary, da. of the late Arthur David Clere Parsons [see E. Rosse, colls.], and widow of the late Capt. Ian Stanley Akers-Douglas, Berks. Yeo. [see V. Chilston, colls.], and has issue living (by 1st marriage) Simon Rhys b. 1949, Veronica Mary b. 1946,—Cynthia Mary, b. 1920: m. 1946, Sidney James Fulton, CMG, of Old Farmhouse, Kingston-St. Mary, Taunton, Somerset, and has issue living, Robert Henry Gervase b. 1948, Ann Elizabeth b. 1947, Jane Louisa b. 1954,—Margaret Daphne, b. 1923; m. 1947, Charles Herbert Fowler Ransom, of Porters Farm, Wyck Rissington, Cheltenham, and has issue living, Andrew Charles D'Oyley b. 1948, Mark Anthony b. 1952, Jeremy Peter Scott b. 1953. *Residence,*—Porters Farm, Wyck Rissington, Cheltenham, Glos.

Hon. Muriel Helen, b. 1887: m. 1916, Major John Edmund Burnet Thornely, O.B.E., sometime RAF, and has issue living, Gervase Michael Cobham (Birksholme, Sedbergh, Yorks.), b. 1918; ed. at Rugby, and at Trin. Hall, Camb. (MA); Headmaster of Sedbergh Sch.: m. 1954, Jennifer Margery, da. of Sir Charles Hilary Scott, of Knowle House, Bishops Walk, Addington, Surrey, and has issue living, Richard Michael Gervase, b. 1957, Charles William Alexander b. 1958, Elizabeth Miranda b. 1960, Jacqueline Sarah b. 1965. *Residence,*—65, Whitelands House, SW3.

WIDOW LIVING OF THIRTEENTH BARON.

CHRISTINA JEAN (*Baroness Cobham*), da. of Albert Edward Honeybone: m. 1923, the 13th Baron, who d. 1951, from whom she had obtained a divorce 1934, and whom she re-married 1949. *Residence*—510, Barren Joey Rd, Avalon, N.S.W.

COBHAM, VISCOUNT. (Lyttelton.) [Viscount G.B. 1718, Bt. E. 1618.]

One God, one king.

CHARLES JOHN LYTTELTON, *KG, GCMG, GCVO, TD, PC,* 10th Viscount and 13th Baronet; *b.* Aug. 8th, 1909; *s.* 1949; ed. at Eton, and at Trin. Coll., Camb. (BA); Lt.-Col. RA, a JP, patron of four livings, and a KStJ; Hon. Col. (Warwicks. and Worcs. Yeo.) Sqdn., The Mercian Yeo. since 1972; Pres. of MCC 1954; Gov.-Gen. and C. in-C. of New Zealand 1957-62; Lord Lt. of Worcs. 1963-74; Lord Steward of HM Household 1967-72; Chancellor of Order of the Garter since 1972; GCMG 1957, KG 1964, PC 1967, GCVO 1972: *m.* 1942, Elizabeth Alison (a CStJ), da. of John Reeder Makeig-Jones, CBE, late ICS, and has issue.

Arms,—Argent, a chevron between three escallops sable. **Crest**—A Moor's head in profile couped at the shoulders proper, wreathed round the temples argent and sable. **Supporters**—Two mermen proper, each holding in the exterior hand a trident or.

Seat,—Hagley Hall, Stourbridge.

SONS LIVING.

Hon. JOHN WILLIAM LEONARD, *b.* June 5th 1943; ed. at Eton, and at Christ's Coll., New Zealand: *m.* 1974, Penelope Ann, el. da. of Roy Cooper, of Moss Farm, Knutsford, Cheshire.

Hon. Christopher Charles, *b.* 1947; ed. at Eton: *m.* 1973, Tessa Mary, da. of the late Col. Alexander George Jeffrey Readmar, DSO, of The Old Rectory, Fairstead, Hatfield Peverel, Essex.

Hon. Richard Cavendish, *b.* 1949; ed. at Eton: *m.* 1971, Romilly, da. of Michael Barker, of 14, Harley Gdns., SW10.

Hon. Nicholas Makeig, *b.* 1951; ed. at Shiplake Court, Oxon.

DAUGHTERS LIVING.

Hon. Juliet Meriel, *b.* 1944: *m.* 1967, John Michael Dugdale, of Birch Farm, Kinlet, Bewdley, and has issue living, Mark Rupert Marshall, *b.* 1968,—Helen Riba, *b.* 1970.

Hon. (Elizabeth) Catherine, *b.* 1946: *m.* 1967, the Hon. (George Cecil) Brooke Weld-Forester, of Willey Park, Broseley, Salop, son of 7th Baron Forester.

Hon. Lucy, *b.* 1954.

Hon. Sarah (twin), *b.* 1954.

SISTERS LIVING.

Hon. Viola Maud (*Duchess of Westminster*), *b.* 1912; late Sqdn. Officer WAAF; a Serving Sister of Order of St. John of Jerusalem; 1939-45 War (despatches): *m.* 1946, the 5th Duke of Westminster. *Residence,*—Ely Lodge, Enniskillen, co. Fermanagh; Eaton, Chester, Cheshire.

Hon. Audrey Lavinia (10, Redland Green Rd., Bristol, BS6 7HE), *b.* 1918: *m.* 1950, as his third wife, David Edzell Thomas Lindsay, who *d.* 1968 [see E. Crawford, colls.].

Hon. Lavinia Mary Yolande, *b.* 1921; European War 1941-5 as Subaltern A.T.S.: *m.* 1st, (Feb.) 1945, Capt. Cecil Francis Burney Rolt, 23rd Hussars, who *d.* (killed in action during European War) (April) 1945; 2ndly, 1949, Major John Edward Dennys, MC, who *d.* 1973, and has issue living, (by 2nd m.) Nicholas Charles Jonathan, *b.* 1951. *Residence,*—50, Chester Row SW1.

UNCLE LIVING. (*Son of 8th Viscount.*)

Hon. Richard Glynne, *b.* 1893; ed. at Eton, and at Trin. Coll., Camb.; 1914-18 War in France as Lieut. R.A. (Croix de Guerre): *m.* 1931, Judith, dau. of the late Lieut.-Col. Percy Archer Clive, M.P., Grenadier Guards, and has issue living, Spencer Clive, *b.* 1939; ed. at Highgate; on staff of Guest Keen & Nettlefold,—Thomas Glynne, *b.* 1940; ed. at Eton and Trin. Coll., Camb.; Assist. Master, Eton. *Residence,*—7, The Grove, Highgate Village, N6 6JU.

WIDOWS LIVING OF SON OF EIGHTH VISCOUNT.

Pamela Marie, dau. of the late Charles Robert Whorwood Adeane, C.B. [B. Leconfield, colls.]: *m.* 1919, the Hon. George William Lyttelton, who *d.* 1962, and has issue living [see colls, infra] *Residence,*—Finndale House, Grundisburgh, Suffolk.

Sibell Eleanor Maud, dau. of the late Charles Robert Whorwood Adeane, C.B., of Babraham, Cambridge [B. Leconfield], and widow of Capt. the Hon. Edward Kay-Shuttleworth [see B. Shuttleworth, colls.]: *m.* 2ndly, 1920. the Rev. the Hon. Charles Lyttelton, M.C., who *d.* 1931 ; 3rdly, 1937, Roger Thomas Baldwin Fulford, CVO. *Residence,*—Barbon Manor, Carnforth, Lancs.

COLLATERAL BRANCHES LIVING.

Issue of the late Hon. George William Lyttelton, 2nd son of 8th Viscount, *b.* 1883, *d.* 1962: *m.* 1919, Pamela Marie (ante) dau. of the late Charles Robert Whorwood Adeane, C.B. [B. Leconfield, colls.] :—

Humphrey Richard Adeane, *b.* 1921: *m.* 1st, 1948 (marriage dissolved 1952), Patricia Mary Braithwaite, dau. of the late J. Wellesley Gaskell; 2ndly, 1952, Elizabeth Jill, dau. of Albert E. Richardson and has issue living, (by 2nd marriage) Anthony Stephen, *b.* 1955,—David George, *b.* 1958,—(by 1st marriage) Henrietta Marie, *b.* 1949,—(by 2nd marriage), Georgina Pamela, *b.* 1963. *Residence,*—Alyn Close, Barnet Rd., Arkley, Herts.——Diana Maud (*Hon. Mrs. Alexander L. Hood*), *C.V.O., b.* 1920; was Assist. Press Sec. to H.M. the late King George VI 1947-52, and to H.M. The Queen 1952-7; M.V.O. (4th Class) 1952, C.V.O. 1957: *m.* 1957, the Hon. Alexander Lambert Hood [see V. Hood]. *Residences,*—67, Chelsea Sq., S.W.3; Loders Court, Bridport, Dorset.——Helena Frances, *b.* 1923: *m.* 1940, Peter Stafford Hayden Lawrence, of Eton College, Windsor, and The Great House, Gt. Milton, Oxford [see Lawrence, Bt., cr. 1867, colls.].——Margaret Rose, *b.* 1926: *m.* 1949, Robert Morice Antony Bourne, an Assist. Master at Eton, of Manor House, Beaminster, Dorset [see E. Cairns].——Mary Pamela, *b.* 1929: *m.* 1953, Brig. Arthur George Ernest Stewart Cox, DFC, RA, and has issue living, Rupert Lyttelton, *b.* 1956,—Jonathan May, *b.* 1957,—Charles Arthur, *b.* 1960,—Belinda Jane, *b.* 1954. *Residence,*—Balscote House, nr. Banbury, Oxon.

Issue of the late Rt. Hon. Sir Neville (Gerald) Lyttelton, G.C.B., G.O.V.O., 3rd son of 4th Baron Lyttelton, *b.* 1845, *d.* 1931: *m.* 1883, Katharine Sarah, who *d.* 1943, dau. of the late Rt. Hon. James Stuart-Wortley, M.P. [E. Wharncliffe, colls.]:—

Lucy Blanche (77, Overstrand Mansions, Battersea Park, SW11), *b.* 1884: *m.* 1908, the Rt. Hon. Charles Frederick Gurney Masterman, PC, who *d.* 1927, and has issue living, Neville Charles (of Bath House, 2, Norton Rd., Mumbles, Swansea), *b.* 1912; is Lecturer in History at Swansea Univ. Coll.: *m.* 1947, Brenda, da. of John William Bywater Tongue, of 11, Tame Rd., Tipton, Staffs, and has issue living, Margaret Elizabeth *b.* 1948, Eleanor Lucy *b.* 1950, Catherine Charlotte Mary *b.* 1957,—Margaret Mary, *b.* 1910: *m.* 1932, Richard Bevan Braithwaite, Fellow of King's Coll. Camb., and has issue living, Lewis Charles (24, Grove St., Leamington Spa), *b.* 1937: *m.* 1968,

Louisette Jane, only da. of H. C. N. Barron, of 3, Ravenscourt Sq., W6, Catherine Lucy, b. 1940,—
Dorothy Hilda, b. 1914; 1939-45 War with ATS (Intelligence).——Mary Hermione, CBE, ARRC,
b. 1894; JP; late County Alderman for Oxon, Chm. of Education Cttee. Oxon, Co. Council, and
Member of Roy. Comm. on Location of Industry; 1914-18 War; QAIMNS (despatches, ARRC);
OBE (Civil) 1950: m. 1919, William Lionel Hichens, who d. (result of enemy action during 1939-45
War) 1940, and has issue living, Mark Lyttelton b. 1926,—Andrew Lionel (North Aston Hall, Oxford)
b. 1936: m. 1968, Anne Goch, of Capetown, S. Africa, and has issue living, Nicholas b. 1970, David
Lionel b. 1974,—Stella b. 1927: m. 1951, Richard Phipps Hornby, MP, of 10, Hereford Sq., SW7;
son of the Rt. Rev. Hugh Leycester Hornby, MC, Suffragan Bishop of Hulme, and has issue living,
John Hugh, b. 1954, Patrick Lionel b. 1958, Simon Richard b. 1960, Juliet b. 1956.—Phoebe Jane
b. 1929: m. 1965, Edward Augur Pearce, of Lower House, N. Aston, Oxford,—Rachel Katherine
b. 1933. Residence,—North Aston Hall, Oxford.

Grandchildren of the late Rt. Rev. the Hon. Arthur Temple Lyttelton, DD, 5th son
of 4th Baron Lyttelton:—
Issue of the late Lieut.-Col. Archer Geoffrey Lyttelton, D.S.O., b. 1884, d. 1959 : m. 1st, 1921,
Mwyndeg Dorothea Winchester, who d. 1951, dau. of Winchester Clowes, formerly of
Hitchin, Herts; 2ndly, 1953, Cynthia Violet, dau. of Edgar Anderson:—
(By 1st marriage) Judith Hazel, b. 1925: m. 1950, Henry James Johnson, OBE, TD, and has issue
living, Rupert Charles Gavin, b. 1954,—Charlotte Mary, b. 1959. Residence,—13, Sloane Av., SW3.

Issue of the late Com. Stephen Clive Lyttelton, O.B.E., D.S.C., b. 1887, d. 1959 : m. 1st, 1919,
Maureen (who obtained a divorce 1933), dau. of Harold Anthony Smith, formerly of
6, Dean's Yard, Westminster, S.W. ; 2ndly, 1938, Mary Cicely, who d. 1945, dau. of
Brig.-Gen. Sir (Ernest) Frederick (Orby) Gascoigne, K.C.V.O., C.M.G., D.S.O. ; 3rdly,
1947, Phoebe Hermione (of Little Ethorpe, Ballards Lane, Limpsfield, Surrey), da. of
A. K. Graham :—
(By 2nd marriage) Edward Gascoigne, b. 1944.——(By 1st marriage) Barbara Meriel, b. 1921 : m. 1947,
Charles Russell Fawcus, and has issue living, Mark Russell, b. 1951,—Meriel Clare, b. 1949. Resi-
dence,—High Drive House, Woldingham, Surrey.——(By 2nd m.) Mary Kathleen, b. 1939: m. 1970,
Malcolm Robert Fraser of Reelig.——(By 3rd m.) Cicely Phoebe Lavinia, b. 1950.

Grandchildren of the late Rt. Hon. Alfred Lyttelton, KC, MP (infra):—
Issue of the late Rt. Hon. Oliver Lyttelton, DSO, MC, PO (Viscount Chandos), b. 1893, d. 1972.
[See V. Chandos].
Issue (by 2nd marriage) of the late Rt. Hon. Alfred Lyttelton, K.C., M.P., 8th son of
4th Baron Lyttelton, b. 1857, d. 1913 : m. 1st, 1885, Laura, who d. 1886, dau. of
Sir Charles Tennant, 1st Bt.; 2ndly, 1892, Dame Edith Sophy, G.B.E., who d.
1948, dau. of the late Archibald Balfour :—
Mary Frances (Lady Craik), b. 1895: m. 1928, Sir George Lillie Craik, MC, 2nd Bt., who d. 1929.
Residence,—5A, Dean's Yard, Westminster, SW1.

PREDECESSORS.—[1] Sir Richard Temple, 4th Bt., of Stowe, a military commander of
renown under the 1st Duke of Marlborough, was cr. Baron Cobham, of Cobham, Kent 1714,
and Baron Cobham, of Cobham, Kent, and Viscount Cobham (peerage of Great Britain) 1718,
with special remainder failing heirs male of his body, to his sister Hester, wife of Richard
Grenville, M.P., and her heirs male, and failing such to his 3rd sister, Christian, wife of Sir
Thomas Lyttelton, 4th Bt. [B. Lyttelton, infra], and her issue male; d. 1749; s. by his sister
[2] HESTER GRENVILLE, cr. Countess of Temple (peerage of Great Britain) 1749, with remainder to
her heirs male; d. 1752; s. by her son [3] RICHARD, K.G., 2nd Earl, a leading statesman, temp.
George III.; d. without issue 1779; s. by his nephew [4] GEORGE, 3rd Earl; was Viceroy of
Ireland 1782 and 1787: m. Mary Elizabeth (who d. 1812, having in 1800 been cr. Baroness
Nugent (peerage of Ireland), with remainder to her 2nd son George, who d. 1850 without issue),
dau. and heiress of Robert, Earl of Nugent, in the peerage of Ireland; assumed by Roy.
licence the additional surnames of Nugent and Temple; was cr. Marquess of Buckingham 1784,
and in 1788 s. by special remainder his father-in-law, as Earl Nugent (peerage of Ireland, cr.
1776); d. 1813; s. by his son [5] RICHARD, K.G., 2nd Marquess; assumed 1799, by Roy.
licence, the additional surnames of Brydges-Chandos; cr. Earl Temple (with remainder to his
granddau. Anne Eliza Mary, afterwards wife of W. H. Powell Gore-Langton, Esq., M.P.),
Marquess of Chandos and Duke of Buckingham (peerage of United Kingdom) 1822; d. 1839;
s. by his son [6] RICHARD PLANTAGENET, K.G., 2nd Duke; d. 1861; s. by his son [7] RICHARD
PLANTAGENET CAMPBELL, 3rd Duke, b. 1823: m. 1st, 1851, Caroline, who d. 1874, dau. of
Robert Harvey, of Langley Hall, Bucks ; 2nd, 1885, Alice Anne, who d. 1931, el. dau. of Sir
Graham Graham-Montgomery, 3rd Bt.; d. 1889, when the Dukedom of Buckingham and the
Earldoms of Temple (cr. 1749) and Nugent became extinct, the Lordship of Kinloss (to which he
had established his right in 1868) devolving on his el. dau., Lady Mary Morgan, the Earldom
of Temple (cr. 1822) on William Stephen Gore-Langton, and the Viscountcy of Cobham (under
special remainder) as heir male of Christian, wife of Sir Thomas Lyttelton, 4th Bt., on [8]
CHARLES GEORGE, 5th Baron Lyttelton [see *⁎* infra], 8th Viscount Cobham, b. 1842; High
Steward of Bewdley; M.P. for Worcestershire, E. (L) 1868-74: m. 1878, the Hon. Mary Susan
Caroline Cavendish, who d. 1937, dau. of 2nd Baron Chesham; d. 1922; s. by his son [9] JOHN
CAVENDISH, K.C.B., T.D., 9th Viscount, b. 1881; Lieut.-Col. R.A. (T.A.), High Steward of
Bewdley, and Lord-Lieut. for City and co. of Worcester: Under-Sec. of State for War 1939-40;
MP for Worcestershire Mid. or Droitwich Div. (U) 1910-16: m. 1908, Violet Yolande, who d. 1966,
dau. of Charles Leonard; d. 1949; s. by his son [10] CHARLES JOHN, 10th Viscount and present
peer; also Baron Cobham, Lord Lyttelton, Baron of Frankley, and Baron Westcote.
⁎ [1] Sir THOMAS Lyttelton, Knt.; Sheriff of Worcester 1613, and M.P. for Worcestershire
1620-8 and 1639-40 (name spelt Littleton in records of Parliament); was a zealous partizan of
Royalty during the Civil Wars, and suffered imprisonment in the Tower; cr. a Baronet 1618;
d. 1650; s. by his el. son [2] Sir HENRY, 2nd Bt.; was imprisoned in the Tower seventeen
months for his attachment to the Royal cause; d.s.p. 1703; s. by his brother [3] Sir CHARLES
3rd Bt., also an active partizan of Royalty; was incarcerated in Colchester; d. 1716; s. by
his son [4] Sir THOMAS, 4th Bt., successively M.P. for Worcestershire and Camelford; a
Lord of the Admiralty 1727-41: m. Christian, dau. of Sir Richard Temple, Bt., of Stowe
(see ante); d. 1751; s. by his son [5] Sir GEORGE, P.C., 5th Bt., M.P. for Okehampton,
Principal Sec. to Prince of Wales 1737, a Lord of the Treasury 1744-55, Cofferer to the House,
hold 1754-5, and Chancellor and Under Treasurer of Court of Exchequer 1755; cr. Lord
Lyttelton, Baron of Frankley, co. Worcester 1756; d. 1773; s. by his son [6] THOMAS, 2nd Baron ;
d.s.p. 1779, when the Barony became extinct, and the Baronetcy devolved upon his uncle [7]
WILLIAM HENRY, 7th Bt.; M.P. for Bewdley 1748-54, Gov. of S. Carolina 1755-60, Gov. of
Jamaica 1760-6, and Envoy Extraor. to Portugal; cr. Baron Westcote, of Balamare, co. Longford (peerage of Ireland) 1766, and Lord Lyttelton, Baron of Frankley (peerage of England) 1794;
d. 1808; s. by his son [8] GEORGE FULKE, 2nd Baron; d. unmarried 1828; s. by his half-
brother [9] WILLIAM HENRY, 3rd Baron; was Lord-Lieut. of co. Worcester; d. 1837; s. by his
son [10] GEORGE WILLIAM, K.C.M.G., P.C., F.R.S., 4th Baron; b. 1817; was Lord-Lieut. of
co. Worcester, Under Sec. for Colonies 1846, and Ch. Commr. of Endowed Schools 1869-74:
m. 1st, 1839, Mary, who d. 1857, dau. of Sir Stephen Richard Glynne, 8th Bt.; 2ndly, 1869,
Sybella Harriet, who d. 1900, dau. of George Clive, and widow of Humphrey Francis
Mildmay; d. 1876; s. by his son [11] CHARLES GEORGE, 5th Baron, who s. (under special
remainder) as 8th Viscount Cobham 1889 (ante).

Cochrane, Lord, son of Earl of Dundonald.

COCHRANE OF CULTS, BARON. (Cochrane.) [Baron U.K. 1919.]

THOMAS CHARLES ANTHONY COCHRANE, 3rd Baron; *b.* Oct. 31st, 1922; *s.* 1968.

Arms,—Quarterly, 1st Argent, a chevron gules between three boars' heads erased azure, armed and langued of the second, within a bordure contre-ermine. *Cochrane;* 2nd, Gules, a fess ermine, a stag's antler or, fessways in chief, *Crawford of Kilbirnie;* 3rd, Gules, a fess chequy argent and azure, in chief three mullets of the second *Lindsay of the Byres;* 4th, Argent, on a saltire sable nine lozenges of the field, in centre chief a mullet gules, *Blair.* Crest,— A horse passant argent, between two stag's attires gules. Supporters,—Two ermines ermine.

Residence,—Balgownie, Buckie, Banffshire.

BROTHERS LIVING.

Hon. RALPH HENRY VERE, *b.* Sept. 20th, 1926; ed. at Eton, and at King's Coll., Camb. (MA): *m.* 1956, Janet Mary Watson, da. of the late William Hunter Watson Cheyne, MB, MRCS, LRCP [see Cheyne, Bt., colls.], and has issue living, Thomas Hunter Vere, *b.* 1957,—Michael Charles Nicholas, *b.* 1959. *Residence,*—Cults, Cupar, Fife. *Club,*—United Service and Royal Aero.

Hon. (John Douglas) Julian (Townend House, Hopton, Derbys.), *b.* 1929; ed. at Eton: *m.* 1965, Vaila Rose, da. of Cdr. Robert Dalby, RN (ret.), of Castle Donington, Leics., and has issue living, John Colin, *b.* 1969,—Julietta Anne, *b.* 1967,—Alice Georgina, *b.* 1974.

UNCLE LIVING. (*Son of 1st Baron*).

Hon. Sir Ralph Alexander, *GBE, KCB, AFC* (Grove Farmhouse, Shipton-under-Wychwood, Oxon. *Club,* Brooks's), *b.* 1895; entered RN 1908; transferred to RAF 1918; Air Ch. Marshal (ret.) RAF; Kurdistan 1923 (despatches), 1939-45 War (despatches twice, CB, KBE); Ch. of Air Staff. RNZAF 1937-39, and an Air ADC to HM 1939-40; appointed Air Officer Comdg.-in-Ch. Transport Command 1945 and Flying Training Command 1948; Vice-Ch. of Air Staff 1950-52; CBE (Mil.) 1939, CB (Mil.) 1943, KBE (Mil.) 1945, KCB (Mil.) 1948, GBE (Mil.) 1950: *m.* 1930, Hilda Frances Holme, da. of the late Francis H. Wiggin, and has issue living, John Alexander (Fairspear House, Leafield, Oxford), *b.* 1935: *m.* 1966, Margaret Minna, da. of the late Sir Charles Henry Rose, 3rd Bt. (cr. 1909), and has issue living, Thomas Hugh *b.* 1973, Phoebe Clare *b.* 1967, Alexandra *b.* 1969,— Malcolm Ralph (Grove Farmhouse, Shipton-under-Wychwood, Oxon.), *b.* 1938: *m.* 1972, Mary Anne, da. of Ralph Scrope [E. Mexborough], and has issue living, William Ralph, *b.* 1974,—Ann Grizel, *b.* 1932: *m.* 1953, Robert Christie Stewart [see Lighton, Bt.].

AUNT LIVING. (*Daughter of 1st Baron*).

Hon. Dame Katherine Elizabeth (*The Dowager Countess of Elgin and Kincardine*), *DBE, b.* 1890; MBE (Civil) 1919, DBE (Civil) 1938: *m.* 1921, the 10th Earl of Elgin and Kincardine, who *d.* 1968. *Residence,* Culross Abbey House, Culross, Dunfermline, Fife.

WIDOW LIVING OF SECOND BARON.

MILLICENT AGNES MARY (*Baroness Cochrane of Cults*), (Château de Bormes, Bormes-les-Mimosas, Var 83, France), da. of the late Alexander Duckham, PhD, and formerly wife of Wilfred Neill Foster, *m.* 1948, as his 2nd wife, the 2nd Baron, who *d.* 1968.

COLLATERAL BRANCH LIVING.

Issue of the late Capt. the Hon. Sir Archibald Douglas Cochrane, 2nd son of 1st Baron, G.C.M.G., K.C.S.I., D.S.O., R.N., *b.* 1885, *d.* 1958: *m.* 1926, the Hon. Julia Dorothy Cornwallis, *CBE,* who *d.* 1971, da. of 1st Baron Cornwallis:—

Douglas Fiennes (of 22, Wilfred St., SW1), *b.* 1928: ed. at Eton, and Trin. Coll., Camb.: *m.* 1969, Patricia Ann, da. of the late Frank Renshaw, of Puddletown, Dorset, and has issue living, Alexander Douglas, *b.* 1972.——Mabel Dorothy, *b.* 1932: *m.* 1958, Col. Geoffrey Douglas Gill, MBE, late King's Regt., of Avenue de Budé 7, 1202, Geneva, and has issue living, Peter Geoffrey Fiennes, *b.* 1966.

PREDECESSORS.—[1] THOMAS HORATIO ARTHUR ERNEST Cochrane, younger son of 11th Earl of Dundonald; *b.* 1857; Major and Hon. Lieut.-Col. 4th Batn. Princess Louise's (Argyll and Sutherland Highlanders); Parliamentary Private Sec. of State for the Colonies 1895-1901, and Under Sec. of State for the Home Depart. 1902-1905; M.P. for Ayrshire, N. Div. (*LU*) 1892-1910; *cr. Baron Cochrane of Cults,* of Crawford Priory, co. Fife (peerage of United Kingdom) 1919: *m.* 1880, Lady Gertrude Julia Georgina Boyle, *O.B.E.,* who *d.* 1950, dau. of 6th Earl of Glasgow; *d.* 1951; *s.* by his son [2] THOMAS GEORGE FREDERICK, *DSO,* 2nd Baron; *b.* 1883; Maj. Black Watch; 1914-18 War: *m.* 1st, 1920, the Hon. Elin Douglas-Pennant, who *d.* 1934, da. of 2nd Baron Penrhyn; 2ndly, 1948, Millicent Agnes Mary, da. of the late Alexander Duckham, PhD, and formerly wife of Wilfred Neill Foster; *d.* 1968; *s.* by his son [3] THOMAS CHARLES ANTHONY, 3rd Baron and present peer.

COHEN, BARONY OF. (Cohen.) [Extinct 1973.]

SONS LIVING OF LIFE BARON.

Hon. Leonard Harold Lionel, *b.* 1922 ; ed. at Eton, and at New Coll., Oxford (B.A. 1945, M.A. 1946) ; Bar. Lincoln's Inn 1948 ; European War 1941-45 with Rifle Brig. (wounded) : *m.* 1949, Eleanor Lucy dau. of the late Philip Q. Henriques, and has issue. *Residence,*—57, Bedford Gdns., Campden Hill, W8. *Clubs,*—White's, St. James'.

Hon. Hugh Lionel, *b.* 1925 ; ed. at Eton, and at New Coll., Oxford ; European War 1943-45 with R.N.V.R.: *m.* 1953, Jane, dau. of the Rt. Hon. Sir Seymour Edward Karminski [Lewis, Bt., cr. 1902, ext.], and has issue. *Residence,*—Ambarrow Wood, Sandhurst, Camberley, Surrey. *Club,* St· James'.

DAUGHTER LIVING OF LIFE BARON

Hon. Elizabeth Adelaide, *b.* 1919 : *m.* 1st, 1940, Capt. Arthur John Pearce-Serocold, Welsh Guards (Supplementary Reserve), who *d.* (killed in action) 1942 [B. Stanley of Alderley]: 2ndly, 1946, The Hon. Peter Montefiore Samuel, MC [see V. Bearsted). *Residences,*—12, Rutland Court, SW7 1BN; Farley Hall, Farley Hill, Reading; Phones, Newtonmore, Inverness-shire.

COHEN OF BIRKENHEAD, BARON. (Cohen.) [Baron U.K. 1956.]

To heal ills ; to harm no one.

HENRY COHEN, *CH, MD,* 1st Baron, son of the late Isaac Cohen; *b.* 1900; ed. at Liverpool Univ. (MD, ChB); FRCP London; Hon. FRCPE, Hon. FRCPS Glasgow, Hon. FRCPI, Hon. FACP, Hon. FRCS, Hon. FRCOG, Hon. FRSM, Hon. FRCGP, Hon. FFR, Hon. FFA, RCS England, Hon. FDS, RCS England, Hon. LLD London, Manchester, Hull, Liverpool, Dublin, Wales; Hon. DCL Oxford; Hon. DSc Nottingham, Sussex, and Nat. Univ. of Ireland; Hon. ScD, Cambridge, Union Univ. NY; Hon. FRICS, Hon. FCS, Hon. FPS, Hon. FAPHA, FSA, FRSA, JP for Liverpool, a DL of Merseyside, Hon. Fellow of Jesus Coll., Camb., Hon. Master of Bench Inner Temple, Asso. KStJ and Hon. Freeman of Liverpool, Birkenhead, and Soc. of Apothecaries; Pres. of BMA 1950-52 (Gold Medal 1967), of Roy. Soc. of Med. 1964-66 (Gold Medal 1971), and of Nat. Soc. for Clean Air, 1961-63, Chm. of Standing Med. Advisory Cttee., Min. of Health 1948-63, and of Central Health Sers. Council 1957-63; Prof. Emeritus of Medicine, Liverpool Univ. since 1965 (Prof. 1934-65), Crown Representative of Gen. Med. Council since 1945; Pres. of Gen. Med. Council 1961-73; a Trustee of Nuffield Provincial Hosps. Trust since 1960; Pres. of BMA Students' Trust, Inst. of Health Education, of Assocn. for Study of Med. Education, of Children's Research Fund, of Nat. Children's Bureau, Roy. Soc. of Health 1958, and of Assocn. of Physicians of Great Britain and N. Ireland 1967-8; Chancellor of Hull Univ. since 1970; Hon. Pres. of International Acad. of History of Medicine Chm. of World Health Foundation (UK), of Liverpool Council of Social Ser. and Pres. of Liverpool Repertory Theatre; *cr.* Knt. 1949, *Baron Cohen of Birkenhead,* of Birkenhead, co. Palatine of Chester (peerage of UK) 1956, and CH 1974.

Arms,—Or a lion passant gules in chief two hands couped at the wrist proper positioned as in the Priestly (Cohanim) Blessing between as many roses of the second barbed and seeded also proper. Crest,—Perched on an open book argent with seven clasps to the sinister or, the pages inscribed with the words Fiat Lux in letters sable a cormorant wings elevated proper holding in the beak a spur gold. Supporters,—Dexter, a representation of Aesculapius supporting in the exterior hand his rod proper; sinister, a representation of Hygeia holding in the interior hand a serpent likewise proper and in the exterior hand a bowl or, both vested in white robes also proper and gorged with a chain gold pendant therefrom an estoile azure.

Residences,—Cornercroft, Glendyke Rd., Liverpool 18; 31, Rodney St., Liverpool, L1 9EH. *Clubs,*—Athenaeum, Savage.

COHEN OF BRIGHTON, BARONY OF. (Cohen.) [Extinct 1966.]

SON LIVING OF LIFE BARON. *(By 1st marriage.)*

Hon. John Christopher Coleman (47, Quickswood, Chalcots Park, NW3), *b.* 1940; ed. at Stowe, and McGill Univ. (PhD): *m.* 1965, Anne-Marie, da. of Eugene Krauss, of Paris, and has issue.

DAUGHTERS LIVING OF LIFE BARON. *(By 1st marriage.)*

Hon. Christine Coleman, *b.* 1942; assumed by deed poll 19— the surname of Coleman in lieu of Coleman-Cohen: *m.* 1965, David Maxwell Park, MRCP, of 13, Belsize Grove, NW3.

Hon. Madeleine Coleman COLEMAN (26, Boydell Court, St. John's Wood Park, NW3), *b.* 1946; assumed by deed poll 19—the surname of Coleman in lieu of Coleman-Cohen.

WIDOW LIVING OF LIFE BARON.

RENIE *(Baroness Cohen of Brighton),* (11F, Bedford Towers, Kings Rd., Brighton, BN1 2JF); JP of Brighton; da. of Simon Frieze, and widow of Leonard Bodlender: *m.* 1961, as his 2nd wife, Baron Cohen of Brighton (Life Baron), who *d.* 1966.

COLE, BARON. (Cole.) [Life Baron 1965.]

GEORGE JAMES COLE, *GBE* son of the late James Francis Cole; *b.* Feb. 3rd, 1906; ed. at Raffles Inst., Singapore; Joint Managing Dir. of The United Africa Co. Ltd., 1952-55, a Dir. of Taylor Woodrow (W. Africa) Ltd., 1947-55, and Chm. of Palm Line Ltd., 1952-55; a Dir. of The Niger Co. Ltd. 1951-70, of Finance Corporation for Industry 1957-73, and of Commonwealth Development Finance Co. Ltd., 1966-70; Chm. of Unilever Ltd. 1960-70 (Vice-Chm. 1956) and Vice-Chm. of Unilever NV 1960-70; Chm. of Leverhulme Trust, a Trustee of Civic Trust, Dep. Chm. of Gov. Body of London Graduate Sch. of Business Studies 1965-70, a Member of Council of Roy. Inst. of Internat. Affairs, and Chm. of Gov. Advisory Cttee. on Appt. of Advertising Agents 1965-71, and a Dir. of Shell Transport & Trading Co., Ltd.; Chm. of Rolls-Royce (1971), Ltd. 1971-72; a Cdr. of Order of Orange Nassau of the Netherlands; *cr. Baron Cole*, of Blackfriars, co. London (Life Baron) 1965, and GBE (Civil) 1973: *m.* 1940, Ruth, da. of the late Edward Stanley Harpham, and has issue.

Arms,—Barry wavy of eight argent and azure, a fess, and supporting it in base a chevron enarched sable. *Crest,*—In front of a palm tree a lymphad sail furled proper, pennon and flags flying gules. *Supporters,*—*Dexter,* an okapi proper; *sinister,* a Malayan deer (Sambar) proper.

Residence,—50, Victoria Rd., W8; Willow Cottage, Holland Rd., Frinton-on-Sea, Essex. *Clubs,*—Athenæum, Travellers', Hurlingham.

SON LIVING.

Hon. Jonathan Dare, *b.* 1946; ed. at Eton, and Hertford Coll., Oxford.

DAUGHTER LIVING.

Hon. Juliet Anthea, *b.* 1951.

Cole, Viscount, son of Earl of Enniskillen.

COLERAINE, BARON. (Law.) [Baron U.K. 1954.]

RICHARD KIDSTON LAW, *P.C.*, 1st Baron, son of the late Rt. Hon. Andrew Bonar Law, M.P.; *b.* Feb. 27th, 1901; ed. at Shrewsbury, and at St. John's Coll., Oxford; High Steward of City and Co. of Kingston-upon-Hull since 1971; Fellow of Roy Postgraduate Med. Sch., and Hon. Treasurer, British Sailors' So.; was Financial Sec. to War Office 1940-41, Parliamentary Under-Sec. of State for Foreign Affairs 1941-43, Min. of State 1943-45, Min. of Educn. May to July 1945, Chm. of Standing Advisory Cttee. on Pay of Higher Civil Ser. 1957-61 and Chm. of Nat. Youth Employment Council 1955-62; MP for SW Div. of Kingston-upon-Hull (*C*) 1931-45, for S. Div. of Kensington 1945-50 and for Haltemprice Div. of Kingston-upon-Hull 1950-54; *cr.* PC 1943, and *Baron Coleraine,* of Haltemprice, E. Riding of Yorks. (peerage of UK) 1954: *m.* 1929, Mary Virginia, yr. da. of the late A. F. Nellis, of Rochester, NY, USA, and has issue.

Thy law my thought.

Arms,—Argent a saltire azure between four cocks proper. *Crest,*—Issuant from a chaplet of maple leaves vert, a demi salmon proper. *Supporters,*—*Dexter,* a Basenji dog; *Sinister,* a kid, both proper.

Residence,—43B, Sloane St., SW1. *Club,*—Carlton; Royal Yacht Squadron.

SONS LIVING.

Hon. JAMES MARTIN BONAR, *b.* Aug. 8th, 1931; ed. at Eton, and at Trin. Coll., Oxford: *m.* 1st, 1958, Emma Elizabeth, from whom he obtained a divorce 1966, only da. of the late Nigel Richards; 2ndly, 1966, Anne Patricia, da. of Maj. Gen. Ralph Henry Farrant, CB, of Wareham, Dorset, and has issue living (by 1st m.), Elizabeth Mary, *b.* 1961,—Sophia Anne, *b.* 1964,—(by 2nd m.) Henrietta Margaret, *b.* 1968,—Juliana Caroline Matilda, *b.* 1971. *Residence,*—3, Cambridge Pl., W8.

Hon. Andrew Bonar, *b.* 1933; ed. at Rugby, and at Trin. Coll., Dublin: *m.* 1961, Joanna Margarette, dau. of Raymond Neill, of Fairview, Delgany, co. Wicklow, and has issue living, Richard Pitcairn Bonar, *b.* 1963,—Charlotte Mary de Montmorency Bonar, *b.* 1964. *Residence,*—Shankill Castle, Shankill, co. Dublin.

COLERIDGE, BARON. (Coleridge.) [Baron U.K. 1873.]

As life so the end.

RICHARD DUKE COLERIDGE, *KBE*, 4th Baron; *b.* Sept. 24th 1905; *s.* 1955; ed. at RNCs, Osborne and Dartmouth; Capt. (ret.) RN; French Gen. Headquarters, Vincennes, France 1940, in War Cabinet Office 1940-41, Dep. Sec. to British Joint Staff and Combined Chiefs of Staff 1941-46, United Kingdom Sec., Mil. Staff Committee of United Nations Organization, New York 1946-48, with British Joint Staff Mission, Washington, USA 1950-51, and Ch. Staff Officer to Marshal of the RAF Lord Tedder 1950-51; represented British Chiefs of Staff on temporary Committee of Council of NATO Paris 1951, Exec. Sec. NATO 1952-70; attended Conferences of Washington, Quebec, Cairo, Malta, and Yalta; Chm. Devon and Exeter Savings Bank; has American Legion of Merit; OBE (Mil.) 1944, CBE (Mil.) 1951, KBE (Civil) 1971: *m.* 1936, Rosamund, el. da. of the late Adm. Sir William Wordsworth Fisher, GCB, GCVO, and has issue.

Arms,—Argent, on a mount vert in base an otter proper, a chief gules, charged with a dove of the first between two crosses patée fitchée or. *Crest,*—On a mount vert therefrom issuing ears of wheat proper, in front of a cross gules an otter also proper. *Supporters,*—*Dexter,* an otter proper; *sinister,* a lion sable ; each gorged with a garland of roses gules, leaved vert.

Seat,—The Chanter's House, Ottery St. Mary, S. Devon.   *Club,*—United Service.

SONS LIVING.

Hon. WILLIAM DUKE (The Chanter's House, Ottery St. Mary, S. Devon), *b.* June 18th, 1937; ed. at Eton; Maj. Coldm. Gds.; Commanded Gds. Ind. Parachute Co. 1970-72: *m.* 1962, Everild Tania, only child of Lt.-Col. Beauchamp Hamborough, of Wispers Farm, Nairobi, Kenya, and has issue living, James Duke, *b.* 1967,—Tania Rosamund *b.* 1966,—Sophia Tamsin, *b.* 1970.
Hon. Samuel John Taylor, *b.* 1942: ed. at Winchester, and at Trin. Coll., Oxford; Maj. Gren. Guards; attached Army Air Corps 1964-68, and 22 Special Air Ser. Regt. 1968-71: *m.* 1973, Patricia Susan, yr. da. of John Basil Edwards, CBE, of Cradley, nr. Malvern, Worcs., and has issue living, Jessica Alice Seymour, *b.* 1974.   *Club,*—Guards'.

BROTHER LIVING.

Hon. John Seymour Duke, *b.* 1908: *m.* 1934, Dora Lovelace, dau. of the late George Coplestone Carter.   *Residence,*—Corner Cottage, 17, St. James Green, Southwold, Suffolk.   *Club,*—English-Speaking Union.

WIDOW LIVING OF SON OF THIRD BARON.

Ursula Mary (Blandford House, Chaffcombe, Chard, Somerset), da. of the late Rev. William Turner Long, of Cheltenham: *m.* 1937, the Hon. Ronald James Duke Coleridge, who *d.* 1972, and has issue living [see colls, infra].

COLLATERAL BRANCHES LIVING.

Issue of the late Hon. Ronald James Duke Coleridge, yst. son of 3rd Baron, *b.* 1911, *d.* 1972: *m.* 1937, Ursula Mary (ante), da. of the late Rev. William Turner Long, of Cheltenham:—
Syndercombe James Duke, *b.* 1941; ed. at King's Sch., Worcester; Lt. RN: *m.* 1st, 1964 (m. diss. 1969), Barbara Jane, da. of F. L. Dawson, of Rio de Janeiro; 2ndly, 1969, Deborah Coburn, da. of The Rev. Marcus Brown Hall, of Vermont, USA, and has issue living (by 1st m.), Christina Joanne, *b.* 1965.——Sara Louise Sidney, *b.* 1945: *m.* 1964, Alexander Arthur Luttrell Reid, PhD, of 9, Barrow Rd., Cambridge, and has issue living, Ann Louise, *b.* 1965,—Katharine Louise, *b.* 1967.

  Grandson of the late John Duke Coleridge, F.R.I.B.A. (infra):—
Issue of the late Peter Duke Coleridge, *b.* 1905, *d.* 1958 : *m.* 1936 (marriage dissolved 1953), Sigrid Stahl Christensen:—
John Duke, *MD, b.* 1940 (Dockagården, Båstad, Sweden); ed. at Univ. of Göteborg Med. Sch.: *m.* 1963, Carin Eva Christina, da. of Karl Olaf Lennart Cassmark, and has issue living, Peter John, *b.* 1966,— Christina *b.* 1964,—Malin Charlotta, *b.* 1970.   *Residence,*—Dockagården, Båstad, Sweden.

  Grandchildren of the late Hon. Stephen (William Buchanan) Coleridge, 2nd son of 1st Baron :—
Issue of the late John Duke Coleridge, F.R.I.B.A., *b.* 1879, *d.* 1934 : *m.* 1904, the Hon. Katharine Euphemia Godley, who *d.* 1941, dau. of 1st Baron Kilbracken:—
Arthur Nicholas, *b.* 1915; ed. at New Coll., Oxford (MA); Bar. Middle Temple 1939; sometime Capt. Irish Guards: *m.* 1941, Lady (Marguerite) Georgina Hay, dau. of 11th Marquess of Tweeddale, and has issue living, Frances Marguerite Katharine, *b.* 1943: *m.* 1964, Neil Lindsay Vaughan Smith, of Park Hill, Appledore, Kent, and has issue living, Julian Arthur Vaughan, *b.* 1969, Candida Louise Vaughan *b.* 1967.   *Residence,*—33, Peel St., W8.——Nancy Katharine, *b.* 1907: *m.* 1928, Maj.-Gen. (Reginald) Llewellyn Brown, CB, CBE, FRICS, MA Oxford, and has issue living, David Arthur Llewellyn (Guston, Chelwood Gate, Sussex), *b.* 1929: *m.* 1954, Priscilla Mary, da. of the late Rev. George Edmund Day, V. of Headington, Oxford, and has issue living, Alexander Edmund Llewellyn *b.* 1956, Richard Arthur Llewellyn *b.* 1957, William David Llewellyn *b.* 1959. *Residence,*—Cricket Hill Cottage. Yateley, Hants.

Issue of the late Capt. Guy Lushington Coleridge, R.N., *b.* 1884, *d.* (on active service during 1939-45 War) 1941: *m.* 1910, Hester Christabel Margaret, who *d.* 1969, only da. of the late Rev. Richard Henry Dickson, R. and V. of Eastchurch, Sheerness:—
Geraldine Margaret Joan, *b.* 1911 : *m.* 1st, 1929 (marriage dissolved 1946), Capt. Cyril Aubrey Hamilton Brooking, C.B.E., R.N., who *d.* 1961 [McMahon, Bt.] ; 2ndly, 1947, Maj.-Gen. (Percival) Napier White, C.B., C.B.E., and has issue living (by 1st marriage), Patrick Guy, *b.* 1937,—Sara Anne, *b.* 1933,—(by 2nd marriage), John Napier, *b.* 1949,—Robert James Napier, *b.* 1952. *Residence,*—Little Langley, Chobham, Surrey.

Issue of the late Paul Humphrey Coleridge, MC, FRIBA, *b.* 1888, *d.* 1955: *m.* 1914, Margaret Frances who *d.* 1964, dau. of the late George Campbell Giffard, J.P., of Bulkeley House, Englefield Green :—
Antony Duke, *b.* 1915 ; Capt. late Queen's Bays; European War 1939-45 (despatches): *m.* 1st, 1942, Kathleen Crozier, dau. of the late Herbert Taylor ; 2ndly, 1947, June Marian, dau. of George Frederick Charles Caswell, and has issue living, (by 2nd marriage) Nicholas Antony *b.* 1955,— David George *b.* 1957,—Geraldine Margaret, *b.* 1948: *m.* 1974, David Roger Leeming. *Residence,*— Chanters, Marlow, Bucks.——James Bernard, *b.* 1919; ed. at King's Coll., Camb. (MA); late Major

Roy. Signals: *m.* 1946, Jane Eveline, da. of Campbell Water Giffard, of 4, Melina Place, NWS, and has issue living, Paul James Duke, *b.* 1949,—Susan Margaret Ethel, *b.* 1947: *m.* 1970, Peter John Cunard,—Lucy Veronica, *b.* 1954. *Residence,*—78, Charlwood Rd., SW15.——Francis Stephen, *DSC, b.* 1920; FRIBA; 1939-45 War as Lieut. RNVR (DSC): *m.* 1948, Jane Dealtry, da. of the late Maj. G. A. Howson, MC, of The Hyde, Hambleden, Bucks., and has issue living, Stephen John, *b.* 1953,—Harriet Sibell, *b.* 1959. *Residence,*—The Hyde, Hambleden, Henley-on-Thames.

PREDECESSORS.—[1] *Rt. Hon.* JOHN DUKE Coleridge, *P.C.,* el. son of the late Rt. Hon. Sir John Taylor Coleridge; *b.* 1820; M.P. for Exeter(*L*) 1865-73; Recorder of Portsmouth 1855-66, Solicitor-Gen. 1868-71, Attorney-Gen. 1871-3, Lord Ch. Justice of Common Pleas 1873-80, and Lord Ch. Justice of England 1880-94; cr. *Baron Coleridge,* of Ottery St. Mary, Devon (peerage of United Kingdom) 1873 : *m.* 1st, 1846, Jane Fortescue, who *d.* 1878, dau. of the Rev. George Turner Seymour, of Farringford Hill, Isle of Wight; 2ndly, 1885, Amy Augusta Jackson, who *d.* 1933, dau. of Henry Baring Lawford, B.C.S.; *d.* 1894: *s.* by his el. son [2] BERNARD JOHN SEYMOUR, 2nd Baron, *b.* 1851 ; M.P. for Sheffield, Attercliffe Div.(*L*) 1885-94 ; was a Judge of High Court of Justice 1907-23 : *m.* 1876, Mary Alethea, who *d.* 1940, dau. of the late Rt. Rev. John Fielder Mackarness, D.D., sometime Lord Bishop of Oxford; *d.* 1927; *s.* by his son [3] GEOFFREY DUKE, 3rd Baron ; *b.* 1877; sometime Capt. Devonshire Regt.: *m.* 1904, Jessie Alethea, who *d.* 1957, dau. of the late Evelyn Mackarness, of Lahard, co. Cavan ; *d.* 1955; *s.* by his son [4] RICHARD DUKE, 4th Baron and present peer.

COLGRAIN, BARON. (Campbell.) [Baron U.K. 1946.]

FAC ET SPERA

Act and Hope

DAVID COLIN CAMPBELL, 3rd Baron; *b.* April 24th, 1920; *s.* 1973; late 9th Lancers: *m.* 1st, 1945 (m. diss. 1964), Veronica Margaret, da. of the late Col. William Leckie Webster, RAMC; 2ndly, 1973, Sheila, da. of the late Robert McLeod Mitchell, and formerly wife of M. M. Hudson, and has issue by 1st m.

Arms,—Gyronny of eight or and sable, on a chief azure a bezant between two crescents of the first. **Crest,—**A boar's head erect and erased azure issuant from a wreath of myrtle leaved and flowered proper. **Supporters,—***Dexter,* a horse argent; *sinister,* a boar azure.

Residences,—51, Winchester St., SW1; Garden Cottage, Everlands, Sevenoaks, Kent.

SON LIVING. (*By 1st m.*).
Hon. ALASTAIR COLIN LECKIE, *b.* Sept. 16th, 1951; ed. at Eton, and Trin. Coll., Camb.

DAUGHTER LIVING. (*By 1st m.*).
Hon. Virginia Charlotte Angela, *b.* 1948: *m.* 1973, Maj. Jonathan Charles Mackay-Lewis, of, 39, Chester Sq., SW1.

BROTHERS LIVING.
Hon. Robert (Robin) Dudley, *b.* 1921; late Scots Guards; Man. Dir. of Balfour Williamson & Co. Ltd. and a Dir. of Bank of London & S. America Ltd.: *m.* 1954, Cecilia Barbara, el da. of the late Com. Alexander Leslie, RN (ret.), of Old Manor Cottage, Lympne Hill, Kent, and has issue living, Lenore Robina Cecilia, *b.* 1957,—Zephyrine Alexandra, *b.* 1967. *Residence,*—15, Porchester Terr., W2. *Club,*—Guards'.

Hon. Neil Donald, *DSC, b.* 1922; late Lt. RN: *m.* 1951, Angela Louise Vereker, da. of the Rt. Hon. Sir Ronald Hibbert Cross, KCMG, KCVO, 1st Bt. (ext.) and has issue living, Andrew Donald *b.* 1954: *m.* 1974, Dominique, el. da. of Peter Juul, of Copenhagen,—Roderick Hugo, *b.* 1960,—Martin Emmott, *b.* 1963,—Joanna Louise, *b.* 1953. *Residence,*—Yorks Hill Farm, Ide Hill, Sevenoaks, Kent.

SISTER LIVING.
Hon. Gillian Margaret, *b.* 1925: *m.* 1951, Peter Scott Young, and has issue living, Robert James Campbell, *b.* 1954,—Mark Peter, *b.* 1961,—Bridget Margaret, *b.* 1952,—Deborah Mary, *b.* 1957. *Residence,*—Stumble Hill, Shipbourne, Tonbridge, Kent.

AUNTS LIVING (*Daughters of 1st Baron.*)
Hon. Marjorie Angela, *b.* 1893. *Residence,*—Eden Croft, Stick Hill, Edenbridge, Kent.

Hon. Rachel Audrey (*Hon. Lady Bosville Macdonald of Sleat*), *b.* 1894 : *m.* 1917, Sir Godfrey Middleton Bosville Macdonald of Sleat, MBE, 15th Bt., who *d.* 1951. *Residence,*—Eden Croft, Stick Hill, Edenbridge, Kent.

WIDOW LIVING OF SON OF FIRST BARON.
Joan Esther Sybella, JP (Doddington Cottage, Nantwich, Ches.), da. of the late Col. Hercules Arthur Pakenham, CMG [see E. Longford, colls.]: *m.* 1926, the Hon. Angus Dudley Campbell, CBE, who *d.* 1967, and has issue living [see colls., infra].

WIDOW LIVING OF SECOND BARON.
MARGARET EMILY (*Madge, Baroness Colgrain*) (Everlands, Sevenoaks, Kent), da. of the late Percy William Carver, of Courtlands, W. Hoathly, Sussex: *m.* 1917, the 2nd Baron, who *d.* 1973.

COLLATERAL BRANCH LIVING.
Issue of the late Hon. Angus Dudley Campbell, CBE, yr. son of 1st Baron, *b.* 1895: *d.* 1967: *m.* 1926, Joan Esther Sybella, JP (ante), da. of the late Col. Hercules Arthur Pakenham, CMG [see E. Longford]:—

Judith Averil, *b.* 1927: *m.* 1954, Lt.-Cdr. Gerard St. John Roden Buxton, RN, of Pitteadie House, Kirkcaldy, Fife [see Buxton, Bt. colls.].——Fiona Mary, *b.* 1930: *m.* 1953, Donald Dundas Scott, JP, DL, of Harsfold Manor, Wisborough Green, Sussex, and has issue living, Roderick Arthur, *b.* 1958,—Angus Malcolm, *b.* 1964.—Henrietta Sara, *b.* 1957,—Rosanna Harriet, *b.* 1962.——Linda Ishbel, *b.* 1934: *m.* 1958, Hugh Guy Cubitt, of Chapel House, W. Humble, Dorking, Surrey [see B. Ashcombe].

PREDECESSORS.—[1] COLIN FREDERICK Campbell, son of George William Campbell; *b.* 1866; Pres. of British Bankers' Asso. 1938-46, and a Director of National Provincial Bank, London Assurance, and other cos.; *cr. Baron Colgrain,* of Everlands, co. Kent (peerage of United Kingdom) 1946: *m.* 1890, Lady Angela Mary Alice Ryder, *M.B.E.,* who *d.* 1939, dau. of 4th Earl of Harrowby ; *d.* 1954; *s.* by his el. son [2] DONALD SWINTON, *MC,* 2nd Baron; *b.* 1891; Chm. of Grindlays Bank 1949 : *m.* 1917, Margaret Emily, da. of the late Percy William Carver, of Courtlands, W. Hoathly, Sussex: *d* 1973: *s.* by his only son [3] DAVID COLIN, 3rd Baron and present peer.

COLLISON, BARON. (Collison.) [Life Baron 1964.]

HAROLD FRANCIS COLLISON, *CBE, b.* May 10th, 1909; ed. at Hay Currie LCC Sch., Poplar, and at Crypt Sch., Gloucester; a Farm Worker 1934-44, Dist. Officer, National Union of Agricultural Workers 1944-46, and National Officer 1946-53, a Member of Pilkington Cttee. on Broadcasting 1960-62; Gen. Sec. of National Union of Agricultural Workers since 1953, a Member of Workers' Side of Agricultural Wages Board, and of Gen. Council of TUC 1953-68 (Chm. 1964-65), Chm. of Social Insurance and Industrial Welfare Cttee. of TUC 1957-68, British Delegate to International Labour Office since 1957, and a Member of Gov. Body 1960-69, a Member of Council on Tribunals since 1959, Pres. of International Federation of Plantation, Agricultural and Allied Workers since 1960, a part-time Member of N. Thames Gas Board since 1961, a Member of Transport Consultative Cttee. (re-elected) 1962-70, and of Agricultural Advisory Council since 1962, Vice-Chm. of Land Settlement Assocn. since 1964, Chm. of Agric. Apprenticeship Council since 1968, and a Member of Roy. Commn. on Trades Unions and Employers' Assocn., of Home Grown Cereals Authority since 1965, of Economic Development Council for Agric., of Industrial Health Advisory Cttee., of Industrial Safety Advisory Council, of National Insurance Advisory Cttee., of Industrial Consultative Approach to Europe, and of Oversea Labour Consultative Cttee.; *cr.* CBE (Civil) 1961, and *Baron Collison,* of Cheshunt, co. Hertford (Life Baron) 1964: *m.* 1946, Ivy Kate, da. of Walter Hanks, of Burleigh, Glos.

Residence,—Honeywood, 163, Old Nazeing Rd., Broxbourne, Herts.

COLVILLE OF CULROSS, VISCOUNT. (Colville.) [Viscount U.K. 1902, Lord precedence S. 1609.]

I can not forget.

JOHN MARK ALEXANDER COLVILLE, 4th Viscount and 13th Lord (cr. 1609); *b.* July 19th, 1933; *s.* 1945; ed. at Rugby, and at New Coll., Oxford (MA); Bar. Lincolns Inn 1960; Lt. Gren. Gds. (Reserve), and a Member of Roy. Co. of Archers Queen's Body Guard for Scotland); Min. of (State Home Office 1972-74: *m.* 1st, 1958 (m. diss. 1973), Mary Elizabeth, dau. of Col. M. H. W. Webb-Bowen, RM, of Camrose, Stockton, Norfolk; 2ndly, 1974, Margaret Birgitta, da. of Maj.-Gen. Cyril Henry Norton, CB, CBE, and formerly wife of 2nd Viscount Davidson, and has issue by 1st m.

Arms.—Quarterly: 1st and 4th argent, a cross moline sable, *Colvill* ; 2nd and 3rd gules, a fesse, checky, argent and azure, *Lindsay.* Crest.—A hind's head couped at the neck argent. Supporters.—*Dexter,* a rhinoceros proper; *sinister,* a savage habited in a bearskin and supporting on his left shoulder with his exterior hand a club all proper.

Residences,—Fawsyde, Kinneff, Montrose, Angus, DD10 0TG; 2, Mitre Court Buildings, Temple, EC4 7BX.

SONS LIVING (By 1st m.)

Hon. CHARLES MARK TOWNSHEND (*Master of Colville*), *b.* Sept. 5th, 1959.

Hon. Richmond James Innys, *b.* 1961.

Hon. Alexander Fergus Gale, *b.* 1964.

Hon. Rupert George Streatfeild, *b.* 1966.

BROTHERS LIVING.

Hon. (Charles) Anthony (Lime Park, Herstmonceux, Sussex), *b.* 1935; ed. at Rugby, and at Magdalen Coll., Oxford (BA); late Sub-Lt. RNR; Solicitor 1969; Overseas Civil Ser., Kenya 1958-64: *m.* 1965, Katherine, da. of the late H. J. Sankey, of Kinangop, Kenya, and has issue living, Robert Quintin Oxnam, *b.* 1971.—Charles Alexander, *b.* 1974.

Hon. Angus Richmond, *b.* 1939; ed. at Rugby; Lt. Grenadier Guards (Reserve); FRICS.

WIDOW LIVING OF THIRD VISCOUNT.

KATHLEEN MYRTLE (*Dowager Viscountess Colville of Culross*), O.B.E., dau. of the late Brig.-Gen. Henry Richmond Gale, C.M.G., R.E. [M. Bute, colls.]; formerly Ch. Commr. for Scotland, Girl Guides Asso.; O.B.E. (Civil) 1961 : *m.* 1931, the 3rd Viscount, who *d.* (killed on active ser. during European War) 1945. *Residence,*—Fawsyde, Kinneff, Montrose, Angus.

COLLATERAL BRANCHES LIVING.

Issue of the late Adm. the Hon. Sir Stanley Cecil James Colville (Vice-Adm. of the United Kingdom), G.C.B., G.C.M.G., G.C.V.O., 2nd son of 1st Viscount, *b.* 1861, *d.* 1939 : *m.* 1902, Lady Adelaide Jane Meade, who *d.* 1960, dau. of 4th Earl of Clanwilliam :—

George Cecil, *C.B.E.*, *b.* 1903; Capt. (ret.) R.N.; appointed an A.D.C. to H.M. 1953; sometime an A.D.C. to Gov.-Gen. of S. Africa; O.B.E. (Mil.) 1942, C.B.E. (Mil.) 1953: *m.* 1935, Gabrielle, dau. of the late Gen. Sir Arthur Power Palmer, G.C.B., G.C.I.E., and widow of Col. Leger Livingstone-Learmonth, of Southover, near Dorchester, and has issue living, Rona Alice Gabrielle (*Hon. Mrs. Thomas R. V. Dixon*), *b.* 1936: *m.* 1959, Maj. the Hon. Thomas Robin Valerian Dixon, MBE, Grenadier Guards [see Glentoran]. *Address,*—c/o Messrs. Coutts & Co., Strand, WC2.——Edward Charles, *C.B.*, *D.S.O.*, *b.* 1905: ed. at Marlborough; Maj.-Gen. (ret.) late Gordon Highlanders; a JP for W. Sussex; a DL for Sussex; sometime an ADC to Gov.-Gen. of Canada; BGS, BAOR, 1952-54, and Ch. of Staff, Far East Land Forces 1954-5, and Gen. Officer Comdg. 51st (Highland) Div. 1955-9; N.-W. Europe 1944-45 (despatches, DSO and Bar), Malaya 1955 (CB); DSO 1944 (Bar 1945), CB (Mil) 1955: *m.* 1934, Barbara Joan, dau. of the late Edward Herry Marland Denny, of Staplefield Place, Staplefield, Sussex, and has issue living, Jane (*HSH Princess Martin Lubomirski*), *b.* 1936: *m.* 1st, 1957 (*m.* diss. 1967), Sir Archibald Bruce Charles Edmonstone, 7th Bt.; 2ndly, 1967, HSH Prince Martin Lubomirski,—Antonia, *b.* 1939: *m.* 1962, (*m.* diss. 1973) Garry Lacon Jock Ropner [see Ropner, Bt. (cr. 1904), colls.]. *Residence,*—Old Bartons, Stoughton, nr. Chichester, Sussex. *Club,*—Army and Navy.——Sir Richard, *KCVO*, *CB*, *DSC* (Inchreed, Jarvis Brook, Sussex), *b.* 1907, *d.* 1975: ed. at Harrow; Cdr. (S.) (ret.) RN; Press Sec. to HM King George VI 1947-52, and to HM Queen Elizabeth II 1952-68; an Extra Equerry to HM since 1968; 1939-45 War (DSC); MVO (4th class) 1950, CVO 1953, CB (Civil) 1960, KCVO 1965: *m.* 1933, Dorothy, who *d.* 1972, da. of Brig.-Gen. Halhead Brodrick Birdwood, and has issue living, Peter Alan (Inchreed, Jarvis Brook, Sussex), *b.* 1935; late Lt. RM: *m.* 1964, Jane, el. da. of the late Capt. Thomas Harland, of Walton House, Kineton, Warwicks, and has issue living, Julia Mary *b.* 1965, Annabel Clare *b.* 1967, Joanna Elizabeth *b.* 1969, Sarah Dorothy Louise *b.* 1972,—Anne Bridget, *b.* 1939: *m.* 1963, Oliver Spankie, late Capt. RM, of Golford Lodge, Cranbrook, Kent, and has issue living, Hugh Nicholas *b.* 1967, Rosemary Bridget *b.* 1964,—June Claire, *b.* 1948.

Issue of the late Hon. George Charles Colville, M.B.E., 3rd son of 1st Viscount, *b.* 1867; *d.* 1943: *m.* 1908, Lady (Helen) Cynthia Crewe-Milnes, *D.C.V.O.*, *D.B.E*, who *d.* 1968, da. of 1st Marquess of Crewe:—

David Richard, *b.* 1909: ed. at Harrow and at Trin. Coll., Camb (MA); a partner in the firm of N. M. Rothschild & Sons; 1939-45 War as Lt. RNVR: *m.* 1933, Lady Joan Child-Villiers, da. of 8th Earl of Jersey, and has issue living, Robert John, *b.* 1941,—James Richard Charles, *b.* 1952,—Sarah Anne, *b.* 1933: *m.* 1968, Maj.-Gen. Robert Anthony Pigot, CB, OBE, of Yew Tree Lodge, Bembridge, I. of Wight [see Pigot, Bt., colls.], Catherine, *b.* 1935: *m.* 1958, Cdr. Warren, L. R. E. Gilchrist, RN, of Rook Hill, Monk Sherborne, Basingstoke,—Mary Julia, *b.* 1947: *m.* 1969, Aubrey Francis Houston Bowden, of 9, Herbert Cres., SW1 [see Bowden, Bt.]. *Residence,*—Old Vicarage, Dorton, nr. Aylesbury, Bucks.: Ducie House, Bembridge, Isle of Wight. *Clubs,*—Brooks's, Pratt's, Royal Yacht Sqn.——Philip Robert *MBE*, *b.* 1910; ed. at Harrow, and at Trin. Coll., Camb. (BA 1932, MA 1935); Maj. Grenadier Guards; N.-W. Europe 1944-45 (despatches, MBE); MBE (Mil.) 1946. *Residence,*—4, Mulberry Walk, SW3. *Clubs,*—Pratt's, White's, Royal Yacht Sqn.——Sir John Rupert, *CB*, *CVO*, *b.* 1915; ed. at Harrow and at Trin. Coll., Camb. (MA); served in Diplo. Ser. 1937-55; was a Page of Honour to HM 1927-31, Private Sec. to Prime Min. 1939-41, and 1943-45, to HM when HRH Princess Elizabeth 1947-49, and again to Prime Min. 1951-55; 1939-45 War as Fl.-Lt. RAF; an Officer of Legion of Honour; CVO 1949, CB (Civil) 1955 Knt. 1974: *m.* 1948, Lady Margaret Egerton, da. of 4th Earl of Ellesmere [see D. Sutherland], and has sissue living, Alexander Georgs, *b.* 1955: a Page of Honour to HM 1968-71,—Rupert Charles, *b.* 1960,—Elizabeth Harriet, *b.* 1952. *Residence,*—The Old Rectory, Stratfield Saye, Reading. *Clubs,*—White's, Pratt's.

PREDECESSORS.—[1] *Sir* JAMES Colville, Knt.; served with distinction in the French War under Henry of Navarre, afterwards Henry IV. of France, and in 1589 received a charter of the Abbey of Culross as a feudal barony, and was cr. (by charter and investiture) *Lord Colville of Culross* 1604 with remainder to his heirs male whatsoever; on the resignation of his kinsman the Commendator of Culross, the Abbey Estates were in 1609 re-erected with a Lordship and he was cr. *Lord Colville of Culross* (peerage of Scotland) 1609, with remainder to heirs male whatsoever; *d.* 1620 ; *s.* by his son [2] JAMES, 2nd Lord, *d.* 1624 ; *s.* by his son [3] WILLIAM, 3rd Lord ; *d.* 1656 ; *s.* by his brother [4] JOHN, 4th Lord ; *s.* by his kinsman [5] ALEXANDER, 5th Lord ; *d.* 1721 ; *s.* by his son [6] JOHN, 6th Lord ; in 1722, at the Gen. Election of Scottish Peers his name was excluded from the Peers' Roll on the ground that it was not on the roll at the time of the Union ; but on petition to the House of Lords, when the Charter of 1609 was the instrument acted on, he was declared, in 1723, to be entitled to the dignity, and his name was placed on the roll as *Lord Colville of Culross* next to Lord Cardross; *d.* 1741 ; *s.* by his el. son [7] ALEXANDER, 7th Lord, a distinguished Vice-Adm. ; *d.* 1770 ; *s.* by his brother [8] JOHN, 8th Lord ; *d.* 1811 ; *s.* by his son [9] JOHN, 9th Lord ; Adm. of the White, and a Representative Peer ; *d.* 1849 ; *s.* by his nephew [10] CHARLES JOHN (son of Gen. Sir Charles Colville, G.C.B., 2nd son of 9th Lord), P.C., K.T., G.C.V.O., 10th Lord, *b.* 1818 ; Lord Chamberlain to Queen Alexandra 1873-1903 ; cr. *Baron Colville of Culross* (peerage of United Kingdom) 1885, and *Viscount Colville of Culross*, co. Perth (peerage of United Kingdom) 1902 : *m.* 1853, Hon. Cecile Katherine Mary Carington, who *d.* 1907, dau. of 2nd Baron Carrington; *d.* 1903 ; *s.* by his el. son [11] CHARLES ROBERT WILLIAM, 2nd Viscount, *b.* 1854 ; Lieut.-Col. late Grenadier Guards ; was Mil. Sec. to Gov.-Gen. of Canada (Baron Stanley of Preston) 1888-92 ; Zulu War 1879 (despatches, medal with clasp) : *m.* 1885, Ruby, who *d.* 1943, dau. of the late Lieut.-Col. Henry Dorrien Streatfeild, of Chiddingstone, Kent ; *d.* 1928 ; *s.* by his son [12] CHARLES ALEXANDER, 3rd Viscount ; *b.* 1888 ; Com. R.N.; European War 1914-19 (despatches), European War 1939-45 : *m.* 1931, Kathleen Myrtle, dau. of the late Brig.-Gen. Henry Richmond Gale, C.M.G., R.E. ; *d.* (killed on active ser. during European War) 1945 ; *s.* by his el. son [13] JOHN MARK ALEXANDER, 4th Viscount and present peer; also Baron Colville of Culross, and Lord Colville of Culross.

COLWYN, BARON. (Smith.) [Baron U.K. 1917, Bt. U.K. 1912.]

I give thanks.

IAN ANTHONY HAMILTON SMITH,
3rd Baron, and 3rd Baronet; b. Jan.
1st, 1942; s. 1966; ed. at Cheltenham,
and at London Univ (BDS), LDS
RCS; m 1964, Sonia Jane, el. da. of
P. H. G. Morgan, of The Eades, Upton-
upon-Severn, Worcs., and has issue.

Arms,—Per chevron gules and argent, in chie
two cocks of the second, in base a whale spouting
proper. Crest,—Upon a whale a cock, both as in
the arms. Supporters,—Dexter, a miner holding
in his exterior hand and resting on his shoulder a
pick-axe, suspended from his belt a miner's lamp, all
proper; sinister, a female weaver holding in her exterior hand a shuttle also proper.

Residences,—Yew Tree Cottage, Dumbleton,
Evesham, Worcs.; Painswick House, Cheltenham;
23, Wimpole St., W1.

SON LIVING.
Hon. CRAIG PETER, b. Oct. 13th, 1968.

DAUGHTER LIVING.
Hon. Jacqueline Jane, b. 1967.

BROTHER LIVING.
Hon. Timothy Hamilton (45, Third Av., Claremont 7700, S. Africa), b. 1944; ed. at Cheltenham;
MA, Oxford: m. 1967, Carolyn, da. of Bernulf Llewelyn Hodge, MRCS, LRCP, of The Old Cottage,
Jac-na-Pare, Polperro, S. Cornwall, and has issue living, Annabel, b. 1972, Fiona, b. 1974.

AUNT LIVING.
Elisabeth Joan Babette Hamilton, b. 1019 : m. 1939, Lieut.-Col. John Baddeley Bagot Ferguson, Roy.
Tank Regt., and has issue, Nicholas John, b. 1941: m. 1965, Karen Elisabeth Svanso, and has issue
living, James Fergus b. 1966, Kate Elisabeth Venetia b. 1967.

GREAT-AUNT LIVING. (Daughter of 1st Baron.)
Hon. Kathleen Whalley, M.B.E.; M.B.E. (Civil)1946 : m. 1945, Robert Cullen Howie. Residence,—
Butts Cottage, Rhinefield Road, Brockenhurst, Hants.

WIDOW LIVING OF SON OF FIRST BARON.
Marjorie Methwold, O.B.E., dau. of the late Arthur Birkett, of Langford Lodge, Southwold, Suffolk;
O.B.E. (Civil) 1957: m. 1917, the Hon. (Hubert) Constantine Smith, who d. 1956, and has issue
living [see colls. infra]. Residence,—Pear Trees Farm, Hermitage Lane, Holmes Chapel, Cheshire.

MOTHER LIVING.
Miriam (Cantley, 32, Bafford Lane, Charlton Kings, Cheltenham), da. of the late Victor Bruce
Ferguson, of Abbotsdene, Cheltenham: m. 1940 (m. diss. 1951), the 2nd Baron, who d. 1966.

WIDOW LIVING OF SECOND BARON.
Beryl (Lady Taylor), da. of the late Harvey Walker, of Heathgates House, Heathgates, Salop, for-
merly wife of Maj. Edward Chorley Cookson, MBE, RE, and widow of Philip Mortimer Reddington,
FRCS: m. 1955, as his 3rd wife, the 2nd Baron, who d. 1966; she m. 4thly, 1969, Sir George Taylor,
FRS, of Belhaven House, Dunbar, E. Lothian, and 142, Harley St., W1.

COLLATERAL BRANCH LIVING.

Issue of the late Hon. (Hubert) Constantine Smith, yr. son of 1st Baron, b. 1890,
d. 1956: m. 1917, Marjorie Methwold, O.B.E. (ante), dau. of the late Arthur
Birkett, of Langford Lodge, Southwold, Suffolk:—
Michael Constantine (Breck Meadow, The Wash, Chapel-en-le-Frith, Derbys.), b. 1919; is Capt. RA:
m. 1st, 1945 (m. diss. 1970), Veronica, only da. of Thomas Flanagan, of Tralee; 2ndly, 1970, Marie
Therese, yr. da. of Patrick Stuart Martin, of Glasgow, and has issue living, (by 1st m.), Christopher
Michael Constantine, b. 1953,—Sally Constantine, b. 1947,—Judy Jennifer Constantine,
b. 1951.——Anthony Methwold Constantine, b. 1923: m. 1955, Susan Muriel, only da.
of Frederick B. Staveacre, of Braeside, Colwyn Bay, and has issue living, David Anthony Con-
stantine, b. 1962,—Caroline Constantine, b. 1957,—Nicola Constantine, b. 1959. Residence,—
Hermitage Farm, Cranage, Holmes Chapel, Cheshire.——Elizabeth Pamela, b. 1918: m. 1945,
Michael William Malim, and has issue living, Flavia Eve, b. 1949,—Lydia Elisabeth, b. 1952,—
Julia Pamela, b. 1955,—Delia, b. 1959. Residence,—Harvard House ,Stock, Essex.

PREDECESSORS–[1] Rt. Hon. FREDERICK HENRY Smith, el. son of the late Joshua
Smith, J.P., of Eccles; b. 1859; was Dep. Chm. of Martin's Bank, Ltd., and a Director of
Railway Cos.; High Sheriff of Carnarvonshire 1917 ; cr. a Baronet 1912, and Baron Colwyn,
of Colwyn Bay, co. Denbigh (peerage of United Kingdom) 1917: m. 1882, Elizabeth Ann, who
d. 1945, dau. of the late Hamilton Savage, of Eccles: d. 1946; s. by his grandson [2]
FREDERICK JOHN VIVIAN (son of the late Hon. Frederick Henry Hamilton Smith, el. son of
1st Baron), 2nd Baron; b. 1914: m. 1st, 1940 (m. diss. 1951), Miriam, da. of the late Victor Ferguson;
2ndly, 1952 (m. diss. 1954), Hermione Sophia O'Bryen, da. of the late Cyril Bertie Edward Hoare
[Hoare, Bt., cr. 1784]; 3rdly, 1955, Beryl (who m. 4thly, 1969, Sir George Taylor, FRS), da. of the
late Harvey Walker, formerly wife of Edward Chorley Cookson, and widow of Mortimer Reddington,
FRCS; d. 1966; s. by his el. son [3] IAN ANTHONY HAMILTON, 3rd Baron.

COLYTON, BARON. (Hopkinson.) [Baron U.K. 1956.]

Look forward.

HENRY LENNOX D'AUBIGNÉ HOP-
KINSON, *C.M.G.*, *P.C.*, 1st Baron,
el. son of the late Sir Henry Lennox
Hopkinson, K.C.V.O.; *b.* Jan. 3rd,
1902; ed. at Eton, and at Trin.
Coll., Camb. (B.A. honours 1923);
appointed 3rd Sec., Washington
1924, 2nd Sec. Foreign Office 1929
and Stockholm 1931, Assist. Private
Sec. to Sec. of State for Foreign
Affairs 1932, 2nd Sec., Cairo 1934,
1st Sec. there 1936, 1st Sec.,
Athens 1938, to War Cabinet Office
1939, Private Sec. to Permanent
Under-Sec. for Foreign Affairs 1940,
Counsellor 1941, and Diplo. Adviser to Min. of State, Cairo 1941,
and Min. Plen., Lisbon 1943; was
Dep. British High Commr., Italy
1944-6; resigned from Diplo. Ser.
1946; Head of Conservative Parliamentary Secretariat, and Joint
Director of Conservative Research Dept. 1946-49; Sec. for Overseas
Trade 1951-52, and Min. of State for Colonial Affairs 1952-55, Delegate to
Consultative Assembly of Council of Europe 1950-52, and to Gen. Assembly of
UN 1952-55, Chm. Anglo-Egyptian Re-settlement Board 1957-60, Joint East
and Central African Board 1960-65; Chm. Tanganyika Concessions Ltd.
1966-72; a Dir. of London Tin Corpn., Union Minière, and other cos.; Roy.
Humane Soc.'s Award for Saving Life from drowning 1919; an OStJ; has
Grand Cross of Order of Prince Henry the Navigator of Portugal, Dato of
Order of Stia Negara of Brunei, Cdr. of Order of Zaire of Zaire; MP for Taunton
Div. of Somerset (*C*) 1950-56; cr. CMG 1944, PC 1952, and *Baron Colyton*, of
Farway, co. Devon, and Taunton, co. Somerset (peerage of UK) 1956: *m.* 1st,
1927, Alice Labouisse, who *d.* 1953, da. of Henry Lane Eno, of Bar Harbour,
Maine, USA; 2ndly, 1956, Mrs. Barbara Estella Addams, da. of the late
Stephen Barb, of New York, USA, and has issue by 1st marriage.

Arms,—Azure, on a chevron argent between three mullets of six points or as many mascles gules
a bordure engrailed of the third. *Crest,*—A demi-lion sable between two mullets of six points or.
Supporters,—On either side an angel proper habited azure winged or, the dexter holding in the exterior
hand a Saxon Crown and the sinister likewise holding a trumpet gold.

Residences,—Netherton Hall, near Colyton, Devon; 27½, Smith Terrace, S.W.3; *Clubs,*—
Buck's, White's, Beefsteak, Royal Cornwall Yacht.

SON LIVING. (*By* 1st *marriage.*)

Hon. NICHOLAS HENRY ENO, *b.* Jan. 18th, 1932; ed. at Eton, and at Trin. Coll. Camb.: *m.*
1957, Fiona Margaret, only dau. of Sir (Thomas) Torquil Alphonso Munro, 5th Bt., and has issue
living, Alisdair John Munro, *b.* 1958,—Charles Henry Kenneth, *b.* 1960. *Residence,*—Maidenhatch
Farm, Tidmarsh, nr. Reading, Berks. *Clubs,*—Buck's, White's, Beefsteak.

COMBERMERE, VISCOUNT. (Stapleton-Cotton.) [Viscount U.K. 1826, Bt. E. 1677.]

[Title pronounced "**Cumbermeer.**"]

Prepared in all circumstances.

MICHAEL   WELLINGTON
STAPLETON-COTTON, 5th Viscount, and 10th Baronet; *b.*
Aug. 8th, 1929; *s.* 1969;
ed. at Eton; BD, MTh Lon-
don; Fl.-Lt. RAF (Reserve);
served Palestine Police Force
1947-48, Roy. Canadian
Mounted Police 1948-50 and
RAF 1950-58: *m.* 1961,
Pamela Elizabeth, da. of the
Rev. Robert Gustavus Coulson, R. of Stansted, Kent, and
has issue.

Arms,—Quarterly: 1st and 4th
azure, a chevron between three hanks of
cotton argent palewise, and in chief pendant from a ribbon gules, a representation of the medal and clasps presented
to the 1st Viscount, *Cotton*; 2nd
and 3rd argent, a lion rampant sable, *Stapleton*. *Crests,*—1st, a falcon, wings expanded and
inverted proper, beaked, membered, and belled or, holding in the dexter claw part of a belt proper,

buckled gold; 2nd, on a mount vert, a dragoon of the 20th Regiment, mounted on a black horse, and in the act of charging, and over the crest in an escrol azure, the word "Salamanca", in gold letters; 3rd, out of a ducal coronet or, a Saracen's head couped at the shoulders affrontée wreathed round the temples, argent and sable. Supporters.—Two falcons, wings expanded and endorsed proper, beaked, membered, and belled or, the *dexter* supporting a spear, also proper, therefrom flowing to the dexter a standard swallow-tailed vert, semée of estoiles or, streamers and tassels of the last, and the *sinister* supporting a like spear, therefrom flowing a yellow standard, swallow-tailed streamers and tassels of the last.

Residence,—46, Smith St., SW3. *Club,*—RAC.

SON LIVING.
Hon. THOMAS ROBERT WELLINGTON, *b.* Aug. 30th, 1969.

DAUGHTERS LIVING.
Hon. Tara Christabel, *b.* 1961.
Hon. Sophia Mary, *b.* 1963.

BROTHER LIVING.
Hon. David Peter Dudley (Papenboom, Newlands, Cape Town, S. Africa), *b.* 1932; ed. at Eton; Lt. Life Guards (Reserve): *m.* 1955, Susan Nomakepu, da. of Sir George Werner Albu, 2nd Bt., and has issue living, Simon, *b.* 1959,—Toby James, *b.* 1966,—Nicola Caroline Louisa, *b.* 1957,—Polly, *b.* 1961.

COLLATERAL BRANCHES LIVING.
(In remainder to Baronetcy only.)

Grandchildren of the late Rev. Henry James Cotton, son of the late Rev. George Cotton, LL.D., 3rd son of 4th Bt.:—

Issue of the late Rev. James Stapleton Cotton, *b.* 1849, *d.* 1932: *m.* 1880, Louisa Jessie, who *d.* 1922, dau. of the late Colin Minton Campbell, of Woodseat, Uttoxeter [Cave-Browne-Cave, Bt., colls.]:—

Rev. Canon Henry Wilmot Stapleton, *b.* 1894; ed. at Radley, and at Queens' Coll., Camb. (BA 1920, MA 1923): is Canon of St. Edmundsbury; 1914-18 War as Capt. Cheshire Regt. (wounded, despatches); Chap. Indian Ecclesiastical Establishment 1925-46, and Archdeacon of Lucknow 1937-47; R. of Bredfield with Boulge, and Debach, Suffolk 1947-52, and of Lavenham, 1952-64: *m.* 1923, Elaine Christine Isobel, who *d.* 1969, da. of Joseph Henry Iredale, of Rock Ferry. *Residence,*—The Moorings, Hindhead, Surrey.——Hester Evelyn, *b.* 1897. *Residence,*—Heritage, Cowbeech, Hailsham, Sussex.

Grandchildren of the late Rev. James Stapleton Cotton, son of the late Rev. Henry James Cotton (ante):—

Issue of the late Capt. Frederick Arthur Stapleton Cotton, *b.* 1884, *d.* 1927: *m.* 1912, Evelyn Mary, who *d.* 1968, da. of the late Col. Samuel Ormsby Rogers, Army Ordnance Corps:—

Hugh Philip Stapleton (19, Old Millmeads, Horsham, Sussex) *b.* 1913; ed. at Felsted; 1939-45 War as Capt. RA: *m.* 1938, Mary Josephine, da. of Frederick Thomas Wheeler, and has issue living, Stephen Hugh Stapleton (c/o Barclays Bank, Horsham, Sussex), *b.* 1949; ed. at Tonbridge and Reading Univ. (BSc. Estate Management); ARICS: *m.* 1970, Josephine Katharina, da. of Owen Eric Goddard, HM British Consul in Zürich, of 8703, Erlenbach ZH, Drusbergstrasse, 31, Switzerland, and has issue living, Gabriele Pippa *b.* 1974,—Jennifer Mary, *b.* 1943: *m.* 1964, Peter Ivan Chettle, of Oakside, Little Browns Lane, Edenbridge, Kent, and has issue living, Dominic Mark *b.* 1967, Deborah Jane Emma *b.* 1970,—Marilyn Elizabeth, *b.* 1946.——Sheila Evelyn Ormsby, *b.* 1915: *m.* 1940, Maj. Arthur Richard Burch, DSO, RM, who *d.* 1964, and has issue living, Peter Ronald, *b.* 1946; Lt. RN,—David John, *b.* 1949,—Sally Louise, *b.* 1943: *m.* 1972, David John North. *Residence,*—Hilington House, Saltburn by the Sea, Yorks.

Granddaughter of the late Rt. Rev. George Edward Lynch Cotton, son of the late Capt. Thomas Davenant Cotton, 3rd son of the late Rev. George Cotton, LL.D. (ante):—

Issue of the late Col. Sir Edward Thomas Davenant COTTON-JODRELL, K.C.B., *b.* 1847, *d.* 1917. having assumed by Roy. licence 1890 the additional surname of Jodrell: *m.* 1878, Mary Rennell, *O.B.E.,* who *d.* 1932, dau. of the late William Rennell Coleridge, of Salston, Devon:—

Olive Harriet, *O.B.E., b.* 1883 : O.B.E. (Civil) 1920 : *m.* 1910, Adm. Richard Greville Arthur Wellington Stapleton-Cotton, C.B., C.B.E., M.V.O., who *d.* 1953, son of the late Col. the Hon. Richard Southwell George Stapleton-Cotton (ante). *Residence,*—Icen House, Wareham, Dorset.

Grandchildren of the late Charles Calveley Cotton, el. son of the late Charles Robert Cotton, son of the late Henry Calveley Cotton (*b.* 1750), 6th son of 4th Bt.:—

Issue of the late Lieut.-Col. Ronald Egerton Cotton, D.S.O., *b.* 1876, *d.* 1932: *m.* 1917, Hilda, who *d.* 1967, da. of the late Capt. Charles Dickson Inglis, RN, of Grianach, Nairn:—

Patricia Daphne, *b.* 1920. *Residence,*—Higher Meerhay Farm, Beaminster, Dorset.

Issue of the late Lt.-Col. Arthur Egerton Cotton, D.S.O., *b.* (twin) 1876; *d.* 1922; *m.* 1909, Beryl Marie, who *d.* 1966 (having *m.* 2ndly, 1922, John Lee Booker, JP, who *d.* 1942), da. of the late Henry Jack Cumming, of Foston Hall, Derby:—

Elizabeth Egerton, *b.* 1910: *m.* 1st, 1934, Francis Mortimer Montgomery, from whom she obtained a divorce 1949; 2ndly, 1951, Stafford William Somerfield, and has issue living, (by 1st marriage) Jon Ayrton (14, Steeple Close, Church Gate, SW6), *b.* 1935: *m.* 1971, Susan Moore, and has issue living, Alexander Stafford *b.* 1972. *Residence,*—Panfield, Denne Park, Horsham.——Anne Rebecca (Cookes St., Edgar Town, Marthas Vineyard, Mass., USA), *b.* 1912: *m.* 1943, Auriol Magor, who *d.* 19—, and from whom she had obtained a divorce 19—.——Diana Sara, *b.* 1914: *m.* 1936, Ernest Addenbrooke Crutchley, who assumed by deed poll 1945, the name of Brooke in lieu of his christian names of Ernest Addenbrooke, and has issue living, Edward Brooke, *b.* 1950.——Christopher Miles, *b.* 1951,—Anna Maria, *b.* 1954. *Residence,* 2, Courtyards, Little Shelford, Cambs.

Issue of the late Lt.-Col. Vere Egerton Cotton, CBE, TD, *b.* 1888; *d.* 1970: *m.* 1922, Elfreda Helen, JP (Langdale, Grassendale Park, Liverpool, 19), da. of William Francis Moore:—
Simon Arthur (28, Sauncey Av., Harpenden, Herts) *b.* 1924; ed. at Repton, and Magdalene Coll., Camb. (Scholar, BA); Bar. Gray's Inn 1951; late Lt. RA (TA); 1939-45 War in India: *m.* 1960, Barbara Helen Ralston, da. of the late Albert James Sutcliffe, of Dodleston, Ches., and has issue living, William Andrew Calveley, *b.* 1962,—Emma Jane, *b.* 1961,—Helen Clare, *b.* 1965.——Robert Charles (The Cherry Orchard, Badgemore, Henley on Thames), *b.* 1925; ed. at Repton, and Magdalene Coll., Camb. (BA); formerly Lt. RE, and Lt. RA (TA): *m.* 1954, Nicolette Anne, da. of Capt. Robert Lionel Brooke Cunliffe, CBE, RN [see Cunliffe, Bt., colls.], and has issue living, Richard Robert, *b.* 1956; ed. at Bradfield,—Philip Egerton, *b.* 1960,—Penelope Clare, *b.* 1957.——Caroline Harriet, *b.* 1963.——Henry Egerton (Norwood, Grassendale Park, Liverpool, 19—), *b.* 1929; ed. at Rugby, and Magdalene Coll., Camb. (BA); late Lt. RA (TA): *m.* 1955, Elizabeth Margaret Susan, da. of the late O. James Peard, of N. Curry, Som., and has issue living, Timothy James Egerton, *b.* 1958,—Catherine Susan, *b.* 1956.

Grandchildren of Maj. Francis Egerton Cotton, 2nd son of Charles Robert Cotton, 5th son of Henry Calverley Cotton (b. 1750), (ante):—
Issue of the late Maj. Gilbert Francis Egerton Cotton, b. 1880, d. 1971: m. 1913, Nora, who d. 1956, da. of Mathew Williams:—

Francis Brian Egerton (Low Houses, nr. Brampton, Cumberland), b. 1916; ed. at Eton; Maj. (ret.) RWF: m. 1955, Ruth, da. of the late Richard Stratton, OBE, of Kingston Deverill, Wilts., and has issue living, Charles Egerton, b. 1958.——Helen Viola Egerton, b. 1917: m. 1st, 1940, Capt. Sir John Hargreaves Pigott-Brown, 2nd Bt. Coldm. Gds., who d. (killed in action) 1942; 2ndly, 1948, Capt. Charles Raymond Radclyffe, late R. Scots Greys, of Lew, Oxon., and has issue living, (by 1st m.) [see Pigott-Brown, Bt.],—(by 2nd m.) Sarah, b. 1950.

Granddaughter of the late William Gordon Lynch Cotton, M.I.C.E., son of the late Col. Hugh Calveley Cotton, 6th son of Henry Calveley Cotton (b. 1750) (ante).
Issue of the late Hugh Gordon Cotton, b. 1869, d. 1942: m. 1903, Gertrude Mary, dau. of the late Charles Parsons:—
Vivien Mary, b. 1903. Residence,—

PREDECESSORS.—[1] Sir ROBERT Cotton, M.P. for Cheshire; cr. a Baronet 1677; d. 1712. s. by his son [2] Sir THOMAS, 2nd Bt. ; s. by his el. son [3] Sir ROBERT SALUSBURY, 3rd Bt.; M.P. for Cheshire; d.s.p.; s. by his brother [4] Sir LYNCH SALUSBURY, M.P., 4th Bt.; d. 1775; s. by his son [5] Sir ROBERT SALUSBURY, 5th Bt., M.P. for Cheshire; d. 1807; s. by his son [6] Sir STAPLETON, G.C.B., G.C.H., K.S.I., b. 1772; served with remarkable distinction in Peninsular War 1791-1814. and at siege of Bhurtpore 1826, when Com. in Ch. in India; was a Field-Marshal, Constable of the Tower, Lord-Lieut. of Tower Hamlets, Gold Stick-in-Waiting and Col. 1st Life Guards; cr. Baron Combermere, of Combermere, co. Chester (peerage of United Kingdom) 1814, and Viscount Combermere, of Bhurtpore, E. Indies, and of Combermere, co. Chester (peerage of United Kingdom) 1827: m. 2ndly, 1814, Caroline, dau. of William Fulke Greville; d. 1865; s. by his son [7] WELLINGTON HENRY, 2nd Viscount, b. 1818; M.P. for Carrickfergus (C) 1847-57: m. 1844, Susan Alice, who d. 1869, dau. of Sir George Sitwell, 2nd Bt.; d. 1891; s. by his el. son [8] ROBERT WELLINGTON, 3rd Viscount, b. 1845: m. 1st, 1866, Charlotte Anne (who obtained a divorce 1879), only child to the late J. Fletcher Ellis Fletcher, of Pool Isabel, Lancashire; 2ndly, 1880, Isabel Marian. who d. 1930, youngest dau. of Sir Viscount; b. 1887: m. 1st, 1913, Hazel Louisa, who d. 1943 (having obtained a divorce 1926), da. of the late Henry de Courcy Agnew, [Agnew, Bt., cr. 1629, colls.]; 2ndly, 1927, Constance Marie Katherine, who d. 1968, da. of the late Lt.-Col. Sir Francis Dudley Williams-Drummond, KBE, of Hafodneddyn, Carmarthenshire, [Williams-Drummond, Bt., colls.]: d. 1969; s. by his son [10] MICHAEL WELLINGTON, 5th Viscount and present peer; also Baron Combermere.

Compton, Earl, son of Marquess of Northampton.

CONESFORD, BARONY OF. (Strauss.) [Extinct 1974.]
[Title pronounced "Connisford."]

WIDOW LIVING OF FIRST BARON.
ANNE SADELBIA MARY (Baroness Conesford), (25, Cheyne Walk, SW3), yr. da. of the late John Bowyer Nichols, FSA, of Lawford Hall, nr. Manningtree, Essex: m. 1927, the 1st Baron, who d. 1974, when the title became ext.

CONGLETON, BARON. (Parnell.) [Baron U.K. 1841, Bt. I. 1766.]

TE DIGNA·SEQVERE

Honours have followed thee.

CHRISTOPHER PATRICK PARNELL, 8th Baron, and 11th Baronet; b. March 11th, 1930; s. 1967; ed. at Eton, and at New Coll., Oxford: m. 1955, Anna Hedvig, da. of G. A. Sommerfelt, of Oslo, Norway, and has issue.

Arms,—Gules: two chevronels, and in chief three escallops argent. Crest,—A boar's head erased or, between two wings gules, each charged with two chevronels argent. Supporters,—Dexter, an angel vested argent, wings and the head radiated gold; sinister, a hermit vested, the exterior hand supporting his staff proper. the hat ensigned with an escallop or.

Residence,—West End Farm, Ebbesbourne Wake, Salisbury, Wilts.

SONS LIVING
Hon. JOHN PATRICK CHRISTIAN, b. March 17th, 1959.
Hon. Thomas David Howard, b. 1963.

DAUGHTERS LIVING.
Hon. Anne Cathrine, b. 1956.
Hon. Elizabeth Dagny, b. 1960.
Hon. Mary Clare, b. 1965.

SISTERS LIVING.
Hon. Mary Elizabeth, b. 1919: m. 1956, Percy Turnbull. Residence,—West Broomers, Broomers Hill, Pulborough, Sussex.
Hon. Jean Margaret. b. 1922: m. 1952, as his second wife, Lieut.-Col. Frederick Henry Howard. D.S.O., MC, late 3rd Hussars [see E. Carlisle, colls.]. Residence,—Isle of Gometra, by Mull, Argyll.
Hon. Sheila Helen, b. 1923: m. 1959, Roger Henry Duvollet, and has issue living, Annette Frances, b. 1961. Residence,—River House, Golant, Fowey, Cornwall.
Hon. Ann Bridget, b. 1927: m. 1947, Major Derek Campbell Russell, R.E. Residence,—Lyscombe, Piddletrenthide, Dorset.
Hon. Heather Doreen, b. 1929: m. 1960, Robert Peter Mangin Bell, and has issue living, Robert Simon Parnell, b. 1961,—Aidan William George, b. 1967,—Penelope Edith, b. 1963. Residence,—Bindon House, St. Cross, Winchester.

WIDOW LIVING OF SON OF THIRD BARON.
Marjorie Gore, dau. of William Millar, formerly of Southport, Lancashire: m. 1899, the Hon. Lionel Charles Nugent Parnell, who d. 1940, and has issue living [see colls., infra].
Residence,—

WIDOW LIVING OF SIXTH BARON.

Hon. EDITH MARY PALMER *CONGLETON, M.B.E.,* dau. of the late Baroness Strathcona and Mount Royal (in her own right); assumed by deed poll 1951 the surname of Congleton in lieu of that of Aldridge; formerly Assist. Co. Organiser for S. Hampshire Women's Vol. Sers., and a Co. Councillor for Hants; has Order of Mercy with bar; M.B.E. (Civil) 1941: *m.* 1st, 1918, the 6th Baron, who *d.* 1932; 2ndly, 1946, Flight-Lieut. Alfred Eric Rowland Aldridge, who *d.* 1950. *Residence,*— 61, Furzecroft, George Street .W.1; Ulva House. Isle of Ulva, by Mull, Argyll.

COLLATERAL BRANCHES LIVING.

Grandson of the late Bertram Damer Parnell (infra):—
Issue of the late Desmond Damer Parnell, *b.* 1900, *d.* 1972: *m.* 1930, Ivy Maude, who *d.* 1972, da. of late Mark Hunt Harding:—
John Desmond (32, Orchard Gate, Greenford, Middlesex) *b.* 1930: *m.* 1961, Barbara Jean, da. of Laurence Chapell, of Leeds, and formerly wife of Coleson John King and has issue living, Sally Dee, *b.* 1966.

Grandchildren of the late Col. the Hon. Arthur Parnell, 3rd son of 3rd Baron:
Issue of the late Bertram Damer Parnell, *b.* 1876, *d.* 1960: *m.* 1st, 1899, Madeleine, who *d.* 1929, dau. of the late James Byrne; 2ndly, 1930, Lucy Margaret, dau. of the late John Hersohn, of S. Africa:—
Myles Bligh Damer FARMILOE (of Little Brookwood, Woodfield Lane, Ashtead, Surrey), *b.* 1903; in 1929 assumed by deed poll the surname of Farmiloe in lieu of his patronymic: *m.* 1929, Cynthia Joyce, da. of Maj. H. R. Holt, and has issue living, Michael John (Newlands, First Av., Felpham, Sussex), *b.* 1931: *m.* 1953, Mary Elizabeth, only da. of the late Ewart Berry, of 118, Berkeley Court, NW1, and has issue living, Simon Charles *b.* 1961, Sarah Elizabeth *b.* 1959.——Timothy Miles *b.* 1935.——Nancy Stewart (78B, London Rd., Deal, Kent), *b.* 1901.——Mary Margaret (78B, London Rd., Deal, Kent), *b.* 1906.

Issue of the late Harold Stewart Parnell, *b.* 1880, *d.* 1945: *m.* 1919, Marjorie Eva (8, Leys Rd., Cambridge), da. of the late H. D. Summers, formerly Commr. Chinese Postal Ser.:—
Joan Letitia Brooke, *b.* 1920: *m.* 1945, Richard Bencraft Joly, who *d.* 1956, and has issue living, Antony Stewart Bencraft, *b.* 1949; ed. at Christ's Hosp.: *m.* 1970, Carolyn Averil, da. of J. S. Hughes, of Timberly, Reigate, Surrey,—Simon Michael Bencraft, *b.* 1952; ed. at Christ's Hosp., and Corpus Christi Coll., Camb. (BA Hons); FRCO. *Residence,* 8 Leys Rd., Cambridge.

Issue of the late Hon. Lionel Charles Nugent Parnell, 7th son of 3rd Baron, *b.* 1864, *d.* 1940: *m.* 1899, Marjorie Gore (ante), dau. of William Millar, formerly of Southport, Lancashire:—
Francis Hugh, *b.* 1904.——Evelyn Molley, *b.* 1906.——Louisa Catherine, *b.* 1910. *Residence,*—
(*In remainder to Baronetcy only.*)

Grandchildren of the late John Henry Parnell, son of the late William PARNELL-HAYES, 3rd son of 2nd Baronet:—
Issue of the late Henry Tudor Parnell, *b.* 1850, *d.* 1915: *m.* 1882, Penelope, dau. of the late Rev. Thomas Luby, D.D.:—
Harold de Mowbray, *b.* 1889.——Maud Yolan Howard, *b.* 1886. *Residence,*—

PREDECESSORS.—[1] JOHN Parnell, *M.P.* for Maryborough 1761; cr. a *Baronet* 1766; *d.* 1782; *s.* by his son [2] Sir JOHN, *P.C.,* 2nd Bt., M.P. for Queen's co. 1783-1801, Chancellor of the Exchequer in Ireland 1787, and a Lord of the Treasury 1793-9; *d.* 1801; *s.* by his el. son [3] Sir JOHN AUGUSTUS, 3rd Bt.; *d.s.p.* 1812; *s.* by his brother [4] Sir HENRY BROOKE, 4th Bt.; *s.* to the paternal estates by special Act of Parliament 1789, upon the demise of his father; was M.P. for Maryborough 1797, Queen's Co. 1802-6, and Dundee (*L*) 1833-41, a Lord of the Treasury, Sec. at War 1831-2. Paymaster-Gen. of the Forces, and Treasurer of the Navy and Ordnance 1835-41; cr. *Baron Congleton,* of Congleton, Cheshire (peerage of United Kingdom) 1841: *m.* 1801, Lady Caroline Elizabeth Dawson, dau. of the 1st Earl of Portarlington; *d.* 1842; *s.* by his el. son [2] JOHN VESEY, 2nd Baron, *b.* 1805: *d.* 1883; *s.* by his brother [3] HENRY WILLIAM, 3rd Baron, *b.* 1809; present as Midshipman at battle of Navarino: *m.* 1st, 1835, Sophia, who *d.* 1846, dau. of the late Col. the Hon. William Bligh; 2ndly, 1851, the Hon. Caroline Margaret, who *d.* 1912 (sometime a Maid of Honour to H.M. Queen Victoria), dau. of the late Hon. Lionel Charles Dawson; *d.* 1896; *s.* by his el. surviving son [4] HENRY, *C.B.,* 4th Baron, *b.* 1839; Maj.-Gen. in Army; served during Zulu Campaign 1879, Comdg. 3rd Batn. Buffs, E. Kent Regt. (despatches, C.B.): *m.* 1885, Elizabeth Peter, who *d.* 1931, youngest dau. of the late Dugald Dove, of Nutshill, co. Renfrew; *d.* 1906; *s.* by his son [5] HENRY BLIGH FORTESCUE, 5th Baron, *b.* 1890; Lieut. Grenadier Guards; *d.* (killed in action during European War at first battle of Ypres) Nov. 1914 (despatches); *s.* by his brother [6] JOHN BROOKE MOLESWORTH, 6th Baron, *b.* 1892: *m.* 1918, the Hon. Edith Mary Palmer Howard, dau. of the late Baroness Strathcona and Mount Royal (in her own right)· *d.* 1932; *s.* by his son [7] WILLIAM JARED, *RN,* 7th Baron, *b.* 1925; *d.* 1967; *s.* by his brother [8] CHRISTOPHER PATRICK, 8th Baron and present peer.

CONSTANTINE, BARONY OF. (Constantine.) [Extinct 1971.]

DAUGHTER LIVING OF LIFE BARON.

Hon. Gloria, *b.* 1928; ed. at St. Andrew's Univ. (MA), and Inst. of Education, London Univ.: *m.* 1954, André Valère, barrister, of Upper School St., Carenage, Trinidad and Tobago, and has issue.

CONYNGHAM, MARQUESS. (Conyngham.) [Marquess I. 1816.] Sits as BARON MINSTER (U.K. 1821).

[Title pronounced "**Cunningham.**"]

FREDERICK WILLIAM HENRY FRANCIS CONYNGHAM, 7th Marquess; *b.* March 13th, 1924; *s.* 1974; ed. at Eton; late Capt. Irish Gds.; patron of one living: *m.* 1st 1950 (m. diss. 1970), Eileen Wren, da. of Capt. Clement Wren Newsam, of Ashfield, Beauparc, co. Meath; 2ndly, 1971, Elizabeth Ann, yr. da. of the late Frederick Molyneux Hughes, of Fareham, Hants., and formerly wife of David Sutherland Rudd, and has issue by 1st m.

Arms,—Argent, a shake fork between three mullets sable. **Crest,**—A unicorn's head erased argent, armed or crined and tufted sable. **Supporters**—*Dexter,* a horse argent, hoofs and mane or, and charged on the breast with an eagle displayed or; *sinister,* a stag, proper, attired, unguled and charged on the breast with a griffin's head erased or.

Residence,—Slane Castle, co. Meath.

Club.—Boodle's.

SONS LIVING. (By 1st m.)

HENRY VIVIAN PIERPOINT (Earl of Mount Charles), b. May 23rd, 1951; ed. at Harrow: m. 1971, Juliet
Ann, yr. da. of Robert R. B. Kitson, of Churchtown, Morval, Cornwall, and has issue.
SON LIVING,—Alexander Burton (Viscount Slane), b. Jan. 30th, 1975.
Lord Simon Charles Eveleigh Wren, b. 1953; ed. at Harrow.
Lord Frederick William Patrick, b. 1959.

WIDOW LIVING OF SON OF SIXTH MARQUESS.

Olivia Phoebe (Hon. Mrs. Francis A. I. Eveleigh-Ross-de-Moleyns) (317, The Water Gdns., Hyde
Park, W2), da. of the late Capt. Percy Neave Leathers, of Fayre Cottage, Robertsbridge, Sussex:
m. 1st, 1950, Lord John Victor Albert Blosse Conyngham, who d. 1963; 2ndly, 1963, Hon. Francis
Alexander Innys Eveleigh-Ross-de-Moleyns, who d. 1964 [see B. Ventry].

WIDOW LIVING OF SIXTH MARQUESS.

STELLA (Dowager Marchioness Conyngham) (Les Prés, St. Lawrence, Jersey), el. da. of the late Francis
Barrallier Thompson, MRCS, LRCP, and widow of Robert Newton Tory: m. 1966, as his 3rd wife,
the 6th Marquess, who d. 1974.

COLLATERAL BRANCH LIVING.

Descendants of the late Lord Albert Conyngham, K.C.H., F.R.S. (3rd son of 1st
Marquess), was cr. Baron Londesborough 1850 [see B. Londesborough].

PREDECESSORS.—[1] Rt. Hon. HENRY Conyngham, P.C., M.P. 1737-53, Vice-Adm. of
Ulster and Gov. of cos. Donegal and Londonderry; cr. Baron Conyngham (peerage of Ireland)
1753, Viscount Conyngham (peerage of Ireland) 1756, Earl Conyngham (peerage of Ireland)
1781, and Baron Conyngham (peerage of Ireland) 1781, with remainder to his nephew Francis
Pierpont-Burton, M.P.; d. 1781; s. by his nephew (ante) [2] FRANCIS Pierpont-Burton, 2nd
Baron, who assumed by Roy. licence the surname and arms of Conyngham; d. 1787; s. by his
son [3] HENRY, K.P., 3rd Baron; was a Gen. in the Army and a Representative Peer for
Ireland; cr. Viscount Conyngham (peerage of Ireland) 1789, Viscount Mount Charles, and Earl
of Conyngham (peerage of Ireland) 1797, Viscount Slane, Earl of Mount Charles and Marquess
Conyngham (peerage of Ireland) 1816, and Baron Minster (peerage of United Kingdom) 1821;
d. 1832; s. by his son [4] FRANCIS NATHANIEL, K.P., P.C., G.C.H., 2nd Marquess; a Gen. in
the Army and Lord-Lieut. of co. Meath; d. 1876; s. by his son [5] GEORGE HENRY, 3rd
Marquess, b. 1825; was a Lieut.-Gen. in the Army, a J.P. for Kent, and Hon. Col. E. Kent
Yeo. Cav.: m. 1854, Lady Jane St. Maur Blanche Stanhope, dau. of 4th Earl of Harrington;
d. June 2nd, 1882: s. by his son [6] HENRY FRANCIS, 4th Marquess, b. 1857: m. 1882, the Hon.
Frances Elizabeth Sarah Eveleigh-de Moleyns, who d. 1939, (having m. 2ndly 1899, Major
John Russell Bedford Cameron), dau. of 4th Baron Ventry; d. 1897; s. by his el. son [7]
VICTOR GEORGE HENRY FRANCIS, 5th Marquess, b. 1883: d. 1918; s. by his brother [8]
FREDERICK WILLIAM BURTON, 6th Marquess, b. 1890: m. 1st, 1914 (m. diss. 1921) Elizabeth Alice,
who d. 1933, da. of the late William Andrew Tobin, of Australia; 2ndly, 1922, Antoinette Winifred,
who d. 1966, da. of John William Howard Thompson; 3rdly, 1966, Stella, el. da. of the late Francis
Barrallier Thompson, MRCS, LRCP, and widow of Robert Newton Tory; d. 1974; s. by his son [9]
FREDERICK HENRY FRANCIS, 7th Marquess and present peer; also Earl Conyngham, Earl
of Mount Charles, Viscount Slane, Viscount Mount Charles, Viscount Conyngham, Baron Conyng
ham, and Baron Minster.

COOPER OF STOCKTON HEATH, BARON. (Cooper.) [Life Baron 1966.]|

JOHN COOPER, son of the late John Ainsworth Cooper, of Warrington; b.
June 7th, 1908; ed. at Stockton Heath Council Sch., and Lymn Gram. Sch.;
MA, Oxford; a Councillor, Manchester City Council 1936-42, and LCC 1949-53
(Alderman 1952); a Member of Nat. Exec. Cttee. of Labour Party 1952-57;
Dist. Sec. Nat. Union of Gen. and Municipal Workers, S. Dist., 1944-61 (Chm.
1952-62) since when Gen. Sec. and Treasurer of Nat. Union of Gen. and
Municipal Workers; a Member of Metropolitan Water Board 1948-65 (Chm.
1964-65), of Thames Conservancy since 1955, of TUC Gen. Council since 1959
(Chm. of TUC 1970), of Nat. Economic Development Council since 1964;
Chm. British Productivity Council 1965-66; a Gov. of London Grad. Sch. of
Business Studies, Ditchley Foundations, and Ruskin Coll.; cr. Baron Cooper
of Stockton Heath, of Stockton Heath, co. Palatine of Chester (Life Baron) 1966:
m. 1st 1934 (m. diss. 1969), Nellie, da. of the late Paul Spencer; 2ndly, 1969,
Mrs. Joan Rogers, and has issue by 1st. m.

Address,—Room 43, Ruxley Towers, Claygate, Esher, Surrey.

DAUGHTERS LIVING. (By 1st m.)
Hon. Brenda, b. 1937: m. 1st, 1958, (m. diss. 1967), John Abbott; 2ndly, 1968, Pereric Astrom, of 50,
Ullswater Rd., Handforth, Wilmslow, Cheshire.
Hon. Marjorie (12, Kings Drive, Thames Ditton, Surrey), b. 1941: m. 1959 (m. diss. 1969), Neville
Finch.
Hon. Jacqueline, b. 1946: m. 1972, J. Bradford Thomas.

COPE, BARONY OF. (Cope.) [Extinct 1946.]

DAUGHTER LIVING.
Hon. Helen Margaret Letitia, b. 1903 : m. 1940, Stephen John Valentine Simpson.   Residence,—Spitch-
wick Manor, Poundsgate, Newton Abbot, Devon.

CORK and ORRERY, EARL OF. (Boyle.) **Sits as BARON BOYLE OF MARSTON** (G.B. 1711). [Earl I. 1620.]

PATRICK REGINALD BOYLE, 13th Earl; *b.* Feb. 7th, 1910; *s.* 1967; ed. at Harrow and RMC; Hereditary Life Gov. of Christian Faith Soc., Vice-Pres. and Chm. of Exec. Cttee, British Council, and a Member of Grand Council, Cancer Research Campaign; a Dep. Chm. of Cttees., House of Lords since 1973; 1939-45 War with R. Ulster Rifles and Parachute Regt.; S.-E. Asia 1941-45 with Burma Rifles and as Maj. Cameronians (Scottish Rifles (severely wounded)): *m.* 1952, Mrs. Dorothy Kate Scelsi, only da. of the late Robert Ramsden, of Meltham, Yorks.

Arms,—Per bend embattled argent and gules Crest,—Out of a ducal coronet or, a lion's head per pale embattled, argent and gules. Supporters—Two lions, the *dexter* per pale embattled, gules and argent; the *sinister*, per pale embattled, argent and gules.
Residence,—Flint House, Heyshott, Midhurst, Sussex.

BROTHER LIVING. *(Raised to the rank of an Earl's son 1967.)*

Hon. JOHN WILLIAM, *DSC* (Craigantaggart, Dunkeld, Perthshire, PH8 0HQ). *Club,*—Royal Thames Yacht), *b.* May 12th, 1916; ed. at Harrow, and King's Coll., London (BSc); FICE; 1939-45 War as Lt. Cdr. RNVR (despatches twice, DSC): *m.* 1943, Mary Leslie, da. of the late Gen. Sir Robert Gordon Finlayson, KCB, CMG, DSO, and has issue living, John Richard (Hawthorn Cottage, Newtown, Fareham, Hants.), *b.* 1945; ed at Harrow, and RNC Dartmouth; Lt. RN: *m.* 1973, The Hon. Rebecca Juliet Noble, da. of Baron Glenkinglas,—Robert William, *b.* 1948; ed. at Harrow, and Ch. Ch., Oxford (BA); ACA,—Charles Reginald, *b.* 1957; ed. at Harrow.

SISTER LIVING. *(Raised to the rank of an Earl's daughter 1967.)*

Lady Elizabeth Theresa, '*b.* 1920: *m.* 1947, Capt. Adrian Noble Dodd-Noble, RE [By Kirkley, ext.], of Rands, High Roding, Dunmow, Essex, and has issue living, Adrian Michael, *b.* 1948,—Patrick Robin, *b.* 1951,—Simon Thomas Antony, *b.* 1955,—Antony William, *b.* 1961,—Joanna Susan, *b.* 1950.

HALF-AUNT LIVING. *(Raised to the rank of an Earl's daughter 1935.)*

Lady Geraldine Lillian, *b.* 1899. *Residence,*—38, Strand Court, Topsham, Exeter.

COLLATERAL BRANCHES LIVING.

Grandson of the late Rev. the Hon. Richard Cavendish Boyle, 4th son of 8th Earl:—
Issue of the late Major Charles John Boyle, *b.* 1849, *d.* 1922: *m.* 1885, Lilian Kennedy, who *d.* 1953, dau. of the late Charles Pochin, H.E.I.C.S., of Barkby Hall, Leicestershire:—
Edmund Michael Gordon Loeventhorpe, *b.* 1895; Capt. (ret.) RN: *m.* 1927, Maida Cecil, da. of the late Lt.-Col. the Hon. Percy Cecil Evans-Freke [see B. Carbery, colls.], and has issue living, George Hamilton (Bisbrooke Hall, Uppingham), *b.* 1928; BSc 1953; an Asso. Roy. Sch. of Mines; High Sheriff of Rutland 1964: *m.* 1953, Alathea Henriette Mary, da. of John Adrian Frederick March Phillipps de Lisle, of Stockerston Hall, Leics., and has issue living, Robert Edmund John *b.* 1954, Richard William *b.* 1959, Rupert Lancelot Cavendish *b.* 1960,—Stephen Crispin, *b.* 1935. *Residence,*—Bisbrooke Hall, Uppingham, Rutland.

Grandson of the late Major Charles John Boyle (*b.* 1849) (ante):—
Issue of the late Capt. Richard Frederick Robert Pochin Boyle, Oxfordshire and Bucks LI, *b.* 1888, *d.* 1953: *m.* 1918, Marion, who *d.* 1969, da. of the late Maj.-Gen. Hill Wallace, OB:—
Richard Michael Charles, *b.* 1918. *Residence,*—Prospect, Birdswell Lane, Berrynarbor, Devon.

Grandchildren of the late Charles John Boyle, son of the late Vice-Adm. the Hon. Sir Courtenay Boyle, K.C.H., 3rd son of 7th Earl:—
Issue of the late Col. Lionel Richard Cavendish Boyle, O.M.G., M.V.O., *b.* 1851, *d.* 1920: *m.* 1883, Alice, dau. of the late Rev. Richard Pulteney, of Ashley, Northamptonshire:—
Richard Courtenay, *DSO, b.* 1902; Capt. RN (ret.); 1939-40 War (DSO): *m.* 1936, Gwendolen Mabel Maclean, da. of the late Lt.-Col. Edward Hugh Griffith, CBE, and has issue living, John Richard (40, Drayton Gdns., SW10), *b.* 1938: *m.* 1964, Jeannine Mary, da. of Capt. Timothy John Gurney, Coldstream Guards, of The White House, Hare St., Buntingford, Herts. [see De Bathe, Bt., ext.], and has issue living, Richard Burlington *b.* 1966, Charles Robert *b.* 1969, Patrick William *b.* 1971,—William, *b.* 1944,—Belinda, *b.* 1940: *m.* 1963, Lt.-Col. Thomas Neil McMicking, The Black Watch, Miltonise, New Luce, Wigtownshire, DG8 0LY, and has issue living, Charles Neil *b.* 1965, James Richard *b.* 1968, Henrietta Sophia *b.* 1972. *Residence,*—Pegsdon Barns, Hexton, Hitchin, Herts.——Audrey Janet (The Flat, Old Brewery House, Malmesbury, Wilts.), *b.* 1888: *m.* 1st, 1916, Maj. Hedworth George Ailwyn Fellowes, MC, who *d.* (killed in action during 1914-18 War) 1917 [see B. Ailwyn]; 2ndly 1922, Wilfrid Valentine Denison, and has issue living, (by 2nd m.) Elizabeth; (South Wing, Rodmarton Manor, Cirencester), *b.* 1923: *m.* 1946, Capt. Terence D'Arcy-Muirhead, MC, 3rd Hussars, who *d.* 1969, and has issue living, Robert Maxim D'Arcy *b.* 1953, Zara *b.* 1947, Deborah *b.* 1949.

PREDECESSORS.—[1] *Rt. Hon. Sir* RICHARD Boyle, *P.C.*, embarked for Ireland as an adventurer, and having eventually amassed considerable wealth, sat as M.P. for Lismore 1615; was knighted 1603, and cr. *Baron Boyle of Youghal* (peerage of Ireland) 1616, and *Viscount Dungarvan* and *Earl of Cork* (peerage of Ireland) 1620, and was afterwards Lord High Treasurer of Ireland, and known as the "Great Earl"; Cromwell is reported to have said of him that "if there had been an Earl of Cork in every province, it would have been impossible for the Irish to have raised a rebellion"; *d.* 1643; *s.* by his son [2] RICHARD, 2nd Earl, who in 1642 had by special remainder *s.* his brother Lewis as 2nd *Baron of Bandon Bridge* and *Viscount Boyle of Kinalmeaky* (peerage of Ireland), cr. 1627: *m.* Elizabeth, da. and heiress of Henry Clifford, 5th and last Earl of Cumberland, who had in 1628 been summoned by writ as Baron Clifford : he was cr. *Baron Clifford*, of Lanesborough, co. York (peerage of England) 1644, and *Earl of Burlington* (peerage of England) 1664; *d.* 1697; *s.* by his grandson [3] CHARLES, 3rd Earl; *d.* 1703; *s.* by his son [4] RICHARD, 4th Earl; an eminent patron of literature and the fine arts; claimed and was allowed the Barony of Clifford by writ, cr. 1628 ; *d.* 1753, without male issue, when the Barony of Clifford, cr. 1628, devolved upon his dau. Charlotte, wife of William Marquess of Hartington, afterwards 4th Duke of Devonshire ; the Barony of Clifford of Lanesborough, cr. 1644, and the Earldom of Burlington became extinct, and the Irish honours reverted to his kinsman [5] JOHN, 5th Earl, who had in 1731 s. as 5th *Earl of Orrery*, 5th *Lord Boyle, Baron of Broghill*, and 2nd *Baron Boyle of Marston* (see *⁎* infra); *d.* 1762; *s.* by his son [6] HAMILTON, 6th Earl; *d.s.p.* 1764; *s.* by his half-brother [7] EDMUND, 7th Earl; *d.* 1798; *s.* by his son [8] EDMUND, K.P.; a Gen. in the Army; *d.* 1856; *s.* by his grandson [9] RICHARD EDMUND ST. LAWRENCE, K.P. P.C., (son of Charles, Viscount Dungarvan, by Lady Katherine St. Lawrence, dau. of 2nd Earl of Howth), 9th Earl; *b.* 1829; Lord-Lieut. of Somerset; Master of the Buckhounds 1866, 1868, and 1880-85, and Master of the Horse 1886 and 1894-5 : *m.* 1853, Lady Emily Charlotte De Burgh, who, *d.* 1912, dau. of 1st Marquess of Clanricarde, K.P.; *d.* 1904; *s.* by his son [10] CHARLES SPENCER CANNING, 10th Earl, *b.* 1861 : *m.* 1918, Rosalie Gray, who *d.* 1930, dau. of William Waterman de Villiers, of Romsey, Hants; *d.* 1925 ; *s.* by his brother [11] ROBERT JOHN LASCELLES, 11th Earl, *b.* 1864 : *m.* 1890, Josephine Catherine, who *d.* 1953, dau. of J. P. Hale, of San Francisco, U.S.A.; *d.* 1934; *s.* by his kinsman, [12] WILLIAM HENRY DUDLEY, GCB, GCVO, son of the late Col. Gerald Edmund Boyle [by Lady Elizabeth Theresa Pepys, da. of 1st Earl of Cottenham], grandson of 8th Earl), 12th Earl, *b.* 1873; Adm. of the Fleet; C. in C. Home Fleet 1933-35, and at Portsmouth 1937-39; commanded combined expedition for capture of Narvik 1940 : *m.* 1902, Lady Florence Cecilia Keppel, who *d.* 1963, da. of 7th Earl of Albemarle; *d.* 1967, *s.* by his nephew [13] PATRICK REGINALD (son of Maj. the Hon. Reginald Courtney Boyle, MBE, MC), 13th Earl, and present peer; also Viscount Dungarvan, Viscount Boyle of Kinalmeaky, Baron Boyle of Youghal, Baron of Bandon Bridge, and Lord Boyle, Baron of Broghill, and Baron Boyle of Marston.

⁎ [1] *Sir* ROGER Boyle, *P.C.*, 3rd son of 1st Earl of Cork, cr. when seven years of age *Baron Boyle of Broghill* (peerage of Ireland) 1621, with remainder to heirs of his father ; was sometime M.P. for co. Cork and for Arundel ; substantially assisted to quell the rebellion in Ireland 1642-3, and after the death of Cromwell planned the restoration of Charles II. in Ireland ; cr. *Earl of Orrery* (peerage of Ireland) 1660; *d.* 1679; *s.* by his son [2] ROGER, 2nd Earl; *d.* 1682; *s.* by his son [3] LIONEL, 3rd Earl; attainted by Parliament of James II. 1689 ; sometime M.P. for E. Grinstead, Sussex : *d.s.p.* 1703: *s.* by his brother [4] CHARLES, *KT*, 4th Earl; a Lt.-Gen. in the Army, MP for Huntingdon 1700, Ambassador to Brabant and, Flanders, and a Lord of the Bedchamber to George I. ; cr. *Baron Boyle of Marston*, Somerset 1711 ; in 1722 was imprisoned for six months in the Tower on suspicion of high treason ; the astronomical instrument invented by George Graham was named " Orrery " after this peer: *d.* 1731; *s.* by his son [5] JOHN, 5th Earl, who *s.* as 5th Earl of Cork (ante).

CORNWALLIS, BARON.　(Cornwallis.)　[Baron U.K.| 1927.]

Virtue overcomes envy.

WYKEHAM STANLEY CORNWALLIS, KCVO, KBE, MC, 2nd Baron; *b.* March 14th, 1892; *s.* 1935; ed. at Eton, and RMC; Hon. DCL, Kent; Capt. (ret. Scots Greys; Lord-Lt. of Kent 1944-72; a JP for Kent (Chm. of Co. Council 1935-36), a Lt. for City of London, 1944-72; Lord-Lt. for City and Co. of Canterbury, 1944-72; Pro-Chancellor, Kent Univ., 1965-72; Vice-Pres. of SE Area of TAVR, 1970-72 of Kent TA and AF Assoc., and Vice-Patron of Kent Co. So.; Chm. of Kent War Agric. Exec. Cttee. 1939-46; Pres. MCC 1947-48 (Hon. Life Vice-Pres.); a KGStJ, and a Knight Com. of Order of Dannebrog of Denmark; formerly Hon. Col., 8th Bn. (T) The Queen's Regt. TAVR (W. Kent), Hon. Col. 415th Coast Regt. (Thames & Medway) RA (TA), and 5th Bn. Buffs (R East Kent Regt.) TA; 1914-18 War in France and Belgium (wounded, despatches, MC, 1914 star, two medals); KBE (Civil) 1945, KCVO 1968: *m.* 1st, 1917, Cecily Etha Mary, who *d.* 1943, da. of Sir James Heron Walker, 3rd Bt. (cr. 1868); 2ndly, 1948, Esme Ethel Alice, who *d.* 1969, da. of the late Capt. J. Montgomerency de Beaumont, 5th Royal Irish Lancers, of Hove, Sussex, and widow of Maj. Sir Robert James Milo Walker, 4th Bt. (cr. 1868) and has issue by 1st m.

Arms,—Quarterly 1st and 4th, sable, guttée d'eau, on a fesse argent three martlets of the field, *Cornwallis*; 2nd and 3rd, sable on a fesse embattled counter-embattled between three goats passant argent, as many pellets, *Mann.* **Crest,**—On a mount vert, a stag lodged reguardant argent, attired or, vulned in the shoulder proper, and gorged with a wreath of laurel also proper. **Supporters,**—On either side a stag argent, attired or and gorged with a chaplet of oak fructed vert.

Residences,—Ashurst Park, Fordcombe, Tunbridge Wells, Kent; Dundurn House, St. Fillans, Perthshire.

SON LIVING.　(*By 1st marriage.*)

Hon. FIENNES NEIL WYKEHAM, *OBE*, *b.* June 29th, 1921; ed. at Eton; formerly in Coldm. Gds. Pres., National Assocn. of Agric. Contractors 1958-63; Founder, Past Chm., and Hon. Life Pres. County Quality Bacon Fedn.; Chm. Planet Building Soc., a Dir., Checkers, Ltd., County Quality (Promotion & Marketing Ltd.), and Northinvest, Ltd., OBE (Civil) 1963: *m.* 1st, 1942 (m) diss. 1948), only da. of Lt.-Col. Lacy Scott, of Ashcroft, Wadhurst Sussex; 2ndly, 1951, Agnes Jean, yr. da. of Capt. H. Russell Landale, of Ewell Manor, W. Farleigh, Maidstone, and has issue living, (by 1st m.) Fiennes Wykeham Jeremy (The Down House, Kilndown, Tonbridge, Kent), *b.* 1946: *m.* 1969, Sara Gray de Neufville, da. of Lt.-Col. Nigel Stockwell, of Benenden, Kent, and has issue living, Anna Julia Gray *b.* 1971, Charlotte Louise *b.* 1972—(by 2nd m.) Patrick Wykeham David, *b.* 1952,—Cecily Mary Clare, *b.* 1954,—Vanessa Rachel, *b.* 1958,)—Susan Patricia Rose, *b.* 1963. *Residences,*— Ruck Farm, Horsmonden, Tonbridge, Kent; 7, Launceston Place, W8.

SISTERS LIVING.

Hon. Yvonne, *b.* 1896: *m.* 1923, Com. the Hon. Henry Mitford Amherst Cecil, O.B.E., R.N., who *d.* 1962 [see B. Amherst of Hackney]. *Residence,*—Greenoaks, Bishop's Waltham, Hants.

Hon. Bridget Frances Kate, *b.* 1900: *m.* 1921, Lieut.-Col. John Cecil Petherick, O.B.E., M.C., 3rd Hussars (retired), and has issue living, Vivienne Bridget, *b.* 1922,—Pamela Susan, *b.* 1929: *m.* 1950, Ian Malcolm Clark, and has issue living, Andrew *b.* 1951, Simon Alistair *b.* 1954, Nicholas John *b.* 1957, Jacqueline Iona, *b.* 1962. *Residence,*—Hextall Court, Peckham Bush, nr. Tonbridge, Kent.

COLLATERAL BRANCH LIVING.

Issue of the late Capt. the Hon. Oswald Wykeham Cornwallis, OBE, yst. son of 1st Baron; *b.* 1894, *d.* 1974: *m.* 1923, the Hon. Venetia Jane Digby, who *d.* 1956, da. of 10th Baron Digby:—

Michael Wykeham (10, Ravelston House Rd., Edinburgh, EH4 3LW), *b.* 1924: ed. at Eton; Lt.-Cdr. RN (ret.): *m.* 1953, Margaret Dorothy, da. of the late J. W. Cannon, MB, ChB, and has issue living, Richard Wykeham, *b.* 1959,—Diana Margaret, *b.* 1957.——Charles Wykeham, *b.* 1937.——Venetia Mabel, *b.* 1928: *m.* 1956, Lt.-Cdr. Geoffrey Arthur George Brooke, DSC, RN [see Brooke, Bt., colls. cr. 1903].

PREDECESSOR.—[1] FIENNES STANLEY WYKEHAM Cornwallis, *C.B.E.*, son of the late Major Fiennes Cornwallis, of Chacombe Priory, near Banbury; *b.* 1864; was Col. late W. Kent Imperial Yeo., a J.P. and D.L. for Kent (Chm. of County Council 1910-30), and M.P. for Maidstone (*C*) 1888-95 and 1898-1900; *cr. Baron Cornwallis* of Linton, co. Kent (peerage of United Kingdom) 1927: *m.* 1886, Mabel, who *d.* 1957, dau. of the late Capt. Oswald Peter Leigh, of Belmont Hall, Cheshire; *d.* 1935; *s.* by his son [2] WYKEHAM STANLEY, 2nd Baron and present peer.

Corvedale, Viscount, son of Earl Baldwin of Bewdley.

COTTENHAM, EARL OF. (Pepys.) [Earl U.K. 1850, Bt. G.B. 1784, and U.K. 1801.]

[Name pronounced "Pepp-iss."]

·MENS·CUJUSQUE·IS·EST·QUISQUE·

Mind makes the man.

KENELM CHARLES EVERARD DIGBY PEPYS, 8th Earl, and 11th Baronet (cr. 1784) and 10th (cr. 1801); *b.* Nov. 27th, 1948; *s.* 1968; ed. at Eton: *m.* 1975, Sarah, yr. da of Capt. S. Lombard-Hobson.

Arms.—Sable, on a bend or, between two nags' heads erased argent, three fleurs-de-lis of the field. **Crest.**—A camel's head erased or, bridled, lined, ringed, and gorged with a ducal coronet sable. **Supporters.**—On either side a horse argent, bridled, and gorged with a ducal coronet sable; pendent therefrom an escutcheon or, charged with a fleur-de-lis of the second.

Residence,—3, Bourne St., SW1.

SISTER LIVING.

Lady Gillian Angela (*Baroness McGowan*), *b.* 1941: *m.* 1962, the 3rd Baron McGowan. *Residence,*—Highway House, Lower Froyle, Alton, Hants.

WIDOW LIVING OF SEVENTH EARL.

Lady ANGELA ISABEL NELLIE NEVILL (*Countess of Cottenham*) (The Hollies, Eridge Green, Tunbridge Wells), da. of 4th Marquess of Abergavenny: *m.* 1933, the 7th Earl, who *d,* 1968.

DAUGHTERS LIVING OF SIXTH EARL.

Lady Rose Edith Idina (Flat B, 101, Earls Court Rd., W8), *b.* 1927.

Lady Paulina Mary Louise, *b.* 1930: *m.* 1973, Denis Bernard Hadley, of 23, Ruscombe Rd., Twyford, Reading, Berks.

COLLATERAL BRANCHES LIVING.

Issue of the late Hon. Everard Digby Pepys, 2nd son of 3rd Earl, *b.* 1876, *d.* 1943 : *m.* 1897, Katherine, who *d.* 1959, dau. of the late Charles Diehl :—

Honor Mary Evelyn (12, Roper's Orchard, Danvers St., SW3), *b.* 1899: *m.* 1923, Brig. (Thomas Denis Daly, CBE, MC, late Roy. Welch Fusiliers, who *d.* 1956.——Yolande Katharine Rosabelle. *b.* 1902: *m.* 1928, Christopher Reginald Turnor, who *d.* 1971, and has issue living, Clive Christopher, *b.* 1929,—Gillian Yolande, *b.* 1931. *Residence,*—Norman Street House, Ide Hill, Kent.——Audrey Marion-Caroline, *b.* 1906: *m.* 1928, Humphrey Charles Vaughan Jones, son of Sir Francis Adolphus Jones, KBE, CB, and has issue living, Janet Katherine Vaughan, *b.* 1930: *m.* 1951, Cdr. Julian Richards, RN, of 327, Woodstock Rd., Oxford, and has issue living, Charles Oliver *b.* 1955, Lucinda Mary *b.* 1953, Frances Julia *b.* 1958, Katharine Anne *b.* 1963,—Philip Charles, *b.* 1933,—Barbara Caroline, *b.* 1935. *Residence,*—Mulberry House, Slindon, Sussex.

Grandchildren of the late Hon. Henry Leslie Pepys, 3rd son of 1st Earl:—
Issue of the late Lieut.-Col. Arthur Guy Leslie Pepys, M.C., Essex Regt., b. 1875, d. 1953:
m. 1915, Olive Grace, who d. 1961, dau. of the late John Frederick Starkey, J.P., D.L.,
of Bodicote House, Banbury :—
Iris Leslie, b. 1918; late Flight Officer WRAF: m. 1953, Wing-Com. Norman Maxwell Boffee, DFC,
RAF (ret.), and has issue living, Mark Guy, b. 1956. Residence,—Sheppey House, Laleham, Middx.
Issue of the late Col. Gerald Leslie Pepys, C.B., D.S.O., b. 1879, d. 1936 : m. 1907,
Charlotte Helen, who d. 1965, da. of the late Charles W. Lambe Forbes, formerly of
Auchrannie, Forfarshire:—
CHARLES DONALD LESLIE, b. Sept. 25th, 1909; ed. at Radley; Lt.-Col. KOYLI: m. 1941, the Hon.
(Pamela Sophia) Nadine Stonor, da. of 5th Baron Camoys. Residence, Brightling Pl.,
Robertsbridge, Sussex. Club,—United Service.——John Evelyn Leslie, b. 1911; ed. at Sherborne
Sch., and at Corpus Christi Coll., Oxford (MA); formerly Headmaster of Colet Court Sch.,
Baron's Court, W6, and of St. Peter's Sch., Trinidad; 1939-45 War as Capt. Recon-
naissance Corps: m. 1943, Zita Mary, da. of His Honour the late Robert Emilius Noble, Puisne
Judge of Leeward Islands. Residence,—10, The Hall, 23A, Grove End Rd., NW8.——Peter Andrew
Leslie (Warwick Castle, Warwick), b. 1914; ed. at Sherborne Sch.; formerly Maj. Indian Army;
Librarian, Warwick Castle.——Geraldine Mary Leslie, b. 1908: m. 1935, Lt.-Col. William Louis
Barnard, Oxford and Bucks LI, who d. 1953, and has issue living, Simon William Leslie (92B, Under-
hill Rd., SE22), b. 1938: m. 1962, Joy, da. of Thomas Frank Prior Pavely, and has issue living,
Jonathan James b. 1969, Emma Louise b. 1966. Residence,—4, Lakeview, Bishop's Down Park Rd.,
Tunbridge Wells, Kent.

Granddaughters of the late Hon. George Pepys, 4th son of 1st Earl:—
Issue of the late George Digby Pepys, C.B.E., b. 1868, d. 1957 : m. 1902, Margaret Mary
Humphrey, who d. 1954, dau. of the late George Walter Davidson, of 167, Queen's Gate,
S.W. :—
Mary Joyce, b. 1903. Residence,—Little Mead, Sparsholt, Winchester.——Anna Margaret, b. 1906:
m. 1931, Peter Pryor, and has issue living, Roderick (of Little Horkesley Priory, Colchester, Essex),
b. 1932: m. 1959, Carolyn Vaughan, el. dau. of Donald Smith of Old Hill House, Sandwich, Kent,
and has issue living, Peter David b. 1965, Louise Margaret b. 1960, Victoria Jane b. 1962,—George
(Fairclough Hall Farm, Weston, Hitchin), b. 1936: m. 1960, Virginia Anne, da. of the Rev. Charles
M. Jones, of Chapel Hill, N. Carolina, USA, and has issue living, Richard b. 1965, Mark b. 1967,
Catherine Eleanor b. 1970,—Clova Margaret, b. 1935: m. 1960, Glyn Tudor, of Brook House, Sutton,
Sandy, Beds., and has issue living, Adam b. 1966, Anna Morwena b. 1962, Gay Elizabeth b. 1964,—
Mary, b. 1944: m. 1969, Roy Hodges, of The Old Rectory, Potsgrove, Bletchley, Bucks, and has
issue living, Jeremy George b. 1972. Residence,—Weston Lodge, Hitchin, Herts.

Grandchildren of the late Rev. Charles Sidney Pepys, BD (infra):—
Issue of the late Rt. Rev. George Christopher Cutts Pepys, Bishop of Buckingham, b. 1914,
d. 1974: m. 1947, Elizabeth Margaret (10, Conegra Rd., High Wycombe, Bucks), da. of
Maj.-Gen. Roger Gillies Ekin, CIE :—
Charles Richard Ekin, b. 1951.——Caroline Elizabeth, b. 1948.——Sarah Priscilla, b. 1950.——Frances
Mary, b. 1954.——Anna Margaret, b. 1956.

Granddaughters of the late Hon. George Pepys (ante):—
Issue of the late Rev. Charles Sidney Pepys, B.D., b. 1875, d. 1927 : m. 1913, Adelaide
Mary Elizabeth, who d. 1968, da. of the late Charles Duncan Cutts, of Buenos Aires:—
Elizabeth Sidney, b. 1915: m. 1939, the Rev. Arthur Guy St. John Daniel, and has issue living, Nicholas
Guy, b. 1942: m. 1974, Menna Matthews,—Timothy Peter Charles, b. 1944: m. 1974, Rosalie Horner.
Residence,—The Vicarage, Colnbrook, Bucks.——Ursula Mary Evelyn, b. 1917: m. 1941, Leighton
Erie Gray, HM Civil Ser. (ret.), and has issue living, Paul Leighton, b. 1958,—Mary Ann, b. 1943:
m. 19—, Alan Oliver Bryan Harris, MA, EEC Comn., of 6 Av. Edouard Lacomblé, Brussels 1040, and
has issue living, Mark b. 1966, Charles b. 1967, Jane b. 1970. Residence,—31, Banders Rise, Merrow,
Guildford, Surrey.——Phyllis Anne Jennifer, b. 1924: m. 1947, Alexander Paton, MD, FRCP, and
has issue living, Alexander, b. 1948,—Anthony Grimwood, b. 1954, Clare Jennifer, b. 1952: m. 1972,
Terence Patrick Mead, of Twickenham,—Rachel Mary, b. 1953. Residence,—15, Charlotte Rd.,
Edgbaston, Birmingham, 15.——Alison Margaret, b. 1927: m. 1955, Peter Harold Edwin Courtenay,
MB, BS, FRCS, and has issue living, Stephen Harold Pepys, b. 1956,—Simon Charles, b. 1958,—
Michael Peter, b. 1962,—Ann Elizabeth, b. 1963. Residence,—1129, Devonshire Rd., Windsor,
Ont., Canada.

Grandchildren of the late Hon. Walter Courtenay Pepys, 6th son of 1st Earl:—
Issue of the late Amy Theresa Pepys, b. 1878, d. 1963: m. 1901, Gerard Tarver Whiteley,
who d. 1944:—
George) Derek Pepys (Magdalene Coll., Camb.; Oxford and Cambridge Univ. Club, and Univ. Pitt
(Camb.) Club), b. 1906; ed. at Sherborne, and at King's Coll., Camb. (MA); Bar. Middle Temple
1931; Author, and contributor to Dictionary of National Biography, Country Life, and other publications; Dep. Pepys Librarian, Magdalene Coll., Camb. 1964-70: m. 1936 (m. diss. 1946) Frances
Georgette Coningsby, el. da. of the late Capt. George Ashmead-Bartlett.——Pamela Helen
(26, St. Margaret's Rd., Girton, Cambridge), b. 1905: m. 1927, the Rev. Albert George Porter,
late Lt.-Col. Indian Army, who d. 1951, and has issue living.

(In remainder to Baronetcy only.)

Grandson of the late Rev. Herbert George Pepys, son of the late Rev. Henry
Pepys, D.D., Bishop of Worcester, 3rd son of 1st Baronet :—
Issue of the late Herbert Frederick Pepys b. 1865, d. 1944: m. 1901, Alice Neame, who
d. 1951, dau. of the late John L. Oliver, formerly of Highgate, Middlesex:—
Frederick Courtenay, b. 1904 : m. 1935. Mary Caroline Bradley, of Los Angeles, California,
USA, and has issue living, Eric Courtenay, b. 1936: m. 1964, Shirley Ann Dietrich, and has issue
living, Noel Dietrich b. 1970, Renée Catherine b. 1964, Tiffany Ann b. 1968,—Mark Bradley (6065
Via Sonoma, Rancho Palos Verdes, Calif. 90274, USA), b. 1937: m. 1970, Anne Claire Bowden, and
has issue living, Craig Brian, b. 1974,—Keith Alan, b. 1948,—Christine, b. 1939: m. 1960, Ronald
Vincent Heusser, and has issue living, Melinda Christine, b. 1965, Noelle Pepys b. 1968, Hillary
Dawn b. 1971,—Mary Noel, b. 1946. Residence,—555, Santa Anita Av., San Marino, California,
USA.

PREDECESSORS.—[1] WILLIAM WELLER Pepys, a Master in Chancery; cr. a Baronet 1801
of Wimpole Street; d. 1825; s. by his son [2] WILLIAM WELLER, 2nd Bt.; d.s.p. 1845; s. by his
brother [3] Sir CHARLES CHRISTOPHER, P.C., K.B., D.C.L., 3rd Bt.; an eminent lawyer,
was Queen's Solicitor-Gen. 1830, Solicitor-Gen. 1834, Master of the Rolls 1834. High Commr.
of the Great Seal 1835, and Lord High Chancellor 1836-41 and 1846-50; cr. Baron Cottenham
(peerage of United Kingdom) 1836; by special remainder s. his cousin, Sir Henry (Pepys)
Leslie, as 4th Bt., cr. 1784 (of Upper Brook Street); cr. Viscount Crowhurst and Earl
of Cottenham 1850 : m. 1821, Caroline Elizabeth, dau. of William Wingfield-Baker, Q.C.; d. 1851 ;
s. by his son [4] CHARLES EDWARD, 2nd Earl; d.s.p. 1863; s. by his brother [5] WILLIAM
JOHN, 3rd Earl; b. 1825: m. 1870, Theodosia Selina, who d. 1919, dau. of Sir Robert Charles
Dallas, 2nd Bt.; d. 1881; s. by his son [6] KENELM CHARLES EDWARD, 4th Earl; b. 1874: m.
1st, 1899, Lady Rose, who d. 1913, dau. of 1st Marquess of Abergavenny; 2ndly, 1916, Patricia,
who d. 1962, dau. of the late John Humphry Burke, of Galway and California; d. 1919; s. by his
el. son [7] KENELM CHARLES FRANCIS, 5th Earl; b. 1901, d. 1922, s. by his brother [8] MARK EVERARD,
6th Earl; b. 1903: m. 1927, Sybil Venetia (from whom he obtained a divorce 1939), dau. of Capt.

John Vickris Taylor, of North Aston Manor, Oxford; *d.* 1943; *s.* by his brother [9] JOHN DIGBY THOMAS, 7th Earl; *b.* 1907: *m.* 1933, Lady Angela Isabel Nellie Nevill, da. of 4th Marquess of Abergavenny; *d.* 1968; *s.* by his son [10] KENELM CHARLES EVERARD DIGBY, 8th Earl and present peer; also Viscount Crowhurst, and Baron Cottenham.

COTTESLOE, BARON. (Fremantle.) [Baron U.K. 1874, Bt. U.K. 1821.]
Title pronounced "Cotslo."]

Neither by entreaty nor bribery.

JOHN WALGRAVE HALFORD FREMANTLE, *G.B.E.*, *T.D.*, 4th Baron, 4th Baronet, and a Baron of the Austrian Empire ; *b.* March 2nd, 1900 ; *s.* 1956 ; ed. at Eton, and at Trin. Coll., Camb. (MA); late Lt.-Col. RA (TA Reserve); a DL co. London, Chm. of South Bank Theatre Board, Gov. of King Edward's Hosp. Fund for London, and Dep. Pres. Nat. Rifle Assocn. (Member of Council since 1932, Vice Chm. 1948-60, Chm. 1960-72); a Trustee of Tate Gallery 1953-60 (Chm. 1959-60), Chm. of Arts Council of Gt. Britain 1960-65, of Advisory Council and Reviewing Cttee. on Export of Works of Art 1954-72, of N-W Metropolitan Regional Hosp. Board 1953-60, of Hammersmith Hosp. 1966-74 of Roy. Postgraduate Med. Sch. 1949-58, and of British Postgraduate Med. Fedn. 1958-72; a Member of Hampstead Borough Council 1945-51, and of LCC 1945-55; Chm. of DLs' Cttees. in Bermondsey and Deptford; a Member of Port of London Authority 1949-67 (Vice-Chm. 1955-67); Pres. of Leander Club 1957-62; a Steward of Henley Regatta; 1939-45 War as a GSO (I), a Senior Mil. Liaison Officer, and Lt.-Col. Comdg. 20th Light Anti-Aircraft Regt., RA (TA); GBE 1960: *m.* 1st, 1926, Lady Elizabeth Harris, from whom he obtained a divorce 1944, only da. of 5th Earl of Malmesbury; 2ndly, 1959, Gloria Jean Irene Dunn, adopted da. of the late W. E. Hill, of Barnstaple, N. Devon, and has issue by 1st and 2nd marriages.

Arms.—Vert. three bars ermine, surmounted by a lion rampant gules, murally crowned or and in chief two plates. **Crest.**—Out of a mural coronet or, a demi-lion gules, charged on the shoulder with a plate and holding in the paws a banner quarterly argent and vert. **Supporters.**—Two eagles, wings expanded inverted, sable.

Residences.—21, Lyndhurst Rd., Hampstead, NW3 5NX; Folly, Winsford Hill, Somerset. *Club,*—Travellers'.

SONS LIVING. (By 1st marriage.)
Hon. JOHN TAPLING, *b.* Jan. 22nd, 1927; ed. at Eton; Cdr. RN (ret.); High Sheriff of Bucks; Vice-Chm. CLA Game Fair 1971, and Bucks. co. Show 1972/73, Pres. Buckingham and Winslow Dist. Scout Assocn. Vice-Pres. Winslow Branch, British Legion, and a Member of Winslow RDC: *m.* 1958, Elizabeth Ann, el. da. of the late Lt.-Col. Henry Shelley Barker, DSO, of Walcote House, nr. Rugby, and has issue living, Thomas Francis Henry, *b.* 1966,—Elizabeth Wynne, *b.* 1959,—Frances Ann, *b.* 1961. *Residence,*—The Old House, Swanbourne, Milton Keynes, Bucks, MK17 0SM. *Clubs,*—Travellers', RN (Portsmouth).

(By 2nd marriage.)
Hon. Edward Walgrave, *b.* 1961.

DAUGHTERS LIVING. (By 1st marriage.)
Hon. Ann, *b.* 1930: *m.* 1951, Timothy Gerald Martin Brooks [see B. Crawshaw, colls.]. *Residence,*—Wistow, Leicester.

(By 2nd marriage.)
Hon. Cecilia Jane, *b.* 1962.
Hon. Flora Catherine, *b.* 1967.

BROTHER LIVING.
Hon. Christopher Evelyn, *b.* 1906; ed. at Eton, and at Balliol Coll., Oxford (B.A.): *m.* 1930, Anne Marie Huth, dau. of the late Rt. Hon. Frederick Huth Jackson [see Mather-Jackson, Bt., colls.], and has issue living, Adam Augustus, *b.* 1934; ed. at Eton, at Balliol Coll., Oxford (MA), and Fordham Univ. NYC (LLB); Bar. Inner Temple 1957; *m.* 1963, Mary Christine, da. of Prince Paul Saphieha, and has issue living, Christopher *b.* 1965, Paul Zachary *b.* 1968,—Richard Christian Wynne (via Matteo Palmieri, Florence 50122, Italy), *b.* 1936; ed. at Portsmouth Priory, Rhode Island, and at Columbia Univ., USA (MA): *m.* 1971, Chloë Sa abella, yr. da. of Sir Geoffrey Cecil Ryves Eley, CBE [see Walker Bt., colls., cr. 1856],—Dominic Christopher Hugh (Privada del Santismo 19, Mexico 20, DF), *b.* 1944; ed. at Georgetown Univ., USA (BA). *Residence,*—San Bernabé, Mexico DF. *Club,*—Arts.

SISTERS LIVING.
Hon. Margaret Augusta (*Baroness Florey*), *b.* 1904; ed. at Oxford Univ. (MA, DM); Univ. Lecturer in Pathology, Oxford Univ. 1945-72, and a Fellow of Lady Margaret Hall, Oxford 1952-72: *m.* 1st, 1930 (m. diss. 1946), Denys Arthur Jennings, BM BCh; 2ndly, 1967, Baron Florey (Life Peer), who *d.* 1968. *Residence,*—4, Elsfield Rd., Old Marston, Oxford. *Club,*—University Women's.
Hon. Bride Faith Louisa, *b.* 1910; ed. at Girton Coll., Camb. (B.A. 1935, M.A. 1938): *m.* 1936, John Berry, CBE, PhD, and has issue living, William (27, Saxe Coburg Place, Edinburgh 3), *b.* 1939; ed at Eton; MA, LLB, WS: *m.* 1973, Elizabeth Margery, da. of Sir Edward Redston Warner, KCMG, OBE, of 16, Lennox St., Edinburgh 4,—Peter Fremantle (58, Pyrland Rd., N3), *b.* 1944; BA (Oxon): *m.* 1972, Paola, da. of the late Giovanni Padovani, and has issue living, Sara *b.* 1974,—Margaret Wilhelmina, *b.* 1937; Dip. Arch. Edinburgh: *m.* 1962, Ronald Lindsay Alexander, ARIBA, of 81,

Balfour Rd., N5, and has issue living, Adam George b. 1971, Jane Louise b. 1969. *Residence,*—
Tayfield, Newport-on-Tay, Fife.
Hon. Katharine Dorothy Honor, b. 1919; ed. at Girton Coll., Camb. (B.A. 1941); Ph.D. London
1956. *Residence,*—Dennenlaan 48, Hollandsche Rading, Netherlands.

COLLATERAL BRANCHES LIVING.

Issue of the late Hon. Reginald Scott Fremantle, 2nd son of 2nd Baron b. 1863,
d. 1956: *m.* 1900, Hilda Lucy, who d. 1953, da. of the late E. M. Barry, RA:—
Rosamund Beatrice (29, Woodlands Rd., Witney, Oxon.), b. 1902: *m.* 1931, Thomas Gilbert Standing,
who d. 1942, of Education Dept., S. Rhodesia, and Capt. Nigeria Regt., and has issue living, Roderick
Fremantle, b. 1932,—Caspar Vernon, b. 1933,—Lionel Gilbert (29, Woodlands Rd., Witney, Oxon.)
b. 1940——Joan Lucy, b. 1904: *m.* 1930, Caleb Henry Trevor, and has issue living, Malcolm Henry,
b. 1932. *Residence,*—72, Talbot Rd., Highgate, N6.

Grandchildren of the late Sir Francis Edward Fremantle, OBE, TD, MD, MCh,
FRCS, FRCP, DPH, MP, 4th son of the Very Rev. the Hon. William Henry
Fremantle (Dean of Ripon) 2nd son of 1st Baron):—
Issue of the late Lt.-Col. Francis David Eardley Fremantle, TD, b. 1906, d. 1968: *m.* 1936,
Emmeline Amy, who *m.* 2ndly, 1973, Lt.-Col. Edward Peter Fletcher Boughey, OBE, of
Ashdown House, Hare St. nr., Buntingford, Herts [see Boughey, Bt., colls.], da. of the late
Brig.-Gen. Vigant William de Falbe, CMG, DSO, of Whittington House, Lichfield:—
Edward Vigant Eardley, b. 1942; ed. at Eton, and Balliol Coll., Oxford (BA): ACA: *m.* 1973, Sarah
Maud, yst. da. of Col. William Henry Whitbread, TD, of Warren Mere, Thursley, Godalming—
Thomas David (28 Tite St., SW3), b. 1944; ed. at Eton. and RNC, Dartmouth; late Lt. RN: *m.* 1971,
Alice Marion, da. of Cyril Reginald Egerton, of Hall Farm, Newmarket [see D. Sutherland, cclls.]—
Richard Francis, b. 1946; ed. at Eton, and Keble Coll., Oxford——Marion Jane, b. 1948: *m.* 1972,
David Christopher Hanbury of The Old Rectory, Ruckinge, nr. Ashford, Kent, and has issue living,
Jonathan Christopher, b. 1975.

Grandson of the late Ronald Aubrey Fremantle (infra):—
Issue of the late Maj. Maurice Alan Fremantle, b. 1900, d. 1972: *m.* 1928, Ida Thelma Gordon
(Castleton Court, 9, Castleton Cres., Newton Mearns, Renfrewshire), da. of the late Edward
Reginald Stirling Bloxsome, of the Rangers, Copthorne, Sussex:—
Robin Patrick (Ladyton, Galston, Ayrshire), b. 1930: ed. at Wellington Coll.; Capt. late 4th Queen's
Own Hussars, and Ayrshire (ECO) Yeo. (TA); a Dir. of Weir Construction Ltd.: *m.* 1962, June
Helen, da. of Brig. Ereld Boteler Winfield Cardiff, of Easton Court, Ludlow, Salop, and has issue
living, Charles Ereld Patrick, b. 1964,—Serena Katherine, b. 1967.

Granddaughters of the late Hon. Sir Charles William Fremantle, KCB, 3rd son of
1st Baron:—
Issue of the late Ronald Aubrey Fremantle, b. 1872, d. 1947: *m.* 1899, Eleanor Susan,
who d. 1946, dau. of Charles John Fletcher, of Dale Park, Madehurst, Arundel:—
Helen Antonia Theresa Susan, b. 1914: *m.* 1940, John Miller. *Residence,*—Dorrien's Farm, Buckland
Common, Tring, Herts.

Issue of the late Capt. Charles Albert Fremantle, D.S.O., R.N., b. 1878, d. 1952: *m.* 1906,
Margaret Griselda, who d. 1918, dau. of Sir William Wedderburn, 4th Bt.:—
Priscilla Jane, b. 1911: *m.* 1938, Henry Bourdillon Imlach Bett, and has issue living, Michael Henry
Archdale, b. 1939,—Giovanna Audrey, b. 1948. *Residence,*—Burnham Market, King's Lynn,
Norfolk.

Grandchildren of the late Adm. the Hon. Sir Edmund Robert Fremantle, G.C.B.,
G.C.V.O., C.M.G., 4th son of 1st Baron :—
Issue of the late Sir Sydney Robert Fremantle, G.C.B., M.V.O., b. 1867, d. 1958 : *m.* 1st, 1896,
Leila Hope, who d. 1930, dau. of the late Lieut. Delvin Fremantle, R.N. ; 2ndly, 1931,
Geraldine, who d. 1974, dau. of Col. William Cooke-Collis, CMG, DL, and widow of Lieut.-Col.
J. S. Fitzgerald:—
By 1st m.) Edmund Seymour Denis, *DSC* (Redlands, Hookhills Rd., Churston Ferrers, Paignton,
Devon), b. 1904; Cdr. (ret.) RN; 1939-45 War (despatches twice, DSC): *m.* 1st, 1928, Dorothy
Clare Haldane (from whom he obtained a divorce 1944), da. of Maj. W. M. Sinclair, RM; 2ndly,
1946, Mrs. Edna Lyddon, and has issue living, (by 1st m.) Charles Alan (The White House, Don-
nington, Cichester, W. Sussex), b. 1935; Lt.-Cdr. RN; Member Nautical Inst.: *m.* 1960, Caroline
Mary, da. of Cdr. Sydney Andrew Boyd Morant, OBE, DSC, RN, and has issue living, Timothy
Charles b. 1967, James Justin b. 1971, Naomi Juliet b. 1961,—Sydney Walter (4, Strafford Rd.,
Twickenham, Middx.), b. 1936: *m.* 1961, Susan Delia Aiton, da. of the late Brig. John Aiton Bell
CBE, and has issue living, Samuel Patrick b. 1967, Joanna Mary Aiton b. 1964,—(by 2nd m.) Richard
William, b. 1948,—Stephen Antony (The Coach House, Littlehampton, Totnes, Devon), b. 1950:
m. 1972, Hanna Elizabeth Fiona, da. of K. Sierakowski, of Bickley, Kent, and has issue living,
Melanie Leila b. 1973,—(by 1st m.) Ann Penelope, b. 1931: *m.* 1966, Sirio Morgia.——David Robert,
b. 1906; Lt.-Cdr. (ret.) RNVR; 1939-45 War: *m.* 1st, 1939 (m. diss. 1951), Patience Ann, da. of the
late Lt.-Cdr. Evelyn Culme-Seymour [see Culme-Seymour, Bt., colls.]; 2ndly, 1954, Mrs. Rosabel
Stewart-Liberty, da. of the late Arthur H. Fynn, of Helston, Cornwall, and has issue living, (by
1st m.) Francesca Mary, b. 1941. *Residence,*—101, Park Rd., Chiswick, W4 3ER——Barbara
Sybil, b. 1898: *m.* 1923, Capt. Douglas J. Claris, RN, who d. 1959, and has issue living. *Residence.*—
Heather Field End, Buriton, Petersfield, Hants.——Margery Hilda (*Margery Lady Sebright*), b. 1900:
m. 1st, 1921, Raymond Massey, of Toronto, from whom she obtained a divorce 1929: 2ndly, 1929,
Lt.-Col. Sir Giles Edward Sebright, CBE, 13th Bt., who d. 1954, and has issue living, (by 1st m.),
(by 2nd m.) [see Sebright, Bt.]. *Residence,*—Rivermeet House, Topsham, S. Devon.

Granddaughter of the late Alfred Ernest Albert Fremantle, youngest son of the late
Adm. the Hon. Sir Edmund Robert Fremantle, G.C.B., G.C.V.O., C.M.G.,
(ante):—
Issue of the late Major Paris Oscar Francesco Réné Fremantle, b. 1908, d. (of wounds received
in action), 1944: *m.* 1934, Rosamond Carnegia of 4, Ravens Court, St. John's Rd., Eastbourne, who *m.* 2ndly, 1947, Brig. Gordon de Bruyne, OBE, late 60 Rifles (who d. 1972),
da. of the late Arthur Knox, of Fairfield, Wargrave, Berks:—
Valerie Rosamond Christina, b. 1942.

PREDECESSORS.—[1] *Rt. Hon.* THOMAS FRANCIS FREMANTLE, *P.C.*, son of Vice Adm. Sir
Thomas Francis Fremantle, G.C.B. (cr. Baron of Austrian Empire 1816); b. 1798; sat as M.P. for
Buckingham (*C*) 1827-46, and was successively Sec. of the Treasury, Sec. at War, Ch. Sec. for Ireland,
and Chm. of Board of Customs; received Roy. licence for himself and issue to bear his father's Austrian
title of Baron 1822; cr. a *Baronet* 1821, and *Baron Cottesloe*, of Swanbourne and Hardwick, co. Bucks
(peerage of United Kingdom) 1874: *m.* 1824, Louisa Elizabeth, who d. 1875, dau. of F.-M. Sir
George Nugent, G.C.B., 1st Bt.; d. 1890; *s.* by his el. son [2] THOMAS FRANCIS, 2nd Baron ;
b. 1830; M.P. for Buckinghamshire (*C*) 1876-85; sometime Chm. of London, Brighton and
South Coast Railway: *m.* 1859, Lady Augusta Henrietta Scott, who d. 1906, dau. of 2nd
Earl of Eldon ; d. 1918; *s.* by his el. son [3] THOMAS FRANCIS, *C.B.*, *V.D.*, *T.D.*, 3rd Baron ; b.
1862; Hon. Col. (formerly Lieut.-Col. Comdg.) Bucks Batn., Oxfordshire and Buckinghamshire
L.I. ; Assist. Sec. to Sec. of State for War (Rt. Hon. W. St. J. Brodrick, M.P.) 1900-1903 ; Lord
Lieut. of Bucks 1923-54 : *m.* 1896, Florence, who d. 1956, dau. of the late Thomas Tapling, of
Kingswood, Dulwich; d. 1956; *s.* by his el. surviving son [4] JOHN WALGRAVE HALFORD, 4th
Baron, and present peer.

Courtenay, Lord, son of Earl of Devon.

COURTHOPE, BARONY OF. (Courthope.) [Extinct 1955.]

DAUGHTER LIVING OF FIRST BARON. (*By 1st marriage.*)

Hon. Elinor Daphne, *OBE, b.* 1902; Chm. E. Sussex Co. Council 1967-70; OBE (Civil) 1963. *Residence,*—Whiligh, Wadhurst, Sussex.

COURTOWN, EARL OF. (Stopford.) Sits as BARON SALTERSFORD (G.B. 1796) [Earl I. 1762.]

Faithful to an unhappy country.

JAMES PATRICK MONTAGU BURGOYNE WINTHROP STOPFORD, 9th Earl; *b.* March 19th, 1954; *s.* 1975; ed. at Eton, and Berkshire Coll. of Agric.

Arms,—Azure, semée of cross crosslets and three lozenges or. **Crest,**—A wyvern, wings elevated proper. **Supporters,**—Two stags proper, plain collared and chained, and each charged on the shoulder with a lozenge or.

Residences,—Beechshade, Cambridge Road, Beaconsfield, Bucks ; Marlfield, Gorey, co. Wexford.

BROTHER LIVING.

Hon. Jeremy Neville, *b.* June 22nd, 1958; ed. at Eton.

HALF SISTERS LIVING.

Lady Mary Christina, *b.* 1936: *m.* 1959, Geoffrey Jermyn Holborow, and has issue living, Crispin David Jermyn, *b.* 1963,—Katharine Mary, *b.* 1961. *Residence,*—Ladock House, Ladock, Truro, Cornwall.

Lady Elizabeth Cameron, *b.* 1939: *m.* 1962, Alan Anthony Colleton Godsal, and has issue living, Hugh Colleton, *b.* 1965,—Lucy Violet, *b.* 1964,—Laura Christina, *b.* 1968. *Residence,*—Haines Hill, Twyford, Berks.

Lady Felicity Aileen Ann, *b.* 1951.

UNCLES LIVING. (*Sons of 7th Earl.*)

Hon. Edward Richard Barrington, *b.* 1914; ed. at Stowe; formerly Capt. Roy. Norfolk Regt.: *m.* 1946, Ann Marie Elizabeth Douglas, only da. of the late Brig. Harold Gordon Henderson, CBE of Hyde House, Chalford, Glos., and has issue living, Michael James Patrick, *b.* 1950,—Christopher Gordon Edward *b.* 1953—Penelope Ann, *b.* 1948. *Residence,*—40, Perry St., Wendover, Bucks.

Hon. Terence Victor (Lake End House, Dorney, Windsor), *b.* 1918; ed. at Eton; Capt. RN (ret.); Assist. Naval Adviser to UK High Commr. in Canada 1959-60, Assist. Dir. of Underwater Weapons, Admiralty 1961-63, and Capt. Inshore Flotilla Far East Fleet, and Cmdg. HMS *Manxman* 1963-64 ; Ch. of Staff to C-in-C Naval Home Command 1965-67, and Ch. Staff Officer to Flag Officer Gibraltar 1967-69; Naval ADC to HM 1969: *m.* 1951, Sheila Adèle, only da. of the late Philip Page, and has issue living, Henry Philip Terence, *b.* 1953; ed. at Eton,—Robert Edward James, *b.* 1958,—James Richard Hugh, *b.* 1961,—Catherine Mary Adéle, *b.* 1965.

AUNTS LIVING. (*Daughters of 7th Earl.*)

Lady Patricia Mary, *b.* 1906: *m.* 1934, Maurice John Hayward, Malayan Civil Ser., only son of the late Sir Maurice Henry Weston Hayward, KCSI, Four Oaks, Sutton Coldfield), *b.* 1939: *m.* 1968, Christina, da. of Matthew Hyland, of the Glebe, Coolrain, co. Leix, and has issue living, David Maurice *b.* 1970, Jane Margaret *b.* 1969,— Bridget Mary, *b.* 1935: *m* 1964, John Everard Kitchin (54, Natcroft Grove, Fetcham, Leatherhead, Surrey), and has issue living, Hugh Everard *b.* 1965, Simon John *b.* 1967,—Caroline Patricia, *b.* 1936 : *m.* 1960, Myles Anthony Clive Saker, of 11, Stonor Rd., Kuala Lumpur, Malaysia, and has issue living, John Anthony *b.* 1962, Deborah Ann *b.* 1967,—Sarah Elizabeth, *b.* 1946. *Residence,*—White Hart House, Haddenham, Bucks.

Lady Rosemary Katharine, *b.* 1911; formerly 2nd Officer, W.R.N.S. *Residence,*—Christmas Cottage, Southview Road, Felpham, Bognor Regis, Sussex.

Lady Moyra Charlotte, *b.* 1917 : *m.* 1943, Lieut.-Com. David Henry Champion Streatfeild, R.N., and has issue living, David Anthony (63, Inglethorpe St., SW6), *b.* 1945: *m.* 1971, Jill Katherine, da. of William Macfarlane, of The Old Cottage, Potters Lane, Send, Surrey and has issue living, Katherine *b.* 1975,—Timothy James, *b.* 1947,—Peter Stopford, *b.* 1954,—Cicely Mary, *b.* 1950. *Residence,*—Redberry House, Bierton, Aylesbury, Bucks.

Lady Cecilia Norah (twin), *b.* 1917 ; formerly Junior Com. A.T.S. : *m.* 1947, Com. Thomas Philip Frederick Urquhart Page, R.N., son of the late Sir Leo Francis Page, and has issue living, Nicholas Leo Thomas, *b.* 1948: *m.* 1971, Sarah June, el. da. of Leslie Bramhall, of Carrick House, Feock, Cornwall,—Victoria Cecilia, *b.* 1951,—Juliet Mary, *b.* 1955. *Residence,*—Road Farm, Churt, Surrey.

GREAT AUNTS LIVING (*Daughters of 6th Earl.*)

Lady Eileen, *b.* 1887 : *m.* 1924, Major Montagu Richard William Duberly, O.B.E., Indian Army (retired), and Capt. Auxiliary Mil. Pioneer Corps. *Residence,*—5, Rivermead Court, Ranelagh Gardens, S.W.6.

Lady Alma, *b.* 1889 : *m.* 1922, Lieut.-Col. Geoffrey Lennard Hoare, C.B.E. [Lennard, Bt.], who *d.* 1960, and has issue living, Richard Geoffrey Stopford (of 46, Pembroke Road, W.8), *b.* 1923 ; Capt. RA (TA Reserve): *m.* 1952, Gillian Mary, da. of the late Maj. G. L. Vivian, and has issue living, Anthony Richard Vivian *b.* 1953, Patricia Gill *b.* 1956, Joanna Vivienne *b.* 1957,—Alma Barbara, *b* 1925: *m.* 1950, Capt. Peter Frederick Warren Clarke, RE, and has issue living, Patrick Warren ....., Jacqueline Mary *b.* 1953, Elizabeth Ann *b.* 1958, Susan Margaret *b.* 1963,—Myra Jean (c/o C. Hoare & Co., 67, Park Lane, W1), *b.* 1930: *m.* 1952, Col. Henry Blackwood Hallowes Waring OBE, late Queen's Own Buffs, R. Kent Regt., and has issue living, Richard Blackwood *b.* 1955, Michael Geoffrey *b.* 1959, Sarah Elizabeth *b.* 1956. *Residence,*—Little Barn, Benenden, Cranbrook, Kent.

Lady Edith Mary, *b.* 1890 ; formerly Co. Com. Auxiliary Territorial Ser. : *m.* 1923, as his second wife, Brigadier Walter Headfort Brooke, C.B.E., M.C., and has issue living, Diana Gertrude, *b.* 1925: *m.* 1951, J. G. S. Coaker, of Sherberton, Princetown, S. Devon, and has issue living, Peter John Brooke *b.* 1954, Anthony James Richard *b.* 1964, Susan Elizabeth *b.* 1960. *Residence,*—12, Roborough Lane, Ashburton, Newton Abbot, Devon.

Lady Marjorie Gertrude, *b.* 1904. *Residence,*—Bournemead, Herkomer Road, Bushey, Herts.

WIDOWS LIVING OF SONS OF SIXTH EARL.

Elsa, dau. of the late William Edward Hinke, of Gothenburg, Sweden, and widow of Carl von Wendt, of Abo, Finland : *m.* 1932, as his second wife, Vice-Adm. the Hon. Arthur Stopford, C.M.G., who *d.* 1955. *Residence,*—8, Scotts Avenue, Shortlands, Bromley, Kent.

Rosalinde Cecil, *M.B.E.*, dau. of the late Rev. Charles Francis Townley, C.B.E.; Senior Com. A.T.S. 1940-41 ; M.B.E. (Civil) 1919 : *m.* 1923, Capt. the Hon. Guy Stopford, R.N. (retired), who *d.* 1954. *Residence,*—Fulbourn Manor, Cambridge.

WIDOW LIVING OF EIGHTH EARL.

Patricia (*Countess of Courtown*) (Beechshade, Cambridge Rd., Beaconsfield, Bucks; Marlfield, Gorey, co. Wexford), da. of the late Harry Stephen Winthrop, of Auckland, N.Z.: *m.* 1951, as his 2nd wife, the 8th Earl, who *d.* 1975.

COLLATERAL BRANCHES LIVING.

Issue of the late Vice-Adm. the Hon. Arthur Stopford, C.M.G., 2nd son of 6th Earl, *b.* 1879, *d.* 1955 : *m.* 1st, 1908, Mary Augusta Grace (who obtained a divorce 1924), dau. of the late Godfrey Cornewall Chester Master, of Rangeworthy Court, Yate, Gloucestershire [Pollock, Bt.] ; 2ndly, 1932, Elsa (ante), dau. of the late William Edward Hinke, of Gothenburg, Sweden, and widow of Carl von Wendt, of Abo, Finland :—

(By 1st marriage) Godfrey Vyvyan, *b.* 1909 ; ed. at Radley, and at New Coll., Oxford ; Capt. R.A. (T.A.): *m.* 1934, Marjorie Alice, younger dau. of Alan Cecil Lupton [Burrell, Bt.]. *Residence,—* The Old Post Office, Cheriton, Hants.

Grandson of the late Capt. the Hon. Edward Barrington Lewis Henry Stopford (infra):—
Issue of the late Lieut.-Com. Barrington George Dashwood Stopford, R.N., *b.* 1889, *d.* 1930 : *m.* 1918, Muriel Florence Mary (5, St. James St., Southover, Lewes, Sussex), el. da. of the late Rev. Nathaniel Nicholas Lewarne, formerly V. of Yealmpton, S. Devon:—
Brian Barrington Dashwood, *MVO*, *b.* 1923; ed. at Stowe, and Trin. Coll., Camb. (BA); Solicitor 1948; Solicitor to Duchy of Cornwall 1954-72; MVO 4th class 1971: *m.* 1948, Alison Honor, da. of the late Maurice Sylvester Gibb, CBE, and has issue living, Justin Montagu Dashwood, *b.* 1949; ed. at Salford Univ.: *m.* 1972, Gillian, da. of Eric Heatherington, of Kendal—Yolande Honor, *b.* 1951; ed. at Dartford Coll. of Ed. *Residence,—*23, St. Anne's Cres., Lewes, Sussex. *Club,—*English-Speaking Union.

Issue of the late Capt. the Hon. Edward Barrington Lewis Henry Stopford, 2nd son of 5th Earl, *b.* 1858, *d.* 1909 : *m.* 1st, 1888, Isabel Alice, who *d.* 1890, dau. of the late Capt. Barrington Dashwood ; 2ndly, 1895, Alice Maud Pashley, who *d.* 1942, dau. of the late J. P. Burbeary, and widow of the Rev. E. F. Haviland :—

(By 2nd m), Patricia Eileen (614, Elm St., Monroe, Connecticut, USA), *b.* 1896: *m.* 1916, Alec Ernest Saxton, formerly Lieut. Duke of Cornwall's L.I., who *d.* 1973, and has issue living, Natalie Moyra, *b.* 1922: *m.* 1940, George Weaver Schroeder, of Edge Hill Rd., Prospect, Kentucky, USA, and has issue living, Peter Saxton *b.* 1940, Wendy Moyra *b.* 1943,—Doreen Patricia, *b.* 1926: *m.* 1st, 1948, Paul Walton Jones, late Lt. U.S. Army Reserve, who *d.* 1972; 2ndly, 1973, Carrington Williams, attorney, of 3543, Half Moon Circle, Falls Church, Va., USA, and has issue living, (by 1st m.) Sheila Heath *b.* 1953, Patricia Doreen *b.* 1956.——Violet Elizabeth, *b.* 1902: *m.* 1931, Capt. John Cameron, CIE, RIN (ret.), who *d.* 1969.——Yolande Valerie (West Lawn, Audley Park Rd., Bath), *b.* 1904: *m.* 1938, S. T. Colvin Turner, and has issue living, Michael James Stopford, *b.* 1945: *m.* 1968, Elizabeth Combes,—Angela Yolande, *b.* 1939: *m.* 1959, James Barry Colquhoun, of Honeyborough House, Neyland, Milford Haven, and has issue living, James Timothy *b.* 1961, Charles Stopford *b.* 1965, Philip *b.* 1967,—Elizabeth Alice, *b.* 1940: *m.* 1963, Hamish John Mackenzie, of 28, Oxshott Way, Cobham, Surrey, and has issue living, Alasdair Hamish *b.* 1966, Arabella Jane *b.* 1968.

Grandchildren of the late Hon. George Frederick William Stopford (infra):—
Issue of the late George Christian Noel Stopford, *b.* 1891, *d.* 1969: *m.* 1915, Mary Georgina, who *d.* 1967, da. of the late Rev. Canon Edward Newland, of Buncara, co. Donegal:—
Edward Montagu (Bargara, Qld.), *b.* 1917; late Ch. Yeoman of Signals RAN: *m.* 1941, Dora, da. of the late—Flood, of Warwick, Qld., and has issue living, Peter, *b.* 1942: *m.* 19—, Lorraine Dawn, da. of Percy Dinman, of Cairns, N. Qld., and has issue living, Tracey Dawn *b.* 1966,—Robin, *b.* 1946,—Wendy, *b.* 1944: *m.* 19—, Allan David Stephens, of Dalby, Qld., and has issue living, a son *b.* 19—, a da. *b.* 19—.——Claire, *b.* 1922: *m.* 1948, James Gordon McIlwraith (27, Judea Rd., Tauranga, NZ), and has issue living, James, *b.* 1955,—Duncan, *b.* 1956,—Margaret Anne, *b.* 1951,—Janet, *b.* 1953,—Judith Pamela, *b.* 1958.

Issue of the late Hon. George Frederick William Stopford, 3rd son of 5th Earl, *b.* 1859, *d.* 1933 : *m.* 1889, Marie Clare, who *d.* 1952, dau. of Capt. Henry Segrave, formerly of Kiltymon, co. Wicklow, and Cabra, co. Dublin :—
Montagu Henry Aubrey, *b.* 1894; ed. at Tonbridge Sch.; formerly Capt. Special Cav.; 1914-18 War: *m.* 1926, Nancy Pauline, da. of the late Paul Hunt, of Kilfera, Kilkenny. *Residence,—*Kilfera, Kilkenny.——Cynthia Mareli Mabel, *b.* 1899. *Residence,—*160, Oakdale Av., Stanground, Peterborough.

Issue of the late Rear-Adm. the Hon. Walter George Stopford, 6th son of 4th Earl *b.* 1855, *d.* 1918 : *m.* 1893, Florence Mary, who *d.* 1950, dau. of the late Hon Loran E. Baker, M.L.C., of Beacon House, Yarmouth, Nova Scotia :—

Walter John, *M.C.*, *b.* 1897 ; ed. at Winchester ; Lieut.-Col. (retired) R.A., and a Com. of Order of the Nile; European War 1915-18 (M.C.), European War 1939-44 in Middle East (despatches:) *m.* 1931, Renfra, da. of the late Adm. Sir Rudolf Walter Bentinck, KCB, KCMG.——Frederick, Victor, *CBE*, *b.* 1900; Rear Adm. (ret.) 1914-18 War; 1939-44 War; CBE (Mil) 1952: *m.* 1924, Mary Guise, da. of Capt. Frederick Charles Ulick Vernon-Wentworth, CB, RN [Guise, Vt., colls.] and has issue living, John Walter (Amberley, N. Canterbury, NZ), *b.* 1926; Capt. R. Canadian Armd. Corps. (ret.): *m.* 1960, Barbara, only da. of Maj. W. H. McHaffie, of Aberdour on Spey, and has issue living, Michael John *b.* 1966, Susan Caroline *b.* 1961, Jennifer Claire *b.* 1965,—Robin Frederick (4, Park Homer Rd., Colehill, Wimborne, Dorset), *b.* 1929: *m.* 1960, Patricia Ann, el. da. of Lt.-Col. Leo Dominic Gleeson, DSO, and has issue living, Jonathan Paul Michael *b.* 1964, Sarah Frances Ann *b.* 1969,—Timothy Patrick, *b.* 1935.—Catherine Jill, *b.* 1939: *m.* 1961, Garry Joseph Oman, of 1, Appledale Rd., Islington, Ont., Canada, and has issue living, Christopher David *b.* 1966, Catherine Mary *b.* 1964, Elizabeth Frances Anne *b.* 1972. *Residence,—*Ash Farm House, Grenofen, Tavistock, Devon.

Grandchildren of the late Rev. Frederick Manners Stopford, son of the late Lieut.-Col. the Hon. Edward Stopford, 2nd son of 3rd Earl:—
Issue of the late Francis Powys Stopford, *b.* 1861, *d.* 1935 : *m.* 1894, Kathleen Edith, who *d.* 1956, dau. of Henry James Coulby Gompertz, of Madras :—
Mary Horatia, *b.* 1896: *m.* 1933, Reginald Cuthbert Stockdale Ellison, Bar.-at-law, of 39, St. Mary's Mansions, St. Mary's Terrace, W.2, and has issue living, Luke Antony, *b.* 1936,—John Michael Cuthbert, *b.* 1938,—Catharine Monica Mary, *b.* 1935,—Lucy Eleanor Mary, *b.* 1937.——Kathleen Stewart (of Spring, Hill, Conghurst Lane, Hawkhurst, Kent), *b.* 1900.——Eleanor Montagu (twin) (of Spring Hill, Conghurst Lane, Hawkhurst, Kent), *b.* 1900.

Issue of the late Walter Montagu Stopford, *b.* 1874, *d.* 1933: *m.* 1919, Mary Josephine (of Greenville, Enniscorthy, co. Wexford), dau. of the late Patrick O'Neill, of Enniscorthy, co. Wexford:—
Lionel Frederick John, *b.* 1921 ; European War 1944-5 in Welsh Guards : *m.* 1950, Violet Eira, dau. of Harold Dart, of Cefn, Murch Road, Dinas Powis, Glamorgan, and has issue living, John Martin, *b.* 1958,—Linda Mary, *b.* 1951,—Wendy Margaret, *b.* 1953. *Residence,*

Grandson of the late Adm. the Hon. Sir Montagu Stopford, KCB, 6th son of 3rd Earl:—
Issue of the late Maj.-Gen. Sir Lionel Arthur Montagu Stopford, K.C.V.O., C.B., *b.* 1860, *d.* 1942 : *m.* 1891, Mabel Georgina Emily, who *d.* 1951, dau. of the late George Alexander Mackenzie, of Applecross. Ross-shire :—
Lionel Montagu Phipps, *b.* 1897; ed. at Wellington Coll.; formerly Capt. Seaforth Highlanders, 1914-18 War: *m.* 1934, Sheila Frances, M.B.E., dau. of Gen. Sir Cecil Francis Romer, G.C.B.; KBE, CMG, and has issue living, Robert Cecil Montagu (29A, Priestfields, Rochester), *b.* 1935: *m.* 1958, Elizabeth Ann, da. of the late Alexander Krott, and has issue living, Andrew

Alexander Montagu *b.* 1959, Sara Elizabeth Fiona *b.* 1967. *Residence,*—12, Coxhill Lane, Potterne, Devizes, Wilts. *Club,*—United Service.

Grandchildren of the late Adm. Robert Fanshawe Stopford, son of the late Adm the Hon. Robert Stopford, G.C.B., 3rd son of 2nd Earl :—
Issue of the late Vice-Adm. Frederick George Stopford, b. 1852, d. 1928 : m. 1889, Maria Mary, who d. 1915, dau. of the late Rev. Thomas Frederick Bigg, formerly R. of St. Andrew's, Deal :—
Robin Edward Wilbraham (28, St. Peters' Rd., W. Mersea, Colchester), *b.* 1897; *m.* 1925, Alicia Ellen Saunders, who d. 1967, and has issue living, Mona, *b.* 1926.——Emily Wilbraham (28, St. Peter's Rd., W. Mersea, Colchester), *b.* 1894: *m.* 1st, 1915, Lt.-Cdr. John W. Pugh, RN, who *d.* 1933, having assumed by deed poll 1923, the surname of Stopford, for himself and his issue: 2ndly, 1939, James William Livingston, who *d.* 1969, and has issue living (by 1st m.) John Desmond STOPFORD (Deegard, St. Peter's Rd., W. Mersea, Colchester), *b.* 1918: *m.* 1942, Dorothy Catherine Barber, and has issue living, John Francis *b.* 1944, Christopher George *b.* 1956, Margaret Catherine *b.* 1943: *m.* 1962, Malcolm Bennett,—Brian Michael STOPFORD (4, Coliemore Villas, Dalkey, co. Dublin), *b.* 1921: *m.* 1944, Dorothy Eleanor Bradley, and has issue living, Thomas Michael *b.* 1947: *m.* 1971, Mary Kerrigan Hoy, of NZ, Peter John *b.* 1949: *m.* 1972, Joy Goulding, of Mount Merrion, Dublin, Rosemary Eleanor Merrill *b.* 1945: *m.* 1966, David Beckett, Caroline Ann *b.* 1950: *m.* 1972, Dermot Smurfit, of Foxrock, co. Dublin,—Robert Hugh STOPFORD (23, Seventh Av., Walmer, Port Elizabeth, S. Africa), *b.* 1928: *m.* 1954, Iona Marie Raw, and has issue living, Desmond Robert *b.* 1958, Clare Iona *b.* 1955, Wendy Anne *b.* 1961.

Grandchildren of the late Col. Lionel Richard Stopford Sackville (infra):—
Issue of the late Col. Nigel Victor Stopford Sackville, OBE, TD, b. 1901, d. 1972: m. 1st, 1929 (m. diss. 1943), Beatrix Helen Constance, da. of the late Col. Hercules Arthur Pakenham, CMG [see E. Longford, colls.]: 2ndly, 1946, Lilah Mary (Park Road, Lowick, Kettering), da. of the late Capt. Percy Richard Hare [see E. Listowel, colls.], and formerly wife of Maj. George Seton Wills, R. Wilts Yeo [see Wills, Bt., cr. 1904]:—

(By 1st m.) Lionel Geoffrey (Drayton House, Lowick, Kettering; White's Club), *b.* 1932: *m,* 1960, Susan J. only da. of the late Jenkin Coles, of the Abbey, Knaresborough, Yorks., and has issue living, Charles Lionel, *b.* 1961,—Thomas Nigel, *b.* 1968,—Lucinda Mary, *b.* 1963.——Venetia Mary (32, Stanhope Gdns., SW7), *b.* 1930: *m.* 1952 (m. diss. 1968), Maj. Benjamin Robert Chetwynd Talbot, TD, and has issue living, Benjamin Simon Robert, *b.* 1956,—Victoria Mary, *b.* 1958.

Granddaughter of the late William Bruce Stopford Sackville (who assumed by Roy. Licence 1870 the additional surname and arms of Sackville), son of the late Rev. the Hon. Richard Bruce Stopford, 4th son of 2nd Earl :—
Issue of the late Col. Lionel Richard Stopford Sackville, b. 1845, d. 1906 : m. 1887, Constance Evelyn, who d. 1945, dau. of the late Major George Gosling :—
Elinor Beryl, *b.* 1888. *Residence,*—12, Brunswick Gdns., W8.

Grandsons of the late James Sydney Stopford, son of the late Rev. the Hon. Richard Bruce Stopford (ante) :—
Issue of the late Major Heneage Frank Stopford, b. 1877, d. (killed in action during European War) 1916 : m. 1908, Margaret Amelia, who d. 1960, dau. of the late Edward Briggs Kennedy [M. Ailsa, colls.] :—
James Coverley, *O.B.E., R.N., b.* 1909 ; is Capt. ; European War 1939-45 (O.B.E.); O.B.E.(Mil.) 1940, *m.* 1936, Sheila, dau. of the late Capt. G. C. S. MacLeod, Black Watch, and has issue living, Robert Heneage, *b.* 1945,—Christopher George, *b.* 1947,—Serena Margaret, *b.* 1939: *m.* 1964, Christopher Holmes, Fl. Lt. RAF, and has issue living, Andrew David *b.* 1965, Richard Mark *b.* 1967, Bridget Constantia (twin) *b.* 1967.——Edward Kennedy, *CB, b.* 1911; ed. at Winchester, and at New Coll., Oxford (BA); an Under-Sec. Min. of Defence 1964-71; (CB (Civil) 1955: *m.* 1952, Patricia Iona Mary, da. of the late W. Howard Carrick, and widow of the late Duncan George Stewart, CMG, and has issue living, Michael John, *b.* 1953. *Residence,*—The Folly, Fifield, Oxford.

Issue of the late Capt. Wyndham Horace Stopford, b. 1878, d. 1903 : m. 1903, Dorothy Eleanor (who m. 2ndly, 1906, Col. Frank Truscott Phillips, RMLL, who d. 1936), da. of the late Rev. Wilfrid Nevill Leeson, BD, of Albany House, Hove, Sussex:—
Wyndham Horace (posthumous), *b.* 1904: *m.* 1928, May, dau. of Col. John White Craig, of Manila, Philippine Islands, and has issue living, Nevill Craig, *b.* 1932,—Craig, *b.* 1939,—Ann, *b.* 1935. *Address,*—

Grandson of the late Robert Stopford, son of the late Rev. the Hon. Richard Bruce Stopford (ante):—
Issue of the late Lieut.-Col. Horace Robert Stopford, b. 1855, Coldstream Guards, d. (killed in action during S. African War) 1899 : m. 1886, Marguerite Louisa Greathed, who d. 1944, dau. of the late Professor B. MacDowel, of Trinity College, Dublin:—
Robert Maurice, *DSC* (Mulberry Cottage, Barhatch Rd., Cranleigh, Surrey; Army and Navy Club), *b.* 1890; Cdr. (ret.) RN: *m.* 1920, Elsie, who *d.* 1967, da. of the late Capt. Francis William Lawson, Connaught Rangers, and has issue living, Michael Robert Horace (8, Miller's Court, Chiswick Mall, W4, and 59, Old Mill St., Mosta, Malta), *b.* 1921; Maj. (ret.) Queen's R. Surrey Regt.: *m.* 1945, Megan, da. of the late Arthur Reyner Williams, and has issue living, Robert Michael Hastings *b.* 1949, Charles Michael Reyner (Cavalry Club), *b.* 1950; Lt. 9/12 R. Lancers, Laura Cecilia Mary *b.* 1947: *m.* 1969, Lt. Kenneth Andrès Courtenay, RN, of Thatchet Cottage, Frampton, Dorchester, Dorset (and has issue living, Edward Michael Andrès *b.* 1970, Tamsin Mary Andres *b.* 1972), Teresa Megan Marguerite *b.* 1955: *m.* 1975, Nigel A. S. Healey,—Stephen Robert Anthony, *MBE* (c/o Child & Co., 1, Fleet St. EC4; Cavalry Club), *b.* 1934; Lt.-Col. R. Scots Dragoon Gds.; MBE (Mil) 1971: *m.* 1963, Vanessa, da. of Theodore Baron, of 18, Rex Pl., W1,—Rosemary Dolores, *b.* 1926: *m.* 1963, John Walter Mills, TD, of Geary's Place, Lower Maes-Coed, Pontrilas, Herefords.

PREDECESSORS.—[1] JAMES Stopford, son of the late James Stopford, M.P., of Courtown, M.P. for co. Wexford 1721-7, and for Fethard 1727-58 ; cr. *Baron Courtown*, of co. Wexford (peerage of Ireland) 1758, and *Viscount Stopford* and *Earl of Courtown* (peerage of Ireland) 1762 ; *d.* 1770 ; *s.* by his son [2] JAMES, 2nd Earl ; cr. *Baron Saltersford*, of Saltersford, co. Chester (peerage of Great Britain) 1796; *d.* 1810 ; *s.* by his son [3] JAMES GEORGE, *K.P., P.C.,* 3rd Earl ; *d.* 1835 ; *s.* by his son [4] JAMES THOMAS, 4th Earl ; *b.* 1794: *m.* 1st, 1822, Lady Charlotte Montagu-Scott, who *d.* 1828, dau. of the 4th Duke of Buccleuch ; 2ndly, 1850, Dora, who *d.* 1859, Jau. of the late Right Hon. Edward Pennefather, Ch. Justice of the Queen's Bench in Ireland ; *d.* 1858 ; *s.* by his son [5] JAMES GEORGE HENRY, 5th Earl ; *b.* 1823 : *m.* 1846, the Hon. Elizabeth Frances Milles, who *d.* 1894, 2nd dau. of 4th Baron Sondes ; *d.* 1914 ; *s.* by his el. son [6] JAMES WALTER MILLES, 6th Earl, *b.* 1853 ; High Sheriff of co. Wexford 1877, and of co. Carlow 1878, and Lieut. for co. Wexford 1901 : *m.* 1st, 1876, the Hon. Catherine Elizabeth Neville, who *d.* 1884, dau. of 4th Baron Braybrooke ; 2ndly, 1886, Gertrude, who *d.* 1934, dau. of the late Gen. Charles James Conway Mills, of Cardington, Beds ; *d.* 1933 ; *s.* by his el. son [7] JAMES RICHARD NEVILLE, *O.B.E.,* 7th Earl ; *b.* 1877 ; Major, Gen. List ; S. Africa 1900-1901, European War 1915-19, Mayor of Aylesbury 1927-8, D.A.A.G., War Office 1941-7 : *m.* 1905, Cicely Mary, *OBE, JP,* who *d.* 1973, yr. da. of the late John Arden Birch; *d.* 1957; *s.* by his el. son [8] JAMES MONTAGU BURGOYNE, *OBE, TD,* 8th Earl; *b.* 1908; Lt. Col. and Brevet Col. London Irish Rifles, R. Ulster Rifles; N. Africa 1943 and Italy 1943-45: *m.* 1st, 1934, Christina Margaret (m. diss. 1946), da of Adm. John Ewen Cameron CB, MVO, of Brunton House, Christon Bank, Northumberland; 2ndly, 1951, Patricia, da of Harry Stephen Winthrop, of Auckland, NZ; *d.* 1975; *s.* by his el. son [9], JAMES PATRICK MONTAGU BURGOYNE WINTHROP, 9th Earl, and present peer; also Viscount Stopford, Baron Courtown, and Baron Saltersford.

COUTANCHE, BARONY OF. (Coutanche.) [Extinct 1973.]

SON LIVING OF LIFE PEER.

Hon. John Alexander Gore, *b.* 1925; is Lt.-Cdr. RNR: *m.* 1949, Jean Veronica, da. of the late Alexander Thomson Dawson, of Portelet House, Jersey. *Residence,*—Clos Des Tours, St. Aubin, Jersey.

COVENTRY, EARL OF. (Coventry.) [Earl E. 1697.]

Candidly and constantly.

GEORGE WILLIAM COVENTRY, 11th Earl; *b.* Jan. 25th, 1934; *s.* 1940; ed. at Eton; late 2nd Lieut. Grenadier Guards: *m.* 1st 1955 (m. diss. 1963), Marie Farquhar, da. of William Sherman Medart, of St. Louis, USA; 2ndly, 1969 (m. diss. 1975) Ann, da. of Frederick William James Cripps, of Bickley, Kent, and has issue by 1st m.

Arms.—Sable, a fesse ermine, between three crescents or. Crest,—A cock gules, comb, wattles, and legs or, standing on a garb fessewise or. Supporters.—Two eagles, wings expanded and inverted argent, beaked and membered or.

Seat.—Earls Croome Court, Earls Croome, Worcester.   *Residence,*—Earls Croome, Worcester.

SON LIVING. (*By 1st m.*)
EDWARD   GEORGE   WILLIAM   OMAR (*Viscount Deerhurst*), *b.* Sept. 24th, 1957.

SISTERS LIVING.
Lady Anne Donne, *b.* 1922.
Lady Maria Alice COVENTRY (Severn Bank, Severn Stoke, Worcester), *b.* 1931; resumed her maiden name of Coventry 1968: *m.* 1954, (m. diss. 1968), John Richard Lewes.

WIDOW LIVING OF TENTH EARL.
Hon. NESTA DONNE PHILIPPS, da. of 1st Baron Kylsant (ext.); a DL of Carmarthenshire; 1939-45 War as Ch. Com. ATS: *m.* 1st, 1921, the 10th Earl, who *d.* (killed in action during European War) 1940; 2ndly, 1953, Maj. Terrance Vincent Fisher-Hoch, RA. *Residence,*—Plâs Llanstephan, Carmarthen, Dyfed SA33 5JP.

COLLATERAL BRANCHES LIVING.
     Issue of the late Col. the Hon. Charles John Coventry, 2nd son of 9th Earl, CB, *b.* 1867, *d.* 1929: *m.* 1900, Lily, who *d.* 1970, yr. da. of the late Fitz Hugh Whitehouse, of Eastbourne Lodge, Newport, USA:—
Francis Henry, *b.* 1912; ed. at Eton, and at New Coll., Oxford (B.A. 1934); is Lieut.-Com. R.N.V.R.; formerly Lieut. Worcestershire Yeo. (T.A.): *m.* 1945, Yolande Lucienne, dau. of P. di Benedetto, of Alexandria and has issue living, Patricia Caroline Mary, *b.* 1950: *m.* 1969, Antonio Morisani, of Viale Val Padana 15, Rome, and has issue living Gian-Marco *b.* 1970. *Residence,*— 6987, Caslano, Switzerland.——Pamela Elizabeth (*Pamela, Countess of Aylesford*), *b.* 1901: *m.* 1st, 1928, Lt.-Cdr. James George Greville Dugdale, RN [E. Warwick], who *d.* 1964, and from whom she obtained a divorce 1940; 2ndly, (April) 1940, the 9th Earl of Aylesford, who *d.* (killed in action) 1940, and has issue living, (by 1st m.) Mary Judy (*Lady Millard*), *b.* 1929: *m.* 1964, Sir Guy Elwin Millard, KCMG, CVO, of Fyfield Manor, Southrop, Cirencester. *Residence.*—105, Dorset House, Gloucester Pl., NW1.——Diana Bruen COVENTRY (Odos Athinas 36, Ano Voula, Athens), *b.* 1910; assumed by deed poll 1970, the surname of Coventry: *m.* 1933 (m. diss. 1969), John Sidney Mason, Lt. Gren. Guards.

     Issue of the late Hon. Henry Thomas Coventry, 3rd son of 9th Earl, *b.* 1868, *d.* 1934: *m.* 1907, Edith, who *d.* 1949, dau. of the late Col. Lawrence Kip, of New York:—
Victor Henry, *b.* 1909; ed. at Eton: *m.* 1943, Winifred Louise, da. of the late Arthur E. Cooper.

     Issue of the late Hon. Sir Reginald William Coventry, K.C., 4th son of 9th Earl, *b.* 1869, *d.* 1940: *m.* 1st, 1911, Gwenllian Pascoe, who *d.* 1925, dau. of Edward Vaughan Morgan, formerly of 22, Harrington Gardens, S.W. ; 2ndly, 1926, Frances Constance, who *d.* 1943, widow of Walter P. Jeffreys, of Cynghordy :—
(By 1st m.) Arthur Reginald, *b.* 1919; formerly 2nd Lt. Coldstream Guards.——Mary Gwenllian, *b.* 1912: *m.* 1935, George Albert Finegan, LRCPI, LRCSI, who *d.* 1965, and has issue living, Barbara Jane, *b.* 1936,—Sonia Mary, *b.* 1939. *Residence,*—274, Cooden Drive, Bexhill, Sussex.——Joan Bettine Gwenllian, *b.* 1916: *m.* 1945, Capt. Simon Birch, Coldstream Guards [E. Hardwicke], and has issue living, Julian Wyndham, *b.* 1950,—James Lovell, *b.* 1956,—Jacqueline Anne, *b.* 1946. *Residence,*—22, Prince Albert Rd., Regent's Park, NW1.

     Issue of the late Hon. Thomas George Coventry, yst. son of 9th Earl, *b.* 1885, *d.* 1972: *m.* 1910, Alice, who *d.* 1961, da. of Thomas Ward, of Hasketon, Woodbridge, Suffolk:—
William Thomas (Suite 407, 1516, Davie Str., Vancouver, BC, Canada), *b.* 1911: *m.* 1st, 1940, Gwendolyn V. Burton; 2ndly, 19—, Irene Muriel Shea.——Victor Gerald CD (2491, Mowat St., Victoria, BC V8R 5T1, Canada), *b.* 1917; Lt. (QW) Cdn. Militia, Sup. Customs-Excise, Govt. of Canada: *m.* 1943, Constance Hilda, da. of the late Henry Edward Green, of S. Tottenham, N15, and has issue living, Angela Barbara, *b.* 1944: *m.* 1974, Robert Arthur Chapman, of 553, Schoolhouse, Coquitlam, BC, V3J 5P2, Canada.

          Granddaughter of the late Hon. Thomas George Coventry (ante):—
     Issue of the late Flight-Lieut. Robert George Coventry, R.A.F., *b.* 1913, *d.* (killed in action during European War) 1940: *m.* 1936, Olga (The Green, Pwllmeyrie, Chepstow, Mon.), only da. of the late John Henry Warhurst:—
Monica Anne (c/o National Westminster Bank, 27, Cannon St., EC4), *b.* 1939: *m.* 1967, James Stuart Underhill.

          Granddaughters of the late Henry Robert Beauclerk Coventry, only son of the late Capt. Henry Amelius Beauclerk Coventry, son of the late Hon. Henry Amelius Coventry, 2nd son of 8th Earl:—

Issue of the late Capt. Arthur Beauclerk Coventry, OBE, DSC, RN, *b.* 1900, *d.* 1971: *m.* 1928, Muriel Ethel Francis (Spring House, Golden Common, Winchester), da. of the late Hugh B. Craven, of Wheathills House, Kirk Langley, Derbys.:—
Sara Mary, *b.* 1929.——Auriol Susan, *b.* 1932: *m.* 1966, Wallace McMillan Reid, of 36, St. Peter's Sq., W6, and has issue living, Caspar James Beauclerk, *b.* 1970,—Frances Elizabeth, *b.* 1967.

Grandchildren of the late William George Coventry, son of the late Hon. William James Coventry, 4th son of 7th Earl :—
Issue of the late Gilbert William Coventry, *b.* 1868; *d.* 1947: *m.* 1st, 1902, Georgina Blanche, who *d.* 1922, dau. of the late Major William H. P. G. Bluett (formerly Lincolnshire Regt.), of Paignton; 2ndly, 1923, Margaret Charlotte, widow of Major G. D'Arcy Elliott-Cooper:—
(By 1st marriage) William George (248, Second Av., Kamloops, BC, Canada), *b.* 1903; formerly Lt. Indian Army; formerly U.K. Trade Commr., Winnipeg, Man., Canada: *m,* 1st, 1928 (m. diss. 19—), Charlotte Dorothy, who *d.* 1966, only da. of the late Verner G. Lyman, of Shanghai, China and Nebraska, USA; 2ndly, 1968, Ethel Olive Louise, da. of the late Benjamin Metcalfe, and widow of Ross Harvey Wilmot.——Gilbert Hugo Gordon, *b.* 1911; formerly Lt.-Cdr. Roy. Indian Navy; is a Rubber Planter; formerly Manager of Eng. Kee Kundong Estates, Tangkah, Jahore, Malaya: *m.* 1st, 1948 (divorce 1953), Alice, widow of Frank Tabrum; 2ndly, 19—, Mary Graham, of Mile End House, Aberdeen.——(By 2nd marriage) Anne, *b.* 1925: *m.* 1951, Stanley A. Peter Keevil, and has issue living, Sarah Anne, *b.* 1952,—Charlotte Fiona, *b.* 1956. *Residence,*—Ogwell Barton, nr. Newton Abbot, S. Devon.

Grandchildren of the late Gilbert William Coventry (ante):—
Issue of the late Com. Cecil Dick Bluett Coventry, D.S.C., R.D., R.N.R., *b.* 1905, *d.* 1952 : *m.* 1939, Anne Josephine Hale, who *d.* 1974, da. of the late Major H. J. Sherwood, RE:—
George William (21, Malvern Rd., Hampton, Middx.), *b.* 1939: *m.* 1965, Gillian Frances, da. of Frank W. R. Randall, of Wyke Regis, Weymouth, Dorset.——Peter Harold Sherwood (The Oaks, Lower Densome Wood, Wood Green, nr. Fordingbridge, Hants.), *b.* 1941: *m.* 1969, Kay Sandra, da. of the late Lt.-Cdr. Roy S. Baker-Faulkner, and has issue living, David Duncan Sherwood, *b.* 1973, Lynn Karen Sherwood, *b.* 1970.

Issue of the late Arthur John Clifford Coventry, *b.* 1909; *d.* 1965: *m.* 1st, 1937 (m. diss. 1947), Dulcie Alice Saxon; 2ndly, 1952, Margaret Nancy (29, Munro Rd., Queanbeyan, NSW), da. of W. Gell, of Gosford, NSW:—
(By 1st marriage) Gilbert John Henry, *b.* 1939.——Geoffrey Robert, *b.* 1941.——Margaret Elaine *b.* 1943.——(by 2nd marriage) Richard William, *b.* 1953.——Elizabeth Nancy, *b.* 1955.

Grandchildren of the late Rev. Henry William Coventry, son of Hon. William James Coventry (ante):—
Issue of the late Fulwar Cecil Ashton Coventry, O.B.E., *b.* 1874, *d.* 1944: *m.* 1917, Lorna Mary, who *d.* 1965, da. of the late Capt. Peregrine H. T. Fellowes, Ch. Constable of Hants:—
Digby Colquitt (120, Beaufort St., SW3), *b.* 1919; 1939-45 War (despatches, Chevalier of Order of, Leopold with palm, Belgian Croix de Guerre with palm): *m.* 1946, Marina von Wahl, and has issue living, Sebastian (81, Sinclair Rd., W14), *b.* 1946: *m.* 1965, Helen Kozlow of Paris, and has issue living, Adrian *b.* 1967, Alexandra *b.* 1966, Christine *b.* 1971,—Mark, *b.* 1952,—Elizabeth, *b.* 1947: *m.* 1967, Henry Pauwels, of 90, Avenue Mesens, Brussels,—Xenia, *b.* 1949.——Lorna Peggy Maria, *b.* 1922.

Granddaughter of the late Com. St. John Coventry, R.N., 2nd son of the late Frederick Coventry, el. son of the late Hon. John Coventry, 2nd son of 6th Earl:—
Issue of the late Capt. St. John Halford Coventry, *b.* 1866, *d.* 1920: *m.* 1895, Lilian Emmeline (who *d.* 1948, having *m.* 2ndly, 1921, Charles E. Allen), dau. of the late George Russell [D. Bedford, colls.]:—
Laura, *b.* 1899 : *m.* 1st, 1919, as his second wife, the Hon. William Arthur Horsley-Beresford, who *d.* 1949, having obtained a divorce 1928 [see B. Decies]; 2ndly, 1932 (marriage dissolved 1946), Reginald Robert Nicholls, who (together with his wife) assumed by Roy. Licence 1933 the surname of Coventry in lieu of his patronymic; 3rdly, 1950, John Hamilton Hamilton, who *d.* 1958.

Grandchildren of the late Harry Coventry (infra):—
Issue of the late St. John Coventry, *b.* 1901, *d.* 1963: *m.* 1930, Caroline Gertrude Hocking (Selwyn Village, Target St., Auckland, NZ):—
Henry John (7, Kim St., Khandallah, Wellington, NZ), *b.* 1932; Sqdn.-Ldr. RNZAF; Queen's Commendation 1964: *m.* 1958, Frances Winifred Clarke, and has issue living, Simon St. John, *b.* 1963,—David Henry Halford, *b.* 1969,—Rosalyn Barbara, *b.* 1959,—Adrienne Claire, *b.* 1960,—Anna Louise *b.* 1967.——Roger Michael (Awadale, Private Bag Masterton, NZ), *b.* 1934; an Asso. of Roy. Soc. of Health: *m.* 1961, Margaret Ann Cooke, and has issue living, Geoffrey Alan, *b.* 1969,—Jennifer Beryl *b.* 1965,—Sylvia Ann, *b.* 1967,—Marilyn Gay, *b.* 1968.——Alan Francis (1, Scott Cres., Mt. Isa, Qld., Aust. 4825), *b.* 1940; a Radio Technician: *m.* 1st, 1961 (m. diss. 1972), Patrina Rathbride, da. of Patrick Francis Dwan; 2ndly, 1972, Alison Leslie, da. of Dallas Evans, and has issue living (by 1st wife), Charles Raymond St. John, *b.* 1963,—Andrew Patrick Francis, *b.* 1964,—Charmaine Louise, *b.* 1961 (by 2nd wife) Richard Alan Penrose, *b.* 1971,—Katherine Margaret, *b.* 1973.——Bernadine Helen Mary, *b.* 1945: *m.* 1964, Enda Francis McBride, of 28B, Ebdentown St., Upper Hutt, NZ.

Grandchildren of the late Henry Halford Coventry, OE, yst. son of the late Frederick Coventry (ante):—
Issue of the late Harry Coventry, *b.* 1858, *d.* 1943: *m.* 1896, Evangeline who *d.* 1963, da. of Gustav August Hermann Hohenzollern (Rockel), of Carnarvon, Feilding, NZ:—
Frederick Halford, *b.* 1905: *m.* 1940, Dolores Rosamund Christine, younger dau. of the late Léon Dominic Ashton, of Cairo, Egypt, and has issue living, Edward Bernard Halford St. John, *b.* 1943; BSc London,—Elizabeth Mary Hephzibah, *b.* 1947; Dip. A. D.: *m.* 1968, Terence Carville of 3, Avon Walk, Shenley Hill Rd., Leighton Buzzard, Beds. *Residence,*—49, Brunswick Gdns., W8.

Grandchildren of the late John Coventry, *b.* 1845 (infra):—
Issue of the late John Joseph Coventry, *b.* 1882, *d.* 1950 : *m.* 1910, Margaret Camilla (who *d.* 1958, having *m.* 2ndly, 1955, Adrian Leonard Moreton, M.S., F.R.C.S., of Wilton House, Hungerford, Berks), dau. of C. H. H. Macartney, formerly of Foxhold, Newbury :—
Angela Mary Camilla (6, Princes House, Kensington Park Rd., W11), *b.* 1911: *m.* 1936, Herman George March, who *d.* 1955, and has issue living, Maxwell James, *b.* 1947,—Clare Elizabeth, *b.* 1939: *m.* 1960, Nigel Warrack, of Rectory Farm House, Church Enstone, Oxon., and has issue living, Richard Sebastian, *b.* 1963, Camilla Valentine, *b.* 1961, Tamsin Julia, *b.* 1967.——Barbara Mary St. John, *MBE, MB, BS, b.* 1912; MRCS England 1952, and LRCP London 1952, MB and BS London 1952; 1939-45 War as Junior Com. ATS (MBE); MBE (Mil.) 1945. *Residence,*—7, Westlands Grove, Portchester, Hants.——Catherine Margaret Mary, *b.* 1915: *m.* 1936, Herbert Alan Jones, and has issue living, Charles Alan (10, Rodway Rd., SW15), *b.* 1937: *m.* 1961, Margaret Elizabeth Cowper, and has issue living, Timothy Charles, *b.* 1963, Nicholas Alan, *b.* 1967, Patricia Margaret, *b.* 1965,—Celia Margaret, *b.* 1948. *Residence,*—4, Earls Court Gdns., SW5.——Dorothea Olivia, *b.* 1918: *m.* 1937 (m. diss. 1952), Adrian Charles Enthoven, and has issue living, Stephen Andrew (29, Thurloe Sq., SW7), *b.* 1939,—John Christopher, *b.* 1945. *Residence,*—

Issue of the late Bernard Seton Coventry, *b.* 1887, *d.* 1965: *m.* 1910, Annie, who *d.* 1960, da. of the late James Cunningham, MICE, of Cyprus:—
Rev. John Joseph Seton (Heythrop College; 11, Cavendish Sq., W1), *b.* 1915; ed. at Oxford Univ. (MA); in Holy Orders Roman Catholic Ch.

Grandson of Bernard Seton Coventry (ante):—
Issue of the late Anthony James Seton Coventry, *b.* 1913, *d.* 1955: *m.* 1942, Mollie Rosina
    (of End House, St. James' Close, Yarmouth, Isle of Wight), who *m.* 2ndly, 1961, Harold J.
    Hayles, who *d.* 1972, da. of J. Grummett, of St. Abbs Head, Coldingham, Berwickshire:—
John James Seton, *b.* 1955.

Grandchildren of the late John Coventry (*b.* 1793), 2nd son of the late Hon. John
    Coventry (ante):—
Issue of the late Bernard Coventry, C.I.E., *b.* 1859, *d.* 1929 : *m.* 1892, Ella Gordon, who *d.*
    1951, dau. of the late Edward Dalgliesh, formerly of Brook, Witley, Surrey :—
Muriel Mary, *b.* 1895.——Isabelle Mary, *b.* 1905. *Residence,*—Hawthorne Cottage, Frogham Fording-
bridge, Hants.

Issue of the late Francis Martin Coventry, *b.* 1863, *d.* 1917 : *m.* 1896, Amy Maud, who *d.* 1949,
    dau. of Henry W. J. Hill, formerly of 17, Cleveland Square, W., and Turcoliah, Bengal:—
Gerald Leslie, *b.* 1900; is a lay brother of Redemptorist Order. *Address,*—St. Joseph's, Bishop's
    Stortford, Herts.——Catherine Nora, *b.* 1906 : *m.* 1926, Hubert de Burgh Williams, and has issue
    living, Evan John, *b.* 1926 : *m.* 1952, Janet, dau. of Boyd Hill, of Ross-on-Wye, and has issue living,
    Alan Christopher *b.* 1956, Sheila Anne *b.* 1954,—Hubert Michael, *b.* 1927.

Grandchildren of the late Gilbert Walter Coventry (infra) :—
Issue of the late Francis Gilbert Coventry, *b.* 1892, *d.* 1960: *m.* 1929, Clara Dorothy, who
    d. 1970, da. of the late Robert Charles Brown:—
Noel, *b.* 1933 : *m.* 1960, Nola Elsie May, dau. of Robert Archibald Lindsay. *Residence,*—26, Corbett
    St., Paeroa, New Zealand.——Francis Henry, *b.* 1934: *m.* 1961, Shirley Ann, dau. of the late
    Thomas Henry Lionel Turner.——Clara Doreen , *b.* 1930. *Residence,*—5, Francis St., Paeroa,
    New Zealand.

Grandchildren of the late Thomas William Coventry, son of the late Hon.
    Thomas William Coventry, 3rd son of 6th Earl :—
Issue of the late Gilbert Walter Coventry, *b.* 1837, *d.* 1909: *m.* 1880, Margaret, who
    d. 1894, dau. of the late Hugh Milligan :—
Arthur Roger, *b.* 1894. *Residence,*—15, Rawhiti Street, Nelson, Tahuna, New Zealand.——Olivia
    Beryl, *b.* 1889.——Bathilda Adele, *b.* 1890. *Residence,*—

PREDECESSORS.—[1] *Sir* Thomas Coventry, K.B. (whose ancestor John Coventry was
    Lord Mayor of London 1426), Recorder of London 1615, Solicitor and Attorney-Gen. 1616,
    and Lord Keeper of the Great Seal 1625; cr. *Baron Coventry,* of Aylesborough, co.
    Worcester (peerage of England) 1628; *d.* 1640; *s.* by his son [2] Thomas, 2nd Baron; *s.*
    1661; *s.* by his son [3] George, 3rd Baron; *s.* by his son [4] John, 4th Baron; *d.* unmarried
    1687; *s.* by his uncle [5] Thomas, 5th Baron, 2nd son of 2nd Baron; cr. *Viscount Deerhurst*
    and *Earl of Coventry* (peerage of England) 1697, with limitation to the grandsons of Walter,
    youngest brother of 1st Baron; *d.* 1699; *s.* by his son [6] Thomas, 2nd Earl; *d.* 1710; *s.* by
    his son [7] Thomas, 3rd Earl; *d.* a minor 1712; *s.* by his uncle [8] Gilbert, 4th Earl, 2nd son
    of 1st Earl; *d.s.p.* 1719, when the Barony became extinct, and the other honours reverted to
    his kinsman [9] William, P.C., 5th Earl, grandson of Walter Coventry (ante); succes-
    sively a Clerk of the Green Cloth, M.P. for Bridport, and Lord-Lieut. of Worcestershire: *d.*
    1751; *s.* by his son [10] George William, 6th Earl; *d.* 1809; *s.* by his son [11] George
    William, 7th Earl; Recorder of Worcester and High Steward of Tewkesbury; *d.* 1831; *s.* by
    his son [12] George William, 8th Earl; Lord-Lieut. of Worcestershire; *d.* 1843; *s.* by his
    grandson [13] George William, P.C. (son of George William, Viscount Deerhurst, el. son
    of 8th Earl), 9th Earl *b.* 1838 ; Capt. and Gold Stick of Corps of Gentlemen at Arms 1877-80
    and 1880-85, Master of the Buckhounds 1886-92 and 1895-1990, and Lord-Lieut. of Worcester-
    shire 1891-1903 : *m.* 1865, Blanche, who *d.* 1930, dau. of 2nd Earl of Craven, *d.* 1930 ; *s.* by his
    grandson [14] George William Reginald Victor (son of the late George William, Viscount
    Deerhurst, el. son of 9th Earl), 10th Earl, *b.* 1900 : *m.* 1921, the Hon. Nesta Donne Philipps (who
    m. 2ndly, 1953, Major Terence Vincent Fisher-Hoch), dau. of 1st Baron Kylsant (ext.); *d.* (killed
    in action during European War) 1940 ; *s.* by his only son [15] George William, 11th Earl and
    present peer; also Viscount Deerhurst.

COVENTRY, LORD BISHOP OF.   (Bardsley.)

Rt. Rev. Cuthbert Killick Norman Bards-
ley, *C.B.E.,* son of the late Rev. Canon J. U. N.
Bardsley ; *b.* March 28th, 1907 ; ed. at Eton
and at New Coll., Oxford (B.A. 1929, M.A. 1934);
was Curate of All Hallows, Barking-by-the-
Tower 1932-4, R. of Woolwich 1940-44, Provost
of Southwark Cathedral, and R. of St. Saviour's,
Southwark 1944-7, and Archbishop's Episcopal
Representative to the Armed Forces 1947 ;
Hon. Canon of Canterbury 1948 ; consecrated
Bishop of Croydon (Suffragan for Diocese of
Canterbury) 1947 ; translated 5th Lord Bishop
of Coventry (2nd Foundation) 1956; CBE:
m. 1972, Ellen Mitchell.

Patron of sixty on-six livings, and a further thirteen in
conjunction with other patrons, two Archdeaconries, a provostship, and fifteen Hon. Canonries.

Episcopal Signature—"Cuthbert Coventry."

Arms of the See.—Gules, a cross potent quadrate in the
centre argent, within a bordure of the last charged with
eight torteaux.

This See, which prior to 1836 was united to the See of
Lichfield, was refounded in 1918.

Residence,—The Bishop's House, 23, Davenport Rd., Coventry. *Club,*—United Service.

COWDRAY, VISCOUNT. (Pearson.) [Viscount U.K. 1917, Bt. U.K. 1894.]

WEETMAN JOHN CHURCHILL PEARSON, *T.D.*, 3rd Viscount and 3rd Baronet; *b.* Feb. 27th, 1910 ; *s.* 1933 ; ed. at Eton, and at Ch. Ch., Oxford ; formerly Capt. 98th (Surrey and Sussex) Field Regt. R.A. (T.A.) ; is a D.L. for Sussex ; European War 1939-40 (severely wounded) ; was Parliamentary Private Sec. to Under-Sec. of State for Air 1941-42: *m.* 1st, 1939, Lady Anne Pamela Bridgeman, from whom he obtained a divorce 1950, dau. of 5th Earl of Bradford ; 2ndly, 1953, Elizabeth Georgiana Mather, 2nd dau. of Anthony Henry Mather Jackson [see Mather-Jackson, Bt.], and has issue by 1st and 2nd marriages.

Arms,—Per fesse indented gules and or, in chief two suns in splendour and in base a demi-gryphon couped, all counter-changed. Crest,—In front of a demi-gryphon gules holding between its claws a millstone proper thereon a mill-rind sable, a sun in splendour. Supporters,—*Dexter*, a diver holding in his exterior hand his helmet ; *sinister*, a Mexican peon ; both proper.

Seats,—Cowdray Park, Midhurst : Dunecht, Aberdeenshire. Address,—17th Floor, Millbank Tower, Millbank, SW1.

SONS LIVING. (*By 1st marriage.*)
Hon. MICHAEL ORLANDO WEETMAN, *b.* June 17th, 1944 ; ed. at Gordonstoun.
(*By 2nd marriage.*)
Hon. Charles Anthony, *b.* 1956.

DAUGHTERS LIVING. (*By 1st marriage.*)
Hon. Mary Teresa, *b.* 1940.
Hon. Liza Jane, *b.* 1942 : *m.* 1967, Malcolm MacNaughton, of 1302, Canada Rd., Woodside, Cal., USA 94062, and has issue living, Justin John, *b.* 1972,—Natasha Anne, *b.* 1969.
(*By 2nd marriage.*)
Hon. Lucy, *b.* 1954 : *m.* 1972, the Hon. Luis Hector Juan Sosa-Basualdo, of 1, Sosa, Argentina, and 156, East 65th St., New York, NY, 10021, USA, and has issue living, Charlotte Pearson, *b.* 1974.
Hon. Rosanna, *b.* 1959.

SISTERS LIVING.
Hon. Daisy Yoskyl Consuelo (*Baroness McCorquodale of Newton*), *b.* 1906 : *m.* 1st, 1932, Lieut. the Hon. Robert Brampton (Robin) Gurdon, who *d.* (killed in action during European War) 1942, el. son of 2nd Baron Cranworth ; 2ndly, 1944, Lieut.-Col. Alistair Monteith Gibb, Hon. Col. Roy. Wilts Yeo., who *d.* 1955, son of Sir Alexander Gibb, G.B.E., C.B., F.R.S.; 3rdly, 1962, the 1st Baron McCorquodale of Newton, who *d.* 1971, when the title became ext., and has issue living, (by 1st m.) [see B. Cranworth],—(by 2nd m.) Jane Elizabeth Angela (*Countess of Aboyne*), *b.* 1946 : *m.* 1972, Granville Charles Gomer Gordon, Earl of Aboyne, son of 12th Marquess of Huntly. *Residences*,—50E, Cornwall Gdns., SW7 ; Cotswold Park, Cirencester, Glos.
Hon. (Beryl) Nancy (*Viscountess Blakenham*), *b.* 1908 : *m.* 1934, the 1st Viscount Blakenham. *Residences*,—10, Holland Park, W11 3TH ; Cottage Farm, Little Blakenham, nr. Ipswich.
Hon. Angela (twin), *b.* 1910 : *m.* 1st, 1930, Lieut.-Col. George Anthony Murray, R.A., who *d.* (killed in action in Italy) 1945 [see D. Atholl] ; 2ndly, 1950, Lieut.-Col. Robert Modan Thorne Campbell-Preston, OBE, MC, and has issue living, (by 1st m.), [see D. Atholl], (by 2nd m.), Sarah Hope, *b.* 1951 : *m.* 1973, James Michael Troughton. *Residences*,—31, Marlborough Hill, NW8 ; Ardchattan Priory, Connel, Argyll.
Hon. Brenda Ruby, *b.* 1912 : *m.* 1st, 1934, Group-Capt. Paul Willert, R.A.F., who obtained a divorce 1948 [Simpson. Bt., ext] ; 2ndly, 1948, Hugh Carter, and has issue living, (by 1st marriage) Wanda Catherine, *b.* 1936 : *m.* 1958, John George Rodway Rix, of Wodehouse, Headley, Bordon, Hants., and has issue living, Jeremy Hugh Rodway *b.* 1962, David John Rodway *b.* 1965, Sally Elizabeth, *b.* 1959,—Pauline, *b.* 1944 : *m.* 1974, John Dorman, son of Sir Maurice Henry Dorman, GCMG, GCVO,—(by 2nd marriage) Hugh Harold John, *b.* 1952. *Residences*, 34, Prince's Court, Knightsbridge, SW3 ; Wakeham, Rogate, Petersfield, Hants.
Hon. (Helena) Daphne. *b.* 1918 : *m.* 1939, Lieut.-Col. John Lakin. T.D., late Warwickshire Yeo. [see Lakin, Bt. colls.]. *Residence*,—Hammerwood House, Iping, Midhurst, Sussex.

WIDOW LIVING OF SON OF FIRST VISCOUNT.
Ethel Elizabeth PEARSON, dau. of John J. Lewis, of Hove ; resumed surname of Pearson 1926: *m.* 1st, 1909, the (Francis) Geoffrey Pearson, who *d.* (killed in action) 1914 ; 2ndly, 1918, Air-Commodore Henry John Francis Hunter, C.B.E., M.C., R.A.F., from whom she obtained a divorce 1926 [B. Dormer], and has issue living by 1st marriage [see colls., infra]. *Residence*,—506, Beatty House, Dolphin Sq., S.W.1. *Club*,—Curzon House.

COLLATERAL BRANCHES LIVING.
Issue of the late Hon. (Bernard) Clive Pearson, 2nd son of 1st Viscount, *b.* 1887, *d.* 1965: *m.* 1915, the Hon. Alicia Mary Dorothea Knatchbull-Hugessen, who *d.* 1974, da. of 1st Baron Brabourne:—
Veronica Mary, *b.* 1916: *m.* 1st, 1940, Albert Marcus Rueff, 2nd Lt. Tower Hamlets Rifles (TA), who *d.* (killed in action) 1941 ; 2ndly, 1950, Patrick Arthur Tritton, of Parham Park, Pulborough, Sussex.——Lavinia, *b.* 1919: *m.* 1939, Maj. (Charles) Michael Smiley, late Rifle Bde, of Castle Fraser, Sauchen, Aberdeenshire [see Smiley, Bt., colls.].——Elisabeth Dione (*Baroness Gibson*), *b.* 1920: *m.* 1945, Baron Gibson (Life Baron), of Penn's Rocks, Groombridge, Sussex.

Issue of the late Hon. Francis Geoffrey Pearson, 3rd son of 1st Viscount, *b.* 1891, *d.* (killed in action) 1914 : *m.* 1909, Ethel Elizabeth PEARSON [(ante) ; she *m.* 2ndly, 1918, Group-Capt. Henry John Francis Hunter, M.C., R.A.F. [B. Dormer], from whom she obtained a divorce 1926], dau. of John Lewis, of Hove :—
Joan Cinnetta, *b.* 1912 : *m.* 1932, William Antony Acton, and has issue living, Caroline Jane, *b.* 1933: *m.* 1955, Major Hugh Halliday Trevor Dawson, late Scots Guards, of 3, Mulberry Walk, SW3, only son of Com. Sir Hugh Trevor Dawson, 2nd Bt., CBE, RN. *Residence*,—La Foscarina, Komeno, Gouvia, Corfu, Greece.

PREDECESSORS.—[1] *Right Hon. Sir* WEETMAN DICKINSON Pearson, G.C.V.O., P.C., son of the late George Pearson, of Brickendonbury, Hertford ; *b.* 1856 ; was Pres. of the firm of S. Pearson

& Son, Ltd., of Westminster, S.W., and High Steward of Colchester 1897-1927 ; Pres. of Air
Board Jan to Nov. 1917; M.P. for Colchester (L)1895 to 1910 ; Lord Rector of Aberdeen Univ.
1918-21; Hon. Freeman of Aberdeen and Colchester; cr. a *Baronet* 1894, *Baron Cowdray*, of
Midhurst, co. Sussex (peerage of United Kingdom) 1910, and *Viscount Cowdray*, of Cowdray,
Sussex (peerage of United Kingdom) 1917 : *m.* 1881, Annie, *G.B.E.*, who *d.* 1932, dau. of the
late Sir John Cass, of Bradford, Yorkshire ; *d.* 1927 ; *s.* by his son [2] WEETMAN HAROLD
MILLER, 2nd Viscount, *b.* 1882 ; M.P. for N.-E., or Eye, Div. of Suffolk (L) 1906-18 : *m.* 1905.
Agnes Beryl, who *d.* 1948, dau. of the late Lord Edward Spencer-Churchill; *d.* 1933 ; *s.* by his
only son [3] WEETMAN JOHN CHURCHILL, 3rd Viscount and present peer; also Baron Cowdray.

COWLEY, EARL.   (Wellesley.)   [Earl U.K. 1857.]

Moreover, one thing is necessary.

PORRO UNUM
NECESSARIUM
EST

RICHARD FRANCIS WELLESLEY, 6th
Earl; *b.* June 12th, 1946; *s.* 1968; ed. at
Eton, and Birmingham Univ.; a Lord-in-
Waiting (Political) to HM Jan. to March
1974: *m.* 1971, Maria Delia, yr. da. of
Enrique Buenaño, of Vicente Lopez,
2602 7°A, Buenos Aires, and has issue.

Arms,—Quarterly: 1st and 4th gules, a cross
argent, between twenty plates, five in each quarter
saltirewise, *Wellesley;* 2nd and 3rd or, a lion rampant gules, ducally gorged gold, *Cowley.* Crest,—Out
of a ducal coronet or, a demi-lion rampant gules,
holding a spear erect proper, and thereon flowing a
pennon argent, charged with the cross of St. George.
Supporters,—Two lions, gules, ducally gorged and
chained or, and charged on the shoulder with an
annulet for difference.

Residence,—5, Stanhope Gdns., SW7 5RG.

DAUGHTER LIVING.
Lady Alexia Anne Elizabeth, *b.* 1973.

UNCLES LIVING.   (*Sons of 4th Earl.*)
Hon. GARRET GRAHAM; Harvard (San Francisco) Club;
b. July 30th, 1934; ed. at Univ. of S. California (BS),
and at Harvard Univ. (MBA); US Army Counter,
Intelligence Corps 1957-60; an investment counsel
with Dodge & Cox, San Francisco: *m.* 1960, Elizabeth Suzanne, da. of the late Haynes Lennon of
S. Carolina, and has issue living, Garret Graham,
b. 1965,—Tara Lennon, *b.* 1962.

Hon. Brian Timothy (4752, La Villa Marina, Marina Del Rey, Cal., USA), *b.* 1938 ; ed. at Arizona
State Coll., Denver Univ., Colorado, and Nevada Univ. (BS); Management Official, US Treas.
Dept., Los Angeles: *m.* 1st, 1961, (*m.* diss. in Reno 1964), Patricia Tribby; 2ndly (in Reno)
1966, Karen Elizabeth Bradbury, of Reno, Nevada, USA.

AUNT LIVING.   (*Daughter of 4th Earl.*)
Lady Colleen, *b.* 1925: *m.* 1945, Paul A. Hanlon, MD, late Capt. US Army, and has issue living,
Paul Christian, *b.* 1946,—Gavin Edward, *b.* 1948,—Christopher Peter, *b.* 1951,—Timothy Patrick,
b. 1955,—Richard Francis, *b.* 1957,—Colleen Patricia, *b.* 1958,—Jennifer Mary, *b.* 1960. *Residence*,
—543, Westmoreland Avenue, Kingston, Pennsylvania, U.S.A.

GREAT UNCLE LIVING.   (*Son of 3rd Earl.*)
Ho ı. (Henry) Gerald Valerian Francis, *b.* 1907, ed. at Harrow: *m.* 1st, 1929 (marriage dissolved 1953),
Sabia, dau. of the late Edward Robert Kennedy [see Kennedy, Bt., colls.] ; 2ndly, 1954 (marriage
annulled 1955), Nancy Joan, only da. of B. C. Hilliam. *Residence*,—

GREAT AUNT LIVING.   (*Daughter of 3rd Earl.*)
Lady Diana Mary (*Baroness Glentoran*), *b.* 1914: *m.* 1933, the 2nd Baron Glentoran. *Residence*,—
Drumadarragh House, Doagh, co. Antrim.

MOTHER LIVING.
Elizabeth Anne (P.O. Box 285, Paget, Bermuda), da. of the late Pelham Rawstorn Papillon, DSO,
of Crowhurst, Sussex, and widow of Fl.-Lt. Stephen Alers Hankey, RAF: *m.* 1944 (m. diss. 1950),
Denis Arthur, Viscount Dangan (later the 5th Earl), who *d.* 1968.

WIDOWS LIVING OF FOURTH AND FIFTH EARLS
MARY ELSIE (HIMES) (*Mary, Countess Cowley*), of San Francisco, California, USA: *m.* 1933, the 4th
Earl, who *d.* 1962. *Residence*,—25, Biltmore Estates, Phœnix, Arizona, USA; Crystal Bay, Lake
Tahoe, Nevada, USA.
JANET ELIZABETH MARY (*Janet, Countess Cowley*), da. of Ramiah Doraswamy Aiya, FRCS, of Ystrad,
Denbigh, N. Wales: *m.* 1961, as his 3rd wife, the 5th Earl, who *d.* 1968.

COLLATERAL BRANCH LIVING. (*In remainder to Barony of Cowley of Wellesley.*

Grandson of the late Gerald Edward Wellesley, son of the late Hon. William Henry
George Wellesley, 2nd son of 1st Baron Cowley of Wellesley:—
Issue of the late Capt. Gerald Valerian Wellesley, MC, *b.* 1885, *d.* 1961: *m.* 1931, Mrs. Elizabeth
Thornton Gilbey, (who m. 3rdly, 1965, Basil Harvey) (2, Douro Place, W8), da. of Otho
Ball, of Chicago, USA:—
Julian Valerian, *b.* 1933: *m.* 1965, Mrs. Elizabeth Joan Hall, da. of Cyril Stocken, and has issue living,
William Valerian, *b.* 1966,—Kate Elizabeth, *b.* 1970. *Residences*,—6, Hale House ,34 .De Vere
Gdns., W8; Tidebrook Manor, Wadhurst, Sussex.

PREDECESSORS.—[1] *Hon. Sir* HENRY Wellesley, *G.C.B.*, 5th son of 1st Earl of Mornington, and brother of Marquess Wellesley and 1st Duke of Wellington: *b.* 1773: an eminent
diplomatist; cr. *Baron Cowley of Wellesley* (peerage of United Kingdom) 1828: *m.* 1st, 1803, Lady
Charlotte Cadogan, who *d.* 1853 (and from whom he had obtained a divorce 1810); she *m.* 2ndly,
1810, the 1st Marquess of Anglesey), da. of 1st Earl Cadogan; 2ndly, 1816, Lady Georgiana Charlotte
Augusta Cecil, who *d.* 1860, da. of 1st Marquess of Salisbury; *d.* 1847; *s.* by his son [2] HENRY
RICHARD CHARLES, 2nd Baron, *KG*, *GCB*, *PC*, *DCL*; *b.* 1804; was Min. Plen. in Switzerland 1848-49;
Envoy Extraor. and Min. Plen. at Frankfort 1849-51, and to Germanic Confederation 1851-52, and
Ambassador Extraor. and Min. Plen. to France 1852-67; cr. *Viscount Dangan* and *Earl Cowley*
(peerage of United Kingdom) 1857: *m.* 1833, the Hon. Olivia Cecilia Fitzgerald de Ros, who *d.* 1885,
dau. of Charlotte (in her own right), Baroness de Ros; *d.* July 15th, 1884; *s.* by his son [3] WILLIAM
HENRY WELLESLEY, 2nd Earl, *b.* 1834; Lieut.-Col. Coldstream Guards: *m.* 1863, Emily Gwendolin,
who *d.* 1932, dau. of Col. Thomas Peers Williams, M.P., of Temple House, Great Marlow; *d.* 1895;
s. by his son [4] HENRY ARTHUR MORNINGTON, 3rd Earl, *b.* 1866: *m.* 1st, 1889, Lady Violet Nevill,
who *d.* 1910 (having obtained a divorce 1897), dau. of 1st Marquess of Abergavenny; 2ndly, 1905, the

Hon. Millicent Florence Eleanor, who obtained a divorce 1913, da. of the 1st Baron Nunburnholme, and formerly wife of Sir Charles Edward Cradock-Hartopp, 5th Bt.; 3rdly, 1914, Clare Florence Mary, who d. 1949, da. of Sir Francis George Stapleton, 8th Bt.; d. 1919; s. by his son [5] CHRISTIAN ARTHUR, 4th Earl, b. 1890: m. 1st (in New York, USA), 1914, Mae Pickard (an actress), of Memphis, Tennessee, USA, who d. 1946, and from whom he had obtained a divorce (at Reno, Nevada) 1933; 2ndly, (at Reno, Nevada) 1933, Mary Elsie HIMES, of San Francisco, Calif., USA; d. 1962; s. by his son [6] DENIS ARTHUR, BEM, 5th Earl, b. 1921; Chm. and Managing Dir. of City Prudential Building Soc. 1962-65: m. 1st, 1944 (m. diss. 1950) Elizabeth Anne, da. of the late Pelham Rawstorn Papillon, DSO, of Crowhurst, Sussex, and widow of Fl.-Lt. Stephen Alers Hankey, RAF; 2ndly, 1950, Mrs. Annette Nancy Doughty Simmonds, who d. 1959, da. of Maj. J. J. O'Hara; 3rdly, 1961, Janet Elizabeth Mary, da. of Ramiah Doraswamy Aiyar, FRCS, of Ystrad, Denbigh, N. Wales; d. 1968; s. by his only son [7] RICHARD FRANCIS, 6th Earl, and present peer; also Viscount Dangan, and Baron Cowley of Wellesley.

COZENS-HARDY, BARON. (Cozens-Hardy.) [Baron U.K. 1914.]
[Title and Name pronounced "Kuzzens-Hardy."]

HERBERT ARTHUR COZENS-HARDY, OBE, 4th Baron; b. June 8th, 1907; s. 1956; ed. at Winchester, and Worcester Coll., Oxford; a JP and a DL for Merseyside; GCStJ; Chm. of Council of Order of St. John for Lancs. since 1947 and Bailiff of Egle, Order of St. John since 1971, and Chm. of Lancs. Magistrates' Courts Cttee. 1952-74; OBE (Civil) 1966.

Arms,—Quarterly, 1st and 4th per chevron argent and or, in chief two fireballs sable, fired proper, *Hardy;* 2nd and 3rd azure, a lion rampant or, gorged with a ducal coronet of the field, in chief two barrulets of the second, *Cozens.* **Crests,—**1st, a dexter arm embowed holding in the hand an eagle's head erased fessewise proper, *Hardy;* 2nd, a lion rampant or, vulned at the shoulder proper, and gorged with a ducal coronet azure, *Cozens.* **Supporters,** —*Dexter,* an eagle argent, wings endorsed gules, holding in the beak a rose argent, leaved and slipped proper; *sinister,* a winged lion queue fourchée argent, wings endorsed gules. **Second Motto,—**Je sers.

Badge,—Upon a field azure diaper of mascles and fleurs-de-lys or, an estoc or thrusting sword, the blade enfiled with a Baron's coronet proper, the guillons terminating on fleurs-de-lys or, the *hilt* also proper, and the pomel or thereon a rose argent.

Seat,—Letheringsett Hall, Holt, Norfolk. *Residence,*—Parkside, Knowsley Park, Prescot, Merseyside.

SISTERS LIVING.

Hon. Beryl Gladys, OBE, b. 1911; JP for Norfolk; Chm. of World Cttee., World Assocn. of Girl Guides and Girl Scouts since 1972; OBE (Civil) 1971. *Residence,*—Letheringsett Hall, Holt, Norfolk.

Hon. Helen Rosemary, b. 1918: m. 1953, Brigadier Douglas Vandeleur Phelps, T.D., J.P., D.L., of Bayfield Hall, Holt, Norfolk.

DAUGHTER LIVING OF SECOND BARON.

Hon. Irma (Warborough House, Stiffkey, Wells next Sea, Norfolk), b. 1896: m. 1921, Lt.-Col. Frederick Marshman Bailey, CIE, who d. 1967.

PREDECESSORS.—[1] *Rt. Hon. Sir* HERBERT HARDY Cozens-Hardy, P.C., 2nd son of the late William Hardy Cozens-Hardy, J.P., of Letheringsett Hall, Holt, Norfolk; b. 1838; Commr. of the Great Seal 1913; M.P. for Norfolk, N. Div. (L) 1885-99; Judge of the High Court of Justice 1899-1901, a Lord Justice of Appeal 1901-7, and Master of the Rolls 1907-18; cr. *Baron Cozens-Hardy* of Letheringsett, Norfolk (peerage of United Kingdom) 1914: m. 1866, Maria, who d. 1886, dau. of Thomas Hepburn, J.P., of Clapham Common; d. 1920; s. by his el. son [2] WILLIAM HEPBURN, K.C., 2nd Baron, b. 1868; European War 1915-18 as Com. R.N.V.R.; M.P. for S. Div. of Norfolk (Co. L) 1918-20: m. 1895, Constance Gertrude Lilian, who d. 1957, dau. of the late Col. Sir William Everett, K.C.M.G.; d. 1924; s. by his brother [3] EDWARD HERBERT, 3rd Baron; b. 1873: m. 1906, Gladys Lily, who d. 1975, of the late Arthur Wrigley Cozens-Hardy, of Cley Hall, Norfolk; d. 1956; s. by his son [4] HERBERT ARTHUR, 4th baron and present peer.

CRAIGAVON, VISCOUNT. (Craig.) [Viscount U.K. 1927, Bt. U.K. 1918.]
[Title pronounced "Craigavvon."]

JANRIC FRASER CRAIG, 3rd Viscount, and 3rd Baronet; b. June 9th, 1944; s. 1974; ed. at Eton, and London Univ. (BA); ACA.

Arms,—Gules, a fesse ermine between three bridges of as many arches proper. **Crest,—**A demi-lion rampant per fesse gules and sable, holding in the dexter paw a mullet or. **Supporters,—***Dexter,* a Constable of the Ulster Special Constabulary, his hand resting on a rifle; *sinister,* a Private of the Royal Ulster Rifles, armed and accontred, both proper.

Residence,—Flat 13, 65, Courtfield Gdns., SW5 0NQ.

SISTERS LIVING.

Hon. Janitha Stormont, b. 1940: m. 1965, Gordon Robert MacInnes, ACIS, AIB, of 22, Grosvenor Rd., Richmond, Surrey, TW10 6PB, and has issue living, Avila, b. 1967,—Córdova, b. 1971,—Jimena, b. 1975.

Hon. Jacaranda Fiona, b. 1949: m. 1972, Dudley Francis MacDonald, of 25, Chase Court, Beaufort Gdns., SW3.

AUNT LIVING. (*Daughter of 1st Viscount.*)

Hon. Ellinor Aileen Cecil (West Lodge, Cluny Castle, Sauchen, Aberdeenshire), *b.* 1907: *m.* 1929 (m. diss. 1943), Capt. Robert Gordon Hood Linzee, CB, CBE, RN, and has issue living, Robert Alexander Craig LINZEE GORDON (Cluny Castle, Sauchen, Aberdeenshire), *b.* 1930; assumed, by decree of Lyon Court 1967 the name of Gordon: *m.* 1958, Frances Sheena, yr. da. of Colin Maclennan of Woodend Farm, Sauchen, Aberdeenshire, and has issue living, Robert James Nicholas *b.* 1959, Philip Alexander Hood *b.* 1962, Andrew Damian *b.* 1966, Frances Susanna (twin) *b.* 1966.

WIDOW LIVING OF SECOND VISCOUNT.

(ANGELA) FIONA (*Viscountess Craigavon*), (27, Launceston Place, W8), da. of the late Percy Tatchell, MRCS, LRCP: *m.* 1939, the 2nd Viscount, who *d.* 1974.

COLLATERAL BRANCH LIVING.

　Issue of the late Maj. the Hon. (Patrick William) Dennis Craig, MBE, yr. son of 1st Viscount, *b.* 1906, *d.* 1972: *m.* 1st, 1931 (m. diss. 1935), Aline, Margaret Mary McLaren, da. of the late J. Cumming; 2ndly, 1947, Marjorie Joy, who *d.* 1974, da. of Algernon Cecil Newton, RA:—

(By 1st m.) Deirdre (48, St. John's Rd., Eastbourne), *b.* 1931: *m.* 1st 1951 (m. diss. 1959), Jonathan Craven, late 9L; 2ndly, 1959, Cyril Vernon Connolly, CBE, writer, who *d.* 1974, and has issue living (by 1st. m.), Simon James, *b.* 1954; ed. at Eton,—Sarah, *b.* 1952,—(by 2nd m.), Matthew Vernon, *b.* 1970,—Cressida Louisa Vernon, *b.* 1960.

PREDECESSORS.—[1] JAMES CRAIG, PC, LLD, DCL, DL, 6th son of the late James Craig, JP, of Craigavon and Tyrella, co. Down; *b.* 1871; was Treasurer of HM Household 1916-18, Parliamentary Sec. to Min. of Pensions 1919-20, Financial Sec. to Admiralty 1920-21, and Prime Min. of N. Ireland 1921-40; sat as M.P. for E. Down Div. of Down Co. (*U* and *Tariff Reformer*) 1906-18, and for Mid. Div. thereof 1918-21, and for Down Co. (*U*) in Parliament of N. Ireland 1921-29, and for N. Down Div. of Down Co. 1929-40; cr. a *Baronet* 1918, and *Viscount Craigavon*, of Stormont, co. Down (peerage of United Kingdom) 1927: *m.* 1905, Dame Cecil Mary Nowell Dering, *D.B.E.*, who *d.* 1960, dau. of the late Sir Daniel Alfred Anley Tupper, M.V.O., formerly Assist. Comptroller of Lord Chamberlain's Depart. and Sergeant-at-Arms to H.M. King George V; *d.* 1940; *s.* by his son [2] JAMES, 2nd Viscount; *b.* 1906: *m.* 1939, (Angela) Fiona, da. of the late Percy Tatchell, MRCS, LRCP, of 29, Barkston Gdns., SW5; *d.* 1974; *s.* by his son [3] JANRIC FRASER, 3rd Viscount and present peer.

CRAIGMYLE, BARON. (Shaw.) [Baron U.K. 1929.]

Mercy, Fidelity, Right.

THOMAS DONALD MACKAY SHAW, 3rd Baron; *b.* Nov. 17th, 1923; *s.* 1944; ed. at Eton, and at Trin. Coll., Oxford; 1939-45 War as Sub-Lt. (A.) R.N.V.R.: *m.* 1955, Anthea Esther Christine Theresa, dau. of the late Edward Charles Rich, of 31, Yeomans Row, S.W.3, and has issue.

Arms,—Ermine, a fir tree growing out of a mount in base proper, between two piles azure, issuing from a chief gules charged with a scroll argent, its seal pendant proper between two lymphads or. Crest,—A demi-savage holding in his dexter hand a club resting on his shoulder proper. Supporters,—*Dexter*, a lion rampant gules; *sinister*, a kangaroo proper.

Residences,—18, The Boltons, SW10 9SY Scottas, Knoydart, Inverness-shire.

SONS LIVING.

Hon. THOMAS COLUMBA, *b.* Oct. 19th, 1960.
Hon. Justin Edward Magnus, *b.* 1965.
Hon. Alexander Joseph Ranald, *b.* 1971.

DAUGHTERS LIVING.

Hon. Alison Margaret, *b.* 1956.
Hon. Catriona Mary, *b.* 1958.
Hon. Madeleine Claire, *b.* 1963.

SISTERS LIVING.

Hon. (Margaret) Jean, *b.* 1915 : *m.* 1949, Shirl Mussell, who *d.* 1956, and has issue living, Anabe Margaret, *b.* 1954,—Lisabel Jean, *b.* 1956. *Residence*,—Dyke Croft, Ravenglass, Cumbria.

Hon. Thalia Mary, *b.* 1918 : *m.* 1939, Winton Basil Dean, and has issue living, Stephen Nicholas Winton, *b.* 1946. *Residence*,—Hambledon Hurst, Godalming, Surrey.

Hon. Elspeth Ruth, *b.* 1921: *m.* 1945, Archibald James Florence Macdonald, J.P., and has issue living, Michael Christopher Archibald, *b.* 1947,—Ian Alexander James, *b.* 1950. *Residence*,—22, Heath Drive, Hampstead, N.W.3.

AUNT LIVING. (*Daughter of 1st Baron.*)

Hon. Isabel: *m.* 1915, Capt. Richard H. Vaughan-Thompson, Roy. Fusiliers (City of London Regt.), who *d.* (killed in action during European War) 1916. *Residence*,—Inglewood, East Hill Rd., Oxted, Surrey.

PREDECESSORS.—[1] *Rt. Hon.* THOMAS Shaw, *P.C., K.C., LL.D.*, son of Alexander Shaw, of Dunfermline, Fifeshire; *b.* 1850; was Solicitor-Gen. for Scotland 1894-5, and Lord Advocate 1905-9, M.P. for Hawick (*L*) 1892-1909; became a Lord of Appeal in Ordinary with title of *Baron Shaw of Dunfermline*, co. Fife (Life Baron) 1909; cr. *Baron Craigmyle*, of Craigmyle, co. Aberdeen (Peerage of United Kingdom) 1929: *m.* 1879, Elsie Stephen, who *d.* 1939, dau. of George Forrest, of Ludquharn, Aberdeenshire; *d.* 1937; *s.* by his son [2] ALEXANDER, 2nd Baron; *b.* 1883; sat as M.P. for Kilmarnock Dist. (*L*) 1915-18, and for Kilmarnock Div. of Buteshire and Ayrshire 1918-23 : *m.* 1913, Lady Margaret Cargill Mackay, who *d.* 1958, el. dau. of 1st Earl of Inchcape; *d.* 1944; *s.* by his son [3] THOMAS DONALD MACKAY, 3rd Baron and present peer

CRAIGTON, BARON. (Browne.) [Life Baron 1959.]

(JACK) NIXON BROWNE, C.B.E., P.C., son of Edwin Gilbert Izod, of Rugby, and Johannesburg, S. Africa : b. Sept. 3rd, 1904; assumed the surname of Browne, in lieu of his patronymic 1920; ed. at Cheltenham; Joint Parl. Under-Sec. of State for Scotland, 1955-59, Min. of State, Scottish Office, Sept. 1959-64; Pres. City of Westminster Chamber of Commerce 1966 (Chm. 1954-55); Chm. Cttee. for Environmental Conservation; Vice-Chm. Fauna Preservation Soc., Trustee and Member of Managing Cttee. of World Wild-life Fund (British National Appeal); 1939-45 War as Group Capt. AAF with Balloon Command; MP for Govan Div. of Glasgow (C) 1950-55, and for Craigton Burgh Div. of Glasgow 1955-59; CBE (Mil) 1945, and *Baron Craigton*, of Renfield, co. of City of Glasgow (Life Baron) 1959, and PC 1961:

m. 1st, 1936 (m. diss. 1949), Helen Anne, da. of the late G. J. Inglis, of Glasgow; 2ndly, 1950, Eileen Humphrey, da. of Henry Whitford Nolan, of London, and has issue by 1st m.

Arms,—Per pale argent and or, on a pale sable between, dexter three leopards' faces vert and sinister as many leopards faces gules, a lion rampant of the first armed and langued of the fifth. **Crest,**—A demi-knight in tilting armour argent garnished vert and helmet grilled or with wreath of these liveries argent and vert and thereon for crest a plume of five feathers, gules, argent, gules, argent, gules, holding in his dexter hand a crossbow bolt or feathered argent and in his sinister hand a garb or banded vert across his sinister shoulder. **Supporters,**—Two knights in tilting armour argent garnished vert their helmets grilled or and on a wreath of the liveries argent and vert plumes as in the crest, that on the dexter holding in his dexter hand a crossbow bolt or feathered argent and that on the sinister sustaining with his sinister hand a garb or banded vert resting upon his sinister shoulder.

Residence,—Friary House, Friary Island, Wraysbury, Bucks. *Club,*—Buck's.

SON LIVING. (*By 1st marriage.*)
Hon. John Nixon (357, Belsize Drive, Toronto, Ont., Canada), *b.* 1937; ed. at Kelvinside Acad.; TV Producer; Canadian Broadcasting Corpn. 1968: *m.* 1964, Mrs. Jean Athalie van Blommestein, da. of the late Eben Alec Hendry.

Cranborne, Viscount, son of Marquess of Salisbury.

CRANBROOK, EARL OF. (Gathorne-Hardy.) [Earl U.K. 1892.]
[Name pronounced "Gaythorn-Hardy."]

Armed with hardy faith.

JOHN DAVID GATHORNE-HARDY, C.B.E., 4th Earl ; *b.* April 15th 1900 ; *s.* 1915 ; ed. at Eton ; Hon. M.A. Camb. 1949 ; Gunner, R.F.A. 1918-19 ; Lieut. R.A. 1921-32 ; a County Alderman for London 1928-30 ; was Parliamentary Private Sec. to First Commr. of Works 1927-8, Dep. Regional Commr. for E. Civil Defence Region 1940-45, Chm. of E. Anglian Regional Hospital Board 1947-59, and Hon. Air Commodore 3619 (Suffolk) Fighter Control Unit, R. Aux. A.F. 1950-61 ; a JP and DL for Suffolk ; E. Suffolk Co. Council 1934-74 (Chm. 1950-57), and a KStJ ; Treasurer of Linnean Soc. 1958-70 ; a Trustee of British Museum (Natural History) 1964-72 ; a Member of Nature Conservancy 1967-73 ; CBE (Civil) 1955 : *m.* 1st, 1926, his cousin. Bridget Cicely (who obtained a divorce 1931), da. of Rupert D'Oyly Carte (infra) ; 2ndly, 1932, Fidelity, OBE, JP, da. of Hugh Exton Seebohm, JP, of Poynders End, Hitchin, and has issue by 2nd marriage.

Arms,—Quarterly, 1st and 4th argent, on a bend invected plain, cottised gules, three catherine wheels or; on a chief of the second as many leopards' faces of the third, *Hardy*; 2nd and 3rd, per pale argent and or, a bend compony azure and gules between two pellets, each within an annulet sable, *Gathorne*. Crests,—1st, a dexter arm embowed in armour proper, garnished or entwined with a branch of oak vert, charged with two catherine wheels, the one above and the other below the elbow gules, the hand grasping a dragon's head erased proper, *Hardy*; 2nd, in front of a wolf's head erased argent, a staff reguly fessewise or, *Gathorne*. Supporters,—On either side a leopard guardant proper, gorged with a collar gules, therefrom auspended an escutcheon of the last, charged with a catherine wheel or.

Residence,—Red House Farm, Great Glemham, Saxmundham, Suffolk.

SONS LIVING. (*By 2nd marriage.*)

GATHORNE (*Lord Medway*) (c/o Nat. Westminster Bank, 1, St. James's Sq, SW1), *b.* June 20th, 1933; ed. at Eton, and at Corpus Christi Coll., Camb., (BA 1956, MA 1960); PhD Birmingham 1960; late Lt. RA (TA); an O.St.J., a FLS and a FZS; Assist., Sarawak Museum 1956-58, and Fellow, Jajasan Siswa Lokantara, Indonesia 1960-61, and Lect. in Zoology, Univ. of Malaya, Kuala Lumpur 1961-70: *m.* 1967, Caroline, da. of the late Col. Ralph George Edward Jarvis, of Doddington Hall, Lincoln [E. Clanwilliam, colls.], and has issue.
    SONS LIVING.—*Hon.* John Jason, *b.* Oct. 26th, 1968. *Hon.* Argus Edward, *b.* 1973.
    DAUGHTER LIVING.—*Hon.* Flora, *b.* 1971.
Hon. Hugh, *b.* 1941; ed. at Eton, and at Corpus Christi Coll., Camb. (BA): *m.* 1971, Caroline Elisabeth, da. of William Nigel Ritchie, of Village House, Bradfield, Berks. [see B. Ritchie of Dundee, colls.], and has issue living, Frederick Jasper, *b.* 1972.

DAUGHTERS LIVING. (*By 2nd marriage.*)

Lady Juliet (The White House, Rooks Hill, Underriver, Sevenoaks, Kent), *b.* 1934: *m.* 1958 (m. diss. 1972), Charles Colin Simpson, TD, and has issue living, Charles Duncan, *b.* 1962,—Edward Colin, *b.* 1965,—Fidelity Anne, *b.* 1960,—Amanda Juliet, *b.* 1964.
Lady Sophia Catherine, *b.* 1936: *m.* 1957, Simon Robert Jasper Meade, of Pen-y-lan, Meifod, Montgomeryshire [see E. Clanwilliam, colls.].
Lady Christina, *b.* 1940: *m.* 1967, Stanley Edward Letanka, MRCS, LRCP, of 98, Park Av., Ruislip, Middx., and has issue living, Stella, *b.* 1968,—Ruth, *b.* 1969.

BROTHERS LIVING.

Hon. Ralph Edward, *b.* 1901; ed. at Eton, and at Ch. Ch., Oxford. *Residence*,—Odos Democharos 53, Flat 13, Athens 601, Greece.
Hon. Antony Gathorne, *MB*, *ChB*, *b.* 1907; ed. at Eton and at Edinburgh Univ. (MB and ChB 1935); is Surg.-Com. RN and an OStJ: *m.* 1st 1931, Ruth Elizabeth, who *d.* 1973, da. of Com. Arthur Penton Napier Thorowgood, DSO [Hunter-Blair, Bt., colls.]; 2ndly, 1974, Mary Catherine, da. of the late Bernard Joseph Smartt, and has issue living (by 1st m.), Jonathan Gathorne (West Lodge, Compton Bassett, Calne, Wilts.), *b.* 1933: *m.* 1963, Sabrina Viola, da. of the late Hon. David Francis Tennant, of El Palomar, Mijas, Malaga, Spain [see B. Glenconner, colls.], and has issue living, Benjamin *b.* 1967, Jenny *b.* 1965,—Samuel Gathorne (South Estate, Carey Island, Port Klang, Selangor, W. Malaysia), *b.* 1936: *m.* 1965, Grace D'Cruz, and has issue living, Robert Dee, *b.* 1973, Lydia *b.* 1964, Penelope Rose *b.* 1965,—Elizabeth Rose, *b.* 1949: *m.* 1974, Ian Richmond Battye, MB, BS, and has issue living, Thomas Gathorne *b.* 1975. *Residence*,—18, Hartington Rd., Aldeburgh, Suffolk.

SISTER LIVING.

Lady Anne Catherine Dorothy, *b.* 1911: *m.* 1938, George Heywood Hill, of Snape Priory, Saxmundham, Suffolk [Johnstone, Bt., colls.], and has issue living, Harriet, *b.* 1943: *m.* 1963, Timothy Behrens, of La Bertinga, Lecchi-in-Chianti 53010, Siena, Italy, and has issue living, Algernon Kenneth *b.* 1966, Frances Anne *b.* 1963,—Lucy, *b.* 1946: *m.* 1970, George James Redpath, of Low Farm House, Hoxne, Diss, Norfolk, and has issue living, Justin Abdulla, *b.* 1971.

AUNT LIVING. (*Daughter of 2nd Earl.*)

Lady Dorothy Milner, *b.* 1889: *m.* 1st, 1907, Rupert D'Oyly Carte, who *d.* 1948, having obtained a divorce 1942; 2ndly, 1942, St. Yves de Verteuil, who *d.* 1963, and has issue living, (by 1st marriage) Bridget D'OYLY CARTE (of 1, Savoy Hill, W.C.2), *b.* 1908: *m.* 1926, the 4th Earl of Cranbrook (ante), from whom she obtained a divorce 1931, and re-assumed by deed poll 1932 her maiden name of D'Oyly Carte, and relinquished her second Christian name of Cicely. *Resides*,—Scarborough, Tobago, West Indies.

COLLATERAL BRANCH LIVING.

Issue of the late Lieut.-Col. the Hon. Nigel Charles Gathorne-Hardy, D.S.O., youngest son of 2nd Earl, *b.* 1880, *d.* 1958: *m.* 1910, Doris Cecilia Featherston, who *d.* 1973, da. of the late Hon. Sir Charles John Johnston, MLC, of Karori, Wellington, New Zealand:—
Margaret Doris (*Lady Cameron of Lochiel*), *b.* 1913: *m.* 1939, Col. Sir Donald Hamish Cameron of Lochiel, KT, CVO, TD, late Comdg. Lovat Scouts [see D. Montrose]. *Residence*,—Achnacarry, Spean Bridge, Inverness-shire.

PREDECESSORS.—[1] Right Hon. GATHORNE Gathorne-Hardy, G.C.S.I. P.C., D.C.L., LL.D. 3rd son of the late John Hardy, M.P.; *b.* 1814; Under-Sec. of State for Home Depart. 1858-9, Pres. of Poor Law Board 1866-7, Sec. of State for Home Depart. 1867-8, for War 1874-8, and for India 1878-80, and Lord Pres. of the Council 1885-6 and 1886-92; assumed in 1878, by Roy. licence, the additional surname of Gathorne; M.P. for Leominster (*C*) 1856-65, and for Univ. of Oxford 1865-78; G.C.S.I. 1880; cr. *Viscount Cranbrook*, of Hemsted, co. Kent (peerage of United Kingdom) 1878, and *Earl of Cranbrook* and *Baron Medway*, of Hemsted, co. Kent (peerage of United Kingdom) 1892: *m.* 1838, Jane, *C.I.*, who *d.* 1897, dau. of James Orr, of Hollywood House, co. Down; *d.* 1906; *s.* by his el. son [2] JOHN STEWART, 2nd Earl, *b.* 1839; M.P. for Rye (*C*) 1868-80, for Mid-Kent 1884-5, and for Kent, Mid, or Medway, Div. 1885-92: *m.* 1867, Cicely Marguerite Wilhelmina, who *d.* 1931, dau. and heiress of the late Joseph Ridgway, of Fairlawn, Kent: *d.* 1911: *s.* by his el. son [3] GATHORNE, 3rd Earl; *b.* 1870: *m.* 1899, Lady Dorothy Montagu Boyle, who *d.* 1968, da. of 7th Earl of Glasgow; *d.* 1915; *s.* by his el. son [4] JOHN DAVID, 4th Earl and present peer; also Viscount Cranbrook, and Baron Medway.

Cranley, Viscount, son of Earl of Onslow.

CRANWORTH, BARON. (Gurdon.) [Baron U.K. 1899.]

Virtue flourishes in dangers.

PHILIP BERTRAM GURDON, 3rd Baron; b. May 24th, 1940; s. 1964; ed. at Eton, and at Magdalene Coll., Camb.; late Lt. R. Wilts Yeo: m. 1968, Frances Henrietta, da. of the late Lord William Walter Montagu-Douglas-Scott, MC [see D. Buccleuch, colls.], and has issue.

Arms.—Sable, three leopards' faces jessant-de-lis or. *Crest.*—A goat climbing up a rock, all proper. *Supporters*—On either side a rock thereon a goat proper, collared gemelle or.
Seat,—Grundisburgh Hall, Woodbridge, Suffolk.

SONS LIVING.
Hon. SACHA WILLIAM ROBIN, b. Aug. 12th, 1970.
Hon. Brampton Charles, b. 1975.

DAUGHTER LIVING.
Hon. Louisa-Jane, b. 1969.

SISTER LIVING.
(Raised to the rank of a Baron's daughter 1964.)
Hon. Jeryl Marcia Sarah, b. 1932: m. 1952, Charles Mortimer Tollemache Smith-Ryland [B. Tollemache, colls.], of Sherbourne Park, Warwick, and has issue living, Robin Charles, b. 1953,—David James, b. 1961,—Sarah Yoskyl, b. 1955,—Joanna, b. 1959,—Petra Louisa, b. 1970.

AUNTS LIVING.
Hon. Camilla, b. 1909: m. 1932, George Marcus Tomline Pretyman [E. Bradford], and has issue living, Gillian Enid, b. 1934: m. 1965, Mark Bence-Jones, of Glenville Park, Glenville, co. Cork, and has issue living, Nicholas George Winthrop b. 1966, Miranda Beatrice May b. 1971. *Residence,*—Orwell Park House, Ipswich.
Hon. Judith Florence, b. 1914: m. 1943, Thomas Henry Bull, late Lt. R.A. *Residence,*—Park Farm, Grundisburgh, Suffolk.

MOTHER LIVING.
Hon. Daisy Yoskyl Consuelo Pearson (*Baroness McCorquodale of Newton*) (of Cotswold Park, Cirencester, Glos., and 50E, Cornwall Gdns., SW7), da. of 2nd Viscount Cowdray: m. 1st, 1932, the Hon. Robert Brampton Gurdon, Lt. Coldstream Guards, who d. (killed in action during European War) 1942; 2ndly, 1944, Lt.-Col. Alistair Gibb, late Roy. Wilts. Yeo., who d. 1955, son of Sir Alexander Gibb, GBE, CB, FRS; 3rdly, 1962, the 1st Baron McCorquodale of Newton, who d. 1971, when the title became ext.

PREDECESSORS.—[1] ROBERT THORNHAGH Gurdon, el. son of the late Brampton Gurdon, MP, of Letton Hall, Norfolk, and Grundisburgh, Suffolk; b. 1829; MP for S. Norfolk (*L*) 1880-85, and for Norfolk Mid Div. (*L*) 1885-6, and (*LU*) 1886-92 and April to July 1895; cr. Baron Cranworth, of Letton and Cranworth, co. Norfolk (peerage of U.K.) 1899: m. 1st, 1862, Harriott Ellin, who d. 1864, da. of Sir William Miles, MP, 1st Bt.; 2ndly, 1874, Emily Frances, who d. 1934. dau. of Robert Boothby Heathcote; d. 1902; s. by his son [2] BERTRAM FRANCIS, KG, MC, 2nd Baron; b. 1877; Vice-Lieut. for Suffolk 1947-64: m. 1903, Vera Emily, OBE, who d. 1966, el. da. of the late Arthur William Ridley [V. Ridley, colls.]; d. 1964; s. by his grandson [3] PHILIP BERTRAM (yr. son of the late Hon. Robert Brampton Gurdon), 3rd Baron, and present peer.

CRATHORNE, BARON. (Dugdale.) [Baron U.K. 1959, Bt. U.K. 1945.]

By persevering.

THOMAS LIONEL DUGDALE, T.D., P.C., 1st Baron, and 1st Baronet, son of the late James Lionel Dugdale, of Crathorne, Yorkshire; b. July 20th, 1897; ed. at Eton and RMC; Capt. R. Scots Greys (Reserve) and Maj. Yorkshire Hussars (Alexandra, Princess of Wales's Own) Yeo. (T.A.), and a J.P. and Vice-Lieut. for N. Riding of Yorkshire; was Parliamentary Private Sec. to Rt. Hon. Sir Philip Cunliffe-Lister, M.P. 1931-35, and to Rt. Hon. Stanley Baldwin, M.P. 1935-37, a Junior Lord of the Treasury 1937-40, Dep. Ch. Govt. Whip and Vice-Chairman of Conservative Party Organization 1941-42, Chm. of Conservative Party Organization 1942-44, Min. of Agriculture and Fisheries 1951-54, U.K. Member of Gen. Assembly of Council of Europe 1958-9, and again 1961-65 (Vice-Pres. 1962-64), and a Member of Advisory Commn. on Central Africa 1960; a Member of Standing Cttee. of N.A.T.O. Parliamentarians Conference 1958-68 (Pres. 1963), and Chm., N. England Advisory Cttee. for Civil Aviation 1964-72; Steward of Jockey Club 1960-2, and Senior Steward 1962, and a Member of Horse Racing Levy Board since 1963; 1914-18 War in France and Belgium with Roy. Scots Greys (two medals); 1939-45 War in Middle East with Yorkshire Hussars; MP for Richmond Div. of N. Riding of Yorkshire (*C*) 1929-59; cr. a Baronet 1945, P.C. 1951, and Baron Crathorne, N. Riding of Yorkshire (peerage of United Kingdom) 1959: m. 1936, Nancy (GATES), OBE, who d. 1969, da. of Sir Charles Tennant, 1st Bt. [B. Glenconner], and has issue.

Arms.—Ermine a cross moline gules between four hurts. *Crest.*—A gryphon's head ermine wings endorsed erminois gorged with a collar azure therefrom pendant a cross moline gules. *Supporters.*—*Dexter,* a crow sable beaked and membered or in the beak a sprig of blackthorn flowered proper; *sinister,* a stag also sable attired unguled and gorged with a mural crown gold charged on the shoulder with a thistle slipped and leaved also proper.

Residence,—Crathorne Hall, Yarm, Cleveland.   *Clubs,*—Jockey, Carlton, White's, Bucks's.

SONS LIVING.
Hon. CHARLES JAMES (Crathorne Hall, Yarm, Cleveland), *b.* Sept. 12th, 1939; *ed.* at Eton, and at Trin. Coll., Camb.: *m.* 1970, Sylvia Mary, yr. da. of Brig. Arthur Herbert Montgomery, OBE, TD [see Montgomery, Bt., colls.], and has issue living, Charlotte, *b.* 1972.
Hon. David John (Crown Farm, Dishforth, Thirsk, N Yorks.), *b.* 1942; *ed.* at Eton, and at Trin. Coll., Camb.: *m.* 1972, Susan Louise, yr. da. of the late Lewis A. Powell.

CRAVEN, EARL OF. (Craven.) [Earl U.K. 1801.]

THOMAS ROBERT DOUGLAS CRAVEN, 7th Earl; *b.* Aug. 24th, 1957; *s.* 1965; *ed.* at Downside.

Arms,—Argent, a fesse, between six cross crosslets fitchée, gules.   **Crest,**—On a chapeau gules, turned up ermine, a griffin statant wings elevated ermine, beaked and membered or.   **Supporters,**—Two griffins, wings elevated ermine, beaked and membered or.
Seat,—Hamstead Marshall, Newbury, Berks.

BROTHER LIVING.
Hon. SIMON GEORGE, *b.* Sept. 16th, 1961.

HALF-SISTER LIVING.
Lady Sarah Jane, *b.* 1940: *m.* 1961, David John Trail Thomson Glover, of Brookfield, Box 53, Elgin, Cape Province, and has issue living, Suzanne Gwendoline, *b.* 1964,—Vanessa Kate, *b.* 1972.

SISTER LIVING.
Lady Ann Mary Elizabeth, *b.* 1959.

WIDOW LIVING OF SIXTH EARL
ELIZABETH GWENDOLEN TERESA (The Dower House, Hamstead Marshall, Newbury), da. of the late Robert Sholto Johnstone-Douglas [see M. Queensberry, colls.]: *m.* 1st, 1954, as his 2nd wife, the 6th Earl, who *d.* 1965; 2ndly, 1966, Kenneth Harmood Banner, of Peelings Manor, Pevensey, Sussex.

VIRTUS·IN·ACTIONE·CONSISTIT
Virtue consists in action.

COLLATERAL BRANCHES LIVING.
Issue of the late Major the Hon. Rupert Cecil Craven, O.B.E., 2nd son of 3rd Earl, *b.* 1870, *d.* 1959 : *m.* 1st, 1898, Inez (from whom he obtained a divorce 1908), dau. of George Broom; 2ndly, 1925, Josephine Marguerite, who *d.* 1971, da. of José Reixach, and widow of Capt. Charles William Banbury [B. Banbury]:—
(By 2nd marriage) Rupert José Evelyn (Swordly, Bettyhill, Thurso, Caithness), *b.* 1926; a JP of Hants; Lt.-Cdr. RN: *m.* 1955, Margaret Campbell, da. of Alexander Smith, MBE, of Glasgow, and Alness.
(In Special remainder to Barony only.)

Grandchildren of the late Edmund Filmer Craven, grandson of the late Fulwar-Craven (*b.* 1782), grandson of the late Charles Craven, brother of 2nd Baron:—
Issue of the late Fulwar Craven, *b.* 1873, *d.* 1956: *m.* 1916, Elizabeth A. Wheatley:—
Edmund Filmer (11, Buckley Av., Mount Isa 4825, Cloncurry, Qld.), *b.* 1917; late RAAF: *m.* 1944, Ada Clemence Adelaide, da. of C. Richardson, of Cloncurry, Qld., and has issue living, John Edmund, *b.* 1946.——Evelyn Caroline, *b.* 1929: *m.* 1952, Donald Leslie Whitehouse, of 58, Alma Rd., Clayfield, Brisbane 4011, Qld., Aust., and has issue living, Gregory Thomas, *b.* 1954,—Jennifer Lynette, *b.* 1953.

Grandchildren of the late Capt. Charles Craven, **son of the late Charles John Craven**, grandson of the late Charles Craven (ante):—
Issue of the late Alfred Eugène Craven, *b.* 1848, *d.* 1936 : *m.* 1st, 1881, Edith (who obtained a divorce 1897), dau. of the late Frederick Urban Sartoris, of Rushden Hall, Rushden ; 2ndly, 1898, Sarah Annie, who *d.* 1931, dau. of Walter Carey, formerly of The Drive, Thornton Heath:—
(By 1st m.) Harold Evelyn Andrew, *b.* 1885; *ed.* at Rugby; late 2nd Lt. RASC; 1914-18 War: *m.* 1914, Florence Mary Jackson (who obtained a divorce 1932), da. of Capt. J. Moore.——Thyra, *b.* 1882. *Residence,*—

PREDECESSORS.—[1] *Sir* WILLIAM Craven, Knt., a soldier of renown in the Netherlands under Henry, Prince of Orange, under Gustavus Adolphus, King of Sweden, and in the service of the States of Holland, was a zealous partizan of Charles I. and Charles II. ; *cr. Baron Craven,* of Hamstead Marshall, co. Berks (peerage of England) 1626, with remainder to his brothers, John and Thomas, *Viscount Craven,* of Uffington, co. Berks, with remainder to Sir William Craven, Knt., and Sir Anthony Craven, *Earl of Craven* (peerage of England), 1663, and *Baron Craven,* of Hamstead Marshall, Berks, 1665, with remainder to Sir William Craven, Knt., of Combe Abbey, Warwickshire, son of Thomas Craven, brother of Sir Anthony (ante ; *d.* unmarried 1697, when all the peerages became extinct except the cr. of 1665, which devolved upon [2], WILLIAM, 2nd Baron, son of Sir William, Knt. (ante); *d.* 1711; *s.* by his son [3] WILLIAM, 3rd Baron; *d.s.p.* 1739; *s.* by his brother [4] FULWAR, 4th Baron; *d.* unmarried; *s.* by his cousin [5] WILLIAM 5th Baron, son of John, 2nd son of 2nd Baron; *d.* 1769; *s.* by his nephew [6] WILLIAM, 6th Baron; *d.* 1791; *s.* by his son [7] WILLIAM, 7th Baron; a Maj.-Gen. in the Army, and Lord-Lieut. of Berks; *cr. Viscount Uffington* and *Earl of Craven* (peerage of Great Britain (1801); *d.* 1825; *s.* by his son [8] WILLIAM, 2nd Earl; *b.* 1809; Lord-Lieut. of Warwickshire; *d.* 1866; *s.* by his son [9] GEORGE GRIMSTON, 3rd Earl; *b.* 1841; Lord-Lieut. of Berks: *m.* 1867, the Hon. Evelyn Laura, who *d.* 1924, dau. of 7th Viscount Barrington; *d.* 1883; *s.* by his son [10] WILLIAM GEORGE ROBERT, 4th Earl; *b.* 1868; Lord-Lieut. of Warwickshire : *m.* 1893, Cornelia, who *d.* 1961, dau. of the late Bradley Martin, of New York, U.S.A.; *d.* 1921; *s.* by his son[11] WILLIAM GEORGE BRADLEY, 5th Earl, *b.* 1897 ; European War 1915-18, as Lieut., Hampshire Regt. (wounded): *m.* 1916, Wilhelmina Mary, who *d.* 1974, da. of William George, OBE, JP, Town Clerk of Invergordon, Scotland; *d.* 1932; *s.* by his son [12] WILLIAM ROBERT BRADLEY, 6th Earl, *b.* 1917: *m.* 1st, 1939, Irene (who obtained a divorce 1954) da. of the late Ferdinand Richard Holmes Meyrick, MD, of 59, Kensington Court, W8; 2ndly, 1954, Elizabeth Gwendolen Teresa (who *m.* 2ndly, 1966, Kenneth Harmood Banner), da. of the late Robert Sholto Johnstone-Douglas [M. Queensberry, colls.]; *d.* 1965; *s.* by his el. son [13] THOMAS ROBERT DOUGLAS, 7th Earl and present peer; also Viscount Uffington, and Baron Craven.

CRAWFORD and BALCARRES, EARL OF. (Lindsay.) [Earl S. 1398 and 1651.]

DAVID ALEXANDER ROBERT LINDSAY, K.T., G.B.E., 28th Earl of Crawford (Premier Earl on Union Roll of Scotland) and 11th Earl of Balcarres; b. Nov. 20th, 1900; s. 1940; ed. at Eton, and at Magdalen Coll., Oxford (B.A. Honours 1922, Hon. D.C.L. 1951); Hon. LL.D. St. Andrews 19—, and Camb. 1955; Hon. Litt.D. Manchester 19—; Hon. D.Litt. Exeter 1956; was Parliamentary Private Sec. (unpaid) to Min. of Agriculture and Fisheries 1924-25, to Sec. to Depart. of Overseas Trade 1931, and to Min. of Health 1931-40, a Trustee of Tate Gallery 1932-41, and of National Gallery 1935-44 and again since 1945 (Chm. 1938-41 and 1945-49), and Chm. of Roy. Fine Art Commn. 1943-57; has been a Trustee of British Museum since 1940, of National Galleries of Scotland since 1947, and of Pilgrim Trust since 1949; is Chm. of National Trust and of National Art Collections Fund, a F.S.A., and an Hon. F.R.I.B.A.; appointed a Member of Standing Commn. on Museums and Galleries 1937, and Chm. of Board of Trustees of National Library or Scotland 1944-74; R. of St. Andrews Univ. 1952-5; unsuccessfully contested Wigan (U) Dec. 1923; sat as MP for Lancashire, Lonsdale Div. Oct. 1924 to March 1940; GBE (Civil) 1951, K.T. 1955: m. 1925, Mary Katharine, da. of the late Col. Rt. Hon. Lord Richard Frederick Cavendish, CB, CMG. [see D. Devonshire, colls.], and has issue.

Arms,—Quarterly: 1st and 4th gules, a fesse checky argent and azure, Lindsay; 2nd and 3rd or, a lion rampant gules, debruised of a ribbon in bend sable, Abernethy. Crest,—Out of an antique ducal coronet a swan's neck and wings proper. Supporters,—Two lions rampant guardant gules.

Seat,—Balcarres, Colinsburgh, Fife. Clubs,—Travellers', Athenæum.

SONS LIVING.

ROBERT ALEXANDER (Baron Balniel), PC, b. Mar. 5th, 1927; ed. at Eton, and Trin. Coll. Camb.; late Lieut. Grenadier Guards; late Hon. Attaché, British Embassy, Paris; was Parliamentary Private Sec. to Financial Sec. to the Treasury 1955-7 ,and to Min. of Housing and Local Govt. 1957-59, Pres., Rural Dist. Council Asso. 1959-65; Chm., National Assocn. of Mental Health 1963-70, Min. of State, Defence 1970-72, Min. of State Foreign and Commonwealth Office 1972-74, and MP for Hertford Div. of Herts. (C) 1955 to Feb. 1974, and for Welwyn and Hatfield Feb. to Oct. 1974; cr. PC 1972, and Baron Balniel, of Pitcorthie, co. Fife (Life Baron) (Dec.) 1974: m. 1949, Ruth Beatrice da. of Leo Meyer-Bechtler, of 49, Keltenstrasse, Zurich, Switzerland, and has issue:—
SONS LIVING,—Hon. Anthony Robert (Master of Lindsay), b. Nov. 24th, 1958.
Hon. Alexander Walter, b. 1961.
DAUGHTERS LIVING,—Hon. Bettina Mary, b. 1950.
Hon. Iona Sina, b. 1957.
Residence,—107, Frognal, NW3.
Hon. Patrick, b. 1928; ed. at Eton, and at Magdalen Coll., Oxford; late 2nd Lieut. Scots Guards: m. 1955, Lady Amabel Mary Maud Yorke, dau. of 9th Earl of Hardwicke, and has issue living, Ludovic Alexander, b. 1957,—James Richard, b. 1961,—Valentine b. 1962,—Laura Mary, b. 1956. Residence,—12, Lansdowne Rd., W.11. Clubs,—Brook's, White's, and Royal Yacht Squadron.
Hon. Thomas Richard, b. 1937; ed. at Eton; late 2nd Lieut. Scots Guards: m. 1961, Sarah Virginia, only dau. of George Nigel Capel Cure, T.D., D.L., J.P. [see Barry, Bt., colls.], and has issue living, Ivan James, b. 1962,—Constantine David, b. 1966,—Jason Richard, b. 1968,—Alexandra Mary, b. 1964,—Sophia Victoria, b. 1971. Residence,—3, Netherton Grove, SW10. Club,—Brook's.

BROTHER LIVING.

Hon. James Louis, b. 1906; ed. at Eton, and at Magdalen Coll., Oxford; formerly Major King's Roy. Rifle Corps; unsuccessfully contested S.-E. Div. of Bristol (C) Nov. 1950, and Oct. 1951; sat as M.P. for N. Div. of Devon May 1955 to Sept. 1959; defeated there Oct. 1959: m. 1933, the Hon. Bronwen Mary Scott-Ellis, dau. of 8th Baron Howard de Walden, and has issue living, Hugh John Alexander (of 91, Lansdowne Rd., W11), b. 1934; ed. at Eton, and at Magdalen Coll., Oxford; a Chartered Accountant; late 2nd Lt. Black Watch: m. 1961, Constance Carolyn, yr. da. of Sir Charles James Buchanan, 4th Bt., and has issue living, David Charles b. 1962, Alastair James b. 1964, Robert Hugh b. 1967, Serena Clare b. 1970,—Alexander Thomas (c/o Drummonds Bank, 49, Charing Cross, SW1; Cavalry Club), b. 1936; ed. at Eton, and at Magdalen Coll., Oxford; Maj. 17th/21st Lancers: m. 1966, Jessie Miranda Cecilia, da. of Col. John Anthony Tristram Barstow, DSO, TD, DL, and has issue living, James Alexander Tristram b. 1968, Roderick Charles b. 1970, Felix Thomas b. 1973,—Stephen James (c/o Drummonds Bank, 49, Charing Cross, SW1), b. 1940; ed. at Eton; Maj. Black Watch: m. 1966, Margaret Ann, da. of the late Maj. J. H. C. Powell, and has issue living, Richard Stephen b. 1969, Charles Ludovic b. 1974, Jane Margaret b. 1966,—Julia Margaret, b. 1941: m. 1963, Peter Barton of Primrose Hill, Hawkhurst, Kent, and has issue living, Henry James b. 1967, Christopher Charles, b. 1970, Fenella Jane b. 1965. Residence,—Througham Slad, Bisley, Stroud, Glos. Club,—Travellers'.

SISTERS LIVING.

Lady Margaret Cynthia, A.R.R.C., b. 1902: m. 1928, Lieut.-Col. Henry Cyril Harker Illingworth, M.C., J.P., late King's Roy. Rifle Corps (an Officer of Order of the Crown of Roumania). Residence, —Headon Lodge, Brompton-by-Sawdon, Scarborough, Yorkshire.
Lady (Cynthia) Anne, b. 1904: m. 1st, 1931, Per Erik Folke Arnander, who d. 1933, 1st Sec., Swedish Legation, Rome; 2ndly, 1934, Giovanni Fummi, who d. 1970, and has issue living (by 1st m.) Christopher James Folke (21, Campden Hill Sq., W8), b. 1932: m. 1961, Pamela Primrose, da. of David McKenna, CBE [see E. Albemarle], and has issue living, Conrad David Folke b. 1963, Michael Theodore Per b. 1964, Magnus Thomas William b. 1967, Katharine Louise b. 1967,—(by 2nd m.) Francesca Giovanna Maria, b. 1935: m. 1961, Christopher Robin St. Quintin Wall, of The Apple Orchard, Bradenham, High Wycombe, Bucks. [E. Peel, colls.], and has issue living, Dominic John

St. Quintin *b.* 1964, Camilla Mary *b.* 1962. *Residence,*—10, Lochmore House, Cundy St. Flats, Ebury St., SW1.

Lady Mary Lilian (*Viscountess Dilhorne*), *b.* 1910: *m.* 1930, the 1st Viscount Dilhorne. *Residences,*— 6, King's Bench Walk, Temple, EC4; Horninghold Manor, Market Harborough.

Lady Barbara, *b.* 1915: *m.* 1939, Col. Richard Lumley Hurst, Roy. Sussex Regt. T.A., Bar.-at-law who *d.* 1962, son of Sir Cecil James Barrington Hurst, G.C.M.G., K.C.B., and has issue living, Robert Andrew, *b.* 1945,—Elizabeth, *b.* 1940: *m.* 1967, Angus Hugh Gilroy of 58, Scarsdale Villas, W8 6PP,—Cecilia Barbara, *b.* 1944: *m.* 1968, Alastair Robertson Goodlad, MP, of 70, Drayton Gdns., SW10 9SB,—Katharine Constance, *b.* 1948. *Residence,*—Rusper Nunnery, Horsham, Sussex, RH12 4QT.

COLLATERAL BRANCHES LIVING.

    Granddaughter of the late Hon. Walter Patrick Lindsay, 2nd son of 26th Earl of Crawford:—

Issue of the late Kenneth Andrew Lindsay, *b.* 1903, *d.* 1970: *m.* 1928, Kathleen Mary (7, Pearson Park, Pearson Av., Kenilworth, Cape Town), da. of H. E. Lovemore, formerly of Queenstown, S. Africa:—
Patricia Jane, *b.* 1932: *m.* 1956, Noël Gwynne Harpur, of Edzell, Sheerness Rd., Kenilworth, Cape Town, and has issue living, Patrick Leslie Gwynne, *b.* 1957,—Colin Andrew Lindsay, *b.* 1959.

    Issue of the late Major the Hon. Robert Hamilton Lindsay, 3rd son of 26th Earl of Crawford, *b.* **1874,** *d.* **1911 :** *m.* **1903, Mary Janet, who** *d.* **1960, dau. of Sir William John Clarke, 1st Bt. :—**
Robert William Ludovic, *OBE* (Derriweit, Mount Macedon, Vic. 34 42, Aust.), *b.* 1905; ed. at Eton; a Member of House of Representatives of Commonwealth of Australia 1954-66; ret. 1966; 1940-45 War as Maj. Grenadier Guards and Trans-Jordan Frontier Force; OBE (Civil) 1971: *m.* 1946, Romsemary Catherine Marion, only da. of Sir Robert Wilson Knox [Clarke, Bt., cr. 1882], and has issue living, Andrew William Michael, *b.* 1949,—Ian Alexander, *b.* 1957,—James Malcolm, *b.* 1961. *Clubs,*—Guards, Melbourne (Vic.).——Joyce Emily, (The Old Cottage, 10, Arnulds Rd., SW16 3EP), *b.* 1904: *m.* 1932 (m. diss. 1967), Sir Martin Alexander Lindsay, 1st Bt., CBE, DSO.

Issue of the late Hon. Lionel Lindsay, MC, son of 26th Earl of Crawford, *b.* 1879, *d.* 1965: *m.* 1921, Kathleen Yone, who *d.* 1970, da. of the late Sir John Gordon Kennedy, KCMG [M. Ailsa, colls.]:—
Colin Paul (Hambrook House, Chichester. *Clubs,* Travellers' and Royal Ocean Racing), *b.* 1922; ed. at Eton, and at New Coll., Oxford; is a FCA: *m.* 1955, Jennifer Ann, da. of the late Capt. Thomas Marcus Brownrigg, CBE, DSO, RN (ret.), and has issue living, Christopher Ronald, *b.* 1957,—Andrew Mark, *b.* 1962.

    Grandchildren of the late Lt.-Col. Henry Edith Arthur Lindsay, OBE, son of Col. the Hon. Charles Hugh Lindsay, CB, 3rd son of 24th Earl of Crawford:—
Issue of the late Lt.-Col. (David Ludovic) Peter Lindsay, DSO, *b.* 1900, *d.* 1971: *m.* 1st, 1940, Ursula Jane (who obtained a divorce 1946), da. of the late Robert Orlando Rodolph Kenyon-Slaney [see B. Kenyon, colls.];   2ndly, 1950, Barbara J. (Méribel, Les Allues, Savoie, France), da. of Edward Dunn:—
(By 2nd m.) David Michael, *b.* 1956.——Jane Caroline, *b.* 1951.——Sarah Jacqueline, *b.* 1952.

    Grandchildren of the late Major Francis Howard Lindsay, 4th son of 24th Earl of Crawford:—
Issue of the late Major John Stewart LINDSAY-MACDOUGALL, **D.S.O., M.C., Argyll and Sutherland Highlanders,** *b.* **1911,** *d.* **(of wounds whilst a prisoner in Italy) 1943, having assumed the additional surname of MacDougall 1922 :** *m.* **1934, Sheila Marion Roma** (who *m.* 2ndly, 1949, Lieut.-Col. Aubrey Wynter Gibbon, O.B.E., Argyll and Sutherland Highlanders, of West Baravoulin, Ardfern, by Lochgilphead, Argyll, da. of the late Capt. J. W. L. Sprot, Black Watch:—
Colin John Francis (of Lunga, Ardfern, Locugilpheaa, Argyll), *b.* 1939; ed. at Radley: *m.* 1961, the Hon. Frances Phœbe, dau. of the late Capt. the Hon. Anthony Francis Phillimore [see B. Phillimore], and has issue living, James Alexander, *b.* 1964,—Lucien Coll, *b,* 1966,—Aidan John, *b.* 1968,—Antonia Frances, *b.* 1961,—Joanna Theresa, *b.* 1962.——Cecilia Anne, *b.* 1941; ed. at Benenden, and Girton Coll., Camb. (MA, MB, BChir): *m.* 1972, Jonathan Coram, of 43, Ashley Rd., Bristol 6, and has issue living, Brendan John, *b.* 1973.

    Granddaughter of the late William Alexander Lindsay, CVO, KC, el. son of the late Hon. Colin Lindsay (infra):—
Issue of the late Major Francis Howard Lindsay, *b.* 1876; *d.* (killed in action during European War) 1916: *m.* 1910, Helen Margaret, who *d.* 1941, el. dau. and co-heir of the late Lieut.-Col. Stewart MacDougall, Gordon Highlanders (formerly Major Argyll and Sutherland Highlanders), one of H.M.'s Corps of Gentlemen-at-Arms, of Lunga, Ardfern, Argyll :—
Katherine Frances LINDSAY-MACDOUGALL, *b.* 1915; ed. at St. Hilda's Coll., Oxford (MA, BLitt); Curator of Manuscripts, Nat. Maritime Museum, Greenwich 1949-59; educational work in Zambia 1964-69; 1939-45 War as 1st Officer WRNS; assumed the additional surname of MacDougall 1949. *Residence,*—Innisaig, Ardfern, Argyll.

    Grandson of the late Alfred Lindsay (infra):—
Issue of the late Maj. Sir George Humphrey Maurice BROUN-LINDSAY, *DSO, b.* 1888, *d.* 1964: *m.* 1921, Edith Christian Broun-Baird (Colstoun, Haddington), dau. of the late John George Alexander Baird, of Wellwood, Muirkirk, when he assumed the additional surname of Broun [Fergusson, Bt., *cr.* 1703]:—
Colin George (Colstoun, Haddington), *b.* 1926: *m.* 1952, Countess Beatrice Marie Thérèse Ferdinande Yvonne Ghislaine, da. of Count Conrad Marie Joseph Gaspard Melchior Baltasar Ghislain d'Ursel, of Château de Moulbaix, Belgium, and has issue living, Ludovic David, *b.* 1954,—Christian Georgiana, *b.* 1956.

    Granddaughter of the late Hon. Colin Lindsay, 4th son of 24th Earl of Crawford:—
Issue of the late Alfred Lindsay, *b.* 1853, *d.* 1901: *m.* 1882, Isabel Catherine, who *d.* 1935, da. of the late Rev. George Barons Northcote, R. of Feniton, Honiton:—
Violet Harriet Isabella (1, Chester Place, Norwich), *b.* 1886: *m.* 1915, Arnold Churchill, who *d.* 1964.

    Grandchildren of Col. Henry Edzell Morgan Lindsay, CB (infra):—
Issue of the late Claud Frederic Thomas Lindsay, *b.* 1892; Capt. and Acting Maj. RFA; *d.* (killed in action 1918): *m.* 1915, Dorothy Lindsay, who *d.* 1969; she *m.* 2ndly, 1923, Lt.-Col. Eric Denis Corkery, MC, Devonshire Regt., who *d.* (killed in action) 1942, da. of the late Sir Henry James Forde, of The Manor of St. John, Waterford:—
George Morgan Thomas, *b.* (*posthumous*) 1918; ed. at Wellington Coll.; Maj. R.A. (ret.): *m.* 1954, Jennifer Mary, only da. of the late Col. J. G. Ferry, RA (ret.), of Wymering Lodge, Farnborough, and has issue living, David Charles Thomas, *b.* 1955,—William George Thomas, *b.* 1958. *Residences,*— Glanmor, Southerndown, nr. Bridgend, Glamorgan; Lane End Cottage, Porton, Salisbury.

Issue of the late David Edzell Thomas Lindsay, *b.* 1910, *d.* 1968: *m.* 1st, 1933, Kathleen Mary, who obtained a divorce 1939, da. Austin Green; 2ndly, 1940, Eleanor Margaret, from whom he obtained a divorce 1947, da. of Kenneth Campbell; 3rdly, 1950, the Hon. Audrey Lavinia Lyttelton (10, Redland Green Rd., Bristol), da. of 9th Viscount Cobham:—

(By 1st m.) David Claud (38, Bassingham Rd., SW18 3AG), *b.* 1934; ed. at Eton: *m.* 1964, Sheela Mary, da. of the late Michael Edward FitzGerald.——(by 3rd m.) Hugh Charles Lyttelton, *b.* 1953. ——Andrew Edzell Thomas, *b.* 1956.——Emma Katrina, *b.* 1955.

Granddaughters of the late Lt.-Col. Henry Gore Lindsay, son of the late George Hayward Lindsay, son of the late Rt. Rev. the Hon. Charles Dalrymple Lindsay, Bishop of Kildare, 6th son of 5th Earl of Balcarres:—

Issue of the late Col. Henry Edzell Morgan Lindsay, C.B., *b.* 1857, *d.* 1935 : *m.* 1889, Ellen Katherine, who *d.* 1937, el. dau. and co-heiress of the late George Thomas, of Ystrad Mynach, Glamorgan:—

Ellen Blanche, *BEM, b.* 1893: *m.* 1921, Maj. Richard Cope Wilson, MBE, who *d.* 1949. *Residence,—* 38, Bassingham Rd., SW18 3AG.

Issue of the late Major David Balcarres Lindsay, *b.* 1863, *d.* 1943: *m.* 1898, Grace Maud, who *d.* 1945, dau. of George Miller, of Brentry House, Westbury-on-Trym:—

Madeline, *b.* 1899: *m.* 1936, Thomas Morgan, and has issue living, John Patrick, *b.* 1937: *m.* 1968, Raine, da. of G. F. Tredwell,—Bernard Lawrence, *b.* 1938: *m.* 1960, Chong Siew Yong, of Kuala Lumpur, Malaysia, and has issue living, Michael Gary *b.* 1963, David *b.* 1965, Susan Jane *b.* 1961. *Residence,—*Ivy Lodge, Letcombe Bassett, Berks.——Juliet Mary, *b.* 1904: *m.* 1st, 1930, the 7th Marquess of Waterford, who *d.* 1934; 2ndly, 1946, Lt.-Col. John Eric Durnford Silcock. *Residence,—*Newtown Anner, Clonmel, co. Tipperary.——Winifred Laura, *b.* 1907. *Residence,—* Newton Anner, Clonmel co. Tipperary.

Issue of the late Col. Walter Charles Lindsay, M.V.O., *b.* 1866, *d.* 1929; *m.* 1897, Lady Kathleen Butler, *O.B.E.,* who *d.* 1953, dau. of 6th Earl of Carrick :—

Doreen, *CVO, b.* 1899; MVO (4th class) 1954, CVO 1969: *m.* 1929, Maj. Richard Archer Houblon, DSO, RHA, who *d.* 1957. *Residence,—*Kilmurry, Thomastown, co. Kilkenny.——Kathleen, *b.* 1902: *m.* 1924, Lt. Cdr. Denys Royds Brocklebank, late RN, who *d.* 1947, and has issue living, Ralph Wilfrid (of Orland, Clent, Worcestershire), *b.* 1927: *m.* 1954, Beryl Seabury, and has issue living, Guy Philip *b.* 1954,—Ann, *b.* 1926: *m.* 1st, 1952 (m. diss. 1960), John Ronald Lindsay Antrobus [see Antrobus, Bt., colls.]; 2ndly, 1967, Maurice Stanley Gooding, of Hackthorn, Beaminster, Dorset, —Eve, *b.* 1929: *m.* 1952, Anthony Victor Kaye, of Dunsdale, Forest Row, Sussex,—Una, *b.* 1930: *m.* 1960, Christopher John Lewers, of Wynstones, Brookthorpe, Gloucester. *Residence,—*Kilmurry, Thomastown, co. Kilkenny.

Issue of the late Maj.-Gen. George Mackintosh Lindsay, CB, CMG, CBE, DSO, *b.* 1880, *d.* 1956: *m.* 1907, Constance who *d.* 1974, da. of George Stewart Hamilton:—

Joan Mary, *b.* 1911: *m.* 1938, Charles Holwell Thomas, OBE [E. Lauderdale, colls.], and has issue living, Robert Heriot Lindsay, *b.* 1941,—David Charles Morgan, *b.* 1942: *m.* 1970, Ann Tresina, da. of R. H. B. Benger, of Johannesburg, and has issue living, Rupert James Morgan *b.* 1972,—George Francis Maitland, *b.* 1944,—Sarah Elizabeth Lindsay, *b.* 1946: *m.* 1971, Henry Charles Alfred Rowe, of Winfrith House, Winfrith, Newburgh, Dorset, and has issue living, Charles Edward Kingsley *b.* 1973. *Residence,—*Southwick House, Kirkcudbrightshire.

PREDECESSORS.—[1] WALTER de Lindesay (1113); *s.* by his son, or brother [2] WILLIAM, of Ercildun, 2nd Lord of his name; *s.* by his son [3] WALTER, 3rd Lord ; *s.* by his son [4] WILLIAM, 4th Lord; *s.* by his son [5] WALTER, 5th Lord (Lord of Lamberton) ; *s.* by his son [6] WILLIAM, 6th Lord (1247); *s.* by his son [7] WALTER, 7th Lord ; *s.* by his son [8] WILLIAM, 8th Lord (1282) ; *s.* by his kinsman [9] Sir ALEXANDER, 9th Lord (grandson of Sir David of Brenevil and the Byres, a Regent of Scotland 1255), companion of King Robert Bruce, and a Baron 1308; *s.* by his son [10] Sir DAVID, 10th Lord, one of the Barons who signed the famous letter to Pope John XXII. asserting the independence of Scotland; *s.* by his son [11] Sir JAMES, 11th Lord; *s.* by his son [12] Sir JAMES, 12th Lord, High Justiciary of Scotland; *s.* by his cousin [13] Sir DAVID, 13th Lord, a valiant knight, was cr., proclaimed and belted *Earl of Crawford* (peerage of Scotland) at Perth, April 21, 1398, his lordship being at the same time erected into a regality; was Ambassador to England 1406 ; *s.* by his son [14] ALEXANDER, 2nd Earl ; a Commr. to treat for the release of James I.; was detained as a hostage for his ransom 1424-7; *s.* by his son [15] DAVID, 3rd Earl; killed 1446, while endeavouring to prevent the Battle of Arbroath ; *s.* by his son [16] ALEXANDER, 4th Earl; Hereditary Sheriff of Aberdeenshire; fought in rebellion at Battle of Brechin 1452; was attainted and afterwards restored ; *s.* by his son [17] DAVID, 5th Earl; having held numerous high offices, was cr. *Duke of Montrose* (peerage of Scotland) 1488, a dignity that has not since been assumed by any of his successors ; *d.* 1495; *s.* by his 2nd son [18] JOHN, 6th Earl ; accused of murdering his el. brother, but was killed at Flodden before the accusation was heard ; *s.* by his uncle [19] ALEXANDER, 7th Earl ; *s.* by his son [20] DAVID, 8th Earl; his son Alexander being found guilty of constructive parricide, was by the law of Scotland attainted; *s.* by his kinsman [21] DAVID, 9th Earl, grandson of Walter, son of 3rd Earl; by consent of the crown he reconveyed his earldom to the son of Alexander (ante), but in failure of his issue the title to be in remainder to his son, Sir David (Lord Edzell), a Lord of Session ; John, the 2nd son of this peer, Lord Menmuir, a Lord of Session, had issue, David, cr. 1st Lord Lindsay of Balcarres (infra): *s.* by his grandson [22] DAVID, 10th Earl; a faithful adherent of Queen Mary's cause; *s.* by his son [23] DAVID, 11th Earl; *s.* by his son [24] DAVID, 12th Earl, who alienated the greater portion of the estates; *s.* by his uncle [25] HENRY, 13th Earl, son of 10th Earl; *s.* by his son [26] GEORGE, 14th Earl; *s.* by his half-brother [27] ALEXANDER, 15th Earl; *s.* by his brother [28] LUDOVIC, 16th Earl; during the Civil Wars commanded a Regt. of Horse, and fought at Marston Moor, Philiphaugh, and Newcastle, where he was taken prisoner, and in exchange, it is supposed, for his liberty, resigned with the sanction of the Crown, his Earldom to Charles 1. for a re-grant (failing his own issue) to John, 10th Earl of Lindsay, with remainder to his own collateral heirs: *d.s.p.*, when the Earldom passed to John, 10th Earl of Lindsay, in whose family it continued until 1808, when the line failed (see E. Lindsay). [29] DAVID, son of Lord Menmuir (refer to 9th Earl), was cr. *Lord Lindsay of Balcarres* (peerage of Scotland) 1633; *s.* by his son [30] ALEXANDER, 2nd Lord; rendered valuable service to the royal cause; cr. *Lord Lindsay and Balniel* and *Earl of Balcarres* (peerage of Scotland) 1651; for taking part with the Earl of Glencairn his estates were sequestrated; *s.* by his son [31] CHARLES, 2nd Earl of Balcarres; *d.* unm. 1662; *s.* by his brother [32] COLIN, a staunch Royalist; *s.* by his son [33] ALEXANDER, 4th Earl of Balcarres; became in 1744, on the death of David Lindsay of Edzell, *de jure* Lord Lindsay of Crawford, and Chief of his house: *m.* 1718, Elizabeth, who *d.* 1768, dau. of David Scott, of Scotstarvet; *d.* 1746; *s.* by his brother [34] JAMES, 5th Earl of Balcarres; *d.* 1768; *s.* by his son [35] ALEXANDER, 6th Earl of Balcarres; a Representative Peer, a Gen. in the Army and Gov. of Jamaica; in 1808, *s.* as 32nd Earl of Crawford; *d.* 1828; *s.* by his son [36] JAMES, 24th Earl of Crawford and 7th of Balcarres; *b.* 1783: *m.* 1811, the Hon. Maria Margaret Frances Pennington, who *d.* 1850, dau. of 1st Baron Muncaster; cr. *Baron Wigan,* of Haigh Hall, co. Lancaster (peerage of United Kingdom) 1826, and had Earldom of Crawford and Lordship of Lindsay confirmed to him 1848; *d.* 1869; *s.* by his son [37] ALEXANDER WILLIAM CRAWFORD, 25th Earl of Crawford and 8th of Balcarres, and 33rd Lord Lindsay of Crawford; *b.* 1912: *m.* 1846, Margaret, who *d.* 1909, da. of Lt.-Gen. James Lindsay, of Balcarres; *d.* 1880: *s.* by his son [38] JAMES LUDOVIC, *KT, LLD, FRS,* 26th Earl of Crawford and 9th of Balcarres; *b.* 1847; MP for Wigan (C) 1874-80; acted as Dep. for Great Steward of Scotland at Coronations of King Edward VII, and King George V: *m.* 1869, Emily Florence, who *d.* 1934, da. of the late Col. the Hon. Edward Bootle-Wilbraham; *d.* 1913; *s.* by his el. son [39] DAVID ALEXANDER EDWARD, *KT, PC, DCL,* 27th Earl of Crawford and 10th of Balcarres; *b.* 1871; was a Junior Lord of the Treasury 1903-5, Pres. of Board of Agriculture and Fisheries July to Dec. 1916, Lord Privy Seal 1916-19, Chancellor of Duchy of Lancaster 1919-21, First Commr. of Works 1921-2 and Min. of Transport 1922 ; M.P. for Lancashire (N.), Chorley Div. (C.) 1895-1913: *m.* 1900, Constance Lilian, who *d.* 1947, dau. of Sir Henry Carstairs Pelly, M.P., 3rd Bt. ; *d.* 1940 ; *s.* by his el. son [40] DAVID ALEXANDER ROBERT, 28th Earl of Crawford and 11th Earl of Balcarres and present peer: also Lord Lindsay (of Crawford), Lord Lindsay of Balcarres, Lord Lindsay and Balniel and Baron Wigan.

CRAWSHAW, BARON. (Brooks.) [Baron U.K. 1892, Bt. U.K. 1891.]

WILLIAM MICHAEL CLIFTON BROOKS, 4th
Baron and 4th Baronet; *b.* March 25th, 1933;
s. 1946; ed. at Eton, and at Ch. Ch., Oxford;
Lord of the Manor of Long Whatton; Treasurer
Loughborough Div. Conservative Assocn.
1954-8, since when Co. Commr., Leics. Boy
Scouts.

Arms,—Argent, three bars wavy azure, a cross fleury
erminois, in chief a fountain. Crest,—A demi-lion proper,
maned argent, charged on the shoulder with a fountain, and
holding in the paws a pheon in bend sinister proper, stringed
or. Supporters,—Dexter, a stag argent; sinister, a horse
argent; each collared wavy azure, and suspended from the
collar an escutcheon erminois charged with a fountain.

Seat,—Whatton, Loughborough, Leicestershire.

FINEM RESPICE
Consider the end.

BROTHERS LIVING.
Hon. DAVID GERALD, *b.* Sept. 14th, 1934; ed. at Eton, and
Roy. Agric. Coll., Cirencester: *m.* 1970, Belinda Mary, da.
of George Burgess, of 14, Kirkwood Av., Sandringham,
Melbourne, Aust., and has issue living, Susanna Jane, *b.* 1974.

Hon. John Patrick (25, Cadogan St., SW3), *b.* 1938; ed. at Loughborough Coll.: *m.* 1967, Rosemary
Vans Agnew, only da. of the late C. Vans Agnew Frank, of Greenways, Hunmanby, E. Yorks., and
has issue living, Edward Samuel, *b.* 1969,—Caroline Miranda, *b.* 1972.

SISTER LIVING.
Hon. Mary Altheia, *b.* 1931.

COLLATERAL BRANCHES LIVING.

Issue of the late Herbert William Brooks, son of 2nd Baron, *b.* 1890, *d* 1974: *m.* 1922,
Hilda Muriel, who *d.* 1967, da. of the late A. G. Steel, K.C.:—
Christopher John (Puesta Del Sol, Guadarranque, San Roque, Cadiz, Spain), *b.* 1925; late Capt.
Coldstream Guards: *m.* 1st, 1951 (m. diss. 1957), Patricia Evelyn Beverley, el. da of John William
Matthews, FRCS, of Heathercroft, Hertford Heath, Herts.; 2ndly, 1958, Gwendoline Helen, el. da.
of Louis D. Evans, and has issue living, (by 1st m.) Sarah Jane, *b.* 1956,—(by 2nd m.) Timothy
Allan William, *b.* 1962,—Georgina Helen, *b.* 1960.——Timothy Gerald Martin (of Wistow, Leicester),
b. 1929; NDA; a Member of Roy. Agric. Coll., and a JP of Leics.: *m.* 1951, the Hon. Ann Fremantle,
da. of 4th Baron Cottesloe, and has issue living, Richard Allan Halford, *b.* 1958,—Andrew Herbert
John, *b.* 1966,—Michael Julian, *b.* 1969,—Lucinda Jane, *b.* 1953,—Nicola Frances, *b.* 1955.

Grandson of the late Hon. Marshall Jones Brooks (infra):—
Issue of the late Lt.-Col. Thomas Marshall Brooks, MC, TD; *b.* 1893; *d.* 1967: *m.* 1920,
Evelyn Sylvia, who *d.* 1967, da. of the Rev. the Hon. Archibald Parker, Preb. of Lichfield
[E. Macclesfield, colls.]:—
Ronald Marshall (Heath Hill, Bourton-on-the-Water, Glos.), *b.* 1924; ed. at Eton; 1939-45 War as
Lt. Queen's Bays: *m.* 1950, Dorothy Valerie, da. of Geoffrey Freer, of Ditchford Hill, Moreton-in-
Marsh, Glos.

Issue of the late Hon. Marshall Jones Brooks, 2nd son of 1st Baron, *b.* 1855, *d.* 1944:
m. 1889, Florence, CBE, JP, who *d.* 1934, da. of the late Frederick Freeman
Thomas, MP [V. Hampden]:—
Noel Brand, MC, TD, *b.* 1896; ed. at Eton, and at New Coll., Oxford; Maj. Cheshire Yeo.; 1914-18
War (MC): *m.* 1921, Joan Margaret, JP, da. of Brig.-Gen. Sir Edward Thomas Le Marchant,
C.B., C.B.E., 4th Bt., and has issue living, Robert Noel Brand (Castle Barn, Churchill, Oxon.),
b. 1927: *m.* 1955, Caroline Diana Todd, and has issue living, Christopher George *b.* 1959, Charles
Patrick Evelyn *b.* 1963, Annabel Joan *b.* 1958,—Anne, *b.* 1922,—Betty Rosamond, *b.* 1924:
m. 1950, Maj. Nigel Steuart Kearsley, late Welsh Guards, of The Mill House, Coln St. Aldwyns,
Cirencester [Ramsay Bt., colls., *cr.* 1806], and has issue living, Rosamond Joanna *b.* 1955, Grania
Anne *b.* 1957. Residence,—Fairgreen Farm, Churchill, Oxford——Dorothy (Hillside House,
Loxley, Warwick), *b.* 1890: *m.* 1911, Maj. Charles Hugh Gregory-Hood, formerly The Buffs (E.
Kent Regt.), who *d.* 1951 [see V. Hood, colls.].——Marjorie Nell (Baroness Ashton of Hyde), *b.* 1901;
is a J.P. for Gloucestershire: *m.* 1925, the 2nd Baron Ashton of Hyde. Residence,—Broadwell
Hill, Moreton-in-Marsh, Glos.

PREDECESSORS.—[1] THOMAS Brooks, son of the late John Brooks, of Crawshaw Hall,
Lancashire, *b.* 1825; High Sheriff of Lancashire 1884; *cr.* a Baronet 1891, and Baron
Crawshaw, of Crawshaw, co. Lancaster and of Whatton, co. Leicester (peerage of the United
Kingdom) 1892: *m.* 1851, Catherine, who *d.* 1917, dau. of the late John Jones, of Kilsall Hall,
Shropshire; *d.* 1908; *s.* by his son [2] WILLIAM, 2nd Baron, *b.* 1853: *m.* 1882, Mary Ethel,
who *d.* 1914, dau. of Sir Michael Hicks-Beach, 8th Bt.; *d* 1929; *s.* by his son [3] GERALD
BEACH, 3rd Baron, *b.* 1884: *m.* 1930, Marjory Shella, dau. of the late Lieut.-Col. Percy Robert
Clifton, C.M.G., D.S.O., T.D.: *d.* 1946; *s.* by his son [4] WILLIAM MICHAEL CLIFTON, 4th Baron
and present peer.

CREWE, MARQUESSATE OF. (Crewe-Milnes.) [Extinct 1945.]

DAUGHTERS LIVING OF FIRST MARQUESS. (By 1st marriage.)

Lady Celia Hermione, *b.* 1884; is a J.P.: *m.* 1906, Capt. Sir Edward Clive Milnes-Coates, 2nd Bt.,
OBE, who *d.* 1971, having assumed the additional surname of Milnes 1946. Residence,—Helperby
Hall, Helperby, Yorks, YO6 2QP.

(By 2nd marriage.)

Lady Mary Evelyn Hungerford, *b.* 1915; bore the Queen's Canopy at Coronation of King George VI:
m. 1935, the 9th Duke of Roxburghe, who *d.* 1974, and from whom she obtained a divorce 1953.
Residence,—15, Hyde Park Gardens, W.2.

Crichton, Viscount, son of Earl Erne.

CROFT, BARON. (Croft.) [Baron U.K. 1940, Bt. U.K. 1924.]

MICHAEL HENRY GLENDOWER PAGE CROFT, 2nd Baron, and 2nd Baronet; b. Aug. 20th, 1916; s. 1947; ed. at Eton, and at Trin. Hall, Camb. (BA); Bar. Inner Temple 1952; OStJ; FRSA; 1939-45 War; Hon. Capt RASC: m. 1948, Lady Antoinette Fredericka Hersey Cecilia Conyngham, who d. 1959, da. of 6th Marquess Conyngham, and has issue.

Arms,—Quarterly per fesse indented azure and argent; in the 1st quarter a lion passant guardant or. Crests,—1st, a lion passant guardant argent; 2nd, a wyvern sable vulned in the side gules. Supporters,—Dexter, a lion rampant quarterly per fesse indented azure and argent; sinister, a wyvern sable, vulned in the side gules.
Seat,—Croft Castle, Leominster, Herefordshire. Residence,—8, Hereford Square, S.W.7. Clubs,—Athenaeum, Bath.

To be rather than to seem.

SON LIVING.
Hon. BERNARD WILLIAM HENRY PAGE, b. Aug. 28th, 1949; ed. at Stowe, and Wales Univ. (BSc Econ.).

DAUGHTER LIVING.
Hon. Charlotte Elizabeth Ann, b. 1952; ed. at Benenden: m. 1975, Emrys Thomas Devonald, of 2, Cherry Tree Dell, Chorleywood Common, Chorleywood, Herts.

SISTERS LIVING.
Hon. Hilda Elizabeth Mary, b. 1909: m. 1934, Richard Hayter Bayford, Bar.-at-Law, Capt. Roy. Berks Regt., and has issue living, Robert Michael Croft, b. 1936,—Gillian Sara Carolyn, b. 1935: m. 1958, Flight-Lieut. Michael Holmes, R.A.F.,—Mary Elizabeth, b. 1944. Residence,—Upper Bowden, near Pangbourne, Berks.
Hon. Nancy Diana Joyce, b. 1912: m. 1936, Manfred Uhlman. and has issue living, Francis Raymond Croft, b. 1943,—Caroline Ann, b. 1940: m. 1966, Albert Charles Compton, and has issue living Tristram Ludovic Archer b. 1968. Residence,—47, Downshire Hill, Hampstead, NW3.
Hon. Anne Rosemary Dorothea, b. 1918: m. 1946, Flight-Lieut. Herbert Edmund Poole, R.A.F., and has issue living, Herbert Benyon, b. 1947,—Jeremy Henry Borwick, b. 1949,—Hugo Edmund, b. 1952. Residence,—Knight's Hill, Sawbridgeworth, Herts.

PREDECESSOR.—[1] Rt. Hon. Sir HENRY PAGE Croft, C.M.G., T.D., P.C., son of the late Richard Benyon Croft, of Fanhams Hall, Ware [see Croft, Bt., cr. 1671, colls.]; b. 1881; European War 1914-16 as Brig.-Gen. late Herts Regt. (C.M.G.); was Joint Under-Sec. of State for War 1940-45; sat as M.P. for Christchurch (C) 1910-18, and for Bournemouth 1918-40; cr. a Baronet 1924, and Baron Croft, of Bournemouth, co. Southampton (peerage of United Kingdom) 1940: m. 1907, the Hon. Nancy Beatrice Borwick, who d. 1949, youngest dau. of 1st Baron Borwick; d. 1947; s. by his son [2] MICHAEL HENRY GLENDOWER PAGE, 2nd Baron and present peer.

CROFTON, BARON. (Crofton.) [Baron I. 1797, Bt. I. 1758.]

CHARLES EDWARD PIERS CROFTON, 6th Baron, and 9th Baronet; b. April 27th, 1949; s. 1974.

Arms,—Per pale indented or and azure, a lion passant guardant counterchanged. Crest,—Seven ears of wheat growing on one stalk or. Supporters—Dexter, a lion azure; sinister, a stag proper.
Residence,—Ballina Park, Ashford, co. Wicklow.

God gives the increase.

BROTHERS LIVING.
Hon. GUY PATRICK GILBERT, b. June 17th, 1951.
Hon. Arthur Blaise Adrian, b. 1957.

SISTER LIVING.
Hon. Georgiana Ann, b. 1955.

AUNT LIVING. (Raised to the rank of a Baron's daughter 1948.)
Hon. Diana Marie Faith, b. 1927: m. 1st, 1949, Com. Hugh May, RN; 2ndly, 1963, Cdr. Edward Michael George Hewitt, RN, of Mote Cottage, 25, The Dell, Kingsclere, Newbury, Berks., and has issue living, (by 1st m.) Peter Seaburne, b. 1952,—Antonia Kinbarra, b. 1950: m. 1974, Michael David Rayment,—(by 2nd m.) David Edward, b. 1965,—Gemma Francis, b. 1963.

WIDOW LIVING OF SON OF FOURTH BARON.
Madeleine Barbara (PRATT), dau. of the late William James Heath, of London: m. 1951, as his 4th wife, the Hon. (Arthur) Marcus Lowther Crofton, Maj., Irish Guards, who d. 1962. Residence,—

MOTHER LIVING.
Ann Pamela, da. of Gp. Capt. Charles Herbert Tighe, OBE, DFC, RAF (ret.): m. 1st, 1948 (m. diss. 1963), the 5th Baron Crofton, who d. 1974; 2ndly 1964 (m. diss 1972), Robert Thomas Francis Flach, Bar.-at-law; 3rdly, 1973, Guy Brooke, of 829 Park Avenue, New York, NY, USA.

WIDOW LIVING OF FIFTH BARON.

MARY (*Baroness Crofton*) (Fowey Lodge, Fowey, Cornwall), el. da. of the late Maj. James Irvine Hatfield Friend, OBE, MC, DL, of Northdown, Thanet, Kent, and formerly wife of Robert T. Flach: *m.* 1964, as his 2nd wife, the 5th Baron, who *d.* 1974.

COLLATERAL BRANCHES LIVING. (*In remainder to Barony and Baronetcy.*)
Grandchildren of the late Capt. the Hon. Francis George Crofton, RN, yr. brother of 3rd Baron:—
Issue of the late George Crofton, *b.* 1881, *d.* 1943 : *m.* 1910, Elina, dau. of the late K. Smith :—
Francis George, *b.* 1915. *Residence,—*
Issue of the late Alfred Gerald Crofton, *b.* 1882, *d.* 1942 : *m.* 1903, Frances Nona, who *d.* 1951, dau. of the Rev. Edward Wilson :—
Dermott Kenneth (Winfrith, Ganges, BC, Canada), *b.* 1904: *m.* 1934, Doris Livingstone, el. da. of the late J. W. Taylor, of Belfast, and has issue living, Patrick Dermott, *b.* 1935; Lt.-Cdr. (S) CAF (ret.): *m* , 1958, Patricia Judith Mary, only da. of Capt. Trevor Williams, of Folly, The Walled Garden, Wargrave, Berks., and has issue living, Marietta Susan Annëtte *b.* 1959, Virginia Margaret Adele *b.* 1961, Susanne Catherine Mary *b.* 1962, Tessa Penelope Sarah *b.* 1965,—Marcus Livingstone (11, Duncraggan Drive, Dartmouth, Nova Scotia), *b.* 1937; Lt. Cdr. CAF: *m.* 1966, Elizabeth Jane, da. of Lt.-Col. G. A. Churchill, of Vic., BC, and has issue living, Dermott Marcus Churchill *b.* 1970, Geoffrey Patrick *b.* 1973, Laura Elizabeth *b.* 1967, Jenny Livingstone *b.* 1969,—Sharron Diana, *b.* 1940: *m.* 1964 (m. diss. 1970), Robert Montagu Scott, and has issue living, Ian Dermott Montagu *b.* 1967, Andrea Gillian *b.* 1966.——Desmond Gerald, *ED* (RRI, Spring Corner, PO Box 432, Ganges, BC), *b.* 1905; NW Europe 1944-45 as Lt.-Col. Canadian Scottish (wounded, despatches, Order of Lion of the Netherlands): *m.* 1st, 1925, Ida, who *d.* 1970, da. of the late F. Hardcastle, and widow of Maj. F. Harvey Corbett, RFA; 2ndly, 1971, Dorothea Harriet, yst. da. of Arthur George Wilson, and widow of Keith Edward Hook, and has issue living, (by 1st m.) John Edward, *b.* 1925; Lt.-Col. CAF: *m.* 1950, Marie White, and has issue living, Desmond *b.* 1951, Kevin *b.* 1954, Neil *b.* 1956,— Sylvia Ida, *b.* 1928: *m.* 1954, Maj. Arthur Leake Gale, QD, Princess Patricia's Canadian LI, and has issue living, Reginald Derek Leake *b.* 1956, Rupert Arthur Leake *b.* 1962, Deirdre Sylvia Leake *b.* 1957.——Donovan Patrick (of 3026, Oakdowne Rd., Vic., BC), *b.* 1915; Italy and NW Europe 1943-45 as Maj. Princess Patricia's Canadian LI (despatches): *m.* 1946, Anne B., da. of Harry Marshall Erskine Evans, OBE, of Edmonton, Alberta, and has issue living, Cameron P. L., *b.* 1947,— Barry Gerald, *b.* 1953.——Doreen Sheila, *b.* 1911: *m.* 1939, Frederick A. E. Morris, and has issue living, Robert Frederick, *b.* 1942,—James R., *b.* 1949,—Wendy P., *b.* 1940.——Denise Frances, *b.* 1913.

Issue of the late Francis Lowther Crofton, *b.* 1883, *d.* 1971: *m.* 1st, 1917, Annie Rebecca, MM, who *d.* 1956, da. of the late Robert Colhoun, of Londonderry; 2ndly, 1957, Nancy Esten (2530, Windsor Rd., Victoria, BC, Canada), da. of H. H. Nash, and widow of F. Arthur Inglis:—

(By 1st m.) Francis David (Box 1124, Station A, Surrey, BC, Canada), *b.* 1919; ed. at McGill Univ. (MD); late Capt. RCAMC: *m.* 1948, Marguerite, da. of Earl Hines, of Halifax, Nova Scotia, and has issue living, Catherine Elizabeth Ellen, *b.* 1950.

(*In remainder to Baronetcy only.*)

Grandchildren of the late Major George Lowther Crofton, son of the late Frederick Charles Edward Lowther Crofton, son of the late Frederick Lowther Crofton, grandson of the late Capt. John Frederick Crofton, 2nd son of 1st baronet:—
Issue of the late Frederick Norris Lowther Crofton, *b.* 1870, *d.* 1947: *m.* 1896, Edith, who *d.* 1951, dau. of the late Hastings Cuningham, of Windermere, N.S. Wales [Fairlie-Cuninghame, Bt.]:—

George Lowther (Walter Cres., Banora Point, Tweed River, NSW), *b.* 1905: *m.* 1928, Nea, da, o the Rev. A. P. Cameron (Moderator of Ch. of Scotland, NSW), of The Manse, Glen Innes, NSW, and has issue living, Judith Mary, *b.* 1932: *m.* 1st, 1957 (m. diss. 1968), Les Hayna; 2ndly, 1970, Edgar Allen, of MS 108, Windermere Rd., Bundaberg, Qld. 4670, and has issue living (by 1st m.), Christine Nea *b.* 1957 (by 2nd m.) Geoffrey Edgar Howell *b.* 1971, William George John (twin) *b.* 1971,—Clare Edith, *b.* 1936: *m.* 1956, Alex Barry Mitchell, of Ellerslie, Glen Innes, NSW, and has issue living, Steven George *b.* 1957, Brian Alex *b.* 1961, Glenn Cameron *b.* 1965, Jennifer Jean *b.* 1959.——Ellen Marjorie Lowther, *b.* 1897. *Residence,—*79, Hunter St., Glen Innes, NSW.

PREDECESSORS.—[1] Catherine, dau. of Sir Edward Crofton, M.P., 4th Bt., of the Mot[e] (which title, cr. 1661, became extinct on the death of the 5th Bt. 1780): *m.* MARCUS Lowther M.P. for Roscommon, who assumed the surname of Crofton and was cr. a Bt. 1758; *d.* 1774; *s.* by his son [2, 3] Sir Edward, 2nd Bt.; M.P. for co. Roscommon: *m.* Anne, dau. and heir of Thomas Croker, of Baxtown, co. Kildare; *d.* Sept. 30, 1797, having a short time before his death been offered a peerage; on Dec. 1 of the same year his widow ANNE, was cr. *Baroness Crofton* (peerage of Ireland); she *d.* 1817, and was *s.* by her grandson ; Sir Edward was *s.* by his son [4] Edward, 3rd Bt.; *d.* 1816; *s.* by his son [5] Edward, 4th Bt., *b.* 1806; *s.* his grandmother as 2nd Baron 1817; a Representative Peer, and a Lord-in-Waiting to H.M. Queen Victoria: *m.* 1833, Lady Georgiana Paget, dau. of 1st Marquess of Anglesey; *d.* 1869; *s.* by his son [6] Edward Henry Churchill, 3rd Baron; *b.* 1834; a Representative Peer; Gentleman of the Bedchamber (1866-8) and State Steward (1880) to Viceroy of Ireland; *d.* 1912; *s.* by his nephew [7] Arthur Edward Lowther, 4th Baron, *b.* 1866 ; a Representative Peer : *m.* 1893, Jessie Castle, who *d.* 1923, dau. of J. Hewitson and widow of Neville Paddon; *d.* 1942; *s.* by his grandson [8] Edward Blaise (son of the late Hon. Edward Charles Crofton, el. son of 4th Baron), 5th Baron, *b.* 1926: *m.* 1st, 1948 (m. diss. 1963) Anna Pamela, da. of Gp. Capt. Charles Herbert Tighe, OBE, DFC, RAF (ret.); 2ndly, 1964, Mary, el. da. of the late Maj. James Irvine Hatfield Friend, OBE, MC, and formerly wife of Robert W. Flach; *d.* 1974; *s.* by his el. son [9], CHARLES EDWARD PIERS, 6th Baron and present peer.

CROMARTIE, EARL OF. (Mackenzie.) [Earl U.K. 1861.]
I shine not burn.

RODERICK GRANT FRANCIS MAC-KENZIE, M.C., T.D., 4th Earl, *b.* Oct. 24th, 1904 ; *s.* 1962 ; ed. at Charterhouse, and RMC Sandhurst; Maj. (ret.) Seaforth Highlanders (TA); commissioned Seaforth Highlanders 1924; served in N. Ireland and India 1924-27; attached Nigeria Regt., RWAFF 1929; N.W. Frontier, India 1930-31 (medal); RARO 1933; joined 4th/ 5th Bns. Seaforth Highlanders (TA) 1935; 1939-45 War as Maj., 4th Bn. in France (prisoner 1940-45); JP and Hon. Sheriff of Ross and Cromarty (Co. Councillor 1935-39 and since 1963); Vice-Convener co. Ross and Cromarty 1970-71, since when Convener; FSAS; Sec. Scottish Peers

Assocn., House of Lords; discontinued the use of the surname of Blunt for himself and son: *m.* 1st, 1933, Dorothy (PORTER) (who obtained a divorce 1945), da. of B. G. Downing, of Kentucky, USA; 2ndly, 1947 (m. diss. 1962), Olga (MENDOZA), da. of Stewart Laurance; 3rdly, 1962, Lilias Janet Garvie, da. of Prof. James Walter McLeod, OBE, FRS, and has issue by 1st and 2nd m.

Arms,—Quarterly, 1st; or a mountain azure in flames proper (*Macleod of Lewis*); 2nd, azure a buck's head cabossed or (*Mackenzie*); 3rd, gules three legs of a man armed proper, conjoined in the centre at the upper part of two of the thighs, flexed in triangle, garnished and spurred, or (*Isle of Man*); 4th, argent, on a pale sable an Imperial Crown proper, within a double tressure flowered and counter-flowered with fleur de lys gules (*Erskine of Innerteall*). **Crest,**—The sun in his splendour. **Supporters,**—*Dexter,* a wild man wreathed about the loins with oak, holding a club resting on the exterior shoulder proper; *sinister,* a greyhound argent, collared gules.

Seat,—Castle Leod, Strathpeffer, Ross-shire. *Clubs,*—Pratt's, Army and Navy.

SON LIVING. (*By 2nd marriage.*)
JOHN RUARIDH BLUNT GRANT (*Viscount Tarbat*), *b.* June 12th, 1948: *m.* 1973, Helen, da. of John Murray.

DAUGHTERS LIVING. (*By 1st marriage.*)
Lady Sibell Anne Julia BLUNT-MACKENZIE, *b.* 1934: *m.* 1953, Francis Edward Lascelles-Hadwen, from whom she obtained a divorce 1961, and has issue living, James Brian Mackenzie, *b.* 1957,— Georgina Frances, *b.* 1959. *Residence,*—
Lady Gilean Frances BLUNT-MACKENZIE, *b.* 1936: *m.* 1959 (m. diss. 1973), René Eugene Welter, and has issue living, Michael George, *b.* 1964,—Nadia-Christine, *b.* 1960. *Residence,*—52, South Edwardes Sq., W8.

SISTER LIVING.
Lady Isobel, *b.* 1911: *m.* 1947, Capt. Oscar Linda. *Residence,*—Assynt House, Evanton, Ross-shire.

WIDOW LIVING OF SON OF SIBELL LILIAN, COUNTESS OF CROMARTIE.
Mary, dau. of T. D. Hix: *m.* 1st, 1946, as his second wife, the Hon. Walter Osra Blunt-Mackenzie, who *d.* 1951; 2ndly, 1964, Maj. Clement Victor Palmer, P.O. Box 14, White River, E. Transvaal, S. Africa, and has issue living (by 1st marriage) [see colls., infra].

COLLATERAL BRANCHES LIVING.
Issue of the late Hon. Walter Osra BLUNT-MACKENZIE, 2nd son of Sibell Lilian, Countess of Cromartie, *b.* 1906, *d.* 1951: *m.* 1st, 1934, Pamela Lilian Ursula Oliver, from whom he obtained a divorce 1940; 2ndly, 1946, Mary (ante) (who *m.* 2ndly, 1964, Maj. Clement Victor Palmer), dau. of T. D. Hix:—
By 2nd marriage) Roderick, *b.* 1947.

Grandchildren of the late Lady Florence Leveson-Gower, el. dau. of Anne, Duchess of Sutherland (Countess of Cromartie) *b.* 1855, *d.* 1881: *m.* 1876, the Rt. Hon. Henry Chaplin, afterwards 1st Viscount Chaplin[see that title.].

PREDECESSORS.—[1] ANNE, *V.A.*, only child of John Hay Mackenzie of Cromartie, in direct descent from the 3rd Earl of Cromartie who was attainted in 1746: *m.* 1849, the 3rd Duke of Sutherland, and was cr. *Countess of Cromartie, Viscountess Tarbat of Tarbat Baroness Castlehaven, of Castlehaven,* and *Baroness MacLeod, of Leod* (peerage of United Kingdom 1861), with remainder (1) to her second surviving son, Francis, and the heirs male of his body, (2) to each other of her younger sons in like manner in priority of birth, (3) to said Francis and the heirs of his body, (4) to each other her younger sons in like manner in priority of birth, (5) to her daughter Florence and the heirs of her body, and (6) to each other of her daughters in like manner in priority of birth] ; she *d.* 1888, when the Earldom of Cromartie devolved, in accordance with the special remainder, upon her second surviving son [2] FRANCIS, *b.* 1852: *m.* 1876, the Hon. Lilian Janet, who *d.* 1926, dau. of 5th Baron Macdonald; *d.* 1893, when the title fell into abeyance between his two surviving daus., Sibell Lilian and Constance, and so remained until the abeyance was terminated in 1895 in favour of his el. dau. and the heirs of her body, when the honours were confirmed to [3] SIBELL LILIAN, as Countess of Cromartie in her own right; *b.* 1878: *m.* 1899, Lieut.-Col. Edward Walter Blunt, D.L., who *d.* 1949, having assumed the additional surname of Mackenzie 1905; she subsequently discontinued the surname of Blunt; *d.* 1962; *s.* by her el. son [4] RODERICK GRANT FRANCIS, 4th Earl, and present peer, and Viscount Tarbat, Baron Castlehaven, and Baron Macleod.

CROMER, EARL OF. (Baring.) [Earl U.K. 1901.]

By probity and industry.

GEORGE ROWLAND STANLEY BARING, GCMG, MBE, PC, 3rd Earl; *b.* July 28th, 1918; *s.* 1953; ed. at Eton, and Trin. Coll., Camb.; Hon. LLD, NY; one of HM Lieuts. of City of London since 1967, and a DL of Kent since 1968; Senior Partner and Managing Dir., Baring Brothers & Co. Ltd., of 8, Bishopsgate, EC2 1948-60, and again 1967-70; a Member of Inter-Parliamentary Delegation to Brazil 1954; Economic Min. and Head of UK Treasury and Supply Delegation, Wash., USA, UK Executive Dir. of International Monetary Fund, and of International Bank for Reconstruction and Development, and UK Dir. of International Finance Corp. 1959-61; Gov. of Bank of England 1961-66; Dir. of Bank of Internat. Settlements 1961-64; Ambassador to USA 1971-74; Chm. of Churchill Memorial Trust since 1968, and a Gov. of Ditchley Foundation since 1971; late Lt.-Col. Gren. Gds.; NW Europe 1944-45 (despatches, MBE); a Page of Honour to HM 1931-35; MBE (Mil) 1945, PC 1966, KCMG 1971, GCMG 1974: *m.* 1942, the Hon. Esme Mary Gabrielle Harmsworth, da. of 2nd Viscount Rothermere, and has issue.

Arms,—Quarterly, 1st and 4th azure, a fesse or, in chief a bear's head proper, muzzled and ringed or, differenced by an escallop azure; 2nd and 3rd gules, a cross-patée fitchée or between three fish haurient argent within an orle of eight cross-crosslets of the second. **Crest.**—A mullet erminois between two wings argent. **Supporters,**—Two bears proper, muzzled or, the dexter collared checky, argent and azure and charged on the shoulder with a lion's head erased or, the sinister collared azure, and charged on the shoulder with an escallop or.

Residence,—French Street Farm, Westerham, Kent. *Address,*—88 Leadenhall St., EC3A 3DT.

SONS LIVING.

EVELYN ROWLAND ESMOND (*Viscount Errington*), *b.* June 3rd, 1946.

Hon. Vivian John Rowland, *b.* 1950: *m.* 1974, Lavinia Gweneth, el. da. of Mark Baring, CVO [see colls., infra].

SISTERS LIVING.

Lady Rosemary Ethel, *b.* 1908: *m.* 1932, Lieut.-Col. John David Hills, M.C., formerly Headmaster of Bradfield Coll., and has issue living, John Evelyn Baring (Upper Ostaig House, Sleat, Isle of Skye). *b.* 1939; Maj. 17/21st Lancers: *m.* 1964, Katherine Adrian, yst. da. of the late G. F. Alderson-Smith, of Bishopric Court, Horsham, and has issue living, John George Baring *b.* 1966, Veronica Adrian Harriet *b.* 1968,—Jean Adini (*Hon. Mrs. H. E. Christopher Willoughby*), *b.* 1933: *m.* 1955, Lt.-Col. the Hon. (Henry Ernest) Christopher Willoughby, Coldstream Guards, of Buckhold Farm, Pangbourne, Berks. [see B. Middleton],—Margaret-Ruby, *b.* 1934: *m.* 1960, Michael Giles Neish Walker, of Shanwell, Milnathort, Kinross-shire [see Nairn, Bt.]. *Residence,*—House by the Dyke, Chirk, Wrexham, Denbighshire.

Lady Violet Mary, *b.* 1911: *m.* 1937, Major Mervyn Sydney Bobus Vernon, M.V.O., Grenadier Guards [see B. Lyveden, colls.]. *Residence,*—Bowldown, Tetbury, Gloucestershire.

WIDOW LIVING OF SON OF FIRST EARL.

Lady Gweneth Frida Ponsonby, dau. of 8th Earl of Bessborough ; is a J.P.; has Order of Mercy ; *m.* 1st. 1913, the Hon. Windham Baring, who *d.* 1922; 2ndly, 1926, Col. Ralph Henry Voltelin Cavendish, CBE, MVO, DL, who *d.* 1968 [D. Devonshire, colls.], and has issue living, (by 1st m.) [see colls., infra]. *Residence,*—Yaldham Manor, Kemsing, Kent.

COLLATERAL BRANCH LIVING.

Issue of the late Hon. Windham Baring, 2nd son of 1st Earl, *b.* 1880, *d.* 1922 : *m.* 1913, Lady Gweneth Frida Ponsonby [(ante) she *m.* 2ndly, 1926, Col. Ralph Henry Voltelin Cavendish, CBE, MVO, who *d.* 1968 [D. Devonshire, colls.]], da. of 8th Earl of Bessborough :—

Robin Windham, *b.* 1914, *TD*; ed. at Eton, and at Trin. Coll., Camb.; is a Member of London Stock Exchange, and an OStJ; 1939-45 War in N. Africa, Italy and NW Europe as Capt. RA (TA): *m.* 1954, Anne Elizabeth, JP, el. da. of Maj. W. F. Husband, and has issue living, James Windham. *b.* 1957,—Clarissa, *b.* 1955,—Rosemary Anne *b.* 1960, Katherine Claire *b.* 1963. *Residence,*—Went House, West Malling, Kent.——Mark, *CVO, b.* 1916; ed. at Eton, and at Trin. Coll., Camb.; a Dir. of Seccombe Marshall & Campion Ltd., discount brokers, and a JP for co. London; late Maj. Grenadier Guards; Mil. Liaison Officer, HM's Embassy, Rome 1945-46; Gen. Comnr. of Income Tax, City of London, since 1966; Exec. Chm. King Edward VII's Hosp. for Officers 1969; 1939-45 War in Italy; CVO 1970: *m.* 1949, Victoria Winifred, da. of Col. Reginald Edmund Maghlin Russell, CVO, OBE, DSO, and has issue living, Lavinia Gweneth (*Hon. Mrs. Vivian J. R. Baring*), *b.* 1951: *m.* 1974, the Hon. Vivian John Rowland Baring [ante],—Juliet Victoria, *b.* 1953. *Residence,*—18 Thurloe Sq., SW7.

Issue of the late Hon Sir Evelyn Baring, KG, CMG, KCVO (who was a *Baron Howick of Glendale* 1960), yst son of 1st Earl [see that title.].

PREDECESSORS.—[1] *Rt. Hon. Sir* **EVELYN** Baring, *G.C.B., O.M., G.C.M.G., K.C.S.I., C.I.E.*, younger son of the late Henry Baring, M.P. [see B. Northbrook, colls.']; was Commr. of Egyptian Public Debt 1877-9, Comptroller-Gen. in Egypt 1879-80, Financial Member of Council of Viceroy of India 1880-83, and Agent and Consul-Gen. in Egypt and a Min. Plen. in Diplo. Ser. 1883-1907 (granted £50,000 by Parliament) ; cr. *Baron Cromer,* of Cromer, co. Norfolk (peerage of United Kingdom) 1892, *Viscount Cromer,* co. Norfolk (peerage of United Kingdom) 1899, and *Viscount Errington,* of Hexham, co. Northumberland, and *Earl of Cromer,* co. Norfolk (peerage of United Kingdom) 1901: *m,* 1st, 1876, Ethel Stanley, who *d.* 1898, dau. of Sir Rowland Stanley Errington, 11th Bt. ; 2ndly, 1901, Lady Katherine Georgiana Louisa Thynne, who *d.* 1933, dau. of 4th Marquess of Bath ; *d.* 1917 ; *s.* by his el. son [2] ROWLAND THOMAS, *G.C.B., G.C.I.E., G.C.V.O., P.C.,* 2nd Earl, *b.* 1877; in Diplo. Ser. 1900-11; Private Sec. on successive Permanent Under-Secs. of State for Foreign Affairs (Lord Hardinge of Penshurst, and Lord Carnock) 1907-11, A.D.C. to successive Viceroys and Govs.-Gen. of India (Lord Hardinge of Penshurst, and Viscount Chelmsford) 1915-16, Equerry and Assist. Private Sec. to H.M. 1916-20, and an Extra Equerry 1920-53; Ch. of Staff to H.R.H. the Duke of Connaught during visit to India 1920-21 (K.C.I.E.), and to H.R.H. the Prince of Wales during tour of India 1921-22 ; Lord Chamberlain of the Household 1922-38 ; a Permanent Lord-in-Waiting 1938-53 ; Pres. of Marylebone Cricket Club 1934-35; Chm. Joint Red Cross and St. John War Organisation 1939-40; Receiver-Gen. of Order of St. John of Jerusalem 1943-47 ; a British Govt. Director of Suez Canal 1926-50 : *m.* 1908, Lady Ruby Florence Mary Elliot (a. G.C.St.J.), who *d.* 1961, dau. of 4th Earl of Minto ; *d.* 1953 ; *s.* by his only son [3] GEORGE ROWLAND STANLEY, 3rd Earl and present peer; also Viscount Cromer, Viscount Errington, and Baron Cromer.

CROMWELL, BARON. (Bewicke-Copley.) [Baron E. 1375.]

DAVID GODFREY BEWICKE-COPLEY, 6th Baron; *b.* May 29th, 1929; *s.* 1966; ed. at Eton, and at Magdalene Coll., Camb.; Bar. Inner Temple 1956: *m.* 1954, Doris Vivian, yst. da. of Hugh de Lisle Penfold, of Isle of Man, and has issue.

Arms,—1st and 4th, argent, a chief gules, over all a bend azure, *Cromwell;* 2nd and 3rd, chequy or and gules, a chief ermine, *Tateshall;* on an escutcheon of pretence, quarterly, 1st and 4th, argent a cross-moline sable, *Copley;* 2nd and 3rd, argent five lozenges conjoined in fesse gules, each charged with a mullet of the field, between three bears' heads erased sable, *Bewicke.* **Crests,**—1st, out of a ducal coronet or five ostrich feathers argent, *Copley;* 2nd, a goat's head erased at the neck argent, armed, maned and gorged with a mural crown gules, *Bewicke.* **Supporters,**—On either side a lion sable charged on the shoulder with a representation of the Treasurer's Purse (being the Badge of Ralph, 3rd Baron Cromwell). *Residence,*—The Manor House, Great Milton, Oxford.

I conquer by the cross.

SONS LIVING.
Hon. GODFREY JOHN, *b.* March 4th, 1960.
Hon. Thomas David, *b.* 1964.

DAUGHTERS LIVING.
Hon. Anne Elizabeth, *b.* 1955.
Hon. Davina Mary, *b.* 1958.

SISTER LIVING.
Hon. Philippa Selina, *b.* 1925: *m.* 1951, Lt.-Col. David Carol MacDonell Mather, MC, MP, Welsh Guards (ret.), and has issue living, Nicholas David, *b.* 1958,—Selina Jane, *b.* 1952,—Rose Amabel, *b.* 1954,—Alice Victoria, *b.* 1960. *Residence,*—Brookfield, Horton, Bucks.

AUNT LIVING. (*Raised to the rank of a Baron's daughter* 1923.)
Hon. Dorothy Albreda: *m.* 1926, Lieut.-Col. Philip Albert Meldon, D.S.O., R.A. (retired), who *d.* 1942, son of the late Sir Albert Meldon, D.L. *Residence,*—7, Editha Mansions, Edith Grove. S.W.10.

WIDOW LIVING OF FIFTH BARON.
FREDA CONSTANCE (*Freda, Baroness Cromwell*) (Gullivers Lodge, Guilsborough, Northampton), da. of the late Maj. Sir Frederick William Beresford Cripps, DSO, of Ampney Park, Cirencester: *m.* 1925, the 5th Baron, who *d.* 1966.

PREDECESSORS.—[1] RALPH de Cromwell ; summoned to Parliament 1375-97 : *m.* 1366, Maud, dau. of John Bernake, of Tattershall ; *d.* 1398 ; *s.* by his son [2] RALPH, 2nd Baron ; summoned to Parliament 1399-1417 : *m.* a widow (Joan), who *d.* 1434'; *d.* 1417 ; *s.* by his son [3] RALPH, P.C., 3rd Baron ; summoned to Parliament 1422-55 ; Lord High Treasurer 1433-43, Master of the Kings' Mews and Falcons 1436, and Constable of Nottingham Castle 1444-5 : *m.* 1424, Margaret, dau. of John, Lord Deincourt ; *d.* 1454, when the Barony fell into abeyance between the co-heirs, his nieces Maud, widow of Robert, Lord Willoughby de Broke, and Joan, wife of Sir Humphrey, Bourchier ; on the death of the latter without issue in 1490, the Barony devolved upon the former [4] MAUD ; *d.s.p.* 1497, when the Barony again passed into abeyance between co-heirs descendants of the daus. of the 1st Baron, and so remained until 1922, when the Committee for Privileges of the House of Lords reported in favour of the petition of Selina Frances, wife of Brig.-Gen. Sir Robert Calverley Alington Bewicke-Copley, K.B.E., C.B., who *d.* 1923 (she was dau. of Sir Charles Watson Copley, 3rd Bt. [Watson, Bt., cr. 1700], and one of the co-heirs of William Fitzwilliam, sole heir of Maud, wife of Sir William Fitzwilliam, of Sprotborough, and a dau. of the 1st Baron), for the determination of the abeyance ; she *d.* 1923, and the Barony was in July 1923 called out of abeyance in favour of her son [5] ROBERT GODFREY WOLSELEY Bewicke-Copley, DSO, MC, 5th Baron, *b.* 1893; Lord Lieut. of Leics. 1949-65: *m.* 1925, Freda Constance, da. of Maj. Sir Frederick William Beresford Cripps, DSO, of Ampney Park Glos.; *d.* 1966; *s.* by his only son [6] DAVID GODFREY, 6th Baron, and present peer.

CROOK, BARON. (Crook.) [Baron U.K. 1947.]

The cross a shield.

REGINALD DOUGLAS CROOK, 1st Baron son of the late Percy Edwin Crook ; *b.* March 2nd, 1901; ed. at Strand Sch.; Chm. of National Dock Labour Board, Dep. Chm. of Cttees., and Speaker, House of Lords, Founder and Pres. of Cystic Fibrosis Research Foundation Trust, Pres. of Pre-Retirement Assocn., Vice-Pres. of Roy. Soc. for Prevention of Accidents, Livery-man of City of London, Apothecary, Past Master of Spectacle Makers' Co., a Life Member of Court of Guild of Free-men (Master 1972-3), a KStJ, a Member of Chapter-Gen. of Order of St. John, and a JP for Surrey; formerly Gen. Sec. of Min. of Labour Staff Asso., and Editor of *Civil Service Argus*; Delegate to United Nations Assembly, New York 1950, Chm. of Cttee. of Inquiry, Optical Services 1949-62, a Member of Cttee. of Inquiry into Police Pay 1951, Chm. of National Dock Labour Board 1951-65, and Vice-Pres. of Administrative Tribunal, UN 1951-71, and Pres. of Nat. Assocn. of Industrial Editors 1956-62; a Member of Ecclesiastical Cttee. of Parliament since 1948, Pres. of Cystic Fibrosis Research Foundation since 1964; Dir of General Practice Finance Corpn. since 1966, Chm. of London Electricity Consultative Council and a Member of London Electricity Board 1967-72; Fellow and Vice-Pres. of Inst. of Municipal Safety Officers; *cr. Baron Crook*, of Carshalton, co. Surrey (peerage of United Kingdom) 1947: *m.* 1922, Ida Gertrude, da. of Joseph Haddon, and has issue.

Arms,—Or, on a bend vert between in chief two Tudor roses barbed and seeded proper, and in base a sprig of oak slipped and fructed of the second, a shepherd's crook of the field. **Crest,**—Two crooks in saltire or, surmounted by a Tudor rose barbed and seeded proper. **Supporters,**—*Dexter,* an antelope gorged with a collar of Tudor roses leaved proper; *sinister,* a greyhound argent collared or, with line reflexed over the back, the collar charged with three cross crosslets gules.

Residence,—Breedene, 25, Princes Avenue, Carshalton, Surrey.

SON LIVING.

Hon. DOUGLAS EDWIN, *b.* Nov. 19th, 1926; ed. at Whitgift Sch., Croydon, and Imperial Coll. of Science and Technology; BSc 1947; MICE: *m.* 1954, Ellenor, da. of the late Robert Rouse, and has issue living, Robert Douglas Edwin, *b.* 1955,—Catherine Hilary, *b.* 1960.

CROSS, VISCOUNT. (Cross.) [Viscount U.K. 1886.]

ASSHETON HENRY CROSS, 3rd Viscount; *b.* May 7th, 1920; *s.* 1932; ed. at Shrewsbury, and at Magdalene Coll., Camb.; formerly Capt. Scots Guards: *m.* 1st, 1952 (m. diss. 1957), Patricia Mary, el. da. of Edward Pearson Hewetson, of The Craig, Windermere, Westmorland; 2ndly, 1972, Victoria, da. of , and formerly wife of Webb, and has issue (by 1st m.).

Trust in the Cross

Arms,—Gules, a cross flory argent, charged with five passion nails sable, a bordure of the second. **Crest.**—A griffin's head, erased argent, gorged with a double chain gold, therefrom pendant a mullet pierced sable, in the beak a passion nail also sabie. **Supporters**—On either side a pegasus argent, holding in the mouth a passion nail sable, the dexter gorged with a chain or, therefrom pendant a cross flory gules, the sinister gorged with a double chain or, therefrom pendant a mullet pierced sable.

Residence,—Delph Cottage, Itchenor, Sussex. *Club,*—Guards'.

DAUGHTERS LIVING (*By 1st m.*

Hon. Venetia Clare, *b.* 1953. *Hon.* Nicola, *b.* 1954.

SISTER LIVING.

Hon. Idonea Mary Ellice, *b.* 1918 : *m.* 1946. Lieut.-Col. William Preston Ashton Shuttleworth, RCT, late Roy. Norfolk Regt. (ret.) (Manor Lodge, Milford, Surrey, and 8, Culford Mansions, Culford Gdns., SW3) [Preston, Bt., colls.], and has issue living, Hugh Ashton John (26, Alfriston Rd., Clapham Common, West Side, SW11), *b.* 1948: *m.* 1972, Kirsten Judith, da. of Eric S. Greenwood, of Wester Croachy, Aberarder, Inverness,—William Richard Ashton, *b.* 1958,—Celia Mary Ashton, *b.* 1951: *m.* 1975, Anthony Shaun Tobin,—Rosamond Ashton, *b.* 1953.

SISTER LIVING OF SECOND VISCOUNT. (*Raised to the rank of a Viscount's daughter* 1914.)

Hon. Ellinor Frances, *b.* 1891.

WIDOW LIVING OF SON OF SECOND VISCOUNT.

Sybil Anne, dau. of Thomas Prain Douglas Murray, M.B.E., T.D., D.L., J.P., of Templewood, Brechin, Angus: *m.* 1st, 1950, the Hon. John Michael Inigo Cross, who *d.* 1951; 2ndly, 1956, Lt.-Cdr. James Parker-Jervis, RN (ret.) [see V. St. Vincent, colls.], and has issue living, (by 1st marriage) [see colls, infra]. *Residence,*—Orchard Hey, Runcton, Chichester, Sussex.

WIDOW LIVING OF SECOND VISCOUNT.

MAUD EVELYN INIGO, dau. of the late Maj.-Gen. Inigo Richmond Jones, C.V.O., C.B. [E. Wemyss, colls.] : *m.* 1st, 1918, the 2nd Viscount, who *d.* 1932; 2ndly, 1944, as his second wife, Guy Hope Coldwell, who *d.* 1948. *Residence,*—Stoke Lodge, Ludlow, Shropshire.

COLLATERAL BRANCHES LIVING.

Issue of the late Hon. John Michael Inigo Cross, youngest son of 2nd Viscount, *b.* 1923, *d.* 1951: *m.* 1950, Sybil Anne [(ante); she *m.* 2ndly, 1956, Lieut.-Com. James Parker-Jervis, R.N. (see V. St. Vincent, colls.)], dau. of Thomas Prain Douglas Murray, M.B.E., T.D., D.L., J.P., of Templewood, Brechin, Angus :—

Mary Beatrice (*posthumous*), *b.* 1951.

Issue of the late Hon. John Edward Cross, 3rd son of 1st Viscount, *b.* 1858, *d.* 1921: *m.* 1st, 1889, Katherine Ellen, who *d.* 1891, dau. of the late Rev. Francis Haden-Cope (formerly V. of N. Malvern, Worcestershire, and Rural Dean), of Bartestree Court, Hereford; 2ndly, 1895, Sophy Katherine Mary, who *d.* 1946, dau. of the late Henry Robertson Sandbach, J.P., D.L., of Hafodunos, Abergele, N. Wales:—

(By 1st m.) Katherine Madge, *b.* 1891: *m.* 1923, Capt. Basil Richard Brooke, DSO, RN (ret.), who *d.* 1929 [E. Dartmouth]. *Residence.*—The Cottage, High Wray, Ambleside.

PREDECESSORS.—[1] *Rt. Hon. Sir* RICHARD ASSHETON CROSS, *G.C.B., G.C.S.I. P.C., D.C.L LL.D., F.R.S.,* 3rd son of the late William Cross, D.L., of Red Scar, Preston ; *b.* 1823 ; Sec. of State for Home Depart. 1874-80 and 1885-6, one of the Committee of Council on Education in Scotland Aug. 1885 to Jan 1886, Sec. of State for India July 1886 to Aug. 1892, and Lord Privy Seal June 1895 to Oct. 1900 ; M.P. for Preston (*C*) 1857-62, for S.W. Lancashire 1868-85, and for Newton Div. of S.W. Lancashire 1885-6 ; cr. *Viscount Cross,* of Broughton-in-Furness (peerage of United Kingdom) 1886: *m.* 1852, Georgiana, *C.I.,* who *d.* 1907, dau. of the late Thomas Lyon, J.P., D.L., of Appleton Hall, Cheshire ; *d.* 1914 ; *s.* by his grandson [2] RICHARD ASSHETON, 2nd Viscount (only son of the late Hon. William Henry Cross, M.P., 2nd son of 1st Viscount), by Mary dau. of the late William Lewthwaite, J.P., D.L. of Broadgate, Cumberland, *b.* 1882 ; acted as Private Sec. to successive Permanent Secs. to the Treasury 1912-17, and was a Principal there 1917-32 : *m.* 1918, Maud Evelyn Inigo (who *m.* 2ndly, 1944, as his second wife, Guy Hope Coldwell, who *d.* 1948), dau. of the late Maj.-Gen. Inigo Richmond Jones, C.V.O., C.B.; *d.* 1932 ; *s.* by his son [3] ASSHETON HENRY, 3rd Viscount and present peer.

CROSS OF CHELSEA, BARON. (Cross.) [Life Baron 1971.]

ARTHUR GEOFFREY NEALE CROSS, *PC*, son of the late Arthur George Cross; *b*. Dec. 1st, 1904; ed. at Westminster, and Trin. Coll., Camb.; Bar. Middle Temple 1930, KC 1949, and Bencher 1959; a Judge of High Court of Justice (Chancery Div.) 1960-69, a Lord Justice of Appeal 1969-71, and a Lord of Appeal in Ordinary 1971-75; Chancellor of Co. Palatine of Durham 1959; *cr*. Knt. 1960, PC 1969, and *Baron Cross of Chelsea*, of Roy. Borough of Kensington and Chelsea (Life Baron) 1971: *m*. 1952, Mildred Joan, da. of the late Lt.-Col. Theodore Eardley-Wilmot, DSO [see Eardley-Wilmot, Bt., colls.], and widow of Thomas Walton Davies, and has issue.

To be astonished at nothing

Arms,—Gules within a cross voided between four cross crosslets or a griffin's head argent, a chief engrailed ermine. **Crest,**—A Staffordshire bull terrier's head couped proper collared gules gemelled and charged with a cross voided or.

Residence,—66, Oakwood Court, W14.

DAUGHTER LIVING.

Hon. Julia, *b*. 1953: *m*. 1973, Barney Walker.

CROWTHER, BARONY OF (Crowther.) [Extinct 1972]

SONS LIVING OF LIFE BARON.

Hon. Charles Worth (Bourne Bank, Bourne End, Bucks.), *b*. 1939: *m*. 1963, Barbara, yr. da. of Prof. Norman Merrett Hancox, MD, of Barn End, Moorside Lane, Neston, Wirrall, Cheshire, and has issue.
Hon. David Richard Geoffrey, *b*. 1943: *m*. 1974, Martina, da. of Martin Menn-Fink, of Ilanz, Switzerland.

DAUGHTERS LIVING OF LIFE BARON.

Hon. Anne Hallowell, *b*. 1937: *m*. 1958, Jonathan Sofer, Bar.-at-Law, of 46, Regent's Park Rd., NW1, and has issue.
Hon. Felicity Margaret, *b*. 1947.
Hon. Nicola Mary, *b*. 1950.

WIDOW LIVING OF LIFE BARON.

MARGARET (*Baroness Crowther*) (43, Meadowbank, NW3), da. of Edward Hallowell Worth, of Claymont, Delaware, USA: *m*. 1932, the 1st Baron (Life Peer), who *d*. 1972, when the title became ext.

CROWTHER-HUNT, BARON. (Crowther-Hunt.) [Life Baron 1973.]

NORMAN CROWTHER CROWTHER-HUNT, son of the late Ernest Angus Hunt, of Bradford; *b*. March 13th, 1920; assumed by deed poll 1973, the surname of Crowther-Hunt; ed. at Sidney Sussex Coll., Camb. (MA, PhD); a Fellow and Lecturer in Politics, Exeter Coll., Oxford since 1952; a Member of Council Headington Sch., Oxford since 1966, of Commn. on the Constitution since 1969, and of Civil Ser. Coll. Advisory Council since 1970; Constitutional Adviser to Govt. Feb. to Oct. 1974, since when, Min. of State, Dept. of Education and Science; Resident Fellow, Sidney Sussex Coll., Camb. 1949-51; Commonwealth Fund Fellow Princeton Univ., USA 1951-52; Domestic Bursar, Exeter Coll., Oxford 1954-70; a Member of Fulton Cttee. on Civil Ser. 1966-68 (Leader of Management Consultancy Group); 1939-45 war with RA; *cr*. *Baron Crowther-Hunt*, of Eccleshill, W. Riding of Yorks. (Life Baron) 1973: *m*. 1944, Joyce, da. of the late Rev. Joseph Stackhouse, of Walsall Wood, Staffs., and has issue.

Residences.—14, Apsley Rd., Oxford; Exeter College, Oxford.

DAUGHTERS LIVING

Hon. Elizabeth Anne, *b*. 1947.
Hon. Rosamund Shirley, *b*. 1950.
Hon. Penelope Carol, *b*. 1955.

CUDLIPP, BARON. (Cudlipp.) [Life Baron 1974.]

HUGH KINSMAN CUDLIPP, *OBE*, son of William Cudlipp, of Cardiff; *b*. Aug. 28th, 1913; ed. at Howard Gardens Sch., Cardiff; 1939-45 War; Features Editor *Sunday Chronicle*, London, 1932-35; Features Editor *Daily Mirror* 1935-37; Editor *Sunday Pictorial* 1937-40, and again 1946-49; Man. Editor *Sunday Express* 1950-52; Joint Man. Dir. *Daily Mirror* and *Sunday Pictorial* 1959-63 (Editorial Dir. 1952-63), Chm. Odhams Press Ltd. 1961-63, of Daily Mirror Newspapers Ltd. 1963-68, of Internat. Publishing Corpn. 1968-73 (Dep. Chm. 1964-68), and of Internat. Publishing Corpn. Newspaper Div. 1970-73; Dep. Chm. (editorial) Reed Internat. Board 1970-73; a Dir. of Asso. Television Ltd. 1956-73; author of " Publish and be Damned!" 1955, and " At Your Peril " 1962; *cr*. OBE (Civil) 1945, Knt. 1973, and *Baron Cudlipp*, of Aldingbourne, co. W. Sussex (Life Baron) 1974: *m*. 1st, 19—; 2ndly, 1945, Eileen Ascroft, who *d*. 1962; 3rdly, 1963, Jodi, da. of the late John L. Hyland, of Palm Beach, Fla., USA.

Residence.—The Dene ,Hook Lane, Aldingbourne, W. Sussex.

CULLEN OF ASHBOURNE, BARON. (Cokayne.) [Baron U.K. 1920.]

Courage in Adversity.

CHARLES BORLASE MARSHAM COKAYNE, *M.B.E.*, 2nd Baron; *b.* Oct. 6th, 1912; *s.* 1932; ed. at Eton; is Major Roy. Corps of Signals (T.A.); M.B.E. (Mil.) 1945: *m.* 1st, 1942, Valerie Catharine Mary, dau. of the late W. H. Collbran; 2ndly, 1948, Patricia Mary, el. dau. of the late Col. S. Clulow-Gray, and has issue by 1st marriage.

𝔄rms,—Argent, three cocks gules, armed crested, and jelloped sable. 𝔠rest,—A cock's head erased gules, beaked, crested, and jelloped sable. 𝔖upporters,—*Dexter*, a lion guardant party per fesse or and argent; *sinister*, an ostrich argent holding in its beak a horseshoe proper; each gorged with a collar pendant therefrom an escutcheon argent, charged with two bars vert.
Residence,—75, Cadogan Gardens, S.W.3.

DAUGHTER LIVING. (*By 1st marriage*)
Hon. Julia Collbran, *b.* 1943: *m.* 1968, Don Francesco Costa Sanseverino, of 75, Cadogan Gdns., SW3, and has issue living, Edoardo, *b.* 1969—Alessandro, *b.* 1971.

BROTHERS LIVING.
Hon. EDMUND WILLOUGHBY MARSHAM; *b.* May 18th, 1916; ed. at Eton; late Flight Lieut. R.A.F.: *m.* 1943, Janet (MANSON), dau. of the late William Douglas Watson, of Canterbury. *Address*,—Box 1254, Merritt, BC, Canada.
Hon. John O'Brien Marsham, *b.* 1920; ed. at Eton: *m.* 1948, Anne Frances, who *d.* 1971, da. of the late Bertram Clayton, of Wakefield, Yorkshire, and has issue living, Michael John, *b.* 1950. *Residence*,— 14, St. Omer Rd., Cowley, Oxford.

SISTERS LIVING.
Hon. Barbara Mary, *b.* 1905: *m.* 1929, Maj. Gilbert Edgar Francis Van der Noot, late Irish Guards, and has issue living, Anthea Caroline, *b.* 1936: *m.* 1963, John Michael Ryan, of Flat 7. 19, Cadogan Place, S.W.1. *Residence*,—Oak Cottage, Hartley Wintney, Hants. *Club*,—Guards
Hon. Dorothy Grace (c/o Barclays Bank, Roehampton, SW15), *b.* 1907.
Hon. Ruth Margaret, *b.* 1909: *m.* 1st, 1939, Capt. Robert William Alfred Moore, RA, who *d.* (killed in action during European War) 1940; 2ndly, 1949, the Rev. David Henry Aitcheson Williams, who *d.* 1955, and has issue living, (by 1st marriage) Elizabeth Virginia (posthumous), *b.* 1940: *m.* 1973, Donald Franklin Hoover, of Vancouver, BC.

PREDECESSOR.—[1] *Sir* BRIEN IBRICAN Cokayne, *K.B.E.*, son of the late George Edward Cokayne, F.S.A., Clarenceux King of Arms; *b.* 1864; a partner in the firm of Anthony Gibbs and Sons, merchants and bankers; appointed a Director of the Bank of England 1902, and was Dep. Gov. **1915-18**, and Gov. **1918-20**; cr. *Baron Cullen of Ashbourne*, of Roehampton, co. Surrey (peerage of United Kingdom) 1920: *m.* 1904, Grace Margaret, who *d.* 1971, da. of the late Rev. the Hon. John Marsham; *d.* 1932; *s.* by his son [2] CHARLES BORLASE MARSHAM, 2nd Baron and present peer.

CUNLIFFE, BARON. (Cunliffe.) [Baron U.K. 1914.]

Faithfully.

ROGER CUNLIFFE, 3rd Baron; *b.* Jan. 12th, 1932; *s.* 1963; ed. at Eton, and at Trin. Coll., Camb. (MA); RIBA; AA Dipl.: *m.* 1957, Clemency Ann, el. da. of Maj. Geoffrey Benyon Hoare, of Clover House, Aldeburgh, Suffolk, and has issue.

𝔄rms,—Per chevron or and sable, three conies courant counterchanged. 𝔠rest,—Upon a rock a greyhound sejant sable, collared or. 𝔖upporters,—On either side a figure habited as a Gate Porter of the Bank of England, supporting in the exterior hand his staff of office.
Residence,—1, Hurst Av., N6 5TX.

SONS LIVING.
Hon. HENRY, *b.* March 9th, 1962.
Hon. Luke, *b.* 1965.

DAUGHTER LIVING.
Hon. Rachel Henrietta, *b.* 1960.

BROTHER LIVING.
Hon. Merlin (42, Lambeth Av., Armadale, Victoria 3143, Australia), *b.* 1935; ed. at Eton: *m.* 1960, Deborah Rutherford Grimwade, and has issue living, Tamsin Elizabeth, *b.* 1963,—Sophia Catherine, *b.* 1966.

SISTERS LIVING.
Hon. Shirley Cynthia, *b.* 1926: *m.* 1959, Alan Desmond Wilson, and has issue living, Matthew Crispin, *b.* 1961,—Richenda Catherine, *b.* 1963. *Residence*,—40, Sutherland Place, W2.
Hon. Corinna, *b.* 1929: *m.* 1957, Frederick Starr Wildman, and has issue living, Tarik Charles, *b.* 1959. *Residence*,—100, Milton Park, Highgate, N6.

UNCLE LIVING. (*Son of 1st Baron.*)

Hon. Geoffrey, *b.* 1903; ed. at Eton, and at Trin. Coll., Camb.; was Controller of Aluminium, Min. of Supply and Min. of Aircraft Production 1939-41; formerly a Member of Industrial and Export Council, Board of Trade: *m.* 1st, 1922, Patrick Sidney, who *d.* 1940, dau. of the late Robert B. Frend, of Ardsallagh, co. Tipperary; 2ndly, 1941, Gavrelle (from whom he obtained a divorce 1947), widow of Christopher Hobhouse; 3rdly, 1947, Barbara Waring, dau. of the late Dr. J. A. Gibb, of Maidstone, Kent, and has issue living, (by 1st marriage) Peter, *b.* 1925: *m.* 1955, Barbara Marion, dau. of H. F. Phillips, of Sous La Hougue, Jersey,—(by 2nd marriage) Adam, *b.* 1946,— Carol, *b.* 1944. *Residence,*—Poyntzfield House, Conon Bridge, Ross-shire.

AUNTS LIVING. (*Daughters of 1st Baron.*)

Hon. Mary Betty, *b.* 1898: *m.* 1921, Lt.-Col. Otho Stuart Irwin Northcote, late Suffolk Regt., who *d.* 1966, and has issue living, Ann Patricia, *b.* 1925. *Residence,*—24, Broadway Av., Newlands, Cape Province, S. Africa.

*Hon.*Ann Madeline, *b.* 1901: *m.* 1922, Brigadier John Wedderburn-Maxwell, D.S.O., M.C. [see Ogilvy-Wedderburn, Bt., colls.]. *Residence,*—The Granary, St. George's Hill, Weybridge.

Hon. Ethel Peggy (*Hon. Lady Southby*), *b.* 1910: *m.* 1st, 1932, Brig. Bernard Lorenzo de Robeck, MC, RA, who *d.* 1957; 2ndly, 1964, Lt.-Col. Sir (Archibald) Richard Charles Southby, OBE, 2nd Bt., of Montgomery Farm, Box 396, Sinoia, Rhodesia, and has issue living, (by 1st m.) Bryan Michael (23, Hartington Rd., Chiswick, W4), *b.* 1936,—Hugh, *b.* 1941.

MOTHER LIVING.

Joan Catherine (of 12A, St. Olave's Court, St. Petersburgh Place, W.2), dau. of the late Cecil Lubbock [see B. Avebury, colls.]: *m.* 1925 (marriage dissolved 1952), the 2nd Baron Cunliffe.

WIDOW LIVING OF SECOND BARON.

KATHLEEN ELSIE (*Kathleen, Lady Cunliffe*) (The Old Rectory, Waterperry, Oxford), da. of Ernest Brownfield Pope, of Wargrave, Berks., and widow of Capt. Philip Robinson, R.A.M.C., of Trinidad: *m.* 1952, as his 2nd wife, the 2nd Baron, who *d.* 1963.

PREDECESSORS.—[1] Sir WALTER Cunliffe, *G.B.E.*, son of the late Roger Cunliffe, of Tyrrell Wood, Surrey; *b.* 1855; was head of the firm of Cunliffe Bros. (afterwards Goschens and Cunliffe), of 12, Austin Friars, E.C.; Dep.-Gov. of Bank of England 1911-13, and Gov. 1913-18; cr. *Baron Cunliffe*, of Headley, co. Surrey (Peerage of United Kingdom) 1914: *m.* 1st, 1890, Mary Agnes, who *d.* 1893, dau. of the late Robert Henderson, of Randalls Park, Leatherhead; 2ndly, 1896, Edith Cunningham, who *d.* 1965, da. of Col. Robert Tod Boothby, of St. Andrews, Fife; *d.* 1920; *s.* by his el. son [2] ROLF, *b.* 1899; Wing-Cdr. RAFVR: *m.* 1st, 1925 (m. diss. 1952), Joan Catherine, dau. of the late Cecil Lubbock [B. Avebury, colls.]; 2ndly, 1952, Kathleen Elsie, dau. of Ernest Brownfield Pope, of Wargrave, Berks., and widow of Capt. Philip Robinson, R.A.M.C., of Trinidad; *d.* 1963; *s.* by his el. son [3] ROGER, 3rd Baron and present peer.

CUNNINGHAM OF HYNDHOPE, VISCOUNTCY OF. (Cunningham.) [Extinct 1963.]

WIDOW LIVING OF FIRST VISCOUNT.

NONA (*Viscountess Cunningham of Hyndhope*) (Claytons, Bishop's Waltham, Hants.), da. of Horace Byatt, of Midhurst, Sussex; a CStJ: *m.* 1929, the 1st Viscount, who *d.* 1963, when the title became extinct.

CURZON OF KEDLESTON, MARQUESSATE OF. (Curzon.) [Extinct 1925.]

DAUGHTER LIVING OF FIRST MARQUESS.

See B. Ravensdale].

DACRE, BARONESS, (Douglas-Home.) [Baron E 1321.]

RACHEL LEILA DOUGLAS-HOME, (*Baroness Dacre*); *b.* Oct. 24th, 1929; da. of 4th Viscount Hampden; *s.* (on termination of abeyance) 1970: *m.* 1951, the Hon. William Douglas-Home [see B. Home of the Hirsel], and has issue.

Arms,—Not exemplified at time of going to press. *Residence,*—Drayton House, East Meon, Hants.

SON LIVING.

Hon. JAMES THOMAS ARCHIBALD, *b.* May 16th, 1952.

DAUGHTERS LIVING.

Hon. Sarah, *b.* 1954.
Hon. Gian Leila, *b.* 1958.
Hon. Dinah Lilian, *b.* 1964.

SISTER LIVING.

Hon. Tessa Mary, *b.* 1934: *m.* 1956, Julian Ogilvie Thompson, of Froome, Froome St., Athol Extension, Johannesburg, S. Africa, and has issue living, Christopher William, *b.* 1958,—Anthony Thomas, *b.* 1964,—Rachel Amanda, *b.* 1960,—Katharine Leila, *b.* 1965.

PREDECESSORS.—[1] Sir RANDOLF de Dacre, son and heir of Sir William de Dacre of Dacre, Cumberland; summoned to Parliament 1321-38, whereby he is held to have become Lord Dacre: *m.* Margaret, da. and heir of Thomas de Multon of Gilsland, Cumberland; *d.* 1339; *s.* by his son [2] WILLIAM, 2nd Baron: *m.* Katherine, da. of Sir Ralph Neville of Raby, co. Durham; *d.* 1361; *s.* by his brother [3] RANDOLF, 3rd Baron; *b.* about 1322; murdered 1375; *s.* by his brother [4] HUGH, 4th Baron: *m.* 1354/55, Elizabeth, widow of Sir William Douglas, Earl of Atholl; *d.* 1383; *s.* by his son [5] WILLIAM, 5th Baron: (said to have married first, Joan Douglas): *m.* Mary, *d.* 1399; *s.* by his son [6] THOMAS, 6th Baron; *b.* 1387: *m.* Philippa, da. of Ralph Neville, Earl of Westmorland; *d.* 1458; *s.* by his grand-da. [7] JOAN (da. of Sir Thomas Dacre): *m.* 1446 Sir Richard Fiennes, who was summoned to Parliament as Baron Dacre 1459; he *d.* 1483 and his widow *d.* 1486; he was *s* by his grandson, [8] THOMAS (son of Sir John Fiennes), 8th Baron; KB 1494: *m.* about 1492 Anne da. of Sir Humphrey Bourchier; *d.* 1533; *s.* by his grandson [9] THOMAS (son of Sir Thomas Fiennes)

9th Baron: *m.* 1536, Mary, da. of George Nevill, Lord Abergavenny; having taken part in a deer hunt at Laughton Park, Sussex, when a park keeper was killed, he was found guilty of murder, hanged at Tyburn 1541, and his honours forfeited; his son [10] GREGORY, 10th Baron (whose elder brother Thomas, *d.* 1553 aged 15, would have succeeded but for his father's forfeiture) was restored to his honours 1558: *m.* about 1558, Anne Sackville, sister of 1st Earl of Dorset; *d.* 1594; *s.* by his sister [11] MARGARET, *b.* 1541: *m.* 1564 Sampson Lennard, who *d.* 1615; *d.* 1612; *s.* by her son [12] HENRY, 12th Baron; *b.* 1570: *m.* 1589, Chrysogona, da. of Sir Richard Baker of Sissinghurst; *d.* 1616; *s.* by his son [13] RICHARD, 13th Baron; *b.* 1596: *m.* 1st, 1617, Elizabeth, da. of Sir Arthur Throckmorton; 2ndly, 1625, Dorothy North, da. of 3rd Lord North; *d.* 1630; *s.* by his son [14] FRANCIS, 14th Baron; *b.* 1619: *m.* 1641, Elizabeth Bayning (who was cr. Viscountess of Shepey for life 1680), da. of Paul 1st Viscount Bayning of Sudbury; *d.* 1662; *s.* by his son [15] THOMAS, 15th Baron; *b.* 1654; cr. *Earl of Sussex* 1674: *m.* 1674, Anne Palmer or FitzRoy, da. of Barbara Duchess of Cleveland; *d.* 1715, when the Earldom became ext. and the Barony of Dacre fell into abeyance between his two das., until 1741, when the yr [16] ANNE *s.* on the death without issue of her sister Barbara; *b.* 1684: *m.* 1st, 1716, Richard Barrett of Belhus, Essex, who *d.* 1716; 2ndly, 1718, Henry Roper, 8th Baron Teynham, who *d.* 1723; 3rdly, 1725 the Hon. Robert Moore, son of 3rd Earl of Drogheda who *d.* 1762; she *d.* 1755; *s.* by her son [17] THOMAS Barrett-Lennard, 17th Baron; *b.* 1717: *m.* 1739, Anna Maria, sister of 1st Earl Camden; *d.* 1786; *s.* by his nephew [18] TREVOR CHARLES Roper (son of the Hon. Charles Roper), 18th Baron; *b.* 1745: *m.* 1773, Mary, da. and heir of Sir Thomas Fludyer of Lee, Kent; *d.* 1794; *s.* by his sister [19] GERTRUDE; *b.* 1750: *m.* 1771, Thomas Brand, who *d.* 1794; *d.* 1819; *s.* by her son [20] THOMAS, 20th Baron; *b.* 1774: *m.* 1819 Barbarina, da. of Adm. Sir Chaloner Ogle, 1st Bt., and widow of Valentine Henry Wilmot, *d.* 1851; *s.* by his brother [21] HENRY OTWAY Trevor, 21st Baron; *b.* 1777; Gen. in the Army; assumed by Roy. licence 1824 the surname of Trevor in lieu of Brand: *m.* 1806, Pyne Crosbie, sister and co-heir of William, 4th Baron Brandon; *d.* 1853; *s.* by his son [22] THOMAS CROSBIE WILLIAM Trevor, 22nd Baron; *b.* 1808; assumed by Roy. licence 1851 the surname of Trevor in lieu of Brand: *m.* 1837, the Hon. Susan Sophia Cavendish, da. of 1st Baron Chesham; *d.* 1890; *s.* by his brother [23] HENRY BOUVERIE WILLIAM, GCB, PC, 23rd Baron; Speaker of the House of Commons, who in 1884 was cr. *Viscount Hampden*, of Glynde, Sussex (peerage of UK); from that time the Barony of Dacre descended with the Viscountcy of Hampden [25-27] until the death of the 4th Viscount and 27th Baron in 1965, when the Barony fell into abeyance between his two das., the Hon. Mrs. Rachel Lelia Douglas-Home, and the Hon. Mrs. Tessa Mary Thompson, and so continued until 1970, when the abeyance was terminated in favour of the el. [28] RACHEL LEILA, present peeress.

DALHOUSIE, EARL OF.   (Ramsay.)   [Earl S. 1633.]

Pray and labour.

SIMON RAMSAY, *KT, GBE, MC,* 16th Earl; *b.* Oct. 17th, 1914; *s.* 1950; ed. at Eton, and at Ch. Ch., Oxford; Lord-Lieut. of Angus, and a KStJ; late Major 4th/5th Batn. Black Watch (T.A.); Gov.-Gen. of Federation of Rhodesia and Nyasaland 1957-63; Lord Chamberlain to H.M. Queen Elizabeth the Queen Mother since 1965, and Lord Lt. of co. Angus since 1967; Hon. LLD Dalhousie Univ., Halifax, Nova Scotia, and Dundee; 1939-45 War (MC); an additional Conservative Whip 1946-50; MP for Forfarshire (*C*) 1945-50; GBE (Civil) 1957, KT 1971: *m.* 1940, Margaret Elizabeth Mary, da. of the late Brig.-Gen. Archibald Stirling of Keir [see Stirling-Maxwell, Bt., colls.], and has issue.

Arms,—Argent, an eagle displayed sable, beaked and membered gules. Crest.—An unicorn's head, couped at the neck argent, armed, maned, and tufted or. Supporters,—*Dexter,* a griffin argent; *sinister,* a greyhound argent, gorged with a collar gules, charged with three escallops of the first.

Seats,—Brechin Castle, Brechin, Angus; Dalhousie Castle, Bonnyrigg, Midlothian.
Clubs,—White's and Puffin's.

SONS LIVING.

JAMES HUBERT (*Lord Ramsay*), *b.* Jan. 17th, 1948; ed. at Ampleforth; late 2nd Lt. Coldstream Guards: *m.* 1973, Marilyn Davina, da. of Maj. David Henry Butter, MC [see Wernher, Bt.].
Hon. Anthony, *b.* 1949; ed. at Ampleforth, and Magdalen Coll., Oxford: *m.* 1973, Georgina Mary, da. of the Hon. Michael Langhorne Astor [see V. Astor].
Hon. John Patrick, *b.* 1952; ed. at Ampleforth.

DAUGHTERS LIVING.

Lady Elizabeth (*Countess of Scarbrough*), *b.* 1941: *m.* 1970, the 12th Earl of Scarbrough. *Residence,*—Sandbeck Park, Rotherham.
Lady Sarah, *b.* 1945: *m.* 1966, Chippendale Keswick, of 1A, Ilchester Pl., W14.

SISTERS LIVING.

Lady Ida Mary, *b.* 1906: *m.* 1938, Maj.-Gen. Sir George Frederick Johnson, K.C.V.O., C.B., C.B.E., DSO, late Scots Guards, and has issue living, Peter David, *b.* 1940; ed. at Eton; Maj. Scots Gds.,— Robert George, *b.* 1946; ed. at Eton,—Sheena Margaret, *b.* 1938. *Residence,*—Castlesteads, Brampton, Cumberland.
Lady Jean (Maule), *b.* 1909 : *m.* 1945, Lieut.-Col. David McNeil Campbell Rose, D.S.O., Black Watch, and has issue living, Hugh Ramsay, *b.* 1946,—Mary Janet, *b.* 1948. *Residence,*—Huntingtower House, Perth.

COLLATERAL BRANCHES LIVING.

Issue of the late Hon. Sir Patrick William Maule Ramsay, K.C.M.G., 2nd son of 13th Earl, *b.* 1879, *d.* 1962: *m.* 1917, Cynthia, who *d.* 1957, dau. of the late Brig.-Gen. Sir Herbert Conyers Surtees, C.B., and widow of Christopher Cecil Tower, of Weald Hall, Essex:— David Patrick Maule, *b.* 1919, *m.* 1948, Hélène, dau. of Leonidas Arvanitidi, of Paris, and has issue living, Patricia Silvia, *b.* 19—. *Residence,*—41, Diego de Leon, Madrid, Spain.

Issue of the late Adm. the Hon. Sir Alexander Robert Maule Ramsay, GCVO, KCB, DSO, 3rd son of 13th Earl, *b.* 1881, *d.* 1972: *m.* 1919, HRH Princess (Victoria) Patricia Helena Elizabeth, VA, CI, who *d.* 1974 (who on her marriage renounced by Roy. permission the style and title of "HRH" and "Princess", and adopted that of "Lady", with precedence before Marchionesses of England), yr. da. of HRH the 1st Duke of Connaught and Strathearn [see ROYAL FAMILY]:— Alexander Arthur Alfonso David Maule RAMSAY OF MAR, (Cairnbuig Castle, Fraserburgh, Aberdeenshire, AB4 5TN; Mar Estate Office, Braemar, Aberdeenshire, AB3 5YB; 21 Cadogan Gdns., SW3 2RW). *Clubs,*—Guards', New (Edinburgh), Puffin's (Edinburgh), Turf; *b.* 1919; ed. at Eton, and at Trin. Coll., Oxford (MA); FRICS; DL of Aberdeenshire; Baron of Kellie; Capt. Gren. Gds. (ret.); served 1938-47, 1939-45 War (wounded Tunisia 1943); an ADC to HRH the Duke of Gloucester whilst Gov.-Gen. of Australia 1944-47; a Page of Honour at Coronation of King George VI; Chm. of Exec. Cttee. of Scottish Life Boat Council, RNLI since 1965; Vice-Patron of RNMPSF, and of Braemar Roy. Highland Soc.: *m.* 1956, the Hon. Flora Marjory Fraser, da. and heir of 19th Lord Saltoun, and has issue living, Katherine Ingrid Mary Isabel FRASER, *b.* 1957; assumed 1973 the name and arms of Fraser by Warrant of Lord Lyon King of Arms,—Alice Elizabeth Margaret, *b.* 1961,— Elizabeth Alexandra Mary, *b.* 1963.

Grandchildren of the late Lieut.-Col. Henry Lushington Ramsay (infra)— Issue of the late Capt. Archibald Henry Maule Ramsay, *b.* 1894, *d.* 1955: *m.* 1917, the Hon. Ismay Lucretia Mary, who *d.* 1975, da. of 14th Viscount Gormanston, and widow of Lord Ninian Edward Crichton-Stuart [M. Bute]:— Robert John Maule, *b.* 1920; ed. at Cheltenham; Member of Inst. of Quarrying: *m.* 1st, 1948 (m. diss. 1961), Theodora Jean, da. of Martyn Hewlett, of Granham Hall, Little Waltham; 2ndly, 1961, Elizabeth Frances, who *d.* 1972, da. of the late A. F. Bultitude, and has issue living, (by 1st m.) Theodora Alice Maule, *b.* 1950,—Christian Ismay Maule, *b.* 1952,—Charlotte Maule, *b.* 1954.— George Patrick Maule (Kellie House, London Rd., Sunningdale, Ascot, Berks., SL5 0EY), *b.* 1922; ed. at Eton; Col. late Scots Gds.: *m.* 1947, Patricia Mary, da. of Dr. J. J. Morrin, and has issue living, Alexander John Patrick Maule, *b.* 1948,—Patrick William Maule, *b.* 1951,—Catherine Mary Maule, *b.* 1950: *m.* 1972, Capt. Peter Ralph Leopold Walker-Okeover, Blues and Royals, el. son of Lt.-Col. Sir Ian Peter Andrew Monro Walker-Okeover, DSO, TD, 3rd Bt.,—Diana Mary Maule, *b.* 1957,— Fiona Elisabeth Maule, *b.* 1964.——*Rev.* John Charles Maule (St. Alexander's, 100, Stirling St., Stirlingshire, FK6 6DL), *b.* 1926; ed. at Eton, and at Pontifical Beda Coll., Rome; late Maj. Scots Gds.; Roman Catholic priest.

Granddaughters of the late Gen. the Hon. Sir Henry Ramsay, KCSI, CB brother of 12th Earl:— Issue of the late Lieut.-Col. Henry Lushington Ramsay, *b.* 1854, *d.* 1928: *m.* 1893, Sophia, who *d.* 1946, dau. of the late J. P. Thomas, of Warneford Place, Wilts, and Calcutta:— Maud Evelyn, *b.* 1895: *m.* 1925, Col. Richard Augustus Spencer. D.S.O., O.B.E., R.A. (retired), who *d.* 1956, [see V. Churchill, colls.]. *Residence,*—Flat 16, Melton Court, SW3.——Vera Edith (Peach Cottage, Walberton, Arundel, Sussex), *b.* 1900.

PREDECESSORS.—[1] *Sir* GEORGE Ramsay of Dalhousie, Knt.; on his own resignation had a charter of the Barony of Dalhousie; also of the Barony of Melrose on the resignation of John Ramsay, Earl of Holderness; cr. *Lord Ramsay of Melrose* (peerage of Scotland) by charter 1618, but not liking the title obtained a letter from James VI. to change it to *Lord Ramsay of Dalhousie* (with precedence of 1618); *d.* 1629; *s.* by his el. son [2] WILLIAM, 2nd Lord; raised a Regt. in Army of the Covenant, which he commanded at Marston Moor and Philliphaugh; cr. *Lord Ramsay and Carrington,* and *Earl of Dalhousie* (peerage of Scotland) 1633; *d.* 1674; *s.* by his son [3] GEORGE, 2nd Earl; *d.* 1675; *s.* by his son [4] WILLIAM, 3rd Earl; 2nd in command of Earl of Mar's Regt. at Bothwell Brig 1679; *d.* 1682; *s.* by his son [5] GEORGE, 4th Earl; *d.* (killed in duel) 1696 unmarried; *s.* by his brother [6] WILLIAM, 5th Earl; Col. Scots Guards; *d.* (while on active ser. in Spain during War of Succession) 1710; *s.* by his kinsman [7] WILLIAM, 6th Earl, son of John, 2nd son of 1st Earl; *d.* 1739; *s.* by his grandson [8] CHARLES, 7th Earl; *d.* 1764 unmarried; *s.* by his brother [9] GEORGE, 8th Earl; an Advocate; Lord High Commr. to Gen. Assembly of Church of Scotland 1777-82, and a Representative Peer 1774-87 (his 2nd son, William, cr. *Baron Panmure,* peerage of United Kingdom 1831, assumed the surname and arms of Maule and *d.* 1852); *d.* 1787; *s.* by his el. son [10] GEORGE, *G.C.B.,* 9th Earl; a Gen. in the Army; served with distinction in Peninsular War, and commanded 7th and 6th Divs. at Vittoria; Gov.-Gen. of Canada 1819-28, and Com.-in-Ch. in India 1829-32; cr. *Baron Dalhousie,* of Dalhousie Castle, co. Edinburgh (peerage of United Kingdom) 1815; *d.* 1838; *s.* by his son [11] JAMES ANDREW, *K.T., P.C.,* 10th Earl; Gov.-Gen. of India 1847-56, Constable of Dover Castle, Lord Warden of the Cinque Ports, &c.; assumed the additional surname of Broun of Coulstoun on succession to the Coulstoun estate; cr. *Marquess of Dalhousie,* of Dalhousie Castle, co. Edinburgh, and of the Punjab (peerage of United Kingdom) 1849; *d.* 1860, when the U.K. Barony of Dalhousie and the Marquessate became ext.; *s.* in Scottish honours by his cousin [12] Fox, *K.T., G.C.B., P.C.,* 11th Earl, who had in 1852 *s.* his father as 2nd Baron Panmure; was an Under-Sec. of State 1835-41, Vice-Pres. of Board of Trade 1841, Sec. at War 1846-52 and 1855-8, Lord-Lieut. of co. Forfar, and Keeper of the Privy Seal of Scotland, &c., assumed the surname and arms of Ramsay after that of Maule; *d.s.p.* 1874, when the U.K. Barony of Panmure expired; *s.* by his cousin [13] GEORGE, *C.B.,* 12th Earl, son of the Hon. John Ramsay, 4th son of 8th Earl, *b.* 1806; was an Adm.; cr. *Baron Ramsay,* of Glenmark, co. Forfar (peerage of United Kingdom) 1875: *m.* 1845, Sarah Frances, dau. of William Robertson, of Logan House, N.B.; *d.* 1880; *s.* by his son [14] JOHN WILLIAM, *K.T., P.C.,* 13th Earl, *b.* 1847: *m.* 1877, Lady Ida Louisa Bennett, who *d.* 1887, dau. of 6th Earl of Tankerville: *d.* 1887; *s.* by his el. son [15] Arthur George Maule, 14th Earl, *b.* 1878; Capt. Scots Guards, and Hon. Col. R.G.A. (T.A.): *m.* 1903, Lady Mary Adelaide Heathcote-Drummond-Willoughby, who *d.* 1960, youngest dau. of 1st Earl of Ancaster; *d.* 1928; *s.* by his son [16] JOHN GILBERT, 15th Earl; *b.* 1904, *d.* 1950; *s.* by his brother [17] SIMON, 16th Earl and present peer; also Lord Ramsay of Dalhousie, Lord Ramsay and Carrington, and Baron Ramsay (of Glenmark).

Dalkeith, Earl of, son of Duke of Buccleuch.

Dalmeny, Lord, son of Earl of Rosebery.

Dalrymple, Viscount, son of Earl of Stair.

DARCY DE KNAYTH, BARONESS. (Ingrams.) [Baroness E. 1332.]

DAVINA MARCIA INGRAMS (*Baroness Darcy de Knayth*), *b.* July 10th, 1938 ; *s.* 1943 : *m.* 1960, Rupert George Ingrams, who *d.* 1964 [Reid, Bt. *cr.* 1897], and has issue.

Arms.—Per pale azure and gules, three lions rampant argent. *Supporters.—Dexter*, an heraldic tiger argent; *sinister*, a bull sable.
Residence,—Camley Corner, Stubbings, Maidenhead, Berks.

SON LIVING.
Hon. CASPAR DAVID, *b.* Jan. 5th, 1962.

DAUGHTERS LIVING.
Hon. Miranda, *b.* 1960.
Hon. Catriona, *b.* 1963.

AUNT LIVING. (*Daughter of 4th Earl of Powis.*)
Lady Hermione Gwladys, *b.* 1900: *m.* 1924, Roberto Lucchesi Palli, 11th Duke della Grazia, and 13th Prince of Campofranco. Bailiff Grand Cross of the Sovereign, Mil. Order of Malta, and has issue living, Violet Maria Carolina Sidonie, *b.* 1930.

Residence,—Le Point de Vue, Chemin des Oisillons, 1012 Pully (Vaud), Switzerland.

WIDOW LIVING OF SEVENTEENTH BARON.
VIDA, only dau. of the late Capt. James Harold Cuthbert, D.S.O., Scots Guards; is an O.St.J.; appointed a Lady-in-Waiting to H.R.H. the Duchess of Gloucester 1944: *m.* 1st, 1934, the 17th Baron (also Viscount Clive), who *d.* (killed on active ser. during European War) 1943: 2ndly, 1945, Brig. Derek Shuldham Schreiber, MVO, who *d.* 1972, [B. Faringdon]. *Residences,*—Fir Hill, Droxford, Hants.; 59, Cadogan Pl., SW1.

PREDECESSORS.—[1] JOHN DARCY DE KNAYTH was summoned to Parliament of England as "*Johanni Darcy le Cosin*" 1332 ; *d.* 1347 ; *s.* by his son [2] JOHN ; summoned to Parliament as *Lord Darcy de Knayth* : *m.* Elizabeth, in her own right *Baroness Meinill* (who *d.* 1368), only child of Nicholas Lord Meinill ; *d.* 1356, and was *s.* by his son [3] JOHN, 3rd Baron ; *d.* unmarried, and *vita matris* ; *s.* by his brother [4] PHILIP, Lord Darcy de Knayth and Meinill ; *d.* 1398 ; *s.* by his son [5] JOHN ; *d.* 1411 ; *s.* by his el. son [6] PHILIP, Lord Darcy de Knayth and Meinill, at whose death in 1418 the Baronies of Darcy de Knayth and Meinill fell into abeyance between his daus., of whom the younger, Margery, *m.* Sir John Conyers of Hornby, and had a son Sir John Conyers of Hornby, who *m.* Alice, dau. and co-heir of William Nevill, Earl of Kent, and Lord Fauconberg (by Joan his wife *suo jure* Baroness Fauconberg) [see under B. Conyers]; they had issue William, 1st Lord Conyers [see By. of Fauconberg and Conyers*₀*], whose great-great-grandson [7] CONYERS DARCY (son of Thomas Darcy by Elizabeth, dau. and co-heir of the 3rd Baron Conyers) received in 1641 Letters Patent determining in his favour the abeyances then existing in the Baronies of Darcy de Knayth and Conyers ; *d.* 1653 ; *s.* by his son [8] CONYERS, Baron Darcy de Knayth and Conyers ; *cr.* *Earl of Holdernesse* 1682 ; *d.* 1688 ; *s.* by his son [9] CONYERS, 2nd Earl ; *d.* 1692 ; by his grandson [10] ROBERT 3rd Earl ; *d.* 1722 ; *s.* by his son [11] ROBERT 4th Earl ; *d.* 1778, when the Earldom became ext., but the Baronies passed to his dau. [12] AMELIA, wife of 5th Duke of Leeds ; *d.* 1784 ; *s.* by her son [13] GEORGE WILLIAM FREDERICK, 6th Duke ; *d.* 1838 ; *s.* by his son [14] FRANCIS GODOLPHIN DARCY, 7th Duke ; *d.* 1859 ; *s.* by his nephew [15] SACKVILLE GEORGE (son of Sackville Walter Lane Fox, Esq., M.P.), *b.* 1827 : in 1859 established his right to Barony of Conyers only, and was known by that title, his right to the Barony of Darcy de Knayth being established posthumously in 1903 : *m.* 1860, Mary, Lady Darcy de Knayth and Conyers, who *d.* 1921, el. dau. of Reginald Curteis, of Windmill Hill, Sussex ; *d.* 1888, when the Baronies fell into abeyance, this being determined as to the Barony of Conyers in 1892 in favour of the elder dau. Marcia Amelia Mary, Countess of Yarborough (in whose favour also the abeyance existing in the Barony of Fauconberg was determined 1903), and as to the Barony of Darcy de Knayth in 1903 in favour of the younger dau. [16] VIOLET IDA EVELYN, Countess of Powis, *b.* 1865 : *m.* 1890, the 4th Earl of Powis, who *d.* 1952 ; *d.* 1929 ; *s.* by her younger son [17] MERVYN HORATIO, 17th Baron ; *b.* 1904 ; Squadron-Leader R.A.F.: *m.* 1934, Vida, only dau. of the late Capt. James Harold Cuthbert, D.S.O.; *d.* (killed on active ser. during European War) 1943 ; *s.* by his only child [18] DAVINA MARCIA, present peeress.

DARESBURY, BARON. (Greenall.) [Baron U.K. 1927, Bt. U.K. 1876.]
[Title pronounced "Darsbury."]

EDWARD GREENALL, 2nd Baron, and 3rd Baronet ; *b.* Oct. 12th, 1902 ; *s.* 1938; ed. at Wixenford, and at Eton ; Lieut. late Reserve of Officers (Life Guards) : *m.* 1st, 1925, Joan Madeline, who *d.* 1926, el. dau. of the late Capt. Robert Thomas Oliver Sheriffe, of Goadby Hall, Melton Mowbray ; 2ndly, 1927, Josephine, who *d.* 1958, youngest dau. of Brig.-Gen. Sir Joseph Frederick Laycock, K.C.M.G., D.S.O. [E. Listowel, colls.]; 3rdly, 1966, Lady Helena Albreda Marie Gabriella, who *d.* 1970, da. of 7th Earl Fitzwilliam, and widow of Maj. Chetwode Charles Hamilton Hilton-Green, and has issue by 2nd m.

Arms,—1st and 4th or, on a bend benuly vert three bugle-horns stringed of the field, *Greenall*; 2nd and 3rd argent, five pallets sable, the centre pallet charged with an ermine spot of the field, *Griffith.* Crest,—Between two wings or, a pomme surmounted by a bugle-horn as in the arms. Supporters,—*Dexter*, a bull proper ; *sinister*, a bay mare, mane and tail sable, charged on the shoulder with a sprig of two oak leaves or.

I seek to rise.

Residence,—Clonshire. Limreick House, Adare, co.

SON LIVING. (*By 2nd marriage.*)

Hon. EDWARD GILBERT, *b.* Nov. 27th, 1928; *ed.* at Eton: *m.* 1952, Margaret Ada, yst. da. of the late Charles John Crawford, [Anson, Bt.], and has issue living, Peter Gilbert, *b.* 1953,—Gilbert, *b.* 1954,—John Edward, *b.* 1960,—Susan Rosemary, *b.* 1956. *Residence,*—Crossbow House, Trinity, Jersey.

WIDOW LIVING OF ELDER SON OF FIRST BARON.

Betty Isobel, el. dau. of the late J. S. Crawford, of Thorpe Satchville Hall, Melton Mowbray, *m.* 1st, 1924, the Hon. Gilbert Greenall; Lieut. The Life Guards, who *d.* 1928; 2ndly, 1933. Reginald Arthur Farquhar, who *d.* 1937 [Farquhar, Bt.]. *Residence,*—Ardsallagh, Fethard, oo. Tipperary.

PREDECESSORS.—[1] GILBERT Greenall, 6th son of the late Edward Greenall, of Wilderspool co. Chester, *b.* 1806; M.P. for Warrington (*C.*) 1847-68, 1874-80, and 1885-92; *cr.* a *Baronet* 1876, *m.* 1st, 1836, Mary, who *d.* 1861, dau. of David Claughton, of Haydock, Lancashire; 2ndly, 1864; Susannah, who *d.* 1896, dau. of John Louis Rapp; *d.* 1894; *s.* by his only son [2] *Sir* GILBERT, *C.V.O.,* 2nd Bt., *b.* 1867; High Sheriff for Cheshire 1907; *cr. Baron Daresbury* of Walton, co. Chester (peerage of United Kingdom) 1927: *m.* 1900, Frances Eliza, *J.P.,* who *d.* 1953, dau. of the late Capt. Edward Wynne Griffith, formerly 1st Roy. Dragoons; *d.* 1938; *s.* by his only surviving son [3] EDWARD, 2nd Baron and present peer.

DARLING, BARON. (Darling.) [Baron U.K. 1924.]

The gift of God.

ROBERT CHARLES HENRY DARLING. 2nd Baron; *b.* May 15th, 1919; *s.* 1936; *ed.* at Wellington Coll.; Major (retired) Somerset LI; DL for Avon; Ch. Exec., Bath and West and Southern Cos. So.: *m.* 1942, Bridget Rosemary Whishaw, da. of the Rev Francis Cyprian Dickson, formerly V. of Emery Down, Lyndhurst, Hants, and has issue.

Arms.—Argent, on a chevron engrailed between three flesh-pots sable a stirrup leathered or. **Crest,** —In front of a dexter cubit arm proper holding in the hand a heart gules a chaplet of laurel vert. **Supporters,**—On either side a Pegasus argent, charged on each wing with a chevron engrailed sable. **Badge.**—A sprig of heather and a sprig of gorse in saltire proper, enfiled by a Baron's coronet.

Residence,—Puckpits, Limpley Stoke, Bath, Somerset.

SON LIVING.

Hon. ROBERT JULIAN HENRY (Bowles Farm, Freeland, Oxon.), *b.* April 29th, 1944; *ed.* at Wellington: *m.* 1970, Janet, yr. da. of Mrs. D. M. E. Mallinson, of Richmond, Yorks., and has issue living, Robert James Cyprian, *b.* 1972,— Rachel Pollyanna Margaret, *b.* 1974.

DAUGHTERS LIVING.

Hon. Anna Josephine Bridget, *b.* 1946: *m.* 1971, Anthony Robert Pardoe.

Hon. Lucinda Mary Joan, *b.* 1958.

MOTHER LIVING.

Eleanor Joan Martin, dau. of the late H. Martin Powell, of Wilverley Park, Lyndhurst: *m.* 1st, 1918, Major the Hon. John Clive Darling, D.S.O., who *d.* 1933; 2ndly, 1945, as his second wife, the Rev. Francis Cyprian Dickson, formerly V. of Emery Down, Lyndhurst. *Residence,*—Forest Mead, Lyndhurst, Hants.

PREDECESSOR.—[1] *Rt. Hon. Sir* CHARLES JOHN Darling, *P.C.,* el. son of the late Charles Darling, of Langham Hall, Essex; *b.* 1849; M.P. for Deptford (*C*) 1888-97; Judge of the High Court of Justice 1897-1923; *cr. Baron Darling,* of Langham, Essex (peerage of United Kingdom) 1924: *m.* 1885, Mary Caroline, who *d.* 1913, el. dau. of the late Maj.-Gen. Wilberforce Harris Greathed, C.B.; *d.* 1936; *s.* by his grandson [2] ROBERT CHARLES HENRY (son of the late Major the Hon. John Clive Darling, D.S.O., only son of 1st Baron), 2nd Baron and present peer.

DARLING OF HILLSBOROUGH, BARON. (Darling.) [Life Baron 1974.]

GEORGE DARLING, *PC,* son of Frederick William Darling; *b.* July 20th, 1905; ed. at Liverpool and Camb. Univs.; a Member of Council National Fund for Research into Crippling Diseases; Hon. Pres. of Inst. of Trading Standards, and of Industrial Materials Recovery Assocn., and a Dir. of Hallam Radio; Min. of State, Board of Trade 1964-68; Vice-Pres., Council of Europe 1970-74; MP for Hillsborough Div. of Sheffield (*Lab. and Co-op.*) 1950-74; *cr.* PC 1966, and *Baron Darling of Hillsborough,* of Crewe in Cheshire (Life Baron) 1974: *m.* 1932, Dorothy, da. of Thomas William Hodge, and has issue.

Residence,—17, Amersham Rd., Beaconsfield, Bucks.

SON LIVING.

Hon. Peter George, *b.* 1950.

DAUGHTER LIVING.

Hon. Isabel, *b.* 1948.

DARNLEY, EARL OF. (Bligh.) Sits as BARON CLIFTON OF LEIGHTON
BROMSWOLD. [E. 1608.] [Earl I. 1725.]
[Name pronounced " Bly."]

PETER STUART BLIGH, 10th Earl ; *b.* Oct. 1st,
1915; *s.* 1955; ed. at Eton ; Major (retired)
King's Dragoon Guards; European War
1939-40 (prisoner).

Arms,—Azure, a griffin segreant or, armed and langued
gules, between three crescents argent. **Crest,**—A griffin's
head erased or. **Supporters.**—Two griffins, wings expanded
or, ducally gorged and chained azure.

Residence,—Puckle Hill, Shorne, near Gravesend, Kent.

Look to the end.

HALF-BROTHER LIVING.

Hon. ADAM IVO STUART (Hambledon House, nr. Ports-
mouth, Hants.), *b.* Nov. 8th, 1941; ed. at Harrow and
Ch. Ch., Oxford: *m.* 1965, Susan Elaine, da. of the late Sir
Donald Forsyth Anderson [see Llewellyn, Bt., *cr.* 1922],
and has issue living, Ivo Donald Stuart, *b.* 1968,—
Katherine Amanda, *b.* 1971.

SISTER LIVING.

Lady Marguerite Rose, *b.* 1913: *m.* 1st, 1934, Claud Dobrée Strickland, Flying Officer Auxiliary
Air Force, who *d.* (killed in action during European War) (Oct.) 1941, having obtained a
divorce (Feb.) 1941 [Strickland-Constable, Bt., colls.]; 2ndly, 1942, Wing-Com. Gordon Hay-
wood, R.A.F., from whom she obtained a divorce 1951 ; 3rdly, 1951, as his second wife, Nigel
Trevithick Tangye, from whom she obtained a divorce 1964, and has issue living, (by 2nd marriage)
Gareth Peter, *b.* 1943: *m.* 1965 (m. diss. 1969), Zehra Ipek, da. of Prof. Semseddin Talip Diler, of
Taksim, Istanbul,—Lucinda March (twin), *b.* 1943: *m.* 1964, James Hilary Glyn, of 57, Lower
Straithe, Hartingdon Rd., Chiswick, W4 [see B. Wolverton, colls.]. *Residence,*—30, Coleherne Rd.
SW10.

HALF-SISTERS LIVING.

Lady Rose Amanda, *b.* 1935 : *m.* 1961, Thomas Hare, only son of Sir Ralph Leigh Hare, 4th Bt.
Residence,—Stow Bardolph, King's Lynn, Norfolk.
Lady Melissa Geraldine Florence, *b.* 1945: *m.* 1965, Don Manuel Torrado y de Fontcuberta, of 180
Via Augusta, Barcelona, and has issue living, Manuel Ivo, *b.* 1966,—Maria Melissa, *b.* 1968,—
Victoria Irene, *b.* 1973.
Lady Harriet Esme Ghislaine, *b.* 1949; ed. at Cobham Hall, and Somerville Coll., Oxford.

UNCLE LIVING. (*Son of 8th Earl.*)

Hon. Noel Gervase, *D.S.O., b.* 1888; ed. at Eton; is temporary Lieut.-Col. Pioneer Corps;
formerly Lieut.-Col. Rifle Brig. (Prince Consort's Own); 1914-18 War (despatches) D.S.O.),
1940-45 War ; D.S.O. 1918 : *m.* 1st, 1912 (m. diss. 1934), Mary Jack, who *d.* 1940, dau. of the late
Capt. George Alfred Frost, RA; 2ndly, 1934, Dorothy Millicent Isabella (MUNROE), who *d.* 1972,
da. of the late Hubert Lee Bevan; 3rdly, 1973, Mrs. Kathleen Weatherill Strickland, and has issue
living, (by 1st m.) Jasmine Lydia, *b.* 1913, appointed Announcer-Hostess, Directorate of Television,
BBC 1936: *m.* 1st, 1940, as his second wife, Major John Paley Johnson (afterwards 6th Bt.), R.A.;
2ndly, 1948, Frank Hugh Shirley Fox,—Susan Rachel, *b.* 1916: *m.* 1940, Lieut.-Col. William Joseph
Stirling of Keir, Scots Guards [see Stirling-Maxwell, Bt., colls.]. *Address,*—c/o Lloyds Bank, 6,
Pall Mall, S.W.1.

AUNT LIVING. (*Daughter of 8th Earl.*)

Lady Dorothy Violet, *b.* 1893 : *m.* 1916, Capt. Daniel Spencer Peploe, 20th Hussars, who *d.* 1958, and
has issue living, Anthony Daniel Keith (The Garden Cottage, Shoreham, Sevenoaks, Kent), *b.* 1918;
Capt. RA: *m.* 1940, Anne Cecilia, only da. of the late Maj. Geoffrey Lee Compton-Smith, DSO, and
has issue living, Anthony Noel *b.* 1948, Ivo John *b.* 1952, Rupert Lee *b.* 1961, Jennifer Mary Anne
b. 1941,—Diana Felicity Jane, *b.* 1917: *m.* 1955, Lt.-Col. Anthony Swynfen Jervis, MBE, RA, of
Verlands, Erwood, Builth Wells, Breconshire. *Residence,*—Squirrels, Weald Rd., Sevenoaks, Kent.

WIDOW LIVING OF NINTH EARL

ROSEMARY, da. of the late Basil Potter: *m.* 1st, 1940, as his third wife, the 9th Earl, who *d.* 1955;
2ndly, 1963, as his second wife, Pierre Trasenster, who *d.* 1968. *Residence,*—Meadow House,
Cobham, Kent.

COLLATERAL BRANCHES LIVING.

Grandchildren of the late Major Lodovick Edward Bligh (infra):—
Issue of the late Algernon Stuart Bligh, *b.* 1888, *d.* 1952 : *m.* 1st, 1922 (divorce 1937), Dora
Joan, da. of T. Lovelace, of Bratton Court, Minehead; 2ndly, 1938, Dorothy, da. of the
late J. F. V. Larway (Amberley, Lower Park, Minehead, Som.):—
(By 1st marriage) Noel Edward, *b.* 1926; late Capt. R.A.S.C., and Lt. R.N.: *m.* 1961, Jane Mary,
dau. of Trevor Seymour-Smith, and has issue living, Victoria Joan, *b.* 1962. *Residence,*—Court
Barton, Yarnscombe, Barnstaple, N. Devon.——Audrey Diana, *b.* 1924: *m.* 1947, John Sefton
Spencer Hawkins, and has issue living, Nigel Bligh Spencer, *b.* 1954,—David Stuart Spencer, *b.* 1956.
Residence,—Osbornes, Upper Dicker, Hailsham, Sussex.——(By 2nd m.) Jennifer Wendy, *b.* 1942:
m. 1st 1963 (m. diss. 1974), Ronald Colin Board Webber; 2ndly, 1975, Alan Thomas Wormell, of
Thatched Cottage, Stowey, Timberscombe, Minehead, Som., and has issue living (by 1st m.), Katrina
Jane, *b.* 1964.——Heather Rosalind, *b.* 1945: *m.* 1968, Arthur Keith Amor, of Huntersmead, Hele,
Taunton, and has issue living, Jason Keith Bligh, *b.* 1970,—Lucinda Jane Bligh, *b.* 1969.

Granddaughter of the late Rev. the Hon. Edward Vesey Bligh, 2nd son of 5th Earl:—
Issue of the late Major Lodovick Edward Bligh, *b.* 1854, *d.* 1924: *m.* 1886, Marion
Louisa, who *d.* 1925, dau. of the late Rev. Frederick Alexander Stewart-Savile, of
Hollanden Park, Tonbridge.
Rose Marion, *b.* 1896: *m.* 1923, Stanley Hosegood, who *d.* 1969, and has issue living, Jack Bligh (White
Gates Lodge, Roborough, Barnstaple, N. Devon), *b.* 1925; European War 1943-45 with Grenadier
Guards (despatches): *m.* 1st, 1946 (m. diss. 1961), Pamela Lea-Smith; 2ndly, 1961, Enid Phyllis
Webber, and has issue living, (by 1st marriage) David Bligh *b.* 1949, John Stanley *b.* 1955, Anne
Elizabeth *b.* 1947: *m.* 1969, Malcolm Richard Seyfried, (and has issue living, Paul Digby *b.* 1971),
(by 2nd m.) Amanda Jayne *b.* 1964,—Michael Ian, *RN* (Tinker's Warren, Woodlands Av., Ems-
worth, Hants.), *b.* 1927; is Lt.-Cdr.; 1944-45 War: *m.* 1955, Rosemary da. of the late Lt.-Col.
W. J. Best, Indian Army, and has issue living, Sheenagh Mary *b.* 1956, Alison Bridget *b.* 1959, Celia
Ann *b.* 1962. *Residence,*—28, Northfield Park, Pilton, Barnstaple, N. Devon.

PREDECESSORS.—[1] JOHN Bligh, *M.P.* for Athboy 1709-21; *cr. Baron Clifton of Rathmore*
(peerage of Ireland) 1721, *Viscount Darnley* (peerage of Ireland) 1723, and *Earl of Darnley*
(peerage of Ireland) 1725 ; *d.* 1728 ; *s.* by his son [2] EDWARD, 2nd Earl, who in 1722 had *s.* his
mother as *Baron Clifton of Leighton Bromswold* (peerage of England) by writ of summons
1608 ; *d.* unmarried 1747 ; *s.* by his brother [3] JOHN, 3rd Earl; M.P. for Maidstone ; *d.* 1781 ;
s. by his son [4] JOHN, 4th Earl; in 1829 claimed as heir-gen. the Scottish Dukedom of
Lennox, but the House of Lords did not come to any decision ; *d.* 1831 ; *s.* by his son [5]

EDWARD, 5th Earl; *b.* 1795; sat as M.P. for Canterbury 1818-30; was Lord Lieut. of co. Meath: *m.* 1825, Emma Jane, who *d.* 1884, dau. of 1st Baron Congleton; *d.* 1835; *s.* by his son [6] JOHN STUART, 6th Earl, *b.* 1827: *m.* 1850, Lady Harriet Mary Pelham, el. dau. of 3rd Earl of Chichester; *d.* 1896; *s.* by his el. son [7] EDWARD HENRY STUART, 7th Earl, *b.* 1851: *m.* 1899, Miss Jemima Adeline Blackwood; *d.* 1900, when the Barony of Clifton of Leighton Bromswold passed to his dau. and only child Elizabeth Adeline Mary (see infra *₄*), who *d.* 1937, while he was *s.* in the Earldom by his brother [8] IVO FRANCIS WALTER, 8th Earl; *b.* 1859; a Representative Peer for Ireland: *m.* 1884, Dame Florence Rose, *D.B.E.*, who *d.* 1944, dau. of the late Stephen Morphy, of Beechworth, Victoria; *d.* 1927; *s.* by his son [9] ESME IVO, 9th Earl; *b.* 1886: *m.* 1912, Daphne Rachel (who *d.* 1948, having obtained a divorce 1920), dau. of the late Hon. Alfred John Mulholland; 2ndly, 1923, Nancy (from whom he obtained a divorce, 1936), dau. of the late Capt. Glen Kidston, 3rd Batn. Black Watch; 3rdly, 1940, Rosemary, dau. of the late Basil Potter; *d.* 1955; *s.* by his el. son [10] PETER STUART, 10th Earl, and present peer; also Viscount Darnley, Baron Clifton of Rathmore, and Baron Clifton of Leighton Bromswold.

₄ [1] *Sir* GERVASE Clifton, son of Sir John Clifton, of Barrington, Somerset, was summoned to Parliament as *Baron Clifton of Leighton Bromswold* (peerage of England) 1608: *d.* 1618; *s.* by his dau. [2] CATHERINE: *m.* Lord Esme Stuart who was cr. *Baron Stuart* of Leighton Bromswold (in her right), and *Earl of March* 1619, and *s.* as 3rd Duke of Lennox, 1624; *d.* 1637; *s.* by her son [3] JAMES, 4th Duke of Lennox; *d.* 1655; *s.* by his son [4] ESME, 5th Duke; *d.* 1660; *s.* by his sister [5] MARY Butler, Countess of Arran; *d.* 1667; *s.* by her cousin [6] CHARLES, 6th Duke of Lennox; *d.* 1672; *s.* by his sister [7] CATHERINE O'Brien (wife of Henry, el. son of 7th Earl of Thomond), who claimed and was allowed the barony in 1674 as grand-dau. of Catherine, dau. of 1st Baron; she *m.* 2ndly, Sir Joseph Williamson; *d.* 1702; *s.* by her dau. [8] CATHERINE Hyde, Viscountess Cornbury; *d.* 1706; *s.* by her son [9] EDWARD, Viscount Cornbury; *d.* 1712; *s.* by his sister [10] THEODOSIA: *m.* John Bligh, of Rathmore, co. Meath, who was cr. *Baron Clifton of Rathmore* (peerage of Ireland) 1721, *Viscount Darnley* (peerage of Ireland) 1723, and *Earl of Darnley* (peerage of Ireland) 1725; *d.* 1722; *s.* by her son [11] EDWARD, 2nd Earl of Darnley, who in 1722 had *s.* his mother as *Baron Clifton of Leighton Bromswold* (peerage of England) by writ of summons 1608; *d.* unmarried 1747; *s.* by his brother [12] JOHN, 3rd Earl; M.P. for Maidstone; *d.* 1781; *s.* by his son [13] JOHN, 4th Earl; in 1829 claimed as heir-gen. the Scottish Dukedom of Lennox, but the House of Lords did not come to any decision; *d.* 1831; *s.* by his son [14] EDWARD, 5th Earl; *b.* 1795; sat as M.P. for Canterbury 1818-30; was Lord-Lieut. of co. Meath: *m.* 1825, Emma Jane, who *d.* 1884, dau. of 1st Baron Congleton; *d.* 1835; *s.* by his son [15] JOHN STUART, 6th Earl; *b.* 1827: *m.* 1850, Lady Harriet Mary Pelham, who *d.* 1905, el. dau. of 3rd Earl of Chichester; *d.* 1896; *s.* by his el. son [16] EDWARD HENRY STUART, 7th Earl; *b.* 1851: *m.* 1899, Miss Jemima Adeline Blackwood; *d.* 1900, when the Earldom of Darnley passed to his brother, while he was *s.* in the Barony of Clifton of Leighton Bromswold by his dau. and only child [17] ELIZABETH ADELINE MARY, Baroness Clifton of Leighton Bromswold; *b.* 1900; *d.* 1937; *s.* by her cousin [18] ESME IVO 9th Earl of Darnley (ante).

DARTMOUTH, EARL OF. (Legge.) [Earl G.B. 1711.]

GERALD HUMPHRY LEGGE, 9th Earl; *b.* April 26th, 1924; *s.* 1962; ed. at Eton; an F.C.A.; Hon. LLD Dartmouth Coll.; Italy 1944-5, as Capt. Coldstream Guards (despatches): *m.* 1948, Raine, da. of the late Alexander George McCorquodale, of The White Lodge, Speen, Berks., and has issue.

Arms,—Azure, a buck's head cabossed argent. **Crest,**—Out of a ducal coronet or, a plume of five ostrich feathers argent and azure alternately. **Supporters.**—*Dexter,* a lion argent semée of fleurs-de-lis sable, ducally crowned or, and issuing from the coronet a plume of five ostrich feathers argent and azure, alternately; *sinister,* a stag argent, unguled or, and semee of mullets gules.

Residence,—40A, Hill St., W.1.

Virtue rejoices in trial.

SONS LIVING.

WILLIAM (*Viscount Lewisham*), *b.* Sept. 23rd, 1949; ed. at Eton, and Ch. Ch., Oxford.
Hon. Rupert, *b.* 1951; ed. at Eton.
Hon. Henry, *b.* 1968.

DAUGHTER LIVING.

Lady Charlotte, *b.* 1963.

SISTER LIVING.

Lady Heather Margaret Mary (*Baroness Herschell*), *b.* 1925: *m.* 1948, the 3rd Baron Herschell, *Residence,*—Westfield House, Ardington, Wantage, Berks.

DAUGHTERS LIVING OF SEVENTH EARL.

Lady Mary Cecilia, *b.* 1906: *m.* 1929, Com. Noel Charles Mansfeldt Findlay, RN (ret.), son of Sir Mansfeldt de Cardonnel Findlay, GBE, KCMG, CB, and has issue living, Jonathan Mansfeld (Eden Lodge, Droxford, Hants), *b.* 1933; Cdr, RN: *m.* 1962, Jutta, da. of Gen. Karl von Graffent and has issue living, Christopher Mansfeldt Karl, *b.* 1967, Caroline Ilse *b.* 1962, Angela Mary *b.* 1964,—Martin Charles (Ledburn Manor, Leighton Buzzard, Beds.), *b.* 1935: *m.* 1966, Davina Margaret, da. of Maj. Sir Thomas Calderwood Dundas, MBE, 7th Bt. [cr. 1898] (ext.), and has issue living, Mark Simon *b.* 1967, Adam James *b.* 1969,—Jane Elizabeth, *b.* 1930: *m.* 1961, Jeremy Debenham, of Reeds Farm, Sayers Common, Hassocks, Sussex, and has issue living, Catherine Mary *b.* 1962, Henrietta Jane *b.* 1965, Susannah Elizabeth *b.* 1968. *Residence,*—Court Lodge, Hastingleigh, Ashford, Kent.
Lady Elizabeth (67, Cottesmore Court, Stanford Rd., W8), *b.* 1908; appointed an Extra Woman of the Bedchamber to HM Queen Elizabeth the Queen Mother 1955: *m.* 1931, Ronald Lambart Basset, who *d.* 1972 [Salusbury-Trelawny, Bt.], and has issue living, Bryan Ronald (10, Stack House, Cundy St., SW1; and Quarles, Wells-next-Sea, Norfolk), *b.* 1932: *m.* 1960, Lady Carey Elizabeth Coke, da. of 5th Earl of Leicester, and has issue living, David Francis *b.* 1961, Michael James *b.* 1963, James Bryan, *b.* 1968.
Lady Barbara, *b.* 1916; formerly in First Aid Nursing Yeo.: *m.* 1945, Adam Kwiatkowski, Lieut. Polish Army, and has issue living, Jan Witold (The Bothy, Patshull Park, Burnhill Green, Wolverhampton), *b.* 1945: *m.* 1968, Sarah Hope, da. of Christopher Challis, of Pineways, Grays Park, Stoke Poges, Bucks, and has issue living, Adam Witold *b.* 1972, Daniel Christopher *b.* 1974,—Marek William, *b.* 1947,—Christopher, *b.* 1951,—Michael Andrew Adam, *b.* 1955. *Residence,*—Butler's House, Patshull, Park, Wolverhampton.

Lady Josceline Gabrielle (*Marchioness of Donegall*), *b.* 1918; is in First Aid Nursing Yeo.: *m.* 1946, the 7th Marquess of Donegall. *Residence,*—Dunbrody Park, Arthurstown, co. Wexford.

WIDOW LIVING OF EIGHTH EARL.

ROMA ERNESTINE (*Roma, Countess of Dartmouth*) (15B, Bedford Towers, Brighton), da. of Sir Ernest Burford Horlick, 2nd Bt.: *m.* 1923, the 8th Earl, who *d.* 1962.

COLLATERAL BRANCHES LIVING.

Grandchildren of the late Nigel Walter Henry LEGGE-BOURKE, only son of the late Col. the Hon. Sir Henry Charles Legge, GCVO, 2nd son of 5th Earl:—
Issue of the late Sir (Edward Alexander) Henry Legge-Bourke, KBE, MP, *b.* 1914, *d.* 1973, *m.* 1938, Catherine Jean (9, Wilbraham Place, SW1), da. of Col. Sir Arthur Grant, 10th Bt, CBE, DSO:—
William Nigel Henry (Glanusk Park, Crickhowell, Powys), *b.* 1939; ed. at Eton and Magdalene Coll. Camb. (MA); late Capt. RHG (The Blues): *m.* 1964, the Hon. (Elizabeth) Shân (Josephine) Bailey da. of 3rd Baron Glanusk, and has issue living Harry Russell, *b.* 1972,—Alexandra (Shân), *b.* 1965,—Zara (Victoria), *b.* 1966.——Heneage, *b.* 1948; a Page of Honour to HM 1963-64.——Victoria Lindsay, *b.* 1950; appointed a Lady in Waiting to HRH the Princess Anne, Mrs. Mark Phillips, 1974.

Grandson of the late Rev. the Hon. George Barrington Legge, 2nd son of 4th Earl:—
Issue of the late Rev. Hugh Legge, *b.* 1870, *d.* 1944 : *m.* 1917, Bessie, who *d.* 1950, dau. of Richard Pether, formerly of Sandford-on-Thames :—
John Barrington, *b.* 1918 ; ed. at Haileybury ; Major (retired) R.A.; European War 1939-42 (wounded): *m.* 1940, Gertrude Sarah, dau. of Frederick Wood, of Little Preston Capes, Northants, and has issue living, Hugh, *b.* 1945; ed. at Haileybury; late Lt. RA,—Jane, *b.* 1941,—Hannah, *b.* 1947. *Residence,*—The Porch House, Dodford, Northants.

Granddaughter of the late Lt.-Col. the Hon. Edward Henry Legge (infra) :—
Issue of the late John Douglas Legge, MC, *b.* 1886, *d.* 1954: *m.* 1917, Haroldine, who *d.* 1970, da. of the late Harold S. Peck, of Chicago, USA:—
Virginia Lois (*Hon. Mrs. Nial A. R. O'Neill*), *b.* 1922: *m.* 1966, Maj. the Hon. Nial Arthur Ramleh, O'Neill, of Mill of Syde, Kennethmont, Huntly, Aberdeenshire [see B. Rathcavan].

Issue of the late Lieut.-Col. the Hon. Edward Henry Legge, 3rd son of the 4th Earl, *b.* 1834, *d.* 1900 : *m.* 1873, Cordelia Twysden, who *d.* 1915, 3rd dau. of the late Walter Hele Molesworth [Molesworth-St. Aubyn, Bt., colls.]:—
Cecilia Katharine, *b.* 1895 : *m.* 1916, Capt. Reginald Hugh Errington, R.N. (retired), and has issue living, Janetta Lois (*Baroness Huntingfield*), *b.* 1917: *m.* 1941, the 6th Baron Huntingfield,—Cordelia (*Hon. Mrs. Peter B. R. Vanneck*), *b.* 1922: *m.* 1943, Air Commodore the Hon. Peter Beckford Rutgers Vanneck, CB, OBE, AFC, of White Lodge, Waldringfield, Suffolk, and 25, Elvaston Pl., SW7 [see B. Huntingfield]. *Residence,*—Tostock Old Hall, Bury St. Edmunds.

Grandchildren of the late Rt. Rev. the Hon. Augustus Legge, DD, Bishop of Lichfield, 5th son of 4th Earl:—
Issue of the late Francis Augustus Legge, *b.* 1880, *d.* 1966: *m.* 1909, Mabel Clara Arden, who *d.* 1963, da. of the late Charles Lucena, of Westwick, Easthampstead:—
Christopher Augustus Sackville (20, Ipswich Rd., Woodbridge, Suffolk), *b.* 1911; ed. at Eton, and Worcester Coll., Oxford (MA); Bar. Inner Temple 1936: *m.* 1952, Kari, who *d.* 1971, da. of the late Walther Brebeck, Pres. of Senate, of Eutin, Germany, and has issue living, Robert Augustus, *b.* 1953,—Christopher Walter, *b.* 1955,—Barbara Ingrid, *b.* 1960.——Fanny Angela Mary (Meon House, Droxford, Hants.), *b.* 1912: *m.* 1940, Lt.-Col. Philip Lewis, SLI, who *d.* 1968, and has issue living, Christopher Julian Arden, *b.* 1941: *m.* 1972, Caroline Dyson,—Lavinia Zaria, *b.* 1943: *m.* 1969, Maj. (Murray Bernard) Neville Cyprian Howard, Coldm. Gds. [see D. Norfolk, colls.].

Grandchildren of the late Hon. Charles Gounter Legge, 6th son of 4th Earl :—
Issue of the late Brig.-Gen. William Kaye Legge, C.M.G., D.S.O., *b.* 1869, *d.* 1946: *m.* 1902, Constance Adeline, who *d.* 1964, dau. of the late Hon. James David Palmer, of Bloemfontein, Orange Free State Province. S. Africa:—
Peter (2, Church St., St. Ives, Huntingdon, PE17 4DG), *b.* 1910; ed. at Wellington Coll.; Wing-Cdr. (ret.) RAF; 1939-45 War (despatches twice): *m.* 1st, 1937 (m. diss. 1953), Mary Claire, da. of William Dwyer, of Elmville, Rushbrooke, co. Cork; 2ndly, 1955, Violet Bertha, da. of the late George Wallace, and has issue living, (by 1st m.) Michael William, *b.* 1938; ed. at Downside,—David Anthony, *b.* 1941; ed. at Downside,—Susan Noelle Ann, *b.* 1943.

Issue of the late Lieut.-Com. John Augustus Legge, R.D., R.N.R., *b.* 1871, *d.* 1945 : *m.* 1908, Grace Margaret, who *d.* 1957, dau. of the late Alexander Henderson Dunsmure, of 46, Egerton Crescent, S.W.3 :—
John Michael Derek, *b.* 1913; ed. at Eton: *m.* 1945, Esmé Edith, da. of the late Vice-Adm. Cyril St· Clair Cameron, CBE, and has issue living, Derek Rupert Spicer, *b.* 1949,—Elizabeth Angela, *b.* 1946. *Residence,*—Little Combe, Whatley, Frome, Som.——David Alexander Keppel, CBE. *b.* 1916; ed. at Eton; Col. R. Fus. (ret.); 1939-45 War (wounded); MBE (Mil.) 1953, CBE (Mil.) 1970: *m.* 1944, Patria, da. of the late Lt.-Col. C. B. R. Hornung, DL, JP, of Ivorys, Cowfold, and has issue living, Richard Charles Gounter, *b.* 1948: *m.* 1972, Lesley Mayfield Finch, da. of Frederick Ledger, of Brompton House, Malvern,—Anthea Frances, *b.* 1946: *m.* 1969, Richard Charles Roundell, of Dorfold Hall, Nantwich, Ches. [Os. Dysart, colls.]. *Residence,*—Sandwell, Marston Magna, Yeovil, Som.——Margaret Elizabeth, *b.* 1908. *Residence,*—Tutton Hill House, Colerne, Wilts.

Issue of the late Thomas Charles Legge, *b.* 1872, *d.* 1949: *m.* 1904, Ivy Emily, who *d.* 1961, youngest dau. of J. Reid, of Zeerust, Transvaal :—
Gounter Heneage Hugh, *b.* 1909; ed. at Witwatersrand Univ. (BSc(Eng) ; FICE; FASCE: *m.* 1936, Joyce Kathleen, BA, da. of the late Thomas Angus Brown, and has issue living, Traver Francis Hugh, *b.* 1942; assumed the christian name of Traver in lieu of Thomas; ed. at Witwatersrand Univ. (BSc(Eng.)) and Imperial Coll., London (DIC, MSc): *m.* 1972, Helen, da. of Jack Downie, of Johannesburg. *Residence,*—1, St. David Rd., Houghton, Johannesburg, S. Africa. *Clubs,*—Rand, Country (Johannesburg).——Mary Charlotte Lois, *b.* 1905; BCom: *m.* 1934, George Wilson Low, Colonial Vet. Ser. *Address,*—c/o National & Grindlays Bank, Mombasa, Kenya.

Grandchildren of the late Capt. Ronald George Legge, 7th son of the late Hon. Charles Gounter Legge (ante) :—
Issue of the late Major Rupert Mortimer Legge, Roy. Fusiliers, *b.* 1911, *d.* (killed in action in Italy) 1944: *m.* 1940, Anne (Nether House, Pebmarsh, Essex), da. of the late Sir James Adam, CBE, KC:—
Rupert James (4, Hollins Walk, Reading, Berks.), *b.* 1944; ed. at Wellington: *m.* 1968, Jacqueline Hope, da. of the late Maj. E. T. H. Ubsdell, and has issue living, a son, *b.* 1971,—a da., *b.* 1972 ——Christian Anne Victoria, *b.* 1942.

PREDECESSORS.—[1] *Rt. Hon.* GEORGE Legge, an eminent naval commander, and Col. of a regt. of Foot; Gov. of Portsmouth, Master of the Ordnance, and Master of the Horse and Gentleman of the Bedchamber to James, Duke of York, &c.; cr. *Baron Dartmouth,* of Devon (peerage of England) 1682; during the reign of James II. held several important offices, but falling with his party at the Revolution, and having been suspected of plotting against William III., was imprisoned in the Tower, where he *d.* 1691 ; *s.* by his son [2] *Rt. Hon.* WILLIAM,

2nd Baron ; Sec. of State 1710 ; Lord Privy Seal 1713, and after the death of Queen Anne, one of the Lords Justices of Great Britain ; cr. *Viscount Lewisham* and *Earl of Dartmouth* (peerage of Great Britain) 1711 ; *d.* 1750 ; *s.* by his grandson [3] WILLIAM, 2nd Earl; *d.* July 1801 ; *s.* by his son [4] GEORGE, *K.G.*, 3rd Earl, summoned to Parliament in his father's barony June 1801 ; *d.* 1810 ; *s.* by his son [5] WILLIAM, *F.R.S., D.C.L.*, 4th Earl ; *b.* 1784 : *m.* 1st, 1821, the Lady Frances Charlotte, who *d.* 1823, dau. of 2nd Earl Talbot ; 2ndly, the Hon. Frances, who *d.* 1849, dau. of 5th Viscount Barrington ; *d.* Nov. 22, 1853 ; *s.* by his son [6] WILLIAM WALTER, 5th Earl, *b.* 1823; M.P. for S. Staffordshire (*C*) 1849-53 ; Lord-Lieut. of Staffordshire : *m.* 1846, Lady Augusta Finch, who *d.* 1900, el. dau. of 5th Earl of Aylesford ; *d.* 1891 ; *s.* by his el. son [7] *Rt. Hon.* WILLIAM HENEAGE, *G.C.V.O., K.C.B., V.D., T.D.*, 6th Earl, *b.* 1851 ; Vice-Chamberlain of H.M. Queen Victoria's Household 1885-6, and 1886-91, and Lord-Lieut. of Staffs 1891-1927 ; M.P. for W. Kent (*C*) 1878-85, and for Lewisham 1885-91 : *m.* 1879, Lady Mary Coke, *C.B.E.*, who *d.* 1929, dau. of 2nd Earl of Leicester ; *d.* 1936 ; *s.* by his el. son [8] WILLIAM, *G.C.V.O., T.D.*, 7th Earl ; *b.* 1881 ; Co. Councillor for London, 1907-10, Hon. Col. Duke of Wellington's (W. Riding) Regt. and Staffordshire Yeo. ; M.P. for West Bromwich (*C*) 1910-18 ; upon death of Marquess of Lincolnshire appointed 1928 by H.M. King George V to execute office of Lord Great Chamberlain for remainder of his reign: *m.* 1905, Lady Ruperta Wynn-Carrington, who *d.* 1963, dau. of 1st Marquess of Lincolnshire; *d.* 1958; *s.* by his brother [9] HUMPHRY, *CVO, DSO*, 8th Earl; *b.* 1888; Cdr. RN; present at Jutland 1916; Assist. Ch. Constable of Staffs. 1929-32, and Ch. Constable of Berks. 1932-54: *m.* 1923, Roma Ernestine, dau. of Sir Ernest Burford Horlick, 2nd Bt.; *d.* 1962; *s.* by his only son [10] GERALD HUMPHRY, 9th Earl and present peer; also Viscount Lewisham and Baron Dartmouth.

DARTREY, EARLDOM OF. (Dawson.) [Extinct 1933.]

DAUGHTER LIVING OF THIRD EARL.

Lady Eleanor Charlotte Augusta, *b.* 1885 : *m.* 1st, 1906, Capt. Aubrey Nugent Wade Palmer, from whom she obtained a divorce 1920 ; 2ndly, 1920, János Orsolya Kiss, who *d.* 1932; 3rdly, 1934, Frigyes Szántó (Dr. of Politics), who *d.* 1947; 4thly, 1951, Judge Syed Waris Ameer Ali, CIE, IOS (ret.), who *d.* 1975, and has issue living, (by 1st m.) Barbara Madeline WADE-PALMER (Myrtle, Quickley Lane, Chorleywood, Herts.), *b.* 1907: *m.* 1923, Col. Béla Domjan de Domjanszeg, of Hungary, from whom she obtained a divorce 1936, and has issue living, Robert (Dene Hill, Beechenlea Lane, Swanley Village, Kent), *b.* 1924; Div. Man. Dir. of Steetley Ltd.: *m.* 1956, Countess Heilwig Freda Anna Helene Christa Hildegard, da. of Count Gerhart von Budingen, and has issue living, Nicholas Charles Robert *b.* 1960,—Ismé Ruth, *b.* 1908: *m.* 1934, Capt. Christian Satzger de Bálványos, from whom she obtained a divorce 1941. *Residence,*—1, Alexandra Court, Queen's Gate, SW7.

COLLATERAL BRANCHES LIVING.

Grandchildren of Lady Edith Anne Windham-Dawson, da. of 2nd Earl (ante):—
Issue of the late Lt.-Cdr. Charles William Windham, RN : *m.* 1st, 1939, Sheila Mairi (from whom he obtained a divorce 1953), only da. of Capt. L. C. W. Harrington, RN ; 2ndly, 19—, Margaret Elizabeth (The Grange, Bradford Abbas, Dorset), only da. of the late Very Rev. E. C. Bigger, Dean of Clogher:—
(By 1st m.) Charles Richard Dawson, *b.* 1948.——Elizabeth Anne Dawson, *b.* 1940: *m.* 1968, Kenneth Paul Ward, and has issue living, Alexandra Grace Windham, *b.* 1970.——Gillian Julia Dawson, *b.* 1943: *m.* 1970, Bernard Joseph Keegan, of Chilworth House, Wheatley, Oxon., and has issue living, Damian Cremorne Dawson, *b.* 1973,—Melody Mary Dawson, *b.* 1970.

Issue of the late Capt. the Hon. Edward Stanley Dawson, R.N., 2nd son of 1st Earl, *b.* 1843, *d.* 1919 : *m.* 1898, Lady Elizabeth Selina Meade, who *d.* 1924, dau. of 4th Earl of Clanwilliam :—
Kaitilin Elizabeth Anne (*Kaitilin, Countess of Lucan*), *b.* 1900: *m.* 1929, the 6th Earl of Lucan, who *d.* 1964. *Residence,*—73, Lords View, NW8

DARWEN, BARON. (Davies.) [Baron U.K. 1946.]

CEDRIC PERCIVAL DAVIES, 2nd Baron ; *b.* Feb. 18th, 1915 ; *s.* 1950 ; ed. at Sidcot Sch., and at Manchester Univ. (B.A. Honours 1947) : *m.* 1934, Kathleen Dora, dau. of George Sharples Walker, and has issue.

Residence,—White Lodge, Sandelswood End, Beaconsfield, Bucks.

SONS LIVING.

Hon. ROGER MICHAEL (Labourer's Rest, Green St., Pleshey, Chelmsford), *b.* June 28th, 1938; ed. at Bootham Sch., York: *m.* 1961, Gillian Irene, da. of Eric G. Hardy, of Bristol, and has issue living, Paul, *b.* 1962.—Benjamin, *b.* 1966, Sarah *b.* 1963,—Naomi, *b.* 1965,—Mary, *b.* 1969.
Hon. Stephen Humphrey, *b.* 1945: *m.* 1968, Kathleen Prestwood, and has issue living, Timothy Prestwood, *b.* 1970,—Ruth Mary, *b.* 1972.
Hon. Philip Cedric Mark, *b.* 1951.

DAUGHTER LIVING.

Hon. Catherine Joy, *b.* 1948: *m.* 19—, Robert Nienhuis.

BROTHERS LIVING.

Hon. Thomas Barratt (18, St. Winifreds, Rd., Bournemouth), *b.* 1916; ed. at Bootham Sch., Coll. of Art, Liverpool: *m.* 1941, Doreen, da. of Arthur James Allen, and has issue living, Alan John Barry, *b.* 1949,—Barbara Jean, *b.* 1944,—Frances Hilary, *b.* 1947,—Judith Ann (twin), *b.* 1949.
Hon. (Francis) Ronald, *b.* 1920; ed. at Bootham Sch., and at Queen's Coll., Oxford (B.A. 1942, M.A. 1946); Bar. Gray's Inn 1948 : *m.* 1942, Margaret Phyllis, dau. of John George Cocksworth, and has issue living, Daniel Watson, *b.* 1943,—John Russell, *b.* 1950,—Helen Brouwen, *b.* 1954. *Residence,* —39, Parkside, Mill Hill, N.W.7.

SISTERS LIVING.

Hon. Joan Kathleen, *b.* 1917: *m.* 1940, Walter Higham Brindle, MBE, TD, and has issue living, Michael Patrick, *b.* 1943,—Alison Lesley, *b.* 1947. *Residence,*—Cottonwood, 20 Firs Rd., Edwalton, Nottingham, NG12 4BX.
Hon. Marjorie Heather, *b.* 1923: *m.* 1944, Frederick Joseph Adams, and has issue living, Christopher Stephen, *b.* 1946. *Residence,*—Witches Barn, Llancarfan, Barry, S. Glamorgan.

PREDECESSOR.—[1] JOHN PERCIVAL Davies, son of the late Thomas Pearce Davies, of Heatherfield, Darwen, and Pengarth, Grange-over-Sands ; *b.* 1885 ; a Cotton Manufacturer ; a Lord-in-Waiting to H.M. 1949-50 ; cr. *Baron Darwen*, of Heys-in-Bowland, W. Riding of Yorkshire (peerage of U.K.) 1946: *m.* 1914, Mary Kathleen, who *d.* 1964, dau. of Alfred Kemp Brown, B.D.; *d.* 1950; *s.* by his son [2] CEDRIC PERCIVAL, 2nd Baron and present peer.

DARYNGTON, BARON. (Pease.) [Baron U.K. 1923.]

Peace and hope

JOCELYN ARTHUR PIKE PEASE, 2nd Baron; *b.* May 30th, 1908; *s.* 1949; ed. at Eton, and at Trin. Coll., Camb. (B.A. 1928, M.A. 1931).

Arms,—Azure, a fesse between in chief two lambs passant argent, and in base a wreath of laurel or. Crest,—Upon the capital of an Ionic column a dove rising, holding in the beak a pea stalk, all proper. Supporters,—On either side a dove wings addorsed, holding in the beak a pea stalk, all proper.
Residence,—Vincent's Cottage, Monks Eleigh near Ipswich.

SISTERS LIVING.

Hon. Ruth Evelyn, *b.* 1900: *m.* 1925, Norman Ernest Archer, CMG, OBE, who *d.* 1970, [D. Atholl colls.], and has issue living, Ronald Walter (Oldfield, High Cross, Ware, Herts.), *b.* 1929: *m.* 1959, Catherine Mary, el. da. of the late Marcus R. C. Overton and has issue living, James Norman *b.* 1960, Michael Marcus *b.* 1962, Edward John Harold *b.* 1964, Mary Ruth Elizabeth *b.* 1966,—Esther Joy, *b.* 1926: *m.* 1952, Robert Blackburn, of 14, Woodsyre, Sydenham Hill, SE26, and has issue living, Kari Ruth *b.* 1954, Lucy Patricia *b.* 1956. *Residence,*—Oldfield, Wadesmill Ware, Herts.
Hon. Phyllis Helen, *b.* 1904; ed. at Camb. Univ. (BA). *Residence,*—7, Stocks Mead, Washington, Sussex.

PREDECESSOR.—[1] *Rt. Hon.* HERBERT PIKE Pease, *P.C.*, 2nd son of the late Arthur Pease M.P. [brother of Sir Joseph Whitwell Pease, 1st Bt. (cr. 1882)]; *b.* 1867; an Ecclesiastica, Commr., and Pres. of Church Army; sometime Chm. of House of Laity of National Church Assembly; a Church Estates Commr. 1926-48; Joint Treasurer of Queen Anne's Bounty 1935-9; appointed Whip to Liberal Unionist Party 1906; was Assist. Postmaster-Gen. 1915-22; sat as M.P. for Darlington (*LU*) 1898-1910, and 1910-23; cr. *Baron Daryngton*, of Witley, Surrey (peerage of United Kingdom) 1923: *m.* 1894, Alice Mortimer, who *d.* 1948, dau. of the late Very Rev. Herbert Mortimer Luckock, D.D., Dean of Lichfield: *d.* 1949; *s.* by his son [2] JOCELYN ARTHUR PIKE, 2nd Baron and present peer.

DAVENTRY, VISCOUNT. (FitzRoy.) [Viscount U.K. 1943.]

The ornament and recompense of virtue.

(ROBERT) OLIVER FITZROY, 2nd Viscount; *b.* Jan. 10th, 1893; *s.* 1962; Capt. R.N. (ret.); High Sheriff of Rutland 1956; European War 1914-18; European War 1939-45 (despatches): *m.* 1916, Grace Zöe, dau. of the late Claude Hume Campbell Guinness [E. Westmeath, colls.], and has issue.

Arms,—Quarterly: 1st and 4th, France and England quarterly; 2nd, Scotland; 3rd, Ireland; the whole debruised by a baton sinister compony argent and azure. Crest,—On a chapeau gules, turned up ermine, a lion statant guardant or, ducally crowned azure, and gorged with a collar counter compony argent and azure. Supporters,—*Dexter,* a lion rampant guardant or, crowned azure; *sinister,* a greyhound argent; both gorged with a collar gobony ermine and azure a mullet argent in the azure, each collar edged also azure.

Residence,—Stoke Dry House, Uppingham, Rutland. *Club,*—Carlton.

DAUGHTERS LIVING.

Hon. Mary Angela, *b.* 1919: *m.* 1st, 1940, Major Anthony Dermot Melloney Musker, Coldstream Guards who *d.* 1959; 2ndly, 1962, Richard Mayon Mayon-White, MD, PhD, FRCP, and has issue living, (by 1st marriage) Charles Dermot FitzRoy (The College, Rashford, Thetford, Norfolk), *b.* 1941: *m.* 1963, Caroline Theresa, only da. of the late Hon. Robert Henry Digby [see B. Digby, colls.],— Herbert Oliver Fitzroy, *b.* 1948,—Robert Anthony FitzRoy, *b.* 1952,—Belinda Mary, *b.* 1942: *m.* 1st, 1966, John Aspinall; 2ndly, 1972, Stuart Wyndham Murray Thriepland,—Fiona Zoë, *b.* 1944. *Residence,*—Baylham House, Baylham, Ipswich.
Hon. Katherine Susan (47, Four Gables, Sandown Park, Sandown, Johannesburg), *b.* 1923; late Cadet Ensign First Aid Nursing Yeo.: *m.* 1st, 1945 (m. diss. 1958), Phil John Turner; 2ndly, 1958, Anthony Woodington Boardley, who *d.* 1967, and has issue living, (by 2nd m.) Kevan Anthony FitzRoy, *b.* 1961.
Hon. Barbara Helen, *b.* 1928: *m.* 1952, Major Peter Charles Ormrod, M.C., 8th King's Roy. Irish Hussars. *Residence,*—Pen-y-Lan, Ruabon, N. Wales.
Hon. Amelia Grace, *b.* 1930; *m.* 1950, Capt. David Charles George Jessel, Coldstream Guards of Collyers, Steep, Petersfield, Hants.[see Jessel, Bt.].

BROTHER LIVING.

Hon. JOHN MAURICE *FITZROY NEWDEGATE, b.* March 20th, 1897; Com. R.N. (retired); European War 1914-18, European War 1939-45; assumed by Roy. licence 1936, the additional surname and Arms of Newdegate: *m.* 1919, Lucia Charlotte Susan, *O.B.E.* (a C.St.J., and a J.P.), dau. of the late Sir Francis Alexander Newdigate-Newdegate, G.C.M.G. [B. Bagot], and has issue living, Francis Humphrey Maurice (of Temple House, Arbury, Nuneaton, Warwickshire), *b.* 1921; ed. at Eton: formerly Capt. Coldstream Guards (wounded); High Sheriff of Warwicks. 1970: *m.* 1959, the Hon. Rosemary Norrie, da. of 1st Baron Norrie, and has issue living, James Edward *b.* 1960, Hugh Francis, *b.* 1962, Joanna Norrie *b.* 1964,—Lucia Anne, *b.* 1920: *m.* 1942, Maj. Timothy Stuart Lewis, Roy. Scots Greys, of Inchdura House, N. Berwick, and has issue living, Caroline Anne (*Lady Thomson*), *b.* 1946: *m.* 1967, Sir Frederick Douglas David Thomson, 3rd Bt., of Glenbrook House, Balerno, Midlothian,—Jocelyne, *b.* 1929: *m.* 1st, 1952 (m. annulled 1953), Richard John Barton; 2ndly, 1957, Maj. Henry John Allfrey, RA (ret.), of Four Acre House, West Green, Hartley Wintney, Hants, and has issue living, (by 2nd m.) Henry David *b.* 1959, Charles John *b.* 1963, Lucia Susan: *b.* 1961. *Residence,*—Arbury, Nuneaton, Warwicks.

SISTER LIVING.

Hon. Nancy Jean, *B.E.M., b.* 1894 ; was Sergeant Dispenser V.A.D. 1939-46 [B.E.M. (Mil.)]. *Residence,*—Greenways, Kingswood Common, Henley-on-Thames.

PREDECESSOR.—[1] Muriel, *C.B.E.,* dau. of the late Lt.-Col. the Hon. Archibald Charles Henry Douglas-Pennant [B. Penrhyn, colls.], *b.* 1869; cr. *Viscountess Daventry,* of Daventry, co. of Northampton (peerage of U.K.) 1943: *m.* 1891, Capt. the Rt. Hon. Edward Algernon FitzRoy, M.P. (Speaker of House of Commons 1928-43), who *d.* 1943 (two months before he was to have received a Viscountcy) [B. Southampton, colls.) ; *d.* 1962; *s.* by her el. son [2] (ROBERT) OLIVER, 2nd Viscount and present peer.

DAVIDSON, VISCOUNT. (Davidson.) [Viscount U.K. 1937.]

JOHN ANDREW DAVIDSON, 2nd Viscount; *b.* Dec. 22nd, 1928; *s.* 1970; ed. at Westminster, and Pembroke Coll., Camb.: *m.* 1st, 1956 (m. diss. 1974), Margaret Birgitta, da. of Maj.-Gen. Cyril Henry Norton, CB, CBE, DSO; 2ndly, 1975, Mrs. Pamela Joy Dobb, da. of John Vergette, and has issue, by 1st m.

Arms,—Argent, on a fesse sable between in chief two pheons azure and in base a boar's head erased of the second a portcullis chained or. Crest,—A lion passant gules charged on the shoulder with a pheon or and holding in the dexter paw a torch inflamed proper. Supporters,—*Dexter,* a horse argent charged on the shoulder with a rose gules, barbed and seeded proper; *sinister,* a horse sable charged on the shoulder with a martlet or.

LUX EX TENEBRIS

Residence,—The Hill Farm, Thorpe Morieux Bury St. Edmunds. *Club,*—Farmers'.

DAUGHTERS LIVING. (*By* 1*st m*).
Hon. Alexandra Frances Margaret, *b.* 1957.

Hon. Georgina Caroline, *b.* 1958.
Hon. Camilla Birgitta, *b.* 1963.
Hon. Kristina Louise (twin), *b.* 1963.

BROTHER LIVING.
Hon. MALCOLM WILLIAM MACKENZIE, *b.* Aug. 28th, 1934; ed. at Westminster, and Pembroke Coll., Camb.: *m.* 1970, Mrs. Evelyn Ann Carew Perfect, yr. da. of William Blackmore Storey [M. Queensberry, colls.], and has issue living, John Nicolas Alexander, *b.* 1971,—Sophie Ann Francis, *b.* 1973. *Residence,*—Widden Hill House, Horton, Chipping Sodbury, Avon. *Club,*—Travellers'.

SISTERS LIVING.
Hon. Margaret Joan, *b.* 1922: *m.* 1943, the Ven. Benjamin George Burton Fox, MC, TD, Archdeacon of Wisbech, and has issue living, Colin George, *b.* 1946,—Elizabeth Angela, *b.* 1944,—Catherine of Wisbech, and has issue living, Colin George, *b.* 1946,—Elizabeth Angela, *b.* 1944: *m.* 1973, Prof. Anthony R. Mellows, TD, LLD, of 22, Devereux Court, Temple Bar, WC2R 3JJ,—Catherine Anne, *b.* 1950,—Penelope Margaret, *b.* 1953,—Rosemary Marjorie (twin), *b.* 1953. *Residence,*—The Vicarage, Haddenham, Ely.
Hon. Jean Elizabeth, *b.* 1924; late Capt. W.R.A.C. (T.A.): *m.* 1952, the Hon. Charles Richard Strutt [see B. Rayleigh]. *Residence,*—Berwick Place, Hatfield Peverel, Chelmsford, Essex.

WIDOW LIVING OF FIRST VISCOUNT.
Hon. Dame FRANCES JOAN, *DBE* (*Dowager Viscountess Davidson*), (16, Lord North St., Westminster, SW1); MP, Hemel Hempstead Div. of Herts. (*U*) 1937-59; OBE (Civil) 1920, DBE (Civil) 1952, and *Baroness Northchurch* (Life Baroness) 1963; da. of the 1st Baron Dickinson: *m.* 1919, the 1st Viscount, who *d.* 1970.

PREDECESSOR.—[1] *Rt. Hon. Sir* JOHN COLIN CAMPBELL Davidson, *GCVO, CH, CB, PC,* son of the late Sir James Mackenzie Davidson, MB, *b.* 1889; MP for Hemel Hempstead (*U*) 1920-23 and 1924-37; Chancellor of Duchy of Lancaster 1923-24 and 1931-37; Chm. of Conservative and Unionist Party Organisation 1926-30; cr. *Viscount Davidson,* of Little Gaddesden, co. Hertford (peerage of UK) 1937: *m.* 1919, the Hon. Dame Frances Joan Dickinson, DBE (*Baroness Northchurch*), da. of the 1st Baron Dickinson; *d.* 1970; *s.* by his el. son [2] JOHN ANDREW, 2nd Viscount, and present peer.

DAVIES, BARON.   (Davies.)   [Baron U.K. 1932.]

DAVID DAVIES, 3rd Baron, *b.* Oct. 2nd, 1940;
s. 1944; ed. at Eton, and at King's Coll., Camb.
m. 972, Beryl, da. of W. J. Oliver, of Harborne, Birmingham, and has issue.

Arms,—Or, a lion rampant gules, between two fleurs-de-li
in fesse azure; on a chief azure, two pickaxes fessewise. Crest
—An arm embowed proper, vested to the elbow argent, hold
ing in the hand a miner's safety lamp proper.
Seat,—Plâs Dinam, Llandinam, Montgomeryshire.

DAUGHTER LIVING.
Hon. Eldrydd Jane, *b.* 1973.

BROTHER LIVING.
Hon. JONATHAN HUGH (Stonehill House, Abingdon,
Berks), *b.* Jan. 25th, 1944; ed. at Eton, and Univ. Coll.,
Oxford: *m.* 1966, Mary Veronica, da. of Sir (William)
Godfrey Agnew, KCVO, of Pinehurst, S. Ascot, Berks, and
has issue living, Michael Edward, *b.* 1968,—Alexander
William, *b.* 1972,—Ruth Gwendoline, *b.* 1969,—Gwendoline
Christianne Mary, *b.* 1975.

UNCLES LIVING.
Hon. Edward David Grant, *b.* 1925; ed. at Gordonstoun, and
at King's Coll., Camb.; late R.A.F.: *m.* 1949, Patricia, dau.
of O. R. Musto, of Salisbury, Rhodesia, and has issue
living, David Edmund Clifford, *b.* 1958,—Mary Ann Margaret,
b. 1949,—Patricia Jean, *b.* 1951,—Penelope Eldrydd, *b.* 1955.
Residence,—Cefngwyfed, Tregynon, Montgomeryshire.
Hon. Islwyn Edmund Evan, *b.* 1926; ed. at Gordonstoun;
is a J.P. for Montgomeryshire: *m.* 1959, Camilla Anne, el.
da. of Col. L. W. Coulden, of 14, Portsea Place, W2, and has
issue living, Robin, *b.* 1961,—Christopher William, *b.* 1963,—
Richard Edward, *b.* 1965.   *Residence*,—Berthddu, Llandinam, Montgomeryshire.

AUNTS LIVING.
Hon. Mary Myfanwy, *b.* 1923; formerly in Women's Roy.
Canadian Naval Ser.; is a O.St.J.: *m.* 1958, Hugh MacAskill
Noble, and has issue living, Robert David, *b.* 1961. *Resi-
dence*,—Craigton, Fintry, Stirlingshire.
Hon. Gwendoline Rita Jean, *b.* 1929: *m.* 1950, John McRae Cormack, A.F.C., and has issue living.
Michael John, *b.* 1962,—Shara Jane, *b.* 1955,—Amanda Caroline, *b.* 1957,—Teresa Mary, *b.* 1959,
Residence,—Littleton, Reigate Heath, Surrey.

PREDECESSORS.—[1] DAVID Davies, only son of the late Edward Davies, of Plâs Dinam,
Llandinam; *b.* 1880; a Director of Great Western Railway, and of Midland Bank; sat as
M.P. for Montgomeryshire (*L*) 1906-29; cr. *Baron Davies*, of Llandinam, co. Montgomery
(peerage of United Kingdom), 1932; *m.* 1st, 1910, Amy, who *d.* 1918, dau. of J. T. Penman, of
Broadwood Park, Lanchester, and Gateshead; 2ndly, 1922, Henrietta Margaret, who *d.* 1948,
dau. of the late James Grant Fergusson, of Baledmund; *d.* June 1944; *s.* by his son [2] DAVID,
2nd Baron; *b.* 1915; Maj. R. Welch Fusiliers (TA): *m.* 1939, Ruth Eldrydd, who *d.* 1966, da. of
the late Maj. W. M. Dugdale, of Glanyrafon Hall, Llanyblodwell, Salop; *d.* (killed in action) Sept.
1944; *s.* by his son [3] DAVID, 3rd Baron and present peer.

DAVIES OF LEEK, BARON. (Davies.) [Life Baron 1970.]

HAROLD DAVIES, *PC,* son of William Davies; *b,* July 31st, 1904; ed. at
Lewis' Gram. Sch., Pengam, Glam., and London Univ.; FRGS; Joint Parl.
Sec. to Min. of Pensions and Nat. Insurance 1964-66, and to Min. of Social
Security 1966-67, and PPS to Prime Min. 1967-70; MP for Leek, Staffs. (*Lab.*)
1945-70; cr. PC 1969, and *Baron Davies of Leek,* of Leek, co. Stafford (Life
Baron) 1970: *m.* 1925, Jessie Elizabeth, BSc, da. of George Bateman, and has
issue.
Residence,—36, Cleveden Mansions, Lissenden Gdns., NW5; 81, Trentham Rd., Longton, Stoke-
on-Trent.

DAUGHTER LIVING.
Hon. Harriet Olivia, *b.* 1930; BScEcon. London: *m.* 1950, Derek Shephard, of 36, Clevenden Mansions,
Lissenden Gdns., NW5.

DAVIES OF PENRHYS, BARON. (Davies.) [Life Baron 1974.]

GWILYM ELFED DAVIES, son of David Davies; *b.* Oct. 9th, 1913; ed. at
Tylorstown Boys' Sch.; Branch Official Tylorstown Lodge, National Union of
Mineworkers 1935-59; a Co. Councillor Glamorgan 1954-61, Chm. Local Govt.
Cttee. 1959-61, PPS to Min. of Labour 1964-68, and to Min. of Power 1968;
MP for Rhondda East (*Lab.*) 1959-74; cr. *Baron Davies of Penrhys,* of Rhondda,
co. Mid Glamorgan (Life Baron) 1974: *m.* 1940, Gwyneth, da. of Daniel Rees,
of Trealaw, Rhondda, and has issue.
Residence,—Maes-y-Ffrwd, Ferndale Rd., Tylorstown, Rhondda, Mid-Glam.

SONS LIVING.
Hon. Gwynfor, *b.* 1942: *m.* 1969, Linda, da. of the late Anthony Henry, of Port Talbot, Glam., and has
issue.
Hon. David Daniel, *b.* 1944: *m.* 1969, Cheryl, da. of Thomas Herbert, of Tylorstown, Rhondda, and
has issue.

DAUGHTER LIVING.
Hon. Beryl, *b.* 1947: *m.* 1965, Colin James Powell, of Maesgwyn, Ton Pentre, Rhondda, and has issue.

Davies, see Baron Llewelyn-Davies.

Davies, see Baron Lovell-Davies.

Dawick, Viscount, son of Earl Haig.

Dawnay, Baron, title of Viscount Downe of Roll of H.L.

DAWSON OF PENN, VISCOUNTCY OF. (Dawson.) [Extinct 1945.]
DAUGHTERS LIVING OF FIRST VISCOUNT.

Hon. Sybil Frances Dawson (Viscountess Eccles), b. 1904; assumed by deed poll 1929, the additional Christian name of Dawson: m. 1928, 1st Viscount Eccles. Residence,—Dean Farm, Upper Chute, near Andover.

Hon. Ursula Margaret (Hon. Lady Bowater), b. 1907: m. 1927, Lt.-Col. Sir Ian Frank Bowater, GBE, DSO, RA (TA) [see Bowater, Bt., cr. 1939]. Residence,—Hasker House, Woolley Firs, Maidenhead Thicket, Berks.

Hon. Rosemary Monica (Hon. Lady Wrightson), b. 1913: m. 1939, Maj. Sir John Garmondsway Wrightson, 3rd Bt., late Durham L.I. (T.A.). Residence,—Neasham Hall, near Darlington.

DE BLAQUIERE, BARONY OF. (de Blaquiere.) [Extinct 1920.]
DAUGHTER LIVING OF SIXTH BARON.

Hon. Kathleen (Baroness Dorchester), b. 1891: m. 1911, the 2nd Baron Dorchester, who d. 1963, when the title became extinct. Residence,—The Dower House, Greywell, Basingstoke, Hants.

DECIES, BARON. (de la Poer Beresford.) [Baron I. 1812.]
[Title pronounced "Deeshies."]

Nothing without the Cross.

ARTHUR GEORGE MARCUS DOUGLAS DE LA POER BERESFORD, 6th Baron, b. April 24th, 1915; s. 1944; European War 1939-45 as Flying Officer R.A.F. Vol. Reserve (American D.F.C.): m. 1st, 1937, Ann Christina, who d. (March) 1945, dau. of the late Sidney Walter Trevor, of Camperdown, Victoria, Australia; 2ndly, (Sept.) 1945, Diana (GALSWORTHY), dau. of Wing-Com. G. Turner Cain, and has issue by 2nd marriage.

Arms,—Quarterly: 1st and 4th argent-semée of cross-crosslets fitchée, three fleurs-de-lis within a bordure engrailed, all sable-Beresford; 2nd and 3rd argent, a chief indented sable, de la Poer; a mullet argent for difference. Crest,—A dragon's head erased azure, transfixed in the neck with a broken tilting spear or, the point broken off argent transfixing the upper jaw, charged with a mullet for difference. Supporters,—Two angels proper, vested argent, crined and winged or, each holding in the exterior hand a sword erect of the first, pommel and hilt gold and charged on the breast with a mullet for difference.

Residence, Chateau de Bétouzet, Andrein, Sauveterre de Bearn, Pyrenees Atlantiques, France.

SON LIVING. (By 2nd marriage.)
Hon. MARCUS HUGH TRISTAM DE LA POER, b. Aug. 5th, 1948; ed. at St. Columba's Coll. and Dublin Univ.: m. 1970, (m. diss. 1974), Sarah Jane, only da. of Col. Basil Gunnell.

DAUGHTERS LIVING. (By 2nd marriage.)
Hon. Sarah Ann Vivien de la Poer, b. 1949.
Hon. Clare Antoinette Gabrielle de la Poer, b. 1956.

WIDOW LIVING OF SON OF THIRD BARON
Ida Kaye: m. 1941, as his fourth wife the Hon. William Arthur Horsley-Beresford, who d. 1949, and has issue living [see colls., infra.]. Residence,—53, Overstrand Mansions, Prince of Wales Drive, S.W.11.

COLLATERAL BRANCHES LIVING.

Grandchildren of the late Hon. William Arthur de la Poer Horsley-Beresford (infra):—
Issue of the late George Graham Horsley-Beresford, b. 1903, d. 1974: m. 1938, Sherman (Frederiksted, Isle of St. Croix, US Virgin Islands), da. of Frank Olmsted of New York, NY, USA:—
Marcus Hughes (7, Essex Lane, Willingboro', NJ, USA), b. 1943; late Capt. USAF; Pilot Eastern Airlines: m. 1962, Lynne Green, of East Millstone, NJ., USA, and has issue living, Marcus Tyler de la Power, b. 1963,—Teresa Leigh, b. 1965.——Peter Graham de la Power, b. 1956.——Holley Audrey, b. 1939.

Issue of the late Hon. William Arthur de la Poer Horsley-Beresford, yst. son of 3rd Baron, b. 1878; d. 1949: m. 1st, 1901, Florence (who d. 1969, having obtained a divorce 1919), da. of Gardner L. Miller, M.D., of Providence, Rhode Island, U.S.A.; 2ndly, 1919, Laura (from whom he obtained a divorce 1928), dau. of the late Capt. St. John Halford Coventry [see E. Coventry, colls.]; 3rdly, 1933, Georgina Leonora (from whom he obtained a divorce 1940), only dau. of the late Richard Frederik Hendrik Mosselmans, of the Hague, and formerly wife of Count Fernand de Bertier de Sauvigny; 4thly, 1941, Ida Kaye (ante):—

John Duncan (Box 610, Sandia Park, New Mexico, USA), *b.* 1904: *m.* 1934, Aina, who *d.* 1974, da. of Blaine R. Richard, of Miami Beach, Flor., USA, and has issue living, Sheila Kathleen, *b.* 1941.—— (By 2nd m.) Patrick George, *b.* 1924: *m.* 1st, 1953 (m. diss. in USA 1956), Miriam Morton, of Philadelphia, USA; 2ndly, 1959, Lesley Yvonne, da. of the late Leslie Robert McCaskey, of Wellington, NZ.——Hazel, *b.* 1920: *m.* 1940, Gerald Herbert Incledon (PO Box 38, Nottingham Rd., Natal, S. Africa) and has issue living, Jonathan Guy, *b.* 1963,—Margaret Anne, *b.* 1941: *m.* 1961, Anthony E. Hodson, of Hazlehead, 41, Woodend Drive, Ascot, Berks., and has issue living, Christopher James *b.* 1963, Lucy Alice *b.* 1967,—Heather, *b.* 1943: *m.* 1966, Christopher C. E. Stamford, of Grassmere, Mid St., S. Nutfield, Surrey, and has issue living, Daniel Charles *b.* 1967, Charlotte Anne *b.* 1970, Louise Emma *b.* 1975,—Susan Amber, *b.* 1945: *m.* 1968, David Ellis Green, MBE, R. Regt. Fus., of 12 Dulwich Common, SE21,—Amanda Elizabeth, *b.* 1947,—Moya Catherine, *b.* 1956.——(By 4th m.) Peter, *b.* 1945.——Maureen, *b.* 1942.

Grandchildren of the late Henry Tristram Beresford, son of the Rev. George Hamilton de la Poer Beresford, 3rd son of the Rev. The Hon. George Beresford, 2nd son of 1st Baron.

Issue of the late Maj.-Gen. Sir George de la Poer Beresford, C.B., M.C., *b.* 1885, *d.* 1964: *m.* 1916, Margaret Ethel Granville, who *d.* 1963, dau. of the late Rev. Arthur Christopher Thynne [M. Bath, colls.]:—

Benedict Henry de la Poer (of 3, Cambridge Cottages, Kew, Richmond, Surrey), *b.* 1917; 1939-45 War with Roy. Armoured Corps: *m.* 1949, Dorothy Kate, dau. of George Cooper, of Gt. Bedwyn, Wilts., and has issue living, Margaret Jane, *b.* 1963.——Stephen Marcus de la Poer, *D.S.C.* (of Murranumbla, Dalgety, N.S. Wales), *b.* 1920; Lt.-Com. R.N. (ret.); 1939-45 War (D.S.C.): *m.* 1952, Susan Wendy, da. of the late Maj. Tom Lees Dearbergh, of Hollywood Cottage, Lymington, Hants., and has issue living, Diana Margaret, *b.* 1953,—Angela Susan (twin), *b.* 1953.

Issue of the late William Coventry de la Poer Beresford, *b.* 1887, *d.* 1938: *m.* 1921, Jessie, who *d.* 1931, dau. of J. Rowling, of N.S. Wales:—

Charles Marcus Tristram de la Poer (Mobla, Binnaway, NSW), *b.* 1923; 1942-45 War with RAAF: *m.* 1948, Mary Frances, who *d.* 1972, da. of Hugh Buckingham Loveband, of Blenheim, Coonabarabran, NSW, and has issue living, Roslyn de la Poer, *b.* 1949,—Julie de la Poer, *b.* 1952.——Patricia de la Poer, *b.* 1922: *m.* 1953, R. S. Meares of 450, Auburn St., Goulburn, NSW, and has issue living, Richard Grant, *b.* 1955,—Philip Marcus, *b.* 1960.

Issue of the late Marcus Gervais de la Poer Beresford, *b.* 1888, *d.* 1967: *m.* Susan Mildred (3, Hovel St. Manuka, ACT 2603, Aust.), da of the late Edward Charles Campbell:—

Barrington Henry de la Poer (9, Melrose Av., Sylvania, NSW), *b.* 1928: *m.* 1952, Fleur Marie, dau. of the late John Chrisp, of Corowa, N.S. Wales, and has issue living, Amanda de la Poer, *b.* 1956,— Sean Anthony de la Poer, *b.* 1962.

PREDECESSORS.—[1] *Rev. the Hon.* WILLIAM Beresford, 3rd son of 1st Earl of Tyrone and brother of 1st Marquess of Waterford; Bishop of Dromore 1780-2. Bishop of Ossory 1782-94, and Archbishop of Tuam 1794-1819: cr. *Baron Decies* (peerage of Ireland) 1812; *d.* 1819; *s.* by his son [2] JOHN, 2nd Baron; *b.* 1773: *m.* 1810, Charlotte Philadelphia, only dau. and heiress of Robert Horsley, of Bolam House, Morpeth, when he assumed the additional surname of Horsley; *d.* March 1st, 1855; *s.* by his son [3] WILLIAM ROBERT JOHN DE LA POER, 3rd Baron, *b.* 1811 : *m.* 1860, Catherine Anne, who *d.* 1941, dau. of William Dent Dent, of Shortflatt Tower, Belsay; *d.* 1893; *s.* by his el. son [4] WILLIAM MARCUS DE LA POER, 4th Baron, *b.* 1865 : *m.* 1901, Maria Gertrude, who *d.* 1939, dau. of Sir John Pollard Willoughby, 4th Bt., *d.* 1910: *s.* by his brother [5] JOHN GRAHAM HOPE DE LA POER, *P.C.*, *D.S O.*, 5th Baron, *b.* 1866; Major (retired) 7th Hussars; Matabeleland 1896, S. Africa 1902, Somaliland 1903-4 (D.S.O.); Ch. Press Censor in Ireland 1916-19 : *m.* 1st, 1911, Helen Vivien, who *d.* 1931, dau. of the late George Jay Gould, of New York, U.S.A.; 2ndly, 1936, Elizabeth, who *d.* 1944, dau. of George Drexel, and widow of Henry Symes Lehr; *d.* 1944; *s.* by his son [6] ARTHUR GEORGE MARCUS DOUGLAS DE LA POER, 6th Baron and present peer.

DE CLIFFORD, BARON. (Russell.) [Baron E. 1299.]

What will be, will be.

EDWARD SOUTHWELL RUSSELL. *O.B.E..T.D.,* 26th Baron ; *b.* Jan. 31st, 1907; *s.* 1909 ; ed. at Eton; Col. (ret.) REME, late R. Gloucestershire Hussars (TA); OBE (Mil) 1955: *m.* 1st, 1926 (m. diss. 1973), Dorothy Evelyn, da. of the late Ferdinand Richard Holmes Meyrick, MD, of 59, Kensington Court, W8; 2ndly, 1973, Mina Margaret, only da. of George Edward Sands, and has issue, by 1st m.

Arms.—Argent, a lion rampant gules, on a chief sable three escallops of the first. **Crest.**—A goat statant argent, armed and unguled or. **Supporters.**— *Dexter,* a wyvern gules; *sinister,* a monkey proper, ringed round the loins and lined or.

Residence.—The Birches, Silvington, Cleobury Mortimer, Kidderminster, Worcs.

SONS LIVING (By 1st m.)

Hon. JOHN EDWARD SOUTHWELL, *b.* June 8th, 1928 ; ed. at Eton : *m.* 1959, Bridget Jennifer, youngest da. of Duncan Robertson, of Llantysilio, Hall, Llangollen, Denbighshire [see Williams-Wynn, Bt.] *Residence,*—Cliff House, Sheepy, Atherstone, Warwickshire.

Hon. William Southwell (of Christopher's, Newney Green, Writtle, Essex), *b.* 1930; ed. at Eton, and at King's Coll., Camb.: *m.* 1961, Jean Brodie, dau. of Neil Brodie Henderson, of Glebe House, Little Hormead, Buntingford, Herts. [see Madden, Bt.], and has issue living, Miles Edward Southwell, *b.* 1966,—Mary-Jane Sophia, *b.* 1963,—Joanna Clare, *b.* 1965.

SISTER LIVING.

Hon. Diana Katharine, *b.* 1909 : *m.* 1st, 1933, Mervyn Hesseltine Taylor, from whom she obtained a divorce 1948; 2ndly, 1948, His Honour Judge Thomas Elder-Jones, and has issue living, (by 1st m.) Christopher John (East Cottage, Bourton on the Hill, Morton in Marsh, Glos.), *b.* 1934: *m.* 1st, 1959 (m. diss. 1971), Sarah Mary, only da. of the late Ewan Mews; 2ndly, 1972, Jane Seymour, yst. da. of the late George Macdonald Brown, and has issue living (by 1st m.), Vernon Edmund Christopher *b.* 1965, Claire Virginia Mary *b.* 1962,—Virginia Carol ELDER-JONES, *b.* 1945; adopted by her mother and her stepfather, whose surname she assumed 1956.

WIDOW LIVING OF TWENTY-FIFTH BARON.

Evelyn Victoria Anne, dau. of Walter Robert Chandler: *m.* 1st, 1906, the 25th Baron, who *d.* 1909; 2ndly, 1913, Capt. Arthur Boy Stock, 2nd Ayrshire Yeo., who *d.* 1915 ; 3rdly, 1922, George Vernon Tate, M.C., who *d.* 1955 [see Tate, Bt., colls.]. *Residence,*—7, Princes Gate, S.W.7.

COLLATERAL BRANCHES LIVING.

Descendants of Frances Sophia Cholmondeley, (da. of George James Cholmondeley, by the Hon. Mary Elizabeth, da. of John Thomas Townshend, 2nd Viscount Sydney, by his 1st wife, the Hon. Sophia Southwell, da. of 20th Baron): m. 1846, the Rev. Charles Riddell, of whom the Rev. John Charles Riddell was father of 11th Bt.:—
[see Riddell, Bt.].

Descendants of Robert Marsham-Townshend, only son of 2nd Earl of Romney, by his 2nd wife, the Hon. Mary Elizabeth Townshend, da. of 2nd Viscount Sydney, and widow of George James Cholmondeley (ante):—
see E. Romney, colls.].

Descendants of the Hon. Elizabeth Southwell, da. of 20th Baron: m. 1792 as his 1st wife, the 4th Earl of Albemarle:—
[see E. Albemarle].

PREDECESSORS.—[1] ROGER de Clifford: m. Isabel, el. dau. and co-heiress of Robert de Vipont, Lord of Westmorland, and in 1277 acknowledged the service of two fees and a half, for a moiety of the Barony of Westmorland ; d. 1282 ; s. by his son [2] ROBERT, 2nd Lord of Westmorland, and 1st Baron de Clifford; summoned to Parliament of England 1299-1313; Earl Marshal of England 1307, Warden of Scotland 1308 ; killed at Bannockburn 1314; s. by his son [3] ROGER, 2nd Baron ; d.s.p. 1327 ; s. by his brother [4] ROBERT, 3rd Baron ; d. 1344 ; s. by his son [5] ROBERT, 4th Baron ; d.s.p. 1362 ; s. by his brother [6] ROGER, 5th Baron ; d. 1390 ; s. by his son [7] THOMAS, 6th Baron ; d. 1392 ; s. by his son [8] JOHN, 7th Baron; d. 1422 ; s by his son [9] THOMAS, 8th Baron ; d. 1455; s. by his son [10] JOHN, 9th Baron; d. 1461 ; s. by his son [11] HENRY, 10th Baron ; d. 1524; s. by his son [12] HENRY, 11th Baron ; cr. Earl of Cumberland (peerage of England) 1525 ; obtained large grants out of the monastic spoliations and had a principal command in the army which invaded Scotland ; d. 1543; s. by his son [13] HENRY, K.B., 2nd Earl ; d. 1569 ; s. by his son [14] GEORGE, K.G., 3rd Earl, an eminent naval commander and an ardent sportsman ; d. 1605, leaving issue one dau. [15] ANNE, wife of Richard Sackville, 2nd Earl of Dorset ; in 1628 the Countess of Dorset claimed the title, but the House of Lords postponed the hearing, and the Barony remained dormant until 1691, when it was allowed to [16] NICHOLAS, 15th Baron, and 3rd Earl of Thanet, son of John, 2nd Earl of Thanet, by Lady Margaret, dau. of Anne, Countess of Dorset (ante) ; s. by his brother [17] JOHN, 16th Baron, and 4th Earl of Thanet : s. by his brother [18] RICHARD, 17th Baron, and 5th Earl of Thanet ; s. by his brother [19] THOMAS, 18th Baron, and 6th Earl of Thanet ; d. 1721, when the Earldom of Thanet devolved upon his nephew, and the Barony of de Clifford went into abeyance between his five daus., and remained so until 1734, when the crown terminated it in favour of the 3rd dau. [20] MARGARET, wife of Thomas Coke, 1st Baron Lovel, who in 1744 was cr. Earl of Leicester; d. 1775, when the Barony again became abeyant, and it remained so until 1776, when it was terminated in favour of [21] EDWARD Southwell, 20th Baron (M.P. for co. Gloucester), son of Edward Southwell, by the Hon. Catherine, dau. of Edward, Viscount Sondes (el. son of 1st Earl of Rockingham) and Lady Catherine, el. dau. of 6th Earl of Thanet; d 1777 ; s. by his son [22] EDWARD, 21st Baron ; d.s.p. 1832, when the Barony became abeyant between his sisters, and remained so until 1833, when it was terminated in favour of the surviving issue of his el. sister Catherine, by Col. George Coussmaker, viz. [23] SOPHIA, wife of Capt. John Russell, R.N. [see D. Bedford. colls.]; d. 1874, s. by her son [24] EDWARD SOUTHWELL, 23rd Baron ; b. 1824 ; M.P. for Tavistock (L) 1847-58: m. 1853, Harriet Agnes, who d. 1896, dau. of the late Adm. Sir Charles Elliot, K.C.B.; d. 1877; s. by his son [25] EDWARD SOUTHWELL, 24th Baron; b. 1855: m. 1879, Hilda, who d. 1895, dau. of Charles Balfour, of Easthampstead, Berks; d. 1894; s. by his son [26] JACK SOUTHWELL, 25th Baron; b. 1884: m. 1906, Evelyn Victoria Anne, dau. of Walter Robert Chandler; d. 1909; s. by his son [27] EDWARD SOUTHWELL, 26th Baron and present peer.

Deerhurst, Viscount, son of Earl of Coventry.

MALO MORI QUAM FOEDARI

I had rather die than be dishonoured.

DE FREYNE, BARON. (French.) [Baron U.K. 1851.]

FRANCIS ARTHUR JOHN FRENCH, 7th Baron ; b. Sept. 3rd, 1927 ; s. 1935 ; is a Knight of Sovereign Order of Malta : m. 1954, Shirley Ann, dau. of the late D. R. Pobjoy, of Box Farm House, Woodmancote, Gloucestershire, and has issue.

Arms,—Ermine, a chevron sable. Crest,— A dolphin embowed proper. Supporters,—Dexter an ancient Irish warrior habited, supporting with his dexter hand a battle-axe, head downwards and bearing on his sinister arm a shield, all proper; sinister, a female figure vested proper and scarf flowing argent.
Residence,—Craigewilliam, Maynooth, co. Kildare. Clubs,—Kildare St., St. James'.

SONS LIVING.

Hon. FULKE CHARLES ARTHUR JOHN, b. April 21st, 1957.
Hon. Patrick Dominick Fitzstephen Jude, b. 1969.

DAUGHTER LIVING.

Hon. Vanessa Rose Bradbury, b. 1958.

SISTERS LIVING.

Hon. Patricia Mary, b. 1917 : m. 1941, Reginald Johnson, who d. 1958, and has issue living, Michael Reginald, b. 1943,—Diana Mary, b. 1942: m. 1972, Frederick Robert Robinson, of 58, Stafford Rd., Caterham, Surrey. Residence,—80, Idmiston Rd., SE27.

Hon. Patience Veronica, b. 1922: m. 1952, Arthur Rickards, Lt.-Cdr. RN (ret.), and has issue living, Luana Veronica, b. 1957,—Edwina, b. 1958. Residences,—Kirkmichael Old Manse, Ballindalloch, Banffshire; The Fishery Office, Strathnaver, Kinbrace, Sutherland.

AUNT LIVING. (Daughter of 4th Baron)

Hon. Muriel May, b. 1891: m. 1920 (m. diss. 1947), Major William Alexander(Alëx) Came Wilkinson MC, Coldstream Guards. Residence,—

WIDOWS LIVING OF SONS OF FOURTH BARON.

Victoria Louise Dalglish (Beech House, Sturminster Newton, Dorset), da. of the late William Dalglish Bellasis, JP: *m.* 1920, Capt. the Hon. William Joseph French, who *d.* 1974, and has issue living [see colls., infra].

Mary Frances (Stychfield, Bletchingley, Surrey), da. of Charles Hasslacher, of 3, Kensington Park Gdns., W8: *m.* 1937, the Hon. Hubert John French, who *d.* 1961, and has issue living [see colls., infra].

COLLATERAL BRANCHES LIVING.

Issue of the late Capt. Hon. William Joseph French, 3rd son of 4th Baron, *b.* 1885, *d.* 1974: *m.* 1920, Victoria Louise Dalglish (ante), da. of the late William Dalglish Bellasis, JP:—

Marie Isobel (*Lady Weldon*), *b.* 1923: *m.* 1942, Capt. Sir Thomas Brian Weldon, 8th Bt., of Eastcote House, Dogmersfield, Basingstoke.——Eleanor Mary, *b.* 1925: *m.* 1946, Capt. Patrick Munro of Foulis, Seaforth Highlanders, of Foulis Castle, Evanton, Ross-shire [see Munro, Bt., cr. 1634].

Issue of the late Hon. Louis Richard French, 5th son of 4th Baron, *b.* 1888, *d.* 1957 : *m.* 1922, Margaret Eleanor, who *d.* 1972, da. of the late Capt. Maurice Kirk, 4th King's Own (Roy. Lancaster) Regt.:—

Peter John Maurice, *b.* 1923.——Sheila Mary, *b.* 1924 : *m.* 1948, John Benedict Stilwell, Lieut. Coldstream Guards (Reserve), and has issue living, Mark Andrew, *b.* 1949,—Christopher John, *b.* 1952,—John William, *b.* 1954,—Charles Louis, *b.* 1957,—Philippa Ann, *b.* 1950. *Residence,—* 18, Travessa de S. Antonio A Santos, Lisbon, Portugal.——Eleanor Georgina, *b.* 1928 : *m.* 1954, Robert Macalaster Symington, and has issue living, Nicholas Maurice, *b.* 1954,—Richard Andrew, *b.* 1955,—Anthony Macalaster, *b.* 1958. *Residence,*—Casal dos Três Cantos, Ranholas, Sintra, Portugal.

Issue of the late Hon. Hubert John French, 8th son of 4th Baron, *b.* 1896, *d.* 1961, *m.* 1937, Mary Frances (ante), dau. of Charles Hasslacher, of 3, Kensington Park Gardens, W.8:—

Christopher John (of Brewerstreet Farm, Bletchingley, Surrey), *b.* 1943: *m.* 1966, Sacha, da. of Robert Wild, of Hartsridge, Godstone, Surrey, and has issue living, Philip John, *b.* 1968,—Julia Winifred, *b.* 1971.——Richard Charles (Rua Freitas Reis 32, Cascais, Portugal), *b.* 1945: *m.* 1969, Hilda Mary Felicity, el. da. of Lt.-Col. J. J. Pearson, of Tandridge, Surrey, and has issue living, Charles Peter, *b.* 1974,—Helen Mary Luise, *b.* 1969,—Susanna Francis (twin), *b.* 1974.——Jane Mary, *b.* 1938: *m.* 1966, Donald John Lawlor, of 3, College Close, Camberley, Surrey, and has issue living, Bernard John, *b.* 1969,—Timothy Charles, *b.* 1970,—Elizabeth Mary, *b.* 1967.——Sarah Anne, *b.* 1940: *m.* 1971, Clement Henry Lutterodt, PhD, of Ghana, and has issue living, Tobias Henry *b.* 1973.

Issue of the late Hon. Bertram Leo French, 9th son of 4th Baron, *b.* 1900, *d.* 1941: *m.* 1927, Maud Mary, who *d.* 1974, only da. of the late Edmund FitzLaurence Dease [B. Stafford, colls.]:—

Maurice Aloysius (71, East St., Warminster, Wilts.), *b.* 1930; Maj. R. Regt. Fus.; Korea 1952 (despatches): *m.* 1st, 1958 (m. diss. 1965) Heather Stewart, da. of the late A. C. Tarbutt; 2ndly, 1965, Lavinia Mary, da. of the late Maj. Patrick Anthony Henry Burke, of Stackallen, co. Meath, and has issue living, (by 1st m.) Dominic Arthur, *b.* 1959,—Nicola Anne, *b.* 1960,—(by 2nd m.), Patrick Rollo, *b.* 1966,—Claudia Rosemary, *b.* 1973.——Arthur Edmund (85, Abingdon Villas, W8), *b.* 1933; ed. at Trin. Coll., Camb. (BA 1957); Bar. Inner Temple 1962; is Lt. Irish Gds. (Reserve).——Lavinia Marie, *b.* 1928: *m.* 1971, Maj. John Watson, of Pannetts, Shipley, Horsham, Sussex.

PREDECESSORS.—[1] ARTHUR French, *M.P.*, great-grandson of the late Arthur French, of French Park, who *d.* 1769 ; cr. *Baron de Freyne,* of Artagh (peerage of United Kingdom) 1839, and *Baron de Freyne,* of Coolavin (peerage of United Kingdom) 1851, with remainder to his brothers ; *d.* 1856, when the 1st peerage expired ; *s.* in Barony of 1851 by his brother [2] *Rev.* JOHN, 2nd Baron ; *d.* 1863 ; *s.* by his brother [3] CHARLES, 3rd Baron : *m.* 1851, by a Roman Catholic priest, to Catherine, dau. of Luke Maree ; a question having arisen as to the validity of that marriage, she being a Roman Catholic and he a Protestant, they were again married in 1854 in the Established Church, having at that time had issue, Charles, M.P. for co. Roscommon 1873–80, *b.* 1851 (who *d.* 1925), John *b.* 1853 (who *d.* 1916), and William *b.* 1854 ; *d.* 1868 ; *s.* by his el. son born after the marriage of 1854 [4] ARTHUR, 4th Baron ; *b.* 1855: *m.* 1st, 1877, Lady Laura Octavia Dundas, who *d.* 1881, sister of 3rd Earl of Zetland ; 2ndly, 1882, Marie Georgiana, who *d.* 1923, dau. of the late Richard Westbrook Lamb, of West Denton, Northumberland ; *d.* 1913 ; *s.* by his son [5] ARTHUR REGINALD, 5th Baron; *b.* 1879; Capt. 3rd Batn. S. Wales Borderers: *m.* 1902, Annabel, who *d.* 1962, dau. of William Angus; *d.* (killed in action during European War) 1915 (despatches); *s.* by his half-brother [6] FRANCIS CHARLES, 6th Baron, *b.* 1884: *m.* 1916, Lina Victoria, who *d.* 1974, da. of Sir John Alexander Arnott, 2nd Bt.; *d.* 1935; *s.* by his son [7] FRANCIS ARTHUR JOHN, 7th Baron and present peer.

DELACOURT-SMITH, BARONY of.　(Delacourt-Smith.)　[Extinct 1972.]

SON LIVING OF LIFE BARON.

Hon. Stephen DELACOURT-SMITH (4, Weech Hall, Fortune Green Rd., NW6), *b.* 1946.

DAUGHTERS LIVING OF LIFE BARON.

Hon. Carolyn DELACOURT-SMITH, *b.* 1944: *m.* 1969, Roger Martin Pudney, of 10, Mulgrave Rd., Ealing, W5.

Hon. Lesley DELACOURT-SMITH (13, Thornfield Rd., W12), *b.* 1948.

WIDOW LIVING OF LIFE BARON.

MARGARET ROSALIND (*Baroness Delacourt-Smith of Alteryn*) (56, Aberdare Gdns., NW6), da. of Frederick James Hando of Newport, Mon.; cr. a Life Baroness 1974: *m.* 1939, Baron Delacourt-Smith (Life Peer) who *d.* 1972.

DELACOURT-SMITH OF ALTERYN, BARONESS.　(Delacourt-Smith.)
[Life Baroness 1974.]

MARGARET ROSALIND DELACOURT-SMITH, da. of Frederick James Hando, of Newport, Mon.; *b.* April 5th, 1916; ed. at Newport High Sch., and St. Anne's Coll., Oxford (MA); Councillor of Roy. Borough of New Windsor 1962-65, and a JP 1962-67; cr. *Baroness Delacourt-Smith of Alteryn*, of Alteryn, in co. of Gwent (Life Baroness) 1974: *m.* 1939, Baron Delacourt-Smith (Life Peer) who *d.* 1972, and has issue [see that title].

*Residence,—*56, Aberdare Gdns., NW6.

DELAMERE, BARON. (Cholmondeley.) [Baron U.K. 1821.]
[Name pronounced "**Chumley.**"]

Virtue is the safest helmet.

THOMAS PITT HAMILTON CHOLMONDELEY, 4th Baron; *b.* Aug. 19th, 1900; *s.* 1931; ed. at Eton ; is Capt. Welsh Guards, and patron of two livings; unsuccessfully contested Staffordshire, Leek Div. (*U*) Oct. 1924: *m.* 1st, 1924, Phyllis Anne (who obtained a divorce 1944), dau. of the late Lieut.-Col. Lord George William Montagu-Douglas-Scott, O.B.E. [see D. Buccleuch, colls.]; 2ndly, 1944, the Hon. (Ruth) Mary Clarisse (GARDNER), who obtained divorce 1955, dau. of 1st Baron Mount-Temple (ext.); 3rdly, 1955, Diana (COLVILLE), da. of the late Seymour Caldwell, of Hove, Sussex, and has issue by 1st marriage.

Arms,—Gules, two esquires' helmets in chief proper, and in base a garb or. **Crest,**—A demi-griffin sejeant sable, beaked, membered, ducally gorged, and wings elevated or, holding between the claws a helmet, as in the arms. **Supporters,**—Two griffins sable, beaked, membered, and wings elevated, ducally gorged and chained or.
Residence,—Soysambu, Elmenteita, Kenya. *Clubs,*—White's, St. James', Muthaiga (Nairobi).

SON LIVING. (*By 1st marriage.*)
Hon. HUGH GEORGE, *b.* Jan. 18th, 1934; ed. at Eton, and at Magdalene Coll., Camb. (MA Agric.): *m.* 1964, Ann (WILLOUGHBY TINNE), only da. of Sir Patrick Muir Renison, GCMG, and has issue living, Thomas Patrick Gilbert, *b.* 1968. *Residence,*—Sugonoi Farm, Soysambu, Elmenteita, Kenya.

DAUGHTERS LIVING. (*By 1st marriage.*)
Hon. Elizabeth Florence Marion *b.* 1925 : *m.* 1st, 1947, Sir Evelyn Delves Broughton, 12th Bt., who obtained a divorce 1953; 2ndly, 1953, Peter Alexander Barrington, of 36A, Gratton Rd., W14.
Hon. Anne Jeanetta Essex, *b.* 1927: *m.* 1951, Conrad Peter Almeric Garnett, of Hillgarth, Coggleshall Rd., Earles Colne, Essex, and 119, Maryvale Rd., Westville, Natal 3630, and has issue living, Jeremy Paul, *b.* 1953,—David Michael, *b.* 1956.

COLLATERAL BRANCHES LIVING.
Granddaughter of the late Hon. Thomas Grenville Cholmondeley, 2nd son of 1st Baron:—
Issue of the late Brig.-Gen. Hugh Cecil Cholmondeley, C.B., C.B.E., *b.* 1852, *d.* 1941: *m.* 1st, 1885, Mary Stewart, who *d.* 1929, dau. of the late Horace Payne Townshend ; 2ndly, 1931, Violet Maud, *J.P.,* (of Lee Old Hall, Ellesmere, Salop), dau. of the late Rev. the Hon. Archibald Parker [see E. Macclesfield, colls.]:—
(By 2nd m.) Violet Essex, *b.* 1932: *m.* 1964, Maj. William James Pinney,'11th Hussars, of Chartknolle, Stoke Abbott, Beaminster, Dorset, and has issue living, Hugh Charles William, *b.* 1966.

Issue of the late Henry Arthur Cholmondeley, *b.* 1855, *d.* 1952 : *m.* 1920, Helen Mary, who *d.* 1923, dau. of Harold Wrigley, of Ganton Hall, Scarborough :—
Essex Lucy (*Countess of Cavan*), *b.* 1921 : *m.* 1947, the 12th Earl of Cavan. *Residence,*—Waters Upton Manor, Wellington, Salop.

Grandchildren of the late Rev. the Hon. Henry Pitt Cholmondeley, 3rd son of 1st Baron :—
Issue of the late Major Henry Reginald Cholmondeley, D.S.O., *b.* 1862, *d.* 1947 : *m.* 1903, Cordelia Mercy, who *d.* 1949, dau. of the late J. Cross Ormrod, of Wyresdale Park, Lancashire :—
Anthony Pitt (Mendham Old Vicarage, Harleston, Norfolk), *b.* 1908; Maj. (ret.) Glos. Regt.; 1939-45 War (prisoner): *m.* 1936, Monica Irene, da. of the late Rev. Albert Ernest Snow, and has issue living, Anne, *b.* 1938,—Gillian, *b.* 1951,—Faith *b.* 1953.——Diana Mercy, *b.* 1904: *m.* 1934, Henry Lawrence Gill, and has issue living, John Lawrence, *b.* 1938,—Anthony Henry, *b.* 1940. *Residence,*—Chastleton Hill Farm, Moreton-in-Marsh.

PREDECESSORS.—[1] THOMAS Cholmondeley ; *b.* 1767; cr. *Baron Delamere,* of Vale Royal, co Chester (peerage of United Kingdom) 1821: *m.* 1810, Henrietta Elizabeth, dau. of Sir Watkin Williams-Wynn, 4th Bt; *d.* 1855; *s.* by his son [2] HUGH, 2nd Baron, *b.* 1811; sat as M.P. for Denbighshire (*C*) 1840-1, and for Montgomery 1841-7: *m.* 1st, 1848, Lady Sarah Hay, who *d.* 1859, dau. of 10th Earl of Kinnoull: 2ndly, 1860, Augusta Emily, who *d.* 1911, el. dau. of the late Rt. Hon. Sir George Hamilton Seymour, G.C.B., G.C.H., P.C.; *d.* 1887; *s.* by his son [3] HUGH, K.C.M.G., 3rd Baron ; *b.* 1870; sometime a M.L.C. of Kenya Colony : *m.* 1st, 1899, Lady Florence Ame Cole, who *d.* 1914, dau. of 4th Earl of Enniskillen ; 2ndly, 1928, Gwladys Helen, who *d.* 1943, dau. of the Hon. Rupert Evelyn Beckett; *d.* 1931; *s.* by his son [4] THOMAS PITT HAMILTON, 4th Baron and present peer.

DE LA WARR, EARL. (Sackville.) [Earl G.B. 1761.]
[Title pronounced "**De la Ware.**"]

Day of my life!

HERBRAND EDWARD DUNDONALD BRASSEY SACKVILLE, *G.B.E., P.C.,* 9th Earl ; *b.* June 20th, 1900 ; *s.* 1915; ed. at Eton, and at Magdalen Coll., Oxford; is patron of four livings, and an Hon. Member of Incorporated So. of Auctioneers and Landed Property Agents; European War 1918 in R.N.R.; was a Lord-in-Waiting to H.M. Feb. to Nov. 1924; appointed Under-Sec. of State for War June 1929; again a Lord-in-Waiting to H.M. July 1929 to June 1930, Parliamentary Sec. to Min. of Agriculture and Dep. Min. of Fisheries June 1930 to Aug. 1931, and a Member of Council of Duchy of Lancaster 1931 ; re-appointed Parliamentary Sec. to Min. of Agriculture and Dep. Min. of Fisheries (in National Govt.) Nov. 1931 ; became Parliamentary Sec. to Board of Education Nov. 1935, Parliamentary Under-Sec. of State for Colonies July 1936,

Lord Privy Seal May 1937, and Pres. of Board of Education Oct. 1938 ; First
Commr. of Works April to May 1940; Postmaster-Gen. Oct. 1951 to April 1955;
Chm. National Labour Party 1931-39; Dep. Regional Commr. 1940-45; Dir.
of Home Flax Production, Min. of Supply and Chm. of Agric. Res. Council
1943-49, and of Nat. Trust Estates Cttee. 1949-51 and 1955; elected Mayor of
Bexhill 1932, 1933. and 1934 ; Chm. of Joint E. and Central Africa Board
1956, and of Roy. Commonwealth So. 1958; a Dir. of Olympia Ltd.; JP and
DL for Sussex; PC 1936, GBE (Civil) 1956: *m.* 1st, 1920, Diana, who *d.* 1966,
da. of the late Capt. Henry Gerard Leigh [Antrobus, Bt., colls.]; 2ndly, 1968,
Dame Sylvia Margaret, DBE, da. of William Harrison, of Liverpool, and
widow of 1st Earl of Kilmuir, and has issue (by 1st m.).

Arms,—Quarterly, 1st, argent, a fesse dancettée sable, *West*; 2nd, azure, three leopards' heads
reversed jessant de lys or, *Cantelupe*; 3rd gules erusilly and a lion argent, *la Warr*; 4th, quarterly
or and gules, a bend vaire, *Sackville*. *Crests,*—1st, issuant from a ducal coronet or a griffin's
head azure, beaked and eared gold, *West.*; 2nd, upon a coronet composed of fleurs-de-lis or,
an estoile argent, *Sackville.* *Supporters* - *Dexter,* a wolf coward argent gorged with a collar
or ; *sinister,* a cockatrice or, winged azure. *Badge,*—A crampet or, the inside per pale azure and
gules, charged with the letter *r*.

Residences,—Fishers Gate, Withyham, Hartfield, Sussex; 1, Buckingham Mews, Stafford
Place, SW1.

SON LIVING. (*By 1st m.*)
WILLIAM HERBRAND (*Lord Buckhurst*), *b.* Oct. 16th, 1921; ed. at Eton; formerly Capt. Parachute
Regt.: *m.* 1946, Anne Rachel, only dau. of Geoffrey Devas, of Hunton Court, Maidstone, and has
issue:—

    SONS LIVING,—*Hon.* William Herbrand, *b.* April 10th, 1948; ed. at Eton.
    Hon. Thomas Geoffrey, *b.* 1950; ed. at Eton.

    DAUGHTER LIVING,—*Hon.* Arabella Avice Diana, *b.* 1958.
Residences,—Buckhurst Park, Withyham, Sussex; 93, Eaton Pl., SW1.

DAUGHTER LIVING. (*By 1st m.*)
Lady Katharine Pamela, *b.* 1926 : *m.* 1946, Frank Thomas Robertson Giles, and has issue living,
Henry Frank Sebastian, *b.* 1952,—Sarah Elizabeth, *b.* 1950: *m.* 1972, Rodolphe d'Erlanger,—
Belinda Susan Mary, *b.* 1958. *Residence,*—42, Blomfield Rd., W9.

SISTER LIVING.
Lady Avice Ela Muriel (Spye Park, Chippenham, Wilts.), *b.* 1897: *m.* 1st, 1918 (m. diss. 1931), Maj.-
Gen. Sir Stewart Graham Menzies, KCB, KCMG, DSO, who *d.* 1968; 2ndly, 1931, Capt. Frank
Fitzroy Fane Spicer, DSO, who *d.* 1973.

COLLATERAL BRANCH LIVING.

    Descendants of Lt.-Col. the Hon. William Edward SACKVILLE-WEST, 6th son of
    5th Earl, *b.* 1830, *d.* 1905: *m.* 1860, Georgina, who *d.* 1883, da. of the late George
    Dodwell, of Kevinsfort, Sligo [see B. Sackville].

PREDECESSORS.—[1] Sir THOMAS West, Knt., accompanied Edward III. to France 1329, and
also in the wars with David Bruce, King of Scotland ; summoned to Parliament of England as
Baron West 1342 ; *d.* 1342; *s.* by his son [2] THOMAS, 2nd Baron; was not summoned to Parliament; served at Crecy 1346 ; *s.* by his son [3] THOMAS, 3rd Baron; summoned to Parliament
1402 ; *d.* 1405; *s.* by his son [4] THOMAS, 4th Baron ; took a distinguished part in the French
wars of Henry V.; *d.s.p.* 1415; *s.* by his brother [5] REGINALD, 5th Baron: summoned to
English Parliament as 6th *Baron De La Warr* on the death of his uncle 1426 (see note *₊* infra);
d. 1451 ; *s.* by his son [6] RICHARD, 7th Baron, a staunch supporter of the House of Lancaster
in the War of the Roses; *d.* 1497; *s.* by his son [7] THOMAS, K.G., 8th Baron; *d.* 1525; *s.* by
his son [8] THOMAS, 9th Baron; not having male issue he adopted as his heir William, son of
his half-brother Sir George West; his nephew, however, having attempted to poison his uncle,
was debarred by Act of Parliament from succeeding to his uncle's honours or estates; *d.* 1554,
when the baronies of West and De La Warr fell into abeyance. [9] WILLIAM West (ante), nephew
of the 9th Baron, having served in the English Army at Picardy, was knighted Feb. 1568, fully
restored in blood by Act of Parliament in March following, and cr. *Baron De La Warr* 1570 ; *d.*
1595; *s.* by his son [10] THOMAS, 11th Baron ; restored to the place and precedence of his
ancestors; *s.* by his son [11] THOMAS, 12th Baron; Gov. and Capt.-Gen. of Virginia; *d.*
1618 ; *s.* by his son [12] HENRY, 13th Baron; *d.* 1628; *s.* by his son [13] CHARLES, 14th Baron ;
s. by his son [14] JOHN, 15th Baron; *d.* 1723; *s.* by his son [15] JOHN, *K.B.*, *P.C.*, 16th Baron;
a Gen. in the Army, Lord of the Bedchamber to George I., Gov. and Capt.-Gen. of New York;
cr. *Viscount Cantelupe* and *Earl De La Warr* (peerage of Great Britain) 1761; *d.* 1766; *s.* by his
son [16] JOHN, 2nd Earl ; a Lt.-Gen. in the Army, Master of the Horse, and Vice-Chamberlain
to the Queen ; *d.* 1777; *s.* by his el. son [17] WILLIAM AUGUSTUS, 3rd Earl ; *d.* unmarried 1783;
s. by his brother [18] JOHN RICHARD, 4th Earl; *d.* 1795; *s.* by his son [19] GEORGE JOHN,
P.C., *D.C.L.*, 5th Earl; *b.* 1791; Lord Chamberlain 1858-9; assumed by Roy. licence 1845 the
additional surname of Sackville: *m.* 1813, Lady Elizabeth Sackville, who *d.* 1870, younger dau.
and co-heir of 3rd Duke of Dorset (title extinct) ; this lady was in 1864 cr. *Baroness Buckhurst;*
of Buckhurst, co. Sussex (peerage of United Kingdom), with remainder to her younger sons
and their male issue, but with a proviso that upon any Baron Buckhurst succeeding to the
Earldom of Delaware, the said Barony should devolve upon the heir next entitled to succeed,
if the person having so succeeded to the Earldom of De La Warr had died without male issue ;
d. 1869; *s.* by his son [19] CHARLES RICHARD, K.C.B., 6th Earl ; a Maj.-Gen. in the Army
distinguished himself in India and in the Crimea; *d.* unmarried 1873, *s.* by his brother [20]
Rev. REGINALD WINDSOR, 7th Earl, who in 1870 had *s.* his mother as 2nd Baron Buckhurs,
but a claim to that Barony under the above-mentioned proviso by his next brother was un-
successful, and it has remained merged in the Earldom ; *b.* 1817 ; assumed by Roy. licence 1871
the surname of Sackville only in lieu of Sackville-West: *m.* 1867, the Hon. Constance Mary
Elizabeth, who *d.* 1929, el. dau. of 1st Baron Lamington; *d.* 1896; *s.* by his second son [21]
GILBERT GEORGE REGINALD, 8th Earl ; *b.* 1869: *m.* 1st, 1891, Lady Muriel Agnes, who *d.* 1930
(having obtained a divorce 1902), dau. of 1st Earl Brassey; 2ndly, 1903, Hilda Mary Claveriny
(who *d.* 1963, having *m.* 2ndly, 1922, John William Dennis, sometime M.P.), dau. of the late
Col. C. Lennox Tredcroft, of Glen Ancrum, Guildford; *d.* (while on active ser. as Lieut.
R.N.V.R. during European War) 1915 ; *s.* by his only son [22] HERBRAND EDWARD DUNDONALD
BRASSEY, 9th Earl and present peer : also Viscount Cantelupe. Baron De La Warr, and Baron
Buckhurst.

₊ [1] ROGER La Warr, summoned to English Parliament 1299-1311; *d.* 1329; *s.* by his son
[2] JOHN, *K.B.*, 2nd Baron, a valiant soldier: summoned to Parliament of England 1307-47;
d. 1347; *s.* by his son [3] ROGER, 3rd Baron; a renowned soldier, was present at Poictiers
when John, King of France, surrendered to him and Sir John Pelham, in commemoration of
which the crampet, or chape, of the king's sword was given to him as a badge: *m.* 2ndly,
Alianore, dau. of John, 2nd Baron Mowbray, and had an only dau., Joanna, wife of 3rd Baron
West, who had issue Thomas 4th Baron West, and Richard 5th Baron West and 6th Baron
De La Warr; *d.* 1370; *s.* by his son [4] JOHN, 4th Baron, summoned to Parliament 1370-97; *d.*
1398; *s.* by his brother [5] THOMAS, 5th Baron ; Rector of the Parish Church of Manchester;
d. 1426; *s.* by his half-sister's son [6] REGINALD, 5th Baron West (ante).

DE L'ISLE, VISCOUNT. (Sidney.) [Viscount U.K. 1956, Bt.U.K. 1806 and 1818.
[Title pronounced "De Lyle."]

Whither the Fates call me.

WILLIAM PHILIP SIDNEY, VC,
KG, GCMG, GCVO, PC, 1st
Viscount, and 9th Baronet of Castle
Goring (cr. 1806) and 7th Baronet
of Penshurst Place (cr. 1818); b. May
23rd, 1909; s. as 6th Baron De L'Isle
and Dudley 1945, and as 9th
Baronet (cr. 1806) 1965; ed. at Eton
and at Magdalene Coll., Camb. (Hon.
Fellow 1955); Hon. LLD Sydney;
Hon Fellow RIBA; late Capt.
Grenadier Guards (Reserve); a DL
for Kent, a Chartered Accountant,
a KStJ; a Trustee of Winston
Churchill Memorial Trust and RAF
Museum; Chm. of Phoenix Assurance
Co., First Nat. Finance Corpn. Ltd.,
and a Dir. of Phoenix Assurance Co.
of New York, Glens Falls Insurance
Co. of New York, Save & Prosper
Group Ltd., and Yorkshire Bank,
Ltd.; Parl. Sec. to Min. of Pensions, May to July 1945, Sec. of State for Air
1951-55, and Gov.-Gen. of Aust. 1961-65; Chancellor of Order of St. Michael
and St. George since 1968; 1939-45 War in France and Italy (VC); MP for
Chelsea (C) Oct. 1944 to June 1945; PC 1951, and Viscount De L'Isle, of
Penshurst, co. Kent (peerage of United Kingdom) 1956, GCMG 1961, GCVO
1963, KG 1968: m. 1st, 1940, the Hon. Jacqueline Corinne Yvonne Vereker,
who d. 1962, da. of F-M 6th Viscount Gort, VC, GCB, CBE, DSO, MVO, MC;
2ndly, 1966, Margaret Eldrydd, da. of the late Maj.-Gen. Thomas Herbert
Shoubridge, CB, CMG, DSO, and widow of the 3rd Baron Glanusk, and has
issue by 1st marriage.

Arms,—Quarterly: 1st and 4th or, a pheon azure, Sidney; 2nd and 3rd sable, on a fesse
engrailed, between three whelk shells or, a mullet for difference, Shelley. Crests,—1st, a porcupine
statant azure, quills, collar, and chain or; 2nd, a griffin's head erased argent, ducally gorged or.
Supporters,—Dexter, a porcupine azure, quills, collar, and chain or; sinister, a lion queue fourchée
vert.

Seat,—Penshurst Place, Tonbridge, Kent.

SON LIVING. (By 1st marriage.)
Hon. PHILIP JOHN ALGERNON, b. April 21st, 1945; Capt. Gren. Guards.

DAUGHTERS LIVING. (By 1st marriage.)
Hon. Elizabeth Sophia, b. 1941: m. 1st, 1959 (m. diss. 1966) George Silver Oliver Annesley Colthurst
[see Colthurst, Bt.], 2ndly, 1966 (m. diss. 1971) Sir (Edward) Humphry Tyrell Wakefield, 2nd Bt.;
3rdly, 1972, Capt. James Silvester Rattray of Rattray, of Craighall-Rattray, Blairgowrie, Perthshire.
Hon. Catherine Mary, b. 1942: m. 1964, (Martin) John Wilbraham, of Kerminoham House, Holmes
Chapel, Ches., and has issue living, Alexander John, b. 1965,—Rupert Edward Robert, b. 1967,—
Jocelyn Thomas Ralph, b. 1970.
Hon. Anne Marjorie, b. 1947: m. 1967, David Alexander Harries, of Hayselden Manor, Sissinghurst
Kent, el. son of Rear-Adm. David Hugh Harries, CB, CBE, and has issue living, David Henry
b. 1970,—James Hugh, b. 1972,—Alexandra Victoria Corinna, b. 1968.
Hon. Lucy Corinna Agneta, b. 1953: m. 1974, the Hon. Michael Charles James Willoughby, el. son of
12th Baron Middleton.

COLLATERAL BRANCHES LIVING.
Issue of the late Capt. George Ernest Shelley, brother of 5th baronet of Castle
Goring, b. 1840, d. 1910: m. 1889, Anne Janet, who d. 1955, da. of the late
E. Andrewes:—
Gwendolin Evelyn: m. 1st, 1913, the Rev. Frank Shelley-Mills, who d. 1961, having obtained a
divorce 1930; 2ndly, 1930, Eric Tregear Williams, Malayan Civil Ser., who d. 1971, and has issue
living by 1st and 2nd m. Residence,—25, Maudlin Drive, Teignmouth, S. Devon, TQ14 8RZ.

Granddaughters of the late Capt. George Ernest Shelley (ante):—
Issue of the late Maj. George Edward Shelley, MBE, b. 1891, d. 1961: m. 1st, 1920, Cicely
Alice Colquhoun (who d. 1954, having obtained a divorce 1935), el. da. of the late Lt.-Col.
Lionel Arthur Bosanquet; 2ndly, 1935, the Hon. Lucy Gwen (who d. 1957, and from
whom he had obtained a divorce 1941), da. of Baron Atkin (Life Peer); 3rdly, 1951,
Freda Victoria (OHLSON) (of Cherry Orchard, Dean Way, Chalfont St. Giles, Bucks.), yr.
da. of the late F. J. L. Jeffery:—
(By 1st m.) Rosemary Eveline, Brook House, Flat 17, 23, Roland Gdns., SW7 3PF), b. 1921; Subaltern
ATS (later WRAC 1941-50)——Iris Gwendolin, b. 1927: m. 1954, Maj. Philip Gordon Tanner, RA,
and has issue living, Nicholas Shelley, b. 1955,—Clare Theresa, b. 1958. Residence,—Corner Farm,
Stowupland, nr. Stowmarket, Suffolk, IP14 4AN.

PREDECESSORS,—[1] Sir JOHN Shelley-Sidney; cr. a Baronet 1818; assumed additional
surname of Sidney by Roy. licence 1793 on succeeding to the estate of his maternal grandmother, Elizabeth (who m. William Perry), dau. of the Hon. Thomas Sidney, 4th son of 6th
Earl of Leicester; d. 1849; s. by his son [2] PHILIP CHARLES, G.C.H., D.C.L., who had
in 1835 been cr. Baron De L'Isle and Dudley (peerage of United Kingdom); b. 1800;
discontinued the surname of Shelley: m. 1825, Lady Sophia Fitzclarence, natural dau. of King
William IV., and sister of 1st Earl of Munster: d. March 4, 1851; s. by his son [3] PHILIP, 2nd
Baron, b. 1828: m. 1st, 1850, Mary, who d. 1891, dau. of Sir William Foulis, 8th Bt.; 2ndly,
1893, Emily Frances, who d. 1926, el. dau. of the late William Fermor Ramsay; d. 1898; s. by

his el. son [4] PHILIP, 3rd Baron, b. 1853: m. 1902, the Hon. Elizabeth Maria, dau. of 4th
Viscount Gort, and widow of William Harvey Astell, J.P., D.L. (sometime Grenadier Guards),
of Woodbury Hall, Beds ; d. 1922 ; s. by his brother [5] ALGERNON, 4th Baron, b. 1854; some
time Lieut.-Col. and Brevet Col. R.A.; d. April 1945 ; s. by his brother [6] WILLIAM, 5th Baron,
b. 1859 ; Bar. Inner Temple 1886 ; Mayor of Chelsea 1906 and 1907 and a County Councillor
for London 1922-34 : m. 1905, Winifred Agneta Yorke, who d. 1959, dau. of the late Roland Yorke
Bevan, d. June, 1945 ; s. by his son [6] WILLIAM PHILIP, 1st Viscount and present peer ; also Baron
De L'Isle and Dudley [see infra*₊*].

₊[1] Sir BYSSHE Shelley, of Castle Goring, Sussex .son of Timothy Shelley, 7th in descent
from Edward Shelley of Worminghurst Park, Sussex, yr. son of John Shelley, of Michel-
grove (d. 1526) [see Shelley Bt., cr. 1611]; b. 1731; cr. a Baronet 1806: m. 1st, Mary Catherine,
who d. 1760, da. and heir of the Rev. Theobald Mitchell; 2ndly, 1769, Elizabeth Jane Sidney,
who d. 1781, da. and heir of William Perry by Elizabeth Sidney, heir of Penshurst Place, Kent;
d. 1815; s. by his el. son [2] Sir TIMOTHY, 2nd Bt., b. 1753: m. 1791, Elizabeth, da. of Charles
Pilfold, of Effingham, Surrey; d. 1844; s. by his grandson [3] Sir PERCY FLORENCE, 3rd Bt. (son
of Percy Bysshe Shelley the poet, who was drowned 1822); b. 1819: m. 1848, Jane, who d. 1899,
da. of Thomas Gibson, and widow of the Hon. Charles Robert St. John; d. 1889; s. by his
cousin [4] Sir EDWARD, 4th Bt.; b. 1827; Capt. 16th Lancers: m. 1866, Mary, who d. 1886, da.
of Henry Mitchell Smyth; d. 1890; s. by his brother [5] Sir CHARLES, 5th Bt.; b. 1838; Lt.-Col.
Scots Fus. Guards: m. 1869, Lady Mary Jane Jemina Stopford, who d. 1937, da. of 3rd Earl of
Courtown; d. 1902; s. by his el. son [6] Sir JOHN COURTOWN EDWARD, 6th Bt., b. 1871; Capt.
Scots Guards: m. 1898, the Hon. Eleanor Georgiana Rolls, who d. 1961, da. and heir of 1st and
last Baron Llangattock; they assumed by Royal Licence 1917, the additional name and arms
of Rolls; d. 1951; s. by his brother [7] Sir PERCY BYSSHE, 7th Bt., b. 1872, d. 1953; s. by his
brother [8] Sir SIDNEY PATRICK, 8th Bt.; Capt. Hampshire Yeo.; d. 1965; s. by his kinsman
[9] the 1st Viscount De L'Isle, descendant of Sir John Shelley-Sidney, 1st Bt. (cr. 1818), only
son of 1st Bt. (cr. 1806) by his 2nd wife (ante).

Delvin, Lord, son of Earl of Westmeath.

DE MAULEY, BARON. (Ponsonby.) [Baron U.K. 1838.]

[Name pronounced "Punsonby."]

GERALD JOHN PONSONBY, 6th Baron; b.
Dec. 19th, 1921; s. 1962; ed. at Eton, and at
Ch. Ch., Oxford (B.A. 1941, M.A. 1947); Bar.
Middle Temple 1949; formerly Lieut. Leicester-
shire Yeo., and Capt. R.A.; European War
1939-45: m. 1954, Helen Alice, dau. of the late
Hon. Charles William Sholto Douglas [see E.
Morton, colls.], and widow of Lieut.-Col.
Bryan Lynch Leslie Abdy Collins, O.B.E.,
M.C., R.E.

Arms,—Gules, a chevron between three combs argent.
Crest,—Out of a ducal coronet or three arrows, points
downwards, one in pale and two in saltire, entwined at
the intersection by a snake proper. Supporters,—Dexter,
For the king, the law, and the people. a lion reguardant proper; sinister, a bull sable, armed,
unguled, tufted, and ducally gorged or.

Residence,—Langford House, Little Faringdon, Lechlade, Glos.

BROTHER LIVING.

Hon. THOMAS MAURICE, TD, b. Aug. 2nd, 1930; ed. at Eton; Lt.-Col. The Wessex Yeo; D.L. for
Glos.: m. 1956, Maxine Henrietta, da. of the late William Dudley Keith Thellusson, and has issue
living, Rupert Charles, b. 1957,—Ashley George, b. 1959. Residence,—The Common, Little Faringdon, Lechlade, Glos.

SISTERS LIVING.

Hon. June Mary, b. 1924: m. 1949, the Hon. Robert Walter Sigismund Grimston, el. son of 1st Baron
Grimston of Westbury. Residence,—The Old Rectory, Westwell, Burford, Oxon.
Hon. Elizabeth Winifred, b. 1928: m. 1950, Christopher Boot Holman [see By. Trent]. Residences,—
Foxcote, Shipston-on-Stour, Warwickshire ; Shellbridge, Acharacle, Argyllshire.

WIDOW LIVING OF FIFTH BARON.

ELGIVA MARGARET (Dowager Baroness de Mauley), da. of the late Hon. Cospatrick Thomas Dundas
[see M. Zetland, colls]: m. 1920, the 5th Baron, who d. 1962. Residence,—The New House, Little
Faringdon, Lechlade, Glos.

COLLATERAL BRANCHES LIVING.

Issue of the late Hon. Edwin Charles William Ponsonby, 5th son of 2nd Baron,
b. 1851, d. 1939: m. 1st, 1878, Dora, who d. 1897, dau. of the late Octavius
Edward Coope, M.P., of Rochetts, South Weald, Brentwood ; 2ndly, 1906, Hilda
who d. 1943, dau. of the late Robert Smith, of Goldings, Hertford :—
(By 1st marriage) Sir Charles Edward, Bt., T.D, b. 1879 ; cr. a Baronet 1956 [see " BARONETAGE "].

Grandchildren of the late Hon. Edwin Charles William Ponsonby (ante):—
Issue of the late Rev. Maurice George Jesser Ponsonby, M.C., b. 1880, d. 1943: m. 1918,
Lady Phyllis Sydney Buxton, O.B.E., who d. 1942, dau. of 1st Earl Buxton:—
Elizabeth, b. 1922; m. 1952, John Lionel Clay, T.D., Bar.-at-law, and has issue living, Andrew John
Buxton, b. 1962,—Fiona Elizabeth, b. 1954,—Catriona Mary, b. 1955,—Joanna Penelope, b. 1958.
Residence,—Newtimber Place, Hassocks, Sussex.——Mary Veronica, b. 1927: m. 1961, William
Peter Ward Barnes, and has issue living, Peter Denis Ponsonby, b. 1962,—Thomas William Pon-
sonby, b. 1965,—Susanna Barbara, b. 1963. Residence,—28, Park Village East, NW1.
Issue of the late Capt. Victor Coope Ponsonby, MC, b. 1887, d. 1966: m. 1923, Gladys Edith,
who d. 1964, da. of the late Godfrey Walter, of Malshanger, Basingstoke:—
Myles Walter, CBE (c/o FCO (Ulan Batar), King Charles St., SW1; Springs Cottage, Bullingstone
Lane, Speldhurst, Tunbridge Wells), b. 1924; ed. at Eton; late Capt. KRRC; HM Consul-Gen. at
Hanoi 1964-65; Ambassador to Mongolian People's Republic since 1974; 1939-45 War; CBE (Civil)
1966: m. 1950, Ann Veronica Theresa, da. of Brig. Francis Herbert Maynard, CB, DSO, MC, and
has issue living, John Maurice Maynard, b. 1955,—Belinda Mary, b. 1951,—Emma Christina, b. 1959.
——Sheila Mary, b. 1927: m. 1952, Cdr. Michael Edward St. Quintin Wall, RN [E. Peel, colls.],
and has issue living, Hugo St. Quintin, b. 1954,—Sarah Fenella, b. 1955.

Grandchildren of the late Claude **Ashley** Charles Ponsonby (infra) :—
Issue of the late Harold Ashley Curzon Ponsonby, *b.* 1891, *d.* 1950: *m.* 1941, **Ruth Margaret**
(c/o Royds, Rawstorne & Co., 46, Bedford Sq., WC1), only da. of James Miller, of
Chippenham, Wilts.:—
John Ashley Charles, *b.* 1948.——Sarah Haller, *b.* 1944.——Jane Caroline, *b.* 1946: *m.* 1966, (m. diss.
1969) Stephen Thornton Parr, and has issue living, Sally Jane Thornton, *b.* 1965.

Granddaughter of the late Capt. the Hon. Ashley George John Ponsonby, **2nd son**
of 1st Baron :—
Issue of the late Claude Ashley Charles Ponsonby, *b.* 1859, *d.* 1935 : *m.* 1891, **Haller**,
who *d.* 1932 (having obtained a divorce 1907), dau. of the late Orville Horwitz, of
Baltimore, Maryland, U.S.A. :—
Moyra Blanche May Diana (c/o Royds, Rawstorne & Co., 46, Bedford Sq., W.C.1), *b.* 1901: *m.* **1st**
1932, Hans Henning; 2ndly, 1947, Maurice Heriot Nicolls, who *d.* 1954, and has issue living,
(by 1st m.) Peter Ronald KNAPP-FISHER (88, Elgin Cres., W11), *b.* 1933; adopted the surname of
Knapp-Fisher 1947: *m.* 1972, Clare Ward,—Jacqueline Haller, *b.* 1935: *m.* 1966, Dr. Carl-Rudolf
Vidal, of 1475, Kendall Drive, Table Mesa, Boulder, Colorado 80302, USA, and has issue living,
Martin *b.* 1967, Stefan Matthias *b.* 1971, Rudolf Leonard (twin) *b.* 1971, Silvia Natalia *b.* 1970,—
Moyra Christine, *b.* 1938: *m.* 1964, Alexander Hendry, of 76B, St. James Lane, N10, and has issue
living, Katherine, *b.* 1967, Louise *b.* 1969.

PREDECESSORS.—[1] *Hon.* WILLIAM FRANCIS SPENCER Ponsonby, 3rd son of 3rd **Earl of
Bessborough**, *b.* 1787: *m.* 1814, Lady Barbara Ashley-Cooper, dau. of 5th Earl of Shaftesbury
(a co-heir to Barony of Mauley cr. 1295 ; cr. *Baron de Mauley*, of Canford, co. Dorset (**peerage**
of United Kingdom) 1838; *d.* 1855; *s.* by his son [2] CHARLES FREDERICK ASHLEY COOPER,
2nd Baron, *b.* 1815 ; M.P. for Poole (*L*) 1837-47 and for Dungarvan 1851-2: *m.* 1838, Lady Maria
Jane Elizabeth Ponsonby, dau. of 4th Earl of Bessborough; *d.* 1896; *s.* by his el. son [3]
WILLIAM ASHLEY WEBB, 3rd Baron ; *b.* 1843; *d.* 1918; *s.* by his brother [4] *Rev.* MAURICE
JOHN GEORGE, 4th Baron, *b.* 1846; sometime V. of Wantage: *m.* 1875, the Hon. Madeleine
Emily Augusta Hanbury-Tracy, who *d.* 1938, dau. of 2nd Baron Sudeley; *d.* 1945; *s.* by his
son [5] HUBERT WILLIAM, 5th Baron; Capt. Gloucester Yeo., 1914-18 War; *d.* 1962; *s.* by his
son [6] GERALD JOHN, 6th Baron and present peer.

DENBIGH AND DESMOND, EARL OF. (Feilding.) [Earl E. 1622.]

WILLIAM RUDOLPH MICHAEL FEILD-
ING, 11th Earl; *b.* Aug. 2nd, 1943; *s.*
1966; ed. at Eton: *m.* 1965, Caroline
Judith Vivienne, da. of Lt.-Col.
Geoffrey Cooke, and has issue.

Arms—Argent, on a fesse azure, three
lozenges or. **Crest**—A nuthatch pecking at a
hazel branch, all proper. **Supporters**—Two
stags proper, attired and unguled or.

Residence,—Pailton House, Rugby.

SON LIVING.
ALEXANDER STEPHEN RUDOLPH, (*Viscount
Feilding*), *b.* Nov. 4th, 1970.

DAUGHTERS LIVING.
Lady Samantha Clare Barbara, *b.* 1966.
Lady Louisa Helen, *b.* 1969.

SISTER LIVING.
Lady (Imelda) Clare, *b.* 1941: *m.* 1966, **David**
Rodney Doig (PO Box 441, Kiambu, Kenya),
and has issue living, Andrew William David,
b. 1969,—Rowena Helen, *b.* 1967—Zoe Claire
b. 1971.

Honour is the reward of virtue.

UNCLES LIVING.
Hon. Hugh Richard, *b.* 1920; ed. at Ampleforth Coll.; FCA; late Sqd. Ldr. RAF VR; 1939-45 War
(despatches): *m.* 1944, Sheila Katharine, only da. of the late Brig. Charles Arthur Bolton, CBE, and
has issue living, John Henry Christopher, *b.* 1945; ed. at Ampleforth: *m.* 1971, Veronica, 2nd da. of
John Farmer, of 36, Iverna Gdns., W8, and has issue living, Michael *b.* 1975, Natasia Frances
Katharine *b.* 1973. *Residence,*—Home Farm, Bainton, Driffield, E. Yorks. *Club,*—RAF.
Hon. Henry Anthony, *M.C., b.* 1924 ; ed. at Ampleforth Coll., and at King's Coll., Camb. (B.A. 19—,
M.A. 1952) ; late Capt. Coldstream Guards; European War 1944-45 (M.C.): *m.* 1950, **Dunia
Maureen**, dau. of the late Gordon Spencer, M.D., of Putley, near Ledbury, Herefordshire, and has
issue living, Jasper Simon, *b.* 1953,—Penelope Dunia, *b.* 1954. *Residence,*—Manor Farm, Pailton,
near Rugby.
GREAT AUNTS LIVING. (*Daughters of 9th Earl.*)
Lady Marjorie Mary Winifrede, *b.* 1892: *m.* 1st, 1915, Capt. Edward Dudley Hanly (**sometime**
Roy. Inniskilling Fusiliers), who *d.* 1951, having obtained a divorce 1923 , 2ndly, 1923, **Capt. Robert**
Arthur Heath, who *d.* 1943 [E. Peel, colls.], and has issue living (by 2nd m.) Andrew Robert (George's
Plot, Church Rd., Abbots Leigh, Bristol), *b.* 1921; *m.* 1st, 1953 (m. diss. 1966), Sarah Joanna Evelyn
Helen, who *d.* 1970, da. of the Rt. Hon. (Maurice) Harold Macmillan [D. Devonshire]; 2ndly, 1966,
Judith Clare Silver, and has issue living (by 2nd m.) William Robert Michael *b.* 1966, Rachel Clare
b. 1968,—Elizabeth Beatrice (PO Box 83, Ocho Rios, Jamaica), *b.* 1923: *m.* 1946 (m. diss. 1961)
Ian R. Millar, and has issue living, Simon, *b.* 1947, Timothy Ian *b.* 1950, Belinda Jane *b.* 1953.
Residence,—The Old Cottage, Frog Lane, Rotherwick, Basingstoke, Hants.
Lady Bettie Mary, *b.* 1899 : *m.* 1926, Eric George Sherbrooke Walker, M.C., formerly R.A.F.,
and has issue living, Honor Sherbrooke, *b.* 1929 : *m.* 1956, Maurice George Dermot Hurly, M.B.,
BCh (PO Box 20, Whitianga, N2), and has issue living, Dermot Sherbrooke Fitzmaurice *b.* 1958,
Robert Conway *b.* 1966, Anne Elizabeth, *b.* 1959, Cecilia Florence *b.* 1962,—Susan Conway *b.* 1944,—
Susan Mary, *b.* 1931: *m.* 1956, Richard McDonald Hodgson, DSM, of 4, Bert Webster St., Estcourt,
Natal, and has issue living, Simon Eric *b.* 1957, Paul Reuben *b.* 1960, Sonja Margaret *b.* 1958. *Resi-
dence,*—Ca's Fidavé, Calle Isabel II, 110, Sóller, Majorca. *Clubs,*—United Service, Muthaiga

Lady Victoria Mary Dolores (c/o Sirrima Ltd., PO Naro Moru, Kenya) *b.* 1901: *m.* 1933, Walter Miles Fletcher, and has issue living, Christopher Everard, *b.* 1935: *m.* 1970, Pamela Catherine Wilson, da. of James Wilson Hogg (Trinity Gram. Sch., Summer Hill, NSW), and has issue living, Alistair Miles *b.* 1975,—Simon (c/o Sirrima Ltd., PO Naro Moru, Kenya), *b.* 1937: *m.* 1966, Jane, da. of D. Pell Smith, of Molo, Kenya, and has issue living, Graham Miles *b.* 1968, Jennifer Elisabeth *b.* 1970.

WIDOW LIVING OF BROTHER OF TENTH EARL.

Elizabeth (Newnham Paddox, Rugby), da. of the late William Fletcher, of Cumberland: *m.* 1938, the Hon. David Charles Feilding, who *d.* 1966, and has issue living [see cols. infra].

WIDOW LIVING OF BROTHER OF TENTH EARL.

Rosemary (The Park Cottage, Newnham Paddox, Rugby), da. of the late Cdr. (Frederick) Neville Eardley-Wilmot, RN (ret.) [see Eardley-Wilmot, Bt.]: *m.* 1939, Capt. the Hon. Basil Egerton Feilding, who *d.* 1970, and has issue living [see colls. infra].

WIDOW LIVING OF TENTH EARL.

VERENA BARBARA (*Betty, Countess of Denbigh and Desmond*), (Pailton House, Rugby), da. of William Edward Price, and widow of Lt.-Col. Thomas Paget Fielding Johnson: *m.* 1940, the 10th Earl, who *d.* 1966.

COLLATERAL BRANCHES LIVING.

Issue of the late Hon. David Charles Feilding (2nd son of the late Lt.-Col. Rudolph Edmund Aloysius, Viscount Feilding, CMG, DSO, el. son of 9th Earl), *b.* 1913, *d.* 1966: *m.* 1938, Elizabeth (ante), da. of the late William Fletcher, of Cumberland:—

William David, *b.* 1939; ed. at Downside.——Michael Henry (13, Cochrane Rd., SW19 3QP), *b.* 1946; ed. at Downside, and Oxford Univ. (BSc): *m.* 1970, Linnet, da. of William Hale, of The Island, Hurstbourne Priors, Hants , and has issue living, Emily Linnet, *b.* 1973.——Charles Richard, *b.* 1949; ed. at Downside, and Fordham Univ., New York: *m.* 1972, Jeanne, da. of Eugene Tanzillo, of New York.

Issue of the late Capt. the Hon. Basil Egerton Feilding (3rd son of the late Lt.-Col. Rudolph Edmund Aloysius, Viscount Feilding, CMG, DSO, el. son of 9th Earl), *b.* 1916, *d.* 1970: *m.* 1939, Rosemary (ante), da. of the late Cdr. (Frederick) Neville Eardley-Wilmot, RN (ret.) [see Eardley-Wilmot, Bt.]:—

Peter Rudolph (127, London Rd., Burgess Hill, Sussex), *b.* 1941; ed. at Ampleforth: *m.* 1968, Diana Mourne, only da. of C. C. Cox, of Sandfield House, Coleshill St., Sutton Coldfield and has issue living , Basil James, *b.* 1974,——Chloe Louise, *b.* 1972.——Giles Anthony, *b.* 1950.——Crispin Everard, *b.* 1960.——Jennifer Mary FEILDING, *b.* 1947; resumed surname of Feilding by deed poll 1971: *m.* 1st, 1968 (m. diss. 1971), Graham F. Bond; 2ndly, 1974, Charles Eliot Crawley.——Imelda Jane, *b.* 1958.

Grandchildren of the late Gen. the Hon. Sir Percy Robert Basil Feilding, K.C.B., 2nd son of 7th Earl:—

Issue of the late Percy Henry Feilding, *b.* 1867, *d.* 1929: *m.* 1904, Clotilde, who *d.* 1937, only dau. of Henry Brewster, of The Palazzo Mattei, Rome:—

Basil Percy Terence Henry (of Beckley Park, Oxford), *b.* 1907: *m.* 1931, Margaret Mary, dau. of Lt.-Col. Rowland Charles Feilding, DSO (infra), and has issue living, Jocelyn Rupert Roland Geoffrey (9, Sion Rd., Twickenham, Middlesex), *b.* 1940; ed. at Downside: *m.* 1963, Rowena Marion, dau. of Capt. Simon Harvey Combe, M.C., of The Manor House, Burnham Thorpe, Norfolk [see E. Leicester], and has issue living, Emma Mary Clothilde *b.* 1964, Lucy Silvia Margaret *b.* 1966,—Julia Felicity Maria Gabrielle, *b.* 1933; Dip. Arch. Oxford 19—; an ARIBA: *m.* 1st, 1957 (m. diss. 1963), Leslie Rebanks; 2ndly, 1963, Donald Rhind Morrison, ARIBA, of Bridge End House, Dorchester-on-Thames, and has issue living, (by 1st m.) Leander Piers John *b.* 1960, Alexander Basil *b.* 1961, (by 2nd m.) Justin Guy Stuart Feilding *b.* 1964, Zuleika Jane Feilding *b.* 1963,—Chloë Mary Antonia (16, London Place, Oxford), *b.* 1936: *m.* 1962 (m. diss. 1973), David Coombes, and has issue living, Victoria Roque-Rebecca *b.* 1963,—Amanda Claire Marian, *b.* 1943.——Susan Louisa Mary, *b.* 1906: *m.* 1926, Maj.-Gen. Hugh Hibbert, DSO, late King's Own Yorks LI, of Sunton House, Collingbourne Ducis, Wilts., and has issue living, Robert Hugh *b.* 1929,—Evelyn Valery, *b.* 1927: *m.* 1952, Andrew D. H. Hingston (who assumed by deed poll 1969 the surname of Hibbert-Hingston), of Kilsall Hall, Shifnal, Salop, and has issue living, Mark Andrew Tilden *b.* 1953, James Hugh Trevillion *b.* 1960, Teresa Clotilde *b.* 1956.

Grandchildren of the late Rev. the Hon. Charles William Alexander Feilding, 4th son of 7th Earl:—

Issue of the late John Basil Feilding, *b.* 1868, *d.* 1942 : *m.* 1897, Emily Margaret, who *d*, 1955, dau. of Ewen Monteith Tod :—

Rev. Charles Rudolph. *S.T.D.*, *b.* 190?; ed. at Upper Canada Coll., at McGill Univ., at King's Coll., Nova Scotia (B.A. 1926), and at Gen. Theological Seminary, New York (B.D. 1931, Hon. Dr. of Sacred Theology 1949); was Fellow and Tutor of Gen. Theological Seminary, New York 1929-35, R. of St. Mary's Church, Staten Island, New York 1935-40, Prof. of Moral Theo., Trin. Coll., Toronto 1940-70, and Dean of Divinity 1947-61, since when Prof. Emeritus of Divinity: *m.* 1935, Ann, only da. of the late Ernest Truslow, of Southport, Connecticut, USA, and has issue living, Geoffrey Truslow (500, Gilmour St., Peterborough, Ont., Canada), *b.* 1939: *m.* 1966, Martha Anne, da. of John S. Corrigan, of Toronto, and has issue living, Charles Corrigan *b.* 1968,—Jonathan Corrigan *b.* 1970,—Goodith Mary, *b.* 1936: *m.* 1956, the Rev. Brian Heeney, DPhil, Master of Champlain Coll., Trent Univ., Peterborough, Ont., Canada, and has issue living, Michael Feilding *b.* 1957, Timothy Charles *b.* 1966, Matthew Macleod *b.* 1968, Ann *b.* 1961. *Residence,*—Suite 803, 10, Avoca Av., Toronto, M4T 2B7, Canada.

Issue of the late Lieut.-Col. Rowland Charles Feilding, D.S.O., *b.* 1871, *d.* 1945: *m.* 1903, Edith Mary, who *d.* 1961, dau. of the late Frederick Stapleton-Bretherton, of The Hall, Rainhill, Lancs. [B. Petre]:—

Joan Mary, *b.* 1904 : *m.* 1926, Brigadier Ian Robert Craufurd George Mary Bruce, D.S.O., M.B.E. (Cameron Highlanders) who *d.* 1956 [see Bruce, Bt., cr. 1628, colls.]. *Residence,*—Hampton Court Palace, East Molesey, Surrey.——Anita Mary, *b.* 1907 : *m.* 1931 (marriage dissolved 1949), Sir Basil Antony Trevor Mostyn (afterwards 13th Bt.), who *d.* 1956. *Residence,*—6, London Place, Oxford.——Margaret Mary, *b.* 1908 : *m.* 1931, Basil Percy Terence Henry Feilding (ante).——Prunella Mary Patricia, *b.* 1916 ; late Junior Com. A.T.S.: *m.* 1942, Charles Neil Howard, M.C., late Major Black Watch, and has issue living, Simon Neil. *b.* 1951,—Caroline Edith Mary, *b.* 1947,—Harriet Prunella Mary, *b.* 1948. *Residence,*—Lodge Farm, Stowood, Beckley, Oxon.

Grandchildren of the late Allen Fielding, son of the late Rev. Henry Fielding, el. son of the late Rev. Allen Fielding (son of the famous novelist), grandson of the late Rev. the Hon. John Fielding, D.D., son of 1st Earl of Desmond and brother of 3rd Earl of Denbigh:—

Issue of the late Henry Fielding, M.B.E. *b.* 1861, *d.* 1926: *m.* 1892, Amy Emma Cooper, who *d.* 1947 :—

Barbara, *b.* 1896: *m.* 1927, James Evelyn Thoresby, and has issue living, Henry Fielding, *b.* 1936; ed. at Harrow, and LSE (BSc); Bar. Middle Temple 1969; Legal Branch, Dept. of the Environment since 1971: *m.* 1971, Laura, da. of Julius Adams Stratton, of 800, Park Av., New York. *Residence,*—14, Lin 1 House Basil St. SW3.——Mary *b.* 1901 *m* 1933 Ma Reginald Horace Mould RA, who assumed by deed poll 1935, the surname of Fielding, in addition to and before that of Mould Resid nce,—Prestbury House, Smarden, nr. Ashford, Kent.

　　Issue of the late Geoffrey Kenmil Fielding, b. 1884, d. 1960: m. 1917, Elsie, da. of the late John Edward Watkins, of Shrewsbury:—
Allen Henry, b. 1919; ARIBA, ARAIA; 1939-45 War as Capt. R. Sussex Regt.: m. 1943, Estelle Teague, of The Old Hall, Builth, and has issue living, David Henry, b. 1944,—Barbara Ann, b. 1950: m. 1972, William Henderson, of Brunnel, Pastoral Co., Morven, Qld. 4468. Residence,—15, Peuno Parade North, Belair, Adelaide, S. Australia.——John Henry (twin), b. 1919; 1939-45 War as Lt. RA: m. 1948, Pamela Mary, only da. of John Alfred Spurdel Barnard, and has issue living, Simon Henry, b. 1949,—Geoffrey John, b. 1950. Residence,—14, Oakfield Gardens, Beckenham, Kent.

Grandchildren of the late Rev. George Frederick Marshall Fielding (infra):—
　　Issue of the late George Basil Feilding, b. 1889, d. 1959: m. 1st, 1918, Esmé (who d. 1961, having obtained a divorce 1932), dau. of the late Outram Kellie McCallum; 2ndly, 1932· Gertrude (of 24, New Metropole Hotel, The Leas, Folkestone, Kent), widow of G. A, Vickers:—
(By 1st marriage) Cecil Dolores, b. 1922: m. 1944, Major Charles William Auchmuty, late Indian Army, of Wood Cottage, Church Rd., Fleet, Hants, and has issue living, Susan Ann Esmé, b. 1950: m. 1972, David André Wavre,—Jane Dolores, b. 1955.

　　Issue of the late Henry Armitage Fielding, b. 1892, d. 1965: m. 1914, Ethel Mary Baldock (606, Rochester Way, Eltham, SE9):—
Henry George (132, Court Rd., Eltham, SE9), b. 1916: m. 1st, 1940, Anne Scargill, who d. 1965; 2ndly, 1965, Eirene Helen Sell, and has issue living, by (1st m.) Henry Michael Clive MSc (Flat 8, 22, Roslyn Gdns., Sydney, NSW), b. 1944: m. 1971, Lorraine Patricia Kirton,—George Peter Keith (101, Winthrop Rd., Bury St. Edmunds), b. 1945; Lt. RNAS: m. 1968, Gillian Margaret Stearn, and has issue living, Sarah Anne b. 1970, Emma Jade b. 1972,—John David Barry (Flat 8, 22, Roslyn Gdns., Sydney, NSW), b. 1946: m. 1968, Pamela Margaret Cann, and has issue living, Maxine Anne b. 1969,—Anthony Robert Max, b. 1948; Sub Lt. RNAS——Barbara Jean, b. 1917: m. 1st, 1940, Frank St. Omer, from whom she obtained a divorce 1952; 2ndly, 1952, Godfrey Aalten Allen Sweet, of 606, Rochester Way, Eltham, SE9 1RL, and has issue living, (by 1st m.) Judy Mary, b. 1942: m. 1970, Martin Moseling, of 28, Grange Rd., Gravesend, Kent, and has issue living, Mark Christian b. 1973, Emma June b. 1972,—(by 2nd m.) John Simon, b. 1954.

Granddaughter of the late George Fielding, son of the late Rev. Charles Fielding LL.B., son of the late Rev. Allen Fielding (ante):—
　　Issue of the late Rev. George Frederick Marshall Fielding, b. 1851, d. 1914 : m. 1888, Elizabeth, who d. 1950, dau. of John Armitage:—
Rosa, b. 1891: m. 1918, George Harold Whiteman, who d. 1957, formerly Ch. Officer, London Salvage Corps, and has issue living, Angela Beatrice, b. 1919: m. 1952, Lt.-Col. Clement Swetenham, MC, RE (ret.), of Kelmscott, Branksomewood Rd., Fleet, Hants., and has issue living, Richard Clement b. 1953, Elizabeth Angela b. 1954. Residence,—11, Hillside Court, Hythe, Kent.

　　Issue of the late Percy Fielding, b. 1866, d. 1950 : m. 1889, Alice, who d. 1935, dau. of the late George Webber, of Broken Hill, N.S. Wales:—
George Rudolph, b. 1889 ; European War 1914-19 in Canadian Forces: m. 1926, Marya Nagazina and has issue living, Ernest Rudolf, b. 1928,—Rosa Alice, b. 1927: m. 1944, John Boyd, of Drumheller' Alberta, and has issue living, Kathleen Anne b. 1945, Gloria Jean b. 1947,—Vera Marie, b. 1929: m. 1946, John Mackenzie Adamson, and has issue living, Carol Anne b. 1948, Gary Wesley b. 1951: Residence,—1770, 5th Av., Prince George, British Columbia.——Rosa Dorothy Mary, b. 1893, m. 1915, Edmund John Golledge, and has issue living, Arthur George, b. 1916,—Cyril Frank, b. 1918,—Robert Gerald, b. 1921. Residence,—Long Beach, California, U.S.A.

Granddaughters of the late Sir Charles William Fielding, KBE (infra):—
　　Issue of the late Rudolph Burton Fielding, b. 1902, d. 1970: m. 1939, Frances Adelaide (Okehurst, Billingshurst, Sussex), da. of George Green, of Dublin:—
Daphne Claire, b. 1942; MA Oxon; BA Camb.——Jean Eleanora Leckie, b. 1946: m. 1966, Terence Michael O'Flynn, of Hey House, Steeple Ashton, Wilts., and has issue living, Caspar Michael, b. 1969,—Emma Frances, b. 1966.

Granddaughters of the late Thomas Mantell Fielding, son of the late Rev. Charles Fielding, LL.B. (ante):—
　　Issue of the late Sir Charles William Fielding, K.B.E., b. 1863 ; d. 1941 : m. 1899, Florence, who d. 1958, dau. of the late James Willis Dixon, of Hillsborough Hall. Sheffield:—
Jean Kathleen Mary, b. 1900: m. 1st, 1925, Lt. Hugh Neville Clegg, RN, who d. 1929; 2ndly, 1944, Windsor Holden White, of Cleveland, Ohio, USA. Residences, 10, Lowndes Court, SW1; Polo Cottage, Midhurst, Sussex.——Pamela, b. 1906: m. 1937, as his second wife, Maj. William Walter Brough Scott, 1st Roy. Dragoons [see Scott, Bt., cr. 1907, colls.]. Residence,—Folly House, Bampton, Oxford.

Grandson of the late Rev. George Hanbury Fielding, son of the late Rev. Georg Fielding, son of the late Rev. Allen Fielding (ante):—
　　Issue of the late Major George Rudolf Fielding, Sherwood Foresters (Notts. and Derbyshire Regt.), b. 1881, d. (killed in action during European War) 1915 : m. 1914, Evelyn Carlota, dau. of Edward Jewell, formerly of Clifton Court, Bournemouth:—
George Rudolf Hanbury, D.S.O., b. 1915; ed. at Shrewsbury; Major (retired) 3rd King's Own Hussars; European War 1939-45 (wounded, D.S.O.): D.S.O. 1945 : m. 1946, Beatrice Georgina, da. of Maj. Maurice Pope, and has issue living, Martin George Rudolf, b. 1945; ed. at Eton; Capt. (ret.) Queen's Own Hussars,—Sarah Georgina (Hon. Mrs. Guy B. Norrie), b. 1947: m. 1968, the Honl Guy Bainbridge Norrie, of 21, Radipole Rd., Fulham, SW6 5DN [see B. Norrie]. Address,—Vat D'ogoz, Chateau d'Oex, Vaud, Switzerland.

PREDECESSORS.—[1] Sir WILLIAM Feilding, Knt., was cr. Baron Feilding, of Newnham Paddox, Warwickshire, Viscount Feilding (peerage of England) 1620, and Earl of Denbigh (peerage of England) 1622; a faithful adherent of Charles I.; killed in a skirmish near Birmingham 1643; his 2nd son Sir George, K.B., was in 1622 cr. Baron Feilding, of Lecaghe, Viscount Callan and Earl of Desmond (peerage of Ireland); s. by his el. son [2] BASIL, 2nd Earl, was one of the most eminent of the Parliament's Mil. Commanders; cr. after the restoration of the monarchy Baron St. Liz 1663, with remainder to the male issue of his father ; d.s.p. 1675: s. by his nephew [3] WILLIAM, 3rd Earl, who had in 1665 s. his father George (ante) as 2nd Earl of Desmond; d. 1685; s. by his son [4] BASIL, 4th Earl; d. 1717; s. by his son [5] WILLIAM 5th Earl; d. 1755; s. by his son [6] BASIL, 6th Earl, b. 1719: m. 1757, Mary, who d. 1782, 3rd dau. of Sir John Bruce Cotton, 6th Bt. ; d. 1800; s. by his grandson [7] WILLIAM BASIL PERCY, D.C.L. (el. son of William Robert Basil, Viscount Feilding, el. son of 6th Earl), 7th Earl, b. 1796 ; Master of the Horse to Queen Adelaide: m. 1822, Mary Elizabeth Kitty, who d. 1842, el. dau. of 1st Earl of Ducie; d. 1865 ; s. by his son [8] RUDOLPH WILLIAM BASIL, 8th Earl, b. 1823 : m. 1st, 1846, Louise, who d. 1853, dau. of David Pennant, of Downing, Flint; 2ndly, 1857, Mary, who d. 1901, dau. of Robert Berkeley; d. 1892; s. by his el. son [9] RUDOLPH ROBERT BASIL ALOYSIUS AUGUSTINE, G.C.V.O., 9th Earl, b. 1859;

Col. T.A. (retired); a Lord-in-Waiting to H.M. Queen Victoria 1897-1901 and to H.M. King Edward VII. 1901-1905: *m.* 1st, 1884, the Hon. Cecilia Mary Clifford, who *d.* 1919, dau. of 8th Baron Clifford of Chudleigh; 2ndly, 1923, Kathleen, who *d.* 1952, dau. of the late Thomas Addis Emmet, of New York, U.S.A.; *d.* 1939; *s.* by his grandson [10] WILLIAM RUDOLPH STEPHEN (el. son of the late Lieut.-Col. Rudolph Edmund Aloysius, Viscount Feilding, C.M.G., D.S.O., el. son of 9th Earl), 10th Earl of Denbigh and 9th Earl of Desmond, *b.* 1912: *m.* 1940, Verena Barbara, da. of William Edward Price, and widow of Lt.-Col. Thomas Paget Fielding Johnson; *d.* 1966; *s.* by his only son [11]WILLIAM RUDOLPH MICHAEL, 11th Earl of Denbigh and 10th Earl of Desmond and present peer; also Viscount Callan, Viscount Feilding, Baron Feilding, and Baron St. Liz.

DENHAM, BARON. (Bowyer.) [Baron U.K. 1937, Bt. England 1660 and U.K. 1933.]

Contentment surpasses riches.

BERTRAM STANLEY MITFORD BOW-YER, 2nd Baron, 10th Baronet of Denham, and 2nd Baronet of Weston Underwood; *b.* Oct. 3rd, 1927; *s.* to the Barony and Baronetcy of Bowyer of Weston Underwood (cr. 1933) 1948, and to the Baronetcy of Bowyer of Denham (cr.1660) 1950; ed. at Eton, and at King's Coll., Camb.; late Lieut. Oxford and Bucks L.I.; a Lord-in-Waiting to HM 1961-64, and again 1970-71; Capt. of Yeomen of the Guard and Dep. Ch. Whip 1971-74; *m.* 1956, Jean, only da. of Kenneth McCorquodale, MC, TD, of Fambridge Hall, White Notley, Essex, and has issue.

Arms,—Or, a bend vaire cottised sable. *Crest,*—A falcon rising, belled or. *Supporters,*— *Dexter,* a golden retriever; *sinister,* a black greyhound proper, each charged on the shoulder with a portcullis or.

Residence,—The Laundry Cottage, Weston Underwood, Olney, Bucks. *Clubs,*—White's, Pratt's.

SONS LIVING.
Hon. RICHARD GRENVILLE GEORGE, *b.* Feb. 8th, 1959.
Hon. Henry Martin Mitford, *b.* 1963.
Hon. George Philip Paul, *b.* 1964.

DAUGHTER LIVING.
Hon. Jocelyn Jane, *b.* 1957.

SISTER LIVING.
Hon. Peggy, *b.* 1925: *m.* 1947 .Cdr. John David Latimer Repard, OBE, DSC, RN, and has issue living, Jennifer Ann, *b.* 1948: *m.* 1970, Peter William Allen, of Chearsley, Bucks., and has issue living, William John Kenneth *b.* 1974,—Susan Elisabeth, *b.* 1950,—Melinda Louise, *b.* 1955. *Residence,*—Pheasant Lodge, The Common, Berkhamsted, Herts.

WIDOW LIVING OF FIRST BARON.
Hon. DAPHNE FREEMAN-MITFORD (*Dowager Baroness Denham*), da. of 1st Baron Redesdale: *m.* 1919, the 1st Baron, who *d.* 1948. *Residence,*—10, West St., Olney, Bucks.

COLLATERAL BRANCH LIVING. (*In remainder to Baronetcy of Bowyer of Denham* [*cr.* 1660] *only.*)

Grandchildren of the late Lt.-Col. Wentworth Grenville Bowyer, 2nd son of the late Rev. William Henry Wentworth Atkins-Bowyer, 2nd son of the late Maj. William Atkins-Bowyer, el. son of the late Richard Atkins-Bowyer, 5th son of 3rd baronet of Denham:—
Issue of the late Lt.-Cdr. John Francis Bowyer, CB, RN (Emergency List), *b.* 1893, *d.* 1974: *m.* 1919, Violet (1, Avenue Lodge, Avenue Rd., NW8), da. of Maj.-Gen. George Robert James Shakespear, Indian Army, and widow of Maj. Egerton Lowndes Wright, MC:—
Peter George Grenville (7, Foxhill Rd., Scarborough, Ontario, Canada), *b.* 1920, late Fl. Lt., RAF: *m.* 1951, Mary Bayliss, of Toronto, Canada.——Hugh Edward Wentworth, *b.* 1921; Bar. Inner Temple 1947; late Maj. Rifle Brig.: *m.* 1942, Suzette, da. of Capt. Peter Longton, of Heatherwold, Burgh-clere, Newbury, and has issue living, James David Ross, *b.* 1949,—Sally Ann, *b.* 1945.——John Robert Patrick (Rectory Farm House, W. Hanney, Wantage, Berks.), *b.* 1924: *m.* 1948, Diana, da. of the late J. P. Longland, of Olney, Bucks., and has issue living, David Hugh, *b.* 1950,—Sabrina Violet, *b.* 1949,—Sarah Joy, *b.* 1958,—Diana Jane, *b.* 1965.——Michael Christopher (149, Rivermead Court, SW6), *b.* 1926: *m.* 1952, Elizabeth Anne, da. of Cdr. Stuart J. Layton Bennett, RN.—— Penelope Rosemary Joy MOUNTLANGEN (twin) (Ockenden, White Rose Lane, Woking, Surrey), *b.* 1926; assumed by deed poll 1968, the surname of Mountlangen: *m.* 1955 (m. annulled 1963), Derek Langenberg.

PREDECESSORS.—[1] GEORGE EDWARD WENTWORTH Bowyer, *M.C.*, son of the late Lieut.-Col. Wentworth Grenville Bowyer, el. son of the late Rev. William Henry Wentworth Atkins-Bowyer, great-grandson of 3rd Bt. of Denham (cr. 1660); *b.* 1886; Major late Oxfordshire and Bucks L.I.; Parliamentary Private Sec. (unpaid) to Pres. of Board of Trade 1921-24; Conservative Party Whip in House of Commons 1925-35, Vice-Chm. Conservative and Unionist Party Organisation 1930-36, a Junior Lord of the Treasury 1926-29, Comptroller of H.M.'s Household June to Dec. 1935, and Parliamentary Sec. to Min. of Agriculture and Fisheries 1939-40; a Conservative Whip in House of Lords 1945-47; European War 1914-18 (wounded, despatches, M.C.); sat as M.P. for Buckingham Div. of Buckinghamshire (*U*) 1918-37; cr. a Knt. 1929, a *Baronet* 1933, and *Baron Denham* of Weston Underwood, co. Buckingham (peerage of United Kingdom) 1937: *m.* 1919, the Hon. Daphne Freeman-Mitford, dau. of 1st Baron Redesdale; *d.* 1948: *s.* by his son [2] BERTRAM STANLEY MITFORD, 2nd Baron and present peer.

,°[1] *Sir* WILLIAM Bowyer, el. son of Sir Henry Bowyer, of Denham Court, Bucks; *b.* 1612; M.P. for Bucks 1659-60, and 1661-79 (Sheriff 1646-47); cr. a *Baronet* 1660: *m.* 1634, Margaret, who *d.* 1678, dau. of John Weld, of Arnolds, Edmonton, Middlesex: *d.* 1679; *s.* by his el. son [2] WILLIAM, 2nd Bt.; *b.* 1639: *m.* 1679, the Hon. Frances, who *d.* 1723, dau. of Charles Cecil, Viscount Cran-borne, son of 2nd Earl of Salisbury; *d.* 1722; *s.* by his grandson [3] WILLIAM (el. son of the late Cecil Bowyer, el. son of 2nd Bt.), 3rd Bt.; *b.* 1710: *m.* 1733, Anne, who *d.* 1785, dau. of the Rt. Hon.

Sir John Stonhouse, M.P., 7th and 4th Bt. of Radley, Berks; *d.* 1767: *s.* by his el. son [4] WILLIAM
4th Bt., *b.* 1736; Capt. The Guards: *m.* 1776, Anne, who *d.* 1802, dau. of — Carey, and widow of
Capt. James Baker, R.N.; *d.* 1799; *s.* by his brother [5] GEORGE, 5th Bt., *b.* 1739; Adm.; M.P. for
Queenborough 1784-90; distinguished himself in Lord Howe's naval victory over the French, June
1st, 1794, for which he was rewarded with an annual pension of £1,000, and was cr. a *Baronet* 1794 (of
Radley, Berks.): *m.* 1st, 1768, Margaret, who *d.* 1778, dau. of the Rev. — Price, curate of Barrington, Gloucestershire, and widow of Sir Jacob Garrard Downing, 4th Bt.; 2ndly, 1782, Henrietta,
who *d.* 1845, dau. of Adm. Sir Piercy Brett, of Beckenham, Kent; *d.* 1799; *s.* by his el. son [6]
GEORGE, 6th Bt., *b.* 1783; M.P. for Malmesbury 1807-10, and for Abingdon 1811-18: *m.* 1808,
Anne Hammond, who *d.* 1844, dau. of Capt. Sir Andrew Snape Douglas, R.N.; *d.* 1860; *s.* by his
el. son [7] GEORGE, 7th Bt., *b.* 1811; M.P. (*L*) for Dundalk 1852-68, and for Wexford 1874-80; *d.*
1883; *s.* by his brother [8] WILLIAM, 8th Bt., *b.* 1812: *m.* 1857, Ellen Sarah, who *d.* 1899, dau. of
Shirley Foster Woolmer, Bar.-at-law; *d.* 1893; *s.* by his nephew [9] GEORGE HENRY (only son of
the late Henry George Bowyer, youngest son of 6th Bt.), 9th Bt.; *b.* 1870; Lieut. Cheshire Mil.:
m. 1899, Ethel (from whom he obtained a divorce 1900), dau. of Francis Hawkins; *d.* 1950; *s.* by
his kinsman [10] BERTRAM STANLEY MITFORD (ante).

DENMAN, BARON. (Denman.) [Baron UK 1834, Bt. UK 1945.]

CHARLES SPENCER DENMAN, *MC*, 5th
Baron, and 2nd Baronet (of Staffield, co.
Cumberland); *b.* July 7th, 1916; *s.* as
2nd Bt. 1957, and as 5th Baron, 1971;
ed. at Shrewsbury; late Maj. DCLI
(TA); 1939-45 War in Middle East
(MC): *m.* 1943, Shelia Anne, da. of the
late Lt.-Col. Algernon Bingham Anstruther Stewart, DSC [see E. Galloway,
colls.], and has issue.

Arms.—Argent, on a chevron between three
lions' heads erased gules, as many ermine spots or.
Crest.—A raven rising proper, in the beak an
annulet or. *Supporters.*—On either side a lion
gules, charged on the body with five ermine spots in
cross or.

Residence,—Highden House, Washington,
Sussex.

SONS LIVING.
Hon. RICHARD THOMAS STEWART, *b.* Oct. 4th, 1946;
ed. at Milton Abbey.
Hon. James Stewart, *b.* 1954.
Hon. Christopher John, *b.* 1955.

DAUGHTER LIVING.
Hon. Gillian Patricia, *b.* 1944: *m.* 1971, William K. McCall, of Caitloch, Moniaivie, Dumfries-shire,
and has issue living, Hamish Spencer Murray, *b.* 1972.

BROTHERS LIVING.
Harold (4, Selwood Terr., SW1), *b.* 1922; ed. at Repton, and Balliol Coll., Oxford (BA); 1939-45 War
with RA.
George (5, Scarsdale Villas, W8), *b.* 1925; 1939-45 War with Border Regt.: *m.* 1960, Linda Louisa,
yr. da. of David Fortune Landale, of Dalswinton, Dumfries, and has issue living, Louisa Anne,
b. 1961,—Carola Jane, *b.* 1963,—Davina, *b.* 1968.

SISTERS LIVING.
Phyllis (1, Hazel Grove, Arundel, Sussex), *b.* 1919; MRCS England and LRCP London.
Catherine (c/o Barclays Bank, Carlisle), *b.* 1920: *m.* 1957, Philip Musgrave Cowburn, and has issue
living, Stephen Denman, *b.* 1959,—Anne Clare, *b.* 1962.

DAUGHTER LIVING OF THIRD BARON.
Hon. Anne Judith (*Hon. Lady Burrell*), *OBE, b.* 1907; ed. at Camb. Univ. (BA 1929); formerly Chm. of
Women's Land Army, W. Sussex, Vice-Pres. of Family Planning Assocn., OBE (Civil) 1947: *m.* 1931,
Lt.-Col. Sir Walter Raymond Burrell, CBE, TD, DL, 8th Bt. *Residence,*—Knepp Castle, Horsham.

COLLATERAL BRANCHES LIVING.
(*Not in remainder to the Baronetcy.*)

Grandchildren of the late *Hon.* Richard Denman, 3rd son of 1st Baron:—
Issue of the late Thomas Hugh Anderson Denman, *b.* 1855, *d.* 1918: *m.* 1896, Margaret
Evelyn, who *d.* 1933, dau. of the late Charles Watson Townley, of Fulbourn Manor,
Cambridge:—
Margaret Cecil, *b.* 1898: *m.* 1927, Charles Seymour Eastwood, M.C. [E. Shrewsbury, colls.], and has
issue living, Richard Seymour (Orchard Bank, South St., Broadchalke, Salisbury), *b.* 1932: is
Maj. RA: *m.* 1957, Alice Brenda, da. of Herbert Hall, of Fenwick, and has issue living, Elizabeth
Jane *b.* 1959, Katherine Mary Cecil *b.* 1961, Helen Margaret *b.* 1965,—Mary Cecil, *MBE* (9D, Observa-
tory Gdns., W8), *b.* 1927; MBE (Civil) 1961,—Ann Bridget, *b.* 1930: *m.* 1957, David Gordon Rix
Bentliff, of 5, Eversley Rd., SE19, and has issue living, Caroline Sarah *b.* 1958, Georgina Mary
b. 1960. *Residence,*—Tree House, Plaxtol, nr. Sevenoaks.

Grandchildren of the late Sir Arthur Denman, 2nd son of the late Rt. Hon. George
Denman, 4th son of 1st Baron:—
Issue of the late Lieut.-Col. Roderick Peter George Denman, Roy. Corps of Signals,
b. 1894, *d.* (killed in action during European War) 1941: *m.* 1922, Charlotte Marie
Mathilde, *M.B.E.* (of Monmouth House, 24, Lawrence Street, S.W.3), dau. of the late
Baron Raphael d'Erlanger [Blennerhassett, Bt.]:—
Peter Frederick Arthur, *b.* 1923; ed. at Eton, and at Trin. Coll., Camb. (B.A. 19—): *m.* 1957, Cornelia
Rowena (JANSON), dau. of the late Hon. (Oscar) Montague Guest [see V. Wimborne, colls.], and has
issue living, Philip Roderick, *b.* 1961,—Benedict Raphael, *b.* 1970,—Francesca Marie-Carola, *b.* 1959.
Residence,—Duke's House, 23, Lawrence St., SW3.——Carol Antonia Rosaline, *b.* 1928.

Issue of the late Henry du Bourg Denman, b. 1918, d. 1938: m. 1936, Joy, dau. of George
        Henry Hatton:—
Carol Julian du Bourg (son), b. 1938. Residence,—

Grandchildren of the late Lewis William Eden Denman (infra):—
Issue of the late Joseph Alban Denman, b. 1890, d. 1965: m. 1919, Annie Mary, who d. 1954
        da. of Thomas Spicer, of Sask., Canada:—
George Lewis (Cartin RR1, Notch Hill, BC, Canada), b. 1920: m. 1st, 1949, Emily Woodgate who
        d. 1956; 2ndly, 1963, Catherine Woodgate, da. of W. A. C. Batchelor, of Water Valley, Alberta,
        and has issue living, (by 1st marriage) Robert John, b. 1952,—Ronald Dean, b. 1954,—Dorothy
        Louisa, b. 1951: m. 1971, Robert Honeyman.——David Keith (Box 20, RR1, Prince George, BC,
        Canada), b. 1937: m. 1957, Helen Balko, and has issue living, Stephen Lawrence, b. 1961,—Stacey
        Eldon, b. 1968,—Shaun Lewis Eden, b. 1973,—Debra Ann, b. 1958,—Denise Josephine, b. 1965.——
        Joan Gwendoline, b. 1925: m. 1959, Maurice J. Parfitt.

Granddaughter of the late Rev. the Hon. Lewis William Denman, 5th son of
        1st Baron:—
Issue of the late Lewis William Eden Denman, b. 1857, d. 1947: m. 1889, Emma, who d.
        1936, dau. of Charles Rainbow:—
Theodosia Victoria, b. 1897. Residence,—The Elms, Church Norton, Selsey, Chichester.

PREDECESSORS.—[1] Sir THOMAS Denman, b. 1779; M.P. for Nottingham, Attorney-Gen.
        1830-2 and Lord Ch. Justice of England 1832-50; cr. Baron Denman, of Dovedale (peerage of
        United Kingdom) 1834: m. 1804, Theodosia Anne, dau. of the late Rev. Richard Vevers,
        Rector of Saxby; d. 1854; s. by his son [2] THOMAS, 2nd Baron, b. 1805; Bar. Lincoln's Inn
        1833; Marshal and Associate to his father 1832-50; assumed by Roy. licence 1876 the additional
        surname of Aitchison: m. 1st, 1829, Georgiana, who d. 1871, el. dau. of the late Rev. Thomas
        Roe; 2ndly, 1871, Marion, who d. 1902, el. dau. and co-heiress of James Aitchison, of Alderston
        and Morham, N.B.; d. 1894; s. by his great nephew [3] THOMAS, G.C.M.G., K.C.V.O., P.C., (el. son
        of the late Richard Denman, grandson of 1st Baron), 3rd Baron; b. 1874; was a Lord-in-Waiting to
        King Edward VII 1905-7, Capt. of H.M.'s Hon. Corps of Gentlemen-at-Arms 1907-11, Dep. Speaker
        in House of Lords, 1909, and Gov.-Gen. of Commonwealth of Australia 1911-14: m. 1903, the Hon.
        Dame Gertrude Mary Pearson, G.B.E., who d. 1954, dau. of 1st Viscount Cowdray; d. 1954: s. by
        his only son [4] THOMAS, 4th Baron; b. 1905; d. 1971; s. by his cousin [5] CHARLES SPENCER (el. son
        of the Hon. Sir Richard Douglas Denman, who was cr. a Baronet (UK) 1945), 5th Baron, and present
        peer.

DENNING, BARON. (Denning.) [Life Baron 1957.]

ALFRED THOMPSON DENNING, P.C., son of the late Charles Denning, of
Whitchurch, Hants ; b. Jan. 23rd, 1899 ; ed. at Magdalen Coll., Oxford (Hon.
Fellow 1948) ; Hon. LL.D. Ottawa 1955, Glasgow and Southampton 1959,
London 1960, Camb. 1963, Leeds 1964, McGill 1967, Dallas 1969, and Dalhousie
1970 ; Hon. DCL Oxford, 1965 ; Bar. Lincoln's Inn 1923, a KC 1938, and a
Bencher 1944 ; Chancellor of Diocese of Southwark 1937-44, and of London
1942-44, a Judge of the High Court of Justice 1944-48, a Lord Justice of
Appeal 1948-57, and a Lord of Appeal in Ordinary 1957-62, since when Master
of the Rolls ; conducted Profumo Inquiry 1963 ; 1914-18 War in France with
RE ; cr. Knt. 1944, PC 1948, and Baron Denning, of Whitchurch, co. Southamp-
ton (Life Baron) 1957: m. 1st, 1932, Mary, who d. 1941, da. of the late Rev.
F. N. Harvey, R. of Fawley, Hants.; 2ndly, 1945, Joan Daria, da. of John
Vinings Elliott Taylor, and widow of John Matthew Blackwood Stuart,
CIE, and has issue by 1st m.

Residence,—The Lawn, Whitchurch, Hants. Club,—Athenæum.

SON LIVING. (By 1st marriage.)
Hon. Robert Gordon, b. 1938; ed. at Winchester, and at Magdalen Coll., Oxford (Fellow 1968): m. 1967,
        Elizabeth Carlyle Margaret, da. of E. R. Chilton, of Oxford, and has issue.

DERAMORE, BARON. (de Yarburgh-Bateson.) [Baron U.K. 1885, Bt. U.K. 1818.]

We fly by night.

RICHARD ARTHUR DE YARBURGH-
BATESON, 6th Baron, and 7th
Baronet; b. April 9th, 1911; s.
1964; ed. at Harrow, and at St.
John's Coll., Camb. (MA); 1939-45
War as Fl.-Lt. RAFVR: m. 1948,
Janet Mary, da. of the late John
Ware, MD, of Nether Close, Askam-
in-Furness, and has issue.

Arms.—Quarterly, 1st and 4th grand
quarters, 1st and 4th argent, three bats' wings
erect sable, on a chief gules, a lion passant or,
Bateson; 2nd and 3rd per pale argent and azure,
a chevron between three chaplets counterchanged, de Yarburgh. 2nd and 3rd grand
quarters, argent three lions dormant in pale
sable between two flaunches of the last, each
charged with three mullets palewise of the first,
Lloyd. Crests.—1st, a bat's wing as in the arms;
2nd, a falcon close or, belled gold, preying on a
mallard proper. Supporters—Two lions or,
each gorged with a collar gemel gules, and
pendant therefrom an escutcheon ermine, that on
the dexter charged with a bat's wing as in the
arms, and that on the sinister with a raven
proper. Second Motto,—" Non est sine pulvere
palma" (The prize is not won without dust).

Residence,—Heslington House, Aislaby, Pickering, Yorks.

DAUGHTER LIVING.
Hon. Ann Katharine, b. 1950.

DAUGHTER LIVING OF FIFTH BARON.

Hon. Jane Faith (Baroness Mowbray, Segrave and Stourton), b. 1933: m. 1952, the 26th Baron Mowbray, Seagrave and Stourton. Residences,—23, Warwick Sq., S.W.1; Marcus, by Forfar, Angus.

DAUGHTER LIVING OF FOURTH BARON.

Hon. Judith Katharine, b. 1909. Residence,—Heslington House, Aislaby, Pickering, Yorks.

DAUGHTER LIVING OF THIRD BARON.

Hon. Moira Faith Lilian, b. 1898 : m. 1st, 1919 (marriage annulled on her petition 1923), John Robert Rankin Fullerton, sometime Lieut. 19th Hussars ; 2ndly, 1924, as his second wife, Sir Edward George Chichester, 10th Bt., who d. 1940, and from whom she had obtained a divorce 1935. Residences,—16, Rutland Gate, Knightsbridge, SW7; 3, Metropole Court, Regency Sq., Brighton, 1.

WIDOW LIVING OF SON OF SECOND BARON.

Elsie Florence, dau. of the late H. Jones, and widow of Capt. Charles Cottam, M.C., Hampshire Regt.: m. 1927, the Hon. Eustace de Yarburgh-Bateson, who d. 1958. Residence,—Blackboro' Lodge, Lincoln Sq., Hunstanton, Norfolk.

WIDOW LIVING OF FIFTH BARON

NINA MARION, OBE (Nina Baroness Deramore) (6, Eaton Place, SW1), da. of the late Alastair Macpherson-Grant [see Macpherson-Grant, Bt., colls.]; a CStJ, and Branch Patron of British Red Cross Soc., Humberside; OBE (Civil) 1956: m. 1929, the 5th Baron, who d. 1964.

PREDECESSORS.—[1] ROBERT BATESON; M.P. for Londonderry (C) 1830-42; cr. a Baronet 1818; b. 1782: m. 1811, Catherine, dau. of the late Samuel Dickson, of Ballynaguile, Limerick; d. 1863; s. by his son [2] Sir THOMAS, 2nd Bt., who was cr. Baron Deramore, of Belvoir, co. Down (peerage of United Kingdom) 1885, with remainder to his younger brother, George William Bateson-de Yarburgh; b. 1819; sat as M.P. for Londonderry (C) 1844-57, and for Devizes 1864-85; a Lord of the Treasury 1852: m. 1849, the Hon. Caroline Elizabeth Anne Rice-Trevor, who d. 1887, dau. of 4th Baron Dinevor; d. 1890; s. by his brother [3] GEORGE WILLIAM, 2nd Baron; b. 1823; assumed by Roy. licence 1876, the additional surname of de Yarburgh, and in 1892 the surname of Bateson after that of de Yarburgh: m. 1862, Mary Elizabeth, who d. 1884, dau. of George John Yarburgh, of Heslington Hall, York: d. 1893; s. by his el. son [4] ROBERT WILFRID, T.D., 3rd Baron; b. 1865; Lord-Lieut. for E. Riding of Yorkshire, and Lieut.-Col. late Yorkshire Hussars Yeo. : m. 1st, 1897, Lucy Caroline, who d. 1901, dau. of the late William Henry Fife, of Lee Hall, Northumberland; 2ndly, 1907, Blanche Violet, who d. 1972, el. da. of Col. Philip Saltmarshe, formerly RA, of Saltmarshe, East Yorkshire; d. 1936; s. by his brother [5] GEORGE NICHOLAS, 4th Baron: b. 1870; m. 1900, Muriel Katharine, who d. 1960, da. of the late Arthur Grey; d. 1943, s. by his el. son [6] STEPHEN NICHOLAS, 5th Baron, b. 1903: m. 1929, Nina Marion, OBE, da. of the late Alastair Macpherson-Grant; d. 1964, s. by his brother [7] RICHARD ARTHUR, 6th Baron and present peer.

DE RAMSEY, BARON. (Fellowes.)   [Baron U.K. 1887.]

Patience and perseverance with magnanimity.

AILWYN EDWARD FELLOWES, KBE, 3rd Baron; b. March 16th, 1910; s. 1925; ed. at Oundle; is Capt. RA (TA), and patron of four livings; Lord-Lt. of Hunts. 1947-65, and of Huntingdon and Peterborough 1965-68; 1939-45 War (prisoner); KBE (Civil) 1974: m. 1937, Lilah Helen Suzanne, da. of the late Francis Anthony Labouchere [Stirling, Bt., cr. 1800 (ext.)], and has issue.

Arms,—Azure, a fesse dancettée ermine between three lions' heads erased or, murally crowned argent. Crest,—A lion's head as in the arms, charged with a fesse dancettée ermine. Supporters.—On either side a ram proper gorged with a chain or, pendant herefrom an escutcheon ermine charged with ram's eye also proper.

Residence,—Abbots Ripton Hall, Huntingdon.

SONS LIVING.

Hon. JOHN AILWYN (Abbey House, Ramsey, Huntingdon), b. Feb. 27th, 1942; ed. at Winchester: m. 1973, Phyllida Mary, yr. da. of Philip Athelstan Forsyth, MRCS, LRCP, of The Poplars, Wickhambrook, Suffolk.

Hon. Andrew Edward (Bodsey House, Ramsey, Huntingdon), b. 1950: m. 1974, Anne Mary, da. of Roy Tweedy, of Mungle, North Star; NSW.

DAUGHTERS LIVING.

Hon. Sarah, b. 1938.

Hon. Jennifer Julia, b. 1940: m. 1964, John Frederick Moxon, of Roundwood, Bury Rd., Ramsey, Huntingdon, and has issue living, Simon John, b. 1965,—Matthew Sebastian, b. 1967,—Christian Frederick, b. 1974,—Alice Lavinia, b. 1966,—Emily Faith Martha, b. 1972.

HALF-BROTHER LIVING. (Raised to the rank of a Baron's son 1933.)

Hon. (John) David Coulson (12, Birkirkara Hill, St. Julians, Malta, G.C.), b. 1915; ed. at Eton, and at Univ. Coll., Oxford (BA); ed. 2nd Lieut. Rifle Brig.: 1939-45 War in France (wounded, despatches, prisoner): m. 1st, 1946, Louise (MACKAY) (m. diss. 1962), da. of Lt. Sir James Henry Domville, RN, 5th Bt.; 2ndly, 1963, Joan Lynette (NEAME), who d. 1965, only da. of Edgar G. Rees, of Llanelli, and has issue living, (by 1st m.) Peter Reginald, b. 1948.—Jacqueline Denise, b. 1955.

COLLATERAL BRANCHES LIVING.

Issue of the late Hon. Reginald Ailwyn Fellowes, 2nd son of 2nd Baron, b. 1884, d. 1953: m. 1919, Marguerite, who d. 1962, dau. of 4th Duc Decazes, and widow of Prince Jean de Broglie:—

Rosamond Daisy, b. 1921: m. 1st, 1941 (divorce 1945), James Gustavus Gladstone, Lieut. King's Own Scottish Borderers [E. Shrewsbury, colls.]; 2ndly, 1952, Tadeusz Maria Wiszniewski, and has issue living, (by 1st m.) Reginald James, *b.* 1943; ed. at Eton: *m.* 1965, Mary Valentine, da. of the late L. A. Chiodetti, of Orondall, Surrey,—(by 2nd m.) Diana Marguerite, *b.* 1953. *Address,*— R.R.2, Newmarket, Ontario, Canada.

Issue of the late Rt. Hon. Sir Ailwyn Edward Fellowes, K.C.V.O., K.B.E. (2nd **son** of 1st Baron), who was cr. *Baron Ailwyn* 1921 [see that title].

PREDECESSORS.—[1] Edward Fellowes, *b.* 1809 ; M.P. for Huntingdonshire (*C*) 1837-80; cr. *Baron De Ramsey*, of Ramsey Abbey, Huntingdon (peerage of United Kingdom), July 5th, 1887 : *m.* 1845, Hon. Mary Julia Milles, el. dau. of 4th Baron Sondes; *d.* Aug. 9th, 1887; *s.* by his el. son [2] William Henry, 2nd Baron, *b.* 1848 ; M.P. for Huntingdonshire (*C*) 1880-85, and for N., or Ramsey, Div. of Huntingdonshire 1885-7 ; a Lord-in-Waiting to Queen Victoria 1890-92 : *m.* 1877, Lady Rosamond Jane Frances Spencer-Churchill, who *d.* 1920, dau. of 7th Duke of Marlborough, K.G.; *d.* 1925 ; *s.* by his grandson [3] Ailwyn Edward (son of the late Capt. the Hon. Coulson Churchill Fellowes, 1st Life Guards, el. son of 2nd Baron), 3rd Baron and present peer.

DERBY, EARL OF. (Stanley.) [Earl E. 1485, Bt. E. 1627.]

Without changing.

Edward John Stanley, *M.C.,* 18th Earl, and 12th Baronet : *b.* April 21st, 1918 ; *s.* 1948 ; ed. at Eton and at Oxford Univ. ; late Maj. Gren. Gds. (Res.); Hon. Col. 5th/ 8th (Vol.) Bn., King's Regt. (Comdg.) 5th Bn. 1947-51, Hon. Col. 1951-67 and 4th (Vol.) Bn., Queen's Lancashire Regt. TAVR Hon. Col. 1st and 2nd Bn. Lancastrian Vols. 1967-75; Hon. Capt. Mersey Div., RNR; Hon. LLD Liverpool and Lancaster, Pres. of Cotton Research Corpn. since 1957, and Merseyside Chamber of Commerce 1972. Lord-Lt. of co. Lancaster 1951-68; Pro-Chancellor of Univ. of Lancaster 1964-71; Pres. of N-W Prov. Area Council of National Union of Conservative Assocns. 1969-72; Constable of Lancaster Castle since 1972; 1939-45 War in Italy (MC): *m.* 1948, Lady Isabel, da. of the late Henry Augustus Mills-Lade [see E. Sondes]. **Arms,**—Argent, on a bend azure, three bucks' heads, cabossed or. **Crest,**—On a chapeau gules, turned up ermine, an eagle wings extended, or, preying on a child proper, swaddled gules, in a cradle laced or.

Supporters,—*Dexter,* a griffin, wings elevated, or, ducally collared, and line reflexed over the back azure ; *sinister,* a stag, or, collared and lined as the dexter.
Seats,—Knowsley, Prescot ; Stanley House, Newmarket.

BROTHER LIVING.

Hon. RICHARD OLIVER, *b.* Jan. 29th, 1920; ed. at Eton, and at Trin. Coll., Camb.; is Chm. Lancashire and Cheshire Federation of Boys' Clubs, and of the Lancashire Playing Fields Assocn.; 1939-45 War as Capt. Grenadier Guards; MP for N. Fylde Div. of Lancashire (*C*) 1950-66; Joint Treasurer Conservative Party 1963-66: *m.* 1965 Susan Mary Fynvola, only da. of Lt.-Col. Sir John Henry Lancelot Aubrey-Fletcher 7th Bt. *Residence,*—New England Stud, Newmarket, Suffolk.

WIDOW LIVING OF GRANDSON OF SEVENTEENTH EARL.

Mary Rose (47, Flood St., SW3), da. of Charles Francis Birch, of Rhodesia: *m.* 1st, 1961, the Hon. Hugh Henry Montagu Stanley, who *d.* 1971; 2ndly, 1973, A. William A. Spiegelberg, of Shuttlingstow, Wildboarclough, Macclesfield, Cheshire, and has issue living (by 1st m.) [see colls. infra].

COLLATERAL BRANCHES LIVING.

Grandsons of the late Rt. Hon. Edward Montagu Cavendish Stanley, MC (*Lord Stanley*), el. son of 17th Earl:—

Issue of the late Hon. Hugh Henry Montagu Stanley, *b.* 1926, *d.* 1971: *m.* 1961, Mary Rose (ante), (who *m.* 2ndly, 1973, A. William A. Spiegelberg), da. of Charles Francis Birch, of Rhodesia:—

Edward Richard William, *b.* 1962.——Peter Hugh Charles, *b.* 1964.

Issue of the late Rt. Hon. Oliver Frederick George Stanley, M.C., M.P., 2nd son of 17th Earl, *b.* 1896, *d.* 1950 : *m.* 1920, Lady Maureen Helena Vane-Tempest-Stewart, who *d.* 1942, dau. of 7th Marquess of Londonderry :—

Michael Charles, *MBE*, *b.* 1921; ed. at Eton, and at Trinity Coll., Camb. (MA); Capt. R. Signals, (RARO), CEng, MIEE; High Sheriff of Westmorland 1959-60, and Vice-Lt. 1965-74; DL of Cumbria; 1939-45 War in N. Africa and Italy (MBE); MBE (Mil.) 1945: *m.* 1951, Aileen Fortune Hugh, da. of Owen Hugh Smith, of Old Hall, Langham, Rutland, and has issue living, Oliver Hugh, *b.* 1952,— Nicholas Charles, *b.* 1954. *Residence,*—Halecat, Witherslack, Grange-over-Sands, Lancashire.—— Kathryn Edith Helen, CVO, *b.* 1923; a JP for Salop; a Woman of the Bedchamber (temporary) to HM the Queen 1955-61; Woman of the Bedchamber since 1972; Cdr. of Roy. Order of North Star of Sweden 1956, since when an Extra Woman of the Bedchamber; 1939-45 in WRNS; CVO 1973: *m.* 1956, John Robert Stratford Dugdale [see Dugdale, Bt., cr. 1936]. *Residence,*—Tickwood Hall, Much Wenlock, Salop.

Issue of the late Adm. the Hon. Sir Victor Albert Stanley, K.C.B., M.V.O., 2nd son of 16th Earl, *b.* 1867, *d.* 1934: *m.* 1896, Annie Bickerton, who *d.* 1962, dau. of the late Hon. C. E. Pooley, K.C., Pres. of British Columbia Executive Council:—

Rosemary Constance, *b.* 1905: *m.* 1943, George Pelham Ritchie, of 13, Pelham Pl., SW7.

Issue of the late Brig.-Gen. the Hon. Ferdinand Charles Stanley, C.M.G., D.S.O., 5th son of 16th Earl, *b.* 1871, *d.* 1935: *m.* 1904, the Hon. Alexandra Frances Anne Fellowes, who *d.* 1955, el. dau. of 2nd Baron De Ramsey :—

Frederick Arthur, *O.B.E.*, *T.D.*, *b.* 1905; ed. at Wellington Coll.; is Col. Cameron Highlanders (T.A.); France 1940, N.-W. Europe 1944-5 (O.B.E.) ; O.B.E. (Mil.) 1945: *m.* 1932, Annie Jane, dau. of the late Col. William Fellowes Collins, D.S.O. [D. Roxburghe], and has issue living, Peter Henry Arthur (29, Roedean Cres., SW15), *b.* 1933: *m.* 1965, Countess Gunilla Douglas, and has issue living, Robin James *b.* 1967, Louisa Charlotte Ann *b.* 1966,—Sarah, *b.* 1935: *m.* 1962, Simon Hawkshaw Creswell, of 96, Eaton Terr., SW1, and has issue living, Alexander John Peter 1965, Miranda Anne Louise *b.* 1963, Sophia Alice Chrystal *b.* 1969. *Residence,*—Bramshott Lodge, Liphook, Hants.——Henry Ferdinand, *MC*, *b.* 1911; ed. at Wellington Coll.; is Maj. Grenadier Guards; 1939-45 War (MC): *m.* 1949, Grizel (SYKES), da. of Air Vice-Marshal Sir Norman Duckworth Kerr MacEwen, CB, CMG, DSO. *Residence,*—Binfield Priory, Bracknell, Berks. *Clubs,*—Brooks's, Guards', Royal Automobile.

      Issue of the late Lieut.-Col. the Rt. Hon. Sir George Frederick Stanley, G.C.S.I., G.C.I.E., C.M.G., 6th son of 16th Earl, *b.* 1872, *d.* 1938 : *m.* 1903, Lady Beatrix Taylour, C.I., C.B.E., who *d.* 1944, dau. of 4th Marquess of Headfort:—
Barbara Helen (*Lady Buchanan*), *b.* 1906; past Pres. Notts. Branch BRC: *m.* 1932, Maj. Sir Charles James Buchanan, 4th Bt. *Residence,*—St. Anne's Manor, Sutton Bonington, Loughborough.

      Issue of the late Col. the Hon. Algernon Francis Stanley, D.S.O., 7th son of 16th Earl, *b.* 1874: *m.* 1918, Lady Mary Cavendish Grosvenor, who *d.* 1959, dau. of 1st Duke of Westminster, and widow of Viscount Crichton, M.V.O., D.S.O. [E. Erne]:—
Constance Mary, *b.* 1919: *m.* 1946, Malcolm Weaver, Lieut. US Army, and has issue living, Mark *b.* 1960,—Mary Constance, *b.* 1954. *Residence,*—Center, Texas, USA.

      Issue of the late Lieut.-Col. the Hon. (Frederick) William Stanley, D.S.O.. 8th son of 16th Earl, *b.* 1878, *d.* 1942: *m.* 1905, Lady Alexandra Louise Elizabeth Acheson, who *d.* 1958, el. dau. of 4th Earl of Gosford :—
David William, *b.* 1906; ed. at Wellington Coll., and at Trin. Coll., Camb.; European War 1939-45 in Middle East, N. Africa and Italy as Major R.E.M.E.: *m.* 1937. Marjorie, only dau. of the late Douglas K. Homan, and has issue living, William Douglas (P.O. Rivonia, Transvaal), *b.* 1938: *m.* 1963, Sally, da. of S. H. Read, of Johannesburg, and has issue living, David Andrew *b.* 1964; Clare Alexandra *b.* 1967, Nicola Avory *b.* 1969, Fiona Anne *b.* 1972,—Patrick (833, Portman Rd., Bryanston, Transvaal), *b.* 1943: *m.* 1968, Jane, el. da. of D. Evers, of Four Winds, Wolverley, Kidderminster, and has issue living, Andrew *b.* 1969, Deborah *b.* 19—, a da. *b.* 1973,—Caroline, *b.* 1940: *m.* 1968, Nigel Proddow, of 64, Chiswick Staithe, W4, and has issue living, Charles *b.* 1969. *Residence,*—Summit Rd., Morningside, Johannesburg, S. Africa.——Olivia Mary Beatrice, *b.* 1908: *m.* 1st, 1937, Capt. John Galloway Rankin, who *d.* 1949 [Rankin, Bt., cr. 1898, colls.]; 2ndly, 1950, Brig. Archer Francis Lawrence Clive, DSO, MC, DL, JP, late Gren. Gds. [Buxton, Bt., colls.]. *Residence,*—Perrystone, Hereford.——Diana Margaret, *b.* 1909: *m.* 1954, Prof. Charles Aubrey Pannett, FRCS, who *d.* 1969. *Residence,*—39, Cliddesden Rd., Basingstoke, Hants.

      Grandson of the late Col. the Hon. Charles James Fox Stanley, 3rd son of 13th Earl :—
      Issue of the late Lieut.-Col. Charles Edward Henry Stanley, *b.* 1843. *d.* 1909: *m.* 1874, Frederica Lucy Phipps, who *d.* 1936, dau. of the late Capt. Phipps Hornby, R.E.:—
Charles Douglas, *b.* 1878 ; ed. at Eton : *m.* 1909, Adela Grace, who *d.* 1950, dau. of F. A. Walker-Jones, J.P., formerly of Beddgelert, Caernarvonshire, and has issue living, Charles John Geoffrey (of Oxbourne House, Shoreham, Sevenoaks, Kent), *b.* 1918; ed. at Eton, and at St. John's Coll., Camb. (B.A. 1940); formerly Capt. Roy. Armoured Corps; France 1940, N.-W. Europe 1944-5: *m.* 1942, Marjorie Laura Awdry, dau. of J. F. Awdry Ball, and has issue living, Christopher Geoffrey Awdry *b.* 1949; ed. at Radley and London Univ. (BSc(Econ): *m.* 1974, Anita Jane Keogh, Martin John Llewelyn *b.* 1952; ed. at Radley, and St. John's Coll., Oxford. *Residence,*—Applethwaite Lodge, Windermere.

      Grandsons of the late Capt. Charles Geoffrey Stanley, 2nd son of the Hon. Henry Thomas Stanley, MP, 2nd son of 13th Earl:—
      Issue of the late Charles Henry Stanley, D.S.M., *b.* 1863, *d.* 1945: *m.* 1st, 1883, Mary Massy, dau. of the late Charles Nason, of Cork; 2ndly, 1898, Belinda Ottley; 3rdly, 19—, Mabel Johnson:—
(By 1st marriage) *Very Rev.* Charles Geoffrey Nason (of 19, Kingston College, Mitchelstown, co. Cork), *b.* 1884; ed. at Trin. Coll. Dublin (B.A. 1906); Dean of Lismore 1934-61, and Rural Dean of Waterford 1951-61: *m.* 1st, 1914, Eileen Chapman, who *d.* 1928; 2ndly, 1931, Violet Claire Baldwin, and has issue living, (by 1st m.) *Rev.* Canon Eric William (St. Mary's Rectory, Nenagh, co. Tipperary): *b.* 1922, ed. at Trin. Coll., Dublin (MA), Rural Dean of Lower Ormonde: *m.* 1949, Phœbe Elizabeth Mary Pollard, and has issue living, Joy *b.* 1950, Katherine *b.* 1953,—(by 2nd m.) *Rev.* Arthur Patrick (c/o Glyn, Mills & Co., Kirkland House, Whitehall, SW1), *b.* 1932; ed. at Trin. Coll., Dublin (MA); Chap. to the Forces: *m.* 1958, Kathleen Marjorie Ethel Earl, and has issue living, Stephen Patrick *b.* 1961, Belinda Susan *b.* 1959,—Sylvia Penelope *b.* 1936: *m.* 1956, the Rev. William George Stanley Spence, of 6, Dundela Gdns., Belfast, BT4 3DH, and has issue living, Peter Edward, *b.* 1959, Janet, *b.* 1962,—Hazel Claire, *b.* 1940: *m.* 1963, Richard John Armstrong (Dr.Phil.), of Nedre Markveg 1, Tromso, Norway, and has issue living, Geoffrey James *b.* 1966, Charles Ivan *b.* 1969, Niall John *b.* 1974, Claire Winifred *b.* 1964.——Frederick George (of 10, Royston Av., Wallington, Surrey), *b.* 1888: *m.* 1931, Grace Evelyn Thrower, and has issue living, Helen Audrey, *b.* 1936: *m.* 1966, George Watts, of 32, Maylands Rd., Oxhey, Watford.——(by 2nd m.) Henry William (of 45, George Lane, Lewisham, SE13), *b.* 1903: *m.* 1930, Kathleen May Hardwick, and has issue living, Leslie Hugh (18, Heather Av., Bearsden, Glasgow), *b.* 1931: *m.* 1956, Marjorie Green, and has issue living, Christopher John *b.* 1958, Geoffrey Hugh *b.* 1962, Lissa Rachel *b.* 1963,—Norman Edward (Carraghan, Church St., Alcombe, Minehead, Som., TA24 6AJ), *b.* 1937: *m.* 1961, Maxime Wyness, and has issue living, Adam *b.* 1969, Dominique *b.* 1965, Mia *b.* 1966.

      Grandsons of the late Edward James Stanley, 5th in descent from Peter Stanley, yr. son of Sir Thomas Stanley, 2nd Bt., and great-uncle of 11th Earl:—
      Issue of the late Capt. Edward Arthur Vesey Stanley, *b.* 1879, *d.* 1941 : *m.* 1st, 1919, Sybil (from whom he obtained a divorce 1932), dau. of the late Major Heathfield Butler Dodgson, D.S.O. [B. Vivian, colls.] ; 2ndly, 1936, Marjorie Beatrice (who *m.* 2ndly, 1942, Charles L. Sidey, da. of the late A. R., Booth:—
(By 1st m.) Peter Vivian (24, Main Rd., Crick, Rugby), *b.* 1921; ed. at Eton: *m.* 1960, Kay, da. of R. S Wybrow, of Chobham, Surrey.——David Norman Sidney, *b.* 1928——(By 2nd m.) John Alexander, *b.* 1938; ed. at Repton.

      Granddaughters of the late Adm. Edward Stanley, son of the Rev. James Stanley, 5th in descent from Henry Stanley, 2nd son of Sir Thomas Stanley, 1st Bt., and great great uncle of 11th Earl:—
      Issue of the late Edward James Stanley, *b.* 1857, *d.* 1933 : *m.* 1st, 1885, Catherine Mary Maud, who *d.* 1896, dau. of William Kidger ; 2ndly, 1902, Annie Clifford, who *d.* 1949, dau. of Richard Cawood :—
(By 1st marriage) Irene, *b.* 1886: *m.* 1916, (Frederick) Charles Pope, who *d.* 1948, and has issue living, Francis Stanley (of Marsh Moor, Molteno, Cape Province, S. Africa), *b.* 1916: *m.* 1943, Sybil Ross Scott, and has issue living, Charles William Scott *b.* 1946: *m.* 1971, Lynette Mary Watkin, (and has issue living, Bevin Scott *b.* 1971), Steven Charles *b.* 1972), Elizabeth Ann *b.* 1944: *m.* 1st, 1967 (m. diss. 1969), Geoffrey Leyden Keith; 2ndly, 1972, Lt. Harold Arthur Mockford, of 9, Mareola Way, Pinelands, Cape Town 8001, S. Africa, (and has issue living, Belinda Anne *b.* 1972, Penelope Jane *b.* 1973), Sheryl Margaret *b.* 1950: *m.* 1972, Charles John Broster, of Broughton, Molteno, Cape Prov., (and has issue living, Nicola Jane *b.* 1973), Rosemary Lynn *b.* 1954,—Nancy Stanley, *b.* 1921: *m.* 1952, Lionel Ronald Mortlock, of Willow Park PO, Birds' River Siding, via Sterkstroom, Cape Prov. 5425, S. Africa, and has issue living, Peter Frederick

b. 1954, Irene Stanley, *b.* 1953: *m.* 1974, Daniel Booyens, Kathleen Anne *b.* 1957,—Kathleen Stanley, *b.* 1924: *m.* 1947, Geoffrey Rowland Chase, of Brandon, Indwe, Cape Province, S. Africa, and has issue living, Michael Ernest *b.* 1950, Allan Frederick *b.* 1953, Sydney Philip *b.* 1955, Rena Pope *b.* 1948, Vanessa Tess *b.* 1959.

Issue of the late Alphonse Frederick Stanley, *b.* 1869, *d.* 19—: *m.* 18—, Ruth, dau. of Robert Jagge:—

Dorothy, *b.* 1894.——Constance, *b.* 1900.

(*In remainder to the Barony of Stanley (cr.* 1456) *only*) [see Css. Loudoun.]

Descendants of the late Sir Thomas Stanley (el. son of Sir Thomas Stanley 5th in descent from the Hon. Sir John Stanley, 3rd son of 1st Baron Stanley), who was cr. a Baronet 1660. [See B. Stanley of Alderley].

PREDECESSORS.—[1] *Sir* THOMAS Stanley, *K.G.*; successively Lord Dep. and Lord-Lieut. of Ireland, and Knight of the Shire of Lancashire 1447-51 and 1453-4; summoned to Parliament on England as *Baron Stanley* 1456; *d.* 1458-9; *s.* by his son [2] THOMAS, *K.G.*, 2nd Baron; Justice of Chester 1463-85, Steward of the Household 1474, and Constable of England for life; for the services he rendered at Bosworth Field, where he placed the crown of Richard III. on the head of the victorious Richmond (Henry VII.), was cr. *Earl of Derby* (peerage of England) 1485; *d.* 1504; *s.* by his grandson [3] THOMAS, 2nd Earl, who in 1488 had *s.* as 2nd *Baron Strange*, his father having been summoned to Parliament in right of his wife as Baron Strange of Knockyn 1482-97; *d.* 1522; *s.* by his son [4] EDWARD, *K.G.*, 3rd Earl; Lord High Steward at coronation of Queen Mary; celebrated for his magnificence and liberality; *d.* 1593; *s.* by his son [5] HENRY, *K.G.*; one of the peers who sat upon the trial of Mary, Queen of Scots; *d.* 1593; *s.* by his el. son [6] FERDINANDO, 5th Earl; is supposed to have been poisoned by certain conspirators who had suggested he should assume the title of king in right of his grandmother, a proposal he had indignantly rejected; *d.* 1594, when the Baronies of Stanley and Strange fell into abeyance among his daus., and the earldom devolved upon his brother [7] WILLIAM, *K.G.*, 6th Earl; purchased from his nieces their claims on the Isle of Man; *d.* 1642; *s.* by his son [8] JAMES, *KG*, 7th Earl, who in 1628 had been summoned to Parliament as Baron Strange under the impression that such a barony was enjoyed by his father; the summons cr. ai new peerage [see B. Strange]; during the Civil Wars was attached to the royal cause, and his wife Charlotte, dau. of Claude de la Trémouille, Duke of Thouars, is famed for her defence of Latham House when besieged by the Parliamentarians 1644, and for her energetic protection of the Isle of Man 1651; falling into the hands of the enemy after the battle of Worcester was decapitated at Bolton 1651; *s.* by his son [9] CHARLES, 8th Earl; *d.* 1672; *s.* by his son [10] WILLIAM GEORGE RICHARD, 9th Earl; *d.* 1702; *s.* by his brother [11] JAMES, 10th Earl; *d.s.p.* 1736 when the Isle of Man and the Barony of Strange, cr. 1627, devolved upon the 2nd Duke of Atholl, the other baronies became abeyant between the co-heirs of the 5th Earl, and the earldom reverted to his kinsman [12] *Sir* EDWARD Stanley, 11th Earl and 5th Bt. (see note *⁎* infra); *d.* 1776, *s.* by his grandson [13] EDWARD, 12th Earl: Lord-Lieut. of Lancashire; *d.* 1834; *s.* by his son [14] EDWARD SMITH, *K.G.*, 13th Earl; Lord-Lieut. of Lancashire; cr. *Baron Stanley,* of Bickerstaffe (peerage of United Kingdom) 1832; *d.* 1851; *s.* by his son [15] EDWARD GEOFFREY, *K.G., G.C.M.G., P.C., D.C.L.,* 14th Earl; *b.* 1799; an eminent orator, scholar and statesman; M.P. for Stockbridge (C) 1820-6, for Preston 1826-30, for Windsor 1830-2, and for N. Lancashire 1832-46; Ch. Sec. for Ireland 1830-3, Sec. of State for Colonies and for War 1833-4 and 1841-5, First Lord of the Treasury 1852, 1858-9 and 1866-8, Chancellor of Univ. of Oxford, &c.; called to House of Lords in his father's Barony of Stanley 1846: *m.* 1825, the Hon. Emma Caroline Wilbraham, who *d.* 1876, dau. of 1st Baron Skelmersdale; *d.* Oct. 28, 1869; *s.* by his son [16] EDWARD HENRY, *K.G., P.C.,* 15th Earl; *b.* 1826; M.P. for Lynn Regis (C) 1848-69; Under-Sec. for Foreign Affairs 1852, Sec. for Colonies 1858, Pres. of Board of Control 1858, Sec. of State for India 1858-9, for Foreign Affairs 1866-8 and 1874-8, and Sec. of State for the Colonies 1882-5: *m.* 1870, Mary Catherine, who *d.* 1900, dau. of 5th Earl Delawarr, and widow of 2nd Marquess of Salisbury; *d.* 1893; *s.* by his brother [17] FREDERICK ARTHUR, *K.G., G.C.B., G.C.V.O., P.C.,* 16th Earl; *b.* 1841; Lord-Lieut. of Lancashire; a Civil Lord of the Admiralty Aug. to Nov. 1868, Financial Sec. to War Office 1874-7, Sec. to Treasury 1877-8, Sec. of State for War 1878-80, Sec. of State for Colonies 1885-6, Pres. of Board of Trade 1886-8, and Gov.-Gen. of Canada and Com.-in-Ch. of Prince Edward Island 1888-93; M.P. for Preston (C) 1865-8 for N. Lancashire 1868-85, and for Blackpool Div. of Lancashire N. 1885-6; cr. *Baron Stanly of Preston* (peerage of United Kingdom) 1886: *m.* 1864, Lady Constance Villiers, who *d.* 1922, el. dau. of 4th Earl of Clarendon; *d.* 1908; *s.* by his el. son [18] EDWARD GEORGE VILLIERS, *K.G., G.C.B., G.C.V.O., T.D., P.C.,* 17th Earl; *b.* 1865; Lord-Lieut. of Lancashire; was a Junior Lord of the Treasury 1895-1900, Financial Sec. to War Office 1900-1903, Postmaster-Gen. 1903-1905, Under-Sec. of State for War 1916, Sec. of State for War 1916-18, Ambassador Extraor. and Plen. to France 1918-20, and again Sec. of State for War 1922-4; sat as M P. for Lancashire (S.E.) Westhoughton Div. 1892-6: *m.* 1889, Lady Alice Maud Olivia Montagu, who *d.* 1957, dau. of 7th Duke of Manchester; *d.* 1948; *s.* by his grandson [19] EDWARD JOHN (son of the late Edward Montagu Cavendish, Lord Stanley, P.C., M.C., M P., el. son of 17th Earl), 18th Earl and present peer; also Baron Stanley of Bickerstaffe, and Baron Stanley of Preston.

 *[1] EDWARD, of Bickerstaffe, great-grandson of the Hon. Sir James Stanley, Knt., brother of 3rd Earl; cr. a Baronet 1627; *s.* by his son [2] *Sir* THOMAS, 2nd Bt.; *d.* 1653; *s.* by his son [3] *Sir* EDWARD, 3rd Bt.; *d.* 1671; *s.* by his son [4] *Sir* THOMAS, 4th Bt.; *d.* 1714; *s.* by his son [5] EDWARD, 11th Earl of Derby and 5th Bt. (see ante).

DERBY, LORD BISHOP OF. (Bowles.)

Rt. Rev. CYRIL WILLIAM JOHNSTON BOWLES, son of the late William Cullen Allen Bowles, of West Ham; *b.* May 9th, 1916; ed. at Brentwood Sch., and Emmanuel and Jesus Colls., Camb. (MA); Curate of Barking 1939-41, Chap. of Ridley Hall, Camb. 1942-44, Vice-Prin. 1944-51, and Prin. 1951-63; Hon. Canon of Ely Cathedral 1959-63; Select Preacher Camb. 1945, 1953, 1958 and 1963, Oxford 1961, and Dublin 1961; Archdeacon of Swindon 1963-69, since when 4th Bishop of Derby: *m.* 1965, Florence Joan, da. of the late John Eastaugh, of Windlesham.

This See was founded July 1927.

Episcopal Signature,—"Cyril Derby."

ARMS OF THE SEE.—Purpure, a cross quadrate potent argent, in chief three fountains.

Residence,—Bishop's House Turnditch, Derby, DE5 2LH

DE ROS, BARONESS (Maxwell.) [Baron E. 1264.]

[Title pronounced "de Roos."]

GEORGIANA ANGELA MAXWELL, *Baroness de Ros* in her own right (Premier Barony of England); *b.* May 2nd, 1933; *s.* (on termination of abeyance) 1958: *m.* 1954, Cdr. John David Maxwell, RN, and has issue.

Arms,—Quarterly, 1st and 4th, Argent a saltire gules, *Fitzgerald*, 2nd and 3rd, gules, three water bougets argent *de Ros*. Supporters,—Two falcons wings expanded and inverted proper

Residence,—Old Court, Strangford, co. Down.

SON LIVING.

Hon. PETER TREVOR, *b.* Dec. 23rd, 1958; ed. at Headfort Sch., Kells.

DAUGHTER LIVING.

Hon. Diana Elizabeth, *b.* 1957.

SISTER LIVING.

Rosemary ROSS, *b.* 1937: *m.* 1973, Beresford George Edward sborne, MIPA of Heddon House, Crowcombe, Dorset. *Residence,*—Luckington Court, Chippenham, Wilts.

UNCLE LIVING (*Son of Una Mary, Baroness de Ros.*)

Hon. Charles Dudley Anthony ROSS, *b.* 1907; ed. at Shrewsbury, and at Camb. Univ.: *m.* 1st, 1940 Lady Elizabeth (ANNESLEY) (who obtained a divorce 1949), dau. of 8th Earl of Roden; 2ndly 1953, Mary Margaret, da. of the late Thomas Graham, of Monaghan, and has issue living, (by 1st m.) Anthony Arthur (Casa Zabara, Brendon Av., Morningside Manor, PO Rivonici, Transvaal), *b.* 1941: ed. at Winchester ACA: *m.* 1969, Joan, da. of Herbert Cahn, of Highlands North Johannesburg, and has issue living, Zara Gail *b.* 1971, Deborah Kim *b.* 1972. *Residence,*—67, Seafield Rd., Southbourne, Bournemouth.

GREAT-AUNT LIVING. (*Daughter o Mary Frances, Baroness de Ros and 3rd Earl of Dartrey.*)

See E. Dar trey, [ext.].

MOTHER LIVING.

Hon. Angela Ierne Evelyn Dixon, da. of 1st Baron Glentoran: *m.* 1st, 1929, Lt.-Cdr. Peter Ross RN, who *d.* (killed in action) 1940, el son of Una Mary, Baroness de Ros; 2ndly, 1943, Lt.-Col. Trevor Langdale Horn, MC, 16th/5th Lancers, who *d.* 1966, and has issue living, (by 2nd m.) June Victoria Langdale *b.* 1946. *Residence,* Luckington Court, Chippenham, Wilts.

PREDECESSORS.—[1] ROBERT de ROS took an active part against Henry III. and was one of the principal barons summoned to Parliament of England in the king's name 1264; was also again summoned as *Baron de Ros* 1285; *d.* 1285; *s.* by his son [2] WILLIAM, 2nd Baron; unsuccessfully competed for the crown of Scotland 1292 and 1296; *d.* 1316; *s.* by his son [3] WILLIAM, 3rd Baron; *d.* 1343; *s.* by his son [4] WILLIAM, 4th Baron; led a division of the English Army at Crecy; *d.* in Palestine 1352; *s.* by his brother [5] THOMAS, 5th Baron; *d.* 1384; *s.* by his son [6] JOHN, 6th Baron; *d.* 1394; *s.* by his brother [7] WILLIAM, K.G., 7th Baron : Lord High Treasurer of England 1403; *d.* 1414; *s.* by his son [8] JOHN, 8th Baron; killed at battle of Baugé 1421; *s.* by his brother [9] THOMAS, 9th Baron; *d.* 1431; *s.* by his son [10] THOMAS, 10th Baron; summoned to Parliament 1449-60; was attainted 1461 and his honours forfeited; *s.* by his son [11] EDMUND, 11th Baron; obtained a reversal of attainder 1485, but was not summoned to Parliament; *d.* 1508, when the title became abeyant between his two sisters; the abeyance was terminated 15— in favour of [12] GEORGE Manners (son of Eleanor, the el. sister by Sir Robert Manners, Knt.), 12th Baron; was not summoned to Parliament; *d.* 1513; *s.* by his son [13] THOMAS, K.G., 13th Baron; summoned to Parliament 1515, and cr. *Earl of Rutland* (peerage of England) 1525: *d.* 1543; *s.* by his son [14] HENRY, K.G., 2nd Earl; *d.* 1563; *s.* by his son [15] EDWARD, 15th Baron; *d.* 1587, when the earldom reverted to his brother [see D. Rutland], and the barony devolved upon his dau. [16] ELIZABETH, wife of William Cecil, afterwards 2nd Earl of Exeter; *d.* 1591; *s.* by her son [17] WILLIAM Cecil, 17th Baron; *d.s.p.* before his father 1618; *s.* by his cousin [18] FRANCIS Manners, 18th Baron and 6th Earl of Rutland: cr. *Baron Ros*, of Hamlake 1616; *d.* 1632 without male issue, when the Barony of Ros, of Hamlake, expired, the earldom reverted to his brother, and the old barony devolved upon his dau. [19] KATHARINE: *m.* 1620, the 1st Duke of Buckingham, who was assassinated 1628; 2ndly, 1635, the 1st Marquess of Antrim; *d.* 1666; *s.* by her son [20] GEORGE, K.G., 20th Baron and 2nd Duke; noted for his profligacy and his wit; *d.* 1687, when the dukedom expired, and the Barony of de Ros went into abeyance between the descendants of Bridget and Frances, daus. of John, 4th Earl of Rutland, and remained so until 1806, when it was terminated in favour of [21] CHARLOTTE [a descendant of Frances (ante), and dau. of the Hon. Robert Boyle-Walsingham, 5th son of 1st Earl of Shannon]: *m.* 1791, Lord Henry FitzGerald, son of 1st Duke of Leinster: assumed by Roy. licence 1806 the additional surname of de Ros; *d.* 1831; *s.* by her son [22] HENRY WILLIAM, 22nd Baron; *d.* 1839; *s.* by his brother [23] WILLIAM LENNOX LASCELLES, P.C., 23rd Baron, *b.* 1797; a Gen. in the Army, Capt. Yeomen of the Guard 1852 and 1858-9, and Lieut.-Gov. of the Tower of London 1852-74, &c. : *m.* 1824, Georgiana, who *d.* 1891, dau. of 4th Duke of Richmond; *d.* 1874; *s.* by his son [24] DUDLEY CHARLES, K.P., K.C.V.O., 24th Baron, *b.* 1827: Equerry to the Prince Consort 1853-61, and to Queen Victoria 1861-92, and a Lord-in-Waiting 1874-80, 1885-6, and 1886-92 : *m.* 1st, 1853, Lady Elizabeth Egerton, who *d.* 1892, el. dau. of 2nd Earl of Wilton, G.C.H.; 2ndly, 1896, Mary Geraldine, who *d.* 1921, dau. of the Rev. Sir William Vesey Ross Mahon, 4th Bt. ; *d.* 1907 ; *s.* by his only dau. [25] MARY FRANCES, *b.* 1854 : *m.* 1878, the 3rd Earl of Dartrey (who *d.* 1933) ; she *d.* 1939, when the Barony again fell into abeyance between her three daughters and so remained until 1943, when it was terminated in favour of the el. [26] UNA MARY ROSS, *b.* 1879 : *m.* 1904, Arthur John Ross, who *d.* (killed in action during European War) 1917 ; *d.* 1956, when the Barony again fell into abeyance between her two granddaughters, and so remained until 1958, when it was terminated in favour of the el. [27] GEORGIANA ANGELA (dau. of the late Lieut.-Com. Peter Ross R.N., el. son of Una Mary, Baroness de Ros), present peeress.

DERWENT, BARON. (Vanden-Bempde-Johnstone.) [Baron U.K. 1881, Bt. G.B. 1795.]

[Title pronounced "**Darwent.**"]

NUNQUAM NON PARATUS
Never unready.

PATRICK ROBIN GILBERT VANDEN-BEMPDE-JOHNSTONE, *CBE*, 4th Baron, and 6th Baronet; *b.* Oct. 26th, 1901; *s.* 1949; Junior Conservative Whip in House of Lords 1950-51, and Dep. Speaker 1970; Chm. of British Road Federation 1954-62, Min. of State, Board of Trade 1962-63, and Min. of State, Home Office 1963-64; Dep. Speaker House of Lords since 1970; late Maj. KRRC; CBE (Civil) 1974: *m.* 1929, Marie-Louise Henriette (MYBURGH), da. of the late Albert Picard, of Paris, and has issue.

Arms,—Quarterly: 1st and 4th argent, a saltire sable, in base a human heart ensigned with a regal crown or, on a chief gules, three woolpacks of the third; 2nd and 3rd per fesse, the 1st or, and the last per pale gules and vert, a demi-eagle with two heads displayed, issuing in chief sable, the dexter base charged with a tower, the sinister with five towers in saltire of the first, the gate and portcullis of each proper. Crests,—1st, a winged spur erect or, straps gules, buckles argent; 2nd, out of the battlements a tower argent, issuant therefrom a demi-eagle with two heads displayed sable. Supporters,—Dexter, a lion ermine, crowned or, and charged on the breast with an escutcheon or, thereon a winged spur gules; sinister, A horse ermine, bridled and saddled gules, and charged on the shoulder as the dexter.

Residences,—Hackness Hall, Scarborough, Yorkshire; 48, Cadogan Pl., SW1.

SON LIVING.

Hon. ROBIN EVELYN LEO, *M.V.O., b.* Oct. 30th, 1930; ed. at Winchester, and at Clare Coll., Camb.; late 2nd Lieut. King's Roy. Rifle Corps, and Lieut. Queen Victoria's Rifles (T.A. Reserve); 3rd Sec. Foreign Office 1954-5, and at Paris (Private Sec. to British Ambassador) 1955-8, 2nd Sec. 1958, at Foreign Office 1958-61, at Mexico City 1961-65, 1st Sec. 1962, Washington 1965-68, and Foreign Office 1968-69; a Merchant Banker; Chev. of Legion of Honour; MVO (4th class) 1957: *m.* 1957, Sybille Marie Louise Marcelle, da. of Vicomte de Simard de Pitray, and has issue living, Francis Patrick Harcourt, *b.* 1965,—Emmeline Veronica Louise, *b.* 1958,—Joanna Louise Claudia, *b.* 1962,— Isabelle Catherine Sophie, *b.* 1968. *Residences,*—Low Hall, Hackness, Scarborough, Yorks.; 27, The Crescent, Barnes, SW13. *C ub,*—Garrick.

COLLATERAL BRANCHES LIVING.

Grandchildren of the late Hon. Louis Vanden-Bempde-Johnstone (infra):—
Issue of the late Lt.-Col. Granville Henry Vanden-Bempde-Johnstone, DSO, RA, *b.* 1891, *d.* 1969: *m.* 1923, Margarita Ruby who *d.* 1972, da. of the late Arthur Vernon O'Connell, of Buenos Aires:—
John Louis (61, Salisbury Rd., Farnborough, Hants.), *b.* 1928; ed. at Eastbourne Coll.; late Capt. RA: *m.* 1964, Eltis, da. of W. Robinson, and has issue living, Louise Dorothy Ann, *b.* 1967.——Elizabeth Mary, *b.* 1924: *m.* 1945, Lt.-Col. Richard McCaig, MC, RA (ret.), of 15, Gorselands, Andover Rd., Newbury, and has issue living, David John, *b.* 1949,—Mark Richard, *b.* 1959,—Susan Mary, *b.* 1951: *m.* 1974, Capt. Jeremy Turner, RTR.

Issue of the late Hon. Louis-Bempde-Johnstone, 5th son of 1st Baron, *b.* 1862, *d.* 1922: *m.* 1891, Gwendoline Mary Elizabeth, da. of the late Major Henry Charles Talbot [who *d.* 1969, E. Shrewsbury, colls.]:—
Robin Talbot, *b.* 1901; ed. at Eton, and at Christ's Coll., Camb.: *m.* 1st, 1927, Vivian Patricia (who obtained a divorce 1936), da. of the late Rupert Marais, of Brooklyn, Pretoria; 2ndly, 1936, Louise, da. of Guy Chalkley, of Folly Farm, White River, E. Transvaal; 3rdly, 1951 (m. diss. 1959), Betty, da. of Michael Cooper, and widow of Frank van Zwanenberg; 4thly, 1960, Mrs. Elsa Ann Zillah Mann, da. of Maj. James Eland Buchanan, of Hales Hall, Market Drayton.——Joan Gwendoline, *b.* 1895: *m.* 1st, 1915, William Robert Younger (who obtained a divorce 1923), later Sir William Robert Younger, 2nd Bt., who *d.* 1973; 2ndly, 1923, Capt. Hubert Lachlan Pelham-Burn, Gordon Highlanders, who *d.* 1927; 3rdly, 1931, Dennis Yates Wheatley, and has issue living, (by 1st m.) [see Younger, Bt.],—(by 2nd m.) Colin Louis St. Hubert (Boundstone House, Boundstone, Farnham, Surrey), *b.* 1926; late Maj. Coldstream Guards: *m.* 1956, Pamela Mary, only da. of the late Lt.-Col. Matthew Carrington-Sykes, MC, late RA, and has issue living, Andrew Louis *b.* 1959, Fiona Mary *b.* 1957. *Residence,*—60, Cadogan Sq., SW1.

Grandchildren of the late Hon. Gilbert Vanden-Bempde-Johnstone, yst. son of 1st Baron:—
Issue of the late Lieut.-Col. Mark Vanden-Bempde-Johnstone, *b.* 1900, *d.* 1956: *m.* (Jan.) 1928, Susan (of Latimer Cottage, St. Helens, Isle of Wight), dau. of the late Geoffrey Head, O.B.E. [Pauncefort-Duncombe, Bt.]:—
Virginia Susan (of 17, Lennox Gdns. S.W.1), *b.* (Oct.) 1928.
Issue of the late Cdr. Felix Gilbert Vanden-Bempde-Johnstone, RN, *b.* 1904, *d.* 1964: *m.* 1st, 1938, Mrs. June Estcourt, da. of the late H. W. Looker; 2ndly, 1945, Frances Elizabeth (Cricket Green House, Hartley Wintney, Hants.), da. of the late Charles McIntyre Brown:—
(By 1st marriage) Sarah June, *b.* 1939: *m.* 1961, Peter George Glossop, of Penlan Hall, Fordham, Colchester, and has issue living, Nicholas George, *b.* 1971,—Georgemma Sarah, *b.* 1963,—Lucy Maria, *b.* 1966,—Camilla June, *b.* 1969.——(By 2nd m.) Philippa Rachel (147, Gloucester Rd., SW7; Far Hill, Llanishen, Mon.), *b.* 1946.

(*In remainder to the Baronetcy only.*)

Grandchildren of the late Capt. Charles Johnstone-Scott (infra):—
Issue of the late Ronald Johnstone-Scott, *b.* 1911, *d.* 1967: *m.* 1937, Winifred Joan Peck, of 19, Boleyn Drive, Eastcote, Ruislip, Middlesex:—
Richard Anthony (Howletts Private Zoo, Bekesbourne, Canterbury, Kent), *b.* 1946: *m.* 1968, Jennifer Le Lerre, and has issue living, Iain Richard, *b.* 1972,—Emma Louise, *b.* 1970.——Bruce Roger, *b.* 1956. ——Gillian Fenton, *b.* 1938: *m.* 1960, David Godfrey Kimsey, of 34, Kent Gdns., Eastcote, Ruislip,

Middx., and has issue living, Stephen David, *b.* 1962,—Mark Fenton, *b.* 1967,—Deborah Gillian, *b.* 1964,—Sarah Cressida, *b.* 1972.——Sandra Elizabeth Louise, *b.* 1952: *m.* 1974, Ivor Owen Tomrley, of 26, Hatherleigh Rd., Ruislip, Middx.

Descendants of the late Col. John Johnstone, 2nd son of 2nd baronet of Westerhall (cr. 1700):—

Grandchildren of the late Henry Richard JOHNSTONE-SCOTT, 2nd son of 2nd baronet of Hackness (cr. 1795), who assumed the additional surname of Scott by Roy. licence 1860.
Issue of the late Capt. Charles JOHNSTONE-SCOTT, S. African Forces, *b.* 1870, *d.* 1948: *m.* 1907, Elizabeth Irvine Matheson-Warrack, who *d.* 1956 :—
Charles Hugh, *b.* 1913.——Aline, *b.* 1908.——Margaret Cressida, *b.* 1915: *m.* 1947, Richard Melville Brooker, of The Burrells, Appleby, Westmorland, and has issue living, Robin Nicholas, *b.* 1948,— Richard David, *b.* 1949.

Grandson of the late Rev. Vanden Bempde Johnstone, son of the late Charles Philipps Johnstone, 2nd son of Charles John Johnstone, brother of 1st baronet :—
Issue of the late Charles Julius Johnstone, *b.* 1857, *d.* 1904 : *m.* 1885, Mary Gertrude, who *d.* 1930, dau. of G. Madoc-Jones, formerly of Glentworth, Oswestry :—
Richard Noel, *b.* 1896; Com. RN (ret.): *m.* 1933, Mary Edmée, da. of the late Charles William Campbell, CMG, and has issue living, Susan Mary, *b.* 1935. *Residence,*—Birch Cottage, Woodchurch, Kent.
——William Robert Parke, *b.* 1900; ed. at Repton, and at New Coll., Oxford: *m.* 1938, Mary, da. of the late Peter Robinson, of Waresley, Bedfordshire. *Residence,*—Dunlichity Lodge, Farr Inverness.

Grandson of the late Frederick Charles Johnstone, son of the late Richard James Johnstone, son of the late Charles Johnstone, brother of 1st baronet:—
Issue of the late Frederick Alexander Johnstone, *b.* 1865, *d.* 1939 : *m.* 1890, Grace Margaret, who *d.* 1927, dau. of Finlay Cameron, of Edinburgh :—
Frederick John Finlay, *b.* 1898 : *m.* 1933, Yvonne, dau. of the late Colin Frederick Murray Campbell, of Halston, Westmeath. *Residence,*—Broom Hill, Benenden, Kent.

PREDECESSORS.—[1] RICHARD Johnstone (son of the late Col. John Johnstone, 2nd son of Sir William Johnstone, 2nd Bt., of Westerhall), *M.P.* for Weymouth 1790-96; assumed by Act of Parliament 1793, the surnames of Vanden-Bempde, and in 1795 was authorized by Roy. licence to resume the name of Johnstone; cr. a *Baronet* 1795, under the name of Bempde-Johnstone, with remainder to the male issue of his brother Charles John; *d.* 1807; *s.* by his son [2] *Sir* JOHN, successively M.P. for Yorkshire and Scarborough; *b.* 1799: *m.* 1825, Louisa Augusta Venables-Vernon, dau. of the Most Rev. Edward Harcourt, Archbishop of York [B. Vernon], *d.* 1869; *s.* by his son [3] *Sir* HARCOURT, 3rd Bt.: *b.* 1829; M.P. for Scarborough (*L*) 1869-80; cr. *Baron Derwent,* of Hackness, co. York (peerage of United Kingdom) 1881 : *m.* 1850, Charlotte Mills, who *d.* 1903, sister of 1st Baron Hillingdon; *d.* 1916; *s.* by his son [4] *Sir* FRANCIS, 2nd Baron, *b.* 1851: *m.* 1880, Ethel, who *d.* 1891, dau. of Henry Strickland-Constable; *d.* 1929; *s.* by his nephew [5] GEORGE HARCOURT (son of the late Hon. Edward Henry Vanden-Bempde-Johnstone, 2nd son of 1st Baron), 3rd Baron, *b.* 1899; Hon Attaché at Warsaw 1923, at Brussels 1927, at Madrid 1928, and at Berne 1939: *m.* 1929, Comtesse Sabine Ozaykowska, who *d.* 1941, dau. of Gen. D. Iliesco (formerly Ch. of Gen. Staff, Rumanian Army), of 12, Rue Alexandre Lahovary, Bucharest, Rumania; *d.* 1949; *s.* by his brother [6] PATRICK ROBIN GILBERT, 4th Baron and present peer.

DE SAUMAREZ, BARON. (Saumarez.) [Baron U.K. 1831, Bt. U.K. 1801.]
[Title and Name pronounced "Sommerez."]

I hope in God.

JAMES VICTOR BROKE SAUMAREZ, 6th Baron, and 6th Baronet (Premier Baronet of U.K. creation); *b.* April 28th, 1924; *s.* 1969; ed. at Eton, and Magdalene Coll., Camb. (MA); 1939-45 War with Life Guards: *m.* 1953, Joan Beryl (Julia), da. of Douglas Raymond Charlton, of Windlesham, and has issue.

Arms.—Argent, on a chevron gules, between three leopards' faces sable, as many castles triple-towered or. **Crest.**—A falcon, displayed proper. **Supporters.**—*Dexter,* an unicorn, tail between the legs argent, navally gorged azure, charged on the shoulder with a castle triple-towered or; *sinister,* a greyhound argent, collared gules, rimmed or, charged on the shoulder with a wreath of laurel vert, encircling an anchor sable.

Residence,—Shrubland Vista, Coddenham, Ipswich.

SONS LIVING.
Hon. ERIC DOUGLAS, *b.* Aug. 13th, 1956.
Hon. Victor Thomas, (twin), *b.* 1956.

DAUGHTER LIVING.
Hon. Louisa, *b.* 1955.

SISTERS LIVING.
Hon. Veronica, *b.* 1915 ; European War 1943-5 with A.T.S. : *m.* 1945, Brigadier Anthony William Allen Llewellen Palmer, D.S.O., M.C., King's Dragoon Guards [M. Lincolnshire ext.]. *Residence,*— Great Somerford Manor, Chippenham, Wilts.
Hon. Christine. *b.* 1916; European War 1943-5 with W.R.N.S. : *m.* 1944, Lieut.-Col. Henry Morton Llewellyn, OBE, DL, Warwickshire Yeo. [see Llewellyn, Bt., cr. 1922]. *Residence,*—Llanvair Grange, nr. Abergavenny, Mon.

AUNT LIVING. (*Daughter of 4th Baron.*)
Hon. Marion, *b.* 1885. *Residence*,—Orion, Coton Road, Grantchester, Cambridge.

WIDOW LIVING OF FIFTH BARON.

GUNHILD (*Gunhild, Baroness De Saumarez*) (Ratal River Estate, Bredasdorp, Cape Prov.), da. of the late Maj.-Gen. Viktor Gustaf Balck, KCMG, of Stockholm: *m.* 1914, the 5th Baron, who *d.* 1969.

PREDECESSORS.—[1] *Sir* JAMES Saumarez, *G.C.B.*, 3rd son of the late Matthew Saumarez; *b.* 1757; Adm. of the Red, Gen. of the Marine Forces, and a most distinguished naval commander; 2nd in command at the battle of Nile; cr. a *Baronet* 1801, and *Baron de Saumarez*, of Saumarez, Guernsey (peerage of United Kingdom) 1831: *m.* 1788, Martha, who *d.* 1849, dau. of Thomas Le Marchant, of Guernsey; *d.* 1836; *s.* by his son [2] *Rev.* JAMES, 2nd Baron, *b.* 1789; Rector of Huggate, co. York: *m.* 1814, Mary, who *d.* 1849, dau. of Vice-Adm. Lechmere, of Steeple Aston, Oxon; *d.s.p.* 1863; *s.* by his brother [3] JOHN ST. VINCENT, 3rd Baron, *b.* 1806: *m.* 1st, 1838, Caroline Esther, who *d.* 1846, el. dau. of William Rhodes, of Kirskill and Bramhope Halls, York: *m.* 2ndly, 1850, Margaret Antoinette, dau. of William Richard Hopkyns Northey, of Oving House, Bucks; *d.* 1891; *s.* by his el. son [4] JAMES ST. VINCENT, 4th Baron, *b.* 1843: *m.* 1882, Jane Anne, *O.B.E.*, who *d.* 1933, dau. of the late Capt. Charles Acton Vere-Broke, R.E.; *d.* 1937; *s.* by his son [5] JAMES ST. VINCENT BROKE, 5th Baron; *b.* 1889; Capt. Scots Guards; Founded Rhodesia Fairbridge Coll. 1946: *m.* 1914, Gunhild, da. of the late Maj.-Gen. Viktor Gustaf Balck, KCMG, of Stockholm; *d.* 1969; *s.* by his son [6] JAMES VICTOR BROKE, 6th Baron and present peer.

Desmond, Earl of, see Earl of Denbigh and Desmond.

DE VESCI, VISCOUNT. (Vesey.) [Viscount I. 1776, Baron I, 1750, Bt. I. 1698.]
[Name pronounced "Veezy."]

JOHN EUSTACE VESEY, 6th Viscount, 8th Baronet; *b.* Feb. 25th, 1919; *s.* 1958; ed. at Eton, and at Trin. Coll., Camb.; FRICS; is Lt. Irish Guards (Supplementary Reserve); 1939-45 War in Norway, N. Africa and Italy (wounded, prisoner): *m.* 1950, Susan Anne, da. of the late Ronald Owen Lloyd Armstrong-Jones, MBE, QC, and has issue.

Arms,—Or, on a cross sable, a patriarchal cross of the field. Crest,—A dexter hand erect in armour holding a laurel branch proper. Supporters,—Two figures of Hercules, each clad in a lion's skin, and holding a club over the exterior shoulder proper.

Seat,—Abbey Leix, co. Leix. *Clubs*,—Turf, White's.

SON LIVING.
Hon. THOMAS EUSTACE, *b.* Oct. 8th, 1955.

DAUGHTERS LIVING.
Hon. Emma Francis, *b.* 1951.
Hon. Catherine Anne, *b.* 1953.

SISTERS LIVING.
Margaret Constance, *b.* 1912: *m.* 1946, Herbert William Quinton, of 6, Forest Field, Horsham, Sussex, and has issue living, Thomas William, *b.* 1947,—Christopher John, *b.* 1948: *m.* 1969, Carol, da. of Clifford Green, and has issue living, Catherine Sara *b.* 1969,—Peter Valentine, *b.* 1953,—Caroline Mary, *b.* 1950.
Bridget Georgiana (*Lady Airey*), *b.* 1915: *m.* 1947, Lieut.-Gen. Sir Terence Sydney Airey, K.C.M.G., C.B., C.B.E. *Residence*,—Fritton Old Rectory, Fritton, near Norwich.

MOTHER LIVING.
Lady Cecily Kathleen Browne, dau. of 5th Earl of Kenmare; was a Lady-in-Waiting to H.R.H. the Duchess of Gloucester 1947-51, and a Woman of the Bedchamber to H.M. Queen Mary 1951-53, since when Extra Lady-in-Waiting to H.R.H. the Duchess of Gloucester: *m.* 1911, Col. the Hon. Thomas Eustace Vesey, who *d.* 1946. *Residence*,—The Red House, Sunningdale, Berks.

WIDOW LIVING OF FIFTH VISCOUNT.
FRANCES) LOIS (*Lois, Viscountess de Vesci*), dau. of Sir Cecil Edmund Lister-Kaye, 4th Bt., and widow of 5th Earl of Rosse: *m.* 1920, as his second wife, the 5th Viscount, who *d.* 1958. *Residence*, —Womersley Park, Doncaster.

COLLATERAL BRANCHES LIVING.
Issue of the late Lieut.-Col. the Hon. Sir Osbert Eustace Vesey, K.C.V.O., C.M.G., C.B.E., brother of 5th Viscount, *b.* 1884, *d.* 1957: *m.* 1910, Dorothy, who *d.* 1961, dau. of the late William Morison Strachan, of Strood Park, Horsham :—
Elisabeth, *b.* 1910: *m.* 1931, Lieut.-Col. William Dudley Henry Charles Forbes of Callendar, C.B.E., late Coldstream Guards [B. Hotham, colls.], and has issue living, William Frederick Eustace (of Dinning House, Gargunnock, by Stirling), *b.* 1932; ed. at Eton; late Capt. Coldstream Guards: *m.* 1956, the Hon. Pamela Susan McCorquodale, da. of 1st Baron McCorquodale of Newton, (ext.)—

John William Arthur (The Cottage, Newton Mill, Brechin, Angus), *b.* 1935; ed. at Eton; late Capt 9/12 R. Lancers: *m.* 1961, Rosemary Jane, da. of Andrew Usher, and has issue living, Angus William Andrew *b.* 1964, Victoria Jane Elizabeth *b.* 1962. *Residences,*—Whinfell, Bridge of Allan, Stirlingshire; Earlstoun Lodge, Dalry, Castle Douglas, Kirkcudbrightshire.——Anne, *b.* 1914: *m.* 1937, Maj. Lord Roderic Armyne Gordon, MBE, RA (TA), from whom she obtained a divorce 1949 [see M. Huntly]. *Residence,*—Bridge House, Constantine, Falmouth, Cornwall.

Granddaughter of the late Maj.-Gen. George Henry Vesey, 5th son of Rev. the Hon. Arthur Vesey, 2nd son of 1st Viscount:—
Issue of the late Lieut.-Col. Charles Edward Gore Vesey, *b.* 1871, *d.* 1958: *m.* 1920, Mary Dorothea, who *d.* 1966, da. of Arthur Henry Loring:—
Claudine Mary Rosalind, *b.* 1925; MRCS England and LRCP London 1950, DCH England 1954: *m.* 1959, William Anthony Barry Brown, LDS, DOrth RCS, MSc, PhD, of Redwing, South Park, Sevenoaks, Kent, and has issue living, Martin Thomas Vesey, *b.* 1960,—James Benedict, *b.* 1961,— Adrian Walter, *b.* 1963,—Susan Mary Loring, *b.* 1965.

Grandsons of Gen. Sir Ivo Lucius Beresford Vesey, KCB, KBE, CMG, DSO, yst. son of Maj.-Gen. George Henry Vesey (ante):—
Issue of the late Major Christopher Thomas Vesey, MC, RHA, *b.* 1916, *d.* 1956: *m.* 1952, Helen Cynthia Mary (who *m.* 2ndly, 1969, Brig. Ferdinand Shaw Eiloart, OBE, of Vinesse Farm, Little Horkesley, Colchester, Essex), da. of Brig. Wilfred Algernon Ebsworth, CB, CBE:—
Nicholas Ivo, *b.* 1954.——Thomas Wilfrid, *b.* 1956.

PREDECESSORS.—[1] *Right Rev.* THOMAS Vesey; successively Bishop of Killaloe and Ossory; cr. *Baronet* 1698; *d.* 1730; *s.* by his son [2] *Sir* JOHN DENNY, 2nd Bt., MP for Newtown, co. Down, and Custos Rotulorum of Queen's Co.; cr. *Baron Knapton* (peerage of Ireland) 1750; *d.* 1761; *s.* by his son [3] THOMAS, 2nd Baron: cr. *Viscount de Vesci* of Abbeyleix, Queen's Co. (peerage of Ireland) 1776; *d.* 1804; *s.* by his son [4] JOHN, 2nd Viscount: Lord-Lieut. of Queen's Co., and a Representative Peer; *d.* 1855; *s.* by his son [5] THOMAS, 3rd Viscount; *b.* 1803; MP for Queen's Co. (*C*) 1835-7; a Representative Peer: *m.* 1839, Lady Emma Herbert, da. of 11th Earl of Pembroke; *d.* 1875; *s.* by his son [6] JOHN ROBERT WILLIAM, 4th Viscount, cr. *Baron de Vesci*, of Abbey Leix, Queen's Co. (peerage of United Kingdom) 1884; *b.* 1844: *m.* 1872, Lady Evelyn Charteris, who *d.* 1939, da. of 8th Earl of Wemyss and March; *d.* 1903, when the Barony became ext. and he was *s.* in the Irish dignities by his nephew [7] IVO RICHARD (son of the late Capt. the Hon. Eustace Vesey, 2nd son of 3rd Viscount), 5th Viscount; *b.* 1881; Major Irish Guards; an Irish Representative Peer: *m.* 1st, 1906, Georgiana Victoria, who *d.* 1930 (having obtained a divorce 1919), da. of the late Gerald Edward Wellesley [E. Cowley, colls.]; 2ndly, 1920, Frances Lois, da. of Sir Cecil Edmund Lister-Kaye, 4th B., and widow of 5th Earl of Rosse; *d.* 1958; *s.* by his nephew [8] JOHN EUSTACE (son of the late Col. the Hon. Thomas Eustace Vesey, brother of 5th Viscount), 6th Viscount and present peer; also Baron Knapton.

DE VILLIERS, BARON. (de Villiers.) [Baron U.K. 1910.]

ARTHUR PERCY DE VILLIERS, 3rd Baron; *b.* Dec. 17th, 1911; *s.* 1934; ed. at Magdalen Coll., Oxford (B.A. 1936); Bar. Inner Temple 1938: *m.* 1939 (marriage dissolved 1958), Edna Alexis Lovett, el. dau. of the late Rev. Dr. A. D. MacKinnon, of Peachland, British Columbia, and has issue.

Arms.—Azure, a bend enhanced argent, on a mount in base a Paschal Lamb proper. *Crest,*—Issuant from a circlet of gold embellished with nine pearls raised upon points, a dexter arm in armour embowed grasping in the hand a seax argent. *Supporters.*—On either side a springbok proper, gorged with a circlet of gold, embellished with nine pearls raised upon points.
Address,—RD1, Kumeu, Auckland, NZ.

The hand to the work.

SON LIVING.
Hon. ALEXANDER CHARLES, *b.* Dec. 29th, 1940: *m.* 1966.

DAUGHTERS LIVING.
Hon. Celia Yvonne Lovett, *b.* 1942: *m.* 1968, Robin Hastings Sancroft Beck, of Mountain Rd., Somerset West, Cape Province, S. Africa, and has issue living, Donovan Henry, *b.* 1969,—Robert Arthur, *b.* 1974,— Honor Alexa Catherine, *b.* 1970.
Hon. Rosemary Aletta, *b.* 1946: *m.* 1967, Robin Anderson Elliott, TD, of 52, St. John Rd., Houghton, Johannesburg, and Sangar Hill Farm, Magaliesburg, Transvaal, and has issue living, Robert Alexander Blyth, *b.* 1970.— Hector de Villiers James, *b.* 1973,—Conrad Lovat Johnston, *b.* 1974.

BROTHER LIVING
Hon. John Maurice, *b.* 1915; ed. at Wadham Coll., Oxford, and Univ. of Cape Town (BA 1947); admitted a Solicitor 1950; consultant to the legal firm of Cloete & Partners, of 117, St. Georges' St., Cape Town, S. Africa; late Fl.-Lt. RAF: *m.* 1946, Christine Mary, da. of A. C. Buller, of Dwarsriviershoek, Stellenbosch, S. Africa, and has issue living, Jeanne Clair, *b.* 1947: *m.* 1st 1968, Peter Puttick; 2ndly, 1972, Patrick Grierson,—Michèle Jacqueline, *b.* 1950. *Residence,*—Blue Mountains, Durbanville, Cape Province, S. Africa.

SISTER LIVING.

Hon. Yvonne Aletta, *b.* 1913; ed. at Lady Margaret Hall, Oxford: *m.* 1939, James Kenneth Hill, and has issue living, Antony James de Villiers, *b.* 1940,—Richard Lansley, *b.* 1946,—Hamish Robert, *b.* 1949,—Susan Felicity, *b.* 1942. *Residence,*—Edgehill, 22, Wynhdorn Av., Buderim, Qld., Australia.

PREDECESSORS.—[1] *Rt. Hon. Sir* JOHN HENRY de Villiers, *K.C.M.G.*, **son of Charles** Christian de Villiers. of Paarl, Cape of Good Hope; *b.* 1842; Attorney-Gen. of Cape Colony 1872-4, and Ch. Justice of Cape of Good Hope 1874-1910, and first Ch. Justice of Union of South Africa 1910-14; *cr. Baron de Villiers,* of Wynberg, Province of Cape of Good Hope and Union of South Africa (peerage of United Kingdom) 1910: *m.* 1871, Aletta Johanna, who *d.* 1922, dau. of Jan Pieter Jordaan, of Worcester, Cape of Good Hope; *d.* 1914; *s.* by his son [2] CHARLES PERCY, 2nd Baron, *b.* 1871: *m.* (Jan.) 1911, Adelheid Helen Selma, who *d.* 1968, da. of Henri Christian Koch, formerly an Assist. Judge, Supreme Court, Natal, of Pietermaritzburg, Natal; *d.* 1934; *s.* by his el. son [3] ARTHUR PERCY, 3rd Baron and present peer.

DEVLIN, BARON.   (Devlin.) [Life Baron U.K. 1961.]

PATRICK ARTHUR DEVLIN, *P.C.*, son of William John Devlin; *b.* Nov. 25th, 1905; ed. at Stonyhurst, and Christ's Coll., Camb.; Bar. Gray's Inn 1929, a K.C. 1945, a Bencher 1947, and Treasurer 1963; appointed Attorney-Gen. to Duchy of Cornwall 1947, a Judge of High Court of Justice (King's Bench Div.) 1948, a Lord Justice of Appeal 1960, and a Lord of Appeal in Ordinary 1961; ret. 1964; Chm., of Press Council 1964–69, and of Court of Quarter Sessions for Wilts since 1964; *cr.* Knt. 1948, P.C. 1960, and *Baron Devlin,* of West Wick, co. Wilts (Life Baron) 1961: *m.* 1932, Madeleine Hilda, *J.P.*, dau. of Sir Bernard Oppenheimer, 1st Bt., and has issue.

Residence,—West Wick House, Pewsey, Wilts.

SONS LIVING.

Hon. Gilpatrick (19, 1st Av., East, Johannesburg), *b.* 1938; ed. at Winchester: *m.* 1967, Glenna, da. of John Parry-Evans, MRCS, of Colwyn Bay, and has issue.
Hon. Dominick (4, Chemin de Chaumont, 1232 Confignon, Switzerland), *b.* 1942; ed. at Winchester, and Univ. Coll., London (LLB): *m.* 1967, Carla, da. of Lamberto Fulloni, of Rome, and has issue.
Hon. Timothy, *b.* 1944; ed. at Winchester, and at Univ. Coll., Oxford: *m.* 1967, Angela, da. of A. J. G. Laramy, and has issue.
Hon. Matthew, *b.* 1946; ed. at Winchester, and at New Coll., Oxford: *m.* Rosemary Joan Boutcher, da. of Lt.-Col. E. C. Van der Kiste, of The Old Rectory, Durrington, Wilts., and has issue.

DAUGHTERS LIVING.

Hon. Clare, *b.* 1940 : *m.* 1961, Julian Reginald Desgrand Jermy Gwyn, of 484, Highland Av., Ottawa, 13, Canada, Prof. in History, Univ. of Ottawa, and has issue.
Hon. Virginia (twin), *b.* 1940: *m.* 1965, Paul Kennedy, QC, of Rydal, 11A, Kent Rd., Harrogate, and has issue.

DEVON, EARL OF.   (Courtenay.) [Earl E. 1553, Bt. I. 1644.]

Where have I fallen, what have I done?

CHARLES CHRISTOPHER COURTENAY, 17th Earl, and 13th Baronet; *b.* July 13th, 1916; *s.* 1935; ed. at Winchester; is patron of four livings; is Capt. Coldstream Guards (Regular Army Reserve): European War 1939-43 (wounded, despatches): *m.* 1939, Sybil Venetia, dau. of the late Capt. John Vickris Taylor (formerly Welsh Guards), of North Aston Manor, Oxford, and formerly wife of 6th Earl of Cottenham, and has issue.

Arms,—Quarterly: 1st and 4th or, three torteaux, *Courtenay*; 2nd and 3rd or, a lion rampant azure, *Redvers, Earl of Devon.* Crests,— 1st, out of a ducal coronet or, a plume of seven ostrich feathers four and three argent; 2nd, a dolphin embowed proper. Supporters,—Two boars argent, tusked, crined, and unguled or.

Seat,—Powderham Castle, near Exeter.

SON LIVING.

HUGH RUPERT (*Lord Courtenay*) (The Stables House, Powderham, Exeter), *b.* May 5th, 1942; ed. at Winchester, and at Magdalene Coll., Camb.: *m.* 1967, Dianna Frances, el. da. of Jack Watherston, of Menslaws, Jedburgh, Roxburghshire, and has issue:—
   SON LIVING—*Hon.* Charles Peregrine, *b.* Aug. 14th, 1975.
   DAUGHTERS LIVING—*Hon.* Rebecca Eildon, *b.* 1969. *Hon.* Eleonora Venetia, *b.* 1971. *Hon.* Camilla Mary, *b.* 1974.

DAUGHTER LIVING.

Lady Katherine Felicity, *b.* 1940: *m.* 1966, Antony Stephen Pope Watney (c/o Paterson Simons, PO 897, Singapore 1.), and has issue living, Michael Hugh Sanders, *b.* 1966.

SISTERS LIVING.

Lady Evelyn Frances, *b.* 1908 : *m.* 1936, Thomas Anstey, and has issue living, Thomas Michael Courtenay (The Cedars, Lincombe Hill Rd., Torquay, Devon), *b.* 1937: *m.* 1961, Margaret, el. da. of the late Dudley Woodman, of Stratford-upon-Avon, and has issue living, Thomas Dudley *b.* 1965, Henry Michael (twin) *b.* 1965, Angela Margaret *b.* 1964,—Patrick John, *b.* 1942,—Anne Caroline (Heath House, Aylesbeare, Exeter) *b.* 1939: *m.* 1964, Maj. David Lionel Scott Langley, MC, RM, and has issue living, Jeremy David Scott *b.* 1967,—Evelyn Margaret, *b.* 1941: *m.* 1966, Philip-James Bedford Linzee Penfold, of Linzee House, Eakring, Newark. *Residence,*—8, Green Leaves, Clyst St. George, Devon.

Lady Mary Elizabeth, *b.* 1910 ; is a State Registered Nurse. *Residence,*—The Briary, Exton, Exeter.

Lady Marguerite Kathleen, *b.* 1911: *m.* 1933, Col. Eugene St. John Birnie, OBE, Indian Army (ret.), and has issue living, Marguerite Susan, *b.* 1934: *m.* 1958, Jasper Meadows Clutterbuck, of Mottisfont House, nr. Romsey, Hants., and has issue living, Hugh Meadows *b.* 1959, Nichola Marguerite *b.* 1961,—Angela Patricia Jane, *b.* 1936: *m.* 1956, Michael Edmond Joly de Lotbinière, of Rougham House, Bury St. Edmunds [see B. Hylton]. *Residence,*—The Cottage, Longparish, Hants.

Lady Camilla Gabrielle, *b.* 1913. *Residence,*—The Briary, Exton, Exeter.

Lady Angela Leslie, *b.* 1918 : *m.* 1947, Harold Cecil Moreton Horsley, M.B.E., Malayan Civil Ser. (ret.), who *d.* 1969, and has issue living, Richard Geoffrey Courtenay, *b.* 1947,—William Frederick Moreton, *b.* 1949. *Residence,*—Marwood House, Offwell, Honiton, Devon.

PREDECESSORS.—[1] Sir Hugh de Courtenay, Knt., 6th feudal Baron of Okehampto summoned as a Baron to all the Parliaments of Edward II., and to the Parliaments o Edward III. 1327-35; was in 1335 summoned as *Earl of Devonshire* ; *d.* 1340 ; *s.* by his son [2] Hugh, 2nd Earl; *d.* 1377; *s.* by his grandson [3] Edward, 3rd Earl; Earl Marshal; *d.* 1419 : *s.* by his son [4] Hugh, 4th Earl; *d.* 1422; *s.* by his son [5] Thomas, 5th Earl; a faithful adherent to the "Red Rose"; *d.* 1458; *s.* by his son [6] Thomas, 6th Earl, a strenuous upholder of the Lancastrian cause fell into the hands of the Yorkists at Towton Field, and was beheaded April 1462, his honours being attainted ; *s.* by his brother [7] Hugh ; was restored to a part of his ancestral estates, but subsequently engaged in the Lancastrian quarrel, was attainted and beheaded 1466. (The greater part of the Courtenay estates having been conferred upon Humphrey Stafford, Baron Stafford, of Southwicke, he was cr. *Earl of Devon* 1469, and in the same year was beheaded as a traitor, when the earldom expired). Hugh (ante), was *s.* by his brother [8] John, 8th Earl, who was restored to his honours by the Parliament that replaced the crown upon the head of Henry VI.; the subsequent defeat of the Earl of Warwick, at Barnet Field, April 14, 1471, again jeopardised his fortunes, and joining Margaret of Anjou he fell at Tewkesbury, May 14, following, and his honours were attainted. The representation of the family then devolved upon [9] Sir Edward, Knt., grandson of Sir Hugh, next brother of 3rd Earl ; participated in the victory of Bosworth and was cr. *Earl of Devon* 1485, and obtained regrants of the greater part of the estates of Thomas, 6th Earl : *d.* 1509; *s.* by his son [10] Sir William : was attainted 1504 and doomed to incarceration during the reign of Henry VII.; he was released by Henry VIII., but *d.* before being formally restored to earldom his son [11] Henry, 2nd Earl (cr. 1485), was restored in blood and honours, and cr. *Marquess of Exeter* 1525; was subsequently committed to the Tower for conspiring to place Reginald Pole, Dean of Exeter, upon the throne, and was beheaded Jan. 9, 1539, his titles being attainted and his estates annexed to the Duchy of Cornwall ; *s.* by his son [12] Edward ; was committed to the Tower 1539 when twelve years of age, and remained there until 1553, when he was released by Queen Mary, and though restored in blood not any of the attainders were reversed; cr. *Earl of Devon* 1553; was subsequently imprisoned in the Tower and in Fotheringay Castle for an alleged connection with Wyatt's rebellion, but was released on the marriage of the Queen with Philip of Spain ; *d.* unmarried at Padua 1556, when, in consequence of the limitations of the patent not being known, the honours became dormant, and remained so until 1831, when it was revived in favour of [13] William, 3rd *Viscount Courtenay* (see note *∗* infra), who became 9th Earl (of cr. 1553) ; *d.* unmarried 1835, when the viscountcy became extinct and his baronetcy and earldom devolved upon his cousin [14] William, 10th Earl, son of the Right Rev. Henry Reginald, Bishop of Exeter, who was son of Henry Reginald Courtenay, M.P., 2nd son of 2nd Bt. (see note *∗∗* infra); *b.* 1777 : *m.* 1st, 1804, Lady Harriet Leslie, dau. of Sir Lucas Pepys, Bt., and Jane Elizabeth, Countess of Rothes; 2ndly, 1849, Elizabeth Ruth, who *d.* 1914, dau. of the late Rev. John Middleton Scott: *d.* 1859; *s.* by his son [15] William Reginald, P.C., 11th Earl, *b.* 1807; was M.P. for S. Devon (C) 1842-8 : *m.* 1830, Lady Elizabeth Fortescue, who *d.* 1867, dau. of 1st Earl Fortescue ; *d.* 1888 ; *s.* by his son [16] Edward Baldwin, 12th Earl, *b.* 1836: M.P. for Exeter (C) 1864-8, and for Devonshire E. 1868-70; *d.* 1891; *s.* by his uncle [17] *Rev.* Henry Hugh, 13th Earl, *b.* 1811; R. of Powderham : *m.* 1835, Lady Anna Maria Leslie, who *d.* 1897, dau. of the late Henrietta Anne, Countess of Rothes; *d.* 1904; *s.* by his grandson [18] Charles Pepys (son of the late Henry Reginald, Lord Courtenay, el. son of 13th Earl, by Lady Evelyn Pepys, dau. of 1st Earl of Cottenham), 14th Earl ; *b.* 1870 ; an Inspector in Board of Agriculture 1895-1904 ; *d.* 1927 ; *s.* by his brother [19] *Rev.* Henry Hugh, 15th Earl, *b.* 1872 ; was R. of Powderham 1904-27 ; *d.* (Feb.) 1935 ; *s.* by his brother [20] *Rev.* Frederick Leslie, 16th Earl, *b.* 1875; was R. of Honiton : *m.* 1907, Marguerite, who *d.* 1950, dau. of the late John Silva, of Itchen Abbas, Hants; *d.* (June) 1935 ; *s.* by his son [21] Charles Christopher, 17th Earl and present Peer.

∗∗ [1] Sir Philip Courtenay, Knt., 6th son of 2nd Earl of Devon of the original cr., Lord-Lieut. of Ireland 1383-92; *s.* by his son [2] Richard ; Lord Bishop of Norwich ; one of the Ambassadors sent by Henry V. to the King of France to demand the crown of that kingdom; *d.* 1415 ; *s.* by his nephew [3] Sir Philip, Knt.; *s.* by his son [4] Sir William, Knt.; High Sheriff of Devon 1483; *d.* 1485; *s.* by his son [5] Sir William, Knt.: *d.* 1512; *s.* by his son [6] Sir William, Knt.; styled "The Great;" *d.* 1535; *s.* by his grandson [7] Sir William, Knt., *de jure* 2nd Earl; killed at storming of St. Quintin 1557 ; *s.* by his son [8] Sir William, Knt., *de iure* 3rd Earl ; one of the undertakers to send over settlers for the better planting of Ireland ; *d.* 1630 ; *s.* by his son [9] Francis, *de jure* 4th Earl, *d.* 1638 ; *s.* by his son [10] William, *de jure* 5th Earl ; cr. a *Baronet* 1644 (disdaining the title did not assume it, but was always styled "Sir" in commissions sent by the king) ; *d.* 1702 ; *s.* by his son [11] Sir William, 2nd Bt. *de jure* 6th Earl ; M.P. for Devon; *d.* 1736 ; *s.* by his son [12] Sir William, *de jure* 7th Earl; cr. *Viscount Courtenay*, of Powderham Castle, co. Devon (peerage of Great Britain, 1762; *d.* 1762; *s.* by his son [13] William, 2nd Viscount, and *de jure* 8th Earl ; *d.* 1788 ; *s.* by his son [14] William, 3rd Viscount, who established his right to the Earldom of Devon (see ante).

DEVONPORT, VISCOUNT. (Kearley.) [Viscount U.K. 1917, Bt. U.K. 1908.]

Love and Work.

TERENCE KEARLEY, 3rd Viscount, and 3rd Baronet; *b.* Aug. 29th, 1944; *s.* 1973; ed. at Aiglon Coll., Switzerland, and Selwyn Coll., Camb. (MA); Dip Arch RIBA: *m.* 1968, Elizabeth Rosemary, 2nd da. of the late John Gordon Hopton, Solicitor, of Chute Manor, Andover.

Arms,—Azure, in chief two mitres argent garnished or, and in base a square tower of the second. Crest.—An ancient ship or, the mainsail azure charged with a sea lion gold. Supporters,—On either side a sea lion argent, crined, finned, and tufted or, each gorged with a collar gules charged with three roses gold, and each supporting a spear erect proper.

Residence,—Linnhead House, W. Woodburn, Hexham, Northumberland. *Clubs,*—Northern Counties (Newcastle), Beefsteak, and RAC.

SISTER LIVING.
Hon. Marilyn Whitson, *b.* 1939.

UNCLE LIVING. (*Son of 1st Viscount.*)
Hon. MARK HUDSON, *b.* March 3rd, 1895; ed. at Eton, and at Magdalen Coll., Oxford, and exhibitor RA, and co-founder Art Gallery of Greater Victoria, BC; 1914-18 War a civilian prisoner Ruhleben, Germany: *m.* 1928, Mabel Florence, who *d.* 1967, da. of the late John Francis Dagley, and has issue living, Chester Dagley Hugh, *b.* 1932: *m.* 1974, Josefa Mesquida,— Patrick Richard Hudson, *b.* 1935: *m.* 1962, Susanna Brigitta, da. of Carl Erik Ringberg, of Stockholm, and has issue living, Selina Anna-Karin *b.* 1967, Cecilia Laura Anthea *b.* 1974,—Anthea, *b.* 1929: *m.* 1959, Luigi Triossi, of 141, Via del Babuino, Rome, Italy, and has issue living, Amanda Consuelo Fiorenza *b.* 1963. *Residence,*—Chalet du Vallon, Chateau d'Oex, Switzerland.

WIDOW LIVING OF SECOND VISCOUNT.
SHEILA ISABEL (*Sheila, Viscountess Devonport*), (Peasmarsh Place, Sussex), el. da. of the late Col. Charles Hope Murray, of Morishill, Beith, Ayrshire: *m.* 1938, the 2nd Viscount, who *d.* 1973.

PREDECESSORS.—[1] Rt. Hon. HUDSON EWBANKE Kearley, son of George Ewbanke Kearley, of Uxbridge; *b.* 1856; Parl. Sec. to Board of Trade 1905-09, Chm. of Roy. Commn. on Sugar Supply 1917, Food Controller 1916-17, and First Chm. of Port of London Authority 1909-25; sat as MP for Devonport (*L*) July 1892 to Jan. 1910; cr. a Baronet 1908, PC 1909, and Baron Devonport, of Wittington, co. Buckingham (peerage of United Kingdom) 1910, and Viscount Devonport, of Wittington, co. Bucks. (peerage of United Kingdom) 1917: *m.* 1888, Selina, who *d.* 1931, da. of Edward Chester, of Blisworth, Northampton; *d.* 1934; *s.* by his el. son [2] GERALD CHESTER, 2nd Viscount, *b.* 1890: *m.* 1938, Sheila Isabel, da. of the late Col. Charles Hope Murray, of Morishill, Beith, Ayrshire; *d.* 1973; *s.* by his son [3] TERENCE, 3rd Viscount and present peer; also Baron Devonport.

DEVONSHIRE, DUKE OF. (Cavendish.) [Duke E. 1694.]

CAVENDO · TVTVS

Secure by caution.

ANDREW ROBERT BUXTON CAVENDISH, *M.C., P.C.,* 11th Duke; *b.* Jan. 2nd, 1920; *s.* 1950; ed. at Eton, and at Trin. Coll., Camb.; Hon. LL.D., Sheffield 1963; Pres. Derbyshire Boy Scouts Assocn., Vice-Lieut. for Derbyshire, and a K.St.J.; Parliamentary Under-Sec. of State for Commonwealth Relations 1960-62, and Min. of State, Commonwealth Relations Office 1962-64; Chancellor of Manchester Univ. since 1965; 1939-45 War as Capt. Coldstream Guards in Italy (M.C.); P.C. 1964: *m.* 1941, the Hon. Deborah Vivien Freeman-Mitford, dau. of 2nd Baron Redesdale, and has issue.

Arms,—Sable, three bucks' heads cabossed argent. Crest.—A serpent nowed proper. Supporters,—Two bucks proper, each wreathed round the neck with a chaplet of roses, alternately argent and azure.

Seats,—Chatsworth, Bakewell, Derbyshire; Bolton Abbey, Yorks.; Lismore Castle, co. Waterford. *Residence,*—4, Chesterfield St., W.1.

SON LIVING.
PEREGRINE ANDREW MORNY (*Marquess of Hartington*) (Chatsworth, Bakewell, Derbys; 15, Christchurch Rd., SW14), *b* April 27th, 1944; ed. at Eton, and Exeter Coll., Oxford: *m.* 1967, Amanda Carmen, only da. of the late Cdr. Edward Gavin Heywood-Lonsdale, RN, and has issue:—

SON LIVING,—William (*Earl of Burlington*), b. June 6th, 1969.
DAUGHTERS LIVING,—*Lady* Celina, b. 1971.
Lady Jasmin, b. 1973.

DAUGHTERS LIVING.
Lady Emma, b. 1943: m. 1963, the Hon. Tobias William Tennant, of Shaws, Newcastleton, Roxburghshire [see B. Glenconner].
Lady Sophia Louise Sydney, b. 1957.

SISTERS LIVING.
Lady Elizabeth Georgiana Alice, b. 1926 ; is a J.P. ; appointed an Extra Lady-in-Waiting to H.R.H. Princess Margaret 1960. *Residences*,—19, Radnor Walk, S.W.3; Moor View, Edensor, Bakewell, Derbyshire.
Lady Anne Evelyn Beatrice, b. 1927: m. 1949, Michael Lambert Tree, of Flat E, 75 Eaton Sq., SW1

AUNTS LIVING. (*Daughters of 9th Duke.*)
Lady Blanche Katharine, b. 1898; is a DStJ; sometime Senior Comdt. ATS; a JP of Suffolk 1951-66 : m. 1919, Lt-Col. John Murray Cobbold, Scots Guards, who d. (killed on active ser.) 1944 [E. Dunmore], and has issue living, John Cavendish, b. 1927; ed. at Eton; is a Director of Cobbold & Co., Ltd., of Cliff Brewery, Ipswich,—Patrick Mark, b. 1934,—Pamela Maud (Dark Lane House, Easton, Woodbridge, Suffolk), b. 1920: m. 1st, 1943, Capt. William Vernon Hope-Johnstone, Grenadier Guards, from whom she obtained a divorce 1950: 2ndly, 1955, Ambrose Alec Patrick George Cadogan, from whom she obtained a divorce 1971 [see E. Cadogan, colls.], and has issue living, (by 1st m.) Philip William (Dark Lane House, Easton, Woodbridge, Suffolk), b. 1943: m. 1968, Antonia Joy, da. of Jack Yuan Hutton-Potts, of The Old Vicarage, Mentmore, Leighton Buzzard; Charles John Victor b. 1948.—Jean, b. 1921: m. 1951, Roger Hewitt Paul, of Brundish Lodge, Woodbridge, Suffolk, and has issue living, Robert Ivan Hewitt b. 1953, David Victor Hewitt b. 1957, Henrietta Katherine b. 1955, Lavinia Christine b. 1962. *Residence*,—Glemham Hall, Woodbridge, Suffolk.
Lady Rachel (*Dowager Viscountess Stuart of Findhorn*), *OBE* (Elm Cottage, Finchingfield, nr. Braintree, Essex, CM7 4LD), b. 1902; has served in ATS and WAAF; OBE (Civil) 1946: m. 1923, the 1st Viscount Stuart of Findhorn, who d. 1971.
Lady Anne, *MBE* (Kilmore House, Bampton, Oxon.), b. 1909; is a JP; MBE (Civil) 1952: m. 1st 1929, Lt.-Col. Henry Philip Hunloke (from whom she obtained a divorce 1945), son of Maj. Sir Philip Hunloke, KCVO; 2ndly, 1949, Christopher John Holland-Martin, MP, who d. 1960; 3rdly, 1962, as his 2nd wife (m. annulled 1965) Alexander Victor Edward Paulet Montagu (10th Earl of Sandwich until he disclaimed his titles 1964) [see E. Sandwich], and has issue living, (by 1st marriage) Timothy Henry, b. 1932,—Nicholas Victor (52, Walham Grove, SW6), b. 1939: m. 1965, Lady Katharine Victoria Montagu, da. of (Alexander) Victor Edward Paulet Montagu (ante), and has issue living, Edward Perceval b. 1969, Henrietta Yvery b. 1968, Matilda Anne b. 1972,—Philippa Victoria (2, St. Albans Grove, W8), b. 1930: m. 1955, (m. diss. 1960), the 3rd Viscount Astor, who d. 1966.

WIDOW LIVING OF SON OF NINTH DUKE.
Adèle, dau. of Frederic E. Astaire, of U.S.A.: m. 1st.1932, Lord Charles Arthur Francis Cavendish, who d. 1944; 2ndly, 1947, Kingman Douglas, investment banker, of New York, USA, who d. 1971. *Residence*,—41, Biltmore Estates, Phoenix, Arizona, 85016, USA.

WIDOW LIVING OF TENTH DUKE.
MARY ALICE (*Dowager Duchess of Devonshire*), *G.C.V.O.*, *C.B.E.*, dau. of 4th Marquess of Salisbury, Hon. LL.D. Leeds 1954, and Exeter 1956: Mistress of the Robes to H.M. the Queen 1952-66 ; Chancellor of Exeter Univ., 1956-71; CBE (Civil) 1946, GCVO 1955: m. 1917, the 10th Duke, who d. 1950. *Residences*,—107, Eaton Sq., SW1; Moorview, Edensor, Bakewell, Derbys.

COLLATERAL BRANCHES LIVING.
Grandchildren of the late Col. the Rt. Hon. Lord Richard Frederick Cavendish, CB OMG (infra):—
Issue of the late Capt. Richard Edward Osborne Cavendish, JP, DL, b. 1917, d. 1972: m. 1937, Pamela (The Dower House, Holker Hall, Cark-in-Cartmel, Cumbria), da. of the late Hugh Lloyd Thomas, CMG, CVO [see B. Bellew]:—
Richard Hugh (Holker Hall, Cark-in-Cartmel, Cumbria), b. 1941: m. 1970, Grania Mary, da. of Brig. Toby St. George Caulfeild, MBE [see V. Charlemont, colls.], and has issue living, Frederick Richard Toby, b. 1972,—Lucy Georgiana, b. 1973.——Edward Osborne, b. 1955.——Georgina Elisabeth, b. 1939: m. 1968, Andrew Henry Clowes, late Scots Gds., of 37, Ellerby St., SW6 [see M. Lothian, colls.].——Harriet Moyra Aline, b. 1944: m. 1972, Capt. Anthony Peter Coote Sykes [D. Wellington], late R. Scots Greys, of Bickton, Fordingbridge, Hants., and has issue living, Nina Aline, b. 1973.—— Susan Anne, b. 1949: m. 1970, Quentin Hugh Crewe [M. Crewe, ext.] of Netherset Hey, Madeley, Crewe, Ches.

Grandchildren of the late Rt. Hon. Lord Edward Cavendish, M.P., 3rd son of 7th Duke:—
Issue of the late Col. the Rt. Hon. Lord Richard Frederick Cavendish, C.B., C.M.G., b. 1871 (raised to rank of a Duke's son 1908), d. 1946: m. 1895, Lady Moyra de Vere Beauclerk, who d. 1942, dau. of 10th Duke of St. Albans :—
Elizabeth, Vere (*Elizabeth, Marchioness of Salisbury*), b. 1897: m. 1915, the 5th Marquess of Salisbury who d. 1972. *Residences*,—Hatfield House, Herts.; Cranborne Lodge, Cranborne, Dorset; 2, Swan Walk, SW3.——Mary Katherine (*Countess of Crawford and Balcarres*), b. 1930: m. 1925, the 28th Earl of Crawford and 11th Earl of Balcarres. *Residence*,—Balcarres, Colinburgh, Fife.——Diana (*Viscountess Gage*), b. 1909: m. 1st, 1935, Robert John Graham Boothby (from whom she obtained a divorce 1937)—now Baron Boothby; 2ndly, 1942, Lt.-Col. the Hon. Ian Douglas Campbell-Gray, RE, who d. 1946 [see L. Gray]; 3rdly, 1971, the 6th Viscount Gage, of Firle Pl., Lewes——Sybil, b. 1915: m. 1941, the Rev. Laurence Gregson Fell Dykes, R. of Hartfield, Sussex, and has issue living, Michael, b. 1942,—Rose, b. 1946,—Catherine Mary, b. 1948. *Residence*,—The Rectory, Hartfield, Sussex.

Grandchildren of the late Lieut.-Col. William Henry Frederick Cavendish, son of the late Gen. the Hon. Henry Frederick Compton Cavendish, M.P. (infra):—
Issue of the late Capt. Henry Frederick Compton Cavendish, R.N., b. 1854, d. 1928 : m. 1888, Lady Harriet Castalia Godolphin Osborne, who d. 1922, dau. of 9th Duke of Leeds :—
Emily Georgiana Harriett (*Lady Saunders-Pryse*), b. 1890: m. 1938, Sir Pryse Loveden Saunders-Pryse, 5th Bt., who d. 1962, when the title became ext. *Residence*,—Glanrhydw, Kidwelly, Carmarthenshire.——Evelyn Alice Beatrix, b. 1892: m. 1924, Brig. James Erskine Stirling, DSO, Seaforth Highlanders, who d. 1968, and has issue living, William Henry (3, Woodsford Sq., Addison Rd., W14), b. 1926: m. 1st, 1959 (m. diss. 1967), Mariota, yst. da. of Lt.-Col. Ronald Steuart Menzies of Menzies, of Arndilly House, Craigellachie, Banffshire; 2ndly, 1968, Primrose, da. of the late Maj. W. F. Butler, 13th/18th R. Hussars,—Bridget Mary (*Hon. Mrs. David J. Rollo*), b. 1925: m. 1948, Capt. the Hon. David Ian Rollo, MBE, MC, Gren. Gds. [see L. Rollo],—Anne Evelyn, b. 1929: m. 1951, Maj. Claude Glen Kelway-Bamber, MBE, Argyll and Sutherland Highlanders, and has issue living Roderick James b. 1952, Martin Charles b. 1955, Euan Glen b. 1958, Emma Clare b. 1960,—Sarah Caroline, b. 1933: m. 1963, Capt. Patrick Doyne, Rifle Bde., of Northend Manor, Leamington Spa, Warwicks., and has issue living, Timothy Robert Hamish b. 1966, Sarah Lucinda b. 1964. *Residence*,—Westfield, Nairn.
Issue of the late Major Cecil Charles Cavendish, b. 1855, d. 1931 : m. 1890, Maud Henrietta, who d. 1956, dau. of Lieut.-Gen. George Thomas Halliday, Indian Army :—
Charles) Vernon Balfour (120, Queen Alexandra Mansions, Tonbridge St., WCIH 9DW), b. 1902: ed. at Haileybury: m. 1st, 1938 (m. diss. 1950), Nancy Cranswick Neal, da. of Ernest William Redstone;

2ndly, 1963, Eve, widow of Athelstan Douglas Dempster Bonnor, and has issue living (by 1st m.), Susan (152, Balfour Rd., Preston Park, Brighton), *b.* 1939,—Rosalind, *b.* 1945: *m.* 1971, Alan Hugh Davidson.

Grandchildren of the late Major Cecil Charles Cavendish (ante):—
Issue of the late Major Frederick George Cavendish, D.S.O., M.C., *b.* **1891,** *d.* **1936:** *m.* 1919, Milla Jean, dau. of the late W. St. Clair Grant, of Bhagalpur, Bengal :—
Anne, *b.* **1920.**——Jean Caroline, *b.* **1932:** ed. at Lady Margaret Hall, Oxford: *m.* 1954 (*m.* **diss.** 1959) Anthony Richard Champion de Crespigny, and has issue living, Camilla Georgiana, *b.* 1955.
Issue of the late Brigadier Ronald Valentine Cecil Cavendish, O.B.E., M.C., *b.* 1896, *d.* (killed in action in Burma) 1943: *m.* 1923, Violet Helen, who *d.* 1974, el. da. of the late Arthur Sackville Boucher, of Sharpcliffe Hall, Staffordshire:—
Peter Boucher, *OBE,* *b.* 1925; ed. at Winchester; Brig. late 14th/20th King's Hussars, OBE (Mil) 1969; *m.* 1952, Marion Loudon, da. of Robert Alfred Constantine, TD, JP, of Tanton Grange, Stokesley, Yorks, and has issue living, Ronald Simon Constantine, *b.* 1954,—Mark Francis, *b.* 1955,—Rupert William, *b.* 1962.——Robin Francis, *MBE,* *b.* 1930; ed. at Winchester; is late Capt. King's Roy. Rifle Corps; MBE (Civil) 1975: *m.* 1957, Diana Mary, yr. da. of Lt.-Col. Latham Valentine Stewart Blacker, OBE [see E. Peel], and has issue living, Jonathan Stewart, *b.* 1959. *Residence,*—Furlongs, Drayton St. Leonard, Oxford.

Granddaughters of the late Capt. Godfrey Lionel John Cavendish (infra):—
Issue of the late Capt. Godfrey Herbert Richard Cavendish, *b.* 1912, *d.* 1958 : *m.* 1950, Angela Margaret Jervis (37, Dovehouse St., SW3), da. of the late Lt.-Col. William Gerald Officer, late Duke of Wellington's Regt., of 37, Lowndes St., SW1:—
Diana Grace Angela, *b.* 1954: *m.* 1975, F. John Reeves.——Caroline Elizabeth Clare, *b.* 1956.

Grandchildren of the late Reginald Richard Frederick Cavendish (infra):—
Issue of the late Capt. Godfrey Lionel John Cavendish, 97th Deccan Inf., *b.* **1884,** *d.* (of wounds received in action) 1914: *m.* 1911, Cora Grace Graham (who *d.* 1962, having *m.* 2ndly, 1919, Douglas M. Horsford), dau. of Joseph Alphonsus Horsford, M.R.C.S., L.R.C.P., of Long Melford, Suffolk:—
Hubert Gordon Compton, *b.* 1913; late Capt. R.A.S.C.; European War 1939-45 in E. Africa : *m.* 1942, Beaujolois Inez, da. of the late Capt. Philip George Wodehouse, DSO, RN [see E. Kimberley, colls.], and has issue living, Richard Gordon John, *b.* 1949: *m.* 1973, Jill Dare, da. of Frank D. Baker, of Sunbury on Thames, and has issue living, Susanna Lucy *b.* 1974,—Beaujolois Katharine, *b.* 1947. *Residence,*—Merrivale, Constantine, Falmouth, Cornwall.
Issue of the late Dorothy Alice Georgina Cavendish, *b.* 1891, *d.* 1965: *m.* 1918, Maj. Hilary Ralph Hood, MC, formerly RGA, who *d.* 1960:—
Hilary Ollyet Dupuis, *b.* 1920; Maj. (ret.) RA; 1939-45 War in Burma: *m.* 1953, Mrs. Nicandra McCarthy, el. da. of the late Everest Sampson, and has issue living, a son, *b.* 1955,—a da., *b.* 1953. ——Richard Godfrey Palgrave (1290, South Los Robles Av., Pasadena, Cal., USA), *b.* 1929: *m.* 1966, Victoria Louise Butler, of Atlanta, Georgia, USA.——Dorothea Barbara, *b.* 1924: *m.* 1955, Stanley Charles Phipps, of Little Browndreys, Carhampton, Minehead, Somerset.

Grandaughter of the late Francis William Henry Cavendish, son of the late Gen. the Hon. Henry Frederick Compton Cavendish, M.P., 3rd son of 1st Earl of Burlington, who was uncle of 7th Duke:—
Issue of the late Reginald Richard Frederick Cavendish, *b.* **1857,** *d.* **1941:** *m.* **1880,** Mary Constance, who *d.* 1914, dau. of the late Rev. Harry Dupuis, V. of Richmond, Surrey; 2ndly, 1922, Martha Douglas, who *d.* 1963, dau. of the late Thomas Henry Reynolds, and widow of Col. Richard Leigh, Highland L.I.:—
(By 1st marriage) Beatrix Frances Dupuis, *b.* 1888: *m.* 1914, Hugh Molyneux Miller, who *d.* 1942, and has issue living, Robert Charles Patrick (Geldeston Hall, Beccles, Suffolk), *b.* 1916; Lt.-Col. (ret.) Indian Cav.: *m.* 1st, 1950 (m. diss. 1953), Elizabeth Ogilvie Noall; 2ndly, 1955, Lydia Georgina Vaux Miéville, and has issue living, (by 2nd marriage) Emma Anastatia Molyneux, *b.* 1957. *Residence,*—Ellingham Hall, Kirby Lane, Suffolk.

Grandson of the late Ernest Lionel Francis Cavendish, son of the late Francis William Henry Cavendish (ante):—
Issue of the late Major Alwyn Lionel Compton Cavendish, *b.* **1890,** *d.* **1928 :** *m.* 1917, Muriel Cecil Harriotte, who *d.* 1975 having *m.* 3rdly, 1946, the 2nd Baron Forteviot, who *d.* 1947, da. of the late Lt.-Col. Sir Charles Henry Brabazon Heaton-Ellis, OBE, of Wyddiall Hall, Herts, and widow of Richard Charles Graves-Sawle, Lt. Coldm. Gds. [Graves-Sawle, Bt. (ext.]:—
Charles Francis Alwyn Compton, *b.* 1919; ed. at Eton, and at Fettes ; is Lieut. King's Own Scottish Borderers; formerly 2nd Lieut. 8th Hussars and Intelligence Corps; European War 1939-45 in Middle East and N.-W. Europe (wounded): *m.* 1st, 1943 (marriage dissolved 1946), Margaret Savage (Section Officer, W.A.A.F.), who *d.* 1961, dau. of Capt. Philip Clayton Alcock, D.L., J.P., late Gloucester Regt., of Overton Lodge, Ludlow, Salop.; 2ndly, 1947, Esther Marion, only dau. of Col. Chichester de Windt Crookshank, of Johnstounburn, Humbie, East Lothian, and has issue living, (by 2nd marriage) William Alwyn Charles Chichester, *b.* 1956,—Mark Andrew Lionel Compton, *b.* 1958. *Residence,*—Yealscombe, Exford, Minehead, Somerset. *Club,*—Turf.

Grandson of the late William Henry Alexander George Delmar Cavendish (infra):—
Issue of the late Charles Alfred William Delmar Cavendish, *b.* 1878, *d.* 1939 : *m.* 1st, 1914, Ruth Madeline (who obtained a divorce 1926), dau. of the late Henry William Smith, of Sydney, N.S. Wales; 2ndly, 1926, Marguerite Florence, who *d.* 1943, el. dau. of Henri Moreau, of Sydney, N.S. Wales, and Paris:—
(By 1st marriage) Richard Blake Delmar, *b.* 1916.

Grandson of the late William Henry George Cavendish (infra):—
Issue of the late Capt. Edwin Pearson Delmar Cavendish, *b.* 1908, *d.* 1970: *m.* 1943, Daphne Joan (Banchory Cottage, Hinton St. George, Som.), da. of the late Maj. William John Van. de Weyer, MVO [see V. Powerscourt], and widow of Sqdn. Ldr. Charles Richard John Pink, RAF:—
Adrian Delmar, *b.* 1947.

Grandson of the late William Henry Alexander George Delmar Cavendish (infra):—
Issue of the late William Henry George Cavendish, *b.* 1886, *d.* 1964: *m.* 1907, Beatrice, who *d.* 1914, da. of E. Pearson .of Toronto:—
William Delmar (Public Schools Club), *b.* 1911; ed. at Bedford Sch.; 1939-45 War, as Capt. Middx Regt. in Middle East, and NW Europe (twice wounded): *m.* 1943, Luisa, da. of Antonio Fusco, of Catania, Sicily, and has issue living, William Anthony, *b.* 1952,—Jessica Luisa, *b.* 1946.

Granddaughters of the late Capt. George Henry Cavendish, son of the late Gen·ther Hon. Henry Frederick Compton Cavendish, M.P. (ante):—
Issue of the late William Henry Alexander George Delmar Cavendish, *b.* 1849, *d.* 1919: *m.* 1874, Edith Louisa, who *d.* 1902, dau. of Edmund Chivers :—
Edith Emily Ida. *b.* 1881: *m.* 1906, Richard Lucas Chaldecott, who *d.* 1934. *Residence,*—2128, Arbutus, Vancouver, 9, British Columbia.
Descendants of the late Hon. Charles Compton Cavendish (4th son of 1st Earl of Burlington), who was cr. *Baron Chesham* 1858 [see that title].

PREDECESSORS.—[1] *Sir* WILLIAM Cavendish, *K.B.;* cr. *Baron Cavendish,* of Hardwicke (peerage of England) 1605, and *Earl of Devonshire* (peerage of England) 1618; *d.* 1625; *s.* by

his son [2] WILLIAM, 2nd Earl; d. 1628; s. by his son [3] WILLIAM, 3rd Earl; d. 1684; s. by
his son [4] WILLIAM, K.G., P.C., 4th Earl; M.P. for co. Derby, Lord-Lieut. of Derbyshire and
Lord Steward of the Household; cr. Marquess of Hartington, and Duke of Devonshire (peerage
of England) 1694; d. 1707; s. by his son [5] WILLIAM, K.G., 2nd Duke; s. by his son [6]
WILLIAM, K.G., 3rd Duke; Lord Steward of the Household 1729, Lord-Lieut. of Ireland 1737-
44; d. 1755; s. by his son [7] WILLIAM, K.G., 4th Duke; summoned to House of Lords in his
father's Barony of Cavendish 1751; Lord-Lieut. of Ireland 1755, First Lord of the Treasury
1756-7, Master of the Horse, Lord Chamberlain 1757, &c.: m. Charlotte Elizabeth, Baroness
Clifford, dau. of Richard, 4th Earl of Cork, whose claim to the Barony of Clifford, of
Lanesborough (peerage of England, cr. 1628), had been allowed; his 3rd son, George Augustus
Henry, was cr. Earl of Burlington and Baron Cavendish, of Keighley (peerage of United
Kingdom) 1831; d. 1764; s. by his el. son [8] WILLIAM, K.G., 5th Duke, who in 1754 had s.
his mother as Baron Clifford; d. 1811; s. by his son [9] WILLIAM SPENCER, K.G., P.C., 6th
Duke; Lord-Lieut. of co. Derb; ·d. unmarried 1858, when the Barony of Clifford became
abeyant between his two sisters, and the other honours devolved upon [10] WILLIAM, K.G.,
7th Duke, who had in 1834 s. his grandfather as 2nd Earl of Burlington (el. son of the Hon.
William Cavendish, M.P., el. son of 1st Earl of Burlington (ante), by Louisa, el. dau.of 1st
Baron Lismore), b. 1808; Chancellor of London Univ. 1836-56, and of Camb. Univ. 1862-91,
and Lord-Lieut. of Lancashire 1855-8, and of Derbyshire 1858-91; M.P. for Camb. Univ. (L)
1829-31, for Molton 1831, and for N. Derbyshire 1831-4: m. 1829, Lady Blanche Georgiana
Howard, who d. 1840, dau. of 6th Earl of Carlisle, K.G.; d. 1891; s. by his el. son [11]
SPENCER COMPTON, K.G., G.C.V.O., P.C., D.C.L., LL.D., 8th Duke, b. 1833; attached to Earl
Granville's Special Embassy to Russia 1856, and went to St. Petersburg to attend the Corona-
tion of Alexander II. 1857; a Lord of the Admiralty 1863, Under-Sec. for War 1863-6, Sec. of
State for War 1866, Postmaster-Gen. 1868-70, Ch. Sec. for Ireland 1870-74, Lord Rector of
Glasgow Univ. 1877-80, Sec. of State for India 1880-82 and for War 1882-5, Pres. of Board
of Education 1900-1902, and Lord Pres. of the Council and Pres. of Council of National
Defence 1895-1903; Lord-Lieut. of Derbyshire and High Steward of Derby; M.P. for N. Lancashire
1857-68, for New Radnor (L) 1869-80, for Lancashire, N.E. 1880-85, and for Rossendale Div.
of N.E. Lancashire 1885-91 (LU): m. 1892, Louise Frederica Augusta, who d. 1911, dau. of the
late Charles, Count von Alten, of Hanover, and widow of 7th Duke of Manchester, d. 1908;
s. by his nephew [12] VICTOR CHRISTIAN WILLIAM, K.G., G.C.M.G., G.C.V.O., T.D., P.C. (el.
son of the late Lord Edward Cavendish, M.P., 3rd son of the 7th Duke), 9th Duke; b. 1868; was
Treasurer of H.M.'s Household 1900-1903, Financial Sec. to the Treasury 1903-5, a Civil Lord of
the Admiralty 1915, Gov.-Gen. and Com.-in-Ch., Dominion of Canada 1916-21, Sec. of State
for the Colonies 1922-4, and Chm. of Executive Council of British Empire Exhibition 1924
and 1925; sat as M.P. for Derbyshire, W. Div. (LU) 1891-1908; bore Queen Consort's Crown at
Coronation of King George V.: m. 1892, Lady Evelyn Emily Mary Fitzmaurice, G.C.V.O.,
who d. 1960, dau. of 5th Marquess of Lansdowne; d. 1938; s. by his el. son [13] EDWARD WILLIAM
SPENCER, K.G., M.B.E., T.D., 10th Duke; b. 1895; Train Bearer at Coronation of King George V.
1911; was Parliamentary Under-Sec. of State for Dominion Affairs 1936-40, for India and Burma
1940-42, and for the Colonies 1942-45; sat as M.P. for W. Div. of Derbyshire (U) 1923-38: m. 1917,
Lady Mary Alice Gascoyne-Cecil, C.B.E., dau. of 4th Marquess of Salisbury; d. 1950; s. by his only
surviving son [14] ANDREW ROBERT BUXTON, 11th Duke and present peer; also Marquess of
Hartington, Earl of Devonshire, Earl of Burlington, Baron Cavendish of Hardwicke, and Baron
Cavendish of Keighley.

DIAMOND, BARON. (Diamond.) [Life Baron 1970.]

JOHN DIAMOND, PC, son of the late Rev. Solomon Diamond, of Leeds; b.
April 30th, 1907; ed. at Leeds Gram. Sch.; FCA; PPS to Min. of Works
1947, and Chm. of Finance Cttee., Gen. Nursing Council 1947-53; Hon.
Treas. of Fabian Soc. 1950-64; Dir. Sadler's Wells Trust 1957-64; Hon.
Treas. Labour Cttee. for Europe 1961-64; Ch. Sec. to Treasury (and Member
of Cabinet 1968-70) 1964-70; Dep. Chm. of Cttees., House of Lords 1974; Chm.
Roy. Commn. on Distribution of Income and Wealth since 1974; MP for
Blackley, Manchester (Lab.) 1945-51, and for Gloucester 1957-70; cr. PC 1965,
and Baron Diamond, in City of Gloucester (Life Baron) 1970: m. 1st, 1932 (m.
diss. 1947); 2ndly, 1948, Julie —, and has issue by 1st and 2nd m.

Residence,—44, Chenies, Bucks.

SONS LIVING (By 1st m.)

Hon. Derek, b. 1933.
Hon. Martin, b. 1935.

DAUGHTERS LIVING (By 1st m.)

Hon. Ruth, b. 1937.

(By 2nd m.)

Hon. Joan, b. 1949.

DICKINSON, BARON. (Dickinson.) [Baron U.K. 1930.]

RICHARD CLAVERING HYETT DICKIN-
SON, 2nd Baron; b. March 2nd, 1926; s.
1943; ed. at Eton, and at Trin. Coll.,
Oxford; late Capt. Coldstream Guards:
m. 1957, (Margaret) Ann, el. da. of
Brigadier Gilbert Reader McMeekan,
CBE, DSO, and has issue.

Arms,—Or, a bend cottised between two
lions passant gules. Crest,—Issuant from clouds
a dexter cubit arm erect the hand holding an olive
branch fructed all proper. Supporters,—Dexter,
a falcon proper, collared and lined or; sinister,
a dove holding in the beak an olive branch
fructed, both proper.
Residence,—Painswick House, Painswick,
Gloucestershire.

SONS LIVING.
Hon. MARTIN HYETT, b. Jan. 30th, 1961.
Hon. Andrew, b. 1963.

BROTHERS LIVING. (Raised to the rank
of a Baron's sons 1944.)
Hon. Peter Malcolm De Brissac, b. 1927; ed.
at Eton, and at King's Coll., Camb.: m.
1953, Mary Rose, el. dau. of Vice-Adm. Sir

Geoffrey Barnard, K.C.B., C.B.E., D.S.O., and has issue living, John Geoffrey Hyett *b.* 1962, —James Christopher Meade, *b.* 1963,—Philippa Lucy Ann, *b.* 1955,—Dorothy Louise, *b.* 1956. *Residence,*—33, Queensdale Rd., W.11.
Rev the Hon. Hugh Geoffrey (The Vicarage, Old Milverton, nr. Leamington Spa., Warks.), *b.* 1929; ed. at Westminster Sch., and at Trin. and Cuddesdon Colls., Oxford; Chap., Trin. Coll., Camb. 1958-63, and Winchester Coll. 1963-69: *m.* 1963, Jean Marjorie, only da. of Arthur Storey, of 25, Woodbourne Av., Leeds, 17, and has issue living, Benjamin Mark, *b.* 1966,—Teresa, *b.* 1964.
Hon. David Christopher (The Hollins, Utkinton, Tarporley, Ches.), *b.* 1935; ed. at Eton and at Trin. Coll., Oxford: *m.* 1970, Mrs. Caroline Mary Yeoward, da. of the late Arthur Denton Toosey.

AUNTS LIVING. (*Daughters of 1st Baron.*)

Hon. Agnes Désirée, *OBE*, *b.* 1892; a JP; OBE (Civil) 1966: *m.* 1ˡ 2, James Cyril Butterwick, who *d.* 1966, and has issue living, John Newton (Danyells, Sandon, Buntingford, Herts), *b.* 1923; Brevet-Col. (ret.); formerly OC, Queen's Westminsters (TA) and Queen's R. Rifles (TA): *m.* 1956, Marcia, only da. of John Hull Scott, of Pittsburgh, USA, and has issue living, Nicholas Scott *b.* 1959, Christopher Hugh *b.* 1963, William Toby *b.* 1965, Sarah *b.* 1958,—Michael Willoughby (Manor House, Stanton St. John, Oxford), *b.* 1927; formerly Lt. Rifle Brig.: *m.* 1957, Felicity, el. da. of Col. F. W. S. Roberts, and has issue living, Miranda *b.* 1959, Lucy *b.* 1961, Catrina *b.* 1963, Flora *b.* 1966,—Antony James (Pinkneys House, Pinkneys Green, Berks), *b.* 1930; late Capt. Queen's Westminsters (TA): *m.* 1959, Joanna, yr. da. of Col. Hugh Vanderfelt, and has issue living, James Hugo *b.* 1962, Antony Guy *b.* 1966, Henrietta *b.* 1960,—Elizabeth Anne, *b.* 1924: *m.* 1951, John Robertson, of Hillcrest, Burton, Wirral, Cheshire, and has issue living, David *b.* 1954, Jennifer *b.* 1957, Diana *b.* 1959. *Residence,*—Parkside, Beaconsfield, Bucks.
Hon. Frances Joan, *DBE* (*Dowager Viscountess Davidson*), *b.* 1894; MP, Hemel Hempstead Div. of Herts (*U*) 1937-59; OBE (Civil) 1920, DBE (Civil) 1952, and *Baroness Northchurch* (Life Baroness) 1963: *m.* 1919, the 1st Viscount Davidson, who *d.* 1970. *Residence,*—16, Lord North St., Westminster, SW1.

MOTHER LIVING.

May Southey, dau. of Charles Lovemore, of Melsetter, Cape Province, S. Africa; is a J.P.: *m.* 1924, the Hon. Richard Sebastian Willoughby Dickinson, D.S.O., who *d.* 1935, only son of 1st Baron. *Residence,*—The Poultry Court, Painswick, Gloucestershire.

PREDECESSOR.—[1] *Rt. Hon.* WILLOUGHBY HYETT Dickinson, *K.B.E.*, only son of the late Sebastian Stewart Dickinson (M.P. for Stroud), of Brown's Hill, Stroud; *b.* 1859; Chm. of London County Council 1900; sat as M.P. for N. Div. of St. Pancras (*L*) 1906-18; *cr. Baron Dickinson,* of Painswick, co. Gloucester (peerage of United Kingdom) 1930: *m.* 1891, Minnie Elizabeth, who *d.* 1967, da. of the late Gen. Sir Richard John Meade, KCSI, CIE; *d.* 1943; *s.* by his grandson [2] RICHARD CLAVERING HYETT (el. son of the late Hon. Richard Sebastian Willoughby Dickinson, D.S.O., only son of 1st Baron), 2nd Baron and present peer.

DIGBY, BARON. (Digby.) [Baron I. 1620, and G.B. 1765.]

EDWARD HENRY KENELM DIGBY, 12th Baron; *b.* July 24th, 1924; *s.* 1964; ed. at Eton, and at Trin. Coll., Oxford; Capt. late Coldstream Guards; a JP, Vice-Lt., and a Co. Councillor of Dorset; Dept. Chm. of S-W Economic Planning Council, and a Dir. Brooklyns Westbrick, Ltd., ADC to C.-in-C. Far East Land Forces 1950-51, and to C.-in-C., BAOR 1951-52; 1939-45 War; Malaya 1948-50: *m.* 1952, Dione Marian, da. of Rear-Adm. Robert St. Vincent Sherbrooke, VC, CB, DSO, and has issue.

Arms,—Azure, a fleur-de-lis argent. Crest, —An ostrich with a horse-shoe in its beak, all proper. Supporters,—Two monkeys proper, environed round the loins and lined or.

Residence,—Minterne, Dorchester, Dorset. *Club,*—Pratt's.

From God not Fortune.

SONS LIVING.

Hon. HENRY NOEL KENELM, *b.* Jan. 6th, 1954; ed. at Eton.
Hon. Rupert Simon, *b.* 1956; ed. at Eton.

DAUGHTER LIVING.

Hon. Zara Jane, *b.* 1958.

SISTERS LIVING.

Hon. Pamela Beryl, *b.* 1920: *m.* 1st, 1939, Maj. the Hon. Randolph Frederick Edward Spencer Churchill, MBE [see D. Marlborough, colls.]. who *d.* 1968, and from whom she obtained a divorce 1946; 2ndly, 1960, Leland Hayward, who *d.* 1971; 3rdly, 1971, (William) Averell Harriman, of 3038, N St. NW, Washington, DC, 20007, USA.
Hon. Constance Sheila, *b.* 1921; in A.T.S. 1939-40, and with British Security Co-ordination 1943-45, *m.* 1945, Charles Arthur Moore. *Residences,*—135, East 71st St., New York City, USA; Bearforest, Mallow, co. Cork.
Hon. Jaquetta Mary Theresa, *b.* 1928; a Member of Mid-Sussex Hosp. Cttee. 1960-68, and of Dorset Area Health Authority since 1974; Chm., Hamilton Lodge Sch. for Deaf Children, Brighton since 1962: *m.* 1950, David Pelham James, MBE, DSO, MP, el. son of Wing-Com. Sir Archibald William Henry James, KBE, MC, and has issue living, Peter Edward, *b.* 1951,—Michael David Ashworth, *b.* 1955,—Christopher Leslie Donan, *b.* 1957,—Kenelm Henry Thomas, *b.* 1962,—Patricia Bridget Edwina, *b.* 1952,—Diana Mary, *b.* 1953. *Residence,*—Malabar House, Child Okeford, Blandford, Dorset.

UNCLE LIVING. (*Son of 10th Baron.*)

Hon. Albert Elmar, *b.* 1911. *Residence,*—Flat 12, 49 Lowndes Square, S.W.1.

WIDOW LIVING OF ELEVENTH BARON.

Hon. CONSTANCE PAMELA ALICE, *O.B.E.,* (*Pamela, Baroness Digby*) (Cerne Abbey, Dorchester, Dorset), da. of 2nd Baron Aberdare; Co. Comdt. Dorset A.T.S. 1938-9, and Ch. Com. A.T.S. 1939-46; a Member of Council of Queen's Inst. of Dist. Nursing, and a JP for Dorset; a Co. Councillor for Dorset 1943-46, and 1953-57, since when a Co. Alderman; Pres. of Dorset Branch, British Red Cross Soc. 1964-72, since when Hon. Vice-Pres.; has Red Cross Badge of Honour; OBE (Mil.) 1944: *m.* 1919, the 11th Baron, who *d.* 1964.

COLLATERAL BRANCHES LIVING.

Issue of the late Hon. Robert Henry Digby, 2nd son of 10th Baron, *b.* 1903; *d.* 1959: *m.* 1928, Diana Mary, who *d.* 1969, da. of Sir Berkeley Digby George Sheffield, 6th Bt.:—

Henry Berkeley, *b.* 1933; ed. at Eton: *m.* 1960, Jacqueline, el. da. of Charles A. Hussey, of Barking, Essex, and has issue living, Jane Diana, *b.* 1962,—Charlotte Sophia, *b.* 1964.——Caroline Theresa, *b.* 1943: *m.* 1963, Charles Dermot FitzRoy Musker [see V. Daventry].

Issue of the late Hon. Lettice Theresa Digby, da. of 10th Baron, *b.* 1896, *d.* 1967: *m.* 1921, Lt.-Col. Eric Tillyer Tatham:—

Gerald Edward (Mandeville, Jamaica), *b.* 1926; late Lt. KRRC: *m.* 1952, Joan Patricia, da. of the late William Charles Buie, and has issue living, Christopher Nigel Digby, *b.* 1954,—William David Buie, *b.* 1965,— Melinda Gaye, *b.* 1962,—Sandra Joan, *b.* 1964.——Nigel John (Araluen, Hindhead, Surrey), *b.* 1927: *m.* 1951, Elizabeth Anne, da. of Sir William Errington Keville, CBE, and has issue living, Joanna Mary, *b.* 1956,—Caroline Julie Theresa, *b.* 1958,—Edwina Jane, *b.* 1962,— Ailsa Charlotte Elizabeth, *b.* 1966.——Nancye Jean, *b.* 1924: *m.* 1945, Fl.-Lt. Andrew Desmond Pelly, DFC [see Pelly Bt., colls.].

Issue of the late Col. the Hon. Everard Charles Digby, 3rd son of 9th Baron, *b.* 1852, *d.* 1915: *m.* 1886, Lady Emily Louisa Anne Fitzmaurice, who *d.* 1939, dau. of 4th Marquess of Lansdowne :—

Giles Stephen, *b.* 1894.

Grandchildren of the late Sir Kenelm Edward Digby, GCB, KC, el. son of the late Rev. the Hon. Kenelm Henry Digby (infra):—

Issue of the late Com. Edward Aylmer Digby, K.C., *b.* 1883, *d.* 1935: *m.* 1911, Winifred Digby, who *d.* 1967, da. of Arthur George Watson, DCL, JP:—

Kenelm Hubert (8, Patna St., Wellington N4, NZ), *b.* 1912: *m.* 1946, Mutal Agnes Helen, only da. o Bertram E. Fielder, of Glebe Farm, Sherfield English, Romsey, and has issue living, Noel Kenelm *b.* 1946,—Geoffrey Aylmer, *b.* 1957,—Rosalind Clare, *b.* 1948.——Fiona, *b.* 1917.——Monica, *b.* 1920.

Grandson of the late Rev. the Hon. Kenelm Henry Digby, brother of 9th Baron:—

Issue of the late Algernon Digby, *b.* 1849, *d.* 1936: *m.* 1888, Richenda Catherine, who *d.* 1940, dau. of the late Capt. Philip Hamond, 34th Regt. :—

Thomas Hankinson, *b.* 1892; ed. at Marlborough; European War 1914-19 as Capt. (despatches); late Live Stock Officer for E. Suffolk, Min. of Agriculture and Fisheries: *m.* (Jan.) 1938, Diana Broughton, only da. of Capt. Guy Knight, and has issue living, Simon Kenelm (77, Tenterden Drive, Canterbury, Kent), *b.* (Dec.) 1938: *m.* 1st, 1961 (m. diss. 1965), Ann Stallard, da. of the Rev. Geoffrey Walton; 2ndly, 1965, Sylvia Josephine, da. of John Cheers, and has issue living (by 2nd m.), Oliver Francis *b.* 1966, Roland Anthony *b.* 1969,—Patrick Timothy, *b.* 1941,—Robin Paul, *b.* 1944: *m.* 1966, Marja Birgitta, da. of Helmer Hägglöf, of Njurunda, Sweden, and has issue living, Christina Ruth *b.* 1967, Joanna Isabell *b.* 1971. *Residence,*—Hill Drop Cottage, Wiveton, nr. Holt, Norfolk.

PREDECESSORS.—[1] ROBERT Digby, Gov. of King's Co.; cr. *Baron Digby*, of Geashill, King's Co. (peerage of Ireland) 1620; *d* 1642; *s.* by his son [2] KILDARE, 2nd Baron; *s.* by his son [3] ROBERT, 3rd Baron; *s.* by his brother [4] SIMON, 4th Baron; *d.* 1686; *s.* by his brother [5] WILLIAM, 5th Baron; *d.* 1752; *s.* by his grandson [6] EDWARD, 6th Baron; *d.* unmarried 1757; *s.* by his brother [7] HENRY, 7th Baron; cr. *Baron Digby*, of Sherborne (peerage of Great Britain) 1765, with remainder to the issue male of his father, and *Viscount Coleshill* and *Earl Digby* (peerage of Great Britain) 1790; *d.* 1793; *s.* by his son [8] EDWARD, 2nd Earl; Lord-Lieut. of Dorset; *d.* unmarried 1856, when the viscountcy and earldom became extinct, and the baronies devolved upon his kinsman [9] EDWARD ST. VINCENT, 9th Baron, *b.* 1809 · *m.* 1837, Lady Theresa Anne Maria Fox-Strangways, who *d.* 1874, el. dau. of 3rd Earl of Ilchester: *d.* 1889; *s.* by his el. son [10] EDWARD HENRY TRAFALGAR, 10th Baron, *b.* 1846; sat as M.P. for Dorsetshire (C) 1876-85: *m.* 1893, Emily Beryl Sissy, who *d* 1928, dau. of the Hon. Albert Hood; *d.* 1920; *s.* by his el. son [11] EDWARD KENELM, *K.G., D.S.O., M.C., T.D.,* 11th Baron, *b.* 1894; Col. late Coldstream Guards, Lord-Lieut. of Dorset 1952-64, and Chm. of Dorset Co. Council 1955-64: *m.* 1919, the Hon. Constance Pamela Alice Bruce, *O.B.E., J.P.,* da. of 2nd Baron Aberdare *d.* 1964; *s.* by his only son [11] EDWARD HENRY KENELM, 12th Baron and present peer.

DILHORNE, VISCOUNT. (Manningham-Buller.) [Viscount U.K. 1964, Bt. U.K. 1866.]

The eagle does not catch flies.

REGINALD EDWARD MANNINGHAM-BULLER, PC, 1st Viscount, and 4th Baronet; *b.* Aug. 1st, 1905; ed. at Eton, and at Magdalen Coll., Oxford (BA); Bar. Inner Temple 1927, KC 1946, a Bencher 1951, and Reader 1973; Member of Parl Mission to Russia, 1945, and of Anglo-American Palestine Commn. 1946; Parl. Sec., Min. of Works May to July 1945, Solicitor-Gen. 1951-54, Attorney-Gen. 1954-62, Lord High Chancellor 1962-64, and Dep. Leader of Opposition, House of Lords 1964-66; a Lord of Appeal in Ordinary since 1969; MP for Daventry Div. of Northants. (C) 1943-50, and for S. Div. of Northants. and Soke of Peterborough 1950-62; *cr.* Knt. 1951, P.C. 1954, *Baron Dilhorne,* of Towcester, co. Northampton (peerage of U.K.) 1962, and *Viscount Dilhorne,* of Green's Norton, co. Northampton (peerage of U.K.) 1964: *m.* 1930, Lady Mary Lilian Lindsay, da. of 27th Earl of Crawford and Balcarres, and has issue.

Hrms,—Quarterly: 1st and 4th, sable, on a cross argent quarterly pierced of the field, four eagles displayed of the first, *Buller*; 2nd and 3rd, sable, a fesse ermine in chief three griffins' heads erased or, *Manningham*. *Crests,*—1st, a Saracen's head affrontée couped proper; 2nd, out of a ducal coronet gules, a talbot's head or, collared gules, line terminating in a knot sable. *Supporters,*— *Dexter,* An eagle wings elevated and addorsed ermine beaked and legged or gorged with a ducal coronet gules therefrom a line reflexed over the back and terminating in a knot sable; *sinister,* a Pegasus azure winged crined unguled and queued argent both charged on the shoulder with a Portcullis chained gold.

Residences,—6, King's Bench Walk, Temple, EC4; Horninghold Manor, Market Harborough. *Clubs,*—Buck's, Pratt's.

SON LIVING.

Hon. JOHN MERVYN, b. Feb. 28th, 1932; ed. at Eton; formerly Lt. Coldstream Guards; a Fellow of Inst. of Taxation; a Member of Wilts. Co. Council 1967-70: m. 1955 (m. diss. 1973), Gillian Evelyn JP, da. of Col. George Stockwell, and has issue living, James Edward, b. 1956,—Mervyn Reginald, b. 1962,—Mary Louise, b. 1970. *Clubs,*—Buck's, Pratt's, MCC.

DAUGHTERS LIVING.

Hon. Marian Cynthia, b. 1934: m. 1955, Edmund Crispin Stephen James George Brudenell [see M. Ailesbury, colls.]. *Residences,*—Deene Park, Corby, Northants; 18, Laxford House, Ebury St., SW1.
Hon. Elizabeth Lydia, b. 1948.
Hon. Anne Constance, b. 1951.

SISTERS LIVING.

Evelyn Constance, MBE (Easton House, 53, Bodenham Rd., Hereford), b. 1904; MBE (Civil) 1947: m. 1972, Capt. Patrick Mervyn Archdale, RN (ret.), who d. 1974.——Myra (The Stone House, Chelwood Gate, Sussex), b. 1909: m. 1940, Lt.-Col. P. C. Snatt, Roy. Signals, who d. 1961.——Pamela Liliah (Ravenscar, Meadfoot Lane, Torquay), b. 1919: m. 1951, Norman Wilkinson-Cox, who d. 1969, and has issue living, Gavia Lilah, b. 1952.

PREDECESSORS—[1] EDWARD Manningham-Buller, of Dilhorne Hall, Staffs., 3rd son of Sir Francis Buller, 2nd Bt. (cr. 1790) and brother of 1st Baron Churston; b. 1800; assumed by Roy. Licence 1866 the additional surname of Manningham; M.P. for N. Staffs. 1833-42, 1867 and 1874, and for Stafford 1842-47; cr. a Baronet 1866: m. 1st, 1824, Mary Anne, who d. 1860, da. and heir of Maj.-Gen. Coote Manningham; 2ndly, 1863, Georgina Charlotte, who d. 1875, da. and heir of Adm. of the Fleet Sir Charles Edmund Nugent, G.C.M., and widow of the Rt. Hon. George Bankes M.P.; d. 1882; s. by his el. son [2] Sir MORTON EDWARD, 2nd Bt., b. 1825: m. 1865, Mary, who d. 1923, da. of William Davenport, of Maer Hall, Staffs.; d. 1910; s. by his nephew [3] Sir MERVYN EDWARD (only son of Maj.-Gen. Edmund Manningham-Buller), 3rd Bt.; Lt.-Col. Rifle Bde., and M.P. for Kettering 1924-29, and Northampton 1931-40: m. 1903, the Hon. Lilah Constance Cavendish, O.B.E., who d. 1944, da. of 3rd Baron Chesham; d. 1956; s. by his only son [4] Sir REGINALD EDWARD, 4th Bt.. and present peer; also Baron Dilhorne.

DILLON, VISCOUNT.   (Dillon.)   [Viscount I. 1622.]

MICHAEL ERIC DILLON, 20th Viscount; b. Aug. 13th, 1911; s. 1946; ed. at Eton; is *Count Dillon* in France (cr. 1711), Lieut.-Col. (retired) Roy. Horse Guards; sometime Lieut. 15/19th The King's Roy. Hussars; a Vice-Pres. of Roy. Stuart So., an Officer of Order of Orange Nassau of the Netherlands with swords, and a Knight of Sovereign Order of Malta : m. 1939, Irène Marie France, dau. of René Merandon du Plessis, of Whitehall, Mauritius, and has issue.

Arms,—Quarterly : 1st and 4th argent, a lion passant, between three crescents gules, *Dillon*; 2nd and 3rd argent, a fesse between three crescents sable, *Lee*. Crest,—A demi-lion gules, holding in its paws an estoile argent. Supporters,—Two angels proper, vested argent, winged and crined or, each holding in the exterior hand a branch of palm proper, and having a riband over the shoulder of the second.

DUM·SPIRO·SPERO

While I breathe I hope.

Residence,—Rath House, Termonfeckin, Drogheda, co. Louth. *Clubs,*—Kildare St., Challoner.

SONS LIVING.

Hon. CHARLES HENRY ROBERT (83, Talfourd Rd., SE15), b. Jan. 18th, 1945; ed. at Downside, and Roy. Coll. of Art, Kensington: m. 1972, Mary Jane, da. of John Young, of Castle Hill House, Birtle, Lancs., and has issue living, Henry Benedict, b. 1973.
Hon. Richard Arthur Louis (5, Edith Grove, SW10), b. 1948; ed. at Downside: m. 1975, the Hon. Priscilla Frances Hazlerigg, da. of 2nd Baron Hazlerigg.
Hon. Patrick Dominic, b. 1956; ed. at Downside, and Trin. Coll., Dublin.
Hon. Michael Edmond, b. 1957; ed. at Glenstal.

DAUGHTERS LIVING.

Hon. Isabelle Anne Marie Henrietta, b. 1942: m. 1970, Richard Alexander Charles Cobbe, of 9, Templar St., SE5, and has issue living, Thomas Michael, b. 1973,—Frances Henrietta, b. 1971,—Rose Eleanor (twin), b. 1973.
Hon. Inès Marie Jeanne, b. 1952.
Hon. Madeleine Marie (twin), b. 1957.

SISTER LIVING.

Hon. Pamela Louisa Eleanor, b. 1915: m. 1936 (marriage dissolved 1962), the 6th Earl of Onslow. *Residence,*—12, Callcott St., W.8.

AUNT LIVING. (*Raised to the rank of a Viscount's daughter 1934.*)

Hon. Vere Mary, b. 1888: m. 1911, Reginald Edward Marsden (sometime Silviculturist to Govt. of India, and Bursar of Eton), who d. 1960, and has issue living, Hubert Henry, b. 1912; ed. at Eton; formerly Corporal RAF,—(Arthur) John, TD (Oakley Green House, Oakley Green, Windsor), b. 1915; ed. at Eton; PhD; formerly Lt.-Col. Gen. Staff; a Housemaster Eton Coll.; 1939-45 War as a GSO (despatches, American Bronze Star, Croix de Guerre with Palm): m. 1944, Suzanne (m. diss. 1965), da. of Brig.-Gen. Bertram Hewett Hunter Cooke, OMG, OBE, DSO, and widow of A. N. Boyd, Gren. Gds., and has issue living, Robert John b. 1947; ed. at Eton, Mary Frances b. 1950, Gillian Vere b. 1953, Rosemary Ann b. 1958,—Eric Charles, b. 1918 (of Gaddesden Place, Hemel Hempstead, Herts.); ed. at Eton; a JP and a DL of Herts; formerly Capt. Signals; S.-E. Asia 1942 (prisoner): m. 1949, Mary Julia, da. of the late Thomas Selwyn Pryor, MO [see Halsey, Bt.], and has issue living, Thomas Eric b. 1956, Henry Edward b. 1959, Charles Frederick b. 1961, Arthur Hugh b. 1966, William Maurice b. 1968, Elizabeth Mary b. 1950, Margaret Julia b. 1952,—(Mary) Sylvia b. 1920; formerly in WRNS: m. 1951, Greville Courtenay Bartholomew Gidley-Kitchin, of Wybournes, Kemsing, Sevenoaks, Kent, and has issue living, Thomas Edward b. 1954, Dorothy Virginia b. 1955, Penelope Jane b. 1958,—Iris Edrica (*Hon. Mrs. Stephen R. Cawley*), b. 1922; was with United Nations

Secretariat, New York 1949: *m.* 1952, the Hon. Stephen Robert Cawley [see B. Cawley],—Rosemary Joan (twin) (*Baroness Cawley*), *b.* 1922, formerly in WRNS: *m.* 1944, the 3rd Baron Cawley, of Bircher Hall, Leominster, Herefordshire, 0AX HR6. *Residence,*—Bishopsgate Place, Englefield Green, Surrey.

COLLATERAL BRANCHES LIVING.

Issue (by 1st marriage) of the late Hon. Harry Lee Stanton Lee-Dillon (*Comte Henri de Dillon* in France), only son of 17th Viscount (by 1st marriage), *b.* **1874,** *d.* **1923** (having assumed 1892 the surname of Lee before that of Dillon): *m.* 1st, 1904, Brenda Mary, who *d.* 1963, having obtained a divorce 1912 [she *m.* 2ndly, 1929, as his second wife, Lieut.-Col. Lennox Galloway, D.S.O., of Cluden, Northam, N. Devon, who *d.* 1959], el. dau. of the late Thomas Smith, M.R.C.S., L.R.C.P., of Croft Cottage, Crawley, Sussex; 2ndly, 1913, Kathleen Clare, who *d.* 1950 [she *m.* 2ndly, 1924, Lieut.-Com. Robert Francis Lee-Dillon, R.N. (infra)], dau. of the late James Atchison, O.E., of Belfast, and Cardigan, Lavender Bay, Sydney, N.S. Wales:—

Charlotte Henriette, *b.* 1907 : *m.* 1929, Leonard Cundell, who *d.* 1952, and has issue living, Jack Stratton, *b.* 1930,—Robin Osmund (Lincoln Meads, Pietermaritzburg, S. Africa), *b.* 1931: *m.* 1969, Marie-Antoinette Patricia, da. of Patricia Francois Green, of Mahé, Seychelles,—Leonard John Michael (Eliorths Retreat, Pietermaritzburg, S. Africa), *b.* 1943: *m.* 1967 (m. diss. 1973), Diane Nesta, da. of Martin Steward Skillman, and has issue living, Trevor Michael *b.* 1969. *Residence,*— Mahé, Seychelles Islands.

Grandsons of the late Philip Gerald Dillon, son of the late Hon. Constantine Augustus Dillon, 4th son of 13th Viscount :—

Issue of the late Francis Noel Dillon, *b.* **1878;** *d.* **1933:** *m.* **1909, Mildred Edith, who** *d.* **1962, dau. of A. G. Fell, of Wellington, New Zealand:—**

Patrick Philip Lee, *b.* 1912; ed. at Stowe : *m.* 1937, Joan Elfie, dau. of G. C. Williams, of Masterton, NZ, and has issue living, Patrick Francis (Leefield, Blenheim, NZ), *b.* 1946: *m.* 1974, Susan Lee, da. of Dr. Peter Thodey, of Timaru, NZ, and has issue living, Lisa Francis *b.* 1975,— Rachel Anne, *b.* 1939: *m.* 1966, Robert Lionel Savory, of Knoll House, High Cross, Ware, Herts and has issue living, Charlotte Katharine Anne *b.* 1968, Victoria Lucy Lee *b.* 1970, Josephine Elizabeth *b.* 1972,—Joanna Lee, *b.* 1941: *m.* 1963, David Cameron, Waituma, Waikari, North Canterbury, NZ, and has issue living, Timothy Charles *b.* 1967, Andrew Lee *b.* 1970, Nicola Jane *b.* 1965. *Residence,*— Leefield, Blenheim, NZ.——Gerald Francis Lee, *b.* 1917; ed. at Stowe; is Maj. NZ Forces, Middle East 1940-45: *m.* 1946, Mary Ritson, da. of Cdr. T. S. Critchley, RN, of Tirohunga, Blenheim, NZ, and has issue living, David Sandford Lee, *b.* 1946,—Susan Lee, *b.* 1947. *Residence,*—The Throne, Blenheim, NZ.

Grandchildren of the late Francis Noel Dillon (ante):—

Issue of the late Fl-Lt. Michael Lee Dillon, RNZAF, *b.* 1913, *d,* 1968: *m.* 1939, Gwendoline Reay (The Tummil, Blenheim, NZ), da. of J. W. Trolove, of The Shades, Blenheim, NZ:— Richard Lee (The Tummil, Blenheim, NZ), *b.* 1941: *m.* 1965, Elizabeth Campbell, da. of J. B. Hay, of Pigeon Bay, Bank's Peninsular, NZ, and has issue living, Nicolas Lee, *b.* 1966—Samuel Hay, *b.* 1967, —Sarah Elizabeth, *b.* 1971.——James Michael Lee, *b.* 1947.——Sarah Christine, *b.* 1942: *m.* 1965, Peter Wallace Coy, of Salt Creek, Woorndoo, Vic., Aust., and has issue living, Edward Francis Dillon, *b.* 1973,—Rosa Susan, *b.* 1966,—Sally Amanda, *b.* 1968,—Georgina Anne, *b.* 1971.——Rosa Lee, *b.* 1949.

Granddaughters of the late Augustus Henry Fitz-Gibbon, son of the late Hon. Gerald Normanby Fitz-Gibbon (infra) :—

Issue of the late Capt. Gerald Ernest George Fitz-Gibbon, M.C., *b.* 1884, *d.* 1929 : *m.* 1st, 1908, Mary Monica, who *d.* 1930 (from whom he obtained a divorce 1912), dau. of Lieut.-Col. Hugh Marshall Hole, C.M.G., of 2, London Wall Buildings, E.C.2; 2ndly, 1914, Hélène, widow of Strentham Ford, of Cape Town :—

(By 1st m.) Doreen Adele Monica Clare, *b.* 1910: *m.* 1st, 1928 (m. diss. 1937), Wing-Cdr. James Edward Stuart-Lyon, RAF (ret.): 2ndly, 1938, Francis Prideaux Allbutt, Solicitor, who *d.* 1965; 3rdly, 1968, re-married Wing-Cdr. James Edward Stuart-Lyon, RAF (ret.), and has issue living, (by 1st m.) James Alastair Garry (5, Hermit Court, Don Mills, Ont., Canada), *b.* 1934; ed. at Bradfield Coll.; late RN: *m.* 1960, Gillian Mary, da. of Donald Arthur Dawes, of New Milton, Hants, and has issue living, Steven Alastair *b.* 1960, James Alexander *b.* 1962, Jonathon Michael *b.* 1964, Angus Edware Matthew *b.* 1965. *Residence,*—Hurstan-clays North, E. Grinstead, Sussex.——Elizabeth Rosemary, *b.* 1912: *m.* 1934, Henry Bockholst Livingston, CBE, who *d.* 1968, and has issue living, Nicholas Henry, *b.* 1942; ed. at King's Sch., Canterbury, and at King's Coll., Camb. (Foundation Scholar); Foreign Office 1964.——(By 2nd m.) Diana Clare, *b.* 1924: *m.* 1952, Derek Harry Johnson, and has issue living, Gerald Harry, *b.* 1952,—Mary Clare Hélène, *b.* 1958. *Residence,*—Boden Hall, Scholar Green, Stoke-on-Trent.

Granddaughters of the late Hon. Gerald Normanby FITZ-GIBBON, 6th son of 13th Viscount :—

Issue (by 2nd marriage), of the late John Arthur FITZ-GIBBON, *b.* 1854, *d.* 1908 : *m.* 1st, 1882, Louisa Bosville, who *d.* 1883, dau. of the late Sir Belford Hinton Wilson, K.C.B.; 2ndly, 1890, Katherine Maude, who *d.* 1939, dau. of the late Rev. W. C. Randolph, of Yate House, Gloucesterhire :—

Kathleen Beatrice Florence, *b.* 1891. *Residence,*—

Issue of the late Clare Valentine Fitz-Ribbon, *b.* 1859; *d.* 19—; *m.* 1882, Mary Agnes, da. of the late Richard Barrett Bernard :—

Agnes, *b.* 1885. *Residence,*—

Issue of the late Louis Theobald FITZ-GIBBON, Lieut. Oxfordshire L.I., *b.* 1859, *d.* 1913: *m.* 1884, Maria Dolores, who *d.* 1909, dau. of the late Robert Maxwell:—

Olive Geraldine (*Olive, Lady Antrobus*), *b.* 1887: *m.* 1st, 1911, Jordan Dumaresq, of Boston, USA, who *d.* 1915; 2ndly, 1919, Capt. Sir Philip Humphrey Antrobus, MC, 6th Bt., who *d.* 1968. *Residence,*— West Amesbury House, Amesbury, Salisbury.

Grandchildren of the late Louis Theobald FITZ-GIBBON (ante):—

Issue of the late Lieut.-Com. Robert Francis LEE-DILLON, R.N. (*Count Robert F. Lee-Dillon* in France), *b.* 1884, *d.* 1954 : having resumed in 1925 the surnames of Lee-Dillon: *m.* 1st, (Feb.) 1908, Georgette (who *d.* 1972, having obtained a divorce 1923), da. of George Winthrop Folsom, of Lenox, Mass., USA; 2ndly, 1924. Kathleen Clare, who *d.* 1950, da. of the late James Aitchison, CE, of Belfast, and Cardigan, Lavender Bay, Sydn3y, NS Wales, and widow of the Hon. Henry Lee Stanton Lee-Dillon (ante):—

(By 1st m.) (Robert Louis) Constantine FITZ-GIBBON, *b.* 1919; 1939-45 War as Lt. Oxfordshire and Bucks LI; sometime Maj. US Army: *m.* 1st, 1939 (m. diss. 1944), Margaret Aye Moung; 2ndly, 1944, (m. diss. 1960), Theodora Rosling; 3rdly, 1960, Marion Gutmann; 4thly, 1967, Mrs. Marjorie Sutton, da. of Harold Wright Steele, of Cal., USA, and has issue living, (by 3rd m.) Francis George Herbert Dillon, *b.* 1961,—(by 4th m.) Oonagh Louisa Dillon, *b.* 1968. *Residence,*—St. Annes, Killiney Hill Rd., Killiney, co. Dublin.——Frances Hastings, *b.* 1910.——(By 2nd m.) Louis Theobald DILLON FITZGIBBON (of Clare House, 7, Bembridge Drive, Hayling Island, Hants), *b.* 1925; assumed by deed poll 1962, the surnames of Dillon FitzGibbon in lieu of Lee-Dillon; Lt. RN (ret.); Area Pres. of St John Ambulance Bde.; a Knt. of Sovereign Mil. Order of Malta; Cdr. of Order of Restitution of Poland; Polish Gold Cross of Merit: *m.* 1st, 1950 (m. diss. 1962), Mrs. Josephine McDonald, da. of J. H. Webb; 2ndly, 1962, Madeleine Sally Hayward-Surry, and has issue living, (by 2nd m.) James Augustus *b.* 1963,—Simone Frances, *b.* 1962,—Michèle Clare, *b.* 1965.

Grandchildren of the late John Monro Dillon, son of the late Rev. Martin Dillon,
6th in descent from the Hon. Thomas Dillon, 4th son of 1st Viscount:—
Issue of the late Capt. Arnold Michael Dillon, *b.* 1892, *d.* 1955: *m.* 1915, Esther Dorothy,
dau. of William Currie Allen, of London, Ontario :—
Arnold Charles, *b.* 1920: *m.* 1947, Donalda Ruth, da. of Arthur J. Cowie, of Caledonia, Ontario,
Canada, and has issue living, John Michael *b.* 1956,—Dorothy Nina, *b.* 1954.——Mary Louie Margarette, *b.* 1917 : *m.* 1944, Dennis Bishop, late Flying Officer, R.A.F. Vol. Reserve, and has issue
living, Dennis John, *b.* 1945,—Caroline Mary Beverley Anne, *b.* 1952. *Residence,—*

Grandson of the late Rev. Martin Dillon (ante):—
Issue of the late Maurice Ashurst Dillon, *b.* 1856, *d.* 1901: *m.* 1894, Florence, dau. of Henry
Morgan, of Old Abbey, co. Limerick:—
Marmaduke Murray, *M.C., E.D.* (of 842, Wellington St., London, Ont., Canada), *b.* 1894; Brig. (ret.)
Canadian Fusiliers (City of London Regt.); formerly D.Q.M.G., Ottawa; 1914-18 War in France and
Belgium, as Capt. Canadian Machine Gun Corps.) (M.C. with bar, two medals); Silver Jubilee (1935)
and Coronation (1937) medals: *m.* 1st, 1919, Muriel, dau. of the late Rev. Canon Richard Hicks;
2ndly, 1956, Mildred Whitley, widow of Col. Charles W. Jeffers, U.S. Army, and has issue living,
(by 1st marriage) Richard Maurice, *M.C., E.D.* (of 44, Greenacres Drive, London, Ont., Canada),
b. 1920; B.A. 1948; Lt.-Col. (ret.) Canadian Mil.; Dean of Faculty of Eng. Science, W. Ontario
Univ.; 1939-45 War in Sicily and Italy (M.C.); Coronation medal (1953): *m.* 1945, Mary Elizabeth,
dau. of Harry H. Dempsey, of Stratford, Ont., and has issue living, Kelly Elizabeth *b.* 1949, Ann,
Dempsey *b.* 1952, Katherine Talbot *b.* 1955,—Michael Talbot, *CD* (373, Wortley Rd., London,
Ont., Canada), *b.* 1926; BA, MD; Lt.-Col. (ret.), late RCAMC (M): *m.* 1959, Margaret, da. of Roy
Kirk Hamilton, of Arthur, Ont., Canada, and has issue living, Timothy Arthur *n.* 1960, Kirk Fitz-
gerald *b.* 1961, David Morgan *b.* 1963,—Shelagh Muriel, *b.* 1924: *m.* 1945, Neil Archibald Watters,
MD, FRCS (Canada), of 172, Rosedale Heights Drive, Toronto, Canada, and has issue living, Douglas
Bruce *b.*1948, James Murray *b.* 1952, Michael Grant *b.* 1955, Louise Shelagh *b.* 1959,—Diana Mary
Morgan, *b.* 1926; BA, MD, FRCP: *m.* 1956, the Rev. Gerald Cecil Johnson, BA, BTh, of 246, Main
St., Ildeston, Ont., N0M 2AO, Canada, and has issue living, Patrick Bruce *b.* 1965, Kevin Sean (twin)
b. 1965, Michele Ann Jean *b.* 1958, Margaret Rebecca Morgan *b.* 1962.

Grandson of the late Charles Blake Dillon, son of the late Luke Dillon, 4th in descent
from Hon. Thomas Dillon (ante):—
Issue of the late Luke Gerald Dillon, O.B.E., M.D., *b.* 1862, *d.* 1937: *m.* 1900, Elizabeth
Mary, who *d.* 1949, dau. of the late Hon. Hubert Francis Dormer [B. Dormer, colls.]:—
Gerald Dormer Fitzgerald, *b.* 1901; ed. at Downside, and at Balliol Coll., Oxford (B.A.
1st class Lit. Hum. 1922): *m.* 1940, Maureen, dau. of Thomas Stewart, formerly of Cowden-
beath, Fifeshire, and has issue living, Martin Luke Gerald (The White Horse, Green Tye, Much
Hadham, Herts.), *b.* 1942; ed. at Downside, and Queen's Coll., Oxford (BA): *m.* 1965, Diana Mary,
da. of the late Rev. Arthur Robert Botting, BA, and has issue living, Anthony Hugh Patrick Martin
b. 1965, Clare Elizabeth Teresa *b.* 1968. *Residence,—*20, Tedworth Sq., SW3. *Clubs,—*White's,
Garrick.

PREDECESSORS.—[1] *Sir* THEOBALD Dillon, Knt.; Lord Pres. of Connaught; cr. *Viscount
Dillon,* of Costello-Gallen (peerage of Ireland) 1622; *d.* 1624: *s.* by his grandson [2] LUCAS, 2nd
Viscount; *d.* 1629; *s.* by his son [3] THEOBALD, 3rd Viscount; *d.* an infant 1630; *s.* by his uncle
[4] THOMAS, 4th Viscount; *b.* 1615; Joint Commr. of Mayo Nov. 1641, and Joint Pres. of
Connaught and Gov. of Fort Athlone 1645-62 ; exempted from pardon for life by Cromwell
1652 (restored 1660) ; Custos Rotulorum of co. Meath 1662 ; *d.* 1673 ; *s.* by his son [5] THOMAS,
5th Viscount; *d.* 1674; *s.* by his kinsman [6] LUCAS, 6th Viscount; el. son of Sir Theobald,
3rd son of Sir Christopher el. son of 1st Viscount; *d. s. p.* 1682; *s.* by his kinsman [7]
THEOBALD, 7th Viscount, grandson of Sir Lucas, 2nd son of 1st Viscount; attached himself
to the falling fortunes of James II., and was outlawed 1690; *s.* by his son [8] HENRY, 8th
Viscount, in whose favour the outlawry was reversed; *d.* 1713; *s.* by his son [9] RICHARD,
9th Viscount; *d.* 1737; *s.* by his cousin [10] CHARLES, 10th Viscount, el. son of the Hon.
Arthur Dillon (2nd son of 7th Viscount), who was cr. Count Dillon by Louis XIV. 1711,
Earl Dillon by the Old Pretender 1721 and K.T. 1722; *d. s. p.* 1741; *s.* by his brother [11]
HENRY, 11th Viscount; a Col. in the French army; *d.* 1787; *s.* by his son [12] CHARLES,
K.P.,12th Viscount; conformed to the Established Church, and his claim to be 12th Viscount was
allowed by the House of Lords in 1788 in the names of Dillon-Lee, which he had assumed in
1776 in accordance with the will of his maternal uncle, the 3rd Earl of Litchfield ; *d.* 1813 ; *s.* by his
son [13] HENRY AUGUSTUS, 13th Viscount; *b.* 1777: *m.* 1807, Henrietta, dau. of Dominick
Geoffrey Browne, M.P. ; *d.* 1832, *s.* by his el. son [14] CHARLES HENRY, 14th Viscount;
d. 1865; *s.* by his brother [15] THEOBALD DOMINICK GEOFFREY, 15th Viscount; *d.* 1879; *s.* by
his brother [16] ARTHUR EDMUND DENIS, 16th Viscount, *b.* 1812: *m.* 1843, Ellen, da. of James
Adderly; *d.* 1892; *s.* by his el. son [17] HAROLD ARTHUR, *C.H.,* 17th Viscount, *b.* 1844; Pres.
of So. of Antiquaries 1897-1904, Curator of the Tower Armouries 1895-1913, and a Trustee of
British Museum 1897-1932 ; Senior Trustee of the National Portrait Gallery, Antiquary of Roy.
Acad. and an Original Fellow of British Acad.: *m.* 1st, 1870, Julia (Order of Mercy), who *d.*
1925, el. dau. of the late Isaac Brock Stanton, of the Canadian Civil Ser.; 2ndly, 1926, his
cousin, Margaret Louisa Everard, who *d.* 1954 dau. of the late Rev. Henry Edward Ffolkes, and
widow of the Rev. John Erasmus Philipps: *d.* 1932 ; *s.* by his nephew [18] ARTHUR HENRY (el.
son of the Hon. Conrad Adderly Dillon, 2nd son of 16th Viscount), 18th Viscount, *b.* 1875 : *m.*
1907, Hilda, who *d.* 1966, da. of the Rt. Hon. Sir John Tomlinson Brunner, PC, 1st Bt, and widow
of Charles Harold Broadbent, JP; *d.* 1934; *s.* by his brother [19] ERIC FITZGERALD, *CMG, DSO,*
19th Viscount, *b.* 1881; Brig. (ret.) Roy. Munster Fusiliers; S. Africa 1900-01, 1914-18 War (DSO,
CMG), 1939-41 War: *m.* 1907, Norah Juanita Muriel, who *d.* 1962, only child of the late Brig.-Gen.
Charles Edward Beckett, CB; *d.* 1946; *s.* by his son [20] MICHAEL ERIC, 20th Viscount and present
peer.

Dinevor, Baron, see Dynevor.

Dingwall, Lady, see Baroness Lucas of Crudwell and Dingwall.

DIPLOCK, BARON. (Diplock.) [Life Baron 1968.]

WILLIAM JOHN KENNETH DIPLOCK, *PC*, son of William John Hubert Diplock, solicitor, of Croydon; *b.* Dec. 8th, 1907; ed. at Whitgift Sch., and Univ. Coll. Oxford (Hon. Fellow 1958); Hon LL.D Alberta; Bar. Middle Temple 1932, KC 1948, and a Bencher 1956; Sec. to Master of the Rolls 1939-48, a Member of Lord Chancellor's Law Reform Cttee. 1952, Recorder of Oxford 1951-56, a Judge of High Court of Justice (Queen's Bench Div.) 1956-61, and a Lord Justice of Appeal 1961-68, since when a Lord of Appeal in Ordinary; Judge of Restrictive Practices Court 1960 (Pres. 1961), Pres. of National Assocn. of Parish Councils 1962-65, Chm. of Board of Studies Council of Legal Education 1963-69, and Vice-Pres. of British Maritime Law Assocn. 1964; Hon. Member of American and Canadian Bar Assocns., and Hon. Fellow of American Bar Foundation; Chm. of Standing Security Comm. since 1971; 1939-45 War with RAF; cr. Knt. 1956, PC 1961, and *Baron Diplock*, of Wansford, co. of Huntingdon and Peterborough (Life Baron) 1968: *m.* 1938, Margaret Sarah, da. of George Atcheson, of Londonderry.

Arms,—Gules a quintain argent garnished and with a cross beam and Targe double chained towards the base and padlocked or, a bordure ermine. **Crest,**—a demi horse argent maned tailed and hooved or, supporting a pair of keys interlaced at the bows ward downward, one argent the other or. **Supporters,**—On the *dexter* side a fox hound and on the *sinister* side a fox, the whole on a compartment of ploughland between pasture within a hedgerow interspersed with paling all proper.

Residences,—1, Crown Office Row, Temple, EC4; Wansford in England, Peterborough.

DONALDSON OF KINGSBRIDGE, BARON. [(Donaldson.)] [Life Baron 1967.]

JOHN GEORGE STUART DONALDSON, *OBE*, son of the late Rev. Stuart Alexander Donaldson, Master of Magdalene Coll., Camb. [E. Buckinghamshire]; *b.* Oct. 9th, 1907; ed. at Eton, and Trin. Coll., Camb. (MA); a Farmer; a Dir. of Roy. Opera House, Covent Garden since 1959, of Sadlers Wells since 1962, and of British Sugar Corpn. since 1966; a Member of Board of Visitors, HM Prison, Grendon, Bucks., since 1962, Chm. of Nat. Assocn. for the Care and Resettlement of Offenders since 1966, and of Nat. Exec. Cttee. of Family Service Units since 1968; Chm. of Consumer Council 1968-71; Chm. of Fedn. of Zoos since 1971, and of Hotels and Catering NEDO 1972; Parl. Under-Sec. of State N. Ireland Office since 1974; 1939-45 War as Lt.-Col. RE; *cr.* OBE (Mil) 1944, and *Baron Donaldson of Kingsbridge*, of Kingsbridge, co. Buckingham (Life Baron) 1967: *m.* 1935, Frances Annesley, da. of Frederick Lonsdale, and has issue.

Arms,—Or a double headed eagle displayed azure beaked and membered gules, surmounted of a lymphad with two masts sails furled sable flagged on the fore mast with the Banner of Scotland proper (azure a saltire argent) and on the main mast with a pennon, in the dexter chief point a sinister hand couped of the third, and on the sinister chief point a book expanded proper, all within a bordure also of the third. **Crest,**—A dexter hand holding, a sword proper.

Residence,—1, Chalcot Cres., NW1. *Club,*—Brooks's.

SON LIVING.

Hon. Thomas Hay (Cinderella Cottage, Village Way, Little Chalfont, Bucks.), *b.* 1936: *m.* 1962 Natalie, da. of Basil Wadkovsky, and has issue.

DAUGHTERS LIVING.

Hon. Rose Albinia, *b.* 1937: *m.* 1961, Nicholas Deakin, of London, NW3, and has issue.

Hon. Catherine Frances, *b.* 1945: *m.* 1973, G. Mark Jennings.

DONEGALL, MARQUESS OF. (Chichester.) Sits as **BARON FISHERWICK.**
(G.B. 1790). [Marquess I. 1791.]

Dermot Richard Claud Chichester,
7th Marquess; *b.* April 18th, 1916; *s.*
as 5th Baron Templemore 1953, and as
7th Marquess of Donegall 1975; ed.
at Harrow and RMC; Maj. (ret.) late
7th Queen's Own Hussars; a Member of
HM Body Guard of Hon. Corps of
Gentlemen at Arms; Hereditary Lord
High Admiral of Lough Neagh and
Gov. of Carrickfergus Castle; 1939–45
War in Middle East and Italy (prisoner):
m. 1946, Lady Josceline Gabrielle
Legge, da. of 7th Earl of Dartmouth,
and has issue.

Arms,—Quarterly : 1st and 4th checky, or and
gules, a chief vaire, *Chichester;* 2nd and 3rd azure,
fretty argent, *Etchingham.* **Crest,**—A stork, with
an eel in its bill proper. **Supporters,**—Two wolves
gules. ducally collared and chained or.

Seat,—Dunbrody Park, Arthurstown, co. Wexford. *Clubs,*—Cavalry, Kildare St. (Dublin).

SON LIVING.
Arthur Patrick (*Earl of Belfast*), *b.* May 9th, 1952;
ed. at Harrow; Lt. Coldm. Gds.

Honour follows, though unsought for.

DAUGHTERS LIVING.
Lady Jennifer Evelyn, *b.* 1949: *m.* 1971, John Robert
Henry Fowler, of Clegarrow, Enfield, co. Meath.
Lady Juliet Clare, *b.* 1954.

BROTHER LIVING. (*Son of 4th Baron Templemore*).
Hon. Desmond Clive, *MC, b.* 1920; ed. at Harrow, and at Ch. Ch., Oxford (BA 1944, MA 1945); Maj.
Coldm. Gds. (ret.); was ADC to Gov.-Gen. of Canada 1948-50; 1939-45 War in N. Africa and Italy
(despatches MC): *m.* 1st, 1946, Lorna Althea, who *d.* 1948, da. of Capt. Montagu Hamer Ravenhill
[Colleton, Bt.], and widow of (1) Geoffrey Christopher Appleby Holt, Pilot Officer RAF, and (2)
Capt. Richard Cecil Twining, Welsh Gds.; 2ndly, 1951, Felicity Stella, da. of Maj. John Fenwick
Harrison [B. Burnham], and has issue living, (by 1st m.) Desmond Shane Spencer, *b.* 1948,—(by
2nd m.) Dermot Michael Claud, *b.* 1953: *m.* 1975, Francis Jane Berners, da. of Michael Edward
Ranulph Allsopp [see B. Hindlip, colls.]. *Residence,*—Preston Hill, Preston, Hitchin, Herts.
Clubs,—White's, Pratt's, Kildare Street.

WIDOW LIVING OF SIXTH MARQUESS.
Maureen (*Maureen, Marchioness of Donegal*) (Le Priolaz, 1802, Corseaux, Vevey, Vaud, Switzerland),
el. da. of the late Maj. Geoffrey O. Scholfield, MC, of Birkdale, Lancs., and formerly wife of Douglas
McKenzie: *m.* 1968, as his 2nd wife, the 6th Marquess, who *d.* 1975.

COLLATERAL BRANCHES LIVING.

Granddaughter of the late Lord Adolphus John Spencer Churchill Chichester, 3rd
son of 4th Marquess, *b.* 1836, *d.* 1901: *m.* 1872, Mary, who *d.* 1924, only da. of the
late Col. Robert Peel Dawson, MP:—
Issue of the late Lieut.-Col. Robert Peel Dawson Spencer Chichester, M.P., *b.* 1873,
d. 1921: *m.* 1901, Rt. Hon. Dame Dehra Kerr, *GBE, JP* who *d.* 1963, having *m.* 2ndly,
1928, Adm. Henry Wise Parker, C.B., C.M.G., who *d.* 1940], only child of the late James
Kerr Fisher, of The Manor House, Kilrea, Ireland, and Chicago, U.S.A.:—
Marion Caroline Dehra, *b.* 1904: *m.* 1st, 1922, Capt. James Jackson Lenox-Conyngham
Chichester-Clark, D.S.O., R.N. (retired), who *d.* 1933; 2ndly, 1938, Charles Edward
Brackenbury, and has issue living, (by 1st m.) James Dawson (*Baron Moyola*); cr. *Baron Moyola,
Life Baron* 1971; [see that title],—*Sir* Robert, *MP* (Ross House, Kells, co. Antrim; *Club,*—Carlton),
b. 1928; ed. at Magdalene Coll., Camb., MP for Londonderry (*U*) since 1955; an Assist. Govt. Whip
1958-60, a Lord Commr. of the Treasury 1960; Comptroller of Queen's Household 1961-64; Min. of
State, Dept. of Employment 1972-74; Knt. 1974: *m.* 1st, 1953 (m. diss. 1972), Jane Helen, da. of
Air Marshal Sir (Robert) Victor Goddard, KCB, CBE; 2ndly, 1974, Caroline, da. of Anthony Bull,
CBE [see Bull, Bt.], and has issue living (by 1st m.), Mark Jason *b.* 1957, Emma Penelope *b.* 1955,
Sophia Melissa Jane *b.* 1961, (by 2nd m.), Adam Tamniarn *b.* 1975,—Penelope, *b.* 1929: *m.* 1952,
Paul Rodbard Hobhouse, of Hadspen House, Castle Cary, Som., son of the late Sir Arthur Lawrence
Hobhouse [Mather-Jackson, Bt., colls.], and has issue living, Niall Alexander *b.* 1954, David Paul
b. 1957, Georgina Debra Catherine *b.* 1953. *Residence,*—La Maison du Vigneron, 1256, Troinex,
Geneva, Switzerland.

Descendants of the late Arthur Chichester (el. son of the late Lord Spencer Stanley
Chichester, 3rd son of 1st Marquess), who was cr. *Baron Templemore* 1831.

Granddaughters of the late Hon. Frederick Arthur Henry Chichester, 3rd son of
1st Baron Templemore, el. son of Lord Spencer Stanley Chichester, of Dunbrody
Park, co. Wexford, 3rd son of 1st Marquess:—
Issue of the late Maj. Spencer Frederick Chichester, *b.* 1854, *d.* 1931: *m.* 1892, Helen, who *d.*
1948, da. of Archibald Coats, of Woodside, Paisley:—
Doreen Margaret Helen, *b.* 1897: *m.* 1st, 1920, Thomas Peter Murray, from whom she obtained a divorce
1925; 2ndly, 1925, Capt. Lewis Coker, from whom she obtained a divorce 1940; 3rdly, 1940, Thomas
Edmund Fenlon, from whom she obtained a divorce 1946, and has issue living, (by 2nd m.) Denise
Aubrey Doreen, *b.* 1930. *Residence,*—18, Chelsea Park Gdns., SW3.——Verena Frances Elizabeth,
b. 1906: *m.* 1931, Cdr. Derek Howard Secker, MVO, RN and has issue living, Malcolm Chichester,
b. 1934; ed. at Eton.

Grandsons of Hon. Francis Algernon James Chichester, 5th son of 1st Baron Temple-
more:—
Issue of the late Shane Randolph Chichester, OBE, *b.* 1883, *d.* 1969: *m.* 1914, Madeline Herschel
(The Rough, Tilford, Farnham, Surrey), da. of Henry Arthur Whately:—
(Oscar) Richard Herschel (Wiscombe Park, Southleigh, Colyton, Devon; Pratt's Club), *b.* 1915; ed. at
Wellington Coll., and Trin. Coll., Camb. (BA); Maj. (ret.) Rifle Bde. (Prince Consort's Own); ADC to
High Commr. for Palestine 1946-48; Palestine 1939 (medal), 1939-45 War (African star): *m.* 1951,

Margaret Edmondson, da. of Charles Edgar Farr, JP, of Weston Bury, Weston, near Hitchin, Herts, and has issue living, Timothy Arthur Shane, b. 1956,—Jane Caroline Sheelah, b. 1952,—Sara Kathleen Arabella, b. 1958.——Desmond Shane (Newcourt, Downton, Salisbury, Wilts; MCC), b. 1919; ed. at Wellington Coll., and Trin. Coll., Camb (MA); Agent to the Earl of Radnor, a Fellow of Chartered Land Agents' So., and an ARICS; Capt. (ret.) 80th Heavy Anti-Aircraft Regt. RA and N. Irish Horse; 1939-45 War in N. Africa and Italy: m. 1951, Patricia, yr. da. of the late Lt.-Col. Henry George Moreton Pleydell-Railston, DSO [see Mansel, Bt., colls.], and has issue living, Piers Desmond Herschel, b. 1954,—Jonathan Morton (twin), b. 1954,—Adrian George, b. 1955,—Morna Rosemary b. 1952.

(*In remainder to the Earldom of Donegall, Viscountcy of Chichester, and Barony of Chichester of Belfast only.*)

Descendants of the late Rev. Edward Chichester, great-great-grandson of John Chichester, brother of 2nd Earl :—

Descendants of the late Rev. William Chichester [el. son of the late Rev. Edward Chichester (ante)], who was cr. *Baron O'Neill* 1868 [see that title].

Granddaughters of the late Rev. Edward Arthur Chichester (infra):—
Issue of the late Lt.-Col. Arthur O'Neill Cubitt Chichester, OBE, MC, b. 1889, d. 1972: m. 1924, Hilda Grace (Ardvernis Farm, Cullyhackey, co. Antrim; Galgorm Castle, Ballymena, co. Antrim, da. of the late Rt. Hon. William Robert Young [Macnaghten, Bt.]:— Rosemary Hilda (*Viscountess Brookeborough*), (Colebrooke, co. Fermanagh, and Ashbrooke, Brookeborough, co. Fermanagh), b. 1926: m. 1949, the 2nd Viscount Brookeborough.——Deirdre Willa, b. 1928: m. 1951, Col. Rodney Francis Maurice Windsor, OBE, of Byth House, New Byth, Turriff, Aberdeenshire.——Finola Margaret, b. 1932: m. 1st, 1959, William McWilliams, who d. 1963; 2ndly, 1964, D. Herbison, of Ardvernis Farm, Cullyhackey, Ballymena, co. Antrim, and has issue living (by 1st m.) Grace Mildred, b. 1960,—Tracey, b. 1961,—(by 2nd m.) Vivienne R. 19—.

Granddaughter of the late Rev. George Vaughan Chichester, son of the late Rev. Edward Chichester (ante) :—
Issue of the late Rev. Edward Arthur Chichester, b. 1849, d. 1925 : m. 1884, the Hon. Mary Agnes Cubitt, who d. 1944, dau. of 1st Baron Ashcombe :—
Harriet Laura, b. 1887: m. 1915, Brigadier Alexander Henry Delap West, DSO, late RA, who d. 1959. *Residence,*—Sonoma, Easthampstead Rd., Wokingham, Berks.
Issue of the late Lieut.-Col. Alfred Godfrey de Vaud Ohichester, b. 1866, d. 1933 : m. 1901, Agnes Donaldson, who d. 1945, dau. of Col. John Anderson, Army Vet. Depart. :—
Maureen Agnes, b. 1909 : m. 1929, Brigadier George Alexander Bain, O.B.E., 2nd Gurkha Rifles, of Sandy Lodge, Chagford, S. Devon, and has issue living, Mary Anne Chichester (*Lady Campbell*), b. 1930: m. 1952, Sir Colin Moffat Campbell, M.C., 8th Bt.,—Maureen Veronica, b. 1931: m. 1956, Charles Riou Mosse, of East Ash Manor, Whiddon Down, Okehampton, Devon, and has issue living, Charles David Fairless b. 1959, Rosalind Mary b. 1957, Anne Veronica b. 1962.

PREDECESSORS.—*Sir* ARTHUR Chichester, Knt., *PC*, 2nd son of Sir John Chichester of Raleigh, Pilton, Devon, and yr. brother of Sir John, grandfather of 1st Bt. [see Chichester, Bt.]; 1563; Lord Dep. of Ireland 1605-15, Lord Treas. of Ireland 1616-1625, and Ambassador to Palatinate 1622; cr. *Baron Chichester of Belfast* (peerage of Ireland) 1613: m. 1605, Lettice, who d. 1620, da. of Sir John Perrott of Haroldston, Pembrokeshire, Lord Dep. of Ireland, and widow of (i) John Langharne, and (ii) Walter Vaughan, of Golden Grove, Carmarthenshire; d. 1625, when his peerage became ext., but was s. in estates by his next brother [1] *Sir* EDWARD, Knt., *PC*, b. c. 1568; Gov. of Carrickfergus; Joint Commr. of the Treasury, Ireland 1632; cr. *Viscount Chichester of Carrickfergus*, and *Baron Chichester of Belfast*, both in co. Antrim 1625-48: m. 1st, 1605, Anne, who d. 1616, da. and heir of John Coplestone of Eggesford, Devon; 2ndly, 16—, Mary, who d. 1637, da. of — Denham, of Wortham, Devon, and widow of Otwell Hill; d. 1648; s. by his el. son [2] ARTHUR, *PC*, b. 1606; Gov. of Carrickfergus 1660-1675; MP for co. Antrim 1634 and 1640-47; being distinguished in Irish Rebellion, was cr. *Earl of Donegall*, 1647, with remainder to heirs male of his father's body: m. 1st, Dorcas, who d. 1630, da. of John Hill of Honiley, Warwicks.; 2ndly before 1638, Lady Mary Digby, who d. 1648, da. of 1st Earl of Bristol; 3rdly, 1651, Letitia, (who m. 2ndly Sir William Franklin, and d. 1691), da. of Sir William Hicks, 1st Bt.; d. 1675; s. by his nephew [3] ARTHUR, *PC*, 2nd Earl, el. son of Lt.-Col. John Chichester, of Dungannon, co. Tyrone, 2nd son of 1st Viscount), b. 16—; MP for Dungannon 1661-66, joint Clerk of the Pipe Roll 1668-78, and Gov. of Carrickfergus 1675-78: m. 1st, 1660/1, Jane, da. and heir of John Etchingham of Dunbrody, co. Wexford, who d. 1712, having m. 2ndly, Richard Booth of Epsom; d. 1678; s. by his el. son [4] ARTHUR, 3rd Earl; b. 1666; Col. 35th Regt. Foot; Maj. Gen. of Spanish Fofces 1704: m. 1st before 1676, Lady Barbara Boyle, who d. 1682, da. of 1st Earl of Orrery; 2ndly, 1685, Lady Catherine Forbes, who d. 1743, da. of 1st Earl of Granard; Killed at Fort Monjuich 1706: s. by his son, [5] ARTHUR, 4th Earl; b. 1695: m. 1716, Lady Lucy Ridgeway, who d. 1732, da. of 4th Earl of Londonderry; d. 1757; s. by his newphew [6] ARTHUR, 5th Earl, son of the Hon. John, MP, 2nd son of 3rd Earl; b. 1739; cr. *Baron Fisherwick*, of Fisherwick, co. Stafford (peerage of Great Britain) 1790, *Marquess of Donegall*, and *Earl of Belfast* (peerage of Ireland) 1791: m. 1st, 1761, Lady Anne, who d. 1780, da. of 5th Duke of Hamilton; 2ndly, 1788, Charlotte, who d. 1789, da. and co heir of Conway Spencer, of Tremary, co. Down, and widow of Thomas Moore.
3rdly, 1790, Barbara, who d. 1829, da. of the Rev. Luke Godfrey, D.D., R. of Midleton, York, d. 1799; s. by his son [7] GEORGE AUGUSTUS, *K.P.*, 2nd Marquess; b. 1769; Lieut. of co. Donegal: m. 1795, Anna, dau. of Sir Edward May, Bt.; d. 1844; s. by his son [8] GEORGE HAMILTON, *K.P.*, *G.C.H.*,*P.C.*, *F.R.S.*,3rd Marquess; b. 1797; M.P. for Carrickfergus 1818-20, for Belfast 1820-30, and for Antrim (L) 1830-7; Vice-Chamberlain of the Household 1831-4, Capt. of Yeomen of the Guard 1848-52, and Lord-Lieut. of co. Antrim; cr. *Baron Ennishowen and Carrickfergus* (peerage of United Kingdom) 1841 : m. 1st, 1822, Harriet Anne who d. 1860, dau. of 1st Earl of Glengall (ext.); 2ndly, 1862, Harriet, dau. of Sir Bellingham Reginald Graham, 7th Bt., and widow of Lieut.-Gen. Sir Frederick Ashworth, K.C.B.; d. 1883, when the barony of *Ennishowen and Carrickfergus* became extinct; s. in the other honours by his brother [9] EDWARD, 4th Marquess, b. 1799; Dean of Raphoe 1832-73; m. 1821, Amelia Spread Deane, da. of Henry Deane Grady; d. 1889; s. by his el. son [6] GEORGE AUGUSTUS HAMILTON, 5th Marquess, b. 1822; was Clerk of the Peace for co. Antrim: m. 1st, 1859 (marriage annulled 1863), Lucy Elizabeth Virginia, da. of Henry Holt Oliver, of Weston Priory, Somerset; 2ndly, 1865, Mary Ann Williams, who d. 1901, da. of the late Edward Cobb, of Wright's Lane, Kensington, and of Arnold, Kent; 3rdly, 1902, Violet Gertrude, who d. 1952, only da. of the late Henry St. George Twining, of Halifax, Canada; d. 1904; s. by his son [7] EDWARD ARTHUR DONALD ST. GEORGE HAMILTON, 6th Marquess, b. 1903: Lt.-Col. Army Cadet Force; Journalist; War Correspondent 1939-45: m. 1st, 1943 (m. diss. 1968), Gladys Jean, yr. da. of the late Capt. Christian Combe [M. Conyngham]; 2ndly, 1968, Maureen, el. da. of the late Maj. Geoffrey C. Scholfield, MC, of Birkdale, Lancs; d. 1975; s. by his kinsman [see infra*₊*], Dermot Richard Claud, 5th Baron Templemore, (5th in descent from Lord Spencer Stanley Chichester, 2nd son of 1st Marquess), 7th Marquess and present peer; also Earl of Donegall, Earl of Belfast, Viscount Chichester, Baron Chichester of Belfast, and Baron Fisherwick.

₊—[1] ARTHUR Chichester, *MP*, of Durbrody Park, co. Wexford (el. son of Lord Spencer Stanley Chichester, 2nd son of 1st Marquess of Donegall); b. 1797; MP for co. Wexford; Lt.-Col., a Lord of the Bedchamber to William IV, and a Lord-in-Waiting to HM Queen Victoria; cr. *Baron Templemore*, of Templemore, co. Donegal (peerage of United Kingdom) 1831: m. 1820, Lady Augusta Paget, who d. 1872, da. of 1st Marquess of Anglesey; d. 1837; s. by his son [2] HENRY SPENCER, 2nd Baron; b. 1821: m. 1st, 1842, Laura Caroline Jane, who d. 1871, 3rd da. of the late Right Hon. Sir Arthur Paget, *GCB*; 2ndly, 1873, Lady Victoria Elizabeth Ashley, who d. 1927, da. of 7th Earl of Shaftesbury; d. 1906; s. by his son [3] ARTHUR HENRY, 3rd Baron, b. 1854; High Sheriff of co. Wexford 1890: m. 1st, 1879, Evelyn, who d. 1883, da. of the Rev. William James Stracey [Stracey, Bt.,

colls.]; 2ndly, 1885, Alice Elizabeth, who *d.* 1954, da. of the late Clinton George Augustus Dawkins; *d.* 1924; *s.* by his son [4] ARTHUR CLAUD SPENCER, *KCVO, DSO, OBE, PC, b.* 1880; Col. (retired) TA (formerly Comdg. 5/7th Batn. Hampshire Regt.); formerly Major Irish Guards, and Capt. Roy. Fusiliers (City of London Regt.); S. Africa 1902, with Tibet Mission 1904, present at action of Gyantse and march to Lhassa, European War 1915-18; was Private Sec. to Under-Sec. of State for War 1927-28, and to Paymaster-Gen. 1928-29, a Lord-in-Waiting to HM 1929, and 1931-34, and Capt. of Yeomen of the Guard 1934-45; Ch. Whip in House of Lords 1940-45: *m.* 1911, the Hon. Clare Meriel Wingfield, who *d.* 1969, da. of 7th Viscount Powerscourt; *d.* 1953; *s.* by his son [5] DERMOT RICHARD CLAUD, 5th Baron, who *s.* as 7th Marquess of Donegall [see ante].

DONERAILE, VISCOUNT. (St. Leger.) [Viscount I. 1785.]

[Title pronounced "**Dunnaral.**"   Name pronounced "**Sentleger.**"]

RICHARD ST. JOHN ST. LEGER, 9th Viscount; *b.* Oct. 29th, 1923; *s.* 1957: *m.* 1945, Melva Jean Clifton, and has issue.

Arms,—Azure, fretty argent, a chief or
Crest.—A griffin passant or. **Supporters,**—
Two griffins or, wings elevated azure,
fretty argent.

Residence,—

SONS LIVING.
Hon. RICHARD ALLEN, *b.* Aug. 17th, 1946; ed. at Orange Coast Coll., Cal.; Air Traffic Control Specialist, Mississippi Univ.
Hon. David Hugh, *b.* 1950.
Hon. Edward Hayes, *b.* 1960.

DAUGHTERS LIVING.
Hon. Elizabeth Adele, *b.* 1953.
Hon. Karen Jean, *b.* 1955.

AUNT LIVING.
Charlotte Hazel, *b.* 1892: *m.* 1913, Francis Boxwell, who *d.* 1950, and has issue living, Francis St. Leger, *b.* 1922,—Elizabeth Hazel, *b.* 1916: *m.* 1937, Maj. Brian Harry Craig, The Buffs (ret.), of Preshute, Carnew, co. Wicklow [E. Ranfurly, colls.], and has issue living, David Miles *b.* 1939: *m.* 1971, Jane Elizabeth Frazer, Peter Adrian *b.* 1948, Inez Elizabeth *b.* 1946: *m.* 1971, David Bacon Bury Hutton-

Great and good.

Bury, of Charleville Forest, Tullamore, co. Offaly, and has issue living, Caryl Bly Elizabeth *b.* 1972—Phyllis St. Leger, *b.* 1918: *m.* 1949, Col. Evelyn David Vereker Prendergast, MBE, DFC, late RA, of Manor House, Bagber, Sturminster Newton, Dorset, and; has issue living, Hew David Vereker *b.* 1950, Andrew Maurice Dalrymple *b.* 1952,—Hazel Helen, *b.* 1926: *m.* 1952, John Sholto Herries Skrine, MC, Solicitor, of 3791, Gombak Rd., Kuala Lumpur, Malaysia, and has issue living, Anna Hazel *b.* 1953, Nicola Gladys *b.* 1955, Fiona Ruth *b.* 1956, Lorna Helen *b.* 1958,—Patricia Sibyl, *b.* 1930: *m.* 1956, Antony Cameron Dacre Lacy, of Elmcroft, Moorlynch, Bridgwater, Somerset, and has issue living, Susan Cherry *b.* 1957, Julia Patricia *b.* 1959, Joanna Hazel *b.* 1960. *Residence,*—Butlerstown, Tomhaggard, co. Wexford.

WIDOW LIVING OF SEVENTH VISCOUNT.
ISOBEL Mary, *Viscountess Doneraile*), da. of Francis Morice, JP, of Whakapunake, Poverty Bay, New Zealand: *m.* 1920, the 7th Viscount, who *d.* 1956. *Residence,*—Doneraile Court, co. Cork.

PREDECESSORS.—[1] ST. LEGER Aldworth, *M.P.* for Doneraile 1761-76, succeeded in 1767 to the estates of his maternal uncle, Hayes St. Leger, 4th and last Baron Kilmadon, and Viscount Doneraile (cr. 1703), and assumed the surname of St. Leger in lieu of his patronymic; cr. *Baron Doneraile* of Doneraile (peerage of Ireland) 1776, and *Viscount Doneraile* (peerage of Ireland) 1785; *d.* 1797; *s.* by his son [2] HAYES, 2nd Viscount; *d.* 1819; *s.* by his son [3] HAYES, 3rd Viscount; *b.* 1786; a Representative Peer: *m.* 1816, Lady Charlotte Esther Bernard, dau. of 1st Earl of Bandon, *d.* 1854; *s.* by his son [4] HAYES, 4th Viscount; *b.* 1818; a Representative Peer: *m.* 1851, Mary Anne Grace Louisa, who *d.* 1907, dau. of the late George Lenox-Conyngham; *d.* 1887; *s.* by his cousin [5] RICHARD ARTHUR, 5th Viscount, son of the Rev. Richard Thomas Arthur St. Leger, and grandson of Hon. Richard St. Leger M.P., 2nd son of 1st Viscount, *b.* 1825; *d.* 1891; *s.* by his nephew [6] EDWARD (son of the Rev. Edward Frederick St. Leger, and great-grandson of the Hon. Richard St. Leger, 2nd son of 1st Viscount), 6th Viscount, *b.* 1886; Mayor of City of Westminster 1919-20, and Chm. of Metropolitan Asylums Board 1928-30; *d.* 1941; *s.* by his brother [7] HUGH, 7th Viscount ; *b.* 1869; admitted a Solicitor 1893 : *m.* 1920, Mary Isobel, dau. of Francis Morice, J.P., of Whakapunake, Poverty Bay, New Zealand ; *d.* 1956; *s.* by his kinsman, [8] ALGERNON EDWARD (son of the late Richard William St. Leger, grandson of the late Hon. Richard St. Leger, M.P., 2nd son of 1st Viscount), 8th Viscount; *b.* 1878: *m.* 1919, Sylvia Stephenson, who *d.* 19—, da. of Alexander Mitchell; *d.* 1957; *s.* by his only son [9] RICHARD ST. JOHN, 9th Viscount and present peer; also Doneraile.

DONOUGHMORE, EARL OF. (Hely-Hutchinson.) Sits as VISCOUNT HUTCHINSON (U.K. 1821). [Earl I. 1800.]

[Title pronounced "Dunomore."]

JOHN MICHAEL HENRY HELY-HUTCHINSON, 7th Earl; *b.* Nov. 12th, 1902; *s.* 1948; ed. at Winchester, and at Magdalen Coll., Oxford; is Col. late Roy. Armoured Corps (T.A.), and serving in Petroleum Warfare Depart.; sat as M.P. for Peterborough Div. of Northamptonshire (*C*) Oct. 1943 to June 1945; defeated there July 1945: *m.* 1925, Dorothy Jean, *M.B.E.*, dau. of the late John Beaumont Hotham [see B. Hotham, colls.], and has issue.

Arms,—Quarterly: 1st and 4th per pale gules and azure, a lion rampant, between eight cross-crosslets argent, *Hutchinson;* 2nd azure, a fesse between three bucks' heads erased in chief argent, and in base a demi-lion rampant or, *Hely;* 3rd azure, a garb or, between three wolves' heads erased argent, *Nickson.* **Crest.**—Out of a ducal coronet a demi cockatrice, wings elevated azure. **Supporters,**—Two cockatrices, wings elevated or, collared sable, combs and wattles gules, and charged on the breast with a wreath of laure vert.

He bravely bears the cross.

Residence,—Knocklofty Grange, Clonmel, co. Tipperary. *Club,*—Kildare Street (Dublin).

SONS LIVING.

RICHARD MICHAEL JOHN (*Viscount Suirdale*), *b.* Aug. 8th, 1927; ed. at Winchester, and at New Coll., Oxford (MA, BM and BCh); Capt. RAMC: *m.* 1951, Sheila, da. of the late Frank Frederick Parsons, and has issue:—
    SONS LIVING,—*Hon.* John Michael James, *b.* Aug. 7th, 1952.
        Hon. Timothy Mark, *b.* 1953.
        Hon. Nicholas David, *b.* 1955.
        Hon. Ralph Charles, *b.* 1961.
    Residence,—58 bis. Rue du 19 Janvier, 92, Garches, France. *Clubs,*—Hurlingham, Kildare Street.
Hon. Mark, *b.* 1934; ed. at Eton, at Magdalen Coll., Oxford (BSc, MA), and Mass. Inst. of Technology, USA, (SM); late 2nd Lt. Irish Guards: *m.* 1962, Margaret, yr. da. of the late Dr. Robert Rowan Woods. of 3, Fitzwilliam Place, Dublin, 2, and has issue living, Henry Peter, *b.* 1963,—Walter James, *b.* 1966,—Anna Doreen, *b.* 1969. *Residence,*—Larch Hill, Santry, co. Dublin.

DAUGHTER LIVING.

Lady Sara Elena, *b.* 1930: *m.* 1951, William Janson Collins, and has issue living, William Noel, *b.* 1952,—Jane Margarita, *b.* 1954,—Tiffany Anne, *b.* 1964,—Bryony Mary Pierre, *b.* 1974. *Residence* —House of Craigie, by Kilmarnock, Ayrshire.

BROTHER LIVING.

Hon. David Edward, *b.* 1911; ed. at Winchester, and at New Coll., Oxford (B.A. 1932, M.A. 1954); formerly Lieut.-Col. R.A. (T.A.): *m.* 1934, Barbara Mary. dau. of Hugh Wyld, of Essendon Close. Hatfield, and has issue living, Rose Mary, *b.* 1935: *m.* 1959, William Mackinnon Fernie, of Sawley Lodge, Clitheroe, Lancs., and has issue living, James Mackinnon *b.* 1962. Barbara Alison *b.* 1960, Juliet Rose *b.* 1967, Deborah Mary *b.* 1971,—Jean Elena, *b.* 1939: *m.* 1972, Bernard B. D. Kain, of Poplar Farm, Atworth, Melksham, Wilts.,—Pollyann Elise, *b.* 1942: *m.* 1970, Capt. Hamish J. Lochore, R. Scots Greys (ret.) [see Brooke Bt, cr. 1919] of Burgie House, Forres, Moray,—Kathryn Gabriel, *b.* 1944: *m.* 1973, Christopher Brian Amery, of 12, Maunsel St., SW1, and has issue living, Edward, *b.* 1975,—Deborah Jane, *b.* 1949: *m.* 1971, William Backhouse, of Layer Marney Wick, Colchester, Essex, CO5 9UT [see Backhouse, Bt., colls.]. *Residence,*—Middlewick, Corsham, Wilts.; Cranston, North Berwick, E. Lothian. *Clubs,*—Flyfishers', White's, Kildare Street (Dublin).

COLLATERAL BRANCHES LIVING.

Grandchildren of the late Rt. Hon. Sir Walter Francis Hely-Hutchinson, G.C.M.G. (infra):—
    Issue of the late Christopher Douglas Hely-Hutchinson, M.C., *b.* 1885, *d.* 1958: *m.* 1914, Gladys, who *d.* 1974, da. of William Beachy Head, of Johannesburg:—
Frances Anne (*Lady Stevens*), *b.* 1917: *m.* 1940, Sir John Melior Stevens, KCMG, DSO, OBE, who *d.* 1973, and has issue living, John Christopher Courtenay, *b.* 1955,—Jane Frances, *b.* 1945,—Mary Anne Victoria, *b.* 1947. *Residences,*—62, Bedford Gdns., W8; East Worlington House, Crediton, Devon.

    Issue of the late Maurice Robert Hely-Hutchinson, M.C., *b.* 1887, *d.* 1961: *m.* 1920, Melita Agnes Mary (58, Richmond Court, 200, Sloane St., SW1X 9QU), da. of the late Adm. Sir Colin Richard Keppel, GCVO, KCIE, CB, DSO [see E. Albemarle, colls.]:—
Henry Aymar, *b.* 1925; ed. at Eton; late Lieut. Coldstream Guards: *m.* 1957, Maria Anna, da. of the late Charles de Erney, of Zürich, Switzerland, and has issue living, Nicholas Charles, *b.* 1958,—Colin Henry, *b.* 1959,—Melita Louise, *b.* 1962. *Residence,*—23, Alderney St., SW1.——Colin Christopher (twin) (9, Concorde Flats, The Green, Marandellas, Rhodesia), *b.* 1925; ed. at Eton; late Lt. Irish Guards.——Marie Elizabeth, *b.* 1921. *Residence,*—35, Richmond Court, 200, Sloane St., SW1.—— Myrtle Melita (Tighnavlt, Aberfeldy, Perthshire), *b.* 1924: *m.* 1951, Alexander Lindsay Aymer, who *d.* 1972,—Diana Margaret, *b.* 1928: *m.* 1960, Walter von Halle, of 25, Carlyle Sq., SW3.—— Patricia May *b.* 1929: *m.* 1950, Maj. George Burell MacKean, DL, JP, and has issue living, William Muir, *b.* 1954,—Shane Charles Robert, *b.* 1958,—Kirsten Henrietta, *b.* 1951: *m.* 1972, Nicholas Cooper,—Georgia Isabella, *b.* 1961. *Residence,*—Loughanmore, Dunadry, co. Antrim.

    Issue of the late (Christian) Victor (Noel Hope) Hely-Hutchinson, D.Mus., *b.* 1901. *d.* 1947; *m.* 1925, Marjorie Anna (of Ronde Lodge, Doordrift Road, Constantia, Cape Province, S. Africa). dau. of Dr. Dirk de Vos Hugo, of Cape Town, S. Africa:—
John Richard (295, Hay St., Brooklyn, Pretoria, Transvaal) *b.* 1929: BSc, AMIEE: *m.* 1957, Allison Joyce, only da. of Ernest Simpson, of Paarl, S. Africa.——Christopher Adrian, *b.* 1931: Lt.-Cdr. RN (ret.): *m.* 1963, Beatrice Mary, yr. da. of Stephen Harris, of Barbon, Westmorland, and has issue

living, Adam Hugo, *b.* 1968,—Henrietta Lucy, *b.* 1973. *Address,*—c/o Westminster Bank, 14, Sloane Sq., SW1.

Issue of the late Rt. Hon. Sir Walter Francis Hely-Hutchinson, G.C.M.G., 2nd son of 4th Earl, *b.* 1849, *d.* 1913: *m.* 1881, May, who *d.* 1938, dau. of Maj.-Gen. William Clive Justice, C.M.G. :—

Natalie Leila Margaret (Tilhayes, Iwerne Minster, Blandford, Dorset, DT11 8LS), *b.* 1894: *m.* 1916, Gerard Mackworth Mackworth-Young, CIE, who *d.* 1965 [Young, Bt. cr. 1813, colls.].

Grandchildren of the late John Hely-Hutchinson, son of the late Capt. the Hon. Coote Hely-Hutchinson, RN, brother of 3rd Earl:—
Issue of the late Lieut.-Col. Coote Robert Hely-Hutchinson, O.B.E., *b.* 1870, *d.* 1930: *m.* 1914, Julia, who *d.* 1948, dau. of the late William Browne-Clayton, of Browne's Hill, Carlow :—

John, *b.* 1914. *Residence,*—Newport, Donabate, co. Dublin.——Michael (Croft Cottage, New Marton, St. Martins, Oswestry, Salop), *b.* 1916; Maj. (ret.) Roy. Norfolk Regt.; European War 1939-43 in Malaya (prisoner): *m.* 1951, Ruth Somerled, da. of the late Kenneth Mackenzie, MD, FRCS, of Auckland, New Zealand, and has issue living, Caroline Anne, *b.* 1954.——David Coote, *b.* 1918: *m.* 1948, Geraldine Mary, da. of the late Donough Richard O'Brien [see B. Inchiquin, colls.], and has issue living, Fiona Kathryn O'Brien, *b.* 1965. *Residence,*—Parteenalax, Limerick.——Mary Caroline, *b.* (twin) 1914.——Julia Louisa, *b.* 1921.

Issue of the late Col. Richard George Hely-Hutchinson, Roy. Fusiliers, D.S.O., *b.* 1871, *d.* 1953: *m.* 1899, Alice Maud, who *d.* 1962, dau. of the late William Crozier Cunningham, J.P., of Dante House, Whiteabbey, co. Antrim:—
Pamela (Winslade, Sunnyside, Fleet, Hants), *b.* 1909.

PREDECESSORS.—[1] CHRISTIANA, dau. of Abraham Nickson and wife of the Rt. Hon. John Hely-Hutchinson, an eminent lawyer and statesman of Ireland, was cr. *Baroness Donoughmore,* of Knocklofty, co. Tipperary (peerage of Ireland) 1783 ; *d.* 1788 ; *s.* by her son [2] RICHARD HELY, 2nd Baron; a Gen. in the Army; cr. *Viscount Donoughmore* of Knocklofty (peerage of Ireland) 1797, and *Earl of Donoughmore* (peerage of Ireland) 1801, with remainder to the heirs male of his mother, and while a Representative Peer was cr. *Viscount Hutchinson* (peerage of United Kingdom) 1821, with limitation as in peerage of 1801 ; *d.* unmarried, when all the honours devolved upon his brother [3] JOHN, *GCB,* 2nd Earl, who in 1801 had been cr. *Baron Hutchinson,* of Alexandria and Knocklofty peerage of UK) ; *d.* 1832, when the Barony of Hutchinson became ext. and the other honours, devolved upon his nephew [4] JOHN HELY, *K.P.,* 3rd Earl, son of the Hon. Francis Hely, M.P., 3rd son of Baroness Donoughmore; *d.* 1851 ; *s.* by his son [5] RICHARD John, *P.C.,* 4th Earl; *b.* 1823; Pres. of Board of Trade: *m.* 1847, Thomasine Jocelyn, dau. of Walter Steele, of Moynalty, co. Monaghan ; *d.* 1866; *s.* by his son [6] JOHN LUKE GEORGE, *K.C.M.G.,* 5th Earl, *b.* 1848 : *m.* 1874, Frances Isabella, who *d.* 1924, dau. of the late Gen. Stephens, H.E.I.C.S.; *d.* 1900; *s.* by his son [7] RICHARD WALTER JOHN, *K.P., P.C.,* 6th Earl; *b.* 1875; Under-Sec. of State for War 1903-1904, Civil Member of the Army Council 1904-1905, and Chm. of Committees and Dep. Speaker in House of Lords 1911-31; a Member of Senate of S. Ireland 1921; *m.* 1901, Elena Maria, who *d.* 1944, dau. of the late M. P. Grace, of New York, U.S.A.; *d.* 1948: *s.* by his son [8] JOHN MICHAEL HENRY, 7th Earl and present peer; also Viscount Donoughmore, Viscount Hutchinson, and Baron Donoughmore.

DONOVAN, BARONY OF. (Donovan.) [Extinct 1971.]

SONS LIVING OF LIFE BARON.

Hon. Hugh Desmond (Flat 1, Fulham Park House, Fulham Rd., SW6), *b.* 1934; ed. at Harrow and New Coll., Oxford: *m.* 1968, Margaret Mary, el. da. of Hugh Forbes Arbuthnott, of Winterfold House, Chaddesley Corbett, Worcs. [see V. Arbuthnott, colls.], and has issue living, Charles Edward Horatius, *b.* 1974.

Hon. John (23, Brooks Mews, Mayfair, W1), *b.* 1938; ed. at Harrow and Univ. Coll., Oxford: *m.* 1973, Pauline Nicole Christine, yst. da. of H. A. Klene, of Wittenburgerweg 4, Wasennaar, The Hague.

DAUGHTER LIVING OF LIFE BARON.

Hon. Susan Elizabeth, *b.* 1936: *m.* 1960, Gerard Francis Horton, of 27, Weemala Rd., Northbridge, NSW, and has issue.

WIDOW LIVING OF LIFE BARON.

MARJORIE (*Baroness Donovan*) (Lamb Building, Temple, EC4), da. of the late Charles Murray, of Winchester: *m.* 1925, Baron Donovan (Life Peer), who *d.* 1971.

DORCHESTER, BARONY OF. (Carleton.) [Extinct 1963.]

DAUGHTERS LIVING OF SECOND BARON.

Hon. Diana Claudia Patricia (*Countess of Malmesbury*), *b.* 1912 : *m.* 1932, the 6th Earl of Malmesbury. *Residence.*—Greywell Hill, Basingstoke.

Hon. Lorraine Charmian Gabrielle, *b.* 1919 : *m.* 1947, James Metcalfe Knowles, F.R.I.B.A., and has issue living, Thomas James Metcalfe, *b.* 1952,—Elizabeth Charmian Carleton, *b.* 1949. *Residence,*—9, St. Leonards Terrace, S.W.3.

WIDOW OF SECOND BARON.

KATHLEEN (*Baroness Dorchester*) (of The Dower House, Greywell, Basingstoke, Hants), da. of 6th Baron de Blaquiere: *m.* 1911, the 2nd Baron Dorchester, who *d.* 1963, when the title became ext.

DORMER, BARON. (Dormer.) **[Baron E. 1615, Bt. E. 1615.]**

What God wills I will.

CIO CHE DIO VUOLE IO VOGLIO

CHARLES WALTER JAMES DORMER, 15th Baron, and 15th Baronet; *b.* Dec. 20th, 1903; *s.* 1922; ed. at Oratory Sch.; Capt. (ret.) LG an ADC to Gov.-Gen. of NZ 1939-41: *m.* 1944, Lady Maureen Thérèse Josephine Noel, only da. of the 4th Earl of Gainsborough, and has issue. [The 15th Baron *d.* Aug. 27th, 1975].

ᾰrms,—Azure, ten billets, four, three, two, and one, or; on a chief of the second, a demi-lion issuant sable. Crest,—A falcon, wings displayed and inverted argent, beaked, membered, and belled or, standing on a falconer's right-hand glove fesseways argent. Supporters,—Two falcons, wings displayed and inverted argent, beaked, membered, and belled or

Residences, Grove Park, Warwick; 12, Campden House Court, 42, Gloucester Walk, W8.

DAUGHTERS LIVING.

Hon. Jane Maureen Thérèse, *b.* 1945: *m.* 1966, H. A. Samuel Sandbach, of 14, Rutland House, Marloes Rd., W8, and has issue living, James Peter Charles, *b.* 1969,—Emma Pauline, *b.* 1967.

Hon. Catherine Mary, *b.* 1950: *m.* 1973, Christopher J. G. Bird.

BROTHER LIVING.

Hon. JOSEPH SPENCER PHILIP, *b.* Sept. 4th. 1914; ed. at Ampleforth Coll., and at Ch. Ch., Oxford; late Capt. Scots Guards. *Residence,*—Orchard Hill, Birlingham, Pershore, Worcs.

SISTERS LIVING.

Hon. Myrtle Emmeline Theresa, *b.* 1907: *m.* 1927, Robert Wilmot Berkeley, who *d.* 1969, [see Bs. Berkeley, colls.]. *Residences,*—.

Hon. Rosamund Jane, *b.* 1911; JP for Warwickshire. *Residence,*—Ridgeacre Farm, Broad Green, Broadway, Worcester.

COLLATERAL BRANCHES LIVING.

Grandchildren of the late Hon. Hubert Francis Dormer, 3rd son of 11th Baron, *b.* 1837, *d.* 1913: *m.* 1865, Mary, who *d.* 1938, da. of Kenelm Digby:—
    Issue of the late Edward Henry Dormer, *b.* 1870, *d.* 1943: *m.* 1903, the Hon. Vanessa, Margaret, who *d.* 1962, dau. of 1st Baron Borwick:—
Robert Francis Edward Baptist, *b.* 1904; ed. at Eton; European War 1939-45 as Lieut. R.A.S.C.: *m.* 1st, 1928, Ebba (who obtained a divorce 1934), dau. of Niels Stokholm-Hestbeck, of Mors, Denmark; 2ndly, 1934, Barbara (from whom he obtained a divorce 1949), dau. of the late Martin Reed Brierley; 3rdly, 1951, Loris, yr. dau. of John H. Baines, of Hove, Sussex. *Residence,*—Villa Bellocchio, Garavan, Mentone, France, A.M. *Club,*—Travellers'.——Geoffrey Henry, *b.* 1920; ed. at Eton, and at Trin. Coll., Camb.; Lt.-Cdr. RNR; 1939-45 War as Lt. RNVR: *m.* 1947, Janet (who obtained a divorce 1957), dau. of James F. A. Readman, of 16, Lennox Street, Edinburgh; 2ndly, 1958, Pamela, dau. of the late Wallace Levick Simpson, and has issue living, (by 1st marriage) Carol Susan, *b.* 1949,—Sally Ann Vanessa, *b.* 1951,—(by 2nd marriage) William Robert, *b.* 1960, Hugh Richard Cecil, *b.* 1964. *Residence,*—Yew Tree Cottage, Dittisham, Devon. *Club,*—Naval.
    Issue of the late John Hubert Aloysius Dormer, *b.* 1874, *d.* 1946: *m.* 1900, Virginia Sinclair, who *d.* 1956, dau. of the late Charles Tankerville Chamberlaine Bey, of Paris :—
Charles Hubert Aloysius, *b.* 1906: *m.* 1930, Mary Johnson, of Ottawa, Canada.——Richard Joseph Thaddeus, *DSC* (8, Palliser Rd., W14), *b.* 1913; late RNVR.——Mary Louise Isabel, *b.* 1904.——Hélène Venetia Anne, *b.* 1907: *m.* 1937, Frank R. Kelley, and has issue living, Christopher Francis Valentine (66, Dogwood Drive, Easton, Conn. 06612, USA), *b.* 1939: *m.* 1963, Ruth Jordan, and has issue living, Kevin Francis Dormer *b.* 1966, Laura Anne *b.* 1964,—Peter John Dormer, *b.* 1943: *m.* 1967, Patricia F. Ruehle, of Chicago. *Residence,*—7, Ridgewood Lane, Westport, Conn., USA.——Pia Magdalen Virginia, *b.* 1920: *m.* 1945, Col. Henry Thomas Bernard Bellingham Rooke, MBE, Indian Army (ret.) [see Somerville, Bt., colls.]. *Residence.*—Wootton, Woodstock, Oxford.——Louise Cecilia Mary, *b.* 1922: *m.* 1st, 1940 (m. diss. 1954), Capt. Peter Bailward, RA; 2ndly, 1954, Maj. William Goulding Petrie-Hay, RA, and has issue living, (by 1st m) David John Aucher Michael (Lower Bowts Farm, Bowts Lane, Inkberrow, Worcs.), *b.* 1941; ed. at Ampleforth: *m.* 1969, Charlotte Martha Petra, da. of Herbert Frohberg, of Ottawa,—Sarah Jane, *b.* 1944: *m.* 1965, Richard Grahame Dugard Showell, of Old School House, Bishampton, Worcs., and has issue living, Clare Louise Dugard *b.* 1966,—(by 2nd m.) Rufus William, *b.* 1955. *Address,*—Lower Bowts Farm, Inkberrow, Worcs.
    Issue of the late Kenelm Everard Dormer, *b.* 1879, *d.* 1935: *m.* 1910, Josephine, who *d.* 1965, da. of the late Hon. John T. Toohey, of Sydney:—
John Kenelm, *b.* 1915; ed. at Downside; 1939-45 War as Capt. KOYLI.
    Issue of the late Capt. Robert Stanhope Dormer, *b.* 1880, *d.* 1960: *m.* 1927, Ebba, who *d.* 1961, dau. of the late Charles Cecil Beresford Whyte, of Hatley Manor and Newton Manor, co. Leitrim, and widow of Sir Everard Alexander Hambro, K.C.V.O. :—
Michael Henry Stanhope, *b.* 1930; is a Knight of Sovereign Order of Malta: *m.* 1959, Daphne Margaret, el. dau. of the late Capt. O. J. Battine, and has issue living, Merlin Robert Colum Charles, *b.* 1963, —Leanda Xenia Sophia Stanhope, *b.* 1959,—Athena Cecilia Stanhope, *b.* 1961. *Residence,*—Bow-down House, Greenham, Newbury.
    Issue of the late Hon. Hubert Francis Dormer (ante):—
Sir Cecil Francis Joseph, *K.C.M.G., M.V.O., b.* 1883; entered Foreign Office 1905; was Acting 2nd Sec., British Embassy, Constantinople 1911-12; appointed Assist. Private Sec. to Sec. of State for Foreign Affairs (Rt. Hon. Sir E. Grey, Bt., M.P.) 1915, in National Ministry (Rt. Hon. A. J. Balfour, M.P.) 1916, 1st Sec., Diplo. Ser. 1919, Chargé d'Affaires, Caracas 1919-20, 1st Sec. to British Legation to the Holy See 1921, Counsellor to British Embassy at Tokio 1925, and Envoy Extraor. and Min. Plen. at Bangkok 1929, Envoy. Extraor. and Min. Plen. at Oslo 1934-40, and Ambassador to Polish'Gov't. in London 1941-3; retired 1943; has Grand Cross of Order of St. Olav of Norway, and Norwegian War Medal; M.V.O. (4th class) 1923, K.C.M.G. 1937: *m.* 1915, Lady Mary Alice Clare Feilding, who *d.* 1973, da. of 9th Earl of Denbigh. *Address,*—St. Anne's Nursing Home, Wokingham, Berks.

PREDECESSORS.—[1] *Sir* ROBERT Dormer, Knt.; cr. a *Baronet* June 10th, 1615, and *Baron Dormer*, of Wenge (peerage of England) June 20th, 1615; *d.* 1616; *s.* by his grandson [2] ROBERT, 2nd Baron; a Gen. of Horse; cr. *Viscount Ascot* and *Earl of Carnarvon* (peerage of England) 1628; killed at first battle of Newbury 1643; *s.* by his son [3] CHARLES, 2nd Earl; *d.* 1709, when the earldom and viscountcy expired, and the barony reverted to his kinsman [4] ROWLAND, 4th Baron, grandson of the Hon. Anthony, 2nd son of 1st Baron; *d.* 1712; *s.* by his cousin [5] CHARLES, 5th Baron, grandson of the Hon. Robert, 3rd son of 1st Baron; *d.* 1728; *s.* by his son [6] *Rev.* CHARLES, 6th Baron, a Priest of the Church of Rome; did not assume the title; *d.* 1761; *s.* by his brother [7] JOHN, 7th Baron; *d.* 1785; *s.* by his el. son [8] CHARLES, 8th Baron; *d.* 1804; *s.* by his son [9] CHARLES, 9th Baron; *d.* unmarried 1819; *s.* by his half-brother [10] JOHN EVELYN PIERREPONT, 10th Baron; having conformed to the Church of England took his seat in the House of Lords; *d.* 1826; *s.* by his kinsman [11] JOSEPH THADDEUS, 11th Baron, son of John, 2nd son of 7th Baron; *b.* 1790: *m.* 1829, Elizabeth Anne, who *d.* 1883, dau. of Sir Henry Joseph Tichborne, 8th Bt.; at one time an officer of rank in the Austrian service; *d.* 1871; *s.* by his son [12] JOHN BAPTIST JOSEPH, 12th Baron, *b.* 1880: *m.* 1st, 1866, Louisa, who *d.* 1868, dau. of the late Col. Edward King Tenison, of Kilronan Castle, Roscommon; 2ndly, 1871, Leonie, who *d.* 1883, dau. of Mons. Fortamps, a Senator of Belgium, and widow of Count Alfred de Beuren; 3rdly, 1885, Emily Constance Campbell, who *d.* 1919, dau. of John Bald, of Monzie Castle, Perth; *s.* by his nephew [13] ROLAND JOHN, 13th Baron, *b.* 1862; sometime Sub-Director, Secretariat, Egyptian Ministry of Finance: *m.* 1897, Marie Hanem, who *d.* 1964, el. da. of the late F. Eywaz, of Cairo; *d.* 1920; *s.* by his brother [14] CHARLES JOSEPH THADDEUS, *C.B.E.*, 14th Baron; *b.* 1864; Capt. R.N.; a Gentleman Usher to H.M. King George V. 1919-22: *m.* 1903, Caroline Mary, who *d.* 1951, dau. of the late Sir Robert Cavendish Spencer Clifford, 3rd Bt. (ext.); *d.* 1922; *s.* by his el. son [15] CHARLES WALTER JAMES, 15th Baron and present peer.

DOUGLAS OF BARLOCH, BARON. (Douglas) [Baron U.K. 1950].

FRANCIS CAMPBELL ROSS DOUGLAS, *K.C.M.G.*, 1st Baron, son of Francis James Boswell Douglas; *b.* Oct. 21st, 1889; ed. at Grantown-on-Spey Gram. Sch., and at Glasgow Univ. (M.A. honours 1913); LL.D. Malta Univ.; admitted a Solicitor 1924; a KStJ; a Member of Battersea Borough Council 1919-45 (Mayor 1922-23), and a County Councillor for London 1934-46 (Chm. of Finance Cttee. 1940-6); PPS to Min. of Education and Home Sec. (Rt. Hon. J. Chuter Ede) 1940-46, temporary Chm. and Chm. of Standing Cttees. and of Estimates Cttees. of House of Commons 1945-46, Gov. and Com.-in-Ch. of Malta 1946-49, and Dep. Chm. of Corby Development Corporation 1950-62, since when Dep. Speaker of House of Lords; author of "Land Value Rating", and of many papers on land tenure, taxation, soil fertility and nutrition; MP for Battersea, N. Div. (*Lab.*) 1940-46; cr. KCMG 1947, and *Baron Douglas of Barloch*, of Maxfield, co. Sussex (peerage of United Kingdom) 1950: *m.* 1st, 1914, Minnie Findlay, *JP, MA* (C.St.J.), who *d.* 1969, da. of William Smith, JP, of Kirriemuir, Angus; 2ndly, 1971, Adela Elizabeth, widow of Capt. George La Croix Baudains, DSO, MC, and has issue by 1st m.

Arms,—Argent, a bar wavy chequy gules and of the first, cottised azure, between three stars in chief of the last and a heart in base of the second. **Crest,**—An oak tree with a lock hanging on one of the branches, all proper.

Residences,—8, Cambridge Road, S.W.11; Maxfield Manor, Three Oaks, Hastings, Sussex.

DAUGHTER LIVING (By 1st m.).

Hon. Frances Margaret, *M.B., B.S., b.* 1920; M.B. and B.S. London 1943; Fellow of Faculty of Anaesthetists 1957: *m.* 1943, Kenneth Ulyatt, Ph.D., M.Sc., and has issue living, Charles Kenneth, *b.* 1945,—James Francis, *b.* 1950,—Mary Stella Miranda, *b.* 1958. *Residence,*—134, Knights Hill, S.E.27.

DOUGLAS OF KIRTLESIDE, BARONY OF. (Douglas.) [Extinct 1969.]

DAUGHTER LIVING OF FIRST BARON.

Hon. Katharine Ann, *b.* 1957.

WIDOW LIVING OF FIRST BARON.

HAZEL (*Baroness Douglas of Kirtleside*), (Misbourne Cottage, Denham Village, Bucks.), da. of the late George Eric Maas Walker, of Mill Hill, NW, and widow of Capt. W. E. R. Walker: *m.* 1955, as his 3rd wife, the 1st Baron, who *d.* 1969, when the title became ext.

DOUGLASS OF CLEVELAND, BARON. (Douglass.) [Life Baron 1967.]

HARRY DOUGLASS, son of the late John Douglass; *b.* Jan. 1st, 1902; a Member of Nat. Exec., Labour Party 1948-53; Gen. Sec. Iron & Steel Trades Confederation 1953-67; a Member of Gen. Council TUC 1953-67 (Chm. 1967), of Iron and Steel Board 1960-67; and of Nat. Economic Development Council 1962-67; a Member of Electricity Council, and Monopolies Comm. 1967-71; *cr.* Knt. 1964, and *Baron Douglass of Cleveland,* of Cleveland, co. York 1967: *m.* 1926, Edith, da. of Charles Amer, and has issue.

Residence,—5, The Chase, Stanmore, Middlesex.

DAUGHTER LIVING.

Hon. Jean, *b.* 1928: *m.* 1952, Garry Long, FCIS, of 8, The Avenue, Hatch End, Pinner, Middlesex.

Doune, Lord, son of Earl of Moray.

Douro, Marquess of, son of Duke of Wellington.

DOVERDALE, BARONY OF (Partington.) [Extinct 1949.]

DAUGHTER LIVING OF SECOND BARON.

Hon. Aline Emily (*Hon. Lady Hogg*), *b.* 1907 : *m.* 1936, Lieut.-Col. Sir Kenneth Weir Hogg, O.B.E., 6th Bt. *Residence,*—2, Curzon Place, Park Lane .W.1.

DOWDING, BARON. (Dowding.) [Baron U.K. 1943.]

DEREK HUGH TREMENHEERE DOWDING, 2nd Baron; *b.* Jan. 9th, 1919; *s.* 1970; ed. at Winchester; Wing-Cdr. RAF (ret); 1939-45 War: *m.* 1st, 1940 (m. diss. 1946), Joan Myrle, da. of Donald James Stuart, of Nairn; 2ndly, 1947 (m. diss. 1960), Alison Margaret, da. of James Bannerman, LRCP, LRCS, of Norwich, and widow of Maj. R. W. H. Peebles; 3rdly, 1961, Mrs. Odette L. M. S. Hughes, da. of Louis Joseph Houles, and has issue by 2nd m.

§rms,—Argent, three bars gemel sable, over all a fleur-de-lys azure, on a chief of the second, three Doric columns of the first. Crest,—Upon a catherine wheel azure, a falcon rising or, belled and hooded gules. §upporters,—Not recorded at time of going to press.

Residence,—501, Gilbert House, Barbican, EC2Y 8BD. *Club,*—RAF.

LABORARE EST ORARE

To work is to pray.

SONS LIVING. (*By 2nd m.*).

Hon. PIERS HUGH TREMENHEERE, *b.* Feb. 18th, 1948; ed. at Fettes.
Hon. Mark Denis James, *b.* 1949.

WIDOW LIVING OF FIRST BARON.

MURIEL (*Muriel, Baroness Dowding*), (1, Calverley Park, Tunbridge Wells), da. of John Albino, and widow of Maxwell Whiting, P/O RAFVR; Pres. (past Chm.) of Nat. Anti-Vivisection Soc.; Founder and Chm. of " Beauty Without Cruelty ": *m.* 1951, as his 2nd wife, the 1st Baron, who *d.* 1970.

PREDECESSOR.—[1] *Air Ch. Marshal Sir* HUGH CASWALL TREMENHEERE DOWDING, *GCB, GCVO, CMG*, son of Arthur John Caswall Dowding; *b*, 1882; 1914-18 War (despatches); Dir. of Training Air Min. 1926-29, AOC Fighting Area, Air Defence of Gt. Britain 1929-30, a Member of Air Council (Research and Development) 1930-36, and AOC-in-C. Fighter Command 1936-40; *cr. Baron Dowding*, of Bentley Priory, co. Middlesex (peerage of UK) 1943: *m.* 1st, 1918, Clarice Maud, who *d.* 1920, da. of Capt. John Williams; 2ndly, 1951, Muriel, da. of John Albino, and widow of Maxwell Whiting, P/O RAF; *d.* 1970; *s.* by his son [2] DEREK HUGH TREMENHEERE, 2nd Baron, and present peer.

DOWNE, VISCOUNT. (Dawnay.) Sits as BARON DAWNAY (U.K. 1897).

[Viscount I. 1681.]

TIMET · PUDOREM

He fears shame.

JOHN CHRISTIAN GEORGE DAWNAY, 11th Viscount; *b.* Jan. 18th, 1935; *s.* 1965; ed. at Eton and Ch. Ch., Oxford; Lt. Grenadier Guards (Reserve): *m.* 1965, Alison Diana, da. of Ian Francis Henry Sconce, OBE, TD, of The Spinneys, Sevenoaks, and has issue.

Arms,—Argent, on a bend cottised sable, three annulets of the field. **Crest,**—A demi-Saracen in armour couped at the thighs, wreathed about the temples proper, holding in the dexter hand a ring or, stoned azure, and in the sinister a lion's jamb erased gold, armed gules. **Supporters,**—Two lions or, ducally crowned argent, each gorged with a collar cottised sable, charged with three annulets of the second.

Seat,—Wykeham Abbey, Scarborough, Yorkshire.

Residence,—5, Douro Place, W8.

SON LIVING.

Hon. RICHARD HENRY, *b.* April 9th, 1967.

DAUGHTER LIVING.

Hon. Sarah Frances, *b.* 1970.

BROTHER LIVING.

Hon. James Richard (146, Somerset Rd., Wimbledon, SW19), *b.* 1937.

UNCLE LIVING. (*Son of 9th Viscount.*)

Hon. George William ffolkes, *M.C.*, *b.* 1909 ; ed. at Eton ; Major Coldstream Guards, and a D.L. for Norfolk; 1939-45 War (MC): *m.* 1945, Rosemary Helen, who *d.* 1969, da. of the late Lord Edward Arthur Grosvenor [D. Westminster, colls.], and has issue living, Valentine George, *b.* 1948,—Edward William, *b.* 1950,—Elizabeth Rose, *b.* 1946,—Mary Isabel Dorothy, *b.* 1955. *Residence,*—Hillington Hall, King's Lynn, Norfolk.

COLLATERAL BRANCHES LIVING.

Grandchild of the late Maj. the Hon. Hugh Dawnay, DSO (infra):—
Issue of the late Maj.-Gen. Sir David Dawnay, KCVO, CB, DSO, *b.* 1903, *d.* 1971: *m.* 1926, Lady Katharine Nova de la Poer Beresford (Whitfield Court, Waterford), da. of 6th Marquess of Waterford:—
Hugh (Whitfield Court, Waterford), *b.* 1932; ed. at Eton; Maj. (ret.) The R. Hussars: *m.* 1971, Maria Ines, da. of Dr. C. Pellegrini, of Salta, Argentina, and has issue living, David Danton, *b.* 1972.——Peter (twin), *b.* 1932; ed. at Eton, and Ch. Ch., Oxford (BA).——Rachel, *b.* 1929.

Issue of the late Major the Hon. Hugh Dawnay, D.S.O., 2nd son of 8th Viscount, *b.* 1875, *d.* (killed in action) 1914: *m.* 1902, Lady Susan de la Poer Beresford, who *d.* 1947, dau. of 5th Marquess of Waterford :—
Sir Peter, KCVO, CB, DSO, *b.* 1904; Vice-Adm. (ret.); Dep. Controller of the Navy 1956-57 and Flag Officer, Roy. Yachts, 1958-62; an Extra Equerry to HM since 1958; 1939-45 War (DSO); MVO (4th class) 1939, CB (Mil) 1958, KCVO 1961: *m.* 1936, Lady Angela Christine Rose Montagu-Douglas-Scott, da. of 7th Duke of Buccleuch, and has issue living, Charles John, *b.* 1938; Maj. Welsh Guards: *m.* 1968, Adrian Louise, da. of Maj.-Gen. D.S.O. [see Colthurst, Bt.], and has issue living, Henry Marcus *b.* 1969, George Edward *b.* 1970,—Moyra Jane, *b.* 1946: *m.* 1969, Timothy Rupert de Zoete, of 33, Pembridge Villas, W11, and has issue living, Alexandra Margot *b.* 1973. *Residence,*—Hattingley House, Medstead, Alton, Hants. *Clubs,*—White's, United Service.——Ronald, *b.* 1908; is Lt.-Col. Coldstream Guards (ret.); 1939-45 War in Libya (despatches, prisoner): *m.* 1st, 1932, Lady Elizabeth Katherine, who *d.* 1941, da. of 5th Earl Grey; 2ndly, 1949, Sibell Margaret, da. of Ronald Collet-Norman [Collett Bt., ext.], and formerly wife of Maj. the Hon. Archibald Edward Cubitt [see B. Ashcombe], and has issue living, (by 1st m.) Andrew, *b.* 1934,—Ann Josephine, *b.* 1933,—Mary, *b.* 1936; a Lady-in-Waiting to HRH the Princess Anne 1970-74, since when an Extra Lady in Waiting: *m.* 1974 (John) Richard Walter Reginald Carew Pole, of Erth Barton, Saltash, Cornwall, son of Col. Sir John Gawen Carew Pole, DSO, TD, 12th Bt. *Residence,*—Ballydavid, Woodstown, Waterford.

Grandchildren of the late Major the Hon. Hugh Dawnay, D.S.O. (ante):—
Issue of the late Wing-Com. Michael Dawnay, R.A.F., *b.* 1912, *d.* 1946: *m.* 1938, Julian Mary (Orchard House, Foxearth, Sudbury, Suffolk), adopted da. of 1st Baron Brassey of Apethorpe:—

Patrick Julian (The Tower House, Sible Hedingham, Essex), *b.* 1939: *m.* 1966, Julie Katherine, da. of Lt.-Col. William Herbert Olivier, TD, DL, RA [see Jones, Bt., cr. 1919], and has issue living, Michael William, *b.* 1969,—Katharine Julian, *b.* 1968,—Evelyn, *b.* 1974.——Romayne Julian, *b.* 1940: *m.* 1972 Peter Rowland Timms.

(In remainder to Viscountcy only.)

Grandchildren of the late Lieut.-Col. the Hon. Lewis Payan Dawnay, 2nd son of 7th
Viscount :—
Issue of the late Maj.-Gen. Guy Payan Dawnay, C.B., C.M.G., D.S.O., M.V.O., *b.* 1878, *d.* 1952: *m.* 1906, Cecil, who *d.* 1972, yst. da. of the late Frances William Buxton [Buxton, Bt., colls.]:—
Christopher Payan, *C.B.E., M.V.O., b.* 1909 ; ed. at Winchester, and at Magdalen Coll., Oxford ; Lt.-Col. (ret.) Coldstream Guards; 1939-45 War in N. Africa and N.-W. Europe; MBE (Mil.) 1940, OBE (Mil.) 1943, MVO (4th class) 1944, CBE (Mil.) 1946: *m.* 1939, Patricia, da. of the late Maj.-Gen. Sir Hereward Wake, 13th Bt., CB, CMG, DSO, and has issue living, Rupert Payan, *b.* 1940,— Guy Payan, *b.* 1944,—Gillian, *b.* 1942: *m.* 1966, Christopher Butler of 73, Mill St., Old Kidlington, Oxford, and has issue living, Sophie Rosalind *b.* 1968, Josephine Laura *b.* 1970,—Sarah, *b.* 1947: *m.* 1970, Jollyon Combs, Welsh Guards, and has issue living, Arabella *b.* 1971. *Residence,*—Longparish House, Andover, Hants.——Oliver Payan, CVO, *b.* 1920; ed. at Eton, and at Balliol Coll., Oxford; Capt. late Coldstream Guards; NW Europe 1944-45 (despatches); Private Sec. to HM Queen Elizabeth The Queen Mother 1951-56, an Equerry 1953-56, and an Extra Equerry 1956-62; CVO 1953: *m.* 1st, 1944 (m. diss. 1962), Lady Margaret Dorothea Boyle, da. of 8th Earl of Glasgow; 2ndly, 1963, Hon. Iris Irene Adele Peake, MVO, da. of 1st Viscount Ingleby, and has issue living, (by 1st m.) Charles James Payan, *b.* 1946,—Ivo Nicholas Payan, *b.* 1952,—Caroline Margaret, *b.* 1950,—(by 2nd m.) Emma Jane Clarissa, *b.* 1964. *Residences,*—Flat 5, 32, Onslow Sq., SW7; Wexcombe House, nr. Marlborough, Wilts. *Clubs,*—Brooks's, MCC.——Pamela, *b.* 1907.—— Elizabeth Lavender, *b.* 1914: *m.* 1938, Peter Noel Loxley, Diplo. Ser., who *d.* 1945, and has issue living, David Noel, *b.* 1942,—Elizabeth Patricia, *b.* 1939.—*Residence,*—Boswick House, Dudswell, Berkhamsted, Herts.

Issue of the late Maj.-Gen. Alan Geoffrey Charles Dawnay, C.B.E., D.S.O., *b.* 1888, *d.* 1938: *m.* 1914, Elizabeth Sofia, who *d.* 1968 [having *m.* 2ndly, 1949, Lt.-Col. Sir (Walter) Guy Shaw-Stewart, MC, 9th Bt.], da. of J. George Bulteel:—
Denys, *b.* 1921. *Residence,*—Ardgowan, Inverkip, Renfrewshire.

Granddaughters of the late Hon. Eustace Henry Dawnay, 5th son of 7th Viscount:—
Issue of the late Lt.-Col. Cuthbert Henry Dawnay, MC, *b.* 1891, *d.* 1964: *m.* 1921, Marjorie Kathleen (16, Hale House, De Vere Gdns., W8), da. of the late Maj. Reginald Bernard Loder [see Loder, Bt., colls.]:—
Eve Margaret, *b.* 1926.——Delia Mary (*Lady Millar*), *b.* 1931: *m.* 1954, Sir Oliver Nicholas Millar, KCVO, FSA, FBA, Surveyor of HM's Pictures, of Yonder Lodge, Penn, Bucks., and has issue living, Charles James, *b.* 1965.—Cynthia Mary, *b.* 1956,—Lucy Anne, *b.* 1958,—Beatrix Jane, *b.* 1961.—— Verena Joan, *b.* 1936: *m.* 1958, John Antony de la Cour Elliott, of 12, Cathcart Rd., SW10, and has issue living, Davina May, *b.* 1962,—Bridget Victoria, *b.* 1964,—Felicity Jane, *b.* 1966.

Grandchildren of the late Hon. William Frederick Dawnay, 6th son of 7th
Viscount:—
Issue of the late Nigel William Dawnay, *b.* 1942: *m.* 1st, 1903, Daisy Rosalie, who *d.* 1940, only da. of the late Harry Norman Dunnett, of The Kennels, Stratford St. Mary, Suffolk; 2ndly, 1941, Violet Mary Harrison, who *d.* 1965:—
By 1st marriage) Frederick Cecil (2, Spring Grove, Sunningdale, Berks.), *b.* 1905; ed. at Radley: *m.* 1st, 1929 (m. diss. 1955), Margaret Jean, da. of the late William Coats Hutton, of Lexden Grange, Colchester; 2ndly, 1956, Betty Thora, da. of the late Samuel Henry Darling, of Wentworth, Surrey, and has issue living, (by 1st m.) Richard William, *OBE* (The Old Vicarage, Tisbury, Wilts), *b.* 1930; ed. at Sherborne; late Col. Parachute Regt.; OBE (Mil) 1970: *m.* 1962, Penelope Anne, da. of Col. Norman West Finlinson, DSO, and has issue living, Rupert Charles Richard *b.* 1964, Philippa Ruth, *b.* 1963, Deborah Kate *b.* 1966,—Christopher Ronald *b.* 1933: ed. at Sherborne; late Capt. 10th Hussars.——William Richard (of Crouch Farm, Whatfield, Ipswich), *b.* 1910: *m.* 1st, 1940 (m. diss. 1961), Olive Margaret, da. of the late Arthur James Barratt, of The Mile House, Oswestry; 2ndly, 1963, Pamela Lester, and has issue living, (by 1st m.) Diana Margaret, *b.* 1947.——Eric Christopher, *TD* (Grange Farm, Harpole, Northampton) *b.* 1913; ed. at Radley Coll.; Capt. 104th (Essex Yeo.) Regt. RHA (TA); 1939-45 War (prisoner): *m.* 1945, Vera Winifred, da. of the late Arthur James Barratt, of Mile House, Oswestry, and has issue living, David Nigel *b.* 1946,—Michael William *b.* 1950. ——Evelyn Adelaide (*Lady Joly de Lotbiniere*) (of Horringer Manor, Bury St. Edmunds), *b.* 1904: *m.* 1st, 1927, as his third wife, Lt.-Col. James Archibald Innes, DSO, who *d.* 1948; 2ndly, 1954, as his third wife, Lt.-Col. Sir Edmond Joly de Lotbinière, RE, of Brandon Hall, Suffolk, and has issue living, (by 1st m.) David Archibald (Hensill House, Hawkhurst, Kent), *b.* 1931: *m.* 1955, Philippa, da. of Maj. Sir Alexander Penrose Gordon Cumming, MC, 5th Bt, and has issue living, Guy Archibald *b.* 1956, John Hugh *b.* 1959, Davina Evelyn *b.* 1957,—Richard Dawnay (Playford Hall, Ipswich), *b.* 1937: *m.* 1966, Theresa Frances, da. of Marcus Spurway [see Baird Bt. cr. 1809], and has issue living, Antonia *b.* 1966, Sara *b.* 1967, Johanna *b.* 1968, Katherine *b.* 1973,—Delia Mary (*Lady Hall*), *b.* 1933: *m.* 1957, Sir John Bernard Hall, 3rd Bt. (cr. 1919), of Penrose House, Patmore Heath, Albury, Ware, Herts., and Inver House, Lochinver, Lairg, Sutherland.

Granddaughter of the late Capt. the Hon. Geoffrey Nicolas Dawnay (infra):—
Issue of the late Capt. Eris Geoffrey Dawnay, *b.* 1890; *d.* 1970: *m.* 1930, Daisy, who *d.* 1967, da. of the late Lt.-Col. Lewis Butler, of The Wilderness, Earley, Reading:—
Diana Buttercup, *b.* 1931: *m.* 1957, Hugh Rowland Murray Barran, of Hildenley, Malton, Yorks. [see Barran, Bt., colls.].

Issue of the late Capt. the Hon. Geoffrey Nicolas Dawnay, 7th son of 7th
Viscount, *b.* 1852, *d.* 1941 : *m.* 1887, Emily Janie, who *d.* 1935, dau. of John
Bulteel, of Pamflete, Devon :—
Kathleen, *b.* 1892. *Residence,*—The Brows, York Rd., Malton, Yorks.

PREDECESSORS.—[1] Christopher Dawnay; cr. a *Baronet* 1642; *d.* 1644; *s.* by his son [2] Sir Thomas, 2nd Bt.; *d.* 1644, aged 12. His uncle [3] Sir John (M.P. for Yorkshire 1660, and for Pontefract 1661-88) was cr. *Viscount Downe* (peerage of Ireland) 1681, and sat in James's Irish Parliament 1689; *d.* 1695; *s.* by his son [4] Henry, 2nd Viscount, M.P. for Yorkshire in several parliaments; *d.* 1741; *s.* by his grandson [5] Henry Pleydell, 3rd Viscount; M.P. for Yorkshire 1749-51; *d. s. p.* 1760, from wounds received at battle of Campen, near Wesen, when in command of 25th Foot; *s.* by his brother [6] John, 4th Viscount; *d.* 1780; *s.* by his son [7] John Christopher Burton, 5th Viscount; cr. *Baron Dawnay,* of Cowick, co. York (peerage of Great Britain) 1796; *d.* 1832, when the barony expired; *s.* by his brother [8] *Rev.* William Henry, 6th Viscount; Rector of Sessay and Thormanby ; *d.* 1846; *s.* by his son [9] William Henry, 7th Viscount; *b.* 1812: *m.* 1843, Mary Isabel, dau. of the Rt. Rev. the Hon. Richard Bagot, Lord Bishop of Bath and Wells ; *d.* 1857: *s.* by his son [10] Hugh Richard, *K.C.V.O.. C.B., C.I.E.,* 8th Viscount; *b.* 1844 ; Hon. Maj.-Gen. in the Army ; Zulu Campaign 1879 (medal with clasp), and S. Africa 1900, as A.D.C. to F.-M. Lord Roberts, and in charge of Foreign Mil. Attachés (despatches twice, medal with seven clasps, C.B.), and 1901-2, in charge of Remount Depart.; cr. *Baron Dawnay,* of Danby, N. Riding of York (peerage of United Kingdom) 1897: *m.* 1st, 1869, Lady Cecilia Maria Charlotte Molyneux, *V.A.* (sometime Lady of the Bedchamber to H.M. Queen Victoria), who *d.* 1910, dau. of 3rd Earl of

Sefton ; 2ndly, 1911, Florence Faith, who d. 1958, (having m. 2ndly, 1931, the Rev. Arthur Maxwe
Bury, V, of Loose, who d. 1937), dau. of the late Rev. Thomas Henry Dening, formerly V. of Holy
Trinity, Kilburn, N.W., d. 1924 ; s. by his son [11] JOHN, C.M.G., D.S.O., 9th Viscount, b. 1872;
A.D.C. to F.M. Lord French 1915-18, and Mil. Sec. to him in Ireland 1918-19 : m. 1902, Dorothy,
who d. 1957, only dau. of Sir William Hovell Browne ffolkes, 3rd Bt. ; d. 1931 s. by his el. son [12]
RICHARD, OBE, 10th Viscount; b. 1903; Col. and Hon. Brig. 5th Bn. Green Howards; Comdg.
69th Inf. Bde. and Assist. A.-G. W. Africa Command 1939-45 War: m. 1928, Margaret Christine,
who d. 1967, da. of Christian Bahnson, of Passiac, NJ, USA; d. 1965; s. by his el. son [13] JOHN
CHRISTIAN George, 11th Viscount and present peer; also Baron Dawnay.

DOWNSHIRE, MARQUESS OF. (Hill.) Sits as EARL OF HILLSBOROUGH
(G.B. 1772).   [Marquess I. 1789.]

ARTHUR WILLS PERCY WELLINGTON BLUN-
DELL TRUMBULL SANDYS HILL, 7th Marquess ;
b. April 7th, 1894 ; s. 1918 ; ed. at Eton ; is
Hereditary Constable of Hillsborough Fort,
and patron of one living; formerly Lieut.
Berks Yeo.; attached to British Red Cross in
France during European War : m. 1953,
Noreen (GRAY-MILLER) dau. of the late
William Barraclough.

Arms.—Quarterly: 1st sable, on a fesse argent
between three leopards passant guardant or, spotted
of the field, as many escallops gules, Hill; 2nd per
bend sinister ermine and ermines, a lion rampant or,
Trevor; 3rd gules, a quatrefoil or, Rowe; 4th argent,
a chevron azure, between three trefoils slipped, per
pale, gules and vert, Rowe. Crest.—A reindeer's
head couped gules, attired and plain collared or.
Supporters.—Dexter, a leopard or, spotted sable, ducally
collared and chained gules; sinister, a reindeer gules,
attired, unguled, and plain collared or.

Seat,—Murlough, Dundrum, co. Down. Residence,
—21, Wilton Crescent, S.W.1. Club,—Cavalry.

COLLATERAL BRANCHES LIVING.
Issue of the late Capt. Lord (Arthur)
Francis Henry Hill, The Greys
(Reserve), younger son of 6th
Marquess, b. 1895, d. 1953 : m. 1927,
Sheila, who d. 1961, youngest dau. of the late Lieut.-Col. Stewart MacDougall of Lunga :—
(ARTHUR) ROBIN IAN, b. May 10th, 1929; ed. at Eton: m. 1957, the Hon. Juliet Mary Weld-
Forester, dau. of 7th Baron Forester, and has issue living, Arthur Francis Nicholas Wills, b. 1959,—
Anthony Ian, b. 1961,—Georgina Mary, b. 1964. Residences,—Clifton Castle, Ripon; 13, Lowndes
Close, SW1. Club,—Turf.——Venice Marigold (Rosie) (Hon. Mrs. R. Hugh M. Kindersley),
b. 1930: m. 1954, the Hon. Robert Hugh Molesworth Kindersley, of 35, South Eaton Place, SW1,
only son of the 2nd Baron Kindersley.——Caroline Sylvia, b. 1938. Residence,—45, Old Church
St., SW3.

Descendants of the late Lord Arthur Edwin Hill-Trevor, 3rd son of 3rd Marquess,
who was cr. Baron Trevor 1880 [see that title].

Descendants of the late Lord George Augustus Hill, MP, 5th son of 2nd Marquess,
and in remainder to his mother's Barony of Sandys [see that title].

PREDECESSORS.—[1] TREVOR Hill, P.C.; successively M.P. for Aylesbury, Malmesbury
and Downshire, and Lord-Lieut. of co. Down; cr. Baron Hill, of Kilwarlin, and Viscount
Hillsborough (peerage of Ireland) 1717, with remainder to the heirs male of his father; d. 1742;
s. by his son [2] WILLS, P.C., 2nd Viscount; M.P. for Huntingdon, and for Warwick 1742-56,
Comptroller of Household to George II., Joint Postmaster-Gen., Sec. of State for the Colonies
1768-72 and 1779-82, and Registrar of High Court of Chancery, Ireland ; cr. Viscount Kilwarlin
and Earl of Hillsborough (peerage of Ireland) 1751, with remainder to his uncle Arthur
(later Viscount Dungannon), Baron Harwich, of Harwich, co. Essex (peerage of Great Britain,
1756), Viscount Fairford and Earl of Hillsborough (peerage of Great Britain) 1772, and Marquess
of Downshire (peerage of Ireland) 1789; d. 1793; s. by his son [3] ARTHUR, 2nd Marquess; his wife
Mary, da. of the Hon. Martyn Sandys, having succeeded to the estates of Edwin, 2nd and last
Baron Sandys (cr. 1743), was cr. Baroness Sandys, of Ombersley (peerage of United Kingdom)
1802, with remainder to 2nd and younger sons successively; she d. 1836, and was s. by her 2nd son (see
B. Sandys): the Marquess d. 1801; s. by his son [4] ARTHUR BLUNDELL SANDYS TRUMBULL, KP,
DCL, 3rd Marquess; Lord-Lieut. of co. Down; d. 1845; s. by his son [5] ARTHUR WILLS BLUNDELL
SANDYS TRUMBULL WINDSOR, KP, 4th Marquess; d. 1868; s. by his son [6] ARTHUR WILLS BLUN-
DELL, 5th Marquess; b. 1844; m. 1870, Georgina Elizabeth, who d. 1919, da. of John Balfour, of
Balbirnie, co. Fife; d. 1874; s. by his son [7] ARTHUR WILLS JOHN WELLINGTON BLUNDELL TRUM-
BULL, 6th Marquess; b. 1871; m. 1st, 1893, Katherine Mary, who d. 1959, and from whom he had

obtained a divorce 1902, da. of the Hon. Hugh Henry Hare; 2ndly, 1907, Evelyn Grace May, who *d.* 1942, da. of Edmund Benson Foster; *d.* 1918; *s.* by his el. son [8] ARTHUR WILLS PERCY WELLINGTON BLUNDELL TRUMBULL SANDYS, 7th Marquess, and present peer; also Earl of Hillsborough, Viscount Hillsborough, Viscount Fairford, Viscount Kilwarlin, Baron Harwich, and Baron Hill.

DROGHEDA, EARL OF. (Moore.) [Earl I. 1661, Baron U.K. 1954.]
Sits as BARON MOORE (U.K. 1954.)
[Title pronounced "Droyeda."]

FORTIS CADERE — NON POTEST

CEDERE

A brave man may fall but cannot yield.

CHARLES GARRETT PONSONBY MOORE, *KG, KBE,* 11th Earl; *b.* April 23rd, 1910; *s.* 1957; ed. at Eton, and Trin. Coll., Camb.; formerly Capt. (TA); Chm. of Financial Times, Ltd., a Dir. of Economist Newspaper, Ltd., of Pearson Longman Ltd., and of Industrial & Trade Fairs (Hdgs.), Ltd.; Chm. of Financial Times, Ltd. 1971-74 (Man. Dir. 1946-71), of Newspaper Publishers Assocn. 1968-70, and of Roy. Opera House, Covent Garden, Ltd. 1958-74; in Min. of Production 1942; a Com. of Legion of Honour of France, and of Order of Merit of Italy and Grand Officer Order of Leopold II of Belgium; OBE (Civil) 1946, KBE (Civil) 1964, KG 1972: *m.* 1935, Joan Eleanor, da. of the late William Henry Carr, and has issue.

Arms,—Azure, on a chief indented or, three mullets pierced gules. Crest.—Out of a ducal coronet or, a Moor's head in profile proper, wreathed round the temples argent and azure. Supporters.—Two greyhounds argent.

Residence,—Parkside House, Englefield Green, Surrey. *Club,*—White's.

SON LIVING.
(40, Warwick Av., W9), *b.* Jan. 14th, 1937; ed. at Eton, and Trin. Coll., Camb.; late 2nd Lt. Life Guards: *m.* 1968 (m. diss. 1972), Eliza, da. of Stacy Barcroft Lloyd, Jr., of Philadelphia, and St. Croix, Virgin Is. — HENRY DERMOT PONSONBY (*Viscount Moore*)

COLLATERAL BRANCH LIVING.

Granddaughters of the late Col. Francis Moore, gt. grandson of John Moore of Drumbanagher, co. Armagh (*d.* 1809), grandson of the Hon. Arthur Moore, 5th son of 1st Viscount:—

Issue of the late Col. Francis Moore, D.S.O., O.B.E., *b.* 1879, *d.* 1938: *m.* 1916, Anne Early, who *d.* 1964, dau. of William Van Wyck, of New York:—

Mary Van Wyck, *b.* 1917: *m.* 1951, Douglas Arden Lyon Camm. *Residence,*—The Moorings, St. George's Hill, Weybridge, Surrey.——Kathleen Clifford, *b.* 1918: *m* 1942, Lieut.-Col. Stephen Murfin Rose, OBE, R. Fusiliers, and has issue living, Margaret Anne, *b.* 1947: *m.* 1975, Maj. Mark Roberts, R. Regt. of Wales,—Mary Elizabeth, *b.* 1951. *Residence,*—Wingrove House, Chipping Campden, Glos.

PREDECESSORS.—[1] *Sir* GARRETT Moore, Knt., M.P., cr. *Baron Moore,* of Mellefont, co. Louth (peerage of Ireland) 1616, and *Viscount Moore,* of Drogheda (peerage of Ireland) 1621 ; *d.* 1627, *s.* by his son [2] HENRY, 2nd Viscount ; killed at Portlester in service of Charles I. 1643 ; *s.* by his son [3] HENRY, 3rd Viscount ; cr. *Earl of Drogheda* (peerage of Ireland) 1661 ; *s.* by his son [4] CHARLES, 2nd Earl ; *d.* 1679 ; *s.* by his brother [5] HENRY, 3rd Earl ; assumed the name of Hamilton on succeeding to the estates of his brother-in-law Henry, 2nd and last Earl of Clanbrassill ; *d.* 1714 ; *s.* by his grandson [6] HENRY, 4th Earl ; inherited the Monasterevin estates of Arthur, 3rd and last Viscount Loftus, of Elye ; *d. s. p.* 1727 ; *s.* by his brother [7] EDWARD, 5th Earl ; drowned in passage from England to Dublin 1758 ; *s.* by his son [8] CHARLES, K.P. ; cr. *Marquess of Drogheda* (peerage of Ireland) 1791, and *Baron Moore,* of Moore Place, co. Kent (peerage of United Kingdom) 1801 ; *d.* 1821 ; *s.* by his son [9] CHARLES, 2nd Marquess ; *d.* unmarried 1837 ; *s.* by his nephew [10] HENRY FRANCIS SEYMOUR, 3rd Marquess (son of the late Lord Henry Seymour Moore, 2nd son of 1st Marquess), *b.* 1825 ; Vice-Adm. of Ireland, and Lieut. of Kildare : *m.* 1847, the Hon. Mary Caroline Stuart-Wortley, who *d.* 1896, dau. of 2nd Baron Wharncliffe ; *d.* 1892, when the Marquessate of Drogheda (cr. 1791) and Barony of Moore (cr. 1801) became extinct, and the peerages of 1616, 1621 and 1661 devolved upon his cousin [11] PONSONBY WILLIAM (son of the late Ponsonby Arthur Moore, great grandson of 5th Earl), 9th Earl, *b.* 1846 ; a Representative Peer for Ireland : *m.* 1879, Anne Tower, who *d.* 1924, dau. of the late George Moir, LL.D , Sheriff of Stirlingshire ; *d.* 1908 ; *s.* by his son [12] HENRY CHARLES PONSONBY, *K.C.M.G.,* P.C., 10th Earl, *b.* 1884 ; was Lieut. of Co. Kildare 1918-21, a Representative Peer for Ireland 1913-57, Director-Gen. of Min. of Economic Warfare 1942-5, and Chm. of Committees and Dep. Speaker of House of Lords 1946-57 ; cr. *Baron Moore,* of Cobham, co. Surrey (peerage of UK) 1954: *m.* 1st, 1909, Kathleen, *CBE* (who *d.* 1966, having obtained a divorce 1922), da. of the late Charles Maitland Pelham Burn, of Grange Park, Edinburgh ; 2ndly, 1922, Olive Mary (formerly Lady Victor William Paget), who *d* 1947, dau. of George Mestyard : *d.* 1957 ; *s.* by his only son [13] CHARLES GARRETT PONSONBY, 11th Earl and present peer : also Viscount Moore, and Baron Moore (peerage of Ireland 1616, and of U.K. 1954).

DRUMALBYN, BARON. (Macpherson.) [Baron U.K. 1963.]

I will lift up mine eyes unto the hills.

NIALL MALCOLM STEWART MACPHERSON, *KBE, PC*, 1st Baron, 3rd son of the late Sir Thomas Stewart Macpherson, CIE; *b.* Aug. 3rd, 1908; ed. at Edinburgh Acad., at Fettes, and at Trin. Coll., Oxford; NL Scottish Whip 1945-50, Liberal Unionist Scottish Whip 1950-55, Parliamentary Under-Sec. of State for Scotland 1955-60, Parliamentary Sec. Board of Trade 1960-62, Min. of Pensions and National Insurance 1962-63, and Min. of State, Board of Trade 1963-64; Min. without Portfolio 1970-74; 1939-45 War as Maj. Queen's Own Cameron Highlanders (TA); MP for Dumfriesshire (*NL*) 1945-50 (*NL & U*) 1950-63; *cr.* PC 1962, *Baron Drumalbyn*, of Whitesands, Roy. Burgh of Dumfries (peerage of UK) 1963, and KBE (Civil) 1974: *m.* 1937, Margaret Phyllis, da. of the late Julius Joseph Runge, of Kippington Court, Sevenoaks, Kent, and has issue.

Arms,—Per fess or and azure, a galley of the first, masts, oars and tackling proper, flagged gules, in the dexter chief point a hand couped fessways holding a dagger paleways, and in the sinister a cross-crosslet fitchee of the last, over all a fess chequy of the second and ermine; a bordure Argent for difference. Crest,—sejant upon a mount of white heather a cat-a-mountain proper, its dexter paw in a guardant posture. Supporters,—*dexter*, a Cameron Highlander attired in green military jacket, white belt and sporran, red and green hose tops and white spats, and Glengarry bonnet with blue hackle; *sinister*, an Ayrshire bull proper, horned and unguled sable.

Résidence,—High Larch, Iver Heath, Bucks. *Clubs*—Carlton and RAC.

DAUGHTERS LIVING.

Hon. Jean Stewart, *b.* 1938: *m.* 1962, Cdr. James L. Weatherall, RN, of Craig House, Bishop's Waltham, Hants., and has issue living, Anne Norah, *b.* 1974.
Hon. Mary Stewart, *b.* 1942: *m.* 1967, Philip D. Wilson, of 5, Clancarty Rd., SW6.

Drumlanrig, Viscount. son of Marquess of Queensberry.

DUCIE, EARL OF, (Moreton.) [Earl U.K. 1837.]

By persevering.

BASIL HOWARD MORETON, 6th Earl; *b.* Nov. 15th, 1917 ; *s.* 1952 ; is patron of two livings : *m.* 1950, Alison May, dau. of L. A. Bates, of Pialba, Queensland, and has issue.

Arms,—Quarterly : 1st and 4th argent, a chevron gules, between three square buckles sable, *Moreton*; 2nd and 3rd or, two lions passant gules, *Ducie*. Crest.—A moorcock's head or, combed and wattled gules, between two wings displayed azure. Supporters.—Two unicorns argent, armed, unguled, maned, and tufted or, each gorged with a ducal coronet per pale gold and gules.

Seat,—Tortworth, Falfield, Gloucestershire.

SONS LIVING.

DAVID LESLIE (*Lord Moreton*), *b.* Sept. 20th 1951; ed. at Cheltenham: *m.* 1975, Helen, da. of M. L. Duchesne, of Langford, Bristol.
Hon. Douglas Howard, *b.* 1958.
Hon. Robert Matthew, *b.* 1964.

DAUGHTER LIVING.

Hon. Alison Jeannette, *b.* 1954.

SISTERS LIVING.

Dorothy Mildred, *b.* 1916 : *m.* 1945, Sutherland Grant, M.M. *Address,*—Box 121, P.O. Hillston, NSW.
May Reynolds, *b.* 1919. *Residence,*—91, Sherwood Road, Toowong, Brisbane, Queensland.
Joan Eleanor, *b.* 1921 : *m.* 1944, Squadron-Leader Basil Bannister Daish, Roy. Australian Air : : *Residence*, 12, Binnalong Avenue, North Manly, NSW.

DAUGHTER LIVING OF FOURTH EARL.

Lady Irmengarde, *b.* 1879: *m.* 1924, the Rev. John Reginald Stotten, of Long St., Point Verno Queensland

COLLATERAL BRANCHES LIVING.
Grandchildren of the late Henry John Moreton, 2nd son of the late Capt. The Hon.
Reynolds Moreton, RN, 5th son of 2nd Earl:—
Issue of the late Theodore Reynolds Moreton, *b.* 1890, *d.* 19—: *m.* 1921, Marie Ann Josephine,
who *d.* 19—, da. of David O. Anderson, of Duluth, Minnesota, USA:—
David, *b.* 1922.
Issue of the late Hugh Berkeley Moreton, *b.* 1891, *d.* 1935: *m.* 1923, Phyllis Mott, who *d.*
1928:—
Henry John (The Pas, Manitoba, Canada), *b.* 1926: *m.* 19—, Patricia, da. of
and has issue living, John Russell Berkeley, *b.* 1956,—Richard Steven, *b.* 1963,—Brenda Leigh, *b.*
1952,—Patricia Ann, *b.* 1954.——Carrie Ann, *b.* 1924: *m.* 1950, Charles William Schmidt, of 509,
Washington Av., Glencoe, Ill. 60022, USA, and has issue living, Charles William, *b.* 1951,—Stephen
Berkeley, *b.* 1957,—Susan Moreton, *b.* 1953,—Karin Marie, *b.* 1955.

Grandchildren of the late Capt. the Hon. Reynolds Moreton, RN (ante):—
Issue of the late Francis James Moreton, *b.* 1863, *d.* 1915: *m.* 1894, Clara Frances, dau.
of W. H. Smith, of Le Mars, Iowa, U.S.A.:—
Constance, *b.* 1895.——Evelyn Jane, *b.* 1898. *Residence,—*

Issue of the late Reginald Moreton, *b.* 1869, *d.* 1929: *m.* 1907, Mary, who *d.* 1935, dau. of
Edward Beresford [M. Waterford, colls.]:—
Richard Beresford Reynolds. *b.* 1909: *m.* 1929, Irene Beatrice, dau. of Major — Donnithorne,
of Torquay, and has issue, David Buckland, *b.* 1931,—Anthony Reynolds, *b.* 1938,—Jennifer Anne,
b. 1941,——Edward Havelock Erroll, *b.* 1911.

Grandchildren of the late Hon. Seymour Moreton, 8th son of 2nd Earl:—
Issue of the late Douglas Seymour Herbert Moreton, *b.* 1878; *d.* 1948: *m.* 1905, Winifred
Josephine Hilda, who *d.* 1967, da. of the late W. R. Richards, JP, of West Boulder House,
Fimiston, W. Australia:—
Marjory Elizabeth Douglas, *b.* 1907: *m.* 1932, John Albert Lane, who *d.* 1965. *Residence,*—8, Bellevue
Av., Moss Vale, N.S. Wales.——Hilda Jeanette Douglas, *b.* 1909: *m.* 1934, Clifford Ewing Spoule,
and has issue living, Clifford Moreton, *b.* 1939,—Douglas Moreton, *b.* 1944. *Residence,*—19,
Courtenay Road, Rose Bay, N.S. Wales.——Ellen Evelyn Douglas, *b.* 1913 : *m.* 1937, Capt.
James Edward Neville Rolfe, Australian Mil. Force (retired), and has issue living, James Moreton
Neville, *b.* 1939,—Jeremy Evelyn Neville, *b.* 1948. *Residence,*—Hardigreen Park, Burradoo, NSW.

Grandchildren of the late Hon. Percy Moreton, 3rd son of 1st Earl :—
Issue of the late Robert Moreton, *b.* 1850, *d.* 1884: *m.* 1880, Annabella Emily, who *d.*
1915, dau. of the late Edward Thornewill, of Dove Cliff, co. Stafford :—
Maurice Fitzhardinge Reynolds (Sister Dora Rest Home, Milford, Staffs.), *b.* 1884: *m.* 1917, Anna
Margaretta, who *d.* 1971, da. of the late Rev. Edward Brown Charlton, R. of Tatenhill, and has issue
living, Berkeley John Reynolds (Wason House, Castle Caris, Somerset), *b.* 1918: *m.* 1945, Lois,
yr. da. of the late Louis Hardaker, of Ackworth, Yorkshire, and has issue living, Stephen Maurice
b. 1950, John Evelyn *b.* 1952, Jane Mary Margaretta *b.* 1956,—Evelyn Emily Margaretta, *b.* 1921.

Issue of the late Rev. Percy Dundas Moreton, *b.* 1855, *d.* 1939: *m.* 1884, Alti Edith, who
d. 1940, dau. of the late Gen. Sir William Anthony Gib, K.C.B. :—
Muriel Evelyn, *b.* 1887. *Residence,*—Thanet Lodge, Ferndown, Dorset.

Grandchildren of the late Charles Macdonald-Moreton, el. son of the late Hon
Augustus Henry Macdonald-Moreton, MP, 2nd son of 1st Earl:—
Issue of the late John Ronald Moreton-Macdonald, *b.* 1873, *d.* 1921: *m.* 1906, Daisy Maud,
who *d.* 1966, da. of the late Brig.-Gen. Eyre Macdonnell Stewart Crabbe, CB, Grenadier
Guards, of Glen Eyre, Southampton:—
John MAXWELL MACDONALD, *b.* 1908: ed. at Winchester, and at Magdalen Coll., Oxford (BA 1929),
m. 1930, Anne, da. and heir of tailzie of Sir John Maxwell Stirling-Maxwell, KT, 10th Bt., and
assumed the surname of Maxwell Macdonald in lieu of his patronymic 1930, and has issue living,
John Ronald *b.* 1936; is eventual heir to the Baronetcy of Stirling-Maxwell [see that title],—
Donald (Overbury Cottage, Alton, Hants.), *b.* 1938; ed. at Winchester, and Ch. Ch., Oxford: *m.*
1962, Caromy, da. of Robert Jenkins, of The Manor House, Hooton Roberts, Yorks., and has issue
living, James Donald *b.* 1965, Harriet Caromy Anne *b.* 1967. *Residence,*—Largie, Tayinloan,
Argyllshire. *Clubs,*—Travellers', New (Edinburgh), Leander——Simon Foster MACDONALD-
LOCKHART OF THE LEE (Dunsyre House, Dunsyre, Carnwarth, Lanark), *b.* 1916; Maj. and a DL
and JP for Lanarkshire; assumed the surname of Macdonald-Lockhart of The Lee 1946: *m.* 1942,
Caitriona, el. da of Seton Gordon, and has issue living, Angus Hew (Newholm, Dunsyre, Lanark),
b. 1946: *m.* 1970, Susan Elizabeth, da. of the late Hon. William Normand [By. of Normand], and
has issue living, Fiona *b.* 1972,—Simon James (40, Reporton Rd., SW6 7JR), *b.* 1949: *m.* 1973,
Lavinia, da. of the late Col. Peter William Marsham, MBE [see E. Romney colls.],—Norman Philip,
b. 1954,—Mairi Susan, *b.* 1943: *m.* 1st, 1962 (m. diss. 1965), Leslie Swan; 2ndly, 1965, Ian Hamilton
Finlay, of Stonypath, Dunsyre, Lanark, and has issue living, Alexander *b.* 1966, Aileen *b.* 1967.——
Elizabeth, *b.* 1909: *m.* 1932, the Rev. Henry Richard Rogers, and has issue living, Duncan Henry (of
Ellary, Achahoish, Lochgilphead, Argyll), *b.* 1937: *m.* 1962, Dorothee, da. of Rolf Heimbach, of
Walberberg, Germany, and has issue living, Duncan Norman *b.* 1963, Andrew Richard *b.* 1968,
Stephanie Dorothee *b.* 1965,—Angus, *b.* 1948,—Shian Douna Mary, *b.* 1934: *m.* 1952, Donald James
Maclean, of Tullich, Kimelford, Oban, and has issue living, Duncan James *b.* 1953, Nancy Jane
b. 1955,—Nancy, *b.* 1939: *m.* 1961, Richard Fitzgerald Tuthill, of Creag a'Mhadaidh, Achnamara,
Lochgilphead, Argyll, and has issue living, John Fitzgerald *b.* 1964, Caroline Fitzgerald *b.* 1962,
Amanda Fitzgerald *b.* 1966. *Residence,*—Ellary, Achahoish, Lochgilphead, Argyll.——Esher Mary
b. 1920: *m.* 1947, David Stewart Gladstone [E. Shrewsbury, colls.], and has issue living, Colin
Hew, *b.* 1954,—Mary Cecil, *b.* 1948: *m.* 19—, David Cooke,—Elizabeth Jean, *b.* 1951,—Janet
Esther, *b.* 1952: *m.* 1970, Graham Noble. *Residence,*—Glassoch, Newton Stewart, Wigtownshire.

PREDECESSORS.—[1] MATTHEW DUCIE Moreton; cr. *Lord Ducie, Baron of Moreton,* co.
Stafford (peerage of Great Britain) 1720; *d.* 1735; *s.* by his son [2] MATTHEW, 2nd Baron; cr.
Baron Ducie of Tortworth, co. Gloucester (peerage of Great Britain) 1763, with remainder to the
sons of his sister the Hon. Elizabeth Reynolds ; *d.* 1770, when the Barony of Moreton expired,
and the Barony of Ducie devolved upon his nephew [3] THOMAS Reynolds, 2nd Baron ;
assumed the surname of Moreton by Act of Parliament 1771; *d. s. p.* 1785 ; *s.* by his brother
[4] FRANCIS Reynolds, 3rd Baron; assumed the surname of Moreton by Act of Parliament
1786; *d.* 1808; *s.* by his son [5] THOMAS REYNOLDS, 4th Baron; cr. *Baron Moreton,* of
Tortworth, and *Earl of Ducie* (peerage of United Kingdom) 1837; *d.* 1840; *s.* by his son [6]
HENRY GEORGE FRANCIS, 2nd Earl ; *b.* 1802; *m.* 1826, the Hon. Elizabeth Dutton, dau. of 2nd
Baron Sherborne ; *d.* 1853 ; *s.* by his son [7] HENRY JOHN, *G.C.V.O., F.R.S.,* 3rd Earl ; *b.* 1827 ;
M.P. for Stroud (*L*) 1852-53 ; Lord-Lieut. of Gloucestershire 1857-1911, and Lord Warden of the
Stanneries and a Member of Council of Prince of Wales 1888-1908 : *m.* 1849, Julia, who *d.* 1895, dau.
of the late James Haughton Langston, M.P., of Sarsden, Chipping Norton ; *d.* 1921 ; *s.* by his brother
[8] BERKELEY BASIL, 4th Earl, *b.* 1831 ; many years engaged in sheep and cattle farming in Queens-
land ; Postmaster-Gen. of Queensland 1885. Min. of Public Instruction, Queensland 1885-86, and
Colonial Sec. and Min. of Public Instruction 1886-88 : *m.* 1862, Emily Eleanor, who *d.* 1921, dau. of
John Kent, Commr. of Crown Lands, Queensland ; *d.* 1924 ; *s.* by his el. son [9] CAPEL HENRY
BERKELEY, 5th Earl ; *b.* 1875 ; many years engaged in dairy and fruit farming in Australia : *m.* 1903
(Maria) Emma, who *d.* 1958, dau. of Frederick Bryant, of Maryborough, Queensland ; *d.* 1952 ;
s. by his nephew [10] BASIL HOWARD (son of the late Hon. Algernon Howard Moreton, 2nd son of
4th Earl), 6th Earl and present peer ; also Baron Ducie. and Baron Moreton.

DUDLEY, BARONESS.   (Wallace.)   [Baron E. 1439.]

BARBARA AMY FELICITY WALLACE, *Baroness Dudley*; *b.* April 23rd, 1907; *s.* 1972: *m.* 1929, Guy Raymond Hill Wallace, who *d.* 1967, and has issue.

Arms,—not exemplified at time of going to press.

Residence,—Hill House, Kempsey, Worcs.

SONS LIVING.

Hon. JIM ANTHONY HILL (Little Grange, Kempsey, Worcs.), *b.* Nov. 9th, 1930; ed. at Lancing: *m,* 1962, Nicola Jane, da. of Philip William Edward Leslie Dunsterville, and has issue living, Jeremy William Guilford, *b.* 1964,—Nicholas John Hill, *b.* 1967.
Hon. Robin Guy Hill, *b.* 1936; ed. at Malvern: *m.* 1959, Jill Alexandra, da. of the late Herbert Williams, and has issue living, Simon Alexander Hill, *b.* 1962,—Andrew George Hill, *b.* 1964.
Hon. William John Sutton (Beechmount House, Hallow, Worcs.), *b.* 1938; ed. at Malvern: *m.* 1962, Jean Carol Ann, da. of the late Albert Edward Shipton, and has issue living, Guy Edward John Sutton, *b.* 1963,—Piers William Somery, *b.* 1965.

DAUGHTER LIVING.

Hon. Felicity Lilla, *b.* 1944: *m.* 1967, Philip Neil Faram, of Heath Hill, Queenshill, Upton-on-Severn, Worcs., and has issue living, David Stephen, *b.* 1968,—Michael Guy, *b.* 1970.

PREDECESSORS.—[1] Sir JOHN Sutton de Dudley, *K.G.*, son of Sir John Sutton ; *b.* 1400 ; summoned to Parliament 1439-40 ; *d.* 1487 ; *s.* by his grandson [2] EDWARD (son of Sir Edmund Dudley), 2nd Baron ; *b.* 1459 ; knighted 1487 ; summoned to Parliament 1492-1529: *m.* Cicely, dau. of Sir William Willoughby ; *d.* 1531 ; *s.* by his son [3] JOHN, 3rd Baron ; *d.* 1553 ; *s.* by his son [4] EDWARD, 4th Baron ; summoned to Parliament 1584-86 ; Lieut. of Hampnes Castle: *m.* 1st, 1555, Katherine, dau. of 1st Baron Chandos of Sudeley ; 2ndly, Jane, dau. of 3rd Earl of Derby ; 3rdly, Mary, dau. of 1st Baron Howard of Effingham ; *d.* 1586 ; *s.* by his son (by his 2nd marriage) [5] EDWARD, 5th Baron ; *b.* 1567 ; *d.s.p.* 1643 ; *s.* by his granddaughter [6] FRANCES (only dau. of Sir Ferdinando Sutton) ; *b.* 1611: *m.* 1628, Sir Humble Ward, who *d.* 1670, having been cr. *Baron Ward*, of Birmingham, co. Warwick 1643, with remainder to the heirs-male of his body, by his wife, Frances ; *d.* 1697 ; *s.* by her son [7] EDWARD Ward, 7th Lord Dudley and 2nd Baron Ward : *m.* Frances, dau. of Sir William Gretton, 2nd Bt. ; *d.* 1701 ; *s.* by his grandson [8] EDWARD (son of William Ward), 8th Baron Dudley and 3rd Baron Ward ; *b.* 1683 ; *m.* 1703, Diana, dau. of Sir Thomas Howard, of Ashtead, Surrey ; *d.* 1704 ; *s.* by his son [9] EDWARD, 9th Baron Dudley and 4th Baron Ward : *b.* (posthumous) 1704 ; *d.* 1731 ; *s.* by his uncle [10] WILLIAM, 10th Baron Dudley and 5th Baron Ward (younger brother of the 8th Baron) ; *b.* 168- ; *d.* 1740, when the Barony of Ward devolved upon the heir-male, and that of Dudley on the heir-general, his nephew [11] FERDINANDO DUDLEY Lea, 11th Baron (son of William Lea, of Halesowen Grange, by Frances, sister of the 10th Baron) ; *b.* 1710 ; *d.* 1757, when the Barony of Dudley fell into abeyance between his sisters and co-heirs, and so remained until 1916, when the abeyance was determined in favour of the senior co-heir [12] FERDINANDO DUDLEY WILLIAM LEA SMITH (el. and only surviving son of the late Ferdinando Dudley Lea Smith), 12th Baron: *m.* 1904, Sybil Augusta, who *d.* 1958, dau. of the late Rev. Henry William Coventry; *d.* 1936; *s.* by his only son [13] FERDINANDO DUDLEY LEA, 13th Baron, *b.* 1910: *m.* 1941 (m. annulled 1965), Kirsten Laura Hedvig, da. of Lars Anton Albrechtson, of Vibsig, Denmark; *d.* 1972; *s.* by his sister [14] BARBARA AMY FELICITY, Baroness Dudley and present peeress.

DUDLEY, EARL OF.   (Ward.)   [Earl U.K. 1860.]

WILLIAM HUMBLE DAVID WARD, 4th Earl; *b.* Jan. 5th, 1920; *s.* 1969; ed. at Eton, and Ch. Ch., Oxford; late Lt. and temp. Capt. 10th R. Hussars; 1939-45 War in Italy (wounded): *m.* 1st, 1946 (m. diss. 1961), Stella, el. da. of Miguel Angel Carcano, KBE, formerly Argentine Ambassador in London; 2ndly, 1961, Maureen, da. of James Swanson, and has issue by 1st and 2nd m.

Arms,—Checky, or and azure, a bend ermine. **Crest,**—Out of a ducal coronet or, a lion's head azure. **Supporters.**—Two angels proper, hair and wings or, under robe sanguine, upper robe azure.

Residence,—6, Cottesmore Gdns., W8. *Clubs,*—White's, Pratt's, and Royal Yacht Squadron.

SONS LIVING. (By 1st m.)

WILLIAM HUMBLE DAVID JEREMY (*Viscount Ednam*), *b.* March 27th, 1947; ed. at Eton, and Ch. Ch., Oxford: *m.* 1972, Sarah Mary, da. of Sir Alastair Francis Stuart Coats, 4th Bt.
(*By 2nd m.*)
Hon. Leander Grenville Dudley, *b.* 1971.

DAUGHTERS LIVING. (By 1st m.
Lady Rosemary Millicent, *b.* 1955.
Lady Anne-Marie Ines (twin), *b.* 1955.

(*By 2nd m.*)
Lady Susanna Louise, *b.* 1963.
Lady Melissa Patricia Eileen, *b.* 1964.
Lady Victoria Cecilia Larissa, *b.* 1966.
Lady Amelia Maureen Erica, *b.* 1967.
Lady Emma Sophia Cressida, *b.* 1970.

As I was.

BROTHER LIVING.

Hon. Peter Alistair, *b.* 1926; ed. at Eton, at Univ. of British Columbia, and at Ch. Ch., Oxford; 1943-45 War with Roy. Canadian Air Force, and Fleet Air Arm: *m.* 1st, 1956 (m. diss. 1974), Claire Leonora, da. of Amyas Evelyn Giles Baring [see B. Ashburton, colls.]; 2ndly, 1974, Elizabeth Rose, da. of Richard V. C. Westmacott, of Ascona, Switzerland, and has issue living (by 1st m.), Alexander Evelyn Giles, *b.* 1961,—Rachel Claire, *b.* 1957,—Tracy Louise, *b.* 1958,—(by 2nd m.), Jeremy Christopher, *b.* 1975. *Residences,*—29, Egerton Terrace ,SW3; Cornwall Manor, Kingham, Oxon. *Clubs,*—White's and Royal Yacht Squadron.

UNCLES LIVING. (*Sons of 2nd Earl*)

Hon. Edward Frederick, *b.* 1907; ed. at Eton; sometime 2nd Lieut. 10th Roy. Hussars Group Capt. (retired) R.A.F.; European War 1939-45 (despatches): *m.* 1st, 1940, Pauline Katharine (who obtained a divorce 1947), da. of the late Hon. Charles Frederick Winn [see B. St. Oswald, colls.]; 2ndly, 1953, the Hon. Alathea Gwendoline Alys Mary Fitzalan-Howard, da. of 2nd Viscount FitzAlan of Derwent. *Club,*—White's.

Rt. Hon. George Reginald (twin), *b.* 1907 ; *cr. Viscount Ward of Witley* 1960 [see that title].

WIDOW LIVING OF THIRD EARL.

GRACE MARIA (*Grace, Countess of Dudley*), (Greycliff, Nassau, Bahamas), da. of Dr. Michel Kolin, of Dubrovnik, and formerly wife of Prince Stanislas Radziwill: *m.* 1961, as his 3rd wife, the 3rd Earl, who *d.* 1969.

COLLATERAL BRANCHES LIVING.

Issue of the late Lieut.-Col. the Hon. Roderick John Ward, 2nd son of 2nd Earl, *b.* 1902, *d.* 1952 : *m.* 1st, 1928, Eileen Patricia (from whom he obtained a divorce 1936), dau. of Lieut.-Col. Marcus Michael Hartigan, C.M.G., D.S.O.; 2ndly, 1940, Valerie Maud, dau. of R. J. Skelton, of Nairobi, Kenya Colony ; 3rdly, 1947, Charlotte Anne Park, who *d.* 1971, da. of the late Capt. Charles Frederick Osborne, R.D., R.N.R., of Broadstone, Dorset :—
(By 2nd m.) Robert John Christopher BARWICK-WARD, (c/o Midland Bank, High St., Northallerton); *b.* 1942; ed. at Millfield, and Grenoble Univ.; assumed by deed poll 1952, the additional surname of Barwick: *m.* 1968 (m. diss. 1974), Frances Pauline, el. da. of Sqdn.-Ldr. Mathieu Donald Einhorn, JP, RCAF, of Cragg Hill House, Killinghall, Yorks., and has issue living, Annabel Jane, *b.* 1970.——
(By 3rd m.) Rupert Michael (Hyde Tyning Stables, Minchinhampton, Glos.), *b.* 1947: *m.* 1970, Frances Margaret Mary, el. da of J. C. Barry, of Adelaide House, Bruff, co. Limerick, and has issue living, Eric Roderick Humble, *b.* 1973.

Issue of the late Major the Hon. Sir John Hubert Ward, K.C.V.O., 2nd son of 1st Earl, *b.* 1870, *d.* 1938: *m.* 1908, Jean Templeton, *C.B.E.*, who *d.* 1962, only dau. of the late Hon. Whitelaw Reid, American Ambassador in London:—
Edward John Sutton, *M.V.O., M.C., b.* 1909 ; ed. at Eton ; is Col. Life Guards (Reserve); European War 1939-45 (M.C.); M.V.O. (4th class) 1952: *m.* 1934, Susan, el da. of the late Geoffrey Robert Josceline Corbett, D.S.O., of Rossferry, Enniskillen, co. Fermanagh, and has issue living, Gerald John (Chilton Park Farm, Hungerford, Berks.), *b.* 1938: *m.* 1967, Rosalind Elizabeth, da. of the late Hon. Richard Edward Lygon [see E. Beauchamp, colls.], and has issue living, Sarah Patricia *b.* 1968, Margaret Lucy *b.* 1970,—Patricia Elizabeth Marion (Green Acres Farm, RT2 Fordland, Missouri, USA 65652), *b.* 1935: *m.* 1st, 1956 (m. diss. 1964), Kenneth E. Cooper, of Cal., USA ; 2ndly, 1965 (m. diss. 1966), John Gray; 3rdly, 1966 (m. diss. 1971), Frederick Calvin Danner, and has issue living, (by 1st m.) Susan Elizabeth Margaret *b.* 1957, Laura Jean *b.* 1959. *Residence,*—Chilton, Hungerford, Berks.——Alexander Reginald, *b.* 1915; ed. at Eton: *m.* 1st, 1946 (m. diss. 1959), Ilona, only da. of the late Maj. B. Hollos, of Budapest, Hungary; 2ndly, 1967 (m. diss. 1969), Zena Moyra Marshall. *Residences,*—Poughley, Woodlands St. Mary, nr. Newbury, Berks.; Kinnaird Ballinluig, Perthshire; 6, Groom Pl., Belgrave Sq., SW1.

Granddaughters of the late Hon. Robert Arthur Ward, OBE (infra):—
Issue of the late Maj. Julian Humble Dudley Ward, *b.* 1908, *d.* 1971: *m.* 1st, 1946, (m. diss. 1954), Ann Elisabeth, only da. of the late Capt. John Walter Wilson Bridges; 2ndly, 1962, Mary Rebecca Jane (Maryland, Bundanoon, NSW), da. of Albert Edward Morris-Hadwell, of Kidderminster, Worcs., and Ballarat, Vic., Aust., and widow of Col. Harry Latham, RHA :—
(By 1st m.) Patricia Anne, *b.* 1947.—Georgina Mary, *b.* 1950.

Issue of the late Hon. Robert Arthur Ward, O.B.E., 3rd son of 1st Earl, *b.* 1871, *d.* 1942: *m.* 1906, Lady Mary Acheson, who *d.* 1972, da. of 4th Earl of Gosford:—
Lettice Mary, *b.* 1909: *m.* 1934, as his second wife (marriage dissolved 1948), Arthur Thomas Filmer Wilson-Filmer [Filmer, Bt.]. *Residence.*—Grove House, 94, Woodstock Rd. Oxford.

Issue of the late Capt. the Hon. Cyril Augustus Ward, MVP, RN, 5th son of 1st Earl, *b.* 1876, *d.* 1930: *m.* 1904, Baroness Irene de Brienen, who *d.* 1974, having *m.* 2ndly, 1934, Vice-Adm. the Hon Arthur Charles Strutt, CBE [B. Rayleigh], da. of the late Baron de Brienen:—
Margaret Helene Edith, *b.* 1905: *m.* 1929, as his second wife, Count Paul William Alexander Munster, [E. Kinnoull], who *d.* 1968, and has issue living, Peter Cyril Alexander (Allemogne/Thoiry, Ain 01170, France), *b.* 1931: *m.* 1955, Veronica Rosemary, da. of Sir Albert Edward Herbert Naylor-Leyland, 2nd Bt., and has issue living, Alexander Paul *b.* 1961, Sarah Helène *b.* 1957, Marina Claire *b.* 1960. *Residence,*—The Manor House, Rampton, Oxon.——Nicolette Joan (twin), *b.* 1907; is a JP for Berks.: *m.* 1928, Michael Charles St. John Hornby, and has issue living, Simon Michael (8, Ennismore Gdns., SW7), *b.* 1934: *m.* 1968, Sheran, da. of Peter Victor Ferdinand Cazalet, of Fairlawne, Tonbridge,—Charles Nicholas (Hodges, Shipton Moyne, Tetbury, Glos.), *b.* 1939: *m.* 1966, Amanda, da. of the late Maj. Anthony Fitzwilliams Hyde, and has issue living, Nicholas Michael *b.* 1967, Johnathon Anthony *b.* 1969,—Camilla *b.* 1973, Susan Mary, *b.* 1929: *m.* 1st, 1951 (m. diss. 1960), the Marquess of Blandford, now 11th Duke of Marlborough); 2ndly, 1962, Alan Cyril Heber-Percy [see D. Northumberland, colls.]. *Residence,*—Pusey House, Faringdon, Oxon.

Granddaughters of the late William Humble Dudley Ward (infra):—
Issue of the late Rt. Hon. William Dudley Ward, *b.* 1877, *d.* 1946: *m.* 1913, Winifred May [who obtained a divorce 1931 and *m.* 2ndly, 1937, Wing-Com. Marquis de Casa Maury (Spain)], dau. of the late Col. Charles Wilfrid Birkin [see Birkin, Bt.] :—
Penelope Ann Rachel (*Lady Reed*), *b.* 1914 : *m.* 1st, 1930, Anthony Pelissier, Lieut. R.E., from whom she obtained a divorce 1944 ; 2ndly, 1948, Sir Carol Reed, and has issue living, (by 1st marriage) Tracy Clare Compton, *b.* 1941,—(by 2nd marriage) Max, *b.* 1948. *Residence,*—213, King's Road, Chelsea, SW3.——Angela Clare Louise (*Lady Laycock*), *b.* 1916; a DStJ, a JP and Co. Councillor for Notts.: *m.* 1935, Maj.-Gen. Sir Robert Edward Laycock, K.C.M.G., C.B., D.S.O., Roy. Horse Guards, who *d.* 1968, [E. Listowel, colls.], and has issue living, Joseph William, *b.* 1938,—Benjamin Richard, *b.* 1947,—Edwina Ottilie Jane, *b.* 1936: *m.* 1st, 1955 (m. diss. 1963), Lt. (Richard) Mark Walter Agnew, RN [see Agnew, Bt., *cr.* 1895, colls.]; 2ndly, 1963, Sidney Davis, of 217, East 61st St., New York City, USA,—Emma Rose, *b.* 1943: *m.* 1964, Richard Temple, of 29, Artesian Rd., W2, el. son of Sir Richard Antony Purbeck Temple, MC, 4th Bt.—Katherine Martha, *b.* 1949: *m.* 1969, David A. Milnaric, of 33, Tite St., SW3. *Residence,*—24, Sloane Court East, SW3.

Granddaughter of the late Hon. Humble Dudley Ward, 2nd son of 10th Baron Ward :—
Issue of the late William Humble Dudley Ward, *b.* 1849, *d.* 1903: *m.* 1876, the Hon. Eugénie Violet Adèle Brett, who *d.* 1938. dau. of 1st Viscount Esher:—
Enid Violet Ida (*Lady Adair*), *b.* 1897: *m.* 1919, Maj-Gen. Sir Allan Henry Shafto Adair, 6th Bt., GCVO, CB, DSO, MC. *Residences,*—55, Green Street, W1; Holy Hill, co. Tyrone; Ballymena, co. Antrim.

PREDECESSORS.—[1] JOHN de Sutton; *d.* 1359; *s.* by his son [2] JOHN; *d.* 1376; *s.* by his son [3] JOHN; *d.* 1407; *s.* by his son [4] John, *K.G.*; summoned to Parliament as *Baron Dudley*, or *Sutton of Dudley* 1439-87; *d.* 1487; *s.* by his grandson [5] EDWARD, *K.G.*, 2nd Baron; summoned to Parliaments 1492-1529; *d.* 1531; *s.* by his son [6] JOHN, 3rd Baron; never summoned to Parliament; having suffered great pecuniary losses by the machinations of usurers he eventually lost Dudley Castle, and for many years subsisted upon the charity of friends, being styled "Lord Quondam"; *d.* 1553; *s.* by his son [7] EDWARD, *K.B.*, 4th Baron; summoned to Parliaments 1554-86; Queen Mary restored to him by patent Dudley Castle and other lands of great value, which had vested in the crown on the attainder of John Dudley, Duke of Northumberland; *d.* 1586; *s.* by his son [8] EDWARD, 5th Baron, summoned to Parliament 1593-1639; having lavished a large portion of his patrimony in profligacy, gave his grand-dau. and heir in marriage to Humble Ward, son of an opulent goldsmith and jeweller to Charles I.; he *d.* 1643, and was succeeded in the Barony by his grand-dau. (ante) [9] FRANCES Ward, whose husband, Humble Ward, having been knighted was in 1644 cr. *Baron Ward*, of Birmingham (peerage of England); he *d.* 1670; *s.* by his son [10] EDWARD, 2nd Baron Ward, who also became on the death of his mother in 1697 7th Baron Dudley, and was styled Baron Dudley and Ward; *d.* 1701; *s.* by his grandson [11] EDWARD, 8th Baron Dudley and 3rd Baron Ward; *d.* 1704; *s.* by his son [12] EDWARD, 9th Baron Dudley and 4th Baron Ward; *d.* unmarried 1731; *s.* by his uncle [13] WILLIAM, 10th Baron Dudley and 5th Baron Ward; *d.* unmarried 1740, when the Barony of Dudley passed to Ferdinando Dudley, son of his sister Frances, by her marriage with William Lea, and at his death, in 1757, that title fell into abeyance between his sisters [see B. Dudley]; *s.* in Barony of Ward by his kinsman [14] JOHN, 6th Baron Ward, grandson of the Hon. William Ward, 2nd son of 1st Baron Ward; cr. *Viscount Dudley and Ward* (peerage of Great Britain) 1763; *d.* 1774; *s.* by his son [15] JOHN, *LL.D.*, 2nd Viscount; *d. s. p.* 1788; *s.* by his half-brother [16] WILLIAM, 3rd Viscount; *d.* 1823; *s.* by his son [17] JOHN WILLIAM, 4th Viscount; cr. *Viscount Ednam* and *Earl Dudley* (peerage of United Kingdom) 1827; *d.* unmarried 1833, when the Viscountcies and Earldom became extinct, and the Barony of Ward passed to his kinsman [18] *Rev.* WILLIAM HUMBLE, 10th Baron Ward; *b.* 1781; *m.* 1816, Amelia, dau. of William Gooch Pillans, of Bracondale, Norwich; *d.* 1835; *s.* by his son [19] WILLIAM, 11th Baron; *b.* 1817; *m.* 1st, 1851, Selina Constance, who *d.* 1851, dau. of Hubert de Burgh, of West Drayton Manor, Middlesex; 2ndly, 1865, Georgiana Elizabeth, who *d.* 1929, dau. of Sir Thomas Moncreiffe, 7th Bt.; cr. *Viscount Ednam and Earl of Dudley* (peerage of United Kingdom) 1860; *d.* May 7th, 1885; *s.* by his son [20] WILLIAM HUMBLE, 2nd Earl, *G.C.B.*, *G.C.M.G.*, *G.C.V.O.*, *P.C.*, *b.* 1867; Parliamentary Sec. to Board of Trade 1895-1902; Lord-Lieut. of Ireland 1902-5, and Gov.-Gen. of Commonwealth of Australia 1908-1911; *m.* 1st, 1891, Rachel, *C.B.E.*, *R.R.C.*, who *d.* 1920, dau. of the late Charles Gurney; 2ndly, 1924, Gertrude, who *d.* 1952, dau. of John Millar, widow of Lionel Monckton; *d.* 1932; *s.* by his el. son [21] WILLIAM HUMBLE ERIC *MC*, *TD*, 3rd Earl, *b.* 1894; PPS to Under-Sec. of State for India 1922-24; High Sheriff of Worcs. 1930; MP for Hornsey (*C*) 1921-24, and for Wednesbury 1931-32; *m.* 1st, 1919 Lady Rosemary Millicent Sutherland-Leveson-Gower, RRC, who *d.* 1930, da. of 4th Duke of Sutherland; 2ndly, 1943, (m. diss. 1954), Frances Laura, da. of the Hon. Guy Lawrence Charteris [see E. Wemyss]; 3rdly, 1961, Grace Maria, da. of the late Dr. Michel Kolin, of Dubrovnik, and formerly wife of Prince Stanislas Radziwill; *d.* 1969; *s.* by his el. son [22] WILLIAM HUMBLE DAVID, 4th Earl and present peer; also Viscount Ednam, and Baron Ward.

DUFFERIN AND AVA, MARQUESS OF. (Hamilton-Temple-Blackwood.)
[Marquess U.K. 1888, Bt. I. 1763.]

Straight forward.

SHERIDAN FREDERICK TERENCE HAMILTON-TEMPLE-BLACKWOOD, 5th Marquess, and 10th Baronet: *b.* July 9th, 1938: *s.* 1945: ed. at Eton: late 2nd Lt. RHG: a Trustee of the Wallace Collection since 1973: *m.* 1964, Serena Belinda Rosemary, da. of Capt. Thomas Loel Evelyn Bulkeley Guinness, C.B.E., Auxiliary Air Force (Reserve) [see, D. Rutland].

Arms,—Quarterly: 1st and 4th azure, a fesse or, in chief a crescent argent, between two mullets of the second, and in base a mascle of the third, *Blackwood*; 2nd quarterly, 1st and 4th or, an eagle displayed sable, 2nd and 3rd argent, two bars sable, each charged with three martlets or, *Temple*; 3rd gules, three cinquefoils pierced ermine; on a chief or, a lion passant of the field, *Hamilton*. **Crests,**—1st, on a cap of maintenance gules, turned up ermine, a crescent argent; 2nd, on a ducal coronet or, a martlet gold; 3rd, a demi-antelope affronté ermine, attired and unguled or, holding between his hoofs a heart gules. **Supporters,**—*Dexter*, a lion gules, gorged with a tressure flory counterflory or, supporting a staff proper, therefrom flowing to the sinister a flag or, charged with a peacock in its pride also proper; *sinister*, an heraldic tiger ermine, gorged with a tressure flory counterflory gules, and supporting a staff proper, therefrom a flag flying to, and charged as that of the dexter.

Seat,—Clandeboye, co. Down. *Residences,*—4, Holland Villas Rd., W14; The Owl House, nr. Lamberhurst, Kent.

SISTERS LIVING.
Lady Caroline Maureen, *b.* 1931: *m.* 1st, 1953 (marriage dissolved at Juarez, Mexico 1957), Lucian Michael Freud; 2ndly (in New York), 1959, Israel Citkovitz, who *d.* 1974.
Lady Perdita Maureen, *b.* 1934.

DAUGHTERS LIVING OF SECOND MARQUESS.
Lady Doris Gwendolen, *b.* 1895: *m.* 1922, Capt. Cecil Bernard Gunston, M.C., who *d.* 1934, formerly Coldstream Guards [D. Wellington, colls.], and has issue living, Hermione Hamilton, *b.* 1923: *m.* 1942, Lieut.-Col. Geoffrey Walter Fownes Luttrell, M.C., of Court House, East Quantoxhead, Bridgwater, Somerset,—Sonia Helen (*Lady Fairfax of Cameron*) (of Gay's House, Holyport, Maidenhead, Berks), *b.* 1926; a JP of Berks); appointed a Temporary Lady of the Bedchamber to HM 1967: *m.* 1951, the 13th Lord Fairfax of Cameron, who *d.* 1964. *Residence,*—Folly House, Warfield Park, Bracknell, Berks.
Lady Ursula Florence, *b.* 1899: *m.* 1926, Arthur Swithin Newton Horne, formerly Federated Malay States Gov. Sec., who *d.* 1954. *Residence,* 51, Ovington Street, S.W.3.
Lady Patricia Ethel, *b.* 1902: *m.* 1926, Henry Russell, who *d.* 1937. *Residence,*—Aumbry Lodge, Eastry, Sandwich, Kent.

WIDOW LIVING OF FOURTH MARQUESS.
MAUREEN CONSTANCE, dau. of the late Hon. Arthur Ernest Guinness [see E. Iveagh, colls.]: *m.* 1st, 1930, the 4th Marquess, who *d.* (killed in action in Burma) 1945; 2ndly, 1948, Major Harry Alexander

Desmond Buchanan, M.C., from whom she obtained a divorce 1954 ; 3rdly, 1955, His Honour Judge John Cyril Maude, Q.C. [see V. Hawarden, colls.]. *Residences,*—Clandeboye, co. Down ; 4, Hans Crescent, S.W.1.

COLLATERAL BRANCHES LIVING. (*Male line in remainder to Barony and Baronetcy.*)

Granddaughters of the late Rev. the Hon. William Stear Blackwood, 4th son of 2nd Baron Dufferin :—

Issue of the late Major Price Frederick Blackwood, *b.* 1841, *d.* 1930 : *m.* 1880, Henrietta, who *d.* 1936, only child of the late Albemarle Bertie Cator :—
Ursula Henrietta, *M.B.E.*, *b.* 1885; a Member of Roy. Institution; M.B.E. (Civil) 1928. *Residence,*—Craigowrie, Boat of Garten, co. Inverness.

Granddaughter of the late Major Price Frederick Blackwood (ante) :—
Issue of the late Lieut.-Col. Albemarle Price Blackwood, D.S.O. (Border Regt.), *b.* 1881, *d.* 1921 : *m.* 1920, Kyra, who *d.* 1937, elder dau. of the late Albert Llewelyn Hughes, and widow of Serge de Boursac :—
Kyra Henrietta, *b.* 1921 : late Sergeant W.A.A.F.: *m.* 1st, 1945, Samuel Junior Marshall, U.S. Army Air Force, who *d.* 1948; 2ndly, 1951, Iain Gregor Finton Robertson, and has issue living, (by 2nd m.) James Paul, *b.* 1952. *Residence,*—Green Bank Cottage, 9, Langside, E. Linton, E. Lothian.

Descendants of the late Vice-Adm. the Hon. Sir Henry Blackwood, K.C.B. (7th son of the late Baroness Dufferin and Clandeboye), who was cr. a *Baronet* 1814.
Of whom *Sir* FRANCIS ELLIOT TEMPLE, 6th Bt., is *h.p.* to the Barony and Baronetcy.

PREDECESSORS.—[1] ROBERT Blackwood, el. son of the late John Blackwood, of Ballyleidy, co. Down : *m.* 1st, 1721, Joyce, dau. of the late Joseph Leeson ; 2ndly, 1729, Grace, who *d.* 1788, dau. of Isaac Macartney ; cr. a *Baronet* 1763 ; *d.* 1774; *s.* by his son [2] *Sir* JOHN, 2nd Bt.; M.P. in five Parliaments 1761-90; *d.* 1799; in 1800 his widow DORCAS was cr. *Baroness Dufferin and Clandeboye* (peerage of Ireland) ; she *d.* 1808; *s.* by her son [3] JAMES, 2nd Baron, who had in 1799 *s.* his father as 3rd Bt. ; M.P. for Killyleagh in three Parliaments and a Representative Peer; *d.s.p.* 1836; *s.* by his brother [4] HANS, 3rd Baron; *d.* 1839; *s.* by his son [5] PRICE, 4th Baron; *b.* 1794; Capt. R.N. : *m.* 1825, Helen Selina, dau. of the late Thomas Sheridan; *d.* 1841; *s.* by his son [6] FREDERICK TEMPLE, *K.P., G.C.B., G.C.S.I., G.C.M.G., G.C.I.E., P.C., D.C.L., LL.D., F.R.S.,* 5th Baron, *b.* 1826 ; a Lord-in-Waiting to H.M. Queen Victoria 1848-52, and 1854-8, Under-Sec. for India 1864-6, and for War 1866, Chancellor of Duchy of Lancaster and Paymaster-Gen. 1868-72, Gov.-Gen. and Com.-in-Ch. of Canada 1872-8 Ambassador Extraor. and Min. Plen. at St. Petersburg 1879-81, and at Constantinople 1881-4 Viceroy of India 1884-8, Ambassador Extraor. and Plen. at Rome 1888-91, and Ambassador at Paris 1891-6; assumed by Roy. licences 1862 the additional (surname of Hamilton and 1872 that of Temple; cr. *Baron Clandeboye* 1850, and *Viscount Clandeboye* and *Earl of Dufferin* (peerage of UK), 1871, and *Earl of Ava* and *Marquess of Dufferin and Ava,* of co. Down and of Burmah (peerage of UK) 1888: *m.* 1862, Dame Hariot Georgina, *VA, CI. DBE,* who *d.* 1936, el. da. of the late Archibald Rowan Hamilton, of Killyleagh Castle, co. Down; *d.* 1902; *s.* by his son [7] TERENCE TEMPLE, 2nd Marquess; *b.* 1866; a Clerk in Foreign Office 1906-18: *m.* 1893 ("Flora") Florence, who *d.* 1925, da. of John H. Davis, of 24, Washington Square, New York: *d.* 1918; *s.* by his brother [8] FREDERICK TEMPLE, *DSO, PC,* 3rd Marquess, *b.* 1875; S. Africa 1900 (wounded, despatches twice, Queen's medal with nine clasps DSO), European War 1914-17 as Staff-Capt. Household Cav. and with a Guards Div. (twice wounded, 1914-15 star, two medals); Mil. Sec. to Gov.-Gen. of Commonwealth of Australia 1914, Speaker of Senate of N. Ireland June 1921 and 1925-30, and Vice-Adm. of Province of Ulster 1923-30: *m.* 1908, Brenda, who *d.* 1946, only da. of the late Robert Woodhouse, formerly of Orford House, Ugley, Bishop's Stortford; *d.* 1930; *s.* by his son [9] BASIL SHERIDAN, 4th Marquess, *b.* 1909; Capt. Roy. Horse Guards; a Lord-in-Waiting to H.M. 1936-7, and Under-Sec. of State for Colonies 1937-40 : *m.* 1930, Maureen Constance, dau. of the Hon. Arthur Ernest Guinness ; *d.* (killed in action in Burma) 1945; *s.* by his son [10] SHERIDAN FREDERICK TERENCE, 5th Marquess and present peer ; also Earl of Dufferin, Earl of Ava, Viscount Clandeboye, and Baron Dufferin and Clandeboye.

DUGAN OF VICTORIA, BARONY OF. (Dugan.) [Extinct 1951.]
WIDOW LIVING OF FIRST BARON.
RUBY LILIAN (*Baroness Dugan of Victoria*), dau. of the late Charles Abbott, of Abbott Abbey, co. Cork; is a DStJ: *m.* 1912, Maj. Gen. Baron Dugan of Victoria, GCMG, CB, DSO, who *d.* 1951, when the title became ext.

DULVERTON, BARON. (Wills.) [Baron U.K. 1929, Bt. U.K. 1897.]

(FREDERICK) ANTHONY HAMILTON WILLS, *CBE, TD,* 2nd Baron, and 3rd Baronet; *b.* Dec. 19th, 1915; *s.* 1956, ed. at Eton, and at Magdalen Coll., Oxford (MA); late Major Lovat Scouts; Pres. British Deer Soc., Chm. The Dulverton Trust, Vice-Chm. Timber Growers' Organisation, a Member Forestry Cttee. of Great Britain, of Red Deer Commn., and of Scottish Advisory Cttee. Nature Conservancy; CBE (Civil) 1974; *m.* 1st, 1939 (*m.* diss. 1960), Judith Betty, da. of the late Lt.-Col. the Hon. Ian Leslie Melville, TD [see E. Leven and Melville, colls.]; 2ndly, 1962, Ruth Violet Mary (FANSHAWE), da. of Sir Walter Randolph Fitzroy Farquhar, 5th Bt., and has issue by 1st marriage.

Wherever the light leads.

Arms,—Gules, three estoiles flammant fessewise between two griffins passant wings expanded and inverted all or. Crest,—Issuant from an annulet or, a demi-griffin gules, charged with an estoile as in the arms, and holding in the dexter claw a battle-axe also or. Supporters.—*Dexter,* a trumpeter of the Royal North Devon Yeomanry; *sinister,* a huntsman of the Dulverton hunt; both proper.
Seat.—Batsford Park, Moreton-in-Marsh, Gloucestershire. *Residence,*—Fassfern, Fort William, Inverness-shire. *Club,*—Boodle's.

SONS LIVING. (By 1st marriage.)

Hon. GILBERT MICHAEL HAMILTON, b. May 2nd, 1944; ed. at Gordonstoun.
Hon. Robert Ian Hamilton, b. 1948; ed. at Harrow.

DAUGHTERS LIVING. (By 1st marriage.)

Hon. Marion Hamilton, b. 1940: m. 1964, John G. A. Tulloch, of Tundergarth House, Lockerbie, Dumfries-shire, and has issue living, Andrew John Alexander, b. 1965,—Miranda Louise, b. 1968.
Hon. Sarah May Hamilton, b. 1942.

BROTHERS LIVING.

Hon. Edward Robert Hamilton (Farmington Lodge, Northleach, Glos.), b. 1918; ed. at Eton; Maj. late Gren. Gds., 1935-45 War (wounded).

Hon. Victor Patrick Hamilton, b. 1926; ed. at Eton; Lt. late Gren. Gds. (ret.) and Parachute Regt., and a Fellow of Chartered Land Agents' Soc.: m. 1st, 1948 (marriage dissolved 1962), Felicity Betty, dau. of the late Major Aubrey Jonsson, Roy. Irish Rifles; 2ndly, 1963, Jean Felicity (STRUTT), yr. da. of the late Hon. Francis Walter Erskine [see E. Mar and Kellie, colls.], and has issue living, (by 1st marriage) Christopher Aubrey Hamilton, b. 1953,—Jeremy Robert Hamilton, b. 1955,—Penelope Margaret Hamilton, b. 1950. Residence,—Litchfield Down, Whitchurch, Hants.

COLLATERAL BRANCHES LIVING. (In remainder to the Baronetcy only.

Grandsons of the late Frederick Noel Hamilton Wills (infra):—
Issue of the late Capt. Michael Desmond Hamilton Wills, M.C., Coldstream Guards; b. 1915, d. (killed in action in Middle East) 1943 : m. 1939, Mary Margaret (who m. 2ndly, 1947, Col. Martin St. John Valentine Gibbs, CB, DSO, of The Manor House, Ewen, Cirencester, Glos.), da. of Lt.-Col. Philip Mitford [Fowler, Bt., ext.]:—
Michael Thomas Noël Hamilton (The Old Forge, Miserden, Stroud, Glos.), b. 1940; ed. at Eton; Maj. late Coldm. Gds. (ret.).——Frederick Hugh Philip Hamilton (twin) (The Old House, Rendcomb, Cirencester, Glos.; Coulin Lodge, Kinlochewe, Ross-shire), b. 1940; ed. at Eton; Capt. 11th Hussars: m. 1969, Priscilla Annabelle, da. of Capt. Alec Francis, of The Grange, Malmesbury, [see L. Kinloss, colls.], and has issue living, Michael James Hamilton, b. 1972.——Peter John Hamilton (Kirkham Farm, Lower Slaughter, Cheltenham, Glos.), b. 1941; ed. at Eton, and Magdalen Coll., Oxford: m. 1970, Elizabeth Jean, da. of Maj. J. J. Mann, of Oxleaze Farm, Filkins, Lechlade, Glos., and has issue living, Richard Henry, b. 1974,—Grania Sarah, b. 1972.

Issue of the late Frederick Noel Hamilton Wills, 3rd son of 1st baronet, b. 1887, d. 1927 : m. 1912, Margery Hamilton (who m. 2ndly, 1942, Wing-Com. Huntly Macdonald Sinclair, RCAF, of Misarden Park, Stroud), el. da. of the late Hon. Sir Hugh Fraser, JP, a Judge of High Court of Justice, of Stromeferry House, Ross-shire:—
Hugh David Alastair Hamilton, CBE, TD, b. 1917; late Maj. Queen's Own Cameron Highlanders; a DL of Oxford (High Sheriff 1961); 1939-45 War (MBE); MBE (Mil.) 1946, CBE (Civil) 1971: m. 1949, Eva Helen McMorrough, da. of the late Maj. Arthur Thomas McMorrough Kavanagh, MC [see Buxton, Bt., colls.], and has issue living, Martin David Hamilton b. 1952,—Catherine Mary Hamilton, b. 1950. Residences,—Sandford Park, Sandford St. Martin, Oxon; Knockando House, Morayshire. Clubs,—Boodle's, Turf, Beefsteak.——Rosemary Theodora Hamilton (Lady MacLeod), b. 1913: m. 1938, Sir John MacLeod, TD, late Capt. Queen's Own Cameron Highlanders, and has issue living, David John Noel, b. 1939: m. 1972, Wendy Joy, only da. of Edwin Cookson, of Minshull Hall, Nantwich,—Martin Michael Alan, b. 1949,—Carolyn Margery Hamilton (twin), b. 1939: m. 1961, Hugh Petre Barclay, c/o P.O. Menengai, Kenya [B. Petre, colls.], and has issue living, Edward Hugh b. 1963, John Peter b. 1967, Karen Theodora b. 1962, Camilla Patricia b. 1966,—Jocelyn Ishabel Ann, b. 1946: m. 1967, David Algernon Fleming, of Copse Hill, Lower Slaughter, Glos. [see Borthwick, Bt., colls.],—Patricia Mary-Rose, b. 1951. Residences,—Turkdean Manor, Northleach, Glos.; 36, Donovan Court, Drayton Gdns., SW10.——Margery Angela Hamilton, b. 1922: m. 1st, 1948 (m. diss. 1971), Anthony Andrew Francis Tabor, late Capt. Herts. Yeo; 2ndly, 1972, Thomas Anthony Stainton, and has issue living (by 1st m.), Adrian Andrew Hamish, b. 1960,—Marilyn Margery Hamilton, b. 1949,—Nicola Mary Hamilton, b. 1952. Residences,—Coruanan Lodge, Fort William, Inverness-shire, and 20, Godfrey St., SW3.——Audrey Mackenzie Hamilton, b. 1925: m. 1946, Capt. Peter Houldsworth Gibbs, Scots Guards, and has issue living, Peter Noel Houldsworth, b. 1948,—Linda Hamilton, b. 1951: m. 1973, Robert Bruce John Dunipace. Residence,—Combend Manor, Elkstone, Glos.

PREDECESSORS.—[1] FREDERICK Wills, son of the late Henry Overton Wills, J.P., of Bristol, and brother of Sir Edward Payson Wills, K.C.B., 1st Bt. (cr. 1904), b. 1838 ; a Director of Imperial Tobacco Co. (Limited); sat as M.P. for Bristol, N. Div. (LU) 1900-1906 ; cr. a Baronet 1897 : m. 1867, Annie, who d. 1910, el. dau. of the Rev. James Hamilton, D.D., of Longridge, Stonehouse ; d. 1909 ; s. by his son [2] GILBERT ALAN HAMILTON, O.B.E., 2nd Bt. ; b. 1880 ; Pres. of Imperial Tobacco Co. (Limited), Parliamentary Private Sec. to Postmaster-Gen. 1921, High Sheriff of Gloucestershire 1928, M.P. for Taunton (C) 1912-18, and for Weston-super-Mare Div. of Somerset 1918-22 ; cr. Baron Dulverton, of Batsford (peerage of United Kingdom), 1929 : m. 1914, Victoria May, O.B.E., who d. 1968, dau. of Rear-Adm. Sir Edward Chichester, C.B., C.M.G., 9th Bt.; d. 1956; s. by his el. son [3] (FREDERICK) ANTHONY HAMILTON, 2nd Baron, and present peer.

Dumfries, Earl of, son of Marquess of Bute.

DUNALLEY, BARON. (Prittie.) [Baron I. 1800.]

In Omnia Paratus.

Prepared for all things.

HENRY DESMOND GRAHAM PRITTIE, 6th Baron; b. Oct. 14th, 1912; s. 1948; ed. at Stowe, and RMC; Lt.-Col. late Rifle Bde.; served with King's African Rifles 1937-40; 1939-45 War in E. Africa, Middle East, Italy, and Far East: m. 1947, (Mary) Philippa, only child of the late Maj. the Hon. Philip Plantagenet Cary [see V. Falkland, colls.], and has issue.

Arms.—Per pale argent and gules three wolves' heads erased or. Crest,—A wolf's head erased or. Supporters,—Dexter, a man in armour proper, holding a tilting spear in the right hand; sinister, a stag proper, attired, unguled, ducally collared and chained, or.

Residence,—Glendalough Lodge, Recess, co. Galway. Clubs,—Cavalry Kildare Street (Dublin).

SONS LIVING.

Hon. HENRY FRANCIS CORNELIUS, b. May 30th, 1948; ed. at Gordonstoun, and Trin. Coll., Dublin (BA).

Hon. Michael Philip St. John, b. 1961.

DAUGHTER LIVING.

Hon. Mary Rose Madeline, b. 1953.

BROTHER LIVING.

Hon. Terence Cornelius Farmer, MBE, b. 1913; ed. at Stowe, and at Ch. Ch., Oxford, M.A.; Writer and Historian; formerly Cricket, German Correspondent and Diplomatic Correspondent of The Guardian and Lt. Rifle Bde. (SR); 1939-45 War in France (despatches, prisoner); MBE (Mil) 1946: m. 1946, Laura, only child of the late G. D. Dundas, of Colombia, and has issue living, Oliver Alan Graham, b. 1948,—James Hugo Cameron, b. 1950. Residence,—9, Blithfield St., W8.

PREDECESSORS.—[1] HENRY PRITTIE, b. 1743; M.P. for Banagher 1767-8, for Gowran 1769-76, and for co. Tipperary 1776-90; cr. Baron Dunalley, of Kilboy, co. Tipperary (peerage of Ireland) 1800; d. 1801; s. by his el. son [2] HENRY SADLEIR, F.S.A., 2nd Baron, b. 1775; M.P. for Carlow 1798-1801, and for Okehampton 1819-24; a Representative Peer; d. 1854; s. by his nephew [3] HENRY, 3rd Baron, b. 1807: m. 1841, the Hon. Anne Maria Louisa O'Callaghan, who d. 1867, dau. of 1st Viscount Lismore: d. Sept. 10th, 1885: s. by his son [4] HENRY O'CALLAGHAN, 4th Baron; b. 1851; a Representative Peer for Ireland, and Lieut. and Custos Rotulorum of co. Tipperary: m. 1876, Mary Frances, M.B.E., who d. 1929, dau. of the late Maj.-Gen. Reginald Onslow Farmer, R.A., of Grove House, Aspley Guise; d. 1927; s. by his son [5] HENRY CORNELIUS O'CALLAGHAN, D.S.O., 5th Baron; b. 1877: Major late Rifle Brigade; 1914-18 War (DSO): m. 1911, Beatrix Evelyn, who d. 1967, da. of the late James Noble Graham, JP, DL, of Carfin, and Stonebyres, Lanarkshire; d. 1948; s. by his son [6] HENRY DESMOND GRAHAM, 6th Baron and present peer.

DUNBOYNE, BARON. (Butler.) [Baron I. 1324 and 1541.]

Timor Domini Fons Vitæ.

The fear of the Lord is the fountain of life.

PATRICK THEOBALD TOWER BUTLER, 28th Baron (18th by patent); (His Honour Judge the Lord Dunboyne); b. Jan. 27th, 1917; s. 1945; ed. at Winchester, and at Trin. Coll., Camb. (MA, Pres. of Union 1939); Bar. Middle Temple (Harmsworth Scholar) 1949, of Inner Temple 1962, and King's Inns, Dublin 1966, a JP; Foreign Office 1945-46; Dep. Chm. Middlesex Sessions 1963-65; Commissary Gen. of Canterbury Diocese 1959-71; Recorder of Hastings 1961-71; Dep. Chm. Kent Sessions 1963-71, and Inner London Sessions 1971; a Circuit Judge 1972; Lt. late Irish Guards (SR); 1939-45 War (prisoner, repatriated): m. 1950, Anne Marie, da. of Sir Victor Alexander Louis Mallet, GCMG, CVO, and has issue.

Arms.—Or, a chief indented azure, and three escallops in bend counterchanged. Crest—Out of a ducal coronet or, a plume of five ostrich feathers, and issuant therefrom a demi-falcon rising argent. Supporters,—Dexter, a lion guardant argent; sinister, a horse sable, mane. tail, and hoofs or.

Residence,—36, Ormonde Gate, S.W.3. Clubs,—Irish, Pitt (Cambridge), Union (Cambridge), All England Lawn Tennis and Croquet (Wimbledon), and International Lawn Tennis of Great Britain.

SON LIVING.

Hon. JOHN FITZWALTER, b. July 31st, 1951; ed. at Winchester, and Trin. Coll., Camb.: m. 1975, Dianna Caroline, da. of Sir Michael Sanigear Williams, KCMG.

DAUGHTERS LIVING.

Hon. Mary Synolda, b. 1954; ed. at Benenden and Girton Coll., Camb.
Hon. Betty Quenelda, b. 1956; ed. at Benenden and Girton Coll., Camb.
Hon. Victoria Morina, b. 1959; ed. at Benenden.

SISTERS LIVING.

Hon. (Doreen) Synolda Tower, b. 1918: m 1945, Major Atholl Duncan, M.C., R.A. (retired),
and has issue living, Walter Alastair, b. 1947,—Patrick Atholl, b. 1957,—Zara Synolda,
b. 1950,—Lorna Romayne, b. 1956. Residence,—20, Tite Street, S.W.3.
Hon. Maureen Maude Tower, b. 1919: m. 1946, Lieut.-Col. Robert Caradoc Rose Price, D.S.O., O.B.E.,
late Welsh Guards [see Price, Bt., cr. 1815, colls.]. Residence,—Tetworth Hall, Ascot, Berks.
Hon. (Isolde) Sheila Tower, b. 1925 : m. 1949, Com. Penryn Victor Monck, R.N.V.R. [E. Peel], and
has issue living, Rory Penryn, b. 1951,—Tasha Penryn, b. 1950,—Fiona Penryn, b. 1957. Residence,—Yaverland Manor, Sandown, Isle of Wight.

WIDOW LIVING OF SON OF TWENTY-SIXTH BARON.

Hon. Vera Elizabeth Sanders, OBE (Kentisbeare House, Cullompton, Devon), da. of 1st Baron Bayford: m. 1933, Maj.-Gen. the Hon. Theobald Patrick Probyn Butler, DSO, who d. 1970.

WIDOW LIVING OF TWENTY-SEVENTH BARON.

DORA ISOLDE BUTLER (Dowager Baroness Dunboyne), dau. of the late Com. Francis Fitzpatrick Tower,
O.B.E., late R.N.V.R. [Butler, Bt., cr. 1628, colls.]: m. 1915, the 27th Baron, who d. 1945.
Residence,—49, Cheyne Court, S.W.3.

COLLATERAL BRANCHES LIVING.

Issue of the late Brig.-Gen. the Hon. Lesley James Probyn Butler, C.M.G., D.S.O.,
2nd son of 26th Baron, b. 1876, d. 1955 : m. 1907, Mary Christal, J.P., who d.
1951, dau. of Sir John Heathcoat Heathcoat-Amory, 1st Bt. :—
James Dighton,b. 1911 ; ed. at Winchester ; Lieut.-Col. (retired) late 15th/19th King's Roy. Hussars ;
formerly Major Probyn's Horse, Indian Army ; Waziristan 1936-37 (despatches), Middle East and
Persia 1942-43 (despatches): m. 1943, Pamela, dau. of the late William Alfred Pickwoad, OBE, and
widow of Lt.-Col. A. J. F. Sugden, RA, and has issue living, Michael James (Pear Tree Cottage, Nidd,
Ripley, Harrogate, Yorks.), b. 1944; ed. at Eastbourne Coll., and Roy. Agric. Coll., Cirencester
(MRAC); late Lt. 15th/19th King's R. Hussars; Assist. Agent Nidd Estate Office,—Robert Patrick,
b. 1947; ed. at Milton Abbey Sch.; late 2nd Lt. Queen's R. Irish Hussars: m. 1972, Nicola Jane,
da. of P. W. R. Pope, of Tennantrees, W. Stafford, Dorchester, Dorset. Residence,—The Dower
House, Boyton, Warminster, Wilts.——Anne Christal, b. 1909: m. 1948, Gerald Frederic Wigram
[see Wigram, Bt., colls.]. Residence,—Calverleigh Cottage, Tiverton, Devon.

Grandchildren of the late St. John Henry ARCEDECKNE-BUTLER, grandson of the
late Hon. St. John Butler, 2nd son of 23rd Baron:—
Issue of the late Maj.-Gen. St. John Desmond Arcedeckne-Butler, O.B.E., b. 1896, d. 1959 : m.
1929, Ethel Helen Nesbitt, who d. 1953, dau. of the late Col. Reginald Selby Walker,
D.S.O., R.E. :—
St. John Patrick (28, High Oaks Rd., Welwyn Garden City), b. 1930; Maj. (ret.), R. Signals: m. 1956,
Jane (Frances Elizabeth Mary), da. of Lieut.-Col. F. E. Massie, M.C., of W. Ayton, Scarborough,
and has issue living, St. John Terence, b. 1956,—Christopher Michael, b. 1959,—John Patrick, b.
1969,—Mark Piers, b. 1972.——Michael Francis Peel, R.N., b. 1933; Lt.-Cdr.: m. 1961, Jacqueline,
da. of Col. George Leonard Carpenter-Garnier, OBE, of Wickham, Hants, and has issue living,
Timothy Garnier, b. 1962,—Nicola Catherine, b. 1964. Residence,—Outlers, Wickham, Hants.——
Christal Synolda, b. 1938: m. 1961, Geoffrey William Medcalf, of East Rd., Tetford, Horncastle,
Lincs., and has issue living, Richard William Desmond, b. 1966,—David Geoffrey, b. 1969,—Sallie
Jane, b. 1962,—Helen Sheevaun Christal, b. 1963,—Patricia Ann, b. 1964,—Rosemary Janet
Slaney, b. 1970.

Grandchildren of the late Edward Arthur Butler (infra):—
Issue of the late Charles Edward Butler, b. 1874, d. 1960: m. 1919, Alice Elizabeth (Leigh
House, Holcombe, Dawlish, S. Devon), dau. of the late T. J. Worship, of North Walsham:—
Clarence Francis (Ballavagher House, Union Mills, Douglas, Isle of Man), b. 1920; 1939-45 War
as Flight-Lieut. R.A.F. (despatches): m. 1944, Pamela Constance, dau. of the late F. J. Drakard,
of Ingham House, Martlesham, Suffolk, and has issue living, Julia Rosemary, b. 1945,—Denise
Angela b. 1947.——Brian Charles (of Leigh House, Holcombe, Dawlish, Devon), b. 1924: m. 1952,
Joyce Caroline, dau. of G. Hitchcock, of Kenton, Devon, and has issue living, Rosena Marie,
b. 1959.——Rosalinda Maria, b. 1921: m. 1946, Douglas Kyrle Redgrave, of Merrihill, Eastcliff,
Dawlish, Devon, and has issue living, Michael Kyrle, b. 1950,—Diana Lynne, b. 1952.

Grandson of the late Hon. Charles Lennox Butler, 7th son of 23rd Baron:—
Issue of the late Edward Arthur Butler, b. 1843, d. 1916: m. 1872, Clara, who d. 1912,
dau. of Major-Gen. J. T. Francis:—
Henry Francis (Falls Farm, Falls Rd., Warkworth, NZ), b. 1877: m. 1908, Ethel Isabel Marion, da.
of the late Allix Edward Pardoe, of Dawlish, Devon, and has issue living, Sheila Frances, b. 1914:
m. 19—, — Stevens, of No. 1, R.D., Warkworth, Auckland, NZ.

Grandchildren of the late Lieut.-Col. Charles James BUTLER-KEARNEY, D.L., J.P.
son of the late William Butler, great-grandson of the late Theobald Butler, el.
son of the late Richard Butler (b. 1701), grandson of the late James Butler, el.
son of the late Hon. Theobald Butler, 8th son of 12th Baron:—
Issue of the late Theobald William Butler-Kearney, b. 1876, d. 1936: m. 1914, Hester Louise,
who d. 1972, da. of the late Carew Davies Gilbert:—
James Davies Theobald (Jordans, Old Odiham Rd., Alton, Hants.), b. 1916: m. 1951 (m. diss 1954),
Gillian Mary Soltau, el. da. of the late Maj. W. H. Anketell; 2ndly, 1970, Juliet Mary, da. of the late
Rev. Andrew Hunt.——Catherine Mary, b. 1918. Residence,—Spring Cottage, Durcott Rd., Camer-
ton, Bath.
Issue of the late Capt. Trench Frank Butler-Kearney, b. 1877, d. 1954: m. 1920, Shirley,
who d. 1971, da. of the late John Bailey Sequeira:—
Jean, b. 1920.——Norma, b. 1924. Residence,—Greycote, 44, Cornwall Road, Cheam, Surrey.

Grandchildren of the late William Butler (b. 1814), son of the late James Butler
(b. 1785), grandson of the late James Butler, of Park, co. Tipperary, 3rd son of the
late Richard Butler (b. 1701) (ante) :—
Issue of the late Charles Herbert Jackson Butler, b. 1870, d. 1937 : m. 1900, Margaret, dau
of the late Frederick Batten, of Durban, Natal :—
George Herbert, b. 1901 : m. 1929, Irene Rose Sparnon, and has issue living, John Charles Edward,
b. 1935,—June Rose Margaret, b. 1930,—Patricia Colleen, b. 1938. Residence,—

Grandsons of the late Charles Herbert Jackson Butler (ante) :—
Issue of late Frederick William Butler, b. 1903, d. 1946 : m. 1934, Nancy Anne O'Mahony :—
Patrick Barry Webb, b. 1941.——Michael Terence Webb, b. 1943. Residence,—
Issue of the late Henry John BUTLER-LLOYD, b. 1874, d. 1946 (having assumed in 1896,
the surname of Lloyd after his patronymic): m. 1st, 1897, Catherine, who d. 1907,
dau. of the late James Davoran; 2ndly, 1908, Jane (of Cranagh, Templemore, co. Tipperary), el. dau. of the late Capt. W. Headech, 20th Regt :—

By 2nd marriage) Henry John, *b.* 1910: *m.* 1947, Kathleen Leacky of Castleney, Templemore, co. Tipperary, and has issue living, Henry John, *b.* 1948. *Residence,*—Cranagh, Templemore, co. Tipperary.——James, *b.* 1912. *Residence,*—Park Killea, Templemore, co. Tipperary.——Charles, *b.* 1913. *Residence,*—Leicester.——Anne (Tyn y Rhos Hall, Weston Rhyn, Oswestry), *b.* 1908: *m.* 1930, Walter Thompson, and has issue living, Mervyn THOMPSON-BUTLER-LLOYD (Tyn y Rhos Hall, Weston Rhyn, Oswestry), *b.* 1939; assumed by deed poll 1963 the additional surnames of Butler-Lloyd,—Kenneth, *b.* 1946; ed. at Salford Univ. BA: *m.* 1969, Carol, only da. of Sidney Shipton, of Liverpool,—Ivor, *b.* 1947; RN: *m.* 1969, Catherine, da. of Roynald Leishman, of S. Queensferry, W. Lothian, and has issue living, Carol Anne, *b.* 1970.

Grandson of the late Henry John BUTLER-LLOYD (ante):—
Issue of the late William Francis Butler-Lloyd, *b.* 1899, *d.* 1956: *m.* 1930, Mary Margaret (Richmond Templemore, co. Tipperary), da. of Thomas FitzGerald:—
Thomas Henry (Richmond Templemore, co. Tipperary), *b.* 1932: *m.* 1966, Veronica, da. of Patrick Harney, of Manna, Templemore, co. Tipperary, and has issue living, William Francis, *b.* 1969,—Audrey Veronica, *b.* 1972.

Grandchildren of the late Richard John Butler, 2nd son of the late Whitwell Butler (*b.* 1798), 4th son of the late Rev. Richard Butler, DD (infra):—
Issue of the late George Whitwell Butler, *b.* 1888, *d.* 1960: *m.* 1918, Ada Isabel Dering, who *d.* 1961, dau. of Arthur Lucius Cary, of Swords, co. Dublin:—
John Radcliff (57, Britwell Rd., Wylde Green, Sutton Coldfield), *b.* 1921.——Mary Isabel, *b.* 1919: *m.* 1943, Carass Frederick Bladon Topham, of 25, Selwyn Cres., Radley, Abingdon, Oxon., and has issue living, Ronald Bladon, *b.* 1945,—Michael George, *b.* 1947,—John Carass, *b.* 1951,—Pamela Mary (twin), *b.* 1951.——Eileen Synolda, *b.* 1926. *Residence,*—49 Shelley Close, Abingdon, Oxon.

Granddaughter of the late Rev. Edward Butler, son of the late Rev. Richard Butler, D.D., el. son of the late James Butler, of Priestown, co. Meath, el. son of the late Capt. Theobald Butler, 2nd son of the late Pierce Butler, 2nd son of the late Hon. Theobald Butler (ante):—
Issue of the late Edward Butler, *b.* 1851, *d.* 1928 : *m.* 1887, Emily Frances, who *d.* 1951, dau. of Arthur Battiscombe:—
Judith Eileen, *MBE,* *b.* 1895; MBE (Civil) 1966. *Residence,*—Abellynfi, Glasbury, via Hereford.

Grandchildren of the late John Butler, 6th son of the late Rev. Richard Butler, D.D. (ante):—
Issue of the late George Butler, *b.* 1859, *d.* 1941 : *m.* 1898, Harriet Neville, who *d.* 1939, dau. of Marshal Neville Clarke, of Graiguenoe Park, co. Tipperary :—
Hubert Marshal, *b.* 1900 : *m.* 1930, Susan Margaret, dau. of Dr. Thomas Clement Guthrie, of Annaghmakerrig, co. Monaghan, and has issue living, Julia Mary Synolda, *b.* 1935 : *m.* 1959, Dr. Richard Savington Crampton, of 1106, Rugby Rd., Charlottesville, Va., 22903, USA, and has issue living, Thomas William Butler, *b.* 1967,Anne Cordelia, *b.* 1960, Suzanna Louise b. 1963, Katherine Synolda *b.* 1966. *Residence,*—Maiden Hall, Bennettsbridge, co. Kilkenny,——George Gilbert, *b.* 1910: *m.* 1940, Norah Helen Pomeroy, da. of the late George Pomeroy Arthur Colley, of Corkagh House, Dublin [see V. Harberton, colls.], and has issue living, James George, *b.* 1942: *m.* 1972, Diana Gillian, da. of the late John Hedges Becher, of Bagenalstown House, co. Carlow, and has issue living, Thomas George, *b.* 1973, John James b. 1974,—Jessica Harriet (*Baroness Rathdonnell*), *b.* 1940: *m.* 1965, the 5th Baron Rathdonnell. *Residence,*—Scatorish, Bennettsbridge, co. Kilkenny.——Joanna Vernon, *b.* 1903: *m.* 1938, Gerald Lenox-Conyngham, and has issue living, Edward Vere Gerald, *b.* 1942,—Melosina Anne, *b.* 1941,—Eleanor Elizabeth Rita, *b.* 1946: *m.* 1969, Nicholas Grene, of Ballinaclash, co. Wicklow. *Residence,*—Anaverna, Ravensdale, Dundalk, co. Louth.

Grandchildren of the late James Edward Butler (infra):—
Issue of the late Maj. James Whitwell Butler, *b.* 1897, *d.* 1971: *m.* 1927, Hilda Winifred (Flat 1, Shell Cove House, Teignmouth Rd., Dawlish, S. Devon), da. of Charles Nason Haines:—
James Charles, MC (Belgrove, Cobh, co. Cork), *b.* 1928; late Lt. King's R. Irish Hussars; Korea 1951 (MC): *m.* 1959, Margaret Perry, da. of Harold Perry Goodbody, of The Glen, Cobh, co. Cork, and has issue living, James Perry George, *b.* 1960,—Corinna Margaret, *b.* 1962.——Edward Theobald (Tullow, Fethard, co. Tipperary), *b.* 1929: *m.* 1952, Judith, da. of Edward Webb, of Borris-in-Ossory, co. Leix, and has issue living, Jennifer Mary, *b.* 1954,—Diana Elizabeth, *b.* 1956,—Caroline Eve, *b.* 1960.——Hilda Elizabeth, *b.* 1932: w. 1956, Julius Pridden Jameson, of Shell Cove House, Teignmouth Rd., Dawlish, Devon, and has issue living, Robert Julius Whitwell, *b.* 1957,—James Leander, *b.* 1954,—Linda Rose, 1959.

Grandchildren of the late James Butler (*b.* 1820), grandson of the late Whitwell Butler (*b.* 1743), 2nd son of the late Capt. Theobald Butler (ante):—
Issue of the late James Edward Butler, *b.* 1856, *d.* 1905 : *m.* 1897, Mary, who *d.* 1938, dau. of William Goyne Stevens :—
Issue of the late Theobald Butler, I.C.S., *b.* 1857, *d.* 1946 : *m.* 1880 Charlotte Elizabeth, who *d.* 1949, dau. of Richard Bayly, of Green Park, co. Limerick :—
Theobald Richard Fitzwalter, *b.* 1894: ed. at Charterhouse, and at Univ. Coll., Oxford; Bar. Inner Temple 1921, and a Bencher 1960; Recorder of Newark 1945-62, and of Derby 1962-63 Chm., Notts. Quarter Sessions 1954-63 and Dep. and Chm., Middlesex 1959-65; Dep. Chm. of Kent Quarter Sessions 1963, Chm. of Greater London Sessions (S.E. London Area) 1965-67; Chancellor, Diocese of Peterborough since 1962: *m.* 1948, Laura Rachel, da. of the late Sir Vincent Nash, D.L. *Residence,*—Flat 1, 70, Shepherds Hill, Highgate, N.6. *Club,*—Reform.——Arabella Agnes Muriel (*Lady Seeds*), *b.* 1883: *m.* 1911, Sir William Seeds, KCMG, who *d.* 1973, and has issue living, Robert (of 68, Corringham Rd., NW11), *b.* 1914: *m.* 1950, Mary Nafsika, da. of Theodoulos C. Ficardo, of Alexandria, Egypt, and has issue living, Arabella Aphrodite *b.* 1951, Corinna *b.* 1952,—Hugh, *b.* 1917: *m.* 1949, Luise Therese, who *d.* 1965, da. of the late Gottfried Gompertz, of Krefeld, Germany,—Sheila (Durcombe Water, Furzehill, Lynton, N. Devon), *b.* 1912: *m.* 1st, 1934 (m. diss. 1949), Sir John Fisher Wentworth Dilke, 5th Bt.; 2ndly, 1949 (m. diss. 1964), John Constantine Phipps, Metropolitan Stipendiary Magistrate; 3rdly, 1968, Kenneth Northcote Knapp, who *d.* 1968, and has issue living, (by 1st m.) [see Dilke, Bt.], (by 2nd m.) Elizabeth Anne *b.* 1952, Susan Margaret *b.* 1956. *Residence,*—68, Corringham Rd., NW11.

Descendants of the late Hon. Peter (or Pierce) Butler, 2nd son of 10th Baron :—
Issue of the late Theobald Blake Butler, el. son of Theobald Fitzwalter Butler, JP, DL, (infra), *b.* 1888, *d.* 1965: *m.* 1st, 1921 (m. diss. 1930), Mary Gammell Stewart, da. of William Smytton Davidson; 2ndly, 1933 (m. diss. 1942), Catherine Dorothy, da. of Arthur Ashworth; 3rdly, 1962, Elsie, who *d.* 1970, da. of the late Albert Edward Keen:—
(By 1st m.) James Roland Blake FOX-ANDREWS, QC (20, Cheyne Gdns., SW3; *Club,* Hampshire), *b.* 1922; ed. at Stowe, and Camb. Univ. (BA); Bar. Gray's Inn 1949, QC 1968, an ad eundem Member of Middle Temple 1972, and a Bencher, Gray's Inn 1974; Recorder of Winchester 1971, since when Hon. Recorder; Dep. Chm. of Devon Quarter Sessions 1970-71; a Recorder of Crown Court since 1972; assumed the surname of Fox-Andrews in lieu of his patronymic 1939: *m.* 1950, Angela Bridget, da. of Brig. Charles Copley Swift, OBE, MC, and has issue living, Jonathan Mark Piers, *b.* 1952,—Piers Norman James, *b.* 1954.

Grandson of the late Theobald Blake Butler (ante):—
Issue of the late John Stuart Blake Butler, *b.* 1923, *d.* 1957   *m.* 1947, Stephanie Elizabeth
(who *d.* 1970, having *m.* 2ndly, 1963, Guy Green), da. of Thomas Swan:—
Samuel Thomas Blake, *b.* 1949.

Grandson of the late James Blake Butler, JP, great-grandson of the late James
Butler (*d.* 1746), el. son of James Butler of Doon, co. Clare, great-great- grandson
of the late James Butler, el. son of the late Hon. Peter (or Piers) Butler (ante):—
Issue of the late Theobald Fitzwalter Butler, J.P., D.L., *b.* 1845, *d.* 1914 : *m.* 1883, Catherine
Elizabeth, who *d.* 1946, dau. of Major John Barraclough :—
Fitzwalter, *b.* 1889: *m.* 1920 (m. diss. 1930), Doris Emma, who *d.* 1950, da. of Robert Pollok, OBE,
and has issue living, Theobald Fitzwalter (29, Queen St., Henley-on-Thames), *b.* 1921: *m.* 1951,
Patricia Penelope, da. of Richard Lowe, and has issue living, Simon Blake Fitzwalter *b.* 1958,
Judith Margaret *b.* 1953,—John David Blake (33, Bath Rd., W4), *b.* 1924; an actor. *Residence,*—
2, Harbour View, Baston St., Senglea, Malta.

Grandchildren of the late Lieut.-Col. Walter Blake BUTLER-CREAGH (infra):—
Issue of the late Richard BUTLER-CREAGH, *b.* 1890, *d.* 1955 : *m.* 1919, Ada Murray, who
d. 1949 :—
Richard (P.O. Box 8951, Nairobi, Kenya), *b.* 1922: *m.* 1957, Therése Agnes Spoorenberg, and has
issue living, Michelle Edith, *b.* 1957,—Simone Antoinette, *b.* 1960.——Vincent, *b.* 19—.——Walter,
b. 19—.——Mary, *b.* 19—: *m.* 19—, William Witham. —Sheila, *b.* 19—: *m.* 19—, Michael Baines,
solicitor, and has issue living.——Maureen, *b.* 19—. *m.* 19—,—Whittingham, of Shangrila, Salisbury,
Rhodesia.——Clara, *b.* 1929: *m.* 1953, William Craig, and has issue living, Albert, *b.* 1954,—William
Richard, *b.* 1956,—Robert, *b.* 1958.——Ethanna, *b.* 19—: *m.* 1957, William Henry Harris.——Joan,
b. 19—: *m.* 19—, — Finn and has issue living, Anthony Richard, *b.* 19—,—David, *b.* 1956,—Linda,
b. 19—,—Bernardette Marie, *b.* 1952. *Residence,*—

Granddaughter of the late Nicholas Butler, son of the late Walter Butler, el. son of
the late William Butler, of Bunnahow, co. Clare, (*b.* 1759), son of the late Peter
Butler, younger son of the late James Butler, of Doon, co. Clare (ante):—
Issue of the late Lieut.-Col. Walter Blake BUTLER-CREAGH, King's Own Yorkshire L.I., *b.*
1859, *d.* 1943 (having assumed 1889 by Roy. Licence the additional surname and arms of
Creagh after his patronymic): *m.* 1888, Clara, who *d.* 1928, dau. and co-heir of Cornelius
Creagh, of Dangan, co. Clare :—
Mary Gertrude, *b.* 1892. *Residence,*—2, Waterloo Road, Dublin.

PREDECESSORS.—[1] *Sir* Thomas Butler, 3rd son of the late Theobald Butler or Botiller, 4th
hereditary Chief Butler of Ireland (whose 2nd son Edmund was father of 1st Earl of Ormonde) [see
Ormonde, M.], was summoned as *Baron of Dunboyne* to Parliament of Ireland 1324: *m.* 1320, Synolda,
Lady of Dunboyne, dau. and heiress of William le Petit, 6th Baron of Dunboyne (by tenure), who
was summoned to parliament as *Baron of Dunboyne* 1274 ; *d.* 1329 ; *s.* by his son [2] PETER, 2nd
Baron : *m.* before 1353, Katherine, dau. and heiress of John de Bermingham, Lord of Kiltenian ; *d.*
1370 ; *s.* by his son [3] WILLIAM, 3rd Baron : *m.* Elizabeth, dau. of Nicholas le Poer, of Kilmeaden,
co. Waterford ; *d.* 1405; *s.* by his son [4] PETER, 4th Baron, *b.* before 1398 ; *d.* unm. 1415 ; *s.* by
his brother [5] EDMUND, 5th Baron ; *d.* unm. 1419 ; *s.* by his brother [6] JAMES (3rd son of 3rd Baron)
6th Baron: *m.* Morina Brien, of Thomond, who *d.* 1476 ; *d.* 1445 ; *s.* by his son [7] WILLIAM, 7th Baron;
attainted 1455 ; *d.* circa 1459 ; *s.* by his brother [8] EDMOND FITZ-JAMES, 8th Baron ; his dignity
and estates were restored by Act of Parliament 1471/2, and he received large grants from the Crown
for his great services in the Irish Wars : *m.* before 1468/9, Catherine, dau. of Richard Butler Mac-
Richard, of Buolick, co. Tipperary ; *d.* 1498/9 ; *s.* by his son [9] JAMES, 9th Baron : *m.* 1st, Ellnor,
dau. of Sir Laurence Taafe ; 2ndly, Catherine, dau. of Fineen McCarthy Reagh, Chief of Carberry ;
d. 1508 ; *s.* by his son [10] JAMES, 10th Baron : *m.* Lady Joan Butler, dau. of 1st Earl of Ossory and
8th Earl of Ormonde; *d.* 1533 ; *s.* by his son [11] EDMUND, K.B., 11th Baron, *b.* 1520 ; cr. by patent
Baron Dunboyne, of co. Meath (peerage of Ireland) 1541: *m.* before 1551, Cecilia (who *m.* 2ndly,
1568, as his 3rd wife, Richard Bourke, 2nd Earl of Clanricarde), dau. of Cormac Oge Macarty, of
Muskerry ; *d.* 1566 ; *s.* by his son [12] JAMES, 12th Baron ; summoned to Parliament 1569-71 and
1614 : *m.* 1st, about 1580, Margaret FitzPatrick, dau. and heiress of 2nd Baron of Upper Ossory;
2ndly, about 1591, Lady Margaret O'Brien, dau. of 3rd Earl of Thomond ; *d.* 1624 ; *s.* by his grandson [13] EDMOND (son of the late John Butler, son of 9th Baron), 13th Baron : *m.* 1st, 1625,
Margaret Butler, who *d.* 1632, dau. and heiress of 2nd Baron Caher ; 2ndly, about 1637, Lady Ellen
FitzGerald, who *d.* 1660, dau. of 15th Earl of Desmond, and widow of (1) Sir Donough O'Connor, and
(2) Sir Robert Cressy ; *d.* 1640 ; *s.* by his son [14] JAMES, 14th Baron : twice outlawed in 1642 for his
share in the Irish Rebellion 1641 (but the Solicitor-Gen. reported in 1827 that as there were serious
errors in the drawing up of the writs of outlawry, he considered them invalid) : *m.* Ellen Butler, dau.
of 1st Viscount Ikecrin : *d.* 1662 ; *s.* by his cousin [15] PIERCE (only son of the late Edmund Butler,
el. son of the late Piers Butler, 2nd son of 11th Baron), 15th Baron : ostensibly outlawed posthumously 1691 for rebelling against William and Mary's government (which the Lord Chancellor
stated in 1859 was illegal, as such an outlawry could only have been made by the Lord Ch.
Justice acting as Coroner, and in this instance the outlawry was in the wrong Christian name,
and Pierce, Baron Dunboyne, was not involved in this rebellion): *m.* Catherine, dau. of Sir
Thomas Hurley, 1st Bt. ; *d.* 1690 ; *s.* by his son [16] JAMES, *de jure* 16th Baron : *m.* 1686, Elizabeth, dau. of Sir Redmond Everard, Bt. ; *d.* 1701 ; *s.* by his el. son [17] PIERCE, *de jure* 17th Baron:
m. Anna, dau. and heir of Robert Cadell, of Dublin ; *d.* 1718 ; *s.* by his brother [18] EDMOND, *de*
jure 18th Baron : *m.* Anne, dau. of Oliver Grace, of Shanganagh, co. Tipperary, Ch. Remembrancer
of the Exchequer, Ireland, and widow of Richard Nagle ; *d.* 1732 ; *s.* by his el. son [19] JAMES;
de jure 19th Baron ; *d.s.p.* 1768 ; *s.* by his brother [20] PIERCE, *de jure* 20th Baron, *m.* 1775, Maria,
(who *m.* 2ndly, 1775, David Walsh), dau. of George Macnamara, of Cong, co. Mayo; *d.* 1773 ; *s.* by his
son [21] PIERCE EDMOND CREAGH, *de jure* 21st Baron ; *d.* unm. 1785 ; *s.* by his uncle [22] *Right Rev.*
JOHN, *D.D.* (3rd son of 8th Baron), *de jure* 22nd Baron, Roman Catholic Bishop of Cork 1763-86 ;
he resigned his See after succession to the title and demanded from the Pope a dispensation to
marry ; this being refused, he became a Protestant: *m.* 1787, Maria (who *m.* 2ndly, 1801, John Hubert
Moore, of Shannon Grove, King's Co., Bar.-at-law, and *d.* 1860), dau. of Theobald Butler, of Wilford,
co. Tipperary ; *d.* 1800 ; *s.* by his kinsman [23] JAMES (son of the late James Butler, grandson of
the late Edward Butler, grandson of the late Hon. Edward Butler, 6th son of 11th Baron), *de jure* 23rd
Baron ; the outlawries of James, 14th Baron and Pierce, 15th Baron, were reversed by Royal Warrant,
on the grounds of "the errors therein" 1827, and he was confirmed in the peerage: *m.* 1st, 1799, Eleanor,
who *d.* 1817, dau. of David O'Connell, of Cork, 2ndly, 1843, Mary Anne Vincent Vaughan, who *d.* 1847;
d. 1850 ; *s.* by his son [24] THEOBALD FITZ-WALTER, 24th Baron; *b.* 1806; his right to Barony of
Dunboyne was confirmed by Committee of Privileges of House of Lords 1860 ; a Representative
Peer: *m.* 1832, Julia Celestina Maria, dau. of the late William Brander, of Morden Hall,
Surrey ; *d.* 1881 ; *s.* by his son [25] JAMES FITZ-WALTER CLIFFORD, 25th Baron, *b.* 1839 : *m.*
1860, Marion, who *d.* 1919, dau. of Col. Henry Morgan Clifford, of Llantilio Crossenny, Monmouth-
shire, whose surname he assumed in addition to that of Butler; *d.* 1899; *s.* by his brother [26]
ROBERT ST. JOHN FITZ-WALTER, 26th Baron, *b.* 1844 ; a Representative Peer ; sometime Senior
Master of Supreme Court, and King's Remembrancer : *m.* 1869, Caroline Maude Blanche, who *d.*
1927, dau. of the late Capt. George Probyn ; *d.* 1913 ; *s.* by his el. son [27] FITZ-WALTER GEORGE
PROBYN, 27th Baron, *b.* 1874 ; Capt. (retired) R.N. : *m.* 1915, Dora Isolde Butler, dau. of the late
Tom. Francis Fitzpatrick Tower, O.B.E., late R.N.V.R. ; *d.* 1945 ; *s.* by his son [28] PATRICK
CHEOBALD TOWER, 28th Baron(and 18th by patent)and present peer.

DUNCAN-SANDYS, BARON. (Duncan-Sandys.) [Life Baron 1974.]

(EDWIN) DUNCAN SANDYS, *CH*, *PC*, only son of the late Capt. George John Sandys; *b.* Jan. 24th, 1908: assumed by deed poll 1974 the surname of Duncan-Sandys in lieu of his patronymic; ed. at Eton, and Magdalen Coll., Oxford (MA); Hon. FRIBA; Hon. MRTPI; Lt.-Col. late RA (TA); 1939-45 War with RA in Norway (disabled 1941); MP for Norwood Div. of Lambeth (*C*) 1935-45, and for Streatham Div. of Wandsworth 1950-74; a Member of Nat. Exec. Conservative Party 1938-39, Finance Member of Army Council 1941-43, Parl. Sec. Min. of Supply 1943-44, Min. of Works 1944-45, Min. of Supply 1951-54, Min. of Housing and Local Govt. 1954-57, Min. of Defence 1957-59, Min. of Aviation 1959-60, Sec. of State for Commonwealth Relations 1960-64, Sec. of State for the Colonies 1962-64, and Min. responsible for Central African Affairs 1963-64; founded European Movement (Chm. of Internat. Exec. 1947-50, founded Civic Trust (Pres. since 1957), a Member of Gen. Advisory Council of BBC 1947-51, and of European Consultative Assembly 1950-51 and since 1965 (Leader of British Delegation 1970-72); Pres. of Europa Nostra since 1969, and a Member of W. European Union Assembly since 1965 (Vice-Pres. 1970-72); Chm. of Lonrho since 1972; Grand Cross Order of Merit of Italy; cr. PC 1944, CH 1973, and *Baron Duncan-Sandys*, of City of Westminster (Life Baron 1974): *m.* 1st, 1935 (m. diss. 1960) Diana, who *d.* 1963, da. of the late Rt. Hon. Sir Winston Leonard Spencer-Churchill, KG, OM, CH, TD, MP [D. Marlborough, colls.], and formerly wife of John Milner Bailey (afterwards 2nd Bt.); 2ndly, 1962, Marie-Claire, da. of Adrien Schmitt, of Paris, and formerly wife of 2nd Viscount Hudson, and has issue by 1st and 2nd m.

Arms,—not exemplified at time of going to press.

Residence,—86, Vincent Sq., SW1. *Club.*—Carlton.

SON LIVING (*By 1st m.*)

Hon. Julian George Winston (Charnwood, Shackleford, Godalming, Surrey), *b.* 1936; Bar. Inner Temple 1959: *m.* 1970, Elisabeth Jane, only da. of John Besley Martin, JP, of Kenton, and has issue living, Duncan John Winston, *b.* 1973,—Jonathan Martin Edwin, *b.* 1975,—Lucy Diana, *b.* 1971.

DAUGHTERS LIVING (*By 1st m.*)

Hon. Edwina (66, Chester Row, SW1), *b.* 1938: *m.* 1960 (m. diss. 1973), Piers (Pierson John Shirley) Dixon, MP, yst. son of the late Sir Pierson John Dixon, GCMG, CB, and has issue living, Mark Pierson, *b.* 1962,—Hugo Duncan, *b.* 1963.
Hon. Celia Mary, *b.* 1943: *m.* 1st, 1965 (m. diss. 1970), George Michael Kennedy; 2ndly, 1970, Dennis Walters, MBE, MP, of 15, Wilton St., SW1, and has issue living (by 1st m.), Justin, *b.* 1967,—(by 2nd m) Dominic, *b.* 1971.

(*By 2nd m.*)

Hon. Laura Jane, *b.* 1964.

Dundas, Lord, grandson of Marquess of Zetland.

DUNDEE, EARL OF. (Scrymgeour-Wedderburn.) [Earl S. 1660.]

HENRY JAMES SCRYMGEOUR-WEDDERBURN OF WEDDERBURN, P.C., 11th Earl ; b. May 3rd, 1902 ; s. 1924 (claim to Viscountcy of Dudhope admitted by Committee for Privileges of House of Lords 1952, and to Earldom of Dundee 1953) ; ed. at Winchester, and at Balliol Coll., Oxford (B.A. 1925, M.A. 1926) ; LL.D. St. Andrews 1953 ; is Hereditary Roy. Standard Bearer for Scotland, Baron of the Barony of Wedderburn, and a J.P. and D.L. for Fifeshire; was Parl. Under-Sec. of State for Scotland 1936-39, served with the 7th Bn. Black Watch 1939-41, and Additional Parl. Under-Sec. of State, Scottish Office 1941-42, Min. without Portfolio 1958-61, and Min. of State, Foreign Office 1961-63, Dep. Leader of House of Lords 1962-64; bore Roy. Standard of Scotland at Coronations of King George VI 1937, and of Queen Elizabeth II 1953; MP for W. Div. of Renfrew 1931-45; cr. Baron Glassary, of Glassary, co. Argyll (peerage of United Kingdom) 1954, and PC 1959: m. 1946, Patricia Katharine, da. of the late Lt.-Col. Lord Herbert Andrew Montagu-Douglas-Scott, CMG, DSO [see D. Buccleuch, colls.], and widow of (1) Lt.-Col. Walter Douglas Faulkner, MC, Irish Guards, and (2) Lt.-Col. (the Hon.) David Scrymgeour-Wedderburn, DSO, Scots Guards [see infra], and has issue.

Arms,—Quarterly : 1st and 4th argent a chevron between three roses gules, Wedderburn ; 2nd and 3rd gules a lion rampant or armed and langued azure holding in the dexter paw a broadsword proper, Scrymgeour. Crests,—1st, an eagle's head erased proper, Wedderburn ; 2nd, a lion's gamb erased in bend, holding a cutlass, all proper, Scrymgeour. Supporters,—Two greyhounds argent collared gules.

Seat,—Birkhill, Cupar, Fife. Clubs,—Carlton, Travellers', White's, New (Edinburgh).

SON LIVING.

ALEXANDER HENRY (Lord Scrymgeour), b. June 5th, 1949; a Page of Honour to H.M. 1964-65.

WIDOW LIVING OF SON OF DE JURE NINTH EARL.

Joyce, only dau. of the late Col. Robert Henry Jennings, C.S.I., R.E.: m. 1921, Capt. the Hon. William Ogilvy Scrymgeour-Wedderburn, D.S.C., R.N. (retired), who d. 1958, and has issue living [see colls., infra]. Residence,—B13, Sloane Avenue Mansions, Sloane Avenue, SW3 3JG.

COLLATERAL BRANCHES LIVING.

Issue of the late Lieut.-Col. (the Hon.) David Scrymgeour-Wedderburn, D.S.O., Scots Guards, younger son of the de jure 10th Earl, b. 1912 ; d. (of wounds received in action during European War) 1944: m. 1940, Patricia Katharine (Countess of Dundee), (who m. 3rdly, 1946, the 11th Earl of Dundee [ante]), dau. of the late Lieut.-Col. Lord Herbert Andrew Montagu-Douglas-Scott, C.M.G., D.S.O. [see D. Buccleuch, colls.], and widow of Lieut.-Col. Walter Douglas Faulkner, M.C., Irish Guards:—
Janet Mary, b. 1941: m. 1962, Capt. (Edward Arthur) Mervyn Fox-Pitt, Welsh Guards, of Grange Scrymgeour, Cupar, Fife, and has issue living, David William, b. 1964.—Leonie, b. 1962.—Miranda Mary, b. 1968.——Elizabeth (Baroness Teynham), b. 1943: m. 1964, the 20th Baron Teynham, of The Severalls, Hatherop, Cirencester.

Issue of the late (Hon.) Frederick Lewis Scrymgeour-Wedderburn, 2nd son of the de jure 9th Earl, b. 1874, d. 1936 : m. 1913, Zaida Grace, who d. 1943, only dau. of Sir Ffolliott William Erskine, 3rd Bt. (cr. 1821):—
William Alexander, D.F.C., b. 1919 ; European War 1939-45 as Flight-Lieut. R.A.F. (D.F.C. and bar): m. 1st, 1940, Mabel Kathleen, dau. of F. W. Rowe, of Torquay, S. Devon ; 2ndly, 1951, Margaret Emily, da. of William Henry Innes, of Largo, Fife, and has issue living, (by 2nd marriage) John Frederick b. 1955,—Caroline Sarah, b. 1954,—Grace Marion, b. 1959. Residence,—Lesmurdie House, Lower Cabrach, by Huntly, Aberdeenshire.——Cecily Grace, b. 1915; is a Sister of Bethany. Residence,—House of Bethany, Bournemouth.——Marion, b. 1917. Residence,—Innisfail Hospital, Innisfail, N. Queensland.

Issue of the late Hon. Charles Kenneth Scrymgeour-Wedderburn, 3rd son of de jure 9th Earl, b. 1887, d. 1963: m. 1915, Gertrude Louisa Marie, who d. 1957, only dau. of the late James Carnegie Wemyss, younger, of Wemyss Hall:—
Rosemary (Cuil-an-Duin, Ballinluig, Perthshire), b. 1916: m. 1st 1937 (m. diss. 1947), Lt.-Col. Christian Landale Melville, DSO; 2ndly, 1949, Brig. William Noel Roper-Caldbeck, DSO, who d. 1965, and has issue living, (by 1st m.) Robin Kenneth Christian (Druimantavore Lodge, Crieff, Perthshire), b. 1938; ed. at Edinburgh Univ. (LLB); Fl. Lt. RAF (ret): m. 1961, Elisabeth Mary Melville, da. of Capt. Melville Stewart Jameson, and has issue living, James Landale b. 1963, Christian Kenneth Bowring b. 1965,—Edward Charles, WS, (Sherwood, 28, Redford Rd., Edinburgh), b. 1940: WS: m. 1966, Alison Sinclair, da. of Thomas Sinclair Fraser, and has issue living, Peter Charles Fraser b. 1970, Rachel Anne Rosemary b. 1972,—Anthony, b. 1942,—Michael Landale (1st Bn. The Black Watch, Colchester, Essex), b. 1943: Maj. The Black Watch: m. 1971, Susan Louise Margaret, da. of Maj. Edmund Robert Cox, TD, JP, of Strowan, Crieff, Perthshire, and has issue living, Sarah Anne Louise b. 1974.——Lorna Mabel, b. 1918: m. 1966, Ian Miskelly, DSC, JP, Glenara, Methven, Perthshire.——Aimée Elspeth, b. 1920: m. 1945, James Ferrier Macfarlane, of Apt. 509, 3495, Mountain St., Montreal, Quebec, Canada, and has issue living, Charles Ferrier, b. 1946: m. 1970, Kathryn Anne Oppe, and has issue living, James Andrew b. 1973,—Jennifer Elspeth, b. 1948: m. 1975, William Lorne Lindsay.——Susan Mary, b. 1926: m. 1st 1950 (m. diss. 1970), Noel George Moore; 2ndly, 1970, John Frederick Ingleby, of 31, Westbourne Gdns., Hove, and has issue living, (by 1st m.) Mary Louisa, b. 1954.

Issue of the late Capt. the Hon. William Ogilvy Scrymgeour-Wedderburn, D.S.C., R.N. (retired), youngest son of de jure 9th Earl, b. 1894, d. 1958 : m. 1921, Joyce (ante), only dau. of the late Col. Robert Henry Jennings, C.S.I., R.E. :—
Ian Alexander (Merle Wood, Letchworth Lane, Letchworth, Herts.; Army and Navy Club, and MCC), b. 1923; Cdr. RN (ret.): m. 1947, Desirée, da. of the late Col. Richard White, of Church Farm House, Smarden, Kent, and has issue living, James Ian, b. 1951.——Fiona Marigold Joyce, b. 1925: m. 1951, the Rev. James Ainsworth Yates, and has issue living, Katherine Fiona, b. 1958,—Veronica Margaret (twin), b. 1958. Residence,—The Vicarage, Shillington, nr. Hitchin, Herts.

PREDECESSORS.—[1] JOHN Scrymgeour, Hereditary Standard Bearer of Scotland and Constable of Dundee : cr. Viscount Dudhope and Lord Scrymgeour (peerage of Scotland) 1641, with remainder to his heirs male whatsoever : m. 1596, Margaret, dau. of George Seton, of Parbroath ; d. 1643 ; s. by his el. son [2] JAMES, 2nd Viscount, b. 1597 ; commanded a Regt. of Scottish Inf. under the Earl of Leven : m. 1618, Lady Isobel Kerr, 3rd dau. of 3rd Earl of Roxburghe ; d. (from wounds received at Battle of Marston Moor) 1644 ; s. by his el. son [3] Rt. Hon. JOHN, 3rd Viscount, b. 1622 ; Col. of Horse under Duke of Hamilton 1648 in attempt to rescue Charles I; accompanied Charles II at Battle of Worcester 1650, and was taken prisoner by the English ; fought in Middleton's Campaign of 1654 ; cr. Earl of Dundee, and Lord Inverkeithing (peerage of Scotland) 1660, with remainder to heirs male whatsoever : m. 1644, Lady Anne Ramsay, dau. of 1st Earl of Dalhousie ; d. 1668, whereupon all the honours became dormant ; s. (as Viscount Dudhope according to the decision of the Committee for Privileges of House of Lords 1952, and as Earl of Dundee according to the decision of the Committee for Privileges of House of Lords 1953) by his kinsman and heir male, and of line [4] JOHN (son of John Scrymgeour of Kirkton, grandson of John Scrymgeour of Kirkton (d. 1629), great-grandson of James Scrymgeour of Kirkton (d. 1513), grandson of David Scrymgeour, younger son of Sir James Scrymgeour of Dudhope, and brother of Sir John Scrymgeour of Dudhope, great-grandfather of John Scrymgeour (d. 1562), great-grandfather of 1st Viscount Dudhope, de jure 2nd Earl ; b. 1628 ; deprived of the Scrymgeour family estates by the influence of the Duke of Lauderdale with Charles II.: m. 1659, Magdalene, dau. of Alexander Wedderburn of Kingennie ; d. 1698 ; s. by his son [5] JAMES, de jure 3rd Earl, b. 1664 ; d. 1699 ; s. by his brother [6] ALEXANDER, de jure 4th Earl, b. 1669, Lay Professor of Humanity, Philosophy and Theology, St. Andrews Univ.: m. 1697, Janet, only da. of David Falconer, Professor of Divinity, St. Andrews Univ.; d. 1739; s. by his son [7] DAVID, de jure 5th Earl, b. 1702; Advocate and Sheriff Depute of Inverness: m. 1739, Katherine, dau. of Sir Alexander Wedderburn, 4th Bt. of Blackness; d. 1772; s. by his son [8] ALEXANDER Scrymgeour-Wedderburn, de jure 6th Earl, b. 1742; s. to estates, name and arms of Wedderburn of Wedderburn 1778: m. 1771, Elizabeth Ferguson, dau. of Lord Pitfour; d. 1811; s. by his brother [9] HENRY Scrymgeour-Wedderburn, de jure 7th Earl, b. 1755; attended King George IV, as Hereditary Standard Bearer of Scotland at Holyrood 1822: m. 1793, Mary Turner, el. dau. of Capt. the Hon. Frederick Lewis Maitland-R.N., 6th son of 6th Earl of Lauderdale: d. 1841; s. by his only son [10] FREDERICK LEWIS, de jure 8th Earl, b. 1808; a J.P. and D.L.t or Fifeshire: m. 1st, 1839, the Hon. Helen Arbuth, nott, who d. 1840, 5th dau. of 8th Viscount Arbuthnott; 2ndly, 1852, Selina Mary, who d. 1902; dau. of Capt. Thomas Garth, R.N., of Haines Hill, Berks; d. 1874; s. by his el. son [11] HENRY SCRYMGEOUR, de jure 9th Earl; b. 1840; a J.P. and D.L. for Fifeshire and Capt. 17th Regt., his right to the hereditary office of Roy. Standard Bearer for Scotland was admitted by the Court of Claims at Coronation of Edward VII, when he bore the Standard of Scotland, and confirmed by the House of Lords 1910: m. 1869, Juliana, who d. 1921, youngest dau. of Thomas Braddell, of Coolmelagh. co. Wexford; d. 1914; s. by his son [12] HENRY, de jure 10th Earl; b. 1872; Lieut.-Col. late T.A. Reserve and Capt. Gordon Highlanders; bore Standard of Scotland at Coronation of George V in place of his father: m. 1901, Edith, who d. 1968, only da. of John Moffat; d. 1924; s. by his son [13] HENRY JAMES, 11th Earl, and present peer (who established his right to Viscountcy of Dudhope 1952, and to Earldom of Dundee 1953), also Viscount Dudhope, Lord Scrymgeour, Lord Inverkeithing, and Baron Glassary.

DUNDONALD, EARL OF. (Cochrane.) [Earl S. 1669.]

By courage and labour.

IAN DOUGLAS LEONARD COCHRANE, 14th Earl; b. Dec. 6th, 1918; s. 1958; ed. at Wellington and RMC; a Representative Peer for Scotland 1959-63; Maj. (ret.), Black Watch; Chm. of Anglo-Chilean Soc. 1958-65; Chm. de Jersey & Co. (Finland) Ltd., and Pres. of Ayr and Bute Assocn. of Youth Clubs; a member of UK Delegation to Citizens Conference of NATO Nations, Paris, 1962; 1939-45 War in N. Africa, Italy, Sicily and Greece: m. 1960, Aphra Farquhar, who d. 1972, da. of the late Cdr. George Fetherstonhaugh, RNR, of The Beacon, Benenden, Kent and has issue.

Arms,—Argent, a chevron gules, between three boars' heads erased azure. Crest,—A horse passant argent. Supporters,—Two greyhounds argent, collared and lined or.
Seat,—Lochnell Castle, Ledaig, Argyll. Residence,—Beacon Hall, Benenden, Cranbrook, Kent. Club,—Carlton.

SON LIVING.

IAIN ALEXANDER DOUGLAS BLAIR (Lord Cochrane), b. Feb. 17th, 1961.

DAUGHTER LIVING.

Lady Tanya Jean Farquhar, b. 1964.

SISTER LIVING.

(*Raised to the rank of an Earl's daughter* 1960.)

Lady Winifred Anne Grizel, *b.* 1923: *m.* 1967, Alfred Ashford, and has issue living, Alexis, *b.* 1969. *Residence,*—Hole Farm, Blackboys, Uckfield, Sussex.

DAUGHTER LIVING OF TWELFTH EARL.

Lady Grizel Winifred Louise, *b.* 1880: *m.* 1904, Lieut.-Col. the Hon. Ralph Gerard Alexander Hamilton (*Master of Belhaven*), R.F.A., who *d.* (killed in action during European War) 1918, only son of 10th Lord Belhaven and Stenton. *Residence,*—Stowlangtoft Hall, Bury St. Edmunds.

COLLATERAL BRANCHES LIVING.

Issue of the late Hon. Thomas Horatio Arthur Ernest Cochrane (younger son of 11th Earl), who was cr. *Baron Cochrane of Cults* 1919 [see that title].

Grandson of the late Capt. the Hon. Ernest Grey Lambton Cochrane, 4th son of 10th Earl:—
Issue of the late Horace Egerton Cochrane, *b.* 1883, *d.* 1959 : *m.* 1907, Eva Martha Clarke, who *d.* 1945 :—
Richard Ernest Horace, *b.* 1909: *m.* 1939, Alma Josephine, dau. of Albert Helland, of 6308, Cedar Av., Powell River, British Columbia, and has issue living, David Lambton Grey, *b.* 1957,—Gayle Patricia, *b.* 1941,—Myrna Avice Ruth, *b.* 1946. *Residence,*—Red Castle, Lifford, co. Donegal.

Grandchildren of the late Col. William Marshall Cochrane, son of the late Major the Hon. William Erskine Cochrane, 3rd son of 9th Earl:—
Issue of the late Brig.-Gen. William Francis Dundonald Cochrane, C.B., *b.* 1847, *d.* 1927: *m.* 1893, Carola, who *d.* 1936, dau. of the late Enrique Theodoro Möller, of Valparaiso :—
Carola Mary Rosita Isabel, *b.* 1896. *Residence,*—Court Lodge Farm, East Brabourne, Ashford, Kent.

Issue of the late Com. Thomas Erskine Cochrane, *b.* 1849, *d.* 1906: *m.* 1886, Mary, who *d.* 1937, dau. of the late John Bell-Irving [Jardine, Bt., cr. 1885]:—
Jessie Edith, *b.* 1891 : *m.* 1912, Major Walter Peter Stewart, D.S.O., from whom she obtained a divorce 1943, and has issue living, Kenneth Walter Hugh Cochrane (c/o Royal Hong Kong Jockey Club, Hong Kong), *b.* 1916: *m.* 1948, Heather Nagle, of Brisbane, and has issue living, Clarissa Cochrane *b.* 1950, Jane Cochrane *b.* 1951,—Grizel Margaretta Cochrane, *b.* 1914; a CStJ : *m.* 1950, George Williams, MC, of Llanharan House, Llanharan, Glam., and has issue living, Owain Anthony Mervyn, *b.* 1955. *Residence,*—Gt. Maytham Hall, Rolvenden, Kent.——Daisy Bell-Irving, *b.* 1894: *m.* 1916, Edward Ernest Mizen, J.P., formerly Lieut. 2/5th E. Surrey Regt., and has issue living, Patrick Erskine Cochrane, *b.* 1917: *m.* 1945, Norma Margaret Ball, of Auckland, New Zealand, and has issue living, Gary Edward *b.* 1947, Caroline Margaret *b.* 1948, Linda Sue *b.* 1950, Julie Loretta *b.* 1952,—Joan Louise Bell-Irving, *b.* 1919 : *m.* 1st, 1940, David Malpas Snow, who *d.* (killed in action) 1943; 2ndly, 1950, Adrian Rhodes Delamore, RN (ret.), Matiatia Farm, Waiheke Island, NZ, and has issue living, (by 1st marriage) Penelope June *b.* 1940: *m.* 1964, David Paykel, of Waiouru Rd., E. Tamaki, RD, NZ (by 2nd marriage) Robin Cochrane Rhodes *b.* 1951, Nicholas Edward *b.* 1953, Adrian Michael *b.* 1955,—Elizabeth Anne, *b.* 1927: *m.* 1951, John Hugh Newcombe Waymouth, RNZ (ret.), of 14, Turua St., St. Heliers Bay, Auckland, NZ, and has issue living, Peter John Newcombe (11, Bouverie St., N.E. Valley, Dunedin, NZ), *b.* 1952: *m.* 1970, Mary Livesey, of Timaru (and has issue living, Benjamin Newcombe *b.* 1971, Nicholas Newcombe *b.* 1975, Emma Newcombe, *b.* 1972), Christopher Simon Newxombe (13, King St., Grey Lynn, Auckland, NZ), *b.* 1955: *m.* 1973, Joy Carter, of Auckland, (and has issue living, Samuel *b.* 1973). *Residence,*—Kotiri Lodge, Tamamutu St., Taupo, N.Z.

Issue of the late Capt. John Palmer Cochrane, *b.* 1852, *d.* 1921 : *m.* 1882, Frances, who *d.* 1934, dau. of William Gilbert, formerly of Canterbury, Kent :—
Douglas Thomas, *b.* 1900: *m.* 1st, 1926, Ivy, who *d.* 1928, el. da. of G. A. Maasdorp. of Queenstown, Cape Province; 2ndly, 1935, Christine Marie Hammond, and has issue living, (by 1st marriage) Edward Denzil Dundonald (P.O. Box 650, Salisbury, Rhodesia), *b.* 1927: *m.* 1953, Janet Ainslie, only da. of Robert Allan, OBE, MC, DCM, and has issue living, Michael Allan Dundonald *b.* 1957, Susan Elizabeth *b.* 1954,—Blair Douglas Dundonald, (PO Box 101, Karoi, Rhodesia), *b.* 1928, *m.* 1958, Thea Jean. el. da. of Norman R. Stevenson, and has issue living, Ian Dundonald *b.* 1959, Robert Douglas Dundonald *b.* 1961, Jennifer Mary *b.* 1965, Sarah Alyson Jane *b.* 1972,—(by 2nd m), John Robert Collie (P.O. Box 650, Salisbury, Rhodesia), *b.* 1939: *m.* 1960, Rosemary Josephine Anne, da. of G. W. R. Caine, of Salisbury, Rhodesia and has issue living, Jeremy Robert *b.* 1962, Samantha Caroline *b.* 1965,—William Thomas (2, Sofston Close, Lewisham Drive, Lewisham, Highlands, Salisbury, Rhodesia), *b.* 1943: *m.* 1969, Pamela Evelyn, da. of Val Setzkorn, of 46, Danpienaar Drive, Amanzimtoti, Natal, and has issue living, Richard William *b.* 1974, Ingrid Margaret *b.* 1971,—Richard Bruce, *b.* 1948,—Steven David (PO Box 177, Karoi, Rhodesia), *b.* 1951: *m.* 1973, Penelope Jane Randles,—Cecily Mary Elizabeth, *b.* 1935: *m.* 1959, Kenneth Saywood (PO Box 177, Karoi, Rhodesia), and has issue living, Neil Frank *b.* 1960, David *b.* 1961, Peter John *b.* 1966, Michael Anthony *b.* 1970,—Una Patricia Leowina (The Retreat, 4, Harris Rd., Highlands, Salisbury, Rhodesia), *b.* 1937: *m.* 1958 (m. diss. 1975) Kenneth Davies, and has issue living, Patricia-Clare Cochrane *b.* 1959, Andrea-Jane Cochrane *b.* 1962. *Residence,*—The Retreat, Harris Rd., PO Highlands, Salisbury, Rhodesia.

Issue of the late Arthur Henry Douglas Cochrane, *b.* 1856, *d.* 1925: *m.* 1882, Marie Josephine Clegg, who *d.* 1934, 2nd dau. of George Killick, formerly of Kirby Hall, Leicestershire :—
Gladys Cochrane, *b.* 1891; resumed the surname of Cochrane in lieu of Robertson 19— : *m.* 1916, Alexander Cockburn Robertson, who obtained a divorce 1928.——(Ruby) Stella Cochrane, *b.* 1897; resumed the surname of Cochrane in lieu of Coates 1952 : *m.* 1st, 1918, Capt. Ralph Mannering West, late Yeo. ; 2ndly, 1923, Lieut.-Com. Basil William Barrymaine Hallwood, D.S.C., late R.N. from whom she obtained a divorce 1935 ; 3rdly, 1936, Cyril Edmondson Coates, and has issue living, (by 2nd m.) Kenneth Cochrane Coates (c/o New Municipal Offices, Monkton Park, Chippenham), *b.* 1923; assumed the surname of Coates in lieu of his patronymic 1938: *m.* 1963, Jane Oliver, of Arnold, Nottingham, and has issue living, Sarah Katherine *b.* 1967,—(Rowland) Carroll Coates, *b.* 1930; assumed the surname of Coates in lieu of his patronymic 1938: *m.* 1958 (m. dissolved 1962), Elvi Ruottinen, of Helsinki, Finland, and has issue living, Anna Karelia *b.* 1960. *Address,*—c/o P.O. Box 274, U.S.P.O. Laguna Beach, Cal. (92625), U.S.A.

Grandchildren of the late Capt. John Palmer Cochrane (ante):—
Issue of the late Basil William Dundonald Cochrane, *b.* 1891, *d.* 1954: *m.* 1920, Anne, 2nd da. of the late William Robertson, of Edinburgh :—
Elizabeth Anne, *b.* 1926.

Issue of the late Wing-Com. John Erichsen Blair Cochrane, *b.* 1894, *d.* 1949: *m.* 1916, Mary, who *d.* 1958, el. dau. of the late Com. Thomas Erskine Cochrane (ante):—
John Erskine Dundonald, *b.* 1920; formerly Lieut. R.A.: *m.* 1st, 1943 (marriage dissolved 1958), Elizabeth Mary, dau. of the late Capt. Bertram Allgood; 2ndly, 1958, Bela, el. dau. of William Carlton, of Leeds, and has issue living, (by 1st marriage) Ian Michael Dundonald, *b.* 1950,—Alistair Charles Dundonald, *b.* 1956,—Sarah Elizabeth, *b.* 1946.——Basil Thomas Dundonald (P.O. Box 1528, Durban, Natal), *b.* 1924; late RAF: *m.* 1st, 1955 (m. diss. 1973), Sally, only da. of Henry Edmund Hounsell, of Livingstone, Zambia; 2ndly, 1974, Daphne Maureen Joyce, da. of the late Elliot Esmond Baxter, of Camberley, Surrey.

Grandsons of the late Arthur Henry Douglas Cochrane (ante) :—
Issue of the late Arthur Blair Dundonald Cochrane, b. 1888, d. 1936: m. 1918, Nancy, da.
of the late Robert Barber, Bar.-at-Law:—
Hugh Benjamin (61, Carlisle Mansions, Carlisle Place, SW1), b. 1925; late Lt. RE: m. 1953, Anne
Deirdre, el. da. of William Schoener Scott.——Nicholas Baillie, b. 1929; late Capt. King's African
Rifles: m. 1958, Diana Isabel, da. of the late Norman Balfour Craig, and has issue living, Amanda
Elizabeth, b. 1959,—Susan Mary, b. 1962. Residence,—Silver Wood, Wick Hill Lane, Finchamp-
stead, Berks.

Granddaughters of the late Vice-Adm. Basil Edward Cochrane, el. son of the late
Basil Edward Arthur Cochrane, 2nd son of the late Capt. the Hon. Archibald
Cochrane, RN, 4th son of 9th Earl.
Issue of the late Rear-Adm. Archibald Cochrane, C.M.G., b. 1874, d. 1952 : m. 1904, Maye
Amelie Lucile, who d. 1954, dau. of the late Col. Alured de Vere Brooke, R.E. [Brooke, Bt.,
cr. 1662, colls.] :—
Marie Cecilia, b. 1905: m. 1944, Maj. Reginald Joseph Vosser, MBE, Bedfordshire and Herts Regt.,
who d. 1967, and has issue living, Michael Cochrane, b. 1945: m. 1970, Susan Margaret, el. da. of
David Greenwood, of Heathhayne, Woking,—Charles Brooke, b. 1948.——Grizel Rosemary (Lady
Peto), b. 1907: m. 1st, 1941, Maj. Thomas Lionel Ashburner Clapton, Durham LI, who d. (killed
in action in Normandy) 1944; 2ndly, 1948, Cdr. Sir (Henry) Francis Morton Peto, RN,
3rd Bt. (cr. 1855), and has issue living, (by 1st m.) Peter Thomas Archibald, b. 1942; Capt. SG: m.
1972, Sarah Marion, da. of the late J. R. Chrystal,—Thomas Robert (posthumous), b. 1944,—(by
2nd m.) [see Peto, Bt. (cr. 1855)]. Residence,—Balbeg, Straiton, Maybole, Ayrshire.——Monica
Frances Mary, b. 1908: m. 1950, George Worcester, who d. 1969. Residence,—Penny Cottage,
Windlesham, Surrey.——Dorothea Stella, b. 1913; sometime Junior Com. ATS: m. 1951, John
Errington Rothwell Harrison, and has issue living, James Anthony Rothwell, b. 1952,—Anne
Lucile Rothwell, b. 1953. Residence,—102, Lytton Boulevard, Toronto, Canada.

Graddaughter of Rear-Adm. Sir Edward Owen Cochrane, KBE (infra):—
Issue of the late Maj. James Owen Cochrane, MC, RA, b. 1914, d. (killed in action during
European War) 1943: m. 1941, Margaret Angela Clare (who m. 2ndly, 1950, Desmond
Pertwee, of Rookery House, Great Horkesley, nr. Colchester, Essex), da. of Vice-Adm.
Charles Wolfram Round-Turner, CB, CMG:—
Janet Owen, b. 1942: m. 1965, Paul Moore, of 14, Freeland Place, Clifton, Bristol 2, and has issue living,
Thomas Owen, b. 1966,—Amy Clare, b. 1969.

Granddaughter of the late Vice-Adm. Basil Edward Cochrane (ante):—
Issue of the late Rear Adm. Sir Edward Owen Cochrane, KBE, b. 1881, d. 1972: m. 1908,
Mary Lucy (Molly), who d. 1955, da. of S. K. George, of The Brackens, Ascot:—
Susanne Gloria, b. 1918: m. 1957, David Logan Howell, of 3/5, St. George's Sq., SW1.

Grandchildren of the late William Edward Cochrane, 4th son of Basil Edward
Arthur Cochrane (ante):—
Issue of the late Cdr. Arthur FitzGerald Cochrane, RN, b. 1888, d. 1967: m. 1913, Beryl
Irma, who d. 1954, da. of Gen. Charles Frederick Thomas, of Excliffe, Exmouth, and
widow of Percy Hugh Druce:—
Peter William FitzGerald, b. 1916; ed. at Ampleforth, and at the McGill Univ.; 1939-45 War with
Atlantic Ferry Command and as Flying Officer RCAF with Bomber Command: m. 1944, Margaret
Eunice, only da. of Wesley William Rowley, of London, Ontario, Canada, and has issue living,
Richard Arthur Wesley Rowley, b. 1948.——Evelyn Jean FitzGerald, b. 1914.——Sheila Fitz-
Gerald, b. 1917: m. 1942, Lt.-Cdr. John Aarvold Loughlin Stubbs, RNVR, of 10, Dorset Close,
Harrogate, and has issue living, Penelope Anne, b. 1945: m. 1966, Maj Patrick Joseph David
Herberts, Parachute Regt., and has issue living, Andrew John David b. 1970, Alison Philippa b. 1967,
Catherine Elizabeth b. 1972,—Gillian Mary b. 1947.——Cecilia Florence Fitzgerald, b. 1924: m.
1955, John Gray Robertson, of Sunlaws, Parkhead, Dumfries, and has issue living, Peter Arthur
Cochrane, b. 1956,—Philip John Cochrane, b. 1962.

Granddaughter of the late Alexander Dundas Ross Cochrane-Baillie (el. son of the
late Adm. of the Fleet Sir Thomas John Cochrane, G.C.B., M.P., son of Adm.
the Hon. Sir Alexander Forester Inglis Cochrane, G.C.B., M.P., 6th son of 8th
Earl), who was cr. Baron Lamington 1880 [see that title].

PREDECESSORS.—[1] Sir WILLIAM Cochrane (of the family of Cochrane, which had been
settled on the Barony of Cochrane in W. of Scotland for many centuries), P.C., K.B., M.P.
for Ayrshire, and a Col. of Royalist Militia, who assisted in sending the Scots Army into
England, was cr. Lord Cochrane, of Dundonald (peerage of Scotland) 1647, with remainder to
the heirs male of his body, and Earl of Dundonald and Lord Cochrane of Paisley and Ochiltree (peerage of Scotland) 1669, with remainder to his heirs male, whom failing to his heirs female without
division who should bear or assume the name of Cochrane, and in failure to his heirs-gen.; d. 1686 ;
s. by his grandson [2] JOHN, P.C., 2nd Earl; d. 1690; s. by his el. son [3] WILLIAM, 3rd Earl; d.
unmarried 1705 ; s. by his brother [4] JOHN, 4th Earl ; a Representative Peer ; commanded Scottish
Horse Guards 1715; d. 1720; s. by his son [5] WILLIAM, 5th Earl; d. unmarried 1725; s. by his cousin
[6] THOMAS, 6th Earl, grandson of William, Lord Cochrane of Dundonald, el. son of 1stEarl; d.1737; s.
by his son [7] WILLIAM, 7th Earl; killed at siege of Louisburg 1758 ; s. by his cousin [8] THOMAS, 8th
Earl (grandson of Col. the Hon. Sir John Cochrane, 2nd son of 1st Earl), b. 1691 ; sat as M.P. for Renfrewshire 1722-7; d. 1778 ; s. by his son [9] ARCHIBALD, 9th Earl; b. 1748; served in R.N. ; an
eminent scientist, and inventor ; made many beneficial discoveries connected with Chemistry ; s. by
his son [10] THOMAS, G.C.B., 10th Earl; b. 1775; a distinguished Adm., and one of the greatest
Naval Commanders of any age ; conducted attack on French Fleet in Basque Roads, with fire and
explosion ships, 1809, and was also renowned for many daring exploits in the R.N. ; commanded the Chilian and Peruvian Navy (destroying Spanish Naval Power in Pacific), the
Brazilian Navy against Portugal (completely successful), and the Greek Fleet, in the Wars of
Independence of those countries ; sat as M.P. for Westminster, and was an advanced Reformer,
and an eminent scientist and inventor; cr. Marquess of Maranham, in Brazil, 1824; d.
1860 (buried in Westminster Abbey); s. by his son [11] THOMAS BARNES, 11th Earl;
b. 1814; was a Representative Peer, and Q.M.G. to Forces in Chinese War: m. 1847, Louisa
Harriet, who d. 1902, dau. of the late William Alexander-Mackinnon, M.P., of Mackinnon ; d.
1885 ; s. by his son [12] DOUGLAS MACKINNON BAILLIE HAMILTON, K.C.B., K.C.V.O., 13th Earl;
b. 1852; Lieut.-Gen. (retired) ; Nile Expedition 1884-5, S. Africa 1899-1901 at Relief of Ladysmith (promoted Maj.-Gen. for distinguished ser. in the field); sometime a Representative
Peer for Scotland: m. 1878, Winifred, who d. 1924, only child of the late Robert Bamford Hesketh,
of Gwrych Castle, Abergele, N. Wales; d. 1935, s. by his son [13] THOMAS HESKETH DOUGLAS
BLAIR, 13th Earl; b. 1886; was a Representative Peer for Scotland 1941-55; d. 1958; s. by his
nephew [14] IAN DOUGLAS LEONARD, (son of the late Hon. Douglas Robert Hesketh Roger Cochrane,
2nd son of 12th Earl) 14th Earl and present peer; also Lord Cochrane of Dundonald, and Lord
Cochrane of Paisley and Ochiltree.

DUNLEATH, BARON. (Mulholland.) [Baron U.K. 1892.]

Always girt.

CHARLES EDWARD HENRY JOHN MUL-
HOLLAND, *TD*, 4th Baron; *b.* June 23rd, 1933;
s. 1956; ed. at Eton, and at Camb. Univ.;
Lt.-Col. Comdg. N. Irish Horse (T) 1967-69;
DL of co. Down; Member of N.I. Assembly
(*Alliance Party*) 1973-74, and of N.I. Conven-
tion since 1975, Nat. Gov. for N. Ireland, BBC
1967-73; late 2nd Lt. 11th Hussars: *m.* 1959,
Dorinda Margery, da. of the late Lt.-·Gen.
Arthur Ernest Percival, CB, DSO, OBE, MC.

Arms,—Azure, a stag's head erased argent between
three escallops or. Crest,—An escallop gules. Supporters,
—On either side an elk proper, charged on the shoulder with
an escallop or, and holding in the mouth a trefoil slipped vert.

Seat,—Ballywalter Park, Newtownards, co. Down.

WIDOWS LIVING OF SONS OF SECOND BARON.
Lady Hester Joan Byng (*Joan, Countess of Cavan*), *DBE*, da. of 5th Earl of Strafford; Lady-in-Waiting
to HRH Princess Mary 1918-22, and to HM Queen Elizabeth the Queen Mother (when Duchess
of York) during tour of Australia and New Zealand 1927; an Extra Lady-in-Waiting to HRH the
Princess Royal 1932-66; DBE (Civil) 1927: *m.* 1st, 1913, Capt. the Hon. Andrew Edward Somerset
Mulholland, Irish Guards, who *d.* (killed in action) 1914, el. son of 2nd Baron; 2ndly, 1922, as his
second wife, the 10th Earl of Cavan, who *d.* 1946, and has issue living (by 1st marriage) [see colls.
infra]. *Residence,*—39, Knightsbridge Court, Sloane St., SW1.
Hon. Dame Olivia Vernon Harcourt, *DCVO*, da. of 1st Viscount Harcourt; Vice-Chm. of Roy. Free
Hospital 1950-62; Chm. of Elizabeth Garrett Anderson Hospital 1945-72, and a Woman of the Bedchamber to HM Queen Elizabeth the Queen Mother since 1950; CVO 1958, DCVO 1971: *m.* 1923
the Hon. (Godfrey) John Arthur Murray Lyle Mulholland, MC, who *d.* 1948, and has issue living [see
colls., infra]. *Residence,*—Weston Mark, Upton Grey, Hants.

COLLATERAL BRANCHES LIVING.

Issue of the late Capt. the Hon. Andrew Edward Somerset Mulholland, Irish
Guards, el. son of 2nd Baron, *b.* 1882, *d.* (killed in action) 1914: *m.* 1913, Lady
Hester Joan Byng, *D.B.E.* [(ante); she *m.* 2ndly. 1922, as his second wife, the
10th Earl of Cavan, who *d.* 1946], da. of 5th Earl of Strafford:—
Daphne Norah (*Lady Ward*), *b.* (posthumous) 1915; formerly Senior Com. A.T.S.: *m.* 1942, as his
second wife, Sir John Guthrie Ward, GCMG, and has issue living, Jane Mulholland, *b.* 1943: *m.* 1968,
Fabrice Jules Olivier Marie Gauguier,—Joanna Guthrie, *b.* 1950: *m.* 1974, Marco Dal Moro. *Residences,*—Lenox, St. Margaret's Bay, nr. Dover, Kent; 31, Knightsbridge Court, Sloane St., SW1.

Issue of the late Rt. Hon. Sir Henry George Hill Mulholland, Bt., (cr. 1945), 2nd son
of 2nd Baron, *b.* 1888, *d.* 1971: *m.* 1914, Sheelah, da. of Sir Arthur Douglas
Brooke, 4th Bt. (cr. 1822) [see V. Brookeborough]:—
Of whom, *Sir* MICHAEL HENRY, 2nd Bt. is *h.p.*

Issue of the late Hon. (Godfrey) John Arthur Murray Lyle Mulholland, M.C.,
4th son of 2nd Baron, *b.* 1892; *d.* 1948: *m.* 1923, the Hon. Dame Olivia Vernon
Harcourt, *DCVO* (ante), da. of 1st Viscount Harcourt:—
Martin Edward Harcourt, *b.* 1927; formerly Lieut Irish Guards; High Sheriff co. Antrim 1961: *m.* 1953,
Lilian Diana Tindall, only da. of the late Maj. John de Blaquiere Tindall Lucas, MC, and has issue
living, John Martin, *b.* 1953,—Simon Edward, *b.* 1955; a Page of Honour to HM Queen Elizabeth,
The Queen Mother 1969-71,—Giles Alexander, *b.* 1959. *Residence,*—North Hall, E. Chilting-
ton, Lewes.——Mary Norah, *b.* 1924; in WRNS 1943-45: *m.* 1944, John William Owen Elliot, late
Capt. Scots Guards, of East Hoase, Dedham, Colchester [see E. Minto, colls.].——Bridget Olivia,
b. 1930: *m.* 1953, Gerald Cecil Williams [Salusbury-Trelawny, Bt.], and has issue living, Christopher
Harcourt, *b.* 1960,—Carolyn Mary, *b.* 1953,—Anne Olivia *b.* 1955. *Residence,*—Upper Kennards,
Leigh, nr. Tonbridge, Kent.

Issue of the late Hon. Alfred John Mulholland, 3rd son of 1st Baron; *b.* 1856, *d.*
1938: *m.* 1889, Mabel Charlotte, who *d.* 1934, el. dau. of Llewellyn Traherne
Basset Saunderson [E. Clonmel]:—
John Llewellyn, *b.* 1908: *m.* 1st, 1928, Helen (from whom he obtained in Hungary, June 1930,
a dissolution of the marriage), dau. of V. Moss; 2ndly (in Hungary), 1930, Olga (from whom he
obtained a divorce 1937), dau. of Nicolas Kuznetzov; 3rdly (in France) 1937, Colette (from whom
he obtained a divorce 1938), dau. of Georges Mounier; 4thly (in Brazil) 1944, Lucia, dau. of Antonio
Izaquirre, and has issue living, (by 1st m.) John Peter Patrick (Chesterfield, Somerford Rd., Cirencester, Glos.), *b.* 1929; ed. at Berkhamsted, RMC, Trin Coll., Dublin, and Sch. of Slavonic Studies
(BA(Hons)); Bar. Middle Temple 1969; late Brazilian Organiser BBC: *m* 1st 1962 (m. diss. 1970),
Suelly, da. of Olympio José do Lindo; 2ndly, 1973, Rosemary Kathleen Vaughan, only da. of the
late Charles Hawkins, MC, BDS,—(by 2nd m.) Alexander Anatole, *b.* (in Hungary) 1931,—(by 3rd m.)
Christian, *b.* (in France) 1938.——Ivo Alfred, *b.* 1913; late Maj. Bedfordshire and Herts Regt.:
m. 1946, Monica Mary, da. of the late William Lowry Craig Knight, CMG, and has issue living, Mary
Rose, *b.* 1951.

PREDECESSORS.—[1] JOHN Mulholland, *LL.D.*, son of the late Andrew Mulholland, J.P., D.L.,
of Ballywalter Park; *b.* 1819; M.P. for Downpatrick (*C*) 1874-85; cr. *Baron Dunleath*, of Ballywalter, co. Down (peerage of United Kingdom) 1892: *m.* 1851, Frances Louisa, who *d.* 1909, dau.
of Hugh Lyle, of Knocktarna, co. Londonderry; *d.* 1895; *s.* by his second son [2] HENRY LYLE,
2nd Baron, *b.* 1854; M.P. for Londonderry co., N. Derry Div. (*C*) 1885-95: *m.* 1881, Norah
Louisa Fanny, *O.B.E.*, who *d.* 1935, dau. of the late Capt. the Hon. Somerset Richard Hamilton
Augusta Ward; *d.* 1931; *s.* by his son [3] CHARLES HENRY GEORGE, *C.B.E.*, *D.S.O.*, 3rd Baron;
b. 1886; Capt. 11th Hussars; Mil. Sec. to Lord-Lieut. of Ireland 1919-21, and Gov.-Gen. of Australia 1923-5: *m.* 1st, 1920, Sylvia Henrietta, who *d.* 1921, dau. of Sir Arthur Douglas Brooke, 4th
Bt.; 2ndly, 1932, Henrietta Grace, who *d.* 1969, da. of the late Most. Rev. Charles Frederick D'Arcy
[B. Darcy de Knayth, colls.]; *d.* 1956; *s.* by his only son [4] CHARLES EDWARD HENRY JOHN,
4th Baron and present peer.

Dunluce, Viscount, son of Earl of Antrim.

DUNMORE, EARL OF. (Murray.) [Earl S. 1686.]

JOHN ALEXANDER MURRAY, 9th Earl ; *b.* April 3rd, 1939 ; *s.* 1962 ; ed. at Eton; late Lt. Queen's Own Cameron Highlanders; a Member of Inst. of Public Relations: *m.* 1967, Anne Augusta, da. of Thomas Clouston Wallace, of Holodyke, Dounby, Orkney, and has issue.

Arms—Not matriculated at Lyon Office.
Residence,—14, Regent Terr., Edinburgh.

DAUGHTERS LIVING.
Lady Kate Rodel, *b.* 1969. *Lady* Rebecca Moulin, *b.* 1970.

AUNT LIVING. (*Daughter of 8th Earl.*)
Lady Marjorie Hilda, *b.* 1904 : has Order of Mercy : *m.* 1926, Duncan Alexander Stirling, late Capt. Coldstream Guards, and has issue living, Alexander Murray (Hunterswood House, Chipperfield, Herts.), *b.* 1927; ed. at Eton, and New Coll., Oxford; late Lieut. Coldstream Guards: *m.* 1951, Mary, da. of the late Maj. Neville Wakefield, DSO, and has issue living, Robert Alexander *b.* 1959, Oliver John *b.* 1961, Annabel Mary Charlotte *b.* 1963,—Angus Duncan Æneas (of 25, Ladbroke Grove, W.11), *b.* 1933; ed. at Eton, and at Trin. Coll., Camb.: *m.* 1959, Armyne Morar Helen, dau. of William George Broadbent Schofield [see B. Hastings], and has issue living, Duncan William Angus *b.* 1963, Emma Elisabeth *b.* 1960, Candida Helen *b.* 1966. *Residences,*—28, St. James's Place, SW1; Hinton Ampner Place, Alresford, Hants.
Lady (Mary) Elisabeth, *b.* 1918 : *m.* 1937, Major Peter Carlton Oldfield, O.B.E., Warwickshire Yeo., and has issue living, Sara Elisabeth, *b.* 1939: *m.* 1961, William Thomson, late Scots Guards, of East Ilsley Hall, Newbury, Berks., and has issue living, Lucinda *b.* 1965. *Residence,*—50, Clabon Mews, SW1.

MOTHER LIVING.
Hon. Pamela Kate, dau. of the 2nd Baron Wyfold: *m.* 1st, 1938, Capt. Edward David, Viscount Fincastle, who *d.* (killed in action during European War) 1940; 2ndly, 1944, Capt. Follett Watson Bell, R.A. *Residence,*—Dalness House, Glenetive, Ballachulish, Argyll.

COLLATERAL BRANCHES LIVING.

Granddaughter of the late Charles James Murray, son of the late Rt. Hon. Sir Charles Augustus Murray, K.C.B., son of 5th Earl :—
Issue of the late Charles Wadsworth Murray, *b.* 1894, *d.* 1945 : *m.* 1924, Elizabeth (of 3, York Road, Trinity, Edinburgh), dau. of Frank Grant, of Knockie, Inverness :—
Helen Rosemary, *b.* 1928: *m.* 19—.

Grandchildren of the late Reginald Augustus Frederick Murray (infra):—
Issue of the late Virginius Henry Randolph Murray, *b.* 1872, *d.* 1937: *m.* 1910, Alice, who *d.* 1966, da. of William Clarke, MD, of Banff:—
Virginia Margaret, *b.* 1911: *m.* 1942, Alfred Allen Gibbs, Chartered Accountant (Australia), and has issue living, Peter Murray, *b.* 1943,—David Ian, *b.* 1950. *Residence,*—17, Wanda Road, Caulfield, S.E.7, Victoria, Australia.——Patricia Aimee, *b.* 1916: *m.* 1960, Peter Bayard Horne, c/o Trade Commr. Ser., Dept. of Trade, Canberra, A.C.T., Australia.——Judith Dunmore, *b.* 1918: *m.* 1944, Ian Monk, M.B., M.S., F.R.C.S., and has issue living, Virginia Ann, *b.* 1949,—Victoria Jane *b.* 1952,—Serena Dunmore, *b.* 1954. *Residence,*—35 Raglan St., Mosman, Sydney, N.S. Wales.

Issue of the late Arthur Charles Murray, *b.* 1882, *d.* 1964: *m.* 1st, 1909, Susan Maud, who *d.* 1922, da. of Edward Richards, of Tasmania; 2ndly, 1929, Ida Clara Dawe, who *d.* 1970, da. of the late John Mallinson:—
(By 1st m.) REGINALD ARTHUR (Gravelly Beach, W. Tamar, Tasmania), *b.* July 17th, 1911: *m.* 1948, Patricia Mary da. of Frank Coles, of Robingana, W. Tamar, Tasmania, and has issue living, Susan, *b.* 1949,—Elizabeth Mary, *b.* 1951.——Kenneth Randolph (Gravelly Beach, West Tamag, Tasmania), *b.* 1913; late Sergeant 12th/50th Btn. Australian Inf.: *m.* 1938, Margaret Joy, da. of the late P. D. Cousins, of Burnie, Tasmania, and has issue living, Malcolm Kenneth (PO Box 100, East Devonport, Tasmania), *b.* 1946: *m.* 1970, Joy Anne, da. of A. Partridge, 1, South St., Launceston, Tasmania,—Geoffrey Charles (73, Pomona Rd., Riverside, Tasmania), *b.* 1949: *m.* 1974, Margaret Irene, da. of H. Bulloch, of Blackwall, Tasmania.——Alexander Edward (1, Mount Stuart Rd., N. Hobart 7000, Tasmania), *b.* 1917; 1939-45 War as Able Seaman RAN: *m.* 1st, 1940 (m. diss. 19—), June Caroline Lucy, el. da. of B. Rabinovitch, of 21, Pitt St., North Hobart, Tasmania: *m.* 2ndly, 19—, Irene Maude Barwick, of Hobart, Tasmania, and has issue living (by 1st m.), Stephen Alexander, *b.* 1953,—Marilyn Joy, *b.* 1947: *m.* 1964, Michael John Hankin, and has issue living, Brett Michael *b.* 1967, Tania Maree *b.* 1965, Sharon Louise *b.* 1971,—Wendy Lorraine, *b.* 1951: *m.* 1969, Maxwell Kevin Upton, of 122, Brent St., Glenorchy, Hobart, Tasmania, and has issue living, Jason Boaz *b.* 1971.——Lorraine Edith (62, Talbot Rd., S. Launceston, Tasmania), *b.* 1914: *m.* 1st, 1940, Hector Bird, who *d.* 1963; 2ndly, 1966, Stanley Millwood Farquhar, and has issue living, (by 1st m.) Grace Lucinda, *b.* 1950: *m.* 1969, Haydn Peter Borella, of 62, Talbot Rd., Launceston, Tasmania, and has issue living, Paul Andrew *b.* 1973, Angela Jayne *b.* 1971.——Constance Margaret, *b.* 1922: *m.* 1946, John Mallinson, of 12, Munford St., Kings Meadows, Launceston, Tasmania, and has issue living, Edward Arthur John *b.* 1955,—David Andrew *b.* 1957.

Issue of the late Malcolm Fincastle Murray, *b.* 1885, *d.* 1935: *m.* 1915, Rhoda Dorothy, dau. of Richard Davies Hanson, of Adelaide, S. Australia :—
Judith Hanson Fincastle, *b.* 1923.

Grandchildren of the late Capt. Virginius Murray, son of the late Lieut.-Col. the Hon. Alexander Murray (infra):—
Issue of the late Reginald Augustus Frederick Murray, *b.* 1846, *d.* 1925: *m.* 1st, 1869, Jane Louisa Otway, who *d.* 1887, dau. of Henry Ford, of Melbourne, Victoria: 2ndly, 1888, Ethel, who *d.* 1912, dau. of Thomas Tompson Bates, of Melbourne, Australia:—
(By 2nd m.) Reginald Herbert Earn (1/13, Northcote Terr., Medindie, S. Aust. 5081), *b.* 1889; a Fellow of Australian Soc. of Accountants, and of Chartered Inst. of Secretaries; 1914-18 War (despatches): *m.* 1928, Nina Clarendon, da. of Clarendon James Seager, and has issue living, John Dunmore (2, Edwin Terr., Gilberton, S. Aust. 5081), *b.* 1929; ed. at Adelaide Univ. (B.Eng.); MIE Aust.: *m.* 1962, Geraldine Majorie, da. of the late Col. Rupert Edward Fanning, of S. Yarra, Victoria, and has issue living, Catriona Dunmore Stewart *b.* 1965, Bridget Dunmore Stewart *b.* 1967, Vanessa Dunmore Stewart *b.* 1969, Kirsten Dunmore Stewart *b.* 1971.——Christina Dunmore, *b.* 1889: *m.* 1917, Dr. W. W. McLaren, and has issue living, William, *MB*, *b.* 1921; MB 19—; *m.* 1949, Joan Pullman, and has issue living, a son *b.* 19—,—Neil, *b.* 1922; SE Asia 1944-45 (wounded): *m.* 1950, Beatrice Faichney, and has issue living, a da. *b.* 19—,—David Malcolm, *MB*, *b.* 1926; MB 19—: *m.* 1952, Margaret Estelle Rayson, and has issue living, a da. *b.* 1954,—Janet Ruth, BSc, *b.* 1920; BSc 19—. *Residence,*—48, Snowden Av., Caulfield, SE3, Victoria, Australia.——Katrine Elizabeth Alice (Mayflower, 7, Centre Rd., Brighton East, Vic. 3187, Aust.), *b.* 1891: *m.* 1913, the Hon. James Miller Balfour, JP, a MLC, of Victoria, who *d.* 1943, and has issue living, James Charles Murray (of Willow Grove, via Moe, Victoria, Australia) *b.* 1914; is a Farmer, and a MLA, Victoria: *m.* 1937, Mary Emma Savige, and has issue living, Russell Miller *b.* 1939, Peter Murray *b.* 1943, David *b.* 1945, Graeme Charles *b.* 1952,—Daisy Miller, *b.* 1920: *m.* 1947, Lieut.-Col. Geoffrey Mander-Jones, York and Lancaster Regt. (ret.), and has issue living, Robert

Geoffrey *b.* 1949, Angela Margaret *b.* 1953, Susan Elizabeth *b.* 1958,—Bery Miller, *b.* 1922; BA 1942: *m.* 1946, the Rev. Ronald Ian Scott, of 44, Aphrasia St., Newtown, Vic. 3220, Aust., and has issue living, John Balbour *b.* 1946, Katrine Elizabeth *b.* 1947, Margaret Anne *b.* 1950, Virginia Blanche *b.* 1956.——Phyllis Ethel Sheila (Flat 3, 6 Pencarrow St., Mount Eden, Auckland, NZ), *b.* 1901: *m.* 1938, Dr. R. Keenan, who *d.* 1962.

   Issue of the late George Earn Murray, *b.* 1850, *d.* 1902: *m.* 1889, Julia Mary McLeod, who *d.* 1933, second dau. of the late Gen. C. B. Fuller, R.H.A. (Col. Comdt.):—
Dudley Stewart, *b.* 1892.——Gladys, *b.* 1890.——Doris Vivienne (Lucas Hospital, Wokingham, Berks.), *b.* 1894.

   Issue of the late Henry Alexander Murray, *b.* 1857, *d.* 1934: *m.* 1889, Fannie Morris, who *d.* 1940, dau. of Samuel D. Babcock, of New York:—
Henry Alexander, *MD, b.* 1893; formerly Lieut.-Col. USA Med. Corps: *m.* 1st, 1916, Josephine Lee, who *d.* 1962, da. of Neal Rantoul, of Boston, Mass., USA; 2ndly, 1969, Caroline, da. of Alfred Chandler, of Wilmington, Delaware, USA, and has issue living, (by 1st m.) Josephine, *b.* 1921; *Residence*,—22, Francis Av., Cambridge, Mass., USA.——Virginia, *b.* 1890: *m.* 1913, Robert Low Bacon, who *d.* 1938, and has issue living, Virginia Murray, *b.* 1916: *m.* 1949, Byron Thomas, of Woodstock, Vermont, USA, and has issue living, Richard Byron *b.* 1951, Virginia Murray *b.* 1950, Mary Elizabeth *b.* 1953,—Martha, *b.* 1918: *m.* 1942, Creighton Churchill, late Capt. US Army; 2ndly, 1953, James Farley, of Windsor, Vermont, U.S.A., and has issue living, (by 1st m.) Daniel Creighton *b.* 1948, Alexandra *b.* 1946, (by 2nd m.) Kevin Lawlor *b.* 1955, Robert Bacon *b.* 1957, Deirdre Murray *b.* 1953, Sheila Sullivan *b.* 1958. *Residence*,—Westbury, Long Island, USA.

   Grandchildren of the late Henry Alexander Murray (ante):—
   Issue of the late Cecil Dunmore Murray, *b.* 1897, *d.* 1935: *m.* 1921, Veronica (of Harcot, Garrison-on-Hudson, New York, U.S.A.), dau. of Kenneth Frazier, of Garrison, New York:—
Rev. Michael Hunt (Exec. Council, Episcopal Church, 815, 2nd Av., New York, USA), *b.* 1922; late Lt. USA Naval Air Force: *m.* 1st, 1943, Gloria Caruso; 2ndly, 1955, Eliane, da. of Eugene Cadilhac, of Paris, France, and has issue living, (by 1st marriage) Eric Dunmore, *b.* 1945,—Colin Duncan Alexander, *b.* 1949.——Julia Fannie, *b.* 1924: *m.* 1953, Robert Linfield Mackintosh, and has issue living, Amy Rogers, *b.* 1954,—Louisa Linfield, *b.* 1956,—Susan Frazier, *b.* 1958. *Residence*,—Manchester, Mass., USA.

   Grandson of the late Brig.-Gen. Alexander Henry Murray, son of the late Lieut.-Col. the Hon. Alexander Murray, 2nd son of 4th Earl:—
   Issue of the late Charles Stewart Murray, C.I.E., *b.* 1858, *d.* 1903: *m.* (Jan.) 1892, Laura Susan (who *m.* 2ndly, 1914, Maj.-Gen. Charles Edmund Layard, formerly Comdg. E. Yorkshire Regt., who *d.* 1919), dau. of Franklin Prestage, of Darjeeling, Bengal:—
Archie Alastair Stewart, *RN, b.* 1892; Cdr. RN (ret.); Persian Gulf 1914 (medal); 1914-18 War (wounded); 1939-45 War: *m.* 1925, Marie Louise Ravend de Martainville, da. of the late Alfred Taylor Pattison, of New Orleans, USA, and has issue living, Hugh Archie Stewart (Abbot's Lodge, nr. Buckland Monachorum, Yelverton, S. Devon), *b.* 1927; ed. at Stowe, and at Trin. Coll., Oxford; late Lt. Welsh Guards: *m.* 1st, 1955 (m. diss. 1964), Kathleen Mary, only da. of Clive Raymond Hargreaves, of White Barn Lodge, Alderley Edge; 2ndly, 1967, Eileen Alexandra Jane, da. of the late Charles Clements Lockhart Ross. *Residence*,—Abbot's Lodge, nr. Buckland Monachorum, Yelverton, S. Devon.

   Grandchildren of the late Charles Stewart Murray, CIE (ante):—
   Issue of the late Maj. Alastair Donald Stewart Murray, MC, *b.* 1898, *d.* 1966; *m.* 1st, 1922, Joan Ethel, da. of the late Robert Moore McMahon, of Holly Mount, Carlow; 2ndly, 1933 (m. diss. 1948), Marjory, who *d.* 1959, da. of the late Capt. Anthony Standish Thomson, CB, CBE; 3rdly, 1951, Oonah Tighe, only da. of Thomas Tait, of Gatehouse-of-Fleet, Kirkcudbrightshire, and formerly wife of   McKellar:—
(By 3rd m.) Alastair Stewart, *b.* 1952.

   Issue of the late Charles Stewart Murray, *b.* 1900, *d.* 1960: *m.* 1926, Beryta (who obtained a divorce 1933), only dau. of Roland Allport, of Sydney, N.S. Wales:—
Diana Stewart *b.* 1930: *m.* 1st, 1948 (m. diss. 1960), Richard de Graaff Hunter; 2ndly, 1969, Arthur Eustace Farmiloe, of 41, Cumberland St., SW1, and has issue living, (by 1st m.) Sarah Stewart, *b.* 1949.

   Grandchildren of the late Lieut.-Col. Cyril Francis Tyrrell Murray, C.B., M.V.O. son of the late Brig.-Gen. Alexander Henry Murray (ante):—
   Issue of the late Brigadier Cyril Alexander George Octavius Murray, D.S.O., *b.* 1887, *d.* 1960 *m.* 1922, Marjorie Lilias, who *d.* 1965, da. of the late W. Jennings Milles, M.D., F.R.C.S. of Shanghai:—
Blair Cyril (c/o Westminster Bank, 195, Earl's Court Rd., SW5), *b.* 1929; ed. at Winchester, and at Magdalene Coll., Camb. (MA); late Lt. 16th Hussars.——Anne Elizabeth, *b.* 1937.

   Grandson of the late Brig.-Gen. Alexander Henry Murray (ante):—
   Issue of the late Lieut.-Col. Sir Malcolm Donald Murray, G.C.V.O., C.B., C.I.E., *b.* 1867, *d.* 1938: *m.* 1898, Lady Hilda Joanna Gwendolen Finch, who *d.* 1931, dau. of 7th Earl of Aylesford:—
Iain Arthur, *DSO* (The Dower House, Oxonhoath, Tonbridge, Kent), *b.* 1904; ed. at Eton; a Page of Honour to HM 1917-21; 1939-45 War, with Gren. Guards and as Lt.-Col. Glider Pilot Regt.; DSO 1944 (Bar 1945): *m.* 1st, 1932, Angela Houssemayne (who obtained a divorce 1946), da. of the late Lt.-Col. Arthur Houssemayne du Boulay, DSO; 2ndly, 1947 (m. diss. 1957), Anne, da. of the late Vice-Adm. the Hon. Edmund Rupert Drummond, CB, MVO [see E. Perth, colls.] and has issue living, (by 1st m.) Virginia Anne, *b.* 1936: *m.* 1st, 1955 (m. diss. 1963) Anthony Gordon Reid; 2ndly, 1964, D. Ricardo Saenz de Heredia, of 11, Montague Rd., Richmond, Surrey, and has issue living, (by 1st m.) Ian Malcolm Gordon *b.* 1956, (by 2nd m.) Ricardo *b.* 1968, Roberto *b.* 1969, Peter *b.* 1970,—Serena Jane, *b.* 1939: *m.* 1963, Konradin Geotte Vidigal, of Avenida do Brazil, 130 2E, Lisbon 5, Portugal.

PREDECESSORS.—[1] *Rt. Hon. Lord* Charles Murray, 2nd son of 1st Marquess of Athole; Master of the Horse to Queen Mary II. of England; *cr. Lord Murray of Blair, Moulin and Tillimet (Tullimet), Viscount Fincastle* and *Earl of Dunmore* (peerage of Scotland) 1686; *d.* 1710; *s.* by his el. son [2] JOHN, 2nd Earl; a Gen. in the Army, and a Representative Peer; *d.* 1752; *s.* by his brother [3] WILLIAM, 3rd Earl; having taken part in the rebellion of 1745, was in 1746 tried for high treason and pleaded guilty, but obtained the King's pardon; *s.* by his son [4] JOHN, 4th Earl; a Representative Peer 1761-84, Gov. of New York 1769-70, Virginia 1770-76, and Bahamas 1787-96; *d.* 1809; *s.* by his son [5] GEORGE, 5th Earl; *cr. Baron Dunmore*, of Dunmore (peerage of United Kingdom) 1831; *d.* 1836; *s.* by his son [6] ALEXANDER EDWARD, 6th Earl; *b.* 1804: *m.* 1836, Catherine, who *d.* 1886, da. of 11th Earl of Pembroke; *d.* 1845; *s.* by his son [7] CHARLES ADOLPHUS, 7th Earl; *b.* 1841; a Lord-in-Waiting to Queen Victoria 1874-80, and Lord-Lt. of co. Stirling 1875-85: *m.* 1866, Lady Gertrude Coke, who *d.* 1943, da. of 2nd Earl of Leicester; *d.* 1907; *s.* by his son [8] ALEXANDER EDWARD, *VC, DSO, MVO*, 8th Earl; *b.* 1871; Maj. 16th Lancers; served with Soudan Field Force 1896, and Malakand Field Force 1897-98 (VC); S. Africa 1899-1900; Comdg. 31st Batn. Imperial Yeo. 1902; 1915-17 War (twice wounded, DSO); Capt. Hon. Corps. of Gentlemen-at-Arms 1924, and a Lord-in-Waiting to HM 1930-36: *m.* 1904, Lucinda Dorothea, who *d.* 1966, el. da. of the late Col. Horace William Kemble, of Toravaig, Skye [Mackenzie, Bt., cr. 1702, colls.]: *d.* 1962; *s.* by his grandson [9] JOHN ALEXANDER (son of the late Capt. Edward David, Viscount Fincastle, who was *k.* in action 1940, only son of 8th Earl) 9th Earl and present peer; also Viscount Fincastle, Lord Murray of Blair, Moulin and Tillimet (Tullimet), and Baron Dunmore.

DUNRAVEN and MOUNT-EARL, EARL OF. (Wyndham-Quin.) [Earl I. 1822 Bt. G.B. 1781.]

Head of the serpent for ever.

THADY WINDHAM THOMAS WYNDHAM-QUIN, 7th Earl, and 7th Baronet; *b.* Oct. 27th, 1939; *s.* 1965; ed. at Le Rosey: *m.* 1969, Geraldine, da. of Air Commodore Gerard Ward McAleer, CBE, of Wokingham, Berks., and has issue.

Arms.—Quarterly, 1st and 4th gules, a hand couped below the wrist grasping a sword all proper between in base two serpents erect and respecting each other, tails nowed or, in chief two crescents argent, *O'Quin of Munster;* 2nd and 3rd azure, a chevron between three lions' heads erased or, a mullet for difference, *Wyndham.* **Crests,**—1st, wolf's head, erased argent, *Quin;* 2nd, a lion's head erased within a fetter lock and chain or, *Wyndham.* **Supporters,**—Two ravens with wings elevated proper, collared and chained or.

Residence,—Adare Manor, Adare, co. Limerick.
Clubs,—White's, Kildare Street.

DAUGHTER LIVING.

Lady Ana, *b.* 1972.

SISTERS LIVING.

Lady Melissa Eva Caroline, *b.* 1935 : *m.* 1959, Major Sir George Cecil Francis Brooke, M.B.E., 3rd Bt., of Glenbevan, Croom, co. Limerick.

Lady Caroline Olein Geraldine (*Marchioness of Waterford*), *b.* 1936 : *m.* 1957, the 8th Marquess of Waterford, of Curraghmore, Portlaw, co. Waterford, and Glenbride Lodge, Valleymount, co. Wicklow.

UNCLE LIVING. (*Son of 5th Earl.*)

Hon. VALENTINE MAURICE, *R.N., b.* May 22nd, 1890; ed. at Eton; Capt. (ret.); 1914-18 War, European War 1939-44 (despatches four times); appointed Naval Attaché at Buenos Aires 1945: *m.* 1919, Marjorie Elizabeth, who *d.* 1969, da. of the late Rt. Hon. Ernest George Pretyman [E. Bradford], and has issue living, Ursula Eva (*Lady Roderic A. N. Pratt*), *b.* 1921: *m.* 1945, Major, Lord Roderic Arthur Nevill Pratt, son of 4th Marquess Camden,—Marjorie Olein (*Marchioness of Salisbury*), *b.* 1922: *m.* 1945, the 6th Marquess of Salisbury.—Pamela (*Baroness Egremont*) (Petworth House, Sussex; 62, Chester Sq., SW1; Cockermouth Castle, Cumberland), *b.* 1925: *m.* 1947, the 6th Baron Leconfield and 1st Baron Egremont, who *d.* 1972. *Residence,*—66, Cadogan Sq., SW1. *Club,*—White's and Royal Yacht Squadron.

WIDOW LIVING OF SIXTH EARL.

NANCY (*Nancy, Countess of Dunraven and Mount-Earl*), (Kilgobbin, Adare, co. Limerick), da. of Thomas Burks Yuille, of Halifax Co., Virginia, USA: *m.* 1934, as his 2nd wife, the 6th Earl, who *d.* 1965.

PREDECESSORS.—[1] VALENTINE RICHARD Quin ; cr A *Baronet* 1781, *Baron Adare* (peerage of Ireland) 1800, *Viscount Mount-Earl* (peerage of Ireland) 1816, and *Viscount Adare* and *Earl of Dunraven and Mount-Earl* (peerage of Ireland) 1822 ; *d.* 1824 ; *s.* by his son [2] WINDHAM HENRY, 2nd Earl ; assumed the additional surname of Wyndham by Roy. licence 1815 ; a Representative Peer ; *d.* 1850: *s.* by his son [3] EDWIN RICHARD WINDHAM, *K.P.*, 3rd Earl ; *b.* 1812; M.P. for Glamorganshire (*C*) 1836-50 ; Lieut. of co. Limerick ; cr. *Baron Kenry*, of co. Limerick (peerage of United Kingdom) 1866: *m.* 1st, 1836, Augusta, who *d.* 1866, dau. of Thomas Goold, a Master in Chancery ; 2ndly, 1870, Anne, who *d.* 1917, dau. of Henry Lambert, of Carnagh, co. Wexford ; *d.* Oct. 6th, 1871 ; *s.* by his son [4] Rt. Hon. WINDHAM THOMAS, *K.P.*, 4th Earl, *b.* 1841 ; Parliamentary Under-Sec. of State for the Colonies 1885-86, and H.M. Lieut. for co. Limerick 1894-1926 ; a Senator of Irish Free State 1922-6 : *m.* 1869, Florence, who *d.* 1916, dau. of the late Lord Charles Lennox Kerr ; *d.* 1926, when the Barony of Kenry became ext., while the Irish titles and the baronetcy devolved upon his cousin [5] WINDHAM HENRY WYNDHAM-QUIN, *C.B., D.S.O.* (el. son of the late Capt. the Hon. Windham Henry Wyndham-Quin, 2nd son of 2nd Earl), 5th Earl, *b.* 1857 ; Major! 5th Lancers, Capt. and Hon. Major Gloucestershire Yeo. Cav., and Lieut.-Col. Comdg. and Hon. Col. Glamorganshire Yeo.; Transvaal Campaign 1881, S. Africa 1900-01 with Imperial Yeo. (despatches, D.S.O.) ; was A.D.C. and Mil. Sec. to Gov. of Madras 1886-89, and High Sheriff for co. Kilkenny 1914 ; sat as M.P. for Glamorganshire, S. Div. (*C*) 1895-1906 : *m.* 1885, Lady Eva Constance Aline, who *d.* 1940, dau. of 6th Earl of Mayo ; *d.* 1952 ; *s.* by his son [6] RICHARD SOUTHWELL WINDHAM ROBERT, *CB, CBE, MC,* 6th Earl, *b.* 1887; Master of the Horse and Mil. Sec. to Lords Lieut. of Ireland 1918-21: *m.* 1st, 1915, Helen (who *d.* 1962, having obtained a divorce 1932), da. of the late John Swire, of Hillingdon House, Harlow; 2ndly, 1934, Nancy, da. of Thomas Burks Yuille, of Halifax Co., Virginia; *d.* 1965; *s.* by his only son [7] THADY WINDHAM THOMAS, 7th Earl and present peer; also Viscount Mount-Earl, Viscount Adare, and Baron Adare.

DUNROSSIL, VISCOUNT. (Morrison.) [Viscount U.K. 1959.]

JOHN WILLIAM MORRISON, 2nd Viscount ;
b. May 22nd, 1926 ; *s.* 1961 ; ed. at Fettes,
and at Oriel Coll., Oxford (B.A. 1950,
M.A. 1952) ; formerly Flight-Lieut. R.A.F.,
entered Commonwealth Relations Office
1951 ; was Assist. Private Sec. to Sec. of
State 1952-4, 2nd Sec., Canberra 1954-56,
and 1st Sec. and acting Dep. High Commr.,
Dacca, E. Pakistan 1958-60; 1st Sec.,
Pretoria and Capetown 1961-64, and FO
1964-68, and on loan to Intergovern-
mental Maritime Consultative Organisation
1968-70, since when Counsellor and Head
of Chancery, Ottawa: *m.* 1st, 1951 (m.
diss. 1969), Mavis Dawn, da. of A. Llewellyn
Spencer-Payne, LRCP, MRCS, LDS; 2ndly,
1969, Diana Mary Cunliffe, da. of C. M.
Vise, and has issue by 1st and 2nd m.

Arms,—Per bend sinister gules and argent a demi-
lion rampant issuant or armed and langued azure holding
in his paws a battleaxe the shaft curved of the third and
the axehead of the fourth in chief, and in base, issuant
from the sea undy vert and or, a tower sable windows and
port or, over all a bend sinister embattled azure charged
with an open crown or jewelled gules between two
fleurs-de-lys argent ; within a bordure vert for difference.
Crest,—Issuant from waves of the sea azure crested
argent, a mount vert, thereon an embattled wall azure
masoned argent, charged with a portcullis or, and issuant
therefrom a cubit arm naked proper, the hand grasping
a dagger azure hilted or. Supporters,—Two lions regardant or armed and langued gules collared
vert supporting between their exterior forepaws and interior hind paws battleaxes azure, the shafts
embowed.

Residences,—70, Placel Rd., Ottawa 2; 1, Temple Gdns., EC4; Dun Rossail, b Lochmaddy,
N. Uist, Outer Hebrides.

SONS LIVING. (*By 1st m.*)
Hon. ANDREW WILLIAM REGINALD, *b.* Dec. 15th, 1953.
Hon. Ranald John, *b.* 1956.
Hon. Alasdair Godfrey, *b.* 1962.

DAUGHTERS LIVING. (*By 1st m.*)
Hon. Catriona Mary, *b.* 1952.
(*By 2nd m.*)
Hon. Joanna Catherine, *b.* 1971.
Hon. Mary Allison, *b.* 1972.

BROTHERS LIVING.
Hon. Alasdair Andrew Orr, *b.* 1929; ed. at Fettes, and at Balliol Coll., Oxford (MA); PhD, Chicago:
m. 1958, Frances Mary, da. of Wilfrid Rippon Snow, of Adelaide, S. Australia, and has issue living,
William Alasdair Ewing, *b.* 1960,—Alexandra Mary, *b.* 1962,—Joanna Allison, *b.* 1964. *Residence,*—
Maisemore Park, Gloucester.
Rev. the Hon. Nial Ranald, *b.* 1932; ed. at Fettes and at Jesus Coll., Oxford (B.A. 1954, M.A. 1957);
V. of Randwick, Glos. since 1962; *m.* 1959, Dr. Sheila Mary, dau. of Alexander Forbes, of Gloucester,
and has issue living, Neil William Alexander, *b.* 1961,—John Forbes, *b.* 1963,—Hugh Robert Shep-
herd, *b.* 1965,—Alison Mary, *b.* 1960,—Elizabeth Iona, *b.* 1969. *Residence,*—The Vicarage, Rand-
wick, Glos.
Hon. Godfrey Donald, *b.* 1937; ed. at Stowe, and at Balliol Coll., Oxford. *Residence,*—19, Lloyd
Baker St., WC1.

WIDOW LIVING OF FIRST VISCOUNT.
(CATHERINE) ALLISON (*Allison, Viscountess Dunrossil*), dau. of the late Rev. William Swan, D.D.,
Min. of S. Leith Parish; MA, Edinburgh, Bar. Inner Temple 1926, Dep. Pres. of Victoria League for
Commonwealth Friendship, and a CStJ: *m.* 1924, the 1st Viscount, who *d.* 1961. *Residences,*—
Yew Tree Cottage, Withington, Glos.; 1, Temple Gdns., EC4.

PREDECESSOR.—[1] *Rt. Hon.* WILLIAM SHEPHERD Morrison, *G.C.M.G., M.C., P.C., Q.C.*
son of the late John Morrison, of Torinturk, Argyll ; *b.* 1893 ; Recorder of Walsall Feb. to Nov
1935 ; Private Sec. to Solicitor-Gen. 1922-23 and 1924-27, and to Attorney-Gen. 1927-28 ; again
Parliamentary Private Sec. to Attorney-Gen. 1931-5, Financial Sec. to Treasury 1935-6, Min. of
Agriculture and Fisheries 1936, Chancellor of Duchy of Lancaster and Min. of Food 1939-40, and
Postmaster-Gen. 1940-43 ; Min. for Town and Country Planning 1943-45, Speaker of House of
Commons 1951-9, and Gov.-Gen. and Com.-in-Ch. of Commonwealth of Australia 1960-61 ; European War 1914-19 as Capt. R.F.A. (Special Reserve) in France (wounded, despatches thrice, M.C.);
sat as M.P. for Cirencester and Tewkesbury Div. of Gloucestershire 1929-59; cr. *Viscount Dunrossil,*
of Vallaquie, Isle of North Uist, co. Inverness (peerage of United Kingdom) 1959 : *m.* 1924,
(Catherine) Allison (a C.St.J.), dau. of the late Rev. William Swan, D.D., Min. of South Leith Parish,
1961 ; *s.* by his el. son [2] JOHN WILLIAM, 2nd Viscount and present peer.

DUNSANY, BARON OF. (Plunkett.) [Baron I. 1439.]

[Title pronounced "Dunsayny."]

FESTINA LENTE

Quick, without impetuosity

RANDAL ARTHUR HENRY PLUNKETT, 19th Baron ; *b.* Aug. 25th, 1906 ; *s.* 1957 ; ed. at Eton ; Lieut.-Col. (retired) Indian Cav. (Guides) ; N.-W. Frontier of India 1930 (medal with clasp) : *m.* 1st, 1938, Mrs. Vera Bryce (from whom he obtained a divorce 1947), dau. of Senor de Sà Sottomaior, of San Paulo, Brazil ; 2ndly, 1947, Sheila Victoria Katrin, dau. of Capt. Sir Henry Erasmus Edward Philipps, 2nd Bt. [see Foley-Philipps, Bt. (ext.)], and widow of Maj. John Frederick, Foley, Baron de Rutzen, Welsh Guards and has issue by 1st and 2nd marriages.

Arms,—Sable, a bend, and in the sinister chief a tower argent. Crest,—A horse passant argent. Supporters.—*Dexter,* a pegasus per fesse or and argent ; *sinister,* an antelope argent, armed, unguled, plain collared and chained, or.

Seats,—Dunsany Castle, co. Meath ; Dunstall Priory, Shoreham, Kent. *Clubs,*—Beefsteak, Bath, Cavalry, Kildare Street.

SON LIVING. (*By 1st marriage.*)
Hon. EDWARD JOHN CARLOS, *b.* Sept. 10th, 1939 ; ed. at Eton.

DAUGHTER LIVING. (*By 2nd marriage.*)
Hon. Beatrice Mary, *b.* 1948.

WIDOW LIVING OF SON OF SEVENTEENTH BARON.
KATHLEEN (*Hon.* Lady *Plunkett-Ernle-Erle-Drax*) (Charborough Lodge, Wareham), da. of Quintin Chalmers, MD, JP : *m.* 1916, Adm. the Hon. Sir Reginald Aylmer Ranfurly Plunkett-Ernle-Erle-Drax, KCB, DSO, who *d.* 1967, and has issue living (see infra).

COLLATERAL BRANCH LIVING.
Issue of the late Adm. the Hon. Sir Reginald Aylmer Ranfurly PLUNKETT-ERNLE-ERLE-DRAX, KCB, DSO (who assumed by Roy. licence for himself and issue 1916, the additiona surnames and arms of Ernle, Erle and Drax, after that of Plunkett), 2nd son of 17th Baron, *b.* 1880, *d.* 1967 : *m.* 1916, Kathleen (ante), da. of Quintin Chalmers MD, JP :— Henry Walter (Charborough Park, Wareham, Dorset), *b.* 1928 ; Lt.-Cdr. RN (ret.) : *m.* 1957, the Hon. Pamela Rose Weeks, da. of 1st Baron Weeks, and has issue living, Richard Grosvenor, *b.* 1958,—Jeremy Ryton, *b.* 1960,—Charles Ranfurly, *b.* 1962,—Mark Wyndham, *b.* 1967,—Edward Quintin, *b.* 1971.——Kathleen Mary, *b.* 1918 : *m.* 1963, Charles Owen George, of Leys Cottage, Llanblethian, Cowbridge, Glam.——Patricia Doreen, *b.* 1919 : *m.* 1953, Col. Neil Stanley Eustace Maude, RM (ret.), of Westholme House, Pilton, Shepton Mallet, Som., and has issue living, Nicholas John Eustace, *b.* 1953,—Julia Jane, *b.* 1954,—Sarah Anne, *b.* 1956.——Joan Elizabeth, *b.* 1923. ——Mary, *b.* 1925 : *m.* 1948, Robert Gustaf Percy Hollond, of 9, Chelsea Sq., SW3, and has issue living, Thomas Robert, *b.* 1950,—John Ernle, *b.* 1953,—James Nicholas, *b.* 1959,—Eliza Jane, *b.* 1965.

PREDECESSORS.—[1] *Sir* CHRISTOPHER Plunkett, uncle of 1st Baron Killeen [see E. Fingall] ; cr. *Baron of Dunsany* by writ (peerage of Ireland) 1439, and by patent 1461 ; *s.* by his son [2] RICHARD, 2nd Baron ; *s.* by his son [3] JOHN, *K.G.,* 3rd Baron ; *s.* by his son [4] EDWARD, 4th Baron ; *d.* 1521 ; *s.* by his son [5] ROBERT, 5th Baron ; one of the Peers of Parliament held at Dublin 1541 ; *s.* by his son [6] CHRISTOPHER, 6th Baron ; *s.* by his son [7] PATRICK, 7th Baron ; *s.* by his son [8] CHRISTOPHER, 8th Baron ; *s.* by his son [9] PATRICK 9th Baron ; summoned to Parliament 1625 and 1660-6 ; *s.* by his grandson [10] CHRISTOPHER, 10th Baron ; *d.* unmarried ; *s.* by his brother [11] RANDAL, 11th Baron ; for his adherence to James II. was outlawed, but by the treaty of Limerick his estates were restored, but neglecting the forms necessary to re-establish himself in the privileges of the peerage he had not a seat in Parliament ; *d.* 1735 ; *s.* by his son [12] EDWARD, 12th Baron, conformed to the Established Church but took no step to confirm his right to a seat in Parliament ; *d.* 1781 ; *s.* by his son [13] RANDAL, 13th Baron ; claimed and was allowed his seat in Parliament 1791 ; *d.* 1821 ; *s.* by his son [14] EDWARD WADDING, 14th Baron ; *b.* 1773 : *m.* 1st, 1803, Hon. Charlotte Louisa Lawless—who *d.* 1819—dau. of 1st Baron Cloncurry ; 2ndly, 1823, *Hon.* Eliza, dau. of 7th Baron Kinnaird ; *d.* 1848 ; *s.* by his el. son [15] RANDAL EDWARD, 15th Baron ; *d.s.p.* 1852 ; *s.* by his brother [16] EDWARD, 16th Baron, *b.* 1808 ; an Adm. and a Representative Peer : *m.* 1846, the Hon. Anne Constance Dutton, who *d.* 1858 dau. of 2nd Baron Sherborne ; *d.* 1889 ; *s.* by his son [17] JOHN WILLIAM, 17th Baron ; *b.* 1853 ; a Representative Peer for Ireland ; M.P. for Gloucestershire, S., or Thornbury, Div. (*C*) 1886-92 : *m.* 1877, Ernle Elizabeth Louisa Maria Grosvenor, who *d.* 1916 (having assumed by Roy. licence 1906 the surnames of Plunkett-Ernle-Erle-Drax), only child of the late Col. Francis Augustus Plunkett Burton, Coldstream Guards : *d.* 1899 ; *s.* by his el. son [18] EDWARD JOHN MORETON DRAX, 18th Baron ; *b.* 1878 : a Poet, Playwright and Author ; Byron Professor, Athens Univ. 1941, Pres. of Authors' Club 1953-57 : *m.* 1904, Lady Beatrice Child-Villiers, who *d.* 1970, da. of 7th Earl of Jersey ; *d.* 1957 ; *s.* by his only son [19] RANDAL ARTHUR HENRY, 19th Baron and present peer.

DU PARCQ, BARONY OF. (du Parcq.) [Extinct 1949.]

SON LIVING OF LIFE PEER.
Hon. John Renouf (c/o Nat. Westminster Bank, 65, Aldwych, WC2B 4DS), *b.* 1917 ; ed. at Rugby, and at Exeter Coll., Oxford (MA) ; MIEE : *m.* 1940, Elizabeth Anne, da. of the late Evan Skull Poole, and has issue.

DAUGHTERS LIVING OF LIFE PEER.

Hon. Helen: *m.* 1st, 1935 (m. diss. 1948), William Farr; 2ndly, 1948, Alec Andrew Muir, CBE, of Windywalls, Gatehouse-of-Fleet, Kirkcudbrightshire, and has issue.

Hon. Catherine Simonne: *m.* 1939, Leslie Twelvetrees, of 14, Overdale Rd., Leicester, and has issue,

Dupplin, Viscount, son of Earl of Kinnoull.

DURHAM, EARLDOM OF. (Lambton.) [Earl UK 1833, disclaimed 1970.]

ANTONY CLAUD FREDERICK LAMBTON; *b.* July 10th, 1922; *s.* as 6th Earl of Durham, Feb. 4th, 1970; disclaimed his peerages for life Feb. 23rd, 1970; patron of two livings; PPS to Min. of Supply 1954, and to Foreign Sec. 1955-57; an Under-Sec., Min of Defence 1970-73; MP for Berwick-upon-Tweed (C) 1951-73: *m.* 1942, Belinda Bridget, da. of the late Capt. Douglas Holden Blew-Jones, and has issue.

Arms,—Quarterly: 1st sable, a fesse between three lambs passant argent, *Lambton*; 2nd argent, a fesse gules, between three popinjays vert, collared gules, *Lumley*; 3rd argent, an escutcheon sable, within an orle of eight cinquefoils gules, *Hedworth*; 4th argent, three cinquefoils gules, *D'Arcy.* *Crest.*—A ram's head cabossed argent, horns sable. *Supporters*—(borne by Earls of Durham). Two lions, the *dexter* gules, the *sinister* azure, each ducally gorged or, and supporting a flagstaff or, therefrom flowing a banner azure, the dexter charged with a cross patonce and the sinister with a lion passant guardant or.

Seats,—Lambton Castle, Fence Houses, co. Durham; Fenton, Wooler, Northumberland. *Residence,*—Biddick Hall, Lambton Park, Chester-le-Street, co. Durham.

LE JOUR VIENDRA

The day will come.

SON LIVING.

EDWARD RICHARD (*Viscount Lambton*), *b.* Oct. 19th, 1961.

DAUGHTERS LIVING.

Lady Lucinda, *b.* 1943: *m.* 1965, Henry Mark Harrod, el. son of Sir (Henry) Roy Forbes Harrod [see Ffolkes, Bt. colls.]

Lady Beatrix Mary, *b.* 1949.

Lady Rose Diana, *b.* 1952.

Lady Mary Gabrielle Ann, *b.* 1954.

Lady Isabella, *b.* 1958.

HALF-BROTHER LIVING.

Hon. John George, *b.* 1932.

UNCLE LIVING. (*Son of 4th Earl*).

Hon. Claud, *D.S.O.*, *b.* 1888; ed. at Eton; formerly Capt. Yeo. and attached Roy. Scots Fusiliers; European War 1914-18 (wounded, D.S.O.); D.S.O. 1918: *m.* 1916, Olive Isabel Eleanor, who *d.* 1955, dau. of the late William Robert Percival Lockwood [V. Combermere, colls.], and has issue living, Barbara Anne, *b.* 1917. *Residence,*—Westnewton, Wooler, Northumberland.

AUNT LIVING. (*Daughter o 4th Earl*).

Lady Violet (*Countess of Ellesmere*), *b.* 1880; is a DGStJ: *m.* 1905, the 4th Earl of Ellesmere, who *d.* 1944 [see D. Sutherland]. *Residences,*—Stetchworth Park, Newmarket; 26, Hans Cres., SW1.

WIDOW LIVING OF SON OF SECOND EARL.

Lavinia Marion, dau. of the late William Henry Garforth, of The Brow, Malton, Yorkshire [B. Middleton]: *m.* 1912, Brig.-Gen. the Hon. Charles Lambton, D.S.O., who *d.* 1949, and has issue living [see colls., infra]. *Residence,*—Abbey Croft, Mortimer, Berks.

WIDOW LIVING OF FIFTH EARL.

HERMIONE (*Countess of Durham*), (West Marden Hall, Chichester), da. of Sir George Bullough, 1st Bt.: *m.* 1931, as his 2nd wife, The 5th Earl, who *d.* 1970.

COLLATERAL BRANCHES LIVING.

Issue of the late Geoffrey Lambton, Lieut. Coldstream Guards, 2nd son of 4th Bar *b.* 1887, *d.* (killed in action) 1914: *m.* 1914, Dorothy (who *d.* 1965, having, *m.* 2ndly, 1920, Col. Graham Sydney Leventhorpe, DSO, RA), da. of the late Christopher John Leyland, of Haggerston Castle, Northumberland [Cayley, Bt., colls.]:—

Monica Helen, *OBE* (*Baroness Kilmany*), *b.* (posthumous) 1915; late Dist. Administrator, E. Scotland, Women's Vol. Ser.; OBE (Civil) 1946: *m.* 1934, Baron Kilmany (Life Peer). *Residence,*—Kilmany, Cupar, Fife.

Issue of the late Brig.-Gen. the Hon. Charles Lambton, D.S.O., 4th son of 2nd Earl *b.* 1857, *d.* 1949: *m.* 1912, Lavinia Marion (ante), dau. of the late William Henry Garforth, of The Brow, Malton, Yorkshire [B. Middleton]:—

Charles William, *b.* 1921; ed. at Eton; Major (retired) Coldstream Guards: *m.* 1950, Lady Elizabeth Mary Fitzmaurice, dau. of 6th Marquess of Lansdowne, and has issue living, William Henry Charles, *b.* 1951,—Julian Edward, *b.* 1955,—Christopher John, *b.* 1960,—Anne Elizabeth, *b.* 1952. *Residence,* —Mortimer Hill, Mortimer, Reading.——Diana Mary (*Baroness Hailes*), *b.* 1914; is a CStJ: *m.* 1st, 1936, Maj. William Hedworth Williamson, who *d.* (killed in action during European War) 1942 [see Williamson, Bt.]; 2ndly, 1945, the 1st Baron Hailes, who *d.* 1974, when the title became ext. *Residence,*—1, Pelham Pl., SW7.

Grandson of the late Hon. George Lambton (infra):—

Issue of the late John Lambton, Flying Officer R.A.F., *b.* 1909, *d.* (killed on active ser. during European War) 1941: *m.* 1934, Ethel Ruth, only dau. of the late Capt. William Henry Nicholson, R.N.:—

Peter John George, *b.* 1935.

Issue of the late Hon. George Lambton, 5th son of 2nd Earl, *b*. 1860. *d*. 1945 : *m*. 1908, Cecily, who *d*. 1972, da. of the late Sir John (Francis Fortescue) Horner, KCVO:—

Edward George, *b*. 1918 : ed. at Eton ; is Capt. Roy. Horse Guards : *m*. 1949, Anne (RAWNSLEY), dau. of Col. Laurence Lees : *m*. 1959, Pauline Mary, dau. of the late Herbert Coxon Bolton, and formerly wife of Victor Frederick Cochrane Hervey, Earl Jermyn (afterwards 6th Marquess of Bristol), and has issue living, George, *b*. 1962. *Residence*,—Mesnil Warren, Newmarket, Suffolk.——**Ann Katharine Swynford**, *OBE*, *b*. 1912; BA, PhD, DLit, FBA; Prof. of Persian, London Univ.; Press Attaché, British Embassy, Teheran 1939-46; OBE (Civil) 1943.

Issue of the late Hon. Claud Lambton, 7th son of 2nd Earl, *b*. 1865; *d*. 1945: *m*. 1901, Lettice, who *d*. 1945, dau. of Edward Wormald, formerly of 15, Berkeley Square, W. :—

Hedworth, DSO (The Old House, Benhall, Saxmundham), *b*. 1904; is Com. R.N. (ret.); European War 1939-45 (D.S.C.): *m*. 1st, 1935 (marriage dissolved 1963), Mrs. Iris Hewitt; 2ndly, 1963, Olivia, dau. of Reginald Monckton, and widow of Col. D. R. Vachell, M.C., and has issue living, (by 1st marriage) Rosemary Ann, *b*. 1936.——Angela Marjory (*Hon. Mrs. Niall G. Chaplin*) (of Flat 4, 34, Ennismore Gdns., SW7 1AE), *b*. 1902: *m*. 1961, the Hon. Niall Greville Chaplin, who *d*. 1963 [see V. Chaplin].

Grandchildren of the Hon. Claud Lambton (ante):—
Issue of the late D'Arcy Lambton, *b*. 1908, *d*. 1938: *m*. 1933, the Hon. Monica Dorothy Brand (now of Green Close, Copdock, Ipswich), dau. of 3rd Viscount Hampden :—
Michael Charles, *b*. 1934.——Lorna Katherine, *b*. 1938.

Issue of the late Hon. D'Arcy Lambton, 8th son of 2nd Earl, *b*. 1866, *d*. 1954: *m*. 1888, Florence Ethel (who *d*. 1941, and from whom he had obtained a divorce 1899), dau. of A. Sproule, formerly of Goulbourn, N.S. Wales :—
Eileen, MBE, *b*. 1891; a JP for Surrey; MBE (Civil) 1948: *m*. 1st, 1918, Alfred Trevor Barker, who *d*. 1942, and from whom she obtained a divorce 1923; 2ndly, 1931, Charles Leach, who *d*. 1952. *Residence*,—Burpham Court House, Guildford, Surrey.

PREDECESSORS.—[1] *Rt. Hon. Sir* JOHN GEORGE Lambton, *G.C.B.*; M.P. for co. Durham 1813-28, Ambassador to Court of Russia, Lord Privy Seal 1830-33, and Gov.-Gen. of British N. America, &c.; cr. *Baron Durham* (peerage of United Kingdom) 1828, and *Viscount Lambton* and *Earl of Durham* 1833; *d*. 1840; *s*. by his son [2] GEORGE FREDERICK D'ARCY, 2nd Earl; *b*. 1828; Lord-Lieut. of co. Durham; *m*. 1854, Lady Beatrix Frances Hamilton, dau. of 1st Duke of Abercorn; *d*. 1879; *s*. by his son [3] *Rt. Hon.* JOHN GEORGE, *K.G.*, *G.C.V.O.*, 3rd Earl; *b*. 1855; bore Queen Consort's Ivory Rod with Dove at Coronation of King George V. 1911; was Lord High Steward to H.M. during visit to India 1911-12: *m*. 1882, Ethel Elizabeth Louisa, who *d*. 1931, dau. of the late Henry Beilby William Milner; *d*. 1928; *s*. by his twin brother [4] FREDERICK WILLIAM, 4th Earl, *b*. 1855; sat as M.P. for Durham, S. (*L*) 1880-85, and for Durham co., S.-E. Div. (*LU*) 1900-1910: *m*. 1879, Beatrix, who *d*. 1937, dau. of John Bulteel, of Pamflete, Ivybridge; *d*. 1929; *s*. by his el. son [5] JOHN FREDERICK, 5th Earl, *b*. 1884: *m*. 1st, 1919, Diana Mary, who *d*. 1924, da. of the late Granville Frederick Farquhar [Farquhar, Bt.]; 2ndly, 1931, Hermione, da. of Sir George Bullough, 1st Bt.; *d*. 1970; *s*. by his son [6], ANTONY CLAUD FREDERICK, 6th Earl, and Viscount Lambton and Baron Durham until he disclaimed his peerages 1970.

DURHAM, LORD BISHOP OF. (Habgood.)

Rt. Rev. JOHN STAPYLTON HABGOOD, son of Lt.-Col. Arthur Henry Habgood, DSO, MB, BCh [V. Chetwynd, colls.]; *b*. June 23rd, 1927; ed. at Eton, King's Coll., Camb., (MA. PhD, Fellow 1952-55) and Cuddesdon Coll., Oxford; Demonstrator in Pharmacology, Camb. 1950-53; Curate of St. Mary Abbots, Kensington 1954-56; Vice-Prin. of Westcott House, Camb., 1956-62, Examining Chap. to Bishop of Worcester, 1960-73 and to Bishop of Edinburgh 1962-67, R. of St. John's, Jedburgh, 1962-67, and Prin. of Queen's Coll., Birmingham, 1967-73; Hon. Canon of Birmingham Cathedral 1971-73; consecrated 91st Bishop of Durham 1973; author of "Religion and Science" 1964: *m*. 1961, Rosalie Mary Anne, da. of Edward Lansdown Boston, of Deeside House, Neston, Cheshire.

Patron of one hundred and one livings, the Archdeaconries of Durham and Auckland, and all the Canonries in his Cathedral.

This see was first established at Holy Island in 635 ; but on the invasion of the Danes it was removed to Chester-le-Street, where it continued for over 200 years, when it was finally (995) fixed at Durham.

𝔈piscopal 𝔖ignature—"John Dunelm."
ARMS OF THE SEE.—Azure: a cross or, between four lions rampant argent.
Residence—Auckland Castle, Bishop Auckland.

DUVEEN, BARONY OF. (Duveen.) [Extinct 1939.]
DAUGHTER LIVING OF FIRST BARON.

Hon. Dorothy: *m*. 1st, 1931, Lieut.-Com. William Francis Cuthbert Garthwaite, D.S.C., R.N.V.R. (afterwards 2nd Bt.), from whom she obtained a divorce 1937; 2ndly, 1938, Bryan Hartopp Burns FRCS. *Residence*,—6, Chesterfield Hill, W1.

DYNEVOR, BARON. (Rhys.) [Baron G.B. 1780.]

Secret and bold.

RICHARD CHARLES URYAN RHYS,
9th Baron; *b.* June 19th, 1935; *s.* 1962
ed. at Eton, and at Magdalene Coll.,
Camb.: *m.* 1959, Lucy Catherine King,
only dau. of Sir John Knewstub
Maurice Rothenstein, C.B.E., and has
issue.

Arms,—Argent, a chevron between three ravens
sable. Crest.—A raven sable. Supporters—
Dexter, a griffin per fesse or and argent, wings
addorsed and inverted, tail between the legs;
sinister, a talbot argent, collared flory counterflory
gules, ears ermine, and charged on the shoulder
with a trefoil slipped vert.
Residence,—18, Brook Green, W6.

SON LIVING.
Hon. HUGO GRIFFITH URYAN, *b.* Nov. 19th,
1966.

DAUGHTERS LIVING.
Hon. Miranda Jane Caroline, *b.* 1960.
Hon. Sarah Sophia Rhiannon, *b.* 1963
Hon. Susannah Mair Elizabeth, *b.* 1964.

UNCLE LIVING. (*Son of 7th Baron.*)
Hon. David Reginald (of Southwick Court,
Trowbridge, Wilts.; Guards' Club), *b.* 1907;
ed. at Eton: late Capt. Welsh Guards; 1939-45 War (wounded): *m.* 1st, 1933 (m. diss.
1963), Lady Anne Maud Wellesley, only da. of 5th Duke of Wellington; 2ndly, 1963, Sheila Mary
d'Ambrumenil, only da. of the late D. J. Phillips, of Popley Fields, Basingstoke, and has issue living,
(by 1st m.) Llewelyn Arthur (Westaways, Greenham Common, Newbury, Berks.), *b.* 1935: *m.* 1961,
Rosemary Martha Ann, el. da. of the Rev. Canon Robert Victor Sellers, of Burnham-on-Sea, Somerset, and has issue living, Robert David Arthur *b.* 1963, Julian Nicholas James *b.* 1966, Fiona Martha
Alison *b.* 1962,—Elizabeth Maud, *b.* 1937: *m.* 1966, Peter Matthew Doran, Le Bourg, Castel Parish,
Guernsey,—(by 2nd m.) George Dayfdd, *b.* 1965.

AUNT LIVING. (*Daughter of 7th Baron.*)
Hon. Imogen Alice (*Viscountess Hampden*) (Trevor House, Glynde, Lewes), *b.* 1903: *m.* 1936, the
5th Viscount Hampden.

WIDOW LIVING OF SON OF SEVENTH BARON.
Diana Sloane (Beechwood, Barley, Hants.), da. of Maj. Roger Cyril Hans Sloane Stanley: *m.* 1931
Capt. the Hon. Elwyn Villiers Rhys, who *d.* 1966, and has issue living [see colls, infra].

WIDOW LIVING OF EIGHTH BARON.
HOPE MARY WOODBINE (SOAMES) (*Hope, Baroness Dynevor*) (of 16, Upper Brook St., W.1), dau. of
the late Charles Woodbine Parish [L. Torphichen]: *m.* 1934, the 8th Baron, who *d.* 1962.

COLLATERAL BRANCHES LIVING.
Issue of the late Capt the Hon. Elwyn Villiers Rhys, 2nd son of 7th Baron, *b.* 1900,
d. 1966: *m.* 1931, Diana Sloane (ante), da. of Maj. Roger Cyril Hans Sloane
Stanley:—
Daphne Margaret, *b.* 1933: *m.* 1956, Maurice Brain, of Upper Youngs Farm, Whiteparish, Salisbury,
and has issue living, Graham Stephen Maurice, *b.* 1957,—Patrick John Elwyn, *b.* 1959.

Issue of the late Rev. the Hon. William Talbot Rice, 3rd son of 5th Baron; *b.*
1861, *d.* 1945 : *m.* 1887, Marian, who *d.* 1950, dau. of Henry Edmund Gurney.
formerly of Nutwood. Reigate, Surrey :—
Mervyn Gurney Talbot, *b.* 1899; ed. at Charterhouse, and Ch. Ch. Oxford: *m.*, 1st, 1929, Eleanor
Butler Adair, who *d.* 1965, da. of Andrew Williamson, of 6, Wetherby Gdns., SW; 2ndly, 1969,
Esther Lynette Sutherland, da. of Maj. James Reay Sutherland Mackay, of Doune, Perthshire, and
widow of Ronald David Stewart-Brown, QC, and has issue living, (by 1st m.) Andrew Gurney Talbot
(Coombe House, Wheatley, Oxon.), *b.* 1930; ed. at Eton, and at Worcester Coll., Oxford: *m.* 1957,
Helen Lalage (Gay), only da. of Charles Buchanan, of Chesterhill, Newport-on-Tay, Fife, and has
issue living, Richard Bruce *b.* 1957, Jonathan William Gurney *b.* 1961, Julia Margaret *b.* 1959,
Catherine Helen *b.* 1964,—David Mervyn Talbot (19, Ovington Gdns., SW3), *b.* 1935: ed. at Charterhouse, and at Worcester Coll., Oxford,—Nigel Talbot (Beech House, Mayfield Rd., Oxford), *b.* 1938;
ed. at Charterhouse, and Ch. Ch., Oxford (MA, Dip-Ed.): *m.* 1968, Joanna, da. of Air Commodore
Frederick John Manning, CB, CBE, of Myrtle Cottage, Eynsham, Oxford, and has issue living,
Sarah Kate *b.* 1969, Caroline Emma *b.* 1971, Rebecca Mary *b.* 1973,—Margaret Adair Talbot, *b.* 1932:
m. 1956, the Rev. Edward George Humphrey Saunders, and has issue living, Hilary Margaret
b. 1959. *Residence,*—28, East St. Abingdon, Berks.——Winifred Marian, *b.* 1888:
m. 1918, the Rt. Rev. Bishop George Alexander Chambers, OBD, DD, who *d.* 1963, and has issue
living, Talbot Alexander, *b.* 1921,—Roland George, *b.* 1923.——Katheryn Cecil, *b.* 1893. *Residence,*
—Court Cottage, Southmoor, Abingdon, Berks.——Muryell Gladys, *b.* 1895: *m.* 1817, Prof. Patrick
Alfred Buxton, CMG, FRS, MRCS, LRCP, who *d.* 1955 [see Buxton, Bt., colls.]. *Residence,*—
Saunders Close, Bledlow, Aylesbury, Bucks.——Victoria May *b.* 1897.——Lettice Evelyn, *b.* 1901:
m. 1960, Robert Mathew Hale. *Residence,*—Herons Crest, Cross Lanes, Guildford, Surrey.

Grandchildren of the late Capt. Henry Charles Talbot Rice, yr. son of the late Rev.
the Hon. Henry Rice, brother of 5th Baron:—
Issue of the late Major Harry Talbot Rice, late Welsh Guards, *b.* 1889, *d.* 1948: *m.* 1927,
the Hon. Blanche Marion Devereux (now of Castle Weir, Lyonshall, Herefordshire), dau.
of the 17th Viscount Hereford :—
David Arthur Talbot, *b.* 1931; ed. at Eton, and at Ch. Ch., Oxford; Capt. Welsh Guards (Reserve):
m. 1st, 1957 (marriage dissolved 1961), Annabella Frances Serena, dau. of the late Major Cyril
Augustus Drummond [see P. Perth, colls.]; 2ndly, 1961, Sylvia Dorothea, dau. of P. B. Metaxas,
and has issue living, (by 2nd m.) Robert Harry Talbot, *b.* 1963,—Alexander Thomas Talbot, *b.* 1969,
—Victoria Penelope Helen Talbot, *b.* 1961. *Residence,*—47, Argyll Rd., W8. *Clubs,*—Carlton,
Guards'.
Issue of the late Lt.-Col. David Talbot Rice, CBE, TD, *b.* 1903, *d.* 1972: *m.* 1927, Tamara (The
Pigeon House, Fossebridge, Glos.), adopted da. of Boris Abelson, of Paris:—
Nicholas Charles Talbot (Pigeon House, Coln Rogers, Glos., GL54 3LB; Farmers' and Pratt's Clubs),
b. 1944; ed. at Eton, and Ch. Ch., Oxford (BA): *m.* 1973, Jocelyn Mary, da. of Robin Higgens, and
has issue living, David Henry, *b.* 1975,—Sophia Elizabeth, *b.* 1974.——Elizabeth Roussoudana
Talbot, *b.* 1931; ed. at Edinburgh Univ. (MA).——Nina Violet Tamara Talbot, *b.* 1941: *m.* 1966,
Hugh Bredin, of 115, Studdridge St., SW6.

PREDECESSORS.—[1] WILLIAM Talbot, 1st *Earl Talbot* (see E. Shrewsbury) ; cr, *Baron Dinevor*, of Dinevor [usually spelt Dynevor] (peerage of Great Britain) 1780, with remainder to his only dau. and the heirs male of her body; *d.* 1782; *s.* by his dau. [2] *Lady* CECIL, wife of the Rt. Hon. George Rice, P.C., M.P. (10th in descent from Sir Rhys ap Thomas, K.G., who joined the Earl of Richmond, later Henry VII, after his landing and assisted him at Bosworth); assumed the surname of de Cardonnell only by Roy. licence 1787; *d.* 1793; *s.* by her son [3] GEORGE TALBOT, 3rd Baron; assumed the surname of de Cardonnell by Roy. licence 1793, and resumed the name of Rice by Roy. licence 1817; Lord-Lieut. of Carmarthenshire; *d.* 1852; *s.* by his son [4] GEORGE RICE, 4th Baron; assumed the additional surname of Trevor by Roy. licence 1824; *d.* 1869; *s.* by his kinsman [5] *Rev.* FRANCIS WILLIAM, 5th Baron, 2nd son of the Very Rev. the Hon. Edward Rice, 2nd son of Baroness Dynevor; *b.* 1804; V. of Fairford; *d.* 1878; *s.* by his son [6] ARTHUR DE CARDONNEL, 6th Baron; *b.* 1836: *m.* 1869, Selina, who *d.* 1889, dau. of the late Hon. Arthur Lascelles; *d.* 1911; *s.* by his son [7] WALTER FITZ-URYAN, 7th Baron, *b.* 1873; was Assist. Sec. to Sec. of State for India 1899-1903, an Assist. Private Sec. to First Lord of the Admiralty 1903-5, M.P. for Brighton (*C*) 1910-11, a Co. Councillor for Carmarthenshire 1919-35, and Lord Lieut. for Carmarthenshire 1928-49; re-assumed by Roy. licence 1916 for himself and his issue the surname of Rhys in lieu of Rice: *m.* 1898, Lady Margaret Child-Villiers, who *d.* 1959, el. dau. of 7th Earl of Jersey; *d.* 1956; *s.* by his el. son [8] CHARLES ARTHUR URYAN, C.B.E., M.C., 8th Baron; *b.* 1899; Capt. Gren. Guards; MP for Romford (*C*) 1923-29, and Guildford 1931-35; PPS to Financial Sec. to War Office 1924-26, to Under-Sec. of State for the Colonies 1926-27, and to Prime Min. 1927-29; 1939-45 War; Pres. of Univ. Coll. of S. Wales and Monmouth 1960-62: *m.* 1934, Hope Mary Woodbine Soames, dau. of the late Charles Woodbine Parish; *d.* 1962; *s.* by his only son [9] RICHARD CHARLES URYAN, 9th Baron, and present peer.

DYSART, COUNTESS OF. (Greaves.) [Earl S. 1643.]

ROSAMUND AGNES GREAVES, *Countess of Dysart*, *b.* Feb. 15th 1914; *s.* 1975.

Arms,—Azure, an Imperial Crown proper between three mullets argent within a double tressure flory counterflory or. **Supporters,**—Two lions gules collared azure, each collar charged with three mullets argent.

Residence,—Barham House, Higher Fyldon, South Molton, Devon.

SISTER LIVING.

Lady KATHERINE, *b.* June 1st, 1918: *m.* 1941, Lieut.-Col. John Peter Grant of Rothiemurchus, MBE, Lovat Scouts, and has issue living, John Peter, *b.* 1946; ed. at Gordonstoun: *m.* 1971, Wendy Philippa, da. of John Wybergh Chance, of Llanvapley Court, Mon., and has issue living, Louise, *b.* 1975,—Jane Margery, *b.* 1943: *m.* 1965, Andrew Robert Fowell Buxton, of Bentley Park, Ipswich [see Buxton, Bt., colls.]. *Residence*,— Rothiemurchus, Aviemore, Inverness-shire.

COLLATERAL BRANCHES LIVING.

Descendants in the male line of William Tollemache Lord Huntingtower, who was cr. a Bt. 1793, are also in remainder to this Baronetcy.

Issue of the late Lady Mary Greaves, youngest da. of the late Wenefryde Agatha, Countess of Dysart, *b.* 1921, *d.* 1955: *m.* 1942, Capt. Bernard Albert Blanger, Sec. French Legation, Lisbon, who *d.* 1950:—
Brigitte, *b.* 1943: *m.* 1st, 1964 (m. diss. 1967), J. Fotheringham; 2ndly, 1969, Pavlos Athanasacopoulos, of 38, Westbourne Terr., W2.——Beatrice Wenefryde, *b.* 1945.

Grandchildren of the late Lady Agatha Manners Tollemache (sister of 9th Earl) who *d.* 1941, having *m.* 1882, the 3rd Lord Westbury, who *d.* 1930 [see that title].

Grandchildren of the late Caroline Tollemache (only dau. of the late Felix Thomas Tollemache, 2nd son of William Lord Huntingtower, el. son of Louisa Countess of Dysart), who *d.* 1867, having *m.* 1853, as his 1st wife, the Rev. Ralph William Lionel Tollemache-Tollemache (infra):—
Issue of the late Sir Lyonel Felix Carteret Eugene Tollemache, 4th Bt., *b.* 1854, *d.* 1952 [see "BARONETAGE"].

Granddaughter of the late Arthur Lionel Tollemache, son of the late Hon. Arthur Cæsar Tollemache, 3rd son of William, Lord Huntingtower (ante):—
Issue of the late Arthur Frederick Churchill Tollemache, *b.* 1860, *d.* 1923: *m.* 1888. Susan Eleanor, who *d.* 1918, dau. of Capt. James Carter Campbell, R.N. [Vincent, Bt., colls.]:—
Hermione Edith Agnes (Owls Combe, Porlock Weir, Som.), *b.* 1890: *m.* 1918, Guy Edward Pelham-Clinton, M.C., late R.E., who *d.* 1934 [see D. Newcastle, colls.].

Grandson of the late Emily Katherine, da. of Arthur Lionel Tollemache (ante), *b.* 1858, *d.* 1940: *m.* 1888, George Ralph Fitz Roy Cole, who *d.* 1910:—
Issue of the late Derek Arthur Stephen Fitz Roy Cole, MC, *b.* 1895, *d.* 1971: *m.* 1918, Joan Shirley, who *d.* 1971, da. of Walter Octavius Hudson:—
John Derek, (Lynam Court, Rock, nr. Wadebridge, Cornwall), *b.* 1920: *m.* 1st, 1942, (m. diss. 1959), Beryl Portia Black; 2ndly, 1960, Penelope Ann Hyde-Hartley, and has issue living (by 1st m.) Nigel John, *b.* 1943,—Clive Derek, *b.* 1944,—Nicholas Peter, *b.* 1949,—(by 2nd m.) Jeremy Fitz Roy, *b.* 1961,—Alicia Jane, *b.* 1962.

Descendants of the late Melanie Sophia Tollemache (2nd dau. of the late Hon. Arthur Caesar Tollemache, 3rd son of William Lord Huntingtower (ante) *b.* 1823, *d.* 1894, having *m.* 1849, Raymond Louis Abrial.

Descendants of the late Laura Tollemache (4th dau. of the late Hon. Arthur Caesar Tollemache [ante], *b.* 1830, *d.* 1908, having *m.* 1859, Albert, Comte de Lastic St. Jal.

Grandchildren of the late Rev. Ralph William Lionel TOLLEMACHE-TOLLEMACHE, son of Rev. the Hon. Hugh Francis Tollemache, 4th son of William, Lord Huntingtower (ante):—
Issue of the late Sir Lyonel Felix Carteret Eugene Tollemache, 4th Bt. *b.* 1854, *d.* 1952 (ante).

Issue of the late Lyulph Ydwallo Odin Nestor Egbert Lyonel Toedmag Hugh Erchenwyne
Saxon Esa Cromwell Orma Nevill Dysart Plantagenet Tollemache-Tollemache *b.* 1876,
d. 1961 : *m.* 1st, 1897, Winifred Frances, who *d.* 1955, dau. of the late Thomas Goldsbrough
Anderson, of Tauranga, New Zealand ; 2ndly. 1957, Kathleen (of Benteleigh, Otumoetai,
Tauranga, New Zealand), dau. of Michael Hinge, of Northolt, Middlesex, and widow of
Robert William Alexander Geoffrey Gordon, of Huia, New Zealand:—

By 1st m.), Lyulph Thomas, *b.* 1899: *m.* 1st, 1924 (m. diss. 1943), Mavis, da. of the late Rev. Charles
Tuke, of Ellerslie, New Zealand; 2ndly, 1946, his cousin, Phylis Agnes Barham, da. of the late Major
Frederick Pitcairn Nunneley, OBE, MD (infra), and has issue living, (by 1st m.) Lyulph Hugh Tuke
(4, Roland Hill, Glen Eden, Auckland, 7, NZ), *b.* 1933; ed. at Wanganui Collegiate Sch.; MCSP,
London: *m.* 1960, Nadja, el. da. of U. Victor Benziger (infra), and has issue living, Ralph Victor
Hugh Thomas *b.* 1968, Damon Leo *b.* 1969, Nigel Robert Bentley *b.* 1972, Rachel Eva *b.* 1961, Amanda
Beatrice *b.* 1963, Melanie Ruth *b.* 1964, Vanessa Mavis (twin) *b.* 1964, Althea Phyllis Jessica *b.*
1967,—Diana Rosemary, *b.* 1928; ed. at NZ Univ. (BA); a JP, Croydon: *m.* 1949, Saiyad Zarbaft
Shah, of Shalimar, 24, Oakfield Rd., West Croydon, Surrey, and has issue living, Saiyad
Mubarak *b.* 1959, Layla Irene Zarbaft *b.* (Dec.) 1949; ed. at Univ. of Newcastle upon Tyne (BA
Arch. Studies): *m.* 1970, Terry Dawson, BSc Civil Eng., of Jesmond, Newcastle upon Tyne, Shireen
Haseena *b.* 1952. *Residence,*—Toedmag Cottage, The Parade, Bucklands Beach, Auckland, NZ.—
Adrian Francis, *b.* 1903: *m.* 1938, Una Frances (Peggy), da. of Lionel Edward Mackenzie, of Perth,
W. Australia, and has issue living, John Jeffrey, *b.* 1941,—Peter Clive, *b.* 1948,—Joan, *b.* 1944.—
Saxon George (64, Churchill St., Judea, Tauranga, NZ), *b.* 1904: *m.* 1933, Ruth Bell, da. of Frederick
George Wayne, of Parawai, Thames, NZ, and has issue living, John Saxon Manners *b.* 1943: *m.* 1971,
Catherine Mary, da. of Seymour Jack, and has issue living, Mark Seymour Manners *b.* 1975,—
Elizabeth Mary, *b.* 1936: *m.* 1966, Maurice John Arthur Fuller, MSc, of 113, Sunrise Av., Mairangi
Bay, Auckland, NZ, and has issue living, Michael Arthur *b.* 1968, Katherine Ruth *b.* 1969, Louisa
Elizabeth *b.* 1974,—Suzannah Jane *b.* 1940: *m.* 1962, John Brian Miller, PhD, ME, of 11, Chaucer
Court, Ewelme, Oxford and has issue living, Hugh Benjamin Tollemache *b.* 1965, Jane Elizabeth *b.*
1963.——Lyonel Dysart (84, Barrack Rd., Mt. Wellington, Auck., NZ), *b.* 1908: *m.* 1942, Rita Janet
Isabel Rowley, of Auck., and has issue living, Roland Lionel (23, Matangi Rd., Mt. Wellington, Auck,
NZ), *b.* 1948: *m.* 1970, Sara Norris, of Auckland, qnd has issue living, Peter Michael Dysart *b.* 1973,—
Pamela Rita, *b.* 1952.——Archibald Douglas (104, Landscape Rd., Mt. Eden, Auck., NZ), *b.* 1910:
m. 1935, Edna, da. of the late F. C. Willis, of Napier, NZ, and has issue living, Janet Winifred,
b. 1936: *m.* 1957, William Winston Lewins, of 75, Belfast St., Hillsborough, Auckland, NZ, and
has issue living, Robyn Ann *b.* 1963, Denise Gay, *b.* 1965,—Yvonne Dorothy, *b.* 1938: *m.* 1961, John
Walker Robinson, of 63, Peary Rd., Mt. Eden, Auckland, NZ, and has issue living, Tania Anne
b. 1962, Vicki Jan *b.* 1964, Angela Patricia *b.* 1967.——James de Orellana *b.* 1916.——Winifred
Dora, *b.* 1898: *m.* 1926, Laurence Galwey Walker, and has issue living, Peter Robert Tollemache
(2, Arthur St., Oamaru, NZ), *b.* 1928; BA, LLM: *m.* 1961, Yvonne Isabelle, da. of John James
Fleming, of Paeroa, NZ, and has issue living, Robert James Tollemache *b.* 1963, Johnathan William
Lawrence *b.* 1969, Elizabeth Jane Stewart *b.* 1965, Catherine Frances Tollemache *b.* 1966,—Richard
Henry Tollemache, *b.* 1935; B. Civil Eng.: *m.* 1965, Yvonne, da. of Percival Lawrence Le Marquand,
of Timaru, NZ, and has issue living, John Henry *b.* 1968, Caroline Mary *b.* 1966,—Michael Lawrence
Galwey, *b.* 1938; BSc.: *m.* 1961, Kathleen Rosemary, da. of John Norris Buckland of Little River,
Banks Peninsula, NZ, and has issue living, Peter Lawrence Galwey *b.* 1962, Andrew John Morris
b. 1964, Christopher Michael Tollemache *b.* 1966, Michelle Kathleen *b.* 1961, Fiona Marianne *b.* 1968,
—Lyonella Mary Tollemache, *b.* 1933: *m.* 1963, Henry Lynn Thetford, of 403, Harewood Rd.,
Christchurch 5, NZ, and has issue living, John Henry *b.* 1966, David *b.* 1968,—Helen Dora Tollemache, *b.* 1937: *m.* 1959, Colin Pringle Robertson, of Wendonside, No. 7 RD, Gore, NZ, and has
issue living, Colin Laurence *b.* 1961, Maryann Madeline *b.* 1960, Sarah Jane *b.* 1964, Jayne Winifred
b. 1966, Rachel Helen *b.* 1971,——Celia Kathrine Mabel Tollemache (46, McCorveys Rd., Whakatane, NZ), *b.* 1901: *m.* 1935, Charles Tennant Smith, who *d.* 1971, and has issue living, Guthrie
Tennant, *b.* 1935: *m.* 1955, Louise Florence, da. of Clement Auguste Le Lièvre, and has issue living,
Denys Guthrie *b.* 1957, Gregory Tennant *b.* 1963, Marie Terese Rawhiti *b.* 1955, Juliet Louise *b.* 1956.
—— Ethel Mary, *b.* 1906.——Vivian Rosamond, *b.* 1913: *m.* 1934, the Rev. Harold Graham Titter-
ton, V. of St. John the Baptist, of 47, Jocelyn St., Te Puke, NZ, and has issue living, Graham Richard
(12, Maunganui Rd., Mt. Maunganui, NZ) *b.* 1947: *m.* 1974, Gaylene, da. of James Cooper, of Kati
Kati, NZ.—Jennifer Graham, *b.* 1937: *m.* 1964, John Yeeles, of 820, Idylwood Drive SW, NW
Issaquah, Wash., 98027, USA, and has issue living, Christopher John *b.* 1964, Peter Graham *b.* 1967,
Andrew Scott *b.* 1971.——Ruth Lorraine *b.* 1915: *m.* 1944, Ivan Edward Salter Bartlett, of Bente-
leigh, 409, Otumoetai Rd., Tauranga, NZ, and has issue living, Timothy John, *b.* 1951.——Jacqueline
Jane, *b.* 1949: *m.* 1971, John Michael Cochrane Piper, of 481, Gt. King St., Dunedin, NZ.

Issue of the late Capt. Leo [Quintus Tollemache-Tollemache] de Orellana [Plantagenet
Tollemache, *b.* 1879, *d.* (killed in action) 1914 (names in brackets were renounced by deed
poll 1908): *m.* 1906, Jessie Winifred, who *d.* 1967, da. of the late Charles Bryant, of Highbury New Park, N.:—

Rev. Frederick, *b.* 1910; ed. at Keble Coll., Oxford (B.A. 1931); is in Holy Orders of Church of Rome.
Residence.—Instituto S. Francesco Saverio, via del Platano, 4, Livorno, Italy.——*Rev.* Robert, *T.D.*,
b. 1914, sd. at St. Edmund's Coll., Ware, Herts ; is in Holy Orders of Church of Rome, and Parish
Priest of St. Augustine's, Hoddesdon; 1939-45 War in Iceland, and as Senior Catholic Chap. in
Scotland. *Residence,*—St. Augustine's, Hoddesdon, Herts.——Eva, *b.* 1908: *m.* 1935, U. Victor
Benziger, who *d.* 1962, and has issue living, Roderich Rupert Victor Leo, *b.* 1938; ed. at Queen's
Coll., Oxford.—Carl Dietrich Nicholaus Meinrad, *b.* 1939: *m.* 1969, Marjorie Anna Mercedes Webb,
and has issue living, Hugh Rafe de Orellana *b.* 1971,—Stanislaus Quintus Rudolph, *b.* 1945,—Nadja,
b. 1936; ed. at Somerville Coll., Oxford (MA); Bar. Middle Temple 1960: *m.* 1960, Lyulph Hugh
Tuke Tollemache-Tollemache (ante),—Dorothea Rosemary, *b.* 1941: *m.* 1968, Nirmal Kumar
Mazumdar, MS, FRCS, of 29, Ashdown Drive, Wordsley, Stourbridge, Worcs., and has issue living,
Abhigit Victor *b.* 1969, Anita Nadja *b.* 1968, Rosita *b.* 1971. *Residence,*—Cabbages, Gt. Sampford,
Saffron Walden, Essex.

Issue of the late Capt. Leone Sextus Denys Oswolf Fraudati filius Tollemache-Tollemache *d.*
Orellana Plantagenet Tollemache, Leicestershire Regt. *b.* 1884, *d.* (while on active ser-
during European War) 1917: *m.* 1914, Kathleen Mary, who *d.* 1915, dau. of Capt. J. Mills,
formerly 3rd Dragoon Guards, of Acomb Hall, York :—

Denys Herbert George (76, The Mint, Rye, Sussex), *b.* 1915; ed. at Magdalene Coll., Camb. (BA);
late Fl.-Lt. RAF (Reserve): *m.* 1939 (m. diss. 1948), Eileen Frances Mary, da. of the late Owen
Phelim O'Conor, The O'Conor Don, and has issue living, Peter Denys, *b.* 1940,—Nicholas John
b. 1943,—Stephen Patrick, *b.* 1946,—Susan Frances, *b.* 1939,—Linda Mary, *b.* 1945.

Issue of the late Maj. Lyonulph Cospatrick Bruce Berkeley Jermyn Tullibardine Petersham
de Orellana Dysart Plantagenet Tollemache-Tollemache, *b.* 1892, *d.* 1966: *m.* 1914, Lilian
May, who *d.* 1969, da. of the late Ernest T. W. Pearse, Govt. Agent, Kamloops, BC,
Canada:—

Miles de Orellana, *b.* 1918; Lt. RNVR: *m.* 1st, 1942, Diana Muriel, da. of C. C. Hatry; 2ndly, 19—,
Margaret, el. da. of the late Henry Williams, of Llwyn Gern, Pontardulais; 3rdly, 1949, Joan Doreen,
da. of the late G. Saxon, Civil Ser., and has issue living, (by 3rd m.) Timothy Miles Saxon, *b.* 1950,—
Bruce Robert Saxon, *b.* 1951,—Alasdair Murray Saxon, *b.* 1953,—Iain Stuart William Saxon, *b.*
1961,—Elspeth Mary Joan, *b.* 1956.

Issue of the late Lyonesse Matilda Dora Ida Agnes Ernestine Curxon Paulet Wilbraham
Joyce Eugenie Bentley Saxonia Dysart Plantagenet Tollemache, *b.* 1874, *d.* 1944 : *m.* 1897,
Francis William Astley Cooper, who *d.* 1945 :—

See Cooper, Bt., cr. 1821, colls.

Issue of the late Lyona Decima Veronica Esyth Undine Cyssa Hylda Rowena Viola Adele
Thyra Ursula Ysabel Blanche Lelias Dysart Plantagenet Tollemache, *b.* 1878, *d.* 1962:
m. 1909, Major Charles Cecil Stone, late Berks. Yeo., who *d.* 1951:—

Lyonel Frances Tollemache (1122, Nashville Av., New Orleans, La., USA. *Club*,—St. James'), *b*. 1909;
Capt. late Coldstream Guards: *m*. 1st, 1943 (m. diss. 1951), Mathilde, da. of the late G. Henry A.
Thomas of New Orleans, USA; 2ndly 1952 (m. diss. 1966), Marie Lod (MONTELEONE), da. of the
late Frank Marion Attaway, of New Orleans, USA; 3rdly, 1972, Mrs. Christine Claire McRoberts
da. of the late Petrus Marthoud, of Lyons, France and has issue living, (by 1st m.) Michael Tollemache (7806, Jeaunette St., New Orleans, La., USA 70118), *b*. 1949, Mathilde Thomas, *b*. 1945:
m. 1967, Prieur James Leary, of 174, Country Club Drive, New Orleans, La, USA, 70124, and has
issue living, Prieur James *b*. 1968, Ashley Baldwin *b*. 1973, Mathilde Deslonde *b*. 1971.
Issue of the late Lyonella Fredegunda Outhberga Ethelawytha Ideth Ysabel Grace Monica
de Orellana Plantagenet Tollemache-Tollemache, *b*. 1889 *d*. 1959: *m*. 1906, Major
Frederick Pitcairn Nunneley, O.B.E., M.D. (Oxon), who *d*. 1922, formerly Army Med. Ser.:—
Lyonella Joan Tollemache, *b*. 1907: *m*. 1935, Ernest Robin Vladimir Kindersley, of Old Cottage
Mayfield, Sussex, and has issue living, Patricia Dora Mary, *b*. 1936: *m*. 1966, John Pearman Spencer-
Wood, of Coromandel, Salters Green, Mayfield, Sussex, and has issue living, Alexandra Carolina,
b. 1967.——Phyllis Agnes Barham, *b*. 1909: *m*. 1946, as his second wife, her cousin, Lyulph Thomas
Tollemache-Tollemache (ante).
    Issue of the late Lyonetta Edith Regina Valentine Myra Polwarth Avelina Philippa Violantha
    de Orellana Plantagenet Tollemache, *b*. 1887, *d*. 1951 : *m*. 1909, Adolph Paul Oppé, C.B.,
    who *d*. 1957 :—
Denys Lyonel Tollemache, *M.B.E.*, *b*. 1913 : Major Roy. Berks Regt. (T.A.); European War 1939-45
in France, India, and Burma (M.B.E.) ; M.B.E. (Mil.) 1945 : *m*. 1949, Jean Mary, dau. of the late
Charles Struthers White Ogilvie, of Delvine Murthly, Perthshire, and has issue living, John Simon
Tollemache, *b*. 1951,—Lucy Valentine Mary, *b*. 1950,—Charlotte Mary Clare, *b*. 1954,—Mary
Josephine, *b*. 1956. *Residence*,—Manor Farm, Newnham, Basingstoke.——Armide Lyonesse
Tollemache (Bartholomews, Corfe Castle, Wareham, Dorset), *b*. 1910.

    Granddaughter of Hugh Ernest Tollemache, el. son of the Rev. Ernest Celestine
    Tollemache (infra):—
    Issue of the late Maj. John Ernest Tollemache, *b*. 1898, *d*. 1969: *m*. 1921, Violet Edith Gertrude
    (Cherry Tree Cottage, Aveley Lane, Farnham, Surrey), da. of the late W. Rae Sands:—
Lyona Violet Anne Tollemache, *b*. 1929: *m*. 1950, Lt.-Cdr. Richard Milford Power Carne, RN, of
Tresahor Vean, Constantine, Cornwall and Nairobi, Kenya, and has issue living, William Lyonel
Power, *b*. 1957,—Caroline Julia Tollemache, *b*. 1951: *m*. 1970 (m. diss. 1973), D. A. Godley,—Karenza
Lyona Tollemache, *b*. 1953: *m*. 1973, Gordon Taylor (Johannesburg, S. Africa).

    Grandchildren of the late Henry Gilbert Tollemache, 2nd son of the late Rev. Ernest
    Celestine Tollemache (infra):—
    Issue of the late Com. Douglas Hugh Tollemache, R.N., *b*. 1898, *d*. (on active ser. during
    European War) 1941 : *m*. 1931, Alys Kynaston (who *m*. 2ndly, 1943, Com. Richard Tolson,
    D.S.C., R.N., of Trafford House, Morley Green, Wilmslow, Cheshire), dau. of the late Rev.
    John Henry Bebbington, R. of Slinfold, Sussex, and Canon of Chichester :—
Ian Henry Douglas, *b*. 1936.——Sheila Rosemary Edith, *b*. 1939: *m*. 1963, T. Barry Nightingale,
FCA, of The Spinney, 18, Stoughton Lane, Stoughton, Leics. LE2 2FH, and has issue living, Lucy
Frances, *b*. 1964,—Kate Elizabeth, *b*. 1965,—Anna Ruth, *b*. 1967.
    Issue of the late Dorothy Clare Tollemache, *b*. 1895, *d*. 1949: *m*. 1921, Arthur Edward
    Durling:—
John Alfred Osborne (17 Walker Cres., Griffith, Canberra, ACT, Aust.), *b*. 1929: *m*. 1960, Enid Joan
Coling, and has issue living, Paul Edward Porttor *b*. 1962,—Richard John, *b*. 1965,—Jillian Clare,
b. 1969.——Pauline Mary Tollemache, *b*. 1924: *m*. 1954, John Ingham Brooke, and has issue living,
Penelope Anne, *b*. 1955,—Susan Miranda, *b*. 1957. *Residence*,—40, Charlwood Rd., Putney, SW15.

    Granddaughters of the Rev. Ernest Celestine Tollemache, 3rd son of the Rev. the
    Hon. Hugh Francis Tollemache, brother of 8th Earl:—
    Issue of the late Gwendoline Anna Tollemache, *b*. 1872, *d*. 1945 : *m*. 1907, Gilbert Henderson
    Philips, Bar.-at-law, who *d*. 1936 :—
Constance Gwendoline Joyce (196, Foster Hill Rd., Bedford), *b*. 1908: *m*. 1934, the Rev. John William
Harper Faulkner, and has issue living, Alan Henderson (134, Gayton Rd., Kings Lynn, Norfolk),
b. 1938: *m*. 1964, Anita Diana, da. of Harwood Arthur Bence, of Bedford, and has issue living, Lynn
Deborah *b*. 1966, Tracey Jane *b*. 1968.——Rhona Caroline (196, Foster Hill Rd., Bedford), *b*. 1911;
SRN.

    Grandson of the late Capt. Anastasius Eugene Tollemache son of the late Rev. the
    Hon. Hugh Francis Tollemache (ante):—
    Issue of the late Louisa Ethelgiva Rowena, *b*. 1878, *d*. 1962: *m*. 1910, Lieut.-Col. Walter
    Francis Courtenay Chicheley Plowden, who *d*. 1918:—
Cursham Chicheley, *b*. 1911; Capt. (ret.): *m*. 1937, Joan Brown, and has issue living, Robert Henry
Bowland Chicheley, *b*. 1947. *Residence*,—The Old Market Sq., Cartmel, Cumbria.

    Grandchildren of the late Louisa Harrington Tollemache, *b*. 1833 (who *d*. 1928,
    having *m*. 1862, Col. the Rt. Hon. Thomas Edward Taylor, M.P., who *d*. 1883),
    2nd dau. of the late Rev. the Hon. Hugh Francis Tollemache (ante) :—
See M. Headfort, colls.
            Descendants of the late Ada Maria Katherine Tollemache, *b*. 1848 (who
            d. 1928, having *m*. 1868, the 4th Baron Sudeley), younger dau. of the
            late Hon. Frederick James Tollemache, M.P., 5th son of William, Lord
            Huntingtower (ante):—
See B. Sudeley.
            Descendants of the late Louisa Maria Burke, who *d*. 1863 (having *m*.
            1849, the Rev. John Montagu Mason), el. dau. of the late Hon. Louisa
            Grace Tollemache (who *d*. 1830, having *m*. 1816, Sir Joseph Burke,
            11th Bt.' ext.]), el. dau. of William, Lord Huntingtower (ante).
            Descendants of the late Lady Catherine Camilla Tollemache, *b*. 1792'
            (who *d*. 1863, having *m*. 1816, Sir George Sinclair, 2nd Bt.), 2nd dau.
            of William, Lord Huntingtower (ante).
See V. Thurso.
        Grandson of the late William Tollemache, son of the late Hon. Charles
        Tollemache, 3rd son of Louisa (in her own right), Countess of Dysart (ante):—
    Issue of the late Algernon Seymour Tollemache, *b*. 1842, *d*. 1904 : *m*. 1868 [judicially
        separated 1890], Caroline Marianne, dau. of Col. Montriou, of the Bombay Army :—
Algernon Montriou, *b*. 1884; formerly Lt. Lancashire Hussars Yeo. *Residence*,—

        Granddaughters of the late Matilda Jane Tollemache (dau. of William Tollemache
        [ante]), who *d*. 1918, having *m*. 1873, Capt. Marcus Augustus Stanley Hare, R.N.,
        who *d*. 1878 :—
    Issue of the late Ethel Lucy Hare, *b*. 1875, *d*. 1940 : *m*. 1901, Sir Herbert Charles Perrott,
        C.H., C.B., 6th Bt., who *d*. 1922, when the title became ext.:—
See Perrott, Bt. (ext.).
            Descendants of the late Lady Catherine Sophia Tollemache, *b*. 1769,
            who *d*. 1825 (having *m*. 1793, Sir Gilbert Heathcote, 4th Bt.), el. dau.
            of Louisa (in her own right), Countess of Dysart (ante):—
See E. Ancaster.
            Descendants of the late John Jervis Tollemache, M.P. (el. son of the late
            Adm. John Richard Delap Tollemache, who assumed by Roy. Licence
            in 1821 that surname and Arms in lieu of Halliday, el. son of the late
            Lady Jane Halliday, youngest dau. and co-heir of 4th Earl) who was
            cr. *Baron Tollemache* 1876 [see that title].

PREDECESSORS.—[1] WILLIAM Murray, son of the Rev. William Murray, Min. of Dysart co. Fife (grandson of Anthony Murray, of Dollerie, Perthshire, whose elder brother Patrick was ancestor of the Murray baronets of Ochtertyre); M.P. for Fowey 1626, and for E. Looe 1628-9; cr. by patent *Lord Huntingtower* and *Earl of Dysart* (peerage of Scotland) 1643: *m.* 16—, Catherine, dau. of Col. Norman Bruce, of Clackmannan; *d.* 1654; *s.* by his el. dau. [2] ELIZABETH, *Countess of Dysart, b.* 16—; who in 1670 resigned the peerage and received a new grant thereof by patent with precedency of her father, and with remainder to her heirs of the body, failing which to her heirs whatsoever: *m.* 1st, 1647, Sir Lionel Tollemache, 3rd Bt. (cr. 1611), who *d.* 1669; 2ndly, 1672, John Maitland, 1st Duke of Lauderdale, by whom she did not have issue; the Duchess *d.* 1698; *s.* by her el. son [3] LIONEL, 3rd Earl. *b.* 1648; *s.* his father as 4th Bt. in 1669; M.P. for Orford 1678-85 and for Suffolk 1698-1700; declined an English barony upon accession of Queen Anne: *m.* 1680, Grace, who *d.* 1740, dau. of Sir Thomas Wilbraham, 3rd Bt.; *d.* 1727; *s.* by his grandson [4] LIONEL, *K.T.*, 4th Earl (only son of Lionel, Lord Huntingtower), *b.* 1708: *m.* 1729, Hon. Grace Carteret, who *d.* 1755, dau. of 2nd Earl Granville; *d.* 1770; *s.* by his son [5] LIONEL, 5th Earl, *b.* 1734: *m.* 1st, 1760, Charlotte, who *d.* 1789, natural dau. of the Hon. Sir Edward Walpole, K.B.; 2ndly 1791, Magdalene, who *d.* 1823, dau. of David Lewis, of Malvern Hall, Warwickshire; *d.s.p.* 1799; *s.* by his brother [6] WILBRAHAM, 6th Earl, *b.* 1739: *m.* 1773, Anna Maria, who *d.* 1804, dau. of David Lewis (ante); *d.* 1821, when the Baronetcy (cr. 1611) became ext.; *s.* in Earldom and Lordship by his sister [7] LOUISA; *b.* 1745; assumed by Roy. licence 1821 (the surname and Arms of Talmash in lieu of Manners: *m.* 1765, John Manners, M.P., of Grantham Grange, co. Lincoln, who *d.* 1792; *d.* 1840; *s.* by her grandson [8] LIONEL WILLIAM JOHN, 8th Earl (el. son of William, Lord Huntingtower, who in 1793 was cr. a *Baronet*, and in 1821 assumed by Roy. licence the surname and Arms of Talmash only), *b.* 1794; *s.* to his father's Baronetcy 1833: *m.* 1819, Maria Elizabeth, who *d.* 1852, dau. of Sweeney Toone, of Keston Lodge, Kent: *d.* 1878: *s.* by his grandson [9] WILLIAM JOHN MANNERS, 9th Earl (only son of William Lionel Felix, Lord Huntingtower), *b.* 1859: *m.* 1885, Cecilia Florence, who *d.* 1917, dau. of the late George Onslow Newton, of Croxton Park, St. Neots; *d.* 1935; *s.* in the Baronetcy by his kinsman, Lyonel Felix Carteret Eugene Tollemache, and in the Earldom and Lordship by his niece [10] WENEFRYDE AGATHA Greaves (dau. of the late Charles Norman Lindsay Tollemache Scott, by Lady Agnes Mary Manners, who *d.* 1912, da. of William Lionel Felix, Lord Huntingtower), Countess of Dysart, *b.* 1889: *m.* 1913, Maj. Owain Edward Whitehead Greaves, DL, RHG Machine Gun Regt., who *d.* 1941, *d.* 1975, *s.* by her el. da. [11] ROSAMUND AGNES, Countess of Dysart, and present peeress; also Lady Huntingtower.

EBBISHAM, BARON. (Blades.) [Baron U.K. 1928, Bt. U.K. 1922.]

ROWLAND ROBERTS BLADES, *T.D.*, 2nd Baron, and 2nd Baronet; *b.* Sept. 3rd, 1912; *s.* 1953; ed. at Winchester, and at Ch. Ch. Oxford; (M.A.); is a Liveryman of Mercers' Co.; a Common Councilman of City of London since 1947; Pres. of London Chamber of Commerce 1958-61, and of Assocn. of British Chambers of Commerce 1968-69; 1939-45 War as Lieut. 98th (Surrey and Sussex Yeo.) Field Regt. R.A.: *m.* 1949, Flavia Mary, youngest da. of the late Charles Francis Meade [see E. Clanwilliam, colls.], and has issue.

Arms.—Azure, on a saltire between four pheons argent a portcullis chained sable, on a chief or a lion passant gules. **Crest.**—Issuant from a mural crown or a talbot's head sable between two branches of oak fructed proper. **Supporters.**—On either side a talbot sable, charged on the shoulder with a portcullis, chained or, encircled by a chaplet of oak proper, tied gold.

For God, King, and Country.

Residence,—The Old Rectory, Bletchingley, Surrey.

DAUGHTERS LIVING.

Hon. Susan Mary, *b.* 1951.
Hon. Emma Caroline, *b.* 1954.
Hon. Catherine Anne, *b.* 1955.

SISTERS LIVING.

Hon. Margaret Agnes, *b.* 1908: *m.* 1933, Brig. Richard John Penfold Wyatt, MC, TD, DL, JP, late Roy. Sussex Regt. (TA), who *d.* 1954, and has issue living, Hugh Rowland (The Bell House, Ellisfield, Hants), *b.* 1933; ed. at Winchester: *m.* 1959, Jane Ann Elizabeth, da. of Lt.-Col. Robert Laurence Eden, OBE, TD, of Ashley Close, St. Saviour, Jersey, and has issue living, Hugh Geoffrey Robert *b.* 1961, Anne Elizabeth *b.* 1963, Susan Jane *b.* 1965,—John Geoffrey, *b.* 1937; ed. at Winchester, and at Ch. Ch., Oxford. *Residence,*—Cissbury, nr. Worthing, Sussex.
Hon. (Helen) Elizabeth (*Hon. Lady Russell*) (twin), *b.* 1908: *m.* 1939, Adm. the Hon. Sir Guy Herbrand Edward Russell, G.B.E., K.C.B., D.S.O., [see B. Ampthill]. *Residence,*—The Old Vicarage, Shamley Green, Guildford, Surrey.
Hon. Janet Mary, *b.* 1916: *m.* 1952, Rear-Adm. John Edwin Home McBeath, CB, DSO, DSC, DL, and has issue living, John Rowland Blades, *b.* 1954,—Rosemary Diana Jane, *b.* 1957. *Residence,*—Woodbury House, Churt, Surrey.

PREDECESSOR.—[1] (GEORGE) ROWLAND Blades, *G.B.E.*, only son of Rowland Hill Blades, of Sydenham, Kent; *b.* 1868; Master of Gardeners' Co. 1912, of Stationers' Co. 1926, of Shipwrights' Co. 1927, of Broderers' Co. 1930 and 1935, of Wheelwrights' Co. 1932, and of Haberdashers' Co. 1938; formerly an Alderman of City of London (Senior Sheriff 1917-18, Lord Mayor 1926-27); sometime Treasurer of Conservative Party; was Pres. of Federation of British Industries 1928-29, and Hon. Col. 57th (E. Surrey) Anti-Tank Regt. R.A. 1938-47; M.P. for Epsom Div. of Surrey (*U*) 1918-28; cr. a *Baronet* 1922, and *Baron Ebbisham* of Cobham, co. Surrey (peerage of U.K.) 1928: *m.* 1907, Margaret, *M.B.E.*, who *d.* 1965, dau. of the late Arthur Reiner, of Sutton, Surrey; *d.* 1953; *s.* by his only son [2] ROWLAND ROBERTS, 2nd Baron and present peer.

Ebrington, Viscount, son of Earl Fortescue.

EBURY, BARON. (Grosvenor.) [Baron U.K. 1857.]

Virtue, not ancestry.

FRANCIS EGERTON GROSVENOR, 6th
Baron; b. Feb. 8th, 1934; s. 1957; ed. at
Eton; is h.p. to Earldom of Wilton:
m. 1st, 1957 (m. diss. 1962),
Gillian Elfrida, da. of Martin Soames,
of 5, Lowndes Sq., SW1 [see E. Perth,
colls]; 2ndly, 1963 (m. diss. 1973),
Kyra, da. of the late L. L. Aslin;
3rdly, 1974, Suzanne Jean, da. of
Graham Suckling, of Tai Tapu, NZ,
and has issue by 1st and 3rd wives.

Arms.—Azure, a garb or, a mullet for difference. Crest.—A talbot statant or. Supporters—
On either side a talbot reguardant or, collared
azure, charged on the shoulder with a mullet of
the second.
Residence,—5, Landale Rd., Toorak, 3142,
Melbourne, Australia.

SON LIVING. (By 1st wife).
Hon. JULIAN FRANCIS MARTIN, b. June 8th,
1959.
DAUGHTER LIVING (By 3rd wife)
Hon. Georgina Lucy, b. 1973.
BROTHER LIVI G.
Hon. Robert Victor, b. 1936; ed. at Eton, and
Gordonstoun; late 2nd Lt. Life Guards: m. 1959,
Caroline, da. of Ronald Harry Higham [see V.
Hampden] and has issue living, Rachel Egerton,
b. 1963,—Virginia, b. 1965. Residence,—Bennets,
Grafton, Oxon.

HALF-BROTHERS LIVING.

Hon. William Wellesley (The Old Rectory, Eversholt, Beds.), b. 1942; ed. at Eton: m. 1966, Ellen
da. of the late Dr. Gunter Seeliger, of Harlaching, Munich, and has issue living, Alexander Egerton,
b. 1968,—a da., b. 1969.
Hon. Richard Alexander (Bartons Lodge, Eversholt, Bletchley, Bucks.), b. 1946: m. 1970, Gabriella,
da. of Dr. Xavier Speckert, of Bishopsgate House, Englefield Green, Surrey.

HALF-SISTERS LIVING.

Hon. Laura Georgina Kiloran (twin), b. 1946: m. 1969, G. R. Mark Cross.
Hon. Linda Denise, b. 1948: m. 1973, Christopher D. Vane Percy.

UNCLE LIVING. (Son of 4th Baron.)

Hon. Hugh Richard, b. 1919; ed. at Radley Coll.; European War 1939-45 as Capt. King's Shropshire
L.I.: m. 1st, 1939 (marriage dissolved 1952), Margaret, dau. of James L. Jacobs, of Neilsen, Ped-
nolver Terr., St. Ives, Cornwall; 2ndly, 1955, Victoria, only dau. of H. Wright, of Newport, Salop,
and has issue living, (by 2nd marriage) William Peter Wellesley b. 1959,—(by 1st marriage) Margaret
Elizabeth b. 1947. Residence,—River Ridge, Courtlands Park, Carmarthen.

AUNT LIVING. (Daughter of 4th Baron.)

Hon. Maud Elizabeth, b. 1909: m. 1st, 1931, the 2nd Viscount Harcourt, who obtained a divorce
1942; 2ndly, 1942, Lieut.-Col. Edward O'Shaughnessy, and has issue living, (by 1st marriage) [see
V. Harcourt], (by 2nd marriage) Elizabeth Mary, b. 1947,—Caroline Margaret (twin), b. 1947.
Residence,—Bepacama, Tas Swiequi, St. Andrews, Malta, GC.

MOTHER LIVING.

Anne WIGNALL, da. of the late Major Herbert Walter Acland-Troyte, M.C. [see Acland, Bt., cr. 1678,
colls.]; assumed by deed poll 1969 the surname of Wignall; m. 1st, 1933 (m. diss. 1941), the 5th
Baron, who d, 1957; 2ndly, 1941 (m. diss. 1946), as his second wife, Henry Peregrine Rennie Hoare
[M. Bristol]; 3rdly, 1947, as his second wife, Lieut.-Col. Frederick Barton Wignall, Life Guards
(retired), who d. 1956 [Tate, Bt., colls.]; 4thly, 1961 (m. diss. 1973), as his third wife, Anthony Freire
Marreco. Residence,—Huntsham Court, Tiverton, Devon.

WIDOW LIVING OF FIFTH BARON.

SHEILA WINIFRED (ANKER) (Dowager Baroness Ebury), younger dau. of Arthur Edward Dashfield,
of Oxford: m. 1954, as his third wife, the 5th Baron, who d. 1957. Residence,—37, Linkside Av.
Five Mile Drive, Wolvercote, Oxford.

COLLATERAL BRANCH LIVING.

Issue of the late Capt. the Hon. Norman de l'Aigle Grosvenor, 3rd son of 1st Baron,
b. 1845, d. 1898: m. 1881, Caroline Susan Theodora, who d. 1940, dau. of the late
Rt. Hon. James Stuart-Wortley [E. Wharncliffe, colls.]:—
Susan Charlotte (Susan, Baroness Tweedsmuir), b. 1882; is a D.G.St.J.: m. 1907, the 1st Baron Tweedsmuir, who d. 1940. Residence,—Hill House, Burford, Oxon.——Margaret Sophie Kathtrine, b.
1886: m. 1916, Jeremy Peyton-Jones, and has issue living, Jeremy Norman (Rodsall Manor,
Puttenham, Surrey), b. 1919; ed. at Eton; formerly Lieut.-Col. R.A: m. 1st, 1948 (marriage
dissolved 1962), Rhona Gertrude Jean, dau. of the late Major Edmund Walter Hanbury Wood
[see Wood, Bt., cr. 1918, colls., ext.]; 2ndly, 1963, Eva Louise, da. of Singdahl Kjaer, and has issue
living, (by 1st marriage) Julia Caroline b. 1952, Lucinda Margaret b. 1954, (by 2nd marriage)
Katherina Louise b. 1964, Elizabeth Eva b. 1966, Joanna Sophie b. 1969, Marina Caroline (twin) b.
1969,—Margaret Letitia Susan, b. 1922. Residence,—Wendover Dean Farm, Wendover, Bucks.

PREDECESSORS.—[1] Rt. Hon. ROBERT Grosvenor, 3rd son of 1stMarquess of Westminster,
b. 1801; M.P. for Shaftesbury 1822-6, for Chester 1826-47, and for Middlesex (L) 1847-57[;]
Comptroller of H.M.'s Household 1830-34, Treasurer thereof 1846-7, and Groom of the Stole
to the Prince Consort; was cr. Baron Ebury (peerage of United Kingdom) 1857 : m. 1831, the
Hon. Charlotte Arbuthnot Wellesley, who d. 1891, sister of 1st Earl Cowley; d. 1693;
s. by his el. son [2] ROBERT WELLESLEY, 2nd Baron, b. 1834; pt. 1st Life Guards; M.P. for
Westminster (L) 1865-74: m. 1867, the Hon. Emilie Beaujolais White, who d. 1923, dau. of 1st.
Baron Annaly; d. 1918; s. by his el. son [3] ROBERT VICTOR, 3rd Baron, b. 1868: m. 1903,
Florence, who d. 1927, dau. of the late Edward M. Padelford, of Savannah, U.S.A.; d. 1921; s.

by his brother [4] FRANCIS EGERTON, *D.S.O.*, *M.C.*, 4th Baron, *b.* 1883; Chm. Army and Navy Co-operative So., a Director of Union Bank of Australia, and of Roy. Exchange Assurance Co. (West End Branch), and Major Canadian Forces (Reserve of Officers); European War 1914-18. (wounded, despatches four times, M.C. with Bar, D.S.O. with Bar, French Croix de Guerre with Palm): *m.* 1902, Mary Adela, who *d.* 1960, dau. of the late G. Glasson: *d.* 1932; *s.* by his son [5] ROBERT EGERTON, *D.S.O.*, 5th Baron; *b.* 1914; Major Berkshire Yeo.; was a Lord of Waiting to H.M. 1939-40: *m.* 1st, 1933, Anne (who obtained a divorce 1941), dau. of the late Major Herbert Walter Acland-Troyte, M.C.; 2ndly, 1941 (marriage dissolved 1954), the Hon. Denise Margaret Yarde-Buller, dau. of 3rd Baron Churston; 3rdly, 1954, Mrs. Sheila Winifred (ANKER), younger dau. of Arthur Edward Dashfield, of Oxford; *d.* 1957; *s.* by his el. son [6] FRANCIS EGERTON, 6th Baron and present peer.

ECCLES, VISCOUNT. (Eccles.) [Viscount U.K. 1964.]

TRUTH AND BEAUTY

DAVID MCADAM ECCLES, *K.C.V.O.*, *P.C.*, 1st Viscount, *b.* Sept. 18th, 1904; ed. at Winchester, and at New Coll., Oxford Hon. FRIBA; a Trustee of British Museum 1963-70 (Chm. of Trustees 1968-70), Chm. Anglo-Hellenic League 1967-70; in Min. of Economic Warfare 1939-40; Economic Adviser to British Ambassadors at Lisbon and Madrid 1940-42; in Min. of Production 1942-3; Min. of Works 1951, Min. of Education 1954, Pres. of Board of Trade 1957, and again Min. of Education 1959-62; M.P. for Chippenham Div. of Wilts. (*C*) 1943-62; Paymaster Gen. and Min. for The Arts 1970-73, since when Chm. of British Library Board, and Pres. of World Craft Council; *cr.* PC 1951, KCVO 1953, *Baron Eccles*, of Chute, co. Wilts. (peerage of UK) 1962, and *Viscount Eccles*, of Chute, co. Wilts. (peerage of UK) 1964: *m.* 1928, the Hon. Sybil Frances Dawson, da. of 1st Viscount Dawson of Penn, and has issue.

Arms,—Chevronny argent and sable per pale counterchanged two torches erect or enflamed proper. **Crest,**—A three masted ship sails furled pennons and flags flying or, between two wings addorsed sable. **Supporters,**—On either side a wolf sable armed and langued gules gorged with a plain collar attached thereto a chain reflexed over the back and resting the interior hind paw on a portcullis chained or.

Residences,—Dean Farm, Upper Chute, Wilts; 6, Barton St., SW1. *Clubs,*—Brooks's, Roxburghe.

SONS LIVING.

Hon. JOHN DAWSON, *b.* April 20th, 1931; ed. at Winchester, and at Magdalen Coll., Oxford: *m.* 1955, Diana Catherine, da. of Raymond Sturge, of Lords Mead, Ashmore, Salisbury, and has issue living, William David, *b.* 1960,—Alice Belinda, *b.* 1958,—Catherine Sara, *b.* 1963,—Emily Frances, *b.* 1970. *Residence,*—Moulton Hall, Middleton Tyas, Richmond, Yorks.

Hon. Simon Dawson, *b.* 1934; ed. at Repton: *m.* 1961, Sheelin, dau. of Henry E. Ryan, of Long Meadow, Goring on Thames, Oxon., and has issue living, Anthony James, *b.* 1967,—Annabelle Charlotte, *b.* 1964. *Residence,*—5, Little Boltons, SW10.

DAUGHTER LIVING.

Hon. Selina Polly Dawson (*Marchioness of Lansdowne*), *b.* 1937; ed. at Sherborne Sch. for Girls, and London Univ.: *m.* 1st, 1962, (m. diss. 1968) Robin Andrew Duthac Carnegie, late Capt. Queen's Dragoon Guards; 2ndly, 1969, the 8th Marquess of Lansdowne, and has issue living (by 1st m.) Andrew James, *b.* 1973. *Residence,*—63, Warwick Sq., SW1.

Eddisbury, Baron, **see** Baron Sheffield

Eden, Viscount, son of Earl of Avon.

EDINBURGH, DUKE OF, **see** Royal Family.

EDMUND-DAVIES, BARON. (Edmund-Davies.) [Life Baron 1974.]

(HERBERT) EDMUND EDMUND-DAVIES, *PC*, son of Morgan John Davies, of Mountain Ash, Glam.; *b.* July 15th, 1906; assumed by deed poll 1974 the surname of Edmund-Davies in lieu of his patronymic; ed. at King's Coll., London (Life Gov. and Fellow), and Exeter Coll., Oxford (Hon. Fellow); Hon. LLD Univ. of Wales; Bar. Gray's Inn 1929, Bencher 1948, KC 1943, and Treas. 1965; Recorder of Methyr Tydfil 1942-44, Swansea 1944-54, and Cardiff 1953-58; a Judge of High Court of Justice Queen's Bench Div.) 1958-66, a Lord Justice of Appeal 1966-74, since when a Lord of Appeal in Ordinary; Pro-Chancellor, Univ. of Wales since 1974; cr. Knt. 1958, PC 1966, and *Baron Edmund-Davies*, of Aberpennar, co. Mid Glamorgan 1974: *m.* 1935, Eurwen, da. of the late John Williams, JP, of Barry, and has issue.

Arms—not exemplified at time of going to press.
Residence.—5, Gray's Inn Sq., WC1.

DAUGHTERS LIVING.

Hon. Ann, *b.* 1936: *m.* 1959, Frederick Cecil Worlock, MB, BChir, MRCS, LRCP, of The Monastery, Fladbury, Pershore, Worcs. WR10 2QB.

Hon. Elisabeth, *b.* 1939: *m.* 1965, Richard Owen Roberts, of 28, Rosehill Rd., Burnley, Lancs., BB11 2JS.

Hon. Shân, *b.* 1940: *m.* 1964, Wolfram Schüffel, MD, of 7900, Ulm Donau, Burgunderweg 9, W. Germany.

Ednam, Viscount, son of Earl of Dudley.

EFFINGHAM, EARL OF. (Howard.) [Earl U.K 1837.]

MOWBRAY HENRY GORDON HOWARD, 6th Earl, *b.* Nov. 29th, 1905; *s.* (July) 1946; ed. at Lancing; 1939-45 war with RA and 3rd Maritime Regts.: *m.* 1st, 1938 (m. diss. 1946), Maria Malvin Gertler; 2ndly, 1952 (m. diss. 1971), Gladys Irene, da. of the late Capt. William Freeman, Merchant Navy, and formerly wife of Frederick Charles Kerry; 3rdly, 1972, Mabel Suzanne Mingay, da. of the late Maurice Jules-Marie Le Pen of Paris, and widow of Wing-Cdr. Francis Talbot Cragg.

Virtue is worth a thousand shields

Arms.—Quarterly: 1st gules, on a bend between six cross-crosslets fitchée argent an escutcheon or, charged with a demi-lion rampant pierced through the mouth with an arrow gules, within the Royal tressure of Scotland. *Howard*; 2nd England, with a label of three points for difference. *Thomas of Brotherton*; 3rd checky or and azure. *Warren*; 4th gules, a lion rampant argent. *Mowbray*; the whole charged with a mullet for difference. ♂ —On a cheapan gules, turned up ermine, a lion statant guardant or, tail extended, ducally gorged argent, charged with a mullet sable. **Supporters**—Two lions argent, each charged on the shoulder with a mullet for difference.

Address,—House of Lords, SW1.

WIDOW LIVING OF SON OF FIFTH EARL.

Naida Frances (Jacaranda, 4, Chiltley Lane, Liphook, Hants.), da. of Henry Morden Guest, and formerly wife of Hugh Boucher: *m.* 1946, as his 2nd wife, the Hon. John Algernon Frederick Charles Howard, who *d.* 1971, and has issue [see colls. infra.].

COLLATERAL BRANCH LIVING.

Issue of the late Hon. John Algernon Frederick Charles Howard, yr. son of 5th Earl, *b.* 1907, *d.* 1971: *m.* 1st, 1938 (m. diss. 1942), Suzanne Patricia, da. of the late Edgar Macassey; 2ndly, 1946, Naida Francis (ante), da. of Henry Morden Guest, and formerly wife of Hugh Boucher:—

(By 1st m.) DAVID (PETER) MOWBRAY ALGERNON, (Greatford Cottage, Stocking Green, Radwinter, Essex) *b.* April 29th, 1939; ed. at Fettes; Lt. RN: *m.* 1964, Anne Mary, da. of Harrison Sayer, of Seven Dials, Saffron Walden, and has issue living, Edward Mowbray Nicholas, *b.* 1971.——(By 2nd m.) Charles Anthony Frederick, *b.* 1951; ed. at Sherborne, and St. John's Coll., Camb.

PREDECESSORS.—[1] *Lord* WILLIAM Howard, *K.G.*, el. son by his 2nd marriage of Thomas 2nd Duke of Norfolk; in 1542 found guilty of misprision of treason for concealing the misconduct of his niece Catherine, Queen of Henry VIII., and condemned with his wife to perpetual imprisonment (pardoned 1544); Lord Dep. of Calais 1552-3, Lord High Adm. 1553-7, Lord Chamberlain of the Household 1558-72, and Lord Privy Seal 1572; cr. *Baron Howard of Effingham* (peerage of England) 1554, *d.* 1572; *s.* by his son [2] CHARLES, *K.G.*, 2nd Baron; was Com.-in-Ch. of the fleet that destroyed the Spanish Armada 1588; cr. *Earl of Nottingham* (peerage of England) 1596; *d.* 1624; *s.* by his son [3] CHARLES, 2nd Earl; *d.s.p.* 1642; *s.* by his half-brother [4] CHARLES, *K.B.*, 3rd Earl; *d.* 1681, when the earldom expired and the barony reverted to [5] FRANCIS, 5th Baron; *d.* 1694; *s.* by his son [6] THOMAS, 6th Baron; *d.s.p.* 1725; *s.* by his brother [7] FRANCIS, 7th Baron; a distinguished military officer; cr. *Earl of Effingham* (peerage of Great Britain) 1731; *d.* 1743; *s.* by his son [8] THOMAS, 2nd Earl; Dep. Earl

Marshal; *d.* 1763; *s.* by his el. son [9] THOMAS, 3rd Earl; Dep. Earl Marshal; *d.s.p.* 1791; *s.* by his brother [10] RICHARD, 4th Earl; *d.* 1816, when the earldom became extinct, and the barony devolved upon his kinsman [11] KENNETH ALEXANDER, *G.C.B.*, 11th Baron; *b.* 1767; a Gen. in the Army; cr. *Earl of Effingham* (peerage of United Kingdom) 1837 : *m.* 1800, Lady Charlotte Primrose, dau. of 3rd Earl of Rosebery; *d.* 1845; *s.* by his son [12] HENRY, 2nd Earl, *b.* 1806; sat as M.P. for Shaftesbury (*L*) 1841-5 : *m.* 1832, Eliza, dau. of the late Gen. Sir Gordon Drummond, G.C.B.; *d.* 1889; *s.* by his el. son [13] HENRY, 3rd Earl, *b.* 1837 : *m.* 1865, Victoria Francisca, who *d.* 1899, el. dau. of Mons. A. Boyer, of Paris; *d.* 1898 : *s.* by his son [14] HENRY ALEXANDER GORDON, 4th Earl, *b.* 1866: *d.* 1927; *s.* by his cousin [15] GORDON FREDERICK HENRY CHARLES (son of the late Capt. the Hon. Frederick Charles Howard, 2nd son of 2nd Earl), 5th Earl, *b.* 1873 : *m.* 1st, 1904, Rosamond Margaret (who *d.* 1957, having obtained a divorce 1914), dau. of the late Edward H. Hudson, of Scarborough ; 2ndly, 1924, Madeleine (Mrs. Keleher), who *d.* 1958, dau. of William D. Foshay, of U.S.A. ; *d.* 1946 ; *s.* by his son [16] MOWBRAY HENRY GORDON, 6th Earl and present peer ; also Baron Howard of Effingham.

EGLINTON and WINTON, EARL OF. (Montgomerie.)
[Earl S. 1507, and U.K. 1859.]
[Name pronounced " Muntgummery."]

ARCHIBALD GEORGE MONTGOMERIE, 18th Earl; *b.* Aug. 27th, 1939; *s.* 1966; ed. at Eton; Hereditary Sheriff of Renfrew: *m.* 1964, Marion Carolina, only da. of John Henry Dunn-Yarker, of Le Château, 1814 La Tour de Peilz, Vaud, Switzerland, and has issue.

Arms,—Quarterly, 1st and 4th grand quarters counterquartered, 1st and 4th azure, three fleurs-de-lys or, *Montgomerie ;* 2nd and 3rd gules, three annulets or, stoned azure, *Eglinton,* all within a bordure or charged with a double tressure flory counterflory gules ; 2nd and 3rd grand quarters counterquartered, 1st and 4th or, three crescents within a double tressure flory counterflory gules, *Seton ;* 2nd and 3rd azure, three garbs or, *Buchan ;* over all an escutcheon parted per pale gules and azure, the dexter charged with a sword in pale proper, pommelled and hilted or, supporting an imperial crown, the sinister charged with a star of twelve points argent, all within a double tressure flory counterflory gold. **Crests,**—1st, a lady dressed in ancient apparel azure, holding in her dexter hand an anchor or, and in her sinister the head of a savage couped suspended by the hair all proper ; 2nd, a ducal coronet or, issuing therefrom a wyvern vomiting fire, his wings elevated proper. **Supporters,**—Two wyverns vert, vomiting fire proper.

Take good care.

Seat,—Skelmorlie Castle, Ayrshire. *Residence,*—The Dutch House, West Green, Hartley Wintney, Hants.

SONS LIVING.
HUGH ARCHIBALD WILLIAM (*Lord Montgomerie*), *b.* July 24th, 1966.
Hon. William John, *b.* 1968.
Hon. James David, *b.* 1972.
Hon. Robert Seton, *b.* 1975.

SISTERS LIVING
Lady Susanna, *b.* 1941: *m.* 1963, Capt. David Dundas Euing Crawford of Hazyhill, Humbie, E. Lothian, and has issue living, Alexander William Euing, *b.* 1967,—Daniel Dundas Euing (twin), *b.* 1967,—Arabella Sara, *b.* 1965.
Lady Elizabeth Beatrice, *b.* 1945.

HALF-UNCLE LIVING. (*Son of 16th Earl.*)
Hon. Roger Hugh, *DFC, b.* 1923; ed. at Eton, and at New Coll., Oxford (MA); formerly Flight-Lt. RAF; 1939-45 War (DFC). *Residence,*—Rudgwick Manor, nr. Horsham, Sussex.

AUNTS LIVING. (*Daughters of 16th Earl.*)
Lady Barbara Susan (31, Sloane Court West, SW3), *b.* 1909: *m.* 1930, Capt. Christopher Gerald Gore, Coldstream Guards, who *d.* 1954 [E. Sondes], and has issue living, John Temple (35, Flood St., SW3), *b.* 1931: *m.* 1st, 1957 (m. diss. 1969), Serena Margaret, da. of Charles Mounsey, of Yaxley Hall, Eye, Suffolk; 2ndly, 1969, Antonia, da. of Osmond James George McMullen, of 63, Eaton Sq., SW1, and formerly wife of Alan B. Henderson, and has issue living (by 1st m.) Christopher Charles *b.* 1959, Charlotte Sara Jane *b.* 1958, Georgina Susan *b.* 1962,—Susan Sara (Hatts Cottage, Hazeley Heath, Hartley Wintney, Hants.), *b.* 1935: *m.* 1st, 1956 (m. diss. 1963), Basil Ziani de Ferranti, son of Sir Vincent Ziani de Ferranti, MC; 2ndly, 1963, Peter Quixano Henriques who *d.* 1974, and has issue living, (by 1st m.) Jonathan *b.* 1957, Adrian *b.* 1958, Marcus Basil *b.* 1961, (by 2nd m) David Quixano *b.* 1964, Benedict James Quixano *b.* 1967.
Lady Janet Egidia, *b.* 1911 : *m.* 1934, Capt. Lord Robert Crichton-Stuart, Scots Guards [see M. Bute]. *Residence,*—Holmhill, Thornhill, Dumfriesshire.
Lady Betty Mary Seton, *b.* 1912 : *m.* 1933, Capt. George Vane Hay-Drummond, Scots Guards (Reserve)[see E. Kinnoull, colls.]. *Residence,*—Dornoch Mill, Crieff, Perthshire.

WIDOW LIVING OF SEVENTEENTH EARL.
URSULA JOAN (*Ursula Countess of Eglinton and Winton*), (Slaphouse, Monument h Ayr), da. of the Hon. Ronald Bannatyne Watson [By. Watson, ext.]: *m.* 1938, the 17th Earl, who *d.* 1966.

COLLATERAL BRANCHES LIVING.

Grandchildren of the late Alexander Montgomerie (infra):—
    Issue of the late Alexander James Montgomerie, *b.* 1892, *d.* 1945 : *m.* 1919, Winifred Jane (now of High Street, Bulls, New Zealand), dau. of the late George Gifford, of Bulls, Rangitikei, New Zealand :—
Alexander Kelvin (488, Riddell Rd., St. Heliers Bay, Auckland, 5, NZ), *b.* 1922; 1939-45 War with NZ Scottish Regt. and RN: *m.* 1958, Doreen Evelyn, da. of Capt. G. F. Price, 51, Woodfield Av., Farlington, Portsmouth, and has issue living, Alexander Andrew, *b.* 1962,—Stuart Hugh, *b.* 1966.——Seton Eglinton, *b.* 1924: *m.* 1960, Joan, da. of the late Harry Bladen, and has issue living, Seton Bladen *b.* 1962,—Elsa Jane *b.* 1964. *Residence,*—18, Tongariro St., Castlecliff, Wanganui, NZ.——Zona Winnifred, *b.* 1920: *m.* 1943, Norman Claude Nicholson, RNZAF, and has issue living, John Montgomerie, *b.* 1947,—Murray James (21, Molloys Rd., Te Marua, Upper Hutt, NZ), *b.* 1950: *m.* 1971

Joy Louise, da. of V. Frampton, of 1, Mundoora Av., Yattalunga, Gosford, NSW, and has issue living, Mathew James *b.* 1974, Jodie Louise *b.* 1972,—Claudia Michele, *b.* 1945: *m.* 1966, Peter William Fitzsimmons (PO Box 14104, Kilbirnie, Wellington, NZ), and has issue living, Timothy Peter *b.* 1974. *Residence,*—Woodleigh, Jocelyn Cres., Pinehaven, Silverstream, Wellington, NZ.——Rana Maude, *b.* 1929: *m.* 1951, Jack Rogers William Elder, Roy. New Zealand Air Force, and has issue living, David Lawson James, *b.* 1959, Raèwyn Janice, *b.* 1955. *Residence,*—Bellevue Heights, Tauranga, NZ.——Cynthia Beryl June, *b.* 1935.

Issue of the late Archibald William Montgomerie, *b.* 1894, *d.* 1969: *m.* 1942, Barbara Mary (304 Durham Drive, Havelock North, NZ), da. of Samuel Scott Linton:—
David William, *b.* 1944.——Roger Linton, *b.* 1946.——Barbara Mary, *b.* 1942.—— Jeanne Elizabeth, *b.* 1945.——Barbara Hylda, *b.* 1950.

Grandchildren of the late Capt. Alexander Montgomerie, el. son of William Eglinton Montgomerie, el. son of Alexander Montgomerie, brother of 12th Earl:—
Issue of the late Alexander Montgomerie, *b.* 1865, *d.* 1905: *m.* 1892, Emily Bashford .—
John Eglinton (of 101, Koromiko Rd., Gonville, Wanganui, New Zealand), *b.* 1899: *m.* 1921, Irene Agnes, da. of Thomas Ross Cameron, of New Plymouth, New Zealand), and has issue living, Alexander Cameron, *b.* 1926,—Archibald William, *b.* 1931: *m.* 1962, Geraldine Anne, da. of Gerald Cecil Davy, of Turanga, and has issue living, Michael William *b.* 1966, Donna Marie *b.* 1962,—Robert Patrick (24, Ihaia St., Waitara, Taranaki, NZ) *b.* 1934: *m.* 1960, Mhyre Laughton, da. of A. H. Collins, and has issue living, Leighton *b.* 1966, Wilson Bruce *b.* 1968, Patricia Ann *b.* 1961, Kerrie Lyn *b.* 1963, Jillian Beth *b.* 1964,—Ian James (Hursthouse Rd., Inglewood, NZ), *b.* 1935: *m.* 1961, Diana Long, and has issue living, Paul Ian *b.* 1963, Tracy Diana *b.* 1966,—Anita Mary, *b.* 1921: *m.* 1944, David Gordon Harrison, of 15, Whiteley St., New Plymouth, NZ, and has issue living, Errol John *b.* 1945, Ira James *b.* 1948, Peter David *b.* 1950, Patrick Vivian *b.* 1959, Carrol Ann *b.* 1948, Shirley Mary *b.* 1953, Yvonne Joan *b.* 1956,—Nola Joan *b.* 1923: *m.* 1941, Eric William Hopson, of 3 RD, Matamata, NZ, and has issue living, Kevin Eric *b.* 1943, Denis Michael *b.* 1946, Graeme Patrick *b.* 1950, Murray John *b.* 1953, Allan David *b.* 1956, Joan Frances *b.* 1941: *m.* 1962, Peter Bruce Donnison, of 13, Haig St., Morrinsville, NZ (and has issue living, Bruce Stephen *b.* 1962, Paul David *b.* 1963, Gregory James *b.* 1965), Maureen Anne *b.* 1948, Karen Irene *b.* 1960, Diane Marie (twin) *b.* 1960,—Peggy Agnes, *b.* 1924: *m.* 1945, Aubrey Edgar Hopson, of 170, Tukapo St., Westown, Waitara, New Plymouth, NZ, and has issue living, Wayne Leighton *b.* 1946, Brian James *b.* 1948, Valerie Margaret *b.* 1952, Barbara Irene *b.* 1953,—Barbara Winifred, *b.* 1933: *m.* 1954, David Gosling, of 18, Clyde St., New Plymouth, NZ, and has issue living, Ronald David *b.* 1955, Ian Peter *b.* 1957, Claire Annette *b.* 1963.——George Arnulph, *b.* 1901: *m.* 1945, Peggy Patricia Greener, of Wanganui, NZ, and has issue living, Wayne Arnold, *b.* 1947,—Peter John, *b.* 1951. *Residence,*—Parawanui Rd., Bulls, NZ.——Mary Elizabeth, *b.* 1895: *m.* 1924, Jack Staite.—Kathleen Minna, *b.* 1897: *m.* 1925, Rex Cameron Bailey, and has issue living, a son *b.* 19—.

Issue of the late Roger Arnulph Montgomerie, *b.* 1866, *d.* 1936: *m.* 1893, Annie, who *d.* 1958, dau. of the late Archibald Mason, of Tauangatutu, Wanganui, New Zealand :—
Sybil Alexandra, *b.* 1902: *m.* 1925, David Rayney Jackson, of Waverley, NZ who *d.* 1968, and has issue living, David Rayney Montgomerie, *b.* 1929: *m.* 1959, Diana Georgina, yr. da. of the late Frank Galbraith Hyde, of Tarras, Otago, New Zealand, and has issue living, Edward Hyde Rayney *b.* 1963, Sarah Jane Rayney *b.* 1960, Belinda Elizabeth *b.* 1962, Priscilla Rayney Montgomerie *b.* 1926; ed. at Nga Tawa and Otago Univ. (BA). *Residence,*—5, Tulloch St., St. John's Hill, Wanganui, NZ.

Grandchildren of the late Roger Arnulph Montgomerie (ante):—
Issue of the late Roger Oswald Montgomerie, *b.* 1896, *d.* 1965: *m.* 1940, Beryl Victoria (3A, Gonville Av., Wanganui, NZ), da. of the late Guy Carlton Clark, of Melbourne:—
John Clark, *b.* 1943: *m.* 1972, Glenis Erina, only da. of Norman Cameron, of Masterton, NZ.——Roger Clark, *b.* 1945: *m.* 1971, Patricia Clare, only da. of Vincent Kerepehi Donnelly, of Paeroa, NZ.—— Beverley Joan, *b.* 1941: *m.* 1963, Edward William Gudopp, c/o P.O. Kaitoke, Wellington, NZ, and has issue living, David Charles, *b.* 1967,—Deborah Jane, *b.* 1965.——Helen Victoria, *b.* 1959.

Issue of the late Hew Seton Montgomerie, *b.* 1898, *d.* 1969: *m.* 1938, Violet Muriel (11, Apihai St., Orakei, Auckland 5, NZ), da. of the late Donald Harry Rait, MRCVS, of Palmerston N, NZ:—
Susanna Seton, *b.* 1940.——Egidia Seton, *b.* 1942.

Grandchildren of the late Capt. Alexander Montgomerie (ante):—
Issue of the late Hew Winton Montgomerie, *b.* 1872, *d.* 1920: *m.* 1906, Mary Laura, dau. of Charles J. G. de Greenlaw, of Sydney, N.S. Wales:—
Ian Hew de Greenlaw (31, Woodland Rd., Timaru, NZ), *b.* 1913; 1939-45 War with RNZAF in Singapore and Japan: *m.* 1st 1940 (m. diss. 1948) Elizabeth Isabella Gregg Stratford; 2ndly, 1948, Majorie Thelma da. of Albert Eugene Brookes, of Auckland, New Zealand, and has issue living, (by 1st m.) Hew Winton Rowland (48, Tiri Tiri Rd., Birkdale, Auck. 10, NZ), *b.* 1941: *m.* 1967, Carol Leonie, yst. da. of Stanley Rollingston Cromwell, late Headmaster of Whangarei, NZ, and has issue living, Stuart Seton *b.* 1974, Rachael Leonie *b.* 1970,—(by 2nd m) Lynetta Eugene, *b.* 1952: *m.* 1971, Albert John Bainbridge, and has issue living, Sacha Lea *b.* 1975, Tanya Lyh *b.* 1973.—— Barbara de Greenlaw, *b.* 1915: *m.* 1942, Ernest Clement Dawson, and has issue living, Ernest John Linnaeus, *b.* 1945,—Bernard Stanley Winton, *b.* 1953,—Ann Michelle de Greenlaw, *b.* 1943,—Linda Egidia Montgomerie, *b.* 1949. *Residence,*—17, Balgay St., Upper Riccarton, Christchurch, NZ.

Issue of the late Archibald William Eglinton Montgomerie, *b.* 1874, *d.* 1951: *m.* 1901, Elizabeth Grace, who *d.* 1956, dau. of the late Duncan Blair, of Wanganui, New Zealand :—
Nancy Edith, *b.* 1903. *Residence,*—54, Durie St., Durie Hill, Wanganui, New Zealand.——Betty Sybil *b.* 1913: *m.* 1963, Frank Barnard Wingfield of 63, Seine Rd., Milford, Auckland 10, NZ, and has issue living, Blair Winton (24, Imatra Place, Pakuranga, Auckland, NZ), *b.* 1941: *m.* 1970, Jean Patricia Hogland, and has issue living, Seton Barnard *b.* 1973,—Elizabeth Jane, *b.* 1938: *m.* 1963, Francis Vrian Charles Bolt, co NZ Insurance Co., PO Box 186, Wanganui, NZ, and has issue living, Francis Charles Wingfield *b.* 1966, Elizabeth Sarah *b.* 1965.

Issue (by 1st marriage) of the late John Eglinton Montgomerie, *b.* 1878, *d.* 1930: *m.* 1st 1910, Edith Lillian, who *d.* 1921, dau. of the late Hon. George Young, M.L.C., of Melbourne, Australia; 2ndly, 1928, Sarah (who *m.* 2ndly, 19—, George Crowe, of 34, Elliot Street, Arbroath, Angus), dau. of — Mitchell, of Arbroath, Scotland :—
Sheila Elizabeth, *b.* 1911: *m.* 1940, Francis Churtain Triggs, and has issue living, Michael Francis (14, Clarke Rd., Auckland, NZ), *b.* 1942: *m.* 1972, Susan Marlene, da. of James Lincoln Todd, of Auckland, and has issue living, Matthew James *b.* 1975,—Mary Seton *b.* 1946: *m.* 1964, Stafford John Reed, of 12, Avondale Rd., Auckland, NZ, and has issue living, Darren Stafford *b.* 1965, Mark *b.* 1967, Eugene *b.* 1971. *Residence,*—1427, Great North Rd., Avondale, Auck. 7, NZ.——Edith Mary Seton, *b.* 1915: *m.* 1938, Samuel Alan Smith, and has issue living, Alan Graeme *b.* 1939,—Raymond Francis, *b.* 1940,—Bruce Seton, *b.* 1942,—Sandra Mary, *b.* 1948. *Residence,*—13, Adventure St., New Plymouth, NZ.——Bettie Winton, *b.* 1916: *m.* 1940, Thomas Charles Howden, and has issue living, Ann Montgomerie, *b.* 1952,—Janet, *b.* 1955. *Residence,*—103, Nelson Cres., Napier, NZ.

PREDECESSORS.—[1] Sir ALEXANDER Montgomerie, Kut.; cr. *Lord Montgomerie* (peerage of Scotland) 1449; *d.* 1451; *s.* by his grandson [2] ALEXANDER, 2nd Lord; *s.* by his son [3] HUGH, 3rd Lord; nominated after the fall of James IV. at Flodden one of the Queen-

Dowager's Councillors, and was afterwards Justice Gen. of N. parts of Scotland ; cr. *Earl of Eglinton* (peerage of Scotland) 1508: *d.* 1545; *s.* by his grandson [4] HUGH, 2nd Earl; *d.* 1546; *s.* by his son [5] HUGH, 3rd Earl; *d.* 1585; *s.* by his son [6] HUGH, 4th Earl ; assassinated 1586 ; *s.* by his son [7] HUGH, 5th Earl ; obtained a charter settling the earldom upon his cousins, Alexander, Thomas and John, sons of his aunt Margaret, by Robert Seton, 1st Earl of Winton ; *d.* 1611 ; *s.* by his cousin (ante) [7] ALEXANDER Seton, 6th Earl (3rd son of 1st Earl of Winton and 6th Lord Seton); took an active part against the crown, *temp.* Charles I., fought on the Parliament side at Marston Moor ; subsequently attached himself to Charles II., and falling into the hands of the enemy was imprisoned at Berwick 1651-60 ; died 1661 ; *s.* by his son [8] HUGH, 7th Earl; espoused the royal cause during the civil wars and was opposed to his father at Marston Moor; *d.* 1669 ; *s.* by his son [9] ALEXANDER, 8th Earl ; *d.* 1701 ; *s.* by his el. son [10] ALEXANDER, *P.C.*, 9th Earl ; a Representative Peer ; *d.* 1729 ; *s.* by his son [11] ALEXANDER, 10th Earl ; killed during a dispute 1769 by Mungo Campbell, whom the Earl had ordered off his lands and insisted upon the trespasser delivering up his gun; *s.* by his brother [12] ARCHIBALD, 11th Earl ; a Gen. in the Army, M.P. for Ayrshire 1761, Dep. Ranger of Hyde and St. James's Parks, and a Representative Peer 1776-96; *d.* 1796 ; *s.* by his kinsman [13] HUGH, *K.T.*, 12th Earl, great grandson of the Hon. James Seton, 4th son of 6th Earl; M.P. for Ayrshire 1780-9 and 1796, and a Representative Peer 1798-1806; cr. *Baron Ardrossan* (peerage of United Kingdom) 1806; *d.* 1819; *s.* by his grandson [14] ARCHIBALD WILLIAM, *K.T.*, *P.C.*, *D.C.L.*, *LL.D.*; *b.* 1812: in 1840 served heir male of George, 4th Earl of Winton (cr. 1600), and 9th Lord Seton (cr. 1448) (peerage of Scotland) ; cr. *Earl of Winton*, and *Baron Seton and Tranent* (peerage of United Kingdom) 1859 ; Viceroy of Ireland 1852 and 1858-9, and Lord-Lieut. of Ayrshire ; inaugurated and carried out a celebrated tournament at Eglinton Castle 1839 : *m.* 1st, 1841, Theresa, who *d.* 1853, widow of Com. Richard Howe Cockerell, R.N. ; 2ndly, 1858, Lady Adela Capel, who *d.* 1860, dau. of 6th Earl of Essex ; *d.* 1861 ; *s.* by his son [15] ARCHIBALD WILLIAM, 14th Earl, *b.* 1841: *m.* 1862, Lady Sophia Adelaide Theodosia Anderson-Pelham, who *d.* 1886, dau. of 2nd Earl of Yarborough ; *d.* 1892 ; *s.* by his brother [16] GEORGE ARNULPH, 15th Earl, *b.* 1848 , Lord-Lieut. of Ayrshire: *m.* 1873, Dame Janet Lucretia, *D.B.E.*, *LL.D.*, who *d.* 1923, dau. of Boyd Cunninghame, R.N., of Craigends, co. Renfrew ; *d.* 1919: *s.* by his son [17] ARCHIBALD SETON, 16th Earl, *b.* 1880: *m.* 1st, 1908, Lady Beatrice Susan Dalrymple (who *d.* 1962, having obtained a divorce 1922), dau. of 11th Earl of Stair; 2ndly, 1922, Marjorie, dau. of Thomas Walker McIntyre, and widow of Guy Fitzpatrick Vernon; *d.* 1945; *s.* by his son [18] ARCHIBALD WILLIAM ALEXANDER, 17th Earl, *b.* 1914: *m.* 1938, Ursula Joan, da. of the Hon. Ronald Bannatyne Watson [B. Watson, extr.]; *d.* 1966; *s.* by his son [9] ARCHIBALD GEORGE, 18th Earl and present peer; also Earl of Winton Lord Montgomerie , Baron Seton and Tranent, and Baron Ardrossan

EGMONT, EARL OF. (Perceval.) Sits as BARON LOVEL AND HOLLAND (G.B. 1762). [Earl I. 1733, Bt. I. 1661.]

Under the white cross.

FREDERICK GEORGE MOORE PERCEVAL, 11th Earl, and 15th Baronet ; *b.* April 14th, 1914; established his claim to the Earldom 1939: *m.* 1932, Ann Geraldine, dau. of D. G. Moodie, and has issue.

Arms,—Quarterly ; 1st and 4th argent, on a chief indented gules, three crosses patée of the field, *Perceval* ; 2nd and 3rd barry nebulée of six, or and gules, *Lovel*. Crest.—A thistle proper. Supporters,— *Dexter*, an antelope argent, armed, unguled, ducally collared and chained or, holding in the mouth a thistle slipped proper ; *sinister*, a stag sable, attired, unguled, ducally collared and chained or, holding in the mouth a thistle slipped proper.

Residence,—Two-Dot Ranch, Nanton, Alberta Canada.

SON LIVING.

THOMAS FREDERICK GERALD (*Viscount Perceval*), *b.* Aug. 17th, 1934.

DAUGHTER LIVING.
Lady Geraldine Elizabeth Ursula, *b* 1939.

COLLATERAL BRANCHES LIVING.
Grandchildren of the late Charles Spencer Perceval, LL.D., son of the late Dudley Montagu Perceval, son of 4th son of 2nd Earl :—
Issue of the late Dudley Perceval, *b.* 1874, *d.* 1956 : *m.* 1914, the Hon. Mary Elizabeth Massey, who *d.* 1960, dau. of 5th Baron Clarina :—
Philip Edward, *M.D.*, *b.* 1915; ed. at St. John's Coll., Camb. (B.A. 1936, M.A. 1940, M.B. and B.Ch. 1940, M.D. 1950): *m.* 1945, Joan Margaret, dau. of Lieut.-Col. Alfred Hacking, D.S.O., M.C., of Dalmorton, Selsey, Sussex, and has issue living, Elizabeth Margaret, *b.* 1947. *Residence,*—11, Condover Park, Condover, Salop.——Mary Leonora, *b.* 1916. *Residence,*—Dobsons, Sotwell, nr. Wallingford, Berks.

Grandson of the late Frederick James Perceval, 2nd son of the late Rt. Hon. Spencer Perceval. M.P., 7th son of 2nd Earl :—
Issue of the late Charles Augustus Trevelyan Perceval, *b.* 1848, *d.* 1898 : *m.* 1890, Annie, who *d.* 1932, dau. of the late Thomas Evison, of Hornsey, N. :—
Gordon Lawrence, *b.* 1891 : *m.* 1914, Constance Mary Victoria, dau. of Samuel Ernest Yelland, of Dreadnought, Hove, Sussex. *Residence,*—Arden, 51, Kingston Lane, Southwick, Sussex.

PREDECESSORS.—[1] *Rt. Hon. Sir* JOHN PERCEVAL ; cr. a *Baronet* 1661 with the exceptional privilege of allowing the el. son or grandson when twenty-one years of age (and after notice given as provided) to receive the Order of Knighthood and have the rank and precedence of a Bt. concurrently with the father or grandfather ; *d.* 1665 ; *s.* by his el. son [2] *Sir* PHILIP, 2nd Bt.; *d.* unmarried 1680; *s.* by his brother [3] *Sir* JOHN, 3rd Bt.; *d.*

1686; *s.* by his son [4] *Sir* EDWARD, 4th Bt.; *d.* a minor 1691; *s.* by his brother [5] *Rt. Hon. Sir* JOHN, 5th Bt.; successively M.P. for co. Cork and Harwich, and 1st Pres. of Georgia; *cr. Baron Perceval,* of Burton, co. Cork (peerage of Ireland) 1715, with remainder to the heirs male of his father, *Viscount Perceval* (peerage of Ireland) 1722, and *Earl of Egmont* (peerage of Ireland) 1733; *d.* 1748; *s.* by his son [6] *Rt. Hon.* JOHN, 2nd Earl; M.P. 1731-62, Lord High Adm. and Postmaster-Gen.; summoned to Parliament of Great Britain as *Lord Lovel and Holland,* of Enmore, co. Somerset 1762: *m.* 1st, 1737, Catherine who *d.* 1752, dau. of 5th Earl of Salisbury; 2ndly, 1756, Catherine, dau. of the Hon. Charles Compton (M. Northampton); she was *cr. Baroness Arden,* of Lohort Castle, co. Cork (peerage of Ireland) 1770; he *d.* 1772; *s.* by his son [7] JOHN JAMES, 3rd Earl; *d.* 1822; *s.* by his son [8] JOHN, 4th Earl; *d.* 1835; *s.* by his son [9] HENRY FREDERICK JOHN, 5th Earl; *d.* 1841, *s.* by his cousin [10] GEORGE JAMES, 6th Earl (2nd Baron Arden, of Arden), whose father CHARLES GEORGE (Baron Arden, of Lohort), el. son of Catherine, Baroness Arden, of Lohort, had been *cr. Baron Arden,* of Arden, co. Warwick (peerage of United Kingdom) 1802; *d.s.p.* 1874; *s.* by his nephew [11] CHARLES GEORGE (son of the late Rev. the Hon. Charles George Perceval, 4th son of 2nd Baron Arden, of Lohort), 7th Earl, *b.* 1845; M.P. for Midhurst (C) 1874: *m.* 1869, Lucy, who *d.* 1932, dau. of the late Henry King; *d.* 1897; *s.* by his cousin [12] AUGUSTUS ARTHUR (son of the late Charles John Perceval, grandson of 2nd Baron Arden, of Lohort), 8th Earl, *b.* 1856: *m.* 1881, Kate, who *d.* 1926, dau. of the late Warwick Howell, of S. Carolina, U.S.A.; *d.* 1910; *s.* by his brother [13] CHARLES JOHN, 9th Earl, *b.* 1858: *m.* 1890, Florence, who *d.* 1954, youngest dau. of the late George Gibson, M.D.; *d.* 1929, when the title was claimed by [14] FREDERICK JOSEPH TREVELYAN (a descendant of the late Rt. Hon. Spencer Perceval, M.P., 7th son of 2nd Earl), *b.* 1873: *m.* 1911, Cecilia, who *d.* 1916, dau. of James Burns Moore, of Montreal, Canada; *d.* 1932, without having established his claim to the Earldom; his only son [15] FREDERICK GEORGE MOORE, *b.* 1914, established his claim as 11th Earl 1939; also Baron and Viscount Perceval, Baron Arden, and Baron Lovel and Holland.

EGREMONT, BARON LECONFIELD AND (Wyndham.) [Baron U.K. 1859.]

To the just, right.

JOHN MAX HENRY SCAWEN WYNDHAM, (*Baron Egremont*), 7th Baron Leconfield, and 2nd Baron Egremont; *b.* April 21st, 1948; *s.* 1972; ed. at Eton, and Ch. Ch., Oxford.

Arms,—Azure, a chevron between three lions, heads erased or, within a bordure wavy of the last. Crest,—A lion's head erased or, within a fetterlock, the lock gold, and the bow counter-componée or and azure; the head charged with a saltire wavy gules. Supporters,—*Dexter,* a winged lion azure, wings, inverted and plain collared or; *sinister,* a griffin argent, gutté de sang, plain collared, gules.

Residences,—Petworth House, Sussex: Cockermouth Castle, Cumberland.

BROTHER LIVING.
Hon. HARRY HUGH PATRICK, *b.* Sept. 28th, 1957.

SISTER LIVING.
Hon. Caroline Elizabeth, *b.* 1951.

UNCLE LIVING. (*Son of 5th Baron Leconfield*) *Hon.* Mark Hugh, *MC* (Yew Tree Farm, Ascott, Shipston-on-Stour, Warwicks.), *b.* 1921: late Capt. 12th R. Lancers; Chm. of C. of E. Children's Soc.; 1939-45 War in Middle East and Italy (twice wounded, MC): *m.* 1947, Anne, da. of the Hon. Reginald Henry Winn [see B. St. Oswald], and has issue living, Henry Mark, *b.* 1953,—Elizabeth Jane (*Lady Charles G. W. C. Spencer-Churchill*), *b.* 1948: *m.* 1970, Lord Charles George William Colin Spencer-Churchill, of 164, Ebury St., SW1 [see D. Marlborough],—Melissa Anne *b.* 1949.

AUNT LIVING. (*Daughter of 5th Baron Leconfield*).
Hon. Ursula Constance (of Honeyway House, Petworth, Sussex), *b.* 1913.

WIDOW LIVING OF SON OF SECOND BARON LECONFIELD.
Ruth Constance (Caversfield, Bicester, Oxon.), da. of the late Hubert Delaval Astley, of Brinsop Court, Herefordshire [see B. Hastings, colls.]: *m.* 1920, Col. the Hon. Everard Humphrey Wyndham, MC who *d.* 1970, and has issue living [see colls., infra].

WIDOW LIVING OF SIXTH BARON LECONFIELD AND FIRST BARON EGREMONT.
Pamela (*Baroness Egremont*), (Petworth House, Sussex; Cockermouth Castle, Cumberland; 62, Chester Sq., SW1), da. of Capt. The Hon. Valentine Maurice Wyndham Quin, RN [see E. Dunraven]: *m.* 1947, the 6th Baron Leconfield and the 1st Baron Egremont, who *d.* 1972.

COLLATERAL BRANCHES LIVING.
Issue of the late Col. the Hon. Everard Humphrey Wyndham, MC, yst. son of second Baron Leconfield, *b.* 1888, *d.* 1970: *m.* 1920, Ruth Constance (ante), da. of the late Hubert Delaval Astley, of Brinsop Court, Herefordshire [see B. Hastings, colls.]:—

Michael Patrick (21, Hyde Park Gate, SW7), *b.* 1929; late Capt. Life Guards: *m.* 1st, 1957, Mrs. Shelagh Anne Barker, who *d.* 1967, da. of the late Dr. Sydenham Frederick Moore, OBE; 2ndly, 1967, Mrs. Laura Prudence Rosamund Murray, da. of the late Mervyn Stutchbury, and has issue living, (by 1st m.) Samantha Madeline, *b.* 1962,—Georgina Maria, *b.* 1963.——Mary Constance, *b.* 1921: *m.* 1st, 1945, Ralph Hamilton Cobbold, from whom she obtained a divorce 1966; 2ndly, 1966, the Rt. Hon. John Wynne William Peyton, MP, of 32, Chester Terr., NW1, and Lytes Cary, Somerton, Som., and has issue living, (by 1st m.) David Anthony, *b.* 1946,—Charlotte Ruth, *b.* 1949.

410 DEBRETT'S ILLUSTRATED PEERAGE.

Granddaughters of the late Col. Guy Percy Wyndham, CB, MVO (infra):—
Issue of the late Maj. Guy Richard Charles Wyndham, MC, b. 1896, d. 1948: m. 1st, 1920,
Iris Winifred Youell (who obtained a divorce 1925), da. of Andrew Percy Bennett, CMG,
Envoy Extraor. and Min. Plen. to Panama; 2ndly, 1930, Margeretha Wulfsberg, who
obtained a divorce 1941:—
(By 1st m.) Joan Olivia, b. 1921: m. 1st 1947 (m. diss. 1952) Maurice Rowdon; 2ndly, 1952, Alexander
Shivarg, of 34, Wellington Sq., SW3, and has issue living, (by 1st m.) Clare Viola, b. 1947,—(by 2nd
m.) Camilla Gabrielle, b. 1953.——(By 2nd m.) Ingrid Olivia Georgia, b. 1931: m. 1st (m. diss.
1963), the Hon. Jonathan Bryan Guinness, el. son of 2nd Baron Moyne; 2ndly, 1963, (Henry) Paul
Guinness Channon, MP [see E. Iveagh]. Residence,—96, Cheyne Walk, SW10.

Grandsons of the late Capt. the Hon. Percy Scawen Wyndham, 3rd son of 1st
Baron Leconfield:—
Issue of the late Col. Guy Percy Wyndham, CB, MVO, b. 1865, d. 1941: m. 1st, 1892, Edwina
Virginia Joanna, who d. 1919, da. of the Rev. Frederick Fitzpatrick, and widow of John
Monck Brooks [M. Headfort]; 2ndly, 1923, Violet Lutetia (19, Lonsdale Rd., W11), da. of
the late Ernest Leverson:—
(By 2nd marriage) Francis Guy Percy, b. 1924; ed. at Eton, and at Ch. Ch., Oxford.——Hugh Guy
Osbert (of 178, Kensington Park Rd., W11), b. 1926; ed. at Eton, and at Corpus Christi Coll.,
Oxford; Capt. late Coldstream Guards: m. 1961 (m. diss. 1966), Edith Elizabeth Creswick, el. da.
of John Watson, FRIBA, of Old Mains, Giffnock, Glasgow and has issue living, Rachel Olivia
Violet, b. 1963.

PREDECESSORS.—The 7th Duke of Somerset, who inherited the Percy estates, including the lands
of Egremont, Cumberland, from his mother Elizabeth, da. and heir of the 11th Earl of Northumberland, was cr. Earl of Egremont 1749, with special remainder to his maternal nephew Sir Charles
Wyndham, 4th baronet of Orchard Wyndham, Som. The Egremont estates passed to the 1st Earl
of Northumberland (cr. 1377) on his 2nd m. to Maud (who d.s.p.), sister and heir of Anthony, Lord
Lucy. These, and the Sussex estates of the Percys, were devised to the 2nd Earl of Egremont.
[1] Col. GEORGE Wyndham, natural son and adopted heir of George O'Brien, 3rd Earl of Egremont:
b. 1787; a Col. in the Army; cr Baron Leconfield, of Leconfield, E. Riding of York (peerage of
United Kingdom) 1859: m. 1815, Mary Fanny, who d. 1863, da. of the Rev. William Blunt, of
Crabbett, Sussex; d. 1869; s. by his son [2] HENRY, 2nd Baron, b. 1830; MP for W. Sussex
(C) 1854-69: m. 1867, Lady Constance Evelyn Primrose, who d. 1939, having been raised to the
rank of an Earl's da. 1886, 2nd da. of the late Lord Dalmeny; d. 1901; s. by his el. surviving son
[3] CHARLES HENRY, GCVO, 3rd Baron; b. 1872; Co. Comdt. Roy. Sussex Vol. 1917-18, and Lord-
Lt. of Sussex 1917-49: m. 1911, Beatrice Violet, who d. 1956, da. of the late Col. Richard Hamilton
Rawson, MP; d. 1952; s. by his brother [4] HUGH ARCHIBALD, 4th Baron, b. 1877: m. 1908, the
Hon. Maud Mary Lyttleton, who d. 1953, da. of 8th Viscount Cobham; d. 1963; s. by his brother, [5]
EDWARD SCAWEN, DSO, 5th Baron, b. 1883: m. 1907, Gladys Mary, who d. 1971, da. of the late
Fitzroy James Wilberforce Farquhar [Farquhar, Bt., colls.], d. 1967; s. by his son [6] JOHN EDWARD
REGINALD, MBE (who was cr. Baron Egremont, of Petworth, co. Sussex, 1963), 6th Baron, b. 1920;
Private Sec. to P.M. 1957-63; a Trustee of Wallace Collection 1953-72; m. 1947, Pamela, da. of Capt.
the Hon. Valentine Maurice Wyndham Quin, RN [E. Dunraven], d. 1972: s. by his el. son [7] JOHN
MAX HENRY SCAWEN, 7th Baron Leconfield, 2nd Baron Egremont, and present peer.

ELDON, EARL OF. (Scott.) [Earl U.K. 1821.]

JOHN SCOTT, G.C.V.O., 4th Earl ; b. March
29th, 1899 ; s. 1926 ; ed. at Ampleforth Coll.,
and at Magdalen Coll., Oxford; Fl. Lt. No.
930 (Hampshire) Squadron, Auxiliary Air
Force; formerly Lt. Scots Guards; 1914-18
War; a Lord-in-Waiting to HM 1937-68; a
Grand Officer of Legion of Honour; KCVO
1952, GCVO 1963: m. 1934, the Hon. Magdalen Mary Charlotte Fraser, OBE, who d. 1969,
da. of 14th Lord Lovat, and has issue.

Let honour be without stain.

Arms,—Argent, an anchor erect sable, between three
lions' heads erased gules ; on a chief wavy azure, a portcullis with chains or. Crest.—A lion's head erased gules,
gorged with a chain, and pendant therefrom a portcullis or. Supporters,—Two lions guardant proper,
each gorged with a double chain and a portcullis attached thereto gold, pendent from the portcullis
a shield argent, charged with a civic wreath vert.

Residences,—Cardrona House, Innerleithen, Peebleshire; 174, Cranmer Court, Sloane Av., SW3.
Club,—White's.

SONS LIVING.

JOHN JOSEPH NICHOLAS (Viscount Encombe) (2, Coach House Lane, Wimbledon, SW19), b
April 24th, 1937; ed. at Ampleforth Coll., and at Trin. Coll., Oxford; Lt. Scots Guards Army Emer-
gency Reserve: m. 1961, Countess Claudine, yst. da. of Count Franz von Montjoye-Vaufrey and de
la Roche, of 45, Hasenauerstrasse, Vienna, 18, and has issue:—
SON LIVING,—Hon. John Francis Thomas Marie Joseph Columba Fidelis, b. July 9th, 1962.
DAUGHTERS LIVING,—Hon. Tatiana Maria Laura Rose Columba Fidelis, b. 1967.
Hon. Victoria Laura Maria Magdalene, b. 1968.
Hon. Simon Peter (Howe Hills Farm, Mordon, Sedgefield, co. Durham), b. 1939; was a Page of Honour
to HM 1953-56; ed. at Ampleforth Coll., Salamanca and Madrid Univs., and Sorbonne (Paris);
Lt. Scots Guards Army Emergency Reserve: m. 1966, Mary Isabel, da. of the late Andrew Ramon
Dalzell de Bertodano [E. Mexborough], and has issue living, Sebastian Andrew, b. 1967,—Benedict
Simon, b. 1971—James Joseph Michael, b. 1974——Maria Sylvia Rose, b. 1968.

WIDOWS LIVING OF SONS OF THIRD EARL.

Winifred Kathleen Brodrick (Hon. Lady Scott): m. 1941, the Hon. Sir Ernest Stowell Scott, K.C.M.G.,
M.V.O., who d. 1953, and has issue living [see colls., infra]. Residence,—The Manor House, Bradford
Peverell, Dorchester, Dorset.
Dorothie Primrose (Lady Greeson), da. of Maj. C. Murray-Stewart, and widow of Eric Hoy Stuart [see M.
Bute, colls.]: m. 2ndly, 1958, as his third wife, Capt. the Hon. Michael Scott, OBE, who d. 1959; 3rdly,
1969, Surg. Vice-Adm. Sir Clarence Edward Greeson, KBE, CB.

COLLATERAL BRANCHES LIVING.

Grandchildren of the late John, Viscount Encombe, el. son of 3rd Earl:—
Issue of the late Hon. Michael Simon Scott, b. 1900, d. 1938: m. 1928, Ruth [(of Windmill
Farm, Far Hills, New Jersey, U.S.A.) ; she m. 2ndly, 1944, Lieut.-Com. Adams Batcheller
who d. 1950], dau. of the late James Cox Brady :—

John, b. 1929.——Michael Richard (Far Hills, New Jersey, USA) b. 1937: m. 1964, Pamela Hanford Vandeveer.——Sheila Maria, b. 1932: m. 1952, Philip Webster Smith, and has issue living. Residence,—Windmill Farm, Far Hills, New Jersey, USA.

Issue of the late Hon. Sir Ernest Stowell Scott, K.C.M.G., M.V.O., 2nd son of 3rd Earl b. 1872, d. 1953: m. 1941, Winifred Kathleen Brodrick (ante) :—
Margaret Rachel, b. 1943: m. 1964, David Edward Wyndham Tennant [see B. Glenconner, colls.].

Issue of the late Hon. Osmund Scott, 3rd son of 3rd Earl; b. 1876, d. 1948: m. 1906, Mary Cecilia, who d. 1941, dau. of the late Com. Dudley Charles Stuart, R.N. [M. Bute, colls.] :—
Harold Eldon, b. 1907; ed. at Winchester; Lieut.-Col. (ret.) Queen's Own Roy. W. Kent Regt.: m. 1938, Daphne Josephine, dau. of Col. Fitzhardinge Hancock, of Congham Hall, King's Lynn, and has issue living, David Eldon (Arne House, Arne, Wareham, Dorset), b. 1939: m. 1966, Clover Noakes, and has issue living, Rupert Eldon b. 1967, Henry Eldon b. 1969,—Verena Mary, b. 1942: m. 1963, Simon Norman Philips [E. Ducie, colls.], and has issue living, Lucy Jane b. 1964, Sophie Ann b. 1966,—Angela Lindsay, b. 1949,—Susanne, b. 1952. Residence,—Encombe, nr. Wareham, Dorset.——Osmund Stuart, b. 1909; ed. at Bradfield Coll. Residence,—Creg-Ny-Baa, Hartfield, Sussex.——Eric Surtees, MBE, b. 1912; ed. at Bradfield Coll., Lt.-Col. (ret.) The Buffs (Roy. E. Kent Regt.); N.-W. Europe 1944-45 (MBE); MBE (Mil) 1945: m. 1938, Rose Anne, only da. of the late Lt.-Col. C. E. Stewart, RA, and has issue living, Michael Ian Eldon, b. 1941; Maj. Scots Guards; Equerry to H.R.H. the Duke of Gloucester 1965-66: m. 1968, Veronica Mary Daniell, and has issue living, Charles Daniell Eldon b. 1970, Louisa Claire b. 1971,—Veronica Susan b. 1944: m. 1965, Michael Conway Phayre-Mudge, of 72, Campden St., SW8, and has issue living, Marcus Andrew b. 1968, Zoe Catherine b. 1970. Residence,—Bucknowle House, Wareham, Dorset.

Grandchildren of the late Hon. Osmund Scott (ante) :—
Issue of the late Alan Dudley Scott, b. 1910, d. 1951: m. 1936, Dorothy Dulany (Thea), only da. of Lt.-Col. Sefton D. Brancker, of The Croft, Crowborough, Sussex:—
Dudley John Eldon, b. 1939: m. 1961, Irene Florence, da. of F. J. Smith, of 30, Old Lane, Chobham, Surrey, and has issue living, Alan James, b. 1964,—Maria Lynn, b. 1963.——Caroline Edith Mary, b. 1946: m. 1969, Michael John Theobald.——Jennifer Dorothy Dulany, b. 1948.

Issue of the late Maj. Kenneth Bertram Scott, MC, b. 1915; d. (killed in action 1943: m. 1939, Denise Primrose Garnet (who d. 1968, having m. 2ndly, 1952, Alan Blackwell, of Laurel Farm, Little Barningham, Aldborough, nr. Norwich), da. of Garnet Leslie Clark, of The Red Lodge, Tadworth, Surrey:—
John Kenneth Eldon, b. 1940.

Issue of the late Capt. Hon. Denys Scott, 4th son of 3rd Earl, b. 1877, d. 1962: m. 1907, Lillis Amy, who d. 1950, da. of the late Com. Dudley Charles Stuart, RN [M. Bute, colls.]:—
John Ernest Dudley (Roundswell House, Barnstaple, N. Devon), b. 1908: an AFRAeS; formerly Squadron Leader RAFO: m. 1st, 1934, Joan Gwendolen (who obtained a divorce 1937), da. of R. Clayton-Cooper; 2ndly, 1937, Ethel Daphne Smith, who d. 1956; 3rdly, 1957, Margaret Lila Monro Monro, MRCS, LRCP, who d. 1973, and has issue living, (by 1st m.) Peter Denys John, b. 1935; (by 2nd m.) Roger John Stuart, b. 1939,—Georgina Rosemary, b. 1944.——Frederick Denys, b. 1909.—— Eustace Ian, b. 1911: m. 1950, Daphne Ann, da. the late Lt.-Col. Arthur O'Brien ffrench Blake, TD, of Giles Lane, Canterbury. Residence,—Lower Upacott Farm, Tawstock, nr. Barnstaple, N. Devon.

PREDECESSORS.—[1] Rt. Hon. Sir JOHN SCOTT, K.B., one of the most distinguished lawyers of England, was son of a merchant at Newcastle, and younger brother of Baron Stowell (cr. 1821, extinct 1836); was Solicitor-Gen. 1788, Attorney-Gen. 1793, Lord Chief Justice of the Common Pleas 1799-1801, and Lord High Chancellor 1801-6 and 1807-27; cr. Baron Eldon, of Eldon, co. Durham (peerage of Great Britain) 1799, and Viscount Encombe and Earl of Eldon (peerage of United Kingdom) 1821; d. 1838; s. by his grandson [2] JOHN, D.C.L., 2nd Earl, b. 1805; M.P. for Truro 1829-31: m. 1831, the Hon. Louisa Duncombe, dau. of 1st Baron Feversham; d. 1854; s. by his son [3] JOHN, 3rd Earl; b. 1845: m. 1869, Henrietta Minna, who d. 1921, dau. of Capt. Henry Martin Turnor; d. 1926; s. by his grandson [4] JOHN (son of the late John, Viscount Encombe, el. son of 3rd Earl), 4th Earl and present peer; also Viscount Encombe, and Baron Eldon.

ELGIN AND KINCARDINE, EARL OF. (Bruce.)
[Earl S. 1633.]

We have been.

ANDREW DOUGLAS ALEXANDER THOMAS BRUCE, 11th Earl; b. Feb. 17th, 1924; s. 1968; ed. at Eton, and Balliol Coll., Oxford (MA); JP and DL of co. Fife; HM Lt.-Col.; Comdt. Fife Bn., Army Cadet Force 1951-65; Grand Master Mason of Scotland 1961-65; Brig. of Queen's Body Guard for Scotland (Roy. Co. of Archers), and Bde Pres., Boys' Bde.; a Dir. of Dominion Insurance Co., Gurr Johns & Co., Scottish Amicable Life Assurance Soc., and Roy. Highland & Agric. Soc.; Chm., Nat. Savings Cttee. for Scotland; Hon. Col. The Elgin Regt. (Canada); 1939-45 War as Lt. Scots Guards (wounded): m. 1959, Victoria Mary, only da. of Maj. Dudley George Usher, MBE, TD, Scottish Horse [Hunter Blair, Bt., colls.], and has issue.

Arms.—Or, a saltire and chief gules, on a canton argent, a lion rampant azure, armed and langued of the second. Crest.—A lion statant, tail extended azure, armed and langued gules. Supporters—Two wild men, proper, wreathed round the temples and loins with laurel vert.

Residences,—Broomhall, Dunfermline, Fife.; Strathkyle, Ardgay, Ross & Cromarty.

SONS LIVING.
CHARLES EDWARD (Lord Bruce), b. Oct. 19th, 1961.
Hon. Adam Robert, b. 1968.
Hon. Alexander Victor, b. 1971.

DAUGHTERS LIVING.
Lady Georgiana Mary, b. 1960.
Lady Antonia Katherine, b. 1964.

BROTHERS LIVING.

Hon. James Michael Edward, *b.* 1927; ed. at Eton; late Lt. Scots Guards; a JP of Perthshire; Vice-Chm. of Forestry Cttee. of Gt. Britain; a member Home Grown Timber Advisory Cttee.; Chmn. of Scottish Woodland Owners Assen. (Commercial) Ltd.: *m.* 1st, 1950 (m. diss. 1974) the Hon. (Margaret) Jean Dagbjørt Coats, da. of 2nd Baron Glentanar (ext.); 2ndly, 1975, Morven-Anne, da. of Alistair Macdonald, of Gate Fulford, York, and has issue living (by 1st m.), Robert James Thomas, *b.* 1953; ed. at Eton,—John Edward, *b.* 1958,—Michael Andrew, *b.* 1961,—Janet Clare, *b.* 1954. *Residences,*—Park House, Balmanno, by Perth, and at 25, Ann St., Edinburgh. *Club.*—New (Edinburgh).

Hon. Edward David, *b.* 1936; ed. at Eton, and at Balliol Coll., Oxford (B.A. 1960); late Lieut. Intelligence Corps: *m.* 1960, Sara Elisabeth Wallop, younger dau. of the late Capt. Newton James Wallop William-Powlett, DSO, JP, RN [see E. Portsmouth, colls.], and has issue living, Newton Edward John, *b.* 1964,—Anna Catherine *b.* 1962. *Residence,*—Blairhill, Rumbling Bridge, Kinross

SISTERS LIVING.

Lady Martha Veronica, *OBE*, *TD*, *b.* 1921; Gov. HM Prison, Greenock, and a JP for co. Fife; Lady-in-Waiting to HRH the late Princess Royal Jan. to March 1965; OBE (Mil) 1958. *Residence,*— 89, Old Inverkip Rd., Greenock, Renfrewshire.

Lady Jean Christian, *b.* 1923 ; formerly in W.A.A.F.: *m.* 1945, Capt. David Wemyss, late Roy. Corps of Signals [see E. Wemyss, colls.]. *Residence,*—Invermay, Forteviot, Perthshire.

Lady Alison Margaret Katherine Antoinette, *b.* 1931; is a L.R.A.M.: *m.* 1957, Cleveland Stewart-Patterson, and has issue living, David Henry Cleveland, *b.* 1958,—Donald Iain Edward, *b.* 1960, —Christian Mary Lorraine, *b.* 1962. *Residence,*—Drishane Farm, 251, Senneville Rd., Senneville, P.Q., Canada.

UNCLE LIVING. *(Son of 9th Earl).*

Hon. Bernard, *M.C.*, *b.* (*posthumous*) 1917; ed. at Eton, and at New Coll. Oxford (B.A. 1938); Major late Scots Guards ; European War 1939–45 in Middle East and Italy (despatches, M.C.): *m.* 1st, 1958 (m. diss. 1968), Mrs. Mary Coxe Humphreys, da. of Philippus Miller, of Philadelphia, USA; 2ndly, 1970, Georgina, yr. da. of Philip Argenti, of 16, Via Tevere, Rome. *Residences,*— Cauldhame, Dunblane, Perths.; 35, Brompton Square, SW3. *Clubs,*—Pratt's, Brooks's, City of London.

WIDOWS LIVING OF SONS OF NINTH EARL.

Mary Katherine, dau. of the late Maj.-Gen. the Hon. John Edward Lindley [B. Lindley] : *m.* 1910. Major the Hon. Robert Bruce, C.B.E., who *d.* 1959, and has issue living [see colls., infra]. *Residence,* —Glenerney, Dunphail, Morayshire.

Jennet, *OBE* (Ballamor, Brora, Sutherland), da. of the Rt. Rev. Atherton Gwillym Rawstorne, DD, Suffragan Bishop of Whalley, OBE (Civil) 1974: *m.* 1919, Col. the Hon. David Bruce, who *d.* 1964, and has issue living [see colls. infra].

Helen Rachel (Larchwood, Itchen Abbas, Winchester; Clunel Cottage, Sallachy, Lairg), da. of the late Henry Feilden Rawstorne, of Roche Court, Fareham, Hants.: *m.* 1923, Capt. the Hon. John Bernard Bruce, RN, who *d.* 1971, and has issue living [see colls., infra].

WIDOW LIVING OF TENTH EARL.

Hon. Dame KATHERINE ELIZABETH Cochrane *DBE* (*The Dowager Countess of Elgin and Kincardine*), (Culross Abbey House, Culross, Dunfermline, Fife), da. of 1st Baron Cochrane of Cults; MBE (Civil) 1919; DBE (Civil) 1938: *m.* 1921, the 10th Earl, who *d.* 1968.

COLLATERAL BRANCHES LIVING.

Issue of the late Major the Hon. Robert Bruce, C.B.E., 2nd son of 9th Earl, *b.* 1882, *d.* 1959 : *m.* 1910, Mary Katherine (ante), dau. of the late Maj.-Gen. the Hon. John Edward Lindley [B. Lindley] :—

Veronica Mary, *b.* 1911; Director of Cygnet Ballet Sch., Forres.——Isobel Ursula, *b.* 1920; sometime in W.R.N.S. *Residence,*—Glenerney, Dunphail, Morayshire.

Issue of the late Col. the Hon. David Bruce, 4th son of 9th Earl, *b.* 1883, *d.* 1964: *m.* 1919, Jennet, OBE (ante), da. of the Rt. Rev. Atherton Gwillym Rawstorne, DD, Suffragan Bishop of Whalley:—

Rachel Mary, *b.* 1922: *m.* 1967, Rear-Adm. Bryan Cecil Durant, CB, DSO, DSC, of The Old House, Bighton, nr. Alresford, Hants.

Issue of the late Capt. the Hon. John Bernard Bruce, RN, 5th son of 9th Earl, *b.* 1892, *d.* 1971: *m.* 1923, Helen Rachel (ante), da. of the late Henry Feilden Rawstorne, of Roche Court, Fareham, Hants:—

Henry Victor (Barley Down House, Ovington Down, Alresford, Hants., and Sallachy, Lairg, Sutherland; Farmers' and Hampshire County Clubs, and MCC), *b.* 1924; ed. at Eton and Roy. Agric. Coll., Cirencester: Lt.-Cdr. RN (ret.), and a Farmer; JP of Hants., Councillor of Winchester; Itchen Stoke and Ovington with Northington; Chm. of Hants. Co. Scout Council; a Gen. Commr. of Income Tax since 1967: *m.* 1951, Helen Vernon Wallop, da. of Vice-Adm. Sir Peveril Barton Beibey Wallop William-Powlett, KCB, KCMG, CBE, DSO [see E. Portsmouth, colls.], and has issue living, Peveril John, *b.* 1953,—Alastair Andrew, *b.* 1960,—Robina Helen, *b.* 1952,—Lucinda Jane, *b.* 1956. ——*Rev.* Francis Bernard (Croston Rectory, Croston, Lancs.), *b.* 1930; ed. at Eton and Trin. Coll., Oxford (MA); Assist. Curate of Bury 1954-58, and Sherborne Abbey, and Curate in charge of St. Paul's Sherborne 1958–61, since when R. of St. Michael and All Angels, Croston: *m.* 1957, Fiona Jane Beryl, da. of Capt. John Robert Sutherland Haines, CBE, RN, 2nd has issue living, Simon Jock, *b.* 1959,—Jonathan Francis, *b.* 1967,—Emma Cecilia Rachel, *b.* 1960.——Victor Robert (Brook House, Henley Rd., Marlow, Bucks.), *b.* 1932: ed. at Eton; MB, BS London 1956; DRCOG 1958; Surg.Lt. RN (ret.): *m.* 1956, Dorothy May, da. of the late Arthur E. Pavey, and has issue living, Angus Robert John, *b.* 1960,—Hamish Charles Victor, *b.* 1962.——Alexander Rawstorne (9 Av. de Foestraets, 1180 Brussels), *b.* 1936; ed. at Eton: *m.* 1962, Beatrice Germaine, da. of Jacques-Etienne Rossièr, of Champbabaud, Veytaux, Vaud, Switzerland.——Constance Madeleine, *b.* 1927: *m.* 1949, Lt.-Cdr. Godfrey Joseph Hines, RN (ret.), of Crossways, Droxford, Hants., and has issue living, Catherine Angela, *b.* 1950,—Fiona Madeleine, *b.* 1952.——Mabel Cecilia Helen, *b.* 1939: *m.* 1962, Lt.-Cdr. Lachlan Ronald Duncan Mackintosh of Mackintosh, OBE, DL, RN (ret.), of Moy Hall, Tomatin, Inverness-shire, IV13 7YQ, and has issue living, John Lachlan, *b.* 1969,— Louisa Celia, *b.* 1962,—Bridget Margaret, *b.* 1966.

Grandson of the late Hon. Frederick John Bruce (infra) :—

Issue of the late Lewis Bruce, *b.* 1880, *d.* 1961: *m.* 1911, Anne Margaret Macdonald, who *d.* 1961, dau. of the late Robert Burt Ranken, W.S., of Edinburgh:—

John Frederick Lambton, *b.* 1912 : *m.* 1941, his cousin Marjory Katherine Fernie, dau. of Charles Bruce (infra), and has issue living, Penelope Margaret, *b.* 1943,—Juliet Louisa, *b.* 1950,—Janet Marion, *b.* 1956. *Residence,*—Lambda Cottage, Wick Hill, Finchampstead, Berks.——Robert Ri_chard Fernie, *DFC* (Y Gât, Llechryd, Cardigan), *b.* 1915; BMus 1938; 1939-45 War as Fl.-Lt. RA F Vol. Reserve (DFC and Bar): *m.* 1941, Beatrice, da. of A. Tombolini, of 55, Wainfelin Av., Pontypool, and has issue living, Richard Stephen Worthington (47, Woodlands St., Woodlands, W. Australia), *b.* 1942, MB, BS London: FFARCS: *m.* 1st 1965 (m. diss. 1969), Frances Mary, da. of K. G. Morgan, MRCVS, of Llanover Lodge, Chepstow; 2ndly, 1969, Katherine Jane, da. of Mrs. J. A. Hunter, of 1528, Yale St., Santa Monica, Cal., USA, and has issue living (by 1st m.) Katharine Blanche Mary, *b.* 1966,—Anthony James Lewis (25, Snowdon St., Porthmadog, Gwynedd), *b.* 1948; BSc: *m.* 1972, Glenys Vaughan, da. of J. Jones of Caernarvon,—Katharine Anne Russel, *b.* 1945; MCSP: *m.* 1968, John Mervyn Henry Clements, MA, ACA, and has issue living, Timothy Robert Henry *b.* 1968, Charles Richard Edward, *b.* 1971, Victoria Penelope Louise *b.* 1972.——James Alexander, *b.* 1919: *m.* 1952, Joan Beryl Marion Elizabeth, da. of Granville Alexander Silby, and

widow of Group Capt. Walter Donald Butler, RAF, and has issue living, Nige lCharles, *b.* 1954,—
Miranda Veronica, *b.* 1953.——Katharine Anne Doughty (of 2, Moat Side, Hanworth, Middx.,)
b. 1921; ARCM: *m.* 1971, Sidney John Doe.

Grandchildren of the late Capt. Charles Bruce (infra) :—
Issue of the late Lieut. David Charles Richard Bruce, R.N., *b.* 1928 ; *d.* 1957: *m.* 1950,
Georgina (who *m.* 2ndly, 1968, P. J. Bruce-Souster, da. of G. E. Keay, of 5, Erith Rd.,
Bexleyheath, Kent:—
Roland Christopher, *b.* 1956.——Clarissa Jane Fernie, *b.* 1952.——Fiona Geraldine, *b.* 1953.——
Miranda Jacqueline, *b.* 1955.

Granddaughters of the late Hon. Frederick John Bruce, yst. son of 8th Earl:—
Issue of the late Capt. Charles Bruce, *b.* 1883, *d.* 1958: *m.* 1918, Joan (Landmark, Pye Hill,
Finchampstead, Berks.), da. of Isaac Newton Woodiwiss, of Trusthorpe Hall, Lincolnshire:—
Marjory Katherine Fernie, *b.* 1919: *m.* 1941, her cousin, John Frederick Lambton Bruce (ante).
Residence,—Lambda Cottage, Wick Hill, Finchampstead, Berks.——Isobel Seaton, *b.* 1921: *m.*
1956, Joseph Henry Clift, and has issue living, Michael Charles David, *b.* 1957,—Simon Paul,
b. 1963. *Residence,*—Taskus Farm, Leedstown, Hayle, Cornwall.——Zenobie Margaret, *b.* 1922:
m. 1942, Walter Bevan Coulson Tregarthen, and has issue living, Bruce Coulson, *b.* 1943. *Residence,*—Gorran, Canon's Town, Hayle, Cornwall.——Jill Rosalind Dodsworth (The Old Rectory
E. Bridgford, Nottingham), *b.* 1927; BA, Oxford; assumed by deed poll 1972, the surname of Dodsworth: *m.* 1949 (m. diss. 1968), James Mayo Alastair Gunn, and has issue living, Henry Alastair
Bruce, *b.* 1951,—David James Paul, *b.* 1956,—Nicola Fernie, *b.* 1952,—Ann Veronica, *b.* 1954.

Grandchildren of the late Charles Thomas Bruce, el. son of the late Hon. Thomas
Charles Bruce, 5th son of 7th Earl :—
Issue of the late Robert Charles Bruce, M.C., *b.* 1898, *d.* 1953 : *m.* 1919, the Hon. Kate
Mary Maugham, who *d.* 1961, dau. of 1st Viscount Maugham :—
David, *b.* 1920 ; ed. at Eton ; European War 1939-45 as Capt. Welsh Guards (twice wounded) : *m.*
1949 (marriage dissolved 1958), Elizabeth Joan, dau. of the late Maj.-Gen. Philip Saxon Gregson-
Ellis, C.B., O.B.E. [see Lloyd, Bt. (ext.)], and has issue living, Cynthia Penelope Helen, *b.* 1951.
Residence,—Flat 1, 80, Elm Park Gdns., SW10.——Katherine Mary (Garth House, Llangammarch
Wells, Breconshire), *b.* 1928: *m.* 1st, 1948 (m. diss. 1960) John Scott; 2ndly, 1968, Francis Amcotts
Wilson [see Wilson, Bt. (cr. 1874)], and has issue living, (by 1st m.) Caroline Judith, *b.* 1950: *m.*
1970, Michael David Sykes.—Katherine (twin) *b.* 1950: *m.* 1971, John Hunter Pemberton.

PREDECESSORS.—[1] *Sir* EDWARD Bruce, Knt., P.C., a Lord of Session 1597-1603, accompanied
King James to England on his accession 1603, was naturalized that year, and appointed Master of
the Rolls for life; cr. *Lord Kinloss* (peerage of Scotland) 1602, with remainder to his heirs and assigns
whatsoever, and *Lord Bruce of Kinloss* (peerage of Scotland) 1604, with remainder to his heirs male:
d. 1610; *s.* by his el. son (2) EDWARD, *KG,* 2nd Lord; killed in a duel 1613; *s.* by his brother [3]
THOMAS, 3rd Lord; cr. *Earl of Elgin* (peerage of Scotland) 1633 with remainder to heirs male
whatever bearing the name and arms of Bruce, and *Baron Bruce,* of Whorlton, co. York
(peerage of England) 1640; *d.* 1663; *s.* by his son [4] ROBERT, 2nd Earl; cr. *Baron Bruce,*
of Skelton, co. York, *Viscount Bruce,* of Ampthill, Beds, and *Earl of Ailesbury,* co. Bucks
(peerage of England) 1663; Lord Chamberlain 1685; *d.* 1685; *s.* by his son [5] THOMAS,
3rd Earl of Elgin and 2nd Earl of Ailesbury; *d.* 1741; *s.* by his son [6] CHARLES, 4th Earl of Elgin
and 3rd Earl of Ailesbury; cr. *Baron Bruce,* of Tottenham (peerage of Great Britain) 1746, with
remainder to his nephew the Hon. Thomas Brudenell, 4th son of 3rd Earl of Cardigan ; *d.* 1746,
when the Lordship of Kinloss became abeyant (see Ly. Kinloss), the Lordship of Bruce of Kinloss
reverted to his heir male, see M. Ailesbury, and the Earldom of Elgin devolved upon his kinsman and heir male [7] CHARLES BRUCE, 5th Earl, who in 1740 had *s.* as 9th Earl of Kincardine (see
note *⁎*²), assumed the joint title of Earl of Elgin and Kincardine ; *d.* 1771 ; *s.* by his el. son [8]
WILLIAM ROBERT, 6th Earl of Elgin and 10th Earl of Kincardine ; *d.* 1771 ; *s.* by his brother [9]
THOMAS, *P.C.,* 7th Earl of Elgin and 11th Earl of Kincardine ; a Gen. in the Army, a Representative
Peer 1790-1840, and successively Ambassador to Brussels, Berlin, and Constantinople ; the " Elgin
Marbles " deposited in the British Museum were collected by him during his residence in Turkey ;
d. 1841 ; *s.* by his son [10] JAMES, *K.T., G.C.B.,* 8th Earl of Elgin and 12th Earl of Kincardine, *b.*
1811 ; M.P. for Southampton 1841-2, Gov.-Gen. of Jamaica 1842-6, and of Canada 1846, Ambassador
on special missions to China 1850 and 1860, Postmaster-Gen. 1859, and Gov.-Gen. of India 1860-8 ;
cr. *Baron Elgin,* of Elgin (peerage of United Kingdom) 1849 : *m.* 1st, 1841, Elizabeth Mary, who *d.*
1843, dau. of Charles Lennox Cumming-Bruce, M.P., of Dunphail, Morayshire : 2ndly, 1846, Lady
Mary Louisa Lambton, *C.I.,* dau. of 1st Earl of Durham : *d.* 1863 ; *s.* by his son [11] VICTOR
ALEXANDER, *K.G., G.C.S.I., G.C.I.E., P.C.,* 9th Earl of Elgin and 13th Earl of Kincardine, *b.*
1849 ; Treasurer of the Household and Commr. of Works and Buildings 1886, Viceroy of India
1894-9, and Sec. of State for Colonies Dec. 1905 to April 1908 ; Lord-Lieut. of Fife 1886-1917 :
m. 1st, 1876, Lady Constance Mary Carnegie, *C.I.,* who *d.* 1909. dau. of 9th Earl of Southesk, K.T. ;
2ndly, 1913, Gertrude Lilian, who *d.* 1971, da. of the late Com. William Sherbrooke, RN, of Oxton
Hall, Notts, and widow of Capt. Frederick Charles Ashley Ogilvy, RN; *d.* 1917; *s.* by
his el. son [12] EDWARD JAMES, *KT, CMG, TD, CD,* 10th Earl of Elgin and 14th Earl of Kincardine,
b. 1881; Lord High Commr. to Gen. Assembly of Ch. of Scotland 1925-26, Pres. and Chm. of Scottish
Development Council 1931-46; and Lord-Lieut. of Fife 1935-65: *m.* 1921, the Hon. Dame Katherine
Elizabeth Cochrane, DBE, el. da. of 1st Baron Cochrane of Cults; *d.* 1968; *s.* by his son [13]
ANDREW DOUGLAS ALEXANDER THOMAS, 11th Earl of Elgin, and 15th Earl of Kincardine, and
present peer; also Lord Bruce of Kinloss, Lord Bruce of Torry, and Baron Elgin.

⁎⁎ [1] *Sir* EDWARD Bruce, Knt.; cr. *Lord Bruce of Torry,* and *Earl of Kincardine* (peerage of
Scotland) 1647, with remainder to heirs general; *d.s.p.*; *s.* by his brother [2] ALEXANDER,
P.C., 2nd Earl; after the Restoration the Govt. of Scotland was placed in his hands, and he
was appointed an Extraordinary Lord of Session ; *d.* 1680; *s.* by his son [3] ALEXANDER, 3rd
Earl ; *d.* unmarried 1705, when the honours were claimed by his sister Lady Mary Cochrane,
and also by his kinsman only son of Robert Bruce, Esq., uncle of 1st Earl ; the competition
terminated in favour of the latter [4] ALEXANDER, 4th Earl ; *s.* by his el. son [5] ROBERT, 5th
Earl; *d.s.p.*; *s.* by his brother [6] ALEXANDER, 6th Earl, *d.s.p.*; *s.* by his brother [7] THOMAS,
7th Earl; *s.* by his el. son [8] WILLIAM, 8th Earl; *s.* by his son [9] CHARLES, 9th Earl,
who *s.* as 5th Earl of Elgin.

ELIBANK, LORD. (Erskine-Murray.) [Lord S. 1643, Bt. S. 1628.]
[Title pronounced " Ellibank."]

ALAN, D'ARDIS ERSKINE-MURRAY, 14th Lord and 14th Baronet; *b.* Dec.
31st 1923; *s.* 1973 (petition to Lyon Court pending); ed. at Bedford Sch. and
Peterhouse, Camb. (MA); Bar. Middle Temple 1949: *m.* 1962, Valerie Sylvia,
da. of the late Herbert William Dennis, of St. Margarets, Middlesex, and has
issue.

Arms.—Not yet rematriculated in the line of the present Lord.
Residence,—The Coach House, Charters Rd., Sunningdale, Berks.

SONS LIVING.
Hon. ROBERT FRANCIS ALAN, *b.* Oct. 10th, 1964.
Hon. Timothy Alexander Elibank, *b.* 1967.

BROTHER LIVING.
Patrick Elibank (Elmhurst, Station Rd., Bakewell, Derbys.), *b.* 1927; ed. at Bedford Sch. and Pembroke Coll., Camb. (MA); FICE: *m.* 1957, Jenny Mary Margaret, da. of the late John Brown, of Bowbank, Middleton-in-Teesdale, co. Durham, and has issue living, Vivien Mary, *b.* 1958,—Clare Ruth, *b.* 1960,—Hilary Margaret, *b.* 1965.

SISTER LIVING.
Helen Veronica, *b.* 1931, MB, BS London: *m.* 1958, Neil MacDonald, FRCS, of 22, Old Broadway, Manchester, 20, and has issue living, Sally, *b.* 1959,—Fiona *b.* 1961,—Juliet, *b.* 1964.

DAUGHTER LIVING OF FIRST VISCOUNT.
Hon. Evelyn Izme (*Dowager Baroness Mottistone*), *b.* 1886; a JP for Isle of Wight: *m.* 1st, 1906, Capt. George Crosfield Norris Nicholson, Roy. Flying Corps, who *d.* (on active ser. during European War, 1916 [see Nicholson, Bt. (cr. 1912)]; 2ndly, 1917, as his second wife, the 1st Baron Mottistone, who *d.* 1947. *Residence,*—The Dower House, Mottistone Manor, Isle of Wight.

COLLATERAL BRANCHES LIVING.
　　　Issue of the late Capt. the Hon. Edward Oliphant Murray, 2nd son of 1st Viscount, *b.* 1871, *d.* (killed in action in S. Africa) 1901: *m.* 1900, Mary, who *d.* 1943, dau. of the late Henry Christian Allhusen, of Stoke Court, Bucks.:—
Mary Alice Oliphant (*Hon. Mrs. Harry N. Morgan-Grenville*), *b.* 1900: *m.* 1921, Capt. the Hon. Harry Nugent Morgan-Grenville, of 18, Farley Court, Melbury Rd., W14 [see Ly. Kinloss].
　　　Issue of the late Hon. Nina Charlotte Murray, da. of 1st Viscount, *b.* 1875, *d.* 1966: *m.* 1896, Hylton Philipson, who *d.* 1935:—
Oliphant James (Manor House, Everton, Lymington, Hants.), *b.* 1905: *m.* 1st, 1930, Yvonne, da. of Albert Kreglinger, of Antwerp; 2ndly, 1946, Mabel Helen (DOYLE), da. of David Fell.——Nina Clare, *b.* 1899: *m.* 1932, the Rev. Cyril Parkinson Shaw, who *d.* 1972, and has issue living, Christopher John Hylton Murray (Domaine de Migron, Biarritz, BP, France; 2, East 62nd St., New York, USA), *b.* 1938; ed. at Eton; Lt. Gren. Guards: *m.* 1962, Liza, da. of Howard Dietz, of Sands Point, Long Island, NY, USA, and has issue living, Benjamin Howard Stephen Bulkely *b.* 1968, Tanis Murray *b.* 1966.

　　　Grandson of the late Alexander Erskine ERSKINE-MURRAY, son of the late Hon. James Murray, 4th son of 7th Lord:—
　　　Issue of the late Lieut.-Col. Arthur Erskine-Murray, O.B.E., D.S.O. (uncle of 13th Lord), *b.* 1877, *d.* 1948: *m.* 1906, Ena Nelson, who *d.* 1942, dau. of the late Henry Ernest Trestrail, F.R.C.S., M.R.C.P., of Mount Pleasant House, Longton, Staffordshire:—
Arthur Sydney Elibank, *b.* 1909; BSc (Civil Eng.); MICE; a Dir. of Thomas Poole & Gladstone China Ltd., Alfred Clough Ltd., Alfred Clough (Potteries) Ltd., Swithaincote Ltd., S. Newman Ltd., and Bentley Piano Co., Ltd.: *m.* 1940, Florence Duncan, da. of William Duncan Robertson, and has issue living, Ann, *b.* 1942; MA: *m.* 1965, Anthony Peter Bartleet, of Bucklers, Great Tey, Coggeshall, Essex, and has issue living, James Murray *b.* 1967, Thomas Anthony *b.* 1969, William Arthur *b.* 1971,—Susan, *b.* 1945. *Residence,*—The Homestead, Gt. Amwell, Ware, Herts.

　　　Grandchildren of the late Capt. James Pulteney Murray, son of late Lieut. James Edward Ferguson Murray, R.N., el. son of Maj.-Gen. James Patrick Murray, C.B., M.P., el. son of the late Gen. the Hon. James Murray, 5th son of 4th Lord:—
　　　Issue of the late William Harry Elibank Murray, *b.* 1866, *d.* 1937: *m.* 1892, Bertha Delamore, who *d.* 1959, dau. of Patrick Brougham :—
Douglas Elibank, *b.* 1898; European War 1915-18 in Palestine with Australian Light Horse, European War 1939-44 with Australian Light Horse: *m.* 1st, 1935, Rewa (from whom he obtained a divorce 1946), dau. of Joseph Patrick O'Hara; 2ndly, 1948, Ngaio Milva Barnott, and has issue living, (by 1st m.) William Eoin Elibank, (Kennedy and 16th Ave., RR1 Unionville, Ont., Canada) *b.* 1938: *m.* 1970, Sheila Marion, da. of Walter Robert Pont, of E. Maitland, NSW, and has issue living, James Douglas Elibank *b.* 1970, Alexandra Naomi *b.* 1974,—Pamela Anna Elibank, *b.* 1940: *m.* 1967, T. McKenna, of Hamilton, NZ,—Rita Gai Elibank (25/254, Pacific Highway, Lindfield, NSW) *b.* 1942. *Residence,*—Harness Cask, Bostobrick, Dorrigo, North Coast, NSW.——Rita Lindsay (25/254, Pacific Highway, Lindfield, NSW), *b.* 1895: *m.* 1917, John Frederick Wyly, who *d.* 1960.

　　　Issue of the late Brig.-Gen. Edward Rushworth Blakiston Murray, *b.* 1868, *d.* (result of enemy action during European War) 1942 : *m.* 1905, Hilda Dorothea, who *d.* (result of enemy action during European War) 1942, el. dau. of the late Reginald Paul, formerly of Woodgate, Loughborough :—
James Patrick, *C.M.G.*, *b.* 1906; ed. at St. Edward's Sch., Oxford, and at Ch. Ch., Oxford (B.A. 1928); Commr. for N. Rhodesia in U.K. 1961-64; formerly Senior Provincial Commr., N. Rhodesia; C.M.G. 1958: *m.* 1934, Margaret Ruth, dau. of the late Rev. A. E. Buchanan, formerly R. of Pedmore, Worcs., and has issue living, James Alexander Gideon, *b.* 1936; ed. at Trin. Coll., Glenalmond; AOA: *m.* 1965, Gillian Mary, da. of the late H. G. Adcock, of St. Albans, Herts., and has issue living, James Richard *b.* 1967, Andrew Thomas *b.* 1968,—Patrick Edward (Greenhaigh, Woodham Rd., Horsell, Woking, Surrey), *b.* 1939; ed. at Trin. Coll., Glenalmond: *m.* 1963, Marie-Danielle, da. of H. C. du Cladier de Curac, of Durban, S. Africa, and has issue living, Charles Patrick *b.* 1971, Danielle Jeanne *b.* 1964, Diana Ruth *b.* 1965,—Thomas Walter, *b.* 1942; ed. at Trin. Coll., Glenalmond. *Residence,*—Trewen, Shaftesbury Rd., Woking, Surrey.——*Rev.* Thomas Edward Elibank (2, Spottiswoode St., Edinburgh, EH9 1ER), *b.* 1908; ed. at St. Edward's Sch., Oxford; has Diploma of Art, Edinburgh: Hon. Assist. Supernumy Edinburgh Dio 1973; 1939-45 War as Capt. Gordon Highlanders: *m* 1932, Hester Doreen, who *d.* (result of enemy action during 1939-45 War) 1942, da. of the late Capt. C. A. C. Bentley, Roy, Warwicks. Regt.——Elizabeth (2, Spottiswoode St., Edinburgh, EH9 1ER), *b.* 1911.

PREDECESSORS.—[1] PATRICK Murray, el. son of Sir Gideon Murray of Elibank, Lord of Session (3rd son of Andrew Murray of Blackbarony, and uncle of 1st Bt., *cr.* 1628); *cr.* a *Baronet* 1628 and *Lord Elibank*, of Ettrick Forest, co. Selkirk (peerage of Scotland) 1643, with remainder to his heirs male whatsoever; one of the six peers who opposed the delivering up of Charles I. to the Parliament of England; *d.* 1649; *s.* by his son [2] PATRICK, 2nd Lord; *d.* 1661; *s.* by his son [3] PATRICK, 3rd Lord; *d.* 1687; *s.* by his son [4] ALEXANDER, 4th Lord; *d.* 1736; *s.* by his el. son [5] PATRICK, 5th Lord; *d.s.p.* 1778; *s.* by his brother [6] GEORGE, 6th Lord; an Adm.; *d.* 1785; *s.* by his nephew [7] ALEXANDER, 7th Lord, son of the Rev. the Hon. Gideon, D.D. 3rd son of 4th Lord; Lord-Lieut. of co. Peebles; *d.* 1820; *s.* by his son [8] ALEXANDER, 8th Lord; *d.* 1830; *s.* by his son [9] ALEXANDER OLIPHANT, 9th Lord; *b.* 1804: *m.* 1838, Emily Maria, dau. of Archibald Montgomery; *d.* 1871; *s.* by his son [10] MONTOLIEU FOX OLIPHANT, 10th Lord; *b.* 1840; was Lord-Lieut. of Peeblesshire 1896-1908; *cr.* *Viscount Elibank*, of Elibank, co. Selkirk (peerage of United Kingdom) 1911: *m.* 1868, Blanche Alice, who *d.* 1936, dau. of the late Edward John Scott, of Portland Lodge, Southsea; *d.* 1927; *s.* by his son [11] (CHARLES) GIDEON, 2nd Viscount; *b.* 1877; was Private Sec. to Commr. for Native Affairs in S. Africa 1901-2, Assist. Private Sec. to Permanent Under-Sec. of State for the Colonies 1907-9, Administrator of St. Vincent 1909-14, and of St. Lucia 1914-17, and Lord-Lieut. for Peeblesshire 1935-45; sat as M.P. for St. Rollox Div. of Glasgow (*U*) 1918-22: *m.* 1908, Ermine Mary Katherine, *J.P.*, who *d.* 1955, dau. of the late Henry Robarts Madocks, of

Glanywen, Denbigh, and widow of Lieut.-Col. James Henry Aspinwall; d. 1951; s. by his brother [12] ARTHUR CECIL, C.M.G., D.S.O., 3rd Viscount, b. 1879; Capt. King's Own Scottish Borderers and Lt.-Col. Special Reserve Cav.; M.P. for Kincardineshire (L) 1908-23; P.P.S. to Parliamentary Sec. to Board of Trade 1909, to Under-Sec. of State for India 1909-10, and to Sec. of State for Foreign Affairs (Rt. Hon. Sir Edward Grey, Bt., M.P.) 1910-14, and Assist. Mil. Attaché at Washington 1917-18: m. 1931, Faith Celli, who d. 1942 (the dream dau. in Barrie's " Dear Brutus " 1916 and 1922), dau. of the late Francis H. Standing; d. 1962, when the U.K. Viscountcy became ext.; s. in the Lordship by his kinsman [13] JAMES ALASTAIR FREDERICK CAMPBELL Erskine-Murray (son of the late Sqdn. Leader James Robert Erskine-Murray, D.Sc., el. son of the late Alexander Erskine Erskine-Murray, el. son of the late Hon. James Murray, 4th son of 7th Lord), 13th Lord; b. 1902; Maj. HLI, d. 1973, s. by his cousin, [14] ALAN D'ARDIS (son of Maj. Robert Alan Erskine-Murray, OBE, uncle of 13th Lord), 14th Lord and present peer.

Eliot, Lord, son of Earl of St. Germans.

ELLENBOROUGH, BARON. (Law.) [Baron U.K. 1802.]

Law and equity combined.

RICHARD EDWARD CECIL LAW, 8th Baron ; b. Jan. 14th, 1926 ; s. 1945 ; ed. at Eton, and at Magdalene Coll., Camb. ; is Pres., National Union of Ratepayers' Assos. : m. 1953, Rachel Mary, only dau. of the late Major Ivor Hedley, 17th Lancers, and has issue.

Arms,—Ermine, on a bend engrailed, between two cocks gules, three mullets pierced or. Crest.— A cock gules, charged on the breast with a mitre pendant from a chain round the neck or Supporters.—Two eagles, wings elevated sable, each gorged with a chain or, and pendant there from on the breast of the *dexter* supporter a mitre, and on the *sinister* a covered cup gold.

Residence,—Broadfield House, Wadhurst, Sussex. *Clubs*,—Gresham, Turf.

SONS LIVING.

Hon. RUPERT EDWARD HENRY, b. March 28th, 1955; 2nd Lt. Coldm. Gds.
Hon. Edmund Ivor Cecil, b. 1956.
Hon. Charles Adrian Christian Towry, b. 1960.

BROTHER LIVING.

Hon. Cecil Towry Henry, b. 1931 ; ed. at Eton; late Lieut. King's Dragoon Guards (Reserve) and Chm. of Towry Law (Holdings), Ltd., Insurance Brokers, of Towry Law & Co., Ltd., of Towry Law (General Insurance) Ltd., of Towry Law & Co. (Scotland) Ltd., of Towry Law & Co. (Midlands) Ltd., Towry Law & Co. (Northern) Ltd., Towry Law & Co. (Yorkshire), Ltd., Towry Law Trustee Co., Ltd., and Towry Law Investment & Advisory Sers., Ltd.: m. 1957, Daphne Mary Jean, yr. da. of the late Hon. Laurence Paul Methuen-Campbell [see B. Methuen, colls.], and has issue living, Edward Henry Towry, b. 1971,—Cecilia Diana, b. 1958,—Marianne Jean, b. 1960,—Catherine Rose, b. 1962. *Residence*,—6, Sussex Sq., W2. *Club*,—Cavalry.

WIDOW LIVING OF SEVENTH BARON.

HELEN) DOROTHY (*Dorothy, Baroness Ellenborough*), da. of the late H. W. Lovatt, formerly of Tiraun, Newcastle, co. Down; a D.St.J.: m. 1923, the 7th Baron, who d. 1945. *Residence*,—119, Ashley Gdns., SW1.

COLLATERAL BRANCHES LIVING.

Grandsons of the late Thomas Graves Law, LLD, 3rd son of the Hon. William Towry Law (infra):—
Issue of the late Henry Duncan Graves Law, C.I.E., b. 1883, d. 1964: m. 1st, 1909, Jean, who d. 1956, da. of the late Peter Graham, R.A., of Westoun, St. Andrews; 2ndly, 1958, Nancy Olive Legge (c/o Lloyds Bank, Sherborne, Dorset), da. of the late Sir Henry Frederick Oswald Norbury:—
(By 1st marriage) Richard Graham (of 99, Wood Vale, N.10), b. 1918; ed. at Tonbridge, and at Peterhouse, Camb. (B.A. 1940, M.A. 1947); M.B. 1947, M.D. 1952, F.R.C.O.G. 1961: m. 1944, Barbara, M.B., B.S., D.P.H., dau. of Horace Wright, and has issue living, Nigel Graham, b. 1949,—David Jocelyn Wright, b. 1951,—Penelope Jane, b. 1955.——Christopher (of Appleyard, Little Chart, Ashford, Kent), b. 1921; ed. at Tonbridge, and at Peterhouse, Camb.; ARIBA: m. 1954, Alison Mitchell, and has issue living, Jonathan, b. 1958,—Ian Graham, b. 1961,—Fiona Jean, b. 1955,——Michael Haldane (39, St. Paul's Sq., Holgate, York), b. 1925; ed. at Tonbridge, and at Peterhouse, Camb.: m. 1954, Dorothea von Schön-Kreuzenau, and has issue living, Richard Anthony b. 1955,—Peter Andrew, b. 1958,—John Martin, b. 1961,—Stephen Francis, b. 1966.

Granddaughter of the late Hon. William Towry Law, 5th son of 1st Baron:—
Issue of the late Thomas Graves Law, LL.D., b. 1836, d. 1904 : m. 1880, Wilhelmina Frederica who d. 1931, dau. of the late Capt. John James Allen. R.N., of Errol Park, Perth :—
Frances Augusta Laura (The Convent [Guest House], Fulmer Common Rd., Iver Heath, Bucks): m. 1902, John Ayling, who d. 1935, and has issue living, Winifred Rose, b. 1903; is a Nun,—Joan Eleanor, b. 1904: m. 1936, Evan Robert Rees, MD, FRCOG, of 5, Sunnydene Lodge, Bridgewater Rd., Wembley, Middlesex,—Grace Marion Wilfrid (twin) (5, The Grove, Minsterley, Shrewsbury), b. 1904: m. 1934, Capt. Oswald Sebastian Griffin, who d. 1950.

Grandchildren of the late Cdr. Frederick Charles Law, 4th son of the Hon. William Towry Law (ante):—
Issue of the late John Crawford Law, b. 1876, d. 1919: m. 1917, Eleanor Agnes Letitia, dau. of Rupert E. Kingsford, of Toronto:—
Margaret Augusta Eleanor, b. 1918: m. 1st, 1940, Capt. Denys Symons, Roy. Tank Regt.; 2ndly,

1966, Oliver Bosshardt Bennett, CBE, of 14, Graham Terr., SW1, and has issue living, (by 1st m.) Ivor James, *b.* 1944,—Dianna Venetia, *b.* 1940.
  Issue of the late Capt. William Victor Law, *b.* 1880, *d.* 1967: *m.* 1912, Helen Violet who *d.* 1971, da. of the late Henry Morris Watson, Assist. Gen. Manager of Bank of Hamilton:—
Frederick Henry (RRI Sunderland, Ont., Canada, LOC 1HO), *b.* 1912; Lt. RCNVR: *m.* 1937, Ruth, da. of George H. Dill, of Toronto, and has issue living, Stephen Frederick (22, McDonald Drive, Aurora, Ont., Canada), *b.* 1943: *m.* 1966, Julika Fietius,—Sharron Constance, *b.* 1937: *m.* 1955, James Wilfred Brazier, of 106, Hawthorne Av., Stouffville, Ont., Canada, and has issue living, Frederick James *b.* 1955, Danny Allen *b.* 1957, Tomothy Stewart *b.* 1960.——Mary Charlotte Violet (44, Valerie Drive, St. Catherines, Ont., Canada), *b.* 1917: *m.* 1st, 1939, Capt. W. Marshal Cleland, Gov.-Gen's, Horse Guards, Canadian Army, who *d.* 1958; 2ndly, 1960, John Franklin Horne, who *d.* 1974, and has issue living, (by 1st m.) William Marshal (290, St. Clair Av., E. Toronto 290, Ont., Canada), *b.* 1944: *m.* 1967, Sheila, da. of Jack M. Reid, of Kingston, Ont.,—Donald Law (RR2 St. Williams, Ont., Canada), *b.* 1947: *m.* 1974, Katherine, da. of Ward E. Kitchen, of RRI, Vittoria, Ont.,—Calder Bruce (RRI, Paris, Ont.), *b.* 1949: *m.* 1969, Sandra, da. of Louis Melnyle, of Brantford, Ont.,—Peter A., *b.* 1957.
    Issue of the late Maj. Adrian Aloysius Sherwood Law, *b.* 1885, *d.* 1945: *m.* 1914, Maud, who *d.* 1960, da. of the late Hon. Louis Arthur Audette, a Puisne Judge of Exchequer Court, Canada:—
Charles Anthony Francis, *DSC*, *CD*, *b.* 1916; Cdr. RCN (ret.); landscape and seascape painter; artist-in-residence St. Mary's Univ., Halifax, Nova Scotia; 1939-45 War (despatches twice, DSC): *m.* 1942, Jane Brumm Shaw. *Residence*,—8, Halls Rd., Armdale, Halifax, Co., Nova Scotia, Canada, B3P IP3.

    Granddaughter of the late Maj. Adrian Aloysius Sherwood Law (ante):—
    Issue of the late Adrian Augustus Stuart Law, *b.* 1918, *d.* 1968: *m.* 1st, 1942 (m. diss. 1951), Willa Noble Angus; 2ndly, 1952, Muriel Beverley (2582, MacDonald Drive, Victoria, BC, Canada), da. of the late Brooke Vaio:—
Moira Jean (435, Hilson Av., Apt. 2, Ottawa, Ont., Canada), *b.* 1943; SRN.

PREDECESSORS.—[1] Sir EDWARD LAW, *K.B.*, *P.C.*, an eminent lawyer, was Attorney-Gen. 1801-2, and Lord Ch. Justice of England 1802-18 ; cr. *Baron Ellenborough*, of Ellenborough, co. Cumberland (peerage of United Kingdom) 1802 ; *d.* 1818; *s.* by his son [2] EDWARD, 2nd Baron, P.C., G.C.B. ; Lord Privy Seal 1828-9, Pres. of Board of Control 1829-30, 1884-5, 1841 and 1858, Gov.-Gen. of India 1841-4, and First Lord of the Admiralty 1846 ; cr. *Viscount Southam* and *Earl of Ellenborough* (peerage of United Kingdom) 1844; *d.* 1871, when the viscountcy and earldom became extinct and the barony devolved upon his nephew [3] CHARLES EDMUND TOWRY, 3rd Baron (son of the late Hon. Charles Ewan, 2nd son of 1st Baron, by Elizabeth Sophia, dau. of Sir Edward Nightingale, 6th Bt.), *b.* 1820 ; assumed in 1885 by Roy. licence the additional surname of Towry: *m.* 1st, 1840, Lady Eleanor Cecil Howard, who *d.* 1852, dau. of 4th Earl of Wicklow ; 2ndly, 1855, Anna Elizabeth, who *d.* 1860, dau. of the Rev. John Fitzgerald-Day of Beaufort House, Killarney ; 3rdly, 1863, Isabella, who *d.* 1874, dau. of Alexander Ogilby, Esq., of Pelipar, Londonderry ; 4thly, 1874, Beatrice Joanna, who *d.* 1932, dau. of Sir Norton Joseph Knatchbull, 10th Bt. ; *d.* 1890 ; *s.* by his son [4] CHARLES TOWRY HAMILTON, 4th Baron, *b.* 1856 ; *d.s.p.* 1902 ; *s.* by his cousin [5] EDWARD DOWNES, 5th Baron, *b.* 1841 ; Com. R.N. ; served in Baltic during Russian War 1855 in China Expedition 1859-61, and during Ashantee War 1870-74 : *m.* 1906, Hermione Octavia Courtenay, who *d.* 1942, dau. of E. W. H. Schenley (Rifle Brig.), of Little Warsash, S. Hants ; *d.* 1915 ; *s.* by his brother [6] CECIL HENRY, *C.B.*, 6th Baron, *b.* 1849 ; entered 54th Regt. 1869, and retired as Brevet Col. 1906 ; Afghan Campaign 1878-80, S. African War 1900-2: *m.* 1884, Alice Caroline, who *d.* 1916, dau. of the late John Harvey Astell, of Woodbury Hall, Sandy, Beds; *d.* 1931 ; *s.* by his son [7] HENRY ASTELL, *M.C.*, 7th Baron, *b.* 1889 ; Major (retired) King's Own Yorkshire L.I.; European War 1914-18 (M.C.): *m.* 1923, Helen Dorothy, dau. of H. W. Lovatt, formerly of Tiraun, Newcastle, co. Down; *d.* 1945; *s.* by his el. son [8] RICHARD EDWARD CECIL, 8th Baron and present peer.

ELLES, BARONESS.   (Elles.)   [Life Baroness 1972.]

DIANA LOUIE ELLES, da. of the late Col. Stewart Francis Newcombe, DSO; *b.* July 19th, 1921; ed. at London Univ. (BA); Bar. Lincoln's Inn 1956; 1939-45 War as Flight Officer WAAF (Intelligence, Air Ministry); Member of Outside Organization Sub.-Cttee., Conservative Women's Nat. Advisory Cttee. 1960-72, and of Women's Nat. Advisory Cttee. 1961-62, and since 1969 (Chm. Sub-Cttee. on One Parent Families 1970); author of "The Housewife and the Common Market" 1971; Care Cttee. Worker, Kennington SE 1956-72; UK Delegate to UN Gen. Assembly 1972; a Member of UN Sub Commn on Prevention of Discrimination and Protection of Minorities 1973 and 74; Chm. of Conservative Party Central Office, and of European Union of Women since 1973; a Member of UK Delegation to European Parl. since 1973; cr. *Baroness Elles*, of City of Westminster (Life Baroness) 1972: *m.* 1945, Neil Patrick Moncrieff Elles, barrister, and has issue.

    Arms,—Not exemplified at time of going to press.
    Residences,—75, Ashley Gdns., SW1; Villa Fontana, Ponte del Giglio, Lucca, Italy.

SON LIVING.

Hon. James Edmund Moncrieff, *b.* 1949.

DAUGHTER LIVING.

Hon. (Elizabeth) Rosamund, *b.* 1947; ed. at St. Andrews Univ. (MA) and Courtauld Inst., London Univ. (MA): *m.* 1971, Christopher John Lockhart-Mummery, of 127 Abbotsbury Rd., W14.

Ellesmere, Earl of, see Duke of Sutherland.

ELLIOT OF HARWOOD, BARONESS. (Elliot.) [Life Baroness 1958.]

Under 'ull sail.

KATHARINE ELLIOT, D.B.E., dau. of Sir Charles Tennant, 1st Bt. [see B. Glenconner] ; b. Jan. 15th, 1903 ; ed. at Abbot's Hill ; Hon. LLD Glasgow; a JP and a Co. Councillor for Roxburghshire, a Member of Carnegie United Kingdom Trust, and of King George V Jubilee Trust 1937-68, U.K. Delegate to U.N. Gen. Assembly in New York 1954-56, and 1957, and Chm. of National Union of Conservative and Unionist Assos. 1957-58; 1st Chm. of Consumer Council, Board of Trade, 1963-68; Order of Merit of Austrian Federal Republic; CBE (Civil) 1946, DBE (Civil), and *Baroness Elliot of Harwood,* of Rulewater, co. Roxburgh (Life Baroness) 1958; m. 1934, as his second wife, the Rt. Hon. Walter Elliot, CH, MC, MP, FRS, DSc, MB, ChB, who d. 1958.

Arms,—Two coats per pale, *dexter,* gules on a bend or between a holly leaf proper in chief and a portcullis in base of the second a baton azure, *Elliot; sinister* argent, two crescents in fesse and a lymphad in base sable, on a chief gules a boar's head couped of the first, within a bordure compony of the second and first, *Tennant.* Supporters,—*dexter,* a black-faced ram proper, horned gules, gorged of a collar argent, charged with two crescents sable. *Sinister,* a horse argent, hooves or, bridle and reins sable.

Residences,—17, Lord North Street SW1P 3LD; Harwood ,Bonchester Bridge, Hawick Roxburghshire, TD9 9TL.

ELPHINSTONE, LORD. (Elphinstone.) [Lord S. 1509, and Baron U.K. 1885.]

JOHN ALEXANDER ELPHINSTONE, 17th Lord ; b. March 22nd, 1914 ; s. 1955 ; ed. at Eton, and at Ch. Ch., Oxford; is Capt. Queen's Body Guard for Scotland (Roy. Co. of Archers), a D.L. for co. Angus, Pres. of Scottish Assocn. of Boys Clubs, and of Roy. Zoological Soc. of Scotland, and Chm. of Council of Scottish Branch British Red Cross Soc.; 1939-45 War as Capt. Black Watch (prisoner).

Arms,—Quarterly : 1st grand quarter argent, a chevron sable, between three boars' heads erased gules, armed of the field, and langued azure, *Elphinstone ;* 2nd, grand quarter, counterquartered ; 1st, gules, a chevron, within a double tressure, flory counterflory, argent, *Fleming ;* 2nd, azure, three frases argent, *Fraser ;* 3rd, argent, on a chief gules, three pallets or, *Keith ;* 4th, or, three bars wavy gules, *Drummond ;* 3rd grand quarter, argent, a chevron, between three otters' heads erased gules, within a bordure of the last, *Fullerton ;* 4th grand quarter, sable, on a cross argent, square pierced of the field, four eagles, displayed of the first, in the dexter canton an arm embowed proper, issuing out of a naval crown, the hand holding a trident or, *Buller.* Crest,—A lady, from the waist upwards, richly habited in red, her arms extended, the right hand supporting a tower, and the left holding a branch of aurel, all proper. Supporters,—Two wild men, wreathed about the temples and loins with laurel, and holding on their exterior shoulders clubs proper.

Residences,—Drumkilbo, Meigle, Perthshire ; Glenmazeran, Tomatin, Inverness-shire.

SISTERS LIVING.

Hon. Mary Elizabeth, b. 1911. *Residence,*—Llanerchwen, Llandefaelog, Brecon.
Hon. Jean Constance, b. 1915, Extra Lady-in-Waiting to HRH The Princess Margaret, 1970: m.1936, Maj. John Lycett Wills, Life Guards (ret.) [see Wills, Bt., cr. 1904, colls.]. *Resi* —Allanbay Park Binfield, Berks.

Hon. Margaret, *b.* 1925: *m.* 1950, Denys Gravenor Rhodes [B. Plunket], and has issue living, Simon John Gravenor, *b.* 1957; a Page of Honour to HM 1971-73,—Michael Andrew Gravenor, *b.* 1960,— Annabel Margaret, *b.* 1952,—Victoria Ann, *b.* 1953. *Residence,*—

WIDOW LIVING OF SON OF SIXTEENTH LORD.

Jean Frances, CVO, (Maryland, Worplesdon, Guildford, Surrey), da. of the late Capt. Angus Valdimar Hambro, MP, and widow of Capt, the Hon. Vicary Paul Gibbs, Gren. Gds. [see B. Aldenham and Hunsdon of Hunsdon]: *m.* 2ndly, 1946, Rev. The Hon. Andrew Charles Victor Elphinstone, who *d.* 1975, and has issue living, (by 1st m.), [see B. Aldenham and Hunsdon of Hunsdon, colls.], (by 2nd m.), [see colls. infra].

COLLATERAL BRANCH LIVING.

Issue of the late Rev. The Hon. Andrew Charles Victor Elphinstone, yr. son of 16th Lord; *b.* 1918, *d.* 1975: *m.* 1946, Jean Frances, CVO (ante), da. of the late Capt. Angus Valdimar Hambro, MP, and widow of Capt. the Hon. Vicary Paul Gibbs, Gren. Gds. [see B. Aldenham and Hunsdon of Hunsdon]:—

JAMES ALEXANDER, *b.* April 22nd, 1953; ed. at Eton.——Rosemary Elizabeth, *b.* 1947: *m.* 1967, James Pigé Leschallas, of Wittersham Court, Tenterden, Kent, and has issue living, Andrew James, *b.* 1970,—Sophie Elizabeth, *b.* 1968.

PREDECESSORS.—[1] ALEXANDER Elphinstone, son of Sir John Elphinstone, grandson of Sir Henry Elphinstone, of Pittendreich; cr. *Lord Elphinstone*, of Elphinstone, co. Stirling (peerage of Scotland) 1509; fell at Flodden Field 1513; *s.* by his son [2] ALEXANDER, 2nd Lord; slain at Pinkie 1547; *s.* by his son [3] ROBERT, 3rd Lord; *s.* by his son [4] ALEXANDER, 4th Lord; Lord Treasurer of Scotland; *d.* 1638; *s.* by his son [5] ALEXANDER, 5th Lord; *d.* 1648; *s.* by his nephew [6] ALEXANDER, 6th Lord; *d.* 1654; *s.* by his el. son [7] ALEXANDER, 7th Lord; *d.s.p.* 1669; *s.* by his brother [8] JOHN, 8th Lord; *d.* 1720; *s.* by his son [9] CHARLES, 9th Lord; *d.* 1757; *s.* by his son [10] CHARLES, 10th Lord; *d.* 1781; *s.* by his son [11] JOHN, 11th Lord; a Representative Peer 1784-94; *d.* 1794; *s.* by his son [12] JOHN, 12th Lord; a Lt.-Gen. in the Army, Lord-Lieut. of Dunbartonshire, and a Representative Peer 1803-13; *d.* 1813; *s.* by his son [13] JOHN, *G.C.B., G.C.H., P.C.,* 13th Lord; a Representative Peer; was Gov. of Bombay and of Madras during the Mutiny 1857; cr. *Baron Elphinstone,* of Elphinstone, co. Stirling (peerage of United Kingdom) 1859; *d.* 1860, when the barony of 1859 became extinct, and the Scottish Lordship devolved upon his cousin [14] JOHN (el. son of Adm. the Hon. Charles Elphinstone-Fleeming, 2nd son of 11th Lord), 14th Lord; *d.* unmarried 1861; *s.* by his kinsman [15] JOHN (son of Lt.-Col. James Drummond Buller-Fullerton Elphinstone, 4th son of the Hon. William Elphinstone, 3rd son of 10th Lord), 15th Lord, *b.* 1828; a Representative Peer for Scotland 1867-85, and a Lord-in-Waiting to H.M. Queen Victoria 1874-80, 1885-6, and 1886-9; cr. *Baron Elphinstone,* of Elphinstone co. Haddington (peerage of United Kingdom) 1885: *m.* 1864, Lady Constance Euphemia Woronzow Murray, who *d.* 1922. dau. of 6th Earl of Dunmore; *d.* 1893; *s.* by his el. surviving son [16] SIDNEY HERBERT, *K.T.,* 16th Lord, *b.* 1869; Lord High Commr. to Gen. Assembly of Church of Scotland 1923-4, Capt.-Gen. of Queen's Body Guard for Scotland (Roy. Co. of Archers) 1935-52, Clerk Register of Scotland and Keeper of the Signet 1944-55, and Chancellor of Order of the Thistle 1949-55 : *m.* 1910, Lady Mary Frances Bowes-Lyon, *D.C.V.O.,* who *d.* 1961, dau. of 14th Earl of Strathmore; *d.* 1955 ; *s.* by his el. son [17] JOHN ALEXANDER, 17th Lord and present peer.

ELTISLEY, BARONY OF. (Newton.) [Extinct 1942.]

DAUGHTER LIVING OF FIRST BARON.

Hon. Myra Alice (*Hon. Lady Fox*), *b.* 1906: *m.* 1927, Sir Gifford Wheaton Grey Fox, 2nd Bt., who *d.* 1959, and from whom she had obtained a divorce 1952. *Residence,*—Croxton Park, Cambridgeshire.

ELTON, BARON. (Elton.) [Baron U.K. 1934.]

RODNEY ELTON, *TD*, 2nd Baron; *b.* March 2nd, 1930; *s.* 1973; ed. at Eton, and New Coll., Oxford (BA); late Capt. Warwicks. Yeo., and late Maj. Leics. and Derbys. Yeo.; Publisher of Yendor Books; Assist. Master Loughborough Gram. Sch. 1962-67, Fairlawn Comprehensive Sch. for Boys 1967-69, Lecturer Bishops Lonsdale Coll. 1969-72; a Conservative Whip House of Lords: *m.* 1958, Anne Francis, ed. da. of Brig. Robert Adolphus George Tilney, CBE, DSO, TD, DL [Paget, Bt. cr. 1897 (ext.)], and has issue.

Arms,—Paly or and gules a bend and on a chief sable three pierced mullets or. **Crest,**—Between two pierced mullets and out of a wreath of laurel fructed or a dexter arm embowed in mail proper, tied about the elbow a cord or, the gauntlet grasping a scimitar proper hilt and pommel or. **Supporters,**—*Dexter,* a knight in mail and white surcoat supporting with the exterior hand a sword point downwards proper hilt and pommel or; *sinister,* a Viking habited proper mantled azure supporting with the exterior hand a battleaxe head downwards and outwards proper.

Address,—House of Lords, W1.　*Club.*—Cavalry.

SON LIVING.

HON. EDWARD PAGET, *b.* May 28th, 1966.

DAUGHTERS LIVING.

Hon. Annabel, *b.* 1960.
Hon. Jane, *b.* 1962.
Hon. Lucy, *b.* 1963.

SISTERS LIVING.

Hon. Audrey, *b.* 1922: *m.* 1948, the Rev. Brian William Frere Goodrich, formerly Assist. Commr., Singapore Police, of Frant Rectory, Tunbridge Wells, Kent, TN3 9DX, and has issue living, John, *b.* 1952,—Peter, *b.* 1954,—Simon, *b.* 1957,—Justin, *b.* 1962,—Alexander, *b.* 1968,—Sarah, *b.* 1949.

Hon. Rosemary, *b.* 1925: *m.* 1st, 1946 (m. diss. 1955), William Yates; 2ndly, 1955, David Charles Attlee, and has issue living, (by 1st m.) Elizabeth Anne, *b.* 1948: *m.* 1975, Oliver Raymond Greene,—Angela, *b.* 1950,—(by 2nd m.) James Tristam, *b.* 1956,—Helena Rosemary, *b.* 1958. *Residence,*—Greenhill, Egerton, Ashford, Kent.

WIDOW LIVING OF FIRST BARON.
DEDI (*Dedi Baroness Elton*), (The Mount, Adderbury, Banbury, Oxon.), da. of Gustav Hartmann, of Oslo: *m.* 1921, the 1st Baron, who *d.* 1973.

PREDECESSORS.—[1] GODFREY Elton, el. son of the late Edward Fiennes Elton, of Ovington Park, Hants., and Burleigh Court, Glos.; *b.* 1892; Fellow of Queen's Coll., Oxford and Lecturer in Modern History 1919-39, Dean 1921-23; Hon. Political Sec. Nat. Labour Cttee. 1932, and Sec. to Rhodes Trust 1939-59; author of "Life of James Ramsay MacDonald 1866-1919", 1939, and other works, cr. *Baron Elton,* of Headington, co. Oxford (peerage of UK) 1934: *m.* 1921, Dedi, da. of Gustav Hartmann, of Oslo, *d.* 1973, *s.* by his only son [2] RODNEY, *TD,* 2nd Baron and present peer.

Elveden, Viscount, son of Earl of Iveagh.

ELWORTHY, BARON. (Elworthy.) [Life Baron 1972.]

(SAMUEL) CHARLES ELWORTHY, *GCB, CBE, DSO, MVO, DFC, AFC,* el. son of the late Capt. Percy Ashton Elworthy, late 1st Life Gds., of Gordons Valley, Timaru, NZ; *b.* March 23rd, 1911; ed. at Marlborough and Trin. Coll., Camb. (MA); Bar. Lincoln's Inn 1935, Hon. Bencher 1970; Marshal of the RAF; Comdt. RAF Staff Coll. 1957-59, Dep. Ch. of Air Staff 1959-60, C.-in-C. Middle East 1960-63, Ch. of Air Staff 1963-67, and Ch. of Defence Staff 1967-71, since when Constable and Gov. Windsor Castle; Lord Lieut. of Greater London since 1973; 1939-45 War with Bomber Command (despatches, DFC, AFC, DSO); *cr.* DSO 1941, CBE (Mil.) 1946, MVO (4th Class) 1953, CB (Mil.) and KCB (Mil.) 1960, GCB (Mil.) 1962, and *Baron Elworthy,* of Timaru in New Zealand, and of Elworthy, co. Somerset (Life Baron) 1972: *m.* 1936, Audrey, da. of the late Arthur Joseph Hutchinson, OBE, of Auckland, NZ, and has issue.

Arms,—Azure, a lion passant per pale or an argent, between two bars per pale argent and or, in chief three bezants. **Crest,**—A steels cap proper rimmed studded and garnished, and with a comb from the rear to the crown or. **Supporters,**—On either side a New Zealand Kotuku (Eggretta Alba Modesta) proper, each gorged with an astral crown per pale argent and or, pendant therefrom by a ring a double-warded key or.

Residence,—Norman Tower, Windsor Castle, Berks. *Clubs,*—Bath, RAF.

SONS LIVING.
Hon. Timothy Charles (c/o Australia & New Zealand Banking Group Ltd., 20, Crofton St., W1), *b.* 1938; Sqdn.-Ldr. RAF: *m.* 1971, Anabel, da. of the late Reginald Ernest Harding, OBE, and has issue.
Hon. Anthony Arthur (2, Ikendele Rd., Kloof, Natal), *b.* 1940: *m.* 1967, Penelope, da. of A. J. Hendry.
Hon. Christopher Ashton (269, Otipua Rd., Timaru, NZ); *b.* 1946: *m.* 1968, Anne, da. of the late Harry Bell Lewis Johnstone.

DAUGHTER LIVING.
Hon. Clare Louise Katharine, *b.* 1950.

ELWYN JONES, BARON. (Jones.) [Life Baron 1974.]

(FREDERICK) ELWYN JONES, *PC,* son of Frederick Jones, of Llanelli; *b.* Oct. 24th, 1909; ed. at Llanelli Gram. Sch., Univ. of Wales, Aberystwyth, and Gonville and Caius Coll., Camb. (MA); Hon. LLD Wales; Pres. of Univ. Coll., Cardiff, and a Fellow of King's Coll., London since 1970; Bar. Gray's Inn 1935, Bencher 1960, QC 1953, and QC N. Ireland 1958; PPS to Attorney-Gen. 1946-51; Recorder of Methyr Tydfil 1949-53, of Swansea 1953-60, of Cardiff 1960-64, and of Kingston upon Thames 1968-74; Attorney-Gen. 1964-70; Lord Chancellor since 1974; MP for Plaistow Div. of W. Ham (*Lab.*) 1945-50, and for S. Div. of W. Ham 1950-74; *cr. PC* 1964, Knt. 1964, and *Baron Elwyn Jones,* of Llanelli, co. Carmarthen, and Newham, Greater London [Life Baron] 1974: *m.* 1937, Pearl Binder, and has issue.

Arms,—not exemplified at time of going to press.

Residence,—5, Gray's Inn, WC1.

Hon.

SON LIVING

DAUGHTERS LIVING.

Hon. Josephine, *b.* 19—: *m.* 1972, James Francis Gladstone, of 68, Stockwell Park Rd., SW9 [see Gladstone, Bt.].

Hon.

ELY, LORD BISHOP OF. (Roberts.)

Rt. Rev. EDWARD JAMES KEYMER ROBERTS, *DD*, son of the Rev. Arthur Henry Roberts; *b.* April 18th, 1908; ed. at Marlborough, at Corpus Christi Coll., Camb. (DD 1965, MA 1935), and at Cuddesdon Theological Coll.; Curate of All Saints, Margaret St., W. 1931-5, Vice-Prin. of Cuddesdon Theological Coll. 1935-9, Examining Chap. to Bishop of Portsmouth and Commissary, Johannesburg 1936-9, V. of St. Matthew, Southsea 1940-5, Curate-in-Charge of St. Bartholomew, Southsea 1941-45, Examining Chap. to Bishop of Portsmouth 1942-56, Proctor in Convocation, Portsmouth 1944-9, Commissary, N. Rhodesia 1946-51, Hon. Canon of Portsmouth 1947-9, Archdeacon of I. of Wight, V. of Brading, and R. of Yaverland 1949-52, Archdeacon of Portsmouth 1952-6, Suffragan Bishop of Malmesbury 1956-62, Examining Chap. to Bishop of Bristol 1959-62, and Suffragan Bishop of Kensington 1962-4, translated 65th Bishop of Ely 1964: *m.* 1941, Dorothy Frances, dau. of Canon Edwin David Bowser, of Deal.

Patron of ninety-two livings (eleven alternately), three Canonries, twenty Honorary Canonries, and the Archdeaconries of Ely, Huntingdon, and Wisbech.

The Diocese, founded in 1109, now includes the major part of Cambridgeshire and three Rural Deaneries in West Norfolk.

𝕰pis𝕔opal 𝖘ignatur𝕖,—"Edward Elien."

ARMS OF THE SEE,—Gules: three ducal coronets, two and one, or.

Residence,—The Bishop's House, Ely.

ELY, MARQUESS OF. [Tottenham.] Sits as BARON LOFTUS (U.K. 1801).
[Marquess I. 1801, Bt. I. 1780.]

CHARLES JOHN TOTTENHAM, 8th Marquess, and 9th Baronet; *b.* May 30th, 1913; *s.* 1969; ed. Queen's Univ., Kingston, Ontario (BA); Headmaster, Junior Sch., Trin. Coll. Sch., Port Hope, Ontario: *m.* 1938, Katherine Elizabeth, who *d.* 1975, da. of Lt.-Col. W. H. Craig, of Kingston, Ontario, and has issue.

𝕬rms,—Not yet confirmed at the College of Arms for the line of the present Marquess.

Residence,—Trinity College School, Port Hope, Ontario, Canada.

SONS LIVING.

CHARLES JOHN (*Viscount Loftus*), *b.* Feb. 2nd, 1943; ed. at Trin. Coll., Toronto Univ. (MA): *m.* 1969, Judith Marvelle, da. of Dr. J. J. Porter, of Calgary, Alberta.
Lord Timothy Craig, *b.* 1948; ed. at Ottawa Teachers' Coll. : *m.* 1973, Elizabeth Jane, da. of Grant McAllister, of Ottawa, Ont.
Lord Richard Ivor, *b.* 1954.

DAUGHTER LIVING.

Lady Ann Elizabeth, *b.* 1940; ed. at Trin. Coll., Toronto Univ. (BA, STB), and Union Seminary, New York (MTB).

BROTHER LIVING. (*Raised to the Rank of a Marquess's son* 1973)
Lord George Robert (3, West Way, Rickmansworth, Herts.), *b.* 1914; Cdr. RCN (ret.); 1939-45 War: *m.* 1944, Jane Elizabeth, da. of Arthur Martin, and has issue living, Jane Elizabeth, *b.* 1945.

SISTER LIVING. (*Raised to the Rank of a Marquess's daughter* 1973)
Lady Dora Elizabeth (24, The Gateways, SW3), *b.* 1919; ed. at Queen's Univ., Kingston, Ont. (BA); 1939-45 War, as Lt. WRCNS: a JP for London: *m.* 1st, 1946, Lt. (E) Bernard Edgar Hall, RN, who *d.* 1947; 2ndly, 1950, Sir Ivor Thomas Montagu Pink, KCMG, who *d.* 1966, and has issue living, (by 2nd m.) Celia Elizabeth, *b.* 1952.

MOTHER LIVING.
Cecile Elizabeth (Port Hope, Ont., Canada), da. of the late James Salkeld Burra, JP, of Bockhanger, Kennington, Kent: *m.* 1912, George Leonard Tottenham, who *d.* 1928.

WIDOW LIVING OF SEVENTH MARQUESS.
THEA MARGARET GORDON (*Thea, Marchioness of Ely*), (23, The Avenue, Chichester, W. Sussex), da. of the late Lars G. Gronvold, of 36, Wilbury Rd., Hove: *m.* 1928, the 7th Marquess, who *d.* 1969.

COLLATERAL BRANCHES LIVING.
Grandchildren of the late Very Rev. George Tottenham, son of the late *Rt. Rev.* Lord Robert Ponsonby Tottenham, Bishop of Clogher, 2nd son of 1st Marquess:—
Issue of the late Edward Loftus Tottenham, *b.* 1867, *d.* 1949 : *m.* 1899, Jessie Hilda, who *d.* 1938, dau. of the late John Honey Trace :—
George William Loftus, *b.* 1911 : *m.* 1949, Margaret Mary Hamilton, dau. of the late Thomas Valentine Powell, and has issue living, Robert Ashley Christopher, *b.* 1953,—Alison Margaret, *b.* 1951. *Residence,*—Blaney, Enniskillen, co. Fermanagh.——Emily Frances: *m.* 1931, Henry Gordon Sansom, and has issue living. *Residence,*—Main St., Lisbellaw, co. Fermanagh.

Granddaughter of the late Major Robert Loftus Tottenham, son of the late Rev. Robert Loftus Tottenham, 2nd son of the Rt. Rev. Lord Robert Ponsonby Tottenham (ante):—

Issue of the late Lieut.-Col. Robert Loftus Tottenham, *b.* 1865, *d.* 1925 : *m.* 1899, Hilda May, who *d.* 1961, dau. of F. G. Brook Fox, C.E. :—

Lynda Lucy, *b.* 1904: *m.* 1927, Maurice Bernhard Baron ; 2ndly, 1939, Lieut. James Hamilton Martin, R.N.V.R., who *d.* (on active ser. during European War) 1940 [E. Coventry, colls.]; 3rdly, 1947, Capt. Simpson, R.N. [retired], and has issue living, (by 1st marriage) Susan Frances, *b.* 1928. *Residence,*—27, Barnhorn Road, Little Common, Bexhill-on-Sea.

PREDECESSORS.—|1| John Tottenham, *M.P.* for New Ross, &c.; cr. a *Baronet* 1780 ; *d.* 1786 ; *s.* by his son [2] Charles, *K.P., P.C.* (2nd Bt.), who had in 1783 *s.* to the estates of his uncle Henry Loftus (which surname he assumed), K.P., 1st and last Earl of Ely (cr. 1771), and in 1785 had been cr. *Baron Loftus,* of Loftus (peerage of Ireland) ; was Postmaster-Gen. 1789; cr. *Viscount Loftus* (peerage of Ireland) 1789, *Earl of Ely* (peerage of Ireland) 1794, *Marquess of Ely* (peerage of Ireland) 1801, and *Baron Loftus,* of Long Loftus, co. York (peerage of United Kingdom) 1801 ; *d.* 1806; *s.* by his son [3] John, *K.P.,* 2nd Marquess; *d.* 1845 ; *s.* by his son [4] John Henry, 3rd Marquess; *b.* 1814: *m.* 1844, Jane, *V.A.,* dau. of James Hope-Vere, of Craigie and Blackwood, N.B.; *d.* 1857; *s.* by his son [5] John Henry Wellington Graham, 4th Marquess, *b.* 1849: *m.* 1875, Caroline Anne, who *d.* 1917, dau. of the late George Caithness; *d.* 1889; *s.* by his cousin [6] John Henry (el. son of the Rev. Lord Adam Loftus, 3rd son of 2nd Marquess). 5th Marquess, *b.* 1851: *m.* 1895, Margaret Emma, who *d.* 1931, dau. of F. Aldridge Clark, of Lynton Court, Hove, Sussex, and Gracefield, Prince, Risborough, Bucks ; *d.* 1925; *s.* by his brother [6] George Herbert, 6th Marquess, *b.* 1854: *m.* 1st, 1884, Emily Harriet, who *d.* 1886, dau. of Major Arthur Vandeleur, R.A.; 2ndly, 1902, Ethel Beatrice Lemprière, who *d.* 1927, dau. of the late Nigel Gresley, J.P., of Hobart, Tasmania; *d.* 1935; *s.* by his son [7] George Henry Wellington, 7th Marquess, *b.* 1903: *m.* 1928, Thea Margaret Gordon, da. of the late Lars G. Gronvold, of Hove; *d.* 1969; *s.* by his kinsman [8] Charles John (el. son of George Leonard Tottenham, grandson of Charles John Tottenham (*b.* 1808), el. son of the Rt. Rev. Lord Robert Ponsonby Tottenham, Bishop of Clogher (who resumed the name and arms of Tottenham), 2nd son of 1st Marquess), 8th Marquess and present peer; also Earl of Ely, Viscount Loftus, and Baron Loftus.

Emlyn, Viscount, son of Earl Cawdor.

EMMET OF AMBERLEY, BARONESS. (Emmet.) [Life Baroness 1964.]

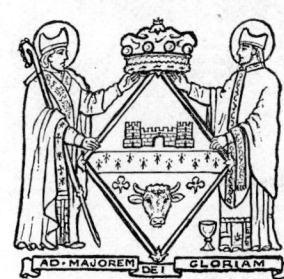

To the greater glory of God.

Evelyn Violet Elizabeth Emmet, da of 1st Baron Rennell; *b.* March 18th, 1899; ed. at Lady Margaret Hall, Oxford (MA); a JP for Sussex 1936-71, a Member of LCC 1925-34, a Co. Councillor for W. Sussex 1944-52 and an Alderman 1952-67; Chm. of Conservative Women's National Advisory Cttee. 1951-54, and of National Union of Conservative and Unionist Assocns. 1955, and UK Delegate to Assembly of UN 1952-53; Chm. of Lord Chancellor's Legal Aid Advisory Cttee., and Dep. Speaker and Chm. of Cttees. House of Lords; MP for E. Grinstead Div. of E. Sussex (*C*) 1955-64; *cr. Baroness Emmet of Amberley,* of Amberley, co. Sussex (Life Baroness) 1964: *m.* 1923, Thomas Addis Emmet, who *d.* 1934, and has issue.

Arms,—Azure a fess ermine in chief a port between two towers argent, and in base a bull's head caboshed between two trefoils slipped. Supporters,—*Dexter,* a representation of St. Wilfrid in processional vestments; *sinister,* a representation of St. Richard of Chichester in mass vestments, at his feet a chalice all proper.
Residences,—Amberley Castle, Amberley, Sussex; 2/3, Grosvenor Cottages, Eaton Terr., SW1.

SONS LIVING.
Hon. Christopher Anthony Robert (Sorrels House, Fittleworth, Petworth, Sussex; 18, Tournay Rd., SW6), *b.* 1925; ed. at Ampleforth, and Balliol Coll., Oxford (MA); a JP for W. Sussex; a Co. Councillor for W. Sussex 1952-62: *m.* 1947, Lady Miranda Mary Fitzalan Howard, da. of 3rd Baron Howard of Glossop, and Baroness Beaumont [see D. Norfolk], and has issue living, Robert Anthony Bernard, *b.* 1958,—Teresa Miriam, *b.* 1949: *m.* 1969, Anthony Andrew Myers, of 21, Chesilton Rd., SW6, and has issue living, Adrian Anthony Geoffrey *b.* 1972, Nicholas Andrew Robert, *b.* 1973, —Catriona Mary, *b.* 1951,—Rowena Mary Gabriel, *b.* 1954: *m.* 1975, Michael F. Hallinan.
Hon. David Alastair Rennell (Louis Vernet 260, San Isidoro, Provincia Buenos Aires, R. Argentina), *b.* 1928; ed. at Ampleforth, and Worcester Coll., Oxford; a Member of British Community Council, Argentina 1964-68: *m.* 1967, Sylvia Delia, da. of the late Willis Knowles, of Buenos Aires, and has issue living, Thomas Ian David, *b.* 1970,—Caroline Ann Gloria *b.* 1968.

DAUGHTERS LIVING.
Hon. Gloria Lavinia Eileen, *b.* 1924: *m.* 1950, Maj. Mark Winton Slane Fleming, 10th R. Hussars (PWO), (ret.) of Ardath, Shamley Green, nr. Guildford, and has issue living, Andrew Gerard James, *b.* 1956,—Mary Georgina, *b.* 1951: *m.* 1972, Michael David Hardinge, and has issue living, Elizabeth Selene *b.* 1972,—Sarah Elizabeth Sophia, *b.* 1953,—Charlotte Ann, *b.* 1955.
Hon. Penelope Ann Clare (Naldrett, Bucks Green, Rudgwick, Sussex), *b.* 1932: *m.* 1951 m. diss. 1965), the Hon. Hugo Nevill Money-Coutts, only son of 7th Baron Latymer.

EMMOTT, BARONY OF. (Emmott.) [Extinct 1926.]
DAUGHTER LIVING OF FIRST BARON.
Hon. Dorothy, *b.* 1890: *m.* 1920, Capt. (Christopher) Neild Barlow, late K.R.R.C., who *d.* 1964, and has issue living, Christopher Edward Emmott (55, Torwood Av., Glen Waverley, Vic. 3150, Aust.), *b.* 1922: *m.* 1957, Marea, da. of the late Eric Hughes, of Melbourne, Australia,—Diana Veronica Ann, *b.* 1925. *Residence,*—Milcombe House, Banbury, Oxon.

Encombe, Viscount, son of Earl of Eldon.

ENERGLYN, BARON. (Evans.) [Life Baron 1968.]

WILLIAM DAVID EVANS, son of David
George Evans, of Energlyn, Caerphilly; *b.*
Dec. 25th, 1912; ed. at Caerphilly Gram.
Sch., and Univ. Coll. Cardiff; DSc Wales,
PhD London; FRGS, FLS, MIME MIMM;
a DL for Notts.; Prof. of Geology, and Head
of Dept., Notts. Univ. since 1948; Dean of
Faculty of Pure Science 1953-57; *cr. Baron
Energlyn*, of Caerphilly, co. Glamorgan (Life
Baron) 1968: *m.* 1942, Jean Thompson, da.
of John Miller, of St. Andrew Cres., Cardiff.

Arms,—Sable a round Norman Tower in bend sinister
masoned proper, on a chief or a book gules between two
quartz crystals vert. Crest,—On a Cap of Maintenance
gules turned up ermine a Dragon sejant gules holding a
cross raguly vert.
Residence,—14, Village Close, Edwalton, Nottingham.
Club,—Reform.

Enfield, Viscount, son of Earl of Strafford.

ENNISKILLEN, EARL OF. (Cole.) Sits as BARON GRINSTEAD (U.K. 1815) [Earl I. 1789.]

DAVID LOWRY COLE, *M.B.E.*,
6th Earl; *b.* Sept. 10th, 1918;
s. 1963; ed. at Eton and Trin. Coll.
Camb. (BA Agric.); DL and JP of
co. Fermanagh; 1939-45 War as
Capt. Irish Guards; MBE (Civil)
1954: *m.* 1st, 1940 (m. diss. 1955)
Sonia, da. of the late Maj. Thomas
Syers, RA; 2ndly, 1955, Nancy
Henderson, da. of the late Dr. John
Alexander MacLennan, of 105, Brooklawn Place, Bridgeport, Conn., USA,
and has issue by 1st m.

Arms,—Argent, a bull passant sable, armed
and hoofed or, within a bordure of the second,
charged with eight bezants; on a canton sinister
per pale gules and azure, a harp of the third,
stringed argent. Crest,—A demi-dragon wings
elevated vert, holding a dart in the dexter paw
and resting the sinister on an antique buckler,
charged as the canton. Supporters,—Two
dragons reguardant vert, each holding in the
inner fore paw a dart.

Worship God; honour the king.

Seat,—Florence Court, Enniskillen, co.
Fermanagh. *Club,*—Carlton.

SON LIVING. (By 1st m.)

ANDREW JOHN GALBRAITH (Viscount Cole) (Stream House, Box 912, Nakuru, Kenya), b. April 28th, 1942; ed. at Eton; late Capt. Irish Guards: m. 1964, Sarah Frances Caroline, only da. of Maj-Gen. John Keith Edwards, CBE, DSO, MC, and has issue.
DAUGHTERS LIVING,—Hon. Amanda Mary, b. 1966.
Hon. Emma Frances, b. 1969.
Hon. Lucy Caroline, b. 1970.

DAUGHTER LIVING (By 1st m.)

Lady Linda Mary, b. 1944: m. 1975, Richard James Kay Muir [see Muir Bt.].

BROTHER LIVING.

Arthur Gerald, b. 1920; ed. at Eton; late Capt. Irish Guards: m. 1949, Prudence Tobina, dau. of the late Algernon Richard Aubrey Cartwright [see Buxton, Bt. colls.], and has issue living, Berkeley Arthur, b. 1949,—Hugh Galbraith, b. 1954,—Richard Lowry, b. 1956,—Marian Rose, b. 1951. Residence,—Kokopey, Gilgil, Kenya.

DAUGHTERS LIVING OF FIFTH EARL.

Lady Frances Jane, b. 1914 ; late Junior Com. A.T.S.: m. 1954, as his second wife, Group Capt. Henry Ivan Hanmer, D.F.C., R.A.F. [see Hanmer, Bt., colls.]. Residence,—Westhorpe Hall, Southwell, Notts.
Lady Kathleen Irene, b. 1919 : m. 1st, 1940 (marriage dissolved 1948), Major Desmond Ralph Lloyd-Verney, who d. 1957 [Verney, Bt., cr. 1818, colls.] ; 2ndly, 1948, Tadeusz Borkowski. Residence,—6, Gloucester Walk, W8.

MOTHER LIVING.

Lady Eleanor Balfour, dau. of 2nd Earl of Balfour : m. 1917, the Hon. Galbraith Lowry Egerton Cole, who d. 1929. Residence,—Kekopey, Box 127, Gilgil, Kenya.

COLLATERAL BRANCHES LIVING.
Grandchildren of the late Hon. Arthur Edward Casamaijor Cole, 3rd son of 3rd Earl:—
Issue of the late Lowry Arthur Casamaijor Cole, M.B.E., b. 1878, d. 1955 : m. 1910, Adelaide Grizel who d. 1965 dau. of the late Frederick Pratt-Barlow [M. Angelesey, colls.]:—
Rev. Arthur Lowry Frederick (c/o Royal Bank of Scotland, 49, Charing Cross, SW1), b. 1911; ed. at Eton; was V. of Wroxham 1954-59, Assist. Priest at St. Paul's, Knightsbridge, SW1, 1959-60, and Bishop's Chap. for Youth, Diocese of Coventry 1960-64; formerly a Chap. to Forces.——Elizabeth Joan, b. 1919.——Florence Margaret, b. 1923: m. 1st, 1948 (m. diss. 1959), John Walter; 2ndly, 1959, Vladimir Georgieff Daskaloff, and has issue living, (by 1st m.) John, b. 1953.

Grandchildren of the late Claud CHALONER (who assumed the surname of Chaloner under the will of his uncle Richard Chaloner) son of Arthur Willoughby Cole-Hamilton, grandson of the late Hon. Arthur Cole-Hamilton, MP, 2nd son of 1st Baron Mountflorence:—
Issue of the late Maj. Claudius Willoughby CHALONER, b. 1882, d. 1963: m. 1918, Winifred Adelaide, who d. 1969, da. of the late Col. Alexander Sinclair Grove, DSO, MSC:—
Desmond Willoughby Richard (Dorton House, Aylesbury), b. 1920 ; ed. at Shrewsbury, and at Trin. Coll., Dublin (B.A.); 1939-45 War as Lt. King's African Rifles.——Nancy Winifred, b. 1921: m. 1st, 1945, Francis G. Cornwall, who d. 1949; 2ndly, 1959, Prof. John Seton Michael Pringle, F.R.C.S., of Rathmore House, Naas, co. Kildare, and has issue living, (by 1st marriage) Francis David Willoughby, b. 1947.—Ann Patricia (posthumous), b. 1950: m. 1973, Robert Tristram Rowan Woods, of 35, St. Kevins Park, Dartry, Dublin 6.

Issue of the late John Cole CHALONER, b. 1889, d. 1940: m. 1922, Monica Katharine (St. Anthony's, Sidmonton Rd., Bray, co. Wicklow), da. of the late Rev. William Ralph Westropp Roberts, DD:—
Charity Patricia, b. 1923: m. 1949, Henry FitzGibbon, MD, of 477, Martin St., Penticton, BC, Canada, and has issue living, John, b. 1951,—Thomas, b. 1952,—Frances, b. 1954,—Pamela Anne, b. 1959.——Mary Frances Jonet, b. 1925: m. 1950, Richard John Shackleton, and has issue living, Richard Chaloner, b. 1953,—Michael Beattie, b. 1959,—Christine Mary, b. 1951,—Jonet Rhoda, b. 1956. Residence,—Anna House, Liffey, Lucan, co. Dublin.——Henrietta Sophia, b. 1930: m. 1959, Robert Frederick Twigg, and has issue living, Robert Chaloner, b. 1960,—Nicola b. 1962,—Fiona, b. 1963,—Sarah b. 1970. Residence,—38, Meadow Grove, Churchtown, co. Dublin.

Granddaughters of the late Capt. William Claude Cole-Hamilton, son of the late Arthur Willoughby Cole-Hamilton (ante) :—
Issue of the late Lieut.-Col. Claud George Cole-Hamilton, C.M.G., D.S.O., b. 1869, d. 1957: m. 1893, Lucy Charlewood, who d. 1951, dau. of the late Reginald Henry Thorold [Thorold, Bt., colls.]:—
Isabel Katherine, b. 1894.——Lucy Alice, b. 1896.——Norah Elizabeth, b. 1899 : m. 1926, James Gordon Mitchell, and has issue living, James Andrew (The Manor, North Huish, South Brent, Devon), b. 1928: Lt.-Cdr. RN (ret.): m. 1951, Venna Agnete Granqvist, of Copenhagen, Denmark,—Gillian Haldane (Field House, Barkham, Wokingham, Berks.) b. 1930: m. 1954, Septimus Booth, who d. 1966, and has issue living, Deborah Ann b. 1956, Elizabeth Jane b. 1958. Residence,—Long Barn, Linton, Ross-on-Wye.

Grandchildren of the late Rev. Arthur Henry Cole-Hamilton, son of the late Arthur Willoughby Cole-Hamilton (ante) :—
Issue of the late George William Cole-Hamilton, b. 1875, d. 1946: m. 1908, Katharine Edith, who d. 1960, da. of the late William Clinton-Baker, of Bayfordbury, Herts.:—
Katharine Letitia b. 1909: m. 1930, Bernard Alleyne Murray, MC, TD, RA, and has issue living, Katharine Elizabeth, b. 1932: m. 1962, Robert Hugh Shirley, of RR2, Vernon, British Columbia,—Mary Bridget (17, Ingram Rd., Thornton Heath, Surrey), b. 1935: BM, BCh, DCH, MRCP: m. 1st, (m. diss. 1974), Randall Clive Smith; 2ndly, 1975, John Robin Edwards. Residence,—37, Bayford Green, Bayford, nr. Hertford, Herts.——Anne (Bell Cottage, Widford, Ware, Herts.), b. 1910: m. 1st, 1938, Lt. David Edmund Cole-Hamilton, DSC, RN [infra], who d. (on active ser. during 1939-45 War) 1942; 2ndly, 1959, O. G. N. Turnbull, MC, who d. 1970.——Mary, TD, b. 1913; formerly Ch. Comm. ATS: m. 1st, 1936 (m. diss. 1952), Lt.-Col. John Carew Jones, late RA (TA); 2ndly, 1952, Col. John Locke Lovibond, TD, MD, FRCP, RAMC (TA), who d. 1954: 3rdly, 1956, Col. Donald Barry Girling, MC, TD, RA (TA). Residence,—Highworth Farm, Charlwood, Surrey.——Elizabeth Peace, b. 1918: m. 1st, 1939, Lt.-Com. Rodney Athelstan Price, RN, who d. (killed in action during 1939-45 War) 1943: 2ndly, 1945, Col. Geoffrey Russell Armstrong, DSO, MC, TD, Hon. Artillery Co., and has issue living, (by 1st m.) David George (Rosehill, Gt. Ouseburn, Yorks.), b. 1940; MA, Camb.: m. 1970, Diana Catherine Symington, da. of Thomas Alastair Symington Davie, of Grangehill, Beith, Ayrshire, and has issue living, Toby Charles Rodney b. 1972, Simon James Edward b. 1974,—(by 2nd m.) Johny, b. 1946; MA, Camb.,—Ruth Margaret, b. 1949. Residence,—Long Copse, Ewhurst, Surrey.

Issue of the late Ven. Richard Mervyn Cole-Hamilton, b. 1877, d. 1959 : m. 1st, 1911, Margaret, J.P., who d. 1954, dau. of the late Edmund Grove Bennett, of The Close, Salisbury; 2ndly, 1955, Elsie Irén (WARNER), who d. 1975, da. of W. H. Pendlebury, of Shrewsbury:—

(By 1st marriage) Richard Arthur, *b.* 1912 ; ed. at Marlborough, and at Worcester Coll., Oxford (M.A. 1962); is 2nd master, Fettes Coll.; formerly Maj. Cameronians (TA): *m.* 1947, Ruth Kathleen Betty, da. of Sir William Lorenzo Parker, 3rd Bt., OBE, and has issue living, Robin, *b.* 1948,— Richard Simon, *b.* 1951,—William Mervyn John, *b.* 1954.   *Residence,*—4, Garscube Terr., Edinburgh.
——Anthony Mervyn, *b.* 1919: Lieut.-Com. RN (retired); 1939-45 War (despatches): *m.* 1st, 1944, Monica Mary (3rd Officer WRNS), who *d.* 1954, da. of the late Lieut.-Col. John Rogers Cartwright, DSO: 2ndly, 1956, Angela Elizabeth (HANSCHELL), da. of J. I. Baeza, FRCS, DPH, of Barbados, and has issue living, (by 1st m.) David John (Oven Cottage, Thundridge, Herts.), *b.* 1948: *m.* 1973, Elizabeth Ann, da. of Bruce Lloyd Brown, of Vic., BC, Canada,—Susan Joan, *b.* 1945: *m.* 1969, Andrew Wallace, of 111, Grove Lane, Camberwell, SE5,—Isobel Margaret, *b.* 1950,—Patricia Anne, *b.* 1952.   *Residence,*—The Moat House, Hertingfordbury, Herts.

         Grandson of the Ven. Richard Mervyn Cole-Hamilton, son of the late Rev. Arthur Henry Cole-Hamilton (ante) :—
Issue of the late Lieut. David Edmund Cole-Hamilton, D.S.C., R.N., *b.* 1914 ; *d.* (on active ser. during European War) 1942 : *m.* 1938, Anne (who *m.* 2ndly, 1959, O. G. N. Turnbull, M.C.), dau. of the late George William Cole-Hamilton (ante) :—
Michael Anthony (The Old Blue Boar, St. John St., Winchester), *b.* 1940: *m.* 1963, Jane Elizabeth Mary, el. da. of Arthur Maurice Stewart-Wallace, MD, FRCP, of The Moot House, Ditchling, Sussex, and has issue living, William Michael David *b.* 1967,—Elen Susannah, *b.* 1965,—Alexandra Jane, *b.* 1971.

         Granddaughter of the late John Isaac Cole-Hamilton, yst. son of the late Arthur Willoughby Cole-Hamilton (ante):—
Issue of the late Air Vice-Marshal John Beresford Cole-Hamilton, C.B., C.B.E., *b.* 1894, *d.* 1945 : *m.* 1928, Hilda Violet Leslie, who *d.* 1945, dau. of the late Charles Leslie Fox, of Rumwell Hall, Taunton:—
Diana Patricia Selina, *b.* 1932: *m.* 1957, (m. diss. 1968), Stephen Wilbraham Ford, and has issue living, Jonathan Hugo, *b.* 1960,—Joanna Margaret Randle, *b.* 1958.   *Residence,*—The Old Vicarage Greywell, Basingstoke.

         Granddaughters of the late Col. Arthur Richard Cole-Hamilton, son of the late Capt. William Claude Cole-Hamilton (ante) :—
Issue of the late Capt. William Moore Cole-Hamilton, late R.A.S.C., *b.* 1883, *d.* 1948 : *m.* 1903, Ada Beatrice, youngest dau. of the late William Peter Huddle, of Dover :—
Nora Kathleen, *b.* 1904 : *m.* 1st, 1926 (marriage dissolved 1944), Carl Rudolf Baltzar von Braun, MRCS, late Capt. RAMC; 2ndly, 1944, John Mathew Shufflebotham.   *Residence,*—.
     Issue of the late Capt. William Andrew Thomas Cole-Hamilton, *b.* 1864, *d.* 1903 *m.* 1891, Lizzie Alexander, who *d.* 1951, dau. of the late Christopher S. Penny, and widow of Capt. Ashton Rendle, M.S.C. :—
Clodagh Madeline Janie, *b.* 1897.   *Address,*—c/o Lloyds Bank, 6, Pall Mall, S.W.1.

PREDECESSORS.—[1] JOHN COLE, *M.P.* for Enniskillen, 4th in descent from Sir William Cole who settled in Co. Fermanagh, temp. James I., was cr. *Baron Mountflorence,* of Florence Court, co. Fermanagh (peerage of Ireland) 1760; *d.* 1767; *s.* by his son [2] WILLIAM WILLOUGHBY, 2nd Baron; cr. *Viscount Enniskillen* (peerage of Ireland), 1776, and *Earl of Enniskillen* (peerage of Ireland) 1789; *d.* 1803; *s.* by his son [3] JOHN WILLOUGHBY, 2nd Earl; *b.* 1768; Lord-Lieut. of co. Fermanagh; cr. *Baron Grinstead,* of Grinstead, Wilts (peerage of United Kingdom) 1815; *d.* 1840; *s.* by his son [4] WILLIAM WILLOUGHBY, *D.C.L., LL.D., F.R.S.*; *b.* 1807; sat as M.P. for Fermanagh (C) 1831-40: *m.* 1st, 1844, Jane, who *d.* 1855, el. dau. of the late James Archibald Casamaijor Esq.; 2ndly, 1865, the Hon. Mary Emma Brodrick, who *d.* 1896, dau. of 6th Viscount Middleton; *d.* Nov. 1886; *s.* by his el. son [5] LOWRY EGERTON, *K.P.*, 4th Earl, *b.* 1845, M.P. for Enniskillen (C) 1880-5: *m.* 1869, Charlotte Marion, who *d.* 1937, dau. of the late Douglas Baird, of Closeburn, N.B.; *d.* 1924; *s.* by his son [6] JOHN HENRY MICHAEL, *C.M.G.*, 5th Earl, *b.* 1876; Lt. 7th Hussars, and Lt.-Col. N. Irish Horse, and Chm. N. Ireland Transport Board: *m.* 1st, 1907 (marriage dissolved 1931) Irene Frances, who *d.* 1937, dau. of Alfred Edward Miller Mundy; 2ndly, 1932, Mary Cecily, dau. of the late Hugh Nevill, and widow of Maj. Thomas Syers, R.A.; *d.* 1963; *s.* by his nephew [7] DAVID LOWRY (son of the late Hon. Galbraith Lowry Egerton Cole, 3rd son of 4th Earl), 6th Earl and present peer; also Viscount Enniskillen, Baron Mountflorence, and Baron Grinstead.

Ennismore, Viscount,   son of Earl of Listowel

Erleigh, Viscount,   son of Marquess of Reading.

ERNE, EARL OF. (Crichton.) Sits as **BARON FERMANAGH (U.K. 1876).**
[Earl I. 1789.]

[Name pronounced " **Cryton.**"]

HENRY GEORGE VICTOR JOHN CRICHTON, 6th Earl; b. July 9th, 1937; s. 1940; ed. at Eton; was a Page of Honour to HM 1952-54; late Lieut. N. Irish Horse; a JP and DL for co. Fermanagh: m. 1958, Camilla Marguerite, el. da. of the late Wing Com. Owen George Endicott Roberts, and has issue.

Arms,—Argent, a lion rampant azure. Crest,—A wyvern's head couped at the neck vert emitting flames proper from the mouth and ears. Supporters.—Two lions azure, on the head of each an earl's coronet proper.
Seat,—Crom Castle, Newtown Butler. co. Fermanagh. Town Residence,—16, Chesham Mews, SW1. Clubs,—White's, Turf, Royal Yacht Squadron.

SON LIVING.
JOHN HENRY MICHAEL NINIAN (Viscount Crichton), b. June 19th, 1971.
DAUGHTERS LIVING.
Lady Cleone Lucinda, b. 1959.
Lady Davina Jane, b. 1961.
Lady Katherine Patricia, b. 1962.
Lady Tara Guinevere, b. 1967.
SISTERS LIVING.
Lady Rosanagh Mary, b. 1932 : m. 1956, Baron Michael Paul Raben-Levetzau, of Belfield House, Kilpedder, co. Wicklow, and has issue living, Siegfried Matthew John, b. 1962,—Alexander Peter Vincent, b. 1964,—Christopher Victor Patrick, b. 1968,—Seamus Julian Henry, b. 1971.

GOD · SEND · GRACE

Lady Antonia Pamela Mary, b. 1934: m. 1953, Timothy William Wardell [see Crossley, Bt.]. Residence.—Williamstown House, Clonsilla, co. Dublin.

AUNT LIVING. (Raised to the rank of an Earl's daughter 1920.)
Lady Mary Kathleen (Duchess of Abercorn), DCVO, b. 1905; Mistress of the Robes to H.M. Queen Elizabeth the Queen Mother since 1964; DCVO 1969: m. 1928, the 4th Duke of Abercorn. Residence,—Barons Court, Omagh, co. Tyrone, N. Ireland.

WIDOW LIVING OF FIFTH EARL.
Lady DAVIDEMA KATHARINE CYNTHIA MARY MILLICENT BULWER-LYTTON, dau. of 2nd Earl of Lytton m. 1st, 1931, the 5th Earl, who d. (of wounds received in action during European War) 1940 ; 2ndly, 1945, Col. the Hon. Christopher Montague Woodhouse, DSO, OBE, MP [see B. Terrington]. Residence,—Bois Mill, Latimer, Bucks.

COLLATERAL BRANCHES LIVING.
Issue of the late Col. the Hon. Sir George Arthur Charles Crichton, G.C.V.O., Coldstream Guards, 2nd son of 4th Earl, b. 1874, d. 1952: m. 1913, Lady Mary Augusta Dawson, J.P., who d. 1961, dau. of 2nd Earl of Dartrey :—

David George MVO, b. 1914; ed. at Eton; late HM Diplo. Ser.; MVO (class 4) 1968; 1939-45 War as Maj. Derbys. Yeo. (TA) (despatches): m. 1941, Joan Fenella, da. of the late Lt.-Col. Douglas Whyte Cleaver, DSO of Park Palace, Monte Carlo, and has issue living, Charles David Blayney, b. 1953; ed at Eton,—Fenella Jane, b. 1948: m. 1969 (m. diss. 1974) the Hon. Anthony Henry Amherst Cecil [see B. Amherst of Hackney). Residences,—77, Cadogan Gdns., SW3; Bois Joli, 06-Cap D'ail, France. Club,—Boodle's.——Richard John Vesey, MC, b. 1916; ed. at Eton; is Col. late Coldstream Guards; appointed a Member of HM's Bodyguard of Hon. Corps of Gentlemen-at-Arms 1966; 1939-45 War (twice wounded, despatches, MC): m. 1948, Yvonne (OLIVER), da. of the late Dr. H. E. Worthington, and has issue living, Vesey George, b. 1949,—Adrian David, b. 1952: m. 1974, Janie, yr. da. of Duncan Wauchope, of 14, Porchester Terr., W2,—Simon Patrick, b. 1956. Residence,—Eglinton Lodge, Hartley Wintney, Hants.——Patrick Henry Douglas, b. 1919; ed. at Eton, and at Oxford Univ.; is Maj. Berks. Yeo. (TA); late Capt. RA (TA); was a Page of Honour to HM 1932-36; 1939-45 War (despatches): m. 1948, Gillian Moyra, da. of the late Rt. Hon. Sir Alexander George Montagu Cadogan, GCMG, KCB [see E. Cadogan, colls.], and has issue living, Hugh Patrick George, b. 1949,—Desmond Cadogan, b. 1953,—Jane Elizabeth (twin), b. 1949. Residence,—Dippenhall Grange, Farnham, Surrey.——Barbara Mary Cynthia, b. 1922: m. 1947, Alastair Malcolm Nicholson, and has issue living, Michael Alastair George, b. 1951,—Jennifer Mary, b. 1949,—Sara Kathleen, b. 1957. Residence,—Tundry House, Dogmersfield, Hants.——Mary Bridget Ann, b. 1927: m. 1951, Maj. John William Burke Cole, Coldstream Guards (ret.) [E. Longford, colls.], and has issue living, James William John, b. 1952,—Michael George, b. 1955,—Elizabeth Anne, b. 1961. Residence,—The Malt House, West Woodhay, Newbury, Berks.

Issue of the late Hon. Arthur Owen Crichton, yst. son of 4th Earl, b. 1876, d. 1970: m. 1906, Katherine Helen Elizabeth, who d. 1964, da. of the late Col. the Hon. Walter Rodolph Trefusis, CB [B. Clinton, colls.]:—
Jean Trefusis, b. 1912: m. 1st, 1933, Lt.-Col. Eion James Henry Merry, MC, R. Horse Guards [V Chetwynd], who d. 1966; 2ndly, 1969, Capt. Montagu William Lowry-Corry, of Clover Farm, Shalden, Alton, Hants., and 11, Holland Villas Rd., W14 [see E. Belmore, colls.], and has issue living (by 1st m.), Davina Jean (Lady Gibbs) b. 1934: m. 1955, Gen. Sir Roland Christopher Gibbs, KCB, CBE, DSO, MC, late 60th Rifles, of Shalden Lodge, Alton, Hants., and has issue living, Aidan Joseph Merry b. 1957, James Roland Melvil b. 1958, Melissa Margaret Jean b. 1966,—Diana, b. 1937.

Granddaughter of Lieut.-Col. the Hon. Charles Ferderick Crichton, 2nd son of 3rd Earl:—
Issue of the late Major Hubert Francis Crichton, b. 1874, d. (killed in action) 1914: m. 1903, Esther Eliza (who m. 2ndly, 1920, Maj.-Gen. Spencer Edmund Hollond, C.B., C.M.G., D.S.O., who d. 1950), dau. of the late Llewellyn Traherne Bassett Saunderson, J.P. [E. Clonmell]:—

Doris Madeline, *b.* 1904: *m.* 1925, Philip Ivan Pease, who *d.* 1964, and has issue living, Nigel Crichton, *b.* 1934; ed. at Eton,—Simon Philip, *b.* 1945,—Bridget, *b.* 1926,—Alison Beatrix, *b.* 1928,—Carol Esther, *b.* 1932: *m.* 1959, William E. A. Fox, of Anmer Hall, King's Lynn, and has issue living, William Philip *b.* 1960, Robert James Ayscough *b.* 1970, Annabel Carol *b.* 1962, Jane Cordelia *b.* 1965.   *Residence,*—Cleatham Hall, Winston, Darlington.

Grandchildren of the late Hon. Sir Henry George Louis Crichton, K.C.B., 3rd son of 3rd Earl:—

Issue of the late Col. Charles William Harry Crichton, D.S.O., *b.* 1872. *d.* 1958: *m.* 1912, Dorothy Maud, who *d.* 1959, dau. of the late Hon. Eustace Henry Dawnay [V. Downe, colls.] :—

Ronald Henry, *b.* 1913 ; ed. at Radley, and at Ch. Ch., Oxford ; late Capt. Rifle Brig.   *Residence,*—Flat 3, 24, Palace Court, W2.   *Club,*—Reform.——Brian John, *b.* 1918; ed. at Radley, and at Trin. Coll., Camb. : *m.* 1953, Anne Radclyffe, younger dau. of the late Lieut.-Col. Thomas Hassard Montgomery, D.S.O., of Cadogan House, Shrewsbury, and has issue living, Susan Jane, *b.* 1955,—Diana Mary, *b.* 1957,—Judith Anne, *b.* 1959.   *Residence,*—Plas Trefor, Llansadwrn, Anglesey.

Issue of the late Capt. Reginald Louis Crichton, R.N., *b.* 1874, *d.* 1929: *m.* 1902, Hester Beatrix, who *d.* 1961, dau. of the late Rev. Richard Allen White, R. of Wing, Rutland :—
Marcus Henry Reginald, *b.* 1904 ; Com. (retired) R.N.; appointed Inspector H.M. Coastguard, E. Scotland Div. 1952 ; European War 1939-45 in Atlantic and Mediterranean : *m.* 1935, Elizabeth Frances, dau. of the late Col. Francis Holland Dorling, D.S.O., of The Crouch, Seaford, Sussex, and has issue living, Catherine Elizabeth, *b.* 1937: *m.* 1969, Christopher Bates, PhD, of 8, Haslingfield Rd., Harston, Cambridge, and has issue living, Gemma Clare Irene *b.* 1974,—Frances Margaret, *b.* 1942: *m.* 1962, Maj. Patrick Lloyd Ker Thompson, of Mongewell Meadow, Wallingford, Berks., and has issue living, James Marcus Crichton, *b.* 1966, Bridget Clare, *b.* 1964,—Madelaine Louise, *b.* 1944: *m.* 1967, Peter George Ridley Dodds, of Heather Lane, Princeton, NJ 08540, USA, and has issue living, George Alexander Crichton *b.* 1970, Lucy Clare *b.* 1972.   *Residence,*—Lochanhead Wood, Loch Rutton, Dumfries.   *Club,*—RN Sailings.——(Francis) Michael, *b.* 1909; is Cdr. (ret.) RN, and a Fellow of Roy. Commonwealth So.; 1939-45 War in Atlantic, Mediterranean, Burma, and the Pacific.   *Residence,*—Commanders, Lisbellaw, co Fermanagh.   *C ubs.*—Royal Cruising, RN Sailing, Royal Norfolk and Suffolk, Island Sailing (Cowes), Lough Erne Yacht.——Elisabeth Hester, *b.* 1914: *m.* 1939, Francis Alfred Lepper, Fellow of Corpus Christi Coll., Oxford, of 3, Merton St., Oxford, and Trewollack House, St. Wenn, Bodmin, Cornwall, and has issue living, Patrick Francis Dalway (Friern Cottage, Doctors Commons Rd., Berkhamstead, Herts.), *b.* 1941: *m.* 1966, Anthea, el. da. of W. Douglas C. Scott, of 1, Holly Pl., NW3, and has issue living, Edward Patrick Robert *b.* 1971, Francesca Eugénie, *b.* 1967,——Jane Helen Veronica, *b.* 1942: *m.* 1970, Roger James Willoughby, of 9, Beechwood Court, Park Rd., W4.——(Patricia) Jane, *b.* 1920: *m.* 1946, John Herbert Mount, who *d.* 1973, and has issue living, John Richard Herbert Crichton, *b.* 1953; ed. at Gordonstoun,—Mark Donald Crichton, *b.* 1957; ed. at King's Sch., Canterbury,—Virginia Jane *b.* 1947: *m.* 1968, Richard Henry Ringrose Latham, of 23, Chancellor House, 17, Hyde Park Gate, SW7, and Mudhole, Bekesbourne, Canterbury [see E. Jellicoe],—(Selina) Clare, *b.* 1950: *m.* 1974, Alexander Brunton Badenock, of 27, De Walden St., SW1.   *Residence,*—Woolton Farm, Bekesbourne, nr. Canterbury.

PREDECESSORS.—[1] ABRAHAM Creighton; cr. *Baron Erne,* of Crom Castle, co. Fermanagh (peerage of Ireland) 1768; *d.* 1772; *s.* by his son [2] JOHN, 2nd Baron ; *b.* 1738 (about); cr. *Viscount Erne* (peerage of Ireland) 1781, and *Earl Erne* (peerage of Ireland) 1789: *m.* 1761, Catherine, dau. of the Rt. Rev. Robert Howard, Lord Bishop of Elphin, and sister of 1st Viscount Wicklow; *d.* 1828; *s.* by his son [3] ABRAHAM, 2nd Earl; *d.* unmarried 1842; *s.* by his nephew [4] JOHN, *K.P.,* 3rd Earl; *b.* 1802 ; changed spelling of name to Crichton; was Lord-Lieut. of co. Fermanagh and a Representative Peer for Ireland ; cr. *Baron Fermanagh,* of Lisnaskea (peerage of United Kingdom) 1872: *m.* 1837, Selina Griselda, who *d.* 1884, dau. of the late Rev. Charles Cobbe Beresford ; *d.* Oct. 2nd, 1885 ; *s.* by his son [5] JOHN HENRY, *K.P., P.C.,* 4th Earl ; Lieut. of co. Fermanagh ; M.P. for Enniskillen (C) 1868-80, and for co. Fermanagh 1880-83 ; a Lord of the Treasury 1876-80 : *m.* 1870, Lady Florence Mary Cole, who *d.* 1924, dau. of 3rd Earl of Enniskillen ; *d.* Dec. 2nd, 1914 ; *s.* by his grandson [6] JOHN HENRY GEORGE (only son of the late Major (Henry William) Viscount Crichton, M.V.O., D.S.O., Roy. Horse Guards (el. son of 4th Earl), who *d.* (killed in action during European War Oct. 31st, 1914), 5th Earl; *b.* 1907 ; Major N. Irish Horse, and Lieut. Roy. Horse Guards (Reserve) ; was a Page of Honour to H.M. 1921-4, and a Lord-in-Waiting to H.M. 1936-9: *m.* 1931, Lady Davidema Katharine Cynthia Mary Millicent Lytton, dau. of 2nd Earl of Lytton ; *d.* (of wounds received in action during European War) 1940; *s.* by his son [7] HENRY GEORGE VICTOR JOHN, 6th Earl and present peer; also Viscount Erne, Baron Erne, and Baron Fermanagh.

ERROLL, COUNTESS OF. (Hay.)
[Earl S. 1452.]

Bear the yoke.

DIANA DENYSE HAY (*Countess of Erroll*), *b.* Jan. 5th, 1926; *s.* 1941; is 27th Hereditary Lord High Constable of Scotland, an O.St.J., and Hon. Pres. '45 Asso.; retains her maiden surname of Hay under Scots Law: *m*, 1st, 1946 (marriage dissolved 1964) Capt. Sir (Rupert) Iain Kay Moncreiffe of that Ilk, 11th Bt.; 2ndly, 1964, Maj. Raymond Alexander Carnegie [see E. Southesk], and has issue by 1st and 2nd marriages.

Ãrms,—Argent, three inescutcheons gules; on either side of the shield an arm gauntleted proper, issuing out of a cloud and grasping a sword in pale argent, hilt and pommel or; behind the shield in saltire, two silver batons tipped with gold at either end (*as Lord High Constable of Scotland*). Crest,—A falcon volant proper, armed, jessed, and belled or. Supporters, —Two savages wreathed about the middle with laurel proper, each bearing on his shoulders an ox yoke proper bows gules.

Residence,—Crimonmogate, Lonmay, Aberdeenshire.

Badge as Chief of the Hays.

SONS LIVING. (*By 1st marriage.*)
MERLIN SERELD VICTOR GILBERT *HAY* (*Lord Hay*) (Turf Club), *b.* April 20th, 1948; ed. at Eton; Rfn. The Queen's R. Rifles (Parachutist).
Hon. Peregrine David Euan Malcolm MONCREIFFE, *b.* 1951; ed. at Eton.

(*By 2nd marriage.*)
Hon. Jocelyn Jacek Alexander Bannerman CARNEGIE, *b.* 1966.

DAUGHTER LIVING. (*By 1st marriage.*)
Lady Alexandra Victoria Caroline Anne HAY, *b.* 1955.

WIDOW LIVING OF SON OF TWENTIETH EARL.
Pamela, dau. of Francis George Burroughes [B. Suffield, and E. Mayo, colls.] : *m.* 1921, Capt. the Hon. Ivan Josslyn Lumley Hay, M.B.E., who *d.* 1936, and has issue living [see colls., infra]. *Residence*,—9, Wellington Place, N.W.8.

COLLATERAL BRANCHES LIVING.
Issue of the late Gilbert Allan Rowland Boyd (who *s.* as 6*th Baron Kilmarnock* 1941), yr. son of 21st Earl, *b.* 1903, *d.* 1975:—
[see that title.]
Issue of the late Lady Rosemary Constance Ferelith, dau. of 21st Earl, *b.* 1904, *d.* 1944 : *m.* 1st, 1924, Lieut.-Col. Rupert Sumner Ryan, C.M.G., D.S.O., who *d.* 1952, and from whom she obtained a divorce 1935 ; 2ndly, 1935, Major James Frank Gresham, D.S.O., Welsh Guards :—
(By 1st marriage) Patrick Victor Charles, *b.* 1925 : *m.* 1949, Rosemary Elizabeth, el. dau. of Francis Rupert Chesterman, of Orford, Tasmania, and has issue living, Dominic Rupert Charles, *b.* 1956.— Siobhan Ferelith, *b.* 1959. *Residence*,—228, Williams Road, Toorak, Victoria, Australia.
Issue of the late Capt. the Hon. Ivan Josslyn Lumley Hay, M.B.E., 3rd son of 20th Earl, *b.* 1884, *d.* 1936: *m.* 1921, Pamela [ante], dau. of Francis George Burroughes [B. Suffield and E. Mayo, colls.]:—
Alexandra Cecilia Mary (Flat 7, 67, Longridge Rd., SW7), *b.* 1922.——Elizabeth Anne, *b.* 1925: formerly in WRNS: *m.* 1945 (m. diss. 1970), Jeremy Christopher Gurney, Lt. RN, and has issue living, Michael Jeremy, *b.* 1946.—William Ivan, *b.* 1948. *Residence*,—22, Lennox Gdns., SW1.—— Penelope Constance, *b.* 1930: *m.* 1957, George Harold Armine Dare [Morris, Bt., cr. 1806], of 9, Launceston Pl., W8, and has issue living, Henry James, *b.* 1959.—Amelia Alexandra Elizabeth *b.* 1961.

PREDECESSORS.—William de la Haye, Butler of Scotland, was granted a charter of feudal Barony of Erroll c. 1178-82; Sir Gilbert de la Haye, 3rd feudal Baron of Erroll, co-Regent of Scotland 1255: *m.* Lady Idoine, dau. of William Comyn, Earl of Buchan, and sister of the Constable of Scotland. Their grandson, Sir Gilbert, was for his long adherence to Bruce cr. by charter hereditary *Great Constable of Scotland* 1314 on the forfeiture of his Comyn cousins (his great-grandson, *Sir* Thomas, 3rd Constable: *m.* Elizabeth, dau. of Robert II, King of Scots); his descendant in the 7th generation was [1] *Sir* WILLIAM Hay, 5th Great Constable of Scotland; cr. *Lord Hay* (peerage of Scotland) 1449, and *Earl of Erroll* and *Lord Slains* (peerage of Scotland) 1452 : *m.* Beatrix, dau. of James, 7th Earl of Douglas; *d.* 1463; *s.* by his el. son [2] NICHOLAS, 2nd Earl; *d.s.p.* 1470; *s.* by his brother [3] WILLIAM, 3rd Earl; *d.* 1506; *s.* by his son [4] WILLIAM, 4th Earl; *d.* (killed at Flodden) 1513; *s.* by his son [5] WILLIAM, 5th Earl; *d.* 1522; *s.* by his son [6] WILLIAM, 6th Earl; *d.* 1541; *s.* by his cousin [7] GEORGE (son of Thomas, 2nd son of 3rd Earl), 7th Earl; Lord Lieut. of all Central Scotland from the Earn to the Spey 1559; *d.* 1573; *s.* by his son [8] ANDREW, 8th Earl; *d.* 1585; *s.* by his son [9] FRANCIS, 9th Earl; exiled for leading a Catholic rebellion 1594; but subsequently pardoned; *d.* 1631; *s.* by his son [10] WILLIAM, 10th Earl; *d.* 1636; *s.* by his son [11] GILBERT, 11th Earl; *d.s.p.* 1674; *s.* by his kinsman [12] JOHN (grandson of Sir George, 4th son of 8th Earl), 12th Earl; *d.* 1704; *s.* by his son [13] CHARLES, 13th Earl; *d.* unmarried 1717; *s.* by his sister [14] MARY, wife of Alexander Falconer (brother of 5th Lord Falconer), who assumed the name of Hay of Delgaty; *d.s.p.* 1758; *s.* by her grand-nephew [15] JAMES (son of William, 4th Earl of Kilmarnock, by Lady Anne Livingstone, dau. of Lady Margaret Hay (wife of James, 5th Earl of Linlithgow), sister of Mary, Countess of Erroll), 15th Earl; was Lord of Police 1767; *d.* 1778; *s.* by his el. son [16] GEORGE, 16th Earl; having let drop a secret of Mr. Pitt, committed suicide 1798; *s.* by his brother [17] WILLIAM, 17th Earl; was Knight-Marischal of Scotland 1805, and Lord High Commr. to Ch. of Scotland; *d.* 1819; *s.* by his son [18] WILLIAM GEORGE, K.T., P.C., G.C.H., 18th Earl, *b.* 1801; was Lord Steward of the Household, Master of the Buckhounds, and Lord-Lieut. of Aberdeenshire; cr. *Baron Kilmarnock*, of Kilmarnock, co. Ayr (peerage of United Kingdom) 1831 : *m*. 1820, Lady Elizabeth Fitzclarence, who *d*. 1856, sister of 1st Earl of Munster; *d*. 1846; *s*. by his son [19] WILLIAM HENRY, 19th Earl, *b*. 1823; Major (retired) Rifle Brig.; Crimea 1854-5 (wounded): *m*. 1848, Eliza Amelia, *V.A.*, who *d*.1916 dau. of the late Gen. the Hon. Sir Charles Gore, G.C.B.   *d*. 1891; *s*. by his son [20] CHARLES GORE, *K.T.*, *C.B.*, *L.L.D.*. 20th Earl, *b*. 1852; Hon. Maj.-Gen. in the Army ; sometime Lieut.-Col. Comdg. Roy. Horse Guards; a Lord-in-Waiting to King Edward VII. 1903-5 : *m*. 1875, Mary Caroline, who *d*. 1934, dau. of the late Edmund L'Estrange, of Tynte Lodge, co. Leitrim ; *d*. 1927; *s*. by his son [21] VICTOR ALEXANDER SERELD, *K.C.M.G.*, 21st Earl, *b*. 1876; acted as Chargé d'Affaires at Berlin 1919-21 ; was British High Commr. of Rhineland Commn.1921-28 : *m*.1900, Mary Lucy Victoria, who *d*.1957, only dau. of Sir Allan Russell Mackenzie, 2nd Bt. (cr. 1890); *d*. 1928; *s*. by his son [22] JOSSLYN VICTOR, 22nd Earl, *b*.1901: *m*. 1st, 1923, Lady (Myra) Idina (GORDON), who *d*. 1955 (having obtained a divorce 1930), dau. of 8th Earl De La Warr ; 2ndly, 1930, Edith Mildred Mary (RAMSAY-HILL), who *d*. 1939, dau. of the late R. W. Maude, of Cleveland, Yorkshire; *d*. 1941 ; *s*. in the Barony of Kilmarnock by his brother the Hon. Gilbert Allan Rowland Hay, and in the Earldom, and Lordships of Hay and Slains by his only child [23] DIANA DENYSE, present peeress, also Lady Hay and Lady Slains.

ERROLL OF HALE, BARON. (Erroll.) [Baron U.K. 1964.]

FREDERICK JAMES ERROLL, *TD, PC*, 1st Baron, son of George Murison Erroll, of Glasgow, and London; *b*. May 27th, 1914; ed. at Oundle, and at Trin. Coll., Camb.; Parl. Sec. to Min. of Supply 1955-56, and to Board of Trade 1956-58, Economic Sec. to HM Treasury 1958-59, Min. of State, Board of Trade, 1959-61, Pres. of Board of Trade 1961-63, and Min. of Power 1963-64, a Member of National Economic Development Council 1962-63, and Pres. of London Chamber of Commerce 1966-69; Dep. Chm. Decimal Currency Board 1966-71; Chm. of Home Office Liquor Licensing Cttee., 1970-72, Pres. Electrical Research Assocn. since 1971, and Chm. of Whessoe, Ltd., Darling since 1970, Bowater Corpn. since 1973, and Automobile Assocn. since 1974; a Dir. of other cos.; MP for Altrincham and Sale (*C*) 1945-64; cr. PC 1960, and *Baron Erroll of Hale*, of Kilmun, co. Argyll (Peerage of UK) 1964: *m*. 1950, Elizabeth, da. of R. Sowton Barrow, of Exmouth, Devon.

Arms,—Per bend azure and gules, on a bend embellished of six electric flashes or a fleur-de-lys and two lozenges sable. Crest,—A chevronel round embattled sable. Supporters,—*Dexter*, an elephant guardant sable; *sinister*, a bear reguardant argent, muzzled azure, and from the muzzle a cord sable, ringed or and reflexed over the back.

Residences,—21, Ilchester Place, W14; Foxholes, Pinkneys Green, Maidenhead, Berks.

Erskine, Baron, see Earl of Buchan.

Erskine, Lord, son of Earl of Mar and Kellie.

ERSKINE OF RERRICK, BARON. (Erskine.) [Baron U.K. 1964, Bt. U.K. 1961.

JOHN MAXWELL ERSKINE, *G.B.E.*, 1st Baron and 1st Baronet, son of John Erskine, of Kirkcudbright; *b*. Dec. 14th, 1893; ed. at Kirkcudbright Acad., and Edinburgh Univ.; Solicitor 1924; Hon. LLD Glasgow, and Belfast; Hon. FRCPE; FRSE; Chm. of Scottish Hosp. Endowment Research Trust 1953-72; a Dir. (Gen. Manager 1932-53) of Nat. Commercial Bank of Scotland Ltd., Edinburgh 1951-69; late Dir. Guardian Assurance Co., Ltd., Caledonian Insurance Co., and other Cos.; Chm. Scottish Savings Cttee. 1945-58, and Pres. 1958-72; Pres. of Inst. of Bankers in Scotland 1937-40, and of Edinburgh Chamber of Commerce and Manufacturers 1941-44, Chm. of Central Cttee. of Scottish Chambers of Commerce 1942-44, Member of Hetherington Department Cttee. on Hosp. Policy in Scotland 1942, and of Cttee. of Management of Roy. Victoria Hosp., Tuberculosis Trust 1945-56, Trustee and a Member of Exec. Cttee. of Carnegie Trust for Scottish Univs. 1944-47, Pres. of Edinburgh Union of Boys' Clubs 1945-56, and of Scottish Council of Social Ser. 1949-57 (Chm. 1945-49), Chm. of Transport Users' Consultative Cttee. for

Scotland 1954-57, a Member of Transport Consultative Cttee. 1953-56, of Scottish Transport Council 1955-56, and of National Arbitration Tribunal for Coal Mining Industry 1956-59, and Chm. of Joint Exchequer Board (Govt. of Ireland Act 1920) 1964-64; Gov. of N. Ireland 1964-68; a KStJ; a Member of Queen's Body Guard for Scotland (Roy. Co. of Archers); a Foundation Member of Thistle Foundation, a Vice-Pres. of Trustee Savings Bank Assocn., a Freeman of Kirkcudbright, and an Hon. Member of Co. of Merchants of City of Edinburgh; *cr.* CBE (Civil) 1946, Knt. 1949, GBE (Civil) 1956, a *Baronet* 1961, and *Baron Erskine of Rerrick,* of Rerrick, Kirkcudbright (peerage of UK) 1964: *m.* 1922, Henrietta (CStJ), da. of the late William Dunnett, of E. Canisbay, Caithness, and has issue.

Arms,—Quarterly: 1st and 4th, argent, a pale sable between two lions rampant azure armed and langued gules, *Erskine*; 2ndly, argent, a saltire sable, in centre chief a label of three points in centre base a mullet gules, *Maxwell of Nether Rerrick*; 3rd, argent, three hurcheons sable, *Herries.* **Crest,**—A cubit arm attired in a manche party sable and azure the hand naked and grasping a partisan bendways all proper. **Supporters,**—Two griffins per fesse gules and sable powdered with ten bezants and armed and beaked, argent.

Residence,—69, Eaton Sq., SW1. *Clubs,*—New (Edinburgh), Caledonian.

SON LIVING.

Hon. IAN MAXWELL (10, Chesham Pl., SW1; Guards' Club), *b.* Jan. 22nd, 1926; ed. at Harrow; Maj. (ret.) Gren. Gds.; a Chevalier of Legion of Honour, and an OStJ; a qualified Pilot, a Member of Inst. of Dirs.; M.Inst.M.; MIPR; Comptroller to Gov.-Gen. of NZ 1960-61, PRO Household Div. in London Dist. HQ. 1964-66; a Professional Photographer, and an Advertising and Public Relations Consultant, an Asso. Dir., Saward Baker Advertising Agency, and Chm. of Guards' Flying Club: *m.* 1st, 1955 (m. diss. 1964), Marie Elizabeth, da. of the late Maj. Richard Burton Allen, 3rd Dragoon Gds.; 2ndly, 1974, Maria Josephine, da. of Dr. Josef Klupt.

DAUGHTER LIVING.

Hon. Elizabeth Olson, *b.* 1923; 1939-45 War as Subaltern ATS: *m.* 1944, Gilbert Butler, of The Croft, 8, Churchfields Av., Weybridge, and has issue living, David John Lister, *b.* 1949; BA,—Brian Robert Erskine, *b.* 1960,—Elizabeth Mary, *b.* 1946.

ESHER, VISCOUNT. (Brett.) [Viscount U K. 1897.]

We have conquered.

LIONEL GORDON BALIOL BRETT, *CBE,* 4th Viscount; *b.* July 18th, 1913; *s.* 1963; ed. at Eton, and at New Coll., Oxford (MA); Hon. DLitt Strathclyde, and York; Hon. Fellow American Inst. of Architects; a Fellow of Inst. of Landscape Architects; a Trusteee of London Museum; Pres. of RIBA 1965-67; a Member of Roy. Fine Art Commn. 1951-69; Rector and Vice-Provost, Roy. Coll. of Art since 1971; 1939-45 War as Maj. RA (despatches); CBE (Civil) 1970: *m.* 1935, Helena Christian Olive Lecky. da. of Col. Ebenezer, John Lecky Pike, CBE, MC, and has issue.

Arms—Quarterly: 1st and 4th or, a lion rampant gules holding in the dexter paw a fasces erect proper, within an orle of crosses bottonée fitchée of the second; 2nd, per pale or and gules three leopards' faces counterchanged; 3rd, azure three bears' heads couped argent, muzzled gules. **Crest,**—A lion passant gules, charged on the shoulder with a cross bottonée fitchée or, and holding in the dexter paw a fasces proper. **Supporters,**—*Dexter,* a boar sable; *sinister,* a lion sable; each charged on the shoulder with a cross bottonée fitchée or, and supporting a fasces proper.

Seat,—Watlington Park, Oxon. *Clubs,*—Athenæum, Garrick.

SONS LIVING.

Hon. CHRISTOPHER LIONEL BALIOL (Watlington Park, Oxon.), *b.* Dec. 23rd, 1936; ed. at Eton, and at Magdalen Coll., Oxford: *m.* 1st 1962 (m. diss. 1970) Camilla Charlotte, da. of Sir (Horace) Anthony Claud Rumbold, KCMG, CB, 10th Bt.; 2ndly, 1971, Valerie Harrington, and has issue living, (by 1st m.) Matthew Christopher Anthony, *b.* 1963,—Miranda Jane, *b.* 1964,—Rebecca Catherine, *b.* 1966,—(by 2nd m.), Oliver Maxwell, *b.* 1972,—Susannah Mary, *b.* 1973,—Clare Christian (twin), *b.* 1973.

Hon. Michael Jeremy Baliol, *b.* 1939; ed. at Eton; ARIBA: *m.* 1971, Sarah Calloway, of Shelbyville, Kentucky, USA.

Hon. Guy Anthony Baliol, *b.* 1942; ed. at Eton.

Hon. Maurice Sebastion Baliol, *b.* 1944; ed. at Eton, and at Trin. Coll., Oxford: *m.* 1968, Pauline R., da. of Lt.-Cdr. Paul Murray-Jones, RN, (ret.), of Cordwainers, Titchfield, Hants.

Hon. Stephen Patrick Baliol, *b.* 1952; ed. at Bryanston.

DAUGHTER LIVING.

Hon. Olivia Clare Teresa, *b.* 1947.

SISTERS LIVING.

Hon. Virginia Charlotte Anne, *b.* 1916.

Hon. Nancy Mildred Gladys (*Hon. Lady Shuckburgh*), *b.* 1918 : *m.* 1937 Sir (Charles Arthur) Evelyn Shuckburgh, GCMG, CB, Diplo. Ser., el. son of Sir John Evelyn Shuckburgh, KCMG, CB, and has issue living, Julian (8, Northumberland Place, W2), *b.* 1940: *m.* 1963, (m. diss. 1970), Faith Beatrice, da. of Paul Wright, and has issue living, Benjamin Evelyn *b.* 1966, Matilda Ann *b.* 1964,—Robin Anthony, *b.* 1948: *m.* 1972, Philippa Mary, da. of Nicholas Spargo, of Maidengrove, Henley-on-Thames,—Catherine, *b.* 1939: *m.* 1961, John Caute. *Residence,*—High Wood, Watling-ton, Oxon.

Hon. Priscilla Léonie Helen (*Hon. Lady Beckett*), *b.* 1921: *m.* 1941, Capt. Sir Martyn Gervase Beckett, M.C., 2nd Bt., Welsh Guards. *Residences,*—3, St. Alban's Grove, W.8; Kirkdale Farm, Nawton, Yorks.

AUNT LIVING. (*Daughter of 2nd Viscount.*)

Hon. Dorothy Eugénie, *b.* 1883 ; is an Artist. *Address,*—Box 214, Taos, New Mexico, U.S.A.

COLLATERAL BRANCH LIVING.

Issue of the late Lieut.-Col. the Hon. Maurice Vyner Baliol Brett, O.B.E., M.V.O., 2nd son of 2nd Viscount, *b.* 1892, *d.* 1934 : *m.* (Jan.) 1911, Florence Hariette Zena (the actress), "Miss Zena Dare"), who *d.* 1975, da. of the late Arthur Albert Dones:—

Antony Reginald Forbes Baliol, *M.B.E.*, *b.* 1913 ; N. Africa and Italy 1943-45 as Major Black Watch (M.B.E.); M.B.E. (Mil.) 1945 : *m.* 1939, Bay Helen, dau. of the late Charles Neville Brownell, of Birkenhead, and has issue living, Simon, *b.* 1943,—Vanessa, *b.* 1947. *Residence,*—St. Bartholomew's Hospital, E.C.1.——Angela Mariel Baliol, *b.* (Oct.) 1911 : *m.* 1934, Kenneth Marcus Thornton, and has issue living, Timothy Kenneth (Linden House, West Drive, Wentworth, Surrey), *b.* 1935; ed. at Eton: *m.* 1966, Mrs. Jacqueline Green, da. of David Hillman, and has issue living, Daniel Timothy *b.* 1968, Katherine *b.* 1970,—Brian Maurice (Stansted House, Stansted, Essex), *b.* 1937; ed. at Eton: *m.* 1959, Verity, da. of the late Guy Gordon Lawrence, of Little Easton Manor, Dunmow, and has issue living, Guy Dominic *b.* 1960, Benjamin Douglas *b.* 1965, Giles Marcus *b.* 1966, Jolyon Kenneth *b.* 1970, Kim Marie *b.* 1961. *Residence,*—Woodside Cottage, Windsor Forest, Berks.—— Marie Louise, *b.* 1916: *m.* 1938, Cdr. Archibald Rider Cheyne, RN, who *d.* 1950, and has issue living, Mark Rider, *b.* 1941; ed. at Rugby,—Angela Zena, *b.* 1947. *Residence,*—Spring Hill, Burleigh Rd., Ascot, Berks.

PREDECESSORS.—[1] Rt. *Hon. Sir* WILLIAM BALIOL BRETT, son of the late Rev. Joseph George Brett, of Ranelagh, Chelsea, S.W.; *b.* 1815 ; M.P. for Helston (*C*) 1866-8 ; Solicitor-Gen. 1868, a Justice of the Common Pleas 1868-75, a Judge of the High Court of Justice (Common Pleas Div.) 1875-6, a Lord Justice of Appeal 1876-83, and Master of the Rolls 1883-97 ; cr. *Baron Esher,* of Esher, co. Surrey (peerage of United Kingdom) 1885, and *Viscount Esher,* of Esher, co. Surrey (peerage of United Kingdom) 1897 : *m.* 1850, Eugenie, who *d.* 1904, dau. of Louis Mäyer ; *d.* 1899 ; *s.* by his eldest son [2] REGINALD BALIOL, G.C.B., G.C.V.O., P.C., 2nd Viscount, *b.* 1852; Private Sec. to Marquess of Hartington 1878-85, MP for Penryn and Falmouth (*L*) 1880-85, Sec. to Office of Works and Public Buildings 1895-1902, Dep. Constable and Lieut.-Gov. of Windsor Castle 1901-28, and Constable thereof 1928-30: *m.* 1879, Eleanor, R.R.C., who *d.* 1940, Court of St. James's; *d.* 1930: *s.* by his son [3] OLIVER SYLVAIN BALIOL, G.B.E., 3rd Viscount, *b.* 1881; Private Sec. to Sec. of State for India 1905-10: *m.* 1911, Antoinette, who *d.* 1965, da. of the late August Heckscher of New York; *d.* 1963; *s.* by his only son [4] LIONEL GORDON BALIOL, 4th Viscount and present peer, also Baron Esher.

ESSENDON, BARON. (Lewis.) [Baron U.K. 1932, Bt. U.K. 1918.]

By courage and faith.

BRIAN EDMUND LEWIS, 2nd Baron, and 2nd Baronet; *b.* Dec. 7th, 1903; *s.* 1944; ed. at Malvern, and at Pembroke Coll., Camb.: *m.* 1938, Mary, dau. of the late G. W. Booker, of Los Angeles, U.S.A., and widow of Albert Duffill.

Arms,—Per chevron sable and argent, in chief two spearheads of the second and in base a lymphad of the first. Crest,—Upon two spears in saltire, argent, headed gules, a bee volant or. Supporters, —Dexter, a dragon gules, gorged with a collar argent charged with a spearhead sable; *sinister,* a seahorse argent, maned, finned and tufted or, gorged with a collar sable charged with a spear-head argent.

Residence,—5, Av. Eglantine, Lausanne, Switzerland.

SISTER LIVING.

Hon. Frieda, *b.* 1897: *m.* 1st, 1927, Ian Patrick Robert Napier, M.C.; 2ndly, 1940, Cecil Warde Mason, and has issue living, (by 1st m.) (Ian Frederick) Malcolm (Falcon House, Kennel Av., Ascot, Berks; Club—MCC) *b.* 1927; ed. at Eton, and at Trin. Coll., Oxford,—Andrew Patrick Forbes (Manor House, Syleham, Diss., Norfolk), *b.* 1932; ed. at Eton, Nautical Coll., Pangbourne, and RMA; Maj. (ret.) Coldm. Gds.: *m.* 1967, Katharine Anne, da. of Col. Sir Robert Eric Sherlock Gooch, DSO, 11th Bt. (cr. 1746), and has issue living, James Frederick Brian *b.* 1968, Katharine Louisa *b.* 1969. *Residences,*—90K, Eaton Sq., SW1; Royal Yacht Sqdn.

PREDECESSOR.—[1] FREDERICK WILLIAM Lewis, only child of the late Edmund Lewis, of W. Hartlepool (by his wife Elizabeth, yst. da. of John Dent, of Weardale), son of William Lewis, of Whitchurch Glam. ; b. 1870; Chm. of Furness, Withy & Co., Ltd., and other shipping cos.; cr. a *Baronet* 1918, and *Baron Essendon*, of Essendon, co. Hertford (peerage of United Kingdom) 1932: m. 1896, Daisy Ellen, who d. 1967, el. da. of Robert Henry Harrison, of West Hartlepool; d. 1944; s. by his son [2] BRIAN EDMUND, 2nd Baron and present peer.

ESSEX, EARL OF. (Capell.) [Earl E. 1661.]

By fidelity and fortitude.

REGINALD GEORGE DE VERE CAPELL, *TD*, 9th Earl; b. Oct. 9th, 1906; s. 1966; ed. at Eton, and Magdalene Coll., Camb., (BA); Hon. Col. Middlesex Yeo. (16th Airborne Signals Regt.) (TA); patron of three livings: m. 1st, 1937, Mary Reeve (who obtained a divorce 1957), da. of the late F. Gibson Ward, of Bermuda, and widow of Col. George Ashton Strutt; 2ndly, 1957, Nona Isobel, da. of David Wilson Miller, of Christchurch, NZ, and widow of Francis Sydney Smythe, of Yew Tree Cottage, Colgate, Sussex.

Arms,—Gules, a lion rampant between three cross-crosslets fitchée or. **Crest,**—A demi-lion rampant holding in the dexter paw a cross-crosslet fitchée gules. **Supporters.**— Two lions or, ducally crowned, gules.

Residence,—Floyds Farm, Wingrave, Aylesbury. *Club,*—Bath.

HALF-AUNTS LIVING. (*Daughters of 7th Earl*)
Lady Iris Mary Athenais de Vere, b. 1895. *Residences,*—17, Hornton Court, W8; Walters Ash, Farnham Common, Bucks.
Lady Rachel Joan de Vere (*Joan Viscountess Ingleby*), b. 1899: m. 1922, the 1st Viscount Ingleby, who d. 1966. *Residences,*—36, Kingston House, SW7; Smilesworth, Osmotherly, Yorks.

WIDOW LIVING OF EIGHTH EARL.
CHRISTINE MARY DAVIS (*Christine Countess of Essex*), (36, Stonehaven Cres., Deakin, Canberra, Aust.): m. 1957, as his 4th wife, the 8th Earl, who d. 1966.

COLLATERAL BRANCHES LIVING.
Granddaughters of the late Capt. the Hon. Algernon Henry Champagne Capell, RN, brother of 6th Earl:—
Issue of Reginald Randolph Algernon CAPEL, b. 1841, d. 1901: m. 1875, Marion, who d. 1937, da. of John Struthers, of Madras:—
Caroline, b. 1880: m. 1899, Thomas Alexander Clapperton, of Tarong Station, Nanango, N. Qld., and has issue living, Thomas Capel, b. 1907,—Roderick Capel, b. 1909,—William Alexander Capel, b. 1915,—Marion Evelyn, b. 1900,—Annie Blanche, b. 1901: m. 1926, William Atkinson, of Brookfield Rd., Brookfield, Brisbane, Qld., and has issue living, Thomas b. 1927, John b. 1930, Jane b. 1937,—Mary Gwendolyn, b. 1902: m. 1925, Stanley Lord, of Illeura, Biggenden, Qld., and has issue living, William b. 1931, Anne b. 1928, Sallie (twin) b. 1931.——Millicent Florence, b. 1892: m. 1913, Henry Knox Paul, of 77 Ray Rd., Epping, Sydney 2121, NSW, and has issue living, Reginald Henry Capel (c/o Burns Philip Ltd., Popondetta, New Guinea), b. 1914: m. 1941, Alison Margaret Barrie, and has issue living, David Barrie Capel b. 1946, Ian Christopher b. 1949, Graham Kenneth b. 1954,—Marion Capel, b. 1917: m. 1942, John William Douglas, of 77, Ray Rd., Epping, Sydney, NSW, and has issue living, Janette Capel b. 1943: m. 1963, John Charles Trinder, of 37 Magnolia Av., Epping, NSW (and has issue living, Philip John b. 1965, Ashley Blair Capel b. 1972), Carolyn Marion b. 1944: m. 1968, Bruce Bryden Smith, of 21, Cocos Av., Eastwood, NSW (and has issue living, Kylie Samone b. 1971, Sancha Natalie b. 1972).

Grandchildren of the late Charles Horatio Algernon Capell, yst. son of the late Capt. the Hon. Algernon Henry Champagne Capell, RN (ante):—
Issue of the late Arthur Algernon de Vere Capell, b. 1869, d. 1924: m. 1st, 1890, Alice Ann, who d. 1913, da. of William Yewett Pine; 2ndly, 1916, Alice Mabel, who d. 1951, da. of James Currie, of Wimbledon, SW:—
(By 1st m.) Alice Maud de Vere (Flat 6, 60, The Drive, Hove), b. 1896: m. 1920, Thomas James Garnham who d. 1963, and has issue living, John Arthur Thomas (205, Burnt Ash Lane, Bromley, Kent), b. 1921: m. 1956, Margaret Gehring, and has issue living, Thomas Hans b. 1957, Michael John b. 1962, Ingrid b. 1959,—Bryan Langton de Vere, b. 1927,—Rosalind Angela, b. 1923: m. 1st, 1944 (m. diss. 1947), Denys Gino Angelo Rogora; 2ndly, 1948, (m. diss. 1953), Francis Harold Newman; 3rdly, 1955 (m. diss. 1960), Roy Joseph Iles; 4thly, 1960, Peter David Stanley Miles Carter, of

Flat 4, 45, Selbourne Rd., Hove 3, and has issue living, (by 2nd m.), Nigel Roger Francis b. 1951. ——Elfreda Beatrice de Vere b. 1892: m. 1915, Rudolph Henry Weston, of Cliff View, Pargolla Rd., Newquay, Cornwall, and has issue living, Marjorie Beatrice b. 1916.——(By 2nd m.) ROBERT EDWARD DE VERE (2, Novak Place, Torrisholme, Morecambe, Lancs.), b. Jan. 13th, 1920; 1939-45 War as Fl. Sgt. RAF: m. 1942, Doris Margaret, da. of George Frederick Tomlinson, of Morecambe Lancs., and has issue living, Frederick Paul de Vere, b. 1944, LLCM; FRSA.——Elsie Elfrida (49, Northmere Drive, Dorset, Parkstone), b. 1921: m. 1943, Ernest Walls, who d. 1968, and has issue living, Derek Arthur, b. 1950,—Jennifer Dawn, b. 1948.

Grandchildren of the late Horace Charles George Arthur Capell (infra) :—
Issue of the late Bladen Ozro Capell, b. 1897, d. 1959 : m. 1st, 1920, Marjora Crawford, of Utah, U.S.A., who d. 1956, having obtained a divorce 1929 ; 2ndly, 19—, Hazel Kruse, of Route 1, Blackfoot, Idaho, U.S.A. :—
(By 1st marriage) Bladen Horace, b. 1922 : m. 1945, Mae Elizabeth, dau. of the late William J. Walley, and has issue living, William Jennings, b. 1952,—Dorita Mae, b. 1948. Residence,—722, Walnut Street, Yuba City, California, U.S.A.——Ada, b. 1924 : m. 1941, Kay Boren, and has issue living, Dennis Kay, b. 1941,—Larry Dean, b. 1943,—Jeffrey Lee, b. 1956,—Toni Carol, b. 1946. Residence, —North 4904, Elm Street, Spokane, Washington, U.S.A.——Helen Lucille, b. 1926 : m. 1945, Leonard A. Simpson, and has issue living, David Andrew, b. 1947.

Grandchildren of the late Lieut.-Col. Algernon Essex Capell, C.B.E., D.S.O. (infra) :—
Issue of the late Algernon Arthur Capell, b. 1903, d. 1950: m. 1933, Violet Mary (Mount Royal, 310, Rhodes Av., Salisbury, Rhodesia), da. of the late Andrew Boyd, of Dumfries:—
Colin Algernon Andrew Essex (Kileture Estate, Shamva, Rhodesia), b. 1935: m. 1957, Cecily Ann, da. of Arend Smith, of Marlborough, Rhodesia, and has issue living, Clint Andrew Devereux, b. 1960,— Craig Robert Lawrence, b. 1962.——Robert Devereux Boyd (1097, Maranzi Rd., PO Chisipite, Salisbury, Rhodesia), b. 1942: m. 1967, Elin Rosemary, da. of the late Alan L. Earle, of Bulawayo, Rhodesia.——Rosemary Susan Lois, b. 1934: m. 1958, Cyril Bryan Hughes, and has issue living, Barry William Vaughan, b. 1961,—Kevin Bryan Vaughan, b. 1962,—Ross Anthony Vaughan, b. 1967,—Susan Anne Vaughan, b. 1969. Address,—PO Box 2, Plumtree, Rhodesia.

Grandchildren of the late Rev. Horatio Bladen Capell (infra) :—
Issue of the late Horace Charles George Arthur Capell, b. 1868, d. 1953 : m. 1896, Clara Isabel, dau. of Ozro Jackson, of Dakin, Nebraska, U.S.A.:—
Ada Lorena b. 1901: m. 1923, Arthur Foster Dagnall, of 1254, E. 23rd Av., Vancouver, 10, BC, Canada
Issue of the late Lieut.-Col. Algernon Essex Capell, C.B.E., D.S.O., b. 1869, d. 1952 : m. 1903 Lois Ethel, who d. 1944, dau. of the late William Slatter, of Stratton, Cirencester :—
Joan Lois, b. 1905: m. 1930, Walter James Evans, and has issue living, Walter Robin (29, Circular Dr. Umtali, Rhodesia), b. 1931: m. 1957, Jennifer Huntly, da. of Huntly Shaw, of Marlborough, Salisbury, Rhodesia, and has issue living, David Huntly b. 1962, Susan Mary b. 1958, Bronwen Gay b. 1959,—David Anthony (P.O. Box 758, Blantyre, Malawi), b. 1932: m. 1st, 1957 (m. diss. 1966), Phyllis Ann, da. of Dr. Desmond Drew, of Mbabane, Swaziland; 2ndly, 1967, Mrs. Monica Frances Burne, da. of the late R. F. Winson, of Bulawayo, and has issue living (by 2nd m.), Richard Warwick, b. 1968, Ashleigh b. 1971, Anthony Capell b. 1972,—Carol Ann, b. 1938: m. 1959, Millar Rankin, of 21, Eileen Rd., Blairgowrie, Randburg, S. Africa, and has issue living, Bruce Ian b. 1961, Lynette Gayle b. 1966. Residence,—66, West Rd., Strathaven, Salisbury, Rhodesia.

Issue of the late Henry Addison Devereux Capell, b. 1873, d. 1925 : m. 1901, Olive Mary, who d. 1937, dau. of the late William Richardson-Bunbury [Richardson-Bunbury Bt., colls.] :—
Robert, b. 1903. Residence,—

Granddaughter of the late Hon. Adolphus Frederick Charles Molyneux Capell, brother of 6th Earl :—
Issue of the late Rev. Horatio Bladen Capell, b. 1839, d. 1933 : m. 1st, 1866, Ada Augusta, who d. 1916, dau. of Theophilus Hawkins, formerly of Newton Abbot ; 2ndly, 1916, Violet Annie, who d. 1960, dau. of Robert Frost, formerly of Snape, Suffolk :—
By 2nd marriage) Beatrix Violet De Vere. b. 1919: m. 1st, 1939, Raymond Smith, from whom she obtained a divorce 1950: 2ndly, 1950, Edward Reginald Tranter, and has issue living, (by 1st marriage) Anthony Capell, b. 1940. Residence,—

Grandson of the late Col. Arthur William Capell, Bengal Cav., el. son of Lt.-Col. Edward Samuel Capell, Bengal Army, yst. son of Rev. the Hon. William Robert Capell, yst. son of 4th Earl:—
Issue of the late Capt. Terence Capell, RFC, b. 1891, d. 1962: m. 1919, Florence Penelope, who d. 1963, da. of William Whitham:—
William Terence (3, Hillgate Place, W8; Cavalry Club), b. 1921; late Capt. 11th Hussars: m. 1963, Petronella, da. of the late Maj. Peter Beale Lewis, MC, late R. Ulster Rifles, and has issue living, Georgina Penelope, b. 1964,—Rosalind Elizabeth Maud, b. 1968.

PREDECESSORS.—[1] ARTHUR Capell ; M.P. for co. Hertford in the Long Parliament; cr. Baron Capell, of Hadham 1641; for his loyalty to the King he was beheaded 1649; s. by his son [2] ARTHUR, 2nd Baron, cr. Viscount Malden and Earl of the co. of Essex (peerage of England, 1661; Viceroy of Ireland 1672-7, and sometime First Commr. of the Treasury; being accused with Lord Russell of connection with "The Fanatic Plot" was committed to the Tower, where he was found with his throat cut 1683; s. by his son [3] ALGERNON, 2nd Earl; a Lt.-Gen. in the Army and Constable of the Tower of London; d. 1709; s. by his son [4] WILLIAM, 3rd Earl; d. 1743; s. by his son [5] WILLIAM ANNE, 4th Earl; d. 1799; s. by his son [6] GEORGE, D.C.L., 5th Earl; assumed the surname of Coningsby; d. 1839; s. by his nephew [7] ARTHUR ALGERNON (son of the Hon. John Thomas, 2nd son of 4th Earl), 6th Earl, b. 1803; assumed in 1880, by Roy. licence, for himself and issue the surname of Capell in lieu of Capel; d. 1892: m. 1st, 1825, Lady Caroline Jeannetta Beauclerk, who d. 1862, dau. of 8th Duke of St. Albans; 2ndly, 1863, Lady Louisa Caroline Elizabeth Boyle, who d. 1876, sister of 9th Earl of Cork. 3rdly, 1881, Louisa, who d. 1914, dau. of the late Charles Fieschi Heneage, and widow of Lord George Augustus Frederick Paget, K.C.B. ; s. by his grandson [8] GEORGE DEVEREUX DE VERE (el. son of Viscount Malden, el. son of 6th Earl), 7th Earl. b. 1857: m. 1st, 1882, Ellenor Harriet Maria, who d. 1885, dau. of the late William Henry Harford, J.P., of Oldown House, Almondsbury, Gloucestershire ; 2ndly, 1893, Adele, who d. 1922, el. dau. of the late Beach Grant, of New York ; d. 1916; s. by his son, [9] ALGERNON GEORGE DE VERE, 8th Earl, b. 1884: m. 1st, 1905 (m. diss. 1926) (Mary) Eveline Stewart, who d. 1955, el. da. of the late William Russell Stewart Freeman, JP, DL, of The Old Manor House, Wingrave, Bucks.; 2ndly, 1926 (m. diss. 1950) Alys Montgomery, da. of Robert Hayes Falkiner, and formerly wife of Ernest Scott Brown; 3rdly, 1950 (m. diss. 1956), Zara Mildred Carson, of Los Angeles, Cal., USA; 4thly, 1957, Christine Mary Davis; d. 1966; s. by his son [10] Reginald George de Vere, TD, 9th Earl and present peer; also Viscount Malden, and Baron Capell.

Ettrick, Baron,   see Lord Napier and Ettrick.

Euston, Earl of, son of Duke of Grafton.

EVANS, BARONY OF, (Evans.). [Extinct 1963.]

DAUGHTER LIVING OF FIRST BARON.

Hon. Jean Rosemary, *b.* 1934: *m.* (Jan.) 1966, Eric Anthony Hathorn, of 51, Netherhall Gdns., NW3, and has issue living, James Horace Vans, *b.* (Dec.) 1966,—Charles Thomas Vans, *b.* 1972,—Helen Angela, *b.* 1970.

EVANS OF HUNGERSHALL, BARON. (Evans.) [Life Baron 1967.]

(BENJAMIN) IFOR EVANS, son of Benjamin Evans, of London; *b.* Aug. 19th, 1899; ed. at Stationers' Co. Sch., and Univ. Coll., London (MA, DLitt); Hon. Dr. Paris; Hon. LLD Manchester; an Author; a Fellow of Univ. Coll., and of Queen Mary Coll., London; Provost of Univ. Coll., London 1951-66; Officer of Legion of Honour, a Chevalier of Order of Crown of Belgium; Cdr. of Order of Orange Nassau of the Netherlands, and a Cdr. of Order of Dannebrog of Denmark; *cr.* Knt. 1955 and *Baron Evans of Hungershall,* of Borough of Royal Tunbridge Wells (Life Baron) 1967: *m.* 1923, Marjorie Ruth, da. of John Measures, of Ifield, Sussex, and has issue.

Residences,—1317, Minister House, St, James Court, Buckingham Gate, SW1; Hungershall Lodge, Tunbridge Wells. *Club,*—Athenaeum.

DAUGHTER LIVING.

Hon. Hilary Ann (Silver Lane End, Stone cum Ebony, Tenterden, Kent), *b.* 1931: *m.* 1954 (m. diss. 1963), William John Barrow, and has issue.

EVERSHED, BARONY OF. (Evershed.) [Extinct 1966.]

WIDOW LIVING OF FIRST BARON.

CICELY ELIZABETH (JOAN) (*Baroness Evershed*) (Tudor House, Castle Acre, King's Lynn); FSA; da. of the late Hon. Sir Charles Alan Bennett; a JP for Norfolk: *m.* 1928, the 1st Baron, who *d.* 1966, when the title became ext.

Orr-Ewing, Baron, see Orr.

EXETER, LORD BISHOP OF.

Right Rev. ERIC ARTHUR JOHN MERCER, son of Ambrose John Mercer, of Walmer, Kent; *b.* Dec. 6th, 1917; ed. at Dover Gram. Sch., and Kelham Theo. Coll.; 1939-45 War as Capt. Sherwood Foresters, in Western Desert, Italy and Palestine and GSO 2 (SD) MEF (despatches); R. St. Thomas, Stockport 1953-59, and St. Bridget with St. Martin, Chester 1959-65; Chester Diocesan Missioner 1959-65, and Hon. Canon Chester Cathedral 1964; consecrated Bishop of Birkenhead (Suffragan for Diocese of Chester) 1965, and translated 68th Bishop of Exeter 1973: *m.* 1951, Rosemary Wilma, da. of John William Denby, of Barrow on Humber.

Patron of one hundred and twenty-one livings and of two alternately with the crown, the Precentorship, Chancellorship, Treasurership, Subdeanery, four Canonries, and twenty-nine Prebends in his Cathedral, and the Archdeaconries of Exeter, Totnes, Barnstaple, and Plymouth.

This See consists of Devon (except seven parishes) and one parish in Somerset.

𝕰piscopal 𝕾ignature—Eric Exon.

ARMS OF THE SEE,—Gules, a sword erect in pale argent, hilted or surmounted by two keys addorsed in saltire of the last.

Residence,—The Palace, Exeter, EX1 1HY.

EXETER, MARQUESS OF. (Cecil.) [Marquess U.K. 1801.]

[Name pronounced "Cissel."]

One heart, one way.

DAVID GEORGE BROWNLOW CECIL,
K.C.M.G., 6th Marquess ; b. Feb. 9th,
1905 ; s. 1956 ; ed. at Eton, and at
Magdalene Coll., Camb. (M.A. 1952),
L.L.D. St. Andrews 1950, Hon.
F.R.C.S. 1964; Lt.-Col. late Grenadier
Guards; is patron of seventeen
livings, Hereditary Grand Almoner,
Lord Paramount of the Soke of
Peterborough, Member of King
George VI Nat. Memorial Fund; Pres.
and Chm. of Internat. Amateur
Athletic Fedn. since 1946, of Amateur
Athletic Asso., and of British Olympic
Assocn., and Doyen Internat. Olym-
pic Cttee. (elected 1933), Chm. of
Birmid-Qualcast, and a Dir. of
National Westminster Bank, of Fire-
stone Tyre and Rubber Co., Ltd., of
Lands Improvement, and of Jun.
Carlton Club, and a KStJ; Master of
Burghley Hunt 1935-39 and 1957-69,
of East Sussex Hunt 1939-53, and
of Old Berkshire Hunt 1953-57; Chm. of Organizing and Exec. Cttees.
Olympic Games in London 1948; Chm. of Jun. Imperial League 1933-37
(Pres. 1939); Pres. British Empire Chambers of Commerce, and of Radio
Industry Council 1952-54, and Vice-Pres. of Internat. Olympic Cttee. 1954-
66; Pres. British Travel Assocn. 1966-69; Assist. Dir. of Tank Supply 1941-42,
Controller of Repair and Overseas Supplies of Aircraft 1942-43, and Gov. and
C-in-C of Bermuda 1943-45; R. of St. Andrews Univ. 1949-52; Leader of UK
Industrial Mission to Pakistan 1950 and to Burma 1954; Mayor of Stamford
1961-62; MP for Peterborough Div. of Northants (C) 1931-43; KCMG 1943:
m. 1929, Lady Mary Theresa Montagu-Douglas-Scott (who obtained a
divorce 1946), da. of 7th Duke of Buccleuch; 2ndly, 1946, Diana Mary, da. of
the late Hon. Arnold Henderson, OBE [see B. Faringdon, colls.], and widow
of Lt.-Col. David Walter Arthur William Forbes, MC, Coldstream Guards
[B. Hotham, colls.], and has issue by 1st and 2nd m.

Arms,—Barry of ten argent and azure, six escutcheons, three, two, and one, sable each
charged with a lion rampant argent. Crest,—On a chapeau gules, turned up with ermine, a
garb or, supported by two lions rampant, the dexter argent, the sinister azure. Supporters,—
Two lions ermine.

Seat,—Burghley House, Stamford, Lincolnshire. Clubs,—Junior Carlton, Pratt's.

DAUGHTERS LIVING. (By 1st marriage.)

Lady Davina Mary (Baroness Barnard), b. 1931; an O.St.J.: m. 1952, the 11th Baron Barnard. Resi-
dence,—Selaby, Gainford, Darlington, co. Durham, DL2 3HF.
Lady Gillian Moyra Katherine, b. 1935: m. 1954, Sir Giles Henry Charles Floyd, 7th Bt. Residence,—
Tinwell Manor, Stamford, Lincolnshire.

Lady Angela Mary Rose, b. 1938: m. 1958, William Richard Michael Oswald, MA, and has issue
living, William Alexander Michael, b. 1962,—Katharine Davina Mary, b. 1959. Residences,—
Flitcham Hall, King's Lynn, Norfolk; Hampton Court Palace, E. Molesey, Surrey.

(By 2nd marriage.)
Lady Victoria Diana, b. 1947: m. 1967, Simon Patrick Leatham, of Hayes House, Corbridge, Northumberland [see By. Buckland].

BROTHER LIVING.

Lord (WILLIAM) MARTIN ALLEYNE, b. April 27th, 1909: m. 1st, 1934, Edith Lilian de Csánady,
who d. 1954, only da. of the late Aurel Csanády de Telegd, of Budapest, Hungary; 2ndly, 1954,
Lillian Jane, da. of R. P. K. Johnson, of Wisconsin, USA, and has issue living, (by 1st m.) William
Michael Anthony, b. 1935; ed. at Eton: m. 1967, Nancy Rose, da. of Lloyd Arthur Meeker, of Box 8
100, Mile House, BC, Canada, and has issue living, Anthony John b. 1970, Angela Kathleen b. 1975,—
(by 2nd m.) Marina June, b. 1956. Residence,—100, Mile House, PO Box 8, British Colombia.

SISTERS LIVING.

Lady Letitia Sibell Winifred (Dowager Baroness Hotham), b. 1903; was a Lady-in-Waiting to HRH
the Duchess of Gloucester 1935-7: m. 1937, the 7th Baron Hotham, who d. 1967. Residences,—
Dalton Hall, Dalton Holme, Beverley, Yorks; Scorborough Hall, Lockington, Driffield, Yorks.
Lady Romayne Elizabeth Algitha, A.R.R.C., b. 1915; late V.A.D. (attached R.N.); European
War 1939-44 (A.R.R.C.): m. 1944, Lieut.-Col. the Hon. Peter Esmé Brassey, Northants Yeo. [see
B. Brassey of Apethorpe]. Residence,—Close House, Barnack, Stamford.

COLLATERAL BRANCHES LIVING.

Granddaughter of the late Lieut. Lord Francis Horace Pierrepoint Cecil, RN, 2nd
son of 3rd Marquess:—

Issue of the late Violet Dorothea Cecil, b. 1878, d. 1953: m. 1st, 1901, Lieut.-Col. Oswald
Henry Ames, who d. 1927, formerly 2nd Life Guards; 2ndly, 1942, as his second wife,
Sir Maurice Bromley-Wilson, 7th Bt. :—

(By 1st m.) Aubretia Phyllis (White House, Cedar Heights, Petersham, Surrey), b. 1909: m. 1928
Count Igor Ouvaroff, who d. 1939, el. son of Count Igor Ouvaroff, of Holm Smolensk, Russia, and
has issue living, Count Stephen (White House, Cedar Heights, Petersham, Surrey. Club,—British
Racing Drivers'), b. 1935; late RAAF: m. 1961, Aprille, el. da. of W. G. Brighton, of Felpham,
Sussex, and has issue living, Count Jason Stephen b. 1965, Count Dominic William b. 1966, Count
Alexander Giles b. 1969, Count Luke Gerard b. 1971, Count Casper Serge b. 1974, Countess Marina
Violet Elizabeth, b. 1931.

Granddaughter of the late Richard William Francis Cecil, son of the late Lieut. Lord Francis Horace Pierrepont Cecil, R.N. (ante) :—
Issue of the late Lieut. Richard Francis Bain Cecil, R.N., *b.* 1902, *d.* 1929 : *m.* 1926, Marjorie Joan (who *m.* 2ndly, 1939, B. Grosvenor Harris, of Monxton Manor, Andover. Hants.), dau. of the late William Lloyd Evans, of Postlip Hall, Gloucestershire :—
Jean Frances, *b.* (*posthumous*) 1929 : *m.* 1952, Com. Henry Walton Jennings, R.N., and has issue living, Dirmuid Brian, *b.* 1957,—Stephen Francis, *b.* 1959. *Address,*—c/o Monxton Manor, Andover, Hants.

Descendants of the late Col. Lord William Cecil, CVO, 3rd son of 3rd Marquess, *b.* 1854, *d.* 1943, who *m.* 1st, 1885, Mary Rothes Margaret, who *d.* 1919 (*Baronesss Amherst of Hackney* in her own right), [see B. Amherst of Hackney].

Issue of the late Col. Lord John Pakenham JOICEY-CECIL, 4th son of 3rd Marquess, *b.* 1867, *d.* 1942, having assumed by Roy. licence 1898 the additional surname of Joicey : *m.* 1896, Isabella Maud, who *d.* 1949, el. dau. of the late Col. John Joicey, M.P., of Newton Hall, Stocksfield-on Tyne :—
Edward Wilfrid George, *b.* 1912 : ed. at Eton : *m.* 1945, Rosemary Lusia, only dau. of the late Capt. the Hon. Fergus Bowes-Lyon, Black Watch [see E. Strathmore, colls.], and has issue living, James David Edward, *b.* 1946,—(Elizabeth) Anne, *b.* 1950: *m.* 1971, Alastair Richard Malcolm, of Hart Hill Farm, Woodfalls, Salisbury, Wilts., and has issue living, Colin Andrew Fergus *b.* 1973. *Residence,* —Braddocks, Solefields, Sevenoaks, Kent.——Maud Lettice Mary, *b.* 1906: *m.* 1930, Maj-Gen. Robert Hallam Studdert, CB, DSO, MC, late RA, who *d.* 1968, and has issue living, Hallam John Cecil (16, Steele's Rd., NW3), *b.* 1931: BA 1953, LLB 1954: *m.* 1961, Lilian Joan Brown,—Moira Winifred, *b.* 1933; BA 1954, LLB 1955, MA 1958: *m.* 1957, Peter Hope, MusB, of 82, Etheldene Av., N10, and has issue living, Roderick Jonathan *b.* 1966, Louisa Dionysia *b.* 1961. *Residence,*—Clonderlaw, Enniskerry, co. Wicklow.

(*In remainder to Barony of Burghley only.*)
Descendants of the late Rt. Hon. Sir Robert Cecil, K.G., (younger son of 1st Baron Burghley), who was cr. *Earl of Salisbury* 1605 [see M. Salisbury].

PREDECESSORS.—[1] *Sir* WILLIAM Cecil, *K.G.*, *K.B.*,*P.C.*, a lawyer and eminent statesman was Sec. of State 1549, 1551, and 1558, Chancellor of Camb. Univ. 1558-98, Master of the Ward, 1561, and Lord High Treasurer 1572-98 ; cr. *Baron of Burghley* (peerage of England) 1571 ; *d.* 1598 ; *s.* by his son [2] THOMAS, *K.G.*, *K.B.* ; M.P. in five Parliaments ; distinguished himself in the wars in the Low Countries; cr. *Earl of Exeter* (peerage of England) 1605 ; *d.* 1622 ; *s.* by his son [3] WILLIAM, *K.G.*, 2nd Earl ; *d.* 1640 ; *s.* by his nephew [4] DAVID, 3rd Earl, son of Sir Richard, M.P., 2nd son of 1st Earl; *d.* 1643 ; *s.* by his son [5] JOHN, 4th Earl; *d.* 1678 ; *s.* by his son [6] JOHN, 5th Earl; *d.* 1700 ; *s.* by his son [7] JOHN, 6th Earl: *d.* 1721, *s.* by his el. son [8] JOHN, 7th Earl; *d.* 1722 ; *s.* by his brother [9] BROWNLOW, 8th Earl; *d.* 1754 ; *s.* by his son [10] BROWNLOW, 9th Earl ; *d.s.p.* 1793; *s.* by his nephew [11] HENRY, 10th Earl, son of the Hon. Thomas Chambers, 2nd son of 8th Earl; cr. *Marquess of Exeter* (peerage of United Kingdom) 1801 ; *d.* 1804 ; *s.* by his son [12] BROWNLOW, *K.G.*, 2nd Marquess ; *b.* 1795; Lord Lieut. of cos. Northampton and Rutland, Groom of the Stole to Prince Albert 1841-6, Lord Chamberlain 1852, and Lord Steward of the Household 1858-9 : *m.* 1824, Isabella, dau. of William Stephen Poyntz, of Cowdray House, Sussex ; *d.* 1867; *s.* by his son [13] WILLIAM ALLEYNE, *P.C.*, 3rd Marquess, *b.* 1825 ; M.P. for S. Lincolnshire (*C*) 1847-57, and for N. Northampton-shire 1857-67; was Treasurer of H.M. Queen Victoria's Household 1866-7, and Capt. of Hon. Corps of Gentlemen-at-Arms 1867-8 and 1874-5 : *m.* 1848, Lady Georgiana Sophia Pakenham, who *d.* 1909, dau. of 2nd Earl of Longford ; *d.* 1895 ; *s.* by his el. son [14] BROWNLOW HENRY GEORGE, *P.C.*, 4th Marquess, *b.* 1849 ; M.P. for Northamptonshire N. (*C*) 1877-85 and for Northamptonshire, N. Div. 1885-95 ; Vice-Chamberlain of H.M. Queen Victoria's Household 1891-2: *m.* 1875, Isabella, who *d.* 1917, dau. of Sir Thomas Whichcote, 7th Bt. ; *d.* 1898; *s.* by his son [15] WILLIAM THOMAS BROWNLOW, *K.G.*, *C.M.G.*, *T.D.*, 5th Marquess ; *b.* 1876 ; Col. R.F.A. (T.A.); Chm. of Govs. of Stamford Endowed Schs. 1899-1955, Mayor of Stamford 1909-10, Chm. of Soke of Peterborough County Council 1910-49, Lord Lieut. of Northants 1922-52, an Additional A.D.C. to H.M. 1922-32, and Pres. of County Councils Asso. 1943 and 1945 : *m.* 1901, the Hon. Myra Rowena Sibell Orde-Powlett, who *d.* 1973, only da. of 4th Baron Bolton, *d.* 1956, *s.* by his el. son [16] DAVID GEORGE BROWNLOW, 6th Marquess and present peer: also Earl of Exeter, and Baron of Burghley.

EXMOUTH, VISCOUNT. (Pellew.)   [Viscount U.K. 1816, Bt. G.B. 1796.]
God being my helper.

PAUL EDWARD PELLEW, 10th Viscount, and 10th Baronet; *b.* Oct. 8th, 1940; *s.* 1970; ed. at Downside; patron of one living: *m.* 1964, Maria Krystina de Garay, da. of the late D. Recaredo de Garay y Garay, of Madrid, and has issue.

Arms,—Gules, a lion passant guardant, in chief two civic wreaths or, on a chief of augmentation wavy argent, a representation of Algiers, and on the dexter side a man-of-war bearing the flag of an admiral of the blue, all proper. **Crest.**—Upon waves of the sea the stern of a wrecked ship, inscribed "Dutton" (East Indiaman), upon a rocky shore off Plymouth garrison (*i.e.* in the background a hill, upon the top of which a tower with a flag hoisted), all proper. **Supporters,**—*Dexter,* a lion guardant or, navally crowned azure, his sinister hind paw resting on an increscent argent ; *sinister,* a human figure intended to represent a Christian slave, naked from the waist upwards, a cloth round the loins, and thighs and legs habited in blue and white striped trousers, holding in the right hand a cross or, and in his left fetters broken proper.

Residence,—Canonteign, near Exeter, Devon.

DAUGHTER LIVING.
Hon. Patricia Sofia, *b.* 1966.

BROTHER LIVING.
Hon. PETER IRVING, b. Oct. 20th, 1942; ed. at Downside.

SISTERS LIVING.
Hon. Mary Rose, b. 1938: m. 1974, D. Roman Llanso, of Madrid.
Hon. Mary Elizabeth Josephine, b. 1947: m. 1969, Robin Gerard d'Erlanger, ACA, of Craddock House, Craddock, Cullompton, Devon, son of the late Sir Gerard John Regis Leo d'Erlanger, CBE, and has issue living, Gerard Pownoll, b. 1970,—Josephine Louise, b. 1972,—Marietta Elizabeth, b. 1974.

AUNT LIVING. (Daughter of 8th Viscount.)
Hon. Rose Mary PELLEW, b. 1903; resumed the surname of Pellew in lieu of Van de Goor 1949 : m. 1942 (marriage dissolved 1949), Maurice Van de Goor, and has issue living, Elizabeth, b. 1943,—Fleur (twin), 1943. Residence,—Le Boué, Jurançon, Pau, Basses Pyrénées, France.

WIDOW LIVING OF NINTH VISCOUNT.
MARIA LUISA (Maria Luisa, Viscountess Exmouth), (Marquesa de Olias in Spain cr. 1652; s. 1940), da. of the late Luis de Urquijo, Marques de Amurrio, of Madrid, and widow of Gonzalo Alvarez-Builla: m. 1938, the 9th Viscount, who d. 1970. Residence,—Canonteigh Manor, Lower Ashton, Exeter.

COLLATERAL BRANCHES LIVING.
Grandchildren of the late Fleetwood Hugo Pellew (infra):—
Issue of the late Major Fleetwood Hugo Pellew, b. 1871, d. 1961: m. 1909, Violet, who d. 1964, dau. of the late James Du Pre, of Wilton Parks, Bucks.:—
Fleetwood Hugo, b. 1910 ; Lieut.-Col. (retired) Roy. Signals : m. 1939, Geraldine Mildred, dau. of Major William Gerald Hole, of Parke, Bovey Tracey, S. Devon, and has issue living, Pamela Geraldine, b. 1946. Residence,—Waye Farm, Lustleigh, Devon.——Anthony Pownoll, b. 1911; Cdr. (ret.) RN: m. 1st, 1941, Margaret Julia (from whom he obtained a divorce 1953), da. of Clive Cookson, of Nether Warden, Hexham; 2ndly, 1957, Hilary Frances, da. of Capt. Alfred Garbett Pape, of 20, Northumberland St., Edinburgh, and has issue living, (by 1st m.) Mark Edward (27, Alderney St., SW1), b. 1942: m. 1965, Jill Hosford, da. of Frank Thistlethwaite, of Wood Hall, Hethersett, Norfolk, and has issue living, Adam Lee b. 1966,—Dominic Stephen, b. 1968, —Robert Anthony, b. 1945,—Phoebe Sarah, b. 1947.—(by 2nd m.) Nicholas Charles, b. 1959,—Philip Esmond, b. 1962. Residence,—Woodlands, Woldingham, Surrey.——Myles Addington, b. 1919: m. 1957, Jill Primrose Twentyman, yst. da. of the late Capt. Alfred Maurice Davis, OBE, of 124, Walton St., SW3, and has issue living, Simon Du Pre, b. 1959,—Alexandra Twentyman, b. 1961,—Miranda Frances, b. 1964. Residence,—Pinfold, Walton Heath, Tadworth, Surrey. ——Timothy Winthrop, b. 1921; ed. at Camb. Univ. (MA): m. 1950, Margaret Richmond, da. of the late Edmund George Hamilton Mewburn, of 20, Norfolk House, Courtlands, Richmond, Surrey, and has issue living, Fleetwood Timothy, b. 1952,—Adrian Harold, b. 1954,—Owen Simon, b. 1958,—Colin David, b. 1961,—Mabel Audrey, b. 1955. Residence,—31, Churchill Av., Willowdale, Ontario, Canada.——Anne, b. 1915: m. 1st, 1941, Capt. John Pearce Gould, RASC; 2ndly, 1947, Denis Owen Burns, of Clumps End, Lower Bourne, Farnham, Surrey.

Granddaughter of the late Rev. the Hon. Edward Pellew, 4th son of 1st Viscount:—
Issue of the late Fleetwood Hugo Pellew, b. 1888, d. 1906: m. 1869, Dorothy Mary, who d. 1926, dau. of the Rev. Philip Anderson :—
Constance Langford Frances: m. 1914, H. Camville Layard, and has issue living, Camville Pellew, b. 1924. Residence,—Andmere Drive, RR2, Sidney, British Columbia.

PREDECESSORS.—[1] Sir EDWARD Pellew, G.C.B.: a celebrated Adm.; cr. a Baronet 1796, Baron Exmouth, of Canonteign, co. Devon (peerage of United Kingdom) 1814, and Viscount Exmouth (peerage of United Kingdom) 1816 ; d. 1833 : s. by his son [2] POWNOLL BASTARD, 2nd Viscount; d. 1833; s. by his son [3] EDWARD, 3rd Viscount; d. 1876; s. by his nephew [4] EDWARD FLEETWOOD JOHN, 4th Viscount (son of the Hon. Fleetwood John, 4th son of 2nd Viscount), b. 1861: m. 1884, Edith, who d. 1914, dau. of the late Thomas Hargreaves, of Arborfield Hall, Reading; d. 1899; s. by his son [5] EDWARD ADDINGTON HARGREAVES, 5th Viscount, b. 1890; d. 1922; s. by his cousin [6] HENRY EDWARD (only son of the late Very Rev. the Hon George Pellew, D.D., Dean of Norwich, 3rd son of 1st Viscount, by the Hon. Frances Addington, dau. of 1st Viscount Sidmouth), 6th Viscount : b. 1828 ; a naturalized American: m. 1st, 1858, Eliza, who d. 1869, dau. of the late Hon. William Jay, of Bedford, New York, a Judge in New York; 2ndly, 1873, Augusta, who d. 1917, dau. of the late Hon. William Jay (ante); d. 1923: s. by his son [7] CHARLES ERNEST, 7th Viscount: b. 1863: m. 1st 1886, Margaret, who d. 1922, dau. of the late Professor C. F. Chandler, of New York; 2ndly 1923, Mabel, who d. 1940, dau. of the late Richard Gray, of San Francisco; d. 1945; s. by his kinsman [8] EDWARD IRVING POWNOLL, O.B.E., M.R.C.S., L.R.C.P. (son of the late Capt. Pownoll William Pellew, R.N., son of the Rev. the Hon. Edward Pellew, 4th son of 1st Viscount), 8th Viscount ; b. 1868: m. 1902, Frances, who d. 1963, dau. of Alfred Wells Edwards; d. 1951; s. by his son [9] POWNOLL IRVING EDWARD, 9th Viscount; b. 1908: m. 1938, Maria Luisa (Marquesa de Olias in Spain; cr. 1652; s. 1940), da. of the late Luis de Urquijo, Marques de Amurrio, of Madrid, and widow of Gonzalo Alvarez-Builla; d. 1970; s. by his son [10] PAUL EDWARD, 10th Viscount and present peer; also Baron Exmouth.

FAIRFAX OF CAMERON, LORD. (Fairfax.) [Baron S. 1627]

NICHOLAS JOHN ALBERT FAIRFAX, 14th Lord; b. Jan. 4th, 1956; s. 1964.

Arms,—Or, three bars gemelles gules, surmounted by a lion rampant sable. Crest.—A lion passant guardant sable. Supporters.—Dexter, a lion guardant sable; sinister, a bay horse proper.

Residence,—Gay's House, Holyport, Maidenhead Berks.

BROTHERS LIVING.
Hon. HUGH NIGEL THOMAS, b. March 29th, 1958.
Hon. Rupert Alexander James, b. 1961.

SISTER LIVING.
Hon. Serena Frances, b. 1952.

FARE FAC

Speak and act.

UNCLE LIVING. (Son of 12th Lord.)
Hon. Peregrine John Wishart, b. 1925; ed. at Eton, and at Trin. Coll., Camb.; late Lt. 12th R. Lancers; Northumberland Hussars 1955-61: m. 1965, Virginia Alexandra de L'Etang, da. of the Hon.

Philip Leyland Kindersley [see B. Kindersley], and has issue living, Thomas Philip, b. 1966,—
Doune Alexandra Wishart, b. 1968. *Residence,*—Mindrum, Northumberland. *Clubs,*—Cavalry,
Northern Counties (Newcastle).

WIDOW LIVING OF THIRTEENTH LORD.

SONIA HELEN (*Lady Fairfax of Cameron*) (of Gay's House, Holyport, Maidenhead, Berks.), da. of
the late Capt. Cecil Bernard Gunston, MC [see M. Dufferin and Ava]; a JP of Berks.; a Temporary
Lady of the Bedchamber to H.M. 1967-71: m. 1951, the 13th Lord, who d. 1964.

COLLATERAL BRANCHES LIVING.

Grandchildren of the late Raymond Fairfax, son of the late Hon. Henry Fairfax,
2nd son of 9th Lord :—

Issue of the late Henry Reginald Fairfax, M.D., b. 1875, d. 1955 : m. 1907, Nellie Virginia who
d. 1957, dau of M. O. Randolph, of Williamson, West Virginia, U.S.A. :—

Reginald Randolph, b. 1908 : m. 1934, Genevieve, dau. of J. W. McKee, of Brookhaven, Mississippi,
U.S.A.——Ronald Cary, b. 1915 : m. 1954, Judith Victoria, dau. of Jonathan Breckenridge Stovall,
of Amherst co. Virginia, U.S.A. *Residence,*—Elon Road, Madison Heights, Virginia, U.S.A.——
Marion Avery, b. 1918 : m. 1943, Collin Freeman Baker, M.D. (Junior), and has issue living, Collin
Freeman, b. 1947,—Carey Leigh, b. 1952,—Ann Fairfax, b. 1949. *Residence,*—

Grandchildren of the late William Henry Fairfax, M.D., son of the late Ferdinand
Fairfax, MD, 3rd son of the Hon. Ferdinando Fairfax, 2nd son of 8th Lord:—
Issue of the late Frederick Griffith Fairfax, b. 1867, d. 1948 : m. 1903, his cousin, Mary
Fernando, who d. 1961, dau. of Capt. Edmund Wharton :—

William Henry, b. 1904 : m. 1937, Grace Woodson, of Atlanta, Georgia, U.S.A., and has issue
living, Gloria, b. 1938. *Residence,*—2077, Cascade Road, S.W. Atlanta, Georgia, U.S.A.——
Edmund Wharton, b. 1914 : is in U.S.A. Army: m. 1943, Nancy, dau. of James L. King, of
Pittsburg, U.S.A., and has issue living, Edmund Wharton, b. 1944,—Bryan Griffith, b. 1959,—
Jean Ann, b. 1951,—Barbara Jane, b. 1953. *Residence,*—The Hague, Virginia, U.S.A.——
Frederick Griffith, b. 1916: m. 1st, 1946 (m. diss. 1956) Dorothy Brooke; 2ndly, 1957, Annette
Aiken, of Atlanta, Georgina, and has issue living (by 1st marriage), Frederick Griffith, b. 1947,—
William Henry, b. 1950,—Dorothy Eleanor, b. 1946,—Ada Carter, b. 1949,—Grace Kate, b. 1952,—
(by 2nd marriage) Mary Lynette, b. 1960. *Residence,*—The Hague, Virginia, USA.——Edith
Wharton, b. 1905: m. 1933, Harold Benjamin Lang, of 2805, Shoreview Drive, Naples, Florida
33 940, USA, and has issue living, Ann Fairfax, b. 1936: m. 1958, Virgil A. Ponzoli, MD, of 600,
Riviera Drive, Naples, Florida 33940, USA, and has issue living, Linda Marie b. 1960, Patricia
Ann b. 1961, Susanne Joan b. 1963, Amy Carolyn b. 1968.——Fernado (da.), b. 1908. *Residence,*—
The Hague, Virginia, USA.——Annie Staunton, b. 1911: m. 1933, Edward Greco, and has issue
living, Edward Fairfax (329, Jamestown Rd., Front Royal, Va. 22630, USA), b. 1935: m. 1966,
Barbara Ruth Gomez, of Rio Vista, Cal., USA, and has issue living, Michelle Anne b. 1968, William
Edward Fairfax b. 1972,—Frederick Dominic, (6618, Ivy Hill Drive, McLean, Va. 22101, USA)
b. 1937: m. 1962, Carole Ann Drake, of Falling Waters, W. Va., and has issue living, William Scott
b. 1969, Michael Drake b. 1972. *Residence,*—2314, Grove Av., Falls Church, Virginia, USA.——
Katherine Rambsey (The Hague, Va., USA) b. 1919.

Grandchildren of the late Archibald Carlyle Fairfax, son of the late Com. Archibald
Blair Fairfax, 4th son of the Hon. Ferdinando Fairfax (ante):—
Issue of the late Lieut.-Col. John Carlyle Fairfax, U.S. Army, b. 1874, d. 1944 : m. 1909,
Winifred Mar, who d. 1960, dau. of the late Lieut.-Col. Otis Wheeler Pollock, U.S. Army
(retired), of San Francisco, California :—

John Pollock (2645, Ptarmigan Drive, Walnut Creek, Calif. 94595, USA), b. 1911: m. 1935, Dorothy
Elsa da. of the late Reginald Charles Steeple, of San Mateo, California, USA, and has issue living,
Dorothy Anne, b. 1936: m. 1st, 1956 (m. diss. 1961), Frederick W. Timby; 2ndly, 1961 (m. diss.
1973), Henry Mohr Hermann; 3rdly, 1974, Jack Margolis, of 1520, Middlefield Rd., Palo Alto,
Calif. 94301, USA, and has issue living, (by 1st m.) Jeffrey William Fairfax b. 1957, Christopher
Corey b. 1959, (by 2nd m.) Susan Mohr b. 1963,—Jain Pollock, b. 1937: m. 1st, 1960 (m. diss. 1968),
John Phillip de Angeles; 2ndly, 1968, Terry Ernest Jamison, of 2790, South Reed St., Denver,
Colorado 80227, USA, and has issue living, (by 1st m.) Melissa Jain b. 1962, Jenna Lynne b. 1963.——
Sallie Virginia, b. 1912: m. 1934, Paul Nyeland, of 1509, Bernal Av., Burlingame, Cal., USA, and
has issue living, David Fairfax, b. 1936: m. 1962, Beverly Louise Bachich, and has issue living,
Kristin Louise b. 1968,—Nancy Hoff, b. 1938: m. 1957 (m. diss. 1968), Robert Harlow Leekley,
and has issue living, Robert Bruce Nyeland b. 1959, Philip Cameron Nourse b. 1962, Virginia Carlyle
b. 1957.

PREDECESSORS.

PREDECESSORS.—[1] *Sir* THOMAS Fairfax, Knt; *cr. Lord Fairfax of Cameron* (peerage of
Scotland) 1627 ; *s.* by his son [2] FERDINANDO, *K.B.,* 2nd Lord ; successively M.P. for Borough-
bridge and Yorkshire; as Parliamentary Gen. of the Northern Forces became eminently
distinguished, and had a chief command at the Battle of Marston Moor, where he defeated the
Royal Army ; was subsequently Gov. of York; d. 1647 ; *s.* by his son [3] THOMAS, *K.B.,* 3rd
Lord, a distinguished Republican military leader ; commanded a Cavalry wing at Marston
Moor; appointed Gen. in Ch. of the Parliaments' Army 1645, and in that year gained the
celebrated victory at Naseby ; he afterwards defeated the Royalists in a series of engagements, but did not participate in the execution of the king; in 1650 resigned the command of
the army to Cromwell, and in 1659 zealously assisted to restore the monarchy ; was Constable of
the Tower 1647, and Lord of the Isle of Man 1650, and sat as M.P. for Yorkshire 1660; d. 1671;
s. by his cousin [4] HENRY, 4th Lord, son of the Rev. the Hon. Henry, 2nd son of 1st Lord ;
d. 1685 ; *s.* by his son [5] THOMAS, 5th Lord, M.P. for co. York 1688-1707, when by the Act of
Union he became ineligible ; took an active part in promoting the revolution ; d. 1710; *s.* by
his el. son [6] THOMAS, 6th Lord ; inherited from his mother estates in England which he gave to
his brother, and also inherited about 5,700,000 acres of land in Virginia, upon which he erected two
mansions, where he resided in baronial splendour; d. 1781; *s.* by his brother [7] ROBERT, 7th
Lord ; d. 1793; *s.* by his kinsman [8] BRYAN, 8th Lord, grandson of the Rev. the Hon. Henry, 2nd
son of 4th Lord (title confirmed by House of Lords 1800) ; d. 1802; *s.* by his son [9] THOMAS,
9th Lord ; d. 1846; *s.* by his grandson [10] CHARLES SNOWDEN, 10th Lord, son of the Hon. Albert
el. son of 9th Lord, by Caroline, dau. of Richard Snowden, of Oakland, Maryland ; Speaker of House
of Delegates of State of California 1854-7, and Clerk of Supreme Court of California 1857-62 ; d.
1869 ; *s.* by his brother [11] JOHN CONTEE, *M.D.,* 11th Lord ; b. 1830 : m. 1857, Mary, who d.
1912, dau. of Col. Edmund Kirby, of U.S.A. : d. 1900 : *s.* by his el. son [12] ALBERT KIRBY, 12th
Lord (confirmed by Committee for Privileges of the House of Lords 1908); b. 1870; a Representative
Peer for Scotland: m. 1922, Maude Wishart (who d. 1973, having m. 2ndly, 1947, Maj. Cecil Rook-
herst Wigan, MC, who d. 1958; 3rdly, 1962, Brig. Felix Alexander Vincent Copland-Griffiths, DSO,
MC), da. of James McKelvie, of Ducklys Park, East Grinstead, d. 1939, *s.* by his el son [13] THOMAS
BRIAN MCKELVIE, 13th Lord; b. 1923; Lt. Grenadier Guards; a Representative Peer for
Scotland 1945-63; Assist. Conservative Whip, House of Lords 1947-48, P.P.S. to Lord Pres. of
the Council 1951-53, and to Min. of Materials 1953-54, and a Lord-in-Waiting to H.M. 1954-47: m. 1951,
Sonia Helen, da. of the late Capt. Cecil Bernard Gunston, M.C. [M. Dufferin and Ava]; d. 1964;
s. by his el. son [14], NICHOLAS JOHN ALBERT, 14th Lord and present peer.

FAIRHAVEN, BARON. (Broughton.) [Baron U.K. 1961.]

AILWYN HENRY GEORGE BROUGHTON, 3rd Baron; *b.* Nov. 165h, 1936; *s.* 1973; ed. at Eton, and RMA; Maj. Blues and Royals: *m.* 1960, Kathleen Patricia, el. da. of Col. James Henry Magill, OBE, of Byford House, Ousden, Suffolk, and has issue.

Arms.—Argent, two bars and in the dexter chief point a saltire gules. **Crest.**—In front of a bull's head erased sable, armed and collared and chained or, three fleur-de-lis gold. **Supporters.**—On either side a winged bull sable, each armed and gorged with a chain or, pendant therefrom an escutcheon charged with the Arms of Broughton.

If I can.

Residence,—Anglesey Abbey, Cambridge. *Club,*—Turf.

SONS LIVING.
Hon. JAMES HENRY AILWYN, *b.* May 25th, 1963.
Hon. Huttleston Rupert, *b.* 1970.
Hon. Charles Leander, *b.* 1973.

DAUGHTERS LIVING.
Hon. Diana Cara, *b.* 1961.
Hon. Melanie Frances, *b.* 1966.

WIDOW LIVING OF SECOND BARON.
JOYCE IRENE (*Joyce Baroness Fairhaven*), (South Walsham, nr. Norwich), da. of Edward Arthur Miller, and widow of Rt. Gerald Henry Charles Dickens, RN: *m.* 1952, as his 2nd wife, the 2nd Baron, who *d.* 1973.

PREDECESSORS:—[1] URBAN HUTTLESTON ROGERS Broughton, son of Urban Hanlon Broughton, of Park Close, Englefield Green, Surrey (*b.* 1857, *d.* 1929, before his intended elevation to the Peerage, and who gave Ashridge to Conservative Party), by Cara Leland (who, with her two sons presented Runnymede to the nation 1929, and who was granted by Roy. Warrant 1929 the style and title as if her husband had received the barony of Fairhaven), da. of Henry Huttleston Rogers, of New York; cr. *Baron Fairhaven,* of Lode, co. Camb. (Peerage of UK 1929) with remainder to, heirs male of the body, and *Baron Fairhaven,* of Anglesey Abbey, co. Camb. (Peerage of UK) 1961, with remainder to his yr. brother, and the heirs male of his body; *d.* 1966, when the Barony cr. 1929 became ext.; *s.* in the Barony cr. 1961, by his brother [2] HENRY ROGERS, 2nd Baron, *b.* 1900: *m* 1st, 1932, the Hon. Diana Rosamond, who *d.* 1937, da. of the late Capt. the Hon. Coulson Churchill Fellowes [B. de Ramsey]; 2ndly, 1953, Joyce Irene, da. of Edward Arthur Miller, and widow of Lt.-Gerald Henry Charles Dickens, RN; *d.* 1973; *s.* by his only son [3] AILWYN HENRY GEORGE, 3rd Baron, and present Peer.

FALCONER OF HALKERTON, LORDSHIP OF. (Falconer.) [Dormant 1966.]

The Lordship of Falconer of Halkerton became dormant on the death of the 10th Earl of Kintore and 12th Lord Falconer of Halkerton in 1966. Owing to the Earls of Kintore not having taken any steps to vote as Lords Falconer for over forty years the dignity was removed, by mistake, from the Union Roll after the death of the 7th Earl and 9th Lord in 1844. It will be necessary for the next male heir to the Lordship of Falconer of Halkerton to have this peerage restored to the Union Roll by resolution of the House of Lords.

COLLATERAL BRANCHES LIVING.
Descendant of the late George Falconer (who changed the spelling of his surname to Falconar), brother of 4th Lord:—
Granddaughter of the late George Mercer FALCONAR-STEWART (who assumed the additional surname of Stewart after his patronymic), son of the late George FALCONAR of Carlowrie, great-grandson of the late George Falconer (ante):—
Issue of the late Maj. Cyril Falconar-Stewart, MC, *b.* 1884, *d.* 1962: *m.* 1915, Nita, who *d.* 1968, da. of Bryce Allan, of Wemyss Bay, Renfrewshire:—
Grizel Anne, *b.* 1917: *m.* 1944, Wladyslaw Chlebowski, of 11, Merchiston Park, Edinburgh, EH10 4PW, and has issue living, Jan Ronald Stewart, *b.* 1945,—Victor Tadeusz Stewart, *b.* 1953,—Alexandra Ewa Stewart, *b.* 1948.

Grandchildren of the late John Egerton Falconer, son of Randle Wilbraham Falconer, MD, FRCP, DCL, 6th in descent from Patrick Falconer of Newton, uncle of 1st Lord:—
Issue of the late Thomas Falconer, FRIBA, *b.* 1879, *d.* 1934: *m.* 1912, Florence Edith, who *d.* 1944, da. of the late Henry Campbell Serrell, of Brooke House, Hants.:—
PETER SERRELL (*presumed heir to the Lordship of Falconer of Halkerton*), *b.* March 7th, 1916; ed at Bloxham; is a FRIBA: *m.* 1941, Mary, da. of the late Rev. C. B. Hodson, and has issue living, Thomas Serrell, *b.* 1916,—Richard Alaric, *b.* 1949,—William John, *b.* 1952,—Caroline Elisabeth, *b.* 1942: *m.* 1973, Maj. Paul B. Weller, late Som. Ll. *Residence,*—St. Francis, Minchinhampton, Gloucestershire.——Peggie Florentia, *b.* 1918: *m.* 1941, Douglas Guest, CVO, MA, MusB, Organist and Master of Choristers, Westminster Abbey, and has issue living, Susan Jennifer *b.* 1943: *m.* 1966, Martin Hayward Garrett-Cox, of Shrubbhill, By Dunblane, Perthire, and has issue living, Jeremy Hayward *b.* 1968, Robin Guy *b.* 1970, Sacha Clare *b.* 1973,—Penelope Anne, *b.* 1946: *m.* 1970, Simon de Lange, MB, BS, FFAROS (c/o Groote Schuur Hospital, Cape Town, S. Africa), and has issue living, Care Michelle *b.* 1974. *Residence,*—8, Little Cloister, Westminster Abbey, SW1.

Issue of the late William Wilbraham Phillips Falconer, *b.* 1883, *d.* 1952: *m.* 1912, Gladys, da. of the late David Howard Jones, of Carmarthen:—
John Dalmahoy, *b.* 1914: *m.* 1956, Edna Johanna, da. of Alfred Foulsham Brooks, of Cheam, Surrey. *Residence,*—7B, Russell Gdns., W14.——Elidure Wilbraham, *b.* 1920.——Joan Egerton (twin), *b.* 1920: *m.* 1st, 1940, Maj. Gerrit Geel, Netherlands Army, from whom she obtained a divorce 1944; 2ndly, 1945, Col. James Bouverie-Brine, and has issue living, (by 1st marriage), Marie Ann Falconer,

b. 1943: *m.* 1963, Edward Alexander Caudwell, and has issue living, Edward James *b.* 1966, Alexandra Jane Mare *b.* 1969,—(by 2nd marriage), Christopher James Falconer, *b.* 1946: *m.* 1968, Ellen Agnes Maria Verkroast,—Michael Pusey, *b.* 1959,—Kathleen Joan, *b.* 1948: *m.* 1968, Fl. Lt. Alexander Frederick Paul Rhodes, RAF, and has issue living, Paul William *b.* 1969, Helen Kathleen (twin) *b.* 1949,—Amelia Pusey, *b.* 1953,—Elizabeth, *b.* 1956. *Residence,*—64, Springfield Rd., Trench, Telford, Salop.

Issue of the late John Philip Egerton Falconer (twin), *b.* 1883, *d.* 1970: *m.* 1931, Florence Eleanor, who *d.* 1957, da. of the late Alfred Attwood, of Yeovil, Som.:—

David Dunbar *b.* 1934: *m.* 1959, Gillian Mary, only da. of Wing-Cdr. William Richard Owen, MBE, RAF (ret.), of 10, Sladebrook Rd., Southdown, Bath, and has issue living, Jonathan Randle, *b.* 1961, —Patrick Markham, *b.* 1964.

PREDECESSORS.—[1] *Sir* ALEXANDER Falconer of Halkerton, Kincardineshire, whose family descended from Ranulphus Falconer to William the Lion, from which office he assumed the surname of Falconer, was a Lord of Session 1639, MP for co. Kincardine 1643, and a Commr. of the Treasury 1645; cr. *Lord Falconer of Halkerton* (peerage of Scotland) 1646, with remainder to his heirs male whatsoever: *m.* 1619, Anne Lindsay, only da. and heiress of 8th Lord Lindsay of the Byres; *d.* 1671; *s.* by his son [2] ALEXANDER, 2nd Lord: *m.* 16—, Lady Margaret Ogilvy, da. of 2nd Earl of Airlie; *d.* 1684; *s.* by his son [3] DAVID, 3rd Lord; *d.* unmarried 1724; *s.* by his kinsman [4] DAVID [son of Sir David Falconer of Newton, Lord Newton, Lord Pres. of Court of Session (who *m.* 1678, Mary, da. of George Norvell of Boghall, co. Linlithgow), 2nd son of Sir David Falconer, brother of 1st Lord], 4th Lord: *m.* 1703, Lady Catherine Margaret Keith, el. da. of William, 2nd Earl of Kintore (ante), *d.* 1751; *s.* by his son [5] ALEXANDER, 5th Lord, *b.* 1707: *m.* 1757, Frances, da. of Herbert Mackworth; *d.* 1762; *s.* by his brother [6] WILLIAM, 6th Lord; Col. in Dutch Ser.: *m.* 17—, Rembertina-Maria Idiking; *d.* 1776; *s.* by his son [7] ANTHONY ADRIAN, 7th Lord, who *s.* as 5th Earl of Kintore 1778 (see that title). On the death of ARTHUR GEORGE, 10th Earl and 12th Lord Falconer of Halkerton 1966, the latter peerage became dormant.

FALKENDER, BARONESS. (Faulkender.) [Life Baroness 1974.]

MARCIA MATILDA FALKENDER, *CBE*, da. of Harry Field; *b.* 1932; ed. at Queen Mary Coll., London Univ. (BA); Sec. to Mr. Morgan Phillips, Gen. Sec. Labour Party 1955-56, since when Private Sec. to Rt. Hon. Harold Wilson, OBE, FRS, MP; Assumed by deed poll, 1974 the surname of Falkender in lieu of Williams; cr. CBE (Civil) 1970, and *Baroness Falkender*, of West Haddon, co. Northants. (Life Baroness) 1974: *m.* 1955, (m. diss. 1969), George Edmund Charles Williams.

Residence.—Bow House, Green Lane, Prestwood, Gt. Missenden, Bucks.

FALKLAND, VISCOUNT. (Cary.) [Viscount S. 1620.]

Faithful in both.

LUCIUS HENRY CHARLES PLANTAGENET CARY, 14th Viscount; *b.* Jan. 25th, 1905; *s.* 1961; ed. at Eton; formerly Flying Officer R.A.F. Vol. Reserve : *m.* 1st, 1926, Joan Sylvia (who obtained a divorce 1933), dau. of Charles Bonham Southey ; 2ndly, 1933 (marriage dissolved 1958), Constance Mary, dau. of the late Capt. Edward Berry; 3rdly, 1958 (m. diss. 1974), Charlotte Anne, el. dau. of Bevil Granville, of Chadley, Wellesbourne, Warwickshire [Halsey, Bt.], and has issue by 1st and 2nd m.

Arms.—Quarterly : 1st and 4th argent, on a bend sable, three roses of the field, barbed and seeded proper, *Cary* ; 2nd sable, two bars nebulée ermine. *Spencer of Spencercombe* ; 3rd, France and England quarterly, within a bordure componée argent and azure, *Beaufort*, Duke of Somerset. **Crest.**—A swan, wings elevated proper. **Supporters**—*Dexter,* an unicorn argent, armed, crined, tufted and unguled or; *sinister,* a lion guardant proper, ducally crowned, and gorged with a plain collar or.

Residence,—22, Tower Park, Fowey, Cornwall.

SON LIVING. (By 2nd marriage.)
Hon. LUCIUS EDWARD WILLIAM PLANTAGENET (*Master of Falkland*) (Court House, Winchfield, nr. Basingstoke, Hants.), *b.* May 8th, 1935: ed. at Wellington Coll.: late 2nd Lt. 8th Hussars; a Ch. Exec. C. T. Bowring Trading (Holdings), Ltd.: *m.* 1962, Caroline Anne, only da. of the late Lt. Cdr. Gerald Butler, DSO, RN, and has issue living, Lucius Alexander Plantagenet, *b.* 1963,— Samantha Camilla, *b.* 1973,—Lucinda Mary, *b.* 1974.

DAUGHTERS LIVING. (By 1st marriage.)
Hon. Elizabeth Ann Bevil (*Hon. Lady Nelson*), *b.* 1927 : *m.* 1945, Sir William Vernon Hope Nelson, OBE, 3rd Bt. *Residence,*—.
Hon. Jean Rosemary Vera, *b.* 1928 : *m.* 1950, Capt. Henry Herman Evelyn Montagu Winch. *Residence,*—Castle Barn, Minffordd, Merioneth.

BROTHER LIVING.
Hon. Richard Lorenzo Plantagenet, *b.* 1915; ed. at Repton, and at Downing Coll., Camb.: *m.* 1959, Dorothy Denise Lloyd. *Address,*—c/o 17, Albemarle St., W.1.

SISTERS LIVING.
Hon. Rosemary Sylvia, *b.* 1910: *m.* 1st, 1928, John de Perigault Gurney Mayhew, from whom she obtained a divorce 1936; 2ndly, 1937, Aubrey Esson-Scott, and has issue living, (by 1st marriage, John Alexander Simon Cary (Ballards Wood, Rosemary Lane, Ticehurst, Sussex), *b.* 1931; ed. at Eton; late 2nd Lt. Roy. Norfolk Regt.: *m.* 1st, 1954 (m. diss. 1962), Ann, only da. of Maj. Grant Saunders; 2ndly, 1962, the Hon. Margaret Louise Brock, yst. da. of Baron Brock (Life Baron), and has issue living, (by 1st marriage) Shaun Simon Cary *b.* 1955, Fergus James *b.* 1956, (by 2nd m.) Ella Rose Louise *b.* 1963, Matilda Jane *b.* 1965. *Residence,*—25, Sussex House, Eastbourne.

Hon. Sheila, *b.* 1912: *m.* 1931, William Philip Neville Edwards, OBE, of Hill House, Brockham Lane, Betchworth, Surrey, and has issue living, Timothy William Byron Cary (273, Ladbroke Grove, W10), *b.* 1933; ed. at Bryanston,—Jeremy John Cary (37, Oakley Gdns., Chelsea, SW3), *b.* 1937; ed. at Haileybury: *m.* 1st, 1963, Jenifer, da. of the late Lt.-Col. Cecil Langton Mould, 2nd R. Lancers: 2ndly, 1974, April Phillipa, da. of the late Reginald Ernest Harding, OBE, and has issue living (by 1st m.), Julian Peter Cary *b.* 1967, Venetia Hester *b.* 1964.

WIDOWS LIVING OF SON OF THIRTEENTH VISCOUNT.

Daphne Helen (The Cottage, 26, Dorset Road South, Bexhill-on-Sea), da. of the late Capt. Edward Westcott King, RA: *m.* 1932, the Hon. Byron Godfrey Plantagenet Cary, who *d.* 1971, and has issue [see colls. infra].

COLLATERAL BRANCHES LIVING.

Issue of the late Hon. Byron Godfrey Plantagenet Cary, 2nd son of 13th Viscount,
b. 1908, *d.* 1971: *m.* 1932, Daphne Helen (ante), da. of the late Capt. Edward Westcott King, RA:—

Robert Byron, *b.* 1944; ed. at Repton.——Rosemary Sally (118, High St., Wivenhoe, Essex), *b.* 1935.
——Susan Jane, *b.* 1938: *m.* 1960, Ronald Frederick Featherstone, and has issue living, Angus Frederick, *b.* 1962,—Penelope Helen, *b.* 1961,—Louise, *b.* 1964, Greta Jane, *b.* 1965,—Katy Ann Lorraine, *b.* 1967.

Issue of the late Hon. Philip Plantagenet Cary, yst. son of 12th Viscount, *b.* 1895,
d. 1968: *m.* 1920, Esther Mildred, who *d.* 1972, da. of Sir George Edward Leon, 2nd Bt.:—

(Mary) Philippa (*Baroness Dunalley*), (Glendalough Lodge, Recess, co. Galway), *b.* 1922: 1939-45 War, as 3rd Officer, WRNS: *m.* 1947, the 6th Baron Dunalley.

PREDECESSORS.—[1] *Rt. Hon. Sir* HENRY Carye, *P.C.*, Comptroller of the Household 1617; M.P. for Hertfordshire 1620-1, and Lord Dep. for Ireland 1622-9; cr. *Viscount Falkland* and *Lord Carye* (peerage of Scotland) 1620; *d.* 1633; *s.* by his son [2] LUCIUS, 2nd Viscount; M.P. for Newport, and Sec. of State to Charles I. ; killed at first battle of Newbury 1643; *s.* by his el. son [3] LUCIUS, 3rd Viscount; *d.* 1649; *s.* by his brother [4] HENRY, 4th Viscount; M.P. for Arundell and Lord-Lieut. of co. Oxford; *d.* 1663; *s.* by his son [5] ANTHONY, *P.C.*, 5th Viscount; filled several high offices *temp.* Charles II. and William III.; committed to the Tower in 1693 by the House of Commons, of which he was a member, for begging and receiving £2,000 from H.M., contrary to the ordinary method of issuing and bestowing the King's money; *s.* by his cousin [6] LUCIUS HENRY Cary, 6th Viscount, grandson of the Hon. Patrick Cary, 5th son of 1st Viscount; *d.* 1730; *s.* by his son [7] LUCIUS CHARLES, 7th Viscount; *d.* 1785; *s.* by his grandson [8] HENRY THOMAS, 8th Viscount, el. son of the Hon. Lucius Ferdinand, el. son of 7th Viscount; *d.* unmarried 1796; *s.* by his brother [9] CHARLES JOHN, 9th Viscount; *b.* 1768; killed in a duel 1809; *s.* by his son [10] LUCIUS BENTINCK, *G.C.H.*, *P.C.*, 10th Viscount; *b.* 1803; was a Lord of the Bedchamber to William IV. 1830, a Representative Peer for Scotland 1831-32, Gov. of Nova Scotia 1840-46, Capt. of Yeomen of the Guard 1846-48, and Gov. of Bombay 1848-53; cr. *Baron Hunsdon of Scutterskelfe*, co. York (peerage of United Kingdom) 1832; *d.* 1884, when the Barony of Hunsdon became extinct; *s.* by his brother [11] PLANTAGENET PIERREPONT, 11th Viscount; was an Adm.; *d.* Jan. 31, 1886; *s.* by his nephew [12] BYRON PLANTAGENET (el. son of Capt. the Hon. Byron Charles Ferdinand Plantagenet Cary, 3rd son of 9th Viscount), 12th Viscount, *b.* 1845; a Representative Peer : *m.* 1879, Mary (a Lady of Grace of Order of St. John of Jerusalem in England), who *d.* 1920, dau. of the late Robert Reade, of New York ; *d.* 1922 ; *s.* by his el. son [13] LUCIUS PLANTAGENET, *O.B.E.*, 13th Viscount, *b.* 1880 ; Capt. and Brevet Major Grenadier Guards ; Dep. Gov. of Wandsworth Prison 1910-14; European War 1914-19 (O.B.E.); a Representative Peer for Scotland 1922-31 : *m.* 1904, Ella Louise, who *d.* 1954, dau. of the late E. W. Oatford ; *d.* 1961 ; *s.* by his el. son [14] LUCIUS HENRY CHARLES PLANTAGENET, 14th Viscount and present peer ; also Lord Carye.

FALMOUTH, VISCOUNT. (Boscawen.) [Viscount G.B. **1720**.]

[Name pronounced "Boscowen."]

PATIENCE PASSE SCIENCE

Patience surpasses knowledge.

GEORGE HUGH BOSCAWEN, 9th Viscount ; *b.* Oct. 31st, 1919 ; *s.* 1962 ; ed. at Eton, and at Trin. Coll., Camb. (MA); is Capt. Coldstream Guards, a DL of Cornwall, and patron of five livings; 1939-45 War in Italy (wounded, despatches): *m.* 1953, Elizabeth, el. dau. of A. H. Browne, and has issue.

Arms,—Ermine, a rose gules, barbed and seeded proper. *Crest,*—A falcon close proper. *Supporters,*—Two sea lions erect on their tails argent, gutte de larmes.

Seats,—Tregothnan, Truro; Buston, Hunton, Kent. *Club,*—Athenaeum.

SONS LIVING.

Hon. EVELYN ARTHUR HUGH, *b.* May 13th, 1955.
Hon. Nicholas John, *b.* 1957.
Hon. Charles Richard, *b.* 1958.
Hon. Vere George, *b.* 1964.

BROTHERS LIVING.

Hon. Henry Edward, *b.* 1921 ; ed. at Eton, and at Peterhouse, Camb.; is Lieut. R.E.; European War 1940-45 in Italy and N.-W. Europe : *m.* 1951, Anne Philippa, el. dau. of Col. Sir Edward Courtenay Thomas Warner, D.S.O., M.C., 2nd Bt., and has issue living, Thomas Edward, *b.* 1964,—Sarah Kathleen, *b.* 1958,—Jessica Frances, *b.* 1960. *Residence,*—The High Beeches, Handcross, Sussex.

Hon. Robert Thomas, *MC, MP, b.* 1923; ed. at Eton, and Trin. Coll., Camb.; late Lt. Coldstream Guards; MP for Wells (*C*) since 1970; 1941-45 War in NW Europe (wounded, MC): *m.* 1949, Mary Alice, JP, el. da. of the late Col. Sir Geoffrey Ronald Codrington, KCVO, CB, OMG, DSO, OBE, TD [see Codrington, Bt., cr. 1721], and has issue living, Hugh Geoffrey Robert *b.* 1954,—Dozmary Carolyn Claire, *b.* 1951,—Karenza Pamela Mary, *b.* 1961. *Residence,*—14, Tite St., SW3. *Clubs,*—Pratt's, and Royal Yacht Squadron.

SISTER LIVING.

Hon. Mary Kathleen, *b.* 1926 ; is a J.P. for Cornwall ; European War 1944-5 in W.R.N.S. : *m.* 1948, Lieut.-Com. David Verney [see Verney, Bt., cr. 1946]. *Residence,*—Trevella, St. Erme, Truro, Cornwall.

AUNT LIVING.

Hon. Kathleen Pamela Mary Corona, *b.* 1902: *m.* 1937, Maj. Henry Sherek, Rifle Bde., who *d.* 1967. *Residence,*—89A, Route de Florissant, 1206 Geneva, Switzerland.

WIDOW LIVING OF EIGHTH VISCOUNT.

MARY MARGARET DESIRÉE (*Dowager Viscountess Falmouth*), *C.B.E.*, dau. of the late Hon. Frederick George Lindley Meynell [see E. Halifax, colls.] ; C.B.E. (Civil) 1946 : *m.* 1915, the 8th Viscount, who *d.* 1962. *Residence,*—28, Chelsea Square, S.W.3.

COLLATERAL BRANCHES LIVING.

Issue of the late Major the Hon. John Richard de Clare Boscawen, youngest son of 6th Viscount, *b.* 1860, *d.* 1915 : *m.* 1890, Lady Margaret Florence Lucy, who *d.* 1945, dau. of 2nd Earl of Strafford :—

Catherine Margaret (*Catherine, Lady Rasch*) (of 9, Trevor St., Knightsbridge, S.W.7), *b.* 1891; is a J.P. for Essex: *m.* 1st, 1913, the 16th Baron Petre, who *d.* (wounds in action) 1915; 2ndly, 1921, Sir Frederic Carne Rasch, 2nd Bt., who *d.* 1963.

(In remainder to the Viscountcy only.)

Grandchildren of the late Lieut.-Col. John Hugh Boscawen (infra):—
Issue of the late Capt. Hugh Townshend Boscawen, *b.* 1880, *d.* (killed in action during European War) 1917: *m.* 19—, Kathleen, dau. of Richard Crowe, Education Depart., Auckland, New Zealand :—
Patricia, *b.* 1910. *Residence,*—

Issue of the late Capt. Spencer Boscawen, *b.* 1887, *d.* 1957 : *m.* 1919, Sydney Iris Kelly, of Papatoetoe, near Auckland, New Zealand :—
John Roger, *b.* 1922; Flight Lieut. Roy. New Zealand Territorial Air Force; with New Zealand Shipping Co. Ltd., Auckland, New Zealand; S.-W. Pacific 1943-5 (1939-45 star, Pacific star, two medals). *Residence,*—Ferndale, Brookby Rd., Whitford, Manunewa RD2, Auckland, NZ.—
Owen Tremayne (12, McCullough Av., Papatoetoe, NZ), *b.* 1925; ed. at Otahuhu Coll., and NZ Univ. (BSc, BA, DipEd); Prin. of Otahuhu Coll.; 1939-45 War as LAC, RNZAF: *m.* 1954, Beverley Rose Wheeler, of Papatoetoe, Auckland, NZ, and has issue living, John Spencer, *b.* 1956,—Leanne Kay, *b.* 1960.——Diana Margaret, *b.* 1926: *m.* 1950, Alan Frederick Arlington.——Sydney Joy, *b.* 1931: *m.* 1959, Walter Flatz.——Vanda Vivian, *b.* 1935: *m.* 1958, Clement Henry Harris. *Residence,*—

Issue of the late Valentia Maud Boscawen, *b.* 1877, *d.* 19—: *m.* 1899 (m. diss. 19—) Maj. James Skitt Matthews, VD (1158 Arbutus St., Vancouver 9, B.C.), City Archivist of Vancouver, B.C.:—
James Evelyn Huia Boscawen, *b.* 1899.——Herbert Llewellyn Terua Boscawen (twin) *b.* 1899.—— Edward Hugh Pryce Boscawen, *b.* 1900.

Grandchildren of the late Rev. the Hon. John Townshend Boscawen, brother of 6th Viscount Falmouth :—
Issue of the late Lieut.-Col. John Hugh Boscawen, *b.* 1851, *d.* 1937: *m.* 1st, 1876, Katharine Isabel, who *d.* 1884, dau. of the late Rev. John Williams Conway-Hughes, M.A., of Nydd Vicarage, near Leeds; 2ndly, 1886, Ellen, who *d.* 1895, dau. of the late Henry Parker, of Louth ; 3rdly, 1896, Teresa Catherine, *B.A.*, who *d.* 1949, dau. of C. Gerkens, of Lauder House, Lauderdale Estate, Central Otago, New Zealand :—
(By 3rd marriage) Edward Aroha, *b.* 1898 ; European War 1916-18 in Palestine, as Lieut. New Zealand Mounted Rifles and Camel Corps. *Residence,*—

Issue of the late Rev. Arthur Townshend Boscawen, *b.* 1862, *d.* 1939: *m.* 1902, Christian, who *d.* 1940, el. dau. of the late Chapell Hodge, of Pounds, Plymouth :—
Violet Mary, *b.* 1903 : *m.* 1st, 1929, Lieut.-Com. David Cameron Williams, R.N., who *d.* 1931 [see Williams, Bt., cr. 1866, colls.] ; 2ndly, 1946, Humphrey Douglas Tyringham, and has issue living, (by 1st marriage) Susan Mary, *b.* 1931. *Residence,*—Little Wood, Buckland Monachorum, Yelverton, Devon.——Karenza Margaret, *b.* 1904 : *m.* 1943, R. C. Weatherby, who *d.* 1953. *Residence,*—Nanceglos, Madron, Penzance, Cornwall.

Grandsons of the late Townshend Evelyn Boscawen (infra):—
Issue of the late Maj. John Perceval Townshend Boscawen, MBE, *b.* 1906, *d.* 1972: *m.* 1931, Lady Mary Helen Alma Graham (The Old Rectory, W. Clandon, Guildford, Surrey; Dubbhgharadh Lodge, Isle of Arran), el. da. of 6th Duke of Montrose:—
James Townshend (Killiechassie, Aberfeldy, Perthshire), *b.* 1932; late Lt. Gren. Gds.; a Member of Queen's Body Guard for Scotland (Roy. Co. of Archers): *m.* 1955, Deirdre Elsie Elizabeth, da. of the late (Frederick Henry) Derek Curtis-Bennett, QC, and has issue living, Caroline Elizabeth, *b.* 1959,— Diana Mary, *b.* 1962.——Simon John Evelyn (Jackson's Cottage, Rudgwick, Sussex), *b.* 1936; ed. at Eton: *m.* 1961, Judith, da. of A. G. G. Marshall, of Horseheath Lodge, Linton, Cambridge, and has issue living, Alistair John Evelyn, *b.* 1963,—David Simon Townshend, *b.* 1965,—John Michael Arthur, *b.* 1969.

Granddaughter of the late Rev. the Hon. John Townshend Boscawen (ante):—
Issue of the late Townshend Evelyn Boscawen, *b.* 1864, *d.* 1936 : *m.* 1902, Mary Sophia, who *d.* 1948, el. dau. of Thomas Algernon Dorrien-Smith, of Tresco Abbey, Scilly Isles :—
Edith Joan, *b.* 1909: *m.* 1944, Capt. Peter Henry Cookson, of Manor Farm, Upper Slaughter, Cheltenham, Glos., and has issue living, Robert Edwin, *b.* 1946,—Mary Anne, *b.* 1952.

(In remainder to the Barony of Le Despencer only.)

Descendants of the late Rev. the Hon. Miles John Stapleton, 3rd son of 22nd Baron Le Despencer (infra).

Descendants of the late Rev. the Hon. Francis Jarvis Stapleton (4th son of Sir Thomas Stapleton, 6th Bt. and 22nd Baron Despencer), who *s.* his father in the Baronetcy 1831.
See Stapleton, Bt.

PREDECESSORS.—[1] HUGH Boscawen, P.C., M.P. for Cornwall, Truro, and Penryn, Groom of the Bedchamber to Prince George, Comptroller of the Household, Warden of the Stanneries, and Vice-Treasurer of Ireland; cr. *Baron Boscawen-Rose* and *Viscount Falmouth* (peerage of Great Britain, 1720; *d.* 1734; *s.* by his son [2] HUGH, 2nd Viscount, a Gen. in the Army and Capt. of the Yeomen of the Guard; *d.s.p.* 1782; *s.* by his nephew [3] GEORGE EVELYN, 3rd Viscount, son of Adm. the Hon. Edward, 2nd son of 1st Viscount; Capt. of Band of Gentlemen-at-Arms; *d.* 1808; *s.* by his son [4] EDWARD, 4th Viscount; cr. *Earl of Falmouth* 1821; *d.* 1841; *s.* by his son [5] GEORGE HENRY, 2nd Earl; *d.* 1852, when the earldom became extinct, and the viscountcy devolved upon his cousin [6] EVELYN, 6th Viscount, son of the Rev. the Hon. John Evelyn, 2nd son of 3rd Viscount, *b.* 1819: *m.* 1845, Mary Frances Elizabeth, in her own right Baroness Le Despencer; *d.* 1889; *s.* by his el. son [7] EVELYN EDWARD THOMAS, KCVO, CB, 7th Viscount, *b.* 1847; Maj.-Gen. in the Army; *s.* as 24th Baron Le Despencer 1891 [see *⁎⁎* infra]: *m.* 1886, the Hon. Kathleen Douglas-Pennant, who *d.* 1953, da. of 2nd Baron Penrhyn; *d.* 1918; *s.* by his el. son [8] EVELYN HUGH JOHN, 8th Viscount;

b. 1887; Alderman of London Co. Council 1931-7: m. 1915, Mary Margaret Desirée, CBE, da. of the late Hon. Frederick George Lindley Meynell; d. 1962; s. by his 2nd son [9] GEORGE HUGH, 9th Viscount and present peer; also Baron Boscawen-Rose, and Baron Le Despencer.

₊ [1] HUGH Le Despencer, summoned to Parliament of England 1264 and constituted Justiciary of England; killed at battle of Evesham 1265; s. by his son [2] HUGH, 2nd Baron; summoned to Parliament 1283-1326; cr. Earl of Winchester 1322; was banished the realm 1321; and being subsequently recalled was beheaded Oct. 1326 without the formality of a trial; s. by his son [3] HUGH, Knt., 3rd Baron; summoned to Parliament 1314-25, and cr. Earl of Gloucester; was Lord Chamberlain to Edward II., and Warden of Forest of Dean; in Nov. 1326 he was beheaded, and his honours forfeited; his el. son [4] Hugh, commonly called Lord Glamorgan, was summoned to Parliament 1338-49; d.s.p. 1349; s. by his nephew [5] EDWARD, KG, 5th Baron; summoned to Parliament 1357-72; d. 1375; s. by his son [6] THOMAS, 6th Baron; summoned to Parliament 1396 and cr. Earl of Gloucester 1397; declared a traitor and beheaded 1400 when his honours were forfeited; his sister, [7] ISABEL, m. 1st, Richard Beauchamp, Earl of Worcester and Baron Bergavenny, and 2ndly, Richard, 5th Earl of Warwick; by her 1st marriage she had [8] ELIZABETH, who having obtained a reversal of the attainder became Baroness Le Despencer: m. Sir Edward Neville, KG, 6th son of Ralph, 1st Earl of Westmorland who was summoned to Parliament, in right of his wife, as Baron Bergavenny 1450-72; on the death of [9—11] HENRY, 4th Baron Bergavenny, that barony passed to the heir male and the Barony of Le Despencer reverted to his da. [12] MARY, wife of Sir Thomas Fane, Knt., and in 1604 the barony was confirmed to her by letters patent; d. 1626; s. by her el. son [13—20] FRANCIS, 12th Baron; cr. Baron Burghersh and Earl of Westmorland (peerage of England) 1624; the Barony of Le Despencer was merged in the earldom until 1762 when it became abeyant between the sisters of the 7th Earl; in 1763 the abeyance was terminated in favour of [21] FRANCIS Dashwood, 21st Baron, who had in 1724, s. his father as 2nd Bt.; was Lord-Lieut. of Bucks and Groom of the Stole to HRH the Prince of Wales; d.s.p. 1781, when the barony again became abeyant, and continued so until 1788 when it was terminated in favour of [22] THOMAS Stapleton, 22nd Baron, who had in 1781, s. his father as 6th Bt.; d. 1831; when the baronetcy reverted to his 4th son, and the barony descended to his granddaughter [23] MARY FRANCES ELIZABETH (only child of the Hon. Thomas, el. son of 22nd Baron, by Maria Wynne, da. of Henry Bankes, of Kingston Hall, Dorset), b. 1822: m. 1845, the 6th Viscount Falmouth, who d. 1889; d. 1891; s. by her el. son [24] EVELYN EDWARD THOMAS, KCVO, CB, 7th Viscount Falmouth (ante).

FARINGDON, BARON. (Henderson.)   [Baron U.K. 1916, Bt. U.K. 1902.]

Virtue alone ennobles.

ALEXANDER GAVIN HENDERSON, 2nd Baron, and 2nd Baronet: b. March 20th, 1902; s. 1934; ed. at Eton, and at Ch. Ch., Oxford (MA); a Member of LCC 1958-61, and an Alderman 1961-65; Pres. of British Fire Sers. Assocn., and of Theatres Advisory Council, a Member of Central Housing Advisory Cttee., and of Historic Building Council, and a Trustee of Wallace Collection: m. 1927 (marriage annulled 1931), the Hon. Honor Chedworth Philipps, who d. 1961, da. of 1st Baron Kylsant (ext.).

Arms,—Or, three piles issuant from the sinister vert, on a chief ermine three torteaux. Crest,—A hand holding a torteau charged with a mullet of six points argent. Supporters,— Dexter, a chevalier armed at all points, holding in his dexter hand a lance with his lordship's pennon, bearing the motto "Sursum corda," all proper; sinister, a centaur drawing his bow proper.
Seat,—Buscot Park, Faringdon, Oxon.

BROTHER LIVING (Raised to the rank of a Baron's son 1935).

Hon. Roderic Harold Dalzell, b. 1909; ed. at Eton, and at Camb. Univ. (B.A. 19—); Hon. Attaché Diplo. Ser. 1933-39, Cypher Officer, Montevideo 1939-42, and Private Sec. to H.M.'s A mbassador, Buenos Aires 1943-45. Residences,— Stonenorton, Chester Depot, Vermont, 05144, USA; 565, Tuckerman Av., Middletown, R.I. 02840, USA.

SISTER LIVING. (Raised to the rank of a Baron's daughter 1935.)
Hon. Margaret Violet, b. 1904: m. 1932, Lieut.-Col. Henry Charles Minshull Stockdale, and has issue living, Henry Minshull, (Hill Farm, Mears Ashby, Northampton), b. 1933: m. 1957, Caroline Frances, da. of Cdr. L. Lawrence St. George Rich, DSO, RN, and has issue living, Henry Charles Minshull b. 1960, Charlotte b. 1958,—Rosemary Violet, b. 1934: m. 1954, Anthony John Tennant, of Britwell Priors, Longparish, Hants. [see B. Glenconner, colls.], Margaret Jane, b. 1940: m. 1960, Capt. Richard Hugh Nicholson, late 16th/5th Queen's R. Lancers, of Woodcott House, Whitchurch, Hants. [see B. Sudeley]. Residence,—Mears Ashby Hall, Northampton.

WIDOW LIVING OF BROTHER OF SECOND BARON
Esther Isabelle (GLENDINNING), dau. of the late Alfred Edward Coleman: m. 1948, as his second wife, Lieut.-Col. the Hon. Michael Thomas Henderson, 16/5th Lancers, who d. 1953, and has issue living [see colls. infra]. Residence,—Flat 13, 30, Bramham Gardens, Kensington, S.W.5.

WIDOW LIVING OF SON OF FIRST BARON.
Hon. Sophia Isabelle ("Zoe") Butler-Massey, dau. of 5th Baron Clarina: m. 1910, the Hon. Eric Brand Butler-Henderson, who d. 1953, and has issue living [see colls. infra]. Residence,—Faccombe Manor, Andover, Hants. Club,—Farmers'.

COLLATERAL BRANCHES LIVING.
Issue of the late Lieut.-Col. the Hon. Michael Thomas Henderson, 16th/5th Lancers, brother of 2nd Baron, b. 1906, d. 1953: m. 1st, 1929 (marriage dissolved 1948), Oonagh Evelyn, dau. of the late Lieut.-Col. Harold Ernest Brassey [E. Donoughmore]; 2ndly, 1948, Esther Isabelle (GLENDINNING) (ante), dau. of the late Alfred Edward Coleman:—

By 1st marriage) CHARLES MICHAEL (of Barnsley Park, Cirencester, Glos., and 30 Phillimore Gdns., W.8), b. July 3rd, 1937; ed. at Eton and at Trin. Coll., Camb. (B.A. 1961): m. 1959, Sarah Caroline, dau. of Major John Marjoribanks Askew, Grenadier Guards [see D. Sutherland], and has issue living, James Harold, b. 1961,—Thomas Alexander Gavin, b. 1966,—Angus George, b. 1969,— Susannah Jane, b. 1963.——Brighid Sarah, b. 1929: m. 1958, Timothy John Oswald Mosley, of Vicarage Field, Milton-under-Wychwood, Oxon [see Mosley, Bt., colls.].

Grandchildren of the late Hon. Alec Puleston Henderson (infra):—
Issue of the late Capt. Ian Alexander Henderson, b. 1918, d. 1968: m. 1st, (m. diss. 1955) Patience, da. of the late Lt.-Col. John Charles Brand, DSO, MC [see W. Hampden, colls.]; 2ndly 1955, Sarah Veronica, (Westmeads, Butlers Marston, Kineton, Warwickshire) da. of Cosmo Stafford Crawley [Crawley-Boevey, Bt., colls.]:—
(By 1st m.) Veronica, b. 1946: m. 1967, Oliver Alexander Guy Baring [see B. Ashburton, colls.].——
(by 2nd m.) Shamus Alec, b. 1958.

Issue (by 2nd marriage) of the late Hon. Alec Puleston Henderson, 2nd son of 1st Baron, b. 1876, d. 1931: m. 1st, 1905, Henrietta Emily Cecil, who d. 1913, dau. of the late Capt. Frederick Arthur Bertie [E. Abingdon, colls.]; 2ndly, 1915, Gladys Rhoda, who d. 1953, having m. 2ndly, 1934, as his second wife, Sir Murrough John Wilson, K.B.E., of Cliffe Hall, Darlington (B. Inchiquin, colls.)], only child of the late Major Donald Maclean:—

Adrian Donald, b. 1922; formerly Leading Aircraftman RAF Vol. Reserve: m. 1st, 1944 (m. diss. 1958), Marieluz, da. of Capt. Robert Denistoun-Webster, DSC, RN, of Hurst Grange, nr. Twyford; 2ndly, 1959, Angela Mary Oriana Harrington (POLLEN), el. da. of Capt. Felix John Russi, MC, 5th Roy. Inniskilling Dragoons, and has issue living, (by 1st m.) Gavin Adrian Alexander, b. 1944,—Mark Alistair, b. 1946,—(by 2nd m.) Alexander Jonathan, b. 1962,—Fiona Mary (twin), b. 1962. *Residence,*—Killochan Castle, Girvan, Ayrshire.——Susan Violet, b. 1915: m. 1st 1936, Capt. Mark Leslie Pilkington, MC, Life Guards, who d. (killed in action) 1942; 2ndly, 1943, Fl. Lt. Charles Pretzlik, RAF Vol. Reserve, and has issue living, (by 1st m.) Simon Mark (Flatfield House, Symington, by Kilmarnock, Ayrshire), b. 1938: m. 1963, Angela Mary Monica, da. of the late Lord Patrick Crichton-Stuart [see M. Bute, colls], and has issue living, Rupert Charles b. 1964, Mark Patrick b. 1965, Jane Susan b. 1966, Kate Sophie b. 1970,—(by 2nd m.) Nicholas Charles, (44, Hornton St., W8), b. 1945: m. 1970, Ursula Scheuring, and has issue living, Charles Oliver b. 1971,—Jacqueline Susan, b. 1944: m. 1970, Peter Raine, of 14, Bramerton St., Chelsea, SW3, and has issue living, Simon Patrick Wallace b. 1973, Nancy Susan Wallace b. 1971. *Residence,*—Millers House, Isington, Hants.——Rosemary Gladys, b. 1917: m. 1941, Count Robert Philip Orssich, and has issue living, Paul Alexander, (Pou Nou 101, San Luis, Menorca, Baleares, Spain), b. 1942: m. 1972, Susan Clements, —Christopher Levin (Drove, West Tytherley, Hants.), b. 1948: m. 1971, (Alexandra) Hazel, el. da. o, Antony Gibbs, of Wickenden Farm, Sharpthorne, Sussex,—Susan Rosemary, b. 1943: m. 1963f Richard Lionel Terry, of Pou Nou 55, San Luis, Menorca, Baleares, Spain, and has issue living, Simon Richard Brett b. 1964, Jonathan Paul Brandon b. 1966, Nicholas Damian Blaine b. 1967, Emma-Jane Kate b. 1969. *Residence,*—Poplars Farm, Winkfield, nr. Windsor.

Issue of the late Lieut.-Col. the Hon. Philip Henderson, 4th son of 1st Baron, b. 1881; d. 1939: m. 1908, Rachel Magdaleine Mary, who d. 1953, dau. of the late James Charles Hope-Vere [M. Linlithgow, colls.]:—

David Hope, b. 1912; ed. at Eton: m. 1st, 1935, Alice Reed Rawle (from whom he obtained a divorce 1938), da. of Antony Geyelin, of Philadelphia, USA; 2ndly, 1945, Eleanora Anderson, da. of Maj. David Anderson Spence, VD, Black Watch, of Dunninald Mains, Montrose, and has issue living, (by 2nd m.) Philip David Hope, (40, Bramham Gdns., SW5), b. 1947; ed. at Eton, and Roy. Agric. Coll., Cirencester,—Ian Ramsay Hope (4, Peel St., W8), b. 1949; ed. at Eton, and Edinburgh Univ. (MA, LLB). *Residence,*—Achie Farm, New Galloway, Kirkcudbrightshire. *Club,* St. James'.—— Alistair Philip, b. 1919; Lt. Black Watch; 1939-45 War. *Residence,*—Villa Azzif, 3, Rue d'Ecrosse, Tangiers. *Club,*—New.——Ralph Alexander, b. 1923; ed. at Eton, and at Trin. Coll., Camb.; was 3rd Sec. at British Embassy, Lisbon 1945-46: m. 1950, Myriam, da. of the late Adm. A. de Souza e Silva, Brazilian Navy, of Rio de Janeiro, and has issue living, Ralph Peter, b. 1951,—Charles James (twin), b. 1951,—Lavinia Magdaleine Marie, b. 1954. *Club,*—Boodle's.

Grandchildren of the late Hon. Arnold Henderson, O.B.E. (infra):—
Issue of the late Flight-Lieut. Roger Arnold Henderson, R.A.F. Vol. Reserve, b. 1909, d. (on active ser.) 1941: m. 1934, Judith Violet Christine (who d. 1966, having m. 2ndly, 1946, Robert Edward Manifold, of Wiridgil, Camperdown, Victoria, Australia), da. of ..dmund Thornley, of Gnotuk, Camperdown, Australia:—
David Arnold Thornley (Koorrnong, Tarcutts, N.S. Wales), b. 1937: m. 1962, Sophie Jacqueline Fern Welsh, and has issue living, Roger David, b. 1963,—Nicholas John Welsh, b. 1964,—Anna Jacqueline Judith, b. 1966.——Davina Christine, b. 1935: m. 1st 1961 (m. diss. 1974), Dr. Peter Kaye Bryan; 2ndly, 1974, Richard Lawrence Baillieu, of Clondrisse, Flinders, Vic., Aust., and has issue living (by 1st m.), Roger Jon, b. 1961,—Christopher Peter, b. 1968,—Rebecca Alexandra, b. 1963.

Issue of the late Hon. Arnold Henderson, O.B.E., 5th son of 1st Baron, b. 1883, d. 1933: m. 1908, Helen Madeline, who d. 1961, dau. of Gen. Evans Gordon:—

Diana Mary (*Marchioness of Exeter*), b. 1911: m. 1st, 1931, Lieut.-Col. David Walter Arthur William Forbes, MC, Coldstream Guards, who d. (killed in action 1943) [B. Hotham, colls.]; 2ndly, 1946, the 6th Marquess of Exeter, and has issue living, (by 1st m.) Anthony David Arnold William, Wakerley Manor, Oakham, Leics.), b. 1938: m. 1st, 1962, Virginia June, from whom he obtained a divorce 1973, da. of Sir Leonard Ropner, MC, TD, 1st Bt. (cr. 1952); 2ndly, 1973, Belinda Mary, da. of Sir Hardman Alexander Mort Earle, 5th Bt., and formerly wife of Patrick John Boteler Drury-Lowe, and has issue living (by 1st m.), Jonathan David b. 1964, Susanna Jane b. 1966, Rosemary Davina, b. 1932: m. 1953, Robert Leigh-Pemberton, of Torry Hill, Sittingbourne, Kent [see Payne-Gallwey, Bt.],—(by 2nd m.) [see M. Exeter]. *Residence,*—Burghley House, Stamford, Lincs.

Grandchildren of the late Hon. Eric Brand Butler-Henderson (infra):—
Issue of the late Major Lionel Butler-Henderson, b. 1911, d. 1961: m. 1936, Una (Beckfield Stud Farm, Sandon, Buntingford, Herts), dau. of the late Guy Fenwick:—
Guy (Beckfeld Stud Farm, Sandon, Buntingford, Herts.), b. 1948: m. 1968, Glynis, da. of Kenneth Bladon, of Goodridge, Weston, Hitchin, Herts, and has issue living, Timothy, b. 1971.——Jane, b. 1938: m. 1st, 1957 (m. diss. 1967), John Guy Mercer; 2ndly, 1968, George Frederick Hewitt, of Wheelers Stud, Peasenhall, Suffolk, and has issue living, (by 1st m.) Christopher John, b. 1960,— Belinda, b. 1958,—(by 2nd m.) Antony George, b. 1970.

Issue of the late Hon. Eric Brand BUTLER-HENDERSON, youngest son of 1st Baron, b. 1884, d. 1953, having assumed by deed poll 1910 the additional surname of Butler: m. 1910, the Hon. Sophia Isabelle (" Zoe ") Butler-Massey (ante), dau. of 5th Baron Clarina:—
Patrick, b. 1913; ed. at Eton; late Fl.-Lt. RAFVR: m. 1st, 1943 (m. diss. 1963), Kathleen Rebe Curtis (Section Officer late WAAF), da. of the late Lt.-Col. Herman Curtis Clarke, CBE, DSO; 2ndly, 1968, Mrs. Pamela L. Godrich, and has issue living, (by 1st m.) Eric Alexander, b. 1946: m. 1970, Leslie Halligan,—Christine, b. 1944: m. 1971, Maj. Neil James Cameron Sutherland, Queen's Own

Highlanders, of Ardsheal, Kentallen, Argyll, and has issue living, Rachael Bridget b. 1974,—Amalia Zoe, b. 1945: m. 1970, Capt. Simon Brian Taylor, of Sandside, Reay, Thurso, Caithness [see Smith-Dodsworth, Bt.]. *Residence,*—Buscot Manor, Faringdon, Berks.——Edward, b. 1916; ed. at Eton; late Lt.-Col. 99th (Roy. Bucks. Yeo.) Field Regt., RA (TA): m. 1939, Elizabeth Marjorie Dacres, only da. of the late Henry George Dacres Dixon [see E. Yarborough, colls.], and has issue living, Alan (Whitewalls, Courtaulds Av., Esher, Surrey), b. 1943: m. 1964, Maria Cassy Ugena, and has issue living, David James b. 1967, Elizabeth Cassy b. 1965,—Penelope, b. 1940: m. 1962, Ian Alan Douglas Pilkington, of Warennes Wood, Mortimer, Berks., and has issue living, Rory Ian Douglas b. 1968, Camilla Douglas b. 1966. *Residence,*—Flat 14, 43, Lowndes Sq., SW1.——Kenneth (11, Egerton Place, SW3), b. 1929; ed. at Eton: m. 1952, Phyllis Daphne, da. of the late Lt.-Col. Alfred Edward Cartmel, CIE, MM, of 29, Fanshawe St., Hertford, and has issue living, Julian, b. 1956, —Serina Anne, b. 1953,—Clare, b. 1954.——Mary, b. 1915: m. 1939, Algernon Desmond Wigan, MC, TD, late Maj. 23rd Hussars, of Netherton Farmhouse, nr. Andover, Hants., and has issue living, Desmond, b. 1941: m. 1969, Anne, Louise, da. of Prof. A. Black, and has issue living, Desmond Patrick Neil b. 1970, Zoe Margaret, b. 1972,—Peter, b. 1943: m. 1973, Victoria Mary Riddle, and has issue living, Patrick Claude b. 1974,—Christopher (46, Stockwell Park Rd., SW9), b. 1947: m. 1970, the Hon. Caroline Kinnaird, da. of the 13th Lord Kinnaird, and has issue living, Leila Willow b. 1974, —Susan b. 1945.——Doreen, b. 1920: m. 1st, 1939 (m. diss. 1961), John Gordon Wordsworth, OBE, late Lt.-Col. Suffolk Regt.: 2ndly, 1962, Group Capt. William Digby Blackwood, OBE, DFC, RAF (ret.), of Garsdon House, Garsdon, Malmesbury, Wilts., and has issue living, (by 1st m.) Antony Christopher Curwen (The Lodge, Elsenham, Bishops Stortford, Herts.), b. 1940: m. 1962, Rosamond Anne Summers, and has issue living, Mark Edward Curwen b. 1965, Katherine Lucy b. 1968, Evelyn Mary b. 1972,—Michael (Cornhill House, The Hangers, Bishops Waltham, Southampton), b. 1942: m. 1966, Christine Stella Lear, and has issue living, Giles Patrick John b. 1969, Zara Caroline b. 1972,—Charles William, b. 1946: m. 1968, Maria Reyes Garcia Contillo, and has issue living, Cristina Maria b. 1971,—Peter John, b. 1949.

PREDECESSOR.—[1] ALEXANDER Henderson, *C.H.*, son of the late George Henderson, of Langholm, Dumfries; b. 1850; M.P. for W. Div. of Staffordshire (*LU*) 1898-1906, and for St. George, Hanover Square 1913-15; cr. a *Baronet* 1902, and *Baron Faringdon*, of Buscot Park, co. Berks (peerage of United Kingdom) 1916: m. 1874, Jane Ellen, who d. 1920, dau. of the late Edward William Davis, d. 1934; s. by his grandson [2] ALEXANDER GAVIN (son of the late Lieut.-Col. the Hon. Harold Greenwood Henderson, OVO, el. son of 1st Baron, and the late Lady Violet Charlotte Dalzell, da. of 12th Earl of Carnwath (ext.), 2nd Baron, and present peer.

FARNHAM, BARON. (Maxwell.) [Baron I. 1756, Bt. N.S. 1627.]

I am ready.

BARRY OWEN SOMERSET MAXWELL, 12th Baron and 14th Baronet; b. July 7th, 1931; s. 1957; ed. at Eton, and at Harvard Univ.; late Lieut. Roy. Horse Guards; a Director of Brown, Shipley & Co., Merchant Bankers, E.C.2: m. 1959, Diana Marion, el. dau. of Nigel Eric Murray Gunnis, of Branden, Sissinghurst, Kent [B. Trevor].

Arms,—Quarterly: 1st and 4th, argent, a saltire sable, on a chief of the first three pallets of the second, *Maxwell*, 2nd and 3rd, barry of six argent and gules, *Barry*. Crest,—A buck's head erased proper. Supporters,—Two bucks proper.

Seat,—Farnham, co. Cavan. *Residence,*—11 Earls Court Gdns., SW5. *Clubs,*—Boodle's, Kildare St

BROTHER LIVING. (*Raised to the rank of a Baron's son* 1959.)

Hon. SIMON KENLIS, b. Dec. 12th, 1933; ed. at Eton; is Lieut. 10th Roy. Hussars (Supplementary Reserve): m. 1964, Karol Anne, da. of Maj.-Gen. George Erroll Prior-Palmer, CB, DSO, and has issue living, Robin Somerset, b. 1965,—Mark Erroll, b. 1968,—Lorna Suzanna Katherine (twin) b. 1968. *Residence,*—85, Dovehouse St., SW3.

SISTER LIVING. (*Raised to the rank of a Baron's daughter* 1959.)

Hon. Sheelin Virginia (*Viscountess Knollys*), b. 1937: m. 1959, the 3rd Viscount Knollys. *Residence,*—Bramerton Grange, Norwich, NR14 7HF, Norfolk.

AUNT LIVING. (*Daughter of 11th Baron.*)

Hon. Verena Aileen (*Hon. Lady Milbank*), b. 1907: m. 1st, 1934, Charles Lambart Crawley, who d. 1935; 2ndly, 1938, as his second wife, Maj. Sir Mark Vane Milbank, KCVO, MC, 4th Bt. *Residence,*—Barningham Park, Richmond, Yorks.

WIDOW LIVING OF SON OF TENTH BARON.

Theodora Mary (1, Arlington Row, Umtali, Rhodesia), da. of Arthur Hickling, of Wing Old Hall, Rutland: m. 1923, Vice-Adm. the Hon. Sir Denis Crichton Maxwell, KCB, CBE, who d. 1970, and has issue [see colls., infra.]

COLLATERAL BRANCH LIVING.

Issue of the late Vice-Adm. the Hon. Sir Denis Crichton Maxwell, KCB, CBE, yst. son of 10th Baron, b. 1892, d. 1970: m. 1923, Theodora Mary (ante), da. of Arthur Hickling, of Wing Old Hall, Rutland:—
Elizabeth Crichton, b. 1926: m. 1953, Ivor Mabberley, of Wanborough, Wilts.

PREDECESSORS.—[1] JOHN Maxwell, *M.P.* for co. Cavan 1727-56; cr. *Baron Farnham*, of Farnham, co. Cavan (peerage of Ireland) 1756; d. 1759; s. by his el. son [2] ROBERT, 2nd Baron; cr. *Viscount Farnham* (peerage of Ireland) 1761, and *Earl of Farnham* (peerage of Ireland) 1763; d.s.p. when the Viscountcy and Earldom expired, and the Barony reverted to his brother [3] BARRY, 3rd Baron; cr. *Viscount Farnham* (peerage of Ireland) 1781, and *Earl of Farnham* (peerage of Ireland) 1785; d. 1800; s. by his son [4] JOHN JAMES, 2nd Earl; d.s.p. 1823, when the Viscountcy and Earldom expired, and the Barouy devolved upon his kinsman [5] JOHN MAXWELL BARRY, 5th Baron, el. son of the Most Rev. the Hon. Henry, D.D., P.C., Lord Bishop of Meath, 3rd son of 1st Baron; d.s.p. 1838; s. by his brother [6] *Rev.* HENRY, 6th Baron: m. 1798, Lady Ann Butler, dau. of 2nd Earl of Carrick; d. 1838; s. by his el. son [7] HENRY, 7th Baron; successively M.P. for Cavan, and a Representative Peer; killed with his wife in a dreadful accident on N.W. Railway at Abergele, Aug. 20th, 1868; s. by his brother [8] SOMERSET RICHARD, 8th Baron; b. 1803; was M.P. for Cavan (C) 1838-40; d.s.p. 1884; s.

by his brother [9] JAMES PIERCE, 9th Baron, b. 1813; M.P. for Cavan 1843-65; s. his kinsman as 11th *Baronet* [cr. 1627] of Calderwood 1885; *d.s.p.* 1896; *s.* by his nephew [10] SOMERSET HENRY (son of the late Hon. Richard Maxwell, 7th son of 6th Baron), 10th Baron; b. 1849; Lieut. of co. Cavan, and a Representative Peer for Ireland: *m.* 1875, Lady Florence Jane Taylour, who *d.* 1907, dau. of 3rd Marquess of Headfort: *d.* 1900: *s.* by his son [11] ARTHUR KENLIS, D.S.O., 11th Baron; b. 1879; Lieut.-Col. (retired) late N. Irish Horse, and a Representative Peer: *m.* 1903, Aileen Selina, who *d.* 1964, dau. of the late Charles Purdon Coote [see Coote, Bt., colls.]; *d.* 1957; *s.* by his grandson [12] BARRY OWEN SOMERSET (el. son of the late Lieut.-Col. the Hon. Somerset Arthur Maxwell, M.P.), 12th Baron and present peer.

FARRER, BARONY OF. (Farrer.) [Extinct 1964.]

DAUGHTERS LIVING OF SECOND BARON.

Hon. Dame Frances Margaret, *DBE*, b. 1895; MA, Camb.; Gen. Sec., Nat. Fedn. of Women's Institutes 1929-59, Member of Independent Television Authority 1957-61, and of Post Office Advisory Council 1960-64; DBE (Civil) 1950. *Residence,*—West Hackhurst, Abinger Hammer, nr. Dorking, Surrey.
Hon. Katherine Dianthe (*Katherine, Baroness Bridges*), b. 1896: *m.* 1922, the 1st Baron Bridges, who *d.* 1969. *Residence,*—Goodmans Furze, Headley, Surrey.
Hon. Anne Lucy, b. 1908. *Residence,*—1, Upper Phillimore Gardens, W.8.

WIDOW LIVING OF FOURTH BARON.

Hon. KATHARINE (*Hon. Lady Lyell*), dau. of 1st Viscount Runciman of Doxford: *m.* 1st, 1931, the 4th Baron, who *d.* 1954; 2ndly, 1955, *Hon. Mr. Justice* (Sir Maurice Legat) Lyell. *Residence,*—Puddephat's Farm, Markyate, Herts.

FAUCONBERG AND CONYERS, BARONIES OF. (Pelham.) [Baron E. 1283 and 1509.] [Abeyant 1948.]

SACKVILLE GEORGE PELHAM, 5th Earl of Yarborough, 8th Baron Fauconberg, and 14th Baron Conyers; *d.* 1948, when the Baronies fell into abeyance [see infra].

DAUGHTERS LIVING OF EIGHTH BARON FAUCONBERG AND FOURTEENTH BARON CONYERS (FIFTH EARL OF YARBOROUGH). (*Co-heiresses to the Baronies.*)

Lady DIANA MARY (c/o Rhobank Corporation Ltd., Box 2270, Salisbury, Rhodesia), b. July 5th, 1920; SRN: *m.* 1952, Robert Miller, and has issue living, Marcia Anne LYCETT, b. 1954; adopted by Michael H. L. Lycett [infra], whose surname she assumed, but retains right of succession to the Baronies,—Beatrix Diana, b. 1955.
Lady (JUNE) WENDY, b. June 6th, 1924; late 3rd Officer WRNS; is a JP: *m.* 1959, Michael Hildesley Lycett Lycett, late Maj. Roy. Scots Greys. *Residence,*—West Grange, Scots Gap, Morpeth, Northumberland.

COLLATERAL BRANCHES LIVING.

Grandchildren of the late Charlotte Katherine Marcia Weld-Blundell, daughter of the late Hon. Charles Pierrepont D'Arcy Lane-Fox, brother of 15th Baron Darcy de Knayth and great-grandson of Amelia, Baroness Conyers and *de jure* Baroness Darcy de Knayth :—
Issue of the late Richard Shireburn Weld-Blundell, b. 1887, *d.* 1916: *m.* 1915, Mary Angela [(now of Lisle Combe, St. Lawrence, Isle of Wight); she *m.* 2ndly, 1927, Alfred Noyes, O.B.E., who *d.* 1958], dau. of the late Capt. Jasper Graham Mayne, O.B.E., Ch. Constable of E. Suffolk :—
Agnes Mary (*Lady Grey*), b. 1915: *m.* 1936, Sir Paul Francis Grey, K.C.M.G. [see E. Grey, colls.]. *Residence,*—17, Smith Terr, SW3.

Issue of the late Mary Teresa Weld-Blundell, b. 1885, *d.* 1957 : *m.* 1912, Capt. George Frederick Montagu, R.N. (retired), who assumed by Roy. licence 1923, the surname of Weld-Blundell in lieu of his patronymic [see D. Manchester, colls.].

Issue of the late Alice Mary, b. 1890, *d.* 1947 : *m.* 1923, John Joseph Humphrey Weld, of 32, Weld Road, Birkdale, Lancashire, who assumed by Roy. licence 1923, the additional surname of Blundell :—
Charles Joseph Ignatius (Leagram Park, Chipping, nr. Preston, Lancs), b. 1928: *m.* 1951, Veronica Mary, da. of the late Alfred Noyes, OBE, and has issue living, John Joseph Thomas, b. 1955,—Peter Alfred, b. 1956,—Mary Alice, b. 1952,—Lucy Ann, b. 1953,—Diana Celia, b. 1958.——Theresa Mary Katharine, b. 1926. *Residence,*—12, Cadogan Sq., SW1.——Mary Geraldine, b. 1930.——Anne Mary, b. 1933: *m.* 1960, Thomas Frederick de Pentheny-O'Kelly.

PREDECESSORS.—[1] Walter de Fauconberg, son of Walter de Fauconberg of Ryse; summoned to Parliament by various writs, the earliest being in 1283, signed the famous letter of the Barons to the Pope in 1301; *d.* 1304; *s.* by his son [2] WALTER; summoned to Parliament 1303-1318; *d.* 1318; *s.* by his son [3] JOHN; *d.* 1349; *s.* by his son [4] WALTER; *d.* 1362; *s.* by his son [5] THOMAS: *d.* leaving an only dau. and heiress [6] JOAN, *suo jure* Baroness Fauconberg; *m.* Sir William Nevill, younger son of the Earl of Westmorland, who was summoned to Parliament and sat therein as *Lord Fauconberg* in right of his wife; distinguished himself greatly in the French Wars and at the siege of Orleans; K.G. and Adm. of England; cr. *Earl of Kent* 1461; *d.* without male issue in 1463, when the Earldom became extinct; at the death of his wife (1491) the Barony of Fauconberg fell into abeyance between his daus. and co-heirs, and so remained until 1903, when it was determined by Letters Patent in favour of [7] MARCIA AMELIA MARY, O.B.E., Countess of Yarborough, she and her sister the Countess of Powis (in whose favour the Barony of Darcy de Knayth was at the same time determined) being the sole heirs of Alice, younger dau. and co-heiress of Joan, Lady Fauconberg and Countess of Kent, which Alice *m.* Sir John Conyers of Hornby, and had issue William, 1st Baron Conyers [see *infra*]; b. 1863: *m.* 1886, the 4th Earl of Yarborough; *d.* 1926; *s.* by her younger son [8] SACKVILLE GEORGE, 8th Baron Fauconberg, 14th Baron Conyers, and 5th Earl of Yarborough; b. 1888; Lieut.-Col. Comdg. Notts Yeo. (Sherwood Rangers); European War 1914-19 (M.C.), European War 1939-45: *m.* 1919, Nancye, dau. of the late Alfred Brocklehurst; *d.* 1948, when he was *s.* in the Earldom by his brother and the Baronies of Fauconberg and Conyers fell into abeyance between his two daus. [see ante].

₊ [1] Sir WILLIAM Conyers; served at Flodden Field; summoned to the Parliament of England as *Baron Conyers* 1509; *d.* 1524; *s.* by his son [2] CHRISTOPHER, 2nd Baron; *d.* 1538; *s.* by his son [3] JOHN, 3rd Baron; *d.* without male issue, when the title went into abeyance between his three daughters; the 2nd dau., Elizabeth, *m.* Thomas, 2nd son of Sir Arthur D'Arcy, 2nd son of Thomas, Baron D'Arcy, who was attainted and beheaded 1538, and had with other issue [4] CONYERS, 4th Baron, in whose favour the abeyance in the Baronies of Darcy de Knayth [see Bs Darcy de Knayth] and Conyers were determined by letters patent 1641; *d.* 1653; *s.* by his son [5] CONYERS, 5th Baron; cr. 1682 *Earl of Holderness*; *d.* 1689; *s.* by his son [6] CONYERS, 2nd Earl; *d.* 1692; *s.* by his grandson [7] ROBERT, 3rd Earl; *d.* 1722; *s.* by his son [8] ROBERT, 4th Earl; *d.* 1778, when the Earldom became extinct, and the Barony of Conyers reverted to his daughter [9] AMELIA, wife of 5th Duke of Leeds; *d.* 1784; *s.* by her son [10] GEORGE WILLIAM FREDERICK, 16th Baron Conyers and 6th Duke of Leeds; *d.* 1838; *s.* by his son [11] FRANCIS GODOLPHIN, 11th Baron and 7th Duke; *d.* 1859; *s.* by his nephew [12] SACKVILLE GEORGE, 12th Baron (son of Sackville Walter Lane-Fox, M.P.), *b.* 1827: *m.* 1860, Mary, who *d.* 1921, el. dau. of Reginald Curteis, of Windmill Hill, Sussex; *d.* 1888, when the title remained in abeyance between his two daus., until in 1892 the abeyance was terminated in favour of his el. dau. [13] MARCIA AMELIA MARY, O.B.E., Countess of Yarborough (ante).

FEATHER, BARON. (Feather.) [Life Baron 1974.]

VICTOR GRAYSON HARDIE FEATHER, *CBE*, son of Harry Feather, of Bradford; *b.* April 10th, 1908; Hon. D.Tech. Bradford; Hon. LLD Manchester; Assist. Gen. Sec. of Trades Union Congress 1960-69, and Gen. Sec. 1969-73; *cr.* CBE (Civil) 1961, and *Baron Feather*, of City of Bradford (Life Baron) 1974: *m.* 1930, Alice Helena, da. of John Fernyhough, and has issue.

Residence,—43, Shelley Cres., Heston, Hounslow, Middx.

SON LIVING.
Hon. Harry Alexander (The Mill, Sudborough, Northants), *b.* 1938: *m.* 1972, Patricia Lesley, da. of Gilbert Victor Green.

DAUGHTER LIVING.
Hon. Patricia Margaret, *b.* 1934: *m.* 1957, Stanley Laurence Palmer.

Feilding, Viscount, son of Earl of Denbigh and Desmond.

Fermanagh, Baron, title of Earl Erne on Roll of H.L.

FERMOY, BARON. (Roche.) [Baron I. 1856.]

MON·DIEU·EST·MA·ROCHE

My God is my rock.

EDMUND JAMES BURKE ROCHE, 5th Baron; *b.* March 20th, 1939; *s.* 1955; ed. at Eton, and R.M.A., Sandhurst; late Capt. R. Horse Guards; Chm. Eddington Bindery Ltd.; Hon. Dir. Hawk Trust: *m.* 1964, Lavinia Frances Elizabeth, only da. of the late Capt. John Pitman, of Foxley House, Malmesbury, and has issue.

Arms.—Gules, three roach naiant in pale argent, a canton of the last. Crest,—Standing on a rock proper, an osprey, or sea eagle, with wings displayed argent, collared gemelle azure, membered or, holding a roach in its claw. Supporters—*Dexter*, a lion erminois, gorged with a collar sable, therefrom pendent an escutcheon gules, charged with three roach naiant in pale argent; *sinister*, a greyhound pean, gorged with a collar or, therefrom pendent an escutcheon per pale of the second and gules, charged with three lions passant guardant in pale counterchanged.

Residence,—Eddington House, Hungerford, Berks.

SONS LIVING.
Hon. PATRICK MAURICE BURKE, *b.* Oct. 11th, 1967.
Hon. Edmund Hugh Burke, *b.* 1972.

DAUGHTER LIVING.
Hon. Frances Caroline Burke, *b.* 1965.

SISTERS LIVING
Hon. Mary Cynthia Burke, *b.* 1934: *m.* 1st, 1954, (m. diss. 1966) the Hon. Anthony George Berry, MP [see V. Kemsley]; 2ndly, 1973, Dennis Roche Geoghegan. *Residence,*—40, Chester Terr., Regent's Park, NW1.
Hon. Frances Ruth Burke, *b.* 1936: *m.* 1st 1954, (m. diss. 1969) Viscount Althorp, MVO (later 8th Earl Spencer), son of 7th Earl Spencer; 2ndly, 1969, Peter Shand Kydd, of 69, Cadogan Pl., SW1.

WIDOW LIVING OF FOURTH BARON.
RUTH SYLVIA (*Ruth, Baroness Fermoy*), *CVO, OBE*, da. of the late William Smith Gill, CB, VD, of Dalhebity, Bieldside, Aberdeenshire; an Extra Woman of the Bedchamber to H.M. Queen Elizabeth the Queen Mother 1956-60, since when a Woman of the Bedchamber; Freedom of King's Lynn 1963; OBE (Civil) 1952, CVO 1966: *m.* 1931, the 4th Baron, who *d.* 1955. *Residence,*—36, Eaton Sq., SW1.

COLLATERAL BRANCHES LIVING.

Grandson of the late Hon. Alexis Charles Burke Roche (infra):—
Issue of the late Capt. George Denis Burke Roche, M.C., *b*. 1893, *d*. 1954 : *m*. 1921, Aletta S.,
dau. of M. M. Venter, of Comodoro, Rivadavia, Argentine, and Cape Province :—
Alexis Martinus Burke, *b*. 1922. *Resides* in Argentina.

Issue of the late Hon. Alexis Charles Burke Roche, 3rd son of 1st Baron, *b*. 1853;
d. 1914 : *m*. 1889, the Hon. Lucy Maude, who *d*. 1909, el. dau. of 1st Viscount
Goschen :—
Moira Burke, *b*. 1891: *m*. 1918, Brig. Desmond Henry Sykes Somerville, O.B.E., M.C., late S. Wales
Borderers, and has issue living, Christopher, *b*. 1921 ; formerly Capt. R.A. ; is with British Council:
m. 1949, Celia Penelope, dau. of Major Leonard Maurice Edward Dent, D.S.O., of Hillfields, Burghfield Common, and has issue living, Thomas Clinton *b*. 1952, John Henry *b*. 1956, Harriet Elizabeth
b. 1950,—John Nicholas (Deptford Cottage, Greywell, Hants), *b*. 1924; Brig. late S. Wales Borderers: *m*. 1951, Jenifer Dorothea, da. of Capt. Walter Macdonald Nash, RN, of Point House,
Castletownshend, co. Cork, and has issue living, Robin Nicholas *b*. 1959, Philippa Wren *b*. 1953,
Penelope *b*. 1954. *Residence*,—Drishane House, Castletownshend, co. Cork.

Issue (by 2nd marriage) of the late Col. the Hon. Ulick De Rupé Burke Roche,
C.B., 4th son of 1st Baron, *b*. 1856, *d*. 1919 : *m*. 1st, 1882, Agnes Blair, who *d*.
1905, da. of Col. Jasper Otway Mayne, RE; 2ndly, 1906, Dorothea Blanche, who
d. 1963, having *m*. 2ndly, 1931, Percy William Allday, da. of John Jones, JP, DL,
of Ynysfor, Merionethshire:—
Ulick Edmund Burke, *b*. 1906; Major S. Wales Borderers; a DL of Merioneth: *m*. 1949, Primrose
Eda, da. of Sir John Karslake Thomas Buchan-Hepburn, 5th Bt., and has issue living, Rosemary
Evelyn Sybil Burke, *b*. 1951. *Residence*,—Ynysfor, Penrhyndeudraeth, Merionethshire.

PREDECESSORS.—[1] EDMUND BURKE Roche, *b*. 1815 ; *M.P*. for co. Cork (*L*) 1837-55, and for
Marylebone 1859-65, and Lord Lieut. for co. Cork ; cr. *Baron Fermoy* (peerage of Ireland) 1856:
m. 1848, Elizabeth Caroline, who *d*. 1897, dau. of James B. Boothby, Esq., of Twyford Abbey,
near Acton; *d*. 1874 ; *s*. by his son [2] EDWARD FITZ EDMUND BURKE, 2nd Baron, *b*. 1850 ;
m. 1877, the Hon. Cecilia O'Grady, who *d*. 1919, dau. of 3rd Viscount Guillamore ; *d*. 1920 ;
s. by his brother [3] JAMES BOOTHBY BURKE, 3rd Baron, *b*. 1852 : *m*. 1880, Frances, who *d*.
1947 (divorced 1891, on her petition to Superior Court, Wilmington, Delaware. U.S.A.), dau. of
F. Work, of New York ; *d*. 1920 ; *s*. by his el. son [4] EDMUND MAURICE, 4th Baron ; *b*. 1885 ; sat
as M.P. for King's Lynn Div. of Norfolk (*U*) 1924-35, and 1943-5, and was Mayor of King's Lynn
1931-32: *m*. 1931, Ruth Sylvia, *CVO*, *OBE*, da. of the late Col. William Smith Gill, CB, VD, of
Dalhebity, Bieldside, Aberdeenshire; *d*. 1955; *s*. by his only son [5] EDMUND JAMES BURKE, 5th
Baron and present peer.

Ferrard, Viscount, see Viscount Massereene and Ferrard.

FERRERS, EARL. (Shirley.) [Earl G.B. 1711, Bt. E. 1611.]

Honour is the reward of virtue.

ROBERT WASHINGTON SHIRLEY, 13th Earl,
and 19th Baronet; *b*. June 8th, 1929; *s*. 1954:
ed. at Winchester, and at Magdalene Coll.,
Camb. (M.A. Agriculture); late Lieut.
Coldstream Guards; Malaya 1950; a Lord-
in-Waiting to HM 1962-64, and again 1971-74,
and Parl. Sec. Min. of Agric., Fisheries and
Food Jan. to March 1974; a Trustee of E.
Anglian Trustee Savings Bank (Vice-Chm.
since 1971); a Member of Council, Hurstpierpoint Coll. 1959-68: *m*. 1951, Annabel Mary,
da. of Brig. William Greenwood Carr, CVO,
DSO, of Ditchingham Hall, Norfolk, and has
issue.

Arms,—Paly of six or and azure, a quarter ermine.
Crest,—A Saracen's head in profile, couped at the neck,
proper, wreathed round the temples or and azure. *Supporters*.—*Dexter*, a talbot ermine, the ears
gules, and ducally gorged or ; *sinister*, a reindeer gules, attired and ducally gorged or, billettée and
charged on the shoulder with a horse-shoe argent.
Seat,—Shirley, Brailsford, Derbyshire. *Residence*,—Hedenham Hall, Bungay, Suffolk.

SONS LIVING.
ROBERT WILLIAM SASWALO, (*Viscount Tamworth*), *b*. Dec. 29th, 1952.
Hon. Andrew John Carr Sewallis, *b*. 1965.

DAUGHTERS LIVING.
Lady Angela Mary, *b*. 1954: *m*. 1975; Jonathan Felix Hugo Ellison.
Lady Sallyanne Margaret, *b*. 1957. *Lady* Selina Clare, *b*. 1958.

SISTERS LIVING.
Lady Elizabeth Hermione, *b*. 1923; formerly with WRNS: *m*. 1959, John Fownes Luttrell, of Water-
wynch, Itchen Abbas, nr. Winchester [Ogilvy-Wedderburn, Bt.], and has issue living, Robert Hugh
Courtenay, *b*. 1961.
Lady Jane Penelope Justice, *b*. 1925: *m*. 1944, the Rev. John Maurice Robson, T.D., R. of Brailsford,
and V. of Shirley, Derbyshire, and Rural Dean of Ashbourne, Derbyshire, and has issue living,
David Edward Shirley, *b*. 1947: *m*. 1973, Carol Diana, yr. da. of the late Wilfrid Durose,—Julia
Phillida Shirley, *b*. 1953: *m*. 1972, James Douglas Jermain. *Residence*,—The Rectory, Brailsford,
Derbyshire.

AUNT LIVING. (*Daughter of* 11th *Earl*.)
Lady Phillida, *b*. 1896: is a Nun.

WIDOW LIVING OF SON OF ELEVENTH EARL.
Ethel Muriel, dau. of the late John Henry David Ellis Lewis : *m*. 1927, the Hon. Andrew Shirley,
who *d*. 1958, and has issue living [see colls., infra]. *Residence*,—33A, Highshore Rd., S.E.15.

COLLATERAL BRANCHES LIVING.
Issue of the late Hon. Andrew Shirley, younger son of 11th Earl, *b*. 1900, *d*. 1958 : *m*. 1927,
Ethel Muriel (ante), dau. of the late John Henry David Ellis Lewis:—

Mary Teresa, *b*. (Dec.) 1927. *Residence*,—33, Highshore Rd., S.E.15.
Grandchildren of the late Sewallis Evelyn Shirley (infra):—
Issue of the late Lieut.-Col. Evelyn Charles Shirley, *b*. 1889, *d*. 1956 : *m*. 1921, Kathleen Mary
Phillis (of Harristown House, Ardee, co. Louth), dau. of the late Lieut.-Col. George
Ambrose Cardew, O.M.G., D.S.O. :—
John Evelyn, *b*. 1922; ed. at Eton; Major (ret.) King's Roy. Rifle Corps; 1939-45 War: *m*. 1952,
Judith Margaret, younger dau. of Sir William Francis Stratford Dugdale, 1st Bt. (*cr*. 1936), and has

Issue living, Philip Evelyn, b. 1955,—Hugh Sewallis, b. 1961,—Emily Margaret, b. 1957. Seats,— Ettington Park, Stratford-on-Avon; Lough Fea, Carrickmacross, co. Monaghan.——Mary Louisa Phyllis, b. 1931.

Granddaughters of the late Evelyn Philip Shirley, son of the late Evelyn John Shirley, M.P., D.C.L., son of the late Evelyn Shirley (infra):—
Issue of the late Sewallis Evelyn Shirley, b. 1844, d. 1904: m. 1884, Emily Jeane, who d. 1918, dau. of the late Col. William Macdonald Colquhoun Farquharson Macdonald, of St. Martin's Abbey, Perth:—
Emily Phyllis, b. 1893: m. 1916, her cousin, Capt. Wilfrid Herbert Cecil Brownlow, Northumberland Fusiliers, who d. (killed in action during European War, 1918).——Winifred Mary Frances, b. 1894: m. 1929, Lt.-Col. Julius Francis Chenevix Trench, DSO, OBE, DL, who d. 1948, formerly Comdg. 1st Batn. Northumberland Fusiliers [B. Ashtown, colls.]. Residence,—7, Alexander Sq., SW3.

Granddaughters of the late Rev. William Shirley, son of the late Rev. Arthur George Sewallis Shirley, son of the late Evelyn Shirley, son of the late Hon. George Shirley, 5th surviving son of 1st Earl:—
Issue of the late Col. Sewallis Robert Shirley, MC, b. 1885, d. 1969: m. 1st, 1917, Hilda Grace, da. of Harry Gavin Young, formerly Indian Army; 2ndly, 1940, Edna Blodwen (7, Minster House, Abbey Park Park Rd., Beckenham, Kent), da. of Albert William Laking:—
(By 1st. m.) Eileen Diana, b. 1922: m. 1946, Malcolm Young, of Yeddinges, Woldingham, Surrey, and has issue living, Peter Malcolm Gavin, b. 1947,—Richard William Shirley, b. 1949.——(by 2nd m.) Anne Devereux, b. 1943: m. 1962, Richard Norman Notley, Capt. R. Hampshire Regt. (c/o Barclays Bank, 10, The Square, Petersfield, Hants.), and has issue living, John Norman Devereux, b. 1964,—Diana Phillida, b. 1966.

PREDECESSORS.—[1] GEORGE Shirley; cr. a Baronet 1611; d. 1622; s. by his son [2] Sir HENRY, 2nd Bt.: m. Lady Dorothy, dau. of Robert Devereux, 2nd Earl of Essex (cr. 1572), who became on the death of her brother, Robert, the 3rd and last Earl, youngest co-heir to the Baronies of Ferrers of Chartley, and Bourchier; d. 1632; s. by his el. son [3] Sir CHARLES, 3rd Bt.; d. unmarried 1646; s. by his brother [4] Sir ROBERT, 4th Bt.; d. a prisoner in the Tower, where he had been committed by Cromwell; s. by his el. son [5] Sir SEYMOUR, 5th Bt.: s. at birth by his posthumous son [6] ROBERT, 6th Bt.; d. an infant; s. by his uncle [7] Sir ROBERT, 7th Bt., in whose favour, in 1677, Charles II. terminated the abeyance of one of the peerages of which his grandmother was co-heir (see ante), he thus became Baron Ferrers of Chartley (peerage of England) cr. 1299 [see infra *₊*], while his right to the Barony of Bourchier, cr. 1342, was overlooked; cr. Viscount Tamworth, and Earl Ferrers (peerage of Great Britain) 1711; d. 1717, when the Barony of Ferrers of Chartley, reverted to his granddau. [see infra *₊°*], and the viscountcy and earldom passed to his 2nd son [8] WASHINGTON, 2nd Earl; Lord-Lieut. of Staffordshire; d.s.p.; s. by his brother [9] HENRY, 3rd Earl; d. unmarried 1745; s. by his nephew [10] LAURENCE, 4th Earl, son of the Hon. Laurence, 3rd surviving son of 1st Earl; having in a paroxysm of rage killed Mr. Johnson, his land-steward, was tried and condemned for murder, and executed at Tyburn May 5th, 1760; s. by his brother [11] WASHINGTON, 5th Earl; Vice-Adm.; d.s.p. 1778; s. by his brother [12] ROBERT, 6th Earl; d. 1787; s. by his son [13] ROBERT, 7th Earl; d.s.p. 1827; s. by his brother [14] WASHINGTON, 8th Earl; d. 1842; s. by his grandson [15] WASHINGTON SEWALLIS, 9th Earl, son of Robert William, Viscount Tamworth, el. son of 8th Earl: m. 1844, Lady Augusta Annabella Chichester, who d. 1914, dau. of the 4th Marquess of Donegall; d. 1859; s. by his son [16] SEWALLIS EDWARD, 10th Earl, b. 1847: m. 1885, Lady Ina Maude White, who d. 1907, dau. of 3rd Earl of Bantry (ext.); d. 1912; s. by his kinsman [17] WALTER KNIGHT (great-great grandson of the Rev. the Hon. Walter Shirley, brother of 4th, 5th and 6th Earls), 11th Earl, b. 1864: m. 1890, Mary Jane, who d. 1944, dau. of the late Robert Moon, Bar.-at-law of 10, Prince's Gardens, S.W.: d. 1937; s. by his son [18] ROBERT WALTER, 12th Earl; b. 1894; m. 1922, Hermoine Justice, who d. 1969, da. of the late A. Noel Morley; d. 1954; s. by his only son [19] ROBERT WASHINGTON, 13th Earl and present peer; also Viscount Tamworth.

₊ [1] JOHN de Ferrers, only son of Robert de Ferrers, 8th and last Earl of Derby (cr. 1138) whose title was forfeited, was summoned to Parliament as Baron Ferrers of Chartley, co. Stafford 1299; d. 1312; s. by his son [2] ROBERT, 2nd Baron; summoned to Parliament 1342; s. by his son [3] JOHN, 3rd Baron; never summoned to Parliament; d. 1367; s. by his son [4] ROBERT, 4th Baron; never summoned to Parliament; d. 1413; s. by his son [5] EDMUND, 5th Baron; never summoned to-Parliament; d. 1435; s. by his son [6] WILLIAM, 6th Baron; d. 1450; his da. Anne m. [7] Sir Walter Devereux, who was summoned to Parliament in the dignity of his deceased father-in-law 1461; he d. at Bosworth Field 1485, and was s. by his son [8] JOHN, 8th Baron; summoned to Parliament 1488-95; d. 1499; s. by his son [9] WALTER, 9th Baron; cr. Viscount Hereford [see V. Hereford] in whose family it remained until 1646, when it became abeyant, and remained so until it was terminated in favour of [13] Sir ROBERT Shirley, 7th Bt. (ante); d. 1717; s. by his granddau. [14] ELIZABETH, wife of 5th Earl of Northampton [see M. Northampton].

FERRIER, BARON. (Noel-Paton.) [Life Baron 1958.]

VICTOR FERRIER NOEL-PATON, E.D., son of the late Frederick Waller Ferrier Noel-Paton, of Edinburgh; b. Jan. 29th, 1900; ed. at Edinburgh Acad.; a Member of Queen's Body Guard for Scotland (Roy. Co. of Archers); formerly a MLC Bombay, a Dir. of Imperial Bank of India, and Pres. of Bombay Chamber of Commerce; Maj. (ret.) Bombay Light Horse Aux. Force, India, and Army in India (Reserve), and Hon. ADC to Gov. of Bombay; cr. Baron Ferrier, of Culter, co. Lanark (Life Baron) 1958: m. 1932, Joane Mary, da. of the late Sir Gilbert Wiles, KCIE, CSI, and has issue.

Arms,—Azure a wolf's head erased argent, armed and langued gules, between two crescents in chief and a fleur-de-lys in base or; a bordure argent charged with eight horseshoes sable. Crest,—A dexter hand paleways proper having a passion cross gules on the palm issuant from a crescent or all in front of two doves' wings expanded and erected proper.

Residence,—Bankhead, E. Linton, E. Lothian. Clubs,— Cavalry, Beefsteak, New (Edinburgh).

SON LIVING.

Hon. Frederick Ranald (18, Langford Green, Champion Hill, SE5), *b.* 1938; ed. at Rugby, Haverford Coll., Pa., USA, and McGill Univ.: *m.* 1973, Patricia, da. of the late Gen. Sir William Gurdon Stirling, GCB, CBE, DSO, of Saxham Hall, Bury St. Edmunds, and has issue.

DAUGHTERS LIVING.

Hon. Amanda Mary (*Hon. Lady Fergusson*), *b.* 1933: *m.* 1961, Sir Charles Fergusson, 9th Bt., of Gigmagog, Kilkerran, Maybole, Ayrshire, and has issue.

Hon. Caroline (Kirsty), *b.* 1934: *m.* 1957, Michael Laird, ARIBA, FRIAS, of 22, Moray Place, Edinburgh, 3, and has issue.

Hon. Fiona Margaret, *b.* 1943: *m.* 1967, the Hon. Leslie Bruce Hacking, of Burchetts, Lower Monshill Lane, Milford, Surrey [see B. Hacking].

FEVERSHAM, BARON (Duncombe.) [Baron U.K. 1826.]
[Title pronounced "Fevversham."]

For God, my king, and my country.

(CHARLES ANTONY) PETER DUNCOMBE, 6th Baron; *b.* Jan. 3rd, 1945; *s.* 1963; ed. at Eton; Chm. of Yorks. Arts Assocn., and Standing Conference of Regional Arts Assocns. 1969; author of "A Wolf in Tooth" 1967 and "Great Yachts" 1970: *m.* 1966, Shannon, da. of Sir Thomas Arthur Wyness Foy, CSI, CIS, and has issue.

Arms,—Per chevron engrailed gules and argent three talbots' heads erased, counterchanged. Crest,—Out of a ducal coronet or, a Horse's hind leg sable, hoof upwards, and shod argent. Supporters,—Dexter, a horse of a dark iron gray colour, guttee and ducally gorged or; sinister, a lion argent semée of fleurs-de-lis sable, his head adorned with a plume of six ostrich feathers argent and azure alternatively, issuant from a ducal coronet or. Residence,—Beckdale House, Helmsley, York.

SONS LIVING.

Hon. JASPER ORLANDO SLINGSBY, *b.* March 14th, 1968.

Hon. Jake Barnaby, *b.* 1972.

DAUGHTER LIVING.

Hon. Melissa Rose, *b.* 1973.

DAUGHTER LIVING OF THIRD EARL.

Lady Clarissa, *b.* 1938: *m.* 1966, Nicholas Collin, of Wytherstone House, Pockley, York., and has issue living, Frederick Slingsby, *b.* 1967,—Laura Anne, *b.* 1969.

SISTER LIVING.

Juliet Priscilla Mary, *b.* 1937: *m.* 1960, Wilfred Trevor Woodley, pianist, and has issue living, a da., *b.* 1961.

UNCLE LIVING.

Wilfred George DUNCOMBE-ANDERSON (Hawthorns, White Parish, Salisbury), *b.* Feb. 6th, 1911; ed. at Sherborne, and at Worcester Coll., Oxford; 1939-45 War as Maj. Roy. Corps of Signals (TA): *m.* 1st, 1942, Valerie Pemberton, who *d.* 1969; 2ndly, Mrs. Enid Mary Gabrielle Nicholl, and has issue living, (by 1st m.) David Martin (The Cider House, East Chinnock, Yeovil, Somerset), *b.* 1944: *m.* 1967, Marlene Kathleen, da. of the late Herbert Edwin Peet, and widow of Lt.-Cdr. Earle Peter Weavind, and has issue living, Rachel Katherine Louise *b.* 1972,—Jane Louise Valerie, *b.* 1946: *m.* 1969, Charles Tatton Sykes.

MOTHER LIVING.

Gloranna Georgina Valerie (Knipe's Hall, Helmsley, York), da. of the late Maj. C. E. Irvine McNalty; discontinued by deed poll 1954 for herself and issue the additional surname of Anderson: *m.* 1931, Col. Antony John Duncombe-Anderson, TD, W. Yorks. Regt., who *d.* 1949.

WIDOW LIVING OF THIRD EARL OF FEVERSHAM.

Lady ANNE DOROTHY, *MBE* (*Countess of Feversham*) (Pennyholme, Fadmoor, Yorks.), da. of 1st Earl of Halifax; M.B.E. (Civil) 1950: *m.* 1936, the 3rd Earl of Feversham, who *d.* 1963, when the Earldom became ext.

COLLATERAL BRANCHES LIVING.

Grandchildren of the late Capt. Frederick William Duncombe, 3rd son of the late Adm. the Hon. Arthur Duncombe, 4th son of 1st Baron Feversham:—

Issue of the late Basil Archibald Charles Duncombe, *b.* 1870, *d.* 1930: *m.* 1896, Ida Hope, who *d.* 1935, dau. of the late Alfred Hope Doeg:—

Phyllis Gertrude DUNCOMBE (P.O. Box 189, Wellington, 2820, NSW) *b.* 1897; resumed the surname of Duncombe in lieu of that of Ainsworth-Davis by deed poll 1947: *m.* 1st, 1917, Capt. Cecil Cureton Taylor, formerly York and Lancaster Regt., from whom she obtained a divorce 1930; 2ndly, 1936, John Creyghton Ainsworth-Davis, MD, FRCS, late Wing-Com. RAFVR, from whom she obtained a divorce 1947; 3rdly, 1950, Leslie George Whalan, who *d.* 1969.

Issue of the late Maj. Roland Frederick DUNCOMBE-ANDERSON, *b.* 1908, *d.* (killed in action, 1940): *m.* 1935, Elizabeth Frances (who *m.* 2ndly, 1952, Brig. Howard Greene, OBE, DSO, MC, of Glebe Cottage, Bishopstrow, Warminster, Wilts), da. of the late Algernon Mawson:—

Alastair Guy, *b.* 1938: *m.* 1961, Judith Anne Abbot, and has issue living, Alastair Mark, *b.* 1962,—Nicholas, *b.* 1963,—Timothy Guy, *b.* 1965,—Rebecca Elizabeth, *b.* 1966.

PREDECESSORS.—[1] CHARLES DUNCOMBE, cr. *Baron Feversham* (peerage of United Kingdom) 1826; *d.* 1841; *s.* by his son [2] WILLIAM, 2nd Baron, *b.* 1798; sat as M.P. for Yorkshire 1826-30, and for N. Riding of York (C) 1832-41: *m.* 1823, Lady Louisa Stewart, dau. of 5th Earl of Galloway; *d.* 1867; *s.* by his son [3] WILLIAM, 3rd Baron, *b.* 1829; M.P. for E. Retford (C) 1852-7, and for N. Riding of York 1859-67; cr. *Viscount Helmsley* and *Earl of Feversham* (peerage of United Kingdom) 1868: *m.* 1851, Mabel Violet, who *d.* 1915, dau. of the Rt. Hon. Sir James Graham, G.C.B., P.C., 2nd Bt., of Netherby; *d.* 1915; *s.* by his grandson [4] CHARLES WILLIAM REGINALD (son of the late William Reginald, Viscount Helmsley, el. son of 1st Earl), 2nd Earl, *b.* 1879; Lieut.-Col. King's Roy. Rifle Corps; M.P. for Yorkshire, W. Riding, Thirsk and Malton Div. (C) 1906-15: *m.* 1904, Lady Marjorie Blanche Eva

Greville, dau. of 5th Earl of Warwick ; *d.* (killed in action during European War) 1916 ; *s.* by his el. son [5] CHARLES WILLIAM SLINGSBY, 3rd Earl; *b.* 1906; Lt.-Col. 13th/18th Hussars and Hon. Col. Queen's Own Yorkshire Yeo. 1962-3; a Lord-in-Waiting to H.M. 1934-6, Parl. Sec. Min. of Agriculture and Dep. Min. of Fisheries 1936-9: *m.* 1936, Lady Anne Dorothy Wood, M.B.E., dau. of 1st Earl of Halifax; *d.* 1963 when the Earldom of Feversham and Viscountcy of Helmsley became ext., and the Barony devolved upon [6] (CHARLES ANTONY) PETER (only son of the late Lt.-Col. Anthony John Duncombe-Anderson, T.D., grandson of the late Capt. Frederick William Duncombe, 3rd son of the Hon. Arthur Duncombe, 4th son of 1st Baron), 6th Baron and present peer.

FFRENCH, BARON.   (ffrench.)   [Baron I. 1798, Bt. I. 1779.]

PETER MARTIN JOSEPH CHARLES JOHN FFRENCH, 7th Baron, and 8th Baronet ; *b.* May 2nd, 1926 ; *s.* 1955 : *m.* 1954, Katherine Sonia, da. of the late Maj. Digby Coddington Cayley, late King's Own Scottish Borderers [see Cayley, Bt., colls.], and has issue.

Arms,—Ermine, a chevron sable. **Crest,**—A dolphin embowed proper. **Supporters,**—*Dexter*, a falcon gules, armed, membered, belled, and wings inverted or ; *sinister,* an unicorn gules, armed, unguled, crined, and tufted or, and in its mouth a rose branch thereon, two red roses proper.

I had rather die than be dishonoured.   *Seat,*—Castle ffrench, Ballinasloe, co. Galway.

SON LIVING.

Hon. ROBUCK JOHN PETER CHARLES MARIO, *b.* March 14th, 1956.

DAUGHTERS LIVING.

Hon. Rose Sophia Iris Mary, *b.* 1957.
Hon. Clare Katherine Grace Mary, *b.* 1958.

BROTHER LIVING.

John Charles Mary Joseph Francis (Stockbridge, Mass., USA), *b.* 1928: *m.* 1963, Sara-Primm, da. of James A. Turner, of Stockbridge, Mass., USA, and has issue living, Johanna Felicitas *b.* 1964,— Teodora Crispina, *b.* 1965,—Dorcas Sofia, *b.* 1967.

SISTERS LIVING.

Freida Dora Katherine Mary Josephine, *b.* 1916 : *m.* 1946, Hans Vajda, and has issue living. *Residence,*—16, Wakefield Rd., Tottenham, N.15.
Katherine Mary Margaret Frances Josephine, *b.* 1917 : *m.* 1935, Lieut. Christopher Valerio Edward Paul Banon, R.N., and has issue living. *Residence,*—Glenhaven, Gisbowne, Vic., Aust.
Ellen Frances Anna Maria Josephine, *b.* 1918 : *m.* 1946, Thomas Anderson Courtenay Agnew. *Residence,*—Cregmore, Ardrahan, co. Galway.

MOTHER LIVING.

Sofia, dau. of the late Signor Giovanni Brambilla, of Villa Sucota, Como, Italy : *m.* 1915, Capt. the Hon. John Martin Valentine ffrench, who *d.* 1946. *Residence,*—Castle ffrench, Ballinasloe, co. Galway.

PREDECESSORS.—[1] CHARLES ffrench ; cr. a *Baronet* 1779 ; *d.* 1784 ; his widow, Rose, was in 1798 cr. by patent *Baroness ffrench*, of Castle ffrench, co. Galway (peerage of Ireland), with remainder to the heirs male of her body, by her husband Sir Charles ffrench, Bt.; she *d.* 1805 ; *s.* by her son [2] THOMAS, 2nd Baron, who had in 1784 *s.* his father as 2nd Bt.; *d.* 1814; *s.* by his son [3] CHARLES AUSTIN, 3rd Baron, *b.* 1786: *m.* 1809, Maria, el. dau. of John Browne, of Moyne, co. Galway; *d.* 1860 ; *s.* by his son [4] THOMAS, 4th Baron, *b.* 1810 : *m.* 1851, Mary Anne, who *d.* 1906, dau. and heiress of Richard Thompson, of Stansty Hall, Wrexham ; *d.* 1892 ; *s.* by his brother [5] MARTIN JOSEPH, 5th Baron, *b.* 1813 ; Resident Magistrate for co. Tipperary 1846-82: *m.* 1862, Catherine Mary Anne, who *d.* 1908, only dau. of John O'Shaughnessy, of Birchgrove, co. Roscommon; *d.* 1893; *s.* by his el. son [6] CHARLES AUSTIN THOMAS ROBERT JOHN JOSEPH, 6th Baron ; *b.* 1868 : *m.* 1st, 1892, Mary Margaret, who *d.* 1944, el. dau. of Matthew J. Corbally, J.P., D.L., of Rathbeal Hall, near Swords, co. Dublin ; 2ndly, 1951, Catherine Elizabeth, who *d.* 1960, youngest dau. of the Rt. Hon. Sir Christopher John Nixon, M.D., LL.D., 1st Bt. ; *d.* 1955 ; *s.* by his nephew [7] PETER MARTIN JOSEPH CHARLES JOHN (el. son of the late Capt. the Hon. John Martin Valentine ffrench, younger son of 5th Baron) 7th Baron and present peer.

FIFE, DUKE OF.   (Carnegie.)   [Duke U.K. 1900.]

JAMES GEORGE ALEXANDER BANNERMAN CARNEGIE, 3rd Duke; *b.* Sept. 23rd, 1929 ; *s.* 1959 ; ed. at Gordonstoun ; is *h.a.* to E. of Southesk, a Freeman of City of London, and a Liveryman of Clothworkers' Co. ; Malaya 1948-50 with Scots Guards : *m.* 1956, (m. diss. 1966) the Hon. Caroline Cecily Dewar, el. dau. of 3rd Baron Forteviot, and has issue.

Arms,—Quarterly, 1st grand quarter, or, a lion rampant gules, armed and langued azure, *Dukedom of Fife* ; 2nd grand quarter, counter quartered, 1st and 4th gules, three lions passant guardant in pale or, *England*, 2nd, or, a lion rampant within a double tressure flory counter-flory gules, *Scotland*, 3rd, azure a harp or, stringed argent, *Ireland* ; differenced by a label of five points argent, the points charged with two thistles between three crosses of St. George gules, *Princess Royal, Duchess of Fife, el. daughter of King Edward VII* ; 3rd grand quarter, counter-quartered, 1st and 4th, vert, a fess dancettée ermine between a hart's head cabossed in chief and two escallops in base or, *Duff of Braco* ; 2nd and 3rd, gules, three skeans paleways argent hafted and pommelled or, surmounted of as many wolves' heads couped of the third, *Skene of that Ilk* ; 4th grand quarter, gules, a banner displayed argent charged with a canton azure, a saltire of the second *Bannerman of Elsick*; over all an inescutcheon ensigned of an Earl's coronet, argent, an eagle displayed azure, armed, beaked, and membered gules, on its breast an antique covered cup or differenced as Master of Southesk by a label of three points gules, *Carnegie*. Crests,—*Centre*, a thunderbolt proper, winged or, *Carnegie* ; *dexter*, a knight denoting the ancient MacDuff armed at all points on a horse in full speed, in his dexter hand a sword erected all proper, his jupon argent, on his sinister arm a shield or charged with a lion rampant gules, the visor of his helmet shut, over which, on a wreath of his liveries with a long mantling flowing therefrom behind him and ending in a tassel of the fourth, the doubling of the third is set a lion rampant issuing out of the wreath of the third and fourth, the caparisons of the horse gules, fimbriated or and thereon six shields of the last, each charged with a lion rampant of the fourth, *Dukedom of Fife* ; *sinister*, a man is armour issuing from the loins and wearing a tabard emblazoned of the arms, argent on a fess between three boars' heads erased gules three mascles or, sustaining with his dexter hand a banner developed argent having a canton azure charged with a saltire of the first, Ethel, *Countess of Southesk*. Supporters,—*Dexter*, a lion rampant guardant gules, langued azure, charged with a label of five points argent, the points charged with two thistles between three crosses of St. George gules ; *Sinister*, a talbot argent collared gules, the collar charged with a label of three points argent.

Residence,—Elsick House, Stonehaven, Kincardine. *Clubs*,—Turf, Pratt's, Royal Northern (Aberdeen).

SON LIVING.
DAVID CHARLES (*Earl of Macduff*), *b*. March 3rd, 1961.
DAUGHTER LIVING.
Lady Alexandra Clare, *b*. 1959.

PREDECESSORS.—[1] WILLIAM Duff, *M.P.* for Banffshire 1727-34; cr. *Baron Braco*, of Kilbryde, co. Cavan (peerage of Ireland) 1735, and *Viscount Macduff*, and *Earl Fife* (peerage of Ireland) 1759 ; *d*. 1763 ; *s*. by his el. son [2] JAMES, 2nd Earl; cr. *Baron Fife* (peerage of Great Britain) 1790 ; *d*. 1809, when the Barony of Fife expired, and the Irish honours devolved upon his brother [3] ALEXANDER, 3rd Earl; *d*. 1811; *s*. by his son [4] JAMES, *K.T., G.C.H.*, 4th Earl; a Maj.-Gen. in the Spanish Army during the Peninsular War, MP 1818-26, Lord Lieut. of co. Banff, and a Lord of the Bedchamber; cr. *Baron Fife* (peerage of United Kingdom) 1827; *d*. 1857, when the Barony of Fife expired, and the Irish honours reverted to his nephew [5] JAMES, *K.T.*, 5th Earl, son of Gen. the Hon. Sir Alexander, 2nd son of 3rd Earl; *b*. 1814; M.P. for Banffshire (*L*) 1837-57, Lord-Lieut. of co. Banff 1856-7; cr. *Baron Skene* (peerage of United Kingdom) 1857 ; *d*. 1879 ; *s*. by his son [6] ALEXANDER WILLIAM GEORGE, *K.G., K.T., G.C.V.O., P.C.*, 6th Earl ; *b*. 1849 ; cr. *Earl of Fife* (peerage of United Kingdom) 1885, *Duke of Fife and Marquess of Macduff*, of co. Banff (peerage of United Kingdom) July 29th, 1889, and *Earl of Macduff*, of co. Banff, and *Duke of Fife* (peerage of United Kingdom) 1900, with remainder to the heirs male of his body by his marriage with H.R.H. Princess Louise, and in default of such issue (1) to their el. dau. (*Princess* Alexandra) and her heirs male, (2) in default of such issue to their younger dau. (*Princess* Maud) and her heirs male, and (3) in default of such issue to each of the after-born daus. by H.R.H. Princess Louise and the heirs male of the body and respective bodies of such daus. severally and successively, one after another, as they shall be in seniority of age and priority of birth ; Lord-Lieut. and Custos Rotulorum of co. London ; Lord-Lieut. of Elginshire 1871-1901 ; M.P. for Elgin and Nairn (*L*) 1874-9 ; Capt. and Gold Stick of Corps of Gentlemen-at-Arms 1880-81; acted as Lord High Constable at Coronations of King Edward VII and King George V; had Royal Victorian Chain: *m*, July 27th, 1889, H.R.H. Princess Louise Victoria Alexandra Dagmar (*the Princess Royal*), who *d*. 1931, el. dau. of King Edward VII. [see "ROYAL FAMILY"]; *d*. 1912, when the Irish Honours (Barony of Braco, cr. 1735, and Viscountcy of Macduff and Earldom of Fife, cr. 1759) became dormant or ext., and the Barony of Skene 1857, Earldom of Fife, cr. 1885, and Dukedom of Fife and Marquessate of Macduff, cr. 1889, became ext., while the peerages cr. 1900 devolved under the special remainder upon his el. dau. [7] *H.H. Princess* ALEXANDRA VICTORIA ALBERTA EDWINA LOUISE, *R.R.C.* ; *b*. 1891 ; a G.C.St.J. ; appointed Col.-in-Ch. R.A.P.C. 1939 ; acted as a Counsellor of State during H.M.'s absence abroad 1939, 1943, and 1944 : *m*. 1913, Maj.-Gen. H.R.H. Prince Arthur Frederick Patrick Albert of Connaught, K.G., P.C., K.T., G.C.M.G., G.C.V.O., who *d*. 1938, only son of H.R.H. the 1st Duke of Connaught and Strathearn ; *d*. 1959 ; *s*. by her nephew [8] JAMES GEORGE ALEXANDER BANNERMAN Carnegie (*Lord Carnegie*) (only son of 11th Earl of Southesk and H.H. the late Princess Maud Alexandra Victoria Georgina Bertha, younger dau. of 1st Duke), 3rd Duke, and present peer : also Earl of Macduff.

FINGALL, EARL OF. (Plunkett.) Sits as BARON (U.K. 1831). [Earl I. 1628.]
[Title pronounced "Fingawl."]

OLIVER JAMES HORACE PLUNKETT, *M.C.*, 12th Earl ; *b*. June 17th, 1896 ; *s*. 1929; ed. at Downside Coll., and at R.M.C. ; is Major (retired) 17th/21st Lancers ; European War 1915-18 (MC), 1939-45 War: *m*. 1st, 1926, Jessica, who *d*. 1965, da. of the late Allan Hughes, of Lynch, Allerford, Somerset; 2ndly, 1966, Clair, widow of Frank Richardson, of Geelong, Victoria, Australia.

Arms,—Sable, a bend, and in sinister chief a tower argent. Crest,—A horse passant argent. Supporters.— *Dexter*, a pegasus, per fesse or and argent , *sinister*, an ibex or heraldic antelope argent, armed, maned, tufted, collared, and chained or.

Residence,—The Common, Dunsany, co. Meath.

Quick without impetuosity.

PREDECESSORS.—[1] *Sir* CHRISTOPHER Plunkett, Knt., became in 1403, in right of his wife proprietor of the Barony of Killeen ; *d*. about 1441 ; *s*. by his grandson [2] CHRISTOPHER, *K.B*. (son of John Plunkett, son of Sir Christopher Plunkett), cr. *Baron Killeen* (peerage of Ireland) 1449: *m*. circa 1432, Joan Bellew, *d*. circa 1455 : *s*. by his el. son [3] CHRISTOPHER, 2nd Baron; summoned to Parliaments of 1493 and 1498 : *m.* before 1464, Elizabeth, dau. and co-heir of Sir William Welles, Lord Chancellor, *d.s.p.* 1467; *s.* by his brother [4] EDMUND, 3rd Baron; *s.* by his son [5] JOHN, P.C., K.B., 4th Baron; *s.* by his son [6] CHRISTOPHER, 5th Baron; summoned to Parliament 1509; *s.* by his brother [7] JAMES, 6th Baron; summoned to Parliament 1585; *s.* by his son [8] CHRISTOPHER, 7th Baron; summoned to Parliament 1613; *s.* by his son [9] LUCAS, 8th Baron; *cr. Earl of Fingall* (peerage of Ireland) 1628; *d.* 1637; *s.* by his son [10] CHRISTOPHER, 2nd Earl; taken prisoner at battle of Rathmines 1649, and *d.* in Dublin Castle ten days afterwards; *s.* by his son [11] LUKE, 3rd Earl; restored to his honours and estates; *s.* by his son [12] PETER, 4th Earl; was outlawed 1691-7 for his loyalty to James II.; *s.* by his son [13] JUSTIN, 5th Earl; *d.s.p.*; *s.* by his cousin [14] ROBERT, 6th Earl, grandson of the Hon. George, 2nd son of 1st Earl; *d.* 1738; *s.* by his son [15] ARTHUR JAMES, 7th Earl; *d.* 1793; *s.* by his son [16] ARTHUR JAMES, K.P., 8th Earl; *cr. Baron Fingall,* of Woolhampton, co. Berks (peerage of United Kingdom) 1831; *d.* 1836; *s.* by his son [17] ARTHUR JAMES, K.P., P.C., 9th Earl; Lord-Lieut. of co. Meath, and a Lord-in-Waiting to H.M. Queen Victoria; *d.* 1869; *s.* by his son [18] ARTHUR JAMES, 10th Earl; *b.* 1819: *m.* 1857, Elise Mary, dau. of Mons. Francis Alexis Rio; *d.* 1881; *s.* by his son [19] ARTHUR JAMES FRANCIS, P.C., 11th Earl, *b.* 1859: State Steward to Viceroy of Ireland (Earl Spencer) 1882-5, and Master of the Horse to Lord-Lieut. of Ireland (Earl of Dudley) 1905: *m.* 1883, Elizabeth Mary, who *d.* 1944, dau. of the late George Edmund Burke, J.P., of Danesfield, co. Galway; *d.* 1929; *s.* by his el. son [20] OLIVER JAMES HORACE, 12th Earl and present peer, also Baron Killeen, and Baron Fingall.

FINLAY, VISCOUNTCY OF. (Finlay.) [Extinct 1945.]

DAUGHTER LIVING OF SECOND VISCOUNT.

Hon. Rosalind Mary (*Hon. Lady Hayes*), *b.* 1914 : *m.* 1939, Vice-Adm. Sir John Osler Chattock Hayes, KCB, OBE, and has issue living, Colin John Finlay, *b.* 1943: *m.* 1969, Rosemary Lucie, da. of the Rev. Canon Herbert Naunton Bates, of Blaxhall, Woodbridge, Suffolk, and has issue living, Alexander Finlay *b.* 1971,—Malcolm Lionel FitzRoy, *b.* 1951,—Griselda Mary, *b.* 1954. *Residence,—* Arabella House, by Tain, Ross-shire.

FINTRIE, LORD, grandson of DUKE OF MONTROSE.

FISHER, BARON. (Fisher.) [Baron U.K. 1909.]

JOHN VAVASSEUR FISHER, *D.S.C.,* 3rd Baron; *b.* July 24th, 1921; *s.* 1955; ed. at Stowe, and at Trin. Coll., Camb. (BA); sometime Lieut. RNVR; 1941-45 War (DSC); JP and DL of Norfolk: *m.* 1st, 1949 (m. diss. 1969), Elizabeth Ann Penelope, da. of the late Maj. Herbert Holt, MC, of Nassau, Bahamas; 2ndly, 1970, the Hon. Rosamund Ann Clifford, da. of 12th Baron Clifford of Chudleigh, and formerly wife of Geoffrey Forrester Fairbairn, and has issue by 1st m.

Arms,—Argent, in chief two demi-lions rampant erased gules, and in base the stern of an ancient battleship showing three lanterns proper. Crest,—A dexter hand in mail armour couped at the wrist grasping the head of a trident erect all proper. Supporters,— On either side a sailor of the Royal Navy supporting in the exterior hand an anchor cabled, that to the dexter in bend sinister and that to the sinister in bend dexter, all proper.

Seat,—Kilverstone Hall, Thetford. *Residence,—*Marklye, Rushlake Green, Heathfield, Sussex.

SONS LIVING. (*By 1st m.*).
Hon. PATRICK VAVASSEUR, *b.* June 14th, 1953.
Hon. Benjamin Vavasseur, *b.* 1958.

DAUGHTERS LIVING. (*By 1st m.*).
Hon. Frances Alice, *b.* 1951.
Hon. Bridget Ann, *b.* 1956.

SISTERS LIVING.

Hon. Anna, *b.* 1916: *m.* 1936, Thomas Williams Clark, M.D., and has issue living, Frederic William *b.* 1939,—Hugh Roberts, *b.* 1948,—Jane Morgan, *b.* 1940,—Elizabeth Clark, *b.* 1946. *Residence,—* 6, Moreland Circle, Philadelphia, Pa., USA 19118.
Hon. Katharine(*Baroness Clifford of Chudleigh*), *b.* 1919 : *m.* 1945, 13th Baron Clifford of Chudleigh. *Residence,—*Ugbrooke Park, Chudleigh, S. Devon.
Hon. Barbara, *b.* 1925: *m.* 1961, Leslie Charles Croft Buswell, and has issue living, Gerald John Croft, *b.* 1965,—Pamela Gwendolyn, *b,* 1968. *Residences,—*St. Peter's House, Jersey; Seaton Farm, Stellenbosch, S. Africa.

PREDECESSORS.—[1] *Adm. of the Fleet Sir* JOHN ARBUTHNOT Fisher, *G.C.B., O.M., G.C.V.O., LL.D.,* son of Capt. William Fisher, 78th Highlanders; *b.* 1841; Adm. of the Fleet; Director of Naval Ordnance 1887-91, Adm. Sup. of Portsmouth Dockyard 1891-2, a Lord of the Admiralty and Controller of the Navy 1892-7, Com.-in-Ch. on N. American and W. Indies Station 1897-9, and of Mediterranean Fleet 1899-1902, Second Lord of the Admiralty 1902-3, Com.-in-Ch. at Portsmouth 1903-4, Principal Naval A.D.C. to H.M. 1904-11, First Sea Lord of the Admiralty 1904-10, and again First Sea Lord of the Admiralty 1914-15; *cr. Baron Fisher,* of Kilverstone, co. Norfolk (peerage of United Kingdom) 1909 : *m.* 1866, Frances Katharine Josepha, who *d.* 1918, only dau. of the late Rev. Thomas Delves-Broughton; *d.* 1920; *s.* by his only son [2] CECIL, 2nd Baron; *b.* 1868; assumed by Roy. licence 1909 the additional name of Vavasseur: *m.* 1910, Jane, who *d.* 1955, dau. of Randal Morgan, of Chestnut Hill, Philadelphia, U.S.A., *d.* 1955; *s.* by his only son [3] JOHN VAVASSEUR, 3rd Baron and present peer.

FISHER OF CAMDEN, BARON. (Fisher.) [Life Baron 1974.]

SAMUEL FISHER, son of Barnett Fisher, of London; *b.* Jan. 20th, 1905; ed. at Myrdle Sch., London; Accountant; FCIS; Vice-Pres. of London Diamond Bourse; Pres. Board of Deputies of British Jews since 1973 (Snr. Vice-Pres. 1967-73); Mayor of Stoke Newington 1953-54, and Camden 1965-66; Chm. Metropolitan Water Board, and Chm. Magistrate, W. Central Div., and London Labour Mayors' Assocn.; a JP for Inner London; cr. Knt. 1967, and *Baron Fisher of Camden,* of Camden in Greater London (Life Baron) 1974: *m.* 1930, Millie, da. of Isaac Gluckstein, of London, and has issue.

Residence,—48, Viceroy Court, Prince Albert Rd., NW8 7PR.

DAUGHTER LIVING.
Hon. Marilyn Ruth, *b.* 1940; BA: *m.* 1960, Mervyn Taylor, solicitor, of 4, Springfield Rd., Templeogue, Dublin.

FISHER OF LAMBETH, BARONY. (Fisher.) [Extinct 1972.]

SONS LIVING OF LIFE BARON.
Hon. Sir Henry Arthur Pears, *b.* 1918; ed. at Marlborough and Ch. Ch., Oxford (MA); is Fellow of All Souls Coll., Oxford; Bar. Inner Temple 1947, and a QC 1960; Recorder of Canterbury (1962-67); Chm. of Bar Council 1966-68; a Judge of High Court of Justice (Queen's Bench Div.) 1968-70; Pres. of Wolfson Coll., Oxford, since 1975; a Dir. of Schroder Wagg, and Thomas Tilling; formerly Lt.-Col. R. Leics. Regt.; Burma 1944-45 (despatches); Knt. 1968: *m.* 1948, Felicity, da. of the late Eric Sutton, of 15, Cheyne Pl., SW3, and has issue. *Residence,*—Linchmere House, nr. Haslemere, Surrey.
Hon. Francis Forman, *M.C., b.* 1919 ; ed. at Repton, and at Clare Coll., Camb. (B.A. 1947, M.A. 1951); MA Oxford 1955; late Maj. Sherwood Foresters, TA (Reserve), Warden of St. Edward's Sch., Oxford 1954-66, and Master of Wellington Coll., since 1966; sometime Assist. Master of Repton; 1939-45 War in N. Africa (prisoner, escaped, MC). *Residence,*—The Master's Lodge, Wellington Coll., Crowthorne, Berks.
Hon. Charles Douglas (The Headmaster's House, Geelong Grammer School, Corio, Vic., Aust.), *b.* 1921; ed. at Marlborough, and at Keble Coll., Oxford (MA); late Maj. RA (Res.); an Assist. Master at Harrow 1948-55, at Peterhouse, Rhodesia 1955-61, at Sherborne 1961-2, Headmaster of Scotch Coll., Adelaide 1963-69, and of C. of E. Gram. Sch., Brisbane, 1970-73, and of Geelong Ch. of England Gram. Sch. since 1974; Middle East and Italy 1942-45: *m.* 1952, Anne Gilmour, only da. of the late Ian S. Hammond, of Chidikamwedzi, Umvukwes, Rhodesia, and has issue.
Hon. Humphrey Richmond, *b.* 1923 ; ed. at Repton ; formerly Lieut. R.A. ; a Film Technician and Producer 1946-54, Exec. Producer BBO Television 1954-64, Representative in Aust. and NZ 1964-67, and Head of Science and Features, BBC Television 1967-69, since when Dir. of Television Features Aust. Broadcasting Commn.: *m.* 1959, Diana Beresford, da. of C. Beresford Davis. *Residence,*—32, South St., Edgecliff, N.S.W. 2027, Australia.
Hon. Geoffrey Robert Chevallier, *b.* 1926 ; ed. at Repton, and at Emmanuel Coll., Camb. (B.A. 1947, M.B. and B.Chir. 1949) ; D. (Obst.) R.C.O.G. 1952 ; Surg. Lieut. R.N. (Emergency Reserve): *m.* 1961, Jill Audrey, el. dau. of J. H. Cooper, of 10, Turner Rd., New Malden, Surrey, and has issue. *Residence,*—3, Wendover Drive, New Malden, Surrey.
Hon. Richard Temple (Bilton Grange, Dunchurch, Rugby), *b.* 1930; ed. at St. Edward's Sch., Oxford, and at King's Coll., Camb. (Choral Scholar, MA); Hon. Maj. TA Gen. List, late 16th/5th Queen's R. Lancers; Assist. Master and Housemaster at Repton 1953-69, since when Headmaster of Bilton Grange Prep. Sch.: *m.* 1969, Clare Margaret, da. of J. Lewen Le Fanu, of Newton House, Repton, and has issue.

WIDOW LIVING OF LIFE BARON.
ROSAMOND CHEVALLIER, (*Baroness Fisher of Lambeth*), (Trent Rectory, Sherborne, Dorset), da. of the late Rev. Arthur Francis Emilius Forman: *m.* 1917, the Most Rev. and Rt. Hon. Baron Fisher of Lambeth (Life Peer), who *d.* 1972.

FISHER OF REDNAL, BARONESS. (Fisher.) [Life Baroness 1974.]

DORIS MARY GERTRUDE FISHER, da. of the late Frederick James Satchwell, BEM; *b.* Sept. 13th, 1919; ed. at Tinker's Farm Girls' Sch., Fircroft Coll., and Bournville Day Continuation Coll.; a JP for Birmingham; a City Councillor, Birmingham 1952-74; Nat. Pres. of Co-operative Guild 1961-62; MP for Ladywood Div. of Birmingham (*Lab.*) 1970–74; Member of European Parl., Strasbourg since 1975; cr. *Baroness Fisher of Rednal,* of Rednal in City of Birmingham (Life Baroness) 1974: *m.* 1939, Joseph Fisher, and has issue.

Residence,—36, Irwin Av., Rednal, Birmingham 45.

DAUGHTERS LIVING.
Hon. Pauline Mary, *b.* 1940: *m.* 1961, Michael James Platt, of 2, Shortbutts Lane, Lichfield, Staffs.
Hon. Veronica Mary, *b.* 1945: *m.* 1968, John Adrian Pickering, of 27, Fulton Close, Bromsgrove, Worcs.

Fisherwick, Baron, title of Marquess of Donegall on Roll of H.L.

FISKE, BARON. (Fiske.) [Extinct 1974.]

SON LIVING OF LIFE BARON. (*By 1st. m.*)
Hon. Giles Geoffrey (23, Blenheim Rd., NW8 0LX), *b.* 1935.

DAUGHTER LIVING OF LIFE BARON. (*By 1st m.*)
Hon. Rosemary, *b.* 1931: *m.* 19—, A. Holbrow, of Worcester.

WIDOW LIVING OF LIFE BARON.
JOSEPHINE (*Baroness Fiske*) (23, Blenheim Rd., St. John's Wood, NW8), da. of Alan Coppin, JP, of Hong Kong: *m.* 1955, as his 2nd wife, Baron Fiske (Life Baron), who *d.* 1975.

FITZALAN OF DERWENT, VISCOUNTCY OF. (Fitzalan-Howard.) [Extinct 1962.]

DAUGHTERS LIVING OF SECOND VISCOUNT.
Hon. Alathea Gwendoline Alys Mary, *b.* 1923: *m.* 1953, the Hon. Edward Frederick Ward of 34, Av. des Mousquines, Lausanne, Switzerland [see E. Dudley].
Hon. Elizabeth Anne Marie Gabrielle, *b.* 1934: *m.* 1st, 1952 (m. diss. 1960), Sir Viyan Edward Naylor-Leyland, 3rd Bt.; 2ndly 1975, Stephen Lewis Edmonstone Hastings, MP, of 12A, Ennismore Gdns., SW7.

FITZGERALD, BARONY OF. (FitzGerald.) [Extinct 1889.]
WIDOW LIVING OF SON OF LIFE BARON.
Dorothy (ANDERSON) (of 1, Harbour Close, Haven Rd., Canford Cliffs, Poole), dau. of the late George Walter Constable: *m.* 1936, as his second wife, the Hon. Eustace Robert FitzGerald, who *d.* 1944.

FitzHarris, Viscount, son of Earl of Malmesbury.

FITZWALTER, BARON. (Plumptre.) [Baron E. 1295.]

I will guard.

FITZWALTER BROOK PLUMPTRE, 21st Baron; *b.* Jan. 15th, 1914; *s.* (on termination of abeyance) 1953; ed. at Diocesan Coll., Cape Town, and at Jesus Coll., Camb.; Capt. The Buffs (Reserve), a J.P. for Kent, and a Gov. of King's Sch., Canterbury; European War 1939-45 in N.W. Europe and India: *m.* 1951, Margaret Melesina, younger dau. of Herbert William Deedes, J.P. [B. Ashtown, colls.], and has issue.

Arms,—Argent, a chevron between two mullets pierced in chief, and an annulet in base sable, a crescent sable for difference. Crest,—A phoenix or, out of flames proper. Badge,—An estoile or.

Seat,—Goodnestone Park, Canterbury.

SONS LIVING.
Hon. JULIAN BROOK, *b.* Oct. 18th, 1952; ed. at Radley.
Hon. Henry Bridges, *b.* 1954.
Hon. Wyndham George, *b.* 1956.
Hon. William Edward, *b.* 1959.
Hon. Francis Charles, *b.* 1963.

BROTHER LIVING.
Peter Bridges, *M.B.E.*, *b.* 1916; ed. at Diocesan Coll., Cape Town, and at King's Sch., Canterbury; Major (retired) The Buffs; formerly Capt. RWF, and has issue living, Thomas George Edmund, *b.* 1944, Maude Helen May, dau. of the late Geoffrey Henry Baird, of Goodnestone, Kent, and has issue living, Timothy George, *b.* 1945,—Jeremy Peter, *b.* 1947,—Michael John *b.* 1955,—Rosalin Helen, *b.* 1952. *Address,*—Harford Bridge Caravan Park, Tavistock, S. Devon.

SISTERS LIVING.
Margaretta (Wilan Cottage, Drayton, Banbury, Oxon., OX15 6EH), *b.* 1908.
Judith Patricia (c/o Isle of Man Bank, P.O. Box 13, Douglas, Isle of Man), *b.* 1910.
Elizabeth Mary, *b.* 1912: *m.* 1941, the Rev. Philip Vivian Rogers Pennant, TD, MA, R. of Sutton Bonington, Notts; formerly Capt. RWF, and has issue living, Thomas George Edmund, *b.* 1947, —Philip Pearson, *b.* 1952,—Stephen Owen Falconer, *b.* 1956,—Philippa Berain Elizabeth Plumptre, *b.* 1942: *m.* 1962, Bryan Henry Farr, of Worksop Manor, Worksop, and has issue living, Henry Philip John *b.* 1966, Rosalinde Mary *b.* 1963, Susannah Margaret *b.* 1965,—Sarah Fariana Mary Agnes, *b.* 1944: *m.* 1966, Robert Iain Bescoby Jenkins, of Rose Cottage, Pages Lane, Hornton, Banbury, Oxon., and has issue living, Robert Brook Pennant *b.* 1970, Philip David Alexander *b.* 1971,—Helen Michèle, *b.* 1949. *Residence,*—The Rectory, Sutton Bonington, Loughborough.
Frederica Anne, *b.* 1919: *m.* 1942, Anthony Durnford Gaymer, F.R.I.B.A., late Major R.A., and has issue living, Nigel Anthony Plumptre, *b.* 1944,—Felicity Anne Plumptre, *b.* 1950. *Address,*—P.O. Box 1073, Lusaka, Zambia.

COLLATERAL BRANCHES LIVING.
Grandchildren of the late Margaretta Agnes Wright (infra):—
Issue of the late Edward Fitzwalter Wright, *b.* 1902, *d.* 1957: *m.* 1927, Jane Fairrie Wilson (161, Cranmer Court, SW3), da. of the late Thomas Chalmers McGuffie:—
John Leslie Fitzwalter, *b.* 1934: ed. at Winchester, and at Ch. Ch., Oxford; late 2nd Lieut. Sherwood Foresters: *m.* 1974, Susan Annette, da. of Maj.-Gen. Allan Elton Younger, DSO, OBE, of Southern Haye, Heath Rise, Camberley, Surrey. *Residence,*—Kirby House, Kirby Bedon, Norwich.——Margaretta Jane, *b.* 1928: *m.* 1949 (m. diss. 1965), Cdr. Robert Ian Langlands Pearse, RN, and has issue living, Robert Simon Hugh, *b.* 1950,—Adam Philip, *b.* 1955,—Dominic Walter, *b.* 1959. *Residence,*—Manor Cottage, Meysey Hampton, Cirencester.——Jennifer Marion, *b.* 1930: *m.* 1952, Lt.-Cdr. John Muir Drinkwater, RN (ret.), and has issue living, Jonathan Dominick St. Clair, *b.* 1956,—Jane Fairrie, *b.* 1954,—Joanna Elizabeth, *b.* 1958,—Juliet Caroline Leslie, *b.* 1961,—Jessanda Katherine Jemima, *b.* 1964. *Residence,*—Meysey Hampton Manor, Cirencester.——Caroline Leslie, *b.* 1932. *Residence,*—Rowan Cottage, Tadmarton, Banbury.
Issue of the late Margaretta Agnes Plumptre, el. sister of 20th Baron, who *d.* 1907, having *m.* 1892, Albert Leslie Wright, of Butterley Hall, Derby, who *d.* 1938:—
Margaretta: *m.* 1918, Arthur Philip Coote, JP, who *d.* 1954 [see Coote, Bt., colls.]. *Residence,*—Wylye Head, Kilmington, Warminster, Wilts.
Issue of the late Selina Fanny Plumptre, 2nd sister of 20th Baron, who *d.* 1949, having *m.* 1897, Lionel Sherbrooke Osmaston, who *d.* 1969.:—
Fitzwalter Camplyon, *b.* 1901; ed. at Cheltenham Coll., and at St. John's Coll., Oxford (MA), Univ. Lecturer; formerly Maj. Indian Army; Fellow of St. Cross Coll., Oxford 1965-68; Indian Forest Ser. (ret.); India and Malaya 1939-45 (despatches twice). *Residence,*—The White House, Drayton St. Leonard, Oxford.——Robert Lionel, *MB*, *BCh*, *b.* 1903; ed. at Camb. Univ. (BA 1924, MB, BCh 1932); MRCS England and LRCP London 1927: *m.* 1945, Dorothy, da. of Albert Edward Ward, and has issue living, Margaret Elizabeth, *b.* 1946: *m.* 1968, John Richard Bradley, BDS, LDS, RCS,—Dorothy June, *b.* 1947. *Residence,*—37, Bathwick Hill, Bath.——Gwendolen Selina, *b.* 1905: *m.* 1935, Thomas Gerald Elwin Nash, who *d.* 1963, and has issue living, Stephen Thomas, *b.* 1942. *Residence,*—Forge Cottage, Goodnestone, nr. Canterbury, Kent.——Marion Margaretta, *b.* 1915: *m.* 1st, 1941, Capt. David Harold Archer, MC, Roy. W. Kent Regt., who *d.* (killed in action in Tunisia) 1943; 2ndly, 1973, Lt. Cdr. Frank Williams, RN, of Glion Aalin, Barregarrow, Kirk Michael, I. of Man, and has issue living (by 2nd husband), Sally Elizabeth, *b.* 1954.
Issue of the late Elisabeth Eleanor Plumptre, youngest sister of 20th Baron, who *d.* 1953, having *m.* 1902, Maurice Beresford Wright, O.B.E., M.D., who *d.* 1951:—

Maurice Christopher, *b.* 1906: *m.* 1939, Doris Kaye Puckle.——Nigel, *B.Sc.*, *b.* 1908: *m.* 1948, Patricia, Kidd, and has issue living, Andrew Firman, *b.* 1953,—Susan Jane, *b.* 1951: *m.* 1974, Robert Andrew Allison, of 6, Dickenson Rd., Crouch Hill, N3. *Residence,*—Little Standing, West Lavington, Midhurst, Sussex.——Phyllis Alicia, *b.* 1904. *Residence,*—29, West Mall, Clifton, Bristol 8.——Marjorie Prunella, *b.* 1912: *m.* 1939, Charlie Stuart Grunsell, and has issue living, Robin Nigel Stuart (17, Lowman Rd., N7), *b.* 1946: *m.* 1968, Angela Boulton, and has issue living, Leila *b.* 1973,—Elspeth Ann Grant, *b.* 1940: *m.* 1965, Edward Godfrey Cantrell, MB, MRCP, of 12, Charlotte St., Bristol, and has issue living. Matthew Ross *b.* 1968, Tamsin *b.* 1971,—Susanna, *b.* 1943. *Residence,*—Towerhead House, Banwell, Somerset.

PREDECESSORS.—[1] Sir ROBERT FitzWalter, *b.* 1247 ; Constable of Bere Castle, co. Merioneth and of Hadleigh Castle, Essex ; Capt. and Keeper of the Peace in Essex ; summoned to Parliament 1295-1325: *m.* 1st, Doverguille, who *d.* 1284, dau. and co-heir of Sir John de Burgh ; 2ndly, 1289, Alianore, dau. of Robert de Ferrers, 6th Earl of Derby (cr. 1138) ; 3rdly, 1308, Alice, widow of Sir Warren de l'Isle ; *d.* 1325 ; *s.* by his son by his 2nd marriage [2] ROBERT, 2nd Baron : *m.* Joan, dau. of Thomas Lord Multon ; *d.* 1328 ; *s.* by his son [3] JOHN, 3rd Baron ; summoned to Parliament 1340-60 : *m.* Alianore, dau. of Henry, Lord Percy ; *d.* 1361 ; *s.* by his son [4] WALTER, 4th Baron, *b.* 1345 ; Adm. of the Fleet ; summoned to Parliament 1369-85 : *m.* 1st, Alianore, dau. of Thomas, Lord Dagworth ; 2ndly, 1385, Philippa, who *d.* 1431, dau. of John, Lord Mohun ; *d.* 1386 ; *s.* by his son by his 1st marriage [5] WALTER, 5th Baron, *b.* 1368 ; summoned to Parliament 1390-1404 : *m.* Joan, dau. of John, Lord Devereux, of Dinton, Bucks ; *d.* 1406 ; *s.* by his el. son [6] HUMPHREY, 6th Baron, *b.* 1398 ; *d.* 1415 ; *s.* by his brother [7] WALTER, 7th Baron, *b.* 1400 ; Master of the King's Hart Hounds and Capt. of Vire ; summoned to Parliament 1429-30 : *m.* Elizabeth, dau. of Sir John Chideock, and widow of William Massy ; *d.* 1431 ; *s.* by his only child [8] ELIZABETH, Baroness FitzWalter : *m.* 1st, John Radcliffe ; 2ndly, 1466, John, Lord Dinham ; *d.* 1485 ; *s.* by her son [9] JOHN Radcliffe, 9th Baron, *b.* 1451 ; Steward of the King's Household ; summoned to Parliament in his mother's Barony 1485-95 ; attainted of high treason 1495: *m.* 1st, Anne, sister of Richard Whetehill, of Calais ; 2ndly, Margaret ; beheaded 1496 ; *s.* by his son by his 2nd marriage [10] ROBERT, *K.G.*, 10th Baron ; obtained reversal of attainder by Act of Parliament 1509 ; summoned to Parliament 1511-23 ; cr. *Viscount FitzWalter* 1525, and *Earl of Sussex* 1529: *m.* 1st, Elizabeth, dau. of Henry Stafford, 2nd Duke of Buckingham ; 2ndly, Margaret, dau. of Thomas Stanley, 2nd Earl of Derby ; 3rdly, 1536, Mary, dau. of Sir John Arundell, of Lanherne, Cornwall ; *d.* 1542 ; *s.* by his son [11] HENRY, *K.G.*, 2nd Earl, *b.* 1506: *m.* 1st, 1524, Elizabeth, who *d.* 1537, dau. of Thomas, 2nd Duke of Norfolk ; 2ndly, 1539, Anne (whom he divorced), dau. of Sir Philip Calthorpe ; *d.* 1556 ; *s.* by his el. son [12] THOMAS, *K.G.*, 3rd Earl, *b.* 1525 ; summoned in his father's Barony 1553 : *m.* 1st, 1553, Elizabeth, who *d.* 1554, dau. of 1st Earl of Southampton ; 2ndly, 1555, Frances, dau. of Sir William Sydney ; *d.* 1583 ; *s.* by his brother [13] HENRY, *K.G.*, 4th Earl, *b.* 1530: *m.* 1549, Honora, dau. of Anthony Pound ; *d.* 1593 ; *s.* by his only child [14] ROBERT, *K.G.*, 5th Earl, *b.* 1560 ; Earl Marshal Oct. to Dec. 1597 and Oct. to Dec. 1601: *m.* 1st, 1599, Bridget, who *d.* 1622, dau. of Sir Charles Morrison ; 2ndly, 1623, Frances, dau. of Hercules Meatas, and widow of Edward Shute ; *d.s.p.* legitimate 1629, when the Viscountcy of FitzWalter and Earldom of Sussex (both of which titles became extinct in 1643) passed to his cousin and heir-male Edward Radcliffe, while the Barony of FitzWalter devolved upon the heir-general [15] Sir HENRY Mildmay (descendant of Lady Frances Mildmay, only dau. of 2nd Earl of Sussex), *de jure* 15th Baron, *b.* 1585 ; claimed Barony 1641 and 1645 (no order made to the petition): *m.* Elizabeth, dau. of Thomas Darcy ; *d.* 1654 ; *s.* by his grandson [16] HENRY, *de jure* 16th Baron ; claimed the Barony 1660 ; *d.* 1661 ; *s.* by his brother [17] BENJAMIN, 17th Baron, *b.* 1646 ; petitioned for the Barony 1667 ; and was summoned to House of Lords 1669-70: *m.* 1669, Catherine, dau. of William, 3rd Viscount Fairfax of Emiley ; *d.* 1679 ; *s.* by his son [18] CHARLES, 18th Baron, *b.* 1670 : *m.* 1693, Elizabeth, dau. of the Hon. Charles Bertie ; *d.* 1727 ; *s.* by his brother [19] BENJAMIN, 19th Baron, *b.* 1672 ; Commr. of Essex 1720-28 ; cr. *Viscount Harwich,* co. Essex, and *Earl FitzWalter* 1735 ; Treasurer of the Household 1737-55, and Lord-Lieut. of Essex 1741-56 : *m.* 1724, Frederica, dau. of the 3rd Duke of Schomberg and Duke of Leinster, and widow of Robert Darcy, Earl of Holderness ; *d.* 1756, when the Earldom and Viscountcy became ext., while the Barony fell into abeyance among the daus. of Mary, only sister of the 16th and 17th Barons (ante), and so remained until 1924 when (after petition to the House of Lords) the abeyance was determined in favour of [20] HENRY FITZWALTER Plumptre, 20th Baron [son of the late John Bridges Plumptre, and grandson of Eleanor, wife of the Rev. Henry Western Plumptre, and dau. of Sir Brook William Bridges, 4th Bt. (a descendant of Mary, only sister of 16th and 17th Barons), whose el. son, Sir Brook William Bridges, 5th Bt., having claimed the Barony of FitzWalter in 1842 as a co-heir, was cr. Baron FitzWalter by letters patent 1868, but *d.s.p.* 1875], *b.* 1860 : *m.* 1st, 1892, Maude Dora Gertrude, who *d.* 1893, dau. of the late Capt. Thomas Carpendale Baird (Dorset Regt.), of Flatfield, co. Ayr ; 2ndly, 1908, Emily Harriet Jemima, who *d.* 1951, el. dau. of the late Capt. Thomas Carpendale Baird (ante) ; *d.s.p.* 1932, when the Barony again fell into abeyance and so remained until 1953, when the abeyance was terminated (after petition to H.M. the Queen) in favour of [21] FITZWALTER BROOK Plumptre (son of the late George Beresford Plumptre, younger brother of 20th Baron), 21st Baron and present peer.

FITZWILLIAM, EARL. (Wentworth-Fitzwilliam.) [Earl I. 1716 and G.B. 1746.]

WILLIAM THOMAS GEORGE WENTWORTH-FITZWILLIAM, 10th Earl ; *b.* May 28th, 1904 ; *s.* 1952 ; ed. at Eton and at Magdalene Coll., Camb.; a JP and DL of Peterborough, a Co. Alderman for Soke of Peterborough, and patron of thirty-three livings; 1939-45 War with RA (American Bronze star medal): *m.* 1956, Joyce Elizabeth Mary, da. of the late Lt.-Col. Philip Joseph Langdale, OBE [see B. Mowbray, colls.], and formerly wife of the 2nd Viscount FitzAlan of Derwent.

Let your desires obey your reason.

Arms.—Quarterly : 1st and 4th lozengy argent and gules, *Fitzwilliam* ; 2nd and 3rd sable, a chevron between three leopards' faces or, *Wentworth.* **Crests.**—1st, out of a ducal coronet or, a triple plume of ostrich feathers argent, *Fitzwilliam* ; 2nd, a griffin passant argent, *Wentworth.* **Supporters.**—Two wild men, wreathed about the temples and loins, and each holding in the exterior hand the trunk of a tree (without leaves) eradicated proper, and disposed across the body bendwise, that in the hand of the *dexter* supported in bend sinister, that in the hand of the *sinister* supported in bend dexter.

Seats,—Milton, Peterborough ; Wentworth Woodhouse, Rotherham. *Clubs*,—Boodle's, Pratt's. White's.

DAUGHTER LIVING OF EIGHTH EARL.

Lady (Anne) Juliet Dorothea Maud, *b.* 1935; ed. at St. Hilda's Coll., Oxford (MA); a Co. Director, and a Co. Councillor of W. Suffolk: *m.* 1st, 1960 (m. diss. 1972), as his second wife, the 6th Marquess of Bristol; 2ndly, 1974, Capt. Somerset Struben de Chair, late RHG, of St. Osyth Priory, St. Osyth, Essex, son of the late Admiral Sir Dudley Rawson Stratford de Chair, KCB, KCMG, MVO.

SISTERS LIVING OF EIGHTH EARL.

Lady Maud Lilian Elfrida Mary (*Elfrida, Countess of Wharncliffe*), *b.* 1898 : *m.* 1918, the 3rd Earl of Wharncliffe, who *d.* 1953. *Residence*,—Carlton House, Wortley, Sheffield.

Lady (Marjorie) Joan Mary, *b.* 1900 : *m.* 1st, 1925, Major Grismond Picton Philipps, C.V.O. (Knt. 1953), late Gren. Gds., who *d.* 1967, having obtained a divorce 1949; 2ndly, 1949, Lt.-Col. William Wallace Smith Cuninghame of Caprington, DSO, JP, DL, late Life Gds., who *d.* 1959, and has issue living, (by 1st marriage) Griffith William Grismond (Cwmgwili, Bronwydd Arms, Carmarthen), *b.* 1935; ed. at Eton: *m.* 1964, Ingrid Götilda, da. of Med. Dr. G. von Sydow, of Gothenburg, Sweden, and has issue living, John George Grismond, *b.* 1965, Marianne Sioned *b.* 1967, Charlotte Ingrid *b.* 1969, Ebba Serena *b.* 1971. *Residence*,—La Masseline, St. Martin, Jersey. *Club*,—English-Speaking Union.

WIDOW LIVING OF EIGHTH EARL.

OLIVE DOROTHEA (*Olive, Countess Fitzwilliam*), dau. of the late Most Rev. the Hon. Benjamin John Plunket, D.D. [see B. Plunket, colls.]: *m.* 1933, the 8th Earl, who *d.* 1948. *Residence*,—Coollattin, Shillelagh, co. Wicklow.

PREDECESSORS.—[1] WILLIAM Fitzwilliam, el. son of the late Sir William Fitzwilliam, of Milton, and Gaines Park Hall, Essex; cr. *Baron Fitzwilliam*, of Lifford, co. Donegal (peerage of Ireland) 1620: *m.* 16—, Catherine, dau. of the late William Hyde, of South Denchworth, Berks; *d.* 1634; *s.* by his son [2] WILLIAM, 2nd Baron; *d.* 1658; *s.* by his son [3] WILLIAM, 3rd Baron : cr. *Viscount Milton*, and *Earl Fitzwilliam* (peerage of Ireland), 1716; *d.* 1719; *s.* by his son [4] JOHN, 2nd Earl; *d.* 1728; *s.* by his son [5] WILLIAM, 3rd Earl; cr. *Lord Fitzwilliam, Baron of Milton*, co. Northampton (peerage of Great Britain) 1742, and *Viscount Milton* and *Earl Fitzwilliam*, of Norborough, co. Northampton (peerage of Great Britain) 1746; *d.* 1756; *s.* by his son [6] WILLIAM, 4th Earl; Lord-Lieut. of Ireland 1795; *d.* 1833; *s.* by his son [7] CHARLES WILLIAM, K.G., 5th Earl; *b.* 1786; assumed the additional surname of Wentworth by Roy. licence 1856: *m.* 1806, Mary, dau. of 1st Baron Dundas; *d.* 1857; *s.* by his 2nd son [8] WILLIAM THOMAS SPENCER, K.G., 6th Earl; *b.* 1815; M.P. for Malton (L) 1837-41 and 1846-7, and for Wicklow 1847-57 ; Lord-Lieut. of W. Riding of York 1853-92, and an A.D.C. to H.M. Queen Victoria 1846-94: *m.* 1933, Lady Frances Harriet Douglas, who *d.* 1895, el. dau. of 19th Earl of Morton; *d.* 1902; *s.* by his grandson [9] WILLIAM CHARLES DE MEURON, K.C.V.O., C.B.E., D.S.O. (el. son of the late Viscount Milton, M.P., el. son of 6th Earl), 7th Earl; *b.* 1872; Lieut.-Col. late Grenadier Guards; 4th Earl; Lord-Lieut. Oxford and Bucks L.I. and R.H.A.; S. Africa 1900 (D.S.O.), European War 1914-18 (C.B.E.); M.P. for Wakefield (LU) 1895-1902: *m.* 1896, Lady Maud Frederica Elizabeth Dundas, OBE, who *d.* 1967, da. of 1st Marquess of Zetland; *d.* 1943; *s.* by his son [10] WILLIAM HENRY LAURENCE PETER, DSC, 8th Earl; *b.* 1910; Capt. Grenadier Guards, 1939-45 War (DSC): *m.* 1933, Olive Dorothea, da. of the late Most Rev. the Hon. Benjamin John Plunket, DD; *d.* 1948; *s.* by his kinsman [11] ERIC SPENCER son of the late Capt. the Hon. Sir William Charles Wentworth-Fitzwilliam, G.C.V.O. (4th son of 6th Earl), 9th Earl; *b.* 1883; Lieut. Leicestershire Yeo.: *m.* 1912, Jessie Gertrude (from whom he obtained a divorce 1917), dau. of R. F. Rowlands; *d.* 1952; *s.* by his kinsman [12] WILLIAM THOMAS GEORGE (son of the late George Charles Wentworth-Fitzwilliam, son of the Hon. George Wentworth-Fitzwilliam, M.P., 3rd son of 5th Earl) 10th Earl and present peer; also Viscount Milton, Lord Fitzwilliam, Baron of Milton, and Baron Fitzwilliam (I).

FLETCHER, BARON. (Fletcher) [Life Baron 1970.]

ERIC GEORGE MOLYNEUX FLETCHER, *PC*, son of the late Clarence George Eugene Fletcher, Town Clerk of Islington, N.; *b.* March 26th, 1903; ed. at Radley, and Univ. of London (BA, LLD); FSA; Solicitor 1924; Sen. Partner of Denton, Hall, & Burgin; formerly a Dir. of Assoc. British Picture Corpn. Ltd., and other cos.; a Member of LCC 1934-39 (Chm. of Finance Cttee.); Min. without Portfolio 1964-66, and Dep. Speaker, and Chm. of Ways and Means 1966-68; Pres. of British Archaeological Assocn. 1960-63; Pres. of Selden Soc. 1967-70, a Trustee of British Musum since 1968; MP for E. Islington (*Lab.*) 1945-70; *cr.* Knt. 1964, PC 1967, and *Baron Fletcher,* of Islington, in Greater London (Life Baron) 1970: *m.* 1929, Bessie Winifred, da. of the late James Butt, of Enfield, and has issue.

Arms,—Azure two arrows barbs upward Or, between four crosses moline Or. Crest,—On a cap of maintenance gules doubled ermine, a cubit arm vested sable the shirt cuff of bleached linen proper linked Or, the hand proper grasping a rolled document in bend sinister proper and an arrow in bend barb upward Or. Supporters,—Dexter, a representation of a Saxon Archer of the mid-seventh century; *sinister*, a representation of a Norman archer; each supporting with the exterior hand a bow all proper.

Residence,—9, Robin Grove, Highgate, N6 6PA. *Address*,—3, Gray's Inn Pl., WC1. *Club*,— Athenaeum.

SONS LIVING.

Rev. the Hon. David Clare Molyneux (4, Burfield Rd., Chorleywood, Herts.), *b.* 1932: *m.* 1970, Susan Charlotte Langford.

Rev. the Hon. Jonathan James Molyneux (27, Malcolm Place, King St., Cambridge) *b.* 1942.

DAUGHTER LIVING.

Hon. Elizabeth Jane Molyneux, *b.* 1938: *m.* 1962, David Blair Wilkinson, of The Orchard, Repton, Derbys.

FLOREY, BARONY OF. (Florey.) [Extinct 1968.]

SON LIVING OF LIFE BARON.

Hon. Charles du Vé (c/o Department of Clinical Epidemiology & Social Medicine, St. Thomas's Hosp. Medical School, SE1), *b.* 1934; ed. at Camb. Univ. (BA, MD, BChir); MPH, Yale Univ., USA: *m.* 1966, Susan Hopkins, and has issue.

DAUGHTER LIVING OF LIFE BARON.

Hon. Paquita Mary Joanna, *b.* 1929: *m.* 1955, John McMichael, (90, Inverleith Pl., Edinburgh, EH3 5PA), and has issue.

WIDOW LIVING OF LIFE BARON.

Hon.▮MARGARET AUGUSTA Fremantle, *DM (Baroness Florey)*, (4, Elsfield Rd., Old Marston, Oxford), da. of 3rd Baron Cottesloe, and formerly wife of Denys Arthur Jennings, BM, BCh: *m.* 1967, as his 2nd wife, Baron Florey (Life Peer), who *d.* 1968.

FOLEY, BARON. (Foley.) [Baron G.B. 1776.]

ADRIAN GERALD FOLEY, 8th Baron ; *b.* Aug. 9th, 1923 ; *s.* 1927 ; is a composer and pianist: *m.* 1st 1958 (m. diss. 19—), Patricia (DE MEEK), da. of Joseph Zoellner III, of Pasadena, California, USA; 2ndly, 1972, Ghislaine, only da. of Cornelius Dresselhuys, of Long Island, USA, formerly wife of (1) Maj. Denis James Alexander, 1G, later 6th Earl of Caledon, and (2) the 4th Baron Ashcombe, and has issue by 1st m.

Arms.—Argent, a fesse engrailed, between three cinquefoils, and the whole within a bordure sable. **Crest.**—A lion rampant argent, supporting between the fore paws a shield of the arms of *Foley*. **Supporters.**—Two lions argent, semée of cinquefoils sable.

Address—c/o Marbella Club, Marbella, Malaga, Spain. *Clubs*, White's, Turf

SON LIVING. *(By 1st m.)*
Hon. THOMAS HENRY, *b.* April 1st, 1961.

That I may do good.

DAUGHTER LIVING. *(By 1st m.)*
Hon. Alexandra Mary, *b.* 1960.

AUNT LIVING.
(Raised to the rank of a Baron's daughter 1920.)

Hon. Mildred Caroline, *b.* 1895.

COLLATERAL BRANCHES LIVING.

Grandchildren of the late Paul Henry Foley (infra) :—
Issue of the late Henry Thomas Hamilton Foley, M.B.E., *b.* 1905, *d.* 1959 : *m.* 1936, Helen Constance Margaret (The Vine, Tarrington, Hereford), C St. J, el. da. of Sir Robert Barclay Pearson :—
Andrew Thomas (Stoke Edith Park, Hereford; *Club*, Boodle's) *b.* 1937; ed. at Eton; late Capt. Rifle Bde.: *m.* 1968, Gillian, da. of William Carleton Brown, of Over Alderley, Ches., and has issue living, Rupert Thomas, *b.* 1970,—Ian Richard *b.* 1973.——John Paul (Rock House, Fownhope, Hereford; Cavalry, Special Forces Clubs) *b.* 1939; ed. at Bradfield; Maj. Rifle Bde: *m.* 1972, Ann Rosamond, only da. of John William Humphries, of Coval Court, Sunningdale, Berks., and has issue living, Annabel Frances Helen, *b.* 1973.——Anne Victoria Helen, (The Vine, Tarrington, Hereford), *b.* 1943.

Grandson of the late Henry John Wentworth Hodgetts-Foley, great-grandson of 1st Baron :—
Issue of the late Paul Henry Foley, *b.* 1857, *d.* 1928 : *m.* 1904, Dora, who *d.* 1959, only child of Hamilton W. Langley, of Estancia La Dorita, Argentina :—
Paul Robert, *O.B.E.*, *b.* 1910 ; ed. at Eton, and Ch. Ch., Oxford (B.Sc. 1932) ; sometime Group-Capt. Auxiliary Air Force ; European War 1939-45 (despatches, O.B.E., Officer of American Legion of Merit, Com. of Order of George I. of Greece) ; O.B.E. (Mil.)1945 : *m.* 1st, 1939 (marriage dissolved 1952), Cecilia Margaret Anne Yolande, only dau. of Frank Seddon ; 2ndly, 1954, Oriel Leonie (GREGSON), younger dau. of the late Col. Edward Lucas Scudamore, of Kentchurch Court, Hereford. *Residence*,—Le Dauphin, Quartier de la Tuiliere, Auribeau sur Siagne, 06810, France.

PREDECESSORS.—Thomas Foley, 2nd and last Baron Foley; cr. 1712; *d.* 1766, and his estates passed to his cousin [1] THOMAS Foley ; cr. *Baron Foley*, of Kidderminster (peerage of Great Britain) 1776; *d.* 1777; *s.* by his son [2] THOMAS, 2nd Baron; *d.* 1793; *s.* by his son [3] THOMAS, 3rd Baron; Lord-Lieut. of Worcestershire; *d.* 1833; *s.* by his son [4] THOMAS HENRY, *P.C.*, *b.* 1808; M.P. for Worcestershire W. (*L*) 1830-3; Capt. of Corps of Gentlemen at Arms: *m.* 1849, Lady Mary Charlotte Howard, who *d.* 1897, dau. of 13th Duke of Norfolk ; *d.* 1869; *s.* by his son [5] HENRY THOMAS, 5th Baron, *b.* 1850: *m.* 1899, Evelyn Vaughan, who *d.* 1968, da. of Arthur Radford, JP, of Smalley, Derbyshire, and Bradfield Hall, Berks.; *d.* 1905; *s.* by his brother [6] FITZALAN CHARLES JOHN, 6th Baron; *b.* 1852; *d.* 1918; *s.* by his cousin [7] GERALD HENRY (son of the late Henry St. George Foley, grandson of 3rd son of 3rd Baron], 7th Baron; *b.* 1898: *m.* 1922, Minoru, who *d.* 1968, da. of the late Harry Greenstone, mine-owner, of Johannesburg, S. Africa, *d.* 1927; *s.* by his son [8] ADRIAN GERALD, 8th Baron and present peer.

FOOT, BARON. (Foot.) [Life Baron 1967.]

JOHN MACKINTOSH FOOT, son of the late Rt. Hon. Isaac Foot; *b.* Feb. 17th, 1909; ed. at Bembridge Sch., and Balliol Coll., Oxford (BA); Solicitor 1934; 1939-45 War as Maj. RASC (GSO 111, 43rd Div. and GSO 11 12th Corps., despatches); *cr. Baron Foot, of Buckland Monachorum, co. Devon* (Life Peerage) 1967: *m.* 1936, Anne Bailey, da. of Clifford Bailey Farr, MD, of Bryn Mawr, Pa., USA, and has issue.

Arms,—Or, on a chevron engrailed sable between three lions' gambs erect and erased gules, three wheels or. Crest,—Perching on a tower sable, supported by two lions' gambs erect gules, a Cornish chough proper. Supporters,—*Dexter*, a buck, and *sinister* a Dartmoor pony, each gorged with a wreath of yew proper, and supporting between the legs a sword erect sheathed or, the whole upon a compartment of rock, in the middle thereof a pit proper.

For law and liberty

Residence,—Yew Tree, Crapstone, Yelverton, Devon.

SON LIVING.

Hon. John Winslow, *b.* 1939.

DAUGHTER LIVING.

Hon. Katherine Elliott, *b.* 1937: *m.* 1955, David Stavely Gordon, and has issue.

FORBES, LORD. (Forbes.) [Lord S. 1445.]

NIGEL IVAN FORBES, *KBE*, 23rd Lord and Premier Lord of Scotland; *b.* Feb. 19th, 1918; *s.* 1953; ed. at Harrow, and RMC; a Representative Peer for Scotland 1955-63; Maj. Gren. Gds. (Reserve); Board Member Aberdeen and Dist. Milk Marketing Board 1962-72, Member of Board Sports Council for Scotland 1966-71; Chm. of River Don Dist. Board, 1960-73; Dep. Chm. of Tennent Caledonian Breweries, Ltd., 1964-74; Chm. of Nat. Playing Fields Assocn. (Scottish Branch), and of Rowlawn Turf Growers, Ltd., a Dir. of Grampian Television, Ltd. and of Robert Sibbald Travel Agents, Ltd., Pres. of Scottish Scout Council, and a JP and a DL for Aberdeenshire; Adj. Gren. Guards 1941-43, a Dist. Councillor for Alford 1955-58, a Member of Inter-Parl. Union Delegation to Denmark 1956, to Hungary 1965 and to Ethiopia 1971, Pres. Roy. Highland and Agric. Soc. of Scotland 1958-59, and a Member of Commonwealth Parl. Assocn. Delegation to Canada 1961 and of Parl. Deleg. to Pakistan 1962, Mil. Assist. to High Commr. for Palestine 1947-48, Min. of State, Scottish Office 1958-59, and a Board Member Scottish Cttee. Nature Conservancy 1962-65; 1939-45 War (wounded): KBE (Civil) 1960: *m.* 1942, the Hon. Rosemary Katharine Hamilton-Russell, only da. of 9th Viscount Boyne, and has issue.

Arms,—Azure, three bears' heads couped argent, muzzled gules. Crest,—A stag's head attired with ten tynes proper. Supporters,—Two bloodhounds argent, collared gules. *Seat,*—Castle Forbes, Alford, Aberdeenshire. *Residence.*—Balforbes, Alford, Aberdeenshire. *Clubs,*—Guards', Inst. of Directors.

SONS LIVING.

Hon. MALCOLM NIGEL (*Master of Forbes*), (Finzeauch, Whitehouse, Alford, Aberdeenshire), *b.* May 6th, 1946; ed. at Eton: *m.* 1969, Carole Jennifer Andrée, da. of N. S. Whitehead, of Aberdeen, and has issue living, Neil Malcolm Ross, *b.* 1970,—Joanne Carole, *b.* 1972.
Hon. Jonathan Andrew, *b.* 1947; ed. at Eton; Capt. Grenadier Guards.

DAUGHTER LIVING.

Hon. Gillian Rosemary, b. 1949: m. 1969, Alexander Neil Foster, of Church Farm House, Blakesley, Towcester, Northants., and has issue living, Michael Alexander, b. 1973,—Lucia Katharine, b. 1970.

COLLATERAL BRANCHES LIVING.

Granddaughter of the late Capt. the Hon. Walter Robert Drummond Forbes, 7th son of 19th Lord :—
Issue of the late Sir (Victor) Courtenay Walter Forbes, K.C.M.G., b. 1889, d. 1958 : m. 1st, 1916 (marriage dissolved 1949), Luia, dau. of the late Hon. Sir Henry Herbert Juta; 2ndly, 1950, Mary, who d. 1972, da. of Francis George Olivieri, and widow of Walter Carter Bizley:—
(By 1st m.) Sara Elizabeth Ninita, b. 1917: m. 1938, Hugh Gyle-Thompson, who d. 1972, and has issue living, David Courtenay Gladstone, b. 1943: m. 1970, Penelope Fearnley, and has issue living, Camilla Kate b. 1974,—Elizabeth Helen Donita, b. 1939: m. 1965, George Oliver Papps, of USA, and has issue living, Gillian Sara b. 1967, Luia Elizabeth b. 1970,—Sara Anne Robina, b. 1941: m. 1969, Christopher Watson, and has issue living, Timothy Hugh James b. 1970, Angus Christopher Hugo b. 1972. Residence,—Old Quarry House, North Park, Gerrards Cross, Bucks.

Grandsons of the late Hon. Montagu Ormond Forbes, 8th son of 19th Lord:—
Issue of the late Col. Courtenay Fergus Ochoncar Grey Forbes, late Coldm. Gds., b. 1898, d. 1971: m. 1st, 1924 (m. diss. 1928), Gundrede Mary, da. of the late Capt. Graham Owen Robert Wynne [B. Killanin]; 2ndly, 1929, Mary Shelagh, who d. 1932, da. of the late Col. Arthur Llewellyn, Som. LI; 3rdly, 1933 (m. diss. 1954), Dorothea, da. of His Honour the late Henry Staveley Staveley-Hill, TD; 4thly, 1954, Emilie de Kosenko (Remenham Piece, Henley on Thames, Oxon), da. of the late Mrs. Edward Brooks of New York, and widow of 5th Baron Monteagle of Brandon:—
(By 1st m.) Fergus Patrick, b. 1925: m. 1st, 1950, Margaret Elizabeth, da. of John Percy Wayte; 2ndly, 1967, Jeanette Fendryck, of Baltimore, and has issue living (by 1st m.) Christopher Michael Fergus, b. 1955,—Grania Elizabeth, b. 1950,—Moira Isobel, b. 1957,—(by 2nd m.) a son, b. 1974.——
(By 3rd m.), John Alistair Ponsonby (The Old Rectory, Barford St. Martin, Salisbury, Wilts.; Boodle's Club), b. 1937; late Capt. Coldm. Gds.: m. 1965, Mary Dorothea, da. of Sir William Macnamara Goodenough, 1st Bt., and has issue living, James William Courtenay, b. 1970,—Sophie Louisa Dorothea, b. 1968.

Granddaughter of the late Col. Robert Ochoncar Hawkins Forbes, el. son of the Hon. Robert Forbes, 6th son of 18th Lord:—
Issue of the late Robert Ochoncar Forbes, b. 1859, d. 1913 : m. 1898, Juliana Olga, who d. 1954, dau. of Major John Nevinson, formerly 4th Hussars :—
Rosalie Jessie Olga (15, Sloane Gdns., SW1), b. 1904: m. 1938, Thomas Percival Durant Beighton, who d. 1971.

Granddaughter of the late Rev. Malcolm Forbes (infra):—
Issue of the late Maj. Malcolm Hay Ochoncar Forbes, b. 1891, d. 1973: m. 1st, 1921, Edith Maud, who d. 1962, only da. of G. A. MacMillan; 2ndly, 1966, Mrs. Helen Roslyn Dickson, who d. 1970, da. of A. C. Graham:—
(By 1st m.) Helen Mary Hay, b. 1922: m. 1945, Fl.-Lt. Terence Dudley Thompson, RAAF, of 52, Burlington St., Walkerville, S. Aust., and has issue living, Ian Forbes, b. 1951,—Pamela Forbes, b. 1947,—Jane Forbes, b. 1948,—Georgina Helen Forbes, b. 1968.

Granddaughter of the late Maj. Frederick Murray Hay Forbes, BSC, 2nd son of the late Hon. Robert Forbes (ante):—
Issue of the late Rev. Malcolm Forbes, b. 1860, d. 1941 : m. 1888, Ella Constance Josephine Brenton, who d. 1937, el. dau. of the late Rev. Adolphus Frederick Carey, V. of Brixham, Torbay, Devon :—
Helen Stuart Angus, b. 1889. Residence,—38, Spottiswoode St., Edinburgh, EH9 1DG.

Grandchildren of the late Robert Inglis Forbes, el. son of Col. Henry Twisden Forbes, 3rd son of the Hon. Robert Forbes (ante):—
Issue of the late William Robert Townsend Forbes, b. 1893, d. 1967: m. 1925, Evelyn (Flat 2, 19, Selborne Rd., Hove, BN3 3AJ), da. of the late Very Rev. Preb. H. Erskine-Hill, DD, of Much Dewchurch, Hereford:—
Ian Robert Patrick (75, Hillbury Rd., Warlingham, Surrey), b. 1926: m. 1953, Patricia Heginbotham, of Brighton.——William Michael (Oakmead, Westfield Av., Hayling Is., Hants), b. 1934; Cdr. RN: m. 1957, Wendy Ann Birch, of Southsea, and has issue living, David Charles, b. 1959,—Simon Robert, b. 1964,—Jeremy Andrew, b. 1966,—Anne Lesley, b. 1960.——Rev. Patrick (121, Roydene Rd., SE18 1PZ), b. 1938; Curate in Thamesmead, SE2: m. 1962, Annette Margaret Miller, of Upper Norwood, SE, and has issue living, Stephen Robert, b. 1967.——Elizabeth Anne, b. 1933: m. 1st, 1953 (m. annulled 1955), Tom Richard Denning; 2ndly, 1956, William Lathrop Bauhan, of The James House, Old County Rd., Dublin, NH, USA, and has issue living (by 2nd m.), Patrick Lathrop, b. 1957,—Sarah Forbes, b. 1959.

Grandchildren of the late Col. Henry Twisden Forbes (ante):—
Issue of the late Robert Inglis Forbes, b. 1860, d. 1945 : m. 1892, Helena Eleanor, who d. 1944, dau. of the late Edward Townsend, of co. Galway and Torquay :—
Kenneth Herbert, b. 1899: m. 1st, 1929, Zara Muriel (from whom he obtained a divorce 1938), da. of the late Walter Currie; 2ndly, 1947, Dorothy Joan, da. of the late Alfred Percival Folkard, and has issue living, (by 2nd m.) Colin Kenneth, b. 1956,—(by 1st m.) Susan, b. 1933: m. 1958, Iain Stuart Bain, of New Cottage, Newnham, Baldock, Herts., and has issue living, Christina Mary b. 1962, Catriona Frances b. 1964. Residence,—Orchard Cottage, Coopers Hill Lane, Englefield Green, Surrey.
Issue of the late Herbert Russell Forbes, b. 1863, d. 1920: m. 1896, Amy Ella, who d. 1935, dau. of the late William Duncan Scott, of Graylands, Chiswick :—
Marjorie Alice, b. 1900: m. 1920, John Taylor Porritt, and has issue living, Joan, b. 1921,—Gillian, b. 1927. Residence,—

Granddaughters of the late Charles Twisden Forbes, 3rd son of the late Col. Henry Twisden Forbes (ante):—
Issue of the late Archibald Herbert D'Esterre Forbes, M.C., b. 1899, d. 1956 : m. 1924, Emily Flora (of Lambrook, Bracknell, Berks), dau. of the late S. K. Keyes, of The Dene, Dartford :—
Isla Hamilton, b. 1926: MA 1948: m. 1948, the Rev. Philip Paul Stanley Brownless, MA, of Mattingley Vicarage, Basingstoke, Hants., and has issue living, Andrew Hamilton, b. 1952,—Benjamin Stanley, b.1956,—Alison Kilworth, b.1950; ed. at Bristol Univ. BSc (SocSci).——Rona Kilworth, b. 1928; MA 1951: m. 1952, Raymond Frank Abraham Hunter, MC, and has issue living, Charles William Forbes, b. 1955,—Jolyon Nigel Forbes, b. 1958,—Mark Raymond Forbes, b. 1960,—William John Forbes, b. 1965. Residence,—Hunters, Clarence, Bridgetown, Nova Scotia.

Grandchildren of the late Col. Henry Twisden Forbes (ante):—
Issue of the late Arthur Trevor Forbes, b. 1866, d. 1933: m. 1st, 1890, Caroline Eliza, who d. 1915, dau. of Richard Vicary Gorham, of Yoxford, Suffolk; 2ndly, 1916, Cornelia M., who d. 1956, dau. of the late Rev. Thomas Robert Matthews, of Moviddy, Crookstown, co. Cork:—

(By 1st marriage) Trevor Courtenay, *b.* 1898; formerly Lt. Suffolk Regt.——Edith Marjorie, *b.* 1901: *m.* 1934, Lt.-Col. Graham Brunel Ingle Nokes, R. Indian Army Ser. Corps., of The Lodge, Blackhouse Hill, Hythe, Kent, and has issue living, Daphne Veronica, *b.* 1942.

Granddaughter of the late Francis Sutherland Courtenay Forbes, 2nd son of the late Col. Walter Ernest Forbes, 4th son of the Hon. Robert Forbes (ante):—

Issue of the late Lt.-Cdr. Haydon Marriott Sutherland Forbes, DSC, RN, *b.* 1897, *d.* 1927: *m.* 19—, Cecily, da. of Capt. — Armitage, RN:—
Pamela Patricia, *b.* 1925.

Granddaughters of the late Ernest Colebroke Forbes, yst. son of the late Col. Walter Ernest Forbes (ante):—

Issue of the late Atholl Courtenay Forbes, *b.* 1892, *d.* 1952: *m.* 1926, Veronica (who *d.* 1966, having *m.* 2ndly, 1939, L. A. C. Houston, of 79, Southbourne Gdns., Eastcote, Middlesex), da. of Arthur Willis, of Gisbourne, NZ:—
Pamela Jane, *b.* 1929; formerly a Sister, QARNNS: *m.* 1958, Richard Bostock, of 18, Canford Cliffs Av., Poole, Dorset, and has issue living, John Edward, *b.* 1960,—David Forbes, *b.* 1962,—Julia Elizabeth, *b.* 1965.

Issue of the late Ernest Twisden Forbes, *b.* 1902, *d.* 1966: *m.* 1932, Mavis Amy, who *d.* 1973, da. of Edward Ingham, of Melbourne:—
Barbara Beatrice, *b.* 1934: *m.* 1963, Hubert Andrew Thebo, BS (6116, Temple St., Bethesda, Maryland, USA), and has issue living, Christine Forbes, *b.* 1967.

Grandchildren of the late Arthur St. Quintin Forbes, yst. son of the late Hon. Robert Forbes (ante):—

Issue of the late Bertie St. John Ochoncar Forbes, *b.* 1882, *d.* 1953: *m.* 1902, Margaret Smith, who *d.* 1946:—
Bertie St. John Ochoncar (of 61, Comiston View, Edinburgh 10), *b.* 1918; 1939-45 War as Maj. Indian Army and Roy. Scots.: *m.* 1942, Anne Moore Crozer, and has issue living, Graham Richard, *b.* 1946: *m.* 1971, Anne Catherine Haigh, of Edinburgh, and has issue living, Callum Richard *b.* 1972,—Gillian Margaret, *b.* 1951.——Alice Margaret Whitelaw (of 115, Piersfield Terr., Edinburgh, 8), *b.* 1906: *m.* 1929, Robert Gray Pottinger, who *d.* 1933, and has issue living, Ronald Forbes (115, Piersfield Terr., Edinburgh, 8), *b.* 1933; MB and ChB Edinburgh 1959: *m.* 1960, Marija Ozanic, and has issue living, David Forbes, *b.* 1964.
Descendants of William Forbes (4th in descent from the Hon. Duncan Forbes, 2nd son of 2nd Lord), who was cr. a *Baronet* 1626. *See* Stuart-Forbes, Bt.
Descendants of William Forbes (5th in descent from the Hon. Sir Patrick Forbes, 3rd son of 2nd Lord), who was cr. a *Baronet* 1630 [*See* L. Sempill and Forbes, Bt, cr. 1630].

PREDECESSORS.—[1] *Sir* ALEXANDER de Forbes, of that ilk, feudal baron of Forbes; *cr. Lord Forbes* (peerage of Scotland) about 1445; *d.* 1448; *s.* by his son [2] JAMES, 2nd Lord; *d.* 1460; *s.* by his son [3] WILLIAM, 3rd Lord; *s.* by his el. son [4] ALEXANDER, 4th Lord; *s.* by his brother [5] ARTHUR, 5th Lord; *d.* 1493; *s.* by his brother [6] JOHN, 6th Lord; *d.* 1547; *s.* by his son [7] WILLIAM, 7th Lord; *d.* 1593; *s.* by his son [8] JOHN, 8th Lord; *d.* (June) 1606; *s.* by his 2nd son (by 1st m.) [9] JOHN, *de jure* 9th Lord, Capuchin monk; *d.* (Aug.) 1606; *s.* by his half-brother [10] ARTHUR, 10th Lord; *d.* 1641; *s.* by his son [11] ALEXANDER, 11th Lord; *d.* 1672; *s.* by his son [12] WILLIAM, 12th Lord; *d.* 1691; *s.* by his son [13] WILLIAM, 13th Lord; *d.* 1716; *s.* by his el. son [14] WILLIAM, 14th Lord; *d.* 1730; *s.* by his son [15] FRANCIS, 15th Lord; *d.* a minor 1734; *s.* by his uncle [16] JAMES, 16th Lord; *d.* 1761; *s.* by his son [17] JAMES, 17th Lord, *d.* 1804; *s.* by his son [18] JAMES OCHONCAR, 18th Lord; Gen. in the Army, Repres. Peer, and High Commr. to Gen. Assembly, Ch. of Scotland; *d.* 1843; *s.* by his son [19] WALTER, 19th Lord, *b.* 1798; served at Waterloo: *m.* 1st 1825, Horatia, who *d.* 1862, da. of Sir John Gregory Shaw, Bt.; 2ndly 1864, Louisa, who *d.* 1921, da. of the late James Ormond; *d.* 1868; *s.* by his son [20] HORACE COURTENAY, 20th Lord, *b.* 1829; Repres. Peer 1874-1906; *d.* 1914; *s.* by his brother [21] ATHOLL MONSON, 21st Lord; *b.* 1841: *m.* 1876, Margaret Alice, who *d.* 1943, da. of Sir William Hanmer Dick-Cunnyngham, 8th Bt.; *d.* 1916; *s.* by his son [22] ATHOLL LAURENCE CUNYNGHAM, 22nd Lord ; *b.* 1882; Maj. Gren. Gds.; Repres. Peer 1917-24: *m.* 1914, Lady Mabel Anson, who *d.* 1972, da. of the 3rd. Earl of Lichfield; *d.* 1953; *s.* by his son [23] NIGEL IVAN, 23rd Lord, and present peer.

★FORESTER, BARON. (Weld-Forester.) [Baron U.K. 1821.]

Always the same.

CECIL GEORGE WILFRID WELD-FORESTER, 7th Baron; *b.* July 12th, 1899; *s.* 1932; ed. at Armstrong Coll., Durham; Col. (ret.) late Comdg. Roy. Horse Guards; is a D.L. for co. Salop, a K.St.J., and patron of three livings; has been an Alderman of Wenlock since 1943 (Mayor 1936, and 1961), and a Co. Alderman of Salop since 1960; European War 1918 in France and Belgium (two medals), European War 1941-5 as G.S.O. in Middle East, N. Africa, Italy, and France (despatches); was A.D.C. to Gov. Gen. and Com.-in-Ch. Union of S. Africa 1924-7: *m.* 1931, Marie Louise Priscilla (a D.St.J.), dau. of Sir Herbert Charles Perrott, 6th Bt., C.H., C.B. (ext.), and has issue.

𝔄rms.—Quarterly: 1st and 4th quarterly, per fesse indented argent and sable, in the 1st and 4th quarters, a bugle horn of the 2nd, *Forester*; 2nd and 3rd azure, a fesse nebulée between three crescents ermine, and in the centre chief point a cross crosslet fitchée or, *Weld*.   ℭrests, —1st, a talbot passant argent, collared sable, and line reflexed or; 2nd, a wyvern sable, guttée, collared and lined, and wings elevated or, on the wing an escallop of the first.   𝔖upporters,—

★ This nobleman has in his possession a licence of the time of Henry VIII, giving to John Forester of Watling St., co Salop, the privilege of wearing his hat in the Royal presence.

Two talbots argent, collared sable, lined or, and pendent from the collar a bugle horn of the
second.
 Seat,—The Old Hall, Willey, Broseley, Shropshire. *Residence*,—Marasha, Banket, Rhodesia.

SON LIVING.

Hon. (GEORGE CECIL) BROOKE (Willey Park, Broseley, Shropshire), *b.* Feb. 20th, 1938: *m.*
1967, the Hon. (Elizabeth) Catherine Lyttelton, da. of 10th Viscount Cobham, and has issue living,
Charles Richard George, *b.* July 8th, 1975,—Selina Lucy, *b.* 1968,—Alice Sophie, *b.* 1969,—Alexandra Elizabeth, *b.* 1973.

DAUGHTERS LIVING.

Hon. Christine Helena (*Baroness Bolton*), *b.* 1932: *m.* 1951, the 7th Baron Bolton. *Residence*,—Bolton
Hall, Leyburn, Yorkshire.
Hon. Juliet Mary, *b.* 1934: *m.* 1957, (Arthur) Robin Iain Hill [see M. Downshire]. *Residences*,—13,
Lowndes Close, S.W.1; Clifton Castle, Ripon.
Hon. Kythe Priscilla, *b.* 1941.
Hon. (Mary Angela) Fiona (*Hon. Lady Barttelot*) *b.* 1944: *m.* 1969, Capt. Sir Brian Walter de Stopham
Barttelot, 5th Bt.

COLLATERAL BRANCHES LIVING.

  Grandchildren of the late Hon. Charles Cecil Orlando Weld-Forester, 2nd son of
  5th Baron :—
  Issue of the late Lieut.-Com. Wolstan Beaumont Charles Weld-Forester, O.B.E., R.N.
  b. 1899, *d.* 1961: *m.* 1932, Anne Grace Christian (c/o Coutts & Co., Strand, W.C.2), dau.
  of the late Capt. William Augustus Stirling-Home-Drummond-Moray [B. Kensington]:—
Wolstan William, *b.* 1941.——Beatrice Nicola Grace (*Marchioness of Bute*), *b.* 1933 : *m.* 1955, the
6th Marquess of Bute. *Residences*,—Mount Rothesay, Isle of Bute ; Dumfries House, Cumnock,
Ayrshire; 7, Upper Phillimore Gdns., W8.
  Issue of the late Lieut.-Col. the Hon. Francis Henry Cecil Weld-Forester, 3rd son
  of 5th Baron, *b.* 1871, *d.* 1952 : *m.* 1st, 1901, Alexina Josephine Arbuthnott, who
  d. 1934, dau. of the late Major Frederick Wellaston, 6th Dragoons, of Shenton
  Hall, Leicester [V. Arbuthnott, colls.]; 2ndly, 1937, Grace, who *d.* 1973, da. of
  the late Archibald Peel [E. Peel, colls.]:—
(By 1st marriage) Katherine Georgina Josephine, *b.* 1902 : *m.* 1924, Vice-Adm. Cecil Dacre Staveley
Raikes, O.B.E., who *d.* 1947 [B. Teynham], and has issue living, Francis Arthur Alexander Daore
(c/o The Borneo Co. Ltd., Bangkok, Thailand), *b.* 1925; Man. Dir. of The Borneo Co. Ltd.; Order of
The Crown of Thailand,—Cecilia Heather, *b.* 1927: *m.* 1st, 1949 (m. diss. 1955), James Fleming,
The Black Watch; 2ndly, 1956, John Power George, of Fernhurst Cottage, Pinkneys Green, Maiden-
head, Berks. *Residence*,—Clare House, Dudsbury Av., Ferndown, Dorset.
  Issue of the late Maj. the Hon. Edric Alfred Cecil Weld-Forester, O.V.O., 6th son of
  5th Baron, *b.* 1880, *d.* 1963: *m.* 1916, Lady Victoria Alexandrina, who *d.* 1966,
  da. of 1st Marquess of Lincolnshire, and widow of Nigel Walter Henry Legge-
  Bourke [E. Dartmouth]:—
Charles Robert Cecil (of The Lodge, Laverton, nr. Broadway, Worcs., WR12 7NA), *b.* 1919; ed. at
Stowe; Lt. Rifle Brig.: 1939-40 War in France (despatches twice, prisoner): *m.* 1st, 1940
(m. diss. 1947), Lady Moyra Rosamond Butler, who *d.* 1959, da. of 5th Marquess of Ormonde;
2ndly, 1948 (m. diss. 1962), Venetia Dawn, el. da. of Lt.-Col. Sir (Ernest) Edward de Winton Wills,
4th Bt. (cr. 1904); 3rdly, 1963, Delia (KEITH), yr. da. of the late Col. Guy H. Buxton and has issue
living, (by 1st m.) Piers Edric, *b.* 1946: *m.* 1973, Georgina, who *d.* 1974, da. of the Ven. John Ross
Youens, CB, OBE, MC, Chap. Gen. to Army,—(by 2nd m.) Anthony Edward, *b.* 1954,—Mary,
b. 1957.——Mary Cecilia Georgina (*Hon. Mrs. W. Nicholas S. L. H. Villiers*), *b.* 1917: *m.* 1939,
Major the Hon. (William) Nicholas Somers Laurence Hyde Villiers, Grenadier Guards [see E.
Clarendon].——Elizabeth Rosalind, *b.* 1923: *m.* 1942, Major Francis Holdsworth Hunt, late Coldm.
Gds. (36, Burton Court, SW3), and has issue living, Charles Edric Holdsworth (c/o Williams &
Glyn's Bank, 1, Fleet St., EC4), *b.* 1943; Capt. Coldm. Gds.: *m.* 1968, Sarah Mary, da. of Maj.
Anthony Peter Howorth Greenly, late R. Berks. Regt. [see Gibson, Bt., cr. 1926], and has issue living,
Guy Edric Holdsworth *b.* 1970, Charles Edward Holdsworth *b.* 1972, a da. *b.* 1975,—Elizabeth,
b. 1947: *m.* 1969, Maj. Conway John Edward Seymour, Gren. Gds. [see M. Hertford, colls.]
  Issue of the late Rev. the Hon. Orlando St. Maur Weld-Forester, 2nd son of
  4th Baron, *b.* 1877, *d.* 1944: *m.* 1913, Dorothy Salome Wynne, who *d.* 1963, dau.
  of the late Rev. William Wynne Willson :—
John Orlando (Hunter's Thatch, Wambrook, Chard, Som.), *b.* 1913; Lieut. (ret.) 2nd N. Rhodesia Regt.
entered Colonial Education Ser. 1938; Assist. Director of African Education, N. Rhodesia 1959-61,
and Assist. Sec. 1961-4: *m.* 1938, Lydia Gertrude, younger dau. of the late Rev. Stephen Harold
Wingfield Digby, Canon of Salisbury, Wilts., and of Mombasa, Kenya, and has issue living, Priscilla
Mary, *b.* 1939: *m.* 1974, Neville Henry Prendergast Vereker, of 17, Holland Villas Rd., W14 [see
V. Gort, colls.],—Elizabeth *b.* 1941: *m.* 1962, John Jeremy Inskip Hawkins, of Felbridge, Nursery
Lane, Fairwarp, Uckfield, Sussex, and has issue living, John Edward Inskip *b.* 1963, Bruce James
Orlando *b.* 1965, Veronica Caroline *b.* 1967, Sarah Elizabeth *b.* 1969,—Dorothy Katharine, *b.* 1944:
m. 1967, John Wyndham Simson, of The Cottage, Netley Park, Gomshall, Guildford, Surrey, and
has issue living, Christopher Adhémar *b.* 1969, Henrietta Katharine *b.* 1971, Penelope Anne *b.* 1974,—
Caroline Lydia, *b.* 1948: *m.* 1970, Frank John Montague Wakefield, of Well Cottage, Cliddesden,
Basingstoke, Hants., and has issue living, Anna Charlotte *b.* 1972, Holly Christina *b.* 1974,—Rosa-
mund Eleanor, *b.* 1950: *m.* 1971, Raymond James Edmonds, of 91, Gloucester Rd., Exeter, Devon.
——Katharine Dorothy, *b.* 1916: *m.* 1956, Sydney Herbert Brenan, of Fron Ganol, Pentrecelyn,
Ruthin, Denbighshire, LL15 2HR.

PREDECESSORS.—[1] CECIL Weld-Forester, *b.* 1767 ; assumed by Roy. licence 1811, the
additional surname of Weld ; cr. *Baron Forester*, of Willey Park, co. Salop (peerage of
United Kingdom) 1821 : *m.* 1800, Lady Katharine Mary Manners, dau. of 4th Duke of
Rutland ; *d.* 1828; *s.* by his el. son [2] JOHN GEORGE WELD, *P.C.*, 2nd Baron; M.P. or
Wenlock 1826-8, and Capt. of Corps of Gentlemen at Arms 1841-6 ; *d.* 1874 ; *s.* by his brother [3]
GEORGE CECIL WELD, *P.C.*, 3rd Baron; was Comptroller of H.M. Queen Victoria's Household
1852 and 1858-9; sat as M.P. for Wenlock (*C*) 1828-74; *d.* Feb. 14th, 1886; *s.* by his brother
[4] *Rev.* ORLANDO WATKIN WELD, 4th Baron, *b.* 1813; Canon Residentiary and Preb. of
York: *m.* 1st, 1840, Sophia Elizabeth, who *d.* 1872, dau. of Richard Norman; 2ndly, 1875,
Emma Maria, who *d.* 1898, el. dau. of the late William Tollemache; *d.* 1894; *s.* by his el. son
[5] CECIL THEODORE WELD, 5th Baron, *b.* 1842 ; M.P. for Wenlock (*C*) 1874-85 : *m.* 1866, Emma
Georgina who *d.* 1922, dau. of Sir Willoughby Wolstan Dixie, 8th Bt.; *d.* 1917 ; *s.* by his el. son
[6], GEORGE CECIL BEAUMONT WELD, 6th Baron, *b.* 1867 ; Capt. Roy. Horse Guards; Mayor of
Wenlock 1920-21 and 1921-22 : *m.* 1896, Christine Isabel, who *d.* 1948, dau. of the late Lieut.-
Col. Duncan Henry Caithness Reay Davidson ; *d.* 1932 ; *s.* by his son [7] CECIL GEORGE WILFRID,
7th Baron and present peer.

FORRES, BARON. (Williamson). [Baron U.K. 1922, Bt. U.K. 1909.]

Little is made larger by little.

JOHN ARCHIBALD HARFORD WILLIAMSON, 3rd Baron, and 3rd Baronet; b. Oct. 30th, 1922; s. 1954; ed. at Eton and Trin. Coll., Camb.; Capt. Black Watch; a Dir. of Lobitos Oilfields, Ltd. 1954-65, and of Bank of London & S. America, Ltd., 1961-68; UK representative Pacific Internat. Trade Fair in Peru 1961; Pres. Roy. Forest Agric. Assocn., Windsor 1963-64; a Dir. of Balfour Williamson & Co., Ltd., and other cos.; 1939-45 War in Middle East, Sicily, Italy and Normandy (despatches); ADC to Cdr. 6th (British) Armoured Div. 1944-45: m. 1st, 1945 (m. diss. 1967), Gillian Ann Maclean, da. of Maj. John Maclean Grant, RA; 2ndly, 1969 (m. diss. 1974), Cecily Josephine, da. of Maj. Sir Alexander Penrose Gordon-Cumming, MC, 5th Bt., and widow of the 2nd Earl of Woolton and has issue by 1st marriage.

Arms,—Argent, a saltire wavy between a mullet in chief and another in base and as many boars' heads couped in the flanks sable.
Crest,—A garb or.   Supporters (as recorded at Lyon Office),—On either side a condor proper.
Residences.—Glenogil, by Forfar, Angus; 31 Tite St., SW3.   Clubs,—Brooks's, Pratt's.

SON LIVING.   (By 1st marriage.)
Hon. ALASTAIR STEPHEN GRANT (Clear Springs, Collins Creek, Kyogle 2474, NSW; Brooks's Club), b. May 16th, 1946; ed. at Eton: m. 1969, Margaret, da. of the late G. J. Mallam, of Mullumbimby, NSW, and has issue living, George Archibald Mallam, b. 1972,—Guthrie John, b. 1975.

DAUGHTERS LIVING.   (By 1st marriage.)
Hon. Juliet Ann, b. 1949: m. 1972, Nigel John Eldon Bankes, of Broadwater Cottage, Furners Green, Uckfield, Sussex, and has issue living, William Nigel Wynne, b. 1974.
Hon. Astrid Signe, b. 1951.

BROTHER LIVING.
Hon. Angus Stephen, b. 1929.   Residence,—Old Forge Cottage, Mildenhall, Marlborough, Wilts.

SISTER LIVING.
Hon. Jean Mary, b. 1919: m. 1941, Wing-Com. William James Maitland Longmore, OBE [Maitland, Bt., colls.], and has issue living, Virginia Marjorie, b. 1945: m. 1973, Henry D. N. B. Candy, of Kingstone Warren, Wantage, Berks., and has issue living, Emma Juliet b. 1974,—Carolyn Mary, b. 1946: m. 1966, Michael E. Denison, of Streete End House, Bishops Waltham, Hants., and has issue living, James Edward b. 1968, Lucinda Mary b. 1971,—Jennifer Maitland, b. 1953: m. 1975, Capt. Patrick J. R. Snowball, 4/7th R. Dragoon Gds.   Residence,—Gracious Pond Farm, Chobham, Woking, Surrey.

COLLATERAL BRANCH LIVING.
Issue of the late Capt. the Hon. Gerald Hayne Guthrie Williamson, yr. son of 1st Baron, b. 1893, d. 1966: m. 1917, Christian Alicia Hersey, who d. 1958, da. of the late Edmund Batten Forbes [Stuart-Forbes, Bt, colls.]:—
Alexander Fergus Forbes (Alvie, Kincraig, by Kingussie, Inverness-shire, PH21 1NE. Clubs,—Highland (Inverness), Bath, Lansdowne, and New (Edinburgh)), b. 1919; ed. at Eton; late Lt. RNVR; DL for Inverness-shire; Dir. of Fergus Williamson & Co. Ltd., Albany Meat Products Ltd., Ham Packers Ltd., Spey Fishing Trust Ltd., and Cairngorm Winter Sports Development Board Ltd.: m. 1943, Sabina Ann, only da. of the late Col. Sir Dermot McMorrough Kavanagh, GCVO, and has issue living, James David Alexander, b. 1947,—Dermot Fergus, b. 1950,—Caroline Ann, b. 1945: m. 1968, Lt.-Cdr. Colin Laird MacGregor, RN of The Dairy House, Corton Denham, nr. Sherborne,— Rolline Charlotte, b. 1956.——David Archibald Forbes, MC (33, Fifth Av., San Francisco, Calif., USA). Clubs,—Cavalry, Pacific Union (San Francisco), b. 1922; ed. at Eton; is a Dir. of Avenal Land & Oil Co. Incorp.; formerly Capt. 11th Hussars: m. 1953, Elizabeth Wilbur, da. of Roy Case, of Seattle, USA, and has issue living, David Staphen Charles, b. 1958,—Alexander Fergus Case, b. 1960,—Charlotte Mary, b. 1955.——Hersey Caroline Ann (Newington House, Winkfield, Windsor, Berks), b. 1920; Jun. Cdr. ATS: m. 1st, 1943, Oliver Beakwell, who d. (killed in action in N. Africa) 1943; 2ndly, 1945 (m. diss. 1973), Maj. Donald Struan Robertson, SG, only surviving son of the Rt. Hon. Sir Malcolm Arnold Robertson, GCMG, KBE, and has issue living, (by 2nd m.) Christian Sarah Hersey, b. 1948,—Alexandra Charlotte, b. 1952,—Lucinda Margaret Ann, b. 1960.——Jane Christian Forbes, b. 1931.

PREDECESSORS.—[1] Rt. Hon. ARCHIBALD Williamson, P.C., el. son of the late Stephen Williamson (M.P. for St. Andrews Dist. 1880-85, and Kilmarnock Dist. 1886-95), of Copley, Thornton Hough, Cheshire, and Glenogil, Forfar; b. 1860: a partner in Balfour, Williamson & Co., and Chm. of Lobitos Oilfields, and of Central Argentine Railway, and other cos.; Parliamentary Financial Sec. to War Office 1919-21; M.P. for Elginshire and Nairnshire (L) Jan. 1906 to Nov. 1918 and for Moray and Nairn Dec. 1918 to June 1922; cr. a Baronet 1909, P.C. 1918, and Baron Forres, of Glenogil, co. Forfar (peerage of United Kingdom) 1922: m. 1st, 1887, Caroline Maria, who d. 1911, dau. of the late James Charles Hayne; 2ndly, 1912, the Hon. Agnes Freda, O.B.E., who d. 1942, dau. of 1st Baron Herschell; d. 1931; s. by his el. son [2] STEPHEN KENNETH GUTHRIE, 2nd Baron; b. 1888; Chm. of Lobitos Oilfields, and Anglo-Ecuadorian Oilfields; Director of Office Machinery, Board of Trade 1942-45: m. 1918, Jessica, who d. 1972, da. of the late William Alfred Harford, JP, of Petty France, Badminton, Gloucestershire; d. 1954; s. by his el. son [3] JOHN ARCHIBALD HARFORD, 3rd Baron and present peer.

FORSTER, BARONY OF. (Forster.) [Extinct 1936.]
DAUGHTERS LIVING OF FIRST BARON.
Hon. Dorothy Charlotte (*Baroness Wardington*), *b.* 1891: *m.* 1st, 1914, Capt. the Hon. Harold Fox Pitt Lubbock, Grenadier Guards, who *d.* (killed in action during European War) 1918 [see B. Avebury]; 2ndly, 1923, the 1st Baron Wardington, who *d.* 1950. *Residence,*—Lepe House, Exbury, Southampton.

Hon. Emily Rachel, *b.* 1896: *m.* 1915, Capt. George Henry Lane Fox-Pitt-Rivers, R. Dragoons, who *d.* 1966, and from whom she obtained a divorce 1930 [M. Bath], and has issue living, Michael Angustus (of King John's House, Tollard Royal, Wilts.), *b.* 1917; ed. at Eton; formerly Maj. Welsh Guards: *m.* 1958 (m. diss. 1965), Sonia Mary Brownell, widow of Eric Blair ("George Orwell", the author),—Julian Alfred (19, Lansdowne Walk, W11, and Château du Roc, Fons, Lot, France), *b.* 1919; ed. at Eton; formerly Capt. R. Dragoons: *m.* 1st, 1946 (m. diss. 1953), Pauline Laetitia, el. da. of the late Hon. David Tennant [see B. Glenconner, colls.]; 2ndly, 1955 (m. diss. 1971), Margarita Larios, da. of the Marques de Marzales and formerly wife of the late Miguel, Duke of Primo de Rivera; 3rdly, 1971, Françoise, da. of the late Marcel Geoffroy. *Residence,*—19, Lansdowne Walk, Holland Park, W11.

FORSTER OF HARRABY, BARONY OF. (Forster.) [Extinct 1972.]
DAUGHTER LIVING OF FIRST BARON.
Hon. Pamela, *b.* 1921: *m.* 1948, Peter Hitcham Palmer. *Residence,*—34, Albemarle Rd., Beckenham, Kent.

WIDOW LIVING OF FIRST BARON.
MURIEL (*Baroness Forster of Harraby*), (84, Albemarle Rd., Beckenham, Kent; Brick Court, Temple, EC4), da. of the late Samuel Vosper, of Devonport: *m.* 1917, the 1st Baron, who *d.* 1972, when the title became ext.

FORTESCUE, EARL. (Fortescue.) [Earl G.B. 1789.]

DENZIL GEORGE FORTESCUE, *M.C.*, *T.D.*, 6th Earl; *b.* June 13th, 1893; *s.* 1958; ed. at Eton, and at New Coll., Oxford; Col. T.A.; European War 1914-18 (M.C.), European War 1939-45: *m.* 1st, 1920, Marjorie Ellinor *O.B.E.* (who obtained a divorce 1941), dau. of the late Col. Charles William Trotter, C.B. [B. Hamilton of Dalzell]; 2ndly, 1941, the Hon. Sybil Mary Hardinge, dau. of 3rd Viscount Hardinge, and has issue by 1st and 2nd marriages.

Arms,—Azure, a bend engrailed argent, plain cottised or. *Crest,*—An heraldic tiger statant argent, armed, maned, and tufted or, *Supporters.*—Two greyhounds argent, ducally gorged and lined gules.
Seat,—Ebrington Manor, Chipping Campden, Gloucestershire. *Club,* Boodle's.

A strong shield is the salvation of leaders.

SONS LIVING. (*By 1st marriage.*)
RICHARD ARCHIBALD (*Viscount Ebrington*), *b.* 1922; ed. at Eton, and at Ch. Ch., Oxford; is Capt. Coldstream Guards (Reserve): *m.* 1st, 1949, Penelope Jane, who *d.* 1959, dau. of the late Robert Evelyn Henderson (Clerke, Bt.]; 2ndly, 1961, Margaret Anne, dau. of Charles Michael Stratton, of The Cottage, Mote Park, Maidstone [see E. Perth colls.], and has issue by 1st and 2nd marriages:—
    SON LIVING (*By 1st marriage*),—Hon. Charles Hugh Richard, *b.* May 10th, 1951; ed. at Eton.
    DAUGHTERS LIVING (*By 1st marriage*),—Hon. Celia Anne, *b.* 1957.
        (*By 2nd marriage*),—Hon. Laura Margaret, *b.* 1962.
        —Hon. Sarah Jane, *b.* 1963.
  Residence,—The Old Farm, Swinbrook, Burford, Oxon.
Hon. Martin Denzil, *b.* 1924; ed. at Eton; is Lieut., R.N. (Emergency List): *m.* 1954, Prudence Luisa, dau. of Sir Charles Samuel Rowley, T.D., 6th Bt. (cr. 1786), and has issue living, John Andrew Francis, *b.* 1955,—Anthony William, *b.* 1962,—Katharine, *b.* 1956,—Georgina Elizabeth, *b.* 1958. *Residence,*—Wincombe Park, Shaftesbury, Dorset.

    (*By 2nd marriage.*)
Hon. Seymour Henry (7, The Terrace, Barnes, SW13), *b.* 1942; ed. at Eton, Trin. Coll., Camb., and London Graduate Sch. of Business Studies: *m.* 1966, Julia, da. of Sir John Arthur Pilcher, KCMG, and has issue living, Marissa Clare, *b.* 1973.

DAUGHTER LIVING. (*By 1st marriage.*)
Lady Bridget Ellinor, *b.* 1927: *m.* 1952, Wing-Com. Gordon Leonard Sinclair, D.F.C., and has issue living, Alan Gordon William, *b.* 1956,—Robert Alistair, *b.* 1965,—Caroline Fiona, *b.* 1958,—Joanna Rosalind, *b.* 1963. *Residence,*—Mary Monks Close, Whitchurch, Aylesbury.

DAUGHTERS LIVING OF FIFTH EARL.
Lady Margaret FORTESCUE, *b.* 1923; resumed 1966 the surname of Fortescue: *m.* 1948 (m. diss. 1968), Bernard van Cutsem, and has issue living, Eleanor (*Viscountess Sudley*), *b.* 1949: *m.* 1974, Arthur (Desmond) Colquhoun, Viscount Sudley, son of 8th Earl of Arran,—Rosamund Isabelle, *b.* 1952: *m.* 1975, Thomas William Fellowes, son of Sir William Albemarle Fellowes, KCVO [see V. Hampden, colls.]. *Residence,*—Castle Hill, Barnstaple, N. Devon.
Lady Elizabeth Joan, *b.* 1926: *m.* 1946, Major William Lloyd (John) Baxendale, Coldstream Guards, and has issue living, David Hugh, *b.* 1952,—Peter Anthony, *b.* 1955,—Lucinda Margaret, *b.* 1958. *Residence,*—Hailwell House, Framfield, Uckfield, Sussex.

COLLATERAL BRANCHES LIVING.

Grandchildren of the late Capt. the Hon. Arthur Grenville Fortescue, 4th son of 3rd Earl:—

Issue of the late Capt. **Grenville** Fortescue, Rifle Brig. (Prince Consort's Own), *b.* 1887, *d.* (killed in action) 1915: *m.* 1912, Adelaide [(now of **Thorney Wood House, Bransgore,** Hants.); she *m.* 2ndly, 1930, Brigadier Robin Leslie Hutchins, MC, who *d.* 1973], el. da. of the late Henry Jephson, of 4, Cornwall Gardens, SW [Crampton, Bt.]:—

Arthur Henry Grenville, *MBE, MC* (Walnut Tree Cottage, Skirmett, Bucks.), *b.* 1913; ed. at Winchester, and at Ch. Ch., Oxford; Brig. late Coldstream Guards; 1939-45 War (wounded, despatches, MC, MBE); MBE (Mil.) 1946: *m.* 1946, Rosita Anne, da. of the late Maj.-Gen. John Charles Campbell, VC, DSO, MC, and has issue living, Mark Charles Grenville, *b.* 1947: *m.* 1971, Mrs. Virginia R. Berens,—Nicholas Cecil John, *b.* 1953.——Diana FORTESCUE, *b.* 1915; resumed in 1947 her maiden surname of Fortescue: *m.* 1945 (marriage annulled on her petition 1947), Lieut.-Col. Charles Murray Floyd, OBE, RE, wh o *d.* 1971 [see Floyd, Bt., colls.]. *Residence,*—Thorney Wood House, Bransgore, Hants.

Issue of the late Brig.-Gen. Hon. the Charles Granville Fortescue, CB, CMG, DSO, 6th son of 3rd Earl, *b.* 1861, *d.* 1951: *m.* 1906, Æthel Rosa, who *d.* 1967, da. of Gen. Sir Charles Mansfield Clarke, 3rd Bt., GCB, GCVO, and widow of Capt. Ernest George Campbell, 3rd Batn. Rifle Brig. (Prince Consort's Own) [V. Barrington):—

Anne Mary, *b.* 1910: *m.* 1929, Henry Reginald Aked Garnett, who *d.* 1944, and has issue living, Adrian John Fortescue (Bradley Court, Wotton-under-Edge, Glos.), *b.* 1930; ed. at Eton: *m.* 1967, Polly, da. of T. F. Devlin, of Sessia, Coagh, co. Tyrone, and has issue living, Rose Penelope *b.* 1970, Daisy Domenico *b.* 1972, Louise Agatha *b.* 1973. *Residence,*—7 Seymour Walk, SW10.——Lilah Rose, *TD, b.* 1912; formerly Capt. WRAC (TA), 1939-45 War in Middle East and Germany. *Residences,*— Angell's, Merseyhampton, Glos.; 7, Seymour Walk, SW10.

Grandchildren of the late John Bevill Fortescue, yst. son of the late Hon. George Matthew Fortescue, MP, 2nd son of 1st Earl:—

Issue of the late Lt. Col. John Grenville Fortescue, *b.* 1896; *d.* 1969: *m.* 1917, Daphne Marjorie, who *d,* 1962, da. of the late Hon. Algernon Henry Bourke [E. Mayo, colls.]: John Desmond Grenville (The Stewardry, Boconnoc, Lostwithiel, Cornwall), *b.* 1919; ed. at Eton; Coldstream Guards; a DL and JP; High Sheriff of Cornwall 1966-67; 1939-45 War: *m.* 1942, Nina, da. of the late E. Kendall-Lane of Sask., Canada, and has issue living, Anthony Desmond Grenville, *b.* 1946,—Anne Desnia, *b.* 1948: *m.* 1970, Capt. Iain Anthony Mackie, 15/19 H.——Rosemary Sylvia, *b.* 1920: *m.* 1944, Douglas Frederick Thomas White, of The Manor, Berwick Bassett, Swindon, Wilts., and has issue living, John Frederick Fortescue, *b.* 1946: *m.* 1972, Rosemary Kathleen, da. of Maj. Edward Palmer, of Fernvale, Northam, N. Devon,—David Grenville, *b.* 1948; *m.* 1970, Diana Penelope, da. of Peter Werden Wilson, of The Manor, Clyffe Pypard, Wilts.,—April Rosemary, *b.* 1950: *m.* 1971, Robert Edward Simpson, of 14, Rothesay Place, Edinburgh.——June Diana, *b.* 1924: *m.* 1952, Derek Alistair Bigham, of Woodside, Horsegate Drive, S. Ascot, and has issue living, Diana Susan, *b.* 1954,—Julia Rosemary *b.* 1959.

(In remainder to Barony of Fortescue only).

Grandchildren of the late William Archer IRVINE-FORTESCUE, son of the late Archer Irvine-Fortescue (infra) :—

Issue of the late Col. Archer Irvine-Fortescue, DSO, *b.* 1880; *d.* 1959: *m.* 1916, Ruth Olive, who *d.* 1971, da. of the late Henry Boddington, JP, of Pownall Hall, Wilmslow, Cheshire:— James William, *b.* 1917 ; ed. at Edinburgh Acad., and at Aberdeen Univ. (M.A. honours 1937); CA 1948; 1939-45 War as Maj. and Staff Paymaster RAPC; a member of Kincardine Co. Council 1952-8 and 1964-73, a JP for Kincardineshire: *m.* 1953, Margaret Guise, da. of the late Lt.-Col. G. D. Yates, of Tohillwood, Canonbie, Dumfriesshire, and has issue living, Grenville Archer, *b.* 1954; ed. at Fettes; 2nd Lt. Gordon Highlanders,—Henry Boswell, *b.* 1958,—James Robert, *b.* 1960,— Rachel Sarah, *b.* 1956. *Residence,*—Kingcausie, Maryculter, Aberdeen.——Agnes Virginia FORTESCUE, *b.* 1922; Mus. Bac., Cape Town; LRAM: *m.* 1st, 1944, Donald Spenser Nuttall, Lieut. RA, who *d.* (killed in action in Burma) 1945; 2ndly, 1949 (m. diss. 1964), Jerzy Wladislaw Jaholkowski; 3rdly, 1973, Eric Atwell (160 Church Rd., Walmer, Port Elizabeth, Cape Prov., S. Africa).

Grandson of the late Archer IRVINE-FORTESCUE, son of the Rev. William Fortescue, LL.B., 2nd son of Capt. the Hon. Matthew Fortescue, 2nd son of 2nd Baron :—

Issue of the late William Archer IRVINE-FORTESCUE, *b.* 1851, *d.* 1941 : *m.* 1877, Edith Virginia, who *d.* 1946, dau. of the late John Robert Duguid, of Gibraltar :— William Grenville, *M.C.*, *b.* 1897 ; Lieut.-Col. (retired) R.E.; European War 1915-19 (despatches, M.C. and Bar), European War 1939-45 : *m.* 1st, 1921 (marriage dissolved 1929), Joan Evelyn Mary, dau. of the late Henry Sydney Powell, of Pocklington, Yorkshire ; 2ndly, 1941, Sheila, dau. of the late Dr. W. Bennett Jones, of Liverpool, and has issue living, (by 1st marriage) Henry (of The Old Dairy House, Trentham, Staffs), *b.* 1922 ; ed. at Cheltenham ; Major (retired) Roy. Tank Regt. ; European War 1941-45, Korea 1953, Malaya 1955, Cyprus 1957 : *m.* 1951, Bridget Unity, dau. of Col. Edmund Portman Awdry, M.C., T.D., D.L., of Chippenham, Wilts, and has issue living, Alexander Ramsay *b.* 1952; ed. at Wellington, Ian Henry *b.* 1954; ed. at Wellington, Victoria Awdry *b.* 1957,—(by 2nd m.) William Archer, *b.* 1945; ed. at Wellington, and Wadham Coll., Oxford,—(by 1st m.) Valerie Faith *b.* 1925,—(by 2nd m.) Margaret Anne, *b.* 1944; ed. at Aberdeen Univ. (MA) *Residence,*—111, Craigleith Rd., Edinburgh, 4.

Grandchildren of the late William Archer IRVINE-FORTESCUE (ante) :— Issue of the late Rev. John Faithful IRVINE-FORTESCUE, *b.* 1883, *d.* 1957 : *m.* 1917, Anne (of 5, Seton Place, Edinburgh, 9), dau. of the late J. Brockhurst Souter, of Newhaven :— Hugh William (12, Alameda Rd., Ampthill, Beds.), *b.* 1930; ed. at Glasgow Acad., and at Glasgow Univ. (BSc); MIEE; late Lt., RAPC: *m.* 1967, Patricia Anne Elizabeth, da. of F. J. Dudgeon, of Kingsknowe, Edinburgh, and has issue living, John Hugh, *b.* 1968,—Caroline Anne Patricia, *b.* 1971, —Katherine Helen Isobel, *b.* 1974.——Edith Caroline, *b.* 1921; ed. at Glasgow Univ. (MA honours 1942). *Residence,* 5, Seton Place, Edinburgh, 9.

PREDECESSORS.—[1] *Sir* HUGH Fortescue; summoned to Parliament 1721 in right of his maternal grandmother, as 14th *Baron Clinton* (peerage of England), and cr. *Baron Fortescue* of Castle Hill, co. Devon, with remainder to his half-brother Mathew, and *Earl of Clinton* (peerage of Great Britain) 1746 ; was a Lord of the Bedchamber; *d.s.p.* 1751, when the earldom expired, the Barony of Clinton fell into abeyance, and the Barony of Fortescue passed to his half-brother [2] MATHEW, 2nd Baron ; *d.* 1785 ; *s.* by his son [3] HUGH, *D.C.L.*, 3rd Baron ; cr. *Viscount Ebrington* and *Earl Fortescue* (peerage of Great Britain) 1789; *d.* 1841 ; *s.* by his son [4] HUGH, *K.G.*, 2nd Earl, *b.* 1783; summoned to House of Lords in his father's Barony of Fortescue 1839, Lord-Lieut. of Ireland 1839 41: *m.* 1st, 1817, Lady Susan Ryder, who *d.* 1827, dau. of 1st Earl of Harrowby; 2ndly, 1841, Elizabeth, dau. of Piers Geale, and widow of Sir Marcus Somerville, M.P., 4th Bt.: *d.* 1861; *s.* by his son [5] HUGH, 3rd Earl, *b.* 1818; summoned to House of Peers in his father's Barony of Fortescue 1859 ; sat as M.P. for Plymouth (*L*) 1841-52, and for Marylebone 1854-9 ; a Lord of the Treasury, 1846-7, and Sec. to Poor Law Board 1847-51 ; *m.* 1847, Georgiana Augusta Charlotte Caroline, who *d.* 1866, el. dau. of the late Right Hon. George Lionel Dawson-Damer ; *d.* 1905 ; *s.* by his son [6] HUGH, 4th Earl, *b.* 1854; Lord-Lieut. of Devonshire 1904-28; M.P. for Tiverton (*L*) 1881-5, and for W., or Tavistock, Div. of Devonshire 1885-92: *m.* 1886, the Hon. Emily Ormsby-Gore, *C.B.E.*, who *d.* 1929 (an Extra Lady of the Bedchamber to Queen Mary), dau. of 2nd Baron Harlech ; *d.* 1932 ; *s.* by his son [7] HUGH WILLIAM, *K.G.*, *C.B.*, *O.B.E.*, *M.C.*, P.C., 5th Earl ; *b.* 1888; was Col. Comdt. Hon. Artillery Co. 1935-41. Capt. of the Hon. Corps of Gentlemen-at-Arms April to July 1945, and 1951-8, Lord-in-Waiting to H.M. 1936-45, and Ch. Opposition Whip in House of Lords 1945-51 : *m.* 1917, the Hon. Margaret Helen Beaumont, *C.B.E.*, who *d.* 1958, dau. of 1st Viscount ; *d.* 1958, *s.* by his brother [8] DENZIL GEORGE, 6th Earl and present peer; also Viscount Ebrington, and Baron Fortescue.

FORTEVIOT, BARON. (Dewar.) [Baron U.K. 1917, Bt. U.K. 1907.]

HENRY EVELYN ALEXANDER DEWAR, M.B.E., 3rd Baron, and 3rd Baronet; *b.* Feb. 23rd, 1906 ; *s.* 1947; ed. at Eton, and at St. John's Coll., Oxford (B.A. 1929); is temporary Major Black Watch (T.A.), a Member of Queen's Body Guard for Scotland (Roy. Co. of Archers), Chm. of John Dewar & Sons, Ltd., a Director of Buchanan-Dewar, Ltd., and of Distillers Co. Ltd., and a J.P. and D.L. for Perthshire ; European War 1939-45 (M.B.E.) ; M.B.E. (Mil.) 1943 : *m.* 1933, Cynthia Monica, el. dau. of the late Piers Cecil Le Gendre Starkie [de Hoghton, Bt.], and has issue.

Arms,—Or, on a pale vert the crozier of St. Fillan proper, on a chief engrailed gules a holy lamb passant reguardant, staff and cross argent with the banner of St. Andrew proper, between two stalks of barley slipped also proper. **Crest,**— A cock proper. **Supporters** (as recorded at Lyon Office),—*Dexter*, the figure of St. Fillan holding in his exterior hand his crozier proper ; *sinister*, an eagle, wings erected proper.

Seat,—Dupplin Castle, Perth. *Clubs,*—Brooks's, Royal (Perth).

SONS LIVING.

Hon. JOHN JAMES EVELYN (6, Holland Villas Rd., W14), *b.* April 5th, 1938; ed. at Eton: *m.* 1963, Lady Elisabeth Jeronima Waldegrave, 3rd da. of 12th Earl Waldegrave, and has issue living, Alexander John Edward, *b.* 1971,—Mary-Emma Jeronima, *b.* 1965,—Miranda Phoebe, *b.* 1968,— Henrietta Cynthia, *b.* 1970.
Hon. Simon Thomas (Terling Park, Moree, NSW), *b.* 1941: *m.* 1970, (m. diss. 1973), Helen Elizabeth, da. of W. N. Bassett, of Karoola Park, Roma, Qld.

DAUGHTERS LIVING.

Hon. Caroline Cecily (14, Cheyne Gdns., SW3), *b.* 1934: *m.* 1956 (*m.* diss. 1966), the 3rd Duke of Fife.
Hon. Penelope Cynthia, *b.* 1935 : *m.* 1959, Norman Frank Paul Butler, and has issue living, Paul, *b.* 1960,—Sean, *b.* 1963,—Tracey Penelope, *b.* 1961. *Residence,*—

SISTER LIVING.

Hon. Irene Margareta, *b.* 1908 : *m.* 1934, Lieut.-Col. Hugh Littleton Dewhurst, R.A., and has issue living, Jeremy Hugh (Woodend, Madderty, Crieff), *b.* 1934: *m.* 1958, Angela Rachel, yr. da. of Col. Sir William Giles Newsom Walker, TD, of Pitlair, Cupar, Fife,—Susan Margaret, *b.* 1936: *m.* 1958, Alick Michael Rankin, Lt. Scots Guards [see Rankin, Bt., colls. cr. 1898].—Fiona Mary, *b.* 1942: *m.* 1968, David Alexander Whitaker. *Residence,*—Dungarthill, Dunkeld, Perthshire.

HALF-SISTER LIVING.

Hon. Janet Bertha (*Hon. Lady Stainton*), *b.* 1895 : *m.* 1918, Sir John Armitage Stainton, K.C.B., K.B.E., Q.C., who *d.* 1957, and has issue living, John David Adam, *b.* 1921,—Andrew Thomas (Coombe Manor, Hastingleigh, Ashford, Kent), *b.* 1925: *m.* 1956, Mikaela, da. of Constantine Lykiardopulos, of Athens, and has issue living, John Andrew, *b.* 1968, Deborah Leila *b.* 1957, Joanna Natalie *b.* 1959, Antigone Maria *b.* 1962,—Nancy Pauline (*Hon. Mrs. Richard A. O. Henniker-Major*), *b.* 1919: *m.* 1946, the Hon. Richard Arthur Otway Henniker-Major [see B. Henniker],—Sheila Catherine, *b.* 1929. *Residence,*—Crundale House, Crundale, Canterbury.

PREDECESSORS.—[1] JOHN ALEXANDER Dewar, son of the late John Dewar, distiller, of Perth ; *b.* 1856; Chm. of John Dewar and Sons (Limited) ; a Director of Buchanan-Dewar (Limited), and of Distillers Co. (Limited); twice Lord Provost of Perth; M.P. for Inverness-shire (*L*) 1900-1916 : cr. a *Baronet* 1907, and *Baron Forteviot*, of Dupplin, Perthshire (peerage of United Kingdom) 1917 : *m.* 1st, 1884, Johann, who *d.* 1899, dau. of William Tod, of Gospetry, Kinross-shire ; 2ndly, 1905, Margaret Elizabeth, who *d.* 1940, el. dau. of the late Henry Holland ; *d.* 1929 ; *s.* by his el. son [2] JOHN, 2nd Baron, *b.* 1885 ; Lieut.-Col. and Brevet Col. late 6th/7th Batn. Black Watch (T.A.), Chm. of Distillers Co., Ltd., and Brigadier Roy. Co. of Archers (King's Body Guard for Scotland) ; Lord Provost of Perth 1922-5; European War 1914-19 (M.C.): *m.* 1st, 1919, Marjory Winton Isobel, *A.R.R.C.*, who *d.* 1945, 2nd dau. of the late Lieut.-Col. Sir Charles Henry Brabazon Heaton-Ellis, O.B.E., of Wyddiall Hall, Herts ; 2ndly, 1946, Muriel Cecil Harriotte, who *d.* 1975, da. of the late Lt.-Col. Sir Charles Henry Brabazon Heaton-Ellis, CBE and widow of (1) Richard Charles Grave-Sawle [Graves-Sawle, Bt.], and (2) Major Alwyn Lionel Compton Cavendish [D. Devonshire, colls.]; *d.* 1947; *s.* by his half-brother [3] HENRY EVELYN ALEXANDER, *b.* 1906, 3rd Baron and present peer.

Foxford, Baron, title of Earl of Limerick on Roll of H.L.

FRANCIS-WILLIAMS, BARONY OF. (Williams.) [Extinct 1970.]

SON LIVING OF LIFE BARON

Hon. John Melville, *b.* 1931; ed. at St. Christopher Sch., Letchworth, and at St. John's Coll., Camb., Bar. Inner Temple 1955: *m.* 1955, Jean Margaret. dau. of Harold Lucas, of Huddersfield, and has issue. *Residence,*—Deers Hill, Abinger Hammer Dorking, Surrey.

DAUGHTER LIVING OF LIFE BARON.

Hon. Elizabeth Frances, *b.* 19—: *m.* 1963, George Alexander Thomson, of 27, Haverfield Gdns., Kew, Richmond, Surrey, and has issue.

WIDOW LIVING OF LIFE BARON.

JESSIE MELVILLE (*Baroness Francis-Williams*), (Russetts, The Paddock, Westcott, Dorking, Surrey), da. of E. Hopkins, of Leeds: *m.* 1926, Baron Francis-Williams (Life Peer), who *d.* 1970.

FRANKS, BARON.   (Franks.)   [Life Baron U.K. 1962.]

To be rather than to seem to be

OLIVER SHEWELL FRANKS, *G.C.M.G.*, *K.C.B.*, *C.B.E.*, *P.C.*, son of the Rev. Robert Sleightholme Franks, of Leppington, Winscombe, Somerset; *b.* Feb. 16th, 1905; ed. at Bristol Gram. Sch., and at Queen's Coll., Oxford (B.A. 1927, M.A. 1930, Hon. Fellow 1948); Hon. D.C.L. Oxford 1952; Hon. LLD Camb.; Reading, and St. Andrews; Provost of Queen's Coll., Oxford 1946-8, Ambassador to U.S.A. 1948-52, Chm. of Lloyds Bank 1954-62 and of Board of Govs. of United Hosps. 1958-64; a Trustee of Pilgrim Trust since 1947, Provost of Worcester Coll., Oxford since 1962, a Member of Prince's Council, Duchy of Cornwall since 1965, and Chancellor of Univ. East Anglia since 1966; *cr.* C.B.E. (Civil) 1942, K.C.B. (Civil) 1946, P.C. 1949, C.M.G. 1952, and *Baron Franks*, of Headington, co. Oxford (Life Baron) 1962: *m.* 1931, Barbara Mary, dau. of H. G. Tanner, and has issue.

Arms,—Argent on a chevron engrailed azure between in chief two eagles displayed, and in base three martlets gules three bezants. Crest,—A fountain charged with a martlet rising gules bezanty. Supporters,—*Dexter*, a Protestant minister habited in a Geneva gown proper clasping in the exterior hand a Bible proper; *sinister*, a sea horse (hippocampus) proper.

Residence,—The Provost's Lodgings, Worcester College, Oxford.   *Club*,—Athenæum.

DAUGHTERS LIVING.

Hon. Caroline Lesley, *b.* 1939: *m.* 1962, John Rowland Dinwiddy (Little St Anne's Coach House, Bakeham Lane, Englefield Green, Surrey), and has issue.
Hon. Alison Elizabeth, *b.* 1945.

FRASER OF ALLANDER, BARONY OF.   (Fraser.)   [Baron U.K. 1964, disclaimed 1966, Bt. U.K. 1961.]

Sir HUGH FRASER, 2nd *Baronet*; *b.* Dec. 18th, 1936; *s.* as 2nd Baron Fraser of Allander Nov. 6th, 1966; disclaimed his peerage for life Dec. 7th, 1966; ed. at St. Mary's, Melrose, and Kelvinside Acad.; Chm. and Man. Dir. of House of Fraser, of Scottish Universal Investments, Ltd., and George Outram and Co., Ltd. since 1966; Chm. W.of Scotland Cttee. of the Scottish Council (Development & Industry); a Dir. of Noble Grossart, Ltd., and Highland Tourist (Cairngorm Development), Ltd.: *m.* 1st, 1962 (*m.* diss. 1971), Patricia Mary, el. da. of John Bowie; 2ndly, 1973, Aileen Margaret, da. of George Paterson Ross, and has issue by 1st m.

Arms,—Per fess azue and argent, a fess enwreathed or and gules between three fraises of the second in chief and an antique crown in base gules. Crest,—A stag's head erased proper, attired azure, and gorged of a collar consisting of a torse enwreathed or and gules. Supporters—(borne by Barons Fraser of Allander)—Two Labrador dogs sable, langued gules.
Residence,—Dineiddwg, Mugdock, Stirlingshire.

DAUGHTERS LIVING.   (By 1st *m.*)
Hon. Patricia Lydia, *b.* 1963.
Hon. Belinda Ann, *b.* 1964.
Hon. Caroline Emily, *b.* 1966.

SISTER LIVING.
Hon. Ann Lewis, *b.* 1932.

WIDOW LIVING OF FIRST BARON.

KATIE HUTCHEON (*Baroness Fraser of Allander*) (Allander Lodge, Milngavie, Dunbartonshire), da. of the late Sir Andrew Jopp Williams Lewis, LLD: *m.* 1931, the 1st Baron, who *d.* 1966.

PREDECESSOR.—[1] *Sir* HUGH Fraser, son of Hugh Fraser, *b.* 1903: Chm. and Managing Dir. House of Fraser, Ltd.; cr. a *Baronet* 1961, and *Baron Fraser of Allander*, of Dineiddwg, co. Stirling (peerage of UK) 1964: *m.* 1931, Katie Hutcheon, da. of Sir Andrew Jopp Williams Lewis, LLD; *d.* 1966; *s.* by his only son [2| Hugh, 2nd Baron, until he disclaimed his peerage, and 2nd baronet.

FRASER OF KILMORACK, BARON. (Fraser.) [Life Baron 1974.]

(RICHARD) MICHAEL FRASER, *CBE*, yr. son of the late Col. Thomas Fraser, CBE, DSO, TD, DL, LLD, of 16, Albyn Place, Aberdeen; *b.* Oct. 28th, 1915; ed. at Fettes Coll., and King's Coll., Camb. (MA.); entered Conservative Research Dept. 1946 (Head of Home Affairs Section 1950-51, Dir. 1951-64, Chm. since 1970); Sec. to the Conservative Party's Advisory Cttee. on Policy 1951-64, and Dep. Chm. since 1970; Sec. to Conservative Leader's Consultative Cttee. 1964-70, and since 1974; Dep. Chm. Conservative Party Orgn. since 1964; 1939-45 War as Lt.-Col. RA (MBE); cr. MBE (Mil) 1945, CBE (Civil) 1955, Knt. 1962, *Baron Fraser of Kilmorack*, of Rubislaw, in Co. of City of Aberdeen (Life Baron) 1974: *m.* 1944, Elizabeth Chloe, el. da. of Brig. Cyril Alexander Fraser Drummond, OBE, of Little Knoll, Portishead, Somerset, and has issue.

Arms,—not exemplified at time of going to press.

Residence.—18, Drayton Court, SW10. *Clubs.*—Carlton, St. James'.

SON LIVING.

Hon. Angus Simon James (4, Rue Collas, 92310-Sèvres, France), *b.* 1945: *m.* 1970, Jennifer Ann, da. of Colin McKean Craig, FRCS, and has issue.

FRASER OF LONSDALE, BARONY OF. (Fraser.) [Extinct 1974.]

DAUGHTER LIVING OF LIFE BARON.

Hon. Margaret Joan, *b.* 1920: *m.* 1939, Arthur Edward McDonald, and has issue. *Residence,*—Meads Farm, East Orchard, Shaftesbury, Dorset.

WIDOW LIVING OF LIFE BARON.

IRENE GLADYS (*Baroness Fraser of Lonsdale*), *CBE* (St. John's Lodge, Inner Circle, Regent's Park, NW1; Low Wood House, Haverthwaite, Ulverston, Lancs.; Fraser House, Wepener, Orange Free State, S. Africa), da. of the late George Frederick Mace, of Chipping Norton, Oxon; OBE (Civil) 1920: *m.* 1918, Baron Fraser of Lonsdale (Life Baron) who *d.* 1974.

FRASER OF NORTH CAPE, BARON. (Fraser.) [Baron U.K. 1946.]

BRUCE AUSTIN FRASER, *G.C.B., K.B.E.*, 1st Baron, son of the late Gen. Alexander Fraser, C.B.; *b.* Feb. 5th, 1888; ed. at Bradfield Coll.; D.C.L. Oxford 1947; Hon. LL.D. Wales 1955; is Adm. of the Fleet; European War 1914-19 (O.B.E.), European War 1939-45 (K.B.E., K.C.B., G.C.B., cr. Baron, Grand Officer of Order of Orange Nassau of the Netherlands, Chevalier of Legion of Honour, Croix de Guerre with palm, Order of St. Olav. of Norway, 1st class Order of Suvarov of Russia, American D.S.M.); appointed an A.D.C. to H.M. 1936, and Ch. of Staff to Com.-in-Ch. Mediterranean Fleet 1938; was Third Sea Lord of the Admiralty and Controller of the Navy 1939-42, Com.-in-Ch., Home Fleet 1943-44, Eastern Fleet 1944-5, British Pacific Fleet 1945-7, and Portsmouth 1947-8, and First Sea Lord of the Admiralty and Ch. of Naval Staff 1948-51; First and Principal Naval A.D.C. to H.M. 1946-8; an Hon. Freeman of Shipwrights' Co.; cr. O.B.E. (Mil.) 1919, C.B. (Mil.) 1939, K.B.E. (Mil.) 1941, K.C.B. (Mil.) 1943, G.C.B. (Mil.) 1944, and *Baron Fraser of North Cape*, of Molesey, co. Surrey (peerage of United Kingdom), 1946.

Residence,—18, Wolsey Road, East Molesey, Surrey. *Club,*—United Service.

FRASER OF TULLYBELTON, BARON. (Fraser.) [Life Baron 1975.]

WALTER IAN REID FRASER, *PC*, son of the late Alexander Reid Fraser, stockbroker, of Glasgow; *b.* Feb. 3rd, 1911; ed. at Repton, and Balliol Coll., Oxford (Scholar, BA); LLD Glasgow; Advocate Scotland 1936, QC 1953; Lecturer in Constitutional Law, Glasgow Univ. 1936, and Edinburgh Univ. 1948, Dean of Faculty of Advocates 1959-64, and a Member of R. Commn. on Police 1960; a Member of Queen's Body Guard for Scotland (R. Co. of Archers); 1939-45 War with RA, in UK, and Burma; a Lord of Session with title of Lord Fraser 1964-75, and a Lord of Appeal in Ordinary with title of *Baron Fraser of Tullybelton*, of Bankfoot, co. Perth (Life Baron) 1975: *m.* 1943, (Mary Ursula) Cynthia (Gwendolen), da. of Col. Ian Harrison Macdonell, DSO, late Highland L.I. and has issue.

Residence.—Tullybelton House, Bankfoot, Perthshire, PH1 4DH. *Clubs.*—New (Edinburgh), Western (Glasgow).

SON LIVING.

Hon. Alexander Andrew Macdonell, *b.* 1946.

FREYBERG, BARON. (Freyberg.) [Baron U.K. 1951.]

PAUL RICHARD FREYBERG, *OBE*, *MC*, 2nd Baron, *b*. May 27th, 1923; *s*. 1963; ed. at Eton; Col. late Grenadier Guards; Greece and W. Desert 1940-42 with New Zealand Expeditionary Force; N. Africa and Italy 1942-45 with Grenadier Guards (MC); Palestine 1947-48, Cyprus 1956-58, and Cameroons 1961; AAG, HQ London District 1962-65, Comd. HAC Inf. Bn. 1965-68, on Defence Policy Staff, Min. of Defence 1968-71; and Col. Gen. Staff to Dir. Territorials, Volunteers & Cadets 1971-75; OBE (Mil.) 1965: *m*. 1960, Ivry Perronelle Katharine, only da. of Cyril Harrower Guild, of Aspall Hall, nr. Debenham, Suffolk, and has issue.

Arms,—Or, on a chief sable four mullets of the field. Crest,—A demi lion gules holding between the paws an eagle displayed sable. Supporters,—On either side a salamander proper. *Residence,*—Munstead House, Godalming, Surrey. *Clubs,*—Boodle's, RAC.

SON LIVING.
Hon. VALERIAN BERNARD, *b*. Dec. 15, 1970.

DAUGHTERS LIVING.
Hon. Annabel Pauline, *b*. 1961.
Hon. Venetia Rose, *b*. 1963.
Hon. Christina Marie Gabriel, *b*. 1967.

PREDECESSOR.—[1] *Sir* BERNARD CYRIL Freyberg, *V.C.*, *G.C.M.G.*, *K.C.B.*, *K.B.E.*, *D.S.O.*, son of J. Freyberg, of Wellington, New Zealand; *b*. 1889; Lt.-Gen. late Grenadier Guards and Manchester. Regt.; G.O.C., New Zealand Expeditionary Force 1939-45, and Gov.-Gen. and C.-in-C. of New Zealand 1946-52, and Dep. Constable and Lt.-Gov. of Windsor Castle 1953-63; cr. *Baron Freyberg*, of Wellington, New Zealand, and of Munstead, co. Surrey (peerage of U.K.) 1951: *m*. 1922, Dame Barbara, GBE, who *d*. 1973, da. of Sir Herbert Jekyll, KCMG, and widow of the Hon. Francis Walter Stafford MacLaren, MP [B. Aberconway]; *d*. 1963; *s*. by his only son [2] PAUL RICHARD, 2nd Baron and present peer.

FULTON, BARON. (Fulton.) [Life Baron 1966.]

JOHN SCOTT FULTON, son of the late Angus Robertson Fulton, LLD, DSc, of Dundee; *b*. May 27th, 1902; ed. at Dundee High Sch., at St. Andrew's Univ. (MA), and at Balliol Coll., Oxford (MA); Fellow and Tutor in Philosophy and Politics, Balliol Coll., Oxford 1928-45, of Univ. Coll. of Swansea 1947-59, and Vice-Chancellor of Univ. of Sussex 1959-67; Prin. Assist. Sec. Min. of Fuel and Power 1942-44; Chm. of Commn. Educational Requirements Sierra Leone 1954, of Nat. Advisory Council Training Supply of Teachers 1959-63, of Univs. Central Council on Admissions 1961-64, of Commn. on Establishment of second Univ. in Hong Kong 1962, of Inter-Univ. Council Higher Education Overseas 1964-68, of Cttee. on Civil Ser. 1966-68; Chm. of British Council, 1968-71, and of Tavistock Inst. of Human Relations since 1968, and Vice-Chm. BBC 1965-70; cr. Knt. 1964, and *Baron Fulton*, of Falmer, co. Sussex (Life Baron) 1966: *m*. 1939, Jacqueline, da. of Kenneth Edward Towler Wilkinson, of York, and has issue.

Residence,—Brook House, Thornton-le-Dale, Yorks. *Club,*—Athenæum.

SONS LIVING.
Hon. (Kenneth Angus) Oliver, *b*. 1941; ed. at Eton, Balliol Coll., Oxford (BA) and Univ. of California.
Hon. Alan Scott, *b*. 1946; ed. at Eton and Balliol Coll., Oxford.
Hon. Duncan John Rowntree, *b*. 1949; ed. at Eton and Balliol Coll., Oxford.

DAUGHTER LIVING.
Hon. Charity Marion Anne, *b*. 1951.

FURNESS, VISCOUNT. (Furness.) [Viscount U.K. 1918.]

WILLIAM ANTHONY FURNESS, 2nd Viscount; *b.* March 31st, 1929; *s.* 1940; ed. at Downside, and in U.S.A.; Chm. and Managing Dir. of United & Gen. Trust, Ltd., and a Dir. of other cos., and a Record Producer; formerly Gdsm. Welsh Guards (invalided); Knt. Grand Cross of Obedience and Grand Officer of Merit, Sovereign Mil. Order of Malta, Grand Officer Order of Merit of Italy, Knt. Cdr., with Star, Order of St. Gregory the Great; K.St.J.; Delegate to 42nd, 43rd, 44th, 48th, 50th and 52nd Inter-Parl. Union Conferences, Washington 1953, Vienna 1954 Helsinki 1955, Warsaw 1959, Brussels 1961 and Belgrade 1963; Founder Chm. of Anglo-Mongolian Soc. 1963-67; Vice-Pres. of London Univ. Catholic Chaplaincy Assocn. since 1952, and Sec. Gen. of British Assocn. of Sovereign Mil. Order of Malta since 1965 (Sec. 1956-65, a Member of Sovereign Council 1960-62), and Pres. of Employment Agents Federation of Great Britain since 1966; Chm. of Council of Soc. of St. Augustine of Canterbury 1964-73, a Member of Council of Hansard Soc. for Parl. Govt. 1955-67; Pres. of Aged Poor Soc.

Arms,—Or, a talbot sejant sable, in chief three fountains proper. *Crest,*—Issuant from a chaplet of cinquefoils vert a bear's paw erect argent grasping a javelin in bend sinister sable, pendant therefrom by the straps two spurs or. *Supporters,*—On either side a sea dog reguardant proper gutte d'eau.

Addresses,—60, St. James St., SW1; 508, North Alpine Drive, Beverly Hills, Cal., USA 90210. *Clubs,*—Boodle's, Carlton, American, Travellers' (Paris).

PREDECESSORS.—[1] CHRISTOPHER Furness, seventh son of the late John Furness, of West Hartlepool, by Averill, dau. of John Wilson, of Naisbet Hall, co. Durham ; *b.* 1852; a Shipowner, Shipbuilder, and Engine-builder, and founder of the " Furness Line" of Steamships ; M.P. for Hartlepool (*L*) Jan. 1891 to June 1895 and Oct. 1900 to May 1910; *cr. Baron Furness,* of Grantley, W. Riding of co. York (peerage of United Kingdom) 1910 : *m.* 1876, Jane Annette, who *d.* 1930, dau. of the late Henry Suggitt, of Brierton, co. Durham; *d.* 1912; *s.* by his only son [2] MARMADUKE, 2nd Baron; *b.* 1883; a Shipbuilder and an Iron and Steel Works and Colliery Proprietor ; *cr. Viscount Furness,* of Grantley, W. Riding of co. York (peerage of United Kingdom) 1918 : *m.* 1st, 1904, Daisy, who *d.* 1921, dau. of G. J. H. Hogg, of Seaton Carew, co. Durham : 2ndly, 1926. Mrs. Thelma CONVERSE (who *d.* 1970, having obtained a divorce 1933), da. of the late Harry Hays Morgan, US Consul-Gen. at Buenos Aires; 3rdly, 1933, Enid Maud (who *d.* 1973, having *m.* 4thly, as his 2nd wife, the 6th Earl of Kenmare), da. of Charles Lindeman, of Sydney, and widow of (1) Roderick Cameron, of New York, and (2) Brig.-Gen. Frederick William Lawrence Sheppard Hart Cavendish, CMG, DSO [see B. Waterpark, colls.]; *d.* 1940; *s.* by his only surviving son [3] WILLIAM ANTHONY, 2nd Viscount and present peer; also Baron Furness.

FURNIVALL, BARONY OF. (Dent.) [Baron E. 1295.]
[Abeyant 1968.]

DAUGHTERS LIVING OF MARY FRANCES KATHERINE DENT, BARONESS FURNIVALL (*Co-heiresses to the Barony.*)
Hon. ROSAMOND MARY (Sister Ancilla, OSB, of St. Mildred's Abbey, Minster, Ramsgate), *b.* June 3rd, 1933.
Hon. PATRICIA MARY (Trotwood, 11, Gresham Rd., Limpsfield, Oxted, Surrey), *b.* April 4th, 1935: *m.* 1st, 1956 (m. diss. 1963), Capt. Thomas Hornsby, late Durham LI, who *d.* 1967; 2ndly, 1970, Roger Bence, and has issue living, (by 1st m.), Walton Petre, *b.* 1958,—Clare Mary Petre, *b.* 1957,— (by 2nd m.) Katharine Rosamund Petre, *b.* 1971.

GAGE, VISCOUNT.   (Gage.)   Sits as BARON (G.B. 1790)
[Viscount I. 1720, Bt. E 1622]

Courage without fear.

HENRY RAINALD GAGE, K.C.V.O., 6th
Viscount, and 13th Baronet; b. Dec.
30th, 1895; s. 1912; ed. at Eton; is
Vice-Lieut.for Sussex, a member of E.
Sussex Co. Council (formerly Chm.),
and Patron Nat. Federation of
Housing Socs.; 1914-18 War
in France and Belgium (wounded,
1914-15 star, two medals), European
War 1939-45 with Coldstream Guards
and on Staff; was a Lord-in-Waiting
to H.M. 1924-9, and again 1931-9;
Hon. Col. 58th (Home Counties) Field
Brig. R.A. (T.A.) 1936-45; K.C.V.O.
1939:   m.   1st,   1931,   the   Hon.
Alexandra Imogen Clair Grenfell,
who d. 1969, da. of 1st Baron Desborough (ext.) [see Bs. Lucas of Crud-
well]; 2ndly, 1971, Diana, da. of the
late Col. the Rt. Hon. Lord Richard Frederick Cavendish, CB, CMG [see D.
Devonshire, colls.], formerly wife of Robert John Graham Boothby,—afterwards Baron Boothby, and widow of Lt.-Col. the Hon. Ian Douglas-Campbell-
Gray [see L. Gray], and has issue by 1st m.

Arms,—Quarterly: 1st and 4th, per saltire argent and azure, a saltire gules, Gage; 2nd and 3rd
azure, a sun in splendour or, St. Clere.   Crest,—A ram statant argent, armed and unguled or.
Supporters,,—Two greyhounds of a light brown colour, proper, gorged with plain collars, adorned on
their upper edges with fleurs-de-lis or.
Seat,—Firle Place, Lewes.

SONS LIVING.   (By 1st m.).
Hon. GEORGE JOHN ST. CLERE, b. July 8th, 1932; ed. at Eton: m. 1971, Valerie Ann, da. of J. E.
Dutch, of Horam, Sussex.
Hon. Henry Nicolas, b. 1934; ed. at Eton, and at Ch. Ch., Oxford; late 2nd Lt. Coldstream Guards.

DAUGHTER LIVING.   (By 1st m.).
Hon. Camilla Jane, b. 1937: m. 1965, Edward Stephen Cazalet, Bar.-at-Law, of 31, Chelsea Sq.,
SW3, and has issue living, David Benedict, b. 1967,—Henry Pelham, b. 1969,—Lara Imogen Leonora,
b. 1973.

SISTERS LIVING.
Hon. Irene Adelaide, b. 1898: m. 1st, 1923 (marriage annulled on his petition 1928), Capt.
Murray Shuldham Shuldham-Legh, The Queen's Roy. Regt. [V. Elibank, colls.]: 2ndly,
1928, Major Frederick Cecil Bull, R.H.A., from whom she obtained a divorce 1950; 3rdly, 1950,
Ernest William Dalrymple Tennant, OBE, who d. 1962, and has issue living, (by 2nd marriage)
David John Frederick, b. 1929,—Diana Margaret Leila b. 1931: m. 1966, Gabor Justus von Liebig,
of Hungary.   Residence,—Grove House, Gt. Bardfield, Essex.
Hon. Vera Benedicta, b. 1899: m. 1919, Francis Lyall Birch, C.M.G., O.B.E., who d. 1956 [E. Courtown,
colls.].   Residence,—40, Pont Street, S.W.1.

COLLATERAL BRANCHES LIVING.
    Grandchildren of the late Lt.-Col. Ælla Molyneux Berkeley Gage, son of the late
    Lt.-Gen. the Hon. Edward Thomas Gage, CB (infra):—
Issue of the late John Fitzhardinge Berkeley Gage, b. 1901, d. 1967: m. 1st, 1923 (m. diss.
1927), Olivia Beth, adopted da. of the late Brig.-Gen. Ronald Maclachlan, Rifle Bde.;
2ndly, 1931 (m. diss. 1937), Griselda Margaret, da. of the late Rear-Adm. Sir Godfrey
Marshall Paine, KCB, MVO; 3rdly, 19—, Jenny (Gibraltar), da. of   :—
(By 2nd m.) John Grenville Berkeley (45, Kew Rd., Richmond, Surrey), b. 1933; ed. at Eton: m. 1961,
Pauline, da. of Antony Paul Pape, and has issue living, Aëlla Rupert Fitzhardinge Berkeley, b. 1966,
—Cassandra Griselda Louise, b. 1961,—Emma Leonora Falaise, b. 1963.——Thomas Aella Godfrey
(Yard Farm, Stogumber, Taunton), b. 1935; ed. at Eton: m. 19—, Dorothy Isobel Margaret, da. of
John Baxter Wylie, and has issue living, Andrew Thomas Berkeley, b. 1961,—John Duncan Godfrey,
b. 1962,—Caroline Margaret, b. 1966,—Amber Camilla, b. 1969.——Malcolm Edward Fitzhardinge,
b. 1936; ed. at Eton: m. 1971, Venessa Smith.——Dawn Falaise, n. 1932: m. 1st, 1952 (m. diss.
1963), John Kershaw Sanders; 2ndly, 1963, Cdr. John Pym Loughnan, RN, of Old Farm House,
Steep, Hants, and has issue living, (by 1st m.) John James Godfrey, b. 1953,—Guy Dominic Robson,
b. 1955,—Hugo Thomas Kershaw, b. 1957.
    Grandchildren of the late Lieut.-Gen. the Hon. Edward Thomas Gage, C.B., 3rd
    son of 4th Viscount:—
Issue of the late Brig.-Gen. Moreton Foley Gage, D.S.O., late 5th Dragoon Guards, b. 1873,
d. 1953: m. 1st, 1902, Anne Massie, who d. 1915, ed. dau. of William Everard Strong, of
New York City, U.S.A.; 2ndly, 1916, Frances, who d. 1955, dau. of Senator Henry P.
Lippitt, of Providence, Rhode Island, U.S.A.:—
(By 1st m.) Sir Berkeley Everard Foley, KCMG (24, Ovington Gdns, SW3; Boodle's, Buck's and
Beefsteak Clubs), b. 1904; ed. at Eton, and at Trin. Coll., Camb. (BA); Ambassador to Thailand
1954-57, and to Peru 1957-63; Chm. of Cttee. for Exports to Latin America of British Nat. Export
Council and a Member of Council for Volunteers Overseas 1964-66; Chm. of Anglo-Peruvian Soc.
1969-71: a Member of Council of Fauna Preservation Soc. 1968-73; Grand Cross Order of Sun of
Peru: CMG 1949, KCMG 1955: m. 1st, 1931 (m. diss. 1954), Maria, da. of Carl von Chappuis, 2ndly,
1954, Mrs. Lillian Riggs, Miller, and has issue living, (by 1st m.) Anthony St. Clere Berkeley (Little
Triton, Bluebury, Oxon.) b. 1931: m. 1965, Virginia Mary, da. of Denis H. Ferens, of Bilver, Ipplepen,
S. Devon, and has issue living, Benjamin Francis, b. 1969, Gregory Bernard, b. 1971, Oliver, b.
1973,—Ulick Charles Christopher (Moff in Av., Darlington, W. Aust. 6070), b. 1938; ed. at Eton,
and St. John's Coll., Camb. (MA); late 2nd Lt. 12th Lancers: m. 1964, Helen Mary Janet, da.
of Air Vice-Marshal Evelyn Michael Thomas Howell, CBE, and has issue living, Marius Berkeley
b. 1966, Ulicia Mary b. 1965.——Edward Fitzhardinge Peyton, b. 1906; ed. at Eton, and at Ch.
Ch., Oxford (BA); formerly Maj. Coldm. Gds.; Sheriff of Salop, 1963: m. 1931, Thailia Westcott, da. of Stephen Caldwell Millett, and has issue living, Robert Westcott Moreton (59, Cadogan
Sq., SW1), (Buck's Club), b. 1934; ed. at Eton, and at Ch. Ch., Oxford; late Lt. Life Gds.: m.
1964, Maria Teresa Francisca, da. of the late Don Emilio Maria Diaz-Caneja, and has issue living,
Henry St. Clere Rokewood b. 1966, Dolores Isabella b. 1965,—Ann Caroline Thalia (Hon. Mrs.
Robin A. Baring), b. 1931; ed. at Oxford Univ. (BA 1953): m. 1960, the Hon. Robin Alexander
Baring [see B. Ashburton],—Elizabeth Estling (72, Cadogan Sq., SW3), b. 1937: m. 1st,

1957: (m. diss. 1965), David V. Russell; 2ndly, 1970, David Bruce Douglas Lowe. *Residence.*—Chateau de Combecave, 82, Touffailles, Tarn et Garonne, France.———(By 2nd m.) Quentin Henry Moreton (of Chalvington House, Chalvington, nr. Hailsham, Sussex), *b.* 1920; ed. at Eton, and at Ch. Ch., Oxford; formerly Maj. Gren. Gds.; 1939-45 War (wounded): *m.* 1949, Hazel Swinton, da. of Col. George Archibald Swinton Home, DSO, OBE, late 5th Dragoon Gds., and has issue living, Jonathan Moreton, *b.* 1954,—Deborah Pamela, *b.* 1950. *Club,*—Guards'.——Dorothy Louise, *b.* 1917: *m.* 1941, Maj. Anthony George Akers-Douglas, late 13th/18th Hussars [see V. Chilston, colls.]. *Residence,*—Roe Downs, Medstead, Alton, Hants.

PREDECESSORS.—[1] THOMAS Gage; cr. a *Baronet* 1622; *d.* 1633; *s.* by his son [2] *Sir* THOMAS, 2nd Bt.; *d.* 1655; *s.* by his el. son [3] *Sir* THOMAS, 3rd Bt.; *d.* unmarried 1660; *s.* by his brother [4] *Sir* JOHN, 4th Bt.; *s.* by his el. son [5] *Sir* JOHN, 5th Bt.; *d.* 1700; *s.* by his brother [6] *Sir* THOMAS, 6th Bt.; *d.* 1713; *s.* by his brother [7] *Sir* WILLIAM, *K.C.B.*, 7th Bt., M.P. for Seaford; *d.* unmarried 1744; *s.* by his cousin [8] THOMAS, 8th Bt., el. son of Joseph, 4th son of 2nd Bt.; M.P. for Tewkesbury, Verderer of the Forest of Dean and Steward of the Household to Frederick, Prince of Wales; cr. prior to his succession to the baronetcy *Baron Gage,* of Castlebar, and *Viscount Gage* (peerage of Ireland) 1720; *d.* 1754; *s.* by his son [9] WILLIAM HALL, 2nd Viscount; cr. *Baron Gage.* of Firle, co. Sussex (peerage of Great Britain) 1780, and *Baron Gage,* of High Meadow, co. Gloucester (peerage of Great Britain) 1790, with remainder to his nephew, heir presamptive to the peerage of 1720 and to the baronetcy; *d.* 1791, when the Barony of Gage, of Firle became extinct, and the peerages of 1720 and 1790 devolved upon his nephew [10] HENRY, 3rd Viscount, el. son of Gen. the Hon. Thomas, 2nd son of 1st Viscount; a Major-Gen. in the Army; *d.* 1808; *s.* by his son [11] HENRY HALL, 4th Viscount; *d.* 1877; *s.* by his grandson [12] HENRY CHARLES [son of the Hon. Henry Edward Hall Gage (el. son of 4th Viscount), and Sophia Selina, who *d.* 1886, dau. of Sir Charles Knightley, 2nd Bt.], 5th Viscount, *b.* 1854: *m.* 1894, Leila Georgina, who *d.* 1916, dau. of the Rev. Frederick Peel; *d.* 1912; *s.* by his only son [13] HENRY RAINALD, 6th Viscount and present peer; also Baron Gage.

GAINFORD, BARON. (Pease.) [Baron U.K. 1917.]

Peace and hope.

JOSEPH EDWARD PEASE, 3rd Baron; *b.* Dec. 25th, 1921; *s.* 1971; ed. at Eton, and Gordonstoun; FRGS; MSST; 1939-45 War as Sgt. RAF: *m.* 1953, Margaret Theophila Radcliffe, da. of the late Henry Edmund Guise Tyndale, of Winchester Coll., and has issue.

Arms,—Per fesse azure and gules, a fesse nebuly ermine between two lambs passant in chief argent, and in base upon a mount proper a dove rising argent, holding in the beak a pea stalk, the blossom and pods proper. Crest.—Upon the capital of an Ionic column a dove rising, holding in the beak a pea stalk as in the arms. Supporters,—On either side a Barbary wild sheep ram guardant or. *Residence,*—60, Lansdowne Rd., W11.

DAUGHTERS LIVING.

Hon. Joanna Ruth Miriam, *b.* 1959.
Hon. Virginia Claire Margaret, *b.* 1960.

BROTHERS LIVING.

Hon. GEORGE, *b.* April 20th, 1926; ed. at Eton; ARIBA; MRTPI; 1939-45 War in RNVR: *m.* 1958, Flora Daphne, da. of the late Dr. N. A. Dyce-Sharp, and has issue living, Adrian Christopher, *b.* 1960, —Matthew Edward, *b.* 1962,—Olivia Daphne, *b.* 1958,—Samantha Rachel, *b.* 1965. *Residence,*— Maryburgh Cottage, Maryburgh, Ross-shire.
Hon. John Michael (of Auchentenavil, Tayvallich, Lochgilphead, Argyll), *b.* 1930; ed. at Gordonstoun: *m.* 1962, Catherine Margaret, da. of Duncan F. Shaw, and has issue living, David Michael, *b.* 1964,—. Andrew Joseph, *b.* 1967,—Daniel John, *b.* 1973.

WIDOW LIVING OF SECOND BARON.

VERONICA MARGARET (*Veronica Baroness Gainford*), Duntaynish, Tayvallich, Lochgilphead, Argyll, da. of Sir George John William Noble, 2nd Bt. (*cr.* 1902): *m.* 1921, the 2nd Baron, who *d.* 1971.

PREDECESSORS.—[1] *Rt. Hon.* JOSEPH ALBERT Pease, second son of Sir Joseph Whitwell Pease, 1st Bt. (*cr.* 1882); *b,* 1860; appointed Junior Liberal Whip 1897, a Junior Lord of the Treasury Dec. 1905, Parliamentary (Patronage) Sec. to the Treasury and Ch. Liberal Whip May 1908, Chancellor of Duchy of Lancaster (with a seat in the Cabinet) Feb. 1910, Pres. of Board of Education Oct. 1911, and a Member of Committee of Science Council 1915; was Postmaster-Gen. Jan. to Dec. 1916, Chm. of British Broadcasting Co. 1922-6, and Dep. Chm. 1926-31; M.P. for Northumberland, Tyneside Div. (*L*) 1892-1900, for Essex, N., or Saffron walden, Div. May 1901 to Jan. 1910, and for Rotherham Div. of S. Part of W. Riding of York-shire March 1910 to Dec. 1916; cr. *Baron Gainford,* of Headlam, co. Durham (peerage of United Kingdom) 1917: *m.* 1886, Ethel, who *d.* 1941, only dau. of Lieut.-Gen. Sir Henry Mershman Havelock-Allan, G.C.B., V.C., M.P., 1st Bt.; *d.* 1943; *s.* by his son [2] JOSEPH, *TD,* 2nd Baron, *b.* 1889: *m.* 1921, Veronica Margaret, da. of Sir George John William Noble, 2nd Bt. (*cr.* 1902); *d.* 1971; *s.* by his el. son [3] Joseph Edward, 3rd Baron and present pee

GAINSBOROUGH, EARL OF. (Noel.) [Earl U.K. 1841, Bt. G.B. 1781.]

All well, or nothing.

ANTHONY GERARD EDWARD NOEL, 5th Earl, and 7th Baronet; *b.* Oct. 24th, 1923; *s.* 1927; ed. at Worth, Sussex, and at Georgetown, Maryland, U.S.A.; is patron of four livings (but being a Roman Catholic cannot present), a J.P. for Rutland, and a Bailiff Grand Cross of Sovereign Order of Malta (Pres. of British Assocn. 1968-74); Chm. of Rutland co. Council 1970-73: *m.* 1947, Mary, da. of the Hon. John Joseph Stourton, TD [see B. Mowbray], and has issue.

ᴀrms.—Or, fretty gules, and a canton ermine. Crest.—A buck at gaze argent, attired or. Supporters.—On either side a bull argent, armed and unguled proper, gorged with a naval crown azure, therefrom a chain reflexed over the back gold, pendent from the crown an escutcheon, also azure, charged with an anchor erect, encircled by a wreath of laurel or.

Seat,—Exton Park, Oakham, Rutland. *Clubs,*—Boodle's, Brooks's, Royal Yacht Squadron, Bembridge Sailing.

SONS LIVING

ANTHONY BAPTIST (*Viscount Campden*) (Top House, Exton, Oakham, Rutland), *b.* Jan. 16th, 1950; ed. at Ampleforth, and Roy. Agric. Coll., Cirencester: *m.* 1972, Sarah Rose, el. da. of Col. Thomas Foley Churchil Winnington, MBE [see Winnington, Bt.]

Hon. Gerard Edward Joseph, *b.* 1955; ed. at Ampleforth.
Hon. Thomas, *b.* 1958; ed. at Ampleforth.
Hon. Edward Andrew, *b.* 1960; ed. at Ampleforth.

DAUGHTERS LIVING.

Lady Juliana Mary Alice (*Countess of Liverpool*) (The Grange Farm, Exton, Oakham, Rutland), *b.* 1949: *m.* 1970, the 5th Earl of Liverpool.
Lady Maria, *b.* 1951: *m.* 1971, Robert Pridden, of Fort Henry House, Exton, Oakham, Rutland, and has issue living, Benedict John Anthony, *b.* 1973.
Lady Celestria Magdalen Mary, *b.* 1954.

BROTHER LIVING.

Hon. Gerard Eyre Wriothesley, *b.* 1926 ; ed. at Georgetown, Maryland, U.S.A., and at Exeter Coll., Oxford; Bar. Inner Temple 1952; Editor of *Catholic Herald* 1971-74: *m.* 1958, Adèle Julie Patricia, only da. of Maj. Bonville Were, of Carrington House, Hertford St., W1, and has issue living, Philip Arthur Nicholas, *b.* 1959,—Robert John Baptist, *b.* 1962,—Elizabeth Mary Alice, *b.* 1967. *Residences,*—105, Cadogan Gdns., SW3; Green Dragons, Campden, Glos.

SISTER LIVING.

Lady Maureen Thérèse Josephine (*Baroness Dormer*), *b.* 1917: *m.* 1944, the 15th Baron Dormer, who *d.* 1975. *Residences,*—Grove Park Warwick; 12, Campden House Court, 42, Gloucester Walk, W8.

COLLATERAL BRANCHES LIVING.

Issue of the late Major the Hon. Charles Hubert Francis Noel, O.B.E., son of 3rd Earl, *b.* 1885; *d.* 1947: *m.* 1912, May, who *d.* 1964, el. da. and heir of the late Brig.-Gen. Archibald Campbell Douglas Dick, C.B., C.M.G., of Pitkerro, Angus.
Archibald Charles William *MC* (15, Abbotsbury Close, W14), *b.* 1914; ed. at Oratory Sch.; is Col. late Welsh Guards; 1939-45 War in France (MC, prisoner): *m.* 1945, Bridget Mary, only da. of the late Brig. William Albany Fetherstonhaugh, CB, CBE, DSO [Cayley, Bt.], and has issue living, Charles William, *b.* 1948; ed. at Ampleforth, and Trin. Coll., Camb.,—Edward Albany, *b.* 1956.—Douglas Robert George, *b.* 1924; ed. at Oratory Sch.; Mag. Cold. Gds.; Italy 1943-45: *m.* 1949, Susan, da. of the late Brig. George Edward Younghusband, CBE, and has issue living, James Douglas George, *b.* 1950,—William Edward Douglas, *b.* 1953,—Caroline Mary Jane, *b.* 1956. *Residence,*—25, Broomhouse Road, SW6——Carola Mary, *b.* 1916: *m.* 1936, Maj. Thomas Steuart Fothringham, MC, Black Watch, of The Lagg, Aberfeldy, Perthshire, PH15 2EE, and has issue living, Robert (Fothringham, Forfar, Angus), *b.* 1937: *m.* 1962, Elizabeth Mary Charlotte, el. da. of T. H. Brendan Lawther, of 20, Coleherne Court, SW5, and has issue living, Thomas *b.* 1971, Lionel *b.* 1973, Mariana *b.* 1966, Ilona *b.* 1969,—Walter (Kennacoil House, Dunkeld, Perthshire), *b.* 1939: *m.* 1972, Patricia Anne, el. da. of Sir David Charles Watherston, KBE, CMG, and has issue living, Teresa Catherine Frances, *b.* 1975,—Henry (Grantully Castle, Aberfeldy, Perthshire), *b.* 1944: *m.* 1972, Cherry Linnhe, only child of Brig. Ian MacAlister Stewart, of Achnacone, Appin, Argyll, and has issue living, Patrick Donald *b.* 1973, Charles Henry, *b.* 1974.
Grandson of the late Lt.-Col. the Hon. Edward Noel, 2nd son of 2nd Earl (infra):—
Issue of the late Lt.-Col. Edward William Charles Noel, CIE, DSO, *b.* 1886, *d.* 1974: *m.* 1st, 1923, Katherine Florence, who *d.* 1952, da. of the late Robert Leighton Ross; 2ndly, 1961, Simone, who *d.* 1974, da. of Prof. Jean Corbiau, of Louvaine Univ.:—
(By 1st m.) Denys Edward (Brooklands, Goose Green, Lyndhurst, Hants.), *b.* 1926: *m.* 1947, Petronelle Moore, only da. of C. Austin Bostock, of Cambridge, and has issue living, Julian Rodern Bostock, *b.* 1949,—Laura Frances, *b.* 1951.
Issue of the late Lieut.-Col. the Hon. Edward Noel, 2nd son of 2nd Earl, *b.* 1852; *d.* 1917: *m.* 1884, Ruth, who *d.* 1926, da. of the late W. H. Lucas, of Treniffle, Cornwall:—
John Baptist Lucius, *b.* 1890; ed. at RMC; late Capt. E. Yorkshire Regt.; 1914-18 War, 1939-45 War as Staff Officer Intelligence Corps.; accompanied Mount Everest Expeditions 1922 and 1924 as Official Photographer; a FRSA, a Life FRGS, and Asso. of Roy. Photographic Soc., and an Hon. Life Member of American Museum of Natural History of New York; MInst.PI; assumed additional Christian name of John by deed poll 1908: *m.* 1st, 1915, Sybil Graham, who *d.* 1939; 2ndly, 1941, Mary Sullivan, and has issue living, (by 2nd m.) Sandra Ruth Catherine, *b.* 1943. *Address,*—c/o Royal Geographical Society, Kensington Gore, SW7.
Grandchildren of the late Hon. Henry Lewis Noel, 3rd son of 1st Earl:—
Issue of the late Major Gerard Thomas Noel, *b.* 1856, *d.* 1941: *m.* 1888, Edith Mary, who *d.* 1917, dau. of the late Rev. the Hon. William Byron [B. Byron, colls.] :—
Mary Cecily, *b.* 1888: *m.* 1921, Major Alan Charles Grenville Luther, MC, formerly KOYLI, who *d.* 1961, and has issue living, David John (of Ofcolaco, N. Transvaal), *b.* 1924; ed. at Eton; late Capt. RE: *m.* 1951, Moyra Anne Margaret, da. of the late John Watson Simpson, MB [see Stirling-Hamilton, Bt., colls.], and has issue living, Charles Anthony *b.* 1951, Robert Guy *b.* 1955, Carola Mary *b.* 1959.
Issue of the late Hugh Middleton Noel, *b.* 1862, *d.* 1956: *m.* 1901, Helen Winnefred, dau. of Robert Gibbs, of 32, St. Augustine's Road, Bedford:—
Geoffrey Francis Middleton, *b.* 1902. *Residence,*—1421, McDonald Av., Santa Rosa, Cal., USA.——

Leland Hugh Wriothesley, *b.* 1906; is a Landscape Artist: *m.* 1941, Barbara Jean, el. da. of A. H. Meier, of Chico, Cal., USA, and has issue living, William Hugh, *b.* 1950,—Palela Lee, *b.* 1948. *Residence,*—1421, McDonald Av., Santa Rosa, Cal., USA.——Diana Catharine (1526, Shoreline Drive, Santa Barbara, Cal., USA), *b.* 1914: *m.* 1942, Hollis H. Parker, who *d.* 1948, Sgt. AA Artillery, and has issue living, Geoffrey Hollis, *b.* 1944; USA Coast Guard: *m.* 1965, Patricia Edwards,— Stephen Hugh Anderson, *b.* 1946; ed. at Hawaii Univ., and Cal. State Coll., Long Beach.

Issue of the late Henry Hamlyn Noel, *b.* 1864, *d.* 1941 : *m.* 1897, Mary Neame, who *d.* 1942, dau. of John Lauer Oliver :—
Mildred Mary Hamlyn, *b.* 1904: *m.* 1929, Lieut.-Col. Norman Leslie Crozier Irwin, DSO (and Bar), Indian Army (ret)., who *d.* 1972. *Residence,*—Squirrels Hall, Stratford St. Mary, Colchester.

Grandchildren of the late Major Gerard Thomas Noel (ante) :—
Issue of the late William Henry Middleton Noel, *b.* 1898, *d.* 1954 : *m.* 1934, Jacqueline Naomi (now of Bemborough, P.O. Ofcolaco, N. Transvaal, S. Africa), younger dau. of R. Bendall, of Ofcolaco, N. Transvaal :—
Gerard Roland (c/o Land & Survey, Kuching, Sarawak), *b.* 1936.——Michael John, *b.* 1944: *m.* 1973, Amand Jane, only da. of the late Wing-Cdr. A. B. Corfe, RAF.——Christopher William, *b.* 1947: *m.* 1971, Rhoda, only da. of H. Allen, of Trichardt, E. Transvaal, and has issue living, Gillian Frances, *b.* 1973.——Wilfred Byron, *b.* 1949: *m.* 1975, Patricia Maud, 2nd da. of W. D. J. Van Niekerk, of Johannesburg.——Margaret Celestria, *b.* 1939: *m.* 1963, Hugh Boswell Brown, of Crake Valley Farm, PO Box 3025, Umtali, Rhodesia, and has issue living, Robert Jason, *b.* 1969,—Catherine Ann, *b.* 1964,—Joan Cécile, *b.* 1965,—Nicola Noel, *b.* 1971.

Grandchildren of the late Henry Hamlyn Noel (ante) :—
Issue of the late Major Edward Francis Hamlyn Noel, M.R.C.V.S., Indian Army, *b.* 1899, *d.* 1953: *m.* 1926, Doris Marie (Westway, Stratford St. Mary, Suffolk), da. of Albert Claude Verrières, CIE :—
Gerard John Hamlyn (Frostwood House, East Lane, Dedham, Essex), *b.* 1930; ed. at Wellington Coll.; Capt. (ret.) RE: *m.* 1963, Gillian Ralphia, only da. of W. T. B. Head, of Frinton-on-Sea, Essex, and has issue living, Richard Gerard Hamlyn, *b.* 1965,—Victoria Gillian Emilia, *b.* 1969.——Penelope Noel, *BD*, *b.* 1934: *m.* 1962, the Rev. Colin Scott Lee, of Ludgershall Rectory, Aylesbury, and has issue living, Jonathan Noel, *b.* 1963,—Mary Penelope, *b.* 1965.——Lyn Noel, *b.* 1947: *m.* 1968, Ian Thomas Kennedy, of 83. Loom Lane, Radlett, Herts., and has issue living, Gordon Noel, *b.* 1971, —James Edward, *b.* 1972.

Granddaughter of the late Hon. Roden Berkeley Wriothesley Noel, 4th son of 1st Earl :—
Issue of the late Rev. Conrad le Despencer Roden Noel, *b.* 1869, *d.* 1942 : *m.* 1895, Miriam, who *d.* 1961, dau. of James Greenwood :—
Barbara, *b.* 1897: *m.* 1921, the Rev. John Cyril Putterill, of 43, West Rd., Saffron Walden, Essex, and has issue living, Sylvia, *b.* 1922: *m.* 1952, Desmond Butterworth Heath, of 60, Esmond Road, Bedford Park, Chiswick, W4, and has issue living, Martin Christopher *b.* 1955, Jenny Clare *b.* 1953, Sally Christine *b.* 1959,—Cecilia Rosemary, *b.* 1929: *m.* 1952, Vernon John Curtis, of East Grove, Marsham Way, Gerrard's Cross, Bucks., and has issue living, Matthew John Stephen *b.* 1964, Victoria Jane *b.* 1954, Katherine Anne *b.* 1965.

Descendants of the late Sir Gerard Noel Noel, 2nd Bt. (father of 1st Earl of Gainsborough), by his wife Diana, in her own right, Baroness Barham :—
Granddaughters of the late Adm. of the Fleet Sir Gerard Henry Uctred Noel, G.C.B., K.C.M.G., son of the late Rev. Augustus William Noel, son of the late Capt. the Hon. Frederic Noel, R.N., 6th son of Diana Baroness Barham :—
Issue of the late Francis Arthur Gerard Noel, O.B.E., *b.* 1880, *d.* 1955: *m.* 1913, Evelyn (now of Hopton Hall, Great Yarmouth, Norfolk), dau. of the late Benjamin Bond Cabbell, of Cromer Hall Norfolk :—
Evelyn Diana (*Lady Lethbridge*), *b.* 1914 : *m.* 1st, 1936, Major John Vivian Bailey, Roy. Scots Fusiliers, who *d.* killed in action during European War) 1943 ; 2ndly, 1946, Capt. Sir Hector Wroth Lethbridge, 6th Bt., and has issue living, (by 1st marriage) Lucy, *b.* 1938: *m.* 1962, Thomas Harry Farthing, of Coombe Park, Lynton, N. Devon, and has issue living, Harry Vivian Stuart *b.* 1964, Isabella Jane *b.* 1968,—(by 2nd m.) [see Lethbridge, Bt.]. *Residence,*—Long Sutton House, Langport, Somerset.——Susan Rachel, *b.* 1917.

(In remainder to Barony of Barham, and to the Baronetcy.)
Grandsons of the late Col. William Frederick Noel Noel (infra) :—
Issue of the late Lieut.-Col. Maurice Waldegrave Noel, A.F.C., The King's (Liverpool) Regt., *b.* 1888, *d.* 1958 : *m.* 1920, Elisabeth Christine Edith (of The Redlands, Minsterworth, Gloucestershire), el. dau. of the late Charles Gairdner, of Rangoon, and Tower of Lethendy, Perthshire :—
Peter Maurice William, *b.* 1922 ; ed. at Malvern, and at London Univ. (Diploma of Imperial Coll.) ; is an A.M.I.Mech.E., and an Asso. F.R.Ae.S.; Lt. (E) R.N. (ret.): *m.* 1946, Patricia Margaret youngest dau. of A. C. W. Hill, of Mosman, Sydney, N.S. Wales, and has issue living, Diana Margaret, *b.*1947,—Susan Elizabeth Gay, *b.* 1951. *Residence,*—7, Merton Street, Ivanhoe, Victoria, Australia, ——Robert Gerard Charles (17, Greenhill, Hook, Swindon), *b.* 1928; ed. at Malvern: late Lt. RM (invalided): *m.* 1961, Gillian Margaret Halse.

Granddaughters of the late Col. Edward Andrew Noel, son of the late Rev. the Hon. Francis James Noel, 7th son of Sir Gerard Noel Noel, 2nd Bt., and Diana, Baroness Barham :—
Issue of the late Col. William Frederick Noel Noel, *b.* 1849, *d.* 1923 : *m.* 1st, 1879, Josephine Annie (from whom he obtained a divorce 1883), who *d.* 1904, dau. of Joseph Watts Halliwell, of Stratford Park, Stroud ; 2ndly, 1885, Beatrice Elizabeth, who *d.* 1988, dau. of the late Rev. Joseph Christopher Bradney, R. of Greet, Salop; 3rdly, 1689, Laura Carolina, who *d.* 1897, dau. of the late Charles Henry Beilby :—
(By 2nd marriage) Sarah Dorothy Beatrice, *b.* 1886 ; is a J.P. : *m.* 1911, Col. Malby Crofton, D.S.O., who *d.* 1948 [see Crofton, Bt., cr. 1838, colls.]. *Residence,*—33, Trevor Place, S.W.7.——(By 3rd marriage) Audrey Beilby Noel, *b.* 1897 : *m.* 1924, Richard Francis Orme Grafton, late Capt. R.E., and has issue living, John Gerard Noel, *b.* 1929; ed. at Shrewsbury; formerly in RAF: *m.* 1956, Annette Mary, yr. da. of Maj. William Anderson, MBE, DCM, RA (ret.),—Elizabeth Audrey Noel, *b.* 1925; sometime in WRNS: *m.* 1953, Derek Edward Thomas Towle, and has issue living, Richard Derek *b.* 1959, Phillipa Elizabeth *b.* 1954, Caroline Daphne *b.* 1955. *Residence,*—

Grandchildren of the late Adm. Francis Charles Methuen Noel, 3rd son of Col. Edward Andrew Noel (ante):—
Issue of the late Com. Montague Wriothesley Noel, *b.* 1892, *d.* (killed in action during European War) 1941 : *m.* 1926, Christabel Florence Arthur, who *d.* 1965, dau. of the late Rev. Henry Startin, V. of Horrabridge, Devon :—
Henry Methuen Noel (Hill House, Kirby-le-Soken, Essex: City University, and Sackville Clubs), *b.* 1927; ed. at Marlborough Coll., and at New Coll., Oxford (MA); FCIS; Capt. Queen Victoria's Rifles (TA Reserve) (ret.): *m.* 1963, Helen Elizabeth Anne, da. of the late Sir William Oliphant Hutchison, of Cholmondeley Lodge, Richmond, Surrey, and has issue living, Robert Montague, *b.* 1964,—William Gerard, *b.* 1965,—Emma Margery, *b.* 1969.——Gerard Lionel Gordon (twin) (c/o National Trust, Attingham Park, Shrewsbury), *b.* 1927; ed. at Marlborough Coll., and at Trin. Hall, Camb. (MA); late RE; FRICS: *m.* 1965, Caroline Patricia, da. of Brig. Eric Llewellyn Griffith Griffith-Williams, CBE, DSO, MC, of Rockbeare Manor, Exeter, Devon, and has issue living, Andrew Francis Methuen, *b.* 1966,—Thomas Charles Eric, *b.* 1970,—Delia Christabel Mary, *b.* 1967,—Mathilda Theresa Caroline, *b.* 1972. *Club,*—Royal Ocean Racing.——Montague Geoffrey Bickersteth (11, Shaftsbury Av., Bedford), *b.* 1931; ed. at Marlborough Coll., and at Trin. Hall, Camb. (BA), MRCS and LCRP; late Lt. Roy. Signals: *m.* (Jan.) 1958, Audrey Mavis, da. of Allan Metcalf, of Wingerworth, Chesterfield, Derbys., and has issue living, David Charles, *b.* 1963,—Peter, *b.* 1966,—Michael (twin), *b.* 1966,—Jennifer Anne, *b.* (Dec.) 1958.——Celestria Wilmot Rosalie, *b.* 1935: *m.* (Jan.) 1960,

David Jeffrey Bell, 15, North Rd., Berkhamsted, Herts. and has issue living, Charles Montague Jeffrey, *b.* 1974,—Caroline Barbara Penelope, *b.* (Dec.) 1960,—Joanna Elizabeth Gelcairn *b.* 1962,—Alice Christabel Ann, *b.* 1967,—Christina Mary Noel, *b.* 1968.

Grandchildren of the late Capt. Robert Lascelles Gambier Noel, R.N. (infra):—
Issue of the late Gambier Baptist Edward Noel, *b.* 1888, *d.* 1957 : *m.* 1st, 1914, Beatrice Eva Tytler (who *d.* 1966, and from whom he obtained a divorce 1922), da. of the late Rear-Adm. John Clarke Byng [V. Torrington, colls.]; 2ndly, 1924, Rosalie Sibyl (from whom he obtained a divorce 1931), da. of Major S. S. Flower, late Northumberland Fusiliers, and formerly wife of Capt. W. L. Aplin Harrison, MC.:—
(By 1st m.) Gambier John Byng, *CB, b.* 1914; Rear-Adm. (ret.) 1939-45 War (despatches twice): *m.* 1936, Joan, da. of the late Percy Herbert Stevens, and has issue living, Caroline Byng, *b.* 1936,—Penelope Byng, *b.* 1939: *m.* 1st, 1960 (m. diss. 1967), Anthony Henry John Rawlinson, (now 5th Bt.); 2ndly, 1967, Count Axel Du Monceau de Bergendal, of Rue de L'Ecole 33, 1460, Ittre, Belgium,—Virginia Byng, *b.* 1943,—Vanessa Jane (twin), *b.* 1943. *Residence,*—Olivers, Haslemere, Surrey.——Beatrice Louise Frances, *b.* 1915; formerly Assist. Section Officer WAAF: *m.* 1943, William Falcon Skelton, only son of Engineer Vice-Adm. Sir Reginald William Skelton, KCB, CBE, DSO, and has issue living, Peter, *b.* 1950,—Sally, *b.* 1944,—Judy, *b.* 1946. *Residence,*—Boughton Cottage, Green Lane, Henley-on-Thames, Oxon.
Issue of the late Capt. John Andrew Vernatti Noel, *b.* 1893, *d.* 1966: *m.* 1923, Marion Shanks, who *d.* 1959, da. of the late John Shanks Wylie of Edinburgh:—
Anthony Robert Alistair (University of Natal, Pietermaritzburg, S. Africa), *b.* 1927; BSc honours, London; PhD London; a FRHort.S; Prof. Dr. Univ. of Natal: *m.* 1958, Marthina Cornelia Rousseau, of Roodepoort, Transvaal, and has issue living, Darwin John Robert, *b.* 1959.
Grandson of the late Col. Edward Andrew Noel (ante):—
Issue of the late Capt. Robert Lascelles Gambier Noel, R.N., *b.* 1855, *d.* 1935 : *m.* 1887, Letitia Louisa Carmela, who *d.* 1940, dau. of the Rev. S. Koelle, D.Ph.:—
Norman Philpot Robert, *b.* 1891 ; ed. at Cheltenham Coll.; European War 1914-18 as Capt. R.F.A. (wounded twice, despatches, Croix de Guerre): *m.* 1927, Jane Jones. *Residence,*—56A, Lewin Rd., SW16.

Granddaughter of Capt. John Andrew Vernatti Noel (ante):—
Issue of the late John Edward Barham Noel, *b.* 1929; *d.* 1954: *m.* 1952, Grace Vera (who *m.* 2ndly, 1966, Anthony Maurice Thomas, of 10, Archery Gdns., Woolston, Southampton), yst. da. of A. Paul, of Herne Hill, SE:—
Jacqueline Susan, *b.* 1953: *m.* 1972, Victor Clive Hayton, of Middleholms, Langholm, Dumfriesshire.
Grandson of the late Col. Edward Andrew Noel (ante):—
Issue of Matilda Catherine Noel, *b.* 1857, *d.* 1923: *m.* 1893, Col. John Charles Griffith, VD, JP:—
Edward Noel, *CBE* (Little Hallingbury Park, Bishop's Stortford, Herts.), *b.* 1896; FRAgS, CIAgE; *cr.* CBE (Civil) 1969: *m.* 1st, 1917, Margery Joan Wesley-Smith, who *d.* 1918; 2ndly, 1919, Maude Lyle, OBE, JP, who *d.* 1970, da. of the late Capt. Henry Brereton Hooper, and widow of Lt. Reay Parkinson, RN, and has issue living (by 2nd m.) Madeleine *b.* 1920: *m.* 1945, Maj. Thomas Barraclough, MC, 4/7th R. Dragoon Gds., who *d.* 1963, and has issue living, Anthony Noel *b.* 1945: *m.* 1969, Prudence Hawkesworth Norris (and has issue living, Annabelle Juliet *b.* 1972), Thomas James *b.* 1948, William Mackay *b.* 1950: *m.* 1973, Georgina Reynell Moran, (and has issue living, Thomas Edward *b.* 1974.).

Grandson of the late Berkeley Plantagenet Guildford Charles Noel, son of the late Hon. Berkeley Octavius Noel, 8th son of Sir Gerard Noel Noel, 2nd Bt., and of Diana, Baroness Barham:—
Issue of the late Rev. Edward Henry Noel, *b.* 1859, *d.* 1941 : *m.* 1907, Caroline Ethel, who *d.* 1956, dau. of James Crowley :—
Arthur Edward, *b.* 1908 ; late R.E. *Residence,*—

Granddaughter of the late Albert Leland Noel, 3rd son of the late Rev. the Hon. Baptist Wriothesley Noel, 10th son of Diana, Baroness Barham:—
Issue of the late Barham Molyneux Noel, *b.* 1868, *d.* 1932: *m.* 1895, Dorothy, who *d.* 1948, dau. of Spencer Brunton:—
Audrey Baillie (c/o Barclays Bank, (D.C. & O.), Adderley St., Cape Town, S. Africa), *b.* 1896: *m.* 1920, Maj.-Gen. François Henry Theron, CB, CBE, who *d.* 1967, and has issue living, Jacqueline Marie, *b.* 1923: *m.* 1947 (m. diss. 1967), Angus Christian Edward Malcolm, CMG, who *d.* 1971, and has issue living, Caroline Jeanne *b.* 1948, Christina Noel *b.* 1950, Sophie Louisa *b.* 1954, Anne Victoria Mary Christian *b.* 1957.

Granddaughter of the late Eugene Frederic Noel, yst. son of the late Rev. the Hon. Baptist Wriothesley Noel (ante).:—
Issue of the late Evan Baillie Noel, *b.* 1879, *d.* 1928 : *m.* 1906, Marjorie, who *d.* 1955, dau. of the late R. Deane Sweeting, M.D., Bar.-at-law, Senior Med. Inspector H.M. Local Govt. Board :—
Susan Diana Barham, *b.* 1912: *m.* 1940, Prof. Geoffrey Frederic Powell, DSO, Solicitor and late Sq.-Ldr. RAFVR. *Residences,*—175A, High St., Lee-on-the-Solent, Hants; Fortune House, San Pawl Tat-Targa, Malta.

PREDECESSORS.—[1] *Rt. Hon.* Sir CHARLES Middleton, *P.C.,* Adm. of the Red, M.P. for Rochester and First Lord of the Admiralty, &c. ; *cr.* a *Baronet* 1781 with remainder to his son-in-law, Gerard Noel Edwards (who in 1798 assumed the surname of Noel), nephew of Henry Noel, 6th Earl of Gainsborough (cr. 1682), 9th Viscount Campden (cr. 1628), and 4th Baron Noel (cr. 1617); *cr. Baron Barham* (peerage of United Kingdom) 1805, with remainder to his dau. Diana, wife of Gerard Noel Noel, Esq. (ante); *d.* 1813 ; *s.* in baronetcy by his son-in-law (ante) and in barony by his dau. [2] DIANA; *d.* 1823; *s.* by her el. son [3] CHARLES, 3rd Baron; *s.* to his father's baronetcy 1838, and *cr. Baron Noel, Viscount Campden,* and *Earl of Gainsborough* (peerage of United Kingdom) 1841 ; *d.* 1866 ; *s.* by his el. son [4] CHARLES GEORGE, 2nd Earl, *b.* 1818 ; Lord-Lieut. of Rutland : *m.* 1841, Lady Ida Harriet Augusta, dau. of 16th Earl of Erroll ; *d.* 1881 ; *s.* by his son [5] CHARLES WILLIAM FRANCIS, 3rd Earl, *b.* 1850: *m.* 1st, 1876, Augusta Mary Catherine, who *d.* 1877, dau. of the late Robert Berkeley, of Spetchley Park, Worcester; 2ndly, 1880, Mary Elizabeth, who *d.* 1937, dau. of the late James Arthur Dease, of Turbotston, co. Westmeath ; *d.* 1926 ; *s.* by his son [6] ARTHUR EDWARD JOSEPH, *O.B.E.,* 4th Earl, *b.* 1884 : Private Chamberlain to Pope Benedict XV. and Pope Pius XI. ; an Hon. Attache in Norway and Sweden 1908-12, and at Washington, USA 1913-14: *m.* 1915, Alice Mary, who *d.* 1970, da. of Edward Eyre, of Gloucester House, Park Lane, W.; *d.* 1927 ; *s.* by his son [7] ANTHONY GERARD EDWARD, 5th Earl and present peer; also Viscount Campden, Baron Barham, and Baron Noel.

GAITSKELL, BARONESS. (Gaitskell.) [Life Baroness 1963.]

ANNA DORA GAITSKELL, da. of Leon Creditor; *b.* 19—; *cr. Baroness Gaitskell,* of Egremont, co. Cumberland [Life Baroness] 1963: *m.* 1st, 1921 (m. diss. 1937), David Frost; 2ndly, 1937, Rt. Hon. Hugh Todd-Naylor Gaitskell, CBE, MP, who *d.* 1963, and has issue by 1st and 2nd marriages.
Address,—c/o House of Lords, SW1.

SON LIVING. (*By 1st marriage.*)
Hon. Raymond Frost (5506, Wilson Lane, Bethesda, Maryland, USA), *b.* 1924; ed. at Oundle, and Worcester Coll., Oxford: *m.* 1958, June Virginia Johnston, da. of the late Ing. Eduardo Gonzalez Rodriquez del Rey, and has issue.

DAUGHTERS LIVING. (*By 2nd marriage.*)
Hon. Julia, *b.* 1939; ed. at Somerville Coll., Oxford: *m.* 1969, George Peter McNeal, of 4, Talbot Pl., SE3, and has issue.
Hon. Cressida (18, Frognal Gdns., Hampstead, NW3), *b.* 1942; ed. at Somerville Coll., Oxford (MA): *m.* 1964, Gordon Joshua Wasserman, Economic Adviser to Home Office, and has issue.

GALLOWAY, EARL OF. (Stewart.)
Valour strengthens from a wound.

[Earl S. 1623, Bt. S. 1627 and 1687.]
Randolph Algernon Ronald Stew-art, 12th Earl, and 11th Baronet of Corsewell, and 9th of Burray; *b.* Nov. 21st, 1892; *s.* 1920; ed. at Harrow; Col. (retired) King's Own Scottish Borderers, Capt. late Scots Guards, and a J.P. and Lord-Lieut. of Stewartry of Kirkcudbright; European War 1914 in France and Belgium (prisoner, 1914 star, two medals): *m.* 1924, Philippa Fendall, who *d.* 1974, da. of the late Jacob Wendell, of New York, and has issue.

Arms,—Or, a fesse checky argent and azure, surmounted of a bend engrailed gules, within a double tressure flory counterflory of the last. Crest,—A pelican in nest, vulning herself argent, winged or. Supporters,—*Dexter*, a savage man, wreathed about the head and middle with laurel, and holding in the right hand a club resting on the shoulder, all proper; *sinister*, a lion gules.

Seat,—Cumloden, Newton Stewart, Wigtown-shire. *Clubs,*—St. James', Carlton, New (Edinburgh).

SON LIVING.
Randolph Keith Reginald (*Lord Garlies*), *b.* Oct. 14th, 1928; ed. at Harrow.

DAUGHTER LIVING.
Lady Antonia Marian Amy Isabel, *b.* 1925: *m.* 1946, Sir (Charles) Mark Dalrymple, 3rd Bt., who *d.* 1971, when the title became ext. *Residence,*—Newhailes, Musselburgh, Midlothian.

COLLATERAL BRANCHES LIVING.
Grandsons of the late Maj.-Gen. the Hon. Alexander Stewart, 3rd son of 9th Earl:—
Issue of the late Lieut.-Col. Walter Robert Stewart, DSO, MC, *b.* 1888, *d.* (killed in action during European War) 1918: *m.* (Jan.) 1914, Esmé Winifred Mary (who *d.* 1975, having *m.* 2ndly, 1929, Major Joseph Anthony Douglas Bell, late RASC, who *d.* 1956, da. of Riversdale Francis John Grenfell [B. Avebury, colls.]:—
Alexander David, *M.B.E., T.D., b.* 1914; ed. at Eton; late Major City of London Yeo.; M.B.E. (Mil.) 1945: *m.* 1948, Daphne Marion, only dau. of Sir Reginald Bonsor, 2nd Bt., and widow of Clyde Euan Miles Graham, Flying Officer, R.A.F. [E. Peel, colls.], and has issue living, Andrew Clyde, *b.* 1949,—David Mark, *b.* 1960,—Rosemary Zara, *b.* 1952. *Residence,*—North Green, Kelsale, Saxmundham, Suffolk.

Grandchildren of the late Lt.-Col. Walter Robert Stewart, DSO, MC (ante):—
Issue of the late Capt. Ian Michael Stewart, *b.* 1917, *d.* 1973: *m.* 1941 (*m.* diss. 1952), Peggy Spencer, who *d.* 1957, twin da. of Spencer Thornton:—
Alastair Grenfell (Orchard Farm, Thenford, Banbury, Oxon.), *b.* 1944: *m.* 1973, Sarah Monica Scott.
——Carolyn Mary, *b.* 1942: *m.* 1963, Alec Charles Hinchcliff Bond, of Clay House, Marston St. Lawrence, Banbury, Oxon., and has issue living, William David Hinchcliff, *b.* 1970.

Granddaughters of the late Rev. James Stewart, 2nd son of the Hon. Montgomery Granville John Stewart, MP, 6th son of 7th Earl:—
Issue of the late Horatio George Willoughby Stewart, *b.* 1877, *d.* 1943: *m.* 1929, Beatrice Maud (of Pengar, 52, St. Stephen's Rd., Saltash, Cornwall), dau. of the late James Bedson:—
Flora Margaret, *b.* 1930: *m.* 1951, Richard Arthur Revell, of 16, Bellencroft Gdns., Merry Hill, Wolver-hampton, and has issue living, Nicholas Stewart, *b.* 1952,—Clare Victoria, *b.* 1956,—Jennifer Mary, *b.* 1968.——Daphne Isabel, *b.* 1932: *m.* 1956, Neville Tasker, of 15, Georgina Av., Elanora Heights, NSW 2101, Aust., and has issue living, Sheryl Ann, *b.* 1959,—Melanie Jane, *b.* 1963.

Granddaughter of the late Maj.-Gen. Sir Herbert Stewart, KCB, el. son of the late Rev. Edward Stewart, el. son of the Hon. Edward Richard Stewart, 7th son of 7th Earl:—
Issue of the late Major Geoffrey Stewart, *b.* 1878, *d.* (killed in action) 1914: *m.* 1908, Violet [who *d.* 1968, having *m.* 2ndly, 1922, the Rev. Harold Omer Cavalier, who *d.* 1936, V. of St. Stephen's, St. Albans], da. of the late William Clarence Watson, of Colworth, Bedfordshire:—
Jean Violet, *b.* 1909: *m.* 1940, Maj.-Gen. Michael Prynne, CB, CBE, late RE, and has issue living, Andrew Geoffrey Lockyer, *b.* 1953,—Bridget Mary, *b.* 1941: *m.* 1965, Donald Ian Spence, of South Lodge, Redleaf, Penshurst, Kent, and has issue living, Robert Ian James *b.* 1969, Arabella Jean *b.* 1967,—Caroline Anne *b.* 1943: *m.* 1965, Terence Michael Kehoe, of Jasminstrasse 6, 8 Munich 45, Germany, and has issue living, Susanna, Jane *b.* 1966, Catherine Jenny *b.* 1973,—Celia Jane, *b.* 1947. *m.* 1971, David Greenberg, of Bull Cottage, Balsham, Cambridge. *Residence,*—4, Victoria Rd., W8 5RD.

Granddaughters of the late Col. Charles Edward Stewart, C.B., C.M.G., C.I.E., son of the late Algernon Stewart, yr. son of the late Hon. Edward Richard Stewart (ante):—
Issue of the late Lieut.-Col. Algernon Bingham Anstruther Stewart, D.S.O., *b.* 1869, *d.* (killed in action during European War) 1916: *m.* 1911, Edith Evelyn, who *d.* 1932 (having *m.* 2ndly, 1922, Henry de Grey Lennox [D. Richmond, colls.]), dau. of the late Sir Arthur Pendarves Vivian, K.C.B. [B. Swansea, colls.]:—
Sheila Anne (*Baroness Denman*), *b.* 1915: *m.* 1943, the 5th Baron Denman. *Residence,*—Highden House, Washington, Pulborough, Sussex.——Barbara Jean (twin), *b.* 1915: *m.* 1939, Maj. George De Pree, King's Roy. Rifle Corps, and has issue living, Andrew Hugo Stewart, *b.* 1946: *m.* 1972, Victoria, only da. of David Neilson, of Catton Hall, Burton-on-Trent,—Jane Mary, *b.* 1940: *m.* 1961, Giles William Pitman, of Heath House, Patmore Heath, Albury, Ware, Herts., and has issue living, George Eustace, *b.* 1963, John Struan *b.* 1969, Kate Jane *b.* 1965,—Rachel Anne, *b.* 1950: *m.* 1970, James Edward Cory Liddell, of Cottonworth House, Fullerton, Andover, Hants. [see B. Ravensworth, colls.]. *Residence,*—Little Knelle Farm, Beckley, Rye, Sussex.

Grandchildren of the late Charles Patrick Stewart, son of the late Lt.-Col. the Hon James Henry Keith Stewart, C.B., M.P., 8th son of 7th Earl:—
Issue of the late Charles Nigel Stewart, *b.* 1864, *d.* 1915 : *m.* 1895, Edith Mabel, dau. of the late Julius Miller, M.D., M.R.C.S. :—
Herbert Nigel, *b.* 1896. *Residence,*—
Issue of the late Alan Keith Stewart, *b.* 1860, *d.* 1897 : *m.* 1889, Louisa Jane, who *d.* 1950, dau. of John Moreton Marchinton:—
Frances Evelyn, *b.* 1896 : *m.* 1916, Leon Richmond Leuty, and has issue living, Cecil Richmond (of 56, Broadgate Lane, Horsforth, Leeds), *b.* 1918 ; European War 1939-45 with R.A. in Middle East (prisoner),—Sheila Arthington, *b.* 1923 ; is an Architect : *m.* 1950, David Eric Jennings, architect. *Residence,*—
Issue of the late Capt. Arthur Courtenay Stewart, O.B.E., R.N., *b.* 1871, *d.* 1958 : *m.* (Jan.) 1911, Gwendolyn Marion, who *d.* 1961, dau. of Waldo Story:—
Ivor Courtenay, *b.* 1916.——Fiammetta Maud Courtenay, *b.* (Oct.) 1911: *m.* 1939, Squadron-Leader Gordon Addison Hope Kent, R.A.F., and has issue living, Nigel Courtenay, *b.* 1947,—Sarah Penelope, *b.* 1945. *Residence,*—Hopcote, Stratton, Cirencester, Glos.

Grandson of the late John Leveson Douglas Stewart (*b.* 1842), grandson of Leveson Douglas Stewart (*b.* 1786), 2nd son of Adm. the Hon. Keith Stewart, 3rd son of 6th Earl:—
Issue of the late Lieut.-Col. John Stewart, D.S.O., *b.* 1869 ; *d.* 1931 : *m.* 1892, Valentia, who *d.* 1947, dau. of the late William Worship:—
Keith Ian Douglas, O.B.E., *b.* 1904 ; ed. at Radley ; Lieut.-Col. (retired) R.A.P.C., a Member of Queen's Body Guard for Scotland (Roy. Co. of Archers), and a J.P. ; formerly Capt. Black Watch (Roy. Highlanders); 1939-45 War in N. Africa, Italy and N.-W. Europe (OBE); OBE (Mil.) 1945: *m.* 1st, 1930, Helena, who *d.* 1940, da. of Edward Ashton St. Hill; 2ndly, 1940, Philippa North, who *d.* 1966, el. da. of the late Robert Nairn, of Hastings, NZ; 3rdly, 1967, Frances Auckland Louise Bogue, da. of the late Francis Joseph Hieronymus-Jones, and has issue living, (by 1st m.) John Edward Hamish Keith, *b.* 1935,—Jennifer Mary Hamilton, *b.* 1931. *Residence,*—Quinta das Laranjeiras, Loures, Portugal. *Clubs,*—New (Edinburgh), United Hunts, Royal British (Lisbon), Turf (Lisbon).

Granddaughter of the late Leveson Douglas Stewart (*b.* 1844), el. son of George, Stewart (infra):—
Issue of the late Leveson Douglas Stewart, *b.* 1873, *d.* 1905: *m.* 18—, Elizabeth, dau. of ———— :—
Elizabeth Leveson Douglas. *Residence,*—Ottawa, Canada.

Grandchildren of the late George Stewart, son of the late Leveson Douglas Stewart (*b.* 1786), (ante):—
Issue of the late Leveson Douglas Stewart, *b.* 1844, *d.* 1916: *m.* 1872, Kate, who *d.* 1915, dau. of J. Gillone:—
Keith, *b.* 1877; with Canadian Expeditionary Force during 1914-18 War: *m.* 1919, Margaret, da. of the late Nicholas Fox, master mariner, of Dublin, and has issue living, Ian Keith, *b.* 1923,—Allan Galloway, *b.* 1928,—Barbara, *b.* 1921,—Isobel Evelyn, *b.* 1925.——Thomas Corrie, *b.* 1879.——John, *b.* 1882: *m.* 1912, and has issue living, Mary Frances, *b.* 191-.——Randolph Douglas, *b.* 1884: *m.* 1916, Ellen Tullagher, of Edge Hill, Liverpool.
Issue of the late Thomas Corrie Stewart, *b.* 1846, *d.* 1907 : *m.* 18—, Maria, dau. of William Cook :—
Several children (both sons and daus.). *Resident* in Natal.

PREDECESSORS.—[1] Sir ALEXANDER Stewart, *K.B., P.C.* (descended from Sir William Stewart, of Jedworth—second son of Sir Alexander Stewart of Darnley and one of the leading men of Scotland during the reigns of his kinsmen, the two first Stewart Kings—whose son Sir John Stewart, *m.* Marion, dau. of Sir Walter Stewart, of Dalswinton); cr. *Lord Garlies* (peerage of Scotland) 1607, with remainder to the heirs male of his body succeeding to the estates of Garlies, and *Earl of Galloway* (peerage of Scotland) 1623, with remainder to his heirs male bearing the name and arms of Stewart ; *d.* 1649; *s.* by his son [2] JAMES, 2nd Earl, who in 1627 had been cr. a *Baronet* (of Corsewell); for his loyalty to the Roy. cause in 1654 was fined £4,000 by Cromwell; *d.* 1671; *s.* by his el. son [3] ALEXANDER, 3rd Earl; *s.* by his brother [4] ALEXANDER, 4th Earl; *d.* unmarried 1694; *s.* by his brother [5] JAMES, *P.C.*, 5th Earl; an able statesman *temp.* Queen Anne; *d.* 1746 ; *s.* by his son [6] ALEXANDER, 6th Earl ; a Lord of Police; served heir male as 4th Bt. to Sir Archibald Stewart, 2nd Bt. (cr. 1687, of Burray, with remainder to heirs male whatsoever); *d.* 1773; *s.* by his el. son [7] JOHN, *K.T.*, 7th Earl; M.P. for Morpeth, &c., a Lord of the Bedchamber to George III. and a Representative Peer 1774-96 ; cr. *Baron Stewart of Garlies* (peerage of Great Britain) 1796 ; *d.* 1806; *s.* by his son [8] GEORGE, *K.T.*, 8th Earl; an Adm., M.P. for Cockermouth, &c., and a Lord of the Admiralty ; *d.* 1834; *s.* by his son [9] RANDOLPH, 9th Earl, *b.* 1800; M.P. for Cockermouth 1826-31 ; Lord-Lieut. of co. Kirkcudbright 1828-45 and of co. Wigtown 1828-51 ; *m.* 1833, Lady Harriet Blanche, who *d.* 1885, dau. of 6th Duke of Beaufort; *d.* 1873; *s.* by his son [10] ALAN PLANTAGENET, *K.T.*, 10th Earl: *b.* 1835 ; M.P. for Wigtownshire 1868-78 ; Lord High Commr. to Gen. Assembly for Ch. of Scotland 1876-7 : *m.* 1872, Lady Mary Arabella Arthur, who *d.* 1903. dau. of 2nd Marquess of Salisbury ; *d.* 1901 ; *s.* by his brother [11] RANDOLPH HENRY, 11th Earl; *b.* 1836; Crimean Campaign 1855, and Indian Mutiny Campaign 1857-9 : *m.* 1891, Amy Mary Pauline, who *d.* 1942, dau. of the late Anthony John Cliffe, of Belle Vue, co. Wexford; *d.* 1920 : *s.* by his son [12] RANDOLPH ALGERNON RONALD, *b.* 1892, 12th Earl and present peer ; also Lord Garlies, and Baron Stewart of Garlies.

GALWAY, VISCOUNT. (Monckton-Arundell.) [Viscount I. 1727.]
(Title pronounced " Gaulway." Name pronounced " Munkton-Arundell."]

WILLIAM ARUNDELL MONCKTON-ARUNDELL,
10th Viscount; b. Sept. 24th, 1894; s. 1971; ed.
at Trin. Coll., Camb.; late Lt. 2nd Bn. R.
Jersey LI (Mil): m. 1939, Joan, who d. 1973,
only child of the late Maj. G. A. Williams, S.
Staffs. Regt., of Morelands, Purbrook, Hants.

Arms,—Quarterly: 1st and 4th sable, six swallows,
three, two, and one, argent, Arundell; 2nd and 3rd sable,
on a chevron between three martlets or, as many
mullets of the field, Monckton. Crests,—1st, on a chapeau
azure, turned up ermine, a swallow argent; 2nd, a
martlet or. Supporters,—Two unicorns ermine, crined,
armed and unguled, and each gorged with an Eastern
coronet or.

To extend my fame by deeds.
Address,—c/o National Westminster Bank, 1, Lombard St., EC3.

BROTHER LIVING. [Raised to the rank of a Viscounts' son 1973].
Hon. EDMUND SAVILE MONCKTON (Simons Close, Richmond Rd., Bath), b. Sept. 11th, 1900; ed. at
Charterhouse, and Clare Coll., Camb. (MA); Solicitor (Honours) 1930: m. 1927, Kathleen Joyce,
who d. 1975, da. of the late James Musgrave [Musgrave, Bt., cr. 1782], and has issue living, Rose
Wynsome, b. 1937.

SISTER LIVING. [Raised to the rank of a Viscounts' daughter 1973].
Hon. Rosamond Vere, b. 1892: m. 1922, Vice-Adm. Arthur Duncan Read, CB, of Brewer's Wood, Shorne,
Kent, and has issue living, Elisabeth Hermione Rosamond, b. 1924,—Rose Ethel, b. 1925: m. 1951,
Michael Louis Maude Chavasse, QC, of Park House, Chevening, Kent, and has issue living, Camilla
Rose b. 1958, Julia Catherine b. 1962, Sarah Elizabeth, b. 1965,—Pamela Vere, b. 1927: m. 1961,
Maj.-Gen. Marston Eustace Tickell, CBE, MC, MA, FICE, of Shaw Top House, Chipstead, Seven-
oaks, Kent, son of the late Maj.-Gen. Sir Eustace Francis Tickell, KBE, CB, MC.

DAUGHTER LIVING OF NINTH VISCOUNT.
Hon. Charlotte Anne, b. 1955.

DAUGHTERS LIVING OF EIGHTH VISCOUNT.
Hon. Mary Victoria, b. 1924: m. 1st, 1947 (m. diss. 1972), David Henry Fetherstonhaugh, Coldm.
Gds.; 2ndly, 1974, Maj. Robert Patricius Chaworth-Musters, of Felley Priory, Jacksdale, Notts.,
and has issue living (by 1st m.), Hugh Simon, b. 1949: m. 1971, Louise, adopted da. of Hon. (Richard)
Hanning Philipps [B. Milford],—Henry George, b. 1954,—Victoria Bronwen, b. 1951.
Hon. Celia Ella Vere MONCKTON (Hon. Lady Rowley), b. 1925: m. 1959, Sir Joshua Francis Rowley,
7th Bt., of Holbecks, Hadleigh, Suffolk; appointed an Extra Lady-in-Waiting to HRH Princess
Alexandra, the Hon. Mrs. Angus Ogilvy 1970.
Hon. Isabel Cynthia MONCKTON, b. 1926: m. 1970 John Leonard King, of Wartnaby, Melton Mowbray,
Leics.

WIDOW LIVING OF EIGHTH VISCOUNT.
LUCIA EMILY MARGARET (Dowager Viscountess Galway), dau. of 3rd Baron Annaly: was a Maid of
Honour to Queen Alexandra 1919-22; European War 1914-18 with Red Cross (Bronze Medal):
m. 1922, the 8th Viscount, who d. 1943. Residence,—Serlby Hall, Bawtry, Doncaster, Yorkshire.

WIDOW LIVING OF NINTH VISCOUNT.
Lady TERESA JANE FOX-STRANGWAYS (Melbury House, Dorchester, Dorset; Bishopfield House,
Bawtry, Doncaster), da. of the 7th Earl of Ilchester: m. 1st, 1953, the 9th Viscount, who d. 1971;
2ndly, 1972, Mark Agnew.

COLLATERAL BRANCHES LIVING.
Issue of the late Joan Frances Monckton, sister of 10th Viscount, b. 1889, d. 1959:
m. 1914, Capt. Frederick Thomas de Mallet Morgan, CBE, RN, who d. 1959.
Geoffrey Thomas Monckton de Mallet, MC (Cowford House, Fridge, Sussex), b. 1919, Maj. (ret.) RA:
m. 1945, Violet, da. of J. Watkins, and has issue living, Thomas Michael John, b. 1948,—David
Geoffrey, b. 1950,—Mark James, b. 1952,—Georgina Ann, b. 1946: m. 1974, Richard Penticost,—
Eironwy Elizabeth, b. 1949.——Rosemary Edith de Mallet, b. 1915: m. 1940, Lt.-Col. John John-
ston Dingwall, DSO, RTR (ret.), of Lyford Grange, Wantage, Berks, and has issue living, Charles
Berkeley Johnston, b. 1946: m. 1971, Jennifer Davina da. of Edward Dorrien Dudley Ryder [see
E. Harrowby colls.] and has issue living, Sophie b. 1972,—Maryrose Danvers, b. 1941: m. 1964,
Nicholas Westendarp.of Broomvale, Gt. Blakenham, nr. Ipswich, Suffolk, and has issue living, Charles
John James b. 1971, Joanna Caroline Danvers b. 1965, Annabel Rosemary Abdy b. 1974,—Nony
Caroline Vatcher, b. 1944: m. 1969, Hugh Charles Stanley Buchanan, [see Buchanan Bt.], Anthea
Rochfort, b. 1974, d. 1974, having m. 1973, Colin Stranach Sinclair.——Faith Joan de Mallet, b. 1927:
m. 1957, Maj. Henry Walrond Lancelot Vatcher, MBE, RE (ret.), of Badbury House, Swed, Wilts.,
and has issue living, Henry Nigel Christopher, b. 1958,—Robert Lancelot b. 1962,—Rupert, (twin),
b. 1962,—Simon Philip Monckton, b. 1970.

Grandchildren of the late Marmaduke John Monckton, 3rd son of the late Hon.
Edmund Gambier Monckton, 4th son of 5th Viscount:—
Issue of the late Philip Marmaduke Monckton, b. 1892, d. 1965: m. 1918, Lavender (Apt. 405,
505, Rupert St., Victoria, BC, Canada), da. of the late W. J. O'Hara:—
George Rupert (672, Berkshire Drive, London, Ont., Canada), b. 1922; Lt.-Cdr. RCN (ret.): m. 1944,
Fiona Margaret, da. of Capt. W. de P. Taylor, of Sooke, BC, Canada, and has issue living, John,
Philip, b. 1952,—Sheelagh Margaret, b. 1945: m. 1967, William Arthur Herd, of 361, Queens Av.,
Apt. 9, London 14, Ontario, Canada,—Fiona Marilyn, b. 1947,—Rachel Jean, b. 1957.——Sylvia
Margaret, b. 1921: m. 1947, Thomas Bruce Wilson, late Lt.-Cdr. RCN, of 1815, West 30th Av.,
Vancouver, 9, BC, Canada, and has issue living, Patrick John, b. 1957,—Kathleen Elizabeth, b. 1948:
m. 1969, Roland R. Stephen, of 14, Rue des Artisans, Port Grimaud 83, France,—Rosemary Jean,
b. 1949: m. 1971, Niels Bols, 504, 100, Maitland St., Toronto 5, Ont., Canada.

Grandchildren of the late Gen. Henry Monckton, 4th son of the late Hon. Edward
Monckton, 5th son of 1st Viscount:—
Issue of the late Francis Monckton, b. 1841, d. 1926: m. 1889, Evelyn Mary, who d. 1941,
dau. of the late Algernon Charles Heber-Percy [see D. Northumberland, colls.]:—
Reginald Francis Percy, TD, b. 1896; ed. at Eton; Maj. (ret.) Staffordshire Yeo., TA, and a DL
for Staffordshire (High Sheriff 1937); a member of House of Laity, Church Assembly 1950-70,
and Church Commr. 1958-68; 1914-18 War in Egypt and Palestine (two medals), 1939-45 War
in Middle East (four medals); sometime ADC to High Commr. and Com.-in-Ch., Palestine: m. 1931,
Sheila, JP, da. of H. G. Stobart, of Thornton-le-Dale, Pickering, and has issue living, Alan Stobart
(of Bishopswood House, Bishopswood, Stafford), b. 1934; FRICS; High Sheriff of Staffs., 1975;
a Bridge Life Master, and a Dir. of Penk, Ltd., Penk Holdings, Ltd., Penk Products, Ltd., and Halifax
Building Soc.: m. 1961, Joanna Mary, el. da. of G. C. Bird, of Appleton, Abingdon, Berks., and has
issue living, Piers Alastair Carlos b. 1962, Toby Philip Carlos b. 1970, Davina Claire b. 1964, Sophie

Louise (twin), *b.* 1967,—Daphne Alice Cavil, *b.* 1937: *m.* 1958, Nigel John Lincoln Estlick, Maj. RM, of Kent House, Amesbury, Wilts., and has issue living, Robin Monckton *b.* 1968, Caroline Rosemary *b.* 1962, Marian Heather *b.* 1965. *Residence,*—Stretton Hall, Stafford.——Violet Maud Frances, *b.* 1894: *m.* 1925, Sidney James Farrer, JP, who *d.* 1946. *Residence,*—Winton, The Close, Saltwood, Hythe, Kent.

Issue of the late Arthur Monckton, *b.* 1845, *d.* 1917: *m.* 1896, Lady Gertrude Pleydell Bouverie, who *d.* 1940, dau. of 4th Earl of Radnor:—

Marmaduke, *b.* 1899; ed. at Eton, and at Balliol Coll., Oxford; European War 1918 in France. *Residence,*—38, Oompayne Gardens, N.W.6.——Mary, *b.* 1897; formerly 2nd Officer W.R.N.S. : *m.* 1959, Geoffrey Palgrave Barker, F.S.A., Major Suffolk Yeo. (retired). *Residence,*—15, Neville Court, Abbey Road, N.W.8.——Nora, *b.* 1901. *Residence,*—38, Oompayne Gardens, N.W.6.

Grandchildren of the late Lieut.-Col. Edward Philip Monckton (infra) :—
Issue of the late George Edward Monckton, *b.* 1868, *d.* 1936: *m.* 1896, Marguerite Edith Evelyn Eleanor, dau. of the late James Marigold, of Park House, Edgbaston :—

Cavil Grace Mary, *b.* 1903: *m.* 1925, Sydney Lipscomb Elborne, MBE, MA, JP, Bar.-at-Law, of Water Newton, Peterborough, and has issue living, Robert Edward Monckton (20, Ranelagh Av., SW6 3PS), *b.* 1926; ed. at Eton, and Trin. Coll., Camb.; Bar. Inner Temple 1950; Solicitor 1958, formerly Lt. Life Guards, and Inns of Court Regt. (TA): *m.* 1953, Vivienne, yr. da. of Lt.-Gen. Sir Ernest Wood, KBE, CB, CIE, MC, and has issue living, Mark Edward Monckton *b.* 1958; ed. at Eton, William Henry Alexander *b.* 1966, Charlotte Julia Mary *b.* 1956,—Margaret *b.* 1931: *m.* 1st, 1955, Maj. J. R. M. Laird, RA; 2ndly, 1967, Edward William Ingram, of 9, Grange Rd., Eastbourne, Sussex, and has issue living, (by 1st m.) Duncan John Alexander *b.* 1958, Caroline Margaret Ann *b.* 1956, (by 2nd m.) Claire Constance Cavil *b.* 1968.

Issue of the late Philip Tunnard Monckton, *b.* 1870, *d.* 1928 : *m.* 1901, Agnes Carr, who *d.* 1956, dau. of Maxwell Smith, of Darjeeling, India :—
Philip Anthony, *b.* 1913; ed. at Sherborne; formerly Pilot Officer R.A.F. Vol. Reserve.—— Sybil Carr, *b.* 1902: *m.* 1st, 1927, Ronald Charles Keith Smith; 2ndly, 1955, Capt. George Lardner-Clarke, late King's Regt.——Mary Philippa, *b.* 1912 : *m.* 1st, 1934, William Michael Gambier Bandwith, Sup. of Police, Kenya ; 2ndly, 1948, Walter John Smail, and has issue living, (by 1st marriage) Caroline Ann, *b.* 1938. *Residence.*—

Granddaughter of the late Capt. Noel Monckton, son of the late Lieut.-Col. Edward Philip Monckton, son of the late Edward Henry Cradock Monckton (infra):—
Issue of the late Cecily Flora Noel, who *d.* 1950 (she assumed by deed poll 1944, the additional surname of Monckton), having *m.* 1922, Com. George Evelyn Paget How, R.N. (retired), from whom she obtained a divorce 1940 :—

Rachel MONCKTON-HOW, *b.* 1928: *m.* 1961, Peter Hutchinson, MB, BS. *Residence,*—7, Highfield Rd., Westerhope, Newcastle upon Tyne.

Grandson of the late Edward Henry Cradock Monckton, son of the late Philip Monckton, 5th son of the late Hon. Edward Monckton (ante):—
Issue of the late Lieut.-Col. William Parry Monckton, *b.* 1846, *d.* 1914 : *m.* 1891, Florence Georgina Sybella, who *d.* 1927, dau. of James Sawrey Cookson, of Neasham Hall, Darlington, and Broughton Towers, Lancashire :—

Ivor Parry, *b.* 1892; ed. at Sherborne; is an Engineer; formerly Lieut. R.A.S.C.: *m.* 1921, Olive, da. of William Bassett and has issue living, Dennahouse Parry (Hillhead, Nether Wallop, Stockbridge, Hants.), *b.* 1930; ed. at Sherborne; Maj. RCT: *m.* 1966, Mary Elizabeth Doreen, da. of James Carson. *Residence,*—Stone Court, Berkeley, Glos.

Grandchildren of the late Hugh Monckton, yst. son of the late Edward Henry Cradock-Monckton (ante):—
Issue of the late Hugh Claud Monckton, *b.* 1881, *d.* 1970: *m.* 1st, 1910, Emily Sophia Ray, who *d.* 1945, da. of E. C. Gibson; 2ndly, 1946, Helen Atherton, who *d.* 1974, da. of the late P. A. Morris, of Sydney, NSW :—

(By 1st m.) Basil Robert (38 Creswell St., Campbell, ACT), *b.* 1917; ed. at NZ Univ. (BE); ME Adelaide: MICE; MIEAust.; Ch. Engineer, Overseas Property Bureau, Dept. of Foreign Affairs, Canberra (formerly of S. Aust.), and a Town Engineer, Suva, Fiji: *m.* 1943, Audrey Constance, da. of Arthur Charles Tribe, of Auckland, NZ, and has issue living, Robert Parry (c/o Friedrick Meischer Institut, PO Box 273, Basel CH 4002, Switzerland, *b.* 1948; ed. at Flinders Univ., Adelaide (BSc), Aust. National Univ. (BSc Hons., PhD), and Friedrich Miescher Inst., Basel, Switzerland,—David Christopher, *b.* 1951; ed. at Canberra Coll. of Advanced Education (Bach. of Applied Science),— Peter Charles, *b.* 1955.——Hugh Noel Campbell (17, Hinton Av., Hamilton, NZ), *b.* 1923; ed. at NZ Univ. (BE); MNZIE, AMICE, MPCI, MACI; a Consulting Architect: *m.* 1950, Elizabeth Rubi Young, da. of Arthur Boswell, of Torbay, NZ, and has issue living, Hugh Geoffrey, *b.* 1954,— Roger John, *b.* 1958,—Elizabeth Anne, *b.* 1953.——Sybil Dorothy (116, Southern River Rd., Gosnells, W. Aust. 6110), *b.* 1916; resumed the surname of Canard 1962: *m.* 1st, 1940, Ernest Herbert Canard, P/O RAF, who *d.* (killed on active ser. in S. Africa) 1942; 2ndly, 1957 (m. diss. 1962), Nils A. A. H. Gyllenberg; 3rdly, 1966, Frederick Alma Gearing, 116, Southern River Rd., Gosnells, W. Aust., 6110, and has issue living, (by 1st m.) Hugh Jason Paul (17, Whareora Terr., Christchurch, NZ), *b.* 1942; ed. at Rutherford Coll. of Tech. (IHVE), Newcastle upon Tyne: *m.* 1968, Elizabeth Frances Wildridge, and has issue living, Jamie Duncan *b.* 1971, Dugal Stephen *b.* 1972.
Issue of the late Eric Parry Monckton, *b.* 1883, *d.* 1953: *m.* 1917, Minna (14, Jackson St., Balgowlah, NSW 2093), da. of the late H. Erhard, of Sydney, N.S. Wales:—
James Hugh, *b.* 1921.——Joan Harriette, *b.* 1918: *m.* 1940, Jack Anderson Stackpool, who *d.* 1971, and has issue living, Michael John, *b.* 1946 ACIV, QRV, AREI,—Susan Jane, *b.* 1947: *m.* 1969, Stephen Charles Bowden, of 32, The Crescent, Dee Way, Sydney, NSW. *Residence,*—14, Jackson Street, Balgowlah, NSW 2093.

Grandchildren of the late Henry Monckton, B.C.S., son of the late William Monckton (infra):—
Issue of the late Henry Grant Monckton, *b.* 1860, *d.* 1917: *m.* 1890, Maud Lilian, who *d.* 1895, dau. of the late Rev. John W. Hallowell, R. of Oranmore, co. Galway:—

Frederick Hardy, *b.* 1892; ed. at Camb. Univ. (BA honours 1914); Maj. (ret.) RE; MICE: *m.* 1941, Frances, who *d.* 1967, da. of Paul Ryan, of Dublin, and has issue living, Henry William (Bursden Court, Bursden Close, Glenfield, Leicester), *b.* 1945; BA Camb.,—Michael Frederick, *b.* 1947; ed. at Manchester Univ. (BSc). *Residence,*—122, Poplar Av., Hillyfields, Bedford.——Maud Lillian Seaflower, *b.* 1895.

Issue of the late Rev. William Gawler Monckton, *b.* 1866, *d.* 1934 : *m.* 1902, Sophie Mary, who *d.* 1957, dau. of Henry Oldham, of Napier, New Zealand ; she *m.* 2ndly, 1937, Robert Millen, who *d.* 1949 :—

Violet Arundell, *b.* 1905 : *m.* 1933, Paul Jay, J.P., and has issue living, Christopher Laurence Monckton (2, Putsborough Close, Georgeham, nr. Braunton, N. Devon), *b.* 1942: *m.* 1968, Mary Margaret, da. of Ronald Holbrook, of Tring, and has issue living, Madeleine Victoria Elizabeth *b.* 1973,—Rosalind Mary Monckton, *b.* 1934: *m.* 1st, 1955 (m. diss. 1963) Anthony David Mayes, who assumed by deed poll 1956, the additional surname of Monckton before his patronymic; 2ndly, 1965, Ronald William Inkpen, c/o County Police Station, Slough. *Residence,*—Coleshill House, Berkhamsted, Herts.

Grandchildren of the late Frederick Edward Monckton, son of the late William
Monckton, 8th son of the late Hon. Edward Monckton (ante):—
Issue of the late Rev. James Frederick Monckton, *b*. 1858, *d*. 1946: *m*. 1885, Alice Australia,
who *d*. 1931, dau. of Neil Harper:—

James Frederick Edward, *b*. 1892; ed. at Gonville and Caius Coll., Camb. (MA); late Capt. Northants
Regt.; 1914-18 War: *m*. 1917, Dorothy Verrinder, who *d*. 1975, 2nd da. of the late George Willson,
of Upper Sydenham, SE, and has issue living, Georgina Elspeth, *b*. 1917: *m*. 1st, 1938, Capt. Peter
Wilkinson Swift, Green Howards, who *d*. (killed in action during European War) 1942; 2ndly, 1946,
Godfrey Walter Thrift, of 2, Mill Lawn, Wray Common Rd., Reigate, Surrey, and has issue living,
(by 2nd marriage) Peter Walter Monckton *b*. 1949, (by 1st marriage) Patricia Elspeth *b*. 1940: *m*. 1962,
Robin William Langford Gritton, of Birkheads Cottage, Birkheads Rd., Reigate, Surrey, and has
issue living, Peter William *b*. 1963, Susan Mary *b*. 1965, Lucy Belinda *b*. 1970,—Patricia Penn *b*. 1920:
m. 1942, Richard James Ellis, late Lt. RAN, of Sinnington, 3, Burfitt Parade, Glenbrook, NSW, 2773,
and has issue living, Peter Francis Monckton *b*. 1947, Michael Richard Penn *b*. 1952, Timothy Willson
b. 1961, Susan Patricia *b*. 1943: *m*. 1970, Geoffrey John Lawson, Dep. Headmaster, Papunya Native
Settlement, N.T., Aust. (and has issue living, Josephine Emily *b*. 1972), Jennifer Ann *b*. 1949, Winifred
Jill *b*. 1958,—Jean Mary, *b*. 1927: *m*. 1948, Edward Richard Taylor, BE, of 18A, Morella Av.,
Mosman, NSW, and has issue living James Edward Monckton *b*. 1950: *m*. 19—, Anne Alison, da.
of Prof. Stalley, of Manly, NSW, Richard *b*. 1955, Matthew (twin) *b*. 1955; Catherine, Elizabeth
Monckton *b*. 1949: *m*. 1973, Donald Ross Kennedy, BSc, of Kalgoorlie, W. Aust. (and has issue living,
Rebecca Jean *b*. 1974). *Residence*,—Nabiac, IO, NSW.——Gordon Cecil ,*b*. 1902, ed. at St. Cath-
arine's Coll, Camb. (BA 1924, MA 1932); formerly in Nigerian Civil Ser.: Lt.-Col. late Northants
Regt.; was Senior Control Officer, Control Commn. for Germany, and British Resident in Germany
1947-51: *m*. 1st, 1928 (m. diss. 1948), Mary Catherine, da. of the late Hugh McCaffrey, of Clones, co.
Monaghan; 2ndly, 1948, Thérèse, da. of Stephen Minarovic, of Loimersdorf, Marchfeld, Austria,
and has issue living, (by 1st m.) Elizabeth Ann, *b*. 1930: *m*. 1962, Martin Rosoff, PhD, of 15, Wellesley
Av., Yonkers, NY 10705, USA, and has issue living, David *b*. 1965,—(by 2nd m.) James Edward
(Trevarth Vean, Lanner Moor, Redruth, Cornwall), *b*. 1951: *m*. 1971, Jacqueline Ann, only da. of
N. Conner, and has issue living, Timothy Norman *b*. 1975,—Evelyn Stephanie, *b*. 1948: *m*. 1972,
David John Penman,—Valentine Penn (a da.), *b*. 1950,—Helen Marina, *b*. 1953. *Residence*,—Fern-
side, Old Wokingham Rd., Crowthorne, Berks.——Alice Elizabeth, *b*. 1895; BA London Univ. 1922:
m. 1927, Thomas Evan Ryves, MRCS, and has issue living, Thomas Bruno (Rusland, Gloucester
Rd., Kingston Hill, Surrey), *b*. 1930; ed. at Trin. Coll., Oxford (BA 1952): *m*. 1954, Ann Catherine,
da. of J. Bertram Roberts, of Kingston Hill, Surrey, and has issue living, Alun Thomas McKellar
b. 1958, William Jonathan *b*. 1964, Mary Ann McKellar *b*. 1962,—Margaret Elizabeth (twin), *b*. 1930;
ed. at Newnham Coll., Camb. (BA 1952). *Residence*,—Rusland, Gloucester Rd., Kingston Hill,
Surrey.

Issue of the late Walter Hillary Monckton, *b*. 1861, *d*. 1924: *m*. 1888, Jeannie Bruce, wh
d. 1939, dau. of Alexander Bruce Webster:—
Hilary James, *b*. 1889; ed. at Sydney Gram. Sch. ; was Controlling Wool Appraiser, N.S Wales
1939-46 : *m*. 1915, Ruby Rose, dau. of John Crisp, of Cooma, N.S. Wales, and has issue living,
Walter John Bruce, *b*. 1918 : *m*. 1942, Betty Allen, dau. of C. W. Keele, of Bellevue Hill, Sydney,
N.S. Wales, and has issue living, Robin Anne *b*. 1944, Rosemary Joan *b*. 1946, Frances Anne *b*. 1951,
—Jean Winifred (The Kopje, 2, Cromwell St., Cooma, NSW), *b*. 1916: *m*. 1940, Maj. Charles Cuth-
bert Wolfe, R . Aust. Engineers, who *d*. 1969, and has issue living, Edwin Monckton *b*. 1941, Peter
Hilary *b*. 1943, Elizabeth Jean *b*. 1955. *Residence*,—139, Victoria Rd., Bellevue Hill, Sydney,
NSW——Basil Bruce, *b*. 1894: *m*. 1st, 1929 (m. diss. 1949), Edna, da. of E. N. R. McMillan, of
Rockdale, NSW; 2ndly, 1949, Violet Lillian, da. of P. S. O'Donnell, of Mosman, NSW, and has issue
living (by 1st m.) Margaret Heather, *b*. 1930; *m*. 1952, Keith Willoughby Payne, Architect, and has
issue living, Geoffrey William *b*. 1953, David Bruce *b*. 1956, Robyn Louise *b*. 1959. *Residence*,—
15, Allan St., Roseville, NSW.

Issue of the late Cecil Charles Fisk Monckton, *b*. 1867, *d*. 1954 : *m*. 1902, Dorothy Tatham
(now of Portelet Cottage, Jersey), younger dau. of the late Walter Tatham Hughes, I.S.O.,
of 12, Somerset Place, Bath :—
Edward Walter, *O.B.E.*, *R.N.*, *b*. 1903; is Lieut.-Com. and acting Com.; O.B.E. (Mil.) 1944: *m*. 1932,
Margaret Frances, dau. of Brig.-Gen. Frederick Walter Radcliffe, C.M.G., C.I.E., O.B.E., of White-
croft, Buxton Road, Weymouth, and has issue living, Christopher John Edward, *b*. 1942.—Hugh
Francis, *b*. 1948. *Residence*,—42, Ottoline Drive, Troon, Ayrshire.——Charles Tatham (Portelet
Cottage, Jersey), *b*. 1913; late Capt. 4th/7th R. Dragoon Gds.: *m*. 1946, Ruth Elizabeth Blandy,
and has issue living, Timothy James (10, Glebe Close, Flowerpot Lane, Long Stratton, NOR 72W),
b. 1947: *m*. 1971, Mary, da. of John Mcleod, of Blackburn,—Richard Charles, *b*. 1960,—Felicity
Ruth, *b*. 1950.

PREDECESSORS.—[1] JOHN Monckton, M.P. for Clitheroe 1722-33, and for Pontefract 1734-
51, a Commr. of Revenue in Ireland 1734-47, and Surveyor Gen. of Woods and Forests in
England and Wales 1748-51; cr. *Baron Killard*, of co. Clare, and *Viscount Galway* (peerage of
Ireland) 1727; *d*. 1751; *s*. by his son [2] WILLIAM, 2nd Viscount; M.P. for Pontefract and
Thirsk, and Receiver of Crown Rents, &c.; assumed by Roy. licence 1769 the additional surname of Arundell; *d*. 1772; *s*. by his el. son [3] HENRY WILLIAM, 3rd Viscount ; sat as M.P.
for Pontefract; *d*. 1774; *s*. by his brother [4] ROBERT MONCKTON ARUNDELL, *P.C.*, *K.B.*;
M.P. for York, Pontefract, and Thirsk in several Parliaments; *d*. 1810; *s*. by his son [5]
WILLIAM GEORGE, 5th Viscount ; discontinued the surname of Arundell by Roy. licence 1826,
and obtained permission for each successive holders of the title and his eldest son to use the
surnames of Monckton-Arundell, while the younger branches of the family should use the
surname of Monckton only; *d*. 1834; *s*. by his son [6] GEORGE EDWARD ARUNDELL, 6th
Viscount, *b*. 1805; M.P. for E. Retford (C) 1847-76, and a Lord-in-Waiting to H.M. Queen
Victoria 1852: *m*. 1838, Henrietta Eliza, dau. of Robert Pemberton Milnes, Esq. and sister of
1st Baron Houghton: *d*. 1876: *s*. by his son [7] GEORGE EDMUND MILNES, C.B. 7th Viscount-
b. 1844 ; was A.D.C. to Queen Victoria 1897-1901, to King Edward VII. 1901-10 and to King
George V. 1910-20, and was Lord High Steward of Retford ; sat as M.P. for Nottinghamshire
North (C) 1872-85 : cr. *Baron Monckton*, of Serlby, co. Nottingham (peerage of United
Kingdom) 1887 : *m*. 1879, Vere, who *d*. 1921, only dau. of the late Ellis Gosling, of Busbridge
Hall, Godalming ; *d*. 1931 ; *s*. by his son [8] VERE ARUNDELL, *G.C.M.G.*, *D.S.O.*, *O.B.E.*, *P.C.*
8th Viscount, *b*. 1882 ; Lieut.-Col. late Life Guards; was Gov.-Gen. and Com.-in-Ch. of New
Zealand 1935-41 : European War 1914-19 (D.S.O., O.B.E.): *m*. 1922, the Hon. Lucia Emily
Margaret White, da. of 3rd Baron Annaly; *d*. 1943; *s*. by his only son [9] SIMON GEORGE ROBERT
9th Viscount, *b*. 1929: *m*. 1953, Lady Teresa Jane Fox-Strangways (who *m*. 2ndly, 1972, Mark
Agnew), da. of 7th Earl of Ilchester; *d*. 1971, when the UK Barony of Monckton (cr. 1887) became
ext.; *s*. in his other peerages by his kinsman [10] WILLIAM ARUNDELL, who adopted the additional
surname of Arundell on succession (el. son of William Henry Monckton, el. son of the Hon. Edmund
Gambier Monckton, 4th son of 5th Viscount), 10th Viscount and present peer; also Baron Killard.

GARDINER, BARON. (Gardiner.) [Life Baron 1963.]

Trust in God, act rightly.

GERALD AUSTIN GARDINER, *CH*, *PC*, son of the late Sir Robert Septimus Gardiner; *b.* May 30th, 1900; ed. at Harrow, and at Magdalen Coll., Oxford (MA); Bar. Inner Temple 1925, a KC 1948, and a Bencher 1955; Pres. of Oxford Union and O.U.D.S. 1924; a Member of Cttee. on Supreme Court Practice and Procedure 1947-53, and of Lord Chancellor's Law Reform Cttee. 1952-63; Chm. of Gen. Council of the Bar 1958 and 1959; an Alderman of London Co. Council 1961-63; Lord High Chancellor 1964-70; elected to International Commn. of Jurists 1971; Chancellor designate of Open Univ. 1972; 1914-18 War as 2nd Lt. Coldm. Gds.; *cr.* Baron Gardiner, of Kittisford, co. Somerset (Life Baron) 1963, PC 1964, and CH 1975; *m.* 1st, 1925, Lesly, who *d.* 1966, da. of Edwin Trouson, JP; 2ndly, 1970, Muriel, da. of Charles Baker, and formerly wife of Sydney Box, and has issue by 1st m.

Arms,—Gules a plain fess with cottises engrailed argent between four roses, three in chief and one in base, of the last. **Crest,**—A stag proper, gorged with a collar argent, charged with three lozenges conjoined gules and supporting with the dexter leg an escutcheon also argent charged with four lozenges conjoined in fess gules between two barrulets sable and in chief a rose also gules. **Supporters,—** *Dexter,* a pegasus argent; *sinister,* a dragon gules.
Address,—House of Lords, SW1. *Club,*—Garrick.

DAUGHTER LIVING. (*By 1st m.*).
Hon. Carol (109, East 89th St., New York 10028), *b.* 1929

GARDNER, BARONY OF. (Gardner.) [Dormant 1883.]
COLLATERAL BRANCHES LIVING.

Grandchildren of the late Stewart William Gardner, son of the late Rear-Adm. the Hon. Francis Ffarington Gardner, 2nd son of 1st Baron:—
Issue of the late Alan Hyde Gardner (who claimed the title, styling himself Lord Gardner), *b.* 1836, *d.* 1891: *m.* March 12th, 1879, by a Methodist minister in the house of his father, to Jane (a native Indian), who *d.* 1899, dau. of Unjem Shikó, of Roy. House of Delhi:—
Alan Legge (*claims the title*), *b.* Oct. 25th, 1881 ; ed. at Allahabad Govt. Sch. ; formerly in Govt. Secretariat, United Provinces, India : *m.* 1st (Jan.), 1908, Christiana Jane, who *d.* 1918, dau. of D. Wilson Gardner, Zamindar, of Village Arroopore, Dist. Etah, United Provinces, India ; 2ndly, 1918, Ellen Orde, and has issue living, (by 1st marriage) Alan William, *b.* (Dec.) 1908 : *m.* 19—, Ethel Lydia, dau. of the late James Valentine Gardner, Zamindar, Village Fatehpore, Dist. Etah, United Provinces, India, and has issue living, Julian James *b.* 1942, Archibald Horace *b.* 1945, Barbara Christian *b.* 1939. *Residence,*—Village Bhnowta, Dadri, Dist. Bulandshahr, United Provinces, India.

Issue of the late William Rickard Gardner, *b.* 1852, *d.* 1915: *m.* 1879:—
Francis ffarington, *b.* 1880 : *m.* 1897, his cousin, Henrietta, who *d.* 1943, dau. of Edward Gardner. ——Wellington, *b.* 1881 : *m.* 1916, Dorothy, dau. of Edward Gardner, and has issue living, Richard (of Village Manota, P.O. Nadrai (Etah), United Provinces, India) ; *b.* 1919 : *m.* 1945, Daisy Margaret, dau. of the late Benjamin Gardner [infra], and has issue living, Kendrick Navill *b.* 1946, Regine Wellington *b.* 1950, Edgar Terance *b.* 1953, Beryl Dorothy *b.* 1955.—Leslie Clifford, *b.* 1926 : *m.* 1952, Vida, dau. of Benjamin Gardner, and has issue living, Dulcie Vida *b.* 1953.——Jane Constance, *b.* 1898 : *m.* 1916, Gilbert Gardner, and has issue living, Oswald Gilbert, *b.* 1919,——Dulcie Barbara, *b.* 1917.—Olive Sheila, *b.* 1923. *Residence,*—

Grandchildren of the late Edward Gardner, son of the late Stewart William Gardner (ante):—

Issue of the late Charles van Straubenzee Gardner, *b.* 1885, *d.* 1951: *m.* 1900, his cousin Ellen, who *d.* 1952, dau. of the late William Rickard Gardner (ante):—
Henry, *b.* 1911; ed. at Colvin Sch., Allahabad : *m.* 1941, Emma, dau. of Harry Gardner, and has issue living,—David Francis, *b.* 1945,—Charles Straubenzee, *b.* 1951,—Suzon, *b.* 1942,—Evelyn, *b.* 1948.——Edward Kingston, *b.* 1917 : *m.* 1946, Mary Ciclia, dau. of G. A. De Silva, and has issue living, Frederick Anthony, *b.* 1946,—Terrance Lewis, *b.* 1952,—Jennet Ciclia, *b.* 1949. *Residence,*—Village Manota, P.O. Nadrai (Etah), United Provinces, India.——Francis Robert, *b.* 1920 : *m.* 1953, Irene Martin, and has issue living, George Washington, *b.* 1954.——Mary, *b.* 1901: *m.* 1920, Walter Vernon Mackenzie, Inspector of Police, Simla, Punjab, and has issue living, Vernon Charles, *b.* 1923,—Louisa Ellen, *b.* 1921,—Dulcie Olga, *b.* 192-.——Lily, *b.* 1903 : *m.* 1922, the Rev. Patrick Solomon Gardner, a Methodist Min., who *d.* 1954, and has issue living, Hubert Stanley (50, Broxholm Rd., SE27), *b.* 1926 : *m.* 1956, Nell Gwendoline Rosemeyer, and has issue living, Royce Sherman Frederick *b.* 1957, Andre Alroy Michael *b.* 1961, Hubert Barney *b.* 1967, Beverley Sue Ann *b.* 1960,—Bartholomew Florian, *b.* 1936,—Robert Sidney, *b.* 1939,—Mildred Julia, *b.* 1922,—Gladys Annie, *b.* 1924: *m.* 1946, Percy Earnest Gardner, Finger Print Inspector, Eastern Railway, Dinapore, Bihar, and has issue living, Greer Gwendoline Lillian *b.* 1948: *m.* 1973, Paul Henry Kibble, Patricia Marian Zarina *b.* 1952,—Phyllis Mary, *b.* 1928,—Sylvia Agnes, *b.* 1933,—Carol Alice, *b.* 1914: *m.* 1946, Edward Albert Batchelor, and has issue living, Deborrah Marjorie *b.* 1965. *Address,*—11/27, Civil Lines, Kanpur, UP, India.——Catherine, *b.* 1907: *m.* 1924, Harry Newton, and has issue living, Baldwin Charles (Wynberg Allen Sch., Mussoorie, UP, India), *b.* 1936; artist: *m.* 1934, Shirley Hatfield, and has issue living, Richard *b.* 1966, Beverley Ann *b.* 1964,—Alfred Richard, *b.* 1940,—Rose Delight, *b.* 1938: *m.* 1965, J. C. Dass, c/o Wynberg Allen School, Mussoorie, UP, India, and has issue living, Rohit *b.* 1966. *Residence,*—3, Barrow Rd., Lal Bagh, Lucknow, India.——Cherry Martha, *b.* 1913: *m.* 1935, Alfred Samuel Tupper, who *d.* 1953, and has issue living, Albert Jasbir Samuel, *b.* 1936,—Arthur Alexander, *b.* 1942,—Ezekiel Habib, *b.* 1948,—Rexey, *b.* 1951,—Margaret Shirin, *b.* 1938,—Maybelle Iris, *b.* 1940.——Ruby Maggie, *b.* 1915: *m.* 1943, James Gideon, and has issue living, a son, *b.* 1944,—a son, *b.* 19—,—a a da., *b.* 19,—da., *b.* 19—,—a da, *b.* 19—,—a da., *b.* 19—.——Majory Julia, *b.* 1925: *m.* 1947, Kenneth Charles Johnson. *Residence,*—

Issue of the late Benjamin Gardner, *b*. 1889, *d*. 1937 : *m*. 1914, Sophia Shiko, who *d*. 1936 :—
Daniel, *b*. 1919 : *m*. 1946, Irene Coal, and has issue living, Noel, *b*. 1946,—Iviwin, *b*. 1949.——Caroline,
b. 1915.——Maggie, *b*. 1917 : *m*. 1935, Lenis Gardner, and has issue living, Albert, *b*. 1938,—Malwni,
b. 1943,—Mickey, *b*. 1945,—Princeton, *b*. 1947,—Elizabeth, *b*. 1939,—Maran, *b*. 1941. *Residence*—
Nadrai Road, near Mission Hospital, Kasganj, District Etah, Uttar Pradesh, India.——Queenie, *b*.
1921 : *m*. 1941, Augustine Paul, and has issue living, Noel, *b*. 1943,—George, *b*. 1945,—Ugin, *b*.
1947,—Joyce, *b*. 1949.——Daisy Margaret, *b*. 1924 : *m*. 1945, Richard Gardner [ante].——Harold,
b. 1928.——Mervin, *b*. 1930.——Lion, *b*. 1932.——Hazel, *b*. 1926.

Grandchildren of the late Alan Hyde Gardner (ante) :—

Issue of the late Major Charles Phillips Gardner, *b*. 1883, *d*. 1932: *m*. 1st, 1910, Dorothy
Margaret, who *d*. 1921, 2nd dau. of William Mullock, formerly of Llantarnam, Mon-
mouth; 2ndly, 1924, Constance Eillen, who *d*. 1975, da. of the late Major Charles Hay Cox,
W. Yorkshire Regt.:—

(By 1st marriage) David William Hyde, *R.N.*, *b*. 1913 ; is Lieut.-Com. : *m*. 1st, 1936 (divorce 1957),
Edith Margaret, dau. of William Henry Wroth ; 2ndly, 1958, Susanne Willeter, dau. of John L.
Bagshaw, of The Manor House, Uttoxeter, Staffs, and has issue living, (by 1st marriage) Alan David
Hyde, *b*. 1939: *m*. 1973,—John Henry Wroth, *b*. 1946: *m*. 1973,—Gillian Margaret, *b*. 1941:
m. 1962, John Seager Green, and has issue living:—(by 2nd marriage) William Patrick Hyde,
b. 1960,—James Francis ffarington *b*. 1962. *Residence*,—The Oaklands, Bramshall, near Uttoxeter,
Staffs. *Club*,—United Hunts.——Rosamund Dorothy (8339, Terrace Drive, El. Cerito, Cal.,
USA), *b*. 1915.——(By 2nd marriage) Susannah Caroline Hyde (*Viscountess Hawarden*), *b*. 1927:
m. 1957, the 8th Viscount Hawarden. *Residences*,—Wingham Court, nr. Canterbury; 39, Shawfield
St., SW3. *Club*—Guards.

Grandchildren the late Capt. Herbert Calthorpe Gardner, son of the late Gen.
the Hon. William Henry Gardner, 3rd son of 1st Baron :—
Issue of the late Herbert Prescott Gardner, *b*. 1854, *d*. 1938 : *m*. 1906, Ethel Mary, who *d*.
1954, dau. of the late Henry Crouch :—

Alan Henry, *b*. 1914: *m*. 1942, Gemma Elizabeth, dau. of the late E. K. McCord, of Coonambula,
Eidsvold, Queensland, and has issue living, Alan Peter Prescott, *b*. 1944,—Shane McCord, *b*.
1946,—Mark McCord, *b*. 1954. *Residence*.—Coal Creek, Toogoolawah, Queensland.——Olivera
Graham, *b*. 1911: *m*. 1939, Jack Christian Richards, and has issue living, Roger Gardner, *b*. 1940:
m. 1966, Annabel Gee, of Launceston, Tasmania,—Alan Gardner, *b*. 1941,—Hew Gardner, *b*. 1946,—
Susanna, *b*. 1944. *Residence*,—416 Wattle Tree Rd., E. Malvern, Victoria, Australia.——Helen
Prescott, *b*. 1912: *m*. 1939, Lt.-Col. James Peile Love, and has issue living, Antony James (48,
Miles St., Wooloowin, Brisbane, Qld.), *b*. 1946: *m*. 1971, Margot Elizabeth, da. of J. G. Moore, of
Toowoomba, Qld., and has issue living, Nicholas James *b*. 1973,—Judith Prescott, *b*. 1940: *m*. 1962,
Dr. John Noble of High View Court, Prince Henry Heights, Toowoomba, Qld. 4350, and has issue
living, Andrew James *b*. 1963, Cameron Charles *b*. 1968, Louise Annabelle *b*. 1965,—Rosalind
Prescott, *b*. 1943: *m*. 1970, Michael Ian Minchin, of Cremorne, Tasmania, and has issue living,
Anna Prescott *b*. 1971. *Residence*,—109, Virginia Av., Hawthorne, Brisbane, Qld.

PREDECESSORS.—[1] ALAN Gardner, Adm. of the Blue, and Maj.-Gen. Marine Forces;
successively M.P. for Plymouth and Westminster ; was cr. a *Baronet* 1794, *Baron Gardner*, of
Uttoxeter (peerage of Ireland) 1800, and *Baron Gardner*, of Uttoxeter, co. Stafford (peerage of
United Kingdom) 1806 ; *d*. 1809; *s*. by his son [2] ALAN HYDE, *K.C.B.*, 2nd Baron ; was an
Adm. ; gazetted a Viscount Sept. 30, 1815, and *d*. Dec. 27th following, before the patent had
passed the Great Seal ; *s*. by his son [3] ALAN LEGGE, 3rd Baron ; was a Lord-in-Waiting 1832-41;
d. 1883, since when the title has remained dormant.

Garlies, Lord, son of Earl of Galloway.

Garmoyle, Viscount, son of Earl Cairns.

GARNER, BARON. (Garner.) [Life Baron 1969.]

JOSEPH JOHN SAVILLE GARNER, *GCMG*, son of the late Joseph Garner, of
Highgate, N6; *b*. Feb. 14th, 1908; ed. at Highgate Sch., and Jesus Coll.,
Camb. (MA); Hon. LLD Toronto and BC; Private Sec. to Sec. of State for
Dominion Affairs 1940-43, Senior Sec. Office of UK High Commr. at Ottawa
1943-46, Dep. High Commr. there 1946-48, Assist. Under-Sec. of State
Commonwealth Relations Office 1948-51, Dep. High Commr. for UK in India
1951-53, Dep. Under-Sec. of State Commonwealth Relations Office 1953-56,
High Commr. for UK in Canada 1956-61, Permanent Under-Sec. of State
Commonwealth Office 1962-68, and Head of Diplo. Ser. 1965-68; Chm. of
Inst. of Commonwealth Studies, and of Commonwealth Scholarship Commn.,
and of London Board, Bank of Adelaide; *cr*. CMG 1948, KCMG 1954, GCMG
1965, and *Baron Garner*, of Chiddingly, co. Sussex (Life Baron) 1969: *m*. 1938,
Margaret, da. of the late Herman Beckman, of Cedar Lake, Indiana, USA, and
has issue.

Residences,—Highdown Farm House, Horam, Sussex: 1, Courtenay Sq., SE11 5PG. *Club*,—RAC.

SONS LIVING.

Hon. Christopher John Saville (11, Stokewood Rd., Bournemouth), *b*. 1939: *m*. 1962, Janet, only
da. of Maj. Harold Vaughan Rees, of Winnersh, Wokingham, Berks., and has issue.
Hon. Joseph Jonathan (44, Holmewood Rd., SW2), *b*. 1940: *m*. 1969, Brigitte, da. of M. Pittet, of
Sens, France, and has issue.

DAUGHTER LIVING.
Hon. Helena Geneva, *b*. 1947.

Garnock, Viscount, son of Earl of Lindsay.

GARNSWORTHY, BARONY OF. (Garnsworthy.) [Extinct 1974.]

SON LIVING OF LIFE BARON (*by 2nd m.*)
Hon. Charles Edyvean, *b*. 1974.

WIDOW LIVING OF LIFE BARON.
SUE (*Baroness Garnsworthy*) (Little Dormers, Smithy Lane, Lower Kingswood, Tadworth, Surrey,
da. of Harold Taylor, and formerly wife of Michael Farley: *m*. 1973, as his 2nd wife, Baron Garnsworthy (Life Peer), who *d*. 1974.

GARVAGH, BARON. (Canning.) [Baron I. 1818.]

Yield not to misfortunes, but oppose them.

3rd a demi-griffin segreant. **Supporters.**—*Dexter*, a griffin reguardant, wings elevated and expanded azure, guttée d'or; *sinister*, an eagle reguardant, wings elevated and expanded sable.

(ALEXANDER LEOPOLD IVOR) GEORGE CANNING, 5th Baron; *b.* Oct. 6th, 1920; *s.* 1956; Capt. late Indian Army; MBIM; Fellow of Inst. of Dirs., a Member Inst. of Exports; Chm. and Managing Dir. of The Lord Garvagh and Assos., Ltd., Consultants, London, of Indep. Chartering, Ltd., of Camco Machinery, Ltd., of Intersal Commodities, Ltd., and Anglo Brazilian Investments, Ltd., a Dir. of AODC (UK), Ltd., Campden Research & Sales, Ltd., The Lord Garvagh & Partners, Ltd., Stonehaven Tankers, Ltd., and Seaways (London), Ltd.; 1939-45 War (despatches): m. 1st, 1947 (m. diss. 1973), Edith Christine, da. of the late Jack Cooper, of Little Bridley, Worplesdon; 2ndly, 1974, Cynthia, da. of the late Eric Ernest Falk Pretty, CMG, and has issue by 1st m.

Arms.—Quarterly of six: 1st and 6th argent, three Moors' heads, couped in profile, proper, wreathed round the temples, argent and azure, *Canning*: 2nd gules, three spears' heads palewise in fesse argent, *Salmon*; 3rd gules, a goat salient or, *Marshall*; 4th argent, three bendlets azure, within a bordure gules, *Newburg*; 5th, per pale argent and sable, a fesse nebulée, between three griffins' heads erased, all counterchanged, and within a bordure engrailed also counterchanged, of the field, *Spencer.* **Crests.**—1st a demi-lion rampant argent, charged with three trefoils vert, holding in the dexter paw an arrow, pheoned and flighted proper, shaft or: 2nd a demi-lion rampant, holding in the dexter paw a battle-axe;

Residences,—2, Porchester Gdns., W2; Lyzzick Gate, Keswick, Cumbria. *Clubs,*—Bath, No. 10.

SON LIVING (By 1st m.)
Hon. SPENCER GEORGE STRATFORD DE REDCLIFFE, *b.* Feb. 12th, 1953.

DAUGHTERS LIVING. (By 1st m.)
Hon. (Christine) Alexandra, *b.* 1949: *m.* 1971, Louis David Lawrence.
Hon. Louise Eleanor Alice, *b.* 1951: *m.* 1975, Mark Lawrence.

SISTERS LIVING.
Hon. (Dora) Valerie Patricia, *b.* 1919 : *m.* 1st, 1942, Philip Anthony Wellesley Colley, Lieut. R.A., who *d.* (killed in action during European War) 1944 : 2ndly, 1950. Peter Sutcliffe. and has issue living, (by 1st m.) Angela, *b.* 1942: *m.* 1973, David Campbell Anderson, of 2, Dunbar Rd., Toronto, Canada, —Elizabeth Jane (posthumous), *b.* 1945: *m.* 1966, Peter John Wilson, of 30, The High St., Charing, Kent, and has issue living, Camilla Jane *b.* 1969, Sarah Louise *b.* 1970, Henrietta *b.* 1973,—(by 2nd m.) James, *b.* 1953. *Residence,*—Crow Tree Cottage, Louth, Lincolnshire.
Hon. Daphne Rose, *b.* 1922 : *m.* 1950, Bancroft Svenningson, and has issue living, Victor Stratford de Redcliffe, *b.* 1954,—Jennifer, *b.* 1955,—Andrea, *b.* 1960. *Residence,*—Svendon, Westwood Lane, Thornhill, Ontario, Canada.

WIDOW LIVING OF FOURTH BARON.
GLADYS DORA MAY, (*Dora, Baroness Garvagh*), dau. of Bayley Parker, of Edgbaston, and widow of Lieut.-Col. D. M. Dimmer, V.C.: *m.* 1919, as his second wife, the 4th Baron, who *d.* 1956. *Residence,* —Lyzzick Gate, Millbeck, Keswick.

PREDECESSORS.—[1] GEORGE Canning, *F.R.S.*, Lord-Lieut. of co. Londonderry ; *cr. Baron Garvagh*, of Garvagh, co. Londonderry (peerage of Ireland) 1818 ; *d.* 1840 ; *s.* by his son [2] CHARLES HENRY SPENCER GEORGE, 2nd Baron, *b.* 1826 ; Capt. 10th Hussars : *m.* 1851, Cecilia Susannah, who *d.* 1898, dau. of John Ruggles-Brise, of Spains Hall, Brentwood ; *d.* 1871 ; *s.* by his son [3] CHARLES JOHN SPENCER GEORGE, 3rd Baron ; *b.* 1852 : *m.* 1877, Florence Alice, *M.B.E.*, who *d.* 1926, dau. of Baron Joseph de Bretton, of Copenhagen ; *d.* 1915 ; *s.* by his son [4] LEOPOLD ERNEST STRATFORD GEORGE, 4th Baron ; *b.* 1878 : *m.* 1st, 1906 (marriage annulled 1909), Caroline Grace Elizabeth, only dau. of Charles Ernest Rube ; 2ndly, 1919, Gladys Dora May, dau. of Bayley Parker, of Edgbaston, and widow of Lieut.-Col. D. M. Dimmer, V.C., *d.* 1956 ; *s.* by his son [5] (ALEXANDER LEOPOLD IVOR) GEORGE, 5th Baron and present peer.

GEDDES, BARON. (Geddes.) [Baron U.K. 1942.]

Strive to hold fast to the greater things.

EUAN MICHAEL ROSS GEDDES, 3rd Baron; b. Sept. 3rd, 1937; s. 1975; ed. at Rugby, Gonville and Caius Coll., Camb. (MA), and Harvard Business Sch.; Lt.-Cdr. RNR (ret.): m. 1966, Gillian, da. of William Arthur Butler, of Staple House, Peppard Common, Henley-on-Thames, and has issue.

Arms,—Azure three geds naiant or, on a chief engrailed of the last as many boars' heads couped sable, armed argent, langued gules. Crest,—A demi-pike hauriant environed of the circlet of a Lord Baron's coronet all proper. Supporters,—On a compartment semée of sea-pinks, two geds proper.

Residence,—Briar House, Odiham, Basingstoke, Hants.

SON LIVING.
Hon. JAMES GEORGE NEIL, b. Sept. 10th, 1969.

DAUGHTER LIVING.
Hon. Margaret Clair, b. 1967.

SISTER LIVING.
Hon. Margaret Ross, b. 1934 ; ed. at Benenden ; is a Member of Asso. of Occupational Therapists : m. 1961, Ralph Emilius Quintus van Koetsveld, and has issue living, Michael William, b. 1963,—Antony Guy Hans, b. 1964,—Christopher Dirk, b. 1969. *Residence,*—Northacre, Sackleford, Godalming, Surrey.

UNCLES LIVING. (*Sons of 1st Baron.*)
Hon. John Reay Campbell, *TD,* b. 1915; ed. at Stowe, and at Edinburgh and London Univs.; late Capt. R. Glos. Hussars (TA), and Maj. RTR; Adviser to Chm. of Pearson Longman Ltd.; 1939-45 War: m. 1944, Diana Elizabeth, JP (GLC Streatham), da. of Brig. Charles Copley Swift, OBE, MC, and has issue living, Hugh John Reay (12, Camden Sq., NW1; Nanty-reglwys, Llanboidy, Dyfed), b. 1945: m. 1972, Harriet Diana Christabel, da. of the late Sqdn. Ldr. the Hon John Francis McLaren RAF, and has issue living, Luke John McLaren b. 1974 [see B. Aberconway, colls.]. *Residence,*—15, Merrick Sq., Southwark, SE1 4JD. *Club,*—Brooks's.
Hon. David Campbell, *TD,* b. 1917; ed. at Stowe, and at Gonville and Caius Coll., Camb. (MA); a FRGS; late Capt. Roy. Hong Kong Defence Force, and Maj. RA; with FCO Overseas Development Administration: m. 1948, Gerda, da. of the late Gerdt Meyer Brunn, of Bergen, Norway, and has issue living, Jane b. 1950,—Harriet, b. 1953. *Residence,*—Oldhouse Farm, Hildenborough, Kent. *Clubs.*—Brooks's.

AUNT LIVING. (*Daughter of 1st Baron.*)
Hon. Margaret Campbell (*H.R.H. the Princess of Hesse and the Rhine*), b. 1913 : m. 1937, H.R.H. Prince Louis Hermann Alexander Chlodwig, of Hesse and the Rhine, who d. 1968. *Residence,*—Wolfsgarten, 607 Langen, Hessen, Germany.

WIDOW LIVING OF SON OF FIRST BARON.
Altgräfin Marie-Anne Helena Emanuela (Petersham Lodge, Richmond, Surrey, and Beach House, Green Island, Jersey), da. of HSH the 6th Prince (Franz Joseph) of Salm-Reifferscheidt, Krautheim und Dyck: m. 1964, as his 2nd wife, Col. the Hon. Alexander Campbell Geddes, OBE, MC, TD, who d. 1972, and has issue [see colls. infra].

WIDOW LIVING OF SECOND BARON.
ENID MARY (*Enid, Lady Geddes*) [Nagshead Field, Lymington, Hants.), da. of Clarance Howell Butler, of Tenterden, Kent: m. 1931, the 2nd Baron, who d. 1975.

COLLATERAL BRANCH LIVING.
Issue of the late Col. the Hon. Alexander Campbell Geddes, OBE, MC, TD, 2nd son of 1st Baron, b. 1910, d. 1972: m. 1st, 1934 (m. diss. 1964), Margaret Kathleen, da. of the late Sir Charles (Stewart) Addis, KCMG; 2ndly, 1964, Altgräfin Marie-Anne Helena Emanuela (ante), da. of HSH the 6th Prince (Franz Joseph) of Salm-Reifferscheidt, Krautheim und Dyck:—
(By 1st m.) Andrew Campbell (12, Dawson Place, Notting Hill, W11), b. 1943: m. 1974, Jacqueline, 2nd da. of Emil Tan-Bunzel.——Alexander James Campbell (29, Hugo Rd., N19), b. 1948: m. 1971; Vivien, only da. of F. H. Salter, of 55, Danycoed Rd., Cyncoed, Cardiff.——Margaret Campbell, b. 1947: m. 1960, Peter Gross, of 3904, Legation St., NW, Washington, DC, and has issue living, James Jonathan Geddes, b. 1964,—Daniel Paul Geddes, b. 1970,—Adam John Geddes, b. 1972,—Sarah Anne, b. 1967.——Christina Helen Campbell, b. 1939: m. 1965, Roy Kenneth Horrell, of Zermatt, 14, Linkoping Rd., Rondebosch 7700, Cape, S. Africa, and has issue living, Jasper Mark Geddes, b. 1968,—Hamish Harry Geddes, b. 1970,—Eliza-Jane Geddes, b. 1966,—Emma Clare Geddes, b. 1972.——Jean Campbell, b. 1940: m. 1963, Christopher Lubbock Verity, of Boundary House, Brimpton Common, Berks., and has issue living, Richard Christopher Geddes, b. 1965.——Jonathan William Geddes, b. 1967.——Caroline Anne Campbell, b. 1947: m. 1970, David Kelly, of 8, Crooms Hill, Greenwich, SE10; and has issue living, Alexandra Mary b. 1972.——Diana Elizabeth Campbell (twin), b. 1947.——(by 2nd m.) Stephen George, b. 1969.——Camilla Joanna Isabella, b. 1966.

PREDECESSORS,—[1] Rt. Hon. Sir AUCKLAND CAMPBELL GEDDES, GCMG, KCB, TD, MD, second son of the late Acland Geddes, of Edinburgh; b. 1879; sometime Professor of Anatomy at Roy. Coll. of Surgs., Ireland, and at McGill Univ., Montreal; S. African War 1901-2, European War 1914-18 on Staff at Gen. Headquarters, France (Brevet Lieut.-Col., Hon.Brig.-Gen.) ; was Director of Recruiting, War Office 1916-17 (with rank of Brig.-Gen.), Min. of National Ser. 1917-18, Pres. of Local Govt. Board 1918-19, Min. of Reconstruction Jan. to May 1919, Pres. Board of Trade 1919-20 (with a seat in the Cabinet), Ambassador Extraor. and Plen. to Washington 1920-24, and Commr. for Civil Defence for S.-E. Region 1939-41, and for N.-W. Region 1941-2 ; sat as M.P. for N., of Basingstoke, Div. of Hampshire (*U*) 1917-18, and for Basingstoke Div. thereof 1918-20 ; cr. *Baron Geddes,* of Rolvenden, co. Kent, (peerage of UK) 1942: m. 1906, Isabella Gamble, who d. 1962, da. of the late William A. Ross, of Staten Island, New York; d. 1954; s. by his el. son [2] ROSS CAMPBELL 2nd Baron, b. 1907; Pres. of Chamber of Shipping of UK 1968: m. 1931, Enid Mary, da. of Clarance Howell Butler; d. 1975; s. by his yr. son [3] EUAN MICHAEL ROSS, 3rd Baron and present peer.

GEDDES OF EPSOM, BARON. (Geddes.) [Life Baron 1958.]

CHARLES JOHN GEDDES, *C.B.E.*, son of Thomas Varney Geddes; *b.* March 1st, 1897; formerly Gen. Sec., Union of Post Office Workers; European War 1914-18 as Lieut. R.F.C.; C.B.E. (Civil) 1950, Knt. 1957, and *Baron Geddes of Epsom*, of Epsom, co. Surrey (Life Baron) 1958: *m.* 1920, Julia, dau. of Cornelius Burke, and has issue.

Residence,—28, Parkhill Court, Addiscombe Rd., Croydon, CR0 5PJ.

DAUGHTER LIVING.

Hon. Pamela Margaret (North Cottage, Pump Lane, Framfield, Sussex), *b.* 1925: *m.* 1957 (m. diss. 1966), Louis Patrick Taylor.

GEOFFREY-LLOYD, BARON. (Lloyd.) [Life Baron 1974.]

GEOFFREY WILLIAM LLOYD, *PC*, son of the late G. W. A. Lloyd, of Andover House, Newbury; *b.* Jan. 17th, 1902; ed. at Harrow, and Trin. Coll., Camb. (MA); MP for Ladywood Div. of Birmingham (*C*) 1931-45, for King's Norton Div. of Birmingham 1950-55, and for Sutton Coldfield 1955-74; PPS to Rt. Hon. Stanley Baldwin (Lord Pres. of the Council 1931-34, and PM 1935), Parl. Under-Sec. of State, Home Office 1935-39, Sec. for Mines 1939-40, Sec. for Petroleum 1940-42, Petroleum Warfare Min. 1940-45, Parl. Sec. (Petroleum) Min. of Fuel and Power 1942-45, Min. of Information May to July 1945, a Gov. of BBC 1946-49, Min. of Fuel and Power 1951-55, and Min. of Education 1957-59; Pres. of Birmingham Conservative and Unionist Assocn.; cr. PC 1943, and *Baron Geoffrey-Lloyd*, of Broomfield, co. Kent (Life Baron) 1974.

Arms,—not exemplified at time of going to press.
Residence.—77, Chester Sq., SW1W 9DY.

GEORGE-BROWN, BARON. (George-Brown.) [Life Baron 1970.]

GEORGE ALFRED GEORGE-BROWN, *PC,* son of George Brown; *b.* Sept. 2nd 1914; assumed by deed poll 1970 the surname of George-Brown in lieu of his patronymic; PPS to Min. of Labour and Nat. Ser. 1945-47, and to Chancellor of the Exchequer 1947, Joint Parl. Sec., Min. of Agric. & Fisheries 1947-51, Min. of Works April to Oct. 1951, First Sec. of State, Sec. of State for Economic Affairs, and Chm. of NEDC 1964-66, and Sec. of State for Foreign Affairs 1966-68; Dep. Leader, Labour Party 1960-70; MP for Belper. (*Lab.*) 1945-70; Industrial Counsellor, Courtaulds Ltd., 1968-73; a Dir. of First Fortune Holdings, and Chm. of Stewart Title Guarantee Co. (UK), Ltd. since 1973; cr. PC 1951, and *Baron George-Brown*, of Jevington, co. Sussex (Life Baron) 1970: *m.* 1937, Sophie, da. of Solomon Levene, JP, and has issue.

Residence,—Sharon, Jevington, Sussex.

DAUGHTERS LIVING.

Hon. Frieda Mary, *b.* 1938: *m.* 1964, Brian Warman.
Hon. Patricia Janet, *b.* 1942: *m.* 1967, Derek Knowles.

George, see Earl Lloyd George of Dwyfor.

GERARD, BARON. (Gerard.) [Baron U.K. 1876, Bt. E. 1611.]

In God is my hope.

ROBERT WILLIAM FREDERICK ALWYN GERARD, 4th Baron, and 16th Baronet; *b.* May 23rd, 1918; *s.* 1953; ed. at Ampleforth.

Arms,—Argent, a saltire gules. Crests,—1st, a monkey statant proper, environed round the loins and chained argent; 2nd, a lion rampant ermine, ducally crowned or and charged on the shoulder with a saltire couped gules. Supporters.—On either side a lion ermine, ducally crowned or, with a collar gemell, and supporting a tilting spear proper.

Residence, Blakesware, Ware, Herts.

SISTERS LIVING.

Hon. Heloise Katherine Marie, *b.* 1911.
Hon. Mary Dorothy Fresia, *b.* 1922: *m.* 1st 1946 (m. diss. 1958), Maj. Eric George Davies, who *d.* 1968; 2ndly, 1959), Sean Stevenson, of Old Court Bungalow, Henley Rd., Misterton, Crewkerne, Som., and has issue living, (by 1st m.), Mark Edwin, *b.* 1947.

COLLATERAL BRANCHES LIVING.
Grandsons of the late Capt. the Hon. Robert Joseph Gerard-Dicconson (infra):—
Issue of the late Lt.-Col. Charles Robert Tolver Michael GERARD, DSO, OBE, *b.* 1894, *d.* 1971:
m. 1st, 1915, Aimee Gwendolyn (who obtained a divorce 1930), da. of Sir Rupert Turner
Havelock Clarke, 2nd Bt. (cr. 1882); 2ndly, 1930, Norma Gertrude (Doone, Sunningdale,
Berks.; Wrightington, Wigan), da. of the late Amos Frankford Rogers, MD, of Ottawa:—
(By 1st m.) RUPERT CHARLES FREDERICK, *MBE* (The Stone Cottage, Bernardsville, New Jersey, USA),
b. Oct. 6th, 1916; ed. at Eton, and Trin. Coll., Camb.: Maj. Gren. Gds.; MBE (Mil) 1946: *m.* 1948
(m. diss. 1969), Huguette Reiss-Brian, da. of the late Hugo Reiss, of Brazil, and has issue living,
Anthony Robert Hugo, *b.* 1949,—Peter Charles Robert, *b.* 1951: *m.* 1973, Sophie, da. of Irenée
du Pont May, of Wilmington, Delaware, USA.——(Robert) Guy (Standish) (Thélème, Chemin du
Crêt Ministre, 1602 La Croix sur Lutry, Switzerland), *b.* 1921; Capt. Gren. Gds.: *m.* 1st, 1948
(m. diss. 1964), Barbara, da. of Leonard J. Stone, of Constant Spring, Jamaica: 2ndly, 1964, Ursula
Cogswell, da. of Andrew Mackenzie, of Vancouver, and has issue living (by 1st m.) Susan Roberta
Caroline, *b.* 1951,—Diana Sarah, *b.* 1952.
Issue of the late Capt. the Hon. Robert Joseph Gerard-Dicconson, 2nd son of
1st Baron, *b.* 1857, *d.* 1918, having assumed the additional surname and arms
of Dicconson by Roy. licence 1896: *m.* 1888, Eleanor, who *d.* 1953 (having *m.*
2ndly, 1925, as his second wife, Mark Fenwick, J.P., who *d.* 1945), granddau. of
the late Meyrick Bankes, of Winstanley Hall, near Wigan:—
Winefride Mary, *b*, 1888: *m.* 1st, 1908, Maj.-Gen. Sir Thompson Capper, KCMG, CB, DSO,
who *d.* (wounds in action) 1915; 2ndly, 1920, Godfrey Newall Graburn. *Residence.*—Westridge,
House, Crowborough, Sussex.

PREDECESSORS.—[1] Sir THOMAS Gerard, Knt.; cr. a *Baronet* 1611; the £1,000 he paid for
the dignity was returned to him in consideration of the sufferings of his father in the cause of
Mary, Queen of Scots; *s.* by his son [2] Sir THOMAS, 2nd Bt.; *s.* by his son [3] Sir WILLIAM, 3rd
Bt., a zealous royalist who expended a large estate in the cause of Charles I.; *s.* by his son [4]
Sir WILLIAM, 4th Bt.; *s.* by his el. son [5] Sir WILLIAM, 5th Bt.; *d.* 1721; *s.* by his el. son [6]
Sir WILLIAM, 6th Bt.; *d.* 1732; *s.* by his brother [7] Sir WILLIAM, 7th Bt.; *d.* a minor 1740;
s. by his brother [8] Sir THOMAS, 8th Bt.; *d.* 1780; *s.* by his brother [9] Sir ROBERT, 9th Bt.; *d.*
1784; *s.* by his el. son [10] Sir ROBERT, 10th Bt.; *d.* a minor 1791; *s.* by his brother [11] Sir
WILLIAM, 11th Bt.; *d.* 1826; *s.* by his nephew [12] JOHN, 12th Bt., el. son of John, 3rd son of
9th Bt., by Elizabeth, dau. of Edward Ferrers, of Baddesley Clinton, co. Warwick; *d.s.p.* 1854;
s. by his brother [13] ROBERT TOLVER, 13th Bt.; cr. *Baron Gerard* (peerage of United Kingdom,
1876: *m.* 1849, Harriet, who *d.* 1888, dau. of the late Edward Clifton, of Lytham Hall, Lancashire;
d. 1887; *s.* by his son [14] WILLIAM CANSFIELD, *D.S.O.*, 2nd Baron; *b.* 1851: *m.* 1877, Mary
Emmeline Laura, who *d.* 1918, dau. of the late Henry Beilby Milner, of West Retford; *d.* 1902;
s. by his son [15] FREDERIC JOHN, *M.C.*, 3rd Baron; *b.* 1883; European War 1914-17 as Capt.
Roy. Horse Guards (twice wounded, M.C.): *m.* 1906, his cousin, Mary Frances Emma, who *d.* 1954,
dau. of the late Sir Martin Le Marchant Hadsley Gosselin, G.C.V.O., K.C.M.G., C.B.; *d.* 1953; *s.*
by his only son [16] ROBERT WILLIAM FREDERICK ALWYN, 4th Baron and present peer.

GIBSON, BARON. (Gibson.) [Life Baron 1975.]

RICHARD PATRICK TALLENTYRE GIBSON,
son of Thornely Carbutt Gibson; *b.* Feb. 5th,
1916; ed. at Eton, and Magdalen Coll.,
Oxford (MA); 1939-45 War as Maj., with
Middx. Yeo.; N. Africa 1940-41, POW
1941-43, Special Ops. Exec. 1943-45, Political
Intelligence FO 1945-46; Chm. of Pearson
Longman Ltd., since 1967, of Advisory
Council of Victoria and Albert Museum
since 1970, of Arts Council of Great Britain
since 1972, and of Financial Times Ltd.
since 1975; Vice-Chm. of Westminster Press
since 1953, and Dep. Chm. of S. Pearson and
Son Ltd. since 1969; cr. *Baron Gibson*, of
Penn's Rocks, co. E. Sussex (Life Baron)
1975: *m.* 1945. Elizabeth Dione, da. of the
late Hon. (Bernard) Clive Pearson [see V.
Cowdray, colls.], and has issue.

Arms,—Azure, a chevron or, surmounted by another gules, thereon three pheons of the second
between as many storks, wings expanded proper. **Crest,**—Out of an antique crown or, a lion's gamb
erect proper, grasping a club gules, spiked also or **Supporters,**—Not exemplified at time of going to
press. **Motto,**—Recte et fideliter.

Residences.—Penn's Rocks, Groombridge, Sussex; 4, Swan Walk, SW3. *Clubs.*—Garrick,
Brooks's.

SONS LIVING.
Hon. Hugh Marcus Thornely (The Fold, Parwich, Ashbourne, Derbys.), *b.* 1946: *m.* 1967, the Hon.
Frances Towneley Strachey, da. of the late Hon. (Thomas) Anthony Edward Towneley Strachey
[see B. O'Hagan], and has issue living, Jasper Tallentyre, *b.* 1975,—Effie Dione, *b.* 1970,—Amelia
Mary, *b.* 1972.
Hon. Clive Patrick (7, Chelsea, Sq. SW3), *b.* 1948: *m.* 1974, Anne Marie Jeanne, da. of the late Comte
Jacques de Chauvigny de Blot, and has issue.
Hon. William Knatchbull (11, Paultons Sq., SW3), *b.* 1951.
Hon. Piers Nathaniel, *b.* 1956.

GIFFORD, BARON. (Gifford.) [Baron U.K. 1824.]
[Name and Title pronounced "Jifford."]

ANTHONY MAURICE GIFFORD, 6th Baron; b. May 1st, 1940; s. 1961; ed. at Winchester, and at King's Coll., Camb.; Bar. Middle Temple 1962: m. 1965, Katherine Anne, da. of Dr. Max Mundy, of 52, Hornton St., W8., and has issue.

Arms,—Azure, a chevron between three stirrups, with leathers or, within a bordure engrailed argent, pelletée. Crest,—A panther's head couped at the neck and affrontée, between two branches of oak proper. Supporters—Dexter, a bay horse proper, charged on the shoulder with a portcullis or; sinister, a greyhound, argent, charged on the body with three ermine spots. Residence,—1, Gledmow Gdns., SW5.

NON-SINE-NUMINE ·i·

Not without God's assistance.

SON LIVING.
Hon. THOMAS ADAM, b. Dec. 1st, 1967.
DAUGHTER LIVING.
Hon. Polly Anna, b. 1969.
AUNT LIVING.
(Raised to the rank of a Baron's daughters 1937.)
Hon. Diana Frederica, (1, Devon Flats, Devon Cres., Redhill, Surrey.) b. 1901 : m. 1924 (m. diss. 1953), Leslie Frederick Talbot Price [see Price, Bt., cr. 1815, colls.].
DAUGHTER LIVING OF FOURTH BARON.
Hon. Serena Mary, b. 1919 : m. 1st, 1940 (marriage dissolved 1945), Patrick de Gruchy Vignoles Crawshay Warren; 2ndly, 1951, Arthur Reginald Danks, and has issue living, (by 1st marriage) Edgar Jeremy, b. 1941,—(by 2nd marriage) John Francis Reginald, b. 1954,—Fenella Christian Mary, b. 1952. Residence,—Lealands Cottage, Box, Minchinhampton, Stroud, Glos.

WIDOW LIVING OF FIFTH BARON.
ELLICE MARGARET (Margaret Baroness Gifford), da. of the late Arthur Wigram Allen, of Merioola, Woollahra, Sydney, N.S. Wales: m. 1939, the 5th Baron, who d. 1961. Residence,—Merioola, Highclere, Newbury.

PREDECESSORS.—[1] Rt. Hon. Sir ROBERT Gifford, P.C.; appointed Solicitor-Gen. 1817, Attorney-Gen. 1819, and Lord Ch. Justice of Common Pleas Jan. 1824; cr. Baron Gifford, of St. Leonard's, Devon (peerage of United Kingdom) 1824, and was afterwards Master of the Rolls and Dep. Speaker of the House of Lords; d. 1826; s. by his son [2] ROBERT FRANCIS, 2nd Baron, b. 1817: m. 1845, Frederica Charlotte, who d. 1920, el. dau. of 1st Baron Fitz-Hardinge; d. 1872; s. by his son [3] EDRIC FREDERICK, V.C., 3rd Baron, b. 1849; served with Ashanti Expedition, 1873-4 (medal with clasp, V.C.), and in Zulu War 1879 (medal with clasp): on Staff of Sir Garnet Wolseley, Gov. of Natal 1874 and 1879-80; Colonial Sec. for W. Australia, and M.L.C. 1880-3, and Colonial Sec. at Gibraltar 1883-8: m. 1880, Sophie Catherine, who d. 1947, dau. of the late Gen. John Alfred Street, C.B.: d. 1911; s. by his brother [4] EDGAR BERKELEY, 4th Baron, b. 1857: m. 1st, 1879, Mary, who d. 1913, dau. of John Osborne, Q.C., and widow of Thomas Booth, of West Ashby Manor, Horncastle; 2ndly, 1918, Anne Maud, who d. 1956, dau. of the late Col. Aitchison, Scots Fusilier Guards, of Drummore, Musselburgh; d. 1937; s. by his nephew [5] CHARLES MAURICE ELTON (son of the late Hon. Maurice Raymond Gifford, C.M.G., 4th son of 2nd Baron), 5th Baron; b. 1899; Chm. of Challis & Benson, Ltd.; late Com. R.N. and Flight Lieut. R.A.F.; A.D.C. to Gov. of N.S. Wales 1930-35: m. 1939, Ellice Margaret, dau. of the late Arthur Wigram Allen, of Merioola, Woollahra, Sydney, N.S. Wales; d. 1961; s. by his only son [6] ANTHONY MAURICE, 6th Baron and present peer.

Gifford, Earl of, son of Marquess of Tweedsdale.

GISBOROUGH, BARON. (Chaloner.) [Baron U.K. 1917.]

Frugality is the left hand of fortune, and diligence the right.

THOMAS RICHARD JOHN LONG CHALONER, 3rd Baron; b. July 1st, 1927; s. 1951; ed. at Eton; late Capt. Northumberland Hussars, and Lt. 16th/15th Lancers; Lt.-Col. Green Howards Territorials 1967-69; Co. Councillor for N. Riding of Yorks. 1964-74, since when of Cleveland; a DL of Cleveland: m. 1960, Shane, el. da. of Sidney A. Newton, [see Newton, Bt., colls., cr. 1924], and has issue.

Arms,—Sable, a chevron between three cherubims or. Crest,—A demi sea-wolf or. Supporters,—On either side a kneeling angel, wings elevated, inverted and endorsed, each ensigned on the head with a cross, all or.
Seat,—Gisborough House, Guisborough, Cleveland. Club,—Northern Counties (Newcastle).

SONS LIVING.
Hon. THOMAS PEREGRINE LONG, b. Jan. 17th, 1961.
Hon. Robert Toby Long, b. 1966.

SISTER LIVING.
Hon. Angela Mary (Geranium Cottage Ditchling, Sussex), b. 1925: m. 1946 (m. diss. 1973), Roderick Edward Faure

Walker, late Maj. Coldstream Guards, and has issue living, Rupert Roderick (14, Brechin Place, SW7), b. 1947; ed. at Eton and Bristol Univ. (BSc): m. 1975, Sally, da. of J. Sidebottom, of Augusta House, Castle Hedingham, Halstead, Essex,—James Edward Bruce (22, Almedia St., N1), b. 1948; ed. at Eton: m. 1973, Caryn Lois, da. of Dr. Robert Becker, of 1701, York Av., New York, USA,— Camilla Mary, b. 1953: m. 1974, Timothy J. P. Coghlan, of 19, Thurlow Rd., NW3.

AUNTS LIVING. (*Daughters of 1st Baron.*)

Hon. Ursula Violet. *Residence,*—Wood Cottage, Earls Common, Droitwich, Worcestershire.

Hon. Honora Elizabeth Dundas; is a J.P. for Salop; has Kaisar-i-Hind Silver medal: m. 1929, Col. Frank Drummond Shuttleworth Field, O.B.E., M.C., Indian Army, who d. 1958. *Residence,*— Stocking Cottage, Balsham, Cambs.

WIDOW LIVING OF ELDEST SON OF FIRST BARON.

Evelyn Maud, younger dau. of A. Benyon, of Ashe, Windsor; raised to rank and precedence of widow of el. son of a Baron 1917 (so long as she remained a widow); is a J.P.: m. 1st, 1914, Capt. Richard Godolphin Hume Chaloner, Wiltshire Regt., who d. (killed abroad during European War) 1917; 2ndly, 1918, Lieut.-Col. John Clement Wolstan Francis, 15/19th Hussars (retired). and has issue living (by 1st marriage) (infra). *Residence,*—Quy Hall, Cambridge.

COLLATERAL BRANCH LIVING.

Issue of the late Capt. Richard Godolphin Hume Chaloner, Wiltshire Regt., el. son of 1st Baron, b. 1883, d. (killed abroad during European War) April 1917: m. 1914, Evelyn Maud, J.P. [(ante): she m. 2ndly, 1918, Lieut.-Col. John Clement Wolstan Francis, 15/19th Hussars (retired)], younger dau. of A. Benyon, of Ashe, Windsor:—

Diana Margaret Bruce: m. 1948, Ian Melville Wright, who d. 1971.

PREDECESSORS.—[1] RICHARD GODOLPHIN WALMESLEY Chaloner, second son of the late Richard Penruddocke Long, M.P., of Rood Ashton, Wilts.; b. 1856; assumed by Roy. licence 1888 the surname of Chaloner in lieu of his patronymic (under the will of his maternal grand-uncle, Adm. Thomas Chaloner, CB, who inherited the Gisborough Estates through his mother, who was a descendant, through her grandmother, Margaret Bruce of Kennet, (of Robert de Brus, Lord of Skelton, who founded Gisborough Priory 1119); Afghan War 1879-80, S. Africa 1900; MP for W. or Westbury Div. of Wilts. (C) 1895-1900, and for Abercromby Div. of Liverpool 1910-17; cr. *Baron Gisborough,* of Cleveland, Yorkshire (peerage of UK) 1917: m. 1882, Margaret Brocklesby, who d. 1941, el. da. of the late Rev. Weston Brocklesby Davis, V. of Ramsbury, Wilts.; d. 1938; s. by his second but only surviving son [2] THOMAS WESTON PEEL LONG, TD, 2nd Baron, b. 1889; Maj. (ret.) Green Howards (TA) and Fl.-Lt. (Hon. Capt.) RAF; 1914-18 War in RFC and RAF; 1939-45 War as Fl.-Lt. RAFVR: m. 1923, Esther Isabella Madeleine, who d. 1970, da. of the late Charles Oswin Hall, of Eddlethorpe Hall, Malton, Yorks.; d. 1951; s. by his son [3] THOMAS RICHARD JOHN LONG, 3rd Baron, and present peer.

GLADWYN, BARON. (Jebb.) [Baron U.K. 1960.]

By hope and work.

(HUBERT MILES) GLADWYN JEBB, *G.C.M.G., G.C.V.O., C.B.,* 1st Baron, son of the late Sydney Jebb, of Fir-beck Hall, Rotherham, Yorkshire; b. April 25th, 1900 ; ed. at Eton, and at Magdalen Coll., Oxford (Hon. Fellow 1954); Hon. D.C.L. Oxford; Hon. Dr. Essex; entered Diplo. Ser. 1924; served at Teheran 1924-7, in Foreign Office 1927-31, at Rome 1931-5, and again in Foreign Office 1935-40 (Private Sec. to Parliamentary Under Sec. of State 1929-31 and to Perma-nent Under-Sec. of State 1937-40); appointed Foreign Policy Adviser to Min. of Economic Warfare with temporary rank of Assist. Under-Sec. of State 1940, Head of Economic and Reconstruction Depart., Foreign Office 1942, Executive Sec. of Pre-paratory Commn. of U.N. 1945, acting Sec.-Gen. of U.N. 1946, Dep. to Sec. of State on Council of Foreign Mins. March 1946, Assist. Under-Sec. of State and U.N. Ad-viser May 1946, U.K. Representative on Permanent Commn. of Brussels Treaty with rank of Ambassador March 1948, Dep. Under-Sec. of State Dec. 1948, Permanent Representative of U.K. to U.N. 1950, and Ambassador to France 1954; ret. 1960; a Member of European Parl. since 1973; Pres. of Campaign for Europe, Vice-Pres. of European Movement, of Atlantic Treaty Assocn., of Atlantic Inst., and of UN Assocn.; Dep. Liberal Leader in House of Lords since 1967; author of "the European Idea", "Half-Way to 1984", "De Gaulle's Europe or Why the General Says No", "Europe after De Gaulle", and "The Memoirs of Lord Gladwyn"; Grand Cross of Legion of Honour; CMG 1942, CB (Civil) 1947, KCMG 1949, GCMG 1954, GCVO 1957, and *Baron Gladwyn,* of Bramfield, co. Suffolk (peerage of UK) 1960: m. 1929, Cynthia, da. of Sir Saxton William Armstrong Noble, 3rd Bt. (cr. 1902), and has issue.

Arms,—Quarterly vert and or, in the first quarter a falcon argent with bells of the second, and in the last quarter a lure of the third. Crest,—A lure fessewise argent, and thereon a falcon rising proper with bells or. Supporters,—*Dexter,* a brown bear proper ; *sinister,* a unicorn argent, charged on he shoulder with a patriarchal cross bottony gules.

Residences,—Bramfield Hall, Halesworth, Suffolk; 62, Whitehall Court, S.W.1. *Clubs,*—Garrick, Turf.

SON LIVING.

Hon. MILES ALVERY GLADWYN, *b.* March 3rd, 1930; ed. at Eton, and Magdalen Coll., Oxford (MA); with British Airways. *Residence,*—E1, Albany, Piccadilly, W1.

DAUGHTERS LIVING.

Hon. Vanessa Mary, *b.* 1931: *m.* 1962, Prof. Hugh Swynnerton Thomas, of 29, Ladbroke Grove, W11, and has issue living, Charles Inigo Gladwyn, *b.* 1962,—Henry Isambard Claudio Tobias, *b.* 1964,—Isabella Pandora, *b.* 1966.

Hon. Stella Candida, *b.* 1933: *m.* 1959, Baron Joël de Rosnay, and has issue living, Alexis Marc Louis Joël, *b.* 1967,—(Vanessa) Tatiana Louise, *b.* 1961,—Cecilia Fiona Louise, *b.* 1963. *Residence,*—146, rue de l'Universite, Paris VII, France.

Glamis, Lord, son of Earl of Strathmore and Kinghorne.

Glandine, Viscount, son of Earl of Norbury.

GLANUSK, BARON. (Bailey.) [Baron U.K. 1899, Bt. U.K. 1852.]

Liberty.

DAVID RUSSELL BAILEY, 4th Baron, and 5th Baronet : *b.* Nov. 19th, 1917 ; *s.* 1948; ed. at Eton; Lt.Cdr. (ret.) RN; Managing Dir. of Wandel & Goltermann (UK) Ltd., since 1966: *m.* 1941, Lorna Dorothy, only da. of the late Capt. E. C H. N. Andrews, MBE, RA, and has issue.

Arms,—Argent, between two bars, three annulets in fesse gules between as many martlets of the last. Crest,—A griffin sejant argent, semée of annulets gules. Supporters.—*Dexter,* a collier proper; *sinister,* a smith proper.

Residence,—Sawmill House, Park Farm Rd., High Wycombe, Bucks.

SON LIVING.

Hon. CHRISTOPHER RUSSELL (4, Kings Yard, Kings Ride, Ascot, SL5 8AH), *b.* March 18th, 1942; ed. at Eton, and at Clare Coll., Camb. (BA): *m.* 1974, Frances Elizabeth, MA, da. of Air Marshal Sir Douglas Charles Lowe, KCB, DFC, AFC.

DAUGHTER LIVING.

Hon. Susan Mary, *b.* 1944: *m.* 1970, Peter Mansel Lloyd James, MB, BS, FRCS, of 104, Pottergate, Norwich, Norfolk, and has issue living, David Lloyd, *b.* 1971,—Victoria Mary, *b.* 1974.

SISTERS LIVING. (*Raised to the rank of a Baron's daughters* 1948.)

Hon. Deborah Mary, *b.* 1910: *m.* 1938, Cdr. Anthony Vyvyan Thomas, OBE, RN (ret.), and has issue living, Deborah Willow Vyvyan, *b.* 1940: *m.* 1960, Maj. Peter Kenneth Cracroft, 4th/7th Roy. Dragoon Guards, of Woodsford House, near Dorchester, Dorset, and has issue living, Fenella Jane *b.* 1962, Henrietta Louise *b.* 1966, Miranda Susan (twin) *b.* 1966—Antonia Mary Vyvyan, *b.* 1944: *m.* 1969, Robert Henry Stallibrass Hiscocks, of Gore Cottage, Rayne, Braintree, Essex. *Residence,*—Tretower House, Crickhowell, Breconshire.

Hon. Shirley Joan (Rectory Cottage, Rectory Lane, Ashington, Sussex), *b.* 1912: *m.* 1946, George Dupin Drayson, who *d.* 1969, and has issue living, Charles Dupin, *b.* 1947: *m.* 1974, Rosemary Ann, da. of the late Capt. D. P. Evans, RN.

Hon. Rachel Kathleen, *b.* 1914: *m.* 1940, Brig. Dimitry Zvegintzov, CBE, late Border Regt. (ret.), and has issue living, Ivan Dimitry (c/o Westminster Bank, Salisbury), *b.* 1943; Maj. Coldstream Guards: *m.* 1967, Caroline, da. of Lt.-Col. W. G. Watt, of Jackdaws, N. Waltham, Hants, and has issue living, Piers Ivan Robin *b.* 1968, Tania Arabella *b.* 1970,—Paul David (c/o Lloyds Bank, 6, Pall Mall SW1), *b.* 1945; Capt. 5th Inniskilling Dragoon Gds.: *m.* 1968, Rose Maree, da. of Maj. James Mellor, of Knipoch, by Oban, Argyll, and has issue living, Alexander Dimitry James *b.* 1972,—Elizavietta Mary, *b.* 1942: *m.* 1963, Michael Anthony Robert Oakley, TD, of Fernhill, Farther Common, Liss, Hants., and has issue living, Mathew James *b.* 1967, Frances Rachel *b.* 1971. *Residence.*—Parc-Gwynne, Glasbury-on-Wye.

Hon. Elspeth Lorraine (*Hon. Lady Musson*), *b.* 1915: *m.* 1939, Gen. Sir Geoffrey Randolph Dixon Musson, GCB, CBE, DSO, late KSLI (ret.), and has issue living, Peter Geoffrey Dixon, *b.* 1946,—Penelope Anne, *b.* 1941: *m.* 1962, Capt. William Richard Dudgeon, late The Black Watch, of Old Thatch, Bamber's Green, Takeley, Bishop's Stortford, Herts, and has issue living, Angus Geoffrey Peter *b.* 1963, Deborah Elspeth *b.* 1968. *Residence,*—Provost Hill, Hurstbourne Tarrant, Andover.

DAUGHTER LIVING OF THIRD BARON.

Hon. Elizabeth Shân Josephine, *b.* 1943: *m.* 1964, Capt. William Nigel Henry Legge-Bourke, of Glanusk Park, Crickhowell, Powys [see E. Dartmouth, colls.].

WIDOW LIVING OF THIRD BARON.

MARGARET ELDRYDD (*Viscountess De L'Isle*), da. of the late Maj.-Gen. Thomas Herbert Shoubridge, CB, CMG, DSO; a JP of Breconshire: *m.* 1st, 1942, as his second wife, the 3rd Baron, who *d.* 1948; 2ndly, 1966, as his second wife the 1st Viscount De L'Isle. *Residences,*—Penhurst Place, Tonbridge, Kent; Glanusk Park, Crickhowell, Powys.

COLLATERAL BRANCHES LIVING.

Issue of the late Capt. the Hon. Arthur Bailey, 3rd son of 1st Baron, *b.* 1868, *d.* 1929 : *m.* 1924, Ethel Sophia, who *d.* 1959, dau. of the late James Ledger Hill, J.P., of Bulford Manor, Wilts., and Combe Grove, Bath:—

Carola Mary, *b.* 1925: *m.* 1949, Capt. Hugh Denman Way, MC, RHA, who *d.* 1971, and has issue living, Nigel Arthur Denman, *b.* 1958,—Anthony Hugh Vereist, *b.* 1961. *Residence,*—Fittleton House, Netheravon, Wilts.

Issue of the late Capt. the Hon. John Lancelot Bailey, 5th son of 1st Baron, *b.* 1878, *d.* 1918: *m.* 1903, Vivien Dora, who *d.* 1938, dau. of the late Ferdinand G. Carey, of Guernsey, and Frogmore, Ceylon:—

Joseph Ferdinand (1537, Summerhill Av., Apt. 207, Montreal, Quebec, H3H 1C2, Canada), *b.* 1907 : *m.* 1st, 1935 (divorce 1946), Alicia Cecilia Anne, da. of Oswald Magniac, DL, of Nursling, Hants.; 2ndly, 1948, Evelyn Marie, da. of Robert P. B. Blauveldt, LLB, of Yarmouth, Nova Scotia, and has issue living, (by 1st m.) Lancelot Oswald (c/o PO Box 500 (VAO), General Post Office, Ottawa 2,

Canada), b. 1936: m. 1959, Armelle Francoise, da. of Jean François Le Roux, of Candé, Maine-et-Loire, France, and has issue living, Antoine Lancelot Gwenaél b. 1965,—Vernon Joseph Russell (555, Laird Blvd., Montreal, 305, Quebec), b. 1937: m. 1968, Melanie Frances Moore, and has issue living, Rachel Marjorie b. 1969,—Priscilla Anne b. 1971,—Cynthia Mary, b. 1940: m. 1963, Patrick Joseph Moran, and has issue living, Malachi Joseph b. 1965, Roisin b. 1968, Garett b. 1969, Fiona Mary b. 1964,—(by 2nd m.) Herbert Van Courtlandt, b. 1952,—Josephine Blauveldt, b. 1949,—Deborah Evelyn, b. 1950.——Jacqueline, b. 1905. *Residence,*—2, Grove Cres., Combs Park, Coleford, Glos.——Marjorie Vivienne, b. 1910: m. 1930, Oliver Fowell Lancaster [Buxton, Bt., colls.]. *Residence,*—Daniel Zorrilla 5276, Colon, Montevidao, Uruguay.

(In remainder to the Baronetcy only).

Granddaughter of the late Richard Crawshay Bailey, son of the late Joseph Bailey, el. son of 1st baronet:—

Issue of the late Rev. Canon Charles Henry Bailey, MC, b. 1882, d. 1971: m. 1915, Ethel, who d. 1962, da. of the late George Millward:—

Mabel Anna, b. 1920: m. 1947, Maj. Ronald Patrick Ward, MC, The Border Regt., of Ivall's Farm Cottage, Bentworth, Alton, Hants., and has issue living, Charles Patrick, b. 1949,—Susan, b. 1948: m. 1970, John Grosvenor Phillips,—Deborah Rose, b. 1957.

Granddaughters of the late John Arthur Crawshay Bailey, only son of the late
Capt. John Crawshay Bailey, RN, 3rd son of 1st baronet:—

Issue of the late John Henry Bailey, b. 1889, d. 1966: m. 1913, Ruby, who d. 1972, da. of Edward Giles:—

Margaret Elizabeth (84, Snowden Cres., London, Ont. N6E 1G4, Canada), b. 1915: m. 1939, Derrick Thomas Ashworth Douglas, who d. 1975, and has issue living, Derrick John (31, Harding Cres., London, Ont.), b. 1947: m. 1969, Penelope Elizabeth, da. of Rudi Krause, of Elmira, Ont., and has issue living, Lee Christian b. 1971, Todd Matthew b. 1973,—David Henry (twin), (36, Kettering St., Winnipeg, Manitoba, Canada), b. 1947; constable RCMP: m. 1970, Charlotte, da. of the late Stefan Johannson, of Gimli, Manitoba, and has issue living, Stefan Nathan b. 1971, Jill Elizabeth b. 1974,—Judy Ann, b. 1941: 1971, Herbert Flax (PO Box 369, St. Anthony, Newfoundland), and has issue living, Timothy Aaron b. 1974, Joanna Susan b. 1972.——Josephine Lucy Ann (92, Shrub End Rd., Shrub End, Colchester), b. 1922: m. 1943, Ronald Jenkins, who d. 1968, and has issue living, Susan Ann, b. 1944: m. 1967, Graham Francis Holmes, of Glanusk, Ashfield Rd., Framsdon, Suffolk, and has issue living, Timothy b. 1974.——Barbara, b. 1927: m. 1945, Capt. Ernest Ronald Matthewson of Capac Yupanqui 2745, Lance, Lima, Peru, and has issue living, Michael Derek (Meadow Rd., Berkhamsted, Herts.), b. 1946: m. 1970, Barbara Mary Saunders, and has issue living, Toby b. 1974.

PREDECESSORS.—[1] JOSEPH Bailey, younger son of John Bailey, of Wakefield; sat successively as M.P. for Worcester City and Breconshire; cr. a *Baronet* 1852: m. 1st, 1810, Maria, who d. 1827, dau. of Joseph Latham; 2ndly, 1830, Mary Anne, who d. 1874, dau. of the late John Thomas Hendry Hopper, of Witton Castle, co. Durham; d. 1858; s. by his grandson [2] JOSEPH RUSSELL (son of the late Joseph Bailey, M.P., el. son of 1st Bt.), 2nd Bt., b. 1840; cr. *Baron Glanusk,* of Glanusk Park, co. Brecknock (peerage of United Kingdom) 1899; M.P. for Herefordshire (C) 1865-85, and for Hereford 1886-92; was Lord-Lieut. of Breconshire: m. 1861, Mary Ann, who d. 1935, dau. of Henry Lucas, M.D., of Glan-yr-Afon; d. 1906; s. by his son [3] JOSEPH HENRY RUSSELL, C.B., C.B.E., D.S.O., 2nd Baron, b. 1864; Lord-Lieut. of Breconshire 1905-28: m. 1890, Editha Elma, C.B.E., who d. 1938, dau. of the late Major Warden Sergison; d. 1928; s. by his son [4] WILFRED RUSSELL, D.S.O., 3rd Baron; b. 1891, Lord-Lieut. of Breconshire; late Lieut.-Col. Welsh Guards; European War 1914-19 (D.S.O.): m. 1st, 1919, Victoria Mary Enid Anne (from whom he obtained a divorce 1939), dau. of the late Lieut.-Col. Frank Dugdale, CVO; 2ndly, 1942, Margaret Eldrydd (who m. 2ndly, 1966, the 1st Viscount De Lisle), da. of the late Maj.-Gen. Thomas Herbert Shoubridge, CB, CMG, DSO; d. 1948; s. by his cousin [5] DAVID RUSSELL (son of the late Hon. Herbert Crawshay Bailey, 4th son of 1st Baron), 4th Baron and present peer.

GLASGOW, EARL OF. (Boyle.) [Earl S. 1703.]

DOMINUS PROVIDEBIT

The Lord will provide.

DAVID WILLIAM MAURICE BOYLE, CB, DSC, 9th Earl; b. July 24th, 1910; s. 1963; ed. at Eton; Rear-Adm. (ret.); Capt. of the Fleet, Home Fleet 1957-59, Commodore, R.N. Barracks, Portsmouth 1959-61, and Flag Officer Malta 1961-63; 1939-45 War in Atlantic, Arctic, and Far East, and present at destruction of *Bismarck* (despatches, DSC); a Member of Roy. Co. of Archers (Queen's Body Guard for Scotland); CB (Mil) 1963: m. 1st, 1937 (marriage dissolved 1962), Dorothea, only da. of Col. Sir Archibald Moir Park Lyle, MC, 2nd Bt.; 2ndly, 1962, the Hon. Ursula Vanda Maud, da. of 4th Baron Vivian, and formerly wife of Maj. Sir William Fane Wrixon-Becher, MC, 5th Bt., and has issue by 1st marriage.

Arms.—Quarterly: 1st and 4th or, an eagle with two heads displayed gules, armed and beaked azure; a coat of augmentation for the earldom of *Glasgow;* 2nd and 3rd per bend embattled argent and gules, *Boyle:* over all an escutcheon or, charged with three stags' horns gules, for the paternal coat of *Boyle of Kelburn.* Crest.—An eagle with two heads displayed per pale embattled gules and argent. Supporters.—Dexter, a savage, wreathed round the temples and loins, and holding in the dexter hand a branch of laurel all proper: *sinister,* a lion per pale embattled argent and gules.

Seat,—Kelburn, Fairlie, Ayrshire. *Clubs,*—United Service, St. James'.

SON LIVING. *(By 1st marriage.)*
PATRICK ROBIN ARCHIBALD *(Viscount of Kelburn),* b. July 30th, 1939; ed. at Eton; Sub-Lt. R.N.R.

DAUGHTERS LIVING. (By 1st marriage.)
Lady Sarah Dorothea, b. 1941: m. 1962, John Edward Baily, of 27, Park Walk, S.W.10 [see E. Haddington, colls.].
Lady Nichola Jane Eleanora (Minervina), b. 1946.

SISTERS LIVING.
Lady Hersey Margaret, b. 1914 : m. 1st, 1940, Com. the Hon. John Montagu Granville Walde-grave, R.N., D.S.O., who d. (killed on active ser. during European War) 1944 [see By. Radstock, ext.]; 2ndly, 1947, John Goring, OBE, TD [see Goring, Bt., Colls.]. Residence,—Findon Park House, Findon, Sussex.
Lady Margaret Dorothea, b. 1920: m. 1st, 1944 (m. diss. 1962), Capt. Oliver Payan Dawnay, CVO, Coldstream Gds. [see V. Downe, colls.], 2ndly, 1973, Peter Douglas Miller Stirling—Aird of Kippendaire, TD. of Kippenross House, Dunblane, Stirlingshire, and 26, Sheffield Terr, W8.

WIDOWS LIVING OF SONS OF SEVENTH EARL.
Marie (Dinvin, Portpatrick, Wigtownshire, Stranraer, DG9 8TH); a JP and Co. Councillor for Wigtownshire; da. of John Gibb, of Chillesford, Orford, Suffolk, and formerly wife of George Chettle: m. 1934, as his 2nd wife, Air Commodore the Hon. John David Boyle, CBE, DSO, who d. 1974.
Isabel Julia, dau. of the late Edmund Charles Pendleton Hull, J.P., of Park Gate House, Ham Common, Richmond, Surrey : m. 1916, the Hon. Alan Reginald Boyle, A.F.C., who d. 1958, and has issue living [see colls., infra]. Residence,—8, The Precincts, Canterbury.

WIDOW LIVING OF EIGHTH EARL.
HYACINTHE MARY (Dowager Countess of Glasgow) (of 28, Campden House, Sheffield Terr., W.8), da. of the late William A. Bell, of Pendell Court, Bletchingley: m. 1906, the 8th Earl, who d. 1963.

COLLATERAL BRANCHES LIVING.
Grandsons of the late Capt. the Hon. James Boyle (infra):—
Issue of the late Lieut.-Col. Patrick John Salvin Boyle, Roy. Scots Fusiliers, b. 1910, d. (killed in action during European War) 1944 : m. 1938, Mary Elizabeth (of Great Chalfield, Melksham, Wilts.) (who m. 2ndly, 1948, Lieut.-Col. Charles Murray Floyd OBE, who d. 1971 [see Floyd, B., colls.]), only child of Robert Fleetwood Fuller, of Great Chalfield, Melksham:—
Andrew Robert James (2, Cheltenham Terr., SW3), b. 1939: ed. at Eton: m. 1971, Julia, da. of N. W. Gardener, of Boxted Farm, Hemel Hempstead, Herts., and has issue living, James William, b. 1973,—Olivia Mary, b. 1975.——Simon Hugh Patrick (Meadowbank, Park Lane, Bewdley, Worcs.), b. 1941: ed. at Eton: m. 1970, Catriona, da. of W. G. Gordon, DFC, of Lude, Vlair Atholl, Perths, and has issue living, Alice Catriona Jane, b. 1972, Mary Helen Fenella, b. 1974.——David Thomas Alan (Glassmount, by Kirkcaldy, Fife), b. 1943; ed. at Eton, and Trin. Coll., Camb.: m. 1969, Angela, da. of George Frederick Pinney, CBE [see Lacy, Bt.], and has issue living, Robert John, b. 1970,—Edward George, b. 1972,—Patrick Thomas, b. 1974.

Issue of the late Capt. the Hon. James Boyle, 3rd son of 7th Earl, b. 1886; d. (killed in action) 1914 : m. 1908, Katherine Isabel Salvin, who d. 1960 (having m. 2ndly, 1920, the 1st Viscount Trenchard, who d. 1956), dau. of the late Edward Salvin Bowlby, of Gilston Park, Herts, and Knoydart, Inverness-shire :—
Belinda Margaret Graeme, O.B.E., b. 1913; is Ch. Com. A.T.S.; Middle East 1941-4 ; O.B.E. (Mil.) 1944: m. 1947, Simon Fowell Buxton, who d. 1974 [Buxton, Bt., colls.]. Residence,—Riverside, Wylye, Wilts.

Issue of the late Hon. Alan Reginald Boyle, A.F.C., 5th son of 7th Earl, b. 1886, d. 1958 : m. 1916, Isabel Julia (ante), dau. of the late Edmund Charles Pendleton Hull, J.P., of Park Gate House, Ham Common, Richmond, Surrey :—
Fenella Frances Dora, b. 1918: m. 1954, Robin Halliday Macartney, FRIBA, who d. 1973, yr. son of the late Sir George Macartney, KCIE. Residence,—Caia de Urra, Portalegre, Portugal.——Jean Isabel, b. 1919: m. 1941, Bartholomew Guy Ellison, of Grove House, 94, Woodstock Rd., Oxford, and has issue living, Caroline Anne, b. 1942: m. 1967, John Antony Hobbs, of May Cottage, Alice Bright Lane, Crowborough, Sussex, TN6 3SQ, and has issue living, Jonathan Noel Alan b. 1970, Francesca Agnes b. 1968,—Rosanna Natasha b. 1972,—Joanna Fenella, b. 1945.

(In remainder to Scottish peerages only.)
Granddaughters of the late Col. Patrick David Boyle, son of the late Vice-Adm. Alexander Boyle (infra) :—
Issue of the late Col. Cecil Alexander Boyle, C.I.E., D.S.O., b. 1888, d. 1941 : m. 1923, Gladys (Dulcie) (Maywood St. Luke, Portsmouth Rd., Camberley, Surrey), da. of the late Lt.-Col. Robert Arthur Edward Benn, C.I.E.:—
Mary Grizel, b. 1924; 1939-45 War with WAAF: m. 1947, Lt.-Col. James Berkeley Sackville Hamilton, RE (ret.), of Acklam Grange, Acklam, Malton, Yorks., YO17 9RG [see V. Boyne, colls.].——Patricia, b. 1929: is a State Registered Nurse: m. 1955, Lt.-Col. Jonathan Robert Alford, RE. Address,—c/o National & Grindlays Bank, 13, St. James's Sq., SW1.

Granddaughters of the late Alexander Boyle (infra):—
Issue of the late Alister Patrick Boyle, b. 1905, d. 1973: m. 1st, 1932, Rose Howard, who d. 1933, da. of Howard Tripp, of S. Canterbury, NZ; 2ndly, 1936, Lois Morton (45, Wairarapa Terr., Christchurch, NZ), only da. of the late C. M. Ollivier:—
(By 1st m.) Jennifer Frances, b. 1933: m. 1965, Ian Coutts (Oundle School, Peterborough), and has issue living, Frances, b. 1967,—Rosa, b. 1969.——(by 2nd m.) Mary Montgomerie, b. 1937: m. 1964, Laurence George Holder, who d. 1974, and has issue living, Patrick George, b. 1966,—Bridget Mary, b. 1967,—Alexandra Browning, b. 1969,—Sara Annabel, b. 1972.——Alexandra Montgomerie, (26A, Aubrey Walk. W8), b. 1943.
Granddaughter of the late Vice-Adm. Alexander Boyle, son of the late Rt. Hon. David Boyle, Lord Justice-Gen. of Scotland, 4th son of the late Rev. the Hon. Patrick Boyle, 4th son of 2nd Earl:—
Issue of the late Alexander Boyle, b. 1857, d. 1923 : m. 1883, Fanny, O.B.E., who d. 1930, dau. of the late Michael Studholme:—
Janet, b. 1886: m. 1907, Algar Temple Williams, of 60A, Park Terr., Christchurch, NZ, and has issue living.

Grandsons of the late Henry David Boyle, el. son of John Boyle, 3rd son of the Rt. Hon. David Boyle (ante):—
Issue of the late David Hugh Montgomerie Boyle, CMG, b. 1883, d. 1970: m. 1916, Laura Grant, who d. 1971, da. of the late James Tennant, of Fairlieburne, Fairlie:—
Alasdair David Forbes (241, Nithsdale Rd., Glasgow, G41 5PY), b. 1919; ed. at Wellington Coll., and RMC; Maj. (ret.) Argyll and Sutherland Highlanders; MBIM; Sec. of Scottish Business Sch.; 1939-45 War (wounded, despatches): m. 1st, 1945 (m. diss. 1958), Elizabeth Winifred, da. of the late Cdr. H. R. Kelway-Bamber, RN; 2ndly, 1958, Mrs. Doris Louise Clayton, da. of Victor Eaton Usherwood, of Tunbridge Wells, and has issue living, (by 1st m.) Roderick David Alasdair, b. 1951,—Henrietta Elizabeth Flora (Hon. Mrs. James M. Rollo), b. 1948: m. 1968, the Hon. James Malcolm Rollo, of Corwar House, Barrhill, Girvan, Ayrshire [see L. Rollo].——Ranald Hugh Montgomerie, DSC (Downcraig Ferry, Millport, I. of Cumbrae, Brooks's, RAC, MCC Clubs), b. 1921; ed. at Wellington Coll., and at Exeter Coll., Oxford; late Sudan Govt. Ser., HMOCS Kenya and HM Dip. Ser.; a Dir. of Hambros Bank, and a Member of Queen's Body Guard for Scotland (R. Co. of Archers); 1939-45 War as Lt. RNVR (wounded, DSC): m. 1957, Norma, yst. da. of the late Alexander Gray and has issue living, Fergus David, b. 1958,—Alexander Ranald, b. 1959,—Patrick Mungo, b. 1961,—

John Quentin, *b.* 1964,—Hamish William, *b.* 1970,—Laura Grizel *b.* 1963,—Beatrice Elizabeth, *b.* 1966.

Granddaughter of the late William Henry David Boyle, son of the late Col. William Boyle, C.B., son of the late Rt. Hon. David Boyle (ante) :—
Issue of the late George Frederic Boyle, *b.* 1893, *d.* 1929 : *m.* 1920, Mary Jeffrey [who *d.* 1954, having obtained a divorce 1929, and who *m.* 2ndly, 1929, Douglas Charles Beaumont, M.D., M.R.C.P., of Claywood, Sway, Hants], dau. of Sir Peter Jeffrey Mackie, 1st Bt. :—
Eleanor Mary, *b.* 1921: *m.* 1st, 1945 (marriage dissolved 1962), Capt. the Hon. Arthur Cameron Corbett, Ayrshire Yeo., el. son of 2nd Baron Rowallan; 2ndly, 1963, Col. R. Derek Cardiff, late Scots Gds., Claywood House, Sway, Hants., and has issue living (by 1st m.) [see B. Rowallan], (by 2nd m.) David Richard George, *b.* 1964.

Granddaughter of the late Cdr. Edward Louis Dalrymple Boyle, CMG, RN; 3rd son of Capt. Robert Boyle, RA, 7th son of the Rt. Hon. David Boyle (ante):—
Issue of the late Lt.-Col. Edward Patrick Ogilvie Boyle, MVO, *b.* 1893, *d.* 1966: *m.* 1934, Audrey (17, Grosvenor Court, Sloane St., SW1) (who *m.* 2ndly, 1970, Maj. Clarence J. Henry, who *d.* 1973, da. of the late Lt.-Col. Audley Willis):—
Jennifer Mary, *b.* 1934.

PREDECESSORS.—[1] DAVID BOYLE, *M.P.* for Buteshire 1689-99 ; *cr.* *Lord Boyle*, of Kelburn, Stewartown, Cumbra, Largs and Dalry (peerage of Scotland) 1699, and *Lord Boyle*, *Viscount of Kelburn* and *Earl of Glasgow* (peerage of Scotland) 1703, with remainder to his heirs male whatsoever; Lord High Commr. to Gen. Assembly for Ch. of Scotland 1706-10, a Representative Peer 1707-08, and Lord Registrar of Scotland 1708-14; *d.* 1733; *s.* by his son [2] JOHN, 2nd Earl; *d.* 1740; *s.* by his son [3] JOHN, 3rd Earl; was Lord High Commr. to Ch. of Scotland 1764-72; *d.* 1775; *s.* by his son [4] GEORGE, *G.C.H.*, 4th Earl, *b.* 1766; Lord-Lieut. of Renfrewshire, and a Representative Peer; *cr.* *Baron Ross*, of Hawkhead, co. Renfrew (peerage of United Kingdom) 1815: *m.* 1st, 1788, Lady Augusta Hay, dau. of 14th Earl of Erroll ; 2ndly, 1824, Julia, dau. of the Rt. Hon. Sir John Sinclair, 1st Bt. ; *d.* 1843; *s.* by his 2nd son [5] JAMES, 5th Earl; a Capt. R.N., and Lord Lieut. and Sheriff of Renfrewshire ; assumed, 1822, by Roy. licence the additional surname of *Carr*; *d.* 1869: *s.* by his half-brother [6] GEORGE FREDERICK, 6th Earl, *b.* 1825; M.P. for Buteshire (*C*) 1865, and subsequently Lord Clerk Register of Scotland: *m.* 1856, Montagu, who *d.* 1931, dau. of 3rd Baron Abercromby; *d.* 1890, when the Barony of Ross became extinct, and the Scottish Peerages devolved upon his cousin [7] DAVID, *G.C.M.G.* (son of Patrick Boyle, of Shewalton, co. Ayr, and el. great-grandson of the Hon. Patrick Boyle, 3rd son of 2nd Earl), 7th Earl, *b.* 1833 ; Capt. R.N. ; served in White Sea during Russian War 1854, and in China 1857 ; was Gov. of New Zealand 1892-7 ; *cr.* *Baron Fairlie*, of Fairlie, co. Ayr (peerage of United Kingdom) 1897: *m.* 1873, Dorothea Elizabeth Thomssina, who *d.* 1923, dau. of Sir Edward Hunter-Blair, 4th Bt. ; *d.* 1915; *s.* by his el. son [8] PATRICK JAMES, *DSO*, 8th Earl, *b.* 1874; Capt. R.N.; Convener of Ayr Co. Council 1947-58; *m.* 1906, Hyacinthe Mary, da. of the late William A. Bell, of Pendell Court, Bletchingley; *d.* 1963; *s.* by his el. son [9] DAVID WILLIAM MAURICE, 9th Earl, and present peer; also Viscount of Kelburn, Lord Boyle, and Baron Fairlie.

Glenapp, Viscount,   son of Earl of Incheape.

GLENARTHUR, BARON.   (Arthur.)   [Baron U.K. 1918, Bt. U.K. 1903.]

Do and hope.

MATTHEW ARTHUR, *O.B.E.*, 3rd Baron, and 3rd Baronet; *b.* May 12th, 1909; *s.* 1942, ed. at Winchester, and at Magdalen Coll.; Oxford; is a D.L. for Ayrshire; late Major and temporary Lieut.-Col. Roy. Scots Greys ; European War 1939-45 in Middle East and N.-W. Europe (despatches twice, M.B.E., O.B.E.); M.B.E. (Mil.) 1943, O.B.E. (Mil.) 1945 : *m.* 1st, 1931, Audrey (who obtained a divorce 1939), dau. of George Crompton Lees Milne [B. Glanusk, colls.]; 2ndly, 1939, Margaret Risk, only dau. of the late Capt. H. J. Howie, of Stairaird, Mauchline, Ayrshire, and has issue by 1st and 2nd marriages.

Arms,—Sable, an escarbuncle or, within an orle of besants.   Crest,—On a rock a pelican in her piety proper.   Supporters (as recorded at Lyon Office).—*Dexter*, a bay horse proper ; *sinister*, a lion rampant gules.

Residence,—Stairaird, Mauchline, Ayrshire.

SONS LIVING.   (*By 2nd marriage.*)

Hon. SIMON MARK (Burnham House, Upavon, Pewsey, Wilts.), *b.* Oct. 7th, 1944; ed. at Eton; Maj. The R. Hussars (PWO): *m.* 1969, Susan, da. of Cdr. Hubert Wyndham Barry, RN (ret.) [see Barry, Bt., colls.] and has issue living, Edward Alexander, *b.* 1973.

Hon. Matthew Richard, *b.* 1948; ed. at Eton: *m.* 1974, Veronica Rosemary, yr. da. of Michael Hall, of the Bridge, Kilternan, Co. Dublin.

DAUGHTERS LIVING.   (*By 1st marriage.*)

Hon. Prudence Armorel, *b.* 1932 : *m.* 1953, Major Edwin Rowland Winwood Robinson, and has issue living, Henry Claude Winwood, *b.* 1953,—Nicholas John Winwood, *b.* 1955,—Richard Edwin Winwood, *b.* 1958.   *Residence*,—Moor Wood, Cirencester, Gloucestershire.

(*By 2nd marriage.*)

Hon. Victoria, *b.* 1946.

SISTER LIVING.

Hon. Pamela Helen, b. 1908: m. 1st, 1927, Jack Drummond Rudd; 2ndly, 1944 (marriage dissolved 1951), Lieut.-Com. John Hamilton, R.N.; 3rdly, 1951, William Hamilton Robertson Aikman, of the Ross and Broomelton, and has issue living, (by 1st marriage) John William Glen, b. 1931,— Gillian Sara, b. 1929,—(by 2nd marriage) Sarah Sue Veronica b. 1946. Residence,—The Ross, Hamilton, Lanarkshire.

PREDECESSORS.—[1] Sir MATTHEW Arthur, LL.D., el. son of the late James Arthur, of Carlung, Ayrshire, and Barshaw, Renfrewshire, by Jane, dau. of Thomas Glen, of Thornhill, Renfrewshire; b. 1852; Chm. of Arthur and Co. (Limited), of Glasgow, and of Lochgelly Iron and Coal Co. (Limited), and a Member of Roy. Co. of Archers (King's Body Guard for Scotland); Chm. of Glasgow and S.-W. Railway Co. 1920-22; cr. a Baronet 1903, and Baron Glenarthur, of Carlung, Ayrshire (peerage of United Kingdom) 1918: m. 1879, Janet Stevenson Bennett, O.B.E., who d. 1946, younger dau. of the late Alexander Bennett McGrigor, LL.D., of Cairnoch, Stirlingshire; d. 1928; s. by his son [2] (JAMES) CECIL, 2nd Baron; b. 1883: m. 1907, Evelyn, who d. 1959, el. dau. of the late Henry March-Phillipps, of Tiverton, N. Devon; d. 1942; s. by his son [3] MATTHEW, 3rd Baron and present peer.

GLENAVY, BARON. (Campbell.) [Baron U.K. 1921, Bt. U.K. 1916.]

PATRICK GORDON CAMPBELL, 3rd Baron, and 3rd Baronet; b. June 6th, 1913; s. 1963; ed. at Rossall, and at Pembroke Coll., Oxford, late Irish Marine Force; a Sunday Times columnist, author, and television broadcaster: m. 1st, 1941 (m. diss. 1947), Sylvia, only da. of the late Capt. Kenneth Willoughby Lee, MC, of Muizenberg, S. Africa; 2ndly, 1947 (m. diss. 1966) Cherry Margaret, da. of Maj. George Lowson Monro, Indian Army; 3rdly, 1966, Vivienne, only da. of Charles Knight, MC, of Ipswich, widow of (1) Eric Drake, and formerly wife of (2) Hartley Sharpe, and (3) Charles Orme, and has issue living by 2nd m.

Moderation in all things.

Arms,—Gyronny of eight sable and erminois, on a pale gules a sword erect proper, pommel and hilt or. Crest,— A boar's head fessewise erased erminois. Supporters,— Dexter, a grey owl proper; sinister, a parrot vert, both beaked and membered or.
Residence,—La Tranche, Le Rouret, 06, France.

DAUGHTER LIVING. (By 2nd marriage.)
Hon. Brigid Margaret, b. 1948.

BROTHER LIVING.
Hon. MICHAEL MUSSEN, b. Oct. 25th, 1924; ed. at St. Columba's Coll., and at Trin. Coll., Dublin; Bar. King's Inn, Dublin. Residence,—39, Kendal St., W.2.

WIDOW LIVING OF SON OF FIRST BARON.
Martha Evelyn Audrey (COURTENAY) (Hon. Lady Campbell): m. 1934, as his second wife, the Hon. Sir Cecil James Henry Campbell, K.B.E., C.M.G., who d. 1952. Residence,—17, Sharia Kasr El Nil, Cairo, Egypt.

PREDECESSORS.—[1] Rt. Hon. JAMES HENRY MUSSEN Campbell, youngest son of the late William Mussen Campbell, of Prospect Terenure, co. Dublin; b. 1851; was Solicitor-Gen. for Ireland 1901-5, and Attorney-Gen. Dec. 1905, and 1916, Lord Ch. Justice of Ireland Nov. 1916 to June 1918, and Lord Chancellor of Ireland June 1918 to June 1921; M.P. for St. Stephen's Green Div. of Dublin (C) Jan. 1898 to Oct. 1900, and for Dublin Univ. March 1903 to Nov. 1916; Chm. Irish Free State Senate Dec. 1922 to Nov. 1928; cr. a Baronet 1916, and Baron Glenavy, of Milltown, co. Dublin (peerage of United Kingdom) 1921: m. 1884, Emily, who d. 1939, dau. of the late John MacCullagh, Resident Magistrate, of Newry, co. Down; d. 1931; s. by his son [2] CHARLES HENRY GORDON, 2nd Baron b. 1885; Sec. to Min. of Industry and Commerce, Irish Free State 1922-32: m. 1912, Beatrice Moss, who d. 1970, da. of William Elvery, of Rothbury, Foxrock, co. Dublin; d. 1963; s. by his el. son [3] PATRICK GORDON, 3rd Baron and present peer.

GLENCONNER, BARON (Tennant.) [Baron U.K. 1911, Bt. U.K. 1885.]

CHRISTOPHER GREY TENNANT, 2nd Baron, and 3rd Baronet; b. June 14th, 1899; s. 1920: m. 1st, 1925, Pamela Winefred (who obtained a divorce 1935), dau. of Sir Richard Arthur Surtees Paget, 2nd Bt. (cr. 1886); 2ndly, 1935, Elizabeth, da. of the late Lt.-Col. Evelyn George Harcourt Powell, Grenadier Guards, of 31, Hillgate Place, W8, and has issue by 1st and 2nd marriages.

Arms,—Argent, two crescents in fesse sable, on a chief gules a boar's head couped of the first; a bordure compony of the second and first. Crest,—A mast with a sail hoisted proper. Supporters,—Dexter, a stag proper, gorged with a mural crown or; sinister, a tiger also proper, gorged with a crown palissado also or; each charged on the shoulder with a thistle, eaved and slipped, gold.

God will fill the sails.

Residence,—Rovinia, Liapades, Corfu, Greece.

SONS LIVING. (By 1st marriage.)

Hon. COLIN CHRISTOPHER PAGET, b. Dec. 1st, 1926; ed. at Eton, and at New Coll., Oxford; formerly Lieut. Irish Guards: m. 1956, Lady Anne Veronica Coke, dau. of 5th Earl of Leicester, and has issue living, Charles Edward Pevensey, b. 1957,—Henry Lovell, b. 1960,—Christopher Cary, b. 1967,—Flora May Pamela, b. 1970,—Amy Jasmine Elizabeth (twin), b. 1970. Residences,—35, Tite St., SW3; The Glen, Innerleithen, Peebleshire. Club,—Bath.

Hon. James Grey Herbert, b. 1929; ed. at Eton, and at Trin. Coll., Camb.; formerly 2nd Lieut. Roy. Horse Guards: m. 1st, 1955, Emily Fawaz, from whom he obtained a divorce 1962, da. of George Licos; 2ndly, 1962, Mrs. Elizabeth Marya Romer, da. of James Dales, of W. Vancouver, and has issue living, (by 1st marriage), Alexander David Gabriel, b. 1957. Residence,—25, St. Leonards Terr., SW3. Clubs,—White's, St. James'.

(By 2nd marriage.)

Hon. Tobias William (Shaws, Newcastleton, Roxburghshire), b. 1941: m. 1963, Lady Emma Cavendish, el. da. of 11th Duke of Devonshire, and has issue living, Edward Tobias, b. 1967,—Isabel, b. 1964,—Stella, b. 1970.

DAUGHTERS LIVING. (By 2nd marriage.)

Hon. Emma Christina, b. 1937: m. 1st, 1957 (m. diss. 1962), Sebastian Yorke [see E. Hardwicke, colls.]; 2ndly, 1963 (m. diss. 19——), Christopher John Penrice Booker; 3rdly, 1968, (m. diss. 1973), Alexander Claud Cockburn [see Arbuthnot, Bt., colls., cr. 1823]

Hon. Catherine Elizabeth, b. 1947.

BROTHER LIVING.

Hon. Stephen James Napier, b. 1906. Residence,—Wilsford Manor, Salisbury.

AUNTS LIVING.

Dame Margaret, DBE (Margaret, Baroness Wakehurst), b. 1899; Hon. LL.D. Belfast; a GCStJ; DBE (Civil) 1965: m. 1920, the 2nd Baron Wakehurst, who d. 1970. Residence,—31, Lennox Gdns., SW1.

Dame Katharine, DBE (Baroness Elliot of Harwood), (17, Lord North St., SW1; Harwood, Bonchester Bridge, Hawick, Roxburghshire), b. 1903; cr. Baroness Elliot of Harwood (Life Peerage) 1958 [see that title].

WIDOW LIVING OF SON OF FIRST BARON.

Shelagh Anne (El Palomar, Mijas, Malaga, Spain), da. of Maj. Sean Rainey: m. 1963, as his 3rd wife, the Hon. David Francis Tennant, who d. 1968, and has issue living [see colls., infra].

COLLATERAL BRANCHES LIVING.

Issue of the late Hon. David Francis Tennant, 2nd son of 1st Baron, b. 1902, d. 1968: m. 1st, 1928 (m. diss. 1937), Hermione Youlanda Ruby Clinton, da. of Clinton Baddeley; 2ndly, 1938 (m. diss. 1953), Virginia Penelope, da. of the late Alan Parsons, of The Baas, Broxbourne, Herts.; 3rdly, 1963, Shelagh Anne (ante), da. of Maj. Sean Rainey:—

(By 1st m.) David Edward Wyndham (La Sirena, Mijas, Malaga, Spain. Clubs, White's and St. James'), b. 1930; ed. at Eton: m. 1964, Margaret Rachel, da. of the late Hon. Sir Ernest Stowell Scott, KCMG, MVO [see E. Eldon, colls.], and has issue living, Aubone Christopher, b. 1969,—a son, b. 1970,—Laura Hermione, b. 1967.——Pauline Laetitia, b. 1929: m. 1st, 1946 (m. diss. 1953), Capt. Julian Alfred Fox-Pitt-Rivers, late R. Dragoons [see By. Forster]; 2ndly, 1954, Euan Douglas Graham, [see D. Montrose, colls.].——(by 2nd m.) Annabel Skye, b. 1941.——Sabrina Viola, b. 1943: m. 1963, Jonathan Gathorne-Hardy [see E. Cranbrook].

(In remainder to Baronetcy only.)

Grandchildren of the late Francis John Tennant (infra).—

Issue of the late Group Capt. John Edward Tennant, D.S.O., M.C., R.A.F. Vol. Reserve, b. 1890, d. (on active ser. during European War) 1941: m. 1st, 1918, Georgina Helen (who obtained a divorce 1925), dau. of Gen. Sir George Macaulay Kirkpatrick, K.C.B., KCSI; 2ndly, 1926, Victoria Maud Veronica, MBE, who d. 1967, da. of Sir Robert (Robin) George Vivian Duff, 2nd Bt. (cr. 1911):—

(By 1st marriage) Iain Mark, b. 1919; ed. at Eton, and at Magdalene Coll., Camb.; late Capt. Scots Guards; a JP; Lord Lt. of Morayshire since 1964; a Member of Queen's Body Guard for Scotland (Roy. Co. of Archers); 1939-45 War: m. 1946, Lady Margaret Helen Isla Marion Ogilvy, da. of 12th Earl of Airlie, and has issue living, Mark Edward, b. 1947; Capt. Scots Gds.: m. 1971, Hermione Rosamond, da. of Lt.Col. Maurice W. Howe, and has issue living, Miranda Hermione b. 1974,—Christopher John, b. 1950; a Page of Honour to HM 1964-66,—Emma Margaret b. 1954. Residence,—Innes House, Elgin, Morayshire.——(By 2nd m.) Andrew Duff (13, Stanhope Gdns., SW7; White's and St. James' Clubs), b. 1928; late Scots Gds.; m. 1953 (m. diss. 1967), Lucinda Evelyn, only da. of Arthur Walter James [see B. Northbourne, colls.], and has issue living, Ann Charlotte, b. 1956.——Hugh Rinnes Duff (of 4, Lecky St., SW7), b. 1932; ed. at Eton; formerly Lt. Scots Gds.——Victoria Robina Duff, b. 1927: m. 1956, Alberto Zancan, of San Pedro Claver, 36, Barcelona, Spain, and has issue living, Michael, b. 1961,—Marina, b. 1958.——Laura Duff, b. 1935; a JP of Wilts: m. 1955, Reginald John Richard Arundell [see B. Talbot of Malahide, colls.]. Residence, Hook Manor, Donhead St. Andrew, nr. Shaftesbury, Wilts.

Issue of the late Francis John Tennant, 5th son of 1st baronet, b. 1861, d. 1942: m. 1886, Annie Geraldine, who d. 1956, da. of the late John Marriner Redmayne, JP, of Harewood, co. Durham:—

Kathleen (Dowager Duchess of Rutland), b. 1894; is a JP; bore the Queen's Canopy at Coronation of HM King George VI: m. 1916, the 8th Duke of Rutland, who d. 1940. Residence,—

Grandchildren of the late Rt. Hon. Harold John Tennant (infra):—

Issue of the late Maj. John Tennant, TD, b. 1899, d. 1967: m. 1st, 1929 (m. diss. 1939), the Hon. Antonia Mary Roby Benson, da. of 1st Baron Charnwood; 2ndly, 1948, Rosemary Irene (Budds Farm, Wittersham, Kent), da. of Sir Alfred Theodore Hennessy, KBE:—

(By 1st m.) Anthony John (Britwell Priors, Longparish, Hants), b. 1930; ed. at Eton, and Trin. Coll., Camb. (BA); late Lt. Scots Guards: m. 1954, Rosemary Violet, el. da. of Lt.-Cdr. Henry Charles Minshull Stockdale [see B. Faringdon], and has issue living, Christopher Sebastian, b. 1955,—Patrick Charles, b. 1958.——Mark Iain (30, Abbey Gdns., NW8; Balfluig Castle, by Alford, Aberdeenshire; Brooks's Club), b. 1932; ed. at Eton, and New Coll., Oxford (MA); Bar. Inner Temple 1958; Baron of Balfluig: m. 1965, Lady Harriot Pleydell-Bouverie, da. of 7th Earl of Radnor, and has issue living, Lysander Philip Roby, b. 1968.——Sophia Roby, b. 1967.——(by 2nd m.) Ivo Simon, b. 1955.——Aurea Mary Rose, b. 1949.

Issue of the late Archibald Tennant, b. 1907, d. 1955: m. 1947, Diana Primrose (GIBBS) (now of 12, Victoria Sq., SW1), da. of the late Percy Cuthbert Quilter [see Quilter, Bt., colls.]:—

Veronica Clare, b. 1950.——Pamela Mary Diana, b. 1953.

Issue of the late Rt. Hon. Harold John Tennant, 6th son of 1st baronet, b. 1865, d. 1935: m. 1st, 1889, Helen Elizabeth, who d. 1892, dau. of Major Gordon Duff, of Drummuir, Banffshire; 2ndly, 1896, May Edith, C.H., J.P., who d. 1946, dau. of the late George Whitley Abraham, of Rathgar, co. Dublin:—

(By 2nd m.) Peter, b. 1913; ed. at Eton, and at Trin .Coll., Camb. (BA 1934 , MA 1951): m. 1938, Valerie, da. of the late John S. Nettlefold, of The Manor House, Bampton, Oxfordshire, and has issue living, Alison Valerie, b. 1939: m. 1962, Roger Leon Burnley, of Braes of Greenock, Callander, Perthshire, and has issue living, Julian Lee b. 1969, Andrea Adwoa b. 1968.——Fiona, b. 1940: m. 1964, Neil Graham Douglas Snow, of Beechlawn, Whitbarrow Rd., Lymm, Cheshire, and has issue living, Justin Douglas Tennant b. 1965, Jonathan Peter b. 1968, Catriona Louisa b. 1967, Kirsten Fiona, b. 1970,—Shelia, b. 1946: m. 1970, Edward Findlay Burnett, of Hogwood, Ruskie, Thornhill by Stirling. Residence,—Invertrossachs, Callander, Perthshire.——Alison Margaret, OBE, b. 1903; late

Ch. Com. ATS, a Member of Westminster City Council 1949-59, and 1963-74, of London Co. Council 1955-58, and 1961-65, and of Inner London Exec. Council, Nat. Health Ser. since 1964; OBE (Civil) 1974. *Residence,*—1, Wilton St., SW1X 7AF.

PREDECESSORS.—[1] CHARLES Tennant, son of John Tennant, D.L., J.P., of St. Rollox, Lanark, a descendant of John Tennant of Blairston, Ayrshire (temp. 1635-1728), by his wife Jean McTaggart (temp. 1669-1723): *b.* 1823; M.P. for Glasgow (*L*) 1879-80, and for Peebles and Selkirkshire 1880-86; cr. a *Baronet* 1885: *m.* 1st, 1849, Emma, who *d.* 1895, dau. of Richard Winsloe; 2ndly, 1898, Marguerite Agaranthe, who *d.* 1943, having *m.* 1907, Major Geoffrey Lubbock, who *d.* 1932, dau. of the late Col. Charles Miles, of Burtonhill, Malmesbury; *d.* 1906; *s.* by his fourth son [2] EDWARD PRIAULX, 2nd Bt., *b.* 1859; Lord-Lieut. of Peeblesshire; M.P. for Salisbury (*L*) Jan. 1906 to Jan. 1910; Lord High Commr. to Gen. Assembly of Church of Scotland 1911, 1912, 1913, and 1914; cr. *Baron Glenconner*, of Glen, co. Peebles (peerage of United Kingdom) 1911: *m.* 1895, Pamela Geneviève Adelaide (who *d.* 1928, having *m.* 2ndly, 1922, the 1st Viscount Grey of Fallodon), dau. of the late Hon. Percy Scawen Wyndham; *d.* 1920; *s.* by his second son [3] CHRISTOPHER GREY, 2nd Baron and present peer.

GLENDEVON, BARON. (Hope.) [Baron U.K. 1964.]

My hope is not broken.

JOHN ADRIAN HOPE, *PC*, 1st Baron, 2nd (twin) son of the 2nd Marquess of Linlithgow; *b.* April 7th, 1912; ed. at Eton, and at Ch. Ch., Oxford (MA); Capt. and temporary Maj. Scots Guards (Reserve); Joint Parl. Under-Sec. of State for Foreign Affairs 1954-56, Parl. Under-Sec. of State for Commonwealth Relations 1956-57, Joint Parl. Under-Sec. for Scotland 1957-59, and Min. of Works 1959-62; 1939-45 War in Norway and Italy (despatches): MP for N. Div. of Midlothian and Peebles (*C*) 1945-50, and for Pentlands Div. of Edinburgh 1950-64; cr. PC 1959, and *Baron Glendevon*, of Midhope, co. Linlithgow (peerage of UK) 1964: *m.* 1948, Elizabeth (PARAVICINI), da. of the late William Somerset Maugham, CH, and has issue.

Arms,—Azure, on a chevron or between three bezants as many bay-leaves paleways vert. Crest—A broken sphere surmounted of a rainbow proper issuant from two bay-leaves slipped vert on either side of the sphere. Supporters,—Two female figures denoting Hope, their hair dressed sable and braided vert, garnished or, richly vested Argent garnished of vert, and sustaining bendways in their exterior hands light lifeboat anchors with long shafts azure garnished with chains or, and over their exterior shoulders garlands of white lilies proper.
Residence,—Durham House, Durham Place, SW3.

SONS LIVING.

Hon. JULIAN JOHN SOMERSET, *b.* March 6th, 1950; ed. at Eton and Ch. Ch., Oxford.
Hon. Jonathan Charles, *b.* 1952; ed. at Eton and Ch. Ch., Oxford.

GLENDYNE, BARON. (Nivison.) [Baron U.K. 1922, Bt. U.K. 1914.]

The end proves actions.

ROBERT NIVISON, 3rd Baron, and 3rd Baronet; *b.* Oct. 27th, 1926; *s.* 1967; ed. at Harrow; late Lt. Grenadier Guards; Senior Partner in the firm of R. Nivison & Co., of 25, Austin Friars, EC2; 1939-45 War: *m.* 1953, Elizabeth, yr. da. of the late Sir Stephen Cecil Armitage, CBE, of Hawksworth Manor, Notts., and has issue.

Arms,—Per chevron or and azure, in chief two eagles displayed of the second and in base an eagle rising of the first. Crest,—Upon the battlements of a tower a wolf passant sable, gorged with a collar and with line reflexed over the back or. Supporters,—On either side a wolf sable, gorged with a collar with line reflexed over the back or, and charged on the shoulder with a saltire couped argent.

Residence,—Red Court, Haslemere, Surrey. *Club,*—RAC.

SON LIVING.
Hon. JOHN, *b.* Aug. 13th, 1960.

DAUGHTERS LIVING.
Hon. Linda, *b.* 1954.
Hon. Sarah Jane Moira, *b.* 1957.

SISTERS LIVING.
Hon. Moira Jane, *b.* 1921.
Hon. Pamela Roxane, *b.* 1923: *m.* 1955, Maj.-Gen. David John St. Maur Tabor, MC, late Roy. Horse Guards, and has issue living, Patrick John, *b.* 1957,—Andrew James, *b.* 1959. *Residence,*—Upton Manor, near Andover, Hants.
Hon. Gillian Wightman, *b.* 1931: *m.* 1953, Maj.-Gen. Peter Raymond Leuchars, CBE, late Welsh Guards, and has issue living, Christopher John Raymond, *b.* 1956. *Residence,*—5, Chelsea Sq., SW3.

DAUGHTERS LIVING OF FIRST BARON.
Hon. Alice Jane. *Residence,*—5, Frognal Way, Hampstead, NW3.
Hon. Mabel Gertrude: *m.* 1916, Arthur Ryder Bastard Owen, from whom she obtained a divorce
1936. *Residence,*—White Lodge, Les Merriennes, St. Martin, Guernsey.

PREDECESSORS.—[1] ROBERT Nivison, son of John Nivison, of Sanquhar, Dumfriesshire;
b. 1849; senior partner of R. Nivison and Co.; cr. a *Baronet* 1914, and *Baron Glendyne,* of
Sanquhar, co. Dumfries (peerage of United Kingdom) 1922: *m.* 1877, Jane, who *d.* 1918, dau.
of John Wightman, of Sanquhar, Dumfriesshire; *d.* 1930; *s.* by his son [2] JOHN, 2nd Baron, *b.*
1878; senior partner of R. Nivison & Co.: *m.* 1920, Ivy May, who *d.* 1971, da. of the late J. Rose, of
Bournemouth; *d.* 1967; *s.* by his son [3] ROBERT, 3rd Baron, and present peer.

GLENKINGLAS, BARON. (Noble.) [Life Baron 1974.]

MICHAEL ANTONY CRISTOBAL NOBLE, *PC,*
yst. son of Sir John Henry Brunel Noble, 1st
Bt. (cr. 1923); *b.* March 19th, 1913; ed. at
Eton, and Magdalen Coll., Oxford; 1939-45
War as Sqdn. Ldr. RAFVR; MP for Argyll
(*C*) 1958-74; Govt. Scottish Whip 1960-62,
Sec. of State for Scotland 1962-64, Pres. of
Board of Trade June to Oct. 1970, and Min.
for Trade 1970-72; Chm. of Assoc. Fisheries
Ltd. 1966-70; Chm. of British Agric. Export
Council since 1973; cr. PC 1962, and *Baron
Glenkinglas,* of Cairndow, co. Argyll (Life
Baron) 1974: *m.* 1940, Anne, da. of Sir
Neville Arthur Pearson, 2nd Bt., (cr. 1916),
and has issue.

Arms,—not exemplified at time of going to press.

Residence,—Strone, Cairndow, Argyll.

DAUGHTERS LIVING.
Hon. Catharine Gina Amita, *b.* 1943: *m.* 1964, Peter Conrad Hamilton Vey, of Godsfield Manor,
Alresford, Hants., and has issue living, Rupert Michael Christopher, *b.* 1971,—Tessa Atlanta Louise,
b. 1969.
Hon. Marya Anne, *b.* 1944: *m.* 1969, Peter Egerton-Warburton, of Mulberry House, Bentworth,
Hants. [see Grey-Egerton, Bt., colls.].
Hon. Anastasia Diana, *b.* 1948: *m.* 1967, Jonathan Sinclair Delap, of Little Armsworth, Alresford,
Hants., and has issue living, James Robert Onslow, *b.* 1969,—Michael Jonathan Sinclair, *b.* 1972.
Hon. Rebecca Juliet, *b.* 1950: *m.* 1973, John Richard Boyle, Lt. RN, of Hawthorn Cottage, Newtown,
Fareham, Hants. [see E. Cork and Orrery].

Glenlivet, see Lord Strathavon and Glenlivet.

GLENTANAR, BARONY. (Coats.) [Extinct 1971.]

DAUGHTER LIVING OF SECOND BARON.
Hon. (Margaret) Jean Dagbjørt, *b.* 1928: *m.* 1950 (m. diss. 1974), the Hon. James Michael Edward
Bruce [see E. Elgin and Kincardine]. ffi*Residences,*—Glen Tanar House, Aboyne, Aberdeenshire,
Flat 15, 35, Bryanston Sq., W1.

GLENTORAN, BARON (Dixon.) [Baron U.K. 1939, Bt. U.K. 1903.]

DANIEL STEWART THOMAS BING-
HAM DIXON, *KBE,* 2nd Baron and
4th Baronet; *b.* Jan. 19th, 1912;
s. 1950; ed. at Eton; Lt.-Col. (ret.)
Gren. Gds., and Hon. Col. 6th Bn.
RUR (TA) 1957-62; Lieut. City of
Belfast since 1950; 1939-45 War
(despatches); CSt.J; Member of
House of Commons, N.I. (*U*) 1950-
61; Parl. Sec., Min. of Commerce,
N.I., 1952-53, and Min. of Commerce
1953-61; Min. in Senate 1961-72
(Speaker of Senate 1964-72); PC
(N.I.) 1953, KBE (Civil) 1973: *m.*
1933, Lady Diana Mary Wellesley,
da. of 3rd Earl Cowley. and has
issue.

Arms,—Or, on a chevron vair three
billets of the first, on a chief crenellé gules a
tower proper between two fleurs-de-lis or.
Crest,—A demi-lion rampant azure, charged
on the shoulder with a cross patonce surrounded by a civic crown or. *Supporters,*—
Two war horses argent, unguled or, caparisoned proper, the shabraque sable, broidered of the second.

By fidelity and constancy.

Residence,—Drumadarragh House, Doagh, co. Antrim. *Club,*—Ulster.

SONS LIVING.

Hon. THOMAS ROBIN VALERIAN, *MBE, b.* April 21st, 1935; ed. at Eton; is Maj. Grenadier Guards; MBE (Civil) 1969: *m.* 1959, Rona Alice Gabrielle, da. of Capt. George Cecil Colville, CBE, RN [see V. Colville of Culross, colls.], and has issue living, Daniel George, *b.* 1959,—Andrew, Wynn Valerian, *b.* 1961,—Patrick Anthony, *b.* 1963. *Residence,*—Drumadarragh House, Doagh, co. Antrim
Hon. Peter Herbert, *b.* 1948: *m.* 1975, Jane Blanch, da. of Eric S. Cutler, of Grayshott Hall Farm, Grayshott, Hants.

DAUGHTER LIVING.

Hon. Clare Rosalind, *b.* 1937: *m.* 1965, Rudolph Ion Joseph Agnew, of 29, Queensdale Rd., W11 [see Campbell, Bt., colls., cr. 1815].

SISTERS LIVING.

Hon. Angela Ierne Evelyn, *b.* 1907 : *m.* 1st, 1929, Lieut.-Com. (E.) Peter Ross, R.N., who *d.* (killed in action during European War) 1940 [see Bs. de Ros] ; 2ndly, 1943, Lieut.-Col. Trevor L. Horn, 16th/5th Lancers, who *d.* 1966, and has issue living, (by 1st marriage) [see Bs. de Ros],—(by 2nd marriage) June Victoria Langdale, *b.* 1946. *Residence,*—Luckington Court, Chippenham, Wilts.

Hon. Patricia Clare, *b.* 1919 : *m.* 1940, Lieut.-Com. Adam McLeod Mackinnon, R.N., Fleet Air Arm, and has issue living, Michael Bingham, *b.* 1941,—Ian Dixon, *b.* 1944,—Diana Patricia, *b.* 1950, —Teresa Claire, *b.* 1955,—Zara Lavinia, *b.* 1959. *Residence,*—The Cottage Inn, Maidens Green, Winkfield, Windsor, Berks.

PREDECESSORS.—[1] *Rt. Hon.* DANIEL Dixon, *M.P.,* son of the late Thomas Dixon, of Larne, co. Antrim, *b.* 1844 ; was High Sheriff of co. Down 1896, M.P. for N. Belfast (C) 1905-07, Mayor of Belfast 1892, and Lord Mayor 1893, 1901-3, 1905-6, and 1906-7 ; cr. a *Baronet* 1903 : *m.* 1st, 1867, Lizzie, who *d.* 1868, dau. of the late James Agnew, of Belfast ; 2ndly, 1870, Annie, who *d.* 1918, dau. of James Shaw, of Belfast ; *d.* 1907, *s.* by his el. son [2] *Sir* THOMAS JAMES, 2nd Bt., *b.* 1868 ; High Sheriff co. Antrim 1912, and of co. Down 1913, H.M.'s Lieut. for Co. of City of Belfast, and a Member of Senate of N. Ireland 1924-50 : *m.* 1906, *Dame* Edith Stewart, *D.B.E.,* dau. of the late Stewart Clark, of Dundas Castle, Linlithgowshire ; *d.* (May) 1950 ; *s.* by his brother [3] *Rt. Hon.* HERBERT, *P.C., O.B.E.,* 3rd Bt. ; *b.* 1880 ; High Sheriff of co. Kildare 1916 ; Capt. 6th Inniskilling Dragoons ; S. Africa 1899-1902, European War 1914-19 with Remounts ; Ch. Whip of Unionist Party in Parliament of N. Ireland, and Parliamentary Sec. to Min. of Finance 1921-42, and Min. of Agriculture 1942-3 ; sat as M.P. for Pottinger Div. of Belfast (U) 1918 to 1922, and for Belfast, E. Div. 1922 to 1930 ; also elected for Belfast, E. Div. in Parliament of N. Ireland 1921 and 1925, and for Bloomfield Div. of Belfast 1929, 1945 and 1949 ; cr. *Baron Glentoran,* of Ballyalloly, co. Down (peerage of United Kingdom) 1939 : *m.* 1905, the Hon. Emily Ina Florence Bingham, who *d.* 1957, dau. of 5th Baron Clanmorris, *d.* (July) 1950 ; *s.* by his son [4] DANIEL STEWART THOMAS BINGHAM, 2nd Baron and present peer ; also 4th baronet.

Glentworth, Viscount, son of Earl of Limerick.

Glerawly, Viscount, son of Earl Annesley.

GLOUCESTER, DUKE OF, see Royal Family.

GLOUCESTER, LORD BISHOP OF. [Yates]

Rt. Rev. JOHN YATES, son of the late Frank Yates, of Burslem, *b.* April 17th, 1925; ed. at Battersea and Blackpool Gram. Schs., Jesus Coll., Camb. (MA), and Lincoln Theological Coll.; with RAFVR 1943-47; Princ., Lichfield Theological Coll.; 1966-72; consecrated Bishop of Whitby (Suffragan for Diocese of York) 1972; translated as 37th Bishop of Gloucester 1975: *m.* 1954, Jean Kathleen, da. of William Dover, of London.

Patron of eighty livings, and the Archdeaconries of Gloucester and Cheltenham.

The See of Gloucester (formerly part of the diocese of Worcester), is one of the six Bishoprics created by Henry VIII. in 1541: that of Bristol is another. The two Bishoprics were united in 1836 and separated 1897.

Episcopal Signature,——John Gloucester.

ARMS OF THE SEE,— Azure, two keys endorsed in saltire, the wards upwards or.

Residence,—Palace House, Pitt Street, Gloucester.

GODBER, BARON. (Godber.) [Baron U.K. 1956.]

Strength from Faith

FREDERICK GODBER, 1st Baron, son of Edward Godber; *b.* Nov. 6th, 1888; Hon. Bencher Middle Temple 1954; Chm. of Commonwealth Development Finance Co., Ltd., 1953-68 ; a Trustee of Churchill Coll. Trust Fund, Camb. ; was a Managing Director of Roy. Dutch/Shell Group 1929-46, Chm. of Shell Union Oil Corporation 1937-46, Chm. and Managing Director of Shell Transport and Trading Co., Ltd. 1946-61, and Chm. of Shell Petroleum Co., Ltd. 1946-61 ; during 1939-45 War was Chm. of Overseas Supply Cttee. of Petroleum Board, and a Dir. of Petroleum Board; Hon. Livery-man, Leathersellers' Co.; Hon. Fellow of Inst. of Petroleum; a Grand Officer of Order of Orange Nassau of the Nether-lands; cr. Knt. 1942, *Baron Godber*, of Mayfield, co. Sussex (peerage of U.K.) 1956 : *m.* 1914, Violet Ethel Beatrice, dau. of George Lovesy, of Cheltenham, and has issue.

𝔄rms,—Per chevron argent and gules in chief five martlets two one and two of the last, in base a slip of white may flowered and leaved proper. 𝔠rest,—Between two sprigs of pink may flowered and leaved proper a crane's head and neck erasedor. 𝔖upporters,—On either side a crane or, gorged with a collar gemel gules.

Residence,—Cranesden, Mayfield, Sussex.

DAUGHTERS LIVING.

Hon. Joyce Violet, *b.* 1917: *m.* 1938, Andrew Agnew, and has issue living, Heather Elizabeth, *b.* 1940: *m.* 1966, Dr. Charles John Roderick Lewis, of Old Rectory, Bodiam, Robertsbridge, Sussex, and has issue living, Henry Roderick Andrew *b.* 1968, Richard John *b.* 1972,—Susan Joyce, *b.* 1942: *m.* 1966, David Gwynder Lewis, of 38, Stanford Rd., W8, and has issue living, George David Gwynder *b.* 1972, Alexandra Joy Gwynder *b.* 1969,—Sally Caroline, *b.* 1949. *Residences,*—Sweethaws Farm, Crow-borough, Sussex; Garheugh, Port William, Wigtownshire.
Hon. Daphne Joan, *b.* 1923: *m.* 1942, Archibald Ian Scott Debenham, DFC, and has issue living, Michael George Scott (Homefield, Tandridge Lane, Lingfield, Surrey), *b.* 1943: *m.* 1966, Janine Elizabeth, da. of A. L. Davies, of Railings, Limpsfield, Surrey, and has issue living, Sarah Elizabeth *b.* 1968, Anna Caroline *b.* 1969, Tessa Kate *b.* 1971,—Peter Frederick Scott, *b.* 1957,—Jane Scott *b.* 1945: *m.* 1966, Hamish John Benson Skinner, of Orchards, Merle Common, Oxted, Surrey, and has issue living, Paul Andrew *b.* 1968, Hugh Antony *b.* 1972, Lucy Jane *b.* 1969,—Marye Scott, *b.* 1954. *Residence,*—Pollards Hill, Limpsfield, Surrey, RH8 0QX.

GODDARD, BARONY OF. (Goddard.) [Extinct 1971.]

DAUGHTERS LIVING OF LIFE BARON.

Hon. Pamela Mary Violet, *b.* 1907 ; is a J.P. for Wilts : *m.* 1934, James Burdett Maurice, M.R.C.S., LRCP, and has issue. *Residence,*—Batt's Farm, Wilton, Marlborough, Wilts.
Hon. Janet Margaret (*Hon. Lady Sachs*), *b.* 1909: *m.* 1934, the Rt. Hon. Sir Eric Sachs, MBE, and has issue. *Residence,*—Walland Oast, Wadhurst, Sussex.
Hon. Ruth Evelyn, *b.* 1912; is a JP for Berks: *m.* 1937, Archibald Sands Clayton, a former Member of London Stock Exchange, and has issue. *Residence,*—Lane House, Bracknell, Berks.

GOODMAN, BARON. (Goodman.) [Life Baron 1965.]

To understand all is to pardon all

ARNOLD ABRAHAM GOODMAN, *CH*, son of Joseph Goodman, *b.* Aug. 21st, 1913; ed. at Cambridge Univ. (MA, LLB); Fellow of Univ. Coll., London; Solicitor 1936; Senior Partner, Messrs. Goodman, Derrick & Co., 30, Bouverie St., EC4; Chm. of Arts Council of Gt. Britain 1965-72; Chm. of Council of Newspaper Publishers Assocn. since 1970; Master (designate) of Univ. Coll., Oxford 1976, and of Housing Corpn. and National Building Agency since 1973, and Vice-Chm. British Council since 1974; 1939-45 War as Maj.; *cr. Baron Goodman*, of City of West-minster (Life Peerage) 1965, and CH 1972.

𝔄rms,—Azure a chevron wavy argent between in chief two lyres and in base a torch or enflamed proper. 𝔠rest,—On a cap of maintenance gules turned up ermine two hands couped at the wrists and clasped proper. 𝔖upporters,—*Dexter*, a carrier pigeon, and *sinister* a seagull proper, about the neck of each a chain suspended thereforom a lyre or.

Addresses,—University College, Oxford; Goodman Derrick & Co., 4, Little Essex St., Strand, WC2R 3LD.

Gordon, Duke of, see Duke of Richmond and Gordon.

GORDON-WALKER, RARON. (Gordon Walker.) [Life Baron 1974.]

PATRICK CHRESTIEN GORDON WALKER, *CH, PC,* son of the late Alan Lachlan Gordon Walker, of Supreme Court, Lahore; *b.* April 7th, 1907; ed. at Wellington Coll., and Ch. Ch. Oxford (B.Litt., MA); Organiser of Broadcasts, European Ser. of BBC 1940-44, Ch. Editor, Radio Luxembourg 1944, Assist. German Ser. Dir. BBC 1945; PPS to Lord Pres. of the Council 1946-47, Parl. Under-Sec. of State Commonwealth Relations Office 1950-51, Sec. of State for Foreign Affairs 1964-65, UK Delegate to Council of Europe (Leader of UK Delegation) 1966, Min. without Portfolio 1967, and Sec. of State for Education and Science 1967-68; MP for Smethwick (*Lab.*) 1945-64 and for Leyton 1966-74; Member of European Parl., Swasbourg since 1975; cr. PC 1950, CH 1968, and *Baron Gordon-Walker,* of Leyton in Greater London (Life Baron) 1974: *m.* 1935, Audrey Muriel, da. of Norman Andrew Rudolf, of Hopewell, Jamaica, and has issue.

Arms,—not exemplified at time of going to press.

Residence.—Flat 105/106, Frobisher House, Dolphin Sq., Westminster, SW1V 3LL.

SONS LIVING.

Hon. Alan Rudolf (27, Elgin Cres., W11), *b.* 1946.
Hon. Robin Chrestien (49, Tulsemere Rd., SE27), (twin), *b.* 1946: *m.* 1974, June Patricia, da. of Patrick Barr, of Eversholt, Beds.

DAUGHTERS LIVING.

Hon. Judith Margaret, *b.* 1936; ed. at N. London Collegiate Sch., Lady Margaret Hsll, Oxford (MA), and Univ. Coll., London, (BA, PhD); Lecturer in Psychology, Birkbeck Coll., Univ. of London, since 1966: *m.* 1957, Graham Carleton Greene, of 11, Leverton St., NW5.
Hon. Caroline, *b.* 1937: *m.* 1960, David Brierley, of Old Farm, Harthall Lane, King's Langley, Herts.
Hon. Ann Marguerite, *b.* 1944; ed. at N. London Collegiate Sch., Queen's Coll., Dundee, Univ. of St. Andrews (BSc), and Oxford Univ. (D. Phil): *m.* 1968, Laurence Andrew Ball, of 65, Northwood Rd., Storrs, Conn. 06268, USA.

GORE-BOOTH, BARON. (Gore-Booth.) [Life Baron 1969.]

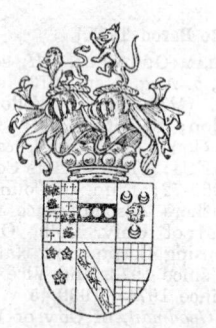

PAUL HENRY GORE-BOOTH, *GCMG, KCVO,* el. son of the late Mordaunt Gore-Booth [see Gore-Booth, Bt., colls.]; *b.* Feb. 3rd, 1909; ed. at Eton, and Balliol Coll., Oxford (MA); Head of European Recovery Dept., Foreign Office 1948-49, Dir. of British Information Sers. in USA 1949-53, Ambassador to Burma 1953-56, Dep. Under Sec. of State for Economic Affairs, Foreign Office 1956-60, British High Commr. in India 1960-65, Perm. Under-Sec. at Foreign Office 1965-68, and Head of Diplo. Ser. 1968-69; Chm. Windsor Music Festival 1971-73; Registrar of Order of St. Michael and St. George, Chm. of Save The Children Fund, a Dir. of Nat. & Grindlays Bank Ltd., and United Kingdom Provident Inst. since 1969; cr. CMG 1949, KCMG 1957, KCVO 1961, GCMG 1965, and *Baron Gore-Booth,* of Maltby, W. Riding, co. York (Life Baron) 1969: *m.* 1940, Patricia Mary, da. of the late Montague Ellerton, and has issue.

Arms—Quarterly of six: 1st quarterly, 1st and 4th, argent three boars heads couped and erect sable; 2nd and 3rd, gules, a fesse between three cross-crosslets or; 2nd, argent, on a fesse sable three bezants; 3rd, argent a lion's head erased between three crescents gules; 4th, gules three cinquefoils argent; 5th, gules on a bend or, three martlets; 6th, checky azure and argent a fesse gules-Crest,—1st, a lion passant, *Booth;* 2nd, a wolf rampant, *Gore.* **Mottoes—over First Crest,—**" Quod ero spero " (*I hope for what I shall be*); **over Second Crest,—**" In hoc signo vinces " (*Under this sign hou shalt conquer*).

Residence,—70 ,Ashley Gdns., SW1P 1QG. *Club,*—Athenaeum.

SONS LIVING.

Hon. David Alwyn (c/o FCO, SW1), *b.* 1943; ed. at Eton, and Ch. Ch., Oxford (MA): *m.* 1964, (m. diss. 1970), Jillian Sarah, yr. da. of James Wyatt Valpy, of 116, Cranmer Court, SW3, and has issue living, James Alwyn Colum, *b.* 1966,—Paul Wyatt Julian, *b.* 1968.
Hon. Christopher Hugh (twin), *b.* 1943; ed. at Eton, and Durham Univ.

DAUGHTERS LIVING.

Hon. Celia Mary, *b.* 1946; ed. at Downe House, and London Acad. of Music and Dramatic Act.
Hon. Joanna Rosamond Georgina, *b.* 1954; ed. at Sherborne Sch., and New Hall, Camb. (BA).

GORELL, BARON. (Barnes.) [Baron U.K. 1909.]

You may break, you shall not bend me.

TIMOTHY JOHN RADCLIFFE BARNES, 4th Baron; *b.* Aug. 2nd, 1927; *s.* 1963; ed. at Eton, and at New Coll., Oxford, Bar. Inner Temple 1951, formerly Lieut. Rifle Bde.; an Exec., Royal Dutch and Shell Group since 1959: *m.* 1954, Joan Marion, yr. da. of John Collins, of Moseley, Birmingham.

Arms.—Azure, two lions passant guardant ermine each holding in the dexter paw a sprig of oak slipped or, between three annulets in pale argent. Crest,— In front of a cubit arm in armour, the hand grasping a broken sword all proper, the wrist encircled by a wreath of oak or, five annulets interlaced and fesseways argent. Supporters.—On either side, a ram proper charged on the shoulder with two annulets interlaced azure.

Residence,—4, Roehampton Gate, SW15.

BROTHER LIVING.

Hon. RONALD ALEXANDER HENRY, *b.* June 28th, 1931; ed. at Harrow, and at New Coll., Oxford; formerly Lieut. Roy. Fusiliers, seconded King's African Rifles: *m.* 1957, Gillian Picton, youngest dau. of the late Picton Hughes-Jones, of Henstridge, Somerset, and has issue living, John Picton Gorell, *b.* 1959,—Elizabeth Gail, *b.* 1961. *Residence,*—Low Barn, Ponjeravah, Constantine, Falmouth, Cornwall.

SISTER LIVING.

Hon. Rosemary Eva Gorell, *b.* 1925; ed. at Bedford Coll., London: *m.* 1960, Peter Douglas Gill, and has issue living, Nicholas Charles Ronald, *b.* 1966,—Katherine Elizabeth Louise, *b.* 1962,— Henrietta Patricia Mary, *b.* 1964. *Residence,*—St. Anne's House, Nun Monkton, York, YO5 8ER.

PREDECESSORS.—[1] *Rt. Hon.* Sir JOHN GORELL Barnes, P.C. (Knt.), el. son of the late Henry Barnes, of Liverpool; *b.* 1848 ; a Judge of the Probate, Divorce, and Admiralty Div. of the High Court of Justice 1892-1905, and Pres. thereof 1905-9 ; cr. *Baron Gorell,* of Brampton, co. Derby (peerage of United Kingdom) 1909: *m.* 1881, Mary Humpston, who *d.* 1918, dau. of the late Thomas Mitchell, of West Arthurlie; *d.* 1913 ; *s.* by his el. son [2] HENRY GORELL, D.S.O., 2nd Baron; *b.* 1882; Major R.F.A. (T.F.); *d.* (killed in action during European War) 1917; *s.* by his brother [3] RONALD GORELL, C.B.E., M.C., 3rd Baron; *b.* 1884; Under-Sec. of State for Air and Vice-Pres. of Air Council 1921-2, Editor of *Cornhill Magazine* 1933-9; Chm. of Prime Min.'s Cttees. on Carlton House Terr. 1933-40, and on Regents Park Terr. 1946-7: *m.* 1922, Maud Elizabeth Furse, who *d.* 1954, dau. of the late Alexander Nelson Radcliffe, of 45, Kensington Sq., W.8; *d.* 1963; *s.* by his el. son [4] TIMOTHY JOHN RADCLIFFE, 4th Baron and present peer.

Gormanston, Baron, title of Viscount Gormanston on Roll of H. L.

GORMANSTON, VISCOUNT. (Preston.) [Viscount I. 1478, Baron I. 1365-70. Sits as Baron (U.K. 1868).

Without stain.

JENICO NICHOLAS DUDLEY PRESTON, 17th Viscount, and Premier Viscount of Ireland; *b.* Nov. 19th, 1939; *s.* 1940: *m.* 1974, Eva Antonie, and has issue.

Arms.—Or, on a chief sable, three crescents of the first. Crest.—On a chapeau gules turned up ermine, a fox passant proper. Supporters,—*Dexter,* a fox proper; *sinister,* a lion rampant proper, armed and langued gules.

Residence,—70, Waterloo Rd., Ballsbridge, Dublin.

SON LIVING.

Hon. JENICO FRANCIS TARA, *b.* April 30th, 1974.

UNCLE LIVING. (*Son of 15th Viscount.*)

Hon. Robert Francis Hubert, *b.* 1915; ed. at Downside; formerly Capt. 11th Hussars; 1939-45 War (wounded); assumed by deed poll 1947 the additional surname of Shaw which he subsequently relinquished: *m.* 1st, 1941, Jean Helen (who obtained a divorce 1955), only child of the late Capt. Charles Henry Shaw, 15th Hussars; 2ndly, 1970, Daphne Helen Anne, da. of the late Col. Robert Hanbury Brudenell-Bruce, DSO [see M. Ailesbury, colls.], and formerly wife of [1] the late Lt.-Cdr. Reginald Hughes-Onslow, RN [see E. Onslow, colls.], and [2] Maj. John Edward Montague Bradish-Ellames, and has issue living (by 1st m.), Jennifer Anne SHAW PRESTON, *b.* 1946. *Residence,*—Bosworth House, Arthingworth, Market Harborough, Leicestershire. *Club,*—Cavalry.

AUNT LIVING. (*Daughter of 15th Viscount.*)

Hon. Eileen Antoinette Mary, *b.* 1912: *m.* 1939, Peter Northcote Lunn, CMG, OBE, of 60, Lebanon Park, Twickenham, Middlesex [E. Iddesleigh], and has issue living, David Christopher John, *b.* 1940; DPhil.: *m.* 1973, Rosemary, da. of R. W. Holmes of 227, Glenfield Rd., Western Park, Leicester,—Stephen Hugh, *b.* 1951,—Bernard Patrick William, *b.* 1954,—Mary, *b.* 1941: *m.* 1965, Dieter Welfonder, of Düsseldorf,—Brigid, *b.* 1944: *m.* 1972, Christopher C. R. Battiscombe,— Elizabeth Catherine Bernadette, *b.* 1948: *m.* 1971, Paul Mostyn [see Mostyn, Bt.].

COLLATERAL BRANCHES LIVING.

Issue of the late Lt.-Col. the Hon. Richard Martin Peter Preston, DSO, 2nd son of 14th Viscount, *b.* 1884, *d.* 1965: *m.* 1st, 1908, Belle, who *d.* 1936, da. of the late Frederick Harcourt Hamblin; 2ndly, 1943, Edith Sheilah, who *d.* 1951, da. of the late Reginald de Crecy Steel, of Walton-on-Thames, and widow of Lt.-Cdr. John Hay Forbes, DSO, RN [see Stuart-Forbes, Bt. colls.]:—

(By 1st m.) Christopher Edward Martin, *DSC* (of Marston House, Priors Marston, Rugby), *b.* 1918; Lt.-Com. RN (ret.): *m.* 1949, Joy Celeste Agata, da. of the late Maj. Hugh Davidson, and has issue living, Philip Martin Jenico, *b.* 1950,—Stephen Richard Hugh, *b.* 1952,—Matthew Christopher Edward, *b.* 1955,—Anthony Thomas Patrick, *b.* 1964,—Camilla Mary Lucy, *b.* 1959.——Ismay Elizabeth, *b.* 1912: *m.* 1942, Denzil Robert Clarke, of Puffins, 8, South Drive, Wokingham, Berks, and has issue living, Michael Richard Neil, *b.* 1946: *m.* 1973, Francine Van Schepdael, and has issue living, Geraldine Anne Danielle *b.* 1973,—Jennifer Roberta Anne, *b.* 1944: *m.* 1968, Simon Anthony Aldridge, of Old Bell Cottage, Langley Upper Green, Saffron Walden, and has issue living, Victoria Helmore Elizabeth *b.* 1969,—Francesca Elizabeth Anne, *b.* 1951.——Diana Mary Bruce (Old Sun House, Riseley, Berks.), *b.* 1914: *m.* 1939, John Francis Colledge, who *d.* 1954, and has issue living, Simon John (The Well Cottage, Mattingley, Basingstoke), *b.* 1940: *m.* 1966, Robina Elizabeth Anne, da. of H. L. Light, of The Grange, Waltham St. Lawrence, Berks, and has issue living, Timothy Andrew John *b.* 1967, Patrick Richard *b.* 1968, Henry Charles Valentine *b.* 1972,—Robert Patrick Francis, *b.* 1950: *m.* 1974, Dena, da. of D. Jones, of Southport, Lancs.,—Sarah Virginia Mary, *b.* 1942,—Judith Cecilia Anne, *b.* 1953: *m.* 1974, James Calderbank.——Ursula Anne Marie, *b.* 1923: *m.* 1952, Cdr. Charles Sheridan Moseley, RN, of Tigh Caldadh, Rosturk, Westport, co. Mayo, and has issue living, Dominic Richard Sheridan, *b.* 1955,—Christopher John Wallace, *b.* 1957,—Justin Robert Patrick, *b.* 1962,—Virginia Clare Diana, *b.* 1954,—Lucy Elizabeth Anne, *b.* 1960.

Issue of the late Capt. the Hon. Hubert Anthony John Preston, M.C., 3rd son of 14th Viscount, *b.* 1885, *d.* 1940: *m.* (Jan.) 1917, Mary, who *d.* 1971, da. of the late Rt. Hon. William Kenny, a Judge of High Court in Ireland, and widow of R. S. Pringle, Queen's Regt.:—

Penelope Sybil Mary, *b.* (Oct.) 1917. *Residence*,—60, Morehampton Rd., Dublin, 4.——Georgina Ismay Mary, *b.* 1919: *m.* 1948, Alfred Stanley Head. *Residence*,—3, Hawthorn Drive, Willowbank, Denham, Bucks.

Grandchildren of the late Capt. the Hon. Charles Preston, 5th son of 12th Viscount:—

Issue of the late Charles Arthur Preston, *b.* 1857, *d.* 1924: *m.* 1889, Miriam, who *d.* 1936, dau. of the late Hon. Charles Alleyne, formerly M.P. for Quebec, and a M.E.C.:—

Arthur, *b.* 1902: *m.* 1928, Marion Blair, dau. of the late John Dean, and has issue living, Richard Dean, *b.* 1929.——Hubert Philip, *b.* 1905: *m.* 1938, Marie Hester, da. of Michale Joseph Aberne, QC, and has issue living, Anthony Ernest Michael, *b.* 1938,—Ronald Thomas Edward, *b.* 1940,— Andrea Margaret, *b.* 1941,—Michelle Joan Adrienne, *b.* 1944,—Ruth Jocelyn Vickie,—*b.* 1945,— Louise Marie Isabel, *b.* 1946.——Oswald, *b.* 1907.——Blanche (600, Laurier Av., Quebec City, Quebec, Canada): *m.* 1st, 1916, Arthur Fitzpatrick, who *d.* 1939, son of the Rt. Hon. Sir Charles Fitzpatrick, GCMG; 2ndly, 1941, George Blaikie, who *d.* 1949, and has issue living, (by 1st m.) Nonie Francis, *b.* 1918: *m.* 1950, Coote Nesbit Shanly, and has issue living, Charles Coote Nisbit, *b.* 1951, John James Arthur, *b.* 1954, Walter Patrick Francis *b.* 1959.——Mary (600, Laurier Av., Quebec City, Quebec, Canada): *m.* 1922, Lt.-Col. Francis M. Stanton, VD, RCA, who *d.* 1969, and has issue living, Mary Frances, *b.* 1937: *m.* 1964, Paul Jackson Johnson, of 22, Randolph Rd., Toronto 352, Canada, and has issue living, John Francis *b.* 1965, Paul Anthony *b.* 1966,—Francesca Anne Margaret *b.* 1971,—Elizabeth Ann, *b.* 1939.

Granddaughter of the late Hon. Thomas Preston, 7th son of 12th Viscount:—

Issue of the late Arthur James Preston, *b.* 1852, *d.* 1896: *m.* 1887, Christina Maria Dundas, who *d.* 1914, dau. of Henry Spencer, formerly of Woodlands, Havant, Hants:—

Marguerite Irene. *Residence*,—Glenbourne Cottage, West End, near Southampton, SO3 3BS.

PREDECESSORS.—[1] *Sir* Robert de Preston (knighted in the field by Lionel, Duke of Clarence, 1361), Lord of Preston in Lancashire, and sometime Lord High Chancellor of Ireland: *m.* Margaret, only dau. of Walter de Bermingham, of Kells: cr. *Lord Gormanston* (peerage of Ireland) about 1365-70; *s.* by his son [2] CHRISTOPHER: *m.* Elizabeth, dau. of William Laundres, Lord of the Barony of Naas; *s.* by his son [3] CHRISTOPHER ; *s.* by his son [4] *Sir* ROBERT Preston, *Knt.*, Dep. to Sir John Dynham, Lord Chancellor of Ireland, and during his minority to Richard, Duke of York, Lord Dep. of Ireland ; cr. *Viscount Gormanston* (peerage of Ireland) 1478; sat in the Parliaments of 1490 and 1493; *d.* 1503 ; *s.* by his son [5] WILLIAM, 2nd Viscount ; Dep. to Lord Treasurer of Ireland 1493, and Lord Justice of Ireland 1525; *s.* by his son [6] JENICO, 3rd Viscount ; sat in Parliament 1559 ; *d.* 1560 ; *s.* by his son [7] CHRISTOPHER, 4th Viscount ; sat in Parliament 1580 ; *d.* 1599 ; *s.* by his son [8] JENICO, 5th Viscount ; sat in Parliament 1613 ; *d.* 1630 ; *s.* by his son [9] NICHOLAS, 6th Viscount ; *s.* by his el. son [10] JENICO, 7th Viscount ; for his adherence to James II. was indicted for high-treason and outlawed 1691; *s.* by his brother [11] JENICO, 8th Viscount *de jure; s.* by his brother [12] ANTHONY, 9th Viscount *de jure ; s.* by his son [13] JENICO, 10th Viscount *de jure; d.* 1757; *s.* by his son [14] ANTHONY, 11th Viscount *de jure; d.* 1786; *s.* by his son [15] JENICO, 12th Viscount; having successfully instituted proceedings for the removal of the outlawry of Nicholas, 6th Viscount, was summoned to take his seat in the Irish House of Peers 1800 ; *d.* 1860; *s.* by his son [16] EDWARD ANTHONY JOHN, 13th Viscount, *b.* 1796; High Sheriff of Dublin 1845 ; cr. *Baron Gormanston*, co. Meath (peerage of United Kingdom) 1868 : *m.* 1836, Lucretia, dau. of the late William Charles Jerningham, next brother of 8th Baron Stafford, *d.* 1876; *s.* by his son [17] JENICO WILLIAM JOSEPH, *G.C.M.G.*, 14th Viscount, *b.* 1837; Chamberlain to Lord-Lieut. of Ireland (Duke of Abercorn, K.G.) 1866-8, Gov. and Com.-in-Ch. of Leeward Islands 1885-7, of British Guiana 1887-93, and Gov. of Tasmania 1893-1900: *m.* 1st, 1861, the Hon. Ismay Louisa Ursula Bellew, who *d.* 1875, dau. of 1st Baron Bellew ; 2ndly, 1878, Georgina, who *d.* 1932, dau. of the late Peter Connellan, of Coolmore, Kilkenny ; *d.* 1907 ; *s.* by his el. son [18] JENICO EDWARD JOSEPH, 15th Viscount, *b.* 1879: *m.* 1911, Eileen (who *d.* 1964, having *m.* 2ndly, 1934, John Black Atkins), da. of the late Lt.-Gen. the Rt. Hon. William Francis Butler, *GCB; d.* 1925; *s.* by his son [19] JENICO WILLIAM RICHARD, 16th Viscount, *b.* 1914; acting Capt. K.O.Y.L.I.: *m.* 1939, Pamela (who *d.* 1975, having *m.* 2ndly, 1943, Maurice Bernard O'Connor, who *d.* 1961), da. of the late Capt. Edward Dudley Hanly; *d.* (killed in action) 1940; *s.* by his son [20] JENICO NICHOLAS DUDLEY, 17th Viscount and present peer; also Baron Gormanston (peerage of Ireland 1365-70, and of U.K. 1868).

GORONWY-ROBERTS, BARON. (Roberts.) [Life Baron 1974.]

GORONWY OWEN ROBERTS, *PC*, son of Elias Edward Roberts, of Bethesda, Caernarvonshire; *b.* Sept. 20th, 1913; ed. at Ogwen Gram. Sch., and Wales (MA, Fellow) and London Univs.; FRSA; Hon. Freeman Roy. Borough of Caernarvon; served in Inf. Regt. 1941; Youth Education Officer to Caernarvonshire Education Authority 1941-44; Min. of State Welsh Office 1964-66, and Dept. of Education and Science 1966-67, and for Foreign Affairs 1967-70; Under-Sec. of State Foreign and Commonwealth Office since 1974; MP for Caernarvonshire (*Lab.*) 1945-50, and for Caernarvon 1950-74; cr. PC 1968, and *Baron Goronwy-Roberts,* of Caernarvon, and of Ogwen, co. Caernarvon (Life Baron) 1974: *m.* 1942, Marian Ann, yr. da. of David Evans, of Tresalem, Aberdare, and has issue.

Address.—c/o House of Lords, SW1. *Residence.*—Plas Newydd, Pwllheli, Gwynedd.

SON LIVING.
Hon. Owen Dafydd, *b.* 1946.

DAUGHTER LIVING.
Hon. Ann Elisabeth, *b.* 1947.

GORT, VISCOUNT. (Vereker.) [Viscount I. 1816.]

Truth conquers.

COLIN LEOPOLD PRENDERGAST VEREKER, 8th Viscount, *b.* June 21st, 1916; *s.* 1975; Lt. Cdr. RNVR; JP of Castletown, Isle of Man; Member of House of Keys, I. of Man Govt. 1966-71; 1939-45 War (despatches): *m.* 1946, Bettine Mary Mackenzie, da. of the late Godfrey Green, of Douglas, and formerly wife of Arthur Henry Jarand, and has issue.

Arms,—Quarterly: 1st and 4th azure, on a chevron or, a chaplet vert, *Vereker;* 2nd and 3rd gules, a saltire vairy or and azure, *Prendergast.* Crest,—Out of a mural crown gules, a stag's head proper. Supporters—*Dexter,* a lion proper; *sinister,* an heraldic antelope proper, each gorged with a plain collar gules, rimmed and chained or, chain reflexed over the back.

Residence,—Westwood, The Crofts, Castletown, Isle of Man.

SONS LIVING.
Hon. FOLEY ROBERT STANDISH PRENDERGAST, *b.* Oct, 24th 1951; ed. at Harrow.
Hon. Nicholas Leopold Prendergast, *b.* 1954.

DAUGHTER LIVING.
Hon. Elizabeth Jane, *b.* 1948.

SISTER LIVING.
Eileen Ivy, *b.* 1920: *m.* 1942, William John Dean, RAF, of 2, Dowlands Rd., Ensbury Park, Bournemouth, and has issue living, Terence Anthony (156, Emlyn Rd., E12), *b.* 1946: *m.* 1970, Mary Glenrose Porteous,—Anne Mary, *b.* 1943: *m.* 1964, Leonard Ernest Ruffell, DMA, of 37, Coombe Gdns., Ensbury Park, Bournemouth, and has issue living, Antonia Marie *b.* 1973.

WIDOW LIVING OF SON OF SIXTH VISCOUNT.
Yvonne Frances, da. of the late Major Geoffrey Arthur Barnett, MBE [see E. Verulam, colls.]: *m.* 1938, the Hon. Charles Standish Vereker, who *d.* 1941. *Residence,*—Serge Hill, Abbots Langley, Herts.

COLLATERAL BRANCHES LIVING.

Grandchildren of the late Capt. the Hon. Foley Charles Prendergast Vereker RN, 2nd son of 4th Viscount:—

Issue of the late Standish Henry Prendergast Vereker, D.C.M., *b.* 1878, *d.* 1953: *m.* 1908, Eleanor Elizabeth, who *d.* 1957, el. dau. of the late Henry Bott, O.B.E., M.R.C.S., of Washenden Manor, Biddenden, Kent:—

Daphne Eleanor, *b.* 1910: *m.* 1933, Com. Sydney Arthur Moorhouse Else, O.B.E., R.N. (retired), and has issue living, Patrick Arthur Henry (20, Deanhill Rd., East Sheen, SW14), *b.* 1934: *m.* 1965, Jane Ann Ickringill, and has issue living, Sarah-Jane *b.* 1966, Sophia Frances *b.* 1969,—Nigel Christopher John (31, Crowtrees Rd., Sabden, Blackburn, Lancs.), *b.* 1939: *m.* 1972, Sandra Whittaker,—Oliver Francis, *b.* 1948; MB, BS: *m.* 1972, Elizabeth Holman, and has issue living, Timothy Stephen *b.* 1974,—Marion Elizabeth, *b.* 1940: *m.* 1963, Lt.-Cdr. Peter Russell Gordon-Smith, RN, of Apple Tree Farm, Prinsted, Emsworth, and has issue living, Russell Guy Morris *b.* 1964, David *b.* 1968, Louise Ann *b.* 1965. *Residence,*—35, Birch Tree Drive, Emsworth, Hants.

Issue of the late Maurice Charles Prendergast Vereker, MC, *b.* 1884, *d.* 1963: *m.* 1928, Winifred Joan (8, Banbury Lane, Byfield, Daventry, Northants.), da. of the late Alberic Arthur Twisleton-Wykeham-Fiennes [see B. Saye and Sele, colls.]:—

Charles John Prendergast (of Ash Court, Overslade Lane, Rugby), *b.* 1935; Lt. RA (TA); a JP and Co. Councillor of Warwickshire.——Jeffrey Maurice Prendergast (Romily, Eathorpe, Leamington Spa, Warwicks), *b.* 1940: *m.* 1972, Denzil Farnsworth, and has issue living, Edward Foley Prendergast, *b.* 1973,—Charlotte Louise, *b.* 1974.——Margaret Joan, *b.* 1929.——Brenda Rosemary, *b.* 1931: *m.* 1965, Harold James Mills, of Glebe House, Bentworth, Alton, Hants, and has issue living, Catherine Joanna, *b.* 1967.

Issue of the late Capt. the Hon. Foley Charles Prendergast Vereker, R.N., 2nd
son of 4th Viscount, *b.* 1850, *d.* 1900: *m.* 1876, Ellen Amelia, who *d.* 1943,
dau. of the late Rev. Henry Michael Myddelton Wilshere, formerly R. of
Simon's Town, Cape of Good Hope:—

Lilian Isolda, *b.* 1883: *m.* 1911, the Rev. Lionel Smithett Lewis, formerly V. of Glastonbury, who
d. 1953. *Residence,*—West View, 8, St. John's Rd., Farnham, Surrey.

    Granddaughter of the late Capt. the Hon. Foley Charles Prendergast Vereker,
R.N. (ante):—

    Issue (by 2nd marriage) of the late Lieut. Foley Gerald Prendergast Vereker, R.N.,
b. 1893, *d.* 1921 : *m.* 1st,1914, Annette Julia Richmond (from whom he obtained a divorce
1919), only child of the late William Scotland Dawson, of Duffield, Derbyshire; 2ndly,
1920, Muriel, who *d.* 1945, dau. of the late Lindsay Horrocks, of 8, Connaught Street, W. :—

Barbara Isma Prendergast (*posthumous*) (18, Prince Arthur Rd., Hampstead, N W3), *b.* (June) 1921

    Grandson of the late Hon. John Prendergast Vereker, 3rd son of 3rd Viscount:—
Issue of the late Capt. George Medlicott Vereker, *b.* 1860, *d.* 1924 : *m.* 1887, Frances Gore,
M.B.E., who *d.* 1931, el. dau. of the late Robert Manders, of Landscape, Dundrum, co.
Dublin :—

Sir (George) Gordon Medlicott, *KCMG, MC, b.* 1889; ed. at Eton, and at Trin. Coll., Camb.; Envoy
Extraor. and Min. Plen to Bolivia 1939-40, to Finland 1940-41, and to Uruguay 1943-44, and
Ambassador Extraor. and Plen there 1944-49; 1914-18 War as Capt. Grenadier Guards (des-
patches, MC); CMG 1942, KCMG 1948: *m.* 1945, Roxana Wentworth Bowen Van Rensselaer,
who *d.* 1968, only child of the late Clarence Winthrop Bowen, of New York City, USA. *Residence,*—
Domaine de Beaumont, Valbonne, France, AM. *Clubs,*—Carlton, Guards', White's.

    Grandchildren of the late Hon. John Prendergast Vereker (ante):—
Issue of the late Major John Medlicott Vereker, *b.* 1863, *d.* 1940: *m.* 1892, Mary Agnes,
who *d.* 1930 (having obtained a divorce 1913), el. dau. of Sir Charles William Cayzer,
1st Bt., of Gartmore, Perthshire :—

Charles William Medlicott (Coloony, Queens Hill Rise, Ascot, Berks.), *b.* 1903; is Cdr. (ret.) RN;
FICS; 1939-45 War and Far East; HM's Vice-consul, Kristiansand, S. Norway 1948-51; an Assist,
Ship's Manager 1951-55; Legal Executive (Admiralty Court) 1957-72: *m.* 1937, Marjorie Hughes.
da. of William Hughes Whatley, and has issue living, Peter William Medlicott (c/o FCO, King Charles
St., SW1): *b.* 1939; ed. at Marlborough, Trin. Coll., Camb. (BA), and at Harvard Univ.; entered
Foreign Ser. 1963: *m.* 1967, Susan Elizabeth Dyball, and has issue living, Connel Charles Medlicott
b. 1971, Toby John Medlicott *b.* 1973,—John Michael Medlicott (32, Inner Park Rd., Wimbledon,
W19), *b.* 1944; ed. at Marlborough, and at Keele Univ: *m.* 1971, Judith Frewen, of Washington,
DC, and has issue living, Andrew Shane Medlicott *b.* 1975, Jennifer *b.* 1973,—Corinna Mary, *b.* 1938:
m. 1961, Maj. John Tadman, R. Anglian Regt., of Pennyone House, Wycombe Rd., Prestwood,
Bucks., and has issue living, Miles William Vereker *b.* 1967, Carey Joanna *b.* 1962, Fenella Jane
b. 1964.——Denis Medlicott, *b.* 1906; ed. at Harrow: *m.* 1927 (m. diss. 1942), Marjory Mary, da.
of Julius A. Fryer, formerly of Port Elizabeth, S. Africa, and has issue living, Moyra Maureen, *b.*
1928: *m.* 1962 (m. diss. 1971), Rodney Graham Smit, CA (S. Africa), ACIS.——Eileen Mamie, *b.* 1897:
m. 1918, Capt. John Clarke Heaton, Victoria Rifles of Canada, of 4, Wilbury Lodge, Eaton Rd.,
Hove.——Kathleen Sybil, *b.* 1904: *m.* 1931, Cdr. Michael George Marriott, RN (ret.), of 76, Woodside
Av., Cowie's Hill, Durban, S. Africa, and has issue living, Jeremy Edward Alan (Carnamah, W.
Aust.), *b.* 1937; Lt. RN: *m.* 1963, Teresa Katherine, da. of Malcolm Francis Ogilvie-Forbes of
Boyndlie, Aberdeenshire, and has issue living, Benedict Michael Andrew *b.* 1963, Peter Malcolm
b. 1966,—Bridget Mary, *b.* 1934: *m.* 1956, Julius Horowitz, of 8, Kernick Av., Melrose North,
Johannesburg, S. Africa, and has issue living, Adam Mark *b.* 1957, Ivan Brandon *b.* 1961, Seth
William (twin) *b.* 1961, Ben Robert *b.* 1964, Robyn Ester *b.* 1956, Yael Tayce *b.* 1959. *Residence,*—

    Granddaughter of the late Lt.-Col. John Cayzer Medlicott Vereker, MC (infra):—
Issue of the late Lieut. John Herbert Radcliffe Medlicott Vereker, R.N., *b.* 1914, *d.* (killed
on active ser. during European War) 1941 : *m.* 1939, Betty Eleanor Grace (who *m.*
2ndly, 1945, Capt. Maurice Milton Jones, U.S. Air Force, of Jackson, Mississippi, U.S.A.),
only child of Charles Edward Shepherd, of Trerice Manor, St. Newlyn East, Cornwall:—
Jocelyn, *b.* 1940.

    Grandchildren of the late Major John Medlicott Vereker (ante):—
Issue of the late Lt.-Col. John Cayzer Medlicott Vereker, MC, *b.* 1895, who *d.* 1962: *m.* 1914,
Dulce Flores Elder, who *d.* 1973, only child of Alexander Randle Skene Radcliffe, formerly
of Dilston, Kentville, Nova Scotia:—

Dulcibella Joy, *b.* 1917: *m.* 1st, 1935 (m. diss. 1946), Capt. Hender Charles Molesworth St. Aubyn
[see Molesworth-St. Aubyn, Bt]; 2ndly, 1948, Wing-Cdr. Harold Frederick Gurney Fry, RAF, and
has issue living (by 1st m.) [see Molesworth-St. Aubyn, Bt.],—(by 2nd m.) Elizabeth Gurney, *b.* 1950.
——Sheela Maureen (Barton Cottage, Rosebery Rd., W. Runton, Cromer), *b.* 1925; late WRNS:
m. 1947 (m. diss. 1971), Hugh Bellasis Martin, MBE, and has issue living, Clive Patrick, *b.* 1955;
ed. at Harrow, and Wadham Coll., Oxford,—Corinna France Avril, *b.* 1948; ed. at St. Margarets
Sch., Bushy, and Homerton Coll., Camb.: *m.* Philip Charles Creasy, BA, of 19, Beacon Rd., King-
standing, Warwickshire, and has issue living, Mathew Henry *b.* 1974.
Issue of the late Capt. Stanley Lloyd Medlicott Vereker, OBE, RN, *b.* 1899, *d.* 1967: *m.*
1925, Elaine Irene (Mottynsden Manor, Burwash, Sussex), da. of the late John Henry
Edwards, of 54, Portland Place, W1:—

John Stanley Herbert Medlicott (Orchard Farm, Tutts Clump, Bradfield, Berks.; 118, Coleherne
Court, SW5), *b.* 1927; ed. at Rugby and Trin. Hall, Camb.: *m.* 1954, Valerie Ann Virginia, da. of
William James Threlfall, CIE, of Skoons, Bembridge, I. of W., and has issue living, Simon Lloyd
William Medlicott, *b.* 1955,—Rupert David Peregrine Medlicott, *b.* 1957,—Hugo Dominic Charles
Medlicott, *b.* 1959.——David William Leslie Edwards (Holton House, Burwash, Sussex), *b.* 1930; ed.
at Eton, and Trin. Hall, Camb. (MA): Lt.-Cdr. RNVR (ret.): *m.* 1965, Jane Elizabeth, da. of Alan
Campbell Gairdner, FRCS, of Branscombe, Whimple, Devon, and has issue living, William David
Lloyd Medlicott, *b.* 1966,—Henry Alan Charles Medlicott, *b.* 1969.

    Grandchildren of the late Hon. Henry Prendergast Vereker, LL.D., 4th son of 3rd
Viscount.

Issue of the late Lieut.-Col. Charles Granville Vereker, *b.* 1869, *d.* 1947: *m.* 1st, 1895,
Adeline Eleanor, who *d.* 1930, dau. of the late Maj.-Gen. Thomas Porter Berthon, R.A.;
2ndly, 1931, Leila Frances Helena, (who *m.* 2ndly, 1973, Robert Hugh Pardoe, of Bridge
House, Bibury, Cirencester), da. of the late F. G. Bosanquet:—

(By 2nd m.) Neville Henry Prendergast (17, Holland Villas Rd., W14 8BT), *b.* 1934; FRICS: *m.* 1974,
Priscilla Mary, el. da. of John Orlando Weld-Forester [see B. Forester, colls.], and has issue living,
John Charles Prendergast, *b.* 1975.——Louise Katherine (8, Addison Rd., W14), *b.* 1933: *m.* 1953
(m. diss. 1961), Geoffrey Whitaker Gotch, and has issue living, Peter Charles Thomas *b.* 1955.
Issue of the late Cdr. Henry Gosset Vereker, RN, *b.* 1871, *d.* 1916: *m.* 1903, Kate Beatrice,
who *d.* 1915, el. da. of the late Frank Herbert:—

Charles Henry (46, South St., Durham; United Univ. Club), *b.* 1913; ed. at Lincoln Coll., Oxford
(MA, DPhil); Prof. of Political Theory and Insts., Durham Univ. since 1966: *m.* 1942, Patricia, da.
of the late S. G. K. Kastelian, MD, and has issue living, Julian Charles Prendergast (15, Churchfields
Rd., Salisbury), *b.* 1945: *m.* 1968, Elizabeth Glascott Wise,—Katherine Elizabeth, *b.* 1949,—
Deirdre Patricia, *b.* 1954.——Vera Kathleen, *b.* 1898: *m.* 1st, 1918 (m. diss. 1943), Albert Durston,
RAF; 2ndly, 1948, Cdr. Geoffrey Cayley Lambert Dalley, RN (ret.), of Stone Cottage, Motcombe,
Shaftesbury, Dorset, and has issue living (by 1st m.), Richard Vereker, *b.* 1934,—Sylvia Vera, *b.*
1919,—Caroline Valerie, *b.* 1937.

PREDECESSORS.—[1] Sir THOMAS Prendergast, a Brig.-Gen. in the Army, and M.P. for Monaghan 1703; cr. a *Baronet* 1699; killed at Malplaquet 1709; *s.* by his son [2] Sir THOMAS P.C., 2nd Bt.; was M.P. for Chichester and Clonmel, and Postmaster-Gen. of Ireland; *d.s.p.* 1760 before the patent creating him Viscount Clonmel had been completed; the baronetcy having expired the estates passed to his nephew [3] JOHN Smyth, 2nd son of Elizabeth (2nd dau. of 1st Bt.), by Charles Smyth, M.P. for Limerick 1731-76; successively M.P. for Carlow and Limerick; assumed the surname of Prendergast in lieu of Smyth 1760, and the additional surname of Smyth 1785; cr. *Baron Kiltarton* (peerage of Ireland) 1810 with remainder to his nephew Charles, son of his sister Juliana, by her marriage with Thomas Vereker, and *Viscount Gort* (peerage of Ireland) 1816, with similar limitation; *d.* 1817; *s.* by his nephew (ante) [4] CHARLES Vereker, P.C., 2nd Viscount; M.P. for Limerick 1790-1817, and afterwards a Representative Peer; *d.* 1842; *s.* by his son [5] JOHN PRENDERGAST, 3rd Viscount, *b.* 1790; successively M.P. for Limerick and a Representative Peer: *m.* 1st, 1814, the Hon. Maria O'Grady, who *d.* 1854, dau. of 1st Viscount Guillamore; 2ndly, 1861, Elizabeth Mary, who *d.* 1880, dau. of John Jones, and widow of George Tudor, M.P. for Barnstaple; *d.* 1865; *s.* by his son [6] STANDISH PRENDERGAST, 4th Viscount, *b.* 1819: *m.* 1847, the Hon. Caroline Harriet Gage, who *d.* 1888, dau. of 4th Viscount Gage, *d.* 1900; *s.* by his el. son [7] JOHN GAGE PRENDERGAST, 5th Viscount, *b.* 1849: *m.* 1885, Eleanor, who *d.* 1933, dau. of the late R. C. Surtees, of Hamsterley Hall, co. Durham; *d.* 1902; *s.* by his el. son [8] JOHN STANDISH SURTEES PRENDERGAST. V.C., G.C.B., C.B.E., D.S.O., M.V.O., M.C., 6th Viscount, *b.* 1886; Field Marshal; C.I.G.S. 1937-9; European War 1914-18 (four times wounded, M.C., D.S.O. with two bars, V.C.), European War 1939-40 as Com.-in-Ch., British Expeditionary Force in France (G.C.B., Grand Cross of Legion of Honour); Inspector-Gen. to Forces for Training 1940-41, Gov. and Com.-in-Ch., Gibraltar 1941-2, and Malta 1942-4, and High Commr. and Com.-in-Ch. Palestine, and High Commr. for Transjordan 1944-5; cr. *Viscount Gort*, of Hamsterley, co. Durham (peerage of United Kingdom) 1946: *m.* 1911, his cousin, Corinna Katharine, who *d.* 1940, and from whom he had obtained a divorce 1925, dau. of the late Capt. George Medlicott Vereker; *d.* 1946, when the United Kingdom Viscountcy became ext. and the Irish Viscountcy and Barony passed to his brother [9] STANDISH ROBERT GAGE PRENDERGAST, MC, 7th Viscount; *b.* 1888; 1914-18 war as Lt. RHA; High Sheriff of Co. Durham 1934: *m.* 1921, Bessy, who *d.* 1972, da. of the late Aubone Alfred Surtees, of Dinsdale Manor, Co. Durham; *d.* 1975; *s.* by his kinsman [10] COLIN LEOPOLD PRENDERGAST (only son of Cdr. Leopold George Prendergast Vereker, 2nd son of Capt. the Hon. Foley Charles Prendergast Vereker, 2nd son of 4th Viscount), 8th Viscount and present peer: also Baron Kiltarton.

GOSCHEN, VISCOUNT. (Goschen.) [Viscount U.K. 1900.]

By peace.

JOHN ALEXANDER GOSCHEN, KBE, 3rd Viscount, *b.* July 7th, 1906; *s.* 1952; ed. at Eton; Col. (retired) late Grenadier Guards; served with British Mil. Mission to Greece 1945-47; Assist. Ch. Whip, House of Lords 1962-64; Capt., Yeomen of the Guard and Dep. Ch. Whip 1970-71; 1939-45 War in N. Africa, Sicily, Italy, and S. France (OBE); OBE (Mil) 1944, KBE (Civil) 1972: *m.* 1st, 1934, Hilda Violet Ursula (from whom he obtained a divorce 1949), da. of the late Col. the Hon. St. Leger Henry Jervis, DSO [see V. St. Vincent, colls.]; 2ndly, 1955, Alvin, yr. da. of the late H. England, of Durban, Natal, and has issue by 2nd m.

Arms,—Argent, a heart fired and transfixed with an arrow bendwise point upwards gules, in chief two anchors erect sable. **Crest,**—On an arrow fessewise, a dove wings endorsed all proper. **Supporters,**—*Dexter*, a sailor; *sinister*, a private of the Royal Marines, both proper, each holding in the exterior hand a flagstaff of the last, therefrom flowing a banner argent, charged with a pale gules thereon an anchor cabled and erect or.

Residence,—Hilton House, Crowthorne, Berks. *Club,*—Guards'.

SON LIVING. (*By 2nd marriage.*)
Hon. GILES JOHN HARRY, *b.* Nov. 16th, 1965.

DAUGHTER LIVING. (*By 2nd marriage.*)
Hon. Caroline Elizabeth, *b.* 1963.

SISTER LIVING. (*Raised to the rank of a Viscount's daughter* 1953.)
Hon. Angela, *b.* 1897: *m.* 1920, Lieut.-Col. John Carne Hargreaves, from whom she obtained a divorce 1939, and has issue living, David William (of The Garden Cottage, Crowthorne, Berks.). *b.* 1926; ed. at Eton; is Col. Lt.-Col. Gren. Gds.: *m.* 1951, Judith Anne, yst. da. of the late Capt. Bertram Currie, of Dingley Hall, Market Harborough, Leicestershire, and has issue living, John Patrick *b.* 1953, Andrew Raikes *b.* 1955,—George Jonathan, *b.* 1931; ed. at Eton, late Grenadier Guards; is with Lloyd's: *m.* 1953, Judy Jane, only child of Air Marshal Sir Hugh Alex Constantine, K.B.E., C.B., D.S.O., and has issue living, David Marcus *b.* 1960,—Geraldine Elizabeth, *b.* 1924: *m.* 1946; Maj. James Sidney Rawdon Scott-Hopkins, late Indian Army, and KOYLI (MP 1959-66), of 53, Markham St., SW3, and Fenterwanson, St. Teath, Bodmin, Cornwall, and has issue living, Richard Michael *b.* 1947, James Barry *b.* 1950, Anthony John *b.* 1952, Jennifer Jane *b.* 1948. *Residence,*—

DAUGHTERS LIVING OF SECOND VISCOUNT.

Hon. Phyllis (Evelyn), (Old Peans, Robertsbridge, Sussex), *b.* 1895; a Lady-in-Waiting to HRH the Princess Royal 1948-65: *m.* 1920, Lt.-Col. Francis Cecil Campbell Balfour, CIE, CVO, CBE, MC, who *d.* 1965 [see E. Balfour, colls.].

Hon. Cicely Winifred, *b.* 1899: *m.* 1926, Maj. Melville Edward Bertram Portal, MBE, late Coldm. Gds., who *d.* 1971 [see Portal, Bt., colls.]. *Residence,*—Redcote, Birch Av., Haywards Heath, Sussex.

PREDECESSORS.—[1] *Rt. Hon.* GEORGE JOACHIM Goschen, son of the late William Henry Goschen, of Austinfriars, E.C., and Templeton House, Roehampton ; *b.* 1831; sometime a partner in firm of Fruhling and Goschen, of Austinfriars, a Director of the Bank of England, and Chm. of Lloyd's; Vice-Pres. of Board of Trade 1865-6, Chancellor of Duchy of Lancaster (with a seat in the Cabinet) 1866, Pres. of Poor Law Board 1868-71, First Lord of the Admiralty 1871-4, Envoy Extraor. and Min. Plen. to Constantinople on a Special Mission 1880-81, an Ecclesiastical Commr. for England 1882-5, Chancellor of the Exchequer Jan. 1887 to Aug. 1892, and again First Lord of the Admiralty 1895-1900 : M.P. for City of London (*L*) 1863-80, for Ripon 1880-85, for E. Div. of Edinburgh Borough 1885-6. and for St. George, Hanover Square (*C*) Feb. 1887 to Nov. 1900; cr. P.C. 1865, and *Viscount Goschen,* of Hawkhurst, co. Kent (peerage of United Kingdom) 1900: *m.* 1857, Lucy, who *d.* 1898, dau. of the late John Dalley ; *d.* 1907 ; *s.* by his [2] son *Rt. Hon.* GEORGE JOACHIM, *G.C.S.I., G.C.I.E., C.B.E., V.D.,* 2nd Viscount, *b.* 1866 ; Private Sec. to Gov. of N.S. Wales (Earl of Jersey) 1890-92 ; sometime a partner in the firm of Goschens and Cunliffe, of 12, Austin Friars, E.C., and Chm. of Med. Research Council; Lieut.-Col. and Hon. Col. (Lieut.-Col. Comdg. 1914-18) a Batn. Buffs (E. Kent Regt.) ; sat as M.P. for N., or E. Grinstead Div. of Sussex (*C*) 1895-1906 ; appointed a Member of Roy. Commn. on King's Bench 1912, and Joint Parliamentary Sec. (unpaid) Board of Agriculture 1918 ; was Controller Labour Div., Food Production Depart. 1918-19 ; Gov. of Madras 1924-29 (acted as Viceroy and Gov.-Gen. of India June to Oct. 1929) : *m.* 1893, Lady Margaret Evelyn Gathorne-Hardy, *C.I.,* who *d.* 1943, dau. of 1st Earl of Cranbrook; *d.* 1952 ; *s.* by his nephew, [3] JOHN ALEXANDER, *O.B.E.* (son of the late Hon. Sir William Henry Goschen, K.B.E., 2nd son of 1st Viscount), 3rd Viscount and present peer.

GOSFORD, EARL OF. (Acheson.) Sits as BARON WORLINGHAM (U.K. 1835) [Earl I. 1806, Bt. N.S. 1628.]

To the watchful.

VIGILANTIBUS

CHARLES DAVID ALEXANDER JOHN SPARROW ACHESON, 7th Earl and 13th Baronet; *b.* July 13th, 1942; *s.* 1966; ed. at Harrow, at Byam Shaw Sch. of Drawing and Painting, and Roy. Acad. Schs.

Arms.—Argent, an eagle with two heads displayed sable, beaked and membered or; on a chief vert two mullets of the third. *Crest.*—A cock gules, standing on a trumpet or. *Supporters.*—Two leopards proper, collared and chained or, the sinister reguardant.
Address.—House of Lords, SW1.

SISTERS LIVING.
Lady (Francesca Georgina) Caroline, *b.* 1940: *m.* 1967, David Wallace Fleming, of 1045, Fifth Av., New York 10028, NY, USA, and has issue living, Alexander Montagu Acheson, *b.* 1968, *Lady* Isabella Augusta, *b.* 1950.

UNCLE LIVING. (*Son of 5th Earl.*)
Hon. PATRICK BERNARD VICTOR MONTAGU, *b.* Feb. 4th, 1915; ed. at Harrow, and at Trin. Coll., Camb. (BA 1937), and at Harvard Univ. (MBA 1939): *m.* 1946, Judith, da. of Mrs. F. B. Bate, of Waterford, Virginia, USA, and has issue living, Nicholas Hope Carter, *b.* 1947,—Christopher, *b.* 1950,—John Alexander Simon, *b.* 1957,—Alexandra Sarah Camilla, *b.* 1962,—Caroline Mary Patricia (twin), *b.* 1962. *Residence,*—Market Hill, Waterford, Va. 22190, USA.

AUNTS LIVING. (*Daughters of 5th Earl.*)
Lady Camilla Mildred Nicola, *b.* 1917 : *m.* 1st, 1937, Baron Hans Christolph Schenk von Stauffenberg; 2ndly, 1950, Baron Axel von dem Bussche-Streithorst, and has issue living, (by 1st marriage) *Baron* John Sebastian Rudolph, *b.* 1940,—*Baron* John Patrick Frederick, *b.* 1941, *Baron* Damian Ignaz Carl, *b.* 1944,—(by 2nd marriage), *Baroness* Nicola Georgina Mildred Jenny, *b.* 1951,—*Baroness* Jane Olivia, *b.* 1955. *Address,*—en Menthon, 1268, Begnins, Switzerland.
Lady Mary Virginia Shirley, *b.* 1919 : *m.* 1941, Fernando Corcuera, and has issue living, Juan Fernando Pedro, *b.* 1948,—Jaime Marcos Pedro, *b.* 1955,—Fernanda Mary, *b.* 1942,—Monica Ana, *b.* 1944,—Marysol Manuela, *b.* 1946. *Residence,*—Hidalgo 14, San Angel, Mexico City.

GREAT-AUNT LIVING. (*Daughter of 4th Earl.*)

Lady Theodosia Louise Augusta, *b.* 1882: *m.* 1912, the Rt. Hon. Sir Alexander George Montagu Cadogan, OM, GCMG, KCB, who *d.* 1968 [see E. Cadogan]. *Residence,*—2, Westminster Gdns., SW1.

MOTHER LIVING.

FRANCESCA AUGUSTA MARIA (14, De Vere Gdns, W8), da. of Francesco Cagiati, of Rome: *m.* 1935 (m. diss. 1960), the 6th Earl, who *d.* 1966.

WIDOW LIVING OF SIXTH EARL.

CYNTHIA MARGARET (*Countess of Gosford*) (Heath Cottage, Camberley, Surrey), da. of the late Capt. H. C. West, and widow of Maj. J. P. Delius, 13th/18th R. Hussars: *m.* 1960, as his second wife the 6th Earl, who *d.* 1966.

COLLATERAL BRANCH LIVING.

Issue of the late Com. the Hon. Patrick Charles George Cavendish Acheson, D.S.O. MVO, yr. son of 4th Earl, *b.* 1883, *d.* 1957: *m.* 1915, Norah, who *d.* 1970, da. of Alfred Jones, formerly of Halifax, Nova Scotia:—

Blanche Theodosia (twin), *b.* 1923 : *m.* 1950, Com. Oliver Russell Moore, R.N. (retired), and has issue living, Susan Theodosia, *b.* 1952,—Victoria Caroline, *b.* 1954,—Patricia Alexandra, *b.* 1956. *Residence,*—Dash Hayes, Kington Magna, Gillingham, Dorset.

PREDECESSORS.—[1] *Sir* ARCHIBALD Acheson of Edinburgh, later of Market Hill, Clonekearney, co. Armagh, successively Solicitor-Gen. for Scotland, a Senator of Justice (with title of Lord Glencairnie), an Extraor. Lord of Session, and Sec. of State for Scotland; cr. a *Baronet* (of Nova Scotia) 1628 with remainder to his heirs male whatsoever: *m.* 1st, c. 1610, Agnes Vernor; 2ndly, 1622, Margaret, da. and heir of the Hon. Sir John Hamilton [D. Abercorn]; *d.* 1634; *s.* by his el. son [2] *Sir* PATRICK, 2nd Bt. (son of 1st m.): *m.* 1634, Martha, da. and heir of William Moore: *d.* 1638; *s.* by his brother [3] *Sir* GEORGE, 3rd Bt.; *b.* 1629: *m.* 1st, 1654, Nichola, da. and co-heir of Sir Robert Hannay, 1st Bt.; 2ndly, 1659, Hon. Margaret Caulfeild, da. of 2nd Baron Charlemont; *d.* 1685; *s.* by his son [4] *Sir* NICHOLAS, 4th Bt. (son of 1st m.); MP for co. Armagh 1695: *m.* 1686, Anne, da. of Thomas Taylor, of Kells; *d.* 1701; *s.* by his son [5] *Sir* ARTHUR, 5th Bt.; *b.* 1688: *m.* 1715, Anne, da. and heir of Rt. Hon. Philip Savage; *d.* 1749; *s.* by his son [6] *Sir* ARCHIBALD, PC; *b.* 1718; successively MP for Dublin Univ., and Enniskillen; cr. *Baron Gosford,* of Market Hill, co. Armagh (peerage of Ireland) 1776, and *Viscount Gosford* (peerage of Ireland) 1785: *m.* 1740, Mary, da. of John Richardson, of Rich Hill, co. Armagh; *d.* 1790: *s.* by his son [7] ARTHUR, 2nd Viscount; *b.* c. 1742, MP for Old Leighlin 1783-90; cr. *Earl of Gosford* (peerage of Ireland) 1806: *m.* 1774, Millicent, da. of Lt.-Gen. Edward Pole, *d.* 1807; *s.* by his son [8] ARCHIBALD, GCB, 2nd Earl; *b.* 1776; Gov. of Canada; cr. *Baron Worlingham* (peerage of UK) 1835: *m.* 1805, Mary, da. of Robert Sparrow of Worlingham Hall, Suffolk; *d.* 1849; *s.* by his son [9] ARCHIBALD, KP, 3rd Earl; *b.* 1806; who in 1847 had been cr. *Baron Acheson of Clancairny,* co. Armagh (peerage of UK): *m.* 1832, Lady Theodosia Brabazon, who *d.* 1876, da. of 10th Earl of Meath; *d.* 1864; *s.* by his son [10] ARCHIBALD BRABAZON SPARROW, 4th Earl; *b.* 1841; Lord of the Bedchamber to HRH the Prince of Wales 1886-1901, and Vice-Chamberlain of the Household to HM Queen Alexandra 1901-22; bore Queen Consort's Ivory Rod at Coronation of King Edward VII 1902: *m.* 1876, Lady Louisa Augusta Beatrice Montagu, DBE, who *d.* 1944, 2nd da. of 7th Duke of Manchester, KP; *d.* 1922; *s.* by his son [11] ARCHIBALD CHARLES MONTAGUE BRABAZON, MC, 5th Earl; *b.* 1877; Col. Coldstream Gds.; S. Africa 1899-1902, 1914-18 War (MC): *m.* 1st, 1910, Mildred (who *d.* 1965, having obtained a divorce 1928), da. of John Ridgely Carter, of Balt., USA, Amer. Min. to the Balkans; 2ndly, 1928, Beatrice Claflin, who *d.* 1967, formerly wife of Robert P. Breese, of New York; *d.* 1954; *s.* by his el. son [12] ARCHIBALD ALEXANDER JOHN STANLEY, OBE, 6th Earl, *b.* 1911; a Lord in Waiting to HM 1957-58: *m.* 1st, 1935 (m. diss. 1960), Francesca Augusta Maria, da. of Francesco Cagiati, of Rome; 2ndly, 1960, Cynthia Margaret, da. of Capt. H. C. West, and widow of Maj. J. P. Delius; *d.* 1966; *s.* by his only son [13] CHARLES DAVID ALEXANDER JOHN SPARROW, 7th Earl and present peer; also Viscount and Baron Gosford, Baron Worlingham and Baron Acheson of Clancairny.

GOUGH, VISCOUNT. (Gough.) [Viscount U.K. 1849, Bt. U.K. 1842.]

[Name and Title pronounced "Goff."]

SHANE HUGH MARYON GOUGH, 5th Viscount and 5th Baronet ; *b.* Aug. 26th, 1941 ; *s.* 1951; ed. at Winchester; late Lt. Irish Guards.

Arms,—Quarterly; 1st and 4th gules, on a mount vert a lion passant guardant or, supporting with his dexter paw the Union flag flowing to the sinister proper, over the same, in chief, the words "China," "India," in letters of gold ; 2nd and 3rd azure, on a fesse argent, between three boars' heads, couped or, a lion passant gules ; in the centre chief point, pendent from a riband argent, fimbriated azure, a representation of the badge of the Spanish order of Charles III. proper, and on a chief, a representation of the east wall of the fortress of Tarifa, with a breach between two turrets, the dexter turret surmounted by the British flag flying, all proper. **Crests,**—1st, a boar's head couped or, motto over "Goojerat" (of augmentation); 2nd, on a mural crown argent, a lion passant guardant or, holding in the dexter paw two flag staves in bend sinister proper, the one being the Union flag of Great Britain and Ireland surmounting the other, the staff thereof broken, with a triangular banner flowing therefrom to represent a Chinese flag, having thereon a dragon, and in an escroll above the word "China"; 3rd. a dexter arm embowed, in facings of 87th Regiment (gules, faced vert), the hand grasping the colour of the said Regiment displayed, and a representation of a French eagle reversed and depressed, the staff broken proper, in an escroll above the word "Barossa." **Supporters,**—*Dexter,* a lion reguardant or, gorged with an Eastern crown gules, the rim inscribed with the word "Punjab" in letters of gold, with chain reflexed over the back, also gold ; *sinister,* a Chinese dragon or, gorged with a mural crown sable, ensorbed with the word "China," and chained gold.

Residences,—Keppoch House, Strathpeffer, Ross-shire; 17, Stanhope Gdns., SW7. *Clubs,*—Guards', White's, MCC.

WIDOW LIVING OF FOURTH VISCOUNT.

MARGARETTA ELIZABETH (*Viscountess Gough*), only dau. of Sir Spencer Pocklington Maryon Maryon-Wilson, 11th Bt. [see Wilson Bt., cr. 1661]: *m.* 1935, the 4th Viscount, who *d.* 1951. *Residences,*—Inchvannie, Strathpeffer, Ross-shire; 26, Markham St., SW3.

PREDECESSORS.—[1] *Field-Marshal the Rt. Hon. Sir* HUGH Gough, *K.P.*, *G.C.B.*, *G.C.S.I*, *P.C.; b.* 1779; an eminent Mil. Com. who achieved brilliant victories in India, and subjugated and annexed the Punjab to the British Dominions: cr. a *Baronet* 1842, *Baron Gough*, of Chinkangfoo, in China and of Maharajpore and the Sutlej, in the East Indies (peerage of United Kingdom) 1846, and *Viscount Gough*, of Goojerat, in the Punjaub, and of the City of Limerick (peerage of United Kingdom) 1849; thrice thanked by Parliament and awarded a pension of £2,000 a-year for three lives: *m.* 1807, Frances Maria, dau. of Gen. Edward Stephens, R.A.; *d.* 1869; *s.* by his son [2] GEORGE STEPHENS, 2nd Viscount, *b.* 1815; Capt. Grenadier Guards: *m.* 1st, 1840, Sarah Elizabeth, who *d.* 1841, dau. of the late Wray Palliser, of Comragh, Waterford; 2ndly, 1846, Jane, who *d.* 1892, dau. of the late George Arbuthnot, of Elderslie, Surrey; *d.* 1895; *s.* by his el. son [3] HUGH, *K.C.V.O.*, 3rd Viscount; *b.* 1849; Min. Resident at Dresden and Coburg, and Chargé d'Affaires at Court of Waldeck 1901-07: *m.* 1889, Lady Georgiana Frances Henrietta Pakenham, who *d.* 1943, dau. of 4th Earl of Longford; *d.* 1919; *s.* by his son [4] HUGH WILLIAM, *M.C.*, 4th Viscount; *b.* 1892; Lieut. Col. Irish Guards; European War 1914-18 (M.C.): *m.* 1935, Margaretta Elizabeth, dau. of Sir Spencer Pocklington Maryon Maryon Wilson, 11th Bt.; *d.* 1951; *s.* by his son [5] SHANE HUGH MARYON, 5th Viscount, and present peer; also Baron Gough.

GOWRIE, EARL OF. (Ruthven.) [Earl U.K. 1945.]

ALEXANDER PATRICK GREYSTEIL RUTHVEN, 2nd Earl; *b.* Nov. 26th, 1939; *s.* to Earldom of Gowrie 1955, and to Barony of Ruthven of Gowrie 1956; ed. at Eton, at Balliol Coll., Oxford, and at Harvard Univ., U.S.A.; officially recognised in the name of Ruthven by Warrant of Lord Lyon King of Arms 1957; a Lord-in-Waiting to HM 1972-74: *m.* 1st 1962 (m. diss. 1974), Xandra, yr. da. of Col. Robert Albert Glanville Bingley, CVO, GSO, OBE; 2ndly, 1974, Countess Adelheid, yst. da. of the late Fritz-Dietlof, Graf von der Schulenburg, and has issue by 1st m.

Arms,—Paly of six, argent and gules. Crest, —A ram's head couped sable armed or. Supporters,—Two goats sable, armed, unguled and ducally gorged or, with chains also or reflexed over the back.

Residences,—34, King St., Covent Gdn., WC2; Dunstall Priory, Shoreham, Kent.

SON LIVING. (By 1st m.)

PATRICK LEO BRER (*Viscount Ruthven of Canberra*), *b.* Feb. 4th, 1964.

BROTHER LIVING.

Malise Walter Maitland Knox Hore RUTHVEN (23, Stockwell Park Rd., SW9), *b.* 1942; ed. at Eton, and at Trin. Coll., Camb.

MOTHER LIVING.

Pamela Margaret, da. of the Rev. A. H. Fletcher, of 87, Cadogan Gdns., S.W.1; was an Extra Woman of the Bedchamber to H.M. the Queen 1948-51; in 1945 was granted rank and precedence of wife of the el. son of an Earl during her widowhood: *m.* 1st, 1938, Major the Hon. (Alexander Harding) Patrick Hore Ruthven, only son of 1st Earl, who *d.* (of wounds received in action in Libya) 1942; 2ndly, 1952, Major Derek Cooper, M.C., The Life Guards. *Residence,*—Dunlewey, Letterkenny, Gweedore, co. Donegal.

PREDECESSOR—[1] *Brig.-Gen. the Rt. Hon. Sir* ALEXANDER GORE ARKWRIGHT Hore Ruthven, *V.C.*, *P.C.*, *G.C.M.G.*, *C.B.*, *D.S.O.*, 2nd son of 8th Lord Ruthven of Freeland; *b.* 1872; Col. and Hon. Brig.-Gen. Welsh Guards; Sudan 1898 (despatches, V.C.), White Nile 1900 (despatches thrice), Somaliland 1903-04, European War 1914-19 in Gallipoli and France (severely wounded, despatches five times, D.S.O. with Bar, French and Belgian Croix de Guerre, C.M.G., C.B.); Gov. of S. Australia 1928-34, Gov. of N.S. Wales 1935-6, and Gov.-Gen. and Com.-in-Ch. of Commonwealth of Australia 1936-44; Lieut.-Gov. and Dep. Constable of Windsor Castle 1945-53; cr. *Baron Gowrie*, of Canberra in the Commonwealth of Australia, and of Dirleton, co. E. Lothian (peerage of United Kingdom) 1935, and *Viscount Ruthven of Canberra*, of Dirleton, co. E. Lothian and *Earl of Gowrie* (peerage of United Kingdom) 1945: *m.* 1908, Zara Eileen, who *d.* 1965, da. of the late John Pollok [B. Clanmorris]; *d.* 1955; *s.* by his grandson [2] ALEXANDER PATRICK GREYSTEIL (el. son of the late Maj. the Hon. (Alexander Harding) Patrick Hore Ruthven, only son of 1st Earl), 2nd Earl and present peer; also Viscount Ruthven of Canberra, Baron Gowrie, and Baron Ruthven of Gowrie (see *₄*₄* infra).

*₄*₄*[1] WALTER JAMES RUTHVEN, 8th Lord Ruthven of Freeland (peerage of Scotland) cr. 1651 [see that title], was cr. *Baron Ruthven of Gowrie* (peerage of United Kingdom) 1919: *m.* 1869, Lady Caroline Annesley Gore, who *d.* 1914, dau. of 4th Earl of Arran; *d.* 1921; *s.* by his el. son [2] WALTER PATRICK, *C.B.*, *C.M.G.*, *D.S.O.*, 2nd Baron, *b.* 1870; Maj.-Gen. late Scots Guards; commanded Bangalore Brig. 1920-24, and London Dist. 1924-8, and was Lieut.-Gov. of Guernsey 1929-34: *m.* 1st, 1895, Jean Leslie, who *d.* 1952, dau. of the late Norman George Lampson [Lampson Bt., colls.]; 2ndly, 1953, Judith Gordon, dau. of the late Bertie E. Bell, of Guernsey; *d.* 1956; *s.* in the Barony of Ruthven of Gowrie (peerage of United Kingdom) by his great-nephew, ALEXANDER PATRICK GREYSTEIL, 3rd Baron, and 2nd Earl of Gowrie (ante).

GRAFTON, DUKE OF. (FitzRoy.) [Duke E. 1675.]

HUGH DENIS CHARLES FITZROY, 11th Duke; *b.* April 3rd, 1919; *s.* 1970; ed. at Eton and Magdalene Coll., Camb.; Hon. FRIBA; late Capt· Gren. Gds.; ADC to Viceroy of India 1943-47; patron of four livings, and Hereditary Ranger of Whittlebury Forest; Chm. of Soc. for Protection of Ancient Bldgs., of Nat. Trust, E. Anglian Regional Cttee., and of Exec. Cttee. of Historic Churches Preservation Trust, a Member of Historic Bldgs. Council for England, of Advisory Cttee. to Min. of Housing and Local Govt., of Cathedrals Advisory Cttee., and of Central Council for Care of Churches, and a Trustee of London Museum, of Sir John Soanes' Museum, and of Nat. Portrait Gallery: *m.* 1946 (Ann) Fortune, DCVO (Mistress of the Robes to HM the Queen), only da. of the late Capt. (Evan Cadogan) Eric Smith, and has issue.

Arms,—The royal arms of Charles II., viz. Quarterly: 1st and 4th, France and England quarterly; 2nd, Scotland; 3rd, Ireland: the whole debruised by a baton sinister-compony of six pieces, argent and azure. **Crest,**—On a chapeau gules, turned up ermine, a lion statant guardant or, ducally crowned azure, and gorged with a collar counter-compony argent and of the 4th. **Supporters,**—Dexter, a lion guardant or, ducally crowned azure; *sinister,* a greyhound argent; each gorged with a collar counter-compony argent and azure.

The ornament and recompense of virtue.

ET·DECUS·ET·PRETIUM·RECTI

Seat,—Euston Hall, Thetford, Norfolk. *Club,*—Boodle's.

SONS LIVING.

JAMES OLIVER CHARLES (*Earl of Euston*) (16, Campden St., W8), *b.* Dec. 13th, 1947; ed. at Eton and Magdalene Coll., Camb.; a Page of Honour to HM 1962-63: *m.* 1972, Lady Clare Annabel Kerr, 3rd da. of 12th Marquess of Lothian, and has issue living.
DAUGHTERS LIVING,—*Lady* Louise Helen, *b.* 1973,—*Lady* Emily Clare, *b.* 1974.
Lord Charles Patrick Hugh, *b.* 1957.

DAUGHTERS LIVING.

Lady Henrietta Fortune Doreen, *b.* 1949.
Lady Virginia Mary Elizabeth, *b.* 1954.
Lady Olivia Rose Mildred, *b.* 1963.

HALF-BROTHER LIVING.

Lord Edward Anthony Charles, *b.* 1928; ed. at Eton; late Capt. Coldm. Gds.; Chm. and Managing Dir. of Ross Poultry Ltd., and a Dir. of Imperial Foods Ltd., and of Beaver Boats Ltd.: *m.* 1956, Veronica Mary, da. of Maj. R. F. Ruttledge, of Moorfield, Ballybrack, co. Dublin, and has issue living, Michael Robert Charles, *b.* 1958,—Joanna Lucy, *b.* 1957,—Shauna Anne, *b.* 1963. *Residence,*—Norton House, Norwich, NR14 6RY. *Club,*—Pratt's.

SISTER LIVING.

Lady Anne Mildred Ismay, *b.* 1920: *m.* 1947, Major Colin Dalziel Mackenzie, M.B.E., M.C., late Seaforth Highlanders, and has issue living, Philip Austin George, *b.* 1949,—Caroline Doreen, *b.* 1952, —Laura Patience Kathleen, *b.* 1954,—Harriet Anne, *b.* 1958. *Residences,*—Farr, Inverness-shire; Bergh Apton Manor, Norwich. *Club,*—Turf.

SISTERS LIVING OF NINTH DUKE. (*Raised to the rank of a Duke's daughters* 1931.)
(*Co-heiresses to the Barony of Arlington, cr.* 1664, *and the Earldom of Arlington, er.* 1672.)

Lady (Margaret) Jane, *b.* 1916: *m.* 1936, Maj. Gen. Sir Eustace John Blois Nelson, KCVO, CB, DSO, MC, late Grenadier Guards [Blois, Bt.], and has issue living, Jennifer Jane, *b.* 1939: *m.* 1964, Rodney Simon Dudley Forwood, Capt. IG, of Wellow House, Wellow, Bath, and has issue living, Patrick John Dudley *b.* 1967, James Roland Nelson *b.* 1969,—Juliet Auriol Sally (*Lady Cholmeley*), *b.* 1940: *m.* 1960, Capt. Sir Montague John Cholmeley, 6th Bt. *Residence,*—Tigh Bhaan, Appin, Argyll.
Lady Mary Rose (*posthumous*), *b.* 1918: *m.* 1945 (m. diss. 1951), Francis Trelawny Williams, late Lieut. KRRC [Salusbury-Trelawny, Bt.], and has issue living, Linda Jane Auriol, *b.* 1947. *Residence,*—Turkdean, North Leach, Gloucestershire.

WIDOW LIVING OF BROTHER OF TENTH DUKE.

Kathleen Ruthar Mary, dau. of the late Rev. Arthur Willoughby Rokeby, of Clifton Manor, Shefford, Bedfordshire: *m.* 1st, 1929, Lord John Percy Samuel FitzRoy, who *d.* 1945; 2ndly, 19—, L. T. Carr ,and has issue living [see colls., infra). *Residence,*—.

COLLATERAL BRANCHES LIVING.

Issue of the late Lord John Percy Samuel FitzRoy, brother of 10th Duke, *b.* 1899, *d.* 1945: *m.* 1929, Kathleen Ruthar Mary [(ante); who *m.* 2ndly, 19—, L. T. Carr], da. of the late Rev. Arthur Willoughby Rokeby, of Clifton Manor, Shefford, Bedfordshire:—
Ismay Diana, *b.* 1933.

Grandson of the late Harold Charles Cavendish FitzRoy (infra):—
Issue of the late Charles Cavendish FitzRoy, *b.* 1900, *d.* 1960: *m.* 1st, 1926, Simone Andrée, who *d.* 1957, dau. of Jules Hennebert; 2ndly, 1957, Norah Bardsley, of 57, Harrow View, Harrow, Middlesex:—
(By 1st m.) Kenneth Cavendish, *b.* 1928: *m.* 1952, Pamela Mary, da. of Leslie Dodson, and has issue living, Ian Charles Cavendish, *b.* 1954,—Susan Pamela, *b.* 1955,—Rosemary Alison, *b.* 1964. *Address,* —c/o National Provincial Bank, Egham, Surrey.

Granddaughter of the late Major Cavendish Charles FitzRoy, son of the late Lieut.-Col. the Rt. Hon. Lord Charles FitzRoy, M.P., 2nd son of 4th Duke :—

Issue of the late Harold Charles Cavendish FitzRoy, *b.* 1870, *d.* 1939 : *m.* 1892, **Eliza Mary,**
who *d.* 1924, dau. of Thomas Butt, formerly of Prior's Court, Worcestershire:—
Mary Georgina Anne, *b.* 1897.   *Residence,*—57, Harrow View, Harrow, Middlesex.

Grandson of the late Rev. Augustus FitzRoy, grandson of 3rd Duke :—
Issue of the late Hugh Maitland FitzRoy, *b.* 1843, *d.* 1903: *m.* 1877, Bertha, who *d.* 1918,
dau. of the late Major Cecil Kearney, 15th Hussars [E. Coventry, colls.] :—
Ronald Hugh, *b.* 1878; late Capt. Scots Guards ; S. African War 1901-2 (medal with four **clasps),**
European War 1914-18 (1914 star, two medals).

Granddaughter of the late Sir Almeric William FitzRoy, KCB, KCVO, el. son of
Francis Horatio FitzRoy (infra):—
Issue of the late Nigel Horatio Trevor FitzRoy, *b.* 1889, *d.* 1953: *m.* 1st, 1917, Constance
(who obtained a divorce 1928), only dau. of the late Capt. Robert Henry Paul, R.N., of
The Highlands, Banbury; 2ndly, 1936, Diana Frances FitzRoy-Yates (Upend Stud
Farm, Newmarket, Suffolk), who *m.* 2ndly, 1958, William Edward Yates, who *d.* 1964),
el. da. of the late Brig. Arthur Francis Gore Pery-Knox-Gore, DSO [see E. Limerick,
colls.]:—
(By 2nd marriage) Susanna Diana Georgina, *b.* 1937: *m.* 1st, 1964 (m. annulled 1966), William Anthony
Coleridge; 2ndly, 1967, George Henry Peter-Hoblyn, of Manton Stables, Marlborough, Wilts.
[see Philipson-Stow, Bt.].

Grandchildren of the late Francis Horatio FitzRoy, son of the late Adm. Lord
William FitzRoy, K.C.B., 5th son of 3rd Duke :—
Issue of the late Cyril Duncombe FitzRoy, *b.* 1861, *d.* 1939: *m.* 1st, 1903, Leila Margaret,
who *d.* 1904, dau. of the late Robert Smith, of Goldings, Hertford; 2ndly, 1908,
Margaret Cuninghame, who *d.* 1948, dau. of the late Rev. James Samuel William
Durham, D.D., R. of Ladbroke, Warwickshire :—
(By 1st marriage) Esmé Leila Gertrude, *b.* 1904: *m.* 1936, Lieut.-Col. Reginald Henry Osgood
Hanbury, MC, 15th/19th KR Hussars, who *d.* 1973.   *Residence,*—Melgate, Slingsby, York.——(By
2nd m.) Charles Francis Mark, *b.* 1909: *m.* 1936, Baroness Irmgard, el. da. of the late Baron Rudolf
von Dincklage, of Hanover, and has issue living, Felix Rudolf, *b.* 1938; MSc, PhD (Heidelberg)—
Christina Margaret, *b.* 1944; BSc: *m.* 1974, Ali Kemâl Caba, of Izmir, Turkey.   *Residence,*—North
Lodge, Crimonmogate, Lonmay, Aberdeenshire.——Elizabeth Anne Horatio, *b.* 1912; Founder of
Catholic Handicapped Children's Fellowship, and Founder-Trustee of the Elizabeth FitzRoy Homes
for the Handicapped Trust; has Papal Cross Pro Ecclesia et Pontifice.   *Residence,*—The Coach
House, Whitegates, Liss, Hants.

Descendants of the late Lieut.-Gen. Charles FitzRoy (2nd son of Lord Augustus
FitzRoy, 2nd son of 2nd Duke), who was cr. *Baron Southampton* 1780 (Barony
disclaimed 1964) [see that title].

(*In special remainder to Earldom of Arlington only.*)
Descendants of the late Sir John Bennet, K.B. (el. brother of 1st Earl of
Arlington), who was cr. *Baron Ossulston* 1682 [see E. Tankerville].

PREDECESSORS.—[1] Henry Charles FitzRoy, *K.G.,* 2nd natural son of King Charles II., by
Barbara Villiers, Duchess of Cleveland ; cr. *Baron of Sudbury, Viscount Ipswich,* and *Earl of
Euston* (peerage of England) 1672, and *Duke of Grafton* (peerage of England) 1675 : *m.* 1682,
Isabella, in her own right Countess of Arlington, who in 1673 had *s.* by special remainder her
father, Henry Bennet, who had been cr. *Baron Arlington* of Arlington, Middlesex (peerage of
England) 1664, with special remainder, failing issue male, to the heirs of his body, and *Baron
Arlington,* of Arlington, Middlesex, *Viscount Thetford,* and *Earl of Arlington* (peerage of
England) 1672 with like special remainder, and in default of heirs of his body, with a further
remainder to his brother, Sir John Bennet, K.B., and the heirs male of his body ; was Lord High
Constable at Coronation of James II., and in 1685 commanded part of H.M.'s forces at the
landing of the Duke of Monmouth ; was afterwards one of the first to desert his royal master
for the Prince of Orange, in whose cause he was wounded in storming the City of Cork, and *d.*
within a fortnight afterwards, Oct. 9th, 1690 ; *s.* by his son [2] Charles, *K.G.,* 2nd Duke, who
in 1723 *s.* to his mother's peerages (ante) : *m.* 1713, Henrietta, sister of 2nd Duke of Beaufort ;
d. 1757 ; *s.* by his grandson [3] Augustus Henry, *K.G.,* 3rd Duke ; a Sec. of State 1765, 1st
Lord of the Treasury 1766, and Lord Privy Seal 1771 : *m.* 1st, 1756 (divorce by Act of Parliament
1769), the Hon. Anne Liddell, dau. of Henry, Baron Ravensworth (ext. 1784) ; 2ndly, 1769,
Elizabeth, dau. of the Very Rev. Sir Richard Wrottesley, 7th Bt.; *d.* 1811 ; *s.* by his el. son [4]
George Henry, *K.G.,* 4th Duke ; Lord-Lieut. of Suffolk : *m.* 1784, Lady Charlotte Maria, dau.
of 2nd Earl Waldegrave ; *d.* 1844 ; *s.* by his son [5] Henry, 5th Duke ; sometime M.P. for
Thetford : *m.* 1812, Mary Caroline, dau. of the late Adm. the Hon. Sir George Berkeley, G.C.B.
[E. Berkeley] ; *d.* 1863 ; *s.* by his el. son [6] William Henry, 6th Duke ; *b.* 1819; M.P. for Thetford (*L*) 1847-63 : *m.* 1858, the Hon. Marie Louisa Anne, who *d.* 1928, dau. of 3rd Baron Ashburton; *d.s.p.* May 21, 1882 ; *s.* by his brother [7] Augustus Charles Lennox, *K.G., C.B.,*
7th Duke, *b.* 1821 ; a Gen. in the Army ; Crimean Campaign 1854 (medal with three clasps,
Sardinian and Turkish medals, and 5th class Medjidie) ; an Equerry to Queen Victoria
1849-82, and an Hon. Equerry to Queen Victoria 1882-1901, to King Edward VII. 1901-10,
and to King George V. 1910-18 : *m.* 1847, Anna, who *d.* 1857, dau. of James Balfour, of
Whittinghame Hall, Berwick; *d.* 1918 ; *s.* by his son [8] Alfred William Maitland, 8th
Duke; *b.* 1850: *m.* 1st, 1875, Margaret Rose, who *d.* 1913, dau. of Eric Carrington Smith, of
Ashfold, Sussex; 2ndly, 1916, Susanna Mary, who *d.* 1961, dau. of Sir Mark John MacTaggart-
Stewart, 1st Bt., and widow of 17th Baron Borthwick; *d.* 1930; *s.* by his grandson [9] John Charles
William (son of William Henry Alfred, Viscount Ipswich), 9th Duke; *d.* 1936, when the
Barony of Arlington (cr. 1664), and the Viscountcy of Thetford and the Earldom of Arlington
(cr. 1672) fell into abeyance between the sisters of the 9th Duke ; *s.* in the Dukedom by his kinsman
[10] Charles Alfred Euston (son of the late Rev. Lord Charles Edward Fitz-Roy, 4th son of
7th Duke), 10th Duke, *b.* 1892: *m.* 1st, 1918, Lady Doreen Maria Josepha Sydney Buxton, who *d.*
1923, dau. of 1st Earl of Buxton; 2ndly, 1924, Lucy Eleanor, who *d.* 1943, da. of Sir George Stapylton
Barnes, KCB, KCSI [Buxton, By. cr. 1840, colls.]; 3rdly, 1944, Rita Emily, who *d.* 1970, da. of the
late John Ralph Stockley Carr-Ellison, and widow of Lt.-Cdr. John Thurburn Currie, RN; *d.* 1970;
s. by his el. son [11] Hugh Denis Charles, 11th Duke, and present peer; also Earl of Euston,
Viscount Ipswich, and Baron Sudbury.

Graham, Marquess of, son of Duke of Montrose.

Granard, Baron, title of Earl of Granard on Roll of H. L.

GRANARD, EARL OF. (Forbes.) Sits as BARON (U.K. 1806). [Earl I. 1684; Bt. S. 1628.]

The incitement to glory is the firebrand of the mind.

ARTHUR PATRICK HASTINGS FORBES, A.F.C., 9th Earl, and 10th Baronet ; b. April 10th, 1915 ; s. 1948 ; ed. at Eton, and at Trin. Coll., Camb. (B.A. 1937) ; is Air Commodore R.A.F. Vol. Reserve ; European War 1939-45 (despatches, AFC, Cdr. of Legion of Honour, Officer of American Legion of Merit, 4th class Order of George I. of Greece with crossed swords, French Croix de Guerre, Polish Cross of Valour): m. 1949, Marie Madeleine Eugène, yst. da. of Jean Maurel of Millau, Aveyron, and formerly wife of the late Prince Humbert de Fauciqny Lucinge, and has issue.

𝕬rms,—Azure, three bears' heads couped at the neck argent, muzzled gules. 𝕮rest,—A bear statant argent, guttée de sang, and muzzled gules. 𝕾upporters,—Dexter, an unicorn erminois, armed, maned, tufted, and unguled or ; sinister, a dragon wings elevated ermine.

Seat,—Castle-Forbes, Newtown Forbes, co. Longford. Residence,—73, Rue de Varenne, Paris. Clubs,—White's, Jockey (France).

DAUGHTERS LIVING.
Lady Moira Beatrice, b. 1951: m. 1971, HH Prince Charles Antoine Louis Lamora de Ligne de La Tremoille, of Chateau d'Antoing, Hainaut, Belgium.
Lady Georgina Ann, b. 1952.

BROTHER LIVING.
Hon. JOHN, b. Oct. 8th, 1920 ; ed. at Eton, and at Trin. Coll., Dublin (B.A. and B.A.I. 1947); is Flight-Lieut. R.A.F.; formerly Lieut. Signal Corps, Eire Army ; European War 1942-45: m. 1947, Peter Arthur Edward Hastings, b. 1957,—Susan, b. 1948,—Patricia Moira, b. 1950,—Caroline Joan, da. of A. Edward Smith, of Sherlockstown House, Sallins, co. Kildare, and has issue living, Mary, b. 1954: m. 1975, Dominick Charles Hamilton. Residences,—Graigueaverne House, Ballybrittas, Portlaoise, co. Leix; 87, Ailesbury Rd., Dublin, 4. Club,—Kildare Street.

SISTERS LIVING.
Lady Moira Mary FORBES, b. 1910: m. 1st, 1934 (marriage dissolved under French civil law 1936), Count Louis de Brantes ; 2ndly, 1942, Count Rossi di Montelera. Residence,—Château de Carpenito, La Loggia, Turin, Italy.
Lady Eileen Beatrice (Dowager Marchioness of Bute), b. 1912 : m. 1932, the 5th Marquess of Bute, who d. 1956. Residence,—Dumfries House, Old Cumnock, Ayrshire.

WIDOW LIVING OF SON OF SEVENTH EARL.
Mary Doreen, dau. of the late Andrew Sherlock Lawson [V. Mountgarret] : m. 1918, Col. the Hon. Donald Alexander Forbes, D.S.O., M.V.O., who d. 1938, and has issue living [see colls., infra]. Residence,—51, South Street. W.1.

COLLATERAL BRANCHES LIVING.
Issue of the late Col. the Hon. Donald Alexander Forbes, D.S.O., M.V.O., 4th son of 7th Earl, b. 1880, d. 1938 : m. 1918, Mary Doreen (ante), dau. of the late Andrew Sherlock Lawson [V. Mountgarret] :—
Rosaleen Frances, b. 1919 : m. 1956, Anthony Rhodes. Residence,—40, Lower Belgrave Street, S.W.1.
——Penelope, b. 1923: m. 1952, Sacheverell Reresby Sitwell, el. son of Sir Sacheverell Sitwell, 6th Bt, Residences,—4, Southwick Place, W2; Renishaw Hall, Derbyshire; Castello di Montegufoni, Florence.

Grandson of the late Col. The Hon. William Francis Forbes, brother of 7th Earl:—
Issue of the late Lieut.-Col. George Francis Reginald Forbes, Comdg. 1st Batn. Roy. Irish Regt., b. 1866, d. (of wounds in action) 1915 : m. 1904, Agnes Margaret, who d. 1944, dau. of the late Walter Ewing Crum :—
Walter Arthur Hastings, b. 1905 ; ed. at Winchester ; is Lieut.-Col. Cameronians (Scottish Rifles) (Reserve); formerly Game Warden, Sudan : m. 1946, Joan Margaret (KEITH MURRAY), el. dau. of Major H. Kettles-Roy, of Nairobi, Kenya, and has issue living, Peter Patrick Spencer, b. 1949,— Rolleen Ann, b. 1947. Residence,—Northcourt Farm, Clanfield, Oxon.

PREDECESSORS.—[1] Sir ARTHUR Forbes, Knt., great-great-grandson of the Hon. Patrick, 3rd son of 2nd Lord Forbes ; cr. a Baronet 1628 ; obtained grants of land in co. Longford ; killed in a duel 1632 ; s. by his son [2] Rt. Hon. Sir ARTHUR, P.C., 2nd Bt. ; Lt.-Gen. in the Army; M.P. for Mullingar 1661 ; having served under Montrose for the Royal Cause in Scotland, was after the Restoration appointed Marshal of the Army in Ireland, and constituted one of the Lords Justices 1671 and 1673 ; raised in 1684 the 18th Royal Irish Regt. ; cr. Baron Clanehugh and Viscount Granard (peerage of Ireland) 1675, and Earl of Granard (peerage of Ireland) 1684 ; d. 1696 ; s. by his son [3] ARTHUR, 2nd Earl ; was deprived of his command of the 18th Royal Irish Regt. and imprisoned in the Tower ; d. 1734 ; s. by his son [4] GEORGE, 3rd Earl ; an eminent Adm. ; Ambassador to Court of Muscovy ; called to House of Peers as Lord Forbes in lifetime of his father ; d. 1765 ; s. by his son [5] GEORGE, 4th Earl ; a Lt.-Gen. in the Army ; d. 1769 ; s. by his son [6] GEORGE, 5th Earl ; d. 1780 ; s. by his son [7] GEORGE, 6th Earl ; a Gen. in the Army, and Clerk of the Crown and Hanaper in Ireland ; cr. Baron Granard, of Castle Donington, co. Leicester (peerage of United Kingdom) 1806 ; d. 1837 ; s. by his grandson [8] GEORGE ARTHUR HASTINGS, K.P., 7th Earl (son of Major-Gen. George, Viscount Forbes, el. son of 6th Earl, by Frances Mary, V.A., dau. of the late William Territt, Esq., LL.D., of Chilton Hall, Suffolk), b. 1836 ; was Lord-Lieut. of co. Leitrim 1856-72 : m. 1st, 1858, Jane Colclough, who d. 1872, dau. of Hamilton Knox Grogan-Morgan, Esq., of Johnstown Castle, Wexford ; 2ndly, 1873, the Hon. Frances Mary, who d. 1920, dau. of 12th Baron Petre ; d. 1889 ; s. by his el. son [9] BERNARD ARTHUR WILLIAM PATRICK HASTINGS, P.C., K.P., G.C.V.O., 8th Earl ; b. 1874 ; Lieut.-Col. 8th Batn. City of London Regt., Lieut.-Col. Reserve of Officers (Scots Guards), Vice-Adm. of Province of Connaught, and a Dep. Speaker of House of Lords ; a Lord-in-Waiting to King Edward VII. 1905, Master of the Horse to King Edward VII. 1905-10, and to King George V. 1910-15 ; Assist. Postmaster-Gen. 1906-9, and again Master of the Horse 1924-36 ; a Member of Senate, S. Ireland June 1921, and of Irish Free State Dec. 1922 to Dec. 1934 ; H.M.'s Comptroller at Ascot 1936-45: m. 1909, Beatrice, O.B.E., who d. 1972, da. of the late Ogden Mills, of East 69th Street, New York, and Staatsburg, Dutchess Co., New York; d. 1948; s. by his el. son [10] ARTHUR PATRICK HASTINGS, 9th Earl and present peer; also Viscount Granard, Baron Clanehugh, and Baron Granard.

Granby, Marquess of, son of Duke of Rutland.

GRANTCHESTER, BARON. (Suenson-Taylor.) [Baron U.K. 1953.]

ALFRED JESSE SUENSON-TAYLOR, O.B.E., 1st Baron, son of the late Alfred George Taylor, of Stowford, Sutton, Surrey; b. Aug. 14th, 1893; ed. at Epsom Coll., and at King's Coll., Camb. (MA); Bar. Middle Temple 1920; a Dir. of London & Manchester Assurance Co. Ltd. 1934-67 (Chm. 1953-61) and of Westminster and County Insurance Offices, Ltd. 1934-68; a Dir. of United Stock-yards Corpn. (of USA), of Canal Randolph Corpn. (of USA), and of Onyx Country Estates Ltd., Vice-Pres. of United Nations Assocn., a Fellow of the Chartered Insurance Institute, a FRSA, a FRGS, a Vice-Pres. of London Insurance Institute, a Member of Roy. Institute of Inter-national Affairs, a Gov. of British Soc. for International Understanding, a Member of Mont Pelerin Soc. (Internat. Economic), and Editor of The Owl; Pres. of Insurance Institute of Kent 1934; Delegate to Council of Europe and W. European Union 1957-66, and a Member of various cttees.; initiated meet-ings of EFTA Parliamentarians at Strasbourg; Pres. Emeritus of London Liberal Party; has Orders of DSLJ, DHBS and DSNS (Brunei); 1914-18 War in Gallipoli and France as Maj. RASC and on Staff (despatches twice, OBE, 1914-15 star, and two French decorations); cr. OBE (Mil) 1919, Knt. 1935, and Baron Grantchester, of Knightsbridge, in the City of Westminster (peerage of UK) 1953: m. 1920, Mara Henrietta (Mamie), da. of the late Albert Suenson, of Copenhagen, and has issue.

Arms,—Quarterly, 1st and 4th sable, on a fesse engrailed between in chief a fleur-de-lys between two annulets or, and in base as many like annulets a lion passant of the field, Taylor; 2nd and 3rd gules, in chief two swans rousant proper each crowned with an antique crown or, and in base barry wavy of six argent and azure, Suenson. Crests,—1st, issuant from a crown palisado or an unicorn's head sable armed and charged on the neck with an annulet gold and holding in the mouth an acorn leaved and slipped proper, Taylor; 2nd, issuant from a coronet composed of eight roses gules seeded argent set upon a rim or, a swan rousant proper crowned with an antique crown gold, Suenson. Supporters,—Dexter, an unicorn sable armed and crined or, gorged with a collar argent, thereon a fesse wavy azure; sinister, a lion or, gorged with a collar of four hearts gules.

Residences,—49, Grosvenor Sq., W1X 9AA; 52, Westminster Mansions, 1, Little Smith St., SW1.

SON LIVING.

Hon. KENNETH BENT, QC, b. Aug. 18th, 1921; ed. at Westminster, and at Christ's Coll., Camb. (BA 1942, MA 1946, LLB 1946, LLM 1955); Bar. Middle Temple, and Lincoln's Inn 1946; QC 1971: m. 1947, Betty, da. of John Moores, and has issue living, Christopher John, b. 1951,—Jeremy Kenneth (twin), b. 1951,—James Gunnar, b. 1955,—Janet Elizabeth Gudrun, b. 1949: m. 1973, Gerald Edgar Grimstone,—Deborah Katherine Louise, b. 1957,—Kirsten Victoria Mary, b. 1961. Residence,—The Gate House, Coombe Wood Road, Kingston Hill, Surrey.

DAUGHTER LIVING.

Hon. Monica Esmé Ebba, b. 1926; ed. at Queen's Coll., London, and Newnham Coll., Camb. (B.A. 1947, MA 1950): m. 1951, (m. diss. 1965) Graeme Spotswood Parish, and has issue living,—Alexandra Francesca Spotswood, b. 1953. Residence,—71, Princes House, Kensington Park Rd., W11.

GRANTLEY, BARON. (Norton.) [Baron G.B. 1782.]

I follow a long line of ancestry.

AVI · NUMERANTUR · AVORUM

JOHN RICHARD BRINSLEY NORTON, *M.C.*, 7th Baron; *b.* July 30th, 1923; *s.* 1954; ed. at Eton, and at New Coll., Oxford; a Member of Lloyd's; a Dir. of Leslie & Godwin, Ltd.; 1939-45 War in Italy as Capt. Grenadier Guards (MC): *m.* 1955, Lady Deirdre Freda Mary Hare, da. of the 5th Earl of Listowel, and has issue.

Arms,—Azure, a maunch ermine, surmounted by a bend gules. Crest,—A Moor's head affrontée, couped at the shoulders proper, wreathed round the temples with laurel, and round the neck a torse, argent and azure. Supporters.—*Dexter*, a lion, and *sinister*, a griffin, both argent and ducally gorged or, and pendent from the coronets, by a red ribbon, a shield of the arms of *Norton*.

Residences,—Markenfield Hall, Ripon; 53, Lower Belgrave St., S.W.1. *Clubs*,—White's, Pratt's.

SONS LIVING.

Hon. RICHARD WILLIAM BRINSLEY, *b.* Jan. 30th, 1956.
Hon. Francis John Hilary, *b.* 1960.

SISTER LIVING.

Hon. Sarah Katharine Elinor (23, Scarsdale Villas, W8), *b.* 1920: *m.* 1st, 1945 (m diss. 1953), the 3rd Viscount Astor, who *d.* 1966; 2ndly, 1953, Maj. Thomas Michael Baring, Derbyshire Yeo., from whom she obtained a divorce 1965 [see B. Northbrook, colls.].

COLLATERAL BRANCH LIVING.

Grandson of the late Capt. Robert Thomas Lowndes-Stone-Norton, son of the late Rev. the Hon. James Norton, brother of 3rd Baron:—
Issue of the late Major Roger Fletcher Earle Lowndes-Stone-Norton, *b.* 1863, *d.* 1934: *m.* 1890, Agnes Selina, who *d.* 1941, dau. of the Rev. William Henry Thornton, formerly R. of N. Bovey, Devon:—
Fletcher William, *b.* 1908; ed. at Eton, and at Ch. Ch., Oxford (B.A. 1932); is a Rubber Planter in Malaysia; European War 1940 in France and Belgium as Major Oxfordshire and Buckinghamshire L.I.: *m.* 1941, Emma Dorothy (from whom he obtained a divorce 1945), dau. of the late Henry Thomas Gager, of New York, U.S.A. *Clubs*,—Naval and Military, Selangor (Kuala Lumpur.)

PREDECESSORS.—[1] Sir FLETCHER Norton, *K.B.*, *P.C.*; M.P. for Appleby 1754-61, and for Wigan 1761-82, Solicitor-Gen. 1761, Attorney-Gen. 1763 and Speaker of the House of Commons 1769-82; cr. *Lord Grantley, Baron of Markenfield*, co. York (peerage of United Kingdom) 1782; *d.* 1789; *s.* by his son [2] WILLIAM, 2nd Baron; *d.* 1822; *s.* by his nephew [3] FLETCHER, 3rd Baron, son of the Hon. Fletcher, 2nd son of 1st Baron; present at Quatre Bras and Waterloo; *d.s.p.* 1875; *s.* by his nephew [4] THOMAS BRINSLEY, 4th Baron, 2nd son of the Hon. George Chapple Norton, brother of 3rd Baron; *b.* 1831: *m.* 1854, Maria Chiara Eliza, who *d.* 1892, dau. of Signor Federigo; *d.* 1877; *s.* by his son [5] JOHN RICHARD BRINSLEY, 5th Baron; *b.* 1855: *m.* 1st, 1879, Katharine, who *d.* 1897, dau. of the late William Henry McVickar, of U.S.A.; 2ndly, 1899, Alice, who *d.* 1942, natural dau. of 7th Viscount Ranelagh; *d.* 1943; *s.* by his son [6] RICHARD HENRY BRINSLEY, 6th Baron; *b.* 1892; *m.* 1919, Jean Mary, who *d.* 1945, dau. of Sir David Alexander Kinloch, O.B., M.V.O., 11th Bt.; *d.* 1954; *s.* by his only son [7] JOHN RICHARD BRINSLEY, 7th Baron and present peer.

GRANVILLE, EARL. (Leveson-Gower.) [Earl U.K. 1833.]

[Name pronounced "Looson-Gore."]

You may break, but you will not bend me.

FRANGAS NON FLECTES

GRANVILLE JAMES LEVESON-GOWER, *M.C.*, 5th Earl; *b.* Dec. 6th, 1918; *s.* 1953; ed. at Eton; Maj. Coldm. Gds. (Supplementary Reserve); a DL for Inverness-shire; Pres. of Navy League 1953-66; 1939-45 War in Tunisia and Italy (twice wounded, despatches, MC): *m.* 1958, Doon Aileen, da. of the late Flight-Lieut. the Hon. Brinsley Sheridan Bushe Plunket, RAF Vol. Reserve [see B. Plunket], and has issue.

Arms,—Quarterly: 1st and 4th, barry of eight, argent and gules, a cross flory sable, *Gower*; 2nd azure, three laurel leaves or, *Leveson*; 3rd gules, three clarions or, *Granville*; in the centre a crescent for difference. Crest.—A wolf passant argent, collared and lined or. Supporters.—Two wolves argent, plain collared, and line reflexed over the back gold, and charged on the shoulder with an escutcheon gules thereon a clarion or.

Residences,—49, Lyall Mews, SW1; Callernish, N. Uist, Inverness-shire.

SONS LIVING.

GRANVILLE GEORGE FERGUS (*Lord Leveson*), *b.* Sept. 10th, 1959; appointed a Page of Honour to HM Queen Elizabeth, The Queen Mother 1973.
Hon. Niall James, *b.* 1963.

DAUGHTER LIVING.

Lady Marcia Rose Aileen, *b.* 1961.

SISTER LIVING.

Lady Mary Cecilia, *b.* 1917: *m.* 1956, Samuel Wittewronge Clayton, son of the late Brig.-Gen. Sir Gilbert Falkingham Clayton, K.C.M.G., K.B.E., C.B., and has issue living, Gilbert Falkingham, *b.* 1958; a page of Honour to HM Queen Elizabeth, The Queen Mother 1973-74,—Rose Cecilia, *b.* 1960. *Residence,*—Borad Lea, Long Martin, Appleby, Westmorland.

COLLATERAL BRANCH LIVING.

Granddaughter of the late Hon. Edward Frederick Leveson-Gower, 3rd son of 1st Earl :—
Issue of the late Sir George Granville Leveson-Gower, K.B.E., *b.* 1858, *d.* 1951 : *m.* 1898, the Hon. Adelaide Violet Cicely, who *d.* 1955, dau. of 8th Baron Monson :—
Edomé Georgiana Lavender, *b.* 1906. *Residence,*

PREDECESSORS.—[1] *Lord* GRANVILLE Leveson-Gower, *G.C.B., P.C.,* youngest son of 1st Marquess of Stafford [see D. Sutherland]; *b.* 1773; was sometime Sec. at War, and successively Ambassador to Russia, Holland and France, cr. *Viscount Granville* (peerage of United Kingdom) 1815, and *Baron Leveson,* of Stone, co. Stafford, and *Earl Granville* (peerage of United Kingdom) 1833: *m.* 1809, Lady Henrietta Elizabeth Cavendish, who *d.* 1862, dau. of 5th Duke of Devonshire; *d.* 1846; *s.* by his son [2] GRANVILLE GEORGE, *K.G., P.C.,* 2nd Earl, *b.* 1815; M.P. for Morpeth (*L*) 1837-40, and for Lichfield 1841-6; was Under-Sec. for Foreign Affairs 1840-41, Vice-Pres. of Board of Trade 1848-51, Sec. of State for Foreign Affairs 1851-2, 1870-74, and 1880-85, Lord Pres. of Council 1852-4, 1855-8, and 1859-66, Chancellor of Duchy of Lancaster 1854-5, Ambassador Extraor. to Russia at coronation of Alexander II, 1856, and Sec. of State for the Colonies 1868-70 and 1886; sometime Constable of Dover Castle, and Lord Warden of the Cinque Ports: *m.* 1st, 1840, Marie Louise Pelline, who *d.* 1860, dau. of Emeric Joseph Duc de Dalberg, and widow of Sir Ferdinand Richard Edward Acton, 7th Bt.; 2ndly, 1865, Castalia Rosalind, who *d.* 1938, dau. of Walter Campbell, of Islay; *d.* 1891; *s.* by his el. son [3] GRANVILLE GEORGE, *G.C.M.G., G.C.V.O., P.C.,* 3rd Earl, *b.* 1872; a Lord-in-Waiting to Queen Victoria 1895-1905, to King Edward VII, 1905-10, and to King George V 1910-15, Envoy Extraor. and Min. Plen. to Greece 1917-21, to Denmark 1921-6, and to the Netherlands 1926-8, and Ambassador Extraor. and Plen. to Belgium and Luxembourg 1928-33: *m.* 1900, Nina Ayesha, who *d.* 1955, dau. of the late Walter Baring; *d.* 1939; *s.* by his brother [4] WILLIAM SPENCER, *K.G., K.C.V.O., C.B., D.S.O.,* 4th Earl; *b.* 1880; Vice-Adm.; Ch. of Staff and Maintenance Capt. the Nore 1924-27, and Rear-Adm. Comdg. Coast of Scotland 1931-33; Lieut.-Gov. of Isle of Man 1937-45, and Gov. of N. Ireland 1945-52; 1914-18 War (D.S.O.) : *m.* 1908, Lady Rose Constance Bowes-Lyon, *G.C.V.O., LL.D.,* who *d.* 1967, dau. of 14th Earl of Strathmore; *d.* 1953; *s.* by his son [5] GRANVILLE JAMES, 5th Earl and present peer; also Viscount Granville, and Baron Leveson.

GRANVILLE OF EYE, BARON. (Granville.) [Life Baron 1967.]

EDGAR LOUIS GRANVILLE, son of Reginald Granville, of Brighton; *b.* Feb. 12th, 1899; ed. at High Wycombe and Melbourne, Australia; Managing Dir. of E. L. Granville & Co. Ltd.; PPS to Sec. of State, Sir Herbert Samuel, first Nat. Govt. 1931, and to Foreign Sec., Sir John Simon, National Govt. 1931-36; MP for Eye Div. of Suffolk (*L.*) 1929-51; joined Labour Party 1951; 1914-18 War with AIF, Gallipoli, Egypt and France; 1939-45, helped to raise 119th Suffolk Battery RA, as acting Capt.; cr. *Baron Granville of Eye,* of Eye, co. Suffolk (Life Baron) 1967: *m.* 1943, Elizabeth, da. of the late Rev. William Cecil Hunter, British Mission Sch., India, and has issue.

Arms.—Tierced in pairle vert purpure and azure, in chief two sea gulls volant proper, and in base a sun in splendour charged with an eye, and on a bordure or eight beech leaves proper in aestival and autumnal tints alternately. Crest,—In front of a mount vert, thereon a beech tree proper, a chaplet of roses argent barbed and seeded proper. Supporters,—*Dexter,* a bay horse, *sinister,* a kangaroo proper.
Residence,—112, Charlton Lane, Cheltenham.

DAUGHTER LIVING.

Hon. Linda, *b.* 1949.

GRANVILLE-WEST, BARON (West.) [Life Baron 1958.]

DANIEL GRANVILLE WEST, son of John West, of Newbridge, Monmouthshire; *b.* March 17th, 1904; admitted a Solicitor 1929; Senior Partner in the firm of D. Granville West, Chivers & Morgan, of Newbridge, and Pontypool; was Parliamentary Private Sec. to Home Sec. 1950-51; a Member of Estimates Committee 1946-51, and of Committee of Public Accounts 1951-9; 1939-45 War with R.A.F. Vol. Reserve; sat as M.P. (*Lab.*) for Pontypool Div. of Monmouthshire July 1946 to July 1953; cr. *Baron Granville-West,* of Pontypool, co. Monmouth (Life Baron) 1958: *m.* 1937, Vera, dau. of J. Hopkins, of Pontypool, and has issue.
Residence,—Brynderwen, Abersychan, Monmouthshire.

SON LIVING.

Hon. Gerald Hugh Granville (Saas Fee, Ffrwyd Rd., Abersychan, Mon, NP4 8PF), *b.* 1942: *m.* 1969, Barbara, da. of Arthur Strath, of Ellwood Dene, Kilndown, Cranbrook, Kent, and has issue.

DAUGHTER LIVING.

Hon. Vera Lesley Meryl, *b.* 1937: *m.* 1959, William Smith, of Hollycroft, Sunnybank Rd., Griffithstown, Mon. and has issue.

GRAVES, BARON. (Graves.) [Baron I. 1794.]

PETER GEORGE WELLESLEY GRAVES, 8th Baron; *b.* Oct. 21st, 1911; *s.* 1963; ed. at Harrow; an Actor: *m.* 1960, Winifred Ruby (the actress Vanessa Lee), dau. of Alfred Moule, and widow of Warde Morgan.

Arms,—Gules, an eagle, displayed or ducally crowned argent, on a canton of the last an anchor proper. Crest,—A demi-eagle, displayed and erased or, encircled round the body and below the wings by a ducal coronet argent. Supporters,—Two royal vultures, wings close proper.

Residence,—11, Sheldrake Place, Duchess of Bedford Walk, W.8.

DAUGHTERS LIVING OF SIXTH BARON.

Hon. Cerise Evelyn Georgina, *b.* 1906. *Residence,*—Halsted, Tilford, Surrey.
Hon. Rosemary Alys Audrey, *b.* 1910: *m.* 1938, Major Herbert Edward Osborne, M.C., who *d.* 1951. *Residence,*—35, Primrose Gdns., N.W.3.

The eagle does not catch flies.
COLLATERAL BRANCHES LIVING.

Grandchildren of the late Hon. Henry Richard Graves, 3rd son of 2nd Baron:—
Issue of the late Augustus Edgar Graves, *b.* 1856, *d.* 1896: *m.* 1889, Josephine, who *d.* 1924, dau. of the late Joseph Robinson, of Lewins, Edenbridge, Kent:—
Millicent Olive, *b.* 1890: *m.* 1912, Capt. Walter Randolph Bernard, R.N. (retired), who *d.* 1950, and has issue living, Peter Graves (37 St. Luke's St., SW3), *b.* 1913: *m.* 1957, Mary Rose, da. of the late John Coleridge Patteson, CMG, and widow of Richard Fox-Linton, and has issue living, John Patteson *b.* 1959, Araminta *b.* 1961, Alexandra *b.* 1964,—Josephine, *b.* 1915: *m.* 1st, 1938 (m. diss. 1945), John Francis Ainsworth (now 3rd Bt.), el. son of Sir Thomas Ainsworth, 2nd Bt.; 2ndly, 1947, Lt. Trevor Russell West, RNVR, of Church Farm House, Hulcott, Aylesbury, Bucks. and has issue living, (by 2nd m.) Jeremy David Trevor *b.* 1948: *m.* 1974, Diana, el. da. of Maj. Sir Philip Digby Pauncefort-Duncombe, 4th Bt., Peta Caroline *b.* 1951: *m.* 1974, Timothy Charles Whitlock,—Patricia Rosemary Hawker (Manyons, Barkway, Royston, Herts.), *b.* 1919: *m.* 1st, 1940, Patrick Robert Cecil Guinness, Sub-Lieut. RN, who *d.* (killed in action) 1941; 2ndly, 1945, Lieut. (A) John Robert Dimsdale, RNVR, who *d.* 1951; 3rdly, 1958, Michael Henry Piercy [B. Forteviot], and has issue living, (by 2nd m.) Jonathan Camplin *b.* 1946, (by 3rd m.) Patrick Basil *b.* 1959, Stephen Michael *b.* 1961. *Residence,*—The Old Forge, Barkway, Royston, Herts.

Grandchildren of the late Hon. Adolphus Edward Paget Graves (infra):—
Issue of the late Alwyn Montague Graves, *b.* 1892, *d.* 1956: *m.* 1924, Kathleen Eleanor Cowley Priest who *d.* 1974:—
EVELYN PAGET, *b.* May 17th, 1926: *m.* 1957, Marjorie Ann, dau. of the late Dr. Sidney Ernest Holder, of Wallingford, Berks, and has issue living, Timothy Evelyn, *b.* 1960,—Simon Paget, *b.* 1963,—Wendy Susan, *b.* 1958,—Philippa Ann, *b.* 1962. *Residence,*—Woodlands, Lemana, Tasmania.—
Diana Wellesley, *b.* 1934: *m.* 1st, 1956 (m. diss. 1974) Edgar Mark Wolfhagen; 2ndly, 1974, Guy Paul Emile Peltzer, of Ravensworth, Longford, Tasmania, and has issue living, (by 1st m.) Julian Mark, *b.* 1957,—Martin Charles, *b.* 1959,—Philip Gerret Wellesley, *b.* 1963,—Quentin Evelyn, *b.* 1969.
Issue of the late Lieut.-Com. Vernon North Graves, D.S.C., R.N., *b.* 1911, *d.* 1960: *m.* 1947, Elizabeth Constance (Linkhurst, Stonegate, Wadhurst, Sussex), da. of the late Capt. R. Uniacke Penrose FitzGerald, RN:—
Janice Penrose Iona (Upper Wenbans Cottage, Wadhurst, Sussex), *b.* 1947: *m.* 1968 (m. diss. 1974), Stephen Van Simons, and has issue living, Isobel Jane, *b.* 1972.—Sarah Frances Paget, *b.* 1950.
Issue of the late Hon. Adolphus Edward Paget Graves (uncle of 6th Baron), son of the late Hon. Henry Richard Graves (ante), *b.* 1855, *d.* 1931: *m.* 1st, 1886, Elaine Mabelle, who *d.* 1887, dau. of the late Robert Leake; 2ndly, 1889, Katherine Louisa, who *d.* 1900, dau. of Col. Henry Constantine Evelyn Ward, CIE; 3rdly, 1909, Hilda May, who *d.* 1966, da. of the late David Cruickshank:—

(By 2nd m.) Irene (The Thatched Cottage, Iffley, Oxford), *b.* 1897: *m.* 1921, Brig. Frederick Ivor de la Poer Garforth, RE, who *d.* 1962, and has issue living, Rosemary Katharine Jane, *b.* 1925: *m.* 1st, 1944 (m. diss. 1953), Richard Lawrence Westinghouse, DFC; 2ndly, 1955, Cdr. Ian Wigram Valentine Browne, RN, of Crabwood Farm House, Crabwood, Winchester, and has issue living (by 1st m.) Timothy Adrian *b.* 1946: *m.* 1970, Virginia Walmisley-Dresser, Tatiana *b.* 1944: *m.* 1,966, Thomas Orde Treadwell, of 25, Edwardes Sq., SW,—Griselda Mary, *b.* 1936: *m.* 1959, Ormonde Maitland Valentine Browne, of 1, Wharf Rd., Longueville, NSW, and has issue living, Polly *b.* 1969.

Granddaughter of the late Capt. the Hon. Adolphus Edward Paget Graves, 4th son of 2nd Baron:—
Issue of the late Cyril Edward Cuthbert Hare Graves, *b.* 1860, *d.* 1946: *m.* 1916, Constance Katherine, who *d.* 1951, dau. of the late François Chrysostom Mouflet, of Leamington:—
Mary Caroline Margot, *b.* 1919: *m.* 1942, Albert Arthur Puddick, of Fishers, New Pound, Wisborough Green, Sussex, and has issue living, Robert Arthur Graves, *b.* 1944,—David Stewart Graves, *b.* 1946.

PREDECESSORS.—[1] THOMAS Graves, 2nd son of the late Rear-Adm. Thomas Graves, of Thanckes, Cornwall; *b.* 1725; Adm. of the White; was second in command under Lord Howe at great Naval Victory of June 1st, 1794 (cr. Baron and granted pension of £1,000 per annum): *m.* 1771, Elizabeth, who *d.* 1827, dau. of the late William Peere Williams, of Cadhay, Devon; *cr. Lord Graves, Baron of Gravesend,* co. Londonderry (peerage of Ireland) 1794; *d.* 1802; *s.* by his son [2] THOMAS NORTH, 2nd Baron; M.P.; a Lord of the Bedchamber and Comptroller of the Household to H.R.H. the Duke of Cumberland: *m.* 1803, Lady Mary Paget, who *d.* 1835, youngest du. of 1st Earl of Uxbridge, and sister of 1st Marquess of Anglesey, K.G.; *d.* 1830, *s.* by his son [3] WILLIAM THOMAS, 3rd Baron, *b.* 1804: *m.* 1st, 1829, Sophie Therese, who *d.* 1833, dau. of Gen. Berthier, and widow of Gen. Count Bruyere; 2ndly, Louise Adèle Malene, who *d.* 1877; *s.* by his son [4] CLARENCE EDWARD, *b.* 1847: *m.* 1870, Katherine Frederica, who *d.* 1926, dau. of Sir Thomas William Clinton Murdoch, K.C.M.G.; *d.* 1904; *s.* by his cousin [5] HENRY CYRIL PERCY (son of the late Hon. Henry Richard Graves, 3rd son of 2nd Baron), 5th Baron, *b.* 1847: *m.* 1870, Elizabeth Ellen, who *d.* 1914, youngest dau. of the late

Henry Craven, of Wickham Hall, Kent: *d.* 1914; *s.* by his son [6] CLARENCE PERCY RIVERS, 6th Baron, *b.* 1871: *m.* 1903, his cousin, Mary Ada Isabel, who *d.* 1962, dau. of the late Edward Corbett Parker; *d.* 1937; *s.* by his cousin [7] HENRY ALGERNON CLAUDE (son of the late Claude Thomas Graves, son of the late Hon. Henry Richard Graves, 3rd son of 2nd Baron), 7th Baron *b.* 1877: *m.* 1909, Vera Blanche Neville, who *d.* 1953, and from whom he obtained a divorce 1922, dau. of the late Alfred Neville Shepp: *d.* 1963: *s.* by his son [8] PETER GEORGE WELLESLEY, 8th Baron and present peer.

GRAY, LORD.　(Campbell-Gray.)　[Lord S. 1445.]

ANGUS DIARMID IAN CAMPBELL-GRAY, 22nd Lord ; *b.* July 3rd, 1931 ; *s.* 1946 ; ed. at Eton : *m.* 1959, Patricia Margaret, only dau. of the late Capt. Philip Sylvester Alexander, 8th Hussars [see E. Caledon, colls.], and has issue.

Arms,—Gules a lion rampant within a bordure engrailed argent, over all a label of two points or, each point charged gyronny of eight or and sable. Crest,— An anchor in pole or. Supporters,—Two lions guardant gules charged with a label as in the arms. *Residence,*—Airds Bay House, Taynuilt, Argyll. *Club,*—Carlton.

SON LIVING.
Hon. ANDREW GODFREY DIARMID STUART (*Master of Gray*), *b.* Sept. 3rd, 1964.

DAUGHTERS LIVING.
Hon. Lucinda Margaret, *b.* 1961.
Hon. Iona Doreen, *b.* 1962.
Hon. Cethlyn Isobell, *b.* 1969.

BROTHER LIVING.
(*Raised to the rank of a Baron's son* 1950.)
Hon. Cailain Douglas (The Old Rectory, Ovington, Alresford, Hants.), *b.* 1934; ed. at Eton: *m.* 1963, Wendy Helen Katharine, yr. da. of W. H. Dunlop, of Doonside, Ayrshire, and has issue living, James Douglas, *b.* 1966,—Charlotte Anne, *b.* 1968.

SISTERS LIVING.
(*Raised to the rank of a Baron's daughters* 1950.)
Hon. Fiona Faith, *b.* 1933: *m.* 1955, Major (Ronald Hugh) Desmond Fabling, R. Dragoons (ret.), who *d.* 1974, and has issue living, Victoria Theresa, *b.* 1958,—Fenella Mary, *b.* 1963. *Residence,*—Victoria House, Ampleforth, Yorks., YO6 4DA.
Hon. Christine Anne, *b.* 1938: *m.* 1960, Brian Joseph Lockhart, Blues and Royals, and has issue living, Crispin Alexander, *b.* 1967. *Residence,*—Hawkesbury, South Drive, Wokingham, Berks.

GREAT-AUNT LIVING.
(*Daughter of Eveleen, Lady Gray.*)
Hon. Kathleen Eileen Moray GRAY, *b.* 1879. *Residence,,*—21, Rue Bonaparte, 75, Paris, VI.

WIDOW LIVING OF SON OF ETHEL EVELEEN, LADY GRAY.
Diana (*Viscountess Gage*), da. of the late Col. the Rt. Hon. Lord Richard Frederick Cavendish, CB, CMG, [see D. Devonshire, colls.]: *m.* 1st, 1935, Robert John Graham Boothby,—afterwards Baron Boothby, from whom she obtained a divorce 1937; 2ndly, 1942, Lt.-Col. the Hon. Ian Douglas Campbell-Gray, who *d.* 1946; 3rdly, 1971, the 6th Viscount Gage, of Firle Pl., Lewes.

COLLATERAL BRANCHES LIVING.
　　Issue of the late Hon. Thora Zelma Grace Gray, da. of Eveleen, Lady Gray, *b.* 1875; *d.* 1966: *m.* 1911, Edward Lorne Frederic Clough-Taylor [D. Argyll], who *d.* 1947:—
Cara Prunella (65, Moore Park Rd., SW6), *b.* 1919

　　Descendants of the late Hon. Archibald Stuart, 2nd son of the late Hon. Jean Gray (el. dau. of 11th Lord), who *m.* 1763, the 9th Earl of Moray [see that title].

PREDECESSORS.—[1] ANDREW, son of Sir Andrew Gray; successively Ambassador to England, Master of the Household to King James II., and a Warden of the Marches; cr. *Lord Gray* (peerage of Scotland), 1444-5, according to Exchequer Rolls; *s.* by his grandson [2] ANDREW, 2nd Lord ; a Justiciary of Scotland ; *s.* by his son [3] PATRICK, 3rd Lord ; *d.* 1541; *s.* by his nephew [4] PATRICK (son of Gilbert Gray, 2nd son of 2nd Lord); *d.* 1584; *s.* by his son [5] PATRICK, 5th Lord, *b.* 1538 ; a Lord of Session; *d.* 1609; *s.* by his son [6] PATRICK, 6th Lord, *b.* 1584; *d.* 1611; *s.* by his son [7] ANDREW, 7th Lord ; obtained a new patent with remainder to William Gray, husband of his only dau. Anne, and his heirs male, and failing which to Sir William Gray, of Pittendrum, father of William Gray (*ante*), and his heirs male whatsoever; *s.* by his grandson [8] PATRICK, 8th Lord, son of Anne and William Gray (*ante*) ; resigned his honours Feb. 1707, and in the same month obtained a new patent with the former precedency with remainder to John Gray, of Crichie, husband of his dau. Marjory, and the heirs of their bodies, and failing which to the el. heir female without division; in virtue of this patent [9] JOHN GRAY (*ante*) became 9th Lord, even during the lifetime of Patrick, 8th Lord ; John *d.* 1724; *s.* by his son [10] JOHN, 10th Lord ; *d.* 1738 ; *s.* by his son [11] JOHN, 11th Lord ; *d.* 1782; *s.* by his third son [12] CHARLES, 12th Lord ; was Capt. 1st Dragoon Guards; *d.* unmarried 1786 ; *s.* by his brother [13] WILLIAM JOHN, 13th Lord ; *d.* unmarried 1807; *s.* by his brother [14] FRANCIS, 14th Lord ; was Postmaster Gen. of Scotland ; *d.* 1842 ; *s.* by his son [15] JOHN, 15th Lord ; a Representative Peer ; *d.s.p.* 1867 ; *s.* by his sister [16] MADELINA ; *d.* unmarried 1869 ; *s.* by her niece [17] MARGARET, dau. of the Hon. Margaret, 2nd dau. of 14th Lord, and wife of the Hon. David Henry Murray, son of 3rd Earl of Mansfield; *d.* 1878 ; *s.* by her cousin [18] GEORGE PHILIP, 14th Earl of Moray (heir male of the Hon. Jean, el. dau. of 11th Lord Gray, *ante*); *b.* 1816 ; *d.* 1895; when the Earldom of Moray and the Baronies of Doune, St. Colme, and Stuart passed to his cousin, Edmund Archibald [see E. Moray], and the Lordship of Gray was adjudged by the Committee for Privileges of the House of Lords to [19] EVELEEN, dau. of the late Lady Jane Pounden, dau. of 10th Earl of Moray, *b.* 1841 : *m.* 1863, James Maclaren Smith, who *d.* 1900, having received Roy. licence 1897 to assume for himself and wife the additional surname and arms of Gray, and for his issue to assume the surname of Gray in lieu of their patronymic with the arms of Gray only); *d.* 1918; *s.*

by her son [20] JAMES MACLAREN STUART, 20th Lord, *b*. 1864; *d*. 1919; *s*. by his sister [21] ETHEL EVELEEN, *b*. 1866: *m*. 1888, Henry Tufnell Campbell, who *d*. 1945, having assumed by Roy. licence 1920, the additional surname of Gray; *d*. 1946 ; *s*. by her grandson [22] ANGUS DIARMID IAN (son of the late Major the Hon. Lindsay Stuart Campbell-Gray, M.C. (*Master of Gray*), el. son of Ethel Eveleen, Lady Gray), 22nd Lord and present peer.

GREENE OF HARROW WEALD, BARON. (Greene.) [Life Baron 1974.]

SIDNEY FRANCIS GREENE, *CBE*, son of Frank James Greene, of London; *b*. Feb. 12th, 1910; Gen. Sec. NUR since 1957; Chm. of TUC 1969-70; a Dir. of Bank of England since 1970; cr. CBE (Civil) 1966, Knt. 1970, and Baron Greene of Harrow Weald, of Harrow, Greater London, (Life Baron) 1974: *m*. 1936, Masel Elizabeth Carter, and has issue, 3 das.

Residence.—26, Kynaston Wood, Boxtree Rd., Harrow Weald, Middx.

GREENHILL, BARON (Greenhill.) [Baron U.K. 1950.]

STANLEY (ERNEST) GREENHILL, *MD*, *DPH*, 2nd Baron; *b*. July 17th, 1917; *s*. 1967; ed. at Kelvinside Acad., Glasgow, and at Glasgow, California and Toronto Univs.; FRSM, FRCP (C), a Fellow of American Coll. of Physicians, and of Roy. Coll. of Physicians and Surgns., Ottawa; Prof. and Chm. of Dept. of Community Medicine; Lecturer in Medicine, Alberta Univ., Assoc. Dir. of University Health Sers., Consultant Physician, Occupational Health, Edmonton, a Fellow of Industrial Med. Assocn. (USA), and of Roy. Soc. of Health, London; 1939-45 War with RAF: *m*. 1946, Margaret Jean, da. of Thomas Newlands, of Hamilton, Ontario, Canada, and has issue.

Residences,—10223, 137th St., Edmonton, Alberta, Canada; 28, Gorselands, Newbury, Berks.

DAUGHTERS LIVING.

Hon. Catherine Elizabeth, *b*. 1948.
Hon. Sheila Anne, *b*. 1951.

BROTHER LIVING.

Hon. MALCOLM (28, Gorselands, Newbury, Berks.), *b*. May 5th, 1924; ed. at Kelvinside Acad., Glasgow, and Glasgow Univ. (BSc); a Chartered Patent Agent; a Member of UK Scientific Mission to Wash., USA 1950-51, and with UK Atomic Energy Authority 1951-73, since when with Min. of Defence.

WIDOW LIVING OF FIRST BARON.

IDA (*Ida, Baroness Greenhill*), (28, Gorselands, Newbury, Berks.), da. of the late Mark Goodman: *m*. 1914, the 1st Baron, who *d*. 1967.

PREDECESSOR.—[1] ERNEST Greenhill, *OBE*, *LLD*, son of the late Maurice Greenhill; *b*. 1887; Councillor, Glasgow Corpn. 1932; cr. *Baron Greenhill*, of Townhead in the City of Glasgow (peerage of UK) 1950: *m*. 1914, Ida, da. of the late Mark Goodman; *d*. 1967; *s*. by his el. son [2] STANLEY (ERNEST), *MD*, 2nd Baron and present peer.

GREENHILL OF HARROW, BARON. (Greenhill.) [Life Baron 1974.]

DENIS ARTHUR GREENHILL, *GCMG, OBE*, son of the late James Greenhill, of Ashfields, Loughton, Essex: *b*. Nov. 7th, 1913; ed. at Bishop's Stortford Coll., and Ch. Ch. Oxford (MA); entered FO 1946, 1st Sec. Sofia 1947-49, and at Washington, DC 1949-52, FO 1952-53, Counsellor to UK Delegation to NATO, Paris 1955-56, and to Office of Commr.-Gen. for SE Asia, Singapore 1956-58, FO 1958-59, Counsellor Washington 1959-62, and Min. there 1962-64, Assist. Under-Sec. FO 1964-66, Dep. Under-Sec. 1966-69, and Permanent Under-Sec. of State FCO, and Head of Diplo Ser. 1969-73; 1939-45 War as Col. RE in Middle East, N. Africa, Italy, India and SE Asia (despatches thrice, OBE); cr. OBE (Mil) 1941, CMG 1960, KCMG 1967, GCMG 1972, and *Baron Greenhill of Harrow*, of Roy. Borough of Kensington and Chelsea (Life Baron) 1974: *m*. 1941, Angela, da. of the late William Leitch McCulloch, and has issue.

Arms.—not exemplified at time of going to press.
Residence.—25, Hamilton House, Vicarage Gate, W8. *Club.*—Travellers'.

SONS LIVING.

Hon. Nigel Denis St. George (31, Spencer Rd., SE24), *b*. 1942.
Hon. Robin James (66A, Hillfield Rd., W. Hampstead, NW6), *b*. 1945: *m*. 1970, Elizabeth, da. of Sir Eric Roll, KCMG, CB.

Greenock, Lord, son of Earl Cathcart.

GREENWAY, BARON. (Greenway.) [Baron U.K. 1927, Bt. 1919.]

Industry and honour.

(CHARLES) PAUL GREENWAY, 3rd Baron, and 3rd Baronet; b. Jan. 31st, 1917; s. 1963; ed. at Winchester, and at Trin. Coll., Camb. (MA); late Maj. Parachute Regt.; 1939-45 War (wounded): m. 1939, Cordelia Mary, dau. of the late Maj. Humfrey Campbell Stephen, J.P., of High Mead, Dormansland, Surrey, and has issue. The 3rd Baron d. Sept 14th, 1975

Arms,—Per pale ermine and ermines, on a chief azure a crescent between two covered cups or. Crest,—A griffin's head, or, erased gules, holding in the beak an anchor sable. Supporters,—On either side a griffin sable, beak and claws or, holding in the beak an anchor and charged on the shoulder with a covered cupgold.
Residence,—703, Collingwood House, Dolphin Sq., SW1. Clubs,—City Livery, Royal London Yacht, Royal Fowey Yacht, Lloyd Yacht, Island Sailing, House of Lords Yacht, Mylor Sailing.

SONS LIVING.

Hon. AMBROSE CHARLES DREXEL, b. May 21st, 1941; ed. at Winchester.

Hon. Mervyn Stephen Kelvynge, b. 1942; ed. at Winchester.

Hon. Nigel Paul, b. 1944; ed. at Winchester.

AUNT LIVING. (Daughter of 1st Baron.)

Hon. Marjorie Phyllis, b. 1892: m. 1915, Lieut.-Col. John Brown Dalzell Hunter, O.B.E., Indian Med. Ser., who d. 1952, and has issue living, Phyllis Morva Dalzell, b. 1917 : m. 1939, Capt. John Ronald Gordon Trechman, R.N., and has issue living, Gavin b. 1942, Frances Ann Gordon b. 1944, Antonia Elspeth Gordon (twin) b. 1944. Residence,—Annesley, Three Gates Lane, Haslemere, Surrey.

COLLATERAL BRANCH LIVING.

Issue of the late Hon. Atheling Kelvynge Brooking Greenway, yr. son of second Baron, b. 1921, d. 1970: m. 1944, (m. diss. 1962), Stella Alice, da. of William Joseph Jennings, of Salisbury, Rhodesia:—
(Neil) Kelvynge Brooking, b. 1945: m. 1970, Floray, da. of Lindsay Glegg, of Salisbury, Rhodesia.

PREDECESSORS.—[1] CHARLES Greenway, son of John David Greenway, of Taunton, Somerset: b. 1857: a Merchant and Banker; cr. a Baronet 1919, and Baron Greenway, of Stanbridge Earls, co. Southampton (peerage of United Kingdom) 1927: m. 1883, Mabel, who d. 1940, dau. of Edwin Augustine Tower; d. 1934; s. by his son [2] CHARLES KELVYNGE, 2nd Baron, b. 1888; Capt., Indian Army: m. 1916, Eileen Constance, who d. 1963, dau. of the late Maj.-Gen. Sir Harry Triscott Brooking, K.C.B., K.C.S.I., K.C.M.G.; d. 1963; s. by his el. son [3] CHARLES PAUL, 3rd Baron and present peer

GREENWOOD, VISCOUNT. (Greenwood.) [Viscount U.K. 1937, Bt. U.K. 1915.]

DAVID HENRY HAMAR GREENWOOD, 2nd Viscount, and 2nd Baronet; b. Oct. 30th, 1914 ; s. 1948.

Arms,—Gules, on a chevron ermine between three saltires as many portcullises or. Crest,—A demi-lion per fesse gules and sable resting the sinister paw on a portcullis or. Supporters,—On either side a lion rampant per fesse gules and sable supporting a staff or, flowing therefrom a banner argent, that on the dexter charged with a rose gules, barbed and seeded proper, and that on the sinister charged with a maple leaf also proper.
Residence,—43, Lennox Gdns., SW1.

BROTHER LIVING.

Hon. MICHAEL GEORGE HAMAR (of 14, Kingston House East, Princes Gate, SW7), b. May 5th, 1923; ed. at Eton, and at Ch. Ch., Oxford; late Roy. Signals.

SISTERS LIVING.

Hon. Angela Margo Hamar, b. 1912: m. 1937, Edward Dudley Delevingne, formerly Capt. R. Fus., who d. 1974, and has issue living, Edward Hamar, b. 1939,—Charles Hamar, b. 1949,—Anne Venetia, b. 1938,—Caroline Felicia, b. 1953. Residence,—52, Sheffield Terr., W8.

Hon. Deborah Hamar, b. 1917; a JP Inner London: m. 1st, 1940 (m. diss. 1970), Patrick David de Laszlo; 2ndly, 1975, Roderick Walter, of 24, Durand Gdns., SW9, and has issue living, (by 1st m.) Damon Patrick (24, Durand Gdns., SW9), b. 1942: m. 1972, the Hon. Sandra Daphne Hacking, da. of the 2nd Baron Hacking,—Stephanie Gay, b. 1945,—Muriel Perpetua, b. 1950,—Grania Tiffany, b. 1953,—Charmian Deborah, b. 1957.

PREDECESSOR.—[1] (THOMAS) HAMAR Greenwood, PC, KC, son of John Hamar Greenwood, Bar.-at-law, Grays Inn; b. 1870; Under-Sec. of State for Home Depart. Jan. 1919, an Additional Under-Sec. of State for Foreign Depart., Additional Parliamentary Sec. to Board of Trade, and Sec. to

Depart. of Overseas Trade July 1919; was last Ch. Sec. for Ireland (with a seat in the Cabinet), and Chancellor of the Order of St. Patrick April 1920 to Oct. 1922; sat as MP for York (L) 1906-10 for Sunderland 1910-22, and for E. Div. of Walthamstow (C) 1924-9; cr. a Baronet 1915, Baron Greenwood, of Llanbister, co. Radnor (peerage of United Kingdom) 1929, and Viscount Greenwood, of Holbourne, co. London (peerage of United Kingdom) 1937: m. 1911, Dame Margery, DBE, who d. 1968, da. of the late Rev. Walter Spencer, of Fownhope Court, Herefordshire; d. 1948; s. by his el. son [2] DAVID HENRY HAMAR, 2nd Viscount and present peer also Baron Greenwood.

GREENWOOD OF ROSSENDALE, BARON. (Greenwood.) [Life Baron 1970.]

(ARTHUR WILLIAM JAMES) ANTHONY GREENWOOD, PC, son of the late Rt. Hon. Arthur Greenwood, CH, MP; b. Sept. 14th, 1911; ed. at Kingston Gram. Sch., Merchant Taylors' Sch., and Balliol Coll., Oxford (MA); JP of co. London; a Member of Hampstead Borough Council 1945-49, Vice-Chm., Parl. Labour Party 1950-51, and a Member of Parl. Cttee. of Labour Party 1951-52 and 1955-60; Colonial Sec. 1964-65, Min. of Overseas Development 1965-66, and Min. of Housing and Local Govt. 1966-70; a Member of Nat. Exec. Cttee., Labour Party 1954-70 (Vice-Chm. 1963, Chm. 1964); a Member of Board of Commonwealth Development Corpn. 1970-73; Pro-Chancellor of Univ. of Lancaster since 1972; Chm. of Local Govt. Staff Commn. 1972, and of Local Govt. Training Board since 1975; 1939-45 War as Fl. Lt. RAF; MP for Heywood and Radcliffe, Lancs. (Lab.) 1946-50, and for Rossendale, Lancs. 1950-70; cr. PC 1964, and Baron Greenwood of Rossendale, of East Mersea, co. Essex (Life Baron) 1970: m. 1940, Gillian, da. of Leslie Crawshay-Williams, of Bridgend [Monkswell, By., colls.], and has issue.

Residences,—38, Downshire Hill, Hampstead, NW3; The Old Ship Cottage, East Mersea, Essex. Clubs,—Savile, RAC.

DAUGHTERS LIVING.

Hon. Susanna Catherine Crawshay, b. 1943: m. 1970, Christopher Gardiner, of 5, Talacre Rd., NW1. Hon. Dinah Karen Crawshay, b. 1946: m. 1970, David Murray, 62, Belsize Park, NW3.

GRENFELL, BARON. (Grenfell.) [Baron U.K. 1902.]

Honest duty.

PASCOE CHRISTIAN VICTOR FRANCIS GRENFELL, CBE, TD, 2nd Baron; b. Dec. 12th, 1905; s. 1925; ed. at Eton; Lt. (ret.) KRRC and Capt. and temporary Lieut.-Col. Queen's Westminsters, KRRC (TA); Hon. Col. 8th Herts and Cambridge Bn., Mobile Defence Corps 1956-59; Middle East 1940-44 (despatches, Officer of American Legion of Merit); Chm. of Finance & G.P. Cttee. Invalid Children's Aid since 1969; CBE (Civil) 1974: m. 1st, 1932, Elizabeth Sarah Polk (" Betty ") (from whom he obtained a divorce 1946), da. of the late Hon. Alfred Thomas Shaughnessy [see B. Shaughnessy, colls.]; 2ndly, 1946, Irene Lilian, da. of H. A. G. Cartwright, of Buenos Aires, Argentina, and has issue by 1st and 2nd marriages.

Arms,—Gules, on a fesse between three organ rests or, a mural crown of the first. Crest,—On the battlements of a tower gules, a griffin passant or, holding in the beak a sprig of laurel. Supporters,—Dexter, An Egyptian cavalryman; sinister, an Egyptian infantryman.

Residence,—13, Liphook Cres., Honor Oak, Forest Hill, SE23 3BN.

SON LIVING. (By 1st marriage.)

Hon. JULIAN PASCOE FRANCIS ST. LEGER (c/o World Bank, 1818, H St., NW, Washington DC, USA), b. May 23rd, 1935; ed. at Eton, and at King's Coll., Camb.; Capt. Queen's Westminsters (KRRC) (TA): m. 1st 1961, Loretta Maria Olga Hildegarde, da. of Alfredo Reali, of 11 Cupolino Florence, Italy, 2ndly, 1970, Gabrielle, only da. of Dr. Ernst Raab. and has issue living, (by 1st m.) Isabella Sarah Frances, b. 1966,—(by 2nd m.) Katharina Elizabeth Anne, b. 1973.

DAUGHTERS LIVING. (By 1st marriage.)

Hon. Caroline Sarah Aline, b. 1933: m. 1965, Zbyszek L. Mieczkowski, Rose Cottage, Henley Park, Henley-on-Thames, and has issue living, Stefan Pascoe St. Leger, b. 1967,—Helena Elizabeth Caroline, b. 1970.

(By 2nd marriage.)

Hon. Aline Mary, b. 1950.

SISTER LIVING.

Hon. Madelina Victoria Margaret, b. 1904: m. 1937, Archibald Julian Lucas, who d. 1946, and has issue living, Virginia Beatrice, b. 1939: m. 1968, Tristram Roger Dymoke Powell [see E. Longford],—Julia Margaret (twin), b. 1939: m. 1968, William Robert Ferdinand Mount, of 17, Ripplevale Grove, N1 [see Mount, Bt.]. Residence,—Mount Pleasant, Goudhurst, Cranbrook, Kent.

WIDOW LIVING OF SON OF FIRST BARON.

Eleanor Dorothy Alice, only dau. of Sir (John) Francis William James, of Tamar Bank, Saltash, Cornwall: *m.* 1st, 1933, Major the Hon. Arthur Bernard John Grenfell, who *d.* (killed in action during European War) 1942; 2ndly, 1944, Capt. Brian Herbert Malyon, 10th Hussars, and has issue living (by 1st *m.*) [see colls., infra].   *Residence,*—The Mill House, Longparish, Andover, Hants.

COLLATERAL BRANCH LIVING.

Issue of the late Major the Hon. Arthur Bernard John Grenfell, 2nd son of 1st Baron, *b.* 1908, *d.* (killed in action during European War) 1942: *m.* 1933, Eleanor Dorothy Alice [(ante): she *m.* 2ndly, 1944, Capt. Brian Herbert Malyon, 10th Hussars], only dau. of Sir (John) Francis William James, of Tamar Bank, Saltash, Cornwall:—

Francis Pascoe John (Middle Coombe, Huntsham, Tiverton, Devon), *b.* 1938; ed. at Eton, and Ch. Ch., Oxford.——John St. Leger (Halfpenny Green, Chudleigh Knighton, Devon), *b.* 1940: *m.* 1965, Pauline Mary Walton, and has issue living, Richard Arthur St. Leger, *b.* 1966,—Julian Francis John, *b.* 1971,—Sarah Marion, *b.* 1968,—Sophie Elizabeth, *b.* 1975.——Margaret, *b.* 1935: *m.* 1960, Capt. Simon Trevor Smail, 11th Hussars [see V. Amory, colls.].   *Address,*—c/o Mrs. Smail, Rock, Exebridge, Dulverton, Som.

PREDECESSOR.—[1] *Field-Marshal the Rt. Hon. Sir* FRANCIS WALLACE Grenfell, *G.C.B., G.C.M.G., P.C.,* son of the late P. St. L. Grenfell, of Maesteg, Glamorgan ; *b.* 1841 ; entered 60th Rifles 1859, and became Field-Marshal 1908 ; raised 1st Brig. Egyptian Army 1883 ; served in Expedition to Griqualand W. 1875, in Kaffir Campaign 1878, in Zulu Campaign 1879 (several times mentioned in despatches, medal with clasp), in Egyptian Expedition 1882, present at battle of Tel-el-Kebir, as A.A.G., Head Quarters (medal with clasp), in Nile Expedition 1884 (3rd class Medjidie, bronze star), and in command of Frontier Field Force, Egypt 1885, a Div. at action of Ginnis 1886, of Anglo-Egyptian Expedition at action of Gamaiza, Suakin 1888, and of Anglo-Egyptian Div. at action of Toski 1889 ; an A.D.C. to H.M. Queen Victoria 1882-9, Sirdir of Egyptian Army 1885-92, D.A.G. for Auxiliary Forces at Headquarters 1892-4, Inspector-Gen. of Auxiliary Forces and of Recruiting 1894-7, in command of Army of Occupation in Egypt 1897-8 (specially thanked by both Houses of Parliament), and Gov. of Malta, and in command of troops there 1898-1902, in command of 4th Army Corps 1902-4, and Gen. Officer Comdg.-in-Ch. the Forces in Ireland 1904-8 ; *cr. Baron Grenfell,* of Kilvey, co. Glamorgan (peerage of United Kingdom) 1902 : *m.* 1st, 1887, Evelyn, who *d.* 1899, dau. of the late Gen. R. Blacher Wood, C.B. ; 2ndly, 1903, the Hon. Margaret Aline, who *d.* 1911, only dau. of the late Lewis Ashurst Majendie, M.P. [E. Crawford] ; *d.* 1925 ; *s.* by his el. son [2] PASCOE CHRISTIAN VICTOR FRANCIS, 2nd Baron and present peer.

GRETTON, BARON. (Gretton.) [Baron U.K. 1944.]

JOHN FREDERIC GRETTON, *O.B.E.,* 2nd Baron ; *b.* Aug. 15th, 1902 ; *s.* 1947 ; ed. at Eton ; appointed Pres. of Institute of Brewing 1960 ; sat as M.P. for Staffordshire, Burton Div. (*C*) July 1943 to June 1945 ; defeated there July 1945 ; O.B.E. (Civil) 1950 : *m.* 1930, Margaret, el. dau. of Capt. Henrik Loeffler, of 51, Grosvenor Square, W.1, and has issue.

Arms.—Quarterly, per fesse indented or and gules, in the second quarter an anchor in bend sinister of the first, in the third an antique lamp also or, fired proper. **Crest.**—An arm embowed proper, vested above the elbow argent, holding in the hand a torch erect fired, a sickle in bend sinister both also proper. **Supporters.**—*Dexter,* a bull sable ; *sinister,* a chestnut horse proper, each gorged with a chain pendent therefrom an anchor or.

STEADFAST

Residences,—Stapleford Park, Melton Mowbray ; 77, Sussex Square, W.2.   *Club,*—Carlton.

SONS LIVING.

Hon. JOHN HENRIK (The Old Rectory, Ufford, nr. Stamford, Lincs.), *b.* Feb. 9th, 1941 ; ed. at Shrewsbury : *m.* 1970, Jennifer, only da. of Edmund Moore, of York, and has issue living, John Lysander, *b.* April 17th, 1975,—Sarah Margaret, *b.* 1971.

Hon. Anthony David Erik, *b.* 1945 ; ed. at Eton.

DAUGHTERS LIVING.

Hon. Mary Ann, *b.* 1939.

Hon. Elizabeth Margaret (twin), *b.* 1945 : *m.* 1968, Christopher Mark Meynell, of 56, Chepstow Rd., W2 [see E. Halifax, colls.].

SISTER LIVING.

Hon. Kathleen Fanny (*Hon. Lady Floyd*): *m.* 1929, Brigadier Sir Henry Robert Kincaid Floyd, 5th Bt., CB, CBE, who *d.* 1968.   *Residence,*—Chearsley Hill House, Aylesbury, Bucks.

PREDECESSOR.—[1] *Rt. Hon.* John Gretton, *P.C., O.B.E., V.D., T.D.,* son of the late John Gretton, of Bladon, Burton-on-Trent ; *b.* 1867 ; Chm. of Bass, Ratcliff & Gretton, Ltd., brewers, of Burton-on-Trent 1908-45 ; Lieut.-Col. and Hon. Col. 6th Batn. Prince of Wales's (N. Staffs Regt.) ; sat as M.P. for S. Derbyshire (*C*) 1895-1906, for Rutland 1907-18, and for Burton Div. of Staffordshire 1918-43 : *cr. Baron Gretton* of Stapleford, co. Leicester (peerage of United Kingdom) 1944 ; *m.* 1900, the Hon. Maud Helen Eveleigh-de-Moleyns, who *d.* 1934, dau. of 4th Baron Ventry ; *d.* 1947 ; *s.* by his son [2] JOHN FREDERIC, 2nd Baron and present peer.

GREVILLE, BARON. (Greville.) [Baron U.K. 1869.]

I scarce call these things our own.

RONALD CHARLES FULKE GREVILLE, 4th Baron ; *b.* April 11th, 1912 ; *s.* 1952 ; ed. at Eton, and at Magdalen Coll., Oxford.

Arms,—Sable, on a cross within a bordure both engrailed or, five pellets. Crest,—Out of a ducal coronet gules, a demi-swan with wings expanded argent. Supporters,—Two swans argent, each ducally gorged gules, and charged on the breast with a pellet.

Residences,—75, Swan Court, Chelsea Manor St., SW3; Cubberley, Ross-on-Wye. *Clubs,*—Bath, Hurlingham.

PREDECESSORS.—[1] FULKE SOUTHWELL Greville, 2nd son of Algernon Greville, a descendant of the 5th Baron Brooke [see E. Warwick]; *b.* 1821; was M.P. for co. Longford (*L*) 1852-69, Lord-Lieut. of co. Westmeath, and Hon. Col. 5th Batn. Prince of Wales's Leinster Regt.; assumed by Roy. licence 1866 the additional surname of Nugent; cr. *Baron Greville, of Clonyn* (peerage of United Kingdom) 1869 : *m.* 1840, Lady Rosa Emily Mary Anne Nugent, who *d.* 1883, only dau. of 1st Marquess of Westmeath; *d.* 1883; *s.* by his son [2] ALGERNON WILLIAM FULKE, 2nd Baron, *b.* 1841; Groom in Waiting to Queen Victoria 1868-73, Private Sec. to Rt. Hon. W. E. Gladstone 1872-3, and a Lord of the Treasury 1873-4; M.P. for Westmeath co. (*L*) 1865-74; resumed the surname of Greville only by Roy. licence 1883: *m.* 1863, Lady Beatrice Violet Graham, who *d.* 1932, dau. of 4th Duke of Montrose; *d.* 1909; *s.* by his only son [3] CHARLES BERESFORD FULKE, O.B.E., 3rd Baron, *b.* 1871; A.D.C. to Gov. of Bombay (Baron Northcote) 1900-03, and Mil. Sec. to Gov.-Gen. of Australia (Baron Northcote) 1904-08 : *m.* 1909, Olive Grace, who *d.* 1959, dau. of the late J. W. Grace of Leybourne Grange, Kent, and widow of Henry Kerr, of New York ; *d.* 1952 ; *s.* by his only son [4] RONALD CHARLES FULKE, 4th Baron and present peer.

GREY, EARL. (Grey.) [Earl U.K. 1806, Bt. G.B. 1746.]

To serve the king with good will.

RICHARD FLEMING GEORGE CHARLES GREY, 6th Earl, and 7th Baronet; *b.* March 5th, 1939; *s.* 1963: *m.* 1st, 1966 (m. diss. 1974), Margaret Ann, el. da. of Henry Bradford, of Ashburton, Devon; 2ndly, 1974, Stephanie Caroline, only da. of Donald Gaskell-Brown, of Newton Ferrers, Plymouth, and formerly wife of Surg-Cdr. Neil Leicester Denham, RN.

Arms,—Gules, a lion rampant, within a bordure engrailed, argent, in dexter chief point a mullet of the last. Crest—A scaling ladder or, hooked and pointed sable. Supporters,—*Dexter,* a lion guardant purpure, ducally crowned or; *sinister,* a tiger guardant, proper.

Residences,—40, Compton Av., Mannamead, Plymouth, S. Devon; Rainbow House, Penally Terr., Boscastle, N. Cornwall.

BROTHER LIVING.

PHILIP KENT (Westcroft, Rock, Wadebridge, N. Cornwall), *b.* May 11th, 1940; a Navigating Officer RFA Ser.: *m.* 1968, Ann Catherine, yst. da. of Cecil Applegate, of Shute Farm, South Milton, Kingsbridge, Devon, and has issue living, Alexander, *b.* 1968.

UNCLE LIVING.

Rodney York DE CHARMOY GREY, *b.* 1921; ed. at Queen's Univ., Kingston, Ontario (BA), and Toronto (MA), and London (PhD) Univs.; added the name of de Charmoy before Grey 1970; Assistant Dep. Min. Depart. of Finance, Ottawa, Canada; 1939-45 War with RCAF: *m.* 1st, 1945, Margaret Eileen (who obtained a divorce 1952), da. of Colin Hawley, of Bristol; 2ndly, 1952, Roslyn (who obtained a divorce 1970), da. of Max Marcus, of Rothesay, New Brunswick, Canada; 3rdly, 1970, Cozette, da. of Louis Roger Guy d'Emmerez de Charmoy, and has issue living, (by 1st m.) Christopher John, *b.* 1946,—David York, *b.* 1947,—(by 2nd m.) Simon Alexander, *b.* 1958,—Marcus Edward, *b.* 1960.

AUNTS LIVING.

Diana Sybil, *b.* 1906: *m.* 1957, Lawrence Frederick Burford, Box 174, Postal Station Q, 27, St. Clair Av. East, Toronto 7, Canada.

Janice Evelyn (27, Park Av., Windsor, Conn. 06095, USA), *b.* 1909: *m.* 1936, Com. Boris Luts, U.S. Navy, who *d.* 1956, and has issue living, Boris Michael, *b.* 1937: *m.* 1960, Sandra Lynne, da. of the late Edward Lee Burch, of Pampa, Texas, and has issue living, Indrik Edward *b.* 1963, Tania Lynne *b.* 1961,—Dorothy Tania Jane, *b.* 1944.

Margery Mary Maitland, *b.* 1910: *m.* 1933, Edgar Cunliffe Price, of 9, Woodhead Drive, Hale, Cheshire, and has issue living, Rodney Fredrick Walter (Meadowbank, Hilton, Carrigrohane, co. Cork), *b.* 1940; ed. at St. Bees, and Manchester Univ. (BSc): *m.* 1967, Diane Vivien, da. of the late Douglas Wren Vaughan, of Hale, Cheshire, and has issue living, Richard John Douglas *b.* 1968, Catherine Mary, *b.* 1971.

GREAT-AUNT LIVING.
Mary Stuart *b.* 1888: *m.* 19—, H. James, of Edinburgh.

DAUGHTER LIVING OF FIFTH EARL.
Lady Mary Cecil (*Lady Mary Howick*), *b.* 1907: *m.* 1935, the 1st Baron Howick of Glendale, who *d.* 1973. *Residence,*—Howick, Alnwick, Northumberland.

COLLATERAL BRANCHES LIVING.
Descendants of the late Capt. the Hon Sir George Grey, K.C.B., R.N. (3rd son of 1st Earl), who was cr. a *Baronet* 1814:—
See Grey, Bt., cr. 1814.

Grandchildren of the late Frederick William Grey (infra):—
Issue of the late Frederick Arthur Herbert Grey, *b.* 1895, *d.* 1973: *m.* 1919, Adelaide Suchan, who *d.* 1949:—
Frederick, *b.* 1921.——Beverly, *b.* 1924.
Issue of the late Leopold John Grey, *b.* 1905, *d.* 1968: *m.* 1929, Ruth Aline (137, Camino San Clemente, San Clemente, Cal., USA), da. of Charles Christian Elmiger:—
Ronald John (25331, Posada Lane, Mission Viejo, Calif., USA), *b.* 1930: *m.* 1954, Nell Hope, only da. of John Adams, of Port Charlotte, Florida, USA, and has issue living, Kenneth Alan, *b.* 1962,—Julia Lynn, *b.* 1959.——Joel Edward (4977, North Ridge Drive, Citrus Heights, Cal., USA), *b.* 1944: *m.* 1968, Kathryn Lee, da. of Paul Fralic, and has issue living, Adam Brady, *b.* 1973.

Grandchildren of the late Col. Leopold John Herbert Grey, C.S.I., only son of the late Leopold James Henry Grey, 3rd son of the late Rt. Rev. the Hon. Edward Grey, Bishop of Hereford (5th son of 1st Earl:—
Issue of the late Frederick William Grey, *b.* 1873, *d.* 1950: *m.* 1st, 1892, Agnes Annie, who *d.* 1917, dau. of Peter Gow, M.P., and Sheriff of Wellington County, Ontario, Canada ; 2ndly, 1919, Mary Harriet, el. da. of Edward Moissant, of Santa Amelia, San Salvador:—
(By 1st m) Robert Maxwell, *b.* 1903: *m.* 1928, May Dawn, da. of Joseph George Washington Brand, and has issue living, Barbara Ann, *b.* 1934: *m.* 1951, Durwood Freeman Anderson, of Nederland, Texas, USA, and has issue living, Rebecca Ann *b.* 1956,—Jane Ellen, *b.* 1940,—Joyce Elaine (twin), *b.* 1940. *Residence,*—609, S. 12th Street, Nederland, Texas, USA.——Henry James, *b.* 1906: *m.* 1930, Alice Mary, da. of Alphonse Joseph Samson, and has issue living, Doris Arlene, *b.* 1932,— Harriet Alice, *b.* 1940.——(By 2nd m.) Mary Catherine, *b.* 1923: *m.* 1943, Capt. Archibald Bauer MacDonald, US Navy (ret.), and has issue living, Bruce Grey, *b.* 1946,—James Douglas, *b.* 1948,— John Mark, *b.* 1962,—Craig William, *b.* 1962,—Ellen Mary, *b.* 1952.
Issue of the late Lt.-Col. Arthur James Herbert Grey, *b.* 1880, *d.* 1960: *m.* 1st, 1911 (divorce obtained in French Courts 1924), Cecile Ruth, dau. of the late François Pogaceniq, Lt. Italian Army; 2ndly, 1925, Anna (who *m.* 2ndly, 1963, Cyril Denzil Branch, Bar.-at-law), dau. of Axel Vennersten, Grand Marshal to Court of Sweden, and has issue living:—
(By 2nd m). *Rev.* Axel Robert Henry (Moravian Church, Bruderheim, Alberta, Canada), *b.* 1933; ed. at Wellington Coll., at St. Andrew's Coll., S. Africa, and at St. Paul's Theological Coll., S. Africa (LTh 1958): *m.* 1954, Zenith Catherine, da. of James Gallagher, and has issue living, Paul, *b.* 1958.

Grandson of the late William Francis Hungerford Grey (infra):—
Issue of the late Capt. William Archibald Swinton Grey, *b.* 1883, *d.* 1942: *m.* 1919, Kathleen Elsie, who *d.* 1949, dau. of W. Paulson, of Mountsorrel, Leicestershire:—
William Ronald, *b.* 1920: *m.* 1945, Florence Margaret, dau. of John Martin, and has issue living, David Swinton, *b.* 1946,—Margaret Ann, *b.* 1949,—Jennifer Francis, *b.* 1951.

Granddaughters of the late Sir William Grey, K.C.S.I., youngest son of the late Right Rev. the Hon. Edward Grey, Bishop of Hereford (ante):—
Issue of the late Lieut.-Col. Leopold James Henry Grey, *b.* 1847, *d.* 1891: *m.* 1871, Clare, who *d.* 1879, dau. of Maj.-Gen. George Verner:—
Clare : *m.* 1909, Lieut.-Col. John Arthur Claude Kreyer, D.S.O., who *d.* 1950, late Indian Army, and has with other issue living, Robin Grey, *b.* 19—: *m.* 1940, Jean Atkinson Ellis. *Residence,*—
Issue of the late William Francis Hungerford Grey, *b.* 1849, *d.* 1929: *m.* 1879, Isabella Harriett, who *d.* 1922, dau. of Archibald Adam Swinton, formerly of B.C.S.:—
Lilian Mary, *b.* 1884: *m.* 1921, Francis Ashburner Richards.

Grandchildren of the late Col. Arthur Grey, C.I.E. (infra):—
Issue of the late Francis Temple Grey, M.B., Ch.M., M.R.C.P., Bar.-at-law, *b.* 1886, *d.* 1941: *m.* 1928, Eglantine Ellice (Sundial, Cripps Corner, Staple Cross, Sussex), da. of the late Major Edward Charles Ellice, DSO:—
Egerton Francis, *b.* 1930; ed. at St. Edward's Sch., Oxford; Capt. (retired) Queen's Own Cameron Highlanders: *m.* 1961, Elizabeth Mary Blackburn, and has issue living, Simon Temple, *b.* 1962,— John Egerton, *b.* 1966,—Frances Mary, *b.* 1963,—Jane Elizabeth Catherine, *b.* 1965. *Residence,*— Garry Gualach, Invergarry, Inverness-shire.——Robin Douglas (84, St. Dionis Rd., SW6), *b.* 1931; ed. at Eastbourne Coll., and at London Univ. (LLB); Bar. Gray's Inn 1957: *m.* 1st, 1968 (m. diss. 1972), Gillian, da. of the late Maj. Esme Austin Reeves Porch; 2ndly, 1972, Berenice Anna, da. of Denis Wheatley, of 9, Nightingale Cres., W. Horsley, and has issue living (by 2nd m.), Louise Katherine, *b.* 1973.——John Edward (Acharn, Duror of Appin, Argyll), *b.* 1932; ed. at Epsom Coll.: *m.* 1965, Elizabeth Anne, only da. of the late Lt.-Col. Francis Patrick St. Maur Shiel, DSO, and has issue living, Patrick John, *b.* 1966,—Seumas Edward, *b.* 1971,—Claire Alexandra, *b.* 1967.——Alan Arthur (Slatrach, Isle of Kerrera, Argyll), *b.* 1934; ed. at Epsom Coll., and Univ. of Newcastle upon Tyne (BSc): *m.* 1966, Jocelyn Elizabeth, da. of John Anthony Cooper, of The Old Croft of Tighphuirst, Glencoe, Argyll [Eden, Bt., colls.], and has issue living, Melanie Jane, *b.* 1967,—Rebecca Frances, *b.* 1968,—Iona Marau, *b.* 1972.——Harry George, *b.* 1937; ed. at Allhallows Sch.—— Alexander (15, Rollscourt Av., SE24 0EA), *b.* 1939; ed. at Eastbourne Coll., and at Oxford Univ, (MA): *m.* 1966, Eleanor, da. of Leonard White, of 42, Highcroft Gdns., NW11, and has issue living. Thomas, *b.* 1972,—Anna, *b.* 1967,—Lucy, *b.* 1969.——Elisabeth Adair, *b.* 1929; ed. at Bryn Mawr Coll., Pennsylvania (BA 1950).——Joane Eglantine, *b.* 1935; ed. at Edinburgh Univ. (MA 1961): *m.* 1956, Michael Mervyn Whitmore, BSc, MRCVS, who *d.* 1959, and has issue living, James Temple, *b.* 1958,—William Rupert, *b.* 1959. *Residence,*—

Grandchildren of the late Lieut.-Col. Francis Douglas Grey, son of the late Rt. Rev. the Hon. Edward Grey, Bishop of Hereford (ante):—
Issue of the late Col. Arthur Grey, C.I.E., *b.* 1855, *d.* 1924: *m.* 1st (in U.S.A.), 1834, Florence Intaglio Donlevy Duncan; 2ndly (in India), 1895, Julia (Mrs. W. H. Stopford), who *d.* 1900, dau. of Granado Chester, H.E.I.C.S. ; 3rdly (in London), 1907, Margaret Rosalie Teresa Mary, who *d.* 1945, el. dau. of the late Rev. Arthur Osborne Gibbs Alleyne, R. of St. Edmund's, Exeter :—

(By 3rd marriage) *Sir* Paul Francis, *K.C.M.G.*, *b.* 1908; ed. at Charterhouse, and at Ch. Ch., Oxford; entered Diplo. Ser. 1933; appointed a Counsellor, Foreign Office 1947, Counsellor at Lisbon 1949, H.M.'s Min. at Moscow 1951, Assist. Under-Sec. of State, Foreign Office 1954, and Ambassador in Czechoslovakia 1957-60, and in Switzerland 1960-64; CMG 1951, KCMG 1963: *m.* 1936, Agnes Mary, da. of the late Richard Shireburn Weld-Blundell [see By. Fauconberg and Conyers, colls.], and has issue living, Nicholas Richard (Avenue des Lievres, 22, 1970 Wezembeek, Belgium), *b.* 1937: *m.* 1964, Mary Cecilia, da. of F. H. Hughes, of 2, Kingsway, Fenham, Newcastle-upon-Tyne, and has issue living, Stephen Hugh Francis *b.* 1968, Benedick Justin *b.* 1971, Clare Philomena *b.* 1965, Eleanor Mary Grace *b.* 1966,—Richard Charles Edward (The Old Farmhouse, Elstead, Godalming, Surrey), *b.* 1939: *m.* 1964, Hilary Marguerite Térèse, da. of Sq. Ldr. Malcolm Francis Ogilvie Forbes, and has issue living, Demitri Malcolm Paul *b.* 1965, Malcolm Dominic Antony *b.* 1967, Eloise Teresa Mary *b.* 1968, Annabel Lucy *b.* 1971,—Timothy, *b.* 1943. *Residence*,—17, Smith Terr., SW3. *Club*,—Brooks's.—— Arthur Christopher, *BM*, *BCh* (9, Abingdon Rd., Kensington, W8 6AH), *b.* 1911; ed. at Wellington Coll., and at Brasenose Coll., Oxford (BA 1932, BM and BSch); LRCP and MRCS England 1937; Hon. RCM; Physician to Imperial Coll. of Science and to Roy. Coll. of Music; late Lt.-Col. RAMC: *m.* 1st, 1941, Diana Marjorie, who *d.* 1971, da. of the late Rupert Sackville Gwynne, MP, JP, and RCM; [V. Ridley], 2ndly, 1973, Diana, JP, da. of Ewen Cameron Bruce, DSO, MC, and widow of Anthony Saymour Bellville, and has issue living (by 1st m.) (Rupert) Christopher, *b.* 1946; ed. at Wellington Coll. and Univ. Coll., London (LLB); Roy. Humane Soc., Bellum Award 1963;— Jonathan, *b.* 1951; ed. at Wellington Coll., and Architectural Assocn.,—Stephen, *b.* 1954; ed. at Wellington Coll., and Brunel Univ., Christopher Edward, *b.* 1957; ed. at Wellington Coll.,—Diana Christabel, *b.* 1952; ed. at Francis Holland Sch., SW1.——Martin, *b.* 1913; ed. at Wellington Coll.; Solicitor 1936; late Maj. RASC; 1939-45 War (despatches twice): *m.* 1943, Wendy Ursula, da. of Charles Creasy Wray, and has issue living, David Anthony, *b.* 1946; ed. at Allhallows Sch.; a chartered architect,—Priscilla Jane, *b.* 1949: *m.* 1974, David John Dyer Lewis. *Residence*,—East End House, Ditchling, Sussex.——Douglas, *OBE* (Villa Pins Noirs, 19, Avenue des Pins Noirs, Brussels 1050), *b.* 1915; ed. at Wellington Coll.; Commercial Dir. of BEA, and a Member of Inst. of Transport, a Dir. of Cyprus Airways, Gibraltar Airways, Sovereign Group Hotels Ltd., Golden Sands Hotels Ltd., and British Airways Associate Cos. Ltd.; OBE (Civil) 1960: *m.* 1st, 1935 (divorce 1945), Elinor Violet,da. of Lt.-Col. D'Arcy Hemsworth Kay, DSO; 2ndly, 1950, Anne Clementine Francoise, da. of the late Hector Leon Marie van Coppenolle, of Belgium. *Residence*,—

Grandchildren of the late Egerton Spencer Grey (infra):— Issue of the late Nigel Francis Egerton Grey, *b.* 1891, *d.* 1974: *m.* 1st, 1921 (m. diss. 1949), Eileen Sybil Lyttleton, who *d.* 1960, da. of the late Francis Ludlow Holt; 2ndly, 1949, Mary Rose (Thesiger), who *d.* 1962, da. of the late Hon. Guy Laurence Charteris [E. Wemyss and March]; 3rdly, 1970, Marion, who *d.* 1971, da. of the late Cdr. Robert Tennant-Park, OBE, RNR, and widow of Anthony Alfred Harmsworth Marlowe, QC:— (By 1st m.) Ann, *b.* 1922: *m.* 1955, Pierre Staheyeff, of Parsonage House, Helions Bumpstead, Haver-hill, Suffolk, and has issue living, Nicholas Peter, *b.* 1957,—Michael Peter, *b.* 1961.—(by 2nd m.) Francis John, *b.* 1951.

Grandchildren of the late Lt.-Col. Francis Douglas Grey (ante):— Issue of the late Egerton Spencer Grey, C.B., *b.* 1863, *d.* 1950: *m.* 1890, Ethel Harriet, who *d.* 1949, dau. of Sir Frederick Wigan, 1st Bt. :—

Cecil Charles Frederick, *b.* 1893; Lt.-Cdr. (ret.) RN. *Residence*,—Ardmore, Gillard Rd., Brixham, S. Devon.——Aubrey Arthur Douglas (36, Laurensford Rd., Somerset W., Cape, S. Africa), *b.* 1894; Lt.-Cdr. RN (ret.); in Min. of Works; 1914-18 War (wounded, prisoner); Roy. Humane Soc's silver medal and Stanhope gold medal: *m.* 1928, Joan Fabian, da. of the late O. H. Dickinson, and has issue living, Aubrey Jeremy Spenser (The Coach House, Beech Av., Worcester), *b.* 1929; late Maj. Lancs. Fus. (TA): *m.* 1958, Jennifer M., da. of V. J. Keyte, of Lime Cottage, Beaudesert Park, Minchinhampton, Glos., and has issue living, Charles Spenser *b.* 1959, James Aubrey *b.* 1961, Annabel Clare *b.* 1963,—Timothy Bryan Richard (Border Cottage, Elghast Green, Newport, Essex), *b.* 1931: *m.* 1st, 1955 (m. diss. 1959) Pamela Anne, da. of Col. Denys Fitzgerald Murphy, MC; 2ndly, 1960, Gillian A., da. of E. R. Hillman, of 14, Marshallswick Lane, St. Albans, and has issue living (by 2nd m.) Richard Nicholas Aubrey *b.* 1961, Susannah Emma Jane *b.* 1963,—Michael Francis Adair, *b.* 1940. ——Geoffrey Ernest Adair, *CBE*, *MC*, *b.* 1895; formerly Capt. RFA and Assist. Sec., HM Treasury; 1914-18 War (twice wounded, despatches twice, MC); CBE (Civil) 1954: *m.* 1931, Marjorie Myburgh, da. of Arthur Henderson, formerly of Cobham. *Residence*,—Spring Cottage, W. Byfleet, Surrey.—— John (68, Abingdon Villas, W8), *b.* 1899; late 2nd Lt. Rifle Bde.; a Chartered Architect: *m.* 1926, Nancy Augusta, da. of the late Vivian Nickalls, of The High House, Newbury, Berks, and has issue living, John Egerton (86, Station Rd., Burnham-on-Crouch, Essex), *b.* 1929; Bar. Inner Temple 1954; Clerk Assistant, House of Lords: *m.* 1961, Patricia, da. of the late Col. Walter Francis Hanna, MC, RE (infra).——Kathleen Ethel Madeline, *b.* 1897: *m.* 1923, Col. Walter Francis Hanna, MC, RE, who *d.* 1963, and has issue living, Rosemary Grey, *b.* 1925,—Patricia Grey, *b.* 1927: *m.* 1961, John Egerton Grey (ante). *Residence*,—10, Wilson-Valkenburg Court, Speen, Newbury, Berks.

PREDECESSORS.—[1] Rt. *Hon Sir* CHARLES Grey, K.B., 4th son of Sir Henry Grey, 1st Bt. (infra), *b.* 1729; Gen., wounded at Minden 1759; C.-in-C. W. Indies 1793, reducing Martinique, St. Lucia and Guadeloupe; Gov. of Guernsey 1797-1807; cr. *Baron Grey of Howick*, Northumberland (peerage of UK 1801), and *Viscount Howick* and *Earl Grey* (peerage of UK) 1806: *m.* 1762, Elizabeth, who *d.* 1822, dau. of George Grey, of Southwick, co. Durham; *d.* 1807; *s.* by his 2nd son [2] CHARLES K.G., 2nd Earl; *b.* 1764; *s.* his uncle Sir Henry Grey as 3rd Bt. 1808 [see *•₊•* infra]; First Lord of the Admiralty 1806, Foreign Sec. 1806-7, and First Lord of the Treasury 1830-4: *m.* 1794, Hon. Mary Elizabeth Ponsonby, who *d.* 1861, dau. of 1st Baron Ponsonby; *d.* 1845; *s.* by his son [3] Rt. *Hon.* HENRY GEORGE, K.G., G.C.M.G., 3rd Earl, *b.* 1802; M.P. for Winchilsea (L) 1826-30, for Higham Ferrers 1831, for Northumberland 1831-3, for N. Northumberland 1833-41, and for Sunder-land 1841-5; Lord-Lieut. of Northumberland 1847-77; Under-Sec. for Colonies 1830-33, for Home Depart. 1834, and Sec. of State for War 1835-9, and for Colonies 1846-52: *m.* 1832, Maria, who *d.* 1879, dau. of Sir Joseph Copley, 3rd Bt.; *d.* 1894; *s.* by his nephew [4] Rt. *Hon.* ALBERT HENRY GEORGE, G.C.B., G.C.M.G., G.C.V.O. (son of the late Gen. the Hon. Charles Grey, M.P., 2nd son of 2nd Earl), 4th Earl; *b.* 1851; Administrator of Rhodesia 1894-7; Lord-Lieut. of Northumberland 1899-1904, and Chancellor of Order of St. Michael and St. George 1916-17; M.P. for Northumberland S. 1880-85, and for Tyneside Div. of Northumberland 1885-6; Gov.-Gen. of Canada 1904-11: *m.* 1877, Alice, who *d.* 1944, dau. of the late Robert Stayner Holford; *d.* 1917; *s.* by his only son [5] CHARLES ROBERT, 5th Earl, *b.* 1879; Lt. 1st Life Guards, Maj. in the Army, and Hon. Col. Comdt., Northumberland Vol. Regt.: *m.* 1906, Lady Mabel Laura Georgiana Palmer, C.B.E., who *d.* 1958, dau. of 2nd Earl of Selborne; *d.* 1963; *s.* by his kinsman [6] RICHARD FLEMING GEORGE CHARLES (el. son of the late Albert Harry George Campbell Grey, el. son of the late Adm. the Hon. George Grey, 4th son of 2nd Earl), 6th Earl and present peer; also Viscount Howick, and Baron Grey of Howick. *•₊•* [1] *Sir* HENRY Grey, of Howick, Northumberland, descendant of an ancient family in that Co., 8th in descent from Sir Thomas Grey of Heton, el. brother of Sir John Grey, K.G., who received the Anglo-Norman Earldom of Tankerville 1419, and 5th in descent from Sir Edward Grey, of Howick, uncle of 1st Baron Grey of Warke (cr. 1623, ext. on death of 4th Baron 1706), cr. a Baronet 1746: *m.* 1720, Hannah, who *d.* 1764, dau. of Thomas Wood, of Falloden; *d.* 1749; *s.* by his el. son [2] *Sir* HENRY, 2nd Bt., *b.* 1727; M.P. for Northumberland 1754-68; *d.* unm. 1808; *s.* by his nephew [3] CHARLES, 2nd Earl Grey (ante).

GREY DE RUTHYN, BARONY OF. [Baron E. 1324.] [Abeyant 1963.]

COLLATERAL BRANCHES LIVING. (*Representatives of the daughters of Barbara, Baroness Grey de Ruthyn, wife of the 2nd Marquess of Hastings, are co-heirs of this Barony.*)
Descendants of the late Lady Edith Maud Rawdon-Hastings (el. dau. of Barbara, Baroness Grey de Ruthyn, by her 1st husband, the 2nd Marquess of Hastings), who *s.* her brother as *Countess of Loudoun* [see that title].
Grandson of the late Lady Victoria Mary Louisa Rawdon-Hastings (3rd da. of Barbara, Baroness Grey de Ruthyn, by her 1st husband, the 2nd Marquess of Hastings): *m.* 1859, John Forbes Stratford Kirwan, who *d.* 1892 of 1, Richmond Gardens, Bournemouth :—

  Issue of the late May Evelyn Bertha Emily, *b.* 1861, *d.* 1902: *m.* 1895, Count Louis Lubienski Bodenham, J.P., D.L., of Rotherwas, Hereford, and Bullingham Manor, Hereford, who *d.* 1909 :—
  (*Count*) Stanislas (twin), *b.* 1899; co-heir to Barony of Grey de Ruthyn (quarter share); late Lt. Irish Gds.: *m.* 1928, Elizabeth, who *d.* 1941, da. of the late George Lawson, of Forth House, Aberfoyle, and has issue living, Charles Henry (22, Allingham Court, Haverstock Hill, NW3), *b.* 1935; ed. at Beaumont, and at Gordonstoun: *m.* 1964, Lia Zappala, and has issue living, Paul *b.* 1965, Elizabeth *b.* 1972, Monica (twin) *b.* 1972. *Residence,*—Little Odiam, Bethersden, Kent.
Descendants of the late Lady Frances Augusta Constance Rawdon-Hastings (4th dau. of Barbara, Baroness Grey de Ruthyn, by her 1st husband, the 2nd Marquess of Hastings): *m.* 1863, the 4th Earl of Romney, who *d.* 1905 [see that title].
Descendants of the late Hon. Barbara Yelverton (only dau. of Barbara, Baroness Grey de Ruthyn, by her 2nd husband, Adm. Sir Hastings Reginald Henry Yelverton, G.C.B.); *m.* 1872, the 2nd Baron Churston, who *d.* 1910 [see that title].

GREY OF NAUNTON, BARON. (Grey.) [Life Baron 1968.]

RALPH FRANCIS ALNWICK GREY, *GCMG, GCVO, OBE,* son of the late Francis Arthur Grey; *b.* April 15th, 1910; ed. at Wellington Coll., NZ, Auckland Univ. Coll. (LLB), and Pembroke Coll., Camb.; Hon. LLD, Belfast; Bar. and Solicitor NZ 1932; a KStJ (Kt. Cdr. of the Commandery of Ards); entered Admin. Ser., Nigeria 1937; Assist. Financial Sec. 1949-52, Development Sec. 1952-54, Sec. to Gov.-Gen. and Council of Mins. 1954, Ch. Sec. of Federation 1955-57; and Dep. Gov.-Gen. 1957-59; Gov. and C.-in-C. British Guiana 1959-64, Gov. of Bahamas 1964-68, of Turks and Caicos Islands 1965-68, and Gov. of N. Ireland 1968-73, since when Dep. Chm. of Commonwealth Development Corpn.; Hon. Bencher Inn of Court, N. Ireland; Hon. Freeman of Belfast; *cr.* OBE (Civil) 1951, CMG 1955, KCVO 1956, KCMG 1959, GCMG 1964, *Baron Grey of Naunton,* of Naunton, co. of Gloucester (Life Baron) 1968, and GCVO 1973: *m.* 1944, Esme Mae (CStJ), da. of the late Albert Victor Kerry Burcher, of Remuera, Auckland, NZ, and widow of PO Kenneth Kirkcaldie, RAFVR, and has issue.

Arms,—Bendy argent and azure two lions' faces in pale, issuing from either flank of the shield a cross formy flory dimidiated gules. **Crest,**—A sheathed sword erect gules garnished hilt and pommel or, each quillon ending in a kiwi's head erased gold the scabbard supported by two lions' gambs erased gules winged azure semy of bees volant or. **Supporters,**—*Dexter,* a lion or, *sinister,* a crested crane proper, each gorged with an ancient crown flowing therefrom a mantle gules lined vair.
Residence,—Overbrook, Naunton, Glos.   *Club,*—Travellers'.

SONS LIVING.

Hon. Jolyon Kenneth Alnwick (36, Octavia St., SW11), *b.* 1946; ed. at Marlborough, and Pembroke Coll., Camb. (MA); Bar. Inner Temple, 1968: *m.* 1971, Sarah Jane, da. of Lt.-Col. Samuel Brian Digby Hood, TD [see V. Hood, colls.], and has issue living, Tobias Alnwick, *b.* 1973.
Hon. Jeremy Francis Alnwick, *b.* 1949; ed. at Marlborough, and Roy. Agric. Coll., Cirencester; 2nd Lt. 14th/20th King's Hussars: *m.* 1973, Susan Elizabeth Louise, da. of Duncan Richard Fraser, CBE, of Corner House, Burnaston, Etwall, Derby.

DAUGHTER LIVING.

Hon. Amanda Mary Alnwick, *b.* 1951; ed. at St. Mary's Sch., Calne, and Bedford Coll., Univ. of London (BA (Hons.)): *m.* 1975, José das Neves.

GRIDLEY, BARON. (Gridley.) [Baron U.K. 1955.]

ARNOLD HUDSON GRIDLEY, 2nd Baron; *b.* May 26th, 1906; *s.* 1965; ed. at Oundle; entered Colonial Ser., Malaya 1928; interned by Japanese in Changi Gaol, Malaya 1941-45; Acting Dep. Comptroller, Fedn. of Malaya 1956; ret. 1957; a Member of Council of HM Overseas Ser. Pensions Assocn. 1966, and of Somerset Co. Council Local Valuation Panel 1966; Chm. of Centralised Audio Systems Ltd. 1971, and of Board of Govs. of Hall Sch., Bratten Seymour, Somerset 1974; a Dir. of Lawdon Ltd. 1968; a Govt. Trustee of Far East (POW & Internee) Fund 1973; Knt. 1957: *m.* 1948, (Edna) Lesley, el. da. of the late Leslie Richard Wheen, Shanghai, and has issue.

Arms,—Gules three bendlets enhanced and in base a portcullis chained or. Crest,—A wyvern azure semee of lozenges or, resting the dexter claw on a grid iron gules. Supporters,—Dexter, a wyvern azure semee of lozenges or: sinister, a lion gules semee of grid irons gold.

Residence,—Coneygore, Stoke Triste, Wincanton, Somerset. *Club,*—Royal Overseas League.

SON LIVING.
Hon. RICHARD DAVID ARNOLD, *b.* Aug. 22nd, 1956

DAUGHTERS LIVING.
Hon. Susan Lesley, *b.* 1950.
Hon. Alison Elizabeth Vivienne, *b.* 1953.
Hon. Vivienne Nicola, *b.* 1955.

SISTERS LIVING.
Hon. Enid Kathleen, *b.* 1909: *m.* 1936, as his second wife, Alec Frederic Plummer, MC, who *d.* 1974. *Residence,*—Bonners, Pepperstock, nr. Luton, Beds.
Hon. Geraldine, *b.* 1918: *m.* 1939, Col. Norman John Lascelles Field, OBE, Roy. Fusiliers, and has issue living, Richard Clive, *b.* 1947,—Anne Jacqueline, *b.* 1942: *m.* 1967, Anthony E. Vicars-Miles (c/o Shell Centre, SE1), and has issue living, Sarah Elizabeth *b.* 1969, Katherine Juliet *b.* 1972. *Residence,*—Fair Acres, White Hill, Bilting, nr. Ashford, Kent.

PREDECESSOR—[1] *Sir* ARNOLD BABB Gridley, KBE, son of Edward Gridley of Abbey Dore, Herefordshire; *b.* 1878; a consulting Engineer; MP for Stockport (*C*) 1935-50, and Stockport S. 1950-55; *cr.* *Baron Gridley* of Stockport, co. Palatine of Chester (peerage of UK) 1955: *m.* 1905, Mabel, who *d.* 1955, da. of Oliver Hudson, of Fakenham; *d.* 1965; *s.* by his el. son [2] ARNOLD HUDSON, 2nd Baron and present peer.

GRIMSTON OF WESTBURY, BARON. (Grimston) [Baron U.K. 1964, Bt. U.K. 1952.]

Moderate things are stable.

ROBERT VILLIERS GRIMSTON, 1st Baron, and 1st Baronet, el. son of the late Rev. Canon the Hon. Robert Grimston [see E. Verulam, colls.]; *b.* June 8th, 1897; *h.p.* to Earldom of Verulam; ed. at Repton, and at London Univ. (BSc Eng.); ACGI; P.P.S to Rt. Hon. Douglas Hacking when Parl. Under-Sec. of State, Home Office 1933-34, when Financial Sec. to War Office 1934-35, and when Under-Sec. for Dominions 1935-36, to H. Ramsbotham when Min. of Pensions 1936, an Assist. Govt. Whip May-Oct. 1937, a Junior Lord of The Treasury 1937-38, Vice-Chamberlain of HM Household 1938-39, Treasurer of the Household 1939-42, Assist. Postmaster-Gen. 1942-45, Parl. Sec. to Min. of Supply May-July 1945, Member of UK Delegation to Gen. Assembly of UN 1960, and Dep. Chm. of Ways and Means, House of Commons 1962-64; Pres. of Urban Dist. Councils Assocn. 1949-71; 1914-18 War as Lt. RGA. in Salonika and Palestine; MP for Westbury Div. of Wilts. (*C*) 1931-64; *cr.* *Baron Grimston of Westbury*, of Westbury, co. Wilts. (peerage of UK) 1964: *m.* 1923, Sybil Rose, da. of Sir Sigmund Neumann, 1st Bt. [see Newman, Bt., cr. 1912], and has issue.

Arms.—Quarterly: 1st and 4th argent, on a fesse sable, three rowels of six points or pierced gules; in the dexter chief an ermine spot sable, *Grimston*; 2nd sable, a fesse dancettée between two leopards' faces or, *Luckyn*; 3rd argent, three bugle horns sable, stringed gules, *Forrester*.   **Crest,**—A stag's head erased proper, attired or.   **Supporters,**—*Dexter,* a stag reguardant proper attired or; *sinister,* a horse reguardant argent.

Address,—4, Cadogan Sq., SW1.   *Club,*—Carlton.

SONS LIVING.
Hon. ROBERT WALTER SIGISMUND (The Old Rectory, Westwell, nr. Burford, Oxon.; Bath, and City of London Clubs, and MCC), *b.* June 14th, 1925; ed. at Eton; formerly Lt. Scots Guards; N.-W. Europe 1944-45: *m.* 1949, the Hon. June Mary Ponsonby, da. of 5th Baron de Mauley, and has issue living, Robert John Sylvester, *b.* 1951; ed. at Eton, and Reading Univ. (BSc); Lt. R. Hussars (PWO),—Gerald Charles Walter, *b.* 1953; ed. at Eton,—Georgiana Mary, *b.* 1961.
Hon. Cecil Antony Sylvester (Wellington Vane, nr. Lewes, Sussex, BN8 5SN; Bath Club, MCC), *b.* 1927; ed. at Eton, and at Camb. Univ. (MA); FRICS, FRSA; late Coldm. Gds.: *m.* 1958, Dawn Monica Ann, da. of Guy Janson, of Fair Hall, Southover, Lewes, and has issue living, Guy Anthony Edward, *b.* 1963,—John Lionel Charles, *b.* 1968.
Hon. Michael John Harbottle (Penny Hill, Bryanston, S. Africa; Turf Club), *b.* 1932; ed. at Eton; *m.* 1957, Julia Mary, da. of Sir George Albu, 2nd Bt., and has issue living, Simon Harbottle, *b.* 1960,—Giles Villiers, *b.* 1961,—Katherine Flavia, *b.* 1962,—Sybella Jane, *b.* 1966.

DAUGHTERS LIVING.
Hon. Rosemary Sybella Violet, *b.* 1929: *m.* 1953 (m. diss. 1964), Charles Edward Underdown.
Hon. Ella Zia, *b.* 1937: *m.* 1972, Humphrey K. Humphreys.

GRIMTHORPE, BARON.   (Beckett.)   [Baron U.K. 1886, Bt. U.K. 1813.]

To benefit the State.

CHRISTOPHER JOHN BECKETT, *O.B.E.*, 4th Baron and 8th Baronet; *b.* Sept. 16th, 1915; *s.* 1963; ed. at Eton; patron of two livings; Brig. (ret.) late 9th Queen's R. Lancers; Col. Comdg. 9th Queen's R. Lancers 1955-58; Col. 9th/12th Lancers (PWO) since 1973; Brig. R. Armoured Corps, HQ, Western Command 1961-64, and Dep.-Cdr. Malta and Libya 1964-67; ADC to HM 1964-68; a DL, E. Riding of Yorks.; OBE (Mil.) 1958: *m.* (Feb.) 1954, Lady Elizabeth Lumley, da. of 11th Earl of Scarbrough, and has issue.

Arms,—Gules, a fesse between three boars' head couped erminois.   **Crest,**—A boar's head couped or pierced by a cross patée fitchée erect gules.   **Supporters,** —Two sangliers erminois, each gorged with a collar and pendant therefrom an escutcheon gules, charged with a cross patée fitchée or.

Seat,—Westow Hall, York.   *Club,*—Cavalry.

SONS LIVING.
Hon. EDWARD JOHN, *b.* Nov. 20th, 1954.
Hon. Ralph Daniel, *b.* 1957.

DAUGHTER LIVING.
Hon. Harriet Lucy, *b.* 1961.

BROTHER LIVING.
Hon. Oliver Ralph, *b.* 1918; ed. at Eton: *m.* 1944, Helene Agnes (TASKER-EVANS), dau. of Constantine Fessas, of 2, Chalfont Court, Baker St., W1, and has issue living, Sarah Christine, *b.* 1946: *m.* 1966, Jonathan Crook, and has issue living, John Henry *b.* 1967,—Juliet Mary, *b.* 1949.

HALF-BROTHER LIVING.
Hon. William Ernest (8, Elthiron Rd., SW6; Cavalry Club), *b.* 1945; ed. at Eton; 2nd Lt. 9th/12th R. Lancers: *m.* 1968, Virginia Helen, only da. of Michael Clark Hutchison, MP, of 16, Maunsel St., SW1, and has issue living, Ralph Michael, *b.* 1971,—Serena Angela Anne, *b.* 1974.

SISTER LIVING.
Hon. Lucy Clare, *b.* 1926: *m.* 1957, Wilson Peregrine Nicholas Crewdson, and has issue living, Giles Wilson Mervyn, *b.* 1959,—Diana Constance Mary (twin), *b.* 1959,—Virginia Clare, *b.* 1964. *Residence,* —Wherstead Old Hall, Ipswich.

AUNT LIVING.   (*Daughter of 2nd Baron.*)
Hon. Lucy (Lucile) Katherine, *b.* 1884; re-naturalised 1922, and resumed by deed poll 1922 her maiden surname of Beckett: *m.* 1st, 1903 (judicial separation in Austrian Courts 1914, and decree of divorce in Czecho-Slovakian Courts 1920), Count Otto Czernin, sometime Austrian Min. Plen. to Sofia; 2ndly, 1926, Capt. Oliver Harry Frost, MBE, MC, formerly Middx. Regt., and RAF, from whom she obtained a divorce 1940, and has issue living, (by 1st marriage) *Count* Edmund Theobald Douglas Friedrich Ferdinand, *b.* 1907; ed. at Univ. Coll., Oxford (MA 1935). *Residence,*—Madresilva, Birre, Cascais, Portugal.

WIDOW LIVING OF THIRD BARON.
ANGELA (GREEN) (*Angela, Baroness Grimthorpe*) (The Old Farm House, Ramsbury, Marlborough, Wilts.), da. of Edward Hubert Courage, of Kirkby Fleetham Hall, Bedale, Yorks.: *m.* 1945, as his second wife, the 3rd Baron, who *d.* 1963.

COLLATERAL BRANCH LIVING.   (*In special remainder.*)
Issue of the late Hon. (William) Gervase Beckett (2nd son of the late William, Beckett-Denison, and brother of 2nd Baron), who was cr. a *Baronet* 1921:—
See Beckett, Bt., cr. 1921.

PREDECESSORS.—[1] *Sir* JOHN Beckett, of Leeds and Somerby Park, Lincs., *b.* 1743; cr. a *Baronet* 1813: *m.* 1774, Mary, who *d.* 1833, dau. of Christopher Wilson, Bishop of London; *d.* 1826; *s.* by his el. son [2] JOHN, *P.C., M.P., F.R.S.,* 2nd Bt.; *b.* 1775; M.P. for Cockermouth (*C*) 1820-21, Haslemere 1826-32, and Leeds 1835-7; Judge-Advocate-Gen.: *m.* 1817, Lady Anne Lowther, who *d.* 1871, dau. of 1st Earl of Lonsdale; *d.s.p.* 1847; *s.* by his brother [3] THOMAS, 3rd Bt.; *b.* 1779; *m.* 1829, his cousin Caroline, who *d.* 1878, dau. of Joseph Beckett, of Barnsley; *d.* 1872; *s.* by his brother [4] EDMUND, 4th Bt.; *b.* 1787; M.P. for W. Riding of York (*C*) 1841-59; assumed the name and arms of Denison by Roy. licence 1816, and resumed his patronymic on succeeding to the Baronetcy: *m.* 1814, Maria, who *d.* 1874, dau. of William Beverley, and great-niece and heir of Anne Smithson, wife of Sir Thomas Denison, Justice of King's Bench 1742; *d.* 1874; *s.* by his el. son [5] EDMUND, LL.D., K.C., 5th Bt.; *b.* 1816; resumed surname of Beckett in lieu of Deniston 1874; Vicar-Gen. and Chancellor of York; cr. *Baron Grimthorpe,* of Grimthorpe, co. York (peerage of U.K.) 1886, with remainder to the issue male of his father: *m.* 1845, Fanny Catharine, who *d.* 1901, dau. of the late Right Rev. John Lonsdale, D.D., Lord Bishop of Lichfield; *d.* 1905; *s.* under special remainder by his nephew [6] ERNEST WILLIAM, 2nd Baron (son of the late William Beckett, M.P., brother of 1st Baron), *b.* 1856; M.P. for Whitby Div. of N. R. of York (*C*) 1885-1905; partner in banking firm of Beckett & Co., of Leeds: *m.* 1883, Lucy Tracy, who *d.* 1891, dau. of the late William P. Lee, of New York; *d.* 1917; *s.* by his son [7] RALPH WILLIAM ERNEST, *T.D.,* 3rd Baron; *b.* 1891; Lt.-Col. (Comdg. 1936-40) Yorkshire Hussars T.A., and partner in banking firm of Beckett & Co., of Leeds; P.P.S. to Under Sec. of State for War 1919-21: *m.* 1st, 1914 (marriage dissolved 1945), Mary Alice, who *d.* 1962, dau. of Col. Mervyn Henry Archdale, 12th Lancers; 2ndly, 1945, Angela (GREEN), dau. of Edward Hubert Courage, of Kirkby Fleetham Hall, Bedale, Yorks.; *d.* 1963; *s.* by his el. son [8] CHRISTOPHER JOHN, 4th Baron and present peer.

Grinstead, Baron, title of Earl of Enniskillen on Roll of H. L.

Grosvenor, Earl, son of Duke of Westminster.

Guernsey, Baron, son of Earl of Aylesford.

GUEST, BARON. (Guest.) [Life Baron 1961.]

CHRISTOPHER WILLIAM GRAHAM GUEST, *P.C.,* son of the late Edward Graham Guest, of Edinburgh; *b.* Nov. 7th, 1901: ed. at Merchiston Castle Sch., and at Clare Coll., Camb. (LLB. MA, Hon. Fellow 1971); LLB Edinburgh 1924; Hon. LLB Dundee; Advocate Scotland 1925, Bar. Inner Temple 1929, a KC 1945, and a Bencher 1961; Sheriff of Ayr and Bute 1952-54, and of Perth and Angus 1954-55: Dean of Faculty of Advocates 1955-57, a Lord of Session with title of *Lord Guest* 1957-61, and a Lord of Appeal in Ordinary 1961-71; 1939-45 War as 2nd Lieut. RA (TA) and Maj. Judge Advocate Gen.'s Branch, War Office; *cr. Baron Guest,* of Graden, co. Berwick (Life Baron) 1961, P.C. 1962: *m.* 1st, 1928, Constance Jessie (from whom he obtained a divorce 1940), da. of Finlay Ramage, SSC; 2ndly, 1941, Catharine Geraldine, da. of the late John Beaumont Hotham [see B. Hotham, colls.], and has issue by 1st and 2nd marriages.

Residences,—3, Ainslie Place, Edinburgh; Woodend, Dirleton, East Lothian. *Clubs,*—Buck's and New (Edinburgh).

SONS LIVING. (*By 1st marriage.*)
Hon. Christopher John Graham (20, Cathcart Rd., SW10), *b.* 1929; ed. at Eton, and Clare Coll., Camb.: *m.* 1960, Myrna Dukes, and has issue living, Christopher Caspar Graham, *b.* 1967,—Amanda Ruth Graham, *b.* 1964.

(*By 2nd marriage.*)
Hon. David William Graham, *b.* 1943; ed. at Charterhouse and Clare Coll., Camb. (BA; CA).
Hon. Simon Edward Graham, *b.* 1949; ed. at Charterhouse, and Dundee Univ. (LLB).
Hon. Andrew Beaumont Graham, *b.* 1951; ed. at Charterhouse, and St. Andrew's Univ. (MA).

DAUGHTER LIVING. (*By 2nd marriage.*)
Hon. Elizabeth Jane Graham, *b.* 1945: *m.* 1968, George Willing Pepper, of 128, Springton ake Rd., Media, Pa., USA.

Guest, see Baron Haden Guest

GUILDFORD, LORD BISHOP OF. (Brown.)

Right Rev. DAVID ALAN BROWN, son of Russell Alan Brown; *b.* July 11th, 1922; ed. at London Univ. (BD, MTheo, BA); CMS Mission Yambio Dio Sudan 1952-54, Prin. Bishop Gwynne Coll., Mundri 1955-60, Canon Missionary Khartoum Cathedral 1960-63, Missionary Amman 1963-66, Curate of St. John the Evangelist Bromley 1966-67, V. of Herne Bay, 1967-73, and Rural Dean, Reculver 1972-73; consecrated 6th Bishop of Guildford 1973: *m.* 1954, Elizabeth Mary, da. of the late Dr. John Warwick Hele, of Silloth, Carlisle, Cumberland.

Patron of the Archdeaconries of Dorking and Surrey, and of sixty-nine livings.
This See was founded in May 1927.
Episcopal Signature—"David Guildford."

ARMS OF THE SEE—Gules, two keys conjoined, wards outwards in bend the uppermost or, the other argent, a sword of the third pommeled and hilted of the second interposed between them in bend sinister, all within a bordure azure charged with ten woolpacks also argent.

Residence,—Willow Grange, Stringers Common, Guildford, Surrey.

GUILFORD, EARL OF. (North.) [Earl G.B. 1752.]

EDWARD FRANCIS NORTH, 9th Earl; *b.* Sept.
22nd, 1933; *s.* 1949; ed. at Eton; a JP for
Kent; is patron of three livings: *m.* 1956,
Osyth Vere Napier, da. of Cyril Napier Leeston,
of Trottiscliffe, West Malling, Kent, and has
issue.

Arms,— Azure, a lion passant or, between three
fleurs-de-lis argent. Crest,—A dragon's head erased sable,
ducally gorged and chained or. Supporters,—Two mastiffs
proper.

Residence,—Waldershare Park, Dover.

With courage and fidelity.

SON LIVING.
PIERS EDWARD BROWNLOW (*Lord North*), *b.* March 9th,
1971.

SISTERS LIVING.
(*Raised to the rank of an Earl's daughters* 1950.)
Lady Barbara Joan, *b.* 1928 ; is an O.St.J.: *m.* 1951,
Maj. the Hon. Sir Clive Bossom, 2nd Bt. *Residences,*—3, Eaton Mansions, SW1; Parson's Orchard,
Eastnor, nr. Ledbury, Herefordshire.
Lady Angela Mary, *b.* 1931 : *m.* 1955, Peter John Henry Whiteley, of 95, Eaton Place, S.W.1, and has
issue living, Simon William Alastair, *b.* 1958,—Justin Henry Francis, *b.* 1964,—Emma Louise,
b. 1959.

UNCLES LIVING. (*Sons of 8th Earl.*)
Hon. John Montagu William, *b.* 1905 : *m.* 1st, 1927, Muriel Norton (who obtained a divorce
1939), dau. of Sir William Norton Bicking, 1st Bt. [see North, Bt.]; 2ndly, 1939, Marion Dyer.
dau. of Frank Erving Chase, of Boston, Mass., U.S.A., and has issue living, (by 1st marriage)
Sir William Jonathan Frederick, 2nd Bt., *b.* 1931 [see "BARONETAGE"],—Georgiana Mary, *b.*
1928: *m.* 1960, Esmond Unwin Butler, CVO, Sec. to Gov.-Gen. of Canada, of Rideau Cottage,
Government House, Ottawa, Canada, and has issue living, Mark William *b.* 1961, Clare Martine
b. 1963. *Residence,*—57, Montagu Square, W1.
Hon. Charles Evelyn, *b.* 1918; ed. at Eton, and at London Univ. (B.Sc. 1939) ; European War,
1939-45 as Flight-Lieut. R.A.F. : *m.* 1st., 1942, Maureen O'Callaghan (from whom he obtained a
divorce 1957), dau. of Major F. C. B. Baldwin, of Malmo, Park Avenue, Gillingham ; 2ndly, 1959,
Joan Aston, dau. of Major F. B. Booker, and has issue living, (by 1st marriage) Peter David, *b.* 1943,
—Susan Caroline, *b.* 1947. *Residence,*—Park End House, Eythorne, near Dover.

MOTHER LIVING.
Joan Louise, dau. of Sir Merrik Raymond Burrell, C.B.E., 7th Bt.: *m.* 1st, 1927, Major Lord
North, who *d.* 1940, el. son of 8th Earl; 2ndly, 1947, Charles Harman Hunt. *Residence,*—Ockenden
Garden House, Cuckfield, Sussex.

COLLATERAL BRANCHES LIVING.
Issue of the late Hon. Morton William North, brother of 7th Earl, *b.* 1852, *d.*
1895 : *m.* 1879, Hylda Hylton, who *d.* 1902, dau. of the late Capt. Hylton
Jolliffe [B. Hylton, colls.] :—
Roger, *b.* 1888 : *m.* 1912, Alice Amy Le Gros. *Residence,*—

        Grandson of the late Charles Augustus North, el. son of the late Brownlow North,
        only son of the late Rev. Charles Augustus North, brother of 6th Earl :—
Issue of the late Frederic Dudley North, C.M.G., *b.* 1866, *d.* 1921 : *m.* 1886, Flora Frances,
who *d.* 1950, dau. of the late Edward Hamersley, of Pyrton, W. Australia :—
Charles Frederic John, *b.* 1887 ; ed. at Rugby, and at Oriel Coll., Oxford (B.A. 1909) ; Bar. Middle
Temple 1912, and W. Australia 19— ; European War 1914-19 as Capt. R.A.F. ; has been a
M.L.A. (for Claremont) of W. Australia since 1924 (Speaker 1948-53): *m.* 1916, Bessie, dau. of
William Saddington, of Cheshire, and has issue living, Muriel Elvia Joan, *b.* 1917: *m.* 1942, Roy
Wilson Parr (R. 1, Box 56A, Hopewell, Ohio, 43746, USA),—Mary Rachael June, *b.* 1930: *m.* 1st,
1955 (m. diss. 1966), Garth Murray Denny; 2ndly, 1967, Thomas Nolan Cassidy, of 6F, Florence St.,
Cottesloe, 6011, Perth, W. Aust., and has issue living, David North Murray *b.* 1958, Julie Elizabeth
b. 1961. *Residence,*—Kulahea, Cottesloe, W. Australia.
        Granddaughter of the late Frederic Dudley North. C.M.G. (ante) :—
Issue of the late George Eustace Dudley North, *b.* 1893. *d.* 1960: *m.* 1920, Florence Ethel
Yeo, of Mount Street, Perth, W. Australia:—
Mary Elizabeth, *b.* 1925 : *m.* 1948, Geoffrey Norris Russell, and has issue living, John Norris Grant,
b. 1951,—Francis Guilford, *b.* 1953,—Philip Brownlow, *b.* 1959. *Residence,*—Dunkathel, Glanmire,
co. Cork.
        Grandchildren of the late Brownlow John Jarvis North, 2nd son of the late Brown-
        low North (ante) :—
Issue of the late Brownlow Hamilton North, *b.* 1854, *d.* 1886: *m.* 1879, Elizabeth
Martha, who *d.* 1947, dau. of John Warren Ryan, of Wynaad :—
Brownlow John Frederic, *b.* 1883.——George Dudley Guilford, *b.* 1884.——Elizabeth Grace
Margaret, *b.* 1831.—— Violet Hope O'Ryan, *b.* 1882. *Residence,*—

PREDECESSORS.—[1] *Sir* EDWARD North, an eminent lawyer, M.P. for Cambridgeshire
1541-2, Lord-Lieut. of Cambridgeshire, and one of the executors of Henry VIII.; summoned to
Parliament as *Baron North,* of Kirtling, co. Cambridge (peerage of England) 1554; *d.* 1564 ; *s.*
by his son [2] *Rt. Hon.* ROGER, K.B., 2nd Baron, Ambassador to France and Treasurer of Queen
Elizabeth's Household ; *d.* 1600; *s.* by his grandson [3] DUDLEY, 3rd Baron ; *d.* 1666 ; *s.* by his
son [4] DUDLEY, K.B., 4th Baron ; *d.* 1677 : *s.* by his son [5] CHARLES, 5th Baron; summoned
to Parliament during his father's lifetime as *Baron Grey,* of Rolleston, co. Stafford (peerage of
England) 1673 ; *d.* 1690; *s.* by his son [6] WILLIAM, 6th Baron North and 2nd Baron Grey ;
d.s.p. 1734, when the Barony of Grey expired and the Barony of North devolved upon his
cousin [7] FRANCIS, 7th Baron North, who had in 1729 *s.* as 3rd *Baron Guilford,* of Guildford,
co. Surrey (peerage of England, cr. 1683), a peerage that had been conferred upon the Hon. Sir
Francis, Lord Ch. Justice of the Common Pleas, 2nd son of 4th Baron North; cr. *Earl of
Guilford* (peerage of Great Britain) 1752 ; *d.* 1790 ; *s.* by his el. son [8] *Rt. Hon.* FREDERICK, K.G.,
2nd Earl; an eminent statesman who (when Lord North) held high official positions 1759-83,
and was Prime Minister 1770-81; *d.* 1792; *s.* by his son [9] GEORGE AUGUSTUS, 3rd Earl; *d.*
1802, when the Barony of North became abeyant (see B. North), and the earldom devolved
upon his brother [10] FRANCIS, 4th Earl; *d.s.p.* 1817; *s.* by his brother [11] FREDERICK, 5th
Earl; *d.s.p.* 1827 ; *s.* by his cousin [12] *Rev.* Francis, 6th Earl ; *d.* 1861; *s.* by his grandson [13]
DUDLEY FRANCIS (el. son of the late Dudley, Lord North, el. son of 6th Earl), 7th Earl, *b.* 1851 :
m. 1874, Georgiana, who *d.* 1931, dau. of Sir George Chetwynd, 3rd Bt.; *d.* 1885: *s.* by his
son [14] FREDERICK GEORGE, T.D., 8th Earl, *b.* 1876 ; Lieut.-Col. Roy. E. Kent Yeo.: *m.* 1901,
Mary Violet, who *d.* 1947, el. dau. of the late William Hargrave Pawson; *d.* 1949 ; *s.* by his
grandson [15] EDWARD FRANCIS (only son of the late Francis George, Lord North, el. son of 8th
Earl), 9th Earl and present peer ; also Baron Guilford.

GUILLAMORE, VISCOUNTCY OF. (O'Grady.) [Extinct 1955.]

DAUGHTER LIVING OF SIXTH VISCOUNT.

Hon. Kathleen Gertrude, *b.* 1914; late Junior Com. A.T.S.: *m.* 1945. Capt. Geoffrey Hearn, Somersetshire L.I., and has issue living, Timothy Charles, *b.* 1947. *Residence,*—Badgers Mount, Bottle Sq. Lane, Radnage, Bucks.

Gwynedd, Viscount, son of Earl Lloyd George of Dwyfor.

HACKING, BARON. (Hacking.) [Baron U.K. 1945, Bt. U.K. 1938.]

DOUGLAS DAVID HACKING, 3rd Baron, and 3rd Baronet; *b.* April 17th, 1938; *s.* 1971; ed. at Charterhouse, and Clare Coll., Camb. (MA); Bar. Middle Temple 1963; Pres. of Assocn. of Lancastrians in London 1971-72; Freeman. Merchant Taylors' Co., and City of London; Lt. RNR (ret): *m.* 1965, Rosemary Anne, el. da. of Frank Penrose Forrest, FRCSE, of Lytchett Matravers, Dorset, and has issue.

Arms,—Argent, on a chevron azure between three roses gules barbed and seeded proper, two bird bolts of the field, feathered or. Crest,—In front of an oak tree eradicated, two axes in saltire all proper. Supporters,—On either side a griffin gules, on the shoulder an escutcheon argent charged with a blue-bottle (Cyanus), stalked and leaved proper.

Residence,—Forrest Hill, Roxmoor, Herts. HP3 0BD.

SONS LIVING.

Hon. DOUGLAS FRANCIS, *b.* Aug. 8th, 1968.
Hon. Daniel Robert, *b.* 1972.

DAUGHTER LIVING.

Hon. Belinda Anne, *b.* 1966.

BROTHER LIVING.

Hon. Leslie Bruce (Burchetts, Lower Moushill Lane, Milford, Surrey), *b.* 1940; ed. at Eton; Freeman, Haberdashers' Co., and City of London: *m.* 1967, the Hon. Fiona Margaret Noel-Paton, yst. da. of Baron Ferrier (Life Peer), and has issue living, Matthew Bruce, *b.* 1969,—Joanna, *b.* 1972.

SISTERS LIVING.

Hon. Sandra Daphne, *b.* 1950: *m.* 1972, Damon Patrick de Laszlo [see V. Greenwood].
Hon. Carina Gillian, *b.* 1956.

UNCLE LIVING. (*Son of 1st Baron.*)

Hon. Edgar Bolton, *M.B E., T.D.*, *b.* 1912; ed. at Charterhouse, and at Clare Coll., Camb. (B.A. 1983, M.A. 1937, M.B. and B.Ch. 1937); M.R.C.S. England and L.R.C.P. London 1936; Diploma in Anæsthesia Roy. Coll. of Physicians and Roy. Coll. of Surgs. 1946; a Member of Faculty of Anæsthetists, Roy. Coll. of Surgs. 1949, a Fellow of Asso. of Anæsthetists 1951 and a Fellow of Faculty of Anæsthetists, Roy. Coll. of Surgs. 1954, formerly Senior Assist. Anæsthetist, Groote Schuur Hospital. Cape Town; European War 1939-45 as Major R.A.M.C. (M.B.E.); M.B.E. (Mil.) 1943: *m.* 1st, 1943 (marriage dissolved 1950), Winifred Mary, dau. of John Christie Kelly, of S. Africa; 2ndly, 1950, Evangeline Grace, dau. of Percy Burtsal Shearing, of S. Africa, and has issue living, (by 1s, m.) Elizabeth Anne, *b.* 1944,—Susan Margaret, *b.* 1946,—(by 2nd m.) Douglas Percival Bolton, *b.* 1955,—Geoffrey Edgar Bolton, *b.* 1958,—Margery Ethel, *b.* 1952. *Residence,*—Leeming, Alice Rd., Claremont, Cape, S. Africa.

AUNT LIVING (*Daughter of 1st Baron*).

Hon. Elizabeth Margery (*Hon. Lady Waller*), *b.* 1916; is a JP: *m.* 1936, Hon. Mr Justice (Sir George Stanley) Waller, OBE, and has issue living, George Mark, *b.* 1940, LLB; Bar. Grays Inn, 1964: *m.* 1967, Rachel Elizabeth, da. of Judge Christopher Beaumont, of 13, King's Bench Walk, Temple, EC4,—James Irvin (c/o Dir. of Research, Solicitor Gen. of Canada); *b.* 1944: *m.* 1966, Myriam, da. of Prof. Pierre de Bie, of 2, Chaussée de Namur, Blanden, Belgium,—Elizabeth Tessa, *b.* 1937: *m.* 1959, John Hedley-Whyte. *Residence,*—Hatch Hill, Kingsley Green, Haslemere, Surrey.

WIDOWS LIVING OF FIRST AND SECOND BARONS.

MARGERY ALLEN (*Dowager Baroness Hacking*),*Q.B.E.*, el. dau. of H. H. Bolton, J.P., of Newchurch-in-Rossendale; OBE (Civil) 1956: *m.* 1909, the 1st Baron, who *d.* 1950. *Residence,*—8, Dorchester Court, Sloane Street, S.W.1.
DAPHNE VIOLET (*Daphne, Baroness Hacking*), el. da. of the late Robert Leslie Finnis, of Kensington, W.: *m.* 1936, the 2nd Baron, who *d.* 1971.

PREDECESSORS—[1] DOUGLAS HEWITT Hacking, *OBE, PC*, son of Joshua Hacking, JP, of Clayton-le-Moors, Lancs., *b.* 1884; Financial Sec. to War Office and a Member of Army Council 1934-35, and Under-Sec. of State for Dominions 1935-36; founded Travel Assoc. of Great Britain and Ireland 1928; Chm. of Conservative Party 1936-42; MP for Chorley (*U*) 1918 to 1945; cr. a *Baronet* 1938, and *Baron Hacking*, of Chorley, co. Lancaster (peerage of UK) 1945: *m.* 1909, Margery Allen, el. da. of H. H. Bolton, JP, of Newchurch-in-Rossendale; *d.* 1950; *s.* by his el. son [2] DOUGLAS ERIC, 2nd Baron, *b.* 1910; Chm. of Council Trust Houses 1965-70 and Trust Houses Forte Hotel and Catering Group 1970-71; 1939-45 War as Maj. RA: *m.* 1936, Daphne Violet, el. da. of the late Robert Leslie Finnis, of Kensington, W, *d.* 1971; *s.* by his el. son [3] DOUGLAS DAVID, 3rd Baron and present peer; also 3rd baronet.

HADDINGTON, EARL OF.
I undertake   Virtue is greater
and persevere.   than splendour.

(Baillie-Hamilton.) [Earl S. 1619.]
GEORGE BAILLIE-HAMILTON, K.T.,
M.C., T.D., 12th Earl; b. Sept. 18th,
1894; s. 1917; ed. at Eton; Hon. LL.D.
Glasgow 1957; a Representative Peer for
Scotland 1922-63; is Capt. late Scots
Greys (Reserve), Major late 19th (Lothians
and Border Horse) Armoured Car Co.
Roy. Tank Corps (T.A. Reserve), and a
Lt. of Queen's Body Guard for Scot-
land (Roy. Co. of Archers); Lord-Lt. of
Berwickshire 1952-69; sometime on
Staff of Gov.-Gen. of Canada; 1914-18
War in France and Belgium (wounded,
M.C., 1914-15 star, two medals), 1939-45
War in France; bore Ivory Rod of the
Queen at Coronation of King George VI;
K.T. 1951: m. 1923, Sarah, da. of the
late G. W. Cook, of Montreal, and has issue.

Arms,—Quarterly: 1st and 4th grand quarters, 1st and 4th gules, on a chevron between three
cinquefoils argent, a buckle azure, between two ermine spots, all within a bordure or, charged
with eight thistles vert, Hamilton of Byres; 2nd and 3rd argent, a fesse wavy between three roses
gules barbed and seeded proper, Melrose; 2nd and 3rd grand quarters sable, the sun in his glory
betwixt nine stars, three, two, three, and one, argent, Baillie of Jerviswoode. Crests,—1st, two
dexter hands issuing out of clouds, conjoined fessewise and holding betwixt them a branch
of laurel erect, all proper; 2nd, a crescent or. Supporters,—Two talbots argent, plain collared
gules.
Seat,—Tyninghame, Prestonkirk, East Lothian.

SON LIVING.
JOHN GEORGE (Lord Binning), b. Dec. 21st, 1941; ed. at Ampleforth: m. 1975, Prudence Elizabeth,
da. of Andrew Rutherford Hayles, of Bowerchalke, Wilts.

DAUGHTER LIVING.
Lady Mary, b. 1934; m. 1st, 1954 (m. diss. 1965), John Adrian Bailey; 2ndly, 1965, David Russell,
and has issue living, (by 1st marriage) William Anthony, b. 1957,—Philip Graham, b. 1959,—Arabella
Sarah Lucy, b. 1955,—(by 2nd m.) Jason Dominic, b. 1966,—Mariana, b. 1968. Residence,—23,
Edwardes Sq., W8.

COLLATERAL BRANCHES LIVING.
Grandson of the late Rev. the Hon. John Baillie, brother of 10th Earl :—
Issue (by 1st marriage) of the late Hugh John Baillie, b. 1838, d. 1923: m. 1st, 1873, Sarah,
who d. 1890, dau. of J. Heather ; 2ndly, 1902, Maria, dau. of W. N. Wallace, J.P.,
D.L., and widow of Donald Ross, F.R.S.E. :—
John Cecil George, b. 1888. Residence,—
Grandchildren of the late Rev. Thomas George Baillie (infra):—
Issue of the late Charles Jarviswoode Baillie, b. 1882, d. 1974: m. 1914, Dora Dunn, who d.
1974:—
Robert Alastair (4308, West 14th Av., Vancouver, BC, Canada), b. 1919; a Collector of Customs and
Excise 1960-63; 1939-45 War with Seaforth Highlanders of Canada (despatches): m. 1945, Elizabeth
Amy, da. of Alexi Chernoff, of Tiflis Russia and Kelowna, BC, and has issue living, Dexter Robert,
b. 1958,—Eve Sylvia, b. 1946,—Angeline Cecelia, b. 1950.——Barbara, b. 1914: m. 1945, Maurice
W. Brown.
Issue of the late Richard George HAMILTON-BAILLIE, b. 1869, d. 1945: m. 1915, Maud
Gertrude, who d. 1952, only dau. of the late Edward Hadley, Bar.-at-Law :—
John Robert Edward, M.C., b. 1919; ed. at Camb. Univ. (MA); Brig. (ret.) late RE, MICE; 1939-45 War
(MC): m. 1947, Lettice Mary, da. of the late C. E. Pumphrey, of Belsay, Northumberland, and has
issue living, Thomas Richard, b. 1948; ed. at Winchester, and London Univ. (BA); Capt. R. Green
Jackets: m. 1975, Marina J.A.S., da. of General Major Dr. Ferdinand von Senger und Etterlin, of
5 Kohn-Marienburg Germany,—Benjamin Robert, b. 1955,—Griselda Mary, b. 1950,—Katherine
Maud, b. 1957. Residence,—Rectory House, Stanford-in-the-Vale, Faringdon, Oxon.

Granddaughter of the Rev. the Hon. John Baillie (ante):—
Issue of the late Rev. Thomas George Baillie, b. 1842, d. 1917: m. 1st, 1867, Ellen
Isabella, who d. 1909, dau. of Richard Gregson, of Sydney, N.S.W.; 2ndly, 1911,
Violet Amy Kate, dau. of F. W. Dunn:—
(By 2nd m.) Violet Georgina Eila, b. 1912: m. 1931, Albert Ranney Chewett, who d. 1965.
Residence,—Reveley Lodge, Bushey Heath, Herts.
Grandchildren of the late Capt. Peregrine Charles Baillie-Hamilton, son of the late
Charles John Baillie-Hamilton, M.P., 2nd son of the late Ven. Charles Baillie-
Hamilton, 2nd son of the late Hon. George Baillie, brother of 7th Earl :—
Issue of the late Rev. George James Baillie-Hamilton, b. 1851, d. 1904: m. 1875, Eliza, who
d. 1931, dau. of the late Rev. Lucius Fry, of Croft, Leicestershire :—
George Leslie, b. 1877; has been Capt. 13th Batn. Roy. Scots (Lothian Regt.): m. 1st, 1906,
Florence Maud Robinson, who d. 1912; 2ndly, 1918, Katherine Ida Pennicard, and has issue
living, (by 1st marriage) George Leslie, b. 1909,—(by 2nd marriage) David Lincoln, b. 1922,—
Ella Faith b. 1919,—Jean Elizabeth, b. 1921.——Arthur Vivian, b. 1881 : m. 1906, Ida Mand
Harrison.——Lucius Hugh Noel, b. 1886.——Patrick Stephen, b. 1890.——Edith Mary, b. 1876 :
m. 1919, James Herbert Crompton, who d. 1944.——Aline Melrose, b. 1879.——Madeline Violet, b.
1888 : m. 1913, Arthur Hammond Jones, and has issue living, Margaret Elizabeth, b. 1914. Resi-
dence,—Sandringham Estate, Agrapatana, Ceylon.
Grandchildren of the late Violet Mary King (who m. 1898, Algernon Christian
Baily), da. of the late Harriet Eleanor Baillie-Hamilton (who m. 1863, Henry
Samuel King, J.P.), da. of the late Adm. William Alexander Baillie-Hamilton,
grandson of the late Hon. George Baillie (ante):—
Issue of the late Brigadier Michael Henry Hamilton Baily, D.S.O., b. 1901, d. 1950: m. 1935,
Elizabeth Helena (now of Hampton Court Palace, East Molesey, Surrey), dau. of Julian
Cornes, J.P., of Layston House, Buntingford, Herts:—
John Edward (of 27, Park Walk, S.W.10), b. 1936; ed. at Eton, and at Corpus Christi Coll., Oxon.: m.
1962, Lady Sarah Dorothea Boyle, da. of 9th Earl of Glasgow, and has issue living, Michael, b. 1963,—
Peter, b. 1967,—Tanya Jane, b. 1965,—Polly Anne, b. 1972.——Mark Richard Henry (3, Smith
Terr., SW3), b. 1940; ed. at Eton, and at Ch. Ch., Oxford (MA); Solicitor 1966: m. 1971, Penelope
Mary, da. of Henry Cooper, of Stockwell House, Silverton, Devon, and has issue living, James
Edward Hugo, b. 1972,—Alexander Mark Henry, b. 1975.

Grandsons of the late John BUCHANAN-BAILLIE-HAMILTON (infra):—
Issue of the late John Edmondstone BUCHANAN-BAILLIE-HAMILTON, *b.* 1874, *d.* 1957: *m.*
1925, Bridgett Everett, who *d.* 1971, da. of John E. Baker, formerly of Cambridge:—
John Neil, *b.* 1926 ; ed. at Winchester ; Capt. (retired) late Black Watch : *m.* 1955, the Hon. Caroline
Barbara Coupar Barrie, da. of 1st Baron Abertay, and has issue living, John Michael, *b.* 1958,—
Alexander Neil *b.* 1963. *Residence,*—Cambusmore, Callander, Perthshire.——James Angus, *b.*
1927; late Lt. R.N.; is a Farmer: *m.* 1954, Prudence, only da. of Cdr. Wenman Humfry Wykeham-
Musgrave, R.N.(Ret.) [E. Grey, colls.], of The Dower House, Barnsley, Cirencester, Gloucestershire,
and has issue living, Charles Wenman, *b.* 1957,—Simon James, *b.* 1963,—Jane, *b.* 1955,—Sally, *b.*
1961. *Residence,*—South Farm, Shipton Oliffe, nr. Cheltenham, Gloucestershire.——Alexander,
b. 1932; ed. at Glenalmond, and at Aberdeen Univ. (MB and ChB); Diploma of Industrial Medicine,
London 1959: *m.* 1964, Mrs. Lilia Julia Mary Eaton, da. of the late Alan Peter, of St. Lucia, W.
Indies, and has issue living, Fiona Mary, *b.* 1966,—Alexandra Helen, *b.* 1969. *Residence,*—Knowle
Croft, Shoppenhangers, Maidenhead, Berks.

Granddaughter of the late Capt. Gerard Baillie-Hamilton, 6th son of the late
Ven. Charles Baillie (ante):—
Issue of the late John BUCHANAN-BAILLIE-HAMILTON, *b.* 1837, *d.* 1908 : *m.* 1869, Catherine
Elizabeth Grace, who *d.* 1932, dau. and heiress of the late Alexander Buchanan, of Arnprior,
whose name he assumed :—
Grisell Baillie, *b.* 1886. *Residence,*—Auchleshie, Callander, Perthshire.

Granddaughter and sole heiress of the late Thomas Baillie-Hamilton, son of the
late Capt. Gerard Baillie-Hamilton (ante):—
Issue of the late Augusta Emmeline Baillie-Hamilton, *b.* 1879, *d.* 1957 : *m.* 1906, Major
Arthur Claude Willcocks, T.D., A.M.I.C.E.:—
Violet Baillie, *b.* 1908: *m.* 1944, the Rev. John Francis Walmsley, MA, Chap. RN, of Elsted Rectory,
Midhurst, Sussex, and has issue living, John Gerard, *b.* 1945; ed. at Rossall; Lt. RN: *m.* 1972, Marie
Evelyn, da. of the late Roger Kenworthy, of Sydney, NSW.

PREDECESSORS.—[1] *Sir* THOMAS Hamilton, successively a Lord of Session (as Lord Drumcairn), a Commr. to treat of a Union with England, Lord Clerk Register of Scotland, Sec. of
State, Pres. of Court of Session, and Keeper of the Privy Seal; cr. *Lord Binning* (peerage of
Scotland) 1613, *Earl of Melrose,* and *Lord Byres and Binning* (peerage of Scotland) 1619; the
title of Melrose was changed in 1627, and he was cr. *Earl of Haddington* (peerage of Scotland)
with precedence of 1619 and limitation to his heirs male bearing the name of Hamilton; *d.* 1637,
leaving one of the largest fortunes of his time; *s.* by his son [2] THOMAS, 2nd Earl; a zealous
Covenanter; was killed by an explosion at the Castle of Dunglas, of which he was Gov., 1640; *s.*
by his el. son [3] THOMAS, 3rd Earl; *d.s.p.* 1645; *s.* by his brother [4] JOHN, 4th Earl; *d.* 1669;
s. by his son [5] CHARLES, 5th Earl; *m.* 1674, Lady Margaret Leslie, dau. of 1st Duke of Rothes,
who on the death of her father became in her own right by charter Countess of Rothes; in 1689
was granted a patent confirming the terms of the marriage contract, by which the Earldom of
Rothes was to descend to the el. son, and the Earldom of Haddington and Lordship of Binning
were to revert to the 2nd son; the Countess *d.* 1702, and was *s.* by her el. son (see Rothes); the
Earl *d.* 1681, and was *s.* by his 2nd son [6] THOMAS, 6th Earl; obtained a charter of the Earldom, and appointed Hereditary Keeper of Holyrood Palace; a Representative Peer 1716-35; *d.*
1735 ; *s.* by his grandson [7] THOMAS, 7th Earl; el. son of Charles, Lord Binning; *d.* 1794; *s.*
by his son [8] CHARLES, 8th Earl; a Representative Peer, and Lord-Lieut. of Haddingtonshire ;
d. 1828; *s.* by his son [9] THOMAS, *K.T., P.C.,* 9th Earl; Lord-Lieut. of Ireland 1833-4; cr.
Baron Melrose, of Tyninghame (peerage of United Kingdom) 1827; in 1843 resigned the office of
Hereditary Keeper of Holyrood Palace for the consideration of £40,000 ; *d.* 1858, when the Barony
of Melrose became extinct, and the Scottish honours devolved upon his cousin [10] GEORGE,
10th Earl, son of George Baillie, nephew of 7th Earl; *b.* 1802; was a Lord-in-Waiting to
H.M. 1867-8, a Representative Peer, and High Commr. to Gen. Assembly of Ch. of Scotland;
assumed by Roy. licence 1859 the additional surname of Hamilton to that of Baillie, which
had been assumed in lieu of Hamilton by his grandfather: *m.* 1824, Georgina, dau. of the Ven.
Robert Markham, Archdeacon of York; *d.* 1870; *s.* by his son [11] GEORGE, *K.T.,* 11th Earl;
b. 1827 ; Vice-Lieut. of co. Berwick 1873-1917, and Lord-Lieut. of co. Haddington 1896-1917;
assumed by Roy. licence, 1858, the additional surname of Arden after that of Baillie-
Hamilton: *m.* 1854, Helen Catherine, who *d.* 1889, dau. of Sir John Warrender, 5th Bt.; *d.*
1917; *s.* by his grandson [12] GEORGE (son of the late Brig.-Gen. George, Lord Binning, C.B.,
M.V.O., el. son of 11th Earl), 12th Earl and present peer; also Lord Binning, and Lord Byres
and Binning.

HADEN-GUEST, BARON. (Haden-Guest.) [Baron U.K .1950.]

RICHARD HADEN HADEN-GUEST, 3rd Baron; *b.* July 20th, 1904; *s.* 1974:
m. 1st, 1926 (m. diss. 1934), Hilda, da. of the late Dr. Thomas Russell-Cruise;
2ndly, 1934, Olive Maria, da. of the late Anders Gotfrid Nilsson; 3rdly, 1951,
Marjorie Douglas, da. of the late Dr. Douglas Kennard, and has issue by
1st m.

Residence,—Le Cédre, Route des Fryards, Versoix, Geneva, Switzerland.

DAUGHTER LIVING. (*By 1st m.*)
Hon. Susan Josephine Gabrielle Haden, *b.* 1930: *m.* 1953, John Orr Stanley, of Granary House, Holly
Hill, NW3, and has issue living, Charles Orr Nicholas, *b.* 1954,—Martin David Anthony, *b.* 1956,—
Shaun Richard, *b.* 1958,—Philip Thomas, *b.* 1962.

HALF-BROTHER LIVING.
Hon. PETER HADEN, *b.* 1913; ed. at City of London Sch., and New Coll., Oxford (MA); Senior Editorial
Control Officer, Office of Conference Sers., UN Secretariat, New York; 1939-45 War as Lt. RCNVR:
m. 1945, Jean, da. of the late Dr. Albert George Hindes, of 190, Waverly Place, New York City,
USA, and has issue living, Christopher, *b.* 1948,—Nichols, *b.* 1951,—Elissa, *b.* 1953. *Residences.*—
86, MacDougal St., New York 10012, NY, USA; 12, Belsize Rd., St. John's Wood, NW6.

DAUGHTER LIVING OF SECOND BARON.
Hon. Hadley (1148, Fifth Av., New York City, NY, USA), *b.* 1949.

WIDOW LIVING OF FIRST BARON.
EDITH EDGAR (*Edith, Baroness Haden-Guest*) (The University, Glasgow), da. of the late George Macqueen, of Montrose; MA, 1922, PhD St. Andrews, 1927; Commonwealth Fund Fellow, Yale:
m. 1944, as his third wife, the 1st Baron, who *d.* 1960.

WIDOW LIVING OF SECOND BARON.
DOROTHY (*Dorothy, Baroness Haden-Guest*) (105, Bayard Lane, Princeton, New Jersey 08540, USA),
da. of Thomas Roseberry Good; late of Princeton, New Jersey: *m.* 1968, as his second wife, the
2nd Baron, who *d.* 1974.
PREDECESSORS.—[1] LESLIE HADEN Haden-Guest, *MC, MRCS, LRCP,* son of the late Alexander
Haden-Guest, Surg. and Physician of Manchester; *b.* 1877; a Lord-in-Waiting to HM Feb. to Oct.
1951; sat as MP for N. Div. of Southwark (*Lab*) 1923-7, and for N. Div. of Islington 1937-50; cr.
Baron Haden-Guest, of Saling, co. Essex (peerage of United Kingdom) 1950: *m.* 1st, 1898 (m. diss
1909), Edith, who *d.* 1944, da. of Max Low, of London; 2ndly, 1910, Muriel Carmel, who *d.* 1943,

da. of the late Col. Albert Goldsmid, MVO; 3rdly 1944, Edith Edgar, da. of the late George Macqueen, of Montrose; *d.* 1960; *s.* by his el. son [2] STEPHEN HADEN, 2nd Baron *b.* 1902; editor and translator: *m.* 1st, 1948 (m. diss. 1954), Barbara Ann, da. of James Harvey Pinson, of W. Virginia, USA; 2ndly, 1968, Dorothy da. of Thomas Roseberry Good, late of Princeton, New Jersey; *d.* 1974; *s.* by his brother [3] RICHARD HADEN, 3rd Baron and present peer.

HAIG, EARL. (Haig.) [Earl U.K. 1919.]

GEORGE ALEXANDER EUGENE DOUGLAS HAIG, *OBE*, 2nd Earl (*30th Laird of Bemersyde*); *b.* March 15th, 1918: *s.* 1928; ed. at Stowe, and at Ch. Ch., Oxford (MA); Capt. Roy. Scots Greys; is a Member of Queen's Body Guard for Scotland (Roy. Co. of Archers), a DL for Berwicks. (Vice-Lt. 1967-70); Pres. Scottish Craft Centre, Chm. SE Scotland Disablement Advisory Cttee., a Member of Soc. of Scottish Artists, of Scottish Arts Council, and of Council of Earl Haig Fund and Officers' Assocn. (Scottish Cttee), a Trustee of Scottish National War Memorial; of National Gallery of Scotland 1962-72; FRSA; Chm. of British Legion, Scotland 1962-65; 1939-45 War (prisoner); was a Train Bearer at Coronation of King George VI; OBE (Civil) 1966: *m.* 1956, Adrienne Thérèse, da. of Derrick Morley, of Quaives, Wickhambreaux, Kent, and has issue.

Arms,—Azure, a saltire between a mullet in chief and another in base, a decrescent and an in crescent in the flanks argent. **Crest,**—A rock proper. **Supporters,**—*Dexter,* a bay horse caparisoned thereon mounted a Private of the 7th (Queen's Own) Hussars, habited, armed and accoutred; *sinister* a bay horse, caparisoned, thereon mounted a Lancer of the 17th (Duke of Cambridge's Own) Lancers habited, armed and accoutred all proper.

Seat —Bemersyde, Melrose, Roxburghshire. *Clubs,*—White's, Cavalry, Puffin's, New.

SON LIVING.
ALEXANDER DOUGLAS DERRICK (*Viscount Dawick*), *b.* June 30th, 1961.

DAUGHTERS LIVING.
Lady Adrienne Rainà, *b.* 1958.
Lady Elizabeth Vivienne Thérèse, *b.* 1959.

SISTERS LIVING.
Lady Alexandra Henrietta Louisa, *b.* 1907: *m.* 1st, 1941 (marriage dissolved 1954), Rear Adm. Clarence Dinsmore Howard-Johnston, C.B., D.S.O., D.S.C.; 2ndly, 1954, Hugh Redwald Trevor-Roper [see B. Teynham, colls.], and has issue living, (by 1st marriage) James Douglas, *b.* 1942.—Philip Peter Dawyck, *b.* 1950,—Xenia, *b.* 1944. *Residences,*—8, St. Aldate's, Oxford; Chiefswood, Melrose, Roxburghshire.
Lady Victoria Doris Rachel (The Pavilion, Park Rd., Isleworth, Middlesex, TW7 6BD), *b.* 1908: *m.* 1929, Brig. Claud Andrew Montagu-Douglas-Scott, DSO, Irish Guards (Reserve) [see D. Buccleuch], who *d.* 1971, and from whom she obtained a divorce 1951.
Lady Irene Violet Freesia Janet Augusta (*Baroness Astor of Hever*), *b.* 1919: *m.* 1945, the 2nd Baron Astor of Hever. *Residences,*—Hever Castle, Edenbridge, Kent; 11, Lyall St., S.W.1; Tillypronie, Tarland, Aberdeenshire.

PREDECESSOR.—[1] *Field-Marshal Sir* DOUGLAS Haig, *K.T., G.C.B., O.M., G.C.V.O., K.C.I.E.,* son of the late John Haig, of Cameronbridge, Fife, *b.* 1861; Nile Expedition 1898, present at battles of Atbara and Khartoum (despatches, Egyptian medal with two clasps, Brevet Major), in S. Africa 1899-1902 on the Staff, present at battles of Elandslaagte, operations around Colesberg, relief of Kimberley, and battles of Paardeberg and Belfast, and in command of Mounted Columns with rank of Col. (despatches twice, Brevet Lieut.-Col. and Col., C.B.), European War 1914-18, first in command of 1st Army Corps, secondly of 1st Army, and thirdly of British Expeditionary Force in France and Flanders (despatches thrice, promoted Gen., Grand Officer Legion of Honour, G.C.B., G.C.V.O., Field-Marshal, K.T., Obilitch medal, Croix de Guerre, Italian Order of St. Maurice and St. Lazarus, 4th class of Russian Order of St. George, and of Michael the Brave of Roumania, Serbian Order of Karageorge with Swords, Order of Tower and Sword of Portugal, Medaille Militaire, American Cross of Honour, Grand Cordon of Japanese Order of the Rising Sun with Paulowina, and 1st class Order of Chia Ho of China, Gold Medal of La Solidaridad of Panama, American D.S.M., thanked by Parliament, cr. Earl, granted £100,000, presented by people of British Empire with house and fishings of Bemersyde); attached to Egyptian Army 1897-8; appointed an Extra A.D.C. to H.M. 1902, Inspector-Gen. of Cav. in India 1903, Director of Mil. Training at Head Quarters 1906, Director of Staff Duties there 1907, Ch. of the Staff in India and a Member of Council of Gov.-Gen. of India 1909, an A.D.C. Gen. to H.M. 1914, Gen. Officer Comdg.-in-Ch., Aldershot 1912, and Gen. Officer Comdg.-in-Ch., Great Britain 1919; cr. *Earl Haig, Viscount Dawick,* and *Baron Haig,* of Bemersyde, co. Berwick (peerage of United Kingdom) 1919: *m.* 1905, the Hon. Dorothy Maud Vivian (a D.G.St.J.), who *d.* 1939, dau. of 3rd Baron Vivian; *d.* 1928; *s.* by his son [2] GEORGE ALEXANDER EUGENE DOUGLAS, 2nd Earl and present peer; also Viscount Dawick, and Baron Haig.

HAILES, BARONY OF. (Buchan-Hepburn.) [Extinct 1974.]
WIDOW LIVING OF FIRST BARON.

DIANA MARY (*Baroness Hailes*), (Lane House, Mortimer, Reading), da. of the late Brig.-Gen. the Hon. Charles Lambton, DSO [see E. Durham colls.], and widow of Maj. William Hedworth Williamson [see Williamson, Bt., colls.]: *m.* 1945, the 1st Baron, who *d.* 1974, when the title became ext.

HAILSHAM, VISCOUNTCY OF, see Baron Hailsham of St. Marylebone.

HAILSHAM OF ST MARYLEBONE, BARON. (Hogg). [Viscount UK 1929, disclaimed 1963, Life Baron 1970.]

QUINTIN McGAREL HOGG, *CH, PC, FRS; b.* Oct. 9th, 1907; *s.* as 2nd Viscount Hailsham Aug. 16th, 1950; ed. at Eton, and Ch. Ch., Oxford (MA, Hon. Student); Hon. DCL Oxford; FRS; Fellow of All Souls Coll., Oxford 1931-38, and since 1962; Bar. Lincoln's Inn 1932, QC 1953, and Bencher 1956; Hon. LLD Camb.; 1939-45 War as Maj. Rifle Bde. (TA) (wounded); Joint Under-Sec. of State for Air April to July 1945, First Lord of the Admiralty 1956-57, Min. of Educ. Jan. to Sept. 1957, Dep. Leader of House of Lords 1957-60, Lord Pres. of the Council 1957-59, and again 1960-64, Lord Privy Seal 1959-60, Leader of House of Lords 1960-63, Min. for Science and Tech. 1959-64, and Lord Chancellor 1970-74; elected R. of Glasgow Univ. 1959; MP for Oxford City (*C*) 1938-58, and for St. Marylebone 1963-70; cr. PC 1956; disclaimed his peerage for life Nov. 20th, 1963; cr. PC 1956, *Baron Hailsham of St. Marylebone,* of Herstmonceux, co. Sussex (Life Baron) 1970, and CH 1974: *m.* 1st, 1931, Natalie Antoinette (from whom he obtained a divorce 1943), da. of Alan Sullivan, of Sheerland House, Pluckley, Kent; 2ndly, 1944, Mary Evelyn, only child of Richard Martin, of 46, Wynnstay Gdns., W8, and has issue by 2nd m.

Arms,—Argent, three boars' heads erased azure, langued gules, between two flaunches azure each charged with a crescent of the field. **Crest,**—Out of an eastern crown argent, an oak-tree fructed proper, and pendent therefrom an escutcheon azure, charged with a dexter arm embowed in armour, the hand grasping an arrow in bend sinister, the point downwards, also proper. **Supporters,**—On either side a ram argent armed and unguled or, gorged with a baron's coronet, the *dexter* supporting a representation of the Lord High Chancellor's mace, and the *sinister,* a representation of the Lord High Chancellor's purse, with the initials of Her Majesty Queen Elizabeth II, proper.

Residence,—The Corner House, 13, Heathview Gdns., Putney Heath, SW15.

SONS LIVING. (*By 2nd marriage.*)

Hon. DOUGLAS MARTIN (11, Mallord St., SW3), *b.* Feb. 5th, 1945; *h.a.* to Viscountcy of Hailsham; ed. at Eton, and at Ch. Ch., Oxford; Bar. Lincoln's Inn 1968: *m.* 1968, the Hon. Sarah Elizabeth Mary, yr. da. of Baron Boyd-Carpenter, and has issue living, Quintin John Neil Martin, *b.* 1973,— Charlotte Mary, *b.* 1970.
Hon. James Richard Martin, *b.* 1951; ed. at Eton; Capt. Gren. Gds.

DAUGHTERS LIVING. (*By 2nd marriage.*)

Hon. Mary Claire, *b.* 1947; Bar. Lincoln's Inn 1968.
Hon. Frances Evelyn, *b.* 1949: *m.* 1970, Richard Quintin Hoare, of Garden House, Logan Place, W8, and has issue living, Alexander Richard Quintin, *b.* 1973.
Hon. Katharine Amelia, *b.* 1962.

BROTHER LIVING

Hon. William Neil McGarel, *b.* 1910; ed. at Eton; HM's Diplo. Ser. (ret.). *Address,*—Hotel Seeburg, 6008 Lucerne, Switzerland.

PREDECESSOR—[1] *Rt. Hon. Sir* DOUGLAS McGAREL Hogg, *PC,* son of Quintin Hogg [see Hogg Br, cr. 1846, colls.]; *b.* 1872; Bar. Lincoln's Inn, 1902, a KC 1917, and a Bencher 1920; Attorney Gen. to HRH the Prince of Wales and a Member of Council of Duchy of Cornwall 1920-22, Attorney-Gen. (with a seat in the Cabinet) 1924-28, Lord High Chancellor 1928-29 (acted as Prime Min. 1928), and Leader of Opposition in House of Lords June to Aug. 1931; appointed Sec. of State for War (National Govt.) and Leader of the House of Lords 1931, and again Lord High Chancellor 1935; Lord President of the Council March to Oct. 1938 ; Recorder of Kingston-upon-Thames 1924-28 ; sat as M.P. for St. Marylebone (*U*) 1922-28 ; *cr. Baron Hailsham,* of Hailsham, co. Sussex (peerage of United Kingdom) 1928, and *Viscount Hailsham,* of Hailsham, co. Sussex (peerage of United Kingdom) 1929 : *m.* 1st, 1905, Elizabeth, who *d.* 1925, dau. of the late Judge James Trimble Brown, of Nashville, Tennesee, U.S.A., and widow of the Hon. Archibald John Majoribanks ; 2ndly, 1929, Mildred Margaret, who *d.* 1964, da. of the late Rev. Edward Parker Dew, R. and Patron of Breamore, Hants, and widow of the Hon. Alfred Clive Lawrence [B. Trevethin & Oaksey]; *d.* 1950; *s.* by his el. son [2] QUINTIN McGAREL, 2nd Viscount, until he disclaimed his peerages 1963; *cr. Baron Hailsham of St. Marylebone* (Life Baron) 1970.

HAIRE OF WHITEABBEY, BARONY OF. (Haire.) [Extinct 1966.]
SONS LIVING OF LIFE BARON.

Hon. Michael John Kemeny, *b.* 1945
Hon. Christopher Peter, *b.* 1951.

WIDOW LIVING OF LIFE BARON.

SUZANNE ELIZABETH (*Baroness Haire of Whiteabbey*); Lynford Hall, Mundford, Norfolk; White-abbey House, Belfast), da. of Dr. Eugene Kemeny, of Hatvan: *m.* 1939, Baron Haire of Whiteabbey (Life Peer), who *d.* 1966.

HALE, BARON. (Hale.) [Life Baron 1972.]

(CHARLES) LESLIE HALE, son of Benjamin George Hale; *b.* July 13th, 1902; ed. at Ashby-de-la-Zouch Boys' Gram. Sch.; Solicitor 1923; Member of Leics. County Council 1925-50; a Freeman of Oldham 1969; 1939-45 War with RA; MP for Oldham (*Lab.*) 1945-50, and for Oldham West 1950-68; *cr. Baron Hale,* of Oldham, co. Palatine of Lancaster (Life Baron) 1972; *m.* 1926, Dorothy Ann, who *d.* 1971, da. of Joseph Latham, and has issue.

Residence,—92, College Rd., SE21.   *Club,*—RAC.

SON LIVING.

Hon. Ian William Percy, *b.* 1930.

DAUGHTER LIVING.

Hon. Dorothy Lesley, *b.* 1927.

HALIFAX, EARL OF. (Wood.) [Viscount U.K. 1866, Baron U.K. 1925, Earl U.K. 1944, Bt. G.B. 1784.]

CHARLES INGRAM COURTENAY WOOD, 2nd Earl and 6th Baronet, *b.* Oct. 3rd, 1912 ; *s.* 1959 ; ed. at Eton, and at Ch. Ch., Oxford (BA 1934); Capt. R. Horse Guards; Lord-Lt. for E. Riding of Yorks 1968-74, since when of Humberside (JP 1963-68, DL 1955-68) and Chm. of E. Riding of Yorks Co. Council since 1968; High Steward of York Minster 1970; 1939-45 War; MP for York (*U*) 1937-45: *m.* 1936, Ruth Alice Hannah Mary, da. of the late Capt. the Rt. Hon. Neil James Archibald Primrose, MC, MP [see E. Rosebery, colls.], and has issue.

Arms,—1st and 4th azure, three naked savages ambulant in fesse proper, in the dexter hand of each a shield argent, charged with a cross gules, and in the sinister a club resting on the shoulder also proper, on a canton ermine three lozenges conjoined in fesse sable ; 2nd and 3rd palybendy or and azure, a canton ermine. **Crest,**—A savage as in the arms, the shield sable charged with a griffin's head erased argent. **Supporters,**—On either side a griffin sable, gorged with a collar and pendant therefrom a portcullis or.

Seat,—Garrowby, York.   *Residence,*—Swynford Paddocks, Six Mile Bottom, Cambridgeshire. *Clubs,*—Turf, White's.

SON LIVING.

CHARLES EDWARD PETER NEIL (*Lord Irwin*), *b.* March 14th, 1944; ed. at Eton, and at Ch. Ch., Oxford.

DAUGHTERS LIVING.

Lady Caroline Victoria, *b.* 1937: *m.* 1st, 1958 (m. diss. 1970), Randle Joseph Feilden, son of Maj.-Gen. Sir Randle Guy Feilden, KCVO, CB, CBE (see V. Hampden, colls.]; 2ndly, 1970, John Gosling, of The Claw, Brushford, Dulverton, Somerset.
Lady Susan Diana, *b.* 1938 : *m.* 1959, Brigadier Ian Darsie Watson, O.B.E., T.D., and has issue living, David Charles Darsie, *b.* 1960,—Richard Ian, *b.* 1962. *Residence,*—Bossall, Barton-le-Willows, York, YO6 7NT.

BROTHER LIVING.

Rt. Hon. Richard Frederick, *M.P.*, *b.* 1920; ed. at Eton, and at New Coll., Oxford; Hon. LL.D. Sheffield 1963; late Lt. KRRC; Hon. Col. Queen's Roy. Rifles 1962-67, since when Hon. Col. 4th (Vol.) Bn. R. Green Jackets, T & AVR; appointed Parl. Sec. to Min. of Pensions and National Insurance 1955, and to Min. of Labour and National Ser. 1958; Min. of Power 1959-63 and Min. of Pensions and Nat. Insur. 1963-64; Min. for Overseas Development 1970-74; 1939-45 War in Middle East (severely wounded); as MP for Bridlington Div. of E. Riding of Yorks. (*U*) since Feb. 1950; a DL for E. Riding; PC 1959: *m.* 1947, Diana, only da. of the late Col. Edward Orlando Kellett, DSO, MP, and has issue living, Edward Orlando Charles, *b.* 1951,—Emma Myrtle Mary Anne, *b.* 1949: *m.* 1970, Capt. Edward Nicholas Brooksbank, son of Lt.-Col. Sir Edward William Brooksbank, 2nd Bt. *Residences,*—Flat Top House, Bishop Wilton, York; 49, Cadogan Place, SW1.

SISTER LIVING.

Lady Anne Dorothy, *M.B.E.* (twin) (*Countess of Feversham*), *b.* 1910 : M.B.E. (Civil) 1950 : *m.* 1936, the 3rd Earl of Feversham, who *d.* 1963. *Residence,*—Pennyholme, Fadmoor, Yorks.

WIDOW LIVING OF FIRST EARL.

DOROTHY EVELYN AUGUSTA ONSLOW (*Dowager Countess of Halifax*), *C.I., D.C.V.O., LL.D.*, younger dau. of 4th Earl of Onslow; Hon. LL.D. Leeds 1939 ; is a D.St.J., and a J.P. for E. and W. Riding of Yorkshire ; appointed a Lady-in-Waiting to H.M. the Queen 1937, and an Extra Lady-in-Waiting 1946; CI 1926, DCVO 1953: *m.* 1909, the 1st Earl, who *d.* 1959. *Residence,*—Bugthorpe, York.

COLLATERAL BRANCHES LIVING. (*In remainder to Viscountcy and Baronetcy only.*)

Grandchildren of the late Lieut.-Col. Francis Hugo Lindley Meynell (infra):—
Issue of the late Col. Hugo Meynell, M.C., *b.* 1909, *d.* 1960 : *m.* 1936, Dorothy Jean (of Hollybush Park, Newborough, Burton-on-Trent), dau. of Sir Edward Henry Goschen, 2nd Bt. :—
Nicholas Edward Hugo (Hollybush Park, Newborough, Burton-on-Trent), *b.* 1937: *m.* 1966, the Hon. Alexandra Rachel Catherine Mary Lampson, da. of 2nd Baron Killearn, and has issue living, Hugo Graham Nicholas, *b.* 1970,—Alexander Frederick Miles, *b.* 1972.——David Christian Francis, *b.* 1940: *m.* 1962, Susan Lesley, da. of George Garfield-Jones, of The Mount, Shrewsbury and has issue living, Charles, *b.* 1964,—a son, *b.* 1971.——Frederick James, *b.* 1944: *m.* 1969 (m. diss. 1973), Charmian Joy, da. of Maj. Harcourt Michael Scudamore Gold, MC [see By. of Trent].——Karen Elizabeth Mary (*Hon. Mrs. George C. D. Jeffreys*), *b.* 1947: *m.* 1967, Capt. the Hon. George Christian Darell Jeffreys, of Willoughby House, Rugby, Warwicks [see B. Jeffreys].——Alexandra Dorothy Jean (*Baroness Tollemache*), *b.* 1949: *m.* 1970, the 5th Baron Tollemache, of 43, Belgrave Mews North, SW1.

Grandchildren of the late Hon. Frederick George Lindley MEYNELL (infra):—
Issue of the late Lieut.-Col. Francis Hugo Lindley Meynell, D.S.O., *b.* 1880, *d.* 1941:
  m. 1907, Lady Dorothy Legge, *OBE*, who *d.* 1974, da. of 6th Earl of Dartmouth:—
Rev. Mark (The Vicarage, Leamington Hastings, Rugby), *b.* 1914; ed. at Eton, and Ch. Ch., Oxford:
  m. 1940, Diana Mary, da. of Col. Sir Charles Edward Ponsonby, TD, 1st Bt., and has issue living,
  Christopher Mark (56, Chepstow Rd., W2), *b.* 1941: *m.* 1968, ¨¨. Hon. Elizabeth Margaret Gretton,
  twin da. of 2nd Baron Gretton, and has issue living, Mark John Henryk *b.* 1970, Guy Francis *b.* 1973,
  —Andrew Francis, *b.* 1943: *m.* 1971, Caroline Anne, da. of the late Rt. Hon. Sir John Gardiner
  Sumner Hobson, OBE, TD, QC, MP,—Peter John, *b.* 1947,—Anna Mary Barbara, *b.* 1960.——Dorothy
  Emily, *CVO*, *b.* 1908; is an Extra Lady-in-waiting to HRH the Duchess of Gloucester; MVO (4th
  Class) 1955, CVO 1959. *Residence,*—3, Courtenay Sq., SE11.——Rachel, *b.* 1917: *m.* 1941, John
  Kift Winter, and has issue living, Mark John, *b.* 1948,—Giles Meynell, *b.* 1950,—Julia, *b.* 1944:
  m. 1975, Ali Dehir Akel, of Istanbul. *Residence,*—Scotts Hall, Beyton, Bury St. Edmunds.
      Issue of the late Sir Everard Charles Lindley MEYNELL, O.B.E., M.C., *b.* 1885, *d.* 1956 : *m.*
  1914, Rose (15, Grosvenor Sq., W1), da. of Lionel Bulteel, of 13, Gloucester Place, W:—
Francis Everard, *MBE*, *b.* 1917; ed. at Eton; Lt.-Cdr. R.N. (ret.); MBE (Mil) 1962: *m.* 1956, Jane
  Penelope, da. of the late Engineer-Rear-Adm. Albert Kingsley Dibley, CB, and has issue living
  Rosemary Janet, *b.* 1960,—Elizabeth Anne, *b.* 1961,—Anne Penelope, *b.* 1964. *Residence,*—
  Valbona, Hohenort, Constantia, Cape Province, S. Africa.——Clare, *b.* 1932: *m.* 1956, John Marsham
  Hallward, of 3150, Trafalgar Av., Montreal, Quebec, H27 1H7, Canada [see By. Atholstan].——
  Mary, *b.* 1935: *m.* 1974, Robert Leonard Clother, of Martlets, Rodmell, Lewes.
      Issue of the late Hon. Frederick George Lindley MEYNELL, 4th son of 1st Viscount,
  b. 1846, *d.* 1910 (having assumed by Roy. licence 1905 for himself and issue the
  surname and arms of Meynell in lieu of his patronymic): *m.* 1878, Lady Mary
      Susan Felicie Lindsay, who *d.* 1937, da. of 25th Earl of Crawford:—
Charles Wilfrid Lindley, *b.* 1890; Capt. R.N. (retired); European War 1914-19, European
  War 1939-45 (despatches): *m.* 1917, Ida Beatrice, dau. of the late Rt. Hon. Ernest George Pretyman,
  M.P. [H. Bradford], and has issue living, Richard Walter (of Merrywood House, Honingham,
  Norfolk, NOR 55X), *b.* 1923; is a FCA; 1939-45 War: *m.* 1950, Countess Ilse Teresa, da. of
  Lt.-Gen. Count Theodor von Sponeck, and has issue living, Anthony Charles *b.* 1952, Charles
  Humphrey, *b.* 1954, Patricia Rose *b.* 1960,—Beatrice Mary, *b.* 1918: *m.* 1945, Major John Whit-
  combe, RA, of 7, Astell St., SW3, and has issue living, Sarah Rose, *b.* 1946: *m.* 1972, the Rev. Barry
  Thorley, of Kingsley Holt, Staffs., Clarissa Beatrice *b.* 1949: *m.* 1969, Robert Anthony Gosling, of
  Pulham Cottage, Wetherden, Stowmarket [see B. Ampthill, colls.]. *Residence,*—Berry Hall,
  Honingham, Norwich.——Mary Margaret Desirée (*Dowager Viscountess Falmouth*), *CBE*, *b.* 1894;
  was a Vice-Chm. of Conservative Party Organization 1931-39, and Chm. Council of British Socs. for
  Relief Abroad 1948-50, and Dep. Chm. of British Red Cross Soc. 1952; CBE (Civil) 1946: *m.* 1915,
  Capt. the 8th Viscount Falmouth, who *d.* 1962. *Residence,*—28, Chelsea Sq., SW3.

PREDECESSORS.—[1] FRANCIS Wood, 2nd son of the late Francis Wood, J.P., D.L., of
  Barnsley; *b.* 1728 ; cr. a *Baronet* 1784, with remainder to his el. brother, the Rev. Henry, D.D.,
  V. of Halifax, and failing him to the sons of his younger brother, Charles, of Bowling Hall;
  m. 1779, Elizabeth, who *d.* 1796, dau. and heiress of Anthony Ewer, of The Lea, and Bushey
  Hall, Herts ; *d.* 1795; *s.* by his nephew [2] Sir FRANCIS LINDLEY, 2nd Bt. [son of Charles
  (ante)]; *b.* 1771; High Sheriff of Yorkshire 1814-15: *m.* 1798, Anne, who *d.* 1841, dau. of Samuel
  Buck, Recorder of Leeds; *d.* 1846; *s.* by his son [3] CHARLES, G.C.B., P.C., 3rd Bt.; *b.* 1800 ;
  was Chancellor of the Exchequer 1846-52, Pres. of Board of Control 1852-5, First Lord of the
  Admiralty 1855-8, Sec. of State for India 1859-66, and Lord Privy Seal 1870-74 ; sat as M.P. for
  Grimsby (L) 1826-31, for Wareham 1831-2, for Halifax 1832-65, and for Ripon 1865-6; cr.
  Viscount Halifax, of Monk Bretton, co. York (peerage of United Kingdom) 1866: *m.* 1829.
  Lady Mary Grey, C.I., who *d.* 1884, dau. of 2nd Earl Grey: *d.* 1885; *s.* by his el. son [4] CHARLES
  LINDLEY, *b.* 1839 ; Pres. of English Church Union 1869-1919 and 1921-33 : *m.* 1869, Lady Agnes
  Elizabeth Courtenay, who *d.* 1919, only dau. of 11th Earl of Devon: *d.* 1934 ; *s.* by his only
  surviving son [5] EDWARD FREDERICK LINDLEY, K.G., O.M., G.C.S.I., G.C.M.G., G.C.I.E., T.D.,
  P.C., 1st Earl, *b.* 1881 ; formerly Lieut.-Col. Yorkshire Dragoons Yeo. (Hon. Col. 1935-60);
  sometime Chm. Med. Research Council ; was Assist. Sec. Min. of National Ser. 1917-18, and a
  British Delegate to League of Nations Assembly 1923 ; appointed Under-Sec. of State for the
  Colonies 1921 ; Pres. of Board of Education 1922-4, Min. of Agriculture and Fisheries 1924-5,
  Pres. of Board of Education (in National Govt.) 1932-5, Sec. of State for War June to Nov. 1935,
  Lord Privy Seal 1935-7, Leader of the House of Lords 1935-8, Lord Pres. of the Council 1937-8,
  Sec. of State for Foreign Affairs 1938 to 1940 (also again Leader of the House of Lords Oct. to
  Dec. 1940), and Ambassador Extraor. and Plen. at Washington 1941-6 ; a Vice-Pres. E. India
  Asso. 1931 ; was Viceroy and Gov.-Gen. of India 1926-31 ; elected Chancellor of Oxford Univ.
  1933, and of Sheffield Univ. 1947 ; appointed Chancellor of Order of the Garter 1943, Chm. of Gen.
  Advisory Council of British Broadcasting Corporation 1947, and Grand Master of Order of St.
  Michael and St. George 1957 ; became High Steward of Westminster 1947 ; bore St. Edward's
  Staff at Coronation of King George VI. ; sat as M.P. for Yorkshire, W. Riding, E. Part, Ripon
  Div. (C) 1910-18, and for Ripon Div. of W. Riding of Yorkshire 1918-25 ; cr. *Baron Irwin*, of Kirby
  Underdale, co. York (peerage of United Kingdom) 1925, and *Earl of Halifax* (peerage of United
  Kingdom) 1944 : *m.* 1909, Lady Dorothy Evelyn Augusta Onslow, C.I.. D.C.V.O., LL.D., younger
  dau. of 4th Earl of Onslow ; *d.* 1959 ; *s.* by his el. son [6] CHARLE INGRAM COURTENAY 2nd Earl
  and present peer, also Viscount Halifax and Baron Irwin.

HALL, VISCOUNT. (Hall.) [Viscount U.K. 1946.]

Truth and Strength.

(WILLIAM GEORGE) LEONARD HALL, 2nd
Viscount; *b.* March 9th, 1913; *s.* 1965; MRCS
England, and LRCP London; Dir. of Invest-
ments, Africa, Asia and Middle East, Inter-
national Finance Corpn., an affiliate of
International Bank for Reconstruction and
Development (World Bank), Washington, DC,
USA, 1962; Advisor for Special Projects,
International Finance Corpn., Washing-
ton, DC, USA, 1963; Chm. of Post Office
Corpn. 1969-70; 1939-45 War as Surg.
Lt.-Cdr. RNVR: *m.* 1st, 1935, Joan Mar-
garet, who *d.* 1962, da. of William
Griffiths; 2ndly, 1963, Constance Ann
Gathorne, who *d.* 1972, da. of Rupert
Gathorne Hardy; 3rdly, 1974, Marie-Colette, da. of the late Col. Henri Bach.,
and has issue by 1st m.

Arms,—Lozengy argent and sable on a pile reversed azure between in chief two talbots' heads
erased an anchor fouled or. **Crest,**—A demi talbot lozengy argent and sable supporting between the
paws a leek proper. **Supporters,**—*Dexter,* a pegasus; *sinister,* a griffin azure winged or. **Badge,**—
Within a reef knot azure a talbot's head erased or.

Residences,—Belgrave Cottage, Upper Belgrave St., SW1X 8AA; Solvain, 41210 St. Viatre, Loiret Cher, France.

DAUGHTER LIVING, (*By 1st marriage.*)
Hon. Lena Margaret, *b.* 1950.
Hon. Georgina Anne, *b.* 1953.

WIDOW LIVING OF FIRST VISCOUNT.
ALICE MARTHA, *OBE* (*Alice, Viscountess Hall*), (Stanton House, 2, Glenville Av., Glen Parva, Leicester), da. of the late Ben Walker, of Brenklow, Rugby; OBE (Civil) 1962: *m.* 1964, as his 2nd wife, the 1st Viscount, who *d.* 1965.

PREDECESSOR.—GEORGE HENRY HALL, *PC*, son of George Hall, of Marshfield, Glos.; *b.* 1881; Miners' Official; Civil Lord of the Admiralty 1929-31; Parl. Under-Sec. of State, Colonial Office 1940-42, Financial Sec. to Admiralty 1942-44, Parl. Under-Sec. of State for Foreign Affairs 1944-45, Sec. of State for Colonies 1945-46 and First Lord of the Admiralty 1946-51; MP for Merthyr Tydfil (*Lab.*) 1922-46; cr. *Viscount Hall,* of Cynon Valley, co. Glamorgan (peerage of UK 1946): *m.* 1st, 1910, Margaret, who *d.* 1941, da. of William Jones of Ynysybwl; 2ndly, 1964, Alice Martha *OBE,* da. of the late Ben Walker; *d.* 1965; *s.* by his el. son [2] (WILLIAM GEORGE) LEONARD, 2nd Viscount and present peer.

Hall, see Barony of King-Hall

HALSBURY, EARL OF. (Giffard.) [Earl U.K. 1898.]
[Title pronounced "Haulsbury."]

JOHN ANTHONY HARDINGE GIFFARD, 3rd Earl; *b.* June 4th, 1908; *s.* 1943; ed. at Eton; FRS; first Chancellor of Brunel Univ. 1966: *m.* 1st, 1930, Ismay Catharine (who obtained a divorce 1936), da. of the late Lt.-Col. Lord Ninian Edward Crichton-Stuart [see M. Bute, colls.]; 2ndly, 1936, Elizabeth Adeline Faith, da. of the late Maj. Harry Crewe Godley, DSO [E. Annesley, colls.], and has issue by 1st and 2nd m.

Form no vile wish.

Arms.—Sable, three losenges conjoined in fesse ermine. Supporters,—Two swans ermine, beaked and legged gules, each having pendant from the neck by a ribbon of the last a shield charged as the arms.

NE·VILE·VELIS

Residence,—4, Campden House, 29, Sheffield Terr., W8.

SON LIVING. (*By 1st marriage.*)
ADAM EDWARD (*Viscount Tiverton*), (140, Sullivan St., New York 10012, USA), *b.* June 3rd, 1934; ed. at Stowe, and at Jesus Coll., Camb.; late 2nd Lt. Seaforth Highlanders: *m.* 1963, Mrs. Ellen Huxley, da. of the late Brynjolf Hovde.

DAUGHTERS LIVING. (*By 2nd marriage.*)
Lady (Elisabeth) Caroline (Elinor Evelyn), *b.* 1939: *m.* 1968, Rodney John Derek Blois, of Cockfield Hall, Yoxford, Saxmundham, Suffolk [see Blois, Bt.].
Lady Clare Rohais Antonia Elizabeth, *b.* 1944: *m.* 1964, Maj. Oliver John Martin Lindsay, of Brookwood House, Brookwood, Surrey [see Lindsay, Bt.].

SISTER LIVING.
Lady Flavia Joan Lucy, *b.* 1910: *m.* 1933, James Alasdair Anderson of Tullichewan, of 39, Royal Terr., Edinburgh, 7, and has issue living, Douglas Hardinge, *b.* 1934: *m.* 1st, 1962 (m. diss. 1969), Mary Elizabeth Siani, da. of John Jenkins, 2ndly, 1974, Veronica Margaret da. of John Edward Markes, of Recess House, Recess, Co. Galway, and has issue living (by 1st m.), James Henry Wallace *b.* 1964, Lucy, Elizabeth *b.* 1962,—Margaret Minette Ronais (*Lady Campbell*), *b.* 1937: *m.* 1961, Sir Ilay Mark Campbell, 7th Bt. (cr. 1808), of Crarae Lodge, by Inveraray, Argyll, and Lennell, Coldstream, Berwickshire.

PREDECESSORS.—[1] *Rt. Hon. Sir* HARDINGE STANLEY Giffard *P.C.,* son of the late Stanley Lees Giffard, LL.D.; *b.* 1823; was Solicitor-Gen. 1875-80, and Lord High Chancellor of England June 1885 to Jan. 1886, July 1886 to Aug. 1892, and June 1895 to Dec. 1905; M.P. for Launceston (*C*) 1877-85, Constable of Launceston Castle 1883-1919; cr. Knt. 1875, P.C. 1885, *Baron Halsbury,* of Halsbury, co. Devon (peerage of United Kingdom) 1885, and *Viscount Tiverton,* of Tiverton, co. Devon and *Earl of Halsbury,* in co. Devon (peerage of United Kingdom) 1898: *m.* 1st, 1852, Caroline, who *d.* 1873, dau. of W. C. Humphreys, of Wood Green, Middlesex ; 2ndly, 1874, Wilhelmina, who *d.* 1927, dau. of the late Henry Woodfall ; *d.* 1921 : *s.* by his son [2] HARDINGE GOULBURN, *K.C.,* 2nd Earl, *b.* 1880; was Recorder of Carmarthen 1923-35: *m.* 1907, Esmé, who *d.* 1973, da. of the late James Stewart Wallace; *d.* 1943; *s.* by his son [3] JOHN ANTHONY HARDINGE, 3rd Earl and present peer; also Viscount Tiverton, and Baron Halsbury.

HAMBLEDEN, VISCOUNT. (Smith.) [Viscount U.K. 1891.]

Relying on God, not on fortune.

[DEO NON FORTUNA FRETUS]

WILLIAM HERBERT SMITH, 4th Viscount; *b.* April 2nd, 1930; *s.* 1948; ed. at Eton: *m.* 1955, Maria Carmela Attolico di Adelfia, dau. of the late Count Bernardo Attolico, of 15, Via Porta Latina, Rome, Italy, and has issue.

Arms,—Argent, on a chevron azure between three oak leaves vert, each charged with an acorn or as many leopards' faces jessant-de-lis of the field. Crest,—A cubit arm erect habited azure, cuffed and charged with three mascles in chevron argent holding in the hand proper three branches of oak vert, fructed or. Supporters—*Dexter*, a sea-lion vert langued gules semée of escallops and gorged with a collar or, pendant therefrom by a gold chain a portcullis of the third; *sinister*, a wyvern gules, langued azure, semée of mullets or, and gorged with a gold chain, thorefrom pendant a portcullis of the third.

Seat,—The Manor House, Hambleden, Henley-on-Thames. *Town Residence,*—9, Chester Square, S.W.1.

SONS LIVING.

Hon. WILLIAM HENRY, *b.* Nov. 18th, 1955.
Hon. Bernardo James, *b.* 1957.
Hon. Alexander David, *b.* 1959.
Hon. Nicolas Robin Bartolomeo, *b.* 1960.
Hon. Lorenzo Patrick Harold, *b.* 1962.

BROTHERS LIVING.
Hon. Richard Edward, *b.* 1937: *m.* 1973, Christine Hickey.
Hon. Philip Reginald, *b.* 1945, ed. at Eton; Maj. (ret.) R. Green Jackets (despatches): *m.* 1973, Mary, yst. da. of John Roberts, of Bottom Farm, Checkendon, Oxon, and has issue living, Clare Elizabeth, *b.* 1974.

SISTERS LIVING.
Hon. Laura Caroline Beatrice, *b.* 1931: *m.* 1953, Michael Charles Brand, Lieut. Coldstream Guards [see V. Hampden, colls.]. *Residence,*—10, Upper Phillimore Gardens, W.8.
Hon. Katherine Patricia, *b.* 1933: *m.* 1st, 1961, Ivan Moffat; 2ndly, 1973, Peter Robert Gascoigne Townend, and has issue living (by 1st m.), Jonathan David, *b.* 1964,—Patrick Nicholas, *b.* 1968.

UNCLES LIVING. (*Sons of 2nd Viscount.*)
Hon. James Frederick Arthur, *O.B.E.*, *b.* 1906; ed. at Eton, and at Oxford Univ.; late Lieut.-Col. Gen. List; CStJ, and an Hon FRCM; N.-W. Europe 1944-45 (despatches, OBE); OBE (Mil) 1945. *Residence,*—21, Cadogan Lane, SW1. *Clubs,*—Brooks's, Garrick.
Hon. David John, *CBE,* *b.* 1907; ed. at Eton, and at Oxford Univ.; Hon DLitt.; formerly Maj. RA (TA); Chm. of W. H. Smith & Son (Holdings), Ltd. 1948-72; appointed Lord-Lt. of Berks 1959; CBE (Civil) 1964: *m.* 1931, Lady Helen Pleydell-Bouverie, *OBE,* da. of 6th Earl of Radnor, and has issue living, Julian David (6, The Hermitage, Barnes, SW13), *b.* 1932: *m.* 1966, Eleanor, da. of John Eustace Blyth, MBE, of Ham Common, Surrey, and has issue living, Dickon Julian Henry *b.* 1972, Alexandra Esther Helen *b.* 1969,—Anthony Frederick (Penelup Farms, Denbarker, W. Aust.), *b.* 1937; ed. at Eton: *m.* 1962, Alison Priscilla, da. of Lt.-Col. John Clark Pyper, OBE, IMS (ret.), of Westbury, Tasmania, and has issue living, James Antony David *b.* 1962, Philip John *b.* 1964, Harriet Frances *b.* 1967, Helen Sarah *b.* 1969,—Peter Henry (The Stone House, Newnham, Daventry, Northants), *b.* 1939: *m.* 1967, Scilla Ann, el. da. of Peter Bennett, of Kingston Manor, Lewes, and has issue living, Charles Henry *b.* 1968, Clare Scilla *b.* 1971,—David Michael, *b.* 1947: *m.* 1970, Caroline, el. da. of R. H. Ardill, of Broummana, Lebanon, and has issue living, Rachel Charlotte *b.* 1973,—Esther Joanna, *b.* 1934. *Residence,*—King's Copse House, Bucklebury, Berks. *Club,*—White's.

AUNT LIVING. (*Daughter of 2nd Viscount.*)
Hon. Margaret Esther Lucie (*Baroness Margadale*), *b.* 1908: *m.* 1928, 1st Baron Margadale. *Residences,*—Fonthill House, Tisbury, Wilts; Islay House, Islay, Argyll.

WIDOW LIVING OF THIRD VISCOUNT.
Lady PATRICIA (*Dowager Viscountess Hambleden*), *DCVO,* da. of 15th Earl of Pembroke; a Lady-in-Waiting to HM the Queen (now HM Queen Elizabeth the Queen Mother) since 1937; DCVO 1953: *m.* 1928, the 3rd Viscount, who *d.* 1948. *Residence,*—The Old Rectory, Ewelme, Oxon.

PREDECESSORS.—[1] EMILY Smith, el. dau. of the late Frederick Dawes Danvers, of the Duchy of Lancaster; *b.* 1828; cr. *Viscountess Hambleden*, of Hambleden, Bucks (peerage of United Kingdom) 1891, with remainder to the heirs male of her body by the 2nd marriage: *m.* 1st, 1854, Benjamin Auber Leach, who *d.* 1855; 2ndly, 1858, the Rt. Hon. William Henry Smith, P.C. (M.P. for Westminster (C) 1868-85, and for Strand 1885-91), who *d.* 1891, First Lord of the Treasury, Lord Warden of the Cinque Ports, and Leader of the House of Commons; *d.* 1913; *s.* by her son [2] WILLIAM FREDERICK DANVERS, 2nd Viscount, *b.* 1868; senior partner in the firm of W. H. Smith and Son, of Strand House, Portugal Street, W.C.; European War 1914-17 (despatches); sat as M.P. for Strand (C) Oct. 1891 to Jan. 1910: *m.* 1894, Lady Esther Caroline Georgiana Gore, who *d.* 1955, dau. of 5th Earl of Arran; *d.* 1928; *s.* by his son [3] WILLIAM HENRY, 3rd Viscount; *b.* 1903; Chm. of W. H. Smith & Son, Ltd., of Strand House, Portugal Street, W.C.: *m.* 1928, Lady Patricia Herbert, dau. of 15th Earl of Pembroke; *d.* 1948; *s.* by his son [4] WILLIAM HERBERT, 4th Viscount and present peer.

Hamilton, Marquess of, son of Duke of Abercorn.

HAMILTON AND BRANDON, DUKE OF. (Douglas-Hamilton.)
[Duke S. 1643 and G.B. 1711.]
ANGUS ALAN DOUGLAS DOUGLAS-HAMILTON, 15th Duke of Hamilton, 12th Duke of Brandon, and Premier Peer of Scotland; *b.* Sept. 13th, 1938; *s.* 1973; ed. at Eton, and Balliol Coll., Oxford (BA); is Hereditary Keeper of Palace of Holyrood House; Fl. Lt. RAF: *m.* 1972, Sarah Jane, da. of Sir Walter Scott, 4th Bt. (cr. 1907), and has issue.

Arms,—Quarterly: 1st and 4th grand quarter counter-quartered, 1st and 4th gules, three cinque foils ermine, *Hamilton;* 2nd and 3rd argent, a lymphad with the sails furled proper; flagged gules, *Arran;* 2nd and 3rd, grand quarters, argent, a man's heart gules, ensigned with an imperial crown proper, on a chief azure, three mullets of the first, *Douglas.* **Crests,—1st,** on a ducal coronet an oak tree, fructed and penetrated transversely in the main stem by a frame saw proper, the frame or, *Hamilton;* 2nd, on a chapeau gules turned up ermine, a salamander in flames proper, *Douglas.* **Supporters,—**Two antelopes argent, armed, unguled, ducally gorged and chained or.

Seat,—Lennoxlove, Haddington, E. Lothian.

DAUGHTER LIVING.

Lady Eleanor, *b.* 1973.

BROTHERS LIVING.

Lord JAMES ALEXANDER, *b.* July 31st, 1942; ed. at Eton, Balliol Coll., Oxford (MA), and Edinburgh Univ. (LLB); Lt. Cameronians (RARO); Advocate 1967; Pres. of Oxford Union 1964: *m.* 1974, the Hon. Priscilla Susan Buchan, da. of the 2nd Baron Tweedsmuir.
Lord Hugh Malcolm, *b.* 1946; ed. at Eton: *m.* 1971, June Mary Curtis, and has issue living, Brendan Thomas, *b.* 1974.
Lord Patrick George, *b.* 1950; ed. at Lancing.
Lord David Stephen, *b.* 1952; ed. at Eton.

UNCLE LIVING. (*Son of* 13*th Duke.*)

Lord (George) Nigel (*Earl of Selkirk*), G.C.M.G., O.B.E., A.F.C., Q.C., *b.* 1906; s. as 10th *Earl of Selkirk* 1940 [see that title].

AUNTS LIVING. (*Daughters of* 13*th Duke.*)

Lady Jean, *b.* 1904; *m.* 1st, 1927 (marriage dissolved 1946), Charles Ernest Whistler Mackintosh ; 2ndly, 1947, Major Leo Zinovieff, MICE, who d. 1951; 3rdly, 1972, Wing Cdr. Vivian Norton Bell, and has issue living, (by 1st m.), Christopher Douglas (Ivy Lea, Lansdowne, Ontario), *b.* 1931: *m.* 1958, Anne Elizabeth, da. of Anson C.McKim, of Montreal, and has issue living, David Douglas *b.* 1961, James Douglas *b.* 1962, Graham Douglas *b.* 1964—Charlach Rob Douglas (3627-6th St., SW, Calgary, Alberta, Canada), *b.* 1935: *m.* 1960, Sheila Elizabeth Walters, and has issue living Christopher Geordie Douglas *b.* 1962, Robin Douglas *b.* 1968, Sarah Elizabeth Douglas *b.* 1961,—Asthore Sheena Douglas, *b.* 1928: *m.* 1952, Ruaraidh Edward Macleod Robertson Hilleary of Tarras Farm, Forres, Morayshire, and has issue living, Alasdair Malcolm Douglas MacLeod *b.* 1954, Duncan Ruaraidh Douglas Macleod *b.* 1959, Dhileas Vairi Flora Douglas Macleod *b.* 1953,— Vora June Douglas, *b.* 1929: *m.* 1955, John William Archibald Shaw-Stewart, of Linplum House, Haddington, E. Lothian [see Shaw-Stewart, Bt., colls.]. *Residence,*—Hacienda, Montevideo, Alhaurin el Grande Malaga, Spain.
Lady Margaret, *b.* 1907: *m.* 1930, Major James Drummond-Hay of Seggieden, Coldstream Guards [Stewart-Richardson, Bt.], and has issue living, Malcolm James, *b.* 1932; ed. at Trin. Coll., Glenalmond, and Toronto Univ. (MD): *m.* 1958, and has issue living, Kathleen *b.* 19—,—Andrew Douglas, *b.* 1946,—Jane Mairi Margaset, *b.* 1931: *m.* 1955, Richard Timothy Whiteley, of Warren Farm, Finmere, Buckingham, and has issue living, Christopher James *b.* 1958, Nicola Mairi *b.* 1956, Clarissa Jane *b.* 1959,—Elizabeth Ann, *b.* 1937,—Christine Lilias, *b.* 1943: *m.* 1968, Nigel Buchan Watt, and has issue living,—Mary Nina Benita, *b.* 1947. *Residence,*—P.O. Box 69219, Bryanston, Johannesburg, S. Africa.

WIDOWS LIVING OF SONS OF THIRTEENTH DUKE.

Natalie, *CBE* (Apart. 10, 174 East 74th St., New York, USA), da. of Maj. Nathaniel Brackett Wales, of New York, and Boston, USA, and widow of Edward Bragg Paine, of New York, USA: *m.* 1953, as his 2nd wife, Lord Malcolm Avondale Douglas-Hamilton, OBE , DFC, who d. 1964 [see colls., infra].
Ann Prunella, dau. of the late Capt. Edward Hugh Bagot Stack, Indian Army : *m.* 1st, 1938, Squadron-Leader Lord David Douglas-Hamilton, R.A.F. Vol. Reserve, who d. (killed on flying operations during European War) 1944; 2ndly, 1950, Alfred G. Albers, who d. 1951; 3rdly, 1964, Brian St. Quentin Power, and has issue living, (by 1st marriage) [see colls., infra]. *Residence,*—Buckham Hill House, Uckfield, Sussex.

WIDOW LIVING OF FOURTEENTH DUKE.

Lady ELIZABETH IVY Percy (*Elizabeth, Duchess of Hamilton and Brandon*) Lennoxlove, Haddington, E. Lothian, da. of 8th Duke of Northumberland: *m.* 1937, the 14th Duke, who d. 1973.

COLLATERAL BRANCHES LIVING.

Issue of the late Lord Malcolm Avondale Douglas-Hamilton, OBE, DFC, 3rd son of 13th Duke, *b.* 1909, *d.* 1964: *m.* 1st, 1931 (m. diss. 1952), (Clodagh) Pamela, only child of the late Lt.-Col. the Hon. Malcolm Bowes-Lyon, CBE [see E. Strathmore, colls.]; 2ndly, 1953, Natalie, CBE (ante), da. of Maj. Nathaniel Brackett Wales, of New York, and Boston, USA, and widow of Edward Bragg Paine, of New York:—
(By 1st m.) Alasdair Malcolm (*Master of Selkirk*) (The Old Manse, Fountainhall, Pencaitland, E. Lothian), *b.* 1939; ed. at Gordonstoun, and Edinburgh Univ.: is *h.p.* to Earldom of Selkirk: *m.* 1965, Angela Kathleen, 2nd da. of James Molony Longley, of The Old Rectory, W. Knoyle, Wilts., and has issue living, Angus Gavin, *b.* 1968,—Geordie Fergus, *b.* 1969,—Fenella Mairi, *b.* 1966.—— Diana Mairi, *b.* 1933: *m.* 1955, Gavin William Younger, of Chapel-on-Leader, Earlston, Berwicks., and has issue living, Douglas Henry, *b.* 1956,—Hugh Patrick, *b.* 1958,—Malcolm James, *b.* 1959,— Robert William, *b.* 1964,—Alexandra Anna, *b.* 1963.——Fiona Margaret, *b.* 1935: *m.* 1973, Jeremy Blackstone Wise.
Issue of the late Squadron-Leader Lord David Douglas-Hamilton, R.A.F. Vol. Reserve, 4th son of 13th Duke, *b.* 1912, *d.* (killed on flying operations during 1939-45 War) 1944: *m.* 1938, Ann Prunella [(ante); she *m.* 2ndly, 1950, Alfred G. Albers, who d. 1951; 3rdly, 1964, Brian St. Quentin Power], da. of the late Capt. Edward Hugh Bagot Stack, Indian Army:—
Diarmaid Hugh (39, Pinckney St., Boston, Mass., USA 02114), *b.* 1940: ed. at Gordonstoun, Balliol Coll., Oxford, and Harvard Univ.: *m.* 1967, Margaret Barlow, only da of Dr. William Matthew Hambrecht, of Lakeville, Conn., USA.——Iain (Department of Zoology, Oxford University, Oxford), *b.* 1942; ed. at Gordonstoun and at Oriel Coll., Oxford: *m.* 1971, Oria, 2nd da. of Lt.-Col. Mario Rocco, of Dominio di Doriano, Naivasha, Kenya, and has issue living, Iassa Saba, *b.* 1970,—Mara Dudu, *b.* 1971.

Grandchildren of the late Algernon Percy Douglas-Hamilton, 2nd son of Col. Francis Seymour Douglas-Hamilton, RA, uncle of 13th Duke.—

Issue of the late Percy Seymour Douglas-Hamilton, *b.* 1875, *d.* 1940: *m.* 1st, 1901, Edith Annie Hamilton, who *d.* 1927, el. dau. of Sir Frederick Wills, 1st Bt.: 2ndly, 1929, Barbara Margherita (who *d.* 1974 having *m.* 2ndly, 1946, David George Arbuthnot [Arbuthnot, Bt., colls.]), da. of Francis Chiappini, JP, of Wynberg, Cape Province, S. Africa:—
(By 2nd marriage) John Percy, *b.* 1930 : *m.* 1955, June Mary Clifton Michler, of Rondesbosch, Cape Province, S. Africa, and has issue living, John Gavin, *b.* 1957,—Tessa Jeanne, *b.* 1958,—Debra Anne, *b.* 1959,—Diane Barbara (twin), *b.* 1959. *Residence,*—Elandspad Farm, Wydgeldegen, Bredasdorp, Cape Province, S. Africa.——Diana Barbara, *b.* 1932 : *m.* 1954, Ian Emslie Austin,

of Klein Constantia, Constantia, Cape Prov., S. Africa, and has issue living, Christopher James, b. 1955,—Philip Ian, b. 1959,—David Douglas, b. 1961,—Gillian Barbara, b. 1957.

Grandchildren of the late Aubrey Reginald Douglas-Hamilton, 3rd son of the late Algernon Percy Douglas Hamilton (ante):—
Issue of the late Herbert Eustace Seymour Douglas Hamilton, b. 1886, d. 1963: m. 1912, Ruth, who d. 1974, da. of the late Cuthbert Harrison.
Cecil Seymour (Box 77047, Station S. Vancouver, BC., Canada, V5R 5T4), b. 1916; Fl. Lt. RCAF (ret.): m. 1943, Ada Louise, da. of the late Orie Donily.——Doreen (2401, 28th Av., Vernon, BC, VIT IV5, b. 1914: m. 1941 (m. diss. 1962), Alan Ogg Davidson, and has issue living, Ian Hamilton, b. 1945,— Shelia Margaret, b. 1944: m. 1965, Hugh Charles Statham, of 35, Bradene Pl., RR1, Victoria, BC, V8X 3W9, and has isue living, Grant Douglas b. 1969, Craig Hugh b. 1972,—Joan Lesley, b. 1952.

Issue of the late Claud Archibald Aubrey Douglas-Hamilton, M.B.E., b. 1889, d. 1961: m. 1915, Evelyn Addison, who d. 1975, only da. of the late Thomas Addison Chater, of 51 Addison Avenue, Kensington, W., and Chesham Bois, Bucks:—

Evelyn Daphne, b. 1916 : m. 1st, 1940, the Rev. Jack Rawlins, Chap. to the Forces, who d. 1946; 2ndly, 1956, Hedley Boardman, M.B., Ch.B., D.P.H., of The Poplars, Melbourne, Derby, and has issue living, (by 1st m.) Prof. Michael David (The White House, 5, Front St., Tynemouth, Northumberland), b. 1941; BSc London; MD, BS, MRCP: m. 1963, Elizabeth Cadbury, only da. of Edmund Henry Hambly, MB, BS, FRCS, and has issue living, Victoria Jane b. 1964, Lucy Sarah b. 1965, Susannah Clara b. 1972,—Christopher John (21, Lawday Link, Folly Hill, Farnham, Surrey), b. 1945; BSc London; LRIC: m. 1969, Mary Joan, only da. of Donovan William Goodchild, and has issue living, Jeremy Mark b. 1974, Sarah Elizabeth b. 1972. Residences,—The Poplars, Melbourne, Derby; 49, Chatsworth Court, Pembroke Road, W8.

Granddaughters of the late Maj.-Gen. Octavius Douglas-Hamilton, uncle of 13th Duke:—
Issue (by 1st marriage) of the late Rev. Hamilton Anne Douglas-Hamilton, b. 1853, d. 1929 m. 1st, 1875, Lillie, who d. 1918, dau. of J. Bowles; 2ndly, 1922, the Hon. Agnes Rosamund Bateman-Hanbury, who d. 1947, dau. of 2nd Baron Bateman :—
Mary Hamilton, b. 1885: m. 1915, Maj. Christopher Martin Ingoldby, RAMC, who d. 1927, and has issue living, Christopher William Hamilton (of 11, Watling St., St. Albans. Club,—Junior Carlton), b. 1916; MRCS London and LRCP England 1940; late Capt. RAMC: m. 1945, Alice Maisie Chesher, and has issue living, Christopher John Hamilton b. 1948, Rosmund Mary Hamilton b. 1946, Catherine Anne Hamilton b. 1953. Residence,—11, Watling St., St. Albans, Herts.
Issue of the late Capt. Charles Reginald Sydney Douglas-Hamilton, b. 1856, d. 1935: m. 1890, Mary Isabel Hammond, who d. 1948, dau. of the late Capt. George Alexander Whitla, Roy. Antrim Rifles :—
Elsie Muriel, b. 1891. Residence,—The Old House, Fleet, Hants.

PREDECESSORS.— [1] JAMES, K.G., P.C., 3rd Marquess of Hamilton, and 2nd Earl of Cambridge, Gentleman of the Bedchamber, Master of the Horse, &c., or. Lord Aven and Innerdale, Earl of Arran and Cambridge, Marquess of Clydesdale, and Duke of Hamilton (peerage of Scotland) 1643, with remainder to the heirs male of his body, and in default to his brother William, Earl of Lanark, and his male issue, and in default thereof to his own el. dau., Anne, and her issue male; appointed Hereditary Keeper of the Palace of Holyrood; commanded the Army raised in Scotland for the relief of Charles I., and being defeated at Preston he surrendered and was beheaded on March 9, 1649; s. by his brother [2] WILLIAM, 2nd Duke, who had in 1639 been cr. Lord Machansire and Polmont, and Earl of Lanark (peerage of Scotland); killed at the battle of Worcester 1651, when his own honours expired and the Dukedom descended to his sister [3] ANNE, wife of William, K.G., 1st Earl of Selkirk (ante), who in 1660 was cr. Duke of Hamilton for life; the Duchess surrendered her honours in favour of her el. son [4] JAMES, K.G., K.T., 4th Duke, who in 1698 received a novodamus of the titles of Lord Aven Polmont, Machansire. and Innerdale, Earl of Arran, Lanark, and Cambridge, Marquess of Clydesdale and Duke of Hamilton (peerage of Scotland) with precedence of 1643, and in 1711 was cr. Baron Dutton and Duke of Brandon (peerage of GB); upon applying for his seat in the House of Peers, the House decided that after the union no peer of Scotland could be cr. a peer of England; killed in a duel 1712 ; s. by his son [5] JAMES, K.T., 5th Duke of Hamilton and 2nd of Brandon ; a Lord of the Bedchamber; d. 1743; s. by his el. son [6] JAMES, K.T., 6th Duke of Hamilton and 3rd of Brandon; d. 1758; s. by his son [7] JAMES GEORGE, 7th Duke of Hamilton and 4th of Brandon , s. to the Marquessate of Douglas and Earldom of Angus [see infra *₊*] 1761 ; d. unmarried 1769; s. by his brother [8] DOUGLAS, 8th Duke of Hamilton and 5th of Brandon ; was summoned to House of Lords as Duke of Brandon; d.s.p. 1799; s. by his uncle [9] ARCHIBALD, 9th Duke of Hamilton and 6th of Brandon; M.P. for Lancashire 1768-72; d. 1819; s. by his son [10] ALEXANDER, K.G., P.C., 10th Duke of Hamilton and 7th of Brandon; Ambassador to St. Petersburg; MP for Lancashire 1802; summoned to House of Lords in his father's Barony of Dutton 1806; Lord-Lieut. of Lanarkshire; d. 1852; s. by his son [11] WILLIAM ALEXANDER ARCHIBALD, 11th Duke of Hamilton and 8th of Brandon; b. 1811; was Lord-Lieut. of Lanarkshire: m. 1843, the Princess Mary of Baden, dau. of Charles Louis Frederick, late reigning Grand Duke of Baden, and cousin of H.I.M. Napoleon III.; d. 1862, s. by his son [12] WILLIAM ALEXANDER LOUIS STEPHEN, K.T., 12th Duke of Hamilton and 9th Duke of Brandon; b. 1845; granted Dukedom of Chatellerault by Imperial decree of Napoleon III., dated April 20th, 1864 [see D. Abercorn], and s. to the Earldom of Selkirk under special remainder 1886: m. 1873, Lady Mary Louise Elizabeth Montagu, O.B.E., who d. 1934, dau. of 7th Duke of Manchester; d. 1895; s. by his cousin [13] ALFRED DOUGLAS (great-grandson of Adm. Charles Powell Douglas-Hamilton, 2nd son of Lord Anne Douglas-Hamilton, 3rd son of 4th Duke), 13th Duke, b. 1862: m. 1901, Nina Mary Benita, who d. 1951, dau. of the late Major Robert Poore; d. 1940; when he was s. in the Earldom of Selkirk (under the terms of special destination) by his second son. Lord (George) Nigel Douglas-Hamilton, and in the Dukedom and other peerages by his el. son [14] DOUGLAS, KT, GCVO, AFC, PC, 14th Duke, b. 1903; Ch. Pilot Mount Everest Flight Expedition 1933; Lord High Commr. to Gen. Assembly of Church of Scotland, 1953-55 and 1958; Lord Steward of the Household 1940-64; Chancellor of St. Andrews Univ. 1948-73: MP for E. Renfrewshire, (C) 1930-40: m. 1937, Lady Elizabeth Ivy Percy, da. of 8th Duke of Northumberland; d. 1973; s. by his el. son [15] ANGUS ALAN DOUGLAS, 15th Duke and present peer: also Duke of Brandon, Marquess of Douglas, Marquess of Clydesdale, Earl of Angus, Earl of Arran, Lanark, and Cambridge, Lord Abernethy and Jedburgh Forest, Lord Aven and Innerdale, Lord Machansire and Polmont, and Baron Dutton.

*₊*William Douglas, cr. Earl of Douglas (peerage of Scotland) 1358 (title attainted 1455):m. 3rdly, Lady Margaret Stewart (dau. of Thomas, 2nd Earl of Angus, and on the decease of her brother the 3rd Earl), Countess of Angus in her own right, and had issue [1] GEORGE, who in 1389 obtained a grant of his mother's earldom and became Earl of Angus (peerage of Scotland): m. Princess Mary, dau. of Robert III. by whom he was granted charters of considerable lands; d. 1402; s. by his son [2] WILLIAM, 2nd Earl; d. 1437; s. by his son [3] JAMES, 3rd Earl; betrothed to Princess Jean, 3rd dau. of James I. (of Scotland), but d. 146, before the marriage took place; s. by his uncle [4] GEORGE, 4th Earl, 2nd son of 14st Earl; received a grant of the forfeited Lordship of Douglas 1457; when Henry VI. took refuge in Scotland, the Earl offered the King substantial aid and was promised an English dukedom; s. by his son [5] ARCHIBALD, P.C., 5th Earl; styled the "Great Earl" and "Bell the Cat;" a powerful noble who was High Chancellor of Scotland 1493-8; d. 1514; s. by his grandson [6] ARCHIBALD, 6th Earl: m. the Princess Margaret of England and Queen Dowager of James IV. of Scotland; d. before Jan. 22nd, 1557 ; s. by his nephew [7] DAVID, 7th Earl; d. June 1557; s. by his son [8] ARCHIBALD, 8th Earl, who in 1585 s. his uncle as 5th Earl

of Morton (peerage of Scotland, cr. 1458) ; *d.* 1588; when the Earldom of Morton devolved on Sir William Douglas, of Lochleven, though there were other representatives in a more direct line; *s.* in Earldom of Angus by his kinsman [9] WILLIAM, *K.B.*, 9th Earl, descendant of Sir William, 2nd son of 5th Earl; obtained in 1591 from James VI. a charter confirming to himself and his heirs male the ancient privileges of the Douglas family, viz. "The first vote in Parliament or Council; to be the king's Hereditary Lieutenant; to have the leading of the van of the army in the day of battle; and to carry the crown at coronations"; *d.* 1591: *s.* by his son [10] WILLIAM, 10th Earl; obtained a charter in 1602 under the great seal confirming the charter granted to his father (ante); *d.* 1611; *s.* by his son [11] WILLIAM. 11th Earl; cr. *Lord Abernethy and Jedburgh Forest* and *Marquess of Douglas* (peerage of Scotland) 1633; *m.* 1st, Margaret Hamilton, dau. of 1st Baron Paisley and sister to 1st Earl of Abercorn; 2ndly, Lady Mary Gordon, dau. of 1st Marquess of Huntly; had with other issue by 1st marriage Archibald, cr. 1651 *Lord Bothwell and Hartside,* and *Earl of Ormond,* with remainder to the heirs male of his 2nd marriage; and by 2nd marriage William, cr. *Lord Daer and Shortcleuch,* and *Earl of Selkirk* (peerage of Scotland) 1646, which peerages he resigned into the King's hands, who in 1688 re-conferred them with precedency of 1646 on his 3rd and younger sons primogeniturely provided that, if any of their representatives succeeded to the Dukedom of Hamilton, cr. 1648, the Earldom should pass to the then Duke's next brother), and with further remainder to the heirs male Grace's other heirs male; he *m.* Anne, in her own right, Duchess of Hamilton (see ante), and was himself created *Duke of Hamilton* for life; *d.* 1660; *s.* by his grandson [12] JAMES, 2nd Marquess, who had in 1655 *s.* his father (ante) as 2nd Earl of Ormond; *d.* 1700; *s.* by his son [13] ARCHIBALD, 3rd Marquess; cr. *Lord Douglas of Bonkill, Viscount of Jedburgh Forest, Marquess of Angus and Abernethy,* and *Duke of Douglas* (peerage of Scotland) 1703, all of which honours expired at his death in 1761, and the Marquessate of Douglas devolved upon James George, 7th Duke of Hamilton [see ante], and the Duke of Douglas's nephew, Archibald Stewart, was returned heir of line to the Duke of Douglas. The Duke of Hamilton disputed the return on the ground of Mr. Stewart's birth being surreptitious, the Scottish Courts decided in favour of the Duke, but in 1769 the House of Lords reversed the Scottish judgement and awarded the estates to Mr. Stewart, who assumed the name of Douglas. He was cr. *Lord Douglas,* of Douglas Castle (peerage of Scotland) 1790 (ext. 1857) [see E. Home].

HAMILTON OF DALZELL, BARON. (Hamilton.) [Baron U.K. 1886.]

[Title pronounced "Hamilton of Dee-el."]

Who will oppose.

JOHN D'HENIN HAMILTON, *M.C.*, 3rd Baron ; *b.* May 1st, 1911 ; *s.* 1952; ed. at Eton; Major late Coldstream Guards; a JP for Guildford; Lord Lt. of Surrey since 1973 (Vice-Lt. 1957-74); Chm. Surrey Co. Agricultural Exec. Cttee. 1957-68, Liaison Officer to Min. of Agriculture 1961-64, a Member, Council on Tribunals, 1964-72; Pres., National Assocn. of Probation Officers 1964, a Lord-in-Waiting to HM 1968, and a member of Lord Chancellor's Advisory Cttee. on Legal Aid 1971 (Chm. 1972); 1939-45 War (MC): *m.* 1935, Rosemary Olive, da. of the late Maj. the Hon. Sir John Spencer Coke, KCVO [see E. Leicester, colls.], and has issue.

Arms,—Gules, an annulet or between three cinquefoils pierced ermine. Crest,—An antelope proper, attired and hoofed or. Supporters,—*Dexter,* an antelope proper, ducally gorged and chained, the chain reflexed over the back or; *sinister,* a wild man proper, wreathed about the temples and loins with laurel, and holding over the sinister shoulder a club or.

Residence,—Snowdenham House, Bramley, Surrey. *Club,*—Guards'.

SONS LIVING.

Hon. JAMES LESLIE (of 19, St. Petersburgh Place, W2), *b.* Feb. 11th, 1938; ed. at Eton; late Coldstream Guards: *m.* 1967, (Ann) Corinna (Helena), yr. da. of the late Sir Pierson John Dixon, GCMG, CB, and has issue living, Gavin Goulburn, *b.* 1968,—Robert Pierson, *b.* 1971,—John Duff (twin), *b.* 1971,—Benjamin James, *b.* 1974.

Hon. Archibald Gavin (7, Portland Rd., W11), *b.* 1941: ed. at Eton; late Coldstream Guards: *m.* 1968, Anne Catharine, da. of the late Com. Trevylan Napier, DSO, RN, and has issue living, Laura Katherine, *b.* 1970,—Iona Janet, *b.* 1971,—Alice Rose Alethea, *b.* 1974.

DAUGHTER LIVING.

Hon. Janet, *b.* 1936: *m.* 1960, Richard Sackville Lane Fox [see By. Bingley]. *Residence,*—17, Princedale Rd., W11.

PREDECESSORS.—[1] JOHN GLENCAIRN CARTER Hamilton, son of the late A. J. Hamilton of Dalzell; *b* 1829; a Lord-in-Waiting to H.M. Queen Victoria 1892-4; M.P. for Falkirk Burgh, (L) 1857-9, for S. Lanarkshire 1868-74 and 1880-85 and for Lanarkshire, S. Div 1885-6; cr. *Baron Hamilton of Dalzell* co. Lanark (peerage of United Kingdom 1886 : *m.* 1864, Lady Emily Eleanor, who *d.* 1882, 4th dau. of 10th Earl of Leven and Melville ; *d.* 1900 : *s.* by his el. surviving son [2] GAVIN GEORGE, *K.T., C.V.O., M.C.,* 2nd Baron ; *b.* 1872 : Major (retired) Scots Guards ; Lord-in-Waiting to F.M. H.R.H. Duke of Connaught 1910, to H.M. King Edward VII. 1905-10, and to H.M. King George V. 1910-11 : *m.* 1912, Sybil Mary, who *d.* 1933, dau. of the late Lieut.-Gen. Sir Frederick Marshall, K.C.M.G. ; *d.* 1952 : *s.* by his nephew [3] JOHN D'HENIN (son of the late Major the Hon. Leslie d'Henin Hamilton, M.V.O., Coldstream Guards, 3rd son of 1st Baron), 3rd Baron, and present peer.

HAMNETT, BARON (Hamnett.) [Life Baron 1970.]

CYRIL HAMNETT, son of James Henry Hamnett; *b.* May 20th, 1906; ed. at Manchester Tech. Sch.; a JP of Manchester City; Engineering Journalist; Editor and Publicity Officer to Union of Shop, Distributive & Allied Workers 1937-52, and Admin. Officer 1953-66; Chm. of *Reynolds News* and *Sunday Citizen* 1953-67, a Member of Newspaper Proprietors' Assocn. 1953-67, and of British Press Council 1956-65; a Dir. of NW Co-operative Soc. Ltd. since 1946, and of Co-operative Press Ltd. since 1947 (Chm. since 1952); Chm. Parl. Cttee., Co-operative Union since 1959; a Member of Licensing Planning

Cttee. since 1960, and Chm. of Licensing Cttee. Manchester City Magistrates 1962-65, and since 1968; a Member of Industrial Tribunals; *cr. Baron Hamnett*, of Warrington, co. Palatine of Lancaster (Life Baron) 1970: *m.* 1929, Elsie, who *d.* 1970, da. of James Cox, and has issue.

Residence,—11, Bolton Av., Manchester, M19 1RP.

DAUGHTER LIVING.

Hon. Sheila, *b.* 1933: *m.* 1962, Eric Layland, of 31, Sevenoaks Av., Heaton Moor, Stockport, Ches.

HAMPDEN, VISCOUNT. (Brand.) [Viscount U.K. 1884.]

[Title pronounced "Hamden."]

DAVID FRANCIS BRAND, 5th Viscount; *b.* June 14th 1902; *s.* 1965; ed. at Eton, and at Trin. Coll. Camb.; Lt.-Col. Hertfordshire Regt.; 1939-45 War (despatches): *m.* 1936, the Hon. Imogen Alice Rhys, da. of 7th Baron Dynevor, and has issue. [The 5th Viscount *d.* Sept. 4th, 1975.]

Arms,—Azure, two swords in saltire points, upwards argent, pommels and hilts or, between three escallops of the last. Crest,—Out of a crown vallory or, a leopard's head argent, semée of escallops and gorged with a gemel gules.
Residence,—Trevor House, Glynde, Lewes, Sussex.

SON LIVING.

Hon. ANTHONY DAVID (Glynde Combe, Glynde, Lewes, Sussex), *b.* May 7th, 1937; ed. at Eton: *m.* 1969, Caroline Fiona, da. of Capt. Claud Proby [see Proby, Bt.], and has issue living, Francis Anthony, *b.* 1970,—Saracha Mary, *b.* 1973.

DAUGHTERS LIVING.

Hon. Jean Margaret, *b.* 1938.
Hon. Philippa Mary Imogen (*Hon. Mrs. Chetwode*), *b.* 1942: *m.* 1961, the Hon. Christopher Roger Chetwode, of Hockley House, Cheriton, Alresford, Hants.

BROTHER LIVING.

Hon. Charles Andrew, *b.* 1920; ed. at Eton; is Capt. Irish Guards; Italy 1943-5 (despatches). *Residence,*—

SISTERS LIVING.

Hon. Joan Louisa (*Hon. Lady Hill-Wood*) (of Knipton Lodge, Grantham, Lincs.), *b.* 1904: *m.* 1925, Sir Basil Samuel Hill Hill-Wood, 2nd Bt., who *d.* 1954.
Hon. Barbara Constance, *b.* 1907: *m.* 1934, Ronald Harry Higham, who *d.* 1966, and has issue living, Robin David, *b.* 1939,—Caroline (*Hon. Mrs. Robert V. Grosvenor*), *b.* 1936: *m.* 1959, the Hon. Robert Victor Grosvenor, of Bennets Grafton, Oxon. [see B. Ebury]. *Residence,*—
Hon. Elizabeth Margaret, *b.* 1911: *m.* 1935, Cecil Lomax, formerly Major 9th Lancers, and has issue living, Fiona Valerie, *b.* 1936: *m.* 1957, Simon H. M. Bradley,—Dinah Patricia, *b.* 1946,— Camilla Elizabeth, *b.* 1948. *Residence,*—Codicote Mill, Hitchin, Herts.
Hon. Monica Dorothy, *b.* 1914: *m.* 1933, D'Arcy Lambton, who *d.* 1938 [see E. Durham, colls.]. *Residence,*—Green Close, Copdock, Ipswich.

DAUGHTERS LIVING OF FOURTH VISCOUNT.

See Bs. Dacre.

WIDOW LIVING OF SON OF SECOND VISCOUNT.

Muriel H. L., dau. of H. B. Montgomery: *m.* 1913, Brig.-Gen. the Hon. Roger Brand, C.M.G., D.S.O., who *d.* 1945, and has issue living [see colls, infra]. *Residence,*—10, Dorchester Court, Sloane Street, S.W.1.

WIDOW LIVING OF FOURTH VISCOUNT.

LEILA EMILY (*Leila, Viscountess Hampden*), (Mill Court, Alton, Hants), da. of the late Lt.-Col. Frank Evelyn Seely [see Seely Bt., colls.]: *m.* 1923, the 4th Viscount, who *d.* 1965, and has issue living [see Bs. Dacre].

COLLATERAL BRANCHES LIVING.

Issue of the late Hon. Robert Henry Brand (4th son of 2nd Viscount), who was *cr.* Baron Brand 1946 [see that title].

(*In remainder to Barony of Dacre only.*)

Issue of the late Adm. the Hon. Sir Hubert George Brand, G.C.B., K.C.M.G., K.C.V.O., 2nd son of 2nd Viscount, *b.* 1870, *d.* 1955 : *m.* 1914, Norah Conyngham, who *d.* 1924, dau. of the late Rt. Hon. Sir (William) Conyngham Greene, K.C.B., Ambassador Extraor. and Min. Plen. to Japan :—
Elizabeth Norah, *b.* 1915: *m.* 1940, Major John Edward Seymour, Gren. Gds., who *d.* 1972 [see M. Hertford, colls.]. *Residence,*—Upper Chilland House, Martyr Worthy, Winchester.

Issue of the late Brig.-Gen. the Hon. Roger Brand, C.M.G., D.S.O., 5th son of 2nd Viscount, *b.* 1880 ; *d.* 1945: *m.* 1913, Muriel H. L. (ante), dau. of H. B. Montgomery:—
Patricia Helen Winifred, *b.* 1926: *m.* 1st, 1950, John Ralph Lubbock, who obtained a divorce 1957 [see B. Avebury, colls.]; 2ndly, 1957, Pierre Micheletto, of Ch. Coudrette 3, Lausanne, Switzerland. Grandson of the late Hon. Margaret Ferguson (infra):—
Issue of the late Col. Andrew Henry Ferguson, Life Guards, *b.* 1899, *d.* 1966: *m.* 1927, Marian Louisa (The Cottage, Dummer, Basingstoke) (who *m.* 2ndly, 1968, Air Marshal Sir Thomas Walker Elmhirst, KBE, CB, AFC), da. of the late Lt.-Col. Lord Herbert Andrew Montagu-Douglas-Scott, CMG, DSO [see D. Buccleuch]:—
Ronald Ivor (Dummer Down House, Dummer, Basingstoke), *b.* 1931; ed. at Eton; Maj. Life Guards: *m.* 1956, Susan Mary, da. of FitzHerbert Wright, [see V. Powerscourt], and has issue living, Jane Louisa, *b.* 1957,—Sarah, *b.* 1959.
Issue of the late Hon. Margaret Brand, el. da. of 2nd Viscount, *b.* 1873, *d.* 1948: *m.* 1897, Brig.-Gen. Algernon Francis Holford Ferguson who *d.* 1943 :—
Jane Charlotte (*Lady Fellowes*), *b.* 1912: *m.* 1934, Capt. Sir William Albemarle Fellowes, KCVO, and has issue living, Robert, *b.* 1941.—Thomas William (21, Princedale Rd., W11), *b.* 1945: *m.* 1st, 1968 (m. diss. 1972), Caroline Moira, da. of Capt. Richard Ker, MC, DL [see E. Suffolk, colls.], 2ndly 1975, Rosamund Isabelle da. of Bernard Van Cutsem [see E. Fortescue],—Susan Mary, *b.* 1936: *m.* 1960, Michael Cole, of The Old Rectory, Little Gransden, Sandy, Beds.,—Rachel, *b.* 1939: *m.* 1959, Joseph Gilfred Studholme [see Studholme, Bt.]. *Residence,*—Flitcham House, Flitcham, King's Lynn, Norfolk.
Issue of the late Hon. Dorothy Louisa Brand, youngest dau. of 2nd Viscount, *b.* 1877, *d.* 1959 : *m.* 1902, Major Percy Henry Guy Feilden, J.P., D.L., late King's Roy. Rifle Corps who *d.* 1944 :—

Sir Randle Guy, *KCVO, CB, CBE, b.* 1904; Maj.-Gen. (ret.) late Coldm. Gds.; Pres. of Queen Elizabeth's Training Coll. for the Disabled since 1965: *m.* 1929, Mary Joyce, da. of Sir John Frecheville Ramsden, 6th Bt. [see Pennington-Ramsden, Bt.], and has issue living, Randle Joseph (of The Old Rectory, Sheering, Bishop's Stortford, Herts), *b.* 1931: *m.* 1958 (m. diss. 1970), Lady Caroline Victoria Wood, el. da. of 2nd Earl of Halifax, and has issue living, Randle Charles Roderick *b.* 1961, Virginia Mary *b.* 1959, Fiona Caroline *b.* 1965,—Andrew James, *b.* 1941. *Residences,*— The Old Manor, Minster Lovell, Oxon.; 3, Kingston House South, Ennismore Gdns., SW7.—— Cecil Henry, *b.* 1907; ed. at Shrewsbury, and at Magdalene Coll., Camb.; is Maj. Coldstream Guards (Supplementary Reserve): *m.* 1941, Olivia Constance Leonora, da. of the late Lt.-Col. the Hon. Guy Victor Baring, MP [see B. Ashburton, colls.], and has issue living, Victoria Rose, *b.* 1942: *m.* 1971, Gerald Hugo Cropper Wakefield [see Wakefield, Bt.],—Mary Henrietta, *b.* 1944. *Residence,*— Bramdean House, Alresford, Hants.——Dorothy Priscilla, *b.* 1909: *m.* 1941, Lt.-Col. John Wilson Seton Galbraith, 11th Hussars, and has issue living, Jonathan Charles, *b.* 1942,—Arthur Guy, *b.* 1947,—Joanna Katherine, *b.* 1943: *m.* 1967, Capt. John William Nelson Mitchell, of Parkend, Lockerbie, Dumfries-shire, and has issue living, Mark Alaistair Nelson *b.* 1969, Katrina Mary *b.* 1972. Miranda Janet *b.* 1973. *Residence,*—Foxwood, Parkgate, Dumfries.

(Male line in remainder to Viscountcy)
Grandchildren of the late Maj. the Hon. Charles Brand, 4th son of 1st Viscount:—
Issue of the late Lieut.-Col. John Charles Brand, D.S.O., M.C., *b.* 1885, *d.* 1929: *m.* 1916, Lady Rosabelle Millicent, who *d.* 1956, dau. of 5th Earl of Rosslyn, and widow of David Cecil Bingham [see E. Lucan, colls.]:—
Michael Charles, *b.* 1925; European War 1943-5 as Lieut. Coldstream Guards (wounded): *m.* 1953, the Hon. Laura Caroline Beatrice Smith, dau. of 3rd Viscount Hambleden, and has issue living, Charles David William, *b.* 1954,—Charlotte Katharine, *b.* 1961,—Rosabelle Patricia, *b.* 1965. *Residence,*— 10, Upper Phillimore Gdns., W8.——Patience, *b.* 1922: *m.* 1945 (m. diss. 1955), Capt. Ian Alexander Henderson, late R. Horse Guards, who *d.* 1968 [see B. Faringdon, colls.]. *Residences,*—Swan Cottage, Swan Walk, SW3; Oxleaze Farm, Uffington, Berks.
Issue of the late Ruth Brand (*Baroness Monk Bretton*), *b.* 1882, *d.* 1967: *m.* 1911, the 2nd Baron Monk Bretton, who *d.* 1933 [see that title].
Grandchildren of the late Evelyn Brand, Lady Crerar (infra):—
Issue of the late David James Crerar late Fl. Lt. RAFVR, *b.* 1922, *d.* 1974: *m.* 1949, Eileen Chester Walsh, who *d.* 1974:—
Peter John, *b.* 1955.——Roy James, *b.* 1958.——Jonathan David, *b.* 1963.——Catherine (12, Glengeary Av., Dun Loaghaire, Co. Dublin), granddaughter of the late Maj. the Hon. Charles Brand (ante):—
Issue of the late Evelyn Brand (*Lady Crerar*), *b.* 1883, *d.* 1954: *m.* 1916, Sir James Crerar, K.C.S.I., C.I.E., who *d.* 1960:—
Elizabeth Jean, *b.* 1918: *m.* 1946, Hugh Evelyn Lockhart-Mummery, MD, MChir, FRCS, of 5, Hereford Sq., SW7, and has issue living, Christopher John, *b.* 1947.

PREDECESSORS—[1] *Hon.* HENRY BOUVERIE WILLIAM BRAND, *GCB, PC,* 2nd son of 21st Baron Dacre, *b.* 1814; Speaker of House of Commons 1872-84; cr. *Viscount Hampden,* of Glynde, co. Sussex 1884 (peerage of UK); *s.* his brother as 23rd Baron Dacre 1890: *m.* 1838, Eliza, da. of Gen. Robert Ellice; *d.* 1892; *s.* by his el. son [2] HENRY ROBERT, *GCMG,* 2nd Viscount, *b.* 1841; Gov. of NSW 1895-99: *m.* 1st, 1864, Victoria, who *d.* 1865, da. of M. Jean Sylvain Van de Weyer; 2ndly, 1868, Susan Henrietta, who *d.* 1909, da. of the late Lord George Henry Cavendish, MP; *d.* 1906; *s.* by his el. son [3] THOMAS WALTER, *GCVO, KCB, CMG,* 3rd Viscount; *b.* 1869; a Lord in Waiting to HM 1924-36: *m.* 1899, Lady Katharine Mary Montagu-Douglas-Scott, who *d.* 1951, da. of 6th Duke of Buccleuch; *d.* 1958; *s.* by his el. son [4] THOMAS HENRY, *CMG,* 4th Viscount, *b.* 1900: *m.* 1923, Leila Emily, da. of the late Lt.-Col. Frank Evelyn Seely [Seely, Bt. colls.], *d.* 1965, when the Barony of Dacre fell into abeyance [see Bs. Dacre]; *s.* in the Viscountcy by his brother [5] DAVID FRANCIS, 5th Viscount and present peer.

HAMPTON, BARON. (Pakington.) [Baron U.K. 1874, Bt. U.K. 1846.]
[Name pronounced **"Packington."**]

RICHARD HUMPHREY RUSSELL PAKINGTON, 6th Baron, and 6th Baronet; *b.* May 25th, 1925; *s.* 1974; served RNVR 1944-47: *m.* 1958, Jane Elizabeth Farquharson, da. of the late Thomas Frank Arnott, OBE, TD, MB, ChB, and has issue.

Arms,—Per chevron sable and argent, in chief three mullets pierced or, in base as many garbs gules. **Crest,**—A demi-hare azure charged on the shoulder with a quatrefoil argent. **Supporters,**—*Dexter,* an elephant or, charged on the shoulder with a mullet pierced sable; *sinister,* a talbot argent, charged as the dexter.

Valour equals strength.

PAR VIRIBUS VIRTUS

Residence,—Palace Farmhouse, Upton-on-Severn, Worcester.

SON LIVING.
Hon. JOHN HUMPHREY ARNOTT, *b.* Dec. 24th, 1964.

DAUGHTERS LIVING.
Hon. Catharine Mary Grace, *b.* 1960.
Hon. Sarah Jane Auriol, *b.* 1961.

SISTERS LIVING.
Hon. Hilary Evelyn Spicer, *b.* 1914: *m.* 1938, David John Vaughan Bevan, TD, BA, of Kingsland, Bledington, Oxford, OX7 6UX, and has issue living, Timothy David Vaughan (c/o Lloyds Bank, Pride Hill, Shrewsbury), *b.* 1939; Maj. 3LI: *m.* 1964, Jill, el. da. of Leslie Murrell, of Hapford, nr. Sidmouth, Devon, and has issue living, Simon David Vaughan *b.* 1970, Charlotte Hilary Vaughan *b.* 1968,—Nicholas Vaughan, *b.* 1942: *m.* 1967, Penelope Jane, da. of Col. D. H. Tildesley, of Tettenhall Court, Tettenhall, Staffs., and has issue living, Edward Duder Vaughan *b.* 1971, Katherine Jane Vaughan, *b.* 1969,—Richard Vaughan, *b.* 1943: *m.* 1972, Christine, da. of B. G. Harte, of Hill Cottage, Rostrevor, co. Down,—Jennifer Jill Vaughan, *b.* 1946,—Margaret Hilary Vaughan, *b.* 1953.
Hon. Anne, *b.* 1919.
Hon. Auriol Mary Grace, *b.* 1922.

PREDECESSORS.—[1] JOHN SOMERSET Russell, *G.C.B., P.C.,* son of the late William Russel, of Powick, by Elizabeth, el. dau. of Sir Herbert Perrott Pakington, 7th Bt.; *b.* 1799; *s.* in 1830 to the estates of his uncle Sir John Pakington, 8th and last Bt., and assumed the surname of Pakington in lieu of his patronymic; sat as M.P. for Droitwich (C) 1837-74; Sec. of State for Colonies 1852, First Lord of the Admiralty 1858-9 and 1866-7, Sec. of State for War 1867-8, and First Civil Ser. Commr. 1876-80; cr. a *Baronet* 1846, and *Baron Hampton,* of Hampton Lovett and of Westwood, co. Worcester (peerage of United Kingdom) 1874: *m.* 1st, 1822, Mary, who *d.* 1843, dau. of Moreton Aglionby Slaney; 2ndly, 1844, Augusta Anne, who *d.* 1848, dau. of the late Rt. Rev. George Murray, D.D., Bishop of Rochester; 3rdly, 1851, Augusta, dau. of Thomas Champion de Crespigny, and widow of Col. Henry Davies, M.P.

of Elmley Park, Worcester; *d.* April 1880; *s.* by his son [2] JOHN SLANEY, 2nd Baron, *b.* 1826: *m.* 1849, Lady Diana Boyle, who *d.* 1877, dau. of 4th Earl of Glasgow; *d.* 1893; *s.* by his half-brother [3] HERBERT PERROTT MURRAY, 3rd Baron, *b.* 1848: *m.* 1877, Evelyn Nina Frances, who *d.* 1904, dau. of Sir George Baker, 3rd Bt.; *d.* 1906: *s.* by his son [4] HERBERT STUART, *C.B.E., D.S.O.,* 4th Baron, *b.* 1883; Maj. Worcestershire Yeo., *d.* 1962; *s.* by his brother [5] HUMPHREY ARTHUR, *OBE, FRIBA,* 5th Baron, *b.* 1888; Cdr. RN: *m.* 1913, Grace Dykes, who *d.* 1959, da. of the Rt. Hon. Sir Albert Spicer, 1st Bt.; *d.* 1974; *s.* by his son [6] RICHARD HUMPHREY RUSSELL, 6th Baron and present peer.

HANKEY, BARON. (Hankey.) [Baron U.K. 1939.]

ROBERT MAURICE ALERS HANKEY, *K.C.M.G., K.C.V.O.,* 2nd Baron; *b.* July 4th, 1905; *s.* 1963; ed. at Rugby, and at New Coll., Oxford (B.A. 1926); H.M.'s Chargé d'Affaires in Spain 1949-51, Min. to Hungary 1951-53, and Ambassador to Sweden 1954-60, U.K. Delegate to Organization for European Economic Co-operation, Paris, 1960, and to Organization for Economic Co-operation and Development 1961-65; Vice-Pres. of European Inst. of Business Admin., Fontainbleau since 1962; a Member of Internat. Council of United World Colls., and of Council of Internat. Baccalaureati Orgn., Geneva; a Dir. of Alliance Building Soc.; Pres. of Anglo Swedish Soc.; Grand Cross of Order of the North Star of Sweden; CMG 1947, KCMG 1955, KCVO 1956: *m.* 1st, 1930, Frances Bevyl, who *d.* 1957, da. of the late Walter Erskine Stuart-Menteth [Stuart-Menteth, Bt., colls.]; 2ndly, 1962, Joanna Riddall, da. of the late Rev. James Johnstone Wright, and has issue.

Arms,—Per pale azure and gules, a wolf salient erminois vulned on the shoulder of the second, a bordure wavy of the third.

Crest,—A wolf's head erased at the neck erminois, gorged with a collar wavy azure.

Residence,—Hethe House, Cowden, Edenbridge, Kent. *Club,*—Royal Commonwealth Society.

SONS LIVING.

Hon. DONALD ROBIN ALERS (41, Grandison Rd., SW11), *b.* June 12th, 1938; ed. at Rugby, and at Univ Coll., London (Dip. Arch), RIBA: *m.* 1st, 1963 (m. diss. 1974), Margaretha, yr. da. of Cand. Jur. H. Thorndahl of Copenhagen; 2ndly, 1974, Eileen Désirée, yr. da. of Maj.-Gen. Stuart Hedley Molesworth Battye, CB, of Fensacre House, Ascot, Berks.

Hon. Alexander Maurice Alers, *b.* 1947; ed. at Rugby, Trin. Coll., Camb., and Mass. Inst. of Tech.: *m.* 1970, Deborah, da. of Myron Benson, of 141, Greenwood St., Newton, Mass., USA.

DAUGHTERS LIVING.

Hon. Juliet Alers, *b.* 1931: *m.* 1957, Peter John Wrensted Alchin, of Parkstone, Clenches Farm Rd., Sevenoaks, and has issue living, Gordon David, *b.* 1961,—Vanessa Frances, *b.* 1962,—Chloe Sylvia, *b.* 1965.

Hon. Adele Bevyl Alers, *b.* 1933: *m.* 1964, Dr. Erik Emil Ånggård, of Drottvägen 9A, Djursholm, Sweden, and has issue living, John Mikael, *b.* 1967,—Eola Anni, *b.* 1965,—Malin Adele, *b.* 1970.

BROTHERS LIVING.

Hon. Christopher Alers, *O.B.E.* (of New Cottage, French Street, nr. Westerham, Kent), *b.* 1911; ed. at Rugby, at Oxford (BA honours in History 1932, MA 1947), and London (BSc Eng. honours 1939) Univs.; Prin. Min. of Overseas Development 1964-72; 1939-45 War s Major RM; OBE (Civil) 1958: *m.* 1st, 1945, Prudence May (from whom he obtained a divorce 1957), da. of Keith Brodribb, of Frodsley, Tasmania; 2ndly, 1958, Helen Christine, yr. da. of the late A. J. Cassavetti, of Puckshott, Oxted, Surrey, and has issue living, (by 2nd m.) Rupert Christopher Alers, *b.* 1960,—(by 1st m.) Felicity Laura Alers, *b.* 1947.

Hon. Henry Arthur Alers, *CMG, CVO* (Hosey Croft, Westerham, Kent; United Univ. Club), *b.* 1914; ed. at Rugby, and at New Coll., Oxford; Ambassador to Panama 1966-69; CVO 1959, CMG 1960: *m.* 1941, Vronwy, only da. of the late Rev. T. F. Fisher, and has issue living, Christopher Ceri Alers (56, Fitzjohns Av., NW3), *b.* 1944: *m.* 1970, Eleanor, only da. of C. J. C. Beckett, of Danemore House, S. Godstone, Surrey,—Maurice Peregrine Alers (The Stables, Touchbridge Farm, Bearstall, nr. Aylesbury), *b.* 1945: *m.* 1970, Juliet, da. of Antony Ross Moore, CMG,—Peter John Alers, *b.* 1951, —Veronica Vronwy Alers, *b.* 1957.

SISTER LIVING.

Hon. Ursula Helen Alers (*Hon. Lady Benn*), *b.* 1909: *m.* 1929, Sir John Andrews Benn, 3rd Bt., of High Field, Limpsfield, Surrey.

WIDOW LIVING OF FIRST BARON.

Adeline Hermine Gertrude Ernestine (*Adeline, Baroness Hankey*) (of Highstead, Limpsfield, Surrey), dau. of the late Abraham de Smidt, formerly Surveyor-Gen. of Cape Colony: *m.* 1903, the 1st Baron, who *d.* 1963.

PREDECESSOR..—[1] *Sir* MAURICE PASCAL ALERS Hankey, *G.C.B., G.C.M.G., G.C.V.O., P.C., LL.D.,* son of the late Robert Alers Hankey of Warcowie, S. Australia and Brighton (whose grandfather, William Alers, of City of London, was authorized to assume the surname of Hankey in addition to Alers and to bear the arms of Hankey only with difference by Roy. Licence 1815); *b.* 1877; Col. R.M.A.; Sec., War Cabinet 1916-7, and Imperial War Cabinet 1917-18, British Sec. to Peace Conference 1919, Sec. to Cabinet 1920-38, Sec. to Imperial Conferences 1921, 1923, 1926, 1930, and 1937, Sec.-Gen. Hague Conference 1929-30, London Naval Conference 1930, and Lausanne Reparation Conference 1932, Clerk to P.C. 1923-38; Min. without Portfolio in War Cabinet 1939-40; Chancellor of Duchy of Lancaster 1940-41, Paymaster-Gen. 1941-2, and Chm. of Technical Personnel Cttee. 1941-52; cr. *Baron Hankey,* of The Chart, Surrey (peerage of U.K.), and a P.C. 1939: *m.* 1903, Adeline, dau. of the late Abraham de Smidt, Surveyor-Gen. of Cape Colony; *d.* 1963; *s.* by his el. son [2] ROBERT MAURICE ALERS, 2nd Baron and present peer.

HANWORTH, VISCOUNT. (Pollock.) [Viscount U.K. 1936, Bt. U.K. 1922.]

DAVID BERTRAM POLLOCK, 2nd Viscount, and 2nd Baronet; *b.* Aug. 1st, 1916; *s.* 1936; ed. at Wellington Coll., and at Trin. Coll., Camb. (B.A. 1939); Bar. Inner Temple 1958; Lt.-Col. (ret.) RE; CEng; MIMechE; FIEE, FIQA, FRPS, and author of books on colour photography; Tech. Adviser to Consumers' Assocn.: *m.* 1940, Isolda Rosamond, da. of the late Geoffrey Parker [see E. Macclesfield, colls.], and has issue.

Arms,—Azure, three fleurs-de-lis within a bordure engrailed or, on a chief ermine two portcullises of the second. **Crest,**—A boar passant quarterly or and vert, pierced through the sinister shoulder with an arrow proper. **Supporters** (hereditary),—On either side a bear or, muzzled, collared, and chain sable.

Residence,—Folly Hill, Ewhurst, Cranleigh Surrey. *Club,*—Athenæum.

Boldly and strenuously.

SONS LIVING.

Hon. DAVID STEPHEN GEOFFREY, *b.* Feb. 16th, 1946; ed. at Wellington, Guildford Tech. Coll., and Sussex Univ.; Lecturer, Econometrics, London Univ.: *m.* 1968, Elizabeth, da. of Lawrence Vambe, of 59, Nags Head Rd., Enfield, and has issue living, Cecile Abigail Shona, *b.* 1971.
Hon. Richard Charles Standish, *b.* 1951; ed. at Wellington Coll., and Trin. Coll., Camb.

DAUGHTER LIVING.

Hon. Gillian Isolda Josephine, *b.* 1944: *m.* 1963, Timothy von Weber Sarson, of 36, Hilldrop Rd., N7, and has issue living, Cosmo Harold Antony, *b.* 1971,—Emma Isolda, *b.* 1964.

AUNT LIVING. (*Daughter of 1st Viscount.*)

Hon. Marjorie Laura (*Hon. Lady Farrer*), *b.* 1895: *m.* 1926, Sir (Walter) Leslie Farrer, KCVO, and has issue living, Charles Matthew, *CVO* (of 6, Priory Av., W4), *b.* 1929; ed. at Bryanston and Balliol Coll. Oxford; Solicitor 1956; Private Solicitor to HM since 1965; *CVO* 1973: *m.* 1962, Johanna Creszentia Maria Dorothea, da. of Prof. Hans-Hermann Bennhold, of Tübingen, Germany, and has issue living, Jennett Mabella *b.* 1965,—Laura Leslie Jenett, *b.* 1932: *m.* 1961, Edward James Clarke Garden, of Norwood, Beech Rd., Lenzie, Glasgow. *Residence,*—Charlwood Place Farm, Charlwood, Surrey.

PREDECESSOR.—[1] *Rt. Hon. Sir* ERNEST MURRAY Pollock, *K.B.E., P.C.*, son of the late George Frederick Pollock [Pollock, Bt., colls.]: *b.* 1861; was Solicitor-Gen. 1919-22, and Master of the Rolls 1923-35; M.P. for Warwick and Leamington (C) 1910-18, and for Warwick and Leamington Div. of Warwickshire 1918-23; cr. a *Baronet* 1922, *Baron Hanworth* of Hanworth, co. Middlesex (peerage of United Kingdom) 1926, and *Viscount Hanworth* of Hanworth, co. Middlesex (peerage of United Kingdom) 1936: *m.* 1887, Laura Helen, who *d.* 1954, el. dau. of Sir Thomas Salt, 1st Bt. (cr. 1899); *d.* 1936; *s.* by his grandson [2] DAVID BERTRAM (only son of the late Capt. Charles Thomas Anderdon Pollock (only son of 1st Viscount), who *d.* (killed in action during European War 1918), 2nd Viscount and present peer, also Baron Hanworth.

HARBERTON, VISCOUNT. (Pomeroy.) [Viscount I. 1791.]

HENRY RALPH MARTYN POMEROY, 9th Viscount; *b.* Oct. 12th, 1908; *s.* 1956; ed. at Eton.

Arms,—Or, a lion rampant gules, armed and langued azure, holding between the fore paws an apple proper. **Crest,**—A lion rampant as in the arms. **Supporters,**—Two wolves, the *dexter* proper, the *sinister* argent; both collared and chained or.

Residence,—38, Thurloe Sq., SW7.

BROTHERS LIVING.

Hon. THOMAS DE VAUTORT, *b.* Oct. 19th, 1910; ed. at Eton; Lieut.-Col. (retired) R.A.O.C.; formerly in Welsh Guards: *m.* 1st, 1939 (marriage dissolved 1946), Nancy Ellen, dau. of the late C. A. Penoyer, of San Francisco; 2ndly, 1950, Pauline Stafford, who *d.* 1971, da. of the late Wilfred Sidney Baker, of Stoke, Plymouth. *Residence,*—Calle Presidente Alvear 32, Las Palmas, Canary Islands, Spain. *Club,*—Guards'.

Hon. Robert William, *b.* 1916; ed. at Eton; Maj. (ret.) Welsh Guards: *m.* 1953, Winifred Anne, second dau. of the late Sir Arthur Colegate, M.P. [Worsley, Bt.], and has issue living, Henry Robert, *b.* 1958,—Richard Arthur, *b.* 1960. *Residence,*—Rockfield House, Nunney, nr. Frome, Somerset. *Club,*—Boodle's.

Fortune is the companion of valour.

SISTER LIVING.

Hon. Rosamond Mary (38, Thurloe Sq., SW7, and The Cottage in Swains Lane, Bembridge, Isle of Wight; United Hunts, and Bembridge Sailing Clubs) (*twin*), *b.* 1916; 1944-45 War in France and Germany with A.T.S.

COLLATERAL BRANCHES LIVING.

Grandchildren of the late John Arthur Pomeroy, el. son of the Rev. the Hon. Arthur William Pomeroy, 2nd son of 4th Viscount:—
Issue of the late Major Francis Knox Pomeroy, *b.* 1876, *d.* 1962: *m.* 1906, Helen, who *d.* 1955, da. of Arthur Cinnamond, formerly of St. Helens, Belfast:—
Arthur John Cinnamond (Butternut Alley Farm, River Rd., Cantley, P.Q., Canada; Naval and Military Club), *b.* 1907; ed. at Rugby; Com. (ret.) RNVR, and in Roy. Canadian Mint, Ottawa, Canada: *m.*

1962, Rowena Mary Vesey, da. of the late Vice-Adm. Reginald Vesey Holt, CB, DSO, MVO, and has issue living, Hugh Reginald Arthur, b. 1963,—John Francis Vesey, b. 1965.——Jocelyn Francis Brian (The Old House, Sutton Courtenay, Abingdon, Oxon.), b. 1912; ed. at Rugby: m. 1940, Lucy Margaret, da. of Robert Hayne, of Osmington, Weymouth, and has issue living, Thomas (Avon House, Hartley Wintney, Hants.), b. 1941; ed. at Eton, and at Trin. Coll., Camb. (BA): m. 1967, Belinda Jane, da. of Maj.-Gen. John Sheffield, CBE, and has issue living, Helen Emily Jane b. 1971, Rosalind Lucy b. 1973, Laura Patience (twin) b. 1973,—Simon Robert Valentine (Chapel House, Priddy, Wells, Som.), b. 1943; ed. at Eton, and at Keble Coll., Oxford (BA); ACA: m. 1972, Ursula Jean, yr. da. of the late John Stephen Barclay,—Frances Louise, b. 1947: m. 1972, Ian Heathcoat-Amory [see V. Amory].——Helen Mary Ursula, b. 1909; late Junior Com. ATS: m. 1943, Archibald Richard Sanford Hodgson, DSC, late Lt.-Cdr. RNVR, and has issue living, Nicholas Pomeroy Sanford, b. 1945: m. 1974, Melissa, yr. da. of Donald B. Prouty, of 32, Foster St., Littleton, Mass., USA,—Helen Rose Sanford, b. 1947,—Ursula Virginia Sanford, b. 1952. Residence,—The Cottage, Compton, Guildford.

Issue of the late Lieut.-Col. Edmund John Pomeroy, D.S.O., b. 1871, d. 1945: m. 1911, Dorothy Maud, who d. 1949, dau. of the Hon. A. E. Wigan, of Highfield, Spanish Town, Jamaica:—
Alice Letitia, b. 1922. Address,—P.O. Redhouse, Cape Province, S. Africa.

Grandsons of the late George Pomeroy Arthur COLLEY (infra):—
Issue of the late George Dudley Pomeroy COLLEY, b. 1911, d. 1959: m. 1947, Ann Patricia (The Mill House, Kilmatead, Clondalkin, co. Dublin), da. of the late William Burns:—
Finlay FitzGeorge, b. 1948.——Anthony William Pomeroy (Bracken, Rathmore, Naas, co. Kildare b. 1951: m. 1973, Mary, da. of Hugh Kelly.

Granddaughters of the late Henry FitzGeorge COLLEY, son of the late Hon. George Francis COLLEY (who assumed the name of Colley in lieu of his patronymic 1830), 3rd son of 4th Viscount :—
Issue of the late George Pomeroy Arthur COLLEY, b. 1866, d. 1933: m. 1909, Edith Maude Olivia, who d. 1975, da. of the late Col. Henry Thomas Finlay, DL [V. Bangor, colls.]:—
Norah Helen Pomeroy, b. 1910: m. 1940, George Gilbert Butler [see B. Dunboyne, colls]. Residence,—Scatorish, Bennets Bridge, co. Kilkenny.——Veronica Maud Pomeroy, b. 1913: m. 1st, 1935 (m. diss. 1968), Maj. Jeffry Arden Patrick Lefroy, MBE, Yorkshire Dragoons; 2ndly, 1972, Lt.-Col. Derrick Arthur Hall-Dare, OBE, of 1, Park Hill, Wheatley, Oxon., and has issue living (by 1st m.) Jeffry George (Cambria House, Lechlade, Glos), b. 1936; Maj. R. Irish Rangers: m. 1964, Teresa Margaret, da. of Henry Alwyn White, DL, of Orange Hill, Tanderagee, co. Armagh, and has issue living, Jeffry Peter Langlois b. 1965, Edward Christian Perceval b. 1967,—Laetitia Mary, b. 1937.——Valerie Edith Pomeroy, b. 1915: m. 1947, William Patrick Hone, MC, and has issue living, Christopher Patrick George, b. 1949. Residence,—Kilmatead, Clondalkin, co. Dublin.——Rosemary Pomeroy b. 1916: m. 1947, Henry Nicholas Crocker, and has issue living, Henry Alistair b. 1949,—Roderic John, b. 1954,—Virginia Helen, b. 1948: m. 1971, F/L James Edward Malcolm Mustard, RAF, of Churchers, Upper Farringdon, Alton, Hants. Residence,—The Cottage, Portishead, Bristol.

Issue of the late Rev. William Wingfield Colley, b. 1868, d. 1947: m. 1915, Helen Isabel who d. 1974, da. of the late Rev. Duncan John Brownlow:—
Elisabeth Margaret, b. 1918.——Esmé Florence Helen, b. 1920. Residence,—Carberry, 12, Albany Court, Ballybrack, co. Dublin.

Issue of the late Gerald Henry Pomeroy COLLEY, b. 1870, d. 1923: m. 1906, Dorothy Evelyn, who d. 1929, dau. of the late Col. James Addie, formerly of Calder Park, Lanarkshire :—
Patricia Pomeroy, b. 1907: m. 1930, Kenneth Hastings Nethersole, and has issue living, Shelagh Elizabeth, b. 1931: m. 1952, John Franklin Lisle Worsley,—June Rosalie, b. 1933: m. 1956, Phillip John Hosford. Residence,—Springfield, Melsetter, Rhodesia.

PREDECESSORS.—[1] ARTHUR Pomeroy, son of the late Rev. John Pomeroy; b. 1723; was M.P. for co. Kildare 1761-83; cr. Baron Harberton of Carbery (peerage of Ireland) 1783, and Viscount Harberton (peerage of Ireland) 1791: m. 1747, Mary, dau. of Henry Colley, of Castle Carbery, co. Kildare; d. 1798; s. by his el. son [2] HENRY, 2nd Viscount; b. 1749: m. 1778, Mary, who d. 1823, dau of Nicholas Grady, of Grange, co. Limerick; d. 1829; s. by his brother [3] ARTHUR JAMES, 3rd Viscount, b. 1753: m. 1800, Elizabeth, who d. 1862, dau. of Thomas Kinsley; d. 1832; s. by his brother [4] Rev. JOHN, 4th Viscount; b. 1758: Preb. of St. Patrick's Cathedral, Dublin 1783-1822: m. 1785, Esther, who d. 1840, dau. of James Spencer; d. 1833; s. by his son [5] JOHN JAMES, 5th Viscount: b. 1790: m. 1822, Caroline, who d. 1886, dau. of the Rev. Sir John Robinson, 1st Bt. (cr. 1819); d. 1862; s. by his son [6] JAMES SPENCER, 6th Viscount; b. 1836: m. 1861, Florence Wallace, who d. 1911, dau. of William Wallace Legge, D.L., of Malone House, co. Antrim; d. 1912; s. by his el. son [7] ERNEST ARTHUR GEORGE, 7th Viscount; b. 1867; sometime Lieut. 20th Hussars and Capt. Roy. Dublin Fusiliers; S. Africa 1900 (Queen's medal): m. 1932, Fairlie, who d. 1945, dau. of the late Col. Charles D'Oyly Harmar, of Ramridge, Andover; d. 1944; s. by his brother [8] RALPH LEGGE, O.B.E., 8th Viscount; b. 1869; Major Reserve of Officers (Dragoon Guards); S. African War 1899-1902 (severely wounded) 1914-18 War: m. 1907, Mary Katherine, who d. 1971, da. of Arthur Leatham, formerly of Smallfield Place, Surrey; d. 1956; s. by his son [9] HENRY RALPH MARTYN, 9th Viscount and present peer ; also Baron Harberton.

HARCOURT, VISCOUNT (Harcourt.) [Viscount U.K. 1917.]

Le bon temps viendra

The good time will come.

WILLIAM EDWARD HARCOURT, K.C.M.G., O.B.E., 2nd Viscount; b. Oct. 5th, 1908; s. 1922; ed. at Eton, and at Ch. Ch., Oxford (B.A. 1930, M.A. 1954); Hon. Fellow St. Antony's Coll., Oxford; h.p. to Barony of Vernon; Vice-Lt. of Oxfordshire 1963: Chm. of Legal & General Assurance Soc., Ltd., of Gresham Fire & Accident Insurance Soc., Ltd., and of British & Commonwealth Insurance Co., Ltd.; Chm. of Rhodes Trust, and of Oxford Preservation Trust; Chm. of Trustees of London Museum, and of Board of Govs. of Museum of London; Min. (Economic), British Embassy, Washington, and Head of UK Treasury Delegation in USA, UK Executive Director of International Bank for Reconstruction and Development and of International Monetary Fund 1954-57, a Member of Departmental (Radcliffe) Cttee. on Monetary and Credit Policy 1957-59, and Departmental Plowden Cttee. on Overseas

Sers. 1962-64; 1939-45 War in Middle East and Mediterranean with 63rd (Oxford Yeo.) Anti-Tank Regt. RA (TA), and as Lt.-Col. and GSO; MBE (Mil) 1943, OBE (Mil) 1945, KCMG 1957: *m.* 1st, 1931 (m. diss. 1942), the Hon. Maud Elizabeth Grosvenor, da. of 4th Baron Ebury; 2ndly, 1946, Elizabeth Sonia, who *d.* 1959, da. of the late Sir Harold Edward Snagge, KBE [B. Avebury, colls.], and widow of Capt. Lionel Gibbs, and has issue by 1st m.

𝔄rms,—Gules, two bars or.   ℭrest,—Out of a ducal coronet or a peacock close proper. 𝔖upporters,—On either side a lion rampant or, gorged with a collar gemel gules.

Seat,—Stanton Harcourt, Oxon. Residence,—23, Culross Street, W.1.

DAUGHTERS LIVING. *(By 1st marriage.)*

Hon. (Elizabeth) Ann, *b.* 1932: *m.* 1954, Crispin Gascoigne (of Ronans, Winkfield Row, Bracknell, Berks.), only son of Maj.-Gen. Sir Julian Alvery Gascoigne, K.C.M.G., K.C.V.O., C.B., D.S.O. [see Newman Bt., cr. 1836].

Hon. Penelope Mary, *b.* 1933: *m.* 1954, Capt. Anthony David Motion, late 9th Queen's Roy. Lancers, of 7, Jaraba Av., Kalamunda, W. Aust., and has issue living, Stephen Anthony, *b.* 1967.

SISTERS LIVING.

Hon. Doris Mary Thérèse *(Baroness Ashburton)*, *b.* 1900: *m.* 1924, the 6th Baron Ashburton. Residence,—Itchen Stoke House, Alresford, Hants.

Hon. Olivia Vernon, *DCVO, b.* 1902; ed. at Notting Hill High Sch., and at Lady Margaret Hall, Oxford; Vice-Chm. of Roy. Free Hosp. 1950-62; Chm. of Elizabeth Garrett Anderson Hosp. 1945-72; a Woman of the Bedchamber to HM the Queen (now HM Queen Elizabeth the Queen Mother) since 1950; CVO 1958, DCVO 1971: *m.* 1923, the Hon. (Godfrey) John Arthur Murray Lyle Mulholland, MC, who *d.* 1948 [see B. Dunleath, colls.]. Residence,—Weston Mark, Upton Grey, Hants.

PREDECESSOR.—[1] Lewis Harcourt, son of the late Rt. Hon. Sir William George Granville Venables-Vernon-Harcourt, P.C. [see B. Vernon, colls.]; *b.* 1863; Private Sec. to his father (Home Sec.) 1884-5 and (Chancellor of the Exchequer) 1886 and 1892-5, First Commr. of Works 1905 to Nov. 1910 (with a seat in the Cabinet from 1907). Sec. of State for the Colonies Nov. 1910 to May 1915, and again First Commr. of Works (with a seat in the Cabinet) 1915-16; M.P. for Rossendale Div. of Lancashire (N.-E.) *(L)* March 1904 to Dec. 1916; assumed by Roy. licence for himself and issue the surname and arms of Harcourt only 1905; cr. *Baron Nuneham*, of Nuneham Courtenay, and *Viscount Harcourt*, of Stanton Harcourt, Oxford (peerage of United Kingdom) 1917: *m.* 1899, Dame Mary Ethel, *G.B.E.*, who *d.* 1961, dau. of the late Walter Hayes Burns, of New York, and North Mymms Park, Hatfield; *d.* 1922; *s.* by his son [2] WILLIAM EDWARD, 2nd Viscount and present peer; also Baron Nuneham.

HARDING OF PETHERTON, BARON. (Harding.) [Baron U.K. 1958.]

ALLAN FRANCIS (JOHN) HARDING, *G.C.B., C.B.E., D.S.O., M.C.*, 1st Baron, son of the late Francis E. Harding, of Compton Way, South Petherton, Somerset; *b.* Feb. 10th, 1896; ed. at Ilminster Gram. Sch.; Hon. D.C.L. Durham 1959; Field-Marshal, late Somerset L.I.; ADC Gen. to H.M. King George VI 1950, and to H.M. The Queen 1952-53; Hon. Col. N. Somerset Yeo. 1950-57, Col. 6th Queen Elizabeth's Own Gurkha Rifles 1951-61, Somerset Light Inf. 1953-59, SCLI 1959-60, and Life Guards 1957-64, and Chm. of Horserace Betting Levy Board 1961-67; a Dir. of Western Gazette Co. Ltd., of The Plessey Co. Ltd. (Dep. Chm. 1964-67, Chm. 1967-70); GOC-in-C, S. Command 1947-49, C-in-C, Far East Land Forces 1949-51, and BAOR 1951-52, CIGS 1952-55, Gov. and C-in-C of Cyprus 1955-57, and Gold Stick to HM 1957-64; 1914-18 War in Gallipoli and Egypt (twice wounded, despatches, MC, 1914-15 star, two medals), 1939-45 War in Middle East and Italy (wounded, despatches thrice, CBE, DSO, and two bars, KCB); a KStJ; cr. CBE (Mil) and DSO 1941, Bar to DSO 1942, 2nd Bar 1943, KCB (Mil) 1944, GCB (Mil) 1951, and *Baron Harding of Petherton,* of Nether Compton, co. Dorset (peerage of UK) 1958: *m.* 1927, Mary Gertrude Mabel (a CStJ), da. of the late Joseph Wilson Rooke, JP, of Knutsford, Ches., and has issue.

𝔄rms,—Argent on a bend azure between two lions passant guardant gules as many kukris in saltire proper between two martlets or. ℭrest,—Out of a mural crown gules a cubit arm in armour the hand gauntleted grasping a Field Marshal's baton in bend sinister proper. 𝔖upporters,—Dexter, a Private of 1st Life Guards of early nineteenth century; sinister, a Somerset Light Infantryman of the late eighteenth century; both habited and accoutred proper.

Residence,—Nether Compton, Sherborne, Dorset.

SON LIVING.

Hon. JOHN CHARLES (The Vine House, Nether Common, Sherborne, Dorset), *b.* Feb. 12th, 1928; ed. at Marlborough, and at Worcester Coll., Oxford; Maj. (ret.) 11th Hussars: *m.* 1966, Harriet, da. of the late Maj.-Gen. James Francis Hare, CB, DSO, and has issue living, William Allan John, *b.* 1969,—Diana Mary, *b.* 1967.

HARDINGE, VISCOUNT. (Hardinge.) [Viscount U.K. 1846.]
[Name and Title pronounced "Harding."]

CARYL NICHOLAS CHARLES HARD-
INGE, *M.B.E.*, 4th Viscount; *b.* Dec.
25th, 1905; *s.* 1924; ed. at Harrow;
Major 7th Hussars; was an A.D.C. to
Gov.-Gen. of Canada 1926-8, and Mil.
Assist. to A.G. to Forces 1941-5;
M.B.E. (Mil.) 1946: *m.* 1928, Mar-
garet Elizabeth Arnot, dau. of the late
Hugh Fleming, of Wynyards, Rock-
cliffe, Ottawa, and has issue.

Arms,—Gules, on a chevron argent, fimbriated or, three escallops sable. Crest,—A mitre
gules, charged with a chevron, as in the arms.
Supporters,—On either side a lion proper, that on
the dexter murally crowned, supporting a flag
flowing to the dexter or, and that on the sinister
crowned with an Eastern crown, supporting a
flag flowing to the sinister or.

Residence,—1523, Summerhill Avenue, Montreal, Canada. *Club,*—Turf.

MENS ÆQUA REBUS IN ARDUIS
An equal mind in difficulties.

SON LIVING.

Hon. (HENRY) NICHOLAS PAUL (422,
Roslyn Av., Montreal 6, Quebec, Canada;
Cavalry Club), *b.* Aug. 15th,1929; ed. at Harrow;
late Lt. 7th Hussars: *m.* 1955, Zoë Ann, da. of Hartland de Montarville Molson, OBE, of Montreal.
Senator of Canada, and has issue living, Charles Henry Nicholas, *b.* 1956,—Andrew Hartland,
b. 1960,—Maximilian Evelyn *b.* 1969.

DAUGHTERS LIVING.
Hon. Carolyn Wynyard, *b.* 1932: *m.* 1954, John Arthington Worsley (RR2, Uxbridge, Ont., Canada)
[see Worsley, Bt.].
Hon. Gay, *b.* 1938: *m.* 1963, Pierre Raymond, of Warden, Quebec, Canada, and has issue living, a son,
b. 1965.

SISTERS LIVING.
Hon. Ruby, *b.* 1897: *m.* 1928, as his second wife, Maj.-Gen. Frederick George Beaumont-Nesbitt,
CVO, CBE, MC, late Gren. Gds., who *d.* 1971, and has issue living, Dermot Patrick (Baddow Park
Lodge, Gt. Baddow, Chelmsford, Essex), *b.* 1931; ed. at Gordonstoun,—Brian Charles (38, Lisburne
Rd., NW3), *b.* 1932; ed. at Eton: *m.* 1965, Patricia, da. of the late G. G. K. McBarnet, and has
issue living, Jake Kellie *b.* 1967, Lucia Clare *b.* 1965,—June, *b.* 1929: *m.* 1st, 1959 (m. diss. 1975), Ivor
Barry Skrine; 2ndly, 1975, Robin Leslie, of Glebe House, Langham, Colchester, and has issue living,
(by 1st m.) Rupert Charles *b.* 1960. *Residence,*—10, Clifton Court, NW8.
Hon. Sybil Mary (*Countess Fortescue*), *b.* 1898; is an O.St.J.: *m.* 1st, 1922, the 4th Baron Penrhyn,
who *d.* 1949, and from whom she had obtained a divorce 1941; 2ndly, 1941, the 6th Earl Fortescue.
Residence,— Ebrington Manor, Chipping Campden, Gloucestershire.

COLLATERAL BRANCHES LIVING.
Issue of the late Rt. Hon. Charles Hardinge, K.G., G.C.B., G.C.S.I., G.C.M.G.,
G.C.I.E., G.C.V.O., I.S.O. (2nd son of 2nd Viscount), who was cr. *Baron Hardinge
of Penshurst* 1910 [see that title].

Granddaughter of the late Gen. the Hon. Sir Arthur Edward Hardinge, K.C.B.,
C.I.E., son of 1st Viscount :—
Issue of the late Rt. Hon. Sir Arthur Henry Hardinge, G.C.M.G., K.C.B., *b.* 1859,
d. 1933: *m.* 1899, Alexandra Mina, who *d.* 1949, dau. of the late Maj.-Gen. Sir Arthur
Edward Augustus Ellis. G.C.V.O., C.S.I. [B. Howard de Walden, colls.]:—
Mary Pamela, *b.* 1907; Bar. Inner Temple 1940.
Issue of the late Hon. Mary Hilda Madelina Hardinge, da. of 2nd Viscount; *b.* 1862,
d. 1936: *m.* 1890, the Rev. Ernest John Wild, MA, who *d.* 1931 :—
Gladys Lavinia Mary, *b.* 1897: *m.* 1934, Cdr. Piercy Glyn Ormsby Langley, RN (ret.), of 93, Christchurch Rd., East Sheen, SW14 7AT, and has issue living Robin Patrick, *b.* 1942; ed. at Charterhouse, and Roy. Coll. of Music; Music Editor, Oxford Univ. Press.——Joan Mary, *b.* 1900: *m.* 1931,
the Rev. George Mostyn Prichard of 24, Palace Court, W2, formerly R. of Whippingham, IOW, and
Chap. to HRH the late Princess Beatrice and has issue living, Preston Caradoc Hardinge Mostyn
(44, Earls Court Sq., SW5), *b.* 1932; ed. at Radley, and Pembroke Coll., Oxford: *m.* 1969, Barbara
Joan Shellah, da. of Lt.-Col. Wilmot Smyth Caulfeild, MC [see V. Charlemont, colls.], and has issue
living, Julian Caulfeild Mostyn *b.* 1970, Diana Mostyn *b.* 1973,—David Colville Mostyn, *b.* 1934; ed.
at Radley, and Pembroke Coll., Oxford; Headmaster of Port Regis Sch., Motcombe Park, Shaftesbury, Dorset.

PREDECESSORS.—[1] *Field-Marshal the Rt. Hon. Sir* HENRY Hardinge, *G.C.B., P.C.,* son o
the Rev. Henry Hardinge, R. of Stanhope, whose heirs male are in special remainder to the
Baronetcy (cr. 1801); *b.* 1785; entered the Army at an early age and was present at all engagements throughout the Peninsular War; became Field-Marshal 1855; sat as MP for
Launceston (C) 1826-41; was Clerk of the Ordnance 1823, Sec. at War 1828, Ch. Sec. of
Ireland 1830 and 1834, again Sec. at War 1841, Gov.-Gen. of India 1844-8, Master-Gen. of the
Ordnance 1852, and Gen. Com. in Ch. 1852-6; cr. *Viscount Hardinge* (peerage of United Kingdom)
1846 : twice thanked by Parliament for his military and civil services, and awarded a pension
of £3,000 a year for three lives: *m.* 1821, Lady Emily Jane Stewart, who *d.* 1865, dau. of 1st
Marquess of Londonderry, K.G., and widow of John James: *d.* 1856; *s.* by his son [2]
CHARLES STEWART, 2nd Viscount, *b.* 1822; M.P. for Downpatrick 1851-6. *m.* 1856, Lady
Lavinia Bingham, who *d.* 1864, dau. of 3rd Earl of Lucan; *d.* 1894; *s.* by his el. son [3] HENRY
CHARLES, *C.B.*, 3rd Viscount; *b.* 1857; Capt. Rifle Brig.: *m.* 1891, Mary Frances (who *d.* 1954,
having *m.* 2ndly, 1928, as his 3rd wife, the 3rd Marquess of Abergavenny), dau. of the late Hon.
Ralph Pelham Nevill; *d.* 1924; *s.* by his son [4] CARYL NICHOLAS CHARLES, 4th Viscount and
present peer.

HARDINGE OF PENSHURST, BARON. (Hardinge.) [Baron U.K. 1910.]

[Name and Title pronounced "Harding."]

GEORGE EDWARD CHARLES HARDINGE, 3rd Baron; b. Oct. 31st, 1921; s. 1960; ed. at Eton; Lieut.-Com. (retired) R.N.; was a Page of Honour to H.M. 1933-38; a Train Bearer at Coronation of King George VI: m. 1st 1944 (m. diss. 1962), Janet Christine Goschen, who d. 1970, da. of the late Lt.-Col. Francis Cecil Campbell Balfour, CIE, CBE, MC [E. Balfour, colls.]; 2ndly, 1966, Mrs. Margaret Trezise, da. of William Thomas Jerrum, and has issue by 1st and 2nd m.

Arms,—Gules, on a chevron argent fimbriated or three escallops sable; a chief wavy argent, thereon the representation of a French frigate wholly dismasted, towed towards the dexter by an English frigate in a shattered state. Crests,—1st, a dexter hand couped in naval uniform grasping a sword, surmounting a Dutch and French flag in saltire, on the former inscribed "Atalanta," on the latter "Piedmontaise," the sword passing through a wreath of laurel near the point and a little below through one of cypress, all proper; 2nd, a mitre gules, thereon a chevron argent fimbriated or charged with three escallops sable. Supporters,—Dexter, a bear proper; sinister, a Bengal tiger proper.
Residence,—Hunts Barn, Mayfield, Sussex. Clubs,—Brooks's, Savile.

For King and Country.

SONS LIVING. (By 1st m.)
Hon. JULIAN ALEXANDER, b. Aug. 23rd, 1945; ed. at Eton, and at Trin. Coll., Camb.; a Page of Honour to H.M. 1952-62.
Hon. Hugh Francis, b. 1948; ed. at Eton.
Hon. Edward Frederick, b. 1958.

(By 2nd m.)
Hon. Charles Alexander, b. 1967.

SISTERS LIVING.
Hon. Winifred Mary, b. 1923; late W.R.N.S.: m. 1943, Major John Anthony Jerningham Murray, late Grenadier Guards [Jerningham, Bt. (ext.)], and has issue living, George Alexander John, b. 1947: m. 1975, Caroline, da. of John Miller. Residence,—Woodmancote Manor, Cirencester, Gloucestershire.
Hon. Elizabeth Rosemary, b. 1927; late WRNS; JP for Berks.: m. 1949, Lt.-Col. John Frederick Dame Johnston, MVO, MC, late Gren. Gds., a Member of HM Household, and has issue living, Christopher Michael, b. 1951,—Joanna Elizabeth, b. 1953. Residences,—Adelaide Cottage, Windsor Home Park, Berks.; Stone Hill, Newport, Pembrokeshire.

WIDOW LIVING OF SECOND BARON.
HELEN MARY (Helen, Baroness Hardinge of Penshurst), only surviving child of the late Lord Edward Herbert Gascoyne-Cecil, K.C.M.G., D.S.O. [see M. Salisbury, colls.]: m. 1921, the 2nd Baron, who d. 1960. Residence,—South Park, Penshurst, Kent.

PREDECESSORS.—[1] Rt. Hon. CHARLES HARDINGE, K.G., G.C.B., G.C.S.I., G.C.M.G., G.C.I.E., G.C.V.O., I.S.O., 2nd son of 2nd Viscount Hardinge, b. 1858; was an Assist. Under-Sec. of State for Foreign Affairs 1903-4, Ambassador at St. Petersburg 1904-6, Permanent Under-Sec. of State for Foreign Affairs 1906-10, Viceroy of India 1910-16, again Permanent Under-Sec. of State for Foreign Affairs 1916-20, and Ambassador Extraor. and Plen. in Paris 1920-23; cr. Baron Hardinge of Penshurst, co. Kent (peerage of United Kingdom) 1910: m. 1890, the Hon. Winifred Sturt, C.I., who d. 1914, dau. of 1st Baron Alington; d. 1944; s. by his second and only surviving son [2] ALEXANDER HENRY LOUIS, G.C.B., G.C.V.O., M.C., P.C., 2nd Baron, b. 1894; Major Grenadier Guards (retired); was an A.D.C. to Viceroy and Gov.-Gen. of India 1915-16; an Equerry in Ord. and an Assist. Private Sec. to H.M. 1920-36 (Assist. Keeper of H.M.'s Privy Purse 1935-6), and an Extra Equerry to H.M. 1936-60, Private Sec. to King Edward VIII. 1936, and to King George VI. 1936-43; European War 1914-18 (wounded, M.C.); a Gov. of St. Bartholomew's Hospital, and King's Sch., Canterbury: m. 1921, Helen Mary, dau. of the late Lord Edward Herbert Gascoyne-Cecil, K.C.M.G., D.S.O. [M. Salisbury, colls.]; d. 1960; s. by his only son [3] GEORGE EDWARD CHARLES, 3rd Baron and present peer.

HARDWICKE, EARL OF. (Yorke.) [Earl G.B. 1754.]

JOSEPH PHILIP SEBASTIAN YORKE, 10th Earl; b. Feb. 3rd, 1971; s. 1974.

Arms,—Argent, a saltire azure charged with a bezant. Crest,—A lion's head erased proper, gorged with a plain collar gules, charged on the collar with a bezant. Supporters,—Dexter, a lion guardant or, gorged with a plain collar gules, the collar charged with a bezant; sinister, a stag proper, attired or, and collared as the lion.

SISTER LIVING.
Hon. Jemima Rose, b. 1969.

AUNTS LIVING.
Lady Amabel Mary Maud, b. 1935: m. 1955, Hon. Patrick Lindsay, of 12, Lansdowne Rd., W11 [see E. Crawford].
Lady Victoria Mary Verenia Braganza, b. 1947.
Lady Rose Mary Sydney, b. 1951.

Neither covet nor fear.

DAUGHTER LIVING OF EIGHTH EARL.

Lady Elizabeth Mary, *DCVO* (*Countess of Leicester*), *b.* 1912; a Lady of the Bedchamber to HM the Queen 1953-73; CVO 1965, DCVO 1973: *m.* 1931, the 5th Earl of Leicester. *Residence,*—The Parsonage House, Burnham Thorpe, Kings Lynn, Norfolk.

MOTHER LIVING.

Virginia Anne (*Viscountess Royston*) (9, Fernshaw Rd., SW10), da. of Geoffrey Lyon, of Hydon End, Hambledon, Surrey; *m.* 1968, Philip Simon Prospero Rupert Lindley, Viscount Royston, who *d.* 1973.

WIDOW OF NINTH EARL.

ENID MUNNICK (*Countess of Hardwicke*), formerly wife of Roy Boulting: *m.* 1970, as his 2nd wife, the 9th Earl, who *d.* 1974.

COLLATERAL BRANCHES LIVING.

Issue of the late Hon. Claud John Yorke, 3rd son of 7th Earl, *b.* 1872, *d.* 1940: *m.* 1914, Fay, who *d.* 1928, dau. of John Michael Zarifi, of 6, Norfolk Street, Park Lane, W.:—

RICHARD CHARLES JOHN *b.* July 25th, 1916.——David John Napier Edward *b.* 1919; ed. at Eton and at Jesus Coll., Camb.; Bar. Middle Temple 1949; a JP of W. Sussex; an Underwriting Member of Lloyd's: *m.* 1950, Anne Margaret, da. of Denis George Mackail [Burne-Jones, Bt. (ext.)], and has issue living, Charles Edward, *b.* 1951; ed. at Eton,—James Alexander, *b.* 1954; ed. at Eton. *Residence,*—Gatewick, Steyning, Sussex.

Grandson of the late John Reginald Yorke, son of the late Joseph Yorke, el. brother of the late Capt. James Charles Yorke (*b.* 1816) (infra):—

Issue of the late Vincent Wodehouse Yorke, *b.* 1869, *d.* 1957: *m.* 1899, the Hon. Maud Evelyn Wyndham, who *d.* 1963, dau. of 2nd Baron Leconfield:—

Gerald Joseph, *b.* 1901; ed. at Eton, and at Trin. Coll., Camb. (BA 1st class History 19—); is Major 21st (Gloucester Hussars) Armoured Car Co., Royal Tank Corps (TA), and Major Roy. Norfolk Regt. : *m.* 1937, Angela Vivien, el. dau. of Maj.-Gen. Sir John Duncan, K.C.B., C.M.G., CVO, DSO, and has issue living, John Sarne (37, St. Peter's Sq., W6), *b.* 1938: *m.* 1967, Jean Victoria, da. of Anthony Reynolds, of Sintra, Portugal, and has issue living, Anabel *b.* 1971, Sara *b.* 1974,—Vincent James (65, Blenheim Cres, W11 2EG), *b.* 1942: *m.* 1970, Francine Caroline, da. of the late F. W. Barker, of Hythe, and has issue living, Griselda Rose *b.* 1973, Hester Mary *b.* 1974,—Michael Piers (15, Wyndham Place, W1), *b.* 1944: *m.* 1972, Valerie Margaret, da. of H. Peter B. Cox, of Chislehurst, Kent. *Residence,*—Forthampton Court, Gloucester.

Grandson of the late Vincent Wodehouse Yorke (ante):—

Issue of the late Henry Vincent Yorke, *b.* 1905, *d.* 1974: *m.* 1929, the Hon. Adelaide Mary Biddulph (30, Wilton Place, SW1), da. of 2nd Baron Biddulph:—

Sebastian, *b.* 1934: *m.* 1957 (m. diss. 1962), the Hon. Emma Christina Tennant, da. of 2nd Baron Glenconnor, and has issue living, Matthew Henry, *b.* 1958.

Granddaughter of the late John Reginald Yorke (ante):—

Issue of the late Brig.-Gen. Ralph Maximilian Yorke, C.M.G., D.S.O., *b.* 1874, *d.* 1951: *m.* 1906, the Hon. Muriel Fanny, who *d.* 1956, dau. of 1st Baron Herschell :—

Adela Sophie, *b.* 1907. *Residence,*—Little Grange, St. Michaels, Tenterden, Kent.——Daphne Elizabeth, *b.* 1910: *m.* 1948, David Alan Fullerton, who *d.* 1965. *Residence,*—Mill Farm House, Tenterden, Kent.

Grandchildren of the late Capt. James Hamilton Langdon Yorke, M.C. (infra):—

Issue of the late James John Simon Yorke, D.S.O., R.N.. *b.* 1912, *d.* 1963: *m.* 1938, Bridget Essex (Constant, Nevern, Newport, Pembrokeshire), da. of Adm. Sir Alban Thomas Buckley Curteis, KCB:—

James Hamilton Simon, *b.* 1939, Lt.-Cdr. RN: *m.* 1966, Elizabeth Ann, da. of Col. John Leeper Anketell Macafee, OBE, of Grove House, Bredhurst, Kent, and has issue living, Simon Anketell Hamilton, *b.* 1967,—Patrick James Langdon, *b.* 1968,—Rebecca Mary Amabel, *b.* 1970,—Amabel Lucy Elizabeth, *b.* 1972.——Nicholas Roger, *b.* 1944: *m.* 1969, Kathleen Prentice, da. of Kent Sanger, of Duxbury, Mass., USA.——Philippa Mary, *b.* 1947: *m.* 1968, Roger Morrall, and has issue living, Bridget Essex, *b.* 1974.

Granddaughters of James Charles Yorke (*b.* 1847) (infra):—

Issue of the late Capt. James Hamilton Langdon Yorke, M.C., *b.* 1884, *d.* (killed in action during European War) 1917: *m.* 1910, Violet Mary, who *d.* 1963, dau. of the late James E. Vincent, Chancellor of Diocese of Bangor:—

Susannah Mary, *b.* 1915: *m.* 1st, 1934, Major Gerald Hartas FitzGerald, I.M.S., whc *d.* 1937; 2ndly, 1938, Allan Forbes Malcolmson, and has issue living, (by 1st marriage) Anne Sara, *b.* 1935: *m.* 1959, Richard Michael Johnston Eastham, and has issue living, Cedric Gerald *b.* 1960, Jane Francesca *b.* 1962,—(by 2nd m.) Jean Sheila, *b.* 1942: *m.* 1971, Peter Robjant, and has issue living, David Allan *b.* 1973. *Residence,*—Wingates, Wood Lane, Bramdean, Hants.

Issue of the late Com. Joseph Hugh Langdon Yorke, R.N., *b.* 1888, *d.* 1936: *m.* 1916, Ursula Mary Vere, who *d.* 1959, dau. of the late Col. Robert Oliver Lloyd, C.B. (formerly R.E.), of Treffgarne Hall, Pembrokeshire :—

Josephine Mary, *b.* 1917: *m.* 1st, 1945, Maurice Newton, who *d.* 1949; 2ndly, 1959, Luis Nicolin y Martinez Del Campo. *Address,*—c/o British Embassy, Mexico City, Mexico.——April Ursula, *b.* 1919; is a Carmelite Nun.

Issue of the late Capt. Philip Cecil Langdon Yorke, OBE, RN, *b.* 1903, *d.* 1970: *m.* 1st, 1936, Elsie Margaret, who *d.* 1945, da. of the late F. Davis, of Barnwood, Glos.; 2ndly, 1946 (*m.* diss. 1960), Violet Helen, da. of C. Ormonde Trew, of Little Rough, Hindhead; 3rdly, 1961, Rose, who *d.* 1966, da. of A. Rubinstein, of London:—

(By 2nd m.) Clare Amabel, *b.* 1948: *m.* 1969, Jonathan Robert Barclay, of Larks Hill, Stoke Holy Cross, Norwich, NOR 55W [see Barclay, Bt.].

Grandchildren of the late Capt. James Charles Yorke, son of the late Joseph Yorke, el. son of the late Rt. Rev. the Hon. James Yorke, Bishop of Ely, 5th son of 1st Earl :—

Issue of the late James Charles Yorke, *b.* 1847, *d.* 1932: *m.* 1878, Katherine Ellen, who *d.* 1935, dau. of Robert Langdon, J.P. of New Zealand :—

Worthington Langdon, *b.* 1901: *m.* 1934, Irene Rebecca, dau. of George O. Britney, of Manyberries, Alberta, Canada, and has issue living, Frederick Alton, *b.* 1935,—Katharine Anne, *b.* 1937,—Diane Marie, *b.* 1945.——Katherine Olive (*Lady Ford*), *b.* 1893: *m.* 1918, (Sir Francis Charles) Rupert Ford, 5th Bt., who *d.* 1948 [see St. Clair-Ford, Bt.]. *Residence,*—Trecwn, Wilfred Rd., Boscombe, Hants.

Grandchildren of the late Hon. Mr. Justice (Robert Langdon) Yorke, son of the late James Charles Yorke (ante):—

Issue of the late Major Patrick Langdon Yorke, Roy. Corps of Signals, *b.* 1916, *d.* (of wounds received in action in N.-W. Europe) 1945: *m.* 1939, Pamela Mary (who *m.* 2ndly 1950, Robert Michael Olive, of Clarendon, East Lennox Drive, Helensburgh, Dunbartonshire), dau. of the late Lieut.-Col. Harold Rudgard, O.B.E., of 22, Orchard Drive, Watford :—

Robert Anthony *b.* 1944; ed. at Marlborough, and Clare Coll., Camb. (MA): *m.* 1975, Morag, da. of John S. McD. Dow, of Helensburgh.——Caroline Ann *b.* 1941: *m.* 1969, Peter Roy Chamberlain, of West House, The Leys School, Cambridge, and has issue living, Juliet Catherine, *b.* 1970,—Rachel Claire, *b.* 1972.

Grandchildren of the late Reginald Somers Yorke, 2nd son of Capt. James Charles
Yorke (ante):—
Issue of the late Reginald Henry Crofton Yorke, *b.* 1897, *d.* 1947 : *m.* 1927, **Gwendolen**
Maude (45, West Park, Minehead, Som.), da. of the late Frank Watkinson:—
John Reginald (9, Mornington Rd., Chingford, E.4), *b.* 1928: *m.* 1959, Catherine Stewart, da. of the late
Frank William Borthwick, of West Ham, and has issue living, Margaret Helen, *b.* 1967,—Jennifer
Frances, *b.* 1970.

Grandsons of the late Capt. James Charles Yorke (ante):—
Issue of the late Algernon Joseph Yorke, *b.* 1856, *d.* 1932 : *m.* 1888, **Violet Lucy Grahame,**
who *d.* 1926, dau. of the late James Henry Spring Branson, Advocate-Gen., Madras.
Simon Algernon, *b.* 1889; ed. at Harrow, and at Clare Coll., Camb.; 1914-19 War as Capt.
Canadian Forces, 1939-44 War in France and India as Lt.-Col. Anti-Aircraft RA (TA):
m. 1920, Annie Paton, da. of the late J. P. Fyfe, JP, of Craigielea, Greenock,
and has issue living, Joseph Algernon, *b.* 1922 : *m.* 1945, Mary Robertson, dau. of Alexander Brown,
of Dunshelt, Fife, and has issue living, Marianne Alexandra *b.* 1946, Josephine Mary Bunty *b.* 1948.
——Vivian Joseph, *b.* 1895: *m.* 1929, Elizabeth Selina Thérèsa Frances Witcher.

Granddaughters of the late Algernon Joseph Yorke (ante):—
Issue of the late Harold Branson Yorke, *b.* 1890, *d.* 1949: *m.* 1920, Stella Catharine, who *d.*
1968, da. of the late Rear-Adm. Henry Compton Aitchison, of Shrubs Hill, Lyndhurst:—
Thérèse, *b.* 1925.——Joan Felicity, *b.* 1933 : *m.* 1957, Count Mario Bizzarri, and has issue living,
Flaminia Stella Giovanna Maria, *b.* 1958,—Alessandra Luisa Teresa Cristina Maria, *b.* 1959,—
Paola Maria Augusta Audreina Giovanna, *b.* 1960. *Residence,*—63, Vle. Parioli, Rome, Italy.——
Christine Anne, *b.* 1935: *m.* 1958, Alan Neville White, and has issue living, Richard Neville, *b.* 1964,
—Margaret Lesley, *b.* 1959,—Helen Mary, *b.* 1960. *Residence,*—41, Woodfields, Chipstead, Seven-
oaks, Kent.

Grandsons of Lt.-Col. Philip Charles Yorke, el. son of the Rev. Charles Isaac Yorke,
2nd son of the Rev. Philip Yorke, 2nd son of the Rt. Rev. the Hon. James Yorke,
5th son of 1st Earl:—
Issue of the late Major Henry Reginald Yorke, M.C., *b.* 1874, *d.* 1944 : *m.* 1903, **Beatrix**
Victoire, who *d.* 1960, dau. of Capt. Lynch-Staunton, formerly 14th Hussars :—
Philip (c/o Barclays Bank, 16, Whitehall, SW1) *b.* 1905; ed. at Harrow: *m.* 1945, Elsie May Heasman.
——David Christopher, *DSO, b.* 1913; Group-Capt. RAF; 1939-44 War latterly in SE Asia (des-
patches, DSO); DSO 1940. *Residence,*—8, Challoner Mansions, W. Kensington, W14.

Grandchildren of the late Brig. Philip Gerard Yorke, DSO (infra):—
Issue of the late Lt.-Col. Arthur Philip Denys Yorke, MC, *b.* 1915, *d.* 1971: *m.* 1957, Mary
Elizabeth (Brooke House, Ipplepen, Newton Abbot), da. of John Henry Glasbrook, of
Childe Okeford Manor, Blandford:—
Michael Philip, *b.* 1959.——Nicholas Simon, *b.* 1961.——Delia Mary, *b.* 1964.

Granddaughter of Lt.-Col. Philip Charles Yorke (ante):—
Issue of the late Brig. Philip Gerard Yorke, DSO, *b.* 1882, *d.* 1968: *m.* 1914, Beryl Emelia
(Marycourt, Childe Okeford, Blandord), da. of the late Brig.-Gen. Arthur Henry Croker
Phillpotts, formerly RHA [Brady, Bt.]:—
Amabel Marion, *b.* 1924: *m.* 1963, Brig. Robert Michael Carr, MBE, DFC, RA, Fairfield House, Mar-
garetting, Essex.

PREDECESSORS.—[1] Sir PHILIP Yorke, having been Solicitor-Gen. and Attorney-Gen., was
in 1733 appointed Lord Ch. Justice of the King's Bench and cr. *Baron Hardwicke,* of Hardwicke
co. Gloucester (peerage of Great Britain); one of the Lords Justices for Administering the
Govt. during the king's absences; promoted to be Lord High Chancellor 1737, and cr. *Viscount*
Royston and *Earl of Hardwicke* (peerage of Great Britain) 1754; resigned the Great Seal
1756 ; *d.* 1764 ; *s.* by his son [2] PHILIP, 2nd Earl : *m.* 1740, Lady Jemima Campbell (only
dau. of 3rd Earl of Breadalbane), and afterwards in her own right Baroness Lucas of Crudwell (cr.
1663), and Marchioness de Grey (cr. 1740, extinct); the Marchioness *d.* 1779 when the Marquessate expired, and the Barony of Lucas of Crudwell devolved upon her dau. Amabel;
the Earl *d.* 1796 without male issue; *s.* by his nephew [3] PHILIP, K.G., 3rd Earl, el. son of the
Hon. Charles, 2nd son of 1st Earl, who had been appointed Lord High Chancellor, and *d.* 1770
before the patent conferring upon him the title of Baron Morden was completed; was Viceroy of
Ireland 1801-6; *d.* without surviving male issue 1834 ; *s.* by his nephew [4] CHARLES PHILIP, *P.C.,*
4th Earl, son of Vice-Adm. Sir Joseph Sydney, K.C.B., M.P., 3rd son of the Hon. Charles (ante);
b. 1779; was a Vice-Adm.; sat as M.P. for Reigate (*C*) 1831, and for Cambridgeshire 1831-4;
Lord-Lieut. of Cambridgeshire, Postmaster-Gen. 1852, Lord Privy Seal 1858-9, and sometime
a Lord-in-Waiting to H.M. Queen Victoria: *m.* 1833, the Hon. Susan, who *d.* 1886, dau. of 1st
Baron Ravensworth; *d.* 1873; *s.* by his son [5] CHARLES PHILIP, 5th Earl, *b.* 1836; Comp-
troller of the Household 1866-8, and Master of the Buckhounds 1874-8; M.P. for Cambridge-
shire (*C*) 1865-73: *m.* 1863, Lady Sophie Georgiana Robertine, who *d.* 1923, dau. of 1st Earl
Cowley; *d.* 1897; *s.* by his son [6] ALBERT EDWARD PHILIP HENRY, 6th Earl; *b.* 1867; Under
Sec. of State for India 1900-1902, Under Sec. of State for War 1902-3, and again Under Sec. of
State for India 1903-4; *d.* 1904; *s.* by his uncle [7] JOHN MANNERS, 7th Earl; *b.* 1840; Capt.
R.N. : *m.* 1869, Edith, who *d.* 1930, dau. of the late Alexander Oswald, of Auchencruive, Scotland;
d. 1909: *s.* by his el. son [8] CHARLES ALEXANDER, 8th Earl; *b.* 1869: *m.* 1st, 1911, Ellen,
CBE (who *d.* 1968, having obtained a divorce 1927), da. of the late James Russell, of Auckland,
NZ; 2ndly, 1930, Mary Radley, who *d.* 1938 (having *m.* 2ndly, 1933, W. E. L. Jennings, Dist.
Officer of Dedza, Nyasaland), da. of Edward Robert Twist, of Liverpool; *d.* 1936; *s.*
by his nephew [9] PHILIP GRANTHAM (son of the late Hon. Alfred Ernest Frederick Yorke, 2nd
son of 7th Earl), 9th Earl; *b.* 1906; late Lt. LG; 1939-45 War with City of London Yeo, and as Maj.
SAS: *m.* 1st, 1934, Sarah Katharine, who *d.* 1965, da. of the Rt. Hon. Sir Francis Oswald Lindley,
GCMG, CB, CBE; 2ndly, 1970, Enid Munnick, of S. Africa, formerly wife of Roy Boulting; *d.* 1974;
s. by his grandson, JOSEPH PHILIP SEBASTIAN (only son of the late Joseph Philip Sebastian, Viscount
Royston, only son of 9th Earl), 10th Earl and present peer; also Viscount Royston, and Baron
Hardwicke.

HAREWOOD, EARL OF. (Lascelles.) [Earl U.K. 1812.]
[Title pronounced "Harwood."]

Salvation in God alone.

GEORGE HENRY HUBERT LAS-
CELLES, 7th Earl; *b.* Feb. 7th,
1923; *s.* 1947; ed. at Eton, and
at King's Coll., Camb. (BA);
Hon. LL.D. Leeds 1959 and
Aberdeen 1966; Hon. Dr. Music,
Hull 1962; Capt late Grenadier
Guards; was Editor of magazine
" Opera " 1950-53, a Dir. of R.
Opera House, Covent Garden
1951-53, Admin. Executive
thereof 1953-60, Artistic Dir of.
Edinburgh Festival 1961-65, Chan-
cellor of York Univ. 1963-67;
Dir. of Leeds Festival 1958-74;
and Artistic Adviser to New
Philharmonia Orchestra 1966-72;
Man. Dir. of Sadler's Wells Opera
(now English Nat. Opera) since
1972; Chm. of Music Advisory
Panel of Arts Council and Pres. of
English Opera Group, Manchester
Coll. of Music, and Leeds United
AFC; a Train Bearer at Corona-
tion of King George VI; an
ADC to Gov.-Gen. of Canada
1945-46; acted as a Counsellor of
State during HM King George
VI's absence abroad 1947, and during HM Queen Elizabeth II's absence
abroad 1953-54 and 1956; 1939-45 War in Italy (wounded, prisoner): *m.* 1st
1949, Maria Donata Nanetta Paulina Gustava Erwina Wilhelmina (Marion),
who obtained a divorce 1967, da. of the late Erwin Stein; 2ndly, 1967,
Patricia Elizabeth, only da. of Charles Tuckwell of Sydney, Aust., and
formerly wife of Athol Shmith, and has issue.

Arms,—Sable, a cross patonce within a bordure or. **Crest,**—A bear's head couped at the neck
ermine, muzzled gules, buckled or, and gorged with a collar of the second, rimmed and studded gold.
Supporters,—Two bears ermine; each muzzled gules, buckled or, gorged with a collar of the second,
rimmed and studded, and with a chain reflexed over the back gold ; pendant from the collar an
estucheon sable, charged with a cross patonce or.
    Seat,—Harewood House, Leeds, LS17 9LG. *Town Residence,*—3, Clifton Hill, NW8 0QE.

SONS LIVING. (*By 1st wife.*)
DAVID HENRY GEORGE (*Viscount Lascelles*), *b.* Oct. 21st, 1950; ed. at Westminster.
Hon. James Edward, *b.* Oct. 5th, 1953; ed. at Westminster: *m.* 1973, Fredericka Ann Duhrrson.
Hon. Robert Jeremy Hugh, *b.* Feb. 14th, 1955; ed. at Westminster.
    (*By 2nd wife.*)
Hon. Mark Hubert, *b.* July 5th, 1964.

BROTHER LIVING.
Hon. Gerald David, *b.* Aug. 21st, 1924; ed. at Eton; late Capt. Rifle Bde.; 1944-45 War; Pres. Inst. of
Motor Industry 1969-73; Pres. of British Racing Drivers' Club since 1964: *m.* 1952, Angela, da. of the
late Charles Stanley Dowding, and has issue living, Henry Ulick, *b.* May 19th, 1953. *Residences,*—
Fort Belvedere, Sunningdale, Berks; 95, Sloane St., SW1.

AUNT LIVING. (*Daughter of 5th Earl.*)
Lady Margaret Selina (*Dowager Viscountess Boyne*), *C.B.E., LL.D., b.* 1883 ; Hon. LL.D. Leeds 1951 ;
is a D.G.St.J., a J.P., and an Alderman of Salop Co. Council ; C.B.E. (Civil) 1920 : *m.* 1906, **the**
9th Viscount Boyne, who *d.* 1942. *Residence,*—Dower House, Burwarton, Bridgnorth, Salop.

COLLATERAL BRANCHES LIVING.
    Issue of the late Com. the Hon. Frederick Canning Lascelles, 2nd son of 4th Earl
    b. 1848, *d.* 1928 : *m.* 1878, Frederica Maria, who *d.* 1891, dau. of the late Hon
    Sir Adolphus Frederick Octavius Liddell, K.C.B., Q.C. [E. Ravensworth]:—

Rt. Hon. Sir Alan Frederick, *G.C.B., G.C.V.O., C.M.G., M.C.* (of Kensington Palace, W.8; Brooks's
Club), *b.* 1887; ed. at Marlborough, and at Trin. Coll., Oxford (BA 1909, MA 1915,
Hon. Fellow 1968); Hon. LL.D. Bristol 1954, and Durham 1958; Hon. F.R.A.M. 1961; Hon. D.C.L.
Oxford 1963; Capt. (ret.) 105th (Bedfordshire Yeo.) Field Brig. R. A. (T.A.), an Extra Equerry to
H.M., Chm. of Pilgrim Trust, and a Director of Midland Bank, and of Midland Bank Executor and
Trustee Co.; sometime A.D.C. to Gov. of Bombay; 1914-18 War (despatches, M.C.); was Assist.
Private Sec. to H.R.H. Prince of Wales 1920-29, Sec. to Gov.-Gen. of Canada 1931-35, and Assist.
Private Sec. to H.M. King George VI 1935-43, and Private Sec. 1943-52, and Private Sec. to H.M.
Queen Elizabeth II 1952-53; appointed Keeper of H.M.'s Archives 1945, and Chm. of Historic
Buildings Council for England 1953; M.V.O. (4th class) 1926, C.M.G. 1933, C.B. (Civil) 1937,
K.C.V.O. 1939, P.C. 1943, K.C.B. (Civil) 1944, G.C.V.O. 1947, G.C.B. (Civil) 1953: *m.* 1920, **the**
Hon. Joan Frances Vere Thesiger, who *d.* 1971, da. of 1st Viscount Chelmsford, and has issue living,
Lavinia Joan, *b.* 1923: *m.* 1st, 1946, Maj. Edward W. Renton, Black Watch, from whom she obtained
a divorce 1960; 2ndly (m. diss. 1964), 1962, Gavin Maxwell, who *d.* 1969, [Maxwell, Bt., cr. 1681];
3rdly, 1969, David Hankinson, RN, and has issue living (by 1st m.) Nicholas John *b.* 1946, Simon
Anthony *b.* 1948,—Caroline Mary, (*Viscountess Chandos*), *b.* 1928: *m.* 1949, the 2nd Viscount
Chandos, of The Vine, Sherborne St. John, Basingstoke.

    Issue of the late Maj. the Hon. George Algernon Lascelles, 7th son of 4th Earl
    b. 1865, *d.* 1932 : *m.* 1905, Mabel, who *d.* 1951, dau. of the late Francis Elcock,
    Massey, of Poole Hall, Nantwich :—
Sybil Mary, *b.* 1907: *m.* 1935, Col. Humphrey Bradshaw Mellor Wright, late RA. *Residence,*—
Conyers Place, Marnhull, Dorset.

    Issue of the late Hon. William Horace Lascelles, 8th son of 4th Earl, *b.* 1868, *d.*
    1949 : *m.* 1899, Madeline, who *d.* 1950, dau. of the late Rev. Gerard Barton, of
    Fundenhall, Norfolk :—

Mary Madge, *b.* 1900; ed. at Lady Margaret Hall, Oxford (BA 1922, BLitt, 1927, MA 1931);   Fellow
of Somerville Coll., Oxford 1932;   FBA 1962.——Pamela Diana (twin), *b.* 1902.——Susan Olivia, *b.*
1907.   *Residence,*—Cley-next-Sea, Holt, Norfolk.

Grandchildren of the late Hon. George Edwin Lascelles, 3rd son of 3rd Earl :—
Issue of the late Hon. Sir Alfred (George) Lascelles, *b.* 1857, *d.* 1952: *m.* 1911, Isabel Carteret,
   who *d.* 1965, da. of the late Francis John Thynne [M. Bath, colls.]:—
Ursula, *b.* 1914 : *m.* 1946, Alan George Ross Ormiston, and has issue living, James Christopher Ross,
   b. 1949,—Lavinia Anne Ross, *b.* 1952.   *Residence,*—Holford House, North Chailey, Sussex.——
Kathleen Louisa Isabel, *b.* 1916 : *m.* 1940 (marriage dissolved 1953), Brigadier Robert Hugh Bellamy,
   CBE, DSO, late DCLI, who *d.* 1972, and has issue living, Martin Hugh, *b.* 1946,—Vivien Patricia, *b.*
   1943.   *Residence,*—Manor Cottage, Coln St. Aldwyns, Cirencester.
Issue of the late Edward George Lascelles, *b.* 1859, *d.* 1938:   *m.* 1891, Minna, who *d.* 1950,
   dau. of the late Rev. John Boyle, V. of Ashby Folville, Leicestershire :—
Evelyn Herbert (25, Balcha St., Holland Park, Brisbane 2, Qld.), *b.* 1893;   1914-18 War as Lt. KRRC
   and attached to RFC (wounded): *m.* 1923, Colleen Una, da. of the late John Taylor, of Rockwood
   Station, Qld., and has issue living, Geoffrey George (35, Mitchell St., Sunnybank, Qld.), *b.* 1927;
   1939-45 in RAN: *m.* 1951, Gwen Martin, of Yandina, Qld., and has issue living, Scott *b.* 1952, Kent
   b. 1954, Fiona Jane *b.* 1962.
Grandchildren of Evelyn Herbert Lascelles (ante):—
Issue of the late John Edward Lascelles, *b.* 1923, *d.* 1975: *m.* 1946, Isabelle Christine Graham
   Maxwell, of Gordonvale, N. Qld.:—
David John, *b.* 1948.——Peter James, *b.* 1952.——Stephen Charles, *b.* 1954.——Isabelle Diana, *b.* 1957.

Granddaughters of the late Rev. the Hon. James Walter Lascelles, 6th son of
   3rd Earl :—
Issue of the late Cecil Henry Lascelles, *b.* 1865, *d.* 1899 : *m.* 1892, Euphemia Carr, who *d.*
   1954, dau. of W. Robison :—
Cecil Elizabeth, *b.* 1894 : *m.* 1927 (marriage dissolved 1936), Conrad Hal Waddington, C.B.E., and has
   issue living, Cecil Jacob, *b.* 1929.——Ruth Carr, *b.* 1895.   *Residence,*—Seadown, 28, Sullington
   Gdns., Worthing.

Granddaughter of the late Rt. Hon. Sir Frank Cavendish Lascelles, GCB, GCMG,
   GCVO, son of the Rt. Hon. William Saunders Sebright Lascelles, MP (infra):—
Issue of the late Major William Frank Lascelles, *b.* 1868, *d.* 1913 : *m.* 1899, Lady Sybil
   Evelyn de Vere Beauclerk, who *d.* 1910, dau. of 10th Duke of St. Albans :—
Vreda Esther Mary (*Mary, Duchess of Buccleuch*), *b.* 1900; bore the Queen's Canopy at Coronation of
   King George VI: *m.* 1921, the 8th Duke of Buccleuch, who *d.* 1973.   *Residences,*—Bowhill, Selkirk;
   Boughton House, Kettering; Drumlanrig Castle, Thornhill, Dumfriesshire.

Grandson of the late Rt. Hon. William Saunders Sebright Lascelles, M.P., 3rd
   son of 2nd Earl:—
Issue of the late Lieut.-Col. Henry Arthur Lascelles, M.V.O., *b.* 1842, *d.* 1913 : *m.* 1883,
   Caroline Maria, who *d.* 1945, dau. of the late Hon. Charles Alexander Gore [E.
   Arran, colls.] :—
Sir Francis William, K.C.B., M.C., *b.* 1890; ed. at Ch. Ch., Oxford (B.A. 1914, M.A. 1953), sometime
   Major Sussex Yeo ; was Clerk of the Parliaments, House of Lords 1953-8 ; European War 1914-18
   (wounded, M.C.) ; C.B. (Civil) 1937, K.C.B. (Civil) 1954 : *m.* 1924, Esmée Marion, dau. of the late
   C. A. Bury, of Downings, Salins, co. Kildare, and has issue living, Charles Brian (Bank House,
   Glenfarg, Perthshire), *b.* 1926: *m.* 1953, Elizabeth Mary, only da. of the late Lt.-Cdr. Geoffrey
   Grenfell, RN, and has issue living, Charles Riversdale *b.* 1954, James Dominic *b.* 1956, Tobias Francis
   b. 1965,—Henry Giles Francis (Hillwatering Farm, Langham, Bury St. Edmunds), *b.* 1931: *m.* 1957,
   Caroline Venetia, da. of the late Esmond Charles Baring, OBE [see B. Ashburton, colls.], and has
   issue living, Hugo Giles *b.* 1958, Peregrine Simon *b.* 1962, Sophie Caroline (twin) *b.* 1958.   *Residence,*—
   Field House, Orford, Woodbridge, Suffolk.

Grandchildren of the late Lieut.-Col. Henry Arthur Lascelles, M.V.O. (ante) :—
Issue of the late Edward Charles Ponsonby Lascelles, O.B.E., *b.* 1884, *d.* 1956 : *m.* 1911,
   Leila Winifred Leonor (a DGStJ) (The Plough, Redford, Midhurst, Sussex), da. of the late
   Sir Vincent Kennett-Barrington:—
Henry Anthony, CB, CBE, DSO, *b.* 1912; ed. at Winchester, and Oriel Coll., Oxford (BA); Maj.-Gen.
   (ret.) late RTR;   Maj.-Gen., Gen. Staff, HQ Far East Land Forces 1964-66;   Dir.-Gen. of Winston
   Churchill Trust since 1967; 1939-45 War in Middle East and Italy (despatches twice, DSO, OBE);
   DSO and OBE (Mil) 1945, OBE (Mil) 1962, CB (Mil) 1967: *m.* 1941, Ethne Hyde Ussher, da. of the
   late Norman Charles.   *Residence,*—Manor Farm Cottage, Hedgerley Green, Bucks.——Alice Leila
   b. 1914;   ed. at London Univ. (BSc Economics 1936).   *Residence,*—The Plough, Redford, Midhurst,
   Sussex.

Issue of the late Henry Francis Lascelles, *b.* 1886, *d.* 1937: *m.* 1918, Rose Caroline Georgiana
   (43, Cadogan Place, SW1), da. of the late Col. Frederick Arthur Aylmer [see B. Aylmer,
   colls.]:—
Oliver, *MBE, DSC, b.* 1921, Cdr. RN;   1939-45 War (DSC);   MBE (Mil) 1950: *m.* 1963, Pamela
   Margaret Enid, da. of the late Robert Whillis, and has issue living, Harriet Caroline, *b.* 1964.——
   Nicola Jane, *b.* 1966.   *Residence,*—The Old Rectory, Thurston, Bury St. Edmunds.——Anthea
   Caroline, *b.* 1930: *m.* 1950, William Ralph Merton, son of the late Sir Thomas Ralph Merton, KBE,
   and has issue living, Michael Ralph, *b.* 1951,—Rupert Ralph, *b.* 1953,—Jeremy Ralph, *b.* 1961.
   Residence,—Flat 7, 97, Cadogan Gdns., SW3.

Granddaughters of the late Col. Walter Richard Lascelles (infra) :—
Issue of the late Captain Walter Edward Lascelles, *b.* 1862, *d.* 1897: *m.* 1891, Mabel
   Gwendoline, who *d.* 1931, dau. of the late Lieut.-Col. R. Hasell Thursby, Coldstream
   Guards :—
Constance Gertrude, *b.* 1894: *m.* 1922, James Ogilvy Fairlie, who *d.* 1960, and has issue living, David
   Ogilvy (of Myres Castle, Auchtermuchty, Fife), *b.* 1923; ed. at Ampleforth, and at Oriel Coll.,
   Oxford; late Capt. R. Signals; a Member of Queen's Body Guard for Scotland (Roy. Col of Archers);
   DL of Fife; Co. Commr. Scouts for Fife 1966; 1939-45 War, Java and Malaya 1944-45, Korea
   1951-52: *m.* 1969, Ann Constance, da. of the late Francis Dermot Bolger, of Madeira.   *Residence,*—
   Myres Castle, Auchtermuchty, Fife.

Issue of the late Lieut.-Col. George Reginald Lascelles, C.V.O., O.B.E., *b.* 1864; *d.* 1939:
   m. 1895, Beatrice, who *d.* 1953, dau. of the late Rev. R. T. Pulteney, R. of Ashley,
   Northants:—
Joan, *b.* 1896.   *Residence,*—12B, Hornton Street, Kensington, W.8.——Barbara Judith, *b.* 1903: *m.*
   1925, Edward William Seymour [see D. Somerset, colls.].   *Residence,*—Tarrant Abbey, Blandford,
   Dorset.
Grandson of the late Lieut.-Col. George Reginald Lascelles, C.V.O., O.B.E.
   (ante) :—
Issue of the late Lieut.-Col. John Norman Pulteney Lascelles, *b.* 1898, *d.* (on active ser.
   during European War) 1939 : *m.* 1932, Elizabeth Katharine Joan (now of Saywell Farm,
   Bedmonton, Sittingbourne, Kent), da. of the late Lieut.-Col. Lord Robert William Orlando
   Manners, C.M.G.. D.S.O. [see D. Rutland, colls.]:—
Rupert John Orlando, *b.* 1935; late Coldstream Guards: *m.* 1963, Jeanne Gordon, da. of Norman
   Gordon Farquharson, of Bryanston, Johannesburg, and has issue living, Robert Norman, *b.* 1965,
   —Frances Sarah Elizabeth, *b.* 1970.   *Residence,*—2, Ormonde House, Ormonde Gate, SW3.

Granddaughter of the late Col. Walter Richard Lascelles, son of the late Hon. Arthur
Lascelles, 5th son of 2nd Earl :—
Issue of the late Lieut.-Col. Ernest Lascelles, O.B.E., Rifle Brig., *b.* 1870, *d.* 1948 : *m.*
1895, Flora Evelyn, who *d.* 1956, dau. of the late John Bulteel, of Pamfleet, Ivybridge,
Devon :—
Faith Evelyn, *b.* 1903. *Residence,—*Paradise House, Yealmpton, Devon.

PREDECESSORS.—[1] EDWARD Lascelles, heir at law of Edwin Lascelles, 1st and last
Baron Harewood, of Harewood Castle, co. York, having sat as MP for Northallerton in several
Parliaments was cr. *Baron Harewood,* of Harewood, co. York (peerage of Great Britain) 1796,
and *Viscount Lascelles* and *Earl of Harewood* (peerage of United Kingdom) 1812; *d.* 1820; *s.*
by his son [2] HENRY, 2nd Earl ; Lord-Lieut. of W. Riding of York; *d.* 1841; *s.* by his son [3]
HENRY, 3rd Earl; *b.* 1797; Lord-Lieut. of W. Riding of York: *m.* 1823, Lady Louisa Thynne, dau.
of 2nd Marquess of Bath; *d.* 1857; *s.* by his son [4] HENRY THYNNE, 4th Earl, *b.* 1824: *m.* 1st.
1845, Lady Elizabeth Joan De Burgh, who *d.* 1854, dau. of 1st Marquess of Clanricarde; 2ndly,
1858, Diana Elizabeth Matilda, who *d.* 1904, dau. of John George Smythe, of Heath Hall,
Wakefield; *d.* 1892; *s.* by his el. son [5] HENRY ULICK, *G.C.V.O.,* 5th Earl, *b.* 1846 ; Lord,
Lieut. of W. Riding of Yorkshire 1904-27; sometime an A.D.C. to King George V. : *m.* 1881,
Lady Florence Katherine Bridgeman, who *d.* 1943, dau. of 3rd Earl of Bradford; *d.* 1929;
s. by his el. son [6] HENRY GEORGE CHARLES, *K.G., G.C.V.O., D.S.O., T.D.,* 6th Earl, *b.*
1882; a Personal A.D.C. to H.M.; Lord-Lieut. of W. Riding of Yorkshire 1927-47; Chancellor
of Sheffield Univ. 1944 ; European War 1914-19 with Grenadier Guards (D.S.O.): *m.* Feb. 28th,
1922, *H.R.H. Princess* (Victoria Alexandra Alice) Mary *(The Princess Royal), C.I., G.C.V.O.
G.B.E., R.R.C., T.D., C.D.,* who *d.* March 28th, 1965, only da. of H.M. King George V. [see
" ROYAL FAMILY "]; *d.* 1947; *s.* by his son [7] GEORGE HENRY HUBERT, 7th Earl and present
peer; also Viscount Lascelles, and Baron Harewood.

HARLECH, BARON. (Ormsby-Gore.) [Baron U.K. 1876.]

Under this sign thou shalt conquer.

(WILLIAM) DAVID ORMSBY-GORE,
KCMG, PC, 5th Baron; *b.* May 20th,
1918; *s.* 1964; ed. at Eton, and at
New Coll., Oxford (Hon. Fellow 1964);
Hon. DCL Pittsburgh; Hon. LLD
Brown Univ., Rhode Island, New York
Univ., William and Mary Coll., Fairleigh,
Dickinson Univ., and Manchester; Maj.
RA (TA), and a DL for Salop; PPS to
Min. of State, Foreign Office 1951-54, and
a Memb. of Exec. Cttee. of National Trust
1954-56, and 1965-70, and of British
Council 1954-56; Joint Parl. Under-Sec.
of State, Foreign Office 1956-57, and Min.
of State for Foreign Affairs 1957-61,
Ambassador to USA 1961-65, and Dep.
Leader of the Opposition House of Lords
1966-67, since when Chm. of Harlech
TV; Pres. of Pilgrims Soc., and of
British Board of Film Censors, Chm. of Kennedy Memorial Trust, of Pilgrim
Trust, and of Papworth-Enham Village Settlements; a Trustee of Tate Gallery,
and Gov. of Yehudi Menuhin Sch.; a KStJ; MP for Oswestry Div. of Salop (*U*)
1950-61; PC 1957, KCMG 1961: *m.* 1st, 1940, Sylvia, who *d.* 1967, da. of the
late Hugh Lloyd Thomas, CMG, CVO [B. Bellew]; 2ndly, 1969, Pamela, only
da. of Ralph F. Colin, of New York City, and has issue, by 1st and 2nd m.

Arms,—Quarterly : 1st and 4th gules, a fesse between three cross-crosslets fitchée or, *Gore ;*
2nd and 3rd gules, a bend between six cross-crosslets or, *Ormsby.* **Crests,—**1st, an heraldic tiger
rampant argent; 2nd, a dexter arm embowed in armour proper, holding in the hand a man's leg
also in armour, couped at the thigh. **Supporters,—***Dexter,* an heraldic tiger argent, maned and
tufted sable, ducally gorged or; *sinister,* a lion or.

*Residences,—*Glyn, Talsarnau, Merioneth; 14A, Ladbroke Rd., W11 3NJ.

SON LIVING (*By* 1*st m.*)
Hon. FRANCIS DAVID, *b.* March 13th, 1954.

DAUGHTERS LIVING (*By* 1*st m.*)
Hon. Jane Teresa Denyse, *b.* 1942: *m.* 1966, Michael Sean O'Dare Rainey, Ty Baen, Llanfechain,
Montgomeryshire, and has issue living, Saffron (son), *b.* 1967,—Gawaine O'Dare, *b.* 1971,—Rose
Soley, *b.* 1969,—Ramona Alba, *b.* 1973.
Hon. Victoria Mary, *b.* 1946: *m.* 1972, Julian Richard Leslie Lloyd, [see V. Chetwynd, colls.].
Hon. Alice Magdalen Sarah, *b.* 1952.

(*By* 2*nd m.*)
Hon. Pandora Beatrice, *b.* 1972.

BROTHER LIVING.
Hon. John Julian, *b.* 1925; ed. at Eton, and at New Coll., Oxford; late Capt. Coldstream Guards.

SISTERS LIVING.
Hon. Mary Hermione (*Hon. Lady Mayall*), *b.* 1914: *m.* 1st, 1936 (m. diss. 1946), Capt. Robin Francis
Campbell, DSO, only son of the late Rt. Hon. Sir Ronald Hugh Campbell, GCMG; 2ndly, 1947, Sir
Alexander Lees Mayall, CMG, KCVO, and has issue living, (by 1st m.) Gerard Francis (491, Fulham
Rd., SW6), *b.* 1937: *m.* 1964, Theadora Elizabeth, da. of Col. Sir Roderick (Napoleon) Brinckman,
5th Bt., and has issue living, Tarquin *b.* 1966, Caspar *b.* 1967,—Charles, *b.* 1939: *m.* 1963, Philippa,
da. of J. C. H. Le B. Croke, and has issue living, Phineas *b.* 1965, Orlando *b.* 1967,—(by 2nd m.)
Robert George Lees, *b.* 1954,—Cordelia Isobel, *b.* 1947: *m.* 1969, John Nelson Summerscale, of 15,
Sydney Rd., Muswell Hill, N10, son of Sir John Percival Summerscale, KBE, and has issue living,
Aaron Piers *b.* 1969,—Alexandra Beatrice, *b.* 1949: *m.* 1971, John Culme-Seymour. *Residence,—*
Sturford Mead, Warminster, Wilts.
Hon. Dame Katharine Margaret Alice, *DBE, b.* 1921; DBE (Civil) 1974: *m.* 1942, the Rt. Hon.
Maurice Victor Macmillan, MP, of Highgrove, Tetbury, Glos., and has issue living, Alexander Daniel
Alan, *b.* 1943,—Adam Julian Robert, *b.* 1948,—David Maurice Benjamin, *b.* 1957,—Rachel Mary
Georgiana, *b.* 1955.

Hon. Elizabeth Jane, *b.* 1929: *m.* 1962, the Hon. William Simon Pease, of 72, Ladbroke Rd., W.11 [see B. Wardington].

WIDOW LIVING OF FOURTH BARON.

Lady BEATRICE EDITH MILDRED Gascoyne-Cecil, (*Dowager Baroness Harlech*), *DCVO* (of 14, Ladbroke Rd., W.11), da. of the 4th Marquess of Salisbury; a Lady of the Bedchamber to H. M. the Queen 1941-46, and an Extra Lady of the Bedchamber 1946-49; an Extra Lady of the Bedchamber to H.M. Queen Elizabeth the Queen Mother since 1953; DCVO 1947: *m.* 1913, the 4th Baron, who *d.* 1964.

PREDECESSORS.—William Gore [see E. Arran, colls.]; M.P. for Leitrim, for Carnarvon Borough, and for N. Shropshire: *m.* 1815, Mary Jane, dau. and heiress of Owen Ormsby, whose name he assumed; *d.* 1860 leaving issue [1] JOHN RALPH Ormsby-Gore, M.P. for Carnarvonshire (C) 1837-41, and for N. Salop 1859-75 ; a Groom-in-Waiting to H.M. 1841-59; cr. *Baron Harlech,* of Harlech, co. Merioneth (peerage of United Kingdom) 1876, with remainder to his brother: *m.* 1844, Sarah, who *d.* 1898, dau. and co-heir of Sir John Tyssen Tyrell, 2nd Bt.; *d.* 1876; *s.* by his brother [2] WILLIAM RICHARD, 2nd Baron, *b.* 1819 ; Lieut. of co. Leitrim ; M.P. for Sligo (C) 1841-52, and for co. Leitrim 1858-76 : *m.* 1850, Lady Emily Charlotte, who *d.* 1892, dau. of the late Adm. Sir George Francis Seymour, G.C.B. ; *d.* 1904 ; *s.* by his el. surviving son [3] GEORGE RALPH CHARLES, 3rd Baron, *b.* 1855 ; appointed Lieut. of co. Leitrim 1904, and Lord-Lieut. of Merionethshire and Constable of Harlech Castle 1927 ; M.P. for Shropshire W., or Oswestry Div. (C) 1901-4: *m.* 1881, Lady Margaret Ethel Gordon, who *d.* 1950, dau. of 10th Marquess of Huntly ; *d.* 1938 ; *s.* by his son [4] WILLIAM GEORGE ARTHUR, KG, GCMG, PC, 4th Baron; *b.* 1885; MP for Denbigh Dist. (C) 1910-18, and Stafford 1918-38; Under-Sec. of State for Colonies 1922-24, and 1924-29, Postmaster-Gen. Sept. to Nov. 1931, First Commr. of Works 1931-36, and Sec. of State for the Colonies 1936-38, High Commr. for Bechuanaland, Basutoland and Swaziland, and High Commr. in Union of S. Africa 1941-44, Lord Lt. of Merionethshire 1938-57, Constable of Harlech Castle 1938-64, and Caernarvon Castle 1945-63, Pro-Chancellor of Univ. of Wales 1945-56: *m.* 1913, Lady Beatrice Edith Mildred Gascoyne-Cecil, DCVO, da. of 4th Marquess of Salisbury; *d.* 1964; *s.* by his yr. son [5] WILLIAM DAVID, 5th Baron and present peer.

HARMAR-NICHOLLS, BARON. (Harmar-Nicholls.) [Life Baron 1974, Bt. U.K. 1960.]

HARMAR HARMAR-NICHOLLS, *Life Baron,* and 1st *Baronet,* son of Charles Edward Craddock Nicholls, of Walsall, Staffs.; *b.* Nov. 1st, 1912; assumed by deed poll the surname of Harmar-Nicholls in lieu of his patronymic; ed. at Queen Mary's Gram. Sch., Walsall; 1939-45 War as Lt. RE in India and Burma; a Dir. of J. & H. Nicholls (Paints) Ltd., of Nicholls and Hennessy Group Ltd., of Radio Luxembourg (London) Ltd., of Cannon Insurance, Ltd., and of Malvanon Insurance Co., Ltd.; Chm. of Pleasurama Ltd., and of Malvern Festival Theatre Trust; an Underwriter at Lloyd's and a JP for Staffs.; PPS to Assist. Postmaster-Gen. 1951-55, Parl. Sec. Min. of Agric. Fisheries and Food 1955-57, and to Min. of Works 1957-60; MP for Peterborough Div. of Northants. (C) 1950-74; cr. a Baronet, of Darlaston, co. Stafford (UK) 1960 and *Baron Harmar-Nicholls,* of Peterborough, Cambridgeshire: *m.* 1940, Dorothy Elsie, el. da. of James Edwards, of Tipton, Staffs., and has issue.

Arms,—Per pale and per chevron gules and sable, two arrows with broad heads pilewise, the shafts argent, the feathers and heads or overall a chevron engrailed gold. **Crest,**—Gules and sable two keys in saltire wards upwards argent supporting a Davey lamp proper, all tied about with a Stafford knot, the strands gules and sable, the tassels also gules.

Residence,—Abbeylands, Weston, Stafford. *Clubs,*—Constitutional, St. Stephen's, Unionist City, and Counties (Peterborough).

DAUGHTERS LIVING.

Hon. Judith Ann, *b.* 1941: *m.* 1973, Alan Aspden.
Hon. Susan Frances Nicholls, *b.* 1943.

HARMSWORTH, BARON. (Harmsworth.) [Baron U.K. 1939.]

CECIL DESMOND BERNARD HARMSWORTH, 2nd Baron; *b.* Aug. 19th, 1903; *s.* 1948; ed. at Eton, and at Ch. Ch., Oxford (B.A. 19—, M.A. 19—): *m.* 1926, Dorothy Alexander, dau. of the Hon. J. C. Heinlein (sometime a State Senator), of Bridgeport, Ohio, U.S.A., and has issue.

Arms,—Azure, two rolls of paper in saltire or, banded in the centre gules, between two bees volant in pale and as many trefoils in fesse of the second. **Crest,**—A cubit arm erect, the hand holding a roll of paper fessewise proper between two ostrich feathers or. **Supporters,**—On either side a deep sea fisherman proper.

Residence,—Lime Lodge, Egham, Surrey.

DAUGHTER LIVING.

Hon. Margaret Askew Alexander, *b.* 1928: *m.* 1960, Frank Gibson Phillips, and has issue living, Dan Eric, *b.* 19—,—Kevin Desmond *b.* 19—.

BROTHER LIVING.

Hon. ERIC BEAUCHAMP NORTHCLIFFE, *b.* Aug. 28th, 1905; ed. at Eton, and at Ch. Ch. Oxford (MA): *m.* 1st, 1935, Hélène, who *d.* 1962,

He does well who works diligently.

da. of Col. Jules-Raymond Dehove, of Paris; 2ndly, 1964, Helen Gordon (HUDSON), da. of the late Maj.-Gen. Granville George Loch, CB, CMG, CBE, DSO, and has issue living, (by 1st marriage) Thomas Harold Raymond (108, Walton St., SW3 2JJ), b. 1939; ed. at Eton and Ch. Ch. Oxford; Lt. RHG: m. 1971, Patricia Palmer, da. of the late M. P. Horsley, of Waltham House, Brough, Yorks., and has issue living, Dominic Michael Eric b. 1973, Philomena Helène Olivia b. 1975,— Madeleine Thérèse Margaret, b. 1941. *Residence*, 27, Hartington Rd., Chiswick, W4.

SISTER LIVING.
Hon. Daphne Cecil Rosemary, b. 1901: m. 1st, 1928, Capt. Colin David Brodie, late Middlesex Regt. who obtained a divorce 1937; 2ndly, 1938, Lieut.-Col. Harold Macneile Dixon, R.A.S.C., and has issue living (by 2nd m.) Patricia Rosemary, b. 1941,—Mary Lalage b. 1943: m. 1972, John Christopher Gibson. *Residence,*—Lagham Manor, S. Godstone, Surrey.

PREDECESSOR.—[1] CECIL BISSHOPP Harmsworth, 3rd son of the late Alfred Harmsworth, Bar.-at-Law [see also V. Northcliffe (ext.) and V. Rothermere]; b. 1869; was Parliamentary Private Sec. (unpaid) to Pres. of Board of Agriculture and Fisheries (Rt. Hon. W. Runciman, M.P.) 1911-15; Parliamentary Under-Sec. of State, Home Depart. 1915-19, and for Foreign Affairs 1919-22; in Prime Min.'s Secretariat 1917-19; sat as M.P. for Worcestershire Mid., or Droitwich Div. (L) 1906-10, for S., or Luton Div. of Bedfordshire 1911-18, and for Luton Div. thereof 1918-22; cr. *Baron Harmsworth*, of Egham, co. Surrey (peerage of UK) 1939: m. 1897, Emilie Alberta, who d. 1942, da. of William Hamilton Maffett, Bar.-at-Law, formerly of St. Helena, Finglas, co. Dublin; d. 1948; s. by his el. son [2] CECIL DESMOND BERNARD, 2nd Baron and present peer.

HARRINGTON, EARL OF. (Stanhope.) [Earl G.B. 1742.]

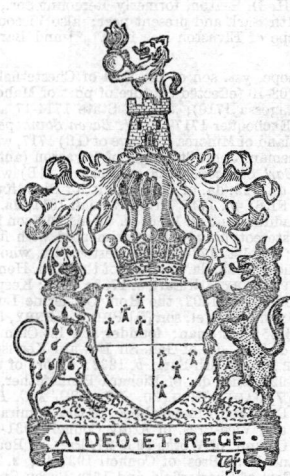

From God and the king.

WILLIAM HENRY LEICESTER STANHOPE, 11th Earl; b. Aug. 24th, 1922; *s.* 1929 to the Earldom of Harrington, Viscountcy of Petersham and Barony of Harrington; and 1967 to Viscountcy of Stanhope of Mahon and Barony of Stanhope of Elvaston; ed. at Eton; Capt. 15th/19th King's R. Hussars: m. 1st, 1942, Eileen (from whom he obtained a divorce 1946), only da. of Sir John Foley Grey, 8th Bt. [see Lambert, Bt.]; 2ndly, 1947, Anne Theodora from whom he obtained a divorce 1962), only da. of the late Maj. Richard Arenbourg Blennerhassett Chute; 3rdly, 1964, Priscilla Margarete da. of the late Hon. Archibald Edward Cubitt [see B. Ashcombe, colls.], and has issue by 1st, 2nd and 3rd m.

Arms,—Quarterly; ermine and gules **Crest,**—A tower azure, a demi-lion rampant issuant from the battlements or, in the paws a bomb fired proper. *Supporters,—Dexter,* a talbot guardant argent, guttée de poix; *sinister,* a wolf erminois; each gorged with a chaplet of oak proper.

Seats,—Dooneen, Patrickswell, co. Limerick, Greenmount, Patrickswell, co. Limerick.

SONS LIVING (*By 1st m.*)
CHARLES HENRY LEICESTER (*Viscount Petersham*), b. July 20th, 1945; ed. at Eton: m. 1966, Virginia Alleyne Freeman, da. of Capt. Harry Freeman Jackson, of Cool-na-Grena, co. Cork, and has issue:—
    SON LIVING—*Hon.* William Henry Leicester, b. Oct. 14th, 1967.
    DAUGHTER LIVING—*Hon.* Serena Alleyne, b. 1970.

(*By 2nd m.*)
Hon. Steven Francis Lincoln, b. 1951.

(*By 3rd m.*)
Hon. John Fitzroy, b. 1965.

DAUGHTERS LIVING (*By 1st m.*)
Lady Avena Margaret Clare, b. 1944: m. 1969, Adrian J. Maxwell, of South Lodge, Carrick-on-Suir, co. Tipperary, and has issue living, Sacha Jane, b. 1974.

(*By 2nd m.*)
Lady Trina Maria, b. 1947.
Lady Sarah Sue (twin), b. 1951: m. 1970, Robert John Barry, of Stonepark, Bruff, co. Limerick, and has issue living, Mark James, b. 1972,—Tristan James, b. 1975,—Guy William (twin), b. 1975.

(*By 3rd m.*)
Lady Isabella Rachel, b. 1966.

COLLATERAL BRANCHES LIVING.
    Issue of the late Hon. Lincoln Edwin Stanhope, 3rd son of 8th Earl, b. 1849, d. 1902: m. 1885, Hélène, who d. 1919, dau. of the Countess de Galve by her first husband, Mons. Leon de Bravura :—
Eva Barbara Edwina, b. 1890: m. 1921, Bertram Marion-Crawford, who d. 1952. *Residence,—* 6, Egerton Court, S.W.7.

    Grandchildren of the late Russell Charles Stanhope (*infra*):—
    Issue of the late Aubrey Charles Stanhope, b. 1895, d. 1953: m. 1st, 1919, Paulette Bordier du Raincy, of France, who d. 1922; 2ndly, 1931, Evelyn Wadsworth:—
(By 1st m.) Aubrey Charles, *DFC* (Bristol, Maine 04539, USA) b. 1920; Lt.-Col. USAF (ret.); 1939-45 War, DSC (USA): m. 1941, Muriel Grace, da. of William Anderson Lauther, of 5, Rushout Av., Harrow, and has issue living, Paulette Beatrice, b. 1946: m. 1968, Gilbert Mark Rollo [see L. Rollo, colls.].—Marie Annick, b. 1921: m. 1953, Lt.-Col. Richard Davis, USAF (ret.).—(by 2nd m.), Noel, b. 1946.

    Grandchildren of the late Russell Charles Stanhope, son of the late Hon. Sir Francis Charles Stanhope, K.C.H., 5th son of 3rd Earl :—
    Issue of the late Russell Charles Stanhope, b. 1866, d. 1945 : m. 1894, Augustine Madeleine Thompson, of U.S.A., who d. 1916 :—
Russell Charles, b. 1899: m. 1934, Jean Kennedy, of New York, and has issue living, Michelle, b. 1945,—Celeste, b. 1946.——Leicester de Macklot, b. 1901: m. 1930, Rose Mary Farnham, of New

York, and has issue living, Leicester, *b.* 1932,—Phillip, *b.* 1939,—Nina, *b.* 1931.——Violet Augustina *b.* 1912: *m.* 1936, Major Robert Duncan Rollo, Suffolk Regt. [see L. Rollo, colls.].   *Residence,—* Harrowsley, Heath Rd., Weybridge, Surrey.

PREDECESSORS.—[1] *Rt. Hon.* WILLIAM Stanhope (son of John Stanhope of Elvaston, Derbys; grandson of Sir John Stanhope of Elvaston, yr. half-brother of 1st Earl of Chesterfield, (infra). *b.* about 1683; Ambassador to Spain 1721-27 and 1729-30, Prin. Sec. of State 1738-42, Lord Pres. of Council 1742-45 and Lord Lt. of Ireland 1746-50; in consideration of his services for negotiating Treaty of Seville, *cr. Baron Harrington,* of Harrington, co. Northampton (peerage of GB) 1730, and *Viscount Petersham* and *Earl of Harrington* (peerage of GB) 1742: *m.* 1718, Anne, who *d.* 1719, da. and heir of Col. Edward Griffith; *d.* 1756; *s.* by his son [2] WILLIAM, 2nd Earl; *b.* 1719; Gen.: *m.* 1746, Lady Caroline FitzRoy, who *d.* 1784, da. of 2nd Duke of Grafton; *d.* 1799; *s.* by his son [3] CHARLES, GCH, 3rd Earl; *b.* 1753; Gen. and Col. 1st Life Guards; Gov. and Constable of Windsor Castle 1812-29: *m.* 1779, Jane, who *d.* 1824, da. and co-heir of Sir John Fleming, 1st Bt. of Brompton Park, Middlesex; *d.* 1829; *s.* by his el. son [4] CHARLES, 4th Earl; *b.* 1780; Col.: *m.* 1831, Maria (actress), who *d.* 1867, da. of Samuel Foote; *d.* 1851; *s.* by his brother [5] LEICESTER FITZGERALD CHARLES, *CB,* 5th Earl; *b.* 1784; Col.: *m.* 1831, Elizabeth Williams, who *d.* 1898, da. and heir of William Green, of Trelawney, Jamaica; *d.* 1862; *s.* by his son [6] SEYMOUR SYDNEY HYDE, 6th Earl; *b.* 1845; *d.* 1866; *s.* by his cousin [7] CHARLES WYNDHAM, 7th Earl; son of the Very Rev. the Hon. FitzRoy Henry Richard, 4th son of 3rd Earl; *b.* 1809: *m.* 1839, Elizabeth Still, who *d.* 1912 da. of Robert Lucas de Pearsall; *d.* 1881; *s.* by his son [8] CHARLES AUGUSTUS, 8th Earl, *b.* 1844: *m.* 1869, the Hon. Eva Elizabeth Carington, who *d.* 1919, da. of 2nd Baron Carrington; *d.* 1917; *s.* by his brother [9] DUDLEY HENRY EDEN, 9th Earl; *b.* 1859: *m.* 1883, Kathleen, who *d.* 1948, da. of J. Carter Wood, of Weybourne Hall, Weybourne, Norfolk; *d.* 1928 ; *s.* by his son [10] CHARLES JOSEPH LEICESTER, *MC,* 10th Earl, *b.* 1887; Bt. Maj. 15th Hussars: *m.* 1919, Margaret Trelawney (Susan), who *d.* 1952, (having *m.* 2ndly, 1934, Luke Theodore Lillingston of Ulverscroft, Leics., and 3rdly, 1949, Maj. Stephen C. Johnston), da. of Maj. H. H. D. Seaton, formerly Remount Ser., *d.* 1929; *s.* by his son [11] WILLIAM HENRY LEICESTER, 11th Earl, and present peer; also Viscount Stanhope of Mahon, Viscount Petersham, Baron Stanhope of Elvaston [see infra*₀*] and Baron Harrington.

•₀ [1] JAMES Stanhope, el. son of Hon. Alexander Stanhope, yst. son of 1st Earl of Chesterfield; *b.* 1673; Lt. Gen.; C.-in-C. of British Forces in Spain 1708-10 (effected capture of port of Mahon, Minorca 1708) and gained victories of Almenara and Saragossa 1710); Sec. of State 1714-17 and 1718-21, 1st Lord of the Treasury and Chancellor of the Exchequer 1717-18; *cr. Baron Stanhope of Elvaston,* co. Derby, and *Viscount Stanhope of Mahon,* in island of Minorca (peerage of GB) 1717, with remainder to the descendants in the male line of his kinsman, John Stanhope of Elvaston (ante), (whose son William was cr. Earl of Harrington); *cr. Earl Stanhope* 1718 (peerage of GB) with remainder to heirs male of his body: *m.* 1713, Lucy, who *d.* 1723, da. of Thomas Pitt of Blandford; *d.* 1721; *s.* by his el. son [2] PHILIP, 2nd Earl; *b.* 1714; FRS; *m.* 1745, Grisel, who *d.* 1811, da. of Charles Hamilton, Lord Binning, el. son of 6th Earl of Haddington; *d.* 1786; *s.* by his 2nd son [3] CHARLES, 3rd Earl, *b.* 1753, FRS; perfected process of stereotyping and experimented with fire-proof buildings, steam vessels and calculating machines: *m.* 1st, 1774, Lady Hester Pitt, who *d.* 1780, da. of 1st Earl of Chatham; 2ndly, 1781, Louisa, who *d.* 1829, da. and heir of the Hon. Henry Grenville [E. Temple]; *d.* 1816; *s.* by his el. son [4] PHILIP HENRY, 4th Earl, *b.* 1782; FRS; Keeper of the Records, Bermingham Tower, Dublin Castle 1805-55: *m.* 1803, the Hon. Catherine Lucy Smith, who *d.* 1843, da. of 1st Baron Carrington; *d.* 1855; *s.* by his el. son [5] PHILIP HENRY, 5th Earl; *b.* 1805, FRS; Under Sec. for Foreign Affairs 1834-35; historian; founder and 1st Chm. of National Portrait Gallery: *m.* 1834, Emily Harriet, who *d.* 1874, da. of Gen. Sir Edward Kerrison, GCH, KCB, 1st Bt.; *d.* 1875; *s.* by his el. son [6] ARTHUR PHILIP, 6th Earl; *b.* 1838; a Lord of the Treasury 1874-75: *m.* 1869, Evelyn Henrietta, who *d.* 1923, only da. of Richard Pennefather, of Knockeevan, co. Tipperary; *d.* 1905; *s.* by his el. son [7] JAMES RICHARD, KG, DSO, MC, PC, 7th Earl; *b.* 1880; Civil Lord of the Admiralty 1924-29, Parl. and Financial Sec. to the Admiralty and Civil Lord 1931, Parl. Under Sec. of State for War and Vice-Pres. of Army Council 1931-34, Parl. Under Sec. of State for Foreign Affairs 1934-36, 1st Commr. of Works 1936-37, Pres. of Board of Education 1937-38, 1st Lord of Admiralty 1938-39, and Lord Pres. of Council 1939-40; *s.* his kinsman, Edward Henry Scudamore-Stanhope, as 13th Earl of Chesterfield and 13th Baron Stanhope of Shelford 1952 (but did not apply for writ of summons): *m.* 1921, Lady Eileen Agatha Browne, who *d.* 1940, da. of 6th Marquess of Sligo; *d.* 1967, when the Earldoms of Chesterfield and Stanhope, and the Barony of Stanhope of Shelford became ext., and the Viscountcy of Stanhope of Mahon and the Barony of Stanhope of Elvaston devolved upon the 11th Earl of Harrington (ante), who thereupon became the representative of the Stanhope family.

HARRIS, BARON. (Harris.) [Baron U.K. 1815.]

GEORGE ST. VINCENT HARRIS, *CBE, MC,* 5th Baron; *b.* Sept. 3rd, 1889; *s.* 1932; ed. at Eton, and at Ch. Ch., Oxford (MA 1968); Capt. (ret.) Yeo., Chm. of Kent Police Authority 1945-64; a JP and Vice-Lt. for Kent 1944-72; a Gov. of King's Sch., Canterbury and a K.St.J.; Co. Commr. for Kent, St. John Ambulance Brig. 1940–45; 1914-18 War (wounded, despatches, MC); CBE (Civil) 1972: *m.* 1918, Dorothy Mary (has Order of Mercy, Ch. Comdt. ATS 1938-40), da. of the Rev. John William Crookes, formerly V. of Borden, Sittingbourne, and has issue.

𝔄rms.—Vert, on a chevron embattled erminois, between three hedgehogs or, as many bombs sable, fired proper; on a chief of augmentation, a representation of the gates and fortress of Seringapatam, the drawbridge let down, and the Union flag of Great Britain and Ireland hoisted above the standard of Tippoo Sahib, all proper. 𝔈rest,—On a mural crown or, a royal tiger passant guardant vert, striped or, spotted of the first, pierced in the breast with an arrow of the last, vulned gules, and charged on the forehead with the Persian character implying "Hyder," and crowned with an Eastern coronet both of the first. 𝔖upporters,—*Dexter,* a grenadier in uniform of 73rd Foot, supporting with the exterior hand a flag staff, thereon hoisted the Union Flag of

Great Britain and Ireland flying towards the dexter over the standard of Tippoo Sultan; and below the same tricoloured flag of the French Republic depressed and furled all proper; *sinister*, a Sepoy of the Madras Establishment of the East India Company, supporting with the exterior hand a flag staff thereon hoisted the flag of the said Company, flying over that of Tippoo Sultan towards the sinister; and below same the tricoloured flag of the French Republic as in the dexter.

Seat,—Belmont Park, Faversham, Kent.

SON LIVING.

Hon. GEORGE ROBERT JOHN, *b.* April 17th, 1920; ed. at Eton, and at Ch. Ch., Oxford; Capt. R.A. (ret.). *Residence,*—Huntingfield, Eastling, near Faversham, Kent.

COLLATERAL BRANCHES LIVING.

Grandchildren of the late Capt. the Hon. Arthur Ernest TEMPLE (who in 1900 assumed by Roy. licence the surname of Temple in lieu of his patronymic), 4th son of 2nd Baron :—
Issue of the late Arthur Reginald HARRIS-TEMPLE, *b.* 1874, *d.* 1928: *m.* 1898, Clare, who *d.* 1951, dau. of Allan Cameron, formerly Assist. Inspector-Gen. Roy. Irish Constabulary:—
Arthur Temple, *b.* 1904; ed. at Radley; 1939-45 War as Lt. R.A. (1939-45 star, Burma star): *m.* 1946, Thelma (CRAFTER), dau. of John Lester, of Springfield, Massachusetts, U.S.A.——Nilah Clare, *b.* 1899: *m.* 1921, Capt. Arthur Vivian Wood, Border Regt.

Grandson of the late Lieut.-Col. Thomas Harris, el. son of Thomas Inglis Parish Harris (infra):—
Issue of the late Maj. Thomas Guy Marriott Harris, OBE, *b.* 1882, *d.* 1955: *m.* 1912, Beryl, who *d.* 1960, dau. of Col. Frederick Alexander Wilson, formerly Indian Army:—
Derek Marshall, *b.* 1916; Maj. Duke of Wellington's Regt. (ret.): *m.* 1938, Laura Cecilia, da. of the late Maj. Edward Thomas William McCausland, Indian Army, and has issue living, Anthony, *b.* 1942,—Amanda, *b.* 1953.

Grandchildren of the late Thomas Inglis Parish Harris, el. son of the late Hon. Michael Thomas Harris, 2nd son of 1st Baron:—
Issue of the late Lieut.-Col. Thomas Harris, *b.* 1845, *d.* 1918: *m.* 1880, Lilias Annie, dau. of William Turner Cole :—
George Scott, *b.* 1883.——Lilias Olive, *b.* 1892. *Residence,*—31, Blenheim Rd., W.4.
Issue of the late Lieut.-Col. Charles Walter Harris, *b.* 1856, *d.* 1905: *m.* 1897, Edith, dau. of Capt. F. W. Crohan, formerly I.S.C. :—
Monica Fay, *b.* 1898. *Residence,*—

Grandchildren of the late George Lucian Taylor Harris (infra) :—
Issue of the late George Temple James Harris, *b.* 1876, *d.* 1929: *m.* 1910, Eva, who *d.* 1942; she *m.* 2ndly, 1933, Randle North Kenyon, who *d.* 1968 [B. Kenyon, colls.], da. of the late Lt.-Col. Henry Green Wilkinson [B. Bateman]:—
Ronald George Temple (Glebe Cottage, Buckerell, Honiton), *b.* 1911; formerly Capt. Air Transport Auxiliary: *m.* 1st, 1936 (m. diss. 1958), Simone Hogbin, of Folkestone; 2ndly, 1958, Beryl, el. da. of George Brown, of, 8, Holt Rd., Fakenham.——Antony John Temple, *OBE, b.* 1915; Cdr. RN; OBE (Mil) 1963: *m.* 1940, Doris, only child of F. D. Drake, of Winter Park, Florida, USA, and has issue living, Michael George Temple (The White House, Severn Stars Lane, Tamerton Foliot, Plymouth), *b.* 1941; Cdr. RN: *m.* 1970, Caroline Sandra Pietre Katrina, da. of Gp. Capt. Patrick George Chichester, OBE [see Chichester, Bt., colls.], and has issue living, Tamsin Caroline Temple *b.* 1971, Rebecca Eva Temple *b.* 1974,—John Frank Temple (193, White Cross, Abingdon), *b.* 1944: *m.* 1972, Sandra Dobson, da. of C. Stones, of Bishop Auckland. *Residence,*—Hawthorns, Wickham, Hants.——June Rosemary Temple (22, Winterbourne Close, Southover, Lewes), *b.* 1928.

Grandchildren of the late George Anstruther Harris, son of the Hon. Michael Thomas Harris (ante) :—
Issue of the late Hermann Gundert Harris, *b.* 1859, *d.* 1950 : *m.* 1895, Alice Uniacke, who *d.* 1927. dau. of the late William Uniacke Townsend, of Ardbrae, Bray [Coote, Bt., cr. 1621, colls.] :—
Eric Townsend (1550, Hayworth St., Hollywood, Cal., USA), *b.* 1902; 1914-18 War with Canadian Expeditionary Force: *m.* 1st, 1920 (m. diss. 1927), Marjorie Peggy, da. of the late Charles Vokes, of Winnipeg; 2ndly, 1946, Helen, da. of the late Howard Francis Bidwell, of Boston, Mass., USA, and has issue living, (by 1st m.) Joan Patricia, *b.* 1922,—Elizabeth Anne, *b.* 1926,—(by 2nd m.), Patricia Anne, *b.* 1950.——George Rutherford (5338, Patterson Av. S., Burnaby, 1, B.C., Canada), *b.* 1903: *m.* 1927, Olive Hall, of Lestock, Saskatchewan, Canada, and has issue living, Gerald Rutherford, *b.* 1928: *m.* 1955, Venetia Harris, and has issue living, Scott *b.* 1960, Shelley Ann *b.* 1957,—Alfred James, *b.* 1942; RCM Police: *m.* 1965, Alexandra Konopelka, and has issue living, Dwayne Stephen *b.* 1966, Suzanne Marie *b.* 1967,—Lucille Olive Iona *b.* 1930: *m.* 1951, William A. Spaidal, of 1044, Charland St., New Westminster, BC, Canada, and has issue living, Richard Arnold *b.* 1952, William Randle *b.* 1957, Robert Matthew *b.* 1968,—Joyce Violet, *b.* 1935: *m.* 1959, Donald Watkins, of 612, Vermouth Av., Cooksville, Ont., Canada.——Doris Emma: *m.* 1918, Albert O. Snook, of 409, Oak St., New Westminster, British Columbia, and has issue living, William Hermann (Point Roberts, Washington, USA), *b.* 1922; 1939-45 War with RCN: *m.* 1961, Phyllis Gurney,——Glen Townsend (15608, Buena Vista Av., White Rock, BC, Canada), *b.* 1924; 1939-45 War with RCN: *m.* 1950, Mae Miller, da. of Charles Pihan, of Langley, BC.

Granddaughter of the late Col. Charles John Birch Harris (ante) :—
Issue of the late Hugh Anstruther Harris, *b.* 1882, *d.* 1951: *m.* 1922, Ada Miller, who *d.* 1966:—
Nina Denise, *b.* 1924 : *m.* 1946, Donald R. Miller, and has issue living, Michael Jeffrey, *b.* 1947,—Gary Lee, *b.* 1949,—Jeffrey Hugh, *b.* 1952,—Wendy Louise, *b.* 1954,—Julie Diane *b.* 1962. *Residence,*—6655, S.W. Preslynn Drive, Portland, Oregon, USA.

Grandsons of the late George Anstruther Harris (ante) :—
Issue of the late Alfred Herschell Harris, *b.* 1863, *d.* 1953 : *m.* 1894, Amèlie, who *d.* 1955, dau. of the late E. B. Anstie :—
Robert Louis Anstruther, *b.* 1900; ed. at Sherborne, and at New Coll., Oxford; is an Actor. *Residence,*—18, Pitt St., W8. *Club,*—Garrick.——Christopher Money, *b.* 1907; ed. at Trin. Coll., Oxford (MA); a JP of Glos., and a Fellow of Soc. of Forestry; formerly Forest Research Officer, Uganda; 1939-45 War with RAFO: *m.* 1935, Ruth Cunliffe, da. of the late George Harwood, MP, of Bolton, and has issue living, Robert Julian Brownlow, *b.* 1943: *m.* 1971, Lady Camilla Dorothy Godolphin Osborne, da. of the 11th Duke of Leeds, and has issue living, Emily Kate Godolphin *b.* 1972,—Phoebe Georgina *b.* 1950: *m.* 1970, Guy Rudolph Bentinck, of The Country Elephant, Painswick, Glos. *Residence,*—Swerford Park, Oxon. *Club,*—Travellers'.

PREDECESSORS.—[1] *Sir* GEORGE Harris, *G.C.B.*, a Gen. in the Army and Col. 73rd Regt. was Com. in Ch. at siege and capture of Seringapatam and conquest of Mysore 1799; cr. *Baron Harris*, of Seringapatam and Mysore, E. Indies, and of Belmont, co. Kent (peerage of United Kingdom) 1815; *d.* 1829; *s.* by his son [2] WILLIAM GEORGE, *K.C.H.*, *C.B.*, 2nd Baron, a Lt.-Gen. in the Army and Col. 73rd Foot; *d.* 1845; *s.* by his son [3] GEORGE FRANCIS ROBERT, *G.C.S.I.*, 3rd Baron; *b.* 1810; was Gov. of Trinidad 1846-54, and of Madras 1854-9, a Lord in Waiting to H.M. Queen Victoria 1860-3, and Chamberlain to Princess of Wales 1863-71; *m.* 1850, Sarah, who *d.* 1853, dau. of the Ven. George Cummins, Archdeacon of Trinidad; *d.* 1872 *s.* by his son [4] GEORGE ROBERT CANNING, *G.C.S.I.*, *G.C.I.E.*, *C.B.*, 4th Baron, *b.* 1852;

Under-Sec. for India 1885-6, Under-Sec. for War 1886-9, Gov. of Bombay 1890-95, a Lord-in-Waiting to Queen Victoria 1895-1900, Vice-Lieut. of Kent 1914-15; bore Queen Consort's Scepter with Dove at Coronation of King Edward VII.: *m.* 1874, the Hon. Lucy Ada Jervis, *C.I.*, who *d* 1930, da. of 3rd Viscount St. Vincent; *d.* 1932; *s.* by his son [5] GEORGE ST. VINCENT, *CBE, MC,* 5th Baron and present peer.

HARRIS OF GREENWICH, BARON. (Harris.) [Life Baron 1974.]

JOHN HENRY HARRIS, son of Alfred George Harris; *b.* April 5th, 1930; ed. at Pinner Gram. Sch., Middx.; Personal Assist. to Leader of the Opposition 1959; Dir. of Publicity, Labour Party 1962-64, Special Assist. to Foreign Sec. 1964-66, to Home Sec. 1966-67, and to Chancellor of the Exchequer 1967-70, and a Min. of State, Home Office since 1974; a Political Correspondent with *The Economist* 1970-74; *cr.* Baron Harris of Greenwich, of Greenwich in Greater London (Life Baron) 1974: *m.* 1952, Patricia Margaret, da. of George Neuby Alstrom, and has issue.

Address,—c/o House of Lords, SW1.   *Club,*—Reform.

SON LIVING.

Hon. Francis Oliver Alstrom, *b.* 1961.

DAUGHTER LIVING.

Hon. Deborah Jane Alstrom, *b.* 1958.

HARROWBY, EARL OF. (Ryder.) [Earl U.K. 1809.]

The promise made to the ashes of my forefathers has been kept.

DUDLEY RYDER, 6th Earl; *b.* Oct. 11th, 1892; *s.* 1956; ed. at Eton and at Ch. Ch., Oxford (BA, Hon D Litt); Maj. R.A. (T.A.); is a D.L. and J.P. for Staffordshire, and patron of five livings; Author of "Geography of Everyday Things," and "England at Worship"; European War 1914-18 (wounded), European War 1939-45; Assist. Private Sec. (unpaid) to Sec. of State for the Colonies 1919-20 and Parliamentary Private Sec. to Sec. of State for Air 1922-23; was an Alderman of London County Council 1932-37 and a Member 1937-40; Col. Comdt. Staffordshire Army Cadet Force 1946-50; a Member of Commn. on Historical Manuscripts 1935-66; MP for Salop, Shrewsbury Div. (*C*) 1922-23, and 1924-29: *m.* 1922, Lady Helena Blanche Coventry, who *d.* 1974, da. of the late George William, Viscount Deerhurst [see E. Coventry], and has issue.

Arms,—Azure, three crescents or, each charged with an ermine spot sable. Crest,—Out of a mural coronet a dragon's head argent, charged on the neck with an ermine spot sable. Supporters,—Two griffins, wings elevated, argent, each charged on the shoulder with an ermine spot sable, gorged with a plain collar azure, thereon three crescents or, and affixed thereto a chain reflexed over the back, of the last.

Seat,—Sandon Hall, Stafford.   *Club,*—Travellers'.

SONS LIVING.

DUDLEY DANVERS GRANVILLE COUTTS, *TD, (Viscount Sandon), b.* Dec. 20th, 1922; ed. at Eton; Dep. Chm. Coutts & Co. since 1970, and Nat. Westminster Bank since 1971; a Dir. of UK Provident Instn. (Dep. Chm. 1956-64), and of Olympia Gp. (Chm. 1971-73); a member of Lord Chancellor's Advisory Investment Cttees. for Court of Protection, and cttee. for Public Trustee; Chm. Inst. of Psychiatry 1965-73, and of Bethlem Roy. & Maudsley (Postgraduate Teaching) Hosps. 1965-73; Dep. Chm. Teaching Hosps. Assocn., London Postgraduate Cttee. 1968-69; Pres. Staffs. Soc. 1957-59; Chm. Cttee. for Standardization and Control of Biological Substances since 1973; a Member of Kensington Borough Council 1950-65, and of Kensington and Chelsea Borough Council 1965-71; TA (City of London) Regt RA 1947-64 (Lt.-Col. comdg. 1962-64); Pres. Wolverhampton S.-W. Conservative Assocn. 1959-68, Member Exec. Cttee. London Area. Conservative Assocn. 1949-50. a Member of Court of Assists., Goldsmiths' Co.; 1939-45 War in N.-W. Europe (wounded), India, and Java (Political Officer); *m.* 1949, Jeannette Rosalthé, da. of the late Capt. Peter Johnston-Saint, and has issue.

SON LIVING,—*Hon.* Dudley Adrian Conroy, *b.* March, 18th, 1951.
DAUGHTER LIVING,—*Hon.* Rosalthé Frances, *b.* 1954.
Residences,—5, Tregunter Rd., SW10; Sandon Hall, Stafford, Burnt Norton, Campden, Glos.

Hon. John Stuart Terrick Dudley, *b.* 1924; ed. at Eton; formerly Warrant Officer Pilot, R.A.F., European War 1942-45 (wounded): *m.* 1946, Dorothy Ethel, dau. of J. T. Swallow, of Mansfield, and has issue living, John Robert, *b.* 1947: *m.* 1970, Rosemary Rita Tester, and has issue living, Claire Jane *b.* 1970, Sara Helena Louise *b.* 1973,—David Anthony, *b.* 1951: *m.* 1973, Judith Sinclair, of Sydney, NSW. *Residence,*—Sandon Hall, Stafford.

DAUGHTER LIVING.

Lady Frances Virginia Susan, *b.* 1926; ed. at St. Hugh's Coll., Oxford: *m.* 1949, Frank Ernest Berendt, and has issue living, Anthony Peregrine Dudley, *b.* 1957,—Susan Venetia, *b.* 1952. *Residence,*—8, Stormont Road, N.6.

COLLATERAL BRANCHES LIVING.

Issue of the late Hon. Archibald Dudley Ryder, 2nd son of 4th Earl, *b.* 1867, *d.* 1950 ; *m.* 1898, Eleanor Frederica, who *d.* 1958, el. dau. of Edward R. Fisher-Rowe [B. Ravensworth] :—
Archibald Stuart Dudley (Briarsfield, Hotfield Common, Ashford, Kent), *b.* 1899; Com. (ret.) RN; was a Member of Naval Mission to Turkey 1941-43, Harbour Master and Marine Court Magistrate, Hongkong 1945-47, and acting British Consul, Formosa, China 1947-48; 1915-19 War; present at battle of Jutland, 1939-45 War in Middle East, India, and Ceylon (despatches): *m.* 1936, Viola Maria,

da. of Jano Kántor, of Budapest, Hungary.——Richard Dudley, *OBE* (Lion House, W. Milton, Dorset), *b*. 1904; ed. at Eton; OBE (Civil) 1947: *m*. 1945, Pamela Gertrude, da. of A. H. Ford, and has issue living, Victoria, *b*. 1948.——Douglas Dudley (PO Rocky Ridge, nr. Port Elizabeth, Cape Province), *b*. 1905; is a JP: *m*. 1931, Sheilah Moore, da. of S. H. Gillespie, of Carrick Cradock, S. Africa, and has issue living, Hugh Donald Dudley (44, Princes Rd., Claremont, Cape Town), *b*. 1936: *m*. 1st, 1963 (m. diss. 1969), Pamela Joan, da. of S. O. Butow, of East London, Cape; 2ndly, 1969, Maria, da. of Max Pitterman, of Bielefeld, W. Germany, and has issue living, (by 2nd m.), Axel Dudley *b*. 1970, Douglas Dudley *b*. 1971,—Atholl Graham Dudley (11, Ralston Rd., Fernglen, Port Elizabeth, Cape, S. Africa), *b*. 1938: *m*. 1964, Iréne, da. of J. J. van Duuren, of Port Elizabeth, Cape Province, and has issue living, Gary Dudley *b*. 1966, Peter Dudley *b*. 1968.——Atholl Dudley (1340, Ridgewood Drive, Sarnia, Ontario, Canada), *b*. 1909: *m*. 1940, Kathleen, yst. da. of the late Robert Pearson, of London, Ontario, and has issue living, Peter Douglas Dudley, *b*. 1952.——Peter Hugh Dudley, *MBE*, *b*. 1913; Hon. Lt.-Col. late R. Armoured Corps; sometime in Political Intell. Dept., Foreign Office; MBE (Civil) 1944: *m*. 1940, Susannah Sarah, da. of the late Geoffrey Francis Bowes-Lyon [see E. Strathmore, colls.], and has issue living, Adrian Dudley, *b*. 1941,—Bruce Dudley (Crix, Hatfield Peverel, Essex), *b*. 1942: *m*. 1969, Charlotte Olivia, da. of Mark Frederic Strutt, MC, TD [see B. Rayleigh, colls.] and has issue living, Mark Reedham Dudley, *b*. 1970, Oliver Hugh Dudley, *b*. 1974,—Sandra Anne *b*. 1954. *Residence*,—The Spanish House, Wardija, Malta, GC.——Sarah, *b*. 1908; a JP for Northumberland; Chm. of Berwick upon Tweed Conservative Constituency Assocn. 1966-68: *m*. 1936, Group-Capt. Cuthbert John Collingwood, OBE, DFC, RAF, and has issue living, Susan Anne *b*. 1939: *m*. 1961, Ewen Samuel Murdoch Cameron of Auchengillan, Blanefield, Stirlingshire, and has issue living, Angus Edward *b*. 1965, Katherine Anne *b*. 1963. *Residence*,—Lilburn Tower, Alnwick, Northumberland.

Grandchildren of the late Hon. Edward Alan Dudley Ryder (infra) :—

Issue of the late Major Henry Dudley Ryder, M.C., *b*. 1894; *d*. 1958: *m*. 1918, Dorothy Marion (12, Cranmer Court, Sloane Av., SW3), da. of Sidney Streatfeild:—
Edward Dorrien Dudley, *b*. 1924 : *m*. 1948, Valerie Nina, only dau. of the late J. B. Soames, **of Kenya** and has issue living, Nicholas Henry Dudley, *b*. 1960,—Jennifer Davina, *b*. 1949: *m*. 1971, Charles Berkeley Johnston Dingwall [see V. Galway, colls.],—Vanessa, *b*. 1951. *Residence*,—Yew Tree Hall, Coleman's Hatch, Sussex.——Maud Marion, *b*. 1919. *Residence*,—The Splash, Coleman's Hatch, Sussex.——Dorothy Joan, *b*. 1921: *m*. 1951, Alan Williams Horton, and has issue living, James McAfee *b*. 1954,—Edward Alan Douglas, *b*. 1957,—Carol Ryder, *b*. 1952. *Residence*,—Lyme, New Hampshire, USA.

Issue of the late Hon. Edward Alan Dudley Ryder, 3rd son of 4th Earl, *b*. 1866, *d*. 1949 : *m*. 1893, Lady (Mary) Maud Anson, *O.B.E.*, who *d*. 1961, 3rd dau. of 2nd Earl of Lichfield :—

Katharine (*Hon. Mrs. Reginald Coke*), *b*. 1899 : *m*. 1924, Capt. the Hon. Reginald Coke, DSO, who *d*. 1969 [see E. Leicester]. *Residence*, 14, Chesham Place, SW1.

Issue of the late Major the Hon. Robert Nathaniel Dudley Ryder, 4th son of 4th Earl, *b*. 1882, *d*. (killed in action during European War) 1917 : *m*. 1908, Beryl [who *d*. 1970, having *m*. 2ndly, 1945, Lt.-Col. William Baring Du Pre, DL, JP, who *d*. 1946], dau. of Charles Angas, of Lindsay Park, Angaston, S. Australia :—
Rosemary Beryl (*Lady Loehnis*) (twin), *b*. 1909: *m*. 1929, Com. Sir Clive Loehnis, K.C.M.G., R.N. (ret.), and has issue living, Anthony David (8, St. Peter's Sq., W6), *b*. 1936: *m*. 1965, Jennifer Forsyth, da. of the late Sir Donald Forsyth Anderson [see Llewellyn Bt., *cr*. 1922], and has issue living, Dominic Anthony *b*. 1967, Alexander Garrett *b*. 1969, Barnaby David *b*. 1971,—Serena Jane (*Baroness Remnant*) (Bear Place, Hare Hatch, Reading, Berks.), *b*. 1932: *m*. 1953, the 3rd Baron Remnant. *Residence*,—12, Eaton Pl., SW1.

Grandchildren of the late Dudley Henry Ryder, son of the late Hon. Granville Dudley Ryder, M.P., 2nd son of 1st Earl :—

Issue of the late Capt. Cyril John Ryder, *b*. 1863, *d*. 1907: *m*. 1897, Lady Isobel Frances Ulrica Iris Douglas-Hamilton, who *d*. 1941, sister of 13th Duke of Hamilton and Brandon :—
Dudley Claud Douglas, *b*. 1901 ; ed. at Sherborne. and at Pembroke Coll., Camb. (B.A. 1923) ; is Major 5th Batn. Dorset Regt. (T.A.), and a J.P. for Dorset ; was a Forest Officer 1925-31 : *m*. 1st, 1927, Nancy Edith (from whom he obtained a divorce 1938), dau. of E. M. Baker, late Federated Malay States Civil Ser. ; 2ndly, 1938, Vera Mary, dau. of Sir Herbert Frederick Cook, 3rd Bt., and has issue living, (by 1st m.) James Calcraft Dudley, (Rempstone Hall, Corfe Castle, Dorset), *b*. 1934; late 2nd Lt. King's Own Regt.: *m*. 1966, Sarah Victoria Bircham, and has issue living, Lara Caroline *b*. 1968, Melonie Isobel *b*. 1970, Emma Katherine *b*. 1974,—Benjamin Guy Dudley (twin) (Vitower Farm, Corfe Castle, Dorset), *b*. 1934: *m*. 1960, Philippa Cunningham, and has issue living, Douglas Alan Dudley *b*. 1963, Guy *b*. 1968, Vanessa Frances *b*. 1965,—Gabriel Nancy, *b*. 1928: *m*. 1958, Egerton James Nevill Tobias Coghill [see Coghill, Bt.],—Jenifer Cherry, *b*. 1929: *m*. 1953, Jeremy Charles Browne, of Higher Houghton, Blandford, Dorset, and has issue living, Simon Jeremy *b*. 1957, Katherine Richenda *b*. 1956, Sarah Caroline *b*. 1960, Emily Charlotte *b*. 1965,—Jacqueline Iris (Jays, Hammer Lane, Bramshot, Hindhead) *b*. 1930: *m*. 1957, Thomas Ralph Winser, from whom she obtained a div. 1969, and has issue living, Hugh James *b*. 1958, Polly Joan *b*. 1959, Tamsin Jacqueline *b*. 1962,—(by 2nd m.) Richard Hood Jack Dudley, *b*. 1940; ed. at Camb. Univ. (MA) 1963. *Residence*,—Bushey House, Rempstone, Corfe Castle, Dorset.——Iris Katherine (64, Alumhurst Rd., Westbourne, Bournemouth), *b*. 1899.

Grandson of the late William Henry Ryder, 3rd son of the late Dudley Henry Ryder (ante):—

Issue of the late Cdr. Frederick Granville Dudley Ryder, RNVR, *b*. 1905, *d*. 1970: *m*. 1st, 1929, Gillian Eleanor (who obtained a divorce 1934), da. of C. H. B. Quennell; 2ndly, 1939, Muriel Eleanor, who *d*. 1975, da. of William S. Corby, of Wash., USA:—
(By 1st m.) Richard Peter Guy Dudley (Hardway House, 3411, Poinciana Av., Miami, Florida, USA), *b*. (Dec.) 1929: *m*. 1955, Angela Jiovanna, da. of Morris M. Melotti, of Johnstown, Pa., USA, and has issue living, Christopher Frederick Dudley, *b*. 1959,—Mark Campbell Dudley, *b*. 1963.

Granddaughters of the late Rev. Algernon Charles Dudley Ryder (infra):—

Issue of the late Major Algernon Frederick Roland Dudley Ryder, M.C., *b*. 1891, *d*. 1957: *m*. 1921, Olive, who *d*. 1973, da. of John Baillie, of Montreal:—
Dione Frances, *b*. 1924: *m*. 1954, (Claud Andrew) James Graham-Watson, and has issue living, Frederick Paul, *b*. 1957,—Iona Mary, *b*. 1955,—Sanda Susan, *b*. 1959. *Residence*,—Falconers, Shipley, Horsham, Sussex.——Xanthe Veronica, *b*. 1926 : *m*. 1949, Michael Dalglish, and has issue living, James, *b*. 1950,—Charles, *b*. 1953,—Clare, *b*. 1956. *Residence*,—142, Priory Lane, Roehampton, S.W.15.——Charis Elizabeth, *b*. 1930.

Grandchildren of the late Hon. Frederick Dudley Ryder, 3rd son of 1st Earl:—

Issue of the late Rev. Algernon Charles Dudley Ryder, *b*. 1847, *d*. 1943 : *m*. 1889, Constance Eugenia, who *d*. 1915, dau. of the late Rowland Smith, of Duffield Hall, Derby, and 131, Queen's Gate, S.W.:—
Hugh Granville Leveson Dudley, *T.D.*, *b*. 1900 ; ed. at Eton ; formerly Lieut.-Col. R.A. (T.A.); was Assist. Mil. Attaché, British Embassy, Greece 1943-45 ; European War 1939-45 in Middle East (despatches) : *m*. 1st, 1926, Diana Vivian, who *d*. 1951, da. of Sir Paul Augustine Makins, 2nd Bt.; 2ndly, 1955, Patricia Geraldine, dau. of the late Gerald Macleay Browne, O.B.E., and widow of Major (Basil Arthur) John Peto, King's Dragoon Gds. [see Peto, Bt., colls. *cr*. 1927], and has issue living, (by 1st m.) Jane Christine, *b*. 1927: *m*. 1955, Denzil Walter Hugh Ffennell, of Martyr Worthy Pl., Winchester, and has issue living, Simon *b*. 1956, Diana Elizabeth *b*. 1963. *Residence*,—47, Burton Court, Franklins Row, SW3. *Clubs*,—Pratt's, Army and Navy.——Mary Constance Eugenia

(Nuneham Courtenay, Oxford), *b.* 1890: *m.* 1921; the Rev. Maurice Rooke Kingsford, BLitt, FRHistS, who *d.* 1973, and has issue living, Eugenia Mary Dorothy, *b.* 1922; formerly in ATS,—Lucy Ruth Cecily, *b.* 1927: *m.* 1959, Peter Vandermin, of 32, Kensington Mansions, Trebovir Rd, SW5.——Philippa Constance Marian, *b.* 1895; is a JP.   *Residence,*—Ghyls Plat, Fairwarp, Uckfield, Sussex.——Joan Florence Helena, *b.* 1897: *m.* 1928, the Rt. Rev. Bertram Pollock, KCVO, DD, who *d.* 1943, Lord Bishop of Norwich 1910-42 [see Pollock, Bt., colls.]. *Residences,*—Bickers End, Wenbaston, Suffolk; Balneath Manor, South Chailey, Sussex.——Dorothy Evelyn Frances (*Lady Ross*), *b.* (twin) 1900: *m.* 1921, Lieut.-Col. Sir Ronal Deane Ross, MC, 2nd Bt., who *d.* 1958, when the title became ext.   *Residences,*—Dunmoyle, Omagh, co. Tyrone; 49, Morpeth Mansions, SW1.

Granddaughters of the late Lieut.-Col. Spencer Charles Dudley Ryder, B.S.C., **son of the late Right Rev. the Hon. Henry Ryder, Bishop of Lichfield and Coventry, 3rd son of 1st Baron Harrowby:—**
Issue of the late Lieut.-Col. Wilfred Ironside Ryder, *b.* 1866, *d.* 1948: *m.* 1901, Tempé Rosa Ridehalgh, who *d.* 1942, dau. of the late Maj.-Gen. James Edmund Bacon Parsons. of The Gables, Southbourne-on-Sea. Hants :—
Joan Tempé, *b.* 1902: *m.* 1945, Francis Edward Maitland, who *d.* 1963.   *Residence,*—Pullens End, Headington Hill, Oxford.——Margery Julia, *b.* 1904: *m.* 1934 (marriage annulled 1948), Capt. Charles Oliver Meeres, late RA. *Residence,*—Boult's Lodge, Boult's Lane, Marston, Oxford.

Grandchildren of the late Col. Charles Henry Dudley Ryder, C.B., C.I.E., D.S.O. **(infra) :—**
Issue of the late Major Lisle Charles Dudley Ryder, Roy. Norfolk Regt., *b.* 1902, *d.* (killed in action in France) 1940: *m.* 1938, Enid Helen Constance (Butlers, Broomfield, Essex), only child of the late Maj. Robert Ralston-Patrick, of Trearne, Ayrshire:—
Ralston Patrick Dudley, *b.* 1939; ed. at Harrow.   *Residence,*—Butlers, Broomfield, Essex.

Issue of the late Major Ernle Terrick Dudley Ryder, Indian Army, *b.* 1906, *d.* (killed in action off Sumatra) 1942: *m.* 1936, Daphne Joan Pillans, only child of the late John Greig, of Rosewood, Ascot, Berks:—
Elizabeth Jean *b.* 1938: *m.* 1959, James John Vernon, MA, of Hordle House, Milford-on-Sea, Lymington, Hants. SO4 0NW, and has issue living, James Michael, *b.* 1960,—Peter John, *b.* 1963,—William Ernle Hardy, *b.* 1965,—Julia Elizabeth, *b.* 1961.——Anthea Daphne, *b.* 1940.

Grandchildren of the late Lieut.-Col.Spencer Charles Dudley Ryder, B.S.C₄(ante):—
Issue of the late Col. Charles Henry Dudley Ryder, C.B., C.I.E., D.S.O., *b.* 1868, *d.* 1945: *m.* 1892, Ida Josephine, who *d.* 1948, el. dau. of the late Lieut.-Col. Edward Evans Grigg, I.S.C., of Orchard Court, Stevenage, Herts:—
Robert Edward Dudley, V.C., *b.* 1908; ed. at Cheltenham Coll.; Capt. R.N. (retired); British Graham Land Expedition 1934 and 1935-7 (Polar medal with clasp), European War 1939-45, commanded Naval Forces in attack on St. Nazaire (despatches four times, V.C., Chevalier of Legion of Honour, Croix de Guerre with palm); MP for Merton and Morden (*U*) 1950-55: *m.* 1941 (Constance) Hilaré Myfanwy, da. of the Rev. Lumley Cecil Green-Wilkinson [Edwards, Bt., cr. 1907], and has issue living, Lisle Robert Dudley, *b.* 1943,—Susan Myfanwy Prudence, *b.* 1944: *m.* 1965, Martin Graves Bates, of Hill Farm, Elmsett, Ipswich [see Bates, Bt., colls., cr. 1880].   *Residence,*—The Old Rectory, Wolferton, King's Lynn.——Violet Constance, *b.* 1898: *m.* 1931, Lt.-Col. Geoffrey Walter Lawson, formerly Somerset LI, and has issue living, Julian Richard, *b.* 1933.   *Residence,*—Knap Cottage, Ramsbury, Wilts.

PREDECESSORS.—Sir Dudley Ryder, Knt. (**great grandson of Robert Ryder, of Wisbech**) Lord Ch. Justice of the King's Bench 1754-6, was offered a peerage by the King on May 24th 1756, but *d.* the following day, before the patent was completed; *s.* by his son [1] NATHANIEL, M.P.for Tiverton; cr. *Baron Harrowby,* of Harrowby, co. Lincoln (peerage of Great Britain) 1776; *d.* 1803; *s.* by his son [2] DUDLEY, P.C., 2nd Baron; *b.* 1762; cr. *Viscount Sandon* and *Earl of Harrowby* (peerage of United Kingdom) 1809; was successively Sec. of State for Foreign Affairs and Lord Pres. of the Council; *d.* 1847; *s.* by his son [3] DUDLEY, K.G., D.C.L., 2nd Earl; *b.* 1798; sat as M.P. for Tiverton (*C*) 1819-31, and for Liverpool 1831-47, was Chancellor of Duchy of Lancaster 1854-5, and Lord Privy Seal 1855-7: *m.* 1823, Lady Frances Stuart, dau. of 1st Marquess of Bute; *d.* 1882; *s.* by his son [4] DUDLEY FRANCIS STUART. P.C., 3rd Earl, *b.* 1831 ; M.P. for Lichfield (*C*) 1856-9,and for Liverpool 1868-82 ; was Vice-Pres. of Committee of Council on Education 1874-5, Pres. of Board of Trade 1878-80, and Lord Privy Seal 1885-6: *m.* 1861, Lady Mary Frances Cecil, who *d.* 1917, dau. of 2nd Marquess of Exeter; *d.* 1900: *s.* by his brother [5] HENRY DUDLEY, 4th Earl, *b.* 1836: *m.* 1859, Susan Juliana Maria Hamilton, who *d.* 1913, dau. of the late Villiers Dent, of Barton Court, Lymington; *d.* 1900; *s.* by his el. son [6] JOHN HERBERT DUDLEY, 5th Earl; *b.* 1864; Lord High Steward of Newcastle under Lyme; Lord-Lieut. of Staffordshire 1927-48; M.P. for Gravesend(*C*) 1898-1900: *m.* 1887, the Hon. Dame Mabel Smith, D.B.E., who *d.* 1956, dau. of Emily, Viscountess Hambleden; *d.* 1956; *s.* by his son [7] DUDLEY, 6th Earl and present peer; also Viscount Sandon and Baron Harrowby.

Hartington, Marquess of, son of Duke of Devonshire.

Hartismere, Baron, title of Baron Henniker on Roll of H. L.

HARTWELL, BARON. (Berry.) [Life Baron 1968.]

(WILLIAM) MICHAEL BERRY, *MBE, TD,* 2nd son of 1st Viscount Camrose; *b.* May 18th, 1911; *h.p.* to Viscountcy of Camrose; ed. at Eton, and Ch. Ch. Oxford (MA); Chm. and Editor-in-Ch. of *The Daily Telegraph* and *Sunday Telegraph*; 2nd Lt. 11th (City of London Yeo.) Light Anti-Aircraft Regt. RA (TA) 1938, Maj. 1940, Lt.-Col. Gen. Staff 1944; 1939-45 War (despatches twice, MBE); *cr.* MBE (Mil) 1945, and *Baron Hartwell,* of Peterborough Court, City of London (Life Baron) 1968: *m.* 1936, Lady Pamela Margaret Elizabeth Smith, yr. da. of 1st Earl of Birkenhead, and has issue.

Arms,—Argent, three bars gules, over all a pile ermine.   *Crest,*—A griffin sejant reguardant sable, collared or. *Supporters,*—*Dexter,* a stag and *Sinister* a wolf proper, both collared or, and standing on a compartment with a well between paving to the dexter and grass to the sinister proper.
Residences,—Oving House, Whitchurch, nr. Aylesbury; 18, Cowley St., SW1. *Clubs,*—White's, Beefsteak, Royal Yacht Squadron.

SONS LIVING.
Hon. Adrian Michael (11, Cottesmore Gdns., W8), *b.* 1937; ed. at Eton, and Ch. Ch., Oxford: *m.* 1967, Marina Beatrice, da. of Cyrus Sulzberger, of 2 ter, Avenue de Ségur, Paris, and has issue living, Jonathan William, *b.* 1970,—Jessica Margaret, *b.* 1968.
Hon. Nicholas William, *b.* 1942; ed. at Eton, and Ch. Ch., Oxford.

DAUGHTERS LIVING.
Hon. Harriet Mary Margaret, *b.* 1944.
Hon. Eleanor Agnes, *b.* 1950.

HARVEY OF PRESTBURY, BARON. (Harvey.) [Life Baron 1971.]

ARTHUR VERE HARVEY, *CBE*, son of the late Arthur William Harvey, of Kessingland, Suffolk; *b.* Jan. 31st, 1906; ed. at Framlingham Coll.; Air Commodore RAuxAF; Dir. of Far East Aviation Co. Ltd., and Far East Flying Training Sch. Ltd., Hong Kong 1930-35; Adviser to S. Chinese Air Forces with hon. rank of Maj.-Gen. 1932-35; 1939-45 War, command 615 Co. of Surrey Sqdn. in France (despatches twice); a Member of Board of CIBA-GEIGY AG; a Dir. of Philips Electronic and Assoc. Industries Ltd., Mullard Ltd., and Mullard Overseas Ltd., and Tradewinds Airways Ltd., Vice-Pres. of British Air Line Pilots Assocn.; MP for Macclesfield (*C*) 1945-71; Hon. Freeman of Macclesfield and Congleton; Cdr. Order of Orange Nassau of the Netherlands; cr. CBE (Mil) 1942, Knt. 1957, and *Baron Harvey of Prestbury*, of Prestbury, co. Palatine of Chester (Life Baron) 1971: *m.* 1st, 1940 (m. diss. 1954), Jacqueline Anne, only da. of W. H. Dunnett; 2ndly, 1955, Hilary Charmian, da. of the late David Charles, and formerly wife of Lt.-Col. Brian Robertson Williams, and has issue by 1st m.

Arms,—Per pale argent and sable, a chevron counterchanged between two lions passant respectant, the dexter azure, the sinister or, in chief a tun counterchanged, in base on a chief vert a garb between two fleurs de lys or. **Crest,**—A rounded gules, charged with a rounded argent, thereon a rounded azure, charged with two fleurs de lys in fess or. **Supporters,**—On either side a rabbit argent, charged on the shoulder with a fleur de lys vert.

Residence,—Villa Wardija, Malta. *Clubs,*—Buck's, Royal Yacht Squadron.

SONS LIVING (*By 1st m.*)
Hon. Philip William Vere, *b.* 1942.
Hon. Guy Alan Vere, *b.* 1947.

HARVEY OF TASBURGH, BARON. (Harvey.) [Baron U.K. 1954, Bt. U.K. 1868.

PETER CHARLES OLIVER HARVEY, 2nd Baron and 5th Baronet; *b.* Jan. 28th, 1921; *s.* 1968; ed. at Eton and Trin. Coll., Camb.; 1939-45 War with RA in N. Africa and Italy: *m.* 1957, Penelope Anne, yr. da. of the late Lt.-Col. Sir William Vivian Makins, 3rd Bt., and has issue.

Arms,—Erminois, on a chief indented gules between two crescents argent, a representation of the gold medal presented to Sir Robert John Harvey, by command of HRH the Prince Regent, for his services at the battle of Orthes, pendent from a riband gules, fimbriated azure, beneath it the word "*Orthes*"; a canton ermine charged with a representation of the insignia of a Knight of the Royal Portuguese order of the Tower and Sword, pendent from a riband azure. **Crest,**—Out of a mural crown or, above a dexter cubit arm erect, proper, a crescent argent between two branches of laurel also proper. **Supporters,**—*Dexter,* a lion or.; *sinister,* a cock or.

Residence,—2, Halsey St., SW3. *Club,*—Brooks's.

DAUGHTERS LIVING.
Hon. Juliet Annora Christine, *b.* 1958.
Hon. Miranda Jean, *b.* 1960.

BROTHER LIVING.
Hon. JOHN WYNN, *b.* Nov. 4th, 1923; ed. at Eton, at Westminster, and at Camb. Univ.; 1941-45 War with King's Roy. Rifle Corps and Essex Regt.: *m.* 1950, Elena Maria-Teresa, dau. of the late Giambattista, Marchese Curtopassi, and has issue living, Charles John Giuseppe, *b.* 1951,—Robert Lambart, *b.* 1953,—Antonella Sophia Gabrielle Maria, *b.* 1957. *Residence,*—55, Addison Rd., W.14.

DAUGHTER LIVING OF THIRD BARONET.
Dorothy (c/o Midland Bank, 22, Victoria St., SW1), b. 1892.

WIDOW LIVING OF THIRD BARONET.
LYDIA (Lady Harvey), el. dau. of Alexis Konshine, of Petrograd, Russia: m. 1921, as his second wife,
Sir Charles Robert Lambart Edward Harvey, 3rd Bt., who d. 1954. Address,—

PREDECESSORS.—[1] ROBERT JOHN Harvey, el. son of the late Gen. Sir Robert John Harvey
K.O.B., of Mousehold House, Norwich : b. 1817; M.P. for Thetford 1865-8 ; cr. a Baronet 1868:
m. 1845, Lady Henrietta Augusta Lambart, who d. 1874, sister of 8th Earl of Cavan ; d. 1870;
s. by his son [2] CHARLES, 2nd Bt.; b. 1849; Col. 4th Batn. Norfolk Regt. and a J.P.: m. 1st,
1870, Jane Ann, who d. 1891, dau. of Benjamin Green, of Newcastle; 2ndly, 1893, Mary Anne
Edith, who d. 1929, dau. of G. F. Cooke, of Holmewood, Norwich; d. 1928 ; s. by his son [3] CHARLES
ROBERT LAMBART EDWARD, 3rd Bt.; b. 1871: m. 1st, 1891, Jessie, who d. 1913, da. of the late
E. Turnbull, of Smedley, Lancashire; 2ndly, 1921, Lydia, dau. of Alexis Konshine, of Petrograd,
Russia; d. 1954; s. by his half-brother [4] OLIVER CHARLES, GCMG, GCVO, CB, 4th Bt., b. 1893;
cr. Baron Harvey of Tasburgh, of Tasburgh, co. Norfolk (peerage of UK) 1954; Dep. Under-Sec. of
State, Foreign Office 1946-48; Ambassador to France 1948-54: m. 1920, Maud Annora, who d. 1970,
da. of the late Arthur Watkin Williams-Wynn [Williams-Wynn, Bt., colls.]; d. 1968; s. by his son
[5] PETER CHARLES OLIVER, 2nd Baron and present peer.

HARVINGTON, BARON.　(Grant-Ferris.)　[Life Baron 1974.]

ROBERT GRANT GRANT-FERRIS, PC, son
of the late Robert Francis Ferris, MB, ChB;
b. Dec. 30th, 1907; ed. at Douai Sch.; Bar.
Inner Temple 1937; Pres. of Southdown
Sheep Soc. of England 1950-52, 1959-60 and
1973; Pres. National Sheep Breeders'
Assocn. 1956-58, and Smithfield Club 1970
(Vice-Pres. 1964); a Member of Speaker's
Panel of Chm. 1962-70, and Chm. of Ways
and Means, and Dep. Speaker of House of
Commons 1970-74; 1939-45 War as Wing
Cdr. R. Aux. AF in Europe, Malta, Egypt
and India (Air Effic. Award 1942); KStJ;
Cdr. Order of Leopold II of Belgium; MP
for N. St. Pancras (C) 1937-45, and for
Nantwich 1955-74; cr. Knt 1969, PC 1971,
and Baron Harvington, of Nantwich, Cheshire
(Life Baron) 1974: m. 1930, Florence, da.
of the late Maj. William Brennan De Vine,
MC, of St. John's, Angmering-on-Sea, Sussex,
and has issue.

Arms,—Gules, three antique crowns or, within an orle of eight horseshoes, argent.　Crest,—
A comb fessewise argent between two hazel branches fruited proper.

Residences.—16, Stafford Place, SW1; 8, Dysart Buildings, Nantwich, Cheshire.　Clubs,—Carlton,
Royal Thames Yacht.

SON LIVING.
Hon. Henry Michael Piers, b. 1933; ed. at Ampleforth; OSB.

DAUGHTER LIVING.
Hon. Greta Sheira Bernadette, b. 1937: m. 1st, 19—, John Frederick Edward Trehearne; 2ndly, 19—,
Christopher Mark Henry Murray.

HASTINGS, BARON.　(Astley.)　[Baron E. 1290, Bt. E. 1660.]

EDWARD DELAVAL HENRY ASTLEY,
22nd Baron, and 12th Baronet ; b. April
14th, 1912; s. 1956; ed. at Eton; is
Major Coldstream Guards (Reserve), and
patron of seven livings; a Lord in Waiting
to H.M. 1961-62, and Joint Parl.
Sec. to Min. of Housing and Local
Government 1962-64; Grand Officer of
Order of Merit of Italy: m. 1954, Catherine (Cecilia) Rosaline Ratcliffe (COATS),
yr. da. of the late Capt. Harold Virgo
Hinton, and has issue.

Arms,—Quarterly: 1st azure, a cinquefoil pierced
ermine, within a bordure engrailed or, Astley; 2nd
argent, a lion rampant gules, ducally crowned or,
Constable of Melton; 3rd gules, two lions passant
argent, Le Strange; 4th or, a maunch gules,
Hastings.　Crest.—Out of a ducal coronet or, a
plume of five feathers argent.　Supporters.—On
either side a lion gules, ducally crowned, and
gorged with a plain collar or, pendant therefrom
an escutcheon of the arms of Hastings.
Seat,—Seaton Delaval Hall, Whitley Bay, Northumberland.　Residence,—Fulmodeston Hall, Fakenham, Norfolk.　Clubs,—St. James', Northern Counties, Norfolk.

Tenacious of justice.

SONS LIVING.
Hon. DELAVAL THOMAS HAROLD, b. April 25th, 1960.
Hon. Justin Edward, b. 1968.

DAUGHTER LIVING.
Hon. Harriet Marguerite, *b.* 1958.

SISTERS LIVING.
Hon. Helen Elizabeth Delaval, *b.* 1907 : *m.* 1st, 1930 (marriage dissolved 1940), Ian Bulloch ; **2ndly,** 1941, George Field, who *d.* 1941 ; 3rdly, 1948, John David Haw, and has issue living, (by 1st marriage) Donald Ian, *b.* 1931,—James Angus, *b.* 1935,—Alasdair, *b.* 1937.
Hon. Armyne Margaret, *b.* 1909 : *m.* 1933, William George Broadbent Schofield, **and has issue living,** Armyne Morar Helen, *b.* 1934 : *m.* 1959, Angus Duncan Æneas Stirling, of 25, Ladbroke Grove, W11 [see E. Dunmore],—Ann Blackstone, *b.* 1935: *m.* 1959, Kinnaird St. Clair Cunningham, of 11, Napier Rd., Edinburgh, 10,—Marigold Elizabeth, *b.* 1937: *m.* 1962, Capt. John Anthony Warrington (ret.), Green Howards, of The Grange, Kirkby Malzeard, Ripon, and has issue living, George Simon Cromek *b.* 1964, Patrick William Cromek *b.* 1966, Olivia Sarah *b.* 1963,—Cicely Rose, *b.* 1941: *m.* 1972, Harold Irvin Golden, of 1801, Centinela, Santa Monica, Cal., USA. *Residence,—* Low Burton Hall, Masham, Yorks.
Hon. Jean, *b.* 1917; formerly in W.R.N.S.: *m.* 1945, Lieut.-Com. Mark Napier, R.N., who *d.* 1962 [see L. Napier and Ettrick, colls.]. *Residence,—*Compass House, West Meon, Hants.

AUNT LIVING. (*Daughter of* 20th *Baron.*)
Hon. Hester Winifred, *b.* 1899: *m.* 1923, Alan Houghton Brodrick, who *d.* 1973, and has issue living, John Alan St. John, *b.* 1924. *Resides in* Connecticut, USA.

WIDOW LIVING OF SON OF TWENTY-FIRST BARON.
Lady Joan Patricia Quirk, da. of 1st Earl Wavell: *m.* 1st, 1943, Maj. the Hon. Simon Nevill Astley who *d.* 1946; 2ndly, 1948, Harry Alastair Gordon, who *d.* 1965; 3rdly, 1973, Maj. Donald Struan Robertson, Scots Gds., of Winkfield Plain Farm, Winkfield, Windsor, Berks., SL4 4QU, son of the late Rt. Hon. Sir Malcolm Arnold Robertson, GCMG, KBE, and has issue living, (by 1st m.) [see colls., infra].

COLLATERAL BRANCHES LIVING.

Issue of the late Maj. the Hon. Simon Neville Astley, 2nd son of 21st Baron, *b.* 1919, *d.* 1946: *m.* 1943, Lady Joan Patricia Quirk (ante) (she *m.* 2ndly, 1948, Maj. Harry Alastair Gordon, Gordon Highlanders, who *d.* 1965, and 3rdly, 1973, Maj. Donald Struan Robertson, of Winkfield Plain Farm, Winkfield, Windsor, Berks., son of the late Rt. Hon. Sir Malcolm Arnold Robertson, GCMG, KBE), da. of 1st Earl Wavell:—
Diana Jane, *b.* 1943: *m.* 1975, Capt. Robert I. W. Kellie, RA.

Issue of the late Capt. the Hon. (Charles) Melton Astley, **youngest son of 20th** Baron, *b.* 1885, *d.* 1960: *m.* 1914, Evelyn Vere, who *d.* 1969, el. da. of the late Gen. George Augustus Strover, and widow of Leonard Stevens :—
George Delaval (84, Drayton Gdns., SW10 9SD, and Swanthorpe Farm, nr. Crondall, Hants), *b.* 1915; ed. at Haileybury; Maj. (ret.) R. Fus.; Chevalier, Order of Merit of France, and Officer, Order of Arts and Letters of France: *m.* 1st, 1942 (m. diss. 1946) Hope, da. of the late Lt.-Col. Francis Holden Shuttleworth Rendall, DSO, Duke of Cornwall's LI; 2ndly, 1949, Diana Christian, only da. of the late Brig.-Gen. Robert Hugh Hare, CB, CMG, DSO, MVO, and has issue living, (by 2nd m.) Delaval Hugh, *b.* 1950,—Caroline Susan, *b.* 1951: *m.* 1974, Charles Philip Barrington Woollett, of 20, Atherston Mews, SW7.

Granddaughter of the late Frederick Bernard Astley, son of the late Lt.-Col. Francis L'Estrange Astley (infra):—
Issue of the late Major Delaval Graham L'Estrange Astley, C.B., *b.* 1868, *d.* 1951: *m.* 1897, Kate, who *d.* 1961, dau. of the late John Kerr Clark, of Ghoolendaadi, New South Wales; and Beaumont, Lansdown, Bath:—
Joan Doreen, *b.* 1901 : *m.* 1928 (marriage dissolved 19—), Gerald Josselyn Royce Tomkin, and has issue, Iona, *b.* 1930: *m.* 1954, Maj. David Vandeleur, c/o Nat. Westminster Bank, 161, Brompton Rd., SW3, and has issue living, Simon *b.* 1956, Alexander *b.* 1963, Christina *b.* 1958.

Granddaughter of the late Lieut.-Col. Francis L'Estrange Astley, **brother of 16th** Baron :—
Issue of the late Bertram Frankland FRANKLAND-RUSSELL-ASTLEY, *b.* 1857, *d.* 1904, having assumed the additional surnames of Frankland-Russell: *m.* 1887, Lady Florence Conyngham (who *d.* 1946, having *m.* 2ndly, 1905, Lieut.-Col. the Hon. Claud Heathcote-Drummond-Willoughby, who *d.* 1950 [E. Ancaster]), dau. of 3rd Marquess Conyngham :—
Olive Joan, *b.* 1893: *m.* 1927, George Grenville Fortescue, who *d.* 1967 [E. Fortescue, colls.]. *Residence*—Ethy House, Lerryn, Lostwithiel, Cornwall.

Grandson of the late Hubert Delaval Astley (infra) :—
Issue of the late Col. Philip Reginald Astley, C.B.E., M.C., *b.* 1896, *d.* 1958 : *m.* 1st, 1931, Edith Madeleine (who obtained a divorce 1940), dau. of the late John Carroll; 2ndly, 1949, Penelope Joan McKerrow, *OBE* (119, Old Church St., SW3), da. of the late Trevor Bright of Freshford, Bath:—
(By 2nd m.) Richard Jacob, *b.* 1950; ed. at Eton and Bedford Coll., London: *m.* 1974, Rosanna, el. da. of (John) Anthony Quayle, CBE.

Granddaughter of the late Lieut.-Col. Francis L'Estrange Astley (ante):—
Issue of the late Hubert Delaval Astley, *b.* 1860, *d.* 1925: *m.* 1895, Constance Edith, who *d.* 1940, dau. of Sir Vincent Rowland Corbet, **3rd** Bt., and widow of Sir Richard Francis Sutton, 5th Bt. :—
Ruth Constance (*Hon. Mrs. E. Humphrey Wyndham*), *b.* 1900: *m.* 1920, Col. the Hon. Everard Humphrey Wyndham, MC, late 1st Life Guards, who *d.* 1970 [see B. Egremont]. *Residence,—*Caversfield, Bicester.

PREDECESSORS.—*Sir* Isaac Astley, cr. a Bt. 1641 (nephew of Jacob, 1st Baron Astley of Reading, cr. 1644, ext. 1668); *d.* without issue 1659, when the Baronetcy expired, and his estates passed to his nephew [1] *Sir* JACOB Astley, Knt., 40 years M.P. for Norfolk; cr. a *Baronet* 1660; *d.* 1729; *s.* by his son [2] *Sir* PHILIP, 2nd Bt.; *d.* 1739; *s.* by his son [3] *Sir* JACOB, 3rd Bt.; *d.* 1760; *s.* by his son [4] *Sir* EDWARD, 4th Bt.; 24 years M.P. for Norfolk; *d.* 1802; *s.* by his son [5] *Sir* JACOB HENRY, 5th Bt.; 20 years M.P. for Norfolk; *d.* 1817; *s.* by his son [6] *Sir* JACOB, 6th Bt.; summoned to Parliament by writ and became 16th Baron Hastings 1841, the abeyance [see **** infra] having been terminated in his favour; *d.* 1859; *s.* by his el. son [7] JACOB HENRY DELAVAL, 17th Baron; *d.* 1871; *s.* by his brother [8] *Rev.* DELAVAL LOFTUS, 18th Baron; *b.* 1825: *m.* 1848, the Hon. Frances Diana Manners Sutton, dau. of 1st Viscount Canterbury; *d.* 1872; *s.* by his el. son [9] BERNARD EDWARD DELAVAL, 19th Baron; *b.* 1855; *d.* 1875; *s.* by his brother [10] GEORGE MANNERS, 20th Baron; *b.* 1857: *m.* 1880, the Hon. Elizabeth Evelyn Harbord, who *d.* 1957, dau. of 5th Baron Suffield; *d.* 1904; *s.* by his son [11] ALBERT EDWARD DELAVAL, 21st Baron; *b.* 1882; Lieut.-Col. late 7th Hussars; High Steward of Norwich Cathedral; bore one of the Golden Spurs at Coronations of King George VI and Queen Elizabeth II: *m.* 1907, Lady Marguerite Helen Nevill, who *d.* 1975, da. of 3rd Marquess of Abergavenny; *d.* 1956; *s.* by his son [12] EDWARD DELAVAL HENRY, 22nd Baron and present peer.

⁎⁎⁎[1] *Sir* JOHN Hastings, who in right of his mother and by tenure of the Castle of Bergavenny was Baron Bergavenny, was summoned to Parliament as *Baron Hastings* 1290-1313; assisted in the Scottish Wars of Edward I., and received in 1273 from the King a grant of the whole co. of Menteth, with the Isles and also all the manors and lands of Alan; 6th Earl of Menteth, then declared a rebel; was seneschal of Aquitaine, and in 1290 a competitor for the Crown of Scotland: *m.* 1st, 1275, Isabel de Valence, who *d.* 1305, dau. of William, Earl of Pembroke; 2ndly, 13—, Isabella Despencer, dau. of 1st Earl of Winchester; *d.* 1313; *s.* by his son **[2]** JOHN, 2nd Baron; summoned to Parliament 1313-25; served in the Scottish Wars of Edward II., and was sometime Gov. of Kenilworth Castle: *m.* 13—, Juliana (who *m.* 2ndly, 1326, Sir Thomas Blount, and 3rdly, 1327, William, Lord Clinton, and *d.* 1367), dau. of Sir Thomas Leybourne; *d.* 1325; *s.* by his son **[3]** LAURENCE, 3rd Baron; *b.* 1320; cr. *Earl of Pembroke* (peerage of England) 1339; served with valour in the French Wars of Edward III.: *m.* 1328, Agnes Mortimer (who *m.* 2ndly, 13—, John Hakelut, and *d.* 1368), dau. of 1st Earl of March; *d.* 1348; *s.* by his son **[4]** JOHN, *K.G.*, 2nd Earl; *b.* 1347; was sent as Lieut. into Aquitaine with a fleet of ships, but no sooner had he got his vessels within the harbour of La Rochelle than he was suddenly attacked by the Spanish fleet, and having suffered a signal defeat was taken prisoner and detained four years in captivity: *m.* 1st, 1359, Margaret, who *d.* 1361, dau. of Edward III.; 2ndly, 1363, Anne, who *d.* 1384, dau. of Walter, 1st Lord Manny; *d.* 1375; *s.* by his son **[5]** JOHN, 3rd Earl; *b.* 1372: *m.* 1st, 1380 (marriage dissolved 1383), Elizabeth, dau. of John of Gaunt, Duke of Lancaster; 2ndly, 13—, Philippa Mortimer (who *m.* 2ndly, 13—, Richard FitzAlan, 15th Earl of Arundel, and 3rdly, 1399, Thomas Poynings, 5th Lord St. John of Basing, and *d.* 1401), dau. of the 3rd Earl of March; *d.* 1391, when 17 years of age, from a wound received in tilting, from the lance of Sir John St. John, when the earldom became ext. and he was *s.* in the barony (according to the decision of the House of Lords 1841) by his kinsman **[6]** *Sir* JOHN, *de jure* 6th Baron (el. son of Sir Hugh Hastings, son of 1st Baron), *b.* 1328, *d.* 1393; *s.* by his great-nephew **[7]** *Sir* Hugh (grandson of Sir Hugh Hastings, brother of *de jure* 6th Baron) *de jure* 7th Baron, *b.* 1376: *m.* 13— Constance (who *m.* 2ndly, 14—, Sir John Sutton, of Dudley, Staffs), dau. of Walter Blount, of Barton Blount, Derbyshire; *d.* 1396; *s.* by his brother **[8]** *Sir* EDWARD, *de jure* 8th Baron, *b.* 1382; unsuccessfully claimed to carry the Second Sword before the King at Henry IV.'s Coronation, and to carry Great Gilt Spurs, and to perform the office of Ch. Napperer: *m.* 1st, 14—, Muriel, dau. of Sir John de Dinham, of Hartland, Devon; 2ndly, 14—, Margery (who *m.* 2ndly, 14—, John Wyndham, of Felbridge, Norfolk, and *d.* 1456), dau. of Sir Robert Clifton, of Bokenham, Norfolk; *d.* 1438; *s.* by his son **[9]**, JOHN, *de jure* 9th Baron, *b.* 1412; Constable of Norwich Castle and Gaol 1441, *m.* 1434, Anne, who *d.* 1471, dau. of Thomas Morley, Lord Morley; *d.* 1477; *s.* by his son **[10]** *Sir* HUGH, *de jure* 10th Baron, *b.* 1447; Sheriff of Yorkshire 1479-80: *m.* 1455, Anne, dau. of Sir William Gascoigne, of Gawthorpe, Yorkshire; *d.* 1488; *s.* by his son **[11]** *Sir* JOHN, *de jure* 11th Baron, *b.* 1466: *m.* 1st, 14—, Isabel, who *d.* 1495, dau. and heir of Sir Ralph Babthorpe, of Babthorpe, Yorkshire; 2ndly, 14—, Katherine, dau. of Sir John Aske, of Aughton Yorkshire; *d.* 1504; *s.* by his brother **[12]** *Sir* GEORGE, *de jure* 12th Baron; *b.* 1474: *m.* 1493 Joan, dau. and co-heir of Roger Brabazon, of Eastwell, Leicestershire; *d.* 1511; *s.* by his son **[13]** JOHN, *de jure* 13th Baron, *b.* 1498; *d.* 1514; *s.* by his brother **[14]** *Sir* HUGH, *de jure* 14th Baron, *b.* 1505: *m.* 1523, Katherine (who *m.* 2ndly, 1554, Thomas Gawdy, Serjeant-at-Law, and *d.* 1558), dau. of Robert L'Estrange, of Winfarthing, Norfolk; *d.* 1540; *s.* by his son **[15]** JOHN *de jure* 15th Baron, *b.* 1530; *d.* unm. 1542, when the Barony fell into abeyance between his sisters (i)Anne, wife of William Browne, of Elsing, Norfolk, and (ii) Elizabeth, wife of Hamon L'Estrange of Hunstanton, Norfolk, and so remained until 1841, when the House of Lords reported that the co-heirs were Frances Berney, widow of the Rev. Richard Browne, Henry L'Estrange Styleman le Strange, of Hunstanton, co. Norfolk, and Sir Jacob Astley, 6th Bt., whereupon the abeyance was terminated in favour of the last-named, who was 9th in descent from Elizabeth L'Estrange(ante).

HATHERTON, BARON.　(Littleton.)　[Baron U.K. 1835.]

UNG·DIEU·ET·UNG·ROY
One God, and one king.

THOMAS CHARLES TASMAN LITTLETON, *TD*, 7th Baron; *b.* Oct. 6th, 1907; *s.* 1973; Capt. (ret.) RA (TA): *m.* 1933, Ann Scott, da. of the late Lt.-Cdr. Thomas MacLeod, RN, and has issue.

Arms,—Argent, a chevron between three escallops sable.　**Crest,**—A stag's head cabossed sable, attired or; between the attires a bugle horn of the first, garnished and pendant from two annulets conjoined gold.　**Supporters,**—*Dexter,* a stag proper, plain collared or, and suspended therefrom an escutcheon argent, charged with a bugle stringed sable; *sinister,* a lion gules, ducally gorged, and suspended from the coronet an escutcheon, charged as in the dexter.

Residence,—Walhouse, Hutton Henery, Hartlepool, Cleveland, TS27 4RH.

DAUGHTER LIVING.
Hon. Hyacinthe Anne, *b.* 1934: *m.* 1954, Patrick Peterken, of Claypool Farm, Hutton Henery, Castle Eden, co. Durham, and has issue living, Patrick James Littleton, *b.* 1957,—Nicholas John Littleton, *b.* 1960,—Frances Josephine, *b.* 1962.

SONS LIVING OF SIXTH BARON (*by 2nd wife.*)
Hon. Richard Brownlow, *b.* 1949.
Hon. Jonathan Lloyd (twin), *b.* 1949.

DAUGHTERS LIVING OF SIXTH BARON (*by 1st wife.*)
Hon. Moonyeen Meriel, *b.* 1933.
Hon. Modwena Louise, *b.* 1947: *m.* 1969, Edward Willison, of 40 Coton Manor, Shrewsbury, and has issue living, Tricia, *b.* 1970,—Rachael, *b.* 1971.

DAUGHTERS LIVING OF 5th BARON.

Hon. Joanna Ida Louisa, *b.* 1926: *m.* 1948, Robert Westby Perceval, of Sandlea Court, Datchet, Bucks, and has issue living, Antony Robin Walhouse, Westby LITTLETON, *b.* 1950; ed. at Eton; adopted by Roy. Licence 1971 the surname of Littleton,—Sara Jane Modwena, *b.* 1954,—Diana Mary, *b.* 1959.

Hon. Jane Anne Caroline, *b.* 1929: *m.* 1967, the Rev. Charles Piachaud Wright, of Lyddington Vicarage, Uppingham, Rutland.

SISTERS LIVING.

Hon. Norah Hyacinthe, *b.* 1899: *m.* 1923, Samuel Ranulph Allsopp, CBE, who *d.* 1975 [see B. Hindlip, colls.]. *Residence,*—Alsa Lodge, Stansted, Essex.

Hon. Leila Cecilia, *b.* 1902: *m.* 1922 (m. diss. 1949), Stuart Sandbach Harrison, MC, late Lieut. Irish Guards, and has issue living, Rupert, *b.* 1924: *m.* 1947, Hazel Price, and has issue living, Roger *b.* 1948, Philip *b.* 1949,—Desmond, *b.* 1926: *m.* 1950, Doreen Chappell, and has issue living, Stephen *b.* 1951, Gillian Lilah *b.* 1953,—Youla Cecilia, *b.* 1927: *m.* 1947, Claude Vauz Mieville, of Orchard House, Wattisfield, Norfolk, and has issue living, Dominic Peter *b.* 1951, Claudia Cecilia *b.* 1949. *Residence,*—La Brétche, Roquebrune, Cap Martin, France, AM.

Hon. Youla Edithe WELLSLEY (Farley, Oakamoor, Stoke-on-Trent), *b.* 1904; assumed by deed poll 1939, the surname of Wellsley in lieu of that of Harris: *m.* 1927, (m. diss. 1938) John Elvine Harris, who *d.* 1965, and has issue living, Nigel John Littleton, *b.* 1928; ed. at Winchester; R. Signals 1946-49,—Jeremy Mark Littleton (Zilverdenenlaan 21, 3762, Gellick, Belgium, and Brookside, Aston Hall Lane, Aston-by-Stone, Staffs.), *b.* 1930; ed. at Lancing; late 2nd Lt. RA: *m.* 1956, Pauline, da. of Col. Gilbert Howson, OBE, TD, of Stoke-on-Trent, and has issue living, Charles Jeremy Howson *b.* 1957, Richard Paul Howson *b.* 1960, John Benjamin Howson *b.* 1966,—Colin Andrew Littleton (Sandon Lodge, Stafford), *b.* 1931: ed. at Winchester: *m.* 1967, Patricia Anne, da. of Neville Lucas Elliott, TD, of Four Oaks, Warwicks, and has issue living, Lea Eunomia *b.* 1969, Alison Youla *b.* 1971.

Hon. Hester Mary Modwena (Pitt Manor Cottage, Winchester), *b.* 1912; 1939-45 with WTS/FANY.

AUNTS LIVING. *(Daughters of 3rd Baron.)*

Hon. Mary Cecilia, *b.* 1884. *Residence,*—Pebbly Croft, Bucklebury, Reading.

Hon. Edith Modwena, *A.R.R.C., b.* 1888; a Nurse in Mil. Hospital, France, during European War 1914-19 (despatches, A.R.R.C.). *Residence,*—Pebbly Croft, Bucklebury, Reading.

WIDOWS LIVING OF FIFTH AND SIXTH BARONS.

KATHLEEN MAY (*Kathleen, Baroness Hatherton*), (Hatherton Hall, Cannock, Staffs.; 55, Lancaster Court, Kingsway, Hove), only da. of the late Clarence Ernest Orlando Whitechurch of Esher, and formerly wife of Maj. Oscar Westendarp: *m.* 1952 as his 2nd wife, the 5th Baron, who *d.* 1969.

MARY ALICE (*Mary, Baroness Hatherton*), (Madeira House, Church Stretton, Salop); Capt. (ret.) QAIMNS; da. of John Roberts, of Ruthin, Denbighshire: *m.* 1955, as his 2nd wife, the 6th Baron, who *d.* 1973.

COLLATERAL BRANCHES LIVING.

Grandchildren of the late Lieut.-Col. the Hon Charles Christopher Josceline Littleton, D.S.O., 3rd son of 3rd Baron:—
Issue of the late Mervyn Cecil Littleton, *b.* 1908, *d.* 1970: *m.* 1940, Margaret Ann (Apertdo 3358, San José, Costa Rica), da. of Frank Sheehy:—
EDWARD CHARLES, *b.* May 24th, 1950.——Aileen Pamela Hyacinthe, *b.* 1941: *m.* 1964, Giovanni Sosto Peralta, of San José, Costa Rica, and has issue living, Giovanni, *b.* 1967,—Eugenio, *b.* 1971,—Carlo, *b.* 1972,—Alexandra Eugenia, *b.* 1968.——Cynthia Ann, *b.* 1943: *m.* 1963, Roberto Padilla Odor, of San José, Costa Rica, and has issue living, Roberto, *b.* 1964,—Andres, *b.* 1968,—Mervyn, *b.* 1971.

Issue of the late Major the Hon. William Hugh Littleton, 4th son of 3rd Baron, *b.* 1882, *d.* 1956 : *m.* 1920, Lilian, who *d.* 1954, dau. of Charles E. Davis, of Clifton, Bristol :—
John William, *b.* 1924; ed. at Canford; 1939-45 War in France, Belgium, Holland and Germany with RASC: *m.* 1956, Hilda Ruth, only da. of J. Pardy, of Christchurch, Hants, and has issue living, Deborah Jayne, *b.* 1960,—Susan Jennifer, *b.* 1965. *Residence,*—The Bridges, 92, King's Av., Christchurch, Hants.——Margaret Hyacinthe, *b.* 1921; 1939-45 War in VAD: *m.* 1948, Edward Roderick Dew. *Residence,*—Highdown, Chulmleigh, N. Devon.

Grandchildren of the late Rear-Adm. the Hon. Algernon Charles Littleton, 2nd son of 2nd Baron:—
Issue of the late Capt. Algernon Edward Percy Littleton, *b.* 1881, *d.* 1943: *m.* 1912, Violet Agnes Lætitia SALUSBURY-TRELAWNY, who *d.* 1973, da. of Sir John William Salusbury-Trelawny, 11th Bt.:—
Leonard Vere Algernon, *b.* 1913; ed. at Malvern; European War 1939-45 as Capt. R.A.: *m.* 1941, Sheila Miriam, da. of the late Stanley Couldrey, of Tunbridge Wells. *Residence,*—82, London Rd., Tunbridge Wells, Kent.——Robert Jocelyn Henry, *D.F.C.* (of 45, Erlesmere Gdns., Ealing, W.13), *b.* 1915; ed. at Malvern; Flight-Lt. R.A.F.; 1939-45 War (D.F.C.): *m.* 1946, Wendy, dau. of the late S. Stevens, and has issue living, Susan Elaine, *b.* 1952,—Zoë Annette, *b.* 1955.

Issue of the late Lt.-Col. Josceline William Littleton, MC, ED, *b.* 1886, *d.* 1969: *m.* 1920, Annie McKerrell, who *d.* 1961, da. of Lt.-Col. Arthur George Wolley-Dod:—
Margaret Anne (1345, W. Tulare Av., Visalia, Cal. 93277), *b.* 1921: *m.* 1st, 1943 (m. diss. 1948), Fl.-Lt. Alfred John Smitz, DFC, RAF; 2ndly, 1948 (m. diss. 1963) Robert Leech; 3rdly, 1967 (m. diss. 1974), Arthur Dale Harder, and has issue living (by 1st m.) Peter Gerard Littleton, *b.* 1944; a Trooper, Lord Strathcona's Horse: *m.* 1965, Carol Thew, of Richmond Hill, Ont.,—(by 2nd m.) Robert Timothy, *b.* 1961,—Martha Anne, *b.* 1951: *m.* 1969, Kerry Wayne King,—Josceline Henrietta, *b.* 1952: *m.* 1971, Mark S. Wingo, and has issue living, Jason Marcus *b.* 1973.

Issue of the late Com. Richard Charles Arthur Littleton, R.N. (retired), *b.* 1888, *d.* 1945: *m.* 1934, Lucy Veronica (now of Luesdon, Blackheath, Guildford, Surrey), dau. of the Rev. Robert Cecil Salmon, R. of Chiddingstone, Kent:—
Joanna Veronica, *b.* 1935.——Marilyn Eve, *b.* 1937.

Issue of the late Capt. Cecil Francis Henry Littleton, *b.* 1890, *d.* (wounds in action during European War) 1917: *m.* 1913, Brenda (who *d.* 1972, having *m.* 2ndly, 1919, Arthur Alexander Baillie, and 3rdly, 1922 (m. diss, 1934), Alwyne R. M. Scrase-Dickins), da. of the late George Southby Hewitt, of 26A, North Audley, St., W1:—
Diana, *b.* 1915: *m.* 19—,—Earley, of 27, Parkside, Cuddesdon, Oxford.

PREDECESSORS.—*Sir* Edward Littleton, 4th and last Bt., of Pillaton, cr. 1627, devised his estates to his grand-nephew [1] EDWARD JOHN Walhouse, *P.C.* (M.P. for Staffordshire 1812-35), who thereupon assumed the surname of Littleton in lieu of his patronymic; *b.* 1791; was Ch. Sec. for Ireland 1834, and Lord-Lieut. of Staffordshire 1854-62: cr. *Baron Hatherton*, of Hatherton, co. Stafford, 1835: *m.* 1st, 1812, Hyacinthe Mary, natural dau. of 1st Marquess Wellesley; 2ndly, 1852, Caroline Anne, who *d.* 1897, dau. of Richard Hurt, of Worksworth, and widow of Edward Davies Davonport, of Capesthorne, Cheshire, *d.* 1863 ; *s.* by his son [2] EDWARD RICHARD, *C.B.*, 2nd Baron, *b.* 1815; sat as M.P. for Walsall (*L*) 1847-52, and for S. Staffordshire 1853-7: *m.* 1841, Lady Margaret Percy, who *d.* 1897, dau. of 5th Duke of Northumberland; *d.* 1888; *s.* by his el. son [3] EDWARD GEORGE PERCY, *C.M.G.* 3rd Baron, *b.* 1842; was Sec. and Mil. Sec. to Earl of Dufferin (Gov.-Gen. of Canada) 1875-8, Mil. Sec. to Marquess of Lorne 1878-9, and an Hon. Commr. in Lunacy 1890-98: *m.* 1867, Charlotte Louisa, who *d.* 1923, dau. of Sir Charles Robert Rowley, 4th Bt.; *d.* 1930; *s.* by his el. son [4] EDWARD

CHARLES ROWLEY, 4th Baron; b. 1868; formerly Lieut. 3rd Batn. N. Staffordshire Regt.; in Ser. of Raja of Sarawak 1890-96: m. 1897, Hester Edith, who d. 1947, dau. of the late Thomas Tarrant Hoskins. M.D., J.P., of Tasmania: d. 1944; s. by his el. son [5] EDWARD THOMAS. WALHOUSE, 5th Baron, b. 1900; Lt. Cdr. RN: m. 1st, 1925 (m. diss. 1951), Ida Guendolen, da. of Robin Legge; 2ndly, Kathleen May, da. of Clarence Ernest Orlando Whitechurch, and formerly wife of Maj. Oscar Westendarp; d. 1969; s. by his brother, [6] JOHN WALTER STUART, 6th Baron; b. 1906: m. 1st, 1932, Nora Evelyn, who d. 1955, da. of R. O. Smith, of Edgbaston; 2ndly, 1955, Mary Alice, Capt. (ret.) QAIMNS, da. of John Roberts, of Ruthin, Denbighshire; d. 1973; s. by his brother [7] THOMAS CHARLES TASMAN, TD, 7th Baron and present peer.

HAWARDEN, VISCOUNT. (Maude.) [Viscount I. 1793, Bt. I. 1705.]

[Title pronounced "Haywarden."]

VIRTVTE SECVRVS

Safe by manliness.

ROBERT LESLIE EUSTACE MAUDE, 8th Viscount, and 10th Baronet ; b. March 26th, 1926 ; s. 1958 ; ed. at Winchester, and at Ch. Ch. Oxford ; European War 1945 in Coldstream Guards (invalided) : m. 1957, Susannah Caroline Hyde, dau. of the late Major Charles Phillips Gardner [see By. Gardner, colls.], and has issue.

Arms.—Quarterly: 1st and 4th azure, a lion rampant argent, Maude; 2nd and 3rd argent, three bars gemelles sable, over all a lion rampant gules, charged on the shoulder with a cross-crosslet fitchée or. Crest,—A lion's jamb erased erect proper, grasping a sprig of oak leaves slipped vert. Supporters.—Two lions gules, each charged on the shoulder with a cross-crosslet fitchée or.

Residences,—Wingham Court, nr. Canterbury; 39, Shawfield St., SW3.

SONS LIVING.

Hon. ROBERT CONNAN WYNDHAM LESLIE, b. May 23rd, 1961.
Hon. Thomas Patrick Cornwallis, b. 1964.

DAUGHTER LIVING.

Hon. Sophia-Rose Eileen, b. 1959.

BROTHER LIVING.

Hon. Henry Cornwallis, b. 1928 ; ed. at Marlborough, and at Worcester Coll., Oxford (B.A. 1953, MA 1957); 1939-45 War with Queen's R. Regt. and as Sergeant Educational Corps: m. 1964, Elizabeth Georgina, only da. of David McNaught Lockie, of La Tour de Peilz, Switzerland, and has issue living, Francis Hugh Cornwallis, b. 1966,—Anthony Eustace David, b. 1972,—Elizabeth Arabella Marion, b. 1967,—Diana Caroline Alice, b. 1971. Residence,—Home Farm House, Draughton, Northampton.

SISTER LIVING.

Hon. Helen Margaretta, b. 1921 : m. 1947, Walter Peter Baxter, and has issue living, Charles Peter, b. 1950: m. 1974, Nicola Caroline, el. da. of the late Maj. N. S. John, of Warminster, Wilts.,—Joanna Rosamond, b. 1948: m. 1970, Michael George Patrick Falkiner of Globeman Hall, Ferns, co. Wexford [see Falkiner, Bt.],—Margaretta Helena, b. 1954,—Victoria Marion, b. 1956. Residence,—The Old House, Milton-on-Stour, Gillingham, Dorset.

COLLATERAL BRANCHES LIVING.

Grandchildren of the late Cdr. Eustace Downman Maude, RN (infra):—
Issue of the late George Ashley Maude, b. 1889, d. 1973: m. 1921, Ruth (Fulford Harbour, Salt Spring Island, BC, Canada), da. of Cdr. M. Updegraff, US Navy:—
George Ashley (Fulford Harbour, Salt Spring Island, BC, Canada), b. 1925: m. 1952, Nancy Mary, da. of John Ingvard Reitan, and has issue living, Anthony John Ashley, b. 1954,—Christopher George, b. 1957,—David Philip, b. 1964.——Alison Beauclerk, b. 1923.

Granddaughters of the late Lt.-Col. Sir George Ashley Maude, KCB, son of the late Rev. the Hon. John Charles Maude, 5th son of 1st Viscount:—
Issue of the late Com. Eustace Downman Maude, R.N., b. 1848, d. 1930 : m. 1885, Amy, who d. 1946, dau. of Oliver Williams:—
Cyrene Marie, b. 1891: m. 1913, Lt.-Com. Cecil Hulton-Sams, formerly RN, who d. 1931, and has issue living, Valerie Beauclerk, b. 1916: m. 1948, William Duncan McClure, MC, of Flat B, 44, Queens Gate Gdn., SW7,—Cyrene Diana, b. 1920: m. 1948, Michael Henry Clarmont Phillips, DFC, of The White House, Church Lane, Eastergate, Sussex, and has issue living, Robert Henry Clarmont b. 1953, James Stephen Beauclerk b. 1954. Residence,—Manor Cottage, Havant.——Valerie Beauclerk: m. 1925, Capt. Humfrey Greenwood Hopper, DSO, RN, and has issue living, John Oliver de Montalt (Corazon-De Maria 21/807, Madrid, Spain), b. 1929: m. 1965 (m. diss. 1972), Nelly Galiatsato, of Paris, and has issue living, Edward Charles de Montalt b. 1968,—Elizabeth Valerie Beauclerk, b. 1930: m. 1952, Donald Furneaux Sweeting, of Hill Farm, Little Rissington, Gloucestershire, and has issue living, James Donald Furneaux b. 1954, Gerard John Cornwallis b. 1958, Henrietta Maria Beauclerk b. 1953. Residence,—55, Cadogan Place, SW1.

Granddaughters of the late Lt.-Col. Aubrey Maurice Maude (infra):—
Issue of the late Brig. Christian George Maude, DSO, OBE, MC, b. 1884, d. 1971: m. 1st, 1920, the Hon. Patience Kemp (who d. 1935, and from whom he obtained a divorce 1930), da. of 1st Baron Rochdale; 2ndly, 1931, Joan (The Downs, Broad Oak, Heathfield, Sussex), da. of the late Charles Augustus Egerton, of Mountfield Court, Robertsbridge, Sussex:—
(By 1st m.) Bridget Diana, b. 1921: m. 1946, Lt.-Col. Hugh Michael Allan Knight, MC, RAOC, late Indian Army, of The Parsonage, Talkin, Brampton, Cumberland, and has issue living, Simon Fairfax, b. 1950,—Jeremy Christian, b. 1955,—Richard Peter, b. 1957,—Cunita Amanda Egerton, b. 1947.—— (by 2nd m.) Gillian Mabelle Beauclerk, b. 1932: m. 1960, Maj. Estcourt Richard Cresswell, MC, MA (ret.), 15th/19th King's R. Hussars, of Charingworth Manor, Chipping Campden, Glos.——Priscilla Douglas, b. 1934: m. 1962, Michael Frederick Tremain Maude (infra).——Elizabeth Joan, b. 1940: m. 1967, Capt. Christopher Evelyn Twiston-Davies, late 4th/7th R. Dragoon Gds., of Drax House, Tilshead, Salisbury, Wilts., son of the late Sir Leonard Twiston-Davies, KBE, and has issue living, William Ashley, b. 1969,—Benjamin James, b. 1971.

Granddaughter of the late Brig. Christian George Maude, DSO, OBE, MC (ante):—
Issue of the late Capt. Peter George Egerton Maude, b. 1926, d. 1957: m. 1952, Olivia Elizabeth (who m. 2ndly, 1961, Brig. Hugh Marlborough Hale Ley, CBE, of Alt Grange, Hightown, Liverpool), el. da. of Lt.-Col. H. O. Wright, of Windlesham, Surrey:—
Sarah Patience, b. 1954.

Granddaughters of the late Lt.-Col. Sir George Ashley Maude, KCB (ante):—
Issue of the late Frederick William Maude, b. 1857, d. 1923: m. 1878, Ellen Maud, who d. 1938, dau. of Sir John Kelk, 1st Bt. (ext.) :—
Norah Diana HANBURY-KELK, b. 1889; assumed by deed poll 1934 the additional surname of Kelk: m. 1912, Arthur Marcus Hanbury (from whom she obtained a divorce 1929), and has issue living, Nicholas John Capel (of 35, Upper Addison Gardens, W.14), b. 1913: m. 1946, Eileen, da. of Richard Conway, and has issue living, John Capel, b. 1953, Danielle b. 1947,— Benedict Frederick Philip, b. 1924,—Diana Martha Germaine HANBURY, b. 1916 (assumed by deed poll 1974 her maiden name of Hanbury: m. 1st, 1939 (m. diss. 1962) Arthur Henry Morris; 2ndly, 1963 (m. diss. 1972) David Russell Thompson, and has issue living (by 1st m.) Charles b. 1943, Dinah b. 1940: m. 1963 (m. diss. 1971) Patrick Wiener (and has issue living, Daniel Patrick b. 1964, Barnaby Mark b. 1967),—Jan Beauclerk (twin), b. 1924: m. 1st, 1952, William Hislop, from whom she obtained a divorce 1957; 2ndly, 1962, Arthur Henry Morris (ante), of The Old Rectory, Alphetonl Sudbury, Suffolk, and has issue living, (by 1st m.) Cordelia Margaret Beauclerk b. 1953, Rache, Norah Ceely b. 1954. *Residence,*—The Gate House, Risby, Bury St. Edmunds.——Katharine Elizabeth, b. 1892: m. 1915, Col. Thomas Hubert Harker, DSO, and bar, who d. 1938, and has issue living, Paul Thomas Borton (127, Junction Rd., N19), b. 1920: m. 1947, Maureen, who d. 1973, da. of J. G. Hoatson, and widow of Maj. Peter J. A. Hankey, RHA, and has issue living, Andrew Peter Thomas b. 1952 (15, Cadogan Court, Draycott Av., SW3 3BX), Sara Jane b. 1949,—Matthew (7, Cadogan Court, Draycott Av., SW3), b. 1924; Capt. (ret.) 60th Rifles: m. 1951, Ann Powell, da. of Noel Clifton, of Hambledon, Surrey, and has issue living, James b. 1954, Simon b. 1957. *Residence,*— 157, Cranmer Court, Draycott Av., SW3 3BX.

Grandchildren of the late Maurice Ceely Maude, 3rd son of the Rev. the Hon. John Charles Maude, 5th son of 1st Viscount:—
Issue of the late Capt. Anthony Fritz Maude, b. 1862, d. 1935 : m. 1895, Eva Emily, who d. 1960, dau. of the late Major Henry Marcus Beresford, 9th Regt.[M. Waterford, colls.]:—
Hugh Arthur Cornwallis (of Hardymount House, Tullow, co. Carlow), b. 1904.——Monica Ruth Lisalie, b. 1905: m. 1929, William Eric Horsburgh-Porter [see Horsburgh-Porter, Bt., colls.]. *Residence,*— Glen Heste, Carrickmines, co. Dublin.

Issue of the late Ralph Alexander Maude, b. 1864, d. 1946: m. 1910, Sarah Adelaide, who d. 1922, 2nd dau. of Robert John Burt, formerly of Vicar's Moor, Winchmore Hill, N.:—
Lisalie Marion, b. 1912: m. 1954, Campbell Singer, actor. *Residences,*—11, Bolton Gdns., SW5 0AL; Bullfinches, Nutley, Sussex.

Issue of the late Christopher Hugh Maude, b. 1867, d. 1942: m. 1924, Mary Elizabeth Christiana, who d. 1952, dau. of the Rt. Rev. James Macmanaway, D.D., 91st Bishop of Clogher:—
Maurice Christopher (Middle Venton, Drewsteignton, Devon), b. 1925; late Capt. KRRC: m. 1st, 1954 (m. diss. 1963), Venetia, da. of William Patterson Doyle, of Kuwait; 2ndly, 1967, Susan Frances, da. of George Lepper, of Blacknest, Alton, Hants., and has issue living (by 2nd m.), Christopher George, b. 1969.

Issue of the late Ceely Maude, b. 1870, d. 1929 : m. 1901, Jane Marion, who d. 1949, dau. of the late C. W. O'Hara, J.P., D.L., of Annaghmore, and Coopers Hill, co. Sligo :—
Kathleen Lisalie, b. 1902: m. 1928, Francis Mervyn Cook, and has issue living, John Patrick Mervyn (The Old Manse, Childrey, Wantage, Berks.), b. 1941: m. 1963, Margaret Susan, da. of Michael Walter Hoare, and has issue living, Nicholas John Mervyn b. 1964, Julian Michael Patrick b. 1966, Lucinda Margaret Venetia b. 1973,—Ann Veronica, b. 1929: m. 1960, Michael Kenneth Maurice Spackman, of Enton Mill, Witley, Godalming, Surrey, and has issue living, Henrietta Louise b. (Nov.) 1960, Catriona Venetia b. 1962. *Residence,*—Lillebo, Fulbrook, Burford, Oxon.—— Venetia Marion Ceely, b. 1905. *Residence,*—142A, Ashley Gdns., SW1.

Grandchildren of the late Gen. Sir Frederick Francis Maude, V.C., G.C.B., 4th son of the late Rev. the Hon. John Charles Maude (ante):—
Issue of the late Lieut.-Gen. Sir Frederick Stanley Maude, K.C.B., C.M.G., D.S.O., b. 1864, d. (on active ser. while Comdg. troops in Mesopotamia) 1917 : m. 1893, Cecil Cornelia Marianne St. Leger, who d. 1942, dau. of the late Col. the Rt. Hon. Thomas Edward Taylor, M.P. [M. Headfort, colls.]:—
Edward Frederick, O.B.E., b. 1897; ed. at Lancing Coll.; Brigadier (retired) late R.A.; Comdt. Bermuda Militia 1936-41, O.C., 98th Field Regt. R.A. 1943-45, and Brig. R.A., S. Command, India 1945; European War 1917-8 in France and Belgium (two medals); has Coronation medal (1937); O.B.E. (Mil.) 1944: m. 1929, Sylvia, dau. of the late Robert Brewster, of New York, U.S.A., and has issue living, Michael Frederick Tremain (Etchilhampton House, Etchilhampton, Devizes, Wilts.), (Club,—Bath), b. 1935: m. 1962, Priscilla Douglas, da. of the late Brig. Christian George Maude, DSO, OBE, MC (ante), and has issue living, Rupert Frederick b. 1965, Andrew Tremain b. 1967, Alexandra b. 1963, Victoria b. 1970,—Eileen b. 1931,—Barbara, b. 1932: m. 1958, William Clarkson Marshall, and has issue living, Thomas Alan b. 1963, Cynthia b. 1959. *Residence,*—Harford Hill Farm, Fallston, Maryland, U.S.A. Club,—Bath.——Stella Cecil Evelyn, b. 1894: m. 1928, Lt.-Col. Arthur Abercromby Scott Duff, C.I.E., M.V.O., who d. 1951, and has issue living, Helen Rosemary (53, Harrington Gdns., SW7), b. 1930: m. 1st, 1955 (m. diss. 1959), Maj. Anthony Greville-Bell, DSO, Army Air Corps; 2ndly, 1966, Kim G. F. B. Howe, and has issue living (by 2nd m.) Guy Arthur b. 1966,—Margaret Abercromby, b. 1932: m. 1972, Hans William Kertess, of 27 East 65th St., New York, NY, 10021. *Residence,*—132, Cranmer Court, SW3.——Beryl Mary, b. 1896.

Granddaughter of the late Lieut.-Gen. Cornwallis Oswald Maude, son of the late Rev. the Hon. John Charles Maude (ante):—
Issue (by 1st marriage) of the late Maurice Oswald Maude, b. 1854, d. 1921: m. 1893, Euphemia Marcella, who d. 1952, dau. of Charles McLean, formerly of Caldara, Bourke Street, Goulburn, N.S. Wales:—
Emily Ord Archdall, b. 1896. *Residence,*—Duart, 262, Bourke Street, Goulburn, N.S. Wales.

Grandson of the late Col. Francis Cornwallis Maude, V.C., C.B., el. son of the late Capt. the Hon. Francis Maude, R.N., 6th son of 1st Viscount :—
Issue of the late Major Francis Sterling de Montalt Maude, b. 1867, d. 1940: m. 1898, Violet Brenda, who d. 1952, dau. of the late John Howarth Ashton, J.P., D.L., of Hatfield Court, Herefordshire :—
Francis Alan de Montalt, b. 1901 : m. 1929 (marriage dissolved 1952), Mary, dau. of Matthew Donohoe Grey, M.D., of Drumlish, co. Longford. *Residence,*—

Grandchildren of the late Capt. Charles Henry Maude, 2nd son of the late Capt. the Hon. Francis Maude, R.N. (ante) :—
Issue of the late Cyril Francis Maude (the well-known actor-manager), b. 1862, d. 1951: m. 1st, 1888, Isabel Winifred (a well-known actress), who d. 1924, dau. of Samuel Anderson Emery; 2ndly, 1927, Beatrice Mary (now of Dundrum, Lower Woodfield Road, Torquay) dau. of the late Rev. John Ellis, V. of Hungarton, Leicester, and widow of P. H. Trew, of Gotham Wood, Bexhill-on-Sea :—
By 1st marriage) *His Honour Judge* John Cyril, QC, b. 1901; ed. at Eton, and at Ch. Ch., Oxford; M.A. Lambeth 1948; Bar. Middle Temple 1925, a K.C. 1943, and a Bencher 1952; European War 1939-45 as Acting Major Intelligence Corps; appointed Prosecuting Counsel to Post Office at Central Criminal Court 1935, and Recorder of Devizes 1939, and of Plymouth 1944; Junior Prosecuting

Counsel to Treasury, Central Criminal Court 1942-43, and Chancellor of Diocese of Bristol 1948-50; has been an additional Judge of Mayor's and City of London Court since 1954; is a F.R.S.L.; sat as M.P. for Exeter (C) July 1945 to Oct. 1951: *m.* 1st, 1927, Rosamond Willing, dau. of Dr. Morris Murray, of 21, Marlborough Street, Boston, Mass., U.S.A.; 2ndly, 1955, Maureen Constance (BUCHANAN), dau. of the late Hon. Arthur Ernest Guinness [see E. Iveagh, colls.], and widow of the 4th Marquess of Dufferin and Ava, and has issue living, (by 1st marriage) Anne, Murray, *b.* 1929: *m.* 1950, Michael Hilary George Bradstock, of Donnington Castle House, Newbury, Berks., and has issue living, James Michael Murray *b.* 1951, Rupert John *b.* 1958, Alantair George *b.* 1961, Sarah Anne *b.* 1954. *Residences,*—4, Hans Cres., SW1; Clandeboye, co. Down. *Clubs,*— Garrick, Beefsteak.——Margery Kathleen, *b.* 1889: *m.* 1917, Joseph Warren Burden, and has issue living, Winifred Emery, *b.* 1922: *m.* 1945, Lt.-Col. Richard Gowen Collins, MBE, Duke of Wellington's Regt., of 4, Dryburgh Mansions, Putney, SW15, and has issue living, Robert Gowen *b.* 1947: *m.* 1973, Miriam, da. of A. T. de B. Wilmot, of Stone St., Kent, Peter Burden *b.* 1949,—Pamela Maude, *b.* 1926: *m.* 1959, James Milholland, Jr., of Long Meadow Rd., Bedford, NY, USA, and has issue living, James *b.* 1960, Peter Burden *b.* 1962. *Residence,*—10, East 85th St., New York 10028, USA.——Pamela Cynthia (*Hon. Mrs. William Fraser*), *b.* 1893: *m.* 1st, 1916, Maj. William La Touche-Congreve, VC, DSO, MC, Rifle Bde. (Prince Consort's Own), who *d.* (killed in action) 1916; 2ndly, 1919, Brig. the Hon. William Fraser, DSO, MC, who *d.* 1964 [see L. Saltoun], and has issue living, (by 1st m.) Mary Gloria CONGREVE (*posthumous*) (La Virginia, Cascada de Camojan, Marbella (Malaga), Spain), *b.* 1917; resumed by deed poll 1958 her maiden surname of Congreve in lieu of that of Stephenson: *m.* 1939, Augustus William Stephenson (who obtained a divorce 1956), son of the late Sir Guy Stephenson, CB [E. Shrewsbury, colls.], and has issue living, Timothy Congreve (Longhgall, co. Armagh), *b.* 1940: *m.* 1966, Nerena Anne Hyde, da. of Maj. the Hon. William Nicholas Somers Laurence Hyde Villiers [see E. Clarendon] (and has issue living, Guy Congreve *b.* 1969, Lucinda Mary Pamela *b.* 1967), Martin Guy (Telegraph Hill, Currawang, NSW 2580; Brooks's Club) *b.* 1942: *m.* 1st, 1966 (*m.* diss. 1970), Zara Nina, da. of the Rt. Hon. Sir (Harold) Anthony Nutting 3rd Bt.; 2ndly, 1973, Sonia Miller of Sydney, NSW (and has issue living, by 1st m., Katya, *b.* 1967), William Benedict, *b.* 1948: Bar Inner Temple 1973,—(by 2nd m.) [see L. Saltoun]. *Residence,*— La Virginia, Cascada de Camojan, Marbella (Malaga), Spain.

Issue of the late Alwyn Julian Maude, *b.* 1867, *d.* 1911: *m.* 1893, Mabel, dau. of James Torpy:—

Dudley Jack, *MB, ChM, b.* 1898; Ophthalmic Surg.: FRACP, MB, ChM, DOMS London, D.Obst. Oxford: *m.* 1925, Marcia, da. of the late John Williamson, solicitor, of Sydney, and has issue living, John Alwyn (4, Garnet St., Killara, NSW), *b.* 1930: *m.* 1955, Susan Theresa Gidley, da. of George Gidley King, of Sydney, NSW, and has issue living, John Philip Cornwallis *b.* 1959, Lisa Margaret, *b.* 1960, Jessica Mary *b.* 1970,—Jacqueline Mary, *b.* 1927: *m.* 1956, Llewellyn Daniel Wheeler, Surg., of 36, Newcastle St., Rose Bay, NSW, and has issue living, Andrew John *b.* 1957, Daniel Julian *b.* 1959, Frances Llewellyn Maude *b.* 1961. *Residence,*—22/366, Edgecliff Rd., Woollahra,NSW 2025.

Issue of the late Maurice Douglas Maude, *b.* 1868, *d.* 1953: *m.* 1906, Zima Irene Lily, who *d.* 1952, dau. of John Godfrey Koch, F.S.L., formerly Assist. Sup. of Surveys, Perak, Malaya:—

Valerie Blanche, *b.* 1908: *m.* 1939, John Chichester Longhurst, who *d.* 1957. *Residence,*—April Cottage, Ripe, Sussex.——Cicely, *b.* 1918: *m.* 1948, Roland Cumberbatch, MB, of Middle Farm House, Sutton, Ditcheat, Shepton-Mallet, Somerset, and has issue living, Toby John, *b.* 1949.— Judith Mary, *b.* 1952,—Hyacinth Anne, *b.* 1954.

Issue of the late Major Ralph Walter Maude, D.S.O., *b.* 1873, *d.* 1922: *m.* 1905, Alice (from whom he obtained a divorce 1915), only dau. of Noël Herford Thomson, of Dinan, France:—

Rev. Ralph Henry Evelyn, *b.* 1909; ed. at St. Peter's Hall, Oxford (MA): *m.* 1933, Marjorie Cecilia Emily, da. of the late Rev. Philip Harold Rogers, and hass issue living, Roger Philip (23 King's Paddock, Park Close, Hampton, Middlesex), *b.* 1937: *m.* 1972, Penelope Joy, da. of the late Christopher Rowe, Solicitor,—Rachel Anne, *b.* 1934: *m.* 1954, John Donald Collum (14, Manor Park Tockington, Bristol), and has issue living, Simon Richard *b.* 1967, Joanna Margaret *b.* 1969.—*Residence,*—6, Titan Barrow, Bathford, Bath.

Granddaughters of the late Raymond William de Latham Maude, son of the late Capt. the Hon. Francis Maude, R.N. (ante):—

Issue of the late Lieut.-Col. Charles Raymond Maude, O.B.E., M.C., *b.* 1882, *d.* 1943: *m.* 1907, Lilian Nancy Bache, CBE, who *d.* 1970, da. of the late William Henry Price, of Rockmount, Kinver, Stourbridge:—

Joan Nancy, *b.* 1908: *m.* 1st, 1933, Frank Henry Waters, who *d.* 1954; 2ndly, 1956, Oliver Frederick John Bradley Woods, MC, who *d.* 1972, and has issue living, (by 1st m.) Sarah Jenny, *b.* 1938: *m.* 1963, Maj. James Alexander Dunsmure, Scots Guards. *Residence,*—6 Southover, High St., Lewes. ——Elizabeth Meriel, *b.* 1912. *Residence,*—Turville Cottage, Turville Heath, nr. Henley-on-Thames.

PREDECESSORS.—[1] ROBERT Maude, *M.P.* for Gowran 1703, St. Canice 1715, and Bangor 1729, was cr. a *Baronet* 1705; *d.* 1750; *s.* by his el. son [2] *Sir* THOMAS, 2nd Bt., M.P. for co. Tipperary 1761; cr. *Baron de Montalt,* of Hawarden, co. Tipperary (peerage of Ireland) 1776; *d.* 1777, when the barony expired and the baronetcy devolved upon his brother [3] *Sir* CORNWALLIS, 3rd Bt., M.P. for Roscommon; cr. *Baron de Montalt,* of Hawarden, co. Tipperary (peerage of Ireland) 1785, and *Viscount Hawarden* (peerage of Ireland) 1793; *d.* 1803; *s.* by his el. son [4] THOMAS RALPH, 2nd Viscount; *d.* 1807, without issue; *s.* by his half-brother [5] CORNWALLIS, 3rd Viscount; *b.* 1780; *m.* 1811, Jane, who *d.* 1852, dau. of Patrick Crawford Bruce, of TaplowLodge, Bucks; *d.* 1856; *s.* by his son [6] CORNWALLIS, 4th Viscount; *b.* 1817; a Lord-in-Waiting to Queen Victoria 1866-8 and 1874-80; cr. *Earl de Montalt,* of Dundrum, co. Tipperary (peerage of United Kingdom) 1886: *m.* 1845, Clementina, who *d.* 1865, el. dau. and co-heir of the late Adm. the Hon. Charles Elphinstone-Fleeming; *d.* 1905, when the Earldom of De Montalt became ext., and he was *s.* in the other honours by his cousin [7] ROBERT HENRY, son of the late Very Rev. the Hon. Robert William Henry Maude, Dean of Clogher, 2nd son of 1st Viscount), 5th Viscount; *b.* 1842: *m.* 1881, Caroline, who *d.* 1930, dau. of the late Major Arthur Ogle; *d.* 1908; *s.* by his son [8] ROBERT CORNWALLIS, 6th Viscount, *b.* 1890; Lieut. Coldstream Guards; *d.* (killed in action) 1914; *s.* by his cousin [9] EUSTACE WYNDHAM (son of the late Ludlow Eustace Maude, son of the late Very Rev. the Hon. Robert William Henry Maude, 2nd son of 1st Viscount), 7th Viscount; *b.* 1877; Major (retired) Queen's Roy. Regt.: *m.* 1920, Marion, who *d.* 1974, da. of the late Albert Leslie Wright [B. Fitzwalter]; *d.* 1958; *s.* by his el. son [10] ROBERT LESLIE EUSTACE, 8th Viscount and present peer; also Baron de Montalt.

HAWKE, BARON. (Hawke.) [Baron G.B. 1776.]

BLADEN WILMER HAWKE, 9th Baron; *b.* Dec. 31st, 1901; *s.* 1939; ed. at Winchester, and at King's Coll., Camb. (B.A. 1923, M.A. 1946); was a Lord-in-Waiting to HM 1953-57, and a Church Commr. 1958-74; a Member of House of Laity, Church Assembly since 1955: *m.* 1934, Ina Mary Faure, da. of the late Henry Faure Walker, of Highley Manor, Balcombe, Sussex, and has issue.

Arms,—Argent, a chevron erminois, between three pilgrims' staves purpure. Crest,—A hawk rising ermine, belled, and charged on the breast with a fleur-de-lis or. Supporters,—Dexter, a figure of Neptune, his mantle vert, edged argent, crowned with an eastern crown or, his dexter arm erect and holding in the act of striking, a trident sable, point downwards silver, and resting his left foot on a dolphin proper; sinister, a sea horse or, holding between the fore fins a banner argent, the staff broken sable.

Residence,—Faygate Place, Faygate, Sussex, Club,—Carlton.

DAUGHTERS LIVING.

Hon. Caroline Ina Maude, *b.* 1937 ; Bar. Middle Temple 1959: *m.* 1960, John Francis Easton, Bar.-a law, and has issue living, Nicholas John, *b.* 1961,—Ina Frances, *b.* 1964. *Residence,*—The Old Hall Barley, nr. Royston, Herts.
Hon. Annabel, *b.* 1940: *m.* 1961, Nicholas Adam Ridley, and has issue living, Caspar Hawke Michael, *b.* 1967,—Celia Kirstin, *b.* 1964,—Harriet Clare, *b.* 1970. *Residence,*—29, Richmond Hill, Richmond, Surrey.
Hon. Cecilia Anne (12, Anhalt Rd., SW11), *b.* 1943: *m.* 1963, Peter Hannay Bailey Tapsell, MP (m. diss. 1971), and has issue living, James Hawke, *b.* 1966.
Hon. Lavinia Mary, *b.* 1945: *m.* 1965, Maj. Nicholas Maclean Verity Bristol, KOSB, of Breacachadh Castle, Isle of Coll., Argyll, and 22, Whittlesey St., SE1, and has issue living, Charles Bladen Maclean, *b.* 1967,—Alexander Stanhope Maclean, *b.* 1970,—Lauchlan Neil Maclean, *b.* 1974.
Hon. Rowena Margaret, *b.* 1948: *m.* 1971, Philip William Leatham, of Burleigh Hall, Brimscombe, Glos. [see By. Buckland].
Hon. Prunella Jane, *b.* 1951.
Hon. Olivia Mary, *b.* 1955.

BROTHER LIVING.

Hon. JULIAN STANHOPE THEODORE, *b.* Oct. 19th, 1904; ed. at Eton, and at King's Coll. Camb. (B.A. 1926); is Squadron-Leader, Auxiliary Air Force: *m.* 1st, 1933, Angela Margaret Griselda dau. of the late Capt. Edmund W. Bury; 2ndly, 1947, Georgette Margaret, dau. of George S. Davidson, of 73, Eaton Square, S.W., and has issue living, (by 1st marriage) Sarah Elisabeth Jane, *b.* 1935: *m.* 1957, John Norris Fennell, of Flint Cottage, East Harting, Petersfield, Hants., and has issue living, Adrian Martin Alexander *b.* 1963, Olivia Louise *b.* 1961,—Catherine Mary, *b.* 1940: *m.* 1963, Charles Groves Darvill Brook, of 7, The Hermitage, Richmond, Surrey, and has issue living, Charlotte Griselda Mary, *b.* 1965, Henrietta Diana Darvill *b.* 1968,—(by 2nd m.) Edward George, *b.* 1950,—Nicola Frances, *b.* 1949,—Vanessa Nathalie Mary, *b.* 1957,—Julia Georgette, *b.* 1960. *Residence,*—Old Mill House, Cuddington, Ches.

SISTER LIVING

Hon. Veronica Margery, *b.* 1915: *m.* 1940, Jack Briscoe Masefield, MA, and has issue living, Delphinia Frances Annie, *b.* 1947: *m.* 1969, Richard James Hall, of 12, King Henry's Rd., NW3, and has issue living , Leander Arthur Casper *b.* 1973, Hereward Ambrose Bertram *b.* 1974. *Residence,*—Down Lodge , East Harting, Petersfield, Hants.

PREDECESSORS.—[1] *Adm. Sir* EDWARD HAWKE, *K.C.B.*, son of the late Edward Hawke, Bar. at law, of Lincoln's Inn ; *b.* 1710 ; a celebrated Naval commander ; signally defeated the French off Bellisle 1759 (thanked by Parliament, rewarded with a pension of £2,000 a year) ; was First Lord of the Admiralty 1766-71 ; cr. *Baron Hawke,* of Towton, co. York (peerage of Great Britain), 1776 ; *d.* 1781 ; *s.* by his son [2] MARTIN BLADEN, *LL.D.*, 2nd Baron ; *d.* 1805 ; *s.* by his son [3] EDWARD, 3rd Baron ; assumed the additional surname of Harvey ; *d.* 1824 ; *s.* by his el. son [4] EDWARD WILLIAM, 4th Baron ; *d.* 1867 ; *s.* by his brother [5] STANHOPE, 5th Baron ; *d.* unmarried 1870 ; *s.* by his cousin [6] *Rev.* EDWARD HENRY JULIUS, 6th Baron, son of the late Hon. Martin Bladen Edward, 2nd son of 2nd Baron, by Hannah, dau. of Thomas Nisbet, of Mersington, *b.* 1815 ; *m.* 1857, Jane, who *d.* 1915, dau. of the late Henry Dowker, of Laysthorpe, York ; *d.* 1887 ; *s.* by his son [7] MARTIN BLADEN, 7th Baron, *b.* 1860: *m.* 1916, Maude, who *d.* 1936, dau. of the late William Peacock Edwards, J.P., and widow of Arthur Graham Cross ; *d.* 1938 ; *s.* by his brother [8] EDWARD JULIAN, 8th Baron ; *b.* 1873 ; *m.* 1900, Frances Alice, who *d.* 1959, dau. of the late Col. John Randal Wilmer, Indian Army ; *d.* 1939 ; *s.* by his son [9] BLADEN WILMER, 9th Baron and present peer.

Hawkesbury, Viscount, son of Earl of Liverpool.

Hay, Lord, son of Countess of Erroll.

HAYTER, BARON. (Chubb.) [Baron U.K. 1927, Bt. U.K. 1909.]

Safe by being cautious.

GEORGE CHARLES HAYTER CHUBB, 3rd Baron, and 3rd Baronet; *b.* April 25th, 1911; *s.* 1967; ed. at Leys Sch., and Trin. Coll., Camb. (MA); Chm. of Chubb & Son's Lock & Safe Co. Ltd.: *m.* 1940, Elizabeth Anne, MBE, only da. of the late Thomas Arthur Rumbold [see Rumbold, Bt., colls.], and has issue.

Arms,—Quarterly : 1st and 4th azure, a cross erminois between in first and fourth quarters a bezant and in second and third quarters a rose or, *Chubb*, 2nd and 3rd azure, a chevron between two bulls' heads couped in chief, and in base an escallop all or, *Hayter.* Crest,— In front of a demi lion rampant azure supporting between the paws a bezant charged with a rose gules, a key fesse-wise wards upwards or. Supporters,—On either side a lion azure, holding in the mouth a rose gules, barbed seeded, leaved and slipped proper, and charged on the shoulder with a key pale-wise wards downwards and to the dexter or.
Residence,—Ashtead House, Ashtead, Surrey.

SONS LIVING.
Hon. GEORGE WILLIAM MICHAEL, *b.* Oct. 9th, 1943; ed. at Marlborough and Nottingham Univ. (BSc).
Hon. John Andrew, *b.* 1946; ed. at Marlborough and Southampton Univ.
Hon. Charles Henry Thomas, *b.* 1949; ed. at Marlborough, and King's Coll., Camb.

DAUGHTER LIVING.
Hon. Sarah, *b.* 1941: *m.* 1963, the Rev. David Humphrey Clark, Priest in charge of St. George, Colegate and Industrial Chap., of St. Pauls Vicarage, Mill Lane, Norwich, NOR 55P, and has issue living, Andrew David, *b.* 1964,—Alison Tamsen, *b.* 1967.

BROTHER LIVING.
Hon. David William Early (19, Cadogan Place, SW1; St. Mary's Cottage, Broughton, Hants.) *b.* 1914; Cdr. RN (ret.); Far East 1939-45 (despatches, prisoner): *m.* 1939, Veronica, da. of W. Clifton, of Shanghai, and has issue living, Jeremy David Knyvett, *b.* 1941.

WIDOW LIVING OF SECOND BARON.
MARGARET ALISON (*Alison, Baroness Hayter*), (Old Housing, Woodgreen, Witney, Oxon), da. of J. G. Pickard, of Leicester: *m.* 1949, as his 2nd wife, the 2nd Baron, who *d.* 1967.

PREDECESSORS.—GEORGE HAYTER Chubb, 2nd son of the late John Chubb; *b.* 1848; a lock and safe manufacturer: *m.* 1870, Sarah Vanner, who *d.* 1940, dau. of the late Charles Early, J.P., of Witney, Oxon: *cr.* a Baronet 1900, and *Baron Hayter*, of Chislehurst, co. Kent (peerage of United Kingdom) 1927; *d.* 1946; *s.* by his son [2] CHARLES ARCHIBALD, 2nd Baron, *b.* 1871; Managing Dir. of Chubb & Sons Lock & Safe Co. Ltd.: *m.* 1st, 1898, Mary, who *d.* 1948, el. da. of John F. Haworth, JP, of Manchester; 2ndly, 1949, Margaret Alison, da. of J. G. Pickard, of Leicester; *d.* 1967; *s.* by his el. son [3] GEORGE CHARLES HAYTER, 3rd Baron and present peer.

HAZLERIGG, BARON. (Hazlerigg.) [Baron U.K. 1945, Bt. E. 1622.]

For our altars and our hearths.

ARTHUR GREY HAZLERIGG, *M.C.*, 2nd Baron, and 14th Baronet; *b.* Feb. 24th, 1910; *s.* 1949; ed. at Eton, and at Trin. Coll., Camb. (B.A. 1932); is Major R.A. (T.A.), and a J.P. and D.L. ; European War 1939-45 (MC): *m.* 1945, Patricia, who *d.* 1972. da. of the late John Pullar, of Durban, Natal, and has issue.

Arms,—Argent, a chevron sable between three hazel leaves vert. Crest,—Issuant from a cap of maintenance gules turned up ermine a Scot's head and shoulders couped proper. Supporters,—*Dexter*, a Cromwellian soldier holding in his exterior hand a sword point downwards; *sinister*, a Coldstream Guardsman of the seventeenth century supporting with his exterior hand by the muzzle a musket all proper.
Seat,—Noseley Hall, Billesdon, Leicester, LE7 9EH.

SON LIVING.
Hon. ARTHUR GREY, *b.* May 5th, 1951.

DAUGHTERS LIVING.
Hon. Angela Christine, *b.* 1946: *m.* 1969, Timothy Effingham MacDowel, of 14, Hazlewell Rd., Putney SW15 6HL, and has issue living, Benjamin St. George, *b.* 1970,—Richard Arthur, *b.* 1973.
Hon. Priscilla Frances, *b.* 1952: *m.* 1975, the Hon. Richard Arthur Louis Dillon [see V. Dillon].

BROTHERS LIVING.
Hon. Thomas Heron (Cafilda, Klosters, Switzerland), *b.* 1914; ed. at Eton, and at Trin. Coll., Camb. (BA); late Maj. Leicestershire Yeo.; formerly Flying-Officer RAF Reserve: *m.* 1st, 1942 (m. diss. 1956), Audrey Cecil, da. of the late Maj. Cecil Robert Bates, DSO, MC [see Bates, Bt., *cr.* 1880]; 2ndly, 1957 (m. diss. 1974), Doussa (CAYZER), da. of Fanbey Bey Wissa, of Ramleh, Egypt, and has issue living, (by 1st m.) Rupert Heron, *b.* 1943; ed. at Eton,—Simon Martival, *b.* 1945; ed. at Eton; Capt. 15th/19th King's R. Hussars (TA).
Hon. Robert Maynard, *b.* 1916; ed. at Eton, and at Trin. Coll., Camb. (BA 1938); is Maj. RA (TA): *m.* 1942, Rose, da. of Charles Cox, and has issue living, Rosemary, *b.* 1942: *m.* 1965, Malcolm Connell, of 49, Huntingdon St., N1, and has issue living, Emma *b.* 1972,—Gillian, *b.* 1946. *Residence,*— Cottonsfield Farm, Three Gates, Billesdon, Leicester.

SISTERS LIVING.

Hon. Rachel Elizabeth, *b.* 1904: *m.* 1928, Col. Anthony Charles Ward Kimpton, Herts Yeo., and has issue living, Anthony Andrew Ward (Beech Knoll House, Aldbourne, Wilts.), *b.* 1931; ed. at Eton, and Trin. Coll., Camb.; late Lt. Irish Gds.: *m.* 1964, Kathleen Margaret, yr. da. of the late Maj. J. S. Sinnott, of Tetbury, Glos., and has issue living, Archibald James Sinnott *b.* 1969, Melissa Emily *b.* 1967,—Rosamond Mary, *b.* 1929: *m.* 1950, Neil McLay Mills, of Upton Grey House, Upton Grey, Basingstoke, and has issue living, Mark Oliver McLay *b.* 1955, Titus Neil Archibald McLay *b.* 1970, Jemima Rachel McLay *b.* 1953: *m.* 1973, Edward George Trotter [see M. Tweeddale] Rosamond Cornelia McLay *b.* 1957,—Diana Rachel (twin), *b.* 1931: *m.* 1955, the Rev. John Theodore Cameron Bucke Collins, of Canford Magna Vicarage, Wimborne, Dorset, and has issue living, Andrew Dominic John Bucke *b.* 1956, Richenda Rachel *b.* 1959. *Residence,*—Sarunds House, Farnham, Blandford, Dorset.

Hon. Edith Bridget, *b.* 1908 ; is a J.P. for Leicestershire ; European War 1939-45 as Senior Com. ATS. *Residence,*—Church Cottage, Carlton Curlieu, Leicester.

COLLATERAL BRANCHES LIVING. (*In remainder to Baronetcy only.*)

Grandsons of the late Maj.-Gen. Thomas Maynard Hazlerigg, 2nd son of 12th baronet :—

Issue of the late Lieut.-Col. Thomas Hazlerigg, D.S.O., *b.* 1877, *d.* 1935: *m.* 1903, Edith Violet, who *d.* 1959, dau. of the late Lieut.-Col. W. H. McCheane, R.M.L.I. :—

Arthur William *b.* 1904; ed. at Uppingham; MA Camb. 1947; Lt.-Col. RA (ret.); Univ. Draftsman and Sen. Assist. Registrary, Camb. 1947-71; 1939-45 War: *m.* 1st, 1935, Marjorie Dorothea (who obtained a divorce 1946), da. of the late Col. George Frederick Brown Turner, DSO, of Blackheath, SE3; 2ndly, 1947, Jane, da. of the late David Wilson, OBE, and has issue living, (by 1st marriage) Arthur Robert (Paddock Lodge, Whitchurch, Pangbourne, Berks.), *b.* 1936; ed. at Leys Sch., and Coll. of Estate Management (BSc); ARICS; ARVA; Capt. RHA (ret.): *m.* 1963, Hermione, da. of Edward Simpson Anderson, MBE, and has issue living, Catrina Louise *b.* 1964. *Residence,*—Lordship Farm, Melbourn, nr. Royston, Herts.

Issue of the late Capt. Greville Hazlerigg, *b.* 1881, *d.* 1944 : *m.* 1908, Helen Margaret, who *d.* 1949, dau. of the late Maj.-Gen. N. T. Parsons, 101st and 103rd Fusiliers :—

Arthur Greville Maynard, *b.* 1910; formerly in P.W.D., Nigeria ; formerly Capt. Roy. Norfolk Regt. and RASC; 1939-45 War (1939-43 star): *m.* 1941, Nancy, da. of the late Capt. J. A. Ingles, RN, and has issue living, Arthur Patrick, *b.* 1943; ed. at Milton Abbey; Capt. RA,—Diana Elizabeth (c/o National and Grindlays Bank, 13, St. James's Sq., SW1), *b.* 1947: *m.* 1971, Capt. Anthony Michael Thomas Moody, R. Irish Rangers,—Sheelagh Marion, *b.* 1952. *Residence,*—Sehore, Tekels Av., Camberley, Surrey.

Granddaughter of the late Rev. William Greville Hazlerigg, 4th son of 12th Bt.:—

Issue of the late Roger Greville Hazlerigg, *b.* 1877, *d.* 1952 : *m.* 1919, Esther Rosamond, dau. of Lacey Nussey Everett, of Rushmere Lodge, Pool, near Leeds :—

Jean Mary, *b.* 1921 : *m.* 1947, Major Kenneth Leonard Perrin. *Residence,*—The Old Rectory, Great Comberton, near Pershore, Worcestershire.

Grandson of the late Allen Martival Hazlerigg, yst. son of 12th baronet:—

Issue of the late Martival Grey Hazlerigg, *b.* 1884, *d.* 1971: *m.* 1925, Marian (Flat 2, 22, Gloucester Rd., New Barnet, Herts.), da. of the late Michael Ray:—

Martival Spencer Woolf (19, Sandford Leaze, Avening, Terbury, Glos.), *b.* 1927: *m.* 1947, Kitty, da. of William Johnson Bowhill, of Wray Cres., N4, and has issue living, Marilyn Kay, *b.* 1952,—Martine Grey, *b.* 1957.

Grandchildren of the late Rev. Grey Hazlerigg (infra):—

Issue of the late Grey Hazlerigg, O.B.E., *b.* 1879, *d.* 1948 : *m.* 1st, 1908, Sarah Dorothy (who *d.* 1965, having obtained a divorce 1924), da. of the late Herbert Bakewell Whetstone, JP, formerly of Ilketshall Hall, Bungay, Suffolk; 2ndly, 1933, Fannie, who *d.* 1949, widow of Frederick Hardy, late of Staunton Hall, Notts:—

(**By 1st marriage**) Herbert William Grey, *b.* 1910 ; 2nd Lieut. late Indian Army (Unattached List). ——Alexander Maynard, *b.* 1914 ; ed. at Lewes County Sch.; entered Colonial Civil Ser. 1935; appointed Sub-Inspector of Constabulary, Trinidad 1937.——Dorothy Mary Louise, *b.* 1912.

Issue of the late Thomas Maynard Hazlerigg, O.B.E., M.C., *b.* 1882, *d.* 1961: *m.* 1st, 1905, Violet Isabella, who *d.* 1941, da. of H. J. Price; 2ndly, 1941, Gladys May, BEM (Broomhill, Ryton, Shrewsbury), da. of T. Cotton:—

(**By 1st marriage**) Diana Margaret, *b.* 1914: *m.* 1946, Robert Edward Hope-Falkner, late Malayan Police, of, Avenida Virgen del Carmen 31, Algeciras, Prov. de Cadiz, Spain, and has issue living, John Alexander, *b.* 1947,—Patrick Miles (8, Park Rd., Hampton Wick, Surrey), *b.* 1949: *m.* 1972, Wendy, el. da. of the late J. D. Mallinson, of Southampton.

Issue of the late Rev. Grey Hazlerigg, 3rd son of 11th baronet, *b.* 1818, *d.* 1912: *m.* 1873, Sarah Ann, who *d.* 1901, el. dau. of the late Thomas Clarke, of 25, Forest Road, Loughborough :—

Dorothy Frances (64, Beach Rd., Weston-super-Mare): *m.* 1903, Wilfred Tyler, who *d.* 1943.

Granddaughter of the late Arthur Hesilrige, Lieut. 59th Regt., son of the late Rev. Charles Maynard Hesilrige, brother of 11th baronet :—

Issue of the late Arthur George Maynard Hesilrige, Editor of *Debrett* 1887-1935, *b.* (posthumous) 1863, *d.* 1953 : *m.* 1889, Amy Florence, who *d.* 1947, dau. of the late M. S. Myers, of Thorney Hedge, High Road, Chiswick, W.4 :—

Violet Maynard, *b.* 1900: *m.* 1943, Maj. George Reginald Jackson, RASC, late Reserve of Officers, who *d.* 1954. *Residence,*—6, Sunstar Lane, Polegate, Sussex.

Grandchildren of the late Thomas Greville Hesilrige, son of the late Rev. Charles Maynard Hesilrige (ante):—

Issue of the late Thomas Greville Hesilrige, *b.* 1878, *d.*1955: *m.* 1st, 1901, Florence Elizabeth, who *d.* 1919, dau. of Edwin Henry Griffiths, formerly of Mount Pleasant, Shrewsbury; 2ndly, 1921, Gertrude May (of The Cherries, 166, Rugby Rd., Binley Woods, Coventry), da. of William Downs, formerly of Uplands, Coventry:—

(**By 2nd marriage**) Roger Greville, *b.* 1932 : *m.* 1957, Barbara Shirley, dau. of Henry Edward Daniel, of 80, Manor Estate, Wolston, near Coventry, and has issue living, Charles Greville, *b.* 1958. *Residence,*—168, Rugby Rd., Binley Woods, Coventry.——(By 1st marriage) Dorothy Greville, *b.* 1903: *m.* 1926, Thomas Gilbert Hodgett, of 2, Rosscolban Av., Kesh, co. Fermanagh.

Issue of the late Robert Maynard Hesilrige, *b.* 1884, *d.* 1951: *m.* 1914, Dora, who *d.* 1969, da. of Thomas Cope, of The Lount Farm, Osbaston:—

Isabel Maynard, *b.* 1916 : *m.* 1938, Reginald Gerald Watts, and has issue living, Richard Maynard *b.* 1941. *Residence,*—Hillcrest, 89, Pioneer Avenue, Desborough, Kettering.

PREDECESSORS.—[1] THOMAS Hesilrige, son of the late Thomas Hesilrige, of Noseley Hall, Leicestershire ; *b.* 1564; M.P. for Leicestershire 1614 and 1624-5 (Sheriff 1612-13 ; cr. a *Barone*, 1622 : *m.* 16—, Frances, who *d.* 1638, dau. of the late Sir William Gorges, of Alderton ; *d.* 1629 ; *s.* by his son [2] ARTHUR, 2nd Bt.; *b.* 16— ; M.P. for Leicestershire 1640-45 and for Leicester 1654-9 ; sometime Gov. of Newcastle; during Civil War, in which he rendered signal sers., was Col. in Parliamentary Army Comdg. a Regt. of Cuirassiers (known as the Lobsters): *m.* 1st, 1625, Frances, who *d.* 1632, dau. of the late Thomas Elmes ; 2ndly, 16—, Dorothy, who *d.* 1650, dau. of the late FulkeGreville, and sister of 2nd Baron Brooke (cr. 1620) ; *d.* (whilst a prisoner in Tower of London) 1660 ; *s.* by his el. son [3] THOMAS, 3rd Bt. ; *b.* 1625 : *m.* 1664, Elizabeth, who *d.* 1673, dau. of the late George Fenwick, of Brunton Hall, Northumberland ; *d.* 1680 ; *s.* by his only son [4] THOMAS, 4th Bt. ; *b.* 1664 ; M.P. for Leicestershire 1690-95 (Sheriff 1686-7) ; *d.* 1700 ; *s.* by his uncle [5] ROBERT (only surviving son of 2nd Bt.), 5th Bt. ; *b.* 1640 : *m.* 1664, Bridget, who *d.* 1697, dau. of the late Sir Samuel Rolle, of Heanton, Devon ; *d.* 1713 ; *s.* by his son [6] ROBERT

6th Bt.; *b.* 1668; Sheriff of Leicestershire 1715-16: *m.* 1696, the Hon. Dorothy Maynard, who *d.* 1748, dau. of 3rd Baron Maynard (cr. I. 1620); *d.* 1721; *s.* by his only son [7] ARTHUR, 7th Bt.; *b.* 17—: *m.* 1725, Hannah Sturges, who *d.* 1765; *d.* 1763; *s.* by his son [8] ROBERT, 8th Bt.; *b.* 17—: *m.* 17—, Sarah, who *d.* 17—, dau. of the late Nathaniel Waller, of Roxburgh, New England, U.S.A.; *d.* 17—; *s.* by his son [9] ARTHUR, 9th Bt.; *b.* 17—; sometime in H.E.I.C.S.: *m.* 1st, 17—, Elizabeth Charnand, of Smyrna, who *d.* 1797; 2ndly, 17—, Charlotte Elizabeth, who *d.* 1817 (having *m.* 2ndly, 1805, Capt. Henry William Wilkinson), dau. of Capt. F. E. S. Gray; *d.* 1805; *s.* by his uncle [10] THOMAS MAYNARD (3rd son of 7th Bt.), 10th Bt.: *b.* 17—: *m.* 1st, 1805, Mary, who *d.* 1809, dau. of the late Edmund Tyrrell, of Gipping Hall, Suffolk; 2ndly, 1811, the Hon. Letitia Wodehouse, who *d.* 1864 (havng *m.* 2ndly, 1842, Frederick Fielding, Bar.-at-Law), dau. of 1st Baron Wodehouse; *d.* 1817; *s.* by his nephew [11] ARTHUR GREY (el. son of Col. Grey Hesilrige, 5th son of 7th Bt.), 11th Bt., *b.* 17—; assumed by Roy. licence 1818 the surname of Hazlerigg in lieu of his patronymic: *m.* 1811, Henrietta Anne, who *d.* 1868, dau. of the late John Bourne, of Stanch Hall, Hants; *d.* 1819; *s.* by his el. son [12] ARTHUR GREY, 12th Bt.; *b.* 1812; Sheriff of Leicestershire 1837: *m.* 1835, Henrietta, who *d.* 1883, dau. of the late Charles Allen Phillipps, of St. Bride's Hill, Pembrokeshire; *d.* 1890; *s.* by his grandson [13] ARTHUR GREY (only son of Lieut.-Col. Arthur Grey Hazlerigg, el. son of 12th Bt.), '13th Bt.; *b.* 1878; was Lord Lieut. and Custos Rotulorum for Leicestershire (High Sheriff 1909); cr. *Baron Hazlerigg,* of Noseley, co. Leicester (peerage of United Kingdom) 1945: *m.* 1903, Dorothy Rachel, who *d.* 1972, el. da. of the late John Henry Buxton, JP, DL, of Easneye, Ware; *d.* 1949; *s.* by his son [14] ARTHUR GREY, 2nd Baron and present peer.

HEAD, VISCOUNT. (Head.) [Viscount U.K. 1960.]

ANTONY HENRY HEAD, *G.C.M.G., C.B.E., M.C., P.C.,* 1st Viscount, son of the late Geoffrey Head, of 51, South Street, W.1; *b,* Dec. 19th, 1906; ed. at Eton; Brig. (ret.) Life Guards; Assist. Sec., Committee of Imperial Defence 1940-41, G.S.O.2, Guards Armoured Div. 1942, Ch. Mil. Planner, Combined Operations 1942-43, and Representative (Brig.) with Directors of Plans for Amphibious Operations 1943-46; Sec. of State for War Oct. 1951 to Oct. 1956, Min. of Defence Oct. 1956 to Jan. 1957, High Commr. for U.K. in Fed. of Nigeria 1960-63, and in Fed. of Malaysia 1963-66; a Member of Board of Trustees of Thomson Foundation since 1967, and Chm. of Roy. National Inst. for Blind since 1968; Col. Comdt. Special Air Ser. Regt. 1968; MP for Carshalton Div. of Surrey (*C*) 1945-60; cr. CBE (Mil) 1946, PC 1951, *Viscount Head,* of Throope, co. Wilts. and KCMG 1960, and GCMG 1963: *m.* 1935, Lady Dorothea Louise Ashley-Cooper, da. of 9th Earl of Shaftesbury, and has issue.

Arms,—Sable a chevron argent between two unicorns' heads couped in chief, and in base as many arrows in saltire and filed by a ducal crown or. **Crest,**—A unicorn's head couped sable armed and erined or, between two arrows erect, points downward of the last. **Supporters,**—On either side a Staffordshire terrier sable gorged with a dog collar or.

Residence,—Throope Manor, Bishopstone, Salisbury. *Club,*—White's.

SONS LIVING.

Hon. RICHARD ANTONY (Rhonehurst, Lambourn, Newbury), *b.* Feb. 27th, 1937; ed. at Eton and RMA Sandhurst; late Capt. Life Guards: *m.* 1974, Alicia Brigid, el. da. of Julian Salmond, of Maidford, Norton, Malmesbury, Wilts.

Hon. Simon Andrew, *b.* 1944; ed. at Eton, Ch. Ch., Oxford, and Berkeley Univ., Cal., USA.

DAUGHTER LIVING.

Hon. Tresa Mary, *b.* 1938: *m.* 1972, Richard Deacon Haddon, of 2, Savile House, Eton College, Windsor, Bucks., and has issue living, Edward Antony Deacon, *b.* 1973,—Joseph Richard, *b.* 1974,—Alice Mary (twin), *b.* 1974.

HEADFORT, MARQUESS OF. (Taylour.) Sits as BARON KENLIS (U.K. 1831). [Marquess I. 1800, Bt. I. 1704.]

[Name pronounced "Taylor."]

He attains whatever he seeks.

THOMAS GEOFFREY CHARLES MICHAEL TAYLOUR, 6th Marquess, and 9th Baronet; *b.* Jan. 20th, 1932; *s.* 1960; ed. at Stowe, and at Christ's Coll., Camb. (MA); ARICS, holds Commercial Pilots' Licence; Freeman of Guild of Air Pilots and Air Navigators; late 2nd Lt. Life Guards, and acting P.O., RAFVR: *m.* 1st, 1958 (m. diss. 1969), the Hon. Elizabeth Angela Veronica Rose Nall-Cain, da. of 2nd Baron Brocket; 2ndly, 1972, Virginia, da. of the late Mr. Justice Nable, of Manila, and has issue by 1st m.

Arms,—Quarterly: 1st and 4th ermine, on a chief gules a fleur-de-lys between two boars' heads couped and erect or; 2nd vert, a Pegasus courant, wings endorsed ermine, a chief or a crescent for difference, *Quin*; 3rd argent, two bendlets gules, on a chief azure a lion passant of the first. **Crest,**—A naked arm couped at the shoulder embowed, holding an arrow proper. **Supporters,**—*Dexter,* a lion guardant or; *sinister,* a leopard guardant proper, both collared and chained argent.

Residence,—Ellerslie, Crosby, IOM. *Clubs,*—Cavalry, Royal Aero, Kildare Street, RAF Reserve, Lansdowne.

SON LIVING. (*By* 1*st m.*)
THOMAS MICHAEL RONALD CHRISTOPHER (*Earl of Bective*), *b.* Feb. 10th, 1959.

DAUGHTERS LIVING. (*By* 1*st m.*)
Lady Rosanagh Elizabeth Angela Mary, *b.* 1961.
Lady Olivia Sheelin Davina Anne, *b.* 1963.

SISTER LIVING.
Lady Olivia Elsie June, *b.* 1929: *m.* 1955, Victor Echevarri Waldron, and has issue living, Sarah Rose
Echevarri, *b.* 1956,—Virginia Elizabeth Echevarri, *b.* 1957. *Residence,*—Ascot Cottage, Winkfield,
Berks.

UNCLE LIVING. (*Son of* 4*th Marquess.*)
Lord William Desmond, *b.* 1904; ed. at Harrow, and at Trin. Coll., Camb. (B.A. 1949, M.A. 1953,
Ph.D. 1955); is a F.S.A.; late Capt. 2nd Derbyshire Yeo. (T.A.). *Residence,*—St. Aubyns 2,
Woodlands Rd., Great Shelford, Cambridge. *Club,*—Bath.

AUNT LIVING. (*Daughter of* 4*th Marquess.*)
Lady Millicent Olivia Mary TAYLOUR, *b.* 1907; resumed the surname of Taylour in lieu of Tiarks
1941: *m.* 1930, Henry Frederic Tiarks, from whom she obtained a divorce 1936. *Address,*—
Heathervale, Oakleigh Park North, Whetstone, N.20.

COLLATERAL BRANCHES LIVING.

Descendants of the late Hon. Clotworthy Taylor (4th son of 1st Earl of Bective),
who was cr. *Baron Langford* 1800 [see that title].

Grandson of the late Capt. Basil Reginald Hamilton TAYLOUR, RN, yr. son of Col.
The Rt. Hon. Thomas Edward Taylor (infra):—
Issue of the late Basil Richard Henry Osgood Taylour, *b.* 1904, *d.* 1969: *m.* 1935, Gwendoline
Edith Marion, who *d.* 1975, da. of His Honour the late William Evans:—
Douglas Terence William Lenthall (105, Penhill Estate, PO Eerste River, Cape Prov., S. Africa),
b. 1939: *m.* 1964,—, and has issue living, Edward, *b.* 1966,—Robert, *b.* 1969,—Kenlis, *b.* 1965.

Granddaughters of the late Col. the Rt. Hon. Thomas Edward Taylor, MP, son of
the late Rev. the Hon. Henry Edward Taylor, 5th son of 1st Earl:—
Issue of the late Wilfrid Doneraile Stanhope Taylor, *b.* 1868, *d.* 1954: *m.* 1892, Margaret
Annie, who *d.* 1940, da. of Arthur William Follett Halcombe, of Urenui, Taranaki, NZ:—
Lois Cecil Beatrix: *m.* 1st, 1914 (marriage dissolved 1919), Frederick Charles Kent; 2ndly, 1933
(marriage dissolved 1944), Samuel Aldenton, and has issue living, (by 2nd marriage) Peter Pearce
Malcolm (14, Moss Clos , E. Bridgford, Notts), *b.* 1923: *m.* 1949, Veronica, da. of R. Saunt,
of Batley, Yorks., and has issue living, Jonathan Simon Peter, *b.* 1949, Cynthia Gabrielle
Peta *b.* 1951,—(by 1st marriage), Hermione Clifforde, *b.* 1915: *m.* 1940, James Cooke, of 67, Cott-
more Av., Walton-on-Thames, Surrey, and has issue living, Barry James *b.* 1950, Patricia Anne
b. 1947: *m.* 1967, Brian Joss, of 70, Campbell Rd., Woodley, Reading, (and has issue living, Amanda
Helen *b.* 1971). *Residence,*—Hill Crest, Ragnal Lane, Nailsworth, Glos.——Ailleen Marjorie, RRC
(PO Box 116, Mangonui, Northland, NZ), *b.* 1895; formerly Matron QARNNS; has 1939-45 Star and
two war medals.——Enid Dorothy (32, Meend Garden Terr., Church Rd., Cinderford, Glos.), *b.* 1897:
m. 1922, Dr. Noel Whitton, MC, who *d.* 1924, and has issue living, Mark James (Coutts & Co., 440,
Strand, WC2), *b.* 1923: late Lt. RM: *m.* 1951, Elsie Chau Yung, who *d.* 1968, el. da. of Chung
Twian Siong, of Jesselton, British N. Borneo, and has issue living, Mark Stuart *b.* 1953, Patrick
James *b.* 1955, Timothy Michael *b.* 1964.——Edith Daphne Eunice, *b.* 1901: *m.* 1922, Group
Capt. Edward Morton Drummond, RAF (ret.) [see E. Perth, colls.]. *Residence,*—Pleasant, The
Ridge, Cold Ash, Newbury, Berks.

PREDECESSORS.—[1] *Rt. Hon.* THOMAS Taylor, son of the late Thomas Taylor, of Kells,
co. Meath; *b.* 1662; sometime M.P. for Kells; cr. a *Baronet* 1704: *m.* 1682, Anne, who
d. 1710, dau. of Sir Robert Cotton, 1st Bt.; *d.* 1736; *s.* by his son [2] *Sir* THOMAS, *P.C.,* 2nd
Bt., *b.* 1686; M.P. for Kells 1711; *s.* by his son [3] *Sir* THOMAS, *K.P., P.C.,* 3rd Bt., *b.*
1724; M.P. for Kells 1747; cr. *Baron Headfort,* of Headfort, co. Meath (peerage of Ireland)
1760, *Viscount Headfort* (peerage of Ireland) 1762, and *Earl of Bective* (peerage of Ireland)
1766; *d.* 1795; *s.* by his son [4] THOMAS, *K.P.,* 2nd Earl, *b.* 1757; a Lord of the Bedchamber;
assumed the surname of Taylour in lieu of his patronymic; cr. *Marquess of Headfort* (peerage
of Ireland) 1800; *d.* 1829; *s.* by his son [5] THOMAS, *K.P., P.C.,* 2nd Marquess; *b.* 1787;
was a Lord-in-Waiting to H.M. Queen Victoria 1837-41, and Lord-Lieut. of co. Cavan; cr.
Baron Kenlis, of Kenlis, co. Meath (peerage of United Kingdom), 1831: *m.* 1st, 1822, Olivia,
who *d.* 1834, el. dau. of Sir John Stevenson; *d.* 1870; *s.* by his son [6] THOMAS, *K.P., P.C.,*
3rd Marquess, *b.* 1822; M.P. for Westmoreland (C) 1854-70; Lord-Lieut. of co. Meath: *m.* 1st,
1842, Amelia, who *d.* 1864, only dau. of the late W. Thompson, M.P., of Underley Hall, Westmoreland; 2ndly, 1875, Emily Constantia, who *d.* 1926, dau. of the late Rev. Lord John
Thynne, D.D., and widow of Capt. Eustace John Wilson-Patten; *d.* 1894; *s.* by his younger
son [7] GEOFFREY THOMAS, 4th Marquess, *b.* 1878; a Senator of Irish Free State 1922-8: *m.*
1901, Rose, who *d.* 1958, dau. of Charles Boote; *d.* 1943; *s.* by his el. son [8] TERENCE GEOFFREY
THOMAS, *T.D.,* 5th Marquess: *b.* 1902; Capt. Warwick Yeo. (T.A.); was A.D.C. to Gov. of S.
Australia 1939-40: *m.* 1928, Elsie Florence, who *d.* 1972, da. of James Partridge Tucker, of Devon,
and widow of Sir Rupert Turner Havelock Clarke, 2nd Bt. (cr. 1882); *d.* 1960; *s.* by his only son [9]
THOMAS GEOFFREY CHARLES MICHAEL, 6th Marquess and present peer; also Earl of Bective, Viscount
Headfort, Baron Headfort, and Baron Kenlis.

HEADLEY, BARON. (Allanson-Winn.) [Baron I. 1797, Bt. E. 1660 and
G.B. 1776.]

CHARLES ROWLAND ALLANSON-WINN, 7th
Baron, and 13th Baronet of Nostell and 7th of
Little Warley; *b.* May 19th, 1902; *s.* 1969;
ed. at Bedford Sch.: *m.* 1927, Hilda May,
da. of the late Thomas Wells Thorpe, of
52, Redington Rd., NW, and has issue.

Arms,—Paly wavy of six or and azure, on a chief
gules, a lion passant guardant or. *Crest,*—Issuant
from a mount vert, a demi-lion guardant or, holding in
the paws a cross gules. *Supporters,*—*Dexter,* an eagle
By valour and labour. wings inverted, or, ducally gorged ermine; *sinister*
a lion guardant or, holding in the dexter paw a cross gules.

Seat,—Aghadoe, Killarney, co. Kerry. *Residence,*—Torton Top, Torton Hill, Arundel, Sussex.

SON LIVING.
Hon. JOHN ROWLAND, *b.* Oct. 14th, 1934; ed. at Canford Sch.

DAUGHTERS LIVING.
Hon. Pamela Jean, *b.* 1928: *m.* 1948, Ivan Beshoff, and has issue living, David Rowland, *b.* 1950.
Hon. Janet Diana (Gamekeeper's Cottage, Commonside, Gt. Bookham, Surrey), *b.* 1932: *m.* 1955, Antony John Vlassopulos, Bar.-at-law, from whom she obtained a divorce 1969, and has issue living, Christopher John Antony, *b.* 1958,—Mark Charles Antony, *b.* 1959.
Hon. Susan Ethel, *b.* 1936.

BROTHER LIVING.
Hon. Owain Gwynedd, *b.* 1906; ed. at Bedford Sch.: *m.* 1938, Ruth (PEARSON), da. of the late Cecil Orpin, of Strand House, Youghal, co. Cork. *Residence,*—Gwydyr, Witfontein Rd., George, Cape Prov., S. Africa.

WIDOW LIVING OF SON OF FIFTH BARON.
Barbara Muriel (Flat 2, 37, Hastie St., Bunbury, W. Aust. 6230), da. of the late Owen Sparks, of Bridgetown, W. Aust.: *m.* 1942, the Hon. John Valentine Allanson-Winn, who *d.* 1972.

WIDOW LIVING OF SIXTH BARON.
EDITH JANE (*Edith, Baroness Headley*) (Haworth House, Turnberry, Ayrshire), yst. da. of the late Rev. George Dods, DD, Min. of Barr, Ayrshire: *m.* 1936, the 6th Baron, who *d.* 1969.

PREDECESSORS.—[1] GEORGE Winn, English Baron of the Court of Exchequer in Scotland was cr. a *Baronet,* of Little Warley, Essex 1776, and *Lord Headley, Baron Allanson and Winn,* of Aghadoe, co. Kerry (peerage of Ireland) 1797; assumed the surname and arms of Allanson only by Roy. licence 1777, but appears to have used the double surname of Allanson-Winn; *d.* 1798; *s.* by his son [2] CHARLES, 2nd Baron; *s.* his kinsman as 8th Bt., of Nostell (see *.*.* infra); *d.s.p.* 1840; *s.* by his nephew [3] CHARLES ALLANSON, 3rd Baron, son of the Hon. George Mark Arthur Way, *M.P.,* 2nd son of 1st Baron; *b.* 1810; a Representative Peer: *m.* 1841, Maria Margaret, dau. of the late Major d'Arley; *d.* 1877; *s.* by his son [4] CHARLES MARK ALLANSON, 4th Baron; *b.* 1845; a Representative Peer; used the surname of Winn only: *m.* 1867, Elizabeth Housemayne, who *d.* 1928, dau. of the Rev. John Blennerhassett, R. of Rymecum-Hermitage; *d.* 1913; *s.* by his cousin [5] ROWLAND GEORGE ALLANSON, 5th Baron, only son of the late Hon. Rowland Allanson-Winn (who used without Roy. licence the double surname of Allanson-Winn); *b.* 1855; Pres. of British Muslim So. (made Pilgrimage to Mecca 1923—entitled to prefix " Al Haj "): *m.* 1st, 1899, Teresa St. Josephine, who *d.* 1919, dau. of the late W. H. Johnson, formerly Gov. of Leh and Jammu; 2ndly, 1921, Barbara Janet Ainsleigh, who *d.* 1929, dau. of Robert Lawrence Kilpatrick, and widow of Thomas Baynton; 3rdly, 1929, Catharine, who *d.* 1947, dau. of the late Joseph Williams Lovibond, of Lake House, Wilts, and widow of Major Lindsay Bashford, O.B.E., R.A.M.C.: *d.* 1935; *s.* by his el. son [6] ROWLAND PATRICK JOHN GEORGE, 6th Baron, *b.* 1901: *m.* 1936, Edith Jane, yst. da. of the late Rev. George Dods, BD, Min. of Barr, Ayrshire; *d.* 1969; *s.* by his brother [7] CHARLES ROWLAND, 7th Baron and present peer.

..* [1] GEORGE Winn, a zealous adherent of Charles I., was cr. a *Baronet,* of Nostell, co. York 1660; *d.* 1667; *s.* by his son [2] *Sir* EDMUND, 2nd Bt.; *d.* 1694; *s.* by his son [3] *Sir* ROWLAND 3rd Bt.; *d.* 1721; *s.* by his son [4] *Sir* ROWLAND, 4th Bt.; *d.* 1765; *s.* by his son [5] *Sir* ROWLAND, 5th Bt.; *d.* 1785; *s.* by his son [6] *Sir* ROWLAND, 6th Bt.; *d.* unmarried and intestate, when his estates passed to his sister, Esther Sabina, wife of John Williamson, and the baronetcy devolved upon his kinsman [7] *Sir* EDMUND Mark, 7th Bt.; *d.* 1833; *s.* by his kinsman [8] CHARLES, 8th Bt. who had previously *s.* as 2nd Baron Headley (ante).

HELSBY, BARON. (Helsby.) [Life Baron 1968.]

LAURENCE NORMAN HELSBY, *GCB, KBE,* son of the late Wilfred Helsby, of Liverpool; *b.* April 27th, 1908; ed. at Sedbergh, and Keble Coll., Oxford (MA, Hon. Fellow 1959); Hon. LLD Exeter, and Hon. DCL Durham; Lecturer in Economics, Univ. Coll. of S.-W. 1930-31, and Durham Colls., Durham Univ. 1931-45, Censor of Hatfield Coll. 1936-38, temporary Senior Clerk, House of Commons 1940-41, temporary Admin. Officer Treasury 1941-45, Assist. Sec., Treasury 1946, Prin. Private Sec. to Prime Min. 1947-50, Dep. Sec. Min. of Food 1950-54, 1st Civil Ser. Commr. 1954-59, Permanent Sec. to Min. of Labour 1959-62, and Joint Permanent Sec. to Treasury and Head of Home Civil Ser. 1962-68; a Dir. of Rank Orgn., Imperial Group, and Midland Bank; Chm. of Midland Bank Trust Co.; *cr.* CB (Civil) 1950, KBE (Civil) 1955, GCB (Civil) 1963, and *Baron Helsby,* of Logmore, co. Surrey (Life Baron) 1968: *m.* 1938, Wilmett Mary, yr. da. of the late W. G. Maddison, of Durham, and has issue.

Arms,—Or a saltire sable and a chief checky or and sable. **Crest,**—A horse salient argent flowing from the neck a mantle checky or and sable.
Residence,—Logmore Farm, Dorking, Surrey, RH4 3JN.

SON LIVING.
Hon. Nigel Charles (Abbots Wood, The Street, Salcott-cum-Virley, Maldon, Essex, CM9 8HL), *b.* 1941: *m.* 1969, Sylvia Rosena, da. of Ronald Brown, of Burnham-on-Crouch, and has issue.

DAUGHTER LIVING.
Hon. Margaret Wilmett, *b.* 1939: *m.* 1960 (John Frederick) Keith St. Pier, of Chadhurst Farm Coldharbour Lane, Dorking, Surrey, and has issue.

HEMINGFORD, BARON. (Herbert.) [Baron U.K. 1943.]

DENNIS GEORGE RUDDOCK HERBERT, 2nd Baron; *b.* March 25th, 1904; *s.* 1947; ed. at Oundle, and at Brasenose Coll., Oxford; a JP for Cambs; Lord-Merit of Huntingdon and Peterborough 1968-74, since when of Cambs.; Head Master of King's Coll., Budo, Uganda 1939-47, Rector of Achimota Training Coll., Gold Coast 1948-51, Chm. of Africa Bureau 1952-63; Chm. of Hunts. Co. Council 1961-65, and of Huntingdon and Peterborough Co. Council 1967-71: *m.* 1932, Elizabeth McClare, da. of the late Col. John McClare Clark, TD, of Haltwhistle, Northumberland, and has issue.
Residence,—The Old Rectory, Hemingford Abbots, Huntingdon, Cambs.

SON LIVING.

Hon. DENNIS NICHOLAS, *b.* July 25th, 1934; ed. at Oundle, and at Clare Coll., Camb. (MA): *m.* 1958, Jennifer Mary Toresen, da. of Frederick William Bailey, of 24, Kent Rd., Harrogate, and has issue living, Christopher Dennis Charles, *b.* 1973,—Elizabeth Frances Toresen, *b.* 1963,—Caroline Mary Louise, *b.* 1964,—Alice Christine Emma, *b.* 1968. *Residence,*—Broad Green, Stonebridge Lane, Fulbourn, Cambridge.

DAUGHTERS LIVING.

Hon. Celia McClare, *b.* 1939; ed. at Oxford Univ. (MA): *m.* 1966, William Howard Goodhart, of 43, Campden Hill Sq., W8, and has issue living, Benjamin Herbert, *b.* 1972,—Annabel Frances, *b.* 1967,—Laura Christabel, *b.* 1970.
Hon. Catherine Grevile, *b.* 1942: *m.* 1962, Harry Treherne Moggridge (The New House, Shilton, Oxon.), and has issue living, Geoffrey Dillwyn, *b.* 1967,—Lawrence Weston, *b.* 1970,—Harriet Fearne, *b.* 1965.

BROTHERS LIVING.

Hon. Valentine Henry Okes, *b.* 1905; ed. at Oundle; 1939-45 War as Lt.-Col. RA: *m.* 1st, 1931, Winifred Mabel, who *d.* 1955, da. of the late Sir Herbert Grayhurst Pearson; 2ndly, 1956, Janet, da. of the late Rev. Gerrard Edmund Wigram [see Wigram Bt., colls.], and has issue living, (by 1st m.), Timothy William Okes, *b.* 1936,—Rosemary Ann, *b.* 1932: *m.* 1957, William George Rhyll Turner, Duke of Edinburgh's Roy. Regt., and has issue living, Valerie Jane *b.* 1958, Penelope May *b.* 1960, Susan Diana *b.* 1964,—Sylvia Valentine, *b.* 1948. *Residence,*—Foxdown, Tile Barn, Woolton Hill, Newbury, Berks., RG15 9UX. *Club,*—Oriental.
Hon. Oliver Hayley Dennis. *b.* 1919; ed. at Oundle. and at Wadham Coll., Oxford ; formerly Major Queen's Roy Regt., attached Indian Army. *Residence,*—75, King Henry's Rd., NW3.

PREDECESSOR.—[1] *Rt. Hon.* Sir DENNIS HENRY Herbert, *K.B.E.,* el. son of the late Rev. Henry Herbert, R. of Hemingford Abbots, Huntingdon; *b.* 1869; was Dep. Chm. of Ways and Means in House of Commons 1928-9, and Chm. of Ways and Means and Dep. Speaker 1931-43; sat as M.P. for Watford Div. of Herts (*U*) 1918-43; *cr. Baron Hemingford.* of Watford, co. Hertford (peerag of United Kingdom) 1943: *m.* 1903, Mary Graeme, who *d.* 1966, da. of the late Valentine Graeme Bell, CMG; *d.* 1947; *s.* by his son [2] DENNIS GEORGE RUDDOCK, 2nd Baron and present peer.

HEMPHILL, BARON. (Martyn-Hemphill.) [Baron U.K. 1906.]

PETER PATRICK FITZROY MARTYN MARTYN-HEMPHILL, 5th Baron ; *b.* Sept. 5th, 1928 ; *s.* 1957 ; ed. at Downside, and at Brasenose Coll., Oxford (B.A. 19—, M.A. 19—); assumed by deed poll 1959 the additional surname of Martyn : *m.* 1952, Olivia Anne, el. dau. of Major Robert Francis Ruttledge, M.C., of Cloonee, Ballinrobe, co. Mayo, and has issue.

Arms,—Or, on a fesse gules between two chevronels and three stars, as many trefoils slipped of the field. Crest,—A boar passant gules charged with a chevron and a portcullis or. Supporters,—On either side an Irish wolfhound gorged with a plain collar or.

Residence,—Tulira Castle, Ardrahan, co. Galway. *Clubs,*—Kildare Street, White's, Royal Automobile, County (Galway).

Steadily and fearlessly.

CONSTANTER·AC NON·TIMIDE

SON LIVING.

Hon. CHARLES ANDREW MARTYN, *b.* Oct. 8th, 1954; ed. at Downside.

DAUGHTERS LIVING.

Hon. Angela Mary Martyn, *b.* 1953.
Hon. Mary Anne, *b.* 1958.

MOTHER LIVING.

Emily, da. of the late F. Irving Sears, of Webster, Mass., U.S.A.: *m.* 1st, 1927 (marriage dissolved in Reno, U.S.A. 1945), the 4th Baron, who *d.* 1957 ; 2ndly, 1945, Ion Henry FitzGerald Villiers-Stuart, of Dromana, co. Waterford, who *d.* 1948. *Residence,*—89, Onslow Sq., SW7.

PREDECESSORS.—[1] CHARLES HARE Hemphill, *P.C.,* son of the late John Hemphill, of Cashel, and Rathkenny, co. Tipperary ; *b.* 1821; M.P. for N. Div. of Tyrone co. (*L*) 1895-1905; Solicitor-Gen. for Ireland 1892-5; *cr. Baron Hemphill,* of Rathkenny and of Cashel, co. Tipperary (peerage of United Kingdom) 1906: *m.* 1849, Augusta Mary, who *d.* 1899, dau. of the late Major the Hon. Sir Francis Charles Stanhope, K.C.H.; *d.* 1908; *s.* by his el. son [2] STANHOPE CHARLES JOHN, 2nd Baron, *b.* 1853: sometime Crown Prosecutor for co. Wicklow: *m.* 1913, the Hon. May Clarke Mary Nisbet Hamilton, who *d.* 1970, da. of 9th Lord Belhaven and Stenton; *d.* 1919; *s.* by his brother [3] FITZROY, 3rd Baron, *b.* 1860; Dep. Chm. of London Co. Council 1907-8: *m.* 1897, Mary, who *d.* 1958, da. of the late Andrew Martyn, of Spiddal, co. Galway; *d.* 1930; *s.* by his son [4] MARTYN CHARLES ANDREWS, 4th Baron; *b.* 1901; Bar. King's Inns, Dublin and Middle Temple: *m.* 1927, Emily (who obtained a divorce in Reno, USA 1945), da. of F. Irving Sears, of Webster, Massachusetts, USA; *d.* 1957; *s.* by his only son [5] PETER PATRICK FITZROY MARTYN, 5th Baron and present peer.

HENDERSON, BARON. (Henderson.) [Baron U.K. 1945.]

WILLIAM WATSON HENDERSON, *P.C.,* 1st Baron, 2nd son of the late Rt. Hon. Arthur Henderson ; *b.* Aug. 8th, 1891 ; ed. at Queen Elizabeth Gram. Sch., Darlington ; formerly Head of Press and Publicity Depart. of Labour Party; PPS to Sec. of State for India 1929-31, Personal Assist. to Min. without Portfolio 1940-42, a Lord-in-Waiting to HM and an Additional Member of Air Council 1945-47, and Joint Under-Sec. of State for Foreign Affairs 1948-51; Chm. of Alliance Building Soc. 1966-72; Pres. of UN Parl. Gp., and Pres. of Westminster Branch, UN Assoen.; MP for Enfield Div. of Middlesex (*Lab.*) 1923-24, and 1929-31; *cr. Baron Henderson,* of Westgate, in the City and Co. of Newcastle-on-Tyne (peerage of UK) 1945, and PC 1950.

Residence,—707, Collingwood House, Dolphin Square, Westminster, S.W.1.

HENDERSON OF ARDWICK BARONY OF. (Henderson.) [Extinct 1950.]

DAUGHTER LIVING OF FIRST BARON.

Hon. Marjorie, b. 1910: m. 1937, George Taylor Irwin, JP, FCSA, and has issue living, Janet Elizabeth, b. 1940: m. 1962, John William Smith, BA. Residence,—33, Morningside, Coventry.

HENLEY, BARON. (Eden.) Sits as BARON NORTHINGTON (U.K. 1885). [Baron I. 1799.]

SI SIT PRVDENTIA

If there be prudence.

MICHAEL FRANCIS EDEN, 7th Baron; b. Aug. 13th, 1914; s. 1962; ed. at Eton, and at Balliol Coll., Oxford (B.A. 1936, M.A. 1952); formerly Capt. Life Guards; is a Chartered Surveyor: m. 1st, 1943 (m. diss. 1947), Elizabeth, da. of Sir Arthur Lawrence Hobhouse [Mather-Jackson, Bt., colls.]; 2ndly, 1949 (m. diss. 1975), Nancy Mary, only da. of Stanley Walton, of The Hill, Gilsland, Carlisle, and has issue by 1st and 2nd m.

Arms,—Quarterly : 1st and 4th gules, on a chevron argent, between three garbs or, banded vert, as many escallops sable, Eden; 2nd and 3rd azure, a lion rampant argent, ducally crowned or, within a bordure of the second, charged with eight torteaux, Henley. Crest,—A dexter arm in armour couped at the shoulder proper, and grasping a garb or. Supporters,—Dexter, a lion argent, semée of torteaux, ducally crowned or, having a plain collar of the last rimmed azure, on the collar three escallops sable, and pendent therefrom a shield gold, charged with an eagle displayed with two heads sable: sinister, a stag argent, semée of torteaux, attired or, and gorged with a plain collar of the last rimmed azure, and charged with three escallops sable, pendent therefrom an escutcheon also or, charged with an eagle displayed with one head also sable.

Residence,—Scaleby Castle, Carlisle.   Clubs,—Brooks's, Pratt's.

SONS LIVING. (By 2nd marriage.)
Hon. OLIVER MICHAEL ROBERT, b. Nov. 22nd, 1953.
Hon. Andrew Francis, b. 1955.

DAUGHTERS LIVING. (By 1st marriage.)
Hon. Victoria Catherine Elizabeth, b. 1944: m. 1965, the Hon. John Hedworth Jolliffe, of Potticks House, Bradford-on-Avon [see B. Hylton].

(By 2nd marriage.)
Hon. Ursula Nancy, b. 1950.
Hon. Ingaret Barbara, b. 1951.
Hon. Rose Griselda, b. 1957.

BROTHER LIVING.
Hon. Roger Quentin Eden, b. 1922 ; ed. at Rugby ; is an A.F.R.Ae.S.; formerly Flying-Officer R.A.F. Vol. Reserve : m. 1946, Carys Wynne, dau. of I. H. D. Davies, of Camwy, Penrhyndeudraeth, Merionethshire, and has issue living, Morton Roger, b. 1949 : m. Sally L., da. of W. H. Brittain, of Redcar, Cleveland,—Elvyn Alexander, b. 1954,—Carol Rosamond, b. 1947,—Jane Rebecca, b. 1956. Seat,—Askerton Castle, Brampton, Cumberland. Residence,—29A, Hamilton Terrace, NW8.

SISTERS LIVING.
Hon. Barbara Dorothy, b. 1915 : m. 1938, Peter Calvocoressi, formerly Wing-Com. R.A.F. Vol. Reserve, and has issue living, Paul Peter, b. 1939,—David Sebastian, b. 1941: m. 1971, Dzagbe Cudjoe, of Accra, Ghana. Residences,—Guise House, Aspley Guise ,Bedfordshire; 42, William IV Street, WC2.
Hon. Griselda Rosalind, b. 1917: m. 1939 (m. diss. 1964), John Buckman, late Sqdn. Ldr. RAFVR, and has issue living, Christopher Simon, b. 1940: m. 1970, Gwendola, da. of Comte de Kersaintgilly, of Poizay les Ormes, France,—Jennifer Susan, b. 1944: m. 1963, John Jellis Ashby, of The Limes, Watford, Rugby, and has issue living, Jeremy Robert, b. 1964, Sarah Charlotte, b. 1966. Residence,—8, High St., W. Haddon, Rugby.
Hon. Nancy Clare, b. 1918: m. 1941, Edmund Ernest Wynne, Lt. Reconnaissance Corps, and has issue living, Robert Edmund, b. 1956,—Rosalind Clare, b. 1942: m. 1965, David Gow, of Casilla 435, Cuzco, Peru, and has issue living, Donovan Fergus b. 1970, Caitlin Fiona b. 1972,—Deborah Dorothy, b. 1944: m. 1968, Michael Stagonakis, of 67, Mikas Asias, Athens, Greece,—Clare Catherine, b. 1946: m. 1969, Colin Smith, of 3, Roseway, Blackpool, and has issue living, Christian b. 1971,—Marilyn Anne, b. 1947: m. 1967, Stephen Padgett, of 1, England Lane, Knottingley, Yorks., and has issue living, Christopher Stephen b. 1969, Richard Anthony b. 1970,—Alexandra Mary, b. 1953. Residence,—580, Lytham Rd., Blackpool.

DAUGHTER LIVING OF FIFTH BARON.
Hon. Joan Beryl, b. 1893: m. 1914, Kildare Stukeley Meager, formerly Lieut. R.A.S.C., and has issue living, John Neil, b. 1926; ed. at King's Sch., Canterbury: m. 19—,—Elizabeth Beryl, b. 1922. Residence,—.

WIDOW LIVING OF SON OF THIRD BARON.
Hon. Sylvia Laura, OBE, da. of 4th Baron Sheffield [see B. Stanley of Alderley]: m. 1906, Brig.-Gen. the Hon. Anthony Morton Henley, CMG, DSO, who d. 1925, and has issue living [see colls., infra]. Residence,—39, Melton Court, SW7.

COLLATERAL BRANCHES LIVING.
Issue of the late Brig.-Gen. the Hon. Anthony Morton Henley, C.M.G., D.S.O., 3rd son of 3rd Baron, b. 1873, d. 1925: m. 1906, the Hon. Sylvia Laura Stanley, OBE (ante), da. of 4th Baron Sheffield [see B. Stanley of Alderley]:—
Rosalind Venetia, b. 1907, is a F.R.S. : m. 1931, as his second wife, Captain George Henry Lane Fox Pitt-Rivers, late Dragoons [M. Bath, colls.], and has issue living, George Anthony, b. 1932. Residence,—23A, Lyndhurst Rd., N.W.3.——Mary Katherine, b. 1908: m. 1936, Evan Kennedy Morton. Residence,—3, Chalcot Sq., NW1.——Juliet Olive, b. 1917: m. 1944 (m. diss. 1965), Stuart Daniel, Bar.-at-law, and has issue living, Laura, b. 1947. Residence,—20, Fitzroy Gdns., SE19.

Grandchildren of the late Rev. the Hon. Robert Henley, 2nd son of 2nd Baron:—
Issue of the late Capt. Charles Beauclerk Henley, Roy. Indian Navy (retired), b. 1869,
d. 1945 : m. 1910, Nellie Barbara, who d. 1961, dau. of the late E. F. Stranack :—
Robert Stephen, OBE, DSC, b. 1917; Cdr. RN; 1939-45 War (DSO); OBE (Mil) 1969: m. 1940,
Noreen, only da. of Eric Hudson, of 29, Curzon Ave., Horsham, Sussex, and has issue living, Robert
Anthony Nigel (42, Chiswick Staithe, W4) b. 1942: m. 1968, Celia, only da. of Leslie Ford, and has
issue living, Robert Alexander b. 1973, Deborah Lucie b. 1971,—Timothy David (4, Derby Rd.,
Wimbledon, SW19 1LP), b. 1945: m. 1972, Jane Hughes, da. of John Fisher, of Chiswick Staithe,
W4, and has issue living, Sarah Margaret b. 1975,—Christopher Basil Patrick, b. 1953,—Jonathan
Paul Sebastian, b. 1956. Residence,—Eden Lodge, Liss, Hants.——David Beauclerk, (Alphina, 36,
Bruce Av., Worthing, BN11 5JU), b. 1923: m. 1950, Eileen Fuller.——Elizabeth Barbara, b. 1911.
Residence,—Ty Hên, Prion, nr. Denbigh.——Violet Hope, b. 1914: m. 1937, Owen Davis, and has
issue living, Nicholas Austen (10, Sutcliffe Close, NW11), b. 1940: m. 1965, Mieke Jongebreur, and
has issue living, Austen Peter b. 1966, Christa Ann b. 1968,—Anthony Simon, b. 1942: m. 1967,
Carol Ann Neibert, and has issue living, Christopher Anthony b. 1968, Amy Katharine b. 1970.
Residence,—20, Neville Drive, N2.

Grandchildren of the late Lt. William Gaven Eden, RN, el. son of the late Rev.
Arthur Eden (infra):—
Issue of the late Cecil Eden, b. 1876, d. 1963: m. 1914, Inez Gilmour (of Estancia Santa Inez.
Marie Teresa, Argentina), da. of William Orr:—
Cecil Gilmour Orr, b. 1921: m. 1953, Ann Mabel, da. of George Bridger, and has issue living, Robert
Gilmour, b. 1954,—David Arthur, b. 1961,—Joanna Inez. b. 1957,—Margaret Alice (twin), b. 1961.
——Constance Edna, b. 1924: m. 1956, Geoffrey Arthur Lees, of Santa Inez, Maria Teresa, Prov.
Santa Fe, Argentina, and has issue living, John Arthur, b. 1960,—Elizabeth Inez, b. 1958.——
Patricia Alice, b. 1926: m. 1954, George Page, of 25, de Mayo 555, Venado Tuerto, FCNGBM,
Argentina, and has issue living, Christine Sheila, b. 1955,—Angela Jean, b. 1957.

Granddaughter of the late Rev. Arthur Eden, son of the late Rev. the Hon. William
Eden, 2nd son of 1st Baron:—
Issue of the late Arthur Yelverton Eden, b. 1856, d. 1922: m. 1888, Fanny Spencer, who
d. 1934, dau. of the late John Theodore Louis Le Blanch, of Beechfield, Cheshire :—
Lelgarde Edith Eleanor, b. 1893: m. 1918, Geoffrey Ronald Aubert Buckland, CB, who d. 1968, and
has issue living, Ronald John Denys Eden, CB, MBE (c/o HQ UK Land Forces, Wilton, Salisbury,
Wilts, SP2 0AG), b. 1920; Maj.-Gen. late Coldstream Gds.; MBE (Mil) 1956: m. 1968, Judith
Margaret Coxhead. Residence,—28, Esmond Court, Thackeray St., W8.

Grandchildren of the late Robert Charles Eden, yst. son of the late Rev. the Hon.
William Eden (ante):—
Issue of the late Morton Edward Eden, b. 1867 d. 1914: m. 1894, Marie Elizabeth, who d.
1900, dau. of the late James Stewart, of Dansville, New York, U.S.A.:—
Robert Henley Stuart, b. 1896. Residence,—

Issue of the late Reginald Yelverton Eden, b. 1871, d. 1949: m. 18—, Sophie, dau. of T.
Hart, of Warren, U.S.A.:—
Anne Louise: m. 19—, Lurelle van Arsdale Guild, and has issue living, Cynthia Eden, b. 1938.——
Beatrice Elizabeth, b. 1902. Residence,—

PREDECESSORS.—[1] MORTON Eden, 8th son of Sir Robert Eden, 3rd Bt.; Min. at Vienna and
Madrid; cr. Baron Henley, of Chardstock (peerage of Ireland) 1799; d. 1830: m. 1783, Lady
Elizabeth Henley, who d. 1821, yst. da. of 1st Earl of Northington, Lord Chancellor, and sister and
co-heir of the 2nd Earl; s. by his son [2] ROBERT Henley, 2nd Baron; b. 1789; was a Master
in Chancery ; assumed by Roy. licence 1831 the surname of Henley in lieu of his patronymic :
m. 1823, Harriet, who d. 1869, dau. of Sir Robert Peel, 1st Bt. ; d. 1841 ; s. by his son [3]
ANTHONY HENLEY, 3rd Baron, b. 1825 ; M.P. for Northampton (L) 1859-74; cr. Baron
Northington, of Watford, co. Northampton (peerage of U.K.) 1885: m. 1st, 1846,
Julia Emily Augusta, who d. 1862, da. of the late Very Rev. John Peel, D.D., Dean of Worcester ;
2ndly, 1870, Clara Campbell Lucy, who d. 1922, dau. of the late Joseph H. S. Jekyll ; d. 1898 ;
s. by his el. son [4] FREDERIC, 4th Baron, b. 1849 : m. 1900, Augusta Frederica, who d. 1905,
dau. of the late Herbert Langham ; d. 1923 : s. by his brother [5] ANTHONY ERNEST, 5th Baron,
b. 1858: m. 1st, 1882, Georgiana Caroline Mary. who d. 1888, dau. of the late Lieut.-Col.
Richard Michael Williams; 2ndly, 1889, Emmeline Stuart, who d. 1933, dau. of the late
George (Gammie) Maitland, of Shotover Park, Oxon ; d. 1925 ; s. by his half-brother [6] FRANCIS
ROBERT, 6th Baron, b. 1877; Chm. of Northants. Co. Council 1945-9; assumed by deed poll (en-
rolled at College of Arms) 1925, the surname of Eden in lieu of Henley: m. 1913, Lady Dorothy
Georgiana Howard, who d. 1968, da. of the 9th Earl of Carlisle; d. 1962; s. by his son [7] MICHAEL
FRANCIS, 7th Baron and present peer; also Baron Northington.

HENNIKER, BARON. (Henniker-Major.) Sits as BARON HARTISMERE.
(U.K. 1866). [Baron I. 1800, Bt. G.B. 1765.]

JOHN ERNEST DE GREY HENNIKER-MAJOR,
7th Baron, and 8th Baronet; b. Jan. 18th,
1883 ; s. 1956 ; ed. at Radley, and at Roy.
Agricultural Coll., Cirencester (Honours Diploma) ; is Patron of four livings, and a Fellow
of Land Agents' So. ; was a Page of Honour
to Queen Victoria 1895-9 ; European War
1914-19, as a Staff-Lieut., and in R.A.F.
(Croix de Guerre) : m. 1914, Molly, who d.
1953, dau. of the late Sir Robert William
Burnet, K.C.V.O., M.D., and has issue.

Arms,—Quarterly : 1st and 4th azure, three Corinthian
columns, two and one palewise or, each having on the
capital a golden ball, Major ; 2nd and 3rd or, on a chevron
gules, between two crescents in chief and an escallop
in base azure, three estoiles argent, Henniker. Crests,—
1st, a dexter arm embowed, habited azure, cuffed argent,
and charged on the elbow with a plate ; the hand proper,
holding a baton or ; 2nd, an escallop or, charged with
an estoile gules. Supporters,—Dexter, a stag argent,
God the greater support.
attired and unguled or, gorged with a chaplet of oak proper, fructed gold, and pendant therefrom
an escutcheon azure, charged with the crest of Henniker ; sinister, an otter argent, gorged with a ducal
coronet or, and pendant therefrom an escutcheon of the arms of Major.
Residence,—Thornham Hall, Eye, Suffolk.

SONS LIVING.

Hon. Sir JOHN PATRICK EDWARD CHANDOS, *KCMG, CVO, MC, b.* Feb. 1916; ed. at Stowe and at Trin. Coll., Camb. (BA 1937); Maj. (ret.) Rifle Bde.; Ambassador to Jordan 1960-62, and to Denmark 1962-66; Dir.-Gen. of British Council 1968-72, since when Dir. of Wates Foundation; 1939-45 War (wounded, MC); CMG 1956, CVO 1960, KCMG 1965: *m.* 1946, Margaret Osla, who *d.* 1974, da. of the late James William Benning, of Montreal, and has issue living, Mark Ian Philip Chandos, *b.* 1947: *m.* 1973, Mrs. Lseley Antionette Masterton-Smith, da. of Wing Cdr. G. W. Foskett, of Ferndale, Qld.—Charles John Giles, *b.* 1949,—Jane Elizabeth, *b.* 1954. *Residence,*—11, Campden Hill Rd., W8.

Hon. Richard Arthur Otway (6, Berkeley Gdns., W8), *b.* 1917; ed. at Stowe and Magdalene Coll., Camb. (BA); admitted a Solicitor 1948; Lieut. (ret.) RA; 1939-45 War (prisoner): *m.* 1946, Nancy Pauline, da. of the late Sir John Armitage Stainton, KCB, KBE, QC [see B. Forteviot], and has issue living, David Richard, *b.* 1949: *m.* 1973, Valerie Ann, el. da. of Francis Martin Lanigan-O'Keeffe, MD, of 10, Priory Rd., Kenilworth, Warks.,—John Alexander, *b.* 1952,—Susan Rose, *b.* 1947.

COLLATERAL BRANCHES LIVING.

Grandsons of the late Capt. Frederick Henniker, yst. son of Rear-Adm. the Hon. Maj. Jacob Henniker, brother of 3rd Baron:—

Issue of Charles Henry Henniker, *b.* 1880, *d.* 1966: *m.* 1914, Dorothy Albinia Cecil, who *d.* 1959, da. of the late Rev. Cecil Locke:—

Charles John Chandos (16, Clos de Verrières, 91, Verrières le Buisson, France), *b.* 1916; ed. at Univ. of BC (B.Ap.Sc.), and Washington (PhD) Univs.: *m.* 1954, Madeleine Adèle, da. of Albert Caton, chartered accountant, of Marseilles, France, and has issue living, Hélène Dorothy, *b.* 1957,—Eve Alice, *b.* 1962.

Issue of the late Capt. Augustus Major Henniker, *b.* 1884, *d.* 1957: *m.* 1910, Dorothy Roche, who *d.* 1956, dau. of Lieut.-Col. Roche Rahilly, formerly R.A.M.C.:—

Anthony Trecothic Major, *b.* 1912; European War 1939-40 in France as Pilot-Officer R.A.F.: *m.* 1950, Ann Elizabeth Gwinnell, el. da. of Lt.-Col. G. C. G. Grey, OBE, late R.A., and has issue living, Christopher Anthony Major, *b.* 1952; ed. at Manchester Univ. (LLB). *Residence,*—7, Evans Av., Allestree, Derby.

Descendants of the late Lieut.-Gen. the Hon. Sir Brydges Trecothic Henniker (youngest son of 1st Baron), who was cr. a *Baronet* 1813 :—

See Henniker, Bt.

PREDECESSORS.—[1] JOHN Major, *M.P.* for Scarborough 1761, and senior Elder Brother of the Trinity House 1741-81, was cr. a *Baronet* 1765, with remainder to John Henniker, husband of his dau. Anne; *d.* 1781; *s.* by his son-in-law [2] JOHN Henniker, 2nd Bt., successively M.P. for Sudbury and Dover; cr. *Baron Henniker,* of Stratford-upon-Slaney, co. Wicklow (peerage of Ireland) 1800; *d.* 1803; *s.* by his son [3] JOHN, 2nd Baron; M.P. 1777-1802; assumed the surname of Major by Roy. licence 1792: *d.s.p.* 1821; *s.* by his nephew [4] JOHN MINET, 3rd Baron, son of the Hon. Major Henniker, 2nd son of 1st Baron; assumed the additional surname of Major by Roy. licence 1822; *d.* 1832; *s.* by his son [5] JOHN, 4th Baron; sat as M.P. for E. Suffolk 1832-47 and 1856-66; cr. *Baron Hartismere,* of Hartismere, co. Suffolk (peerage of United Kingdom) 1866: *m.* 1837, Anna, who *d.* 1889, dau. of Lieut.-Gen. Sir Edward Kerrison, G.C.H., K.C.B., 1st Bt. (*ext.*); *d.* 1870; *s.* by his son [6] JOHN MAJOR, 5th Baron; *b.* 1842; M.P. for E. Suffolk (*C*) 1866-70; a Lord-in-Waiting to Queen Victoria 1877-80, 1885-6, 1886-92, and July to Nov. 1895, and Lieut.-Gov. of Isle of Man 1895-1902: *m.* 1864, Lady Alice Mary, who *d.* 1893, dau. of 3rd Earl of Desart; *d.* 1902; *s.* by his el. surviving son [7] CHARLES HENRY CHANDOS, 6th Baron; *b.* 1872; Col. Rifle Brig.; *d.* 1956; *s.* by his brother [8] JOHN ERNEST DE GREY, 7th Baron and present peer; also Baron Hartismere.

HEREFORD, LORD BISHOP OF. (Eastaugh.)

Right Rev. JOHN RICHARD GORDON EASTAUGH, son of Gordon Eastaugh; *b.* March 11th, 1920; ed. at Leeds Univ. (BA); Curate of All Saints, Poplar 1944-51, R. of W. Hackney 1951-56, Curate in Charge, St. Barnabas, Shacklewell 1954-55, R. of Poplar 1956-63, and V. of Heston 1963-67 and St. Peter, Eaton Sq., London 1967-74; Archdeacon of Middlesex 1966-74; consecrated 102nd Bishop of Hereford 1974: *m.* 1963, Bridget Nicola, da. of Sir (William) Hugh (Stobart) Chance, CBE [see Chance Bt.].

Patron of sixty-four livings, the three Canonries, the Archdeaconries of Hereford and Ludlow, and the Prebends of his Cathedral.

This See was founded 676.

*Episcopal Signature—*John Hereford.

ARMS OF THE SEE,—Gules : three leopards' faces jessant-de-lis reversed or, two and one.

Residence,—The Bishop's House, The Palace, Hereford, HR4 9BN.

HEREFORD, VISCOUNT. (Devereux.) [Viscount E. 1550, Bt. E. 1611.]
[Name pronounced " Deverooks."]

VIRTUTIS INVIDIA COMES

Envy is the attendant of virtue.

ROBERT MILO LEICESTER DEV-
EREUX, 18th Viscount, Premier Viscount of England, and 15th Baronet;
b. Nov. 4th, 1932; s. 1952; ed. at
Eton; O.St.J.: m. 1969, Susan Mary,
only child of Maj. Maurice Godley, of
Idle Hill, Kent, and has issue.

Arms,—Argent, a fesse gules, in chief three
torteaux. *Crest,*—Out of a ducal coronet or, a
talbot's head argent, eared gules. *Supporters,*—
Dexter, a talbot argent, eared gules, ducally
gorged of the last; *sinister,* a reindeer gules,
attired, gorged with a ducal coronet, and lined
or.

Residence,—Haseley Court, Little Haseley,
Oxon. OXG FLT. *Clubs,*—House of Lords
Yacht, Anglo-American Sporting, Lloyd's Yacht.

SON LIVING.
Hon.——*b.* Oct. 11th, 1975.

SISTER LIVING.
(Raised to the rank of a Viscount's daughter 1953.)
Hon. Diana Bridget, *b.* 1931: *m.* 1967, Maj.
Samuel Charles Casamaijor Gaussen, Welsh
Guards, of 22, St. Mary Abbot's Terr., W14,
and Pegglesworth House, Andoversford, Glos.,
and has issue living, Robert Casamaijor, *b.*
1968,—Mariana Diana, *b.* 1971.

AUNT LIVING. *(Daughter of 17th Viscount.)*
Hon. Blanche Marion, *b.* 1893; is an O.St.J.: *m.*
1927, Major Harry Talbot Rice, formerly
Welsh Guards, who *d.* 1948 [see B. Dynevor,
colls.]. *Residence,*—Castle Weir, Lyonshall,
Herefordshire.

MOTHER LIVING.
Audrey Maureen Leslie *(Audrey, Countess o
Lisburne),* yst. da. of the late James Meakin, of
Westwood Manor, Staffordshire; is a D.St.J.: *m.* 1st, 1923, the Hon. Robert Godfrey de Bohun
Devereux, who *d.* 1934: 2ndly. 1961, as his second wife the 7th Earl of Lisburne, who *d.* 1965.
Residences,—Flat 7, 1, St. James's St., SW1; Villa Malet, Moyenne Corniche, Cap d'Ail, France, AM.

COLLATERAL BRANCHES LIVING.

Granddaughters of the late Humphrey Bourchier Devereux (ante):—
Issue of the late Rupert Montague Devereux, *b.* 1907, *d.* 1974: *m.* 1940, Joan Ursula (Flat 3,
14, Tennyson Av., Takapuna, Auckland, NZ), da. of D. W. Thomas:—
Blanche Rosemary, *b.* 1943: *m.* 1966, Harvey Nausbaum, of 72, Seatoun Heights Rd., Seatoun, Wellington, NZ, and has issue living, Aaron, *b.* 1972.——Susan Ursula, *b.* 1947: *m.* 1967, Terrence
Adrian Currie, of 70, Pembroke Rd., Northland, Wellington, NZ, and has issue living, Simon Zane,
b. 1967,—Bridget Susan, *b.* 1971.

Grandchildren of the late Hon. Henry de Bohun Devereux (infra):—
Issue of the late Humphrey Bourchier Devereux, *b.* 1873, *d.* 1920: *m.* 1900, Winifred
Christiana, who *d.* 1937, dau. of George Hosking, of Auckland, New Zealand:—
George Makgill de Bohun, *b.* March, 1909: *m.* 1937, Olga Christina, da. of Karl S. Larsen, of Auckland,
NZ, and has issue living, Colin de Bohun, *b.* 1941: *m.* 1964, Helen Ann, da. of K. Buchanan, of
Takanini, NZ,—Dorothy Wynn, *b.* 1938: *m.* 1958, Graham Leaning, 164, Rowandale Av., Homai,
Manurewa, NZ, and has issue living, Karl Stuart *b.* 1964, Christine Ann *b.* 1961,—Marilyn Joan
b. 1948. *Residence,*—3, Mays Rd., Onehunga, Auckland, SE5, NZ.——Dorothy Maud Amelia,
b. 1902.——Blanche Bourchier, *b.* 1916: *m.* 1955, Henry Francis Schoen, and has issue living, Pauline
Anne, *b.* 1957. *Residence,*—4, Bell Rd., Henderson, Auckland, NZ.

Issue of the late Hon. Henry de Bohun Devereux, 2nd son of 15th Viscount,
b. 1848, *d.* 1909: *m.* 1872, Maud Philippa, who *d.* 1934, dau. of the late Edward
Salamon, of Sydney:—
Godfrey Vaughan, *b.* 1893: *m.* 1925, Ellen, dau. of the late John Black, of Keri Keri, Bay of Islands,
New Zealand, and has issue living, Robin Geoffrey (of 8, Howe Street, Howick, New Zealand),
b. 1927; is Capt. Roy. New Zealand Armoured Corps: *m.* 1953, Glennis Fyfe, dau. of T. F. Kerr,
and has issue living, Susan Lee, *b.* 1956, Vicki Anne *b.* 1959,—David de Bohun (1, Tui St., Kaikohe
NZ), *b.* 1928: *m.* 1951, Roberta Barbara, da. of F. G. R. Souness, and has issue living, Malcolm
Fergus (c/o RNZAF Base, Whenuapai, Auckland, NZ), *b.* 1952; F/O RNZAF, Wendy Anne *b.* 1956,—
Francis Richard, *b.* 1937,—Jennifer Mary, *b.* 1933: *m.* 1959, Maj. George Scott Finlayson, RNZ
Corps of Signals, of Maunu, Whangarei, NZ, and has issue living, George Robert *b.* 1960, James
Scott *b.* 1963, Helen Mary *b.* 1966, Judith Anne *b.* 1970. *Residence,*—56, Bleakhouse Rd., Howick,
NZ.

Grandson of the late Rear-Adm. the Hon. Walter Bourchier Devereux, 3rd son of
14th Viscount :—
Issue of the late Walter de Laci Devereux, *b.* 1864, *d.* 1959 : *m.* 1893, Blanche Isobel, who *d.*
1949, dau. of the late W. H. Johnston, of 13, Kent Gardens, Ealing, W. :—
Robert de Bohun, *b.* 1897 : *ed.* at R.M.C. ; Lieut.-Col. Roy. Scots (The Royal Regt.) ; European War
1915-19 in France, Belgium, the Balkans, and Russia (despatches twice, 1914-15 star, two medals) :
m. 1925, Enid Marion, dau. of the late Gen. Sir Henry Bulkley Burlton Watkis, K.C.B., and has issue
living, Robert Humphrey Bourchier, *b.* 1930 : *m.* 1954, Barbara, dau. of Mrs. G. V. Heywood, of
Fairholme, Guildford,—Marion Blanche, *b.* 1927 : *m.* 1958, Timothy Hollis. *Residence,*—Abbeyfields,
Farnborough, Hants.

PREDECESSORS.—[1] WALTER Devereux, K.G.; in 1500 *s.* his father as 10th *Baron Ferrers,* of
Chartley (peerage of England, cr. 1299, see E. Ferrers) ; *cr. Viscount Hereford* (peerage of England) 1550 ; distinguished himself in the French Wars of Henry VIII. ; was Justice of S.Wales 1524
d. 1558 ; *s.* by his grandson [2] WALTER, K.G., 2nd Viscount, son of Sir Richard, 2nd son of 1st
Viscount; *s.* 1570, in right of his gt.-grandmother, as 8th *Baron Bourchier* (peerage of England,
cr. 1342, see *** infra); cr. *Earl of Essex* (peerage of England) 1572 ; was Field-Marshal of the
Forces sent to suppress the Rebellion of the Earls of Northumberland and Westmoreland ; was
also Earl Marshal of Ireland ; *d.* 1576 ; *s.* by his son [3] ROBERT, K.G., *P.C.,* 2nd Earl ; was Lord
Lieut. of Ireland and Earl Marshal of England ; well known in history as the unfortunate
favourite of Queen Elizabeth ; was Master of the Horse, Earl Marshal of England, Lord Dep. of
Ireland, and Chancellor of Cambridge Univ. ; having conspired against the Queen he made a
fruitless effort at insurrection, was taken prisoner, convicted of high treason, and beheaded on
Tower Hill Feb. 25th, 1601 ; *s.* by his son [4] ROBERT, K.G., who in 1603 was restored in blood
and became 3rd Earl ; was attached to the Royal cause until 1642, when he accepted a commission in the Parliament army, and afterwards distinguished himself as a Parliamentary General-

issimo; *d.* 1646; interred with national obsequies in Westminster Abbey, the two Houses o Parliament attending the funeral; at his death the Earldom of Essex expired, the Barony of Ferrers became abeyant (abeyance terminated 1677, see E. Ferrers), the Barony of Bourchier became abeyant (and still remains so), and the Viscountcy of Hereford devolved upon his kinsman [5] WALTER, 5th Viscount, son of Sir Edward Devereux (cr. *Baronet* 1611 and *d.* 1622), who was 4th son of 1st Viscount; *s.* by his son [6] LEICESTER, 6th Viscount; *d.* 1676; *s.* by his el. son [7] LEICESTER, 7th Viscount; *d.* aged 9 years 1683; *s.* by his brother [8] EDWARD, 8th Viscount; *d.s.p.* 1700; *s.* by his kinsman [9] PRICE, 9th Viscount, great-grandson of Sir George, Knt., brother of 5th Viscount; *d.* 1740; *s.* by his son [10] PRICE, 10th Viscount; *d.* 1748, without male issue; *s.* by his kinsman [11] EDWARD, 11th Viscount, descendant in the 4th generation of Sir George, Knt. (ante); *d.* 1760; *s.* by his el. son [12] EDWARD, 12th Viscount; *d.s.p.* 1783; *s.* by his brother [13] GEORGE, 13th Viscount; *d.* 1804; *s.* by his son [14] HENRY FLEMING LEA, *P.C.*, 14th Viscount; was Capt. of Hon. Corps of Gentlemen-at-Arms; *d.* 1843; *s.* by his son [15] *Rev.* ROBERT, 15th Viscount; *b.* 1809; was an Hon. Canon of Durham: *m.* 1841, Emma Jemima, who *d.* 1870 (having *m.* 2ndly, 1857, Lieut.-Col. John Ireland-Blackburne), dau. of George Ravenscroft; *d.* 1855; *s.* by his son [16] ROBERT, 16th Viscount; *b.* 1843: *m.* 1863, the Hon. Mary Anna Morgan, who *d.* 1934, dau. of 1st Baron Tredegar; *d.* 1930; *s.* by his son [17] ROBERT CHARLES, 17th Viscount; *b.* 1865; was Capt. 1st (Breconshire) Vol. Batn. S. Wales Borderers, and Chm. of Breconshire Quarter Sessions 1907-27: *m.* 1892, Ethel Mildred, who *d.* 1945, dau. of the late John Shaw, of Welburn Hall, Kirkby Moorside; *d.* 1952; *s.* by his grandson [18] ROBERT MILO LEICESTER (only son of the late Hon. Robert Godfrey de Bohun Devereux, only son of 17th Viscount), 18th Viscount and present peer.

⁎⁎⁎ [1] ROBERT de Bourchier, sometime Lord Chancellor of England, afterwards distinguished himself at Crecy; summoned to English Parliament as *Baron Bourchier* 1342-9; *d.* 1349; *s.* by his son [2] JOHN, *K.G.*, 2nd Baron; summoned to Parliament 1381-99; was engaged for many years in the French Wars of Edward III. and Richard II., and was sometime Ch. Gov. of Flanders; *d.* 1400; *s.* by his son [3] BARTHOLOMEW, 3rd Baron; summoned to Parliament 1400-9; *d.* 1409; *s.* by his only dau. [4] ELIZABETH; she *m.* 1st, Sir Hugh Stafford, K.B.. and 2ndly, Sir Lewis Robsart, K.G., each of whom on his marriage assumed the dignity of Lord Bourchier, but was only summoned to Parliament in his own name; *d.* without issue 1432; *s.* by her cousin [5] HENRY, 5th Baron, grandson of William, 2nd son of 1st Baron, and son of William Bourchier, 1st Count of Eu, in Normandy, by Anne, heiress of Thomas of Woodstock, Duke of Gloucester, (youngest son of Edward III.) and his wife Allianore de Bohun, el. co-heir of the last Earl of Hereford, Essex, and Northampton; he had previously *as* his father *as* 2nd Count of Eu, in Normandy title created by Henry V.; summoned to Parliament as "Count of Ewe" 1435, and as Viscount Bourchier 1446, and constituted Lord Treasurer of England 1455; subsequently espoused the interests of the Earls of March and Warwick, and was, on the accession of Edward IV., re-invested with the Lord Treasureship, and shared largely in the confiscated estates of the attainted Earls of Warwick and Wiltshire and Lord Roos; cr. *Earl of Essex* (peerage of England) 1461; *d.* 1483; *s.* by his grandson [6] HENRY, 2nd Earl; had a principal command at the Battle of Blackheath; at the famous tournament held by Henry VIII., on May 19-20, 1516, he answered all comers; accompanied H.M. to France, and assisted at the pageantry in the King's interview with Francis I. upon the Field of the Cloth of Gold; *d.* 1539, when the Earldom of Essex and the Viscountcy of Bourchier expired, and the Barony of Bourchier devolved upon his only dau. [7] ANNE, Lady Parr; *d.* 1570, but her issue being illegitimated (by Act of Parliament 5th of Edward VI.), the Barony passed to [8] WALTER Devereux, 2nd Viscount Hereford (ante).

HERRIES OF TERREGLES, LADY. (Fitzalan-Howard.) [Lordship S. 1490.]

ANNE ELIZABETH FITZALAN-HOWARD, el. da. of the 16th Duke of Norfolk; *b.* June 12th, 1938; *s.* 1975.

Arms,—not exemplified at time of going to press.

Seat,—Everingham Park, York.

SISTERS LIVING.

See D. Norfolk, of whom *Lady* MARY KATHARINE FITZ-ALAN-HOWARD is *h.p.*

COLLATERAL BRANCHES LIVING.

Grandchildren of the late Hon. Joseph CONSTABLE-MAXWELL-SCOTT, 3rd son of 10th Lord:—
Issue of the late Maj.-Gen. Sir Walter Joseph Constable-Maxwell-Scott, Bt, CB, DSO, who was cr. a *Baronet* 1932:—
See Constable-Maxwell-Scott, Bt. (ext.)

Issue of the late Rear-Adm. Malcolm Joseph Raphael Constable-Maxwell-Scott, DSO RN, *b.* 1883, *d.* 1938: *m.* 1918, Fearga Victoria Mary, who *d.* 1969, da. of the late Rt. Hon. Sir Nicholas Roderick O'Connor, GCB, GCMG [M. Linlithgow colls.]:—
See Constable-Maxwell-Scott, Bt. (cr. 1642).

Issue of the late Herbert Francis Joseph Constable-Maxwell-Scott, *b.* 1891, *d.* 1962: *m.* 1924, Eileen Josephine, da. of the late Henry Smail, of Donhead Lodge, Wimbledon, SW:—
Simon Malcolm (Foss House, Strensall, York.), *b.* 1939: *m.* 1962, Moyna, da. of S. Y. Gore, of Calcutta, India, and has issue living, Amanda Mary, *b.* 1962,—Fiona Anne, *b.* 1964,—Joanna Jane, *b.* 1965,——David Darragh (44, Denmark Rd., Wimbledon, SW19), *b.* 1944: *m.* 1969, H. Isabel, da. of Leonard Caplan, QC, of 1, Pump Court, Temple, EC4.——Aurea Mary Josephine, *b.* 1926: *m.* 1947, Peter Humphrey Williams, of 5, Glensgrove Avenue West, Toronto, Canada, and has issue living, Michael Humphrey, *b.* 1948,—Ian Maxwell, *b.* 1951,—David Andrew, *b.* 1953,—Elizabeth Anne, *b.* 1953,—Sheila Mary, *b.* 1956,—Joanna Susan, *b.* 1958,—Pamela Jane, *b.* 1961,—Susan Mary, *b.* 1931.——Mary Monica, *b.* 1945.

Issue of the late Hon. Bernard CONSTABLE-MAXWELL, 4th son of 10th Lord, *b.* 1848, *d.* 1938: *m.* 1st, 1881, Matilda, who *d.* 1882, da. of the late Alfred D. Jessup, of Philadelphia; 2ndly, 1890, the Hon. Alice Charlotte Fraser, who *d.* 1958, da. of 15th Lord Lovat:—
(By 2nd m.) Ian Simon Joseph, *b.* 1891; *d.* 1975; ed. as Trin. Coll., Camb (MA); Capt. Queen's Own Cameron Highlanders and RAF; 1914-18 War (wounded, 1914 star): *m.* 1937, Jean, who *d.* 1944, da. of Lt.-Col. Wilfrid Francis Ricardo, DSO, and has issue living, Jeanette Alice Norah (Farlie House, Beauly, Inverness-shire), *b.* 1942.——David TURVILLE-CONSTABLE-MAXWELL, *TD*, *b.* 1904; Maj. (ret.) RA late Lovat Scouts; assumed 1960 the additional surname of Turville before his patronymic; Sheriff of Leicestershire 1958; is a Knight of Sovereign Mil. Order of Malta; 1939-45 War:

m. 1930, Mary Alethea Elizabeth Evelyn, da. of the late Lt.-Col. Oswald Henry Philip Turville-Petre [see B. Petre, colls.], and has issue living, Robert John (Whitewood House, Yoxall, Burton-on-Trent; Pratt's and Guards' Clubs), *b.* 1933; ed. at Ampleforth; late Grenadier Guards: *m.* 1960, Susan Mary, da. of the late Capt. Stephen Francis Gaisford-St. Lawrence, RN [see Mostyn, Bt., colls.], and has issue living, Anthony Nicholas *b.* 1961, Stephen Bernard *b.* 1963, Alice Marion *b.* 1969,— Christopher Thomas Bernard (Harfield Farm, Chilcombe, Winchester, Hants; Guards' Club), *b.* 1940; ed. at Ampleforth; late Lt. Scots Gds.: *m.* 1963, Lavinia Moira, only da. of Hubert Arthur George Howard [see E. Carlisle, colls.], and has issue living, Simon Hubert *b.* 1965, Gavin Herries *b.* 1967,—Mary Belinda (*Countess of Carrick*), *b.* 1931: *m.* 1951, 9th Earl of Carrick,—Jennifer Mary, *b.* 1937: *m.* 1970, Christopher David Newton, TD, JP (Bosworth Hall, Husbands Bosworth, Lutterworth, Leics.; Cavalry Club), and has issue living, James Nicholas Turville *b.* 1971, Lucinda Rosalinde Mary *b.* 1975.—Marcia Helen (*Lady Radcliffe*) (Château de Cheseaux, 1033, Cheseaux, Vaud, Switzerland), *b.* 1947: *m.* 1968, Capt. Sir (Joseph Benedict) Everard Henry Radcliffe, 6th Bt., MC, who *d.* 1975. *Residence*,—Bosworth Hall, Husbands Bosworth, Lutterworth, Leics.——Andrew Bernard, *MBE, MC* (c/o Plaza Hotel, Brussels; White's, Turf, Guards', Pratt's, Brook (NY), and Travellers (Paris) Clubs), *b.* 1906; late 2nd Lt. Lovat Scouts (TA) and Lt.-Col. Scots Guards (Reserve); Knt. of Sovereign Mil. Order of Malta; 1939-45 War in Middle East and Yugoslavia (MC, MBE); MBE (Mil) 1945: *m.* 1949, Militza, da. of Mark Kerkes, of USA, and has issue living, Andreina Philomena, *b.* 1950.——Michael Hugh CONSTABLE MAXWELL, *DSO, DFC* (Theobalds Manor, Waltham Cross, Herts.; Newton House, Kirkhill, Inverness-shire), *b.* 1917; ed. at Ampleforth Coll., and at Hertford Coll., Oxford (MA); Wing-Cdr. RAF (ret.); a Member of Queen's Body Guard for Scotland (Roy. Co. of Archers), and a Knt. of Sovereign Mil. Order of Malta; formerly Lt. 4th Bn. Queen's Own Cameron Highlanders (TA); 1939-45 War, Battle of Britain (DFC, DSO), Netherlands E. Indies 1945-46 (despatches); DSO 1944: *m.* 1962, Susan Joan, da. of W. Trevor Davies, of Gianrhiw, Oakdale, nr. Blackwood, Mon., and has issue living, Hugh Peter, *b.* 1963,—Thomas Bernard, *b.* 1966. *Residence*,—Theobalds Manor, Waltham Cross, Herts. *Club*,—RAF.—— Margaret Mary Ethelreda, *b.* 1897.——Winifride Mary Ethelreda, *b.* 1898: *m.* 1923, Capt. Ronald Arthur Charteris Foster, late Rifle Bde., and has issue living, David Philip, *b.* 1924,—Giles Anthony, *b.* 1927. *Residence*,—Dallinghoo Hall, Woodbridge, Suffolk.——Joan (*Hon. Mrs. Henry G. O. Bridgeman*), (50, Lennox Gdns., SW1) *b.* 1901: *m.* 1930, Lt.-Col. the Hon. Henry George Orlando Bridgeman, DSO, MC who *d.* 1972 [see E. Bradford].——Elizabeth Mary Alice (Farlie House, Beauly, Inverness-shire; 27 Moray Place, Edinburgh) *b.* 1907.——Ursula Marcia Mary, *b.* 1911: *m.* 1960, Chalmers Davidson, FRCP. *Residences*,—28, Moray Place, Edinburgh; Farlie House, Beauly, Inverness-shire.

Grandchildren of the late Hon. Bernard Constable-Maxwell (ante):—
Issue of the late Wing Com. Gerald Joseph Constable-Maxwell, MC, DFC, AFC, *b.* 1895, *d.* 1959; *m.* 1920 Caroline Burns (of Old Alresford House, Alresford, Hants.), da. of George Alexander Carden, of New York:—
Peter George (Swann Cottage, Alresford, Hants.), *b.* 1944; ed. at Ampleforth and New Coll., Oxford; Lt. Gren. Guards: *m.* 1973, Virginia Ann, da. of Lt.-Col. John Ewart, and has issue living, Laura Katherine, *b.* 1974.——Anne Mary Teresa (*Duchess of Norfolk*), *b.* 1927: *m.* 1949, the 17th Duke of Norfolk. *Residences*,—Arundel Castle, Sussex; Carlton Towers, Goole, Humberside; Bacres, Hambleden, Henley-on-Thames, Oxon.; Burpham Lodge, Burpham, Arundel, Sussex.——Veronica (Diana) Margaret, *b.* 1930: *m.* 1960, Timothy Lawrie Boyd-Wilson, Scots Guards (Reserve), of Gregorys Cottage, Bletchingley, Surrey, and has issue living, William, *b.* 1963,—Lucy, *b.* 1961,— Magdalen, *b.* 1966.——Carolyn Mary, *b.* 1938: *m.* 1960, Maj. Count Charles John de Salis, Scots Guards (Reserve), of Yarlington House, Wincanton, Somerset, and Bondo Promontagno, Grisons, Switzerland, and has issue living, Isobel Oriane Clare, *b.* 1961,—Frances Mary Josephine, *b.* 1963,— Julia Mary Blanche, *b.* 1968,—Theresa Mary Bridget, *b.* 1970.——Rosemary Isabel, *b.* 1941: *m.* 1965, Antony Craven Chambers, Gren. Gds., of the Lake Cottage, Alresford, Hants., and has issue living, Dominic Peter Craven *b.* 1966,—Sebastian George Craven, *b.* 1967,—Antonia Mary Craven, *b.* 1974.

Grandchildren of the late Edmund Joseph Constable-Maxwell-Stuart (infra):—
Issue of the late Capt. Francis Joseph Constable-Maxwell-Stuart, *b.* 1886, *d.* 1962: *m.* 1917, Dorothy Mary (of Traquair Bank, Innerleithen, Peeblesshire), da. of the late J. D'Arcy Hartley, of Billesdon Coplow, Leics.:—
Peter D'Arcy John Joseph, *b.* 1922; formerly Capt. Indian Army: *m.* 1956, Flora, da. of Sir Alexander Morris Carr-Saunders, KBE, and has issue living, Catherine Margaret Mary, *b.* 1964. *Residences*,— Traquair House, Innerleithen, Peeblesshire; 51, Brompton Sq., SW3.——Michael Joseph Edmund, *b.* 1932: *m.* 1970, Kirsty, el. da. of the late Capt. H. K. Salvesen, of Inveralmond, Edinburgh, and has issue living, Justin, *b.* 1973,—Laura Mary, *b.* 1971.——Madeleine Mary Josephine, *b.* 1918: *m.* 1946, John Sherbrooke, and has issue living, Simon, *b.* 1947,—Hugh, *b.* 1948,—Alexander, *b.* 1957,— Elizabeth, *b.* 1959. *Residence*,—Whitecliff Manor, Swanage, Dorset.——Joan Margaret Mary, *b.* 1920: *m.* 1943, Charles Erik Paterson and has issue living, David, *b.* 1944,—Michael, *b.* 1948,— Caroline, *b.* 1945. *Residence*,—

Issue of the late William Joseph Peter Constable-Maxwell-Stuart, *b.* 1895, *d.* 1964: *m.* 1st, 1932, Ruth Patricia Craven, who *d.* 1952, da. of the late Charles Craven Sykes, of 15, Oval Rd., Regent's Park, NW; 2ndly, 1955, Anne Christine, da. of the late Peter John Williamson, of 42, East Claremont St., Edinburgh:—
(By 2nd m.) Joseph Peter, *b.* (Jan.) 1956.——Julian Francis, *b.* (Dec.) 1956.

Grandchildren of the late Hon. Henry Constable-Maxwell-Stuart, brother of 10th Lord:—
Issue of the late Edmund Joseph Constable-Maxwell-Stuart, *b.* 1858, *d.* 1924: *m.* 1884, the Hon. Mary Anne Constable-Maxwell, who *d.* 1941, da. of 10th Baron Herries of Terregles:—
Philip Joseph, *b.* 1903.——Florence Mary (twin), *b.* 1886; is a Nun.

Grandchildren of the late Edmund Constable-Maxwell-Stuart (ante):—
Issue of the late Mary Josephine Constable-Maxwell-Stuart, *b.* 1885, *d.* 1973: *m.* 1918, Capt. Hamish Morton Anderson, MB, ChB, formerly RAMC:—
Patricia Maria, *b.* 1919.

Issue of the late Marcia Mary Gertrude Constable-Maxwell-Stuart, *b.* 1888, *d.* 1956: *m.* 1920, Douglas Christopher Leng, who *d.* 1930:—
Christopher Anthony William (of Juniper Bank, Walkerburn, Peeblesshire), *b.* 1922; ed. at Downside, and at Hertford Coll., Oxford (BA 1947, MA 1947); European War 1939-45 as Capt. 27th Lancers in Middle East, and in Italy (despatches) and Burma: *m.* 1953, Patricia, da. of W. Edmund Lillywhite, of Pilgrims, Chilham, Kent, and has issue living, Malcolm Simon Christopher, *b.* 1959,— Rupert William, *b.* 1961,—Fiona Anne, *b.* 1954,—Teresa Madeleine, *b.* 1955.——David Joseph Timothy, *b.* 1924; ed. at Downside, and at New Coll., Oxford (BA 1948); European War 1940-45, as Capt. 4th Batn. Grenadier Guards: *m.* 1951, Dorothy Lucie, da. of the late C. Seymour, of Folkestone, and has issue living, Felicity Mary, *b.* 1952,—Leonara Rosemary, *b.* 1956. *Residence*,—

Grandchildren of the late Hon. Henry Constable-Maxwell-Stuart (ante):—
Issue of the late Henry Joseph Constable-Maxwell-Stuart, *b.* 1861, *d.* 1932: *m.* 1908, Florence, da. of William Wickham, of Chestnut Grove, Yorkshire:—
Charles Joseph, *b.* 1913; is a Benedictine Monk.——Alice Mary, *b.* 1909. *Residence*,—White Gates, Thorp Arch, Boston Spa, Yorkshire.——Clare Mary, *b.* 1915: *m.* 1938, Squadron Leader James Patrick Cafferkey, RAF (ret.), and has issue living, Patrick Charles, *b.* 1941. *Residence*,—White Gates, Thorp Arch, Boston Spa, Yorkshire.

PREDECESSORS.—[1] HERBERT Herries, was summoned to Parliament of Scotland as *Lord Herries of Terregles* 1490; *s.* by his son [2] ANDREW, 2nd Lord; *d.* 1513; *s.* by his son [3] WILLIAM, 3rd Lord; *s.* by his el. da. [4] AGNES: *m.* Sir John Maxwell, 2nd son of 5th Lord Maxwell (cr. 1440), who became *jure uxoris* Lord Herries of Terregles; *d.* 1582; *s.* by his son [5] WILLIAM, 5th Lord, *d.* 1603; *s.* by his son [6] JOHN Maxwell, 6th Lord; *d.* 1631; *s.* by his son [7] JOHN, 7th Lord: who in 1667 *s.* by special remainder his kinsman as 3rd Earl Nithsdale (the 1st Earl, Robert, 9th Baron Maxwell, was cr. *Lord Maxwell, Eskdale and Carlyle*, and *Earl of Nithsdale*, with remainder to his heirs male, and precedence of 1581); *s.* by his son [8] ROBERT, 4th Earl; *d.* 1685; *s.* by his son [9] WILLIAM, 5th Earl; celebrated for effecting his escape from the Tower of London the night before his execution, through the agency of his wife; peerages attainted; *d.* 1744, leaving a son WILLIAM (6th Earl but for the attainder); *d.* 1776, leaving a da. WINIFRED (who but for the attainder would have inherited the Lordship): *m.* William Haggerston-Constable (2nd son of Sir Carnaby Haggerston, 3rd Bt.); *d.* 1801; her son MARMADUKE WILLIAM Constable-Maxwell; *d.* 1819; *s.* by his son [10] WILLIAM, who became 10th Lord by decision of House of Lords 1858 (the descendants of the 5th Earl of Nithsdale having been restored in blood by Act of Parliament 1848); *b.* 1804: *m.* 1835, Marcia, who *d.* 1883, da. of the Hon. Sir Edward Marmaduke Joseph Vavasour, 1st Bt., *d.* 1876; *s.* by his son [11] MARMADUKE FRANCIS, 11th Lord; *b.* 1837; Lord-Lieut. of Kirkcudbrightshire and of E. Riding of York; cr. *Baron Herries*, of Carlaverock Castle, co. Dumfries (peerage of UK) 1884: *m.* 1875, the Hon. Angela Mary Charlotte Fitzalan-Howard, who *d.* 1919, da. of 1st Baron Howard of Glossop; *d.* 1908, when the UK Barony became ext. and the Scottish Lordship devolved upon his el. da. [12] GWENDOLEN MARY, *b.* 1877: *m.* 1904, the 15th Duke of Norfolk, who *d.* 1917; *d.* 1945; *s.* by her only son [13] BERNARD MARMADUKE, KG, GCVO, GBE, TD, PC, 13th Lord, who had *s.* as 16th Duke of Norfolk 1917; see that title; *b.* 1908; *d.* 1975, *s.* by his el. da. [14] ANNE ELIZABETH, present peeress.

HERSCHELL, BARON. (Herschell.) [Baron U.K. 1886.]

ROGNVALD RICHARD FARRER HERSCHELL, 3rd Baron; *b.* Sept. 13th, 1923; *s.* 1929; a Page of Honour to H.M. 1935-40; was a Train Bearer at Coronation of King George VI.; formerly Capt. Coldstream Guards has Coronation medal (1937): *m.* 1948, Lady Heather Margaret Mary, dau. of 8th Earl of Dartmouth, and has issue.

Arms,—Per fesse azure and sable, in fesse a fasces proper between three stags' heads couped or. Crest.—On a mount vert a stag proper, gorged with a collar gemel azure, and supporting with its dexter fore-foot a fasces in bend or. Supporters,—On either side a stag proper, collared azure, standing on a fasces or.

Residence,—Westfield House, Ardington, Wantage, Berks.

CELERITER.

Quickly.

DAUGHTER LIVING.
Hon. Arabella Jane, *b.* 1955.

PREDECESSORS.—[1] FARRER Herschell, G.C.B.,P.C., son of the late Rev. Ridley Herschell; *b.* 1837; Recorder of Carlisle 1873-80, Solicitor-Gen. 1880-85, and Lord High Chancellor Feb. to July 1886 and Aug. 1892 to June 1895; M.P. for Durham (*L*) 1874-85; cr. *Baron Herschell*, of Durham (peerage of United Kingdom) 1886: *m.* 1876, Agnes Adela, dau. of Edward Leigh Kindersley, of Clyffe, Dorset; *d.* 1899; *s.* by his only son [2] RICHARD FARRER, G.C.V.O., 2nd Baron; *b.* 1878; Private Sec. to Lord-Lieut. of Ireland (Earl of Aberdeen) Dec. 1905 to Aug. 1907, and a Lord-in-Waiting to King Edward VII. 1907-10. and to King George V. 1910-19, and 1924-29: *m.* 1919, Annie Vera Violet, who *d.* 1961, dau. of Sir Arthur Thomas Bennett Nicolson, 10th Bt.; *d.* 1929; *s.* by his son [3] ROGNVALD RICHARD FARRER, 3rd Baron, and present peer.

HERTFORD, MARQUESS OF. (Seymour.) [Marquess G.B. 1793.]

[Title pronounced "Harford" and name "Seamer."]

HUGH EDWARD CONWAY SEYMOUR, 8th Marquess; *b.* March 29th, 1930; *s.* 1940; ed. at Eton; Lt. (ret.) Grenadier Guards, and patron of three livings: *m.* 1956, Countess Pamela Therese Louise de Caraman-Chimay, only da. of the late Lt.-Col. Prince Alphonse de Chimay, TD [see D. Abercorn, colls.], and has issue.

Arms,—Quarterly: 1st and 4th sable, on a bend cotised argent, a rose gules between two annulets of the first, *Conway;* 2nd and 3rd quarterly, 1st and 4th or, a pile gules, charged with three lions of England between six fleurs-de-lis azure; 2nd and 3rd gules, two wings conjoined in lure or, *Seymour.* Crest.—1st, the bust of a Moor in profile couped at the shoulders proper and wreathed about the temples argent and azure, *Conway;* 2nd, out of a ducal coronet a demi-phœnix in flames, *Seymour.* Supporters,—Two Blackamoors proper, wreathed about the temples or and sable, habited in a short garment or, adorned about their waists and shoulders with green and red feathers and buskins gold; each resting his exterior hand on an antique shield azure, adorned gold; that of the *dexter* supporter charged with the sun in splendour, and that of the *sinister* with a crescent.

FIDE ET AMORE

By faith and love.

Seat,—Ragley Hall, Alcester, Warwickshire.   *Club,*—Turf.

SON LIVING.
HENRY JOCELYN (*Earl of Yarmouth*), *b.* July 6th, 1958.

DAUGHTERS LIVING.
Lady Carolyn Mary, *b.* 1960.
Lady Diana Helen, *b.* 1963.
Lady Anne Katherine, *b.* 1966.

COLLATERAL BRANCHES LIVING.

Grandsons of the late Com. Lord George Frederick Seymour, R.N. (infra):—
Issue of the late Squadron-Leader Paul de Grey Horatio Seymour, R.A.F., *b.* 1911, *d.* (killed in action during European War) 1942: *m.* 1937, Hilary (who *m.* 2ndly, 1948, Ian Hamilton Barrett, of Church Hill House, S. Cave, Brough, E. Yorks), dau. of the late Douglas Crickmay, O.B.E.:—
Andrew Conway Paul, *b.* 1939; ed. at Stowe; Sqdn. Ldr. RAF: *m.* 1964, June Ann, da. of Frederick Gardner, and has issue living, Elizabeth Jane, *b.* 1972. *Residence,*—Church Hill House, S. Cave, Brough, E. Yorks.

Issue of the late Lieut.-Col. George Victor Seymour, M.C., Roy. Scots Fusiliers, *b.* 1912, *d.* 1953: *m.* 1946, Mrs. Hilda Elizabeth Kemp (West Wing, Poxwell House, nr. Dorchester, Dorset), da. of the late Harold Lionel Phillips [see Phillips, Bt., cr. 1912]:—
Nicholas George Mark (posthumous), *b.* 1953.

Issue of the late Com. Lord George Frederick Seymour, R.N., 4th son of 6th Marquess, *b.* 1881, *d.* 1940 : *m.* 1906, Norah, who *d.* 1959, dau. of the late Archibald Peyton Skipwith [Skipwith, Bt., colls.] :—
Edith Patricia Mary SEYMOUR (Coachmans Cottage, West Walks, Dorchester, Dorset), *b.* 1913; reverted to her maiden name by deed poll 1972: *m.* 1933 (m. diss. 1972), the Rev. Emmanuel Casdagli, and has issue living, David Seymour Emmanuel (c/o Midland Bank, Cornhill, Dorchester), *b.* 1934: *m.* 1965, Christine Ethne, only da. of Brig. H. H. Cottier.

Grandchildren of the late Col. Lord Albert Charles Seymour, 2nd son of 5th Marquess:—
Issue of the late Lieut.-Col. Charles Hugh Napier Seymour, D.S.O., *b.* 1874, *d.* 1933 : **m.** 1905, Mary Adelaide (now of 127, Cranmer Court, Sloane Avenue, S.W.3), dau. of William Morton Philips [E. urtown, colls.] :—
William Napier, *b.* 1914 ; ed. at Eton ; Major (retired) Scots Guards ; Palestine 1936, Burma 1941-43 (despatches), Palestine 1946, Malaya 1948 : *m.* 1945, Rachel Mary, dau. of the late Capt. Angus V. Hambro, of Milton Abbas, Dorset, and has issue living, Carolyn Sarah, *b.* 1946: *m.* 1967, Simon Thomas Cecil Hanbury, late Life Gds., of The Red House, Binfield, Bracknell, Berks., and has issue living, Serena Mary *b.* 1970, Melissa Jane *b.* 1971,—Sarah Jane, *b.* 1947: *m.* 1974, Richard David O'Mahony Page, of Rathcon, co. Wicklow,—Arabella Mary, *b.* 1952: *m.* 1973, Christopher Elwes. *Residence,*—Falconer's House, Crichel, Wimborne. Dorset.

Issue of the late Brig.-Gen. William Walter Seymour, *b.* 1878, *d.* 1940: *m.* 1906, Muriel, who *d.* 1946, dau. of Lieut.-Col. C. Walter Campbell, of The Ivy House, Hampton Court, and widow of Alfred Corkran Campbell:—
Jane, *b.* 1907: *m.* 1933, Michael A. Unwin-Heathcote, and has issue living, Peter Michael, *b.* 1942,—Oliver Hugh, *b.* 1945,—Elizabeth Anne, *b.* 1934,—Sarah, *b.* 1936 : *m.* 1958, Philip Colin Chasemore, and has issue living, Philip Michael *b.* 1961, Amanda Mary *b.* 1959. *Residence,*—Kitale, Kenya.

Issue of the late Major Edward Victor Francis Seymour, Indian Army, *b.* 1887, *d.* 1927 : *m.* 1915, Grace Florence Harriette (Elfin Cottage, 6, Rossetti Rd., Birchington, Kent), dau. of the late Travers Blackley :—
Jane, *b.* 1917: *m.* 1951, Charles Christopher Dudley Short, and has issue living, Camilla Jane, *b.* 1953: *m.* 1974, Brent Mallory Heatley, of 20, Worcester St., Wilton, Wellington, NZ,—Marguerite Grace, *b.* 1956. *Residence,*—75, Epple Bay Rd., Birchington, Kent.

Issue of the late Lord Ernest James Seymour, 3rd son of 5th Marquess, *b.* 1850, *d.* 1930: *m.* 1877, Lady Georgiana Seymour Fortescue, who *d.* 1915, dau. of 3rd Earl Fortescue:—
Ruth (of 6, Wyndham House, Sloane Sq., S.W.1), *b.* 1881 : *m.* 1911, Bertram Edward Petre, who *d.* 1962 [see B. Petre, colls.].

Grandchildren of the late Rev. Lord Victor Alexander Seymour (infra):—
Issue of the late Major Conway Hugh Seymour, M.C., *b.* 1886, *d.* 1931 : *m.* 1916, Kathleen Louisa, who *d.* 1950, dau. of Lieut.-Col. Francis John Paul Butler, of Wyck Hill, Gloucestershire :—
Adrian John Conway, *b.* 1918; ed. at Radley, and at Ch. Ch., Oxford (MA); Col. (ret.) Scots Guards; Lt.-Col. Comdg. Scots Guards 1962-64; 1939-45 War (despatches): *m.* 1953, Elizabeth Ann, da. of Lieut.-Gen. Sir Edwin Otway Herbert, KBE, CB, DSO, and has issue living, Virginia Kathleen, *b.* 1955,—Angela Mary, *b.* 1957. *Residence,*—Wantsley Farm, Broadwindsor, Dorset.—Francis Hugh, *b.* 1922; ed. at Radley: *m.* 1951, Helen Elizabeth, da. of the Rev. Canon David J. Cornish, of Port Dover, Ont., Canada, and has issue living, William Thomas, *b.* 1955,—Margaret Louise, *b.* 1953. *Residence,*—Crescent Road, Qualicum Beach, British Columbia.

Issue of the late Cdr. William John Seymour, RN, *b.* 1900, *d.* 1967: *m.* 1930, Wilma (11, Marne St., South Yarra 3142, Melbourne, Vic., Aust.), da. of the late W. J. T. Clarke, of Winmarleigh, Toorak, Vic., Aust.:—
Conway William Hugh (Kiandra, Brit Brit, Vic., Australia), *b.* 1934: *m.* 1959, Susan Evizel, da. of R. R. McKay, of Coonabarabran, NSW, and has issue living, Conway Ronald Hugh, *b.* 1962,—Kristin Susan, *b.* 1960,—Jane Evizel, *b.* 1965.——Sarah Gardenia, *b.* 1939.

Issue of the late Rev. Lord Victor Alexander Seymour, 4th son of 5th Marquess *b.* 1859, *d.* 1935 : *m.* 1885, Elizabeth Margaret, who *d.* 1958, dau. of the late Albemarle Cator, of Woodbastwick Hall, Norwich :—
Anne Christian, *b.* 1896: *m.* 1st, 1920, Capt. Cajetan Louis Victor Marno, who *d.* 1930; 2ndly, 1934, Victor Frederick Engleheart, who *d.* 1949, and has issue living, (by 1st m.) John Seymour (of Scotts House, Hunton, Kent), *b.* 1921; formerly Capt. Irish Gds.: *m.* 1943, Diana Dunell, and has issue living, Peter Cajetan Seymour *b.* 1948, Julia Mary Christian *b.* 1945,—Edward Charles, *b.* 1923; late Rifle Bde. (invalided): *m.* 1947 (m. diss. 1957), Joan Chrysogon, da. of Brig. Edward William Drummond Vaughan, CB, DSO, MC, of White Knights, Newick, Sussex, and has issue living, Phyllida Jane, *b.* 1951,—William Victor (Nant y Mwyn House, Rhandirmwyn, Llandovery, Carms.), *b.* 1925; late Capt. RA: *m.* 1st, 1952 (m. diss. 1968), Cressida Doyle Jones; 2ndly, 1969, Hazel Dorothy Westley, and has issue living, (by 1st m.), Nicholas Douglas *b.* 1961, Madeleine Sarah *b.* 1954, Denise Barbara *b.* 1955, Alison Jane *b.* 1958,—(by 2nd m.), Lowri *b.* 1973. *Residence,*—The Old Rectory, Little Blakenham, Ipswich.

Grandson of the late Hugh Horatio Seymour, son of the late Lt.-Col. Hugh Henry Seymour, MP, 2nd son of the late Adm. Lord Hugh Seymour, 5th son of 1st Marquess:—

Issue of the late Hugh Francis Seymour, *b.* 1855, *d.* 1930 : *m.* 1884, Rachel Blanche, who *d.* 1946, dau. of the late Rev. the Hon. James Walter Lascelles [E. Harewood, colls.] :—
Sir Horace James, *G.C.M.G., C.V.O., b.* 1885 ; ed. at Eton, and at Trin. Coll., Camb. ; was Principal Private Sec. to Sec. of State for Foreign Affairs 1932-6, Envoy Extraor. and Min. Plen. to Irán 1936-9, Assist. Under-Sec. of State at Foreign Office 1939-42, and Ambassador Extraor. and Plen. to China 1942-6 ; C.M.G. 1927, C.V.O. 1936, K.C.M.G. 1939, G.C.M.G. 1946 : *m.* 1917, Violet Amy, dau. of the late Thomas Edward Erskine [see E. Buchan, colls.], and has issue living, Hugh Francis (Luccombe Mill, Bratton, Westbury, Wilts), *b.* 1926: *m.* 1954, Mary Elizabeth, da. of T. H. Roberts, of Pucklechurch House, nr. Bristol, and has issue living, Hugh James *b.* 1956, Julian *b.* 1961, Francis Benedict *b.* 1966, Charlotte *b.* 1957, Sarah Catherine *b.* 1962,—Virginia (*Lady Stourton*), *b.* 1919: *m.* 1945, as his second wife, Sir Ivo Herbert Evelyn Joseph Stourton CMG, OBE [see B. Mowbray, colls.].—Joan (Caringle, Four Mile Creek, Orange, NSW), *b.* 1920: *m.* 1945, Flight-Lt. Clive Gordon Thompson, DFC, RAAF, who *d.* 1969, and has issue living, Anthony Seymour *b.* 1946, Nicholas Austen *b.* 1948, Jeremy *b.* 1950. *Residence,*—Bratton House, Westbury, Wilts.

Grandchildren of the late Frederick Charles William Seymour, 5th son of the late Adm. Lord Hugh Seymour (ante):—
Issue of the late Horace Alfred Damer Seymour, O.B., *b.* 1843, *d.* 1902 (having been nominated, but not invested, a K.C.B.): *m.* 1880, Elizabeth Mary (raised to the rank of a Knight's Widow 1902), who *d.* 1950, dau. of the late Col. Frederick Romilly :—
Leopold Robert, *b.* 1888; sometime in Depart. of Pensions and National Health. Canada; 1914-18 War as Pte. 31st Bn. Canadian Expeditionary Force (wounded): *m.* 1914, Mary Elizabeth, who *d.* 1955, da. of the late Thomas Frayer. *Residence,*—1716, 5A Street, S.W., Calgary, Alberta. Canada.——Margaret Lily Winifred, *b.* 1891: *m.* 1916, Maj. Cecil Francis Aleck Walker, MC, Grenadier Guards, who *d.* 1925. *Residence,*—

Grandchildren of the late Lt.-Col. Leopold Richard Seymour, 2nd son of the Rt. Hon. Sir George Hamilton Seymour, GCB, GCH, el. son of Lord George Seymour, MP, 7th son of 1st Marquess:—
Issue of the late Richard Sturgis Seymour, M.V.O., *b.* 1875, *d.* 1959 : *m.* 1911, Lady Victoria Alexandrina Mabel, who *d.* 1969, da. of the late Rev. Lord Charles Edward FitzRoy [D. Grafton]:—
Leopold Richard, *b.* 1912; late Capt. Grenadier Guards; High Sheriff of Herts. 1964: *m.* 1940, Sheila, da. of Lt.-Col. Charles Butler, and has issue living, Hugh Leopold, *b.* 1943: *m.* 1971, Emma Mary, da. of the late Robert Evelyn Henderson [see Clerke, Bt.],—Charles Richard, *b.* 1955,—Anthea Rosemary (*Hon. Mrs. David E. H. Bigham*), *b.* 1941: *m.* 1965, the Hon. David Edward Hugh Bigham, of 24, Argyll Rd., W8, [see V. Mersey),—Sarah Victoria Frances, *b.* 1952,—Lavinia Sheila, *b.* 1954. *Residence,*—Little Hadham Pl., Much Hadham, Herts. *Club,*—Brooks's.——George FitzRoy, *b.* 1923; ed. at Winchester; Lord of the Manor of Thrumpton, a JP and DL of Notts. (High Sheriff 1966), and patron of one living; 1939-45 War with KRRC (invalided): *m.* 1946, the Hon. Rosemary Nest Scott-Ellis, da. of 8th Baron Howard de Walden, and has issue living, Thomas Oliver, *b.* 1952,—Miranda, *b.* 1948: *m.* 1972, Andrew Annandale Sinclair, of 15, Hanover Terr., NW1. *Residences,*—Thrumpton Hall, Notts.; 38, Molyneux St., W1; 2, The Crescent, Cromer. *Club,*— Brooks's.——Alexandra Victoria, *b.* 1914: *m.* 1939, Capt. Samuel Edmund Gurney, of Heggatt Farm House, Horstead, Norfolk, son of the late Sir Eustace Gurney, and has issue living, Richard Eustace Thomas (Heggatt Hall, Horstead, Norfolk), *b.* 1943,—Jane Mary Alexandra, *b.* 1948: *m.* 1970, Simon Warren Macfarlane, of White House Farm, Sprowston, Norfolk.

Grandsons of the late Maj. Sir Edward Seymour, KCVO, DSO, OBE, (infra):—
Issue of the late Maj. John Edward Seymour, *b.* 1915, *d.* 1972: *m.* 1940, Elizabeth Norah (Upper Chilland House, Martyr Worthy, Winchester), only child of the late Adm. the Hon. Sir Hubert George Brand, GCB, KCMG, KCVO [see V. Hampden, colls.]:—
Conway John Edward, *b.* 1941 ; Maj. Gren. Gds.: *m.* 1969, Elizabeth, da. of Maj. Francis Holdsworth Hunt, late Coldm. Gds. [see B. Forester, colls.], and has issue living, Harry Edward, *b.* 1971,—Arabella Elizabeth, *b.* 1974.——Richard Hubert, *b.* 1947.

Grandchildren of the late Lt.-Col. Leopold Richard Seymour (ante):—
Issue of the late Major Sir Edward Seymour, K.C.V.O., D.S.O., O.B.E., *b.* 1877, *d.* 1948 : *m.* 1905, Lady Blanche Frances Conyngham, who *d.* 1956, dau. of 4th Marquess Conyngham :—
Verena Mary, *b.* 1906: *m.* 1932 (m. diss. 1945), Lt.-Col. Robert Harry Doyne, Oxfordshire and Bucks LI, who *d.* 1965, and has issue living, Patrick, *b.* 1936; ed. at Eton,—Diana Mary, *b.* 1933. *Residence,*—Upper Chilland House, Martyr Worthy, Winchester.

Issue of the late Maj. Beauchamp Seymour, *b.* 1878, *d.* 1965: *m.* 1928, Eva Douglas, who *d.* 1949, da. of the late Rev. Herbert Brown, R. of St. Lawrence, Southminster, Essex:—
Julian Conway (23, Princedale Rd., W11), *b.* 1934; ed. at Eton: *m.* 1st, 1958, Alexandra, only da. of Douglas MacLeod, of The Mill House, Stratton, Dorchester; 2ndly, 1971, Lavinia Margaret, el. da. of Sir William Lawrence, 4th Bt., and has issue living (by 1st m.) Leopold Conway, *b.* 1959,—Mark Hamilton, *b.* 1960,—(by 2nd m.) Harry William, *b.* 1974,—Camilla Jane, *b.* 1973.——Jane Mary Naomi, *b.* 1929: *m.* 1954, Maj. Desmond Eric Renforth Scarr, 14th/20th King's Hussars, of Lane House, The Avenue, Chobham, Surrey, and has issue living, Edward Desmond Renforth, *b.* 1958,— Susan Renforth, *b.* 1956,—Sarah Anne Renforth, *b.* 1960.——Anne Victoria (twin), *b.* 1929: *m.* 1951, Maj. Henry Robert Mansel Porter, MBE, 60th Rifles, of Brockham, Birlingham, Pershore, Worcs., and has issue living, Henry Christopher Mansel, *b.* 1953,—Michael Beauchamp Mansel, *b.* 1954.

Grandchildren of the late George Evelyn Seymour, 4th son of the late Right Hon. Sir George Hamilton Seymour, G.C.B., G.C.H. (ante):—
Issue of the late Brig.-Gen. Archibald George Seymour, D.S.O., M.V.O., *b.* 1875, *d.* 1933 : *m.* 1907, Ellen Mary, who *d.* 1973, da. of the late R. Corfield Bucknall, of 13, Grenville Place, SW:—
Evelyn) Roger, *OBE, TD, b.* 1908; Lt.-Col. (ret.), RA (TA); N-W Europe 1944-45 (OBE), OBE (Mil) 1946: *m.* 1936, Rosemary Evelyn, da. of the late Major Horace John Flower, DSO, MC, 60th Rifles, and has issue living, (Archibald) John (Bingham's Park, Water End, Herts.), *b.* 1937: *m.* 1961, (Lavinia Mary) Louise, da. of Christopher York, of South Park, Long Marston, York, and has issue living, Charlotte Louise *b.* 1963, Susanna Clare *b.* 1966, Melinda (Nell) *b.* 1969,— Julian Roger, *b.* 1945. *Residence,*—Sakins, Roydon, Essex.——Christopher George, *b.* 1913; ed. at Radley; formerly Maj. 10th Hussars; 1939-45 War (wounded, despatches): *m.* 1940, Honor, da. of the late Capt. Cecil Leatham, of Redbourn House, Wentworth, and has issue living, Christopher Mark, *b.* 1942: *m.* 1968, Carol, yr. da. of Peter Pitman, of Muirfield Wood, Gullane, E. Lothian, and has issue living, Thomas *b.* 1972, Katherine Louise *b.* 1970,—Penelope Jane, *b.* 1944: *m.* 1966, R. A. Neon Reynolds. *Residence,*—Pamplins, Bentley, Farnham, Surrey.

Issue of the late Lieut.-Col. Sir Reginald Henry Seymour, K.C.V.O., *b.* 1878 ; *d.* 1938 : *m.* 1st, 1922, Winifred Boyd-Rochfort, who *d.* 1925, dau. of the late John Bathurst Akroyd ; 2ndly, 1930, Lady Katharine Hamilton, D.C.V.O. (now of Strettington House, Chichester, Sussex), dau. of 3rd Duke of Abercorn :—
(By 1st m.) George Raymond, *MVO, b.* 1923; is Major King's Roy. Rifle Corps; appointed a Page of Honour to H.M. King George VI. 1935, and an Extra Equerry to H.M. Queen Elizabeth the Queen Mother 1956; was a Train Bearer at Coronation of King George VI; MVO (Class IV) 1972: *m.* 1957, the Hon. Mary Quenelda Ismay, da. of 1st Baron Ismay, and widow of Peter Mervyn Fitz Finnis, and has issue living, Katharine Margaret Lucy, *b.* 1959. *Residence,*—54, Chelsea Sq., SW3

Club,—Turf.——(By 2nd m.) Henry Charles (9A, Bathurst St., W2) *b.* 1936; ed. at Eton; was a Page of Honour to HM King George VI 1949-52, and to HM Queen Elizabeth II 1952-53: *m.* 1st, 1960 (m. diss. 1965) Yolande, da. of Richard Murray, of Banheok, Stellenbosch, S. Africa; 2ndly, 1966, Alexandra Mary Hilda, da. of Maj. Sir Victor Basil John Seely, 4th Bt., and has issue living, (by 2nd m.) Conway Seely Reginald, *b.* 1968.——Mary Virginia, *b.* 1932.

Issue of the late Capt. Charles Evelyn Seymour, *b.* 1882, *d.* 1943 : *m.* 1st, 1909, Gladys Edith Muriel, who *d.* 1913, dau. of the late Walter Henry Hadow [E. Kinnoull]; 2ndly, 1919, Eugénie Sybil, who *d.* 1950, dau. of the late William Humble Dudley Ward [E. Dudley, colls.], and widow of (1) Capt. Dermot Howard Blundell-Hollinshead-Blundell, M.V.O., and (2) Major Maximillian David Francis Wood, D.S.O.:—
(By 1st marriage) Michael Henry, *b.* 1912 ; European War 1939-45 with Roy. Fusiliers (prisoner) : *m.* 1950, Dorothy Mary (DEAN), 2nd dau. of Henry Arthur Dennis, of Overhill Road, Dulwich, S.E. *Residence,*—6, Lynton Court, Cedar Rd., Sutton, Surrey.

PREDECESSORS.—[1] *Rt. Hon.* FRANCIS Seymour, *P.C.,* 4th son of the Rt. Hon. Sir Edward Seymour, P.C., 4th Bt. (cr. 1611) [see D. Somerset]; *b.* 1679; at the death of his el. brother, *s.* to the estates of his cousin, Edward, 1st and last Earl of Conway ; M.P. for Bramber 1701-02 and Gov. of Carrickfergus 1728-32 ; assumed the additional surname of Conway ; cr. *Lord Conway, Baron Conway of Ragley,* co. Warwick (peerage of England) 1703, and *Baron Conway of Killultagh,* co. Antrim (peerage of Ireland) 1712: *m.* 1st, 1703, Lady Mary Hyde, who *d.* 1708, dau. of 1st Earl of Rochester; 2ndly, 1716, Charlotte, who *d.* 1733, dau. of John Shorter of Bybrook, Kent ; *d.* 1732 ; *s.* by his son [2] FRANCIS, *K.G.,* 2nd Baron, *b.* 1718 ; was successively Lord-Lieut. of co. Warwick, Viceroy of Ireland, Master of the Horse, and Vice-Chamberlain of the Household ; cr. *Viscount Beauchamp* and *Earl of Hertford* (peerage of Great Britain) 1750, and *Earl of Yarmouth* and *Marquess of Hertford* (peerage of Great Britain) 1793 : *m.* 1741, Lady Isabella FitzRoy, who *d.* 1782, youngest dau. of 2nd Duke of Grafton ; *d.* 1794 ; *s.* by his son [3] FRANCIS, *K.G., P.C.,* 2nd Marquess ; *b.* 1743 ; was successively Lord Chamberlain of the Household, Lord-Lieut. of co. Warwick, and Gov. of Antrim ; assumed by Roy. licence the additional surname of Ingram: *m.* 1768, the Hon. Alice Elizabeth Windsor, who *d.* 1772, dau. of 2nd Viscount Windsor ; 2ndly, 1776, the Hon. Isabella Anne Ingram Shepherd, who *d.* 1836, dau. of 9th Viscount Irvine ; *d.* 1822 ; *s.* by his son [4] FRANCIS CHARLES, *K.G., P.C.,* 3rd Marquess ; *b.* 1777 ; Warden of the Stannaries and Ch. Steward and Vice-Adm. of the Duchy of Cornwall : *m.* 1798, Maria Emily Fagniani, who *d.* 1856 ; *d.* 1842 ; *s.* by his son [5] RICHARD, *K.G.,* 4th Marquess ; *b.* 1800 ; *d.* 1870 ; M.P. for co. Antrim (*C.*) 1822-6; *s.* by his cousin [6] FRANCIS HUGH GEORGE, *G.C.B., G.C.H.,* el. son of Adm. Lord Hugh Seymour, 5th son of 1st Marquess), 5th Marquess ; *b.* 1812 ; was a Gen. in the Army, and Lord Chamberlain of the Household 1874-9 : *m.* 1839, Lady Emily Murray, who *d.* 1902, dau. of 3rd Earl of Mansfield ; *d.* 1884 ; *s.* by his son [7] HUGH DE GREY, *C.B., P.C.,* 6th Marquess ; *b.* 1843 ; Lord-Lieut. of Warwickshire; Comptroller of Queen Victoria's Household 1879-80 : *m.* 1868, the Hon. Mary Hood, who *d.* 1909, da. of 1st Viscount Bridport; *d.* 1912: *s.* by his el. son [8] GEORGE FRANCIS ALEXANDER, 7th Marquess ; *b.* 1871 : *m.* 1903, Alice Cornelia (marriage annulled on her petition 1908), dau. of the late William Thaw, of Pittsburg, U.S.A. ; *d.* 1940 ; *s.* by his nephew [9] HUGH EDWARD CONWAY (son of the late Brig.-Gen. Lord Henry Charles Seymour, D.S.O., 2nd son of 6th Marquess), 8th Marquess and present peer ; also Earl of Hertford, Earl of Yarmouth, Viscount Beauchamp, Lord Conway, Baron Conway of Ragley, and Baron Conway of Killultagh.

HESKETH, BARON. (Fermor-Hesketh.) [Baron U.K. 1935, Bt. G.B. 1761.]

THOMAS ALEXANDER FERMOR-HESKETH, 3rd Baron, and 10th Baronet ; *b.* Oct. 28th, 1950; *s.* 1955; ed. at Ampleforth.

Arms,—1st and 4th, argent, on a bend sable three garbs or, *Hesketh* ; 2nd and 3rd, argent, a fesse sable between three lions' heads erased gules, *Fermor.* Crests,—A garb or banded azure ; 2nd, out of a ducal coronet or, a cock's head gules, combed and wattled or. Supporters,—On either side a griffin or, gorged with a collar gules, thereon a fleur-de-lis gold, and charged on the shoulders with a rose also gules barbed and seeded proper.

Seat,—Easton Neston, Towcester, Northants.

BROTHERS LIVING.
Hon. ROBERT, *b.* Nov. 1st, 1951; ed. at Ampleforth.
Hon. John, *b.* 1953; ed. at Ampleforth.

AUNT LIVING. (*Daughter of 1st Baron.*)
Hon. Louise (*Hon. Lady Stockdale*), *b.* 1911 : *m.* 1937, Sir Edmund Villiers Minshull Stockdale, 1st Bt. *Residence,*—Hoddington House, Upton Grey, Basingstoke.

Now and always.

WIDOW LIVING OF SON OF FIRST BARON.
Joan Isabel (EDRIDGE) (Said House, Chiswick Mall, W4 2PL), da. of Vernon James Reveley: *m.* 2ndly, 1958, as his second wife, the Hon. John Breckinridge Fermor-Hesketh, who *d.* 1961; 3rdly, 1966, Michael Frederick Laud Robinson, who *d.* 1971, only son of Sir Frederick Villiers Laud Robinson, MC, 10th baronet (cr. 1660), who *d.* 1975.

WIDOW LIVING OF SECOND BARON.
CHRISTIAN MARY (*Baroness Hesketh*) only da. of Sir John Helias Finnie McEwen, 1st Bt., DL, JP, LL.D.: *m.* 1949, the 2nd Baron, who *d.* 1955. *Residences.*—Easton Neston, Towcester, Northants; 20a, Tregunter Rd., SW10.

PREDECESSORS.—[1] THOMAS Hesketh, el. surviving son of the late Thomas Hesketh, of Rufford, Lancashire, whose family had been settled in Lancashire since the 13th century (a Robert Hesketh being knighted by Henry VIII, and a Thomas by Queen Elizabeth I.); cr. a *Baronet* 1761, with special remainder, failing heirs male of his body, to his brother, Robert : *m.* Harriett, who *d.* 1807, dau. of Ashley Cowper; *d.* 1778; *s.* (under special remainder) by his brother [2] ROBERT, 2nd Bt.; *b.* 1729; obtained permission 1792, to assume the surname and arms of his maternal great-grandfather, Sir William Juxon, Bt. ; *m.* 1748, Sarah, who *d.* 1792, dau. of the late William Plumbe, of Wavertree, Lancashire ; *d.* 1796 ; *s.* by his grandson [3] THOMAS DALRYMPLE, 3rd Bt. ; *b.* 1777 : *m.* 1798, Sophia, who *d.* 1817, dau. of the late Rev. Nathaniel Hinde ; *d.* 1842 ; *s.* by his el. son [4] THOMAS HENRY, 4th Bt. ; *b.* 1799: *m.* 1824, Annette Maria, who *d.* 1879, el. dau. of Robert Bomford, of Rahinstown House, Meath; *d.* 1843; *s.* by his son [5] THOMAS GEORGE, 5th Bt. ; *b.* 1825; M.P. for Preston (*C*); assumed by Roy. licence 1867 for himself, and his 2nd son (later 7th Bt.) the surname of Fermor before Hesketh and the arms of Fermor and Hesketh quarterly : *m.* 1846, Lady Anna Maria Arabella Fermor who inherited Easton Neston and who *d.* 1870, sister and heiress of George

5th and last Earl of Pomfret (ext.); *d.* 1872; *s.* by his el. son [6] THOMAS HENRY, 6th Bt.; *b.* 1847; *d.* 1876; *s.* by his brother [7] THOMAS GEORGE, 7th Bt.; *b.* 1849: *m.* 1880, Florence Emily, who *d.* 1924, da. of William Sharon; *d.* 1924; *s.* by his only surviving son [8] THOMAS, 8th Bt.; *b.* 1881; MP for Enfield Div. of Middlesex (*C*) 1922-23 ; cr. *Baron Hesketh*, of Hesketh, co. Palatine of Lancaster (peerage of United Kingdom) 1935 :| *m.* 1909, Florence Louise, who *d.* 1956, da. of the late John Witherspoon Breckinridge, of San Francisco, USA; *d.* 1944; *s.* by his el. surviving son [9] FREDERICK, 2nd Baron; *b.* 1916; Major (ret.) Scots Guards and a DL for Northants: *m.* 1949, Christian Mary, only da. of Sir John Helias Finnie McEwen, 1st Bt., DL, JP, LLD; *d.* 1955; *s.* by his el. son [10] THOMAS ALEXANDER, 3rd Baron and present peer.

HEWART, VISCOUNTCY OF. (Hewart.) [Extinct 1964.]

DAUGHTER LIVING OF FIRST VISCOUNT. (*By 1st marriage.*)

Hon. Katharine Mary, *b.* 1907 : *m.* 1929, Eliot Hodgkin, and has issue living, Gordon Howard Eliot, *b.* 1932,—Ann, *b.* 1930. *Residence,*—Shelley's Hare Hatch, Twyford, Berks.

WIDOW LIVING OF FIRST VISCOUNT.

JEAN (*Viscountess Hewart*), yr. da. of the late James Reid Stewart, of Wanganui, New Zealand: *m.* 1934, as his second wife, the 1st Viscount, who *d.* 1943. *Residence,*—197, Queen's Gate, S.W.7

HEWLETT, BARON. (Hewlett.) [Life Baron 1972.]

(THOMAS) CLYDE HEWLETT, *CBE,* son of the late Thomas Henry Hewlett, JP; *b.* Aug. 4th, 1923; ed. at Clifton, and Magdalene Coll., Camb. (MA); JP of Manchester; Fellow Instn. of Rubber Industry; FBIM; Chm. Anchor Chemical Co. Ltd. since 1971 (Man. Dir. since 1965, and Dep. Chm. 1968-71), Anchor Chemical Developments Ltd., Anchor Italiana Spa, Anchor Chemical Co. (Pty.) Aust. Ltd., Anchor Chemical Co. S. Africa (Pty.), Ltd., and Borg Warner Chemicals UK, Ltd.; a Member Manchester City Council 1949-56; Chm. NW Area, Young Conservatives 1951-53; Chm. NW Area Conservatives 1961-66, and Pres. 1966-69; Nat. Vice-Chm., Young Conservatives 1953; Chm. Exec. Cttee. Nat. Union of Conservative and Unionist Assocn. 1965-71; Chm. NW Industrialists' Council 1971; 1939-45 War as Lt. RM; *cr.* CBE (Civil) 1959, Knt. 1964, and *Baron Hewlett,* of Swettenham, co. Chester: *m.* 1949, Millicent, da. of Sir John William Taylor, KBE, CMG, and has issue.

Arms,—Or an anchor azure between three roses gules, barbed and seeded proper, on a chief sable a three masted ship in full sail also proper. **Crest,**—On two sprigs of willow in saltire vert, an owl affronte wings expanded or. **Supporters,**—*Dexter,* a kingfisher proper; *sinister,* a lesser spotted woodpecker proper.

Residence,—Dane Edge, Swettenham, Congleton, Cheshire, CW12 2LQ. *Clubs,*—Carlton, Constitutional, Cambridge Union.

SONS LIVING.

Hon. (Thomas) Anthony, *b.* 1952; ed. at Magdalene Coll., Camb.
Hon. (John) Richard, *b.* 1955; ed. at Oundle, and Bath Acad. of Art.

HEYCOCK, BARON. (Heycock.) [Life Baron 1967.]

LLEWELLYN HEYCOCK, *CBE,* son of William Heycock, of Taibach, Port Talbot; *b.* Aug. 12th, 1905; ed. at Eastern Sch., Port Talbot; Hon. LLD Univ. of Wales; a JP and a DL of Glamorgan; Chm. of Glamorgan Co. Council 1962-63; Chm. of Glamorgan Education Cttee. since 1946 ; a CStJ and an Hon. Member of Gorsedd of Bards; Pres. of Univ. of Wales Inst. of Science and Tech., and of Harlech Coll., Chm. Welsh Joint Education Cttee., and a Member of Univ. of Wales Council; *cr.* CBE (Civil) 1959, and *Baron Heycock,* of Taibach, in Borough of Port Talbot (Life Baron) 1967: *m.* 1930, Elizabeth Olive, da. of E. Rees, of Port Talbot, and has issue.

Arms,—Or, on a chevron gules between three wheels winged sable two chevronels argent, on a chief azure between two cockatrices heads erased or, on an open book proper bearing the word "Scientia" in letters sable. **Crest,**—On a copy of maintenance gules turned up ermine, a demi dragon gules holding a wheel or charged in the centre with a rose gules, thereon a rose argent barbed and seeded proper. **Supporters,**—*Dexter,* a dragon gules gorged with a baron's coronet proper, pendent therefrom by a ring or a winged wheel sable; *sinister,* a cockatrice gules, gorged with a baron's coronet proper, pendent therefrom by a ring a portcullis chained or.

Residence,—1, Llewellyn Close, Taibach, Port Talbot, Glam.

SON LIVING

Hon. Clayton Rees, (6, Tanygroes Place, Taibach, Port Talbot); *b.* 1941.

HEYTESBURY, BARON. (Holmes à Court.) [Baron U.K. 1828, Bt. G.B. 1795.

GRANDESCUNT·AUCTA·LABORE

Increased by labour, they grow large

FRANCIS WILLIAM HOLMES A COURT, 6th Baron, and 7th Baronet; *b.* Nov. 8th, 1931; *s.* 1971; ed. at Bryanston, and Pembroke Coll., Camb. (BA): *m.* 1962, Alison J., el. da. of Michael Graham Balfour, CBE, of 5B, Prince Arthur Rd., NW3, and has issue.

Arms,—Quarterly: 1st and 4th, barry wavy of six, or and azure; on a canton gules, a lion of England, *Holmes;* 2nd and 3rd per fesse or and paly of six erminois and azure, in chief an eagle displayed sable, beaked and membered gules, charged on the body with two chevronels argent, à *Court.* Crests,—1st, out of a naval crown or, an arm embowed in armour, the hand proper, grasping a trident azure, headed or; 2nd, an eagle displayed sable, charged on the body with two chevronels or, and holding in the beak a lily slipped proper. Supporters,—Two eagles, wings elevated and displayed sable, beaked and membered gules, each holding in the beak a lily slipped proper.

Residence,—

SON LIVING.

Hon. JAMES WILLIAM, *b.* July 30th, 1967.

DAUGHTER LIVING
Hon. Sarah Camilla, *b.* 1965.

AUNT LIVING. (*Daughter of 4th Baron*).
Hon. Betty Mary, *b.* 1902; formerly Co. Assist. A.T.S.; assumed the additional surname of à Court 1946: *m.* 1st, 1923, Com. Vivian John Robinson, R.N., from whom she obtained a divorce 1946; 2ndly, 1956, Alfred Esmond Robinson, O.B.E., M.C., and has issue living, (by 1st marriage) Anthony Leonard à Court, *b.* 1927: *m.* 1952, Sheila Ann, dau. of the late Capt. Richard Stratford Lovatt, O.B.E., R.N., and has issue living, Anthony Henry *b.* 1957, Ann Sophia *b.* 1953, Caroline Jane *b.* 1960,—Kenyon John à Court, *b.* 1929,—Jill à Court, *b.* 1924: assumed the surname of à Court 1968: *m.* 1st, 1947, (m. diss. 1968), Robert William Burt; 2ndly, 1969, Edward Fitzgerald Lawrence, of 14, Mortimer Rd., Clifton, Bristol, and has issue living (by 1st m.) Benjamin William *b.* 1948, Daniel Robert *b.* 1949, Nancy Elizabeth *b.* 1951, Sally Jane *b.* 1953. *Residence,*—Eastfield, Flax Bourton, Bristol.

COLLATERAL BRANCHES LIVING.
Issue of the late Hon. Alfred Holmes à Court, brother of 3rd and 4th Barons; *b.* 1870, *d.* 1941: *m.* 1900, Constance Isabel, who *d.* 1963, el. dau. of Charles John Newton:—
Bridget, *OBE,* (Henstridge, Somerset), *b.* 1901; sometime temporary Ch. Com. ATS; OBE(Mil) 1944.
Issue of the late Hon. Henry Worsley Holmes à Court, brother of 4th Baron. *b.* 1871, *d.* 1924: *m.* 1901, Evelyn Spencer, who *d.* 1947, dau. of W. Edward Woolley, of The Red House, Loughborough:—
Robert Anthony Pierce (P.O. Box 10665, Johannesburg, S. Africa), *b.* 1905; 1939-45 War in S. African Forces: *m.* 1930, Edith Clarice (Mrs. Mason), da. of J. W. Elworthy.——Marjorie Sophia, *MBE,* *b.* 1903; is Gen. Sec., British Council for Aid to Refugees; MBE (Civil) 1960. *Residence,—*

Grandsons of the late Hon. Henry Worsley Holmes à Court (ante):—
Issue of the late Peter Worsley Holmes à Court, *b.* 1912, *d.* 1966: *m.* 1st, 1936 (m. diss. 1950), Ethnée Celia, da. of the late H. R. Cumming, of Christmas Gift, Gwelo, Rhodesia; 2ndly, 1951, Hildè Rosa Hunt (Little Heytesbury, Telford Rd., Fortunes Gate, Bulawayo; c/o P.O. Box 503, Bulawayo):—
Michael Robert Hamilton (6, Osborne Parade, Cottesloe 6011, W. Aust.), *b.* 1937; ed. at Michaelhouse, Natal, and Univ. of W. Aust. (LLB): *m.* 1966, Janet Lee, BSc, da. of F. H. Ranford, of Perth, W. Aust., and has issue living, Peter Michael Hamilton, *b.* 1968.—Simon Antony, *b.* 1972,—Paul William, *b.* 1973,—Catherine Elizabeth, *b.* 1969.——Simon Roger (Heytesbury Stud, Keysbrook 6206, W. Aust.), *b.* 1939; ed. at Michaelhouse, Natal.

Grandchildren of the late Capt. William Alexander Russell Holmes à Court (infra):—
Issue of the late William Charles Holmes à Court, *b.* 1918, *d.* 1967: *m.* 1st, 1943 (m. diss. 1946), Joan Patricia, only da. of J. Lindsay Ellis, of Sutton, Surrey; 2ndly, 1946, Elisabeth Anne (Box 327, Minnedosa, Manitoba), yr. da. of Eric Tayleur, of Winnipeg, Canada:—
(By 2nd *m.*) William Walter (c/o College of Emmanuel & St. Chads, Sask. Univ., Saskatoun, Sask., Canada), *b.* 1948.——Phillip John, *b.* 1960.——Eric Robert, *b.* 1963.——Margaret Anne, *b.* 1951.—— Deborah Mary, *b.* 1953.——Barbara Jane, *b.* 1955.

Grandchildren of the late Hon. Arthur Wyndham Holmes à Court, 6th son of 2nd Baron:—
Issue of the late Capt. William Alexander Russell Holmes à Court, Canadian Mil., *b.* 1878, *d.* 1942: *m.* 1916, Priscilla (who *d.* 1955, having *m.* 2ndly 1954, Reginald Victor Miles), dau. of Charles Grey, of Bosham, Sussex:—
Priscilla Anne, *b.* 1917: *m.* 1948, Herbert Samuel McClay, and has issue living, Samuel Boyd, *b.* 1952,— Russell Alexander, *b.* 1954,—James Andrew, *b.* 1959,—Constance Gail, *b.* 1961. *Address,*—RR 1, Prince Albert, Saskatchewan, Canada.
Issue of the late Thomas Edward Holmes à Court, *b.* 1879, *d.* 1943: *m.* 1918, Violet Constance, dau. of Templeton Blackwell, of Poona, India:—
Constance Ann Berkeley, *b.* 1924.
Issue of the late Leonard Wyndham Daly Holmes à Court, M.B.E., *b.* 1881, *d.* 1934: *m.* 1909, Helen Marjorie Berkeley (who *d.* 19—, having *m.* 2ndly, 1947, W. Walwyn, of Estridge, St. Kitts, British W. Indies), dau. of Robert Allman Hardtman:—
(By 1st *m.*) Robert Douglas Hardtman (Heytesbury Lodge, Tokai Rd., Tokai, 7945, Cape Prov., S. Africa), *b.* 1913; ed. at Haileybury; Senior Assist. Commr. of Police, Malawi; Colonial and Queen's Police medals: *m.* 1941, Sheila Gwendolyn, da. of the late Hugo Hauffman Gibbon, of Trinidad, and has issue living, Robert Leonard, *b.* 1946; ed. at Haileybury, and Univ. of Cape Town (MSc Elec. Eng.),—Sheila Lou, *b.* 1942: *m.* 1964, Nigel Gordon Armstrong, 46, Eldon Rd., Luton, Beds., LU4 0AU.——Dorothy Kathleen, *b.* 1911; late Petty Officer, WRNS.

Grandchildren of the late Hon. Charles George Holmes a Court, 4th son of 2nd
Baron:—
Issue of the late Capt. Reginald Ashe Holmes à Court, MC, b. 1879, d. 1973: m. 1911, Gwladys
Mary Eyre, who d. 1971, da. of Henry Ralfe, Bar.-at-law, of Tasmania:—
Mary Gwladys Vaughan Ashe, b. 1913: m. 1936, John William Jocelyn McClintock, of Little Norton
Mill, Norton-sub-Hamdon, Somerset, and has issue living, William Ashe, b. 1942,—John Neill, b.
1948,—Peter Miles, b. 1950.——Ruth Vaughan Ashe (The Old Rectory, Warmwell, Dorchester,
Dorset), b. 1915; 1939-45 War as Jr. Cdr. ATS: m. 1944, Maj.-Gen. George Peregrine Walsh, CB,
CBE, DSO, who d. 1972, and has issue living, David Peregrine, b. 1949,—Jonathan à Court Peregrine,
b. 1950,—Anne à Court Peregrine, b. 1952.
Issue of the late Lieut.-Col. Alan Worsley Holmes à Court, M.D., b. 1887, d. 1957 : m. 1913,
Eileen who d. 1971, da. of Arthur Rouse, of Sydney, NS Wales:—
Peter, b. 1925 ; ed. at Sydney Univ. (Bachelor of Engineering 1950); late Roy. Australian Air Force:
m. 1950, Margaret Browne, dau. of Col. Eric Campbell, D.S.O., of Billaboola, Young, N.S. Wales,
and has issue living, Alan William, b. 1953,—Campbell Worsley, b. 1958,—Penelope, b. 1951,—
Juliet Helen, b. 1955.   Residence,—Taunton Street, Pymole, Sydney, Australia.——Pamela, b.
1921: m. 1945, Mark Russell Glasson, R.A.A.F., and has issue living, David Alan Russell, b. 1949,—
Anne Russell, b. 1946: m. 1968, William Howard Pendrill Charles, of Kydrabah, Nimmitabel,
NSW, and has issue living, Andrew Mark Pendrill b. 1973, Sally Pendrill b. 1971,—Jillian Russell,
b. 1951. Residence,—Jimenbuan, Dalgety, NS Wales.

Granddaughter of the late Hon. Edward Alexander Holmes à Court, 5th son of 2nd
Baron :—
Issue of the late Col. Rupert Edward Holmes à Court, D.S.O., b. 1882, d. 1958 : m. 1917, Linda
Katharine Cecil, who d. 1935, dau. of the late Rev. Cecil E. Smith :—
Linda Rosemary, b. 1919 : m. 1940, Major Richard Paton Pollitt, Shropshire Yeo., and has issue
living, George Edward Paton, b. 1947,—Andrew Gerald Paton, b. 1949,—Linda Susan, b. 1941,—
Rosemary Caroline, b. 1943. Residence,—Makalanga, Mazoe, Rhodesia.

Granddaughter of the late Lt.-Col. Charles à Court Repington, CMG, grandson
of Lt.-Gen. Charles Ashe à Court Repington, CB, KH, MP, 3rd son of 1st baronet.
Issue of the late Elizabeth Frances à Court Repington, b. 1892, d. 1950 : m. 1923, Thomas
Henry Ratliffe :—
Elizabeth Hermione à Court, b. 1925: m. 1947, John Jenner Marchant, of Old Barn House, Milton-
under-Wychwood, Oxon, and has issue living, Anthony John, b. 1948,—Richard Ratliffe, b. 1952,—
Nigel Francis, b. 1955,—Edward Nicholas, b. 1958.

PREDECESSORS.—[1] WILLIAM PIERCE ASHE à Court, M.P. for Heytesbury 1781-1806, and
Col. in the Army; cr. a Baronet 1795; d. 1817; s. by his son [2] Sir WILLIAM, G.C.B., P.C., 2nd
Bt.; b. 1779: M.P. for Dorchester 1812-14; cr. Baron Heytesbury, of Heytesbury, co. Wilts
(peerage of United Kingdom) 1828; was Ambassador to St. Petersburg 1828-32, and Viceroy of
Ireland 1844-6: m. 1808, Maria Rebecca, dau. of the Hon. William Henry Bouverie [E. Radnor],
d. 1860 ; s. by his son [3] WILLIAM HENRY ASHE, 2nd Baron, b. 1809 ; M.P. for Isle of Wight
(C) 1837-47; assumed the additional surname of Holmes, on his marriage, 1833, with Elizabeth,
who d. 1874, dau. of the late Sir Leonard Worsley Holmes, Bt.; d. 1891; s. by his grandson
[4] WILLIAM FREDERICK (son of the late Hon. William Leonard Holmes à Court, el. son of 2nd
Baron, by Isabella Sophia, who d. 1908, dau. of the late Rev. Richard à Court Beadon), b.
1862 : m. 1887, Margaret Anna, who d. 1920, dau. of the late J. N. Harman, of Tadmarton,
Oxford ; d. 1903 ; s. by his brother [5] LEONARD, 4th Baron, b. 1863 ; Major (retired) Wiltshire
Regt., and Col. late Special Reserve: m. 1896, Sybil Mary, who d. 1937, dau. of the late Capt.
Frank B. Morris, Bengal Army; d. 1949; s. by his son [6] WILLIAM LEONARD FRANK. 5th
Baron, b. 1906: m. 1926, Beryl, who d. 1968, yst. da. of Albert Edward Bredin Crawford, DCL, LLD,
of Aston Clinton House, Bucks.; d. 1971; s. by his son [7] FRANCIS WILLIAM, 6th Baron and present
peer.

HEYWORTH, BARONY. (Heyworth.) Extinct 1974.
WIDOW LIVING OF FIRST BARON

LOIS (Baroness Heyworth), (29, Sussex Sq., W2), da. of Stevenson Dunlop,
of Woodstock, Ont., Canada: m. 1924, the 1st Baron Heyworth, who d. 1974,
when the title became ext.

HILL, VISCOUNT. (Clegg-Hill.) [Viscount U.K. 1842, Bt. G.B. 1727.]

ANTONY ROWLAND CLEGG-HILL, 8th
Viscount, and 10th Baronet; b. March 19th,
1931; s. 1974; ed. at Kelly Coll. and RMA;
late Capt. RA; has freedom of Shrewsbury:
m. 1963, Juanita Phyllis, da. of John W.
Pertwee, of White Gates, Cross Oak Lane,
Salfords, Surrey.

Arms,—Quarterly: 1st and 4th, ermine, a fesse
sable, charged with a castle, triple towered argent,
Hill; 2nd and 3rd, per pale sable and azure a cross-
crosslet crossed between two acorns in bend dexter,
and as many fleurs-de-lys in bend sinister argent, Clegg.
Crests.—1st, a tower argent, issuant from the battlements
a wreath of laurel, all proper, Hill; 2nd, in front of two
branches of oak in saltire, fructed proper, a cross-
crosslet crossed or, Clegg. Supporters,—Dexter, a lion
argent, murally crowned or and gorged with a wreath of
oak fructed proper: sinister, a horse argent, bridled and
saddled, and gorged with a mural crown gules.

Forward.   Residence,—

WIDOWS LIVING OF SONS OF THIRD AND SIXTH VISCOUNTS.
Dorothy, dau. of the Rev. Sir George Boughey, 5th Bt. : m. 1907, Capt. the Hon. Gerald Spencer
Clegg-Hill, J.P., who d. 1930, and has issue living, [see colls., infra]. Residence,—119, Grange Road,
Ealing, W.5.
Alice Dorothy, da. of the late Rear-Adm. Cuthbert Godfrey Chapman, MVO [B. Newborough]: m.
1938, Major the Hon. Frederick Raymond Clegg-Hill, King's Shropshire LI, who d. (killed in action
in Germany) 1945, and has issue living [see colls., infra.] Residence,—Dingley Hill, Bradfield, Berks.

WIDOW LIVING OF SEVENTH VISCOUNT.
CATHERINE MARY (MOLLY), (Molly, Viscountess Hill), da. of Dr. Rowland Venables Lloyd-Williams
of Maiford, Denbigh: m. 1942, as his 2nd wife, the 7th Viscount, who d. 1974.

COLLATERAL BRANCHES LIVING.

Issue of the late Major the Hon. Frederick Raymond Clegg-Hill, King's Shropshire L.I., 2nd son of 6th Viscount, *b.* 1909, *d.* (killed in action in Germany)
1945: *m.* 1938, Alice Dorothy (ante), dau. of the late Rear-Adm. Cuthbert
    Godfrey Chapman, MVO [B. Newborough]:—
PETER DAVID RAYMOND CHARLES Oct. 17th (posthumous), *b.* 1945: *m.* 1973, Sharon Ruth Deane,
of Kaikohe, NZ.
    Issue of the late Capt. the Hon. Gerald Spencer Clegg-Hill J.P., 5th son of 3rd
Viscount, *b.* 1879, *d.* 1930 : *m.* 1907, Dorothy (ante), dau. of the Rev. Sir George
    Boughey, 5th Bt. :—
Anne Selina Elizabeth, *b.* 1915: *m.* 1st, 1940, Edward Hanbury Carington David Lloyd-Davies
from whom she obtained a divorce 1947 ; 2ndly, 1947, Janusz Maria Stanislaw Eugeniusz Juhre,
late 2nd Lieut. Polish Army, of Lwow, Poland, and has issue living, (by 2nd marriage) Tadeusz
Maria Gerald Alexander *b.* 1951,—Maria Jadwiga Teresa, *b.* 1948: *m.* 1973, Andrew Maryniak,—
Jadwiga Maria Teresa Celina, *b.* 1949: *m.* 1972, Richard Seller,—Anna Zofia Maria, *b.* 1954. *Residence,*
—Aqualate Hall, Newport, Salop.
    (In remainder to Barony and Baronetcy.)
    Grandchildren of the late John Hill, son of the late Rev. John Hill (infra) :—
    Issue of the late John Kenyon Hill, *b.* 1869, *d.* 1945 : *m.* 1906, Mary Ruby, dau. of Frank
    Watkins, of Parklands, Nairobi, Kenya :—
Mary Sybil, *b.* 1909: *m.* 1935 (m. diss. 1947), Sq.-Ldr. Colin Alexander MacKenzie, RAFVR, and has
issue living, Ewen Rowland Francis, *b.* 1936.——Muriel Rachel, *b.* 1911: *m.* 1934, John Wilson
Lichfield Harris, and has issue living, Charles John, *b.* 1935,—David Lichfield, *b.* 1942,—Mary
Victoria, *b.* 1940. *Residence,*—Garsden, Subukia, Kenya.——Helen Georgina, *b.* 1913: *m.* 1941,
Patrick Campbell MacDougall Watson. *Residence,*—Heriot, George, Cape Province, S. Africa.
    Issue of the late Frederick Rowland Hill, *b.* 1870, *d.* 1947 : *m.* 1910, Theodora Ann, who
    d. 1961, dau. of the late Rev. R. H. Quick :—
Rev. Preb. Richard Hebert, *b.* 1911; ed. at Wrekin Coll.; is R. and Rural Dean of Ledbury, Preb. of
Hereford Cathedral, and a Freeman of Shrewsbury; 1939–45 War: *m.* 1945, Suzanne, da. of the late
Dr. Horace Gooch, of Ragleth House, Church Stretton, and has issue living, Frederick Peter Gooch,
b. 1946,—Richard Stephen, *b.* 1949. *Residence,*—The Rectory, Ledbury, Herefordshire.——
Rev. Canon Rowland Edward, *b.* 1913; ed. at Shrewsbury, and at Trin. Coll., Oxford (MA 1940);
V. of Cirencester, Hon. Canon of Gloucester Cathedral, and a Freeman of Shrewsbury; 1939–45 War
as Chap. to the Forces: *m.* 1939, Elizabeth, da. of the late Roland Maddison Vaisey, of Tring, Herts.
and has issue living, David Rowland (63, Jalan Templar, Petaling Jaya, Malaysia), *b.* 1940; ed. at
Trin. Coll., Glenalmond and Keble Coll., Oxford (MA); *Freeman* of Shrewsbury: *m.* 1969, Sonya,
da. of Stuart McClusky, and has issue living, Charlotte Ruth *b.* 1973,—Nigel John (36, Bellevue Rd.,
Ealing, W13), *b.* 1943; ed. at Trin Coll., Glenalmond, and Univ. Coll., Durham (BA): Sgt. Met.
Police; Freeman of Shrewsbury: *m.* 1968, Gillian Mary, yr. da. of Ian Heath Stock, MC, and has
issue living, Oliver Rowland Vaisey, *b.* 1972, Clarissa Mary *b.* 1969,—James Geoffrey (20 Melville
Rd., Edgbaston, Birmingham 16), *b.* 1948; ed. at Trin. Coll., Glenalmond, and Univ. Coll., Durham
(BA); Surg. Sub. Lt. RN; Freeman of Shrewsbury: *m.* 1974, Eileen Frances Rachel, da. of the late
Charles Rodney Webster, WS, of Edinburgh,—Andrew Valsey (52, Foyle Rd., Blackheath, SE3),
b. 1950; ed. at Shrewsbury, and Univ. Coll., Durham (BA); Freeman of Shrewsbury: *m.* 1974,
Zaria Caroline Annabel, da. of the late Maj. Joseph Theodore Knowles, Wilts. Regt. *Residence,*—
The Vicarage, Cirencester, Glos.——*Rev.* James Carthew, *b.* 1915; ed. at Shrewsbury; R. of Newport,
Salop, Rural Dean of Edgmond, and a Freeman of Shrewsbury: *m.* 1954, Muriel Beatrice, da. of the
Rev. Roland James Peake, MBE, of Aylesford, Kent. *Residence,*—The Rectory, Newport, Salop.

    Grandchildren of the late Rev. John Hill, son of the late Col. John Hill, father
    of 2nd Viscount :—
    Issue of the late Vice-Adm. George William Hill, *b.* 1843, *d.* 1905: *m.* 1st, 1882, Mary
    Caroline, who *d.* 1896, dau. of Vice-Adm. Morgan Singer, of Emsworth, Hants;
    2ndly, 1898, Helen Maud, who *d.* 1955, dau. of the late Frederick Woodman, of Bedford
    House, Upper Deal, Kent :—
(By 1st m.) Eileen Edith Singer, *b.* 1896: *m.* 1931, the Rev. Brian Golland Crowley, and has issue
living, John Christopher Golland (The View, Vicarage Rd., Penn, Wolverhampton, WV4 5JB),
b. 1933: *m.* 1961, Elisabeth Julia Donkin Read, and has issue living Jonathan Mark *b.* 1963, Catherine
Elisabeth *b.* 1965,—Brian Nicholas Hill (7, Shires Way, Yateley, Camberley, Surrey), *b.* 1942:
m. 1965, Celia Robson, and has issue living, Nicola Louise Hill, *b.* 1969, Philippa Charlotte Hill
b. 1973,—Mary Elspeth Singer, *b.* 1935: *m.* 1962, David Hyde Langford, of 23, Cooper Rd., Westbury-
on-Trym, Bristol, and has issue living, Robin Charles *b.* 1964, Sarah Caroline *b.* 1967. *Residence,*—
39, Peterdale Drive, Penn, Wolverhampton.
    Issue (by 2nd marriage) of the late Sir Clement Lloyd Hill, K.C.B., K.C.M.G., M.P.,
    b. 1845, *d.* 1913: *m.* 1st, 1889, Charlotte Eliza Mary Jane, who *d.* 1900, dau. of Sir
    George William Denys, 2nd Bt., and widow of Charles Waring; 2ndly, 1906, Muriel
    Mary, who *d.* 1958, dau. of the late Colin Glencairn Campbell, of 34, Lower Belgrave
    Street, S.W. [Macnaghten, Bt.] :—
Clement Walter Rowland (Lower Woodside, Hatfield, Herts.; Hawkstone Park, Shrewsbury), *b.* 1909;
ed. at Eton; Major Queen's Own Cameron Highlanders; 1939–45 War (wounded): *m.* 1st, 1935, (*m.*
diss. 1941), Violet, el. da. of Charles Phillimore, of The Old Farm, Swinbrook, Oxford; 2ndly, 1947,
Elizabeth Theresa, who *d.* 1970, da. of the late Capt. J. J. J. de Knoop, and formerly wife of the late
John Henry Hambro, CMG; 3rdly, 1971, Kathleen, da. of Frank Dickie, of Truro, Nova Scotia,
and widow of Norman Walduck, and has issue living, (by 1st m.) Carolyn Mary, *b.* 1937: *m.* 1968,
Edward Lockwood, and has issue living, Richard Rowland *b.* 1971, Louisa Elizabeth *b.* 1969,—
Joanna Clementine, *b.* 1939: *m.* 1965, Charles C. Bastin (c/o Coutts & Co., 440, Strand, WC2), and
has issue living, Alexander Charles *b.* 1969, Nicholas Rowland *b.* 1970.

    Grandson of the late Henry Philip Hill (infra) :—
    Issue of the late Henry Alan Hill, *b.* 1877, *d.* 1940: *m.* 1920, Marjory Stewart (now of
    El Refugio, E. Carbo, F.N.G.U., Argentina), da. of the late James Tyhurst:—
Henry James, *b.* 1921 ; ed. at Wellington Coll. ; Italy 1943–5 as Lieut. 17th/21st Lancers and Lothian
and Border Regt.: *m.* 1953, Ina Philpott, and has issue living, Henry John, *b.* 1962,—Virginia, *b.*
1954,—Margaret Ina, *b.* 1956,—Christine, *b.* 1959. *Residence,*—El Refugio, E. Carbo, F.N.G.U.,
Argentina.

    Grandchildren of the late Lieut.-Col. Richard Frederick Hill, 3rd son of the late
    Col. John Hill (ante) :—
    Issue of the late Henry Philip Hill, *b.* 1845, *d.* 1924 : *m.* 1870, Nora Alice, who *d.* 1928, dau. of
    Major H. A. Scott:—
Rowland Philip, *b.* 1888 : *m.* 1912, Ruth, dau. of C. H. Stott, and has issue living, Brian Henry
Rowland (of 7, Thompson Road, Napier, New Zealand), *b.* 1917 ; ed. at Christ's Coll., Christ-
church, New Zealand, and at Otago Univ. (M.B. and Ch.B. 1943); D.D.M. Sydney 1950 ;
Middle East 1945 with Roy. New Zealand Med. Corps: *m.* 1945, Marjorie Virginia, dau. of Capt.
Euan Dickson, D.S.C., D.F.C., late R.F.C., of Auckland, New Zealand, and has issue living,
Heathcote Henry Rowland *b.* 1949, Simon Philip *b.* 1951, Angela Francesca *b.* 1946. *Residence,*—
Lucknow Road, Havelock North, New Zealand.——Alice Isabel, *b.* 1874 : *m.* 1910, Gerald Mark-
ham Bowen, who *d.* 1930, son of the late Hon. Sir Charles Christopher Bowen, K.C.M.G., and has
issue living, Norah Chrystobel Hill, *b.* 1911. *Residence,*—14, Drayton Gdns., SW10.
    [In remainder to Baronetcy.]
    Grandchildren of the late Capt. Alfred Edward Hill, 2nd son of the late Sir Robert
    Chambre Hill, C.B., 4th son of 3rd Baronet :—
    Issue of the late Robert Hill, *b.* 1847, *d.* 1930 : *m.* 1894, Ethel Murdoch, who *d.* 1930,
    dau. of W. F. Brabant :—

Alfred Brabant, *b.* 1896 : *m.* 1933, Frances, el. dau. of the late Edward Pooley, and has issue living,
John Richard, *b.* 1935; ed. at British Columbia Univ (BSc),—Peter Robert (2509, Laured Rd.,
Jacksonville, Fla., USA), *b.* 1937; ed. at British Columbia Univ. (BA, Sc): *m.* 1968, Mary Lynn, da. of
the late Keller Smith, and has issue living, Peter Brabant *b.* 1970, Molly Cochran *b.* 1972. *Residence,*
—6408, West Saanich Rd., R.R. No. 7, Victoria, BC.——Margaret Anne, *b.* 1894: *m.* 1946, Edwin
W. Fletcher, who *d.* 1964.

Grandchildren of the late Lt.-Gen. Percy Hill, O.B., late Rifle Bde., 3rd son of the late Sir Robert Chambre Hill, O.B. (ante):—

Issue of the late Capt. Percy Graham Hill, Rifle Brig., *b.* 1848, *d.* 1923 : *m.* 1st, 1872, Margaret
Anne Hamilton, who *d.* 1879, dau. of Lieut. Charles Stuart; 2ndly, 1892, Alice Margaret,
who *d.* 1897, da. of Rev. Canon Henry Brown; 3rdly, 1901, Elizabeth Ann (who *d.*
1960, having *m.* 2ndly, 1927, Charles Beaufoy Wright, who *d.* 1944), da. of George
Raworth:—
(By 3rd marriage) Rowland Graham, *O.B.E.*, *b.* 1912; Lieut.-Col. (retired) Dorset Regt.
M.B.E. (Mil.) 1943, O.B.E. (Mil.) 1956 : *m.* 1941, Doris Lucy Frances (EDYE), dau. of the late Sir
Francis Dundas Couchman, K.B.E. *Residence,*—Merevale, Upper High St., Taunton. *Club,*—
Army and Navy.——Florence Cecilia, *b.* 1906: *m.* 1926, Lt.-Col. Julian Edward Wright, Sherwood
Foresters, who *d.* 1967, and has issue living, Juliet Ann Cecilia (6, Cannongate Gdns., Hythe, Kent),
b. 1928: *m.* 1960 (m. diss. 1974), Peter Oswald Richard Gatehouse, and has issue living, James Peter
Wright *b.* 1963, Elizabeth Ann Cecilia *b.* 1965. *Residence,*—3, Cherry Garden Av., Folkestone.

Granddaughters of the late Clement John Hill, son of the late Robert Greene Hill (b 1801):—

Issue of the late Robert Greene Hill, *b.* 1858, *d.* 1943: *m.* 1887, Minna Field Orchard,
who *d.* 1933 :—
vy Ellen Greene, *b.* 1888: *m.* 1910, Robert Bloy, who *d.* 1959, and has issue living, Ivy Hope, *b.* 1911:
m. 1952, Alfred Edwin Harrison, of Sunwich Port, P.O. Anerley, S. Coast, Natal,—Dorothy Minnie
Eileen. *b.* 1914: *m.* 1936. Howard Foss, who *d.* (killed in action in Italy) 1944, and has issue living,
Robert George (Pietermaritzburg, Natal) *b.* 1937: *m.* 1961, Charmione Dennis (and has issue living,
Jennifer Renée *b.* 1963, Eileen Beverley *b.* 1965)—Noel Howard (Pietermaritzburg, Natal) *b.* 1942:
m. 1962, Barbara Reed, (and has issue living, Clive Howard *b.* 1968, Graham Clifton *b.* 1972, Hazel
Margaret *b.* 1971).——Gladys Irene, *b.* 1892.——Vivenne Constance *b.* 1893: *m.* 1919, Douglas
Wise, who *d.* 1966, and has issue living, Vivenne Daphne, *b.* 1923: *m.* 1956, Melvyn Pigg, who *d.* 1968.
Residence,—Silver Lining, Himeville, Natal.
Issue of the late Henry Daniel Hill, *b.* 1844, *d.* 1920: *m.* 1868, Elizabeth Harriet, dau. of
John Speakman, of Nantwich, and widow of William Salmon :—
Katherine Harriete, *b.* 1881.——Mary Wilbraham, *b.* 1884.

Grandchildren of the late Henry Daniel Hill (infra):—

Issue of the late Roger Wilbraham Hill, *b.* 1883, *d.* 1962: *m.* 1912, Mary Ann, who *d.* 1971,
da. of James Sadler, of Acton, Chester:—
Gerald Roger (Hough Gates, Hough, Crewe), *b.* 1921; *m.* 1953, Jane Elizabeth, da. of Frank Haighton,
of Elm House, Nantwich, and has issue living, Gerald Robert Wilbraham, *b.* 1958,—Elizabeth
Mary *b.* 1955.——Sheila Mary, *b.* 1913.

Grandchildren of the late Francis Robert Wilbraham Hill (infra):—

Issue of the late John Francis Hill, *b.* 1882, *d.* 1948: *m.* 1916, Natalie Ivy, who *d.* 1967, da.
of Thomas Payne St. James:—
Alaric Bryan, *b.* 1921; 1939-45 War in S. African Air Force: *m.* 1948, Elizabeth Margaret Allen,
and has issue living, Dallas John, *b.* 1950,—Carol Elizabeth, *b.* 1953: *m.* 1974, Gordon Redvers Bell
(Kruispruit, PO Box 69, Kokstad, E. Griqualand, S. Africa), and has issue living, Cherié Elizabeth
b. 1974. *Address,*—Kruispruit, PO Box 69, Kokstad, S. Africa.——Ellen Maryan, *b.* 1920; *m.* 1946,
Thomas Duncan MacMillan, ACIS, formerly 2nd Transvaal Scottish, and has issue living, Bruce
Warwick Hugh, *b.* 1951; BSc,—Brenda Caroline Dale, *b.* 1955. *Residence,*—42, Rarangi Rd., St.
Heliers Bay, Auckland, 5, NZ.——Vivette Natalie, *b.* 1925: *m.* 1949, Johan Heinrich Moll, BSc,
AMIMechE, of 15, Straker Av., Gun Hill, Salisbury, Rhodesia, and has issue living, Victor Ferek,
b. 1954,—Coleen Yvonne, *b.* 1951.

Grandson of the late Robert Greene Hill (b. 1801), son of the late Rev. Robert Wilbral ham Bromhall Hill, el. son of the late Rev. Robert Hill, 4th son of 1st baronet:—

Issue of the late Francis Robert Wilbraham Hill, *b.* 1852, *d.* 1936: *m.* 1880, Mary
Anne Bennett, who *d.* 1912, dau. of the late Daniel Boote, of Edstaston Hall, Salop :—
Robert Wilbraham, *b.* 1886. *Address,*—c/o Lintlaw Post Office, Saskatchewan, Canada.

Grandchildren of the late Lieut.-Gen. George Mytton Hill, son of the late Richard Hill, 5th son of the late Rev. Robert Hill (ante) :—

Issue of the late Lieut.-Col. George Michell Devereux Hill, *b.* 1845, *d.* 1889: *m.* 1874, Miss
Kate Gough Glynn:—
Mary Glynn Mytton, *b.* 1875. *Residence,*—

Issue of the late Col. Arthur Hill, Cheshire Regt., *b.* 1851, *d.* 1950: *m.* 1879, Katharine
Emily, who *d.* 1949, dau. of the late Thomas Morris, M.D., of Hayes Common, Kent :—
Harold Brian Cunningham (c/o St. George's Hotel, St. George's Rd., Truro), *b.* 1887; ed. at Harrow; Lt.
Indian Cav.; 1914-19 War: *m.* 1920, Elsie, who *d.* 1971, da. of J. Jeppe, JP (Consul-Gen. for Greece
and for Roumania, and Senior Roy. Danish Consul in S. Africa), of 68, Shortmarket St., Cape Town,
and has issue living, Noel Brian, *b.* 1926; ed. at Eastbourne Coll.: *m.* 1958, Gladys Rosa, da. of the
late Sidney George West, OBE, and has issue living, Nicola Anne *b.* 1959, Philippa Jane *b.* 1962,—
Julian (Pleasant Farm, Fairwarp, nr. Uckfield, Sussex; Little Ship Club; MCC), *b.* 1932; ed. at
Eastbourne Coll.: *m.* 1956, Ruth Monica, yst. da. of the late Paul Sekvens Toll, of 10, Villagatan,
Stockholm, and has issue living, Rowland Paul *b.* 1956; ed. at Eastbourne Coll. and King's Coll.,
London, Michael Mytton *b.* 1960; ed. at Eastbourne Coll., Louise Anne *b.* 1963.——Reginald Herbert,
b. 1889; ed at. Wellington Coll.: *m.* 1st, 1914, Elizabeth Wallace, da. of the late A. S. Coubrough, JP,
Blanefield, Stirlingshire; 2ndly, 1931, Gertrude, da. of J. Perry, of Tavistock, Devon, and has issue
living, (by 2nd m.) Arthur Brian Montague (18, Ripple Court, Sacramento, Cal. 95831, USA), *b.* 1932:
m. 1960, Brenda Margaret, da. of W. A. Murray, of Bebington, Ches., and has issue living, George
Mytton *b.* 1969,—(by 1st m.) Kathleen Agnes, *b.* 1916: *m.* 1946, George Elden Burrell, of 2760,
Burdick, Av., Victoria, British Columbia, and has issue living, Robin Elden Adair *b.* 1951, Keith
Edgar *b.* 1953, Wendy Evelyn *b.* 1948,—Winifred Evelyn, *b.* 1920: *m.* 1945, Charles M. Humphrys,
of 6187, McCleery St., Vancouver, British Columbia, and has issue living, Daphne Mary *b.* 1946,
Sheila Elizabeth *b.* 1947, Brenda Ann *b.* 1953, Nancy Maureen *b.* 1958. *Residence,*—Mediterranean
Village, 920, 43rd Av., R67, Sacramento, Cal. 95831, USA.

Granddaughters of the late Col. Arthur Hill (ante):—

Issue of the late Major Arthur Rowland Hill, *b.* 1880, *d.* (killed in action during European
War) 1915: *m.* 1908, Kathleen, dau. of C. Todd :—
Christian Mary (*Baroness Riverdale*), *b.* 1909 : *m.* 1933, as his second wife, the 2nd Baron Riverdale.
Residence,—Ropes, Grindleford, via Sheffield.——Alison Kathleen, *b.* 1911: *m.* 1934, Henry Seaward
Morley, MD, FRCP, who *d.* 1961, and has issue living, John Henry (Derwent Lodge, Oldfield Rd.,
Maidenhead, Berks.), *b.* 1936; ed. at Wellington, and Downing Coll., Camb. (MA): *m.* 1963, Felicity
Faith Beryl, el. da. of John Peile, of Grindleford, Sheffield,—Timothy Rowland *b.* 1939; ed. at
Wellington, and Downing Coll., Camb. (MA); MB, BCh, FRCS, LRCP: *m.* 1966, Mary Elspeth
Holborn, da. of Noel F. Adeney, of Bournemouth. *Residence,*—Church Cottage, Midhurst, Sussex.

Issue of the late Cdr. George Mytton Hill, RN, *b.* 1883, *d.* 1935: *m.* 1919, Olive Odell, who
d. 1966, da. of W. Millar, of Eskbank:—

Doreen Odell, *b.* 1920: *m.* 1950, Major Hector McNeill Tytler Reith, R.A. (ret.), of 78B, Granville Rd., Sevenoaks, Kent, and has issue living, Douglas McNeill Mytton, *b.* 1953.

PREDECESSORS.—*Sir* Richard Hill, P.C., an eminent statesman and diplomatist; *d.* unmarried, and devised his Hawkstone estates to his nephew [1] ROWLAND HILL, who in consideration of his uncle's important sers. was cr. a *Baronet* 1727, with remainder to his cousins Samuel Hill, of Shenstone, Thomas Hill, of Tern, whose el. son was cr. Baron Berwick, and to Rowland Hill, brother of Thomas (ante); sat as M.P. for Lichfield 1734; *d.* 1783; *s.* by his el. son [2] *Sir* RICHARD, 2nd Bt., M.P. for co. Salop 1780-1802; *d.* unmarried 1809; *s.* by his brother [3] *Sir* JOHN, 3rd Bt., M.P. for Shrewsbury 1784-1802; his 2nd son Rowland, G.C.B., a distinguished Gen. and Com. in Ch. 1828-42, was cr. *Baron Hill,* of Almarez and of Hawkstone, co. Salop (peerage of United Kingdom) 1814, and *Viscount Hill* (peerage of United Kingdom) 1842, with remainder in each instance to the issue of his el. brother John; Sir John *d.* 1824, and was *s.* by his grandson [4] ROWLAND, 4th Bt., son of John (ante); in 1842 *s.* his uncle (ante) as 2nd Viscount Hill; *b.* 1800; was M.P. for Shropshire 1821-32 and for N. Shropshire (C) 1832-42, and Lord Lieut. of Salop: *m.* 1831, Anne, only child of Joseph Clegg, of Peplow Hall, Salop, and sole heir of Arthur Clegg; *d.* 1875; *s.* by his son [5] ROWLAND CLEGG, 3rd Viscount, *b.* 1833; M.P. for N. Shropshire (C) 1857-65; assumed in 1875 the additional surname of Clegg: *m.* 1st, 1855, Mary, who *d.* 1874, dau. of William Madax; 2ndly, 1875, the Hon. Isabella Elizabeth Wynn, who *d.* 1898, dau. of 3rd Baron Newborough; *d.* 1895; *s.* by his el. son [6] ROWLAND RICHARD, 4th Viscount, *b.* 1853; was Master of Spectacle Makers' Co.: *m.* 1890, Annie Edith, who *d.* 1937, dau. of the late William Irwin, of Tandrago, co. Sligo; *d.* 1923; *s.* by his brother [7] FRANCIS WILLIAM, 5th Viscount, *b.* 1866: *m.* 1905, Caroline Anna, who *d.* 1941, dau. of the late Capt. Frank Corbett, of Greenfield, Presteign, Radnorshire; *d.* 1924; *s.* by his half-brother [8] CHARLES ROWLAND, D.S.O., 6th Viscount. *b.* 1876; Lieut.-Col. late Roy. Welch Fusiliers: *m.* 1st, 1903, Mildred, who *d.* 1936, dau. of Thomas Bulteel; 2ndly, 1936, Berthe Maria Emilie, who *d.* 1959, dau. of the late A. Schmidt-Immer, of Strasbourg, Alsace-Lorraine; *d.* 1957; *s.* by his son [9] GERALD ROWLAND, 7th Viscount, *b.* 1904: *m.* 1st, 1930, Elisabeth Flora, who *d.* 1967, having obtained a divorce 1942, da. of Brig.-Gen. George Nowell Thomas Smyth-Osbourne, CB, CMG, DSO, DL, of Ash, Iddlesleigh, N. Devon; 2ndly, 1942, Catherine Mary (Molly), da. of Dr. Rowland Venables Lloyd-Williams, of Maiford, Denbigh; *d.* 1974; *s.* by his el. son [10] ANTONY ROWLAND, 8th Viscount and present peer; also Baron Hill.

HILL OF LUTON, BARON (Hill.) [Life Baron 1963.]

CHARLES HILL, *P.C.*, son of Charles Hill, of London; *b.* Jan. 15th, 1904; ed. at St. Olave's Sch., and at Trin. Coll., Camb. (MA, MD and BChir, Hon. LLD 1947); MRCS England and LRCP London 1927; DPH England 1931; Sec. of British Med. Assocn. 1944-50, Pres. of World Med. Assocn. 1949-50, Parl. Sec. of Min. of Food 1951-55, Postmaster-Gen. 1955-57, Chancellor of Duchy of Lancaster 1957-61, and Min. of Housing and Local Govt., and Min. for Welsh Affairs 1961-62; Chm. of ITA 1963-67, and of Board of Govs. of BBC 1967-72; Indep. Chm., Nat. Joint Council for Local Authorities' Admin. Professional, Tech. and Clerical Sers., and Dep. Chm. Abbey National Building Soc.; MP for Luton (C and L) 1950-63; cr. PC 1955, and *Baron Hill of Luton,* of Harpenden, co. Hertford [Life Baron] 1963: *m.* 1931, Marion Spencer, da. of M. Wallace, of Halifax, and has issue.

Residence,—5, Bamville Wood, E. Common, Harpenden, Herts.

SONS LIVING.
Hon. Robert (of Model Farm, Crewe Green, Cheshire), *b.* 1938; ed. at Epsom, and Harpur Adams Agricultural Coll.: *m.* 1960, Ann, da. of E. Williamson, of Southampton, and has issue.
Hon. John (5, Bamville Wood, E. Common, Harpenden, Herts.), *b.* 1945; ed. at Epsom, and Camb. Univ.

DAUGHTERS LIVING.
Hon. Jennifer, *b.* 1933: *m.* 1960, Robert Duncan Barnaby Leicester, MB, of 15, William St., Brighton, Vic. 3186, Aust., and has issue.
Hon. Elizabeth, *b.* 1935: *m.* 1964, David Maxwell Morris, of Herons View, Hatchford, Cobham, Surrey, and has issue.
Hon. Susan, *b.* 1936: *m.* 1958, David Ritchie Fairbairn, of 7, Marlow Mills, Mill Lane, Marlow, Bucks., and has issue.

HILL OF WIVENHOE, BARONY OF. (Hill.) [Extinct 1969.]
WIDOW LIVING OF LIFE BARON.

HANNAH (*Baroness Hill of Wivenhoe*) (3, Eskdale Av., Kings Rd. Estate, Wallsend, Northumberland.); da. of Usher Rosen, of Newcastle upon Tyne, and formerly wife of Colin Crowther: *m.* 1960, as his 2nd wife, Baron Hill of Wivenhoe (Life Peer), who *d.* 1969.

HILLINGDON, BARON. (Mills.) [Baron U.K. 1886, Bt. U.K. 1868.]

CHARLES HEDWORTH MILLS, 4th Baron, and 5th Baronet; *b.* Jan. 12th, 1922; *s.* 1952; ed. at Eton; is Lieut. Life Guards: *m.* 1947, Lady Sarah Gray Stuart, da. of the 18th Earl of Moray, and has issue.

Conscious of no evil in himself.

Arms,—Gyronny of eight azure and argent, a mill-rind sable. *Crest,*—A demi-lion reguardant or, gorged with a collar gemel azure, between the paws a mill-rind sable. *Supporters,*—Two lions reguardant or, each gorged with a collar gemel azure, and charged on the shoulder with a cross fleury.

Residence,—Messing Park, Kelvedon, Essex. *Clubs,*—White's, Buck's.

SON LIVING.
Hon. CHARLES JAMES, *b.* March 8th, 1951.

DAUGHTERS LIVING.
Hon. Victoria Elizabeth, *b.* 1948: *m.* 1971, Anthony Roff.
Hon. Jessica Anne, *b.* 1957.
Hon. Catherine Gray, *b.* 1963.

SISTERS LIVING.

Hon. Penelope Ann, *b.* 1917: *m.* 1940, Evelyn Lennox Napier Sturt, who *d.* 1945, and has issue living, Gerard Philip Napier, *b.* 1945,—Caroline Susan, *b.* 1941,—Pamela Mary, *b.* 1943. *Residence,—*
Hon. Ursula Sybil, *b.* 1918.
Hon. Marygold, *b.* 1924.

WIDOW LIVING OF SON OF FIRST BARON.

Hilda Susan Ellen, dau. of Sir Daniel Cooper, 2nd Bt. (cr. 1863), and widow of Thomas Uchter Caulfeild, Viscount Northland [see E. Ranfurly]: *m.* 2ndly, 1917, as his second wife, Com. the Hon. Geoffrey Edward Mills, R.N.V.R. who *d.* (on active ser. during European War) 1917; 3rdly, 1918, Capt. Michael Wardell (late 10th Hussars), from whom she obtained a divorce 1929; 4thly, 1929, Julien Joseph Lezard, Bar.-at-law. *Residence,—*Mill House, Great Missenden, Bucks.

COLLATERAL BRANCHES LIVING.

Granddaughter of the late Hon. Algernon Henry Mills, 2nd son of 1st Baron :—
Issue of the late Henry Christian George Mills, *b.* 1886, *d.* 1940: *m.* 1st, 1910, Alice, who *d.* 1912, dau. of W. R. Robinson, formerly of Toowoomba, Queensland ; 2ndly, 1913, Hilma, who *d.* 1961, dau. of August Ohman, of Brisbane:—
(By 2nd m.) Diana Mary Christian (*Countess St. Aldwyn*), *b.* 1915: *m.* 1st, 1939 (m. annulled 1942), Capt. Richard Patrick Pilkington Smyly, MC, 13th/18th R. Hussars; 2ndly, 1948, the 2nd Earl St. Aldwyn. *Residences,—*Williamstrip Park, Cirencester, Gloucestershire; 13, Upper Belgrave St., SW1. *Club,—*Guards'.

Issue (by 1st marriage) of the late Com. the Hon. Geoffrey Edward Mills, R.N.V.R., 6th son of 1st Baron, *b.* 1875, *d.* (on active ser. during European War) 1917: *m.* 1st, 1901, Grace Victoria (who obtained a divorce 1913), dau. of the Hon. Hungerford Tudor Boddam, a Judge of High Court, Madras; 2ndly, 1917, Hilda Susan Ellen (of The Mill House, Great Missenden, Bucks ; she *m.* 3rdly, 1918, Capt. Michael Wardell, late 10th Hussars, from whom she obtained a divorce 1929 ; 4thly, 1929, Julien Joseph Lezard, Bar.-at-law), dau. of Sir Daniel Cooper, 2nd Bt. (cr. 1863), and widow of Thomas Uchter Caulfeild, Viscount Northland[see E. Ranfurly]:
Patrick Charles, *M.C.*, *T.D.*, *b.* 1906 ; Lieut.-Col. (retired) and Brevet Col. Kent Yeo. ; European War 1939-45, in France, Middle East, and Italy with Kent Yeo. (M.C.): *m.* 1st, 1931, Nancy Elizabeth (from whom he obtained a divorce 1939), dau. of Brinsley Nixon, of Seafield, Westward Ho! ; 2ndly, 1945, Mary Miriam, dau. of W. Hoare-Ward, of Brighton, and has issue living (by 1st marriage) Sarah Patricia, *b.* 1933: *m.* 1955, Maj. Jonathan Balcon, TD, Inns of Court and City Yeo., of The Grey House, Seal, Sevenoaks, only son of Sir Michael Elias Balcon, and has issue living, Deborah Kate *b.* 1956, Sarah Clair *b.* 1957, Henrietta Beatrice *b.* 1960,—Jennefer Chrystal, *b.* 1934. *Residence,—*The Tod House, Seal, Sevenoaks, Kent.

PREDECESSORS.—[1] CHARLES Mills, many years a Director of the H.E.I.C., and sometime a Member of Council of India; cr. a *Baronet* 1868: *m.* 1825, Emily, who *d.* 1884, dau. of Richard Henry Cox, of Hillingdon; *d.* 1872; *s.* by his only son [2] CHARLES HENRY, 2nd Bt., *b.* 1830; M.P. for Northallerton (*C*) 1865-6, and for W. Kent 1868-85: cr. *Baron Hillingdon* (peerage of United Kingdom) 1886 ; *m.* 1853, Lady Louisa Isabella Lascelles, dau. of 3rd Earl of Harewood *d.* 1898; *s.* by his el. son [3] CHARLES WILLIAM, 2nd Baron, *b.* 1855; was a partner in the banking firm of Glyn, Mills, and Co. ; sat as M.P. for W., or Sevenoaks, Div. of Kent (*C*) 1885-92: *m.* 1886, the Hon. Alice Marion Harbord, *O.B.E.*, who *d.* 1940, dau. of 5th Baron Suffield ; *d.* 1919 ; *s.* by his son[4] ARTHUR ROBERT, 3rd Baron, *b.* 1891 ; Lieut. R.N.V.R; European War 1914-16 in Gallipoli as Lieut. W. Kent Yeo.: M.P. for Uxbridge Div. of Middlesex (*C*) 1915-18: *m.* 1916, the *Hon.* Dame Edith Mary Winifred Cadogan, *DBE*, who *d.* 1969, da. of the late Henry Arthur, Viscount Chelsea [E. Cadogan]; *d.* 1952; *s.* by his son [5] CHARLES HEDWORTH, 4th Baron and present peer.

Hillsborough, Earl of,   title of Marquess of Downshire on Roll of H. L

HILTON OF UPTON, BARON. (Hilton.) [Life Baron 1965.]

ALBERT VICTOR HILTON, son of Thomas Hilton, of S. Walsham, Norfolk; *b.* Feb. 14th, 1908; ed. at Upton Elementary Sch., Norfolk; a JP of Norfolk; a Lord-in-Waiting to HM 1966-70; Vice-Pres. of National Union of Agricultural Workers since 1960, and a Member of Labour Party Nat. Exec. Cttee. 1961-65; a Member of E. Anglia Economic Planning Council; MP for SW Norfolk (*Lab.*) 1959-64; 1939-45 War as Cpl. RASC; cr. *Baron Hilton of Upton,* of Swaffham, co. Norfolk (Life Peerage) 1965: *m.* 1944, Nelly, da. of Thomas Simmons, of London.
*Residence,—*9, Spinners Lane, Swaffham, Norfolk.

HINDLIP, BARON. (Allsopp.) [Baron U.K. 1886, Bt. U.K. 1880.]

HENRY RICHARD ALLSOPP, 5th Baron, and 5th Baronet; *b.* July 1st, 1912; *s.* 1966; ed. at Eton and RMC; Maj. (ret.) Coldstream Guards; a JP and a DL for Wilts; American Bronze Star Medal: *m.* 1939, Cecily Valentine Jane, da. of the late Lt.-Col. Malcolm Borwick, DSO, of Hazlebech Hill, Northampton, and has issue.

Arms,—Sable, three pheons in chevron or, between as many doves rising argent, each holding in the beak a wheat-ear or. Crest,—A plover, holding in beak a wheat-ear or, standing on a pheon also gold. Supporters—Two foxhounds, each gorged with a pair of couples proper.

Hasten slowly.

*Residence,—*Verne Leaze, Calne, Wilts. *Clubs,—*White's, Pratt's, Turf.

SONS LIVING.

Hon. CHARLES HENRY (34, Campden Hill Court, W8; Westbrook House, Boxford, Newbury, Berks), *b.* Aug. 5th, 1940; ed. at Eton; late Lt. Coldstream Guards: *m.* 1968, Fiona Victoria Jean Atherley, da. of the Hon. William Johnston McGowan [see B. McGowan.], and has issue living, Henry William, *b.* 1973,—Kirsty Mary, *b.* 1971.
Hon. John Peter, *b.* 1942; ed. at Eton.

DAUGHTER LIVING.

Hon. Sarah Cecily, *b.* 1944: *m.* 1967, Hugh Robert Myddelton, of 66, Palace Gdns. Terr., W8 [see M. Lansdowne].

SISTERS LIVING.

Hon. Diana Joan (*Hon. Lady Hardy*), *b.* 1908 : *m.* 1930 Lieut.-Col. Sir Rupert John Hardy, 4th Bt. Life Guards (retired). *Residence,*—Spratton House, Northampton.
Hon. Nancy Marion, *b.* 1910 : *m.* 1936, Peter Geoffrey Brooke, and has issue living, Michael Peter, *b.* 1937; Maj. 16th/5th Lancers: *m.* 1970, Susan Rhona Martin, yr. da. of A. W. Peacop, of Blue Hills, Finchampstead, Berks. *Residence,*—Glengiblin, Mallow, co. Cork.

DAUGHTERS LIVING OF FOURTH BARON.

Hon. Penelope Jane, *b.* 1940: *m.* 1965, Theodore D. Velissaropoulos, c/o First National City Bank, Athens 118, Greece.
Hon. Elizabeth Tulla, *b.* 1942.

WIDOW LIVING OF FOURTH BARON.

HANSINA CECILIA ELFRIDA (*Tulla Lady Hindlip*), (Botches, Wivelsfield Green, Haywards Heath, Sussex), da. of the late Frederick William Harris: *m.* 1939, as his second wife, the 4th Baron, who *d.* 1966.

COLLATERAL BRANCHES LIVING.

Issue of the late Lieut.-Col. the Hon. Ranulph Allsopp, 4th son of 1st Baron, *b.* 1848, *d.* 1911 : *m.* 1898, Margaret, who *d.* 1941, dau. of the late William Whitbread :—
Sybil Maud Elizabeth, *b.* 1901; late Senior Comd. ATS: *m.* 1924 (Frederick) Ronald Oliver, formerly Grenadier Guards, and has issue living, Audrey Muriel, *b.* 1925; late WRNS: *m.* 1952, Capt. Lancelot Philip Aubrey-Fletcher, Grenadier Guards (ret.) [see Aubrey-Fletcher, Bt.]. *Residence,*— 2, Cornerways, Daylesford Av., Roehampton, SW15 5QR.

Grandchildren of the late Lt.-Col. the Hon. Ranulph Allsopp (ante):—
Issue of the late Samuel Ranulph Allsopp, CBE, *b.* 1899, *d.* 1975: *m.* 1923, the Hon. Norah Hyacinthe Littleton (Alsa Lodge, Stansted, Essex), da. of 4th Baron Hatherton:—
Michael Edward Ranulph (Little Coxwell Grove, Faringdon, Oxon.; White's and Pratt's Clubs), *b.* 1930; ed. at Eton: *m.* 1953, Patricia, da. of the late Geoffrey H. Berners, of Little Coxwell Grove, Faringdon, Oxon., and has issue living, Frances Jane Berners, *b.* 1955: *m.* 1975, Dermot Michael Claud Chichester [see M. Donegall],—Carolyn Anne Berners, *b.* 1957,—Davina Hyacinthe Berners, *b.* 1960,—Jessica Elizabeth Berners (twin), *b.* 1960.—David Samuel (11, Millers Court, W4), *b.* 1933; ed. at Eton: *m.* 1st, 1960 (m. diss. 1966) Tan Doris May, da. of Frederick J. Arnold, of Turbary Rd., Parkstone, Dorset; 2ndly, 1972, Sally, da. of the late V. H. Thirkell, of High Tilt Farm, Cranbrook, Kent, and has issue living (by 2nd m.), James Samuel, *b.* 1972.——Juliet Modwena, *b.* 1925: formerly WRNS: *m.* 1952, Samuel Arthur Scott, of Low Pasture House, Nunnington, N. Riding [see Scott, Bt. cr. 1962].——Charmain Hyacinthe, *b.* 1926: *m.* 1962, the Rev. David Henry FitzHerbert [see FitzHerbert, Bt.].

Issue of the late Capt. John Ranulph Allsopp, *b.* 1908, *d.* (killed in action in N. Africa) 1943 : *m.* 1934, Audrey Carteret Priaulx (who *d.* 1960, having *m.* 2ndly, 1944, Oliver Van Oss, of The Master's Lodge, Charterhouse Sq., EC1), da. of the late Major E. G. Fellows, of Barberry Cottage, Cheapside, Ascot:—
Mark Ranulph (Colne Park, Colne Engaine, Essex), *b.* 1938; ed. at Eton: *m.* 1960, Tania Anna, da. of the late J. Eustace-Smith, of Thrunton, Whittingham, Northumberland, and has issue living, Jonathan Ranulph, *b.* 1962,—Richard Mark, *b.* 1963,—Charles Samuel, *b.* 1970,—Arabella Sarah Georgianna, *b.* 1972.——Peter William (Mill Barn, Mill Lane, Bramley, Surrey), *b.* 1940; ed. at Eton: *m.* 1962, Pepita, da. of P. E. Mason, of Barnetts Cottage, Redford, Midhurst, Sussex, and has issue living, Amanda Caroline, *b.* 1964,—Sophie Victoria, *b.* 1967,—Katherine Pepita, *b.* 1970.

PREDECESSORS.—[1] Sir HENRY Allsopp, 3rd son of the late Samuel Allsopp, of Burton-on-Trent *b.* 1811; sat as M.P. for E. Worcestershire (C) 1874-80; cr. a *Baronet* 1880, and *Baron Hindlip*, of Hindlip. co. Worcester and of Alsop-en-le-Dale, co. Derby (peerage of United Kingdom) 1886: *m.* 1939, Elizabeth, who *d.* 1906, da. of William Tongue, of Comberforf Hall, Tamworth; *d.* 1887; *s.* by his son [2] SAMUEL CHARLES, 2nd Baron; *b.* 1842; MP for E. Staffordshire (C) 1873-80, and for Taunton 1882-7: *m.* 1868, Georgiana Millicent, who *d.* 1939, da. of the late Charles Rowland Palmer-Morewood, of Alfreton, Derbyshire; *d.* 1897; *s.* by his son [3] CHARLES, OBE, 3rd Baron, *b.* 1877; S. Africa 1900, European War 1914-18 (despatches, twice, OBE, Legion of Honour); Junior Unionist Whip in House of Lords 1907-14: *m.* 1904, Agatha Lilian, who *d.* 1963, da. of the late John Charles Thynne [M. Bath, colls.], *d.* 1931; *s.* by his el. son [4] CHARLES SAMUEL VICTOR, 4th Baron, *b.* 1906: *m.* 1st, 1932, Bridget (who obtained a divorce 1934), da. of the late Harold Nickols; 2ndly, 1939, Hansina Cecilia Elfrida, da. of the late Frederick William Harris; *d.* 1966; *s.* by his brother [5] HENRY RICHARD, 5th Baron.

HINTON OF BANKSIDE, BARON. (Hinton) [Life Baron 1965.]

CHRISTOPHER HINTON, *KBE*, son of the late Frederick Henry Hinton, of Lacock, Wilts.; *b.* May 12th, 1901; ed. at Chippenham Gram. Sch., and at Trin. Coll., Camb. (MA, Hon. Fellow 1957); Hon. D.Eng. Liverpool; Hon. D.Sc. (Eng.) London; Hon. D.Sc. Oxford, Southampton, Durham, and Bath; Hon. LLD Edinburgh; Hon. ScD Camb.; Hon. Assoc. of Manchester Coll. of Science and Technology; a FRS, FRSA, FIChemE, Hon. FICE, FIMechE (Pres. 1966-67), FIEE of Inst. of Metals, of Inst. of Gas Engineers, and of Inst. of Welding; Dep. Dir. Gen. of Roy. Ordnance Filling Factories 1940-45, Dep. Controller of Production (Atomic Energy), Min. of Supply, and Managing Dir. of Industrial Group UK Atomic Energy Authority 1946-57, and Chm. of Central Electricity Generating Board 1957-64; Special Adviser to World Bank 1965-70; Dep. Chm. of Electricity Supply Research Council since 1965, and Chancellor of Bath Univ. since 1966; James Clayton prize of Inst. of Mech. Engineers 1954, Castner gold medal of Soc. of Chemical Industries, Churchill medal of Soc. of Engineers, and Exner medal of Austrian Trade Assocn. 1956, and Albert medal of Roy. Soc. of Arts, Melchett medal of Inst. of Fuel, Silver medal of Instn. of Marine Engineers, Axel Johnson medal of Swedish Acad. of Engineers 1957, Silver medal of Roy. Soc. of Arts 1960, Rumford medal of Roy. Soc. 1971 and James Watt Internat. Medal of IMechE 1973; Imperial Order of Rising Sun of Japan; *cr.* Knt. 1951, KBE (Civil)

1957, and *Baron Hinton of Bankside*, of Dulwich, co. London (Life Baron) 1965: *m.* 1931, Lillian, who *d.* 1973, da. of Thomas Boyer, of Winnington, Cheshire, and has issue.

Arms,—Azure, on a pile or between seven roses argent, barbed and seeded proper, three barrulets dancetty gules. Crest,—A demi talbot argent, gorged with an ancient crown or, in the mouth a baton or, tipped sable. Supporters,—*Dexter*, a pantheon gules semy of mullets or; *sinister*, a male griffin gules, armed langued and rayed or, each gorged with an ancient crown, affixed thereto a chain reflexed over the back or.
Residence,—Tiverton Lodge, Dulwich Common, SE21.

DAUGHTER LIVING.
Hon. Susan Mary, *b.* 1932: *m.* 1957: Arthur Charles Mole, of Polurrian, 30, Rydens Av., Walton-on-Thames, son of the late Sir Charles John Mole, KBE, MVO, and has issue.

HIRSHFIELD, BARON. (Hirshfield.) [Life Baron 1967.]

DESMOND BAREL HIRSHFIELD, son of the late Leopold Hirshfield; *b.* May 17th, 1913; ed. at City of London Sch.; FCA; Home Office Aliens Tribunal (Beds.) 1940-42; Senior Partner, Hesketh, Hardy, Hirshfield & Co., Chartered Accountants, and of Horwath & Horwath (UK); Founder and Chm. of Trades Union Unit Trust Managers Ltd., since 1961, Founder and Dir. of Foundation on Automation and Human Development since 1962; Dep. Chm., Northampton (New Town) Development Corpn. and of MLH Consultants Ltd., and a Member of Board of Trade Cttee. on Consumer Credit 1968-71; a Gov. of London Sch. of Econ. and Political Science; *cr. Baron Hirshfield*, of Holborn in Greater London (Life Baron) 1967: *m.* 1951, Bronia, da. of Joseph Eisen.

Arms,—Azure a menorah between two flaunches or, on each an oak leaf vert charged with a bezant, on a chief or a dexter hand apaume, couped at the wrist articulated of steel proper representing the hand of an automatom, between two cog-wheels gules each charged with a human heart argent. Crest,—On a mount vert, a demi lion guardant and a demi-hart at gaze proper supporting between them a balance, argent. Supporters,—*Dexter* a lion rampant guardant proper, crowned with an eastern crown or; *sinister*, a hart at gaze proper, gorged with an eastern crown or; the whole on a grassy mount with two madonna lilies slipped and leaved proper.
Residence,—13, Southampton Place, WC1. Club,—RAC.

HIRST, BARONY OF. (Hirst.) [Extinct 1943.]
GRANDDAUGHTER OF FIRST BARON.

Issue of the late Harold Hugh Hirst (Lt. 21st Manchester Regt., attached RE Signals), son of 1st Baron, *b.* 1893, *d.* 1919: *m.* 1917, Carol Iris, MBE (by whom he had an only son, Harold Hugh Hirst, Pilot Officer RAFVR, *b.* 1919, *k.* 1941, while on operational duties), da. of the late Lewis Lindon, of Sussex Sq., W; she *m.* 2ndly, 1926, Maurice Theodore Alexander Dreyfus, and *d.* 1966:—
Hon. Pamela Muriel Dorine, *b.* 1918 ; late Junior Com. A.T.S.; raised to rank of a Baron's daughter 1943; a Member of Godstone RDC 1955-74 (Chm. 1969-72) since when of Tandridge Council; Chm. of Lingfield Parish Council 1957-69: *m.* 1st, 1940 (m. diss. 1947), Capt. Arthur George Bevington Colyer, RA; 2ndly, 1949, Roy Edward Goodale, who *d.* 1969, and has issue living (by 2nd m.).

DAUGHTER LIVING OF FIRST BARON.

Hon. Irene Phyllis, *CBE*, *b.* 1901; was a Co. Councillor for London 1952-58, and again 1961-65; O.B.E. (Civil) 1961 : *m.* 1922, Group-Capt. Trevor Felix David Rose, R.A.F. Vol. Reserve and late Major R.F.A. and R.H.A., who *d.* 1946, and has issue living, Veronica Phyllis, *b.* 1924 : *m.* 1943, Major Timothy Ellis, King's Shropshire L.I. (retired) of Mendham Mill, Harleston, Norfolk, and has issue living, Jonathan Felix Hugh *b.* 1951, Jennifer Bryony *b.* 1946: *m.* 1966, Anthony Gibson, of High Clear, Slaley, Northumberland (and has issue living, Benjamin Timothy *b.* 1968, Toby *b.* 1969, Richard (twin) *b.* 1969),—Evelyn Felicity, *b.* 1927: *m.* 1947, Maj. H. Dan Bailey, late Welsh Guards, of Marston Meysey Manor, Cricklade, Wilts, and has issue living, Patrick Robin *b.* 1953, Sandra Caroline *b.* 1948. Residences,—Pear Tree Cottage, Cranleigh, Surrey; 54, Marsham Court, SW1.

HIVES, BARON. (Hives.) [Baron U.K. 1950.]

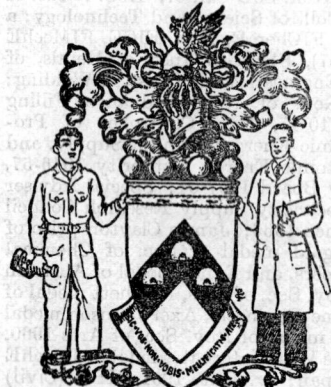

JOHN WARWICK HIVES, 2nd Baron; *b.* Nov. 26th, 1913; *s.* 1965; ed. at Derby Sch.; a farmer: *m.* 1st, 1937, Olwen Protheroe Llewellin, who *d.* 1972; 2ndly, 1972, Gladys Mary, da. of Alfred Seals.

Arms,—Or on a chevron sable, three bee hives of the field. Crest,—In front of a sun in splendour or, an eagle rising proper. Supporters,—*Dexter*, the figure of a mechanic proper overalls azure, holding in the exterior hand a micrometer; *sinister*, the figure of a draughtsman proper coat argent holding under the exterior arm a set square and a T square also proper.

Residence,—The Bendalls, Milton, Derbys.

BROTHERS LIVING.

Hon. Michael Bruce, *b.* 1926; ed. at Repton: *m.* 1951, Janet Rosemary, da. of the late W. E. Gee, of Lynngarth, Duffield, Derby, and has issue living, Robert George, *b.* 1953,—Paul, *b.* 1963,— Jillian Sarah, *b.* 1955. *Residence,*—Fairfield, The Pastures, Duffield, Derbys.

Hon. David Benjamin, *b.* 1931; ed. at Repton: Wing Cdr. RAF: *m.* 1954, Shirley, da. of the late Harold Walker, of Cumberland House, Duffield, Derby, and has issue living, Nigel Ian Edward, *b.* 1960,— Sally Margaret, *b.* 1955,—Sandra Dawn, *b.* 1958. *Residence,*—Halfacre, 28, St. Peter's Way, Chorley Wood, Herts.

SISTERS LIVING.

Hon. Joan Mary, *b.* 1917: *m.* 1939, Adrian Gee, and has issue living, Wendy Elizabeth, *b.* 1943; *m.* 1963, Thomas Neville, of Beech Tree House, Audlem, Cheshire, and has issue living, Alexander William *b.* 1965, Sally Anne *b.* 1968,—Jane Anne, *b.* 1945: *m.* 1967, John Hodgson Berry of 4, Boswell Close, Kinoulton, Notts., and has issue living, Duncan Gee *b.* 1968, Nicholas Gee *b.* 1970. *Residence,*—The Laurels, Duffield, Derbys.

Hon. Ruth Margaret, *b.* 1922: *m.* 1941, Joseph Graham Riley, and has issue living, Michael Edward, *b.* 1947,—John Andrew (twin), *b.* 1947,—David Ernest, *b.* 1951. *Residence,*—7, Avenue Rd., Duffield, Derbys.

Hon. Phillippa Ann, *b.* 1928.

WIDOW LIVING OF SON OF FIRST BARON.

Dinah (Harmer Garry, Harmer Green Lane, Welwyn, Herts.), da. of F. Wilson-North, of Walcott, Norfolk: *m.* 1956, the Hon. Peter Anthony Hives, who *d.* 1974, and has issue living [see colls., infra].

COLLATERAL BRANCH LIVING.

Issue of the late Hon. Peter Anthony Hives, Lt. RNVR, el. son of 1st Baron, *b.* 1921, *d.* 1974: *m.* 1956, Dinah (ante), da. of F. Wilson-North, of Walcott, Norfolk:—

MATTHEW PETER, *b.* May. 25th, 1971.——Julie Laura, *b.* 1957.——Lisa Joanna, *b.* 1963.——Sophie Josephine, *b.* 1964.

PREDECESSOR.—[1] ERNEST WALTER HIVES, CH, MBE, son of John Hives, of Reading; *b.* 1886; Chm. and Managing Dir. of Rolls-Royce Ltd.; *cr. Baron Hives,* of Duffield, co. Derby (peerage of UK) 1950: *m.* 1913, Gertrude Ethel, who *d.* 1961, da. of John Warwick, of Derby; *d.* 1965; , by his el. son [2] JOHN WARWICK, 2nd Baron and present peer.

HOBSON, BARONY OF. (Hobson) [Extinct 1966.]

DAUGHTER LIVING OF LIFE BARON.

Hon. Marian Elizabeth, *b.* 1942; ed. at Newnham Coll., Camb. (MA, PhD): *m.* 1968, Michel Jeanneret, MA, Dr. ès L, of 115, Dewsbury Rd., NW10, and has issue.

WIDOW LIVING OF LIFE BARON.

DORIS MARY (*Baroness Hobson*), (115, Dewsbury Rd., NW10), da. of Fred Spink, of Kensington: *m.* 1933, Baron Hobson (Life Baron), who *d.* 1966.

HODSON, BARON. (Hodson.) [Life Baron 1960.]

(FRANCIS LORD) CHARLTON HODSON, *M.C., P.C.,* son of the Rev. Thomas Hodson, R. of Oddington, Gloucestershire ; *b.* Sept. 17th, 1895 ; ed. at Cheltenham Coll., and at Wadham Coll., Oxford (B.A. 1920, M.A. 1938, Hon. Fellow 1939) ; Bar. Inner Temple 1921, and a KC 1937; a Member of Permanent Court of Arbitration at The Hague 1949-73; Junior Counsel to Treasury (Probate) 1935-37, a Judge of High Court of Justice (Probate, Divorce and Admiralty Div.) 1937-51, a Lord Justice of Appeal 1951-60, and a Lord of Appeal in Ordinary 1960-71; 1914-19 War in Gallipoli, and Mesopotamia as Capt. Gloucestershire Regt. (wounded, M.C., Cavalier of Order of Crown of Italy, 1914-15 star, two medals ; Knt. 1937, P.C. 1951, and *Baron Hodson,* of Rotherfield Greys, co. Oxford (Life Baron) 1960 : *m.* 1918, Susan Mary, who *d.* 1965, dau. of Major William Greaves Blake, D.L., Scots Greys, and 9th Lancers, and has issue.

Arms,—Barry nebuly of six argent and azure, a Lymphad or mainsail furled fore and aft sails argent flags flying gules. Crest.—Upon the apex of a Pyramid a dove holding in the beak a sprig of olive proper.

Residence,—Fishers, Rotherfield Greys, Oxon.

SON LIVING.

Hon. Charles Christopher Philip (Stoney Hall, Hannington, Hants.), *b.* 1922: *m.* 1953, Rose, da. of Sir Charles Markham, 2nd Bt., and has issue living, Rupert Charles, *b.* 1956,—Mary Anne, *b.* 1954, —Caroline Rose, *b.* 1959,—Rosemary Jane, *b.* 1960.

DAUGHTER LIVING.

Hon. Anthea Esther, *b.* 1924: *m.* 1st, 1950, Michael Joseph, who *d.* 1958; 2ndly, 1963, Macdonald Hastings, of Brown's Farm, Old Basing, Hants., and has issue living, (by 1st marriage) Hugh Michael *b.* 1954,—Charlotte, *b.* 1952 (by 2nd m.) Susan Harriet Selina, *b.* 1964.

HOLDEN, BARONY OF. (Holden.) [Extinct 1951.]

DAUGHTER LIVING OF SECOND BARON.

Hon. Donna Diana, *b.* 1916.   *Residence,*—4, Georgian Court, Babbacombe Rd., Torquay.

HOLFORD, BARON. (Holford.) [Life Baron 1965.]

WILLIAM GRAHAM HOLFORD, son of the late William George Holford, of London and Johannesburg; *b.* March 22nd, 1907; ed. at Diocesan Coll., Rondebosch, Capetown, and at Liverpool Univ. (B.Arch., MA, LL.D); Rome Scholar in Arch. 1930; RA; Hon. DLitt Oxford; Hon. DCL Durham; Ch. Technical Officer, Min. of Town and Country Planning 1943-47, Pres. of Town Planning Inst. 1953-54, and of Roy. Inst. of British Architects 1960-62; a part-time Member of Central Electricity Generating Board since 1957, a Trustee of British Museum since 1969, Prof. Emeritus of Town Planning, London Univ. since 1970, and a Dir. of Leverhulme Trust since 1972; Roy. gold medal for Architecture 1963; *cr.* Knt. 1953, and *Baron Holford,* of Kemp Town, co. Sussex (Life Baron) 1965: *m.* 1933, Marjorie, da. of the late John Bunyan Smedley Brooks, of Icklesham, Sussex.

Residences,—Portland House, 133, Marine Parade, Brighton; 20, Eccleston Sq., SW1.   *Clubs,*—Athenæum, Savile, University (Liverpool).

HOLLENDEN, BARON. (Hope-Morley.) [Baron U.K. 1912.]

GEOFFREY HOPE HOPE-MORLEY, 2nd Baron; *b.* Jan. 28th, 1885; *s.* 1929; ed. at Eton; a J.P. for Kent; was High Sheriff of co. London 1917; Prime Warden of Fishmongers' Co. 1938-9; assumed by deed poll (enrolled at College of Arms) the additional surname of Hope in 1923: *m.* 1st, 1914, the Hon. Mary Sidney Katherine Almina Gardner (from whom he obtained a divorce 1928), dau. of 1st Baron Burghclere; 2ndly, 1929, Muriel Ivy, who *d.* 1962, youngest dau. of Sir John Evelyn Gladstone, 4th Bt.; 3rdly, 1963, Violet Norris, widow of Dr. Frank Howitt, and has issue by 1st marriage.

Arms.—Argent, a leopard's face jessant de lis sable between three griffins heads erased gules. Crest.—A demi-griffin argent, wings elevated ermine, holding between the claws a leopard's face jessant-de-lis as in the arms. Supporters,—On either side a stag proper, chained around the neck and suspended therefrom an anchor or.

Tenacious of purpose.

Seat,—Ravensbourne, Stoke Fleming, Dartmouth, Devon.

DAUGHTERS LIVING. (*By 1st marriage.*)

Hon. Mary Joan Fenella Hope, *b.* 1915: *m.* 1st, 1941 (m. diss. 1965), David Babington Smith, son of the late Sir Henry Babington Smith, GBE, CH, KCB, CSI [E. Elgin]; 2ndly, 1966, Geoffrey John, of Lime House, Kintbury, Newbury, Berks., and has issue living (by 1st m.), Catherine Babington, *b.* 1952.

Hon. Elspeth Rachel Marianne Winifred Hope, *b.* 1917: *m.* 1942, David Francis Muirhead, CMG, CVO, Ambassador to Portugal, and has issue living, David Nicholas Geoffrey, *b.* 1946; ed. at Eastbourne Coll.: *m.* 1969, Emma Cecilia Borrero, of Cali, Colombia,—Mark Robert Gavin, *b.* 1951; ed. at Lancing, and Markham Coll., Lima, Peru,—Mary Elizabeth Janet, *b.* 1949: *m.* 1969, Enrico Gambetta de Petrantonio, of Lima, Peru. *Residences,*—British Embassy, Lisbon, Portugal; 16, Pitt St., W8.

COLLATERAL BRANCH LIVING.

Issue of the late Capt. the Hon. Claude Hope Hope-Morley, yr. son of 1st Baron; *b.* 1887; assumed by deed poll 1923, the additional surname of Hope; *d.* 1968: *m.* 1911, Lady Dorothy Edith Isabel Hobart-Hampden-Mercer-Henderson, who *d.* 1972, da. of 7th Earl of Buckinghamshire.

GORDON HOPE (19, Chelsea Sq., SW3), *b.* Jan. 8th, 1914; ed. at Eton; formerly Maj. Black Watch; 1939-45 War: *m.* 1945, Sonja, da. of the late Thorolf Sundt. of Bergen, Norway, and has issue living, Ian Hampden, *b.* 1946; ed. at Eton,—Robin Gordon, *b.* 1949,—Andrew James Sundt, *b.* 1952; ed. at Eton.——Ann Rosemary Hope (*Lady Newman*), *b.* 1916; 1939-45 War, as Junior Cdr. ATS: *m.* 1946, Sir Ralph Alured Newman, 5th Bt.——Stella Hope, *b.* 1919; 1939-45 war as 2nd Officer WRNS: *m.* 1950, Neville Whiteoak Robinson, of 107, Old Church St., Chelsea, SW3, and has issue living, Anthony David Whiteoak, *b.* 1953,—Brian Robert Whiteoak, *b.* 1956,—Julia Mary, *b.* 1954.——Lorna Margaret Dorothy (*Lady Hanley*), *b.* 1929; a JP of High Wycombe: *m.* 1957, Sir Michael Bowen Hanley, KCB, c/o Ministry of Defence, SW1).

PREDECESSOR.—[1] Samuel Hope Morley, el. son of the late Samuel Morley, J.P., D.L. (M.P. for Nottingham 1865-6, and for Bristol 1868-85), by his wife, Rebekah Maria, dau. of Samuel Hope, of Liverpool; *b.* 1845; a partner in the firm of I. and R. Morley, of Wood Street, E.C.; was a Gov. of the Bank of England 1903-5; cr. *Baron Hollenden,* of Leigh, Kent (peerage of United Kingdom) 1912: *m.* 1884, Laura Marianne, who *d.* 1945, dau. of the late Rev. G. Royds Birch; *d.* 1929; *s.* by his son [2] Geoffrey Hope Hope-Morley, 2nd Baron and present peer.

HOLM PATRICK, BARON. (Hamilton.) [Baron U.K. 1897.]

James Hans Hamilton, 3rd Baron; *b.* Nov. 29th, 1928; *s.* 1942; ed. at Eton; late Lieut. 16/5th Lancers: *m.* 1954, Anne Loys Roche, only dau. of Com. Ernest Padwick Brass, R.N. (retired), of Haroldston House, Haverfordwest, Pembrokeshire, and has issue.

Arms,—Gules, three cinquefoils ermine, a mullet argent for difference; on a chief or, a heart gules. **Crest,**—A demiantelope argent, hoofed and armed or, holding a heart gules, and charged on the shoulder with a mullet of the last. **Supporters,**—*Dexter,* an antelope argent gorged with a collar flory counterflory or, pendent therefrom an escutcheon ermine charged with a heart gules; *sinister,* a lion gules gorged with a collar flory counterflory or, pendent therefrom an escutcheon ermine, charged with a heart of the first.

The same as from the beginning. *Residence,*—Tara Beg, Dunsany, co. Meath.

SONS LIVING.

Hon. HANS JAMES DAVID, *b.* March 15th, 1955.
Hon. Ion Henry James, *b.* 1956.
Hon. Evelyn William James, *b.* 1961.

SISTER LIVING.

Hon. Caroline, *b.* 1926: *m.* 1951, Major John Henry Hamilton Bonham, and has issue living, Oliver John Hans, *b.* 1954,—Francis Richard Hamilton, *b.* 1956,—John Arthur Norris, *b.* 1961. *Residence,* —Trumroe, Castlepollard, co. Westmeath.

PREDECESSORS.—[1] Ion Trant Hamilton, P.C., son of the late James Hans Hamilton, M.P. for co. Dublin 1841-63; *b.* 1839; Lord-Lieut. and Custos Rotulorum of co. Dublin; M.P. for Dublin co. (*C*) 1863-85; cr. *Baron HolmPatrick,* of HolmPatrick, co. Dublin (peerage of United Kingdom), 1897: *m.* 1877, Lady Victoria Alexandrina Wellesley, who *d.* 1933, sister of 3rd and 4th Dukes of Wellington; *d.* 1898; *s.* by his only son [2] Hans Wellesley, D.S.O., M.C., 2nd Baron; *b.* 1886; late Capt. 16th Lancers and Bde. Maj.; 1914-18 War (MO, DSO): *m.* 1925, Lady Edina Dorothy Hope, who *d.* 1964, da. of 4th Marquess Conyngham; *d.* 1942; *s.* by his only son [3] James Hans, 3rd Baron and present peer.

HOME, EARLDOM OF, see Baron Home of the Hirsel.

HOME OF THE HIRSEL, BARON. (Douglas-Home.)
(Earl S. 1605, disclaimed 1963.) [Life Baron 1974.]
(Name pronounced "**Hume.**")

Alexander Frederick Douglas-Home, *KT, PC*; *b.* July 2nd, 1903; *s.* as 14th Earl of Home July 11th, 1951; ed. at Eton; Hon. DCL Oxford 1960, and Hon. Student of Ch. Ch., Oxford 1962; Maj. Lanark Yeo. (TA Reserve), Brig. Roy Co. of Archers (Queen's Body Guard for Scotland), and a DL for Lanarkshire, appointed PPS to Parliamentary Sec. to Min. of Labour 1935-36, to Chancellor of the Exchequer 1936-37 and to Prime Min. 1937-40; Joint Under-Sec. of State for Foreign Affairs May to July 1945, Min. of State, Scottish Office Oct. 1951 to April 1955, Sec. of State for Commonwealth Relations April 1955 to July 1960 (also Lord Pres. of the Council Jan. to Sept. 1957 and again Oct. 1959 to July 1960), Leader of House of Lords 1957-60, Sec. of State for Foreign Affairs July 1960 to Oct. 1963, Prime Min. and First Lord of the Treasury 1963-64, and Leader of the Opposition 1964-65; Sec. of State for Foreign and Commonwealth Affairs 1970-74; Grand Master of Primrose League and first Chancellor of Heriot-Watt Univ. Edinburgh since 1966; Pres. of the MCC 1966; Pres. of NATO Council 1974; Chancellor of Order of the Thistle since 1973; Freeman of Selkirk, Edinburgh, Coldstream and Crieff; bore Second Sword at Coronation of Queen Elizabeth II; MP for Lanark Div. of Lanarkshire (*C*) 1931-45, and 1950-51, and for Kinross and W. Perth Div. of Perthshire and Kinross-shire 1963-74; PC 1951, KT 1962; disclaimed his peerages for life Oct. 23rd., 1963, and cr. *Baron Home of the Hirsel,* of Coldstream, co. Berwick (Life Baron) 1974: *m.* 1936, Elizabeth Hester, da. of the late Very Rev. Cyril Argentine Alington, DD, Dean of Durham [V. Cobham], and has issue.

Arms,—Quarterly: 1st and 4th grand quarters counter quartered, 1st and 4th vert, a lion rampant argent, armed and langued gules, *Home;* 2nd and 3rd argent, three popinjays vert, beaked and membered gules, *Pepdie;* over all an escutcheon or, charged with an orle azure, *Landale;* 2nd and 3rd grand quarters counter-quartered, 1st azure, a lion rampant argent, armed and langued gules, crowned with an imperial crown or, *Lordship of Galloway;* 2nd or, a lion rampant gules, armed and langued azure, debruised of a ribbon sable, *Abernethy;* 3rd argent, three piles gules, *Lordship o*

Brechin; 4th or, a fesse checky azure and argent, surmounted of a bend sable, charged with three buckles of the field, *Stewart of Bonkhill;* over all on an escutcheon argent, a man's heart, ensigned with an imperial crown proper, and a chief azure, charged with three mullets of the field, *Douglas.* Crests,— 1st, on a cap of maintenance proper, a lion's head erased argent, *Home;* 2nd, on a cap of maintenance proper, a salamander vert, encircled with flames of fire proper. Supporters,—Two lions argent, armed and angued gules.

Seats,—The Hirsel, Coldstream, Berwickshire; Castlemains, Douglas, Lanarkshire. *Clubs,*— Traveller's, Carlton, Buck's.

SON LIVING.

Hon. DAVID ALEXANDER COSPATRICK, *b.* Nov. 20th, 1943; styled *Lord Dunglass* 1951-63, when he discontinued the use of this courtesy title, and obtained official recognition at Lyon Court in his new name; ed. at Eton, and Ch. Ch. Oxford; Dir. Margan Grenfell & Co. Ltd.: *m.* 1972, Jane Margaret, da. of Col. John Francis Williams-Wynne, CBE, DSO [see Williams-Wynn, Bt., colls.].

DAUGHTERS LIVING.

(All of whom discontinued the prefix of *Lady* and obtained official recognition at Lyon Court in their new names 1963)
Hon. Lavinia Caroline, *b.* 1937; a Woman of he Bedchamber to HM Queen Elizabeth the Queen Mother 1963-65; a Lady in Waiting to HRH the Duchess of Kent 1966-67, since when an Extra Lady in Waiting.
Hon. Meriel Kathleen, *b.* 1939: *m.* 1964, Adrian Marten George Darby, Fellow and Bursar of Keble Coll., Oxford, of Kemerton Court, Tewkesbury, and 12, Park Town, Oxford, and has issue living, Matthew George, *b.* 1967,—Catherine Monica, *b.* 1964.
Hon. Diana Lucy, *b.* 1940: *m.* 1963, James Archibald Wolfe Murray [see Murray, Bt. cr. 1628), colls.], of 12, Cambridge Rd., SW20.

BROTHERS LIVING.

Hon. Henry Montagu, *M.B.E.*, *b.* 1907; ed. at Eton, and at Ch. Ch., Oxford; Major (ret.) Gen. List, M.B.E. (Mil.) 1954: *m.* 1st, 1931, Lady Alexandra Margaret Elizabeth Spencer (who obtained a divorce 1947), da. of 6th Earl Spencer : 2ndly, 1947, Vera (JOHANSEN), who *d.* 1963, da. of the late Carl Herman Jensen, of Oslo; 3rdly, 1966, Felicity Betty, da. of the late Maj. Aubrey Jonsson, and formerly wife of the Hon. Victor Patrick Hamilton Wills [see B. Dulverton], and has issue living, (by 1st m.) Charles Cospatrick (18, Mortimer Cres., NW6) *b.* 1937; ed. at Eton; Defence Correspondent *The Times* 1965-70, Features Editor 1970-73, since when Home Editor: *m.* 1966, Jessica Violet, da. of Maj. John Nevile Wake Gwynne, RA, [see Morrison-Bell, Bt., *cr.* 1923, ext.], and has issue living, Tara John *b.* 1969, Luke Cospatrick *b.* 1971,—(by 2nd m.) George Erik Montagu, *b.* 1948,—(by 3rd m.) Peregrine Montagu, *b.* 1967,—(by 1st m.) Fiona Margaret, *b.* 1936: *m.* 1962, Gregory Martin, and has issue living, Kezia Alexandra Lilian *b.* 1970. *Residence,*—Old Greenlaw, Berwickshire. *Club,*—Puffins (Edinburgh).
Hon. William, *b.* 1912: ed. at Eton and at New Coll., Oxford (B.A. 1934); formerly Capt. Roy. Armoured Corps; unsuccessfully contested Cathcart Div. of Glasgow (*Progressive Ind.*) April 1942, Windsor Div. of Berks June 1942, Clay Cross Div. of Derbyshire (*Atlantic Charter*) April 1944, and S. Div. of Edinburgh (*L*) May 1957 and Oct. 1959: *m.* 1951, Rachel Leila, Baroness Dacre, and has issue living, *Hon.* James Thomas Archibald, *b.* 1952,—*Hon.* Sarah, *b.* 1954,—*Hon.* Gian Leila, *b.* 1958,—*Hon.* Dinah Lilian, *b.* 1964. *Residence,*—Drayton House, East Meon, Hants. *Club,*— Travellers'.
Hon. Edward Charles, *b.* 1920; ed. at Eton; 2nd Lt. R.A.; 1939-45 War (wounded, prisoner): *m.* 1946, Nancy Rose, only dau. of Sir Thomas Dalrymple Straker-Smith, of Carham Hall, Cornhill-on-Tweed, and has issue living, Simon, *b.* 1947: *m.* 1971, Sally Beard, and has issue living, Joanna *b.* 1973,— Andrew, *b.* 1950,—Mark, *b.* 1951. *Residence,*—Easter Langlee, Galashiels.

SISTERS LIVING.

Lady Bridget, *b.* 1905. *Residence,*—Springhill, Coldstream, Berwickshire.
Lady Rachel (*Lady William W. Montagu-Douglas-Scott*), *b.* 1910: *m.* 1937, Lt.-Col. Lord William Walter Montagu-Douglas-Scott, M.C., who *d.* 1958 [see D. Buccleuch]. *Residence,*—Beechwood, Melrose.

COLLATERAL BRANCH LIVING.

Grandson of Maj. the Hon. Henry Montagu Douglas-Home, MBE, (ante), 2nd son of 13th Earl:—
Issue of the late Capt. (Cecil) Robin Douglas-Home, *b.* 1932, *d.* 1968; *m.* 1959 (m. diss. 1965), Sandra Clare, yr. da. of the late Dr. Savile Paul:—
Alexander Sholto, *b.* 1962.

PREDECESSORS.

—[1] *Sir* ALEXANDER Home, of Home, Berwickshire, Baron of Dunglass, (el. son of Sir Alexander Home who was killed at Battle of Verneuil 1424): Ambassador to England 1459; cr. *Lord Home* (peerage of Scotland) 1473; *m.* 1st, before 1424, Marion, dau. and heir of John Lauder; 2ndly, before 1467 Margaret, dau. of Alexander Momtgomerie, Master of Montgomerie; *d.* 1491; *s.* by his grandson [2] ALEXANDER, 2nd Lord (son of Alexander Home, and Agnes, dau. of Sir Adam Hepburn of Hailes: *m.* 1st, Isabel Douglas (annulled on grounds of consanguinity 1476); 2ndly, before March 1493, Nichola (who *d.* 1527/28 having *m.* 2ndly, Sir Alexander Ramsay of Dalhousie), dau. of George Ker of Samuelston, Haddington; *d.* 1506; *s.* by his son [3] ALEXANDER, 3rd Lord, commanded the van with the 4th Earl of Huntly at Flodden, and was one of the few surviving commanders of that battle; afterwards embraced the English interest in opposition to the Regent Albany; whilst visiting the Court in 1516 was taken prisoner, and after a hasty trial was executed, and his titles and estates declared forfeit; these were restored in 1522 to his brother [4] GEORGE, 4th Lord: *m.* 1531, Mariot Halyburton, who *d.* about 1563, dau. and co-heir of the 5th Lord Dirletoun; *k.* in a skirmish at Fauside two days before battle of Pinkie 1547; *s.* by his son [5] ALEXANDER, 5th Lord; supported Mary Queen of Scots; convicted of treason 1573 and his title and estates forfeited: *m.* 1st, Margaret, dau. of Sir Walter Kerr; 2ndly, Agnes (who *m.* 3rdly, Sir Thomas Lyon, Master of Glamis), dau. of 4th Lord Gray, and widow of Sir Robert Logan of Restalrig; *s.* by his son (by 2nd wife) [6] ALEXANDER, 6th Lord; *b.* about 1566; cr. *Lord Dunglass* and *Earl of Home* (peerage of Scotland) 1605 with remainder to his heirs male whatsoever: *m.* 1st, 1586, Christian, dau. of 6th Earl of Morton, and widow of Laurence, Master of Oliphant; 2ndly, before June 1607, Mary Sutton, who *d.* 1645, dau. of 9th Baron Dudley; *d.* 1619; *s.* by his son (by 2nd wife) [7] JAMES, 2nd Earl; *b.* about 1607: *m.* 1st, 1622, the Hon. Katherine Cary, dau. of 1st Viscount Falkland; 2ndly, Lady Grace Fane, dau. of 1st Earl of Westmorland; *d.s.p.* 1633; *s.* by his kinsman [8] JAMES, 3rd Earl, only son of Sir James Home of Whitrig (by Lady Anna *₊* el. dau. and co-heir of George Home, 1st Earl of Dunbar and 1st Lord Home (or Hume) of Berwick), el. son of Sir John Home of Cowdenknows, great grandson of Mungo Home, el. son of John, yr. brother of 2nd Lord: *m.* 1640, Lady Jean Douglas, who *d.* 1666, dau. of 7th Earl of Morton; *d.* 1666; *s.* by his el. son [9] ALEXANDER, 4th Earl: *m.* 1671, Lady Anne Sackville, who *d.* 1672, dau. of 5th Earl of Dorset; *d.* 1674; *s.* by his brother [10] JAMES, 5th Earl: *m.* Lady Anne Ramsay, dau. of 2nd Earl of Dalhousie; *d.* 1687; *s.* by his brother [11] CHARLES, 6th Earl: *m.* about 1680, Anne, dau. of Sir William Purves of Purves, Bt.; *d.* 1706; *s.* by his son [12] ALEXANDER, 7th Earl; imprisoned in Edinburgh Castle 1715-16 on suspicion of being involved in Jacobite rising: *m.* Lady Anne Kerr (who *d.* 1727, having *m.* 2ndly, Henry Ogle), dau. of 2nd Marquess of Lothian; *d.* 1720; *s.* by his el. son [13] WILLIAM, 8th Earl; Lt.-Gen.; Gov. of Gibraltar 1757-61: *m.* 1742, Elizabeth, who *d.* 1784, da. and heir of William Gibbons, and widow of James Lawes; *d.* 1761; *s.* by his brother (14) *Rev.* ALEXANDER, 9th Earl: *m.* 1st, the Hon. Primrose Elphinstone, who *d.* 1759, dau. of 9th Lord Elphinstone; 2ndly, Marion, who *d.* 1765, dau. of his uncle the Hon. James Home; 3rdly, 1768, Abigail Browne, who *d.* 1814, dau. and co-heir of John Ramey, of Yarmouth; *d.* 1786; *s.* by his son [15] ALEXANDER, 10th Earl; *b.* 1769; assumed by Royal Licence the additional surname of Ramey 1814: *m.* 1798, Lady Elizabeth Scott, who *d.* 1837, dau. of 3rd Duke of Buccleuch; *d.* 1841; *s.* by his son [16] COSPATRICK ALEXANDER, 11th Earl; *b.* 1799; Under-Sec. for Foreign Affairs 1828-30, a Representative Peer 1842-74, Lt.-Gen. of Royal Co. of Archers, and Keeper of the Great Seal of Scotland; on death of his mother 1877 took the additional surname of Douglas of Douglas under deed of entail of Douglas estates; *cr. Baron Douglas,* of Douglas, co. Lanark (peerage of United Kingdom), 1875: *m.* 1832, Hon. Lucy Elizabeth, who *d.* 1877, el. dau. of 2nd and last Baron Montagu of Boughton; by Jane Margaret, dau. of Archibald Douglas (formerly Stewart) 1st Baron Douglas of Douglas (*cr.* 1790, ext. 1857); *d.* 1881; *s.* by his son [17] CHARLES ALEXANDER, *K.T.,* 12th Earl, *b.* 1834: *m.* 1870, Maria, who *d.* 1919, dau. of the late Capt. Charles Conrad Grey, R.N.; *d.* 1918; *s.* by his son [18] CHARLES COSPATRICK ARCHIBALD, *K.T., T.D.,* 13th Earl; *b.* 1873; Brig. of King's Body Guard for Scotland (Roy. Co. of Archers): *m.* 1902, Lady Lilian Lambton, who *d.* 1966, da. of 4th Earl of Durham; *d.* 1951; *s.* by his son [19] ALEXANDER FREDERICK, 14th Earl, and Lord Home, Lord Dunglass, and Baron Douglas, until he disclaimed his peerage 1963.

⁂ The Lordship of Home (or Hume) of Berwick, *cr.* by patent 1604, with remainder to his heirs for ever, is held to have descended to the Earls of Home through Lady Anna Home. Whether this was and English Barony, as thought by Dugdale, or a Scottish Lordship, which is though more likely in view of the remainder, is uncertain.

HOOD, VISCOUNT. (Hood.)

With favourable winds.

| Viscount G.B. 1796, Bt. G.B. 1778.]

SAMUEL HOOD, *GCMG,* 6th Viscount, and 6th Baronet; *b.* Oct. 15th, 1910; *s.* 1933; ed. at Eton, and at Trin. Coll., Camb.; was Assist. Private Sec. to Sec. of State for India 1936-39, Private Sec. to Min. of Information 1939-41, 1st Sec. Madrid 1947-48, Counsellor at British Embassy, Paris 1948-51, and Min. at British Embassy, Washington, USA, 1958-62; Dep. Under-Sec., Foreign Office 1962-69; CMG 1953, KCMG 1960, GCMG 1969.

𝔄rms,—Azure, a frette argent, on a chief or three crescents sable. 𝔠rest,—A Cornish chough sable, in front of an anchor in bend sinister or. 𝔖upporters,—*Dexter,* a merman, holding in the right hand a trident; *sinister,* a mermaid, holding in the left hand a looking-glass.

Residence,—80, Eaton Sq., SW1. *Clubs,*—Brooks's, Travellers', Turf.

BROTHER LIVING. (*Raised to the rank of a Viscount's son 1934.*)

Hon. ALEXANDER LAMBERT, *b.* March 11th, 1914; ed. at Trin. Coll., Camb. (MA), and at Harvard (BA); Lt.-Cdr. RNVR; Dep.-Chm. of Tilbury Contracting Group Ltd.; a Dir of J. Henry Schroder, Wagg & Co. Ltd., Continental & Industrial Trust, Ltd. (Chm. since 1971), George Wimpey & Co., Ltd., and Tanganyika Concessions, Ltd., and of other cos.: *m.* 1957, Diana Maud, *CVO,* el. da. of the late Hon. George William Lyttelton [see V. Cobham, colls.], and has issue living, Henry Lyttelton Alexander, *b.* 1958,—John Samuel, *b.* 1959,—James Francis Touzalin, *b.* 1962. *Residences,* Loders Court, Bridport, Dorset; 67, Chelsea Sq., SW3. *Club,*—Brooks's.

WIDOW LIVING OF SON OF FOURTH VISCOUNT.

Helen Kendell Mouncey, el. dau. of the late Col. the Hon. Edward Gawler Prior (a P.C. of Canada, and sometime Lieut.-Gov. of British Columbia), of Victoria, British Columbia: *m.* 1904, Col. the Hon. Francis George Hood, who *d.* 1949, and has issue living [see colls., infra]. *Address,*—2501, Shannon Place, Victoria, British Columbia.

COLLATERAL BRANCHES LIVING.

Granddaughters of Lt.-Col. the Hon. Neville Albert Hood, CMG, DSO, RGA (infra):—

Issue of the late Peter Neville Hood, *b.* 1913, *d.* 1969: *m.* 1936, Nancy Warrington, who *d.* 1968, da. of the late Tristram W. Haward, JP, of Abbey Lands, Alnwick, Northumberland:—

Sally Penelope, *b.* 1937: *m.* 1959, Edward Martin Amphlett Thompson, of The Bolt Hole, Six Ashes, Bridgnorth, Salop [E. Coventry, colls.], and has issue living, Stephen Peter, *b.* 1960,—Sarah Ann, *b.* 1965,—Rosemary Claire, *b.* 1969,—Mary Jane, *b.* 1963.——Anna Rosemary, *b.* 1940: *m.* 1968, Peter Christopher Glazebrook, of 116, Woodstock Rd., Oxford.——Eveline Jane Venetia, *b.* 1957.

Issue of the late Lieut.-Col. the Hon. Neville Albert Hood, C.M.G., D.S.O., R.G.A., 4th son of 4th Viscount, *b.* 1872, *d.* 1948: *m.* 1908, Eveline Mary, who *d.* 1967, da. of the late Herman Usticke Broad (who subsequently assumed the surname of Pender), of Tresilian, Falmouth:—

Edith Rosemary (1673, Wisconsin Av. NW, Washington DC 20007, USA), *b.* 1909: *m.* 1st, 1931 (m. diss. 1947), Martin Ayerst Ingram, late Lt. RNVR; 2ndly, 1947 (m. diss. 1956), Capt. Donald Grant Macleod, late Black Watch, and has issue living, (by 1st m.) Margot Faye, *b.* 1934: *m.* 1959, John A. H. Shober, of 30E, Sunset Av., Philadelphia, USA, 19118, and has issue living John Andrews Harris *b.* 1961, Martin Pemberton *b.* 1966, Cintora Suzanne *b.* 1964,—(by 2nd m.) Carole Alice Grant, *b.* 1948.——Eveline Suzanne, *b.* 1917: *m.* 1945, as his second wife, Henry Arthur Frederick Hohler, CMG [V.Gort], and has issue living, Katharine Elizabeth *b.* 1948,—Edith Mabel, *b.* 1952.——Catherine Mary *b.* 1919: *m.* 1940, Graham Charles George Cheverton, and has issue living, Neville Courtenay, *b.* 1949,—Genevieve Sonia, *b.* 1945: *m.* 1966 (m. diss. 1972), David Maxwell Martin. *Residence,*—Quartrieme, Les Mouriaux, Alderney.

Grandchildren of Edith Rosemary Macleod (ante):—

Issue of the late Annabelle Ingram, *b.* 1933, *d.* 1967: *m.* 1963, Julian Payne Freret (5507, Parkston Rd., Maryland 20016, USA):—

Mary Suzanne, *b.* 1964.——Carole Arthemise, *b.* 1965.

Issue of the late Col. the Hon. Francis George Hood, youngest son of 4th Viscount, *b.* 1880, *d.* 1949: *m.* 1904, Helen Kendell Mouncey (ante), el. dau. of the late Col. the Hon. Edward Gawler Prior (a P.C. of Canada, and sometime Lieut.-Gov. of British Columbia), of Victoria, British Columbia:—

Francis Basil, *b.* 1905: *m.* 1934, Catherine Anna, dau. of the late Hon. Sir Richard McBride, KCMG, KC, and has issue living, John Francis Alexander (c/o Bank of Nova Scotia, Vancouver, BC, Canada), *b.* 1935: *m.* 1963, Barbara Anne, yr. da. of the late Cyril Turner, of Victoria, BC, and has issue living, Valery Anne *b.* 1966. *Residence,*—2501, Shannon Pl., Victoria, BC.

Grandchildren of the late Hon. Albert Hood, 2nd son of 3rd Viscount:—

Issue of the late Samuel Wynn Hornby Hood, *b.* 1869, *d.* 1935: *m.* 1906, Ethel Norah Smith, who *d.* 1956, step-dau. of the late J. S. Moss, of Wintershill Hall, Bishops Waltham:—

Evelyn Rosemary Jane, *b.* 1910: *m.* 1937, Brigadier Brian Webb-Carter, D.S.O., O.B.E., Duke of Wellington's Regt., and has issue living, David Brian Wynn, *MC, b.* 1940; ed. at Eton; Maj.

Irish Gds.: *m.* 1973, Felicity, da. of W. L. R. de B. Young,—Evelyn John (10, Neate House, Lupus
St., SW1), *b.* 1946; ed. at Wellington Coll.; Capt. Gren. Gds.: *m.* 1973, the Hon. Anne Cecilia
Wigram, yr. da. of 2nd Baron Wigram, and has issue living, Alexander Clive *b.* 1975. *Residence,*—
Ashton Cottage, Bishops Waltham, Hants.

Issue of the late Capt. Albert Oscar Hood, Irish Guards, *b.* 1870 ,*d.* 1952: *m.* 1912, Theresa
Emily Margery, who *d.* 1970, da. of the late Col. the Hon. Everard Charles Digby [B. Digby,
colls.]:—

John Oscar Everard, *b.* 1913 ; ed. at Eton, and at Worcester Coll., Oxford ; Middle East 1940-45 with
Sudan Defence Force (despatches): *m.* 1953, Winifred Mary Milne. *Residence,*—La Garenne, Mont
Mallet, Gorey, Jersey.——Georgina Mary, *b.* 1915: *m.* 1944, Anthony Morley, Lt. Life Guards,
and has issue living, Andrew Mark, *b.* 1945,—Geoffrey John, *b.* 1948. *Residence,*—Shanks House,
Wincanton, Somerset.

Issue of the late Capt. Alexander Frank Hood, *b.* 1874, *d.* 1923: *m.* 1905, Gladys Ursula,
who *d.* 1968, 3rd da. of the late Edward C. Youell, of Galatz, Roumania:—

Albert Edward (11, Ryder Close, Bushey, Herts), *b.* 1906.——Samuel Brian Digby, *TD, b.* 1910; late
Lieut.-Col. Middlesex Yeo.; 1939-45 War (despatches twice): *m.* 1937, Myrtle Baron, niece and
adopted da. of Sir Louis Bernhard Baron, 1st Bt. (ext.), and has issue living, Alexander Robert
(Archers Farm, The Leigh, Cricklade, Wilts.), *b.* 1945; ed. at Eton: late Rifle Bde.: *m.* 1967, Ann
Marie Donovan, and has issue living, Samuel *b.* 1967, Padraig *b.* 1971, Jane *b.* 1969, Sarah *b.* 1972,—
Sarah Jane (twin) (*Hon. Mrs. Jolyon K. A. Grey*), *b.* 1945: *m.* 1971, the Hon. Jolyon Kenneth
Alnwick Grey, of 36, Octavia St., SW11. [see B. Grey of Naunton]. *Residence,*—Upper Swell Farm,
Stow-on-the-Wold, Glos. *Club,*—Cavalry.——John Michael Alexander (11, Shoremore Hill,
Merroitt, Somerset), *b.* 1919.

Issue of the late Robert Valentine Hood, *b.* 1876, *d.* 1942: *m.* 1917, Mignon, who *d.* 1973,
da. of the late John E. Cooke:—

Robin Julian Patrick (50 Pont St. Mews, SW1), *b.* 1919; ed. at Eton.

Grandchildren of the late Hon. Alexander Frederick GREGORY (who assumed by
Roy. licence in 1910 the surname of Gregory in lieu of his patronymic, and the
arms of Gregory quarterly with his family arms), 3rd son of 3rd viscount:—

Issue of the late Major Charles Hugh GREGORY-HOOD, The Buffs (retired), *b.* 1877, *d.* 1951
(having assumed by deed poll 1927 (enrolled at College of Arms) the additional surname of
Gregory): *m.* 1911, Dorothy (Hillside House, Loxley, Warwick), da. of the late Hon. Marshall Jones Brooks [see B. Crawshaw, colls.]:—

Alexander Marshall Horace, *O.B.E., M.C., b.* 1915; ed. at Winchester; Col. (ret.) late Grenadier
Guards; M.B.E. (Mil.) 1954, O.B.E. (Mil.) 1959; European War 1939-45 (despatches, wounded,
M.C. and Bar): *m.* 1943, Diana (who obtained a divorce 1949), dau. of Major Sir John Little Gilmour, 2nd Bt. (cr. 1926), and has issue living, Peter Charles Freeman (126, Woodsford Sq., W14)
b. 1943; Diplo. Ser.: *m.* 1966, Camilla, da. of Richard Anthony Bethell [see E. Radnor], and has
issue living, Clare *b.* 1968, Carolyn Jane *b.* 1970, Lucy *b.* 1973,—Jane, *b.* 1946: *m.* 1965, Brian A.
FitzGerald of 9, Abbotsbury Rd., W14, and has issue living, Richard Derek *b.* 1967, Sarah Jane *b.*
1968. *Residence,*—Loxley Hall, Warwick.——Rosemary, *b.* 1913; *m.* 1st, 1932 (m. diss. 1937)
Peter Kenneth Chance; 2ndly, 1937 (m. diss. 1943), Capt. Jack Brittain-Jones, CBE who *d.* 1975;
3rdly, 1943, James Lavery; 4thly, 1951, as his third wife (m. diss. 1959), Alfred James McAlpine
Bt., colls.]. *Residence,*—16, Caroline Pl., Bayswater, W2.

Descendants of the late Hon. Samuel Hood (2nd son of 2nd Viscount), and
grand-nephew of Sir Alexander Hood, M.P. (brother of 1st Viscount), who was
cr. *Baron Bridport* (peerage of Ireland) 1794, *Baron Bridport* (peerage of
Great Britain) 1769, and *Viscount Bridport* (peerage of United Kingdom) 1800,
and whom he *s.* (under special remainder) in the Irish Barony [see V.
Bridport].

PREDECESSORS.—[1] *Adm. Sir* SAMUEL Hood, *G.C.B.,* a celebrated Naval Com.; or. a
Baronet 1778, *Baron Hood,* of Catherington, co. Hants (peerage of Ireland) 1782, and *Viscount
Hood* (peerage of Great Britain) 1796; his wife Susannah, who *d.* 1806, dau. of Edward Linzee
of Portsmouth, was cr. *Baroness Hood,* of Catherington, co. Hants (peerage of Great Britain)
1795; *d.* 1816; *s.* by his son [2] HENRY, 2nd Viscount, who had in 1806 *s.* his mother as 2nd
Baron Hood (cr. 1795); *d.* 1836; *s.* by his grandson [3] HENRY, 3rd Viscount; *b.* 1808; as-
sumed the additional name of Tibbits by Roy. licence 1840: *m.* 1837, Mary Isabella, dau. and
heiress of Richard John Tibbits, of Barton Seagrave; *d.* 1846; *s.* by his son [4] FRANCIS
WHELER, 4th Viscount; *b.* 1838: *m.* 1865, Edith Lydia Drummond, who *d.* 1911, dau. of
Arthur W. Ward of Calverley, Tunbridge Wells; *d.* 1907; *s.* by his el. son [5] GROSVENOR
ARTHUR ALEXANDER, *O.B.E.,* 5th Viscount ; *b.* 1868 ; sometime Major Grenadier Guards and
Lieut.-Col. Comdg. 7th Batn. London Regt.: *m.* 1st, 1911, Jane Primrose, who *d.* 1919, dau. of
Col. the Hon. Richard Southwell George Stapleton-Cotton ; 2ndly, 1928, his cousin, Marguerite
(Margot) Jenny, who *d.* 1966, da. of the Hon. Albert Hood; *d.* 1933; *s.* by his nephew [6] SAMUEL
(son of the late Rear-Adm. the Hon. Horace Lambert Alexander Hood, MVO, DSO, 3rd son of
4th Viscount), 6th Viscount and present peer; also Baron Hood.

Hopetoun, Earl of,   son of Marquess of Linlithgow.

HORDER, BARON.   (Horder.)   [Baron U.K. 1933, Bt. U.K. 1923.]

THOMAS MERVYN HORDER, 2nd Baron, and
2nd Baronet ; *b.* Dec. 8th, 1910 ; *s.* 1955;
ed. at Winchester, and at Trin. Coll., Camb. (B.A.
1932, M.A. 1937) ; Wing-Com. R.A.F. Vol.
Reserve: *m.* 1946 (m. diss. 1957), Mary Ross,
da. of the late Dr. W. S. McDougall, of Wallington, Surrey.

Arms,—Per chevron argent and sable bezantée, in chief a
male griffin passant of the second. Crest,—Issuant from a rock
proper a demi-male griffin sable. Supporters,—Not recorded
at time of going to press
Town Address,—Ashford Chase, Petersfield, Hants.

SISTER LIVING.

Hon. Dorothea Joy, *b.* 1905: *m.* 1930, Edward Revill Cullinan,
OBE, MD, FRCP, who *d.* 1965, and has issue living, Edward
Horder (62, Camden Mews, NW1), *b.* 1931; ARIBA: *m.*
1961, Rosalind Sylvia, yst. da. of the late V. M. Yeates, and
has issue living, Thomas Edward *b.* 1965, Emma *b.* 1962,
Kate *b.* 1963,—Timothy Revill, *b.* 1932: *m.* 1956, Helen
Veronica, yst. dau. of Brig. Edmund James Paton-Walsh, and
has issue living, Paul *b.* 1957, Dominic *b.* 1960, Charlotte *b.*
1959,—Paul Anthony, *b.* 1935,—Susan Joy, *b.* 1937: *m.*
1959, John Murray Owen, of The Orchard, Ford, Chippenham, Wilts., and has issue living, Clare Joy *b.* 1960, Joanna
b. 1961, Phillipa *b.* 1963, Lucy *b.* 1965. *Residence,*—10,
Camden Mews, NW1.

PREDECESSOR.—[1] *Sir* THOMAS JEEVES Horder, *G.C.V.O.*, *M.D.*, son of Albert Horder, *b.* 1871; was Physician-in-Ord. to H.R.H. the Prince of Wales 1923-36, to King Edward VIII. 1936, and to King George VI. 1936-49, and Extra Physician to King George VI. 1949-52, and to Queen Elizabeth II. 1952-5; cr. a *Baronet* 1923, and *Baron Horder*, of Ashford, co. Southampton (peerage of United Kingdom) 1933: *m.* 1902, Geraldine, who *d.* 1954, dau. of the late Arthur Doggett: *d.* 1955; *s.* by his son [2] THOMAS MERVYN, 2nd Baron and present peer.

HORE-BELISHA, BARONY OF. (Hore-Belisha.) [Extinct 1957.]
WIDOW LIVING OF FIRST BARON.
CYNTHIA SOPHIE, *B.E.M.*, dau. of the late Gilbert Compton Elliot [see E. Minto, colls.]: *m.* 1st, 1944, the 1st Baron, who *d.* 1957, when the title became ext.; 2ndly, 1957, Major Ian Victor Major DSO, RM (ret.). *Residence,*—Belle-Rive au Lac, 1162, Saint-Prex, Vaud, Switzerland.

HORNSBY-SMITH, BARONESS. (Hornsby-Smith.) [Life Baroness 1974.]
(MARGARET) PATRICIA HORNSBY-SMITH, *DBE*, *PC*, only da. of the late Frederick Charles Hornsby-Smith, of East Sheen, SW14; *b.* March 17th, 1914; FRSA; Parl. Sec. Min. of Health 1951-57, Joint Parl. Under-Sec. of State, Home Office 1957-59, and Joint Parl. Sec. Min. of Pensions and National Insurance 1959-61; UK delegate to UN Assembly 1958, and led Commonwealth Parl. Delegation, Aust. 1962, and Kenya 1972; MP for Chislehurst Div. of Kent (*C*) 1950-66, and 1970-74; cr. PC 1959, DBE (Civil) 1961, and *Baroness Hornsby-Smith*, of Chislehurst in Greater London (Life Baroness) 1974.

Residence,—31, Stafford Mansions, Stafford Place, SW1.
Clubs,—Constitutional, Cowdray, Special Forces.

HOTHAM, BARON. (Hotham.) [Baron I. 1797, Bt. E. 1622.]
[Name and Title pronounced "Hutham."]

For my country.

LEAD ON

HENRY DURAND HOTHAM, 8th Baron, and 18th Baronet; *b.* May 3rd, 1940; *s.* 1967; ed. at Eton; late Lt. Grenadier Guards; patron of one living; ADC to Gov. of Tasmania 1963-66: *m.* 1972, Alexandra Mary, 2nd da. of the late Maj. Andrew Charles Stirling Home Drummond Moray, and has issue.

Arms,—Barry of ten argent and azure, on a canton or, a Cornish chough proper. **Crest,**—Out of waves of the sea a demi-man naked, holding a sword erect proper, and having on the left arm a shield of the arms of Hotham. **Supporters,**—Two sailors habited proper, and resting their exterior hands on a cutlass point downwards.

Seats,—Dalton Hall, Dalton Holme, Beverley, Yorks.; Scorborough Hall, Driffield, Yorks.

SONS LIVING.
Hon. WILLIAM BEAUMONT, *b.* Oct. 13th, 1972.
Hon. George Andrew, *b.* 1974.

BROTHERS LIVING.
Hon. Peter William, *b.* 1944; ed. at Eton, and Ch. Ch. Oxford (BA).
Hon. Nicholas Charles Frederick, *b.* 1947; ed. at Eton: *m.* 1974, Jane Brydon, of Thurley Beck Farm, Harwood Dale, Scarborough, Yorks.

UNCLE LIVING. (*Raised to the rank of a Baron's son* 1924.)
Hon. Peter, *b.* 1904; ed. at Winchester; formerly Major King's Own Yorkshire L.I.: *m.* 1934, Margaret, dau. of Col. Sir Robert William Herbert Watkin Williams-Wynn, 9th Bt., K.C.B., DSO, TD, and has issue living, Edward Durand, *b.* 1944; late Lt. 15th/19th King's R. Hussars,— Caroline Alathea, *b.* 1937: *m.* 1959, Lt.-Col. Harry Llewellyn Davies, RA (National Westminster Bank, 63, Piccadilly, W1), and has issue living, Catherine Margaret *b.* 1962, Thora Lucinda *b.* 1965,— Mary Elizabeth, *b.* 1940: *m.* 1964, Maj. Peter Harman, 14th/20th King's Hussars, and has issue living, Andrew Charles *b.* 1967, Nicola Jane *b.* 1969. *Residence,*—Plas Newydd, Glascoed, Abergele, N. Wales.

AUNT LIVING. (*Raised to the rank of a Baron's daughter* 1924.)
Hon. Catherine Muriel (*Hon. Lady Bower*), *b.* 1908: *m.* 1939, Lieut.-Gen. Sir Roger Herbert Bower, K.C.B., K.B.E., late King's Own Yorkshire L.I., of Hill House, St. Mary Bourne, Andover, Hants., and has issue living, Anne Catherine, *b.* 1940: *m.* 1972, Robert Riseley.

DAUGHTERS LIVING OF SIXTH BARON.
Hon. Sylvia Benita Francis (*Baroness Clitheroe*), *b.* 1903; FRICS, a Gov. of Westminster Hosp., and a Member of Council of Lancaster Univ.; a Member of Lancs. War Agricultural Exec. Cttee. 1941-48, and of Agricultural Exec. Cttee. 1948-59: *m.* 1924, the 1st Baron Clitheroe. *Residences,*—Downham Hall, Clitheroe, Lancs.; 17, Chelsea Park Gdns., SW3.
Hon. Jocelyne Mary Emma, *b.* 1908. *Residence,*—Ridout Cottage, Tarrant Gunville, Blandford, Dorset.

WIDOW LIVING OF BROTHER OF SEVENTH BARON.

Aileen, da. of the late Capt. Harry Coates, Durham LI: *m.* 1st, 1939, Lieut.-Com. the Hon. John David Hotham, DSC, RN, who *d.* 1962 (having been raised to the rank of a Baron's son 1924); 2ndly, 1969, Cdr. Colin Hugh Smith, RN, of The Manor, Grendon Underwood, Aylesbury, and has issue living by 1st m. [see colls., infra.].

WIDOW LIVING OF SEVENTH BARON

Lady LETITIA SIBELL WINIFRED CECIL (*Dowager Baroness Hotham*), (Dalton Hall, Dalton Holme, Beverley, Yorks.), da. of 5th Marquess of Exeter: *m.* 1937, the 7th Baron, who *d.* 1967.

COLLATERAL BRANCHES LIVING.

Issue of the late Lieut.-Com. the Hon. John David Hotham, D.S.C., R.N., brother of 7th Baron, *b.* 1911, *d.* 1962: *m.* 1939, Aileen (ante) (she *m.* 2ndly 1969, Cdr. Colin Hugh Smith, RN), da. of the late Capt. Harry Coates, Durham LI:—
Martin Patrick (Old Bloxhall House, Hitcham, Suffolk), *b.* 1941: *m.* 1965, Erica Antoinette, twin da. of the late Lt.-Col. B. M. Strang, of Maes Heulyn, Denbigh, and has issue living, Charles Beaumont David, *b.* 1969,—Henry Ralph, *b.* 1974,—Sophia Henrietta, *b.* 1967,—Amelia Oriana Philadelphia, *b.* 1971.——Henrietta Elizabeth *b.* 1944: *m.* 1967, Maj. Philip A. J. Wright, Grenadier Guards, son of the late Sir Andrew Barkworth Wright, KCMG, CBE, MC.——Georgina Rose, *b.* 1947: *m.* 1971, Maj. John V. E. F. O'Connell.

Granddaughter of the late Rev. Frederick Harry Hotham, 2nd son of the late Vice-Adm. the Hon. Sir Henry Hotham, G.C.M.G., K.C.B., 3rd son of 2nd Baron :—
Issue of the late Capt. Algernon John Hotham, R.N., *b.* 1863, *d.* 1913: *m.* 1906, **Grace** Adeline Rous, who *d.* 1963, dau. of the late Adm. Sir Algernon Frederick Rous de Horsey, K.C.B., of Melcombe House, Cowes, I. of Wight.
Rachel Muriel, *b.* 1909; ed. at Oxford Univ. (MA); Lambeth Diploma in Theology 1953; Assoc. Member of Roy. Yacht Sqdn. *Residence,*—Rosetta Cottage, Cowes, I.o.W.

Grandchildren of the late Adm. of the Fleet Sir Charles Frederick Hotham, GCB, GCVO, el. son of Capt. John Hotham, 4th son of Lt.-Col. George Hotham, el. son of Gen. George Hotham, brother of 1st Baron:—
Issue of the late John Beaumont Hotham, *b.* 1874, *d.* 1924: *m.* 1905, Gladys Mary, who *d.* 1972, 2nd da. of the late Col. John Gerald Wilson, CB, of Cliffe Hall, Yorkshire [B. Inchiquin, colls.]:—
John David Durand, *b.* 1917; ed. at Eton, and at New Coll., Oxford; formerly Lieut. Roy. Armoured Corps (TA): *m.* 1954, Marianne Becker, of Vienna. *Residence,*—Milne Graden, Coldstream, Berwickshire.——Dorothy Jean (*Countess of Donoughmore*), *MBE, b.* 1906; is Vice-Pres., Co. London Branch, British Red Cross Soc., and a Serving Sister of Order of St. John of Jerusalem; MBE (Civil) 1947: *m.* 1925, the 7th Earl of Donoughmore. *Residence,*—Knocklofty, Grange, Clonmel, co. Tipperary.——Anne (*Baroness Howard of Penrith*), *b.* 1913: *m.* 1st, 1934, Anthony Gardner Bazley, who *d.* 1937 [see Bazley, Bt., colls.]; 2ndly, 1944, the 2nd Baron Howard of Penrith. *Residence,*—Dean Farm, Hatherop, Gloucestershire.——Catharine Geraldine (*Baroness Guest*), *b.* 1915: *m.* 1941, Baron Guest, a Lord of Appeal in Ordinary (Life Peer). *Residences,*—3, Ainslie Place, Edinburgh; Dirleton, E. Lothian.

Grandchildren of the late Capt. John Hotham (ante):—
Issue of the late Brig.-Gen. John Hotham, C.B., *b.* 1851, *d.* 1932: *m.* 1889, **Rose Florence,** who *d.* 1944, dau. of the late Lieut.-Gen. the Hon. Bernard Matthew Ward, C.B. [V. Bangor, colls.]:—
Angela Rose Emily, *b.* 1902: *m.* 1939, Brigadier Rintoul Edward George Carolin, Essex Regt. (retired). *Residence,*—Berry Horn House, Odiham, near Basingstoke.

Issue of the late George Hotham, *b.* 1856, *d.* 1943: *m.* 1896, **Louisa** Hildegarde Neumeister, of Le Mar, Plymouth Co., Iowa, U.S.A. :—
George Edward, *b.* 1896. *Residence,*—Le Mar, Plymouth Co., Iowa, U.S.A.

Grandchildren of the late Capt. William Charles Hotham, son of the late Rev. Edwin Hotham (infra) :—
Issue of the late Lieut.-Col. John Clarence Hotham, *b.* 1882, *d.* 1959: *m.* 1909, **Margaret Emily Anne,** who *d.* 1952, el. dau. of Horace Wilmer, formerly of Church House, Brede, Sussex :—
Diana, *b.* 1918 : *m.* 1948, John Calkin Whately-Smith, and has issue living, David John, *b.* 1949,—Jeremy William, *b.* 1956,—Susan Jane, *b.* 1950,—Charlotte Anne, *b.* 1952. *Residence,*—Hordle House, Milford-on-Sea, Hants.

Issue of the late Com. William Montagu Hotham, Roy. Canadian Navy, *b.* 1884, *d.* 1951: *m.* 1905, **Margaret** Browne:—
Ronald St. Vincent Carew, *b.* 1911; ed. at St. Michael's Sch., Victoria: *m.* 1936, Muriel Eva Maria Sheather.——Alan Geoffrey (of 1130, Channel Drive, Santa Barbara, California, USA), *b.* 1921; ed. at Brentwood Sch., and at British Columbia Univ. (BASc); 1939-45 War in Research Branch, RCAF: *m.* 1951, Kathleen Cramer-Coxhead, and has issue living, Peter Alan, *b.* 1952,—Daryl, *b.* 1953,—Lisa, *b.* 1955.

Grandsons of the late Rev. Edwin Hotham, el. son of the late Adm. Sir William Hotham, G.C.B., 2nd son of the late Gen. George Hotham (ante) :—
Issue of the late Montagu Conyers Hotham, *b.* 1850, *d.* 1931: *m.* 1883, **Francisca Rosa** Pizarro:—
Edwin, *b.* 1887.——George, *b.* 1899: *m.* 1932, Adriana Maria Franco, and has issue living, Charles Edward, *b.* 1934,—Richard Alan, *b.* 1936. *Residence,*—

PREDECESSORS.—[1] *Sir* JOHN Hotham, Knt. ; Gov. of Hull, *temp.* Charles I. ; cr. a *Baronet* 1622; he and his el. son being discovered in correspondence with the Royalists were tried by Court Martial at the Guildhall, sentenced to death and beheaded on Tower Hill 1644; *s.* by his grandson [2] *Sir* JOHN, 2nd Bt.; *d.* 1689; *s.* by his son [3] *Sir* JOHN, 3rd Bt. ; *d.* 1691; *s.* by his cousin [4] *Sir* CHARLES, 4th Bt.; M.P. for Beverley ; *s.* by his son [5] *Sir* CHARLES, 5th Bt.; M.P. for Beverley, and a Groom of the Bedchamber ; *d.* 1737 ; *s.* by his son [6] *Sir* CHARLES, 6th Bt. ; a Groom of the Bedchamber ; *d.* 1767 ; *s.* by his uncle [7] *Sir* BEAUMONT, 7th Bt. ; *d.* 1771; *s.* by his el. son [8] *Sir* CHARLES Hotham-Thompson, *K.B.,* 8th Bt. ; assumed the additional surname of Thompson ; *d.* 1794 ; *s.* by his brother [9] *Rt. Rev.* Sir JOHN Hotham, 9th Bt. ; Lord Bishop of Clogher; *d.* 1795 ; *s.* by his son [10] *Sir* CHARLES, 10th Bt. ; *s.* by his uncle [11] WILLIAM, 11th Bt., 3rd son of 7th Bt.; a distinguished Adm. ; cr. *Baron Hotham,* of South Dalton (peerage of Ireland) 1797, with remainder to the heirs male of his father ; *d.* unmarried 1813 ; *s.* by his brother [12] BEAUMONT, *K.B.,* 2nd Baron ; a Baron of the Court of Exchequer ; *d.* 1814 ; *s.* by his grandson [13] BEAUMONT, 3rd Baron ; a Gen. in the Army ; served at Waterloo; M.P. for Leominster 1820-41, and for E. Riding of York 1841-68 ; *d.* unmarried 1870 ; *s.* by his nephew [14] CHARLES, 4th Baron, son of Rear-Adm. George Frederick (brother of 3rd Baron), by Lady Susan Maria O'Bryen, el. dau. and co-heir of 2nd Marquess of Thomond ; served with 18th Foot in Crimean Campaign 1855 (wounded); *d.* unmarried 1872 ; *s.* by his brother [15] JOHN, 5th Baron ; *b.* 1838 ; *d. unm.* 1907 ; *s.* by his cousin [16] FREDERICK WILLIAM, 6th Baron (son of the late Rev. William Francis Hotham, son of 2nd son of 2nd Baron), *b.* 1863 : *m.* 1902, Benita, who *d.* 1954, dau. of the late Thomas Sanders, of Sanders Park, Charleville, co. Cork ; *d.* 1923; *s.* by his cousin [17] HENRY FREDERICK, *CBE,* (el. son of the late Capt. Henry Hotham, son of the late Rev. Frederick Harry Hotham, son of 3rd son of 2nd Baron), 7th Baron, b. 1899; Maj. Grenadier Guards; Hon. Col. 440th LAA.: m. 1937, Lady Letitia Sibell Winifred Cecil, da. of 5th Marquess of Exeter; d. 1967; s. by his 3rd son [18] HENRY DURAND, 8th Baron and present peer.

HOTHFIELD, BARON. (Tufton.) [Baron U.K. 1881, Bt. U.K. 1851.]

THOMAS SACKVILLE TUFTON, 4th Baron and 5th Baronet ; b. July 20th 1916 ; s. 1961 ; ed. at Eton, and at Camb. Univ.

Arms,—Sable, an eagle displayed ermine, within a bordure wavy or. Crest.—A sea lion sejant argent, debruised by a bendlet wavy sable. Supporters.—On either side an eagle ermine, gorged with a collar gules pendent therefrom an escutcheon of the arms of Tufton. Address,—Broome Park Hotel, Barham, Canterbury, Kent.

The bird flies to its own.

SISTER LIVING.
Diana Mary, b. 1917 : m. 1947, Lieut-Col. Charles Henry Freeman Coaker, R.A. (retired). Residence, —Manor Cottage, Woodborough, Pewsey, Wilts.

DAUGHTERS LIVING OF SECOND BARON.
Hon. Patricia Ierne Wilmot (c/o Lloyds Bank, 6, Pall Mall, S.W.1), b. 1900: m. 1921, Lt.-Col. the Hon. George Chenevix Hill, late Wilts. Regt. who d. 1963 [see B. Sandys].
Hon. (Noreen Rosamond) Anne, b. 1903: m. 1928, Lieut.-Col. Owen Frederick Morton Tudor, 3rd King's Own Hussars. and has issue living, (Rosamunde Ierne) Idonea, b. 1932 : m. 1954, Baron Nils Otto Taube, of The Old Rectory, Gt. Wigborough, Colchester, and has issue living, Simon Axel Robin b. 1957, Owen Rupert b. 1959, Martin Quentin Nils b. 1962,—Carole Anne, b. 1934: m. 1963, Henry John William Phillips, of 46 Horton St., W8 4NT, and has issue living, Francesca Camilla Roberta Ierne b. 1964. Residence,—Ash Court, Hothfield, Ashford, Kent.

WIDOW LIVING OF SON OF SECOND BARON.
Alice Mary Julia (CHITTY), dau. of Brig.-Gen. Arthur Montagu Perreau : m. 1944, the Hon. Peter John Sackville Tufton, who d. 1956. Residence,—Turner's Cottage, Hothfield, Ashford, Kent.

WIDOW LIVING OF THIRD BARON.
DOROTHY (Baroness Hothfield), el. dau. of the late William George Raphael, of 9, Connaught Place, W.2.[Goldsmid, Bt.] : m. 1918, the 3rd Baron, who d. 1961. Residence,—Castle Hill, Englefield Green, Surrey.

COLLATERAL BRANCHES LIVING.
Issue of the late Hon. Charles Henry Tufton, C.M.G., 3rd son of 1st Baron, b. 1879, d. 1923 : m. 1903, Stella Josephine Faudel, O.B.E., who d. 1958, dau. of Sir George Faudel Faudel-Phillips, G.C.I.E., 1st Bt.:—
GEORGE WILLIAM ANTHONY, T.D., b. Oct. 28th, 1904 ; ed. at Eton, and at Hertford Coll., Oxford (B.A. 1927); Lt.-Col. (ret.) R.A. (T.A.); a D.L. for Herts.: m. 1936, Evelyn Margarette, el. dau. of the late Eustace Charles Mordaunt [see Mordaunt, Bt.], and has issue living, Anthony Charles Sackville, b. 1939; ed. at Eton, and at Magdalene Coll., Camb. (MA): m. 1975, Lucinda Marjorie, da. of Capt. Timothy John Gurney [see de Bathe Bt.], and formerly wife of Capt. Graham Morison Vere Nicoll [see Madden, Bt.],—Nicholas William Sackville, b. 1946; ed. at Eton., and Roy. Agric. Coll., Cirencester,—Jennifer Margaret, b. 1937: m. 1965, Edward Robert Raikes, of Parsonage Oasts, Yalding, Kent, and has issue living, Jason Alexander b. 1966, Benedick Arthur b. 1969, Stella Mary Evelyn b. 1972. Residence,—The Red House, Barkway, Royston, Herts.——Francis Charles Sackville, VRD, b. 1913; ed. at Eton, and at Trin Coll., Oxford (MA), Lt.-Cdr. (ret.) RNVR; a Knight of Order of Dannebrog of Denmark: m. 1942, Eileen Joyce Clara, da. of Sir Edward Henry Goschen, 2nd Bt. (cr. 1916), and has issue living, Edward Philip Sackville, b. 1948; ed. at Eton, and Magdalene Coll., Camb.,—Mary Josephine, b. 1943. Residence,—Crowbury, Watton-at-Stone, Herts.——Susan Stella, b. 1908; a JP for Kesteven, Lincs.: m. 1936, Col. Thomas Alexander Hamilton Coltman, OBE, RA, DL, and has issue living, Timothy Charles (Boundry House, Kingswood, Wotton-under-Edge, Glos.), b. 1939; ed. at Eton, and at Trin. Coll., Camb. (BA): m. 1964, Joanna Mary, only da. of John Richard Bergne-Coupland, of Skellingthorpe Hall, nr. Lincoln, and has issue living, Sarah Elizabeth b. 1966, Mary Jane b. 1968,—David Alexander (13, Manson Mews, SW7 5AF), b. 1942; ed. at Eton: m. 1972, Mary Cecilia, 3rd da. of the Rt. Hon. William Stephan Ian Whitelaw, CH, MC, MP, of Ennim, Penrith. [see Hay. Bt., cr. 1635]. Residence,—Laigh Aldons, Girvan, Ayrshire KA26 0TB.

(In remainder to Baronetcy only.)

Grandchildren of the late Alfred Charles Tufton, brother of 1st Baron:—
Issue of the late Cecil George Tufton, b. 1880, d. 1957 : m. 1st, 1912, Agatha Vere Ripley, who d. 1928, dau. of the late Edward Ripley Dalton, Bar.-at-law, of 184, Gloucester Terrace. Hyde Park. W.: 2ndly, 1930, Vera Mary. who d. 1932, dau. of T. P. W. Barnes:—
(By 1st m.) Richard Cecil (2, Selkwood House, The Street, Selborne, Alton, Hants.), b. 1914; formerly Capt. RAMC, and Med. Officer (ret.), Peninsular & Oriental Steam Navigation Co.

Issue of the late Alfred Guy Tufton, b. 1889, d. 1968: m. 1916, Marjorie Neville, (Toketon House, Southdown Rd., Seaford, Sussex), da. of the late Frederick Charles Thompson, of 40, Porchester Sq., W2:—
Rev. Colin Charles Guy (All Saints Vicarage, Maidstone), b. 1924; ed. at Oriel Coll., Oxford (MA); late Lt. RM; V. of All Saints with St. Philip, and Holy Trinity, Maidstone; Hon. Canon of Canterbury Cathedral 1968.——Barbara Marjorie, b. 1920.

PREDECESSORS.—[1] RICHARD Tufton, b. at Verdun, France, 1813; s. by devise to the estates of Henry, 11th and last Earl Thanet; naturalized, with his family, 1849 ; cr. a Baronet 1851: m. 1843, Adelaide Amelie Lacour; d. 1871; s. by his son [2] Sir HENRY JAMES, 2nd Bt., b. 1844; naturalized by Act of Parliament 1851; s. as 2nd Baronet 1871, and cr. Baron Hothfield, of Hothfield, co. Kent (peerage of United Kingdom) 1881; Lord-Lieut. of Westmorland 1881-1926, Vice-Admiral of Coast of Cumberland and Westmorland 1883-1926, and a Lord-in-Waiting to Queen Victoria 1886 : m. 1872, Alice Harriet Argyll, who d. 1914, dau. of the late Rev. William James Stracey-Clitherow; d. 1926; s. by his son [3] JOHN SACKVILLE RICHARD, D.S.O., 2nd Baron, b. 1873 ; Lieut. 1st Life Guards, and Major Roy. Sussex Regt.; Mayor of Appleby 1937-44; S. Africa 1901-2, European War 1915-18 (D.S.O.): m. 1st, 1896, Lady Ierne Louisa Arundel Hastings, who d. 1935, dau. of 13th Earl of Huntingdon ; 2ndly, 1935, Sybil Augusta, who d. 1950, dau. of John Sant ; d. 1952 ; s. by his son [4] HENRY HASTINGS SACKVILLE THANET, 3rd Baron, b. 1897 ; Lieut. 15th/19th Hussars ; appointed Assist. Director of Public Relations, Home Forces 1942 : m. 1918, Dorothy, el. dau. of the late William George Raphael, of 9, Connaught Place, W.2 ; d. 1961 ; s. by his cousin [5] THOMAS SACKVILLE (only son of the late Hon. Sackville Philip Tufton, 2nd son of 1st Baron), 4th Baron and present peer.

HOUGHTON OF SOWERBY, BARON. (Houghton.) [Life Baron 1974.]

ARTHUR LESLIE NOEL DOUGLAS HOUGH-
TON, *CH, PC,* son of the late John Houghton,
of Long Eaton, Derbys.; *b.* Aug. 11th, 1898;
Sec. Inland Revenue Staff Fedn. 1922-60;
Broadcaster, BBC 1941-64, an Alderman,
London Co. Council 1947-49, a Member of
Gen. Council TUC 1952-60, Chm. (Staff Side)
Civil Ser. National Whitley Council 1956-58,
and of Public Accounts Cttee. 1963-64,
Chancellor of Duchy of Lancaster 1964-66,
Min. without Portfolio 1966-67, and Chm. of
Parl. Labour Party 1967-74; MP for Sowerby
Div. of W. Riding of Yorks. (*Lab.*) 1949-74;
cr. PC 1964, CH 1967, and *Baron Houghton
of Sowerby,* of Sowerby in Co. of W. Yorks.
(Life Baron) 1974: *m.* 1939, Vera, da. of
John Travis, of Southall, Middx.

Arms,—not exemplified at time of going to press.

Residences,—110, Marsham Court, SW1; Becks Cottage, White Hill Lane, Bletchingley, Surrey.

HOWARD DE WALDEN AND SEAFORD, BARON. (Scott-Ellis.)
[Baron E. 1597 and U.K. 1826.]

Light in darkness.

Not by whom, but in what manner.

JOHN OSMAEL SCOTT-ELLIS, 9th Baron
Howard de Walden, and 5th Baron Seaford;
b. Nov. 27th, 1912 ; *s.* 1946 ; ed. at Eton, and
at Magdalene Coll., Camb. (B.A. 1934); is
Major Westminster Dragoons (T.A.): *m.*
1934, Countess Irene Harrach, who *d.* 1975,
yst. da. of Count Hans Albrecht Harrach,
and has issue.

Arms,—Quarterly: 1st and 4th erminois, a cross
sable, charged with five crescents argent, *Ellis;* 2nd
and 3rd or, on a bend azure a star betwixt two
crescents of the field, in chief a crescent gules, all
within a bordure engrailed of the last, *Scott.*
Crests,—1st, on a mount vert, a goat's head erased
argent, *Ellis ;* 2nd, a dexter hand issuing out of the
wreath holding an annulet or in which is set a
carbuncle proper, *Scott.* **Supporters,**—Two lions
argent, each charged on the neck with three trefoils
slipped vert, within a collar gules.

Residences,—Ormeley Lodge, Ham Common,
Richmond, Surrey; Avington Manor, Hungerford,
Berks. *Clubs,*—Turf, Royal Yacht Squadron, Jockey.

DAUGHTERS LIVING. (*Co-heiresses to the Barony of Howard de Walden.*)

Hon. (MARY) HAZEL CARIDWEN, *b.* Aug. 12th, 1935: *m.* 1957, Joseph Czernin, son of the late
Count Franz Josef Czernin, and has issue living, Peter John Joseph, 1966,—Charlotte Mary Sidonia,
b. 1958,—Henrietta Mary Rosario, *b.* 1960,—Alexandra Mary Romana, *b.* 1961,—Philippa Mary
Loretta, *b.* 1963,—Isabelle Mary Benedicta, *b.* 1967. *Residences,*—2, The Boltons, SW10; Chieveley House, Chieveley, Newbury, Berks.

Hon. (BLANCHE) SUSAN FIONODBHAR, *b.* Oct. 6th, 1937 : *m.* 1961, Capt. David William Sinclair
Buchan of Auchmacoy [E. Caithness], and has issue living, (John) Charles Augustus David, *b.* 1963,—
James Alexander Stephen, *b.* 1964,—Thomas Richard Sinclair, *b.* 1966,—Robert Edward William,
b. 1968,—Sophia Jane Elizabeth, *b.* 1962. *Residences,*—Auchmacoy House, Ellon, Aberdeenshire;
28, The Little Boltons, SW10.

Hon. JESSICA JANE VRONWY, *b.* Aug. 6th, 1941: *m.* 1966, Adrian Tancred White, 17, Pelham
Place, SW7 [see Lawson-Tancred, Bt., colls.], and has issue living, Nicholas John Sebastian, *b.* 1967,—
Simon James Alexander, *b.* 1968,—Richard Dominic Edward, *b.* 1970.

Hon. CAMILLA ANNE BRONWEN (Alderley Grange, Wotton Under Edge, Glos., GL12 FQT), *b.*
April 1st, 1947: *m.* 1971, Guy Acloque.

SISTERS LIVING.

Hon. Bronwen Mary (*twin*), *b.* 1912 : *m.* 1933, the Hon. James Louis Lindsay [see E. Crawford].
Residence,—Througham Slad, Bisley, Stroud, Glos.

Hon. Elizabeth Gwendolen, *b.* 1914 : *m.* 1st, 1935, Lieut.-Com. Count Serge Orloff-Davidoff, R.N.V.R.,
who *d.* (on active ser. in Germany) 1945 ; 2ndly, 1959, Dr. Bernard Wheeler Robinson, and has issue
living, (by 1st m.) Tatiana, *b.* 1936: *m.* 1972, William John Whitworth Mallinson, MB, MRCP, of 5,
Halsey St., SW3,—Marina (*Viscountess Bury*) (Piazza di Bellosquardo 10, 50124, Florence, Italy),
b. 1937; ARIBA; AA Dip.: *m.* 1964, as his 2nd wife, Derek, William Charles, Viscount Bury, who *d.*
1968, el. son of 9th Earl of Albermarle. *Residences,*—Pigotts, North Dean, Hughenden, High
Wycombe; 366, Goldhawk Rd., W6.

Hon. Essylt Priscilla, *b.* 1916: *m.* 1945 (m. diss. 1972), Don José Luis de Vilallonga, and has issue living,
Juan Alfonso, *b.* 1946,—(Susanna) Carmen Beatrice, *b.* 1947. *Residences,*—Auribeau-sur-Siagne,
France, A.M.; The Viva, Chelsea Yacht and Boat Co., Cheyne Walk, SW10.

Hon. Margaret Irène Gaenor, *b.* 1919 : *m.* 1938, Richard Frank Heathcoat-Amory, who *d.* 1957 [see
Heathcoat-Amory, Bt., colls.]. *Residences,*—Hele Manor, Dulverton, Somerset; 88, Cadogan
Place, SW1.

Hon. Rosemary Nest, *b.* 1922 : *m.* 1946, George FitzRoy Seymour [see M. Hertford, colls.]
Residences,—Thrumpton Hall, Notts.; 38, Molyneux St., W1; 2, The Crescent, Cromer, Norfolk.

COLLATERAL BRANCHES LIVING.

Grandchildren of the late Rev. the Hon. William Charles Ellis, 2nd son of 6th Baron:—
Issue of the late Henry Guysulf Bertram Ellis, *b.* 1875 ; *d.* 1947: *m.* 1911, **Kathleen** Roberta, who *d.* 1940, only dau. of William Charles Mitchell, formerly of Marmont, co. Down:—
WILLIAM FELTON, *b.* Nov. 27th, 1912 ; ed. at Cheltenham, and at Trin. Coll., Camb. (B.A. 1936) ; is Major R.A.S.C., and *h.p.* to Barony of Seaford : *m.* 1940, Edwina, dau. of the late Major R. E. Bond, Indian Army, and has issue living, Colin Humphrey Felton (Erls Farm, Belchalwell, Dorset), *b.* 1946: *m.* 1971, Susan Magill, and has issue living, Harriet Fay *b.* 1973,—Jill Kathleen, *b.* 1944: *m.* 1968, Jeremy Dudgeon Anderson, of 1, Claremont Av., St. Saviour, Jersey, and has issue living, William Maurice *b.* 1973, Kathleen Fleur *b.* 1971. *Residence,*—Motts, Eridge, Sussex.——Henrietta Roberta, Elizabeth, *b.* 1911: *m.* 1943, Thomas Stewart Lewis Russell, and has issue living, David Guysulf, *b.* 1944,—Peter Stuart, *b.* 1948,—Michael Roland, *b.* 1950. *Residence,*— Green Acres, Dawlish, Devon.——Catherine Rosemary, *b.* 1918: *m.* 1945, Douglas Alexander Clarke-Smith, who *d.* 1959, and has issue living, Humphrey Douglas Bevis, *b.* 1948,—Lucinda Mary, *b.* 1946,—Susan, *b.* 1950. *Residence,*—Old Buckhurst, Withyham, Sussex.

Grandchildren of the Hon. Evelyn Henry Ellis, 5th son of 6th Baron:—
Issue of the late Mary Ellis, OBE, *b.* 1888, *d.* 1971: *m.* 1916, Maj. Denis Granville Coskey Critchley Salmonson, MC, RSF, who *d.* 1943:—
John Albert Miles (The Manor House, Gt. Barton, Bury St. Edmunds), *b.* 1916; Maj. (ret.) 12th R. Lancers: *m.* 1946, Joan, da. of Col. Robert Henry Haseldine, DSO, OBE, and has issue living Denis Patrick Antony, *b.* 1953; ed. at Downside; 2nd Lt. Coldm. Gds.,—Mary Clare *b.* 1947,— Antonia Isabella Mary, *b.* 1949: *m.* 1973, Christopher Tregoning,—Henrietta Margaret Mary, *b.* 1959.——Peter Evelyn George (The Green Mountain, Ascension Island, S. Atlantic), *b.* 1919; a Farmer; 1939-45 War as Lt. RIF, and Fl.-Lt. RAF: *m.* 1948, Grace, da. of Col. J. L. Oliver, and has issue living, Michael Shavin, *b.* 1952,—Kim Hardinge, *b.* 1954,—Peter Kerr, *b.* 1957,— Mark Nicholas, *b.* 1959.——Denise Irene Mary, *b.* 1918.

PREDECESSORS.—[1] *Lord* Thomas Howard, K.G., P.C., el. son of 4th Duke of Norfolk by his 2nd marriage with Margaret, dau. and heiress of Thomas, K.G., 1st and last Baron Audley of Walden; summoned to Parliament of England as *Baron Howard of Walden* 1597, and cr. *Earl of Suffolk* (peerage of England) 1603 (see E. Suffolk); *d.* 1626; *s.* by his son [2] THEO-PHILUS, K.G., P.C., 2nd Earl; *d.* 1640; *s.* by his son [3] JAMES, K.B. 3rd Earl; *d.* without male issue, when the earldom devolved upon his brother, and the barony became abeyant between his daus. Essex and Elizabeth; in 1784 the abeyance was terminated in favour of the descendant of Essex [4] *Field-Marshal Sir* JOHN GRIFFIN Whitwell-Griffin, K.B., 4th Baron; cr. *Baron Braybrooke* (peerage of Great Britain) 1788; twice *m.*, but *d.s.p.* 1797, when the Barony of Braybrooke devolved in terms of the remainder upon his kinsman [see B. Braybrooke), and the Barony of Howard of Walden reverted to the heir male of Elizabeth (ante) [5] *The Right Rev.* FREDERICK AUGUSTUS Hervey, 4th Earl of Bristol (see M. Bristol) ; *d.* 1803; when the earldom passed to his 2nd son, and the Barony of Howard of Walden reverted to his great-grandson [6] CHARLES AUGUSTUS, G.C.B., 6th Baron, grandson of John Augustus, Lord Hervey, whose dau. Elizabeth Catherine Caroline *m.* Charles Rose Ellis, who *d.* 1845 having been cr. *Baron Seaford*, of Seaford, co. Sussex (peerage of United Kingdom) 1826; *b.* 1799; was Min. Plen. at Stockholm 1832-3, at Lisbon 1833-46, and at Brussels 1846-68 : *m.* 1828, Lady Lucy Cavendish-Bentinck, dau. of 4th Duke of Portland; *d.* 1868; *s.* by his son [7] FREDERICK GEORGE, 7th Baron Howard de Walden, and 3rd Baron Seaford, *b.* 1830 : *m.* 1876, Blanche, who *d.* 1911 (having obtained a judicial separation 1893, and having *m.* 2ndly 1903, the 2nd Baron Ludlow), dau. of the late William Holden, of Palace House, Lancashire; *d.* 1899; *s.* by his son [8] THOMAS EVELYN, 8th Baron Howard de Walden and 4th Baron Seaford, *b.* 1880; Hon. Col. Westminster Dragoons, and Pres. of Queen Charlotte's Hospital; assumed by Roy. licence 1917 the additional surname and arms of Scott: *m.* 1912, Margherita, CBE, who *d.* 1974, da. of the late Charles Van Raalte, of Brownsea Island, Dorset; *d.* 1946; *s.* by his son [9] JOHN OSMAEL, 9th Baron and present peer; also Baron Seaford.

HOWARD OF PENRITH, BARON. (Howard.) [Baron U.K. 1930.]

FRANCIS PHILIP HOWARD, 2nd Baron: *b.* Oct. 5th, 1905 ; *s.* 1939 ; ed. at Downside, and Trin. Coll., Camb. (BA); Bar. Middle Temple 1931; Capt. RA; 1939-43 War: *m.* 1944, Anne da. of the late John Beaumont Hotham [see B. Hotham, colls.], and widow of Anthony Gardner Bazley [see Bazley, Bt., colls.], and has issue.

Arms,—Quarterly, 1st, gules, a bend between six cross-crosslets fitchée argent; on the bend an escutcheon or, charged with a demi-lion rampant, pierced through the mouth with an arrow, within a double tressure flory counterflory all gules, *Howard ;* 2nd, gules three lions passant guardant in pale or, and in chief a label of three points argent, *Brotherton ;* 3rd, checky or and azure, *Warren ;* 4th, gules, a lion rampant or, *Fitzalan.* **Crests,**—1st, issuant from a ducal coronet or, a pair of wings gules, each charged with a bend between six cross-crosslets fitchée argent; 2nd, on a chapeau gules, turned up ermine, a lion statant guardant with tail extended or, ducally gorged argent; 3rd, on a mount vert a horse passant argent, holding in the mouth a slip of oak fructed proper. **Supporters,**—*Dexter*, a lion argent; *sinister*, a horse argent, holding in the mouth a sprig of oak fructed proper; each charged on the shoulder with an escutcheon barry of six argent and azure, three chaplets gules.

Virtue alone is unconquerable.

Residence,—Dean Farm, Hatherop, Gloucestershire.

SONS LIVING.
Hon. PHILIP ESME (4, Charlwood Terr., SW15), *b.* May 1st, 1945: *m.* 1969, Sarah, da. of the late
Barclay Walker, and has issue living, Thomas Philip, *b.* 1974,—Natasha Mary, *b.* 1970.
Hon. Michael Edmund, *b.* 1947.
Hon. David Francis, *b.* 1949.　　　　　*Hon.* William John, *b.* 1953.

BROTHERS LIVING.
Hon. Hubert John Edward Dominic, *b.* 1907; ed. at Downside, and at Trin. Coll., Camb. (B.A.
1928): *m.* 1951, Donna Lelia Calista Ada Caetani, only dau. of 18th Duke of Sermoneta. *Residences,*—Palazzo Caetani, Rome, Italy; Lyulph's Tower, Ullswater, Cumberland.
Hon. Edmund Bernard Carlo, *CMG, MVO, b.* 1909; ed. at Downside, and New Coll., Oxford (BA); Bar.
Middle Temple 1934; 2nd Sec. (Information) Rome 1947-51, and in Foreign Office 1951-53, 1st
Sec. Madrid 1953-57, Head of Chancery Bogota 1957-59, Consul-Gen., San Marino and Florence,
1960-61, Counsellor Rome 1961-65, and Consul-Gen. Genoa 1965-69, MVO (4th class) 1961, CMG
1969: *m.* 1936, Cécile, da. of Charles Geoffroy-Dechaume, of Valmondois, France, and has issue
living, Esme Francis (35, Wymond St., SW15), *b.* 1938; ed. at Downside, and New Coll., Oxford (BA):
m. 1963 (m. diss. 1973), Tessa Longhurst, da. of the late Maj. Kenneth Evan Meredith, Dorset Regt.,
and has issue living, Dominic William *b.* 1964, Stephen *b.* 1966, Elizabeth Anne *b.* 1965,—John
Edmund *b.* 1940; ed. at Downside, and New Coll., Oxford (BA): *m.* 1971, Gloria Cano, of Medellin,
Colombia, and has issue living, Alejandro *b.* 1973, Patricia Anita *b.* 1972,—Anthony Richard, *b.* 1947;
ed. at Downside, and Guildhall Sch. of Music and Drama,—Katherine Isabella, *b.* 1952. *Residence,*—
Jerome Cottage, Marlow Common, Bucks., SL7 2QR.
Hon. Henry Anthony Camillo, *CMG, b.* 1913; ed. at Downside; Lt.-Col. Coldstream Guards (Reserve);
Administrator of St. Kitts, Nevis and Anguilla 1956-65; 1939-45 War (despatches); CMG 1960:
m. 1937, Adèle Le Bourgois, da. of the late Reese Denny Alsop, of New York City,
U.S.A., and has issue living, Mary Rosalind, *b.* 1938: *m.* 1961, Ian Harlowe Lowe, of Far End,
Kingham, Oxon., and has issue living, Esme Charles Harlowe, *b.* 1962,—Joan Dacre, *b.* 1946: *m.*
1966, William Lacey, of New York City, and has issue living, William John *b.* 1967,—Adèle Cristina
Sophia, *b.* 1952,—Charlotte Fell, *b.* 1953. *Residence,*—Bushby House, Greystoke, Penrith, Cumbria.

PREDECESSOR—[1] ESME WILLIAM Howard, *G.C.B., G.C.M.G., C.V.O.,* 4th son of the
late Henry Howard, M.P., of Greystoke, Cumberland [D. Norfolk, colls.]; *b.* 1863; was
Envoy Extraor. and Min. Plen. to Swiss Confederation 1911-13, and to Sweden 1913-19, and
Ambassador Extraor. and Plen. to Spain 1919-23, and to Washington 1923-30; cr. *Baron*
Howard of Penrith, of Gowbarrow, co. Cumberland (peerage of United Kingdom) 1930: *m.*
1898, Lady (Maria) Isabella Giovanna Gioacchina Giustiniani-Bandini, who *d.* 1963, da. of 8th
Earl of Newburgh; *d.* 1939; *s.* by his second but el. surviving son [2] FRANCIS PHILIP, 2nd Baron
and present peer.

HOWE, EARL. (Curzon.) [Earl U.K. 1821.]

EDWARD RICHARD ASSHETON PENN
CURZON, *CBE,* 6th Earl; *b.* Aug. 7th,
1908; *s.* 1964; ed. at Eton, and at
Corpus Christi Coll., Camb.; a JP, a
DL, and Co. Councillor of Bucks.,
Vice-Chm. RAC (Member of RAC
Cttee., Public Policy and Competitions
Cttees.), Pres. of British Automobile
Racing Club, of Assocn. of British
Motor Clubs, of Inst. of Road Trans-
port Engineers, and of Chesham and
Amersham Conservative Assocn., a
Member of Cttee. Arethusa Training
Ship, a Trustee of King William IV Naval Asylum, CStJ, and patron of eight
livings; a Co. Councillor for London 1937-46, and Commr. of Bucks. St. John
Ambulance Bde. 1954-56; 1939-45 War as Lt.-Cdr. RNVR; CBE (Civil) 1961;
m. 1st, 1935, Priscilla Crystal Frances Blundell (from whom he obtained a
divorce 1943), only da. of Sir (William Ernest George) Archibald Weigall,
1st Bt., KCMG; 2ndly, 1946, Grace Lilian (BARKER) (OStJ), da. of the
late Stephen Frederick Wakeling, of Durban, and has issue by 1st and 2nd
marriages.

Arms,—Quarterly: 1st and 4th or, a fesse between three wolves' heads couped sable, Howe;
2nd and 3rd argent, on a bend sable, three popinjays or, collared gules, Curzon. **Crests,**—1st, out of
a ducal coronet or, a plume of five ostrich feathers azure, Howe; 2nd, a popinjay wings displayed
and inverted or, collared gules, Curzon. **Supporters,**—On either side a Cornish chough proper,
around the neck a plain gold chain.

Seat,—Penn House, Penn St., Amersham, Bucks. *Residence,*—20, Pitts Head Mews, Curzon St.,
W1. *Clubs,*—1900, RNVR.

DAUGHTERS LIVING. *(By 1st marriage.)*
Lady Priscilla Mary Rose, *b.* 1940: *m.* 1962, Charles William Lyle Keen, of Beesthorpe Hall, Caunton,
Notts., and has issue living, William Walter Maurice, *b.* 1970,—Laura Mary Catherine, *b.* 1963,—
Eleanor Margaret, *b.* 1965,—Alice Priscilla, *b.* 1966.
Lady Jennifer Jane, *b.* 1941: *m.* 1962, Alan Joseph Ponté, (Ardeley Bury, nr. Stevenage, Herts.), and
has issue living, David Joseph Marcus Blundell, *b.* 1964,—Gideon Léo FitzRoy, *b.* 1965,—Joshua
Albert Coriat *b.* 1970,—Luke Antony Archibald, *b.* 1974,—Rebecca Kate Priscilla Clara, *b.* 1967.

(By 2nd marriage.)
Lady Mary Gaye Georgiana Lorna, *b.* 1947: *m.* 1971, (Kevin) Esmond (Peter) Cooper-Key, of 41,
Chepstow Place, W2 [see V. Rothermere].
Lady Charlotte Elizabeth Anne, *b.* 1948.

SISTER LIVING.
Lady Georgiana Mary CURZON, *b.* 1910; assumed the surname of Curzon in lieu of Kidston by deed
poll 1944: *m.* 1st, 1935, Lt. Home Ronald Archibald Kidston, R.N., from whom she obtained a
divorce 1943: 2ndly, 1957, Lt.-Col. Lewis Stanton Starkey, and has issue living, (by 1st marriage)
Glen, *b.* 1937. *Residences,*—Huttons Ambo Hall, York; 30, Radnor Walk, S.W.3.

HALF SISTERS LIVING.
Lady Frances Esmee, *b.* 1939: *m.* 1962, Derek Alan Whiting, of Bowyer House, Denham Village,
Bucks., and has issue living, Alexander, *b.* 1967,—Francis, *b.* 1965.
Lady Sarah Marguerite, *b.* 1945: *m.* 1st, 1966, Piers Raymond Courage, who *d.* 1970; 2ndly, 1972
John Victor Aspinall, of 1, Lyall St., SW1, and has issue living, (by 1st m.) Jason Piers, *b.* 1967,—
Amos Edward Sebastian, *b.* 1969,—(by 2nd m.) Bassa Wulfhere, *b.* 1972.

WIDOW LIVING OF FIFTH EARL.

SYBIL BOYTER (Jesters, Kings Legend, Aldeburgh, Suffolk), only child of the late Capt. Francis Johnson, of Palmeira Sq., Hove, and formerly wife of the late Maj. Ernest Duncombe Shafto: *m.* 1st, 1944, as his third wife, the 5th Earl, who *d.* 1964; 2ndly, 1972, Graham Goodson.

COLLATERAL BRANCHES LIVING.

Issue of the late Hon. Frederick Graham Curzon, 2nd son of 3rd Earl, *b.* 1868, *d.* 1920: *m.* 1894, Minnie Gertrude Ellis (Ellis Jeffreys), who *d.* 1943 (having obtained a divorce 1903, and having *m.* 2ndly, 19—, Herbert Sleath Skelton), dau. of the late Capt. Dodsworth Jeffreys:—

CHAMBRÉ (GEORGE) (WILLIAM PENN), *b.* Oct. 18th, 1898; Cdr. RN (ret.); actor; 1914-18 War (despatches, 1914 star); 1939-45 War: *m.* 1st, 1927, Louise Merrill Rowe, who *d.* 1942, da. of the late A. Jackson-Stone, formerly of 27, Rue Théry, Paris; 2ndly, 1950, Enid Jane Victoria, from whom he obtained a divorce 1965, da. of the late Malcolm Mackenzie Fergusson, of Toronto, Canada, and has issue living, (by 2nd m.) Frederick Richard Penn, *b.* 1951; ed. at Rugby, and Ch. Ch., Oxford,—Enid Emma Charlotte, *b.* 1953. *Address,*—c/o Lloyds Bank, 39, Piccadilly, W1. *Club,*—Garrick.——Ellis Evelyn Isabella, *b.* 1897. *Residence,*—Chobham Farm, Chobham, Surrey.

Grandchildren of the late Major Ernest Charles Penn Curzon, son of the late Col. the Hon. Ernest George Curzon (infra) :—
Issue of the late Charles Ernest Basset Lothian Curzon, *b.* 1885, *d.* 1952 : *m.* 1917, Geraldine Fosbery, who *d.* 1962, dau. of Sir James Mills, K.C.M.G.:—

James Quintin Penn (Saplinbrae, Mintlaw Station, Aberdeenshire), *b.* 1923; is Capt. Gordon Highlanders (Reserve): *m.* 1966, Jennifer Anne, da. of Percy Douglas Harrison of Southsea, and has issue living, Charles Mark Penn *b.* 1967,—Camilla Mary, *b.* 1969.——Mary Eleanora Basset, *b.* 1920: *m.* 1941, Maj. James Malcolm Hay, Gordon Highlanders [see M. Tweeddale, colls.]. *Residence,*—Edinglassie, Huntly, Aberdeenshire.

Grandsons of the late Col. the Hon. Ernest George Curzon, 6th son of 1st Earl :—
Issue of the late Mary Ellen Curzon, *b.* 1866, *d.* 1940 : *m.* 1888, the Rev. Arthur Lewis Whitfeld, who *d.* 1937 :—

Ernest Hamilton, *M.C.*, *b.* 1894 ; Lieut.-Col. (retired) Oxfordshire and Bucks L.I.; European War 1915-19 in France and Belgium (wounded, despatches twice, M.C., 1914-15 star, two medals), Burma 1930-32 (medal with clasp) European War 1939-45: *m.* 1935, Iris Esme, second dau. of T. A. Scully, and has issue living, David, *b.* 1936,—Michael (8, Scarsdale Villas, W8), *b.* 1939: *m.* 1966, the Hon. Deborah Mary Vaughan-Morgan, yr. da. of Baron Reigate (Life Peer), and has issue living, Nicholas John *b.* 1968, Mark David *b.* 1971. *Residence,*—St. Ann's, Mere, Wilts.——Gerald Herbert Penn, *OBE*, *MC*, *b.* 1896; Brig. (ret.) late Roy. Ulster Rifles; DL of Herts; 1914-18 War in France and Belgium (wounded, despatches, MC, two medals), Palestine 1936-39 (medal with clasp), 1939-45 War (OBE); OBE (Mil.) 1940: *m.* 1922, Joan Marguerite, da. of the late Capt. Reginald Hughes D'Aeth [E. Cranbrook], and has issue living, Angela, *b.* 1927,—Anthony *b.* 1940. *Residence,*—The Red House, Hartsbourne Av., Bushey Heath, Herts.

Grandchildren of the late Adm. the Hon. Sir Assheton Gore Curzon-Howe, G.C.V.O., K.C.B., C.M.G. (infra) :—
Issue of the late Capt. Leicester Charles Assheton St, John CURZON-HOWE, M.V.O., R.N., *b.* 1894, *d.* (on active ser. during European War) 1941: *m.* 1923, Marguerite Graham, da. of A. Allan Mackenzie of Montreal:—

Anne Rita, *b.* 1923: late WRNS: *m.* 1st, 1955, as his second wife, the 19th Baron Teynham, who *d.* 1972; 2ndly, 1975, Dr. Ian Edwards. *Residence,*—Inwood House, Sarisbury Green, Hants.

Issue of the late Lieut.-Col. Assheton Penn CURZON-HOWE-HERRICK, R.A., *b.* 1898, *d.* 1959, having assumed by Roy. licence 1946, the additional surname and arms of Herrick : *m.* 1930, Joan Henrietta, OBE (The Hermitage, Thornton Watlass, Ripon), da. of the late James Windsor Lewis, of Llwydcoed, Glam.:—

Assheton Montagu Windsor (Le Chastanet, Collonges, Corrèze, France), *b.* 1939.——Marigold Mary (48, Thurloe Sq., SW7), *b.* 1934; SRN.

Issue of the late Adm. the Hon. Sir Assheton Gore CURZON-HOWE, G.C.V.O., K.C.B., C.M.G., 9th son of 1st Earl, *b.* 1850, *d.* 1911: *m.* 1892, Alice Anne, who *d.* 1948, dau. of the late Maj.-Gen. the Rt. Hon. Sir John Clayton Cowell, P.C., K.C.B. :—

Joyce Mary, *b.* 1906: *m.* 1st, 1934, Lieut.-Col. Thomas Ethelston Hussey, R.A., who *d.* (killed in action in France) 1944 ; 2ndly, 1950, Rear-Adm. Robert Kirk Dickson, C.B., D.S.O., who *d.* 1952. *Residence,*—Shadings, Hangersley Hill, Ringwood, Hants.——Elizabeth Anne, *O.B.E.*, *b.* 1909; late Second-in-Com. Women's Transport Ser. (First Aid Nursing Yeo.) ; O.B.E. (Civil) 1946 : *m.* 1939, Brig. David Arthur Hunt, DSO, OBE, RA, who *d.* 1967, and has issue living, Sarah Constance Curzon, *b.* 1942: *m.* 1962, Maj. Michael Roland Dangerfield, 4th/7th Roy. Dragoon Guards, of Hoe Barn, Peaslake, Guildford, and has issue living, Roland Charles David *b.* 1969, Georgina Sarah, *b.* 1967. *Residence,*—Burton House, Masham, nr. Ripon, Yorks.

PREDECESSORS.—[1] ASSHETON Curzon, 2nd son of Sir Nathaniel Curzon, 4th Bt. [see B Scarsdale]; M.P. for Clitheroe 1754-77 and 1790-4; cr. *Baron Curzon*, of Penn, co. Bucks (peerage of Great Britain) 1794, and *Viscount Curzon* (peerage of United Kingdom) 1802; his only son, Assheton, M.P., *d.* 1797, having *m.* SOPHIA CHARLOTTE, who in 1799 on the death of her father, Richard, K.G., 1st and last Earl Howe (cr. 1788 *Baron Howe*, of Langar, co. Notts. peerage of Great Britain, with remainder to his daus.), became Baroness Howe; [2—3] Assheton had by his marriage with the Baroness one son RICHARD WILLIAM PENN, *P.C.*, *G.C.H.*, who in 1820 *s.* his grandfather as 2nd Viscount and Baron Curzon, and in 1836 *s.* his mother as 3rd Baron Howe; assumed the additional name of Howe by Roy. licence 1821; cr. *Earl Howe* (peerage of United Kingdom) 1821; was Lord Chamberlain to Queen Adelaide: *m.* 1st, 1820, Harriet Georgiana, who *d.* 1836, dau. of 6th Earl of Cardigan; 2ndly, 1845, Anne, who *d.* 1877, dau. of the late Adm. Sir John Gore; *d.* 1870; *s.* by his son [4] GEORGE AUGUSTUS FREDERICK LOUIS, 2nd Earl; *b.* 1821; sat as M.P. for S. Leicestershire (C) 1857-70; *d.* 1876; *s.* by his brother [5] RICHARD WILLIAM PENN, G.C.V.O., C.B., 3rd Earl, *b.* 1822; a Gen. in the Army; Mil. Sec. to Com.-in-Ch. in India 1854, and sometime A.D.C. to H.R.H. the Duke of Cambridge: *m.* 1858, Isabella Katherine, who *d.* 1922, dau. of the late Maj.-Gen. the Hon. George Anson; *d.* 1900 : *s.* by his el. son [6] RICHARD GEORGE PENN, G.C.V.O., 4th Earl, *b.* 1861 ; Treasurer of Queen Victoria's Household 1896-1900, a Lord-in-Waiting to Queen Victoria Oct. 1900 to Jan. 1901, and to King Edward VII. Jan. 1901 to Sept. 1903, and Lord Chamberlain to the late Queen Alexandra Sept. 1903 to Nov. 1925 ; M.P. for S., or Wycombe, Div. of Bucks (C) 1885-1900 ; received Roy. Victorian Chain 1925 : *m.* 1st, 1883, Lady Georgiana Elizabeth Spencer, Churchill, who *d.* 1906, dau. of 7th Duke of Marlborough ; 2ndly, 1919, Florence ("Flora"), who *d.* 1925, dau. of John H. Davis, of 24, Washington Square, New York, and widow of 2nd Marquess of Dufferin and Ava ; 3rdly, 1927, Lorna Katherine, who *d.* 1961, dau. of Major Ernest Charles Penn Curzon, and widow of Capt. Quintin Dick, D.L. ; *d.* 1929 ; *s.* by his son [6] FRANCIS RICHARD HENRY PENN, C.B.E., V.D., P.C., 5th Earl, *b.* 1884; Chm. of Roy. National Life-Boat Instn.: *m.* 1st, 1907 (marriage dissolved 1937), his cousin Mary, who *d.* 1962, da. of Col. the Hon. Montagu Curzon, 8th son of 1st Earl Howe; 2ndly, 1937 (marriage dissolved 1943), Joyce Mary McLean, da. of Charles McLean Jack, of Johannesburg; 3rdly, 1944, Sybil Boyter (who m 3rdly 1972 Graham Goodman), da. of Capt. Francis Johnson, of Edinburgh, and formerly wife of the late Maj. Ernest Duncombe Shafto; *d.* 1964; *s.* by his only son [7] EDWARD RICHARD ASSHETON PENN, 6th Earl and present peer; also Viscount Curzon, Baron Curzon, and Baron Howe.

HOWICK OF GLENDALE, BARON.

To serve the King with goodwill.

(Baring.) [Baron U.K. 1960.]

CHARLES EVELYN BARING, 2nd
Baron; *b.* Dec. 30th, 1937; *s.* 1973;
ed. at Eton, and New Coll., Oxford:
m. 1964, Clare Nicolette, yr. da. of
Col. Cyril Darby, MC, of Kemerton
Court, Tewkesbury, Glos., and has
issue.

Arms,—Azure, a fesse or, in chief a bear's
head proper muzzled and ringed or, differenced
by an eastern crown azure. Crest,—A mullet
erminois between two wings argent.
Supporters,—*Dexter*, a tiger guardant proper
gorged with an Eastern crown or; *Sinister*,
a lion guardant purpure crowned with a ducal
coronet or, and gorged with an eastern crown or.
Residence,—Howick, Alnwick, Northumberland.

DAUGHTERS LIVING.
Hon. Rachel Monica, *b.* 1967.
Hon. Jessica Mary Clare, *b.* 1969.
Hon. Alice Olivia, *b.* 1971.

SISTERS LIVING.
Hon. Katherine Mary Alice (*Hon. Lady Wakefield*), *b.* 1936: *m.* 1974, as his 3rd wife, Sir (Edward)
Humphry Tyrrell Wakefield, 2nd Bt.
Hon. Elizabeth Beatrice, *b.* 1940: *m.* 1962. Capt. Nicholas Albany Gibbs, c/o International Bank,
1818, H. St. N.W., Washington 25 DC, USA, and has issue living, Andrew Lionel John, *b.* 1966,—
Mary Camilla, *b.* 1964,—Eliza Jane, *b.* 1968.

WIDOW LIVING OF FIRST BARON.
Lady MARY CECIL Grey (*Lady Mary Howick*), (Howick, Alnwick, Northumberland), da. of 5th Ear
k Grey: *m.* 1935, the 1st Baron, who *d.* 1973.

PREDECESSOR.—[1] *Hon. Sir* EVELYN Baring, *KG, GCMG, KCVO*, yst. son of 1st Earl of Cromer,
b. 1903; Gov. of S. Rhodesia 1942-44, UK High Commr. in Union of S. Africa, and for Basutoland,
Bechuanaland and Swaziland 1944-51, and Gov. of Kenya 1952-59; *cr. Baron Howick of Glendale,*
of Howick, co. Northumberland 1960: *m.* 1935, Lady Mary Cecil Grey, da. of 5th Earl Grey; *d.*
1973; *s.* by his son [2] CHARLES EVELYN, 2nd Baron, and present peer.

Howland, Baron, grandson of Duke of Bedford.

HOY, BARON. (Hoy.) [Life Baron 1970.]

JAMES HUTCHISON HOY, *PC,* son of William Hoy, of Edinburgh; *b.* Jan.
21st, 1909; ed. at Causewayside and Sciennes Public Schs., Edinburgh; a
DL Edinburgh; Vice-Pres. Trustee Savings Bank Assocn. since 1957; PPS to
Sec. of State for Scotland 1947-50; Joint Parl. Sec., Min. of Agric. Fisheries
and Food 1964-70; MP for Leith (*Lab.*) 1945-50, and for Leith Div. of Edinburgh 1950-70; 1939-45 War as Cpl. R. Signals in Middle East and Europe;
cr. PC 1969, and *Baron Hoy,* of Leith, in Co. of City of Edinburgh (Life Baron)
1970: *m.* 1942, Nancy Hamlyn Rae, da. of John McArthur, and has issue.
Residence,—77, Orchard Rd., Edinburgh, EH4 2EX. *Clubs,*—Beefsteak, Royal Scots (Edinburgh).

SON LIVING.
Hon. Ian Richard, *b.* 1945.

HUDSON, VISCOUNTCY OF. (Hudson.) [Extinct 1963.]

DAUGHTER LIVING OF SECOND VISCOUNT.
Hon. Annabel Jocelyne (8, Moncorvo Close, SW7), *b.* 1952: *m.* 1970, Anthony Juan Garton, and has
issue living, Anthony William, *b.* 1974,—Angela Maria Annabel, *b.* 1972.

HUGHES, BARON. (Hughes.) [Life Baron 1961.]

WILLIAM HUGHES, *CBE, PC,* son of the late Joseph Hughes ; *b.* Jan. 22nd,
1911 ; ed. at Balfour Street Sch., Dundee, and at Dundee Technical Coll.;
Hon. LL.D. St. Andrews 1960; Vice-Chm. of Advisory Cttee. of King
George VI. Memorial Club for Old People, Dundee, Hon. Vice-Pres. of Dundee
Old People's Welfare Cttee., of Help the Aged Housing Assocn. (Scotland),
of Boy Scouts' Assocn., Co. of City of Dundee, of Dundee Union of Boys'
Clubs, and of Dundee Branch, British Red Cross, a DL and JP for co. of City
of Dundee, and a Chevalier of Legion of Honour; formerly a Member of Dundee
Town Council (Lord Provost and Lord-Lt. of co. of City of Dundee 1954-60);
Chm. of E. Regional Hosp. Board (Scotland) 1948-60 and a Member of Court of
St. Andrews Univ. 1954-63 and of Council of Queen's Coll., Dundee 1954-63,

Chm. of Glenrothes Development Corporation 1960-64, and a Member of N Scotland Hydro-Electric Board 1956-64; a Parl. Under-Sec. of State, Scottish Office 1964-69, and Min. of State, Scottish Office 1969-70, and 1974-75; India, Borneo and Burma 1944-46 as Capt. RAOC; *cr.* OBE (Civil) 1942, CBE (Civil) 1956, *Baron Hughes,* of Hawkhill, co. of City of Dundee (Life Baron) 1961, and PC 1970: *m.* 1951, Christian Clacher, da. of the late James Gordon, and has issue.

Residence,—East Claverhouse, Dundee.

DAUGHTERS LIVING.

Hon. Christian Alison, *b.* 1952; ed. at Strathclyde Univ. (BSc): *m.* 1973, Alan Cameron Cassels Henry of 88, Balmuildy Rd., Bishopbriggs, Glasgow.
Hon. Janet Margaret, *b.* 1956.

Hunsdon of Hunsdon, Baron, see Baron Aldenham.

HUNT, BARON. (Hunt.) [Life Baron 1966.]

(HENRY CECIL) JOHN HUNT, *CBE, DSO,* son of the late Capt. C. E. Hunt, MC, Indian Army; *b.* June 22nd, 1910; ed. at Marlborough, and RMC; Hon. DCL Durham, and Hon. LLD Aberdeen and London; Col. and Hon. Brig. late KRRC; Comd. 11th Indian Inf. Bde. in Europe 1944-46, and GSO at HQ Allied Staff Central European Command 1949-52; Leader of British Expedition to Mount Everest 1952-53; Assist. Comdt. Staff Coll., Camberley 1953-55, Rector of Aberdeen Univ. 1964-66, and Dir. of Duke of Edinburgh's Award Scheme 1956-67; Chm. of Parole Board for England and Wales 1967-74; Pres. of Council for Volunteers Overseas 1968-74; Head of Relief Missions to Nigeria 1968-70; Chm. Advisory Cttee. on Police in N. Ireland 1969; Member of Roy. Commn. on the Press, and Pres. Nat. Assocn. of Probation Officers since 1974; 1939-45 War in Middle East, India, Greece and Italy; *cr.* DSO 1944, CBE (Mil) 1945, Knt. 1953, and *Baron Hunt,* of Llanvair Waterdine, co. Salop (Life Baron) 1966: *m.* 1936, Joy Mowbray-Green, and has issue, four daughters.

Residence,—Highway Cottage, Aston, Henley-on-Thames.
Clubs,—Ski Club of Great Britain, Alpine.

HUNT OF FAWLEY, BARON. (Hunt.) [Life Baron 1973.]

JOHN HENDERSON HUNT, *CBE, FRCP, FRCS, FRCPG,* son of the late Edmund Henderson Hunt, MCh, FRCS; *b.* July 3rd, 1905; ed. at Charterhouse, and Balliol Coll., Oxford (BCh, MA, DM); FRCP London; FRCS England; FRCGP; Prin. MO Provident Mutual Life Assurance Assocn. since 1947; Cons. Physician St. Dunstan's 1948-66, and Pres. Roy. Coll. of Gen. Practitioners 1967-70; 1939-45 War as Wing-Cdr. RAF Med. Ser.; *cr.* CBE (Civil) 1970, and *Baron Hunt of Fawley,* of Fawley, co. Buckingham (Life Baron) 1973: *m.* 1941, Elisabeth Ernestine, da. of Norman Evill, FRIBA, and has issue.

Arms,—not exemplified at time of going to press.

Residences,—82, Sloane St., SW1; Seven Steep, Fawley Green, nr. Henley-on-Thames, Oxon.
Clubs,—RAF, and MCC.

SONS LIVING.

Hon. Jonathan Philip Henderson, *b.* 1947; BM, BCh, Oxford.
Hon. Christopher Godfrey Evill (twin) *b.* 1947; MA, MB, BS London; MRCS Eng.; LRCP London; DObst, RCOG.

DAUGHTERS LIVING.

Hon. Rosemary, *b.* 1943; ed. at St. Andrews Univ. (MA): *m.* 1974, Dr. Olive Malcolm Senior, BA, PhD, of 55, Warwick Sq., SW1.
Hon. Gillian Mary, *b.* 1951: *m.* 1972, Paul Andrew Richards, MA, of 78, Overstrand Mansions, Prince of Wales Drive, SW11.

HUNTINGDON, EARL OF. (Hastings.) [Earl E. 1529.]

Victory is in truth.

FRANCIS JOHN CLARENCE WESTENRA
PLANTAGENET HASTINGS, 15th Earl; b. Jan.
30th, 1901; s. 1939; ed. at Eton, and at Ch.
Ch., Oxford (MA); 2nd Lt. TA, RHG; an
Artist; Prof. Sch. of Arts & Crafts,
Camberwell 1938, and Central Sch. of
Arts & Crafts, London; Dep. Controller
of Civil Defence, Andover Rural Dist.
Council 1941-45, and Parl. Sec. to Min. of
Agriculture and Fisheries July 1945 to Nov.
1950, Chm. of Cttee. So. of Mural Painters
1951-58, and Pres. of Solent Protection
Soc. 1958-68; author of "The Golden
Octopus" and "Commonsense about
India"; Artist (exhibitions in London,
Paris, Chicago, San Francisco, etc.): m.
1st, 1925, Cristina (who d. 1953 having
obtained a divorce 1943), da. of Marchese
Casati, of Palazzo Barberini, Rome; 2ndly,
1944, Margaret, da. of the late Harry
George Lane, of Vernham Dean, Andover,
and has issue by 1st and 2nd m.

Arms,—Argent, a maunch sable. Crest,—A bull's
head erased sable, armed and ducally gorged or.
Supporters,—Two man tigers (or lions gua dant with
human faces) or, the faces proper.

Residences.—A15, Albany, Piccadilly, W1; Black-
bridge House, Beaulieu, Hants. Clubs,—Garrick,
House of Lords Yacht.

DAUGHTERS LIVING. (By 1st m.)

Lady Moorea (12, Holland Villas Rd., W14 8BT), b. 1928: m. 1st, 1957 (m. diss. 1966), Woodrow Lyle
Wyatt; 2ndly, 1967, Brinsley Black, and has issue living, (by 1st m.) Pericles Plantagenet James
Casati, b. 1963,—(by 2nd m.) Orlando Irvine Casati, b. 1968.

(By 2nd marriage.)

Lady Selina Shirley, b. 1945.
Lady Caroline Harriet, b. 1946: m. 1970, the Hon. Charles Edward Ernest Shackleton, of 10, Canonbury Grove, N1, only son of the 1st Baron Shackleton.

SISTER LIVING.

Lady Norah Frances (Norah, Countess of Kilmorey), b. 1894 : m. 1920, the 4th Earl of Kilmorey, who
d. 1961. Residence,—Mourne Park, Newry, co. Down.

WIDOW LIVING OF SON OF THIRTEENTH EARL.

Winifred, dau. of T. Forsyth-Forrest, formerly of The Querns, Cirencester: m. 1907, the Hon.
Aubrey Craven Theophilus Robin Hood Hastings, who d. 1929, and has issue living [see colls.,
infra]. Residence,—The Lynches, Kingsclere, Newbury, Berks.

COLLATERAL BRANCHES LIVING.

Issue of the late Capt. the Hon. Osmond William Toone Westenra Hastings, 2nd
son of 13th Earl, b. 1873, d. 1933: m. 1896, Mary Caroline Campbell, who d. 1955,
dau. of the late D. Fox Tarratt, of Ellary, Argyllshire:—
DAVID FOX GODOLPHIN, b. Dec. 13th, 1909; ed. at Eton; 1939-45 War in Middle East and
Far East as Fl.-Lt. R.A.F.: m. 1945, Mary, da. of the late Elystan Charles Jones, of Llanfair Grange,
Llandovery, and widow of Edward Hunter Power, RA. Residence,—Timur Beg, Upper Lambourn,
Newbury.——Robin Hood William Stewart, DSO, OBE, MC, b. 1917; ed. at Stowe, and at Ch.Ch.
Oxford; Lt.-Col. (ret.) late Rifle Brig., 1939-45 War in Middle East and Normandy (wounded,
despatches twice, MC, DSO and Bar, OBE); DSO 1944 (Bar 1945), OBE (Mil.) 1946: m. 1950, Jean
Suzanne (HOLBECH), da. of H. Palethorpe, of Stone Manor, Chaddesley Corbett, Worcestershire, and
has issue living, Lucinda Ileene, b. 1955. Residences,—The Malt House, Bramdean, Alresford,
Hants.; 2, Billing Rd., SW10. Club,—White's.——Ileene Wilmot Fox, b. 1898: m. 1918, Capt.
Gordon Armytage Fairbairn, who d. 1973, and has issue living, Stuart William Hastings (12, Hebron
Av., Mt. Pleasant, NSW 2519), b. 1921; ed. at Melbourne Univ. (BSc honours 1947); 1939-45 War as
Sergt. Roy. Austn. Artillery: m. 1949, Virginia, only da. of Dr. Ronald Stott, of Kooyong, Victoria,
and has issue living, Eleanor Ileene b. 1951, Caroline Mary 1959, Linden Helen b. 1962,—Frederick
Logan (of Mirrambeek, Mortlake, Victoria, Aust.), b. 1929: m. 1951, Mary Annette, 3rd da. of the late
Ernest Austin, MC, of Kenton, Ocean Grove, Victoria, Aust., and has issue living, Frederick William
Ernest b. 1955, Julia Anne Westenra b. 1953. Residence,—Arlington, Ocean Grove, Victoria, Aust.
——Dorothy Isabel Westenra (Marchioness of Cambridge), b. 1899: m. 1923, the 2nd Marquess of
Cambridge. Residence,—The Old House, Little Abington, Cambridge.——Osmonda Mary, b. 1903.
Residence,—Little Toyd Farm, Rockbourne, Fordingbridge, Hants.

Grandchildren of the late Hon. Aubrey Craven Theophilus Robin Hood Hastings
(infra):—
Issue of the late Capt. Peter Robin Hood Hastings-Bass, who assumed by deed poll the
additional surname of Bass 1954, b. 1920, d. 1964: m. 1947, Priscilla Victoria (Wells Head
House, Kingsclere, Newbury), da. of Capt. Sir Malcolm Bullock, 1st Bt., MBE (ext.).
William Edward Robin Hood, b. 1948.——Simon Aubrey Robin Hood, b. 1950.——John Peter Robin

Hood, b. 1954.——Emma Alice Mary, b. 1949: m. 1969, Ian Balding, of The Lynches, Kingsclere, Newbury, and has issue living, Clare Victoria, b. 1971.
Issue of the late Hon. Aubrey Craven Theophilus Robin Hood Hastings, 3rd son of 13th Earl, b. 1878, d. 1929: m. 1907, Winifred (ante), dau. of T. Forsyth-Forrest, formerly of The Querns, Cirencester :—
Diana Wilmot, b. 1914.——Joan, b. 1917: m. 1st, 1942, Thomas Frank Bartlett; 2ndly 19—, Kenneth, Porter, of Hitchcock Lane, Westbury, Long Island, NY, USA.

Grandchildren of the late Vice-Adm. the Hon. George Fowler Hastings, C.B., 2nd son of 11th Earl :—
Issue of the late Hans Francis Hastings, b. 1865, d. 1933 : m. 1900, Edyth Mary, who d. 1959, dau. of the late George O. Spratt, formerly of Lamorna, Gibraltar :—
George Godolphin (4. Market St., Naremburn, Sydney, NSW, 2065) b. 1905: m. 1932, Marjory Harris, of Melbourne, Australia, and has issue living, Warren Francis (The Anchorage, Musgrave St., Mosman, NSW) b. 1938: m. 1968; Elaine Adams,—Edyth Leonie (Date St., Adamstown, NSW), b. 1933: m. 1956, (m. diss. 19—), Ross Ekins, and has issue living, David Ross b. 19—, Russel John b. 19— Linda Margaret b. 19—.——Alice Mary Hamilton (Quainton, Milford-on-Sea, Lymington, Hants.), b. 1901, m. 1923, Col. Colin Wilson, RAMC, who d. 1968, and has issue living, Colin David Hastings (c/o Williams Glyn Bank, Kirkland House, Whitehall, SW1), b. 1926; Col. RA: m. 1951, Eileen Edna Fort, and has issue living, Christopher Colin b. 1953, Brian David b. 1954, Sarah Jane Margaret b. 1963,—Monica Hastings, b. 1924: m. 1950, Lt.-Col. David Travers Worsley Gibson, MBE, Roy. Signals, and has issue living, Peter Worsley b. 1951, Helen Morrish b. 1952.——Edythe Cecile, b. 1910: m. 1930, Col. Geoffrey Anderton, RAMC, and has issue living, Rev. Frederic Michael, b. 1931,— Richard Hastings (46, Shaftesbury Way, Twickenham, Middlesex), b. 1946: m. 1974, Susan Challis Bousfield,—Cecile Mary Frances, b. 1933: m. 1959, Trevor Gerald Townsend, of Grove Farm House, Grove Lane, Iden, Rye, Sussex, and has issue living, Michael John b. 1966, Jane Cecile b. 1963. Residence,—Quainton, Milford-on-Sea, Lymington, Hants.

Granddaughters of the late Adm. Alexander Plantagenet Hastings, CB, 2nd son of the late Capt. the Hon. Edward Plantagenet Robin Hood Hastings, 3rd son of 11th Earl:—
Issue of the late Capt. Edward George Godolphin Hastings, CBE, RN, b. 1887, d. 1973: m. 1922, the Hon. Grisell Annabella Gem Cochrane-Baillie (Baldy's Garden, Cuilfail, Lewes, Sussex), da. of 2nd Baron Lamington:—
Marian Hermione Grisell, b. 1924.——Sheila Felicity Phoebe, b. 1925.——Bridget Anne, b. 1928.

Grandchildren of the late Rev. the Hon. Richard Godolphin Hastings, 4th son o 11th Earl:—
Issue of the late Henry John Churchill Hastings (of Robin Hood Estate, P.O. Box 54, Shamva. Rhodesia), b. 1856, d. 1924: m. 1903, Edith Maria, who d. 1966, da. of the late James Clark, of Pendock Court, Tewkesbury:—
Henry Theophilus James, b. 1910: m. 1941, Muriel Hyde, dau. of Walter Turner, of Athol Place, Banket, Rhodesia, and has issue living, David Walter Theophilus, b. 1947: m. 1971, Margaret Netta Allyson, da. of Douglas Andrew Wilkinson, of Forrester Estate Umvukwes, Rhodesia, and has issue living, Kate Rosemary b. 1973. Address,—Robin Hood Estate, PO Box 54, Shamva, Rhodesia.—— Katharine Edith, b. 1904: m. 1930, Bertie Leighton Henderson, who d. 1962, and has issue living, John Leighton, b. 1935,—Anne Katharine, b. 1930: m. 1955, John Michael Somers-Cox of Somers Lodge, PO Barrowdale, Salisbury, Rhodesia [Nightingale Bt., colls.], and has issue living, Anthony John b. 1956, Jane Katharine b. 1962. Residence,—Vivelkia, P.B. 274A, Salisbury, Rhodesia.

Grandchildren of the late Henry John Churchill Hastings (ante):—
Issue of the late Dorothy Agnes Hastings, b. 1905, d. 1970: m. 1930, Leslie Duncan Henderson, who d. 1961:—
Michael John Duncan (Exe, Norton, Rhodesia), b. 1931: m. 1962, Philippa, da. of the late Philip Cecil Braybrooke, Rhodesia Civil Service, of Enstone, Oxon, and has issue living, Bruce Duncan, b. 1967,— Bryony Lesley, b. 1963.——Derek Duncan, b. 1934.

PREDECESSORS.—[1] Sir WILLIAM de Hastings, Knt. (descent deduced from Robert de Hastings, Dispensator to William the Conqueror}; cr. Baron Hastings, of Ashby de la Zouch (peerage of England) 1461; as Master of the Mints at London and Calais introduced the "Noble," a gold coinage of the value of 8s. 4d.; was Ambassador in France and Lord Chamberlain; subsequently fell a victim to the Protector, Gloucester (Richard III.), and was beheaded at the Tower 1483; s. by his son [2] EDWARD, K.B. 2nd Baron, who in 1482 had been summoned to Parliament of England in right of his wife as Baron Hungerford, she having obtained the reversal of the attainder of her father and grandfather in the baronies of Hungerford (cr. 1462), Botreux (cr. 1368), and De Moleyns (cr. 1347); d. 1507; s. by his son [3] GEORGE, 3rd Baron; attended Henry VIII. 1513 at taking of Terouenne and Tournay; cr. Earl of Huntingdon (peerage of England) 1529; d. 1544; s. by his el. son [4] FRANCIS, K.G., P.C., 2nd Earl; was Lt.-Gen. and Com.-in-Ch. of the Army 1549, Lord-Lieut. of Rutland, Leicester, and Warwick, and Master of the Queen's Hart Hounds; d. 1560; s. by his son [5] HENRY, K.G., 3rd Earl; d. 1595; s. by his brother [6] GEORGE, 4th Earl; d. 1605; s. by his grandson [7] HENRY, 5th Earl; d. 1643; s. by his son [8] FERDINANDO, 6th Earl; d. 1655; s. by his son [9] THEOPHILUS, 7th Earl; d. 1701; s. by his el. son [10] GEORGE, 8th Earl; carried the sceptre at Coronation of Queen Anne 1702; d. 1705; s. by his half-brother [11] THEOPHILUS, 9th Earl; carried the Sword of State at Coronation of George II.; d. 1746 s. by his son [12] FRANCIS, 10th Earl; carried the Sword of State at Coronation of George III.; d. 1789, when the Baronies of Hastings, Botreux, and De Moleyns devolved upon his el. sister, Elizabeth, wife of 1st Earl Moira [see E. Loudoun], and the Earldom became dormant, although it was assumed by the lineal descendant of the 2nd Earl, the Rev. Theophilus Henry Hastings, el. uncle of [13] HANS FRANCIS, b. 1779, who took his seat as 11th Earl 1819; was Gov. of Dominica: m. 1st, 1803, Frances, who d. (March) 1820, dau. of the Rev. Richard Chaloner, R. of Great Marlow, Bucks; 2ndly (Sept.), 1820, Eliza Mary, who d. 1846 (having m. 2ndly, 1838, Col. Sir Thomas Noel Harris, K.H.), dau. of Joseph Bettesworth, of Ryde, Isle of Wight, and widow of Alexander Thistlethwayte; d. 1828; s. by his son [14] FRANCIS THEOPHILUS HENRY, 12th Earl: m. 1835, Elizabeth Anne, who d. 1857, dau. of Richard Power, M.P.; d. 1875; s. by his son [15] FRANCIS POWER PLANTAGENET, 13th Earl, b. 1841: m. 1867, Mary Anne Wilmot, who d. 1894, dau. of the Hon. John Craven Westenra, M.P.; d. 1885; s. by his son [16] WARNER FRANCIS JOHN PLANTAGENET, 14th Earl, b. 1868: m. 1892, Maud Margaret, who d. 1953, dau. of the late Sir Samuel Wilson, of 10, Grosvenor Square, W.; d. 1939; s. by his son [17] FRANCIS JOHN CLARENCE WESTENRA PLANTAGENET, 15th Earl and present peer.

HUNTINGFIELD, BARON. (Vanneck.) [Baron I. 1796, Bt. G.B. 1751.]

GERARD CHARLES ARCEDECKNE VANNECK, 6th Baron, and 7th Baronet; *b.* May 29th, 1915; *s.* 1969; ed. at Stowe, and Trin. Coll., Camb. (MA); with UN Secretariat 1946-75; 1939-45 War as Fl. Sgt. RAFVR: *m.* 1941, Janetta Lois, da. of Capt. Reginald Hugh Errington, RN (ret), [see E. Dartmouth, colls.], and has issue.

Arms.—Argent, three bugle horns, two and one, gules, stringed or, and in the fesse point a torteau. Crest,—A bugle horn gules, between two wings elevated argent, tipped or. Supporters,—Two greyhounds ermine, each gorged with a collar paly of six, gules and or, and chained gold.

Address,—c/o Child's Bank, 1, Fleet St., EC4Y 1BD.

Just and loyal.

SON LIVING.

Hon. JOSHUA CHARLES, *b.* Aug. 10th, 1954; ed. at Eton; 2nd Lt. Scots Dragoon Gds.

DAUGHTERS LIVING

Hon. Sara Anne, *b.* 1944: *m.* 1966, Marcus Binney, of 21, Cambridge St., SW1.
Hon. Christina Louise, *b.* 1946: *m.* 1967, Anthony Darell-Brown, R. Green Jackets, of 29, Underhill Rd., Dulwich, SE22, and has issue living, Mark Philip Anthony, *b.* 1969,—Henry Robert, *b.* 1971,—Juliet Cordelia Diana, *b.* 1973.
Hon. Katharine Grace (twin), *b.* 1954.

BROTHER LIVING.

Hon. Peter Beckford Rutgers, *CB, OBE, AFC, AG, b.* 1922; ed. at Geelong Gram. Sch., Australia, at Stowe, at Trin. Coll., Camb. (MA), and at Harvard Univ., USA; late Lt. (P) RN; late Air Commodore RAuxAF; OO No. 3619 (Suffolk) Fighter Control Unit RAuxAF 1959-61; Inspector, RAuxAF 1962-73; Hon. Inspector-Gen. RAuxAF since 1974; Hon. Air Commodore No. 1 MHU RAuxAF; ADC to HM 1963-73; a Gentleman Usher to HM since 1967, and Alderman of City of London since 1969 (a Sheriff 1974-75); KJStJ; a DL for Gt. London; 1939-45 War in RN; OBE (Mil.) 1963, CB (Mil.) 1973: *m.* 1943, Cordelia, da. of Capt. Reginald Hugh Errington, RN (ret.) [see E. Dartmouth, colls.], and has issue living, Charlotte Susan, *b.* 1947: *m.* 1972, H. Dennistoun Stevenson, of 20, Surrey Sq., SE17, and has issue living, Alexander *b.* 1974. *Residences,*—White Lodge, Waldringfield, Woodbridge, Suffolk; 25, Elvaston Pl., SW7. *Clubs,*—White's, Pratt's, and Royal Yacht Squadron.

SISTERS LIVING.

Hon. Sara Carola, *b.* 1913: *m.* 1936, Major David Arthur Peel, M.C., Irish Guards, who *d.* (killed in action in N-W Europe) 1944 [see E Peel, colls.]. *Residence,*—Huntingfield Hall, Halesworth, Suffolk, IP19 0QA.
Hon. Anne Margaret Theodosia, *b.* 1918: *m.* 1940, Peter Moro, F.R.I.B.A., and has issue living, Frances, *b.* 1945: *m.* 1966, John Barnes, of 61, Annandale Rd., SE10, and has issue living, Samuel *b.* 1968, Jessie *b.* 1972,—Alice, *b.* 1948,—Dinah, *b.* 1960. *Residence,*—20, Blackheath Park, Greenwich, SE3.

AUNT LIVING. (*Raised to the rank of a Baron's daughter* 1922.)

Hon. Anne Mary Chaloner (*Countess of Leitrim*), *b.* 1893: *m.* 1st, 1915, Major Percy Rygate Borrett, formerly Scots Guards, from whom she obtained a divorce 1939; 2ndly, 1939, the 5th Earl of Leitrim, who *d.* 1952, when the title became ext., and has issue living, (by 1st m.) Aurea Janet Arcedeckne, *b.* 1916: *m.* 1947, Maj. Owen Courtney Weeks, MBE, RA, of Saxtead Lodge, Woodbridge, Suffolk, and has issue living, Susan Jane Aurea *b.* 1949: *m.* 1970 Adam Duncan Paul, of Parham Hall, Woodbridge, and has issue living, Jonathan Duncan *b.* 1973, Frances Louise *b.* 1974),—Patricia Anne Courtney, *b.* 1953. *Residence,*—Mulroy, co. Donegal.

WIDOW LIVING OF BROTHER OF FIFTH BARON.

Britta (Sylchester, 2/4, Trahlee Rd., Bellevue Hill, Sydney 2023, Aust.), da. of Count Nils Bonde, of Stockholm: *m.* 1939, as his 2nd wife, the late Hon. Andrew Nicolas Armstrong Vanneck, MC, who was raised to the rank of a Baron's son 1922, and *d.* 1965, and has issue living [see colls. infra].

COLLATERAL BRANCHES LIVING.

Issue of the late Hon. Andrew Nicolas Armstrong Vanneck, MC, 3rd son of the Hon. William Arcedeckne Vanneck, 2nd son of 3rd Baron, *b.* 1890, *d.* 1965: *m.* 1st, 1930, Louise (who *d.* 1970, having obtained a divorce 1933), da. of Henry Clews, of The Chateau of La Napoule, France, AM; 2ndly, 1939, Britta (ante), only da. of Count Nils Bonde, of Stockholm, Sweden:—
(By 2nd m.) William Bonde (Trinkey Station, Quirindi, NSW 2343), *b.* 1943: *m.* 1971, Jane Blanton.
——Margita, *b.* 1940: *m.* 1961, David Michael Wheeler, of 124, Avenue Victor Hugo, Paris XVI, France, and has issue living, Andrew Michael, *b.* 1963,—James Nicholas, *b.* 1960.

Issue of the late Hon. Walter Vanneck, 4th son of 3rd Baron, *b.* 1849, *d.* 1931: *m.* 1877, Catherine Medora, who *d.* 1932, dau. of William Armstrong, M.R.C.S., of Toowoomba, Queensland :—
Ralph Wyndham, *b.* 1891: *m.* 1945, Emily Sarah, da. of the late E. A. Bellow.

Grandchildren of the late John Torrance Vanneck, grandson of the late Hon. Tompson Vanneck, 3rd son of 1st Baron:—
Issue of the late John Vanneck, *b.* 1906, *d.* 1974: *m.* 1930, Barbara (Parsonage Point, Rye, NY, USA), da. of Frank Bailey:—
John Bailey (12, East 81st St., New York, NY 10028, USA), *b.* 1938: *m.* 1965, Isabelle Adele Knipe, and has issue living, F. Bailey, *b.* 1970,—Alexandra Knipe, *b.* 1965,—Cynthia Gordon, *b.* 1967.——

William Prentice (Hilltop Pl., Rye, NY, USA), *b.* 1941: *m.* 1962, Nancy Buck, and has issue living, John Lanphear, *b.* 1963,—Richard Prentice, *b.* 1966,—Christine Walker (twin), *b.* 1963,—Sandra Brookman, *b.* 1967.——Marion Louise, *b.* 1937: *m.* 1959, Raymond Robert Konopka, of Plymouth Rd., Rye, NY 10580, USA, and has issue living, Raymond Robert, *b.* 1961,—Lee Bailey, *b.* 1963,— Steven Bailey, *b.* 1966,—Suzanne Louise, *b.* 1959.——Barbara Anne, *b.* 1946: *m.* 1968, James S. May, of Nichols Hill Rd., Dorset, Vermont, USA, and has issue living, Wendy Bailey, *b.* 1968,— Tanya Sheridan, *b.* 1973.

PREDECESSORS.—[1] JOSHUA Vanneck, an eminent London merchant; cr. a *Baronet* 1751; *d.* 1777; *s.* by his el. son [2] Sir GERARD, *M.P.*, 2nd Bt.; *d.* unmarried 1791, *s.* by his brother [3] Sir JOSHUA, 3rd Bt., M.P. for Dunwich; cr. *Baron Huntingfield*, of Heveningham Hall (peerage of Ireland) 1796; *d.* 1816; *s.* by his el. son [4] JOSHUA, 2nd Baron; *b.* 1778: *m.* 1st, 1810, Catherine, dau. of Chaloner Arcedeckne of Glevering Hall, co. Suffolk; 2ndly, 1817, Lucy Anne, who *d.* 1889, dau. of Sir Charles Blois, Bt.; *d.* 1844; *s.* by his son [5] CHARLES ANDREW, 3rd Baron, *b.* 1818: *m.* 1839, Louisa, who *d.* 1898, dau. of the late Andrew Arcedeckne, ef Glevering Hall, Suffolk; *d.* 1897; *s.* by his el. son [6] JOSHUA CHARLES, 4th Baron; *b.* 1842; *d.* 1915; *s.* by his nehpew [7] WILLIAM CHARLES ARCEDECKNE, *KCMG*, son of the Hon. William Arcedeckne Vanneck, 2nd son of 3rd Baron), 5th Baron, 1883; MP for Eye Div., E. Suffolk (*C*) 1923-29; Gov. of Vic., Aust. 1934-39: *m.* 1st, 1912, Margaret Eleanor (CStJ), who *d.* 1943, only da. of the late Judge Ernest Crosby, of New York; 2ndly, 1944, Muriel May Georgina, who *d.* 1953, da. of the late Col. Jemmet Duke, 17th Lancers, and widow of 1st Baron Eltisley; *d.* 1969; *s.* by his el. son [8] GERARD CHARLES ARCEDECKNE, 6th Baron and present peer.

HUNTLY, MARQUESS OF. (Gordon.) [Marquess S. 1599.]

Abiding.

By courage, not by stratagem.

DOUGLAS CHARLES LINDSEY GORDON, 12th Marquess, and Premier Marquess of Scotland; *b.* Feb. 3rd, 1908; *s.* 1937; formerly Lieut. Gordon Highlanders (T.A.): *m.* 1941 (m. diss. 1965), the Hon. (Mary) Pamela Berry, da. of 1st Viscount Kemsley, and has issue.

Arms,—Quarterly: 1st azure, three boars' heads couped or, *Gordon*; 2nd or, three lions' heads erased gules, langued azure, *Badenoch*; 3rd or, three crescents within a double tressure flory counter-flory gules, *Seton*; 4th azure, three fraises argent, *Frazer*. Crest,—Issuing from a ducal coronet or, a hart's head and neck affrontée proper, attired with ten tynes of the first. Supporters,—Two deer-hounds argent, each gorged with a collar gules, the collars charged with three buckles or.

Seat.—Aboyne Castle, Aberdeenshire. *Residence,*—Killigarth House, Devoran, nr. Truro, Cornwall. *Club,*—Puffin's.

SON LIVING.

GRANVILLE CHARLES GOMER (*Earl of Aboyne*) *b.* (Aboyne Castle Home Farm, Aberdeenshire) *b.* Feb. 4th, 1944; ed. at Gordonstoun: *m.* 1972, Jane Elizabeth Angela, da. of the late Lt.-Col. Alistair Monteith Gibb, R. Wilts. Yeo. [see V. Cowdray], and has issue:—
SON LIVING,—Alistair Granville (*Lord Strathavon and Glenlivet*), *b.* July 26th, 1973.

DAUGHTER LIVING.

Lady (Pamela) Lemina, *b.* 1942: *m.* 1970, the Hon. Ian Henry Calthorpe Lawson-Johnston, of Hawkslaw, Coldstream, Berwickshire [see B. Luke].

BROTHERS LIVING. *(Raised to the rank of Marquess's sons, 1937.)*

Lord Adam Granville, *K.C.V.O.*, *M.B.E.*, *b.* 1909; ed. at Eton; is Major R.A. (T.A.), and a Member of Queen's Body Guard for Scotland (Roy. Co. of Archers); Comptroller of the Household to HM Queen Elizabeth the Queen Mother 1953-74, since when an Extra Equerry to HM Queen Elizabeth the Queen Mother; 1939-45 War in N. Africa and Italy (despatches, MBE); MBE (Mil) 1945, CVO 1960, KCVO 1970: *m.* 1947, Pamela, da. of Alexander Herriot Bowhill, CBE, of Inchmarlo, Banchory, Kincardineshire, and has issue living, Adam Alexander, *b.* 1948,—Douglas Herriot, *b.* 1951; a Page of Hon. to HM 1965-67. *Residence,*—Hethersett, Littleworth Cross, Seale, Farnham, Surrey.

Lord Roderic Armyne, *M.B.E.*, *T.D.*, *b.* 1914; ed. at Stowe; is Major 72nd (Hampshire) Anti-Aircraft Brig. R.A. (T.A.); N. Africa 1943 (M.B.E.): M.B.E. (Mil.) 1943: *m.* 1st, 1937, Anne (who obtained a divorce 1949), younger dau. of the late Lieut.-Col. the Hon. Sir Osbert Eustace Vesey, K.C.V.O., C.M.G., O.B.E. [see V. De Vesci, colls.]; 2ndly, 1949, Baroness Joana Alexandra de Stuers, and has issue living, (by 1st m.) David Esmé Douglas (The House by The Water, Shiplake, Henley-on-Thames), *b.* 1937: *m.* 1st 1959 (m. diss. 1962) Audrey Diana, da. of Dermot Carey, of Knutsford, Ches.; 2ndly, 1962, Valerie Elizabeth, da. of Henry Charles Guy Owen, and has issue living, (by 2nd m.) Samantha *b.* 1962,—Angus Lindsay Eustace, *b.* 1941. *Residence,*—Shady Springs Farm, Bentley, Alberta, Canada.

Lord Douglas Claude Alexander, *DSO*, *b.* 1916; ed. at Eton; Lt.-Col. Black Watch, and a Member of Queen's Body Guard for Scotland (Roy. Co. of Archers); Italy 1943-45 (D.S.O.); was a Page of Honour to HM 1930-33; DSO 1945: *m.* 1st, 1940 (m. diss. 1961), Suzanne, da. of the late Lt.-Col. Arthur Houssemayne du Boulay, DSO; 2ndly, 1962, Mrs. Bridget Hutchison, da. of the late Gerald Bryan Ingram, and has issue living, (by 1st m.) Andrew Granville Douglas, *b.* 1942; ed. at Eton; a Page of Honour to HM 1957-60: *m.* 19—, Gillian Thorne, and has issue living, David *b.* 1963, Jamie *b.* 1965,—Douglas George Alexander, *b.* 1947: *m.* 1975, Celina d'Orey, da. of Peter Landsberg, of Rio de Janeiro, Brazil,—Jane Elizabeth, (*Lady Robert H. Mercer Nairne*), *b.* 1950: *m.* 1972, Lord Robert Harold Mercer Nairne [see M. Lansdowne],—(by 2nd m.) Sarah Alexandra, *b.* 1963. *Residence,*—Penpol House Point, Devoran, Truro, Cornwall. *Club,*—Army and Navy.

COLLATERAL BRANCHES LIVING.

Granddaughters of the late Lieut.-Col. George Grant Gordon, C.V.O., C.B., son of the late Lieut.-Col. Lord Francis Arthur Gordon, 6th son of 9th Marquess:—
Issue of the late Brig.-Gen. Laurence George Frank Gordon, C.B., D.S.O., *b.* 1864, *d.* 1943: *m.* 1st, 1895, Florence Juliette, who *d.* 1924, dau. of C. A. Walters, and widow of Alexander McHinch, CIE; 2ndly, 1926, Violet, who *d.* 1970, da. of the late Charles Townshend Murdoch, MP, and widow of Ambrose Yarburgh Lethbridge [see Lethbridge, Bt., colls.]:—

(By 1st m.) Thelma Esme Florence, *b.* 1900: *m.* 1st, 1918 (m. diss. 1921), Sydney Robert Robertson; 2ndly, 1923, Group-Capt. Leslie Acton Kingsford Butt, RAF, who *d.* 1973, and from whom she obtained a divorce 1940; 3rdly, 1940, Leonard Charles Hopwood Coventon, and has issue living, (by 2nd m.) Sonia, *b.* 1924: *m.* *Residence,*—Adastra, Hookwood, Horley, Surrey.

Issue of the late Christian Frederic Gordon, *b.* 1866, *d.* 1934: *m.* 1st, 1894, Margaret (who *d.* 1920, and from whom he had obtained a divorce 1901), widow of Frederick Brooks Close; 2ndly, 1909, Kate Elizabeth, who *d.* 1969, da. of the late Henry Frederick Swan, CB:—
(By 1st marriage) Cicely Margot, *b.* 1899: *m.* 1923, Dr. Alix Lefort, of Paris.——(By 2nd m.) Kittie Ernestine Muriel (Hinton House, Hinton St. Mary, Sturminster Newton, Dorset), *b.* 1911; re-assumed the surname of Gordon in lieu of Loam 1948: *m.* 1st, 1934,—Loam; 2ndly, 1948, Paul Edward Weldon, who *d.* 1972, and has issue living, (by 1st m.) Penelope Jenifer WELDON, *b.* 1939 (legally adopted by her step-father): *m.* 1959, Michael John Brown, and has issue living, Simon Nicholas *b.* 1962, Nichola Kate *b.* 1964,—(by 2nd m.) Paul Frederic Edward (Bittenham Springs, Ewen, nr. Cirencester), *b.* 1948.

PREDECESSORS.—Sir Adam Gordon, Knt., of Huntly, being slain at the battle of Homildon 1402, was *s.* in his estates by his dau. [1] ELIZABETH, wife of Alexander Seton, who in conjunction with her husband obtained in 1408 from Robert, Duke of Albany, a charter of the lands of Gordon, etc., with remainder to their joint heirs; *s.* by their son [2] ALEXANDER Seton; cr. *Earl of Huntly* (peerage of Scotland) 1445; employed in various negotiations to the Court of England 1451-8; defeated the Earl of Crawford then in rebellion at Brechin 1452; *s.* by his son [3] GEORGE, 2nd Earl; *d.* 1470; *s.* by his son [4] ALEXANDER, P.C., 3rd Earl; commanded with Lord Home the left wing of the Scottish Army at Flodden Field; was one of the Council of Regency 1517; *d.* 1523; *s.* by his grandson [5] GEORGE, 4th Earl; constituted Lord Chancellor of Scotland 1546; was killed at the retreat at the battle of Corrichie 1562; his body was afterwards produced in Parliament and in 1563 an Act of Attainder was passed whereby all his honours became forfeited; *s.* by his son [6] GEORGE, 5th Earl; condemned to death for high treason in 1563; was subsequently pardoned, and in 1565 was constituted Lord Chancellor of Scotland ; procured a reversal of his father's attainder 1567; *d.* 1576; *s.* by his son [7] GEORGE, 6th Earl; engaged in a treasonable correspondence with Court of Spain 1588, erected the standard of rebellion in the North 1589, and surrendered to James VI.; tried and found guilty of treason, but was released shortly afterwards on the occasion of the King's marriage; in 1593 his honours were forfeited for complicity in the Spanish and Jesuit Conspiracy ; in conjunction with the Earl of Errol defeated the Royal Army at Strathaven 1594; in 1597 his honours were restored ; cr. *Marquess of Huntly, Earl of Enzie,* and *Lord Gordon of Badenoch* (peerage of Scotland) 1599; *d.* 1636; *s.* by his son [7] GEORGE, 2nd Marquess, who in 1611 had received a charter of the Lordship of Badenoch and in 1632 had been cr. *Viscount Aboyne* with special remainder to his second son ; was a zealous adherent of Charles I., and in consequence was beheaded and his honours attainted in 1649; *s.* by his son [8] LEWIS, 3rd Marquess; in 1651 was granted by the King remission of the attainder of 1649; *s.* by his son [9] GEORGE, 4th Marquess; in 1661 the attainder of 1649 (which had been remitted by the King in 1651) was reversed by Act of Parliament ; cr. *Duke of Gordon, Marquess of Huntly, Earl of Huntly and Enzie, Viscount of Inverness, Lord Badenoch, Lochaber, Strathavon, Balmore, Auchindoun, Garthie, and Kincardine* (peerage of Scotland) 1684; *d.* 1716; *s.* by his son [10] ALEXANDER, 2nd Duke; an earnest partisan of the Chevalier St. George, 1715; *d.* 1728; *s.* by his son [11] COSMO GEORGE, K.T., 3rd Duke; a Representative Peer; *d.* 1752; *s.* by his son [12] ALEXANDER, K.T., 4th Duke; cr. *Baron Gordon of Huntly* and *Earl of Norwich* (peerage of Great Britain) 1784; inherited (through his grandmother) the Barony of Mordaunt of Turvey (cr. 1532), and possibly that of Beauchamp of Bletsoe (cr. 1363); *d.* 1827; *s.* by his son [13] GEORGE, G.C.B., 5th Duke; a Gen. in the Army, &c.; *d.* 1836, when the Dukedom of Gordon (with its accompanying titles, cr. 1684), the Earldom of Norwich, and the Barony of Gordon of Huntly became ext., the Baronies of Mordaunt of Turvey and Beauchamp of Bletsoe became abeyant, and he was *s.* in the Marquessate (cr. 1599) by his kinsman (who also claimed the Earldom of Enzie and the Lordship of Gordon of Badenoch, but whose claim to the Marquessate only was allowed) [14] GEORGE, K.T., 9th Marquess (see note *₊* infra); a Representative Peer 1796-1807; *d.* 1853; *s.* by his son [15] CHARLES, 10th Marquess; *b.* 1792; M.P. for East Grinstead: *m.* 1st, 1826, Elizabeth Henrietta, who *d.* 1839, dau. of 1st Marquess of Conyngham; 2ndly, 1844, Maria Antoinette, who *d.* 1893, dau. of the Rev. Peter William Pegus, and his wife Susannah Elizabeth, Countess Dowager of Lindsey; *d.* 1863; *s.* by his son [16] CHARLES, P.C., 11th Marquess, *b.* 1847; was a Lord-in-Waiting to H.M. Queen Victoria 1870-73, and Capt. of Hon. Corps of Gentlemen-at-Arms 1881: *m.* 1st, 1869, Amy, who *d.* 1920, dau. of Sir William Cunliffe Brooks, 1st and last Bt.; 2ndly, 1922, Charlotte Isabella, who *d.* 1939, dau. of the late John H. Fallon, and widow of James Macdonald, of Cincinatti, Ohio, U.S.A.: *d.* 1937; *s.* by his great-nephew [17] DOUGLAS CHARLES LINDSEY, son of the late Lieut.-Col. (Granville Cecil) Douglas Gordon, C.V.O., D.S.O., son of the late Lord Granville Armyne Gordon, 6th son of 10th Marquess, 12th Marquess and present peer; also Earl of Aboyne, Lord Gordon of Strathavon and Glenlivet, and Baron Meldrum.

₊ [1] Lord CHARLES Gordon, 4th son of 2nd Marquess ; cr. *Earl of Aboyne,* and *Lord Gordon of Strathaven and Glenlivet* (peerage of Scotland) 1660; *d.* 1681; *s.* by his son [2] CHARLES, 2nd Earl; *d.* 1702; *s.* by his son [3] JOHN, 3rd Earl; *d.* 1732; *s.* by his son [4] CHARLES, 4th Earl; *d.* 1794; *s.* by his son [5] GEORGE, 5th Earl; cr. *Baron Meldrum,* of Morven, co. Aberdeen (peerage of United Kingdom) 1815; *s.* his kinsman as 9th Marquess of Huntly (ante).

HURCOMB, BARONY OF. (Hurcomb.) [Extinct 1975.]
DAUGHTERS LIVING OF FIRST AND LAST BARON.
Hon. Cicely Joan, *b.* 1912: *m.* 1940, Cuthbert Antony Norris, of Brookend House, Welland, Worcs., and has issue living, Susan Elizabeth ffiske, *b.* 1946: *m.* 1975, Neil Warbrick, and has issue living, Ada, *b.* 1975,—Teona Felicity, *b.* 1949: *m.* 1974, Paul N. Champkins.
Hon. Pamela, *b.* 1915.

HURD, BARONY OF. (Hurd.) [Extinct 1966.]
SONS LIVING OF LIFE PEER.
Hon. Douglas Richard, CBE, MP (Old Rectory, Alvescot, Oxon.), *b.* 1930; ed. at Eton, and Trin. Coll., Camb.; Dip. Ser. 1952-66, Private Sec. to Leader of Opposition 1968-70, Political Sec. to Prime Min. 1970-74; MP (C) for Mid Oxon since 1974; CBE (Civil) 1974: *m.* 1960, Tatiana Elizabeth Michelle, da. of A. C. Benedict Eyre, of West Burton House, Bury, Sussex, and has issue.

Hon. Stephen Anthony (Browns Farm, Marlborough), *b.* 1933; ed. at Winchester, and at Magdalene Coll., Camb.: *m.* 1973, Pepita, yr. da. of Lt.-Col. Walter Hingston, of The Old Vicarage, Ramsbury Marlborough.

WIDOW LIVING OF LIFE PEER.
STEPHANIE FRANCES (*Baroness Hurd*) (The Old Oxyard, Oare, Marlborough, Wilts.), da. of Edred M. Corner, FRCS: *m.* 1928, Baron Hurd (Life Baron), who *d.* 1966.

Hutchinson, Viscount,   title of Earl of Donoughmore on Roll of H. L.

HUTCHISON OF MONTROSE, BARONY OF. (Hutchison.)
[Extinct 1950.]
WIDOW LIVING OF FIRST BARON.

ALMA, widow, of J. C. Drysdale : *m.* 1st. 1942, as his second wife, the 1st Baron, who *d.* 1950, when the title became ext.; 2ndly, 1954, Brig. Ian Leo William Douglas Laurie, OBE, who *d.* 1970. *Residence,*—Kilrie, Kirkcaldy, Fife.

HYLTON, BARON. (Jolliffe.) [Baron U.K. 1866, Bt. U.K. 1821.]

RAYMOND HERVEY JOLLIFFE, 5th, Baron, and 5th Baronet; *b.* June 13th, 1932; *s.* 1967; ed. at Eton (King's Scholar), and at Trin. Coll.; Oxford (MA); Lt. Coldstream Guards (Reserve); ARICS; Assist. Private Sec. to Gov.-Gen. of Canada 1960-62; a Member of Housing Cttee. LCC 1964-65; Chm. Catholic Housing Aid Soc. 1972-73, a Trustee of Shelter Housing Aid Centre 1969, Vice-Pres. Age Concern (Nat. Old People's Welfare Council) 1971, and Chm. Nat. Fedn. of Housing Assocns. 1973; a Dir. of Christian Industrial Enterprises, Ltd.; DL for Som.: *m.* 1966, Joanna Elizabeth, da. of the late Andrew de Bertodano [E. Mexborough], and has issue.

As much as I can.

Residence,—Ammerdown, Radstock, Bath.

Arms,—Quarterly: 1st and 4th argent, on a pile vert, three dexter hands proper, *Jolliffe:* 2nd and 3rd argent, two bars azure, *Hylton.* Crest,—A cubit arm erect, the hand grasping a scimitar proper, vested vert, cuffed argent, on the sleeve a pile of the last Supporters,—Two lions guardant azure, each charged on the shoulder with three annulets, two and one, or

SONS LIVING.

Hon. WILLIAM HENRY MARTIN, *b.* April 1st, 1967.
Hon. Andrew Thomas Peter, *b.* 1969.
Hon. Alexander John Charles Martin, *b.* 1973.

DAUGHTER LIVING.

Hon. Emily Sylvia Rose Elizabeth, *b.* 1975.

BROTHER LIVING.

Hon. John Hedworth (Potticks House, Bradford-on-Avon), *b.* 1935; ed. at Eton (King's Scholar), and at Ch. Ch., Oxford (BA); a Dir of Cos., Bristol: *m.* 1965, the Hon. Victoria Catherine Elizabeth Eden, el. da. of 7th Baron Henley, and has issue living, Hugo Conrad William, *b.* 1966,—Robert Francis Raymond, *b.* 1968,—Benedict Thomas Aldhelm, *b.* 1970.

SISTER LIVING.

Hon. (Mary) Alice, *b.* 1937 : *m.* 1st 1959 (m. diss. 1969), John Paget Chancellor [see Paget, Bt., cr. 1886]; 2ndly, 1969, the Hon. Richard Archer Alan Windsor-Clive, of Combe, Nettlecombe, Taunton [see E. Plymouth].

AUNT LIVING. *(Daughter of 3rd Baron).*

Hon. Elizabeth Alice Cecilia, *b.* 1906: *m.* 1st, 1928, Lt.-Col. Edmond Joly de Lotbinière (ret.) R.E. (Knt. 1964), from whom she obtained a divorce 1937; 2ndly, 1938 (m. diss. 1946), Hilary Beecham Duke-Woolley, DFC, R.A.F. [see Beecham, Bt.], and has issue living, (by 1st marriage) Thomas Henry (Barmoor House, Bletchingley, Surrey, RH1 4QE), *b.* 1929: *m.* 1953, Prudence Mary, da. of Thomas Richard Bevan, and has issue living, Nicholas Henry *b.* 1955, Lucy Miranda *b.* 1957, Henrietta Romaine *b.* 1960,—Michael Edmond (Rougham House, Bury St. Edmunds), *b.* 1932: *m.* 1956, Angela Patricia Jane, da. of Col. Eugene St. John Birnie [see E. Devon], and has issue living, Christopher David *b.* 1957, Giles Antony *b.* 1959, Tessa Jane *b.* 1962. *Residence,*—

WIDOW LIVING OF FOURTH BARON

Lady PERDITA ROSE MARY ASQUITH *(Dowager Baroness Hylton),* (Ammerdown Park, Radstock, Bath), sister of 2nd Earl of Oxford and Asquith: *m.* 1931, the 4th Baron, who *d.* 1967.

COLLATERAL BRANCH LIVING.

Grandchildren of the late Capt. the Hon. William Sydney Hylton Jolliffe, 4th son of 1st Baron :—
Issue of the late Major Berkeley Gerald Jolliffe, *b.* 1878, *d.* 1956: *m.* 1919, Mary Viola, dau. of Capt. John Douglas Maude Guthrie, of Guthrie Castle, Scotland:—
John Neil Hylton (Barratts Farm, Corton Denham, Sherborne, Dorset) *b.* 1923: *m.* 1957, Eileen Mary, da. of the late Col. George Harold Absell Ing, CMG, DSO, and has issue living, Sarah *b.* 1960,—Lucy, *b.* 1962.——Cynthia Myra, *b.* 1920.——Eileen Daphne, *b.* 1921: *m.* 1st, 1946 (m. diss. 1955), Arthur Harold Morse; 2ndly, 1955, Richard Arthur Edwards, of Tuddenham House, Tuddenham, Ipswich, Suffolk, and has issue living, (by 1st m.) Simon Arthur Davidson, *b.* 1952,—Lavinia May, *b.* 1947,— (by 2nd m.) Chloë Annabel, *b.* 1956,—Miranda Bridget, *b.* 1961.

PREDECESSORS.—[1] WILLIAM GEORGE HYLTON Jolliffe, *P.C.,* son of the late Rev. William John Jolliffe, son of William Jolliffe, M.P. and his wife Eleanor, dau. and heir of Sir Richard Hylton Bt. of Hayton Castle, Cumberland (by Anne, his wife, sister and co-heir of John Hylton, of Hylton Castle, co. Durham); *b.* 1800; sat as M.P. for Petersfield (C) 1830-1 and 1837-66; Under-Sec. for Home Depart. 1852, and Joint Sec. of Treasury 1858-9; cr. a *Baronet* 1821, and *Baron Hylton,* of Hylton Castle, co. Durham, and of Petersfield, co. Southampton (peerage of United Kingdom) 1866, being heir representative of Barony of Hylton or Hilton [cr. 1295]: *m.* 1st, 1825, Eleanor, who *d.* 1862, dau. of the Hon. Berkeley Paget; 2ndly, 1867, Sophia Penelope, who *d.* 1882, dau. of Sir Robert Sheffield, 4th Bt., and widow of 4th Earl of Ilchester; *d.* 1876; *s.* by his son [2] HEDWORTH HYLTON, *b.* 1829 ; M.P. for Wells (C) 1855-68 ; *m.* 1st, 1858, Lady Agnes Mary Georgiana Byng, who *d.* 1878, dau. of 2nd Earl of Strafford ; 2ndly, 1879, Anne, who *d.* 1917, dau. of Henry Lambert, of Carnagh, co. Wexford, and widow of 3rd Earl of Dunraven and Mount Earl; *d.* 1899 ; *s.* by his el. son [3] HYLTON GEORGE HYLTON, 3rd Baron, *b.* 1862 ; in Diplo. Ser. 1888-95 ; M.P. for Wells Div. of Somerset (C) 1895-9 ; was Lord-in-Waiting to H.M. 1915-18, Joint Ch. Govt. Whip in House of Lords 1916-22, and Capt. of Yeomen of the Guard 1918-24 : *m.* 1896, Lady Alice Adeliza Hervey, who *d.* 1962, dau. and co-heir of 3rd Marquess of Bristol; *d.* 1945; *s.* by his son [4] WILLIAM GEORGE HERVEY, 4th Baron, *b.* 1898; Lt.-Col. Coldstream Guards; Lord-Lieut. of Somerset 1949-67: *m.* 1931, Lady Perdita Rose Mary Asquith, sister of 2nd Earl of Oxford and; Asquith; *d.* 1967; *s.* by his son [5] RAYMOND HERVEY, 5th Baron.

HYLTON-FOSTER, BARONESS. (Hylton-Foster.) [Life Baroness 1965.]

AUDREY PELLEW HYLTON-FOSTER, da. of 1st Viscount Ruffside (ext.); b May 19th, 1908; ed. at St. George's, Ascot, and at Ivy House, Wimbledon, Pres. of Co. London Branch British Red Cross Soc. 1960-73 (Dir. of Chelsea Div. 1950-60, and Chm. London Branch 1974); a Member of National Council and Exec. Cttee.; *cr. Baroness Hylton-Foster,* of City of Westminster (Life Baroness 1965): *m.* 1931, the Rt. Hon. Sir Harry Braustyn Hylton Hylton-Foster, QC, MP, Speaker of House of Commons 1959-65, who *d.* 1965.

Residence,—The Coach House, Tanhurst, Leith Hill, Holmbury St. Mary, Dorking, Surrey, RH5 6LQ.

HYNDLEY, VISCOUNTCY OF. (Hindley.) [Extinct 1963.]

DAUGHTERS LIVING OF FIRST VISCOUNT.

Hon. Elizabeth Cairns, *b.* 1912.   *Hon.* Millicent Joyce, *b.* 1914.

IDDESLEIGH, EARL OF. (Northcote.) [Earl U.K. 1885, Bt. E. 1641.]

[Title pronounced "Idsly." Name pronounced "Northcut."]

STAFFORD HENRY NORTHCOTE, 4th Earl and 11th Baronet; *b.* July 14th, 1932; *s.* 1970; ed. at Downside; late 2nd Lt. Irish Gds.; Knt. of Honour and Devotion Sovereign Mil. Order of Malta: *m.* 1955, Maria Luisa (Mima) Alvarez-Builla y Urquijo (Condesa del Real Agrado in Spain, *cr.* 1771), only da. of the late Don Gonzalo Alvarez-Builla y Alvera, and Maria Luisa, Viscountess Exmouth, and has issue.

The Cross of Christ is my Light.

Arms,—Argent, three cross-crosslets in bend sable. **Crest,**—Upon a chapeau gules, a stag trippant argent. **Supporters.**—Two stags proper, and pendant from the neck of each by a gold chain an escutcheon ermine, charged with a fir-cone or.

Seat,—Pynes, Exeter, EX5 5EF. *Residence,*—Shillands House, Upton Pyne, Exeter, EX5 5EB; Royal Yacht Squadron.

SON LIVING.

JOHN STAFFORD (*Viscount* St. Cyres), *b.* Feb. 15th, 1957; ed. at Downside.

DAUGHTER LIVING.

Lady Mary Louise, *b.* 1959.

BROTHER LIVING.

Hon. Edward Frederic, *b.* 1934; ed. at Downside, and at Trin. Coll., Oxford (MA); Maj. Intelligence Corps (T & AVR); Cyprus 1957; Assocn. of Inst. of Cost and Works Accountants; a Prin. Officer HM Treasury 1969-71: *m.* 1963, Vivien Sheena, da. of Col. Robert John Augustine Hornby, OBE, [see Bruce, Bt., colls., *cr.* 1628], and has issue living, Edward Bede Robert Hornby, *b.* 1964,— Alexander Benet Paul Hornby, *b.* 1971,—Modwenna Vivien Hornby, *b.* 1968. *Residence,*—91, Cottenham Park Rd., Wimbledon, SW20 0DS.

SISTERS LIVING.

Lady Catherine Cecilia Mary, *b.* 1931 ; is a Religious of the Assumption.
Lady Hilda Susan Mary, *b.* 1937: *m.* 1957, Conrad Marshall John Fisher Swan, PhD, York Herald, and has issue living, Andrew Conrad Henry Joseph, *b.* 1964,—Mary Elizabeth Magdalen, *b.* 1959,— Hilda Juliana Mary, *b.* 1961,—Catherine Sylveria Mary, *b.* 1962,—Anastasia Cecilia Mary, *b.* 1966. *Residence,*—Boxford House, Boxford, nr. Colchester.

WIDOW LIVING OF THIRD EARL.

ELIZABETH (*Dowager Countess of Iddesleigh*), (Pynes, Exeter EX5 5EF), da. of the late Frederic Sawrey Archibald Lowndes, of 9, Barton St., Westminster, SW1: *m.* 1930, the 3rd Earl, who *d.* 1970.

COLLATERAL BRANCHES LIVING.

Issue of the late Rev. the Hon. Arthur Francis Northcote, 4th son of 1st Earl, *b.* 1852, *d.* 1943 : *m.* 1st, 1877, Alice Caroline, who *d.* 1878, dau. of Edward R. Owen, of Oxford; 2ndly, 1880, Mary Arabella, who *d.* 1888, dau. of the late S. Bush Toller, Q.C.; 3rdly, 1892, Emily Catharine, who *d.* 1931, dau. of the late Col. Samuel Blomfield Kekewich, of Tiverton, Devon :—

(By 3rd m.) Evelyn Olivia Stafford, *b.* 1893: *m.* 1938, Ronald Frederick Green. *Residence,*—10, Golden Miller Lane, Polegate, Sussex.

Grandchildren of the late Rev. the Hon. Arthur Francis Northcote (ante):—

Issue of the late Sir Geoffry Alexander Stafford Northcote, K.C.M.G., *b.* 1881, *d.* 1948 : *m.* 1910, Edith Juliet Mary, who *d.* 1958, dau. of the late Rev. James Williams Adams, V.C. [Wilshire, Bt.] :—

Maxwell Adams Stafford, *b.* 1911; ed. at King's Sch., Canterbury, and at Balliol Coll., Oxford: *m.* 1958, Katharine, youngest dau. of the late Charles Campbell Sheild, of Taumarunui, New Zealand. *Address,*—P.O. Box 827, Nairobi, Kenya.

Issue of the late Dorothea Mary Northcote, *b.* 1882, *d.* 1964: *m.* 1914, Bryan Hook, *d.* 1925:—

Ivan (5, Harmsworth Rd., Tadley, Basingstoke), *b.* 1915; late Sqdn. Leader RAF: *m.* 1949, Glacie Lucille, da. of the late Arthur Howard Watts, and has issue living, Jaqueta Carolyn *b.* 1953, Bryony Claire *b.* 1956: *m.* 1975, Alistair James Paton, of 312, Kings Rd., Reading, Berks.— Stafford, *OBE* (986, Coral Drive, Pebble Beach, Cal., USA), *b.* 1916; Cdr. RN (ret.); 1939-45 War (despatches, prisoner); OBE (Mil) 1940: *m.* 1945, Manie Montrose, da. of Col. J. M. Graham, of Pebble Beach, Cal., USA, and has issue living, Malcolm Stafford Graham, *b.* 1947, Lucy Elizabeth Hilary *b.* 1950.——Hilary (Kiserian, Box 45, Kiganjo, Kenya; Cavalry Club), *b.* 1917; Col. late 7th Queen's Own Hussars; Mil. Attaché, Khartoum 1962: *m.* 1951, Jane Ann, da. of Maj. T. A. G. Budgen, MC, and has issue living, Simon David George, *b.* 1956,—Charles Harry, *b.* 1959.

Granddaughter of the late Sir Geoffry Alexander Stafford Northcote, K.C.M.G.
(ante):—
Issue of the late Major Amyas Henry Stafford Northcote, M.C., *b.* 1916, *d.* (killed in
action in Burma) 1944: *m.* 1941, Mollie Gordon Buchanan (who *m.* 2ndly, 1947,
Antony Smallwood), dau. of Major Gordon Buchanan Scott, of Zaria, Horsham:—
Sylvia Rosalind Stafford, *b.* 1942: *m.* 1968, Antony Cokayne Doulton, of 41, Hans Place, SW1, and
has issue living, Natasha Ophelia Stafford, *b.* 1971.

Granddaughter of the late Hon. Hugh Oliver Northcote, 5th son of 1st Earl :—
Issue of the late Hugh Hamilton Stafford Northcote, *b.* 1887, *d.* 1929: *m.* 1925, Josephine,
who *d.* 1928, dau. of the late Thomas O'Shaughnessy, of Killacolla, Glin, ∞.
Limerick :—
Mary Edith, (c/o Lloyds Bank, 16, St. James's St., S.W.1), *b.* 1926.

Issue of the late Hon. Amyas Stafford Northcote, 7th son of 1st Earl, *b.* 1864, *d.*
1923: *m.* 1890, Helen May, who *d.* 1936, dau. of the late James Garrard Dudley,
of Frankfort, Kentucky, U.S.A. :—
Cecilia Helen, *b.* 1894. *Residence,*—Bracken, Bucklebury Common, Berks.

(*In remainder to Baronetcy, cr.* 1641 *only.*)

Grandchildren of the late Rev. Henry Moubray Northcote, brother of 8th Bt.:—
Issue of the late James Alfred Northcote, M.B.E., *b.* 1861, *d.* 1928: *m.* 1893, Edith
Marion, who *d.* 1905, dau. of James Dupre Lance, of Canterbury, New Zealand :—
Thomas Francis, *b.* 1894: *m.* 1924, Frances Vera, dau. of Arthur Hope, of Tumanako, Timaru,
New Zealand, and has issue living, Peter Stafford, *b.* 1928 : *m.* 1957, Geraldine Margaret, dau. of
Gerald Murray, of Glenmore, Lake Tekapo, NZ, and has issue living, Hugh Stafford *b.* 1960, Michael
John *b.* 1962, Margaret Anne *b.* 1959,—George Arthur (32, Merivale Lane, Christchurch 1, NZ), *b.*
1929: *m.* 1960, Julia Elvira Morton Watkins, and has issue living, Charles Moubray *b.* 1961, Cynthia
Jane *b.* 1962, Diana Mary *b.* 1964,—Frances Roma, *b.* 1931: *m.* 1956, John Endell Wanklyn, of
Mount Alexander, Hawarden, NZ, and has issue living, David Endell *b.* 1959, Catherine *b.* 1957,
Jaquetta *b.* 1958. *Residence,*—Highfield, Waipara, NZ.——Elizabeth Marion *b.* 1896: *m.* 1924, Stuart
Cameron Heard, and has issue living, Richard Kemp (of Hawk Hills, Kaikoura, Marlborough, NZ), *b.*
1925: *m.* 1953, Margaret Elizabeth, da. of George McLaughlin, of St. Leonards, Culverdun, NZ, and
has issue living, David James Stuart, *b.* 1958, Henry Richard George *b.* 1960, Sally Elizabeth *b.* 1955,
Lucinda Mary *b.* 1957, Benita Evelyn *b.* 1962,—James Stuart (Dunbars Rd., Halswell, Christchurch 3,
NZ), *b.* 1928: *m.* 1959, Barbara, da. of Geoffrey Smith, of Christchurch, NZ, and has issue living,
Geoffrey Stephen *b.* 1961, Michael James *b.* 1963,—Garry Antony, *b.* 1932: *m.* 1954, Rosemary Ruth,
da. of Lyndon Peter, of Kaikoura, NZ, and has issue living, Guy Antony *b.* 1958, Nicola Jane *b.* 1955,
Belinda Anne *b.* 1959,—Roderick Cameron, *b.* 1935: *m.* 1960, Perena Avril, da. of the late R. C.
Royston, of Sotik, Kenya, and has issue living, Andrew Roderick Richard *b.* 1962, Avril Perena
Elizabeth *b.* 1964, Lydia Suzanne *b.* 1968. *Residence,*—Kaikoura, Marlborough, NZ.

Grandchildren of the late Capt. Lewis Stafford Northcote, only son of the late
Rev. Stafford Charles Northcote, 3rd son of 7th Bt.:—
Issue of the late Cecil Stafford Northcote, *b.* 1870, *d.* 1912: *m.* 1906, Ida Sybil Mary,
who *d.* 1963, dau. of Capt. Joseph Boulderson:—
Lewis Stafford, *b.* 1907; European War 1939-45 as Capt. R.A.: *m.* 1935 Esmé, dau. of Capt. Lyon-
Campbell, of Stockhill, Settle, Yorks., and has issue living, Sarah Caroline Patricia, *b.* 1936: *m.* 1962,
Cdr. Patrick Timothy Sheehan, AMIBM, RN, and has issue living, Timothy Patrick *b.* 1966, Clare
Anne *b.* 1963, Joanna Mary *b.* 1965,—Jacqueta, *b.* 1937. *Residence,*—St. Catherine's, East Hendred,
Wantage, Oxon.——Cecil Henry (*posthumous*), *b.* 1912: ed. at Douai, and at Queen's Coll., Oxford
(BA 19—, MA 1937); is Headmaster of St. Bede's Sch., Bishton Hall, Staffs., a Co. Councillor of
Staffs., a Gov. of King Edward VI Gram. Sch. Stafford and Church of England Sch., Colwich,
Staffs., and a Knight of Honour and Devotion of Sovereign Order of Malta: a Rural Dist. Councillor:
m. 1936, Freda, da. of the late Frederic Williams and has issue living, Amyas Henry Stafford, *b.*
1937; ed. at Ch. Ch., Oxford (MA); a JP of Staffs.,—Hugh Cecil Camden, *b.* 1938; ed. at Trin. Coll.,
Camb. (MA): *m.* 1974, Hilary Jane, yr. da. of Col. R. J. C. Evans, of Cage Hill, Stowe-by-Chartley,
—Julia Marguerite Mary, *b.* 1941. *Residence,*—Bishton Hall, Staffs.——Sybil Mary, *b.* 1910: *m.*
1952, George Hudson, who *d.* 1970, and has issue living, Mary Agnes, *b.* 1955. *Residence,*—Icknield,
East Hendred, Wantage, Oxon.

Issue of the late Ernest Alfred Stafford Northcote, *b.* 1875, *d.* 1944: *m.* 1900, Sarah Potwin,
who *d.* 1911, dau. of the late Col. Gilbert Dwight Munson, Judge and Lawyer,
Ohio, U.S.A.:—
Oliver Stafford (650, South Grand Av., Los Angeles, Cal. 90017. USA), *b.* 1906; ed. at Stanford Univ.
Cal. (AB, LLB); Bar. Cal., 1933; a member of legal firm of Chandler, Wright, Tyler & Ward, of
Los Angeles, USA, and of American, Californian and Los Angeles Bar. Assos., and Lt.-Cdr. USNR;
Lt USN 1942-45: *m.* 1933, Dorothy Lucille, da. of James A. Ham, and has issue living, Philip,
Stafford (2964, Java Rd., Costa Mesa, Cal. 92626, USA), *b.* 1937: *m.* 19—, , da. of
Embajadores Lane, Mission Viejo, Cal. 92675, (USA), *b.* 1937: *m.* 1964, Sharon Ann, da. of Vachel
Conn Foree, Jr., and has issue living Douglas Stafford *b.* 1971,—John Stafford (6709, Hickory Av.,
Orangeville, [Cal. 95662, USA), *b.* 1940: *m.* 1966, Virginia Lee Camden, da. of the late William
Henry Wright.

Grandchildren of the late Stafford Charles Northcote, el. son of Stafford Henry
Northcote (*b.* 1813), son of Stafford Northcote, 2nd son of Henry Northcote,
2nd son of 5th Bt.:—
Issue of the late Stafford Henry Northcote, *b.* 1872, *d.* 1950: *m.* 1st, 1907, Elizabeth Helène
Louise, who *d.*1914, el. dau. of the late Robert Philip Heilgers, formerly Austro-Hungarian
Consul at Calcutta ; 2ndly, 1921, Lucy May, who *d.* 1971, widow of Herbert Laurence
Vaughan, of Bournemouth :—
(By 1st m.) Stafford Charles Robert (43, St. James's Close, Prince Albert Rd., NW8), *b.* 1909; ed. at
Brighton Coll.; late Ch. Gen. Manager, Chartered Bank: *m.* 1st, 1907, Helen Isabel, who *d.* 1965,
da. of Herbert Nelson Hawker, of Christchurch, NZ; 2ndly, 1972, Sheila Mary, widow of Dr. Paul
H. Sandifer, and has issue living (by 1st m.), Stafford Robert (182, London Rd., Deal, Kent, CT14
9PT), *b.* 1948: *m.* 1969, Penelope Anne Tracy, da. of (Thomas) Michael Eastham, QC,—Helena
Ann Stafford, *b.* 1951.——Elizabeth Joy Stafford, *b.* 1907: *m.* 1933 (m. diss. 1953), Lt.-Col. Arthur
Neville Browning, Artists' Rifles, and has issue living, Jonathan Neville, *b.* 1944,—Carolyn Neville,
b. 1940. *Residence,*—Flat B, Ratton Court, Ratton Drive, Willingdon, Eastbourne.

Grandchildren of the late Stafford Henry Northcote (*b.* 1872) (ante):—
Issue of the late Geoffrey Stafford Northcote, *b.* 1912, *d.* 1968: *m.* 1938, Rhoda C. Ruth
(60, Rosetta Rd., Raumati South, NZ), da. of the late A. McNeill, of Auckland, NZ:—
Robert Stafford, 38, Cooper Place, Beaumont, SA 5066, *b.* 1939; ed. at Univ. of Wellington (MSc),
and Univ. of Adelaide (PhD); Man. Internat. Computers Ltd., Adelaide: *m.* 1963, Patricia Margaret,
da. of the late Arthur Baillie, of Adelaide, and has issue living, Roger Stafford, *b.* 1966,—Bruce
Stephen, *b.* 1969,— Michelle Patricia, *b.* 1972.——Alan McNeill (40, Abbott St., Wellington, N4, NZ),
b. 1940; ed. at Univ. of Wellington (B.Com.), ARANZ: *m.* 1963 Marie Vesey, da. of E. A. Zambra, of
Napier, NZ, and has issue living, Peter Bruce, *b.* 1964,—Stuart Paul, *b.* 1966,—Susan Mary, *b.* 1967.
——Geoffrey John, *b.* 1947.——Margaret Moralee, *b.* 1950: *m.* 1971, Wallace Donald Thomson, of
Christchurch, NZ.

Grandchildren of the late Cyril Charles Stafford Northcote (infra):—
Issue of the late John Wilfrid Cyril Stafford Northcote, *b*. 1904, *d*. 1970: *m*. 1st, 1933, Mary
Caroline (who obtained a divorce 1937), yr. da. of the late Robert Collier, FRIBA; 2ndly,
1938, Grace Carruthers, da. of E. Carruthers Webb, of Mill Hill, Middx.; 3rdly, 1952, Janet
(c/o Barclays Bank, 191, Earls Court Rd., SW5), el. da. of Ronald Grose, of Manor Rd.,
Taunton:—
(By 1st m.) Jennifer Anne Stafford, *b*. 1935: *m*. 1955, John Morley, of 18, The Parkway, Leabrook,
Adelaide, S. Aust., and has issue living, Robert, *b*. 1956,—Peter, *b*. 1957,—Jasper, *b*. 1959,—David
John, *b*. 1964,—Amanda Caroline, *b*. 1966.——(by 3rd m.) Martin Charles Stafford, *b*. 1953.——
Nigel John Stafford, *b*. 1960.——Andrew Alexander Stafford, *b*. 1964.——Gillian Stafford, *b*. 1954.

Grandchildren of the late Stafford Charles Northcote (ante):—
Issue of the late Cyril Charles Stafford Northcote, *b*. 1874, *d*. 1946: *m*. 1903, Adela, who *d*.
1963, dau. of the late Sir William Bowyer-Smijth, 11th Bt.[Bowyer-Smyth, Bt.]:—
Joan Annette Fechnie Stafford (The Studio, 3, Challoner Cres., W14), *b*. 1907: *m*. 1951, Robert Steuart-
Clark, who *d*. 1953.

Issue of the late Major Leonard Augustus Stafford Northcote, *b*. 1879, *d*. 1942: *m*. 1st,
1903, Lilian Cora (who obtained a divorce 1914), dau. of the late J. van Praagh,
formerly of 209, Maida Vale, W.; 2ndly, 1916, Ida (of Nelson House, Strand St., Sandwich,
Kent), dau. of the 5th Marquis Testaferrata-Olivier du Puget (Maltese Nobility):—
(By 1st marriage) Denis Leonard Stafford, *b*. 1904; ed. at Clifton; Major (retired) late R.A.: *m*. 1929,
Sylvia, dau. of the late Col. J. Manners Smith, V.C., Indian Army, and has issue living, Sylvia Alison,
b. 1930,—William John, *b*. 1939,—Veronica Phyllis, *b*. 1932, *Address*,—c/o National Provincial
Bank, Salisbury, Wilts.——Iris Blanche Stafford, *b*. 1909: *m*. 1928, Maurice Ashley Brown.——
(By 2nd marriage) Henry James, *b*. 1922; ed. at Downside; is a Film Technician: *m*. 1949
(marriage dissolved 1961), Sheila, da. of Capt. John Manahan. *Residence*,—Nelson House, Strand
St., Sandwich, Kent.

Issue of the late Major Arthur Frederick Stafford Northcote, D.S.O., *b*. 1881, *d*. 1949: *m*.
1st, 1905, Constance Fanny (who *d*. 19—, having obtained a divorce 1930), da. of the late.
Col. William Henry Salmon, Indian Army (ret.); 2ndly, 1930, Dora, who *d*. 1932, da. of
Congreve Jackson, OBE; 3rdly, 1938, Beryl (Applegarth, 2, Forest Hills, Camberley, Surrey),
da. of the late Rev. W. H. Weekes, of Devizes:—
(By 2nd marriage) Annette Stafford, *b*. 1931: *m*. 1952 Harry Alexander Thomas. *Residence*,—

Grandchildren of Leonard Beauchamp Northcote, yst. son of the late Stafford
Henry Northcote (*b*. 1813) (ante):—
Issue of the late Henry Peter Northcote, *b*. 1891, *d*. 1971: *m*. 1924, Eileen (Alwin, The Green,
Jordans, Beaconsfield, Bucks.), da. of Edwin Charles Irish:—
Edwin Charles Stafford (Alwin, The Green, Jordans, Beaconsfield, Bucks.), *b*. 1926; ed. at Blundell's
Sch.: *m*. 1956 (m. diss. 1974), Angela, da. of James Edward Hutton, and has issue living, Ashley
James Stafford, *b*. 1959,—Belinda Susan, *b*. 1965.——Anne, *b*. 1936.

Issue of the late Frederick Beauchamp Northcote, *b*. 1893, *d*. 1937: *m*. 1923, Jessie Florence
(70, Clapham Court, Gloucester), da. of William James:—
Leon Frederick James (of 29, Orchard Rd., Longlevens, Gloucester), *b*. 1924: *m*. 1951, Valerie May,
dau. of Victor Thomas George Bennett, and has issue, Richard Leon Stafford, *b*. 1952,—Susan
Elizabeth, *b*. 1954.

Grandchildren of the late Ellen Jane Gresham (infra):—
Issue of the late Arthur Seilyard Gresham, *b*. 1881, *d*. 1945: *m*. 1910, Mary Catherine, who *d*.
1963, dau. of the late Joseph Lowery Ewing:—
Thomas Ewing, *b*. 1912; is a Bank Manager; *m*. 1938, Doreen, dau. of the late Virney Comer.
Address,—c/o Bank of New Zealand, Mount Manganui, New Zealand.——Betty Mary Madeleine,
b. 1915: *m*. 1st, 1938, Eric Arthur Brainsby, from whom she obtained a divorce 19—; 2ndly, 19—,
Deryk Olive Fisher, and has issue living, (by 1st marriage) Anthony Gresham, *b*. 1939,—Elizabeth
Mary, *b*. 1941,—Priscilla Sally, *b*. 1948. *Residence*,—13, Egremont St., Belmont, Takapuna,
Auckland, New Zealand.

Grandson of the late Stafford Henry Northcote (*b*. 1813) (ante):—
Issue of the late Ellen Jane Northcote, *b*. 1846, *d*. 1938: *m*. 18—, Thomas Gresham, who
d. 1920:—
Garnet Stafford, *b*. 1886 ; is a Dental Surg.: *m*. 1915, Nina Cavaye, and has issue living, June, *b*. 19—:
m. 19—, —— Holland, and has issue living, a son *b*. 19—, a son *b*. 19—.

Grandchildren of the late Edward Northcote (infra):—
Issue of the late Gilbert Charles Northcote, *b*. 1903, *d*. 1967: *m*. 1930, Marguetite Muriel
(Mahonga Park, Rand, NSW), da. of Joseph William Nicholas:—
Mildred Reynell, *b*. 1931: *m*. 1961, Alexander Walter English, of Redbank, Deniliquin, NSW, and has
issue living, Alexander Northcote, *b*. 1966,—Jean Constance Northcote, *b*. 1962,—Marguerite Louise
Northcote, *b*. 1964.——Gillian Mary Stafford, *b*. 1932: *m*. 1954, Mardi Walker, of Murray Heights,
Jingellic, NSW, and has issue living, Rowena Marius, *b*. 1960.

Issue of Gladys Mary Northcote, *b*. 1888, *d*. 1956: *m*. 1918, Edward Rowden White, MD, of
Pynes, 1, Douglas St., Toorak, Melbourne, Aust.:—
James Northcote Rowden, *b*. 1921; AIF; *d*. (on active ser.) 1942.——Elizabeth Rowden, *b*. 1923: *m*.
1949, H. A. L. Moran, of Pynes, 1, Douglas St., Toorak, Melbourne, Aust., and has issue living,
Andrew Rowden, *b*. 1952,—Timothy Edward, *b*. 1955,—Georgina Reynell, *b*. 1950.

Granddaughter of the late Gilbert Charles Northcote, 7th son of the late Stafford
Northcote (ante):—
Issue of the late Edward Northcote, *b*. 1854, *d*. 1926: *m*. 1884, Mary Georgina Howard, who
d. 1932. dau. of Henry Reynell:—
Doris (twin), *b*. 1888: *m*. 1924, David Taylor, who *d*. 1946, and has issue living, David (of St. John-
stone, Campbell Town, Tasmania), *b*. 1924: *m*. 1950, Elizabeth Jean, da. of Allan Mackinnon, of
Dalness, Evendale, Tasmania, and has issue living, David *b*. 1951, Gilbert Allan *b*. 1963, Catherine
Margaret *b*. 1953, Marguerite Jean *b*. 1954, Marian Reynell *b*. 1957, Elizabeth Northcote (twin) *b*.
1957,—Arminell Judith Reynell, *b*. 1926: *m*. 1948, Allan McLean Mackinnon, of Glen Esk, Conara,
Tasmania, and has issue living, Ian McLean *b*. 1949, David McLean *b*. 1951, Roy McLean *b*. 1952.
Residence,—Glen Esk, Conara, Tasmania.

Grandchildren of the late Horace Northcote (infra):—
Issue of the late Ronald Cecil Northcote, OBE, MM, *b*. 1895, *d*. 1972: *m*. 1934, Joan Eileen
(Quadrant House, Ferry Quay, Woodbridge, Suffolk), da. of John Everard Grafton
Grattan:—
Geoffrey Malcolm (Ferry Quay, Woodbridge, Suffolk), *b*. 1942: *m*. 1969 (m. diss. 1974), Diana Maria,
da. of the late Edmund Maria Hellmer, of Vienna, and has issue living, Lara Veronica, *b*. 1970.——
Veronica Stella (17 Quay St., Woodbridge, Suffolk), *b*. 1940.

Issue of the late Capt. Malcolm Philip Northcote, *b*. 1908, *d*. 1971: *m*. 1st, 1933, Eileen Natalie
Colt, from whom he obtained a divorce 1954, da. of Edward Walter David Colt Williams,
MC, Bar.-at-law; 2ndly, 1956, Moya (Flat F, 25, Eaton Sq., SW1), yr. da of the late William
Maidment, of Parrett Lodge, Bridgwater, Som.:—
(By 2nd m) Amanda Louise, *b*. 1958.——Vanessa Jane (twin), *b*. 1958.

Granddaughters of the late Gilbert Charles Northcote (ante):—
Issue of the late Horace Nothcote, b. 1865, d. 1914: m. 1890, Stella Louisa, who d. 1931, dau.
of the late Charles James Reynolds:—
Audrey Margery, b. 1897: m. 1924, Robert Cuthbert Lee, and has issue living, Ivan Robert Douglas,
b. 1929,—Moira Dawn Audreen, b. 1923: m. 1961, John Godfrey, of 98, Goswell End Rd., Harlingnot,
Dunstable,—Maureen Audrey Wendy, b. 1928. Residence,—St. Cyres, 79, Newport Rd., Woburn
Sands, Milton Keynes, Bucks., MK17 8UN.——Guinevere Olga, b. 1900: m. 1st, 1927, Leslie Ernst
Wintersgill, who d. 1969, and from whom she obtained a divorce 1946; 2ndly, 1952, John Collier, and
has issue living, (by 1st m.) Temple Robin Ernst (51, Granville Place, High Rd., N12), b. 1928;
assumed the surname of Northcote in lieu of his patronymic by deed poll 1949; late WO RE: m.
1950, Eira Marion, da. of the late Leonard Walter Johnson, and has issue living, Ifor Alan Temple,
b. 1952, Kim Norman Austin b. 1957,—Diana Guinevere, b. 1930: m. 1952, Brian James Dobbie, of
1, West Leith, Duckmore Lane, Tring, Herts., and has issue living, Janet Marion b. 1956, Gillian
Patricia b. 1958, Katherine Ann b. 1965. Residence,—3, Lansdowne Rd., Finchley, N3.

PREDECESSORS.—[1] JOHN NORTHCOTE, M.P. for Ashburton 1640-48, for Devon 1654-60, and
for Barnstaple 1667-76, cr. a Baronet 1641; d. 1676; s. by his son [2] ARTHUR, 2nd Bt.; d. 1688;
s. by his son [3] FRANCIS, 3rd Bt.; d.s.p. 1709; s. by his brother [4] HENRY, M.D., 4th
Bt.; d. 1729; s. by his son [5] HENRY, 5th Bt., M.P. for Exeter 1734-43; d. 1743; s. by
his son [6] STAFFORD, 6th Bt.; d. 1771; s. by his son [7] STAFFORD HENRY, 7th Bt.; d.
1851; s. by his grandson [8] STAFFORD HENRY, G.C.B., D.C.L., P.C., 8th Bt., son of the
late Henry Stafford Northcote, Esq. (el. son of 7th Bt.); b. 1818; was Pres. of Board of Trade
1866-7, Sec. of State for India 1867-8, Chancellor of the Exchequer 1874-80, First Lord of
the Treasury 1885-6, Sec. of State for Foreign Affairs 1886-7, and Lord-Lieut. of Devonshire; sat as M.P. for Dudley (C) 1855-7, for Stamford 1858-66, and for N. Devon 1866-85;
cr. Viscount St. Cyres, of Newton St. Cyres, co. Devon, and Earl of Iddesleigh (peerage of
United Kingdom) 1885: m. 1843, Cecilia Frances, C.I., who d. 1910, sister of 1st Baron Farrer,
d. Jan. 12th, 1887; s. by his el. son [9] WALTER STAFFORD, C.B., 2nd Earl, b. 1845; Private
Sec. to his father 1867-8, and 1874-7, Commr. of Inland Revenue 1877-86, Dep. Chm. thereof
1886-92, and Chm. 1892: m. 1868, Elizabeth Lucy, who d. 1928, dau. of Sir Harry Stephen
Meysey-Thompson, 1st Bt.; d. 1927; s. by his nephew [10] HENRY STAFFORD (youngest son of
the late Rev. the Hon. John Stafford Northcote, 3rd son of 1st Earl), 3rd Earl, b. 1901: m. 1930,
Elizabeth, JP, da. of the late Frederic Sawrey Archibald Lowndes, of 9, Barton St., Westminster,
SW1; d. 1970; s. by his son [11] STAFFORD HENRY, 4th Earl and present peer; also Viscount
St. Cyres.

Ikerrin, Viscount, son of Earl of Carrick.

ILCHESTER, EARL OF. (Fox-Strangways.) [Earl G.B. 1756.]

MAURICE VIVIAN DE TOUFFREVILLE
Fox-Strangways, 9th Earl; b. April 1st,
1920; s. 1970; ed. at Kingsbridge Sch.;
Group Capt. RAF; CEng, AFRAeS,
FSE, FINucE, FRSA, MBIM: m.
1941, Diana Mary Elizabeth, el. da. of
the late George Frederick Simpson, of
Cassington, Oxon.

Arms,—Quarterly: 1st and 4th sable, two lions
passant paly of six argent and gules, Strangways;
2nd and 3rd ermine, on a chevron azure, three foxes'
heads erased or, a canton of the 2nd, charged
with a fleur-de-lis of the 3rd, Fox. Crest.—On a
chapeau azure, turned up ermine, a fox sejant or.

Deeds without words.

Supporters.—Dexter, a fox ermine, frette or, collared dovetail azure, and the collar charged with
three fleurs-de-lis gold : sinister, a fox proper, collared as the dexter.
Address,—c/o Lloyds Bank, 6, Pall Mall, SW1. Clubs,—Brooks's, RAF.

BROTHER LIVING.
Hon. RAYMOND GEORGE (Downes, Cherry Orchard, Trull, Taunton), b. Nov. 11th, 1921; ed. at Exeter
Sch., and Seale Hayne Agric. Coll.; with Gov. Communications Radio Staff: 1939-45 War in RAF:
m. 1941, Margaret Vera, da. of the late James Force, of North Surrey, BC, and has issue living,
Robin Maurice (32, Beech Close, Southam, Warks.), b. 1942; ed. at Loughborough Coll., with Lloyds
Bank: m. 1969, Margaret Elizabeth, da. of the late Geoffrey Miles, of Camberley, Surrey, and has
issue living, Simon James b. 1972,—Charlotte Helen b. 1974,—Paul André (Downes, Cherry Orchard,
Trull, Taunton), b. 1950; ed. at Loughborough Coll.; with Exec. and Trustee Depart. Lloyds Bank.

SISTER LIVING.
Lady Jeanne Doreen, b. 1931: m. 1958, Peter Skelton, publisher, from whom she obtained a divorce
1969. Residence,—St. Anthony, Higher Woodfield Rd., Torquay.

AUNTS LIVING.
Sylvia (of Puddavine, Totnes, Devon), b. 1890.
Elinor (of Puddavine, Totnes, Devon), b. 1893.

DAUGHTER LIVING OF SEVENTH EARL.
Lady Teresa Jane, b. 1932: m. 1st, 1953, the 9th Viscount Galway, who d. 1971; 2ndly, 1972, Mark
Agnew. Residences,—Melbury House, Dorchester, Dorset; Bishopfield House, Bawtry, Doncaster,
Yorks.

DAUGHTER LIVING OF SIXTH EARL.
Lady Mabel Edith (Dowager Viscountess Wimborne), b. 1918: m. 1938, the 2nd Viscount Wimborne,
who d. 1967. Residence,—Rozel, Mount Durand, St. Peter Port, Guernsey.

COLLATERAL BRANCHES LIVING.

Granddaughter of the late Rev. Henry Fox-Strangways (b. 1828), el. son of the late
Rev. Henry Fox-Strangways (b. 1793), son of the late Rev. the Hon. Charles
Redlynch Fox-Strangways, 3rd son of 1st Earl :—
Issue of the late Major Theodore Stephen Fox-Strangways, b. 1862, d. 1917: m. 1898,
Rosamund Cleere, who d. 1958, dau. of the late Charles Edmund Newton, of Mickleover
Manor, near Derby :—
Pamela Mary, b. 1907. Residence,—Hunterswood, Galmpton, Brixham, S. Devon.

Granddaughter of the late Col. Walter Aston Fox-Strangways, RA, son of the
late Rev. Henry Fox-Strangways (ante) :—
Issue of the late Lieut.-Col. Harold Stephen Fox-Strangways, b. 1864, d. 1912: m. 1891,
Beatrice Talbot, who d. 1939, dau. of the late Maj.-Gen. William Howey, Bengal Inf. :—

Marjorie, b. 1894: m. 1st, 1917, Capt. Wilfred Harold Swift, Indian Army, who d. (killed in action)
1917; 2ndly, 1919, Capt. Harry Thomas Ridlington, formerly Indian Army, who d. 1956, and from
whom she had obtained a divorce 1936, and has issue living, (by 2nd m.) Jack Harry, b. 1920; Maj.
Gloucestershire Regt.; 1939-45 War in Italy (wounded); Korea 1951-52 (despatches, wounded):
m. 1941, Brigid Mary, da. of T. Myers, and has issue living, Michael John b. 1942: m. 19—, Rosemary
Ann, da. of the late Lt.-Col. Robin Charles Burleigh Stuart [see E. Castle Stewart, colls.], Peter
Charles b. 1954, Denise Mary b. 1944, Pauline Ann, b. 1946, Jacqueline Brigid b. 1955,—Peter Harold
(Junior Army and Navy Club), b. 1927; ed. at King Edward VI Sch., Stourbridge; Maj. Roy.
Signals late Roy. Army Educational Corps,—Stella Mary, b. 1922: m. 1948, William Proctor Bell,
and has issue living, Rosemary Annette b. 1951, Priscilla Mary b. 1956. Residence,—358, Ewell Rd.,
Surbiton, Surrey.

PREDECESSORS.—[1] STEPHEN FOX, MP for Shaftesbury 1726-41; cr. Lord Ilchester, of Ilchester,
co. Somerset, Baron of Woodford, Strangways, co Dorset (peerage of Great Britain) 1941, Lord
Ilchester and Stavordale, Baron of Redlynch, co. Somerset (peerage of Great Britain) 1747, with
remainder to the issue male of his brother Henry, and Earl of Ilchester (peerage of Great Britain)
1756, with like remainder; assumed the additional surname of Strangways 1758; d. 1776; s. by
his son [2] HENRY THOMAS, 2nd Earl; d. 1802; s. by his son [3] HENRY STEPHEN, DCL, 3rd Earl;
Capt. of Yeomen of the Guard; d. without surviving male issue 1858; s. by his half-brother [4]
WILLIAM THOMAS HORNER, 4th Earl; b. 1795; was Under Sec. of State for Foreign Affairs 1835 and
Ambassador to German Confederation 1840-9; d.s.p. 1865; s. by his nephew [5] HENRY EDWARD
(son of the Hon. John George Charles, 4th son of 2nd Earl, by Amelia, who d. 1886, sister of 1st
Baron Tweedmouth), 5th Earl; b. 1847; Capt. of HM Queen Victoria's Corps of Gentlemen-at-Arms
1873-4, and Lord-Lieut. of Dorsetshire: m. 1872, Lady Mary Eleanor Anne Dawson, who d. 1935,
only da. of 1st Earl of Dartrey; d. 1905; s. by his son [6] GILES STEPHEN HOLLAND, GBE, 6th Earl;
b. 1874; Chm. of Trustees of National Portrait Gallery, a Trustee of British Museum, Chm. of Roy.
Commn. on Historical Documents (England), and a FSA; Pres. of Roy. Literary Fund 1940-50:
m. 1902, Lady Helen Mary Theresa Vane-Tempest-Stewart, who d. 1956, da. of 6th Marquess of
Londonderry; d. 1959; s. by his el. son [7] EDWARD HENRY CHARLES JAMES, 7th Earl: b. 1905:
m. 1931, Helen Elizabeth, who d. 1970, da. of the late Capt. the Hon. Cyril Augustus Ward, MVO [E.
Dudley]; d. 1964; s. by his kinsman [8] WALTER ANGELO (el. son of Maurice Walter Fox-Strangways,
CSI, 2nd son of Col. Walter Fox-Strangways, great-grandson of the Rev. the Hon. Charles Fox-
Strangways, 3rd son of 1st Earl), 8th Earl, b. 1887: m. 1916, Laure Georgine Emilie, who d. 1970, da.
of the late Evanghelos Georgios Mazaraki, Treasurer, Suez Canal Co.; d. 1970; s. by his el. son [9]
MAURICE VIVIAN DE TOUFFREVILLE, 9th Earl and present peer; also Baron Ilchester, Baron Strang-
ways, and Baron Ilchester and Stavordale.

ILFORD, BARONY OF. [Hutchinson.] [Extinct] 1974]
WIDOW LIVING OF LIFE BARON

JANET BIDLAKE (Baroness Ilford), (12, Church Row, Hampstead, NW3),
da. of the late Henry Frederick Keep, of Edgbaston: m. 1919, Baron Ilford
(Life Baron), who d. 1974, when the title became ext.

ILIFFE. BARON. (Iliffe.) [Baron U.K. 1933.]

Live, that you may live.

EDWARD LANGTON ILIFFE, 2nd Baron ; b.
Jan. 25th, 1908 ; s. 1960 ; ed. at Sherborne,
and at Clare Coll., Camb.; Vice-Chm. Bir-
mingham Post & Mail, Ltd., Chm., Coventry
Evening Telegraph, a Gov. of Roy. Shakespeare
Theatre, Stratford-on-Avon, and a Trustee of
Shakespeare's Birthplace; High Sheriff, Berks.
1957; 1939-45 War in R.A.F. Vol. Reserve
(despatches): m. 1938, Renée da. of R.
Merandon du Plessis, of Mauritius.

Arms.—Sable, a lion rampant double-queued between
four crosses pattée flory or. Crest,—In front of a demi-lion
rampant double-queued sable, collared or, three crosses as in
the arms. Supporters—Dexter, a scribe holding in the exterior
hand an open parchment proper; sinister, a printer of the time
of Caxton holding in the exterior hand in front of his body a
composing stick proper.

Seat,—Basildon House, Lower Basildon, Reading, RG8
9NR.

SISTER LIVING.

Hon. Kathleen, b. 1904 : m. 1926, Leslie Frederick Laurence,
and has issue living, Elizabeth, b. 1928. Address,—P.O. Box
1202, Nassau, Bahamas.

WIDOW LIVING OF SON OF FIRST BARON.

Christine Marie, dau. of Alfred Eaton Baker, M.D., of Hastings, Sussex: m. 1940, the Hon.
William Henry Richard Iliffe, who d. 1959, and has issue living [see colls. infra]. Residence,—
Croftdown, Aldworth, Reading, Berks.

COLLATERAL BRANCH LIVING.

Issue of the late Hon. William Henry Richard Iliffe, younger son of 1st Baron, b. 1911, d.
1959: m. 1940, Christine Marie (ante), dau. of Alfred Eaton Baker, M.D., of Hastings,
Sussex :—
ROBERT PETER RICHARD (The Malt House, Yattendon, Berks.), b. Nov. 22nd, 1944: m. 1966,
Rosemary Anne, twin da. of Cdr. Arthur Grey Skipwith, RN [see Skipwith, Bt., colls.], and has issue
living, Edward Richard, b. 1968,—George Langton, b. 1970,—Thomas, b. 1973,—Florence (twin),
b. 1973.——John David, b. 1947.

PREDECESSOR.—[1] EDWARD MAUGER Iliffe, G.B.E., son of the late William Isaac Iliffe, J.P., of
Allesley, near Coventry ; b. 1877 ; Chm. of Guildhall Insurance Co., Ltd., a Director of London
Assurance, Pres. and Principal Proprietor Birmingham Post and Birmingham Mail, Proprietor of
Coventry Evening Telegraph, and Cambridge Daily News, and a Member of Lloyd's ; sometime Chm.
of Kelly's Directories, Ltd., and of Iliffe & Sons, Ltd., Dep. Chm. of Allied Newspapers, Ltd., and
part owner of Daily Telegraph ; Controller of Machine Tool Depart., Min. of Munitions 1917-18;
Pres. of Asso. of British Chambers of Commerce 1932-3, and of Govs. of Shakespeare Memorial

Theatre of Stratford-on-Avon 1933-58, Master of Coach Makers' and Coach Harness Makers' Co. 1936, of Stationers' and Newspapermakers' Co. 1937, and of Clockmakers' Co. 1946 ; Hon. Air-Commodore No. 916/7 Squadron R.A.F. 1939-44 ; Chm. of Duke of Gloucester's Red Cross and St. John Fifty-Seven Million Fund 1939-45 ; sat as M.P. for Warwickshire, Tamworth Div. (U) 1923-9 ; cr. Baron Iliffe, of Yattendon, co. Berks (peerage of United Kingdom) 1933 : m. 1902, Charlotte, who d. 1972, da. of Henry Gilding, JP, of Gateacre, near Liverpool; d. 1960; s. by his el. son [2] EDWARD LANGTON, 2nd Baron and present peer.

ILLINGWORTH, BARONY OF. (Illingworth.) [Extinct 1942.]

WIDOW LIVING OF FIRST BARON.

MARGARET MARY CLARE, A.R.R.C. (Baroness Illingworth), dau. of the late William Basil Wilberforce, of Markington Hall, near Harrogate, Yorkshire ; is Comdt. V.A.D.: m. 1931, as his second wife, the 1st Baron, who d. 1942, when the title became ext. Address,—c/o National Provincial Bank, 12, Mount St., W1.

INCHCAPE, EARL OF. (Mackay.) [Earl U.K. 1929.]

With a strong hand.

·MANU·FORTI·

KENNETH JAMES WILLIAM MACKAY 3rd Earl ; b. Dec. 27th, 1917; s. 1939; ed. at Eton, and at Trin. Coll., Camb. (MA); Chm. of Inchcape & Co., Ltd., since 1958, and of P. & O. Steam Navigation Co. since 1973, a Dir. of Guardian Royal Exchange Assurance Group, of Standard Chartered Banking Group, of British Petroleum Co., Ltd., and of Burmah Oil Co., Ltd., Pres. of Commonwealth Soc. for the Deaf, Dep. Pres. of Roy. Soc. for India, Pakistan and Ceylon; a Freeman of City of London; Prime Warden of Shipwrights' Co. 1967, and Renter Warden of Fishmongers' Co. 1975; Chm. of Council for Middle East Trade 1963-65; 1939-45 War with 12th Lancers in France, as Maj. 27th Lancers in Central Mediterranean, and with Mil. Govt., Vienna: m. 1st, 1941, Aline Thorn (from whom he obtained a divorce 1954), da. of Sir Richard Arthur Pease, 2nd Bt. (cr. 1920), and widow of Patrick Claude Hannay, F.O. AAF; 2ndly, 1965, Caroline Cholmeley, el. da. of Cholmeley Harrison, of Emo Court, co. Leix, and has issue by 1st and 2nd ms.

Arms,—Per chevron azure and argent in chief two lymphads of the last, and in base a Bengal tiger proper. Crest,—A cubit arm holding a falcon proper. Supporters,—Dexter, a lion rampant gules supporting a pendant argent charged with a saltire also gules ; sinister, a Bengal tiger proper supporting a like pendant.

Residences,—Glenapp Castle, Ballantrae, Ayrshire; Quendon Park, Saffron Walden, Essex; Tulchan Lodge, Glenisla, Angus.

SONS LIVING. (By 1st m.).
KENNETH PETER LYLE (Viscount Glenapp) (c/o Inchcape Berhaw Ltd., Singapore), b. Jan. 23rd, 1943; ed. at Eton; AIB: m. 1966, Goergina, da. of S. C. Nisbet, and has issue:—
DAUGHTER LIVING—Hon. Elspeth, b. 1972.
Hon. James Jonathan Thorn (34A, Dorset Sq., NW1), b. 1947; ed. at Eton, and Trin. Coll., Camb. (MA): m. 1970, Mary Caroline, el. da. of Peter Joyce, of Becklands Farm, Whitchurch Canonicorum, Dorset, and has issue living, Sophie, b. 1974.

(By 2nd m.)
Hon. Shane Lyle, b. 1975.

DAUGHTER LIVING. (By 1st m.)
Lady Lucinda Louise, b. 1941; ed. at Edinburgh Univ. (MA).

BROTHER LIVING.
Hon. Alan John Francis, b. 1919 ; ed. at Eton, and at Trin. Coll., Camb. : m. 1st, 1945, Janet Mary Wallis, who obtained a divorce 1947 ; 2ndly, 1948, Sonia, who obtained a divorce 1953, dau. of the late Capt. James Richard Tylden, of Milsted Manor, Kent ; 3rdly, 1955, Countess Lucie Cathinka Christiane Julie, only dau. of Count Curt Ludwig Haugwitz-Hardenberg-Reventlow, of Brahe-Trolleborg, Korinth. Fyn, Denmark, and has issue living, (by 2nd marriage) Siobhan Amanda, b. 1949: m. 1973, Christopher O. B. Carver,—Kristina Mary, b. 1951: m. 1975, Simon M. F. Lamb. Residences,—Enterkine, Annbank, by Ayr; Inishanboe, Oughterard, co. Galway.

HALF-BROTHER LIVING.
Hon. Simon Brooke, (Baron Tanlaw), b. 1934; cr. Baron Tanlaw (Life Baron) 1971 [see that title].

HALF-SISTER LIVING.
Lady Rosemary, b. 1936: m. 1957, Francis Martin French, and has issue living, Ewan Alexander Francis, b. 1959,—Anna-Louise Rosemary, b. 1961,—Nicola Catharine, b. 1967,—Kirsty Elizabeth, b. 19—. Residence,—Little Offley, Hitchin, Herts.

AUNT LIVING. (*Daughter of 1st Earl.*)

Lady Effie, *b.* 1895 ; is an O.St.J. : *m.* 1920, Sir (John Henry) Eugen (Vanderstegen) Millington Drake, KCMG, who. *d.* 1972, and has issue living, James Mackay Henry (The Manor House, Shepperton-on-Thames), *b.* 1928; Lt. RN (Emergency Reserve); Dir of Inchcape & Co., Ltd.: *m.* 1953, Manon, yr. da. of R. Redvers-Bate, and has issue living, Tristan James *b.* 1956, Tarquin Julian *b.* 1965, Manon Regina *b.* 1954, Tamsin Alice *b.* 1962,—Edgar Louis Mackay Vanderstegen, *b.* 1932. *Residence,*—Palazzo Taverna, via di Monte Giordano 36, 00186 Rome, Italy.

WIDOW LIVING OF SECOND EARL.

LEONORA MARGARET, el. dau. of the late H.H. the Rajah (Sir Charles Vyner Brooke), of Sarawak, G.C.M.G. [see V. Esher]: *m.* 1st, 1933, as his second wife, the 2nd Earl, who *d.* 1939; 2ndly, 1946, Col. Francis P. Tompkins, US Army. *Residence,*—27, Highland Rd., Northfield, Vermont, USA.

PREDECESSORS.—[1] JAMES LYLE Mackay, *G.C.S.I., G.C.M.G., K.C.I.E.*, son of the late James Mackay, of Arbroath, Forfarshire, by his wife, Deborah Lyle; *b.* 1852; four years Pres-of Bengal Chamber of Commerce, and a Member of Council of India 1897-1911 : a partner in Mackinnon, Mackenzie and Co., of Calcutta, Bombay, Karachi, Colombo, Hong Kong, and Shanghai, of Gray, Dawes and Co., and of Macdonald, Hamilton and Co. of Australia, a Director of National Provincial Bank, Ltd., Chm. and Managing Director of British India Steam Navigation Co., and P. and O. Steam Navigation Co., Chm. of P. & O. Banking Corporation, and Vice-Pres. of Suez Canal Co. ; *cr.* Baron *Inchcape*, of Strathnaver, co. Sutherland (peerage of United Kingdom) 1911, *Viscount Inchcape*, of Strathnaver, co. Sutherland (peerage of United Kingdom) 1924, *Viscount Glenapp*, of Strathnaver, co. Sutherland, and *Earl of Inchcape* (peerage of United Kingdom) 1929: *m.* 1883, Jane Paterson, who *d.* 1937, el. dau. of the late James Shanks, of Rosely, Arbroath, Forfarshire ; *d.* 1932 ; *s.* by his son [2] KENNETH, 2nd Earl; *b.* 1887 ; a partner in Mackinnon, Mackenzie & Co., Pres. of P. & O. Banking Corporation, and a Director of P. & O. Steam Navigation Co. : *m.* 1st, 1915, Frances Caroline Joan (who *d.* 1983, and from whom he had obtained a divorce 1931), dau. of the late Rt. Hon. John Francis Moriarty, Lord Justice of Appeal ; 2ndly, 1933, Leonora Margaret, el. dau. of H.H. the Rajah (Sir Charles Vyner Brooke) of Sarawak, G.C.M.G. [V. Esher]; *d.* 1939 ; *s.* by his son [3] KENNETH JAMES WILLIAM, 3rd Earl, and present peer, also Baron Inchcape, Viscount Inchcape, and Viscount Glenapp.

INCHIQUIN, BARON. (O'Brien.) [Baron I. 1543, Bt. I. 1686.]

LAMH·LAIDIR·AN·UACHTAR

V·I·G·V·E·V·R   DE·DESSVS

Strength from above.

PHAEDRIG LUCIUS AMBROSE O'BRIEN, 17th Baron, and 9th Baronet; *b.* April 4th, 1900; *s.* 1968; ed. at Eton, Magdalen Coll., Oxford (MA) and Imperial Coll., London Univ.; Maj. (ret.) Rifle Bde.; late Colonial Ser. Overseas Geological Survey; 1939-45 War in Somalia, Abyssinia, and Madagascar, attached E. African Intelligence Corps. (wounded, despatches): *m.* 1945, Vera Maud, da. of the late Rev. Clifton Samuel Winter.

Arms.—Quarterly: 1st and 4th, gules, three lions passant guardant in pale ; per pale or and argent; 2nd, argent, three piles meeting in point issuing from the chief gules ; 3rd, or, a pheon azure. **Crest.**—Issuing from a cloud an arm embowed, brandishing a sword argent, pommel and hilt or. **Supporters.**—Two lions guardant per fesse or and argent.

Residences,—Thomond House, Dromoland, co. Clare; Hanway Lodge, Richards Castle, Ludlow, Salop; Winton House, Dawlish, Devon.

BROTHER LIVING.

Hon. FIONN MYLES MARYONS (36, Florence Court, Roman Way, Andover, Hants., SP10 5HZ), *b.* Oct. 28th, 1903; ed. at Radley, and at Loughborough Engineering Coll., 1939-45 War as Flight-Lt. RAF Vol. Reserve: *m.* 1939, Josephine Reine, da. of the late J. E. Bembaron, of Herne Cottage, Long Ditton, Surrey, and has issue living, Conor Myles John, *b.* 1943; Capt. 14/20th King's Hussars,—Fiona Jane, *b.* 1941: *m.* 1965, Romano Obert de Thieusies, (2nd son of Vicomte Obert de Thieusies), of The White House, Calvert Cres., Dorking, Surrey, and has issue living, Patrick *b.* 1968, Isabelle *b.* 1966, Sophie *b.* 1972.

SISTER LIVING.

Hon. Griselda Ethelreda Clodagh, *b.* 1906 : *m.* 1953, David Clifford Christopherson, D.S.C. *Residence,*—Cherry Tree Cottage, Holmwood, Dorking, Surrey.

AUNT LIVING. (*Daughter of 14th Baron.*)

Hon. Beatrice, *b.* 1882 ; sometime a Lady-in-Waiting to the Queen of Italy : *m.* 1st, 1905 (dissolution of marriage granted in Fiume Feb. 12th, 1924, and confirmed by Italian Court), Senatore Guglielmo Marconi, G.C.V.O., LL.D., D.Sc. (afterwards Marchese), who *d.* 1937: 2ndly, March 1924 (in Italy), Liborio Marignoli, Marquis di Montecorona, who *d.* 1948, and has issue living, (by 1st m.),—Degna, *b.* 1908: *m.* 1938, Gabriele Paresce, Italian Ambassador to Korea (of Italian Embassy, Seoul, Korea), and has issue living, Francesco Leone Guglielmo *b.* 1940,—Gioia Yolanda, *b.* 1916: *m.* 1954, George Atkinson Braga, of Church St., Alpine, New Jersey, USA, and has issue living, Michael George Marconi *b.* 1961, Allegra Beatrice Maud *b.* 1958,—(by 2nd m.) Flaminia (40, Via Mangili Parioli, Rome, 00197) *b.* 1928: *m.* 1st, 1946, Capt. William Lack, USA Army, from whom she obtained a divorce (in Florida, USA) 1955; 2ndly, 1958, Vico Vaccaro, and has ssue living, (by 1st m.) Jeffrey William *b.* 1947, Michael Andrew *b.* 1949, (by 2nd m.) Giorgio *b.* 1959. *Residence,* —40, Via Mangili Parioli, Rome, Italy.

DAUGHTERS LIVING OF SIXTEENTH BARON.

Hon. Deirdre Jane Frances, *b.* 1924: *m.* 1954, Horace Beecher Chapin, MD. *Residences:*—136, East 64th St., New York 21, USA; Quinville Abbey, Quin, co. Clare.

Hon. Grania Rachel, *b.* 1928; was Social Sec. to British Ambassador to Peru 1958-60: *m.* 1973, Hugh William Lindsay Weir, of Ballinakella Lodge, Whitegate, co. Clare.

WIDOWS LIVING OF SONS OF FOURTEENTH BARON.

Rose, dau. of —— and formerly wife of Elie N. Ades, of Alexandria, Egypt : *m.* 1928, as his second wife, the Hon. Donough O'Brien, who *d.* 1953. *Residence,*—51, South Street, W1. *Club,*—English-Speaking Union.

Edith Lawrie (3, Ibris Place, N. Berwick, E. Lothian), widow of T. M. Steele: *m.* 1964, as his 2nd wife, Capt. the Hon. Henry Barnaby O'Brien, who *d.* 1969.

COLLATERAL BRANCHES LIVING.

Issue of the late Lieut.-Col. the Hon. Murrough O'Brien, D.S.O., M.V.O., 2nd son of 14th Baron, *b.* 1866, *d.* 1934: *m.* 1906, Marguerite, who *d.* 1958, dau. of William Lewis, of New York:—

Murrough Richard, *b.* 1910; ed. at Eton, and at Balliol Coll., Oxford; sometime Major Irish Guards; European War 1939-45 : *m.* 1st, 1942, Irene Clarice [formerly wife of (i) the 10th Marquess of Queensberry, and (ii) Sir James Hamet Dunn, 1st Bt. (cr. 1921)], dau. of H. W. Richards, of Regent's Park, NW1; 2ndly, 1952, Joan, da. of Charles Pierre Jenkinson, and widow of Capt. Woolf Barnato, and has issue living, (by 2nd m.) Conor John Anthony, *b.* 1952; ed. at Eton,— Melissa Jane *b.* 1956. *Residences,*—34, Connaught Sq., W2; Primrose Hill, West Drive, Sunningdale, Berks. *Club,*—White's.——Edward Cecil, *OBE, b.* 1915; ed. at Eton; sometime Capt. Irish Guards, and Maj. Parachute Regt.; OBE (Civil) 1959: *m.* 1943 (m. diss. 1968), Elizabeth Margaret, da. of the late Col. Sir William Henry Dyke Acland, 3rd Bt. (cr. 1890), MC, AFC, TD, and has issue living, Lucia Jane, *b.* 1947,—Emily Teresa, *b.* 1952. *Club,*—St. James'.

Issue of the late Hon. Edward Donough O'Brien, 3rd son of 14th Baron, *b.* 1867, *d.* 1943 : *m.* 1899, Lady Beatrice Mary Hare, who *d.* 1960, dau. of 3rd Earl of Listowel :—

Enid Moira, *b.* 1903: *m.* 1st, 1928, Rowland Frank Taaffe Finn, from whom she obtained a divorce 1940; 2ndly, 1941, Walter William Wilkinson, and has issue living, (by 1st marriage) Peter Patrick Taaffe *b.* 1931.

Granddaughters of the late Capt. the Hon. Henry Barnaby O'Brien (infra):—

Issue of the late Desmond Barnaby O'Brien, *b.* 1926, *d.* 1969: *m.* 1955, Cherry Angela Mary (42, Kinnerton St., SW1), yr. da. of the late Lt.-Col. (Frank) James (Wriothesley) Seely [see Seely Bt., colls.];—

Karen, *b.* 1956.——Sara Jane, *b.* 1961.

Issue of the late Capt. the Hon. Henry Barnaby O'Brien, 5th son of 14th Baron, *b.* 1887, *d.* 1969: *m.* 1st, 1925, Lady Helen Baillie-Hamilton, OBE, who *d.* 1959, sister of 12th Earl of Haddington; 2ndly, 1964, Edith Lawrie (ante), widow of T. M. Steele:—

(By 1st m.)—Michael George (Kerfield, Peebles), *b.* 1928; late Irish Guards: *m.* 1955, Susan Mary Matilda, da. of Wing-Cdr. Robert Cecil Talbot Speir, OBE, RAF, and has issue living, Peter Thomond, *b.* 1961,—John Michael, *b.* 1964,—Gillian Ursula Helen, *b.* 1956,—Rebecca, *b.* 1957.

Issue of the late Hon. William Henry Ernest Robert Turlough O'Brien, 3rd son of 13th Baron, *b.* 1863; *d.* 1943: *m.* 1901, Henrietta Ethne, who *d.* 1950, dau. of the late George Robert Browne [M. Sligo, colls.]:—

Turlough George Henry, *b.* 1907; ed. at Harrow; late Lieut. RNVR: *m.* 1939 (m. diss. 1966), Catherine, da. of the late Dr. John Watt Senter, of Edinburgh, and has issue living, Patrick Brian, *b.* 1943, —Diana *b.* 1941: *m.* 1961, Ronald Anthony Ostwald, of 8, Cholmeley Park, Highgate, N.6, and has issue living, Christian Mark Sebastian *b.* 1962. *Residence,*—45, Fitzroy Rd., Regent's Park, NW1.——Ethne Lucia, *b.* 1902: *m.* 1932, Group Capt. Valentine Brice Jephson Jackson, RAF (ret.), of 737, Nell Gwynn House, Sloane Av., SW3.

Grandchildren of the late Edward William O'Brien (infra):—
Issue of the late William Dermod O'Brien, *b.* 1865, *d.* 1945: *m.* 1902, Mabel Emmeline, who *d.* 1942, dau. of the late Sir Philip Crampton Smyly, M.D. [B. Plunket] :—

Brendan Edward, *M.D., F.R.C.P.I., b.* 1903 ; ed. at Dublin Univ. (M.B. and B.Ch. 1935, M.D. 1950) : *m.* 1936, Pamela Kathleen Helen, ARHA, only da. of the late Maj. H. G. Wilmer, Indian Army, and has issue living, Dermod Wilmer (Glenside, Lee Rd., Carrigrohane, co. Cork; Roy. Northern Yacht, and Roy. Cork Yacht, Clubs), *b.* 1941; ed. at Dublin Univ. (BA, BAI): *m.* 1966, Rosalind, da. of Robert G. Service, of Helensburgh, and has issue living, Jeremy William *b.* 1971, Lucia Jane *b.* 1969, Charlotte Elizabeth *b.* 1974,—Anthony Derek *b.* 1947; ed. at Haileybury, and Dublin Univ. (BA): *m.* 1974, Najma Madhavjee. *Residence,*—26, Herbert Park, Dublin 4. *Club,*— Kildare Street.——David Lucius, *MRCVS, b.* 1904; BSc 1929; Maj. (ret.) RAVC; is in Tasmanian Vet. Ser.: *m.* 1st, 1929 (divorce 1946), Mary Katharine Drummond, da. of the Rt. Hon. Sir Arthur Herbert Drummond Ramsay-Steel-Maitland, 1st Bt. (ext.); 2ndly, 1954, Shirley, da. of C. P. Hurford, of Worcester Park, Surrey, and has issue living, (by 1st m.) Michael David, *b.* 1930,—Lucia Margaret, *b.* 1932,—(by 2nd m.) Tasman David, *b.* 1955,—Donough William, *b.* 1956. *Residence,*— Scottsdale, Tasmania.——Horace Donough, *MB, b.* 1911; ed. at Dublin Univ. (MB and BCh 1934); FRCSI 1939; FRACS 1958; Lieut.-Col. (retired) RAMC: *m.* 1st, 1941 (m. diss. 1950), Pamela Charlotte, da. of Capt. Barrington Goodbody; 2ndly, 1950, Lucy Ann Stafford, da. of T. E. Stafford O'Brien, and has issue living, (by 2nd m.) Bartholemew Brendan, *b.* 1953,—Alexander Kennedy, *b.* 1955,—(by 1st m.) Caroline Phyllis Anne, *b.* 1942. *Residence,*—Burnie, Tasmania.—— Mary Elinor, *b.* 1907: BA: *m.* 1934, Bruce Martin Flegg, ARIBA, late Sqdn.-Ldr. RAF, and has issue living, Aubrey Martin, *b.* 1938; BA; PhD: *m.* 1956, Jennifer Condell, MLitt, of Dublin, and has issue living, Nigel Patrick Martin *b.* 1970, Eleanor Minta *b.* 1967,—Katharine Elinor, *b.* 1934; ARCM: *m.* 1964, N. Dimitrakopoulos of Thessaloniki, Greece. *Residence,*—St. Nicholas House, Rostrevor Rd., Dublin 6.——Rosaleen Brigid, *b.* 1909; a Roy. Hibernian Academician: *m.* 1936, Andrew Ganly, MA, FFD, RCSI, BDentSc, and has issue living, Eoghan Timothy, *b.* 1938,— Helen Phillida, *b.* 1939. *Residence,*—5, Rus in Urbe, Lower Glenageary Rd., Dun Laoghaire, co. Dublin.

Grandchildren of the late William Smith O'Brien, M.P., brother of 13th Baron:—
Issue of the late Edward William O'Brien, *b.* 1837, *d.* 1909: *m.* 1st, 1863, Mary, who *d.* 1868, dau. of the late Hon. Stephen Edmond Spring-Rice, son of 1st Baron Monteagle; 2ndly, 1880, Julia Mary Garth, who *d.* 1907, dau. of the late James Garth Marshall, of Monk Coniston, Ambleside:—

(By 2nd marriage) Margaret Ernestine, *b.* 1887 : *m.* 1915, Hugh Murrough Vere O'Brien, who *d.* 1955 (infra).

Issue of the late Very Rev. Lucius Henry O'Brien, *b.* 1842, *d.* 1913: *m.* 1872, Emily Mary Hannah, who *d.* 1942, dau. of Richard Thomas Montgomery, of Beaulieu, Drogheda :—

William Lucius Robert, *b*. 1889 : *m*. 1st, 1913, Jean Graham, who *d*. 1946, dau. of the late Thomas Pollok, of Liverpool, and Mearns, Renfrewshire ; 2ndly, 1957, Violet Fairbrother, widow of G. D. Mayer, and has issue living, (by 1st marriage) Mary Lockhart, *b*. 1914,—Eileen Graham, *b*. 1915 : *m*. 1940, R. David Eastham, of Whins, The Drive, Wonersh Park, near Guildford, Surrey, son of Sir Tom Eastham, QC, and has issue living, Robert Murrough *b*. 1948, Gillian Margaret Jean *b*. 1947. *Residence*,—Wilcot Lodge, Pewsey, Wilts.

Grandchildren of the late Very Rev. Lucius Henry O'Brien (ante) :—

Issue of the late Donough Richard O'Brien, *b*. 1876, *d*. 1938: *m*. 1914, Cecilia Maud (now of Parteen-a-Lax, Limerick), dau. of the late Rev. Frederick Neville Carus-Wilson, of Glenfield, Bath :—
Patricia Cicely, *b*. 1918: *m*. 1939, the Rev. John Benson, and has issue living, Donough O'Brien, *b*. 1940,—Murrough John, *b*. 1946,—Brian Lucius, *b*. 1950.——Geraldine Mary, *b*. 1922 : *m*. 1945, David Coote Hely-Hutchinson [see E. Donoughmore, colls.]. *Residence*,—Parteenalax, Limerick.

Issue of the late Charles Murrough O'Brien, *b*. 1877, *d*. 1939: *m*. 1903, Agnes Purdom, who *d*. 1970, da. of James Wilson, formerly of McLeod, Alberta, Canada:—
Lucius James (7878, Taulbut Av., Box 1113, Mission City, BC, Canada), *b*. 1904: *m*. 1932, Evelyn, da. of James Storey, of McLeod, Alberta, Canada.——Donough Robert Murrough, *b*. 1910: *m*. 1940, Rita Denny, da. of the late Rev. William Musson, of Buckingham, and has issue living, Murrough (1130, Roy Rd., Victoria, BC), *b*. 1947: *m*. 1968, Patricia Arlene, da. of George C. Ellison, of N. Vancouver,—Francine Denny, *b*. 1942: *m*. 1969, Donald Vincent Kissinger, and has issue living, Simon Raven *b*. 1972, Sarah Tsu Emily *b*. 1975. *Residence*,—Maple Bay Rd., Duncan. Vancouver Island, BC.——Eileen Moira Agnes, *b*. 1912: *m*. 1939, Dan Stephenson Heelas, and has issue living, Moira Jessica, *b*. 1942: *m*. 1963, Henry Stephens, of 5184, Westminster Av., Ladnor, Vancouver, BC, and has issue living, Sheryl Lynn *b*. 1963, Yvonne Doreen *b*. 1967,—Joan Zenda, *b*. 1944. *Residence*,—1657, West 59th Av., Vancouver, BC.

Grandchildren of the late Charles Murrough O'Brien (*b*. 1849), son of the late William Smith O'Brien, M.P. (ante):—

Issue of the late Brian O'Brien, MD, *b*. 1872, *d*. 1915: *m*. 1903, Mary Henrietta, who *d*. 1968, da. of the late Maurice Charles Hime, LLD, BL, JP, of Cluain Fóis, Buncrana, co. Donegal:
Charles Murrough, *b*. 1908 ; ed. at Trin. Coll., Dublin (M.B. and B.Ch. 1928) : *m*.1930, Elizabeth Joyce, da. of the late Ven. Gerald W. Peacocke, Archdeacon of Kildare, and has issue living, Brian Murrough Fergus (20, Manchester St., W1. Reform and Kildare St. Clubs), *b*. 193,1; ed. at Bedford Sch., and at Univ. Coll., Oxford (MA); Bar. Lincoln's Inn 1955,—David Donough *b*. 1933: *m*. 1962, Carole June Walters, and has issue living, Nicholas Charles Donough, *b*. 1963; Seamus Timothy Lucius *b*. 1965. *Residence*,—73, Knighton Drive, Leicester.——Mary Grainne, *b*. 1905: *m*. 1935, Ian Galbraith Robson, and has issue living, Michael William *b*. 1948. *Residence*,—Tilol, Kipkabus, Kenya.——Margaret Theodora, *b*. 1916.

Grandchildren of the late Brian O'Brien, MD (ante):—

Issue of the late Brian O'Brien, MD, *b*. 1908, *d*. 1968: *m*. 1938, Dorothea (15, Kilbarry Cres., Ottawa 7), da. of John F. A. Simms, of Combermere, Lifford:—
Brian Dermod, *b*. 1942; ed. at Queen's Univ., Kingston (BSc, MD, LMCC): *m*. 1962, Barbara Eileen, da. of John F. Brennagh, of Ottawa, Ont., and has issue living, Brian David, *b*. 1963,—Patrick John, *b*. 1965,—Christopher Michael, *b*. 1968,—Katherine Jennifer Eileen, *b*. 1971.——George Lucius, *b*. 1944; ed. at Queen's Univ., Kingston (MSc), and Dartmouth Coll., New Hampshire (AM, PhD).——Deirdre, *b*. 1940; Reg.N.: *m*. 1963, James Moxley Shearer, BSc, and has issue living, James O'Brien, *b*. 1965,—George Brodie, *b*. 1969,—Margaret Kathleen, *b*. 1967,—Joan Hilary, *b*. 1968.——Ruth Brigid, *b*. 1946; Reg.N.: *m*. 1969, Peter George Ryan, BComm., CA.

Grandchildren of the late Robert Vere O'Brien, yr. son of the late Hon. Robert O'Brien, brother of 13th Baron:—

Issue of the late Hugh Murrough Vere O'Brien, M.C.. *b*. 1887, *d*. 1955 : *m*. 1915, Margaret Ernestine, who *d*. 1968, da. of the late Edward William O'Brien (ante):—
Murrogh Vere, *b*. 1919 ; ed. at Dublin Univ. (B.A.I. 1940), and at Roy. Sch. of Mines, London (Asso. 1947); B.Sc. London 1947 : *m*. 1945, Zsuzsanna Eva Szeréna Károlyi, of Budapest, Hungary, and has issue living. Colm Murrough Vere, *b*. 1947,—Hugh Stephen Vere. *b*. 1948,—Sylvia Caroline Piroska, *b*. 1946: *m*. 1971, Julian Douglas Reynolds,—Iseult Anne, *b*. 1952,—Charlotte Elinor, *b*. 1962. *Residences*,—Woodtown Park, Rathfarnham, Dublin; Monare, Foynes, co. Limerick. ——Elinor Vere (62, Carroll House, Lancaster Gate, W2), *b*. 1918: *m*. 1956, Reginald Wiltshire, who *d*. 1968.

Grandchildren of the late Edward O'Brien, el. son of the Rev. the Hon. Henry O'Brien, yst. brother of 13th Baron:—

Issue of the late Major Murrough Charles O'Brien, M.D., J.P., Canadian Army Med. Corps, *b*. 1868, *d*. 1955 : *m*. 1901, Margaret Eleanor Barber, who *d*. 1958 :—
Muriel Oclanis, *b*. 1904: *m*. 1932, Hamilton Stewart McKee. *Residence*,—1233, Av. C. North, Saskatoon, Saskatchewan, Canada.

Issue of the late Lieut.-Col. Aubrey John O'Brien, CIE, CBE, *b*. 1870, *d*. 1930: *m*. 1906, Annie Winifred, who *d*. 1936, da. of the late James D'Arcy, of Kew:—
Turlough Aubrey, *CBE*, *b*. 1907; ed. at Charterhouse, and at Ch. Ch., Oxford (MA); late Maj. RA; Assist. to Dir. of Public Relations, Board of Trade 1946-49, and Public Relations Officer, Home Office 1949-53, and Gen. Post Office 1953-68, since when Public Relations Manager Bank of London and S. America; 1939-45 War as Maj. RA; CBE (Civil) 1959: *m*. 1945, Phyllis Mary, twin da. of the late Edward Grosvenor Tew [B. Hawke], and has issue living, Teige Henry Patrick, *b*. 1946,— Brian Edward Nicholas, *b*. 1951,—Corinna Moira, *b*. 1955. *Residence*,—Clare Place, Goose-Rye Rd., Worplesdon, Surrey. *Club*,—United University.——Donough, *b*. 1909; ed. at Stowe and at Exeter Coll., Oxford (BA 1931, MA 1949); Chm. of E. D. O'Brien Organisation, Public Relations Consultants: *m*. 1st, 1936, Sylvia Inchbold, who *d*. 1950, da. of Court Denny, of 30, Addison Rd. W14; 2ndly, 1952, Leonora Thayne, el. da. of Manning Leonard Railton, and has issue living, (by 1st m.) Donough Antony (31, Waterford Rd., SW6), *b*. 1939: *m*. 1969, Clare, da. of Leonard Read,— Natalie Deirdre Teresa, *b*. 1941: *m*. 1964, Roger Henry Brough Whittaker,—Geraldine Moira, *b*. 1945,—(by 2nd m.) Fionn Murrough Manning, *b*. 1953,—Lucius Edward, *b*. 1957. *Residences*,—9, Wellington Sq., SW3; Fryers Hse., Braughing, Bishop's Stortford. *Clubs*,—White's, Oriental, Pratt's, Bucks.——Moira Winifred Oclanis, *b*. 1912: *m*. 1932, John Michael Orpen Barstow, and has issue living, Elizabeth Catherine Oclanis, *b*. 1933: *m*. 1959, Richard Cubitt Bevis, of 3, Granville Rd., Barnet, Herts, and has issue living, Elizabeth Margaret Moira *b*. 1960, Maria Catharine Oclanis *b*. 1962, Alexandra Anne Cecilia *b*. 1963, Lucinda Mary Sophia *b*. 1965,—Anne Moira Olivia (2, Fawn Court, The Ryde, Hatfield, Herts.), *b*. 1940: *m*. 1965, Derek Landale Christie, who *d*. 1974, and has issue living, John Michael Landale *b*. 1966, Edward Hugh Landale *b*. 1968, Annabella Moira Orpen *b*. 1969,—Mary Geraldine Sheila, *b*. 1943: *m*. 1970, Graham McGregor Finch, of 45, College Cross, N1, and has issue living, Henrietta Lucy Anne *b*. 1975,—Henrietta Penelope Rose, *b*. 1945: *m*. 1968, Nicholas Frank Kileen, of 9, Holmdene Av., SE24, and has issue living, Beatrice Caroline Ellen *b*. 1974,—Brigid Evelyn Cecilia, *b*. 1947: *m*. 1973, Charles Michael Brett, of 1, College Grove, Gt. Malvern, Worcs., and has issue living, Aubrey Francis Patrick *b*. 1974. *Residence*,—The Old Rectory, Shipton Oliffe, Cheltenham.——Winifred Mary Sheila, *b*. 1918; is Sister Sheila, Community of St. John Baptist. *Address*,—Convent of St. John Baptist, Windsor, Berks.

Granddaughter of the late Lt.-Col. Henry Eoghan O'Brien, DSO, only son of Murrough John O'Brien, 2nd son of the Rev. the Hon. Henry O'Brien, (ante):—

Issue of the late Lieut.-Com. Brian Eoghan O'Brien, R.N., *b.* 1907; *d.* (killed in action during European War) 1940: *m.* 1936, Elizabeth (who *m.* 2ndly, 1949, P. Dennis), dau. of Stuart Séguin Strahan, M.B., B.Ch., of Hong Kong:—
Olivia Fiona, *b.* 1938: *m.* 1960, Sebastian Robinson, of 22, Athole Gdns., Glasgow, W2, and has issue living, James Lucius O'Brien, *b.* 1962,—Amanda Mary Victoria, *b.* 1961.
Descendants, if any, of the late George O'Brien (*b.* 1821), son of the late Adm. Robert O'Brien, 3rd son of the late Sir Lucius Henry O'Brien 3rd Bt.

PREDECESSORS.—Turlogh, King of Munster and principal King of Ireland, had with other issue, Dermot, King of Munster, from whom descended Conor O'Brien, inaugurated King of Thomond 1528; *d.* 1540, when his son Donough was set aside, the principality being usurped by his brother [1] MURROUGH O'Brien, P.C., who surrendered his royalty to Henry VIII., and was cr. 1543 *Earl of Thomond* (peerage of Ireland), with remainder to his nephew Donough, and *Baron Inchiquin* (peerage of Ireland) to him and the heirs male of his body; *s.* in the Barony by his son [2] DERMOT, 2nd Baron; *d.* 1557; *s.* by his son [3] MURROUGH, 3rd Baron; *d.* 1573: *s.* by his son [4] MURROUGH, 4th Baron; *d.* 1597; *s.* by his son [5] DERMOT, 5th Baron; *d.* 1624; *s.* by his son [6] MURROUGH, 6th Baron; a military officer of great renown; cr. *Earl of Inchiquin* (peerage of Ireland) 1654; *d.* 1674; *s.* by his son [7] WILLIAM, 2nd Earl; Gov. of Jamaica; *d.* 1691; *s.* by his son [8] WILLIAM, 3rd Earl; *d.* 1719; *s.* by his son [9] WILLIAM, 4th Earl; *d.* 1777; *s.* by his nephew and son-in-law [10] MURROUGH, K.P., 5th Earl. son of the Hon. James, M.P.. 3rd son of 3rd Earl; cr. *Marquess of Thomond* (peerage of Ireland), with remainder to the issue male of his brother Edward, and *Baron Thomond*, of Taplow. co. Bucks (peerage of United Kingdom) 1801; *d.* 1808, when the Barony of Thomond expired and the Marquessate and Barony of Inchiquin devolved upon his nephew [11] WILLIAM, K.P., 2nd Marquess, 3rd son of the Hon. Edward, 2nd brother of 2nd Earl; a Representative Peer; cr. *Baron Tadcaster*, of Tadcaster, co. York (peerage of United Kingdom) 1826 ; *d.* 1846, when the barony of Tadcaster expired and the Irish peerages devolved upon his brother [12] JAMES, G.C.H., 3rd Marquess; an Adm.; *d.* 1855, when all the titles became extinct except the Barony of Inchiquin, which descended to [13] LUCIUS O'Brien, 13th Baron and 5th Bart. (see note *₊* infra); *b.* 1800; sat as M.P. for co. Clare (C) 1826-30 and 1847-52; a Representative Peer, and Lord-Lieut. of Clare: *m.* 1st, 1837, Mary, who *d.* 1849, el. dau. of William Fitzgerald ; 2ndly, 1854, Louisa, dau. of Major James Finucane, of Ennistymon House, Clare ; *d.* 1872; *s.* by his son [14] EDWARD DONOUGH, 14th Baron, K.P., *b.* 1839; a Representative Peer, and Lieut. for co. Clare : *m.* 1st, 1862, the Hon. Emily Holmes-a'Court, who *d.* 1868, dau. of 2nd Baron Heytesbury ; 2ndly, 1874, the Hon. Ellen Harriet White, who *d.* 1913, dau. of 2nd Baron Annaly; *d.* 1900; *s.* by his son [15] LUCIUS WILLIAM, 15th Baron ; *b.* 1864 ; a Representative Peer for Ireland: *m.* 1896, Ethel Jane, who *d.* 1940, el. dau. and co-heiress of the late Johnston J. Foster, of Moor Park, Ludlow; *d.* 1929; *s.* by his el. son [16] DONOUGH EDWARD FOSTER, 16th Baron; *b.* 1897; Capt. Rifle Bde.: *m.* 1921, the Hon. Anne Molyneux Thesiger, who, *d.* 1973, da. of 1st Viscount Chelmsford; *d.* 1968; *s.* by his brother [17] PHAEDRIG LUCIUS AMBROSE 17th Baron and present peer.

₊ [1] DONOUGH O'Brien, P.C. and M.P. for co. Clare, was cr. a *Baronet* 1686 ; *d.* 1717 ; *s.* by his grandson [2] Sir EDWARD, 2nd Bt.; was M.P. for Clare; *d.* 1765; *s.* by his son [3] Sir LUCIUS, P.C., 3rd Bt., M.P for co. Clare ; *d.* 1795; *s.* by his son [4] Sir EDWARD, 4th Bt., M.P. for Ennis and co. Clare; *d.* 1837; *s.* by his son [5] Sir LUCIUS, 5th Bt., who *s.* as 13th Baron Inchiquin (ante).

INCHYRA, BARON, (Millar.) [Baron U.K. 1962.]

FREDERICK ROBERT HOYER MILLAR, *G.C.M.G.*, *C.V.O.*, 1st Baron, son of the late Robert Hoyer Millar; *b.* June 6th, 1900; ed. at Wellington, and at New Coll., Oxford (B.A. 1922); Hon. Attaché, Brussels 1922; entered Diplo. Ser. 1923, 3rd Sec. Berlin 1923, and Paris 1924, 2nd Sec., Foreign Office 1928, and Cairo 1930, 1st Sec., Foreign Office 1935; Assist. Private Sec. to Sec. of State for Foreign Affairs 1934-8, 1st Sec. at Washington 1939, acting Counsellor 1941, Sec., British Civil Secretariat, Washington 1943, Counsellor, Foreign Office 1944, Min. Washington 1948, UK Dep., NATO Council 1950, UK Representative thereon 1952, High Commr. German Federal Republic 1953-55, Ambassador 1955-56, and Permanent Under-Sec. of State for Foreign Affairs 1957-61; King of Arms of Order of St. Michael and St. George 1961-75; *cr.* CVO 1938, C.M.G. 1939, K.C.M.G. 1949, G.C.M.G. 1956, and *Baron Inchyra*, of St. Madoes, co. Perth (peerage of U.K. 1962): *m.* 1931, Elizabeth, dau. of the late Jonkheer Reneke de Marees van Swinderen, formerly Netherlands Min. in London, and has issue.

Arms,—Quarterly: 1st, or, a cross moline azure and base barry undy gules and vert, on a chief of the third a lozenge of the first between two spur-revels also of the first, *Millar*; 2nd, per bend argent and vert a lion passant gules, *Hoyer*; 3rd, Azure, a chevron argent between two spur-revels in chief and a demi-moon reversed or, *van Swinderen*; 4th, azure, a cross argent cantoned between four roses or, *de Marees*. Crest,—A cubit arm, the hand erect and in the act of blessing proper. Supporters.—Two blackcock proper.

Residences,—57, Eaton Place, S.W.1; Inchyra House, Glencarse, Perthshire. *Clubs,*—Boodle's, Turf, and Metropolitan (Washington).

SONS LIVING.

Hon. ROBERT CHARLES RENEKE HOYER, *b.* April 4th, 1935; ed. at Eton, and at New Coll., Oxford; late Scots Guards: *m.* 1961, Fiona Mary, dau. of (Edmund Charles) Reginald Sheffield, of Sutton Park, Sutton-on-the-Forest, York [*see* Sheffield, Bt.], and has issue living, Christian James Charles Hoyer, *b.* 1962,—Henrietta Julia Hoyer, *b.* 1964,—Louisa Mary Hoyer, *b.* 1968. *Residence,* —Breamish House, Powburn, Alnwick, Northumberland.

Hon. Alastair James Harold Hoyer, *b.* 1936; ed. at Eton; late Scots Guards: *m.* 1974, Virginia Margaret Diana, da. of William Perine Macauley, of Ballyward House, Manor Kilbride, co. Wicklow [see V. Camrose], and has issue living, Mark Christian Frederick, *b.* 1975. *Residence,*—4, Phillimore Gardens Close, W8.

DAUGHTERS LIVING.

Hon. Elizabeth Anne Hoyer, *b.* 1933: *m.* 1965, William Euan Wallace, of Bagnor Manor, Newbury [E. Lytton, colls.].

Hon. Annabel Alice Hoyer (9, Tite St., SW3), *b.* 1943; a Lady in Waiting to HRH The Princess Margaret, Countess of Snowdon, 1971-75, since when an Extra Lady in Waiting: *m.* 1973, Christopher James Bovill Whitehead.

Ingestre, Viscount, son of Earl of Shrewsbury.

INGLEBY, VISCOUNT. (Peake.) [Viscount U.K. 1956.]

MARTIN RAYMOND PEAKE, 2nd Viscount; *b.* May 31st, 1926: *s.* 1966; ed. at Eton, and Trin. Coll., Oxford; Bar. Inner Temple 1955; late Lt. Coldstream Guards; a Co. Councillor of N. Riding of Yorks 1964-67: *m.* 1952, Susan, da. of Russell Landale, of Ewell Manor, W. Farleigh, Kent, and has issue.

Arms,—Sable three crosses pattee argent within an orle of eight fleurs de lys and a bordure or. Crest,—A heart gules between two wings displayed erminois. Supporters,—On either side a Blackfaced Swaledale ram proper holding in the mouth a rose argent barbed seeded slipped and leaved also proper.

Residences, — Snilesworth, Northallerton Yorks.; Flat 1, 61, Onslow Sq., SW7. *Club,*— Brooks's.

DAUGHTERS LIVING.

Hon. Fiona Catherine, *b.* 1955.
Hon. Sarah Rachel, *b.* 1958.
Hon. Henrietta Cecilia Imogen, *b.* 1961.
Hon. Katherine Emma Charlotte, *b.* 1963.

SISTERS LIVING. (*Daughters of 1st Viscount.*)

Hon. Iris Irene Adele, *M.V.O., b.* 1923; Lady-in-Waiting to H.R.H. Princess Margaret 1952-62, and an Extra Lady-in-Waiting 1962-63; M.V.O. (4th class) 1957: *m.* 1963, Capt. Oliver Payan Dawnay, CVO, of Flat 5, 32, Onslow Sq., SW7, and Wexcombe House, nr. Marlborough, Wilts. [see V. Downe, colls.].

Hon. Sonia Mary, *b.* 1924: *m.* 1st, 1946, Lt. David George Montagu Hay, AM, RNR (now 12th Marquess of Tweeddale), from whom she obtained a divorce 1958; 2ndly, 1966, Maj. Michael William Vernon Hammond-Maude, JP, 5th R. Inniskilling Dragoon Guards (ret.), of Wychwood Lodge, Ramsden, Oxford.

Hon. Mary Rose, *b.* 1940 : *m.* 1959, Major Everard John Robert March Phillipps de Lisle, Roy. Horse Guards (ret.), and has issue living, Charles Andrew Everard, *b.* 1960,—Timothy John, *b.* 1962,— Mary Rosanna, *b.* 1968. *Residences,*—4, Hereford Mansions, Hereford Rd., W2 5BA; Stockerston Hall, Leics.

UNCLES LIVING. (*Not in remainder.*)

Sir Harald, *b.* 1899; ed. at Eton, and at Trin. Coll., Camb.; Air-Commodore (ret.), Aux. AF; Dir. of Aux. AF, Air Min. 1938-40, Dir. of Public Relations 1940-42, and Dir. of Air Force Welfare 1942-43; seconded to Foreign Office 1943; Chm. Steel Co. of Wales Ltd. 1955-62, and Lloyd's Bank, Ltd. 1962-69; Pres. and Chm., Soc. for Health Education since 1963 and RAF Benevolent Fund since 1967; 1914-18 War as 2nd Lt. Coldm. Gds.; Knt. 1973: *m.* 1st, 1933, Countess Resy de Baillet-Latour (from whom he obtained a divorce 1944), da. of Henri, Count Baillet-Latour, of Brussels; 2ndly, 1952, *Dame* Felicity Hyde, *DBE, JP,* da. of the late Col. Humphrey Watts, OBE, TD, and widow of John Charles Mackenzie Hanbury, Pilot Officer RAF, and has issue living, (by 1st m.) David Alphy Edward Raymond (of 15, Ilchester Place, W14), *b.* 1934: *m.* 1962, Susanna, da. of Lt.-Cdr. Sir Cyril Hugh Kleinwort, RNVR [see Kleinwort, Bt.], and has issue living, Edward *b.* 1964, Katharine Sophie *b.* 1965,—(by 2nd marriage) Andrew Charles, *b.* 1956. *Residences,*— Court Farm, Tackley, Oxon, OX5 3AQ; 2, Shepherd's Close, Shepherd's Place, Upper Brook St., W1Y 3RT. *Club.*—Brooks's.

Edward Charles, *b.* 1911; ed. at Eton, and at Trin. Coll., Camb.; Bar. Inner Temple 1939; formerly Flight-Lieut. R.A.F. Vol. Reserve; unsuccessfully contested Blaydon Div. of Durham (C) July 1945, and Cleveland Div. of N. Riding of Yorkshire Feb. 1950 : *m.* 1935, Baroness Maria Santina, dau. of Baron Alfred von Henikstein, of Salzburg, Austria, and has issue living, Henry Alfred. *b.* 1937; ed. at Ampleforth, and Ch. Ch., Oxford,—Robert Alexander (96, Campden Hill Rd., W8) *b.* 1938; ed. at Ampleforth, and Trin. Coll., Dublin: *m.* 1968, Meriel Elizabeth, da. of William Lyon Bowie, of Dublin, and has issue living, Lucy Meriel, *b.* 1972,—Christopher George, *b.* 1951; ed. at Ampleforth, and Queen's Coll., Camb.,—Marianna Clotilde, *b.* 1939,—Christina Maria, *b.* 1949: *m.* 1974, Dr. Peter Francis Leadlay. *Residence,*—Landhaus Parsch, Salzburg, Austria. *Clubs,*— Brooks's, Travellers'.

AUNT LIVING.
Maud Eileen, *b.* 1904. *Residence*,—46, Porchester Terr., W2 3TP.

WIDOW LIVING OF FIRST VISCOUNT.
Lady RACHEL JOAN DE VERE CAPELL (*Joan Viscountess Ingleby*), (36, Kingston House, SW7), da. of 7th Earl of Essex: *m.* 1922, the 1st Viscount, who *d.* 1966.

PREDECESSOR.—[1] OSBERT Peake, PC, son of Maj. George Herbert Peake; *b.* 1897; Under Sec. of State for Home Affairs 1939-44, Financial Sec. to Treasury 1944-45, Min. of National Insurance 1951-55 (and Pensions 1953-55); MP for N. Leeds (*C*) 1929-55, and N.-E. Leeds May to Dec. 1955; cr. *Viscount Ingleby*, of Snilesworth, N. Riding of York (peerage of UK) 1956: *m.* 1922, Lady Rachel Joan de Vere Capell, da. of 7th Earl of Essex; *d.* 1966; *s.* by his only son [2], MARTIN RAYMOND, 2nd Viscount and present peer.

INGLEWOOD, BARON. (Fletcher-Vane.) [Baron U.K. 1964.]

WILLIAM MORGAN FLETCHER-VANE, *TD*, 1st Baron, son of the late Col. the Hon. William Lyonel Vane [see B. Barnard, colls.]; *b.* April 12th, 1909; assumed by deed poll 1931 the surname of Fletcher-Vane in lieu of his patronymic; ed. at Charterhouse, and at Trin Coll., Camb. (MA, Dip. Agric.); a DL for .Westmorland; PPS. to Min. of Agriculture 1951-54, to Joint Under-Sec. for Foreign Affairs 1954-55, and to Min. of Health 1955-56, and Joint Parl. Sec. to Min. of Pensions and National Insurance 1958-60, and to Min. of Agriculture 1960-62; Leader of UK Delegation to World Food Congress (FAO), Washington 1963; 1939-45 War in France and Middle East, Lt.-Col. Durham L.I. (T.A.) (despatches); MP for Westmorland (*C*) 1945-64; cr. *Baron Inglewood*, of Hutton in the Forest, co. Cumberland (Peerage of U.K.) 1964: *m.* 1946, Mary, el. da. of Maj. Sir Richard George Proby, MC, 1st Bt., and has issue.

Arms,—Azure three sinister gauntlets or. Crest,—A dexter hand in armour couped at the wrist proper, holding a sword argent pommel and hilt or. Supporters,—On either side a roebuck proper collared and pendent from the collar a pheon argent.

Residences,—Hutton-in-the-Forest, Penrith; 19, Stack House, Ebury St., SW1. *Club*,—Travellers'.

SONS LIVING.

Hon. WILLIAM RICHARD, *b.* July 31st, 1951; ed. at Eton, and Trin. Coll., Camb.
Hon. Christopher John, *b.* 1953; ed. at Eton, and Trin. Coll., Camb.

INMAN, BARON. (Inman.) [Baron U.K. 1946.]

By Faith, Care and Service.

PHILIP ALBERT INMAN, *P.C.*, 1st Baron, son of Philip Inman, of Knaresborough, Yorkshire; *b.* June 12th, 1892; ed. at Knaresborough, at Headingly Coll., Leeds, and at Leeds Univ.; Pres. of Charing Cross Hosp. (Chm. 1936-66), Chm. of Charing Cross Hosp. Med. Sch., a Fellow Roy. Soc. of Health, Patron, Ind. Hospitals Assocn., Chm. and a Dir. of Hotels, Publishing and Industrial Cos., a JP for Co. London, an Underwriting Member of Lloyd's, a Liveryman of City of London, and a Member of Council of King Edward Hospital Fund; appointed Chm. of Govs. of British Broadcasting Corporation Dec. 1946; was Lord Privy Seal April to Oct. 1947, and Chm. of Hotels Executive of British Transport 1948-51, a Church Commr. 1948-57, and Pres. of So. of Yorkshiremen in London and Yorkshire So. 1953-54; 1915-16

War (invalided): cr. *Baron Inman*, of Knaresborough, W. Riding, co. York (peerage of United Kingdom) 1946, PC 1947: *m.* 1919, May Amelie, da. of Edward Dew, of Harrow, and has issue.

Arms,—Per chevron ermine and azure in chief, two lions rampant combatant or, holding between the forepaws a maltese cross gules surmounted by an annulet argent and in base a triple-towered castle proper. Crest,—A covered cup or between two wyvern's wings azure, both charged with an ermine spot gold. Supporters,—On either side a golden retriever proper, gorged with a collar sable charged with three roses argent barbed and seeded proper.

Residence.—Knaresborough House, Warninglid, Haywards Heath, Sussex. Club,—Athenæum.

DAUGHTER LIVING.

Hon. Rosemary, *b.* 1933 : *m.* 1955, Nickolas Kollitsis, M.D., F.R.C.S., and has issue living, Philip Milton, *b.* 1957,—Marina Christamene, *b.* 1956,—Alexandra, *b.* 1961. Residence,—11, Stasinou St., Engomi, Nicosia, Cyprus.

WIDOW LIVING OF SON OF FIRST BARON.

Judith (c/o Fuengirola Car Hire Ltd., Edificio Mediterraneo, Fuengirola, Malaga, Spain), da. of Albert George James Gibbins, of Mount Pleasant, Stocklane, Langford, Bristol: *m.* 1st, 1966, as his 2nd wife, the Hon. Philip John Inman, who *d.* 1968, only son of 1st Baron; 2ndly, 1970, Jonathan Fitzuryan Rhys Wingfield [see V. Powerscourt, colls.].

COLLATERAL BRANCH LIVING.

Issue of the late Hon. Philip John Inman, only son of 1st Baron, *b.* 1929; *d.* 1968: *m.* 1st, 1952 (m. diss. 1957), Jennifer, da. of George Clark; 2ndly, 1966, Judith (ante), (who *m.* 2ndly, 1970, Jonathan Fitzuryan Rhys Wingfield [see V. Powerscourt, colls.]).

(By 1st m.) Althea Rosalind, *b.* 1954.

INVERCHAPEL, BARONY OF. (Kerr Clark Kerr.) [Extinct 1951.]

WIDOW LIVING OF FIRST BARON.

MARIA TERESA DIAZ SALAS, dau. of Javier Diaz Lira, of Santiago de Chile : *m.* 1st, 1929 (marriage dissolved 1945 ; re-married 1948), the 1st Baron, who *d.* 1951, when the title became ext. ; 2ndly, 19—, Ross O. Treseder. Residence,—165, East 66th Street, New York City, U.S.A.

INVERCLYDE, BARONY OF (Burns.) [Extinct 1956.]

DAUGHTER LIVING OF THIRD BARON.

Hon. Emily Dunbar, *O.B.E.,b.* 1891 ; O.B.E. (Civil) 1919 : *m.* 1922, Lieut.-Com. Gerald Morell Mc-Kenna, R.N., who *d.* 1949. Residence,—Kirtling Tower, Newmarket, Suffolk.

INVERFORTH, BARON. (Weir.) [Baron U.K. 1919.]

ANDREW ALEXANDER MORTON WEIR, 2nd Baron ; *b.* Sept. 12th, 1897 ; *s.* 1955; ed. at St. Paul's Sch.; Pres. (Past Gov. Dir.) of Andrew Weir & Co., Ltd., and a Cdr. Order of Dannebrog of Denmark: *m.* 1929, Iris Beryl, da. of the late Charles Vincent, 4th Bn. The Buffs, and has issue.

Arms,—On a fesse azure, between in chief an escutcheon per bend azure and gules, charged with a bend sinister gules and azure a bend argent, and in base an ancient galley, flags flying to the dexter gules, three mullets of the first. Crest,—A dexter and sinister hand couped at the wrists proper supporting an ancient galley as in the arms. Supporters,—On either side a sailor of the Mercantile Marine.

Residence,—24, Clarence Terr., Regents Park, NW1.

SONS LIVING.

Hon. (ANDREW CHARLES) ROY (27, Hyde Park St., W2), *b.* June 6th, 1932; ed. at Malvern: *m.* 1966, J. Elizabeth, da. of John Ward Thornycroft, CBE, of Steyne, Bembridge, I. of W., and has issue living, Andrew Peter, *b.* 1966,—Clarinda Jane, *b.* 1968.

Hon. John Vincent (Brock House, Gt. Chesterford, Saffron Walden, Essex), *b.* 1935; ed. at Malvern.

Through labour to honour.

SISTER LIVING.

Hon. Annie Forrestdale, *b.* 1891: *m.* 1949, Com. Ronald Langton-Jones, DSO, RN (ret.), who *d.* 1967. Residence,—Flat F, 36, Eaton Sq., SW1.

PREDECESSOR.—[1] *Rt. Hon.* ANDREW WEIR, *P.C.*, *b.* 1865 ; senior partner in the firm of Andrew Weir & Co., shipowners and merchants, Surveyor-Gen. of Supply, War Office and a Member of Army Council 1917-19, and Min. of Munitions 1919-21 ; cr. *Baron Inverforth*, of Southgate, co. Middlesex (peerage of United Kingdom) 1919 : *m.* 1889, Anne, who *d.* 1941, younger dau. of the late Thomas Kay Dowie ; *d.* 1955 ; *s.* by his only son [2] ANDREW ALEXANDER MORTON 2nd Baron and present peer.

INVERURIE, LORD, son of Earl of Kintore.

IRONSIDE, BARON. (Ironside.) [Baron U.K. 1941.]

EDMUND OSLAC IRONSIDE, 2nd Baron; *b.* Sept. 21st, 1924; *s.* 1959; ed. at Tonbridge; Lt. (ret.) RN; has Coronation Medal (1953); 1939-45 War: *m.* 1950, Audrey Marigold, yst. da. of the late Col. the Hon. Thomas George Breadalbane Morgan-Grenville, DSO, OBE, MC [see Ly. Kinloss, colls.], and has issue.

Arms,—Per bend sable and gules, on a bend argent a bendlet wavy azure, in sinister chief a garb or, and in base a lion salient or, and in fess a gauntletted dexter hand grasping a sword paleways argent hilted or. Crest.—A dexter gauntletted hand grasping a sword paleways argent hilted and pommelled or. Supporters,—Two bull terriers proper.

Residence,—Broomwood Manor, Chignal St. James' Chelmsford, Essex.

SON LIVING.
Hon. CHARLES EDMUND GRENVILLE, *b.* July 1st 1956.

DAUGHTER LIVING.
Hon. Fiona Georgina, *b.* 1954.

SISTER LIVING.
Hon. Elspeth Mariot, *b.* 1917: *m.* 1941, Capt. Andrew Gilbert Hendry, Black Watch (Roy. Highland Regt.), and has issue living, Michael Andrew, *b.* 1942,—John Edmund Gordon, *b.* 1949,—David Robert Charles, *b.* 1955. *Residence,*—Gagie, Angus.

WIDOW LIVING OF FIRST BARON.
MARIOT YSABEL (*Mariot, Baroness Ironside*), dau. of the late Lieut. Charles Cheyne, I.S.O.: *m.* 1915, the 1st Baron, who *d.* 1959. *Residence,*—Hampton Court Palace, East Molesey, Surrey.

PREDECESSOR.—[1] *Field Marshal Sir* (WILLIAM) EDMUND Ironside, *G.C.B., C.M.G., D.S.O., LL.D.,* son of the late Surg.-Maj. William Ironside, R.H.A. ; *b.* 1880 ; S. Africa 1899-1902, European War 1914-19, finally as Gen. Officer Comdg.-in-Ch. Allied Forces at Archangel, N. Russia ; Ismid 1920 ; N. Persia 1920-21, in command of British Forces, European War 1939-40 ; was Comdt. of Staff Coll. 1922-6, 2nd Div., Aldershot 1926-8, and Meerut Dist. 1928-31, Lieut. of Tower of London 1931-3, and an A.D.C.-Gen. to H.M. 1937-40 ; appointed Q.M.G. of Army in India 1933, Gen. Officer Comdg.-in-Ch., E. Command 1936, Gov. and Com.-in-Ch., Gibraltar 1938, Inspector-Gen. of Overseas Forces July 1939, and Ch. of Imperial Gen. Staff Sept. 1939 ; Com.-in-Ch. Home Forces, May to July 1940 ; Col. Comdt. R.A. 1932-47 ; cr. *Baron Ironside,* of Archangel, and of Ironside, co. Aberdeen (peerage of United Kingdom) 1941 : *m.* 1915, Mariot Ysabel, dau. of the late Charles Cheyne, I.S.O. ; *d.* 1959 ; *s.* by his only son [2] EDMUND OSLAC, 2nd Baron and present peer.

Irwin, Lord, son of Earl of Halifax.

ISLINGTON, BARONY OF. (Dickson-Poynder.) [Extinct 1936.]
DAUGHTER LIVING OF FIRST BARON.
Hon. Joan Alice Katherine (*Baroness Altrincham*), *b.* 1897: *m.* 1923, the 1st Baron Altrincham, who *d.* 1955. *Residence,*—Tormarton Court, Badminton, Glos.

ISMAY, BARONY OF. (Ismay.) [Extinct 1965.]
DAUGHTERS LIVING OF FIRST BARON.
Hon. Susan Katharine (Wormington Grange, Broadway, Worcs.) *b.* 1922: *m.* 1st, 1942, Maj. Neville Ewart Hyde Chance, from whom she obtained a divorce 1946; 2ndly, 1949, Lieut.-Col. Michael John Evetts, MC, RHF, son of Lt.-Gen. Sir John Fullerton Evetts, CB, CBE, MC, and has issue living, (by 1st m.) Patricia Kathleen, *b.* 1942: *m.* 1963, David Henry Smyly [see By. Buckland],—(by 2nd m.) John Hastings, *b.* 1951,—James Michael Ismay, *b.* 1953.
Hon. Sarah Field (*Viscountess Allendale*), *b.* 1928 : *m.* 1948, the 3rd Viscount Allendale. *Residences,*—Bywell Hall, Stocksfield-on-Tyne, Northumberland ; Allenheads Hall, Allenheads, Northumberland.
Hon. Mary Quenelda, *b.* 1929 : *m.* 1st, 1952, Robert Mervyn Fitz Finnis, who *d.* 1955 ; 2ndly, 1957, Major George Raymond Seymour, MVO [see M. Hertford, colls.], and has issue living, (by 1st m.) Jane Laura, *b.* 1953,—Sarah Lavinia, *b.* 1955,—(by 2nd marriage) [see M. Hertford, colls.] *Residence,*—54, Chelsea Sq., SW3.

WIDOW LIVING OF FIRST BARON.
LAURA KATHLEEN (*Baroness Ismay*) (Wormington Grange, Broadway, Worcs.), dau. of the late H. G. Clegg, of Wormington Grange, Worcs.: *m.* 1921, the 1st Baron, who *d.* 1965, when the title became ext.

IVEAGH, EARL OF.   (Guinness.)   [Earl U.K. 1919, Bt. U.K. 1885.]
[Title pronounced "Iver."]

ARTHUR FRANCIS BENJAMIN GUINNESS, 3rd Earl, and 3rd Baronet; b. May 20th, 1937; s. 1967; ed. at Eton and Trin. Coll., Camb.; Joint Chm. of Guinness Group since 1975: m. 1963, Miranda Daphne Jane, da. of Maj. Charles Michael Smiley, of Castle Fraser, Aberdeenshire [see Smiley, Bt., colls.], and has issue.

Arms,—Quarterly; 1st and 4th, per saltire gules and azure, a lion rampant, or; on a chief ermine a dexter hand couped at the wrist of the first, Guinness; 2nd and 3rd argent, on a fesse between three crescents sable a trefoil slipped or, Lee. Crests,—1st, a boar passant, quarterly or and gules; 2nd, on a pillar argent, encircled by a ducal coronet or, an eagle preying on a bird's leg erased proper. Supporters,— Two stags gules, collared gemmel and attired or, each resting a hind hoof upon an escutcheon vert, charged with a lion rampant or.

SPES MEA IN DEO

My hope is in God.

Seat,—Farmleigh, Castleknock, co. Dublin.   Clubs,—Carlton, White's, Kildare Street and Royal Yacht Squadron.

SONS LIVING.
ARTHUR EDWARD RORY (Viscount Elveden), b. Aug. 10th, 1969.
Hon. Rory Michael Benjamin, b. 1974.
DAUGHTERS LIVING.
Lady Emma Lavinia, b. 1963.
Lady Louisa Jane, b. 1967.
SISTERS LIVING. (Raised to the rank of an Earl's daughter 1969.)
Lady Elizabeth Maria, b. 1939: m. 1960, David Hugh Lavallin Nugent, of Chaddleworth House, Chaddleworth, Newbury; and Ross Castle, Mount Nugent, co. Cavan, [see Nugent, Bt., cr. 1795].
Lady Henrietta (59, Eaton Mews West, SW1), b. 1942.
AUNTS LIVING. (Daughters of 2nd Earl).
Lady Honor Dorothy Mary, b. 1909: m. 1st, 1933, Henry Channon, M.P. (Knt. 1957), who d. 1958, having obtained a divorce 1945; 2ndly, 1946, Flight-Lieut. Frantisek Vaclav Svejdar, R.A.F., and has issue living, (by 1st marriage) Henry Paul Guinness, MP (96, Cheyne Walk, SW10, and Kelvedon Hall, Brentwood, Essex. Clubs,—White's, Buck's), b. 1935; ed. at Eton, and at Ch. Ch., Oxford; late 2nd Lt. Roy. Horse Guards; is a Co. Director; PPS to Min. of Power 1959-60, to Home Sec. 1960-62, to First Sec. of State 1962-63, and to Sec. of State for Foreign Affairs, 1963-64; a Parl. Sec., Min. of Housing and Local Govt. June to Oct. 1970, a Parl. Under-Sec. of State, Dept. of Environment 1970-72, Min. of State N. Ireland March to Nov. 1972, and Min. for Housing and Construction 1972-74; MP for W Div., of Southend-on-Sea (C) since 1999: m. 1963, Mrs. Ingrid Olivia Georgia (GUINNESS), da. of the late Maj. Guy Richard Charles Wyndham, MC [see B. Egremont and Leconfield, colls.], and has issue living, Henry b. 1970, Olivia Gwendolen Violet, b. 1964, Georgia Honor Margarethe, b. 1966.   Residence,—Phibblestown, Clonsilla, co. Dublin.
Lady Patricia Florence Susan (Viscountess Boyd of Merton), b. 1918: m. 1938, the 1st Viscount Boyd of Merton.   Residences,—Ince Castle, Saltash, Cornwall; 6, Iveagh House, Ormond Yard, St. James's, SW1.
Lady Brigid Katharine Rachel, b. 1920: m. 1st, July 30th, 1945, Friedrich Georg Wilhelm Christoph von Preussen (HRH Prince Friedrich Georg Wilhelm Christoph of Prussia), who d. 1966 [see ROYAL FAMILY]; 2ndly, June 3rd, 1967, Maj. Anthony Patrick Ness.   Residences,—Patmore Hall, Hadham, Herts.; Letterellan by Aberfeldy, Perths.; 7, Iveagh House, Ormond Yard, SW1.
MOTHER LIVING.
Lady Elizabeth Cecilia, da. of 4th Earl of Listowel: m. 1st, 1936, Maj. Viscount Elveden, RA (TA), who d. (killed in action) 1945, el. son of 2nd Earl; 2ndly, m. 1947, Edward Rory More O'Ferrall. Residences,—Gloucester Lodge, Regent's Park, NW1; The Old Rectory, Elveden, Suffolk.
COLLATERAL BRANCHES LIVING.
Issue of the late Hon. (Arthur) Ernest Guinness, 2nd son of 1st Earl, b. 1876, d. 1949: m. 1903, Marie Clotilde, who d. 1953, dau. of Sir George Russell, M.P., 4th Bt. (cr. 1812):—
Aileen Sibell Mary PLUNKET, b. 1904: m. 1st, 1927, Flight-Lieut. the Hon. Brinsley Sheridan Bushe Plunket, RAF Vol. Reserve, who d. (on active ser.) 1941, and from whom she had obtained a divorce 1940 [see B. Plunket, colls.]; 2ndly, 1956, Valerian Stux-Rybar. Residence,— Luttrellstown Castle, Clonsilla, co. Dublin.——Maureen Constance, b. 1907: m. 1st, 1930, the 4th Marquess of Dufferin and Ava, who d. (killed in action in Burma) 1945; 2ndly, 1948, Major (Harry Alexander) Desmond Buchanan, M.C., from whom she obtained a divorce 1954; 3rdly, 1955, His Honour Judge John Cyril Maude, [see V. Hawarden, colls.]. Residences,—4, Hans Crescent, S.W.1; Clandeboye, co. Down.——Oonagh, b. 1910: m. 1st, 1929, the Hon. Philip Leyland Kindersley, who obtained a divorce 1936 [see B. Kindersley]; 2ndly, 1936, the 4th Baron Oranmore and Browne, from whom she obtained a divorce 1950; 3rdly, 1957, Miguel Ferreras. Residence,—Luggala, Roundwood, co. Wicklow.
Descendants of the late Rt. Hon. Walter Edward Guinness, DSO (3rd son of 1st Earl), who was cr. Baron Moyne 1932 [see that title].

PREDECESSORS.—[1] Sir EDWARD CECIL Guinness, K.P., G.C.V.O., 3rd son of Sir Benjamin Lee Guinness, M.P., 1st Bt., by Elizabeth, who d. 1865, 3rd dau. of the late Edward Guinness, of Dublin; b. 1847; High Sheriff for Dublin City 1876; cr. a Baronet 1885, Baron Iveagh, of Iveagh, co. Down (peerage of United Kingdom) 1891, K.P. 1897, Viscount Iveagh, of Iveagh, co. Down (peerage of United Kingdom) 1905, G.C.V.O. 1910, and Earl of Iveagh, and Viscount Elveden, of Elveden, co. Suffolk (peerage of United Kingdom) 1919: m. 1873, Adelaide Maria, who d. 1916. dau. of the late Richard Samuel Guinness, M.P. for Barnstaple [B. Ardilaun, colls.]; d. 1927; s. by his son [2] RUPERT EDWARD CECIL LEE, KG, CB, CMG, 2nd Earl; b. 1874; Chm. of Arthur Guinness, Son & Co. 1927-62, Chancellor Dublin Univ. 1927-63; MP for Haggerston Div., Shoreditch (C) 1908-10, S-E Essex 1912-18, and Southend-on-Sea 1918-27; S. Africa 1900 (despatches, medal, CMG): m. 1903, Lady Gwendolen Florence Mary Onslow, CBE, who d. 1966, da. of 4th Earl of Onslow; d. 1967; s. by his grandson [3] ARTHUR FRANCIS BENJAMIN (only son of Maj. Arthur Onslow Edward, Viscount Elveden, 2nd son of 2nd Earl), 3rd Earl and present peer; also Viscount Iveagh, Viscount Elveden, and Baron Iveagh.

JACKSON, BARONY OF.   (Jackson.)   [Extinct 1954.]
WIDOW LIVING OF FIRST BARON.
HOPE HARDY (Baroness Jackson), dau. of Benjamin Waterfall Gilmour, of Glasgow: m. 1923, the 1st Baron, who d. 1954, when the title became ext. Residence,—Stowehill, Peterstow, Ross-on-Wye, Herefordshire.

JACKSON OF BURNLEY, BARONY OF. (Jackson.) [Extinct 1970.]

DAUGHTERS LIVING OF LIFE BARON.

Hon. Anne Boswall, *b.* 1939: *m.* 1967, David Garner Freeston, of Hazel Cottage, North Heath Chieveley, Newbury, Berks.
Hon. Ruth Lesley, *b.* 1945: *m.* 1970, David John Moffatt (19, Overbrook, W. Horsley, Leatherhead, Surrey, KT24 6BH), and has issue.

WIDOW LIVING OF LIFE BARON.

MARY ELIZABETH (*Baroness Jackson of Burnley*), (33, Park Close, Templar Rd., Oxford), da. of Dr. Robert Oliphant Boswall: *m.* 1938, Baron Jackson of Burnley (Life Peerage), who *d.* 1970, when the title became ext.

JACQUES, BARON. (Jacques.) [Life Baron 1968.]

JOHN HENRY JACQUES, son of Thomas Dobson Jacques, of Ashington, Northumberland; *b.* Jan. 11th, 1905; ed. at Co-op. Coll , Manchester, and Victoria Univ , Manchester (BA Com.); a JP of Portsmouth; Managing Sec., Moorsley Co-op. Soc., co. Durham 1925-29, Tutor, Co-op. Coll., Manchester 1929-42, accountant Plymouth Co-op. Soc. 1942-45, and Ch. Exec. Officer, Portsea Island (Portsmouth) Co-op. Soc. 1945-65; Pres. of Co-op. Congress 1961; Chm. of Co-op Union 1964-70; appointed a Lord-in-Waiting to HM 1974; *cr. Baron Jacques,* of Portsea Island, co. Southampton (Life Baron) 1968: *m.* 1929, Constance, da. of Harry White, of Bournville, Birmingham, and has issue.

Residence,—23, Hilltop Cres., Cosham, Portsmouth, PO6 1BB.
Club,—Co-operative (Portsmouth).

SONS LIVING.

Hon. Cecil Philip (48801. Lyra St., Fremont, Cal., USA), *b.* 1930; BSc (Hons.) London: *m.* 1960, Rita Ann Florence Hurford, and has issue.
Hon. Paul (4, Potters Lane, East Leake, Loughborough, Leics.), *b.* 1932; MB, ChBEd: *m.* 1958, Nina Mollie MacKenzie, and has issue.

DAUGHTER LIVING.

Hon. Ann, *b.* 1941.

JAMES OF RUSHOLME, BARON. (James.) [Life Baron 1959.]

ERIC JOHN FRANCIS JAMES, son of the late Francis William James, of Parkstone, Dorset ; *b.* April 13th, 1909 ; ed. at Taunton's Sch., Southampton, and at Queen's Coll., Oxford (B.A. and B.Sc. 1931, M.A. 1933, D.Phil. 1933); Hon. LL.D. McGill and York (Canada); Hon. D.Litt. New Brunswick, D.Univ. York; High Master of Manchester Gram. Sch. 1945-62, and Vice Chancellor of York Univ. 1962-72; Chm. of Headmasters' Conference 1953-54, of Communications Research Cttee. in Building Industry 1963, and of Inquiry into Teacher Training 1971; cr. Knt. 1956, and *Baron James of Rusholme,* of Fallowfield, co. Palatine of Lancaster (Life Baron) 1959: *m.* 1939, Cordelia Mary, da. of Maj.-Gen. FitzGerald Wintour, CB, CBE [see Foster, Bt. (ext.), cr. 1831], and has issue.

Residence,—Penhill Cottage, West Witton, Leyburn, N. Yorks. *Club,*—Athenaeum.

SON LIVING.

Hon. Oliver Francis Wintour (Brewery Cottages, Lambton Park, Chester-le-Street, co. Durham). *b.* 1943; ed. at Winchester, and at Balliol Coll., Oxford: *m.* 1965, Rosanna, el. da. of Maj. Gordon Bentley Foster, of Sleightholme Dale, Fadmoor, York, and has issue.

JANNER, BARON. (Janner.) [Life Baron 1970.]

BARNETT JANNER, son of the late Joseph Janner, of Barry, Glam.; *b.* June 20th, 1892; ed. at Co. Sch., Barry, and Univ. of Wales (BA); Hon. LLD Leeds; FIPM; Solicitor 1919; Pres., Board of Deputies, British Jews 1955-64; a Member of Exec. of British Group Inter-Parl. Union (Past Chm.), Chm. of Parl. Anglo-Benelux Group, and of Anglo-Israel Parl. Group; Pres. of Zionist Fedn. of Great Britain and Ireland; Vice-Pres. of Monash branch, British Legion, of Assocn. of Municipal Corpns., and of Assocn. of Jewish ex-Servicemen and Women; Chm. of House of Lords and House of Commons Solicitors' Group, and Parl. Water Safety Group, and Pres. of Leaseholders Assocn. of Gt. Britain; Freedom of City of Leicester 1971; Cdr. of Order of Orange Nassau of the Netherlands; 1914-18 War with RGA; MP for Whitechapel and St. George's Div. of Stepney (*L*) 1931-35, W. Leicester (*Lab*) 1945-50, and NW Leicester 1950-70; Cdr., Order of Leopold II of Belgium; *cr.* Knt. 1960, and *Baron Janner,* of City of Leicester (Life Baron) 1970: *m.* 1927, Elsie Sybil, CBE, JP, da. of the late Joseph Cohen, and has issue.

Residences,—69, Albert Hall Mansions, SW7; The Jungle, Stone Rd., Broadstairs, Kent.

SON LIVING.

Hon. Greville Ewan, *QC, MP* (2, Linnell Drive, NW11; 1, Garden Court, EC4); *b.* 1928; ed. at Bishop's Coll. Sch. Quebec, St. Paul's Sch., London, and Trin. Hall, Camb. (MA) and Harvard Law Sch.; Bar. Middle Temple 1954; Snr. Vice-Pres. Board of Deputies of British Jews; Vice-Pres. of Assocn. for Jewish Youth; MP for NW Leicester (*Lab.*, 1970 to Feb. 1974, since when of Leicester, West, *m.* 1955, Myra Louise, da. of Emmanuel Sheink, of Melbourne, Vic., and has issue.

DAUGHTER LIVING.

Hon. Ruth Joan Gertrude Rahle (*Baroness Morris of Kenwood*); *b.* 1932; Solicitor 1956: *m.* 1958, the 2nd Baron Morris of Kenwood. *Residence,*—Lawn Cottage, Orchard Rise, Kingston upon Thames, Surrey.

JEFFREYS, BARON. (Jeffreys.) [Baron U.K.. 1952.]

Every gift from God.

MARK GEORGE CHRISTOPHER JEFFREYS,
2nd Baron ; b. Feb. 2nd, 1932 ; s. 1960 ;
ed. at Eton; Maj. late Grenadier Guards,
and Lord of Manor of Burkham : m.
1st 1956 (m. diss. 1967) Sarah Annabella,
only da. of Maj. Henry Garnett, of
Somerton House, Winkfield, Berks.;
2ndly, 1967, Anne-Louise, yr. da. of
His Honour Judge Sir (William) Shirley
Worthington-Evans, 2nd Bt., (ext.), and
has issue by 1st and 2nd m.

Arms,—Ermine a lion rampant sable, and a
canton sable. Crest,—On a wreath ermine and sable
a demi lion or, grasping with the dexter claw a wreath
of laurel vert. Supporters,—On either side a lion
regardant sable crowned with an ancient crown or,
and charged on the shoulder with two swords in
saltire points upwards gold.
Residence,—Marden Grange, Devizes, Wilts.
Clubs,—Guards', Boodle's, White's.

SONS LIVING. (By 1st m.)
Hon. CHRISTOPHER HENRY MARK, b. May 22nd,
1957.
Hon. Alexander Charles Darell, b. 1959.
DAUGHTERS LIVING. (By 1st m.)
Hon. Laura, b. 1961.

Hon. Rose Amanda, b. 1962.
(By 2nd m.)
Hon. Sophie Louise, b. 1972.

BROTHER LIVING. (Raised to rank of a Baron's son 1961.)
Hon. George Christian Darell, b. 1939; ed. at Eton; Capt. Grenadier Guards (ret.): m. 1967, Karen
Elizabeth Mary, el. da. of the late Col. Hugo Meynell, MC, of Hollybush Park, Burton-on-Trent
[see E. Halifax, colls], and has issue living, Zara Serena, b. 1972,—a da. b. 1975. Residence,—
Willoughby House, Rugby, Warwicks. Clubs,—Guards', Bootle's.

MOTHER LIVING.
Lady Rosemary Beatrice Agar, dau. of 4th Earl of Normanton: m. 1931, Capt. Christopher John
Darell Jeffreys, M.V.O., Grenadier Guards, who d. (killed in action during European War) 1940.
Residence,—Chapel Cottage, Bentworth, Alton, Hants.

PREDECESSOR.—[1] Gen. Sir GEORGE DARELL JEFFREYS, K.C.B., K.C.V.O., C.M.G., son of the
late Rt. Hon. Arthur Frederick Jeffreys, M.P., J.P., D.L., of Burkham House, Hants ; b. 1878 ;
Col. of Grenadier Guards 1952-60 ; Comdt. Guards Depot 1911-14 ; Nile Expedition 1898, present
at battle of Khartoum, S. Africa 1900-1902, European War 1914-18 Comdg. successively 2nd Batn.
of his Regt., 58th, 57th, and 1st Guards Brig., and 19th Div. ; in command of Light Div., Army of
the Rhine 1919, and London Dist. 1920-24 ; commanded 43rd (Wessex) Div. T.A. and Wessex
Area 1926-30 ; Gen. Officer Comdg-in-Ch. S. Command, India 1932-36, and A.D.C. Gen. to H.M.
1936-38 ; Chm. of Basingstoke Co. Bench 1925-32, and again 1936-52, Hon. Col. 48th (Hampshire)
Anti-Aircraft Regt. R.A. (T.A.) (now 583rd (Hampshire) Heavy Anti-Aircraft Regt., R.A.) 1938-48,
and Col. of Roy. Hampshire Regt. 1945-48 ; sat as M.P. for Petersfield Div. of Hampshire (C)
1941-51 ; cr. Baron Jeffreys, of Burkham, co. Southampton (peerage of United Kingdom) 1952;
m. 1905, Dorothy, who d. 1953, dau. of John Postle Heseltine, of Walhampton, Lymington, and
widow of Viscount Cantelupe, el. son of 7th Earl De La Warr ; d. 1960 ; s. by his grandson [2]
MARK GEORGE CHRISTOPHER (son of the late Capt. Christopher John Darell Jeffreys, M.V.O., only
son of 1st Baron), 2nd Baron and present peer.

JELLICOE, EARL. (Jellicoe.) [Earl (U.K.) 1925.]

Rt. Hon. GEORGE PATRICK JOHN
RUSHWORTH JELLICOE, D.S.O., M.C.,
P.C., 2nd Earl; b. April 4th, 1918;
s. 1935; ed. at Winchester, and at
Trin. Coll., Camb. (Exhibitioner);
in Foreign Ser. 1947-57; formerly
1st Sec., Washington, D.C., and
Brussels and Dep. Sec.-Gen. Baghdad
Pact; a Lord-in-Waiting to H.M. Feb.
to June 1961, Joint Parliamentary
Sec., Min. of Housing and Local Govt.
1961-62, Min. of State, Home Office
1962-63, and First Lord of Admiralty
1963-64, and Min. of Defence for
RN April to Oct. 1964; Dep. Leader
of Opposition, House of Lords 1967;
Lord Privy Seal, and Leader of House
of Lords 1970-73; a Page of Honour
at Coronation of King George VI;
1939-45 War in Middle East as Lt.-
Col. Coldstream Gds. (wounded, des-
patches thrice, DSO, MC, Legion of Honour, French Croix de Guerre, Greek
Mil Cross); DSO 1942; cr. PC 1963: m. 1st, 1944 (m. diss. 1966), Patricia
Christine, only da. of Jeremiah O'Kane, of Vancouver, Canada; 2ndly, 1966,
Philippa, da. of the late Philip Dunne, of Gatley Park, Leominster, and has
issue by 1st and 2nd m.

Arms,—Argent, three bars wavy azure, over all a whale hauriant sable. Crest,—Out of a crown
or, a demi-wolf azure. Supporters,—On either side a sea griffin or.
Residences,—97, Onslow Sq., SW7; Tidcombe Manor, Tidcombe, nr. Marlborough, Wilts.   Club,—
Brooks's.

SONS LIVING. (By 1st marriage.)
PATRICK JOHN BERNARD (Viscount Brocas), b. Aug. 29th, 1950; ed. at Eton: m. 1971, Geraldine
Ann Jackson, and has issue:—
   SON LIVING.—Hon. Justin Amadeus, b. 1970.
Hon. Nicholas Charles, b. 1953; ed. at Eton.
                              (By 2nd marriage.)
Hon. John Philip, b. 1966.
             DAUGHTERS LIVING. (By 1st marriage.)
Lady Alexandra Patricia Gwendoline, b. 1944: m. 1970, Edward Philip Wilson, of 58, Gibson Sq., N1,
   [see Wilson, Bt., cr. 1874, colls.].
Lady Zara Lison Josephine, b. 1948.
                              (By 2nd marriage.)
Lady Emma Rose, b. 1967.
Lady Daisy, b. 1970.
             SISTERS LIVING. (In special remainder to the Viscountcy only.)
Lady Gwendoline Lucy Constance Rushworth, b. 1903 : m. 1935, Col. Edward Latham, M.C., R.H.A.,
   who d. 1957, and has issue living, John Edward Jellicoe (Harwood's House, Bledington, Oxon. Club,
   —Cavalry), b. 1936; ed. at Eton; late 2nd Lt. RAC: m. 1967, Catherine Patricia, da. of Allan
   William Forsyth Craig, MB, of Greenways, Darlington Place, Bath, and has issue living, Jasper
   Nicholas Jellicoe b. 1970, Gabrielle Jane b. 1971, Rosalind Vaari (twin) b. 1971,—Richard Henry
   Ringrose (23, Chancellor House, 17, Hyde Park Gate, SW7; Stowting Hill House, Ashford; Army
   and Navy Club), b. 1943; ed. at Eton, and Univ. of Paris, late Sub-Lt. RN; MBA Cranfield Inst.
   of Tech.; Lt. RNR: m. 1968, Virginia Jane, el. da. of John Mount [see E. Ernie, colls.], and has
   issue living, Edward George Ringrose b. 1969, Harry John Jellicoe b. 1972,—Susan Phyllida, b. 1938;
   ed. at Lady Margaret Hall, Oxford (BA, PhD): m. 1958, Michael Rose, Solicitor, of Heath Winds,
   Merton Lane, Highgate, N6, and has issue living, David Jacob Edward b. 1959, Bernard John Max
   b. 1960, Philip Thomas Solomon b. 1963, Dinah Gwen Lison b. 1965. Residence,—Oak Knoll,
   Sunningdale, Ascot, Berks.
Lady Norah Beryl Cayzer, b. 1910: m. 1935, Major Edward William Rhys Wingfield, late King's Roy.
   Rifle Corps [see V. Powerscourt, colls.]. Residence,—Salterbridge, Cappoquin, co. Waterford.
Lady Prudence Katharine Patton, b. 1913; is a JP for Co. of Kent: m. 1936, Francis William Hope
   Loudon, and has issue living, James Rushworth Hope, b. 1943; ed. at Eton, and Magdalene Coll.,
   Camb. (BA): m. 1975, Jane Gavina da. of T. La. F. Fryett,—Katharine Louise Frederica, b. 1937:
   m. 1964, William Henry Nairn Wilkinson, of 119, Castlenau, SW13, and has issue living, Matthew
   Loudon Nairn b. 1969, Sophia Louise Prudence b. 1971, Alice Laura Gillian b. 1974,—Annabella
   Constance, b. 1939: m. 1965, Ian Jonathan Scott, of 18, Abingdon Villas, W8, and has issue living,
   Alexander James Jonathan b. 1966, Justin William Erskine b. 1970, Julia Katharine Selina b. 1969.
   Residence,—Olantigh, Wye, nr. Ashford, Kent.

COLLATERAL BRANCH LIVING. (In remainder to Viscountcy only.)
             Issue of the late Lady Myrtle Grace Brocas Jellicoe, 3rd da. of 1st Earl, b. 1908,
             d. 1945: m. 1932, Lionel Maxwell Joachim Balfour, of Grayling House, Amberley,
             Stroud, Glos., who d. 1973.
Christopher John Jellicoe, b. 1934; ed. at Trin. Coll., Camb. (BA); Prin. Careers Officer, London
   Borough of Merton: m. 1960, Ann Schuyler Butlin, and has issue living, Maxwell James, b. 1961,—
   Juliet Ann b. 1963,—Katherine Susan, b. 1968. Residences,—The Twynings, Redmarley, Glos.; 5,
   St. Aubyn's Court, SW19. Club,—Cavalry.——Karen Myrtle, b. 1944: m. 1967, Fabyan Evans, of
   Ebenezer House, Orcop, Herefords., and 9, Westwood Gdns., Barnes Common, SW13, and has issue
   living, Nigel Henley Fabyan, b. 1971,—Jessica Ann b. 1973.

PREDECESSOR.—[1] Adm. of the Fleet Sir JOHN RUSHWORTH Jellicoe, G.C.B., O.M., G.C.V.O.
   son of the late Capt. John Henry Jellicoe, of Northfield, Ryde, Isle of Wight ; b. 1859;
   Egyptian War 1882 (medal, bronze star), China 1900, Comdg. Naval Brig. and as Ch. of Staff to
   Vice-Adm. Sir E. Seymour during attempt to relieve British Legation at Pekin (severely
   wounded, C.B.), European War 1914-16 in command of Grand Fleet, and at battle of Jutland
   (G.C.B., G.C.V.O., O.M., Order of Leopold of Belgium, French and Belgian Croix de Guerre,
   Grand Cross of Legion of Honour, Grand Cross of Military Order of Savoy, Japanese Order of
   the Rising Sun with Paulownia, 3rd class of Russian Order of St. George, American D.S.M., Adm.
   of the Fleet, thanked by Parliament, granted £50,000) ; commander of H.M.S. "Victoria" when
   lost off Tripoli June 1893 ; was Director of Naval Ordnance 1905-7, a Lord of the Admiralty
   and Controller of the Navy 1908-10, in command of Atlantic Fleet 1910-11, and of 2nd Squadron
   of Home Fleet 1911-12, Second Sea Lord of the Admiralty 1912-14, Com.-in.-Ch. of Grand Fleet
   1914-16, and First Sea Lord of the Admiralty (also Ch. of Naval Staff) 1916-17 ; Pres. of British
   Legion 1928-32 ; Gov.-Gen. and Com.-in-Ch. of New Zealand 1920-24 ; cr. Viscount Jellicoe, of
   Scapa, co. Orkney (peerage of United Kingdom) 1917, with remainder to heirs male of his body,
   and in default of such issue with remainder (1) to his el. dau. and to the heirs male of her
   body, and (ii) to every other dau. successively in order of seniority of age and priority of
   birth, and heirs male of their bodies, and Viscount Brocas, of Southampton, co. Southampton,
   and Earl Jellicoe (peerage of U.K.) 1925: m. 1902, Florence Gwendoline, who d. 1964, da. of Sir
   Charles William Cayzer, 1st Bt. (cr. 1904); d. 1935; s. by his son [2] GEORGE PATRICK JOHN
   RUSHWORTH, 2nd Earl and present peer; also Viscount Jellicoe, and Viscount Brocas.

Jermyn, Earl, son of Marquess of Bristol.

JERSEY, EARL OF. (Child-Villiers.) [Earl E. 1697.]
             [Name pronounced "Villers."]

             GEORGE FRANCIS CHILD-VILLIERS, 9th
             Earl; b. Feb. 15th, 1910; s. 1923; ed. at
             Eton, and at Ch. Ch., Oxford ; formerly
             Major R.A. (T.A.) : m. 1st, 1932, Patricia
             Kenneth (who obtained a divorce 1937),
             dau. of Kenneth Richards, of Cootamun-
             dra, N.S. Wales ; 2ndly, 1937, Virginia
             (who obtained a divorce 1946), dau. of
             James Cherrill, of Hollywood, U.S.A. ;
             3rdly, 1947, Bianca Maria Adriana Luci-
             ana, dau. of the late Enrico Mottironi, of
             Via Goffredo Casalis, Turin, Italy, and has
             issue by 1st and 3rd marriages.

             Arms,—Quarterly: 1st and 4th, argent, on a
             cross gules, five escallops or, Villiers; 2nd and 3rd,
             gules, a chevron engrailed ermine, between three
             eaglets argent, ducally gorged or, and in the chief
             point, for distinction, an escallop or, Child. Crests,
             —1st, a lion rampant argent, ducally crowned or;
             2nd, on a rock proper, an eagle rising argent,
             ducally gorged or, holding in the beak an adder
The Cross is the test of faith.   proper, and charged on the breast, for distinction,
             with an ermine spot. Supporters,—Two lions argent,

             FIDEI & CRUX
             NOTICULA

ducally crowned or, and gorged with a plain collar gules, charged with three escallops or.
Residence,—Radier Manor, Longueville, Jersey.

SONS LIVING. (*By 3rd marriage*.)
GEORGE HENRY (*Viscount Villiers*), *b.* Aug. 29th, 1948; late 2nd Lt. 11th Hussars and the Roy.
Hussars: *m.* 1st, 1969 (m. diss. 1973), Verna, da. of K. A. Stott, of Jersey; 2ndly, 1974, Sacha Jane
Hooper, only da. of Peter Hooper Valpy, of Jersey, and formerly wife of K. F. Lauder, and has
issue.

DAUGHTER LIVING (*By 1st m.*).—*Hon.* Sophia Georgiana, *b.* 1971.
Hon. Charles Victor (44, Holland Villas Rd., W14 8DH), *b.* 1952: *m.* 1975, Brigitte Elisabeth Germaine,
da. of Robert Jean Rolland Marchand.

DAUGHTERS LIVING. (*By 1st m.*).
Lady Caroline, *b.* 1934: *m.* 1st, 1952 (m. diss. 1965) Viscount Melgund, MBE (now 6th Earl of Minto);
2ndly, 1969 (m. diss. 1972), the Hon. John Douglas Stuart. son of 1st Viscount Stuart of Findhorn.
Residence,—Sedgebrook Manor, nr. Grantham, Lincs.

(*By 3rd m.*)
Lady Isabella Bianca Rosa, *b.* 1950: *m.* 1974, Peter Edward Harrison, of 13, Paradise Walk, SW3.

BROTHER LIVING.
Hon.(Edward) Mansel, *b.*1913 ; ed. at Eton　Squadron Leader R.A.F. (retired) ; formerly 2nd Lieut.
17th/21st Lancers (SR): *m.* 1st, 1934, Barbara Mary (who obtained a divorce 1940), only da. of the
late Capt. W. J. G. S. Frampton, of Newton Hall, Clitheroe; 2ndly, 1946 (m. diss. 1971), Princess
Maria Gloria, only da. of the late Prince Pignatelli Aragona Cortez, Duke of Terranova, of Rome,
and has issue living, (by 1st m.) Edward John Mansel Hugh Frampton (25, Pelham Place, SW7),
b. 1935: *m.* 1958, Celia Elinor Vadyn, da. of Cyril Hall Green [see Blake, Bt., cr. 1622, colls.], and
has issue living, Alexander *b.* 1961, Roderick Anthony *b.* 1963,—(by 2nd m.) George Anthony
Robert, *b.* 1947,—Mary Ann, *b.* 1951,—Maria Consuelo, *b.* 1953. *Residence*,—Keston, Mont
Matthieu, St. Ouen, Jersey.

SISTERS LIVING.
Lady Joan, *b.* 1911: *m.* 1933, Lieut. David Richard Colville, R.N.V.R. [see V. Colville, colls.].
Residences,—Old Vicarage, Dorton, near Aylesbury, Bucks ; Ducie House, Bembridge, Isle of
Wight.
Lady Ann, *b.* 1916: *m.* 1937, Major Alexander Henry Elliot, late R.A. [see E. Minto, colls.].
Residence,—Broadford, Chobham, Surrey.

COLLATERAL BRANCHES LIVING.
Descendants of the late Hon. Thomas Villiers (2nd son of 2nd Earl of Jersey).
who was cr. *Earl of Clarendon* 1776 [see that title].

PREDECESSORS.—[1] *Sir* OLIVER St. John; cr. *Viscount Grandison* (peerage of Ireland) 1620
with remainder to his niece Barbara, wife of Sir Edward Villiers, el. half-brother of George,
Duke of Buckingham, the celebrated favourite of Charles I.; *d.* 1630 ; *s.* by his el. grand-
nephew [2] WILLIAM Villiers, 2nd Viscount, el. son of Barbara (ante) ; a zealous partisan of
Charles I.; *d.* from wounds received at the battle of Bristol 1643 ; *s.* by his brother [3] JOHN,
3rd Viscount; *d.s.p.*; *s.* by his brother [4] GEORGE, 4th Viscount; *d.* 1699; *s.* by his son [5]
JOHN, 5th Viscount; cr. *Earl Grandison* (peerage of Ireland) 1721 ; *d.* 1766, when the Earldom
became ext., and he was *s.* in the Viscountcy by his kinsman [6] WILLIAM, 3rd Earl of Jersey
(see ****infra); *d.* 1769; *s.* by his son [7] GEORGE BUSSY. 4th Earl; successively a Lord of the
Admiralty, Lord Chamberlain of the Household and Master of the Buckhounds; *d.* 1805; *s.* by
his son [8] GEORGE, 5th Earl; assumed the additional surname of Child by Roy. licence 1819,
was twice Lord Chamberlain to William IV., and twice Master of the Horse to Queen Victoria;
d. 1859; *s.* by his son [9] GEORGE AUGUSTUS FREDERICK, 6th Earl; *b.* 1808; successively M.P.
for Honiton, Weymouth, and Cirencester (*C*): *m.* 1841, Julia, dau. of the Rt. Hon. Sir Robert
Peel, 2nd Bt.; *d.* 1859; *s.* by his son [10] VICTOR ALBERT GEORGE, G.C.B., G.C.M.G., P.C.,
7th Earl, *b.* 1845 ; a partner in the banking firm of Child and Co., Fleet Street, E.C. ; a Lord-
in-Waiting to H.M. Queen Victoria 1875-7; Lord-Lieut. for Oxfordshire 1887-1915 ; Paymaster-Gen. 1889-90; Gov. and Com.-in-Ch. of N.S. Wales 1890-93, and Acting Agent-Gen. for
New South Wales in London 1904-5: *m.* 1872, the Hon. Margaret Elizabeth Leigh, D.B.E., who
d. 1945, dau. of 2nd Baron Leigh ; *d.* 1915; *s.* by his el. son [11] GEORGE HENRY ROBERT
CHILD, 8th Earl, *b.* 1873 ; a partner in the firm of Child and Co., bankers, of Fleet Street, E.C. ;
a Lord-in-Waiting to H.M. Jan. to Aug. 1919 : *m.* 1908, Lady Cynthia Almina Constance Mary,
who *d.* 1947 [having *m.* 2ndly, 1926, Com. William Rodney Slessor, R.N.V.R., who *d.* (on active
ser. during European War) 1945], dau. of 3rd Earl of Kilmorey ; *d.* 1923 : *s.* by his son [12]
GEORGE FRANCIS, 9th Earl and present peer: also Viscount Villiers, Viscount Grandison, and Baron
Villiers of Hoo.

***Sir Edward Villiers, 5th son of Barbara St. John, niece of 1st Viscount Grandison, had with other
issue [1] EDWARD, P.C., Knt., cr. *Baron Villiers of Hoo*, co. Kent, and *Viscount Villiers* (peerage of
England) 1691, and *Earl of the Island of Jersey* (peerage of England) 1697 ; successively Special
Ambassador to the Hague, Ambassador to the States Gen. and to France, Lord Justice of Ireland,
Sec. of State, Master of the Horse, Lord Chamberlain of the Household and Knight Marshal ;
d. 1711 ; *s.* by his son [2] WILLIAM, 2nd Earl ; *d.* 1731 ; *s.* by his son [3] WILLIAM, P.C., 3rd Earl,
who *s.* his kinsman as 6th Viscount Grandison (ante).

JESSEL, BARON. (Jessel.)　[Baron U.K. 1924, Bt. U.K. 1917.]

EDWARD HERBERT JESSEL, *C.B.E.*,
2nd Baron, and 2nd Baronet, *b.* March
25th, 1904; *s.* 1950; ed. at Eton, and at
Ch. Ch., Oxford (B.A. 1926); Bar. Inner
Temple 1926; CBE (Civil) 1963: *m.* 1st,
1935, Lady Helen Maglona Vane-
Tempest-Stewart (from whom he
obtained a divorce 1960), da. of 7th
Marquess of Londonderry; 2ndly, 1960,
Jessica, da. of the late William de Wet,
and has issue by 1st marriage.

Arms,—Azure, a fesse raguly counter-raguly
ermine between three eagles' heads erased argent, in
the chief point a portcullis or. *Crest*,—A torch
fessewise fired proper surmounted by an eagle
collared argent, holding in the beak a pearl also
argent. *Supporters*,—On either side a dark bay
horse charged on the shoulder with a portcullis or.

Residence,—101, Eaton Place, SW1.　*Clubs*,—Garrick, White's.

GRANDDAUGHTER LIVING.

Issue of the late Hon. Timothy Edward Jessel, only son of 2nd Baron, b. 1935, d. 1969: m. 1st, 1961 (m. diss. 1965), Janet Calliope, yr. da. of Maurice Smith, of Bidborough, Kent; 2ndly, 1965, Jill (infra), only da. of G. A. Powell, of Auckland, NZ:—

(By 2nd m.) Annabel Helen, b. 1968.

DAUGHTERS LIVING. (By 1st marriage).

Hon. Camilla Edith Mairi Elizabeth, b. 1940: m. 1960, Don Juan Carlos del Prado y Ruspoli, Marques de Caicedo, and has issue living, Miguel Angel, b. 1961,—Alfonso Segundo, b. 1966. Residence,—9, Martinez Campos, Madrid, 10, Spain.

Hon. Joanna Margaret, b. 1945: m. 1967, Simon L. Butler, of 13, Paulton's St., SW3, and has issue living, Ashley Edward Hubert, b. 1969,—Diarmid John, b. 1970.

SISTERS LIVING.

Hon. Gladys May (Via della Scrota, Rome 117), b. 1896.

Hon. Doreen Maud (Hon. Lady Agnew), b. 1909; ed. at Univ. Coll., London (BA), and at the Courtauld Inst. (Dip.) Univ. of London; Administrative Assist., Offices of War Cabinet 1942-43 and 1944-45; a Dir. of Thomas Agnew & Son, Ltd.: m. 1934, Sir Geoffrey William Gerald Agnew [see Agnew, Bt., cr. 1895, colls.]. Residences,—11, Alexander Sq., SW3; Egmere Farm House, Walsingham, Norfolk.

WIDOW LIVING OF SON OF SECOND BARON.

Jill (12, Chester Row, SW1), da. of the late G. A. Powell, of Auckland, NZ: m. 1965, the Hon. Timothy Edward Jessel, who d. 1969, and has issue living [see ante].

PREDECESSOR.—[1] Sir HERBERT MERTON Jessel, C.B., C.M.G., T.D., youngest son of the late Rt. Hon. Sir George Jessel, Master of the Rolls [see Jessel, Bt., cr. 1883] ; b. 1886 ; Col. late 5th Batn. City of London Regt. ; Mayor of Westminster 1902-3, Dep. Director of Remounts, War Office 1918-19 ; Pres., London Municipal So. (Chm. 1904-15) ; M.P. for St. Pancras, S. Div. (LU) 1896-1906, and (C) 1910-18 ; cr. a Baronet 1917, and Baron Jessel, of Westminster, co. London (peerage of U.K.) 1924: m. 1894, Maud, who d. 1965, fifth da. of the late Rt. Hon. Sir Julian Goldsmid, MP, 3rd Bt.; d. 1950; s. by his only son [2] EDWARD HERBERT, 2nd Baron, and present peer.

Jocelyn, Viscount, son of Earl of Roden.

JOICEY, BARON. (Joicey.) [Baron U.K. 1906, Bt. U.K. 1893.]

MICHAEL EDWARD JOICEY, 4th Baron and 4th Baronet; b. Feb. 28th, 1925; s. 1966; ed. at Eton, and at Ch. Ch. Oxford; late Capt. Coldstream Guards: m. 1952, Elisabeth Marion, da. of the late Lt.-Col. the Hon. Ian Leslie Melville, TD [see E. Leven and Melville, colls.], and has issue.

Arms.—Argent, three lozenges sable within two bendlets invected gules between two miner's picks in bend proper. **Crest.**—A demi-man affrontée in armour proper, garnished or, the helmet adorned with three feathers gules, holding in the dexter hand a scimitar of the first, pommel and hilt gold, supporting with the sinister hand an escutcheon argent, charged with three torteaux within two bendlets invected of the second between two fleurs-de-lis sable. **Supporters.**—On either side a Shetland pony proper, haltered or.

Seats.—Etal Manor, Berwick-on-Tweed; Ford Castle, Berwick-on-Tweed. Residence,—Etal Manor, Berwick-on-Tweed.

OMNE SOLVM FORTI PATRI

Every land is a native country to a brave man.

SONS LIVING.

Hon. JAMES MICHAEL, b. June 28th, 1953; ed. at Eton.
Hon. Andrew Hugh, b. 1955; ed. at Eton.

DAUGHTER LIVING.

Hon. Katherine Jane, b. 1959.

DAUGHTERS LIVING OF SECOND BARON.

Hon. Norah Marguerite, b. 1905: m. 1932, Brigadier Ronald Henry Senior, D.S.O., T.D., and has issue living, Susan, b. 1935: m. 1955, David Ean Coleridge, of Spring Pond, Wispers, Midhurst, Sussex, and has issue living, Nicholas David b. 1957, Timothy Richard b. 1959, Christopher Henry b. 1971,—Deirdre Bridget (Hon. Mrs. Anthony T. S. Montagu), b. 1939: m. 1962, Hon. Anthony Trevor Samuel Montagu, of 78, Chelsea Park Gdns., SW3 [see B. Swaythling]. Residence,—110, Eaton Sq., SW1.

Hon. Sylvia Alice, b. 1908: m. 1934, Lieut.-Col. Richard Ian Griffith Taylor, D.S.O., M.C. [Waldie-Griffith, Bt. (ext.)], from whom she obtained a divorce 1951, and has issue living, Simon James, b. 1936,—Alexander Thomas, b. 1941: m. 1974, Sarah da. of Col. Richard Martin-Bird, of Stockingwood, Chelford, Cheshire,—Valerie, b. 1946: m. 1969, Alan Yuill Walker. Residence,—Barelees, Cornhill-on-Tweed, Northumberland.

PREDECESSORS.—[1] JAMES Joicey, son of George Joicey, of Newcastle-upon-Tyne; b. 1846; M.P. for Durham co., Chester-le-Street Div. (L) 1885-1905; cr. a Baronet 1893, and Baron Joicey of Chester-le-Street, co. Durham (peerage of United Kingdom) 1906: m. 1st, 1879, Amy, who d. 1881, dau. of Joseph Robinson, J.P., of North Shields; 2ndly, 1884, Marguerite Smyles, who d. 1911, dau. of the late Col. Drever, H.E.I.C.S.; d. 1936; s. by his el. son [2] JAMES ARTHUR, 2nd Baron, b. 1880; was High Sheriff of co. Durham 1910: m. 1904, Georgina Wharton, who d. 1952, dau. of Major Augustus Edward Burdon, formerly of Hartford Hall, Bedlington, Northumberland; d. 1940; s. by his brother [3] HUGH EDWARD, 3rd Baron, b. 1881; High Sheriff of Northumberland 1933: m. 1921, Lady Joan Katherine Lambton, who d. 1967, da. of 4th Earl of Durham; d. 1966; s. by his yr. son [4] MICHAEL EDWARD, 4th Baron, and present peer.

Jones, see Baron Wynne-Jones.

JOWITT, EARLDOM OF. (Jowitt.) [Extinct 1957.]

DAUGHTER LIVING OF FIRST EARL.

Lady Penelope, *b.* 1923: *m.* 1943, George Wynn-Williams, FRCS, FRCOG, and has issue living, William Jowitt Dafydd, *b.* 1947: *m.* 1975, Amanda SB., yst. da. of Col. John Childs, of 24, Ovington St., SW3,—Huw James, *b.* 1955,—Lesley-Jane, *b.* 1944: *m.* 1965, William Mortimer Man, of St. Rose, Sway Rd., Lymington, Hants. *Residences,*—39, Hurlingham Court, SW6; The Hall, Isle of Oxney, Wittersham, Kent.

KAHN, BARON. (Kahn.) [Life Baron 1965.]

RICHARD FERDINAND KAHN, *CBE*, son of the late Augustus Kahn, of London; *b.* Aug. 10th, 1905; ed. at St. Paul's Sch., and at King's Coll., Camb. (MA, Fellow); a FBA; Assist. Sec., Board of Trade 1940-41, Assist. Sec., Middle East Supply Centre Economic Adviser to Min. of State, Middle East 1941-43, Assist. Sec., Min. of Supply 1943-44, Head of Div., Min. of Production 1944-45; and Prin. Assist. Sec., Board of Trade 1945-46; Emeritus Prof. of Economics, Camb. since 1967; *cr.* CBE (Civil) 1946, and *Baron Kahn*, of Hampstead, London Borough of Camden (Life Peerage) 1965.

Residence,—King's College, Cambridge, CB2 1ST.   *Club,*—RAC.

KALDOR, BARON. (Kaldor.) [Life Baron 1974.]

NICHOLAS KALDOR, *FBA*, son of the late Dr. Julius Kaldor, of Budapest; *b.* May 12th, 1908; ed. at Model Gymnasium, Budapest, and LSE (BSc, Hon. Fellow 1970); MA Camb.; Hon. Dr. Dijon; Fellow of King's Coll., Camb. since 1949; Assist. Lecturer and Lecturer and Reader in Economics LSE 1932-47, Dir of Research and Planning Div. Economic Commn. for Europe, Geneva 1947-49; Reader in Economics Camb. Univ. 1952-65, since when Prof. of Economics; Advisor on Tax Reform Govt. of India 1956, Economic Advisor, Economic Commn. for Latin America, Santiago, Chile 1956, and Govt. of Ghana 1961, Fiscal Advisor, Govt. of Ceylon 1958, Govt. of Mexico 1960, Govt. of British Guiana 1961, of Turkey 1962, and of Iran 1966; Special Advisor to Chancellor of the Exchequer 1964-68; *cr. Baron Kaldor*, of Newnham, in City of Cambridge (Life Baron) 1974: *m.* 1934, Clarissa Elisabeth, da. of Henry Frederick Goldschmidt, and has issue.

Residences.—27, Egerton Gdns., SW3; King's College, Cambridge; 2, Adams Rd., Cambridge. *Club,*—Reform.

DAUGHTERS LIVING.

Hon. Katharine Margaret, *b.* 1937: *m.* 1958, Anthony Hungerford Hoskyns, of 25, Hamilton Gdns., NW8 [see Hoskyns, Bt.].
Hon. Frances Julia, *b.* 1940: *m.* 1962, Michael John Stewart, of 39, Upper Park Rd., NW3.
Hon. Penelope Jane, *b.* 1942: *m.* 1964, Robert Charles Milsom, of 27, The Dreel, Norfolk Park, Edgbaston, Birmingham, 15.
Hon. Mary Henrietta, *b.* 1946.

KEARTON, BARON. (Kearton) [Life Baron 1970.]

(CHRISTOPHER) FRANK KEARTON, *OBE, FRS*, son of Christopher John Kearton; *b,* Feb. 17th, 1911; ed. at Hanley High Sch., and St. John's Coll., Oxford (Hon. Fellow); Hon. Fellow Manchester Coll. of Science and Tech.; Hon. LLD Leeds; Hon. DSc Bath, Reading, Aston and Keele; a Member of Electricity Supply Research Council since 1954 (Chm. since 1959), of UK Atomic Energy Authority since 1955, of Central Electricity Generating Board since 1974, of Tropical Products Inst., since 1958, Cttee of Advisory Council of Technology 1964-70, and of Nat. Economic Development Council 1965-71; Chm. of Courtaulds 1964-75 and of Industrial Reorganisation Corpn. 1966-68; a Visitor, Science and Research Council (formerly DSIR) 1963-68; First Chm. of British Oil Corpn. since 1975; a Member of Central Advisory Council for Science and Tech. 1969-70; Pres. Soc. of Chemical Industry 1972-74, and of Roy. Soc. for Prevention of Accidents since 1973; *cr.* OBE (Civil) 1946, Knt. 1966, and *Baron Kearton*, of Whitchurch, co. Buckingham (Life Baron) 1970: *m.* 1936, Agnes Kathleen, da. of Samuel Pratt Brander, and has issue living, two sons, and two das.

Residence,—The Old House, Whitchurch, Aylesbury, Bucks.

KEITH OF AVONHOLM, BARONY OF (Keith.) [Extinct 1964.]

SON LIVING OF LIFE BARON.

Hon. Henry Shanks, (*Hon. Lord Keith*), [see SCOTTISH LORDS OF SESSION]: *m.* 1955, Alison Hope Alan, yr. da. of Alan Brown, and has issue.

DAUGHTERS LIVING OF LIFE BARON.

Hon. Elizabeth Hamilton, *b.* 1916 : *m.* 1945, Raymond Alan Lolley, and has issue. *Residence,*—17, Cromer Hyde, Lemsford, Welwyn Garden City, Herts., AL8 7XE.
Hon. Helena Stewart, *b.* 1919 : *m.* 1943, Gerald Outram Mayne, M.B., Ch.B., and has issue. *Residence,*—70, Deepfield way, Coulsdon, Surrey.

WIDOW LIVING OF LIFE BARON.

JEAN MAITLAND (*Baroness Keith of Avonholm*) (of 32, India St., Edinburgh), da. of the late Andrew Bennet, solicitor, of Arbroath: *m.* 1915, the 1st Baron, who *d.* 1964, when the title became ext.

Kelburn, Viscount, son of Earl of Glasgow.

Kellie, Earl of, Earl of Mar and Kellie.

KEMSLEY, VISCOUNT. (Berry.) [Viscount U.K. 1945, Bt. U.K. 1928.]

PERSEVERA ET VINCE

(GEOFFREY) LIONEL BERRY, 2nd Viscount, and 2nd Baronet; b. June 29th, 1909; s. 1968; ed. at Marlborough, and Magdalen Coll., Oxford; FRSA; a KStJ; a DL for Leics. 1972; a Co. Councillor for Northants 1964-70; Dep. Chm., Kemsley Newspapers, Ltd., 1938-59; Master of Spectacle Makers' Co. 1949-51 and 1959-61; 1939-45 War as Capt. Grenadier Guards (invalided out 1942); MP for Buckingham (C) 1943-45; High Sheriff of Leics. 1967: m. 1933, Lady Hélène Candida Hay, OStJ, da. of 11th Marquess of Tweeddale, and has issue.

Arms,—Gules, three bars or, on a pile ermine as many martlets sable. Crest,—A griffin sejant sable, collared and chained, the chain reflexed over the back and resting the dexter claw on a catharine wheel or. Supporters,—On either side a stag guardant or, gorged with a chaplet of mistletoe proper.

Persevere and conquer.

Residence,—Thorpe Lubenham Hall, Market Harborough, Leics. Clubs,—Guards', Carlton, Bath, Turf, Pratt's.

DAUGHTERS LIVING.

Hon. Mary Anne, b. 1934: m. 1960, Charles Henry van Raalte, of Boreland House, Kilmarnock, Ayrshire, and has issue living, Marcus Lionel, b. 1961,—Kristina Beryl, b. 1962,—Ghislaine Sara, b. 1964.
Hon. Pamela Jane Margaret, b. 1937: m. 1961, Gerald Nigel Mobbs, of Boot Farm, Little Kingsmill, Gt. Missenden, Bucks., and has issue living, Christopher William, b. 1965,—Virginia Elizabeth, b. 1968,—Penelope Helen (twin), b. 1968.
Hon. Caroline Helen, b. 1942: m. 1965, John Peter Houison Craufurd of Craufurdland and Braehead, of Craufurdland Castle, Kilmarnock, Ayrshire, and has issue living, John Alexander, b. 1966,—Simon Douglas, b. 1972,—Teresa Eleanor, b. 1967.
Hon. Catherine Francis Lilian, b. 1944: m. 1969, Richard Douglas Fowler Bream, of Long Folly Farm, Peatling Parva, Lutterworth, Leics., LE17 5QA, and has issue living, Tamerlane Douglas Fowler, b. 1971,—Atlanta Mary, b. 1970.

BROTHERS LIVING.

Hon. DENIS GOMER, TD, b. July 11th, 1911; ed. at Marlborough; a KStJ; a Councillor of Hants. and of New Forest RDC 1968-73; Pres. of Hants. Fedn. of Young Farmers' Clubs 1970; Pres. of New Forest Assocn.; formerly a Dir. of Kemsley Newspapers, Ltd.; Master of Coachmakers' and Coach Harness Makers' Co. 1959-60; 1939-45 War as Capt. RA and Maj. Grenadier Guards: m. 1st, 1934, Rosemary Leonora (from whom he obtained a divorce 1942), el. da. of the late Lionel de Rothschild [see B. Rothschild, colls.]; 2ndly, 1947, Pamela (GRANT), el. da. of the late Capt. Lord Richard Wellesley [see D. Wellington, colls.], and has issue living, (by 1st m.) Barbara Marie-Louise Constance b. 1935: m. 1954, Alexander Clement Gilmour, of Denchworth Manor, Wantage, Berks. [see Gilmour, Bt., cr. 1926],—Susan Lilian Constance, b. 1938: m. 1963, Christopher G. F. Harding, of Otterington House, Northallerton, Yorks., and has issue living, Rupert b. 1965, Louise b. 1966,— (by 2nd m.) Richard Gomer, b. 1951,—Anne Denise, b. 1948: m. 1970, Brian Peter Harvey Orange, of Fromans House, Kings Somborne, Hants., and has issue living, Michael Richard b. 1973, Simon George b. 1974. Residence,—Brockenhurst Park, Hants., SO4 7QP. Clubs,—White's, Pratt's, Hampshire (Winchester), Royal Yacht Squadron, and Bembridge Sailing.
Hon. (William) Neville, b. 1914; ed. at Harrow, and at Magdalen Coll., Oxford; Dl., Kemsley Newspapers 1938-59 and London Assurance 1950-59; 1939-45 War as Capt. Grenadier Guards: m. 1951, Christobel (NORRIE), only da. of the late John Wallis More-Molyneux. Residences,—Bermuda, 49, Av. Hector Otto, Monaco; Château St. Georges, 06320, Cap d'Ail, France. Clubs,—White's, Turf, Pratt's, Royal Yacht Squadron, Travellers' (Paris) and The Brook (New York).
Hon. Anthony George, MP, b. 1925; ed. at Eton, and at Ch. Ch., Oxford (MA); formerly a Dir. of Kemsley Newspapers Ltd., and Man. Dir. of Western Mail and Echo Ltd., a Member of W. Area Board British Transport Commn. 1956-58; is a JP for Cardiff, a CStJ; Dep. Chm. of Leopold Joseph & Sons, Ltd., a Dir., Anglo-Welsh Investment Trust, and Pres. of Welsh Games Council; High Sheriff of Glamorgan 1962; PPS to Min. of Housing and Local Govt. 1970, to Sec. of State for the Environment 1970-72, since when to Sec. of State for Trade and Industry; MP for Southgate (C) since 1964; 1939-45 War as Lt. Welsh Guards: m. 1st, 1954, the Hon. Mary Cynthia Burke Roche, from whom he obtained a divorce 1966, da. of 4th Baron Fermoy; 2ndly, 1966, Sarah Anne, da. of Raymond Clifford-Turner, and has issue living, (by 1st m.) Edward Anthony Morys, b. 1960,—Alexandra Mary, b. 1955,—Antonia Ruth, b. 1957,—Joanna Cynthia (twin), b. 1957,—(by 2nd m.) George Raymond Gomer, b. 1967,—Sasha Jane, b. 1969. Residences,—98, Ebury Mews, SW1; Warbrook House, Eversley, Hants. Clubs,—White's, Pratt's, Cardiff and County (Cardiff).

SISTER LIVING.

Hon. (Mary) Pamela (twin) (Pamela, Marchioness of Huntly), b. 1918: m 1941 (m. diss. 1965), the 12th Marquess of Huntly. Residence,—

WIDOW LIVING OF SON OF FIRST VISCOUNT.

Lady Mary Clementine Pratt, da. of 5th Marquess Camden; is a C.St.J.: m. 1st, 1940, the Hon. (Herbert) Oswald Berry, who d. 1952; 2ndly, 1953, (Shafto) Gerald Strachan Pawle (OStJ). Residence,—Trehiven, Madron, Penzance, Cornwall.

WIDOW LIVING OF FIRST VISCOUNT.

EDITH, OBE (Edith, Viscountess Kemsley), (Dropmore, Bucks.; 54, South St., W1), da. of E. N. Merandon du Plessis, of Constance, Flacq, Mauritius, and formerly wife of Cornelius Willem Dresselhuys; a CStJ, a Cdr. of Order of Phoenix of Greece, and a Chevalier of Legion of Honour; OBE (Civil) 1953: m. 1931, as his 2nd wife, the 1st Viscount, who d. 1968.

PREDECESSOR.—[1] (JAMES) GOMER Berry, GBE, son of Alderman John Mathias Berry, JP, of Gwaelodygarth, Merthy Tydfil [V. Camrose], b. 1883; Newspaper proprietor; Chm. of Kemsley Newspapers Ltd., and Editor-in-Ch., Sunday Times, 1937-59; cr. a Baronet 1928, Baron Kemsley, of Farnham Royal, co. Bucks. (peerage of UK) 1936, and Viscount Kemsley, of Dropmore, co. Bucks. (peerage of UK) 1945, GBE (Civil) 1959: m. 1st, 1907, Mary Lilian, who d. 1928, da. of the late Horace George Holmes, JP, of 8, Brondesbury Park, NW6; 2ndly, 1931, Edith, da. of E. N. Merandon du Plessis, of Constance, Flacq, Mauritius, formerly wife of Cornelius Willem Dresselhuys; d. 1968; s. by his el. son [2] (GEOFFREY) LIONEL, 2nd Viscount and present peer; also Baron Kemsley.

KENILWORTH, BARON.   **(Siddeley.)**   [**Baron U.K. 1937.**]

By striding.

JOHN DAVENPORT SIDDELEY, 3rd Baron; *b.* Jan. 24th, 1924; *s.* 1971; ed. at Marlborough, and Magdalene Coll., Camb. (BA); FRSA; Lord of the Manor of Kenilworth; Consultant Designer; Master of Coachmakers' and Coach Harness Makers' Co. 1969: *m.* 1948, Jacqueline Paulette, da. of the late Robert Gelpi, and has issue.

𝔄rms,—Per chevron or and azure in chief two goats' heads erased and in base a triangular castle with three towers, on a chief of the second two wings conjoined in fesse all counterchanged. 𝔠rest,— Issuant out of the battlements of a tower a goat's head argent armed or in front of a rising sun also issuant gold. 𝔖upporters,—On either side a goat or gorged with a collar azure pendent therefrom by a chain gold and escutcheon chequy of the first and second a chief ermine.

Residence,—2, Lexham Walk, W8.

SON LIVING.

Hon. JOHN RANDLE, *b.* June 16th, 1954; ed. at Northease Manor and London Coll. of Furniture.

DAUGHTER LIVING.

Hon. Belinda Jane (5, Manson Place, SW7), *b.* 1950: *m.* 1971 (m. diss. 1974), Christopher Aston James.

UNCLE LIVING.   *(Son of 1st Baron.)*

Hon. Ernest Hall, *b.* 1895 ; ed. at St. Lawrence Coll., Ramsgate ; formerly a Director of Armstrong Siddeley Motors, Ltd., of Coventry ; European War 1914-18 in France with Roy. W. Kent Regt.: *m.* 1921, Muriel, da. of the late John R. Quick, and has issue living, Audrey Joan (Belmont, Barford Rd., Bloxham, Banbury, Oxon., OX15 4EZ), *b.* 1922: *m.* 1st, 1951 (m. diss. 1955), John Main; 2ndly, 1971 (m. diss. 1974), Francis Bermingham. *Residence,*—19, Hale House, De Vere Gdns., W8.

AUNT LIVING.   *(Daughter of 1st Baron.)*

Hon. Joan Murray, *b.* 1904: *m.* 1926, Eric Austyn Reynolds, who *d.* 1969, and has issue living, Michael Austyn (6, Butlers Rd., Birmingham, 20), *b.* 1929,—Paul Siddeley (of Church Farm, Budbrooke, Warwick) *b.* 1931: *m.* 1954, Janet Anne Wyatt, and has issue living, Andrew Paul *b.* 1962, Patricia *b.* 1955, Lucy *b.* 1956, Claire Amy *b.* 1961,—Gerald Alfred John, *b.* 1942,—Sallie Joan, *b.* 1935: *m.* 1957, Joseph Antnony Earle, of The Long House, Gt. Alne, Alcester, Warwicks., and has issue living, Martin John, *b.* 1961, Melanie Joan *b.* 1959.   *Residence,*—Rosedale, Station Rd., Chipping Campden, Glos., CL55 6HY.

WIDOW LIVING OF SON OF FIRST BARON.

Pamela (3, Links Court, Grouville, Jersey), da. of the late G. A. Williams, of Gorey, Jersey: *m.* 1953, as his 2nd wife the Hon. Norman Goodier Siddeley, who *d.* 1971.

WIDOW LIVING OF SECOND BARON.

MARJORIE TENNANT (*Marjorie, Baroness Kenilworth*), (Hotel L'Horizon, St. Brelade's Bay, Jersey), da. of the late Harry Firth, of Dewsbury, Yorks.: *m.* 1919, the 2nd Baron, who *d.* 1971.

COLLATERAL BRANCH LIVING.

Issue of the late Hon. Norman Goodier Siddeley, yst. son of 1st Baron, *b.* 1898, *d.* 1971: *m.* 1st, 1924 (m. diss. 1953), Phyllis Erith, da. of Graham Derry, of Salisbury, Rhodesia; 2ndly, 1953, Pamela (ante), da. of the late G. A. Williams, of Gorey, Jersey:—

By 1st m.) Jane Goodier, *b.* 1928.

PREDECESSORS.—[1] JOHN DAVENPORT Siddeley, *CBE,* son of the late William Siddeley, of Manchester; *b.* 1866 ; a Motor and Aircraft Engineer ; was Chm. and Managing Director of Armstrong-Siddeley Motors, Ltd., of Parkside, Coventry, and of Sir W. G. Armstrong-Whitworth Aircraft, Ltd. ; High Sheriff of Warwickshire 1932 ; cr. *Baron Kenilworth,* of Kenilworth, co. Warwick (peerage of United Kingdom) 1937 : *m.* 1893, Sara Mabel, who *d.* 1953, dau. of the late James Goodier, of Macclesfield; *d.* 1953; *s.* by his el. son [2] CYRIL DAVENPORT, *CBE, TD,* 2nd Baron; *b.* 1894; *d.* 1971; *m.* 1919, Marjorie Tennant, da. of the late Harry Firth, of Dewsbury, Yorks.; *s.* by his son [3] JOHN DAVENPORT, 3rd Baron and present peer.

Kenlis, Baron,   **title of Marquess of Headfort on Roll of H. L.**

KENMARE, EARLDOM OF.   **(Browne.)**   [**Extinct 1952.**]

DAUGHTER LIVING OF FIFTH EARL.

Lady Cecily Kathleen, *b.* 1888 ; was Lady-in-Waiting to H.R.H. the Duchess of Gloucester 1947-51, and Woman of the Bedchamber to H.M. Queen Mary 1951-53, since when Extra Lady-in-Waiting to HRH the Duchess of Gloucester: *m.* 1911, Col. the Hon. Thomas Eustace Vesey, Irish Guards, who *d.* 1946 [see V. de Vesci, colls.]. *Residence,*—The Red House, Sunningdale, Berks.

KENNET, BARON. (Young.) [Baron U.K. 1935.]

In colle domus.

A house on a hill.

WAYLAND HILTON YOUNG, 2nd Baron; *b.* Aug. 2nd, 1923 ; *s.* 1960 ; ed. at Stowe, and at Trin. Coll., Camb.; Hon. FRIBA; Writer; Editor of "Disarmament and Arms Control" 1962-65; a Member of British Delegation, Assemblies W. European Union and Council of Europe 1962-65, and Chm. of UK Cttee. for International Co-operation Year 1965; Parl. Sec., Min. of Housing and Local Govt. 1966-70; Chm. of Advisory Cttee. on Oil Pollution at Sea 1970-74, and of Council for Protection of Rural England 1971-72, and of Internat. Parl. Conferences on the Environment since 1971; Dir. of Europe Plus Thirty 1974; 1939-45 War as Ordinary Seaman and Sub-Lt. RNVR; in Foreign Office 1946-47, and 1949-51: *m.* 1948, Elizabeth Ann, da. of Capt. Bryan Fullerton Adams, DSO, RN, of Cherry Tree, Hacheston, Suffolk, and has issue.

Arms,—Per fesse sable and argent: in chief two lions rampant-guardant, and in base an anchor erect with a cable, all counterchanged. Crest,—A demi-unicorn couped ermine, armed, maned, and hoofed or, gorged with a naval crown azure supporting an anchor erect sable.

Residence,—100, Bayswater Rd., W2.

SON LIVING.
Hon. (WILLIAM ALDUS) THOBY, *b.* May 24th, 1957.

DAUGHTERS LIVING.
Hon. Easter Donatella, *b.* 1949.
Hon. Emily Tacita, *b.* 1951.
Hon. Mopsa Mary, *b.* 1953.
Hon. Audrey Louise, *b.* 1959.
Hon. Alice Matelda Zoe, *b.* 1969.

PREDECESSOR.—[1] EDWARD HILTON Young, *G.B.E.*, *D.S.O.*, *D.S.C.*, *P.C.*, youngest son of Sir George Young, 3rd Bt. (cr. 1813) ; *b.* 1879 ; Bar. Inner Temple 1904 ; European War 1914-19 in H.M.S. "Iron Duke" and "Centaur," with British Naval Mission in Serbia, with Naval Guns in Flanders, at Zeebrugge in "Vindictive", and in N. Russia in charge of Armoured Train ; was Assist. Editor *Economist* 1909-10, and City Editor *Morning Post* 1910-14, Parliamentary Private Sec. to Pres. of Board of Education 1919-21, Financial Sec. to the Treasury 1921-22, Ch. Liberal Whip 1922-3, Parliamentary Sec. to Depart of Overseas Trade (in National Govt.) Sept. to Nov. 1931, and Min. of Health 1931-35 ; a Member of Hague Commn. 1922 ; sat as M.P. for Norwich (*L*) 1915-22, and 1924-29 (*L*, afterwards *C*), and for Sevenoaks Div. of Kent (*C*) 1929-35 ; cr. *Baron Kennet*, of the Dene, co. Wilts (peerage of United Kingdom) 1935 : *m.* 1922, Edith Agnes Kathleen, who *d.* 1947, dau. of the late Rev. Canon Lloyd Stewart Bruce [Bruce, Bt., cr. 1804, colls.], and widow of Capt. Robert Falcon Scott, C.V.O., R.N. ; *d.* 1960; *s.* by his only son [2] WAYLAND HILTON, 2nd Baron and present peer.

KENSINGTON, BARON. (Edwardes.) [Baron I. 1776 and U.K. 1886.]

GARDE LA FOI.

Keep the faith.

WILLIAM EDWARDES, 7th Baron ; *b.* May 15th, 1904 ; *s.* 1938; ed. at Eton; Lieut.-Col. Indian Army (retired); was A.D.C. to Gov. of Punjab 1932-5 ; European War 1939-44 in India, Burma, and Malaya (despatches).

Arms,—Quarterly : 1st and 4th ermine, a lion rampant sable, *Edwardes;* 2nd and 3rd gules, a chevron between three crosses bottony or, *Rich*, Crest,—On a mount vert, a wyvern, wings expanded, argent. Supporters.—Two reindeer proper, armed and unguled or.

Residence,—Mardan, P.O. Bromley, Rhodesia. *Club*, —Cavalry.

BROTHERS LIVING.
Hon. David, *D.S.C.*, *b.* 1907 ; ed. at Eton ; Com. (retired) R.N. ; European War 1939-44 (D.S.O.); *m.* 1939, Elizabeth, youngest dau. of the late Robert Alexander Longman Broadley, of Suddon Farm, Wincanton, Som., and has issue living, Susan, *b.* 1945: *m.* 1967, Capt. Hugh Michael Sandars, The Queen's Own Hussars (c/o National Westminster Bank, 45, Park St., Camberley, Surrey), and has issue living, Andrew George *b.* 1969, Claire Catherine *b.* 1972,—Mary Ann, *b.* 1947: *m.* 1968, Maj. Hugh William Kellow Pye, 9th/12th R. Lancers (Prince of Wales's) of Avenings, Danehill, Sussex, and has issue living, Robert Alec Kellow *b.* 1970,—Victoria Ann *b.* 1973,—Louisa Jane, *b.* 1959. *Residence,*—Suddon Farm, Wincanton, Som.
Hon. Michael George, *M.B.E.*, *b.* 1910 ; ed. at Eton ; Lieut.-Col. (retired) Rifle Brig. ; is a Member of Hon. Corps of Gentlemen-at-Arms ; Middle East 1941-43 (M.B.E.) ; M.B.E. (Mil.) 1944 : *m.* 1946, Sylvia Inez Pakenham, dau. of the late Col. Hope Johnstone, C.B.E., and formerly wife of Major A. J. T. McGaw. *Residence,*—4A, Belgrave Mews West, S.W.1.

WIDOW LIVING OF SON OF SIXTH BARON.
Angela Dorothea, dau. of the late Lieut.-Col. Eustace Shearman, 10th Hussars, and widow of George Benson, 15th/19th Hussars : *m.* 2ndly, 1932, Capt. the Hon. (Hugh) Owen Edwardes, who *d.* 1937 ; 3rdly, 1951, Lieut.-Com. John Hamilton, R.N. (retired), and has issue living, (by 2nd *m.*) [see colls., infra]. *Residence,*—Monkwood, Ayr.

COLLATERAL BRANCHES LIVING.
Issue of the late Capt. the Hon. (Hugh) Owen Edwardes, 2nd son of 6th Baron, *b.* 1905, *d.* 1937 : *m.* 1932, Angela Dorothea [(ante), she *m.* 3rdly, 1951, Lieut.-Com. John Hamilton of Rozelle, R.N. (retired)], dau. of the late Lieut.-Col.

Eustace Shearman, 10th Hussars, and widow of George Benson 15th/19th Hussars:—
HUGH IVOR (Ringwood Farm, Kassier Rd., Assagay, PO Hillcrest, Natal), b. Nov. 24th, 1933: m. 1961, Juliet Elizabeth Massy, da. of the late Alexander Massy Anderson, and has issue living, William Owen Alexander, b. 1964,—Hugh Rupert, b. 1967,—Amanda Louise Massy, b. 1962.——Meriel Davina, b. 1935: m. 1972, D. Andrew Long of Odell Lodge, Odell, Beds., and has issue living, James Philip, b. 1972.

Issue of the late Capt. the Hon. George Henry Edwardes, M.C., 4th son of 4th Baron, b. 1877, d. 1930: m. 1903, Olive, who d. 1968, da. of the late Charles Wyndham Rudolph Kerr [M. Lothian, colls.]:—
George Llewellyn, b. 1906.——Hugh Francis (of 125, Dalling Rd., W.6), b. 1908: m. 1957, Amelia Anne, dau. of the late C. H. Barker, of Barnsley, Yorks.——Olive Isobel, b. 1904.——Gwenllian Violet, b. 1912: m. 1932, Rear-Adm. Peter Douglas Herbert Raymond Pelly, C.B., D.S.O. [see Pelly Bt., colls.]. Residence,—Lowmersland, Les Rochers, Alderney.

Granddaughter of the late Lt.-Col. the Hon. Cuthbert Ellison Edwardes, 2nd son of 3rd Baron:—
Issue of the late Capt. Richard Edwardes, b. 1894, d. 1967: m. 1929, Ada Mary (Litchfields, Cripstead Lane, St. Cross, Winchester), da. of the late William R. MacGeorge, of Glasgow:—
Joan Margaret, b. 1932: m. 1958, John Spencer Clarke, of The Roos, Whitchurch, Hants., and has issue living, Charles Richard Spencer, b. 1960,—James Alured, b. 1964,—Sally Aletta, b. 1959,—Fiona Jane, b. 1963.

Grandchildren of the late Rev. the Hon. Thomas Edwardes, 6th son of 2nd Baron:—
Issue of the late Rev. George Edwardes, b. 1869, d. 1919: m. 1893, Ethel Mary, who d. 1900, da. of Frederick Lassetter, and widow of the Rev. Philip Charles Bicknell, R. of Swilland:—
Anne, b. 1900: m. 1930, Claude Edward New, OBE, who d. 1968, and has issue living, Rev. Thomas (The Vicarage, Banstead, Surrey), b. (Sept.) 1930, ed. at Camb. Univ. (MA): m. 1956, Joan Mary, da. of James Alfred Harding, and has issue living, Katharine Elisabeth b. 1959, Mary Frances b. 1962,—Benedict Edward, b. 1936. Residence,—St. Hugh's, Boxgrove, Chichester, Sussex.

Issue of the late Edward Henry Edwardes, O.B.E., b. 1875, d. 1955: m. 1907, Eleanor Matilda, who d. 1925, dau. of the late Rev. William Nuttall (formerly V. of Atherton, Manchester), of 58, Park Road, Southport:—
William, b. 1908; European War 1940-45 as Major R.A.S.C. in France and Germany (despatches): m. 1st, 1937, Dorothy Robertshaw, only dau. of Aaron Wedgwood, of Worsley, Lancashire; 2ndly, 1943, Joan, only dau. of the late Ernest Topping, of Atherton, Lancashire, and has issue living, (by 2nd m.) David William (41, Redwood Av., Stone, Staffs.), b. 1944: m. 1972, Diana June, yst. da. of William Eden Morton, of London. Residence,—Spinneys, Church St., Eccleshall, Stafford.——John, TD, b. 1914; ed. at Manchester Univ. (BSc Technical 1939); is Capt. W. Somerset Yeo., RA, TA), and an AMIEE; European War 1939-45 as Major REME. Residence,—10, Heckford Rd., Corfe Mullen, Dorset.——Barbara, b. 1909: m. 1939, August Henry Gernaey, of Oakwood House, Birkacre, Chorley, Lancs,. and has issue living, Susan Leonie, b. 1940,—Joanna, b. 1942,—Caroline, b. 1945.——Eleonora, b. 1911: m. 1942, Joseph Hugh Scott Gardner, and has issue living, Hugh Martin, b. 1951,—Sarah, b. 1944. Residence,—Barton House, Broadoak Park, Worsley, Lancashire.

Grandsons of the late Edward Henry Edwardes, OBE (ante):—
Issue of the late Rev. Edward Edwardes, b. 1912, d. 1973: m. 1940, Norah (Willowmead, Sector Lane, Axminster, Devon), only da. of J. W. Watson, of Corbridge, Newcastle:—
Antony, b. 1942.——Nigel Kim (20, Stoney Acres, Yetminster, Dorset), b. 1948: m. 1972, Kay Marjorie, el. da. of S. Barnes, of Pitt Farm, Whitchurch, Canonicorum, Dorset.

PREDECESSORS.—[1] WILLIAM Edwardes, M.P. for Haverfordwest; inherited through his mother on the death of his cousin the 7th Earl of Warwick the estates of the Rich family; cr. Baron Kensington (peerage of Ireland) 1776; d. 1801; s. by his son [2] WILLIAM, 2nd Baron; b. 1777; M.P. for Haverfordwest 1801-18; d. 1852; s. by his son [3] WILLIAM, 3rd Baron Capt. R.N. and Lord-Lieut. of co. Pembroke; m. 1833, Laura Jane, dau. of Cuthbert Ellison, Esq., of Hepburn, Durham: d. 1872; s. by his son [4] WILLIAM, P.C., 4th Baron, b. 1835; Lord-Lieut. of co. Pembroke; M.P. for Haverfordwest (L) 1868-85; a Groom-in-Waiting to H.M. Queen Victoria 1873-4, Comptroller of H.M. Queen Victoria's Household 1880-85, a Lord-in-Waiting to H.M. Queen Victoria 1886, and Capt. of Yeomen of the Guard 1892-5; cr. Baron Kensington, of Kensington, co. Middlesex (peerage of United Kingdom) 1886; m. 1867, Grace Elizabeth, who d. 1910, dau. of the late Robert Johnstone-Douglas, d. 1896; s. by his el. son [5] WILLIAM, 5th Baron, b. 1868; Capt. 2nd Life Guards; d. (of wounds received in S. Africa) 1900; s. by his brother [6] HUGH, C.M.G., D.S.O., T.D., 6th Baron, b. 1873; Col. (retired) T.A.; S. Africa 1900-1901 (D.S.O.), European War 1914-19 (C.M.G.): m. 1903, Mabel Carlisle, who d. 1934, dau. of George Pilkington, of Stoneleigh, Woolton, Lancashire; d. 1938; s. by his son [7] WILLIAM, 7th Baron and present peer.

KENSWOOD, BARON. (Whitfield.) [Baron U.K. 1951.]

Give me wisdom.
Hon. Anna Louise, b. 1964.

JOHN MICHAEL HOWARD WHITFIELD, 2nd Baron, b. April 6th, 1930; s. 1963; ed. at Harrow, at Grenoble Univ., and at Emmanuel Coll., Camb. (B.A. 1952): m. 1951, Deirdre Anna Louise, da. of the late Colin Malcolm Methven, and has issue.

Arms,—Azure an argosy in full sail pennons flying or, a chief argent thereon a lion passant gules holding in the dexter forepaw a thunderbolt proper. Crest,—between two wings or, a sprig of oak fructed proper. Supporters,—Dexter, a figure representing St. Cecilia habited argent cloaked azure with organ-pipes proper in her exterior hand; sinister, a figure representing St. Gregory the Great habited argent cloaked gules holding with his exterior arm a papal staff or and holding in the hand a book proper bound sable.

Residence,—Manor Farm, Roch, Pembrokeshire.

SONS LIVING.

Hon. MICHAEL CHRISTOPHER, b. July 3rd, 1955.
Hon. Anthony John, b. 1957.
Hon. Steven James, b. 1958.
Hon. Benjamin Matthew, b. 1961.

DAUGHTER LIVING.

SISTER LIVING.
Hon. Ann Sophia Madeline, b. 1928: m. 1948, Richard Bethune Buzzard, B.M., B.Ch., of 80, Carlton Hill, N.W.8 [see B. Monkswell, colls.].

WIDOW LIVING OF FIRST BARON.
CATHERINE (CHILVER-STAINER) (Catherine, Baroness Kenswood) (c/o Barclays Bank, 5, Oxford St., W1), da. of Frank Luxton: m. 1962, as his second wife, the 1st Baron, who d. 1963.

PREDECESSOR.—[1] ERNEST ALBERT Whitfield, son of John Henry Whitfield, of London; b. 1887; professional violinist; ret. from concert platform 1935; a Gov. of B.B.C. 1946-50; Pres., National Federation of Blind 1951-4: m. 1st, 1920, Sophie Madeline, who d. 1961, dau. of Ernest Walters Howard; 2ndly, 1962, Mrs. Catherine Chilver-Stainer, da. of Frank Luxton; cr. Baron Kenswood, of St. Marylebone, co. London (peerage of UK) 1951; d. 1963; s. by his only son [2] JOHN MICHAEL HOWARD, 2nd Baron and present peer.

KENT, DUKE OF, see Royal Family.

KENYON, BARON. (Tyrell-Kenyon.) [Baron G.B. 1788, Bt. G.B. 1784.]

Sustain the Cross with magnanimity.

LLOYD TYRELL-KENYON, CBE, 5th Baron, and 5th Baronet; b. Sept. 13th, 1917; s. 1927; ed. at Eton, and at Magdalene Coll., Camb. (BA); Hon. LL.D. Wales 1958; FSA; Capt. RA (TA), a JP and a DL for Flintshire, an OStJ, and patron of one living, a Dir. of Lloyds Bank; a Member of Flint Co. Council 1945-55 (Chm. 1954-55), and Pres. of National Museum of Wales 1952-57; Ch. Commr. Boy Scouts for Wales 1948-66, and a Member of Standing Commn. on Museums and Art Galleries 1953-60; Pres. of Univ. Coll., N. Wales since 1947; Gov. of Welbeck Coll. 1952; and a Trustee of National Portrait Gallery 1953 (Chm. 1966); Chm. of Wrexham Powys and Mawddach Hosp. Management Cttee. 1960-74; and a Member of Roy. Commn. on Historical MSS since 1966; CBE (Civil) 1972: m. 1946, Leila Mary, da. of Com. John Wyndham Cookson, RN (ret.) [Colquhoun, Bt.], and widow of Hugh William Jardine Ethelston Peel, Lt. Welsh Guards [Buchanan-Jardine, Bt.], and has issue.

Arms,—Quarterly: 1st and 4th sable, a chevron engrailed or, between three crosses-flory argent, Kenyon; 2nd and 3rd argent, two chevronels azure, within a bordure engrailed gules, Tyrell. **Crests,**—1st, a lion sejant proper, resting the dexter fore paw on a cross flory argent; 2nd, a boar's head couped and erect argent, and issuing from the mouth a peacock's tail proper. **Supporters,**—On either side a tiger reguardant ¦proper, round the neck a chain or pendent therefrom an escutcheon of the arms of Tyrell.

Seat,—Gredington, nr. Whitchurch, Shropshire.

SONS LIVING.
Hon. LLOYD (The Green Cottage, Haughton, Tarporley, Cheshire), b. July 13th, 1947; ed. at Eton and Magdalene Coll., Camb.: m. 1971, Sally Carolyn, el. da. of J. F. P. Matthews, of The Firs, Thurston, Bury St. Edmunds, and has issue living, Lloyd Nicholas, b. 1972.
Hon. Richard, (The Cumbers, Hanmer, Whitchurch, Salop), b. 1948; ed. at Eton, and Seale Hayne Coll.: m. 1970, Davina Jane, da. of David Charles George Jessel [see Jessel, Bt.], and has issue living, Vanessa Zoë, b. 1974.
Hon. Thomas, b, 1954.

DAUGHTER LIVING.
Hon. Katherine, b. 1959.

SISTER LIVING.
Hon. Sarah Myfida Mary, MBE (twin), b. 1917; formerly in VAD; MBE (Civil) 1952: m. 1966, Col. Desmond Aubrey Robert Bancroft Cooke, late 13th/18th Hussars, of 10, Guthrie St., SW3.

COLLATERAL BRANCHES LIVING.
Grandchildren of the late Rev. the Hon. William Trevor Kenyon, 5th son of 3rd Baron:—
Issue of the late Gordon Lloyd Trevor Kenyon, b. 1873, d. 1951: m. 1909, Dorothy Charlotte, who d. 1961, dau. of the late D. J. Wood, Mus.D., F.R.C.O., of The Close, Exeter :—
Lloyd Gordon Trevor, b. 1911: m. 1939, Joyce Alma, dau. of the late F. J. Parker, and has issue living, Roger Lloyd, b. 1960.—Pamela Joan, b. 1940: m. 1963, Barry Thomas Gouldstone, of The Homestead, 105, Slough Rd., Datchet, Berks., and has issue living, Jeremy Thomas b. 1964, Penelope Joan b. 1968,—Carol Ann, b. 1944. Residence,—31, Frays Av., W. Drayton, Middlesex.——
Elizabeth Alis Georgina, b. 1910: m. 1935, Geoffrey Basset Wardell-Yerburgh, who d. 1944, and has issue living, Oswald Kenyon (of Orchard Leigh, Hockett Lane, Cookham Dean, Berks.), b. 1936; ed. at Eton; late 10th Roy. Hussars: m. 1960, Daphne Anne, da. of Arthur Whitley, of Hampton Hill, Middlesex, and has issue living, Peter Geoffrey b. 1964, Susan Elizabeth b. 1961. Residence,—Meadow View, Westbury Leigh, Wilts.

Granddaughter of the late Lt.-Col. Herbert Edward Kenyon, DSO (infra):—
Issue of the late Kenneth Herbert Kenyon, b. 1908, d. 1970: m. 1934, Barbara Joan (White Cottage, Westerland, Marldon, Paignton, S. Devon), da. of the late J. E. M. Urry, of Homedene, Cranley Gdns., N10:—
Anne Judith, b. 1939.

Grandchildren of the late Maj.-Gen. Edward Ranulph Kenyon, C.B., C.M.G. (infra):—
Issue of the late Lieut.-Col. Herbert Edward Kenyon, D.S.O., b. 1881, d. 1958: m. 1907, Gwendoline Ethel Graham, who d. 1958, dau. of the late F. G. Ommanney, of Sheen House, Walmer:—

Lloyd Douglas, b, 1912; ed. at Framlingham Coll.: m. 1929, Joan, da. of the late R. Appleby, of Geraldine, New Zealand, and has issue living, Gwendoline Jane ,b. 1942: m. 1964, Trevor William Payton, of 72, Campbell Rd., Pine Hill, Dunedin, NZ, and has issue living, Kim Maree b. 1966, Jill Michelle b. 1967, Raeleen Jan b. 1971,—Sally Mavourneen, b. 1944: m. 1966, David George Drayton, of 102, Huntsbury Av., Christchurch 2, NZ, and has issue living, Tania May b. 1970, Leanne Mavourneen b. 1971. Residence,—5 Oxford St., Waimate, S. Canterbury, NZ.——John Frederick, OBE. MC, b. 1921; ed. at Marlborough; Col. (ret.) RA and Gen. Staff, Mil. Asst. to C. in C. Far East Land Forces 1962-64, and Defence, Naval and Mil. Attaché, Brussels and Luxembourg 1971-73; SE Asia 1943-45 (MC); OBE (Mil.) 1970: m. 1st, 1947 (m. diss. 1960), Jean Molyneux, da. of Howard Godfrey, MC; 2ndly, 1960, Mrs. Margaret Bowker Franks, da. of the late Mrs. C. C. B. Remington, of Wadham, Horsell, Surrey, and has issue living, (by 1st m.) John Robert (12, Hartley Court, 40, Glen Eyre Rd., Bassett, Southampton), b. 1948; ed. at St. Edward's Sch., Oxford: m. 1973, Christine Ann, da. of Mrs. E. M. Green, of Lightcliffe, Yorks., and has issue living, Philippa Mary b. 1974,— Richard Howard Trevor, b. 1951; ed. at St. Edward's Sch., Oxford, and Harper Adams Agric. Coll. Residence,—Pradoe, Oswestry, Salop. Club,—Farmers.——Margaret Gwendoline, b. 1918; 1939-45 War with VAD (Defence and War Medals): m. 1945, Stanley Steven Baronoski, of 65, Clark St., Wolcott, Conn., USA 06716, and has issue living, Robert Steven, b. 1947; S/Sgt. US Marines; Okinawa and Viet Nam: m. 1971, Kyoko Nakama, and has issue living, Stanley Steven b. 1972, Margaret Gwendoline b. 1971,—Michael John, b. 1948,—David Stanley, b. 1953: m. 1972, Alana Sue Jones, and has issue living, Jeremy David b. 1973,—Peter Kenyon, b. 1955,—Richard Lloyd, b. 1957,—Kenneth Owen, b. 1963,—Gwendoline Mary, b. 1949,—Heather Joy, b. 1956.——Irene Patricia, b. 1923, late WAAF (War medal): m. 1953, Keith Louis Kerr, and has issue living, Graham Keith, b. 1954,—Patricia Louise, b. 1956. Residence,—Dumbarton RD, Millers Flat, Otago, NZ.

Grandchildren of the late John Robert Kenyon, Q.C., D.C.L. (infra) :—

Issue of the late Maj.-Gen. Edward Ranulph Kenyon, C.B., C.M.G., b. 1854; d. 1937: m. 1880, Katharine Mary McCrea, who d. 1908, dau. of the late Maj.-Gen. John Cromie Blackwood De Butts, R.E.:—

Katharine Mary Rose, b. 1887. Residence,—1, The Drove, Twyford, nr. Winchester.——Winifred Lilian, b. 1892: m. 1921, Herbert Stansfield Williamson, ICS (ret.), who d. 1955, and has issue living, Paul Kenyon (Staplegrove House, Taunton, Somerset), b. 1925; ed. at Rugby, and at Trin. Coll., Camb.: m. 1956, Gillian Anderson, da. of Lt.-Col. John Anderson Smith, OBE, RA, of Leamington Spa, and has issue living, Michael Paul b. 1957, Peter John 1958, Clare Honor b. 1961,— Mark Herbert (The Old House, Fulford, York), b. 1928; ed. at Rugby, and at Ch. Ch., Oxford; Prof. of Biol. Univ. of York: m. 1958, Charlotte, da. of the late Hugh Macdonald, of Fyfield, Abingdon, and has issue living, Hugh Thomas Saumarez b. 1961, Emma Charlotte Mary b. 1963, Sophia Louisa Harriet b. 1965,—Ann Katherine, b. 1922; ed. at Lady Margaret Hall, Oxford (MA): m. 1948, John Angus Macbeth Mitchell, CVO, MC, of 20, Regent Terr., Edinburgh, 7, and has issue living, Jonathan James b. 1951; ed. at Marlborough, New Coll., Oxford (BA), and Edinburgh Univ., Andrew Macbeth b. 1958; ed. at Edin Acad., Isabel Charlotte b. 1953; ed. at St. George's, Edinburgh, and Birmingham Coll. of Art & Design: m. 1972, Martin Charles Mooney, of 35, Broughton St., Edinburgh, Catherine Olivia b. 1956; ed. at St. George's Edinburgh, and Robt. Gordon's Inst. of Tech., Aberdeen. Residence,—Redstone, Pound Lane,Bishops Lydeard, Som.——Frances Margaret, MRCS, LRCP, b. 1894; formerly Assist. Co. Med. Officer for Westmorland: m. 1927, Geoffrey Fausitt Taylor, MRCP, MB, BCh, IMS, from whom she obtained a divorce 1941, and has issue living, Robert Julian Fausitt, b. 1929; ed. at Oundle, and at Trin. Coll., Camb. (BA 1st class honours); a FRGS; late 2nd Lt. The R. Scots; is a Member of British Ornithological Union; served with Falkland Islands Dependencies Survey 1953-56 (Polar Medal); a Dir. of Blue Funnel Line, Liverpool: m. 1954, Jacqueline Castaing, and has issue living, Lucien Giles b. 1966, Adrian Piers b. 1967,— Humphrey John Fausitt (25, Springfield Rd., St. John's Wood, NW8), b. 1934; ed. at Gordonstoun, and at Trin. Coll., Camb. (BA); late 2nd Lt. King's African Rifles; late Assist. Dist. Commr., Ngara, Tanganyika; Man. Dir. of Opinion Research Centre, London; m. 1970, Penelope Helen Spathis, and has issue living, Zanthe Fiona Margaret b. 1971, Helena Beatrice b. 1973,—Mary Venetia Fausitt, b. 1928; BA 1st class honours 1951; Carmelite Nun,—Elisabeth Joy Fausitt, b. 1932; ed. at Somerville Coll., Oxford (BA 1954): m. 1954, the Rt. Rev. Geoffrey Hewlett Thompson, MA, Sulfragan Bishop of Willesden, of 173, Willesden Lane, NW6 4YY, and has issue living, Andrew Hewlett b. 1957, Benjamin John b. 1963, Mary Clare b. 1955, Louise Margaret b. 1961. Residence,—Low Broomrigg, Warcop, Appleby, Cumbria.

Issue of the late Eustace Alban Kenyon, b. 1859, d. 1920 : m. 1896, Caroline Ethel Jane, who d. 1950, dau. of the late Rev. William Cornish Hunt, R. of Odell, Bedfordshire :—

William Patrick, MC, b. 1898; ed. at Marlborough; Lieut.-Col. (ret.) Roy. Welch Fusiliers European War 1917-18 (wounded, MC, Italian silver medal), Waziristan 1921-3 (medal with two clasps), European War 1939-45 in France, N. Africa, and Italy (despatches): m. 1928, Joan Mary, da. of the late Allan Edward Batchelor, JP [Makins, Bt.], and has issue living, Martin Robert (Club,— Travellers.), b. 1929; ed. at Eton, and at Corpus Christi Coll., Oxford; late 2nd Lieut. Roy. Welch Fusiliers; Exec. Sec., Overseas Students Trust since 1962: m. 1975, Mary Ann, da. of Lt.-Cdr. Patrick Henry James Southby, RN (ret.) [see Southby, Bt.],—Eustace Allan Michael, b. 1931; ed. at St. Edward's Sch., Oxford; late Lt. RWF; Manager of Nicolton Orchards, Suffolk,—Thomas David, b. 1932; ed. at Wellington; Maj. RWF; Malaya 1954 (wounded), Cyprus 1958. Residence,—Lydbury House, Lydbury North, Shropshire.——Violet Mary, b. 1899: m. 1951, Cedric William de Mesurier Croll. Residence,—Lady Whincups, Rendham, Saxmundham, Suffolk.—— Irene Helen, OBE, b. 1902; OBE (Civil) 1959: m. 1925, Basil Herbert Bright, MC, formerly Capt. Worcestershire Regt. (TF), and has issue living, William Frederick (of Oakdene, Russell Lane, Danbury, Essex), b. 1926; ed. at Halleybury; formerly Gunner RA: m. 1950, Eleanore Ann Lee,— Richard Kenyon (Southlands, Ulting Farm, Ulting, Maldon, Essex), b. 1934; ed. at St. Edward's Sch., Oxford; is Lt. Suffolk Yeo., RA (TA): m. 1963, Maureen Hill,—Elizabeth Ruth, b. 1930: m. 1952, Geoffrey Donald Sharpe, of 11, Netheroyd Hill Rd., Huddersfield, Yorks., and has issue living, Julian Donald b. 1953, Nigel Anthony b. 1955,—Penelope Jane Desborough, b. 1936: m. 1962, Peter Herbert Wilkins, Roy. Malaysia Police, and has issue living, Philip Kenyon b. 1963, Richard Desborough b. 1965. Residence,—32, Beeleigh Rd., Maldon, Essex.

Grandchildren of the late Eustace Alban Kenyon (ante) :—

Issue of the late Rowland Lloyd Kenyon, b. 1901; d. 1959: m. 1936 (m. diss. 1950), Gwendoline Doris Dorman of Trimulgherry, Ipswich Rd., Brantham, Manningtree, Essex, [who m. 2ndly, 1954 (m. diss. 1969), Major Leslie Dunn, Coldstream Gds. and E. Surrey Regt. (ret.)] :—

Peter Rowland (PO Box 144, Bahrain), b. 1937; late RAF; with Internat. Aeradio Ltd.: m. 1962, Wilma, da. of Ludwig Pranger of Pöttsching (Burgenland), Siedlung, 16, Austria, and has issue living, Rupert Peter, b. 1968,—Berenice Sofia, b. 1964,—Rebecca Louise, b. 1966.——Robert Nicholas Andrew (8, Aubre Cres., Noble Park, Vic. 3174, Aust.), b. 1939; formerly in RE.

Granddaughter of the late Maj.-Gen. Lionel Richard Kenyon, C.B., son of the late John Robert Kenyon, Q.C., D.C.L. (infra) :—

Issue of the late Major Harold Anthony Kenyon, M.C., b. 1897, d. 1934 : m. 1931, Iris Veronica Margaret (who m. 2ndly, 1936, as his second wife, Maj.-Gen. Mervyn Savile Wheatley, CB, CBE, of 5, Heathfield Court, Fleet Rd., Fleet, Hants.), da. of the late Lt.-Col. M. McL. Corbyn, of Little Grange, Woodbridge, Suffolk:—

Elisabeth Veronica, b. 1931: m. 1953 (m. diss. 1974), Robert Arthur David Shutes, and has issue living, Anthony David, b. 1955,—Caroline Ann Veronica, b. 1954. Residence,—Ford Cottage, Send, nr. Guildford, Surrey.

Grandchildren of the late John Robert Kenyon, Q.C., D.C.L., son of the late Hon. Thomas Kenyon, 3rd son of 1st Baron :—

Issue of the late Sir Frederic George Kenyon, G.B.E., K.C.B., T.D., b. 1863, d. 1952: m. 1891, Amy, who d. 1938, dau. of the late Rowland Hunt, of Boreatton Park, Shropshire:—

Dame Kathleen Mary, CBE, b. 1906; ed. St. Paul's Girls' Sch., and at Somerville Coll., Oxford (MA), DLit, London 1952, DLitt Oxford 1964; Hon. DLitt Exeter 1969; LHD, Kenyon Coll., Ohio, 1959, Sec., Institute of Archaeology, London Univ. 1935-47, Lecturer in Palestine Archaeology, London Univ. 1947-62, Dir. of British Sch. of Archaeology in Jerusalem 1951-66, and Principal of St. Hugh's Coll., Oxford since 1962; a FSA and a FBA; CBE (Civil) 1954, DBE (Civil) 1973. Residence,—Old Brand's Lodge, Terriers, High Wycombe, Bucks.——Nora Gwendolen Margaret, b. 1908; ed. at St. Paul's Girls' Sch., and at Somerville Coll., Oxford (MA): m. 1936, John Ritchie, MBE, Master of Supreme Court (Queen's Bench Div.), and has issue living, Jeremy Kenyon Tod (59, Church Av., SW14), b. 1942; ed. at Winchester, and Magdalen Coll., Oxford (BA): m. 1971, Barbara Ann Blackwell, and has issue living, Simon John b. 1974,—Janet Margaret Amy, b. 1939: m. 1963, Alan Seward Penson Heath, of The Hollies, Thrussington, Leics., and has issue living, Nicholas Gordon John b. 1966, Christopher Frederic William b. 1968, Caroline Margaret Janet b. 1971,—Elspeth Nora Watson, b. 1948; ed. at St. Hugh's Coll., Oxford (BA): m. 1972, Giulio Nevio Panichi (Viale Ammiraglio del Bond 56, 00056, Ostia Lido, Rome, Italy). Residence,—Kirkstead, Godstone, Surrey.

Issue of the late Maj.-Gen. Lionel Richard Kenyon, C.B., b. 1867, d. 1952: m. 1896, Elizabeth Jane, who d. 1946, dau. of the late Peter Cormack Sutherland, M.D., of Pietermaritzburg, Natal:—

Lionel Frederic Robert, DSO, b. 1900; ed. at Wellington; Brig. (ret.) late R.E.; late Sec. T.A. Assocn. W. Lancs, and a Member of E. Anglian TA & VR Assocn.; E. Suffolk Co. Council 1963-74; Suffolk Co. Council since 1973; Waziristan 1922-23 (despatches, medal with clasp), Khajuri Plain 1930-31 (despatches, clasp); 1939-45 War in Middle East and Italy (despatches, DSO, 1939-45 star, Africa star, Italy star, France and Germany star, Defence and War medals); DSO 1945: m. 1933, Venice, da. of Maj. William John Corbett-Winder, JP, of Vaynor Park, Berriew, Montgomeryshire. Residence,—The Valley House, Stratford St. Mary, Colchester.

Grandchildren of the late Col. the Rt. Hon. William Slaney Kenyon-Slaney, MP. el. son of Col. William Kenyon-Slaney, 5th son of the Hon. Thomas Kenyon, (ante):—

Issue of the late Maj. Robert Orlando Rodolph Kenyon-Slaney, b. 1892, d. 1965: m. 1st, 1917, Lady Mary Cecilia Rhodesia Hamilton (from whom he obtained a divorce 1930), da. of 3rd Duke of Abercorn; 2ndly, 1931, Nesta, who d. 1947, da. of Sir George Ferdinand Forestier-Walker, 3rd Bt. (cr. 1835):—

(By 1st m.) Robert Ivan (Hatton Grange, Shifnal, Salop; White's and Pratts Clubs), b. 1926; ed. at Eton; Lt. Grenadier Guards (Reserve), a JP of Salop; High Sheriff Salop 1973; Regional Dir. Lloyds Bank, and Member Exec. Cttee. CLA: m. 1964, Meriel Rose, da. of the late Capt. Joseph Gurney Fowell Buxton [see Buxton, Bt. colls.], and has issue living, Rupert David, b. 1965,—Thomas Alexander, b. 1966,—Natasha Vivien, b. 1969.——Ursula Jane, b. 1920: m. 1st, 1940, Lt.-Col. David Ludovic Peter Lindsay, DSO, Irish Guards, from whom she obtained a divorce 1946 [see E. Crawford, colls.]; 2ndly, 1946, as his second wife (m. diss. 1950), Group Capt. the Hon. (John William) Maxwell Aitken, DSO, DFC, now Sir (John William) Maxwell Aitken, DSO, DFC, 2nd Bt. [see By. Beaverbrook]; 3rdly, 1951, Robert Edward John Compton [see M. Northampton, colls.].——(by 2nd m.) William Simon Rodolph (Chyknell, Bridgnorth, Salop), b. 1932; ed. at Eton; Lt. Gren. Gds. (Reserve); FRICS; JP of Salop: m. 1960, Mary Helena, el. da. of the late Lt.-Col. the Hon. Henry George Orlando Bridgeman, DSO, MC [see E. Bradford, colls.], and has issue living, Henry James Rodolph, b. 1961,—Andrew William Orlando, b. 1965,—Francis Alan, b. 1966.

Grandchildren of the late Percy Robert Kenyon-Slaney (infra):—

Issue of the late Gerald William Kenyon-Slaney, O.B.E., b. 1899, d. 1953: m. 1928, Barbara Nannette (The Garth, St. Margaret's Bay, Kent; 16, Smith Terr., SW3), da. of the late Rev. Granville Gore Skipwith [see Skipwith, Bt., colls.]:—

Orlando Michael Philip, b. 1929; ed. at Winchester and at Ch. Ch., Oxford (B.A. 1953): m. 1960, Philippa Margaret, da. of Sir Thomas Claude Harris Lea, 3rd Bt., and has issue living, Jeremy Francis Gerald, b. 1966,—Philip Thomas Christopher, b. 1969. Residence,—Oakwood, St. Michael's, Tenterden, Kent.——Gerald Timothy Granville (The Garth, St. Margaret's Bay, Kent), b. 1937; ed. at Bradfield Coll.; late Grenadier Guards.——Thomasina Angela Jane (16, Smith Terr., SW3), b. 1933: m. 1954 (m. diss. 1968), Maj. Thomas David Ogilvy Codner, late Coldstream Guards, and has issue living, Vivien Ogilvy, b. 1957,—Clare Jane, b. 1959.

Grandchildren of the late Col. William Kenyon-Slaney (ante):—

Issue of the late Percy Robert Kenyon-Slaney, b. 1861, d. 1911: m. 1895, Geraldine Ellen Georgina, who d. 1947, dau. of the late Rev. George Whitmore:—

Frances Diamond Sara, b. 1897: m. 1924, Colin Spencer James, who d. 1971, and has issue living, Philip Kenyon (of Langworthy, Broadbury, Okehampton, Devon), b. 1928: m. 1951, Adela Mary Hawtrey, da. of the late John Edward Samuel Long, of Rimpton School, Broadstairs, Kent, and has issue living, Robert Kenyon b. 1958, Philippa Anne b. 1952: m. 1972, Timothy Mansford Newsholme, of Oldfield Cottage, Portishead, Bristol,—Helen Frances b. 1954, Diana Madge b. 1960. Residence,—Bannadon, Broadbury, Okehampton, N. Devon.——Ruth Stella (Nant-y-Lladron Barn, Wrexham), b. 1909: m. 1st 1928, Lt.-Cdr. John Francis Crofton Barker-Hahlo, RN (ret.) who d. (killed in action during European War) 1941, and from whom she had obtained a divorce 1939; 2ndly, 1939, Sir (William) Patrick McMahon, 7th Bt., who obtained a divorce 1960, and has issue living, (by 1st m.) Derek Kenyon (Dishcombe, S. Tawton, Okehampton, Devon), b. 1931: m. 1961, Teresa Clare Cunningham, da. of Capt. Ronald Cunningham Wield, OBE, RN, and has issue living, John William b. (Jan.) 1963, David Julian Neil b. (Dec.) 1963, Robin Douglas b. 1966, Kirstie Isabelle b. 1965,—(by 2nd m.) [see McMahon, Bt.].

Granddaughters of the late Charles Robert Kenyon, el. son of the late Rev. Charles Orlando Kenyon, 6th son of the late Hon. Thomas Kenyon (ante):—

Issue of the late Charles Orlando Kenyon, b. 1886, d. 1973: m. 1st, 1915, Marguerite Laura, who d. 1948, da. of Alexander Kealman, of Santos, Brazil; 2ndly, 1950, Sarah (Santos, Brazil), da. of :—

By 1st m.) Dorothy Beatrice, b. 1917; 1939-45 War with WAAF (Defence Medal): m. 1946, Donald Stanford Egremont, of Pasture Cottage, Redlynch, Salisbury, Wilts., and has issue living, Christopher Andrew, b. 1948,—Donald Alexander, b. 1955.——Elizabeth Matilda, b. 1920: m. 1st, 1942 (m. diss. 1945), ; 2ndly, 1947, Robert F. Dennison, of Lagos, Portugal, and has issue living (by 2nd m.), Robert Kenyon, b. 1948,—William Alexander, b. 1951,—John Keasbey, b. 1958. ——(by 2nd m.) Sylvia Elena, b. 1952.

Granddaughter of the late Arthur Richard Kenyon, yst. son of the late Hon. Thomas Kenyon (ante):—

Issue of the late Arthur Augustus Kenyon, b. 1868, d. 1944: m. 1900, Agnes, who d. 1937, dau. of the late W. A. Oliver-Rutherfurd, of Edgerston, Jedburgh, N.B. :—

May Patricia Agatha, b. 1908: m. 19—, W. Morton, c/o Box 13, Glendo, Wyoming, USA, and has issue living, a son, b. 19—,—a da., b. 19—,—a da., b. 19—.

PREDECESSORS.—[1] Sir Lloyd Kenyon, K.B.; Ch. Justice of Chester 1780, Attorney-Gen. 1782, Master of the Rolls 1784, and Lord Ch. Justice of England 1788; cr. a Baronet 1784, and Lord Kenyon, Baron of Gredington, co. Flint (peerage of Great Britain) 1788; d. 1802; s. by his son [2] George, 2nd Baron; d. 1855; s. by his son [3] Lloyd, 3rd Baron; b. 1805; d. 1869; s. by his grandson [4] Lloyd (son of the late Hon. Lloyd, el. son of 3rd Baron), 4th Baron, *b.* 1864; Lord-Lieut. of Denbighshire, and Registrar of Priory of Order of St. John for Wales; a Lord-in-Waiting to Queen Victoria and King Edward VII. 1900-1905, and to King George V. 1916-18; assumed by Roy. licence 1912 the additional surname of Tyrell: *m.* 1916, Gwladys **Julia**, who *d.* 1965, da. of the late Col. Henry Richard Lloyd Howard, O.B.;‖*d.* 1927; *s.* by his only son [5] LLOYD, 5th Baron and present peer.

KERSHAW, BARON. (Kershaw.) [Baron U.K. 1947.]

EDWARD JOHN KERSHAW, 4th Baron; *b.* May 12th, 1936; *s.* 1962; ed. at Selhurst Gram. Sch., Croydon; R.A.F. 1955-57; Chartered Accountant 1964: *m.* 1963, Rosalind, da. of Ian Strachan Rutherford, of 16, Castlegate, Richmond, and has issue.

Residence,—

SON LIVING.
Hon. JOHN CHARLES EDWARD, *b.* Dec. 23rd, 1971.

DAUGHTERS LIVING.
Hon. Victoria Anne, *b.* 1964.
Hon. Isobel Mary, *b.* 1967.

SISTER LIVING.
Hon. Patricia Margaret, *b.* 1943: *m.* 1968, David Anniss Pickett, BSc, of 21, Lych Gate, Garston, Watford, and has issue, Caroline Mary, *b.* 1969.

UNCLES LIVING. (Sons of the 1st Baron.)
Hon. Donald Arthur, *b.* 1915; Solicitor 1939, a JP for SW London: *m.* 1942, Barbara Edith, da. of Lt.-Col. Cecil Graham Ford, of Richmond, and has issue living, Ian Graham Frederick, *b.* 1948,— Mark Nigel, *b.* 1951. *Residence,—*32, Hans Rd., SW3.
Hon. Peter John, *b.* 1924; ed. at Queen Elizabeth's Sch., Barnet, and at King's Coll., London (B.Sc. 1948); FICE; Sub-Lieut. RNVR 1944-45: *m.* 1948, Brenda Margaret, da. of James Austin Smith, of Brighton, and has issue living, Michael James, *b.* 1951. *Residence,—*22, Orchard Rise, Richmond, Surrey, TW10 5BX.

WIDOWS LIVING OF SECOND AND THIRD BARONS.
CISSIE BURNESS (*Cissie, Baroness Kershaw*), dau. of Charles E. Smyth, of Friern Barnet: *m.* 1933, the 2nd Baron, who *d.* (July) 1961. *Residence,—*29, St. Ann's Rd., Newquay, Cornwall.
KATHARINE DOROTHEA (*Katharine, Baroness Kershaw*), dau. of Charles H. Staines, of Clapham, SW: *m.* 1935, the 3rd Baron, who *d.* 1962. *Residence,—*32, Downs Way, Oxted, Surrey.

PREDECESSORS.—[1] FRED KERSHAW, O.B.E., son of John Joseph Kershaw, of Prestwich, Lancashire; *b.* 1881; a Dep. Speaker House of Lords, a Gov. of Westminster Hospital, Chm. of Gordon Hospital, and of Marie Curie Memorial, a Co. Director, Vice-Pres. of Workers' Temperance League, and Founder Member of Manor House Hospital; a Lord-in-Waiting to H.M. King George VI. 1949-51; cr. *Baron Kershaw*, of Prestwich, co. Palatine of Lancaster (peerage of United Kingdom) 1947: *m.* 1903, Frances Edith, who *d.* 1960, dau. of James Thomas Wigmore, of Hereford; *d.* (Feb.) 1961; *s.* by his el. son [2] HERBERT, 2nd Baron; *b.* 1904; European War and Far East 1939-45 as Sub Lieut. R.N.V.R.: *m.* 1933, Cissie Burness, dau. of Charles E. Smyth, of Friern Barnet; *d.* (July) 1961; *s.* by his brother [3] EDWARD AUBREY, 3rd Baron; *b.* 1906: *m.* 1935, Katharine Dorothea, dau. of Charles H. Staines, of Clapham, S.W.; *d.* 1962; *s.* by his son [4] EDWARD JOHN, 4th Baron and present peer.

KESTEVEN, BARONY OF. (Trollope.) [Extinct 1915.]

SISTER LIVING OF THIRD BARON. (Raised to the rank of a Baron's daughter 1916.)
Hon. Dorothy Nesta, *b.* 1888: *m.* 1918, Col. Froude Dillon Bellew, D.S.O., O.B.E., M.C., D.L., who *d.* 1959 (having assumed by Roy. licence 1920 the additional surname and arms of Trollope), and has issue living, Thomas Fleming (The Cottage, Crowcombe, Taunton, Som.), *b.* 1920; Maj. (ret.) R. Lincolnshire Regt.: *m.* 1951, Daphne Modwen, da. of M. C. Wainwright, of Northfields House, Stamford, Lincolnshire, and has issue living, Anthony Henry *b.* 1953, Thomas Martin *b.* 1956. *Residence,—*Casewick, Stamford.

KEYES, BARON. (Keyes.) [Baron U.K. 1943, Bt. U.K. 1919.]

ROGER GEORGE BOWLBY KEYES, 2nd Baron and 2nd Baronet, *b.* March 14th, 1919; *s.* 1945; Lieut. R.N. (retired); European War 1939-45 in N. Sea and Mediterranean: *m.* 1947, Grizelda Mary, dau. of the late Lieut.-Col. William Vere Packe, D.S.O., and has issue.

Arms,—Per chevron gules and sable, three keys or, the wards of the two in chief facing each other, and of the one in base to the sinister, on a canton argent a lion rampant of the first. **Crest,**—An open hand couped at the wrist proper, holding between the fore-finger and thumb a key or. **Supporters** (hereditary),—*Dexter*, a sailor of the Royal Navy in blue working rig proper, supporting in the exterior hand a staff argent ensigned with a naval crown or, and flying the banner of Saint George also proper; *sinister*, a Royal Marine in field service dress, armed and equipped for trench raiding, all proper.
*Residence,—*Sansomes House, Ellens Green, Rudgwick, Sussex, RH12 3AR.

Acquired by virtue.

SONS LIVING.
Hon. CHARLES WILLIAM PACKE, *b.* Dec. 8th, 1951; ed. at Eton.
Hon. Leopold Roger John, *b.* 1956.
Hon. Adrian Christopher Noel, *b.* 1962.

DAUGHTERS LIVING.
Hon. Virginia Clementine, *b.* 1950: *m.* 1972, Roger Martyn Crompton.
Hon. Josephine Mary, *b.* 1958.

SISTERS LIVING.
Hon. Diana Margaret, *b.* 1910: *m.* 1936, Col. James Robert Johnson, DSO, OBE, MC, Roy. Welch Fusiliers, and has issue living, Robin Edward Roger, *b.* 1937,—James Andrew David, *b.* 1945: *m.* 1st, 1969 (m. diss. 1971), Alison Laing, da. of Hector Laing Waugh, of Edinburgh; 2ndly, 1972, Susan Winifred, da. of Ronald Edmonds, of Bishopstone, Swansea, and has issue living (by 2nd m.), Benjamin Andrew James *b.* 1973,—Sara Anne Margaret, *b.* 1941. *Residence,*—Tingewick House, Buckingham.
Hon. Katherine Elizabeth, *b.* 1911: *m.* 1935, Major Peter de Barton Vernon Wallop William-Powlett, M.C., 3rd Hussars (Reserve) [see E. Portsmouth, colls.]. *Residence,*—22, St. Leonard's Terrace, S.W.3.
Hon. Elizabeth Mary, *b.* 1915; European War 1939-45 with VAD (RN). *Residence,*—Wood Lane Cottage, Tingewick, Buckingham, MK18 4QS.

PREDECESSOR.—[1] *Sir* ROGER JOHN BROWNLOW Keyes, *G.C.B., K.C.V.O., C.M.G., D.S.O., D.C.L., LL.D.,* son of the late Gen. Sir Charles Patton Keyes, G.C.B.; *b.* 1872; entered R.N. 1885, and became Adm. of the Fleet 1930; E. Africa 1890, China 1900, European War 1914-19 as Commodore Submarines, subsequently as Ch. of Staff, E. Mediterranean Squadron, Capt. and Rear-Adm. Grand Fleet, Director of Plans at Admiralty, and Acting Vice-Adm. Comdg. Dover Patrol (despatches, C.M.G., D.S.O., Com. Legion of Honour, K.C.B., K.C.V.O., thanked by War Cabinet, Belgian and French Croix de Guerre Grand Cordon of Order of Leopold of Belgium, Grand Officer Legion of Honour, Com. of Order of St. Maurice and St. Lazarus of Italy, American D.S.M., thanked by Parliament, cr. Baronet, granted £10,000); a Lord of the Admiralty and Dep.-Ch. of Naval Staff, Admiralty 1921-5; commanded Mediterranean Fleet 1925-8; Com.-in-Ch. Portsmouth 1929-31; Hon. Col. Comdt., Portsmouth Div., R.M. 1932-42; 1st Ch. of Combined Operations 1940-41; Special Liaison Officer to King of the Belgians May 1940; sat as M.P. for N. Div. of Portsmouth (C) 1934-43; cr. a Baronet 1919, and *Baron* Keyes, of Zeebrugge, and of Dover, co. Kent 1943: *m.* 1906, Eva Mary Salvin, who *d.* 1973, da. of the late Edward Salvin Bowlby, DL, of Gilston Park, Herts, and Knoydart, Inverness-shire (his el. son, Lt.-Col. Geoffrey Charles Tasker, VC, MC, Roy. Scots Greys (*b.* 1917) was killed on leading Commando raid on General Rommel's HQ at Sidi Rafa, Libya 1941, for which he was awarded a posthumous V.C.); *d.* 1945; *s.* by his only surviving son [2] ROGER GEORGE BOWLBY, 2nd Baron and present peer.

KEYNES, BARONY OF. (Keynes.) [Extinct 1946.]

WIDOW LIVING OF FIRST BARON.
LYDIA (*Baroness Keynes*), dau. of the late Vassili Lopokoff: *m.* 1925, the 1st Baron, who *d.* 1946, when the title became ext. *Residences,*—46, Gordon Square, W.C.; Tilton, Firle, Sussex.

KILBRACKEN, BARON. (Godley.) [Baron U.K. 1909.]

Without God nothing.

JOHN RAYMOND GODLEY, *D.S.C.*, 3rd Baron; *b.* Oct. 17th, 1920; *s.* 1950; ed. at Eton, and at Balliol Coll., Oxford (B.A. and M.A. 1948); is an Author and Journalist; European War 1940-45 as Lieut.-Com. (Air Branch) R.N.V.R. (D.S.C.): *m.* 1943 (divorce 1949), Penelope Anne, youngest dau. of the late Rear-Adm. Sir Cecil Nugent Reyne, K.B.E., and has issue.

Arms,—Argent, three unicorns' heads erased sable, horned gules, two and one, and three trefoils slipped vert, one and two. *Crest.*—A unicorn's head erased argent, horned gules, charged with three trefoils slipped vert. *Supporters,*—Dexter, a griffin sable charged with four stars argent in cross; *sinister,* a lion argent, charged with four roses gules in cross.

Seat,—Killegar, Cavan.

SON LIVING.
Hon. CHRISTOPHER JOHN (23, The Avenue, Andover, Hants.), *b.* Jan. 1st, 1945; ed. at Rugby and Reading Univ. (BSc Agric.); Agriculturalist: *m.* 1969, Gillian Christine, da. of Lt.-Cdr. S. W. Birse, of Alverstoke, Hants., and has issue living, James John, *b.* 1972,— Louisa Laheen, *b.* 1974.

BROTHER LIVING.
Hon. Wynne Alexander Hugh (Manor Farm House, Brede, Rye, Sussex), *b.* 1926; ed. at Rugby, and at New Coll., Oxford (BA 1947); Fellow of King's Coll., Camb.: *m.* 1955, Mrs. Kathleen Eleanora (Kitty) Freud, da. of the late Sir Jacob Epstein, KBE, and has issue living, Eve Katharine, *b.* 1967.

SISTER LIVING.

Hon. Katharine Mary, *b.* 1923; BSc (Soc.): *m.* 1944, Capt. Peter Komierowski, and has issue living, Paul James Alexander, *b.* 1945,—Mary Teresa, *b.* 1947: *m.* 1968 (m. diss. 1974), Richard Michael O'Connell, and has issue living, Daniel Wynne *b.* 1968, Bridget Emily Katharine *b.* 1974. *Residence,* —4, Stanley Mansions, Park Walk, SW10.

PREDECESSORS.—[1] *Sir* JOHN ARTHUR Godley, *G.C.B.*, son of the late John Robert Godley, of Killegar; *b.* 1847; Commr. of Inland Revenue 1882-3, and Permanent Under-Sec. for India 1882-1909; cr. *Baron Kilbracken*, of Killegar, co. Leitrim (peerage of United Kingdom) 1909 : *m.* 1871, the Hon. Sarah James, who *d.* 1921, dau. of 1st Baron Northbourne; *d.* 1932 ; *s.* by his son [2] HUGH JOHN, *C.B., K.C.*, 2nd Baron ; *b.* 1877; Assist. Parliamentary Counsel to the Treasury 1917-22, and Counsel to Chm. of Committees, House of Lords 1922-44 : *m.* 1st, 1919, Elizabeth Helen Monteith (who *d.* 1958, having obtained a divorce 1936), dau. of Vereker Monteith Hamilton, and widow of Com. N. F. Usborne, R.N.; 2ndly, 1936, Rhoda Leonora, who *d* 1948, dau. of Percy Taylor; *d.* 1950 ; *s.* by his el. son [3] JOHN RAYMOND, 3rd Baron and present peer.

KILBRANDON, BARON. (Shaw.) [Life Baron 1971.]

CHARLES JAMES DALRYMPLE SHAW, *PC*, son of James Edward Shaw, DL, of High Greenan, Ayr; *b.* Aug. 15th, 1906; ed. at Charterhouse and Balliol Coll., Oxford; Advocate Scotland 1932, and KC 1949; Sheriff of Ayr and Bute 1954-57, and Perth and Angus 1957-58; Dean of Faculty of Advocates 1957-59; a Lord of Session with title of *Lord Kilbrandon* 1959-71, since when a Lord of Appeal in Ordinary; Chm. of Scottish Law Commn. 1965-71; cr. *Baron Kilbrandon*, of Kilbrandon, co. Argyll (Life Baron) 1971, and PC 1971: *m.* 1937, Ruth Caroline, da. of Frank Morrison Seafield Grant, of Knockie, Inverness, and has issue.

ᬀrms.—Not matriculated at Lyon Court at time of going to press.

Residences.—2, Raymond Buildings, Gray's Inn, WC1; Kilbrandon House, Balvicar, by Oban, Argyll.

SONS LIVING.

Hon. Patrick James (Highfield, Taynuilt, Argyll), *b.* 1938: *m.* 1964, Elisabeth Gibson.
Hon. Michael Frank, *b.* 1944.

DAUGHTERS LIVING.

Hon. Teresa Caroline, *b.* 1940: *m.* 1969, Christopher Orme-Smith (Monte do Casal, 5, Ramao, S. Bras de Alportel, Portugal).
Hon. Mary Anna, *b.* 1946: *m.* 1971, Thomas H. C. Shephard.
Hon. Elizabeth Cecilia, *b.* 1948.

KILLANIN, BARON. (Morris.) [Baron U.K. 1900, Bt. U.K. 1885.]

[Title pronounced "Kil-lan-in."]

MICHAEL MORRIS, *M.B.E.*, *T.D.*, 3rd Baron, and 3rd Baronet ; *b.* July 30th, 1914 ; *s.* 1927 ; ed. at Eton, at Sorbonne, Paris, and at Magdalene Coll., Camb. (MA); Hon. LLD, Nat. Univ. Ireland; Author, Film Producer, MRIA, a Fellow of Roy. So. of Arts.; Pres. of Olympic Council of Ireland 1950-73; Pres. of Internat. Olympic Cttee. since 1972; Chm. of Dublin Theatre Festival 1960-70; a Member of Nat. Monuments Advisory Council of Ireland (Chm. 1960-65), of International Olympic Cttee. (Pres. 1972), and of Irish Nat. Hunt Steeplechase, Vice-Pres. RNLI, a Dir. of Irish Shell and B.P., Ltd., Bovril (Ireland), Ltd., Ulster Bank, Ltd., Lombard & *Si Deus nobiscum quis* Ulster Banking (Ireland) Ltd., and Ulster Investment *contra nos.* Bank, Chubb Safe & Lock of Ireland, Ltd., and other If God be with us, who is Cos., a Trustee of Irish Sailors and Soldiers Land Trust, against us? Hon. Consul-Gen. for Monaco in Ireland; Pres. of Irish Club, London 1947-65; formerly Maj. KRRC; NW Europe 1944-45 (MBE); a Knight of Sovereign Order of Malta, and a Com. of Order of the Grimaldi of Monaco; Order of Sacred Treasure of Japan; Grand Cross of Order of Merit of Germany; Grand Officer of Italian Order of Merit; Officer of the Legion of Honour; has 1st class Order of Olympic Merit of Finland, Star of Italy (1st class) and Austrian Olympic Medal; decorations from Dominican Republic, Colombia, Brazil, and USSR; MBE (Mil.) 1945: *m.* 1945, Mary Sheila Cathcart, *MBE*, da. of the Rev. Canon Douglas Dunlop, of Oughterard, co. Galway, and has issue.

ᬀrms,—Ermine, a fesse indented sable, in base a lion rampant of the last armed and langued gules. Crest.—On a fasces fessewise proper, a lion's head erased argent, gutté de sang. Supporters.—Not yet granted.

Seat,—St. Annins, Spiddal, co. Galway. *Residence,*—30, Lansdowne Road, Dublin, 4. *Clubs,*— Garrick, Beefsteak, Stephen's Green (Dublin), County (Galway).

SONS LIVING.

Hon. GEORGE REDMOND FITZPATRICK, *b.* Jan. 26, 1947; ed. at Gonzaga Coll., Dublin, Ample-forth, and Trin. Coll., Dublin: *m.* 1972, Pauline, only da. of Geoffrey Horton, of The Lawns, Cabinteely, co. Dublin, and has issue living, Luke Michael Geoffrey, *b.* 1975,—Olivia Rose Elizabeth, *b.* 1974.
Hon. Michael Francis Leo, *b.* 1951; ed. at St. Conleth's Coll., Dublin and Ampleforth.
Hon. John Martin (Ballycroy, Delgany, co. Wicklow), *b.* 1951 (twin); ed. at St. Conleth's Coll., Dublin, and Ampleforth: *m.* 1972, Thelma, da. of Mrs. Mansfield, of Monkstown, co. Dublin.

DAUGHTER LIVING.

Hon. Monica Deborah, b. 1950: m. 1970, William Campbell Rough Bryden, of 8, Learmonth Gdns., Edinburgh 9, and has issue living, Dillon Michael George, b. 1972,—Mary Kate, b. 1975.

PREDECESSORS.—[1] Rt. Hon. MICHAEL Morris, P.C., son of the late Martin Morris, J.P., of Spiddal, co. Galway; b. 1827; M.P. for Galway (LC) 1865-7; Recorder of Galway 1857-65; Solicitor-Gen. for Ireland 1866, Attorney-Gen. 1866-7, Justice of Common Pleas for Ireland 1867-76, Lord Ch. Justice thereof 1876-87, Lord Ch. Justice of Ireland 1887-9, and a Lord of Appeal in Ordinary 1889-1900: cr. a Baronet 1885, Baron Morris (life peerage), of Spiddal, co. Galway 1889, and Baron Killanin, of Galway, co. Galway (peerage of United Kingdom) 1900: m. 1860, Anna, who d. 1906, dau. of the late Hon. H. G. Hughes, a Baron of the Exchequer in Ireland; d. 1901, when the Barony of Morris, being a Life Peerage, expired, and he was s. in the Barony of Killanin by his el. son [2] MARTIN HENRY FITZPATRICK, P.C., 2nd Baron, b. 1867: Member of Senate of Roy. Univ. of Ireland 1904-9, Gov. of Univ. Coll., Galway 1909-22; M.P. for Galway (C) 1900-1; Lieut. and Custos Rotulorum for co. Galway; d. 1927; s. by his nephew [3] MICHAEL (son of the late Lieut.-Col. the Hon. George Henry Morris, younger son of 1st Baron), 3rd Baron and present peer.

KILLEARN, BARON. (Lampson.) [Baron U.K. 1943.]

Persevere and conquer.

GRAHAM CURTIS LAMPSON, 2nd Baron, and 4th Baronet (of Rowfant, Worth, Sussex); b. Oct. 28th, 1919; s. to Barony, 1964, and to Baronetcy 1971; ed. at Eton, and at Magdalen Coll., Oxford (MA); late Maj. Scots Guards (US Bronze Star): m. 1946, Nadine Marie Cathryn, only da. of the late Vice-Adm. Cecil Horace Pilcher, DSO, and has issue.

Arms,—Per saltire argent and gules, two gryphons' heads in fesse and as many escarbuncles in pale counterchanged. Crest,—A gryphon's head erased gules, charged with an escarbuncle argent, between two wings paly of four, argent and gules. Supporters,—Dexter, a camel proper with head stall and rope reflexed over the back gules; sinister, a Chinese dragon also proper.

Residence,—6, Trevor St., SW7 1EB.

DAUGHTERS LIVING.

Hon. Alexandra Rachel Catherine Mary, b. 1947: m. 1966, Nicholas Edward Hugo Meynell, of Hollybush Park, Newborough, Burton-on-Trent [see E. Halifax, colls.].

Hon. Nadine Marisa, b. 1948: m. 1969, Nicholas Cosmo Bonsor, of Burcott Hill House, Wing, Leighton Buzzard, Beds., el. son of Sir Bryan Cosmo Bonzor, MC, TD, 3rd Bt.

HALF-BROTHER LIVING

Hon. VICTOR MILES GEORGE ALDOUS (Franchise Manor, Burwash, Sussex), b. Sept. 9th, 1941; ed. at Eton; late Capt. Scots Guards: m. 1971, Melita Amaryllis Pamela Astrid, 2nd da. of Rear Adm. Morgan Charles Morgan Giles, DSO, OBE, GM, MP, and has issue living, Pamela Camilla Roxana, b. 1973,—Miranda Penelope Amber, b. 1975.

SISTERS LIVING.

Hon. Mary Katharine, b. 1915; a Lady-in-Waiting to H.R.H. the late Princess Royal 1948-51: m. 1952, Lt.-Col. Alexander George Falkiner Monro, of Balmain, Canonbridge, Easter Ross.

Hon. Margaret Miranda, b. 1923: m. 1946, Geoffrey John Eustace Jameson, of 64, Limerston St., SW10, and has issue living, Jonathan Eustace, b. 1947: m. 1972, Elizabeth, yr. da. of the Rt. Rev. Gerald Alexander Ellison, PC, DD, Lord Bishop of London.

HALF-SISTERS LIVING.

Hon. Jacquetta Jean Frederica (Lady Eliot), b. 1943: m. 1964, Peregrine Nicholas Eliot, Lord Eliot, el. son of 9th Earl of St. Germans. Residence,—Port Eliot, St. Germans, Cornwall.

Hon. Roxana Rose Catherine Naila, b. 1945: m. 1966, Ian Cowper Ross, of 60, Westbourne Park Rd., W2, and has issue living, Atticus Matthew Cowper, b. 1968,—Milo Joseph Charles, b. 1970,—Holly Zahava Josephine, b. 1971,—Mia Vanilla Catherine, b. 1973.

WIDOW LIVING OF FIRST BARON.

JACQUELINE ALDINE LESLIE (Dowager Baroness Killearn) (35 Montpelier Sq., SW7; Haremere Hall, Etchingham, Sussex); da. of the late Marchese Senator Aldo Castellani, KCMG, FRCP, FACP, DSc, MD; a CStJ: m. 1934, as his 2nd wife, the 1st Baron, who d. 1964.

DAUGHTER LIVING OF THIRD BARONET.

Sophia Curtis (Mill House Farm, Brightling, Sussex), b. 1935: m. 1955, Ronald J. Milwidsky, BSc(Eng.), AMIEE, who d. 1966, and has issue living, Peter Julian, b. 1960,—Caroline Natasha, b. 1956,—Sarah Janet, b. 1962.

COLLATERAL BRANCHES LIVING.

Granddaughters of the late Norman George Lampson, 3rd son of 1st baronet:—
Issue of the late Curtis Walter Lampson, OBE, b. 1875, d. 1952: m. 1908, Hilda, who d. 1946, da. of Sir David Baird, 3rd Bt. (cr. 1809):—
Elizabeth Miranda, b. 1911: m. 1947, as his 3rd wife, (William) John Rayner, OBE, and has issue living, John Peregrine (Dyffryn Marlais, Llanboidy, Dyfed), b. 1947: m. 1970, Susan Berman, and has issue living, Jessica, b. 1971, Leonie b. 1973, Esther b. 1974,—Robert Anthony, b. 1948,—Anne Casuarina, b. 1950,—Camber Mariana, b. 1953. Residence,—Chart Place, Sutton Valence, Kent.
Issue of the late Maj. Adam Cathcart Lampson, b. 1882, d. 1966: m. 1915, Margueretta Aggie Eileen (The Red House, Court Hill, Chipstead, Surrey), da. of the late John Hutchison, of Laurieston, Kirkcudbright:—
Ursula Agnes, b. 1915: m. 1st, 1939, Peter Anthony Johnstone, The Buffs (E. Kent Regt.); 2ndly, 1946, Duncan Chisholm, of The Cottage, Church Lane, Comberton, Cambridge, and has issue living, (by 1st m.) Anthony Paul, b. 1941: m. 1968, Gloria Cooke,—(by 2nd m.) Angus Dominic, b. 1947: m. 1971, Jeannie Turnbull,—Andrew Cathcart, b. 1949: m. 1971, Carol Hughes.

PREDECESSOR.—[1] Rt. Hon. Sir MILES WEDDERBURN Lampson, GCMG, CB, MVO, 2nd son of the late Norman George Lampson, yst. son of 1st Bt. (infra), b. 1880; Min. to China 1926-33, High Commr. for Egypt and the Sudan 1933-36, Ambassador to Egypt and High Commr. for Sudan 1936-46 and Special Commr. in S.-E. Asia 1946-48; cr. Baron Killearn, of Killearn, co. Stirling (peerage of U.K.) 1943: m. 1st, 1912, Rachel Mary Hele, who d. 1930, da. of William Wilton Phipps; 2ndly, 1934, Jacqueline Aldine Leslie, da. of Marchese Senator Aldo Castellani, KCMG, FRCP, FACP, DSc, MD; d. 1964; s. by his el. son [2] GRAHAM CURTIS, 2nd Baron and present peer.

. [1] Sir CURTIS Lampson (yst. son of William Lampson, of New Haven, Vermont, USA); b. 1806, naturalized British subject 1848; Dep. Chm. Atlantic Telegraph Co. 1865, which Co. laid the first

Atlantic telegraph cable, for which sers. he was cr. a *Baronet* 1866: *m.* 1827, Jane Walter, who *d.* 1891, da. of Gibbs Sibley, of Sutton, Mass., USA; *d.* 1885; *s.* by his el. son [2] *Sir* GEORGE CURTIS, 2nd Bt., *b.* 1833: *m.* 1887, Sophia, who *d.* 1926, yst. da. of Manuel Van Gelderen; *d.* 1899; *s.* by his only son [3] *Sir* CURTIS GEORGE, 3rd Bt.; *b.* 1890; FRGS; explorer in central and W. Africa, author and journalist: *m.* 1920, Maud Lawton, who *d.* 1960, da. of Alfred Wrigley, of Manchester; *d.* 1971; *s.* by his cousin, 2nd Baron Killearn (ante).

KILMAINE, BARON. (Browne.) [Baron I. 1789, Bt. N.S. 1636.]

JOHN FRANCIS ARCHIBALD BROWNE, *C.B.E.*, 6th Baron, and 12th Baronet ; *b.* Sept. 22nd, 1902 ; *s.* 1946 ; ed. at Winchester, and at Magdalen Coll., Oxford (MA); Gov. of Thomas Wall Trust, High Steward of Harwich; Chm. of Charities Investment Managers, Ltd. 1965-74; of Rochester Diocesan Advisory Cttee.; 1939-45 War as Lt.-Col. RASC (despatches twice); Admin. Sec., Univ. Coll., Southampton 1930-33, and Sec. to Oxford Soc. 1933-40, to Pilgrim Trust 1945-67, and to Dulverton Trust 1953-66; Chm. of Oxford Soc. 1949-73; a Trustee of Historic Churches Preservation Trust, and of The Dulverton Trust; Hon. DCL Oxford 1973; CBE (Civil) 1956: *m.* 1930, Wilhelmina Phyllis, only da. of Scott Arnott, of Tanners, Brasted, Kent, and has issue.

Arms,—Sable, in bend three lions passant between two double cotises argent. **Crest,**—An eagle displayed vert. **Supporters,**—Two lions reguardant argent, ducally crowned, plain collared and chained or.

Follow right.

Residence,—The Mount House, Brasted, Kent. *Club,*—Travellers'.

SON LIVING.

Hon. JOHN DAVID HENRY, *b.* April 2nd, 1948; ed. at Eton; a Dir. of Fusion (Bickenhill) Ltd.

DAUGHTERS LIVING.

Hon. Carola, *b.* 1932 : *m.* 1960, John Michael Carlyon Lowry Hudson, and has issue living, John Carlyon, *b.* 1961,—Thomas Christopher, *b.* 1963,—Phyllida, *b.* 1966. *Residence,*—Gwavas Station, Tikokino, Hawkes Bay, NZ.

Hon. Phyllida, *b.* 1935 : *m.* 1959, John Edward Previté, Bar.-at-law, and has issue living, Andrew Capper, *b.* 1961,—Matthew John, *b.* 1963. *Residence,*—The Wilderness, Hampton Wick, Kingston upon Thames, Surrey.

SISTER LIVING.

Hon. Alicia Evelyn, *b.* 1909 : *m.* 1936, Com. Edward St. John Edmonstone, R.N. (retired) [see Edmonstone, Bt]. *Residence,*—Barcombe Old Rectory, near Lewes, Sussex.

COLLATERAL BRANCHES LIVING.

Issue of the late Hon. Arthur Henry Browne, 6th son of 3rd Baron, *b.* 1850, *d.* 1908: *m.* 1885, Clotilde Georgina, who *d.* 1945, dau. of Sir John Don Wauchope, 8th Bt.:—

Gertrude Cicely Juliet, *b.* 1896. *Residence,*—12, Crompton Court, S.W.3.

Grandson of the late Frederick Howe Browne, yst. son of the late George Richard Browne, son of the late Hon. Richard Howe Browne, 5th son of 2nd Baron:—
Issue of the late Noel Francis Howe Browne, *b.* 1884, *d.* 1943: *m.* 1919, Jessie Selwyn Tudhope:—
Peter Kilmaine (Morningside Farm, PO Box 692, Rustenburg, Transvaal), *b.* 1920; late Capt. King's African Rifles: *m.* 1948, Grace Dorothy Robson, of Nakuru, Kenya, and has issue living, Margaret Jess, *b.* 1950,—Joan Selwyn, *b.* 1951.

Grandchildren of the late Rev. William James Caulfeild Browne, son of the late Rev. James Caulfeild Browne, D.C.L., son of the late Hon. George Browne, 3rd son of 1st Baron:—
Issue of the late Capt. Aubrey Caulfeild Browne, *b.* 1860, *d.* 1953 : *m.* 1st, 1888, Caroline Mitchell, who *d.* 1893 ; 2ndly, 1894, Ida B. Graham, who *d.* 1942:—
(By 1st m.) Cecil John Osborne Caulfeild, *b.* 1892; 1914-18 War with AIF in Gallipoli: *m.* 1st, 1923, Gladys Isobel Mason, who *d.* 1962; 2ndly, 1965, Mrs. Madeline Constance Ferguson, of Goulburn, NSW, and has issue living, (by 1st m.) *Rev.* Aubrey Robert Caulfeild; *b.* 1931; ed. at Newington Coll., Sydney, and at Moore Coll., Sydney (ThL); Broadcasts Exec. Officer for United Soc. for Propagation of Gospel, 15, Tufton St., SW1. *Residence,*—15, Caroma Av., Kyeemagh, North Brighton, NSW.——Winifred Victoria Edith, *b.* 1889: *m.* 1908, Ernest Alexander Nash, and has issue living, Ethel Winifred, *b.* 1910: *m.* 1935, Kenrick Rowland Lewis, of 34, Garthland Drive, Barnet, Herts., and has issue living, Brian John Wyndham *b.* 1945, Jillian Margaret *b.* 1939: *m.* 1961, Maurice Henry Jack Ducker, of 2A, Highview Av., Clacton-on-Sea, and has issue living, Jonathan Page *b.* 1962, Suzanne Claire *b.* 1964, Diane Elizabeth *b.* 1942: *m.* 1964 ,David John Chaplin, of 68, Princes Rd., Romford, Essex, and has issue living, Simon David John *b.* 1969, James Henry Alexander *b.* 1970.——(By 2nd m.) Edward *b.* 1903——Norah, *b.* 1896.——Kathleen, *b.* 1898. *Residence,*—

Issue of the late James Cecil Caulfeild Browne, *b.* 1862, *d.* 1917: *m.* 1887, Elsie M., who *d.* 19—, dau. of the late G. Manning, British Consul at San Salvador:—
Edwin Caulfeild, *b.* 1895.——Cecily Caulfeild, *b.* 1891: *m.* 1908, Henry Snell.——Nesta Caulfield, *b.* 1894: *m.* 19—, Gordon Rowe. *Residence,*—
Issue of the late Harold John Caulfeild Browne, *b.* 1864, *d.* 1953 : *m.* 1916, Margaret Delamere Booth, who *d.* 1971, da. of Maj. James Booth Clarkson:—
Edith Margaret, *b.* 1919: *m.* 1955, Thomas Henry Standish Goodlake. *Residence,*—1336, W. King Edward Av., Vancouver, 9, British Columbia.

(In remainder to Baronetcy only).

Descendants of John Browne, M.P., of Westport, co. Mayo (grandson of Col. John Browne, 2nd son of 1st baronet), who was cr. *Earl of Altamont* 1771 [see M. Sligo].

Descendants of John Browne, only son of Peter Browne, el. son of Dominick, 3rd son of 1st baronet :—

Grandchildren of the late Dominick Andrew Browne, great-grandson of Dominick Browne, grandson of Dominick Browne (ante) :—
Issue of the late Major Dominick Sidney Browne, J.P., D.L., *b.* 1866, *d.* 1927 : *m.* 1895, Elizabeth Naomi, who *d.* 1965, having *m.* 2ndly, 1928, as his second wife, Arthur Melville Hood Walrond [see B. Waleran, colls.], el. dau. of the Hon. R. R. Dobell, of Beauvoir Manor, Quebec, Canada :—
Dominick Andrew Sidney, *C.B.E.*, *b.* 1904 ; ed. at Eton ; Brigadier (retired) late Roy. Scots Fusiliers, European War 1939-45 in N. Africa, Sicily, Italy and N.-W. Europe (O.B.E., C.B.E.) ; O.B.E. (Mil.) 1943, C.B.E. (Mil.) 1945 : *m.* 1930, Iris Kathleen, dau. of Gerald H. Deane, of Littleton House, near Winchester, and has issue living, Peter Dominick, *b.* 1949, Capt. R. Green Jackets: *m.* 1974, Sally Jane, el. da. of John Eric Marrett, MRCS, LRCP, of Clare House, Howe Green, Sandon, Essex,— Miriam Dominica, *b.* 1931: *m.* 1st, 1953 (m. diss. 1964), Gavin Campbell Anderson, Grenadier Guards; 2ndly, 1964, Maj. Michael William Giles, late Grenadier Guards, and has issue living, (by 1st m.) Sarah Dominica *b.* 1954: (by 2nd m.) Peter William *b.* 1965,—Fiona Naomi, *b.* 1935: *m.* 1956, Cdr. Hugh Douglas Younger Faulkner, RN, of Grenville Hall, Droxford, Hants., and has issue living, Christopher Gerald *b.* 1958, Anthony Dominick Hugh *b.* 1961,—Anne Patrick, *b.* 1944: *m.* 1967, David Forcey, of 35, Cloncurry St., SW6 6DR, and has issue living, Annabelle Jane *b.* 1971. *Residence,*— Aghade Lodge, Kilbride, co. Carlow. *Clubs,*—Boodle's, Kildare Street.——Noël Sidney (*Lady Bevir*), *b.* 1899: *m.* 1935, Sir Anthony Bevir, KCVO, CBE.——Moyra Rose, *b.* 1903: *m.* 1922, Maj. Guy Percy Lumsden Drake-Brockman, DSO, MC, who *d.* 1952, and has issue living, Guy Dominick, 1925,—Marcia (twin), *b.* 1925: *m.* 1944, Charles Williams, mechanical engineer, and has issue living, Charles Dominick *b.* 1945, Andrew *b.* 1949, Christopher Michael *b.* 1954. *Residence,*—

PREDECESSORS.—[1] JOHN Browne, el. son of Josias Browne, of The Neale; cr. a *Baronet* 1636 ; *d.* 1670 ; *s.* by his son [2] Sir GEORGE, 2nd Bt. ; *d.* 1698 ; *s.* by his son [3] Sir JOHN, 3rd Bt. ; *d.* 1711; *s.* by his el. son [4] Sir GEORGE, 4th Bt. ; *d.s.p.* 1737; *s.* by his brother [5] Sir JOHN, 5th Bt. ; *d.* 1762 ; *s.* by his el. son [6] Sir GEORGE, 6th Bt. ; *d.* 1765; *s.* by his brother [7] Sir JOHN, *M.P.*; 7th Bt.; cr. *Baron Kilmaine*, of The Neale, co. Mayo (peerage of Ireland) 1789; *d.* 1794; *s.* by his el. son [8] JAMES CAULFEILD, 2nd Baron ; *d.* 1825 ; *s.* by his el. son [9] JOHN CAVENDISH, 3rd Baron ; *b.* 1794 ; a Representative Peer : *m.* 2ndly, 1839, Mary, dau. of the Hon. Charles Ewan Law, M.P. [B. Ellenborough]; *d.* 1873 : *s.* by his son [10] FRANCIS WILLIAM, 4th Baron, *b.* 1843 ; a Representative Peer for Ireland : *m.* 1877, Alice Emily, who *d.* 1925, dau. of Col. Deane Shute ; *d.* 1907 ; *s.* by his only son [11] JOHN EDWARD DEANE, 5th Baron, *b.* 1878 ; a Representative Peer: *m.* 1901, Lady Aline Kennedy, who *d.* 1957, dau. of 3rd Marquess of Ailsa; *d.* 1946 ; *s.* by his son [12] JOHN FRANCIS ARCHIBALD, 6th Baron and present peer.

KILMANY, BARON. (Anstruther-Gray.) [Life Baron 1966, Bt. U.K. 1956.]

WILLIAM JOHN ST. CLAIR ANSTRUTHER-GRAY, *MC, PC; Life Baron,* and 1st Baronet, son of the late Lt.-Col. William Anstruther-Gray of Kilmany [see Anstruther, Bt., colls.], *b.* March 5th, 1905; ed. at Eton, and at Ch. Ch., Oxford (MA); Maj. (ret.) Coldstream Guards; a DL of Fife; Lord Lt. of Fife since 1974, a Member of National Hunt Cttee since 1948; Crown Nominee for Scotland on Gen. Med. Council 1952-64; PPS to Sec. of Dept. of Overseas Trade 1935, to Sec. of State for Scotland 1938, Assist. Postmaster Gen. May to July 1945, Dep. Chmn. of Ways and Means, House of Commons 1959-62 and Chm. and Dep. Speaker 1962-64; Chm. of the 1922 Conservative Private Members' Cttee. 1964-66, MP for N. Lanarkshire (*C*) 1931-45, and for Berwick and E. Lothian 1951-66; a Member of Horserace Betting Levy Board 1966-74; 1939-45 War in N. Africa and NW Europe (MC); cr. a *Baronet* 1956, PC 1962, and *Baron Kilmany,* of Kilmany, co. Fife (Life Baron) 1966: *m.* 1934, Monica Helen, OBE, da. of the late Geoffrey Lambton [see E. Durham, colls.], and has issue.

Arms,—Not matriculated at Lyon Court at time of going to press.

Residence,—Kilmany, Cupar, Fife. *Clubs,*—Carlton, Brooks's, Guards', Turf, Jockey, New (Edinburgh).

DAUGHTERS LIVING.

Hon. Diana Mary, *b.* 1936: *m.* 1959, James Charles Macnab of Macnab (The Macnab), of Kinnell House, Killin, Perths., and has issue living, James William Archibald, *b.* 1963,—Geoffrey Charles, *b.* 1965,— Virginia Mary, *b.* 1960,—Katharine Monica, *b.* 1968.
Hon. Jane Caroline, *b.* 1943: *m.* 1962, the Hon. George Anthony Weir, of Fiunary House, Newton Mearns, Renfrewshire, and 20, Royal Avenue House, Royal Av., SW3 [see V. Weir].

KILMARNOCK, BARON. (Boyd.) [Baron U.K. 1831.]

ALASTAIR IVOR GILBERT BOYD, 7th Baron; *b.* May 11th, 1927; *s.* 1975; ed. at Bradfield, and King's Coll., Camb.; Lt. late IG; Chief of Clan Boyd; Page to Lord High Constable of Scotland at Coronation of HM King George VI; author of "Sabbatical Year" 1958, "The Road from Ronda" 1969 and "The Companion Guide to Madrid and Central Spain" 1974; Palestine 1947-48: *m.* 1954 (m. diss. 1969), Diana Mary Grant, only da. of D. Grant Gibson.

I trust.

Arms,—Quarterly: 1st azure a fesse chequy argent and gules, *Boyd*; 2nd argent three in-escutcheons gules, *Hay*; 3rd argent three gillyflowers with a double tressure flory counter flory vert, *Livingston*; 4th sable a bend between six billets or, *Callendar*. **Crest,**—A dexter hand erect in pale having the two outer fingers bowed inwards. **Supporters,**—Two squirrels proper. *Residence,*—Casa de Mondragon, Ronda, Malaga, Spain. *Clubs,*—Boodle's, Pratt's.

BROTHER LIVING.
Hon. ROBIN JORDAN (Flat 5, 2, Brondesbury Rd., NW6), *b.* June 6th, 1941; ed. at Eton, and at Keble Coll., Oxford (MA); MB, BS, LRCP, MRCS, DCH; Page to Lord High Constable of Scotland at Coronation of HM Queen Elizabeth II 1953.

HALF-BROTHERS LIVING.
Hon. Jonathan Aubrey Lewis, *b.* 1956.   *Hon.* Timothy Iain, *b.* 1959.

SISTERS LIVING.
Hon. Laura Alice, *b.* 1934: *m.* 1962, Anthony Hyman, of 38a, Downshire Hill, Hampstead, NW3.
Hon. Caroline Juliet, *b.* 1939: *m.* 1969, Alan Bloss.

WIDOW LIVING OF SIXTH BARON.
DENISE AUBREY DOREEN (*Denise Baroness Kilmarnock*), (28, Eaton Terr., SW1), only da. of the late Maj. Lewis Coker: *m.* 1955, as his 2nd wife, the 6th Baron, who *d.* 1975.

PREDECESSORS.—[1] WILLIAM GEORGE Hay, *K.T., G.C.H., P.C.*, 18th Earl of Erroll; *b.* 1801; was Lord Steward of the Household, Master of the Staghounds, and Lord-Lieut. of Aberdeenshire; cr. *Baron Kilmarnock* of Kilmarnock, co. Ayr (peerage of United Kingdom) 1831: *m.* 1820, Lady Elizabeth Fitzclarence, who *d.* 1856, nat. da. of King William IV; *d.* 1846; *s.* by his son [2] WILLIAM HENRY, 19th Earl, *b.* 1823; Maj. (ret.) Rifle Brig.; Crimea 1854-55: *m.* 1848, Eliza Amelia, *VA*, who *d.* 1916, da. of the late Gen. the Hon. Sir Charles Gore, GCB; *d.* 1891; *s.* by his son [3] CHARLES GORE, *KT, CB, LLD*, 20th Earl, *b.* 1852; Hon. Maj.-Gen. in the Army; a Lord-in-Waiting to King Edward VII, 1903-5: *m.* 1875, Mary Caroline, who *d.* 1934, da. of the late Edmund L'Estrange, of Tynte Lodge, co. Leitrim; *d.* 1927; *s.* by his son (4) VICTOR ALEXANDER SERELD, *KCMG*, 21st Earl, *b.* 1876; acted as Chargé d'Affaires at Berlin 1919-21; was British High Commr. of Rhineland Commn. 1921-23: *m.* 1900, Mary Lucy Victoria, who *d.* 1957, only da. of Sir Allan Russell Mackenzie, 2nd Bt. (cr. 1890); *d.* 1928; *s.* by his son [5] JOSSLYN VICTOR, 22nd Earl; *b.* 1901: *m.* 1923, Lady (Myra) Idina (Gordon) Sackville (who *d.* 1957, having obtained a divorce 1930), da. of 8th Earl De La Warr; 2ndly, 1930, Edith Mildred Mary (RAMSAY-HILL), who *d.* 1939, da. of the late R. W. Maude, of Cleveland, Yorks.; *d.* 1941, when the Earldom of Erroll devolved upon his only dau., and he was *s.* in the Barony of Kilmarnock by his brother [6] GILBERT ALLAN ROWLAND, *MBE, TD*, 6th Baron, *b.* 1903; deputised for Lord High Constable of Scotland at Coronation of HM Queen Elizabeth II 1953; assumed for himself and issue by Warrant of Lord Lyon King of Arms 1941, the surname of Boyd in lieu of that of Hay: *m.* 1st, 1926, the Hon. Rosemary Sibell Guest, who *d.* 1971, having obtained a divorce 1955, da. of 1st Viscount Wimborne; 2ndly 1955, Denise Aubrey Doreen, only da. of the late Maj. Lewis Coker; *d.* 1975; *s.* by his el. son [7] ALASTAIR IVOR GILBERT, 7th Baron and present peer.

KILMOREY, EARL OF. (Needham.) [Earl I. 1822.]

[Title pronounced "**Kilmurry.**"]

FRANCIS JACK RICHARD PATRICK NEEDHAM, 5th Earl; *b.* Oct. 4th, 1915; *s.* 1961; ed. at Stowe; late Major Grenadier Guards; is Hereditary Abbot of the Exempt Jurisdiction of Newry and Mourne; European War 1939-45 (wounded): *m.* 1941, Helen Bridget, dau. of Sir Lionel Lawson Faudel Faudel-Phillips, 3rd Bt., and has issue.

Arms,—Argent, a bend azure, between two bucks' heads cabossed sable. **Crest,**—A demi phœnix proper. **Supporters,**—*Dexter,* a bay horse, mane and tail sable; *sinister,* a stag proper.

Seat,—Mourne Park, Newry, co. Down. *Residence.*—Via San Leonardo 32, Florence, Italy. *Club,*—Turf.

NUNC AUT NUNQUAM — Now, or never.

SONS LIVING.
RICHARD FRANCIS (has not used courtesy title of Viscount Newry and Morne since 1969) (Little Aldon, Yeovil), *b.* Jan. 29th, 1942; a Co. Councillor of Som.: *m.* 1965, Sigrid Juliana Thiessen-Gairdner, only da. of the late Ernst Thiessen, and has issue.
SONS LIVING—*Hon.* Robert Francis John, *b.* May 30th, 1966.
Hon. Andrew Francis, *b.* 1969.
Hon. Christopher David, *b.* 1948: *m.* 1974, Marina, el. da. of Rodi Malvezzi, of Milan.
Hon. Patrick Jonathan, *b.* 1951.

DAUGHTER LIVING OF FOURTH EARL
Lady Hyacinth Kathleen Anne, *b.* 1923: *m.* 1953, John Hubert Gough, and has issue living, Cynthia Jane, *b.* 1954,—Rosaleen Anne, *b.* 1956,—Caroline May, *b.* 1958. *Residence,*—Moore Lodge, Newry, co. Down.

BROTHER LIVING. (*Raised to the rank of an Earl's son 1962.*)
Hon. Arthur Edward Peter, *b.* 1921; Major (retired) late Grenadier Guards; European War 1939-45 (wounded, despatches): *m.* 1951, Janet Beatrice Winifred, youngest dau. of the late Capt. George Taylor Ramsden, M.P., of Bramham, Yorkshire, and has issue living, Robert Arthur John, *b.* 1953, —Thomas Francis, *b.* 1959,—Jane Diana, *b.* 1955: *m.* 1975, John Bell [M. Ailsa]. *Residence,*—The Old Manor House, Helmsley, York.

SISTER LIVING. (*Raised to the rank of an Earl's daughter 1962.*)
Lady, Mary Esther Constance, *b.* 1918: *m.* 1949, Com. Anthony Boyce Combe, R.N. (retired), and has issue living, David Boyce, *b.* 1952,—Peter, *b.* 1955,—John (twin), *b.* 1955,—Anne Romaine, *b.* 1950. *Residence,*—Grove Cottage, South Creake, Fakenham, Norfolk.

WIDOW LIVING OF FOURTH EARL.

NORAH FRANCES Hastings (*Norah, Countess of Kilmorey*), dau. of 14th Earl of Huntingdon : *m.* 1920, the 4th Earl, who *d.* 1961. *Residence,*—Mourne Park, Newry, co. Down.

COLLATERAL BRANCHES LIVING.

Granddaughter of the late Lt.-Col. the Hon. Henry Colville Needham, brother of 3rd Earl.
Issue of the late Maj.-Gen. Henry Needham, CB, CMG, DSO, *b.* 1876, *d.* 1965: *m.* 1902, Violet, who *d.* 1962, da. of the late Capt. H. Andrew, 5th Lancers and 8th Hussars:—
Lina Mary (86, Swan Court, SW3), *b.* 1902.

Granddaughter of the late Francis Henry Needham, 3rd son of the Hon. Francis Henry Needham (infra):—
Issue of the late Francis Charles Needham, *b.* 1889, *d.* 1958: *m.* 1922, Violet, who *d.* 1963, da. of William Kaye Parker:—
Thyra Frances (Unit 196, Park Regis, 27, Park & Castlereagh St., Sydney, NSW) *b.* 1923.

Grandson of the late Hon. Francis Henry Needham, 3rd son of 2nd Earl:—
Issue of the late Alfred Edwin Needham, *b.* 1858, *d.* 1920; *m.* 1890, Katherine, who *d.* 1945, dau. of the late William Pickrell, of St. Leonards-on-Sea:—
Francis Jack, *b.* 1892; Lt. Aust. Forces (Reserve of Officers); FCA Aust.; 1914-19 War: *m.* 1926, Mary Clare, da. of the late Patrick Alban O'Sullivan, of Brisbane, Qld., and has issue living, Patrick Francis Jack (10, Glengariff Av., Killarney Heights, NSW), *b.* 1927: *m.* 1955, Margaret Anne, el. da. of Hilton John Daley, of Monavale Station, Hughenden, Qld., and has issue living, Robert Francis Jack *b.* 1956, John Edward *b.* 1963, Patrick Thomas (twin) *b.* 1963, Mary Margaret *b.* 1958, Judith Anne *b.* 1960,—Robert Cust (of 40, Palm Av., Ascot, Brisbane, Qld.), *b.* 1928: *m.* 1958, Annette Mary Beiers, el. da. of Michael Patrick O'Rourke, of 104, Reeve St., Clayfield, Brisbane, Queensland, and has issue living, Robert Michael *b.* 1963, Michael Francis Jack *b.* 1967, Morna Irene *b.* 1959, Susan Clare *b.* 1961, Lucy Ann *b.* 1969,—Thomas Edwin (Wyvanham Biloela, Qld.), *b.* 1931: *m.* 1964, Julia Elizabeth, da. of William O. Moore, of Shadyside, Longreach, Qld., and has issue living, Deborah Clare *b.* 1970,—Edward Francis (St. Patrick's College, Strathfield, NSW), *b.* 1936. *Residence,*—69, Margate Parade, Redcliffe, Qld.

Grandchildren of the late Frederick William Needham (infra):—
Issue of the late Capt. James Owen Needham, *b.* 1897, *d.* 1975: *m.* 1929, Marjorie Hylda (13, Voltaire, Kew, Surrey), da. of the late Charles George Lumley Cator [Blois, Bt.]:—
Christopher James Blois (Snode Hill House, Beech, Alton, Hants.), *b.* 1931: *m.* 1955, Nicola Anne, only da. of the late Capt. Robert Coles, and has issue living, Henrietta Aeddan, *b.* 1957,—Alicia Claire, *b.* 1959,—Camilla Romaine, *b.* 1961.——David John Manners (Pine Lodge, Cokes Lane, Chalfont St. Giles, Bucks.), *b.* 1934: *m.* 1955, Evelyn Elizabeth (who assumed by deed poll 1965, for herself and her issue the surname of Palmers-Needham), da. of Theodore L. Palmers, Consul Gen. for Nicaragua in London, and has issue living, Katherine Elizabeth Theodora, *b.* 1970.——Patricia Deline, *b.* 1942: *m.* 1968, John Michael Singer, of Fairlawn, Christchurch Rd., Virginia Water, Surrey, and Green Farm House, Western Colville, Cambs., and has issue living, Jeremy James, *b.* 1974,—Caroline Emma Louise, *b.* 1969,—Serena Claire, *b.* 1972.

Granddaughter of the late Hon. Francis Henry Needham (ante):—
Issue of the late Frederick William Needham, *b.* 1861, *d.* 1928 : *m.* 1886, Geraldine, who *d.* 1946, da. of Edmund Arthur Paget, of Thorpe Satchville Hall, Melton Mowbray:—
Audrey Deline, *b.* 1895: *m.* 1918, Capt. Adrian Dura Stoop, MC, TA (ret.), who *d.* 1957, and has issue living, James Richard, *b.* 1920; Sqdn.-Ldr. RAF (ret.),—Michael, *MC* (*Club*),—St. James'), *b.* 1922; ed. at Univ. Coll., Oxford; Maj. (ret.) Gren. Gds.; 1939-45 War (MC): *m.* 1st, 1948 (m. diss. 19—), Micheline, da. of Baron de Posson, of 56, Rue Gachard, Brussels, 2ndly, 19— (m. diss. 19—), Mrs. Diana Buchanan; 3rdly, 1959, Beverley Ann, da. of Herbert Roberts, of Glangwa, Caernarvon, and has issue living, (by 1st m.) Adrian Gaston *b.* 1949, Caroline *b.* 1950. *Residence,*—Half-Tiles, 5, Meadow Lane, Hartley Wintney, Hants.

PREDECESSORS.—[1] *Sir* ROBERT Needham, *K.B.*, one of the Council of the Pres. of Wales; *cr. Viscount Kilmorey* (peerage of Ireland) 1625 ; *d.* 1625 ; *s.* by his el. son [2] ROBERT, 2nd Viscount ; *d.* 1653 ; *s.* by his son [3] Robert, 3rd Viscount ; *d.s.p.* 1657 ; *s.* by his half-brother [4] CHARLES, 4th Viscount ; *d.* 1660 ; *s.* by his el. son [5] ROBERT, 5th Viscount ; *b.* 1655 ; *d.* 1668 ; *s.* by his brother [6] THOMAS, 6th Viscount ; *d.* 1687 ; *s.* by his son [7] ROBERT, 7th Viscount ; *d.* 1710 ; *s.* by his el. son [8] ROBERT, 8th Viscount ; *d.* 1716 ; *s.* by his brother [9] THOMAS, 9th Viscount ; *d.s.p.* 1768 ; *s.* by his brother [10] JOHN, 10th Viscount ; a Col. in the Army ; *d.* 1791 ; *s.* by his el. surviving son [11] ROBERT, 11th Viscount ; *d.* 1818 ; *s.* by his brother [12] FRANCIS, 12th Viscount ; a Gen. in the Army ; *cr. Viscount Newry and Morne* and *Earl of Kilmorey* (peerage of Ireland) 1822 ; *d.* 1832 ; *s.* by his son [13] FRANCIS JACK, 2nd Earl ; M.P. for Newry 1818-26 : *m.* 1st, 1814, Jane, who *d.* 1867, dau. of George Gun Cuninghame, of Mount Kennedy, co. Wicklow ; 2ndly, 1867, Martha, who *d.* 1907, dau. of John Foster, of Lenham, Kent ; *d.* 1880 ; *s.* by his grandson [14] FRANCIS CHARLES, *K.P.* [el. son of Francis Jack (Viscount Newry and Morne), M.P. for Newry 1841-51, by Anne Amelia, dau. of Gen. the Hon. Sir Charles Colville, G.C.B. (B. Colville)], 3rd Earl ; *b.* 1842 ; a Representative Peer ; M.P. for Newry (*C*) 1871-4 : *m.* 1881, Ellen Constance, who *d.* 1920, dau. of the late Edward Holmes Baldock, M.P. for Shrewsbury ; *d.* 1915 ; *s.* by his el. son [15] FRANCIS CHARLES ADELBERT HENRY, *O.B.E., V.R.D., P.C.,* 4th Earl ; *b.* 1883 ; Capt. 1st Life Guards, Capt. Comdg. Ulster Div. R.N.V.R., Lieut. for co. Down, and High Sheriff 1913 ; Vice-Adm. of Ulster 1937-61 : *m.* 1920, Lady Norah Frances Hastings, dau. of 14th Earl of Huntingdon ; *d.* 1961 ; *s.* by his nephew [16] FRANCIS JACK RICHARD PATRICK (son of the late Major the Hon. Francis Edward Needham, M.V.O., 2nd son of 3rd Earl), 5th Earl and present peer ; also Viscount Kilmorey, and Viscount Newry and Morne.

KILMUIR, EARLDOM OF. (Fyfe.) [Extinct 1967.]

DAUGHTERS LIVING OF FIRST EARL.

Lady Pamela Maxwell, *b.* 1928; a JP of Yorks: *m.* 1st, 1950, Olive Wigram, Bar.-at-law, who *d.* 1956; 2ndly, 1957, Courtenay Thomas Gardner Blackmore, and has issue living, (by 1st marriage) Caroline, *b.* 1952,—(by 2nd marriage) Thomas David Maxwell Fyfe, *b.* 1960,—Katharine Fanny, *b.* 1958,—Victoria Jane, *b.* 1965. *Residence,*—55a, Lee Rd., Blackheath, SE3.
Lady Miranda Maxwell, *b.* 1938: *m.* 1960, Michael Ormiston Cormack, and has issue living, David Ormiston, *b.* 1964,—Alistair Kilmuir, *b.* 1970,—Helen Madeleine, *b.* 1963. *Residence,*—31, White Hart Wood, Sevenoaks, Kent.

WIDOW LIVING OF FIRST EARL.

Dame SYLVIA MARGARET, *DBE* (*Countess De la Warr*); DBE (Civil) 1957; (Fishers Gate, Withyham, Hartfield, Sussex; 1, Buckingham Mews, Stafford Place, SW1), da. of William Harrison, of Liverpool: *m.* 1st, 1925, the 1st Earl who *d.* 1967, when the title became ext.; 2ndly, 1968, as his 2nd wife, the 9th Earl De la Warr.

KIMBERLEY, EARL OF. (Wodehouse.) [Earl U.K. 1866, Bt. E. 1611.]

Strike hard.

JOHN WODEHOUSE, 4th Earl, and 11th Baronet; *b.* May 12th, 1924; *s.* 1941; ed. at Eton, and at Magdalene Coll., Camb.; is Lieut. **Grenadier Guards (Reserve)** *m.* 1st, 1945, Diana Evelyn (who obtained a divorce 1948), only dau. of the late Lieut.-Col. the Hon. Sir Pier; Walter Legh, G.C.V.O., C.M.G., C.I.E., O.B.E. [see B. Newton, colls.]; 2ndly, 1949 (marriage dissolved 1952), Carmel June (DUNNETT), dau. of the late Michael Maguire, of Melbourne, Australia; 3rdly, 1953, Mrs. Cynthia Abdy Westendarp (who obtained a divorce 1960), younger dau. of E. Abdy Collins, F.R.C.S., M.R.C.P., of The Chantrey, Saxmundham, Suffolk; 4thly, 1961 (m. diss. 1965), Margaret, da. of Alby Simons; 5thly, 1970, Gillian, da. of Col. Norman Ireland-Smith, and formerly wife of John Raw, and has issue by 2nd, 3rd and 4th m.

Arms,—Sable, a chevron or, gutté de sang between three cinquefoils ermine. Crest,—A dexter arm couped below the elbow, vested argent, and grasping a club or. Supporters,— Two wild men, wreathed about the loins, and holding in the exterior hand a club, raised in the attitude of striking, sable.

Seat,—Arwenack Manor House, Falmouth. *Residences*,—17A, South Audley St., W.1; 4B, Wadham Gdns., N.W.3; Chilterns, Thames Drive, Twyford, Sonning, Berks. *Clubs*,—Bath, Guards, Norfolk County.

SONS LIVING. *(By 2nd marriage.)*
JOHN ARMINE (*Lord Wodehouse*), *b.* Jan. 15th, 1951; ed. at Eton: *m.* 1973, the Hon. Carol Lylie Palmer, el. da. of 3rd Baron Palmer.

(By 3rd marriage.)
Hon. Edward Abdy, *b.* 1954; ed. at Eton.   Hon. Henry Wyndham, *b.* 1956; ed. at Millfield.

(By 4th marriage.)
Hon. Charles James, *b.* 1963.

COLLATERAL BRANCHES LIVING.

(In remainder to Barony of Wodehouse only.)

Granddaughter of the late Col. the Hon. Berkeley Wodehouse, CMG, 4th son of 2nd Baron:—
Issue of the late Clarence Francis Berkeley Wodehouse, *b.* 1855, *d.* 1945: *m.* 1881, Frances, who *d.* 1937, dau. of A. H. Saunders Davies, of Pentre, co. Pembroke:—
Armine Frances Berkeley (The Manse of The Braes of Cromar, Logie Coldstone, Dinnet, Aberdeenshire), *b.* 1903.

Granddaughter of the late Rev. Algernon Wodehouse, son of the late Rev. the Hon. William Wodehouse, 4th son of 1st Baron:—
Issue of the late Rev. William Wentworth Wodehouse, *b.* 1846, *d.* 1888: *m.* 1878, Helen Maud (judicially separated on her petition 1885), who *d.* 1932, dau. of the late Arthur Brooke [Brooke, Bt., cr. 1662, colls.]:—
Alice Mary, *b.* 1884: *m.* 1909, John Broadwood, who *d.* 1964, and has issue living, Clarice Betty, *b.* 1911. *Residence*,—85, Old Dover Rd., Canterbury.
Issue of the late Thomas Frederick Wodehouse (twin), *b.* 1855, *d.* 1908: *m.* 1896, Alice Caroline, dau. of the late Col. John Ormsby Vandeleur, C.B. [D. St. Albans, colls.]:—
Elinor Alice Hilda, *b.* 1897. *Residence*,—

(In remainder to Baronetcy.)

Granddaughter of the late Rev. Philip John Wodehouse (infra):—
Issue of the late Capt. Philip George Wodehouse, DSO, RN, *b.* 1883, *d.* 1973: *m.* 1st, 1915, Beaujolois Theresa Constance (who obtained a divorce 1928), only da. of the late Arthur George Ridout, of Condercum, Benwell, Northumberland; 2ndly, 1928, Alice Margaret (Ebor House, Park Lane, Barnstaple, N. Devon), da. of the late William Rowe:—
(By 1st m.) Beaujolois Inez, *b.* 1919: *m.* 1942, Capt. Hubert Gordon Compton Cavendish, RASC, of Merrivale, Constantine, Falmouth, Cornwall [see D. Devonshire, colls.].

Granddaughter of the late Col. Philip Wodehouse, el. son of the late Rev. Philip Wodehouse, 2nd son of 5th Bt., and brother of 1st Baron:—
Issue (by 2nd marriage) of the late Rev. Philip John Wodehouse, *b.* 1836, *d.* 1917: *m.* 1st, 1876, Constance Helen, who *d.* 1877, dau. of the late Wade Browne, of Monkton Farley, Wilts; 2ndly, 1879, Marion Bryan, who *d.* 1922, dau. of the late Rev. Gilbert I. Wallas:—
Christine Lucy (c/o Lloyds Bank, Seaton, Devon, EX12 2QS), *b.* 1881.

Granddaughters of the late Col. Charles Wodehouse, CIE, 2nd son of Col. Philip Wodehouse (ante):—
Issue of the late Lieut.-Col. Frederic William Wodehouse, C.I.E., *b.* 1867, *d.* 1961: *m.* 1st, 1893, Mary Helen, who *d.* 1920, dau. of the late George Nugent Lambert, Sup. Engineer Sind; 2ndly, 1940, Hilary Mary, who *d.* 1974, only da. of the late William Henry Pell, of Holme House, Nottinghamshire:—
(By 1st marriage) Kathleen Doris Laetitia, *b.* 1897: *m.* 1922, Air Vice-Marshal Stanley James Goble, CBE, DSO, DSC, RAAF, who *d.* 1948, and has issue living, John Douglas (5, Raglan St., Turramurra, NSW 2074), *b.* 1923; Capt. RAN: *m.* 1953, Annette Margaret, dau. of Col. G. Youl, of

Launceston, Tasmania, and has issue living, James Wodehouse *b.* 1957, Margaret Kate *b.* 1959,—Alan James, *b.* 1925; MB and BS; MD Melbourne; MRACP; MRCP London: *m.* 1950 (m. diss. 1968), Patricia, da. of R. A. Johnston, of Corowa, NSW, and has issue living, David Stanley *b.* 1955, Anne Louise *b.* 1957,—Ivor Norman, *b.* 1929: *m.* 1954, June, da. of A. E. Peart, of Maroona, Victoria, and has issue living, Ann Sally *b.* 1956. *Residence,*—Flat 5, 26, Queen's Rd., Melbourne, SE2, Australia.——Sybil Margaret, *b.* 1899: *m.* 1928, the Rt. Rev. Bishop Claud Thomas Thellusson Wood, MC (Bishop of Bedford 1948-53), who *d.* 1961, and has issue living, John Wedgwood Thellusson (of Home Farm, Bringhurst, Leicestershire), *b.* 1932: *m.* 1956, Cleone Anne, da. of Douglas Cory-Wright [see Cory-Wright, Bt.], and has issue living, Nicholas John Wedgwood *b.* 1961, Amelia Jane *b.* 1959, Rebecca Anne *b.* 1964,—Richard Mountford Theilusson, *MB, BS, FRCSEd* (Flat D) (G/F) 5, Mount Davis Rd., Hong Kong), *b.* 1940: *m.* 1969, Kay, el. da. of K. M. Fenwick, and has issue living, Claudia Margaret *b.* 1970, Susanna Mary *b.* 1973,—Mary Elizabeth Thellusson (72, Townsend Lane, Harpenden, Herts.), *b.* 1929: *m.* 1954 (m. diss. 1962), Allan Ronald Beverley Skertchly, and has issue living, Caroline Patricia Elizabeth *b.* 1954, Louise Beverley Anne *b.* 1957, Mary Bernadette *b.* 1960,—Stella Armine Thellusson *b.* 1935: *m.* 1958, Michael Muschamp, of 34, Sussex St., Brighton, Vic., Aust., and has issue living, Timothy *b.* 1972, Virginia Lucy *b.* 1960, Amanda *b.* 1962, Katherine *b.* 1966. *Residence,*—8, Grange Court Rd., Harpenden, Herts.

Grandsons of the late Rev. Frederic Armine Wodehouse, 3rd son of the late Col. Philip Wodehouse (ante):—
Issue of the late Vice-Adm. Norman Atherton Wodehouse, C.B., R.N., *b.* 1887, *d.* (killed in action during European War) 1941: *m.* 1923, Theodosia Frances, who *d.* 1966, da. of the late Com. Edward Louis Dalrymple Boyle, CMG, RN, and widow of Capt. Douglas William Swire, Shropshire Yeo. [see E. Glasgow, colls.]:—
Armine Boyle (Gladwyns, Sheering, Bishop's Stortford, Herts.), *b.* 1924; ed. at Radley; 1939-45 War with Gren. Gds.: *m.* 1952. Diana Helen Arabella, only dau. of the late Charles Sidney Bowen Wentworth-Stanley, O.B.E. [Brocklebank, Bt., colls.], and has issue living, Armine Mark Robin, *b.* 1960,—Julia Katherine, *b.* 1955,—Victoria Frances, *b.* 1957.——Charles Norman Boyle, *b.* 1927: *m.* 1953, Joyce Marie Williamson, da. of the late John Dobson, MC, and has issue living, Dominic Charles John, *b.* 1968,—Fiona Clare, *b.* 1958,—Charlotte Thea Fleur, *b.* 1962. *Residence,*—17, South Border, Purley, Surrey.

Grandchildren of the late Henry Ernest Wodehouse, CMG, 5th son of the late Col· Philip Wodehouse (ante):—
Issue of the late Ernest Armine Wodehouse, *b.* 1879, *d.* 1936: *m.* 1919, Helen, da. of the late Patrick Harnett:—
Patrick Armine, *b.* 1920; ed. at Cheltenham, and Imperial Coll. of Science and Technology; BSc; ACGI, MIEE; Consultant Eng.; Fl.-Lt. RAuxAF (ret.): *m.* 1947, Joyce Lilian, da. of Charles Champion, and has issue living, Nigel Armine, *b.* 1948.

Issue of the late Richard Lancelot Deane Wodehouse, *b.* 1892, *d.* 1940: *m.* 1st, 1925, Katharine, who *d.* 1932, dau. of W. Wallace Cook, O.B.E.; 2ndly, 1934, Winifred Baker (1, St. Anns Court, Friary Lane, Salisbury, Wilts.), da. of Brig.-Gen. William Baker-Brown, CB, and widow of Robert Arthur Williams:—
(By 1st m.) Ann Elizabeth, *b.* 1930: *m.* 1953, Lt.-Col. Richard Gerald Higgins, RA (c/o Midland Bank, Calne, Wilts.), and has issue living, Andrew Richard, *b.* 1954,—Michael James, *b.* 1956,—John Deane, *b.* 1962.——Katharine Jane Armine, *b.* 1932: *m.* 1955, Graeme Roper Wallace, of Little Grondra, Shirenewton, Chepstow, Mon., and has issue living, Ross Matthew Walker, *b.* 1956,—Neil Richard Deane, *b.* 1958,—Constance Armine Louise, *b.* 1960.

Grandchildren of the late Maj. James Hay Wodehouse *b.* 1824, 2nd son of the Ven. Charles Nourse Wodehouse, 2nd son of the Rev. Philip Wodehouse (ante):—
Issue of the late James Hay Wodehouse, *b.* 1861, *d.* 1913: *m.* 1890, Annie Pauahi, who *d.* 1897, dau. of the Hon. A. S. Cleghorn, of Waikiki, Honolulu:—
James Hay Archibald, *b.* 1895; is Gen. Sup. Kohala Sugar Co. Mill: *m.* 1st, 1916, Florence, who *d.* 1937, dau. of Edward Boyd; 2ndly, 1938, Elizabeth K., dau. of William K. Buchanan, and has issue living, (by 1st marriage) Mildred Pauahi, *b.* 1916: *m.* 1942, Asa Alan Clark, Capt. U.S. Navy, and has issue living, Asa Alan *b.* 1944, Jeffrey Wodehouse *b.* 1947, Bruce Shannon *b.* 1953,—(by 2nd m.) Florence Elizabeth Hay, *b.* 1939: *m.* 1963, George Warren Freeland, Field Engineer, of 94-939, Makaaloha St., Waipahu, Oahu, Hawaii. *Residence,*—Kohala, Hawaii.——Irma Pauahi, *b.* 1897: *m.* 1926, James Jay Rothschild, of 3009, Ocean Drive, Oxnard Beach, Cal., USA, and has issue living, James Jay, *b.* 1927.

Grandchildren of the late Guy Armine Wodehouse (infra):—
Issue of the late Everard Hay Wodehouse, *b.* 1895, *d.* 1970: *m.* 1st, 1927 (m. annulled 1934), Dorothy Eileen, da. of J. G. Cameron, of Santiago, Chile; 2ndly, 1927, Winifred Mary, da. of Reginald Ashton, of Lima, Peru:—
(By 2nd m.) Richard Everard, *b.* 1949.——Diana Elaine, *b.* 1939: *m.* 1964, Donald Ralph Strong (c/o Trans World Radio, Bonaire, Netherlands, Antilles), and has issue living, Everard George, *b.* 1968,—Miriam Ruth, *b.* 1966.——Marilyn Joanna, *b.* 1943: *m.* 1964, Garvin Olaf Muri, of 1616, Avenue E., Bismarck, N. Dakota, USA, and has issue living, Michelle Ingrid, *b.* 1967,—Jenelle, *b.* 1970.

Grandchildren of the late Maj. James Hay Wodehouse (ante):—
Issue of the late Guy Armine Wodehouse, *b.* 1863, *d.* 1926: *m.* 1894, Elisa Millie, who *d.* 1935, dau. of David Millie, of Coquimbo, Chile:—
Lionel von Tempsky, *b.* 1904: *m.* 1930, Ruby, da. of Frederick C. Prain, of Vina del Mar, Chile. *Address,*—Cochrane, 812, Valparaiso, Chile.——Ivy Maud, *b.* 1901: *m.* 1937, Edward James Campbell. *Residence,*—Casella 12, Lo Espejo, Santiago, Chile.

Grandchildren of the late Guy Armine Wodehouse (*b.* 1863) (ante):—
Issue of the late Guy Armine Wodehouse, *b.* 1897, *d.* 1967: *m.* 1925, Marjorie Eileen (Calle Hereberto Covarrubias, 753, Los Guindos, Santiago, Chile), da. of the late Adam Birrell, of Valparaiso:—
Charles Armine Birrell, *b.* 1928: *m.* 1952, Eloise Rae, da. of the late Raymond James Cassie, of Florida, USA.——Valerie Elisa, *b.* 1935.

Issue of the late Ernest Hay Wodehouse, *b.* 1868, *d.* 1957: *m.* 1893, May, who *d.* 1938, da. of Curtis Perry Ward, of Honolulu:—
Cenric Nourse (RR1, Box 260, Holualoa, Kona, Hawaii 96725), *b.* 1909: *m.* 1934, Maude, da. of Walter D. Ackerman, of Kona, Hawaii.

Issue of the late Kenneth Charles Wodehouse, *b.* 1873, *d.* 1928: *m.* 1910, Norah, who *d.* 1967, da. of the late Denis Madden:—
John Hay (Casilla 2133, Santiago, Chile), *b.* 1917: *m.* 1st, 1941, Maria Francisca Garrido, who *d.* 1945; 2ndly, 1947 (m. annulled 1959), Carmen Meza Valdés; 3rdly, 1960, Jeannette Wackenhut, and has issue living, (by 1st m.) Cyprian Gerard, *b.* 1941,—(by 2nd m.) Kenneth John, *b.* 1958.—(by 3rd m.) Roderick Dhu, *b.* 1965,—Sharon Elizabeth, *b.* 1962.

Grandchildren of the late Rear-Admiral Capel Wodehouse, yr. son of the late Rev. Nathaniel Francis Wodehouse, son of the late Thomas Wodehouse, 3rd son of 5th Bt., and brother of 1st Baron:—
Issue of the late Brigadier Edmond Wodehouse, O.B.E., *b.* 1894, *d.* 1959 : *m.* 1935, Persis (Pen-y-Glyn, Overton, Wrexham), only da. of Plumer Rooper, of Min-yr-Afon, Overton Bridge, Wrexham:—

Armine John (c/o Lloyds Bank, 6, Pall Mall, SW1), *b.* 1936; ed. at Winchester; Maj. Roy. Welch Fusiliers: *m.* 1965, Louise Kynaston, da. of Mark Kynaston Mainwaring [Rankin Bt.], of Oteley, Ellesmere, and has issue living, Edmond Armine, *b.* 1968,—Rosemary Louise, *b.* 1966,—Rowena Carolyn, *b.* 1971.——Hugh Capel, *b.* 1945.——Rachel Mary (c/o Midland Bank, Aldershot, Hants.), *b.* 1938: *m.* 1965, Robert Charles Copeman, and has issue living, James Robert, *b.* 1966,—Charlotte Anne, *b.* 1968.——Carolyn Persis, *b.* 1943: *m.* 1968, Michael Oemlyn-Jones, and has issue living, Tara Persis, *b.* 1970,—Jessica Melfis, *b.* 1973.

Issue of the late Dulcibella Wodehouse, *b.* 1891, *d.* 1971: *m.* 1926, Lt.-Col. Edward H. Burton, RASC, of St. Ann's, Sheep Lane, Midhurst, Sussex (who *m.* 2ndly, 1972, Rachel Thornton, da. of the late H. C. S. Tyler, and widow of John Percy Gee, JP):—
Christopher Carleton John, *b.* 1930: *m.* 1960, Sheana, da. of the late Brig. Muirhead, of Yew Tree House, N. Ferriby, Yorks., and has issue living, Kevin Carleton Ronald, *b.* 1964,—Claire Rachel, *b.* 1966.

PREDECESSORS.—[1] *Sir* PHILIP Wodehouse, son of the late Sir Roger Wodehouse, M.P., *b.* 15—; was M.P. for Castle Rising 1586-7 : cr. a *Baronet* 1611 : *m.* 1582, Grizell, who *d.* 1635, dau. of William Yelverton, of Rougham, Norfolk, and widow of Hamon L'Estrange, of Hunstanton, Norfolk ; *d.* 1623 ; *s.* by his son [2] *Sir* THOMAS, 2nd Bt. ; M.P. for Thetford 1640-53; *d.* 1658; *s.* by his son [3] *Sir* PHILIP, 3rd Bt. ; *b.* 1608 : M.P. in Restoration Parliament : *d.* 1681 ; *s.* by his grandson [4] *Sir* JOHN, 4th Bt. ; *b.* 1669; M.P. for Norfolk; *d.* 1754; *s.* by his son [5] *Sir* ARMINE, 5th Bt. ; *b.* 1714; M.P. for Norfolk 1737-67 ; *d.* 1777 ; *s.* by his son [6] *Sir* JOHN, 6th Bt. ; *b.* 1741; M.P. for Norfolk 1784-97; cr. *Baron Wodehouse*, of Kimberley, Norfolk (peerage of Great Britain) 1797 ; *d.* 1834 ; *s.* by his son [7] JOHN 2nd Baron ; *b.* 1771 ; M.P. for Great Bedwyn 1802-6, and Marlborough 1820-26, and Lord-Lieut. of Norfolk, &c.; *d.* 1846; *s.* by his grandson [8] JOHN, K.G., P.C. (son of the Hon. Henry, el. son of 2nd Baron, by Anne, dau. of Theophilus Thornhaugh Gurdon, of Letton, Norfolk), 3rd Baron ; *b.* 1826 ; Under-Sec. for Foreign Affairs 1852-6 and 1859-61, Envoy to Russia 1856-8, Special Envoy to Copenhagen 1863, Under-Sec. for India 1864, Lord-Lieut. of Ireland 1864-6, Lord Privy Seal 1868-70, Sec. of State for Colonies 1870 and 1880-82, Chancellor of Duchy of Lancaster 1882-3, Sec. of State for India 1882-5 and Jan. to July 1886, Sec. of State for India and Lord Pres. of the Council Aug. 1892 to March 1894, and Sec. of State for Foreign Affairs March 1894 to June 1895 ; cr. *Earl of Kimberley* (peerage of United Kingdom) 1866 : *m.* 1847, Lady Florence FitzGibbon, C.I., who *d.* 1895, el. dau. of 3rd and last Earl of Clare (*ext.*) ; *d.* 1902 ; *s.* by his son [9] JOHN, 2nd Earl ; *b.* 1848: *m.* 1875, Isabel Geraldine, who *d.* 1927, dau. of Sir Henry Josias Stracey, 5th Bt. ; *d.* 1932; *s.* by his son [10] JOHN, C.B.E., M.C., 3rd Earl; *b.* 1883 ; M.P. for Norfolk, Mid. Div. (*L*) 1906-10 : *m.* 1922, Frances Margaret, who *d.* 1950, dau. of the late Lieut.-Col. Leonard Howard Loyd Irby ; *d.* (result of enemy action during European War) 1941; *s.* by his only son [11] JOHN, 4th Earl and present peer ; also Baron Wodehouse.

KINDERSLEY, BARON. (Kindersley.) [Baron U.K. 1941.]

With God's assistance.

HUGH KENYON MOLESWORTH KINDERSLEY. *C.B.E.*, *M.C.*, 2nd Baron, *b.* May 7th, 1899 ; *s.* 1954 ; ed. at Eton ; Brig. late Scots Guards; Hon. Fellow since 1959, and Patron since 1960, of Roy. Coll. of Surgs. of England; Chm.. Standing Review Body on Doctors' and Dentists' Remuneration 1962-70, and of Rolls-Royce, Ltd. 1957-68; a Dir. of Lazard Brothers & Co. Ltd. 1927-71, and of Bank of England 1946-66; Gov. of Roy. Exchange Assurance 1955-69; High Sheriff of co. London 1951; 1914-18 War in France (MC, two medals), 1939-45 War (wounded, MBE, CBE); Order of St. Olav. of Norway; MBE (Mil.) 1941, CBE (Mil.) 1945; *m.* 1921, Nancy Farnsworth, da. of Dr. Geoffrey Boyd, of Toronto, Canada, and has issue.

Arms,—Per bend gules and azure, a lion rampant argent, within an orle of cross crosslets and fleurs-de-lis alternately or. *Crest,*—In front of a hawthorn tree proper, charged with an escutcheon azure, thereon a lion rampant argent, a greyhound sejant also argent. *Supporters,*—*Dexter,* a greyhound argent, gorged with a collar azure, charged with three cross crosslets or; *sinister,* a lion argent, gorged with a collar gules, charged as the dexter; each standing on a branch of hawthorn proper.
Residences,—Ramhurst Manor, Leigh, Tonbridge, Kent; 16, Bryanston Court, W1H 7HA. *Clubs,*—Guards', White's.

SON LIVING.

Hon. ROBERT HUGH MOLESWORTH (35, South Eaton Place, SW1), *b.* Aug. 18th, 1929; ed. at Eton, at Trin. Coll., Oxford, and at Harvard Business Sch., USA; Malaya 1948-49 as Lt. Scots Guards: *m.* 1954, Venice Marigold (Rosie), da. of the late Capt. Lord (Arthur) Francis Henry Hill, The Greys (Reserve) [see M. Downshire, colls.], and has issue living, Rupert John Molesworth, *b.* 1955 (Stable Cottage, Ramhurst Manor, Tonbridge, Kent), *b.* 1955: *m.* 1975, Sarah A., da. of the late John D. Warde,—Hugh Francis, *b.* 1956,—Dickon Michael, *b.* 1962,—Anna Lucy, *b.* 1965.

DAUGHTERS LIVING.

Hon. Patricia Nassau (*Hon. Lady Crookenden*), *b.* 1922: *m.* 1948, Lt.-Gen. Sir Napier Crookenden, KCB, DSO, OBE, late Cheshire Regt., and has issue living, James Napier, *b.* 1949,—Charles Stephen Napier, *b.* 1957,—Elizabeth Jane, *b.* 1950: *m.* 1970, Sam G. S. Hughes, of Toronto,—Catharine Nancy, *b.* 1958. *Residence,*—Sissinghurst Place, Cranbrook, Kent.
Hon. Ginette, *b.* 1924 : *m.* 1st, 1945, Dominick Moore Sarsfield, Irish Guards, from whom she obtained a divorce 1949 ; 2ndly, 1953, Henry James Buller Kitson [B. Strathcona and Mount Royal], and has issue living, (by 1st marriage), Simon Patrick, *b.* 1945: *m.* 1967, Sandra, da. of Robert Pearce, of Chichester, Sussex,—Shaun Dominick, *b.* 1947. *Residence,*—Castell Prydydd, Llanfoist, Abergavenny.

BROTHER LIVING.

Hon. Philip Leyland, *b.* 1907; ed. at Eton, and at Oxford Univ.; is Capt. Coldstream Guards; European War 1939-43 in N. Africa (wounded, prisoner): *m.* 1st, 1929, Oonagh (from whom he obtained a divorce 1936), dau. of the Hon. (Arthur) Ernest Guinness [see E. Iveagh]; 2ndly, 1936, Violet Valerie, da. of the late Lt.-Col. the Hon. (Edward) Gerald Fleming French, DSO [see E. Ypres, colls.], and has issue living, (by 1st m.) Gay (of Parsonage Farm, E. Garston, Newbury), *b.* 1930; ed. at Eton: *m.* 1956, Margaret Diana, dau. of Hugh Wakefield, and has issue living, Robin *b.* 1956, Kim *b.* 1960, Catheryn *b.* 1958, Tania *b.* 1967,—(by 2nd marriage), Christian Philip, *b.* 1950: *m.* 1973, Hilary Luise, da. of David Guard, of Ryders Wells House, Lewes, Sussex,—Nicolette Leila, *b.* 1930: *m.* 1963, Robert Nicholas Philipson-Stow, of 23, Drayton Gdns., SW10, [see Philipson-Stow, Bt.]— Virginia Alexandra Alexandra de L'Etang (*Hon. Mrs. Peregrine J. W. Fairfax*) *b.* 1943: *m.* 1965, the Hon. Peregrine John Wishart Fairfax, of Mindrum, Northumberland [see L. Fairfax of Cameron]. *Residence,*—Holford Manor, North Common, Chailey, Sussex. *Club,*—White's.

SISTERS LIVING.

Hon. Margaret Marion, *b.* 1902: *m.* 1st, 1924, Capt. Algernon Spencer Belmont, RA, who *d.* 1944, 2ndly, 1945, Col. Thomas Whicher Boileau, OBE, late R. Signals, and has issue living, (by 1st m. Michael Jeremy Kindersley (Gaunt House, Standlake, Oxon.), *b.* 1930: *m.* 1953, Virginia Ann, da. of the late George Vernon Tate, MC [see Tate, Bt., colls.], and has issue living, Piers Antony Robert *b.* 1954, Antony Vernon Spencer *b.* 1956, Eilsa Ann *b.* 1959,—Robert Jerram (Madrid, Spain), *b.* 1935: *m.* 1961, Caroline Harriette Nares,—Philippa Margaret *b.* 1925: *m.* 1946, Dr. B. Marshall, of The Grange, Bletchingley, Surrey,—Jacqueline Camilla *b.* 1928: *m.* 1950, Henry Robert Hildyard [Bonsor, Bt.], and has issue living, Nicholas Reginald *b.*, 1955, Caroline (*Lady Salt*), *b.* 1951: *m.* 1971, Sir (Thomas) Michael John Salt, 4th Bt. (cr. 1899), Victoria Anne (twin), *b.* 1955. *Residence,*—97, Furze Croft, Furze Hill, Hove, Sussex, BN3 1PE.

Hon. Elizabeth Joan, *b.* 1911: *m.* 1930, Major the Hon. James Perrott Philipps, T.D. [see B. Milford]. *Residence,*—Dalham Hall, Newmarket, Suffolk.

PREDECESSOR.—[1] *Sir* ROBERT MOLESWORTH KINDERSLEY, *G.B.E.*, son of the late Capt. Edward Nassau Molesworth Kindersley, of Sherborne, Dorset; *b.* 1871; was a Director of Bank of England 1916-46, Pres. of National Savings Committee 1920-46 (first Chm. 1916-20), High Sheriff of Sussex 1928-9, and Prime Warden of Fishmongers Co. 1933-4; cr. *Baron Kindersley*, of West Hoathly, co. Sussex (peerage of United Kingdom) 1941: *m.* 1896, Gladys Margaret, who *d.* 1968, da. of the late Maj.-Gen. J. P. Beadle, RE, of 6, Queen's Gate Gdns., SW; *d.* 1954; *s.* by his son [2] HUGH KENYON MOLESWORTH, 2nd Baron and present peer.

King, see Baron Maybray-King.

KING-HALL, BARONY OF. (King-Hall.) [Extinct 1966.]

DAUGHTERS LIVING OF LIFE BARON.

Hon. Ann (11, North Side, Clapham Common, SW4), *b.* 1920.
Hon. Susan (Old Barn, Woldingham, Surrey), *b.* 1927.
Hon. Jane, *b.* 1930: *m.* 1951, Yves Barraud, of Les Saules, Les Cullayes, Vaud, Switzerland.

Kinghorne, Earl of, see Earl of Strathmore and Kinghorne.

Kingsborough, Viscount, son of Earl of Kingston.

KINGSALE, BARON. (de Courcy.) [Baron I. about 1340, precedence 1397.]

Truth conquers all things.

JOHN DE COURCY, *30th Baron, and Premier Baron of Ireland; *b.* Jan. 27th, 1941; *s.* 1969; ed. at Stowe; 2nd Lt. IG.

Arms,—Argent, three eagles, displayed gules, ducally crowned or. Crest,—Out of a ducal coronet or, an eagle displayed with two heads argent. Supporters,—Two unicorns azure, armed unguled, crined and tufted, gorged with collars adorned with crosses pattée and fleurs-de-lis, and chained, all gold.

Residence,—Grove Farm, Bourton, Dorset. *Club,*— Guards'.

SISTER LIVING.

Dione May, *b.* 1937: *m.* 1965, David Kemp Daffin, of Grove Farm, Bourton, Dorset, and has issue living, Miles Irl de Courcy, *b.* 1969,—Thomas Chester de Courcy, *b.* 1971.

AUNTS LIVING. (*Daughters of Twenty-ninth Baron.*)

Hon. Bridget Doreen, *b.* 1915: *m.* 1st, 1938 (m. diss. 1951), the Rev. George Ian Falconer Thomson; 2ndly, 19—, Stephen Watson, of North Blagdon Farm, Ashbury, Okehampton, and has issue living, (by 1st m.), Margaret Doreen Rosemary (Emma), *b.* 1940,—(by 2nd m.), a son, *b.* 19—.

Hon. Eleanor Geraldine, *b.* 1919 : *m.* 1940, John Campbell Clarke, who obtained a divorce 1947, and has issue living, Peter, *b.* 1945. *Residence,*—48, Fore St., North Tawton, Devon.

Hon. Diana Ruth, *b.* 1951.

GREAT-AUNT LIVING. (*Daughter of Twenty-eighth Baron.*)

Hon. Estelle Emily Spencer, *b.* 1889 : *m.* 1916, Wellesley St. George Ashe, late Indian Army, who *d.* 1958, and has issue living, Michael Henry St. George, *b.* 1927: *m.* 1st, 1954, Diana Margaret Campion Dawson, from whom he obtained a divorce 1959; 2ndly, 1962, Norah Ethel Gaussen, from whom he obtained a divorce 1965; 3rdly, 1965, Victoria Edwina Leila Zimmerman,—John de Courcy (twin), *b.* 1927: *m.* 1956, Gillian Margaret Josephine Rickards,—Elizabeth Sheila Lillith, *b.* 1920: *m.* 1946, Humphrey Desmond Juler, late Surg.-Lt. RNVR, of Crinan House, Charlbury, Oxon. *Residence,*— Crinan House, Charlbury, Oxon.

---

* The Barons of Kingsale have claimed the right of remaining covered in the presence of the Sovereign. The first recorded occasion was when Almericus, 18th Lord Kingsale, walked "to and fro with his hat on his head" in the presence chamber before William III, claiming that he was asserting the ancient privilege "granted to John de Courci, Earl of Ulster, and his heirs, by John King of England." There is no evidence that this privilege was granted to Sir John de Courcy (who was not created Earl of Ulster), nor can this family claim descent from him, for he died in 1219 without legitimate issue.

COLLATERAL BRANCHES LIVING.

Granddaughters of the late Hon. Robert Charles Sinclair de Courcy, 4th son of
27th Baron:—
Issue of the late Group-Capt. John Arthur Gerald de Courcy, M.C., R.A.F., b. 1894, d. (on
active ser. during European War) 1940 : m. 1917, Anna Felicia, who d. 1952, dau. of the
late Hon. George Wright, a Judge of High Court of Justice, Ireland [Barrington, Bt.]:—
Fay, b. 1919: m. 1947 (marriage dissolved 1962), Hugh Sykes Davies, Fellow of St. John's Coll.,
Camb., and has issue living, Katharine Felicia, b. 1953.   *Residence,*—6, Barton Close, Cambridge.
——Stella, b. 1921: m. 1948, Paul Kemp-King, of Tudor House, Compton Dundon, Somerton,
Somerset, and has issue living, Stephen de Courcy, b. 1950,—Andrew James de Courcy, b. 1953.——
Suzanne, b. 1923: m. 1948, Edward James Bryant, and has issue living, Edward de Courcy, b. 1951,—
David de Courcy, b. 1954.   *Residence,*—Marsh Morgen, Stradishall, nr. Newmarket.

Grandson of the late Col. Nevinson Willoughby de Courcy, CB, second son of the
late Capt. Nevinson de Courcy, RN, son of Adm. the Hon. Michael de Courcy, 3rd
son of 20th Baron:—
Issue of the late Nevinson William de Courcy, b. 1869, d. 1919: m. 1919, Matilda Hetty
Grace, who d. 1967, da. of the late John B. Russell, of Auckland, NZ:—
NEVINSON RUSSELL (posthumous), b. July 21st, 1920: m. 1954, Nora Lydia, da. of James Arnold Plint,
of Great Crosby, Lancs., and has issue living, Nevinson Mark, b. 1958,—Katherine Grace, b. 1955.
Residence,—15, Market Rd., Remuera, Auckland, 5, NZ.

Grandchildren of the late John Sinclair Bremer de Courcy, 3rd son of the late Capt.
Nevinson de Courcy, RN (ante):—
Issue of the late Rupert John Nevinson de Courcy, b. 1859, d. 1952: m. 1885, Agnes Gordon,
who d. 1953, da. of the late Frederic Brassey:—
Nevinson Egerton, b. 1885: m. 1923, Dorothy Mary, da. of John Bernard Carroll, and has issue
living, Angela Mary, b. 1927: m. 1951, Ian MacDonald Wright, of the Rosary, Lock Island,
Marlow, Bucks, and has issue living, Teresa Dorothy de Courcy b. 1955, Isobel Eileen b. 1958. *Resi-
dence,*—79, Louisville Rd., SW17.——Elaine Bertha, b. 1895: m. 1924, Leslie Ernest Eldridge, of 50,
Berrylands, Surbiton, Surrey, and has issue living, Rosemary de Courcy, b. 1928: m. 1952, the Rev.
Robert Bernard Jones, of The Vicarage, Ringwood, Hants, and has issue living, Jonathan Aubrey
b. 1957, Deborah Ann b. 1954.

Granddaughter of the late Walter Stephen de Courcy (infra):—
Issue of the late John Frederick Manuel de Courcy, b. 1901, d. 1974: m. 1941, Norah de
Courcy (c/o Lloyds Bank, 6, Pall Mall, SW1), el. da. of the late Dr. R. P. Beatty, of Swindon
House, Swindon, Wilts.:—
Mary Kathleen, b. 1947: m. 1967, David Allen Carse.

Descendants of the Hon. James de Courcy, 3rd son of 10th Baron
(according to pedigree recorded at the Office of the Chief Herald of
Ireland):—

Grandson of the late Stephen de Courcy, son of Patrick de Courcy, great grandson
of David de Courcy, 2nd son of James de Courcy, el. son of the Hon. James de
Courcy (ante):—
Issue of the late Walter Stephen de Courcy, b. 1869, d. 1911: m. 1899, Wilhelmina Regina,
who d. 1950, dau. of the late Frederick William Schafer:—
Kenneth Hugh (Seacourt Annex, Hayling Island, Hants.) b. 1909; formerly Lt. Coldstream Guards:
m. 1950 (m. diss. 1973), Rosemary Catherine, only da. of the late Cdr. Henry Leslie Spofforth Baker,
OBE, RN (ret.), of Carrowduff House, Ballymacurly, co. Roscommon, and has issue living,
Joseph Kenneth Charles (Blacklain's Farm, Birdlip, Glos.), b. 1955, ed. at Radley and Oriel Coll. Ox-
ford,—Richard Henry Stephen, b. 1960,—Rosemary Minnie Frances (Blacklain's Farm, Birdlip,
Glos.), b. 1951; ed. at Girton Coll., Camb.,—Catherine Sarah, b. 1952.

PREDECESSORS.—The origin and early descent of this Peerage is obscure. In 1489, when
eleven Irish barons were summoned to Greenwich, this Barony ranked after Athenry and before
Gormanston. "The Complete Peerage" considers that Miles de Courcy, b. about 1286, may have
become *Lord Courcy of Kinsale* about 1340, but adds a footnote "it is more probable that the
family acquired peerage rank 50 years later." In 1397, William de Courcy received a licence,
as *Dominus et Baro de Courcy,* to buy a ship in England and sail it to France. Precedence of the
Barony in the Peerage of Ireland has been given from this date. A list of the Peers present at the
Irish Parliament 1490 includes *Dominus de Kinsale,* but until the 17th century, Lord Courcy, *of
Ringrone and Kinsale* was the style more usually adopted. In 1799 this became the Premier
Barony of Ireland on the extinction or dormancy of the Baronry of Athenry on the death of the
1st (cr. 1759) Earl of Louth. Patrick de Courcy, whose parentage is uncertain, d. before 1261.
His son, Miles d. c. 1290. His son John was killed 1291. His el. son [1] MILES, 1st Baron, b. c.
1286; Sheriff of Cork 1329-32: m. 13— Joan; d. before 1344; s. by his son [2] MILES, 2nd Baron,
d. unm. 1372; s. by his kinsman [3] JOHN, 3rd Baron, (perhaps son of Edmund de Courcy, whose
lineage is uncertain; d. c. 1390; s. by his son [4] WILLIAM, 4th Baron: m. Margaret Peinnel (who
had Robes of the Garter 1399; d. c. 1400; s. by [5] NICHOLAS, 5th Baron, d. c. 1410; s. by [6]
PATRICK, 6th Baron, d. c. 1499: s. by his el. son [7] NICHOLAS, 7th Baron: m. Mary, dau. of More
O'Mahony; d. c. 1475; s. by his el. son [8] JAMES, 8th Baron: m. Ellena Roche, dau. of David,
Baron of Fermoy; d. 1499; s. by his only surviving son [9] EDMUND, 9th Baron, d. c. 1505; s. by
his uncle [10] DAVID, 10th Baron (2nd son of 7th Baron): m. Joan, dau. of Edmund Roche; d. c.
1520; s. by his el. son [11] JOHN, 11th Baron: m. Sarah, dau. of Donogh MacCarthy, of Dowallagh;
d. 1535; s. by his only son [12] GERALD, 12th Baron; commanded an Irish Regt. at siege of Boulogne;
knighted on the field 1567: m. Ellen, dau. of Cormac MacDonogh McCarthy of Carbery; d. 1599;
s. by his kinsman [13] JOHN, 13th Baron (son of Edmund Oge de Courcy, grandson of 10th Baron);
fought against Spaniards at Siege of Kinsale 1601; was a Gentleman of the Bedchamber to King
James I.: m. 1st, Catherine, dau. of William Cogan; 2ndly, Mary, dau. of Cormac O'Cruly, of
Carbery, co. Cork: d. 1628; s. by his el. son [14] GERALD, 14th Baron: m. 16—, Elene, da. of
Sir John FitzGerald, of Dromana, co. Waterford; d. 1642; s. by his brother [15] PATRICK, 15th
Baron: m. 16—, Mary, who d. 1678, dau. of Sir John Fitzgerald (ante); d. c. 1663; s. by his son
[16] JOHN, 16th Baron: m. 16—, Ellen, dau. of Charles MacCarthy Reagh; d. 1667; s. by his el.
son [17] PATRICK, 17th Baron, b. 1660; d. 1669; s. by his brother [18] ALMERICUS, 18th Baron;
outlawed 1691 for his adhesion to the fortunes of James II, but which outlawry was removed 1692:
m. 1698, Anne, dau. of Robert Dring, of Isleworth, Middlesex; d. 1719; s. by his cousin [19] GERALD,
19th Baron (son of Col. the Hon. Miles de Courcy, 3rd son of 15th Baron), b. 1700; P.C. Ireland 1744;
m. 1725, Margaretta, who d. 1750, dau. of John Essington, of Grossington Hall, Glos.; d. 1759;
s. by his kinsman [20] JOHN, 20th Baron (son of Miles de Courcy, of Newport, Rhode Island, N.
America, 2nd son of Anthony de Courcy, of Bandon, co. Cork, only son of the Hon. David de Courcy,
yst. son of 13th Baron); confirmed in the Baronies of Kingsale and Ringrone 1761, and their descent
in the male line: m. 1746, Martha, who d. 1803, dau. of the Rev. William Heron, of Dorchester,
Dorset; d. 1776; s. by his son [21] JOHN, 21st Baron: m. 1763, Susanna, who d. 1819, dau. of
Conway Blennerhassett, of Castle Conway, co. Kerry; d. 1832; s. by his son [22] *Rev.* THOMAS,
22nd Baron, b. 1774; d. 1832; s. by his nephew [23] JOHN STAPLETON, 23rd Baron (son of Capt.
the Hon. Michael de Courcy, R.N., 3rd son of 21st Baron), b. 1805: m. 1825, Sarah, who d. 1883,
dau. of Joseph Chadder, of Portlemouth, Devon; d. 1847; s. by his son [24] JOHN CONSTANTINE,
24th Baron, b. 1827; Capt. E. Devon Mil.: m. 1855, Adelaide, who d. 1885, dau. of Joseph Proctor
Brown-Westhead, of Lea Castle, Worcs.; d. 1865; s. by his brother [25] MICHAEL CONRAD, 25th
Baron, b. 1828; d. 1874; s. by his cousin [26] JOHN FITZROY, 26th Baron (el. son of Lieut.-Col. the

Hon. Gerald de Courcy, 4th son of 20th Baron), *b.* 1821; Maj. in Turkish Contingent during Crimean War 1854-5, and Col. in Federal Army during American Civil War: *m.* 1864, Elia Elizabeth, who *d.* 1893, dau. of C. de François de Ponchalon, of Alençon, France, and widow of C. de Bosque de Beaumont, of Airel, Manche; *d.* 1890; *s.* by his cousin [27] MICHAEL WILLIAM, 27th Baron (el. son of the Rev. Michael de Courcy, D.D., son of Adm. the Hon. Michael de Courcy, 3rd son of 20th Baron), *b.* 1822: *m.* 1st, 1852, Esther Eleanor, who *d.* 1864, dau. of Thomas Williams, of Dublin; 2ndly, 1874, Jessie Maud, who *d.* 1902, dau. of the Rev. Edward Polwhele, sometime R. of Fillaton, *d.* 1895; *s.* by his el. son [28] MICHAEL CONSTANTINE, 28th Baron, *b.* 1855: *m.* 1880, Emily France, Anne, who *d.* 1926, dau. of the late William Sinclair de Courcy, brother of 27th Baron Kingsale, *d.* 1931; *s.* by his son [29] MICHAEL WILLIAM ROBERT, *DSO*, 29th Baron, *b.* 1882: *m.* 1st, 1906, Constance Mary Rancé, who *d.* 1946, da. of the late Maj.-Gen. Sir Tom Percy Woodhouse, *KCMG, CB*; 2ndly, 1947 (m. diss. 1957), Ruth, only child of Herbert Thomas Holmes, OBE; *d.* 1969; *s.* by his grandson [30], JOHN (only surviving son of Lt.-Cdr. the Hon. Michael John Rancé de Courcy, RN, only surviving son of 29th Baron, *b.* 1907, *d.* (killed on active ser.) 1940, who *m.* 1st, 1929, (m. diss. 1933), Glory Elizabeth, da. of Eng.-Cdr. Alfred Claremont Evans, RN (ret.); 2ndly, 1936, Joan, who *d.* 1967, da. of Robert Reid, JP, of Moor Park, nr. Harrogate), *b.* (posthumous) 1941, 30th Baron and present Peer; also Baron of Ringrone.

KINGS NORTON, BARON. (Roxbee Cox). [Life Baron 1965.]

HAROLD ROXBEE COX, son of the late William John Roxbee Cox; *b.* June 6th, 1902; ed. at King's Norton Gram. Sch., and at Imperial Coll. of Science and Technology (BSc, DIC, PhD London, Fellow); Hon. DSc Birmingham and Cranfield, DTech Brunel; Hon; LLD (CNAA); Chm. of Air Registration Board 1966-72. Chm. and Man. Dir. of Power Jets (Research and Development) Ltd. 1944-46, Dir. of Nat. Gas Turbine Establishment 1946-48, Pres. of Roy. Aero. Soc. 1947-49, Chm. of Nat. Council for Technological Awards 1960-64 (Vice-Chm. 1955-60), of Council for Scientific and Industrial Research 1961-65, and of Metal Box Co. Ltd. 1961-67, Chm. of Council for Nat. Academic Awards 1964-71, and of Berger, Jenson & Nicholson Ltd. since 1967, and Pres. of Roy. Institution of Great Britain since 1969; American Medal of Freedom with Silver Palm; *cr.* Knt. 1953, and *Baron Kings Norton*, of Wotton Underwood, co. Bucks. (Life Peerage) 1965: *m.* 1927, (Doris) Marjorie, da. of Ernest Edward Withers, of Northwood, Middx., and has issue.

𝕬rms,—Azure a chevron or between in chief two jet engines palewise, flames downward, and in base a balloon with car proper. 𝕮rest.—A rabbit sejant erect proper in front of two sceptres in saltire, each terminating in a fleur-de-lys or. 𝕾upporters.—On either side a cock standing on a rock proper.

Residences,—3, Upper Harley St., NW1; Westcote House, Chipping Campden, Glos. *Clubs,*— Athenæum, RAC.

SONS LIVING.

Hon. Christopher Withers (52, Southborough Rd., Bickley, Kent), *b.* 1928: *m.* 1955, Rosemary, da. of the late Frederick Day Ardagh, and has issue.
Hon. Jeremy William (1, Rectory Barn, Halton, Lancaster), *b.* 1932: *m.* 1962, Anne, da. of Albert Moore Linton, and has issue.

KINGSTON, EARL OF. (King-Tenison.) [Earl I. 1768, Bt. I. 1682.]

BARCLAY ROBERT EDWIN KING-TENISON, 11th Earl, and 15th Baronet; *b.* Sept. 23rd, 1943; *s.* 1948; ed. at Winchester; late Lt. R. Scots Greys: *m.* 1st, 1965 (m. diss. 1974), Patricia Mary, da. of E. C. Killip, of Beoley Lodge, Uttoxeter, Staffs; 2ndly, 1974, Victoria, only da. of D. C. Edmonds of Northwood, Middlesex, and has issue by 1st m.

𝕬rms,—Quarterly: 1st and 4th gules, on a bend en, grailed or, between two leopards' faces of the last, jessant-de-lis-azure, three crosses-crosslet sable, *Tenison*, 2nd and 3rd gules, two lions rampant combatant; supporting a dexter hand, couped at the wrist and erect all argent, *King*. 𝕮rests,—1st, a leopard's face as in the arms in front of a crozier and a cross-crosslet fitchée in saltire sable, *Tenison*; 2nd, out of a five-leaved ducal coronet or a dexter hand erect, the third and fourth fingers turned down proper, *King*. 𝕾upporters.—Two lions, per fesse argent and gules. ducally crowned of the last.

Residence,—4A, Alwyne Rd., N.1.

Heaven is our highest hope.

SON LIVING (By 1st m.)
ROBERT CHARLES HENRY, (*Viscount Kingsborough*), *b.* March 20th, 1969.

DAUGHTER LIVING (By 1st m.).
Lady Maria Lisette, *b.* 1970.

SISTER LIVING.
Lady Kara Virginia Louisa (White Gates, Old Romsey Rd., Cadnam, Southampton), *b.* 1938: *m.* 1964 (m. diss. 1974), Anthony John Conroy Hawks, MB, BS, DCH, and has issue living, Honor Louise, *b.* 1966.

AUNTS LIVING. (*Daughters of 9th Earl.*)

Lady Sheelah Florence Lisette *b.* 1900; *m.* 1923, Com. Thomas Cleveland Greenway, RN, who *d.* 1959, and has issue living, John Peter Cleveland, *b.* 1925. *Residence,*—The Shieling, Dulverton, Somerset.
Lady Bridget Honor, *b.* 1902. *Club,*—Ladies' Carlton.

WIDOW LIVING OF TENTH EARL.

JEAN SINCLAIR, da. of the late James L. Alexander, of Orkney and Aberdeen: *m.* 1st, 1947, as his second wife, the 10th Earl, who *d.* 1948; 2ndly, 1953, Cecil Geoffrey Monson, who *d.* 1974. *Residence,* Kilronan, Drumlease Rd., Dronmahair, co. Leitrim.

MOTHER LIVING.

Gwyneth (Joan), dau. of William Howard Evans, of Tenby, Pembrokeshire: *m.* 1st, 1937, the 10th Earl, who obtained a divorce 1947, and who *d.* 1948; 2ndly, 1951 (m. diss. 1960), Brig. Edward Maxwell Tyler, DSO, MC, late RA; 3rdly, 1962, Robert Woodford.

COLLATERAL BRANCHES LIVING.

Grandson of the late Hon. Lawrence Harman King-Harman, 2nd son of 1st, Viscount Lorton, and brother of 6th Earl of Kingston :—
Issue of the late Sir Charles Anthony King-Harman, K.C.M.G., *b.* 1851, *d.* 1939: *m.* 1888, Constance, who *d.* 1961, dau. of the late Gen. Sir Robert Biddulph, G.C.B., G.C.M.G.
Robert Douglas, *DSO, DSC, b.* 1891; Capt. RN; Persian Gulf 1913-14, 1914-18 War with Dover Patrol (DSC with Bar), 1939-44 War with Minelayers (DSO); DSO 1941: *m.* 1st, 1916, Lilly (who *d.* 1966, having obtained a divorce 1926), da. of the late Alexander Moffatt, Sheriff-Substitute of Stirlingshire, of Arnotdale, Falkirk; 2ndly, 1927, Bessie Lilian (BULL), who *d.* 1974, da. of the late William James Davis, of Junee Reefs, NSW; 3rdly, 1975, Eva Mary, da. of the late Archdale Stuart Palmer, and has issue living (by 1st m.) Anthony Lawrence (Ouse Manor, Sharnbrook, Beds.; Army and Navy Club), *b.* 1918; ed. at Wellington Coll.; Col. late RA 1939-45 War: *m.* 1944, Jenette Stella Dunkerley, and has issue living, Anthony William *b.* 1946; Capt. RHA, Michael Charles *b.* 1947; ed. at William and Mary Univ., Va. *Residence,*—Jakins, Great Grandsden, Sandy, Beds. *Club,*—Naval and Military.

Granddaughter of the late Col. John Robert King (infra) :—
Issue of the late Capt. Robert Guy Cyril King, Roy. Australian Artillery, *b.* 1877, *d.* 1940: *m.* 1st, 1905, Albertina Millicent, dau. of Philip Steele, of Melbourne ; 2ndly, 1919, Mary Catherine, dau. of John Robert Russell, of Brackly :—
(By 1st m.) Millicent Francklyn (Flat 3, 4, Lansell Rd., Toorak, Aust. 3142), *b.* 1907: *m.* 1st, 1928, Archibald Jennings Ironside, who *d.* 1941; 2ndly, 1942, William Bethel Thompson, Sqdn. Ldr. RAAF, who *d.* 1945, and has issue living, (by 1st m.) Margaret Joan Francklyn, *b.* 1929,—Philip Norman Jennings, *b.* 1931: *m.* 1960, Dorothy Rosemary Joy, da. of Alan Bell, of Melbourne, and has issue living, Andrew Philip *b.* 1962, Alan Francklyn *b.* 1964.

Grandchildren of the late Capt. John Wingfield King, el. son of the late Lt.-Gen. the Hon. Sir Henry King, KCB, 3rd son of 2nd Earl:—
Issue of the late Col. John Robert King, *b.* 1837, *d.* 1898 : *m.* 1872, Kate Elizabeth, dau. of the late Lieut.-Gen. John Henry Francklyn, R.A., C.B. :—
John Francklyn, *b.* 1882 ; is Lieut.-Col. R.A.O.C. (formerly in R.A.); N.-W. Frontier of India 1908 (medal with clasp), European War 1915-19 in Gallipoli, Egypt, France, and Belgium (despatches, 1914-15 star, two medals): *m.* (Jan.) 1914, Mary Elspeth, dau. of Edwin Hellard, and has issue living, Phyllis Mary, *b.* (Nov.) 1914. *Residence,*—

Issue of the late Gerald Fitzgerald King, *b.* 1864, *d.* 1905 : *m.* 1885, Dora, who *d.* 1952, dau. of the late Capt. Charles Launcelot Sandes, of Carrigafoyle Castle, co. Kerry, and Bayview House, Dublin :—
Wingfield Charles Gerald, *b.* 1886; European War 1914-19 in France as Lieut. Canadian Forces (wounded) : *m.* 1st, 1912, Annabell Mae Brown, who *d.* 1914; 2ndly, 1915, Lena Mae Stewart, who *d.* 1934 ; 3rdly, Mamie Green Slusser, of Augusta, Georgia, U.S.A., and has issue living, (by 2nd marriage) John Charles Alwyn Hallowes (of Farm Rd., Sherborn, Mass., U.S.A.), *b.* 1920; ed. at McGill Univ., Canada (B.Eng. 1948), at Columbia Univ., New York (M.Sc. 1958), and at Stuttgart Institute of Technology (DSc 1960); Col. US Army Reserve Engineers; 1939-45 War in Pacific and NW Europe: *m.* 1st, 1942, Mary Parker, da. of Herbert Daniel Casey, of Ozark, Alabama, USA; 2ndly, 1952, Grace Margaret Stanley, Maj. US Women's Army Corps Reserve, and has issue living, (by 1st marriage) Judy Marilyn *b.* 1943, (by 2nd marriage) Carolyn Joan *b.* 1957,—Elizabeth Avarina Joan, *b.* 1926: *m.* 1952, Duane Caldwell, of 827, Pioneer Drive, North Tonawanda, New York, USA, and has issue living, Stewart Duane Sandes *b.* 1953, Deborah Grace *b.* 1955, Gail Heather *b.* 1963. *Residence,*—283, Tyemont St., North Tonawanda, New York, USA.——John Wingfield (6781, Drake St., Powell River, BC, Canada), *b.* 1891: *m.* 1916, Alice Mary Prefontaine, of Vancouver, BC, who *d.* 1974, and has issue living, Gerald Rene Wingfield (1050, Chilco St., Apt. 705, Vancouver, BC), *b.* 1924; Sqdn. Ldr. RCAF; Maj. (ret.) Canadian Armed Forces (War Medal 1939-45), two medals); Airways Inspector, Min. of Transport: *m.* 1958 (m. diss. 1972), Sonia Lanjin, of Yugoslavia,—John Francis Wingfield (RR5, Mono Mills, Orangeville, Ontario, Canada), *b.* 1927.

Issue of the late Percy Wingfield King, *b.* 1868, *d.* 19— : *m.* 18—, Mary Cecelia Foley:—
James, *b.* 1911: *m.* 19—, and has issue living.——Ena, *b.* 1901: *m.* 19—.——Mary, *b.* 1903: *m.* 19—.
——Ida, *b.* 1907: *m.* 19—. *Residence,*—

Granddaughters of the late Percy Wingfield King (ante):—
Issue of the late John Wingfield King, *b.* 1899, *d.* 1963: *m.* 1st, 1922, Margaret Fraser, who *d.* 1941, da. of the late Isaac Van Cleef, of New Jersey, USA; 2ndly, 19—, Alice M— (101, West St., Paul Av., Wildwood Crest, New Jersey, USA), da. of —
(By 1st m.) Jean Margaret, *b.* 1923: *m.* 19—, Raymond Connelly, and has issue living, Robert, *b.* 1948,—
Carol, *b.* 1945.——Elizabeth, *b.* 1925: *m.* 1946, Samuel Hayward Norris, c/o 22, Knox St., Wilkes-Barre, Pa., USA, and has issue living, Samuel, Scott, *b.* 1951.——(by 2nd m.) Patricia Barry, *b.* 19—

Granddaughters of the late Col. Edward Richard King, son of the late Lieut. Gen. the Hon. Sir Henry King, K.C.B. (ante):—
Issue (by 2nd marriage) of the late Lieut.-Col. Robert Ambrose Cecil King, *b.* 1852, *d.* 1897 : *m.* 1st, 1884, Bessie, who *d.* 1892, dau. of the late Rev. J. Mecredy, D.D., R. of Killalan, and widow of Major J. L. Bell, R.A.; 2ndly, 1893, Lilian Walters, dau. of Rochfort Davies, formerly I.C.S.:—
Eileen Mary Fridiswede, *b.* 1894.——Sybil Doreen, *b.* 1896. *Residence,*—

Great-granddaughter of the late Maj.-Gen. George King, son of the late Rev. the Hon. Richard Fitzgerald King, 5th son of 2nd Earl:—
Granddaughter of the late Catherine King, *b.* 1839, *d.* 1915: *m.* 1871, as his 2nd wife, James Clark, of Chapel House, Paisley, who *d.* 1910 :—
Issue of the late Gerald Fitzgerald King-Clark, *b.* 1874, *d.* 1915: *m.* 1902, Maida, who *d.* 1950, da. of the late Bernard Eekhout:—
Maida Katherine King (The Inches, Thornly Park Av., Paisley), *b.* 1903: *m.* 1944, John Cunningham Watt, of Robertland, who *d.* 1954, and has issue living, Maida Cunningham, *b.* 1945: *m.* 1967, James Ingram Watson, MB, ChB, of Dorusduan, 13, Kincarrathie Cres., Perth, and has issue living, Margaret Maida King-Clark *b.* 1969, Helen Caroline Ingram *b.* 1972,—Mabel Hope Geraldine (Dunard, Thornly Park Av., Paisley), *b.* 1906.

PREDECESSORS.—[1] ROBERT King, P.C., M.P. for co. Roscommon; cr. a *Baronet* 1682; *d.* 1708; *s.* by his el. son [2] *Sir* John, 2nd Bt., M.P. for co. Roscommon; *d.s.p.* 1720; *s.* by his brother [3] *Sir* HENRY, P.C., 3rd Bt.; M.P. for co. Roscommon; *m.* 1722, Isabella Wingfield, sister of 1st Viscount Powerscourt; *d.* 1740; *s.* by his el. son [4] *Sir* ROBERT, 4th Bt.; cr. *Baron Kingsborough* (peerage of Ireland) 1748; *d.* unmarried 1755 when the barony expired, and the baronetcy devolved upon his brother [5] *Sir* EDWARD, 5th Bt.; cr. *Baron Kingston of Rockingham,* co. Roscommon (peerage of Ireland) 1764, *Viscount Kingston of Kingsborough,* co. Sligo (peerage of Ireland) 1766, and *Earl of Kingston* (peerage of Ireland) 1768; *d.* 1797; *s.* by his son [6] ROBERT, 2nd Earl; was M.P. for co. Cork; his 2nd son, Robert Edward, a Gen. in the Army, and Lord-Lieut. of Roscommon, was cr. *Baron Erris,* of Boyle, co. Roscommon (peerage of Ireland) 1800, and *Viscount Lorton,* of Boyle, co. Roscommon (peerage of Ireland) 1806; the Earl *d.* 1799; *s.* by his son [7] GEORGE, 3rd Earl: cr. *Baron Kingston of Mitchelstown,* co. Cork (peerage of United Kingdom) 1821; *d.* 1839; *s.* by his el. surviving son [8] ROBERT HENRY, 4th Earl; *d.* 1867; *s.* by his brother [9] JAMES, 5th Earl: *m.* 1860, Anne, dau. of Matthew Brinkley, of Parsonstown, Meath; *d.s.p.* 1869, when the Barony of Kingston of Mitchelstown expired, and the Irish peerages reverted to his cousin [10] ROBERT, 6th Earl, who had in 1854 *s.* his father as 2nd Viscount Lorton; *b.* 1804: *m.* 1829, Anne, dau. of Sir Robert Newcomen Gore-Booth, Bt.; *d.* 1869; *s.* by his el. son [11] ROBERT EDWARD, 7th Earl; *d.* 1871; *s.* by his brother [12] HENRY ERNEST NEWCOMEN, 8th Earl, *b.* 1848; Lord-Lieut. of co. Roscommon, and a Representative Peer for Ireland; assumed by Roy. licence 1883, the additional surname of Tenison: *m.* 1872, Florence Margaret Christine, who *d.* 1907, dau. of the late Col. Edward King-Tenison, of Kilronan Castle; *d.* 1896; *s.* by his only son [13] HENRY EDWYN, 9th Earl, *b.* 1874; a Representative Peer for Ireland; sometime Capt. Irish Guards; S. Africa 1900-02, 1914-18 War (wounded): *m.* 1897, Ethel Lisette, who *d.* 1949, yst. dau. of Sir Andrew Barclay Walker, 1st Bt. (cr. 1886); *d.* 1946; *s.* by his only son [14] ROBERT HENRY ETHELBERT, 10th Earl, *b.* 1897; sometime Lieut. Roy. Scots Greys: *m.* 1st, 1937, Gwyneth (from whom he obtained a divorce 1947), dau. of William Howard Evans, of Tenby, Pembrokeshire; 2ndly, 1947, Jean Sinclair, dau. of the late James L. Alexander, of Orkney and Aberdeen; *d.* 1948; *s.* by his only son [15] BARCLAY ROBERT EDWIN, 11th Earl and present peer; also Viscount Kingston of Kingsborough, Viscount Lorton, Baron Kingston of Rockingham, and Baron Erris.

KINLOSS, LADY. (Freeman-Grenville.) [Lordship S. 1602.]

For God, country and friends.

BEATRICE MARY GRENVILLE FREEMAN-GRENVILLE, *b.* 1922; *s.* 1944; assumption with her husband of the surnames of Freeman-Grenville recognised by decree of Lord Lyon King of Arms 1950: *m.* 1950, Greville Stewart Parker Freeman, DPhil, MA, BLitt (Oxon), FSA, FRAS, Capt. late Roy. Berks Regt. and has issue.

Arms,—Quarterly, 1st vert, on a cross argent five torteaux, *Grenville*; 2nd, paly of six argent and or, a lion rampant reguardant sable, armed and langued gules, charged with a cross-crosslet of the second, between four quatrefoils of the third, *Morgan*; 3rd, or, a pile gules, *Chandos*; 4th, per fess azure and vair-ancient, three fusils in chief, a bordure or for difference, *Freeman*; over all, an escutcheon ensigned with the coronet of a Lord-Baron in the Peerage of Scotland for her Lordship of Kinloss, quarterly 1st and 4th, or, a saltire gules, on a chief of the last three crescents of the first, *Bruce*; 2nd and 3rd, argent, two open crowns in fesse gules and a martlet in base azure, on a chief of the last a mullet of the field, *Kinloss*. **Crest.**—On a chapeau gules furred, ermine a lion passant, tail extended gules, armed and langued azure, supporting with his dexter forepaw a shield emblazoned with the arms of Kinloss, vizt, argent, two open crowns in fess gules, and a martlet in base azure, on a chief of the last a mullet of the field. **Supporters.**—Two savages wreathed about the middle and temples with laurel, supporting in their exterior hands banners floating inwards, that on the dexter having a staff of these liveries or and azure and surmounted of an abbot's mitre, of the ensigns armorial of the abbot of Kinloss, vizt, azure, semée of fleur-de-lys or, an inescutcheon parted per pale, the dexter bendy of six or and azure within a bordure gules, sinister, argent, two open crowns in fesse gules and a martlet in base azure, on a chief of the last a mullet of the field; that on the sinister with a staff of these liveries gules and or, and ensigned with a Baroness's coronet, of the ensigns armorial of Bruce of Kinloss, vizt, or, a saltire gules, on a chief of the last three crescents of the first.

Residence,—North View House, Sheriff Hutton, York. *Club,*—Royal Commonwealth Society.

SON LIVING.

Hon. BEVIL DAVID STEWART CHANDOS (*Master of Kinloss*), *b.* June 20th, 1953.

DAUGHTERS LIVING.

Hon. Teresa Mary Nugent, *b.* 1957.
Hon. Hester Josephine Anne, *b.* 1960.

SISTERS LIVING. (*Raised to the rank of a Baron's daughters* 1947).

Hon. Lilian Anne Grenville, *b.* 1924: *m.* 1st, 1951, Ernest Frederick Harris, CBE, who *d.* 1965; 2ndly, 1965, Maurice Emile Deen, who *d.* 1971. *Residence,*—144B, Château-Périgord, Monte-Carlo, Monaco.
Hon. Caroline Jane Grenville, *b.* 1931 : *m.* 1958, Gordon Glynne-Walton, F.R.G.S., F.R.Met.Soc., F.R.A.S., F.G.S., late Duke of Wellington's Regt., and has issue living, Charlotte Elizabeth Sophia Caroline Louise, *b.* 1961. *Residence—*White Lea Grange, Batley, Yorkshire.

UNCLES LIVING. (*Sons of Mary, Lady Kinloss.*)

Hon. Robert William MORGAN-GRENVILLE, *b.* 1892; ed. at Cheltenham Coll.; formerly Capt. Rifle
Brig. (Prince Consort's Own); 1914-17 War (wounded); is a J.P. for W. Sussex: *m.* 1st, 1915, Irene
Alice Gertrude, who *d.* 1916, dau. of Sir Robert Grenville Harvey, 2nd Bt., of Langley Park, Slough;
2ndly, 1922, Elizabeth Hope Bine, who *d.* 1969, dau. of Sir Charles Bine Renshaw, 1st Bt.,
and widow of Maj. Francis William Lindley Gull [see Gull, Bt.], and has issue living, (by
1st m.) Robert Grenville Plantagenet (PO Box 141, Malindi, Kenya), *b.* 1916: *m.* 1944, Mabel, da. of
Charles Osborne Ellis of Birmingham, and has issue living, Richard Harvey *b.* 1947; ed. at Millfield:
m. 1969, Diana Jane, da. of Ralf Chambler, of 29, Osprey Av., Birdwell, Barnsley, Yorks., Caroline
Irene *b.* 1949: *m.* 1972, Edward James Windham-Belford (BP2248, Lubumbashi, Zaire) (and has
issue living, James Robert Grenville *b.* 1973),—(by 2nd m.) John Richard Bine (of Upperton House,
Petworth, Sussex), *b.* 1927: *m.* 1955, Joan Margaret, 2nd da. of Air Ch. Marshal Sir Wilfred Rhodes
Freeman, 1st Bt., GCB, DSO, MC, and has issue living, Roger Temple *b.* 1959, Joanna Jane *b.* 1957,—
Gerard Wyndham (of Burgate House, Hascombe, Surrey), *b.* 1931; ed. at Eton; late Capt. Rifle
Brig.: *m.* 1955, Virginia Anne, el. da. of the late Major (Basil Arthur) John Peto, King's Dragoon
Guards [see Peto, Bt., cr. 1927, colls.], and has issue living, Hugo George *b.* 1958, George Septimus
b. 1964, Laura Isabel Hester *b.* 1961. *Residence,*—Lower Burgate, Hascombe, Surrey.

Hon. Harry Nugent MORGAN-GRENVILLE, *OBE* (18, Farley Court, Melbury Rd., W14), *b.* 1896; ed. at
Cheltenham Coll., and RMA; late Capt. RE; 1914-18 War (despatches, OBE); OBE (Mil) 1919:
m. 1921, Mary Alice Oliphant, da. of the late Capt. the Hon. Edward Oliphant Murray [see L. Elibank,
colls.], and has issue living, David Bevil (29, Ennerdale Rd., Kew Gardens, Surrey), *b.* 1928: *m.* 1951,
Nancy, el. da. of the late Prof. Seymour Guy Martin, of Washington, USA, and has issue living,
Geoffrey *b.* 1956, Andrew *b.* 1967, Sarah *b.* 1953,—Rosalind Mary, *b.* 1933: *m.* 1955, Maj. Philip I.
Caleb, DFC, AFM, late USAF, of 24, Elm Av., Richford, Vermont, USA, and has issue living,
Caroline Mary *b.* 1956, Penelope Frances *b.* 1963,—Elizabeth Caroline, *b.* 1944: *m.* 1969, John
Kendrick Williams, CEng., MICE, of 4, Brock End, Cuckfield, Haywards Heath, Sussex, and has
issue living, Victoria Caroline Kendrick *b.* 1971, Rachel Mary Kendrick (twin) *b.* 1971.

COLLATERAL BRANCHES LIVING.

Issue of the late Lt.-Col. the Hon. Thomas George Breadalbane MORGAN-GRENVILLE,
DSO, OBE, MC, 3rd son of Mary, Lady Kinloss, *b.* 1891, *d.* 1965: *m.* 1916,
Georgina May St. John, who *d.* 1973, da. of the late Albert St. John Murphy, of
The Island House, Little Island, co. Cork:—
Pamela Mary Ruth, *b.* 1919: *m.* 1944, Capt. Alec David Francis, late Welsh Guards, of The Grange,
Malmesbury, Wilts., and has issue living, Nigel Charles Audley Grenville, *b.* 1949,—Priscilla Anna-
belle, *b.* 1947: *m.* 1969, Frederick Hugh Philip Hamilton Wills, Capt. late 11th Hussars [see B.
Dulverton, colls.].——Cynthia Avril, *b.* 1921: *m.* 1948, Christopher Michael Aliaga-Kelly, of Barna-
vara House, Glanmire, co. Cork, and has issue living, Peter Edward Grenville, *b.* 1956,—Veronica
Ann Cynthia, *b.* 1950.——Audrey Marigold (*Baroness Ironside*), *b.* 1931: *m.* 1950, the 2nd Baron
Ironside, of Broomwood Manor, Chignal St. James, Chelmsford.

Grandchildren of the late Hon. Caroline Mary Elizabeth Grenville Close-Smith
(infra):—
Issue of the late Lt.-Col. Richard Sydney Grenville CLOSE-SMITH, OBE, *b.* 1910, *d.* 1973:
m. 1st., 1935 (m. diss. 1954), Baroness Florence von Ompteda, da. of the late Robert,
Baron Ompteda; 2ndly, 1954, Josephine Judith (Steart Jill, Little Horwood, Milton
Keynes, Bucks.), da. of Vincent Wood Mullins, and widow of Michael Bruce Urquhart
Dewar, of Stagenhoe Park, Hitchin:—
(By 1st m.) Robert Richard (Ashmore Farm, Water Stratford, Buckingham), *b.* 1936: *m.* 1960, Ena
Mary Rooks, and has issue living, Charles Robert, *b.* 1961,—Christopher Paul, *b.* 1925,—Henry
Richard Christian, *b.* 1965.——Venice Mary Grenville, *b.* 1938: *m.* 1959, John Duncan Maitland
Gordon-Colebrooke, of Stagsden, Singleborough, Milton Keynes, Bucks., and has issue living,
James Richard Maitland, *b.* 1961,—Jeremy Patrick Grenville, *b.* 1963,—John Angus Childerstone,
b. 1967.

Issue of the late Hon. Caroline Mary Elizabeth Grenville MORGAN-GRENVILLE,
da. of Mary, Lady Kinloss, *b.* 1886, *d.* 1972: *m.* 1909, Maj. Thomas Close Smith,
who. *d.* 1946:—
Charles Nugent CLOSE-SMITH, *TD* (The Heymersh, Britford, Salisbury, Wilts.), *b.* 1911; late Bucks.
Yeo.; assumed the additional surname of Close: *m.* 1946, Elizabeth Emily Vivien, da. of the late
Maj. William Augustus Cecil Kinsman, DSO, OBE, late R. Inniskilling Fus. (ret.), and has issue
living, Thomas William (16, Ansdell Terr., W8), *b.* 1947: *m.* 1973, Lilian Moire Weston, twin da. of
John Weston Adamson, of Oldstead Hall, Coxwold, York,—Anthony Grenville, *b.* 1950,—Edward
Vivian, *b.* 1951.——Henry Temple CLOSE-SMITH (The Old Vicarage, Messing, Colchester, Essex),
b. 1918; assumed the additional surname of Close: late Welsh Gds.: *m.* 1948, Cicely Margaret
Wingfield, yr. da. of the late Rev. Eustace Hill, and has issue living, Richard Henry, *b.* 1951,—
Caroline Mary, *b.* 1954.

Issue of the late Lady Anne, 2nd dau. of 3rd Duke of Buckingham and Chandos,
b. 1853, *d.* 1890: *m.* 1882, Lieut.-Col. George Rowley Hadaway, J.P., formerly R.A., who *d.* 1926, of Grenville, Godalming:—
Alice Eva (Rose Acre Nursing Home, Priorsfield, Godalming, Surrey), *b.* 1888.

Descendants of the late Lady Anne Eliza Mary, dau. of 2nd Duke of Buckingham
and Chandos, *b.* 1820, *d.* 1879: *m.* 1846, William Henry Powell Gore-Langton,
M.P., who *d.* 1873 [see E. Temple of Stowe].

PREDECESSORS.—[1] *Rt. Hon. Sir* EDWARD Bruce, a Lord of Session 1597-1603, accompanied King James to England on his accession 1603, was naturalized that year, and appointed
Master of the Rolls for life; received charter of Kinloss with title of *Lord Kinloss* (peerage of
Scotland) 1602, with remainder to his heirs and assigns and cr. *Lord Bruce of Kinloss* (peerage
of Scotland) 1604, with remainder to his heirs male whatsoever, and later (1608) with remainder to
heirs male of the body, failing whom to heirs and assigns *d.* 1610; *s.* by his el. son [2] EDWARD,
K.G., 2nd Lord; killed in a duel 1613; *s.* by his brother [3] THOMAS, 3rd Lord; cr. *Earl of Elgin*
(peerage of Scotland) 1633, with remainder to heirs male whatever bearing the name and arms
of Bruce, and *Baron Bruce,* of Whorlton, co. York (peerage of England) 1640, [4—6] in
which title the Lordship of Kinloss was merged until the death of the 6th Earl of Elgin in 1746,
when it devolved (in accordance with the subsequent decision of the House of Lords) on [7]
JAMES, 3rd Duke of Chandos, as *de jure* 7th Lord Kinloss; at his death his dau. [8] ANNA
ELIZA (Duchess of Buckingham and Chandos) became *de jure* Lady Kinloss, and her son [9]
RICHARD PLANTAGENET (Duke of Buckingham and Chandos) *de jure* 9th Lord Kinloss; in 1868
his son [10] RICHARD PLANTAGENET CAMPBELL Temple-Nugent-Brydges-Chandos-Grenville,
G.C.S.I., C.I.E., P.C., D.C.L., 3rd Duke of Buckingham and Chandos [see V. Cobham], established
his right to the title as 10th Lord Kinloss, *b.* 1823; Chm. of Committees and Dep. Speaker in House
of Lords: *m.* 1st, 1851, Caroline, who *d.* 1874, dau. of Robert Harvey, of Langley Park, Bucks;
2ndly, 1885, Alice Anne, who *d.* 1931, el. dau. of Sir Graham Graham-Montgomery, 3rd Bt.; *d.* 1889;
s. by his el. dau. [11] MARY Morgan, *b.* 1852: *m.* 1884, Luis Ferdinand Harry Courthope Morgan, of
Biddlesden Park, Bucks, who *d.* 1896 (having assumed by Roy. licence the additional surname and
arms of Grenville 1890): *d.* 1944; *s.* by her granddaughter [12] BEATRICE MARY GRENVILLE (el.
da. of the late Rev. the Hon. Luis Chandos Francis Temple Morgan-Grenville (*Master of Kinloss*),
2nd and el. surviving son of Mary, Lady Kinloss), present peeress.

KINNAIRD, LORD. (Kinnaird.)
Wandering lights deceive.

ERRANTIA LUMINA FALLUNT

CERTA CRUCE SALUS
Sure salvation by the cross.

[Lord S. 1682, and Baron U.K. 1860.]

GRAHAM CHARLES KINNAIRD, 13th Lord; b. Sept. 15th, 1912; s. 1972; ed. at Eton; F/O RAFVR; late Lt. 4/5th Bn. Black Watch (TA); m. 1st, 1938, Nadia (who obtained a divorce 1940), only child of Harold Augustus Fortington, OBE [see Jardine, Bt., cr. 1919]; 2ndly, 1940, Diana Margaret Elizabeth, yr. da. of the late Robert Shuckburgh Copeman, of Roydon Hall, Diss, Norfolk, and has issue by 2nd m. (of whom his son, Nicholas Charles b. 1946, d. 1951).

Arms,—Quarterly: 1st and 4th or, a fesse wavy between three mullets gules, Kirkcaldy; 2nd and 3rd gules, a saltire between four crescents or, Kinnaird. Crest,—A crescent arising from a cloud, having a star issuing from between its horns, all within two branches of palm disposed in orle proper. Supporters,—Two naked men wreathed about the loins with oak leaves, each holding in his exterior hand a garland of laurel, their interior ankles surrounded by a fetter, and the chain held in the interior hand.

Seat,—Rossie Priory, Inchture, Perthshire
Residence,—Durham House, Durham Place, S W3.

DAUGHTERS LIVING. (By 2nd m.)

Hon. Caroline, b. 1949: m. 1970, Christopher Wigan, of 46, Stockwell Park Rd., SW9 [see B. Faringdon, colls.].
Hon. Anna, b. 1952.
Hon. Susan, b. 1956.
Hon. Mary Clare, b. 1960.

SISTER LIVING.

Hon. Madeline Elisabeth, b. 1908: m. 1929, the Rt. Rev. Hugh Rowlands Gough, CMG, OBE, TD, DD, Primate of Australia 1959-66, and has issue living, Lucy (20, Sion Hill, Bath), b. 1931: m. 1959 (m. diss. 1971), Harold Mervyn Temple-Richards [see Temple, Bt., colls.]. Residence,—21, Sydney Buildings, Bath.

PREDECESSORS.—[1] Sir GEORGE PATRICK Kinnaird, K.B., P.C., M.P. for Perthshire; was a descendant of Reginald Kinnaird, younger son of Sir Richard Kinnaird of that Ilk, founder of the family, who had had a charter of Kinnaird from William the Lion 1172-1184; cr. Lord Kinnaird, of Inchture (peerage of Scotland) 1682; d. 1689: s. by his son [2] PATRICK, 2nd Lord; d. 1701; s. by his son [3] PATRICK, 3rd Lord; d. 1713; s. by his son [4] CHARLES, 4th Lord; d. 1728; s. by his uncle [5] CHARLES, 5th Lord; d. 1758; s. by his kinsman [6] CHARLES, 6th Lord, grandson of the Hon. George, 6th son of 1st Lord; d. 1767; s. by his son [7] GEORGE, 7th Lord; a Representative Peer; d. 1805; s. by his son [8] CHARLES, 8th Lord; b. 1780; M.P. for Leominster 1802-5; elected a Representative Peer 1806: m. 1806, Lady Olivia Letitia Catherine FitzGerald, dau. of 2nd Duke of Leinster, d. 1826; s. by his el. son [9] GEORGE WILLIAM FOX, K.T., 9th Lord; cr. Baron Rossie (peerage of United Kingdom) 1831, and Baron Kinnaird, of Rossie, co. Perth (peerage of United Kingdom) 1860, with remainder to his brother Arthur; d. 1878, when the Barony of Rossie became ext., and the Lordship and Barony of Kinnaird devolved upon his brother [10] ARTHUR WELLESLEY, 10th Lord; b. 1814; M.P. for Perth (L) 1837-9 and 1852-78; d. 1887; s. by his el. son [11] ARTHUR FITZ-GERALD, K.T., 11th Lord; b. 1847; a Director of Barclays Bank (Limited); Lord High Commr. to Church of Scotland 1907, 1908, and 1909: m. 1875, Mary Alma Victoria, who d. 1923, dau. of Sir Andrew Agnew, 8th Bt. (cr. 1629); d. 1923; s. by his son [12] KENNETH FITZ-GERALD, KT. KBE, 12th Lord, b. 1880; Capt. Scottish Horse; Lord High Commr. to Church of Scotland 1936 and 1937; Lord-Lieut. of Perthshire 1942-60: m. 1903, Frances Victoria, JP, who d. 1960, da. of the late Thomas Henry Clifton [Agnew Bt., cr. 1629]; d. 1972; s. by his son [13] GRAHAM CHARLES, 13th Lord and present peer.

KINNOULL, EARL OF. (Hay.) [Earl S. 1633.]

Renew your courage.

RENOVATE ANIMOS

ARTHUR WILLIAM GEORGE PATRICK HAY, 15th Earl; b. March 26th, 1935; s. 1938; ed. at Eton; FRICS; a Member of Agricultural Valuers' Assocn.; a Member, Queen's Body Guard for Scotland (Roy. Co. of Archers) since 1965; Pres. of National Council on Inland Transport since 1964, Junior Conservative Whip, House of Lords 1966-68; Pres. of Scottish Clans Assocn. 1970; Vice-Pres. of Nat. Assocn. of Parish Councils 1971; a Dir. of Property Owners' Building Soc.: m. 1961, Gay Ann, el. da. of Sir Denys Colquhoun Flowerdew Lowson, 1st Bt., and has issue.

Arms,—Quarterly: 1st and 4th grand quarters counterquartered, 1st and 4th azure, an unicorn salient argent, armed, maned, and unguled or, within a bordure of the last, charged with eight half thistles vert, and as many half roses gules joined together per pale as a coat of augmentation, Kinnoull; 2nd and 3rd argent, three escutcheons two and one gules, Hay; 2nd and 3rd grand quarters counterquartered 1st and 4th or, three bars wavy gules, surmounted of a scimitar in pale argent, Drummond; 2nd and 3rd or, a lion's head erased within a double tressure flory counterflory gules, a coat of augmentation, *Strathallan*. **Crest,**—A countryman, couped at the knees, vested grey, his waist-coat gules and bonnet azure, bearing on his right shoulder an ox yoke proper. **Supporters,**—Two countrymen habited as in the crest, the *dexter* holding over his shoulder the coulter, and the *sinister* the paddle of a plough proper.

Residences,—15, Carlyle Sq., SW3; Pier House, Seaview, Isle of Wight. *Clubs,*—Lansdowne, Turf, Pratt's, White's, and MCC.

SON LIVING.
CHARLES WILLIAM HARLEY (*Viscount Dupplin*), *b.* Dec. 20th, 1962.

DAUGHTERS LIVING.
Lady Melissa Ann, *b.* 1964.
Lady Iona Charlotte, *b.* 1967.
Lady Atalanta Rose, *b.* 1974.

SISTERS LIVING.
Lady Venetia Constance Kathleen Luz, *b.* 1929: *m.* 1953, Maj. Joseph Trevor Davies (48, George St., Helensburgh, Dunbartonshire), and has issue living, Nicola Jane, *b.* 1957,—Sally May, *b.* 1960.
Lady June Ann, *b.* 1932: *m.* 1955, Cranley Gordon Douglas Onslow, MP [see E. Onslow, colls.]. *Residence,*—Chobham Park House, Chobham, Surrey.

GREAT-AUNTS LIVING. (*Daughters of* 13th *Earl.*)
Lady Elizabeth Blanche Mary, *b.* 1903: *m.* 1st, 1925, Peter Stanley Chappell, from whom she obtained a divorce 1935 ; 2ndly, 1935, Douglas William Ernest Gordon, who *d.* 1951, having obtained a divorce 1945 ; 3rdly, 1945, William H. S. Dent, M.C., and has issue living, (by 1st marriage) Michael Stanley Fitzroy (760, Grover Av., Coquitlam, New Westminster, BC, Canada), *b.* 1926: *m.* 1952, Eileen Day, of Vancouver, Canada. *Residence,*—Fig Tree Cottage, Northiam, Sussex.
Lady Margaret Florence Grace, *b.* 1907: *m.* 1929, Norman Francis William Haliburton D'Arcy, from whom she obtained a divorce 1942 [Bs. D'Arcy de Knayth, colls.], and has issue living, Philippa, *b.* 1932: *m.* 1st, 1951 (m. diss. 1965) Paul Charles Montagu Curtis-Bennett, son of the late Sir (Francis) Noel Curtis-Bennett, KCVO; 2ndly, 1965, Casper Morten Wilhelm Wilhelmsen Kielland, of 5, Chelsea Embankment, SW3. *Residence,*—7A, Roland Gdns., SW7.

COLLATERAL BRANCHES LIVING.
Grandchildren of the late Lieut.-Col. the Hon. Charles Rowley HAY-DRUMMOND (son of 11th Earl), who *d.* 1918, having assumed in 1900 the additional surname and arms of Drummond on succeeding his brother Arthur in the Cromlix and Innerpeffray estates :—
Issue of the late Col. Arthur William Henry HAY-DRUMMOND, *b.* 1862, *d.* 1953: *m.* 1891, Mary, who *d.* 1948, dau. of Sir Edward Henry Scott, 5th Bt. (cr. 1821) :—
George Vane, *b.* 1910; ed. at Stowe Sch.; is Capt. Scots Guards (Reserve), Capt. late 6th/7th Batn. Black Watch (T.A.), and a Member of Queen's Body Guard for Scotland (Roy. Co. of Archers): *m.* 1933, Lady Betty Mary Seton Montgomerie, dau. of 16th Earl of Eglinton and Winton, and has issue living, Robert Vane (Westridge House, Westridge Green, Streatley, Berks.), *b.* 1936; ed. at Eton; CA (Scot; a Member of Queen's Body Guard for Scotland (R. Co. of Archers)): *m.* 1959, Auriol Fyler, yr. da. of Com. George Martin Pares, of The Old School House, Aldworth, Berks.,—Auriol Vane, *b.* (Oct.) 1933: *m.* 1957, John Anthony Murray, of 7, Inkerman Terr., Allen St., W8, and has issue living, Andrew Henry William Vane, *b.* 1964, Louise Mary, *b.* 1958. *Residence,*—Dornoch Mill, Crieff, Perths.—Violet Vane, *b.* 1897: *m.* 1920, Capt. Sir Anthony St. John-Mildmay, MC, 8th Bt., Grenadier Guards Reserve, who *d.* 1947, and from whom she had obtained a divorce 1933. *Residence,*—Fulford House, Culworth, Banbury.

Descendants of the late Capt. Edward William Auriol Drummond-Hay, son of the late Very Rev. Edward Auriol Hay-Drummond, D.D., Dean of Bocking, brother of 10th Earl :—

Grandchildren of the late Rev. Frederic Drummond-Hay (infra):—
Issue of the late Frederic Edward Drummond-Hay, *b.* 1868, *d.* 1948: *m.* 1st, 1893, Mary Elizabeth, who *d.* 1904, dau. of Henry Stone; 2ndly, 1909, Amy, dau. of the late Francis William Boston, of Croydon :—
(By 1st marriage) Laura Mary Gertrude, *b.* 1895 : *m.* 1919, Frederick Benjamin Nicol, who *d.* 1958, and has issue living, Frederick Edward Drummond-Hay (of Flat 8, 4, Wingate Av., Ascot Vale, Victoria, Australia), *b.* 1926: *m.* 1952, Frances Margaret O'Neil, and has issue living, Debbra Lee *b.* 1955, Amanda Jane *b.* 1959,—William Daniel (1196, Riversdale Rd., Box Hill, Vic. 3128, Australia), *b.* 1933: *m.* 1960, Noela Eastlake, and has issue living, Stephen Gerard *b.* 1961, Marcus Benjamin *b.* 1971, Michael Damian *b.* 1973, Elizabeth Jane *b.* 1963, Andrea Marie *b.* 1965,—Katherine Danielle *b.* 1969,—Geoffrey James (39, Porter St., Eltham 3095, Victoria, Aus.), *b.* 1936: *m.* 1960 Patricia Carmel Harris, and has issue living, Jeremy *b.* 1964, Matthew James *b.* 1968, Felicity Jane *b.* 1962, Kellie Therese *b.* 1966, Lucinda *b.* 1970,—Ruth, *b.* 1932: *m.* 1952, John Thomas Meadth (10, Chirnside Drive, Chirnside Park Est., Lilydale, Vic. 3140, Aust.), and has issue living, Thomas Anthony, *b.* 1953, Terrance Michael *b.* 1954, Patrick John, *b.* 1958, Andrew Gordon *b.* 1961, Kevin Francis *b.* 1963, Margaret Ruth *b.* 1955, Veronica Mary *b.* 1965. *Residence,*—4, King St., Essenden, Victoria, Aust., 3040.

Issue of the late Robert Drummond-Hay, *b.* 1870, *d.* 1907: *m.* 1895, Gertrude Agatha, who *d.* 1924, da. of Thomas Forbutt:—
Robert Augustine Tudor (107, Burnaby Rd., Coventry), *b.* 1897: *m.* 1935, Selina Woodroffe——Geoffrey Francis (19, Buckmans Rd., Crawley, Sussex), *b.* 1898: *m.* 1936, Margaret Fenlon, who *d.* 1959, and has issue living, Peter (40, St. Luke's Rd., W11), *b.* 1943: *m.* 1st, 1966 (m. diss. 1972), Carolyn Macdonald, of Wichita, Kansas, USA; 2ndly, 1972, Celia Humphris, and has issue living (by 1st m.), Samantha *b.* 1966, (by 2nd m.) Luke *b.* 1974,—Alison, *b.* 1946: *m.* 1968, Keith Wills, of Castle Park Cottage, Drummuir by Keith, Banff., AB5 35P, and has issue living, Alexander *b.* 1972.——Ernest Patrick, *b.* 1900: *m.* 19—, and has issue living, a son, *b.* 19—, a da., *b.* 19—,—Barbara May Gertrude, *b.* 1904: *m.* 19—, Peter Drummond-Hay, of 02, Foxhill, Rudd Rd., Illovo, Johannesburg, S. Africa.——Veronica Florence Muriel Aileen (Loyola, 14, Aber Rd., Leicester), *b.* 1907: *m.* 1926, Alfred Camacho, who *d.* 1964.

Grandchildren of the late Sir Robert HAY-DRUMMOND, C.M.G., son of the late Rt. Hon. Sir John Hay Drummond-Hay, G.C.M.G., K.C.B., younger son of the late Capt. Edward William Auriol Drummond-Hay (ante) :—
Issue of the late Edward William HAY-DRUMMOND-HAY, *b.* 1877, *d.* 1941: *m.* 1904, Margaret Alice, who *d.* 1954, dau. of the late E. W. Meade-Waldo, of Stonewall Park, and Hever Castle, Kent :—
John Waldo Edward, *TD*, *b.* 1906; ed. at Marlborough, and at Trin. Coll., Camb.; Major (ret.), Queen's Own Roy. W. Kent Regt. (TA), and attached Indian Army: *m.* 1937, Anne Rachel, who *d.* 1975, da. of W. T. Prideaux, of Elderslie, Ockley, and has issue living, Robert Prideaux (39, Latimer Village, Chesham, Bucks.), *b.* 1941: *m.* 1965, Sally Catherine, da. of Ian Redfern, of Winchester, and has issue living, Robert Simon *b.* 1967, Katherine Louise *b.* 1973, Caroline Sarah *b.* 1974,—Peter Charles, *b.* 1948; ed. at Eton, and Trin. Coll., Camb.,—Auriol Marion, *b.* 1946: *m.* 1968, Donald Alvin Hessemer, of 1219, Eleonore, St., New Orleans, La., USA. *Residence,*—Hill House, Crowhurst, Battle, Sussex.

Issue of the late Cecil Lawrence HAY-DRUMMOND-HAY, *b.* 1882, *d.* 1952: *m.* 1st, 1911, **Jessie** (who *d.* 1961, having obtained a divorce 1924), younger twin dau. of the late Lawrence Munro; 2ndly, 1925, Doris Rachel, who *d.* 1971, da. of the late Dudley Hill, of Christchurch, New Zealand :—
(By 1st m.) Robert Lawrence Munro (Ardfenaig House, by Bunessan, Isle of Mull), *b.* 1912; ed. at Worcester Coll., Oxford (BA 1935, MA 1939).——(By 2nd m.) Annette Alistair, *b.* 1927: *m.* 1948, David Stanford, of Wanganui Rd., Marton, New Zealand.

Grandsons of the late Charles Drummond-Hay (infra):—
Issue of the late Humphry Ringler Drummond-Hay, *b.* 1886, *d.* 1965: *m.* 1st, 1912, May
Katherine (who obtained a divorce 1937), da. of Sir George Bury; 2ndly, 1937, Mrs.
Dorothy Claire Carey, who *d.* 1969, da. of the late Frederick William Heubach, of
Winnipeg:—
(By 1st m.) (Athol) Bury (1189, Matthews Av., Vancouver 9, BC, Canada), *b.* 1913; late Flight-Lt.
RCAF; 1939-45 War (prisoner).——George Thomson (1663, Chickadee Cres., Nanaimo, BC, Canada),
b. 1916; 1939-45 War with Seaforth Highlanders of Canada, and as Capt. 8th Canadian Recon-
naissance Regt.: *m.* 1st, 1939, Elizabeth Barbara Fraser, of Regina, from whom he obtained a
divorce 1949; 2ndly, 1949 (m. diss. 1960), Mrs. Adrienne Ruth Russell, da. of John William Southin,
of Vancouver, BC; 3rdly, 1964, Mrs. Shirlee Marian Montgomery, da. of the late Harry J. Gibbons,
of Sioux City, Iowa, USA, and has issue living, (by 1st m.) Leonard Gordon, *b.* 1940,—Elizabeth
Sandra, *b.* 1945,—(by 2nd m.) Eric Thomson (2084, Monterey Av., Mento Park, Cal., USA), *b.* 1951,—
Charles Webster, *b.* 1952,—Leslie Katherine, *b.* 1954.

Grandchildren of the late Harold Sanford Drummond-Hay (infra):—
Issue of the late Charles Robert Drummond-Hay, late Fl.-Lt. RCAF, *b.* 1917, *d.* 1966: *m.*
1940, Ina Mary (3005, Point Grey Rd., Vancouver, BC, Canada), da. of the late George H.
Disbrow, of Vancouver:—
Humphry Blake, *b.* 1945.——Brian Maxwell, *b.* 1947.——Lee Sanford, *b.* 1950.——Jane Macpherson
(4563, W. Third Av., Vancouver, BC, Canada), *b.* 1953.

Granddaughter of the late Charles Drummond-Hay (infra):—
Issue of the late Harold Sanford Drummond-Hay, *b.* 1890, *d.* 1951: *m.* 1915, Effie Caldwell,
who *d.* 1964, da. of the late Robert Adamson, of Winnipeg:—
Jeanette Audrey (Suite 1202, 1122, Gilford St., Vancouver, BC, Canada), *b.* 1919.

Granddaughter of the late Col. Thomas Robert Hay Drummond-Hay, son of the
late Capt. Edward William Auriol Drummond-Hay (ante):—
Issue of the late Charles Drummond-Hay, *b.* 1856, *d.* 1926 : *m.* 1885, Alena, who *d.* 1952,
dau. of G. Cropley, of Craigielea, Manitoba:—
Doreen Gwendolen (606-595, River Av., Winnipeg, Manitoba, Canada), *b.* 1909.

Grandchildren of the late Sir Francis Ringler Drummond-Hay, 5th son of the late
Capt. Edward William Auriol Drummond-Hay (ante):—
Issue of the late Francis Edward Drummond-Hay, M.V.O., *b.* 1868, *d.* 1943: *m.* 1895,
Eveline Austey, M.B.E., who *d.* 1963, dau. of the late Rev. Edmund Thomas Bennett,
formerly R. of Littleton, Winchester, of Castle Roe, co. Londonderry:—
ClaudeFrancis (c/o The Durban Club, Durban, Natal), *b.* 1898; ed. at Cheltenham Coll.; 1915-18 War
in Salonika and France as Capt. Black Watch (R. Highlanders): *m.* 1st, 1921, Gladys Grant, from
whom he obtained a divorce 1928; 2ndly, 1933, Ellenor, da. of the late G. Carlin, of Cleadon Meadows, Cleadon, Durham; 3rdly, Mrs. Gladys Beatrice Robinson, of Babbacombe Cliffs, Torquay, and
has issue living, (by 2nd m.) John Francis (44, Inanda Rd., Hillcrest, Natal), *b.* 1938: *m.* 1961,
Beverley Ann, da. of Francis Howes, of Hillcrest, Natal, and has issue living, Sean Francis *b.* 1962,
Deborah Joan *b.* 1963,—Jeffrey Derrick Edward, *b.* 1943,—Joan, *b.* 1935.

Issue of the late Frederick William Drummond-Hay, *b.* 1870, *d.* 1923: *m.* 1st, 1894, Ellen
Marion, who *d.* 1896, dau. of the late Major Charles Johnson Anthony Deane, Indian
Army: 2ndly, 1905, Louise Agnese Burke, who *d.* 1920, dau. of Denis Comerford, of
co. Tipperary:—
(By 2nd m.) Rita O'Brien, *b.* 1906: *m.* 1932 (m. diss. 1954), Arthur Harly Whitcomb, and has issue
living, Cheyne, *b.* 1933,—Brenda, *b.* 1935.

Issue of the late Henry Arthur Drummond-Hay, *b.* 1872, *d.* 1918: *m.* 1895, Julia Minnie
St. Barbe, who *d.* 1957, dau. of the late William Robinson Hill, M.D., J.P., of Grosvenor
House, Lymington, Hants:—
Muriel Madelene, *b.* 1897: *m.* 1st, 1922, Sidney Harold Noel Pollack, who *d.* 1926 ; 2ndly,
1936, the Rev. Canon Kenneth Arthur Chaffey, and has issue living, (by 1st marriage) Harry Ronald,
b. 1923,—Francis Donald Edward, *b.* 1925. *Residence*,—All Saints Rectory, Main Rd., Muizenberg,
Cape Province, S. Africa.——Olive Margarita, *b.* 1900: *m.* 1930, Charles William Lockhart-
Barker, who *d.* 1957, and has issue living, Margaret Ann, *b.* 1932,—Patricia Mary, *b.* 1933
Address,—13, da Jama St., Welgemoed, Cape Prov., S. Africa.

PREDECESSORS.—[1] Sir GEORGE Hay, *K.B.*; was successively a Gentleman of the Bedchamber, and Clerk Register of Scotland, and Lord High Chancellor of Scotland 1622-34; cr.
Viscount Dupplin and *Lord Hay of Kinfauns* (peerage of Scotland) 1627, with remainder to
the heirs male of his body, and *Earl of Kinnoull, Viscount Dupplin*, and *Lord Hay of Kinfauns*
with remainder to his heirs male (peerage of Scotland) 1633; *d.* 1634; *s.* by his son [2].
GEORGE, *P.C.*, 2nd Earl; Capt. of Yeomen of the Guard; *d.* 1644; *s.* by his el. son [3] GEORGE,
3rd Earl, of whom "The Scots Peerage," published 1908, says "is not given by the Peerage
writers, but there is undoubted evidence for his existence" ; *d.* about 1650 ; *s.* by his brother [4]
WILLIAM, 4th Earl; became in 1660 proprietor of the Island of Barbados, and in 1661
disposed of it to Charles II.; during the Civil Wars was taken by the Republicans and committed to Edinburgh Castle whence he escaped 1654, and in Nov. of that year was made
prisoner by the English ; *d.* 1677; *s.* by his el. son [5] GEORGE, 5th Earl; *d.* 1687; *s.* by his
brother [6] WILLIAM, 6th Earl; *d.* 1709; after resignation received a regrant of his honours
in 1704, with remainder to his kinsman Thomas, Viscount Dupplin, and heirs male of his
body, whom failing to his heirs of tailzie and provision ; *s.* by the said [7] THOMAS, 7th Earl,
great-grandson of Peter Hay, younger brother of 1st Earl; M.P. for Perthshire 1693-7; had
been cr. *Viscount Dupplin* (peerage of Scotland) 1697 with remainder to heirs male of his
body, whom failing to his heirs of entail; imprisoned in Edinburgh Castle 1715 on breaking
out of rebellion; *d.* 1719; *s.* by his son [8] GEORGE HENRY, 8th Earl, who had in 1711 been
cr. *Baron Hay*, of Pedwardine, co. Hereford (peerage of Great Britain) ; *d.* 1758 ; *s.* by his son
[9] THOMAS, 9th Earl; *d.s.p.* 1787; *s.* by his nephew [10] ROBERT Hay-Drummond, *P.C.*,
10th Earl, son of the Most Rev. the Hon. Robert Hay-Drummond, Archbishop of York, 2nd
son of 8th Earl; assumed for himself the additional surname of Drummond; was Lord Lyon
King of Arms ; *d.* 1804; *s.* by his el. son [11] THOMAS ROBERT, 11th Earl; *b.* 1785; was Lord-
Lieut. of Perthshire, and Lyon King of Arms: *m.* 1824, Louisa Burton, who *d.* 1885, dau. of
Adm. Sir Charles Rowley, G.C.B., 1st Bt. ; *d.* 1866 ; *s.* by his el. son [12] GEORGE, 12th Earl.
b. 1827: *m.* 1848, Lady Emily Blanche Charlotte Somerset, who *d.* 1895, dau. of 7th Duke of
Beaufort, K.G.; *d.* 1897; *s.* by his el. surviving son [13] ARCHIBALD FITZROY GEORGE,
13th Earl; *b.* 1855; served with the late Baker Pasha, as Ch. of his Staff during Campaign
on Red Sea : *m.* 1st, 1879 [judicially separated 1885], Josephine Maria, who *d.* 1900, dau. of
the late John Hawke, solicitor, of Burlington Gardens, W. ; 2ndly, 1903, Florence Mary,
who *d.* 1941 (having *m.* 2ndly, 1919, Major John Joseph Berington, R.M.A.), dau. of the late
Edward Tierney Gilchrist Darell; *d.* 1916; *s.* by his grandson [14] GEORGE HARLEY (only
surviving son of the late Capt. Edmund Alfred Rollo George, Viscount Dupplin, el. son of 13th
Earl), 14th Earl, *b.* 1902: *m.* 1st, 1923, Enid Margaret Hamlyn (who obtained a divorce 1927), only
child of Major Ernest Gaddesden Fellows; 2ndly, 1928, Mary Ethel Isobel, who *d.* 1938, dau.
of the late Ferdinand Richard Holmes Meyrick, M.D., of 59, Kensington Court, W.8 ;
d. 1938; *s.* by his 3rd but only surviving son [15] ARTHUR WILLIAM GEORGE PATRICK, 15th
Earl, and present peer; also Viscount Dupplin, Lord Hay of Kinfauns, and Baron Hay of Pedwardine.

Kinrara, Earl of March and son of Duke of Richmond.

KINROSS, BARON. (Balfour.) [Baron U.K. 1902.]

Nothing rashly.

JOHN PATRICK DOUGLAS BALFOUR, 3rd Baron; *b.* June 25th, 1904; *s.* 1939; ed. at Winchester, and at Balliol Coll., Oxford (B.A. 1925); is an Author and Journalist, and Squadron-Leader R.A.F. Vol. Reserve; European War 1940-44 (despatches); was 1st Sec. in H.M. Diplo. Ser. at Cairo 1944-47: *m.* 1938, Angela Mary (from whom he obtained a divorce 1942), dau. of the late Capt. George Culme-Seymour [see Culme-Seymour, Bt., colls.].

Arms,—Ermine, on a chevron sable between in chief two torteaux and in base an open book, an otter's head proper. Crest,—On a rock a mermaid holding in the dexter hand an otter's head erased, and in the sinister a swan's head erased, all proper. Supporters,—On either side an otter proper, charged on the shoulder with two swords saltirewise, also proper.

Residence,—4, Warwick Avenue, W.2.   *Clubs,*—Travellers', Beefsteak.

BROTHER LIVING.

Hon. DAVID ANDREW, *OBE*, *TD* (58, India St., Edinburgh; Clubs—Army and Navy, and New (Edinburgh)), *b.* March 29th, 1906; ed. at Sherborne, and at Edinburgh Univ.; a WS; Col. RA, and a Member of Queen's Body Guard for Scotland (Roy. Co. of Archers); Hon. Col. 278th (Lowland) Field Regt.; City of Edinburgh Artillery; RA (TA) 1964-67; a DL of City of Edinburgh since 1966; 1939-45 War in Burma; OBE (Civil) 1968: *m.* 1st, 1936, Araminta (from whom he obtained a divorce 1941), da. of the late Lt.-Col. Willoughby Ewart Peel, DSO [Hunter Blair Bt., colls.]; 2ndly, 1948, Helen Anne (PERFECT), who *d.* 1969, da. of the late Alan Welwood Hog, of Edinburgh; 3rdly, 1972, Ruth Beverley, da. of the late William Henry Mill, and formerly wife of Kenneth William Bruce Middleton, and has issue living, (by 2nd m.) Christopher Patrick (23, Glencairn Cres., Edinburgh), *b.* 1949: *m.* 1974, Susan, da. of Ian Robert Pitman, WS—(by 1st m.) Ariadne Maria, *b.* 1939: *m.* 1961, Richard Elliot Nicholson, of Ochiltree Cottage, Linlithgow, W. Lothian, and has issue living, Robert David *b.* 1964, Matthew Charles *b.* 1968, Edward Alan *b.* 1971, Camilla Jane *b.* 1962.

SISTERS LIVING.

Hon. Pamela Lilias, *b.* 1907: *m.* 1933, Humphrey Scott-Plummer, and has issue living, Patrick Joseph, *b.* 1943: *m.* 1970, Elizabeth-Anne, only da. of Lt.-Col. Anthony Way, of 103, Dovehouse St., SW3, and has issue living, Charles Humphrey *b.* 1972, Annabel *b.* 1974,—Julia Elizabeth *b.* 1935: *m.* 1958, Rae Lionel Haggard Lyster, of Malting Green House, Layer de la Haye, Essex, and has issue living, Nicholas Charles, *b.* 1959, Amanda Pamela *b.* 1961, Lucy Caroline *b.* 1963,—Olivia Jane *b.* 1946: *m.* 1968, Thomas Yates Benyon, of The Old Rectory, Adstock, Bucks., and has issue living, Thomas Yates *b.* 1974, Clare Julia Yates *b.* 1969, Camilla Lucinda Joan Yates *b.* 1972. *Residence,*—Mainhouse, Kelso, Roxburghshire.

Hon. Rosemary Jean, *b.* 1910: *m.* 1st, 1934, Alec Maskell Mitchell, who *d.* 1964, and from whom she obtained a divorce 1958; 2ndly, 1958, Robert Monteath McLaren, who *d.* 1969, and has issue living, (by 1st m.) Alexander John (Ocean Sound, Knapton Hill, Smiths Parish, Bermuda), *b.* 1944: *m.* 1969 (m. diss. 1974), Christine Vincent, and has issue living, Vincent Alexander *b.* 1970,—Esther Mary Rose, *b.* 1936: *m.* 1st, 1959 (m. diss. 1968), Richard Alistair Cobbold; 2ndly, 1970, J. C. Lewis, of Glebe Farm, Hinton Waldrist, Faringdon, Berks., and has issue living, Nicholas Philip *b.* 1963, Rowena Sarah Elizabeth *b.* 1961, Catriona Mary Caroline *b.* 1966,—Caroline Jean Balfour, *b.* 1938: *m.* 1960, William Moncrieff Cuthbert, of Old Ballikinrain, Balfron, Stirlingshire, and has issue living, Alan Moncrieff *b.* 1962, Patrick Alick *b.* 1965, Rosemary Louisa *b.* 1961,—Margaret Anne, *b.* 1942: *m.* 1963, Ronald Patrick Thorburn, of Straloch, by Blairgowrie, Perths., and has issue living, Harry Jake *b.* 1970, Maria Alison, *b.* 1965, Lucy Jean *b.* 1967. *Residence,*—4/2 Fettes Rise, East Fettes Av., Edinburgh, EH4 1QH.

Hon. Ursula Nina, *b.* 1914: *m.* 1939, Col. Christopher James York Dallmeyer, D.S.O., W.S., Lothian and Border Horse Yeo., and has issue living, Gavin Richard James (20, Ann St., Edinburgh 4), *b.* 1942: *m.* 1970, Araminta Morgan,—Andrew Victor, *b.* 1945: *m.* 1969, Vivienne Dixon,—James, *b.* 1948,—Rosemary Nina *b.* 1940: *m.* 1962, the Rev. Paul Roderick Nicolson, of Tallents, Kimpton, Hitchin, Herts., and has issue living, Roderick John *b.* 1962, Hugo James *b.* 1965, Thomas Paul *b.* 1966, Claire Katherine *b.* 1968. *Residence,*—Green Corner, Tyninghame, Dunbar, E. Lothian.

COLLATERAL BRANCH LIVING.

Issue of the late Hon. Harry Robert Chichester Balfour, 4th son of 1st Baron, *b.* 1882, *d.* 1964: *m.* 1921, Dorothy Constance, who *d.* 1963, da. of the late Henry Goulburn Willoughby Chetwynd [V. Chetwynd, colls.]:—

Anthony John Chetwynd (38, Cambridge Rd., Ely, Cambs.; RAF and Leander Clubs), *b.* 1926; ed. at Eton, and at King's Coll., Camb. (MA, MB, BChir); Consultant in Pathology, RAF Med. Branch, and a MCPath; Wing-Cdr. RAF: *m.* 1958, Judith Ann Margaret, yr. da. of Leslie Field Anderson, of Pines Av., Worthing, and has issue living, Peter John Torquil, *b.* 1959,—Harry Luke Chetwynd, *b.* 1963,—Helena Clare, *b.* 1961.——Hilary Joan Gwendolen *b.* 1924.

PREDECESSORS.—[1] JOHN BLAIR Balfour, son of the Rev. P. Balfour, Min. of Clackmannan; Solicitor-Gen. for Scotland April 1880 to Aug. 1881, and Lord-Advocate Aug. 1881 to June 1885, Feb. to July 1886, and Aug. 1892 to June 1895; M.P for Clackmannan and Kinross-shire (*L*) Nov. 1880 to Nov. 1899, when he became Lord Justice-General for Scotland (with judicial title of *Lord Blair Balfour*); cr. a P.C. 1883, and *Baron Kinross*, of Glasclune, co. Haddington (peerage of United Kingdom) 1902: *m.* 1st, 1869, Lilias Oswald, who *d.* 1872, dau. of the late Hon. Lord Mackenzie, a Lord of Session; 2ndly, 1877, the Hon. Marianne Eliza, who *d.* 1913, dau. of 1st Baron Moncreiff; *d.* 1905; *s.* by his el. son [2] PATRICK, *K.C.*, 2nd Baron; *b.* 1870; a Brigadier, Roy. Co. of Archers (King's Body Guard for Scotland); Sheriff of Dumfries and Galloway, 1927-39: *m.* 1903, Caroline Elsie, who *d.* 1969, dau. of the late Arthur Henry Johnstone-Douglas [M. Queensberry]; *d.* 1939; *s.* by his son [3] JOHN PATRICK DOUGLAS, 3rd Baron and present peer.

KINTORE, EARL OF.   (Keith.)   [Earl S. 1677.]

(JAMES) IAN KEITH, 12th Earl, 3rd Baronet,
b. July 25th, 1908; *s.* as 2nd Viscount
Stonehaven, 1941; changed his name and
arms from Baird to Keith by Interlocutor
Lyon Court, June 28th, 1967; *s.* his mother
as chief of the name of Keith 1974; ed. at
Eton; Vice-Lt. for Kincardineshire, and an
Asso., Inst. of Structural Engineers; 1939-45
War as Maj. RM: *m.* 1935, Delia, da. of the
late William Lewis Brownlow Loyd, of
Upper House, Shamley Green, Guildford
[B. Brabourne], and has issue.

Arms,—Quarterly; 1st and 4th, argent on a chief,
gules three pallets or, *Keith;* 2nd, azure, a falcon displayed
between three mullets argent, on his breast a man's heart
gules, *Falconer of Halkerton;* 3rd, per pale engrailed gules
and or, a boar passant counterchanged, *Baird of Ury;*
over all, on an inescutcheon gules, a sceptre and sword in
saltire with an Imperial Crown between the upper corners all proper, within an orle of eight thistles
slipped near the head or, ensigned with an Earl's coronet (*being the Coat of Augmentation granted to
John, 1st Earl of Kintore, for his services in the preservation of the Regalia of Scotland*).   **Crests,**—*Dexter,*
a noble lady from the middle richly attired, holding in her right hand a garland proper (*Crest of
Augmentation for Earldom of Kintore*); *Sinister,* a roebuck's head proper, attired or, *Keith.*   **Supporters,**—Two men in complete armour proper, each holding a spear gules banded argent, in posture of
sentinels.

Seat,—Keith Hall, Inverurie, Aberdeenshire.

SONS LIVING.
MICHAEL CANNING WILLIAM JOHN KEITH (*Lord Inverurie, Master of Kintore*), *b.* Feb. 22nd,
1939; ed. at Eton: late Lt. Coldm. Gds.: *m.* 1972, Mary, only da. of the late Sqdn. Ldr. E. G. Plum,
of Rumson, New Jersey.
Hon. Alexander David *BAIRD, b.* 1946.

DAUGHTER LIVING.
Lady Diana Elizabeth Virginia Sydney, *b.* 1937: *m.* 1957, John Francis Holman, OBE, of Glenton
House, Rickarton, Stonehaven, Kincardineshire, and 24, Wellington Sq., SW3 [see By. Trent].

SISTERS LIVING.
Lady Ariel Olivia Winifred, *b.* 1916; appointed Lady-in-Waiting to HRH Princess Alice, Countess of
Athlone 1940: *m.* 1946 (m. diss. 1958), Sir Kenneth Alexander Keith, late Lt.-Col. WG (cr Knt
1969), and has issue living, Alastair James, *b.* 1947,—Camilla Margaret (twin), *b.* 1947: *m.* 1968,
(m. diss. 1972), Sir Rupert Henry Mackeson, 2nd Bt.   *Residence,*—Flat B, 9, Cadogan Sq., SW1.
Lady (Hilda) Ava Fiona Nancy, *b.* 1919:   *m.* 1945, Lt.-Col. Ronald Fulton Lucas Chance, MC, King's
Roy. Rifle Corps, and has issue living, Nicholas John Lucas, *b.* 1946: *m.* 1975, Anne H. G. only da.
of Maj. J. E. V. Rice, of Exhurst Manor, Staplehurst, Kent,—Louise Annette *b.* 1950.   *Residence,*—
Lower Moor Farm, Charlton, Malmesbury, Wilts.
WIDOW LIVING OF SON OF FIRST VISCOUNT STONEEHAVEN AND (ETHEL) SYDNEY,
COUNTESS OF KINTORE.
Dorviegelda Malvina, da. of the late Alexander Ronald MacGregor [see MacGregor of MacGregor,
Bt., colls.]: *m.* 1st, 1939, Sqdn.-Ldr. the Hon. (Robert Alexander) Greville Baird, RAF, who *d.*
(killed in action) 1943; 2ndly, 1947, Sqdn.-Ldr. Algernon Ivan Sladen, DSO, late RAF [E. Dunmore],
and has issue living, (by 1st m.) [see colls., infra].   *Residence,*—Barneheath, Tadley, Basingstoke,
Hants.
COLLATERAL BRANCHES LIVING.
Issue of the late Sqdn.-Ldr. the Hon. (Robert Alexander) Greville BAIRD, RAF.
2nd son of 1st Viscount Stonehaven and (Ethel) Sydney, Countess of Kintore,
b. 1910, *d.* (killed in action) 1943: *m.* 1939, Dorviegelda Malvina [(ante), who
m. 2ndly, 1947, Sqdn.-Ldr. Algernon Ivan Sladen, DSO, late RAF [E. Dunmore],
da. of Alexander Ronald MacGregor [see MacGregor, Bt., cr. 1795]:—
Ceanan Donald, *b.* (*posthumous*) 1943: *m.* 1973, Janet, da. of D. R. Scott.——Rinalda Malvina,
b. 1940: *m.* 1963, Lt.-Col. David Henry Sandford Leslie Maitland-Titterton, 9th/12th R. Lancers,
of Moberty, Airlie, Angus [see E. Lauderdale, colls.].

Grandchildren of the late Lady Blanche Catherine Smith (infra):—
Issue of the late Granville Keith-Falconer Smith, *b.* 1886, *d.* 1914: *m.* 1910, Lady Kathleen
Clements (Postboys, Stoke by Nayland, nr. Colchester), who *m.* 2ndly, 1919, Cdr. Ronald
Granville Studd, DSO, RN, who *d.* 1956 [Studd, Bt.], da. of the 4th Earl of Leitrim:—
Rosemary Winifred, *b.* 1912.——Merial Kathleen, *b.* 1914.
Issue of the late Rev. Roland Audley Smith, *b.* 1887, *d.* 1946: *m.* 1913, Margaret Halcro
Erskine, who *d.* 1965, only da. of the late Robert Alexander Hill, of Coney-Hill House,
Bridge of Allan, Stirlingshire:—
Granville Roland (c/o Bank of Scotland, 57/60, Haymarket, SW1), *b.* 1919; ed. at Eton, and Trin.
Coll., Camb. (MA); 1939-45 War as Lt. RNVR (despatches): *m.* 1944, Aimée Rosemary Patricia,
who *d.* 1963, only da. of the late George Henry Preston Moore-Browne, of Port Stewart Castle, co.
Londonderry, and formerly wife of Dr. John Forbes, and has issue living, Rachel Margaret Pleasance,
b. 1944.——Marion Blanche, *b.* 1915: *m.* 1952, Cdr. Michael Peer-Groves, RN, of Southern Green
House, Rushden, nr. Buntingford, Herts., and has issue living, William Keith, *b.* 1954,—Michael
Roland, *b.* 1957.

Granddaughters of the late Rev. Roland Audley Smith (ante):—
Issue of the late Samuel Erskine Roland Smith, *b.* 1924, *d.* 1963: *m.* 1948, Margaret Anne
(54, Cranwell Park, Weston Rd., Bath, Somerset), el. da. of Brig. John Eric Chippindall,
CBE, MC, of 11, The Royal Cres., Bath:—
Amanda Jane, *b.* 1951.——Vanessa Anne, *b.* 1955.
Issue of the late Lady Blanche Catherine Keith-Falconer, da. of the 8th Earl of Kintore,
b. 1859, *d.* 1922: *m.* 1883, Col. Granville Roland Francis Smith, CVO, CB who *d.* (on
active ser.) 1917:—
Lt.-Gen. Sir Arthur Francis, KCB, KBE, DSO, MC, (Greathed Manor, Lingfield, Surrey); Guards'
and National Clubs.) *b.* 1890; ed. at Eton; Lt.-Gen. late Coldm. Gds.; 1914-18 War (thrice wounded,
despatches five times, MC, French Croix de Guerre, DSO); 1939-45 War (despatches thrice, Order of
Kutuzov of Russia); Brig.-Gen. Staff British Troops in Egypt 1938-39, Ch. of Gen. Staff Middle
East 1940-42, GOC London Dist. and Bde. of Gds. 1942-44, GOC.-in-C. Persia and Iraq 1944-45
and E. Command India 1945, Ch. of Gen. Staff India 1946-47, Comd. of British Forces in India and
Pakistan (after partition) 1947, and Lieut. of Tower of London 1948-51; cr. DSO 1918, CB (Mil)

1941, KBE (Mil) 1942, KCB (Mil) 1946: *m.* 1918, the Hon. Monica Victoria Crossley, da. of 1st Baron Somerleyton, and has issue living, Auriol Blanche, *b.* 1919: *m.* 1944, Maj. Michael Warren Ingram, late Gren. Gds., of Driffield Manor, Cirencester [see Ingram, Bt.],—Susan Monica, *b.* 1921: *m.* 1943, Capt. Thomas Gillespie Browne, late RE, of Misbrooks Cottage, Capel, Surrey, and has issue living, Jennifer Anne *b.* 1944, Hilary Jane *b.* 1945, Monica Jean *b.* 1949,—Hazel Charlotte, *b.* 1924: *m.* 1943, Maj. Peter Gordon Rowley, RA (ret.), of 26, Whittingehame Gdns., Withdean, Brighton, and has issue living, David Gordon *b.* 1946, Wendy Drusilla *b.* 1950, Hazel Jane *b.* 1959.

PREDECESSORS.—[1] *Hon. Sir* JOHN Keith, 3rd son of William, 6th Earl Marischal, **cr. *Lord Keith of Inverurie and Keith Hall,* and *Earl of Kintore* (peerage of Scotland) 1677 with remainder to the heirs male of his body;** in 1694 he resigned his honours and had a **regrant of the titles and estates to him and the heirs male of his body, whom failing to the heirs male of his brother George, Earl Marischal, whom failing to the heirs-general of his own body;** appointed 1660 hereditary Knight-Marischal of Scotland in consideration of his loyalty in preserving the regalia of Scotland from the hands of Cromwell; *d.* 1714; *s.* by his son [2] WILLIAM, 2nd Earl; being engaged in the rebellion of 1715 lost the office of Knight-Marischal; *d.* 1718; *s.* by his el. son [3] JOHN, 3rd Earl; appointed Knight-Marischal; *d.s.p.* 1758; *s.* by his brother [4] WILLIAM, 4th Earl; *d.* 1761, when the estates devolved upon George, 10th Earl Marischal (title attainted 1715), and the peerage remained dormant until his decease 1778, when it passed to his kinsman [5] ANTHONY ADRIAN Falconer, 5th Earl, who in 1776 *s.* as 7th *Lord Falconer of Halkerton* [see that title]; *d.* 1804; *s.* by his son [6] WILLIAM, 6th Earl; *d.* 1812; *s.* by his son [7] ANTHONY ADRIAN, 7th Earl; cr. *Baron Kintore,* of Kintore, co. Aberdeen (peerage of United Kingdom) 1838; *d.* 1844; *s.* by his son [8] FRANCIS ALEXANDER, 8th Earl; *b.* 1828; Lord-Lieut. of co. Kincardine 1856-64, and of co. Aberdeen 1864-80: *m.* 1851, Louisa Madeleine, who *d.* 1916, dau. of Francis Hawkins, Esq.; *d.* 1880; *s.* by his son [9] ALGERNON HAWKINS THOMOND, *K.T., G.C.M.G., P.C.,* 9th Earl; *b.* 1852; a Lord-in-Waiting to Queen Victoria 1885-6, Capt. of the Yeomen of the Guard 1886-9, Gov. of S. Australia 1889-95, again a Lord-in-Waiting to Queen Victoria 1895-1901, and to King Edward VII. 1901-5; a Dep. Speaker House of Lords 1915, and a Member of Select Committee on Peerages in abeyance 1925: *m.* 1873, Lady Sydney Charlotte Montagu, who *d.* 1932, dau. of 6th Duke of Manchester; *d.* 1930; *s.* by his son [10] ARTHUR GEORGE, 10th Earl, *b.* 1879; officially recognised by the name of Keith by Warrant of Lord Lyon King of Arms 1956: *m.* 1937, Helena, who *d.* 1971, da. of Eugene Zimmerman of Cincinnati, USA, and formerly wife of 9th Duke of Manchester; *d.* 1966, when the Barony of Kintore (peerage of UK) became ext., the Lordship of Falconer of Halkerton became dormant [see that title], and the Earldom of Kintore and the Lordship of Keith of Inverurie and Keith Hall devolved on his sister [11] ETHEL SYDNEY, Countess of Kintore, *b.* 1874: *m.* 1905, the 1st Viscount Stonehaven, who *d.* 1941; *d.* 1974, *s.* by her el. son [12] (JAMES) IAN, 12th Earl, and present peer; also Viscount Stonehaven, Baron Stonehaven, and Lord Keith of Inverurie and Keith Hall. [see infra.]

∗∗∗ [1] *Sir* ALEXANDER Baird, *GBE,* son of the late John Baird, of Urie; Lord-Lieut. of Kincardine-shire 1889-1918; cr. a *Baronet* 1897: *m.* 1873, the Hon. Annette Maria, who *d.* 1884, da. of 1st Baron Haldon; *d.* 1920; *s.* by his el. son [2] *Rt. Hon. Sir* JOHN LAWRENCE, *GCMG, DSO, PC,* 2nd Bt., *b,* 1874; European War 1914-15 (despatches, DSO); appointed Parliamentary Private Sec. to the Leader of the Opposition in the House of Commons (Rt. Hon. A. Bonar Law, MP) 1911, Parliamentary Representative of Air Board 1916, Parliamentary Under-Sec. of State to Air Min. 1918, and Joint Parliamentary Sec. to Min. of Munitions 1919 (but declined); was Parliamentary Under-Sec. of State, Home Depart. 1919-22, First Commr. of Works (also Min. of Transport) 1922-4, Gov.-Gen. and Com.-in-Ch. of Commonwealth of Australia 1925-30, and Chm. of Conservative Party 1931-6; sat as MP for Warwickshire, Rugby Div. (C) 1910-22, and for Ayr 1922-5; cr. *Baron Stonehaven,* of Ury, co. Kincardine (peerage of United Kingdom) 1925, and *Viscount Stonehaven,* of Ury, co. Kincardine (peerage of United Kingdom) 1938: *m.* 1905, Lady Ethel Sydney Keith-Falconer, (who *d.* 1974, having *s.* as Countess of Kintore 1966) da. of 9th Earl of Kintore; *d.* 1941, *s.* by his el. son [3] (JAMES) IAN, 2nd Viscount (see ante).

KIRKWOOD, BARON. (Kirkwood.) [Baron U.K. 1951.]

DAVID HARVIE KIRKWOOD, 3rd Baron; *b.* Nov. 24th, 1931; *s.* 1970; ed. at Rugby, and Trin. Hall, Camb. (MA, PhD): *m.* 1965, Judith Rosalie, da. of the late John Hunt, of Leeds, and has issue.

Arms,—Argent, two chevronels round-embattled on their upper edges sable between two oak-sprigs slipped and fructed proper in chief and a cog-wheel azure in base. **Crest,**—The bow of a ship afrontée proper. **Supporters,**—*Dexter,* an Ayrshire bull; *sinister,* a Clydeside stallion, both proper, the latter harnessed or.

Residence,—56, Endcliffe Hall Av., Sheffield.

DAUGHTERS LIVING.

Hon. Ruth Emily, *b.* 1966.
Hon. Anne Judith, *b.* 1969.
Hon. Lucy Jennifer, *b.* 1972.

BROTHER LIVING.

Hon. JAMES STUART (The Cearne, Kent Hatch, Crockham Hill, Edenbridge, Kent), *b.* June 19th, 1937; ed. at Rugby, and at Trin. Hall, Camb. (MA); ARICS: *m.* 1965, Alexander Mary, da. of the late Alec Dyson, of Holt, Norfolk, and has issue living, Kate Victoria, *b.* 1966,—Georgina Grace, *b.* 1969.

UNCLE LIVING. (*Son of 1st Baron.*)

Hon. James Smith, *b.* 1912; ed. at Allan Glens Sch., Glasgow: is an ARIBA, and a JP for Dunbarton-shire; 1939-45 War as Capt. RE in N. Africa, Sicily and Middle East: *m.* 1944, Mary Helen, who *d.* 1970, da. of the late James Marshall, of Elgin, and has issue living, David, *b.* 1945,—James Marshall Smith, *b.* 1954,—Elizabeth Joan, *b.* 1947. *Residence,*—26, Glenburn Rd., Bearsden, Dunbarton-shire.

AUNTS LIVING. (*Daughters of 1st Baron*).

Hon. Elizabeth Smith, *b.* 1908: *m.* 1944, John Archibald Duguid Mair, A.R.I.B.A., and has issue living, David Gordon Kirkwood Duguid, *b.* 1948,—Elizabeth Grace Kirkwood, *b.* 1945,—Janis Duguid Kirkwood, *b.* 1952. *Residence,*—Shieldaig, 12, Iain Road, Bearsden, Dunbartonshire.
Hon. Jean Brown, *b.* 1917: *m.* 1943, William Henderson McGonnigill, and has issue living, Elizabeth Mary Kirkwood, *b.* 1945,—Gillian Fiona Kirkwood, *b.* 1946,—Mairi Seona Kirkwood, *b.* 1952. *Residence,*—Poolfield Farm, Charfield, Wotton-under-Edge, Glos.

WIDOW LIVING OF SECOND BARON.

EILEEN GRACE (*Eileen, Baroness Kirkwood*), (Brasted Hall Cottage, Brasted, Kent), da. of the late Thomas Henry Boalch, of Pill, Bristol: *m.* 1931, the 2nd Baron, who *d.* 1970.

COLLATERAL BRANCHES LIVING.

Issue of the late John Kirkwood, el. son of 1st Baron, *b.* 1900, *d.* 1942 : *m.* 1932, Ellen Florence (now of Lomond, 288, Warwick Road, Olton, Warwickshire), dau. of the late Thomas Peter Haggar, of Witham, Essex :—

Jean, *b.* 1935.

Issue of the late Robert Smith Kirkwood, 2nd son of 1st Baron, *b.* 1901, *d.* 1950: *m.* 1927, Annie Kerr, who *d.* 1963, dau. of John Marshall, of Shettleston, Glasgow:—

Agnes Young (11, Chesterfield Court, Glasgow, W2), *b.* 1930.——Elizabeth Smith, *b.* 1937.

PREDECESSORS.—[1] *Rt. Hon.* DAVID Kirkwood, *P.C.*, son of the late John Kirkwood, of Parkhead Glasgow ; *b.* 1872 ; was Chm. of David Kirkwood and Sons, Ltd., of 9, Woodside Place, Glasgow ; sat as M.P. for Dumbarton Burghs (*Lab.*) 1922-50, and for E. Div. of Dunbartonshire 1950-51 ; cr. *Baron Kirkwood*, of Bearsden, co. Dunbarton (peerage of United Kingdom) 1951: *m.* 1899, Elizabeth, who *d.* 1956, dau. of Robert Smith, of Parkhead, Glasgow; *d.* 1955 ; *s.* by his 3rd (but el. surviving) son [2] DAVID, 2nd Baron; *b.* 1903: *m.* 1931, Eileen Grace, da. of the late Thomas Henry Boalch, of Pill, Bristol; *d.* 1970; *s.* by his el. son [3] DAVID HARVIE, 3rd Baron and present peer.

KISSIN, BARON. (Kissin.) [Life Baron 1974.]

HARRY KISSIN, son of Israel Kissin; *b.* Aug. 23rd, 1912; ed. at Danzig, and Univ. of Basle (LL.D); Exec. Chm., Guinness Peat Gp. Ltd., since 1974 (Joint-Chm. 1973); Chm. of Inst. of Contemporary Art since 1969, a Dir. of Roy. Opera House, Covent Garden, and Chm. of Roy. Opera House Trust since 1973; cr. *Baron Kissin.* of Camden, in Greater London (Life Baron) 1974: *m.* 1935, Ruth Deborah, da. of Siegmund Samuel, of London, and has issue.

Residence,—44, Frognal Lane, Hampstead, NW3. *Clubs.*—Reform, East India, Sports and Public Schools.

SON LIVING.

Hon. Robert David, *b.* 1947.

DAUGHTER LIVING.

Hon. Evelyn Anne, *b.* 1944: *m.* 1972, Dr. Jack Donald Singer, of 45, Campden Hill Court, Campden Hill Rd., W8, and has issue.

KITCHENER OF KHARTOUM AND OF BROOME, EARL. (Kitchener.) [Earl U.K. 1914.]

HENRY HERBERT KITCHENER, *T.D.*, 3rd Earl ; *b.* Feb. 24th, 1919 ; *s.* 1937 ; ed. at Winchester, and at Trin. Coll., Camb.; a Page of Honour at Coronation of King George VI; a DL for Cheshire; Maj. (ret.) R. Signals (TA).

Arms,—Gules, between three bustards close proper a chevron azure, cotised argent. **Crest,**— A stag's head couped, the neck transfixed by an arrow proper between the attires a horseshoe or. **Supporters.**—*Dexter,* a camel proper, bridle trappings and line pendent reflexed over the back gules, gorged with a collar or suspended therefrom an escutcheon paly bendy azure and ermine, a canton of the last charged with a portcullis gold ; *sinister,* a gnu proper gorged with a collar or suspended therefrom an escutcheon ermine charged with a chevron engrailed vert thereon four horseshoes or.

Residence,—56, Elm Park Road, Chelsea, S.W.3. *Club,*—Brooks's.

BROTHER LIVING.
(*Raised to the rank of an Earl's son* 1938.)

Hon. CHARLES EATON, *b.* March 11th, 1920; ed. at Winchester, and at Trin. Coll., Camb : sometime Signalman Roy. Corps of Signals: *m.* 1959, Ursula Hope, dau. of the late Capt. C. M. Luck, Roy. Indian Navy, and has issue living, Emma Joy, *b.* 1963. *Residence,* Croylands, Old Salisbury Lane, Romsey, Hants.

SISTER LIVING. (*Raised to the rank of an Earl's daughter* 1938.)

Lady Kenya Eleanor, *b.* 1923 ; late 3rd Officer W.R.N.S. : *m.* 1947, as his second wife, John Stewart Tatton-Brown, who *d.* 1971, and has issue living, Margaret Caroline, *b.* 1950,—Adela Charlotte, *b.* 1951,—Augusta Kenya, *b.* 1955. *Residence,*—Westergate Wood, nr. Chichester, Sussex.

MOTHER LIVING.

Adela Mary Evelyn (*Viscountess Broome*), dau. of the late John Henry Monins, of Ringwould House, near Dover : *m.* 1916, Capt. Henry Franklin Chevallier, Viscount Broome, R.N., who *d.* 1928, only son of 2nd Earl. *Residence,*—56, Elm Park Rd., SW3.

COLLATERAL BRANCH LIVING. (*In special remainder.*)

Issue of the late Lieut.-Gen. Sir Frederick Walter Kitchener, K.C.B., younger brother of 1st Earl, *b.* 1858, *d.* 1912 : *m.* 1884, Caroline, who *d.* 1901, dau. of Major Fenton. 9th and 53rd Regts. :—

Henry Hamilton (Lynmouth, Melbury Close, W. Byfleet, Surrey), *b.* 1890; late Major and Flight Com RFC, and Sqdn.-Ldr. RAF: *m.* 1st, 1916, Winifred Esther Everest, who *d.* 1959, el. da. of the Hon. A. W. Bluck; 2ndly, 1961, Mrs. Gwynneth Champion, and has issue living, (by 1st m.) Winifred Jean, *b.* 1917: *m.* 1954, Lieut. Peter John Hall, RN, of Clanna Rory, Onslow Rd., Burwood Park, Walton-on-Thames, Surrey and has issue living, Christopher Peter *b.* 1955,—Elizabeth Madge (86 Waller Cres., Campbell, ACT 2601, Aust.), *b.* 1921: *m.* 1946, Louis Cornhill, who *d.* 19—, and has issue living, Peter Robert *b.* 1949, Robert *b.* 1952.——Philippa Chevallier, *b.* 1895: *m.* 1917, Brig. Terence Desmond Murray, CBE, DSO, MC, late Roy. Tank Corps. who *d.* 1961, and has issue living, Molly Patricia, *b.* 1919,—Sybil Madge, *b.* 1921,—Sheila Chevallier, *b.* 1926. *Address,*—c/o Hoare & Co., 37, Fleet St., EC4.

PREDECESSORS.—[1] *Field-Marshal the Rt. Hon. Sir* HORATIO HERBERT Kitchener, *K.G.*, *K.P.*, *G.C.B.*, *O.M.*, *G.C.S.I.*, *G.C.M.G.*, *G.C.I.E.*, second son of the late Lieut.-Col. Henry Horatio Kitchener (13th Dragoons), of Cossington, Leicester; *b.* 1850; served in Soudan Campaign 1883-5, being D.A.A. and Q.M.G. 1884-5 (despatches frequently, medal with clasp, 3rd class Osmanieh), in command of troops at action of Handoub 1888 (severely wounded, 2nd class Medjidie), a Brig. of Soudanese troops at action of Gemaizah, Suakin, 1888 (despatches, clasp), Mounted troops at action of Toski on the Nile 1889 (despatches, clasp, C.B.), Dongola Expedition 1896 (despatches, Grand Cordon Osmanieh, promoted Maj.-Gen.), Nile Expedition 1897 (despatches) and 1898 (despatches), and Soudan Campaign 1898, present at battle of Omdurman, recapture of Khartoum, and subsequent expedition to Fashoda (Khedive's medal with five clasps, peerage, G.C.B., specially thanked by both Houses of Parliament, granted £30,000), and in S. Africa 1899-1902 first as Ch.-of-the-Staff (despatches twice, G.C.M.G.), and subsequently as Com.-in-Ch. (thanked by Parliament, promoted Gen., cr. Viscount, granted £50,000), and acted as High Commr. of S. Africa, and Administrator of Transvaal and of Orange River Colony 1901; employed on Palestine Survey 1874-8, and on Cyprus Survey 1878-9 (awarded Livingstone gold medal 1915); Director of Survey, Cyprus 1880-82, Vice-Consul in Anatolia 1879-80, in command of Egyptian Cavalry 1882-4, H.M. Queen Victoria's Commr. for delimitation of territory of Sultan of Zanzibar 1885, Gov. of Suakin 1886-8 (2nd class Medjidie), A.D.C. to H.M. Queen Victoria 1888-96, and A.G. and 2nd in command of Egyptian Army, as well as Inspector-Gen. of Police 1888-92 (2nd class Osmanieh), Sirdar of Egyptian Army 1892-99 (1st class Medjidie and Osmanieh), Gov.-Gen. of the Soudan 1899, and Com.-in-Ch. in India and a Member of Viceroy's Council 1902-9, Agent and Consul-Gen. in Egypt 1911-14, and Sec. of State for War 1914-16 (forming during European War "Kitchener's Army"); cr. *Baron Kitchener of Khartoum*, and of Aspall, co. Suffolk (peerage of United Kingdom) 1898, and *Viscount Kitchener of Khartoum*, and of the Vaal, Colony of the Transvaal, and of Aspall, co. Suffolk (peerage of United Kingdom) 1902, with remainder to the heirs male of his body, and in default of such issue with remainder (i) to his first daughter and the heirs male of her body, (ii) to his other daughters and the heirs male of their bodies (infra), and (iii) in default of such issue, with remainder to his elder brother, Henry Elliott Chevallier Kitchener, and the heirs male of his body, and (iv) with remainder to his younger brother, Frederick Walter Kitchener, and the heirs male of his body, and *Earl Kitchener of Khartoum and of Broome, Viscount Broome*, of Broome, co. Kent, and *Baron Denton*, of Denton, co. Kent (peerage of United Kingdom) 1914 with similar special remainders to the above-mentioned ; *d.* (on active service during European War) 1916, when the Barony cr. 1898 became ext. and he was *s.* (under the special remainder) in the other peerages by his el. brother **[2]** HENRY ELLIOTT CHEVALLIER, 2nd Earl ; *b.* 1846 ; Col. (retired) ; formerly Lieut.-Col. Duke of Cornwall's L.I. ; France 1870 (medal), Burma 1891 (despatches, medal with clasp), Manipur Expedition 1891 (despatches, clasp), European War 1914-17 (1914 star, two medals, Croix de Guerre) ; was D.A.A.G., Jamaica 1893-8 ; sometime Col. Comdg. W. India Regt. Depôt : *m.* 1877, Eleanor Fanny, who *d.* 1897, only child of the late Lieut.-Col. Franklin Lushington, C.B. : *d.* 1937 ; *s.* by his grandson **[3]** HENRY HERBERT (son of the late Capt. Henry Franklin Chevallier, Viscount Broome, only son of 2nd Earl), 3rd Earl and present peer; also Viscount Kitchener of Khartoum, Viscount Broome, and Baron Denton.

KNARESBOROUGH, BARONY OF. (Meysey-Thompson.) [Extinct 1929.]

DAUGHTER LIVING OF FIRST BARON.

Hon. Gwendolen Carlis (*Hon. Lady Richmond Brown*), *b.* 1903 ; was a Lady-in-Waiting to H.R.H. the Duchess of Gloucester 1938-44: *m.* 1951 (m. diss. 1968), as his second wife, Sir Charles Frederick Richmond Brown, 4th Bt. *Residence,*—Leppington House, Leppington, Malton, N. Yorks.

Knebworth, Viscount, son of Earl of Lytton.

KNOLLYS, VISCOUNT. (Knollys.) [Viscount U.K. 1911.]

[Name and Title pronounced "Noles."]

In every way prepared.

DAVID FRANCIS DUDLEY KNOLLYS, 3rd Viscount; *b.* June 12th, 1931; *s.* 1966; ed. at Eton; late 2nd Lt. Scots Guards: *m.* 1959, the Hon. Sheelin Virginia, da. of the late Lt.-Col. the Hon. Somerset Arthur Maxwell, MP [see B. Farnham], and has issue.

Arms,—Per pale gules and argent a chevron counterchanged and charged with three roses also counterchanged barbed and seeded proper. Crest,—Between two crosses moline per pale azure and or fimbriated counterchanged an elephant statant argent. Supporters,—On either side an Heraldic antelope the dexter argent and sinister or both tufted, horned and unguled sable and charged on the shoulder with a cross as in the Crest.

Residence,—Bramerton Grange, Norwich, NR14 7HF, Norfolk. *Club,*—White's.

SONS LIVING.

Hon. PATRICK NICHOLAS MARK, *b.* March 11th, 1962.
Hon. Christopher Edward, *b.* 1964.
Hon. Michael James George, *b.* 1968.

DAUGHTER LIVING.

Hon. Clarinda Susan, *b.* 1960.

SISTER LIVING.

Hon. Ardyne Mary, *b.* 1929: *m.* 1958, Ronald James Owen, of Paradise Wood, Upper Hartfield, Sussex.

WIDOW LIVING OF SECOND VISCOUNT.

MARGARET MARY JOSEPHINE (*Margaret Viscountess Knollys*) (20, Laxford House, Cundy St., SW1, and Old White's Farm, Forest Row, Sussex), da. of Sir Stuart Auchinloss Coats, 2nd Bt.: *m.* 1928, the 2nd Viscount, who *d.* 1966.

PREDECESSORS.—[1] *Rt. Hon. Sir* FRANCIS Knollys, *GCB*, *GCVO*, *KCMG*, *ISO*, second son of the late Gen. the Rt. Hon. Sir William Thomas Knollys, KCB, PC; *b.* 1837; a Gentleman Usher Quarterly Waiter to Queen Victoria 1868-1901, Groom-in-Waiting to the Prince of Wales 1886-1901, and Private Sec. to Prince of Wales 1870-1901, and to King Edward VII 1901-10, Joint Private Sec. to King George V 1910-13, and a Lord-in-Waiting to Queen Alexandra 1910-24; cr. *Baron Knollys*, of Caversham, co. Oxford (peerage of UK) 1902, and *Viscount Knollys*, of Caversham, co. Oxford (peerage of UK) 1911: *m.* 1887, the Hon. Ardyn, who *d.* 1922, da. of Sir Henry Thomas Tyrwhitt,

3rd Bt.; *d.* 1924, *s.* by his son [2] EDWARD GEORGE WILLIAM TYRWHITT, *GCMG, MBE, DFC,* 2nd Viscount, *b.* 1895; Gov. of Bermuda 1941-43, Chm. of BOAC 1943-47, of Vickers Ltd. 1956-62, and of Northern and Employers Assurance Co. 1954-66: *m.* 1928, Margaret Mary Josephine, da. of Sir Stuart Auchinloss Coats, 2nd Bt.; *d.* 1966, *s.* by his son [3] DAVID FRANCIS DUDLEY, 3rd Viscount, and present peer; also Baron Knollys.

KNUTSFORD, VISCOUNT. (Holland-Hibbert.) [Viscount U.K. 1895, Bt. U.K. 1853.]

Look backwards, look around, look forwards.

THURSTAN HOLLAND-HIBBERT, 4th Viscount, and 5th Baronet ; *b.* June 19th, 1888; *s.*1935; ed.at Eton, and at Trin.Coll., Camb. (B.A. 1911); Bar. Inner Temple 1914; late Capt. Pioneer Corps; European War 1914-19 in France, Egypt, and Gallipoli as Capt. Herts Yeo. and Roy. Scots Greys (1914-15 star, two medals) ; 1939-45 War as Maj. Pioneer Corps: *m.* 1912, Viola Mary, who *d.* 1964, da. of the late Thomas Meadows Clutterbuck, of Putteridge Bury, Herts, and Micklefield Hall, Rickmansworth, Herts, and has issue.

Arms,—Quarterly, 1st and 4th ermine, on a bend nebuly sable three crescents argent, in the sinister chief point a cross bottonée fitchée of the second, *Hibbert ;* 2nd and 3rd per pale argent and azure, semée-de-is, a lion rampant guardant all counterchanged, the whole debruised by a bendlet engrailed gules, *Holland.* Crests,—1st, in front of a dexter cubit arm erect proper, vested azure, cuff ermine, holding in the hand a crescent argent a demi catherine wheel also argent, *Hibbert ;* 2nd, out of a crown vallery or, a demi-lion guardant per bend argent and azure, debruised by a bendlet engrailed countercharged, and holding in the dexter paw a fleur-de-lis of the second, *Holland.* Supporters,—Two lions guardant argent guttée de larmes, each charged on the body with two fleur-de-lis in fesse between bars-geme engrailed azure.

Residence,—Munden, Watford, Herts.

SON LIVING.

Hon. JULIAN THURSTAN, *C.B.E., b.* May 3rd, 1920 ; ed. at Eton and at Trin. Coll., Camb.; late Lieut. Coldstream Guards ; is a Member of National Advisory Council on Employment of the Disabled, an O.St.J., and a J.P. for Herts ; European War 1939-43 (wounded) ; C.B.E. (Civil) 1957. *Residence,*—Munden, Watford, Herts.

DAUGHTER LIVING.

Hon. Diana, *M.B.E., b.* 1914 ; late Senior Com. A.T.S.; European War 1939-45 (M.B.E.). ; M.B.E. (Mil.) 1946. *Residence,*—Munden, Watford, Herts.

DAUGHTERS LIVING OF SECOND VISCOUNT.

Hon. Lucy Katherine HOLLAND, *b.* 1886. *Residence,*—Crowshot Farm, Newbury, Berks.
Hon. Rachael Mary (*Lady Malise Graham*), *b.* 1891: *m.* 1919, Brig. Lord (Douglas) Malise Graham, CB, DSO, MC, who *d.* 1974 [see D. Montrose, colls.]. *Residence,*—Througham Place, Beaulieu, Brockenhurst, Hants.

WIDOW LIVING OF SON OF THIRD VISCOUNT.

Isabel Audrey, dau. of the late Mark Fenwick, of Abbotswood, Stow-on-the-Wold, Gloucestershire : *m.* 1918, the Hon. Wilfrid Holland-Hibbert, who *d.* 1961, and has issue living [see colls., infra]. *Residence,*—Grove House, Beckley, Oxford.

COLLATERAL BRANCHES LIVING.

Issue of the late Hon. Wilfrid Holland-Hibbert, younger son of 3rd Viscount, *b.* 1893, *d.* 1961 : *m.* 1918, Isabel Audrey (ante), dau. of the late Mark Fenwick, of Abbotswood, Stow-on-the-Wold, Gloucestershire :—
Michael, *b.* 1926 ; ed. at Eton, and at Trin. Coll., Camb. ; late Capt. Welsh Guards ; is a local Director of Barclays Bank, Exeter : *m.* 1951, the Hon. Sheila Constance Portman, dau. of 5th Viscount Portman, and has issue living, Henry Thurstan, *b.* 1959.—James Edward, *b.* 1967;—Lucy Katherine, *b.* 1956. *Residence,*—Broadclyst House, Exeter.——Lavinia, *b.* 1919; 1939-45 War as Jun. Com. ATS: *m.* 1953, Maj. Peter John Orde, 15th/19th King's Roy. Hussars (ret.), son of Sir Percy Lancelot Orde, CIE. *Residence,*—Newbrough Park, Hexham, Northumberland.——Delia Mary, *b.* 1922; 1939-45 War as 3rd Officer WRNS: *m.* 1946, Lt.-Col. William McGhie Cunningham, MVO, OBE, MC, late 11th Hussars, and has issue living, Jeremy James, *b.* 1948;—Mark William, *b.* 1950,—Lavinia Mary, *b.* 1952. *Residence,*—Syresham Priory, Brackley, Northants.

Issue of the late Hon. Cecil Trevelyan Holland, 4th son of 1st Viscount, *b.* 1862, *d.* 1941: *m.* 1896, Alice, who *d.* 1946, dau. of the late Gilbert Walker :—
Alice Mary, *b.* 1897: *m.* 1919, Lieut.-Col. Robert Begbie Longridge, formerly 16th Lancers, and has issue living, Dorothy Patricia, *b.* 1920,—Margaret Holland, *b.* 1925,—Elizabeth Mary, *b.* 1926. *Residence,*—

(*In remainder to the Baronetcy only.*)

Grandchildren of the late Rev. Francis James Holland, brother of 1st Viscount :—
Issue of the late Bernard Henry Holland, C.B., *b.* 1856, *d.* 1926 : *m.* 1895, Florence Helen, who *d.* 1933, dau. of the late Rev. William Arthur Duckworth [B. Stratheden]:—
Mary Verena Violet, *b.* 1901; a nun.——Catharine Sibylla (50, Cranley Mews, SW1), *b.* 1903: *m.* 1924, George Anthony Mostyn, who *d.* 1972 [see B. Vaux of Harrowden, colls.].
Issue of the late Capt. Michael James Holland, MC, *b.* 1870, *d.* 1956: *m.* 1911, Marion Ada Flora, who *d.* 1969, da. of the late H. J. T. Broadwood, of Lyne, Horsham, Sussex:—
Antony Francis, *M.C., b.* 1913 ; ed. at Eton, and at Emmanuel Coll., Camb. ; Bar. Middle Temple 1936 ; sometime Crown Counsel, Kenya ; Malaya 1942 with Indian Army (M.C.): *m.* 1946, Ann, dau. of the late Henry Faure Walker, of Highley Manor, Sussex, and has issue living, Thurstan James, *b.* 1948; ed. at Eton and Nottingham Univ.,—Anthea, *b.* 1947: *m.* 1973, John St. Andrew Warde, of Squerryes Court, Westerham, Kent, and has issue living, Charles Antony *b.* 1974,—Arabella Ann, *b.* 1956. *Residence,*—Lullings, Balcombe, Sussex. *Club,*—Muthaiga Country (Nairobi)—— David Cuthbert Lyall, *b.* 1915; ed. at Eton, and at Trin. Coll., Camb.; late Roy, Sussex Regt.; Librarian, House of Commons since 1967: *m.* 1949, Rosemary, da. of David Llewllyn Griffiths,

OBE, and has issue living, Matthew Francis, *b.* 1952; ed. at Eton,—Peter Gwinnell, *b.* 1954,—Lucinda Jane (twin), *b.* 1954. *Residence,*—Trees, Haywards Heath, Sussex. *Club,*—Athenaeum.

PREDECESSORS—[1] Henry Holland; *b.* 1788; Physician in Ordinary to H.M. Queen Victoria 1850-73, and to H.R.H. the Prince Consort 1840-61, was cr. a *Baronet* 1853: *m.* 1st, 1822, Margaret Emma, who *d.* 1830, dau. of James Caldwell of Linley Wood, co. Stafford; 2ndly, 1834, Saba, who *d.* 1866, dau. of the Rev. Sydney Smith, Canon of St. Paul's; *d.* 1873; *s.* by his el. son [2] Henry Thurstan, *G.C.M.G.*, *P.C.*, 2nd baronet; *b.* 1825; Legal Adviser to Colonial Office 1867-70, Assist. Under-Sec. there 1870-74, Financial Sec. to Treasury 1885, Vice-Pres. of Committee of Council on Education Sept. 1885 to Jan. 1886, and July 1886 to Jan. 1887, and Sec. of State for Colonies Jan. 1887 to Aug. 1892; M.P. for Midhurst (*C*) 1874-85, and for Hampstead 1885-8; cr. P.C. 1885, G.C.M.G. 1886, *Baron Knutsford,* of Knutsford, Cheshire (peerage of United Kingdom) 1888, and *Viscount Knutsford,* of Knutsford, Cheshire (peerage of United Kingdom) 1895: *m.* 1st, 1852, Elizabeth Margaret, who *d.* 1855, dau. of Nathaniel Hibbert, of Munden, Watford, Herts; 2ndly, 1858, Margaret Jean (a Lady of Justice of Order of St. John of Jerusalem in England), who *d.* 1906, el. dau. of Sir Charles Edward Trevelyan, K.C.B., 1st Bt.; *d.* 1914; *s.* by his el. son [2] Sydney George, 2nd Viscount, *b.* March 19th, 1855; many years Chm. of London Hospital: *m.* 1883, Lady Mary Ashburnham, who *d.* 1947, dau. of 4th Earl of Ashburnham; *d.* 1931; *s.* by his twin brother [3] Arthur Henry Holland-Hibbert, 3rd Viscount, *b.* (twin) March 19th, 1855; High Sheriff of Herts 1891; assumed by Roy. licence 1876, the additional surname and arms of Hibbert: *m.* 1884, Ellen, who *d.* 1949, el. dau. of Sir Wilfrid Lawson, 2nd Bt. (cr. 1831); *d.* 1935; *s.* by his el. son [4] Thurstan, 4th Viscount and present peer; also Baron Knutsford.

KYLSANT, BARONY OF. (Philipps.) [Extinct 1937.]

DAUGHTERS LIVING OF FIRST BARON.

Hon. Nesta Donne, *b.* 1903; a DL of Carmarthenshire; 1939-45 War as Ch. Com., ATS: *m.* 1st, 1921, the 10th Earl of Cawdor, who *d.* (killed in action during European War) 1940; 2ndly, 1953, Maj. Terrace Vincent Fisher-Hoch, RA. *Residence,*—Plâs Llansteffan, Carmarthen, Dyfed, SA33 5JP.

Hon. Olwen Gwynne, *b.* 1905; is a J.P.: *m.* 1st, 1925, the 7th Baron Suffield, who obtained a divorce 1937; 2ndly, 1937, Lieut.-Col. Frank Richard Peter Barker, who *d.* 1974, and has issue living, (by 2nd m.) Timothy Gwynne (Beadles Hall, Chignal Smealey, Chelmsford, Essex), *b.* 1940: *m.* 1964, Philippa Rachel Mary, da. of Brig. Mervyn Christopher Thursby-Pelham, of Ridgeland House, Finchampstead, Berks., and has issue living, Christopher Gwynne *b.* 1970, Camilla Gwynne *b.* 1968. *Residence,*—Lund Court, Nawton, York.

LAMBERT, VISCOUNT. (Lambert.) [Viscount U.K. 1945.]

George Lambert, *T.D.*, 2nd Viscount; *b.* Nov. 27th, 1909; *s.* 1958; ed. at Harrow, and at New Coll., Oxford; Chm. of Govs. of Seal Hayne Agric. Coll., Devon 1967-70, Chm. of Devon and Exeter Savings Bank 1959-70, and Pres., National Federation of Young Farmers' Clubs 1968-70 (Life Vice-Pres. since 1970); 1939-45 War as Lt.-Col. TA; MP for S. Molton Div. of Devon (*L*) 1945-50, and for Torrington Div. of Devon, 1950-58 (*Nat. L and C*): *m.* 1939, Patricia Mary, da. of J. F. Quinn, and has issue.

Arms,—Azure, a chevron or fretty of the first between, in chief two garbs and in base a fleece of the second. Crest,—Issuant from a mount vert an apple tree fructed proper. Supporters,—On either side a Cornish chough proper collared or.

Residence,—Les Fougères, 1806 St. Légier, Switzerland. *Clubs,*—Carlton, Army and Navy.

DAUGHTER LIVING.

Hon. Louise Barbara, *b.* 1944.

BROTHER LIVING.

Hon. Michael John, *b.* Sept. 29th, 1912: *m.* 1939, Florence Dolores, da. of Nicholas Lechmere Cunningham Macaskie, QC, and has issue living, Sophia Jane, *b.* 1943,—Caelia Anne Georgiana, *b.* 1946: *m.* 1971, Emmanuel Irismar Pereira, and has issue living Antonia Katarina *b.* 1972,—Flavia Mary, *b.* 1949. *Residence,*—2, Aubrey Rd., W8.

SISTERS LIVING.

Hon. Grace Mary, *b.* 1905. *Residence,*—1, St. Germans, Exeter.
Hon. Margaret Barbara, *CMG, b.* 1906; BA Oxon; PhD London; CMG 1965. *Residence,*—39, Thornhill Rd., N.1.

PREDECESSOR.—[1] *Rt. Hon.* George Lambert, son of the late George Lambert; *b.* 1866; Capt. 3rd Batn. Devonshire Regt.; Civil Lord of the Admiralty 1905-15; was a County Councillor for Devonshire 1889-1912, and a County Alderman 1912-52; sat as M.P. for N., or S. Molton, Div., of Devonshire (*L*) 1891-1918, and for S. Molton Div. of Devon 1918-24, and 1929-45; cr. *Viscount Lambert,* of South Molton, co. Devon (peerage of United Kingdom) 1945: *m.* 1904, Barbara, who *d.* 1963, dau. of the late George Stavers, of Morpeth; *d.* 1958; *s.* by his el. son [2] George, 2nd Viscount and present peer.

Lambton, Viscount, see Earldom of Durham.

LAMBURY, BARONY OF (Lord.) [Extinct 1967]

DAUGHTERS LIVING OF FIRST BARON.

Hon. Joan Marguerite, *b.* 1927: *m.* 1st, 1951 (m. diss. 1965), Miles Lucas Breeden; 2ndly, 1966, Angus James Macdonald, and has issue living, (by 1st marriage) Guy Charles, *b.* 1953,—Gail Amanda, *b.* 1956. *Residence*,—113, Century Court, St. John's Wood Rd., NW8.

Hon. Patricia Ann (c/o José Villalonga 52 Bis, El Terreno, Palma de Mallorca), *b.* 1929: *m.* 1951, (m. diss. 1968), Capt. Morfryn James Howard-Smith, RN, and has issue living, Nigel Philip, *b.* 1954,—Susan Merilyn, *b.* 1952.

Hon. Pauline Ruth, *b.* 1931: *m.* 1954, John Pither, and has issue living, Steven Edward, *b.* 1957,—Gary John, *b.* 1959. *Residence*,—Appletree Farmhouse, Chorleywood Common, Herts.

WIDOW LIVING OF FIRST BARON.

ETHEL LILY (*Baroness Lambury*) (The Old Mill House, Loudwater Lane, Rickmansworth, Herts.), da. of George Horton, of Coventry: *m.* 1921, the 1st Baron, who *d.* 1967, when the title became ext.

LAMINGTON, BARONY OF (Cochrane-Baillie.) [Extinct 1951.]

DAUGHTER LIVING OF SECOND BARON.

Hon. Grisell Annabella Gem, *b.* 1898: *m.* 1922, Capt. Edward George Godolphin Hastings, OBE, RN, who *d.* 1973 [see E. Huntingdon, colls.]. *Residence*,—Baldy's Gardens, Ouilfail, Lewes, Sussex.

LANESBOROUGH, EARL OF. (Butler.) [Earl I. 1756.]

DENIS ANTHONY BRIAN BUTLER, T.D., 9th Earl; *b.* Oct. 28th, 1918; *s.* (Aug.) 1950; Maj. R.A. (T.A) a JP and DL for Leics.: *m.* 1939 (marriage dissolved (Sept.) 1950), Bettyne Ione, only dau. of Sir (William) Lindsay Everard, J.P., D.L., M.P. [V. Hawarden, colls.], and has issue.

Arms,—Argent, three covered cups between two bendlets engrailed, sable. Crest,—A demi-cockatrice couped vert, combed, beaked, wattled, and ducally gorged or, wings elevated argent. Supporters,—*Dexter*, a cockatrice vert, wings elevated argent, ducally gorged or, comb, beak, and wattles also gold; *sinister*, a wyvern vert, plain collared and chained or.

Seat,—Swithland Hall, Loughborough.

Liberty entire.

DAUGHTER LIVING.

Lady Denyne Gillian Patricia, *b.* 1945.

HALF-SISTER LIVING.

Lady Freda, *b.* 1895: *m.* 1931, Francis Cyril Oliphant Valentine, M.R.C.P., who *d.* 1957, and has issue living, William Danvers Oliphant (Litigan, by Aberfeldy, Perthshire), *b.* 1933: *m.* 1972, Jennifer, twin da. of A. O. Gill, of House of Strachan, Banchory, Kincardineshire, and has issue living, Alastair Danvers Oliphant *b.* 1974, Clare Margaret Vivien *b.* 1975,—Francis Anthony Brinsley (29, Cornwall Gdns., SW7), *b.* 1935; ed. at Eton. *Residence*,—A11, Albany, W1.

DAUGHTER LIVING OF SEVENTH EARL.

Lady Moyra Elizabeth, *b.* 1899: *m.* 1944, as his second wife, Brigadier John Leslie Weston, C.B.E., D.S.O., who *d.* 1963. *Residence*,—Kingsthorpe, South Hamilton Rd., N. Berwick.

WIDOW LIVING OF EIGHTH EARL.

GRACE LILIAN (*Countess of Lanesborough*), da. of Sir Anthony Charles Sykes Abdy, 3rd Bt.: *m.* 1917, as his second wife, the 8th Earl, who *d.* 1950. *Residence*,—Swithland Hall, Loughborough.

COLLATERAL BRANCHES LIVING.

Issue of the late Capt. the Hon. Francis Almeric Butler, 3rd son of 6th Earl, *b.* 1872, *d.* 1925: *m.* 1902, Madeline Sarah, who *d.* 1961, dau. of the late Richard Birkett Gibbs:—

TERENCE BRINSLEY JOHN DANVERS (c/o Nat. Westminster Bank, Meyrick St., Pembroke Dock) *b.* March 7th, 1913; Cdr. (ret.) RN, and a DL for Pembrokeshire; late HM's Harbour Master, Pembroke Dock; 1939-45 War (prisoner): *m.* 1st, 1937, Hermione, only child of the late Cdr. T. C. H. Williams, RN; 2ndly, 1947, (m. diss. 1970), Beryl (AXTEN), da. of the late George Trotter; 3rdly, 1972, Mrs. Jacqueline Balmer, da. of the late Winthrop Greene, of Washington, DC, and has issue living, (by 1st m.) Valentine Gay (The Poplars, Western Rd., Burgess Hill, Sussex), *b.* 1939: *m.* 1964 (m. diss. 1973), Arthur Clyde Nicholson, of Ponder, Texas, USA, and has issue living, Felicity *b.* 1969—(by 2nd m.) Clemency Anne Susan, *b.* 1949; BA Oxford,—Charlotte Gabrielle, *b.* 1951,—Perryn Joanna, *b.* 1953,—Teresa Jane, *b.* 1959.——Maida Daughne Laurel, *b.* 1906: *m.* 1928, Com. Christopher Bryan Stacey-Clitherow, DSC, RN (ret.) [see Stracey, Bt., colls.]. *Residence*,—Calcot Mount, Curdridge, Botley, Hants.

Grandson of the late Hon. Henry Cavendish Butler, half-brother of 5th Earl:—
Issue of the late Henry Halpin Cavendish Butler, M.B.E., *b.* 1884, *d.* 1966: *m.* 1908, Lucie Sophia Blanche, who *d.* 1974, da. of the late Maj.-Gen. Arthur Hales, late R. Inniskilling Fus., of Lansdown Cres., Bath, and Charmouth, Dorset [Hoare, Bt. cr. 1784, colls.]:—
Henry Arthur Brinsley Cavendish (Silver Hill, Rostrevor, co. Down), *b.* 1909; ed. at Rugby, and at Pembroke Coll., Camb. (BA), Lieut.-Col. (ret.) RE: *m.* 1st, 1940, Ruth Ardyn, who *d.* 1951, only da. of Lieut.-Col. William Hugh Barton, DSO, DL, of The Waterfoot, co. Fermanagh: 2ndly, 1952, Alice Isabella, only da. of the late Rev. G. Watt, BD, of Newry, co. Down.

PREDECESSORS.—[1] *Rt. Hon.* THEOPHILUS Butler, successively M.P. for co. Cavan and for Belturbet; cr. *Baron of Newtown Butler*, of co. Fermanagh (peerage of Ireland) 1715, with remainder to the heirs male of his father; *d.s.p.* 1723; *s.* by his brother [2] BRINSLEY, P.C., 2nd Baron; successively Gentleman Usher of the Black Rod, Col. of the battle-axe Guards, and M.P. for Kells and Belturbet; cr. *Viscount Lanesborough* (peerage of Ireland) 1728; *d.* 1735; *s.* by his son [3] *Rt. Hon.* HUMPHREY, 2nd Viscount; was sometime M.P. for Belturbet, and Dep. Speaker of Irish House of Commons; cr. *Earl of Lanesborough* (peerage of Ireland) 1756; *d.* 1768; *s.* by his son [4] BRINSLEY, 2nd Earl; was Joint Clerk of the Pipe, M.P. for co. Cavan, and Commr. for Revenues; *d.* 1779; *s.* by his son [5] ROBERT HERBERT, 3rd Earl; *d.* 1806; *s.* by his son [6] BRINSLEY, 4th Earl; *d.* unmarried 1847; *s.* by his cousin [7] GEORGE JOHN

DANVERS, 5th Earl, el. son of the late Hon. Augustus Richard, 2nd son of 2nd Earl; *d.* 1866, *s.* by his nephew [8] JOHN VANSITTART DANVERS (son of Capt. the Hon. Charles Augustus, 6th son of the late Hon. Augustus Richard, (ante), by Letitia Rudyerd Ross, da. of the late Col. John W. Freese), 6th Earl, *b.* 1839: *m.* 1864, Anne Elizabeth, who *d.* 1909, da. of the late Rev. John Dixon Clark, of Belford Hall, Northumberland; *d.* 1905; *s.* by his el. son [9] CHARLES JOHN BRINSLEY, *M.V.O.*, 7th Earl, *b.* 1865 ; a Representative Peer for Ireland ; was Assist. Mil. Sec. to Com.-in-Ch., Mediterranean Forces 1907-9, and Mil. Sec. to Gov.-Gen. and Com.-in-Ch. of Dominion of Canada (Earl Grey) 1909-10: *m.* 1st, 1891, Dorothea Gwladys, who *d.* 1920, dau. of the late Maj.-Gen. Sir Henry Tombs, K.C.B., V.C. ; 2ndly, 1922, Dorothy Kate, who *d,* 1935, dau. of the late James Dean Brand (formerly Mrs. Guy Watkins); *d.* 1929 ; *s.* by his brother [10] HENRY CAVENDISH, 8th Earl, *b.* 1868 : *m.* 1st, 1894, Isabel, who *d.* 1905, dau. of the late Ralph Allen Daniell ; 2ndly, 1917, Grace Lilian, dau. of Sir Anthony Charles Sykes Abdy, 3rd Bt. ; *d.* 1950 ; *s.* by his el. son [11] DENIS ANTHONY BRIAN, 9th Earl and present peer; also Viscount Lanesborough, and Baron of Newtown Butler.

LANGFORD, BARON. (Rowley-Conwy.) [Baron I. 1800.]

GEOFFREY ALEXANDER ROWLEY-CONWY, *O.B.E.*, 9th Baron ; *b.* March 8th, 1912; *s.* 1953; ed. at Marlborough ; Lieut.-Col. (retired) R.A.; Hon. Col. 470th Regt. RA (TA) 1961-67; Constable of Rhuddlan Castle, and Lord of the Manor of Rhuddlan; Singapore and Burma 1941-45 (OBE); OBE (Mil) 1943: *m.* 1st, 1939, Ruth St. John (who obtained a divorce 1956), da. of Albert St. John Murphy, of the Island House, Little Island, co. Cork; 2ndly, 1957, Grete, who *d.* 1973, da. of Col. E. T. C. von Freiesleben, Danish Army, of Lille Odinshoj, Aalsgaarde, Denmark; 3rdly, 1975, Susan Denham, and has issue by 2nd m.

Arms.—Quarterly: 1st and 4th argent, on a bend plain cottised gules, three mullets or, *Rowley*; 2nd and 3rd ermine, on a chief gules, a fleur-de-lis, between two boars' heads couped and erect or, *Taylor*. **Crest.**—A wolf's head, erased argent, collared or. **Supporters.**—*Dexter*, a figure of Minerva, armed and vested proper, with a spear in the right hand; *sinister*, a female figure representing Temperance, vested proper, and holding a bridle in her left hand.
Residence,—Bodrhyddan, Flintshire. *Club,*—Naval and Military.

SONS LIVING. *(By 2nd wife.)*
◊Hon. Peter Alexander, *b.* 1951; ed. at Marlborough, and Magdalene Coll., Camb. (BA Archaeology).
◊Hon. John Seymour, *b.* 1955, ed. at Marlborough and Magdalene Coll. Camb.
Hon. OWEN GRENVILLE, *b.* Dec. 27th, 1958; ed. at Marlborough.

SISTER LIVING. *(Raised to the rank of a Baron's daughter 1955.)*
Hon. Rose Marian, *b.* 1915 : *m.* 1938, Ralph Becher Skinner, and has issue living, David Rafe, *b.* 1939, —Meriel Ann, *b.* 1941: *m.* 1963, Jasper M. Garnham, of The Cottage, St. Mary's Way, Chalfont St. Peter, Bucks.,—Rosalind Hope, *b.* 1942. *Residence,*—The Fold, Cwm, Dyserth, Clwyd.

MOTHER LIVING.
Bertha Gabrielle, da. of the late Lt. Alexander Cochran, R.N., of Ashkirk, Selkirkshire: *m.* 1911, Maj. Geoffrey Seymour Rowley-Conwy, who *d.* (killed in action in Gallipoli) 1915. *Residence,*—Bodrhyddan, Rhuddlan, Flintshire.

WIDOWS LIVING OF FOURTH AND SEVENTH BARONS.
MARGARET ANTONIA *(Dowager Baroness Langford)*, dau. of the late Rev. William Mitchell-Carruthers, of Kingham Hill, Kingham, Oxon : *m.* 1915, as his second wife, the 4th Baron, who *d.* 1919. *Residences,*—12, Dorchester Court, Sloane St., S.W.1; Summerhill House, co. Meath.
FLORENCE EILEEN O'DONOVAN *(Florence, Baroness Langford)*, dau. of Isaac Shiel, of Dublin : *m.* 1922, the 7th Baron, who *d.* 1952. *Residences,*—Rose Cottage, Waldemar Rd., Wimbledon, SW19; The Links, Ascot, Berks.

COLLATERAL BRANCH LIVING.

Granddaughters of the late Col. the Hon. Hercules Langford Boyle Rowley, 2nd son of 2nd Baron :—
Issue of the late Hercules Douglas Edward Rowley, *b.* 1859, *d.* 1945 : *m.* 1884, Agnes Mary, who *d.* 1947, only dau. of the late A. Allen, of Devizes:—
Ivy Mabel Armine Douglas; *b.* 1889: *m.* 1910, Reginald Stanley Lewis Boulter, who *d.* 1929. *Residence,*—12A, Sloane Gate Mansions, Sloane Street, S.W.1.—Monica Evelyn Douglas, *b.* 1893; reverted by deed poll 1931 to her maiden name of Rowley: *m.* 1st, 1912, Edward Huskinson, from whom she obtained a divorce 1930 ; 2ndly, 1947, Capt. Guy Hardy MacCaw, MC, who *d.* 1952. *Residence,*—30, Eaton Square, SW1.

PREDECESSORS.—[1] The *Hon.* CLOTWORTHY Taylour, 4th son of 1st Earl of Bective assumed the surname of Rowley, and was cr. *Baron Langford,* of Summerhill, co. Meath (peerage of Ireland) 1800; *d.* 1825; *s.* by his son [2] HERCULES LANGFORD, 2nd Baron ; *d.* 1839; *s.* by his son [3] CLOTWORTHY WELLINGTON WILLIAM ROBERT, 3rd Baron ; *b.* 1824: *m.* 1846, Louisa Augusta, dau. of the late Col. Edward Michael Conolly, M.P.; *d.* 1854; *s.* by his son [4] HERCULES EDWARD ROWLEY, *K.C.V.O.*, 4th Baron, *b.* 1848; State Steward to Viceroy of Ireland 1886-92, and Comptroller of the Household to Lord-Lieut. of Ireland 1895-1902: *m.* 1st, 1889, Georgina Mary, who *d.* 1901, dau. of Sir Richard Sutton, 4th Bt. ; 2ndly, 1915, Margaret Antonia, dau. of the late Rev. William Mitchell-Carruthers, of Kingham Hill, Kingham, Oxon ; *d.* 1919; *s.* by his son [5] JOHN HERCULES WILLIAM, 5th Baron : *b.* 1894 ; *d.* 1922 ; *s.* by his uncle [6] WILLIAM CHAMBRE, 6th Baron, *b.* 1849 : *m.* 1889, the Hon. Mabel Maud Legh, who *d.* 1966, da. of 1st Baron Newton; *d.* 1931; *s.* by his nephew [7] CLOTWORTHY WELLINGTON THOMAS EDWARD (son of the late Hon. Randolfe Thomas Rowley, 3rd son of 3rd Baron), 7th Baron; *b.* 1885: *m.* 1922, Florence Eileen O'Donovan, da. of Isaac Shiel, of Dublin; *d.* 1952; *s.* by his kinsman [8] ARTHUR SHOLTO LANGFORD, *CMG* (son of the late Col. the Hon. Hercules Langford Boyle Rowley, 2nd son of 2nd Baron), 8th Baron; *b.* 1870; H.M.'s Consul-Gen. at Barcelona 1917-23, at Antwerp 1923-30, and at Paris 1930-32: *m.* 1st, 1908, Margareta Ines, who *d.* 1928, da. of Hugh R. F. Jameson, of Iquique, Chile; 2ndly, 1929, Maude Alice, who *d.* 1958, da. of the late Henri Lelacheur, of Guernsey; *d.* 1953; *s.* by his kinsman [9] GEOFFREY ALEXANDER (only son of the late Maj. Geoffrey Seymour Rowley-Conwy, 2nd son of the late Capt. Conwy Grenville Hercules Rowley-Conwy, only son of the late Hon. Richard Thomas Rowley, 2nd son of 1st Baron), 9th Baron and present peer.

LANSDOWNE, MARQUESS OF. (Mercer Nairne Petty-Fitzmaurice.)
[Marquess G.B. 1784.]

By courage, not words.

GEORGE JOHN CHARLES MERCER NAIRNE PETTY-FITZMAURICE, PC, 8th Marquess; b. Nov. 27th, 1912; s. 1944; ed. at Eton, and at Ch. Ch., Oxford; is a Member of Queen's Body Guard for Scotland (Roy. Co. of Archers), a Patron of two livings; a DL for Wilts. 1952-73; 1939-45 War as Capt. Scots Greys and Maj. with French Free Forces (Legion of Honour, Croix de Guerre); appointed Private Sec. to HM's Ambassador in Paris 1944; a Lord-in-Waiting to HM 1957-58, Joint Parl. Under Sec. of State for Foreign Affairs 1958-62, and Min. of State for Colonial Affairs 1962-64; assumption of additional surnames of Petty-Fitzmaurice recognized by decree of Lord Lyon 1947; PC 1964: m. 1st, 1938, Barbara, who d. 1965, da. of Harold Stuart Chase, of Santa Barbara, Calif., USA; 2ndly, 1969, the Hon. Selina Polly Dawson Eccles, da. of 1st Viscount Eccles, and formerly wife of Robin Andrew Duthac Carnegie [see E. Southesk], and has issue (by 1st m.).

Arms,—Quarterly: 1st and 4th, ermine, on a bend azure, a magnetic needle pointing to the polar star or, *Petty*; 2nd and 3rd, argent, a saltire gules, and a chief ermine, *Fitzmaurice*. Crests,—1st. a bee-hive beset with bees, volante, all proper; 2nd, a sagittary passant proper. Supporters,—On either side a pegasus ermine, winged, and unguled or, each charged on the shoulder with a fleur-de-lis azure.

Residence,—63, Warwick Sq., SW1. *Clubs,*—Turf, New (Edinburgh).

SONS LIVING (By 1st m.).
CHARLES MAURICE (*Earl of Shelburne*), b. Feb. 21st, 1941; ed. at Eton; late Kenya Regt., R. Wilts. Yeo. and R. Wessex Yeo.; a Page of Honour to HM 1956-57; Chm. Calne and Chippenham RDC 1972-73; Co. Councillor of Wilts. since 1970; Chm. N. Wilts. Dist. Council since 1973; a Member of S-W Economic Planning Council since 1971; Chm. Population and Settlement Cttee. (SWEPC) since 1972: m. 1965, Lady Frances Helen Mary Eliot, da. of 9th Earl of St. Germans, and has issue:—
  SONS LIVING—Simon Henry George (*Viscount Calne and Calstone*), b. Nov. 24th, 1970.
    Hon. William Nicholas Charles, b. 1973.
  DAUGHTERS LIVING—*Lady* Arabella Helen Mary, b. 1966.
    Lady Rachel Barbara Violet, b. 1968.
  Residences,—Bowood, Calne, Wilts.; 3, Rutland St., SW7.
Lord Robert Harold MERCER NAIRNE (51, Tregunter Rd., SW10), b. 1947; ed. at Gordonstoun, and Univ. of Kent: m. 1972, Jane Elizabeth, el. da. of Lt.-Col. Lord Douglas Claude Alexander Gordon DSO [see M. Huntly], and has issue living, Emily Jane, b. 1974.

DAUGHTER LIVING. (By 1st m.).
Lady Georgina Elizabeth PETTY-FITZMAURICE, b. 1950.

SISTER LIVING. (Raised to the rank of a Marquess's daughter 1946.)
Lady Mary Margaret Elizabeth, b. 1910: m. 1931, Lieut.-Col. Ririd Myddelton, M.V.O., Coldstream Gds. (ret.), and has issue living, David Foulk (Caeaugwynion, Chirk, Wrexham), b. 1932; late Coldstream Gds.: m. 1st, 1965, (m. diss. 1968), Anne, only da. of the late Charles Brotherton, of Kirkham Abbey, York; 2ndly, 1970, Christine Serena Cherry, da. of Arthur Malcolm Morris, OBE, Depart. of External Affairs, Canberra, Aust., and has issue living, (by 1st m.), Guy Charles b. 1966, (by 2nd m.) Mark Ririd b. 1973, Sian Moyra b. 1971.—Hugh Robert (66, Palace Gdns. Terr., W8), b. 1938, late Coldstream Gds.: m. 1967, the Hon. Sarah Cecily Allsopp, da. of 5th Baron Hindlip, and has issue living, Alexander Ririd Henry b. 1969, Claerwen Georgina Margaret b. 1972,—Fiona Violet, b. 1934: appointed a Lady-in Waiting to HRH Princess Margaret 1960: m. 1963, Alastair Sturgis Aird, MVO, Capt. 9th Lancers [see Aird, Bt., coll.]. *Residence,*—Chirk Castle, nr. Wrexham, N. Wales.

DAUGHTERS LIVING OF SIXTH MARQUESS.
Lady Katherine Evelyn Constance (*Viscountess Mersey*), b. 1912; s. as *Lady Nairne* in her own right 1945 [see that title]: m. 1933, the 3rd Viscount Mersey. *Residence,*—Bignor Park, Pulborough, Sussex.

Lady Elizabeth Mary, b. 1927: m. 1950, Major Charles William Lambton, Coldstream Guards (retired) [see E. Durham, colls.]. *Residence,*—Mortimer Hill, Mortimer, Reading, Berks.

COLLATERAL BRANCH LIVING.

Descendants of the late Hon. Thomas FitzMaurice (son of 1st Earl of Shelburne and brother of 1st Marquess of Lansdowne), who m. 1777, Mary, *Countess of Orkney* (in her own right) [see E. Orkney].

PREDECESSORS.—[1] THOMAS FitzMaurice; cr. *Baron of Kerry and Lixnaw* (peerage of Ireland); d. 1280; s. by his son [2] MAURICE, 2nd Baron; sat in Parliament at Dublin 1295; d. 1303; s. by his son [3] NICHOLAS, 3rd Baron; s. by his son [4] MAURICE, 4th Baron; having a dispute with Dermond Oge MacCarthy, killed that chief on the bench before the Judge of Assize at Tralee in 1325, for which he was tried and attainted by the Parliament of Dublin, but was not put to death; his lands were, however, forfeited, but restored after his decease in 1339 to his brother and successor [5] JOHN, 5th Baron; summoned to Parliament 1375; s. by his son [6] MAURICE, 6th Baron; d. 1398; s. by his son [7] PATRICK, 7th Baron; d. 1410; s. by his son [8] EDMUND, 8th Baron; d. 1469; s. by his son [9] EDMUND, 9th Baron; d. 1489; s. by his son [10] EDMUND, 10th Baron; resigned his estates to his el. son and became a lay brother of the Order of St. Francis in the Friary of Ardfert; d. 1543; s. by his son [11] EDMOND, 11th Baron; cr. *Baron Odorney*, of co. Kerry, and *Viscount Kilmaule* (peerage of Ireland) 1537; d. without male issue 1541, when the Baron of Odorney and Viscountcy became extinct, and the Barony of Kerry devolved upon his brother [12] PATRICK, 12th Baron; d. 1547; s. by his el. son [13] THOMAS, 13th Baron; d. a minor 1549; s. by his brother [14] EDMUND, 14th Baron; d. 1549; s. by his uncle [15] GERALD, 15th Baron; d. 1550; s. by hi-brother [16] THOMAS, 16th Baron; served many years in the military service of Emperors of Germany; d. 1590; s. by his son [17] PATRICK, 17th Baron; brought up at Court of Queen Elizabeth, but was in rebellion against H.M. after his succession to title; d. 1600; s. by his son [18] THOMAS, 18th Baron; surrendered his estates to James I., who in 1604 granted him a free pardon, and in 1612, by patent, confirmed his estates to him and his heirs and assigns for ever;

d. 1630; *s.* by his el. son [19] PATRICK, 19th Baron; took his seat in Parliament 1634, and removed to England 1641; *d.* 1660; *s.* by his el. son [20] WILLIAM FITZMAURICE, 20th Baron; *d.* 1697; *s.* by his son [21] *Rt. Hon.* THOMAS, 21st Baron; cr. *Viscount ClanMaurice* and *Earl of Kerry* (peerage of Ireland) 1722; *d.* 1741; *s.* by his son [22] WILLIAM, *P.C.*, 2nd Earl; Gov. of Ross Castle, Col. of Coldstream Guards, and Custos Rotulorum of co. Kerry; *d.* 1747; *s.* by his son [23] FRANCIS THOMAS, 3rd Earl; *d.s.p.* 1818; *s.* by his cousin [24] HENRY Petty-FitzMaurice, K.G., P.C., 3rd *Marquess of Lansdowne* [see *₰*infra]; a distinguished statesman; Lord Lieut. of Wilts, M.P. for Camelford, Chancellor of the Exchequer 1806-7, Lord Pres. of the Council 1830-4 and 1846-52, and a member of the Cabinet without office 1852-8; *d.* 1863; *s.* by his son [25] HENRY, K.G., 4th Marquess; *b.* 1816: sat as M.P. for Calne (*L*) 1847-56; was a Lord of the Treasury 1847, and Under-Sec. for Foreign Affairs 1856-8; summoned to Parliament in his father's Barony of Wycombe: *m.* 1843, Emily Jane Mercer Elphinstone de Flahault, who *d.* 1895, in her own right Lady Nairne (infra): *d.* 1866; *s.* by his son 26] HENRY CHARLES KEITH, K.G., G.C.S.I., G.C.M.G., G.C.I.E., who *s.* as 9th Lord Nairne 1895, 5th Marquess, *b.* 1845; a Commr. of Exchequer of Great Britain, and of Treasury of Ireland 1868-72, Under-Sec. of State for War 1872-4, Under-Sec. for India 1880, Gov.-Gen. of Canada and Com.-in-Ch. of Prince Edward Island 1883-8, Viceroy of India 1888-94, Sec. of State for War 1895-1900, and Sec. of State for Foreign Affairs 1900-1905, and Min. (without portfolio) May 1915 to Dec. 1916; Lord-Lieut. of Wilts 1896-1920; Chancellor of Order of St. Michael and St. George 1917-20; had Roy. Victorian Chain; bore Royal Standard at Coronation of King George V. 1911: *m.* 1869, Lady Maud Evelyn Hamilton, *V.A.*, *C.I.*, *G.B.E.*, *C.H.*, who *d.* 1932, dau. of 1st Duke of Abercorn, K.G.; *d.* 1927; *s.* by his son [27] HENRY WILLIAM EDMOND, D.S.O., M.V.O., 6th Marquess, *b.* 1872; M.P. for W. Div. of Derbyshire (*U*) 1908-18; sometime a Senator of Irish Free State: *m.* 1904, Elizabeth Caroline (who *d.* 1964, having *m.* 2ndly, 1940, Lord Colum Edmund Crichton-Stuart), da. of Sir Edward Stanley Hope, K.C.B.; *d.* 1936: *s.* by his son [28] CHARLES HOPE, 7th Marquess, *b.* 1917; Capt. Roy. Wilts. Yeo. (T.A.); *d.* (killed in action in Italy) Aug. 20th, 1944, when he was *s.* in the Lordship of Nairne by his el. sister, Lady Katherine Evelyn Constance Bigham, and in all the other peerages by his cousin [29] GEORGE JOHN CHARLES MERCER (only son of the late Major Lord Charles George Francis MERCER-NAIRNE, M.V.O., 2nd son of 5th Marquess) 8th Marquess and present peer; also Earl of Wycombe, Viscount Calne and Calstone, Lord Wycombe, Baron of Chipping Wycombe, Earl of Kerry, Earl of Shelburne, Viscount ClanMaurice and FitzMaurice, Baron of Kerry and Lixnaw, and Baron Dunkerron.

₰ [1] The *Hon.* JOHN FitzMaurice, *P.C.*, 2nd son of 1st Earl of Kerry (ante) inherited the estates of his maternal uncle Henry, 1st and last Earl of Shelburne (cr. 1719) whose surname of Petty he assumed; was sole Gov. of co. Kerry, and M.P. for Chipping Wycombe; cr. *Baron Dunkeron* and *Viscount FitzMaurice* (peerage of Ireland) 1751, *Earl of Shelburne* (peerage of Ireland) 1753, and *Baron Wycombe*, of Chipping Wycombe, co. Bucks (peerage of Great Britain) 1760; *d.* 1761; *s.* by his son [2] WILLIAM, K.G., P.C., 2nd Earl: M.P. for Chipping Wycombe 1763, a Lord of Trade, a Major-Gen. in the Army, A.D.C. to H.M. 1760, a Principal Sec. of State 1766, and Prime Minister and First Lord of the Treasury 1782; cr. *Viscount Calne and Calstone, Earl of Wycombe*, and *Marquess of Lansdowne* (peerage of Great Britain) 1784; *d.* 1805; *s.* by his son [3] JOHN HENRY, 2nd Marquess; M.P. for Chipping Wycombe 1786-90; *d.s.p.* 1809; *s.* by his half-brother [4] HENRY, 3rd Marquess (see ante).

Lascelles, Viscount, son of Earl of Harewood.

LATHAM, BARON. (Latham.) [Baron U.K 1942.]

It is good to try.

DOMINIC CHARLES LATHAM, 2nd Baron; *b.* Sept. 20th, 1954; *s.* 1970.

Arms,—Per fesse gules and chequy or and sable a fesse barry wavy argent and azure in chief a seax fessewise point to the sinister cutting edge upwards proper pomel and hilt of the second ensigned with a Saxon crown also of the second. **Crest,**—Two spurs one in bend the other in bend sinister rowels upwards or straps sable with buckles gold. **Supporters,**—On either side a horse sable charged on the shoulder with a plate and gorged with a mural coronet with chain reflexed over the back or.

Residence,—

BROTHER LIVING.
ANTHONY (twin), *b.* Sept. 20th, 1954.

AUNTS LIVING. (*Daughters of 1st Baron*).
Hon. Barbara Wendy, *b.* 1920; 1942-44 War as 1st class Aircraftwoman WAAF: *m.* 1st, 1941 (m. diss. 1945), Capt. Denis Charles Wildish, RASC; 2ndly, 1946 (m. diss. 1951), Peter Anthony Charles Kurt Bruckmann, late Capt. E. Surrey Regt.; 3rdly, 1966, Malcolm Blundell Cole-Fontayn, solicitor, of 54, Eaton Place, SW1, and has issue living, (by 2nd m.) Karin Franchesca, *b.* 1948.
Hon. Jean Helen, (19, Belle Vue Gdns., Brighton, 7) *b.* 1921; WRNS 1940-45: *m.* 1st, 1945 (m. diss. 1961), Sqdn.-Ldr. Ronald Gellatly, RNZAF; 2ndly, 1970, James Oswald Dykes, and has issue living, (by 1st m.), Paul *b.* 1946.
Hon. Diana Dorothy, (Beirut, Lebanon), *b.* 1925.

MOTHER LIVING.
Gabrielle, da. of Dr. S. M. O'Riordan: *m.* 1951, as his third wife, the Hon. Francis Charles Allman Latham, who *d.* 1959. *Residence,—*

GRANDMOTHER LIVING.
Maya Helen, da. of Louis George Allman: *m.* 1913 (m. diss. 1957) the 1st Baron, who *d.* 1970.

WIDOW LIVING OF FIRST BARON.
SYLVIA MAY (*Baroness Latham*), (170, Chiltern Court, Baker St., NW1 5ST), da. of Alexander Newmark, of London, and widow of Alexander Kennard: *m.* 1957, as his 2nd wife, the 1st Baron, who *d.* 1970.

PREDECESSOR.—[1] CHARLES Latham, son of the late George Latham, of Norwich; *b.* 1888, Leader of LCC 1940-47, Chm. of London Transport Exec. 1947-53; Chm. of Finance Cttee. of Metropolitan Water Board 1957-65; Lord Lieut. of Middx. 1945-56; cr. *Baron Latham*, of Hendon, co. Middx (peerage of UK) 1942: *m.* 1st, 1913 (m. diss. 1957) Maya Helen, da of Louis George Allman, of Hendon; 2ndly, 1957, Sylvia May, da. of Alfred Newmark, of London, and widow of Alexander Kennard; *d.* 1970; *s.* by his grandson [2] DOMINIC CHARLES (el. twin son of the Hon. Francis Charles Allman Latham, who *d.* 1959), 2nd Baron and present peer.

LATYMER, BARON. (Money-Coutts.) [Baron E. 1431-2.]

THOMAS BURDETT MONEY-COUTTS, 7th Baron; *b.* Aug. 6th, 1901; *s.* 1949; ed. at Radley, and at Trin. Coll., Oxford; an OStJ; 1939-45 War: *m.* 1925, Patience, da. of the late William Courtenay-Thompson, and has issue.

    Arms,—Quarterly: 1st and 4th, a stag's head erased gules, between the attires a pheon azure, all within a bordure embattled of the last, charged with four buckles or, *Coutts*; 2nd and 3rd or, on a pile azure ten besants, four, three, two, and one, on a chief ermine a lion passant of the second, *Money*. **Crests**,—1st, a man from the middle upwards, shooting an arrow from a bow, all proper, *Coutts*; 2nd, a besant between two wings azure, each semée-de-lis, or, *Money*. **Supporters**,—On either side a griffin or.

    To be, not to seem.

Residence,—Son Rebassa, Moscari, Inca, Mallorca. *Clubs*,—St. James', Carlton.

SON LIVING.

Hon. HUGO NEVILL (Sa Font Garrover, Mancor, Inca, Mallorca), *b.* March 1st, 1926; ed. at Eton: *m.* 1st, 1951 (m. diss. 1965), the Hon. Penelope Ann Clare, da. of the late Thomas Addis Emmet, and Baroness Emmet of Amberley [Life Baroness]; 2ndly, 1965, Jinty, da. of the late Peter George Calvert, and has issue living, (by 1st m.) Crispin James Alan Nevill, *b.* 1955; ed. at Eton,—Giles Thomas Nevill, *b.* 1957,—Clare Louise, *b.* 1952,—(by 2nd m.) Henry Eugene, *b.* 1967,—Vera Dulcie Harriet, *b.* 1972,—Fanny Clara Maria, *b.* 1973.

DAUGHTERS LIVING.

Hon. Joanna Harriet Nevill, *b.* 1928 : *m.* 1951, Pierre Langlais, and has issue living, Eric, *b.* 1952,—Nicole, *b.* 1953,—Louise, *b.* 1954,—Odette, *b.* 1961,—Jacqueline, *b.* 1962. *Residence*,—1340, Avenue Patenaude, Sillery, Province of Quebec, Canada.
Hon. Susan Margaret Nevill, *b.* 1933: *m.* 1st 1956 (m. diss. 1965), Michael John Turner, QC [see By. Schuster, ext.]; 2ndly, 1965, Ian A. K. Dipple, of Nether Walstead, Lindfield, Sussex, and has issue living, (by 1st m.) [see By. Schuster, ext.],—(by 2nd m.) Alexandra Margaret, *b.* 1967,—Joanna Shannon, *b.* 1968.

BROTHERS LIVING.

Hon. Alexander Burdett, O.B.E., *b.* 1902; ed. at Eton, and at New Coll., Oxford; is Lieut.-Col. late 6th Bn. Roy. Scots. Fusiliers; Master of Tobacco Pipe Makers' and Tobacco Blenders' Co. 1964-65; 1939-45 War (OBE); OBE (Mil) 1946: *m.* 1930, Mary Elspeth, da. of Sir Reginald Arthur Hobhouse, 5th Bt., and has issue living, David Burdett (Magpie House, Peppard Common, Henley-on-Thames), *b.* 1931; ed. at Eton, and New Coll., Oxford; late Capt. R. Gloucestershire Hussars: *m.* 1958, Helen Penelope June Utten, da. of the late Cdr. Killingworth Richard Utten Todd, Roy. Indian Navy, and has issue living, Benjamin Burdett *b.* 1961, Harriet St. Bride *b.* 1959, Laura Isabella *b.* 1965. *Residence*,—Askett House, Aylesbury, Bucks. *Club*,—St. James'.
Hon. Godfrey Burdett, *b.* 1905; ed. at Eton; is Major R.E.; European War 1939-45 (despatches): *m.* 1931, Anne Cecilia, who *d.* 1969, da. of the late Hon. Wilfrid James [B. Northbourne, colls.], and has issue living, Julia Jane ST. JOHN AUBIN (15, Gerrard Rd., N1), *b.* 1933; assumed the surname of St. John Aubin 1968: *m.* 1951 (m. diss. 1968), Cdr. Richard John Fisher Turner, RN, and has issue living, Antony Robin Fisher *b.* 1952: *m.* 1973, Barbara Maeve, da. of Harry Stokes of Sevenoaks, Simon John Fisher *b.* 1954, James Michael Fisher *b.* 1956. *Residence*,—Marshborough Cottage, Marshborough, Sandwich, Kent.

SISTER LIVING.

Hon. Mercy Burdett, *b.* 1910; ed. at Lady Margaret Hall, Oxford (B.A. 1933); served with British Red Cross Mission in Greece and Central Mediterranean and with United Nations Relief and Rehabilitation Administration in Crete: *m.* 1947, Michael Seiradhakis, and has issue living, John Hugh, *b.* 1948,—Sophia Hester, *b.* 1949. *Residence*,—19, Odos Seirenon, Byrona, Athens.

COLLATERAL BRANCHES LIVING.

    Issue of the late Hon. Clara Burdett Money-Coutts, el. da. of 5th Baron, *b.* 1877, *d.* 1969: *m.* 1905, the Rev. Melville Watson Patterson, who *d.* 1944:—
Rosamund Margaret, *b.* 1905: *m.* 1934, Selwyn Duruz, of Beacon House, Port Campbell, Victoria, Aust.——Joan Elisabeth, *b.* 1908: *m.* 1st, 1931, Sebastian Max Alexander Myer Clement Salaman, from whom she obtained a divorce 1937; 2ndly, 1947, Raymond Coxon, IG, of Brookfield House, King's Sutton, Banbury, and has issue living, (by 1st m.) Clement Francis (40, Bickerton Rd., N19), *b.* 1932: *m.* 1961, Juliet Nicholson,—Frederick Nicholas (4, Laurel Rd., SW13), *b.* 1936: *m.* 1960, Elisabeth Sclater.——Lindsay Marion, *b.* 1916: *m.* 1939, Humphy Gilbert Bohun Lynch (Orchard House, W. Hagbourne, Didcot, Berks.), and has issue living, Francis Nicholas (64, Huddleston Rd., N7), *b.* 1944: *m.* 1965, Amanda Underwood,—Alison Harriet, *b.* 1955.

    Grandson of the Hon. Joan Burdett Nixon (infra):—
    Issue of the late Arundel James Nixon, *b.* 1907, *d.* 1942: *m.* 1930, Edna Duffy:—
Peter, *b.* 1934. *Residence*,—
    Issue of the late Hon. Joan Burdett Money-Coutts, 3rd da. of 5th Baron, *b.* 1882, *d.* 1968: *m.* 1905, Lt.-Col. James Arundel Nixon, DSO, formerly King's Own (R. Lancaster) Regt., who *d.* 1950, and from whom she obtained a divorce 1941:—
uy John (Les Ecus, King's Rd., St. Peter Port, Guernsey), *b.* 1909: *m.* 1933, Barbara Helen, yr. da. of the late Francis William Whitbourn Morgan, and has issue living, Sara, *b.* 1933: *m.* 1959, John Gordon Mathias, of 19, St. Mark's Court, Barton Rd., Cambridge, and has issue living, Jeremy *b.* 1963, Penelope *b.* 1960.

    Granddaughters of the Hon. Margaret Burdett Still (infra):—
    Issue of the late Robert Still, *b.* 1910, *d.* 1971: *m.* 1944, Elizabeth (Bucklebury Lodge, Bucklebury, Berks.), da. of S. K. Westman, FRCS, of Harley St., W1:—
Susan, *b.* 1945: *m.* 1965, R. C. R. Chesters.——Anthea, *b.* 1947: *m.* 1974, Michael Dillon.——Katharine, *b.* 1949: *m.* 1971, Peter Hyde.——Claudia, *b.* 1954.
    Issue of the late Hon. Margaret Burdett Money-Coutts, yst. da. of 5th Baron, *b.*, 1886, *d.* 1948 : *m.* 1907, Major Francis Churchill Still, late R.G.A., solicitor, who *d.* 1937 :—
Ursula Margaret, *b.* 1913: *m.* 1935, Archibald Walter Bury. *Resides* in Australia.

PREDECESSORS.—[1] *Sir* GEORGE Nevill, 5th son of 1st Earl of Westmorland ; summoned to Parliament by writ as *Baron Latymer* 1431-2: *m.* Elizabeth, dau. of 5th Earl of Warwick ; *d.* 1469 ; *s.* by his grandson [2] RICHARD, *b.* 1468 ; summoned to Parliament 1492-1529 : *m* 1490, Anne, dau. of Sir Humphrey Stafford, of Grafton and Blatherwycke ; *d.* 1530 ; *s.* by his son [3] JOHN, *b.* 1493 ; summoned to Parliament 1533-4 and 1541-2 : *m.* 1st, 1518, Elizabeth, dau. of Sir

Richard Musgrave, of Hartland ; 2ndly, Dorothy, who *d.* 1526-27, dau. of Sir George Vere ; 3rdly Katharine (who subsequently *m.* King Henry VIII.), dau. of Sir Thomas Parr, of Kendal, and widow of Edward, Lord Burgh ; *d.* 1543 ; *s.* by his only son by second marriage [4] JOHN ; summoned to Parliament 1543-80 : *m.* Lucy, dau. of 2nd Earl of Worcester ; *d.* 1577, when the Barony fell into abeyance between his four daus. and co-heirs ; in July 1912, the Committee for Privileges of the House of Lords reported (other co-heirs not appearing) that a claim to the Barony had been made out by [5] FRANCIS BURDETT THOMAS Money-Coutts, 5th Baron, only son of the late Rev. James Drummond Money, by Clara Maria, who *d.* 1899 (having assumed by Roy. licence 1880, for herself and son, the additional surname of Coutts), 4th dau. of Sir Francis Burdett, 5th Bt. (cr. 1618-19) ; *b.* 1852 ; proved his claim to the Barony before the Committee for Privileges of the House of Lords July 1912 [claiming through Frances, el. dau. of Lucy (who *m.* Sir William Cornwallis), 3rd dau. of 4th Baron], and the abeyance was determined in his favour Dec. 1912 ; assumed by Roy. licence 1914, the additional surname and arms of Nevill in lieu of that of Money, and after that of Coutts: *m.* 1875, Edith Ellen, who *d.* 1942, dau. of Charles Churchill, of Weybridge Park, Surrey ; *d.* 1923 ; *s.* by his son [6] HUGH BURDETT Money-Coutts, *T.D.,* 6th Baron ; *b.* 1876; sometime Capt. N. Devon Hussars Yeo. ; European War 1915-17 in Gallipoli and Egypt : *m.* 1900, Hester Frances, who *d.* 1961, dau. of the late Maj.-Gen. John Cecil Russell, O.V.O. ; *d.* 1949 ; *s.* by his son [7] THOMAS BURDETT, 7th Baron and present peer.

LAUDERDALE, EARL OF. (Maitland.) [Earl S. 1624, Bt. S. 1680.]

By wisdom and courage.

PATRICK FRANCIS MAITLAND, 17th Earl, and 13th Baronet; *b.* March 17th, 1911; *s.* 1968; ed. at Lancing, and Brasenose Coll., Oxford (BA); Hereditary Bearer of National Flag of Scotland by decrees of Lord Lyon King of Arms 1790 and 1952; Editor of *The Fleet Street Letter Service,* and *The Whitehall Letter* 1945-58; Pres. of Church Union 1959-62; MP for Lanark (*C*) 1951-59; a Member of Coll. of Guardians of Nat. Shrine of Our Lady of Walsingham, and Founder of Expanding Commonwealth Group of House of Commons (Chm. 1955-61;) Hon. Treasurer of Human Rights Soc. 1969-71; Chm. Civic Education and Research Trust 1972: *m.* 1936, Stanka, da. of Prof. Milivoye Losanitch, of Belgrade, and has issue.

Arms,—Or, a lion rampant gules couped at all his joints of the field, within the Royal tressure azure, in a dexter canton argent a saltire azure, surmounted of an inescutcheon or, charged with a lion rampant within a double tressure flory counterflory gules, behind the shield on staffs in saltire proper two representations of the Sovereign's National Flag of Scotland (Cross of St. Andrew), fringed or, ropes and tassels of the last (Insignia of Office of Bearer for the Sovereign of the Sovereign's National Flag of Scotland). Crest,—A lion sejant affrontee gules, ducally crowned proper, in his dexter paw a sword of the last, hilted and pommelled or, and in his sinister a fleur-de-lis azure. Supporters,—Two eagles proper.

Residences,—12, St. Vincent St., Edinburgh; 10, Ovington Sq., SW3.

SONS LIVING.

IAN (*Master of Lauderdale, Viscount Maitland*) (150, Tachbrook St., SW1), *b.* Nov. 4th, 1937; ed. at Radley and Brasenose Coll., Oxford (MA); Lt. RNR: *m.* 1963, Ann Paule, da. of Geoffrey Clark, of 511, Hood House, Dolphin Sq., SW1, and has issue.
 SON LIVING,—*Hon.* John Douglas (*Master of Maitland*), *b.* 1965.
 DAUGHTER LIVING,—*Hon.* Sarah Caroline, *b.* 1964.
Hon. Sydney Milivoye Patrick, *b.* 1951.

DAUGHTERS LIVING.

Lady (Helen) Olga, *b.* 1944: *m.* 1969, Robin William Patrick Hamilton Hay, of 21, Cloudesley St., N1, and has issue living, Alastair Patrick Hamilton, *b.* 1972,—Camilla Charlotte Hamilton, *b.* 1975.
Lady Caroline Charlotte Militsa, *b.* 1946.

SISTER LIVING (Raised to the rank of an Earl's daughter 1953).

Lady (Ella) Mary, *b.* 1906: *m.* 1932, John Alder Cripps Blumer, late Colonial Civil Ser., Tanganyika, and has issue living, Anthony John Maitland (c/o Container Agencies, PO Box 1059, Kuala Lumpur, Malaysia), *b.* 1936: *m.* 1962, Mary Erica, el. da. of the late Dr. E. J. C. Bockett, and has issue living, Robert John Maitland *b.* 1963, Patrick Neil James *b.* 1965, Elizabeth Mary *b.* 1968,—Peter Robert William, *b.* 1942,—Christopher James Frederick (Melrose, New Rd., Henley-in-Arden, Warwickshire) *b.* 1947: *m.* 1974, Catherine Elizabeth, ed. da. of N. R. Eyres,—Phoebe Mary, *b.* 1933: *m.* 1960, Ralph Hornblower, Junior, of 50, Fairfield Rd., Greenwich, Connecticut, USA, and has issue living, John Greenwood *b.* 1961, David Maitland, *b.* 1963, James Wainwright (twin) *b.* 1963,—Philippa Sydney Isabel, *b.* 1945: *m.* 1975, James C. Bell. *Residence,*—19, Queen's Rd., Cheltenham.

GRANDDAUGHTERS LIVING OF FIFTEENTH EARL (Raised to the rank of an Earl's daughters 1953).

Issue of the late Ivor Colin James (*Viscount Maitland*), Lieut. Roy. Armoured Corps (T.A.), only son of 15th Earl, *b.* 1915, *d.* (killed in action during European War) 1943 : *m.* 1936, Helena Ruth (*infra*), younger dau. of Sir Herbert Charles Perrott, 6th Bt. (ext.), C.H.. C.B. :—
Lady Mary Helena (*Baroness Biddulph*) *b.* 1938: *m.* 1958, the 4th Baron Biddulph, of Makerstoun, Kelso, Roxburghshire.——*Lady* Anne Priscilla, *b.* 1940: *m.* 1968, John Joseph Eyston, of Maple-durham House, Reading [see E. Mexborough].——*Lady* Elizabeth Sylvia, *b.* (posthumous) 1943.

DAUGHTER LIVING OF FIFTEENTH EARL.

Lady Sylvia Gwendoline Eva (*Baroness Carew*), *b.* 1913; is a C.St.J.: *m.* 1937, the 6th Baron Carew. *Residence,*—Mountarmstrong, Donadea, co. Kildare.

WIDOW LIVING OF SON OF FIFTEENTH EARL.

Helena Ruth (*Helena, Viscountess Maitland*), yr. da. of Sir Herbert Charles Perrott, 6th Bt. (ext.), CH, CB; is an OStJ: *m.* 1936, Viscount Maitland, Lt. Roy. Armoured Corps (TA), who *d.* (killed in action during European War) 1943, only son of 15th Earl, and has issue living (see ante). *Residences,*—Flat E, 34, Cadogan Sq., SW1; Park House, Makerstoun, nr. Kelso, Roxburghshire.

WIDOW LIVING OF SIXTEENTH EARL.

IRENE ALICE MAY (*Irene, Countess of Lauderdale*), (S. Raphael, 91, North Lane, E. Preston, Littlehampton, Sussex), da. of the late Rev. C. P. Shipton, of Halsham, Yorks.: *m.* 1940, as his 2nd wife, the 16th Earl, who *d.* 1968.

COLLATERAL BRANCHES LIVING.

Branch from 3rd son of 13th Earl.

Issue of the late Maj. the Hon. Alfred Henry Maitland, 3rd son of 13th Earl, *b.* 1872, *d.* (killed in action) 1914: *m.* 1905, Edith, who *d.* 1963, dau. of the late Sanford George Treweeke Scobell, of Down House, Redmarley, Worcestershire:—
Nora Beatrice, *b.* 1907 : *m.* 1935, Squadron-Leader Peter Yorke, O.B.E., late R.A.F. Vol. Reserve, and has issue living, Cherry Clare, *b.* 1943. *Residence,*—Hatchetts, Old Hall Green, near Ware, Herts.

Branch from 5th son of 6th Darl.

Descendants of the late Gen. the Hon. Sir Alexander Maitland (5th son of 6th Earl), who was cr. a *Baronet* 1818 :—
See Maitland, Bt.

Branch from Charles Maitland of Rankeillour, el. son of 8th son of 6th Earl.

Grandchildren of Maj. Charles Julian Maitland-Makgill-Crichton (infra):—
Issue of the late Maj. Douglas Maitland-Makgill-Crichton, *b.* 1909, *d.* 1968: *m.* 1936, Sybil Frederica Coore (Monzie Castle, Crieff, Perthshire), da. of the late Frederick Lechmere Paton, JP [B. Ashtown, colls.]:—
Charles (Monzie Castle, Crieff, Perthshire; Travellers' Club), *b.* 1942: ed. at Winchester; heir of line of 1st Viscount Frendraught: *m.* 1971, Isla Susan, da. of the late M. F. Gloag, and has issue living, David, *b.* 1972.——Veronica Ann, *b.* 1938.

Grandchildren of the late David Maitland-Makgill-Crichton (*b.* 1854), son of the late Charles Julian Maitland-Makgill-Crichton, el. son of the late David Maitland-Makgill-Crichton (*b.* 1801) (infra):—
Issue of the late Major Charles Julian Maitland-Makgill-Crichton, Gordon Highlanders, *b.* 1880, *d.* (killed in action) 1915 : *m.* 1902, Sybil Twynihoe (The Ibert, Crieff, Perthshire), dau. of the late Twynihoe William Erle, a Master of Supreme Court, of Bramshott Grange, Liphook, Hants :—
Mary Sylvia, *b.* 1905.——Rosemary Julian (37, Clareville Grove, SW7), *b.* 1915: *m.* 1940, James H. L. Musker, Fl. Lt. RAFVR, formerly 7th Hussars, who *d.* 1966, and has issue living, Juliet Alexandra Sarah, *b.* 1941: *m.* 1965, William Edward Barry, of 12, Kensington Park Mews, W11 [see Barry, Bt., colls.].

Issue of the late Lt.-Cdr. James Henry Maitland-Makgill-Crichton, R.N. (ret.), *b.* 1885, *d.* 1948: *m.* 1908, Emily Christina, who *d.* 1972, yr. da. of the late Hugh Weir-MacColl, of Appin, Argyll, and The Woods, Newlands, Cape Province, S. Africa:—
David Hugh, *D.S.O., D.S.C., b.* 1910 ; Com. R.N. (retired), a Com. of Order of Dannebrog, of Denmark, and a Fellow of Institute of Linguists ; European War 1939-44 at Evacuation of Dunkirk and in Atlantic and Mediterranean (wounded, despatches thrice, D.S.O., D.S.O., Polish Naval Commendation); D.S.O. 1942. *Residence,*—High Wray House, 18, Avenue Rd., St. Albans, Herts.——Alice Mary Emily, *b.* 1914: *m.* 1937, Vernon C. Chambers, and has issue living, Virginia, *b.* 1942: *m.* 1968, George Digby MacDougall Dodd, of Sparrow's Barton, Easton, Corsham, Wilts, and has issue living, Tamsin Serena Georgina *b.* 1971, Julian Crichton *b.* 1973,—Vanessa, *b.* 1946. *Residence,*—11, Shouldham St., Bryanston Pl., W1.

Granddaughters of the late Cdr. Coventry Makgill-Crichton-Maitland, RN (infra):—
Issue of the late Col. Henry David Makgill-Crichton-Maitland, OBE, *b.* 1904, *d.* 1970: *m.* 1st, 1930 (m. diss. 1949) Barbara Ellen, da. of the late Brig.-Gen. Sir George Ayscough Armytage, CMG, DSO, 7th Bt.; 2ndly, 1949, Audrey Estelle Ljufing (Gibbons Pl., Ightham, Sevenoaks, Kent), da. of Henry John Hyde-Johnson, and widow of Lt. Peter Thorp Eckersley, RNVR, MP:—
(By 1st m.) Judith Elizabeth, *b.* 1933: *m.* 1965, Anthony John Houssemayne du Boulay, of 110, Fentiman Rd., SW8.——Sarah, *b.* 1936: *m.* 1958, Count Alessandro Monneret de Villard of Il Castello, Via Torre 5, Pombia, Italy, and has issue living, Raffaella, *b.* 1961,—Xenia, *b.* 1965,—Tatiana, *b.* 1970.

Grandchildren of the late Maj.-Gen. David Makgill-Crichton-Maitland (*b.* 1841), (changed the sequence of his surnames 1884), son of the late David Maitland-Makgill-Crichton (*b.* 1801), 2nd son of the late Capt. Charles Maitland, el. son of the Hon. Frederick Lewis Maitland RN, 8th son of 6th Earl:—
Issue of the late Com. Coventry Makgill-Crichton-Maitland, R.N., *b.* 1877, *d.* 1958 : *m.* 1902, Alice Mary, who *d.* 1965, da. of the late Col. Charles Birch-Reynardson [Stracey, Bt., colls.]:—
Jean (Witham House, Gerrards Cross, Bucks.), *b.* 1907: *m.* 1935, Air Commodore James Silvester, CBE, RAF, who *d.* 1956, and has issue living, Anthony James, *b.* 1937,—David Michael (24, St. Peter's Close, Rickmansworth, Herts. WD3 2QY), *b.* 1940; assumed by deed poll 1975 the surname of Silvester Maitland: *m.* 1974, Felicity Ann Hillyard, da. of the late Lt. Cdr. Francis Morgan Stent, RN (ret.).

Issue of the late Col. Mark Edward Makgill-Crichton-Maitland, CVO, DSO, *b.* 1882, *d.* 1972: *m.* 1924, Patience Irene Fleetwood, who *d.* 1974, da. of Sir John Michael Fleetwood Fuller, 1st Bt., KCMG:—
John David (Houston House, Johnstone, Renfrewshire), *b.* 1925; ed. at Eton; Maj. (ret.) Gren. Gds.; Vice-Lt. of Renfrewshire: *m.* 1954, Jean Patricia, da. of the late Maj.-Gen. Sir Michael C'Moore Creagh, KBE, MC [see McGrigor, Bt.], and has issue living, Mark Archibald, *b.* 1955; ed. at Eton,—Mary Elizabeth, *b.* 1962.——Mark Michael (2, Grosvenor Cres., Edinburgh, EH12 5EP), *b.* 1928; Maj. (ret.) Gordon Highlanders.——Irene Margaret, *b.* 1927: *m.* 1953, Maj. Michael Christopher Alfred Codrington, late 16th/5th Lancers of Dene House, Seend, Melksham, Wilts, SN12 6NJ [see Codrington, Bt., cr. 1721, colls.].

Grandchildren of the late Andrew Coventry Maitland-Makgill-Crichton (infra):—
Issue of the late Lieut.-Col. David Edward Maitland-Makgill-Crichton, Queen's Own Cameron Highlanders, *b.* 1879, *d.* 1952: *m.* 1909, Phyllis (53, Evelyn Gdns., SW7), da. of the late Claude Arthur Cuthbert, formerly of Bryn Garth, Much Dewchurch, Herefordshire [Rankin, Bt.]:—
Sir Andrew James (55, Hans Pl., Knightsbridge, SW1; Mill House, Earl Soham, Suffolk), *b.* 1910; ed. at Wellington; Col. late Indian Army; Chm. of Overseas Containers, Ltd.; Dir. of P & O Steam Navigation Co.; Dep. Dir. of Movements GHQ, New Delhi 1944-45, and Chm. Employers' Side, Nat. Joint Council for Port Transport Industry and of Nat. Assocn. of Port Employers 1958-65; an

Arbitrator for Police Council o f Great Britain since 1966; Vice-Chm. Port of London Authority since 1967; *cr.* Knt. 1963: *m.* 1948, Isabel, da. of A. J. McGill, of Sydney, NSW, and widow of John Eric Bain.——Edward, *OBE* (Clive House, Letham, Angus), *b.* 1916; ed. at Bedford Sch. and RMC; Maj.-Gen. late Cameron Highlanders; GOC 51st Highland Div. 1966-68; ret. 1968; Middle East 1940-44 (wounded, despatches), NW Europe 1944-45 (MBE); MBE (Mil.) 1945, OBE (Mil.) 1948: *m.* 1951, Sheila Hibbins, and has issue living, David Edward, *b.* 1952; Lt. Scottish Div., —Andrew James, *b.* 1953,—Charles William, *b.* 1961.——Jean Beatrice (*Baroness Salmon*) *b.* 1912: *m.* 1st, 1933 (m. diss. 1946), the 2nd Baron Morris, who *d.* 1975; 2ndly, 1946, Baron Salmon (Life Peer), of 1, Melina Place, NW8, and The Old Drum, Sandwich, Kent.——Katherine Grizel, *b.* 1930: *m.* 1954, Russell Barton, MRCP, of 1600, South Av., Rochester, New York 14620, USA, and has issue living, Karen Elizabeth, *b.* 1956,—Sarah Muriel, *b.* 1958.

Issue of the late Brigadier Henry Coventry Maitland-Makgill-Crichton, C.B., C.M.G., D.S.O. late Roy. Scots Fusiliers, *b.* 1880, *d.* 1953 : *m.* 1911, Dorothy Margaret (of Hedge Cottage; Kingston Deverill, near Warminster, Wilts), dau. of the late Sir Walter Thorburn, of Glenbreck, Peeblesshire:—

Diana Elizabeth Katherine, *TD*, *b.* 1916. *Residence,*—Hedge Cottage, Kingston Deverell, Warminster, Wilts.

Issue of the late John Denys Maitland-Makgill-Crichton, *b.* 1897, *d.* 1931: *m.* 1930, Denise (of 12, Wanderers Crest, Illovo, Johannesburg, S. Africa); she *m.* 2ndly, 1932, Douglas S. Fraser, from whom she obtained a divorce 1943, and has resumed her former name of Maitland-Makgill-Crichton), dau. of J. H. Crosby:—

Michael John (of Candy Cottage, Rivonia, Johannesburg, S. Africa), *b.* 1931; ed. at Rhodes Univ. (B.A. 1952), at Witwatersrand (LL.B. 1954), and at Oriel Coll., Oxford: *m.* 1958, Euphemia Daphne Joan Hopkins, and has issue living, Anthony John, *b.* 1960,—Philippa Anne, *b.* 1965.

Granddaughters of the late David Maitland-Makgill-Crichton (*b.* 1801) (ante):—

Issue of the late Andrew Coventry Maitland-Makgill-Crichton, *b.* 1845, *d.* 1925 : *m.* 1878, Katharine Charlotte, who *d.* 1941, dau. of Sir Edward Hulse. 5th Bt.:—

Kathleen Esther, *b.* 1886: *m.* 1919, Sidney Gobourn, and has issue living, Peter Charles Crichton, *MBE* (c/o Barclays Bank, High St., Cheltenham), *b.* 1924; Maj. RCT; 1939-45 War (wounded), MBE (Mil.) 1973: *m.* 1953, Elizabeth Barbara Foster, and has issue living, Andrew Denis Crichton *b.* 1960, Guy Richard Crichton *b.* 1964, Catharine Elizabeth Crichton *b.* 1962,—Edward David Crichton (68, Copt Elm Rd., Charlton Kings, Cheltenham), *b.* 1927; 1939-45 War as Fusilier Roy. Fusiliers: *m.* 1955, Shirley Ann Davis Lloyd, and has issue living, Timothy Richard Crichton *b.* 1958, Felicity Mary *b.* 1961. *Residence,*—Segrave Park Place, Cheltenham.——Norah Grizel, *b.* 1889: *m.* 1908, Maj. Charles Noel Lyall, RA, who *d.* 1942, and has issue living, Ronald Crichton, *b.* 1912; ed. at Canford; 1939-45 War as Private Hampshire Regt., and RAOC,—Charles Leslie (Meadowleigh, 4, Weston Rd., Petersfield, Hants.), *b.* 1919, ed. at Charterhouse and Worcester Coll., Oxford: *m.* 1969, Marjorie Yvonne de Burlet,—Marjory Cecil, *b.* 1909,—Barbara Kathleen, *b.* 1911: *m.* 1940, Wilfred Danvers Brinton, DM, FRCP, of Carloway, Sleepers Hill, Winchester [Bowman, Bt., colls.], and has issue living, Veronica Ruth *b.* 1946, Margaret Danvers *b.* 1949. *Residence,*—Ellerslie, Weston Rd., Petersfield, Hants.——Muriel Christian, *b.* 1892: *m.* 1913, Aldred Clement Rowden, Registrar of Sons of the Clergy Corporation, who *d.* 1935, and has issue, Maurice Edward Aldred, *b.* 1918,—Diana Hope, *b.* 1915; Section Officer WAAF (despatches, French Croix de Guerre with star); *d.* (executed at Natzweiler Camp) 1944.

Grandchildren of the late Marie Stuart, dau. of the late David Maitland-Makgill-Crichton (*b.* 1801) (ante), *b.* 1829, *d.* 1895 : *m.* 1849, Vice-Adm. Philip Horatio Townshend Somerville, who *d.* 1881:—

Issue of the late David Maitland Makgill Crichton Somerville, *b.* 1850, *d.* 1915 : *m.* 1884, Alison Clephane, who *d.* 1944, dau. of the late James Macknight, W.S., of Edinburgh :—

Henry Maitland, *b.* 1901.——Helen Elisabeth, *b.* 1890: *m.* 1912, Robert Meynell Stickney, who *d.* 1960, and has issue living, Philip Ambrose Meynell, *b.* 1913,—Helena Alison (Godolphin, Mill Lane West, Elloughton cum Brough, E. Yorks.), *b.* 1914: *m.* 1st, 1939, Wing-Com. Russell Darby Welland, RAF, who *d.* 1974, and has issue living, (by 1st m.) Elizabeth Jennifer *b.* 1941: *m.* 1st, 1961 (m. diss. 1974), Timothy Tugman; 2ndly, 1974, Jonathan Neil Heap Smith, of 1, Weldon Court, Weaponness Park, Scarborough, YO11 2UA (and has issue living by 1st m.), Penelope Claire *b.* 1963, Emma Sue *b.* 1965, Lucy Alison Sophy *b.* 1968,—Agnes Esther, *b.* 1924: *m.* 1951, David Leonard Jowett, of Town Head, Hebden, nr, Skipton, Yorks., and has issue living, Robert Crichton *b.* 1956, Jonathan Paul *b.* 1959, Ian Christopher *b.* 1962, Rosemary Ann *b.* 1954,—Patricia Somerville, *b.* 1935: *m.* 1959, Gordon Hubert Robson, of Westwood Close, Nafferton, nr. Driffield, North Humberside, and has issue living, Sean Philip *b.* 1962, Bridget Stickney *b.* 1961. *Residence,*—14, Bainton Close, New Walk, Beverley, E. Yorks., HU17 7DL.——Esther Maitland, *ARRC*, *b.* 1903: Lt.-Col. (ret.) QARANC; is an OStJ; 1939-45 War (ARRC). *Residence,*—370, Winchester Rd., Southampton.——Christian Eileen, *b.* 1907: *m.* 1934, Col. Patrick Henry Cummins, IMS (ret.) (PO Box 54092, Plimmerton, Wellington, NZ), and has issue living, James Michael (26, Weld St., Wadestown, Wellington, NZ), *b.* 1943, DPhil: *m.* 1973, Erlene Sir Yoong Chun,—Eileen Mary, *b.* 1938: *m.* 1959, Anselm Neison Guise, of Grays Rd., PO Box 54092, Plimmerton, Wellington, NZ [see Guise, Bt., colls.].

Issue of the late Thomas Townshend Somerville, *b.* 1851, *d.* 1914 : *m.* 1873, Elisabeth Frolich, who *d.* 1946, dau. of the late Herr T. J. Wiborg, of Brevik, Norway :—

David Maitland Makgill Crichton, *M.B.E.*, *b.* 1891; British Vice-Consul at Gothenburg, Sweden; MBE (Civil) 1946: *m.* 1918, Harriet Klem, who *d.* 1944, and has issue living, Thomas Townshend, *b.* 1923: *m.* 1st, 1948, Ingrid Wallborg; 2ndly, 1952, Ingrid Birkeland, and has issue living, (by 1st m.) David Maitland Makgill Crichton *b.* 1949, (by 2nd m.) Frederick Lewis Maitland *b.* 1959. *Residence,*—71, Södra Vagen, Gothenburg, Sweden.——Eleanor Julia: *m.* 1905, John Leatham Bright, who *d.* 1947, and has issue living Elaine Maitland: *m.* 1933, John Ellison-Brown, of Broadwater Point, Devoran, Truro, and has issue living, Julia Priscilla Maitland *b.* 1937.——Anna Maitland. *Address,*—BM/STSO, WC1.

Grandchildren of the late Thomas Townshend Somerville (ante):—

Issue of the late Martha Cuninghame Fletcher (Nina), *b.* 1878, *d.* 1956: *m.* 1st, 1899, Sigurd Hoyer Ellefsen, CE, who *d.* 1939; 2ndly, 1908, Earl Johan Wiese, Barrister, of Oslo, who *d.* 1949; 3rdly, 1917, Gen. Carl Erichsen, Norwegian Army, who *d.* 1949:—

(By 1st m.) Thomas Townshend Somerville (Milamores, Loma de Rio Verde, Marbella, Malaga, Spain), *b.* 1900, CE: *m.* 1930, Inez Tenden Michelsen, of New York, USA, and has issue living, Sigurd (Wyngate, PO Box 486, Locust Valley, New York 11560, USA), *b.* 1932; ed. at Mass. Inst. of Tech., Cambridge, Mass. (BS, MS, ScD); resumed by Court Order 1975 for himself, his wife, and issue the surname of Hoyer-Ellefsen instead of Hoyer: *m.* 1959, Astrid Reksten, and has issue living, Thomas Townshend Somerville *b.* 1961, Sigurd Reksten *b.* 1962, Anthony James *b.* 1969, Richard Maitland *b.* 1971, Caroline Elizabeth *b.* 1967,—Dina Beate, *b.* 1935: *m.* 1957, Rolf Reksten, of Avenida Belgica 4, Estoril, Lisbon, Portugal, and has issue living, Rolf *b.* 1965, Inez *b.* 1958, Nina Cecelie *b.* 1960.—Frederick Lewis Maitland, *b.* 1903: *m.* 1st, 1930, Countess Heidi Stewen Steinheil, of Helsingfors, who *d.* 19—; 2ndly, 19—, Vivi ——, and has issue living, (by 1st m.,) Frederick, *b.* 1938,—Nina, *b.* 1932.——Vera, *b.* 1905: *m.* 1929, Tage Jakob Falkenberg, CE, of Øvre Ullern Terrasse 82, Oslo 3, Norway, and has issue living, Carl Tage, *b.* 1934: *m.* 1965, (m. diss. 1968), Francoise Obosinski, and has issue living, Paul Jakob *b.* 1966,—Kerstin, *b.* 1939: *m.* 1964, Arnfinn Pedersen, Lecturer, and has issue living, Annesiv *b.* 1971.——(by 2nd m.) Karl Johan (Ryghs vei 10, Holmenkollen, Oslo), *b.* 1909, a lawyer: *m.* 1937, Sylvia Schou, of Oslo, and has issue living, Karl Johan, *b.* 1940: *m.* 1967, Maud Sylvia ——,—Sylvia, *b.* 1942: *m.* 1964, Ingvar Falk of Hässelby Strandvag 26, Stockholm, and has issue living, Jon Henrik *b.* 1968, Suzanne Sylvia *b.* 1966,—Vera, *b.* 1946.

Grandchildren of the late Rear-Adm. Lewis Maitland, 5th son of the late Charles Maitland (ante):—
Issue of the late Frederick Lewis Maitland, *b.* 1874, *d.* 1915: *m.* 1896, **Constance Zeila**, dau. of the late A. Dewar-Durie, M.D., of Craigluscar, Fife:—
David Randolph, *V.R.D.*, *M.B.*, *Ch.B.*, *F.R.C.P.E.* ; *b.* 1902 ; formerly Surg.-Lieut.-Com. R.N.V.R.; has Diploma of Med. Radiology, Diagnostic : *m.* 1930, **Barbara Mary Carnegie**, dau. of the late Edward Weymss, of Kirkton, Fife, and has issue living, David Lewis, *b.* 1932: *m.* 1st, 1961, Anna Mary Smith, who *d.* 1968, ward of J. de R. Kent, of Valewood, Haslemere, Surrey; 2ndly, 1969, Jennifer Mary Davies, and has issue living (by 1st m.), Lewis Randolph *b.* 1962, Niall David (twin) *b.* 1962, Angus Charles *b.* 1964 (by 2nd m.) Sarah Mary *b.* 1971,—Henry Christopher (Auchengarrich, Comrie, Perthshire), *b.* 1935: *m.* 1968, Charlotte Mary Ross, da. of R. Tod, of 17, South Oswald Rd., Edinburgh, and widow of Lt. J. W. Harvey, RN, and has issue living, Christopher Ross *b.* 1969, Barbara Anne *b.* 1972,—Mary *b.* 1939: *m.* 1962, Peter Lauritz Wang, of Lawhead Loch, Tarbrax, W. Calder, Midlothian, and has issue living, Mark Sigurd Maitland *b.* 1963, Patrick David *b.* 1965, Robert Magnus *b.* 1969. *Residence,*—Halton Hill, Newburgh, Fife.

Issue of the late Anna Lewise Maitland, *b.* 1872, *d.* 1914: *m.* 1893, the Rev. Charles Henry Titterton, B.D., who *d.* 1958 :—
Charles Titterton MAITLAND, *C.B.E.*; *b.* 1894 ; ed. at Univ. Coll. Sch., and at London Univ. (B.Sc. 1915, M.B. and B.S. 1920, M.D. 1921); M.R.C.S. England and L.R.C.P. London 1917 ; M.R.C.P. 1922 ; D.P.H. London 1921 ; F.R.C.P. 1936 ; formerly Principal Med. Officer, Min. of Health; assumed by deed poll 1920, the surname of Maitland (his mother's maiden surname) in lieu of that of Titterton, which he now uses as a forename ; O.B.E. (Civil) 1956 : *m.* 1921, Joyce Muriel Ward, who *d.* 1971, da. of the Rev. Charles Frederick Knight, R. of Frinton, Essex, and has issue living, Allan Charles McLellan, *b.* 1931; ed. at Repton, and at St. John's Coll., Camb. (BA 1956),—Henry Knight, *b.* 1933; ed. at Bradfield, and at Clare Coll., Camb. (BA 1955),—Joan Mary Titterton, *b.* 1926: *m.* 1952, Cdr. Norman Skitt, RN, of Elmgarth, 105, Sussex Rd., Petersfield, Hants., and has issue living, Robin Charles *b.* 1954, Thomas Maitland *b.* 1956, John Richard Knight *b.* 1959,—Esme Elizabeth, *b.* 1929; ed. at London Univ. (BA 1950). *Residence,*—Lethington, Fulmer Way, Gerrards Cross, Bucks.——Lewis Henry, *b.* 1900; ed. at Highgate, and at St. John's Coll., Camb. (BA), and at Harvard Univ.: *m.* 1st, 1929, Nancy, who *d.* 1936, da. of John Evans, of Dayton, Ohio, USA; 2ndly, 1938, Ruth, da. of Frederick Peter Jordan, of Oak Harbour, Ohio, USA, and has issue living, (by 2nd m.) Charles Frederick, *b.* 1941; ed. at St. Marks, and Harvard Univ. (BA); Lt. USN Reserve: *m.* 1969, Kathleen Howard, da. of Walter Howard Malone, of Arlington, Va., USA,—Lewis Henry *b.* 1944; ed. at Choate and Cornell Univ. (BA); Lt. USN Reserve: *m.* 1968, Patricia Ann, da. of the late John Joseph Reddy, of Stamford, Conn., USA, and has issue living, Christopher Maitland *b.* 1970, Jeffrey Jordan *b.* 1972,—Leslie Jordan, *b.* 1946. *Residence,*—RD2, Pound Ridge, NY, USA.——David Maitland MAITLAND-TITTERTON, *TD* (Moberty, Airlie, Angus; Caledonian and Puffins' Clubs) *b.* 1904; ed. at Queens' Coll., Camb. (MA); in Polit. Ser. Nigeria 1928-31; is Maj. late Ayrshire Yeo. and Staff Officer 51st Highland Div.; Falkland Pursuivant Extraor. 1969-72, since when Ormond Pursuivant; 1939-45 War; assumed by deed poll 1926 the additional surname of Maitland before that of Titterton; OStJ: *m.* 1929, Mary Etheldritha, yr. da. of the late Rt. Hon. James Graham Leslie, Senator of N. Ireland, and has issue living, Frederick Lewis Maitland Leslie (c/o Lloyds Bank, 50, Notting Hill Gate, W11), *b.* 1931; ed. at Campbell Coll.; AMBIM; Fl. Lt. RAF: *m.* 1953, Jean, da. of Sydney Webb, and has issue living, Clive Graham *b.* 1958, Anne Leslie *b.* 1955,—David Henry Sandford Leslie (Moberty, Airlie, Angus; Cavalry Club), *b.* 1933; ed. at Campbell Coll.; Lt.-Col. 9th/12th R. Lancers: *m.* 1963, Rinalda Malvina, only da. of the late Sqdn.-Ldr. the Hon. (Robert Alexander) Greville Baird [see E. Kintore, colls.], and has issue living, Rupert Seymour Aulin Leslie *b.* 1965, Shân Gelda Jane *b.* 1967. *Residence,*—Moberty, Airlie, Angus.——John Allan, *TD*, *b.* 1906; ed. at Highgate; Maj. late RA: *m.* 1932, Marion Anstice de Lisle, da. of the late Harold Arthur Mullens, of Acton Turville, Glos., and has issue living, Anna Elizabeth, *b.* 1935: *m.* 1967, Edmund Anthony Cornish Bostock, of 42, Hartington Rd., W4, and has issue living, Richard Anthony Maitland *b.* 1968, Andrew Robert Cornish (twin) *b.* 1968, John Edmund Angus de Lisle *b.* 1970. *Residence,*—1, Fons George Rd., Taunton, Som.——Mary Agnes, *b.* 1896.——Anna Frances, *b.* 1898; BA London 1920. *Residence,*—1, Porchester Rd., Newbury, Berks.

Branch from James Maitland-Heriot of Ramornie, 2nd son of 8th son of 6th Earl.

Granddaughters of the late Andrew Agnew Maitland-Heriot (latterly Heriot-Maitland), el. son of the late Frederick Lewis Maitland-Heriot, el. son of the late James Maitland-Heriot of Ramornie, 2nd son of Capt. the Hon. Frederick Lewis Maitland, RN, 8th son of 6th Earl:—
Issue of the late Frederick Lewis Heriot-Maitland, *b.* 1889, *d.* 1953: *m.* 1919, **Mabel Mary**, who *d.* 1962, dau. of the late James Keenan, of Rosario, Argentina:—
Pamela Gertrude, *b.* 1921 : *m.* 1940, Major Christopher Evelyn Boothby, R.M. [see Boothby, Bt., colls.]. *Residence,*—Corner Cottage, Lower Bourne, Farnham, Surrey.——Jean Ursula, *b.* 1923; 1939-45 with WRNS: *m.* 1st, 1944 (m. diss. 1952), Capt. Alan Seaforth Cox; 2ndly, 1955, John G. Adams, 25, Wilbury Cres., Hove, BN3 6FL, Sussex, and has issue living, (by 1st m.) Andrew Frederick Seaforth (84, Thames St., Weybridge), *b.* 1945: *m.* 1964, Carol Ilott, and has issue living, Oliver *b.* 1967, Emma *b.* 1964, Zoe *b.* 1969,—(by 2nd m.) Sebastian Thomas Maitland, *b.* 1961.

Grandchildren of the late Frederick Maitland-Heriot (infra) :—
Issue of the late Frank de Courcy Maitland-Heriot, *b.* 1882, *d.* 1957 : *m.* 1st (Jan.), 1912, **Marguerita Mary**, who *d.* 1935, dau. of George Duncan Logan, M.D., of Cressfield, Ecclefechan, Dumfriesshire ; 2ndly, 1939, Marion Mercer Moore, of Greystone, Los Cocos, Sierras de Cordoba, Argentina :—
(By 1st m.) Jean, *b.* 1915: *m.* 1935, Henry Ranald Martin, OBE, and has issue living, Ian Duncan (Casilla de Correo 546, Asunción, Paraguay), *b.* 1937: *m.* 1961, June Hope Castleton, and has issue living, Angus Ian *b.* 1973, Virginia Jean *b.* 1963, Anthea Lorraine *b.* 1966, Andrea June *b.* 1968,—Norman, *b.* 1941: *m.* 1965, Jacqueline Ann Booth, and has issue living, Ian Ranald Calvert *b.* 1966, Anthony *b.* 1974,—Nicholas Andrew *b.* 1970,—Alastair Reginald *b.* 1968,—Donald de Courcy (Sao Paulo, Brazil), *b.* 1943: *m.* 1969, Elizabeth Mary Christie, of Montevideo, and has issue living, Angus Donald *b.* 1973, Veronica Ann *b.* 1971,—Adrian Ranald *b.* 1953. *Residence,*—San Lucar 1540, Carrasco, Montevideo, Uruguay.

Issue of the late (Charles) Adrian Maitland-Heriot, D.S.C., *b.* 1886, *d.* 1950: *m.* 1919, **Dorothy** dau. of A. Egerton-Savory, of Eastbourne:—
Audrey Enid, *b.* 1921; 1939-45 War in WAAF: *m.* 1972, John Rogerson, of 95, Ridgmount Gdns., WC1E 7AZ.

Issue of the late Ralph Lionel Maitland-Heriot, M.C., *b.* 1895, *d.* 1935 : *m.* 1927, **Moir** (who *m.* 2ndly, 19—, George Scott, of Buenos Aires, Argentina), dau. of Harry Hugh Jefferies, of Fisherton, Argentina) :—
Ralph Desmond, *b.* 1930: *m.* 1955, Anneslie Atkinson, and has issue living, Richard Patrick, *b.* 1956,—Timothy James, *b.* 1958,—Rosalind Elizabeth, *b.* 1962.——Pamela Avril. *b.* 1928: *m.* 1952, Anthony Benjamin Oliveira, FRCS, of Rosemount, Bellevue Rd., Ryde, I. of Wight, and has issue living, David Benjamin Graeme, *b.* 1955,—Lynette Moira, *b.* 1957.

Grandchildren of the late Frederick Lewis Maitland-Heriot (ante) :—
Issue of the late Frederick Maitland-Heriot, *b.* 1852, *d.* 1925 : *m.* 1882, **Emily Macaulay**, who *d.* 1918, dau. of the late Charles Pelly [Pelly, Bt., colls.] :—
George Vivian (Ville Valle Verde, La Granja, Sierras de Cordoba, Argentina), *b.* 1891; ed. at Rugby; *m.* 1919, Marjorie Kathleen, da. of Edward J. Silcock, MICE, of Roundhay, Leeds, and has issue living, Torrance (Alte Brown 1662, Adrogue Argentina), *b.* 1920; ed. at Lancing; 1939-35 War with RAF (wounded): *m.* 1947, Elda, who *d.* 1963, da. of John Pearson, of Adrogue, Argentina, and

has issue living, Edward John Stevenson *b.* 1950,—Frederick Euan (Vicente Lopez 386, Tigre, Prov. of Buenos Aires, Argentina), *b.* 1924; 1939-45 War with Fleet Air Arm: *m.* 1954, Vera Margaret yst. da. of the late Gavin Greig Watson,—Nigel Hugh (Av. San Lorenzo 57 (E), Concordia FCNGU, Prov. Entre Rios, Argentina), *b.* 1926; 1939-45 War in Far East, with R. Armoured Corps: *m.* 1953, Beryl Francis, el. da. of John Robert Anderson, and has issue living, Christopher John *b.* 1955, Elizabeth Vivian *b.* 1959,—Clare Antoinette, *b.* 1922; 1939-45 War with WAAF.——Gerald Ian, *MC, ED* (of Constantia Hill Farm, Constantia, Cape Province, S. Africa), *b.* 1898; ed. at Sedbergh; Lt.-Col. (ret.) comdg. Calcutta Light Horse; 1914-18 War with RFA (gassed, MC), 1939-45 War attached Indian Army: *m.* 1931, Paula Elsie Barbara, da. of the late Cuthbert Henry Gordon, of Bihar, India, and has issue living, Celia, *b.* 1934: *m.* 1961, Robert Edmund Scott Hanbury, of Drumstinchall, Dalbeattie, Kirkcudbrightshire, and has issue living, Roland William Edmund *b.* 1964, Melanie Rhona *b.* 1967.

Grandchildren of the late Cdr. William Maitland-Dougall (infra):—
Issue of the late Lt.-Col. Wilmot Edward Maitland-Dougall, DSO, MC, *b.* 1890, *d.* 1972: *m.* 1st, 1930, Mary Louisa, who *d.* 1959, da. of Capt. Arthur Schreiber, of Brook's Hall, Ipswich; 2ndly, 1960, Hilda (Mullins Mead, Donhead St. Mary, Shaftesbury, Dorset), widow of Lt.-Col. J. R. H. Baddeley:—
(By 1st m.) Colin (Grangehill, Kinghorn, Fife), *b.* 1933; Lt.-Cdr. RN: *m.* 1964, Philippa Blackstone, da. of Cdr. G. H. Wise, RN, of Titchfield, Hants.——Eve Diana, *b.* 1936: *m.* 1959, Maj. Arthur John French, R. Irish Rangers [E. Lauderdale, colls.], and has issue living, Miles Arthur Maitland, *b.* 1961,—Dominick George Maitland, *b.* 1970,—Amelia Mary Katherine, *b.* 1963.

Granddaughter of the late Adm. William Heriot Maitland-Dougall, 2nd son of James Maitland-Heriot of Ramornie (b. 1774) (ante):—
Issue of the late Cdr. William Maitland-Dougall, *b.* 1852, *d.* 1916: *m.* 1886, Charlotte Isabella, who *d.* 1953, da. of the late Capt. Frederick King [E. Lovelace, colls.]:—
Ethel Clare, *b.* 1898: *m.* 1954, Capt. Evelyn Twysden Wickham, OBE, RN (ret.). *Residence,—*

Branch from 9th son of 6th Earl.

Grandchildren of the late Brig.-Gen. James Dalgleish Heriot-Maitland, CMG, DSO (infra):—
Issue of the late Richard Ogilvy Heriot Maitland, JP, DL, *b.* 1913, *d.* 1972: *m.* 1935, Patricia (Errol Park, Errol, Perthshire), el. da. of the late Lt.-Col. Cecil Bevis:—
Lewis Dalgleish, *b.* 1943; ed. at Winchester.——Patrick Richard, *b.* 1947; ed. at Wellington.——Mary Lorne, *b.* 1945.

Granddaughter of the late Maj.-Gen. Sir James Makgill HERIOT-MAITLAND, KCB, yst. son of James Maitland-Heriot Dalgleish, of Ramornie (b. 1774) (ante):—
Issue of the late Brig.-Gen. James Dalgleish Heriot-Maitland, C.M.G., D.S.O., *b.* 1874, *d.* 1958: *m.* 1903, (Lady) Mary Turner, who *d.* 1937, dau. of the late Henry Scrymgeour-Wedderburn, *de jure* 9th Earl of Dundee (Hereditary Standard Bearer of Scotland), of Birkhill, Fife:—
Joan Margaret, (White House of Aros, Isle of Mull), *b.* 1909.

Grandson of Lt.-Gen. John Maitland, only son of Hon. Patrick Maitland, 7th son of 6th Earl:—
Issue of the late Patrick Lauderdale Maitland, *b.* 1862, *d.* 1939: *m.* 1904: Julia Elizabeth, who *d.* 1953, dau. of the late George May, of Cleveland, Ohio, U.S.A.:—
Lawrence Lauderdale, *b.* 1905; ed. at Ackworth Sch., and at Sheffield Univ.; Major (retired) late Gordon Highlanders, and an Engineer. *Residence,—*The Old Rectory, Thistleton, Oakham, LE15 7RE.

PREDECESSORS.—[1] *Sir* JOHN Maitland, Knt., Keeper of the Privy Seal 1567, and a Lord of Session 1568-70, when his office was forfeited for his adhesion to the Queen's party; appointed a Lord of Session 1581, constituted a Sec. of State for life 1584, and Keeper of the Great Seal of Scotland for life with title of Vice Chancellor 1586; cr. *Lord Maitland of Thirlestane* (peerage of Scotland) 1590; *d.* 1595; *s.* by his son [2] JOHN, 2nd Lord; was a Lord of Session and Pres. of the Council; cr. *Viscount of Lauderdale* (peerage of Scotland) 1616, with remainder to his heirs male and successors in the Lordship of Thirlestane, and *Lord Thirlestane and Boltoun, Viscount Maitland* and *Earl of Lauderdale* (peerage of Scotland), 1624 with remainder to his heirs male bearing the name and arms of Maitland; *d.* 1645; *s.* by his el. son [3] JOHN, 2nd Earl, K.G., P.C., a zealous partizan of Charles II. and one of the historic personages of his time; was a Commr. appointed by the Church of Scotland to meet the assembly of Divines at Westminster 1643, and was several times employed as a Parliamentary Commr.; taken prisoner at battle of Worcester 1651 and was confined in the Tower until 1660; for his fidelity to the king he was made Sec. of State, Pres. of the Council, Heritable High Sheriff of co. Edinburgh, an Extraordinary Lord of Session, First Commr. of the Treasury, Lord High Commr. to the Parliament, and Gov. of Edinburgh Castle; cr. *Marquess of March* and *Duke of Lauderdale* (peerage of Scotland) 1672, and *Baron Petersham* and *Earl of Guilford* (peerage of England) 1674; *d.* 1682, when all the peerages conferred upon himself became extinct and the other honours reverted to his brother [4] CHARLES, 3rd Earl; was Gen. of the Mint, and Dep. Treasurer and a Judge of the Court of Session; *d.* 1691; *s.* by his el. son [5] RICHARD, K.B., P.C., 4th Earl; was Gen. of the Mint, and Lord Justice Gen. 1681-4; outlawed 1694 for his adhesion to the cause of James II.; *d.s.p.* 1695; *s.* by his brother [6] JOHN, 5th Earl; cr. a *Baronet* of Nova Scotia 1680; M.P. for co. Edinburgh 1685; a Lord of Session with title of Lord Ravelrig 1689-1710; *d.* 1710; *s.* by his son [7] CHARLES, 6th Earl, a Representative Peer, Master of the Mint, and Lord-Lieut. of co. Edinburgh; *d.* 1744; *s.* by his son [8] JAMES, 7th Earl, a Representative Peer; *d.* 1789; *s.* by his son [9] JAMES, 8th Earl; cr. *Baron Lauderdale*, of Thirlestane, co. Berwick (peerage of United Kingdom) 1806; *d.* 1839; *s.* by his el. son [10] JAMES, 9th Earl; M.P. for Appleby 1820-31, and Lord-Lieut. of co. Berwick; *d.* unmarried 1860; *s.* by his brother [11] ANTHONY, G.C.B., K.C.M.G., 10th Earl; an Adm. of the Red; *d.* 1863, when the English barony expired, and the other peerages devolved upon his cousin [12] THOMAS, G.C.B., 11th Earl, son of Gen. the Hon. William Mordaunt Maitland, 3rd son of 7th Earl; a Representative Peer, and Adm. of the Fleet, &c.; *d.* 1878; *s.* by his kinsman [13] CHARLES, 12th Earl, who *d.* Aug. 1884; *s.* by his kinsman [14] FREDERICK HENRY (son of the late Gen. Frederick Colthurst Maitland, son of the late Patrick Maitland, 2nd son of Col. the Hon. Richard Maitland, 4th son of 6th Earl), 13th Earl, *b.* 1840; established his claim to the title before Committee for Privileges of the House of Lords, July 1885; Lord-Lieut. of Berwickshire 1889-1901; for 31 years a Representative Peer for Scotland: *m.* 1st, 1864, Charlotte Sarah, who *d.* 1879, dau. of the late Lieut.-Col. Sleigh (77th Regt.); 2ndly, 1883, Ada Twyford, who *d.* 1931, dau. of the late Rev. Henry Trail Simpson, R. of Adel, York; *d.* 1924; *s.* by his son [15] FREDERICK COLIN, O.B.E., 14th Earl, *b.* 1868; a Representative Peer for Scotland, one of H.M.'s Hon, Corps of Gentlemen-of-Arms, and Ensign Roy. Co. of Archers (King's Body Guard for Scotland): *m.* 1890, Gwendoline Lucy, who *d.* 1929, dau. of the late Judge R. Vaughan Williams, of Bodlonfa, Flintshire; *d.* 1931; *s.* by his son [16] IAN COLIN, 15th Earl; *b.* 1891; a Member of Queen's Body Guard for Scotland (Roy. Co. of Archers); was A.D.C. to Viceroy of Ireland 1915-16 and 1918: *m.* 1912, Ethel Mary, who *d.* 1970, dau. of James Jardine Bell-Irving, of Makerstoun House, Kelso; *d.* 1953; *s.* by his cousin [17] *Rev.* ALFRED SYDNEY FREDERICK (son of the late Rev. the Hon. Sydney George William Maitland, 2nd son of

13th Earl), 16th Earl, *b.* 1904: *m.* 1st, 1938, Norah Mary, who *d.* 1938, da. of the late William Henry La Touche; 2ndly, 1940, Irene Alice May, da. of the late Rev. O. P. Shipton, of Halsham, Yorks.; *d.* 1968; *s.* by his brother [18] PATRICK FRANCIS, 17th Earl and present peer; also Viscount of Lauderdale, Viscount Maitland, Lord Maitland of Thirlestane, and Lord Thirlestane and Boltoun.

LAWRENCE, BARON. (Lawrence.) [Baron U.K. 1869, Bt. U.K. 1858.]

BE READY

DAVID JOHN DOWNER LAWRENCE, 5th Baron and 5th Baronet; *b.* Sept. 4th, 1937; *s.* 1968.

Arms,—Ermine, on a cross raguly gules an Eastern crown or ; a chief azure, thereon two swords in saltire proper, pommels and hilts gold, between as many leopards' faces argent. **Crest,**—Out of an Eastern crown or, a cubit arm entwined by a wreath of laurel and holding a dagger all proper. **Supporters,**— *Dexter,* an officer of the Guide Cavalry (Irregulars), of the Pathan tribe, in the province of Peshawar, habited and accoutred proper; *sinister,* an officer of the Sikh Irregular Cavalry, also habited and accoutred proper

Address,—2, Gray's Inn Sq., WC1.

AUNTS LIVING. *(Daughters of 3rd Baron.)*
Hon. Catherine Dorina Mary, *b.* 1910. } *Residence,*—The Lodge, 10, Broadwater Down, Tunbridge
Hon. Sara Honoria Angel, *b.* 1912. } Wells.
Hon. Nona Georgette, *b.* 1922: *m.* 1945, Wing.-Com. Vincent George Byrne, R.A.F., and has issue living, Nicholas John Joseph (Tudor Cottage, Broadoak, Sussex), *b.* 1946: *m.* 1968, Catherine Penelope, da. of Douglas Smith, and has issue living, Kirstie Mary Kate *b.* 1969, Tara Mary *b.* 1971,— James Vincent, *b.* 1950: *m.* 1975, Juliet Elizabeth Anson, da. of John Bailey of Bramshaw Lodge, Lyndhurst,—Vincent Patrick, *b.* 1952.—Dominic Lawrence, *b.* 1959.—Rory Shaun, *b.* 1961.—Teresa Marie, *b.* 1947: *m.* 1968, Robin Herbert Wickham, of Wykeham Oast, Brenchley, Kent, and has issue living, Simon James Wykeham *b.* 1969, Patrick David Wykeham *b.* 1972,—Clare Mary Anne, *b.* 1955,—Fiona Rosaleen Mary, *b.* 1957. *Residence,*—Raughmere Rise, East Lavant, Chichester, W. Sussex, PO18 0AD.

MOTHER LIVING.
Margaret Jean (Ann Cottage, The Circle, E. Preston, Littlehampton), da. of Arthur Downer, of Marshalls, Kirdford, Sussex: *m.* 1st, 1936, the 4th Baron, who *d.* 1968, and from whom she obtained a divorce 1947; 2ndly, 1947, Neil Hartley, and from whom she obtained a divorce 1960.

WIDOW LIVING OF FOURTH BARON.
JOAN ALICE MILDRED, da. of the late Col. Arthur John Lewer, OBE, of Bonchurch, I. of Wight: *m.* 1st, 1948, as his 2nd wife, the 4th Baron, who *d.* 1968; 2ndly, 1969, John Eddison of 143, Longland Drive, Totteridge, N20 8HN.

COLLATERAL BRANCH LIVING.
Issue of the late Gen. the Hon. Sir Herbert Alexander Lawrence, G.C.B., **4th son** of 1st Baron, *b.* 1861, *d.* 1943: *m.* 1892. the Hon. Isabel Mary Mills, who *d.* 1941, el. dau. of 1st Baron Hillingdon:—
Elizabeth Barbara Peace, *b.* 1902; is J.P. for Bucks: *m.* 1923, Major Desmond Abel Smith, MC, Gren. Gds., who *d.* 1974, and has issue living, John Lawrence Abel (Hartwell End House, Hartwell, Northants.), *b.* 1934: *m.* 1970, Caroline Bridget, da. of the late Capt. Howard Bennett Bartlam, and has issue living, Alexander Howard Lawrence *b.* 1971, Oliver Desmond *b.* 1974,—June Isabel, *b.* 1924,—Elisabeth Ann, *b.* 1929: *m.* 1961, Denis H. A. Lewey, who *d.* 1974, son of Sir Arthur Werner Lewey,—Catherine Clare, *b.* 1938: *m.* 1970, Ian Maclean. *Residence,*—Hampden Old Rectory, Gt. Missenden, Bucks.

PREDECESSORS.—[1] *Rt. Hon. Sir* JOHN LAIRD MAIR LAWRENCE, G.C.B., G.C.S.I., P.C. D.C.L., LL.D., 5th son of the late Lieut.-Col. Alexander Lawrence, Gov. of Upton Castle Kent, *b.* 1811; entered Bengal Civil Ser. 1828, and having held numerous minor positions became Commr. of the Jullunder Doab 1846, and was subsequently Member of Board of Administration for the Punjab 1849-52, Chief Commr. of the Punjab 1852-8, First Lt.-Gov. of that province 1858-9, Viceroy of India 1864-8, and Chm. of London School Board 1870-3; cr. a *Baronet* 1858, and *Baron Lawrence,* of the Punjab, and of Grateley, co. Southampton 1869; *m.* 1841, Harriette Katherine, C.I., who *d.* 1917, dau. of the Rev. Richard Hamilton ; *d.* 1879; *s.* by his son [2] JOHN HAMILTON, 2nd Baron, *b.* 1846 ; Lord-in-Waiting to Queen Victoria 1895-1901, and to King Edward VII. 1901-5: *m.* 1872, Mary Caroline Douglas, who *d.* 1938, only dau. of the late Richard Campbell, of Auchinbreck and Glencarradle, Argyllshire; *d.* 1913; *s.* by his son [3] ALEXANDER GRAHAM, 3rd Baron, *b.* 1878: *m.* 1st, 1907, Dorothy Helen, C.B.E., who *d.* 1935, dau. of the late Anthony Pemberton Hobson, many years Inspector-Gen. of Police, St.Vincent, W. Indies: 2ndly, 1935, Jessie, who *d.* 1936, dau. of the late Col. Byron Gordon Daniels, US Army, and widow of William Frederic Lawrence, of Cowesfield House, Wilts; 3rdly, 1938, Catherine Louisa, who *d.* 1965, da. of the late Charles Fernihough, and widow of William Burnet Craigie; *d.* (June) 1947; *s.* by his son [4] JOHN ANTHONY EDWARD, 4th Baron, *b.* 1908: *m.* 1st, 1936 (m. diss. (July) 1947), Margaret Jean, da. of Arthur Downer, of Rotherfield, Kent; 2ndly, 1948, Joan Alice Mildred (who *m.* 2ndly, 1969, John Eddison), da. of Maj. Arthur John Lewer, OBE, of Norwood Green, Middx.; *d.* 1968; *s.* by his son [5] DAVIS JOHN DOWNER, 5th Baron and present peer.

LAWSON, BARONY. (Lawson.) [Extinct 1965.]

DAUGHTERS LIVING OF FIRST AND LAST BARON.

Hon. Irene, *b.* 1909: *m.* 1935, Charles Frederick Campbell Lawson, and has issue living, Ruth Ellison, *b.* 1936,—Elizabeth Graham, *b.* 1943,—Elaine Campbell, *b.* 1944. *Residence,*—Dourene, Park Road North, Chester-le-Street, co. Durham.

Hon. Edna, *b.* 1912: *m.* 19—, D. Brown, and has issue living, David, *b.* 1945. *Residence,*—

Hon. Alma, *b.* 1920.

WIDOW LIVING OF FIRST AND LAST BARON.

ISABELLA (*Baroness Lawson*), (7, Woodside, Beamish, co. Durham), da. of John Scott, of Newcastle: *m.* 1906, the 1st Baron, who *d.* 1965, when the title became ext.

LAYTON, BARON. (Layton.) [Baron U.K. 1947.]

MICHAEL JOHN LAYTON, 2nd Baron; *b.* Sept. 28th, 1912; *s.* 1966; ed. at St. Paul's Sch., and Gonville and Caius Coll., Camb.: *m.* 1938, Dorothy, da. of A. L. Cross, of Rugby, and has issue.

Residence,—6, Old Palace Terr., Richmond Green, Surrey.

SON LIVING.

Hon. GEOFFREY MICHAEL, *b.* July 18th, 1947: *m.* 1969, (m. diss. 1970), Viviane, da. of François Cracco, of Louvain, Belgium.

DAUGHTER LIVING.

Hon. Deanna Christine, *b.* 1938; MB, BS, MRCS, LRCP: *m,* 1964, Melvin Calverley Jennings, MB, FRCS, of 66 Blackborough Rd., Reigate, Surrey.

BROTHERS LIVING.

Hon. David, *MBE* (Syskon Cottage, 18 Grove Terr. Highgate Rd., NW5), *b.* 1914: ed. at Gresham's Sch., Holt, and at Trin. Coll., Camb.; MBE (Mil.) 1946; *m.* 1st, 1939 (m. diss. 1972), Elizabeth, da. of Robert Gray; 2ndly, 1972, Joy Parkinson, and has issue living (by 1st m), Jonathan Francis, *b.* 1942: *m.* 1972, Julie Goodwin,—Mark Oliver, *b.* 1944,—Hilary Ruth, *b.* 1947.

Hon. Christopher Walter, *b.* 1929 ; ed. at Oundle, and at King's Coll., Camb. : *m.* 1st, 1952 (marriage dissolved 1957) Annaliese Margaret, dau. of Joachim von Thadden, of Hanover; 2ndly, 1961. Margaret Ann, dau. of Leslie Moon, of Molesey, Surrey, and has issue living, (by 1st marriage, John Stephen, *b.* 1955,—Diana, *b.* 1953,—(by 2nd m.) Eleanor Rachel, *b.* 1963,—Sarah Jean *b.* 1964,—Lesley Claire, *b.* 1971. *Residence,*—Avenue Albert Lancester, 95 B, 1080, Brussels, Belgium.

SISTERS LIVING.

Hon. Jean Mary, *b.* 1916: *m.* 1944, Paul Eisler, who *d.* 1966, and has issue living, John, *b.* 1946,—Ivan, *b.* 1948: *m.* 1971, Zuzana Tibenska, of Bratislava, Czechoslovakia. *Residences,*—6, Frani Sramka, Prague, 5, Czechoslovakia; 10, Millfield Lane, N6.

Hon. Olive Shirley, *b.* 1918: *m.* 1943, Peter Gellhorn, and has issue living, Martin, *b.* 1945: *m.* 1969, Susanna Elizabeth, da. of Thomas Howard Beauchamp Gladstone, MB, BS, of Ilkeston, Derbys., and has issue living, Catherine *b.* 1969,—Philip, *b.* 1951,—Mary Ann, *b.* 1959,—Barbara Dorothea, *b.* 1960. *Residence,*—33, Leinster Av., SW14.

Hon. Elizabeth Ruth Frances, *b.* 1923: *m.* 1944 (m. diss. 1965), Bobbie Pegna, and has issue living, Robin, *b.* 1945: *m.* 1968, Catherine Bridget Gray, da. of John Henderson, of Greenwood, Frant, Sussex,—Christopher John, *b.* 1956,—Shirley, *b.* 1951. *Residence,*—Whitegates, Chedworth, Cheltenham.

PREDECESSOR.—[1] WALTER THOMAS Layton, *CH, CBE*, son of Alfred John Layton, of Woking, Surrey; *b.* 1884; Editor, *The Economist* 1922-38, and Chm. 1944-63, Chm. News Chronicle Ltd. 1930-50, and Star Newspaper Co. Ltd. 1936-50; Head of Joint War Production Staff and Ch. Adviser on Programmes and Planning, Min. of Production 1942-43, and Vice-Pres. of Assembly of Council of Europe 1949-57: *m.* 1910, Eleanor Dorothea, who *d.* 1959, da. of Francis Beresford Plumtre Osmaston, of Stoneshill, Limpsfield, Surrey: *d.* 1966; *s.* by his el. son [2] MICHAEL JOHN, 2nd Baron and present peer.

LEATHERLAND, BARON. (Leatherland.) [Life Baron 1964.]

CHARLES EDWARD LEATHERLAND, *OBE, MSM,* son of the late John Edward Leatherland, of Churchover, Warwicks.; *b.* April 18th, 1898; ed. at Harborne Sch., Birmingham; a JP of Essex (Alderman 1946-68); Treasurer of Univ. of Essex (D. Univ.), and Vice-Chm. of Univ. of Essex Promotion Cttee.; Assist. Editor of *Daily Herald* 1951-63, and Chm. of Essex co. Council 1960-61 (Vice-Chm. 1952-55 and 1958-60); a Member of Essex T & AF Assocn. 1946-68, and of E. Anglia TA & VR Assocn. 1968; a Member of Basildon New Town Development Corpn. 1967-71; Additional Member of Monopolies Commn. to Consider Newspaper Mergers 1969; 1914-18 War as Co. Sgt. Maj. R. Warwickshire Regt. (MSM despatches); *cr.* OBE (Civil) 1951, and Baron Leatherland, of Dunton, co. Essex (Life Baron) 1964: *m.* 1922, Mary Elizabeth, da. of Joseph Henry Morgan, of Shareshill, Staffs., and has issue.

Arms.—Gules a pen point downwards and a sword point upwards proper hilt and pomel or in saltire between in pale two open books proper edged or bound azure and in fess two roses argent barbed and seeded proper. Crest.—On a chapeau gules turned up ermine, and in front of an arm embowed vested azure cuffed gules the hand proper grasping a trumpet or a seax fesswise proper hilt and pomel or. Supporters,—On either side an heraldic antelope sable armed and crined and unguled or and gorged with a baron's coronet proper with chain reflexed over the back or pendent from the coronet a seax as in the crest.

Residence,—19, Starling Close, Buckhurst Hill, Essex.

SON LIVING.

Hon. John Charles (4, Manor Way, Chingford, E4), *b.* 1929; ed. at Brentwood; *m.* 1954, Esther Stella Steckman, and has issue.

DAUGHTER LIVING.

Hon. Irene Mary, *b.* 1923: *m.* 1961, Douglas Richards, of 19, The Greens Close, Loughton, Essex, and has issue.

LEATHERS, VISCOUNT. (Leathers.) [Viscount U.K. 1954.]

FREDERICK ALAN LEATHERS 2nd Viscount; *b.* April 4th, 1908; *s.* 1965; ed. at Brighton Coll., and at Emmanuel Coll., Camb.; Chm. of Wm. Cory & Son, Ltd.: *m.* 1940, Elspeth Graeme, da. of the late Sir Thomas Alexander Stewart, KCSI, KCIE, and has issue.

Arms,—Azure, a lymphad, sails set or, flags flying to the dexter gules, on a chief of the second three lozenges sable. Crest,—A lozenge sable in front of two anchors in saltire or. Supporters,— *Dexter,* a sea-lion; *sinister,* a sea horse argent gorged with a collar of lozenges conjoined sable.

Residence,—Hills Green, Kirdford, Sussex.

While I breathe I serve.

SONS LIVING.

Hon. CHRISTOPHER GRAEME, *b.* Aug. 31st, 1941: *m.* 1964, Maria Philomena, yr. da. of Michael Merriman, of Charlestown, co. Mayo, and has issue living, James Frederick, *b.* 1969,—Melissa Maria, *b.* 1966.

Hon. Jeremy Baxter (1, Burnsall St., SW3) *b.* 1946: *m.* 1969, Fiona Lesley, el. da. of G. S. Pitt, of Rowbarns Manor, Horsley, Surrey.

DAUGHTERS LIVING.

Hon. Anne Catherine, *b.* 1944.

Hon. Deborah Elspeth, *b.* 1947: *m.* 1966, Thomas Richard Chadbon, of 83, Elm Bank Gdns., Barnes, SW13, and has issue living, Dominic Thomas, *b.* 1966,—Nicholas Richard, *b.* 1968.

BROTHER LIVING.

Hon. Leslie John, *b.* 1911; ed. at Brighton Coll.; admitted a Solicitor 1935; is Maj. late RA: *m.* 1937, Elizabeth Stella, only da. of Thomas Stanley Nash, of Sidcup, and has issue living, Michael John Nash (14, Warrangi St., Turramurra, NSW 2074), *b.* 1938: *m.* 1962, Shelley Matthews, da. of the late Keith Marten, of Gedgrave Hall, Orford, Suffolk, and has issue living, Simon Michael John *b.* 1964, Sean Patrick James *b.* 1966, Richard Anthony *b.* 1968, Benjamin Matthew *b.* 1971,—David Frederick James (14, Holmead Rd., SW6 2JG), *b.* 1942: *m.* 1968, Amanda Elizabeth Ann Vyvyan, da. of Lt.-Col. Arthur Vyvyan Denton, of Dial House, Lower Bourne, Farnham [see Strickland Constable, Bt., colls.], and has issue living, Jonathan James, *b.* 1974,—Rosemary Elizabeth, *b.* 1945: *m.* 1972, Winfried F. W. Bischoff. *Residence,*—Firs House, Lindfield, Sussex.

SISTER LIVING.

Hon. Audrey Mary, *b.* 1915: *m.* 1938, Edward Noel Evans, who *d.* 1964, and has issue living, Richard Edward Craig, *b.* 1945: *m.* 1973, Jillian Sonia, yr. da. of the late H. W. Reid,—Peter James, *b.* 1946,—Jacqueline Mary, *b.* 1940: *m.* 1st, 1961 (m. diss. 1969), Barrington Hugh Lawes; 2ndly, 1969, Michael Hind, of Hill Hall, Little Bardfield, nr. Braintree, Essex, and has issue living, (by 1st m.) Nicholas Hugh *b.* 1962, Suzanna Jane *b.* 1964, (by 2nd m.) Sally Louise *b.* 1970. *Residences,*—28, Hyde Park Gdns., W2; 6, Cunliffe Close, West Wittering, Sussex.

PREDECESSOR,—[1] FREDERICK JAMES Leathers, CH, PC, son of Robert Leathers, of Stowmarket, Suffolk; *b.* 1883; Min. of War Transport 1941-45, and Sec. of State for Co-ordination of Transport Fuel and Power 1951-53; cr. *Baron Leathers,* of Purfleet, co. Essex (Peerage of UK) 1941, and *Viscount Leathers,* of Purfleet, co. Essex (Peerage of UK) 1954: *m.* 1907, Emily Ethel, who *d.* 1971, da. of the late Henry Baxter, of Southend; *d.* 1965; *s.* by his el. son [2] FREDERICK ALAN, 2nd Viscount and present peer; also Baron Leathers.

LECONFIELD, BARON, see Baron Egremont.

LEE OF ASHERIDGE, BARONESS. (Bevan) [Life Baroness 1970.]

JENNIE BEVAN, *PC,* da. of James Lee, of Lochgelly, Fifeshire; *b.* Nov. 3rd, 1904; ed. at Moray House Coll., Beath High Sch., and Edinburgh Univ. (MA, LLB); MP for N. Lanark 1929-31, and for Cannock, Staffs. (*Lab.*) 1945-70; Parl. Sec., Min. of Public Building & Works 1964-65, Parl. Under-Sec. of State, Dept. of Educ. & Science 1965-67, and Min. of State of same 1967-70; Chm. of Nat. Exec. Cttee., Labour Party 1966-67; cr. PC 1966, and *Baroness Lee of Asheridge,* of the City of Westminster, (Life Baroness) 1970: *m.* 1934, the Rt. Hon. Aneurin Bevan, MP, who *d.* 1960.

Residence,—67, Chester Row, SW1.

LEE OF NEWTON, BARON. (Lee.) [Life Baron 1974.]

FREDERICK LEE, *PC,* son of Joseph William Lee; *b.* Aug. 3rd, 1906; ed. at Langworthy Rd. Council of Labour Coll.; a JP for Salford; PPS to Paymaster-Gen., and to Min. of Economic Affairs 1947-48, and to Chancellor of Exchequer 1948-50, Parl. Sec. to Min. of Labour and National Ser. 1950-51, and a Member of UK Delegation to Council of Europe 1949; Min. of Power 1964-66, Sec. of State for the Colonies 1966-67, and Chancellor of Duchy of Lancaster 1967-69; MP for Hulme Div. of Manchester (*Lab.*) 1945-50, and Newton Div. of Lancs. 1950-74; cr. PC 1964, and *Baron Lee of Newton,* of Newton, Co. of Merseyside (Life Baron) 1974: *m.* 1938, Amelia, da. of William Shay, and has issue.

Residence,—52, Ashton Rd., Newton-le-Willows, Merseyside, WA12 0AE.

DAUGHTER LIVING.

Hon. Pamela Margaret, *b.* 1945: *m.* 1965, Rodney Owen Flint, of 36, High St., Newton-le-Willows, Merseyside, EA12 0AE.

LEEDS, DUKEDOM OF. (Osborne.) [Extinct 1964.]

DAUGHTER LIVING OF ELEVENTH DUKE.

Lady Camilla Dorothy Godolphin (21, Markham Sq., SW3), *b.* 1950: *m.* 1971, Robert Julian Brownlow Harris [see B. Harris, colls.].

DAUGHTER LIVING OF TENTH DUKE.

Lady Moira Godolphin (*Lady Moira Lyttelton*), *b.* 1892: *m.* 1920, the 1st Viscount Chandos, who *d.* 1972. *Residence,*—Flat 4, Harrowby Court, Harrowby St., W1.

WIDOW LIVING OF ELEVENTH DUKE.

CAROLINE FLEUR (Flat 1, 34, St. Marks Rd., St. Helier, Jersey; 23, Rue Claude Ydrone, Lectoure, Gers, France), yr. da. of the late Col. Henry Monckton Vatcher, MC, of Valeran, St. Brelade's, Jersey: *m.* 1st, 1955, as his 3rd wife, the 11th Duke, who *d.* 1963; 2ndly, 1968 (m. diss. 1975), Peter Hendrik Peregrine Hoos [see B. Brownlow].

LEICESTER, EARL OF. (Coke.) [Earl U.K. 1837.]

[Name pronounced "**Cook.**"]

THOMAS WILLIAM EDWARD COKE, *M.V.O.*, 5th Earl; *b.* May 16th, 1908; *s.* 1949; ed. at Eton; Maj. (ret.) Scots Guards, Hon. Col. 1st Batn. (Cadets), R. Norfolk Regt.; a DL for Norfolk; an Equerry to HRH Duke of York 1934-36, and an Extra Equerry to HM King George VI 1936-52, since when to HM Queen Elizabeth II; a Dir. of Roy. Insurance Co., and a Gov. of Gresham's Sch.; Pres. Norfolk Agricultural Assocn. 1958, and of Norfolk Branch, Country Landowners' Assocn. 1958-61; 1939-45 War (ADC to F.M. the Earl Wavell, KG, 1941); Order of George 1st of Greece; MVO (4th class) 1937: *m.* 1931, Lady Elizabeth Mary Yorke, DCVO, da. of 8th Earl of Hardwicke, and has issue.

Arms,—Per line gules and azure, three eagles displayed argent. **Crest,**—On a chapeau azure, turned up ermine, an ostrich argent, holding in its mouth a horse-shoe. **Supporters,**—On either side an ostrich argent, that on the *dexter* gorged with a ducal coronet per pale gules and azure, line reflexed over the back of the first; that on the *sinister* gorged with a like coronet, per pale azure and gules, and line reflexed over the back azure.

He is prudent who is patient

Residence,—Holkham Hall, Norfolk.

DAUGHTERS LIVING.

Lady Anne Veronica, *b.* 1932; an Extra Lady-in-Waiting to HRH The Princess Margaret, Countess of Snowdon, since 1971: *m.* 1956, the Hon. Colin Christopher Paget Tennant, el. son of 2nd Baron Glenconner. *Residences,*—35, Tite St., SW3 ; The Glen, Innerleithen, Peeblesshire.

Lady Carey Elizabeth, *b.* 1934: *m.* 1960, Bryan Ronald Basset [see E. Dartmouth]. *Residences,*—10, Stack House, Cundy St., SW1; Quarles, Wells-next-Sea, Norfolk.

Lady Sarah Marion, *b.* 1944: *m.* 1970, Maj. David Finlayson Wylie Hill Walter, late Scots Gds., of Westwood, Balthayock, by Perth, and has issue living, Nicholas Robert, *b.* 1972,—James George, *b.* 1975.

SISTERS LIVING.

Lady Silvia Beatrice (The Manor House, Burnham Thorpe, Kings Lynn), *b.* 1909; is a JP: *m.* 1932, Capt. Simon Harvey Combe, MC, Irish Guards, who *d.* 1965, and has issue living, Robin Harvey (Mill House, Glandford, Holt, Norfolk), *b.* 1934; Lt. RN: *m.* 1960, Olga, da. of R. J. Wise, of Bridgend, Glam., and has issue living, Roger Mark Harvey *b.* 1960, Simon Reginald *b.* 1962, Carey Romaine *b.* 1964, Silvia *b.* 1967,—Rowena Marion, *b.* 1935: *m.* 1963, Jocelyn Rupert Rowland Geoffrey Feilding, of 9, Syon Rd., Twickenham, Middlesex [see E. Denbigh, colls.].

Lady Mary Katherine, *b.* 1920; a Woman of the Bedchamber to H.M. Queen Elizabeth the Queen Mother 1961-63: *m.* 1940, Maj. Thomas Cockayne Harvey, C.V.O., D.S.O., Scots Guards (ret.) [Skipwith, Bt., colls.], and has issue living, David Vincent, *b.* 1941: *m.* 1969, Kathleen, da. of Henry Blaise, of Brussels, and has issue living, Alicia *b.* 1970, Natalie *b.* 1972,—Caroline Susan, *b.* 1943: *m.* 1975, Nicholas Raison,—Juliet Mary Elizabeth, *b.* 1947: *m.* 1969, Maurizio Grana, and has issue living, Francesco Oliver *b.* 1970, Marina *b.* 1973. *Residences,*—Warham House, Warham Wells, Norfolk; 93, Eaton Pl., SW1.

AUNT LIVING. (*Daughter of 3rd Earl.*)

Lady Alexandra Marie Bridget (*Dowager Countess of Airlie*) *b.* 1891: *m.* 1917, the 12th Earl of Airlie, who *d.* 1968. *Residence,*—Airlie Castle, Angus.

WIDOWS LIVING OF SONS OF SECOND EARL.

Elizabeth Vera Catherine Alice (10, Knight St., Walsingham, Norfolk), da. of the late Louis-Leopold M. B. de Beaumont [B. O'Hagan]: *m.* 1932, as his 2nd wife, Maj. the Hon. Richard Coke, who *d.* 1964, and has issue living [see colls. infra].

Katharine (14, Chesham Pl., SW1), da. of the late Hon. Edward Alan Dudley Ryder [see E. Harrowby, colls.]: *m.* 1924, Capt. the Hon. Reginald Coke, DSO, who *d.* 1969, and has issue living [see colls., infra].

WIDOW LIVING OF SON OF THIRD EARL.

Phyllis Hermione (*Lady Howard-Vyse*), dau. of the late Francis Saxham E. Drury, formerly of 50, Pont Street, S.W.: *m.* 1st, 1906, Lieut. the Hon. Arthur George Coke, R.N.V.R., who *d.* (killed in action) 1915, having served in Flanders with Household Cav. 1914 : 2ndly, 1925, Maj.-Gen. Sir Richard Granville Hylton Howard-Vyse, K.C.M.G., D.S.O., who *d.* 1962, and has issue living (by 1st marriage) [see colls., infra]. *Residence,*—60, Kingston House, Prince's Gate, S.W.7.

COLLATERAL BRANCHES LIVING.

Issue of the late Lieut. the Hon. Arthur George Coke, 2nd son of 3rd Earl, *b.* 1882, *d.* (killed in action) 1915: *m.* 1906, Phyllis Hermione [(ante) : she **m.** 2ndly, 1925, Maj.-Gen. Sir Richard Granville Hylton Howard-Vyse, K.C.M.G., D.S.O.], dau. of the late Francis Saxham E. Drury, formerly of 50, Pont Street, S.W.1:—

ANTHONY LOVEL, *b.* Sept. 11th, 1909; 1940-45 War in RAF: *m.* 1st, 1934, Moyra Joan Crossley, who obtained a divorce 1947; 2ndly, 1947, Vera Haigh, of Salisbury, Rhodesia, and has issue living, (by 1st m.) Edward Douglas (The Forge House, Burnham Thorpe, Norfolk), *b.* 1936: *m.* 1962, Valerie, el. da. of the late L. A. Potter, of Berkhamsted, Herts., and has issue living, Thomas Edward *b.* 1965, Laura Jane Elizabeth *b.* 1968,—Wenman John (Box 483, Empangeni, Zululand, S. Africa), *b.* 1940: *m.* 1969, Carolyn May Redler, of Cape Town, and has issue living, Anthony Stuart *b.* 1969, Rosalind Elizabeth *b.* 1971,—Almary Bridget, *b.* 1938: *m.* 1963, Peter Ivens-Ferraz, of 33, Sixth Av., Parktown N., Johannesburg, S. Africa, and has issue living, Robyn Ann *b.* 1964, Bronwen Mary *b.* 1965, Penelope Kate *b.* 1967, Caitlin Tessa *b.* 1970.——Diana Merial, *b.* 1907: *m.* 1930, Trevor Moorhouse, who *d.* 1966, and from whom she obtained a divorce 1938, and has issue living, Carolyn, *b.* 1935: *m.* 1961, Emil Landau, of Marsh House, East Wharf Rd., Madison, Conn. 06443, USA, and has issue living, Alexander James *b.* 1969. *Residence,*—1, Stoke Green Cottages, Slough, Bucks.

Issue of the late Maj. the Hon. Richard Coke, Scots Guards, 3rd son of 2nd Earl, *b.* 1876, *d.* 1964: *m.* 1st, 1907, the Hon. Doreen O'Brien (who *d.* 1960, having obtained a divorce 1927), da. of 14th Baron Inchiquin; 2ndly, 1932, Elizabeth Vera Catherine Alice (ante), da. of the late Louis-Leopold M. B. de Beaumont [see B. O'Hagan]:—
(By 1st m.) Richard Lovel, *DSO*, *MC* (Weasenham Hall, King's Lynn, Norfolk), *b.* 1918; ed. at Stowe; 1939-45 War as Maj. Scots Guards, in Italy (MC, DSO); DSO 1945: *m.* 1951, Molly, yr. da. of W. T. Fletcher, of Dorchester, and has issue living, Richard Townshead, *b.* 1954,—Edward Justin *b.* 1961,—Diana Caroline (*Countess of Caithness*), *b.* 1953: *m.* 1975, the 20th Earl of Caithness. ——Hersey (Crowfield House, Crowfield, Ipswich), *b.* 1915: *m.* 1946, Lt.-Col. Peter William Marsham, MBE, Gren. Gds. (ret.), who *d.* 1970 [see E. Romney, colls.].——Bridget Doreen (*Hon. Mrs. Phelim R. H. O'Neill*), *b.* 1924: *m.* 1st, 1943 (m. diss. 1952), Capt. Thomas Richard Edwards-Moss, who *d.* 1974 [see Edwards-Moss, Bt., colls.]; 2ndly, 1953, the Rt. Hon. Phelim Robert Hugh O'Neill, el. son of 1st Baron Rathcavan.——(by 2nd m.) Henry Francis (19B, Belgrave Mews West, SW1), *b.* 1938: *m.* 1966 (m. diss. 1971), Marie Christina Rosalind, da. of Robert McCrone, of Pitliver, by Dumfermline, Fife, and has issue living, Nicola Katherine, *b.* 1967,—Sarah Victoria Dayas, *b.* 1971. ——Mildred Jeanne Caroline, *b.* 1934: *m.* 1966, David Stephen Harms, of 41, Christchurch Hill, Hampstead, NW2, and has issue living, , *b.* 19—,—Jane Mary, *b.* 1967.——Elizabeth Charmian, *b.* 1935: *m.* 1960, Richard Francis Spickernell [Boothby, Bt., colls.], (Bincknoll House, Wootton Bassett, Swindon, Wilts., SN4 8QR), and has issue living, Godfrey John Wenman, *b.* 1962,— James William Richard, *b.* 1965.

Issue of the late Major the Hon. Sir John Spencer Coke, KCVO, Scots Guards, 5th son of 2nd Earl, *b.* 1880, *d.* 1957: *m.* 1907, the Hon. Dorothy Olive Levy-Lawson, who *d.* 1937, da. of 1st Viscount Burnham:—
Gerald Edward, *CBE*, *b.* 1907; ed. at Eton, and New Coll., Oxford (MA); JP and DL for Hants.; Lt-. Col. Scots Guards (ret.); Dir. Roy. Opera House, Covent Garden 1958-64; Chm. Glyndebourne Arts Trust since 1955, Dir. Roy. Acad. of Music 1957-73; a Gov. of BBC 1961-66; CBE (Civil) 1967: *m.* 1939, Patricia, da. of the late Rt. Hon. Sir Alexander George Montagu Cadogan, GCMG, KCB [see E. Cadogan, colls.], and has issue living, John Alexander, *b.* 1946; ed. at Eton,—David Edward, *b.* 1951,—Lavinia Mary, *b.* 1944: *m.* 1967, Peter Raymond Wilson, of Vale Court, Colerne, Chippenham, Wilts., and has issue living, Nicholas *b.* 1971, Andrew Michael *b.* 1974, Miranda Mary *b.* 1969. *Residence,*—Jenkyn Place, Bentley, Hants.; *Club,* Brooks's.——Rosemary Olive (*Baroness Hamilton of Dalzell*), *b.* 1910: *m.* 1935, the 3rd Baron Hamilton of Dalzell. *Residence,*—Snowdenham House, Bramley, Guildford.——Cecilia Dorothy, *b.* 1919: *m.* 1942, Stamp Godfrey Brooksbank, Capt. Coldm. Gds. [see Brooksbank, Bt.]. *Residence,*—Rock Hill House, Hambledon, Godalming, Surrey.

Issue of the late Capt. the Hon. Reginald Coke, DSO, 8th son of 2nd Earl, *b.* 1883, *d.* 1969: *m.* 1924, Katharine (ante), da. of the late Hon. Edward Alan Dudley Ryder [see E. Harrowby, colls.]:—
Mary Margaret (Augustus House, 21, Tite St., SW3) *b.* 1925.——Katharine Vera, *b.* 1927: *m.* 1951, Peter John Cator, of Rowhook Manor, Rowhook, Horsham, Sussex [B. Mostyn, colls.], and has issue living, Charles Henry, *b.* 1952,—Caroline Sarah, *b.* 1954.

Grandchildren of the late Hon. Henry John Coke, 3rd son of 1st Earl :—
Issue (by 3rd marriage) of the late Reginald Grey Coke, *b.* 1864, *d.* 1930: *m.* 1st, 1887, Elizabeth Wilson, who obtained a divorce 1888; 2ndly, 1892, Phyllis Susan (who *d.* 1939, having obtained a divorce 1908), dau. of the late Francis William Bott, of Somersal, Derby; 3rdly, 1909, Galia, who *d.* 1947, dau. of Michael Hambourg, formerly of 2, Clifton Gardens, W. :—
Henry, *b.* 1912: *m.* 1934, Joyce, da. of Gerald E. Rattigan, and has issue living, Basil, *b.* 1935.—— Stella, *b.* (Dec.) 1910: *m.* 1931, John Michael Ryan, of 43, Westminster Court, St. Stephens Hill, St. Albans, Herts, and has issue living.

PREDECESSORS.—[1] THOMAS WILLIAM Coke, son of the late Wenman Coke (formerly Roberts); *b.* 1754; many years M.P. for co. Norfolk; cr. *Viscount Coke* and *Earl of Leicester* (peerage of United Kingdom) 1837: *m.* 1st, 1775, Jane, who *d.* 1800, dau. of James Dutton; 2ndly, 1822, Lady Anne Amelia Keppel, who *d.* 1844 (having *m.* 2ndly, 1843, the Rt. Hon. Edward Ellice, M.P.), dau. of 4th Earl of Albemarle; *d.* 1842; *s.* by his son [2] THOMAS WILLIAM, *K.G.*, 2nd Earl; *b.* 1822; Lord-Lieut. of Norfolk 1846-1906; sometime a Member of Council of Duchy of Cornwall and Keeper of the Privy Seal: *m.* 1st, 1843, Juliana, who *d.* 1870, dau. of the late Samuel Charles Whitbread, of Southill, Beds; 2ndly, 1875, the Hon. Georgiana Caroline Cavendish, who *d.* 1937, el. dau. of 2nd Baron Chesham; *d.* 1909 : *s.* by his el. son [3] THOMAS WILLIAM, *G.C.V.O.*, *C.M.G.*, 3rd Earl; *b.* 1848; sometime Col. 2nd Batn. Scots Guards; Egypt 1882, Suakin 1885, S. Africa 1901-2 (C.M.G.); Lord-Lieut. of Norfolk 1906-29: *m.* 1879, the Hon. Dame Alice White, *D.B.E.*, who *d.* 1936, dau. of 2nd Baron Annaly; *d.* 1941; *s.* by his el. son [4] THOMAS WILLIAM, 4th Earl; *b.* 1880; Lord-Lieut. of Norfolk 1944-49: *m.* 1905, Marion Gertrude, who *d.* 1955, dau. of the late Col. the Hon. Walter Rodolph Trefusis, C.B.; *d.* 1949; *s.* by his son [5] THOMAS WILLIAM EDWARD, 5th Earl and present peer; also Viscount Coke.

LEICESTER, LORD BISHOP OF. (Williams.)

Rt. Rev. RONALD RALPH WILLIAMS, *D.D.*, son of the late Rev. Ralph Williams ; *b.* Oct. 14th, 1906 ; ed. at Judd Sch., Tonbridge, and at Gonville and Caius Coll. (MA), and Ridley Hall, Camb.; DD Lambeth and Canterbury; Tutor, St. Aidan's Coll., Birkenhead 1928-29, Curate of Leyton Ch. 1929-31, and of St. Andrew the Great, Camb. 1932-33, Chap. of Ridley Hall. 1931-34, and Examining Chap. to Bishop of Chelmsford 1931-53, and to Bishop of Durham 1945-53, Assist., Home Sec. (Education) of Church Missionary Soc. 1934-40, Religious Div., Min. of Information 1940-45, Principal, St. John's Coll., Durham 1945-53, and Hon. Canon, Durham Cathedral 1952-53; consecrated 3rd Lord Bishop of Leicester 1953: *m.* 1934, Cicely Maud, dau. of the late Edward Glanville Kay, of Enfield, Middlesex.

Patron of eighty-four livings, the Archdeaconries of Leicester and Loughborough, and twenty-one Hon. Canonries.

The present Diocese was founded by Act of Parliament Nov. 1926, but an earlier Diocese of Leicester was in existence from about 680 to 874, during which period nine Bishops occupied the See.

Arms,—Gules a pierced cinquefoil ermine, in a chief passant guardant grasping in the dexter forepaw a cross crosslet fitchée or.

Episcopal Signature,—" Ronald Leicester."

Residence,—Bishop's Lodge, Springfield Rd., Leicester, LE2 3BD.

LEIGH, BARON. (Leigh.) [Baron U.K. 1839.]

RUPERT WILLIAM DUDLEY LEIGH, *T.D.*, 4th Baron; *b.* March 14th, 1908; *s.* 1938; ed. at Eton, and RMC; High Steward of Sutton Coldfield, and a DL for Warwicks.; formerly Lieut. 11th Hussars, and Lieut.-Col. 1st Roy. Gloucestershire Hussars: *m.* 1931, Anne, dau. of the late Ellis Hicks Beach [see E. St. Aldwyn, colls.], and has issue.

Arms,—Gules, a cross engrailed argent and in the first quarter a lozenge argent. Crest,—An unicorn's head erased, armed and crined or. Supporters,—On either side an unicorn, armed, maned, tufted and unguled or, gorged with a ducal coronet gules, pendant therefrom an escutcheon charged with the arms of *Brydges*, viz. argent, a cross sable, thereon a leopard's face or.

All comes from God.

Seat,—Stoneleigh Abbey, Kenilworth. *Residence,*—Adlestrop House, Moreton-in-Marsh, Glos. *Club,*—Cavalry.

SONS LIVING.

Hon. JOHN PIERS, *b.* Sept. 11th, 1935 ; ed at Eton, at Oriel Coll., Oxford, and at London Univ.: *m.* 1957 (m. diss. 1974), Cecilia Poppy, yst. da. of the late Robert Cecil Jackson, of Redlynch, Wilts, and has issue living, Christopher Dudley Piers, *b.* 1960,—Camilla Anne, *b.* 1962. *Residence,*—1, Grecian Lodge, Stoneleigh Abbey, Kenilworth, Warwickshire.

Hon. William Rupert, *b.* 1938; ed. at Eton, and RMA Sandhurst; late Lt. 11th Hussars: *m.* 1965, Priscilla Elizabeth, yr. da. of Lt.-Cdr. Edward Francis Patrick Cooper, RN (ret.), of Markree Castle, co. Sligo [B. Castlemaine, colls.], and has issue living, James Rupert, *b.* 1967,—Edward William, *b.* 1968.

Hon. Benjamin Chandos, *b.* 1942; ed. at Eton; late Lt. 11th Hussars.

Hon. Michael James, *b.* 1945; ed. at Eton, and Keble Coll., Oxford: *m.* 1972, Cherry Rosalind, da. of the late David Long-Price.

PREDECESSORS.—[1] CHANDOS Leigh, son of the late James Henry Leigh, *b.* 1791; gained favourable reputation as a poet; cr. *Baron Leigh*, of Stoneleigh, co. Warwick (peerage of United Kingdom) 1839: *m.* 1819, Margarette, who *d.* 1860, dau. of the late Rev. William Shippen Willes, of Astrop House, Northamptonshire, *d.* 1850; *s.* by his son [2] Rt. Hon. WILLIAM HENRY, *LL.D.*, 2nd Baron; *b.* 1824; Lord-Lieut. and a High Steward of Sutton Cold-field *m.* 1848, Lady Caroline Amelia Grosvenor who *d.* 1906, dau. of 2nd Marquess of Westminster; *d.* 1905; *s.* by his son [3] FRANCIS DUDLEY, 3rd Baron; Lord-Lieut. of co. Warwick: *m.* 1st, 1890, Frances Hélène Forbes, who *d.* 1909, dau. of the late Hon. N. M. Beckwith, of New York; 2ndly, 1923, Marie, who *d.* 1949, dau. of the late Alexander Campbell, of New York; *d.* 1938; *s.* by his nephew [4] RUPERT WILLIAM DUDLEY (only son of the late Major the Hon. Rupert Leigh, 3rd son of 2nd Baron), 4th Baron and present peer.

LEIGHTON OF ST. MELLONS, BARON. (Seager.) [Baron U.K. 1962, Bt. U.K. 1952.]

JOHN LEIGHTON SEAGER, 2nd Baron and 2nd Baronet; *b.* Jan. 11th, 1922; *s.* 1963; ed. at Leys Sch., Camb.: *m.* 1953, Elizabeth Rosita, only dau. of the late Henry Hopgood, and has issue.

Arms,—Azure a cross moline between in bend dexter two lymphads and in bend sinister as many mullets all argent. Crest.—Between two wings azure each charged with a mullet a cross moline argent. Supporters.—*Dexter*, a sea-horse (hippocampus) azure; *sinister*, a dragon segreant gules.

Residence,—

SONS LIVING.

Hon. ROBERT WILLIAM HENRY LEIGHTON, *b.* Sept. 28th, 1955.

Hon. Simon John Leighton, *b.* 1957.

DAUGHTER LIVING.

Hon. Carole Mary Leighton, *b.* 1958.

BROTHER LIVING.

By Courage and Faith.

Hon. Douglas Leighton (Leighton House, 5929 Hudson, Vancouver BC, Canada), *b.* 1925: *m.* 1960, Gillian Claire, da. of L. W. Greenwood, of Abberley Hall, Worcester, and has issue living, Nicola Claire Leighton, *b.* 1961,—Wendy Elizabeth Leighton, *b.* 1963,—Michelle Leighton, *b.* 1967.

SISTERS LIVING.

Hon. Thelma Margaret, *b.* 1923: *m.* 1951, Michael Leighton Edmonds, of Darenth Lodge, Shoreham. Sevenoaks, Kent, and has issue living, Christopher Leighton, *b.* 1958,—Susan Leighton, *b.* 1952,— Jane Leighton, *b.* 1954.

Hon. Zoë Leighton, *b.* 1928: *m.* 1955, Malcolm James Peniston, of Dellside, 1, Greatfield Way, Rowlands Castle, Hants., and has issue living, Douglas James, *b.* 1959,—Angela Clare, *b.* 1956,—Rosemary Leighton, *b.* 1964.

WIDOW LIVING OF FIRST BARON.

MARJORIE (*Marjorie,* Baroness Leighton *of St. Mellons*) (of Marleigh Lodge, St. Mellons, nr. Cardiff), da. of William Henry Gimson, of Breconshire; a JP for Mon.: *m.* 1921, the 1st Baron, who *d.* 1963.

PREDECESSOR.—[1] Sir (GEORGE) LEIGHTON SEAGER, *C.B.E.* (son of Sir William Henry Seager, of Lynwood, Cardiff, founder of the firm of W. H. Seager & Co., shipowners and managers, and ships' suppliers); *b.* 1896; an underwriting member of Lloyd's, Pres. of Cardiff Chamber of Commerce 1934-35, and of Council of Shipping 1944; High Sheriff of Monmouthshire 1938-39 and Vice-Lieut. 1957-63; *cr.* a Knt. 1938, a *Baronet* 1952 and *Baron Leighton of St. Mellons,* of St. Mellons, co. Monmouth 1962: *m.* 1921, Marjorie, dau. of William Henry Gimson, of Breconshire, *d.* 1963; *s.* by his son [2] JOHN LEIGHTON, 2nd Baron and present peer.

LEINSTER, DUKE OF. (FitzGerald.) Sits as VISCOUNT (G.B. 1747).
[Duke I. 1766.]
[Title pronounced "Linster."]

Crom to Victory.

EDWARD FITZGERALD, 7th Duke and Premier Duke, Marquess, and Earl of Ireland; *b.* May 6th, 1892; *s.* 1922; ed. at Eton; formerly Lieut. Argyll and Sutherland Highlanders; Lieut. Duke of Wellington's (W. Riding Regt.), and 2nd Lieut. Irish Guards; European War 1914-15 (wounded): *m.* 1st, 1913, May (who *d.* 1935, and from whom he had obtained a divorce in the Scottish Courts 1930), dau. of the late Jesse Etheridge; 2ndly, 1932, Rafaelle (VAN NECK) (who obtained a divorce 1946), dau. of Robert Davidson Kennedy; 3rdly, 1946, Jessie, who *d.* 1960, dau. of the late Alfred John Smither, and formerly wife of (1) the 3rd Baron Churston, and (2) Theodore Wessel; 4thly, 1965, Vivien Irene, da. of the late Thomas Albert Felton, of London, and formerly wife of George William Conner, and has issue by 1st m.

Arms,—Argent, a saltire gules. **Crest,**— A monkey statant proper, environed round the loins and chained or. **Supporters,**—Two monkeys proper environed round the loins and chained or.

Residence,—Ford Manor, Dormansland, Lingfield, Surrey, RH7 6NZ.

SON LIVING. (*By 1st marriage.*)

GERALD (*Marquess of Kildare*), *b.* May 27th, 1914; ed. at Eton; formerly Major 5th Roy. Inniskilling Dragoon Guards; European War 1939-45 (wounded): *m.* 1st, 1936, Joane (who obtained a divorce 1946), el. dau. of the late Major Arthur Thomas MacMurrough Kavanagh, M.C. [see Buxton, Bt., colls.]; 2ndly 1946, Anne, younger dau. of the late Lieut.-Col. Philip Eustace Smith, M.C., and has issue by 1st and 2nd marriages:—

SONS LIVING (*By 2nd m.*)—Maurice (*Earl of Offaly*) (The Garden Cottage, Langston House, Chadlington, Oxon.), *b.* April 7th, 1948; ed. at Millfield: *m.* 1972, Fiona Mary Francesca, da. of Harry Hollick, of Thames Cottage, Wargrave, Berks., and has issue living, Thomas (*Viscount Leinster*), *b.* Jan. 12th, 1974.

Lord John, *b.* 1952; Lt. 5th Inniskilling Dragoon Gds.

DAUGHTERS LIVING (*By 1st m.*)—Lady Rosemary Ann, *b.* 1939; ed. at Lady Margaret Hall, Oxford: *m.* 1963 (m. diss. 1967), Mark Killigrew Wait.

Lady Nesta, *b.* 1942.

Residence,—Langston House, Chadlington, Oxon.

COLLATERAL BRANCHES LIVING.

Grandchildren of the late Lord Maurice FitzGerald, 2nd son of 4th Duke :—

Issue of the late Geraldine Mary FitzGerald, *b.* 1881, *d.* 1954 : *m.* 1907, Gerald More O'Ferrall, who *d.* 1951 :—

Edward George (6, Haigh Terr., Dun Laoghaire, co. Dublin; Kildare Street Club), *b.* 1908.—— Pamela Adelaide (c/o Munster & Leinster Bank, Ltd., Pembroke Branch, Upper Baggot St., Dublin), *b.* 1910: *m.* 1st, 1938, Fl. Lt. Rowan Sydney Howe, RAF, who *d.* 1938; 2ndly, 1940, Joseph P. Kenny, BL, who *d.* 1965, and has issue living, (by 2nd m.) Gerald Joseph (Caltra, Royal Terr. West, Dun Laoghaire, co. Dublin), *b.* 1941: *m.* 1966, Maire Assumpta Hogan, and has issue living, Garret Joseph Michael *b.* 1970, Ciara Pamela Brid, *b.* 1968.——Marjorie Geraldine, *b.* 1912: *m.* 1937, Clement Mervyn Scott Yates, Indian Police, who *d.* 1968, and has issue living, James Mervyn Gerald, *b.* 1944,—Susan Geraldine Margaret, *b.* 1938: *m.* 1964, Michael Emanuel Reynolds, of Maple Down, Main Drive, Gerrards Cross, Bucks., and has issue living, Amanda Jane *b.* 1965, Michelle Henrietta *b.* 1967,—Joy Natalia (3, Oaken Lane, Claygate, Surrey), *b.* 1942: *m.* 1st, 1963 (m. diss. 1967) Frank Jansen Beasley, 1968, Terence Clifford Medcalf, and has issue living, (by 1st m.) Christopher Frank Nell *b.* 1963, (by 2nd m.) Lucy Patricia *b.* 1970. *Residence,*—13, Homington Court, Albany Park Rd., Kingston upon Thames.

Grandchildren of the late Lord Charles FitzGerald (infra):—
Issue of the late Rupert Augustus FitzGerald, b. 1900, d. 1969: m. 1st, 1924, Irene (from whom he obtained a divorce 1932), da. of J. Jennings, of Melbourne, Vic., Aust.; 2ndly, 1936, Ivy, who d. 1945, da. of the late J. Simmons, of Melbourne, Aust.:—
(By 1st m.) Peter Charles (35, York St., Prahran, Vic., Aust.), b. 1925: 1939-45 War with AMF: m. 1950, June, da. of W. Murray, of East St. Kilda, Vic., Aust., and has issue living, Stephen Peter, b. 1953,—Lynette Pamela, b. 1951.——(by 2nd m.) Elizabeth Mary, b. 1937: m. 1958, Ronald Smith, of 24, Ireland Av., Doncaster East, Vic., Aust., and has issue living, Gary Ronald, b. 1960,—Amanda Elizabeth, b. 1962.

Issue of the late Lord Charles FitzGerald, 5th son of 4th Duke, b. 1859, d. 1928: m. 1887, Alice, who d. 1909, da. of M. Claudius:—
Mabel Geraldine, b. 1891: m. 1914, Robert Alan McCracken, who d. 1967, and has issue living, Charles Coiler, b. 1921; 1939-45 War as Capt. AIF: m. 1946, Joan, da. of the late Charles Mercer, of Ranfurlie Cres., Glen Iris, Vict., Aust., and has issue living, Geoffrey b. 1947, Robert b. 1949, David b. 1952. Residence,—28, Avenel Rd., Kooyong, Melbourne, Australia.

Issue of the late Lord Henry FitzGerald, 7th son of 4th Duke, b. 1863, d. 1955: m. 1891, Inez, who d. 1967, da. of the late Cdr. William John Casberd-Boteler, RN, of Eastry Kent:—
Brian Boteler, b. 1908; ed. at Eton: m. 1936, Elizabeth Dorothea Maud, dau. of Charles Hesket, Fleetwood-Hesketh, J.P., D.L., [Brocklebank, Bt.]. Residence,—23, Godfrey Street, S.W.3.—
Denis Henry, D.S.O., O.B.E., b. 1911; ed. at Eton; was A.D.C. to Gen. Officer Comdg. N. Ireland Dist. 1938-39, and G.S.O., Headquarters Guards Armoured Div. 1941-42, Instructor at Staff Coll., Camberley 1942-43, and G.S.O. at Headquarters 30th Corps 1944, A.Q.M.G., War Office 1949-50, and Headquarters, London Dist. 1950-51, Col. Comdg. Irish Guards 1951-52, Brigadier Comdg. 4th Guards Brig. 1953-55, and Director of Plans 1957-58 ; European War 1939-45 in Norway and N-W Europe (DSO), Palestine 1947; DSO, 1945, OBE (Mil) 1951. Residences,—18, Stack House, Ebury St., SW1; Glenshelane Hse., Cappoquin, co. Waterford.

PREDECESSORS.—[1] GERALD FitzGerald; cr. Baron of Offaly, co. Kildare, before 1203; d. about 1203; s. by his son [2] MAURICE, 2nd Baron; Lord Ch. Justice of Ireland; introduced into Ireland 1216 the Order of the Franciscans, and in 1229 the Order of the Dominicans, built in 1231 the Franciscan Abbey of Youghal, where he d. 1257; s. by his son [3] MAURICE, 3rd Baron; was Ch. Gov. of Ireland; d. 1277; s. by his son [4] GERALD, 4th Baron; founded the Franciscan Order at Clane 1271; d. 1287; s. by his cousin [5] MAURICE, 5th Baron; d.s.p.; s. by his cousin [6] JOHN, 6th Baron; a valiant soldier who assisted Edward I. in his Scottish compaigns 1296, 1299, and 1301, and afterwards dispersed the rebels in Munster, and opposed Robert Bruce who had entered the N. of Ireland with 6,000 men, cr. Earl of Kildare (peerage of Ireland) 1316; there is a tradition that the Earl while an infant was asleep at Woodstock Castle, near Athy, when an alarm of fire was raised; in the confusion the child was forgotten, and on the servants returning to search for him they found the room in which he had lain to be in ruins; soon after, hearing a strange noise in one of the towers, they looked up and saw an ape, which was usually kept chained, carefully holding the child in his arms; he afterwards in gratitude for his preservation adopted a monkey for his crest; d. 1316; s. by his son [7] THOMAS, 2nd Earl; was three times Lord Justice of Ireland; d. 1328; s. by his son [8] RICHARD, 3rd Earl; d. 1329; s. by his brother [9] MAURICE, K.B., 4th Earl; present at siege of Calais; d. 1390; s. by his son [10] GERALD, 5th Earl; was Lord Dep. to Thomas, Duke of Gloucester, Lord-Lieut. of Ireland; d. 1410; s. by his brother [11] JOHN, 6th Earl; strengthened and enlarged the Castle of Maynooth; d. 1427; s. by his son [12] THOMAS, 7th Earl; was Lord Dep. of Ireland 1454-9, and Lord Chancellor of Ireland 1468; being involved with the Earl of Desmond he was attainted, but subsequently pardoned, released, restored in blood by Act of Parliament, and appointed Lord Justice of Ireland 1471; d. 1477; s. by his son [13] GERALD, K.G., 8th Earl: Lord Dep. and Lord Justice of Ireland for thirty-three years, an eminent military commander who invaded Ulster, took numerous castles, and in 1504 obtained a complete victory over the Irish chiefs of Connaught; d. 1513; s. by his son [14] GERALD, 9th Earl; Lord Dep. of Ireland, was deprived of his high office, and with his five half-brothers was committed to the Tower and sentenced to be executed as a traitor; d. a prisoner 1534; s. by his son [15] THOMAS, 10th Earl; having heard that his father was to be beheaded he threw off all allegiance to the English crown; he eventually surrendered on the promise of receiving a full pardon; this promise was violated by Henry VIII., and in 1537 he, together with his five uncles, was hanged, drawn and quartered at Tyburn, and his honours were attainted; s. by his half-brother [16] GERALD, 11th Earl; was ed. at Rome by his kinsman Cardinal Pole, and subsequently became Master of the Horse to Cosmo de Medici, Duke of Florence; returned to England after the death of Henry VIII. and received Knighthood from Edward VI., and a regrant of all the Irish family estates, and Queen Mary restored to him all his ancestral honours; d. 1585; s. by his son [17] HENRY, 12th Earl; d. 1597; s. by his brother [18] WILLIAM, 13th Earl; lost at sea 1599; s. by his cousin [19] GERALD, 14th Earl; d. 1612; s. by his son [20] GERALD, 15th Earl; d. 1620; s. by his cousin [21] GEORGE, 16th Earl; d. 1655; s. by his son [22] WENTWORTH, 17th Earl; d. 1664; s. by his son [23] JOHN, 18th Earl; d.s.p. 1707; s. by his cousin [24] ROBERT, 19th Earl; an eminent statesman; d. 1744; s. by his son [25] JAMES, 20th Earl; Master-Gen. of the Ordnance in Ireland; cr. Viscount Leinster (peerage of Great Britain) 1747, Earl of Offaly and Marquess of Kildare (peerage of Ireland) 1761, and Duke of Leinster (peerage of Ireland) 1766; d. 1773; s. by his son [26] WILLIAM ROBERT, KP, 2nd Duke; d. 1804; s. by his son [27] AUGUSTUS FREDERICK, PC, 3rd Duke; b. 1791; HM Lieut. of co. Kildare: m. 1818, Charlotte Augusta Stanhope, da. of 3rd Earl of Harrington; d. 1874; s. by his son [28] CHARLES WILLIAM, P.C., 4th Duke; b. 1819; sat as M.P. for Kildare 1847-52; cr. (in the lifetime of his father) Baron Kildare (peerage of United Kingdom) 1870: m. 1847, Lady Caroline Sutherland Leveson-Gower, dau. of 2nd Duke of Sutherland; d. 1887; s. by his son [29] GERALD, PC, 5th Duke, b. 1851; HM Lieut. of co. Kildare: m. 1884, Lady Hermione Wilhelmina Duncombe, who d. 1895, da. of 1st Earl of Feversham; d. 1893; s. by his el. son [30] MAURICE, 6th Duke, b. 1887; d. 1922; s. by his brother [31] EDWARD, 7th Duke and present peer; also Marquess of Kildare, Earl of Kildare, Earl and Baron of Offaly, Viscount Leinster, and Baron Kildare.

Leinster, Viscount, great-grandson of Duke of Leinster.

LEITRIM, EARLDOM OF. (Clements.) [Extinct 1952.]

[Earl I. 1795.]

DAUGHTER LIVING OF FOURTH EARL.

Lady Kathleen, b. 1888 : m. 1st, 1910, Granville Keith-Falconer Smith, Lieut. Coldstream Guards, who d. (killed in action) 1914 [E. Kintore]; 2ndly, 1919, Com. Ronald Granville Studd, D.S.O., RN, who d. 1956 [Studd, Bt.], and has issue living, (by 1st m.) [see Cs. Kintore, colls.]. Residence,—Postboys, Stoke by Nayland, nr. Colchester.

WIDOW LIVING OF FIFTH EARL.

ANNE MARY CHALONER (Countess of Leitrim), sister of 5th Baron Huntingfield, and formerly wife of Major Percy Rygate Borrett : m. 1939, as his second wife, the 5th Earl, who d. 1952, when the title became ext. Residence,—Mulroy, co. Donegal.

Lennox, Duke of, see Duke of Richmond and Gordon.

Leslie, Lord, son of Earl of Rothes.

LEVEN and MELVILLE, EARL OF. (Leslie Melville.) [Earl S. 1641 and 1690.]

For King | Heaven
and country. | at last.

ALEXANDER ROBERT LESLIE MEL-VILLE, 14th Earl of Leven and 13th Earl of Melville; *b.* May 13th, 1924; *s.* 1947; ed. at Eton; Capt. (ret.) Coldstream Guards; a DL for Nairn; Lord Lieut. for Nairn since 1969; ADC to Gov.-Gen. of NZ 1951-52: *m.* 1953, Susan, da. of Lieut.-Col. Ronald Steuart-Menzies of Menzies, of Arndilly House, Craigellachie, Banffshire, and has issue.

Arms,—Quarterly: 1st, azure, a thistle slipped proper, ensigned with an Imperial Crown or, a coat of augmentation to the arms of *Leslie*; 2nd, gules, three crescents within a bordure argent, charged with eight roses of the first, *Melville*; 3rd, argent, a fesse gules, *Melville of Raith*; 4th, argent, on a bend azure, three buckles or, *Leslie*. **Crests,**—1st, a demi-chevalier in complete armour, holding in his right hand a dagger point downwards proper, pommel and hilt or, *Leslie*; 2nd, a ratchhound's head erased proper, collared gules, *Melville*. **Supporters,**—*Dexter*, a knight in complete armour, holding in his dexter hand the banner of Scotland, all proper, *Leslie*; *sinister*, a ratchhound proper, collared gules, *Melville*.

Seat,—Glenferness, Nairn. *Clubs,*—Naval and Military, Pratt's, New (Edinburgh).

SONS LIVING.

DAVID ALEXANDER (*Lord Balgonie*), *b.* Jan. 26th, 1954; ed. at Eton; 2nd Lt. Queen's Own Highlanders.
Hon. Archibald Ronald, *b.* 1957.

DAUGHTER LIVING.

Lady Jane Catherine, *b.* 1956.

BROTHERS LIVING.

Hon. George David (twin), *b.* 1924; ed. at Eton, and at Trin. Coll., Camb. (BA); Maj. Black Watch (TA Reserve), FRICS, FLAS, FAI; 1942-45 War as Capt. Rifle Bde. in N.-W. Europe (wounded): *m.* 1955, Diana Mary, da. of the late Brig. Sir Henry Walter Houldsworth, KBE, DSO, MC, TD [see E. Morton, colls.], and has issue living, James Hugh, *b.* 1960,—Annabel Clare, *b.* 1956. *Residence,*—Kirkton House, Skene, Aberdeenshire. *Club,*—Naval and Military.
Hon. Ronald Joscelyn, *b.* 1926; ed. at Eton, and at Worcester Coll., Oxford (B.A. 1950): *m.* 1962, Ruth, only da. of the late John Duckworth, and has issue living, Roderick Justice, *b.* 1965,—Robert Jeffrey, *b.* 1967, Angus Jack, *b.* 1968,—Rosamond Joscelyn, *b.* 1962. *Residence,*—Balgarrock, Aberlemno, Forfar, Angus. *Club,*—Brooks's.
Hon. Alan Duncan, *b.* 1928; ed. at Eton; Capt. (ret.) Rifle Bde. *Residence,*—Collielaw, Lauder, Berwickshire.

SISTER LIVING.

Lady Jean Elizabeth (Pathways, Sedgeberrow, Evesham), *b.* 1921.

COLLATERAL BRANCHES LIVING.
Issue of the late Hon. David William Leslie Melville, M.B.E., 3rd son of 11th Earl, *b.* 1892, *d.* 1938: *m.* 1st, 1914, Susanna Elizabeth Johanna (who obtained a divorce 1928), dau. of Francis Sleigh, of Cape Town. S. Africa; 2ndly, 1929, Eleanor Mary, who *d.* 1974, having *m.* 2ndly, 1939, Capt. Arthur Miller, who *d.* on active ser. during 1942, da. of Arthur John Abrahall, formerly of Shustoke, near Coleshill, Warwickshire, and has issue living:—
(By 2nd marriage) John David, *b.* 1933: *m.* 1961 (marriage dissolved 1964), Lady Zinnia Rosemary (COMINS), da. of 4th Earl of Londesborough [see B. Londesborough].——Gillian Mary, *b.* 1930: *m.* 1st, 1950 (marriage dissolved 19—), Peter Riley; 2ndly, 19—.

Issue of the late Lt.-Col. the Hon. Ian Leslie Melville, TD, yst. son of 11th Earl, *b.* 1894, *d.* 1967: *m.* 1915, Charlotte Isabel, who *d.* 1968, da. of the late Maj. William Stirling, of Fairburn, Ross-shire:—
Michael Ian, *TD* (Bridgelands, Selkirk; New (Edinburgh) Club), *b.* 1918; ed. at Eton, and, Balliol Coll., Oxford (MA); Maj. Lovat Scouts (Reserve), a DL for Selkirk, a Member of Queen's Body Guard for Scotland (Roy. Co. of Archers); FRICS: *m.* 1943, Cynthia, da. of Sir Charles Jocelyn Hambro, KBE, MC, and has issue living, Ian Hamish (61, Hartington Rd., W4; Turf Club), *b.* 1944; ed. at Eton, and Ch. Ch., Oxford (MA): *m.* 1968, Lady Elizabeth Compton, yr. da. of 6th Marquess of Northampton, and has issue living, James Ian *b.* 1969, Henry Bingham *b.* 1975,—Pamela, *b.* 1947,—Fiona Evelyn, *b.* 1950: *m.* 1973, James Campbell David Brodie, yr. son of the late Maj. David James Brodie of Lethen, and has issue living, Alexander *b.* 1974.——Judith Betty (8, Montrose Court, Princes Gate, SW7, and Hamswell Hse., Bath), *b.* 1916: *m.* 1939 (m. diss. 1960) the 2nd Baron Dulverton.——Elisabeth Marion (*Baroness Joicey*), *b.* 1928: *m.* 1952, the 4th Baron Joicey. *Residence,*—Etal Manor, Berwick-on-Tweed.

Granddaughters of the late Galfrid John Leslie Melville (infra):—
Issue of the late Norman Victor Leslie Melville, *b.* 1896, *d.* 1974: *m.* 1918, Dorothea (Forty Cottage, Ampney St. Mary, Cirencester), da. of the late Walter Stead:—
Xenia Winifred, *b.* 1919: *m.* 1939, John Michael Richmond Paton, of Haypark, Stow, Midlothian, and has issue living, Alasdair Donald, *b.* 1952,—Frances Dorothea Richmond, *b.* 1948: *m.* 1968, Harold Abbott, of 5, Marchmont Terr., Glasgow, and has issue living, John Anthony *b.* 1970, Clare *b.* 1969,—Fiona Jacqueline, *b.* 1951.——Joan Frances Ruth, *b.* 1922: *m.* 1st, 1941, Norman Henry Gibbs, DPh, from whom she obtained a divorce 1954; 2ndly, 1955, Richard John Marshall Amphlett, of The Close, Fairford, Glos., and has issue living, (by 1st m.) Kathleen Vanessa, *b.* 1942: *m.* 1965, Peter John Quarrell, of 6, Agden Rd., Sheffield 7, and has issue living, Rachel Emma Louise *b.* 1968, Philippa Katherine *b.* 1970,—Judith Rowena, *b.* 1946: *m.* 1967, William Rupert Brent Pelly, of Old Tracey, Fairford, Glos. [see Pelly, Bt., colls.].——Anne, *b.* 1929.

Granddaughter of the late Capt. the Hon. Norman Leslie Melville, 4th son of 9th Earl:—

Issue of the late Galfrid John Leslie Melville, *b.* 1863, *d.* 1910: *m.* 1895, **Nora French,** who *d.* 1924 (having *m.* 2ndly. 1913, Arnold Ceresole, of Lausanne, Switzerland); dau. of the late George Ambler Stead, of Pool, near Leeds :—
Sylvia Beryl, *b.* 1889: *m.* 1924, René Lara, Editor of the " Gaulois " (France), who *d.* 1944, and has issue living, Francis Melville, *b.* 1925. *Residence,*—

Granddaughters of the late Rev. Frederick Abel Leslie Melville, 5th son of the late Hon. Alexander Leslie Melville, youngest son of 7th Earl:—
Issue of the late Malcolm Alexander Leslie Melville, *b.* 1882. *d.* 1946 : *m.* 1924, Ruth Ellen, who *m.* 2ndly, 1951, Arthur Ernest Mallett, who *d.* 1960), da. of James Dowker, of Mount Tolmie, Victoria, BC:—
Eleanor Constance, *b.* 1926 : *m.* 1953, David William Metcalfe, and has issue living, Margaret Rose, *b.* 1955,—Sandra Gail, *b.* 1957,—Heather May, *b.* 1965. *Residence,*—640, Fernhill Rd., Victoria, British Columbia.——Margaret Wardlaw (1833, West 37th Av., Vancouver 13, British Columbia), *b.* 1928.

PREDECESSORS.—[1] *Sir* ROBERT Melville, *K.B., P.C.,* was twice Ambassador to England, Hereditary Keeper of Linlithgow Palace Vice-Chancellor and Treasurer depute, and an **Extraordinary** Lord of Session with title of Lord Murdocarnie 1594-1601 ; **cr.** *Lord Melville of Monymaill* (peerage of Scotland), 1616, with remainder to heirs male of his brother John; *d.* 1621, *s.* by his son [2] ROBERT, *P.C., K.B.,* 2nd Lord ; an Extraordinary Lord of Session as Lord Burntisland 1601-8 ; in 1627 obtained a new charter of the lordship with remainders to his heirs general bearing the name of Melville ; *d.* 1635 ; *s.* by his cousin [3] JOHN, 3rd Lord, son of John (ante), brother of 1st Lord ; *d.* 1643 ; *s.* by his son [4] GEORGE, 4th Lord ; being involved in the rebellion of the Duke of Monmouth he was attainted by Act of Parliament 1685 ; he escaped to Holland, from whence in 1688 he returned to England with the Prince of Orange (William III.); in the following year the attainder was rescinded, and in 1690 he was cr. *Lord Raith, Monymaill and Balwearie, Viscount Kirkaldie and Earl of Melville* (peerage of Scotland) 1690; Sec. of State 1690-1, High Commr. to Parliament 1690, Keeper of the Privy Seal 1691-6, and Pres. of the Council 1696: *m.* Lady Catherine Leslie, dau. of 2nd Earl of Leven; *d.* 1707; *s.* by his son [5] DAVID, *P.C.,* 2nd Earl, who had in 1682 *s.* as 3rd Earl of Leven (see note *₊*infra) ; was Gov. of Edinburgh Castle, Gen. of the Ordnance, Lieut.-Gen. and Com. in Ch. in Scotland, a Commr. of the Union, and a Representative Peer ; *d.* 1728 ; *s.* by his grandson [6] DAVID, 4th Earl of Leven and 3rd Earl of Melville; *d.* a minor 1729; *s.* by his uncle [7] ALEXANDER, 5th and 4th Earl; was a Lord of Session, a Representative Peer 1747, and High Commr. to Church of Scotland 1741-3; *d.* 1745 ; *s.* by his son [8] DAVID, 6th and 5th Earl; High Commr. to Gen. Assembly 1783-1801 ; *d.* 1802; *s.* by his son [9] ALEXANDER, 7th and 6th Earl; *d.* 1820; *s.* by his el. son [10] DAVID, 8th and 7th Earl; a Rear-Adm., Comptroller of the Customs in Scotland, and a Representative Peer; *d.* 1860; *s.* by his brother [11] JOHN THORNTON, 9th and 8th Earl; *b.* 1786; a Representative Peer: *m.* 1st, 1812, Harriet, who *d.* 1832, dau. of Samuel Thornton, M.P., of Albury Park and Clapham ; 2ndly, 1834, Sophia, who *d.* 1887, dau. of Henry Thornton, of Battersea, Surrey; *d.* 1876; *s.* by his son [12] ALEXANDER, 10th and 9th Earl, *b.* 1817; a Representative Peer; *d.* 1889; *s.* by his half-brother ⌊13⌋ RONALD RUTHVEN, *P.C., K.T.,* 11th and 10th Earl, *b.* 1835 ; a Representative Peer and Lord Keeper of the Privy Seal of Scotland ; Lord High Commr. to Gen. Assembly of Church of Scotland 1898, 1899, 1900, 1901, 1902, 1903, 1904, and 1905: *m.* 1885, the Hon. Emma Selina, who *d.* 1941, dau. of 2nd Viscount Portman ; *d.* 1906 ; *s.* by his el. son [14] JOHN DAVID, 12th and 11th Earl, *b.* 1886; a Representative Peer; *d.* 1913; *s.* by his brother [15] ARCHIBALD ALEXANDER, 13th and 12th Earl, *b.* 1890; a Representative Peer, Lieut.-Col. and Brevet-Col. (retired) Lovat Scouts, and Lord Lieut. of Nairnshire: *m.* 1918, Lady Rosamond Sylvia Diana Mary Foljambe, who *d.* 1974, da. of 1st Earl of Liverpool (cr. 1905); *d.* 1947; *s.* by his son [16] ALEXANDER ROBERT, 14th and 13th Earl and present peer; also Viscount Kirkaldie, Lord Melville of Monymaill, Lord Raith, Monymaill and Balwearie.

₊ [1] *Sir* ALEXANDER Leslie, having served with distinction in the Swedish Army, in which service he attained the rank of Field-Marshal in 1638, took command of the Covenanters' Army and defeated the King's troops in various engagements; at the treaty of peace signed at Ripon 1641 the King cr. him *Lord Balgonie* and *Earl of Leven* (peerage of Scotland) 1641, with remainder to his heirs whatsoever; he subsequently joined the Parliamentary Army with 21,000 men, and defeated the Royalists at Marston Moor 1644, but after the execution of the King he served against the Parliamentarians and joined in the cause of the Restoration; he was in 1651 surprised and taken prisoner by Gen. Monk, and incarcerated in the Tower, from whence he was released at the intercession of Christina, Queen of Sweden; *d.* 1661; *s.* by his grandson [2] ALEXANDER, 2nd Earl; who obtained in 1665 a charter with remainder to (i) the heirs male of his body, (ii) the heirs female of his body, (iii) the 2nd son of John, 6th Earl of Rothes, (iv) the heirs male of George, 4th Lord Melville (ante), (v) the 2nd son of David, 2nd Earl of Wemyss, (vi) his own heirs male whatsoever, and (vii) to his heirs and assignees whatsoever; *d.* without male issue 1663; *s.* by his el. dau. [3] MARGARET, *d.s.p.* 1674; *s.* by her sister [4] KATHERINE; *d.* 1682; *s.* by her kinsman [5] DAVID, 3rd Earl (see 2nd Earl of Melville (ante)), the three first remainders having failed.

LEVER, BARON. (Lever.) [Life Baron 1975.)

LESLIE MAURICE LEVER, son of the late Bernard Lever; *b.* April 29th, 1905; ed. at Manchester Gram. Sch., and Univ. of Leeds (LLB Hons.) Hon. LLD Leeds; FRSA; Solicitor 1927; Snr. Partner in firm of Leslie M. Lever & Co., Solicitors; a JP of Manchester (Alderman 1949-74, Lord Mayor 1957-58); MP for Ardwick Div. of Manchester (*Lab.*) 1950-70; a Member Board of Govs. Manchester Univ., and Manchester Gram. Sch.; Coronation Medal 1953, Assoc. SBStJ, Kt. Grand Cross of Order of St. Gregory the Great; cr. Knt. 1970, and *Baron Lever,* of Ardwick in City of Manchester 1975: *m.* 1939, Ray Rosalia, JP, of Lancs., only child of Dr. Leonard Levene, of Leicester, and has issue.

Arms,—Gules, within an orle of bees volant, a pair of scales between three inescutcheons two and one or, each charged with a rose gules, barbed and seeded proper.   **Crest,**—Within a mural crown gules masoned or, a globe thereon a pair of keys addorsed wards outwards or, rising between the bows thereof a sun gules.   **Supporters,**—*Dexter,* a lion sejant or, mane and tail tuft sable; *sinister,* a bear sejant proper; both gorged with a collar gules, thereon pine cones proper.

Residence,—27, Pine Rd., Didsbury, Manchester, M20 0UZ.   *Club,*—Manchester Press.

SON LIVING.

Hon. Bernard Lewis (27, Pine Rd., Didsbury, Manchester, M20 0UZ), *b.* 1951; ed. at Clifton, and Queen's Coll., Oxon; Bar. Middle Temple 1975.

DAUGHTER LIVING.

Hon. June A., *b.* 1940: *m.* 1962, Emanuel S. Rosen, MD, FRCS, FRPS, of 18A, Torkington Rd., Wilmslow, Cheshire, and has issue.

LEVERHULME, VISCOUNT. (Lever.)   [Viscount U.K. 1922, Bt. U.K. 1911.]
[Title pronounced "Leverhume."]

PHILIP WILLIAM BRYCE LEVER, *T.D.,* 3rd Viscount, and 3rd Baronet ; *b.* July 1st, 1915 ; *s.* 1949 ; ed. at Eton, and at Trin. Coll., Camb.; Hon. Col. (Cheshire Yeo. Sqdn.) The Queen's Own Yeo., RAC, TAVR since 1972. Advisory Dir. of Unilever, Ltd., a JP and a KStJ; Lord-Lieut. of Cheshire since 1949; senior steward of Jockey Club since 1973: *m.* 1937, Margaret Ann, who *d.* 1973, only child of John Moon, of Tiverton, Devon, and has issue.

Arms,—Quarterly, 1st and 4th, per pale argent and barry of eight or and azure, two bendlets sable, the upper one engrailed ; 2nd and 3rd, per chevron or and gules, in chief two chaplets of roses and in base a lion's head all counterchanged **Crest,**—A trumpet fessewise, thereon a cock proper, charged on the breast with a rose as in the arms. **Supporters,**—On either side an elephant or, the dexter charged on the shoulder with a rose gules and the sinister with a chaplet of roses also gules.

I scorn to change or fear.

Residences,—Thornton Manor, Thornton Hough, Wirral, Cheshire; Badanloch, Kinbrace, Sutherland. *Clubs,*—Boodle's, Jockey.

DAUGHTERS LIVING.

Hon. Susan Elizabeth Moon (9, Mulberry Walk, SW3 6DZ), *b.* 1938: *m.* 1957 (m. diss. 1973), Hercules Michael Roland Pakenham [see E. Longford, colls.].

Hon. Victoria Marion Ann (44, Edwardes Sq., W8), *b.* 1945: *m.* 1966 (m. diss. 1973), John Richard Walter Reginald Carew Pole, only son of Sir John Gawen Carew Pole, DSO, TD, 12th baronet.

Hon. Margaret Jane, *b.* 1947: *m.* 1966, Algernon Eustace Hugh Heber-Percy, of Hodnet Hall, Market Drayton, Salop [see D. Northumberland, colls.].

SISTER LIVING.

Hon. Rosemary Gertrude Alexandra, *b.* 1919: *m.* 1938, Lieut.-Col. William Erskine Stobart Whetherly, formerly King's Dragoon Guards, and has issue living, Dennis William Stobart, *b.* 1940,—Robin Christopher Philip (22, Hasker St., SW3) *b.* 1947; late RHG: *m.* 1971, Sally Ann, da. of Maj. R. C. S. Price, of Birdhurst, Alderbury, Wilts.—Dawn Elizabeth Evelyn, *b.* 1946: *m.* 1967, Andrew James Little, of Wadley Manor, Farington, Oxon, and has issue living, Mark William Douglas *b.* 1969, Emma Louise *b.* 1973.   *Residence,*—Hallam, Ogbourne St. George, Marlborough, Wilts.

MOTHER LIVING.

Marion Beatrice, dau. of the late Bryce Smith, of Whalley and Manchester: *m.* 1st, 1912, the 2nd Viscount, who *d.* 1949, having obtained a divorce 1936 ; 2ndly, 1937, Wing-Com. Selden Herbert Long, DSO, MC, who *d.* 1952. *Residence,*—Flat 8, 7, Princess Gate, SW7.

PREDECESSORS.—[1] WILLIAM HESKETH Lever, son of the late James Lever, of Bolton, Lancashire ; *b.* 1851 ; founder of Port Sunlight, and Chm. of Lever Bros. (Limited); High Sheriff of Lancashire 1917-18 ; M.P. for Wirral Div. of Cheshire (*L*) Jan. 1906 to Dec. 1909 ; cr. a *Baronet* 1911, *Baron Leverhulme,* of Bolton-le-Moors, co. Palatine of Lancaster (peerage of United Kingdom) 1917, and *Viscount Leverhulme,* of The Western Isles, in the cos. of Inverness and Ross and Cromarty (peerage of United Kingdom) 1922: *m.* 1874, Elizabeth Ellen, who *d.* 1913, dau. of Crompton Hulme, of Bolton; *d.* 1925; *s.* by his son [2] WILLIAM HULME, 2nd, Viscount, *b.* 1888; Gov. of Lever Bros., and of Unilever, Ltd.; High Sheriff of Cheshire 1923; Pres. of London Chamber of Commerce 1931-4, of Institution of Chemical Engineers 1932-4, of Roy. Warrant Holders' Asso. 1933, and of So. of Chemical Industry 1936-8; was Pro-Chancellor Liverpool Univ. 1932-6; Charter Mayor of Bebington 1937 (first Hon. Freeman 1945): *m.* 1st, 1912, Marion Beatrice (from whom he obtained a divorce 1936), dau. of the late Bryce Smith, of Whalley and Manchester; 2ndly, 1937, Winifred Agnes (LEE-MORRIS), who *d.* 1966, yr. da. of Lt.-Col. Lloyd, of Brentwood, Bidston, Cheshire; *d.* 1949; *s.* by his son [3] PHILIP WILLIAM BRYCE, 3rd Viscount and present peer; also Baron Leverhulme.

Leveson, Lord,   son of Earl Granville.

Lewisham, Viscount, son of Earl of Dartmouth.

LICHFIELD, EARL OF. (Anson.) [Earl U.K. 1831.]

NIL ✛ DESPERANDUM

Despair of nothing.

THOMAS PATRICK JOHN ANSON, 5th Earl; *b.* April 25th, 1939; *s.* 1960; ed. at Harrow; late Lt. Grenadier Guards; Photographer; FIIP; FRPS: *m.* 1975, Lady Leonora Mary Grosvenor, el. da. of the 5th Duke of Westminster.

Arms,—Quarterly : 1st, argent, three bends engrailed and in the sinister chief point a crescent gules, *Anson*; 2nd, ermine, three cats-a-mountain passant guardant, in pale sable, *Adams;* 3rd, azure, three salmon naiant in pale, per pale or and argent, *Sambrooke;* 4th, sable, a bend or, between three spears' heads argent, *Carrier.* Crests,—1st, out of a ducal coronet or, a spear head proper; 2nd, a greyhound's head erased ermines, gorged with a collar, double gemelle or. Supporters,—*Dexter,* a sea-horse; *sinister,* a lion guardant, both proper and each gorged with a collar double gemelle or. *Residences,*—Shugborough Hall, Stafford; 22, Clarence Terr., Regents Park, NW1. *Studio,*—20, Aubrey Walk, W8.

SISTER LIVING. (*Raised to the rank of an Earl's daughter* 1961.)

Lady Elizabeth Georgiana, 1941: *m.* 1972, as his 2nd wife, Sir Geoffrey Adam Shakerley, 6th Bt., of 56, Ladbroke Grove, W11 2PB.

AUNT LIVING. (*Daughter of 4th Earl.*)

Lady Betty Marjorie, *b.* 1917: *m.* 1944, Col. Thomas Foley Churchill Winnington, M.B.E., Grenadier Guards [see Winnington, Bt.]. *Residence,*—9, Westminster Gdns., SW1.

MOTHER LIVING.

Anne Ferelith (*H.H. Princess Anne of Denmark*), dau. of the late Hon. John Herbert Bowes-Lyon [see E. Strathmore, colls.]: *m.* 1st, 1938, Thomas William Arnold, Viscount Anson, from whom she obtained a divorce 1948; 2ndly, 1950, HH Prince Georg of Denmark, CVO, of 81, Carlisle Mansions, SW1.

WIDOW LIVING OF FOURTH EARL.

Violet Margaret (PHILIPS) (*Margaret, Countess of Lichfield*), da. of the late Henry Dawson Dawson-Greene, JP, of Slyne, and Whittington Hall, Lancashire: *m.* 1949, as his second wife, the 4th Earl, who *d.* 1960. *Residence,*—17, Strand Court, Topsham, Devon.

COLLATERAL BRANCHES LIVING.

Issue of the late Capt. the Hon. Rupert Anson, yst. son of 3rd Earl, *b.* 1889, *d.* 1966: *m.* 1919, Marion Emma Ruthven, who *d.* 1965, da. of James Halliday, of Harrow-on-the-Hill:—

GEOFFREY RUPERT (1029, 23rd Av. West, Spencer, Iowa 51301, USA), *b.* Jan. 28th, 1929: *m.* 1957, Verna Grace Hall, and has issue living, George Rupert, *b.* 1960,—Christopher Leonard, *b.* 1963,—Edward Peter, *b.* 1965,—Jennifer Marion *b.* 1961.——Thomas Peter (Field Grove House, Durweston, Blandford, Dorset), *b.* 1933; Lt.-Col. Queen's R. Irish Hussars: *m.* 1964, Jufith Hilary, da. of the late Capt. John Nicholl Kennard, RN, and has issue living, Henry James, *b.* 1967,—Patrick John, *b.* 1969.——Anne Rosemary (c/o Coutts & Co., 440, Strand, WC2R 0GS), *b.* 1924: *m.* 1946 (m. diss. 1974), Capt. Paul Coombe, and has issue living, Geoffrey Paul, *b.* 1951,—Michael Anthony, *b.* 1955, Diana Mary, *b.* 1947: *m.* 1967, Timothy Gaines, and has issue living, David Allan *b.* 1970, Daniel Anson *b.* 1972, Devon Ashley *b.* 1974.——Felicity Marion, *b.* 1927: *m.* 1952, John Arbon Woodhouse, of The Old Ford House, Blandford, Dorset, and has issue living, Mark John Michael, *b.* 1955,—Andrew Harold Rupert, *b.* 1957,—Clare Marian, *b.* 1956.

Granddaughters of the late Lt.-Col. the Hon. Sir George Augustus Anson, KCB, CBE, MVO, 2nd son of 2nd Earl:—

Issue of Claud Ronald Anson, *b.* 1895, *d.* 1965: *m.* 1st, 1915, Frederica Heath, who *d.* 1941, da. of the late Frederic James Harrison, of Maer Hall, Staffs.; 2ndly, 1944, Mrs. Lilian Gallia Meiklejohn, da. of the late David George Davies, of New York; 3rdly, 1949, Mrs. Noreen Stella Cross, da. of the late H. G. Barlow:—

(By 1st marriage) Yvonne (Gurston Manor, Broadchalke, Salisbury), *b.* 1916: *m.* 1941, Brig. Francis Edward Buckland, late RAMC, who *d.* 1965, and has issue living, Francis John, *b.* 1944,—Frances Mary, *b.* 1942.——Mary (Weston Meres, Maer, Newcastle, Staffs., and Lyons Hill, Minterne Magna Dorchester, Dorset), *b.* 1918: *m.* 1940 (m. diss. 1960), Lt.-Col. John Anthony Dene, Duke of Cornwall's LI, and has issue living, John Michael, *b.* 1946,—David Frederick, *b.* 1948,—Margaret Katharine, *b.* 1942: *m.* 1962, Michael Charles Power, of The Court House, Congresbury, Bristol, and has issue living, Anthony George Bertram, *b.* 1968,—Katharine Mary *b.* 1965,—Erica Margaret *b.* 1967,—Joan (of Enton Hatch, Godalming, Surrey), *b.* 1919: *m.* 1945, Maj. J. C. Lee, Roy. Netherlands Army, who *d.* 1963.

Issue (by 1st marriage) of the late Hon. Frederic William Anson, 4th son of 2nd Earl, *b.* 1862, *d.* 1917: *m.* 1st, 1886, Florence Louisa Jane, who *d.* 1908, el. dau. of the late Lieut.-Col. John Henry Bagot Lane, of King's Bromley Manor, Lichfield [Vincent, Bt., colls.]; 2ndly, 1915, Edith, who *d.* 1961, dau. of S. E. Rowland, of Slinfold, Sussex:—

Beryl Susan, *b.* 1904: *m.* 1st, 1928, Claude A. Outbill; 2ndly, 1938, Capt. Harold Winchester Sanderson, Grenadier Guards, from whom she obtained a divorce 1948; 3rdly, 1952, Arthur Temple Thorne. *Residence,*—Hill House, Sunninghill, Ascot, Berks.

Issue of the late Hon. Claud Anson, 5th son of 2nd Earl, *b.* 1864, *d.* 1947: *m.* 1901, Lady Clodagh de la Poer Beresford, who *d.* 1957, dau. of 5th Marquess of Waterford:—
Anthony John, *b.* 1904; European War 1941-45 with Roy. Corps of Signals: *m.* 1926, Rosalind Désirée, da. of Rear-Adm. Sir Robert Keith Arbuthnot, CB, MVO, 4th Bt., and has issue living, John Anthony Robert (75, West Hill Rd., SW18), *b.* 1927: *m.* 1962, Fiona Brook, da. of the late Colin Frederick George Wills, and has issue living, Martin Anthony Wills *b.* 1963, Annabel Frances Rosalind *b.* 1967,—Colin Shane, *b.* 1931,—Sarah Rose, *b.* 1944: *m.* 1969, Lt. Cdr. Robin Gifford Kerr, RN, 3, Lansdown Place East, Bath, and has issue living, Bryony Charlotte *b.* 1972, Julia Emily, *b.* 1974. *Residence,*—Highdown, Horam, Sussex.——Hugo Edward, *b.* 1908; Maj. (ret.) Rifle Bde.: *m.* 1st. 1935, Elizabeth (who obtained a divorce 1946), el. da. of Capt. Sir Harold George Campbell, KCVO, DSO, RN (ret.) [E. Leven and Melville, colls.]; 2ndly, 1946, Duchessa Annina Badoglio, da. of Marchese Sili, and widow of Duca Paolo Badoglio, and has issue living, (by 1st m.) Michael (The Glebe House, Bourton-on-the-Water, Glos.) *b.* 1937; a Page of Honour to HM 1950-53: *m.* 1963, Claire-Elizabeth Seymour, da. of Lt.-Col. Frederick Arthur Morris, of St. Katherine's, Cradley, Malvern, Worcs., and has issue living, Alexandra Albinia *b.* 1965, Josephine Emma *b.* 1968, Catherine Elizabeth *b.* 1971,—(by 2nd m.) Bernard Antony, *b.* 1948, Andrew Victor *b.* 1951. *Residence,*— Via Nicolò Porpora, 12, Rome, Italy.——Clodagh Blanche, *b.* 1902. *Residence,*—Ballyin, Lismore, co. Waterford.

Grandchildren of the late Hon. Francis Anson (infra):—
Issue of the late Wing-Com. Henry Adelbert Anson, R.A.F., *b.* 1895, *d.* 1955: *m.* 1st, 1927, Hilda Suzanne (who obtained a divorce 1930). dau. of S. Carson Allen, of 39, Circus Road, St. John's Wood, NW8; 2ndly, 1930, Muriel Irene, da. of Edgar C. Smith:—
(By 1st m.) David Richard, *b.* 1929.——(By 2nd m.) Vanessa Irene, *b.* 1940: *m.* 1962, John Edward Robert Wauchope, of The Old Rectory, Ripe, Lewes, and has issue living, Andrew Charles Anson, *b.* 1974,—Arabella Jane, *b.* 1963,—Lucy Anne Margaret, *b.* 1965,—Alexandra Gladys, *b.* 1968.

Issue of the late Major William Alfred Anson, *b.* 1897, *d.* 1952: *m.* 1919 Dorothy Helme, (now of Ronan's Lea, Brailes, nr. Banbury), da. of the late Richard Mashiter, of 22, Princes Gate, SW, and Hillend, Glamorgan:—
Francis Richard (15, Ridgeway South, Highlands, Rhodesia), *b.* 1926; late Lt. 13th/18th R. Hussars: *m.* 1st, 1948 (m. diss. 1960), Ann, da. of Sir John Lionel Armytage, 8th Bt.; 2ndly, 1960, Bridgett Ann, only da. of Dudley Gerald David Greenhough, of 25, Aldford House, Park Lane, W1, and has issue living, (by 1st m.) Anthony Francis, *b.* 1951,—Amanda Jane, *b.* 1950,—(by 2nd marriage) Juliet May, *b.* 1961,—Emma Louise, *b.* 1963.——Edward William, *b.* 1929.——Harriet Louise, *b.* 1924.

Issue of the late Capt. the Hon. William Anson, 7th son of 2nd Earl, *b.* 1872, *d.* 1926: *m.* 1917, Louisa Goddard, who *d.* 1952, dau. of Frederick De Voe Van Wagenen, of Fulton, New York:—
Edith, *b.* 1921: *m.* 1st, 1943, Capt. Alfred Ryland Howard, who *d.* (killed in action in Normandy), 1944; 2ndly, 1947, Lieut.-Col. Ford Millspaugh Boulware, and has issue living, (by 1st marriage) Alfred Ryland, *b.* 1944. *Residence,*—Head-of-the-River Ranch, Christoval, Texas, U.S.A.

PREDECESSORS.—[1] THOMAS Anson; *M.P.* for Lichfield 1789-1806; cr. *Baron Soberton,* co. Southampton, and *Viscount Anson* (peerage of United Kingdom) 1806; *d.* 1818; *s.* by his son [2] THOMAS WILLIAM, P.C., 2nd Viscount; *b.* 1795; cr. *Earl of Lichfield* (peerage of United Kingdom) 1831; Master of the Buckhounds 1830-34, and Postmaster-Gen. 1835-41: *m.* 1819, Louisa Barbara Catherine, who *d.* 1879, dau. of Nathaniel Phillips, of Slebech Hall, co. Pembroke; *d.* 1854; *s.* by his son [3] THOMAS GEORGE, 2nd Earl, *b.* 1825; M.P. for Lichfield 1847-54, and Lord-Lieut. of Staffordshire 1863-71; *m.* 1855, Lady Harriet Georgiana Louisa Hamilton, who *d.* 1913, el. dau. of 1st Duke of Abercorn, K.G.; *d.* 1892; *s.* by his el. son [4] THOMAS FRANCIS, 3rd Earl, *b.* 1856: *m.* 1878, Lady Mildred Coke, who *d.* 1941, dau. of 2nd Earl of Leicester; *d.* 1918; *s.* by his son [5] THOMAS EDWARD, 4th Earl; *b.* 1883; Capt. London Regt.; A.D.C. and Acting Master of the Horse to Lord-Lieut. of Ireland (Earl of Aberdeen 1906-10); Lord High Steward of Borough of Stafford 1933: *m.* 1st, 1911, Evelyn Maud, who *d.* 1945, dau. of the late Col. Edward George Keppel, M.V.O.; 2ndly, 1949, Violet Margaret (PHILIPS), dau. of the late Henry Dawson Dawson-Greene, J.P., of Slyne, and Whittington Hall, Lancashire; *d.* 1960; *s.* by his grandson [6] THOMAS PATRICK JOHN (son of the late Lieut.-Col. Thomas William Arnold, Viscount Anson, el. son of 4th Earl), 5th Earl and present peer; also Viscount Anson, and Baron Soberton.

LICHFIELD, LORD BISHOP OF. (Skelton.)

Rt. Rev. KENNETH JOHN FRASER SKELTON, *CBE*, son of Henry Edmund Skelton; *b.* May 16th, 1918; ed. at Dulwich Coll., and Corpus Christi Coll., Camb. (MA); R. of Walton-on-the-Hill, Liverpool 1955-62, Bishop of Matabeleland 1962-70, and Assist. Bishop of Durham, Rural Dean of Wearmouth, and R. of Bishopwearmouth 1970-75; translated 96th Bishop of Lichfield 1975; CBE (Civil) 1972: *m.* 1945, Phyllis Barbara, yst. da. of James Emerton.

Patron of one hundred and thirty-four livings, the Canonries and Prebends in his Cathedral, and the Archdeaconries of Stafford, Salop and Stoke-upon-Trent.

This See was founded by Oswy, king of Mercia, 656; in 1075 it was removed to Chester, in 1102 to Coventry; and finally to its original foundation at Lichfield.

Episcopal Signature,—" Kenneth Lichfield."

ARMS OF THE SEE,—Party per pale gules and argent, a cross potent quadrate in the centre between four crosses patée all counterchanged.

Residence,—Bishop's House, The Close, Lichfield, Staffs., WS13 7LG.

LIFFORD, VISCOUNT.　(Hewitt.)　[Viscount I. 1781.]

ALAN WILLIAM WINGFIELD HEWITT, 8th Viscount；　b. Dec. 11th, 1900; s. 1954；ed. at Winchester；sometime Lieut. Hampshire Regt.：　m. 1935, Alison Mary Patricia, dau. of T. W. Ashton, of The Cottage, Hursley, near Winchester, and has issue.

Arms,—Gules, a chevron engrailed, between three owls argent. Crest,—On a stump of a tree, with one branch growing thereon, an low proper. Supporters,—Dexter, a vulture, proper, wings inverted, gorged with a plain collar sable, thereon three bezants；sinister, a griffin, proper, wings elevated, gorged as the dexter.

Residence,—Field House, Hursley, Hants.

SON LIVING.

Hon. EDWARD JAMES WINGFIELD, b. Jan. 27th, 1949.

DAUGHTERS LIVING.

Hon. Lydia Mary, b. 1938：m. 1965, Michael Christopher Swann, of Foxhanger, Burwash, Sussex, el. son of Sir Anthony Charles Christopher Swann, CMG, OBE, 3rd Bt.
Hon. Belinda Anne, b. 1939：m. 1963 the Rev. Piers Eliot de Dutton Warburton, Chap.Bermuda Regt. 1969-71, of The Rectory, Sherborne St. John, Basingstoke, and has issue living, Piers Richard Grove, b. 1964,—Elizabeth Jane, b. 1967.
Hon. Flora Elizabeth, b. 1947：m. 1965, Edward Bell Henderson, and has issue living, Saman, b. 1967,—a da., b. 1971.

DAUGHTER LIVING OF SIXTH VISCOUNT.

Hon. Norah, b. 1879. Residence,—Monmouth House, Lymington, Hants.

COLLATERAL BRANCHES LIVING.

Grandsons of the late James Francis Katharinus Hewitt, 3rd son of the late Rev. the Hon. James John Pratt Hewitt, 2nd son of 2nd Viscount:—

Issue of the late John Stanley Hewitt, b. 1875, d. 1937：m. 1909, Avice Alurade, who d. 1939, dau. of the late Rev. Arthur Langdale Langdale-Smith, R. of Holton, Wheatley, Oxon:—
Terence John Lifford, b. 1911；European War 1940-45 as Lieut. Gurkha Rifles (prisoner)：m. 1946, Rowena Edith Mabel, second dau. of the late Ernest Taylor England, of 26, Field Park, Newbridge, Monmouthshire, and has issue living, Anthea Avice Yvonne, b. 1947：m. 1970, Richard Geoffrey Horsford Kemp. Residence,—Holton Cottage, Holton, Oxon.——Theodore Denis, b. 1918；1940-45 War as Lt. and acting Capt. Gurkha Rifles. Address,—c/o National and Grindlays Bank, 54, Parliament St., SW1.

Issue of the late Cdr. Brian Lifford Hewitt, OBE, b. 1881, d. 1962；m. 1914, Roie (11 Ely Av., Remuera, Auckland, NZ, da. of the late Alfred Nathan, of Wickford, Auckland, New Zealand:—
Michael James Alfred Lifford (of 724, Gladstone Rd., Gisborne, New Zealand), b. 1916：m. 1947, Sybil Grace, youngest dau. of the late William Arthur Izard [E. Eglinton and Winton, colls.], and has issue living, Peter Lifford, b. 1948,—Anthony James, b. 1951,—Rosemary Ruth, b. 1949,— Elizabeth Grace, b. 1956.——Patrick Francis (of 31, Dell Av., Remuera, Auckland, New Zealand), b. 1921：m. 1st, 1944 (marriage dissolved 19—), Mary, dau. of Trevor N. Holmden, of Remuera, Auckland, New Zealand; 2ndly, 1954, Judith, dau. of the late John Hellaby, of 5, Ridings Rd., Remuera, Auckland, New Zealand, and has issue living, (by 1st m.) Brian James Lifford (24, Waipapa Rd., Hataitai, Wellington, NZ) b. 1945；Capt.：m. 1972, Erin Margaret, el. da. of Keith Charles Walshe, of Te Anau, NZ.

Grandchildren of the late Capt. James Dudley Ryder Hewitt, R.N., (infra):—
Issue of the late John Edward Hewitt, b. 1874, d. 1949：m. 1901, Ellen Edith, who d. 1958, dau. of V. T. Hitchings, formerly of Woodstock Levin, New Zealand:—
William Robert Riddiford, b. 1903：m. 1930, Nancy Charlotte Ellen, el. dau. of Sydney Arthur Robert Mair, of Wharekuru, Hunterville, New Zealand, and has issue living, Ian Robert, b. 1931,—Peter David (Margamaire, Pahiatna, NZ), b. 1937：m. 1963, Heather Jean, da. of Robert Allen Donald, of Papataki, NZ, and has issue living, James Donald b. 1965, Peter John b. 1967, Timothy David b. 1968, Teena Anne b. 1964,—Judith Ann, b. 1936：m. 1965, John Henry Armstrong, of Koro Koro, Wellington, NZ, and has issue living, Jane Margaret b. 1966. Residence,—Massey College, Palmerston North, NZ.——Helen Mary Gervais, b. 1902：m. 1926, Thomas Westbury Abraham, who d. 1967, and has issue living, David Thomas (Tainui, RD3, Marton, NZ), b. 1937： m. 1963, Susan Winifred Nelson, and has issue living, Thomas Nelson b. 1968, Nicola Jane b. 1967,— Brian Lionel John, b. 1940：m. 1968, Diana Margaret Cranstone, and has issue living, Andrew James b. 1973, Julia Margaret b. 1970,—Mary Helen, b. 1932：m. 1957, John Ernest Collier, of 17, Higgins St., Marewa, Napier, NZ, and has issue living, David b. 1961, Susan Mary b. 1959. Residence,— 89, Essex St., Masterton, NZ.

Issue of the late Lt.-Col. Dudley Riddiford Hewitt, CIE, b. 1877, d. 1971：m. 1913, Marjorie Middlemas, who d. 1954, yr. da. of the late William Fleming Inglis, of Shanghai:—
Dorothy Mary Riddiford, b. 1914：m. 1942, Capt. William James Lysley, 11th Hussars, of The Old Rectory, West Stow, Bury St. Edmunds, and has issue living, Rachel Marjorie Sarah Anne, b. 1949. ——Patricia Frances Thomasine (PO Box 40111, Nairobi, Kenya), b. 1916：m. 1st, 1940, Capt. Herbert Eldon Hope, RA, who d. 1946; 2ndly, 1948 (m. diss. 1958) Maj. Gilbert Hannington, REME; 3rdly, 1959, Col. Brian Charles Lascelles Tayleur, OBE, 14th/20th King's Hussars, and has issue living, (by 1st m.) Michael Lifford Ashworth (c/o Lloyds Bank, Wincanton, Som.), b. 1942； Capt. 14th/20th King's Hussars：m. 1966 (m. diss. 1972), Alison, da. of Brig. E. S. Lough, and has issue living, Simon Ashworth b. 1967, Justin William Ashworth b. 1969,—Jeremy Fleming Ashworth (c/o Lloyds Bank, Wincanton, Som.), b. 1944；Capt. 14th/20th King's Hussars：m. 1966, Rosemary Ann, da. of the late F/O C. D. Gough, and has issue living, Lucy Nicola b. 1970,—Sally Patricia Ashworth (twin), b. 1944：m. 1965, Christopher John Russell (4, The Newlands, Studley, Warwicks., BS0 7QD), and has issue living, Simon Rupert b. 1972, Kimberley Hope b. 1967, Samantha b. 1969.

Issue of the late Charles Gervais Hewitt, b. 1885, d. 1970：m. 1911, Elsie Mary, who d. 1974, el. da. of Herbert Pryce, of Rangitawa, Halcombe, NZ:—
Cushla Mary (Ngakouka, Carterton, Wellington, NZ), b. 1916.——Ruth Lifford, b. 1918.

Granddaughter of the late Rev. the Hon. James John Pratt Hewitt (ante):—
Issue of the late Capt. James Dudley Ryder Hewitt, R.N., *b.* 1840, *d.* 1913: *m.* 1873,
Thomasine, who *d.* 1942, dau. of Daniel Riddiford, of Woburn, New Zealand:—
Alice Margaret, *b.* 1883.

Grandchildren of the late Capt. James Dudley Ryder Hewitt, R.N. (ante):—
Issue of the late James Francis Daniel Hewitt, *b.* 1881, *d.* 1963: *m.* 1st, 1908, Ellen West-
bury, who *d.* 1938, dau. of R. S. Abraham, of Palmerston North, New Zealand); 2ndly,
1942, May Evelyn, da. of E. J. Wright, of Kerikeri, New Zealand:—
(By 1st m.) Richard Walter (Taratanui, Ponatahi, Carterton, Wellington, NZ), *b.* 1909: *m.* 1951,
Joan Millicent, el. da. of Thomas Edward Holdgate, of Timaru, NZ, and has issue living, Timothy
James, *b.* 1954,—Mary Ellen *b.* 1952.——June Lifford, *b.* 1910: *m.* 1934, Robert Oswald Young, of
14, Matenga St., Waikanae, NZ, and has issue living, Robin Slingsby, *b.* 1935,—Simon Vivian Riddiford, *b.* 1936,—James Francis, *b.* 1940,—Thomas Lifford, *b.* 1945,—Ellen Jennifer, *b.* 1938.

PREDECESSORS.—[1] James Hewitt, *P.C.*; was a Justice of the King's Bench in England
1766-8, and Lord Chancellor of Ireland 1768-82; cr. *Baron Lifford*, of Lifford, co. Donegal
(peerage of Ireland) 1768, and *Viscount Lifford* (peerage of Ireland) 1781; *d.* 1789; *s.* by his
son [2] JAMES, *D.D.*, 2nd Viscount; was Dean of Armagh; *d.* 1830; *s.* by his son [3] JAMES,
3rd Viscount; *b.* 1783: *m.* 1809, the Hon. Mary Anne Maude, who *d.* 1877, dau. of 1st Viscount
Hawarden; *d.* 1855; *s.* by his son [4] JAMES, 4th Viscount, *b.* 1811: was a Representative
Peer: *m.* 1st, 1835, Lady Mary Acheson, who *d.* 1850, el. dau. of 2nd Earl of Gosford; 2ndly,
1851, Lydia Lucy, who *d.* 1919, el. dau. of the Rev. John Digby Wingfield Digby, V. of Coleshill,
and widow of Charles Purdon-Coote; *d.* 1887; *s.* by his el. son [5] James Wilfrid, 5th
Viscount; *b.* 1837: *m.* 1867, Annie Frances, who *d.* 1927, el. dau. of the late Sir Arthur
Hodgson, K.C.M.G., of Clopton House, Stratford-on-Avon; *d.* 1913; *s.* by his brother [6]
ARCHIBALD ROBERT, 6th Viscount, *b.* 1844; Capt. R.N.: *m.* 1878, Helen Blanche, who *d.* 1942,
only dau. of the late Charles S. Geach; *d.* 1925; *s.* by his son [7] EVELYN JAMES, *D.S.O.*, 7th
Viscount; *b.* 1880; Lieut.-Col. (retired) Dorsetshire Regt.; S. Africa 1902, European War 1914-18
(D.S.O. and Bar): *m.* 1919, Charlotte Rankine, who *d.* 1954, dau. of the late Sir Robert Maule, and
widow of Capt. Edgar Walker; *d.* 1954; *s.* by his cousin [8] ALAN WILLIAM WINGFIELD (son of the
late Hon. George Wyldbore Hewitt, 7th son of 4th Viscount), 8th Viscount and present peer; also
Baron Lifford.

LILFORD, BARON. (Powys.) [Baron G.B. 1797.]

[Name pronounced "Poe-is."]

GEORGE VERNON POWYS, 7th Baron; *b.*
Jan. 8th, 1931; *s.* 1949; ed. at Stonyhurst:
m. 1st, 1954, Mrs. Eve Bird; 2ndly, 1957
(m. diss. 1958), Anuta, only da. of L. F.
Merritt, of Johannesburg, S. Africa; 3rdly,
1958 (m. diss. 1961), Norma Yvonne, only
da. of V. Shell, of Johannesburg, S. Africa;
4thly, 1961 (m. diss. 1969), Mrs. Muriel
Spottiswoode; 5thly, 1969, Margaret, da.
of A. Penman, of Roslin, Midlothian, and
has issue living by 4th and 5th m.

To maintain acquired possessions.

Arms.—Or, a bear's jamb erased in bend dexter, between two cross crosslets fitchée in bend
sinister, gules. *Crest.*—A lion's jamb couped and erect gules, holding a staff headed with a fleur-de-
lis, also erect or. *Supporters—Dexter*, a reaper habited in a loose shirt, leather breeches loose at
the knees, white stockings, and black hat and shoes; in his hat ears of corn, in his right hand a reaping-
hook, and at his feet a garb, all proper; *sinister*, a man in the uniform of the Northamptonshire
Yeomanry Cavalry, viz. a green long coat, ornamented on the cuffs and button-holes with gold lace,
yellow waistcoat and breeches, and black top boots; a black stock; a round hat; adorned with a
white feather in front and a green one behind, the sword-belt inscribed with the letters N.Y. and the
exterior hand resting on his sword sheathed and point downwards.
Seat,—Bank Hall, Bretherton, Preston, Lancs. *Residence,*—Bowerswood, Nateby, Preston,
Lancs.

DAUGHTERS LIVING. (By 4th m.)
Hon. Clare Lynette, *b.* 1962.
Hon. Emma-Jane, *b.* 1964.

(By 5th m.)
Hon. Sarah Margaret, *b.* 1971.
Hon. Hannah Victoria, *b.* 1974.

SISTERS LIVING.
Hilary Betty (68, Scott Av., Orkney, W. Transvaal), *b.* 1929: *m.* 1950, Philip Donald Millar, who *d*
1967, and has issue living, Christopher, *b.* 1960,—Philipa Ann, *b.* 1958.
Beryl Irene, *b.* 1932.

AUNTS LIVING.
Magdalen, *b.* 1890.   Nesta, *b.* 1896.

MOTHER LIVING.
Vera Grace Bryant: *m.* 1926, Robert Horace Powys, who *d.* 1940 [see PREDECESSORS]. *Residence,*—
Crossford Lodge, Back Hall Drive, Bretherton, Preston.

COLLATERAL BRANCHES LIVING.
Grandson of the late Henry Littleton Powys, el. son of the late Robert Horace
Powys, 2nd son of 2nd Baron:—
Issue of the late Frank Lilford Powys, *b.* 1902, *d.* 1972: *m.* 1929. Gertrude Frances Elizabeth
(Erensrust, 3, Hilltop Rd., Hillcrest, Natal), da. of G. G. F. Meyer:—
ROBERT CHARLES LILFORD (Lilford Lodge, 10, Langwood Rd., Pinetown, Natal), *b.* Aug. 15th,
1930: *m.* 1st, 1957 (m. diss. 1972), Charlotte Webb; 2ndly, 1973, Janet Wightwick, and has issue
living, (by 2nd m.), Matthew Robert Lilford, *b.* 1974.

Grandchildren of the late Wilfred Owen Powys (infra):—
Issue of the late Horace Victor Powys, *b.* 1907, *d.* 1956: *m.* 1928, Olive Maude Peets, of
Durban, S. Africa:—
Michael John (5, Saturn Rd., Westville, Natal), *b.* 1934: *m.* 1957, Lynette Bernice Hodges, of Durban,
Natal, and has issue living, Victor Michael, *b.* 1961,—Andrew John, *b.* 1970,—Susan Lynn, *b.* 1958.
——Pamela Ann, *b.* 1929: *m.* 1st, 1949 (m. diss. 1959), Ian Falconer; 2ndly, 1959, Harry Rowntree,
of Umbogintwini, Natal, and has issue living, (by 1st m.) Malcolm, *b.* 1950,—Donald, *b.* 1952,—
Colin, *b.* 1955,—Neil, *b.* 1956,—(by 2nd m.) Mark, *b.* 1960,—Anne, *b.* 1961.

Granddaughter of the late Robert Horace Powys (ante):—
Issue of the late Wilfred Owen Powys *b.* 1873, *d.* 1944: *m.* 1905, Constance Mary, who *d.*
1948, dau. of Robert Michael Bradford:—
Marjorie Gladys, *b.* 1911: *m.* 1933, Cecil Wilme Collier, of 10, Ashford Place, Durban, Natal, and has
issue living, Frank Wilme, *b.* 1942: *m.* 1969, Christine Dewar, of Vryheid, Natal, and has issue living
Andrew Blaine *b.* 1972, Claire *b.* 1974,—David Owen, *b.* 1947: *m.* 1970, Fay McKenzie, of Richmond,
Natal, and has issue living, Vicki *b.* 1974.

Grandchildren of the late Rev. the Hon. Atherton Legh Powys, 4th son of 2nd, Baron :—
Issue of the late Richard Atherton Norman Powys, *b.* 1844, *d.* 1913: *m.* 1882, Florence Martha Hussey, who *d.* 1905:—
Atherton Richard Norman, *b.* 1888; admitted Solicitor 1912 : *m.* 1915, Elsie Dyus, who *d.* 1957, dau. of the late Frederick Robert Mattingly, and has issue living, John Frederick Atherton, *b.* 1916,—Richard Atherton Legh, *b.* 1923: *m.* 1962, Ann Patricia Blanchard, and has issue living, Anthony Richard Atherton *b.* 1963, David John Atherton *b.* 1965, Christopher James Atherton *b.* 1967, Michael Paul Atherton *b.* 1970, Nicholas *b.* 1971,—Mary Elizabeth Anne, *b.* 1921. *Residence,—* 5, Albert Terr., NW1.

Grandsons of the late Thomas Charles Leycester Powys-Keck, el. son of the late Thomas Bancho Powys-Keck (infra) :—
Issue of the late Thomas Leycester POWYS-KECK, *b.* 1919, *d.* 1959: *m.* 1949, Joyce (Kingston Gorse House, Kingston Gorse, Littlehampton, Sussex), da. of Albert Hills, of Worthing, Sussex:—
Thomas Charles Leycester, *b.* 1951.——Piers Anthony Leycester, *b.* 1954.

Granddaughter of the late Thomas Bancho Powys-Keck, son of the late Maj. the Hon. Henry Littleton Powys-Keck, 5th son of 2nd Baron :—
Issue of the late Capt. Horatio James POWYS, King's Roy· Rifle Corps, *b.* 1873, *d.* 1952, having resumed in 1930 for himself only the family name of Powys only in lieu of Powys-Keck: *m.* 1902, Edith Mary POWYS-KECK, who *d.* 1971, da. of Alexander Harvey, of St. John's, Newfoundland:—
(Gwladys Margarita) Joan, *b.* 1911; has discontinued the use of the Christian names of Gwladys Margarita, and is known as Malta Joan: *m.* 1933 (marriage diss. 1959), David Fenwick, and has issue living, Anthony Benedict Xavier (Sholebroke, Towcester, Northants), *b.* 1934; ed. at Ampleforth: *m.* 1958, Susan Deirdre, yr. da. of Lt.-Col. Peter Heber-Percy, OBE [see D. Northumberland, colls.], and has issue living, Alexius John Benedict *b.* 1959, Celestria Chantal Arabella *b.* 1963,—Charles Christopher Sebastian, *b.* 1946,—Timothy Dominic Ignatius, *b.* 1947: *m.* 1971, Jeanne Marie Julienne, only da. of Joseph Marechal, of Bastogne, Belgium,—Justin Francis Quintus, *b.* 1949,—Sebastian Edmund Stephen, *b.* 1953,—Serena Mary (Hope Cottage, Gerrards Cross, Bucks.), *b.* 1944. *Residence,—*36, Cloncurry St., SW6.

PREDECESSORS.—[1] THOMAS POWYS, *M.P.* for Northamptonshire 1774-97 ; *cr. Baron Lilford*, of Lilford, co. Northampton (peerage of Great Britain) 1797 ; *d.* 1800; *s.* by his son [2] THOMAS, 2nd Baron; *d.* 1825; *s.* by his son [3] THOMAS ATHERTON, 3rd Baron ; was a Lord-in-Waiting to H.M. Queen Victoria: *m.* the Hon. Mary Elizabeth Fox, dau. of 3rd Baron Holland ; *d.* 1861, *s.* by his son [4] THOMAS LITTLETON, 4th Baron, *b.* 1833 : *m.* 1st, 1859, Emma Elizabeth, who *d.* 1884, dau. of Robert William Brandling, of Low Gosforth, Northumberland; 2ndly, 1885, Clementina Georgiana, who *d.* 1929, dau. of the late Ker Baillie-Hamilton, C.B. ; *d.* 1896 ; *s.* by his el. surviving son [5] JOHN, 5th Baron, *b.* 1863: *m.* 1894, Milly Louisa, who *d.* 1940, dau. of the late George William Culme Soltau-Symons, of Chaddlewood, Plympton : *d.* 1945 ; *s.* by his brother [6] STEPHEN, 6th Baron, *b.* 1869; *d.* 1949 ; *s.* by his kinsman [7] GEORGE VERNON (son of the late Robert Horace Powys, only son of the late Robert Vernon Powys, 2nd son of the late Robert Horace Powys, el. son of the late Hon. Robert Vernon Powys, 2nd son of 2nd Baron), 7th Baron and present peer.

LIMERICK, EARL OF.   (Pery.)   Sits as BARON FOXFORD (U K 1815).
[Earl I. 1803.]

By courage, not by craft.

PATRICK EDMUND PERY, 6th Earl, *b.* April 12th, 1930; *s.* 1967; ed. at Eton, and New Coll., Oxford (MA); late Maj. City of London Yeo (TA); CA; Dir. Kleinwort Benson, Ltd.; Pres. of Assocn. of British Chambers of Commerce, and a Council Member of London Chamber of Commerce; Dep. Chm., Cttee. for Middle East Trade, and a Member of British Overseas Trade Board; Pres. of Ski Club of Gt. Britain; Parl. Under-Sec. Trade 1972-74: *m.* 1961, Sylvia Rosalind, MA, el. da. of Brig. Maurice Stanley Lush, CB, CBE, MC, and has issue.

Arms—Quarterly: gules and or, on a bend argent three lions passant sable. Crest,—A fawn's head erased proper. Supporters,—*Dexter*, a lion ermine; *sinister*, a fawn proper, ducally collared and chained or.

Residences,—Chiddinglye, West Hoathly, East Grinstead, Sussex; 30, Victoria Rd., W8.

SONS LIVING.

EDMUND CHRISTOPHER (*Viscount Glentworth*), *b.* Feb. 10th, 1963.
Hon. Adrian Patrick, *b.* 1967.

DAUGHTER LIVING.

Lady Alison Dora *b.* 1964.

BROTHER LIVING.

Hon. Michael Henry Colquhoun (Kilmaronaig, Connel, Argyll), *b.* 1937; ed. at Eton, and at New Coll., Oxford (BA 1960); late Lt. Inns. of Court and City Yeo.; Man. Dir., Alginate Industries, Ltd.; *m.* 1963, Jennifer Mary, el. da. of J. A. Stuart-Williams, of Causeway House, Braughing, Herts., and has issue living, Marcus Alexander Kemal, *b.* 1965,—Fergus Anthony Colquhoun, *b.* 1967,—Pervaneh Frances, *b.* 1969,—Azelle Fiona, *b.* 1971.

SISTER LIVING.

Lady Anne Patricia, *b.* 1928; ed. at North Foreland Lodge, and at St. Hugh's Coll., Oxford (MA, DPhil); Senior Lecturer and Senior Tutor, Imperial Coll. of Science and Tech.: *m.* 1959, Lt.-Col. Peter Francis Thorne, CBE, yst. son of the late Gen. Sir (Augustus Francis) Andrew Nicol Thorne, KCB, CMG, DSO, DL, and has issue living, Andrew Henry, *b.* 1965,—Bridget Iolanthe, *b.* 1961,—Meriel Patricia, *b.* 1963,—Janet Melinda, *b.* 1968. *Residence,—*Speaker's Green, House of Commons, SW1.

WIDOW LIVING OF FIFTH EARL.

ANGELA OLIVIA, GBE, CH (*Angela, Countess of Limerick*) (Chiddinglye, West Hoathly, East Grinstead, Sussex), da. of the late Lt.-Col. Sir Henry Trotter, KCMG, CB [D. Wellington, colls.]; Hon LLD, Manchester and Leeds; past Chm. of Standing Commn. of Internat. Red Cross, Vice-Chm. of British Red Cross Soc., and of League of Red Cross Socs.; D.St.J.; Austrian Order of Merit; 1914-18 War with VAD; OBE (Civil) 1942, DBE (Civil) 1946, GBE (Civil) 1954, CH 1974: *m.* 1926, the 5th Earl, who *d.* 1967.

COLLATERAL BRANCHES LIVING.

Grandchildren of the late Hon. Edmond Aubrey Templar Pery (Sub-Lt. RN), 3rd son of 2nd Earl:—
Issue of the late Harry Reddall de Vere Pery, b. 1877, d. 1937: m. 1907, Bertha, who d. 1936, da. of John Edward Fouscha:—
Lyndon de Vere (Lot 39, Mathew Flinders Drive, Port Macquarie, NSW), b. 1914: m. 1934, Eileen May, da. of Henry Ernest Reid, and has issue living, Barry Lyndon de Vere, b. 1935,—Carol Ann, b. 1942.——Claudia Thelma de Vere, b. 1909: m. 1933, James Hewitt, of 12, Junction Rd., Summer Hill, NSW, and has issue living, Thelma, b. 1938,—Roslyn, b. 1940.——Gretta de Vere, b. 1911: m. 1944, Daniel John Foster (P.O. Box 36, Ulladulla, NSW).

Granddaughter of the late Hon. Cecil Standish Stackpole Pery, 4th son of 2nd Earl:—
Issue of the late Neville John Tenison Pery, b. 1877, d. 1958: m. 1905, Dolores Harriett, dau. of Harvey Davis, of Upton Hall, Worcester.
Kathleen Dolores de Vere, b. 1906: m. 1937, Kenneth Campbell-Watson, of An Droma, 2-310, Bedford Highway, Rockingham, Halifax, Nova Scotia, and has issue living, Kenneth David Campbell, b. 1944,—Cayleen Elizabeth Hinshaw b. 1939,—Katherine Louise, b. 1940.

Grandchildren of Edmond Arthur Gore PERY-KNOX-GORE, el. son of Edmond Henry Cokayne PERY-KNOX-GORE (infra):—
Issue of the late Maj. Edmond Myles PERY-KNOX-GORE, b. 1904, d. 1965: m. 1st, 1929 (m. diss. 1948), Gundrede Mary, da. of the late Capt. Graham Owen Robert Wynne [B. Killanin] 2ndly, 1948, Ingrid Margaret Mary, da. of the late Henry MacDermot, KC, of 19, Fitz-william Sq., Dublin, and widow of Capt. Francis Holdsworth ffrench-Davis, RASC [B. Mowbray, colls.]:—
(By 1st m.) Simon, b. 1927: m. 1961, Moira, da. of Thomas Jarlath Egan, of The Rise, Sevenoaks, Kent, and has issue living, Myles, b. 1970,—Caroline, b. 1962,—Katherine Lucy, b. 1964,—Siobhan, b. 1966.——(by 2nd m.) Mark, b. 1955.——Sarah, b. 1950.

Grandchildren of the late Edmond Henry Cokayne PERY-KNOX-GORE, el. son of the Hon. Edmond Sexten Pery, 4th son of 1st Earl:—
Issue of the late Brigadier Arthur Francis Gore PERY-KNOX-GORE, C.B., D.S.O., late RASC, b. 1880, d. 1954: m. 1909, Evangeline, who d. 1967, da. of the late Capt. John William St. John Hughes, [Hughes, Bt., cr. 1773, colls.]:—
Diana Frances FITZROY-YATES (Upend Stud Farm, Newmarket, Suffolk), b. 1914, assumed by deed poll 1965 the surname of FitzRoy-Yates: m. 1st, 1936, as his 2nd wife, Nigel Horatio Trevor Fitz-Roy, who d. 1953 [see D. Grafton, colls.]; 2ndly, 1958, William Edward Yates, who d. 1964.——Mary Agnes, b. 1923: m. 1949, Anthony Richard Barrowclough, Bar.-at-Law, and has issue living, Richard Edmond, b. 1953,—Claire Cecilia, b. 1956. Residences,—Spencer Cottage, Spencer Walk, Putney, SW15 and The Old Vicarage, Winsford, Minehead, Som.
Issue of the late Major Aubrey Edmond Pery-Knox-Gore, O.B.E., b. 1883, d. 1960: m. 1916, Monica, who d. 1973, da. of Capt. John Strachan Bridges [E. Courtown]:—
Cullen (P.O. Box 35, St. Michaels-on-Sea, S. Coast, Natal), b. 1917: m. 1st, 1942, Barbara, who d. (at sea, result of enemy action) 1942, only da. of G. L. Stuart, of Dalkeith, Bramhall, Cheshire; 2ndly, 1948, Priscilla Wendy, da. of J. S. Corr, of Johannesburg, S. Africa, and has issue living, (by 2nd m.) Janet Barbara, b. 1950,—Dianna Wendy, b. 1951.——David Edmond Strachan, b. 1920; is Lt. RNVR; 1940-45 War (despatches): m. 1948, Molly, da. of the late A. Daly, of Pretoria, S. Africa, and widow of Maj. Frank Robertson, S. African Air Force. Residence,—

PREDECESSORS.—[1] Right Rev. WILLIAM CECIL Pery (younger brother of Edmond Sexten Pery, cr. Viscount Pery 1785, ext. 1800), successively Bishop of Killala and Limerick; cr. Baron Glentworth, of Mallow (peerage of Ireland) 1790; d. 1794; s. by his son [2] EDMOND HENRY, 2nd Baron; M.P. for Limerick City 1785-94; cr. Viscount Limerick (peerage of Ireland, 1800, Earl of Limerick (peerage of Ireland) 1803, and Baron Foxford, of Stackpole Court, co. Limerick (peerage of United Kingdom) 1815; d. 1844; s. by his grandson [3] WILLIAM HENRY TENNISON, 2nd Earl; b. 1812: m. 1st, 1838, Susannah, dau. of William Sheaffe, of Cornwall; 2ndly, 1842, Margaret Jane, dau. of Capt. Nicholas Horsley. 96th Regt.; d. 1866; s. by his son [4] WILLIAM HALE JOHN CHARLES, K.P., P.C., 3rd Earl; b. 1840; a Lord-in-Waiting to H.M. Queen Victoria 1886-9, and Capt. of the Yeomen of the Guard 1889-92 and 1895-6: m. 1st, 1862, Caroline Maria, who d. 1877, dau. of the late Rev. Henry Gray; 2ndly, 1877, Isabella, who d, 1927, dau. of the late Chevalier James Colquhoun; d. 1896; s. by his el. son [5] WILLIAM HENRY EDMOND DE VERE SHEAFFE, 4th Earl; b. 1863: m. 1890, May Imelda Josephine, C.B.E., who d. 1943, dau. of the late Joseph Burke Irwin, formerly Resident Magistrate, of Stelleen House, Drogheda; d. 1929; s. by his half-brother [6] EDMUND COLQUHOUN, GBE, CH, KCB, DSO, TD, 5th Earl; b. 1888; Brevet Col. RHA (TA) and Comdg. 11th Bde.; Pres. of Med. Research Council 1952-60, and Council of T & AF A 1954-56: m. 1926, Angela Olivia, GBE, CH, da. of Lt.-Col. Sir Henry Trotter, KCMG, CB, d. 1967; s. by his el. son [7] PATRICK EDMUND, 6th Earl and present peer; also Viscount Limerick, Baron Glentworth, and Baron Foxford.

LINCOLN, LORD BISHOP OF. (Phipps.)

Rt. Rev. SIMON WILTON PHIPPS, MC, son of the late Capt. William Duncan Phipps, CVO, RN; b. July 6th, 1921; ed. at Eton, Trin. Coll., Camb. (MA), and West-cott House, Camb.; 1939-45 War as Capt. Coldm. Gds. (MC); Mil. Assist. (Maj.) to Adjt. Gen. to the Forces, War Office 1946; Curate of Huddersfield Parish Church 1950-53; Chap. of Trin. Coll., Camb. 1953-58; Industrial Chap. Coventry Diocese 1958-68; Chap. of Coventry Cathedral 1958-68 (Hon. Canon 1965-68); consecrated Bishop of Horsham (Suffragan for Diocese of Chichester) 1968, and translated 69th Bishop of Lincoln 1974: m. 1973, Mary, da. of the late Sir (Charles) Eric Palmer, of Shinfield Grange, Berks., and widow of the Rev. Dr. James Welch.

Patron of 154 livings, and of 21 alternately, and 14 by turns or jointly, the Canonries, Precentorship, Chancellorship, Sub-Deanery, the Arch-deaconries of Stow, Lincoln, and Lindsey; and Prebendal Stalls in his Cathedral.
This See was founded out of two ancient Sees, that of Lindisfan, whose See was at Sidnacester, and that of the Middle Angles at Leicester. These were united into one Diocese under the See of Leicester which was removed to Dorchester, and after the Conquest, to Lincoln.

Episcopal Signature,—" Simon Lincoln ".

ARMS OF THE SEE,—Gules: two lions passant guardant or, on a chief azure, the Virgin ducally crowned, sitting on a throne, issuant from the chief, on her dexter arm the infant Jesus, and in her sinister hand a sceptre all or.
Residence,—Bishop's House, Eastgate, Lincoln.

LINDGREN, BARONY OF. (Lindgren.) [Extinct 1971.]

SON LIVING OF LIFE BARON.

Hon. Graham Alastair, *b.* 1928: *m.* 1953, Gwendolyne Mary, da. of the late Arthur Miller. *Residence*, —43, Westley Wood, Welwyn Garden City, Herts.

WIDOW LIVING OF LIFE BARON.

ELSIE OLIVE (*Baroness Lindgren*) (4, Attimore Close, Welwyn Garden City, Herts.), da. of the late Frank Reed: *m.* 1926, the 1st Baron, who *d.* 1971, when the title became ext.

LINDSAY, EARL OF. (Lindesay-Bethune.) [Earl S. 1633.]

[Name pronounced "Beeton."]

I love.

WILLIAM TUCKER LINDESAY-BETHUNE, 14th Earl; *b.* April 28th, 1901; *s.* 1943; ed. at Groton, U.S.A., and at Brasenose Coll., Oxford; Major late Scots Guards; Hon. Col., Fife and Forfar Yeo., Scottish Horse 1957-62; a Member of Queen's Body Guard for Scotland (Roy. Co. of Archers), and a D.L. for co. Fife; was Prior of the Order of St. John of Jerusalem in Scotland 1947-50, and a Representative Peer 1947-59; Zone Comnr. for N. Civil Defence Zone of Scotland 1963-69; Pres. of Shipwrecked Fishermen and Mariners Roy. Benevolent Soc. since 1966; 1939-45 War (wounded); assumed for himself and issue the additional surname of Bethune 1939: *m.* 1925, Marjory (a D.St.J.), da. of the late Arthur Graham Cross, and has issue.

Arms.—Quarterly, 1st and 4th gules, fesse checky argent and azure, in chief three mullets of the second: 2nd and 3rd, counter quartered, 1st and 4th azure, a fess between three lozenges or; 2nd and 3rd argent, on a chevron sable an otter's head erased of the first, all within a bordure embattled gold. Crest,—A swan with wings expanded proper. Supporters,—Two griffins gules, armed and beaked or.

Residences,—Lahill, Upper Largo, Fife, KY8 6JE; 6, Denbigh House, Hans Pl., SW1. *Clubs,*—Guards, Portland, Leander.

SONS LIVING.

DAVID BETHUNE (*Viscount Garnock*), *b.* Feb. 9th, 1926; ed. at Eton and at Magdalene Coll., Camb.; formerly Scots Guards; a Member of Queen's Body Guard for Scotland (Roy. Co. of Archers), and an OStJ; with Assocn. of American Railroads 1948-49; Vice-Chm. (Canada) British Overseas Trade Board, N. America; a Dir. of John Crossley Carpet Trades Holdings, Ltd., of Halifax, and other Cos., Abbey Life Canada and other Canadian Cos., and Festiniog Railway Co. and other railway Cos.: *m.* 1st, 1953 (*m.* diss. 1968), the Hon. Mary Clare Douglas-Scott-Montagu, yst. da. of 2nd Baron Montagu of Beaulieu; 2ndly, 1969, Penelope Georgina, da. of the late Anthony Crommelin Crossley, MP, and formerly wife of Maj. Henry Ronald Burn Callander, MC [see Crossley, Bt.], and has issue by 1st m.

SON LIVING.—*Hon.* James Randolph (*Master of Garnock*), *b.* Nov. 19th, 1955.
DAUGHTER LIVING.—*Hon.* Caroline Janet, *b.* 1957.
Residences,—The Slack, Heptonstall, Hebden Bridge, Yorks.; Combermere Abbey, Whitchurch, Salop. *Club,*—Bath.

Hon. John Martin, *b.* 1929; ed. at Eton, and at Trin. Hall, Camb.; late Lieut. Scots Guards: *m.* 1953, Enriqueta Mary Jeanne, only dau. of Peter Koch de Gooreynd [see M. Queensberry, colls.] and has issue living, Nicholas John, *b.* 1956,—Jonathan Patrick, *b.* 1959,—Simon Charles, *b.* 1962,— Sally Alexandra Jane, *b.* 1954. *Residence,*—King's Cottage, Kew Green, Richmond, Surrey. *Club,*—Guards.

DAUGHTERS LIVING.

Lady Elizabeth Marjory Beatrice, *b.* 1932: *m.* 1960 (*m.* diss. 1971), Maj. David Laurence Greenacre, late Welsh Gds., and has issue living, Philip Laurence, *b.* 1961,—Andrew Lindsay, *b.* 1969,—Louise Caroline, *b.* 1967. *Residence,*—Selby House, Ham Common, Richmond, Surrey.
Lady Mary Bethune, *b.* 1935: *m.* 1956, Capt. Owen Buckingham Varney, late Scots Guards, and has issue living, Mark Lindesay Buckingham, *b.* 1958,—Guy Nicholas Buckingham, *b.* 1962,—Georgina Mary Bethune, *b.* 1960. *Residence,*—Hill House, Dedham, nr. Colchester, Essex.

COLLATERAL BRANCHES LIVING.

Grandchildren of the late Eric de Sioblade Sutherland Rudd-Clarke (infra):—
Issue of the late Eric Sinclair James Sutherland Rudd-Clarke, *b.* 1904, *d.* 1962: *m.* 1st, 1927, Ella Mary Gavin (who obtained a divorce 1935), dau. of Col. A. L. Lindesay, late Indian Army; 2ndly, 1936 (marriage dissolved 1942), Pamela Helen Moyle, only dau. of George Magor, of Chygwidden, Lelant, Cornwall; 3rdly, 1948 (marriage dissolved 1951), Mrs. Iren Neuwirth, of Goya, Hungary:—
(By 2nd m.) Simon George Sinclair (The Corner House, Smethcote, Church Stretton, Salop), *b.* 1937; Maj. The Light Inf.: *m.* 1965 (*m.* diss. 1972), Susan, da. of Laurence King, and has issue living, Emma Victoria, *b.* 1967,—Camilla, *b.* 1970.——(By 1st m.) Veronica, *b.* 1928: *m.* 1950, Air Vice-Marshal John Nicol Stacey, CBE, DSO, DFC, of Riseden Cottage, Kilndown, Goudhurst, Kent, and has issue living, Amanda Mary Anne, *b.* 1953,—Caroline Jane, *b.* 1956.

Grandsons of the late Emilia, sister of 11th Earl:—
Issue of the late Eric de Sioblade Sutherland RUDD-CLARKE, b. 1864, d. 1925, having
assumed by Roy. licence 1913, for himself and issue, the additional surname and
arms of Clarke, and matriculated the arms of Rudd-Clarke with a quartering for
Sutherland, Lord Duffus 1919: m. 1903, Jessie Forrester (who d. 1951, having m. 2ndly
1933, the Rev. Arthur Waring, V. of Howden, Yorkshire), youngest dau. of the late James
MacArthur Moir, of Hillfoot, Dollar, and Milton, Argyllshire:—
Ian Forrester Sutherland (9, Brownsea View Av., Lilliput, Poole, Dorset), b. 1906: 1939-45 War as
Lieut. RM: m. 1934, Elizabeth Mary Alexandra Rose, da. of Edward Henry Hillman, and has issue
living, Lindesay, b. 1935: m. 1960, Margaret June, yr. da. of Ronald Alsford, of Salisbury, and has
issue living. Timothy b. 1961, Amanda Anne b. 1963,—Penelope Jane, b. 1940: m. 1962, Raymond Tremlett, and has issue living, Wendie b. 1964, Kerstern b. 1967,—Charlotte Nessa, b. 1946:
m. 1972, Philip Stanley.

Granddaughters of the late Maj. Henry Bethune Lindesay, descendant of 4th
Lord:—
Issue of the late Henry George Lindesay, b. 1842, d. 1915: m. 1886, Jane Edith, who d.
1932, da. of the late Edward Fisher, of Spring Dale, Huddersfield [Philipps, Bt., cr. 1887]:—
Jane Kathleen Mary, b. 1888.——Constance Norah Edith, b. 1889: m. 1926, Arthur John Grin-
field Cresswell, and has issue living, Kathleen Susan Lindesay, b. 1929. Residence,—

PREDECESSORS.—[1] Sir William Lindsay, a celebrated knight, 4th son of David 6th Lord
Crawford, obtained the Barony of the Byres by charter 1366 on the resignation of his elder brother
Sir Alexander, of Glenesk, from whom descends the present Earl of Crawford and Balcarres:
m. Christian, dau. of Sir William More, of Abercorn; s. by his son [2] Sir William, 2nd of the
Byres (and Lord of Abercorn); s. by his son [3] Sir John, Justiciary of Scotland N. of the Forth
1457; cr. Lord Lindsay of the Byres (peerage of Scotland) 1445; s. by his el. son [4] DAVID, 2nd
Lord; noted in history as having presented the "great grey horse" to James III. on the eve
of the battle of Sauchieburn 1488; d.s.p. 1492; s. by his brother [5] JOHN, 3rd Lord, surnamed
"John out with the Sword"; d. without male issue 1497; s. by his brother [6] PATRICK, 4th
Lord; a celebrated advocate; had a grant of the Sheriffdom of Fife to himself, his son and grandson; d. 1526; s. by his grandson [7] JOHN, 5th Lord; one of the four nobles to whom the charge
of the infant Queen Mary was committed in 1542, and whose mediation between the Lords of the
Congregation and the Regent, Mary of Guise, led to the pacification of 1559; d. 1563; s. by his
son [8] PATRICK, 6th Lord; an ardent Reformer and Lord of the Congregation; remembered for
his share in the murder of Rizzio, the deposition of Queen Mary, and his challenge to Bothwell at
Carbery Hill; appointed hereditary bailie of the regality of the Archbishopric of St. Andrews;
s. by his son [9] JAMES, 7th Lord; d. 1601; s. by his el. son [10] JOHN, 8th Lord; d. 1609; s. by
his brother [11] ROBERT, 9th Lord; s. by his son [12] JOHN, 10th Lord; cr. Lord Parbroath and
Earl of Lindsay (peerage of Scotland) 1633, with remainder to his heirs male, and being described in
the patent as "one of the most ancient of the Scottish nobility, and the first in the rank of the
greater Barons and Lords of Parliament"; Ludovic, 16th Earl of Crawford, having no children
resigned in 1642 the Earldom of Crawford into the hands of Charles I. for a re-grant in favour of
John, Earl of Lindsay, and the heirs male of his body, and failing which with remainder to Earl
Ludovic's collateral heirs male; sentence of forfeiture having been passed on Earl Ludovic by
Parliament in rebellion 1644, John, 10th Lord Lindsay was during Earl Ludovic's lifetime (he
d. 1652), put in possession of the dignity as 17th Earl of Crawford (peerage of Scotland, cr. 1398),
and he and his five next successors each assumed the style of "Earl of Crawford-Lindsay"; he
was one of the leading spirits of the Covenant, High Treasurer of Scotland 1644, and President
of the Parliament 1645; opposed the surrender of Charles I. to the English 1647, and joined the
engagement for the King's rescue 1648; taken prisoner by Cromwell 1651, and confined in the
Tower and Windsor until the Restoration 1660, when he was reconstituted Treasurer-President
of Parliament and Extraordinary Lord of Session; retired into private life 1663; d. 1676; s. by
his son [13] WILLIAM, 18th Earl of Crawford, 2nd Earl of Lindsay, and 11th Lord Lindsay; known
as "the great and good Earl of Crawford"; an ardent Presbyterian; concurred in the Revolution
of 1688; was President of the Council 1689; d. 1698; s. by his son [14] JOHN, 19th and 3rd Earl
and 12th Lord; a Gen. in the Army, and a Representative Peer; d. 1713; s. by his son [15]
JOHN, 20th and 4th Earl, and 13th Lord; a celebrated military commander; was the first
officer to command the Black Watch (Royal Highlanders, then known as "Lord Crawford-
Lindsay's Highlanders"); d. 1749, from the effects of a wound received at the battle of Krotzka
in 1738; s. by his kinsman [16] GEORGE, 21st and 14th Earl, and 14th Lord, who had in 1738,
s. as 4th Viscount Garnock (see *.* infra); d. 1778; s. by his son [17] GEORGE, 22nd Earl of
Crawford, 6th Earl of Lindsay, 5th Viscount Garnock, and 15th Lord Lindsay; a Maj.-Gen. in
the Army; d. 1808, when the Earldom of Crawford devolved upon Alexander, 6th Earl of Balcarres as heir male of Ludovic, 16th Earl of Crawford (see E. of Crawford and Balcarres) and
the Earldom of Lindsay and minor honours reverted to his kinsman [18] DAVID, de jure 7th Earl
of Lindsay, 6th Viscount Garnock, and 16th Lord Lindsay (the descendant of David, brother of
5th Lord Lindsay); was a Sergeant in the Perths. Militia; several noblemen offered money to
enable him to establish his claim to the peerage, and the Duke of York offered him a commission if his claim succeeded; d. 1809; s. by his kinsman [19] PATRICK, K.B., de jure 8th
Earl, 7th Viscount, and 17th Lord; a distinguished Gen.: d.s.p. 1839; s. by his kinsman [20]
HENRY Lindsay-Bethune, de jure 9th Earl, 8th Viscount, and 18th Lord, the heir male of William,
2nd son of 4th Lord Lindsay; b. 1787; served with remarkable distinction as Commander of
the Persian forces against Russia 1804-19, and against the rebel Zulli Sultan 1834-6; cr. a Bt.
1836, at the request of the Shah; assumed the additional surname of Bethune 1816; m. 1822,
Coutts, dau. of John Trotter, of Dyrham Park; d. 1851; s. by his son [21] JOHN TROTTER,
10th Earl, 9th Viscount, and 19th Lord, b. 1827; s. as 2nd Bart. 1857, and established his right
to the Earldom of Lindsay and minor honours 1878: m. 1858, Jeanne Eudoxie, dau. of Mons.
J. V. Duval, of Bordeaux; d. 1894, when the Baronetcy became extinct, and he was succeeded
in the other titles by his cousin [22] DAVID CLARK Lindesay (son of the late David Aytone Lindesay,
a descendant of 4th Lord), 11th Earl, b. 1832; assumed (without official authority) the surname
and arms of Bethune in lieu of those of Lindesay: m. 1866, Emily Marian, who d. 1920, dau. of the
late Robert Crosse, of Doctors' Commons, and widow of Capt. Edmund Charles Barnes (of H.M.'s
late St. Helena Regt.); d. 1917; s. by his son [23] REGINALD BETHUNE Lindesay-Bethune, 12th
Earl, b. 1867; was a Representative Peer for Scotland 1917-39; matriculated the Arms and
additional surname of Lindesay 1918: m. 1892, Beatrice Mary, who d. 1944, dau. of the late John
Shaw, of Welburn Hall, Kirbymoorside, Yorkshire; d. 1939; s. by his brother [24] ARCHIBALD
LIONEL, 13th Earl, b. 1872: m. 1900, Ethel, who d. 1942, dau. of W. A. Tucker, of Bay State Road,
Boston, U.S.A.; d. 1943; s. by his son [25] WILLIAM TUCKER, 14th Earl, and present peer; also
Viscount Garnock, Lord Parbroath, Lord Kilbirnie, Kingsburn and Drumry, and Lord Lindsay
of the Byres.

. [1] JOHN Lindsay, son of Patrick, 2nd son of 1st Earl of Lindsay; cr. Lord Kilbirnie, Kingsburn, and Drumry, and Viscount Garnock (peerage of Scotland) 1703; d. 1709; s. by his son [2]
PATRICK, 2nd Viscount; d. 1735; s. by his el. son [3] JOHN, 3rd Viscount; d.s.p. 1738; s. by his
brother [4] GEORGE, 4th Viscount; s. as 21st Earl of Crawford (ante).

LINDSAY OF BIRKER, BARON. (Lindsay.) [Baron U.K. 1945.]

MICHAEL FRANCIS MORRIS LINDSAY, 2nd Baron; b. Feb. 24th, 1909; s.
1952; ed. at Gresham's Sch., Holt, and at Balliol Coll., Oxford; was a Tutor,

Yenching Univ., Peking 1937, Press Attaché, British Embassy, Chungking 1940, Visiting Lecturer, Harvard Univ. 1946-47, Lecturer Univ. Coll., Hull 1948-51, and Reader, Australian National Univ., Canberra 1951-9, since when Professor of Far Eastern Studies, American Univ., Washington, D.C., U.S.A.: *m.* 1941, Hsiao Li, dau. of Col. Li Wen Chi, Chinese Army, of Lishih, Shansi, China, and has issue.

Residence,—6812, Delaware St., Chevy Chase, Maryland 20015, USA.

SON LIVING.

Hon. JAMES FRANCIS, *b.* Jan. 29th, 1945; ed. at Geelong Gram. Sch. and Keele Univ.

DAUGHTERS LIVING.

Hon. Erica Susan, *b.* 1942.   Hon. Mary Muriel, *b.* 1951.

BROTHER LIVING.

Hon. Thomas Martin, *M.B.E.*, *b.* 1915 ; ed. at Sidcot Sch., and at Edinburgh Univ.; is Major Sherwood Rangers; European War 1939-45 (despatches); M.B.E. (Mil.) 1946 : *m.* 1st, 1939 (marriage dissolved 1951), Denise Theresa, dau. of Gerald Albert Vaughan; 2ndly, 1951 (marriage dissolved 1961), Felicitas, dau. of Dr. Martin Lange; 3rdly, Erica, dau. of Maj. Eric Thirkell-Cooper, and has issue living, (by 1st marriage) Alexander Sebastian, *b.* 1940,—Thomas Martin, *b.* 1942,—Teresa, *b.* 1945,—(by 2nd marriage) Stuart Martin, *b.* 1951,—Alexander Gordon, *b.* 1952,—(by 3rd marriage) Benjamin Martin *b.* 1962,—Robert William, *b.* 1967. *Residence,*—

SISTER LIVING.

Hon. Anna Drusilla (*Hon. Lady Scott*), *b.* 1911: *m.* 1937, Sir Ian Dixon Scott, KCMG, KCVO, CIE, and has issue living, Peter John Lindsay, *b.* 1948,—Mary Pauline, *b.* 1939,—Rachel Erica, *b.* 1940,—Ann Catherine, *b.* 1942,—Monica Margaret, *b.* 1947. *Residence,*—Ash House, Alde Lane, Aldeburgh, Suffolk.

PREDECESSOR.—[1] ALEXANDER DUNLOP Lindsay, *C.B.E.*, *LL.D.*, son of the late Rev. T. M. Lindsay, D.D., Principal of United Free Church Coll., Glasgow ; *b.* 1879 ; Fellow and Classical Tutor, Balliol Coll. 1906, Jowett Lecturer in Philosophy 1910, and Professor of Moral Philosophy, Glasgow Univ. 1922 ; Master of Balliol Coll., Oxford 1924-49, Vice-Chancellor of Oxford Univ. 1935-38, and Principal of Univ. Coll., N. Staffs. 1949-52 ; cr. *Baron Lindsay of Birker*, of Low Ground, co. Cumberland (peerage of United Kingdom) 1945: *m.* 1907, Erica Violet, who *d.* 1962, dau. of F. Storr; *d.* 1952; *s.* by his el. son [2] MICHAEL FRANCIS MORRIS, 2nd Baron and present Peer.

LINDSEY AND ABINGDON, EARL OF. (Bertie.) [Earl E. 1626 and 1682.]

[Name pronounced "Barty."]

Valour is stronger than a battering ram.

RICHARD HENRY RUPERT BERTIE, 14th Earl of Lindsey and 9th Earl of Abingdon, *b.* June 28th, 1931; *s.* 1963; ed. at Ampleforth; Lt., Roy. Norfolk Regt. (Supplementary Reserve); an Underwriting Member of Lloyd's; High Steward of Abingdon since 1963: *m.* 1957, Norah Elizabeth Farquhar-Oliver, da. of Mark Oliver, O.B.E. [see Farquhar, Bt., colls.], and has issue.

Arms,—Argent, three battering rams essewise in pale proper, armed and garnished azure. Crest,—A Saracen's head affrontée, couped at the shoulders proper, ducally crowned or, and charged on the chest with a fret azure. Supporters,—*Dexter*, a friar habited in russet grey, with a crutch and rosary, all proper; *sinister*, a savage proper wreathed about the temples and waist with oak leaves vert; each charged on the breast with a fret azure.
Residence,—Hunsdonbury, Hunsdon, Ware, Herts. *Clubs,*—Turf, White's.

SONS LIVING.

HENRY MARK WILLOUGHBY (*Lord Norreys of Rycote*), *b.* June 6th, 1958.
Hon. Alexander Michael Richard, *b.* 1970.

DAUGHTER LIVING.

Lady Annabel Frances Rose *b.* 1969.

AUNT LIVING. (*Daughter of 7th Earl of Abingdon.*)

Lady Elizabeth (Betty) Constance, *O.B.E.*, *b.* 1895; Senior Comdt. (retired) A.T.S.; O.B.E. (Civil) 1938 : *m.* 1st, 1914, Major Sigismund William Joseph Trafford, Rifle Brig. (Prince Consort's Own), who *d.* 1953 ; 2ndly, 1956, Col. Henry Antrobus Cartwright, C.M.G., M.C., who *d.* 1957, and has issue living, (by 1st marriage) Edward Willoughby (of Broad House, Wroxham, Norfolk), *b.* 1924 ; late Scots Guards; a Knight of Honour and Devotion of Sovereign Mil. Order of Malta: *m.* 1952, June Imelda, dau. of Richard Harding, of Echo Valley, Springbrook, Queensland, and has issue living, Michael Francis *b.* 1953, Bernard Edward *b.* 1955, Andrew Martin *b.* 1960, Amanda Gabrielle Mary *b.* 1959,—Helen Mary, *b.* 1915: *m.* 1936, Capt. Peter Evelyn Fanshawe, CBE, DSC, RN [E. Erne, colls.], of 12, Lincoln Av., Wimbledon, SW19, 5JT, and has issue living, Richard Henry (12, Kensington Place, W8), *b.* 1939 : *m.* 1966, the Hon. Maura Clare Evans-Freke, da. of 11th Baron Carbery, Veronica Evelyn *b.* 1947,—Sophie Mary (*Baroness Lyell*), *b.* 1916: *m.* 1938, the 2nd Baron Lyell, who *d.* (killed in action during 1939-45 War) 1943,—Diana Rosemary, *b.* 1920: *m.* 1951, John Reford, of Montreal, Canada. *Residence,*—30, Lennox Gdns., SW1.

DAUGHTER LIVING OF TWELFTH EARL OF LINDSEY.

Lady Muriel Felicia Vere, *b.* 1893 ; is a D.J.St.J.; European War 1914-19 (medals): *m.* 1st, 1922, Capt. Henry Herbert Liddell-Grainger, D.L., Scots Guards, who *d.* 1935 ; 2ndly, 1938, as his second wife, Col. Sir Charles Malcolm Barclay-Harvey, KCMG, who *d.* 1969, and has issue living, (by 1st m.) David Ian (Ayton Castle, Berwickshire; New, and Northern Counties (Newcastle upon Tyne)

Clubs, MCC), *b*. 1930; ed. at St. Peter's Coll., Adelaide, S. Aust., and at Eton; late Scots Guards; is a Member of Queen's Body Guard for Scotland (Roy. Co. of Archers), a DL of Berwickshire, a LStJ and FSA (Scot.): *m*. 1957, Anne Mary Sibylla, da. of Col. Sir Henry Abel Smith, KCMG, KCVO, DSO [see E. Athlone], and has issue living, Ian Richard Peregrine *b*. 1959, Charles Montagu *b*. 1960, Simon Rupert *b*. 1962, Malcolm Henry *b*. 1967, Alice Mary *b*. 1965. *Residences*,—Uffington House, Stamford; Dinnet, Aberdeenshire.

STEP MOTHER LIVING.

Lillian Isabel (Flat 2, The Albany, Main St., St. Julians, Malta, GC), da. of the late Charles Edward Joseph Cary-Elwes, of Staithe House, Beccles, Suffolk, and widow of Lt.-Cdr. Francis Dayrell Montague Crackanthorpe, RN: *m*. 1949, as his second wife, Lt.-Col. the Hon. Arthur Michel Bertie, DSO, MC, who *d*. 1957.

WIDOW LIVING OF SON OF SEVENTH EARL OF ABINGDON.

Lady JEAN CRICHTON-STUART (*Lady Jean Bertie*), (Casa de Piro, Attard, Malta), da. of 4th Marquess of Bute: *m*. 1928, Lt.-Cdr. the Hon. James Willoughby Bertie, RN, 3rd son of 7th Earl of Abingdon, who *d*. 1966, and has issue [see infra]:—

WIDOW LIVING OF THIRTEENTH EARL OF LINDSEY AND EIGHTH EARL OF ABINGDON.

ELIZABETH VALETTA (*Elizabeth, Countess of Lindsey and Abingdon*) (of 2, Curzon Place, W.1), da. of the late Maj.-Gen. the Hon. Edward James Montagu-Stuart-Wortley, C.B., C.M.G., D.S.O. [see E. Wharncliffe, colls.]; a Chevalier of Legion of Honour: *m*. 1928, the 13th Earl of Lindsey and 8th Earl of Abingdon, who *d*. 1963.

COLLATERAL BRANCHES LIVING

Issue of the late Lt.-Cdr. the Hon. James Willoughby Bertie, RN, 3rd son of 7th Earl of Abingdon, *b*. 1901, *d*. 1966: *m*. 1928, Lady Jean Crichton-Stuart (ante), da. of 4th Marquess of Bute:—

Andrew Willoughby Ninian (Worth School, Turners Hill, Crawley, Sussex), *b*. 1929; Lt. Scots Guards (SR), and a Knt. of Obedience of Sovereign Mil. Order of Malta.——Charles Peregrine Albemarle (Brockdale House, Warfield, Berks.), *b*. 1932; Capt. Scots Guards (SR), and a Knt. of Honour and Devotion of Sovereign Mil. Order of Malta: *m*. 1960, Susan Griselda Ann Lyon, el. da. of Maj. John Lycett Wills, Life Guards (ret.) [see Wills, Bt., cr. 1904], and has issue living, David Montagu Albemarle, *b*. 1963,—Caroline Georgina Rose, *b*. 1965.

> (*In remainder to Barony of Norreys of Rycote only.*)

Issue of the late Lady Mary Caroline Bertie, dau. of 7th Earl of Abingdon, *b*. 1859, *d*. 1938 : *m*. 1879, the 1st Viscount Fitz Alan of Derwent who *d*. 1947. [See that title.]

Issue of the late Lady Alice Josephine Bertie, dau. of 7th Earl of Abingdon, *b*. 1865, *d*. 1950 : *m*. 1st, 1890, Sir Gerald Herbert Portal, K.C.M.G., C.B., who *d*. 1894; 2ndly, 1897, Major Robert Reyntiens, who *d*. 1913 :—

(By 2nd marriage) Priscilla Cecilia Maria (*Baroness Norman*), *C.B.E.*; *b*. 1899; is a J.P., C.B.E. (Civil) 1963: *m*. 1st, 1921, Alexander Koch de Gooreynd (who assumed by deed poll 1923, the surname of Worsthorne in lieu of de Gooreynd), from whom she obtained a divorce 1929 ; 2ndly, 1933, the 1st Baron Norman, who *d*. 1950, and has issue living, (by 1st m.) Simon Peter Edmund Cosmo William TOWNELEY (Dyneley, Burnley, Lancs), *b*. 1921; Lt. KRRC, JP and DL; Co. Councillor for Lancs. 1961-64, High Sheriff 1971-72; 1939-45 War (prisoner); assumed by deed poll 1945 the additional surname of Towneley before his patronymic, and by Roy. Licence 1955 the arms of Towneley, and relinquished by deed poll 1955 the surname of Worsthorne: *m*. 1955, Mary, da. of Cuthbert Fitzherbert, and has issue living, Peregrine Henry *b*. 1962, Alice Mary *b*. 1956, Charlotte Mary *b*. 1957, Katharine Mary *b*. 1958, Victoria Mary *b*. 1964, Cosima Cecilia *b*. 1967, Frances Teresa *b*. 1969,—Peregrine Gerard (6, Kempson St., SW6), *b*. 1923; Lt. Oxford and Bucks LI attached Liaison Regt.; 1939-45 War: *m*. 1950, Mrs. Claudia Baynham, and has issue living, Dominique Elizabeth Priscilla, *b*. 1952. *Residence*,—Aubrey Lodge, Aubrey Rd., W8.

Issue of the late Lady Gwendeline Theresa Mary Bertie, da. of 7th Earl of Abingdon, *b*. 1885, *d*. 1941: *m*. 1908, Maj. John Strange Spencer-Churchill, DSO, who *d*. 1947. [See D. Marlborough, colls.].

> (*In remainder to the Earldoms and Barony.*)

Grandchildren of the late Rev. the Hon. Alberic Edward Bertie (infra):—
Issue of the late Lieut.-Com. Aubrey Charles Bertie, R.N., *b*. 1882, *d*. 1944: *m*. 1916, Jeanne, dau. of M. A. Vissers:—

Albert Arnaud, *b*. 1919: *m*. 1950, Joan, da. of A. E. Sidery, and has issue living, John Peregrine, *b*. 1952,—Peter Mark, *b*. 1959.——Christine Caroline, *b*. 1917.

Issue of the late Schomberg Montagu Bertie, *b*. 1888; *d*. 1937: *m*. 1922, Edith Mary (who *m*. 2ndly, 1941, Harry August Anders, of 22, Lowanna St., Kenmore, Brisbane, Qld. 4069), da. of John England:—

Caroline Edith (6, Burley Griffin Place, Heidelberg, Melbourne, Aust.), *b*. 1923: *m*. 1952, Gordon Ernest Ross, who *d*. 1971, and has issue living, Alan Gordon Schomberg, *b*. 1955,—Dagmar Caroline Edith, *b*. 1953,—Hilary, *b*. 1960.——Rose Patricia, *b*. 1926; ed. at Queensland Univ. (MSc Agr): *m*. 1951, Harold Edwin Kleinschmidt, of 45, Kersley Rd., Kenmore, Brisbane, Qld., and has issue living, Christopher Montague, *b*. 1963,—Felicity Rose, *b*, 1965,—Elise Caroline, *b*. 1970.

Issue of the late Capt. Alberic Willoughby Bertie, MC, *b*. 1891, *d*. 1969: *m*. 1922, Maria Flore, who *d*. 1925, da. of Philippe Reinhort:—

Marie Lucette: *m*. 1943, Capt. Ronald Frank Kershaw, late 60th Rifles, of Firs House, Ramsdell, Basingstoke, and has issue living, Martin John, *b*. 1954,—Clarissa Mary, *b*. 1944: *m*. 1970, Capt. Peter Malcolm Roe, The R. Hussars (PWO), of 79, Wellesley Rd., W4,—Serena Jane, *b*. 1948: *m*. 1975, James Fergus Surtees Graham [see Graham Bt, cr. 1783],—Gabrielle Lavinia, *b*. 1951.

Issue of the late Rev. the Hon. Alberic Edward Bertie, 3rd son of 6th Earl of Abingdon, *b*. 1846, *d*. 1928 : *m*. 1881, Lady Caroline Elizabeth McDonnell, who *d*. 1930, dau. of 5th Earl of Antrim (of 2nd creation) :—

Lavinia May (Moreton Hall, Bury St. Edmunds), *b*. 1887: *m*. 1921, Theodore Hubbard, who *d*. 1934, and has issue living, Theodore Bernard Peregrine, (of Moreton Hall, Bury St. Edmunds, Suffolk), *b*. 1923; Lt.-Com. (ret.) RN; 1939-45 War: *m*. 1952, Lady Miriam Fitzalan Howard, da. of 3rd Baron Howard of Glossop and Baroness Beaumont [see D. Norfolk], and has issue living, Martin Peregrine Thomas *b*. 1954, Theodore Bernard Peter *b*. 1959, Mary-Miranda Josephine *b*. (Jan.) 1956: *m*. 1974, Roger John Pratt, of Badwell Ash, Bury St. Edmunds, Lucinda Mary Lavinia *b*. (Dec.) 1956, Vanessa Mary Teresa *b*. 1958,—Thomas Francis (15, rue Cler, Paris VII), *b*. 1925; ed. at Wadham Coll., Oxford (BA 1949); Sub-Lt. (ret.), RN; 1939-45 War: *m*. 1954, Melise de Merindol, da. of the late Marquis de Merindol, and has issue living, John Francis *b*. 1955, Mark Fernand *b*. 1957, Richard Peter *b*. 1959.——Olivia Bridget (8, Harris Court, Harpes Rd., Summertown, Oxford), *b*. 1900.

Issue of the late Lieut. Col. the Hon. George Aubrey Vere Bertie 4th son of 6th Earl of Abingdon, *b*. 1850, *d*. 1926 : *m*. 1885, Harriet Blanche Elizabeth, who *d*. 1923, dau. of Sir Walter Rockliff Farquhar, 3rd Bt.:—

Margaret Adine, *b*. 1888. *Residence*,—The Gatehouse, Long Crendon Manor, Aylesbury.

Granddaughters of the late Rev. the Hon. Frederic Bertie, 4th son of 4th Earl of Abingdon :—

Issue of the late Capt. Frederic Arthur Bertie, b. 1837, d. 1885: m. 1873, Rose Emily who d. 1935, dau. of the late John de Montmorency, of Castle Morres, co. Kilkenny :— Margaret Grace, b. 1883 : m. 1914, Lieut.-Col. Hugh Cleivion Jagger, O.B.E., who d. 1931, late R.A.V.C. (T.A.)[S. Africa 1899-1901, European War 1915-19 (despatches twice)], and has issue living, Margaret Rosemary Helen, b. 1922 ; formerly in W.R.N.S. : m. 1950, Drayton Wiltshire, of Mount Pumps Farm, Hurst Green, Sussex, and has issue living, Richard Drayton b. 1951, Robin Cleivion b. 1956. *Residence*,—Mount Pumps, Hurst Green, Sussex.

Issue of the late Albemarle Henry Bertie, 17th Foot, b. 1847, d. 1906: m. 1888, Rose, who d. 1913, dau. of the late Henry Weston, Notary Public, of Montreal :— Adela Harriet Blossom, b. 1889. *Residence,—*

PREDECESSORS.—[1] ROBERT Bertie, K.G., 12th Baron Willoughby de Eresby (for his predecessors see E. Ancaster); was Gov. of Berwick and Lord High Adm. of England; established his claim in right of his mother to the hereditary office of Lord Great Chamberlain of England ; cr. *Earl of Lindsey* (peerage of England) 1626 ; killed at battle of Edgehill when in command of a division of the King's army 1642 ; s. by his son [2] MONTAGUE, K.G., P.C., 2nd Earl; surrendered himself a prisoner at Edgehill, in order to attend upon his mortally wounded father ; subsequently fought at both battles of Newbury, and at Naseby, &c. ; was a Lord of the Bedchamber to Charles I., and Lord-Lieut. of Oxfordshire ; his el. son by his 2nd marriage was cr. Earl of Abingdon ; d. 1666 ; s. by his el. son [3] ROBERT, 3rd Earl ; d. 1701 ; s. by his son [4] ROBERT, P.C., 4th Earl ; summoned to Parliament in his father's lifetime as Baron Willoughby de Eresby ; was Lord Lieut. of co. Lincoln and one of the Lords Justices before the arrival of George I.; cr. *Marquess of Lindsey* (peerage of Great Britain) 1706, and *Duke of Ancaster and Kesteven* (peerage of Great Britain) 1715; d. 1723 ; s. by his son [5] PEREGRINE, P.C., 2nd Duke ; summoned to Parliament in his father's Barony of Willoughby de Eresby; was Lord-Lieut. of Lincolnshire and Lord Warden of all H.M.'s parks, chasse, forests, &c., North of the Trent; d. 1742; s. by his son [6] PEREGRINE, 3rd Duke; was a Gen. in the Army, Master of the Horse, and Recorder of Lincoln ; officiated as Lord Great Chamberlain at the Coronation of George III.; d. 1778; s. by his son [7] ROBERT, 4th Duke; d. unmarried 1779, when the Barony of Willoughby de Eresby became abeyant between his sister, Priscilla (afterwards Baroness Willoughby de Eresby) and Georgiana (Marchioness of Cholmondeley), the Lord Great Chamberlainship devolved jointly upon those ladies, and the dukedom reverted to his uncle [8] BROWNLOW, 5th Duke; d. without male issue 1809, when the dukedom and marquessate became extinct, and the earldom devolved upon his kinsman [9] ALBEMARLE, 9th Earl, great-grandson of the Hon. Charles Bertie, of Uffington, 5th son of 2nd Earl : b. 1744; was a Gen. in the Army, Col. 89th Regt., Gov. of Blackness Castle, and sometime M.P. for Stamford: m. 1809, Charlotte Susannah Elizabeth, dau. of the Very Rev. Charles P. Lavard, Dean of Bristol; d. 1818; s. by his el. son [10] GEORGE AUGUSTUS FREDERICK ALBEMARLE, 10th Earl; d. unmarried 1877; s. by his brother [11] MONTAGUE PEREGRINE, 11th Earl. b. 1815 : m. 1854, Felicia Elizabeth, who d. 1927, dau. of the late Rev. John Earle Welby; d. 1899; s. by his only son [12] MONTAGU PEREGRINE ALBEMARLE, 12th Earl, b. 1861 : m. 1890, Millicent, who d. 1931, el. dau. of J. C. Cox, formerly of Craig Cruich, Sydney, N.S. Wales; d. 1938 ; s. by his kinsman [13] MONTAGU HENRY EDMUND CECIL, 13th Earl (who had s. as 8th Earl of Abingdon 1928) [see *·* infra]; succession recognized 1951; b, 1887; Capt. Gren. Gds.; High Steward of Abingdon: m. 1928, Elizabeth Valetta, da. of the late Maj.-Gen. the Hon. Edward James Montagu-Stuart-Wortley, CB, CMG, DSO [E. Wharncliffe, colls.]; d. 1963; s. by his cousin [14] RICHARD HENRY RUPERT (son of the late Lt.-Col. the Hon. Arthur Michael Bertie, DSO, MC, 2nd son of 7th Earl of Abingdon), 14th Earl of Lindsey, 9th Earl of Abingdon, and present peer; also Baron Norreys of Rycote.

· [1] *Sir* HENRY NORRIS, KB, Ambassador to France, was summoned to Parliament 1572-97; d. 1600; s. by his grandson [2] FRANCIS, 2nd Baron; cr. *Viscount Thame* and *Earl of Berkshire* (peerage of England) 1620, and d. the same year without male issue when the Viscountcy and Earldom became extinct; his only da. had issue, one da., who m. as his second wife the 2nd Earl of Lindsey, by whom she had [3] JAMES BERTIE, summoned to Parliament of England 1675 as *Baron Norreys of Rycote* (with precedence of 1572), and cr. *Earl of Abingdon* (peerage of England) 1682; was Lord-Lieut. of Oxfordshire 1674-97; d. 1699; s. by his son [4] MONTAGU, 2nd Earl; assumed by Roy. licence 1687 the additional surname of Venables; d. 1743; s. by his nephew [5] WILLOUGHBY, 3rd Earl, el. son of the Hon. James, 2nd son of 1st Earl; d. 1760; s. by his el. son [6] WILLOUGHBY, 4th Earl; d. 1799; s. by his son [7] MONTAGU, DCL, 5th Earl, b. 1784; was Lord-Lieut. of Berkshire, and officiated as cup-bearer at the coronation of George IV.; d. Oct. 16th, 1854; s. by his el. son [8] MONTAGU, DCL, 6th Earl, b. 1808; sat as MP for Oxfordshire 1830 and 1832-52, and for Abingdon (LC) 1852-54; was Lord-Lieut. of Berks. 1855-81: m. 1835, Elizabeth Lavinia, who d. 1858, da. of the late George Granville Vernon-Harcourt, MP, of Nuneham Park, Oxfordshire; d. 1884; s. by his el. son [9] MONTAGU ARTHUR, 7th Earl; b. 1836; High Steward of Abingdon: m. 1st, 1858, Caroline Theresa, who d. 1873, da. of the late Charles Towneley, of Towneley, Lancs.; 2ndly, 1883, Gwendeline Mary, who d. 1942, da. of the late Lt.-Gen. the Hon. Sir James Charlemagne Dormer, KCB; d. 1928; s. by his grandson [10] MONTAGU HENRY EDMUND CECIL [son of the late Capt. Montagu Charles Francis, Lord Norreys, el. son of 7th Earl), who s. as 13th Earl of Lindsey 1938 (succession recognised 1951], 8th Earl.

Linley, Viscount, son of Earl of Snowdon.

LINLITHGOW, MARQUESS OF. (Hope.) [Marquess U.K. 1902, Bt. N.S. 1698.]

But my hope is not broken.

AT · SPES · NON · FRACTA

CHARLES WILLIAM FREDERICK HOPE, MC, 3rd Marquess, and 11th Baronet; b. April 7th, 1912; s. 1952; ed. at Eton, and at Ch. Ch., Oxford (BA 1936); Capt. (ret.) Lothians and Border Horse, Roy. Armoured Corps (TA), Lt. Scots Gds. (Reserve), and Lord Lt. of W. Lothian; 1939-45 War (prisoner): m. 1st, 1939, Vivien, who d. 1963, da. of Capt. Robert Orlando Rodolph Kenyon-Slaney [B. Kenyon, colls.]; 2ndly, 1965, Judith, da. of the late Stanley Matthew Lawson, of Cincinnati, USA, and widow of Lt.-Col. Esmond Charles Baring, OBE [see B. Ashburton, colls.], and has issue by 1st m.

ꝶrms,—Azure, on a chevron or, between three bezants, a laurel leaf vert. Crest,—A broken terrestrial globe, surmounted by a rain-bow proper. Supporters,—Two female figures representing "Hope" habited in loose garments and with hair dishevelled each resting the exterior hand on an anchor all proper-

Seats,—Hopetoun House, South Queensferry, W. Lothian.

SON LIVING. (By 1st m.)

ADRIAN JOHN CHARLES (Earl of Hopetoun) (36, Edwardes Sq., W8), b. July 1st, 1946: m. 1968, Anne, da. of Arthur Leveson, of Hall Pl., Ropley, Hants., and has issue.
SONS LIVING,—Andrew Victor Arthur Charles, (Viscount Aithrie), b. May 22nd, 1969.
Hon. Alexander John Adrian, b. 1971.

DAUGHTER LIVING. (By 1st m.)

Lady Mary Sarah Jane, b. 1940: m. 1967, Michael Gordon Learoyd, of Mounthooly, Jedburgh, Roxburghshire and has issue living, Jeremy, b. 1971.

BROTHER LIVING.

Lord John Adrian, PC (Baron Glendevon) (twin), b. 1912; cr. Baron Glendevon 1964 [see that title].

SISTERS LIVING.

Lady Anne Adeline, b. 1914: m. 1939, Lt.-Com. Patrick Henry James Southby, RN [see Southby, Bt.]. Address,—Los Castaños, 48, Casasola, Guadalmina, San Pedro de Alcantara, Malaga, Spain.
Lady Joan Isabella, b. 1915: m. 1952, Col. Ian William Gore-Langton, MBE, Coldstream Gds., and has issue living, Mary Jane, b. 1955. Residence,—Southpark, Robertsbridge, Sussex.
Lady Doreen Hersey Winifred, b. 1920: m. 1948, Maj.-Gen. George Erroll Prior-Palmer, CB, DSO, 9th Lancers, and has issue living, Simon Erroll, b. 1951,—Lucinda Jane, b. 1953. Residence,—Appleshaw House, Andover, Hants.

AUNT LIVING. (Daughter of 1st Marquess.)

Lady Mary Dorothea (Mary, Countess of Pembroke and Montgomery), CVO, b. 1903; is Hon. 1st Officer WRNS; a Lady-in-Waiting to HRH the Duchess of Kent 1934-49 and an Extra Lady-in-Waiting 1949-68; CVO 1947: m. 1936, the 16th Earl of Pembroke and Montgomery, who d. 1969. Residence, —The Old Rectory, Wilton, Salisbury.

COLLATERAL BRANCHES LIVING. (In remainder to the Earldom.)

Grandchildren of the late John George Frederick Hope-Wallace, el. son of Lt.-Col. the Hon. James Hope-Wallace, MP, 2nd son of 4th Earl of Hopetoun:—
Issue of the late James Hope-Wallace, Lt. Northumberland Fusiliers, b. 1872, d. (killed in action) 1917: m. 1909, the Hon. Ursula Mary Addington, who d. 1962, da. of 4th Viscount Sidmouth:—
Ruth, b. 1911: m. 1937, Capt. Eric Cairns, Roy. Northumberland Fusiliers, and has issue living, Jane, b. 1939: m. 1965, Peter Butcher,—Clare, b. 1947. Residence,—Hallbank Head, Featherstone, Haltwhistle, Northumberland.——Ann, b. 1914: m. 1944, Capt. Robert Byrt Jordan, Roy. Armoured Corps, of 13, Harrop Rd., Hale, Cheshire, and has issue living, Richard, b. 1945,—Mary, b. 1947.—Margaret, b. 1949.

Issue of the late Charles Nugent Hope-Wallace, MBE, b. 1877; d. 1953: m. 1905, Mabel, who d. 1970, da. of the late Col. Allan Chaplin, formerly Madras Army:—
Philip Adrian, CBE, b. 1911; ed. at Charterhouse, and Balliol Coll., Oxford (BA); Music and Dramatic Critic, The Guardian since 1946. Residence,—22, St. Ann's Ter., NW8.——Nina Mary (Nina, Mary (Nina, Lady Hoare), b. 1905: m. 1932, Maj. Sir Edward O'Bryen Hoare, 7th Bt., RASC (ret.), who d. 1969. Residence,—61, Flask Walk, Hampstead, NW3.——Dorothy Jaqueline, CBE, b. 1909; ed. at Lady Margaret Hall, Oxford (BA); Under-Sec., Nat. Assistance Board 1958-64, and Min. of Housing and Local Govt. 1965-69; ret. 1969; a Commonwealth Fellow 1952-53; CBE (Civil) 1958. Residence,—22, St. Ann's Ter., NW8.

Grandchildren of the late James Louis Alexander HOPE, 2nd son of the late Lt.-Col. the Hon. James Hope-Wallace, MP (ante):—
Issue of the late Capt. Laurence Nugent Hope, b. 1890, d. 1973: m. 1st, 1939, Hilda Mary, who d. 1938, only da. of the late Michael Joseph Hunter, JP, of Stoke Hall, Derbyss.; who d. 1938, only da. of the late Michael Joseph Hunter, JP, of Stoke Hall, Derbys.; 2ndly, 1941, Constance Elizabeth Shell (Whitney Court, Herefordshire):—
(By 1st m.) John Nugent (84, Three Colt St., E14), b. 1924; ed. at Eton, and Magdelene Coll., Camb.: m. 1953, Polly, el. da. of Lt.-Gen. Sir Hugh Charles Stockwell, GCB, KBE, DSO, and has issue living, Augustine Jason Nugent, b. 1961.——Jocelyn Mary, b. 1922: m. 1948, Michael Fortune Cleghorn.

Grandson of the late Sir Charles Dunbar Hope-Dunbar, 6th Bt. (who proved his claim to the Baronetcy of Dunbar of Baldoon 1916) grandson of the late Hon. Charles Hope, 3rd son of 4th Earl of Hopetoun:—
See Hope-Dunbar, Bt.

Granddaughter of the late Capt. the Hon. Louis Hope, 7th son of 4th Earl of Hopetoun:—
Issue of the late Herbert George Hope, MBE, b. 1875, d. 1956: m. 1920, May Winifred, who d. 1960, da. of the late Lt.-Col. F. F. Sheppee, RA, and widow of John Harley:—
Isabel Susan, b. 1922: m. 1955, Peter Haviland Hiley, son of the late Col. Sir (Ernest) Haviland Hiley, KBE, and has issue living, William John Haviland, b. 1960. Residence,—King's Holt, Blackmoor, Liss, Hants.

Grandchildren of the late Henry Walter Hope, 2nd son of the late George William Hope, MP, 2nd son of the late Hon. Sir Alexander Hope, GCB, 4th son of 2nd Earl:—
Issue of the late Capt. George Everard Hope, MC, Gren. Gds., b. 1886, d. (killed in action during 1914-18 War) 1917: m. 1911, Margaret, who d. 1923 (having m. 2ndly, 1919, Lionel Clement Erskine Clark), da. of the late John Curwen Cockton, JP, of Kirkborough, Cumberland:—
Archibald John George, MBE, b. 1912; ed. at Eton; Col. (ret.) late RA; Burma 1943-45 (despatches, MBE); MBE (Mil) 1946: m. 1937, Mary Pilar Elizabeth, yr. da. of the late Brig.-Gen. Alister Fraser Gordon, CMG, DSO [B. Stafford, colls.], and has issue living, George Archibald, b. 1938,—Margaret Mary Lucy, b. 1940,—Mary Catherine Elizabeth, b. 1943,—Elizabeth Caroline, b. 1948, Cecilia, b. 1952. Residence,—Lamarck House, Le Mont Saint, St. Saviours, Guernsey.——Wilhelmine Mary Margaret, b. 1911; is a nun.

Grandsons of the late Sir Edward Stanley Hope, KCB, 5th son of the late George William Hope (ante):—
Issue of the late Maj. John Alexander Henry Hope, b. 1882, d. 1938: m. 1st, 1907, Elizabeth Maude (who obtained a divorce 1923), da. of the late Hon. James Dunsmuir, Lt.-Gov. of British Columbia; 2ndly, 1929, Amelia Madeleine Wise, da. of Robert Martin:—
(By 1st m.) Edward James, MC, b. 1911; ed. at Eton, and at McGill Univ., Canada; late Maj. Scots Gds.; a JP for Oxon.; NW Europe 1944-45 (MC): m. 1st, 1937, Enid (who obtained a divorce 1950), da. of the late Robert Gunther, of Parkwood, Englefield Green; 2ndly, 1952, Winifred Gwendolyne Marie, el. da. of the late Maj. John Byng Paget, and has issue living, (by 1st m.) Sarah Elizabeth, b. 1942: m. 1964, Benjamin L. C. Wordsworth, of Steepways, Nether Lypiatt, Glos., and has issue living, Marcia b. 1965, Lucy (twin) b. 1965, Rebecca b. 1967. Residence,—Ibstock Close, Little Tew, Oxon. Club,—St. James'.——Alexander Douglas Byng, b. 1918; ed. at Eton, and at Balliol Coll., Oxford; Ch. Assist., Head of Talks and Current Affairs (Radio), BBC; 1939-45 War as Maj. R. Hussars (despatches): m. 1951, Florence Leslie, JP, da. of Graham St. Clair-Keith. Residence,—Fiddler's Croft, Little Hadham, Herts. Clubs,—St. James', Royal Burnham Yacht.

Grandchildren of the late James Robert Hope-Scott, QC, 3rd son of the late Hon.
Sir Alexander Hope, GCB (ante):—
Issue of the late Rt. Hon. James Fitzalan Hope (*Baron Rankeillour*), *b.* 1870, *d.* 1949; cr.
Baron Rankeillour 1932 [see that title].

Grandson of the late Lt.-Col. James Charles Hope-Vere (infra):—
Issue of the late Ralph Jean James Hope-Vere, OBE, AFC, *b.* 1887, *d.* 1959: *m.* 1928,
Esmé (Little Fosse, Nettleton, Chippenham, Wilts.), el. da. of the late Lt.-Col. H. Crabbe,
Scots Greys, of Duncow, Dumfreisshire:—
Adrian Ralph, *b.* 1929. *Residence,*—Little Fosse, Nettleton, Chippenham, Wilts.

Granddaughter of the late William Edward Hope-Vere, son of the late James Joseph
Hope-Vere, MP, son of the late William Hope-Vere, el. son of the late Hon. Charles
Hope-Vere, 2nd son of 1st Earl of Hopetoun:—
Issue of the late Lt.-Col. James Charles Hope-Vere, *b.* 1858, *d.* 1933: *m.* 1st, 1879, the Hon.
Louisa Maud, who *d.* 1882, sister of 2nd Baron Churston, and widow of the Hon. Reginald
James Macartney Greville-Nugent [B. Greville]; 2ndly, 1884, Merie Elizabeth Francoise
(who *d.* 1937, having obtained a divorce 1905), da. of the late Mons. Guillemin, of Chateau de
Gan, Basses Pyrenees, and great-grandda. of the late Maréchal Lannes (Duc de Montebello);
3rdly, 1906, Mabel Ellis, who *d.* 1954, el. da. of Alkinan Henryson Foster-Barham, formerly
of Maryland, Pau., France:—
(By 3rd m.) Rosemary Marguerite (*Lady Brinckman*), *b.* 1907: *m.* 1st, 1930, Lt.-Col. John Drury
Boteler Drury-Lowe, Scots Gds., who *d.* 1960, having obtained a divorce 1933; 2ndly, 1933 (m. diss.
1942), Quintin Holland Gilbey, Gren. Gds. (ret.); 3rdly, 1943, as his second wife, Col. Sir Roderick
Napoleon Brinckman, DSO, MC, 5th Bt., Gren. Gds. (ret.), and has issue living, (by 1st m.) Patrick
John Boteler (Locko Park, Derby), *b.* 1931; Capt. Scots Gds. (Reserve): *m.* 1st, 1959, Belinda Mary,
who obtained a divorce 1968, only da. of Sir Hardman Alexander Morte Earle, 5th Bt.; 2ndly, 1968,
Mrs. Pamela Cayzer, from whom he obtained a divorce 1972, da. of Geoffrey Myers, of Lagos, Nigeria,
and has issue living, (by 1st m.) Lucy Belinda *b.* 1961; Candida Dorothy *b.* 1963,—(by 2nd m.)
Anthony James (13, St. Loo Court, SW3), *b.* 1933; Capt. Gren. Gds. (Reserve): *m.* 1958 (m. diss.
1971) Lenore Shatton, of New York, USA and has issue living, James Dennis *b.* 1959, Paul Alfred
b. 1964, Emma Lenore *b.* 1961, (by 3rd m.) [see Brinckman, Bt.]. *Residence,*—Mornington House,
Wimbledon Common, SW19; Cross Keys, Sandwich, Kent; St. Helena, St. James, Barbados.

Grandchildren of the late Charles Douglas Hope (infra):—
Issue of the late Major Adrian Alexander Hope, Transvaal Scottish, *b.* 1897; *d.* (killed
in action in Italy) 1945: *m.* 1926, Eleanor (now of 42, Richmond Avenue, Johannes-
burg, S. Africa), dau. of Lieut.-Col. George Ritchie Thomson, C.M.G., M.B.:—
William Adrian (42, Rchimond Av., Auckland Park, Johannesburg), *b.* 1927; ed. at Michaelhouse,
Natal, at Witwatersrand Univ. (BA), and at Trin. Coll., Oxford (MA); an Advocate of Johannesburg,
S. Africa, and of Salisbury, Rhodesia; published "A Digest of Rhodesian Mining Law" 1965; 1939-
45 War with S. African Artillery in Italy: *m.* 1960, Hazel, da. of Adelbert Johnstone, of Gwelo,
Rhodesia, and has issue living, Adrian Charles, *b.* 1962,—James Graham, *b.* 1970,—Patricia Anne,
b. 1961,—Sarah Jane, *b.* 1964.——Anne Eleanor (Box 21194, Nairobi, Kenya), *b.* 1930, BA Rhodes
Univ.; Diploma in Education, Oxford.——Joan Alice, *b.* 1931; ed. at Witwatersrand Univ. (BSc):
m. 1954, James Ecclestone Stewart (Chancellor College, PO Box 280, Zomba, Malawi), and has issue
living, John Adrian, *b.* 1955,—Peter Dominic Stephen, *b.* 1956,—Mary Rachel Alice, *b.* 1958,—Clare
Veronica, *b.* 1959,—Alice Martha, *b.* 1963.

Issue of the late James Hope, *b.* 1899, *d.* 1970: *m.* 1937, Doreen (Rostrevor, Arundel Rd.
Rosebank, Cape Town, S. Africa), da. of Prof. Armstrong:—
Christopher James (115, Muckleneuk Lanterns, 162, Bourke St., Pretoria, S. Africa), *b.* 1938.——
Alastair Frederick (5, Malleson Rd., Mowbray, Cape, S. Africa), *b.* 1941: *m.* 1963, Mary Elizabeth,
da. of Arthur Cecil Bilbrough, of Carmunnock, Somerset West, S. Africa, and has issue living,
Charles Andrew, *b.* 1966,—Paul James, *b.* 1968,—Bridget Moira, *b.* 1964.——Angela Ruth Alice,
b. 1939.

Issue of Henry Francis Hope, *b.* 1900, *d.* 1971: *m.* 1930, Aileen Elinor (8, Orchard St., Newlands, Cape Town, S. Africa), da. of the late William Falkiner Harnett, CBE:—
Gillian Margaret, *b.* 1933: *m.* 1955, Neville Price Boyce, of 23, Ashwold Rd., Saxonwold, Johannesburg,
and has issue living, Richard Henry Price, *b.* 1957,—Diana Mary, *b.* 1959,—Margaret Louise, *b.*
1961.——Rosemary Patricia, *b.* 1936: *m.* 1963, Guy Everingham Hitchings, of Spring Bank, Speldhurst, Kent, and has issue living, Charles Robin, *b.* 1967,—Mark Alexander, *b.* 1969,—Andrew
Hope, *b.* 1971,—Alice Elizabeth, *b.* 1965.

Issue of the late Charles Christopher Hope, *b.* 1902, *d.* 1963: *m.* 1937, Una Mainguy (3,
Claverton St., SW1), da. of the late W. P. Le Feuvre, MD, of Kenilworth, Cape Town:—
Charles Richard Christopher (Herald Rd., Sharon RR1, Ont.; Royal Canadian Yacht Club, and Royal
Commonwealth Society), *b.* 1938; ed. at Downside: *m.* 1970, Mary Lou, da. of John Francis Fitz-
patrick of 178, King St., Saint John, New Brunswick, and has issue living, Mary Mainguy, *b.* 1971.

Granddaughters of the late Lieut.-Col. William Hope, VC, el. son of the late Rt.
Hon. John Hope (Lord Justice Clerk of Scotland) el. son of the late Rt. Hon.
Charles Hope (Lord Justice-Gen. of Scotland), el. son of the late John Hope (*b.*
1739), 2nd son of the late Hon. Charles Hope-Vere (ante):—
Issue of the late Charles Douglas Hope, *b.* 1867, *d.* 1947: *m.* 1896, Alice Mary, who *d.* 1947,
dau. of the Hon. A. Wilmot, M.L.C., of Cape Colony:—
Alice Margaret Mary (c/o Barclays Bank, Marygold House, Carfax, Oxford) *b.* 1906.——Patricia Anne
(2642, Ottawa Av., W. Vancouver, BC, Canada), *b.* 1908: *m.* 1937, Capt. Sebastian F. Newdigate,
DSO, RNR, who *d.* 1954, and has issue living, Anne Charlotte, *b.* 1938: *m.* 1960, Humphrey Edward
Waldock, of 3638, Osler St., Vancouver 9, BC, Canada, son of Sir (Claud) Humphrey (Meredith)
Waldock, CMG, OBE, QC, and has issue living, Harold Sebastian *b.* 1961, Henry Bernard *b.* 1962,
Thomas Edward *b.* 1965, Mary Beatrice *b.* 1969, Alice Patricia *b.* 1973,—Lilah Mary Amphelis
(Sister Mary Lucy) (Carmelite Monastery, PO Box 6, Kew, Vic. 3101, Aust.) *b.* 1940;——Mary
Monica (Sister M. Emmanuel, OP) (Mater Admirabilis Convent, Baird St., Uitenhage, Cape, S.
Africa), *b.* 1912.

Grandchildren of the late Rear-Adm. Charles Webley Hope, only son of Rear-Adm.
Charles Hope, second son of the Rt. Hon. Charles Hope (Lord Justice-Gen. of
Scotland), (ante):—
Issue of the late Adm. Sir George Price Webley Hope, K.C.B., K.C.M.G., *b.* 1869, *d.* 1959: *m.*
1899, Arabella Philippa Sutton, who *d.* 1945, dau. of John Sutton Sams :—
Maurice Webley, *D.S.O.,* *b.* 1901 ; ed. at Winchester ; Brigadier (retired) late R.A. ; Middle East
1941, S.-W. Pacific 1942-43, W. Europe 1944-45; DSO 1944: *m.* 1943, Pamela, da. of the
late J. K. Osborne, of NSW, and has issue living, David George Osborne, *b.* 1944. *Residences,*—
1, Paradise Walk, SW3; Ivy Bank, Vinegar Hill, Milford-on-Sea, Hants. *Club,*—Royal Ocean
Racing.——Philippa, *b.* 1900: *m.* 1922, Brig. Alfred Geoffrey Neville, CBE, MC, who *d.* 1955 [see
B. Baybrooke, colls.]. *Residence,*—Summerhaugh Cottage, St. Mary Bourne, Andover, Hants.

Issue of the late Lt.-Col. William Henry Webley Hope, CMG, *b.* 1871, *d.* 1919: *m.* 1900,
Florence, who *d.* 1918, da. of the late Charles Walter Hill, of Clapham, Sussex:—
James Webley, OBE, (Jindalee, Osborne Rd., Bowral, NSW 2576; United Service and Royal Aero
Club), *b.* 1903; Lt.-Col. (ret.) S. Wales Borderers; Waziristan 1937 (despatches), Burma 1945
(despatches, OBE); OBE (Mil.) 1946: *m.* 1st, 1928, Harriet Mary, who *d.* 1931, da. of the late

Henry Louis King DL, JP, of Ballylin, Ferbane, King's co. [V. Bangor, colls.]; 2ndly, 1934, Veda Annie, da. of the late Dr. Alfred Walter Campbell, of Sydney, Australia, and has issue living, (by 2nd m.) Gillian Florence, b. 1935: m. 1961, Lt.-Col. George Mark Chirnside, 13th/18th Hussars.

Issue of the late Col. Adrian Victor Webley Hope, C.I.E., b. 1873, d. 1960 : m. 1920, Ethel Mary, who d. 1938, dau. of the late J. S. Middleton, of Cadamaney, Mysore :—
Margaret Isobel, b. 1921 : m. 1st, 1943, James Veitch Telfer, from whom she obtained a divorce, 1949; 2ndly, 1950, Squadron-Leader James Geoffrey Cutcliffe Hepburn, DFC, and has issue living, (by 1st m.) Alison, b. 1944; BA Oxon.; PhD London: m. 1970, Terence Parry Jones,—Kate, b. 1947; MA Roy. Coll. of Art,—(by 2nd m.) Harriet Rose, b. 1965. Residence,—68, Parliament Hill, Hampstead, NW3.

Issue of the late Adm. Herbert Willes Webley Hope, CB, CVO, DSO, RN, b. 1878, d. 1968: m. 1905, Katherine Maria Antoinette, who d. 1966, da. of the late Rev. Francis Kewley:—
Adrian Price Webley, CB, CBE (Monks Place, Charlton Horethorne, Sherborne, Dorset), b. 1911; Maj.-Gen. (ret.) late KOSB; Middle East 1940-43 (OBE); OBE (Mil.) 1943, CBE (Mil.) 1952, CB (Mil.) 1960: m. 1958, Mary Elizabeth (Mollie), da. of Graham Partridge, of Cotham Lodge, Newport, Pembrokeshire.——Ellen Katherine Webley, b. 1907: m. 1st, 1929, David William Heneker, formerly Lt. RASC (from whom she obtained a divorce 1937), son of the late Lt.-Gen. Sir William Charles Giffard Heneker, KCB, KCMG, DSO; 2ndly, 1941, Lt.-Col. Charles Vaughan King, OBE, Devonshire Regt., of Withern, River View Close, Chilbolton, Stockbridge, Hants., and has issue living, (by 1st m.) Peter David Grenfell, b. 1931,—(by 2nd m.) Adrian Charles Richard, b. 1944.

Granddaughters of the late Lieut.-Col. William Henry Webley Hope, CMG, 3rd son of Rear Adm. Charles Webley Hope (ante):—
Issue of the late Lt.-Cdr. Charles Webley Hope, RN, b. 1902; d. (on active ser.) 1941: m. 1933, Harriott Barbara, who d. 1970, da. of the late Lt.-Col. R. G. E. Locke, DL, JP, of Hartlip House, Hartlip, Kent:—
Mary, b. 1934.——Janet, b. 1937: m. 1960, Richard Wilson Froggatt, of Chessons Farm, Wallcrouch, Wadhurst, Sussex, and has issue living, Ian Wilson, b. 1962,—Peter Webley, b. 1964,—Nigel Thomas, b. 1966,—Eric Charles (twin), b. 1966,—Jenny Patricia (twin), b. 1962,—Alison Clare (twin), b. 1964.

Grandson of the late Charles William Hope, el. son of the late James Hope, 3rd son of the late Rt. Hon. Charles Hope (Lord Justice-Gen. of Scotland) (ante):—
Issue of the late Adrian James Robert Hope, C.I.E., b. 1874, d. 1963: m. 1913, Jessie Newall, who d. 1950, da. of the late David McLellan of Kirkcudbright, and widow of Maj. D. J. Welsh, 2nd Bn. Border Regt.:—
Charles Adrian (of 23, Ann St., Edinburgh, 4), b. 1918; ed. at Edinburgh Acad.; an A.R.I.B.A., and an Asso. Member of Town-planning Institute; 1939-45 War as Lt. Roy. Scots and Capt. R.A.: m. 1951, Susan Elizabeth Rona Kruse, and has issue living, Adrian Kruse Anthony, b. 1953,—James William Drever, b. 1957. Residence,—23, Ann St., Edinburgh, 4.

Grandsons of the late David Boyle Hope, son of the late James Hope (ante):—
Issue of the late James Arthur Hope, W.S., b. 1865, d. 1925: m. 1895, Geraldine Lucy, da. of the late Rev. Charles Hope Robertson, formerly Lt. of Smeeth, Kent:—
Arthur Henry Cecil, O.B.E., T.D., W.S., b. 1896; ed. at Edinburgh Acad., at Rugby, and at Edinburgh Univ. (B.L. 1922); Lieut.-Col. (retired) Roy. Scots (T.A.) and R.A. (T.A.); European War 1914-19 as Capt. Seaforth Highlanders and attached R.A.F. (despatches twice), European War 1939-45; O.B.E. (Mil.) 1939: m. 1937, Muriel Ann Neilson Collie, and has issue living, James Arthur David (34, India St., Edinburgh, 3), b. 1938; ed. at Edinburgh Acad., at Rugby, at St. John's Coll., Camb. (BA), and at Edinburgh Univ. (LLB); late Lt. Seaforth Highlanders: Advocate 1965: m. 1966, Katherine Mary Kerr, and has issue living, William Thomas Arthur b. 1969, James David Louis (twin) b. 1969, Lucy Charlotte Mary b. 1971,—John William Lewis (c/o Chartered Bank, Singapore), b. 1940; ed. at Edinburgh Acad., and at St. Andrews Univ. (MA): m. 1974, Hazel Goh Mei Ling, da. of Goh Ah Hiong, of Kaching,—Alexander Robertson Boyle, b. 1947; ed. at Rugby, Edinburgh Acad., and Durham Univ. (BA.),—Elspeth Mary Neilson (twin), b. 1947: m. 1969, Dolf Andries Mogendorff, of 25a, Carden Place, Aberdeen, and has issue living, Andrew Michael Alexander b. 1972, Richard Arthur John b. 1974,—Angela Muriel Evelyn, b. 1948; SRN. Residence,—28B, Moray Pl., Edinburgh.——James Louis, TD, WS, b. 1906; ed. at Edinburgh Acad., at Rugby, and at Edinburgh Univ. (MA, LLB); Lt.-Col. (ret.) Roy. Scots (TA): m. 1939, Kathleen Colquhoun Sconce, and has issue living, Charles Louis (Cheriton, Ockham Road North, East Horsley, Surrey), b. 1940; ed. Edinburgh Acad., Rugby, and Magdalene Coll., Camb. (BA): m. 1963, Susan Jane Elizabeth McDowall, and has issue living, Joanna Mary, b. 1968, Fiona Jane b. 1972,—Michael Edmund, b. 1943; ed. at Edinburgh Acad., Rugby, Trin. Coll., Dublin (BA) and St. Andrews Univ. (MA). Residence,—34a, Murrayfield Rd., Edinburgh, 12.

Grandchildren of the late Capt. Percy Alexander John Hope-Johnstone, 2nd son of William James Hope-Johnstone, el. son of John James Hope-Johnstone, el. son of Vice-Adm. Sir William Johnstone-Hope, GCB, 3rd son of John Hope (b. 1739), 2nd son of the Hon. Charles Hope-Vere, 2nd son of 1st Earl of Hopetown:—
Issue of the late Evelyn Wentworth Hope-Johnstone, b. 1879, d. 1964: m. 1st, 1905, Eileen, who d. 1909, da. of G. V. Briscoe, formerly of Bellinter, co. Meath; 2ndly, 1916, Marie Eleanor (May) (who d. 1969, and from whom he obtained a divorce 1925), da. of Compton Domville; 3rdly, 1926, Mary Evelyn Beardmore (BATTEN), who d. 1962, da. of the late John Locke, of Kilbeggan, Westmeath:—
(By 1st marriage) Percy Wentworth, TD (of Raehills, Lockerbie, Dumfriesshire), b. 1909; ed. at Sherborne; formerly Lt. 16/5th Lancers, and Maj. Lanarkshire Yeo.; 1939-45 War (prisoner): m. 1st, 1932, Phyllis Athena, dau. of the late Edgar Errol Napier MacDonell, C.M.G.; 2ndly, 1940, Margaret Jane, dau. of H. W. F. Hunter-Arundell, of Barjarg, Auldgirth, Dumfriesshire, and has issue living (by 2nd m.) Patrick Andrew Wentworth (Blackburn House, Johnstonebridge, Lockerbie), b. 1941; ed. at Stowe and Roy. Agric. Coll., Cirencester: m. 1969, Susan, only da. of Col. Walter John Macdonald Ross, CB, OBE, MC, TD, JP, DL, of Netherall, Castle Douglas, and has issue living, David Patrick Wentworth, b. 1971, Julia Clare, b. 1974,—Eileen Elizabeth, b. 1948: m. 1969, Andrew Walter Bryce Duncan, of Newlands, Kirkmahoe, Dumfriesshire, son of Sir Arthur Bryce Duncan, and has issue living, John b. 1971.——(By 2nd m.) Jean Evelyn, b. 1917: m. 1950, Capt. Robert Philip Henry Elwes, MBE, MC, late 16th/5th Lancers, of Ennistown, Kilmessan, co. Meath, and has issue living, Sarah Jane, b. 1951: m. 1975, Arthur Guy Galbraith.

Grandson of the late Charles Cecil Gordon Hope-Johnstone, el. son of George Gordon Hope-Johnstone, son of the late John James Hope-Johnstone (ante):—
Issue of the late George Wentworth Hope-Johnstone, b. 1872, d. 1920: m. 1900, Annie Eleanor, who d. 1957, da. of the late Thomas Hack:—
George Ernest Gordon, b. 1901: m. 1940, Aileen Stephen, da. of the late Alfred Ewing, and has issue living, John Wentworth Gordon, b. 1944.

Granddaughter of the late Robert Gordon Hope-Johnstone, son of John James Hope-Johnstone (ante) :—
Issue of the late Gordon Frank Hope-Johnstone, b. 1861, d. 1913 : m. 1890, Isabel, who d. 1893, dau. of the late — Breden-Kamp :—
Isabel, b. 189-. Residence,—

Grandchildren of the late Capt. William George Hope-Johnstone, R.N., son of the late Capt. George James Hope-Johnstone, R.N., younger brother of the late John James Hope-Johnstone (ante) :—

Issue of the late Charles Henry Edmund Hope-Johnstone, b. 1867, d. 1940: m. 1st, 1901, Elizabeth, who d. 1922, dau. of the late George Samuel Wright, of Brunswick, New Zealand; 2ndly, 1929, Helen Muriel, who d. 1954, dau. of the late Thomas Revell, of Christchurch, New Zealand :—

(By 1st m.) George William (19, MacDonald Rd., Glenview, Hamilton, NZ), b. 1902: m. 1st, 1925, Dorothy Charity (from whom he obtained a divorce 1932), da. of Frederic Beasley-Hartley, of Birkenhead, NZ; 2ndly, 1933, Amelia Daphne (from whom he obtained a divorce 1946), da. of Thomas Henry du Auvergne de Thierry, of Puniho, Taranaki, NZ; 3rdly, 1946, Helen Louisa, da. of the late William Taylor, of Howick, Scotland, and has issue living, (by 2nd m.) Graeme William (Cushen St., Clifton, Invercargill, NZ) b. 1934; RNZR; m. 1961, Robin, da. of the late Edward Herbert, of Sydney, NSW, and has issue living, Gregory William b. 1963, Bruce Edward b. 1968, Trudy Anne b. 1963,—Nerida Mae b. 1972,—Carolyn Ann b. 1938: m. 1960, Gordon John Bracher, of 14, Reiman St., New Lynn, Auckland, NZ, and has issue living, Jonathan Charles b. 1963, Louise Jane b. 1961.——Emily Elizabeth, b. 1903. Residence,—2, Branch Rd., St. Albans.——Florence Muriel, b. 1904: m. 1932, Reginald Percy Castaing, of 43A, Amaru Rd., Onehunga, Auckland 6, NZ, and has issue living, Rodney Francis (59, Ararui Rd., Mt. Wellington, Auckland 6, NZ), b. 1938: m. 1960, Catherine Jean, yr. da. of Alfred Robert James Stewart, of Kumen, Auckland, NZ, and has issue living, Phillip John b. 1963, Jacqueline Rose b. 1961, Cherié Kathrine b. 1969,—Denis Reginald (c/o Brant House, 5540, Woodlawn Av., Chicago, Illinois, 60637, USA), b. 1940; MSc, ThL, MA: m. 1965, Heather Lorna, BSc, el. da. of D. A. Thorburn, of Takapuna, Auckland, NZ, and has issue living, Bryan Denis b. 1971, Frances Heather b. 1969,—Edna Loraine, b. 1934,—Averil Violet b. 1943: m. 1964, Nicholas Peter Burberay Dudman, MSc, PhD, of 588, Milton Rd., Toowong, Brisbane, Qld., 4066, Aust., and has issue living, Peter Christopher b. 1965, Michael John b. 1966.—— Evelyn Violet (58, Tawa Rd., Onehunga, SE5, Auckland, NZ), b. 1906.

Grandson of Charles Henry Edmund Hope-Johnstone (ante):—

Issue of the late Charles James Hope-Johnstone, b. 1907, d. 1964: m. 1933, Ellen Sarah, da. of Henry John Bennett Gason, of Temuka, S. Canterbury, NZ:—

Robyn, b. 1945: m. 1964, Glen Douglas Ireland, of Kaiwaka, NZ, and has issue living, Kim Joanne, b. 1967,—Gina Dianne, b. 1969,—Jodi Hope, b. 1971.

Grandchildren of the late Charles Hope (infra):—

Issue of the late Charles Henry Sawyer Hope, b. 1880, d. 1964: m. 1913, Olive Lois, who d. 1954, da. of the late Arthur Francis Godwin, of 16, Hans Place, S.W.1:—

Jaqueline (42, Telegraph Lane East, Norwich; Royal Overseas League), b. 1914; a State Registered Physiotherapist; 1939-45 War with Naval VAD.——Anne Vere (Royal Overseas League), b. 1918; 1939-45 War with ATS.

Issue of the late George Leonard Nelson Hope, b. 1884, d. 1973: m. 1908 Honoria Mary Victoria, who d. 1968, yst. da. of the late John Giffard Riddell, of Felton Park, Northumberland:—

Sir (Charles) Peter, KCMG, TD, (14, Cleveland Sq., W2. White's Club), b. 1912; ed. at Oratory Sch., and London (BSc), and Camb. Univs.; 1939-45 War as Lt.-Col. RA; HM Foreign Ser. 1946 as 1st Sec. Paris; Assist. Head of UN Dept., FO 1950, Counsellor, Bonn 1953, Head of News Dept., FO 1956, HM Min., Madrid 1959, HM Consul-Gen. for Texas and New Mexico 1963, Alternate British Repres. to UN 1965-68, and Ambassador to Mexico 1968-72; Grand Cross Order of Aztec Eagle of Mexico; CMG 1957, KCMG 1972: m. 1936, Hazel Mary, da. of the late G. L. Turner, and has issue living, (Charles) Jeremy (Netherhill, Awbridge, Romsey, Hants.; White's Club), b. 1937; ed. at Downside; Capt. (ret.) Gren. Gds.: m. 1961, Judith Ann, da. of H. T. Pearce, and has issue living, Dominic Mark b. 1963, Jonathon Paul b. 1965,—Adrian Philip, b. 1942,—Richard Andrew, b. 1947.

Granddaughter of the late Maj.-Gen. Frederick Hope, son of the late Capt. Charles Hope, RN, 4th son of the late Hon. Charles Hope-Vere (ante):—

Issue of the late Charles Hope, b. 1845, d. 1912: m. 1871, Leonora Louisa Isabella, who d. 1901, dau. of the late Rev. Leonard Shafto Orde [B. Bolton, colls.]:—

Charlotte Gwendoline Frances (Doneraile Rest Home, Newton Abbot, Devon) b. 1876: m. 1st 1913, Capt. Francis Hugh Beaufort, Oxfordshire and Bucks. LI, who d. (killed in action) 1915; 2ndly, 1917, Capt. Harvey William Cobbett, RASC, who d. 1972.

PREDECESSORS.—[1] Sir CHARLES HOPE, K.T., grandson of the late Sir James Hope, K.B., 6th son of Sir Thomas Hope, 1st Bt. (cr. 1628); cr. Lord Hope, Viscount Aithrie and Earl of Hopetoun (peerage of Scotland) 1703, with remainder to heirs male and female of his body; d. 1742; s. by his son [2] JOHN, 2nd Earl, in whom the Baronetcy (cr. N.S. 1698) of Kirliston; became vested on the death of the 3rd Bt. 1783; Lord High Commr. to Gen. Assembly of Church of Scotland; d. 1781; s. by his son [3] JAMES, 3rd Earl; Lord-Lieut. of co. Linlithgow, and a Representative Peer 1784-94; in 1792 s. to the estates of his grand-uncle, George, 3rd Marquess of Annandale (title dormant), and assumed the additional surname of Johnstone: cr. Baron Hopetoun, of Hopetoun (peerage of United Kingdom) 1809, with remainder to the heirs male of his father; d. 1817; s. by his half-brother [4] JOHN, G.C.B., 4th Earl; Col. of 42nd Regt., a distinguished Gen. in the Peninsula; cr. Baron Niddry, of Niddry Castle, co. Linlithgow (peerage of the United Kingdom) 1814, with remainder to the male issue of his father; d. 1823; s. by his son [5] JOHN, 5th Earl; Lord-Lieut. of co. Linlithgow; d. 1843; s. by his son [6] JOHN ALEXANDER, 6th Earl; b. 1831; Lord-Lieut. of co. Linlithgow: m. 1860, Ethelred Anne, who d. 1884, dau. of Charles Thomas Samuel Birch-Reynardson, of Holywell Hall, near Stamford; d. 1873; s. by his son [7] JOHN ADRIAN LOUIS, K.T., G.C.M.G., G.C.V.O., P.C., 7th Earl; b. 1860; a Lord-in-Waiting to Queen Victoria 1885-6 and 1886-9, Lord High Commr. of Gen. Assembly of Church of Scotland 1887-9, Gov. of Victoria 1889-95, Paymaster-Gen. 1895-8, Lord Chamberlain of Queen Victoria's Household 1898-1900, first Gov.-Gen. of the Commonwealth of Australia 1900-1902, and Sec. for Scotland and Keeper of the Great Seal of Scotland, with a seat in the Cabinet Feb. to Dec. 1905; cr. Marquess of Linlithgow, co. Linlithgow or West Lothian (peerage of United Kingdom) 1902: m. 1886, the Hon. Hersey Alice Eveleigh-de Moleyns, who d. 1937, dau. of 4th Baron Ventry; d. 1908; s. by his son [8] Rt. Hon. VICTOR ALEXANDER JOHN, K.G., K.T., G.C.S.I., G.C.I.E., O.B.E., T.D., 2nd Marquess; b. 1887; Civil Lord of the Admiralty 1922-24, Viceroy and Gov. of India 1936-43, and Lord High Commr. to Gen. Assembly of Church of Scotland 1944-45; Chancellor of Edinburgh Univ. 1944; Lord-Lieut. of W. Lothian, Capt. King's Body Guard for Scotland (Roy. Co. of Archers), and a P.C.: m. 1911, Doreen Maud, C.I., who d. 1965, yr. da. of the Rt. Hon. Sir Frederick George Milner, 7th Bt.; d. 1952; s. by his son [9] CHARLES WILLIAM FREDERICK, 3rd Marquess, and present peer; also Earl of Hopetoun, Viscount Aithrie, Lord Hope, Baron Hopetoun, and Baron Niddry.

LISBURNE, EARL OF. (Vaughan.) [Earl I. 1776.]

§ NON·REVERTAR·INULTUS
I will not return unavenged.

JOHN DAVID MALET VAUGHAN, 8th
Earl; *b.* Sept. 1st, 1918; *s.* 1965; ed. at
Eton, and at Magdalen Coll., Oxford
(MA); Bar. Inner Temple 1948; patron
of one living; 1939-45 War as Capt.
Welsh Guards: *m.* 1943, Shelagh, da.
of the late T. A. Macauley, of Montreal,
Canada, and has issue.

Arms,—Sable, a chevron between three fleurs-
de-lis argent. Crest,—An arm embowed in armour,
the hand holding a sword, point to the sinister,
all proper. Supporters,—*Dexter*, a dragon
reguardant, armed and langued or, collared sable
and chained gold, the collar charged with three
fleurs-de-lis argent; *sinister*, a unicorn reguardant
argent, the mane, horn and hoofs or, collared and
chained as the other.

Residences,—Plas Treflyn, Tregaron, Cardiganshire; 22, York House, Kensington, W8.

SONS LIVING.

DAVID JOHN FRANCIS MALET (*Viscount
Vaughan*), *b.* June 15th, 1945; ed. at Ampleforth.
Hon. Michael John Wilmot Malet, *b.* 1948; ed. at
Ampleforth.
Hon. John Edward Malet, *b.* 1952; ed. at Ample-
forth.

SISTERS LIVING.

Lady Gloria Regina Malet, *b.* 1916: *m.* 1st, 1935, Maj. Nigel Thomas Loveridge Fisher, MC, MP,
Welsh Guards (from whom she obtained a divorce 1952), son of the late Cdr. Sir Thomas Fisher,
KBE, RN; 2ndly, 1952, Ronald Philip Flower, OBE, of Manor Farm Cottage, Weston Patrick,
nr. Basingstoke, and has issue living, (by 1st m.) Mark Nigel Thomas Vaughan, *b.* 1944: *m.* 1971,
Mrs. Ingrid Hunt, da. of the late James Hoyle Geach,—Amanda Gloria Morvyth Vaughan, *b.* 1939,—
(by 2nd m.) Philip Ronald, *b.* 1953.
Lady Honor Morvyth Malet, *b.* 1919; a JP for Cardiganshire: *m.* 1943, Maj. William Herbert Rhyidan
Llewellyn, MC, Welsh Gds., of Brynreithin, Ffair Rhos, Ystrad Meurig, Cardiganshire [see Llewellyn,
Bt., cr. 1922].
Lady Auriel Rosemary Malet, *b.* 1923.

WIDOW LIVING OF SEVENTH EARL.

AUDREY MAUREEN LESLIE (*Audrey, Countess of Lisburne*), (Flat 7, 1, St. James's St., SW1,
and The Villa Malet, Moyenne Corniche, Cap d'Ail, France, AM); a DStJ; yst. da. of the late
James Meakin, of Westwood Manor, Staffs., and widow of the Hon. Robert Godfrey de Bohun
Devereux [see V. Hereford]: *m.* 1961, as his 2nd wife, the 7th Earl, who *d.* 1965.

COLLATERAL BRANCHES LIVING.

Granddaughter of the late Capt. George Augustus Vaughan, son of the late
Capt. the Hon. George Laurence Vaughan, 3rd son of 3rd Earl:—
Issue of the late Lieut.-Col. Wilmot Charles Vaughan, *b.* 1863, *d.* 1944: *m.* 189-, Nora,
dau. of Frederick Fane:—
Muriel Alice Katherine Evelyn, *b.* 1897: *m.* 1921, John Abbott Bosvile-Boshell, who *d.* 1969. *Residence,*
—430, East 57th St., Sutton Pl., New York, USA.

Grandchildren of the late Edmund Mallet Vaughan, son of the late Hon. William
Mallet Vaughan, 4th son of 3rd Earl:—
Issue of the late Major Eugène Napoléon Ernest Mallet Vaughan, D.S.O., *b.* 1878, *d.*
1934: *m.* 1914, Hilda Winifred (now of Blackladies, Brewood, Stafford, el. dau. of the
late Neville Hanbury Mander, of Penn, Wolverhampton:—
Edmund Bernard Mallet (The Bath Farm, Codsall Wood, Wolverhampton) *b.* 1920; is Major Grenadier
Gds.: *m.* 1950, Jean, only da. of Col. John Walton Nelson, of Brasted, Kent, and has issue living,
David John, *b.* 1953,—Michael Edmund, *b.* 1957,—Diana Mary (twin), *b.* 1953.——Mary Christine
(Blackladies, Brewood, Stafford), *b.* 1916.

PREDECESSORS.—[1] JOHN Vaughan, *M.P.* for Cardiganshire in several Parliaments; cr.
Baron Fethard, of Feathered, co. Tipperary, and *Viscount Lisburne* (peerage of Ireland) 1695: *d.*
1720; *s.* by his el. son [2] JOHN, 2nd Viscount; *d.* 1741; *s.* by his brother [3] WILMOT, 3rd
Viscount; *d.* 1766; *s.* by his son [4] WILMOT, 4th Viscount; was M.P. for Cardiganshire 1755-
61 and 1768-96, Lord-Lieut. of Cardiganshire, a Lord of Trade 1768, and a Lord of the Admiralty
1770-82; cr. *Earl of Lisburne* (peerage of Ireland) 1776; *d.* 1800; *s.* by his el. son [5] WILMOT,
2nd Earl; *d.* 1820; *s.* by his half-brother [6] JOHN, 3rd Earl; Col. in the Army; *d.* 1831; *s.* by
his second son [7] ERNEST AUGUSTUS, 4th Earl; *b.* 1800: *m.* 1st, 1835, Mary, who *d.* 1851, dau.
of Sir Lawrence Palk, 2nd Bt.; 2ndly, 1853, the Hon. Elizabeth Augusta Harriett, who *d.* 1883
(formerly a Maid of Honour to H.M. Queen Adelaide), dau. of Col. Hugh Henry Mitchell; *d.*
1873; *s.* by his son [8] ERNEST AUGUSTUS MALLET, 5th Earl, *b.* 1836: *m.* 1st, 1858, Laura
Gertrude, who *d.* 1865, dau. of Edwyn Burnaby, of Baggrave Hall, Leicester; 2ndly,
Alice Dalton, who *d.* 1933 (having *m.* 2ndly, 1889 as his second wife, the 3rd Earl Amherst,
who *d.* 1910; 3rdly, 1914, H.S.H. Prince Jean Sapieha-Kodenski), dau. of the late Edmund
Probyn, of Huntley Manor, near Gloucester; *d.* 1888; *s.* by his son [9] ERNEST GEORGE
HENRY ARTHUR, 6th Earl; *b.* 1862: *m.* 1888, Evelyn, who *d.* 1931, dau. of the late Edmund
Probyn, of Huntley Manor and Longhope, Gloucester; *d.* 1899; *s.* by his son [10] ERNEST
EDMUND HENRY MALLET, 7th Earl; *b.* 1892; Lord-Lieut. for Cardiganshire 1923-56 (Sheriff 1923):
m. 1st, 1914, Regina, who *d.* 1944, da. of the late Don Julio Bittencourt, Attaché to Chilean
Legation in London; 2ndly, 1961, Audrey Maureen Leslie, yst. da. of the late James Meakin, of
Westwood Manor, Staffs., and widow of the Hon. Robert Godfrey de Bohun Devereux [V. Hereford];
d. 1965; *s.* by his son [11] JOHN DAVID MALET, 8th Earl and present peer; also Viscount Lisburne,
and Baron Fethard.

LISLE, BARON. (Lysaght.) [Baron I. 1758.]

[Title pronounced "Lyle." Name pronounced "Lycett."]

JOHN NICHOLAS HORACE LYSAGHT, 7th Baron, *b.* Aug. 10th, 1903; *s.* 1919: *m.* 1st, 1928, Vivienne; who *d.* 1948 (having obtained a divorce 1939), dau. of the Rev. M. Brew; 2ndly, 1939, Marie Helen, da. of the late A. D. Purgold, of Ebnal Lodge, Gobowen, Shropshire.

Arms,—Argent: three spears erect gules, on a chief azure, a lion passant guardant or. Crest,—A dexter arm embowed in armour, the hand holding a sword proper. Supporters,—Two lions or.

Wars! horrid wars!

Residence,—4, Bramerton St., SW3.

BROTHERS LIVING.

HORACE JAMES WILLIAM (of The Meadows, Mathern, Chepstow, Mon.), *b.* Sept. 22nd, 1908: *m.* 1st, 1930 (marriage dissolved 1951), Joanna Mary, da. of the late Dr. J. S. Nolan, of Bedwas, Mon-2ndly, 1953, Vyrna, da. of J. Jones, of Pontypool, and has issue living, (by 1st marriage) Patrick James (Pentwyn, Llangenny, Breconshire), *b.* 1931; ed. at Shrewsbury; late Lt. Grenadier Guards: *m.* 1957, Mary Louise (SHAW-STEWART), da. of Lt.-Col. Geoffrey Reginald Devereux Shaw [see Durrant, Bt.], and has issue living, John Nicholas Geoffrey *b.* 1960, David James *b.* 1963, Mary-Jane *b.* 1959,—Philip Henry, *b.* 1933,—Dermot Edward (of Woodlands, Dymock, Glos.), *b.* 1935; late 2nd Lt., King's Roy. Irish Hussars: *m.* 1961, Tessa Susan, dau. of Capt. Terence Hugh Back OBE, and has issue living, Cornelius James Terence *b.* 1965, Georgina Mary *b.* 1966,—Roderic Desmond John (c/o Westminster Bank, 185 Sloane St., SW1), *b.* 1940; ed. at King's Sch., Canter-bury: *m.* 1970, Mrs. Josephine Harrison, da. of Joseph Edward Thompson,—(by 2nd m.) Deirdre Elizabeth Jane, *b.* 1954,—Philippa Jane, *b.* 1955.

George Henry, *b.* 1911: *m.* 1935, Pauline Ann, dau. of Patrick J. Dillon, of the Grove, Girley Hills, co. Meath, and has issue living, Horace George, *b.* 1936,—Lawrence George, *b.* 1937, —John Patrick George, *b.* 1939,—Pauline Ann, *b.* 1942,—Mary Margaret, *b.* 1943.

SISTER LIVING.

Alice Amy: *m.* 1930, Henry Lysaght. *Residence,*—

COLLATERAL BRANCHES LIVING.

Grandchildren of the late Rev. the Hon. Henry Lysaght, 4th son of 5th Baron:—
Issue of the late Rev. John Arthur Constantine Lysaght, *b.* 1876, *d.* 1950 : *m.* 1902, Mary Nicholl, who *d.* 1967 da. of Adam Fettiplace Blandy, of The Warren, Abingdon:—
John Charles Fettiplace, *b.* 1909 ; ed. at Clifton Coll.: *m.* 1939, Phyllis Jean, dau. of the late T. H. Massey, of Newcastle, N.S. Wales, and has issue living, John Daniel Blandy, *b.* 1943,—Nicholas Richard Fettiplace, *b.* 1946,—Primrose Mary, *b.* 1940,—Sarah Louise, *b* 1953. *Residence,*—Abingdon, Paradise Av , Balgownie, NSW 2519——Nicholas Henry Lyster, *TD,* (Haford, Ponthir, Newport, Mon), *b.* 1911; ed. at Clifton Coll.; a DL of Mon.; 1939-45 War in N. Africa, and New Guinea as Maj. Australian Inf.: *m.* 1950, Gillian Mary, da. of R. F. Huggett, of Risca, Monmouth-shire, and has issue living, Mary Susan, *b.* 1952,—Philippa Jane, *b.* 1954,—Elizabeth Anne, *b.* 1961.——Christopher David Blandy, *b.* 1919.——Winifred Joyce, *b.* 1903.——Kathleen Mary Lalage, *b.* 1905: *m.* 1938, John St. Barbe Collins, who *d.* 1954, and has issue living, Elisabeth Mary, *b.* 1942: *m.* 1967, Roger Laws Newson, of 12, London Rd., Ascot, Berks,—Sarah Jane (twin) *b.* 1942. *Residence,*—5, Churchill Rd., Shalford, Guildford, Surrey.——Renée Primrose, *b.* 1907: *m.* 1936, Edward Montgomery Miles, who *d.* 1949. *Residence,*—3A, The Street, Shalford, nr. Guildford, Surrey.

Granddaughter of the late Rev. John Arthur Constantine Lysaght (ante) :—
Issue of the late Wing-Com. Philip Michael Vaughan Lysaght, Auxiliary Air Force, *b.* 1914 ; *d.* (killed in action during European War) 1943 : *m.* 1941, Christine (who *d.* 1968, having *m.* 2ndly, 1948, Cdr. C. G. Procter, RN (ret.) (RR9, Wood Lake, Columbus 47201, Indiana, USA), da. of the late W. Mackenzie Edwards, of Inverness:—
Diana Mary Philippa, *b.* 1943: *m.* 1962, Graham Edward Frank Snell, of Wall Cottage, The Creek, Sunbury-on-Thames, Middx., and has issue living, Matthew Michael Charles, *b.* 1965,—Louise Jane, *b.* 1969.

PREDECESSORS.—[1] JOHN Lysaght, M.P. for Charleville 1727; cr. *Baron Lisle,* of Mount North, co. Cork (peerage of Ireland) 1758; *d.* 1781; *s.* by his son [2] JOHN, 2nd Baron; *d.* 1798; *s.* by his el. son [3] JOHN, 3rd Baron; *d.s.p.* 1834; *s.* by his brother [4] GEORGE, 4th Baron; *b.* 1783: *m.* 1st, 1810, Elizabeth, who *d.* 1815, dau. of Samuel Knight; 2ndly, 1816, Elizabeth Anne, who *d.* 1825, dau. of John Davy Foulkes; 3rdly, Elizabeth, dau. of John Church; *d.* 1868; *s.* by his son [5] JOHN ARTHUR, 5th Baron; *b.* 1811: *m.* 1837, Henrietta Anne, who *d.* 1860, dau. of the late John Church; *d.* 1898; *s.* by his el. son [6] GEORGE WILLIAM JAMES, 6th Baron; *b.* 1840; served throughout Maori War 1864-5; *m.* 1868, Amy Emily, who *d.* 1918, dau. of the late Ayliffe Langford, of St. Heliers, Jersey, and Ventnor, Isle of Wight; *d.* 1919 ; *s.* by his grandson [7] JOHN NICHOLAS HORACE (son of the late Hon. Horace George Lysaght, only son of 6th Baron), 7th Baron and present peer.

LISTOWEL, EARL OF. (Hare.) Sits as BARON HARE (U.K. 1869). [Earl I. 1822.]

Rt. Hon. WILLIAM FRANCIS HARE, *G.C.M.G., P.C.,* 5th Earl ; *b.* Sept. 28th, 1906 ; *s.* 1931 ; ed. at Magdalene Coll., Camb. ; is 2nd Lieut. Intelligence Corps.; a Co. Councillor for London since 1937, and Lord Chm. of Cttees. and Dep. Speaker, House of Lords since 1965; Assist. Whip of Labour Party in House of Lords 1940-44, Parl. Under-Sec. of State for India and Burma 1944-45, Postmaster-Gen. 1945-47, Sec. of State for India and Colonial Affairs 1948-50, Parl. Sec. to Min, of Agriculture and Fisheries 1950-51, and Gov.-Gen. and Com.-in-Ch. of Ghana 1957-60 ; P.C.1946, G.C.M.G. 1957 : *m.* 1st, 1933 (marriage dissolved 1945), Judith, dau. of Raoul de

I hate whatever is profane.

Marffy-Mantuano, of Budapest, Hungary; 2ndly, 1958 (marriage dissolved 1963), Stephanie Sandra Yvonne (CURRIE), da. of Samuel Wise, of Toronto, Canada; 3rdly, 1963, Mrs. Pamela Read, and has issue by 1st, 2nd and 3rd marriages.

Arms,—Gules, two bars and a chief indented or. **Crest,**—A demi-lion rampant argent, ducally gorged or. **Supporters,**—Two dragons, ermine.

Residence,—10, Parkside, Knightsbridge, S.W.1.

SONS LIVING. *(By 3rd marriage).*
FRANCIS MICHAEL *(Viscount Ennismore),* b. June 28th, 1964.
Hon. Timothy Patrick, b. 1966.

DAUGHTERS LIVING. *(By 1st marriage.)*
Lady Deirdre Freda Mary *(Baroness Grantley),* b. 1935; ed. at Lady Margaret Hall, Oxford: m. 1955, the 7th Baron Grantley. *Residences,*—Markenfield Hall, Ripon; 53, Lower Belgrave St., S.W.1.

(By 2nd marriage.)
Lady Fiona Eve Akua, b. 1960.
(By 3rd marriage.)
Lady Diana, b. 1965.

BROTHERS LIVING.
Rt. Hon. John Hugh, O.B.E., P.C. *(Viscount Blakenham),* b. 1911; cr. Viscount 1963 [see that title].
Hon. Alan Victor, M.C., b. 1919 ; ed. at Eton, and at New Coll., Oxford ; formerly Major Life Guards ; was 1st Sec., British Embassy, Athens 1957-60 ; European War and Far East 1939-45 (M.C.) : m. 1945, Jill, dau. of Gordon North, and hasi ssue living, Alan Simon Mercury, b. 1948,—Marcia Persephone *(Hon. Mrs. Michael J. Hare),* b. 1946: m. 1965, the Hon. Michael John Hare, only son of 1st Viscount Blakenham. *Residence,*—53, Rutland Gate, SW7. *Clubs,*—White's, Pratt's.

SISTERS LIVING.
Lady (Ethel) Patricia *(Lady Patricia Milnes-Coates),* b. 1912: m. 1st, 1936, Lt.-Col. Charles Thomas Milnes Gaskell, Coldm. Gds., who d. (killed on active ser.) 1943 [E. Ranfurly]; 2ndly, 1945, Lt.-Col. Sir Robert Edward James Clive Milnes-Coates, 3rd Bt., DSO, Coldm. Gds. (ret.), and has issue living, (by 1st m.) James, b. 1937,—Andrew, b. 1939,—Tom, b. 1942,—(by 2nd m.) [see Milnes-Coates, Bt.]. *Residence,*—Moor House Farm, Helperby, York.
Lady Elizabeth Cecilia, b. 1914 : m. 1st, 1936, Major Viscount Elveden, R.A. (T.A.), who d. (killed in action during European War) 1945, son of 2nd Earl of Iveagh; 2ndly, 1947, Edward Rory More O'Ferrall. *Residences,*—The Old Rectory, Elveden, Suffolk; Gloucester Lodge, Regent's Park, N.W.1.

WIDOW LIVING OF SON OF FOURTH EARL.
Dora (Dorich House, Kingston Vale, SW15), da. of the late Mark Gordine, of St. Petersburg, Russia: m. 1936, the Hon. Richard Gilbert Hare, who d. 1966.

COLLATERAL BRANCHES LIVING.
Grandchildren of the late Rear-Adm. the Hon. Richard Hare (infra) :—
Issue of the late Capt. Harry Vivian Hare, b. 1881, d. (killed in action) 1914 : m. 1909, Ellen Louisa Marie, who d. 1968, da. of Sir Edward Hudson Hudson-Kinahan, 1st Bt.:—
Richard George Wyndham, O.B.E., R.N., b. 1910 ; is Capt.; European War 1939-43 (despatches); O.B.E. (Mil.) 1942 : m. 1937, Doreen Chetwode, dau. of the late Rev. Nixon Chetwode Ram, and has issue living, Rosemary Vivian, b. 1939: m. 1961, Roger Philip Laurence Chetwode Clarke, of 68, Roman Bank, Stamford, Lincs., and has issue living, Dominic Windham b. 1963, Cleone Rachel Vivien b. 1964,—Caroline Veronica, b. 1941: m. 1968, Capt. Richard Baden Bradley, R. Fus., of North Lodge, Westwood Park, Gt. Horkesley, Colchester, and has issue living, Robert Edward Baden b. 1969, Virginia Clare Baden b. 1970, Victoria Elizabeth Baden b. 1973,—Shelagh Virginia (twin), b. 1941: m. 1964, James Alan Edward Morshead, and has issue living, Charmian Juliet b. 1966. *Residence,*—Aghern, Conna, co. Cork.—Emily Lavender, b. 1912: m. 1st, 1935, Tom E. Montgomery, who d. (of wounds received in action at Arnhem) 1944; 2ndly, 1948, Ronald Paul Lancaster Rose [see Rose, Bt. cr. 1874, colls.], and has issue living, (by 1st m.) Thomas Carey b. 1937, —Dawn Vivian b. 1936. *Residence,*—Coole Abbey, Fermoy, co. Cork.

Issue of the late Rear-Adm. the Hon. Richard Hare, 2nd son of 2nd Earl, b. 1836, d. 1903 : m. 1874, Caroline Acland, who d. 1942, dau. of the late Capt. George Rideout Pinder:—
Eleanor Mary, b. 1890 : m. 1914, Harold Godfrey Twist, and has issue living, Patrick Hare Vivian (of Spinney Close, Leamington, Hastings, Rugby, Warwickshire), b. 1915 : m. 1947, Diana Helen Kingsley, and has issue living, Jonathan Patrick b. 1952, Sarah Shirley b. 1949,—Honor Valerie, b. 1919 : m. 1948, Richard James Matterson Ballintine, and has issue living, Zoë Honor Caroline, b. 1951. *Residence,*—The Haven Hotel, Dunmore, co. Waterford.

Grandchildren of the late Hon. Henry Hare, 4th son of 2nd Earl:—
Issue of the late Capt. Percy Richard Hare, T.D., b. 1870, d. 1937: m. 1903, Matilda Gertrude who d. 1972, da. of the late Henry F. Tiarks, of Foxbury, Chislehurst:—
Hugh Percy (St. James' Club), b. 1906; ed. at Eton; 1939-45 War as Capt. Intelligence Corps: m. 1948 (m. diss. 1959), Madeleine Marie Louise Tritter, of Asnières, France.—Joan Agnes, b. 1904: m. 1934 (m. diss. 1961), Group-Capt. Peter Warren Johnson, DSO, OBE, DFC, AFC, RAF [see Johnson, Bt., cr. 1775].—Sybil Rika *(Hon. Mrs. Robert E. U. Hermon-Hodge),* b. 1907: m. 1934, the Hon. Robert Edward Udny Hermon-Hodge, who d. 1937 [see B. Wyfold]. *Residence,*—Wyfold Lodge, Reading.—Victoria Katherine, b. 1914: m. 1961, as his second wife, Major George Seton Wills, Roy. Wilts Yeo. [see Wills, Bt., cr. 1904]. *Residence,*—Eastridge, Ramsbury, nr. Marlborough, Wilts.—Lilah Mary, b. 1915: m. 1st, 1935 (m. diss. 1946), Maj. George Seton Wills, Roy. Wilts Yeo (ante); 2ndly, 1946, as his second wife, Col. Nigel Victor Stopford Sackville, CBE, TD, who d. 1972 [see E. Courtown, colls.]. *Residence,*—Drayton House, Lowick, Kettering.
Grandchildren of the late Robert Dillon Hare, son of the late Hon. Robert Hare (infra):—
Issue of the late Brig.-Gen. Robert William Hare, C.M.G., D.S.O., late Norfolk Regt., b. 1872, d. 1953: m. 1908, Helen Mary, who d. 1972, da. of the late Lt.-Col. Guy Newcomen Atkinson, JP [E. Kingston, colls.]:—
Robert Gerald Dillon, b. 1910 ; Lieut.-Col. (retired) Roy. Norfolk Regt. ; A.D.C. to Gov. and Com.-in-Ch., Gibraltar 1937-9 ; European War 1939-45 : m. 1951, Evelyn Nora, dau. of the late Thomas Pratt, and has issue living, Anthony Gerald, b. 1956,—Carolyn Elizabeth, b. 1952. *Residence,*—12, Camberley Road, Norwich. *Club,*—Army and Navy.—Elizabeth *(Lady Shakespeare),* b. 1914 ; Freeman of City of London 1974; Section Officer WAAF 1940-45 (despatches, Bronze Star of USA): m. 1952, as his second wife, the Rt. Hon. Sir Geoffrey Hithersay Shakespeare, 1st B. *Residence,*—Flat 6, Great Ash, Lubbock Road, Chislehurst, Kent.—Nancy Violet, b. 1915: m. 1942, John Meredith Temple, MP, and has issue living, Guy, b. 1946,—Diana, b. 1943: m. 1965, Robert McConnell, of Hampton Hall, Worthen, Salop. *Residence,*—Picton Gorse, Chester.

Granddaughter of the late Hon. Robert Hare, brother of 2nd Earl:—
Issue of the late Thomas George Hare, b. 1850, d. 1915: m. 1895, Catharine Sophia, who d. 1947, dau. of 6th Count de Salis (Holy Roman Empire):—
Adelaide Mary (Pen Maen, St. George's Rd., Menai Bridge, Anglesey), b. 1896.

Grandchildren of the late Henrietta Bowers, dau. of the late Hon. Henry Hare, brother of 2nd Earl:—
Issue of the late Kathleen Douglas Bowers, b. 1875, d. 1909: m. 1898, Rowland Hawthornthwaite Wilson, who d. 1945:—

Douglas Rowland, b. 1909: m. 1937, Isma Pace, da. of Robert Cherer Smith, of George, S. Africa, and has issue living, Evadne Olga, b. 1938; ed. at Rhodes Univ., Grahamstown (BCom Econ): m. 1965, Jórgen Christiansen, of Holstebro, Denmark,—Brenda Kathleen (c/o Nat. Westminster Bank, 41, Lothbury, EC2), b. 1939; ed. at Cape Town Univ. (Teacher's Licentiate Music and Performers Licentiate Diploma): m. 1960, Ian Matthew Buchanan Gray, of Kariba, Rhodesia, and has issue living, Matthew Neil Buchanan b. 1961, Vivienne Evadne Buchanan b. 1964, Fiona Kathleen Buchanan (twin) b. 1964.——Sheila, b. 1901: m. 1922, Harold Harebottle Albort-Morgan, and has issue living, Terence Rowland (of Many Waters, Adelaide, Cape Province, S. Africa), b. 1926; ed. at Kingswood Coll., Grahamstown, and at Stellenbosch Univ., Cape Province: m. 1952, Moira Margaret, da. of Edward Painter, of Charlgrove, Port Beaufort, S. Africa, and has issue living, Harold Bruce b. 1953, Edward Rowland b. 1955, Keith Terence b. 1959, Janine Moira b. 1957,—Vivienne Kathleen, b. 1924: m. 1st, 1947, Burt Calvin Marshall, who d. 1948; 2ndly, 1954, Peter Pel Wium, MB, ChB, FRCOG, of 8, St. David's Rd., East London, S. Africa, and has issue living, (by 1st m.) Barry Ian Calvin b. 1948,—(by 2nd m.) Peter Morgan b. 1956, David Harold b. 1960, Karin Louise b. 1955. Residence,—Pearl Cottage, Kidds Beach, Cape Province, S. Africa.

Issue of the late Capt. Henry HARE-BOWERS, b. 1876, d. 1957:   m. 1910, Mabel Kathleen, who d. 1962, da. of Phillip Coffey, of Waterford:—
Henry Thompson, b. 1912; ed. at Cape Town and S. Africa Univs. (BA 1943); a lecturer at Grahamstown Training Coll., Cape Province, S. Africa: m. 1942, Phyllis May, da. of the Rev. Thomas Stanton, of St. Germains, Cornwall, and Kroonstad, Orange Free State, and has issue living, Peter Stanton, b. 1953,—Glynis, b. 1946. Address,—21, Fitzroy St., Grahamstown, S. Africa.—— Margaret, b. 1917; ed. at Rhodes Univ. Coll., Grahamstown (BA 1938): m. 1943, James Frederick Smith. Residence,—45, Venice Rd., Morningside, Durban, Natal.

PREDECESSORS.—[1] WILLIAM Hare, el. son of the late Richard Hare; M.P. for Cork City 1790-7, and for Athy 1798-1800; cr. Baron Ennismore, co. Kerry (peerage of Ireland) 1800, Viscount Ennismore and Listowel (peerage of Ireland) 1816, and Earl of Listowel (peerage of Ireland) 1822: m. 1st, 1772, Mary, who d. 1810, only dau. of the late Henry Wrixon, of Ballygiblin, co. Cork; 2ndly, 1812, Anne, who d. 1859, dau. of the late John Latham, of Meldrum. co. Tipperary; d. 1837; s. by his grandson [2] WILLIAM, K.P. (son of the late Richard, Viscount Ennismore, el. son of 1st Earl), 2nd Earl; b. 1801; was Vice-Adm. of Munster: m. 1831, Maria Augusta, who d. 1871, dau. of Vice-Adm. William Windham, of Felbrigge Hall, and widow of George Thomas Wyndham, of Cromer Hall, Norfolk: d. 1856; s. by his son [3] WILLIAM, K.P., 3rd Earl; b. 1833; cr. Baron Hare (peerage of United Kingdom) 1869; a Lord-in-Waiting to Queen Victoria in 1880: m. 1865, Lady Ernestine Mary Brudenell-Bruce, who d. 1936, dau. of 3rd Marquess of Ailesbury: d. 1924; s. by his el. son [4], RICHARD GRANVILLE, 4th Earl, b. 1866; sometime in Life Guards: m. 1904, the Hon. Freda Vanden-Bempde-Johnstone, who d. 1968, da. of 2nd Baron Derwent; d. 1931; s. by his el. son [5] WILLIAM FRANCIS, 5th Earl, and present peer; also Viscount Ennismore and Listowel, Baron Ennismore, and Baron Hare.

LIVERPOOL, EARL OF.   (Foljambe.)   [Earl U.K. 1905.]
[Name pronounced "Fulljum."]

EDWARD PETER BERTRAM SAVILE FOLJAMBE, 5th Earl; b. Nov. 14th, 1944; s. 1969; ed. at Shrewsbury: m. 1970, Lady Juliana Mary Alice Noel, el. da. of 5th Earl of Gainsborough, and has issue.

Arms,—Sable, a bend between six escallops or, and as an honourable augmentation (granted Aug. 1906) on the bend in chief, on an escutcheon vert a key surmounted by a baton in saltire or. Crests.—1st (of honourable augmentation granted Aug. 1906), on a chapeau gules turned up ermine a lion rampant of the first, charged on the shoulder with a besant, thereon an eagle displayed sable, and resting the dexter hind paw on a plate charged with a bend azure, thereon three garbs or, and surmounted by an escutcheon argent charged with an eagle displayed also sable, charged on the breast with a fleur-de-lis also or, the lion crowned gold and supporting with the fore paws a man-of-war's church pennant proper; 2nd, a seaweed rock proper, thereon a sea-lion sejant azure resting the dexter paw on an escutcheon per fesse wavy argent and azure, in chief a cormorant sable, beaked and legged gules, holding in the beak a branch of seaweed, called laver, inverted vert (Liverpool), and in base a hawk, wings elevated and addorsed argent (Hawkesbury); 3rd, a man's leg unarmed, couped at the thigh, quarterly or and sable spurred gold. Supporters.—On either side a griffin, wings elevated or, beaked, membered, ducally gorged, and on the wing three fleurs-de-lis one and two all azure, that on the dexter side charged on the breast with a torteau thereon a cross-crosslet fitchée argent (the badge of Howard), and that on the sinister with a pellet thereon a stag's head cabossed also argent (Cavendish).
Residence,—The Grange Farm, Exton, Oakham, Rutland. Clubs,—Turf, Pratt's.

Be steadfast.

SONS LIVING.
LUKE MARMADUKE PETER SAVILE (Viscount Hawkesbury), b. March 26th, 1972.
Hon. Ralph Edward Anthony Savile, b. 1974.

SISTER LIVING.   (Raised to the rank of an Earl's daughter 1970.)
Lady Jane Rosamond Mary, b. 1943.

GREAT AUNT LIVING.   (Daughter of First Earl.)
Lady Constance Blanche Alethea Mary, b. 1885: m. 1911, the Rev. Hezekiah Astley Kemp Hawkins, who d. 1927, V. of Kilburn, York. Residence,—5, Little Russell Street, W.C.1.

MOTHER LIVING.
Elizabeth Joan, da. of the late Maj. Eric Charles Montagu Flint, DSO: m. 1st, 1942, Capt. Peter George William Savile Foljambe, Herts. Regt., who d. (killed in action) 1944; 2ndly, 1947, Maj. Andrew Antony Gibbs, MBE, TD, Herts. Regt. (TA), of Kilvington Hall, Thirsk, Yorks. [see B. Aldenham, colls.].

AUNT LIVING.
Ursula Susan Annette Mary, b. 1916: m. 1939, Maj. Stephen Carrington Smith, TD, of Dawnedge, Aspley Guise, Beds., and has issue living, Nigel Antony Carrington, b. 1943,—Angela Selina Carrington, b. 1948: m. 1971, John Bunker.

WIDOW LIVING OF THIRD EARL.
CONSTANCE ISABELLE (Constance, Countess of Liverpool), only da. of the late John Holden, of Nuttall Temple, Notts.: m. 1909, the 3rd Earl, who d. 1962. Residence,—Stoneleigh House, Longborough, Moreton-in-Marsh, Glos.

PREDECESSORS.—[1] Sir CHARLES Jenkinson, 7th Bt., el. son of Col. Charles Jenkinson (who was 2nd in command of the Blues at Dettingen, and commanded them at Fontenoy, 3rd son of Sir Robert Jenkinson, 2nd Bt.), b. 1729, held many high offices of State, and was cr. Baron Hawkesbury, of co. Gloucester (peerage of Great Britain) 1786, and Earl of Liverpool 1796 ; d. 1808 ; s. by his el. son [2] ROBERT BANKS, K.G., 2nd Earl, b. 1770 ; called to the House of Lords 1803, in the lifetime of his father; Prime Min. and First Lord of the Treasury 1812-27 ; d.s.p. 1828 ; s. by his half-brother [3] CHARLES CECIL COPE, G.C.B., 3rd Earl, b. 1784 ; Lord Steward 1841-6 : m. 1810, Julia Evelyn Medley, who d. 1814, only child of Sir George Shuckburgh-Evelyn, 6th Bt. ; d. 1851, when the peerages became ext. and the baronetcy reverted to his cousin ; the Barony of Hawkesbury was revived 1893, and the Earldom of Liverpool 1905 in the person of his grandson and principal heir [4] CECIL GEORGE SAVILE Foljambe, P.C., el. son of the late George Savile Foljambe, of Osberton, Notts, and Aldwarke, Yorks, by his 2nd wife, Selina Charlotte, 2nd dau. and co. heiress (el. leaving issue) of 3rd Earl of Liverpool (cr. 1796, ext.), and 3rd Baron Hawkesbury (cr. 1786, ext.), and widow of William Charles, Viscount Milton ; b. 1846 ; a Lord-in-Waiting to Queen Victoria 1894-5, and Lord Steward of King Edward VII.'s Household 1905-7 ; M.P. for N. Nottinghamshire (L) 1880-85, and for Notts, Mansfield Div. 1885-92 ; cr. Baron Hawkesbury, of Haselbech, co. Northampton, and of Ollerton, Sherwood Forest, co. Nottingham (peerage of United Kingdom) 1893, and Viscount Hawkesbury, of Kirkham, co. York, and of Mansfield, co. Nottingham, and Earl of Liverpool (peerage of United Kingdom) 1905 ; P.C. 1906 : m. 1st, 1869, Louisa Blanche, who d. 1871, el. dau. of the late Frederick John Howard, of Compton Place, Sussex [E. Carlisle, colls.] ; 2ndly, 1877, Susan Louisa, who d. 1917, el. dau. of the late Lieut.-Col. William Henry Frederick Cavendish, of West Stoke, Sussex, and 47, Cromwell Houses, S.W., 2nd cousin both paternally and maternally of his 1st wife ; d. 1907 ; s. by his el. son [5] ARTHUR WILLIAM DE BRITO SAVILE, G.C.B., G.C.M.G., G.B.E., M.V.O., P.C., 2nd Earl, b. 1870 ; was State Steward and Chamberlain to Lord-Lieut. of Ireland 1906-8, Comptroller of H.M.'s Household 1909-12, Gov. of New Zealand 1912-17, and First Gov.-Gen. of the Dominion of New Zealand 1917-20: m. 1897, the Hon. Annette Louise Monck, G.B.E., who d. 1948, only dau. of 5th Viscount Monck ; d. 1941 ; s. by his half-brother [6] GERALD WILLIAM FREDERICK SAVILE, D.S.O., 3rd Earl b. 1878; Lieut.-Col. King's Roy. Rifle Corps; S. Africa 1899-1902; 1914-18 War as O.O. 21st Bn.: m. 1909, Constance Isabelle, only dau. of John Holden, of Nuttall Temple, Notts; d. 1962; s. by his brother [7] ROBERT ANTHONY EDWARD ST. ANDREW SAVILE, 4th Earl; b. 1887; d. 1969; s. by his great-nephew [8] EDWARD PETER BERTRAM SAVILE (grandson of Maj. the Hon. Bertram Marmaduke Osbert Savile Foljambe, MC, 6th son of 1st Earl), 5th Earl and present peer; also Viscount Hawkesbury, and Baron Hawkesbury.

LIVERPOOL, LORD BISHOP OF. (Sheppard.)

Rt. Rev. DAVID STUART SHEPPARD, son of Stuart Morton Winter Sheppard, Solicitor; b. 1929; ed. at Sherborne, Trin. Hall, Camb. (MA) and Ridley Hall Theological Coll.; Curate of St. Mary, Islington 1955-57; Warden, Mayflower Family Centre, Canning Town, E16, 1957-69; consecrated Bishop of Woolwich (Suffragan for Diocese of Southwark) 1969, and translated as 6th Bishop of Liverpool 1975: m. 1957, Eleanor Grace, da. of Bayan Raymond Isaac.
Patron of fifty-seven livings, and of four alternately with the crown, of twenty-five Canonries of the Cathedral, of the two Arch-deaconries, the Rural Deaneries of the Diocese, and the Chancellorship.
Episcopal Signature—David Liverpool.
ARMS OF THE SEE,—Argent, an eagle with wings expanded sable, around its head a nimbus or, and holding in its dexter claw an ancient ink-horn proper; a chief paly azure and gules, the dexter charged with an open book or, inscribed with the words "Thy Word is Truth"; the sinister with a lymphad or.
Residence,—Bishop's Lodge, Woolton Park, Liverpool, L25 6DT.

LLEWELYN-DAVIES, BARON. (Llewelyn Davies.) [Life Baron 1963.]

RICHARD LLEWELYN DAVIES, son of Crompton Llewelyn Davies; b. Dec. 24th, 1912; ed. at Trin. Coll., Camb. (MA), and at Ecole des Beaux Arts, Paris; a FRIBA, a Member of RTPI; Hon. Fellow of American Inst. of Architects; Sen. partner, Llewelyn-Davies Weeks, Forestier-Walker & Bor, architects and planners; Architect to LMS Railway 1942-48, and Dir. of Div. for Architectural Studies, Nuffield Foundation, London 1953-60; Prof. Architecture, Univ. of London and Head of Bartlett Sch. of Architecture, at Univ. Coll. 1960-69, since when Prof. of Urban Planning; Head of Sch. of Environmental Studies, Univ. Coll., London since 1971; a Member of Royal Fine Art

Comm. 1961-72, Chm., Centre for Environmental Studies since 1967; *cr.*
Baron Llewelyn-Davies, of Hastoe, co. Hertford [Life Baron] 1963: *m.* 1943,
Annie Patricia, *PC (Baroness Llewelyn-Davies of Hastoe)*, [see that title], da.
of C. P. Parry, and has issue.

Arms,—Chevronny of eight argent and azure, a fess bretessed gules. **Crest,**—In front of two
Dragons Wings conjoined in base gules, a pair of compasses erect and extended or. **Supporters.**—
On either side a stag proper attired unguled and gorged with a collar bretessed or.

Residences,—36, Parkhill Rd., NW3; Carpenters Yard, Tring, Herts.
Club,—Brooks's.

DAUGHTERS LIVING.
Hon. Melissa, *b.* 1945: *m.* 1974, Christopher Desmond Curling [see Bonham ,Bt.].
Hon. Harriett Lydia Rose, *b.* 1955.
Hon. Rebecca, *b.* 1957.

LLEWELYN-DAVIES OF HASTOE, BARONESS. (Llewelyn-Davies.)
(Life Baroness 1967)

ANNIE PATRICIA LLEWELYN DAVIES, *PC*, da. of C. P. Parry, of Prenton
Cheshire; *b.* July 16th, 1915; ed. at Liverpool Coll., Huyton, and Girton Coll.
Camb.; Dir. of Africa Educational Trust since 1960, a Member of Board of
Govs. of Hosp. for Sick Children, Great Ormond St., since 1955 (Chm. 1967-69);
a Baroness in Waiting (Govt. Whip) 1969-70; Opposition Ch. Whip since
1973 (Dep. Ch. Whip 1971-72); Ch. Whip House of Lords and Capt. of the
Hon. Corps. of Gentlemen-at-Arms since 1974; *cr. Baroness Llewelyn-Davies of
Hastoe*, of Hastoe, co. Hertford (Life Baroness) 1967, and PC 1975: *m.*
1943, Baron Llewelyn-Davies, Life Peer, and has issue (see that title).

Residences,—36, Parkhill Rd., NW3; Carpenters Yard, Tring, Herts.

LLOYD, BARON. (Lloyd.) [Baron U.K. 1925.]

Be watchful.

ALEXANDER DAVID FREDERICK LLOYD,
M.B.E.; 2nd Baron; *b.* Sept. 30th, 1912; *s.*
1941; ed. at Eton, and at Trin. Coll., Camb.
(MA); is Capt. Welsh Guards (Reserve),
and a DL of Herts, Chm. of National
Bank of NZ Ltd., a Dir. of Lloyds Bank,
Lloyds Bank Internat., and other cos.,
and a Member of Court of Govs., London
Sch. of Hygiene and Tropical Medicine; a
Co. Councillor for London 1949-51, a Lord-
in-Waiting to HM 1951-52, Joint Parlia-
mentary Under-Sec. of State for Home
Affairs (with responsibility for Welsh
Affairs) 1952-54, and Parliamentary Under-
Sec. of State for the Colonies 1954-57;
Pres., Navy League 1948-51, and of Common-
wealth and British Empire Chambers of
Commerce 1957-61; sometime on Staff of
British Council, and Dep. Chm., British
Empire Producers' Organization 1951; a
Member of White Fish Authority and
Herring Board 1963-69; formerly 2nd Lt.
Coldm. Gds. (Suppl. Reserve); 1939-45
War in Palestine, Syria, and NW Europe (MBE); MBE (Mil) 1945: *m.* 1942,
Lady Victoria Jean Marjorie Mabell Ogilvy, da. of 12th Earl of Airlie, and has
issue.

Arms,—Azure, a chevron between three cocks argent, armed, crested and wattled or. **Crest,**—In
front of a fernbrake a goat salient argent, horned and unguled or, gorged with a collar flory counterflory sable. **Supporters,**—On either side a goat argent, horned and unguled or, and gorged with
n Eastern crown also or.

Residence,—Clouds Hill, Offley, Hitchin, Herts.

DAUGHTERS LIVING.
Hon. Davina Margaret, *b.* 1943.   *Hon.* Laura Blanche Bridget, *b.* 1960.

PREDECESSOR.—[1] *Rt. Hon. Sir* GEORGE AMBROSE Lloyd, *G.C.S.I., G.C.I.E., D.S.O.,*
son of the late Sampson S. Lloyd, of the Priory Warwick, and Dolobran, Montgomeryshire; *b.* 1879; was Gov. of Bombay 1918-23, High Commr. for Egypt and the Sudan 1925-9,
and Sec. of State for the Colonies 1940-41; Leader of House of Lords 1941; Founder of Lloyd
Barrage on the Indus and of the Lloyd Dam in the Deccan; 1914-18 War in Egypt, Gallipoli, and
Trans-Jordania as Capt. Warwickshire Yeo.; MP for W. Div. of Staffordshire (U) 1910-18,
and for Eastbourne Div. of E. Sussex 1924-25; *cr. Baron Lloyd,* of Dolobran, co. Montgomery 1925:
m. 1911, the Hon. Blanche Isabella, who *d.* 1969, da. of the late Com. the Hon. Frederick Canning
Lascelles, of Sutton Waldron House, Blandford; *d.* 1941; *s.* by [2] his only son ALEXANDER DAVID
FREDERICK, 2nd Baron and present peer.

LLOYD GEORGE OF DWYFOR, EARL. (Lloyd George.) [Earl U.K. 1945.]

OWEN LLOYD GEORGE, 3rd Earl; *b.* April 28th, 1924; *s.* 1968; ed. at Oundle; an underwriting member of Lloyd's; carried the Sword at Investiture of HRH the Prince of Wales, Caernarvon Castle 1969; a Member of Historic Buildings Council for Wales since 1971; 1939-45 War as Capt. Welsh Guards: *m.* 1949, Ruth Margaret, only da. of the late Richard Coit, of 18, Thurloe Sq., SW7, and has issue.

Arms,—Azure over water barry wavy in base a bridge of one arch proper, on a chief argent a portcullis sable between two daffodils stalked and leaved also proper. Crest,—A demi-dragon gules holding between the claws a portcullis sable. Supporters,—*Dexter*, a dragon or; *sinister*, an eagle wings addorsed or; each gorged with a collar vert.

Residences,—Brimpton Mill, Reading; 43, Cadogan Sq., SW1.

Clubs,—White's, Pratt's, City of London, Garrick.

SONS LIVING.
DAVID RICHARD OWEN (*Viscount Gwynedd*), *b.* Jan. 22nd, 1951; ed. at Eton.
Hon. Robert John Daniel, *b.* 1952; ed. at Eton, and Univ. Coll., Oxford.

DAUGHTER LIVING.
Lady Julia Margaret Violet, *b.* 1958.

SISTER LIVING.
Lady Valerie Davidia, *b.* 1918: *m.* 1940, Sir Goronwy Hopkin Daniel, KCVO, CB, DPhil, and has issue living, David Llewellyn, *b.* 1950,—Anne Margaret, *b.* 1944,—Gwyneth Roberta, *b.* 1946. *Residence,*— Plas Penglais, Aberystwyth, Cards.

AUNT LIVING. (*Daughter of 1st Earl.*)
Lady Olwen Elizabeth, *DBE*, *b.* 1892; DBE (Civil) 1969: *m.* 1917, Maj. Sir Thomas John Carey Evans, MC, FRCS, who *d.* 1947, formerly IMS, and has issue living, Robert Rufus, *DFC* (2a, Fisher Av., Vancluse, Sydney, Aust.), *b.* 1923; Bar. Middle Temple 1949; late Fl.-Lt. RAFVR; 1939-45 War (DFC): *m.* 1968, Elizabeth Margaret Scott, yr. da. of the late Walter Laing, of Sydney, Aust.,— David Lloyd (of Eisteddfa Farm, Criccieth, Caerns.), *b.* 1925; a Farmer; 1939-45 War as Lt. RNVR: *m.* 1959, Annwen, el. da. of W. Williams, of Cae Mawr, Llanerchymedd, and has issue living, Thomas Robert *b.* 1961, William Lloyd *b.* 1962, Richard Huw *b.* 1968, Davina *b.* 1964,—Margaret Lloyd, *b.* 1918: *m.* 1948, Robert Michael Stewart Barrett, 45, Berkeley Sq., W1, formerly Capt. USAF,— Eluned Jane, *b.* 1921: *m.* 1942, Surg.-Lt. Robert Laidlaw Macmillan, Roy. Canadian Naval VR, of 350, Inglewood Drive, Toronto, Canada, and has issue living, Thomas Carey *b.* 1948, Robert David Hugh *b.* 1951, David John *b.* 1953, Margaret Olwen *b.* 1943, Ann Elizabeth *b.* 1946. *Residence,*— Eisteddfa, Criccieth, Caerns.

WIDOW LIVING OF SECOND EARL.
WINIFRED EMILY (*Winifred, Countess Lloyd George of Dwyfor*), da. of the late Thomas William Peedle, and formerly wife of Henry Michael Calve: *m.* 1935, as his 2nd wife, the 2nd Earl, who *d.* 1968.

PREDECESSORS.—*Rt. Hon.* DAVID Lloyd George, *O.M.*, son of the late William George, of Bulford, Pembrokeshire; *b.* 1863; Hon. D.C.L. Oxford 1908 and Durham 1919, Hon. LL.D. Wales 1908, Glasgow 1917, Edinburgh 1918, Cambridge 1920, and Birmingham 1921, Hon. D.Litt. Sheffield 1919, Hon. Fellow Jesus Coll., Oxford 1910; admitted Solicitor 1884; sometime a partner in the legal firm of Lloyd George and George, of Criccieth; a J.P., D.L., and County Alderman for Caernarvonshire (Chm. of Quarter Sessions 1929-38), Prior and Chancellor of the Priory for Wales of Order of St. John of Jerusalem, a K.G.St.J., and a Freeman of many towns; appointed Pres. of the Board of Trade Dec. 1905, Chancellor of the Exchequer April 1908, Min. of Munitions May 1915 (also a Member of Cabinet War Council), and Sec. of State for War and Member of Army Council July 1916; was Prime Minister and First Lord of the Treasury Dec. 1916 to Oct. 1922; elected Lord Rector of Edinburgh Univ. 1920; Sessional Chm. of Parliamentary Liberal Party 1924-31; appointed Constable of Caernarvon Castle 1908; Ch. British Representative at Paris Peace Conference 1919 (1914-15 star, War and Victory medals, Grand Cordon of Legion of Honour, and Italian Order of St. Maurice and St. Lazarus); sat as M.P. for Caernarvon Dist. (*L*) April 1890 to Dec. 1944; cr. *Viscount Gwynedd*, of Dwyfor, co. Caernarvon, and *Earl Lloyd George of Dwyfor* (peerage of United Kingdom) 1945: *m.* 1st, 1888, *Dame* Margaret, *G.B.E., LL.D., J.P.*, who *d.* 1941, dau. of Richard Owen, of Mynydd Ednyfed, Criccieth; 2ndly, 1943, Frances Louise, *CBE*, who *d.* 1972, da. of John Stevenson, of Wallington, Surrey; *d.* 1945; *s.* by his el. son [2] RICHARD, 2nd Earl, *b.* 1889: *m.* 1st, 1917, Roberta Ida Freeman (who *d.* 1966, having obtained a divorce 1933), da. of Sir Robert McAlpine, 1st Bt.; 2ndly, 1935, Winifred Emily, da. of the late Thomas William Peedle, and formerly wife of Henry Michael Calve; *d.* 1968; *s.* by his son [3] OWEN, 3rd Earl and present peer; also Viscount Gwynedd.

LLOYD OF HAMPSTEAD, BARON. (Lloyd.) [Life Baron 1965.]

DENNIS LLOYD, son of Isaac Lloyd, of 22, Stourcliffe Close, W1; *b.* Oct. 22nd, 1915; ed. at Univ. Coll. Sch., and at Univ. Coll., London (LL.B. Fellow), and at Gonville and Caius Coll., Camb. (MA, LL.D); Bar. Inner Temple 1936; Chm. of Nat. Film Sch. Planning Cttee., of Govs. of Nat. Film Sch., and of Council Univ. Coll. Sch., a Member of Law Reform Cttee., of Consolidation Bills Cttee., and of Theatre Censorship Cttee., a Gov. of British Film Inst. (Chm. of Board 1973), and a Member of Conseil de la Fédération

Britannique de l'Alliance Française; Reader in English Law, Univ. of London, 1947-56, Dean of Faculty of Laws, Univ. of London 1962-64; Quain Prof. of Jurisprudence, Univ. of London since 1956; Head of Depart. of Law Univ. Coll., London; author of "Unincorporated Association" 1938, "Public Policy" 1953, "Rent Control" 2nd edition 1955, "Business Lettings" 1956, "The Idea of Law" 1964, "Introduction to Jurisprudence" 3rd edition 1972, and "Law" (Concept Series) 1968; 1939-45 War as Capt. RAOC in Middle East and Italy; cr. *Baron Lloyd of Hampstead*, of Hampstead, London Borough of Camden (Life Peerage) 1965: *m.* 1940, Ruth Emma Cecilia, da. of Carl Tulla, and has issue.

Residence,—18, Hampstead Way, NW11.   *Club,*—Athenæum.

DAUGHTERS LIVING.

Hon. Naomi Katharine, *b.* 1946: *m.* 1967, Peter Campbell Hodges, of 24, Lowther Rd., Barnes, SW13, and has issue.

Hon. Corinne Deborah, *b.* 1951.

LLOYD OF KILGERRAN, BARON. (Lloyd.) [Life Baron 1973.]

RHYS GERRAN LLOYD, *CBE, QC,* son of the late James Griffith Lloyd, of Kilgerran, Pembrokeshire; *b.* Aug. 12th, 1907; ed. at Sloane Sch., and Selwyn Coll., Camb. (MA; Hon. Fellow 1968); BSc London; Bar. Gray's Inn 1939, and Middle Temple 1954, and a QC 1961; Scientific Research Depart. of Air Min. 1939-46; Part time Sec. of Roy. Commn. of Awards to Inventors, 1947-54; Chm. Liberal Party Law Panel 1965-71; Pres. Welsh Liberal Party 1971-74 (Hon. Treasurer 1967-71), and of UK Liberal Party 1973-74; a Dir. of Marton-air Internat., Ltd., Terrapin Internat., Ltd., Aladdin Industries Ltd., and other cos.; a JP for Surrey; cr. CBE (Civil) 1953, and *Baron Lloyd of Kilgerran,* of Llanwenog, co. Cardigan (Life Baron) 1973: *m.* 1940, Phyllis Mary, da. of the late Ronald Shepherd, JP, of Chilworth, Hants., and has issue.

Residence,—15, Haymeads Drive, Esher, Surrey.   *Clubs,*—Reform, City Livery, United Wards, National Liberal, Royal Commonwealth Society.

DAUGHTERS LIVING.

Hon. Elizabeth Mary Gerran, *b.* 1944: *m.* 1968, Daniel Gerard Robins, of 6, Belvedere Grove, Wimbledon, SW19.

Hon. Catherine Gerran, *b.* 1947: *m.* 1972, Philip Gwynfryn Edwards, of 56, Coolhurst Rd., N8.

Lloyd, see Baron Geoffrey-Lloyd.

LOCH, BARON. (Loch.) [Baron U.K. 1895.]

By constant application, not by sloth.

GEORGE HENRY COMPTON LOCH, 3rd Baron; *b.* Feb. 3rd, 1916; *s.* 1942; ed. at Eton ; Major (retired) 11th Hussars: *m.* 1st, 1942, Leila Mary Grace Isabel Hill Mackenzie, who obtained a divorce 1946 ; 2ndly, 1946 (marriage dissolved 1952), Mrs. Betty Castillon du Perron ; 3rdly, 1952, Joan Dorothy Hawthorn Binns; 4thly, 1975, Mrs. Sylvia Beauchamp-Wilson, only da. of A. G. Beauchamp Cameron, of Dalmahoy, Midlothian, and has issue by 1st m.

Arms,—Or, a saltire engrailed sable, between in fesse two swans in water proper, all within a bordure vert. *Crest,*—A swan devouring a perch proper. *Supporters,*—*Dexter,* a Tartar proper, *sinister,* a Zulu proper.

Residence,—Stoke College, Stoke-by-Clare, Suffolk.

DAUGHTER LIVING. (*By 1st marriage.*)

Hon. Jean Margaret, *b.* 1943.

BROTHER LIVING.

Hon. SPENCER DOUGLAS, *M.C., b.* Aug. 12th, 1920 ; ed. at Wellington, and at Trin. Coll., Camb. ; Bar. Lincoln's Inn 1948 ; is Major Grenadier Guards; N.-W. Europe 1944-5 : *m.* 1948, the Hon. Rachel Cooper, dau. of the late Nan Ino, Baroness Lucas of Crudwell, and Dingwall, and has issue living, Edward Granville, *b.* 1951,—Andrew Spencer, *b.* 1955,—Sara Nan, *b.* 1949.   *Residences,* —51, Lennox Gdns., SW1; Lochluichart by Garve, Ross-shire.   *Club,*—Travellers'.

SISTERS LIVING.

Hon. Maysie Elizabeth, *b.* 1906: *m.* 1932, Ian Gordon Lindsay, OBE, RSA, FRIBA, who *d.* 1966, and has issue living, George Hamish, *b.* 1933,—Douglas Michael, *b.* 1941,—David Ian, *b.* 1943,— Margaret Helen, *b.* 1936,—Jane Elizabeth, *b.* 1938: *m.* 1961, James Airlie Bruce Jones,—Mary Ailsa, *b.* 1943.   *Residence,*—59, Dick Place, Edinburgh, 9.

Hon. Jean Sybil, *b.* 1908: *m.* 1930, Guy Arthur Newman [see Newman, Bt.; cr. 1912].   *Residence,*—Stanners Hill Manor, Chobham, Surrey.

Hon. Helen, *b.* 1919: *m.* 1947, G. Ronald Service, who *d.* 1961, and has issue living, James Ronald, *b.* 1948.   *Residence,*—Kinfauns House, Kinfauns, by Perth.

PREDECESSORS.—[1] *Rt. Hon.* Sir HENRY BROUGHAM Loch, *G.C.B., G.C.M.G., P.C.,* son of the late James Loch, M.P., of Drylaw, Midlothian ; *b.* 1827 ; taken prisoner and cruelly treated by Chinese when negotiating under flag of truce 1860, and brought home same year Ratified Treaty of Tien-Tsin and Convention of Pekin ; Lieut. Gov. of Isle of Man 1863-82, a Commr. of Woods and Forests 1882-4, Gov. of Victoria 1884-9, and Gov. of Cape of Good Hope, and H.M.'s High Commr. for S. Africa 1889-95; cr. *Baron Loch,* of Drylaw, Midlothian (peerage of United Kingdom) 1895: *m.* 1862, Elizabeth, who *d.* 1938, dau. of the late Hon. Edward Ernest Villiers, *d.* 1900 ; *s.* by his only son [2] EDWARD DOUGLAS, *C.B., C.M.G., M.V.O., D.S.O., b.* 1873: Maj.-Gen. (retired) ; Nile Expedition 1898 (D.S.O.), S. Africa 1899-1900, European War 1914-19 (C.M.G., C.B.) ; a Lord-in-Waiting to H.M. 1911-14, and Capt. of Yeomen of the Guard Feb. to Nov. 1924, and 1929-31: *m.* 1905, Lady Margaret Louisa Lizzie Compton, who *d.* 1970, da. of 5th Marquess of Northampton, *d.* 1942 ; *s.* by his son [3] GEORGE HENRY COMPTON, 3rd Baron and present peer.

Loftus, Viscount, son of Marquess of Ely.

LONDESBOROUGH, BARON. (Denison.) [Baron U.K. 1850.]

RICHARD JOHN DENISON, 9th
Baron; b. July 2nd, 1959; s. 1968.

Arms,—Quarterly: 1st and 4th ermine, a
bend azure, cotised sable, between an unicorn's head erased in chief and a cross
crosslet fitchée in base gules, Denison; 2nd
and 3rd argent, a shake fork between three
mullets one and two sable, Conyngham.
Crests,—1st, issuant from clouds a dexter arm
in bend proper, vested gules, cuffed ermine,
and charged with a covered cup or, pointing
with the fore finger to an estoile radiated
gold, Denison; 2nd, an unicorn's head erased
argent, armed and maned or, Conyngham.
Supporters,—Dexter, a horse argent, maned,
unguled, and charged on the shoulder with an
eagle displayed or, with a crescent sable for
difference; sinister, a stag argent, attired, unguled, and charged on the shoulder with a
griffin's head erased or, with a crescent sable for
difference.

Residence,—Dragon House, Edgioak, nr.
Redditch, Worcestershire.

ADVERSA VIRTUTE REPELLO

I repel adversity with courage.

SISTER LIVING OF SEVENTH BARON.

Beatrice Mildred (Beatrice, Lady Gore) (Eastgate House, Malmesbury, Wilts.), b. 1887: m. 1st, 1912,
Lt.-Col. Algernon Corbet Turnor, MC, Roy. Horse Gds., who d. 1930 [V. Combermere, colls.]; 2ndly,
1943, Sir Ralph St. George Claude Gore, 10th Bt., who d. 1961, and has issue living, (by 1st marriage)
Anthony Richard, CBE (Foxley Manor, Malmesbury, Wilts.; Army and Navy, and Pall Mall Clubs)
b. 1914; Maj. KRRC; Palestine 1936-37 (medal with clasp), 1939-45 War; OBE (Civil) 1973:
m. 1952, Joyce Winifred, da. of the late William James Osborn, and has issue living, Carey b. 1953,
Richard William Corbet b. 1956,—Angela, b. 1915: m. 1937, Lt.-Col. Edward George Vernon Northey,
KRRC, of Brook House, Norton, Malmesbury, Wilts., son of Maj.-Gen. Sir Edward Northey, GCMG,
CB [Honywood, Bt.], and has issue living, Edward Martin Anthony b. 1944, Celia Rosemary b. 1937:
m. 1959, David William Riland Bedford, of The Malt House, Upton, Andover, and has issue living,
Simon b. 1962, Nicola b. 1964, Caroline Amalia b. 1948: m. 1971, James Heron, of 85, Gowan Av.,
SW6,—Cynthia Evelyn, b. 1918: m. 1949, Lt.-Col. Hugh Alexander Hope, OBE, MC, KRRC, of
Fosters, Mattingley, nr. Basingstoke [see Hope, Bt., cr. 1628],—Daphne, b. 1920: m. 1957, Lt.-Col.
Richard Martin Harry Mansel Grant Thorold, DSO, 11th Hussars, of Pinkney Mill, Malmesbury,
Wilts., and has issue living, Nicholas b. 1958, Sara b. 1962.

DAUGHTER LIVING OF FOURTH EARL.

Lady Zinnia Rosemary (posthumous), b. 1937: m. 1st, 1957 (m. diss. 1961), Peter Comins; 2ndly,
1961 (m. diss. 1964), John David Leslie Melville [see E. Leven and Melville, colls.]; 3rdly, 1964
(m. diss. 1967), Maj. Hugh Cantlie; 4thly, 1968, Ralph John Hamilton Pollock, of 3, West Eaton
Place, SW1, [see Pollock, Bt., colls.], and has issue living, (by 1st m.) Timothy Hugo, b. 1958,—(by
3rd m.) Charles Edgar, b. 1965.

WIDOW LIVING OF FOURTH EARL.

MARIGOLD ROSEMARY JOYCE LONDESBOROUGH, dau. of the late Edgar Lubbock, LL.B.[see B. Avebury,
colls.]; formerly Senior Comdt., Auxiliary Territorial Ser.; assumed by deed Poll 19—, the surname
of Londesborough: m. 1st, 1935, the 4th Earl, who d. 1937, when the Earldom and Viscountcy
became ext. and the Barony passed to a kinsman; 2ndly, 1948 (marriage dissolved 1952), Zygmund
de Lubicz-Bakanowski, formerly 18th Lancers, Polish Army. Residence,—

WIDOWS LIVING OF SEVENTH AND EIGHTH BARONS.

JOCELYN HELEN (Jocelyn Baroness Londesborough), (Anchor Cottage, Bembridge, Isle of Wight),
da. of the late Lt.-Cdr. Hugh Duppa Collins, RN: m. 1952, as his 3rd wife, the 7th Baron, who d.
1967.
ELIZABETH ANN (Baroness Londesborough), (Dragon House, Edgioak, nr. Redditch, Worcs.), da.
of the late Edward Little Sale, ICS, and formerly wife of Thomas Chambers Windsor Roe: m. 1957,
as his 2nd wife, the 8th Baron, who d. 1968.

COLLATERAL BRANCH LIVING.

Granddaughter of the late Hon. Henry Charles Denison, 3rd son of 1st Baron :—
Issue of the late Commodore Edward Conyngham Denison, M.V.O., R.N., b. 1888, d. 1960 :
m. 1919, Maira Amy Brabazon (Jasper, W. Marden, Chichester), da. of the late Lt.-Col.
Sir Charles Henry Brabazon Heaton-Ellis, CBE, of Wyddiall Hall, Buntingford, Herts:—
Sonia Myrtle, b. 1921 : m. 1st, 1940, Major Edgar FitzGerald Heathcoat-Amory, Roy. Devon Yeo.,
who d. (killed in action in Normandy) 1944 [see V. Amory, colls.]; 2ndly, 1947, Brigadier Roderick
Heathcoat-Amory, MC, The Royals [see V. Amory]. Residence,—Oswaldkirk Hall, York.

PREDECESSORS.—[1] Lord ALBERT Conyngham, K.C.H., F.R.S., 2nd surviving son of Henry,
1st Marquess Conyngham, by Elizabeth, dau. of Joseph Denison, of Denbies, co. Surrey ; b.
1805 ; was Vice-Adm. of Yorkshire; assumed the surname of Denison by Roy. licence 1849 :
cr. Baron Londesborough, of Londesborough, co. York (peerage of United Kingdom) 1850 : m.
1st, 1833, Henrietta Maria, who d. 1841, dau. of 1st Baron Forester; 2ndly, 1847, Ursula Lucy
Grace (who d. 1883, having m. 2ndly, the Rt. Hon. Lord Otho Augustus Fitzgerald, P.C.,
M.P., who d. 1882 [D. Leinster]), dau. of Rear-Adm. the Hon. Charles Bridgeman [E. Bradford];
d. 1860 ; s. by his son [2] WILLIAM HENRY FORESTER, 2nd Baron, b. 1834 ; M.P. for Beverley
(L) 1857-9 and for Scarborough 1859-60 ; cr. Viscount Raincliffe, of Raincliffe, co. York, and
Earl of Londesborough (peerage of United Kingdom) 1887 : m. 1863, Lady Edith Frances Wilhel-
mine Somerset, who d. 1915, dau. of 7th Duke of Beaufort ; d. 1900 ; s. by his son [3] WILLIAM
FRANCES HENRY, K.C.V.O., 2nd Earl, b. 1864 : m. 1887, Lady Grace Augusta Fane, who d.
1933, dau. of 12th Earl of Westmorland ; d. 1917 ; s. by his son [4] GEORGE FRANCIS WILLIAM
HENRY, 3rd Earl, b. 1892 ; d. 1920 ; s. by his brother [5] HUGO WILLIAM CECIL, 4th Earl,

b. 1894: *m.* 1935, Marigold Rosemary Joyce (who *m.* 2ndly, 1948, Zygmund de Lubicz-Bakanow-ski), dau. of the late Edgar Lubbock, LL.B. [B. Avebury, colls.]; *d.* 1937, when the Earldom and Viscountcy became ext., and the Barony passed to his kinsman [6] ERNEST WILLIAM, *MBE* (son of the late Rear Adm. the Hon. Albert Denison Somerville Denison, 2nd son of 1st Baron), 6th Baron; *b.* 1876; Capt. R.N.; MBE (Civil) 1946: *m.* 1905, Sybil May, who *d.* 1963, da. of the late Capt. H. T. Anley, of The Firs, Binstead, Isle of Wight; *d.* 1963; *s.* by his cousin [7] CONYNGHAM CHARLES, *DSO, RN* (only son of Cdr. the Hon. Conyngham Albert Denison, RN, 4th son of 1st Baron), 7th Baron, *b.* 1885; Cdr. RN: *m.* 1st 1912 (m. diss. 1925), Vera, da. of the late Francis Hugh Baxendale; 2ndly, 1926, Mabel, who *d.* 1951, da. of Matthew George Megaw; 3rdly, 1952, Jocelyn Helen, da. of the late Lt.-Cdr. Hugh Duppa Collins, RN; *d.* 1967; *s.* by his cousin [8] JOHN ALBERT LISTER, *TD* (only son of the Hon. Harold Albert Denison, 5th son of 1st Baron). 8th Baron; *b.* 1901: *m.* 1st, 1949 (m. diss. 1953), Lesley Maxwell Gordon, OBE, and widow of Lt.-Col. J. H. Woolridge, Indian Army; 2ndly, 1957, Elizabeth Ann, da. of the late Edward Little Sale, ICS, and formerly wife of Thomas Chambers Windsor Roe; *d.* 1968; *s.* by his son [9] RICHARD JOHN, 9th Baron and present peer.

LONDON, LORD BISHOP OF.   (Ellison.)

Rt. Rev. and Rt. Hon. GERALD ALEXANDER ELLISON, *PC, DD,* son of the late Rev. Preb. John Henry Joshua Ellison, CVO, Chap. in Ord. to H.M. and R. of St. Michael's, Cornhill, EC; *b.* Aug. 19th, 1910; ed. at Westminster and New Coll., Oxford (BA 1932, Diploma in Theology 1934, MA 1936, DD 1974); DD Lambeth 1955; Hon. Fellow King's Coll., London and New Coll., Oxford; Curate of Sherbourne 1935-37, Domestic Chap. to Bishop of Winchester 1937-42, and to Archbishop of York 1943-46, V. of St. Mark, Portsea, Hants. 1946-50, and Examining Chap. to Bishop of Portsmouth 1949-50; Canon of Portsmouth 1950; consecrated Bishop of Willesden (Suffragan for Diocese of London) 1950, Curate in Charge St. Botolph, Bishopsgate 1950-53; translated 37th Bishop of Chester 1955, and 115th Bishop of London 1973; Sub-Prelate, Order of St. John of Jerusalem since 1952, Prelate of Order of British Empire and of Imperial Soc. of Knights Bachelor since 1973, and Dean of Chapels Royal since 1973; European War 1939-43 as Chap. RNVR (despatches); PC 1973: *m* 1947, Jane Elizabeth, da. of the late Brig. John Houghton Gibbon, DSO.

Patron of one hundred and sixty livings, and eighteen alternately with others, all the Prebendal Stalls, the Archdeaconries of London, Middlesex, Hampstead and Hackney, the Precentorship, the Chancellorship, and the Treasurership.

The See of London has existed since the first introduction of Christianity into Britain. Restitutus, Bishop of London, was present at the Council of Arles in A.D. 314, and signed the decrees.

Episcopal Signature—" Gerald Londin: "

ARMS OF THE SEE,—Gules, two swords in saltire argent, hilts and pommels or.

Residence,—London House, 19, Cowley St., Westminster, SW1P 3LZ. *Clubs,*—Army and Navy, United Service, Leander.

LONDONDERRY, MARQUESS OF.   (Vane-Tempest-Stewart.)   Sits as   EARL VANE (U.K. 1823). [Marquess I. 1816.]

ALEXANDER CHARLES ROBERT VANE-TEMPEST-STEWART, 9th Marquess; *b.* Sept. 7th, 1937; *s.* 1955; ed. at Eton: *m.* 1st, 1958 (m. diss. 1971), Nicolette, only da. of Michael Harrison, of Nether-hampton House, Netherhampton, Wilts, and 33, Chesham Place, SW1; 2ndly, 1972, Doreen Wells, and has issue by 1st and 2nd m.

Arms,—Quarterly: 1st and 4th or, a bend counter compony argent and azure, between two lions rampant, gules, *Stewart;* 2nd argent, a bend engrailed, between six martlets, three and three, sable, *Tempest;* 3rd azure, three sinister gauntlets, *Vane.* *Crests,*—1st, a dragon statant or, *Stewart;* 2nd, a griffin's head erased, per pale argent and sable, beaked gules, *Tempest;* 3rd, a dexter cubit arm in armour, the hand in a gauntlet proper grasping a sword also proper, pommel and hilt or, *Vane.* *Supporters,*—Dexter, a Moor, wreathed about the temples argent and azure, holding in the exterior hand a shield of the last, garnished or, charged with the sun in splendour gold; *sinister,* a lion or, collared argent, the collar charged with three mullets sable.

Seat,—Wynyard Park, Billingham-on-Tees, Cleveland.

Mesuenda · Corolla · Draconis

The dragon's crest is to be feared.

SON LIVING.   *(By 2nd m.)*
FREDERICK AUBREY   *(Viscount Castlereagh),* *b.* Sept. 6th, 1972.

DAUGHTERS LIVING. (*By 1st m.*)
Lady Sophia Frances Anne, *b.* 1959.
Lady Cosima Maria Gabriella, *b.* 1961.

SISTERS LIVING.
Lady Jane Antonia Frances, *b.* 1932: *m.* 1965, Sir Max Rayne, of 100, George St., W1H 6DJ, and has issue living, Nicholas Alexander, *b.* 1969,—Alexander Philip, *b.* 1973,—Natalie Deborah, *b.* 1966,—Tamara Annabel, *b.* 1970.
Lady Annabel, *b.* 1934: *m.* 1954 (m. diss. 1975), Marcus Oswald Hornby Lecky Birley, son of the late Sir Oswald Hornby Lecky Birley, MC, and has issue living, Rupert Oswald Robin, *b.* 1955,—Robin Marcus, *b.* 1958,—a da., *b.* 1961. *Residence,*—Pelham Cottage, Pelham Street, SW7.

AUNTS LIVING. (*Daughters of 7th Marquess.*)
Lady Helen Maglona, *b.* 1911: *m.* 1st, 1935 (marriage dissolved 1960), the 2nd Baron Jessel; 2ndly, 1960, Dennis Cecil Whittington Walsh, son of the late Sir Cecil Henry Walsh, K.C. *Residence,*—25, Redington Gdns., Hampstead, NW3.
Lady Mairi Elizabeth (*Lady Mairi Bury*), *b.* 1921; is a JP for co. Down: *m.* 1940 (m. diss. 1958), Lt.-Col. Viscount Bury, late 13th/18th Hussars, who *d.* 1968, el. son of 9th Earl of Albemarle. *Residence,*—Mount Stewart, Newtownards, co. Down.

COLLATERAL BRANCHES LIVING.

Grandson of the late Lord Adolphus Frederick Charles William Vane-Tempest, M.P., 3rd son of 3rd Marquess:—
Issue of the late Major Francis Adolphus Vane-Tempest, *b.* 1863, *d.* 1932: *m.* 1901, Gertrude Magdalen, who *d.* 1925, dau. of the late F. A. Elliot:—
Francis Charles Joseph, *b.* 1911; ed. at Downside; 1939-45 War: *m.* 1st, 1931 (m. annulled on her petition 1935), Pamela Mary, who *d.* 1953, da. of Maj. Edwin Abel Smith, formerly of Great Kimble House, Princes Risborough, Bucks.; 2ndly, 1936, Penelope Joan (from whom he obtained a divorce 1952), da. of Edmund Henry Bevan, JP [B. Grantley]. *Residence,*—Anne Boleyn Cottage, New St., Henley-on-Thames.

Grandchildren of the late Charles Henry Vane-Tempest, son of the late Lord Ernest M'Donnell Vane-Tempest, 4th son of 3rd Marquess:—
Issue of the late Ernest Charles William Vane-Tempest, D.S.C., *b.* 1894, *d.* 1957: *m.* 1st, 1918, Aline Mary Loftus (who *d.* 1967, having obtained a divorce 1933), da. of the late Loftus St. George [St. George, Bt., colls.]; 2ndly, 1933, Anne Elizabeth, who *d.* 1968, da. of Capt. Evan Humphreys, of Borth-y-gest, Portmadoc, Caernarvonshire:—
(By 1st marriage) Charles Stewart M'Donnell, *b.* 1921; ed. at Haileybury; European War 1939-45 with R.A.F.: *m.* 1st, 1948 (marriage dissolved 1956), Diana Constance, dau. of Major Kenneth Arthur Seth-Smith; 2ndly, 1957, Maija-Liisa, dau. of Col. Erkki Elias Puomi, and has issue living, (by 1st m.) Charles Stewart Martin St. George (Furzefield House, Wineham, Henfield, Sussex), *b.* 1950: *m.* 1972, Pamela Elizabeth, da. of M. Jenkin, of Myrtlegrove House, Patching, Sussex,—Aline Elizabeth Stewart, *b.* 1952,—(by 2nd m.) Charles Erkki William, *b.* 1958,—Donald John Ernest, *b.* 1961,—Harold Michael St. George, *b.* 1962,—Mary-Anne Elizabeth (twin), *b.* 1962. *Residence,*—Myllkyla, 02940, Finland.——Theresa Anne Mary Stewart, *b.* 1920. *Residence,*—18A, Plough La., Purley, Surrey.

PREDECESSORS.—[1] ROBERT Stewart, *M.P.* for co. Down 1770-89; cr. *Baron Londonderry* (peerage of Ireland) 1789, *Viscount Castlereagh* (peerage of Ireland) 1795, *Earl of Londonderry* (peerage of Ireland) 1796, and *Marquess of Londonderry* (peerage of Ireland) 1816; *d.* 1821; *s.* by his el. son [2] ROBERT, *K.G.*, 2nd Marquess; a distinguished statesman; *d.s.p.* 1822; *s.* by his half-brother [3] CHARLES WILLIAM, *K.G.*, *G.C.B.*, *G.C.H.*, 3rd Marquess, who had in 1814 been cr. *Baron Stewart*, of Stewart's Court and Ballylawn, co. Donegal (peerage of United Kingdom); *b.* 1778; a distinguished general and diplomatist, Lord-Lieut. of co. Durham, Custos Rotulorum of cos. Londonderry and Down, and Col. 2nd Life Guards; cr. *Viscount Seaham* and *Earl Vane* (peerage of United Kingdom) 1823, with remainder to the male issue of his 2nd marriage; *d.* 1854, when the Viscounty of Seaham and Earldom of Vane passed to his 2nd son George Henry (infra), and the marquessate and minor honours devolved upon his el. son [4] FREDERICK WILLIAM, *K.P.*, *P.C.*, 4th Marquess: M.P. for co. Down 1831-52; *d.s.p.* 1872; *s.* by his half-brother [5] GEORGE HENRY ROBERT CHARLES WILLIAM, *K.P.*, *LL.D.*, 5th Marquess who had in 1854 *s.* his father as 2nd Earl Vane: assumed in 1851 the additional surname of Tempest; sat as M.P. for N. Durham (C) 1847-54: was Lord-Lieut. of Durham: *m.* 1846, Mary Cornelia, only dau. of Sir John Edwards, 1st Bt. (*ext.*); *d.* Nov. 6th, 1884; *s.* by his son [6] CHARLES STEWART, *K.G.*, *G.C.V.O.*, *C.B.*, *P.C.*, 6th Marquess, *b.* 1852; Postmaster-Gen. 1900, first Pres. of Board of Education 1902, also Lord Pres. of the Council 1903, Pres. of Committee on Education in Scotland 1905, Lord-Lieut. of Ireland 1886-9, and Lord-Lieut. of co. of City of Belfast 1900-1903; assumed by Roy. licence 1885 the additional and principal surname of Stewart: *m.* 1875, Lady Theresa Susey Helen, who *d.* 1919, el. dau. of 19th Earl of Shrewsbury; *d.* 1915; *s.* by his son [7] CHARLES STEWART HENRY, *K.G.*, *M.V.O.*, *T.D.*, *P.C.*, 7th Marquess; *b.* 1878; Major and Brevet Lieut.-Col. late Life Guards: Lord-Lieut. of co. Durham; was Finance Member of Air Council 1919, Under-Sec. of State for Air and Vice-Pres. of Air Council 1920-21, first Min. of Education in Ulster Parliament 1921-6, a Member of Senate of N. Ireland 1921-9 (Leader 1921-6), First Commr. of Works (England) 1928-9, and (in National Govt.) Aug. to Nov. 1931, Sec. of State for Air 1931-5, and Lord Privy Seal and Leader of House of Lords June to Nov. 1935; appointed Chancellor of Queen's Univ., Belfast 1923, and of Durham Univ. 1930; sat as M.P. for Maidstone (C) 1906-15: *m.* 1899, the Hon Dame Edith Helen Chaplin, *D.B.E.*, who *d.* 1959, dau. of 1st Viscount Chaplin; *d.* 1949; *s.* by his son [8] EDWARD CHARLES STEWART ROBERT, 8th Marquess: *b.* 1902; Hon. Col. 12th Batn. (Cadet) Durham L.I.; Hon. Attaché, British Embassy, Rome 1924-5; sat as M.P. for co. Down (C) 1931-45: *m.* 1931, Romaine, who *d.* 1951, dau. of Major Boyce Combe, of Great Holt, Dockenfield, Surrey; *d.* 1955; *s.* by his son [9] ALEXANDER CHARLES ROBERT, 9th Marquess, and present peer; also Earl of Londonderry, Earl Vane, Viscount Castlereagh, Viscount Seaham, Baron Londonderry, and Baron Stewart.

LONG, VISCOUNT. (Long.) [Viscount U.K. 1921.]

Pious, though valiant.

RICHARD GERARD LONG, 4th Viscount; *b.* Jan. 30th, 1929; *s.* 1967; ed. at Harrow; late Wilts. Regt.; Vice-Pres. Wilts. Roy. British Legion, and Bath Light Operatic Club; Pres. Bath & Wilts. Gliding Club: *m.* 1957, Margaret Frances, da. of Ninian B. Frazer, and has issue.

Arms,—Sable, within two flaunches and semée of cross-crosslets or, a lion rampant argent. Crest,— A lion's head argent, erased or, holding in the mouth a dexter hand erased gules. Supporters,—On either side a lion argent, holding a flag-staff erect proper, flowing therefrom a pennon sable, that on the dexter charged with a portcullis chained and that on the sinister with a fetterlock or.

Residence,—Steeple Ashton Manor, Trowbridge, Wilts. *Club,*—Carlton.

SON LIVING.
Hon. JAMES RICHARD, *b.* Dec. 31st, 1960.

DAUGHTERS LIVING.
Hon. Sarah Victoria, *b.* 1958.
Hon. Charlotte Helen, *b.* 1965.

BROTHER LIVING.
Hon. John Hume, *b.* 1930; ed. at Harrow: *m.* 1957 (m. diss. 1969), Averil Juliet, only da. of Henry Stobart, of Salisbury, Rhodesia, and has issue living, a da. *b.* 1963. *Residence,*—

SISTER LIVING.
Hon. Noreen, *b.* 1921: *m.* 1947, Capt. John Cairns Bartholomew, Roy. Wilts Yeo., and has issue living, a son, *b.* 1951,—a son, *b.* 1956,—a dau., *b.* 1949. *Residence,*—Poulshot House, Poulshot, Devizes, Wilts.

DAUGHTER LIVING OF SECOND VISCOUNT.
Hon. (Antoinette) Sara (Frances Sibell), *b.* 1934: *m.* 1954, the Hon. Charles Andrew Morrison, MP [see B. Margadale]. *Residence,*—Fyfield Manor, Pewsey, Wilts.

PREDECESSORS.—[1] *Rt. Hon.* WALTER HUME Long, son of the late Richard Penruddock Long, M.P.; *b.* 1854; Parliamentary Sec. to Local Govt. Board Aug. 1886 to June 1892, a Member of Roy. Commn. on Agricultural Depression 1893, Pres. of Board of Agriculture (with a seat in the Cabinet) July 1895 to Nov. 1900, Pres. of Local Govt. Board (with a seat in the Cabinet) Nov. 1900 to March 1905, Ch. Sec. for Ireland (with a seat in the Cabinet) March to Dec. 1905 and Lord-Lieut. of Wilts 1920-24; appointed again Pres. of Local Govt. Board May 1915, Sec. of State for the Colonies in National Min. Dec. 1916, and First Lord of the Admiralty Jan. 1917 (resigned Feb. 1921); M.P. for N. Wilts (*C*) April 1880 to Nov. 1886, for Wilts, E., or Devizes, Div. Nov. 1885 to June 1892, for Liverpool, W. Derby Div. Jan. 1893 to Sept. 1900, for Bristol, S. Div. Oct. 1900 to Jan. 1906, for Dublin co., S. Dublin Div. Jan. 1906 to Jan. 1910, for Strand 1910-18, and for St. George's Div. of Westminster 1918 to May 1921; cr. *Viscount Long,* of Wraxall, co. Wilts (peerage of United Kingdom) 1921: *m.* 1878, Lady Dorothy Blanche Boyle, who *d.* 1938, dau. of 9th Earl of Cork and Orrery; *d.* 1924; *s.* by his grandson [2] WALTER FRANCIS DAVID (son of the late Brig.-Gen. Walter Long, C.M.G., D.S.O. (el. son of 1st Viscount), who *d.* (killed in action during European War) 1917, 2nd Viscount, *b.* 1911; Major Coldstream Guards: *m.* 1933, Frances Laura (who obtained a divorce 1943), dau. of the Hon. Guy Lawrence Charteris [E. Wemyss and March]; *d.* (killed in action during European War) 1944; *s.* by his uncle [3] (RICHARD) ERIC (ONSLOW), *TD*, (2nd son of 1st Viscount), 3rd Viscount, *b.* 1892; a JP for Wilts. 1923-67, and a DL 1946-67; MP for Wilts. Westbury Div. (*C*) 1927-31: *m.* 1916, Gwendolyne Hague, who *d.* 1959, da. of the late Thomas Reginald Hague Cook [Elliot, Bt.]; *d.* 1967; *s.* by his el. son [4] RICHARD GERARD, 4th Viscount and present peer.

LONGFORD, EARL OF. (Pakenham.) Sits as BARON PAKENHAM (U.K. 1945). [Earl I. 1785.]

[Name pronounced "*Packenham.*"]

Glory is the shadow of virtue.

FRANCIS AUNGIER PAKENHAM, *KG, PC, b.* Dec. 5th, 1905; cr. *Baron Pakenham,* of Cowley, City of Oxford (peerage of UK) 1945, PC 1948, KG 1971, and *s.* as 7th Earl 1961; ed. at Eton, and at New Coll., Oxford (B.A. 1928, M.A. 1934); was a Lord-in-Waiting to H.M. Oct. 1945 to Oct. 1946, Parliamentary Under-Sec. of State for War Oct. 1946 to April 1947, Chancellor of Duchy of Lancaster April 1947 to May 1948, Min. of Civil Aviation May 1948 to May 1951, First Lord of the Admiralty May to Oct. 1951 and Lord Privy Seal 1964-65, Sec. of State for the Colonies 1965-66, again Lord Privy Seal 1966-68; Chm. of Nat. Youth Employment Council 1968-71, and of Sidgwick & Jackson 1970: *m.* 1931, Elizabeth, CBE, MA, da. of Nathaniel Bishop Harman, FRCS, of 108, Harley St., W1, and has issue.

Arms.—Quarterly: 1st quarterly or and gules, in the first quarter an eagle displayed vert *Pakenham* ; 2nd argent, a bend dancette sable, between two plain cottises azure, the bend charged with three fleurs-de-lis argent, each cottise charged with three bezants, *Cuffe* ; 3rd ermine, a griffin segreant azure, *Aungier* ; 4th per bend embattled argent and gules, *Boyle*. **Crest,**—Out of a mural coronet or, a demi-eagle displayed gules. **Supporters,**—*Dexter*, a lion azure, charged on the shoulder with a carbuncle or ; *sinister*, a griffin azure, wings, elevated ermine, beaked and clawed or.

Residences,—Bernhurst, Hurst Green, Sussex; 18, Chesil Court, Chelsea Manor St., SW3. *Office,*— 42, Museum St., WC1.

SONS LIVING.

THOMAS FRANK DERMOT, (does not use courtesy title) *b*. Aug. 14th 1933; ed. at Ampleforth, and at Magdalen Coll., Oxford: *m*. 1964, Valerie Susan, yst. da. of Maj. Ronald Guthrie McNair Scott, of Huish House, Old Basing, nr. Basingstoke, Hants. [see V. Camrose], and has issue living, Edward Melchior, *b*. 1970,—Frederick Augustus, *b*. 1971,—Anna Maria, *b*. 1965,—Eliza, *b*. 1966. *Residence,*—Tullynally, Castlepollard, co. Westmeath.

Hon. Patrick Maurice (Little Meadow, London Rd., Sunningdale, Berks.) *b*. 1937; ed. at Ampleforth, and at Magdalen Coll., Oxford; Bar. Inner Temple 1962: *m*. 1968, Mary Elizabeth, el. da. of Maj. H. A. J. Plummer, of Winchester, and has issue living, Richard, *b*. 1969,—Guy, *b*. 1970,—Harry Michael, *b*. 1972.

Hon. Michael Aidan, *b*. 1943; ed. at Ampleforth, and at Trin. Coll., Camb.

Hon. Kevin John Toussaint, *b*. 1947; ed. at Ampleforth, and New Coll., Oxford.

DAUGHTERS LIVING.

Lady Antonia, *b*. 1932; ed. at Oxford Univ. (B.A. 1953): *m*. 1956, the Rt. Hon. Hugh Charles Patrick Joseph Fraser, MBE, MP [see L. Lovat].

Judith Elizabeth (does not use style of Lady), *b*. 1940; ed. at Oxford Univ. (BA 1961): *m*. 1963, Alexander John Kazantzis, of 7a, Clarendon Rd., W11, and The Foreman's House, nr. Glynde, Sussex, and has issue living, Arthur Constantine, *b*. 1967,—Miranda Elizabeth, *b*. 1964.

Lady Rachel Mary, *b*. 1942; ed. at London Univ. (BA): *m*. 1967, Kevin Billington, of 30, Addison Av., W11, and The Court House, Poyntington, Dorset, and has issue living, Nathaniel Kevin, *b*. 1970,— Catherine Rose, *b*. 1973.

SISTERS LIVING.

Lady Margaret Pansy Felicia, *b*. 1904 : *m*. 1928, Henry Taylor Lamb, M.C., R.A., who *d*. 1960, son of the late Sir Horace Lamb, LLD, DSc, and has issue living, Valentine Edward Martin, *b*. 1939: *m*. 1970, Anne Graecen, and has issue living, Celia Margaret *b*. 1971, Stephanie Christine *b*. 1972,— Henrietta Frances, *b*. 1931: *m*. 1960, William Anthony Dominic Phipps, of 31, Chepstow Villas, W.11 [see M. Normanby, colls.],—Horatia Mary Felicia, *b*. 1933: *m*. 1958, William H. T. Palmer, and has issue living, Rufus Henry *b*. 1967, Primrose Felicia *b*. 1960, Harriet Eve *b*. 1961. *Residence*, —23, Denbigh Terr., W11.

Lady Mary Katharine, *b*. 1907 : *m* 1939, Major Meysey George Dallas Clive, Grenadier Guards, who *d*. (killed in action during European War) 1943, and has issue living, George Meysey, *b*. 1940,—Alice Mary (*the Hon. Mrs. Simon D. R. N. Lennox-Boyd*), *b*. 1942: *m*. 1962, Hon. Simon Donald Rupert Neville Lennox-Boyd, of 4, Eaton Close, SW1, and Wivelscombe, Saltash, Cornwall [see V. Boyd of Merton]. *Residence,*—Whitfield, Allensmore, Herefordshire.

Lady Violet Georgiana, *b*. 1912: *m*. 1934, Anthony Dymoke Powell, CBE, and has issue living, Tristram Roger Dymoke, *b*. 1940: *m*. 1968, Virginia Beatrice, da. of the late Archibald Julian Lucas [see B. Grenfell], and has issue living, Archibald Thomas Llywelyn *b*. 1970, Georgia *b*. 1969,—John Marmion Anthony, *b*. 1946. *Residence,*—The Chantry, nr. Frome, Som.

WIDOW LIVING OF SIXTH EARL.

CHRISTINE PATTY (*Christine, Countess of Longford*), dau. of the late Richard Trew, of Cheddar, Somerset; MA 1925: *m*. 1925, the 6th Earl, who *d*. 1961. *Residence,*—81, Ailesbury Rd., Dublin 4.

COLLATERAL BRANCHES LIVING.

Grandchildren of the late Col. Hercules Arthur Pakenham, C.M.G. (infra):—
Issue of the late Major Hercules Dermot Wilfrid Pakenham, *b*. 1901, *d*. (of wounds received in action during European War) 1940 : *m*. 1927, Hetty Margaret (who *m*. 2ndly, 1950 (marriage dissolved 1959), Lieut.-Col. Richard Walter Byng Pembroke, O.B.E., late Coldstream Guards [see V. Torrington, colls.], dau. of the late Capt. Roland Stuart Hebeler, The Queen's Roy. Regt. :—
Hercules Michael Roland, *b*. 1935; ed. at Eton: *m*. 1st, 1957 (m. diss. 1973), the Hon. Susan Elizabeth Moon Lever, da. of 3rd Viscount Leverhulme; 2ndly, 1973, Margaret, da. of Charles William Fisher, of Wold Cottage, Upham, Hants. *Residence,*—Wonham House, Bampton, Tiverton, Devon.—— Ann Penelope, *b*. 1928.——Katharine Susan, *b*. 1930.

Granddaughters of the late Lieut.-Gen. Thomas Henry Pakenham, C.B., 3rd son of the late Lieut.-Gen. the Hon. Sir Hercules Pakenham, K.C.B., 3rd son of 2nd Baron:—
Issue of the late Col. Hercules Arthur Pakenham, C.M.G., *b*. 1863, *d*. 1937: *m*. 1895, Lilian Blanche Georgina, who *d*. 1939, dau. of the late Rt. Hon. (Anthony) Evelyn Melbourne Ashley, P.C. [see E. Shaftesbury, colls.]:—
Joan Esther Sybella (*Hon. Mrs. Angus D. Campbell*), *b*. 1904 ; is a J.P. for Cheshire : *m*. 1926, the Hon. Angus Dudley Campbell, CBE, JP, who *d*. 1967 [see B. Colgrain]. *Residence,*—Doddington Cottage, Nantwich, Cheshire.——Beatrix Helen Constance, *b*. 1910: *m*. 1929 (divorce 1943), Col. Nigel Victor Stopford Sackville, OBE, TD who *d*. 1972 [see E. Courtown, colls.]. *Residence,*—3A, Holland Park Rd., W14 8NA.

Granddaughter of the late Henry Sandford Pakenham-Mahon, son of the Very Rev. Henry Pakenham (infra) :—
Issue of the late Capt. Henry Pakenham-Mahon, *b*. 1851, *d*. 1922 : *m*. 1890, May, who *d*. 1944, dau. of the late Lieut.-Col. Sidney Burrard [Burrard, Bt.]:—
Olive, *b*. 1894: *m*. 1st, 1914, Capt. Edward Charles Stafford-King-Harman, Irish Guards, who *d*. (killed in action during European War) 1914, el. son of Sir Thomas Joseph Stafford, C.B., 1st Bt.; 2ndly, 1921, Major Wilfrid Stuart Atherstone Hales, late E. Yorkshire Regt. (who assumed by deed poll 1923, the additional surnames of Pakenham-Mahon), son of Lieut.-Col. Herbert M. Atherstone Hales, late Bedfordshire Regt., and has issue living, (by 1st m.) [see Stafford-King-Harman, Bt., colls.],—(by 2nd m.) Nicholas (Tile House, Chobham; *Club*,—Guards'), *b*. 1926; is Col. late Grenadier Guards: *m*. 1953, Jennifer Batten, and has issue living, Hugh Nicholas *b*. 1957, Henrietta Jennifer *b*. 1956,—Elizabeth Henrietta, *b*. 1923: *m*. 1946, Capt. Leonard Owen-John, Bryncyn Green, Old Churchstoke, Montgomeryshire, and has issue living, Henry Stuart *b*. 1955, Julia Elizabeth *b*. 1949: *m*. 1973, John Campbell MacDougall, DPhil, of 80, Prince's Av., W3. *Residence,*—Strokestown Park, co. Roscommon.

Grandchildren of the late Lieut.-Col. William Wingfield Verner Pakenham, Indian Army, son of the late William Sandford Pakenham (infra) :—
Issue of the late William Henry Verner Pakenham, *b*. 1885, *d*. 1956: *m*. 1905, Alice, who *d*. 1966, da. of Charles Smith, of Fulwood Park, Liverpool:—

William Wingfield Verner, *b.* 1906.——Frances Josephine, *b.* 1919: *m.* 1946, Eric Douglas Rowlands, and has issue living, William Verner Pakenham (Hill Top, Clayton West, nr. Huddersfield), *b.* 1947; BSc; LIM: *m.* 1974, Ann, only da. of John Tyas, of Skelmanthorpe, Yorks.,—Cynthia Jane Olive, *b.* 1951: *m.* 1974, Andrew Fisher, of 54, Waterloo Rd., Waterloo, Huddersfield. *Residence,*— 28, Rafborn Grove, Salendine Nook, Huddersfield.

Grandchildren of the late William Sandford Pakenham, son of the late Very Rev. the Hon. Henry Pakenham, 5th son of 2nd Baron :—
Issue of the late Frederick Edward Sandford Pakenham, *b.*,,1859, *d.* 1950: *m.* 1898, Margarita Louise, who *d.* 1961, dau. of the late Maurice Ceely Maude [V. Hawarden, colls.] :—
Michael Ceely Sandford, *b.* 1903 ; formerly Capt. R.A.S.C.; sometime in Colonial Ser., Uganda: *m.* 1st, 1933, Aline Mary Loftus (VANE-TEMPEST) (who *d.* 1967, having obtained a divorce 1948), da. of the late Loftus St. George [St. George, Bt., colls.]; 2ndly, 1948, Patricia, da. of the late Capt. William Harvey Murray, of Mill House, Boyton, Suffolk, and has issue living, (by 1st m.) Aline Marguerite Constance Sandford, *b.* 1934: *m.* 1959, Keith William Boyd, and has issue living, William Michael Sandford *b.* 1964, Jane Maria Loftus *b.* 1960, Christina Theresa *b.* 1961. *Residence,*— Flint Cottage, Rhympling, Bury St. Edmunds.

Issue of the late Robert Sandford Pakenham, *b.* 1866, *d.* 1959 : *m.* 1st, 1910, Edith Carter, who *d.* 1912 ; 2ndly, 1920, Mildred Alice Armstrong, who *d.* 1940 :—
(By 1st marriage) Robert Wingfield, *b.* 1912; ed. at Malvern, and at Trin. Coll., Camb. (B.A. 1934, M.A. 1938): *m.* 1941, Alice Gwendoline, da. of the late T. H. James, and has issue living, Clive Sykes (22, Lenthay Close, Sherborne, Dorset), *b.* 1947: *m.* 1973, Jane, yst. da. of H. J. Antell, of Sherborne, Dorset, and has issue living, Daniel Nicholas *b.* 1973. *Residence,*—Longthorns, Priestlands, Sherborne, Dorset.

Issue of the late Hamilton Richard Pakenham, MB, BCh, *b.* 1867, *d.* 1957: *m.* 1900, Emily Willis, who *d.* 1975, da. of the late Thomas Stringer, of Merrion, Dublin:—
Richard Hercules Wingfield, *C.B.E.*, *b.* 1906 ; ed. at Monkton Combe Sch., and at Trin. Coll., Camb. (MA); HM Overseas Civil Ser. 1929-56 (Senior Commr., Zanzibar 1948-56); Gen. Sec. Lebanon Evangelical Mission 1956-69; 2nd class Order of Brilliant Star of Zanzibar; MBE (Civil) 1943, OBE (Civil) 1949, CBE (Civil) 1955: *m.* 1947, Eileen Isolde, el. da. of the late Oscar Faber, CBE, DCL, DSc, and has issue living, John Hubert, *b.* 1951. *Residence,*—9, Kirkwick Av., Harpenden, Herts. *Club,*—Royal Overseas League.——Henry Desmond Verner, *CBE,* *b.* 1911 ; British Dep. High Commr., Sydney, NSW 1968-71; CBE (Civil) 1964: *m.* 1st, 1946 (m. diss. 1960), Crystal Elizabeth, da. of the late Lt.-Col. Edward York Brooksbank [see Brooksbank, Bt.]; 2ndly, 1963, Mrs. Venetia Maude, da. of William Patterson Doyle, and has issue living, (by 1st m.) Anthony Edward, *b.* 1952,—Pandora Clare, *b.* 1948: *m.* 1969, Matthieu Millet, of La Levratiére, 38460, Cremieu, France, and has issue living, Alexandre François *b.* 1974,—(by 2nd m.) Mark Edmund, *b.* 1965,—Sarah Catherine, *b.* 1966. *Residence,*—Hatherley Cottage, Preston St. Mary, Suffolk.

Grandchildren of the late Gustavus Conolly Pakenham (infra):—
Issue of the late Thomas Compton Pakenham, M.C., *b.* 1893, *d.* 1957 : *m.* 1st, 1915, Phyllis Mona (who obtained a divorce 1920), dau. of Col. William Price, R.E. ; 2ndly, 1921, Alma Clark ; 3rdly, 1925, Sara (of Coldstream, Blairstown, New Jersey, U.S.A.), dau. of Charles Manning Furman, of Clemson, S. Carolina, U.S.A. :—
(By 1st marriage) Simona Vere, *b.* 1916: *m.* 1938, Noel Iliff, and has issue living, David Anthony (Green Willows, Station Rd., Woodmancote, Cheltenham, Glos.), *b.* 1939: *m.* 1966, Celia Winifred Foot, and has issue living, Stephanie Brigid Laura *b.* 1968,—Alison Deborah Caroline, *b.* 1970. *Residence,*——64, Canonbury Park South, N1.——(By 2nd m.) Compton Christopher (45 East Park St., East Orange, NJ 07017, USA), *b.* 1921: *m.* 1947, Dorothy Rebecca Cullingford, and has issue living, Diane, *b.* 1949,—Monica, *b.* 1954,—Jennifer (twin), *b.* 1954,—(by 3rd m.) Edward Michael, *b.* 1932.——Joan Compton, *b.* 1932.

Granddaughters of the late Capt. George Dent Pakenham, son of the late Thomas Pakenham, 2nd son of the late Adm. the Hon. Sir Thomas Pakenham, GCB, yst. son of 1st Baron Longford and Elizabeth Countess of Longford:—
Issue of the late Gustavus Conolly Pakenham, *b.* 1856, *d.* 1924 : *m.* 1889, Ella Compton, who *d.* 1913, only dau. of William George Bayne:—
Cynthia Hume Barnard, *b.* 1890: *m.* 1912, Gilbert Lyall. *Residence,*—Mortimers Farm, Toppesfield, Halstead, Essex.——Daphne Eliot Araminta, *b.* 1901: *m.* 1926, Geoffrey Charles Kingham, and has issue living, Michael Francis Pakenham (Ridgway House, Runwick, Farnham, Surrey), *b.* 1928; ed. at Marlborough: *m.* 1958, Ann Augusta Cardamine, dau. of the late Edgar Percival Chance, and has issue living, Charles Edgar Justin *b.* 1962, Camilla Lucinda Jane *b.* 1960. *Residence,*—Marguerite Cottage, Golf Lane, Whitehill, Bordon, Hants.

Grandsons of the late Frederick Edward Pakenham (infra):—
Issue of the late Thomas Hume Pakenham *b.* 1907, *d.* 1965: *m.* 1st, 1928, Margaret Olwen (who obtained a divorce 1945), da. of the late Capt. Thomas Corrance, of Ervin, Wigtownshire; 2ndly, 1946, Isabella Nimmo, da. of Archie Cowie, of Airdrie, Lanarkshire:—
(By 1st m.) Thomas David Corrance, *b.* 1929: *m.* 1951, Edith McDerby, and has issue living, Thomas McDerby, *b.* 1961.—James Arthur, *b.* 1962.—Teresa Christine, *b.* 1952,—Jocelyn Patricia, *b.* 1955.— Edith Lorraine, *b.* 1958,—Maria Aline, *b.* 1964.——John Edwin, *b.* 1930: *m.* 1st, 1954 (m. diss. 1959), Wendy Cox; 2ndly, 1962, Gaylynn Evon, da. of Weir Powellson Armstrong, and has issue living, (by 1st m.) Cheryl Olwen, *b.* 1955,—(by 2nd m.) Sean Thomas, *b.* 1963,—Edward Austin Westmoreland, *b.* 1967,—Maja Chrisanna, *b.* 1968.

Issue of the late Frederick Edward Pakenham, *b.* 1869, *d.* 1923 : *m.* 1906, Nancy Jane dau. of Charles Youmans, formerly of Hazleton, British Columbia :—
Arthur Godfrey, *b.* 1910: *m.* 1st, 1938 (divorce 1950), Wanda Hatcher; 2ndly, 1951, Rose Marie; da. of Anton Eberle, and has issue living, (by 2nd m.) Patricia Eve, *b.* 1956. *Residence,*—1210, N.E. 124th Street, Seattle, Washington, 98125, USA.——William Christopher, *b.* 1922: *m.* 1st, 1943 (divorce 1954), Mona May Morris; 2ndly, 1955, Marjorie Jane, da. of the late Duncan Ried Wilson, of Montrose, Scotland, and has issue living, (by 1st marriage) Frederick Edward, *b.* 1944,—(by 2nd marriage) Ronald Arthur, *b.* 1957.——Norma Muriel Doreen, *b.* 1913: *m.* 1938, Donald Holmes, and has issue living. *Residence,*—9545, 4th, N.-W., Seattle, Washington, USA.——Fiona Evelyn, *b.* 1917: *m.* 1939, Gordon Gatenby. *Residence,*—

Grandchildren of the late Wellington Montagu Pakenham, 2nd son of the late Adm. John Pakenham, 4th son of the late Adm. the Hon. Sir Thomas Pakenham, G.C.B. (ante) :—
Issue of the late William Law Pakenham, *b.* 1869, *d.* 1937 : *m.* 1894, Ada Mary, who *d.* 1940, dau. of the late J. Beavan Phillips, J.P., of Llanelly, S. Wales:—
Rev. Thomas Arthur Charles (c/o Barclays Bank, Library Place, St. Helier, Jersey), *b.* 1900; Capt. (ret.) RN; 1914-18 War, 1939-45 War: *m.* 1925, Clara Talbot, da. of the late William Middleton, of Monks Pond, Lymington, and has issue living, William Thomas Talbot, *RN* (of The Croft House, Botley, Hants.), *b.* 1926; Capt. RN; 1944-45 War: *m.* 1957, Antonia Mary, da. of the late Capt. Antony Coleby, RN (ret.), of Hapton House, Hambledon, Hants., and has issue living, Robin Thomas Cliff *b.* 1963, John Neville *b.* 1964, Katherine Clara *b.* 1961,—Rev. Stephen Walter (Donnington Vicarage, Chichester), *b.* 1929; ed. at Camb. Univ. (MA); Lt. RN (ret.); V. of Donnington and Apuldram since 1964; 1968 record singlehanded crossing of Atlantic in 21 days, 15 hrs. and 7 mins. in a 32 ft. ketch: *m.* 1957, Elizabeth Ann, only da. of the Rt. Rev. Kenneth Edward Norman Lamplugh, Suffragan Bishop of Southampton (ret.), and has issue living, Jonathan Hugh Rust *b.* 1958, Marcus Charles *b.* 1960, Olivia Judith Clare *b.* 1963.

Issue of the late Com. Arthur McClellan Pakenham, R.D., R.N.R., *b.* 1876, *d.* 1948 : *m.* 1st, 1910, Ethel Louise, who *d.* 1934, dau. of the late R. A. W. Holwell; 2ndly, 1938, Katharine Joan (who *m.* 2ndly 19—), dau. of Sidney A. Horstman, of Fair Lawn, Bath :— (By 1st marriage) Peter Hugh Percy Holwell, *b.* 1913; formerly Capt. RA: *m.* 1939, Nancy, who *d.* 1966, da. of Herbert George Alexander, of Woodlands, Westoubirt, Gloucester, and has issue living Jeremy Edwin Montagu, *b.* 1948,—Susan Daphne, *b.* 1942.——Patrick Christopher Montagu Holwell, *b.* 1922; formerly Capt. Roy. Signals; Burma 1942-45 (despatches twice).——Daphne Margaret, Holwell (*Lady Peel*), *b.* 1911: *m.*1932, Capt. Sir (Francis Richard) Jonathan Peel, CBE, MC, DL, and has issue living, Edmund Anthony (Elm House, Tolleshunt D'Arcy, Maldon, Essex), *b.* 1933; ed. at Malvern, and at Pembroke Coll., Camb. (MA): *m.* 1964, Marion Julia, yr. da. of Lister Bass, of Five Corners, Wickham Bishops, Esesx, and has issue living, Edmund Richard, *b.* 1969, Verity Jane *b.* 1965,—Angela Daphne, *b.* 1935: *m.* 1956, Ian Roy Marks, of Coppers, Margaretting, Essex, and has issue living, Nicholas John *b.* 1964, Philippa Gillian *b.* 1958, Caroline Daphne *b.* 1960, Joanna Muriel *b.* 1962.   *Residence,*—Cedarholme, 9, Lexden Rd., Colchester.

Grandsons of the late Major Charles Pakenham (*infra*):—
Issue of the late Capt. Robert Edward Michael Pakenham, *b.* 1874, *d.* (of wounds in action during European War) 1915: *m.* 1900, Nancye, who *d.* 1934, dau. of the late William Fowler, of Broadlands, Liverpool :—
Ivo Robert Raymond Lygon, *b.* 1903; ed. at Wellington Coll.; European War 1939-45 as Capt. Roy. Berks Regt.   *Residence,*—47B, Melbury Rd., W14.   *Club,*—St. James'.

Issue of the late Col. George de la Poer Beresford Pakenham, C.M.G., C.B.E., D.S.O., *b.* 1875, *d.* 1960 : *m.* 1st, 1905, Emilie Elsie, who *d.* 1921, dau. of the late William Fowler, of Broadlands, Liverpool; 2ndly, 1923, Marie Marthe Amalie, who *d.* 1968, widow of Capt. Jacques Henri Joucla, French Army:—
(By 1st m.), Raymond Beresford (RAF Club), *b.* 1907; ed. at Haileybury; Lt.-Col. (ret.) Border Regt. and acting Group Capt. RAF: *m.* 1st, 1930, Sheila Barbara Kathleen (who obtained a divorce 1934), da. of the late Joseph Mason [Price, Bt., cr. 1815, colls.]; 2ndly, 1934, Sophie Patricia (who obtained a divorce 1937), da. of the late Capt. R. D. Pollock, of Teign-na-Mara, Bangor, co. Down; 3rdly, 19—, Catherine Lillian Elizabeth, da. of the late H. Smith, of Salisbury.

Grandson of the late Rev. Robert Pakenham, DD, 6th son of Adm. the Hon. Sir Thomas Pakenham, GCB (*ante*):—
Issue of the late Major Charles Pakenham, *b.* 1844, *d.* 1918: *m.* 1872, Emily Blanche, who *d.* 1899, dau. of Charles H. Harrison, of Singapore:—
Hewitt John Havelock (85, Clarence Gate Gdns., NW1), *b.* 1880; late Lt. Coldstream Guards and Capt. E. Lancs. Regt. Reserve of Officers; S. Africa 1902, 1914-18 War in France and Belgium with Lancashire Fusiliers : *m.* 1st, 1906, Claire May, who *d.* 1944, only dau. of the late Edmond Berdoe-Wilkinson, of Eashing, Godalming; 2ndly, 1946, Molly, el. dau. of the late William Henry Cook, of The Old Cross House, Hertford, and widow of Capt. Oswell-Jones, Roy. W. Kent Regt., and has issue living, (by 1st marriage) Arthur John Edmond, *b.* 1907; is Maj. Queen's R. Regt. (W. Surrey) T.A. (Reserve); Burma 1942-45: *m.* 1st, 1932, Sarah (from whom he obtained a divorce 1948), da. of the late Capt. Rowland Alston (late Coldstream Guards), formerly of Odell Castle, Bedfordshire; 2ndly, 1952, Heidi, el. da. of the late Emil Wegmann, of Frauenfeld, Switzerland, and has issue living, (by 2nd marriage) Timothy James Robert *b.* 1961, Christine Catherine *b.* 1953,—Cynthia Marion Blanche, *b.* 1909: *m.* 1st, 1935, Capt. Alexander Glazebrook Acton Pierce, R.A.; 2ndly, 1947, Guy Fothergill Batho, MBE, of The Hollies, 3A, Compton Way, Olivers Battery, Winchester, Hants., and has issue living, (by 2nd m.) William Nicholas Pakenham *b.* 1948; ed. at Canford Sch., and RNC Dartmouth; Lt. RN: *m.* 1973, Jennifer, da. of W. R. Best, of Embleton, Northumberland.

PREDECESSORS.—[1] Thomas Pakenham, *M.P.* for Longford Borough; cr. *Baron Longford* (peerage of Ireland) 1756; he *d.* 1776, and his widow was cr. *Countess of Longford* (peerage of Ireland) 1785; she *d.* 1794; he was *s.* by his el. son [2] Edward Michael, *PC*, 2nd Baron; MP for co. Longford 1765; *d.* 1792; *s.* by his son [3] Thomas, 3rd Baron, who became in 1794, on the death of his grandmother, 2nd Earl of Longford; cr. *Baron Silchester*, of co. Southampton 1821; *b.* 1774: *m.* 1817, Lady Georgiana Emma Charlotte Lygon, da. of 1st Earl Beauchamp; *d.* 1835; *s.* by his ·el. son [4] Edward Michael, 3rd Earl; was Capt. 2nd Life Guards; *d.* unmarried 1860; *s.* by his brother [5] William Lygon, *G.C.B.*, 4th Earl; *b.* 1819; was Col. 1st and 2nd Batns. Northumberland Fusiliers: *m.* 1862, Hon. Selina Rice-Trevor, who *d.* 1918, dau. of 4th Baron Dinevor; *d.* 1887 ; *s.* by his son [6] Thomas, *K.P.*, *M.V.O.*, 5th Earl, *b.* 1864 ; Col. Life Guards; Lieut. and Custos Rotulorum for co. Longford 1887-1915: *m.* 1899, Lady Mary Julia Child Villiers, who *d.* 1933, dau. of 7th Earl of Jersey; *d.* (killed in action at Dardanelles while Brig.-Gen. 2nd S. Midland Mounted Brig.) 1915: *s.* by his el. son [7] Edward Arthur Henry, 6th Earl, *b.* 1902 ; a Senator of Eire 1946-8 : *m.* 1925, Christine Patty, dau. of the late Richard Trew, of Cheddar, Somerset; *d.* 1961; *s.* by his brother [8] Francis Aungier, 7th Earl and present peer ; also Baron Longford (peerage of Ireland), Baron Silchester, and Baron Pakenham.

LONSDALE, EARL OF.   (Lowther.)   [Earl U.K. 1807, Bt. G.B. 1764.]

James Hugh William Lowther, 7th Earl and 8th Baronet; *b.* Nov. 3rd, 1922; *s.* 1953; ed. at Eton; a Farmer, forester, a Dir. of Border Television, of NE Housing Assocn., and of Internat. Life Insurance Co. (UK) Ltd., a Member of Court of Newcastle Univ., of Sports Council and of English Tourist Board; 1939-45 War with RAC and as Capt. E. Riding Yeo. (despatches): *m.* 1st, 1945 (m. diss. 1954),Tuppina Cecily, da. of the late Capt. C. H. Bennett; 2ndly, 1954 (m. diss. 1962), the Hon. Jennifer Lowther, da. of the late Maj. the Hon. Christopher William Lowther [see V. Ullswater]; 3rdly, 1963, Nancy Ruth (Stephenson), da. of the late Thomas Cobbs, of Pacific Palisades, Cal., USA, and has issue by 1st, 2nd and 3rd m.

Arms.—Or, six annulets, three, two, and one sable.   Crest.—A dragon passant argent. Sup= porters,—Two horses argent, gorged with wreaths of laurel vert.

The office shows the man.

Residences,—Askham Hall, Penrith, Cumberland; 33, Westminster Gdns., SW1.   *Clubs,* Carlton, Brooks's.

SONS LIVING. (*By 1st marriage.*)

HUGH CLAYTON (*Viscount Lowther*) (Parkside, Lowther, Penrith), *b.* May 27th, 1949: *m.* 1971, Pamela Middleton.

(*By 2nd marriage.*)

Hon. William James, *b.* 1957.

(*By 3rd marriage.*)

Hon. James Nicholas, *b.* 1964.

DAUGHTERS LIVING. (*By 1st marriage.*)

Lady Jane Helen Harbord (c/o Westminster Bank, 41, King St., Penrith, Cumberland), *b.* 1947: *m.* 1969, Gary Hunter Wooten, of Cal., USA.

(*By 2nd marriage.*)

Lady Miranda, *b.* 1955.   *Lady* Caroline, *b.* 1959.

BROTHER LIVING. (*Raised to the rank of an Earl's son* 1954.)

Hon. Anthony George, *MBE, b.* 1925; ed. at Eton; Capt. (ret.) 12th Roy. Lancers; a Co. Councillor for Westmorland since 1960; DL 1964, and High Sheriff 1964-65; Joint Master, Ullswater Foxhounds since 1957; Palestine 1946-47, and Malaya 1951-54; MBE (Mil) 1954: *m.* 1958, Lavinia, only child of the late Thomas H. Joyce, of San Francisco, USA, and has issue living, Thomas Scott Anthony *b.* 1966,—Camilla Ann, *b.* 1959,—Arabella Mary, *b.* 1962,—Sarah Lavinia, *b.* 1964. *Residence,*—Whitbysteads, Askham, Penrith. *Clubs,*—National Sporting, White's.

UNCLE LIVING. (*Son of 6th Earl.*)

Hon. Timothy Lancelot Edward (Le Vieux Clos., Trinity, Jersey; Shikar Club), *b.* 1925; Lt. RN (ret.); Master Mariner: *m.* 1966, Margaret, Baroness Testaferrata-Abela, el. da. of the late John Herring, MC, of 50, Harley St., W1.

AUNT LIVING. (*Daughter of 6th Earl.*)

Lady Barbara LOWTHER, *b.* 1890; has resumed the surname of Lowther in lieu of Innes; *m.* 1914, as his second wife, Col. James Archibald Innes, D.S.O., who *d.* 1948, having obtained a divorce 1921, and has issue living, James (of Larkenshaw, Chobham, Surrey), *b.* 1915; Lieut.-Col. (retired) Coldstream Guards; European War 1939-45 in France and Germany (despatches): *m.* 1941, the Hon. Veronica Wenefryde Nefertari Bethell, dau. of the late Capt. the Hon. Richard Bethell [see B. Westbury], and has issue living, James Richard *b.* 1943; Maj. Coldm. Gds., Peter David *b.* 1952; 2nd Lt. Coldm. Gds., Elizabeth Mary *b.* 1947: *m.* 1st, 1967 (m. diss. 1972), James Keith Alan Rugge-Price, [see Rugge-Price, Bt.]; 2ndly, 1973, Edward Rice Nicholl, of 55, Cadogan Lane, SW1.—Majorie, *b.* 1917: *m.* 1938, Maj. Nigel Hambro, of East Hollowcombe Farm, Hawkridge, Dulverton, Som., and has issue living, Carl Nigel Ivan *b.* 1946, Olga Diana, *b.* 1944. *Residence,*—Lowther, Penrith.

COLLATERAL BRANCHES LIVING.

Descendants of the late Rt. Hon. Sir James William Lowther, G.C.B. (son of the late Hon. William Lowther, brother of 3rd Earl), who was cr. *Viscount Ullswater* 1921 [see that title].

Granddaughters of the late Hon. William Lowther (ante):—
Issue of the late Rt. Hon. Sir Gerard Augustus Lowther, G.C.M.G., C.B., who was cr. a Baronet 1914.
See Lowther, Bt., cr. 1914 (ext.).

         (*In remainder to Viscountcy only.*)

Descendants of the late John Lowther, M.P. (brother of 1st Earl), who was cr. a Baronet 1824.
See Lowther, Bt., cr. 1824.

PREDECESSORS.—[1] Sir JOHN Lowther, *M.P.* for Westmorland 1660-75; 30th Knight of the family in almost direct succession; cr. a *Baronet* 1640; *d.* 1675, and was *s.* by his grandson [2] Sir JOHN, P.C., 2nd Bt., M.P. for Westmorland 1680-96; was Vice-Chamberlain of the Household, First Lord Commr. of the Treasury, and Lord-Lieut. of Westmorland and Cumberland; cr *Baron Lowther* and *Viscount Lonsdale* (peerage of England) 1696; *d.* 1700; *s.* by his el. son [3] RICHARD, 2nd Viscount; *d.* 1713; *s.* by his brother [4] HENRY, who *d.s.p.* 1750, when the peerages became extinct, and the baronetcy devolved upon [5] Sir JAMES, M.P., 5th Bt., grandson of Richard, 2nd son of 1st Bt.; cr. *Baron Lowther, Baron Kendal, Baron Burgh, Viscount Lowther,* and *Earl of Lonsdale* (peerage of Great Britain) 1784, and *Baron Lowther* and *Viscount Lowther* (peerage of Great Britain) 1797, with remainder to the heirs male of his cousin, the Rev. Sir William Lowther, Bt., of Swillington (cr. 1764); *d.s.p.* 1802; *s.* in the honours of 1797 by his kinsman [6] *Sir* WILLIAM *K.G.,* 2nd Viscount; cr. *Earl of Lonsdale* 1807; *d.* 1844; *s.* by his el. son [7] WILLIAM, P.C., 2nd Earl; *b.* 1787; Lord of the Admiralty 1809, a Commr. for Indian Affairs 1810-18, a Lord of the Treasury 1813-27, Ch. Commr. of Woods and Forests 1828-30, Vice Pres. of Board of Trade and Treasurer of the Navy 1834-5, and Lord Pres. of the Council 1852; *d.* 1872; *s.* by his nephew [8] HENRY, 3rd Earl; *b.* 1818; sometime M.P. for W. Cumberland, Capt. 1st Life Guards, Col. Cumberland and Westmorland Yeo. Cav., and Lord-Lieut. and Custos Rotulorum of Westmorland and Cumberland: *m.* 1852, Emily Susan, who *d.* 1917, dau. of St. George Francis Caulfeild, of Donamon; *d.* 1876; *s.* by his el. son [9] ST. GEORGE HENRY, 4th Earl; *b* 1855; *d.* Feb. 8th, 1882: *s.* by his brother [10] HUGH CECIL, K.G., G.C.V.O., T.D., 5th Earl; *b.* 1857; Lord-Lieut. and Custos Rotulorum of Cumberland, and Chm. of Quarter Sessions for Westmorland; Mayor of Whitehaven 1894 and 1895: *m.* 1878, Lady Grace Cicelie Gordon, *C.B.E.,* who *d.* 1941, dau. of 10th Marquess of Huntly: *d.* 1944; *s.* by his brother [11] LANCELOT EDWARD, *O.B.E.,* 6th Earl, *b.* 1867; European War 1914-19 as Capt. 3rd Batn. Border Regt., and Gen. Staff (O.R.E.): *m.* 1st, 1889, Sophia Gwendoline Alice, who *d.* 1921, el. dau. of Sir Robert Sheffield, 5th Bt.; 2ndly, 1923, Sybil Beatrix, who *d.* 1966, da. of the late Maj.-Gen. Edward Feetham, CB, CMG; *d.* 1953; *s.* by his grandson [12] JAMES HUGH WILLIAM (son of the late Anthony Edward, Viscount Lowther, el. son of 6th Earl), 7th Earl and present peer; also Viscount Lowther and Baron Lowther.

LOTHIAN, MARQUESS OF. (Kerr.) [Marquess S. 1701.]
[Name pronounced "Karr."]

Late, but in earnest.

PETER FRANCIS WALTER KERR, 12th Marquess; *b.* Sept. 8th,1922; *s.* 1940, ed. at Ampleforth Coll., and at Ch. Ch.; Oxford; FRSA; Lt. Scots Guards, a Member of Queen's Body Guard for Scotland (Roy. Co. of Archers), a D.L. of Roxburghshire, Comdt., Roxburgh, Selkirk and Berwickshire Special Constabulary, and a Knight of Sovereign Order of Malta; Joint Parl. Sec. to Min. of Health, April to Oct. 1964; Lord-in-Waiting to HM 1962-64, and again 1972-73; an Under-Sec., Foreign and Commonwealth Office 1970-72: *m.* 1943, Antonella, da. of the late Maj.-Gen. Sir Foster Reuss Newland, KCMG, CB, and has issue.

Arms—Quarterly: 1st and 4th azure, a sun in splendour or, *Lothian;* 2nd and 3rd gules, on a chevron argent three mullets of the field, *Kerr.* Crests—1st, a sun in splendour or; 2nd, a stag's head erased proper. Supporters—*Dexter,* an angel proper, verted azure, surcoat vert, winged and crined or; *sinister,* an unicorn argent armed, unguled, maned, and tufted or.

Seats,—Monteviot, Jedburgh, Roxburghshire; Melbourne Hall, Derby. *Town Residence,*—54, Upper Cheyne Row, SW3. *Clubs,*—Boodle's, Beefsteak, New, Puffin's.

SONS LIVING.
MICHAEL ANDREW FOSTER JUDE (*Earl of Ancram*) (6, Ainslie Place, Edinburgh), *b.* July 7th, 1945; ed. at Ampleforth, and at Ch. Ch., Oxford (BA, LLB); Advocate Edinburgh 1970, MP for Berwick and E. Lothian (*C*) Feb. to Oct., 1974: *m.* 1975, Lady (Theresa) Jane Fitzalan-Howard, da. of 16th Duke of Norfolk.
Lord Ralph William Francis Joseph, *b.* 1957; ed. at Ampleforth.

DAUGHTERS LIVING.
Lady Mary Marianella Anne, *b.* 1944: *m.* 1970, Charles von Westenholz, of Little Blakesware, Widford, Ware, Herts., and has issue living, Alexander Peter Frederik, *b.* 1971,—Mark Henry Cosimo, *b.* 1973.
Lady Cecil Nennella Therese *b.* 1948: *m.* 1974, Donald Angus Cameron of Lochiel, yr. son of Sir Donald Hamish Cameron of Lochiel [see D. Montrose].
Lady Clare Amabel Margaret (*Countess of Euston*), *b.* 1951: *m.* 1972, James Oliver Charles, Earl of Euston, son of 11th Duke of Grafton.
Lady Elizabeth Marian Frances, *b.* 1954.

BROTHER LIVING. (*Raised to the rank of a Marquess's son* 1941.)
Lord John Andrew Christopher, *b.* 1927; ed. at Ampleforth, and at Ch. Ch., Oxford; late Capt. Scots Guards: *m.* 1949, Isabel Marion, dau. of Sir Hugh Gurney, K.C.M.G., M.V.O., [see B. Southesk, colls.], and has issue living, William Walter Raleigh, *b.* 1950,—David John, *b.* 1952, —Andrew Peter Hugh, *b.* 1955,—Marion Isabel, *b.* 1960,—Catherine Richenda Margaret, *b.* 1965. *Residence,*—Holly Bank, Wootton, Woodstock, Oxford. *Clubs,*—Garrick, Beefsteak.

DAUGHTER LIVING OF NINTH MARQUESS.
Lady Isobel Alice Adelaide, *b.* 1881: *m.* 1907, James Cospatrick Hepburne-Scott, who *d.* 1942 [see L. Polwarth, colls.]. *Residence,*—13, Seafield Road, Southbourne, Bournemouth.

MOTHER LIVING.
Marie Constance Annabel, dau. of Capt. William Walter Raleigh Kerr (infra): *m.* 1915, Capt. Andrew William Kerr, R.N., who *d.* 1929. *Residence,*—Melbourne Hall, Derby.

COLLATERAL BRANCHES LIVING.
Grandchildren of the late Francis Ernest Kerr (infra):—
Issue of the late Capt. Henry Francis Hobart Kerr, *b.* 1878, *d.* 1972: *m.* 1915, Gertrude Mary, who *d.* 1969, da. of James Anthony:—
Francis Robert Newsam, OBE, MC (Blanerne, Edrom, Duns, Berwicks.), *b.* 1916; ed. at Ampleforth Coll.; Lt.-Col. R. Scots (TA), and a DL for Berwicks. (Vice-Lieut. 1971); Palestine 1938-39; 1939-45 War in France, E. Africa, and S.E. Asia (wounded, MC); OBE (Mil.) 1961: *m.* 1941, Anne Frederica, da. of William E. Kitson, of Blanerne House, Edrom, Duns, Berwicks., and has issue living, Henry Mark William, *b.* 1946,—David Anthony Francis, *b.* 1953,—Susan Mary, *b.* 1952.——Monica Mary Cecil, *b.* 1917: *m.* 1939, Gp. Capt. William George Devas, CBE, DFC, AFC, RAF, of Brick Kiln Farm House, Chilgrove, Chichester, and has issue living, Christopher William Kerr (Bridge Cottage, N. Fambridge, Chelmsford, Essex), *b.* 1944: *m.* 1970, the Hon. Penelope Anne, da. of Baron O'Neill of The Maine [Life Baron],—John Robin Ambrose, *b.* 1947; AA Dip, ARIBA: *m.* 1970, Rachel Geraldine, da. of Capt. Gerald Seymour Tuck, DSO, RN (ret.).——Anne Margaret D'Arcy, *b.* 1923: *m.* 1948, Christopher Scott, of Gala House, Galashiels, and has issue living, John Philip Henry Schomberg, *b.* 1952,—Dominic Christopher Hugh, *b.* 1956,—Julian Sebastian Frere, *b.* 1956,—Rupert Benjamin Bartle Frere, *b.* 1958,—Sebastian Simon Frere, *b.* 1961.

Granddaughters of the late Rev. Lord Henry Francis Charles Kerr, 2nd son of 6th Marquess:—
Issue of the late Francis Ernest Kerr, *b.* 1840, *d.* 1884: *m.* 1870, Mary Frances, who *d.* 1916, dau. of Robert Monteith, of Carstairs, Lanarkshire:—
Mary Christina, *b.* 1877: *m.* 1906, Capt. Adrian L. Cave, who *d.* 1931, late 10th Hussars, and has issue living, Daniel Adrian Francis (Beacon House, Inkpen, Newbury), *b.* 1906; ed. at Eton; formerly Lt. Somerset LI: *m.* 1934, Marion Margaret Josephine, da. of the late Lt.-Col. Oswald Henry Philip Turville-Petre, [see B. Petre, colls.], and has issue living, Adrian Oswald (25, Webster Gdns., W5) *b.* 1935; AADip; ARIBA: *m.* 1964, Felicity Mary, da. of Martin Cooper (and has issue living, Benedict Blaise *b.* 1967, Zoë Joanna *b.* 1974), Peter Dan Gabriel *b.* 1938,—John Laurence Mark, *TD* (of Roundals Farm, Hambledon, Surrey) *b.* 1910; Maj. (ret.) RA; 1939-45 War in Middle East and Italy as acting Lt.-Col.: *m.* 1936, Georgiana, da. of the late Somerset Charrington, of Bures Manor, Reigate, and has issue living, Jenifer Anne *b.* 1947: *m.* 1968, Capt. Patrick Michael Corbett, Irish Gds., of Little Croft, Chiddingfold, Surrey (and has issue living, Sean Patrick *b.* 1970, Jasper Michael *b.* 1971). *Residence,*—Beacon House, Inkpen, Newbury, Berks.

Granddaughter of the late Lt.-Col. Lord Charles Lennox Kerr, 4th son (el. by 2nd m.) of 6th Marquess):—
Issue of the late Charles Wyndham Rodolph Kerr, b. 1849, d. 1894: m. 1873, Anna Maria Olivia, who d. 1937, da. of the late Adm. Sir George Elliot, KCB [E. Minto, colls.]:—
Helen Cicely (Whitehill, Gordon, Berwickshire), b. 1884: m. 1st, 1910, Capt. Archibald Edward Butter, CMG, who d. 1928; 2ndly, 1939, as his 2nd wife, Brig.-Gen. Edward William David Baird, CBE, who d. 1956, and has issue living, (by 1st m.) Rev Archibald Charles (175, Prince's Av., Benoni, Transvaal), b. 1911: m. 1968, Margaret, da. of the. late Rees William Maddock, and widow of Douglas George Christison,—John Henry, CMG, MBE (Box 246, Abu Dhabi), b. 1916; MBE (Civil) 1946, CMG 1962: m. 1950, Joyce, da. of Wilfred Platt, of Bradford, and has issue living, Ian Peter b. 1952, Andrew Edward b. 1953, David Charles b 1956,—Peter Herbert (Ashfield, Bridge of Weir, Renfrewshire), b. 1921; ed. at Charterhouse, and Balliol Coll., Oxford; Regius Prof. of English Language and Literature, Glasgow Univ.: m. 1958, Bridget, da. of the late Maj. H. Younger, of Baro, Haddington, E. Lothian, and has issue living, Archibald Simon b. 1962, Rachel Mary Cecilia b. 1965, Helen Lucy Catherine b. 1970.

Grandchildren of the late Charles Wyndham Rodolph Kerr (ante):—
Issue of the late Charles Iain Kerr (Baron Teviot), DSO, MC, b. 1874, d. 1968 [see that title].
Issue of the late Major Basil Kerr, D.S.C., b. 1879. d. 1957 : m. (Feb.) 1912, Winifred Katharine, who d. 1974, da. of the late George Blezard [V. Chetwynd]:—
Diana Katharine, b. 1916: m. 1941, Col. Henry Nelson Clowes, DSO, OBE, late Scots Guards [V. Hatherton, colls.], and has issue living, Andrew Henry (37, Ellerby St., SW6), b. 1942: late Capt. Scots Gds.; Equerry to HRH the Duke of Gloucester 1966-68: m. 1968, Georgiana Elisabeth, da. of Capt. Richard Edward Osborne Cavendish [see D. Devonshire, colls.], and has issue living, Richard William Andrew b. 1971. Residence,—30, Burnsall St., SW3.——Elizabeth, b. 1919: m. 1946, Lt.-Col. George Demetriadi, MBE, TD. Residence,—9, Wilton St., SW1.

Grandchildren of the late Arthur Herbert Kerr (infra) :—
Issue of the late Com. Mark Peregrine Charles Kerr, R.N., b. 1891, d. 1951: m. 1918, Mary Catherine (2, The Chestnuts, Old London Rd., Benson, Oxon.) da. of the late Henry Offley Wakeman [see Wakeman, Bt., colls.]:—
Frederic Mark, DFM, b. 1919: ed. at Canford; 1939-45 War as WO RAFVR (prisoner): m. 1st, 1947, Iris Margaret (URQUHART) (m. diss. 1952), da. of the late William Palk Tully; 2ndly, 1952, June, da. of Capt. Lancelot Gerrard Laurence, and has issue living, (by 2nd m.), Peregrine Gerrard Mark, b. 1955,—Christian Anthony Mark, b. 1960.——Mark David (The Five Bells, Eynsford, Dartford, Kent), b. 1921; ed. at Canford; late F/O RAFVR; 1939-45 War (despatches): m. 1959, Diana Law, da. of the late Arthur Fawcett, of Newmarket,——John Anthony, b. 1926; ed. at Radley.—— Andrew Philip (Ruigh Reabrach, Dundonnell, by Garve, Wester Ross) b. 1933; ed. at Radley.—— Elizabeth Mary, b. 1928: m. 1957, Walter Michael Woodin, of Old Farm, Asthall Leigh, Minster Lovell, Oxon., and has issue living, Mark Chandler, b. 1966,—Elizabeth Mary Anne, b. 1960.

Grandchildren of the late Adm. Lord Frederic Herbert Kerr, 5th son of 6th Marquess :—
Issue of the late Arthur Herbert Kerr, b. 1862, d. 1930: m. 1889, Mildred Caroline, who d. 1950, dau. of Sir James Robert Walker, 2nd Bt., of Sand Hutton, co. York :—
Irene Mildred, b. 1896 : m. 1928, H. Watson Pearson, who d. 1946 and has issue living, Sarah Evelyn, b. 1934: m. 1968, Lt.-Cdr. George S. Rae-Fraser, RN (ret.), of Kingsmead, Fulmer Rd., Gerrards Cross, and has issue living, Hugh George b. 1969, Robin Francis b. 1971. Residence,—Middlecave Cottage, Malton, Yorks.

Issue of the late Adm. Mark Edward Frederic Kerr, C.B., M.V.O., b. 1864, d 1944: m. 1906, Rose Margaret, O.BE., who d. 1944, dau. of the late Wilfred Gough, Roy. Dragoons :—
Alix, OBE, b. 1907; OBE (Civil) 1970: m. 1937, Maurice Arthur Liddell, OBE, of Flat F, 3, West Eaton Place, SW1 [see B. Ravensworth, colls.].——Luise Rosemary, b. 1908. Residences,—26, Upper Strand St., Sandwich, Kent; 19, Draycott Av., SW3.

Granddaughters of the late Frederic Walter Kerr, DSO, yst. son of the late Adm. Lord Frederic Herbert Kerr (ante):—
Issue of the late Ronald William Kerr, b. 1906, d. 1972: m. 1939, Barbara Helen (Barnacarry, Kilninver, Oban, Argyll), da. of C. J. Crawford, of Wayside, St. Andrews:—
Patricia Margaret, b. 1940: m. 1965, Robert James Wakeford, of Grove Farm, Barby, Rugby, and has issue living, Mark Robert, b. 1966,—James Richard, b. 1968,—Ian Frederick, b. 1974.——Angela Helen, b. 1942: m. 1971, John James Goddard, of Christchurch, NZ.——Elizabeth Daphne, b. 1949

Descendants of the late Lord Charles Beauchamp Kerr, 2nd son of 5th Marquess :—

Granddaughters of the late Rev. Beauchamp Kerr Warren KERR-PEARSE, son of the late Caroline (who m. 1826 Thomas Pearse), el. dau. of the late Lord Charles Beauchamp Kerr (ante) :—
Issue of the late Major Beauchamp Albert Thomas KERR-PEARSE, C.M.G., M.V.O., b. 1871, d. 1934: m. 1909, Lily, who d. 1969, da. of the late Capt. Cecil George Assheton Drummond [E. Perth, cols]:—
Elizabeth Alice Durbara, b. 1911. Residence,—3, St. Margaret's Court, Grimston Av., Folkestone.

Issue of the late Capt. Charles Henry Cecil Kerr-Pearse, R.N., b. 1873, d. 1957 : m. 1904, Muriel Mary Monica, who d. 1933, da. of the late Hon. Montague Henry-Mostyn [B. Vaux of Harrowden, colls.]:—
Leila Barbara (Lucerne, Garrison, Barbados), b. 1909.——Iris Margaret Georgina Julia (c/o Lloyds Bank, Cox's and King's Branch, 6, Pall Mall, SW1), b. 1912; late HM Foreign Ser.

Descendants of the late Vice-Adm. Lord Mark Robert Kerr (3rd son of 5th Marquess), who m. 1799, Charlotte, Countess of Antrim in her own right [see E. Antrim].

Grandchildren of the late William Walter Raleigh Kerr, son of the late Lieut.-Col. Lord Robert Kerr, 4th son of 5th Marquess :—
Issue of the late Capt. William Walter Raleigh Kerr, b. 1863, d. 1942: m. 1888, Annabel, who d. 1954, dau. of the late Hon. James Jackson Jarves, of Boston, U.S.A.:—
Sir (Louis William) Howard, KCVO, CMG, OBE, b. 1894; ed. at Lower Canada Coll., Montreal, and Trin. Coll., Camb.; Lieut.-Col. 11th Hussars (R. Hussars), and a Chevalier of Order of Leopold of Belgium; 3rd class of Order of Sacred Treasure (Japan), and Roy. Humane So. of Canada's Medal; European War 1914-19; ADC to Lord-Lieut of Ireland 1921-22: accompanied Garter Mission to Japan 1929 (MVO), and HRH the Duke of Gloucester on his tour of Australasia 1934-35 (CMG); was on Staff of HRH the Duke of Gloucester whilst serving in France 1939-40; accompanied HRH on his visit to Gibraltar 1941 and 1942, and Middle East Forces and E. African Command 1942; Ch. of Staff to HRH on his visist to India and Ceylon 1942, and Comptroller 1946-49; appointed Chamberlain to Pope Pius XI. 1928, and an Extra Equerry to H.R.H. the Duke of Gloucester 1959; has Roy. Humane Soc.'s medal, and Roy. Humane Soc. Medal of Canada; OBE (Civil) 1922, MVO (4th class) 1929, CMG 1935, KCVO 1942, KCVO 1948: m. 1928, Christina Stephanie Mary, da. of the late Arthur Ram, of Ramsfort, co. Wexford, and has issue living, Henry Howard Philip Sackville Casamayor Ram, b. 1932,—Andrew Robert Stephen Casamayor, b. 1936,—Julian James Casamayor (5, Newbridge Cres., Shelton Lock, Derby), b. 1941: m. 1966, Glenys Ann, da. of the Rev. Thomas Hugh Roberts, of Grantham, Lincs., and has issue living, Andrew James b. 1967, Philip Hugh b. 1971, Robert Michael b. 1974. Residence,—The

Dower House, Melbourne, Derbys.——Marie Constance Annabel, *b.* 1889: *m.* 1915, Capt. Andrew William Kerr, RN, who *d.* 1929. *Residence*,—Melbourne Hall, Derbyshire.

Grandson of the late Maj. Schomberg Kerr, only son of the late Lt.-Col. Robert Dundas Kerr, RE, 4th son of the late Lt.-Col. Lord Robert Kerr (ante):—
Issue of the late Cdr. Charles Lester Kerr, DSO, RN, *b.* 1886, *d.* 1965: *m.* 1st, 1908, Innes Margaret Annie, who *d.* 1953, da. of the late Col. P. Archer Chapman, RFA; 2ndly, 1953, Dorothea, who *d.* 1970, da. of the late Capt. Isaac Reeves, and widow of Capt. A. Martin Martin-Smith, Worcs. Regt.:—
(By 1st m.) Mark Barrington (c/o Blandy Bros. y Cia, Funchal, Madeira), *b.* 1910; ed. at Downside; 1939-45 War, as Capt. RA.

PREDECESSORS.—[1] MARK Ker (el. son of Mark Ker of Cessford, Commendator or Abbot of Newbottle), an Extraordinary Lord of Session, and Master of Requests, had the Abbey of Newbottle including the Baronies of Newbottle and Prestongrange erected into a barony with title of *Baron* 1587; was cr. *Lord Newbottle* (peerage of Scotland) with remainder to his heirs male and assignees 1591; a Commr. for holding the Parliament 1597; cr. *Earl of Lothian* (peerage of Scotland) with remainder to heirs male of his body 1606; *d.* 1609; *s.* by his el. son [2] ROBERT, 2nd Earl; Master of Requests 1606; not having male issue obtained permission from Crown to transfer titles and estates to el. dau.; *d.* 1624, when the earldom was assumed by his next brother William, who, however, was interdicted from using it by the Lords of Council 1632, and the titles were confirmed to his niece [3] ANNE, Countess of Lothian, who *m.* Sir William Kerr, Knt., of Ancram branch of the Kerrs of Ferniehurst and a zealous covenanter (engaged in all actions of Scottish Army from commencement of differences between King and Parliament till 1643), el. son of Robert Kerr, who in 1633 was cr. *Lord Kerr*, of Nisbet, Longnewton and Dolphinstoun, and *Earl of Ancram* (peerage of Scotland), with remainder to the issue male of his 2nd marriage, and in default of those to his heirs male whatsoever; Sir William was cr. *Lord Newbottle*, and *Earl of Lothian* (peerage of Scotland) 1631: *d.* 1675; *s.* by his el. son [4] ROBERT, *P.C.*, 4th Earl; received in 1678 a patent of the Earldom with original precedence; *s.* his kinsman Charles, 2nd Earl of Ancram, who *d.s.p.*, in Earldom of Ancram and minor honours; was Justice Gen. and in 1692 High Commr. to Gen. Assembly to Church of Scotland; cr. *Lord Ker*, of Newbottle, Oxnam, Jedburgh, Dolphinstoun, and Nisbet, *Viscount of Briene*, *Earl of Ancram*, and *Marquess of Lothian* (peerage of Scotland) 1701, with remainder to heirs of entail succeeding to his estate in all times to come: *d.* 1703; *s.* by his son [5] WILLIAM, *K.T.*, 2nd Marquess, who had in 1692 *s.* by special remainder his kinsman as 4th *Lord Jedburgh* (peerage of Scotland) cr. 1622; was a Representative Peer, Col. 7th Dragoons, and a Lieut.-Gen.; *d.* 1722; *s.* by his son [6] WILLIAM, *K.T.*, 3rd Marquess; was a Representative Peer 1731-60, Lord Clerk Register 1739-56, and Lord High Commr. to Gen. Assembly 1732-8; *d.* 1767; *s.* by his son [7] WILLIAM HENRY, *K.T.*, 4th Marquess; a Gen. in the Army; sat as M.P. for Richmond 1747-60, and was afterwards a Representative Peer: *m.* 1735, Caroline, who *d.* 1778, dau. of 3rd Earl of Holderness; *d.* 1775; *s.* by his son [8] WILLIAM JOHN, *K.T.*, 5th Marquess; a Gen. in the Army, Col. 1st Life Guards, and a Representative Peer 1778-84; *d.* 1815; *s.* by his son [9] WILLIAM, *K.T.*, 6th Marquess, *b.* 1763; Lord-Lieut. of Midlothian and co. Roxburgh; cr. *Baron Ker*, of Kersheugh, co. Roxburgh (peerage of United Kingdom) 1821: *m.* 1st, 1793, Henrietta, who *d.* 1805, dau. of 2nd Earl of Buckinghamshire; 2ndly, 1806, Harriet, who *d.* 1833, dau. of 3rd Duke of Buccleuch and Queensberry; *d.* 1824; *s.* by his el. son [10] JOHN WILLIAM ROBERT, 7th Marquess; *b.* 1794; Lord-Lieut. of co. Roxburgh: *m.* 1831, Lady Cecil Chetwynd Talbot, dau. of 2nd Earl Talbot; *d.* 1841; *s.* by his el. son [11] WILLIAM SCHOMBERG ROBERT, 8th Marquess, *b.* 1832: *m.* 1857, Lady Constance Harriet Mahonesa Talbot, who *d.* 1901, dau. of 18th Earl of Shrewsbury; *d.s.p.* 1870; *s.* by his brother [12] SCHOMBERG HENRY, 9th Marquess; *b.* 1833; sometime in Diplo. Ser.; Sec. for Scotland, Keeper of Great Seal of Scotland, and Vice-Pres. of Scottish Education Depart. 1887-92; Capt.-Gen. of Roy. Co. of Archers and Gold Stick of Scotland, Lord Keeper of Privy Seal of Scotland, and Pres. of So. of Antiquaries of Scotland : *m.* 1865, Lady Victoria Alexandrina Montagu-Douglas-Scott, who *d.* 1938, dau. of 5th Duke of Buccleuch, K.G.; *d.* 1900; *s.* by his only surviving son [13] ROBERT SCHOMBERG, 10th Marquess; *b.* 1874; *d.* 1930; *s.* by his cousin [14] PHILIP HENRY, *K.T.*, *C.H.*, *P.C.* (son of the late Maj.-Gen. Lord Ralph Drury Kerr, K.C.B., 3rd son of 7th Marquess), 11th Marquess; *b.* 1882; Sec. to Prime Min. 1917-21, and to Rhodes Trust 1925-39, Chancellor of Duchy of Lancaster Aug. to Nov. 1931, Under-Sec. of State for India Nov. 1931 to Sept. 1932, and Ambassador Extraor. and Plen. at Washington 1939-40; *d.* 1940; *s.* by his kinsman [15] PETER FRANCIS WALTER (son of the late Capt. Andrew William Kerr, R.N., grandson of 7th Marquess), 12th Marquess and present peer; also Earl of Ancram, Earl of Lothian, Viscount of Briene, Lord Newbottle, Lord Jedburgh, Lord Kerr (cr. 1633), Lord Ker (cr. 1701), and Baron Ker (cr. 1821).

LOUDOUN, COUNTESS OF. (Abney-Hastings.) [Lordship S. 1601 and 1633. Earldom S. 1633.]

BARBARA HUDDLESTON ABNEY-HASTINGS, *Countess of Loudoun* ; *b.* July 3rd, 1919 ; *s.* 1960 ; assumed (with her husband) by deed poll 1955 the surname of Abney-Hastings in lieu of that of Griffiths ; Hereditary Gov. of Repton Sch., and Etwall Hospital ; is a co-heiress (with her sisters) to the Baronies of Botreaux, Stanley (cr. 1456) and Hastings (cr. 1461): *m.* 1st, 1939 (marriage dissolved 1945), Capt. Walter Strickland Lord ; 2ndly, 1945, Capt. Gilbert Frederick Greenwood, who *d.* 1951 ; 3rdly, 1954, Peter Griffiths, who assumed the surname of Abney-Hastings in lieu of his patronymic by deed poll, 1955, and has issue by 1st, 2nd, and 3rd marriages.

Arms,—Quarterly ; 1st and 4th argent, a maunch sable, *Hastings;* 2nd and 3rd or, on a ief gules, a demi-lion issuant argent, *Abney.* **Supporters,**—*Dexter*, a man in armour, plumed on the head with three feathers gules, and holding with the right hand a spear in bend proper; *sinister*, a lady richly apparelled plumed on the head with three feathers argent, and holding in the left hand a letter of challenge.

Seats,—Loudoun Castle, Galston, Ayrshire ; The Manor House, Ashby-de-la-Zouch. *Residence*,— Harpsicord House, Coborg Place, Hastings, Sussex.

SONS LIVING. (By 1st marriage.)
MICHAEL EDWARD *ABNEY-HASTINGS* (*Lord Mauchline*) (45, Nowranie St., Jerilderic, NSW),
   b. July 22nd, 1942; assumed by deed poll 1946 the surname of Abney-Hastings in lieu of his patronymic: m. 1969, Noelene, da. of W. J. McCormack, and has issue living.
      SON LIVING,—*Hon.* Simon, b. 1974.
      DAUGHTERS LIVING,—*Hon.* Amanda Louise, b. 1969.
         Hon. Lisa, b. 1971.
         Hon. Rebecca (twin), b. 1974.
                       (By 2nd marriage.)
Hon. Frederick James ABNEY-HASTINGS, b. 1949.

DAUGHTERS LIVING. (By 2nd marriage.)
Lady Selina Mary ABNEY-HASTINGS, b. 1946: m. 1967, William Newman, of Apsley Cottage, Billings-
   hurst, Sussex, and has issue living, Christopher James Loudoun, b. 1972,—Selina Anne, b. 1968.
                       (By 3rd marriage.)
Lady Margaret Maud ABNEY-HASTINGS, b. 1956.
Lady Mary Joy ABNEY-HASTINGS, b. 1957.
Lady Clare Louise ABNEY-HASTINGS, b. 1958.

SISTERS LIVING. [*co-heiresses to the Baronies of Botreaux, Stanley* (cr. 1456) *and Hastings* (cr. 1461).
Lady Jean Huddleston, b. 1920 : m. 1st, 1940 (marriage dissolved 1949), Edgar Wright Wakefield;
   2ndly, 1954, Capt. Arthur Alexander Hubble, Queen's Bays, and has issue living, (by 1st marriage)
   Sheena, b. 1941,—(by 2nd marriage), Flora Ann Madeleine, b· 1957.   *Seat*,—Loudoun Castle,
   Galston, Ayrshire.
Lady Iona Mary Huddleston, b. 1922 ; formerly in W.A.A.F. : m. 1951, Robert Alexander French,
   TD, who d. 1970.   *Residence*,—The Beeches, Skelmorlie, Ayrshire.
Lady Fiona Huddleston, b. 1923 : m. 1940, Capt. Robert Conray-Robertson, who assumed by deed
   poll 1944 the surname of de Fresnes, in lieu of his patronymic, having *s.* his maternal grandfather
   as Baron de Fresnes (cr. France), and has issue living, Christopher Ian, b. 1942 ; ed. at Ampleforth,—
   Nigel Diarmid, b. 1944,—Vivian Robert James George, b. 1960,—Paulyn Armand, b. 1949,—Iona
   Mary Nicole, b. 1957.   *Residence*,—Cessnock Castle, Galston, Ayrshire.
Lady Edith Huddleston, b. 1925 : m. 1947, Major David Kenneth Maclaren, and has issue living,
   Norman Angus, b. 1948,—Roderic John, b. 1950.   *Residence*,—Ardarrach, Ardgour, by Fort
   William, Inverness-shire.

COLLATERAL BRANCHES LIVING.
      Issue of the late Gilbert Theophilus Clifton, 3rd Baron Donington, brother of
      11th Earl [see B. Donington (ext.)].

      Descendants of the late Lady Victoria Mary Louisa Kirwan, 3rd da. of 2nd Marquess
      of Hastings and 7th Earl of Loudoun [see By. Grey de Ruthyn].

      Descendants of the late Lady Frances Augusta Constance Muir, yst. da. of 2nd
      Marquess of Hastings and 7th Earl of Loudoun, and wife of 4th Earl of Romney
      [see that title].

PREDECESSORS.—[1] *Sir* HUGH Campbell of Loudoun, co. Ayr, PC; cr. *Lord Campbell of Loudoun*
   (peerage of Scot.) 1601; d. 1622; *s.* by his grand-da. [2] MARGARET (el. da. of George, Master of
   Loudoun): m. c. 1620, Sir John Campbell of Lawers, (descended from Campbell of Glenorchy), who
   was cr. *Earl of Loudoun* and *Lord Tarrinzean and Mauchlin* (peerage of Scot.) 1633, with remainder
   to his heirs male, but, since he opposed the crown, the patent was superseded until 1641, when it
   was issued with original precedence; Lord Chancellor of Scot. 1641-1660 and 1st Commr. of the
   Treasury, 1641-44; d. 1662; *s.* by his son [3] JAMES, 2nd Earl: m. 1666, Lady Margaret Montgomerie, da. of 7th Earl of Eglinton; d. 1684; *s.* by his son [4] HUGH, KT, PC, 3rd Earl: resigned
   his titles 1707, and obtained a new patent with remainder to heirs male of his body, heirs gen. of
   1st Earl and heirs male whatsoever of 1st Earl; Lord Keeper of Scot. 1708-13: m. 1700, Lady
   Margaret Dalrymple who d. 1779, da. of 1st Earl of Stair; d. 1731; *s.* by his son [5] JOHN, 4th
   Earl; b. 1705, Gen.; d. unm. 1782; *s.* by his cousin [6] JAMES, Mure-Campbell, 5th Earl (son of
   Hon. Sir James Campbell, 3rd son of 2nd Earl); Maj.-Gen.: m. 1777, Flora, who d. 1780, da. of
   John MacLeod of Raasay; d. 1786; *s.* by his only da. [7] FLORA, Countess of Loudoun; b. 1780:
   m. 1804, Francis Rawdon-Hastings, 2nd Earl of Moira,* who was cr. *Marquess of Hastings* 1816
   and d. 1826; she d. 1840, and was *s.* by her only surv. son [8] GEORGE AUGUSTUS FRANCIS, 7th
   Earl (and 2nd Marquess of Hastings); b. 1808: m. 1831, Barbara, Baroness Grey de Ruthyn, who
   d. 1858, (having m. 2ndly, 1845, Adm. Sir Hastings Reginald Yelverton, GCB); d. 1884; *s.* by his
   el. son [9] PAULYN REGINALD SERLOE, 8th Earl (and 3rd Marquess); b. 1832; d. unm. 1851; *s.* by
   his brother [10] HENRY WEYSFORD CHARLES PLANTAGENET, 9th Earl (and 4th Marquess); b.
   1842; *s.* his mother 1858 as *Baron Grey de Ruthyn*: m. 1864, Lady Florence Cecilia Paget, who
   d. 1907 (having m. 2ndly, 1870, Sir George Chetwynd, 4th Bt.); d. 1868, when the Marquessate of
   Hastings and subsidiary peerages became ext. (except the English Baronies mentioned below), and
   the Scottish peerages devolved upon his el. sister [11] EDITH MAUD; b. 1833: m. 1853, Charles
   Frederick Clifton, who assumed 1859 by Act of Parl. the surname of Abney-Hastings, was cr. *Baron
   Donington* 1880, and d. 1895; she d. 1874; *s.* by her son [12] CHARLES EDWARD HASTINGS, 11th
   Earl; b. 1855; assumed 1887 by Roy. licence the name of Rawdon-Hastings; bore one of the gold
   spurs at Coronations 1902 and 1911: m. 1880, the Hon. Alice Mary Elizabeth Fitzalan-Howard,
   who d. 1915, da. of 1st Baron Howard of Glossop; d. 1920, when the Barony of Donington passed
   to his 2nd brother, and the Scottish peerages to his niece, [13] EDITH MAUD, Countess of Loudoun
   (el. da. of the Hon. Paulyn Francis Cuthbert Rawdon-Hastings); b. 1883: m. 1916, Capt. Reginald
   Mowbray Chichester Huddleston, from whom she obtained a divorce 1947: they assumed by
   Roy. licence 1918 the surname of Abney-Hastings; d. 1960; *s.* by her el. da. [14] BARBARA HUDDLE-
   STON, present peeress, also Lady Campbell of Loudoun, and Lady Tarrinzean and Mauchline.

*⁎*The 1st Marquess of Hastings *s.* in 1808 to the Baronies of Botreaux (cr. 1368), Hungerford (cr.
   1426), Moleyns (cr. 1445), and Hastings (cr. 1461).   They fell into abeyance 1868 between the
   sisters of the 4th Marquess of Hastings, but were called out in 1871 in favour of Edith Maud Countess
   of Loudoun (b. 1833).   They again fell into abeyance in 1920 between Edith Maud Countess of
   Loudoun (b. 1883) and her sisters.   In 1921 the baronies of Botreaux, Stanley (cr. 1456), and
   Hastings were called out of abeyance in favour of the Countess of Loudoun, but on her death in
   1960 they again fell into abeyance between her daughters, of whom the el. is the Countess of
   Loudoun.

Loughborough, Lord,   son of Earl of Rosslyn

LOUTH, BARON. (Plunkett.) [Baron I. 1541.]

Hasten slowly.

PESTINA LENTE

OTWAY MICHAEL JAMES OLIVER PLUNKETT,
16th Baron ; *b.* Aug. 19th, 1929 ; *s.* 1950 ; ed.
at Downside : *m.* 1951, Angela Patricia, dau.
of W. Cullinane, of St. Helier, Jersey, and
has issue.
    Arms,—Sable, a bend, and in the sinister chief a
tower argent. Crest,—A horse passant argent. Supporters.—*Dexter*, a pegasus, wings inverted, per fesse,
or and argent; *sinister*, an antelope argent, armed,
unguled, plain collared and chained or.
    Residence,—Gardone, Holmfield Avenue, St. Brelade,
Jersey.

SONS LIVING.
Hon. JONATHAN OLIVER, *b.* Nov. 4th, 1952.
Hon. Otway Jeremy Oliver, *b.* 1954.
Hon. Timothy James Oliver, *b.* 1956.

DAUGHTERS LIVING.
Hon. Olivia Jane, *b.* 1953.
Hon. Stephanie Patricia, *b.* 1963.

WIDOW LIVING OF SON OF FOURTEENTH BARON.
Gwendoline Mary, dau. of E. A. Cowling, of Torquay : *m.* (Feb.) 1936, the Hon. Randal Patrick
Ralph Oliver Plunkett, who *d.* (July) 1936. *Residence,*—

WIDOW LIVING OF FIFTEENTH BARON.
ETHEL MOLLY (*Ethel, Baroness Louth*), dau. of Walter John Gallichen, of Jersey : *m.* 1927, the 15th
Baron, who *d.* 1950. *Residence,*—

COLLATERAL BRANCHES LIVING.
    Issue (if any) of the late Harry Edward Plunkett, el. son of the late Hon. Edward
        Sydney Plunkett [infra], *b.* 1848, *d.* 1906 : *m.* 1877, Marianne, dau. of George
        Smith, of Dalkey, co. Dublin.

    Grandchildren of the late Charles Seale Plunkett, Lieut. 95th Regt., son of the late
        Major the Hon. Edward Sydney Plunkett, 5th son of 11th Baron :—
    Issue of the late Sydney Wilmott Plunkett, *b.* 1877, *d.* 1955: *m.* 1904, Elizabeth Josephine,
        who *d.* 1960, da. of John Patrick Higgins, of Rathmines, Dublin:—
Charles Seale (180, Perth Street West, Hull), *b.* 1908; 1939-45 War (despatches): *m.* 1934, Julia
    Elizabeth, da. of Walter Brown, of Hull, and has issue living, Merrick Shawe (51, Woodlands Rd.,
    Willerby, Hull), *b.* 1934: *m.* 1956, Eileen, da. of T. Armstrong, of Leeds, and has issue living, Patrick
    Allan *b.* 1958, Glenn Charles *b.* 1966, Angela *b.* 1963.——Norman Dawson, *b.* 1910; ed. at Bishop
    Wordsworth's Sch., Salisbury, at Muresk Agricultural Coll., W. Aust., and at Sch. of Mines and
    Metallurgy, W. Aust.; Founder of Norden Youth Club: *m.* 1932, Caroline, da. of R. Bernhales, of
    Milan, Italy, and has issue living, Terence Norman, *b.* 1933: *m.* 1957, Lilian Elizabeth, da. of John
    Warren, of London, and has issue living, Michael Terence *b.* 1958, Curtis Alan *b.* 1962.——Randal
    Otway (5, Brompton Close, Bricknell Av., Hull, Yorks.), *b.* 1914; 1939-45 War: *m.* 1935, Sylvia
    May, da. of E. Rutherford, of Hull, and has issue living, Anthony Patrick, *b.* 1939,—Eve, *b.* 1935.——
    Oliver Penson, *b.* 1917: *m.* 1947, Jean Elizabeth, da. of H. Hewson, of Hull, and has issue living,
    Sean Patrick, *b.* 1948; ed. at Hull Gram. Sch., and Ealing Tech. Coll. *Residence,*—4, Hartoft Rd.,
    Bricknell Av., Hull, Yorks.——Frances Louisa, *b.* 1905: *m.* 1st, 1925, Walter Grundy; 2ndly, 19—,
    Pridgent, and has issue living (by 1st m.), Frances Mary, *b.* 1940, (by 2nd m.), William, *b.* 19—.
    Residence,—

    Grandchildren of the late Merrick Shawe Plunkett, son of the late Hon. Matthew
        Plunkett, 2nd son of 10th Baron :—
    Issue of the late Mathew Penson Plunkett, *b.* 1872, *d.* 1940: *m.* (Jan.) 1899, Matilda Myfanwy
        who *d.* 1952, da. of the Rev. Samuel Evans, R. of Llysfaen, N. Wales:—
Sydney Penson, *b.* 1903: *m.* 1928 (marriage dissolved 1955). Helen Margaret, only dau. of H. A.
    Pattullo, MB. of Kelsall, Cheshire, and has issue living, Anthony Penson (14, Barrett Rd., Keswick
    Rd., Great Bookham, Surrey), *b.* 1931: *m.* 1956, Anne Malkin White, of Harpenden, Herts., and
    has issue living, Timothy Penson *b.* 1959, Andrew Christopher *b.* 1961,—Jean Margaret, *b.* 1929:
    m. 1955, John Travers Clark, of Manor Cottage, Woodhurst Lane, Oxted, Surrey, and has issue
    living, Charles James Travers *b.* 1961, Caroline Travers *b.* 1957, Bridget Travers *b.* 1959. *Residence,*—
    —17, Fair Meadow, Rye Hill, Rye, Sussex.——Caroline Frances *b.* (Oct.) 1899. *Residence,*—
    17, Fair Meadow, Rye Hill, Rye, Sussex.

PREDECESSORS.—[1] Sir OLIVER Plunkett, Knt.; cr. *Baron Louth* (peerage of Ireland) 1541;
    s. by his son [2] THOMAS, 2nd Baron ; *d.* 1571; *s.* by his el. son [3] PATRICK, 3rd Baron; was
    slain 1575 in endeavouring to recover cattle that had been stolen from him ; *s.* by his brother[4]
    OLIVER, 4th Baron, *d.* 1607; *s.* by his son [5] MATTHEW, 5th Baron ; *d.* 1629; *s.* by his son [6]
    OLIVER, 6th Baron ; joined the Royalists 1639, and served at the siege of Drogheda ; appointed
    Col.-Gen. of all the forces to be raised in co. Louth ; outlawed 1642 ; *d.* 1679; *s.* by his son [7]
    MATTHEW, *P.C.*, 7th Baron ; was restored to his estates after the Restoration, and appointed
    Lord Lieut. of co. Louth ; attached himself to the cause of James II., and was exiled 1689 ; *d.*
    1689 ; *s.* by his son [8] OLIVER, 8th Baron, who however was not permitted to take his seat in
    consequence of his father's outlawry not having been reversed ; *d.* 1707; *s.* by his son [9]
    MATTHEW, 9th Baron ; *d.* 1754; *s.* by his son [10] OLIVER, 10th Baron ; *d.* 1763 ; *s.* by his son
    [11] THOMAS OLIVER, 11th Baron ; procured a reversal of the outlawry, and was restored to
    his ancestral honour 1798: *d.* 1823 ; *s.* by his son [12] THOMAS OLIVER, 12th Baron ; *b.* 1809;
    d. 1849 ; *s.* by his son [13] RANDAL PERCY OTWAY, 13th Baron, *b.* 1832 : *m.* 1st, 1867, Anna Maria
    McGeough, who *d.* 1868, dau. of the late Walter McGeough Bond, of Drumsill and the Argory, co.
    Armagh ; 2ndly, 1877, Elizabeth Lily, who *d.* 1916, dau. of the late John Black, of Ceylon ; *d.* 1883 ;
    s. by his son [14] RANDAL PILGRIM RALPH, 14th Baron, *b.* 1868 : *m.* 1st, 1890, Eugénie de Miarritze
    (who obtained a divorce 1912), dau. of the late Capt. Edmund Hooke Wilson Bellairs, H.M.'s
    Vice-Consul at Biarritz, France; 2ndly, 1913, Dorothy Lettice, who *d.* 1923, dau. of the late Col.
    Thomas Lewis Hampton-Lewis, of Henllys, Anglesey ; 3rdly, 1926, Marie Ethel, who *d.* 1941, dau.
    of the late Charles Read, solicitor, of Hampstead, N.W., and widow of Sir John Prichard-Jones, 1st
    Bt. ; *d.* 1941 ; *s.* by his son [15] OTWAY RANDAL PERCY OLIVER, 15th Baron, *b.* 1892 : *m.* 1927,
    Ethel Molly, dau. of Walter John Gallichen, of Jersey ; *d.* 1950 ; *s.* by his son [16] OTWAY MICHAEL
    JAMES OLIVER, 16th Baron and present peer.

LOVAT, LORD.   (Fraser.)   **[Lord S. 1458-64, Baron U.K. 1837.]**
[Title pronounced "Luvvut."]

I am ready.

SIMON CHRISTOPHER JOSEPH FRASER, DSO, MC, TD, 15th (de facto) Lord and 17th but for the attainder; b. July 9th, 1911; s. 1933; ed. at Ampleforth Coll., and at Magdalen Coll., Oxford (MA); Hon. LL.D. Nova Scotia 1952, and Simon Fraser Univ. 1962, and 1972; 24th Ch. of Clan Fraser; a JP of Inverness; Brig. Army Commandos, Scots Gds., and Lovat Scouts (TA), and a DL for Inverness; OStJ; Knt. of Sovereign Mil. Order of Malta; Joint Under-Sec. of State for Foreign Affairs May to July 1945; 1939-45 War at operations in Norway, at Dieppe and in Normandy (wounded, MC, DSO, Legion of Honour, Croix de Guerre, Order of Suvorov, 3rd class, of USSR, Norwegian Cross); DSO 1942: m. 1938, Rosamond, only da. of Maj. Sir Henry John Delves Broughton, 11th Bt., and has issue.

Arms.—Quarterly: 1st and 4th azure, three cinquefoils argent; 2nd and 3rd argent, three antique crowns gules.   **Crest.**—A buck's head erased, proper.   **Supporters.**—Two bucks, proper.
Seat,—Beaufort Castle, Beauly, Inverness-shire.   **Residence,**—Balblair House, Beauly, Inverness-shire.   **Club,**—Guards'.

___

SONS LIVING.

Hon. SIMON AUGUSTINE (Master of Lovat) (Beaufort Castle, Beauly, Inverness-shire), b. Aug. 28th, 1939; ed. at Ampleforth Coll.; Lieut. Scots Guards: m. 1972, Virginia, da. of David Grose, of 49 Elystan St., SW3, and has issue living, Violet, b. 1972.
Hon. Kim Maurice, b. 1946; ed. at Ampleforth; Lt. Scots Gds.
Hon. Hugh Alastair Joseph, b. 1947; ed. at Ampleforth, and Ch. Ch., Oxford.
Hon. Andrew Roy Matthew, b. 1952; ed. at Ampleforth, and Magdalen Coll., Oxford.

DAUGHTERS LIVING.

Hon. Fiona Mary, b. 1941.
Hon. Annabel Térèse (Lady Reay), b. 1942: m. 1964, the 14th Lord Reay.   Residences,—Ophemert in Gelderland, Holland; 11, Wilton Cres., SW1.

BROTHER LIVING.

Rt. Hon. Hugh Charles Patrick Joseph, M.B.E., M.P., b. 1918; ed. at Ampleforth Coll., and at Balliol Coll., Oxford; Hon. Col. Lovat Scouts (T.A.); P.P.S. to Sec. of State for Colonies 1951-54, Parliamentary Under-Sec. of State for War and Financial Sec. to War Office 1958-60, Parliamentary Under-Sec. of State for the Colonies 1960-62, Sec. of State for Air 1962-64, and Min. of Defence for R.A.F. April to Oct. 1964; Pres. of W. Midlands Conservative and Unionist Assocn. 1967; 1939-45 War (MBE, Order of Leopold II of Belgium, Belgian Croix de Guerre, Order of Orange Nassau of the Netherlands); MP for Stone Div. of Staffordshire (C) 1945-50 and for Stafford and Stone Div. of Staffordshire since 1950; MBE (Mil.) 1945, PC 1962: m. 1956, Lady Antonia Pakenham, da. of 7th Earl of Longford, and has issue living, Benjamin Hugh, b. 1961,—Damian Stafford, b. 1964,—Orlando Gregory, b. 1967,—Rebecca Rose, b. 1957,—Flora Elizabeth, b. 1958,—Natasha Antonia, b. 1963.   Residences,—52, Campden Hill Sq., W8; Eilean Aigas, Beauly, Inverness-shire.

SISTER LIVING.

Hon. Veronica Nell (Hon. Lady Maclean), b. 1920: m. 1st, 1940, Lieut. Alan Phipps, R.N., who d. (killed in action at Leros) 1943 [see M. Normanby, colls.]; 2ndly, 1946, Brigadier Sir Fitzroy Hew Royle Maclean, 1st Bt. (cr. 1957), C.B.E., M.P., and has issue living, (by 1st marriage) [see M. Normanby, colls.],—(by 2nd marriage) [see Maclean, Bt. (cr. 1957)].   Residence,—Strachur House, Argyll.

AUNT LIVING.   (Daughter of 13th Lord.)
Hon. Muriel, b. 1884; is a Sister of St. Vincent de Paul.

COLLATERAL BRANCH LIVING.

Issue of the late Major the Hon. Alastair Thomas Joseph Fraser, D.S.O., Lovat Scouts, son of 13th Lord, b. 1877, d. 1949: m. 1915, Lady Sibyl Grimston, who d. 1968, da. of 3rd Earl of Verulam :—
Alastair Hugh Joseph, MC, b. 1919; ed. at Ampleforth Coll., and at Magdalen Coll., Oxford; Maj. Lovat Scouts; 1939-45 War (MC): m. 1950, Philippa Margaret, da. of the late Sir Anselm William Edward Guise, 6th Bt., and has issue living, Alastair James, b. 1951,—Roderick Joseph, b. 1953,—Christopher James, b. 1954,—Peter Anselm, b. 1957,—Arabella Mary, b. 1959,—Sophia Margaret, b. 1964.   Residences,—Coddenham House, Coddenham, Ipswich; Moniack Castle, Kirkhill, Inverness-shire.——Ian James, CBE, MC (29, Eaton Sq., SW1; South Haddon, Skilgate, Som.), b. 1923; ed. at Ampleforth Coll., and Magdalen Coll., Oxford; Capt. (ret.) Scots Guards; Chm. Rolls-Royce Motors Ltd. since 1971, and Man. Dir., Lazard Bros. & Co. Ltd. since 1972; 1939-45 War (MC); CBE (Civil) 1972: m. 1958, Anne, yr. da. of the late Maj. A. E. Grant, 9th Lancers, of Nutcombe Manor, Clayhanger, Tiverton, and has issue living, Alexander Charles Evelyn, b. 1962,—James Hector Ian, b. 1963,—Consuelo Catherine Sibyl, b. 1959,—Domenica Margaret Anne, b. 1960.——Simon Joseph, b. 1929; ed. at Ampleforth Coll., and Magdalen Coll., Oxford: m. 1956, E. Jane, da. of H. S. Mackintosh, of 37, Cheyne Court, SW6, and has issue living, Rupert James, b. 1958,—Cordelia Jane, b. 1959,—Katharine Julia, b. 1961,—Olivia Mary Juliet, b. 1965,—Perdita Rachel Josephine, b. 1967,—Helena Jane, b. 1972.   Residence,—38, Clarendon Rd., W11.——Frances Mary, b. 1916: m. 1948, Lt.-Col. Humphrey Joseph Giles Weld, MC, The Queen's Bays (ret.), and has issue living, Charles Humphrey Joseph, b. 1949,—Gabrielle Mary Frances, b. 1950,—Lucinda Mary Rose, b. 1952,—Candida Mary Sibyl, b. 1956.   Residence,—Chideock Manor, Dorset.

Grandchildren of Maj. the Hon. Alastair Thomas Joseph Fraser, DSO (ante):—
Issue of the late Roderick Andrew Joseph Fraser, b. 1927, d. 1964: m. 1958, Ethel Mary who m. 2ndly, 1969, Edward Eyre, of Park Farm, Upper Lambourn, Newbury [see B. Acton], da. of Cdr. Charles H. Drage. RN (ret.), of 38, Sheffield Terr., W8:—
Anthony Henry Joseph, b. 1959.——Archibald Ian Charles, b. 1960.——Thomas William Gerard, b. 1964.——Eleanor Clare, b. 1961.

PREDECESSORS.—[1] HUGH Fraser, one of the hostages for the ransom of James I. 1424 was by that monarch granted the Barony of Kinnell, and is sometimes known as Lord Lovat: *d.* 1440; *s.* by his son [2] THOMAS; *d.* 1450; *s.* by his son [3] HUGH; cr. a Lord of Parliament as *Lord Lovat or Lord Fraser of Lovat* 1458-64; *s.* by his son [4] THOMAS, 2nd Lord; *s.* by his son [5] HUGH, 3rd Lord; having resigned his estates, they were incorporated into a Barony, and granted 1539 with remainder to his heirs male whatsoever, failing whom to his heirs whatsoever; *s.* by his son [6] ALEXANDER, 4th Lord; *d.* 1557; *s.* by his son [7] HUGH, 5th Lord, *d.* 1576; *s.* by his son [8] SIMON, 6th Lord; *s.* by his son [9] HUGH, 7th Lord; *d.* 1646; *s.* by his grandson [10] HUGH, 8th Lord; *d.* 1672; *s.* by his son [11] HUGH, 9th Lord; *d.* 1696; *s.* by his great-uncle [12] THOMAS, 10th Lord, 3rd son of 7th Lord; *d.* 1696; *s.* by his son [13] SIMON, 11th Lord; was outlawed in 1701 for having seized the widow of the 9th Lord, getting the marriage ceremony performed, and forcibly consummating the nuptials; returned in 1715 on the breaking out of the Rebellion, and supported the Govt., for which his outlawry was reversed; in 1745 joined the Pretender, who appointed him Gen. of the Highlands, and cr. him Duke of Fraser; was arrested 1746, and being found guilty of treason was beheaded on Tower Hill, April 9th, 1747, his honours and estates being forfeited; his el. son [14] SIMON; obtained a full pardon and subsequently distinguished himself as a British Gen.; *d.* 1782; *s.* by his brother [15] ARCHIBALD CAMPBELL; Col. in the Army; *d.s.p.* 1815; his kinsman [16] THOMAS ALEXANDER, heir male of Thomas, 2nd son of 4th Lord; *b.* 1802; Lieut. and Sheriff Principal of co. Inverness; cr. *Baron Lovat*, of Lovat, co. Inverness (peerage of United Kingdom) 1837; in 1854 obtained the reversal of the 11th Lord's attainder, and in 1857 established his right to be 12th Lord Lovat (peerage of Scotland): *m.* 1823, the Hon. Charlotte Georgina Jerningham, dau. of 7th Baron Stafford; *d.* 1875; *s.* by his son [17] SIMON, 13th Lord; *b.* 1828; Lord-Lieut. of Inverness: *m.* 1866, Alice, who *d.* 1938, dau. of Thomas Weld Blundell, of Ince Blundell Hall, near Liverpool; *d.* 1887; *s.* by his son [18] SIMON JOSEPH, *KT, GCVO, KCMG, CB, DSO, TD*, 14th Lord; *b.* 1871; Hon. Maj.-Gen. (ret.) TA; S. Africa 1900-02, as Capt. Lovat Scouts (which he raised), 1914-18 War, Comdg. Highland Mounted Bde., and as a Dir. of Forestry; Chm. Forestry Commn. 1919-27, and Under-Sec. of State for Dominion Affairs Dec. 1926 to Dec. 1928: *m.* 1910, the Hon. Laura Lister, who *d.* 1965, da. of 4th Baron Ribblesdale (ext.); *d.* 1933; *s.* by his son [19] SIMON CHRISTOPHER JOSEPH, 15th Lord and present peer.

Lovel and Holland, Baron, title of Earl of Egmont on Roll of H.L.

LOVELACE, EARL OF. (King.) [Earl U.K. 1838.]

PETER AXEL WILLIAM LOCKE KING, 5th Earl; *b.* Nov. 26th, 1951; *s.* 1964.

Arms,—Sable, three spear heads argent, imbrued proper, on a chief or as many battleaxes azure. Crest,—A cubit arm vested azure, charged with three ermine spots in fesse or, cuffed argent, grasping in the hand proper, the broken shaft of a spear in bend sinister sable, the butt argent. Supporters,—Two mastiffs reguardant of a black colour with white belly and nose, collared gules.

Residence,—Torridon House, Torridon, Ross-shire.

WIDOW LIVING OF FOURTH EARL.
MANON LIS (*Countess of Lovelace*), (Torridon House, Torridon, Ross-shire), da. of Axel Sigurd Transø, of Copenhagen, Denmark, and widow of Baron von Blixen Finecke: *m.* 1951, as his 2nd wife, the 4th Earl, who *d.* 1964.

COLLATERAL BRANCHES LIVING.

Labour itself is a pleasure.

Granddaughters of the late Capt. Henry King, son of the late Hon. George King, 3rd son of 6th Baron:—
Issue of the late George Henry Maitland King, *b.* 1853; *d.* 1937: *m.* 1883, Maud Giffard, who *d.* 1957, dau. of the late Rev. F. Tate :—
Mysie Caroline Maitland, *O.B.E.*, *b.* 1892; is a J.P. for Norfolk; O.B.E. (Civil) 1941: *m.* 1923, Cyril Grosvenor Sargent, and has issue living, Hugh Peter, *b.* 1925: *m.* 1952, Bridget Katharine Tuker,—Caryl, *b.* 1927: *m.* 1952, Capt. John D'Oyley Hinde, Roy. Ulster Rifles. *Residence,*—Morning-thorpe Manor, Norfolk.

Issue of the late Major Arthur Montague King, *b.* 1869, *d.* (killed in action) 1915: *m.* 1897, Dorothy Lee, who *d.* 1953, dau. of the late William Congreve, of Congreve, and Burton Hall, Cheshire :—
Diana Charlotte, *b.* 1898: *m.* 1934, Geoffrey Desmond Roper, and has issue living, Mark, *b.* 1935,—John Fitzgerald, *b.* 1936.—Christopher, *b.* 1939,—Charlotte Belinda, *b.* 1941 *Residence,*—Forde Abbey, Chard, Somerset.

PREDECESSORS.—[1] Sir PETER King, Knt., *P.C.*; M.P. for Beeralston 1700-14; was successively Recorder of London, Ch. Justice of the Common Pleas, and 1725-33 Lord High Chancellor; cr. *Lord King, Baron of Ockham*, co. Surrey, 1725; *d.* 1734; *s.* by his el. son [2] JOHN, 2nd Baron; was Out Ranger of Windsor Forest; *d.s.p.* 1740; *s.* by his brother [3] PETER, 3rd Baron; *d.* unmarried 1754; *s.* by his brother [4] WILLIAM, 4th Baron; *d.* unmarried 1767; *s.* by his brother [5] THOMAS, 5th Baron; *d.* 1779; *s.* by his son [6] PETER, 6th Baron; *b.* 1793; *s.* by his son [7] PETER, 7th Baron; *b.* 1776: *m.* 1804, Lady Hester Fortescue, dau. of 1st Earl Fortescue; *d.* 1833; *s.* by his son [8] WILLIAM, 8th Baron, *b.* 1805; cr. *Viscount Ockham and Earl of Lovelace* (peerage of United Kingdom) 1838; Lord-Lieut. of Surrey; assumed for himself and issue by Roy. licence 1860, the additional surname and arms of Noel: *m.* 1st, 1835, Augusta Ada, who *d.* 1852, only dau. of 6th Baron Byron; 2ndly, 1865, Jane Crawford, who *d.* 1908, widow of Edward Jenkins, B.C.S.; *d.* 1893; *s.* by his second son [9] RALPH GORDON NOEL Milbanke, 2nd Earl, *b.* 1839; assumed by Roy. licence 1861 the surname of Milbanke in lieu of Noel; in 1862; *s.* as 13th Baron Wentworth [see E. Lytton]: *m.* 1st, 1869, Fannie, who *d.* 1878, 3rd dau. of the late Rev. George Heriot, of Fellow Hills, Berwick; 2ndly, 1880, Mary Caroline, who *d.* 1941, el. dau. of the late Rt. Hon. James Stuart-Wortley; *d.* 1906, when the Barony of Wentworth passed to his only child Ada Mary, while in the other honours he was *s.* by his half-brother [10] LIONEL FORTESCUE, *D.S.O.*, 3rd Earl, *b.* 1865; European War 1915-19 as Major Northumberland Fusiliers, and Staff-Capt.; in 1895 received for himself only, Roy. licence to continue to use the additional surname and arms of Noel, but **resumed by** Roy. licence 1908 the surname and arms of King only for himself and issue: *m.* 1895, Lady Edith Anson, who *d.* 1932, dau. of 2nd Earl of Lichfield; *d.* 1929; *s.* by his son [11] PETER MALCOLM, 4th Earl, *b.* 1905: *m.* 1st, 1939, Doris Evison, who *d.* 1940; 2ndly, 1951, Manon Lis, da. of Axel Sigurd Transo, of Copenhagen, Denmark, and widow of Baron von Blixen Finecke; *d.* 1964; *s.* by his only son [12] PETER AXEL WILLIAM LOCKE, 5th Earl and present peer; also Viscount Ockham, and Lord King, Baron of Ockham.

LOVELL-DAVIS, BARON. (Lovell-Davis.) [Life Baron 1974.]

PETER LOVELL LOVELL-DAVIS, son of William Lovell Davis, *b.* July 8th, 1924; ed. at Christ's Coll., Finchley, King Ecward VI Sch., Stratford-on-Avon, and Jesus Coll., Oxford (BA); 1939-45 War as Fl. Lt., RAF; Man. Dir. of Davis & Harrison Ltd. 1971-73, and of Central Press Features Ltd. 1952-71; a Member of Press Gallery of House of Commons 1951-71; Chm. of The Features Syndicate Ltd. since 1972; a Dir. of other Printing Publishing and Newspaper Cos.; a Lord in Waiting to HM since 1974; cr. *Baron Lovell-Davis, of Highgate,* in Greater London (Life Baron) 1974: *m.* 1950, Jean, da. of the late Peter Foster Graham, and has issue.

Residence,—80, North Rd., Highgate, N6 4AA.

SON LIVING.

Hon. Stephen Lovell, *b.* 1955.

DAUGHTER LIVING.

Hon. Catherine Ruth, *b.* 1958.

Lowther, Viscount, son of Earl of Lonsdale.

LUCAN, EARL OF. (Bingham.) Sits as BARON BINGHAM (U.K. 1934.)
[Earl I. 1795, Baron U.K. 1934, Bt. S. 1634.]

RICHARD JOHN BINGHAM, 7th Earl, 3rd Baron (U.K.), and 13th Baronet; *b.* Dec. 18th, 1934; *s.* 1964; ed. at Eton; Lt. Coldstream Guards (Reserve); Patron of one living: *m.* 1963, Veronica Mary, 3rd da. (el. by 2nd m.) of the late Maj. Charles Moorhouse Duncan, MC, and has issue. [The 7th Earl has been missing since Nov. 7th 1974.]

Arms,—Azure a bend plain cottised between six crosses patee or. **Crest.**—On a mount vert a falcon rising proper, armed, membered, and belled or **Supporters.**—Two wolves azure, plain collared and chained or.

Christ is my hope.

SON LIVING.

GEORGE CHARLES (*Lord Bingham*), *b.* Sept. 21st, 1967.

DAUGHTERS LIVING.

Lady Frances, *b.* 1964.
Lady Camilla, *b.* 1970.

BROTHER LIVING.

Hon. Hugh (6, Gledhow Gdns., SW5), *b.* 1939; ed. at Charterhouse, and at Hertford Coll., Oxford.

SISTERS LIVING.

Lady Jane, *b.* 1932; ed. at Badminton Sch., Bristol; M.B. and B.S. London 1957: *m.* 1960, James D. Griffin, and has issue living, Nicholas Driscoll, *b.* 1962,—John Christopher *b.* 1963,—Benjamin Dawson, *b.* 1966,—Kaitilin Bingham, *b.* 1961. *Residence,*—444, East 66th St., New York, NY 10021, USA.
Lady Sarah, *b.* 1936 ; ed. at Badminton Sch., Bristol : *m.* 1958, the Rev. William Gilbert Gibbs, and has issue living, Oliver John, *b.* 1961,—Marcia Kaitilin, *b.* 1959.—Selina Helen, *b.* 1964, —Madeleine Susannah, *b.* 1965. *Residence,*—The Vicarage, Guilsborough, Northampton.

UNCLE LIVING. (Son of Fifth Earl.)

Hon. John Edward, *b.* 1904; ed. at Eton, and at Trin. Coll., Camb.; served Derbyshire Yeo. and Army Air Corps 1938-45: *m.* 1942, Dorothea, da. of the late Rev. John Kyrle Chatfield, and has issue living, Nicholas Charles, *b.* 1943,—Peter John, *b.* 1945; Lt. RN: *m.* 1971, Penella, only da. of the late Dr. E. O. Herten-Greaven, of Buenos Aires,—David Julian, *b.* 1951. *Residence,*—Hayes Farm, Beckley, Rye, Sussex. *Club,*—Pratt's.

AUNT LIVING. (Daughter of Fifth Earl.)

Lady Margaret Diana, *GBE* (*Dowager Countess Alexander of Tunis*), *b.* 1905; JP, and DL for Berks.; GBE (Civil) 1954: *m.* 1931, the 1st Earl Alexander of Tunis, who *d.* 1969. *Residence,*—Winkfield Lodge, Windsor Forest, Berks.

WIDOW LIVING OF SIXTH EARL.

KAITILIN ELIZABETH ANNE (*Kaitilin, Countess of Lucan*) (73, Lords View, NW8). da. of the late Capt. the Hon. Edward Stanley Dawson, RN [see E. Dartrey, colls.]: *m.* 1929, the 6th Earl, who *d.* 1964.

COLLATERAL BRANCHES LIVING.
Issue of the late Maj.-Gen. the Hon. Sir Cecil Edward Bingham, G.C.V.O.,
K.C.M.G., C.B., 2nd son of 4th Earl, *b.* 1861, *d.* 1934: *m.* 1st, 1884, Rose,
who *d.* 1908, dau. of the late James Guthrie, of Craigie, Forfarshire; 2ndly,
1911, Alys Elizabeth who *d.* 1953, dau. of the late Col. Henry Montgomerie-Carr,
of Kentucky, U.S.A., and widow of Samuel Sloane Chauncey, of New York :—
(By 1st marriage) Ralph Charles, *C.V.O., D.S.O.,* b. 1885; ed. at Eton: is Lieut.-Col. Coldstream
Guards (ret.); 1914-18 War (despatches thrice, D.S.O., Italian Silver medal); appointed an Exon
of H.M.'s Body Guard of Yeomen of the Guard 1937, and Adj. and Clerk of the Cheque 1950; D.S.O.
1917, CVO 1953: *m.* 1913, Dorothy Louisa, who *d.* 1967, da. of the late Edward Roger Murray Pratt
[B. Dunleath], and has issue living, John Nigel (Stone House, Brimpton, Reading), *b.* 1915;
ed. at Eton, and Trin. Coll., Camb. (BA); Capt. Coldstream Guards (Reserve); 1939-45 War
(wounded): *m.* 1943, Elisabeth Rosamund, da. of the late Maj. Sir Algernon Thomas Peyton,
7th Bt., and has issue living, Lavinia Frances *b.* 1949, Veronica Anabel *b.* 1952,—Rachel Cecilia
(*Baroness Alport*), *b.* 1917: *m.* 1945, Baron Alport (Life Baron). *Residence,*—The Cross House,
Layer de la Haye, Colchester. *Club,*—Royal Thames Yacht.
Issue of the late Maj.-Gen the Hon. Sir Francis Richard Bingham, K.C.B.,
K.C.M.G., 3rd son of 4th Earl, *b.* 1863, *d.* 1935: *m.* 1896, Kathleen, who *d.* 1963,
dau. of Gen. Sir Charles Mansfield Clarke, G.C.B., G.C.V.O., 3rd Bt. [cr. 1831]:—
Francis Humphrey, *O.B.E.,* b. 1899; Lieut. R.A. 1918-28; formerly Commr. for Co-operative Develop-
ment, Nyasaland; European War 1918, European War 1939-43 in Somaliland and Abyssinia with
Gold Coast Regt., and as Major E. African Artillery; O.B.E. (Civil) 1953: *m.* 1927, Evangeline
Marguerite Ladys, dau. of Col. William Henry Wilson Elliot, D.S.O., M.B. *Residence,*—Quintons,
East Bergholt, Colchester.

PREDECESSORS.—[1] HENRY Bingham; cr. a *Baronet* 1634; *s.* by his son [2] *Sir* GEORGE, 2nd
Bt.; *s.* by his el. son [3] *Sir* HENRY, 3rd Bt.; *d.s.p.*; *s.* by his half-brother [4] *Sir* GEORGE,
4th Bt.; *s.* by his son [5] *Sir* JOHN, 5th Bt., M.P. for and Gov. of co. Mayo; *d.* 1749; *s.* by
his el. son [6] *Sir* JOHN, 6th Bt., M.P. for co. Mayo; *d.* unmarried 1752; *s.* by his brother [7]
Sir CHARLES, 7th Bt. M.P. for co. Mayo; cr. *Baron Lucan,* of Castlebar (peerage of Ireland)
1776, and *Earl of Lucan* (peerage of Ireland) 1795; *d.* 1799; *s.* by his son [8] RICHARD, 2nd
Earl; *b.* 1764; a Representative Peer: *m.* 1794, Lady Elizabeth Belasyse, dau. and co-heir of
Henry, 2nd Earl Fauconberg, and the divorced wife of Bernard Edward, 12th Duke of Norfolk;
d. 1839; *s.* by his son [9] GEORGE CHARLES, G.C.B., 3rd Earl, *b.* 1800; was Field Marshal in
the Army: *m.* 1829, Lady Anne Brudenell, who *d.* 1877, dau. of 6th Earl of Cardigan; *d.* 1888;
s. by his el. son [10] GEORGE, K.P., 4th Earl, *b.* 1830; a Representative Peer; bore Sceptre
with Dove at Coronation of King Edward VII.; sat as M.P. for Mayo (*LC*) 1865-74; Lieut.
and Custos Rotulorum of co. Mayo, and Vice-Adm. of the Province of Connaught: *m.*
1859, Lady Cecilia Catherine Gordon-Lennox, who *d.* 1910, dau. of the 5th Duke of Richmond,
K.G.; *d.* 1914; *s.* by his el. son [11] GEORGE CHARLES, *G.C.V.O., K.B.E., C.B., T.D., P.C.,* 5th
Earl, *b.* 1860; Hon. Brig.-Gen., a Lord-in-Waiting to H.M. 1920-24, and 1924-9, and Capt. of
Hon. Corps of Gentlemen-at-Arms 1929 and 1931-40; sat as M.P. for N.-W., or Chertsey, Div.
of Surrey (*C*) 1904-06; cr. *Baron Bingham,* of Melcombe Bingham, co. Dorset (peerage of UK) 1934:
m. 1896, Violet Sylvia Blanche, *OBE,* who *d.* 1972, da. of the late J. Spender Clay, of Ford Manor
Lingfield; *d.* 1949; *s.* by his el. son [12] GEORGE CHARLES PATRICK, *MC,* 6th Earl,
b. 1898; Col. Coldstream Guards (O.C., 1st Bn. 1940-42); Capt. of Yeomen of Guard 1950-51;
Parl. Under-Sec. of State for Commonwealth Relations June to Oct. 1951, and Ch. Opposition
Whip, House of Lords 1954-64: *m.* 1929, Kaitilin Elizabeth Anne, da. of the late Capt. the Hon.
Edward Stanley Dawson, R.N. [E. Dartrey, colls.]; *d.* 1964; *s.* by his el. son [13] RICHARD
JOHN, 7th Earl and present peer; also Baron Lucan, and Baron Bingham.

LUCAS OF CHILWORTH, BARON. (Lucas.) [Baron U.K. 1946.]

MICHAEL WILLIAM GEORGE LUCAS,
2nd Baron, *b.* April 26th, 1926; *s.*
1967; ed. at Peter Symond's Sch.,
Winchester; late RTR; TEng (CEI);
FIMI (Council); AMBIM; Pres.,
Inst. of HGV Driving Instructors since
1973: *m.* 1955, Ann-Marie, only da. of
Ronald William Buck, of Southampton,
and has issue.

Arms.—Per fesse wavy or and azure, in chief
between two annulets a rose gules barbed and
seeded proper, and in base two bars wavy argent
surmounted by a bull's head caboshed sable.
Crest.—A representation of Apollo affronte or.
Supporters.—*Dexter,* a lion or; *sinister,* a
Russian bear sable, each resting the interior paw
upon an annulet therein a rose gules barbed and
seeded proper.

Residence,—Connaught Lodge, 59, Brownhill
Rd., Chandlers Ford, Hants., SO5 2EH. *Clubs,*—
Royal Southern Yacht, RAC.

SONS LIVING.
Hon. SIMON WILLIAM, *b.* Feb. 6th, 1957.
Hon. Timothy Michael, *b.* 1959.

DAUGHTER LIVING.
Hon. Rachel Ann, *b.* 1963.

BROTHER LIVING.
Hon. Ivor Thomas Mark, *b.* 1927; ed. at St. Edward's Sch., Oxford, and at Trin. Coll., Oxford (B.A.
1951, M.A. 1956); late R.A.; entered Diplo. Ser. 1951; *m.* 1954, Christine Mallorie, el. da. of
Com. Arthur Mallorie Coleman, O.B.E., D.S.C., R.N. (retired), of 44, Dartmouth Row, S.E.10, and
has issue living, Mark Haselden, *b.* 1955,—Crispin Mallorie, *b.* 1958,—Adrian George, *b.* 1963.
Residence,—63, Parkside, Vanbrugh Park, Blackheath, SE3. *Address,*—c/o FCO, SW1.

SISTERS LIVING.
Hon. Nadia, *b.* 1923: *m.* 1944, Flight Lieut. Hamish Selkirk, D.F.C., R.A.F., and has issue living, Christopher Rattray Lucas, *b.* 1949,—Alastair Hamish Lawson (twin), *b.* 1949,—Lindsay Alexandra, 1945. *Residence,*—
Hon. Tatiana, *b.* 1933: *m.* 1964, Kenneth Bradford (c/o 20, Abchurch La., EC4), and has issue living, Adam George, *b.* 1966,—Justin Nicholas, *b.* 1967.

WIDOW LIVING OF FIRST BARON.
SONIA (*Sonia, Baroness Lucas of Chilworth*) (Flat 41, Brampton Tower, Southampton), da. of Marcus Finkelstein, of Libau, Latvia: *m.* 1917, the 1st Baron, who *d.* 1967.

PREDECESSOR.—[1] GEORGE WILLIAM Lucas, son of Percy William Lucas, of Oxford; *b.* 1896; a Lord-in-Waiting to HM 1948-49, Capt. of Yeomen of the Guard 1949-50, and Parl. Sec. to Min. of Transport 1950-51; *cr. Baron Lucas of Chilworth,* of Chilworth, co., Southampton (peerage of UK) 1946: *m.* 1917, Sonia, da. of Marcus Finkelstein, of Libau, Latvia; *d.* 1967; *s.* by his el. son [2] MICHAEL WILLIAM GEORGE, 2nd Baron and present peer.

LUCAS OF CRUDWELL, AND DINGWALL, BARONESS. (Palmer.)
[Lordship S. 1609 and Barony E. 1663.]

ANNE ROSEMARY PALMER, *Baroness Lucas of Crudwell,* and *Lady Dingwall,* *b.* April 28th, 1919; *s.* 1958; is a co-heir to Barony of Butler: *m.* 1950, Major the Hon. Robert Jocelyn Palmer, M.C., late Coldstream Guards [see E. Selborne], and has issue.

Arms,—Per pale azure and gules three lions rampant argent. Supporters—On either side a wyvern with wings erect or.

Residence,—The Old House, Wonston, Winchester, Hants.

SONS LIVING.
Hon. RALPH MATTHEW, *b.* June 7th, 1951; ed. at Eton, and Balliol Coll., Oxford.
Hon. Timothy John, *b.* 1953; ed. at Eton.

DAUGHTER LIVING.
Hon. Anthea Amabel, *b.* 1956; assumed by deed poll 1963 the additional Christian name of Amabel.

SISTER LIVING.
Hon. Rachel, *b.* 1921: *m.* 1948, Major the Hon. Spencer Douglas Loch, M.C. [see B. Loch], and has issue living, Edward Granville, *b.* 1951,—Andrew Spencer, *b.* 1955,—Sara Nan, *b.* 1949. *Residence,* —51, Lennox Gdns., SW1; Lochluichart, by Garve, Ross-shire.
COLLATERAL BRANCHES LIVING.
(*In remainder to Lordship of Dingwall, and the Baronies Butler and Lucas of Crudwell.*)

Grandchildren of the late Ethel Anne Priscilla Fane, who *m,* 1887, the 1st Baron Desborough, el. da. of the Hon. Julian Henry Charles Fane [E. Westmorland] and Lady Adine Eliza Anne Cowper, sister of 7th Earl Cowper:—
Issue of the late Hon. Monica Margaret Grenfell, *b.* 1893, *d.* 1973: *m.* 1924, as his 2nd wife, Marshal of the RAF Sir John Maitland Salmond, GCB, CMG, CVO, DSO, who *d.* 1968:—
Julian John William (Maidford, Norton, Malmesbury, Wilts.), *b.* 1926: *m.* 1950, Brigid Louise, da. of FitzHerbert Wright (see V. Powers court) and has issue living, David John Julian, *b.* 1969,—Alicia Brigid, *b.* 1951,—Georgiana Monica, *b.* 1952,—Venetia Anne, *b.* 1956,—Rosemary Laura (Ballamin Farm, Bride, Isle of Man), *b.* 1928: *m.* 1947 (m. diss. 1974), the 3rd Baron Ravensdale.

Issue of the late Hon. Alexandra Imogen Clare Grenfell, *b.* 1905, *d.* 1969: *m.* 1931, the 6th Viscount Gage [see V. Gage].

Descendants (*co-heirs to the Barony of Butler*) of the late Lady Amabel Cowper, sister of 7th Earl Cowper, *b.* 1846, *d.* 1906: *m.* 1873, Adm. of the Fleet Lord Walter Talbot Kerr, G.C.B., who *d.* 1927 [see M. Lothian].
(*In remainder to Barony of Lucas of Crudwell only.*)

Descendants of the late Mary Evelyn Compton Vyner, *b.* 1867, *d.* 1957 (having assumed by Roy licence 1915, the additional surname and arms of Vyner), da. of Robert Charles de Grey Vyner, son of Lady Mary Gertrude de Grey, da. of 2nd Earl Grey: *m.* 1886, Capt. Lord Alwyne Frederick Compton, DFSO, who *d.* 1911, son of 4th Marquess of Northampton [see M Northampton. colls.].

PREDECESSORS.—*⁎*⁎*LORDSHIP OF DINGWALL.—[1] *Sir* RICHARD Preston, K.B.; *cr. Lord Dingwall* (peerage of Scotland) 1609, with remainder to his heirs whatsoever; *s.* by his da. [2] ELIZABETH, wife of James, 12th Earl of Ormonde, cr. Duke of Ormonde [see M. of Ormonde]. her el. son, who predeceased his father, was summoned by writ to English Parliament, as *Baron Butler,* of Moore Park, 1666; she *d.* 1684; *s.* by her grandson [3] JAMES, K.G., 2nd Duke of Ormonde, who had in 1680 *s.* as 2nd Baron Butler; was attainted of high treason and deprived of all his honours 1715, and the Lordship of Dingwall and the Barony of Butler remained dormant till 1871, when the attainder was removed and the titles reverted to [4] FRANCIS THOMAS de Grey, 7th Earl Cowper, as heir of Henrietta, Countess Grantham, 2nd dau. of 1st Baron Butler, whose 2nd dau., Lady Henrietta, *m.* the 2nd Earl Cowper; *b.* 1834; Lord-Lieut. of Bedfordshire; Viceroy of Ireland 1880-82: *m.* 1870, Lady Katrine Cecilia Compton, who *d.* 1913, dau. of 4th Marquess of Northampton; *d.* 1905, when the Earldom and Barony of Cowper, Viscountcy of Fordwich, and the Baronetcy became ext., while the Barony of Butler fell into abeyance, and the Lordship of Dingwall and Barony Lucas of Crudwell passed to his nephew [5] AUBERON THOMAS Herbert (son of the late Hon. Auberon Edward William Molyneux Herbert, by Lady Florence Amabel, who *d.* 1888, el. sister of 7th Earl Cowper), 5th Lord Dingwall, and 8th Baron Lucas of Crudwell (right confirmed by Committee for Privileges of House of Lords 1907), *b.* 1876; Parliamentary Under-Sec. of State for War and a Member of Army Council 1908-11, when he became Under-Sec. of State for the Colonies; appointed Parliamentary Sec. of Board of Agriculture and Fisheries Oct. 1911, and Pres. thereof 1914; served during 1914-18 War in Roy. Flying Corps; *d.* (killed in action during 1914-18 War) 1916; *s.* by his sister [6] NAN INO; *b.* 1880; *m.* 1917, Col. Howard Lister Cooper, late RAF, who *d.* 1972; *d.* 1958; *s.* by her da. [7] ANNE ROSEMARY, present Baroness.

BARONY OF LUCAS.—[1] MARY, only child of Sir John Lucas, Knt. (cr. Baron Lucas), was *cr. Baroness Lucas of Crudwell* (peerage of England) 1663, with remainder to her heirs male by Anthony Grey, 11th Earl of Kent, and failing which to her heirs female without division; *d.* 1702; *s.* by her son [2] HENRY GREY, 2nd Baron Lucas and 12th Earl of Kent; *cr. Viscount Goodrich, Earl of Harold,* and *Marquess of Kent* (peerage of Great Britain) 1706, *Duke of Kent* (peerage of Great Britain) 1710, and *Marquess de Grey* (peerage of Great Britain) 1740, with remainder to his grand-dau., Lady Jemima Campbell, dau. of 3rd Earl of Breadalbane; *d.* 1740, when the peerages of 1706 and 1710 became extinct; *s.* in Barony of Lucas by his grand-dau. [3] JEMIMA (ante), who had *s.* to the Marquessate of De Grey on the death of her uncle in 1741: *m.* Philip, 2nd Earl of Hardwicke; *d.* without male issue 1797; *s.* in Barony of Lucas of Crudwell by her dau. [4] AMABEL GREY; cr. *Countess de Grey* (peerage of United Kingdom) 1816, with remainder to her sister, Mary Jemima, wife of 2nd Baron Grantham, and her heirs male [M. Ripon]; *d.* 1833; *s.* by her nephew [5] THOMAS PHILIP, 2nd Earl, 5th Baron Lucas of Crudwell, and 3rd Baron Grantham; *d.* 1859, without male issue ; *s.* in Barony of Lucas of Crudwell by his dau. [6] ANNE FLORENCE: *m.* 1833, George Augustus, 6th Earl Cowper; *d.* 1880; *s.* by her son [7] FRANCIS THOMAS DE GREY, 7th Earl Cowper, 7th Baron Lucas of Crudwell, and 4th Lord Dingwall*₄*(ante).

LUKE, BARON. (Lawson-Johnston.) [Baron U.K. 1929.]

Never unprepared

IAN ST. JOHN LAWSON-JOHNSTON, *T.D.*, 2nd Baron; *b.* June 7th, 1905; *s.* 1943; ed. at Eton, and at Trin. Coll., Camb. (MA); a DL and JP for Bedfordshire, a CStJ., Chm. of Bovril, Ltd., 1943-70; Chm. of Electrolux, Ltd., and of National Playing Fields Assocn., Vice-Chm. of Gateway Building Soc., a Dir. of Ashanti Goldfields Corpn., Ltd., of Lloyds Bank, Ltd., of Lloyds Bank Internat., Ltd., of IBM United Kingdom, Ltd., of IBM United Kingdom Holdings, Ltd., of Aktiebolaget Electrolux, and of Bunhill Holdings, Ltd., and Pres. of Outdoor Advertising Council, and of Inst. of Export; a Member of Internat. Olympic Cttee. since 1951; Hon. Col. 5th Bedfordshire Regt. 1947-62; a Member of Church Assembly (House of Laity) 1935, Chm. of Area Cttee. for National Fitness in Herts. and Bedford-shire 1937-39, of London Hospital Street Collections Central Cttee. 1943-45, of Bedfordshire TA Assocn. 1943-46, and of Duke of Gloucester's Red Cross and St. John Fund 1943-46; a Co. Councillor (Chm. of Standing Joint Cttee. 1943-61) for Bedfordshire 1943-52; Hon. Sec. of Assocn. of British Chambers of Commerce 1944-52; Nat. Vice-Pres. of Roy. British Legion since 1950, Co. Chm., Bedfordshire British Legion 1946-59, and a Member of BBC Central Advisory Council 1947-52; Pres. of London Chamber of Commerce 1952-55, and of Incorporated Sales Managers' Assocn. 1953-56, and of Operation Britain Organization 1957-62; Vice-Pres. of National Fedn. of Young Farmers' Clubs (Eastern Area) 1948-57, and Chm. of Moorfields Eye Hosp. 1947-56; a Warden of Drapers' Co. 1955 (Master 1962-63); Pres. of Advertising Assocn. 1955-58; 1939-45 War as Lt.-Col. Bedfordshire and Herts Regt.: *m.* 1932, Barbara, da. of Sir Fitzroy Hamilton Anstruther-Gough-Calthorpe, 1st Bt., and has issue.

Arms,—Argent, on a saltire sable between four daggers points downwards gules, the sun in his splendour or, on a chief of the third three cushions of the fourth. Crest,—A spur between two wings or. Supporters.—*Dexter*, a heron ; *sinister*, a flamingo; both proper. *Residence,*—Odell Castle, Odell, Bedfordshire, MK43 7BB. *Club,*—Carlton.

SONS LIVING.

Hon. ARTHUR CHARLES ST. JOHN, *b.* Jan. 13th, 1933 ; ed. at Eton, and at Trin. Coll., Camb. (BA); a Co. Councillor for Beds. 1965-70 (Chm. of Staffing Cttee. 1967-70); High Sheriff of Beds. 1969-70; Pres. of Nat. Assocn. of Warehouse-keepers; a Dir. of Pronantica Ltd., and Bunhill Holdings, Ltd., an OStJ; Commr. of St. John Ambulance Bde. in Beds. since 1972: *m.* 1st, 1959 (m. diss. 1971), Silvia Mary, yr. da. of Don Honorio Roigt, former Argentine Ambassador at The Hague; 2ndly, 1971, Sarah Louise, da. of Richard Hearne, OBE, and has issue living, (by 1st m.) Ian James St. John, *b.* 1963,—Rachel Honoria, *b.* 1960,—Sophia Charlotte, *b.* 1966,—(by 2nd m.) Rupert Arthur, *b.* 1972. *Residence,*—Odell Manor, Beds. *Clubs,*—Jockey (Buenos Aires), Royal Southern Yacht.
Hon. Ian Henry Calthorpe (Hawkslaw, Coldstream, Berwickshire) *b.* 1938: *m.* 1970, Lady (Pamela) Lemina Gordon, da. of 12th Marquess of Huntly, and has issue living, Percy FitzRoy, *b.* 1971,—Henrietta Lemina, *b.* 1973.
Hon. George Andrew (Hobbs Green Farm, Odell, Beds.), *b.* 1944: *m.* 1968, Sylvia Josephine Ruth, el. da. of Mchael Richard Lloyd Hayes [see Shelley, Bt., cr. 1611, colls.], and has issue living, Justin, *b.* 1971,—Giles Spencer, *b.* 1974.
Hon. Philip Richard, *b.* 1950; ed. at Eton.

DAUGHTER LIVING.

Hon. Caroline Jean, *b.* 1935 : *m.* 1958, James Bristow, and has issue living, Timothy Dominic Ian James, *b.* 1959,—George Edward FitzRoy, *b.* 1961,—Barnaby James St. John, *b.* 1966.—Melissa Caroline, *b.* 1963. *Residence,*—Biddenham Close, Bedford.

BROTHER LIVING.

Hon. Hugh de Beauchamp, *TD*, *b.* 1914; ed. at Eton, and at Corpus Christi Coll., Camb. (MA); s. Capt. 5th Batn. Bedfordshire Regt. (TA Reserve), Chm. of Cttees. United So. for Christian Literature, Tribune Investment Trust, Ltd. and of Sir Isaac Pitman & Sons, Ltd.; High Sheriff of Beds. 1961-62, and a DL 1964; author of "Argentina Revisited": *m.* 1946, Audrey Warren, da. of the late Col. Frederick Warren Pearl, of 20, Lowndes Sq., SW1, and has issue living, Primrose Pearl, *b.* 1948: *m.* 1975, Martin Arthur Hudson,—Juliet Amy, *b.* 1950,—Marguerite Laura, *b.* 1952. *Residences,*—Flat 1, 28, Lennox Gdns, SW1; Melchbourne Park, Beds.

SISTERS LIVING.

Hon. Olive Elizabeth Helen, *b.* 1904 : European War 1939-45 as Senior Comdt. A.T.S. and subsequently 2nd Officer W.R.N.S.: *m.* 1934 (marriage annulled 1936), Frederick Lothair Lawson-Johnston, who *d.* 1963. *Residence,*—Milton Mews, Aberlady, East Lothian.
Hon. Margaret Beaufort (*Hon. Lady Pitman*), *b.* 1907 ; has Order of Mercy : *m.* 1927 Sir (Isaac) James Pitman, KBE, [B. Dunboyne, colls.], and has issue living, Peter John (of 21, Campden St., W.8), *b.* 1928; ed. at Eton; Capt. R.M. Forces Vol. Reserve, and a Dir. of Sir Isaac Pitman & Sons, Ltd.; formerly Lt. R.M. Commando; Palestine 1948 (wounded): *m.* 1958, Jennifer Joan, el.

dau. of A. R. Holmes, of 37, Berkeley St., Hawthorne, Melbourne, Australia, and has issue living, James Henry b. 1961, John William b. 1966, Joanna Beaufort b. 1963,—Michael Ian, b. 1931; ed. at Eton, and at Ch. Ch., Oxford; late Flying Officer RAF: m. 1959, Ruth, yr. da. of Harold Dyment, of 500, Avenue Rd., Toronto, Canada, and has issue living, David James b. 1963, Sarah Margaret, b. 1961, Jennifer Katherine b. 1964,—David Christian, b. 1936; ed. at Eton, and at Ch. Ch., Oxford; Bar. Middle Temple 1963; Maj. Queen's Roy. Rifles (KRRC), TA: m. 1971, Christina Mary, el. da. of Gerard Brendan Malone-Lee, BM, BCh, of 84, Lawn Rd., Hampstead, NW3.—Margaret, b. 1939: m. 1965, Timothy Duncan Miller, of 63, Addison Rd., W14, and has issue living, Christopher Duncan, b. 1967, Katherine Beaufort Duncan b. 1970, Leila Sarah Duncan b. 1971. Residences,—58, Chelsea Park Gdns., SW3; Holme Wood, Chisbridge Cross, Marlow, Bucks. Club,—Carlton.

Hon. Charlotte Enid, b. 1910: m. 1933, George McCorquodale, and has issue living, Hamish Norman, b. 1945,—Laura Jane, b. 1935: m. 1957, Hugh Dudley Wilbraham, of The Gage, Little Berkhamsted. Herts., and has issue living, Ian Hugh b. 1958, Philip George b. 1960, James Christopher b. 1964, Fiona Laura Mary b. 1967,—Christina, b. 1943: m. 1970, Simon Biddulph [see B. Biddulph, colls.],— Lucy Enid, b. 1948: m. 1975, Charles George Bernett. Residences,—The Malt House, Shenley Church End, Bletchley, Bucks.; Dunan Lodge, Rannoch, Perth.

Hon. Laura Pearl, OBE, b. 1916; a JP for Beds.; County Pres. St. John Ambulance Brig., and an OStJ; OBE (Civil) 1946. Residence,—Melchbourne Park, Beds.

PREDECESSOR.—[1] GEORGE Lawson-Johnston. K.B.E., 2nd son of John Lawson-Johnston, of Kingswood, Kent; b. 1873; a Director of Lloyds Bank, Ltd., and Lord-Lieut., a Co. Councillor, and a J.P. for Bedfordshire (High Sheriff 1924); cr. Baron Luke, of Pavenham, co. Bedford (peerage of United Kingdom) 1929: m. 1902, the Hon. Edith Laura St. John, who d. 1941, dau. of 16th Baron St. John of Bletso; d. 1943; s. by his el. son [2] IAN ST. JOHN, 2nd Baron and present peer.

LURGAN, BARON. (Brownlow.) [Baron U.K. 1839.]

WILLIAM GEORGE EDWARD BROWNLOW, 4th Baron; b. Feb. 22nd, 1902; s. 1937; ed. at Eton.

Arms,—Quarterly, 1st and 4th, per pale or and argent, an escutcheon within an orle of martlets sable, Brownlow; 2nd, Argent a buck at full speed on a chief vert three mullets of the first, O'Dogherty of Derry; 3rd, Gules, a chevron engrailed or, between three escallops argent, Chamberlaine. Crest,—On a chapeau azure, turned up ermine, a greyhound statant gules, collared or. Supporters,—Dexter, a greyhound argent, gorged with a wreath of shamrocks vert; sinister, a Highland soldier in full uniform, with his firelock, al l proper. Address,—E. W. Cooper, Esq., PO Box 161, Dalbridge 404, Natal, S. Africa.

To be, rather than seem to be.

COLLATERAL BRANCH LIVING.
Issue of the late Capt. the Hon. Francis Cecil Brownlow, 3rd son of 2nd Baron, b. 1870, d. 1932: m. 1909, Angela, who d. 1973, da. of the late Samuel Radcliffe Platt, of Werneth Park, Oldham:—

JOHN DESMOND CAVENDISH, O.B.E., b. June 29th, 1911; ed. at Eton; Lieut.-Col. (retired) Grenadier Guards; O.B.E. (Mil.) 1950.——Daphne Angela, b. 1917: m. 1942, Lieut.-Col. Brian Brazier-Creagh, R.A. Residence,—Quarrey House, Charlton Horethorne, near Sherborne, Dorset.

PREDECESSORS.—[1] Rt Hon. CHARLES Brownlow, el. surviving son of the late Lieut.-Col. Charles Brownlow, of Lurgan; b. 1795; M.P. for co. Armagh 1818-33; cr. Baron Lurgan, of Lurgan (peerage of United Kingdom) 1839: m. 1st, 1822, Lady Mary Bligh, who d. 1823, dau. of 4th Earl of Darnley; 2ndly, 1828, Jane, who d. 1878, dau. of Roderick Macneill, of Barra; d. 1847; s. by his son [2] CHARLES, K.P., 2nd Baron; b. 1831; was Lord-Lieut. of Armagh 1864-82, and a Lord-in-Waiting to H.M. Queen Victoria 1869-74: m. 1853, the Hon. Emily Anne Browne, who d. 1923, dau. of 3rd Baron Kilmaine: d. 1882; s. by his son [3] WILLIAM, K.C.V.O., 3rd Baron; b. 1858: m. 1893, Lady Emily Julia, who d. 1909, dau. of 5th Earl Cadogan; d. 1937; s by his son [4] WILLIAM GEORGE EDWARD, 4th Baron and present peer.

This family is paternally descended from Patrick Chamberlaine of Neslerath, co. Louth, who m. Lettice, da. and heir of Sir William Brownlow of Doughcoron (d. 1661) by Elinor, da. and co-heir of John O'Dogherty of Derry. Arthur, son and heir of Patrick and Lettice, as heir of his maternal grandfather, assumed the name and arms of Brownlow.

LYELL, BARON. (Lyell.) [Baron U.K. 1914, Bt. U.K. 1894.]

CHARLES LYELL, 3rd Baron, and 3rd Baronet; b. March 27th, 1939; s. 1943; ed. at Eton and Ch. Ch. Oxford; late 2nd Lt. Scots Guards.

Arms,—Or, a cross parted and fretty azure between four crosses patée gules, all within a bordure of the last. Crest,—Upon a rock a dexter cubit arm erect in armour proper, charged with a cross parted and fretty gules, the hand grasping a sword in bend sinister also proper. Supporters,—Not yet recorded at College of Arms. Seat,—Kinnordy, Kirriemuir, Angus. Residence,—20, Petersham Mews, SW7.

AUNT LIVING.
Margaret Laetitia, b. 1912; BSc Economics (London); Assist. Comm. Sec. British Embassy, Moscow 1944-45: m. 1st, 1937, Maj. the Hon. Francis Alan Stewart-Mackenzie of Seaforth, RA (TA), who d. (killed in action) 1943 [see E. Midleton]; 2ndly, 1944, Charles Henry Pearson Gifford, OBE, and has issue living, (by 2nd m.) Patrick Antony Francis (7, Needham Rd., W11) b. 1945; ed. at Winchester, and Magdalene Coll., Camb. (BA): m. 1969, Mary, da. of John Kilgour, and has issue living, Antony Patrick b. 1971, John Michael b. 1975, Katharine Laetitia b. 1970,—John Vernon (91, West Row, Edinburgh), b. 1946; ed. at Bradfield, and New Coll., Oxford, BLitt,—William Lyell (20, Portland St., Leamington Spa), b. 1950; ed. at Bedales Sch., and Birmingham Univ. (BA): m. 1972, Carolyn, da. of Maj. B. W. Mortimore,—Andrew Graham, b. 1935; ed. at Bedales Sch., and Edinburgh Univ.,—Mary Charlotte, b. 1948; BA: m. 1971, Michael Neumann. Residence,—Cob House, Aldeburgh, Suffolk.

Forti non ignavo.
To the brave, not to the dastardly.

WIDOW LIVING OF SECOND BARON.

SOPHIE MARY (*Baroness Lyell*), dau. of the late Major Sigismund William Joseph Trafford [see E. Lindsey and Abingdon]: *m.* 1938, the 2nd Baron, *VC*, who *d.* (killed in action) 1943. *Residences,*— Kinnordy, Kirriemuir, Angus; Sheil Hill House, by Forfar.

PREDECESSORS.—[1] LEONARD Lyell, el. son of the late Lieut.-Col. Henry Lyell, and nephew and heir of Sir Charles Lyell, 1st Bt. (cr. 1864) (ext.) ; *b.* 1850; M.P. for Orkney and Shetland (*L*) 1885-1900 ; cr. a *Baronet* 1894, and *Baron Lyell*, of Kinnordy, co. Forfar (peerage of United Kingdom) 1914 : *m.* 1874, Mary, who *d.* 1929, dau. of the late Rev. John Mayne Stirling ; *d.* 1926 ; *s.* by his grandson [2] CHARLES ANTONY, *V.C.* (son of the late Major the Hon. Charles Henry Lyell, only son of 1st Baron), 2nd Baron ; *b.* 1913 ; Capt. Scots Guards ; European War 1939-43 (V.C.) : *m.* 1938, Sophie Mary, dau. of Major Sigismund William Joseph Trafford ; *d.* (killed in action during European War) 1943 ; *s.* by his only son [3] CHARLES, 3rd Baron and present peer.

LYLE OF WESTBOURNE, BARON. (Lyle.) [Baron U.K. 1945, Bt. U.K. 1932.]

AN I MAY

CHARLES JOHN LEONARD LYLE, 2nd Baron, and 2nd Baronet ; *b.* March 8th, 1905 ; *s.* 1954 ; ed at Harrow, and at Pembroke Coll., Camb. ; a JP ; was Dep. Director, Min. of Food, Sugar Div. 1939-50 ; Pres. of Office Management Assocn. 1955 : *m.* 1927, Joyce Jeanne, da. of Sir (Joseph) John Jarvis, MP, 1st Bt. ext.

Arms,—Or, a fess gules fretty of the field between in chief two lions rampant azure and in base a lymphad sable, flags flying gules, the sail charged with a thistle slipped and leaved also of the field. *Crest,*—Upon a mascle fesswise or interlaced with two sugar canes a cock proper. *Supporters,*—*Dexter,* a lion azure charged on the shoulder with a rose or; *sinister,* a snow goose wings endorsed proper.

Residence,—Bakersgate, Pirbright, Woking, Surrey.

SISTERS LIVING.

Hon. Nancy Margaret, *b.* 1910: *m.* 1st, 1938, Capt. Philip Foster Glover, RN, who *d.* 1957; 2ndly, 1969, Ryder Gardyne Maltwood, of Lande á Géon, and has issue living (by 1st m.), John Philip Leonard (Windward Lodge, West Kingsdown, Sevenoaks, Kent), *b.* 1940; ed. at Harrow; a Partner in Power-Marine; a Dir. of Moira Investments, Ltd., and Trent Gravels, Ltd., and other cos.: *m.* 1963, Rosemary Beryl, da. of William Peter Manners, of Dunmore House, by Tarbert, Argyll, and has issue living, James Philip John *b.* 1965, Peter Lyle *b.* 1966,—Margaret Ann, *b.* 1942.

Hon. Barbara Suzanne, *b.* 1915: *m.* 1938 (m. diss. 1953), William Thomas Charles Skyrme, CBE, TD, JP, and has issue living, Anthony Lyle, *b.* 1946; ed. at Harrow: *m.* 1972, Carole-June, da. of W. J. Glover, of Sandown House, Belfast,—Carolyn Anne, *b.* 1940: *m.* 1966, Maj. Philip Norman Holbrook, son of Col. Sir Claude Vivian Holbrook, CBE, of Upper Durford, Petersfield, and has issue living, Charles Philip Elstan *b.* 1968, Miranda Carolyn *b.* 1967,—Diana Suzanne, *b.* 1943: *m.* 1965 (James) Gerard Waterlow [see Waterlow, Bt. (cr. 1930)]. *Residences,*—Beechwood House, Nettlebed, Henley-on-Thames; 20, Eaton Place, SW1.

PREDECESSOR.—[1] CHARLES ERNEST LEONARD LYLE, son of the late Charles Lyle, of Brooke Hall, Norwich; *b.* 1882; Pres. of Tate & Lyle, Ltd., sugar refiners; appointed Parliamentary Private Sec. to the Food Controller 1919 ; sat as M.P. for Stratford Div. of West Ham (*Co. U*) 1918-22, for Essex Epping Div. (*U*) 1923-24, and for Bournemouth 1940-45 ; cr. a *Baronet* 1932, and *Baron Lyle of Westbourne,* of Canford Cliffs, co. Dorset (peerage of United Kingdom) 1945 : *m.* 1904, Edith Louise, who *d.* 1942, dau. of John Levy, of Rochester; *d.* 1954 ; *s.* by his only son [2] CHARLES JOHN LEONARD, 2nd Baron and present peer.

Lymington, Viscount, son of Earl of Portsmouth.

LYONS OF BRIGHTON, BARON. (Lyons.) [Life Baron 1974.]

DENNIS BRAHAM JACK LYONS, son of the late Ralph Lyons; *b.* Sept. 11th, 1918; ed. at St. Paul's Sch.; Features Editor of Everybody's Weekly 1946; Man. Dir. of Modern Features Ltd., Fleet St., since 1951, and of Traverse-Healy, Lyons and Partners since 1969; cr. *Baron Lyons of Brighton,* of Brighton, co. E. Sussex (Life Baron) 1974: *m.* 1st, 1940 (m. diss. 1957), Laurie Adele, da. of Leo Lion; 2ndly, 1961, Mary Priscilla, da. of Ernest John Wooley, and has issue by 1st and 2nd ms.

Residence,—2, Clifton Terr., Brighton.

SONS LIVING. (By 1st m.)

Hon. Rodney (3, The Retreat, Gold St., Tiverton, Devon, EX16 6QE), *b.* 1941: *m.* 1963, Cory Frances, da. of William Owen Hassall, of the Manor House, Wheatley, Oxford.

Hon. William (Flat E, 26, Porchester Sq., W2), *b.* 1945: *m.* 1963 Petra Deanna, da. of William Tibble.

DAUGHTER LIVING. (By 2nd m.)

Hon. Deborah, *b.* 1965.

LYTTON, EARL OF. (Lytton.) [Earl U.K. 1880, Bt. U.K. 1838.]

This is the work of valour.

NOEL ANTHONY SCAWEN LYTTON, 4th Earl and 5th Baronet; *b.* April 7th, 1900; *s.* as 4th Earl of Lytton, 1951, and as 17th Baron Wentworth 1957; ed. at Downside; Lieut.-Col. Rifle Brig.; assumed by deed poll 1925 the additional surname of Milbanke after that of Lytton; discontinued by deed poll 1951 the use of this additional surname: *m.* 1946, Clarissa Mary, dau. of the late Brig.-Gen. Cyril Eustace Palmer, CB, CMG, DSO. [Blakiston, Bt., colls.], and has issue.

Arms,—Quarterly: 1st and 4th, ermine on a chief dancettée azure, two ducal coronets or, a canton argent, charged with a rose gules, *Lytton;* 2nd and 3rd gules, on a chevron argent, between three eaglets reguardant or, as many cinquefoils sable, *Bulwer.* **Crests,—**1st a griffin's head erased ermine, eared and maned or; 2nd, a bittern in flags, all proper; 3rd, an eagle, reguardant argent, holding in the beak a branch of laurel vert. **Supporters,—**Two angels proper, each holding an eastern crown or.

*Residences,—*Lillycombe, Porlock, Som.; Keeper Knights, Pound Hill, Crawley, Sussex, RH10 3PB.

SONS LIVING.

JOHN PETER MICHAEL SCAWEN (*Viscount Knebworth*), *b.* June 7th, 1950; ed. at Downside, and Reading Univ.

Hon. Thomas Roland Cyril Lawrence, *b.* 1954.

DAUGHTERS LIVING.

Lady Caroline Mary Noel, *b.* 1947.   Lady Lucy Mary Frances, *b.* 1957.

Lady Sarah Teresa Mary, *b.* 1959.

SISTERS LIVING.

Lady Anne, *b.* 1901; assumed by deed poll 1925, the additional surname of Milbanke after that of Lytton, but discontinued by deed poll 1947 the use of this additional surname. *Residence,—*Newbuildings Place, Southwater, Sussex.

Lady Winifrid (Bidlington, 3, High St., Steyning, Sussex, BN4 3GG, Roy. Overseas League), *b.* 1904: *m.* 1921, Claude F. H. Tryon, MIME, MICE, who *d.* 1949.

DAUGHTERS LIVING OF SECOND EARL.

Lady (Margaret) Hermione (Millicent) (*Baroness Cobbold*), *b.* 1905: *m.* 1930, the 1st Baron Cobbold. *Residence,—*Lake House, Knebworth, Herts.

Lady Davidema Katharine Cynthia Mary Millicent, *b.* 1909: *m.* 1st, 1931, the 5th Earl Erne, who *d.* (of wounds received in action during European War) 1940; 2ndly, 1945, Col. the Hon. Christopher Montagu Woodhouse, DSO, OBE [see B. Terrington]. *Residence,—*Bois Mill, Latimer, Bucks.

WIDOW LIVING OF THIRD EARL.

ROSA ALEXANDRINE FORTEL (*Sandra, Countess of Lytton*): *m.* 1924, as his second wife, the 3rd Earl, who *d.* 1951. *Residence,—*8, Rue du Val de Grace, Paris, V. France.

PREDECESSORS.—[1] Rt. Hon. Sir EDWARD GEORGE EARLE Bulwer-Lytton, GCMG, PC, DCL, LLD; *b.* 1803; a distinguished poet, novelist, orator, and statesman; M.P. for St. Ives 1831, for Lincoln (L) 1832-41, and for Hertfordshire 1852-66; was Sec. of State for the Colonies 1858-9, and Lord Rector of Glasgow Univ. 1856-8; author of numerous popular novels, of well-known poems and dramas, and of essays on general literature and politics; assumed the additional surname of Lytton 1844; cr. a *Baronet* 1838, and *Baron Lytton*, of Knebworth, co. Herts. (peerage of United Kingdom) 1866: *m.* 1827, Rosina, who *d.* 1882, dau. of Francis Massey Wheeler; *d.* 1873; *s.* by his son [2] EDWARD ROBERT LYTTON, GCB, GCSI, CIE, PC, 2nd Baron; *b.* 1831; a distinguished diplomatist and poet; Minister at Lisbon 1874-6, Viceroy and Gov.-Gen. of India 1876-80, and Ambassador at Paris 1887-91; Lord Rector of Glasgow Univ. 1887-90; cr. *Earl of Lytton*, of co. Derby, and *Viscount Knebworth*, of co. Herts, 1880: *m.* 1864, Edith, VA, CI, who *d.* 1936, dau. of the late Hon. Edward Ernest Villiers; *d.* 1891; *s.* by his son [3] VICTOR ALEXANDER GEORGE ROBERT, KG, GCSI, GCIE, PC, 3rd Earl; *b.* 1876; appointed a Civil Lord of the Admiralty 1916, additional Parliamentary Sec. to Admiralty 1917, British Commr. for Propaganda in France 1918, Dep. First Lord of the Admiralty 1918, again Civil Lord of the Admiralty 1919, and Under-Sec. of State for India 1920; was Gov. of Bengal 1922-7 (acted as Viceroy of India and Gov.-Gen. April to Aug. 1925): *m.* 1902, Pamela Frances Audrey, CI, who *d.* 1971, da. of the late Sir Trevor John Chichele Chichele-Plowden, KCSI; *d.* 1947; *s.* by his brother [4] NEVILLE STEPHEN, OBE, 3rd Earl; *b.* 1879; a Portrait and Landscape Painter: *m.* 1st, 1899, Judith Anne Dorothea (*Baroness Wentworth* in her own right), who *d.* 1957, having obtained a divorce 1923; 2ndly, 1924, Rosa Alexandrine Fortel, of St. Rambert-en-Bugey, Ain, France; *d.* 1951: *s.* by his son [5] NOEL ANTHONY SCAWEN, 4th Earl and present peer; also Viscount Knebworth, Baron Wentworth [see ✱✱✱ infra], and Baron Lytton.

✱✱✱[1] Rt. Hon. Sir THOMAS Wentworth, PC, summoned to English Parliament as *Baron Wentworth,* 1529-48; was Lord Chamberlain of the Household; *d.* 1551; *s.* by his son [2] THOMAS, 2nd Baron; *d.* 1584; *s.* by his son [3] HENRY, 3rd Baron; *d.* 1593; *s.* by his son [4] THOMAS, 4th Baron; cr. *Earl of Cleveland,* co. York (peerage of England) 1625; *d.* 1667; *s.* by his son [5] THOMAS, 5th Baron; *b.* 1613; was summoned in his father's Barony of Wentworth 1640; *d.* 1664 in lifetime of his father, who was *s.* by his dau. [6] HENRIETTA; *s.* by her aunt [7] ANNE, wife of 2nd Baron Lovelace; *d.* 1697; *s.* by her granddau. [8] MARTHA, who was confirmed in the Barony 1702; *d.* 1745; *s.* by her kinsman [9] Sir EDWARD Noel, 6th Bt., heir of the Hon. Margaret Noel, dau. of Anne, Baroness Wentworth (ante), who became 9th Baron; cr. *Viscount Wentworth* (peerage of England) 1762; *d.* 1774; *s.* by his son [10] THOMAS, LLD, 2nd Viscount; was a Lord of the Bedchamber; *d.s.p.* 1815, when the viscountcy became extinct, and the barony became abeyant and remained so until 1856, when it was terminated in favour of [11] ANNE ISABELLA, widow of George Gordon, 6th Baron Byron, who in 1822 assumed by Roy. licence the additional surname of Noel; *d.* 1860; *s.* by her grandson [12] BYRON NOEL King-Noel (Viscount Ockham), el. son of the Hon. Augusta Ada, dau. of Anne Isabella, Baroness Wentworth and Byron (ante) by her marriage with William, 1st Earl of Lovelace; *d.* unmarried 1862; *s.* by his brother [13] RALPH GORDON, 13th Baron; *b.* 1839; assumed by Roy. licence 1861 the surname of Milbanke in lieu of Noel in 1893; *s.* as 2nd Earl of Lovelace [see that title]: *m.* 1st, 1869, Fannie, who *d.* 1878, 3rd da. of the late Rev. George Heriot, of Fellow Hills, Berwick; 2ndly, 1880, Mary Caroline, el. dau. of the late Right Hon. James Stuart-Wortley; *d.* 1906, when the Earldom of Lovelace, Viscountcy of Ockham, and Barony of King devolved upon his half-brother, Lionel Fortescue King-Noel, while he was *s.* in the Barony of Wentworth by his only child [14] ADA MARY *b.* 1871; *d.* 1917; *s.* by her aunt [15] ANNE ISABELLA (dau. of 1st Earl of Lovelace), *b.* 1837: *m.* 1869, Wilfrid Scawen Blunt, who *d.* 1922, of Crabbet Park, Crawley, Sussex; *d.* 1917: *s.* by her dau. [16] JUDITH ANNE DOROTHEA, *b.* 1873; assumed by deed poll 1904 the surname of Blunt-Lytton: *m.* 1899, Major the Hon. Neville Stephen Bulwer-Lytton, OBE, who *d.* 1951, and from whom she obtained a divorce 1923—afterwards 3rd Earl of Lytton; *d.* 1957; *s.* by her son [17] NOEL ANTHONY, who has *s.* as 4th Earl of Lytton 1951 (ante), 17th Baron and present peer.

LYVEDEN, BARON. (Vernon.) [Baron U.K. 1859.]

RONALD CECIL VERNON, 6th Baron; *b.* April 10th, 1915; *s.* 1973: *m.* 1938, Queenie Constance, da. of Howard Arden, and has issue.

Arms,—Quarterly: 1st and 4th argent, a fret sable, *Vernon;* 2nd and 3rd gules, three bars gemelles argent a chevron ermine, on a chief of the second three black-amoors' heads proper; a canton of the field, charged with a battle axe or, all within a bordure counter compony of the second and azure, *Smith.* **Crests,**—1st, a boar's head erased sable, ducally gorged or; 2nd, a cubit arm erect, in armour proper, charged with a battle-axe sable, the hand grasping two wreaths of laurel, pendant on either side, also proper. **Supporters,**—*Dexter,* a boar sable, ducally gorged, and suspended therefrom by a chain an escutcheon or, charged with a rose gules slipped proper; *sinister,* a wyvern vert, plain collared, and suspended therefrom by a chain an escutcheon or, charged with a rose, slipped, proper.

Vernon always flourishes.

Residence,—20, Farmer St. Te Aroha, NZ.

SONS LIVING.

Hon. JACK LESLIE (17, Carlton St., Te Aroha, NZ), *b.* Nov. 10th, 1938: *m.* 1961, Lynette June, da. of William Herbert Lilley, and has issue living, Colin Ronald, *b.* Feb. 3rd, 1967,—Wendy Caroline, *b.* 1962,—Karen Marie, *b.* 1964.
Hon. Robert Howard, *b.* 1942: *m.* 1968, Louise Smith, and has issue living, Russell Sydney *b.* 1969.
Hon. Grant, *b.* 1952.

SISTERS LIVING.

Hon. Valda Jean, *b.* 1918: *m.* 1937, Basil George Garrett, of 18, Tarikaka St., Ngaio, NZ, and has issue living, Vernon Richard (25, Pilmuir St., Lower Hutt, NZ), *b.* 1926: *m.* 1951, Coral June Pring, and and has issue living, Shane Laurence *b.* 1965,—Kevin John (Laguna Station, via Augathella, Queensland), *b.* 1943: *m.* 1967, Annette Joyce Selkirk, and has issue living, Trevor John *b.* 1967, Tracy Wayne *b.* 1969,—Beverley Jean, *b.* 1939: *m.* 1959, Colin Roy Hayes, of 39, Tuhikaramea Rd., Frankton, NZ, and has issue living, Carey John *b.* 1967, Rhonda Joy *b.* 1961,—Patricia Dawn, *b.* 1942: *m.* 1959, Angus Malcolm Macintyre, of 22, Mears Rd., St. Andrew's, Hamilton, NZ, and has issue living, Karen Dawn *b.* 1959, Julie Anne *b.* 1962, Bronwyn Vicki *b.* 1964,—Lynnette Joan, *b.* 1946: *m.* 1963, Laurence Stephan Brister, of 45a, Norton Rd., Frankton, NZ, and has issue living, Craig Alun *b.* 1966, Vivienne Lee *b.* 1963.
Hon. Audrey Joan, *b.* 1922: *m.* 1940, Russell Parker and has issue living, Robert Barry (Waipapa, Mangakino, Waikato, NZ), *b.* 1944: *m.* 1965, Helen Wilkinson, and has issue living, Michelle *b.* 1965, —Allan Sydney Russell (12, Argus St., Rotorua, NZ), *b.* 1946: *m.* 1967, Judi Patterson and has issue living, Kerry James *b.* 1968, Grant Allen *b.* 1970,—Raymond John, *b.* 1953,—Barbara Joan, *b.* 1942: *m.* 1961, John Sydney Barnett, and has issue living, Craig John *b.* 1963, Gregory Mark *b.* 1965, Tracy Megan *b.* 1969.
Hon. Maureen Dawn, *b.* 1926: *m.* 1946, Noel Surrell, of 17, Duncan St., Taupo, NZ, and has issue living,—Andrew Gray, *b.* 1952.

AUNT LIVING.

Dorothy Ann (Kiwi St., Lower Hutt, NZ), *b.* 1902: *m.* 1924, Leonard Ross, who *d.* 1970, and has issue living, Vernon Richard (5, Frederick St., Wainui-o-Mata, NZ), *b.* 1926: *m.* 1951, Coral June Pring, and has issue living, Glenn Douglas *b.* 1964, Anne Kathrine *b.* 1953, Helen Ruth *b.* 1955,—Peter John (Ashforth St., Wainui-o-Mata, NZ), *b.* 1934: *m.* 1959, Thea Margaret Baldwin, and has issue living, Gregory John, *b.* 1960, Mark Leonard, *b.* 1963, Susan Lee *b.* 1964.

DAUGHTER LIVING OF THIRD BARON.

Hon. Victoria Wyndham Dorothy, *b.* 1898: *m.* 1919, the Rev. Walter Frift, who *d.* 1938, formerly R. of Irthlingborough. *Residence,*—Ryecroft, Merley Ways, Wimborne, Dorset.

WIDOW LIVING OF THIRD BARON.

ADA (*Dowager Baroness Lyveden*), formerly Mrs. Springate (the actress " Lynda Martell "): *m.* 1925, as his second wife, the 3rd Baron, who *d.* 1926. *Residence,*—

WIDOW LIVING OF FOURTH BARON.

DORIS VIOLET (*Doris, Baroness Lyveden*) (Hunnersley, Burley, Ringwood, Hants.), da. of the late Henry Francis Coghlan White, and widow of Capt. Eric Paterson: *m.* 1949, the 4th Baron, who *d.* 1969.

WIDOW LIVING OF FIFTH BARON.

GLADYS (*Gladys, Baroness Lyveden*) (Day's Bay, nr. Wellington, NZ), widow of John Cassidy: *m.* 1957, as his 2nd wife, the 5th Baron, who *d.* 1973.

COLLATERAL BRANCHES LIVING.

Granddaughters of the late Cecil Sydney Archibald Vernon, 2nd son of the late Hon. Greville Richard Vernon (infra):—
Issue of the late John Lyveden Vernon, *b.* 1895; *d.* 1970: *m.* 1922, Catherine Mary Draffin, who *d.* 1970:—
Bettina Mary Paulinus, *b.* 1926: *m.* 1950, Archibald Reid McLeay, of 81, Charles St., Westshore, Napier, NZ, and has issue living, Eain Dougald John, *b.* 1953,—Jane Imelda, *b.* 1951,—Leah Paule (twin), *b.* 1951,—Victoria Catherine Ethel (twin), *b.* 1953.——Jillyan Imelda, *b.* 1935: *m.* 1955, Charles Woolnough Locke, of 5, Bracken Close, Copthorne, Crawley, Sussex, and has issue living, Gregory Charles Woolnough, *b.* 1957,—Antoinette Marie, *b.* 1956,—Katherine Hélène, *b.* 1961.

Grandchildren of the late Hon. Greville Richard Vernon, 4th son of 1st Baron:—
Issue of the late Capt. Eustace Vernon, *b.* 1871, *d.* 1914: *m.* 1898, Jane, dau. of William Baillie Rankin, M.D., and widow of W. Henry Cutts, M.D.:—
Greville Rupert Eustace, *b.* 1899: *m.* 1925, Frances, dau. of John Henry Little, and has issue living, Greville Richard Eustace, *b.* 1926: *m.* 1953, Nancy Grace Haslam, and has issue living, Jane Suzanne *b.* 1957,—Robert Harcourt, *b.* 1929: *m.* 1954, Isobel Jennifer Miller, and has issue living, Robert Courtenay John *b.* 1955, Hugh Gowran *b.* 1957, David Stuart Lyveden *b.* 1958.——William Baillie, *b.* 1903: *m.* 1925, Dorothy O'Grady. *Residence,*—Bondi, Sydney, N.S. Wales.

Issue of the late Robert Rupert Charles Vernon, DSO, *b.* 1872, *d.* 1940: *m.* 1906, Dorothy Inez Elinor, who *d.* 1965, only da. of George Benjamin Thorneycroft, of Dunston Hall, Stafford:—
Mervyn Sydney Bobus, *M.V.O., b.* 1912: Major Grenadier Guards; European War 1939-45 in N. Africa (despatches); M.V.O. (5th class) 1936 : *m.* 1937, Lady Violet Mary Baring, younger dau. of 2nd Earl of Cromer, and has issue living, Greville Edward Mervyn (Newington House, Kingscote, Glos.), *b.* 1944: *m.* 1969, Fiona Dawn Cory, da. of Lt.-Col. William Handley Ferguson, of Ozleworth Park, Wotton-under-Edge, Glos. [see Cory, Bt.], and has issue living, James Fitzpatrick Greville,

b. 1971, Zara Caroline, *b.* 1973,—Hugh Richard Mervyn, *b.* 1947,—Veronica Elizabeth, *b.* 1938. *Residence,*—Bowldown, Tetbury, Glos.——Susan Diana Mary, *b.* 1915: *m.* 1946, Francis Reitman, MD, who *d.* 1955, and has issue living, Robert Vernon Michael, *b.* 1947; ed. at Radley,—Susan Theresa Maria, *b.* 1950,—Roseanna Mary Blanche *b.* 1953. *Residence,*—Crowcombe House, Crowcombe, Taunton, Som.

PREDECESSORS.—[1] ROBERT Vernon, *P.C., M.P.* for Tralee 1829-31, and for Northampton (*L*) 1831-59; was a Lord of the Treasury 1830-4, Sec. of Board of Control 1835-9, Under-Sec. for the Colonies 1839-41, Sec. of War 1852, and Pres. of Board of Control 1855-8; assumed for his children in 1846 by Roy. licence the surname of Vernon, and in 1859 assumed for himself the surname of Vernon in lieu of his patronymic Smith; cr. *Baron Lyveden,* of Lyveden, co. Northampton (peerage of United Kingdom) 1859; *b.* 1800: *m.* 1823, Emma Mary Fitz Patrick who *d.* 1882, sister of 1st Baron Castletown; *d.* 1873; *s.* by his son [2] FITZ-PATRICK HENRY, 2nd Baron, *b.* 1824; in Diplo. Ser. 1846-50: *m.* 1st, 1853, Lady Albreda Elizabeth Wentworth-FitzWilliam, who *d.* 1891, dau. of 5th Earl FitzWilliam, K.G. ; 2ndly, 1896, Julia Kate, who *d.* 1949, dau. of Albert Emary, of Harold Road, Clive Vale, Hastings; *d.* 1900; *s.* by his nephew [3] COURTENAY ROBERT PERCY (son of the late Rev. the Hon. Courtenay John Vernon, 3rd son of 1st Baron), 3rd Baron; *b.* 1857; a Purser in the Mercantile Marine; European War 1914-18 as Lieut.-Com. R.N.V.R.; a Member of the Dramatic Profession: *m.* 1st, 1890, Fanny Zelie, who *d.* 1924, dau. of the late Major Hill, of Wollaston Hall, near Wellingborough; 2ndly, 1925, MRS. Ada SPRINGATE (the actress Lynda Martell); *d.* 1926; *s.* by his son [4] ROBERT FITZ-PATRICK COURTENAY, 4th Baron, *b.* 1892: *m.* 1949, Doris Violet, da. of the late Henry Francis Coghlan White, and widow of Capt. Eric Paterson; *d.* 1969; *s.* by his kinsman [5] SYDNEY MUNROE ARCHIBALD (grandson of the Hon. Greville Richard Vernon, yst. son of 1st Baron), 5th Baron, *b.* 1888: *m.* 1st, 1912, Ruby, who *d.* 1932, da. of Robert John Shandley; 2ndly, 1957, Gladys, widow of John Cassidy; *d.* 1973; *s.* by his only son [6] RONALD CECIL, 6th Baron and present peer.

MABANE, BARONY OF. (Mabane). [Extinct 1969.]

WIDOW LIVING OF FIRST BARON.

STELLA JANE (*Baroness Mabane*) (Cock Robin Cottage, Bel Royal, Jersey), da. of the late Julian Duggan: *m.* 1944, the 1st Baron, who *d.* 1969, when the title became extinct.

MACANDREW, BARON. (MacAndrew.) [Baron U.K. 1959.]

CHARLES GLEN MACANDREW, *T.D., P.C.,* 1st Baron, son of Francis Glen MacAndrew, of Knock Castle, Largs ; *b.* Jan. 13th, 1888 ; ed. at Uppingham, and at Trin. Coll., Camb ; Hon. LL.D. St. Andrews 1956 ; is Lieut.-Col. and Brevet Col. T.A. Reserve, an O.St.J., and a J.P. and D.L. for co. Ayr ; European War 1914-19 in France and Belgium with Machine Gun Corps (two medals) ; was temporary Chm. of Committees 1934-50, a Member of Racecourse Betting Control Board 1938-61, Dep. Chm. of Ways and Means, House of Commons May to July 1945, and again March 1950 to Oct. 1951, and Chm. Oct. 1951 to Sept. 1959 ; Hon. Col. Ayrshire Yeo. 1951-55 ; sat as M.P. for Kilmarnock Div. of Ayrshire and Bute (*C*) Oct. 1924 to May 1929 (when he was defeated), for Partick Div. of Glasgow Oct. 1931 to Oct. 1935, and for Bute and N. Ayrshire Div. of Ayrshire and Bute Nov. 1935 to Sept. 1959 ; cr. Knt. 1935, P.C. 1952, and *Baron MacAndrew,* of the Firth of Clyde (peerage of United Kingdom) 1959 : *m.* 1st, 1918, Lilian Cathleen (from whom he obtained a divorce 1938), dau. of James Prendergast Curran, of St. Andrews ; 2ndly, 1941, Mona, dau. of J. A. Ralston Mitchell, of Perceton House, by Irvine, and has issue living by 1st and 2nd marriages.

Residence,—The White House, Monkton, Ayrshire. *Clubs,*—Carlton, Royal Yacht Squadron.

SON LIVING. (*By 1st marriage.*)

Hon. COLIN NEVIL GLEN, *b.* Aug. 1st, 1919 ; ed. at Eton, and at Trin. Coll., Camb.: *m.* 1943, Ursula Beatrice, yr. dau. of Capt. Joseph Steel, of Kirkwood, Lockerbie, Dumfriesshire, and has issue living, Christopher Colin, *b.* 1945; ed. at Malvern,—Nicholas, *b.* 1947; ed. at Eton,—Deborah Jane, *b.* 1956. *Residence,*—Dilston, Aldborough, St. John, Yorkshire.

DAUGHTERS LIVING. (*By 1st marriage.*)

Hon. Elizabeth Lilian Graham, *b.* 1929: *m.* 1950, William David Coats, and has issue living, Brian Glen Heyward, *b.* 1951,—Adrian James MacAndrew *b.* 1955,—Frances Alice, *b.* 1958. *Residence,*—The Cottage, Symington, Ayrshire.

(*By 2nd marriage.*)

Hon. Mary Margaret Hastings, *b.* 1942: *m.* 1967, Lt.-Col. Charles Alexander Ramsay, of Rughtrig, Coldstream, Berwickshire [see Ramsay, Bt. (cr. 1806), colls.].

MACCLESFIELD, EARL OF. (Parker.) [Earl G.B. 1721.]

GEORGE LOVEDEN WILLIAM HENRY PARKER, 7th Earl; *b.* May 24th, 1888; *s.* 1896; ed. at Eton, and at Ch. Ch., Oxford; patron of three livings, and Chm. of Oxon Co. Council; Lord-Lieut. of Oxon 1954-63; 1914-18 War as Lt. Yeo., and on Staff: *m.* 1909, Lilian Joanna Vere, who *d.* 1974, da. of the late Maj. Charles John Boyle [E. Cork, colls.], and has issue. [The 7th Earl *d.* Sept. 20th, 1975.]

Dare to be wise.

Arms,—Gules, a chevron between three leopards faces or. *Crest,*—A leopard's head erased at the neck affrontée, or, ducally gorged gules. *Supporters,*—Two leopards reguardant proper, ducally gorged gules.

Seat,—Shirburn Castle, Watlington, Oxon. *Clubs,*—Carlton, Boodle's, Royal Yacht Squadron.

SONS LIVING.

GEORGE ROGER ALEXANDER THOMAS (*Viscount Parker*), *b.* May 6th, 1914; European War 1939-45 as Lieut. R.N.V.R.: *m.* 1938, the Hon. Valerie Mansfield, only dau. of 4th Baron Sandhurst, and has issue :—

SONS LIVING,—*Hon.* Richard Timothy George (Portobello Farm, Shirburn, Watlington, Oxon.), *b.* May 31st, 1943: *m.* 1967, Tatiana Cleone, da. of Maj. Craig Wheaton Smith [see Craig, Bt., ext.], and has issue living, Tanya Susan, *b.* 1971.
Hon. David Jonathan Geoffrey, *b.* 1945: *m.* 1968, Lynne Valerie, da. of George Butler, and has issue living, Timothy George *b.* 1969,—Elizabeth Ann, *b.* 1971,—Katharine Anne, *b.* 1973,—Marian Jane (twin), *b.* 1973.
Residence,—Shirburn Castle, Watlington, Oxon.
Hon. Jocelyn George Dudley, *b.* 1920; European War 1939-45 as Lieut. R.N.V.R.: *m.* 1948, Daphne dau. of the late Major G. Cecil Whitaker, of Britwell House, Watlington, Oxon, and has issue living Robert George, *b.* 1955,—Mary Joanna Isabel, *b.* 1951: *m.* 1973, Peter Robert Boone. *Residence,*—Pyrton Field Farm, Watlington, Oxon.

COLLATERAL BRANCHES LIVING.

Granddaughters of the late Hon. Cecil Thomas Parker, 2nd son of 6th Earl:—
Issue of the late Cecily Mary Parker, O.B.E., *b.* 1875, *d.* 1955: *m.* 1906, Lieut.-Col. William Scott Warley Radcliffe, who *d.* 1954 :—
Cynthia Alice, *b.* 1907: *m.* 1941, Lieut.-Col. Aubrey Roland Hanbury-Bateman, F.R.I.C.S., F.A.I., and has issue living, Aubrey William, *b.* 1946. *Residence,*—Forton House, Longparish, near Andover, Hants.
Issue of the late Geoffrey Parker, *b.* 1880, *d.* 1954: *m.* 1912, Isolda Mabel Cecil, who *d.* 1955, dau. of Sir Charles William Frederick Craufurd, 4th Bt. :—
Cecily Mary Caroline, *b.* 1913.——Isolda Rosamond (*Viscountess Hanworth*), *b.* 1918; formerly Senior Cdr. Auxiliary Territorial Ser.; a J.P. of Surrey: *m.* 1940, the 2nd Viscount Hanworth. *Residence,*—Folly Hill, Ewhurst, Cranleigh, Surrey.

Grandchildren of the late Robert Edward Parker (infra):—
Issue of the late Capt. Robert Kenyon Parker, *b.* 1907, *d.* 1968: *m.* 1st, 1935, Frances Mary, who *d.* 1964, da. of Robert William Gawthropp, of Little Somerford, Wilts.; 2ndly, 1965, Ealga Hester Balgriffin (Water Meadows, Station New Rd., Brundall, Norwich, NOR 86Z), da. of the late Cyril Joseph Kildare Burnell. MA, of co. Dublin:—
(By 1st m.) Nigel Kenyon (3, Hopetoun Terr., Bucksburn, Aberdeen) *b.* 1942: *m.* 1964, Joey, da. of John Jack, and has issue living, Karen, *b.* 1965,—Lisa, *b.* 1969.——Jennifer Elizabeth, *b.* 1938.

Grandchildren of the late Rev. the Hon. Algernon Robert Parker, 3rd son of 6th Earl:—
Issue of the late Robert Edward Parker, *b.* 1878, *d.* 1942: *m.* 1904, Emily, who *d.* 1951, dau. of the late J. J. Dawson Paul, J.P., D.L.:—
Alexander Patrick, *b.* 1910: *m.* 1st, 1949 (m. diss. 1962), Joan Olive, da. of Benjamin Sayer, of Saxlingham Thorpe, Nethergate, Norwich; 2ndly, 1965, Helen Mary, da. of the late John Owen, and has issue living, (by 1st m.) Patrick Edward Benjamin, *b.* 1956,—Tania Lynne, *b.* 1950,—Alexandra Vanessa, *b.* 1952,—Amanda Rose, *b.* 1960. *Residence,*—Algarsthorpe, Marlingford, Norwich.——
Michael Edward (Oriental Club), *b.* 1916; ed. at Eton; 1939-45 War as Lt.-Col. Norfolk Yeo. (RA): *m.* 1st, 1940 (m. diss. 1956), Florence Margaret Catto, da. of James Catto Duffus, OBE, MC; 2ndly, 1958, Estella Mary, da. of H. A. Dalby of York, and widow of George Hall, of Sheriff Hutton, Yorks., and has issue living, (by 1st m.) Timothy Robert Walter, *b.* 1944,—Alexander Michael, *m.* 1950,—Elizabeth Susan, *b.* 1947.——Isobel, *b.* 1905: *m.* 1946, Alfred George Douglas Greenshields, who *d.* 1947.——Elizabeth Mary, *b.* 1914: *m.* 1940, Frederick Colin George Preston, and has issue living Frederick Robert, *b.* 1947,—Anna Susan, *b.* 1943. *Residence,*—Paddock Farm, Mulbarton, Norwich

Issue of the late Hugh Algernon Parker, *b.* 1879, *d.* 1954: *m.* 1911, Averil Frances, who *d.* 1969, da. of the late Brownlow Richard Christopher Tower [B. Brownlow]:—
Camilla Mary, *b.* 1916: *m.* 1st, 1939, Capt. Sir Lionel Francis Phillips, 2nd Bt., who *d.* (killed in action in Italy) 1944; 2ndly, 1950, John G. Pisani, of 21, Chancellor House, 17, Hyde Park Gate, SW7 5DQ.
——Juliet Leonora, *b.* 1920: *m.* 1945, John Frederick Cathers McCreery, late RNVR and HM Overseas Civil Ser., of Little Rowledge House, Rowledge, Farnham, Surrey, and has issue living, Crispin Hugh, *b.* 1953,—Sean Frederick, *b.* 1964.

Issue of the late Eustace BOWLES, *b.* 1884, *d.* 1952, having assumed by Roy. licence 1920, the surname of Bowles in lieu of his patronymic, and the Arms of Bowles quarterly with those of Parker: *m.* 1913, Wilma Mary Garnault, who *d.* 1928, dau. of Col. Sir Henry Ferryman Bowles, 1st Bt. (ext.), of Forty Hall, Enfield :—
Derek Henry Parker (White Oak House, Highclere, Newbury), *b.* 1915; late Roy. Horse Gds.: *m.* 1939, Ann, CBE, el. da. of Sir Humphrey Edmund de Trafford, MC, and has issue living, Andrew Henry, *b.* 1939; Maj. Blues and Royals: *m.* 1973, Camille Rosemary, da. of Maj. Bruce Shand, MC [see B. Ashcombe], and has issue living, Thomas Henry Charles *b.* 1974,—Simon Humphrey, *b.* 1941: *m.* 1974, Carolyn, yr. da. of Sir (William) Ian Potter, of 30, Sargood St., Toorak, Vic., Aust.,—Richard Eustace, *b.* 1947: *m.* 1973, Camilla, da. of Charles Younger, of Gledswood, Melrose, Roxburghshire, and has issue living, Emma Teresa *b.* 1974,—Mary Ann, *b.* 1945: *m.* 1967, Capt. Nicolas Vincent Somerset Paravicini, Life Gds., of Woodside House, Hatton Hill, Windlesham, Surrey and has issue living, Charles Vincent Somerset *b.* 1968, Elizabeth Ann *b.* 1970.——Daphne Wilma Kenyon (38, Pembroke Sq., W8), *b.* 1917: *m.* 1st, 1939, Brig. Algernon George William Heber-Percy, DSO, who *d.* 1961, having obtained a divorce 1950 [see D. Northumberland, colls.]; 2ndly, 1952, as his 2nd wife, the 2nd Baron Poole, from whom she obtained a divorce 1965.

Grandchildren of the late Hon. Francis Parker, 4th son of 6th Earl:—
Issue of the late Capt. Oliver Ivan Parker, *b.* 1891, *d.* 1968: *m.* 1921, Margaret Noel (30, Brompton Sq., SW3), da. of Frederick Kerr, formerly of Twynceri, Barry, Glam.:—
Timothy Oliver (3, Astell St., SW3), *b.* 1924; formerly Capt. Grenadier Guards: *m.* 1952, Rosemary, da. of Maj. John Henry Dent-Brocklehurst, OBE [B. Trevor], and has issue living, Oliver John, *b.* 1953,—Michael Henry, *b.* 1955,—Emma Mary, *b.* 1964.

Issue of the late Ivo Murray Parker, *b.* 1899, *d.* 1957: *m.* 1923, Dulcibella, who *d.* 1974, da. of the late Capt. Charles William Daubeny, of The Brow, Combe Down, Bath:—
Penelope Joan, *b.* 1924: *m.* 1946, Arthur John Hughes, MC, TD, DL, and has issue living, Max Ivo Arthur (The Cottage, Hurstbourne Tarrant, Andover), *b.* 1947; BSc hons.: *m.* 1974, Clara Christabel Harris,—Jane Phillippa, *b.* 1948: *m.* 1972, R. I. W. Ware, of 20, Mill Lane, Welwyn, Herts., and has issue living, Christopher Arthur Corry *b.* 1973. *Residence,*—Vineyards, Welwyn, Herts.

Grandson of the late Hon. Edmund William Parker, 8th son of 6th Earl:—
Issue of the late Wilfred Henry Parker, M.C., *b.* 1888, *d.* 1938 : *m.* 1913, Audrey Elizabeth Peareth, M.B.E., who *d.* 1955, dau. of Thomas Rawson Vickers, J.P., of Hollyberry Hall, near Coventry:—
Michael Cyril Edmund, *b.* 1920; ed. at Eton, and at Corpus Christi Coll., Camb. (MA), formerly Information Officer, Allied High Commn. in Germany; an Underwriting Member of Lloyds; 1939-45 War as Lt. RNVR. *Residence,*—Dar Zambaquia, Ramon y Cajal 24, Tangier, Morocco. *Clubs,*—Boodle's, Pratt's, RNVR, Pitt. (Cambridge).

Grandson of the late Rev. the Hon. Archibald Parker (infra):—
Issue of the late Capt. Charles Edward Parker, M.C., *b.* 1890, *d.* 1962: *m.* 1915, Hilda Margaret (of 19, Lennox Gardens, S.W.1), dau. of Sir John Ralph Starkey, 1st Bt.:—

Charles George Archibald (of 36, Sloane Court West, SW3. *Clubs*, White's, Garrick, Beefsteak), *b.* 1924: ed. at Eton, and at New Coll., Oxford (MA); 1939-45 War as Capt. Rifle Brig.: *m.* 1958, Shirley Follett Rutland, da. of Col. F. Follett Holt, TD, JP.

Issue of the late Rev. the Hon. Archibald Parker, 9th son of 6th Earl, *b.* 1859, *d.* 1931: *m.* 1890, the Hon. Maud Frances Bateman-Hanbury, who *d.* 1932, dau. of 2nd Baron Bateman:—

Frederic Archibald, *b.* 1894; ed. at Eton, and at Trin. Coll., Camb. (B.A. 1919, M.A. 1922); European War 1914-19 as Lieut. 4th Batn. King's Shropshire L.I.: *m.* 1927, his cousin, Evereld Adela, dau. of the late Capt. James Randolph Innes-Hopkins, and has issue living, Archibald Henry (of 24, Trevor Square, Knightsbridge, S.W.7), *b.* 1928: *m.* 1951, Una-Mary, dau. of the late Hugh Power Nepean-Gubbins, of Rumbling Bridge Cottage, Dunkeld, Perthshire, and has issue living, Philip Archibald Reginald *b.* 1955, Una-Mary Diana *b.* 1953,—Joan Sylvia, *b.* 1931: *m.* 1956, Theodore Luke Giffard Landon, of Great Bromley House, nr. Colchester, and has issue living, Mark Eustace Palmer *b.* 1958, Philip James Aislabie *b.* 1962, Benjamin Edward Giffard *b.* 1967, Felicity Juliana Mary *b.* 1960, Rohais Elizabeth Jane *b.* 1964.——Violet Maud, *b.* 1892; is a JP for Salop: *m.* 1931, Brig.-Gen. Hugh Cecil Cholmondeley, CB, OBE, who *d.* 1941 [see B. Delamere, colls.]. *Residence,*— Lee Old Hall, Ellesmere, Salop.

Issue of the late Hon. Henry Parker, 10th son of 6th Earl, *b.* 1860, *d.* 1952: *m.* 1916, Henrietta Judith, who *d.* 1946, dau. of the late Rev. Robert Lowbridge Baker [E. St. Aldwyn] :—

Peter Henry, *b.* 1918; ed. at Eton, and at New Coll., Oxford (MA); Maj. (ret.) KRRC; a JP and a DL for Oxon (High Sheriff 1973); 1939-45 War (prisoner): *m.* 1953, Susan Rosemary, JP, el. da of the late Maj. Mowbray Buller, MC, of Downes, Crediton, Devon [E. Portsmouth], and has issue living, Henry Mowbray *b.* 1957; ed. at Eton,—Belinda Rosemary, *b.* 1955. *Residence,*—The Hays, Ramsden, Oxford, OX7 3BA.

Grandchildren of the late Hon. Alexander Edward Parker, OBE, 11th son of 6th Earl:—

Issue of the late Sidney Alexander Parker, *b.* 1899, *d.* 1969: *m.* 1st, 1937, Adelaide Mary, who *d.* 1947, da. of the late Maj. Sidney George Everitt, RWF; 2ndly, 1951, June Rosemary, who *d.* 1954, da. of the late Rev. Herbert Arthur Woodman, R. of Filleigh, N. Devon; 3rdly, 1955, Rosemary Moon (Harcomb, Chastleton, Moreton-in-Marsh, Glos.), da. of the late Capt. Henry Errington Moon Ord, and widow of Derek Welton:—

(By 1st m.) David Alexander, *b.* 1943; ed. at Wellington.——Anne Mary, *b.* 1940: *m.* 1961, Paul G. E. Clément.——Rosemary Elizabeth, *b.* 1945.

(In special remainder to Earldom.)

Descendants of Elizabeth (dau. of 1st Earl), who *m.* 1720, Sir William Heathcote M.P., 1st Bt. :—

See Heathcote, Bt.

PREDECESSORS.—[1] Sir THOMAS Parker, Knt.; was M.P. for Derby 1705-8, Ch. Justice of Queen's Bench 1710-18, and Lord High Chancellor of Great Britain 1718-25; cr. *Lord Parker, Baron of Macclesfield,* co. Chester (peerage of Great Britain) 1716, *Viscount Parker* and *Earl of Macclesfield* (peerage of Great Britain) 1721, with remainder (in default of male issue) to his dau. Elizabeth, wife of Sir William Heathcote, 1st Bt., of Hursley Park, and her issue male ; the Earl in 1725 was impeached on charges of corruption, and being convicted at the bar of the House of Lords, was, after a trial of twenty-one days, found guilty and sentenced to pay a fine of £30,000; *d.* 1732; *s.* by his son [2] GEORGE, 2nd Earl; was Pres. of Royal So.; *d.* 1764; *s.* by his son [3] THOMAS, 3rd Earl; *d.* 1795; *s.* by his el. son [4] GEORGE, 4th Earl; was Lord-Lieut. of Oxford-shire; *d.* 1842; *s.* by his brother [5] THOMAS, *D.C.L.,* 5th Earl; *b.* 1763: *m.* 1st, 1796, a dau. of Lewis Edwards, of Talgarth, co. Merioneth; 2ndly, 1807, Eliza, who *d.* 1862, dau. of William Breton Wolstenholme, of Hollyhill, Sussex; *d.* 1850; *s.* by his son [6] THOMAS AUGUSTUS WOLSTENHOLME, 6th Earl, *b.* 1811; M.P. for Oxfordshire (C) 1837-41; High Steward of Henley and Vice-Lieut. of Oxfordshire : *m.* 1st, 1839, Henrietta, who *d.* 1839, dau. of Edmund Turnor, of Stoke Rochford, Lincolnshire ; 2ndly, 1842, Lady Mary Frances Grosvenor, who *d.* 1912, dau. of 2nd Marquess of Westminster: *d.* 1896; *s.* by his grandson [7] GEORGE LOVEDEN WILLIAM HENRY (son of George Augustus, Viscount Parker, el. son of 6th Earl), 7th Earl and present peer ; also Viscount and Baron Parker.

McCORQUODALE OF NEWTON, BARONY OF.   (McCorquodale.)   [Extinct 1971.]

DAUGHTERS LIVING OF FIRST BARON.

Hon. Pamela Susan, *b.* 1934: *m.* 1956, William Frederick Eustace Forbes [see V. de Vesci, colls.]. *Residence,*—Dinning House, Gargunnock, by Stirling.

Hon. Prudence Fiona, *b.* 1936: *m.* 1962, Carel Maurits Mosselmans, T.D., and has issue living, Michael Lodowick Stewart, *b.* 1962,—Julian Frederick Willem, *b.* 1964. *Residence,*—15, Chelsea Sq., SW3.

WIDOW LIVING OF FIRST BARON.

Hon. DAISY YOSKYL CONSUELO (*Baroness McCorquodale of Newton*), (50E, Cornwall Gdns., SW7; Cotswold Park, Cirencester, Glos.), da. of 2nd Viscount Cowdray, and widow of (i) Lt. the Hon. Robert Brampton (Robin) Gurdon [see B. Cranworth], and (ii) Lt.-Col. Alaister Monteith Gibb., Hon. Col. Wilts. Yeo.: *m.* 1962, as his 2nd wife, the 1st Baron McCorquodale of Newton, who *d.* 1971, when the title became ext.

MACDERMOTT, BARON.   (MacDermott.)   [Life Baron 1947.]

JOHN CLARKE MACDERMOTT, *M.C., P.C.,* son of the late Rev. John Mac Dermott, of Belmont, Belfast ; *b.* April 12th, 1896 ; ed. at Campbell Coll. Belfast, and at Queen's Univ., Belfast (LLB); Hon. LLD Belfast, Edinburgh, and Camb.; Bar. King's Inns, Dublin 1921, a KC, N. Ireland 1936, a Bencher Inn of Court, N. Ireland 1942, and an Hon. Bencher Grays' Inn 1947; 1914-18 War in France as Lt. Machine Gun Corps (MC); Maj. RA 1939-40; a member of House of Commons of N. Ireland 1938-44; Pro-Chancellor of Queen's Univ., Belfast 1951-69; appointed Min. of Public Security 1940, Attorney-Gen. 1941, a Judge of High Court of N. Ireland 1944, a Lord of

Appeal in Ordinary with title of *Baron MacDermott*, of Belmont, City of Belfast (Life Baron) 1947, and Lord Ch. Justice of N. Ireland 1951-71; PC (N. Ireland) 1940 and (United Kingdom) 1947: *m.* 1926, Louise Palmer, only dau. of the Rev. J. C. Johnston, D.D., and has issue.

Residence,—Glenburn, 8, Cairnburn Rd., Belfast, 4.

SONS LIVING

Hon. Mr Justice John Clarke, *b.* 1927; ed. at Campbell Coll., Belfast, at Trin. Hall, Camb. (BA), and at Queen's Univ., Belfast; Bar. Inner Temple and N. Ireland 1949: QC, N. Ireland 1964; Judge of High Court N.I. 1973: *m.* 1953, Margaret Helen, da. of the late Hugh Dales, of Belfast. *Residence,* —Stanley House, Church Rd., Holywood, co. Down.

Rev. the Hon. Robert William Johnston (46, Crannagh Rd., Rathfarnham, Dublin, 14), *b.* 1934: ed. at Campbell Coll., Belfast, at Trin. Hall, Camb. (BA 1955), at New Coll., Edinburgh (BD), at Assembly's Coll., Belfast, and at Yale Univ. Divinity Sch. (STM).

DAUGHTERS LIVING.

Hon. Edith Louise, *b.* 1930; M.B. and B.Ch. 1954: *m.* 1955, Samuel Barbour Cunningham, of Woodville, Malone Park (Central), Belfast, 9, and has issue.

*Hon.*Lydia Elizabeth Palmer, *b.* 1939; ed. at Wycombe Abbey Sch., and at Belfast Coll. of Art: *m.* 1964, Capt. David McKenzie Chalmers, RAF, of Old School House, Beech Hill, Reading, Berks., RG7 2BE, and has issue.

MACDONALD, BARON. (Macdonald of Macdonald.) [Baron I. 1776.]

By sea and land.

FRAOCH EILEAN

The Heathery Isle.

GODFREY JAMES MACDONALD OF MACDONALD, 8th Baron; *b.* Nov. 28th, 1947; *s.* 1970; ed. at Eton; Chief of the Name and Arms of Macdonald: *m.* 1969, Claire, el. da. of Commodore Thomas Noel Catlow, CBE, RN, of Gabriel Cottage, Tunstall, via Carnforth, Lancs and has issue.

Arms,—Quarterly: 1st argent, a lion rampant gules armed and langued azure; 2nd or, a dexter hand in armour couped fesseways proper holding a cross crosslet fitchée gules; 3rd or, a lymphad, sails furled and oars in action sable, flagged gules; 4th vert, a salmon naiant in fesse proper; over all (as Chief of the Name and Arms of Macdonald), on an inescutcheon en surtout or, an eagle displayed gules, surmounted of a lymphad, sails furled, oars in action sable. **Crest,**—A hand in armour fesseways couped at the elbow proper, holding a crosscrosslet fitchée gules. **Supporters,**—Two leopards propers *Seat,*—Armadale Castle, Isle of Skye.

DAUGHTER LIVING.

Hon. Alexandra Louisa, *b.* 1973.

BROTHER LIVING.

Hon. ALEXANDER DONALD ARCHIBALD, *b.* Sept. 3rd, 1953; ed. at Eton.

SISTER LIVING.

Hon. Janet Anne, *b.* 1946.

WIDOW LIVING OF SEVENTH BARON.

ANNE (*Anne, Baroness Macdonald*) (Armadale Castle, Isle of Skye; Ostaig House, Isle of Skye), only da. of the late Alfred Whitaker: *m.* 1945, the 7th Baron, who *d.* 1970.

PREDECESSORS.—[1] DONALD MacDonald, of Slate; cr. a *Baronet* of Nova Scotia 1625, with a special clause of precedency, placing him second of that order in Scotland; *d.* 1643; *s.* by his son [2] Sir JAMES, 2nd Bt.; joined the Marquess of Montrose 1645, and sent some of his men to assist Charles II. when he marched into England in 1651: *d.* 1678; *s.* by his son [3] Sir DONALD, 3rd Bt.; *d.* 1695; *s.* by his son [4] Sir DONALD, 4th Bt.; joined the Rebellion of 1715, and was attainted; *d.* 1718; *s.* by his son [5] Sir DONALD, 5th Bt.; *d.* unmarried 1720; *s.* by his uncle [6] Sir JAMES, 6th Bt.; *d.* 1723; *s.* by his son [7] Sir ALEXANDER, 7th Bt., for whom as "Alexander Macdonald of Macdonald" the family estates were re-erected into a feudal Barony of Macdonald 1727; *d.* 1746; *s.* by his el. son [8] Sir JAMES, 8th Bt.; *d.* unmarried 1766; *s.* by his brother [9] Sir ALEXANDER, 9th Bt.; cr. *Baron Macdonald,* of Slate, co. Antrim (peerage of Ireland) 1776; *d.* 1795; *s.* by his el. son [10] ALEXANDER WENTWORTH, 2nd Baron; *d.* 1824; *s.* by his brother [11] GODFREY, 3rd Baron; a Maj.-Gen. in the Army; assumed in 1814 by Roy. licence the additional surname of Bosville and discontinued it by Roy. licence 1824; *m.* (in England) Dec. 15th, 1803, Louisa Maria La Coast, who *d.* 1835, ward of Farley Edsir; *d.* 1832, when (according to a decree of the Court of Session in June 1910) the Scottish Baronetcy passed *de jure* to Alexander William Bosville (*b.* Sept. 12th, 1800, before the date of his parents' English marriage, but according to the law of Scotland legitimated by that marriage) [see Bosville Macdonald, Bt.]: *s.* in the Irish peerage by his el. son (born after the marriage) [12] GODFREY WILLIAM WENTWORTH, 4th Baron; *b.* 1809: *m.* 1845, Maria Anne, who *d.* 1892, dau. of George Thomas Wyndham, of Cromer Hall, Norfolk; *d.* 1863; *s.* by his son [13] SOMERLED JAMES BRUDENELL, 5th Baron; *d.* 1874; *s.* by his brother [14] RONALD ARCHIBALD, 6th Baron, *b.* 1853: *m.* 1875, Louisa, who *d.* 1922, dau. of Col. George William Holmes Ross, of Cromarty; *d.* 1947; *s.* by his grandson [15] ALEXANDER GODFREY, *MBE, TD* (son of the late Hon. Godfrey Evan Hugh Macdonald, who *d.* (killed in action) 1914, 7th Baron, *b.* 1909; Maj. Queen's Own Cameron Highlanders; Lord Lieut. for Inverness-shire 1952-70: *m.* 1945, Anne, only da. of the late Alfred Whitaker; *d.* 1970; *s.* by his el. son [16] GODFREY JAMES, 8th Baron and present peer.

MACDONALD OF GWAENYSGOR, BARON. (Macdonald.) [Baron U.K. 1949.]

GORDON RAMSAY MACDONALD, 2nd Baron; *b.* Oct. 16th, 1915; *s.* 1966; ed. at Upholland Gram. Sch., and Manchester Univ. (MA); UK Trade Commr. in Australia 1947-53 and Managing Dir. Tube Investments Ltd. (now Plessey Co.); Ch. Exec., Hayek Engineering and Consultancy Group; 1939-45 War in Burma (despatches), Malaya, India and Middle East as Maj. RA and a GSO: *m.* 1941, Leslie Margaret, da. of John Edward Taylor, of Rainford, Lancs., and has issue.

Residence,—The Lodge, Pyebush Lane, Beaconsfield, Bucks.

DAUGHTERS LIVING.
Hon. Susan, *b.* 1947: *m.* 1968, David Hensley Adair Stride, of 80, Clarendon Drive, Putney, SW15, and has issue living, Toby David Macdonald, *b.* 1972,—Jessica Charlotte Macdonald, *b.* 1970.
Hon. Helen Margaret, *b.* 1950.
Hon. Marylyn Jane, *b.* 1951.

BROTHER LIVING
Hon. KENNETH LEWIS, *b.* Feb. 3rd, 1921; Private Sec. and ADC to Gov. of Newfoundland 1946-50; is a Business Exec., and a Dir. of cos.; 1939-45 War with RAF Coastal Command in N. Africa, Italy, Sicily, Middle East, and NW Europe: *m.* 1952, Maureen, only da. of David Watson-Allan, of Churston Ferrers, Devon, and has issue living, Sarah Margaret *b.* 1954: *m.* 1974, David Henry Waldron,—Laura Jane, *b.* 1966. *Residence,*—5, Thornby Av., Solihull, Warwicks.

SISTERS LIVING.
Hon. Elsie, *b.* 1917; a JP for Cardiff, a Member of BBC Council of Wales, of Board of Welsh Museum, and of British Arts Council Welsh Board, Charity Review Organiser, S. Wales, and CEO, Cancer Education: *m.* 1938, the Rev. Llywelyn Williams, MP, who *d.* 1965, and has issue living, Richard Gareth Macdonald, *b.* 1946,—Margaret Eryl Macdonald, *b.* 1942. *Residence,*—34, Heol Uchaf, Rhiwbina, Cardiff.
Hon. Glenys, *b.* 1923; a JP for Lancs.: *m.* 1949, Robert Fullard, BSc, and has issue living, Judith Mary, *b.* 1952,—Catherine Elizabeth, *b.* 1955. *Residence,*—2, Thornley Lane, Grotton, Oldham.

PREDECESSOR.—[1] *Sir* GORDON Macdonald, *KCMG, PC,* son of Thomas Macdonald, of Gwaenysgor, Flintshire; *b.* 1888; Miners' Agent and Leader, Lancs. and Cheshire Fedn. of Gt. Britain 1924; Chm. of Cttees., House of Commons 1934-41, Gov. of Newfoundland 1946-49, Paymaster-Gen. 1949-51; MP for Ince Div. of Lancs. (*Lab.*) 1929-42: cr. *Baron Macdonald of Gwaenysgor,* of Gwaenysgor, co. Flint (peerage of UK) 1949: *m.* 1913, Mary, who *d.* 1967, da. of William Lewis, of Blaenau Festiniog; *d.* 1966; *s.* by his el. son [2] GORDON RAMSAY, 2nd Baron and present peer.

Macduff, Earl of, son of Duke of Fife.

McFADZEAN, BARON. (McFadzean.) [Life Baron 1966.]

Endeavour

WILLIAM HUNTER McFADZEAN, son of the late Henry McFadzean, of Stranraer; *b.* Dec. 17th, 1903; ed. at Stranraer Acad. and High Sch., and Glasgow Univ.; a Chartered Accountant, and a Comp.I.E.E.; Pres. of F.B.I. 1959-61, British Electrical Power Convention 1961-62, and British Nuclear Forum 1964-66, Vice-Pres. of British-Swedish Chamber of Commerce 1963, and Middle East Assocn. and City of London Soc. 1965, Chm. of Industrial Fedn. of EFTA 1960-63, of Export Council for Europe 1960-64 (Hon. Pres. 1964), and of British National Export Council and Commonwealth Export Council 1964-66 (Pres. 1966-68), a Member of Council of Inst. of Dirs. 1954 (Member of Council 1954-74), of Min. of Labour Advisory Board on Resettlement of Ex-Regulars 1957-60, of Board of Trade Advisory Council on Middle East Trade 1958-60, of Min. of Transport's Shipping Advisory Panel 1962-64, of Court of British Shippers Council 1964, of Council Anglo-Danish Soc. (Chm. 1969), and of Council Confedn. of British Industry 1965, of Advisory Cttee. for the Queen's Award to Industry 1965-67, and of Council Foreign Bondholders 1968; Chm. of British Insulated Callender's Construction Co., Ltd., 1952-64, of British Insulated Callender's Cables, Ltd. (Managing Dir. 1954-61), of British Insulated Callender's (Submarine Cables), Ltd., 1954-73; Hon Life Pres. 1973); of Canada Life Unit Trust Managers, Ltd., 1971, and of British Insulated Callender's Cables Finance, NV 1971-73; Dep. Chm. of RTZ/BICC Aluminium Holdings, Ltd., 1967-73, and of The Canada Life Assurance Co. of Great Britain 1971; a Dir. of Midland Bank, Ltd. since 1959 (Dep. Chm. 1968) of Anglesey Aluminium, Ltd., 1968-73, of Canada Life Assurance Co. 1969, of Midland Bank Executor & Trustee Co. Ltd., 1959-67, of English Electric Co. Ltd. 1966-68, of The Steel Co. of Wales, Ltd. 1966-67, and of Canadian Imperial Bank of Commerce 1967-74; Pres. Coal Trade Benevolent Assocn. 1967-68, of Electrical and Electronic Industries Benevolent Assocn. 1968-69, and of British Shippers, Council 1968-71; Chm. of Review Cttee. for The Queen's Award to Industry for 1970, of Standard Broadcasting Corpn. (UK) Ltd. 1972, of Broadcasting Marketing Sers., and of Scurry Rainbow (UK) Ltd. 1974; JDipMA; Grand Cdr. of Order of Dannebrog, of Denmark; Grand Officer Order of Prince Henry the Navigator of Portugal; *cr.* Knt. 1960 and *Baron McFadzean,* of Woldingham, co. Surrey (Life Baron) 1966: *m.* 1933, Eileen, el. da. of Arthur Gordon, of Blundellsands, Lancs., and has issue.

Arms,—Vert a saltire argent between in chief a thistle slipped and leaved, in base a thunder bolt, and in fess two garbs or banded gules. Crest,—A lion's gamb gules grasping a caduceu or, the serpents vert within an orle of wild flowers proper. Supporters,—On either side a lion ver supporting a caduceus or the serpents vert.

Residences,—Garthland, Woldingham, Surrey, CR3 7DH; 146, Whitehall Court, SWIA 2EL. *Clubs*—Carlton, MCC.

SON LIVING.

Hon. Gordon Barry (Raeburn, Woldingham, Surrey), *b.* 1937; ed. at Winchester, and Ch. Ch., Oxford (MA); FCA: *m.* 1968, Julia Maxine, da. of Max Dillon, of Pymble, Sydney, NSW, and has issue.

DAUGHTER LIVING.

Hon. Angela Caroline, *b.* 1942: *m.* 1963, Robin Vyvyan Carter Donald, of Osborne House, Bathampton, Bath, and has issue.

McGOWAN, BARON. (McGowan.) [Baron U.K. 1937.]

Union is strength.

HARRY DUNCAN CORY McGOWAN, 3rd Baron; *b.* July 20th, 1938; ed. at Eton: *m.* 1962, Lady Gillian Angela Pepys, da. of 7th Earl of Cottenham, and has issue.

Arms,—Per saltire argent and azure two lions rampant in pale gules and as many horseshoes in fesse proper. Crest,—A tower or, between two horseshoes proper. Supporters,—*Dexter*, a figure representing St. Barbara proper, holding in the exterior hand a tower or ; *sinister*, a figure representing St. Kentigern proper, holding in the exterior hand his crozier or.

Residence,—Highway House, Lower Froyle, Alton, Hants. *Club,*—Boodle's.

SON LIVING.

Hon. HARRY JOHN CHARLES, *b.* June 23rd, 1971.

DAUGHTERS LIVING.

Hon. Emma Louise Angela, *b.* 1963.
Hon. Annabel Kate Cory, *b.* 1965.

BROTHERS LIVING.

Hon. Dominic James Wilson, *b.* 1951.
Hon. Mungo Alexander Cansh, *b.* 1956.

SISTERS LIVING.

Hon. Moana Elizabeth Jean, *b.* 1948.
Hon. Catriona Carmen Harriet, *b.* 1953.

UNCLE LIVING. (*Son of 1st Baron.*)

Hon. William Johnston, *TD*, *b.* 1909; ed. at Uppingham, and Clare Coll., Camb.; formerly Capt. Notts Yeo. (Sherwood Rangers); European War 1939-43 (wounded): *m.* 1946, Helen Myrtle Dorothy, *M.B.E.*, *J.P.*, dau. of the late Arthur Atherley, J.P., D.L., of Landguard Manor, Isle of Wight, and widow of Col. Edward Orlando Kellett, D.S.O., M.P., and has issue living, Fiona Victoria Jean Atherley (*Hon. Mrs. Charles H. Allsopp*), *b.* 1947: *m.* 1968, the Hon. Charles Henry Allsopp [see B. Hindlip]. *Residence,*—32, Marlborough Place, NW8. *Club,*—White's.

AUNT LIVING. (*Daughter of 1st Baron.*)

Hon. Agnes Wilson, *b.* 1913: *m.* 1st, 1936 (m. diss. 1949), Maj. Dermot Ralph Daly, Scots Guards [B. Clanmorris, colls.]; 2ndly, 1949, Maj. George Berkeley Sheffield, Queen's Own Yorkshire Dragoons (TA), who *d.* 1968 [see Sheffield, Bt., colls.], and has issue living, (by 1st m.) James Bowes (of Evendine House, Colwall, Malvern, Worcs.), *b.* 1939: *m.* 1962, Carole Mary, da. of Sir Arthur William Milborne-Swinnerton-Pilkington, 13th Bt.—(by 2nd m.) [see Sheffield, Bt., colls.]. *Residence,*—Ramsden House, Ramsden, Oxon., OX7 3AX.

WIDOW LIVING OF SECOND BARON.

CARMEN (*Dowager, Baroness McGowan*) (Bragborough Hall, Rugby; 7, Princes Gate, SW7), da. of Sir (James) Herbert Cory, 1st Bt., cr. 1919: *m.* 1937, the 2nd Baron, who *d.* 1966.

PREDECESSORS.—[1] *Sir* HARRY DUNCAN McGowan, *K.B.E.*, son of the late Henry McGowan, of Glasgow ; *b.* 1874 ; Hon. Pres. (Chm. 1930-50) of Imperial Chemical Industries Ltd., Pres. of So. of Chemical Industry 1931, of Institute of Fuel 1934-5, and of British Standards Institution 1947 ; *cr.* *Baron McGowan,* of Ardeer, co. Ayr (peerage of U.K.) 1937: *m.* 1903, Jean Boyle, who *d.* 1952, dau. of the late William Young, of Paisley; *d.* 1961; *s.* by his el. son [2] HARRY WILSON, 2nd Baron, *b.* 1906: *m.* 1937, Carmen, da. of Sir (James) Herbert Cory, 1st Bt., cr. 1919; *d.* 1966; *s.* by his el. son [3] HARRY DUCAN CORY, 3rd Baron and present peer.

MACKIE OF BENSHIE, BARON. (Mackie) [Life Baron 1974.]

GEORGE YULL MACKIE, *CBE, DSO, DFC*, son of the late Maitland Mackie, OBE; *b.* July 10th, 1919; ed. at Aberdeen Gram. Sch., and Aberdeen Univ.; 1939-45 War with Bomber Command RAF (DSO, DFC); Farmer; Chm. of Scottish Liberal Party 1965-70 (Vice-Chm. 1960-65); MP for Caithness and Sutherland (*L*) 1964-66; Chm. Caithness Glass Ltd., since 1966, and Caithness Cheese since 1969; a Member of National and Local Cttees. for Scotland, of NFU, and of Scottish Advisory Cttee. of British Council; cr. DSO 1944, CBE (Civil) 1971, and *Baron Mackie of Benshie*, of Kirriemuir, co. Angus (Life Baron) 1974: *m.* 1944, Lindsay, da. of the late Alexander Sharp, Advocate, of Aberdeen, and has issue.

Residence,—Ballinshoe, Kirriemuir, Angus, DD8 5QG. *Clubs.*—Garrick, Farmers', Scottish Liberal (Edinburgh).

DAUGHTERS LIVING.

Hon. Lindsay Mary, *b.* 1945.
Hon. Diana Lyall, *b.* 1946: *m.* 1968, John Carlyle Hope, of 3, St. Bernard Cres., Edinburgh.
Hon. Jeannie Felicia, *b.* 1953.

MACKINTOSH OF HALIFAX, VISCOUNT. (Mackintosh.) [Viscount U.K. 1957, Bt. U.K. 1935.]

JOHN MACKINTOSH, 2nd Viscount, and 2nd Baronet, b. Oct. 7th, 1921; s. 1964; ed. at Bedales, and at Trin. Coll., USA; a Dir. of John Mackintosh & Son, Ltd., and of Tom Smith & Co., Ltd., Dist. Member for Nat Savings (Vice-Chm. of E. Regional Industrial Cttee. & Dep. Regional Member), Chm. Norwich Savings Cttee.; Hon. Treasurer, London Cttee. World Council Christian Education; Chm. of Confectioners' Benevolent Fund since 1967, and of Inst. of Dirs. (Norfolk and Suffolk Branch) since 1968: m. 1st, 1946 (m. diss. 1956), Bronda, only da. of the late Louis John Fibiger; 2ndly, 1956, Gwynneth Charlesworth, da. of Charles H. Gledhill, of Glengarth, Rawson Av., Halifax, and has issue by 1st and 2nd m.

Arms,—Or, on a chevron between two lions rampant in chief and a lymphad in base sable, a bezant charged with a representation of the head of St. John the Baptist proper, between two hearts of the field. Crest,—Upon a rock proper, charged with two roses argent, barbed and seeded, a cat sejant also proper, Supporters.—On either side a squirrel proper, suspended from the neck by a cord a purse or.

Residence,—The Old Hall, Barford, Norwich, NR4 4AY.

SONS LIVING. (By 2nd marriage.)
Hon. (JOHN) CLIVE, b. Sept. 9th, 1958.
Hon. Graham Charles, b. 1964.

DAUGHTERS LIVING. (By 1st marriage.)
Hon. Diana Mary, b. 1947.
Hon. Elizabeth Constance, b. 1950: m. 1972, Timothy Cutting.

SISTER LIVING.
Hon. Mary, b. 1927; is a JP for Norfolk: m. 1949, (Charles) Michael Watt, and has issue living, Charles Jonathan, b. 1950,—Henry Donald b. 1962,—Susan Mary, b. 1953. Residence,—Wychwood House, Hethersett, nr. Norwich, Norfolk (NOR 42X).

WIDOW LIVING OF FIRST VISCOUNT.
Constance (Emily) (Constance Viscountess Mackintosh of Halifax), (Thickthorn Hall, Hethersett, Norwich, NOR 44X), da. of the late Edgar Cooper Stoneham, OBE, of Acton, W3: m. 1916, the 1st Viscount, who d. 1964.

PREDECESSOR,—[1] Sir HAROLD VINCENT Mackintosh, son of John Mackintosh, JP, of Greystones, Halifax; b. 1891; Chm. of John Mackintosh & Sons Ltd., toffee manufacturers, of Halifax; Chm. of National Savings Cttee. 1943-64, and Pres. 1958-64; cr. a Baronet 1935, Baron Mackintosh of Halifax, of Hethersett, co. Norfolk (peerage of UK) 1948, and Viscount Mackintosh of Halifax, of Hethersett, co. Norfolk (peerage of UK) 1957: m. 1916, Constance Emily, da. of Edgar Cooper Stoneham, OBE, of Acton, W3; d. 1964; s. by his only son [2] JOHN, 2nd Viscount and present peer; also Baron Mackintosh of Halifax.

MACLAY, BARON. (Maclay.) [Baron U.K. 1922, Bt. U.K. 1914.]

JOSEPH PATON MACLAY, 3rd Baron 3rd Baronet; b. April 11th, 1942; s. 1969; ed. at Winchester; Man. Dir. Denholm Maclay Co., Ltd., and a Dir. of Milton Shipping Co., Ltd.

Arms,—Or, a lion rampant azure, armed and langued gules, resting its sinister paw on an anchor sable, all within an orle of the second. Crest,—A lymphad sails furled sable, flagged proper. Supporters,—Two wolves proper, each gorged with a chain, pendant therefrom an escutcheon argent, charged with a salmon on its back holding a ring in its mouth proper.

Residences,—Duchal, Kilmacolm, Renfrewshire; Milton, Kilmacolm, Renfrewshire.

BROTHERS LIVING.
Hon. DAVID MILTON (12, Langton St., SW10), b. March 21st, 1944; ed. at Winchester: m. 1968, Valerie, da. of the late Lt.-Cdr. J. P. Fyfe, of Kinkell, St. Andrews, Fife, and has issue living, Duncan, b. 1974.
Hon. Angus Grenfell (Westruther Mains, Gordon, Berwicks.), b. 1945; ed. at Winchester: m. 1970, the Hon. Elizabeth Victoria Baillie, el. da. of the 3rd Baron Burton, and has issue living, Robert Michael, b. 1972.

SISTERS LIVING.

Hon. Sarah, *b.* 1937: *m.* 1968, David Richard Hayes, of Factors House, Pityulish, Aviemore, Invernessshire [see Muir, Bt.].

Hon. Lucy, *b.* 1938: *m.* 1966, James Ian Alexander Robertson, of Glenside Farm, Plean, Stirlingshire, and has issue living, Hugh Sebastian, *b.* 1967,—David Ian, *b.* 1969, Dominic James, *b.* 1973,—Anna Marcelle, *b.* 1971.

UNCLE LIVING. (*Son of First Baron.*)

Hon. John Scott, *KT, CH, CMG, PC* (*Viscount Muirshiel*), *b.* 1905; *cr.* Viscount Muirshiel 1964 [see that title].

WIDOW LIVING OF SON OF FIRST BARON.

Dorothy (Apple Trees, St. Annes Fruit Farm, Chapel Row, Bucklebury, RG7 6PB), da. of the late William Lennox, WS: *m.* 1928, the Hon. Walter Symington Maclay, CB, OBE, MD, who *d.* 1964, and has issue living [see colls. infra]:—

WIDOW LIVING OF SECOND BARON.

NANCY MARGARET (*Baroness Maclay*), (Duchal, Kilmacolm, Renfrewshire, and Milton, Kilmacolm, Renfrewshire), da. of Robert Coventry Greig, of Hall of Caldwell, Uplawnmoor, Renfrewshire: *m.* 1936, the 2nd Baron, who *d.* 1969.

COLLATERAL BRANCH LIVING.

Issue of the late Hon. Walter Symington Maclay, CB, OBE, MD, 4th son of 1st Baron, *b.* 1901, *d.* 1964: *m.* 1928, Dorothy (ante), da. of the late William Lennox, WS:—

Walter Strang Symington (Findings, Hambledon, Surrey), *b.* 1931; ed. at Winchester, and at St. John's Coll., Camb. (MA, MB, BChir): *m.* 1956, Elizabeth Ann, el. da. of Willis C. Cooper, of Tintern, Esher Close, Surrey, and has issue living, Andrew Strang, *b.* 1958,—Christopher Willis, *b.* 1964,—Janet Susan, *b.* 1960.——John Lennox Sim (40, Kensington Sq., W8) *b.* 1937.——Mark Paton (Pentridge House, Salisbury, Wilts), *b.* 1943: *m.* 1967, Elizabeth Ruth, da. of Worsfold McClenaghan, of Sladen Green, Binley, Andover, and has issue living, James Paton, *b.* 1971,—Alasdair Worsfold, *b.* 1973.——(Shirley) Georgina, *b.* 1933: *m.* 1955, Robert David Ogden, of Greystones, Badby, Northants, and has issue living, Robert Nicholas, *b.* 1958,—Joseph Jeremy (twin), *b.* 1958,—Benjamin Patrick, *b.* 1966,—Emma Maclay, *b.* 1961.

PREDECESSORS.—[1] *Rt Hon.* JOSEPH PATON Maclay, son of the late Ebenezer Maclay, of Glasgow; *b.* 1857; sometime Chm. of Maclay & Macintyre, Ltd., shipowners, of 21, Bothwell Street, Glasgow; Min. of Shipping and a Member of War Cabinet 1916-21; *cr.* a *Baronet* 1914, and *Baron Maclay*, of Glasgow, co. Lanark (peerage of United Kingdom) 1922: *m.* 1889, Martha, who *d.* 1929, dau. of William Strang, manufacturer of Glasgow; *d.* 1951; *s.* by his el. surviving son [2] JOSEPH PATON, *KBE*, 2nd Baron, *b.* 1899; MP for Paisley (L.) 1931-45: *m.* 1936, Nancy Margaret, da. of Robert Coventry Greig, of Hall of Caldwell, Uplawnmoor, Renfrewshire; *d.* 1969; *s.* by his el. son [3] JOSEPH PATON, 3rd Baron and present peer.

MACLEAN, BARON. (Maclean.) [Life Baron 1971, Bt. (NS) 1631].

CHARLES HECTOR FITZROY MACLEAN, *KT GCVO, KBE, PC, Life Baron,* and 11th *Baronet,* son of the late Maj. Hector Fitzroy Maclean, SG, el. son of 10th baronet; *b.* May 5th, 1916; *s.* to Baronetcy 1936; ed. at Canford Sch., Wimborne; 27th Chief of the Clan Maclean, Maj. (ret.) SG, a JP for co. Argyll, and Brig. of Queen's Body Guard for Scotland (R. Co. of Archers); Lord Lieut. of Argyll since 1954; Chief Scout of the Commonwealth 1959-75; Lord Chamberlain of the Household since 1971; 1939-45 War (despatches); KBE (Civil) 1967, KT 1969, *Baron Maclean,* of Duart and Morvern, co. Argyll (Life Baron) 1971, and PC and GCVO 1971: *m.* 1941, Joan Elizabeth, da. of the late Capt. Francis Thomas Mann [see Mann, Bt., colls.], and has issue.

Arms,—Quarterly: 1st, argent, a rock gules; 2nd argent, a dexter hand fessewise couped gules holding a cross-crosslet fitchée in pale azure; 3rd, or, a lymphad, oars in saltire, sails furled, sable, flagged gules; 4th, argent, a salmon naiant proper, in chief two eagles' heads erased respectant gules. **Crest,**—A tower embattled argent. **Supporters,**—*Dexter,* a seal proper; *sinister,* an ostrich with a horseshoe in its beak proper.

Residences,—St. James's Palace, SW1; Duart Castle, Isle of Mull.　*Clubs,*—Guards', Pratt's, Royal Highland Yacht, Puffin's.

(*In remainder to Baronetcy only.*)

SON LIVING.

Hon. LACHLAN HECTOR CHARLES (Bolehill, Mytchett Place Rd., Mytchett, Camberley, Surrey), *b.* Aug. 25th, 1942; Maj. SG: *m.* 1966, Mary Helen, el. da. of William Gordon Gordon, of Lude, Blair Atholl, Perths., and has issue living, Emma Mary, *b.* 1967.

DAUGHTER LIVING.

Hon. Janet Elizabeth, *b.* 1944: *m.* 1974, Capt. Nicholas M. L. Barnes, Scots Gds.

SISTER LIVING.

Joan Sybil, *b.* 1909: *m.* 1940, Lt.-Col. David Graham-Campbell, late KRRC, son of the late Sir Rollo Frederick Graham-Campbell, and has issue living, John Malcolm, *b.* 1941; ed. at Eton and Trin. Coll., Camb. (MA); ACA: *m.* 1969, Margaret Britton, and has issue living, Katherine Louise *b.* 1971, Harriet Jane *b.* 1974,—James Alastair, *b.* 1947; ed. at Eton and Trin. Coll., Camb. (MA),—Angus Charles David, *b.* 1949, ed. at Eton and Trin. Coll., Camb. (MA). *Residences,*—Fernbank, Crathes, Kincardineshire; Teangue, Isle of Skye.

AUNT LIVING. *(Daughter of 10th baronet).*

Finovola Marianne Eleanor, *b.* 1887: *m.* 1st, 1908, Capt. Roger Cordy-Simpson, W. Kent Yeo., who *d.* 1919; 2ndly, 1922, Brig. Francis William Bullock-Marsham, DSO, MC, who *d.* 1971 [E. Romney, colls.], and has issue living, (by 1st m.) John Roger, *CBE, MC, b.* 1910; Col. 13th/18th R. Hussars since 1968; OBE (Mil) 1953, CBE (Mil) 1958; *m.* 1st, 1939, Ursula, only da. of Maj. A. West, of Barcote Manor, Faringdon, Berks.; 2ndly, 1959, Diana, da. of Maj. Evan David, MC, of Brynderwen, Llandaff. *Residences,*—Overblow, Shorne, Gravesend, Kent; Woodside Cottage, Aros, Isle of Mull.

COLLATERAL BRANCH LIVING.

Issue of the late Capt. Charles Lachlan Maclean, RN, 2nd son of 10th baronet, *b.* 1874, *d.* 1958: *m.* 1st, 1904, the Hon. Philadelphia Sybil Robertson, who *d.* 1945, da. of the late Baron Robertson, a Lord of Appeal in Ordinary; 2ndly, 1952, Christian Mary (of Penare House, Manaccan, Helston, Cornwall), da. of the Rev. M. Taggart, of Lyne, Peebleshire, and widow of Hedley Briggs-Constable:—

(By 1st m.) Philadelphia Constance, *b.* 1905: *m.* 1926, Richard Kennedy Lingard Guthrie, and has issue living, Philadelphia Ann, *b.* 1927,—Joanna Christian, *b.* 1930,—Elisabeth, *b.* 1933. *Residence,*— The Malt House, Ampney Crucis, Cirencester, Glos.——Finovola Sybil, *b.* 1907: *m.* 1929, Henry Norman Wilson, formerly Lt. BlackWatch (Roy. Highlanders), and has issue living, Charles Jeremp, *b.* 1930,—Robert Malcolm, *b,* 1935. *Residence,*—Princeland, Coupar Angus, Perths.

PREDECESSORS.—[1] *Sir* LACHLAN Maclean of Morvern, son and heir of Hector Og Maclean of Duart; a zealous supporter of Charles I; cr. a Bt. 1631, with remainder to his heirs male whatsoever: *m.* Mary, da. of Roderick Macleod of Macleod; *d.* 1649; *s.* by his el. son [2] *Sir* HECTOR, 2nd Bt.; *b.* about 1625; *d.* unm., killed fighting for Royal cause at Innerkeithing 1651; *s.* by his brother [3] *Sir* ALLAN, 3rd Bt.; *b.* about 1637: *m.* Giles, da. of John Macleod of Macleod; *d.* 1674; *s.* by his only son [4] *Sir* JOHN, 4th Bt.; present with his clan at Killiecrankie 1689 and Sheriffmuir 1715: *m.* about 1704 Mary, da. of Sir Aeneas Macpherson of Invereshie; *d.* about 1719; *s.* by his son [5] *Sir* HECTOR, 5th Bt.; *b.* about 1704; imprisoned in Tower of London 1745-47 as a Jacobite; *d.* unm. 1751; *s.* by his kinsman [6] *Sir* ALLAN, 6th Bt., (gt.-grandson of Donald Maclean of Brolas, half-brother of 1st Bt.): *m.* Una, da. of Hector Maclean of Coll; *d.* 1783; *s.* by his kinsman [7] *Sir* HECTOR, 7th Bt. (grandson of Hector Og, gt.-uncle of 6th Bt.); *d.* unm. 1818; *s.* by his half-brother [8] *Sir* FITZROY JEFFREYS GRAFTON, 8th Bt.; Lt.-Gen.; present at capture of Martinique and Guadaloupe: *m.* 1st, 1794, Elizabeth, who *d.* 1832, da. of Charles Kidd, and widow of John Bishop of Barbados; 2ndly, 1838, Frances, who *d.* 1843, da. of the Rev. Henry Watkins, and widow of Henry Campion; *d.* 1847; *s.* by his el. son [9] *Sir* CHARLES FITZROY, 9th Bt.; *b.* 1798; Col.: *m.* 1831, Emily Eleanor, who *d.* 1838, da. of the Rev. Canon the Hon. Jacob Marsham, DD [E. Romney]; *d.* 1883; *s.* by his son [10] *Sir* FITZROY DONALD, *KCB*, 10th Bt., *b.* 1835; Ch. of Clan Maclean; recovered Duart Castle 1910; Comdg. 13 H.; Crimean War: *m.* 1872, Constance Marianne, who *d.* 1920, da. of George Holland Ackers, of Moreton Hall, Ches.; *d.* 1936; *s.* by his grandson, [11] *Sir* CHARLES HECTOR FITZROY, 11th Bt., who was cr. *Baron Maclean,* of Duart and Morvern, 1971, Life Baron and 11th Bt.

McLEAVY, BARON. (McLeavy.) [Life Baron 1967.]

FRANK McLEAVY, son of the late John McLeavy, of Congleton, Cheshire; *b.* Jan. 1st, 1899; ed. at Elementary Sch., and Evening Insts.; a JP (Middlesex Area), of Greater London; Road Passenger Transport Officer 1922-45; co. Councillor 1934-51 and co. Alderman 1938-51 Cheshire; Mayor of Bebington 1939-41; MP for Bradford East (*Lab.*) 1945-66; cr. *Baron McLeavy,* of City of Bradford (Life Baron) 1967: *m.* 1924, Mary, da. of the late George Waring, of Rock Ferry, Birkenhead, and has issue.

Residence,—9, Sheridan Terr., Whitton Avenue West, Northolt, Middlesex.

SON LIVING.

Hon. Frank Waring (23, West End Rise, Horsforth, Leeds), *b.* 1925: *m.* 1954, Verena, da. of Emil Lüscher, of Unterkulm, Switzerland, and has issue.

DAUGHTER LIVING.

Hon. Heather, *b.* 1929: *m.* 1955, Patrick William Rapley, of 7, Salcombe Drive, Earley, Reading, and has issue.

WIDOW LIVING OF SON OF LIFE BARON.

Janet Elizabeth (40, Ruskin Drive, Morecambe, Lancs.), da. of Harry Ogden: *m.* 1958, the Hon. Douglas John McLeavy, who *d.* 1969, and has issue.

MACLEOD OF BORVE, BARONESS. (Macleod.) [Life Baroness 1971.]

EVELYN HESTER MACLEOD, da. of the late Rev. Gervase Vanneck Blois [see Blois, Bt., colls.]; *b.* Feb. 19th, 1915; JP for Middx.; first Chm. of National Gas Consumers' Council since 1972; cr. *Baroness Macleod of Borve,* of Borve, Isle of Lewis (Life Baroness) 1971: *m.* 1st, 1937, Mervyn Charles Mason, who *d.* (killed by enemy action) 1940; 2ndly, 1941, the Rt. Hon. Iain Norman Macleod, MP, who *d.* 1970, and has issue by 2nd m.

Residence,—14, Tufton Court, Westminster, S.W.1.

SON LIVING (By 2nd m.)

Hon. Torquil Anthony Ross, *b.* 1942; ed. at Harrow: *m.* 1967 (m. diss. 1973) (Elizabeth) Meriol, Trevor, and has issue living, Iain Ross, *b.* 1970.

DAUGHTER LIVING (By 2nd m.)

Hon. Diana Hester. *b.* 1944; *m.* 1968 David Heimann, of Hertfordshire House, Coleshill, Bucks., and has issue living, Hugo Iain Philip, *b.* 1973.

MACLEOD OF FUINARY, BARON. (MacLeod.) [Life Baron 1967, Bt. U.K. 1924.]

Very Rev. GEORGE FIELDEN MACLEOD, *MC,
DD, Life Baron* and 4th Baronet; *b.* June 17th,
1895; *s.* to the Baronetcy 1944; ed. at Win-
chester, and Oriel Coll., Oxford (BA, Hon.
Fellow); DD Glasgow; Min. of St. Cuthberts,
Edinburgh 1926-30, and of Govan, Glasgow
1930-38; Leader of Iona Community 1938-67.
Moderator of Gen. Assembly of Church of Scot-
land 1956-57, since when Extra Chap. to HM in
Scotland; 1914-18 War as temp. Capt. Argyll
and Sutherland Highlanders (MC); *cr. Baron
MacLeod of Fuinary,* of Fuinary in Morven, co.
Argyll (Life Baron) 1967: *m.* 1948, Lorna Helen
Janet, da. of the Rev. Donald MacLeod, of
Balvonie of Inshes, Inverness, and has issue.

Arms,—Azure, a castle triple-towered argent, masoned sable, windows and portcullis gules, on a
chief of the second an open book proper, leaved of the fourth.   Crest—A bull's head cabossed sable,
horned or, between two keys wards uppermost of the last.
Residence,—23, Learmonth Terr., Edinburgh, 4.

SONS LIVING.
Hon. JOHN MAXWELL NORMAN, *b.* Feb. 23rd, 1952; *h.a.* to Baronetcy.
Hon. Neil David, *b.* 1959.
DAUGHTER LIVING.
Hon. Eva Mary Ellen, *b.* 1950.
SISTER LIVING.
Ellen, *MBE, b.* 1893; MBE (Civil) 1968: *m.* 1918, the Rev. James Alan Cameron Murray, BD, who
d. 1966, and has issue living, Alan Norman MacLeod, *b.* 1925,—Ellen Catriona Cameron, *b.* 1922.
Residence,—56, Learmouth Court, Edinburgh, 4.
PREDECESSORS.—[1] JOHN MACKINTOSH MacLeod, son of the Very Rev. Norman MacLeod,
DD, of Barony Church, Glasgow, and Dean of the Order of the Thistle; *b.* 1857; MP for Central Div.
of Glasgow (*Co. U.*) 1915-18 and Kelvingrove 1918-22; cr. a Baronet 1924: *m.* 1888, Edith, who *d.*
1942, da. of Joshua Fielden, of Todmorden and Nutfield Priory, Redhill, Surrey; *d.* 1934; *s.* by his
son [2] JOHN MACKINTOSH, 2nd Bt., *b.* 1891; Unicorn Pursuivant of Arms 1925-29 and Rothesay
Herald 1929-39: *m.* 1918, Isa, who *d.* 1968, da. of Francesco Brusati, of Milan, Italy; *d.* 1939; *s.*
by his only son [3] IAN FRANCIS, 3rd Bt.; *b.* 1921; Capt. Intelligence Corps; *d.* (killed on active
service) 1944; *s.* by his uncle [4] *Very Rev.* GEORGE FIELDEN, 4th Bt.; *cr. Baron Macleod of
Fuinary,* of Fuinary in Morven, co. Argyll (Life Baron) 1967.

MACNAGHTEN, BARONY OF. (Macnaghten.) [Extinct 1913.]

WIDOW LIVING OF SON OF LIFE BARON.
Sybil Torbock, dau. of the late Col. Henry Graham, formerly 16th Lancers: *m.* 1st, 1912, Capt
the Hon. Maurice Patrick Macnaghten, who *d.* 1914; 2ndly, 1925, Major Gerald Aylmer, M.C.
who *d.* 1939, formerly Indian Army. *Resides in* South Africa.

McNAIR, BARON. (McNair.) [Baron U.K. 1955.]

(CLEMENT) JOHN McNAIR, 2nd Baron
b. Jan. 11th, 1915; *s.* 1975; ed. at Shrewsbury, and Balliol Coll., Oxford; 1939-45
War as Capt. RA, in Tunis and Italy:
m. 1941, Vera, da. of Theodore James
Faithfull, MRCVS, of Birmingham.
Arms,—Gules, three barrulets wavy argent surmounted of a lion rampant or, armed and langued azure,
between two thistleheads stalked and leved paleways of
the third. Crest—On a wreath of the liveries an ancient
ship under full sail, flagged azure, the sail emblazoned of
ensigns armorial as on the escutcheon. Supporters,—Two
Bedlington terriers proper.
Residence,—Orchard Close, Greenhill Rd., Sandford,
Som.

SONS LIVING.
Hon. DUNCAN JAMES, *b.* June 26th, 1947; ed. at
Bryanston.
Hon. William Samuel Angus, *b.* 1958.
DAUGHTER LIVING.
Hon. Josephine Margaret, *b.* 1949.
SISTERS LIVING.
Hon. Elizabeth Oona, *b.* 1913: *m.* 1939, Group Capt.
John Barrett Altham, CBE, of Ivy Cottage, Little
Shelford, Cambridge, and has issue living, James Edward
John (8A, Canterbury Close, Cambridge), *b.* 1941:
Danger in delay.
m. 1965, Patricia Mary Elizabeth, da. of Robert Gray,
of Holm Close, Baslow, Derbys., and has issue living, Joseph Robert Edward *b.* 1972,—David Thomas
Wale, *b.* 1945,—Jane Henrietta, *b.* 1940: *m.* 1960, Philippe Pierre de Marigny Lagesse, of 15, Queens-
dale Rd., W11, and has issue living, Pierre Arnaud Marc de Marigny *b.* 1963,—Marie Henriette de
Marigny, *b.* 1961,—Elizabeth Georgina, *b.* 1955.
Hon. Sheila Margaret Ramsay, *b.* 1918: *m.* 1946, John Barwell, and has issue living, Hugh John, *b.*
1949: *m.* 1973, Glynis Christine Rolfe,—Alice Marjorie Sheila, *b.* 1947: *m.* 1971, Franklyn Kimmel
Prochaska,—Lucy Elizabeth, *b.* 1951: *m.* 1973, Lloyd Herman Bernstein,—Claire Bridget, *b.* 1953.
Residence,—13, Cranmer Rd., Cambridge.

Hon. Elinor Ruth, *b.* 1924: *m.* 1955, Raymond Hanscomb, and has issue living, Benjamin Douglas *b.* 1956,—George Sebastian, *b.* 1965,—Emma Frances Mary, *b.* 1963. *Residence*,—Rosalie Farm Cowlinge, Newmarket, Suffolk.

PREDECESSOR,—[1] *Sir* ARNOLD DUNCAN McNAIR, *CBE, QC, LLD*, son of the late John McNair, of Court Lane, Dulwich Village, SE; *b.* 1885; Vice-Chancellor of Liverpool Univ. 1937-45; a Judge of Internat. Court of Justice 1946-55 (pres. 1952-55); Pres. Inst. of Internat. Law 1959-60; 1st Pres. of European Rights at Strasbourg 1959-65; *cr. Baron McNair*, of Gleniffer, co. Renfrew (peerage UK) 1955: *m.* 1912, Marjorie, who *d.* 1971, da. of the late Hon. Sir Clement Meacher Bailhache; *d.* 1975; *s.* by his only son [2] (CLEMENT) JOHN, 2nd Baron and present peer.

MACPHERSON OF DRUMOCHTER, BARON. (Macpherson.) [Baron U.K. 1951.]

Touch not this cat but a glove.

(JAMES) GORDON MACPHERSON, 2nd Baron; *b.* Jan. 22nd, 1924; *s.* 1965; ed. at Loretto, and at Wells House, Malvern; FRES, FRSA, FZS, a JP for Essex, and Chm. of Macpherson, Train & Co., Ltd., Food and Produce Importers and Exporters, and subsidiary and Assoc. Cos.; Chm. of West India Cttee, and of A. J. Macpherson & Co., Ltd., Bankers since 1973; Hon. Game Warden for the Sudan since 1974; a Member of London Chamber of Commerce since 1958; Pres. of British Importers Confedn. 1972; a Trustee of Head Injuries Rehabilitation Trust 1970; Freeman of City of London, a Member of Butcher's Co., and a Gov. of Brentwood Sch.; 1939-45 War with RAF: *m.* 1st, 1947, (Dorothy) Ruth, who *d.* 1974, da. of the late Rev. Henry Coulter, of Bellahouston, Glasgow; 2ndly, 1975, Catherine Bridget, only da. of Dr. Desmond MacCarthy, of Queens Rd., Brentwood, and has issue by 1st m.

Arms,—Per fesse or and azure, a lymphad sail furled flags and pennon flying counter-changed between in chief a dexter hand fessewise couped at the wrist grasping a dagger point upwards, and a cross-crosslet fitchée gules, and in base an oak tree eradicated proper fructed or. **Crest**,—A wildcat sejant guardant proper holding a cross-crosslet fitchée gules. **Supporters**,—*Dexter*, a lion gules, gorged with a collar, pendent therefrom an escutcheon or, charged with a garb azure; *sinister*, a bull gules, armed and unguled azure, gorged with a collar pendent therefrom an escutcheon gold charged with a boar's head couped also azure.

Residences,—Normans, Gt. Warley, Brentwood, Essex; Kyllachy, Tomatin, Inverness-shire. *Club*,—Devonshire.

SON LIVING (By 1st m.).

Hon. THOMAS IAN, *b.* July 25th, 1948.

DAUGHTERS LIVING (By 1st m.)

Hon. Wendy Shona Coulter, *b.* 1950: *m.* 1972, Brian Anthony Fountain.
Hon. Shirley Elizabeth, *b.* 1953.

SISTERS LIVING.

Hon. Annie Butcher, *b.* 1920: *m.* 1944, Richard Harries Davies, CBE, and has issue living, Gregory Thomas Harries, *b.* 1946,—Richard Harries, *b.* 1949,—Lucy Anne, *b.* 1956,—Nancy Caroline, *b.* 1958. *Residence*,—Bretton Clough, Whitebarn Rd., Alderley Edge, Ches.
Hon. Shona Catherine Greig, *b.* 1929: *m.* 1952, Donald le Strange Campbell, MC, and has issue living, Donald Bruce le Strange, *b.* 1956,—Victoria Louise, *b.* 1959. *Residence*,—North Dean House, Hughenden, High Wycombe, Bucks.

WIDOW LIVING OF FIRST BARON.

LUCY (*Lucy, Baroness Macpherson of Drumochter*) (Drumochter, Wickham Bishops, Witham), da. of the late Arthur Butcher, of Heybridge Basin, Maldon, Essex: *m.* 1920, the 1st Baron, who *d.* 1965.

PREDECESSOR,—[1] THOMAS Macpherson, son of James Macpherson, of Muirhead, Chryston, Lanarkshire: *b.* 1888; Chm. of Macpherson, Train & Co. Ltd., Food and Produce Importers and Exporters; MP for Romford (*Lab.*) 1945-50; *cr. Baron Macpherson of Drumochter* of Gt. Warley, co. Essex (peerage of UK) 1951: *m.* 1920, Lucy, da. of the late Arthur Butcher, of Heybridge Basin, Maldon, Essex; *d.* 1965; *s.* by his only son [2] JAMES GORDON, 2nd Baron and present peer.

MAELOR, BARON. (Jones.) [Life Baron 1966.]

THOMAS WILLIAM JONES, son of James Jones, of Poncian, Wrexham, Denbighshire; *b.* 1898; ed. at Poncian Boys' Sch., and Bangor Normal Coll.; a JP of Denbighshire; formerly a miner; Welfare Officer and Education Officer for Merseyside and N. Wales Electricity Board in N. Wales, Chm. of N. Wales Labour Federation and of Wrexham Trades Council; MP for Merioneth (*Lab.*) 1951-66 ; *cr. Baron Maelor*, of Rhosllanerchrugog, co. Denbigh (Life Baron) 1966: *m.* 1928, Flossy, da. of Jonathan Thomas, of Birkenhead, and has issue.

Residence,—Ger-y-Llyn, Poncian, Wrexham.

SON LIVING.

Hon. James Glynmore (Police Station, Llanddewi Velfrey, Pembrokeshire), *b.* 19—.

DAUGHTER LIVING.
Hon. Enid Aughard, *b.* 19—: *m.* 19—, E. Jurkiewicz, of 16, Snowdon Drive, Wrexham.

MAENAN, BARONY OF. (Taylor.) [Extinct 1951.]

GRANDCHILDREN LIVING OF FIRST AND LAST BARON.

Issue of the late the Hon. Ermine Mary Kyffin Taylor, da. of 1st Baron, *b.* 1884, *d.* 1975: *m.* 1917, (Arthur) Geoffrey Evans, MD, FRCP, who *d.* 1951.
Ancrum Francis, *TD* (8, Eccleston Sq., SW1V 1NP; Harpley House, Clifton-on-Teme, Worcs., and 81, Governor's St., Gilbraltar), *b.* 1918; FCA; *m.* 1948, Jean Rosemary Lambert, only da. of the late A. C. Roxburgh, MD, FRCP, and has issue living, Rosemary Kyffin, *b.* 1949; ed. at Bristol Univ. (BSc), and Nottingham Univ. (MA),—Auriol Margaret, *b.* 1952,—Catharine Grace, *b.* 1954; BHSAI,—Ermine Susan, *b.* 1959.——Elizabeth Mary Fleming, *b.* 1921.——Anne Alice Kyffin, *b.* 1927: *m.* 1950, Robin Alastair Denniston, of The Hope, Clifton-on-Teme, Worcester, and 40A, Ladbroke Sq., W11, and has issue living, Nicholas Geoffrey Alastair, *b.* 1955; ed. at Ch. Ch. Coll., Oxford,—Susanna Margaret Alice, *b.* 1956,—Candida Clare Kyffin, *b.* 1961.

Grandchildren of the late Hon. Ermine Mary Kyffin Taylor (ante), who *m.* 1917, (Arthur) Geoffrey Evans, MD, FRCP:—
Issue of the late Judith Ermine Evans, *b.* 1923, *d.* 1972: *m.* 1945, Nigel David Cutting, of Gadlas Hall, nr. Ellesmere, Salop:—
Christopher George, *b.* 1946; ACA.——Simon Geoffrey, *b.* 1948.——Edward Maenan, *b.* 1962.——Jocelyn Mary, *b.* 1949; ed. at Bangor Univ.——Frances Margery, *b.* 1951.

Maidstone, Viscount, son of Earl of Winchilsea and Nottingham.

MAIS, BARON. (Mais.) [Life Baron 1967.]

ALAN RAYMOND MAIS, *GBE, ERD, TD*, son of the late Capt. Ernest Mais; *b.* July 7th, 1911; ed. at Banister Court, Hants., and Coll. of Estate Management, London Univ.; CEng, DSc, FICE, FIStructE, FRICS; a JP of City of London, an Alderman since 1963, and a Sheriff 1969-70, and a DL of co. of London; a Dir of Trollope & Colls. Group 1949-68 (Mang. Dir. 1956, Chm. 1963-68), of Roy. Bank of Scotland, of Slag Reduction Co., Ltd., and Sterling Industrial Securities, Ltd. (Chm. 1969), HAY-MSL (Chm. 1970), Sindalls Holdings, and of other cos.; a Member of Marshall Aid Commemoration Commn.; Pres. of Nat. Fedn. of Building Trades Employers, London Region 1963; a Member of Select Cttee. EEC; Chancellor of City Univ. 1972-73; a Member of Council of City Univ. and of Birkbeck Coll., London Univ. since 1973; a Gov. of the Royal Alexandra and Albert Sch., Reigate; Lord Mayor of London 1972-73; a KStJ; Order of Patriotic War (1st class) of USSR (1942) and Order of Aztec Eagle of Mexico (1973); 1939-45 War as Col. RE (RARO), with BEF and in Middle East, Iraq, Persia, Normandy (despatches thrice), and Special Forces; *cr.* OBE (Mil) 1944, *Baron Mais*, of Walbrook, City of London, and GBE (Civil) 1973: *m.* 1936, Lorna Aline, da. of the late Stanley Aspinall Boardman, of Addiscombe, Surrey, and has issue.

Arms—Per pale argent and gules, a chevron engrailed between in chief two cinquefoils, and in base a rose, all counter-changed, on a chief azure a griffen passant or supporting with the dexter claw a paving stone argent. **Crest**,—A demi sea horse per pale argent and gules finned or, the dexter fin grasping a sword gules and resting, the sinister upon an anchor flukes to the sinister sable. **Supporters**,—*Dexter*, a griffin, and *sinister*, a dragon, both gules armed and langued azure winged argen and, gorged with a collar embattled argent charged with a barrulet wavy azure.
Residence,—Chesham House, Wilderness Rd., Chislehurst, Kent.
Clubs,—City Livery, RAC, Special Forces.

SONS LIVING.
Hon. Richard Jeremy Ian (Ystalafera, 82, Springwood, Llanedeyrn, Cardiff, CF2 6OD; Clubs,—AA, and BARC), *b.* 1945; ed. at Stowe; MIOB; a Dir. of Lyon Group (Wales & Western), Ltd.: *m.* 1972 Janice, el. da. of Ralph Dean, of Farm House Grassland Research Institute, Hurley, Berks.
Hon. Jonathan Robert Neal, *b.* 1954; ed. at Hurstpierpoint.

DAUGHTER LIVING.
Hon. Angela Clare, *b.* 1946; ed. at St. Margaret's, Bushey, and House of Citizenship.

Maitland, Viscount, son of Earl of Lauderdale.

MALMESBURY, EARL OF.   (Harris.)   [Earl G.B. 1800.]
                                  [Title pronounced "Marmsbury."]
I will maintain.

WILLIAM JAMES HARRIS, T.D., 6th
Earl; b. Nov. 18th, 1907; s. 1950; ed.
at Eton, and at Trin. Coll., Camb. (BA);
Maj. late R. Hampshire Regt. (TA),
Hon. Col. 65th Signal Regt. TA 1959-66
and of 2nd Bn. Wessex Vols. 1971-74;
ARICS; Chm. Hants & Isle of Wight
T & AF Asscn. 1960-68, and of E. Wessex
TA & VR Assocn. 1968-70; elected a
Co. Councillor for Hants 1952; Personal
Liaison Officer to Min. of Agric. for
W. Cos. for SE Region 1959-64; Master
of Skinners' Co. 1952-53; Chm. of
Hants Agric. Exec. Cttee. 1959-66; Lord
Lt. for co. Southampton since 1973, and
Official Verderer of New Forest 1966-74;
KStJ; a Gold Staff Officer at Coronation
of King George VI; has Coronation
Medals (1937 and 1953): m. 1932, the
Hon. Diana Claudia Patricia Carleton,
da. of 2nd Baron Dorchester, and has
issue.

To remember my country everywhere.

Arms,—Azure, a chevron erminois, between three hedgehogs or, on a chief argent, the black eagle
of Prussia, crowned with an imperial crown, holding in the claws a sceptre and mound, charged on the
breast with the cipher " F.R." and on each wing a trefoil slipped, all gold.   Crest,—A hedgehog or,
charged on the body with three arrows, one erect and two in saltire, sable, and over them a key barwise
azure.   Supporters,—Dexter, an eagle, wings expanded and elevated sable, crowned with an imperial
crown and charged on the breast with the cipher " F.R." and on each wing with a trefoil slipped,
all gold ; sinister, a reindeer proper, attired and hoofed or.

Residence,—Greywell Hill, Basingstoke, Hants.   Club,—Royal Yacht Squadron (Vice-
Commodore).

SON LIVING.

JAMES CARLETON (Viscount FitzHarris) (Amyand House, Park Rd., Winchester), b. June 19th,
1946; ed. at Eton, and Queens Coll., Univ. of St. Andrews: m. 1969, Sally Ann, yr. da. of Sir Richard
Newton Rycroft, 7th Bt., and has issue:—
     SONS LIVING.—Hon. James Hugh Carleton, b. April 29th, 1970.
                    Hon. Charles Edward, b. 1972.
                    Hon. Guy Richard, b. 1975.

DAUGHTERS LIVING.

Lady Sylvia Veronica Anthea, b. 1934: m. 1956, John Newcombe Maltby, son of the late Air Vice-
Marshal Sir Paul Copeland Maltby, KCVO, KBE, CB, DSO, AFC, DL, and has issue living, William
John, b. 1959,—Caroline Jane, b. 1957,—Sophia Louise, b. 1963.   Residence,—Newnham House,
Basingstoke, Hants.
Lady Nell Carleton, b. 1937: m. 1962, Capt. Michael Patrick Radcliffe Boyle, Irish Guards (ret.) [see
E. Shannon, colls.].   Residence,—Ashe Park, nr. Basingstoke, Hants.

SISTER LIVING.

Lady Elizabeth, b. 1906: m. 1st, 1926 (marriage dissolved 1944), Lieut.-Col. the Hon. John
Walgrave Halford Fremantle, R.A. (T.A.), el. son of 3rd Baron Cottesloe; 2ndly, 1944, Lieut.-
Col. Edward Walter Hall Berwick, Roy. Canadian Dragoons, and has issue living (by 1st
m.) [see B. Cottesloe],—(by 2nd m.) Dorothea, b. 1944.   Residence,—17, Montpelier Villas, Brighton,
BN1 3DG.

PREDECESSORS.—[1] Rt. Hon. Sir JAMES Harris, G.C.B., P.C., el. son of James Harris, M.P.,
Sec. and Comptroller to Queen Charlotte (wife of King George III.), b. 1746; an eminent
diplomatist; was Ambassador to Spain 1771, to Berlin 1772, to Russia 1776, to the Hague 1783
and 1788, and to France 1796-7, Lieut. Gov. of the Isle of Wight 1807, and Lord-Lieut. of
Hants ; cr. Baron Malmesbury, of Malmesbury, co. Wilts (peerage of Great Britain) 1788, and
Viscount FitzHarris and Earl of Malmesbury (peerage of Great Britain) 1800 : d. 1820; s. by
his el. son [2] JAMES EDWARD, 2nd Earl, b. 1778; was M.P. for Helston 1802, and for
Heytesbury 1807, a Lord of the Treasury 1804-6, Under-Sec. for Foreign Affairs 1807, and Gov.
of the Isle of Wight: m. 1806, Harriet Susan, who d. 1815, dau. of Francis Bateman Dashwood,
of Well Vale, Lincolnshire; d. 1841; s. by his el. son [3] JAMES HOWARD, G.C.B., P.C., 3rd
Earl, b. 1807; sat as M.P. for Wilton (C) 1841; Sec. for Foreign Affairs 1852, and 1858-9, and
Lord Privy Seal 1866-8, and 1874-6: m. 1st, 1830, Lady Corisande Emma Bennet, who d. 1876,
dau. of 5th Earl of Tankerville; 2ndly, 1880, Susan, who d. 1935 (having m. 2ndly, 1896,
Maj.-Gen. Sir John Charles Ardagh, K.C.M.G., K.C.I.E., C.B., LL.D., R.E., who d. 1907),
dau. of the late John Hamilton, of Fyne Court, Somerset; d.s.p. 1889; s. by his nephew
[4] EDWARD JAMES, 4th Earl (el. son of the late Adm. the Hon. Sir Edward Alfred John
Harris, K.C.B., 2nd son of 2nd Earl), b. 1842; Lieut.-Col. (retired) 2nd Batn. Roy. Irish
Rifles : m. 1870, Sylvia Georgina, who d. 1934, youngest dau. of the late Alexander Stewart, of
Ballyedmond Castle, Rostrevor, co. Down; d. 1899; s. by his el. son [5] JAMES EDWARD,
5th Earl, b. 1872; was Assist. Private Sec. (unpaid) to Under Sec. of State for the Colonies 1901,
a Co. Councillor for London 1904-5, a Lord-in-Waiting to H.M. 1922-24, and Chm. of Hants Co.
Council 1927-38: m. 1905, the Hon. Dorothy Gough Calthorpe, CBE, who d. 1972, yst. dau. of 6th
Baron Calthorpe; d. 1950; s. by his only son [6] WILLIAM JAMES, 6th Earl and present peer; also
Viscount FitzHarris, and Baron Malmesbury.

MALVERN, VISCOUNT. (Huggins.) [Viscount U.K. 1955.]

Let us all persevere together.

JOHN GODFREY HUGGINS, 2nd Viscount; *b.* Oct. 26th, 1922; *s.* 1971; ed. at Winchester; F/Lt. RAF; 1939-45 War: *m.* (Jan.) 1949, Patricia Marjorie, da. of Frank Renwick-Bower, of Durban, and has issue.

Arms,—Argent, on a fesse sable between three hearts gules a lion passant guardant or. **Crest.**—A lion sejant rampant guardant or the sinister paw resting on a fountain. **Supporters,**—*Dexter,* a lion guardant gules grasping in the exterior forepaw a rod of aesculapius proper; *sinister,* a sable antelope guardant proper.

Address,—c/o Standard Bank, Cecil Sq., Salisbury, Rhodesia.

SONS LIVING.
Hon. Michael Patrick John (c/o PO Box AP 50, Salisbury Airport, Rhodesia), *b.* 1946.
Hon. ASHLEY KEVIN GODFREY, *b.* Oct. 26th, 1949.

DAUGHTER LIVING.
Hon. Haoli Elizabeth Jane, *b.* 1953.

BROTHER LIVING.
Hon. (Martin) James, *b.* 1928; ed. at Hilton Coll., Natal; a Farmer. *Residence,*—The Craig, P.O. Highlands, Salisbury, Rhodesia.

WIDOW LIVING OF FIRST VISCOUNT.
BLANCHE ELIZABETH (*Blanche, Viscountess Malvern*), (The Craig, P.O. Highlands, Salisbury, Rhodesia), da. of the late James Slatter, of Pietermaritzburg, Natal: *m.* 1921, The 1st Viscount, who *d.* 1971.

PREDECESSOR.—[1] *Rt. Hon.* Sir GODFREY MARTIN Huggins, *CH, KCMG, FRCS,* son of the late Godfrey Huggins; *b.* 1883; Prime Min. of S. Rhodesia 1933-53 and Fedn. of Rhodesia and Nyasaland 1953-56; *cr. Viscount Malvern,* of Rhodesia and of Bexley, co. Kent (peerage of UK) 1955: *m.* 1921, Blanche Elizabeth, da. of the late James Slatter, of Pietermaritzburg, Natal; *d.* 1971; *s.* by his el. son [2] JOHN GODFREY, 2nd Viscount, and present peer.

MANCHESTER, DUKE OF. (Montagu.) [Duke G.B. 1719.]

By disposing of me, not by changing me.

ALEXANDER GEORGE FRANCIS DROGO MONTAGU, *O.B.E.,* 10th Duke; *b.* Oct. 2nd, 1902; *s.* 1947; Cdr. R.N. (ret.); 1939-45 War (O.B.E.); O.B.E. (Mil.) 1940: *m.* 1st. 1927, Nell Vere, who *d.* 1966, da. of Sidney Vere Stead, of Melbourne; 2ndly 1969, Elizabeth, da. of Samuel Clyde Fullerton of Miami, USA, and formerly wife of W. W. Crocker, and has issue by 1st m.

Arms,—Quarterly: 1st and 4th argent, three lozenges conjoined in fesse gules, within a bordure sable, *Montagu;* 2nd and 3rd or, an eagle displayed vert, beaked and membered gules, *Monthermer.* **Crest,**—A griffin's head couped at the neck or, gorged with a plain collar argent, charged with three lozenges gules between two wings sable. **Supporters,**—*Dexter,* a heraldic antelope, or, armed, unguled, and tufted argent; *sinister,* a griffin, wings elevated or, collared as in the crest.

Residence,—Kapsirowa, Hoey's Bridge, Kenya.

SONS LIVING (by 1st m.)
SIDNEY ARTHUR ROBIN GEORGE DROGO (*Viscount Mandeville*), (Ol Gorashe Farm, PO Subukia, Kenya; *Club,*—Muthaiga (Kenya)), *b.* Feb. 5th, 1929: *m.* 1955, Adrienne Valerie, da. of John Kenneth Christie, of Sedgefield, Cape Prov., S. Africa.

Lord Angus Charles Drogo, *b.* 1938: *m.* 1961 (m. diss. 1970), Mary Eveleen, da. of Walter Gillespie McClure, of Geelong, Vic., Aust., and has issue living, Alexander Charles David Drogo, *b.* 1962,—Kimble, *b.* 1964,—Emma, *b.* 1965. *Residence,*—

COLLATERAL BRANCHES LIVING.
Issue of the late Lord Edward Eugene Fernando Montagu, younger son of 9th Duke, *b.* 1906, *d.* 1954: *m.* 1st, 1929, Norah Macfarlane (who obtained a divorce 1937), dau. of Albert Edward Potter, of Ontario, Canada ; 2ndly, 1937 (marriage dissolved 1947), Dorothy Vera Peters ; 3rdly 1947, Martha Mathews Hatton Bowen, who *d.* 1951 ; 4thly 1953, Roberta Joughin, who *d.* 19—):—
(By 1st m.) Roderick Edward Drogo (24, St. Georges Cres., Edmonton, Alberta, Canada), *b.* 1930: *m.* 1968, Mary Deas.

Grandchildren of the late Lt.-Cdr. Robert Acheson Cromie Montagu, DL, RN, 2nd son of Rt. Hon. Lord Robert Montagu (infra):—
Issue of the late John Michael Cromie Montagu, *b.* 1881, *d.* 1966; *m.* 1907, Libia Maria, da. of the late Senor Martin Montes, of Quilmes, Argentine Republic:—
Robert Alexander, *b.* 1917.——Alicia May JOHNSON MONTAGU (Pentire, Calvert Rd., Dorking, Surrey), *b.* 1919: assumed by Deed Poll 1963 the surname of Johnson Montagu: *m.* 1st, 1941, Fl.-Lt. Stuart James Lovell, RAF, who *d.* (killed in action) 1944; 2ndly, 1946 (m. diss. 1963), John Dobney Johnson, PhD, and has issue living, (by 2nd m.), Adrian Michael Montagu, *b.* 1947,—Warwick Martin Montagu, *b.* 1950: *m.* 1970, Gaye Marina Harding, and has issue living, Melissa Gaye *b.* 1973, Sarah Louise *b.* 1975,—Phillip Leicester Montagu (1, Ivy Walk, Hendford Gdns., Yeovil, Som.), *b.* 1951: *m.* 1973, Fiona Madeleine Williams,—Michèle Veronica Montagu, *b.* 1953: *m.* 1973, Alan Craig Worrell, of 14, Cherrington Av., Hengoed, Glam.

Issue of the late George Frederick WELD-BLUNDELL, RN, *b.* 1883, *d.* 1958, having assumed by Roy. licence 1923 the surname of Weld-Blundell in lieu of his patronymic: *m.* 1912, Mary Teresa, who *d.* 1957, da. of the late Charles Joseph Weld-Blundell [By. of Fauconberg and Conyers, colls.]:—
Frederica Mary MONTAGU, *b.* 1918: *m.* 1966, Jocelyn Philip Pereira, ARCS (Hilton House, Blandford Forum, Dorset; 20, St. Leonards Terr., SW3), son of the late Maj.-Gen. Sir Cecil Edward Pereira, KCB, CMG.

Issue of the late Austin Robert Montagu, b. 1885, d. 1958: m. 1934, Violet Vera, da. of
Charles William Sandles:—
Henry Robert Sanderson, b. 1935. Residence,—St. Illtyds, 14, New Unifield, Maraisburg, Transvaal,
S. Africa.——Cyril John Sanderson, b. 1937.——Gerard Philip Sanderson, b. 1940.

Grandchildren of the late Rt. Hon. Lord Robert Montagu, 2nd son of 6th Duke:—
Issue (by 1st marriage) of the late Lieut.-Com. Robert Acheson Cromie Montagu, D.L.,
R.N., b. 1854, d. 1931: m. 1st, 1880, Annie Margaret, who d. 1916, dau. of the late Gilbert
McMicking, of Miltonise, Wigtownshire; 2ndly, 1917, Edith, who d. 1948, dau. of the
late Col. Eldred Pottinger, C.M.G., of Portrush, co. Antrim·—
Gilbert Paul (2665, Club Mesa Place, Costa Mesa, Cal. 92627, USA), b. 1887: m. 1st, 1918, Frances
Lazarre Aicher, of Mount Stirling, Kentucky, who d. 1929; 2ndly, 1932, Mrs. Beatrice Mendels,
who d. 1973.
Issue of the late Monthermer Stanley Hume Montagu, M.C., b. 1868, d. 1953: m. 1913,
Harriet Jessie, who d. 1959, dau. of the late James Keith Forbes, of Valparaiso :—
Walter Bernard St. John, TD (2, Trigon Rd., SW8), b. 1915; ed. at Canford Sch.; Capt. (ret.) RA (TA);
Kenya Police (Reserve) 1948-53; 1939-45 War (wounded): m. 1948, Doris Jean, da. of J. Albany
Morton, of Culzean, Busby, Lanarkshire, and has issue living, John Charles Monthermer Albany (c/o
Child's Bank, 1, Fleet St., EC4), b. 1951; ed. at Gordonstoun, and Hull Univ. (LLB),—Elizabeth
Anne Kennedy, b. 1949: m. 1971, Victor Bayntun Hippisley, Dip. Phot. (Dist.), of 29, Stapleton
Rd., SW17, and has issue living, Antonia Serena Olivia, b. 1975.——Olivia Millicent Jane, b. 1914;
1939-45 War with Women's Transport Ser. (E. Africa): m. 1943, Edward Rodwell, FRGS. Address,—
Box 82819, Mombassa, Kenya.
Issue of the late Capt. Henry Bernard Montagu, R.N., b. 1872, d. 1941: m. 1922
Rosamond, who d. 1972, da. of the late Dudley Bowditch Fay, of Boston, U.S.A.:—
John Drogo, b. 1923; MROS England and LROP London, 1946; late Surg.-Lieut. RNVR:
m. 1946. Katharine Mary, dau. of the late Brig.-Gen. Noble Fleming Jenkins, C.M.G., C.B.E.,
and has issue living, Robert Drogo (Darenth Cottage, Chevening Rd., Chipstead, nr. Sevenoaks
Kent), b. 1947: m. 1970, Glenis Diane Littaur, and has issue living, James Drogo b. 1975, Rachel
Bernard b. 1974,—Christopher Bernard, b. 1950,—Rosamond Anne, b. 1953. Residence,—Ramblers,
Graffham, Petworth, Sussex.——Katharine Anne, b. 1925.

Grandson of the late Millicent Fenwick (infra) :—
Issue of the late Capt. Keld Robert George Fenwick, Roy. Horse Guards, b. 1892, d. 1934 ;
m. 1st, 1916, Gladys Mary (who d. 1972 having obtained a divorce 1924), da. of Sir William
Nelson, 1st. Bt.; 2ndly, 1925, Anabel Bertha (who obtained a divorce 1928), da. of David
Herbert Greenough, and widow of Albert L. Johnson, Stockbroker, of New York; 3rdly,
1929, Dorothy Kimberley of Walton Hall, Kelso, Roxburghshire, who m. 2ndly, 1955,
Ian Scott Smith, who d. 1972, da. of Walter Duren, banker, of New York:—
(By 3rd marriage) John David Keld, b. 1930 ; late Lieut. Roy. Inniskilling Dragoon Guards : m.
1954, Eugene Pamela, da. of the late James Edward Shaw, of Melbourne, Australia, and has issue
living, Paul Anthony Ian Keld, b. 1955,—Robin James Montagu, b. 1957,—Nicholas Michael Walter,
b. 1960,—Antonia Helen Eugenie, b. 1966. Residence,—Ketton House, Kedington, W. Suffolk.
Club,—Boodle's.

Grandson of the late Rt. Hon. Lord Robert Montagu, P.C. (ante):—
Issue of the late Millicent Montagu, b. 1864, d. 1942: m. 1891, Walter Lionel Fenwick, J.P.,
who d. 1914 :—
Montagu John, b. 1896; a J.P.; 1914-18 War as Lt. R.F.C., R.N.A.S. and R.A.F. (two medals);
1939-49 War as Sqdn.-Ldr. RAFVR: m. 1923, Marguerite Cecily, who d. 1973, da. of the late Hugh
Peacock, of Greatford Hall, Stamford, and has issue living, Anthony Walter (Eaton Grange, Gran-
tham, Lincs.), b. 1928: m. 1953, Caroline Susan, da. of the late Maj. Lawrence Kimball, of Alderholt
Park, Fordingbridge, Hants, and has issue living, Mark John b. 1962, Claire Sonia b. 1954, Tania
Jane b. 1955, Susan Antonia b. 1960,—June Mary, b. 1925: m. 1956, Marcus Richard Kimball,
M.P., of Great Easton Manor, Market Harborough, Leicestershire, and has issue living, Sarah Marcia
b. 1958, Sophie Henrietta b. 1960. Residence,—The Granary, Eaton, Grantham, Lincs., NG32 1ET.
(Not in remainder to Dukedom.)
Descendants of the late Hon. James Montagu, 3rd son of 1st Earl of
Manchester:—
Grandson of the late Gen. Sir Horace William Montagu, K.C.B., son of the late
Rev. George Montagu, second son of the late Gerard Montagu, 3rd in descent
from the late James Montagu, el. son of the late Hon. James Montagu (ante) :—
Issue of the late Col. Edward Montagu, C.B.E., b. 1861, d. 1941 : m. 1894, Charlotte Eva, who
d. 1952, dau. of Edward Kemble, formerly a Judge of Supreme Court, Jamaica :—
Charles Edward, b. 1900 ; ed. at Wellington Coll. ; is Capt. (retired) R.E. : m. 1928, Rachel Alice,
dau. of the late W. H. Martin, of Shrublands, Swaffham, Norfolk, and has issue living, Michael
Drogo (Barnaby Farm, Ringsfield, Beccles, Suffolk), b. 1929; Maj. RA: m. 1955, Verity Jane, da.
of William James Coode, OBE, of Polgooth, St. Austell, Cornwall, and has issue living, Richard
Lionel James b. 1956, Alan Edward b. 1958, James Robert b. 1962,—Ralph Edward (of The
Manor House, Ringsfield, Beccles, Suffolk), b. 1932; m. 1963, June Margaret (Lisa), only da. of
the late James William Finlayson, of Vaucluse, Sydney, Australia, and has issue living, David
Charles b. 1965, Caroline Elizabeth b. 1964, Victoria Jane b. 1967, Katharine Fiona (twin) b. 1967.
Residence,—Cameron House, Ballygate, Suffolk.

Grandson of the late Edgar Montagu, 3rd son of the late Gerard Montagu
(ante):—
Issue of the late Capt. Cecil Edgar Montagu, b. 1851, d. 1923: m. 1883, Alice Ethel, who
d. 1919, only dau. of J. Asheton Crichley, of Stapleton Towers, Annan:—
James Gerard Edgar Drogo, b. 1893; ed. at Eton, and at Trin. Coll., Camb. ; Major (retired)
R.F.A. : European War 1914-19 in France : m. 1st, 1919, Anne Gladys (who obtained a
divorce 1928), dau. of Sir Harry Ross Skinner ; 2ndly, 1929 (marriage annulled 19—), Violet Ada
Lucy, dau. of the late John Henry Fergusson, of Crochmore, Dumfriesshire ; 3rdly, 1948, Mary Rose,
dau. of Robert Grainger, of Munich. Germany, and has issue living, (by 1st marriage) William
Gerard Drogo (Manor Down, Lamberhurst, Tunbridge Wells), b. 1921; ed. at Stowe, and at Chillon
Coll., Switzerland; Lt.-Cdr. (ret.) RN: m. 1950, Charlotte Delma, da. of Frank Calburn, of Cowden,
Kent, and has issue living, Charles Edward Drogo b. 1952, Francis Gerard Drogo (twin) b. 1952,
James William Drogo b. 1954.

Grandchildren of the late Capt. George Edward Montagu, el. son of the late Adm
John William Montagu, son of the late Adm. Sir George Montagu, G.C.B., son
of the late Adm. John Montagu (infra) :—
Issue of the late John William Montagu, b. 1877, d. 1954: m. 1913, Violet Irene, who d. 1970,
da. of James Shuter, late of Little Park, Newbury;—
John Drogo, b. 1916; ed. at Exeter Sch., and RMC Sandhurst; Lt.-Col. (ret.) Indian Army; Far East
1939-45 (despatches): m. 1952, Dorothy Boreham, yr. da. of C. E. Chuter, of Brisbane, Australia.
and has issue living, Michael Charles Drogo, b. 1956,—Nigel Edward, b. 1958,—Richard John, b,
1959,—Sally Ann, b. 1954,—Felicity Jane, b. 1960. Residence,—Badgers Wood, Farnham Common,
Bucks.——James Edward, b. 1920; late Capt. RA; 1939-45 War: m. 19—, Joan, da. of the late
J. McPherson, of Fieldway, Barrow-in-Furness, and has issue living, Philip James, b. 1949,—Robin
William, b. 1953. Residence,—64, Hill Rd., Barrow-in-Furness, Lancashire.——Mary Hamilton,
b. 1914. Residence,—Caesars, Freshwater, Isle of Wight.

Grandsons of the late Edward Vaughan Montagu, 2nd son of the late John Edward
Montagu (infra) :—

Issue of the late John Francis Vaughan Montagu, *b.* 1877, *d.* 1960 : *m.* 1909, Ada Mary, who *d.* 1957, dau. of the late James Dougal Coley, of Claremont, Cape Town, S. Africa :—
John Edward Coley, *b.* 1910 ; European War 1939-45 in Italy as Lieut. 6th S. African Armoured Div. wounded) : *m.* 1st, 1936 (marriage dissolved 1955), Flora Elizabeth, dau. of the late Col. James Robertson-Cumming, of Langrigg, Strathearn, Scotland ; 2ndly, 1958, Anne, dau. of the late Col. Donald Rolfe Hunt, of Swartkopskloof, Natal, S. Africa, and has issue living, (by 1st marriage) John Anthony Francis (3, Kelvin Grove, Beacon Bay, E. London, S. Africa), *b.* 1938: *m.* 1966, Denise, el. da. of the late F. Dallas, of East London, S. Africa, and has issue living, Joanne Catherine *b.* 1969, Leigh Frances *b.* 1971,—David Vaughan, *b.* 1948,—Gillian Denise, *b.* 1940: *m.* 1966, Michael Keyworth Glover, of 35, Esmeralda Cres., Robindale Extn. No. 1, Randburg, Transvaal, and has issue living, Mark Keyworth *b.* 1968, Marguerite Tracey *b.* 1967, Jenny Lynne *b.* 1972. *Residence,—* 16, Abelia Rd., Kloof, Natal.——Denis Vaughan, *b.* 1913: *m.* 1939, Margarieta, da. of Henry Usher Gradwell, of Bloemfontein, S. Africa. *Residence,—*11, Rushell Cres., Selection Park Springs, Transvaal, S. Africa.

Grandchildren of the late Frederick George Montagu (infra):—
Issue of the late Arthur Drogo Turing Montagu, *b.* 1900, *d.* 1969: *m.* 1934, Dorothy Rittener (Hill Crest, Gourley Rd., Eerste River, 7100, S. Africa), el. da. of Harry Taylor Pitt, of Hill-Top, Woodingdean, Brighton:—
John Drogo, *b.* 1935.——William Pitt (P.O. Box 187, Kuilsriver, Cape Province, S. Africa) *b.* 1939: *m.* 1966, Elsa, da. of J. A. Fourie, of Eerste River, Cape, and has issue living, Michelle, *b.* 1969,—Colleen, *b.* 1971,—Wendy (twin) *b.* 1971.——Margaret Helen, *b.* 1937: *m.* 1961, Hendrik De La Rey Winter, of 64, Ninth St., Linden, Johannesburg, and has issue living, Peter Jacobus de la Rey, *b.* 1964,—Arthur Paul, *b.* 1966,—Catherine, *b.* 1962.

Granddaughter of the late John Edward Montagu, el. son of the late John Montagu, son of the late Lieut.-Col. Edward Montagu, 4th son of the late Adm. John Montagu, great-grandson of the late Hon. James Montagu (ante) :—
Issue of the late Frederick George Montagu, *b.* 1856, *d.* 1923: *m.* 1894, Bertha, who *d.* 1936, dau. of Colin Turing Campbell, formerly of Barbreck, Kimberley, S. Africa:—
Helen Bertha Piers Ashburnham, *b.* 1896: *m.* 1918, Capt. Francis Henry Snow, late S. African Army Ser. Corps, who *d.* 1958, and has issue living, Denis Arthur Fairbreck, *b.* 1922: *m.* 1952, Bernadine, 3rd da. of T. R. Robertson, of Parys, Transvaal, S. Africa, and has issue living, Michael David *b.* 1960, Geraldine Helen *b.* 1954, Jillian Anne *b.* 1956,—Harold Leslie (of Montagu, 12, Vincent Place, East London, S. Africa), *b.* 1925: *m.* 1950, Florence Mavis, yst. da. of the late A. E. V. Fairbrother, of Rosebank, Cape Province, S. Africa, and has issue living, Jeffrey Ernest Barrington *b.* 1952, Nigel Allen *b.* 1953, Robert Arthur *b.* 1957, Belinda Helen *b.* 1959. *Residence,—*Montagu, 12, Vincent Place, East London, S. Africa.

Grandchildren of the late Lieut.-Gen. Alfred Worsley Montagu, younger son of the late John Montagu (ante) :—
Issue of the late Alfred Worsley Montagu, *b.* 1860, *d.* 191-: *m.* 1887, Ruth Lily Wallace, of Stawell, Victoria, Australia :—
Herbert Clive, *b.* 1897.——Ruth Mabel Josephine, *b.* 1888.——Jeffie Ina, *b.* 1891.——Vere Faerie, *b.* 1894. *Residence,—*

PREDECESSORS.—[1] *Sir* HENRY Montagu, Knt.; M.P. for London 1604-16, and Recorder of London ; appointed Lord Ch. Justice of the King's Bench 1615, Lord Treasurer of England 1620, and Lord Privy Seal 1626 ; cr. *Baron Montagu,* of Kimbolton, co. Huntingdon, and *Viscount Mandeville* (peerage of England) 1620, and *Earl of Manchester* (peerage of England) 1626 ; *d.* 1642 ; *s.* by his son [2] EDWARD, 2nd Earl, who had previously been summoned to Parliament as *Baron Kimbolton;* was a distinguished Gen. in the Parliamentary army, and gained the celebrated victory at Marston Moor; he refused to sanction the execution of Charles I., and retired from Parliament until 1660, when he voted for the restoration of Charles II., and was deputed by the Lords as their speaker to congratulate the King upon his return to his capital; *d.* 1671 ; *s.* by his son [3] ROBERT, 3rd Earl ; *d.* 1682 ; *s.* by his son [4] CHARLES, *P.C.,* 4th Earl ; served at the battle of the Boyne; was Ambassador to Venice 1696, to France 1699, and to Vienna 1707, Principal Sec. of State 1701, Lord-Lieut. of Huntingdonshire, and a Gentleman of the Bedchamber to George I.; cr. *Duke of Manchester* (peerage of Great Britain) 1719; *d.* 1722; *s.* by his el. son [5] WILLIAM, *K.B.,* 2nd Duke ; *d.* 1739; *s.* by his brother [6] ROBERT, 3rd Duke ; *d.* 1762; *s.* by his son [7] GEORGE, 4th Duke; was Master of the Horse 1780; *d.* 1788; *s.* by his son [8] WILLIAM, 5th Duke; was Gov. of Jamaica 1807-28, Collector of Customs for Port of London, and Lord-Lieut. of Huntingdonshire; *d.* 1843; *s.* by his son [9] GEORGE, 6th Duke ; a Com. R.N.: *m.* 1st, 1822, Millicent, who *d.* 1848, dau. of Gen. R. B. Sparrow; 2ndly, 1850, Harriet Sydney, dau. of Conway Richard Dobbs, of Castle Dobbs, co. Antrim; *d.* 1855; *s.* by his son [10] WILLIAM DROGO, *K.P.,* 7th Duke, *b.* 1823; sat as M.P. for Bewdley (*C*) 1848-52, and for Huntingdonshire 1852-5: *m.* 1852, the Countess Louise Frederica Augusta, who *d.* 1911 (having *m.* 2ndly, 1892, the 8th Duke of Devonshire), dau. of Count von Alten, of Hanover; *d.* 1890; *s.* by his el. son [11] GEORGE VICTOR DROGO, 8th Duke, *b.* 1853 ; M.P. for Huntingdonshire 1877-80: *m.* 1876, Consuelo Yznaga, who *d.* 1909, dau. of Senor Antonio Yznaga de Valle, of Louisiana, U.S.A., and Cuba; *d.* 1892; *s.* by his el. son [12] WILLIAM ANGUS DROGO, *P.C.,* 9th Duke, *b.* 1877: Capt. of Yeomen of the Guard 1906-7: *m.* 1st, 1900. Helena (who *d.* 1971, having obtained a divorce 1931), da. of the late Eugene Zimmerman, of Cincinnati, USA; 2nd, 1931, Kathleen, who *d.* 1966, da. of W. H. Dawes, *d.* 1947; *s.* by his son [13] ALEXANDER GEORGE FRANCIS DROGO, 10th Duke and present peer; also Earl of Manchester, Viscount Mandeville, and Baron Montagu of Kimbolton.

MANCHESTER, LORD BISHOP OF. (Rodger.)

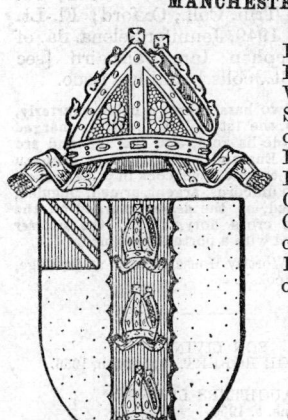

Right Rev. PATRICK CAMPBELL RODGER, son of Patrick Wylie Rodger, *b.* Nov. 28th, 1920; ed. at Rugby, Ch. Ch., Oxford (MA) and Theol. Coll., Westcott House, Camb.; Chap. to Anglican Students in Edinburgh 1951-54, Study Sec., SCM of Gt. Britain and Ireland 1955-58, R. St. Fillan's, Kilmacolm with St. Mary's, Bridge of Weir 1958-61, Exec. Sec. for Faith and Order, World Council of Churches 1961-66, Vice-Provost of St. Mary's Cathedral, Edinburgh 1966-67, and Provost 1967-70; consecrated as 8th Bishop of Manchester 1970: *m.* 1952, Margaret, da. of William Menzies Menzies of Edinburgh.

Patron of 126 livings, and one of patronage trust of 46 livings.

This See was created in 1847.

𝔈piscopal 𝔖ignature,—Patrick Manchester.

ARMS OF THE SEE,—Or, on a pale engrailed gules three mitres of the field, a canton of the second thereon three bendlets enhanced, also of the field.

*Residence,—*Bishopscourt, Bury New Rd., Manchester, M7 0LE.

MANCROFT, BARON. (Mancroft.) [Baron U.K. 1937 Bt. U.K. 1932.]

COURAGE   PATIENCE

STORMONT MANCROFT SAMUEL MANCROFT, K.B.E., T.D., 2nd Baron, b. July 27th, 1914; s. 1942; ed. at Winchester, and at Ch. Ch., Oxford (MA); Bar. Inner Temple 1938 (Member of Bar Council 1947-51); Pres. of London Tourist Board 1963-73; a Dir. of GUS 1958-66, and of Cunard Line Ltd. 1966-71, and Chm. of BNEC Cttee. for Exports to USA 1967-70; a Member of St. Marylebone Borough Council 1947-53, Chancellor of Primrose League 1952-54, and Pres. of St. Marylebone Conservative Assocn. 1961-67; a Lord-in-Waiting to HM 1952-54, Parl. Under-Sec. of State for Home Affairs 1954-57, Parl. Sec., Min. of Defence Jan. to June 1957, and Min. without Portfolio 1957-58; Chm. Horserace Totalisator Board since 1972; a Member of Council on Tribunals; Hon. Col. Comdt. RA since 1970; 1939-45 War as Lt.-Col RA (TA) (despatches twice, MBE, Croix de Guerre); assumed by deed poll 1925 the surname of Mancroft; MBE (Mil) 1945, KBE (Civil) 1959: m. 1951, Diana Elizabeth (QUARRY), only da. of Lt.-Col. Horace Lloyd, DSO, and has issue.

Arms,—Gules, a chevron chequy argent and sable, between in chief two portcullises chained and in base a castle (Farnham) triple towered or, on a chief of the last a lion passant guardant of the third. Crest,—In front of a castle (Norwich) with three cupolas, issuant from each a staff proper flying therefrom a banner argent, charged with a cross gules, a sword sheathed also gules, garnished or, pomel and hilt of the last, and a mace gold in saltire (i.e. a representation of the ancient Crystal Mace and the Sword in the Regalia of the Corporation of the City of Norwich). Supporters,—On either side a Whiffler of the Corporation of the City of Norwich.

Residence,—29, Margaretta Terr., SW3 5NU.

SON LIVING.

Hon. BENJAMIN LLOYD STORMONT, b. May 16th, 1957.

DAUGHTERS LIVING.

Hon. Victoria Lucinda (50, Ebury Mews, SW1W 9NY), b. 1952.
Hon. Jessica Rosetta, b. 1954.

SISTERS LIVING.

Hon. Waveney Mancroft SAMUEL, b. 1916: m. 1950, Anthony William Garthwaite, who d. 1972 [see Garthwaite, Bt., colls.]. Residence,—98, Bickenhall Mansions, W1.

Hon. Rosetta Mancroft SAMUEL, b. 1918: m. 1st, 1947, Alfred John Bostock Hill, late Puisne Judge, Malaya, who d. 1959; 2ndly, 1966, Dr. Cai Christian Holm. Residence,—12, Eaton Place, SW1.

PREDECESSOR.—[1] ARTHUR MICHAEL SAMUEL, el. son of the late Benjamin Samuel, of Norwich; b. 1872; Parliamentary Under-Sec. of State for Foreign Affairs, Parliamentary Sec. to Board of Trade, and Minister for Depart. of Overseas Trade 1924-7, and Financial Sec. to the Treasury 1927-9; Chm. of Public Accounts Committee of House of Commons 1930 and 1931; was Lord Mayor of Norwich 1912-13, received Hon. Freedom of City of Norwich 1928; sat as M.P. for Farnham Div. of Surrey (U) 1918-37: cr. a Baronet 1932, and Baron Mancroft, of Mancroft, in City of Norwich (peerage of UK) 1937: m. 1912, Phoebe, who d. 1969, second da of the late Dr. (George) Alfred Chune Fletcher, Med. Officer to the Charterhouse, London; d. 1942; s. by his son [2] STORMONT MANCROFT, 2nd Baron and present peer.

Mandeville, Viscount, son of Duke of Manchester.

MANNERS, BARON. (Manners.) [Baron U.K. 1807.]

POUR·Y·PARVENIR

In order to accomplish.

JOHN ROBERT CECIL MANNERS, 5th Baron; b. Feb. 13th, 1923; s. 1972; ed. at Eton, and Trin. Coll., Oxford; Fl.-Lt. RAFVR: m. 1949, Jennifer Selena, da. of the late Stephen Ian Fairbairn [see Arbuthnot, Bt., colls.], and has issue.

Arms,—Or, two bars azure, a chief quarterly, azure and gules, the 1st and 4th quarters charged with two fleurs-de-lis gold, and the 2nd and 3rd with a lion of England. Crest,—On a chapeau gules, turned up ermine, a peacock in pride proper. Supporters,—Two unicorns, argent, armed, unguled, crined, and tufted, or, the dexter charged on the shoulder with a cross flory, azure; the sinister similarly charged with a portcullis, sable.

Residence,—Wortley House, Wotton-under-Edge, Glos. Club,—Brooks's.

SON LIVING.

Hon. JOHN HUGH ROBERT, b. May 5th, 1956.

DAUGHTERS LIVING.

Hon. Venetia Jane, b. 1950.
Hon. Selena Mary, b. 1952: m. 1974, Capt. Christopher Jeremy George Langlands, 1st Queen's Dragoon Gds.

BROTHERS LIVING.

Hon. Richard Neville, *b.* 1924; *ed.* at Eton: *m.* 1945, Juliet Mary, da. of the late Col. Sir Edward Hulton Preston ,5th Bt., D.S.O., M.C., and has issue living, Edward Preston, *b.* 1948,—Rupert Francis Henry, *b.* 1950,—Thomas Benjamin *b.* 1954,—Christine Margaret Lavender, *b.* 1946: *m.* 1970, Timothy J. B. Pallister. *Residence,*—Cromer Hall, Norfolk.

Hon. Thomas Jasper, *b.* 1929 ; *ed.* at Eton : *m.* 1955, Sarah, dau. of the late Brigadier Roger Peake, DSO, OBE, and has issue living, Charles Henry, *b.* 1957,—Arthur Roger, *b.* 1959,—Robert Hugh, *b.* 1962. *Residence,*—.

SISTER LIVING.

Hon. Patricia Anne, *b.* 1927: *m.* 1946, John Bonham Kidston, late Lt. Grenadier Guards, who *d.* 196 [Bonham, Bt.], and has issue living, Francis George, *b.* 1947,—Jonathan James, *b.* 1951,—Virginia Lilian, *b.* 1953. *Residence,*—Breach Farm, Dummer, Basingstoke.

WIDOW LIVING OF FOURTH BARON.

MARY EDITH (*Mary Baroness Manners*), (North End House, Avon, Christchurch, Hants,) twin da. of the late Rt. Rev. Lord William Rupert Ernest Gascoyne-Cecil, DD, 65th Bishop of Exeter [see M. Salisbury, colls.]: *m.* 1921, the 4th Baron, who *d.* 1972.

PREDECESSORS.—[1] THOMAS Manners-Sutton, P.C., 5th son of Lord George Manners Sutton (3rd son of 3rd Duke of Rutland and father of 1st Viscount Canterbury) ; was Solicitor Gen. of England 1802-5, a Baron of the Exchequer in England 1805-7, and Lord Chancellor of Ireland 1807 ; cr. *Baron Manners,* of Foston, co. Lincoln (peerage of United Kingdom) 1807 ; *d.* 1842; *s.* by his son [2] JOHN THOMAS, 2nd Baron; *b.* 1818: *m.* 1848, Lydia Sophia, who *d.* 1916, dau. of Vice-Adm. William Bateman Dashwood ; *d.* 1864 ; *s.* by his el. son [3] JOHN THOMAS, 3rd Baron; *b.* 1852 : *m.* 1st, 1885, Constance Edwina, who *d.* 1920, dau. of the late Col. Henry Edward Hamlyn-Fane ; 2ndly, 1922, Zoë Virginie, who *d.* 1953, dau. of the late Albert Llewellyn Nugent, and widow of Claude Hume Campbell Guinness; *d.* 1927 ; *s.* by his son [4] FRANCIS HENRY, MC, 4th Baron; *b.* 1897: *m.* 1921, Mary Edith, da. of the late Rt. Rev. Lord William Rupert Ernest Gascoyne-Cecil, DD, 65th Bishop of Exeter [M. Salisbury]; *d.* 1972; *s.* by his el. son [5] JOHN ROBERT CECIL, 5th Baron, and present peer.

MANSFIELD AND MANSFIELD, EARL OF. (Murray.)
[Earl G.B. 1776 and 1792.]

I hope for better things.

Friendly to virtue alone.

WILLIAM DAVID MUNGO JAMES MURRAY, 8th Earl; *b.* July 7th, 1930; *s.* 1971; ed. at Eton, and Ch. Ch., Oxford; Bar. Inner Temple 1958; Lt. Scots Gds. (Reserve); Malaya 1949-50; Hereditary Keeper of Bruce's Castle of Lochmaben; Hon. Sheriff of Perthshire 1974; a Co. Councillor of Perth, a Member of Tay Salmon Fishery Board, and a Dir. of General Accident Fire & Life Assurance Gp.; a Member of British Delegation to European Parl. since 1973: *m.* 1955, Pamela Joan, da. of William Neill Foster, CBE, and has issue.

Arms,—Quarterly: 1st and 4th, azure, three mullets argent, within a double tressure flory counter flory or, *Murray*; 2nd and 3rd, gules, three crosses patée argent *Barclay*. Crest,—A buck's head couped proper, between his attires a cross patée argent. Supporters,— Two lions gules, armed or.

Residence,—Scone Palace, Perthshire. *Clubs,*— Turf, Pratt's, Garrick.

SONS LIVING

ALEXANDER DAVID MUNGO (*Viscount Stormont*), *b.* Oct. 17th, 1956.

Hon. James William, *b.* 1969.

DAUGHTER LIVING.

Lady Georgina Dorothea Mary, *b.* 1967.

SISTERS LIVING.

Lady Malvina Dorothea (*Countess of Moray*), *b.* 1936: *m.* 1964, the 20th Earl of Moray, of Doune Park, Doune, Perthshire, and Darnaway Castle, Forres, Morayshire.

Lady Mariota Cecilia, *b.* 1945; *m* 1969, the Hon. (Charles) Malcolm Napier [see L. Napier and Ettrick].

WIDOW LIVING OF SEVENTH EARL.

DOROTHEA HELENA (*Dorothea, Countess of Mansfield and Mansfield*), da. of the late Rt. Hon. Sir Lancelot Douglas Carnegie, GCVO, KCMG [see E. Southesk, colls.]: *m.* 1928, the 7th Earl, who *d.* 1971.

COLLATERAL BRANCHES LIVING.

Issue of the late Major the Hon. Alexander David Murray, brother of 6th Earl, *b.* 1871, *d.* 1924: *m.* 1908, Christian Maule, who *d.* 1964, da. of Sir James Thomas Stewart-Richardson, 14th Bt.:—

David John, *T.D.*, *b.* 1919 ; *ed.* at Wellington Coll., and at Magdalene Coll., Camb.; is Major Seaforth Highlanders (T.A. Reserve) ; European War 1939-45 in France, Middle East, Italy and Germany : *m.* 1961, Joanna, dau. of the late Lt. J. G. Lincoln, R.N., and has issue living, Alexander David, *b.* 1962. *Residence,*—Moy House, Forres, Morayshire.——Maryot Louisa (Windyridge, Dunphail, Morayshire) *b.* 1910.——Elizabeth Helen (1, The Colony, Burnham-on-Sea, Somerset), *b.* 1912: *m.* 1937, Lt.-Col. Charles Richard Wynn Brewis, MC, Welch Regt., who *d.* 1967, and from whom she obtained a divorce 1945, and has issue living, Simon David Richard Wynn, *b.* 1941; Maj. Parachute Regt.——Christian Anne, *b.* 1913; late 3rd Officer WRNS.

Granddaughter of the late Charles Archibald Murray (*infra*):—

Issue of the late Archibald John Percy Murray, *b.* 1867, *d.* 1943: *m.* 1907, Dulcibella who *d.* 1949, el. dau. of the late Collingwood Lindsay Wood, of Freeland, Forgandenny:—

Joan Noël, *b.* 1911 : *m.* 1st, 1933, William Neill Graham-Menzies, who *d.* 1943 ; 2ndly, 1950, Lieut.-Col. Michael John Lindsay, D.S.O., 1st King's Dragoon Guards, and has issue living, (by 1st marriage,

Cynthia Lindsay, *b.* 1936: *m.* 1962, Col. Charles Timothy Llewellen Palmer, late 7th Hussars, MO of West Street Farm, Gt. Somerford, Chippenham, Wilts.) [M. Lincolnshire], and has issue living Julian Neil *b.* 1963, Charles Anthony *b.* 1967, Michael Malcolm *b.* 1971, Alexandra Joan *b.* 1964,— (by 2nd m.) William Murray, *b.* 1952. *Residence,*—Hallyburton, Coupar Angus, Perthshire.

Grandchildren of the late Hon. Charles John Murray, 2nd son of 3rd Earl :—
Issue of the late Charles Archibald Murray, *b.* 1836, *d.* 1924: *m.*1st, 1865, Lady Adelaide Emily Feilding, who *d.* 1870, dau. of 7th Earl of Denbigh; 2ndly, 1878, Blanche, who *d* 1926, dau. of Sir Thomas Moncreiffe, 7th Bt. :—
(By 2nd m.) Lilian Edith, *b.* 1884: *m.* 1919, Brig. Harold Senhouse Pinder, CBE, MC, late R. Leics. Regt., who *d.* 1974, and has issue living, John Humphrey Murray (26, Bloomfield Terr., SW1), *b.* 1924: *m.* 1964, Pauline Hawtayne Lewin,—Margaret Lilian (Avington Park House, Winchester), *b.* 1920. *Residence,*—Burghclere Grange, nr. Newbury, Berks.

PREDECESSORS.—[1] *Sir* DAVID Murray, Knt., Cupbearer and Master of the Horse, and Capt. of the Guard to James VI. of Scotland ; accompanied the King to England, and was cr. *Lord Scone* (peerage of Scotland) 1605, and *Viscount Stormont* (peerage of Scotland) 1621, with remainder to Sir Mungo Murray, 4th son of John, 1st Earl of Tullibardine (D. Atholl), to John (Earl of Annandale), and to Andrew Murray, who in 1641 was cr. *Lord Balvaird* (peerage of Scotland &c.; *d.s.p.* 1631; *s.* by [2] *Sir* MUNGO, 2nd Viscount (ante); *d.s.p.* 1642; *s.* by [3] JAMES 3rd Viscount, who had previously *s.* as 2nd *Earl of Annandale; d.s.p.*1658, when the Earldom of Annandale became extinct, and the Lordship of Scone and Viscountcy of Stormont devolved upon [4] DAVID, 4th Viscount, who had previously *s.* his father Andrew Murray (ante) as 2nd *Lord Balvaird* ; was fined £1,500 by Cromwell's Act of grace and pardon 1654 ; *d.* 1668 ; *s.* by his son [5] DAVID, 5th Viscount, opposed the Union, and was called upon to surrender at the breaking out of the Rebellion 1715; *d.* 1731 ; *s.* by his son [6] DAVID, 6th Viscount ; *d.* 1748 ; *s.* by his son [7] DAVID, K.T., P.C., 7th Viscount ; was Justice Gen. of Scotland, Ambassador to Paris and Vienna 1772-8, a Sec. of State 1779-82, Pres. of the Council, and a Representative Peer 1754-90 ; *s.* his uncle as 2nd *Earl of Mansfield* (see *⋆*⋆ infra) 1793 : *m.* 2ndly, 1776, the Hon. Louisa Cathcart (E. Cathcart), who in 1793 *s.* her uncle as Countess of Mansfield under patent of 1776, she *d.* 1843, and was *s.* by her grandson the 4th Earl; *d.* 1796; *s.* by his son [8] WILLIAM, K.T., 3rd Earl ; *b.* 1777; was Lord-Lieut. of Clackmannanshire : *m.* 1797, Frederica, dau. of the Most Rev. William Markham, Archbishop of York; *d.* 1840; *s.* by his son [9] WILLIAM DAVID, K.T., 4th Earl; *b.* 1806; M.P. for Aldborough (*C*) 1830, for Woodstock 1831, for Norwich 1832-7, and for Perthshire 1837-40 ; a Lord of the Treasury 1834-5, and Lord High Commr. of Scottish Gen. Assembly 1852, 1858, and 1859 ; Lord-Lieut. and Sheriff Principal of Clackmannan ; in 1843 *s.* his grandmother (ante) in the Earldom of 1776: *m.* 1829, Louisa, who *d.* 1837, dau. of Cuthbert Ellison, of Hebburn, Durham; *d.* 1898; *s.* by his grandson [10] WILLIAM DAVID, P.C. (son of the late William David, Viscount Stormont), 5th Earl; *b.* 1860; *d.* 1906; *s.* by his brother [6] ALAN DAVID, 6th Earl; *b.* 1864; Gentleman Usher of the Green Rod (Order of the Thistle) 1895-1917 : *m.* 1899, Margaret Helen Mary, who *d.* 1933, dau. of Sir Malcolm MacGregor, 4th Bt. : *d.* 1935 ; *s.* by his son [7] MUNGO DAVID MALCOLM, 7th Earl; *b.* 1900; Gov. of Edinburgh and E. of Scotland Coll. of Agric. 1925-30; Lord High Commr. to Gen. Assembly of Ch. of Scotland 1961-62; Lord Lieut. of Perthshire 1960-71; MP for Perthshire and Kinross 1931-35: *m.* 1928, Dorothea Helena, da. of the late Rt. Hon. Sir Lancelot Douglas Carnegie, GCVO, KCMG [E. Southesk, colls.]; *d.* 1971; *s.* by his son [8] WILLIAM DAVID MUNGO JAMES, 8th Earl and present peer; also Viscount Stormont, Lord Scone, and Lord Balvaird.

⋆⋆ [1] *Hon.* WILLIAM Murray, 3rd son of 5th Viscount Stormont; successively Solicitor-Gen. Attorney-Gen., and Lord Ch. Justice of England ; cr. *Baron Mansfield*, of Mansfield, co. Notts (peerage of Great Britain) 1756, and *Earl of Mansfield*, co. Nottingham (peerage of Great Britain) 1776, with remainder to his niece Louisa, wife of his nephew David, 7th Viscount Stormont, and *Earl of Mansfield*, co. Middlesex (peerage of Great Britain) 1792, with remainder to his nephew David, 7th Viscount Stormont (ante) ; *d.s.p.* 1793, when the Barony of Mansfield expired, and the Earldom of 1776 devolved upon LOUISA (ante), and the Earldom of 1792 upon his nephew DAVID, 7th Viscount Stormont (ante).

MANTON, BARON.   (Watson.)   [Baron U.K. 1922.]

JOSEPH RUPERT ERIC ROBERT WATSON, 3rd Baron; *b.* Jan. 22nd, 1924; *s.* 1968; ed. at Eton; late Capt. 7th Hussars, and Life Guards: *m.* 1951, Mary Elizabeth, da. of the late Maj. Thomas Dennehy Hallinan, of Ashbowne, Glounthaune, co. Cork, and has issue.

𝔄rms,—Argent, on a chevron azure between four martlets, three in chief and one in base sable, a crescent between two roses of the field. 𝔊rest,—A gryphon passant sable in front of an oak tree proper. 𝔖upporters,—On either side a gryphon per fesse azure and argent, charged on the shoulder with a rose also argent.

Residence,—Houghton Hall, Sancton, Yorks.
Clubs,—Cavalry, Jockey.

SONS LIVING.
Hon. MILES RONALD MARCUS, *b.* May 7th, 1958.
Hon. Thomas Philip (triplet), *b.* 1958.

DAUGHTERS LIVING.
Hon. Claire Georgina, *b.* 1952.
Hon. Fiona Caroline Mary, *b.* 1953.
Hon. Victoria Monica (triplet), *b.* 1958.

UNCLES LIVING. *(Son of 1st Baron.)*
Hon. Robert Fraser, *b.* 1900; ed. at Wellington Coll., and at Trin. Coll., Camb.; *m.* 1st, 1928, Angela Blanche, who *d.* 1959, da. of the late Lt.-Col. George Talbot Lake Denniss, Roy. Wifts. Regt.; 2ndly, 1961, Mrs. Enid Cameron, and has issue living, (by 1st m.) Shirley Angela Josephine (5, Campden Hill Court, Campden Hill Rd., W8), *b.* 1932; *m.* 1958 (m. diss. 1974), David T. Chantler, and has issue living, Peter David Robert *b.* 1963, Angela Margaret Jennifer *b.* 1961. *Residences,*—Thankerton House, Windlesham, Surrey; 11, Cadogan Sq., SW1. *Club,*—White's.
Hon. Richard Mark, *b.* 1906; ed. at Eton; 1940-45 War as Flight-Lieut. RAFVR; Attaché at British Embassy, Washington 1930-32, and at Paris 1932-34; Cdr. of Order of Falcon with Star, of Iceland. *Residence,*—55, Brompton Sq., SW3.

WIDOW LIVING OF SON OF FIRST BARON.
Joan, dau. of the late Capt. Philip Wyndham Cobbold [M. Abergavenny colls.]: *m.* 1925, the Hon. Alastair Joseph Watson, who *d.* 1955, and has issue living [see colls., infra]. *Residence,*—Newton Farm, Orford, Suffolk.

MOTHER LIVING.
Alethea Alice Mary Pauline (4, Belgrave Sq., SW1), da. of the late Lt.-Col. Philip Joseph Langdale OBE, JP, DL [see B. Mowbray, colls.]: *m.* 1923, the 2nd Baron Manton, who *d.* 1968, and from whom she obtained a divorce 1936.

WIDOW LIVING OF SECOND BARON.
LEILA JOAN *(Baroness Brownlow)*, (Belton House, Grantham; 2, Belgrave Mews West, SW1; Plumpton Mill, Plumpton, Sussex), da. of the late Maj. Philip Guy Reynolds, DSO, and formerly wife of the late John Dane Player: *m.* 2ndly, 1938, as his 2nd wife, the 2nd Baron, who *d.* 1968; 3rdly, 1969, as his 3rd wife, the 6th Baron Brownlow.

COLLATERAL BRANCH LIVING.
Issue of the late Hon. Alastair Joseph Watson, son of 1st Baron, *b.* 1901, *d.* 1955 : *m.* 1925, Joan (ante), dau. of the late Capt. Philip Wyndham Cobbold [M. Abergavenny, colls.] :—
Michael Oliver, *b.* 1926 : *m.* 1950, Virginia, dau. of the late Eustace Benyon Hoare [E. Coventry], and has issue living, Alastair James, *b* 1958,—George William, *b.* 1962,—Amanda Virginia, *b.* 1956. *Residence,*—Chillesford Lodge, Sudbourne, Woodbridge, Suffolk.—Andrew Philip, *b.* 1930; ed. at Eton, and at Magdalene Coll., Camb. (B.A. 1952, M.A. 1957): *m.* 1957, Annette Mary Helena, dau. of Gerald Wellington Williams, J.P. [see D. Northumberland, colls.], and has issue living, Simon Mark, *b.* 1959,—Nicholas Andrew, *b.* 1961,—Jonathan Philip, *b.* 1965,—Hugh Gerald, *b.* 1968. *Residence,*—Faldonside, Melrose, Roxburghshire. *Club,*—Cavalry.

PREDECESSORS.—[1] JOSEPH Watson, only son of George Watson, of Donisthorpe House, Moor Allerton, Yorkshire; *b.* 1873; Chm. of Joseph Watson and Sons (Limited), and of Olympia Agricultural Co. (Limited), and a Director of London and North-Western Railway; **cr.** *Baron Manton,* of Compton Verney, co. Warwick (peerage of United Kingdom) 1922 : *m.* 1898, Frances Claire, who *d.* 1944, dau. of Harold Nickols, of Sandford House, Kirkstall, near Leeds, and 2, Seamore Place, W. : *d.* 1922; *s.* by his el. son [2] GEORGE MILES, **2nd** Baron, *b.* 1899: *m.* 1st, 1923 (m. diss. 1936), Alethea Alice Mary Pauline, da. of the late Lt.-Col. Philip Joseph Langdale, OBE, JP, DL [B. Mowbray, colls.]; 2ndly, 1938, Leila Joan (who *m.* 3rdly, 1969, as his 3rd wife, the 6th Baron Brownlow), da. of the late Maj. Philip Guy Reynolds, DSO, and formerly wife of the late John Dane Player; *d.* 1968; *s.* by his only son [3] JOSEPH RUPERT ERIC ROBERT, 3rd Baron and present peer.

MANVERS, EARLDOM OF. (Pierrepont.) [Extinct 1955.]
DAUGHTER LIVING OF SIXTH EARL.
Lady (Frederica) Rozelle (Ridgway), *b.* 1925; 1939-5 War as Leading Wren WRNS; a writer: *m.* 1st, 1953 (m. diss. 1961), Maj. Alexander Montgomerie Greaves Beattie, Coldstream Gds; 2ndly, 1965, Richard Hollins Raynes, MB, BS, DPH, MFCM. *Residences,*—Dolphin's Leap, St. Margaret's Bay, Kent; 88, Narrow St., E14.

WIDOW LIVING OF SIXTH EARL.
MARIE LOUISE ROOSEVELT *(Countess Manvers)*, dau. of the late Sir Frederick William Louis (d'Hilliers Roosevelt Theodore) Butterfield, J.P., of Cliffe Castle, Keighley, Yorkshire, and 47, South Street, Mayfair, W1; an artist and painter (under name of M. L. R. Pierrepont): *m.* 1918, the 6th Earl, who *d.* 1955, when the title became ext. *Residences,*—Thoresby Park, Ollerton, Notts.; 22, Woodfall St., SW3.

MAR, COUNTESS OF. (of Mar.) [Earl precedence S. 1404.]
Think more.

MARGARET OF MAR, Countess in her own right (Premier Earldom of Scotland); *b.* Sept. 19th, 1940; *s.* 1975; recognised in the surname of " of Mar " by warrant of Lord Lyon 1967, when she abandoned her second christian name of Alison: *m.* 1959, Edward Noel Artiss, who was recognised in the surname of " of Mar " by Warrant of Lord Lyon 1967.

Hrms,—Azure, a bend between six cross-crosslets fitchée or. Crest—Upon a chapeau gules faced ermine, two wings each of ten pen feathers, erected and addorsed both blazoned as the shield. Supporters,—On either side a grifin argent, armed, beaked and winged or.
Residence,—Corgarff, 10, Cranberry Drive, Stourport-on-Severn, Worcs., DY13 8TH.

DAUGHTER LIVING.
Lady SUSAN HELEN *(Mistress of Mar)*, *b.* May 31st, 1963.
SISTER LIVING.
Lady Janet Helen OF MAR, *b.* 1946; ed. at St. Andrews Univ (MA): *m.* 1969, Laurence Duncan McDiarmid Anderson, MA, Lieut. RN, of 1 Dundonald Rd., Rosyth, Dun-

fermline, Fife, who was recognised in the surname of " of Mar " by warrant of Lord Lyon 1969, and had issue living, Elizabeth, *b.* 1970,—Catherine Jane, *b.* 1971.

AUNT LIVING. (*Raised to the rank of an Earl's daughter* 1967.)

Lady Margaret Isabel, *b.* 1921: *m.* 1943, John Bulley Bray Ayre, TD, late Maj. RA, of 1, Penhurst Park, Pointe Claire, PQ, Canada, and has issue living, Michael Desmonde Erskine (129, Frankl , Beaconsfield, PQ, Canada), *b.* 1944; ed. at Sir George Williams' Univ., Montreal (B.Eng): *m.* 19 , Jane Erica Lock, and has issue living, Nicholas Robert Erskine *b.* 1974,—Rosemary Bray, *b.* 195 ed. at McGill Univ. (BA).

MOTHER LIVING.

Millicent Mary (Corgarff, 10, Cranberry Drive, Stourport-on-Severn, Worcs. DY13 8TH), da. of William Salton: *m.* 1939 (m. diss. 1958), James Clifton Lane (subsequently recognised in the surname of " of Mar " and *s.* as 30th Earl of Mar), who *d.* 1975.

WIDOW LIVING OF THIRTIETH EARL.

MARJORIE AILEEN (*Marjorie, Countess of Mar*) (36, Prince's Court, Brompton Rd., SW3), da. of the late John Reginald Miller, and widow of Maj. C. W. S. Grice, Central Indian Horse, Indian Army: *m.* 1960, as his 2nd wife, the 30th Earl, who *d.* 1975.

COLLATERAL BRANCHES LIVING.

Grandchildren of the late Lady Eliza Philadelphia Erskine Goodeve (who *m.* 1862 the Rev. Edward Maule Cole), sister of 27th Earl:—

Issue of the late Major Seymour Hamilton Maule Cole, V.D., *b.* 1866, *d.* 1938 : *m.* 1892, Lillian May, who *d.* 1952, dau. of Michael Sullivan :—

Douglas Seymour Francis Erskine Maule (56B, Harbour Rd., Southbourne, Bournemouth), *b.* 1898; 1914-18 War as Lt. Dorset Regt., and Capt. Machine Gun Corps and RFC; 1939-45 War as Sqdn-Ldr. RAFVR, and Maj. Indian Army: *m.* 1st, 1924, Iris (who *d.* 1972, having obtained a divorce 1934), da. of the late Col. G. S. Broome, Indian Army (ret.); 2ndly, 1942, Rosa Florence, only da. of the late Lt. Stanley George Bartley, RN, and has issue living, (by 1st m.) Louis Malcolm Erskine (10, Aintree Rd., Furnace Green, Crawley, Sussex), *b.* 1931: *m.* 1955, Kathleen Jarvis, and has issue living, Julia Erskine *b.* 1961, Louise Erskine *b.* 1963,—Iris Erskine, *b.* 1929: *m.* 1950, Roger Harrison, of 8, Roman Cres., Southwick, Sussex, and has issue living, Sally Erskine *b.* 1951: *m.* 1st, 1970, Andrew Aitkenhead, who *d.* 1971; 2ndly, 1973, Grenville Stacey, Victoria Erskine *b.* 1956.——Wilmot OF MAR (19, Ansdell Terr., W8; RNVR Club), *b.* 1903; late Lt. RINVR; matriculated the arms of Mar, Erskine, and Cole, and assumed the additional surname of Erskine (registered in Court of Lord Lyon) 1946; recognised in the surname of " of Mar " by Warrant of Lord Lyon 1961, when he abandoned the Christian names of Edward Robert Erskine Maule and the surname of Cole-Erskine, also matriculated the (unquartered) arms of Mar with a crescent gules in chief of the bend for differ-ence.——Edna Beryl Mavis Erskine (17, Redcliffe Place, SW10), *b.* 1896: *m.* 1919, Constantine Demetriadi, MBE, who *d.* 1951, and has issue living, Michael Anthony, *TD* (Loch-na-brae, by Gare lochhead, Helensburgh, Dunbartonshire, G84 0EN; RAC, and Army and Navy Club), *b.* 1920; ed. at Radley; Col. T & AVR 1968-74, ADC to HM 1974-75, M.Inst.PS; M.Inst.AM; a JP for Dunbartonshire; a Cotton Expert with J. & P. Coats, Ltd., of Glasgow, 1951-75; 1939-45 War as Maj. RWF (wounded, despatches twice, Burma star): *m.* 1948, Nancy Anna, el. da. of Ambrose John Rodocanachi, and has issue living, Peter Michael *b.* 1953; ed. at Radley, and Univ. Coll., London (BA), Philippa Nancy *b.* 1949 : *m.* 1975, Nikos Stamatopoulas of Athens, Antonia Claire *b.* 1959.

Grandchildren of the late Maj. Seymour Hamilton Maule Cole, VD (ante):—

Issue of the late Florence Violet Erskine CLIVE, *b.* 1893; resumed her former surname of Clive 1948, *d.* 19—: *m.* 1st, 1911 (m. diss. 1924), Col. John Alexander Barclay Penn Bowen, RE (ret.); 2ndly, 1925, Maj. Henry William Fitzroy Clive, Indian Army, who *d.* 1932; 3rdly, 1933, Frederick James St. John Croley, from whom she obtained a divorce 1944:—

(By 1st m.) John Erskine Penn, *b.* 1916: *m.* 1939, Kate Molly Faith, da. of Capt. Bernard Arthur Mildmay, Indian Army, and has issue living, Hugh Erskine Penn, *b.* 1945,—Elizabeth Angelo, *b.* 1947,—Halcyon, *b.* 1949.——Barbara, *b.* 1918: *m.* 1941, Raleigh Cornwallis Amesbury, and has issue living, Christopher Raleigh Cornwallis, *b.* 1943,—Bruce Hamilton, *b.* 1944,—Garry John, *b.* 1949,—Stephen Anthony, *b.* 1954,—Valentia, *b.* 1959.——(by 2nd m.) Henry Robert Somerset, *b.* 1926.

Issue of the late Crystal Mary Vera Erskine, *b.* 1895, *d.* 1972: *m.* 1915 (m. diss. 1925), Leonard Charles Simpson, late Indian State Railways :—

Robert Seymour, *b.* 1917: *m.* 19—, Ivy —, and has issue living, Robert, *b.* 19—, — a da., *b.* 19—.—— Yvonne Lilian, *b.* 1919: *m.* 1941, Frank Dator, of 34, Sunnyside Rd., Mahwah, N-J, USA, and has issue living, William Frank *b.* 1943: *m.* 1964, L'ala O'Lear, and has issue living, William Frank *b.* 1971, Lisa Lynn *b.* 1965, Rebecca Ann *b.* 1969,—Raymond James, *b.* 1946: *m.* 1967, Barbara Ann Roosa, and has issue living, Erin Ashley *b.* 1969, Michele Lynn *b.* 1967,—Darryl, *b.* 1947.—— Pamela Bernadene (c/o Lloyds Bank, 6, Pall Mall, SW1), *b.* 1921: *m.* 1st, 1940 (m. diss. 1948), Thomas Wallace Greenwood; 2ndly, 1948, Lt.-Col. Reginald John Isaac, OBE, MC, Intelligence Corps (ret.), and has issue living, (by 1st m.) Patricia Frances, *b.* 1941,—Marilyn Evelyn, *b.* 1946,— (by 2nd m.) James Robert, *b.* 1950,—Lionel Seymour John, *b.* 1954.

Issue of the late Lilian Maude Erskine Cole, *b.* 1900, *d.* 1965: *m.* 1st, 1926, Cyril Ernest Mus grave Ridsdale B.N. Railway, who *d.* 1957, and from whom she obtained a divorce 1933 2ndly, 1933, William, Louis Charles Gerard Cook, OBE (formerly Indian Imperial Police):—

(By 2nd m.) David William Erskine Gerard, *b.* 1936; ed. at Bedford Sch.: *m.* 1960, Joanne Elizabeth, da. of John Fisher, of Sydney, and has issue living, Jonathan David, *b.* 1961,—Jeremy Nicholas, *b.* 1963,—Caroline Louise, *b.* 1965.——(by 1st m.) Suzanne June Toy, *b.* 1928: *m.* 1951, David John Lush, from whom she obtained a divorce 1955; 2ndly, 1957, Claude Guy de la Faye d'Entrains Biard, and has issue living, (by 1st m.) Sarah Jane Judith, *b.* 1953.

Grandchildren of the late Lady Eliza Philadelphia Erskine (ante):—

Issue of the late Beatrice Madeline Erskine Cole, *b.* 1863, *d.* 1936 : *m.* 1884, Henry Tanner Ferguson, M.I.C.E., late of Wolleigh, Bovey Tracey, Devon, who *d.* 1909 :—

Donald Harry, *MC, VD*, *b.* 1890; 1914-18 War with Indian Cav. and Machine Gun Corps (MC, Order of the Nile, Militaire al Valore); formerly in Indian State Railways: *m.* 1st, 1920, Helen Woods, who *d.* 1967, and from whom he obtained a divorce 1927; 2ndly, 1930, Margaret, widow of Algernon G. H. Richards. *Residence,*—Toby Cottage, Sway, Hants.——Roland Edward Stuart (Tangs, Shipley Bridge, South Brent, Devon, TQ10 9ED), *b.* 1899; 1914-18 War with RNAS and RAF; sometime Indian Army (temp. commn.); Indian Imperial Police (ret.); 1939-45 War with RASC: *m.* 1941, Veronica Catherine, yr. da. of Henry Gore Hawker, of Strode, Ermington, Devon, and has issue living, Andrew Stuart, *b.* 1948; Ionsophericist with British Antarctic Survey 1971-74: *m.* 1975, Helen Alice, only da. of Col. P. N. Lodge, RA (ret.), of the Manor House, Compton Abdale, Glos.,— Janet Erskine, *b.* 1946; WRNS 1964-68: *m.* 19—, John Goodwin Fisk, 8th Hussars, of Ermewood Cottage, Harford, nr. Ivybridge, S. Devon, and has issue living, Adrian John Stuart *b.* 1970, Peter Maule Erskine *b.* 1973.——Violet Madeline (c/o English & Scottish & Austn. Bank, 388, Collins St., Melbourne, Anst.), *b.* 1893: *m.* 1919, P. E. Bernard, from whom she obtained a divorce 1926, and has issue living, Barbara Nancy (c/o ANZ Bank, 388, Collins St., Melbourne, Vic., Aust.), *b.* 1920: *m.* 1945, Ronald Hyde, MRCS, LRCP, who *d.* 1965, and has issue living, Timothy David Erskine *b.* 1946, Robin Paul Christopher *b.* 1948; a member of Aust. Inst. of Export: *m.* 1975, Margaret Anne Weichett, Max Anthony John *b.* 1951; ed. at Monash Univ., Vic., Aust. (BA), James Rupert *b.* 1955, Lucy Susan Elizabeth (twin) *b.* 1955.

Grandchildren of the late Beatrice Madeline Erskine Ferguson (ante):—

Issue of the late George Hamilton Ferguson, KPM, *b.* 1896, *d.* 1970: *m.* 1931 (m. diss. 1948), Dorothy Mary Kate Susie Emily Vaughan, da. of the late Sir Robert (Vaughan) Gower, KCVO, OBE, MP:—

Robert Maule Gower, *b.* 1932; ed. at Harrow ——Beatrice Margaret, *b.* 1933: *m.* 1963, Norman Carey Booth Creek, of 2150, W. 49th Av., Vancouver 13, BC, and has issue living, Carey Hamish Ferguson, *b.* 1964,—Benjamin Robert, *b.* 1965,—Nicola Robin, *b.* 1967,—Kanina Susanna Erskine, *b.* 1970.—— Sally Pauline June, *b.* 1941: *m.* 1968, Lt.-Cdr. Ian Cochrane, RN (ret.), of Butts Farm Cottage, Lockerly, Romsey, Hants.

Issue of the late Helen Evelyn Ferguson, *b.* 1886, *d.* 1962: *m.* 1914, Harold Henry Wyndham Newman, who *d.* 1963:—
Durnford Frederick Wyndham (Tanglewood, 67, The Gateway, Woking, Surrey), *b.* 1917; Diploma of Faraday House; CEng, FIEE; Ch. Eng., British Airports Authority, Heathrow Airport, London; late Sqdn.-Leader RAF; 1939-45 War as Capt. RE: *m.* 1948, Joan (Jane) Merriel Hollway, and has issue living, James Richard Wyndham *b.* 1950,—Clare Marian Wyndham, *b.* 1953.

Issue of the late Mary Beatrice Erskine Ferguson, *b.* 1888, *d.* 1970: *m.* 1st, 1912, Maj. Hubert Symons, RFA, who *d.* (killed in action) 1918; 2ndly, 1937, Graham Parsons Earwaker, who *d.* 1971:—
(By 1st m) Jean Erskine, *b.* 1916: *m.* 1940, Maj. Richard Andrew Joscelyne, MC, RTR, of Withycombe, Winsford, Minehead, and has issue living, Andrew Michael Hubert, *b.* 1946; Capt. 2nd Bn. Scots Gds.,—Sarah Anne, *b.* 1941: *m.* 1963, Anthony Owen Blishen, OBE, Diplo. Ser., of 16, Lebanon Park, Twickenham, Middx., and has issue living, James Peter Anthony *b.* 1966, Robert Edward Henry *b.* 1970, David Francis Andrew *b.* 1972, Catherine Annabelle *b.* 1964.

Grandchildren of Mary Beatrice Erskine Earwaker (ante):—
Issue of the late Peter Nicholas Symons, *b.* 1917, *d.* 1951: *m.* 1940, Suzanne Penzer Haynes (*Lady Marshall*) (who *m.* 2ndly, 1953, Cdr. Sir Douglas Marshall, R.N.V.R.), of Hatt, nr. Saltash, Cornwall:—
Heugh Sherwood, *b.* 1949.——Nicola Penn, *b.* 1942: *m.* 1963, John Philip Coverdale, of Brandwood, St. John's Lane, Bewdley, Worcs., and has issue living, Peter John, *b.* 1970,—Anna Frances Mary, *b.* 1966,—Sarah Elizabeth, *b.* 1968.——Celia Mary, *b.* 1947: *m.* 1973, Erich Gerhard Rinagl, of Reitherstrasse 5, A.4060, Leonburg, Austria.——Melanie Anne (twin), *b.* 1947: *m.* 1970, Jeremy John Shales, of 10, Queen Anne's Close, Twickenham, Middx.

Descendants of the late Hon. Henry David Erskine, 3rd son of 24th Earl [see E. Mar and Kellie].

Grandchildren of the late Mary Margaret Anna ZWILCHENBART-ERSKINE, aud. of the late Rev. the Hon. Thomas Erskine (4th son of 24th Earl), *b.* 1829, *d.* 1906 (having assumed the additional name of Erskine for herself and son 1884): *m.* 1864, as his second wife, Rodolph Zwilchenbart, who *d.* 1883:—
Issue of the late Gratney Rodolph ZWILCHENBART-ERSKINE, *b.* 1871, *d.* 1930: *m.* 1896, Theodora, who *d.* 1958, dau. of the late W. H. Laverton, of Leighton, Westbury, Wilts:—
Michael Gratney, *b.* 1914: ed. at Eton.——Helen Mary, *b.* 1901: *m.* 1928, Brigadier Alec Palmer. ffleetwood Churchill, OBE, Indian Army, who *d.* 1947, and has issue living, John ffleetwood (3, Albany Mansions, Albert Bridge Rd., SW11), *b.* 1934; ed. at Wellington Coll., and at Trin. Hall, Camb.: *m.* 1970, Stephanie, da. of H. van den Bergh, of The Hague, Holland, and has issue living, John Edward ffleetwood *b.* 1973,—Charles ffleetwood, *b.* 1937; ed. at Wellington Coll., and at Jesus Coll., Camb. *Residence,*—Givons Grove, North Reading Road, Fleet, Hants.

PREDECESSORS.—According to Lord Hailes the origin of the Earls of Mar is "lost in antiquity". A Mormaer of Mar served as the battle of Clontarf 1014. [1] ROTHRI, Mormaer (or Earl) of Mar witnessed foundation charter of Scone 1114-15, and King David I's charter to Dunfermline Abbey 1124-29; *s.* by [2] MORGUND, who was *s.* by [3] GILCHRIST, *s.* by [4] DUNCAN (son of Morgund), who was *s.* by his son [5] WILLIAM; *s.* by his son [6] DONALD, father of [7] GRATNEY, who *s.* about 1297: *m.* Christian (1st *Lady of Garioch*), sister of King Robert I of Scotland; *d.* before 1305; *s.* by his son [8] DONALD, Regent of Scotland, *d.* 1332; *s.* by his son [9] THOMAS, Great Chamberlain of Scotland; Lordship of Garioch confirmed 1357; *d.s.p.* 1373/4; *s.* by his sister [10] MARGARET, Countess of Mar; *d.* 1390; *s.* by her da. (by her 1st husband William, Earl of Douglas) [11] ISABEL, Countess of Mar; *d.* 1408, having in 1404 granted a life rent in the Earldom to her husband, [12] *Sir* ALEXANDER Stewart, who *d.* 1435; *s.* by [13] ROBERT, 1st Lord Erskine, son of Sir Thomas Erskine, of Alloa and Dun, by his second wife, Janet; returned heir of line of Isabel (ante), and assumed the Earldom; *d.* 1452; *s.* by his son [14] THOMAS, 2nd Lord Erskine (and *de jure* 14th Earl); in 1457 before an Assize of Error the Earldom was found to have devolved upon the Crown, but this was negatived by Queen Mary's restoration and by the ruling of the Court of Session in 1626: he was *s.* by his son [15] ALEXANDER (*de jure* 15th Earl), who was *s.* by his son [16] ROBERT (*de jure* 16th Earl); fell at Flodden 1513; *s.* by his son [17] JOHN (*de jure* 17th Earl); *d.* 1555; *s.* by his son [18] JOHN, 6th Lord Erskine, who was in 1565 *restored* by Queen Mary to the Earldom of Mar and Lordship of Garioch (through Janet, great-granddaughter of Gratney, 7th Earl of Mar [ante]), and of which his ancestor Thomas, 2nd Lord Erskine was declared to have been unjustly dispossessed, and this restoration was confirmed by an Act of Parliament which expressly recognized Robert, 1st Lord Erskine to have been rightfully Earl of Mar, and in the Decreet of Ranking of 1606 (according to the documents then produced) the Earl of Mar was assigned a position conformable to writs of 1393 and 1404: was Regent of Scotland 1571-72; *d.* 1572; *s.* by his son [19] JOHN, *KG*, 19th Earl; attainted 1584 and restored 1585; was Lord Treasurer of Scotland 1616-30; cr. *Lord Cardross* 1610 (with power of nomination); *d.* 1634; *s.* in the Lordship of Cardross (according to nomination) [see E. Buchan], and in the Earldom of Mar by his son, [20] JOHN, *PC*, 20th Earl, an Extraordinary Lord of Session 1620-26 and 1628-30; *d.* 1654; *s.* by his son [21] JOHN, 21st Earl; *d.* 1668; *s.* by his son, [22] CHARLES, *PC*, 22nd Earl; Col. Roy. Scots Fusiliers, which Regt. he raised; *d.* 1689; *s.* by his son, [23] JOHN, *KT, PC*, 23rd Earl; Sec. of State 1706, Keeper of the Signet, and a Representative Peer; having defended the cause of the Stuarts in 1715 his honours were attainted and his estates forfeited; *d.* 1732, and the Alloa property was entailed on his da. Lady Frances Erskine, who but for the attainder would have been Countess of Mar; *s.* by his grandson. [24] JOHN FRANCIS Erskine, 24th Earl, to whom the Earldom was restored by Act of Parliament 1824 through his mother, Lady Frances, as "grandson and lineal representative" of the attainted Earl; *d.* 1825; *s.* by his son [25] JOHN THOMAS, 25th Earl; *d.* 1828; *s.* by his son, [26] JOHN FRANCIS MILLER, 26th Earl; served at Waterloo; successfully claimed to be 11th *Earl of Kellie* 1835; *d.s.p.* 1866, when the Earldom of Kellie devolved upon his cousin, while he was *s.* in the ancient Earldom of Mar by his nephew (the heir-general) [27] JOHN FRANCIS ERSKINE Goodeve-Erskine, 27th Earl [son of Lady Frances Jemina (el. sister of 26th Earl), by her marriage with William James Goodeve, of Clifton]; *b.* 1836; assumed by legal authorization 1866 the additional surname of Erskine; for 36 years a Representative Peer for Scotland: succession to heir-general confirmed with precedence of 1404 by the Declaratory Act of Parliament passed in 1885 (Restitution of Mar Act): *m.* 1866, Alice Mary Sinclair, who *d.* 1924, da. of the late John Hamilton, of Hilston Park, Monmouthshire; *d.* 1930; *s.* by his only son, [28] JOHN FRANCIS HAMILTON SINCLAIR CUNLIFFE BROOKS FORBES, 28th Earl; *m.* 1903, Sibyl May Dominica, who *d.* 1958, only da. of the late Robert Heathcote; *d.* 1932; *s.* by his cousin [29] LIONEL WALTER Young, 29th Earl (grandson of Lady Frances Jemima Erskine Young, el. sister of 27th Earl, *b.* 1891; assumed the additional name of Erskine (registered in Court of Lord Lyon) 1933; *d.* 1965; *s.* by his kinsman, [30] JAMES CLIFTON, 30th Earl (el. son of Charles Macdonald Lane, CSI, el. son of Alice, who *m.* James Horsburgh Lane, da. of Lady Frances Jemima Erskine Young (ante); recognised in the surname of "of Mar" by warrant of Lord Lyon 1959: *m.* 1st, 1939 (m. diss. 1948), Millicent Mary, da. of William Salton; 2ndly, 1960, Marjorie Aileen, da. of the late John Reginald Miller, and widow of Maj. C. W. S. Grice, Indian Army; *d.* 1975; *s.* by his only da. [31] MARGARET, present peeress, and Lady Garioch.

MAR and KELLIE, EARL OF. (Erskine.) [**Earl of Mar S. 1565, Earl of Kellie S. 1616.**]

I think more.   He adds honour to that of his ancestors.

UNIONE·FORTIOR
Strengthened by unity.

JOHN FRANCIS HERVEY ERSKINE, 13th Earl of Mar, and 15th Earl of Kellie, Premier Viscount of Scotland; *b.* Feb. 15th, 1921; *s.* 1955; *ed.* at Eton, and at Trin. Coll., Camb.; a Representative Peer for Scotland 1959-63; Maj. (ret.) Scots Guards and Argyll and Sutherland Highlanders (T.A.); is a Member of Queen's Body Guard for Scotland (Roy. Co. of Archers), Hereditary Keeper of Stirling Castle, Lord-Lt. for Clackmannanshire, an Elder of Church of Scotland, a JP of Clackmannanshire, and a K.St.J.; Vice-Convenor for Clackmannanshire 1961-64; 1939-45 War (despatches, Africa, Italy, and France and Germany stars): *m.* 1948, Pansy Constance, da. of Gen. Sir Augustus Francis) Andrew Nicol Thorne, KCB, CMG, DSO [B. Penrhyn], and has issue.

Arms,—Quarterly: 1st and 4th argent, a pale sable, *Erskine;* 2nd and 3rd azure, a bend between six cross crosslets fitchée or, *Mar:* over all, on ian escutcheon gules, the royal crown of Scotland proper, within a double tressure flory counterflory or, ensigned with an earl's coronet, *Kellie;* behind the shield are placed in saltire a key, wards outwards or, and a baton gules, garnished or, and ensigned with a castle of the last (the insignia of the office of Hereditary Keeper of the Castle of Stirling). Crests,—1st, on a cap of maintenance gules, turned up ermine a dexter hand, holding a skene in pale argent, hilted and pommelled or, over crest "Je pense plus" [I think more]; 2nd, on a cap of maintenance gules, turned up ermine a demi-lion rampant guardant gules, armed argent, over crest "Decori decus addit avito" [He adds honour to the honour of his ancestors]. Supporters,—Two griffins gules, armed, beaked, and winged or.

Seat,—Claremont House, Alloa, Clackmannanshire, FK10 2JF.

SONS LIVING.

JAMES THORNE (*Lord Erskine*), *b.* March 10th, 1949; *ed.* at Eton: *m.* 1974, Mary Irene, yr. da. of Dougal McD. Kirk, and formerly wife of Roderick James Mooney.
Hon. Alexander David, *b.* 1952; *ed.* at Eton, and Pembroke Coll., Cambs. (BA).
Hon. Michael John, *b.* 1956; *ed.* at Eton.

DAUGHTER LIVING.

Lady Fiona (twin), *b.* 1956.

BROTHERS LIVING.

Hon. David Hervey, *b.* 1924; *ed.* at Eton, and at Trin. Coll., Camb. (MA); Bar. Inner Temple 1950; late Capt. Scots Gds.; Co. Councillor, and a JP for Suffolk; Italy and Palestine 1943-45 (Italy star): *m.* 1953, Jean Violet, el. da. of Lt.-Col. Archibald Vivian Campbell Douglas, late Scots Gds. [see de Bunsen, Bt. (ext.)], and has issue living, Janet Cicely, *b.* 1955,—Catherine Marjorie, *b.* 1958,—Mary Viola, *b.* 1962. *Residence,*—Felsham House, Felsham, Bury St. Edmunds. *Club,*—Guards'.
Hon. Robert William Hervey, *b.* 1930; *ed.* at Eton, and at King's Coll., Camb.; late 2nd Lieut. Scots Gds.: *m.* 1st, 1955 (m. diss. 1964), Jennifer Shirley, yr. da. of L. J. Cardew Wood, of Farnham Royal, Bucks.; 2ndly, 1969, Annemarie Alvarez de Toledo, da. of Jean Lattès, of 31, Rue Guinegand, Paris VI, and has issue living, (by 2nd m.) Alister Robert, *b.* 1970. *Residence,*—2, Cambridge Pl., W8. *Club,*—Savile.

COLLATERAL BRANCHES LIVING.

Issue of the late Capt. the Hon. Francis Walter Erskine, yr. son of 12th Earl, *b.* 1899, *d.* 1972: *m.* 1925, Phyllis, who *d.* 1974, da. of the late John F. Burstall, of Quebec, Canada:—
Rosemary Susan, *b.* 1927: *m.* 1947, Mark Alastair Coats, late Lt. Gren. Gds., and has issue living, Nicholas James, *b.* 1952,—Virginia Jane, *b.* 1954.——Jean Felicity (*Hon. Mrs. V. Patrick H. Wills*), *b.* 1931: *m.* 1st, 1951 (m. diss. 1961), Capt. the Hon Desmond Rupert Strutt, late Coldm. Gds. [see B. Belper]; 2ndly, 1963, the Hon. Victor Patrick Hamilton Wills, of Lichfield Down, Whitchurch, Hants. [see B. Dulverton].

Issue of the late Rt. Hon. Sir William Augustus Forbes Erskine, G.C.M.G., M.V.O., 2nd son of 11th Earl, *b.* 1871, *d.* 1952: *m.* 1908, Georgie Viola Eleanor who *d.* 1972, da. of the late William Humble Dudley Ward [E. Dudley, colls.]:—
Cynthia Romola, *b.* 1910: *m.* 1943, Pierre Bressy, former Ambassador, French Diplo. Ser., who *d.* 1973, and has issue living, Francois Pierre Erskine, *b.* 1946,—Catherine Marie Charlotte, *b.* 1945: *m.* 1972, Vicomte Jean-Marie de Bourgoing of 54, Boulevard de la Tour-Maubourg, Paris VII. *Residenc e,*—23, Boulevard Flandrin, Paris XVI.——Margaret Elsie Viola, *b.* 1913: *m.* 1950, Major Denys E rnest Glynn Oglander, and has issue living, William Auberon Erskine, *b.* 1953,—John Peter Er skine, *b.* 1957,—Frances Mary Viola, *b.* 1951,—Mary Theresa Catherine Joan, *b.* 1955. *Resid ence,*—Nunwell Park, Brading, Isle of Wight.

Issue of the late Rev. the Hon. Alexander Penrose Forbes Erskine, 3rd son of 11th Earl, *b.* 1881, *d.* 1925 : *m.* 1916, Irene Annette (who *d.* 1968, having *m.* 2ndly, 1930, the Rt. Rev. Frederic Llewellyn Deane (Bishop of Aberdeen and Orkney 1917-43), who *d.* 1952), dau. of the late Rt. Rev. Archibald Ean Campbell, Bishop of Glasgow and Galloway [E. Midleton]:—
Archibald Walter Forbes, *b.* 1918; *ed.* at Eton, and at New Coll., Oxford (B.M. and B.Ch. 1942, M.A. 1946): *m.* 1958, J. M. Thérèse, el. da. of J. B. Heppel, of 12, Holligrove Rd., Bromley, Kent, and has issue living, James Alexander, *b.* 1959,—Robert John, *b.* 1960,—Benjamin David, *b.* 1971. *Residence,*—130, Walm Lane, NW2.——David Alexander John, *TD, b.* 1921; *ed.* at Eton, and at New Coll., Oxford (BA); formerly Capt. 5th Bn. Queen's Own Cameron Highlanders (TA); 1939-45 War: *m.* 1st, 1947 (m. diss. 19—), Margaret Eleanor, da. of Rear-Adm. Steuart Arnold Pears,

CBE; 2ndly, 1970, Mrs. Joan Mary Gilmour, da. of Brig. James Brindley Bettington, DSO, MC, and has issue living, (by 1st m.) Robin David, b. 1948,—Peter Alexander, b. 1950,—Alistair John, b. 1959. *Residence,*—Les Merriennes, Forest, Guernsey.

Granddaughter of the late Augustus Erskine, el. son of the late Hon. James Augustus Erskine (infra):—
Issue of the late Capt. Bushby Lyons Erskine, b. 1890, d. 1962: m. 1919, Lilian, dau. of Francis William Blenkey, of Beckenham:—
Sheelah Kathleen ERSKINE, b. 1921; resumed surname of Erskine 19—: m. 19—, — Tortonese.

Grandchildren of the late Hon. James Augustus Erskine, brother of 12th Earl of Kellie:—
Issue of the late Edmond Waterton Coningsby Erskine, b 860, d 1926: m. 1st, 1882, Evelina Florence (who d. 1949, having obtained a divorce 1894), dau. of the late George Jones, of Cupar Grange, Trinidad ; 2ndly, 1894, Edith, who d. 1957, dau. of the late Major Alexander Crombie, 72nd Regt.:—
(By 2nd m.) Monica Violet, b. 1897: m. 1st, 1923, Lt.-Col. G. D. Maynard, who d. 1923; 2ndly, 1926, Lt.-Col. Hugh Alan Heber-Percy [see D. Northumberland, colls.]. *Residence,*—Dorset Farm, White River, Transvaal.

Issue of the late Evelyn Pierrepont Erskine, b. 1870, d. 1953: m. 1897, Amy Maria, who d. 1959, da. of Joseph Hough, grazier, of Collie River, W. Aust.:—
Charles Seymour (21, Bellevue Terr., Swanbourne, W. Aust.), b. 1905: m. 1928, Mona Roslynn, da. of Henry Murphy, of co. Cork.——Gratney Pierrepont (12, Devon Rd., Swanbourne, W. Aust.), b. 1911; 1939-45 War with AIF: m. 1st, 1931 (m. diss. 1935), Elsie Evelyn, da. of the late I. Nutall, of W. Aust.); 2ndly, 1940, Beth Rosemary Kenworthy, and has issue living (by 1st m.) Yvonne Constance, b. 1932,—(by 2nd m.) Gratney Evelyn (20, Knight St., Wembley Downs, W. Aust.): m. 1967, Elaine Joy Marchant, of Claremont, W. Aust., and has issue living, Gregory Bryce b. 1972, Janine Gaye b. 1969.——Robert Fallowfield (17, Auburn Grove, Armadale, Vic., Aust. 3143), b. 1913; 1939-45 War with RAAF.——Maime Rhoda Wilhelmina (6, Tasman St., Albany, W. Aust. 6330): m. 1926, Lawrence Ridley Field, who d. 1951, and has issue living, Murray b. 1958, Susan b. 1957, Kay b. 1961,—Barrie Ridley (Crocker Way, Innaloo, W. Aust.), b. 1930: m. 1956, Gwen Murphy, of Victoria Park, W. Aust., and has issue living, Stephen b. 1955, Clinton b. 1958, Bradley b. 1959, Marilyn b. 1954,—Robin Erskine (155, Hare St., Albany, W. Aust.), b. 1938: m. 1960, Lorraine Whitfield, of Albany, W. Aust., and has issue living, Alan b. 1966, Yvonne b. 1963, Beverly b. 1965,— Naomi Laurel Erskine, b. 1928: m. 1949, John O'Keefe, of 4, Tasman St., Albany, W. Aust., and has issue living, Neil b. 1959, Carol b. 1950: m. 19—, Gary Thomas Adams, of Albany, W. Aust. (and has issue living, Tracy Lana b. 1966, Michelle Lisa b. 1968), Linda b. 1952: m. 1970, Kevin Albert Wallinger, of Albany, W. Aust., Diane b. 1954,—Derrice, b. 1933: m. 1953, John Joseph Jones, of Parkerville, W. Aust., and has issue living, Laurence John b. 1955, Mark b. 1957, Matthew b. 1961, Rachel b. 1963.——Azelma Aileen (126, Tribute St., Riverton, W. Aust. 6155), b. 1900.——Alice Amy Mar (126, Tribute St., Riverton, W. Aust. 6155), b. 1906: m. 1927, Wallace Kendal Ross, who d. 1971, and has issue living, Donald John Erskine (7, Windfield Rd., Melville Heights, W. Aust.), b. 1930: m, 1957, Margaret, da. of Colin Melville Thorn, of Langlands, York, W. Aust., and has issue living, Gregory Donald b. 1963, David Colin b. 1966,—Wendy Elizabeth, b. 1936: m. 1956, Ian Wilson, of Balga, W. Aust., and has issue living, Craig Ross b. 1959, Roderick Ian b. 1961, Scott Kendal b. 1964, Tracey Meryl b. 1957, Kellie Jillian b. 1970.

Issue of the late Hugh Bushby Johnson (who assumed by Deed Poll 1952 that surname in lieu of his patronymic), b. 1872, d. 1956: m. 1897, May, who d. 1950, dau. of John Valentine, of Bunbury, W. Australia:—
John William, b. 1899: m. 19—, and has issue living, Hugh Walter Bushby, b. 19—: m. 19—, Doris Gwen Crundwell, and has issue living, Christine Maria, b. 1946.——Kellie Edmund (of Oakley Rd., N. Bondi, NSW), b. 1902: m. 1924, Annie, da. of Robert Knox, and has issue living, Kellie Knox (4, Palermo Place, Allambie Heights, Sydney, NSW), b. 1931: m. 1959, Pamela Ann, da. of the late Alfred Edward Leer, and has issue living, Bryan Andrew b. 1966, Robyn Ann b. 1963.——Hugh Pierrepont Clayhills (6, Frederick St., Randwick, NSW), b. 1903: m. 1935, Edith Wilhelmina, da. of James Ralfs, of Randwick, NSW.——James Keith Brodie (of Cobham Av., West Ryde, NSW), b. 1907: m. 1949, Mary Douglas, da. of Arthur Ernest Savage, of Woolwich, Sydney, NSW, and has issue living, Lynette Mary, b. 1950, Catherine Evelyn, b. 1953,—Joanne Margaret, b. 1960.—— Esmé Mai Lydia (Pitt Town Rd., Kenthurst 2154, NSW), b. 1910: m. 1935, Claude Wentworth Jefferson, late Flt.-Lt. RAAF, who d. 1974, and has issue living, Ian David, b. 1945: m. 1968, Kay Leslie, da. of John Farren Price, of Sydney, NSW, and has issue living, Kalena Ann b. 1971.

PREDECESSORS.—[1] *Sir* ROBERT Erskine, Knt. (son of Sir Thomas Erskine of Alloa and Dun by his second wife, Janet, dau. and heir of Sir Edward Keith, of Synton, and widow of Sir David Barclay, of Brechin), a Commr. to treat for the release of James I. 1421, and one of the hostages for his ransom 1424, sat as *Lord Erskine* in Scottish Parliament 1426 ; served heir of Isabel, Countess of Mar 1438 ; *s.* by his son [2] THOMAS, 2nd Lord ; dispossessed of the Earldom at an Assize of Error 1457 ; sat in Parliament as Lord Erskine 1467 : *m.* Janet Douglas ; *d.* 1493 ; *s.* by his son [3] ALEXANDER, 3rd Lord ; guardian of James IV. ; *d.* 1510 ; *s.* by his son [4] ROBERT, 4th Lord ; killed at Flodden 1513 ; *s.* by his son [5] JOHN, 5th Lord, guardian of James V. ; Ambassador to France 1515 to 1535, and an Extraordinary Lord of Session, &c. ; *d.* 1552 ; *s.* by his son [6] JOHN, P.C., 6th Lord, was Regent of Scotland 1571, and guardian of James VI., &c.; Mary Queen of Scots restored to him the *Earldom of Mar* by charter 1565, though, according to the decision of the Committee of Privileges of the House of Lords in 1875, a new Earldom was created with remainder to heirs male; *d.* 1572; *s.* by his son [7] JOHN, K.G., P.C., 2nd Earl; High Treasurer of Scotland 1615-30; attainted 1584, and restored 1585; Ambassador to England 1603; cr. *Lord Cardross* (peerage of Scotland) 1610, with the right to assign the Lordship to whomsoever he might elect, which right was confirmed by charter in favour of his 2nd son Henry 1618; *d.* 1634; *s.* in Lordship of Cardross by his grandson David (see E. Buchan), and in Earldom by his son [8] JOHN, P.C., K.B., 3rd Earl; an Extraordinary Lord of Session 1620-6 and 1628-30, &c.; *d.* 1654; *s.* by his son [9] JOHN, 4th Earl; *d.* 1668; *s.* by his son [10] CHARLES, 5th Earl; was Col. Roy. Scots Fusiliers 1679-86, which regt. he raised; *d.* 1689; *s.* by his son [11] JOHN, K.T., P.C., 6th Earl; Sec. of State 1706, Keeper of the Signet, and a Representative Peer 1707-13; was attainted by Act of Parliament for having raised the insurrection of 1715; his forfeited estates were purchased by his brother Lord Grange (a Lord of Session) and David Erskine, of Dun, and the Alloa property was entailed on the heirs male of his dau. Lady Frances Erskine, wife of James Erskine, Lord Grange's son; *d.* 1732; *s.* by his grandson [12] JOHN FRANCIS, 7th Earl, who in 1824 was restored to the Earldom by Act of Parliament (but the Lordship of Erskine remains forfeit) as grandson and lineal representative of the attainted Earl; *d.* 1825; *s.* by his son [13] JOHN THOMAS, 8th Earl; *d.* 1828; *s.* by his son [14] JOHN FRANCIS MILLER, 9th Earl, as an officer in the Guards served at Waterloo; in 1835 successfully claimed to be 11th *Earl of Kellie* (see *⁎* infra); *d.s.p.* 1868; *s.* in Earldom of Kellie, the Viscountcy of Fentoun, and Lordship of Erskine of Dirleton, and of Dirleton by his cousin [15] WALTER CONINGSBY, C.B., 12th Earl of Kellie, Viscount Fentoun and Lord Erskine of Dirleton, 3rd son of the Hon. Henry David, 3rd son of 7th Earl of Mar; served in India with distinction, both as a military and a political officer; *d.* 1872; *s.* by his son [16] WALTER HENRY, 13th Earl of Kellie (who in 1875 successfully claimed to be 11th Earl of Mar, cr. 1565); *b.* 1839; was a Representative Peer for Scotland: *m.* 1863, Mary Anne, who *d.* 1927, dau. of the late William Forbes; *d.* 1888; *s.* by his el. son [17] WALTER JOHN FRANCIS, K.T., 12th Earl of Mar, and 14th Earl of Kellie; *b.* 1865; was Lord-Lieut. of Clackmannanshire 1898-1955; appointed Hereditary Keeper of Stirling Castle (with remainder to heirs male) 1923; Lord Clerk Register and Keeper of Signet of Scotland 1936-44, and Chancellor of Order of the Thistle 1933-49: *m.* 1892, Lady Susan Violet Ashley, who *d.* 1938, dau. of 8th Earl of Shaftesbury; *d.* 1955; *s.* by his grandson [18] JOHN FRANCIS HERVEY (el. son of the late John Francis Ashley, Lord Erskine, G.C.S.I., G.C.I.E., el. son of 12th Earl), 13th Earl of Mar, and 15th Earl of Kellie, and present peer; also Viscount Fentoun, Lord Erskine of Dirleton, and Lord Dirleton.

⁎ [1] *Sir* THOMAS Erskine, *K.G.*, 4th son of the Hon. Sir Alexander, 4th son of 5th Lord Erskine ; cr. *Lord Erskine of Dirleton* (peerage of Scotland) 1604, *Viscount Fentoun* and *Lord Dirleton* (peerage of Scotland) 1606, with remainder to his heirs male whatsoever, and *Earl of Kellie* (peerage of Scotland) 1619, with remainder to his heirs male whatsoever bearing the name of Erskine; *d.* 1639; *s.* by his grandson [2] THOMAS (son of Alexander, Viscount Fentoun), 2nd Earl ; *d.* unmarried 1643; *s.* by his brother [3] ALEXANDER, 3rd Earl, whose line failed on the death of [4—7] ALEXANDER, 7th Earl; *d.* 1797; *s.* by his kinsman [8] *Sir* CHARLES Erskine, 8th Earl, descendant of the Hon. Charles, 3rd son of 1st Earl, who in 1666 had been cr. a *Baronet* ; *d.* unmarried 1799; *s.* by his uncle [9] THOMAS, 9th Earl : *m.* 1771, Anne, who *d.* 1829, dau. of Adam Gordon, of Ardoch, *d.* 1828 ; *s.* by his brother [10] METHVEN, 10th Earl : *m.* 1781, Joanna, dau. of Adam Gordon (ante); *d.* 1829 ; *s.* by his kinsman [11] JOHN FRANCIS MILLER, 11th Earl, who had previously *s.* as 9th Earl of Mar (see ante).

March and Kinrara, Earl of (peerage of England), son of Duke of Richmond.

March, Earl of (peerage of Scotland), see Earl of Wemyss and March.

MARCHAMLEY, BARON. (Whiteley.) [Baron U.K. 1908.]

LIVE·TO·LIVE

JOHN WILLIAM TATTERSALL WHITELEY, 3rd Baron; *b.* April 24th, 1922; *s.* 1949; European War 1939-45 as Lieut. Roy. Armoured Corps, attached Indian Army: *m.* 1967, Sonia Kathleen Pedrick, and has issue.

Arms,—Per fesse dancettée sable and gules, in chief a pale or, thereon three bars of the second, in base a fleur-de-lis argent. *Crest*,—A stag's head couped argent, attired or, holding in the mouth a bell gold. *Supporters*, —*Dexter*, a griffin sejant : *sinister*, a hawk ; both per fesse gules and sable, armed and membered or, each charged on the fesse line with a fleur-de-lis argent.

Residence,—Whetcombe, North Huish, South Brent, S. Devon.

SON LIVING.

Hon. WILLIAM FRANCIS, *b.* July 27th, 1968.

SISTER LIVING.

Hon. Alice Tattersall. *b.* 1917; sometime Junior Com. A.T.S.: *m.* 1946, Robert Danby Bradford, and has issue living, Robert William Danby, *b.* 1947.—Andrew Mark Danby, *b.* 1949. *Residence*,—Membland, Haddington, E. Lothian, EH41 4JH.

WIDOW LIVING OF SON OF FIRST BARON.

Marjorie Gordon (*Lady Dreyer*), dau. of Ernest Jukes, of Rickmansworth, Herts: *m.* 1st, 1939, Maj. the Hon. Ronald George Whiteley, O.B.E., who *d.* 1957; 2ndly, 1959, Adm. Sir Desmond Parry Dreyer, GOB, CBE, DSC (ret.). *Residences*,—35, Brompton Sq., SW3; Brook Cottage, Cheriton, Alresford, Hants.

PREDECESSORS.—[1] GEORGE Whiteley, *P.C.*, el. son of the late George Whiteley, J.P., of Woodlands, Blackburn; *b.* 1855 ; Parliamentary (Patronage) Sec. to the Treasury and Ch. Liberal Whip Dec. 1905 to June 1908; M.P. for Stockport (*L*) Feb. 1893 to Sept. 1900, and for Pudsey Div. of E. Part of W. Riding of Yorkshire Oct. 1900 to June 1908; cr. *Baron Marchamley*, of Hawkstone, co. Salop (peerage of United Kingdom) 1908 : *m.* 1881, Alice, who *d.* 1913, only child of the late William Tattersall, J.P., of Quarry Bank, Blackburn, and St. Anthony's, Milnthorpe; *d.* 1925; *s.* by his son [2] WILLIAM TATTERSALL, 2nd Baron; *b.* 1886 ; High Sheriff, co. Southampton 1921; European War 1915-18 as Lieut.-Com. R.N.V.R., European War 1939-45 as Flight-Lieut. RAF: *m.* 1911, Margaret Clara, who *d.* 1974, da. of Thomas Scott Johnstone, formerly of Glenmark, Waipara, New Zealand; *d.* 1949; *s.* by his only son [3] JOHN WILLIAM TATTERSHALL, 3rd Baron and present peer.

MARCHWOOD, VISCOUNT. (Penny.) [Viscount U.K. 1945, Bt. U.K. 1933.]

Always prepared.

PETER GEORGE PENNY, *M.B.E.*, 2nd Viscount, and 2nd Baronet; *b*. Nov. 7th, 1912; *s*. 1955; ed. at Winchester; is Hon. Major R.A.; European War 1939-45; M.B.E. (Mil.) 1944: *m*. 1935, Pamela, only child of John Staveley Colton-Fox, J.P., of Todwick Grange, near Sheffield, and has issue.

Arms,—Gules, six fleurs-de-lis, three, two, and one or, on a chief engrailed of the second, three roses of the first, barbed and seeded proper. Crest,—Issuant from a circlet or, a demi lion gules, collared sable, charged on the shoulder with a rose, and holding in the dexter paw a fleur-de-lis gold. Supporters,—*Dexter*, a Malayan tiger proper; *sinister*, a sea lion proper.

Residence,—Manor House, Cholderton, Salisbury. *Club*,—White's.

SONS LIVING.

Hon. DAVID GEORGE STAVELEY (The Filberts, Aston Tirrold, Didcot, Berks.), *b*. May 22nd, 1936; ed. at Winchester: *m*. 1964, Tessa Jane, da. of W.F. Norris, of Timbers Chase, Chiddingfold, Surrey, and has issue living, Peter George Worsley, *b*. 1965, —Nicholas Mark Staveley, *b*. 1967,—Edward James Frederick, *b*. 1970.

Hon. Patrick Glyn (14, Northumberland Pl., W2), *b*. 1939: *m*. 1968, Sue Eleanor Jane, da. of the late Charles Phipps Brutton, CBE, and has issue living, Sasha Jane, *b*. 1969.

DAUGHTER LIVING.

Hon. Carol Ann, *b*. 1948

PREDECESSOR.—[1] (FREDERICK) GEORGE Penny, *K.C.V.O.*, 2nd son of the late Frederick James Penny, of Sydney Cottage, Bitterne, Hants.; *b*. 1876; a Master Mariner, and Master of Master Mariners' Co. 1941-5; Senior Partner of Fraser & Co., Government exchange brokers, of Singapore; was Parliamentary Private Sec. to Financial Sec. to War Office 1923-4, a Govt. Whip 1926-8, a Junior Lord of the Treasury 1928-9 and (in National Govt.) Sept. to Nov. 1931, Vice-Chamberlain of H.M.'s Household 1931-2, Comptroller of H.M.'s Household 1932-5, and Treasurer of H.M.'s Household 1935-7; sat as M.P. for Kingston-upon-Thames (C) 1922-37; cr. a *Baronet* 1933, *Baron Marchwood* of Penang and of Marchwood, co. Southampton (peerage of United Kingdom) 1937, and *Viscount Marchwood*, of Penang and of Marchwood, co. Southampton (peerage of United Kingdom) 1945: *m*. 1905, Anne Boyle, who *d*. 1957, dau. of the late Sir John Gunn, J.P., of St. Mellons, Cardiff; *d*. 1955; *s*. by his only son [2] PETER GEORGE, 2nd Viscount and present peer; also Baron Marchwood.

MARGADALE, BARON. (Morrison.) [Baron U.K. 1964.]

Margadale).

JOHN GRANVILLE MORRISON, *TD*, 1st Baron, son of the late Hugh Morrison, of Fonthill House, Tisbury, Wilts. [E. Granville]; *b*. Dec. 16th, 1906; ed. at Eton, and at Magdalene Coll., Camb.; KStJ; a JP of Wilts (High Sheriff 1938, DL 1950-69) and Argyll; Lord Lieut. of Wilts. since 1969; MP for Salisbury (C) 1942-64; Chm. of 1922 Cttee. 1955-64, and of Salisbury Div. Conservative Assocn. 1939, and a Member of Nat. Expenditure Cttee. 1945; Hon. Col. R. Wilts Yeo. 1960-72, and R. Yeo. 1965-72; 1935-45 War with R. Wilts. Yeo. in Middle East; cr. Baron *Margadale*, of Islay, co. Argyll (peerage of UK) 1964: *m*. 1928, the Hon. Margaret Esther Lucie Smith, da. of 2nd Viscount Hambleden, and has issue.

Arms,—Tierced in pairle azure, sable and gules, in chief a Saracen's head couped affrontée and in base two Saracens' heads addorsed in profile all argent, and at the fess point an inescutcheon parted per pale dexter per bend sinister embattled gules and or, in dexter chief a battle axe paleways argent, and in sinister base, issuant from a base undy azure and argent, a tower sabre, masoned argent, port gules (*Morrison of Islay*) sinister, vert powdered with bezants, a horse rearing on its hind legs argent, langued and hoofed gules (*Lordship of Margadale*). Crest,—Three Saracens' heads conjoined in one neck one looking to the dexter, one affrontée, and one looking to the sinister all proper. Supporters,—Two Woodcocks proper.

Residences,—Fonthill House, Tisbury, Wilts.; Islay House, Bridgend, Isle of Islay, Argyll. *Clubs*,—Turf, White's, Jockey.

SONS LIVING.

Hon. JAMES IAN, *TD* (Hawking Down, Hindon, Wilts.), *b*. July 17th, 1930; ed. at Eton; Maj. (ret.) R. Wilts. Yeo.; formerly 2nd Lt. Life Guards; a Co. Councillor for Wilts. since 1955 (Alderman 1969-74 and High Sheriff 1971); Chm. of Westbury Conservative Assocn. 1967: *m*. 1952, Clare, da. of Anthony Lister Barclay, of Broad Oak End, Hertford, and has issue living, Alastair John, *b*. 1958,—Hugh, *b*. 1960,—Fiona Elizabeth (*Hon. Mrs. Hugh Trenchard*), *b*. 1954: *m*. 1975, the Hon. Hugh Trenchard, el. son of 2nd Viscount Trenchard.

Hon. Charles Andrew, *MP* (Fyfield Manor, Pewsey, Wilts.), *b.* 1932; ed. at Eton; Capt. (ret.) R. Wilts. Yeo; late 2nd Lt. Life Guards; MP for Devizes Div. of Wilts. (*C*) since May 1964: *m.* 1954, the Hon. (Antoinette) Sara Frances Sibell Long, da. of 2nd Viscount Long, and has issue living, David John, *b.* 1959,—Anabel Laura Dorothy, *b.* 1955.
Hon. Peter Hugh, *MP*, *b.* 1944: ed. at Keble Coll., Oxford; MP for Chester (*C*) since 1974.

DAUGHTER LIVING.
Hon. Mary Anne, *CVO*, *b.* 1937; a Woman of the Bedchamber to HM since 1960; CVO 1970.

MARGESSON, VISCOUNT. (Margesson.) [Viscount U.K. 1942.]

FRANCIS VERE HAMPDEN MARGESSON, 2nd Viscount; *b.* April 17th, 1922; *s.* 1965; ed. at Eton, and Trin. Coll., Oxford; Information Officer, British Consulate-General, New York, 1964-70; 1939-45 War as Lt. RNVR: *m.* 1958, Helena, da. of Heikki Backstrom, of Oulu, Finland, and has issue.

Arms.—Sable, a lion passant guardant argent, a chief engrailed or, thereon between two pallets azure a pale of the last charged with an ostrich feather erect of the second. Crests,—Upon a coronet composed of four roses set upon a rim or, a lion passant guardant sable, collared gold, and charged with a rose argent, barbed and seeded proper. Supporters,—On either side a falcon, wings elevated argent, armed and belled or, and charged with a portcullis chained sable.

Residence,—Stone Ridge, New York 12484, USA.

Loyalty binds me.

SON LIVING.
Hon. RICHARD FRANCIS DAVID, *b.* Dec. 25th, 1960.

DAUGHTERS LIVING.
Hon. Rhoda France, *b.* 1962.
Hon. Sarah Helena, *b.* 1963.
Hon. Jane Henrietta, *b.* 1965.

SISTER LIVING. (*Daughter of 1st Viscount.*)
Hon. (Mary) Gay Hobart (*Hon. Lady Charteris*), *b.* 1919: *m.* 1944, Lt.-Col. the Rt. Hon. Sir Martin Charles Charteris, KCB, KCVO, OBE, late KRRC, of Apart. 25, St. James's Palace, SW1 [see E. Wemyss].

MOTHER LIVING.
Frances (*Mrs. Frances Leggett*) (Ridgely Manor, Stone Ridge, New York, USA), da. of the late Francis H. Leggett, of New York; resumed her maiden surname of Leggett 1941: *m.* 1916 (m. diss. 1940), Capt. the Rt. Hon. Henry David Reginald Margesson, MC, PC (later 1st Viscount), who *d.* 1965.

PREDECESSOR.—[1] HENRY DAVID REGINALD Margesson, MC, PC, el. son of Sir Mortimer Reginald Margesson and Lady Isabel Angusta Hobart-Hampden, sister of 7th Earl of Buckingham; shire; *b.* 1890; Ch. Govt. Whip 1931-40, and Sec. of State for War 1940-42; MP for Upton Div., W. Ham (*C*) 1922-23, and for Rugby 1924-42; cr. *Viscount Margesson,* of Rugby, co. Warwick (peerage of UK) 1942: *m.* 1916 (m. diss. 1940), Frances, da. of Francis H. Leggett, of New York, *d.* 1965; *s.* by his only son, [2] FRANCIS VERE HAMPDEN, 2nd Viscount and present peer.

MARKS OF BROUGHTON, BARON. (Marks.) [Baron U.K. 1961.]

MICHAEL MARKS, 2nd Baron, *b.* Aug. 27th, 1920; *s.* 1964; ed. at St. Paul's and Corpus Christi Coll., Camb.: *m.* 1st, 1949 (m. diss. 1958), Ann Catherine, da. of Maj. Richard James Pinto, MC; 2ndly, 1960, Helene (m. diss. 1965), da. of Gustave Fischer, and has issue by 1st marriage.

Arms,—Pily argent and azure a pair of scales or. Crest,—A dove wings addorsed argent, beaked and membered gules, gorged with an antique crown, and to the beak a gimmel ring cr. Supporters,—On either side a lion or supporting a cornucopia argent the fruit proper, that on the dexter holding aloft with the interior forepaw a red rose slipped and leaved also proper, and that on the sinister two interlaced triangles or.

SON LIVING. (*By 1st marriage.*)
Hon. SIMON RICHARD, *b.* May 3rd, 1950; ed. at Eton, and Balliol Coll., Oxford.

DAUGHTERS LIVING. (*By 1st marriage.*)
Hon. Naomi Anne, *b.* 1952.
Hon. Sarah Elizabeth, *b.* 1953.

SISTER LIVING.
Hon. Hannah Olive, *b.* 1918: *m.* 1st, 1941 (marriage dissolved 1959), Alec Lerner; 2ndly, 1960, Gerald William Harold Marcow, and has issue living, (by 1st marriage) Joel David, *b.* 1942,—Diana Toby, *b.* 1947,—Maureen Ann, *b.* 1952. *Residences,*—The White House, Westwood Rd., Windlesham, Surrey; 15, Eaton Place, S.W.1.

PREDECESSOR—[1] *Sir* SIMON Marks, son of Michael Marks, of Manchester; *b.* 1888; Chm. and joint Managing Dir. of Marks & Spencer Ltd.; cr. *Baron Marks of Broughton,* of Sunningdale, co. Berks. (peerage of UK) 1961: *m.* 1915, Miriam, who *d.* 1971 da. of Ephraim Sieff; *d.* 1964; *s.* by his only son [2] MICHAEL, 2nd Baron and present peer.

MARLBOROUGH, DUKE OF. (Spencer-Churchill.) [Duke England 1702.]
[Title pronounced "Maulbro'."]

FIEL · PERO · DESDICHADO

Faithful, though unfortunate.

JOHN GEORGE VANDERBILT HENRY SPENCER-CHURCHILL, 11th Duke, b. April 13th, 1926; s. 1972; ed. at Eton; late Capt. Life Gds.; JP and a DL of Oxon: m. 1st, 1951 (m. diss. 1960), Susan Mary, only da. of Michael Charles St. John Hornby [see E. Dudley, colls.]; 2ndly, 1961 (m. diss. 1971), Athina (Tina), who d. 1974, da. of the late Stavros G. Livanos, and formerly wife of the late Aristotle Onassis: 3rdly, 1972 (Dagmar) Rosita, (Astri Libertas), da. of the late Count Carl Ludwig Douglas, and has issue by 1st and 3rd m.

Arms,—Quarterly: 1st and 4th sable, a lion rampant argent; on a canton of the second a cross gules, *Churchill*; 2nd and 3rd quarterly argent and gules; on a bend sable, between two frettes or, three escallops of the first, *Spencer*; over all (as an honourable augmentation), in the centre chief point, on an escutcheon argent, the cross of St. George surmounted by another cutcheon azure, charged with three fleurs-de-lis, two and one or. Crests,—1st, a lion couchant and urdant argent, supporting a banner gules, charged with a dexter hand couped argent, *Churchill*; and, out of a ducal coronet or, a griffin's head, gorged with a collar gemelle gules, between two wings expanded, argent, *Spencer*. Supporters,—Two wyverns, wings elevated, gules.
Seat,—Blenheim Palace, Woodstock, Oxon. *Residence,*—Lee Place, Charlbury, Oxon.

SON LIVING. (By 1st m.)
CHARLES JAMES (*Marquess of Blandford*), b. Nov. 24th, 1955.
(By 3rd m.)
Lord Edward Albert Charles, b. 1974.

DAUGHTER LIVING. (By 1st m.)
Lady Henrietta Mary, b. 1958.

BROTHER LIVING.
Lord Charles George William Colin (164, Ebury St., SW1), b. 1940; ed. at Eton: m. 1st, 1965 (m. diss. 1968), Gillian, da. of Andrew Fuller, of New York City, and Fort Worth, Texas, USA; 2ndly, 1970, Elizabeth Jane, el. da. of Capt. the Hon. Mark Hugh Wyndham, MC [see B. Egremont], and has issue living, (by 2nd m.) Rupert John Harold Mark, b. 1971.

SISTERS LIVING.
Lady Sarah Consuelo, b. 1921: m. 1st, 1943 (m. diss. 1966) Lt. Edwin F. Russell, USA Navy; 2ndly, 1966 (m. diss. in Mexico 1967) Guy Burgos, of Santiago, Chile; 3rdly, 1967 (at Philadelphia) Theodorous Roubanis, and has issue living, (by 1st m.) Serena Mary Churchill, b. 1944: m. 1st, 1966 (m. diss. in Mexico 1967), R. Stephen Salant; 2ndly, 1968, Neil A. McConnel, of 12, Sutton Sq., New York, NY, USA,—Consuelo Sarah, b. 1946: m. 1st, 1968 (m. diss. in Mexico 1969), James Toback; 2ndly, 1970, Mark Schulman, of 229, East 79th St., New York City, USA,—Alexandra Brenda, b. 1949: m. 1970, Timothy Biech, of Camp Hill, Penn., USA,—Jacqueline, b. 1958.
Lady Caroline, b. 1923; appointed an Extra Lady in Waiting to HRH Princess Alexandra, the Hon. Mrs. Angus Ogilvy 1970: m. 1946, Maj. (Charles) Hugo Waterhouse, and has issue living, Michael Thomas, b. 1949,—David Charles, b. 1956,—Elizabeth Ann, b. 1951. *Residence,*—Kidmore House, Kidmore End, near Reading.
Lady Rosemary Mildred, b. 1929: m. 1953, Charles Robert Muir, who d. 1972, and has issue living, Alexander Pepys, b. 1954,—Simon Huntly, b. 1959,—Mary A abella, b. 1962. *Residence,*—Billingbear House, Binfield, Bracknell, Berks.

WIDOW LIVING OF SON OF NINTH DUKE.
Betty, dau. of the late J. C. Cunningham, of 27, Culross Street, W.1: m. 1947, Lord Ivor Charles Spencer-Churchill, who d. 1956, and has issue living [see colls., infra]. *Residence,*—Fyning House, Rogate, Petersfield, Hants.

WIDOWS LIVING OF NINTH AND TENTH DUKES.
GLADYS MARIE (*Dowager Duchess of Marlborough*), dau. of Edward Parker Deacon, of Boston, U.S.A., m. 1921, as his second wife, the 9th Duke, who d. 1934. *Residence,*—
(FRANCES) LAURA (*Laura, Duchess of Marlborough*), (58, Portman Towers, George St., W1H 5PN), da. of the late Capt. the Hon. Guy Lawrence Charteris [see E. Wemyss and March, colls.], formerly wife of (1) the 2nd Viscount Long, and (2) the 3rd Earl of Dudley, and widow of Michael Temple Canfield; m. 4thly, 1972, the 10th Duke, who d. 1972.

COLLATERAL BRANCHES LIVING.
Issue of the late Lord Ivor Charles Spencer-Churchill, younger son of 9th Duke, b. 1898, d. 1956: m. 1947, Betty (ante), dau. of the late J. C. Cunningham, of 27, Culross Street, W.1:—
Robert William Charles, b. 1954.

Grandchildren of the late Rt. Hon. Sir Winston Leonard Spencer-Churchill, KG, OM, CH, TD (infra):—
Issue of the late Hon. Randolph Frederick Edward Spencer-Churchill, MBE, b. 1911, d. 1968: m. 1st, 1939, the Hon. Pamela Digby (who obtained a divorce 1946), da. of 11th Baron Digby; 2ndly, 1948 (m. diss. 1961), June Hermione, da. of Col. Rex Hamilton Osborne, DSO:—
(By 1st m.) Winston, MP (Broadwater House, Chailey, Sussex), b. 1940; ed. at Eton, and Ch. Ch., Oxford; Journalist and Writer; MP for Stretford (C) since 1970: m. 1964, Mary Caroline, da. of the late Sir Gerard John Regis d'Erlanger, CBE, and has issue living, Randolph Leonard, b. 1965,—Jennie, b. 1966,—Marina, b. 1967.——(By 2nd m.) Arabella, b. 1949: m. 1972, James J. Barton.

Granddaughters of the late Rt. Hon. Lord Randolph Henry Spencer-Churchill, MP, 3rd son of 7th Duke:—
Issue of the late Rt. Hon. Sir Winston Leonard Spencer-Churchill, KG, OM, CH, TD, Prime Min. 1940-45 and 1951-55, b. Nov. 30th, 1874, d. Jan. 24th, 1965: m. 1908, *Dame* Clementine Ogilvy, GBE (*Baroness Spencer-Churchill*) (Flat 26, 7, Princes Gate, SW7), da. of the late Col. Sir Henry Montagu Hozier, KCB [E. Airlie].

Hon. Sarah Millicent Hermione (*Sarah, Baroness Audley*) (c/o Fladgate & Co., 8, Waterloo Place, Pall Mall, SW1), *b.* 1914; actress, poet and author: *m.* 1st, 1936, Vic Oliver, who *d.* 1964, having obtained a divorce 1954; 2ndly, 1949, Antony Roger Beauchamp, who *d.* 1957; 3rdly, 1962, 23rd Baron Audley, who *d.* 1963.——*Hon.* Mary, *MBE* (*Hon. Lady Soames*), *b.* 1922; formerly Junior Cdr. ATS; MBE (Mil) 1945: *m.* 1947, Rt. Hon. Sir (Arthur) Christopher John Soames, GCMG, GCVO, CBE (Castle Mill House, N. Warnborough, Basingstoke, Hants.), and has issue living, Arthur Nicholas Winston, *b.* 1948; ed. at Eton; 2nd Lt. 11th Hussars; appointed an Extra Equerry to HRH The Prince of Wales 1970,—Jeremy Bernard, *b.* 1952,—Rupert Christopher, *b.* 1959,—Emma Mary, *b.* 1949,—Charlotte Clementine, *b.* 1954: *m.* 1973, (Alexander) Richard Hambro.

                 Grandchildren of the late Rt. Hon. Sir Winston Leonard Spencer-Churchill, KG, OM, CH, TD, MP (ante):—
Issue of the late Diana Spencer-Churchill, *b.* 1909, *d.* 1963: *m.* 1st, 1932, John Milner Bailey (afterwards 2nd Bt.), from whom she obtained a divorce 1935; 2ndly, 1935 (marriage dissolved 1960, the Rt. Hon. (Edwin) Duncan Sandys, PC, MP now Baron Duncan-Sandys, Life Baron:—
(By 2nd m.) [see Baron Duncan-Sandys].

                 Grandchildren of the late Rt. Hon. Lord Randolph Henry Spencer-Churchill, M.P. (ante):—
Issue of the late Major John Strange Spencer-Churchill, D.S.O., *b.* 1880, *d.* 1947: *m.* 1908, Lady Gwendoline Theresa Mary Bertie, who *d.* 1941, dau. of 7th Earl of Abingdon:—
John George (of Place du Cros, Grimaud, Var, France, 83), *b.* 1909; ed. at Harrow, and at Pembroke Coll., Oxford: is a Painter, Sculptor, and Composer; late Maj. R.E.; European War 1939-45 in France, Belgium, and Germany: *m.* 1st, 1934 (marriage dissolved 1938), Angela Mary, dau. of the late Capt. George Culme-Seymour [see Culme-Seymour, Bt., colls.]; 2ndly, 1941 (m. diss. 1952), Mary, dau. of the late Kenneth Cookson, O.B.E. [see Butler, Bt., cr. 1628, colls.]; 3rdly, 1953, Kathlyn Maude Muriel Hall (TANDY), who *d.* 1957, dau. of Maj.-Gen. Walter Samuel Beddall, C.B., O.B.E.; 4thly, 1958, Anna Gunvor Maria, dau. of Johan Janson, of Kristianstad, Sweden, and widow of Granger Boston, and has issue living, (by 1st marriage) Sarah Cornelia, *b.* 1935: *m.* 1957, James Colin Crewe, of 80, Oxford Gdns., W10 [M. Crewe (ext.)], and has issue living, Peregrine John *b.* 1959, Emma *b.* 1962, Annabel Sophia *b.* 1965.——Henry Winston (Peregrine), *b.* 1913; ed. at Harrow, and at Camb. Univ. (BA 1934); is a CE: *m.* 1st, 1954, Patricia Ethel Louisa, who *d.* 1956, da. of the late Thomas March; 2ndly, 1957, Yvonne Henriette Marie, da. of Constant Jéhannin, of Rennes, France. *Residence.*—Holworth House, Warmwell, Dorset.——Clarissa (*Countess of Avon*), *b.* 1920: *m.* 1952, as his second wife, the 1st Earl of Avon. *Residence,*—Manor House, Alvediston, Salisbury, Wilts.

                Descendants of the late Lord Francis Almeric Spencer (2nd son of 4th Duke) who was cr. *Baron Churchill* 1815 [see V. Churchill].

                Grandchildren of the late Rev. Charles Vere Spencer, son of the Rev. Frederick Charles Spencer, son of the late John Spencer, MP, el. son of the late Lord Charles Spencer, MP, 2nd son of 3rd Duke:—
Issue of the late Aubrey John Spencer, *b.* 1853, *d.* 1935: *m.* 1885, Florence Mary, who *d.* 1952, dau. of the late Frederick Halsey Jan-on :—
Frederica Elizabeth, *b.* 1892: *m.* 1919, Thomas Henry Bayley, who *d.* 1937, and has issue living, Christopher Spencer (Durham Ox, Old Town, Kirkby Lonsdale, Westmorland), *b.* 1920; ed. at Christ's Hospital; sometime Capt. RA (E. African Forces); 1939-45 War in Abyssinia, Madagascar, Ceylon, and India (despatches): *m.* 1950, Beryl, el. da. of the late Maj. Robert Jocelyn Rowan Waller, DSO [see B. St. Leonards], and has issue living, Trevor Charles Rowan *b.* 1951; ed. at Marlborough, Anna Penelope *b.* 1953, Caroline Margery *b.* 1955,—Nancy Elizabeth, *b.* 1923: *m.* 1946, George Edward Dixon, MA, BM, BCh, of Victoria House, Battery Row, Old Portsmouth, and has issue living, John Hughes *b.* 1946; ed. at Winchester; MA, BM, BCh Oxford; Fl.-Lt. RAF: *m.* 1972, Jane Clare Cowen, Christopher George *b.* 1948; ed. at Winchester; MB, BS, London; Surg. Lt. RN, Elizabeth Mary *b.* 1951; ed. at Edinburgh Univ. (BSc),—Margaret Audrey, *b.* 1926; ed. at Oxford Univ (BA); Assist. Editor at Oxford University Press. *Residence,*—77, Fairfield Drive, Dorking, Surrey.

             Issue of the late Sir Charles Gordon Spencer, *b.* 1869, *d.* 1934: *m.* 1903, **Edith Mary**, who *d.* 1936, youngest dau. of the late Col. Hugh Pearce Pearson, C.B.:—
John Gray Churchill SPENCER BERNARD, *MA, MD, FRCS, b.* 1907; ed. at Marlborough Coll., and at Magdalene Coll., Camb. (MA, MD); MRCS England and LRCP London, FRCS England; Freedom Research Scholar, London Hospital 1930; late Pathologist, Frenchay Hospital, Bristol; assumed by deed poll 1955 the additional surname of Bernard: *m.* 1933, Elsie Phyllis, *MA,* da. of Ferrand Corley, of Woodside, Witney, and has issue living, Charles Francis Churchill, *b.* 1942: *m.* 1974, Rosalyn Anne, da. of Maj. Patrick Plunkett, of Hazelbury, Plucknett, Som.,—Robert Vere *b.* 1944: *m.* 1975, Katharine Margaret, da. of Lt.-Col. Claud Everard Walter Montagu-Douglas-Scott MC [see D. Buccleuch and Queensberry colls.],—Julia Diana, *b.* 1936: *m.* 1959, John Simon Baskerville Cadwallader Hopton, of Moor Park, Crickhowell, Breconshire, and has issue living, Richard Henry Caldwallader, *b.* 1962, Edward Charles Adams *b.* 1964, Michael John Baskerville *b.* 1972, Isobel Georgiana *b.* 1967,—Clare Rosemary, *b.* 1938: *m.* 1963, Rio Tyrell Arthur Hohler, of Long Crendon Manor, Bucks, and has issue living, Rupert John Frederick *b.* 1972, Harriet Valentine *b.* 1967, Camilla Clare *b.* 1968, Amanda Sophie *b.* 1970. *Residence,*—Nether Winchendon House, Aylesbury, Bucks.——Cynthia Mary, *b.* 1904: *m.* 1928, William H. Peppercorn, of Tudor Cottage, Great Bedwyn, Marlborough, Wilts., and has issue living, John Julian (of 50, Clifton Hill, NW8), *b.* 1935: *m.* 1959, Elizabeth, da. of A. S. Grant, of Roebuck House, SW1, and has issue living, Catherine Elaine *b.* 1960, Margaret Clare *b.* 1963, Penelope Delia *b.* 1965.

             Issue of the Rev. Frederick Augustus Morland Spencer, DD, *b.* 1878, *d.* 1962: *m.* 1913, Gertrude, Lucie, MA, who *d.* 1970, el. da. of the late George John Burke, MICE, of St. Kilda, Melbourne:—
Marion Gertrude (9, Sympson Close, Abingdon), *b.* 1916: *m.* 1940, Kenneth Ninian Hoare, from whom she obtained a divorce 1971, and has issue living, Gillian Shella, *b.* 1947: *m.* 1971, Richard James Kenneth Button (9, Sympson Close, Abingdon, Oxford), and has issue living, Sarah Nicola *b.* 1971, Teresa June *b.* 1974,—Celia Jennifer, *b.* 1952.——Geraldine Mildred (Currony St., Canberra, ACT) *b.* 1920; ed. at Sydney Univ., NSW (BA).

             Grandson of the late Sir Charles Gordon Spencer (ante):—
Issue of the late Charles Bernard Spencer, *b.* 1909, *d.* 1963: *m.* 1st, 1936, Nora Gibbs, who *d.* 1947; 2ndly, 1961, Ann Marjoribanks:—
By 2nd marriage) Piers Bernard, *b.* 1963.

                Descendants of the late John Spencer, M.P. (son of the late Hon. John Spencer, M.P., 3rd son of 3rd Earl of Sunderland), who was cr. *Earl Spencer* 1765 [see that title].

PREDECESSORS.—[1] *Right Hon.* Sir JOHN CHURCHILL, *K.G., P.C.,* **el. son of the late** Sir Winston Churchill; *b.* 1650; the most distinguished Gen. of his time, was cr. *Lord Churchill,* of Eyemouth, co. Berwick (peerage of Scotland) 1682, *Baron Churchill,* of Sandridge, co. Hertford (peerage of England) 1685, *Earl of Marlborough* (peerage of England) 1689, *Marquess of Blandford* and *Duke of Marlborough* (peerage of England) 1702, *Prince of the Holy Roman Empire* 1704 (and to all descendants male and female), and *Prince of Mindelheim* in Suabia 1705; was sometime Ambassador to France from James II., he assisted at the victory of Sedgmoor, and in the Convention Parliament voted in favour of the Prince and Princess of Orange filling the throne; commanded the English troops in the Netherlands 1689; having displeased William III., he was confined for a short time in the Tower; appointed upon the accession of Queen Anne, Capt.-Gen. of all H.M.'s forces in England; in 1702-3 he reduced Venleo, Stevenswaert, Ruremonde, and Liége; in 1704 won the celebrated victory of Blenheim, and afterwards achieved other victories, notably Ramillies 1706, Oudenard 1708, and Malplaquet 1709; for his victories at and before Blenheim he was awarded by Act of Parliament the royal manor of Woodstock, and a splendid palace was erected by H.M.'s orders; in 1706 an Act was passed settling his honours on his posterity and granting him and each successor in the title a pension of £5,000 a year: *m.* 1678, Sarah, who *d.* 1744, dau. and co-heiress of Richard Jennings, of Sandridge, Herts; he had surviving issue Henrietta, wife of Francis, 2nd Earl of Godolphin, and Anne, 2nd wife of Charles Spencer, K.G., 3rd Earl of Sunderland (see infra); *d.* 1722, when the Scottish Barony of Churchill of Eyemouth became ext.; *s.* in his other under the special Act of Parliament by his dau. [2] HENRIETTA (ante); *d.* without surviving male issue 1733; *s.* by her nephew [3] CHARLES, K.G., 3rd Duke, 2nd son of Anne (ante), who had in 1729 *s.* his brother as 5th *Earl of Sunderland* (see *** infra); was Lord-Lieut. of cos. Oxford and Buckingham, and a distinguished military commander; *d.* 1758; *s.* by his son [4] GEORGE, K.G., 4th Duke; Lord Chamberlain of the Household 1762-3, and Lord Privy Seal 1763-5; *d.* 1817; *s.* by his son [5] GEORGE, 5th Duke; M.P. for Oxford 1790 and for Tregony 1804-6; assumed in 1807 by Roy. licence the additional surname of Churchill; called to House of Lords in his father's barony of Spencer 1806; *d.* 1840; *s.* by his son [6] GEORGE, 6th Duke, *b.* 1793; was Lord-Lieut. of Oxfordshire; *d.* 1857; *s.* by his son [7] JOHN WINSTON, K.G., D.C.L., 7th Duke; sat as M.P. for Woodstock (C) 1844-5 and 1847-57; was Lord-Lieut. of co. Oxford, Lord Pres. of the Council 1868, and Viceroy of Ireland 1876-80: *m.* 1843, Lady Frances Anne Emily Vane, dau. of 3rd Marquess of Londonderry; *d.* 1883; *s.* by his son [8] GEORGE CHARLES, 8th Duke, *b.* 1844: *m.* 1st, 1869, Lady Albertha Frances Anne Hamilton, who *d.* 1932 (having divorced him 1883), dau. of 1st Duke of Abercorn, KG; 2ndly, 1888, Lilian Warren da. of (who m. 3rdly 1895, Lord William de la Poer Beresford, VO, KCIE, and *d.* 1909) Cdr. Cicero Price, of US Navy and widow of Louis Hammersley, of New York; *d.* 1892, *s.* by his only son [9] CHARLES RICHARD JOHN, KG, PC, 9th Duke, *b.* 1871; Lord-Lieut. of Oxfordshire; Paymaster-Gen. 1899-1902; acted as Lord High Steward at Coronation of King Edward VII; Under-Sec. of State for Colonies 1903-5, and John Parl. Sec. (unpaid) to Board of Agriculture 1917-18: *m.* 1st, 1895, Consuelo (who *d.* 1964, having obtained a divorce 1920), da. of the late William Kissam Vanderbilt, of New York: 2ndly, 1921, Gladys Marie, da. of Edward Parker Deacon of Boston, USA.: *d.* 1934; *s.* by his el. son [10] JOHN ALBERT EDWARD WILLIAM, 10th Duke, *b.* 1897; Lt.-Col. Life Gds. (Reserve); High Steward of Oxford 1937: *m.* 1st, 1929, the Hon. Alexandra Mary Hilda Cadogan, CBE, JP, who *d.* 1961, da. of the late Henry Arthur, Viscount Chelsea [E. Cadogan]; 2ndly, 1972, Frances Laura, da. of the late Capt. the Hon. Guy Lawrence Charteris [E. Wemyss and March, colls.], formerly wife of (1) the 2nd Viscount Long, and (2) the 3rd Earl of Dudley, and widow of Michael Temple Canfield, *d.* 1972; *s.* by his el. son [11] JOHN GEORGE VANDERBILT HENRY, 115h Duke, and present peer; also Marquess of Blandford, Earl of Sunderland, Earl of Marlborough, Baron Spencer, and Baron Churchill of Sandridge, as well as Prince of the Holy Roman Empire, and Prince of Mindelheim in Suabia.

⁎ [1] Sir ROBERT Spencer, Knt.; cr. *Baron Spencer*, of Wormleighton, co. Northampton (peerage of England) 1603; *d.* 1627; *s.* by his son [2] WILLIAM, 2nd Baron; *d.* 1636; *s.* by his son [3] HENRY, 3rd Baron; cr. *Earl of Sunderland* (peerage of England) 1643; killed at Newbury 1643, fighting for the royal cause; *s.* by his son [4] ROBERT, K.G., 2nd Earl; *d.* 1702; *s.* by his son [5] CHARLES, K.G., 3rd Earl; was a Principal Sec. of State to Queen Anne and George I.; *d* 1722; *s.* by his son [6] ROBERT, 4th Earl; *d.* unmarried 1729; *s.* by his brother [7] CHARLES KG, 5th Earl, who *s.* as 3rd Duke of Marlborough (ante).

MARLEY, BARON. (Aman.) [Baron U.K. 1930.]

GODFREY PELHAM LEIGH AMAN, 2nd Baron; *b.* Sept. 6th, 1913; *s.* 1952; ed. at Bedales Sch., and at Grenoble Univ.; is a Film Producer; European War 1939-44 as Major R.M. (wounded): *m.* 1st, 1938 (marriage dissolved 1948), Lilian Mary, dau. of James Chrystal; 2ndly, 1956, Catherine Doone, dau. of Frank Angwyn Beal, of L'Eden, Cap D'Ail, France, AM.

Residence,—104, Ebury Mews, S.W.1.

PREDECESSOR.—[1] DUDLEY LEIGH AMAN, D.S.C., son of the late Edward Godfrey Aman, of Wassenaar, Farnham; *b.* 1884; Major R.M.A.; was a Lord-in-Waiting to H.M., and Under-Sec. of State for War and Vice-Pres. of Army Council 1930-31, Ch. Labour Whip in House of Lords 1930-37, and a Dep. Speaker in House of Lords 1930-41; attached to Min. of Aircraft Production 1943-45; cr. *Baron Marley*, of Marley, co. Sussex (peerage of United Kingdom) 1930: *m.* 1910, Octable Turquet, *d.* 19—, da. of the late Sir Hugh Gilzean Reid, DL, LLD; *d.* 1952; *s.* by his only son [2] GODFREY PELHAM LEIGH, 2nd Baron and present peer.

MARPLES, BARON. (Marples.) [Life Baron 1974.]

(ALFRED) ERNEST MARPLES, PC, son of the late Alfred Ernest Marples; *b.* Dec. 9th, 1907; ed. at Stretford Gram. Sch.; FCA; FRSA; Hon. Freeman of Wallasey; 1939-45 War with London Scottish, and as Capt. RA (invalided); MP for Wallasey (C) 1945-74; Parl. Sec. Min. of Housing and Local Govt. 1951-54, Min. of Transport 1959-64, and Sponsor Cons. Party Public Sector Research Unit 1967-70; a Dir. Purolator Services Inc., New York; cr. PC 1957, and *Baron Marples*, of Wallasey, co. Merseyside (Life Baron) 1974: *m.* 1st, 1937 (m. diss. 1945), Edna Harwood, of Thornton Heath, Surrey; Inc. 2ndly, 1956, Ruth, da. of the late F. W. Dobson, JP, FSA, of Nottingham.

Residence,—33, Eccleston St., SW1. *Club.*—Carlton.

MARTONMERE, BARON. (Robinson.) [Peerage U.K. 1964.]

(JOHN) ROLAND ROBINSON, *GBE, KCMG, PC,*
1st Baron, son of Roland Walkden Robinson, of
Blackpool; *b.* Feb. 22nd, 1907; ed. at Trin.
Hall, Camb. (MA, LLB); Bar. Lincoln's Inn
1929; Pres. of Assocn. of Health and Pleasure
Resorts 1936-64, and Chm. Conservative Commonwealth Affairs Cttee., House of Commons
1954-64, Chm. of Gen. Council of Commonwealth Parliamentary Assocn. 1960-61 (Dep.
Chm. U.K. Branch 1962-64); Gov. of Bermuda 1964-72; a KStJ; 1939-45 War with
RAF Vol. Reserve (Officer of American Legion
of Merit); MP for Widnes Div. of Lancs. (*C*)
1931-35, for Blackpool 1935-45, and for S. Div.
of Blackpool 1945-64; *cr.* Knt. 1954, PC 1962, *Baron Martonmere,* of Blackpool,
co. Palatine of Lancaster 1964, KCMG 1966, and GBE (Civil) 1973: *m.* 1930,
Maysie (CStJ), da. of the late Clarence Warren Gasque, and has issue.

ᙏrms.—Argent a three masted merchant ship of early eighteenth century date, the mainsails
furled proper, on a chief azure a portcullis chained between two roses or. Ⅽrest.—A lion's head erased
or in the mouth a crescent gules. Supporters.—*Dexter,* a lion or collared flory counterflory gules;
Sinister, a stag gules attired and unguled collared flory counterflory or.

Clubs,—Carlton, Junior Carlton, Royal Yacht Squadron, Royal Bermuda Yacht, Mid-Ocean
(Bermuda), Lyford Cay (Bahamas).

SON LIVING.

Hon. Richard Anthony Gasque (382, Russell Hill Rd., Toronto 7, Ontario), *b.* March 11th, 1935:
m. 1959, Wendy Patricia, da. of James Cecil Blagden, of Bapchild Court, nr. Sittingbourne, Kent,
and has issue living, John Stephen, *b.* 1963,—David Alan, *b.* 1965,—Carolyn Elizabeth, *b.* 1969.

DAUGHTER LIVING.

Hon. Loretta Anne, *b.* 1939: *m.* 1963, Edward Samuel Rogers, of 3, Frybrook Rd., Toronto 7, Ontario,
and has issue living, Edward Samuel, *b.* 1969,—Lisa Anne, *b.* 1967,—Melinda Mary, *b.* 1971,—
Martha, *b.* 1972.

MASHAM OF ILTON, BARONESS. (Cunliffe-Lister.) [Life Baroness 1970.]

SUSAN LILIAN PRIMROSE CUNLIFFE-LISTER
(*Countess of Swinton*), yr. da. of the late Sir
Ronald Norman John Charles Udny Sinclair,
8th Bt., (cr. 1704), *b.* April 14th, 1935; *cr.*
Baroness Masham of Ilton, of Masham in N.
Riding. co. York (Life Baroness) 1970: *m.*
1959, the 2nd Earl of Swinton.

ᙏrms,—Not exemplified at time of going to press.

Residence,—Dykes Hill House, Masham, Ripon,
Yorks.

MASSEREENE AND FERRARD, VISCOUNT. (Skeffington.) Sits as BARON ORIEL (U.K. 1821). [Viscount I. 1660.]

JOHN CLOTWORTHY TALBOT FOSTER
WHYTE-MELVILLE SKEFFINGTON, 13th
Viscount; *b.* Oct. 23rd, 1914; *s.* 1956;
ed. at Eton; is a Co. Director, a
Member of Shipwrights' Co., a Free-
man of City of London, a D.L. for
co. Antrim, and Patron of one living;
European War 1939-44 as Lieut.
Black Watch, and with Small Vessels
Pool: *m.* 1939, Annabelle Kathleen,
dau. of the late Henry D. Lewis, of
Combwell Priory, Hawkhurst, Kent,
and has issue.

ᙏrms,—Quarterly: 1st and 4th, argent,
three bulls' heads erased sable, armed or,
Skeffington; 2nd and 3rd azure a chevron
between three chaplets, or, *Clotworthy.* Ⅽrest,—
A mermaid with comb and mirror, all proper
Supporters,—Two stags sable, attired and unguled
or, each gorged with a chaplet of roses argent.

Seat,—Chilham Castle, Kent.   *Clubs,*—
Carlton, Turf, Pratt's.

Through difficulties to honours.

SON LIVING.

Hon. JOHN DAVID CLOTWORTHY WHYTE-MELVILLE FOSTER, *b.* June 3rd, 1940: *m.* 1970, Anne Denise, da. of the late Norman Rowlandson, and has issue living, Charles, *b.* 1973,—Harriet Denise Margaretta Eileen, *b.* 1975.

DAUGHTER LIVING.

Hon. Oriel Annabelle Diana, *b.* 1950: *m.* 1971, Dominik Luczyc-Wyhowski, of Annagh House, Chilham, Canterbury, and has issue living, Sofia Oriel Laura, *b.* 1973.

WIDOW LIVING OF TWELFTH VISCOUNT.

LORENCE CLEMENTINA VERE (*Florence, Viscountess Massereene and Ferrard*), dau. of the late Hon. Sydney William Foster Skeffington [see colls., infra), and widow of Lieut.-Col. Brenton Laurie : *m.* 1940, as his second wife, the 12th Viscount, who *d.* 1956. *Residence,*—Farholme House, Sutton on Trent, Notts.

COLLATERAL BRANCHES LIVING. (*In remainder to Viscountcy of Massereene and Barony of Loughneagh only.*)

Issue of the late Hon. Norah Florence Margaretta Skeffington, dau. of 11th Viscount, *b.* 1872, *d.* 1944: *m.* 1897, the Rev. Charles Johnston, V. of Eaton Bray, Bedfordshire, who *d.* 1942:—
Reginald John Charles, *b.* 1898: *m.* 1942, Cecilia Ethel d'Anyers, dau. of the late Richard Atherton d'Anyers Willis (infra). *Residence,*—

Grandchildren of the late Hon. Norah Florence Margaretta Johnston, dau. of 11th Viscount (ante):—
Issue of the late Algernon George Henry Johnston, *b.* 1899, *d.* 1948 : *m.* 1926, Eileen Magdalene, dau. of — Kearney, of Doneraile, co. Cork :—
Anthony James Rex, *b.* 1931.——Rosemary Margaretta Norah, *b.* 1929.——Gabrielle, *b.* 1943.

Grandson of the late John Edward Arthur Johnston (infra):—
Issue of the late Michael John Anthony Johnston, *b.* 1939, *d.* 1965: *m.* 1965, Myrtle Stevens, of Springs, S. Africa:—
Craig Alastair, *b.* 1965.

Grandson of the late Hon. Norah Florence Margaretta Johnston (ante):—
Issue of the late John Edward Arthur Johnston, *b.* 1902, *d.* 1958: *m.* 1933, Grietje (Scottburgh, South Coast, Natal), yst. da. of Zelle Zoethout, of Leenwarden, Holland:—
Peter Charles Anthony, *b.* 1945: *m.* 1967, Deborah Jane, da. of John Wilding, of Forest Town, Johannesburg, and has issue living, Christopher John, *b.* 1970,—Katharine Ann, *b.* 1973.

Grandchildren of the late Hon. Ethel Mary Catherine Willis (infra) :—
Issue of the late Maj. Charles Rodolph d'Anyers Willis, *b.* 1907, *d.* 1961: *m.* 1936, Ursula (who *m.* 2ndly, 1963, Maj. E. J. Fitz-Gerald, late Coldstream Guards, of Granton, Mooi River, Natal), only child of the late Brig.-Gen. Sir Robert Harvey Kearsley, KCVO, CMG, DSO [Peto, Bt., cr. 1855, colls.]:—
Martin Atherton d'Anyers, *b.* 1939.——Julian Charles d'Anyers (53, Halford Rd., Durban, S. Africa), *b.* 1945: *m.* 1972, Gillian Curtis, el. da. of Earle Smith, of Pietermaritzburg, and has issue living, Sean d'Anyers, *b.* 1974.——Caroline Ann (2, Sandways Cottage, Bourton, Gillingham, Dorset) *b.* 1937: *m.* 1st, 1960, Col. D. L. G. Carleton Smith, from whom she obtained a divorce 1967; 2ndly 1967 (m. diss. 1971), Richard Courtenay Thorne, and has issue living (by 2nd m), David Courtenay, *b.* 1968.

Issue of the late Hon. Ethel Mary Catherine Skeffington, dau. of 11th Viscount, *b.* 1876, *d.* 1960: *m.* 1904, Richard Atherton d'Anyers Willis, who *d.* 1923, formerly 15th Hussars :—
Cecilia Ethel d'Anyers, *b.* 1905: *m.* 1942, her cousin, Reginald John Charles Johnston (ante).—— Winifred Alice Anyers, *b.* 1910: *m.* 1934, Lieut.-Col. Count Peter Francis de Salis, Coldstream Guards, and has issue living, Richard John, *b.* 1935; Maj. RA: *m.* 1959, Susan Thompson,— Bernard Peter, *b.* 1936; Lt.-Cdr. RN: *m.* 1967, Monica Juanita, da. of Cdr. Robert Tatton Bower, RN [see Strickland, By.].—Nicholas George (104, Blackheath Hill, SE10), *b.* 1938: *m.* 1964, Norma Dennis,—James Anthony, *b.* 1949,—Thomas Peter, *b.* 1950. *Residence,*—Euridge Manor Farm, Colerne, nr. Chippenham, Wilts.

Issue of the late Hon. Sydney William Foster-Skeffington, 3rd son of 10th Viscount Massereene, *b.* 1849, *d.* 1876: *m.* 1872, Clementina Isabella Margaret, who *d.* 1937 (having *m.* 2ndly, 1885, Col. James Craig, J.P., who *d.* 1910), dau. of Archibald Campbell Dennistoun:—
Florence Clementina Vere (*Florence, Viscountess Massereene and Ferrard*), *b.* 1873; assumed by deed poll 1915, the additional surname of Vere; a JP for Notts: *m.* 1st, 1905, Lt.-Col. George Brenton Laurie, R. Irish Rifles, who *d.* (killed in action) 1915; 2ndly, 1940, her cousin, the 12th Viscount Massereene and Ferrard, who *d.* 1956, and has issue living, (by 1st m.) George Halliburton Foster Peel (of Carlton Hall, Carlton-on-Trent, Newark, Notts); *b.* 1906; ed. at Eton; is Lt.-Col. (ret.) 9th Lancers, and a JP and DL for Notts; High Sheriff for Notts 1957; Master of Saddlers' Co. 1965: *m.* 1st, 1932, Caroline Judith, da. of the late Edward Franklin, JP, of Gonalston Hall, Notts.; 2ndly, 1968, Bridget Mary Good, and has issue living, (by 1st m.) George Edward *b.* 1935; ed. at Eton; is Capt. 9th/12th Lancers: *m.* 1962, Georgina, da. of Maj. Anthony Riall, of Rutland Cottage, Rutland Gdns., SW7, Florence Mary *b.* 1939: *m.* 1960, Capt. Christopher Tarleton Feltrim Fagan, late Gren. Guards, of Deane Hill House, Deane, Basingstoke, and has issue living, Christopher Hugh Tarleton Feltrim *b.* 1964, James Tarleton Feltrim *b.* 1965,—Sidney John Athelstan Vere (Farholme House, Sutton-on-Trent, Newark, Notts., and 99, Queen's Gate, SW7), *b.* 1910; Hon. Fellow London Coll. of Music and a Freeman of City of London,—Eleanor Blanche Helen Margaretta, *b.* 1907: *m.* 1932, Andrew Wauchope Johnstone, of Post Box 39, 86, Hazelwood Av., Hudson, Prov. of Quebec, Canada [see Johnstone, Bt., colls.]. *Residence,*—Farholme House, Sutton-on-Trent, Notts.

PREDECESSORS.—[1] Sir JOHN Clotworthy, cr. *Baron Loughneagh* and *Viscount Massereene* (peerage of Ireland) 1660, with remainder to his son-in-law Sir John Skeffington, 5th Bt., of Fisherwick and his issue male, and in default thereof to his heirs-general; *d.* 1665 ; *s.* by [2] Sir JOHN Skeffington (ante) 2nd Viscount; *d.* 1695 ; *s.* by his son [3] CLOTWORTHY, 3rd Viscount; *d.* 1713; *s.* by his son [4] CLOTWORTHY, 4th Viscount; *d.* 1738; *s.* by his son [5] CLOTWORTHY, 5th Viscount; cr. *Earl of Massereene* (peerage of Ireland) 1756; *d.* 1757; *s.* by his el. son [6] CLOTWORTHY, 2nd Earl; *d.s.p.* 1800; *s.* by his brother [7] HENRY, 3rd Earl; *d.* unmarried 1811: *s.* by his brother [8] CHICHESTER, 4th Earl; *d.* 1816, when the Baronetcy and Earldom expired, and the Barony of Loughneagh and the Viscountcy of Massereene devolved upon his dau. [9] HARRIET wife of Thomas Henry Foster, 2nd *Baron Oriel* and 2nd *Viscount Ferrard* (see *⁎⁎* infra); *d.* 1831 ; *s.* by her son [10] JOHN, K.P., 10th Viscount; *b.* 1812 ; assumed the surname of Skeffington in addition to that of Foster 1843 ; *m.* 1835, Olivia Deane, dau. of Henry Deane O'Grady, of Lodge, co. Limerick, and Stillorgan Castle, Dublin; *d.* 1863; *s.* by his son [11] CLOTWORTHY JOHN EYRE, 11th Viscount; *b.* 1842; Lieut. co. Louth and co. and Town of Drogheda *m.* 1870, Florence Elizabeth, who *d.* 1929, only child of the late Major George John Whyte-Melville; *d.* 1905; *s.* by his son [12] ALGERNON WILLIAM JOHN CLOTWORTHY, D.S.O., 12th Viscount; *b.* 1873; Major N. Irish Horse, and 17th Lancers, and Hon. Col. 188th (Antrim) Heavy Battery R.A. (T.A.); S. Africa 1900-2 (wounded, despatches twice, D.S.O.), European War 1914-18 (despatches); Lieut. for co. Antrim 1916-45 ; first Parliamentary Sec. to Prime Min. in Ulster Parliament, and a Member of Senate, N. Ireland 1921-9: *m.* 1st, 1905, Jean Barbara, who *d.* 1937, el. dau. of Sir John Stirling Ainsworth, M.P., 1st Bt.; 2ndly, 1940, his cousin, Florence Clementina Vere, dau. of the late Hon. Sydney William Foster Skeffington, and widow of Lieut.-Col. George Brenton Laurie; *d.* 1956; *s.* by his only son [13] JOHN CLOTWORTHY TALBOT FOSTER WHYTE-MELVILLE, 13th Viscount and present peer; also Baron of Loughneagh, Baron Oriel, of Collon, and Baron Oriel, of Ferrard.

✱✱ [1] JOHN Foster, *P.C.*, *M.P.* for many years, and sometime Speaker of the Irish Parliament was cr. *Baron Oriel,* of Ferrard, co. Louth (peerage of United Kingdom) 1821 : *m.* 1764, Margaret Amelia, cr. *Baroness Oriel,* of Collon (peerage of Ireland) 1790, and *Viscountess Ferrard* (peerage of Ireland) 1797, dau. of Thomas Burgh, of Birt, co. Kildare, she *d.* 1831; *s.* by her son [2] THOMAS HENRY, 2nd Viscount Ferrard [see ante], who had in 1828 *s.* his father as 2nd Baron Oriel, and in 1817 had assumed by Roy. licence the surname of Skeffington in lieu of Foster.

MASSY, BARON. (Massy.) [Baron I. 1776.]

HUGH HAMON JOHN SOMERSET MASSY, 9th Baron; *b.* June 11th, 1921; *s.* 1958; ed. at Clongowes Wood Coll., and at Clayesmore Sch.; European War 1940-45 as Private R.A.O.C.: *m.* 1943, Margaret Elizabeth, dau. of the late John Flower, of Barry, co. Meath, and has issue.

Arms,—Argent, on a chevron between three lozenges sable, a lion passant or. **Crest,**—Out of a ducal coronet or, a bull's head gules, armed sable. **Supporters.**—*Dexter,* a lion; *sinister,* a leopard reguardant; both proper and collared and chained or.

Residence,—

For the liberty of my country.

SONS LIVING.

Hon. DAVID HAMON SOMERSET, *b.* March 4th, 1947; ed. at St. George's Coll., Weybridge.
Hon. John Hugh Somerset, *b.* 1950.
Hon. Graham Ingoldsby Somerset, *b.* 1952.
Hon. Paul Robert, *b.* 1953.

DAUGHTER LIVING.

Hon. Sheila Marie Luise, *b.* 1958.

AUNTS LIVING. (*Daughters of 7th Baron.*)

Hon. Muriel Olive, *b.* 1892.
Hon. Lilian Ierne Susan MASSY-BROWNE, *b.* 1897, resumed her maiden surname of Massy before Browne 19—: *m.* 1929, Herbert Browne, and has issue living, Gordon Anthony Massy, (Clock Tower Bungalow, Whitsbury, nr. Fordingbridge, Hants.), *b.* 1933: *m.* 1968, Hazel Rose, da. of the late E. H. Martin, of Bristol. *Residence,—*35, Seaward Av., Southbourne, Bournemouth.

COLLATERAL BRANCHES LIVING.

Grandchildren of the late Hugh Hamon John Massy, son of the late Hon. George William Massy, 2nd son of 3rd Baron:—
Issue of the late Lt.-Cdr. Hugh Hamon George William Caruthers Massy, R.N., *b.* 1851; *d.* 1916: *m.* 1st, 1882, Agnes Henrietta, who *d.* 1907, dau. of the late John James Edward Hamilton [Hamilton, Bt., cr. 1776]; 2ndly, 1908, Anne Emma Featherstonhaugh, who *d.* 1926, dau. of the late Col. Robert Thomas Thompson:—
(By 2nd m.) Hugh Caruthers, *b.* 1914; ed. at Trin. Coll., Camb.; Maj. (ret.) 4th/7th R. Dragoon Guards; with Kenya Police (Mounted Section) and Game Dept. 1953-59; 1939-45 War: *m.* 1961, Pamela, el. da. of the late John Malcolm Drew, of Eversley, nr. Milnthorpe, Westmorland, and widow of 4th Baron Rathdonnell. *Residence,—*Ballinatray, Youghal, co. Cork.——Narcissa Catherine, *b.* 1910. *Residence,—*Ballyedock, Campile, co. Wexford.

Issue of the late Rollo Dillon Dunham Massy, *b.* 1856, *d.* 1934: *m.* 1884, Emma Augusta, who *d.* 1926, dau. of James Inman, of Lymington :—
Louisa Bythia, *b.* 1887.

Grandchildren of the late Edward Taylor Massy, son of the late Hon. Edward Massy, 2nd son of 2nd Baron:—
Issue of the late Haworth Peel Massy, *b.* 1842, *d.* 1916: *m.* 1873, Anne Justina, dau. of the late Arthur Lloyd Davies Lloyd, of Allty Odin, Cardiganshire :—
Hugh Dillon, *b.* 1880.——Bertie Eroll, *b.* 1883; is Major Cheshire Regt. (Reserve of Officers); European War 1914 (wounded, prisoner): *m.* 1918, Ine van Enst, widow of H. A. Versteegh.——Muriel Kathleen, *b.* 1874. *Residence,—*

Issue of the Rev. Xavier Peel Massy, *b.* 1845, *d.* 1906: *m.* 1872, Harriet Emily, who *d.* 1931, dau. of the late Edward Hurlston, of Warwick :—
Marjory Joan, *b.* 1886: *m.* 1909, Henry Curwen, CBE, MB, ChB, DCH, who *d.* 1946, sometime Principal Mel. Officer, Zanzibar Govt., and has issue living, Henry Massy, *b.* 1912,—Ian Havelock Moncreiff, *b.* 1919,—Marjory Helen, *b.* 1910,—Dorothy Zena, *b.* 1911. *Residence,—*7, Peace Rd., Athlone, Umbogintwini, Natal, S. Africa.

Grandchildren of the late Rev. Xavier Peel Massy (ante) :—
Issue of the late Godfrey Massy, *b.* 1879, *d.* 1953: *m.* 1908, Marianne, who *d.* 1951, dau. of the late Ezra Gooderidge, of Goold, Yorkshire :—
Lawrence Xavier Peel (Box 165, Savona, nr. Kamloops, BC, Canada), *b.* 1909: *m.* 1934, Hazel, da. of Edwin Hartt, of Thelma, Alberta, and has issue living, Marianne Belle, *b.* 1938.——Robert Alastair Peel (Glansevern Hall, Berrien, Welshpool, Montgomeryshire), *b.* 1918: *m.* 1953, Shirley Grania, da. of the late Dr. C. J. Wylde, of Sydenham, SE.

Issue of the late Lieut. Lawrence Peel Massy, D.S.C., R.N.R., *b.* 1883, *d.* 1932: *m.* 1914, Constance Jean Anne, who *d.* 1949, el. dau. of the late John James Galletly, solicitor, of Inchdrewer, Colinton, Midlothian, and Kinnaird, Pitlochry:—
Arthur Lawrence John Peel (18, Ballachrink, Colby, I. of Man) *b.* 1916; Major (ret.) W. Yorkshire Regt.: *m.* 1943, Margaret Alison, da. of the late Rev. E. B. Sharpe, and has issue living, David Lawrence Peel, *b.* 1949; 4th Eng. Officer, RFA,—John Eversdon Peel, *b.* 1954.——Doreen Constance Peel, *b.* 1919; late WRNS: *m.* 1st, 1945 (m. diss. 1956), Conrad Laviolette; 2ndly, 1959, John

Woolls, of Silverdale, Steep Marsh, Petersfield, Hants., and has issue living (by 1st m.) Derry Keith, *b.* 1951; PO, RN,—Lorna Doreen, *b.* 1946; late WRNS: *m.* 1967, Percival N. Skedgell, of 18, Londesborough Rd., Southsea, Hants., PO4 0EX, and has issue living, Elinor Peel *b.* 1971.

Grandchildren of the late Arthur Wellington Massy, 5th son of Edward Taylor Massy (ante):—
Issue of the late Lt.-Gen. **Hugh Royds Stokes Massy,** CB, DSO, MC, *b.* 1884, *d.* 1965, *m.* 1912, Maud Ina Nest, who *d.* 1960, da. of the late Col. Thomas James Roch, JP, DL, of Llether, Pembrokeshire:—
Hugh Peter Stokes (Alderley, School Lane, Briantspuddle, Dorchester, Dorset), *b.* 1914; ed. at Bradfield Coll. Lt.-Col. (ret.) Roy. Tank Regt.; 1939-45 War (despatches): *m.* 1945, Jean H., da. of the late Sqdn. Ldr. M. G. Kidston, of Kamiti Downs, Kahawa, Kenya, and has issue living, Diana, *b.* 1947,—Pauline, *b.* 1951.——Mary Nest, *b.* 1915.
Issue of the late Brig. **Charles Walter Massy,** CBE, DSO, MC, *b.* 1887, *d.* 1973: *m.* 1st, 1920, Muriel Lorna Bell, da. of J. A. Hallinan, of Glandalane, Fermoy; 2ndly, 1958, Irene Gillbee (Rylands, Beckington, Bath, BA3 6ST), da. of the late Richard Gillbee Thorold [see Thorold, Bt., colls.], and widow of Clifford Hackney, MRCS:—
(By 1st m.) Hugh Charles (Cregg Castle, Fermoy, co. Cork), *b.* 1921: *m.* 1970, Janice, da. of the late Maurice de Kay Thompson, of Boston, Mass., and widow of Grenville Goodwin.——John Royds, *MRCS, LRCP* (467, Winchester Rd., Bassett, Southampton), *b.* 1925; MRCS and LRCP 1960: *m.* 1957, Eileen, da. of F. Evans, of Thornfield, Hobb Lane, Hedge End, Southampton, and has issue living, David Hugh, *b.* 1962,—Peter John, *b.* 1964,—Anne Sarah, *b.* 1959,—Clare Muriel, *b.* 1960.

Grandchildren of the late Edward Taylor Massy (ante):—
Issue of the late Rev. **George Eyre Massy,** *b.* 1851, *d.* 1905: *m.* 1877, **Catherine Frances,** who *d.* 1913, only child of Surg.-Major George Frederick Hughes Brown, formerly of Bombay Army:—
Constance, *b.* 1883.

Granddaughter of the late Rev. George Eyre Massy (ante):—
Issue of the late Capt. **Villiers Wilfred Peel Massy,** *b.* 1882, *d.* 1932: *m.* 1915, Beatrice, who *d.* 1952, dau. of the late Carlos Vetter, of 6, Neville Street, S.W.:—
Bridget Ursula Elaine, *b.* 1920: *m.* 1948, Leonard Arthur Hammond Riddett, and has issue living, John Villiers, *b.* 1949,—Patrick Hammond, *b.* 1951,—Philip Peel, *b.* 1957,—Sara Caroline, *b.* 1953. *Residence,*—40, Addison Av., W11.

Grandchildren of Lt.-Col. George Eyre Massy, el. son of Hugh Massy, el. son of the Hon. George Eyre Massy, 3rd son of 2nd Baron:—
Issue of the late Hugh Hamon George Massy, *b.* 1867, *d.* 1918: *m.* 1894, Hortense Mary, who *d.* 1930, da. of Thomas John Pennefather, of Marlow, co. Tipperary:—
Hugh Hamon de Moleyns (Ellisgarty, P.B. Donnybrook, Natal), *b.* 1895; ed. at King Edward VI. Sch., Stratford on Avon, and Trin. Coll., Dublin; late Lt. R. Inniskilling Fusiliers: *m.* 1923, Helen Violet, da. of the late Allen Hamilton Morgan, of Hope Vale, Natal, and has issue living, Hugh Allen Oliver, *b.* 1926,—Evan Eyre Pennefather (PO Hilton, Natal), *b.* 1930: *m.* 1965, Lynette Marion, da. of Arthur Stuart Clark, of Tenby, Hilton, Natal, and has issue living, Jennifer Louise *b.* 1966, Helen Louise *b.* 1969.

Issue of the late Capt. James Eyre Massy, *b.* 1873, *d.* 1952: *m.* 1903, May Evelyn (1, Greenbanks Close, Church Hill, Milford on Sea, Hants.), da. of John Carmichael, JP, of Tracton Park, co. Cork:—
George Eyre (172, Hensman Rd., Subiaco, W. Australia), *b.* 1914: *m.* 1950, Marcella Margaret Helen, da. of the late James McQueen, and has issue living, Timothy James Hamon, *b.* 1953,—Jacqueline Cynthia, *b.* 1952,—Nicola Jane, *b.* 1954.——Beatrice Vera, *b.* 1904: *m.* 19—, H. W. Noyle, of Sunnyway, The Close, Sway, Lymington, Hants.——Theodora Patricia, *b.* 1912: *m.* 1948, Lt.-Col. Humphrey Rawstorne Carmichael, MC, RAOC.——Cynthia Evelyn, *b.* 1916: *m.* 1938, Eric Reade, of Honeysuckle Cottage, Westleigh, Bideford, Devon.

Grandchildren of the late Hugh Massy (ante):—
Issue of the late Robert Harding Massy, *b.* 1826, *d.* 1886: *m.* 1874, **Harriet Elizabeth,** dau. of the late Rev. John Featherstonhaugh:—
Everina Susanna Isabel.——Violet Augusta Mary: *m.* 1902, Thomas Howe, County Inspector Roy. Irish Constabulary, and has issue living, John Victor Massy, *b.* 1905.——Aileen Ismenia: *m.* 1902, Brig.-Gen. Herbert Edward Trevor, C.M.G., D.S.O., who *d.* 1939. *Residence,*—

Grandson of the late Very Rev. John Maunsell Massy-Beresford, son of 4th son of 2nd Baron:—
Issue of the late John George Beresford Massy-Beresford, *b.* 1856, *d.* 1923: *m.* 1892, **the** Hon. Alice Elizabeth Mulholland, who *d.* 1948, dau. of 1st Baron Dunleath:—
Tristram Hugh, *D.S.O. M.C.,* *b.* 1896; ed. at Eton; Brigadier Rifle Brig. (Prince Consort's Own); European War 1914-18 (twice wounded, M.C.); appointed a G.S.O., Roy. Mil. Coll. of Canada 1939; European War **1939-45** in Far East (D.S.O., prisoner); D.S.O. 1945: *m.* 1927, Helen Lindsay, dau. of the late Lindsay Crompton Lawford, of Montreal, and has issue living, Michael James (c/o Lloyds Bank, Fordingbridge, Hants.), *b.* 1935; Maj. R. Green Jackets,—Christopher Kerry, *b.* 1939,—Patricia Nell, *b.* 1931: *m.* 1958, Maj. James Otway George Paton, 13th/18th Hussars, Park Corner Farm, Odiham, Hants., and has issue living, Timothy James *b.* 1964, Nicholas George (twin) *b.* 1968, Penelope Loveday *b.* 1963, Elizabeth Gwendoline *b.* 1967. *Residence,*—New Forest Close, Woodgreen, Fordingbridge, Hants.

Grandchildren of the late Francis Staunton Massy-Dawson, son of the late Francis Dennis Massy-Dawson, son of the late James Hewitt Massy-Dawson, son of the late Hon. James Massy-Dawson, 2nd son of 1st Baron:—
Issue of the late Capt. **Francis Evelyn Massy-Dawson,** D.S.O., R.N., *b.* 1872, *d.* 1939: *m.* 1st, 1922, **Emily Banner Clough,** who *d.* 1928, dau. of Lieut.-Com. Somerset James Somerset-Johnstone, R.N., and widow of Capt. Herbert Algernon Adam, C.B.E., R.N. [Johnstone, Bt., colls.]; 2ndly, 1928, Mary Caroline, who *d.* 1950, dau. of Herbert Taylor, of Holmer, Hereford:—
(By 2nd marriage) Francis Patrick, *b.* 1934: *m.* 1961, Anne Marie, da. of W. H. Heritage, and has issue living, Suzanne, *b.* 1963,—Nicola Jane, *b.* 1965. *Residence,*—Oakleigh, Mary Tavy, Tavistock, Devon.——Rosemarie Julia, *b.* 1933: *m.* 1961, John William Halse. *Address,*— c/o Lloyds Bank, St. Peter Port, Guernsey.

Issue of the late Charles Godfrey Massy-Dawson, *b.* 1873, *d.* 1936: *m.* 1903, **Wilhelmina** Geraldine, el. dau. of the Hon. S. Haughton, Ceylon Civil Ser., formerly of The Old Palace, Kandy, Ceylon:—
Nora St. Clair, *b.* 1904.

Grandchildren of the late William MASSEY, son of the late Robert George MASSEY, el. son of the Hon. George Massy (infra):—
Issue (if any) of the late Hugh Francis Massey, *b.* 1866, *d.* 19—: *m.* 18—.
Issue of the late George William Hughes MASSEY, *b.* 1864, *d.* 1914: *m.* 1st, 1889, Edith Margaret, dau. of John Birrell, of Beech wood, London, Canada; 2ndly, 1912, Marion (*Club,*— Sesame; she *m.* 2ndly, 19—, ————Duke), dau. of the late George Clark, of Petton Grange, Salop:—

(By 2nd marriage) Patrick Godfrey Goolden, *b.* 1913.——(By 1st marriage) Marjorie Geraldine (of 115, Church St., Fredericton, New Brunswick, Canada), *b.* 1890: *m.* 1925, the Hon. Arthur Read Slipp, co. Court Judge, of Fredericton, New Brunswick, who *d.* 1958.——Muriel Frances, *b.* 1891: *m.* 1914, William Morrison McKie, of 117, Church St., Fredericton, New Brunswick, and has issue living, William Massey (of 99, Lemon St., Guelph, Ontario) *b.* 1916: *m.* 1946, Catherine Gladys, da. of T. Dowsley Kennedy, of Owen Sound, Ontario, and has issue living, Robert William Kennedy *b.* 1950, Bruce Dowsley *b.* 1955.

Grandchildren of the late Hugh Massy, son of the Hon. George Massy, 6th son of 1st Baron :—
Issue of the late Beresford Massy, *b.*1840, *d.* 1878: *m.* 1869, Elizabeth Harriet, dau. of the Rev. George H. Reade, of Inniskeen Rectory, Dundalk :—
Sydney Beresford, *b.* 1876.——Frances Mary Georgina.——Eva Constance: *m.* 1916, Frederick J. Smissen, formerly Lieut. Roy. Irish Rifles. *Residence,—*

Issue of the late George Hugh Massy, *b.* 1844, *d.* 1912: *m.* 1880, Georgina, who *d.* 1920, dau. of the late George E. Fenwick, M.D., Professor of Surgery in McGill Univ., Montreal :—
Gordon Eyre, *b.* 1896.——Mary Charlotte Robertson, *b.* 1881.——Ethel Gertrude, *b.* 1882.—— Constance Emily, *b.* 1885.——Marion Edgworth, *b.* 1888.——Evelyn de Hertel, *b.* 1890.—— Georgina Annie Gahan, *b.* 1891. *Residence,—*

PREDECESSORS.—[1] HUGH Massy, M.P. for co. Limerick in several parliaments, was cr. *Baron Massy,* of Duntrileague, co. Limerick (peerage of Ireland) 1776; *d.* 1788; *s.* by his son [2] HUGH, 2nd Baron; M.P. for co. Limerick; *d.* 1790; *s.* by his son [3] HUGH, 3rd Baron; *d.*1812; *s.* by his son [4] HUGH HAMON, 4th Baron; *b.* 1793: *m.* 1826, Matilda, who *d.* 1888, dau. of Luke White, Esq., of Woodlands, co. Dublin; *d.*1836; *s.* by his el. son[5] HUGH HAMON INGOLDSBY, 5th Baron: *m.* 1855, Isabella, who *d.* 1917, dau. of George MacNisbett; *d.s.p.* 1874; *s.* by his brother [6] JOHN THOMAS WILLIAM, 6th Baron, *b.* 1835; a Representative Peer: *m.* 1863, Lady Lucy Maria Butler, who *d.* 1896, dau. of 3rd Earl of Carrick ; *d.* 1915; *s.* by his son [7] HUGH SOMERSET JOHN, 7th Baron, *b.* 1864: *m.* 1886, Ellen Ida Constance, who *d.* 1922, dau. of the late Charles William Wise, of Rochester, Cahir, co. Tipperary ; *d.* 1926; *s.* by his son[8] HUGH HAMON CHARLES GEORGE, 8th Baron, *b.* 1894: *m.* 1919, Margaret, who *d.*1971 dau. of the late Richard Leonard, of Meadsbrook, Ashbourne, co. Limerick, and widow of Dr. — Moran, of Tara, co. Meath; *d.* 1958; *s.* by his only son [9] HUGH HAMON JOHN SOMERSET, 9th Baron, and present peer.

MATHERS, BARONY OF.   (Mathers.)   [Extinct 1965.]
WIDOW LIVING OF FIRST BARON.
JESSIE NEWTON (*Baroness Mathers*), (50, Craiglea Drive, Edinburgh, EH10 5PF), da. of the late George Graham, JP, of Peebles and Edinburgh: *m.* 1940, as his 2nd wife, the 1st Baron, who *d.* 1965, when the title became ext.

Mauchline, Lord, son of Countess of Loudoun.

Maud, see Baron Redcliffe-Maud.

MAUGHAM, VISCOUNT.   (Maugham.)   [Viscount 1939.]

ROBERT CECIL ROMER MAUGHAM, 2nd Viscount ; *b.* May 17th, 1916 ; *s.* 1958 ; ed. at Eton, and at Trin. Hall, Camb. (B.A. 1938) ; Bar. Lincoln's Inn 1944 ; Capt. 4th Co. of London Yeo. ; European War 1939-43 in Middle East (wounded, despatches).

Arms,—Per pale argent and gules a chevron between three roundels all counterchanged. Crest,—A Patriarchal cross reversed conjoined at the chief with two bars saltire enarched and embattled azure.

Residence,—Casa Cala Pada, Santa Eulalia del Rio, Ibiza, Baleares, Spain.

SISTERS LIVING.
Hon. Honor: *m.* 1925, Sebastian Earl, and has issue living, Julian Romer (28, Thurloe Sq., SW7), *b.* 1927: *m.* 1962, Phyllis, da. of Dr. Richard Blum, of New York, and has issue living, Sebastian *b.* 1965, Austin Richard *b.* 1967, Cordelia *b.* 1963,—Quentin Stephen (Church House, Old Headington, Oxford), *b.* 1931: *m.* 1957, Rosemary, da. of Lester Blake-Jolly, Dist. Officer of N. Rhodesia, and has issue living, Colin Raphael *b.* 1958, Mark Justin *b.* 1959, Tristram Andrew *b.* 1962, Jocelyn Malcolm *b.* 1968. *Residences,*—14, South Terr., SW7; Chilland Ford, Martyr Worthy, nr. Winchester.

Hon Diana Julia: *m* 1932, Kenneth Marr-Johnson, and has issue living, Frederick James Maugham (Farrar's Building, Temple, EC4), *b.* 1936: *m.* 1966, Susan, da. of Maj. R. P. H. Eyre, of Winsford, Som., and has issue living, Thomas Maugham *b.* 1966, Helen Rachel *b.* 1969, Clifford Simon Romer (164, Kensington Park Rd., W11), *b.* 1938: *m.* 1966, Catharine Mary, da. of the late Cdr. John Smyth, of Llanbedr, Breconshire, and has issue living, Prosper Henry, *b.* 1967, Alexander Merlin *b.* 1971, Diana Romilly *b.* 1969,—John William (15, Cromwell Rd., SW7) *b.* 1945. *Residence,*—Flat 3, 14, Onslow Sq., SW7

PREDECESSOR.—[1] *Rt. Hon.* Sir FREDERIC HERBERT Maugham, son of the late Robert Ormond Maugham, of Paris; *b.* 1866; appointed a Judge of High Court of Justice (Chancery Div.) 1928, and a Lord Justice of Appeal 1934; was a Lord of Appeal in Ordinary 1935-38, and Lord High Chancellor 1938-39; again a Lord of Appeal in Ordinary 1939-41; cr. *Baron Maugham,* of Hartfield, co. Sussex (Life Baron) 1935, and *Viscount Maugham,* of Hartfield, co. Sussex (peerage of United Kingdom) 1939: *m.* 1896, Helen Mary, who *d.* 1950, da. of the late Rt. Hon. Sir Robert Romer, GCB, a Lord Justice of Appeal; *d.* 1958; *s.* by his only son [2] ROBERT CECIL ROMER, 2nd Viscount and present peer.

MAY, BARON. (May.) [Baron U.K. 1935, Bt. U.K. 1931.

MICHAEL ST. JOHN MAY, 3rd Baron and 3rd Baronet; *b.* Sept. 26th, 1931; *s.* 1950; ed. at Wycliffe Coll., and at Magdalene Coll., Camb.; late Lt. Roy. Signals: *m.* 1st, 1958 (marriage dissolved 1963), Dorothea Catherine Ann, da. of Charles McCarthy, of Boston, U.S.A.; 2ndly, 1963, Jillian Mary, only da. of Albert Edward Shipton, of Wroxton Mill, Wroxton, Oxon., and has issue.

Arms,—Gules, on a chevron between in chief three billets or, and in base an eagle argent, three roses of the field, barbed and seeded proper. Crest,—A demi-leopard proper, holding in the dexter paw a bezant and resting the sinister paw on a terrestrial globe also proper. Supporters,—Dexter, a griffin, and *sinister* a dragon or, each charged on the shoulder with a sprig of mayflower slipped and leaved proper.
  Residence,—Gautherns Barn, Sibford Gower, Oxon.

With God's help work prospers.

SON LIVING.
Hon. JASPER BERTRAM ST. JOHN, *b.* Oct. 24th, 1965.

DAUGHTER LIVING.
Hon. Miranda Jane, *b.* 1968.

SISTER LIVING.
Hon. June Lisette, *b.* 1929 ; ed. at St. Paul's Sch. : *m.* 1958, Raymond Charles Lisser, and has issue living, Aidan Charles, *b.* 1959. *Residences,*—School House, Stanton, Broadway, Worcs.; 6H, Hyde Park Mansions, NW1.

AUNT LIVING. (*Daughter of 1st Baron.*)
Hon. Elizabeth Frances, *b.* 1907 : *m.* 1955, George Leonard Brunton Henderson, M.R.C.V.S., B.Sc., and has issue living, Christopher Iain, *b.* 1959,—Simon Neil, *b.* 1960. *Residence,*—Oak Lodge, Oak Hill Grove, Surbiton, Surrey, KT6 6DS.

WIDOW LIVING OF SON OF FIRST BARON.
(AUDREY) GILLIAN (JACKSON), dau. of Edward Bagot, of Cross Farm, West Coker, Somerset : *m.* 1951, as his second wife, the Hon. Patrick William May, who *d.* 1956, and has issue living [see colls., infra]. *Residence,*—Preston Place Cottage, 28, Worthing Rd., East Preston, Sussex.

WIDOW LIVING OF SECOND BARON.
ELISABETH, dau. of George Ricardo Thoms : *m.* 1st, 1929, as his second wife, the 2nd Baron. who *d.* 1950; 2ndly, 19—, W. H. Hallam, of 2, Drummond Rd., W. Worthing, Sussex.

COLLATERAL BRANCH LIVING.
Issue of the late Hon. Patrick William May, younger son of 1st Baron, *b.* 1911, *d.* 1956: *m.* 1st, 1934, Dorothy Patience (from whom he obtained a divorce 1948), dau. of Francis Du Croz, of Weybridge ; 2ndly, 1951, (Audrey) Gillian (JACKSON) (ante), dau. of Edward Bagot, of Cross Farm, West Coker, Somerset :—
(By 1st m.) Caroline, *b.* 1934: *m.* 19—, Edward Waldman, of 45, Burleigh St., Waterville, Maine, USA.
——Valentine Virginia, *b.* 1938: *m.* 1963, Malcolm Walker MacLeod, of 2A, Ivy Way, Port Washington, New York, 11050, USA, and has issue living, Sarah Walker, *b.* 1965,—Alexandra Louise, *b.* 1968.
——(By 2nd m.) Philippa Jane, *b.* 1952.——Elisabeth Patricia (posthumous), *b.* 1957.

PREDECESSORS.—[1] *Sir* GEORGE ERNEST May, *K.B.E.,* son of William C. May, of Cheshunt, *b.* 1871 ; many years Sec. of Prudential Assurance Co.; sometime Manager of American Dollar Securities Committee; appointed Chm. of Import Duties Advisory Committee 1932 ; cr. a *Baronet* 1931, and *Baron May,* of Weybridge, co. Surrey (peerage of United Kingdom) 1935: *m.* 1903, Lily Julia, *O.B.E.,* who *d.* 1955, younger dau. of G. Strauss; *d.* 1946 ; *s.* by his el. son [2] JOHN LAW-RENCE, 2nd Baron ; *b.* 1904: *m.* 1st, 1925, Cicely Beryl, who *d.* 1928, only child of the late Ernest Fleming, of Raska, Clarendon Road, Watford; 2ndly, 1929, Elisabeth, dau. of George Ricardo Thoms; *d.* 1950; *s.* by his only son [3] MICHAEL ST. JOHN, 3rd Baron and present peer.

MAYBRAY-KING, BARON. (Maybray-King) [Life Baron 1971.]

Suffer little children.

HORACE MAYBRAY MAYBRAY-KING, *PC*, son of the late John William King, of Newcastle upon Tyne; *b*. May 25th, 1901; assumed by deed poll 1970 the surname of Maybray-King in lieu of his patronymic; ed. at Stockton Univ. (BA, PhD): Hon. LLD London, Bath and Durham; Hon. DCL Southampton; Hon. LittD, Loughborough; Hon. DSoc. Sc. Ottawa; an Hon. Alderman of Hants., a Freeman of Southampton and Stockton; Head of English Dept. Taunton's Sch., Southampton 1923-45, and Headmaster Regent's Park Sec. Sch. 1946-50; MP for Test Div. of Southampton (*Lab.*) 1950-55, and for Itchen Div. of Southampton 1955-71; Chm. of Ways and Means, and Dep. Speaker 1964-65, and Speaker of House of Commons 1965-71; Hon. Treas. Help the Aged Assocn. since 1972; cr. PC 1965, and *Baron Maybray-King, of City of Southampton* (Life Baron) 1971: *m*. 1st, 1922, Victoria Florence, who *d*. 1966, da. of George David Harris, of Lewisham, SE13; 2ndly, 1967, Una, da. of William Herbert Porter, of Southampton, and has issue by 1st m.

Arms,—Argent a cherub proper within a chaplet of four roses two in pale argent and two in fess gules barbed seeded and leaved proper. **Crest,**—A mace or and a spade the blade upwards in saltire proper. **Supporters,**—On either side a bittern proper.

Residence,—37, Manor Farm Rd., Bitterne Park, Southampton.

DAUGHTER LIVING. (By 1st m.)

Hon. Margaret Eleanor, *b*. 1926: a JP of Havant: *m*. 1945, Roy Wilson, of 105, Silvester Rd., Cowplain, Portsmouth.

MAYO, EARL OF. (Bourke.) [Earl I. 1785.]
[Name pronounced "Burk."]

Salvation from the Cross.

TERENCE PATRICK BOURKE, 10th Earl; *b*. Aug. 26th, 1929; *s*., 1962; Lt. R.N. (ret.); Managing Dir. of Irish Marble Ltd.; a Councillor of Gosport since 1961: *m*. 1952, Margaret Jane Robinson, only da. of the late Gerald Harrison, DL, of Wetheral, Cumberland, and has issue.

Arms,—Per fesse or and ermine, a cross gules, in the 1st quarter a lion rampant, and in the 2nd a dexter hand erect couped at the wrist, both sable. **Crest,**—A cat-a-mountain sejant guardant proper, collared and chained or. **Supporters,**—Two chevaliers in complete armour, each holding in the exterior hand a pole-axe, proper.

Residence,—Doon House, Maam, co. Galway
Clubs,—R.N.V.R., Galway County.

SONS LIVING.

CHARLES DIARMUIDH JOHN (*Lord Naas*). *b*. June 11th, 1953.
Hon. Patrick Antony, *b*. 1955.
Hon. Harry Richard, *b*. 1960.

SISTER LIVING.

Sheelagh Wilmot, *b*. 1925: *m*. 1955, Frank Merton Trier, of Fairlawn, W. Horsley, Surrey, and has issue living, Terence Anthony Merton, *b*. 1957,—Ysolde Gwynedd, *b*. 1956.

UNCLE LIVING. (Son of 8th Earl.)

Hon. Geoffrey John, *b*. 1900; is a F.R.I.C.S., and a Fellow of Land Agents' So. Pres. 1947-8): *m*. 1926, Nancy Lisette, dau. of the late Douglas T. Thring, Bursar of Merton Coll., Oxford, and has issue living, Elizabeth, *b*. 1928: *m*. 1954, John Anthony Lorimer Auden, of Habshagstrasse 13, 4153, Reinach BL, Switzerland, and has issue living, Christopher John Lorimer, *b*. 1958, Jennifer Mary, *b*. 1956. *Residence,*—167, Russell Court, Woburn Place, WC1.

AUNT LIVING (Daughter of 8th Earl.)

Lady Betty Jocelyne, *b*. 1917: *m*. 1st, 1943, Capt. Ronald Banon, late 60th Rifles, who *d*. 1943: 2ndly, 1953, Samuel Clarke, and has issue living, (by 2nd marriage) Elizabeth Charlotte, *b*. 1955,—Joycelyne Margaret, *b*. 1957. *Residence,*—Cnoc-Na-Curra, Oughterard, co. Galway.

WIDOW LIVING OF SON OF EIGHTH EARL.

Patricia May, el. dau. of the late H. B. Dickinson, M.D., F.R.C.S., of Hereford; is a J.P.: *m*. 1952, as his second wife, Capt. the Hon. Bryan Longley Bourke, who *d*. 1961. *Residence,*—St. Aldhelm, Chapel Amble, Wadebridge, Cornwall.

WIDOW LIVING OF NINTH EARL.

NÖEL JESSIE HALIBURTON (*Nöel, Countess of Mayo*), dau. of the late William James Wilson, of High Park, nr. Kendal: *m*. 1937, the 9th Earl, who *d*. 1962.

COLLATERAL BRANCHES LIVING.

Issue of the late Hon. Terence Theobald Bourke, O.B.E., 4th son of 6th Earl,
b. 1865, *d.* 1923 : *m.* 1896, Eveline Constance, who *d.* 1917, dau. of the late
Col. Thomas William Haines, of Hasketon Manor, Suffolk :—
Myrtle Mercy, *b.* 1899. *Residences,*—Pekes, Hellingly, Sussex; Château Ben Negro, Bizerta, Tunis,

Grandsons of the late Maj. the Hon. Edward Roden Bourke, 6th son of 5th Earl:—
Issue of the late Col. Nigel Edward Jocelyn Bourke, *b.* 1886, *d.* 1970: *m.* 1927, Doris, who *d.*
1949, da. of Allan Wills, of Aberdeen:—
Josslyn Allan Roden, *b.* 1930: *m.* 1951, Barbara Alison, da. of Wilson Braddock, and has issue living,
Alice Grania, *b.* 1954,—Deborah Madeline, *b.* 1958,—Susan Doris, *b.* 1960.

Issue of the late Madeline Emmie Louisa, *b.* 1878, *d.* 1961 : *m.* 1904, Samuel Howard
Whitbread, C.B., who *d.* 1944 [E. Chichester]:—
Simon (of The Mallowry, Riseley, Bedford), *b.* 1904; ed. at Eton, and at Trin. Coll., Camb. (B.A.
1926); Major (retired) King's Roy. Rifle Corps, Lord-Lieut. and Custos Rotulorum for Bedfordshire,
and an O.St.J.: *m.* 1936, Charles Beatrice Margaret, dau. of the late Hon. Robert Henry Hepburn-
Stuart-Forbes-Trefusis [see B. Clinton, colls.], and has issue living, Samuel Charles (of Southill
Park, Biggleswade, Beds.), *b.* 1937; ed. at Eton, and Trin. Coll., Camb.; a CC, a JP, and a DL for
Beds. (High Sheriff 1973-74): *m.* 1961, Jane Mary, da. of Charles Hugh Hayter, and has issue living,
Charles Edward Samuel *b.* 1963, Henry George Simon *b.* 1965, William John Howard *b.* 1966, Vic-
toria Clare Helen *b.* 1969,—Elizabeth Anne (61, Royal Hospital Rd., SW3), *b.* 1939: *m.* 1962, James
Carthew Cavendish Bennett, Diplo. Ser., who *d.* 1969, and has issue living, Nicholas James *b.* 1964,
Simon Patrick *b.* 1965, Charles David *b.* 1969.——Humphrey, *TD, b.* 1912; ed. at Eton, and at
Trin. Coll., Camb. (MA); Maj. (ret.) Queen Victoria's Rifles, King's Roy. Rifle Corps (TA); a DL
of Beds., High Sheriff 1962. *Residence,*—1, Upper Brook St., W1.

Grandson of the late Lt. Hubert Edward Madden BOURKE-BORROWES, RN, son of
Richard Bourke, son of the late Rev. the Hon. George Theobald Bourke (infra):—
Issue of the late Dermot Richard Southwell Bourke-Borrowes, *b.* 1884, *d.* 1968: *m.* 1941,
Mrs. Elizabeth Burton, da. of G. F. Burgess, of Hall Garth, Over Kellett, Lancs.:—
Kildare Hubert (Château des Rêts, Chennevières-sur-Marne, 94, Val de Marne, France), *b.* 1942;
ed. at Wellington and Magdalen Coll., Camb.: *m.* 1971, Pippa Marguerite, yr. da. of Lt.-Col. O. S.
Steel, of Meriden Court, Chelsea Manor St., SW3, and has issue living, Olivia Helene, *b.* 1974.

Grandson of the late Rev. John Bourke, son of the late Rev. the Hon. George,
Theobald Bourke, 4th son of 3rd Earl :—
Issue of the late Arthur Edward Desborough Bourke, *b.* 1852, *d.* 1903: *m.* 1888, Maude
Margaret, who *d.* 1923, dau. of the late Henry Blake Mahon, of Belleville, co. Galway :—
Arthur John Henry, *b.* 1897; is Brigadier (retired) Indian Army; European War 1915-16 in
France and Mesopotamia (wounded twice), Afghanistan 1919, Waziristan 1919-21, N.-W.
Frontier of India 1936-38 and 1940-41 (despatches), Burma 1941-42 (despatches). *Club,*—United
Service.

Granddaughter of the late Maj.-Gen. Sir George Deane Bourke, K.C.M.G., C.B.,
son of the late Lieut.-Col. Thomas Joseph Deane Bourke, son of the late
Rev. the Hon. George Theobald Bourke (ante) :—
Issue of the late Group-Capt. Ulick John Deane Bourke, C.M.G., *b.* 1884, *d.* 1948: *m.*
1917, Irene (from whom he obtained a divorce 1932), dau. of Lewis Ashhurst, of
Norwich :—
Bridget (of 30, French Gate, Richmond, Yorks.), *b.* 1920; Bar. Lincoln's Inn 1956.

This family, formerly of Moneycrower, co. Sligo, descends from John Bourke, 4th son of Sir Thomas
Bourke, 1397 (styled " MacWilliam Eighter ", head of Mayo or Lower Connaught branch, as distinct
from " MacWilliam Oughter " of Galway or Upper Connaught [see M. Sligo]), whose 2nd son Edmund
was ancestor of Viscounts Mayo (cr. 1627, ext. or dormant 1767), and was a branch of the Anglo-
Norman family of de Burgh [1] *Rt. Hon.* JOHN Bourke, of Moneycrower, M.P., First Commr. of
Revenue, Ireland 1749-80; cr. *Baron Naas,* of Naas, co. Kildare 1776, and *Viscount Mayo,* of
Moneycrower, co. Mayo 1781; and *Earl of Mayo* 1785 (all in Peerage of Ireland): *m.* 1726, Mary,
who *d.* 1774, dau. of Rt. Hon. Joseph Deane; *d.* 1790; *s.* by his el. son [2] JOHN, 2nd Earl, *b.* about
1729; M.P.: *m.* 1764, Lady Margaret Leeson, who *d.* 1794, dau. of 1st Earl of Milltown; *d.* 1792;
s. by his brother [3] *Most Rev.* JOSEPH Deane, D.D., 3rd Earl; *b.* 1736; Bishop of Leighlin 1772-82,
and Archbishop of Tuam 1782-94: *m.* 1760, Elizabeth Meade, who *d.* 1807, sister of 1st Earl of
Clanwilliam; *d.* 1794; *s.* by his son [4] JOHN, G.C.H., P.C., 4th Earl; *b.* 1766; a Representative Peer
1816-49: *m.* 1792, Arabella (Lady of the Bedchamber to Queen Adelaide), who *d.* 1843, dau. of
William Mackworth Praed, of Bitton House, Devon; *d.* 1849; *s.* by his nephew [5] ROBERT (only
son of the Rt. Rev. the Hon. Richard Bourke, Bishop of Waterford and Lismore, 2nd son of 3rd
Earl), 5th Earl, *b.* 1797; a Representative Peer 1852-67: *m.* 1820, Anne Charlotte, who *d.* 1867,
dau. of the Hon. John Jocelyn [E. Roden]; *d.* 1867; *s.* by his son [6] *Rt. Hon.* RICHARD SOUTHWELL,
K.P., G.C.M.G., 6th Earl; *b.* 1822; M.P. for Kildare (C) 1847-52, for Coleraine 1852-7, and for
Cockermouth 1857-68; Ch. Sec. for Ireland 1852, 1858, and 1866, and Gov.-Gen. of India 1868-72,
when he was assassinated in the Andaman Islands: *m.* 1848, Blanche Julia, C.I., V.A., who *d.* 1918,
dau. of 1st Baron Leconfield; *s.* by his el. son [7] *Rt. Hon.* DERMOT ROBERT WYNDHAM, K.P., 7th
Earl, *b.* 1851; a Representative Peer for Ireland and Lieut. of co. Kildare; a Member of Senate
of Irish Free State 1922-7: *m.* 1885, Geraldine Sarah, who *d.* 1944, dau. of the late Hon. Gerald
Henry Brabazon Ponsonby; *d.* 1927; *s.* by his cousin [8] WALTER LONGLEY (son of the late Rev.
the Hon. George Wingfield Bourke, 4th son of 5th Earl), 8th Earl; *b.* 1859: *m.* 1st, 1887, Ethel
Kathleen Jane, who *d.* 1913, only dau. of the late Capt. John Freeman, of Rockfield, Herefordshire;
2ndly, 1916, Margaret Anah, dau. of the late Major John Harvey Scott, Indian Army; *d.* 1939;
s. by his son [9] ULICK HENRY, 9th Earl; *b.* 1890; 2nd Lt., King's Roy. Rifle Corps; 1914-18 War
as Lt., King's African Rifles: *m.* 1937, Nöel Jessie Haliburton, dau. of the late William James
Wilson, of High Park, nr. Kendal; *d.* 1962; *s.* by his nephew [10] TERENCE PATRICK (only son of the
late Hon. Bryan Longley Bourke, 3rd son of 8th Earl), 10th Earl and present peer; also Viscount
Mayo, and Baron Naas.

MEATH, EARL OF (Brabazon.) Sits as BARON CHAWORTH (U.K. 1831)
[Earl I. 1627.]
ANTHONY WINDHAM NORMAND BRABAZON,
14th Earl; *b.* Nov. 3rd, 1910; *s.* 1949; ed. at
Eton; European War 1939-45 as Major Grenadier
Guards (wounded): *m.* 1940, Elizabeth Mary
dau. of the late Capt. Geoffrey Vaux Salvin
Bowlby [see V. Valentia], and has issue.

Arms,—Gules: on a bend or, three martlets sable.
Crest,—On a mount vert, a falcon rising or. Supporters,—
Two wyverns or, collared and chained gules.

Residence,—Killruddery, Bray, co. Wicklow.

My life is devoted.

SONS LIVING.

JOHN ANTHONY (*Lord Ardee*), *b.* May 11th, 1941; ed. at Harrow; a Page of Honour to H.M., 1956-58; late Gren. Gds.: *m.* 1973, Xenia, yr. da. of P. Goudime, of Windlesham Park, Surrey, and has issue.

DAUGHTER LIVING,—*Hon.* Corinna Lettice, *b.* 1974.

Hon. David Geoffrey Normand, *b.* 1948: *m.* 1972, Gay Dorothea, yr. da. of Cdr. William (Jock) Whitworth, DSC, RN, of Trudder, co. Wicklow [M. Ely.], and has issue living, a da., *b.* 1973.

DAUGHTERS LIVING.

Lady Romayne Aileen, *b.* 1943: *m.* 1968, Capt. Robert Eben Neil Pike, late Gren. Gds., of 29, Moor Park Rd., SW6 2HU, and has issue living, Harry Eben, *b.* 1974,—Tamsin Lucy, *b.* 1972.
Lady Lavinia Anne, *b.* 1945: *m.* 1969, John Ernest Baron Jobson, of Nasool, Geevagh, co. Sligo, and has issue living, Rebecca Catherine, *b.* 1971,—Charlotte Naomi Marya, *b.* 1973.

SISTERS LIVING.

Lady Maureen Margaret, *b.* 1908: *m.* 1950, the Hon. Laurence Paul Methuen, who *d.* 1970 [see B. Methuen]. *Residence,*—Starlings, Sutton Benger, Chippenham, Wilts.
Lady Meriel Aileen, *b.* 1913: *m.* 1947, Maj. Ernest Gerald Howarth, MBE, who *d.* 1967, and has issue living, Sarah Ann, *b.* 1950: *m.* 1972, Robert A. H. Smeddle, and has issue living, Vanessa Mary *b.* 1974,—Aileen Jane, *b.* 1951,—Elizabeth Meriel, *b.* 1953,—Penelope Susan, *b.* 1958. *Residence,*—Congham Hall, King's Lynn, Norfolk, PE32 1AH.

COLLATERAL BRANCHES LIVING.

Issue of the late Lieut.-Col. the Hon. Claud Maitland Patrick Brabazon, O.B.E., 3rd son of 12th Earl, *b.* 1874, *d.* 1959 : *m.* 1915, Kathleen, who *d.* 1961, dau. of the late Arthur Maitland, of Shudy Camps Park, Cambridgeshire :—
Elizabeth Maitland, *b.* 1915 : *m.* 1942, Lieut.-Col. Evered Mansfield Poole, R.A. (retired) [see By. Ilkeston (ext.)]. *Residence,*—White Lodge, Hill Brow, Liss, Hants.——Felicity Margaretta, *b.* 1917 ; ed. at London Univ. (B.A. honours 1939) ; formerly 1st Officer W.R.N.S. : *m.* 1948, Gilbert Stanley Hodson, who *d.* 1972 [see Hodson, Bt. colls.]. *Residence,*—Luska, Puckana, Nenagh, co. Tipperary.

(*In Special remainder to the Earldom*).

Descendants of the late Hon. Sir Anthony Brabazon, 3rd son of 1st Baron Ardee:—

Grandchildren of the late Anthony Godsell Brabazon, son of the late Rev. James Brabazon, son of the late Anthony Brabazon :—
Issue of the late Charles James Anthony Brabazon, *b.* 1869, *d.* 1944: *m.* 1897, Amy Ruby Victoria, who *d.* 1947, dau. of William McMillan, of Culpraoo, Longreach, Queensland :—
Anthony Godsell, *b.* 1899: *m.* 1925, Margaret Victoria, only da. of the late J. A. Gibson, of Sydney, NSW, and has issue living, Margaret Ann, *b.* 1927; FASA, ACIS, FGAA, and a JP: *m.* 1974, the Rt. Rev. Ian Wotton Allnutt Shevill, Lord Bishop of Newcastle, NSW, of Bishopscourt, Church St., Newcastle 2300, NSW.——Charles Reginald, *b.* 1904: *m.* 1940, Minnie Isabel, da. of James Lennox Arthur, of Quambetook, Nelia, N. Queensland, and has issue living, Charles James Lennox, *b.* 1944; BA, LLB; Lt. Queensland Univ. Regt. CMF,—Richard Anthony, *b.* 1949. *Residence,*—17, Morgan St., Albion Heights, Brisbane, Queensland.——Rupert William (21, Federation Av., Broadbeach, Qld., 4217), *b.* 1908: *m.* 1952, Margaret Cecil Pender, da. of the late Edward Pender Phillott, of Colane, Winton, Queensland, and has issue living, Anthony Edward *b.* 1953,—William Robert, *b.* 1960,—Wendy Pender, *b.* 1955,—Patricia Rain, *b.* 1957.——Ruby Sylvia May (Birrahlee, Ridgelands, Qld.), *b.* 1898: *m.* 1919, William Henry Rudd, who *d.* 1968, and has issue living, Charles Robert Brabazon (17, Amalfi Parade, Isle of Capri, Gold Coast, Qld.), *b.* 1925: *m.* 1950, Eileen, da. of Harold Ellis, of Melbourne, and has issue living, Belinda Anne *b.* 1958,—Frank Brabazon, *b.* 1929: *m.* 1953, Wendy, da. of Reginald Withers, of Rockhampton, Queensland, and has issue living, Peter Brabazon *b.* 1965, Kirsti Sue, *b.* 1954, Kim (da.) *b.* 1958, Amanda Jane *b.* 1961,—Geoffrey Brabazon (73, Kooringal Drive, Tindalee, Brisbane, Qld.), *b.* 1940: *m.* 1967, June Elizabeth, da. of Clement Harold Talbot, of Brisbane, Qld.,—Ruby Patricia, *b.* 1921: *m.* 1946, William George Robertson, of Birrahlee, Wandoan, Queensland, and has issue living, William Robert *b.* 1950, Margaret Patricia *b.* 1947, Susan Jennifer *b.* 1949.——Kathleen Patricia (11, Collin St., Kingston, 4205, Qld.), *b.* 1903.——Eileen Emma, *b.* 1907: *m.* 1929, Bernard Carr Clark, of 5, Mary St., Urangan 4658, S. Qld., and has issue living, Michael George (55, Richmond Terr., Richmond, Victoria, Aust.), *b.* 1930,—Adam Charles (of Bimbadeen, Taroom, Queensland), *b.* 1933: *m.* 1954, Dorothy Isabel, da. of J. S. B. Milne, of Dalby, Queensland, and has issue living, Bruce Robert *b.* 1955, Ian Charles *b.* 1956, Owen Mark *b.* 1967, Kevin Adam *b.* 1969, Wendy Ann *b.* 1961,—Robert Anthony (of Mutation, Clermont, Qld.), *b.* 1936: *m.* 1967, Margot Grant, da. of the late A. F. G. Cameron, of Brisbane, and has issue living, Michael Robert *b.* 1969.

Issue of the late Rupert Levinge Brabazon, *b.* 1871, *d.* 1924 : *m.* 1904, Grace Eva, who *d.* 1948, dau. of Campbell Livingstone Macdonald, of Bromelton, Beaudesert, Queensland :—
Rupert Macdonald, *b.* 1907: *m.* 1934, Moyra Joy, da. of Edgar Joyce, of The Overflow, Beaudesert, Queensland, and has issue living, Margaret Joy, *b.* 1936,—Barbara Joan, *b.* 1938,—Patricia Elizabeth, *b.* 1940. *Residence,*—Waiburra, Gleneagle, Beaudesert, Queensland.
——Campbell Anthony, *b.* 1910: *m.* 1945, Marjorie Seymour Villiers dau. of Villiers Seymour Brown. *Residence,*—5, Anna Street, Beaudesert, Queensland.——Robert Charles, *b.* 1912 : *m.* 1950, Geraldine Hope Gordon, dau. of Robert John Gordon Burrow, and has issue living, Mark Levinge, *b.* 1958. *Residence,* 33, Fraser St., Graceville, Brisbane, Queensland.——Kathleen Grace *b.* 1906.

Grandchildren of the late Rev. Philip Robert Waller Brabazon, son of the late Rev. George Brabazon, brother (*b.* 1780) of the late Anthony Brabazon (ante):—
Issue of the late George Philip Augustus Brabazon, *b.* 1845, *d.* 1912: *m.* 1886, Rhoda Jane, who *d.* 1946, dau. of the late Edmond Nugent, M.D., F.R.C.S.I., of San Diego, California:—
Cecil George Le Normand (of 225, Fig Av., Chula Vista, Cal., U.S.A.), *b.* 1887: *m.* 1927, Gladys May, da. of Nathan Wyman[Downs, of Chula Vista, California, U.S.A., and has issue living, Cora Jane, *b.* 1934: *m.* 1962, Charles F. Ruhr, of 5, Clark Av., White Bear Lake, Minnesota, USA, and has issue living, Christopher Patrick *b.* 1968, Ann Cecilia *b.* 1965.——Edmond Charles Heyland (3953, Eagle St., San Diego, Cal. 92103, USA), *b.* 1893: *m.* 1928, Ann Irene, da. of Edward Ward Young, of Salt Lake City, Utah, USA.——Marian Constance (4460, North Av., San Diego, Cal., USA), *b.* 1900: *m.* 1936, Howard Jonathan Edwards, who *d.* 1950.

Grandson of the late George Philip Augustus Brabazon (ante):—
Issue of the late Montague Philip Le Normand Brabazon, *b.* 1890, *d.* 1967: *m.* 1916, Edwina Meston, da. of the late George T. Smith, of Alpine, San Diego, Cal., USA:—
Keith Elmer (Route 1, Box 528, Alpine, San Diego, Cal., USA), *b.* 1917: *m.* 1963, Clara Carolina, da. of Rudolph Wenger, of Max, N. Dakota, and has issue living, Lee Monte, *b.* 1964.

Granddaughter of the late Anthony Beaufort Brabazon, M.D., brother of the late Rev. Philip Robert Waller Brabazon (ante):—

Issue of the late Lieut.-Col. William Beaufort Brabazon, *b.* 1860, *d.* 1936: *m.* 1894, Mabel, who *d.* 1957, dau. of the late Clement Smith Barter, M.B., of Bath :—
Joan Alexandra Mabel, *b.* 1902. *Residence*,—Wayside, Burnham Overy, King's Lynn, Norfolk.

PREDECESSORS.— [1] *Rt. Hon.* Sir EDWARD Brabazon, *K.T.*, *P.C.*, M.P. for co. Wicklow 1585, and High Sheriff of Staffordshire 1606; cr. *Baron Ardee* (peerage of Ireland) 1616; *d.* 1625; *s.* by his son [2] WILLIAM, *K.B.*, 2nd Baron; cr. *Earl of Meath* (peerage of Ireland) 1627, with remainder to his brother Anthony; *d.* 1675; *s.* by his son [3] EDWARD, 2nd Earl; *d.* 1675, *s.* by his son [4] WILLIAM, 3rd Earl; *d.* 1684; *s.* by his el. son [5] EDWARD, 4th Earl; was Ranger of the Phœnix Park, Dublin; *d.s.p.* 1707; *s.* by his brother [6] CHAMBRE, 5th Earl; *d.* 1715; *s.* by his el. son [7] CHAWORTH, 6th Earl; *d.s.p.* 1758; *s.* by his brother [8] EDWARD, 7th Earl; *d.* 1772; *s.* by his son [9] ANTHONY, 8th Earl; *d.* 1790; *s.* by his el. son [10] WILLIAM, 9th Earl; killed in a duel 1797; *s.* by his brother [11] JOHN CHAMBRE, *K.P.*, 10th Earl; *b.* 1772; Lord-Lieut. of co. Dublin; cr. *Baron Chaworth*, of Eaton Hall, co. Hereford (peerage of United Kingdom) 1831 : *m.* 1801, Lady Melosina Adelaide, who *d.* 1866, dau. of 1st Earl of Clanwilliam ; *d.* 1851 ; *s.* by his son [12] WILLIAM, 11th Earl; *b.* 1803 : *m.* 1873, Harriot, who *d.* 1898, dau. of Sir Richard Brooke, 6th Bt.; *d.* 1887; *s.* by his son [13] REGINALD, *K.P.*, *G.C.V.O.*, *G.B.E.*, *P.C.*, 12th Earl, *b.* 1841; Founder and Chm. of Metropolitan Public Gardens Asso.; Chancellor of Roy. Univ. of Ireland 1902-6: *m.* 1868, Lady Mary Jane Maitland, who *d.* 1918, only dau. of 11th Earl of Lauderdale; *d.* 1929 ; *s.* by his son [14] REGINALD LE NORMAND, *C.B.*, *C.B.E.*, 13th Earl; *b.* 1869; Brig.-Gen. (retired) late Grenadier and Irish Guards ; S. Africa 1900-02, European War 1914-19 (C.B., C.B.E.) : *m.* 1908, Lady Aileen May Wyndham Quin, who *d.* 1962, dau. of the 4th Earl of Dunraven; *d.* 1949; *s.* by his son [15] ANTHONY WINDHAM NORMAND, 14th Earl and present peer; also Baron Ardee, and Baron Chaworth.

Medway, Lord, son of Earl of Cranbrook.

MELCHETT, BARON. (Mond.) [Baron U.K. 1928, Bt. U.K. 1910.]

PETER ROBERT HENRY MOND, 4th Baron, and 4th Baronet; *b.* Feb. 24th, 1948; *s.* 1973; ed. at Eton, Pembroke Coll., Camb., and Keele Univ.; a Lord in Waiting to H.M. since 1974.

Arms,—Quarterly, 1st and 4th, gules, a demi-lion rampant argent between in chief a decrescent and an increscent, and in base a crescent, all or ; on a chief argent an eagle displayed between two mullets sable, *Mond*; 2nd and 3rd, azure, on a pile between three mullets argent, an eagle displayed sable, *Lowenthal*. **Crest**—A demi-bear holding between the paws a fountain, both proper. **Supporters**,—Dexter, a Doctor of Science of the University of Oxford, holding in the exterior hand a chemical measure glass, *sinister*, a labourer, holding in the exterior hand a pick resting on the shoulder all proper.

Residence,—15, Eccleston Sq., SW1.

SISTERS LIVING.
Hon. Kerena Ann, *b.* 1951.
Hon. Pandora Shelley, *b.* 1959.

AUNT LIVING. (*Daughter of 2nd Baron.*)
Hon. Karis Valerie Violet, *b.* 1927: *m.* 1st, 1949 (marriage dissolved 1956), John Hackman Sumner; 2ndly, 1956, Brian Wallace, and has issue living, (by 1st m.) Justin Mark, *b.* 1953,—(by 2nd m.) Jessica Karis, *b.* 1957,—
Arabella Katherine, *b.* 1959. *Residence*,—The Manor, Pertenhall, Beds.

WIDOW LIVING OF SON OF SECOND BARON.
Yvonne Victoria, only child of Capt. T. Douglas Searle, of Cornerways, The Park, Cheltenham: *m.* 1st, 1942, Lt. the Hon. Derek John Henry Mond, RNVR, who *d.* (killed on active ser. during European War) 1945; 2ndly, 1951, Richard Louis Rowe. *Residence*,—4133, Marlowe Av., Montreal 28, Canada.

WIDOWS LIVING OF SECOND AND THIRD BARONS.
AMY GWEN (*Gwen, Baroness Melchett*), dau. of the late John Wilson, of Parktown, Johannesburg, S. Africa : *m.* 1920, the 2nd Baron, who *d.* 1949. *Residence*,—4, Belgrave Square, S.W.1.
SONIA ELIZABETH (*Baroness Melchett*) (16, Tite St., Chelsea, SW3), dau. of the late Col. Roland Harris Graham, RAMC (ret.), of The Lodge, Bridge, Kent: *m.* 1947, the 3rd Baron, who *d.* 1973.

PREDECESSORS—[1] *Rt. Hon.* ALFRED MORITZ Mond, *LL.D.*, *D.Sc.*, *F.R.S.*, son of the late Ludwig Mond, Ph.D., F.R.S., of The Poplars, 20, Avenue Road, St. John's Wood, N.W., and Winnington Hall, Northwich, by his wife, Frieda, who *d.* 1923, dau. of Adolph Meyer Löwenthal, of Cologne ; *b.* 1868 ; first Chm. of Imperial Chemical Industries, Ltd., Chm. of Mond Nickel Co., and of Amalgamated Anthracite Collieries, Ltd., a Director of Westminster Bank, Ltd., Pres. of British Science Guild, Chm. of National Federation of Chemical Employers, and of Council of Jewish Agency for Palestine, and Joint Chm. of Conference on Industrial Reorganisation and Industrial Relations ; was First Commr. of Works 1916-21, and Min. of Health 1921-2; M.P. for Chester (*L*) Jan. 1906 to Jan. 1910, for Swansea, Swansea Town Div. (*L*) Jan. 1910 to Nov. 1918, for W. Div. thereof (*L*) Dec. 1918 to Nov. 1923, and for Carmarthenshire, Carmarthen Div. (*L*) Aug. to Oct. 1924, and (*C*) Oct. 1924 to June 1928 ; cr. a *Baronet*, of Hartford Hill, Great Budworth, co. Chester 1910, and *Baron Melchett*, of Landford, co. Southampton (peerage of United Kingdom) 1928: *m.* 1894, Violet Florence Mabel, who *d.* 1945, *D.B.E.*, dau. of the late James Henry Goetze; *d.* 1930; *s.* by his son [2] HENRY LUDWIG, 2nd Baron; *b.* 1898; was Vice-Chm. of Imperial Chemical Industries Ltd., a Director of International Nickel Co. of Canada, Ltd., of Industrial Finance and Investment Corporation, Ltd., and of Palestine Electric Corporation, Ltd., Chm. of Palestine Plantations, Ltd., etc., and a Trustee of Ramsay Memorial Fellowship ; sat as M.P. for Isle of Ely (*L*) 1923-4, when he was defeated, and for Liverpool, E. Toxteth Div. (*C*) 1929-30 : *m.* 1920, Amy Gwen, dau. of the late John Wilson, of Parktown, Johannesburg, S. Africa; *d.* 1949 ; *s.* by his son [3] JULIAN EDWARD ALFRED, 3rd Baron, *b.* 1925; Chm. of British Steel Corpn. 1967-73, and a Member of NEDC 1969-73: *m.* 1947, Sonia Elizabeth, da. of the late Col. Roland Harris Graham, RAMC (ret.), of the Lodge, Bridge, Kent; *d.* 1973; *s.* by his son [4] PETER ROBERT HENRY, 4th Baron and present peer.

Melgund, Viscount, son of Earl of Minto.

Melville, see Earl of Leven and Melville.

MELVILLE, VISCOUNT. (Dundas.) [Viscount U.K. 1802.]

ROBERT DAVID ROSS DUNDAS, 9th Viscount; *b,* May 28th, 1937; *s.* 1971; at Wellington; late 2nd Lt. Scots Gds.

Arms,—Argent, a lion rampant gules, armed and langued azure, within a bordure of the last charged with three boars' heads couped or, armed proper and langued of the second. Crest,—A lion's head affrontée gules struggling through an oak-bush proper. Supporters,—*Dexter,* a leopard regardant proper; *sinister,* a stag proper attired argent.

Residence,—Melville, Lasswade, Midlothian. *Clubs,*—Guards', Turf, Midlothian County.

AUNT LIVING (*Daughter of 7th Viscount*).
Hon. Diana Pearl, *b.* 1902 : *m.* 1929, Morogh Wyndham Percy Bernard [see E. Bandon, colls.]. *Residence,*—8, Bloomfield Terrace, S.W.1.

WIDOW LIVING OF SON OF SIXTH VISCOUNT.
Mathilde Mary (786, Island Rd., Victoria, BC, Canada), da. of Louis Saxon, of Yorktown, Sask., Canada: *m.* 1926, as his 2nd wife, the Hon. Richard Serle Dundas, who *d.* 1968, and has issue living [see colls., infra].

MOTHER LIVING.
Margaret Connell, da. of the late Percy Cruden Ross, of Mount Charles, Ayrshire: *m.* 1st, 1936, the Hon. Robert Maldred St. John Melville Dundas, who *d.* (killed in action) 1940; 2ndly, 1946, Gerald Bristowe Sanderson. *Residence,*—Keltie Castle, Dunning, Perthshire.

COLLATERAL BRANCHES LIVING.
    Issue of the late Hon. Cospatrick Philip Brooke Dundas, 2nd son of 6th Viscount, *b.* 1879, *d.* 1954: *m.* 1913, Isabella, who *d.* 1969, da. of E. A. W. McKenzie, of Pelly, Saskatchewan, Canada:—
Daphne Roseabella Louise, *b.* 1923.
        Issue of the late Hon. Richard Serle Dundas, 3rd son of 6th Viscount, *b.* 1880, *d.* 1968: *m.* 1st, 1907, Lydia Catherine, who *d.* 1922, da. of E. A. W. R. McKenzie, of Pelly, Saskatchewan, Canada; 2ndly, 1926, Mathilde Mary (ante), da. of Louis Saxon, of York Town, Saskatchewan, Canada:—
By 1st m.) HUGH MCKENZIE (298, Alfred St., Pembroke, Ont., Canada; *Clubs,*—Toronto Royal Canadian Military Institute, and Pembroke Golf and Country), *b.* June 3rd, 1910; ed. at Sask. Univ. (BA); 1939-45 War: *m.* 1939, Catherine Sanderson, da. of the late John Wallace, of Edinburgh, and has issue living, Robert Hugh Sanderson, *b.* 1943; ed. at Sask. Univ. (BA), Carleton Univ. (MA), and Ottawa Univ. (PhD),—Catherine Marion Wallace *b.* 1948; ed. at Carleton Univ. (BA).——Richard Serle, *b.* 1911; 1939-45 War: *m.* 1942, Marianne, da. of the late John Semple, of N. Battleford, Sask., Canada, and has issue living, Richard Semple, *b.* 1948,—James, *b.* 1951,—Dianne, *b.* 1947. ——Kenneth Brooke (1092, Woodside Drive, Dollard Des Ormeaux, Quebec, Canada), *b.* 1913; ed. at Sask. Univ. (BEnd Civil); Tech. Dir. of R. & D. Domtar Chemicals, Ltd., Montreal: *m.* 1942, Dorothy Helen, da. of the late J. A. Walters, of Saskatoon, and has issue living, Anthony John, *b.* 1946; ed. at Queens Univ. Ont., (BA), and Duke Univ. (MA); *m.* 1972, Carol A., da. of R. Brunini of Pointe Claire, Quebec,—Peter Melville, *b.* 1948; ed. at Univ. of Sask. (BA),—Christopher Charles, *b.* 1950; ed. at Queens Univ. (BA) and Univ. of California (MBA),—Dorothy Anne, *b.* 1945.—— Robert Montague (5769, Hudson St., Vancouver, BC, Canada), *b.* 1920; ed. at BC Univ. (BSc App.); Lt.-Cdr. RCN (ret.); 1939-45 War as Lt. RCNVR: *m.* 1953, Shirley Janet, da. of Urwin Finch, of Vancouver, and has issue living, James Unwin, *b.* 1954,—Hugh Montague, *b.* 1959,—Janet Glencora, *b.* 1956,—Patricia Hope, *b.* 1965.——Blanche Constance, *b.* 1908: *m.* 1935, Robert Norfolk, RCMP of 1084, St. David St., Victoria, B.C., Canada, and has issue living, Gillian Blanche Dundas, *b.* 1938; ed. at Carlton Univ. (BA).——Grace Edith Marian, *b.* 1918; ed. at Sask. Univ. (BHSc).——(by 2nd m.) Oenone Judith, *b.* 1927: ed. at BC Univ. (BA), London Univ. (MA); PhD Wisconsin.—— Iris Anne Alayne (414, Roslyn Av., Westmount, PQ), *b.* 1928: *m.* 1952, the Very Rev. Ronald Francis Shepherd, Dean of Montreal, and R. of Christ Church Cathedral, and has issue living, Jeremy Michael, *b.* 1956,—Christopher Patrick, *b.* 1958,—Timothy David, *b.* 1962,—Peter Andrew Dundas, *b.* 1966,— Mary Mathilde, *b.* 1954,—Susan Clare, *b.* 1960.

        Grandchildren of the Hon. Richard Serle Dundas (ante):—
    Issue of the late Gerald Alexander Dundas, *b.* 1916, *d.* 1966: *m.* 1939, Marjorie, (3058 Whitmore Av., Regina, Saskatchewan), da. of Richard Lister, of Pelly, Saskatchewan:—
Richard Melville (Apt. 8, Bldg. 531, Pleasantville, St. John's, Newfoundland), *b.* 1940; RCMP: *m.* 1965, Dorothy Vivian, da. of Alex Bursey, of St. John's, Newfoundland, and has issue living, Karen Anne, *b.* 1965,—Katherine Dawn, *b.* 1969.——Gerald James, *b.* 1959.——Pamela Marion, *b.* 1942; SRN: *m.* 1965, Anthony Braun.

        Issue of the late Lieut. the Hon. Kenneth Robert Dundas (twin), Roy. Naval Vol. Reserve, 4th son of 6th Viscount, *b.* 1882, *d.* (killed in action in Gallipoli) 1915, *m.* 1909, Anne Claudia Whalley, who *d.* 1943 (having *m.* 2ndly, 1922, Lieut.-Col. Auberon Claud Hegan Kennard, formerly Rifle Brig.), dau. of the late Capt. E. C. Foot, R.N.:—
Claud Kenneth Melville (of The Haven, Woodlands Drive, Barnston, Cheshire), *b.* 1911: 1939-45 War: *m.* 1939, Janet, da. of John Donaldson, and has issue living, Kenneth Ninian Melville, *b.* 1943; ed. at Trin. Coll., Glenalmond.

PREDECESSORS.—[1] HENRY DUNDAS, *P.C.* (4th son of Robert Dundas of Arniston, cadet of Dundas of that Ilk), M.P. for co. Edinburgh 1774-90, and for Edinburgh City 1790-1802; was successively Lord Advocate for Scotland, Sec. of State for Home Depart., Pres. of India Board of Control, Keeper of Privy Seal of Scotland, Sec. of State for War, Treasurer of the Navy, and First Lord of the Admiralty; cr. *Baron Duneira*, of co. Perth, and *Viscount Melville* (peerage of United Kingdom) 1802; was impeached by the House of Commons in 1805 of malversation whilst treasurer of the Navy, and being tried by his peers was acquitted; *d.* 1811; *s.* by his son [2] ROBERT, *K.T.*, *P.C.*, 2nd Viscount; *b.* 1771; sat as M.P. for Hastings and co. Edinburgh 1794-1811; was successively Pres. of Indian Board of Control, Ch. Sec. for Ireland, Registrar of Seizins and Lord Privy Seal of Scotland; Gen. and Vice-Pres. of Royal Co. of Archers, an Elder Brother of the Trinity House, &c.; assumed for himself the additional surname of Saunders: *m.* 1796, Anne, dau. of Richard Huck Saunders, M.D.; *d.* 1851; *s.* by his el. son [3] HENRY, *G.C.B.*, 3rd Viscount; a Gen. in the Army, Gov. of Edinburgh Castle, Col. 60th Rifles, and Vice Pres. of Royal Co. of Archers; *d.* unmarried 1876; *s.* by his brother [4] ROBERT, 4th Viscount; *d.* unmarried 1886; *s.* by his nephew [5] HENRY (son of the late Rev. the Hon. Charles Dundas, 4th son of 2nd Viscount, by Louisa Maria, dau. of Sir William Boothby, 9th Bt.), 5th Viscount; *b* 1835: *m.* 1891, the Hon. Violet Marie Louise Cochrane-Baillie, who *d.* 1943, dau. of 1st Baron Lamington; *d.* 1904; *s.* by his brother [6] CHARLES SAUNDERS, *I.S.O.*, 6th Viscount, *b.* 1843; Consul at Santos 1869-77, for Canary Islands 1877-82, and Stettin 1882-5, and Consul-Gen. at Hamburg 1885-97, and at Christiania 1897-1906: *m.* 1st, 1872, Grace Selina Marian, who *d.* 1890, dau. of the late William Scully, of Rio de Janeiro, and formerly of co. Tipperary; 2ndly, 1891, Mary, who *d.* 1919, dau. of the late George Hamilton, M.D., of Falkirk ; 3rdly, 1920, Margaret, who *d.* 1961, dau. of the late William James Todd; *d.* 1926 ; *s.* by his son [7] HENRY CHARLES CLEMENT, 7th Viscount, *b.* 1873 ; was Vice-Consul at Zanzibar 1897-8, at Dar-es-Salaam 1898-1902, at Galatz 1902-6, and at Algiers 1906-7, and Consul for Bolivia 1907-8, for Tahiti 1908-9, for Bahia 1909, and for Corsica 1909-21 : *m.* 1899, Agnes Mary Florence, who *d.* 1954, dau. of the late Henry Brouncker, of Boveridge Park, Cranborne, Dorset; *d.* 1935; *s.* by his son [8] HENRY CHARLES PATRIC BROUNCKER, 8th Viscount, *b.* 1909, *d.* 1971; *s.* by his nephew [9] ROBERT DAVID ROSS (only son of the late Hon. Robert Maldred St. John Melville Dundas, yr. son of 7th Viscount), 9th Viscount and present peer; also Baron Duneira.

Mendip, Baron, title of Viscount Clifden on Roll of H. L.

Mereworth, Baron, title of Baron Oranmore and Browne on Roll of H. L.

MERRIMAN, BARONY OF. (Merriman.) [Extinct 1962.]

DAUGHTERS LIVING OF FIRST BARON.

Hon. Rosemary Catherine (The Mount, W. Stratton, Winchester), *b.* 1908: *m.* 1934, Humphrey Morgan Hughes, who *d.* 1965, and has issue living, Gillian Merriman, *b.* 1938: *m.* 1966, Maj. John Woodforde Deane, XX The Lancashire Fusiliers.

Hon. Violet Grace, *O.B.E.* (c/o Westminster Bank, 195, Earls Court Rd., S.W.5), *b.* 1911; a British Council Officer; O.B.E. (Civil) 1948.

WIDOW LIVING OF FIRST BARON.

JANE LAMB (*Baroness Merriman*), dau. of the late James Stormonth, of Belfast : *m.* 1953, as his third wife, the 1st Baron, who *d.* 1962, when the title became ext. *Residence,*—13, Windsor Av., Bangor, co. Down.

MERRIVALE, BARON. (Duke.) [Baron U.K. 1925.]

JACK HENRY EDMOND DUKE, 3rd Baron; *b.* Jan. 27th, 1917; *s.* 1951; ed. at Dulwich, in France, and at Ecole des Sciences Politiques, Paris; FRSA; Pres. Institute of Traffic Administration, of Railway Development Assocn., and Chm. of Anglo-Malgasy Soc.; (despatches): *m.* 1st, 1939 (m. diss. 1974), Colette, da. of John Douglas Wise; 2ndly, 1975, Betty, widow of Paul Baron, and has issue by 1st m.

Arms,—Argent, an anchor fouled sable between three chaplets, all within a bordure engrailed azure. **Crest,**—Issuant from a chaplet fessewise argent a demi-griffin holding between the claws a fasces erect or. **Supporters,**—On either side a griffin or, the *dexter* gorged with a chain sable, pendant therefrom an escutcheon argent charged with a saltire between four castles sable, and the *sinister* gorged with a like chain suspended therefrom an escutcheon per pale gules and sable, charged with a triple towered castle or.

We conquer by degrees.

Gradatim *vincimus*

Residence,—16, Brompton Lodge, 9-11, Cromwell Road, S.W.7.

SON LIVING (By 1st m.)

Hon. DEREK JOHN PHILIP, *b.* March 16th, 1948.

DAUGHTER LIVING (By 1st m.)

Hon. Elizabeth Anne Marie Violet, *b.* 1939.

SISTER LIVING.

Hon. Elizabeth Suzanne, *b.* 1921 : *m.* 1st, 1942 (marriage dissolved 1953), Capt. Jean Pompei, French Air Force : 2ndly, 1955, Jacques Bechmann, banker, and has issue living, (by 1st marriage) Francois (37 Av. Montebello, 78, Maisons-Laffitte, Paris), *b.* 1944: *m.* 1973, Elizabeth, da. of Christian Dupuy, and has issue living, Antoine *b.* 1975,—Nicole, *b.* 1946: *m.* 1968, Jean Louis Bouchard, of 15, Rue Raynouard, Paris XVI, and has issue living, Robert *b.* 1971, Alexandra *b.* 1969,—(by 2nd m.) Pierre, *b.* 1957. *Residence,*—24 Rue Galilée, Paris XVI, France.

WIDOW LIVING OF SECOND BARON.

META THÉRÈSE (*Dowager Baroness Merrivale*), dau. of Hermann Wolczon, of Danzig : *m.* 1939, as his second wife, the 2nd Baron, who *d.* 1951. *Residence,—*

PREDECESSORS.—[1] *Rt. Hon. Sir* HENRY EDWARD Duke, son of William Edward Duke, granite merchant, of Merrivale, S. Devon ; *b.* 1855; M.P. for Plymouth (*C.*) 1900-1906, and for Exeter 1910-18, Attorney-Gen. and a Member of Council of Duchy of Cornwall 1915, Ch. Sec. for Ireland 1916-18, a Lord Justice of Appeal 1918-19, and Pres. of Probate, Divorce, and Admiralty Div. of High Court of Justice 1919-33 ; cr. *Baron Merrivale*, of Walkhampton, co. Devon (peerage of United Kingdom) 1925 : *m.* 1876, Sarah, who *d.* 1914, dau. of the late John Shorland ; *d.* 1939 ; *s.* by his son [2] EDWARD, *O.B.E.*, 2nd Baron ; *b.* 1883 ; Sec. to Pres. of Probate, Divorce and Admiralty Div. of High Court of Justice 1919-33 ; S. Africa 1901 as Lieut., European War 1914-19 as Capt. (O.B.E.) : *m.* 1st, 1912, Odette (from whom he obtained a divorce 1939), dau. of Edmond Roger, of Paris ; 2ndly, 1939, Meta Thérèse, dau. of Hermann Wolczon, of Danzig; *d.* 1951 ; *s.* by his son [3] JACK HENRY EDMOND, 3rd Baron and present peer.

MERSEY, VISCOUNT. (Bigham.) [Viscount U.K. 1916.]

I advance.

EDWARD CLIVE BIGHAM, 3rd Viscount ; *b.* June 5th, 1906 ; *s.* 1956 ; ed. at Eton, and at Balliol Coll., Oxford (B.A. 1927) ; is a Co. Councillor for W. Sussex; 1939-45 War as Capt. Irish Gds.: *m.* 1933, Katherine Evelyn Constance (*Lady Nairne* in her own right), el. dau. of 6th Marquess of Lansdowne, and has issue.

Arms,—Per bend dancettée azure and or, a bend invected between three crosses patée in chief and as many horseshoes in base all counterchanged. *Crest,*—A horse per pale or and sable, charged on the body with three horseshoes fesseways counterchanged, and resting the dexter foreleg on a cross patée gules. *Supporters,*—On either side a mermaid proper crowned with a naval crown gules, that to the *dexter* supporting with the exterior hand an anchor or, that to the *sinister* an oar argent.

Residence,—Bignor Park, Pulborough, Sussex. *Clubs,*—Brooks's, Pratt's, White's.

SONS LIVING.

Hon. RICHARD MAURICE CLIVE (*Master of Nairne*), *b.* July 8th, 1934 ; ed. at Eton, and at Balliol Coll., Oxford; formerly 2nd Lt. Irish Guards: *m.* 1961, Joanna Dorothy Corsica Grey, el. da. of John Grey Murray, of Cannon Lodge, Cannon Place, NW3 [B. Shuttleworth], and has issue living, Edward John Hallam, *b.* 1966. *Residence,*—1, Rosmead Rd., W11. *Clubs,*—Brooks's, Pratt's.

Hon. David Edward Hugh (24, Argyll Rd., W8), *b.* 1938; ed. at Eton; late Cornet Roy. Horse Guards: *m.* (Jan.) 1965, Anthea Rosemary, el. da. of Capt. Leopold Richard Seymour [see M. Hertford, colls.], and has issue living, Charles Richard Petty, *b.* 1967,—Patrick David Hugh, *b.* 1969,—James Edward Conway, *b.* 1973,—Lucinda Emma, *b.* (Nov.) 1965.

Hon. Andrew Charles, *b.* 1941; ed. at Eton, and late Worcester Coll., Oxford; late 2nd Lt. Irish Gds.

BROTHER LIVING.

Hon. Ralph John, *b.* 1913; ed. at Eton; an O.St.J.: *m.* 1954, Cicely Ruth, yst. da. of the late C. E. Johnson, of Douglas, Isle of Man. *Residence,*—22, Eaton Place, SW1. *Club,*—RAC.

SISTER LIVING.

Hon. Elizabeth Mary (*Baroness Ponsonby of Shulbrede*), *b.* 1905 : *m.* 1929, the 2nd Baron Ponsonby, of Shulbrede. *Residences,*—Shulbrede Priory, Lynchmere, Haslemere, Surrey ; 17. South End, Kensington Square, W.8.

WIDOW LIVING OF SON OF FIRST VISCOUNT.

Edith Ellen (*Hon. Lady Bigham*), dau. of Lieut.-Col. David Drysdale : *m.* 1931, as his second wife, the Hon. Sir (Frank) Trevor Roger Bigham, K.B.E., C.B., who *d.* 1954. *Residence,*—188, Cranmer Court, S.W.3.

COLLATERAL BRANCH LIVING.

Issue of the late Hon. Sir (Frank) Trevor Roger Bigham, K.B.E., C.B., youngest son of 1st Viscount, *b.* 1876, *d.* 1954 : *m.* 1st, 1901, Frances Leonora, who *d.* 1927, dau. of the late J. L. Tomlin ; 2ndly, 1931, Edith Ellen (ante), dau. of Lieut.-Col. David Drysdale :—
(By 1st marriage) Veronica Beatrice, *b.* 1905 : *m.* 1935, as his second wife, James Carew O'Gorman Anderson, who *d.* 1946. *Residence,*—Ballycar, Waterford.——Celia Margaret Hermione, *b.* 1909. *Residence,*—4, Harley Gardens, S.W.10.

PREDECESSORS.—[1] *Rt. Hon. Sir* John Charles Bigham, son of the late John Bigham, merchant, of Liverpool, *b.* 1840 ; M.P. for Liverpool, Exchange Div. (*LU*) 1895-7 ; a Judge of the High Court of Justice 1897-1909 (also Judge in Bankruptcy 1904-8), and Pres. of Probate, Divorce, and Admiralty Div. 1909-10 ; Roy. Commr. for Revision of Martial Law in S. Africa 1902, and Pres. of Railway and Canal Commn. 1904-7 ; Wreck Commr. of United Kingdom 1912, and a Member of Roy. Commn. on Civil Ser. 1915 ; cr. *Baron Mersey*, of Toxteth, co. Palatine of Lancaster (peerage of United Kingdom) 1910, and *Viscount Mersey* of Toxteth, co. Palatine of Lancaster (peerage of United Kingdom) 1916 : *m.* 1871, Georgina Sarah, who *d.* 1925, dau. of John Rogers, of Liverpool ; *d.* 1929 ; *s.* by his el. son [2] Charles Clive, P.C., C.M.G., C.B.E., 2nd Viscount ; *b.* 1872 ; Lieut.-Col. late Grenadier Guards, Dep. Speaker of House of Lords and Dep. Chm. of Committees, and Chm. of Westminster Territorial Committee ; was Hon. Attaché in Diplo. Ser. 1896-1900, A.D.C. to Lord-Lieut. of Ireland 1901-2, and Ch. Liberal Whip in House of Lords 1944-9 ; China 1900 (C.M.G.), European War 1914-18 (C.B.E.) : *m.* 1904, Mary Gertrude, *J.P.*, who *d.* 1973, dau. of the late Horace Alfred Damer Seymour, C.B. (nominated, but not invested, K.C.B.) ; *d.* 1956 ; *s.* by his el. son [3] Edward Clive, 3rd Viscount and present peer, also Baron Mersey.

MERTHYR, BARON. (Lewis.)   [Baron U.K. 1911, Bt. U.K. 1896.]

[Title pronounced "**Merther.**"]

Perseverance.

Do thy duty come what may.

William Brereton Couchman Lewis, *KBE, TD, PC,* 3rd Baron and 3rd Baronet; *b.* Jan. 7th, 1901; *s.* 1932; ed. at Eton, and at Magdalen Coll., Oxford (MA); Bar. Inner Temple 1927; Vice-Pres. Nat. Marriage Guidance Council (Chm. 1951-57), Magistrates Assocn. (Chm. of Council 1952-70), and Family Planning Assocn., a JP for Pembrokeshire, and a CStJ; a Memb. of Pembrokeshire Co. Council 1928-39, of Roy. Commn. on Local Govt. on Tyneside 1936, and of Departmental Cttee. of Justices' Clerks 1938, Chm. of Departmental Cttee. on the Rag Flock Acts 1938, and of Narberth Rural Dist. Council 1939, a Member of Roy. Commn. on Justices of the Peace 1948, Pres. of Roy. Forestry So. of England and Wales 1948-50, Dep. Chm. Haverfordwest Quarter Sessions 1948-51, a Member of Nat. Parks Commn. 1950-53, Chm. of Pembroke-shire Quarter Sessions 1950-71, and of Nat. Marriage Guidance Council 1951-57, Hon. Treasurer of Nat. So. for Prevention of Cruelty to Children 1952-57, Chm. of Departmental Cttee. on Hedgerow and Farm Timber 1953, of Roy. So. for Prevention of Cruelty to Animals 1953-57, and of Constituency Delineation Commn., Malaya 1954, and Nigeria 1957-58, a Vice-Lieut. for Pembrokeshire 1959-74, and Lord Chm. of Cttees. 1957-65, and Dep. Speaker, House of Lords 1957-74; Pres. of Nat. Assocn. of Parish Councils, 1965-73; Chm. of Dyfed Powys Police Authority 1968-72; 1939-45 War as Maj. Pembroke Heavy Regt. RA (TA) (prisoner Hong Kong 1941-45); PC 1964, KBE (Civil) 1969: *m.* 1932, Violet, da. of Brig.-Gen. Sir Frederick Charlton Meyrick, 2nd Bart., CB, CMG, and has issue.

Arms,—Sable, a lion rampant argent, over all a fesse or charged with three bees volant proper. **Crest,**—An eagle displayed azure, charged on the breast with a bee volant or, and holding in the beak a roll of paper argent. **Supporters,**—On either side a lion rampant sable, charged on the shoulder with a bezant thereon a bee volant proper.

Seat,—Churchton, Saundersfoot, Dyfed, SA69 9BB.   *Clubs,*—Oxford and Cambridge, Lansdowne, Royal Cruising, Leander.

SONS LIVING.

Hon. Trevor Oswin (Hean Castle, Saundersfoot, Dyfed, SA69 9AL), *b.* Nov. 29th, 1935; ed. at Eton, at Magdalen Coll., Oxford, and at Magdalene Coll., Camb.: *m.* 1964, Susan Jane, da. of Arthur John Birt-Llewellin, of Boulston Manor, Haverfordwest, and has issue living, Lucy Delia, *b.* 1967,— Elizabeth Anne, *b.* 1970,—Jessamy Jane, *b.* 1972.

Hon. Peter Herbert, *b.* 1937; ed. at Eton; Maj. 15th/19th King's Roy. Hussars: *m.* 1974, Caroline Monica, el. da. of Erik Cadogan, of Wasperton Hill, Barford, Warwick [see E. Cadogan, colls.].

Hon. John Frederick (1, Cedar Hill, Carisbrooke, I. of Wight), *b.* 1938; ed. at Eton, and at St. John's Coll., Camb.: *m.* 1966, Margaret (Gretl), twin da. of Lt.-Col. James William Lewis-Bowen, of Clynflew, Boncath, Dyfed, and has issue living, Deborah, *b.* 1967,—Sarah, *b.* 1968.

Hon. Robin William (Orchard House, Llanstephan, Dyfed), *b.* 1941; ed. at Eton, and at Magdalen Coll., Oxford: *m.* 1967, Judith Ann, da. of Vincent Charles Arthur Giardelli, of Llethr, Pendine, Dyfed, and has issue living, Christopher William, *b.* 1970,—Katharine Ann, *b.* 1972.

Hon. Anthony Thomas (Croesleiky Cottage, St. Bride's-super-Ely, Cardiff), *b.* 1947; ed. at Eton: *m.* 1974, Mary Carola Melton, yr. da. of the Rev. Humphrey John Paine, of Fressingfield Vicarage, Diss, Norfolk.

PREDECESSORS.—[1] *Sir* WILLIAM THOMAS Lewis, *G.C.V.O.*, el. son of the late Thomas William Lewis, of Abercanaid House, Merthyr Tydfil, by Mary Anne, who *d.* 1887, dau. of Watkin John ; *b.* 1837 ; was a large employer of labour in connection with Collieries, Iron and Steel Works, Tinplate Works, and other industries in S. Wales, Founder (many years Chm.) of Monmouthshire and S. Wales Coal Asso., of S. Wales Sliding Scale Committee (18 years Chm.), and of S. Wales Miners' Provident Fund (30 years Chm.) ; cr. a *Baronet* 1896, and *Baron Merthyr,* of Senghenydd, co. Glamorgan (peerage of United Kingdom) 1911 : *m.* 1864, Anne, who *d.* 1902, el. dau. of William Rees. colliery proprietor, of Llettyshenkin, Glamorgan ; *d.* 1914 ; *s.* by his el. son [2] HERBERT CLARK, 2nd Baron, *b.* 1866 : *m.* 1899, Elizabeth Anna, who *d.* 1925, el. dau. of the late Maj.-Gen. Richard Short Couchman, formerly M.S.C., of 117, Victoria Street, S.W. ; *d.* 1932 ; *s.* by his son [3] WILLIAM BRERETON COUCHMAN, 3rd Baron and present peer.

MESTON, BARON. (Meston.) [Baron U.K. 1919.]

In God is my trust.

DOUGALL MESTON, 2nd Baron, *b.* Dec. 17th, 1894; *s.* 1943; ed. at Charterhouse; Bar. Lincoln's Inn 1924; joined S.E. Circuit; late Capt. R.A., and an Hon. Member of Incorporated Assocn. of Architects and Surveyors; 1914-18 War, Afghan War 1919, Waziristan 1919-20: *m.* 1947, Diana Mary Came, only da. of the late Capt. O. S. Doll, of 16, Upper Cheyne Row, S.W.3, and has issue.

Arms,—Argent, a palm tree, eradicated proper, on a chief azure, an Eastern crown between two thistles slipped and leaved or. *Crest,*—An angel proper, habited argent, holding in the dexter hand an Eastern crown as in the arms. *Supporters,*—*Dexter,* a demoiselle crane proper; *sinister,* a stag also proper, charged on the shoulder with a saltire argent.

Seat,—Hurst Place, Cookham Dene, Berks. *Chambers,*—Queen Elizabeth Building, Temple, E.C.4. *Club,*—Reform.

SONS LIVING.

Hon. JAMES, *b.* Feb. 10th, 1950; ed. at Wellington: *m.* 1974, Anne, yr. da. of John Carder, of Stud Farm House, Chalvington, Sussex.

Hon. William Dougall, *b.* 1953; ed. at Wellington.

PREDECESSOR.—[1] *Sir* JAMES SCORGIE Meston, *K.C.S.I.*, son of the late James Meston, of Aberdeen ; *b.* 1865 ; Financial Sec. to Govt. of India 1906-12, and Lieut.-Gov. of United Provinces of Agra and Oudh 1912-18 ; Finance Member of Viceroy's Executive Council 1918-19 ; Chancellor of Aberdeen Univ. 1928 ; *cr. Baron Meston,* of Agra and Dunottar (peerage of United Kingdom) 1919 : *m.* 1891, Jeanie, *C.B.E.* (a D.St.J.), who *d.* 1946, only dau. of the late James McDonald ; *d.* 1943 ; *s.* by his son [2] DOUGALL, 2nd Baron and present peer.

METHUEN, BARON. (Methuen.) [Baron U.K. 1838.]
[Title and Name pronounced "**Methwen.**"]

Virtue is the mark of envy.

b. 1957,—Anne Catriona **Hamilton**, *b.* 1961.

ANTHONY JOHN METHUEN, 6th Baron; *b.* Oct. 26th, 1925; *s.* 1975; ed. at Winchester and Roy. Agric. Coll., Cirencester; ARICS; 1943-47 in Scots Gds. and R. Signals; Land Officer, Air Min. 1951-62.

Arms,—Argent, three wolves' heads erased, proper, borne on the breast of an imperial eagle. *Supporters,*—Two fiery lynxes reguardant proper, collared and lined or. *Residence,*—Corsham Court, Corsham, Wilts.

BROTHER LIVING.

Hon. ROBERT ALEXANDER HOLT (Stoneycroft Farm, Kniveton, Ashbourne, Derbys.), *b.* July 22nd, 1931; ed. at Shrewsbury, and Trin. Coll., Camb.: *m.* 1958, Mary Catharine Jane, da. of the Ven. Charles German Hooper, Archdeacon of Ipswich, and has issue living, Charlotte Mary, *b.* 1964,—Henrietta Christian, *b.* 1965.

SISTER LIVING.

Hon. Elizabeth Penelope, *b.* 1928: *m.* 1956, Malcolm Henry Alastair Fraser, late R.H.G., of Grey Gables, Pilton, Shepton Mallet, Som., and has issue living, Elizabeth Mary Alexandra,

AUNT LIVING. *(Daughter of 3rd Baron.)*
Hon. Ellen Seymour (6, St. Paul's St., Attard, Malta, GC), *b.* 1893: *m.* 1924, Capt. Cyril Gwynne Sedley Barnes, RA, Reserve of Officers, who *d.* 1954, and has issue living, Oliver Evelyn Gwynne, *b.* 1925,—Philip Henry Seymour, *b.* 1927: *m.* 1953, Jonkvrouwe Henriette Constance, da. of the late Jonkheer W. F. van Lennep, of Vorden, Holland, and has issue living, Sarah *b.* 1955, Tanya *b.* 1957, Benjamin Nicholas Sedley (Manor Cottage, Maiden Bradley, Wilts.), *b.* 1931: *m.* 1957, Anne Marie Guilmette Françoise, el. da. of Henri, Comte de Janzé, of 1, Rue Charles Lamoureux, Paris, XVI, France, and has issue living, Christian Marie Sophie *b.* 1957, Annabel Margaret *b.* 1959, Harriet Elizabeth Sedley *b.* 1963.

WIDOW LIVING OF SON OF THIRD BARON.
Lady Maureen Margaret Brabazon (Starlings, Sutton Benger, Chippenham, Wilts.), da. of 13th Earl of Meath: *m.* 1950, as his second wife, the Hon. Laurence Paul METHUEN-CAMPBELL, who *d.* 1970, and has issue living [see colls. infra].

COLLATERAL BRANCHES LIVING.
Issue of the late Hon. Laurence Paul METHUEN, yst. son of 3rd Baron; *b.* 1898; assumed the additional surname of Campbell, which he relinquished by deed poll 1969; *d.* 1970: *m.* 1st, 1927, the Hon. Olive Douglas Campbell, who *d.* 1949, da. of 4th Baron Blythswood (ext.); 2ndly, 1950, Lady Maureen Margaret Brabazon (ante), da. of 13th Earl of Meath:—
(By 1st m.) Christopher Paul Mansel Campbell (Penrice Castle, Reynoldston, Gower, Glam.), *b.* 1928: *m.* 1950, Oona Cecily, da. of John Dalrymple Winn Treherne [see M. Sligo, colls.], and has issue living, James, *b.* 1952,—Joanna Olive, *b.* 1951,—Lucinda Sheela, *b.* 1959,—Catherine Alice Mansel, *b.* 1965. ——David Archibald James, *b.* 1929.——Diana Evelyn, *b.* 1932: *m.* 1953, Capt. Patrick McNair-Wilson, MP, of 5, Kelso Pl., W8, and has issue living, Guy Patrick Adam Campbell, *b.* 1968,— Jennifer Jean, *b.* 1954,—Arabella Jane Campbell, *b.* 1959,—Patricia Ann Campbell, *b.* 1964,—Kate Campbell, *b.* 1975.——Daphne Mary Jean *(Hon. Mrs. Cecil T. H. Law)*, *b.* 1935: *m.* 1957, the Hon. Cecil Towry Henry Law [see B. Ellenborough].——(by 2nd m.) Caroline Aileen METHUEN, *b.* 1936; assumed by deed poll 1969 the surname of Methuen.

Granddaughters of the late Hon. St. John George Paul Methuen, son of 1st Baron:—
Issue of the late Rev. St. John Frederick Charles Methuen, *b.* 1862, *d.* 1953: *m.* 1st, 1892, Louisa Elizabeth, who *d.* 1933, dau. of the late Maj.-Gen. James Hyde Champion; 2ndly, 1940, Millicent Emma Foskett, who *d.* 1970, da. of Samuel George Wittey, of Penzance:—
(By 1st m.) Margaret Dorothea (of Flat 5, Sumner Court, Sumner Rd., Farnham, Surrey), *b.* 1894.—— Kathleen Louisa Mildmay (14, Chesil Court, SW3), *b.* 1896.——Beatrice Ethel Gertrude (Oakhurst, Liphook Rd., Headley, Bordon, Hants.), *b.* 1905.

PREDECESSORS.—PAUL Methuen, *M.P.* for Wiltshire in several parliaments, cr. *Baron Methuene* of Corsham, co. Wilts (peerage of United Kingdom) 1838; *b.* 1779: *m.* 1810, Jane Dorothea, dau. of Sir Henry Paulet St. John Mildmay, 3rd Bt. ; *d.* 1849; *s.* by his son [2] FREDERICK HENRY PAUL, 2nd Baron, *b.* 1818; A.D.C. to H.M. Queen Victoria; was a Lord-in-Waiting to H.M. Queen Victoria 1859-66, 1868-74,1880-85, and 1886: *m.* 1844, Anna Horatia Caroline, dau. of the Rev. John Sanford, of Nynehead, Somerset; *d.* 1891; *s.* by his el. son [3] PAUL SANFORD, 3rd Baron, *G.C.B., G.C.M.G., G.C.V.O., LL.D., b.* 1845 ; a Field-Marshal; Ashantee War 1873-4, as A.A. and Q.M.G. in Egyptian Campaign 1882, as Press Censor during Tirah Expedition 1897, in S. Africa 1899-1902, in command of 1st Inf. Div. at battles of Belmont, Enslin, Modder River, and Magersfontein ; Mil. Sec. Ireland 1877, Mil. Attaché at Berlin 1877-81, A.A. and Q.M.G. Home Dist. 1881-4, D.A.G. Cape of Good Hope 1888-90, in command of Home Dist. 1892-7, of E. Command 1904-8, and of troops in S. Africa 1908-12 (Gov. of Natal 1910), and Gov. and Com.-in-Ch., Malta 1914-19; commanded "Methuen's Horse" in Bechuanaland 1885; was Constable of Tower of London 1920-32: *m.* 1st, 1878, Evelyn, who *d.* 1879, dau. of Sir Frederick Hutchinson Hervey-Bathurst, 3rd Bt.; 2ndly, 1884, Mary Ethel, *C.B.E.*, who *d.* 1941, dau. of the late William Ayshford Sanford, of Nynehead Court, Somerset; *d.* 1932; *s.* by his son [4] PAUL AYSHFORD, 4th Baron, *b.* 1886; FSA; a Trustee of Nat. Gallery, and Tate Gallery 1938-45, and Imperial War Museum 1950-52: *m.* 1915, Eleanor Norah, who *d.* 1958, da. of the late William John Hennessy, of Rudgwick, Sussex; *d.* 1974; *s.* by his brother [5] ANTHONY PAUL, 5th Baron; *b.* 1891; Chartered Architect, 1914-18 War as Capt. Scots Gds.: *m.* 1920, Grace Durning, who *d.* 1972, da. of Sir Richard Durning Holt, 1st Bt. (cr. 1935), *d.* 1975; *s.* by his 2nd son [6] ANTHONY JOHN, 6th Baron, and present peer.

MEXBOROUGH, EARL OF. (Savile.) [Earl I. 1766.]

JOHN RAPHAEL WENTWORTH SAVILE, 7th Earl ; *b.* Oct. 11th, 1906 ; *s.* 1945; ed. at Downside, and at Pembroke Coll., Camb. (MA); a JP for N. Riding of Yorks., and a DL for N. Riding of Yorks.; 1939-45 War as Capt. Intelligence Corps; ADC to Gov. of Bihar 1944-45: *m.* 1930, Josephine Bertha Emily, da. of the late Capt. Andrew Mansel Talbot Fletcher [Winnington, Bt.], and has issue.

Arms,—Argent, on a bend sable, three owls of the field. **Crest,**—An owl argent. **Supporters,**—Two ons proper, collared and chained or.
Seat,—Arden Hall, Helmsley, Yorks.

SONS LIVING.

JOHN CHRISTOPHER GEORGE *(Viscount Pollington)*, *b.* May 16th, 1931; ed. at Eton, and at Worcester Coll., Oxford; late 2nd Lieut. Gren. Gds.: *m.* 1st 1958 (m. diss. 1972), Lady Elisabeth Hariot Grimston, da. of 6th Earl of Verulam; 2ndly, 1972, Catherine Joyce, yst. da. of James Kenneth Hope, CBE, DL, of West Park, Lanchester, co. Durham, and formerly wife of Maj. the Hon. Nicholas Crespigny Laurence Vivian [see B. Vivian], and has issue (by 1st m.):—
SON LIVING *(By 1st m.)*,—*Hon.* John Andrew Bruce, *b.* Nov. 30th, 1959.
DAUGHTERS LIVING *(By 1st m.)*,—*Hon.* Alethea Frances Clare, *b.* 1963.
(By 2nd m.),—*Hon.* Lucinda Sarah Catherine, *b.* 1973.
Residences,—29, Walpole St., SW3, Arden Hall, Hawnby, Yorks. *Clubs,*—Turf, Bath, All England Lawn Tennis.

Hon. Charles Anthony, *b.* 1934; ed. at Eton; late Lt. Grenadier Guards: *m.* 1966, Zita Loretta, da. of Leslie White, and has issue living, Henry Charles, *b.* 1970,—Andrew David, *b.* 1973. *Residence,*—Youngsbury, Ware, Herts.

DAUGHTER LIVING.

Lady Anne Sarah Elizabeth, *b.* 1938: *m.* 1964, Charles Hynman Allanby, of Balblair, Nairn, and has issue living, Henry Hynman, *b.* 1965.

SISTERS LIVING.

Lady Agnes Marjorie Alice Mary, *b.* 1907 : *m.* 1930, Capt. Thomas More Eyston, Roy. Berks Regt., who *d.* (of wounds received in action) 1940, and has issue living, Thomas More, *b.* 1931,—John Joseph (Mapledurham House, Reading), *b.* 1934: *m.* 1968, Lady Anne Priscilla Maitland, da. of the late Viscount Maitland [see E. Lauderdale], and has issue living, Edward Thomas Ivor, *b.* 1969, Katharine Agnes Mary *b.* 1970,—Mary Amicia Helena *b.* 1972,—Mary Amicia (twin), *b.* 1931, —Elizabeth Mary, *b.* 1939. *Residence,*—Hendred House, Wantage, Oxon.
Lady (Anne) Sarah Alethea Marjorie, *b.* 1919 : *m.* 1955, the Hon. Mr. Justice (Hon. Sir James Roualeyn Hovell-Thurlow Cumming-Bruce [see B. Thurlow]. *Residence,*—1, Mulberry Walk, S.W.3.

COLLATERAL BRANCH LIVING.

Granddaughters of the late Rev. the Hon. Philip Yorke Savile, 3rd son of 3rd Earl :—
Issue of the late Rev. William Hale Savile, *b.* 1859, *d.* 1925 : *m.* 1888, Mabel Ann, who *d.* 1947, only dau. of the late Major Count Hippolyte Victor Alexander von Bothmer, a Count of the Holy Roman Empire (naturalized 1857) :—
Venetia Mary Stanley Errington (8, Hawkhurst Way, Bexhill-on-Sea), *b.* 1893: *m.* 1st, 1916, Everard Noel Rye Trentham, CMG, who *d.* 1963, and from whom she obtained a divorce 1926; 2ndly, 1930, Capt. Cecil Hunter Boyd Gowan, R.N. (ret.), who *d.* 1941; 3rdly, 1955, Lt.-Col. Valentine Leathley Armitage, TD, who *d.* 1964.——Violet Irene, *b.* 1899: *m.* 1st, 1921 (marriage annulled 1924), Gordon Brooke Willoughby Hamilton-Gay, formerly Lt. R.G.A.; 2ndly, 1930, William Francis Egginton Briggs. from whom she obtained a divorce 1947; 3rdly, 1956, Col. Christopher Pemberton Worsfold, MC, late RE, who *d.* 1975. *Residence,* —4, Mount Pleasant, Tenterden, Kent.——Veronica Yorke Hélène Cecilia, *b.* 1902: *m.* 1926, Willem Karel Marie de Bruijn, Lord of Gouderack, Belgian Consulate Ser., only son of the late Eduard Rudolf Marie de Bruijn. *Residence,*—Buiten Walevest 6, Dordrecht, Holland.

PREDECESSORS.—[1] *Sir* JOHN Savile, *K.B.*, *b.* 1719; M.P. for Hedon, co. York 1747-54; cr *Baron Pollington*, of Longford, Ireland (peerage of Ireland) 1753, and *Viscount Pollington* and *Earl of Mexborough* (peerage of Ireland) 1766; *d.* 1778; *s.* by his son [2] JOHN, 2nd Earl; *d.* 1830; *s.* by his son [3] JOHN, 3rd Earl; *b.* 1783; M.P. for Pontefract: *m.* 1807, Lady Anne, who *d.* 1870, dau. of 3rd Earl of Hardwicke; *d.* 1860 ; *s.* by his son [4] JOHN CHARLES GEORGE, 4th Earl, *b.* 1810; M.P. for Gatton (*C*) 1831, and for Pontefract 1835-47: *m.* 1st, 1842, Lady Rachel Katherine Walpole, who *d.* 1854, el. dau. of 3rd Earl of Orford; 2ndly, 1861, Agnes Louisa Elizabeth, who *d.* 1898, dau. of John Raphael; *d.* 1899; *s.* by his el. son [5] JOHN HORACE, 5th Earl, *b.* 1843; High Sheriff of Yorkshire 1877: *m.* 1st, 1867, Venetia Stanley, who *d.* 1900, dau. of Sir Rowland Stanley Errington, 11th Bt.; 2ndly, 1906, Donna Sylvia Cecilia Maria, who *d.* 1915, dau. of the Noble Carlo de Ser. Antoni, of Lucca and Naples, and widow of Capt. Claude Clerke, C.I.E. ; 3rdly, 1916, Anne, who *d.* 1943 (having *m.* 3rdly, 1920, as his second wife, Alfred Charlemagne Lambart, who *d.* 1943. and from whom she had obtained a divorce 1926), dau. of the late Rev. Andrew Holmes Belcher, of Fasque, Kincardineshire, and formerly wife of George Bainbridge Ritchie: *d.* 1916; *s.* by his half-brother [6] JOHN HENRY, 6th Earl, *b.* 1868; Hon. Capt. in the Army: *m.* 1905, the Hon. Margaret Eva de Burgh Knatchbull-Hugessen, who *d.* 1957, el. dau. of 2nd Baron Brabourne; *d.* 1945 ; *s.* by his son [7] JOHN RAPHAEL WENTWORTH, 7th Earl and present peer ; also Viscount and Baron Pollington.

MICHELHAM, BARON. (Stern.) [Bt. U.K. 1905, Baron U.K. 1905.]

[Title pronounced " Mitch-lam."]

Perseverance conquers.

HERMAN ALFRED STERN, 2nd Baron, 2nd Baronet, and a Baron of Portugal; *b.* Sept. 5th, 1900 ; *s.* 1919; ed. at Malvern : *m.* 1919, Bertha Isabelle, who *d.* 1961, dau. of the late Arthur Capel.

Arms.—Or, on a bend indented gules, three estoiles of the first. **Crest.**—A demi-unicorn gules. maned and armed or. **Supporters.**—On either side an unicorn gules, maned and hoofed or, and charged on the shoulder with a crescent of the last.

BROTHER LIVING.

Hon. JACK HERBERT *MICHELHAM*, *b.* Dec. 23rd, 1903 ; ed. at Harrow, and at Magdalen Coll., Oxford ; assumed by deed poll 1928, the surname of Michelham in lieu of his patronymic. *Address,* —c/o Coutts & Co., 440, Strand, W.C.2.

PREDECESSOR.—[1] *Sir* HERBERT Stern, *K.C.V.O.*, only son of Baron (Hermann) de Stern, of 4, Hyde Park Gate, W. ; *b.* 1851 ; a well-known philanthropist, and a Baron of Portugal; cr. a *Baronet* July 1905, and *Baron Michelham*, of Hellingly, co. Sussex (peerage of United Kingdom) Dec. 1905: *m.* 1899, Aimée Geraldine, who *d.* 1927, dau. of Octavius Bradshaw, J.P., D.L., of Powderham Castle, Devon ; *d.* 1919 ; *s.* by his el. son [2] HERMANN ALFRED, 2nd Baron and present peer.

MIDDLETON, BARON. (Willoughby.) [Baron G.B. 1711, Bt. E. 1677.]

Truth without fear.

(DIGBY) MICHAEL GODFREY
JOHN WILLOUGHBY, MC, 12th
Baron, and 13th Baronet; *b.*
May 1st, 1921; *s.* 1970; ed. at
Eton, and Trin. Coll., Camb. (MA);
patron of seven livings; a CC
and a JP for E. Riding, and DL
of E. Riding, and Kingston upon
Hull 1964-74, since when a CC for
N. Yorks.; a Member of Yorks.
and Humberside Econ. Planning
Council; 1939-45 War as Maj.
Coldm. Gds. (despatches, MC,
Croix de Guerre): *m.* 1947, Janet,
only da. of Gen. Sir James
Handyside Marshall Cornwall,
KCB, CBE, DSO, MC, and has
issue.

Arms,—Quarterly: 1st and 4th or,
fretty azure, *Willoughby of Parham*; 2nd
and 3rd or, on two bars gules three water
bougets two and one argent, *Willoughby of
Middleton.* Crest,—The bust of a man
couped at the shoulders and affrontée
proper, ducally crowned or. Supporters,—
Dexter, a pilgrim or grey friar in his habit
proper, with his beads, cross, etc., and staff
in his right hand, argent; *sinister,* a savage
with a club in his exterior hand, wreathed
about his temples and middle with laurel all
proper; each supporter holding a banner gules fringed, or ensigned with an owl argent, gorged with a
ducal coronet collared and chained gold, the owl being the crest of *Willoughby of Middleton.*

Residence,—Birdsall House, Malton, N. Yorks. *Club,*—Boodle's.

SONS LIVING.

Hon. MICHAEL CHARLES JAMES (North Grimston House, Malton, N. Yorks.), *b.* July 14th, 1948;
ed. at Eton; late Lt. Coldm. Gds.: *m.* 1974, the Hon. Lucy Corinna Agneta Sidney, yst. da. of 1st
Viscount De L'Isle.
Hon. John Hugh Francis, *b.* 1951; ed. at Eton; Lt. Coldm. Gds.
Hon. Thomas Henry Richard, *b.* 1955; ed. at Harrow.

BROTHER LIVING.

Hon. (Henry Ernest) Christopher, *b.* 1932; ed. at Eton; Lt.-Col. Comdg. 2nd Bn. Coldm. Gds.: *m.* 1955,
Jean Adini, da. of Lt.-Col. John David Hills, MC [see E. Cromer], and has issue living, Guy Nesbit
John, *b.* 1960,—Angela Jane, *b.* 1956,—Caroline Rosemary, *b.* 1957. *Residence,*—Buckhold Farm,
Pangbourne, Berks. *Club,*—Boodles.

SISTERS LIVING.

Hon. Angela Hermione Ida, *b.* 1924: *m.* 1947, Lieut.-Com. the Hon. Charles Henry Romer Wynn, R.N.
[see B. Newborough]. *Residence,*—Bunkersland, Withleigh, Tiverton, Devon.
Hon. Jean Elizabeth Mary, *b.* 1928: *m.* 1952, Major Fergus John Matheson, Coldstream Guards [see
Matheson, Bt.]. *Residence,*—Hedenham, Old Rectory, Bungay, Suffolk.

WIDOW LIVING OF ELEVENTH BARON.

ANGELA FLORENCE ALFREDA (*Angela, Baroness Middleton*), (Foston House, York), da. of the
late Charles Oswin Hall, of Eddlethorpe Hall, Malton, Yorks.: *m.* 1920, the 11th Baron, who *d.* 1970

COLLATERAL BRANCHES LIVING.

Issue of the late Col. the Hon. Claude Henry Comaraich Willoughby, C.V.O., 7th
son of 8th Baron, *b.* 1862, *d.* 1932: *m.* 1904, Sibyl Louise, who *d.* 1957, dau. of
the late Charles James Murray [E. Dunmore, colls.]:—
Mary Bridget (*Lady Howard-Vyse*) (Langton House, Malton, Yorks.), *b.* 1910: *m.* 1940, Lt.-Gen. Sir
Edward Dacre Howard-Vyse, KBE, CB, MC, and has issue living, Richard Edward (Langton,
Malton, Yorks.) *b.* 1941: *m.* 1965, Sally Rosemary, da. of Cdr. R. R. Whalley, of Compton Down,
Winchester, and has issue living, Thomas Norcliffe *b.* 1971,—John Cecil, *b.* 1947: *m.* 1972, Jennifer
Anne, el. da. of Maj.-Gen. Geoffrey de Egglesfield Collin, MC, of Roecliffe, Boroughbridge,—Elizabeth
b. 1945.——Joan Lavinia, *b.* 1913: *m.* 1960, Harry Nettleton, of Rose Cottage, Norton, Malton
Yorks.

Granddaughters of the late Capt. the Hon. Alexander Hugh Willoughby, yst. son
of 8th Baron:—
Issue of the late Wing-Com. James Alexander Willoughby R.A.F., *b.* 1890, *d.* 1955: *m.*
1st, 1918, Dorothea Marion (who obtained a divorce 1926), dau. of the late Richard Hilton
Burbrook, of 7, Buxton Gardens, W.; 2ndly, 1926, Jill, younger dau. of the late David
Denton, F.R.C.O., of Newport Pagnell, Bucks:—
(By 1st marriage) Diana Evelyn Mary, *b.* 1919.——Susan Claire, *b.* 1922.——(by 2nd marriage) Griselda
Mary Honoria, *b.* 1931: *m.* 1955, Lt. Paul Julian David Gifford, R.N., of Holly Lodge, Weathercock
Lane, Woburn Sands, Bucks., and has issue living, Mark Richard Alexander, *b.* 1960,—Nicola
Jane, *b.* 1965.

Issue of the late Capt. Joe Henry Claude Willoughby, RN, *b.* 1892, *d.* 1966: *m.* 1919, Enid
Mary (Dove Cottage, N. Mundham, Chichester), da. of Harry J. Clements, of Somerville
House, Sutton Coldfield.
Ann Honoria Mary, *b.* 1920: *m.* 1st, 1940, Sqdn.-Ldr. P. Campbell Canney, RAF, who *d.* (killed in
action) 1942; 2ndly, 1944 (m. diss. 19—) John Dean; 3rdly, 19—) Wayne Etine, of 3184, Pioneer Rd.,
Medford, Oregon, USA, and has issue living (by 1st m.), Josephine, *b.* 1942.

Granddaughter of the late Maj. Charles Stuart Percival Willoughby, son of the late
Rev. the Hon. Charles James Willoughby (infra):—

Issue of the late Maj. Geoffrey St. Maur Willoughby, Hampshire Regt., *b.* 1881, *d.* 1954: *m.* 1st, 1910, Julia Henrietta Cave, who *d.* 1946, da. of the Rev. Edmund Joseph Francis Johnson (formerly R. of Sarsden, Oxon); 2ndly, 1947, Gwyneth Preston (now of Little Pitt, Wonston, Winchester), only da. of Arthur Henry Willmore, of Oak Ridge, Chandler's Ford, Hants.:—
(By 1st m.) Julia Hermione, *b.* 1913: *m.* 1936, Lt.-Com. (S.) Richard William Chamberlen, RNR. *Residence,*—2, Camino, de C'an Pou, Establiment, Majorca, Spain.

Grandchildren of the late James Frederick Digby Willoughby, OBE (infra):—
Issue of the late Cdr. Ronald James Edward Willoughby, RN (ret.), *b.* 1884, *d.* 1971: *m.* 1930, Constance Louisa (5, Little Anglesey Rd., Alverstoke, Gosport, Hants.), da. of the late Rev. Nevile Sherbrooke:—
Christopher Ronald (I.B.R.D., Washington, DC, USA), *b.* 1938: *m.* 1972, Marie-Anne, el. da. of Emile Normand, of Chamalières, Clermont-Ferrand, France.——Josephine Cicely Alice, *b.* 1931; SRN.—— Nina Mary, *b.* 1933: *m.* 1959, Lt.-Cdr. David Lines, RN, of 3, Clayhall Rd., Alverstoke, Gosport, Hants., PO12 2BB, and has issue living, Charles Willoughby, *b.* 1961,—Patrick Simon, *b.* 1963,— James Michael, *b.* 1965,—Rupert Martin, *b.* 1969,—Vanessa Jane, *b.* 1962.

Issue of the late Com. Archibald Macdonald Willoughby, RN, *b.* 1887, *d.* (on active ser. during 1939-45 War) 1943: *m.* 1st, 1912, Mabel Doris [who *d.* 1956, having obtained a divorce 1935 (she *m.* 2ndly, 1935, Algernon Peter Warren)], *m.* 1st, da. of Sir William Norton Hicking, 1st Bt. [North, Bt.]; 2ndly, 1935, Elizabeth (Flat 11, 68, Elm Park Gdns., SW10; she *m.* 2ndly, 1951, Capt. C. Devaynes Smyth, who *d.* 1962), da. of the late Maj.-Gen. Sir John Hanbury-Williams, GCVO, KCB, CMG:—
By 1st m.) Doris Barbara (Hill Brow, Shilton Rd., Burford, Oxford), *b.* 1913: *m.* 1937, Launcelot Roger Percival, who *d.* 1964, and has issue living, David William, *b.* 1945; ed. at Milton Abbey, Blandford,— Gillian Barbara, *b.* 1938: *m.* 1971, Richard Llewellyn Whitley Hagen, and has issue living, Nicholas Roger John *b.* 1972,—Pamela Mary Norton, *b.* 1916: *m.* 1952, the Rev. Ronald Curnow Parkinson. ——Prudence Joan Mabel, *b.* 1918: *m.* 1949, John Alexander Hannay, and has issue living, Jonathan Howard, *b.* 1951,—Philippa Catherine, *b.* 1953. *Residence,*—37, Downshire Hill, NW3.——Sheila Katherine, *b.* 1921: *m.* 1952, Cdr. Edward Astley-Jones, RN, of Church Farm, Garway, Hereford, and has issue living, Hugh Edward Arthur, *b.* 1953,—Hilary Margaret Doris, *b.* 1958.——Anne Rose-mary, *b.* 1926: *m.* 1956, George Frederick Rothwell, and has issue living, James Peter, *b.* 1958,— Gerald Charles, *b.* 1963,—Charlotte Jane, *b.* 1964,—Frances Elizabeth, *b.* 1966. *Residence,*—Breach House, Cholsey, Oxon.

Grandsons of the late Rev. the Hon. Charles James Willoughby, brother of 8th Baron:—
Issue of the late James Frederick Digby Willoughby, O.B.E., *b.* **1856,** *d.* **1947:** *m.* **1881, Mary Elizabeth, who** *d.* **1927, dau. of the Rev. Edward John Randolph [Rich, Bt., colls.]:—**
Rev. Bernard Digby (Lettergesh, Renvyle, co. Galway), *b.* 1896; ed. at Wellington Coll.; Canon of Tuam Cathedral 1963-73; late R of Knappaugh, co. Mayo; formerly Maj. Indian Army: *m.* 1944, Ruth, da. of W. B. Barber, of Beacon Hill, Hucknall, Notts., and has issue living, Colin James, *b.* 1949,—Elisabeth Grace, *b.* 1945: *m.* 1964, Thomas Miller Ormsby, of Milford, Cloghan's Hill, Tuam, co. Galway, and has issue living, Thomas Anthony *b.* 1969, Lucy Ann *b.* 1966, John Charles *b.* 1971.

Issue of the late Major Leonard Broke Willoughby, *b.* 1860, *d.* 1932 : *m.* 1888, Ada Mary, who *d.* 1960, el. dau. of the late Charles Baxter Causens, of 2, Clanricarde Gardens, Hyde Park, W. :—
Gilbert de Bec, *b.* 1894: *m.* 1923, Queenie Kathleen Lillian, da. of the late Charles William Henry Butts. *Residence,*—Wollaton, 252, Old Shoreham Rd., Southwick, Sussex.

Grandchildren of the late Rev. the Hon. Percival George Willoughby, brother of 8th Baron :—
Issue of the late Col. Herbert Percival Willoughby, *b.* 1853, *d.* 1913: *m.* 1875, Mary Louisa, dau. of T. Allen Brown :—
John Herbert, *b.* 1896; Capt. (ret.) RM.

Issue of the late Rev. Nesbit Edward Willoughby, *b.* 1854, *d.* 1919 : *m.* 1st, 1889, Florence Mary Tottingham, who *d.* 1897, dau. of the Rev. E. Lowe ; 2ndly, 1901, Marjorie Helen, dau. of J. E. Kaye, formerly of Bretton, Wakefield :—
(By 2nd marriage) Guy, *C.B.*, *b.* 1902; Rear-Adm. (ret.); Dir. of Air Warfare and Training, Admiralty, 1945-46, a Member of Australian Commonwealth Navy Board 1948-50, and Flag Officer, Flying Training 1953-56; 1939-45 War; CB (Mil.) 1955: *m.* 1923, Mary, da. of James George Aldridge, AMICE, and has issue living, Hugh Nesbit, *b.* 1925,—Anthea Joan, *b.* 1929. *Residence,*—High Croft, South Woodchester, nr. Stroud, Gloucestershire. *Club.*—United Service.——Lawrence (7807-143A, Edmonton, Alberta, T5R OP8, Canada; *Club,* RNVR), *b.* 1908; MB and ChB Bristol 1940; MRCOG 1951; Surg.-Cdr. (ret.) RNVR, and attending Obstetrician and Gynaecologist, Roy. Alexandra Hospital, Edmonton: *m.* 1st 1936, Dorothy Hughes, who *d.* 1956; 2ndly, 1957, Elizabeth, da. of the late Alexander Sadowski, of Rosko, Poland, and has issue living, (by 2nd m.) Guy Alexander, *b.* 1958,—Digby Edward, *b.* 1959,—Veronica Anne (twin), *b.* 1958.——Anthony (PO Box 75, Round Corner, NSW 2518), *b.* 1911: *m.* 1942, Olive Andrews.——Veronica, *b.* 1903: *m.* 1935, George Alexander Scott, of Kinchellie, Roy Bridge, Inverness-shire, and has issue living, Judith Kate, *b.* 1936: *m.* 1965, Richard Alexander Gordon Stuart, of Colliston Castle, by Arbroath, Angus.——Gwendolen Mary, *RRC* (Pine Cottage, 44, Northend, Bath), *b.* 1905; Lt.-Col. (ret.) QARANC.

PREDECESSORS.—[1] FRANCIS Willoughby ; cr. *Baronet* 1677, with remainder to his only brother ; *d.* 1688 ; *s.* by his brother [2] *Sir* THOMAS, 2nd Bt. ; successively M.P. for Newark and Nottinghamshire ; cr. *Baron Middleton,* of Middleton, co. Warwick (peerage of Great Britain) 1711; *d.* 1729; *s.* by his son [3] FRANCIS, 2nd Baron; *d.* 1758; *s.* by his el. son [4] FRANCIS, 3rd Baron ; *d.* unmarried 1774 ; *s.* by his brother [5] THOMAS, 4th Baron ; *d.* 1781; *s.* by his cousin [6] HENRY, 5th Baron, son of the Hon. Thomas, 2nd son of 1st Baron ; *d.* 1800; *s.* by his son [7] HENRY, 6th Baron ; *d.s.p.* 1835 ; *s.* by his cousin [8] DIGBY, 7th Baron, Capt. R.N., grandson of the late Hon. Thomas, 2nd son of 1st Baron ; *d.* unmarried 1856; *s.* by his cousin [9] HENRY, 8th Baron, great-grandson of the Hon. Thomas, 2nd son of 1st Baron ; *b.* 1817: *m.* 1843, Julia Louisa, dau. of the late Alexander William Bosville, *de jure* 12th Bt., of Thorpe and Gunthwaite, co. York; *d.* 1877 ; *s.* by his el. son [10] DIGBY WENTWORTH BAYARD, 9th Baron, *b.* 1844: *m.* 1860, Eliza Maria, who *d.* 1922, dau. of Sir Alexander Penrose Gordon-Cumming, 3rd Bt. ; *d.* 1922; *s.* by his brother [11] GODFREY ERNEST PERCIVAL, 10th Baron, *b.* 1847; Midshipman R.N.: subsequently entered 9th Lancers and retired as Capt. ; some-time Starter to the Jockey Club : *m.* 1881, Ida Eleanora Constance, who *d.* 1924, dau. of the late George W. H. Ross, of Cromarty House, Cromarty ; *d.* 1924 : *s.* by his second son [12] MICHAEL GUY PERCIVAL, KG, MC, TD, 11th Baron ; *b.* 1887; Chancellor of Hull Univ. 1931-70; Lord-Lt. for E. Riding 1936-68: *m.* 1920, Angela Florence Alfreda, da. of the late Charles Oswin Hall, of Eddle-thorpe Hall, Malton; *d.* 1970; *s.* by his el. son [13] (DIGBY) MICHAEL GODFREY JOHN, MC, 12th Baron.

MIDLETON, EARL OF. (Brodrick.) [Viscount I. 1717, Baron G.B. 1796, Earl U.K. 1920.]

A crown from a lance.

GEORGE ST. JOHN BRODRICK, M.C.
2nd Earl; b. Feb. 21st, 1888; s. 1942; ed.
at Eton, and at Balliol Coll., Oxford;
Capt. Gen. List; sometime Capt.
Surrey Yeo.; 1914-18 War as ADC to
Gen. Comdg. the Forces in Dardanelles
(despatches, MC, Legion of Honour);
ADC to C.-in-C. Home Forces 1939:
m. 1st, 1917, Margaret (who obtained a
divorce 1925), dau. of J. Rush, of
Cromer; 2ndly, 1925 (m. diss. 1975),
Guinivere, dau. of Alexander Sinclair,
of Dublin, widow of George Jay Gould;
3rdly, 1975, Irene Creese (Rene Ray).

Arms,—Argent, on a chief vert, two spears'
heads of the field, erect, and embrued gules.
Crest,—Out of a ducal coronet or, a spear head
argent, embrued gules. Supporters,—Two men in
armour, proper, each holding a spear in the
exterior hand.

Residence,—Martello Lodge, St. Brelade's Bay,
Jersey.

SISTERS LIVING.

Lady Moyra, b. 1897: m. 1922, Gen. Sir Henry Charles Loyd, GCVO, KCB, DSO, MC, DL,
late Coldm. Gds., who d. 1973, and has issue living, Julian St. John (Laycocks, Sandringham,
Norfolk), b. 1926; Land Agent to HM at Sandringham since 1964: m. 1960, Mary Emma, da. of Sir
Christopher Eden Steel, GCMG, MVO, and has issue living, Charles Anthony b. 1963, Alexandra Mary
b. 1961, Mary Rose b. 1967,—Lavinia Gertrude Georgina, b. 1923: m. 1946, Maj. Thomas Anthony
Gore-Browne, late Gren. Gds., of Fryerning House, Ingatestone, Essex, and has issue living, James
Anthony, b, 1947; ed. at Eton, David Charles b. 1952, Patrick Robert b. 1956, Georgina Mary b.
1949: m. 1970, Christopher D. Pilkington. Residence,—Mettingham Pines, Bungay, Suffolk.

WIDOW LIVING OF SON OF FIRST EARL.

Margaret Lætitia, only dau. of the late Major the Hon. Charles Henry Lyell [see B. Lyell];
was Assist. Commercial Sec., British Embassy, Moscow 1944-45: m. 1st, 1937, Major the
Hon. Francis Alan STEWART-MACKENZIE OF SEAFORTH, who d.(killed in action during European
War) 1943, having assumed by declaration 1935 the surname of Stewart-Mackenzie of Seaforth
in lieu of his patronymic; 2ndly, 1944, Charles Henry Pearson Gifford, OBE. Residence,—Cob
House, Aldeburgh, Suffolk.

COLLATERAL BRANCHES LIVING. (Not in remainder to the Earldom.)

Issue of the late Col. the Hon. Arthur Grenville Brodrick, 3rd son of 8th Viscount,
b. 1868, d. 1934: m. 1912, Lesley Venetia, who d. 1954, dau. of the late Lieut.-
Col. Edward Harrison Clough-Taylor, formerly Roy. Welch Fusiliers [D. Argyll]:—
Elisabeth Venetia Marian, b. 1914. Residence,—89, Chatsworth Court, Pembroke Road, W.8.

Granddaughter of the late Rev. the Hon. Alan Brodrick, 5th son of 7th Viscount:—
Issue (by 1st marriage) of the late Alan Melvill Brodrick, b. 1868, d. 1933 : m. 1st, 1898
(marriage dissolved 1901), Beatrice, dau. of Henry Ernst Hall, formerly of Unsted Park,
Godalming; 2ndly, 1912, Diana, who d. 1930, widow of Thomas Davey Peacey :—
Beatrice Mary Alleyne, b. 1899: m. 1945, Alban Churton Roe, Flying Officer, R.A.F. Vol.
Reserve. Residence,—

Grandchildren of the late William Henry Brodrick, OBE (infra):—
Issue of the late Alan Rupert Brodrick, b. 1904, d. 1972: m. 1941, Alice Elizabeth (104,
Fitzjohn's Av., Hampstead, NW3 6NT), da. of the late G. R. Roberts, of Maloya, Purley,
Surrey:—
Alan Henry (10, Ladywell Court, East Heath Rd., Hampstead, NW3), b. 1949.——Susan Margaret,
b. 1945: m. 1971, Robert Andrew Swann, of 25, Denbigh St., SW1, and has issue living, Tabitha
Mary, b. 1972.——Elizabeth Ann, b. 1947: m. 1973, Stephen Kershaw.

Grandchildren of the late Rev. the Hon. Alan Brodrick (ante):—
Issue of the late William John Henry Brodrick, OBE, b. 1874, d. 1964: m. 1902, Blanche
Sophia Emily, who d. 1944, el. da. of the late F. A. Hawker, of Woodend, Wickham, Hants.:—
TREVOR LOWTHER (of Frogmore Cottage, 105, North Rd., Bourne, Lincs.), b. March 7th, 1903,
m. 1940, Sheila Campbell, da. of the late Charles Campbell MacLeod, of Cawthorpe House, Bourne,
Lincs.——Melvill Seymour (Watchoak, 1, Powers Court Rd., Barton-on-Sea, Hants.) b. 1906:
m. 1961, Elizabeth Vaughan, da. of the late Lt.-Col. P. V. Holberton.——His Honour Judge Norman
John Lee, QC (Packhurst Farm House, Clanfield, Hants, PO8 0RR and 19, Old Buildings, Lincoln's
Inn, WC2), b. 1912; ed. at Charterhouse, and at Merton Coll., Oxford (MA); a JP for Hants; Bar.
Lincoln's Inn 1935, a QC 1960 and a Bencher 1965; Recorder of Penzance 1957, of Bridgwater 1959,
of Plymouth 1962, and Portsmouth 1964-67, Regional Chm. of Mental Health Tribunal for Wessex
Region 1960-63, and a Dep. Chm. Middlesex Quarter Sessions 1961-65; Chm. of Departmental Cttee
on Coroners and Certification of Death 1964; Dep. Chm. of I. of Wight Quarter Sessions since 1967
(Chm. 1964-67), Additional Judge at Central Criminal Court since 1967, and a Circuit Judge Western
Circuit since 1972; a Member of Senate of Four Inns of Court 1970: m. 1940, Ruth Severn, da. of
the late Sir Stanley Unwin, KCMG, and has issue living, Michael John Lee, (The Clock House,
Swarraton, Alresford; b. 1941; ed. at Charterhouse and Merton Coll., Oxford (MA); Bar. Lincoln's
Inn, 1965: m. 1969, Valerie Lois, da. of Gerald Stroud, of Brookdean, Liss, Hants., and has issue
living, Robert John Lee b. 1972,—Christopher David, b. 1953,—Peter Matthew, b. 1954,—Frances
Mary Severn, b. 1947: m. 1972, Pedro Prá-Lopez, of 2, West Heath Villas, Sandy Rd., NW3 7EY,
and has issue living, Nicholas Norman Pedro b. 1974.

Issue of the late Mabel Emily Brodrick (Lady Grant), b. 1869, d. 1956, m. 1892, Adm. Sir
(William) Lowther Grant, KCB, who d. 1929:—
Alan Lowther, b. 1896 (570, Park Av., New York City, USA): m. 1st, 1938, Rosemary, who d. 1949,
da. of Edward Horgan, of Buffalo, New York; 2ndly, 1951, Esther Marie, da. of Chauncey
Cochran, of Youngstown, Ohio, and has issue living, (by 1st m.) David Alan (Tuxedo

CUSPIDE CORONA

Park, New York, USA), *b*. 1938; *m*. 1962, Deborah, da. of Robert Jordon of Waban, Mass., and has issue living, Lisa Jordan *b*. 1963, Hilary Lowther *b*. 1966,—Susan, *b*. 1940: *m*. 1963, George Beetle, of 533, Arbutus St., Philadelphia, Pa. 19119, USA, and has issue living, Christopher Bradley *b*. 1971,—Jane, *b*. 1944.——Marjorie Harriet (Warwickdale, Symington, Ayrshire), *b*. 1898: *m*. 1928, Brig. Arthur Nicholas Gosselin, CBE, DSO, who *d*. 1961.

PREDECESSORS.—[1] ALAN Brodrick, Solicitor-Gen. for Ireland 1695, Attorney-Gen. 1707 M.P. for Cork 1692-1709, and for Midhurst 1717-22, sometime Speaker of the House of Commons in Ireland, Ch. Justice of the King's Bench in Ireland 1709-10, Lord Chancellor of Ireland 1714-28, and a Lord Justice of Ireland 1716-17, 1719, and 1723-4; *cr. Baron Brodrick, of* Midleton, co. Cork (peerage of Ireland), 1715, and *Viscount Midleton* (peerage of Ireland) 1717; *d*. 1728; *s*. by his son [2] ALAN, 2nd Viscount; a Commr. of English Customs; *d*. 1747; *s*. by his son [3] GEORGE, 3rd Viscount; M.P. for Ashburton 1754-61; *d*. 1765; *s*. by his son [4] GEORGE, 4th Viscount; M.P. for Whitchurch, Hants 1774-96; *cr. Baron Brodrick*, of Peper Harrow, co. Surrey (peerage of Great Britain) 1796, with remainder to the issue male of his father; *d*. 1836; *s*. by his son [5] GEORGE ALAN, 5th Viscount; *d.s.p*. 1848; *s*. by his cousin [6] CHARLES, 6th Viscount, el. son of the Most Rev. the Hon. Charles, Archbishop of Cashel, 4th son of 3rd Viscount; *d*. 1863; *s*. by his brother [7] WILLIAM JOHN, 7th Viscount; *b*. 1798; was Dean of Exeter and Chaplain to H.M. Queen Victoria: *m*. 1st, 1824, Lady Elizabeth Anne Brudenell, dau. of 6th Earl of Cardigan, and widow of the Hon. John Perceval (E. Egmont); 2ndly, 1829, the Hon. Harriet Brodrick, 3rd dau. of 4th Viscount Midleton; *d*. 1870; *s*. by his son [8] WILLIAM, 8th Viscount; *b*. 1830; Lord High Steward of Kingston 1875-93, and Lord-Lieut. of co. Surrey 1896-1905; M.P. for Mid Surrey (*C*) 1868-70: *m*. 1853, the Hon. Augusta Mary, who *d*. 1903, dau. of 1st Baron Cottesloe; *d*. 1907; *s*. by his el. son [9] WILLIAM ST. JOHN FREMANTLE, *P.C., K.P.*, 9th Viscount; *b*. 1856; an Alderman of London County Council 1907-13; was Financial Sec. to War Office 1886-92, and Under-Sec. of State for War 1895-8, Under-Sec. of State for Foreign Affairs 1898-1900, Sec. of State for War 1900-03, Sec. of State for India 1903-5, and a Member of Irish Convention 1917-18 elected a Member of Senate of S. Ireland June 1921; sat as M.P. for W. Div. of Surrey (*C*) 1880-85, and for S.W. or Guildford, Div. of Surrey 1885-1906; *cr. Viscount Dunsford*, of Dunsford, co Surrey, and *Earl of Midleton* (peerage of UK) 1920: *m*. 1st, 1880, Lady Hilda Charteris, who *d*. 1901, da. of 9th Earl of Wemyss and March; 2ndly, 1903, Madeleine Cecilia Carlyle, who *d*. 1966, da. of the late Lt.-Col. the Hon. John Constantine Stanley; *d*. 1942; *s*. by his el. son [10] GEORGE ST. JOHN, 2nd Earl and present peer; also Viscount Midleton, Viscount Dunsford, Baron Brodrick, of Midleton, and Baron Brodrick, of Peper Harow.

Midlothian, Earl of, see Earl of Rosebery.

MILDMAY OF FLETE, BARONY OF.   (Mildmay.)   [Extinct 1950.]

DAUGHTER LIVING OF FIRST BARON.

Hon. Helen Winifred, *A.R.R.C*., *b*. 1907; is a Nursing Member of V.A.D.: *m*. 1945, Lieut.-Com. Richard John Bramble White, RNVR , who *d*. 1969, having assumed by deed poll 1958 the additional surname of Mildmay before his patronymic, and has issue living, Anthony John Bramble, *b*. 1948,— Richard Francis Bingham, *b*. 1949: *m*. 1973, Sara, da. of the late I. K. Cleland,—Elizabeth Georgiana, *b*. 1947: *m*. 1967, John Valentine Lewthwaite, of 46, Lansdowne Rd., W11. [see Lewthwaite, Bt.]. *Residence*,—Mothecombe House, Holbeton, Plymouth.

MILFORD, BARON.   (Philipps.)   [Baron U.K. 1939, Bt. U.K. 1919.]

WOGAN PHILIPPS, 2nd Baron, and 2nd Baronet, *b*. Feb. 25th, 1902; *s*. 1962; ed. at Eton, and at Magdalen Coll., Oxford; a farmer: *m*. 1st, 1928 (marriage dissolved 1944), Rosamond Nina, dau. of Rudolph Chambers Lehmann, of Fieldhead, Bourne End, Bucks.; 2ndly, 1944, Cristina, who *d*. 1953, dau. of Marchese Casati, of Palazzo Barberini, Rome, and formerly wife of 15th Earl of Huntingdon; 3rdly, 1954, Tamara, widow of William Rust, and has issue by 1st marriage.

Arms,—Argent, a lion rampant sable ducally gorged and chained or. **Crest**,—A lion as in the arms. **Supporters**,—On either side a horse, argent charged on the shoulder with three bars wavy azure.

Residence,—Butlers Farm, Colesbourne, Cheltenham. *Club*,—St. James'.

DUCIT · AMOR · PATRIÆ

Patriotism my motive.

SON LIVING.   (*By 1st marriage*.)
Hon. HUGO JOHN LAURENCE (of 16, Tregunter Rd., S.W.10), *b*. Aug. 27th, 1929; ed. at Eton and at King's Coll., Camb.; a Member of Lloyd's, and a Dir. of Anderson Finch Villiers (Agencies) Ltd., and of Framlington Holdings Ltd.: *m*. 1st, 1951 (m. diss. 1958), Margaret, da. of Capt. Ralph Heathcote, DSO, RN; 2ndly, 1959, the Hon. Mary Makins, el. da. of the 1st Baron Sherfield, and has issue living, (by 1st m.) Anna Margaret, *b*. 1954: *m*. 1975, Christopher Richard James Woodhouse, MB, BS [see B. Terrington], (by 2nd m.) Guy Wogan, *b*. 1961,—Roland Alexander, *b*. 1962,—Ivo Laurence, *b*. 1967,—Katherine Nina, *b*. 1964.

BROTHERS LIVING.

Hon. Richard Hanning, *MBE, b.* 1904; ed. at Eton; Maj. Welsh Gds. (Reserve), Hon. Col. Pembroke Yeo., Hon. Pres. of Schweppes, Ltd., Chm. of Northern Securities Trust, Ltd., and of Milford Haven Conservancy Board, a Member of Civic Trust for Wales, and a JP; Lord-Lt. for Pembrokeshire 1958-74, since when for Dyfed; Keeper of the Rolls for Dyfed since 1974; NW Europe 1944-45; MBE (Mil) 1945: *m.* 1930, Lady Marion Violet Dalrymple, JP, da. of 12th Earl of Stair, and has issue living, Jeremy Hew, *b.* 1931; ed. at Eton; a Member of Lloyds, and Chm. of Laurence Philipps & Co., Ltd.: *m.* 1959, Susan, yr. da. of H. E. B. Gundry, of Grange, Honiton, Devon, and has issue living, Clare Marion *b.* 1961, Nicola *b.* 1964. *Residences,—*Picton Castle, Haverfordwest, Pembrokeshire; 5, Connaught Pl., W2. *Clubs,—*Bootle's, Pratt's.

Hon. James Perrott, *TD, b.* 1905; ed. at Eton, and at Ch. Ch., Oxford; Maj. TA Reserve; Farmer; High Sheriff of Suffolk 1955; 1939-45 War (despatches): *m.* 1930, the Hon. Elizabeth Joan Kindersley, da. of 1st Baron Kindersley, and has issue living, Peter Anthony (of Parsonage Farm, Ugley, nr. Bishop's Stortford, Herts.), *b.* 1933; ed. at Eton, and at Trin. Coll., Camb.; is a Member of London Stock Exchange: *m.* 1957, Susannah Margaret, el. da. of S. W. Eaton, and has issue living, Charles Edward Laurence *b.* 1959, James Anthony Hanning *b.* 1961, Gavin Piers Alexander *b.* 1963,—Penelope Doune, *b.* 1931: *m.* 1950, Capt. Anthony Walsham Neville Lake, of Dove Cliff, Stretton, nr. Burton-on-Trent [see Walsham, Bt., colls.],—Daphne Deirdre (Springfield Maltings, Stogumber, Taunton, Som.), *b.* 1940: *m.* 1963, Robin Hugh Lewes, TD, who *d.* 1969, and has issue living, James Hugh *b.* 1967, Katherine Mary, *b.* 1968, Sarah Jane (twin) *b.* 1968. *Residence,—*Dalham Hall, Newmarket, Suffolk. *Clubs,—*Turf, Jockey, Royal Automobile.

Hon. William Speke (twin), *CBE, b.* 1908; *d.* 1975; formerly Capt. RA (TA); Chm., British National Life Insurance Soc., Ltd., a Freeman of City of London, a Liveryman of Shipwright's Co., and a Dir. of Northern Securities Trust, Ltd.; High Sheriff of Pembrokeshire 1968; 1939-45 War (despatches); CBE (Civil) 1957: *m.* 1939, Lady Jean Meriel McDonnell, da. of 7th Earl of Antrim, and has issue living, Geoffrey Mark, *b.* 1948,—David William, *b.* 1952: *m.* 1971, Stella Katharine Anne, only da. of A. W. Fordham, and has issue living, Frederick William *b.* 1973,—Georgina Rose, *b.* 1942: *m.* 1967, David Llewellyn Pryse Lloyd, and has issue living, Huw Llewellyn *b.* 1971, Jonathan *b.* 1973, Isabel Rose Pryse *b.* 1968, Juliet Ann *b.* 1970,—Theresa Margaret, *b.* 1946: *m.* 1972, Christopher Payne. *Residence,—*Slebech Park, Haverfordwest, Pembrokeshire. *Club—*RAC.

SISTER LIVING.

Hon. Gwenllian, *O.B.E., b.* 1916; formerly Subaltern A.T.S.; is a J.P. for Radnorshire; a Co. Councillor for Radnorshire 1959-64, and High Sheriff 1970-71; OBE (Civil) 1962. *Residence,—* The Old Rectory, Boughrood, Llyswen, Brecon.

PREDECESSOR.—Sir Richard Philipps, 7th Bt. (*cr.* 1621) [see V. St. Davids]; *cr. Baron Milford* 1776, which title became ext. on his death in 1823, and was revived in favour of [1] LAURENCE RICHARD Philipps, 6th son of the Rev. Canon Sir James Erasmus Philipps, 12th Bt.; *b.* 1874; High Sheriff of Hants 1915; a Gov. of Univ. Coll. of Wales and Founder of Paraplegic Hospital in Wales; *cr.* a Bt. 1919, and *Baron Milford*, of Llanstephan, co. Radnor (peerage of U.K.) 1939: *m.* 1901, Ethel Georgina, who *d.* 1971, da. of the late Rev. Benjamin Speke, of Jordans, Somerset; *d.* 1962; *s.* by his el. son, [2] WOGAN, 2nd Baron and present peer.

MILFORD HAVEN, MARQUESS OF. (Mountbatten.) [Marquess U.K. 1917].

GEORGE IVAR LOUIS MOUNTBATTEN, 4th Marquess; *b.* June 6th, 1961; *s.* 1970.

Arms,—Quarterly: 1st and 4th, azure, a lion rampant double-queued barry of ten argent and gules, armed and langued of the last, crowned or, within a bordure compony of the second and third; 2nd and 3rd argent, two pallets sable, charged on the honour point with an escutcheon of the arms of the late *Princess Alice* (*i.e.* the Royal arms differenced with a label of three points argent, the centre point charged with a rose gules barbed vert, and each of the other points with an ermine spot sable. **Crests—**1st, out of a ducal coronet or two horns barry of ten argent and gules, issuing from each three linden leaves vert, and from the outer side of each horn four branches barwise, having three like leaves pendent therefrom of the last, *Hesse*; 2nd, out of a ducal coronet or a plume of four ostrich feathers alternately argent and sable, *Battenberg.* **Supporters,** —On either side a lion double-queued and crowned all or.

*Residence,—*Flat 2, 2, Wilton Terr., SW1.

BROTHER LIVING.
Lord IVAR ALEXANDER MICHAEL, *b.* March 9th, 1963.

AUNT LIVING. (*Daughter of 2nd Marquess.*)
Lady (Elizabeth) Tatiana (Flat 2, 2, Wilton Terr., SW1), *b.* 1917.

GREAT UNCLE LIVING. (*Son of 1st Marquess.*)
Rt. Hon. Lord Louis Francis Albert Victor Nicholas, *KG, GCB, OM, GCSI, GCIE, GCVO, DSO, PC, FRS* (*Earl Mountbatten of Burma*), *b.* June 25th, 1900; *cr. Earl Mountbatten of Burma* 1947 [see that title].

WIDOW LIVING OF THIRD MARQUESS.
JANET MERCEDES (*Marchioness of Milford Haven*), (Flat 2, 2, Wilton Terr., SW1), only da. of the late Maj. Francis Bryce, OBE: *m.* 1960, as his 2nd wife, the 3rd Marquess, who *d.* 1970.

PREDECESSORS.—[1] LOUIS ALEXANDER Mountbatten, *G.C.B., G.C.V.O., K.C.M.G.,* **son** of H.G.D.H. the late Prince Alexander of Hesse, G.C.B., by his morganatic marriage to Julie, Princess of Battenberg; *b.* May 24th, 1854; naturalized 1868 as Prince Louis of Battenberg; Adm. of the Fleet; was Naval Adviser to Inspector-Gen. of Fortifications 1893-4, Assist. Director of Naval Intelligence 1899-1901, Director thereof 1902-5, in Command of second Cruiser Squadron 1905-7, Second in Command of Mediterranean Fleet 1907-8, Com.-in-Ch. of Atlantic Fleet 1908-10, in Command of 3rd and 4th Divs. Home Fleet 1911, Second Sea Lord of the Admiralty 1911-12, and First Sea Lord 1912-14; appointed Hon. A.D.C. to Queen Victoria 1896, and Personal Naval A.D.C. to King Edward VII. 1901 and to King George V. 1910 ; cr. *Viscount Alderney,* co. Southampton, *Earl of Medina,* and *Marquess of Milford Haven* (peerage of the United Kingdom) July 17th, 1917, having by Roy. Warrant, July 14th, 1917, at H.M.'s request, discontinued the use, style and title of "Serene Highness" and "Prince," and appellation of "Battenberg," and assumed for himself and descendants the surname of Mountbatten : *m.* 1884, Victoria Alberta Elizabeth Mathilde Marie, *V.A.,* who *d.* 1950, el. dau. of H.R.H. the late Grand Duke Ludwig IV. of Hesse, K.G., by H.R.H. the late Princess Alice Maud Mary, *V.A.,* 2nd dau. of H.M. the late Queen Victoria ; *d.* 1921 ; *s.* by his el. son [2] GEORGE LOUIS VICTOR HENRY SERGE, *G.C.V.O.,* 2nd Marquess ; *b.* 1892 ; Capt. (retired) R.N. ; European War 1914-18, present at battle of Heligoland, Dogger Bank, and Jutland: *m.* 1916, Countess Nadejda de Torby, who *d.* 1963, yr. dau. of H.I.H. the late Grand Duke Michael Michaelovitch of Russia and the late Countess de Torby; *d.* 1938; *s.* by his only son [3] DAVID MICHAEL, *OBE, DSC,* 3rd Marquess, *b.* 1919: *m.* 1st, 1950, Romaine Dahlgren (from whom he obtained a divorce 1960, she having obtained a divorce at El Paso, Mexico 1954), only da. of the late Vinton Ulric Dahlgren Pierce, and formerly wife of William Simpson; 2ndly, 1960, Janet Mercedes, only da. of the late Maj. Francis Bryce, OBE; *d.* 1970; *s.* by his el. son [4] GEORGE IVAR LOUIS, 4th Marquess and present peer; also Earl of Medina, and Viscount Alderney.

MILLS, VISCOUNT. (Mills.) [Viscount U.K. 1962, Bt. U.K. 1953.]

ROGER CLINTON MILLS, 2nd Viscount, and 2nd Baronet; *b.* June 14th, 1919; *s.* 1968; ed. at Canford and Jesus Coll., Camb.; Bar. Inner Temple 1958; Colonial Ser., Kenya, 1946-63; 1939-45 War as Maj. RA: *m.* 1945, Joan Dorothy, da. of James Shirreff, and has issue.

Arms,—Per chevron azure and argent in chief two millrinds of the last and in base a balance sable. **Crest,**—A bear's gamb erased or, supporting a flint-lock proper. **Supporters.** —On either side a lion or collared and chained azure pendant from the collar an escutcheon of the last charged with a sun in splendour gold.

Residence,—Banbury Cross, 84, Pannal Ash Rd., Harrogate.

SON LIVING.

Hon. CHRISTOPHER PHILIP ROGER, *b.* May 20th, 1956.

DAUGHTERS LIVING.

Hon. Felicity Jane, *b.* 1947: *m.* 1970, Roger B. Pickford.

Hon. Phillipa Susan, *b.* 1950: *m.* 1970, Russell Scott Arthurton, of Riversdale, 253 High St., Boston Spa, Yorks.

SISTER LIVING.

Hon. Beatrice Margaret, *b.* 1916: *m.* 1941, Walter Goodwin Davis. *Residence,*—3, The Dale, Wootton Wawen, Solihull, Warwicks.

PREDECESSOR.—[1] *Rt. Hon.* Sir PERCY HERBERT Mills, *KBE, PC,* son of D. Mills, of Stockton-on-Tees; *b.* 1890; Min. of Power 1957-59; Paymaster-Gen. 1959-61; Min. without Portfolio 1961-62; Controller-Gen. of Machine Tools, Min. of Supply 1940-44; cr. a Baronet 1953, *Baron Mills,* of Studley, co. Warwick 1957, and *Viscount Mills,* of Kensington, co. London 1963: *m.* 1915, Winifred Mary, who *d.* 1974, da. of George Conaty, of Birmingham; *d.* 1968; *s.* by his only son [2] ROGER CLINTON, 2nd Viscount, and present peer; also Baron Mills.

MILLTOWN, EARLDOM OF. (Leeson.) See "Peerages Dormant."

[*This Peerage became dormant since the death of the* 7th *Earl in* 1891, *but the title was claimed by both the late* JOHN LEESON (*who d.* 1905), *and the late* ROBERT WILLIAM FREDERICK LEESON, *who d.* 1906, *son of the late Rev. Joseph Leeson, neither of whom, however, established his right to the dignity. It is now probably extinct.*]

COLLATERAL BRANCH LIVING.

Granddaughter of the late Richard John Leeson-Marshall, son of the late Robert Marshall Leeson, son of the late Hon. Robert Leeson, 4th son of 1st Earl :—

Issue of the late Major Markham Richard Leeson-Marshall, *b.* 1859, *d.* 1939: *m.* 1st, 1890, Mabel Edith, who *d.* 1892, dau. of Sir John Fermor Godfrey, 4th Bt. ; 2ndly, 1907, Meriel Anne, who *d.* 1944, dau. of Sir George Frederick John Hodson, 3rd Bt. :—

(**By 1st marriage**) Mary, *b.* 1891: *m.* 1924, George Annesley Ruth, who *d.* 1947. *Residence,*— Callinafercy, Milltown, co. Kerry.

MILNE, BARON. (Milne.) [Baron U.K. 1933.]

Studies make illustrious.

GEORGE DOUGLASS MILNE, 2nd Baron; *b.* Feb. 10th, 1909; *s.* 1948; ed. at Winchester, and at New Coll., Oxford; a Member of Inst. of Chartered Accountants of Scotland; Master of Grocers' Co. 1961-62; a Member of Lambeth Hosp. Management Cttee. 1947-51; 1939-45 War as Maj. RA (TA) in Norway and Middle East (despatches, wounded, prisoner): *m.* 1940, Cicely, da. of the late Ronald Leslie, and has issue.

Arms,—Or, a cross moline pierced lozengeways of the field between four mullets azure. Crest,—A dexter hand holding up an open book proper, leaved or. Supporters,— *Dexter*, an officer of the Royal Horse Artillery; *sinister*, an officer of the Greek Evzone Guard, both in full dress uniform.

Residence,—33, Lonsdale Road, Barnes, S.W.13.

SONS LIVING.
Hon. GEORGE ALEXANDER, *b.* April 1st, 1941.
Hon. Iain Charles Luis, *b.* 1949.

DAUGHTER LIVING.
Hon. Ann Geraldine, *b.* 1946: *m.* 1969, Ian Frederick Lawrence Straker, of 23, Suffolk Rd., Barnes, SW13.

SISTER LIVING.
Hon. Joan Claire Florence, *b.* 1907: *m.* 1937, as his second wife, James Hart Rutland, who *d.* 1954.
Residence,—53, Drayton Gardens, S.W.10.

PREDECESSOR.—[1] *F.-M. Sir* GEORGE FRANCIS Milne, *G.C.B.*, *G.C.M.G.*, *D.S.O.*, son of the late George Milne, of Westwood, Aberdeen; *b.* 1866; became Field-Marshal 1928; Nile Expedition 1898, S. Africa 1899-1902 (D.S.O.), European War 1914-19 on Staff and as Gen. Officer Comdg. Salonika Army (K.C.B., K.C.M.G., G.C.M.G.); was Lieut. of The Tower 1920-23, Ch. of Imperial Gen. Staff 1926-33, Master Gunner, St. James's Park 1929-46, and Constable of The Tower 1933-8; Grand Pres. of British Empire Ser. League, Chm. Empire Sos. War Hospitality Committee, Pres. of London Fever Hospital, Chm. of Executive Committee of Roy. Cancer Hospital, Patron of Salonika Reunion Asso., and Pres. of Old Contemptibles' Asso., Army Cadet Asso., Roy. Artillery Asso., and Roy. Artillery Memorial Asso.; bore second sword at Coronation of King George VI.; *cr. Baron Milne*, of Salonika and of Rubislaw, co. Aberdeen (peerage of United Kingdom) 1933: *m.* 1905, Claire Marjoribanks, *MBE*, who *d.* 1970, da. of Sir John Nisbet Maitland, 5th Bt.; *d.* 1948; *s.* by his son [2] GEORGE DOUGLASS, 2nd Baron and present peer.

MILNER OF LEEDS, BARON. (Milner) [Baron UK 1951.]

(ARTHUR JAMES) MICHAEL MILNER, *AE*, 2nd Baron; *b.* Sept. 12th, 1923; *s.* 1967; ed. at Oundle, and Trin. Hall, Camb. (MA); Solicitor 1951; partner in the legal firms of Milners, Curry & Gaskell, of London, and J. H. Milner & Son of Leeds; Ft. Lt. 609 (W. Riding) Sqdn. RAuxAF 1947-52; 1939-45 War as Fl. Lt. RAF: *m.* 1951, Sheila Margaret, da. of Gerald Hartley, of Leeds, and has issue.

Arms.—Gules on a chevron ermine between in chief two bits or and in base a rose argent barbed and seeded proper a Teazel sable. Crest.—Perched on a sword with point to the dexter proper and hilt and pomel or an owl also proper, gorged with a collar sable thereon three mullets argent, pendent therefrom a pair of scales and resting on the dexter claw on a portcullis chained or. Supporters.—On either side an owl proper gorged with a collar sable thereon three mullets argent pendent therefrom a portcullis chained or.

Residence,—4, Carlyle Mansions, Cheyne Walk, SW3 5LS.

SON LIVING.
Hon. RICHARD JAMES, *b.* May 16th, 1959.

DAUGHTERS LIVING.
Hon. Geraldine Jane, *b.* 1954.
Hon. Meredith Ann, *b.* 1956.

SISTERS LIVING.
Hon. Lois Elizabeth Florence Zaidée, *b.* 1919. *Residence*,—The Grove, Roundhay, Leeds, 8.
Hon. Shelagh Mary Margaret, *b.* 1925: *m.* 1948, Harry Barker Grimshaw, from whom she obtained a divorce 1965, and has issue living, John Sherwood, *b.* 1950,—Miranda, *b.* 1952. *Residence*,—The Old Forge, Thorner, Yorkshire.

WIDOW LIVING OF FIRST BARON.
LOIS TINSDALE (Lois, Baroness Milner of Leeds), (The Grove, Roundhay, Leeds, 8), da. of Thomas Brown, of Roundhay, Leeds: *m.* 1917, the 1st Baron, who *d.* 1967.

PREDECESSOR.—[1] *Rt. Hon.* JAMES Milner, *MC*, *TD*, *PC*, el. son of the late James Henry Milner of Leeds; *b.* 1889; MP for S.E. Leeds (*Lab.*) 1929-51; Chm. of Ways and Means and Dep. Speaker of House of Commons 1943-45, and 1945-51; *cr. Baron Milner of Leeds*, of Roundhay, City of Leeds (Peerage of UK) 1951: *m.* 1917, Lois Tinsdale, da. of Thomas Brown, of Roundhay, Leeds; *d.* 1967, *s.* by his only son [2] (ARTHUR JAMES) MICHAEL, 2nd Baron, and present peer.

MILVERTON, BARON. (Richards.) [Baron U.K. 1947.]

ARTHUR FREDERICK RICHARDS, *G.C.M.G.*, 1st Baron, son of the late William Richards, of Bristol; *b.* Feb. 21st, 1885; ed. at Clifton Coll., and at Christ Church, Oxford (BA); entered Malayan Civil Ser. 1908; became Under-Sec. to Govt. of Federated Malay States 1926, and Acting Gen. Adviser, Johore 1929; was Gov. of N. Borneo 1930-33, Gov. and Com.-in-Ch. of Gambia 1933-6, Gov. and Com.-in-Ch. of Fiji (also High Commr. for W. Pacific) 1936-8, Capt.-Gen. and Gov.-in-Ch. of Jamaica 1938-43, and Gov. and Com.-in-Ch. of Nigeria 1943-7; is a K.St.J.; has American Medal of Freedom with Silver Palm; cr. C.M.G. 1933, K.C.M.G. 1935, G.C.M.G. 1942, and *Baron Milverton*, of Lagos, and of Clifton, in the City

Mind makes the man.

of Bristol (peerage of United Kingdom) 1947 : *m.* 1927, Noelle Benda (a C.St.J.), dau. of Charles Basil Whitehead, Torquay, and has issue.

Arms,—Argent, three lozenges conjoined in fesse gules between between two barrulets sable, all within two flaunches of the second, both charged with a spearhead of the field. Crest,—A Malay tiger's nead erased proper, gorged with a collar lozengy argent and gules. Supporters,—On either side a Malay tiger proper, gorged with a collar lozengy argent and gules.

Residence,—The Lodge, Cox Green, near Maidenhead, Berks. *Clubs,*—Athenæum, Oxford and Cambridge, West Indian.

SONS LIVING.

Rev. the Hon. FRASER ARTHUR RICHARD, *b.* 1930; ed. at Ridley Coll., Ontario, and at Clifton Coll.; in Roy. Signals 1949-50; in Kenya Police 1952-53; V. of Okewood, Surrey 1963-67, since when of Christian Malford with Sutton Benger and Tytherton Kellaways; Chap. to Wilts. ACF: *m.* 1957, Mary Dorothy, da. of Leslie Fly, of Pulteney St., Bath, and has issue living, Susan Mary, *b.* 1962,—Juliet Elizabeth, *b.* 1964. *Residence,*—The Rectory, Christian Malford, Chippenham, Wilts.

Hon. Michael Hugh, *b.* 1936; ed. at Ridley Coll., Ontario, and at Clifton Coll.; Capt. (ret.) Rifle Bde.; Malaya 1957 (despatches); attached R. Nigerian Army 1962, and a Member of UN Congo Force 1963-65; Man. Dir. of Philip Morris Nigeria Ltd. since 1972: *m.* 1960, E. Leonie B., yst. da. of Col. Leo Steveni, late Indian Army, of 40, Kenilworth Court, Putney, SW15, and has issue living, Arthur Hugh, *b.* 1963. *Residence,*—29, Brandling Park, Newcastle upon Tyne 2. *Club,*—Naval and Military.

DAUGHTER LIVING.

Hon. Diana Benda, *b.* 1928; ed. at Havergal Coll., Toronto, at Cheltenham Ladies' Coll., at London Univ., and at Sorbonne, Paris; Prin. of St. James's Secretarial Coll. (Residential Branch) Bradpole, Bridport, Dorset: *m.* 1960, Sq-Ldr. Glyn John Clement, RAF, and has issue living, Paul Nicholas Arthur, *b.* 1961,—Caroline Benda, *b.* 1966. *Residence,*—The Bell House, Kewstoke Rd., Worle, Weston-super-Mare.

Minster, Baron, title of Marquess Conyngham on Roll of H. L.

MINTO, EARL OF. (Elliot-Murray-Kynynmound.) [Earl U.K. 1813, Bt. S. 1700.]

He needs not the bow.

GILBERT EDWARD GEORGE LARISTON ELLIOT-MURRAY-KYNYNMOUND, *MBE*, 6th Earl, and 9th Baronet; *b.* June 19th, 1928; *s.* 1975; ed. at Eton, and RMA; Capt. Scots. Gds. (Reserve); a Member of Queen's Body Guard for Scotland (Roy. Co. of Archers); JP for Roxburghshire; Chm. of Scottish Council on Alcoholism; a Member of Borders Regional Council (Hermitage Div.) since 1974; ADC to CIGS 1953-55, and to Gov. of Cyprus 1955; MBE (Mil.) 1955: *m.* 1st, 1952 (m. diss. 1965), Lady Caroline Child-Villiers, da. of 9th Earl of Jersey; 2ndly, 1965, Mary Elizabeth, da. of the late Peter Ballantine, of Stonehouse Farm, Gladstone, NJ, USA, and has issue by 1st m.

Arms,—Quarterly: 1st and 4th grand quarters quarterly, 1st and 4th argent, a hunting horn sable, stringed gules, and on a chief azure, three mullets of the field, *Murray*; 2nd and 3rd azure, a chevron argent, between three fleurs-de-lis or, *Kynynmound*; 2nd and 3rd grand quarters gules, within a bordure vair, a bend engrailed or, thereon a baton azure, *Elliot*; above all a chief of augmentation argent, and thereon a Moor's

Mildly but firmly.

head sable, being the arms of the island of Corsica. Crest,—A dexter arm embowed issuant from clouds, throwing a dart, all proper. Supporters,—Dexter, an Indian sheep proper; *sinister*, a fawn proper.

Seat,—Minto, Hawick, Roxburghshire; *Club,*—Puffin's (Edinburgh).

SON LIVING. (*By 1st m.*)
GILBERT TIMOTHY GEORGE LARISTON (*Viscount Melgund*), *b*. Dec. 1st, 1953; ed. at Eton;
Lt. Scots. Gds.

DAUGHTER LIVING. (*By 1st m.*)
Lady Laura, *b*. 1956.

BROTHER LIVING
Hon. George Esmond Dominic ELLIOT (37, Lowndes Sq., SW1; White's and New Club (Edinburgh)),
b. 1931; ed. at Eton, and at Madrid Univ.; formerly Lt. Scots Gds.: *m*. 1962, (m. diss. 1970),
Countess Marianne (Bunny), da. of the late Count Thomas Esterhazy, and has issue living, Alexander,
b. 1963,—Esmond, *b*. 1965.

SISTERS LIVING.
Lady Bridget, *b*. 1921: *m*. 1st, 1944, Lt.-Col. James Averell Clark, Jun., DFC, USAF; 2ndly, 1954
(m. diss. 1963), Maj. Henry Claude Lyon Garnett, CBE; 3rdly, 1966 (m. diss. 1970), Maj. (Edward)
Peter Godfrey Miller Mundy, MC, and has issue living, (by 1st m.) Christopher, *b*. 1949.
Lady Willa ELLIOT, *b*. 1924 : *m*. 1946, Major George David Chetwode, M.B.E., Coldstream Guards
[see B. Chetwode, colls.]. *Residence,*—The Mantles, Blyth, Worksop, Notts.

COLLATERAL BRANCHES LIVING.

Grandson of the late Hon. Arthur Ralph Douglas Elliot, 2nd son of 3rd Earl:—
Issue of the late Capt. Hubert William Arthur Elliot, *b*. 1891, *d*. 1967: *m*. 1st, 1919, Mary
Hester, who *d*. 1945, da. of the late Hon. Sir Langer Meade Loftus Owen, CBE, KC,
formerly Ch. Judge in Divorce, Supreme Court of NSW; 2ndly, 1955, Mrs. Pamela Violet
Cathcart (Dalliotfield, Muthill, Perthshire), da. of the late Lt.-Col. Patrick Douglas Stirling,
OBE, MC, JP, of Kippendavie:—
(By 1st m.) John William Owen (East House, Dedham, Colchester, Essex), *b*. 1921; ed. at Eton,
and at Trin. Coll., Camb.; Capt. late Scots Guards: *m*. 1944, Mary Norah, da. of the late Hon.
(Godfrey) John Arthur Murray Lyle Mulholland, MC [see B. Dunleath, colls.], and has issue living,
Hugh John, *b*. 1946; ed. at Eton, and at Gonville and Caius Coll., Camb. (MA),—Timothy David
b. 1952; ed. at Eton and Bristol Univ.,—Susan Mary *b*. 1948; ed. at Goldsmith's Coll., London
Univ, (Dip.Ed.): *m*. 1969, Patrick Gilbert Dominick Toriglioni del Cassero-Nisbett, Gren. Guards, of
Hanover House, Bray, Berks., and has issue living, Dominick Gilbert *b*. 1972.

Granddaughter of the late Hugh Samuel Roger Elliot, son of the late Hon. Hugh
Frederick Hislop Elliot (infra):—
Issue of the late Herbert Hugh Elliot, Pilot Officer R.A.F., *b*. 1909, *d*. (killed on active
ser.) 1942: *m*. 1939, Kate Marjorie, who *d*. 1972, da. of the late Rev. Vernon Iles, of
South Marston, Swindon, Wilts:—
Patricia, *b*. 1940: *m*. 1964, Maj. Ievan Davies, 11th Hussars, of Poolpark, St. Tudy, Bodmin, Cornwall.

Issue of the late Hon. Hugh Frederick Hislop Elliot, 3rd son of 3rd Earl, *b*. 1848,
d. 1932: *m*. 1879, Mary Euphemia, who *d*. 1934, dau. of the late Col. Samuel
Long, of Bromley Hill:—
Nina Emily (*Lady Russell*) (c/o Coutts & Co., 440, Strand, WC2), *b*. 1882: *m*. 1907, Sir (Charles
Lennox Somerville Russell, who *d*. 1960 [Blomefield, Bt.].

Granddaughters of the late Rt. Hon. Sir Henry George Elliot, G.C.B., 2nd son
of 2nd Earl:—
Issue of the late Sir Francis Edmund Hugh Elliot, G.C.M.G., G.C.V.O., *b*. 1851, *d*. 1940 :
m. 1881, Henrietta Augusta Mary, who *d*. 1938, dau. of the late Rt. Hon. Sir Francis
Clare Ford, P.C., G.C.B., G.C.M.G.:—
Dorothy, *b*. 1888: *m*. 1914, Henry Montesquieu Anthony, CBE, who *d*. 1949, and has issue living,
Lydia Margaret Elliot, *b*. 1918.——Violet Marie, *b*. 1896: *m*. 1920, Lt. Edmond H. O'Connor, RN,
who *d*. 1924.

Grandchildren of the late Frederick Boileau Elliot, son of the late Adm. the
Hon. Sir George Elliot, K.C.B., M.P., 2nd son of 1st Earl:—
Issue of the late Gilbert Compton Elliot, *b*. 1871, *d*. 1931 : *m*. 1910, Marguerita, who *d*. 1955,
dau. of the late Henry Barbey, of New York :—
Alexander Henry, *b*. 1913; ed. at Eton, and at Ch. Ch., Oxford; late Major R.A.: *m*. 1937, Lady
Ann Child-Villiers, dau. of 8th Earl of Jersey, and has issue living, Gilbert Francis, *b*. 1949.—
Victoria Cynthia, *b*. 1938: *m*. 1960, John Robert Hunter, RN (ret.), and has issue living, David John
b. 1961, James Max *b*. 1963, Michael Alexander *b*. 1965,—Patricia Joan, *b*. 1940: *m*. 1964, David
John Curry, RAF, of The Old Rectory, Maltby-le-Marsh, Alford, Lincs., and has issue living, Alex-
ander David Ian *b*. 1974, Georgina Sophie Gay *b*. 1967. *Residence,*—Broadford, Chobham, Surrey.
——Cynthia Sophie, *BEM* (38, Leeward Way, St. Thomas, U.S. Virgin Islands), *b*. 1916; whilst
herself a prisoner, rendered sers. to prisoners in hospitals in Germany during 1939-45 War (BEM):
m. 1st, 1944, the 1st Baron Hore-Belisha, who *d*. 1957; 2ndly, 1957, Maj. Ian Victor Major, DSC,
RM (ret.), who *d*. 1973.

Granddaughter of the late Capt. Amyand Powney Charles Elliot, son of the late
Hon. John Edmund Elliot, M.P. (infra) :—
Issue of the late William Alexander Elliot, *b*. 1851, *d*. 1894 : *m*. 1887, Louisa Margaret, who
d. 1890, el. dau. of Charles M. Russell, M.D.:—
Amy Millicent, *b*. 1888 ; with London Auxiliary Ambulance 1939-45 : *m*. 1st, 1907 (marriage
dissolved 1915), Lieut.-Com. Eric Marsland Groves, formerly R.N., who *d*. 1949 ; 2ndly, 1916
(m. diss. 1932), Lieut.-Com. Paris Graham Singer, RN, who *d*. 1953; 3rdly, 1948, William Henry
Gill, formerly London Scottish, and has issue living, (by 1st marriage) Colin Eric (of La Hêche
St. Martin. Jersey). *b*. 1908: Maj. (ret.) Highland L.I.: *m*. 1938, Dorothea Mary Blamey, and has
issue living, Mary Fay Sylvia *b*. 1940: *m*. 1961, Andrew Sandys Douglas-Bate, of Alwyn Lawn House,
Stone, nr. Aylesbury, Bucks., and has issue living, Rupert Louis Elliot *b*. 1963, Sophie Louise *b*. 1965,
Harriet Mary *b*. 1966. *Residence,*—Paradiso-Mio, Bon Voyage, Roquebrune-Cap Martin, France,
AM.

Issue of the late Capt. Charles Sinclair Elliot, R.N., *b*. 1853, *d*. 1915 : *m*. 1889, Florence
Louisa, who *d*. 1950, el. dau. of the late Frederick Leacroft Dudley :—
Alban Charles, *MC* (865, Pittwater Rd., Collaroy Sydney, NSW), *b*. 1892; Major Australian Forces
(Reserve of Offices); 1914-19 War (MC), 1939-45 War: *m*. 1919, Fanny Compton, da. of Francis
Henry Atherton, of Taunton, Queensland, and has issue living, Charles Atherton (Purchase Rd.,
West Pennants Hills, NSW), *b*. 1921; 1939-45 with AIF: *m*. 19—, Doris May, da. of
Pritchard, of Llansannan, N. Wales, and has issue living, Timothy Charles *b*. 19—, Owen Francis *b*.
19—,—Eileen, *b*. 1924; in Australian Women's Army Ser. during European War 1942-45,—Hilary,
b. 1927; in Australian Women's Army Ser. during European War 1945,——Florence Grace, *b*. 1896:
m. 1922, Reginald Joslin Buckingham, and has issue living, Michael Joslin *b*. 1927,—Joslin Elliot
(twin), *b*. 1927,—Amyand David, *b*. 1930.——Margaret Mildred Norfolk Hope (*Lady Embry*), *b*.
1908: *m*. 1928, Air Ch. Marshal Sir Basil Edward Embry, GCB, KBE, DSO, DFC, AFC, RAF, and
has issue living, Keith, *b*. 1929,—Mark, *b*. 1935,—Patrick Paul, *b*. 1942,—Bridget, *b*. 1931. *Residence,*
—Cape Riche, via Albany, W. Australia.

Grandson of the late Capt. Charles Sinclair Elliot, R.N. (ante) :—
Issue of the late Dudley Sinclair Elliot, *b*. 1890 ; *d*. (killed in action during European
War) 1917 : *m*. 1913, Annie Caroline, dau. of William Hammett Howard, of Sydney,
N.S. Wales:—

Dudley Charles Howard (PO Box 84, Murwillumbah, NSW 2484), *b.* 1918; ed. at Sydney Univ. (LLB); 1939-45 War with RAAF: *m.* 1943, Rosalie Yvonne, da. of the late Francis Walter Vizard, of S. Aust., and has issue living, Gilbert Dennis, *b.* 1947; ed. at Univ. of NSW (Dip. Hosp. Admin.): *m.* 1973, Jane, da. of John Guinane, of NSW,—Victor Roderick, *b.* 1950,—Hugh Kent, *b.* 1953,— Roslyn Kristin, *b.* 1944: *m.* 1966, Ronald Charles Newland, and has issue living.

Grandchildren of the late Ninian Lowis Elliot, 3rd son of Augustus John Elliot (infra):—
Issue of the late Lieut.-Com. Archibald Guthrie Elliot, R.N., *b.* 1898, *d.* 1981: *m.* 1929, Evelyn Agnes, who *d.* 1965, da. of the late Alexander Buchanan:—
John Alexander Ninian (Toroton, Songhor, Kenya), *b.* 1930: *m.* 1962, Jean Patricia, da. of Arthur Willis Winfield Sale, of Pulborough, Sussex.——Margaret Dolores, *b.* (posthumous) 1931: *m.* 1953, Timothy Romer Matthews, of 7, Chislehurst Rd., Richmond, Surrey, and has issue living, Sophia Elizabeth *b.* 1955.

Grandchildren of the late Augustus John Elliot, 4th son of the late Hon. John Edmund Elliot, MP, 3rd son of 1st Earl:—
Issue of the late Archibald Campbell Elliot, *b.* 1864, *d.* 1921: *m.* 1899, Harriet Newcome, who *d.* 1951, dau. of the late J. M. Lowis, B.C.S., of Amery House, Alton, Hants :—
Augustus John (Rose Combe, Furley, Axminister, Devon), *b.* 1901; Lt.-Col. (ret.) Indian Army: *m.* 1st, 1930, Theodora Dorothy (who obtained a divorce 1946), da. of the late Engineer-Com. T. G. J. Harvey, Roy. Indian Marine (ret.); 2ndly, 1946, Ilona, da. of Frederic Charles Wilson Bindley, of Eastbourne, and has issue living, (by 1s m.), Archibald Keith (78, Howard Rd., Queens Park, Bournemouth), *b.* 1932; RAF (ret.): 1957, Pauline Mary, da. of the late Cecil Edwin Pearman Parker, of Watford, Herts., and has issue living, Ross Ian *b.* 1958, Clive Graham *b.* 1960,—Angus Ian (73, Marlene Court, Chelmesley Wood, Birmingham, 37), *b.* 1937: *m.* 1959, Carol Ann, da. of William Henry Evans, and has issue living, Mark Keith *b.* 1960, Jamie Ian *b.* 1964,—Betty Anne, *b.* 1933: *m.* 1956, Jeffrey Edward Power Browning, of Poplar Farm House, Worlingworth, Woodbridge, Suffolk, and has issue living, Charles Richard Power *b.* 1957, Alastair Jeffrey Power *b.* 1960, Philippa Anne Campbell *b.* 1963, Joanna Elizabeth Newcombe *b.* 1967.

Issue of the late Gilbert Augustus Elliot, *b.* 1873, *d.* 1959: *m.* 1905, Phyllis Baret, who *d.* 1972, da. of the late Major Edward William Stokes, 4th King's Own Regt., of Ellel Hall, Lancaster:—
Gilbert Cecil Ninian (Corner Garth, Old Earswick, York) *b.* 1907; is an AMICE: *m.* 1942, Esther Rosamond, da. of the late Capt. Hugh Alfred Cholmley [V. Hill, colls.], and has issue living, Gilbert Hugh Cholmley, *b.* 1947,—Rowland George Cholmley, *b.* 1949,—Jane, *b.* 1943: *m.* 1963, Maj. Iain Alastair McKay, Scots Gds., of Briff Farm, Upper Bucklebury, nr. Newbury, Berks., and has issue living, Alastair James Mark *b.* 1963, Andrew Simon Charles *b.* 1970, Catriona Jane *b.* 1966, Arabella Charlotte *b.* 1968,—Lorna, *b.* 1945: *m.* 1967, John Edward Clive, of Little Cottage, Littleton, Guildford and has issue living, Simon John David *b.* 1970, Edward Thomas *b.* 1974, Sarah Margarita *b.* 1968.——Daphne Patricia, *b.* 1917: *m.* 1949, Maj. Godfrey Carrington Royle, RA (TA), of 61, Cleaver Sq., SE11.

(*Male line in remainder to Baronetcy.*)

Grandchildren of the late Frederick Augustus Hugh Elliot, C.I.E., el. son of the late Edward Francis Elliot, 2nd son of the Rt. Hon. Hugh Elliot (infra) :—
Issue of the late Lieut.-Col. Edward Halhed Hugh Elliot, D.S.O., *b.* 1876, *d.* (result of enemy action during European War) 1944 : *m.* 1911, Ethel Winifred, who *d.* 19—, dau. of the late John Fair:—
Frederick John Hugh, *b.* 1914.——Margaret Elizabeth, *b.* 1912: *m.* 1936, Robert Percival Lawrence, Sub-Lieut. R.N.V.R., who *d.* (killed in action during European War) 1940, and has issue living, Martin, *b.* 1939. *Residence,*—8, St. Margarets Crescent, Putney, S.W.15.

Granddaughter of the late Gilbert Wray Elliot, 2nd son of the late Adm. Sir Charles Elliot, K.C.B., 4th son of the late Rt. Hon. Hugh Elliot, 2nd son of 3rd baronet :—
Issue of the late Launceston Elliot, *b.* 1874, *d.* 1930 : *m.* 1897, Rose Emilia Kathleen, who *d.* 1945, dau. of the late Rev. F. W. Helder, of Lee, Kent:—
Nancy Maud (123, The Parade, Island Bay, Wellington, NZ), *b.* 1901: *m.* 1929, Capt. William Lewis Renwick, Welsh Horse Yeo., who *d.* 1957, and has issue living, Ann Elliot (123, The Parade, Island Bay, Wellington, NZ), *b.* 1940: *m.* 1962 (m. diss. 1972), Garry Eric Smith, and has issue living, Ian Lewis Elliot *b.* 1966.

Grandchildren of the late Frederick Eden Elliot, 3rd son of the late Adm. Sir Charles Elliot, KCB, (ante):—
Issue of the late Major Hugh Elliot, King's Regt., *b.* 1863, *d.* (killed in action during European War) 1915 : *m.* 1888, Alicia Lucy, who *d.* 1954, dau. of the late Rev. William Percy Robinson, D.D., Warden of Glenalmond :—
Charles Francis Desmond (The Street, Raydon, Ipswich, Suffolk), *b.* 1908; is Major late British Gurkha Div.——Clara Lucy, *b.* 1900. *Residence,*—The Street, Raydon, Ipswich, Suffolk.

PREDECESSORS.—[1] GILBERT Elliot, *K.P.*, having been under forfeiture 1685-90 as an accessory to the Rebellion of 1679, received Knighthood ; was afterwards Clerk to P.C., M.P. for Roxburghshire 1702-7, and a Lord of Session (as Lord Minto); cr. a *Baronet* 1700, with remainder to his heirs male; *d.* 1718 ; *s.* by his son [2] Sir GILBERT, 2nd Bt. ; M.P. for Roxburghshire 1722-7 ; was a Lord of Session (as Lord Minto) 1726-33, a Lord of Justiciary 1733-63, and Lord Justice Clerk 1763-6; *d.* 1766 ; *s.* by his son [3] Sir GILBERT, 3rd Bt., M.P. for co. Selkirk 1753-65, and for Roxburghshire 1765-77 ; was Lord of the Admiralty 1756, Treasurer of the Chamber 1762, Keeper of the Signet in Scotland 1767, and Treasurer of the Navy 1770; *d.* 1777 ; *s.* by his son [4] Sir GILBERT, 4th Bt. ; M.P. for co. Roxburgh 1777-84, and for Helston 1790-5 ; was Viceroy of Corsica 1795-7, Envoy Extraor. to Vienna 1799, Pres. of Board of Control India 1806, and Gov.-Gen. of Bengal 1807-13 ; assumed by Roy. licence 1797 the additional surnames of Murray-Kynynmound after that of Elliot; cr. *Baron Minto*, of Minto, co. Roxburgh (peerage of Great Britain) 1797, and *Viscount Melgund* and *Earl of Minto* (peerage of United Kingdom) 1813 ; *d.* 1814 ; *s.* by his son [5] GILBERT, 2nd Earl, *G.C.B., P.C.* ; *b.* 1782 ; was M.P. for Roxburghshire 1812-14, Ambassador to Berlin 1833-4, First Lord of the Admiralty 1835-41, and Lord Privy Seal 1846-52 : *m.* 1806, Mary, who *d.* 1853, dau. of Patrick Brydone, of Lennuel House, Berwick ; *d.* 1859 ; *s.* by his son [6] WILLIAM HUGH, *K.T.*, 3rd Earl, *b.* 1814 ; M.P. for Hythe (*L*) 1837-41, for Greenock 1847-52, and for Clackmannanshire 1857-9 : *m.* 1844, Emma Eleanor Elizabeth, who *d.* 1882, heiress of Gen. Sir Thomas Hislop, Bt. (*ext.*); *d.* 1891; *s.* by his el. son [7] GILBERT JOHN, *K.G., G.C.S.I., G.C.M.G., G.C.I.E., P.C.*, 4th Earl ; *b.* 1845 ; was Gov.-Gen. of Canada 1898-1904, and Viceroy and Gov.-Gen. of India 1905-10 : *m.* 1883, Mary Caroline, *C.I.*, who *d.* 1940, dau. of the late Gen. the Hon. Charles Grey ; *d.* 1914 ; *s.* by his el. son [8] VICTOR GILBERT LARISTON GARNET, 5th Earl, *b.* 1891 ; Capt. Scots Gds.: *m.* 1921, Marion, OBE, who *d.* 1974, da. of George William Cook, of Montreal; *d.* 1975; *s.* by his el son [9] GILBERT EDWARD GEORGE LARISTON, 6th Earl and present peer; also Viscount Melgund, and Baron Minto.

MITCHISON, BARONY OF. (Mitchison.) [Extinct 1970.]

SONS LIVING OF LIFE BARON.

Hon. Denis Anthony (of 14, Marlborough Rd., Richmond, Surrey), *b.* 1919; ed. at Abbotsholme Sch., and at Trin. Coll., Camb. (MB, ChB), MRCP London; Prof. of Bacteriology, London Univ.: *m.* 1940, Ruth Sylvia, MB, BCh, da. of Hubert Gill, and has issue.

Hon. John Murdoch (Great Yew, Ormiston, E. Lothian EH35 5NJ), *b.* 1922; ed. at Winchester, and at Trin. Coll., Camb. (MA, ScD); Prof. of Zoology, Edinburgh Univ.: *m.* 1947, Rosalind Mary, da. of Edward Murray Wrong, and has issue.

Hon. Nicholas Avrion (14, Belitha Villas, N1), *b.* 1928; FRS; Prof. of Zoology, London Univ.: *m.* 1958, Lorna Margaret, da. of Maj.-Gen. John Simson Stuart Martin, CSI, of Husabost, by Dunvegan, Isle of Skye, and has issue.

DAUGHTERS LIVING OF LIFE BARON.

Hon. (Sonja) Lois, *b.* 19—: *m.* 1959, John Godfrey, and has issue.

Hon. Valentine Harriet Isobel Dione *b.* 19—: *m.* 19—, Mark Arnold-Forster, of 50, Clarendon Rd., W11, and has issue.

WIDOW LIVING OF LIFE BARON.

NAOMI MARGARET, (*Baroness Mitchison*), (Carradale House, Carradale, Campbeltown, Argyll), da. of the late John Scott Haldane, CH, FRS; Naomi Mitchison, authoress: *m.* 1916, Baron Mitchison, CBC, QC (Life Peerage) who *d.* 1970, when the title became ext.

MOLESWORTH, VISCOUNT. (Molesworth.) [Viscount I. 1716.]

RICHARD GOSSET MOLESWORTH, 11th Viscount ; *b.* Oct. 31st, 1907 ; *s.* 1961 ; ed. at Lancing ; Middle East 1941-44 with R.A.F. : *m.* 1958, Anne Florence (WOMERSLEY), dau. of John Mark Freeman Cohen, of St. James's Court, SW1, and has issue.

Arms,—Gules, an escutcheon vair, within an orle of eight cross-crosslets or. Crest.—A dexter arm embowed in armour proper, holding a cross crosslet or. Supporters.—*Dexter,* a pegasus argent, wings elevated or ; *sinister,* a pegasus, wings elevated gules, semée of cross crosslets or.

Residence,— Garden Flat, 2, Bishopswood Road, Highgate, N.6.

SONS LIVING.

Hon. ROBERT BYSSE KELHAM, *b.* June 4th, 1959.

Hon. William John Charles, *b.* 1960.

SISTER LIVING.

(Cynthia) Joan (The Chantry, Portinfer Rd., Vele, Guernsey), *b.* 1919; does not use the courtesy title of Honourable.

The love of my country prevails.

VINCIT AMOR PATRIÆ

DAUGHTER LIVING OF NINTH VISCOUNT.

Hon. Cicely Sylvia, *b.* 1902 : *m.* 1927, Guy Haylett Walker Ramsey, who *d.* 1959, and from whom she had obtained a divorce 1937, and has issue living, Valentine Bagot Rudolph Haylett Walker (12, Parkfield, North Parade, Horsham, Sussex), *b.* 1928: *m.* 1959 (m. diss. 1971), Shirley Mary Clare d'Esterre, only da. of Reginald E. Jex, of Barton-on-Sea, Hants., and has issue living, Guy Dominic *b.* 1960, Michelle Elizabeth *b.* 1963. *Residence,*—12, Parkfield, North Parade, Horsham, Sussex.

COLLATERAL BRANCHES LIVING.

Branch from 8th Viscount.

Issue of the late Hon. Arthur Ernest Parnell Molesworth, 3rd son of 8th Viscount, *b.* 1870, *d.* 1951 : *m.* 1910, Nellie Maud, *J.P.*, who *d.* 1956, dau. of George W. Banks, formerly of Wellington, New Zealand, and widow of Dr. George Watson, of S. America :—

Frank Ernest Bysse, *b.* 1911 : *m.* 1st, 1934 (marriage dissolved 1940), Phyllis Margaret Patrick, dau. of the late George Wells ; 2ndly, 1943 (marriage dissolved 1957), Joan, *J.P.*, dau. of A. G. Lethbridge, of Thames Valley and Taranaki, NZ; 3rdly, 1961, Nellie Verdun, da. of the late Edward Hughes, of Hikurangi, NZ, and has issue living, (by 3rd m.) Helen Deirdre Velvet, *b.* 1962. *Address,* —c/o The Northern Advocate, Whangarei, Northland, NZ.——Betty Eleanor Gosset, *b.* 1913, *m.* 1948, Frank Geoffrey Harald Allen, late Wing-Cdr. RAFVR, of Los Barrios, Cadiz Province, Andalucia, Spain.

Branch from brother of 7th Viscount.

Grandson of the late Lionel Charles Molesworth (infra):—

Issue of the late Col. Roger Bevil Molesworth, RA (ret.), *b.* 1901, *d.* 1974: *m.* 1929, Iris (The Croft, St. Clears, Carmarthen), da. of the late Lt.-Col. Roger Lloyd Kennion, CIE, of Durford Wood, Petersfield:—

Allen Henry Neville (31, Norland Sq., W11 4PU), *b.* 1931: *m.* 1970, Gail Cheng Kwai, LRAM, ARCM, LGSM, da. of L. C. Chan, of 10, Holland Rise, Singapore 10.

Grandson of the late Maj. Richard Molesworth, el. son of the late Capt. the Hon. Anthony Oliver Molesworth, RA, brother of 7th Viscount:—

Issue of the late Lionel Charles Molesworth, *b.* 1873, *d.* 1916 : *m.* 1896, Saba Maud, who *d.* 1956, dau. of Sir Henry Delves Broughton, 9th Bt. :—

Hender Delves, *b.* 1907: *m.* 1935, Evelyn Carnegy Helena, da. of the late Malcolm Galloway, of Shelley Hall, Ongar, Essex.

Granddaughter of the late Capt. Morgan Crofton Molesworth, R.E., 2nd son of the late Capt. the Hon. Anthony Oliver Molesworth, R.A. (ante) :—

Issue of the late Major Herbert Crofton St. George Molesworth, *b.* 1863, *d.* 1933 : *m.* 1891, Adeline Stella, who *d.* 1959, dau. of the late C. E. Hutton, of 63, Porchester Terrace, W.:—

Georgina Evelyn Hutton, *b.* 1901. *Residences,*—Green Cottage, Old Newton, Stowmarket, Suffolk; Quinta do Poço dos Passaros, Santa Rita, v. Nova de Cacela, Algarve, Portugal.

Granddaughter of the late Col. William Molesworth, O.I.E., O.B.E., M.B. (infra):—

Issue of the late Lieut.-Col. William Earle Molesworth, M.C., *b.* 1894, *d.* 1955 : *m.* 1918, Dorothy Loftus (of 19, Alexandra Road, Reading), dau. of the late Col. St. George Loftus Steele, O.B., of Cheltenham :—

Pamela, *b.* 1919 : *m.* 1950, Robert Anthony Langham, and has issue living, Peter Anthony, *b.* 1953,—Susan Marie, *b.* 1951. *Residence,*—19, Alexandra Road, Reading, Berks.

Grandchildren of the late Lieut.-Col. Anthony Oliver Molesworth, 4th son of the late Capt. the Hon. Anthony Oliver Molesworth, R.A. (ante) :—
Issue of the late Col. William Molesworth, CIE, CBE, MB, BS, MRCS, LRCP, Indian Med. Ser., *b.* 1865, *d.* 1951: *m.* 1893, Winifred Anne, who *d.* 1960, da. of the late T. E. Weekes, JP, of Hazeldene, Monkstown, Cork :—
Kathleen Winifred, *b.* 1896 : *m.* 1919, Alfred Alyson Fennell Minchin, Indian Forest Ser., and has issue living, Patrick Molesworth (Cruxfield Cottage, Duns, Berwicks.), *b.* 1920; ed. at Charterhouse, and at Merton Coll., Oxford (BA); late Capt. KOSB, attached Indian Army: *m.* 1944, Mary Isobel Penistone, and has issue living, Ronald William, *b.* 1946; ed. at Charterhouse, and RMA; Capt. KOSB. *Residence,*—Cruxfield House, Duns, Berwicks.

Issue of the late Hugh Wilson Molesworth, CBE, *b.* 1870, *d.* 1959: *m.* 1903, Dora Hanbury, who *d.* 1972, only da. of the late Maj. Sir (Robert) Hanbury Brown, KCMG, of Newlands, Crawley Down, Sussex:—
Hugh Mervyn, *b.* 1907 ; ed. at Marlborough, and at Sidney Sussex Coll., Camb. (B.A. honours 1928) ; is a F.C.A.: *m.* 1st, 1934, Mary Langhorne (from whom he obtained a divorce 1936), younger dau. of Henry Langhorne Johnson, CBE, of Hurst Copthorne; 2ndly, 1939, Enid Mary, who *d.* 1969, da. of the late J. U. R. Grave, AMICE, of Manchester, and has issue living, (by 2nd m.) Roger (Oak Apples, Copthorne, Sussex), *b.* 1945; ed. at Marlborough: *m.* 1974, Pauline Fay, da. of Philip Hunt, of Wood Green, N22,—Donald, *b.* 1948; ed. at Embley Park. *Residence,*—Broad Oak, Copthorne, Sussex.——Denys Hope, *MC, b.* 1910; ed. at Marlborough; is Lt.-Col. RA (Reserve); 1939-45 War in Middle East (wounded, MC, prisoner), Malaya 1951 (despatches): *m.* 1945, Dorothy May, yr. da. of the late William C. Johnston, of Calcutta, India, and has issue living, Gillian Tessa, *b.* 1946: *m.* 1972, Juan Planells, of Ibiza, and has issue living, Nicolas Juan *b.* 1973,—Jennifer Margaret, *b.* 1948. *Residence,*—Rory Cottage, Forest Row, Sussex.——Eileen Rose, *b.* 1904: *m.* 1931, Lt.-Col. Basil Woods Ballard, CIE, MBE, Indian Army (Political Ser.), and has issue living, Timothy John (The Cottage, Pilgrims Way, Reigate), *b.* 1932; ed. at Marlborough, and at Sidney Sussex Coll., Camb. (MA); MICE: *m.* 1964, Helen Mary Christopherson, and has issue living, Bridget Anne *b.* 1970,—Jennifer Clare *b.* 1971,—William Richard (Olivers Cottage, Capel St. Mary, Suffolk), *b.* 1933; ed. at Marlborough, and Coll. of Aeronautics, Cranfield (MSc); CEng, AMIMechE, AFRAeS: *m.* 1967, Marianne Jean Elspeth, da. of the late Lt.-Col. Hugh Arbuthnott [see V. Arbuthnott, colls.], and has issue living, Hugh William *b.* 1968. *Residence,*—Shepherds Oak, Crawley Down, Sussex.

Issue of the late Capt. Ernest Kerr Molesworth, *b.* 1878, *d.* 1914 : *m.* 1905, Hilda Rosalie, who *d.* 1943, dau. of the late Lieut.-Gen. Henry Alexander Brownlow, formerly R.E., of 8, Homefield Road, Wimbledon, S.W. :—
Brownlow David, MRCS, LRCP (Hunthay, Axminster, Devon), *b.* 1913; ed. at Emmanuel Coll., Camb. (BA, MB, ChB); late Colonial Med. Ser., Malaya; *m.* 1939, Rosemary Katharine, da. of Lt.-Col. A. W. Moore, RAMC, and has issue living, Patrick David, *b.* 1946,—Anthony Simon, *b.* 1955,—Jenifer Rosemary, *b.* 1940: *m.* 1961, Peter David Rohde, BA, MB, DPM, MANZCP, of 30, Little Bornes, Alleyn Park, Dulwich, SE21, and has issue living, Simon Peter *b.* 1962, Katherine Leslie *b.* 1963,—Sheila, *b.* 1942: *m.* 1967, Jeremy Harvey, MA, of Hill House Flat, The Avenue, Sherborne, Dorset, and has issue living, Rachel Claire *b.* 1969, Joanna Elizabeth *b.* 1970.

Issue of the late Col. Francis Crofton Molesworth, late R.E., *b.* 1880, *d.* 1955 : *m.* 1913, Eileen, who *d.* 1951, dau. of the late Lieut.-Col. Richard Denny [Denny, Bt., colls.] :—
Richard Denny (25, Naunton Way, Cheltenham, Glos.) *b.* 1919; is an Asso. of Institute of Patentees and Inventors: *m.* 1972, Eva Emily Elizabeth Bowler.——Stephen Lindsay, *b.* 1925; 1939-45 War (wounded, despatches); is an ARIBA: *m.* 1959, Eve Lovie, and has issue living, Ivan Alexander, *b.* 1964,—Anna Cordelia, *b.* 1960,—Polly, *b.* 1967. *Residence,*—42, Chalcot Cres., NW1.——Beatrix, *b.* 1917. *Address,*—Chapel Garth, Galphay, Ripon, Yorks.

Issue of the late Rev. Anthony Oliver Molesworth, *b.* 1882, *d.* 1953: *m.* 1907, Melita, who *d.* 1931, dau. of the late Harry Lindsay Tilly, formerly Burma Commn. :—
Elizabeth Melita, *b.* 1911: *m.* 1933 (marriage dissolved 1963), Robert James Neale Lawson, and has issue living, Neale Anthony (Eldersfield, Llanbadoc, Usk, Mon.), *b.* 1935; CEng.; MIEE: *m.* 1964, Jennifer Jill, da. of the late Brig. J. M. C. Hoblyn, and has issue living, Susanna Joy *b.* 1965, Elizabeth Ann *b.* 1968,—Priscilla Joy, *b.* 1938: *m.* 1st, 1957, John Patrick Charles Rucker, who *d.* 1967; 2ndly, 1972, Henry Christopher Moule, and has issue living, (by 1st m.), Prudence Elizabeth *b.* 1958, Nancy Jane *b.* 1960, Venetia Frances *b.* 1963, Sophia Damaris *b.* 1965,—Melita Frances, *b.* 1943; 2nd Officer WRNS: *m.* 1971, Patrick Fenton Moule, of Rock House, Yetminster, Sherborne, Dorset. *Residence,*—Melbury Cottage, Compton Abbas, Shaftesbury, Dorset.

Granddaughter of the late Rev. Anthony Oliver Molesworth (ante) :—
Issue of the late Group Capt. Anthony Oliver Molesworth, RAF, *b.* 1908, *d.* (killed in action during 1939-45 War) 1944: *m.* 1933, Noëlle (B5, Queen Alexandra's Court, Wimbledon, SW19), da. of the late John Richard Holmes, formerly Pres. of District Court, Cyprus:—
Dawn Noëlle, *b.* 1934: *m.* 1955, Simon Jerrard Findlay Muirhead, of 61, Merton Hall Rd., Wimbledon, S.W.19, and has issue living, Anthony Oliver Molesworth, *b.* 1957,—Lauriston Philip, *b.* 1959,—Imogen Jane, *b.* 1963.

Branch from 4th son of 1st Viscount.

Grandchildren of the late Rev. William Nassau Molesworth, LL.D., son of the late Rev. John Edward Nassau Molesworth, D.D., el. son of the late John Molesworth, son of the late Major the Hon. Edward Molesworth, 4th son of 1st Viscount :—
Issue of the late James Murray Molesworth, *b.* 1849, *d.* 1924 : *m.* 1891, Emily Maria, who *d.* 1945, youngest dau. of the late Robert Leech, of 40, Clarendon Square, Leamington :—
Robert Murray Nassau, *b.* 1895 ; ed. at Haileybury ; Lieut. Gordon Highlanders (Reserve) ; European War 1914-16, as Staff-Lieut. Italian Expeditionary Force (wounded); European War 1939-45 with RWF: *m.* 1st, 1916, Lucie Amy Gertrude (who *d.* 1971, having obtained a divorce 1925), da. of the late Edward Lawrence, of Clifton, Bristol; 2ndly, 1926, Nora Madelene, da. of William John Connell, of Sparkhill, Birmingham; 3rdly, 1955, Clare, widow of T. W. Price, and has issue living, (by 2nd m.) Emily Patricia, *b.* 1927. *Residence,*—17, Glen Rise, Kings Heath, Birmingham, 14.

Grandchildren of the late William Nassau Molesworth, 5th son of the late Rev. William Nassau Molesworth, LLD (ante):—
Issue of the late Major William Nassau Molesworth, M.C., Manchester Regt., *b.* 1888, *d.* 1959 : *m.* 1917, Hester Winifred, who *d.* 1966, da. of the late Alfred Watkin, of Danebank, Lymm:—
Rev. Canon Anthony Edward Nassau (The Rectory, Huish Episcopi, Langport, Som.), *b.* 1923; ed. at Haileybury, and at Pembroke Coll., Camb. (MA) and at Coll. of Resurrection, Mirfield; Canon of Pro-Cathedral of St. Michael, Eshowe, Zululand 1963-68, and of Dioc. of Swaziland 1968-71 (Canon Emeritus of Swaziland); R. of Huish Episcopi with Pitney since 1971: *m.* 1969, Susan, SRN, yr. da. of Prof. H. R. B. Fenn, of Weald, Sevenoaks, Kent, and has issue living, Hugh William Nassau, *b.* 1972,—Anna Margaret, *b.* 1970——Gwendolen Clara Nassau (*Lady Lloyd*), *b.* 1919; 1939-45 War in WAAF: *m.* 1947, Sir (John) Peter Daniel Lloyd, and has issue living, David William Molesworth, *b.* 1950,—John Peter Anthony, *b.* 1956,—Judith Mary, *b.* 1947: *m.* 1968, Robert Anthony Hyndes,—Angela Hester Olwen, *b.* 1949: *m.* 1971, John Gipps Knox-Knight,—Penelope, *b.* 1953,—Sarah Jane, *b.* 1955. *Residence,*—6, Earl St., Hobart, Tasmania, 7005.

Grandchildren of the late John Molesworth (*b.* 1858), (infra):—
Issue of the late John Molesworth, *b.* 1894, *d.* 1971; *m.* 1927, Dorothy Josephine Mudge (205,
Foley St., Junction, Texas, USA):—
John Mudge (PO Box 104, Junction, Texas, USA), *b.* 1928: *m.* 1951, Joanne Hill, of New York, USA,
and has issue living, John, *b.* 1952,—Lynn Hill, *b.* 1955,—Cynthia, *b.* 1953.——Fred (Route 3, Box
437B, Amarillo, Texas, USA), *b.* 1931: *m.* 1962, Ann Spoon, of Memphis, Texas, and has issue living,
Fred Vance, *b.* 1963.——Dorothy Patricia, *b.* 1929: *m.* 1949, William Eugene Craft, of Drawer M,
Clarendon, Texas, USA, and has issue living, William Patrick, *b.* 1952,—John Robert, *b.* 1962,—
Catharine, *b.* 1950: *m.* 1974, John Throckmorton Keene, of 4909, Woodstone Drive, Apt. 604, San
Antonio, Texas 78230, USA,—Christine, *b.* 1957.

Grandchildren of the late John Molesworth (*b.* 1818), son of the late Rev. John
Edward Nassau Molesworth, DD (ante):—
Issue of the late John Molesworth, *b.* 1858, *d.* 1947: *m.* 1885, Emily Maude, who *d.* 1941,
dau. of the late Rev. Henry Mitchell, F.S.A., V. of Bosham, Chichester, and Rural Dean:—
Helen (1606-A, South Ong St., Amarillo, Texas 79102, USA), *b.* 1886: *m.* 1921, Lloyd Brown, who *d.*
1968.——Charlotte, *b.* 1902: *m.* 1952, William James Adams. *Residence,*—Clarendon, Texas, USA.

Issue of the late William Mackinnon Molesworth, *b.* 1867, *d.* 1956 : *m.* 1893, Jane Emily
Charlotte, who *d.* 1952, dau. of the Rev. Richard Galbraith, of Montell Uvalde, Texas,
U.S.A. :—
Edward William (of 606, W. Hervey Drive, Roswell, New Mexico, U.S.A.), *b.* 1901: *m.* 1935, Minella
da. of Adolph A. Stadler, of Kent, Ohio——Kathleen, *b.* 1895. *Residence,*—1900, David St.,
Austin, Texas.——Frances Emily, *b.* 1904: *m.* 1st, 1927, Nelson Anderson Sims, who *d.* 1956;
2ndly, 1959, Ernest L. Long, and has issue living, Kathleen Molesworth, *b.* 1936: *m.* 1956, David
Alan Donaldson. *Residence,*—Hobbs, New Mexico, U.S.A.

Grandchildren of the late Rev. Rennell Francis Wynn Molesworth, son of the
late Rev. John Edward Nassau Molesworth, D.D. (ante):—
Issue of the late Francis Hilton Molesworth, *b.* 1854, *d.* 1934: *m.* 1891, Cecilia Michaeliene,
who *d.* 1963, yst. da. of N. Buczkowski, of Seven Hills, S. Australia:—
Reginald Howard Wynn, *b.* 1899; ed. at King's Sch., Canterbury; European War 1939-45 as Lieut.
Roy. Australian Engineers. *Residence,*—1, Jersey Road, Artarmon, Sydney, N.S. Wales.——
Cecilia Frances (39, Tuddenham Rd., Ipswich), *b.* 1892: *m.* 1918, the Rev. Thomas Quigley, who
d. 1964, formerly R. of Foxford, co. Mayo, and has issue living, *Rev.* Thomas Molesworth (c/o Glyn,
Mills and Co., Whitehall, SW1), *b.* 1919; ··d. at London Univ. (BD 1945); formerly a Chap. to
Forces; Malaya 1952 (despatches),—John Molesworth (18, Ashburton Rd., Birkenhead),
b. 1921; ed. at Brasenose Coll., Oxford (MA honours): *m.* 1948, Betty Spafford
Armstrong, and has issue living, Mark Andrew *b.* 1952, Hugh *b.* 1956,—Philip Molesworth
(4874, Côte des Neiges Rd., Montreal, Canada), *b.* 1923; ed. at St. Peter's Hall, Oxford (BA honours);
1939-45 War with RN: *m.* 1958, Jeannine Marie Mirouse, and has issue living, Sophie Anne *b.*
1960,—David Francis Molesworth, *b.* 1926,—Cicely Ruth Molesworth, *b.* 1925: *m.* 1946, Desmond
Campion, of Lower Farm House, Westerfield, Ipswich, and has issue living, Stephen Charles *b.* 1950;
ed. at Hull Univ. (BA), Nicholas Paul *b.* 1953; BA Camb.,—Kathleen Mary Molesworth, *b.* 1928;
ed. at Trin. Coll., Dublin (MA honours); late Capt. WRAC,—Margaret Winifred Molesworth,
b. 1931.

Issue of the late Rev. John Hilton Molesworth, *b.* 1856, *d.* 1921 : *m.* 1908, Everilda Hamer,
who *d.* 1928, el. dau. of the late Rev. Canon James Hamer Rawdon (Hon. Canon of Man-
chester), of The Hermitage, Stockton-on-the-Forest, York :—
Rachel Frances Hilton, *b.* 1912: *m.* 1936, Commodore Neil Alexander Mackinnon, RAN, Tudor House,
Cricket Hill, Yateley, Hants., and has issue living, Peter William Alexander, *b.* 1938,—John Hugh
Molesworth, *b.* 1941; BA Oxon.,—Fiona Margaret, *b.* 1946: *m.* 1970, Ian Horsley, MA, Maj. R.
Green Jackets, of Gundillawah, Tumblong, NSW.——Cecilia Margaret (*Lady Mogg*), *b.* 1914:
m. 1939, Gen. Sir (Herbert) John Mogg, KCB, CBE, DSO, of Church Close, Watlington, Oxon., and
has issue living, John Nigel Ballard (c/o Williams Glyn & Co., Whitehall, SW1), *b.* 1940; Maj. R.
Green Jackets: *m.* 1967, Tessa Elizabeth, da. of F. D. Wright, of Brightwell Park, Brightwell
Baldwin, Oxon., and has issue living, John Peter Francis *b.* 1969,—Richard Julian Charles *b.* 1971,—
Patrick Henry Molesworth, *b.* 1942,—Timothy David Rawdon-Mogg, *b.* 1945. *Residence,*—Church
Close, Watlington, Oxon.

Grandsons of the late Rev. Ernest Hilton Molesworth (infra):—
Issue of the late Eric Mackinnon Molesworth, MB, ChB, *b.* 1890, *d.* 1963: *m.* 1916, Ethel A.
(49, St. Peter's Av., Caversham, Reading, Berks.), da. of the late Isaac Clark Griffith:—
Selwyn Hilton, MRCS, LRCP (Penbryn, Clawton, Holsworthy, Devon), *b.* 1917; ed. at Epsom Coll.,
and Manchester Univ.; MRCS, LRCP; Lt. RA: *m.* 1949, Margaret Seymour, BA da. of Percy
Arthur Smith, of Dormar, Westridge, Bridlington, E. Yorks., and has issue living, Christopher Roger,
b. 1951,—William Hugh, *b.* 1952,—Arthur David, *b.* 1956.——Robert Mackinnon (49, St. Peter's
Av., Caversham, Reading), *b.* 1923; ed. at Oundle and at Magdalene Coll., Camb. (MA); Lt. RNVR,
and an ARIBA: *m.* 1st, 1947 (m. diss. 1967), Ursula, only da. of the late Alwin Julius Jaeger, of
Thalwil-Zürich, Switzerland; 2ndly, 1967, Mary Craig, el. da. of Vice-Adm. Sir Maxwell Richmond,
KBE, CB, DSO, and has issue living, (by 1st m.) Stephen James, *b.* 1961,—(by 2nd m.) Peter Maxwell, *b.* 1974,—Elizabeth Anna, *b.* 1968,—Catherine Julia, *b.* 1969.——David William (170, Pick-
hurst Lane, Hayes, Bromley, Kent), *b.* 1930; ed. at King's Sch., Canterbury; Sqdn.-Ldr. RAF:
m. 1955, Doreen Joyce, da. of George Hunter, of Dunelm, Yarborough Cres., Lincoln, and has issue
living, Caroline Shona, *b.* 1956,—Melanie Susan, *b.* 1958,—Diana Louise, *b.* 1964.

Grandchildren of the late Rev. Rennell Francis Wynn Molesworth (ante):—
Issue of the late Rev. Ernest Hilton Molesworth, *b.* 1858, *d.* 1931 : *m.* 1st, 1886, Adeline,
who *d.* 1908, dau. of the late Rev. Charles King, Canon of Salisbury ; 2ndly, 1909, Hilda,
who *d.* 1940, dau. of the late James Cramp, J.P., of Coventry :—
Dorothea, *b.* 1893: *m.* 1917, Bernard Winthrop Swithinbank, CBE, who *d.* 1958, and has issue living,
Charles Winthrop Molesworth (of 7, Home End, Fulbourn, Cambs.), *b.* 1926; ed. at Bryanston,
and at Pembroke Coll., Oxford (MA, DPhil): *m.* 1960, Mary, da. of Benjamin Duane Stewart, of
Box 881, Sequim, Washington, USA, and widow of Robert Ellsworth Fellows, and has issue living
Kelvin *b.* 1964, Carol *b.* 1962,—Jane, *b.* 1924; ed. at Benenden Sch. and at Camb. Univ. (BA 1947,
MB, BCh 1950, and DCH 1959): *m.* 1949, Brinley Lodwick, MA, of 2, Hill Rd., Lewes, Sussex, and
has issue living, Rhys *b.* 1953, David *b.* 1960, Ceridwen *b.* 1951. *Residence,*—Four Acres, Caring
Lane, Bearsted, Kent.

Issue of the late Rodney Henderson Molesworth, *b.* 1865, *d.* 1944: *m.* 1909, Elonora, da. of
the late Charles Blair, JP, DL, of Glenfoot, Tillicoultry:—
Wynn Blair, *b.* 1911; ed. at King's Sch., Canterbury; formerly in RAF.

Grandson of the late Eric Mackinnon Molesworth (ante):—
Issue of the late Lieut. (E.) Richard Charles Victor Molesworth, RN, *b.* 1919, *d.* (on active
ser.) 1941: *m.* 1940, Doreen Mary, (who m. 2ndly, 1967, Bruce Page (c/o Midland Bank,
59, Old Christchurch Rd., Bournemouth), only da. of Joseph Greenwood:—

Eric Richard (Melbourne, Aust.), *b.* 1942; ed. at Christ's Hospital; 1st Officer, Merchant Navy.

Grandchildren of the late Rev. Rennell Francis Wynn Molesworth (ante):—
Issue of the late Theodore Henderson Molesworth, F.R.C.S., *b.* 1872, *d.* 1955; *m.* 1906,
Ethel Alexandra, who *d.* 1955, dau. of the late Edward Upton, of The Haven, St. Margaret's
Bay, near Dover:—
Michael Henderson, *b.* 1914.——Peter Rennell Henderson, *M.R.C.S., L.R.C.P., b.* 1923; M.R.C.S.
England and L.R.C.P. London 1946: *m.* 1953, Rosemary Ann Gould, and has issue lving, Simon
Peter Henderson, *b.* 1954,—David Rennell Henderson, *b.* 1955,—Nigel Piers Henderson, *b.* 1960.
Address,—P.O. Box 3003, Aden.——Mary Wynne, *b.* 1907 : *m.* 1934, Gerald Dorrett Baxter.——
Elizabeth Theodora, *b.* 1909 : *m.* 1938, Capt. Allan Dunn MacConachie, 7th Gurkha Rifles, and has
issue living, Elspeth, *b.* 1939.——Margaret Ethel, *b.* 1910.——Joan Frances, *b.* 1918 : *m.* 1944,
Lancelot Mitchell Shutte (PO Box 8336, Causeway, Salisbury, Rhodesia), and has issue living, Susan
Frances, *b.* 1952: *m.* 1972, Peter Derek Lapage, BSA Police,—Mary Jane, *b.* 1959.
Issue of the late Walter Henderson Molesworth, *b.* 1873, *d.* 1952 : *m.* 1910, Theodosia Maude,
who *d.* 1920, dau. of John Chapman, formerly of Ramsdale, Hants:—
Ernest Walter (Little Orchard, Hinton St. George, Somerset; RAC, Royal Overseas and Golfers',
Clubs), *b.* 1911; ed. at Dover Coll., and London Univ.; 1939-45 War (prisoner of Japanese): *m.* 1947,
Irene, da. of the Rev. S. F. Whitehead, of Aston Somerville, Glos.——Richard Nassau, *b.* 1913.——
Kathleen Janet, *b.* 1915.——Margery Evelyn, *b.* 1918: *m.* 1st, 1946, Anthony Orde; 2ndly, 1974,
Maj. Phineas Arthur Jackson, of 70, Creighton Av., N10 1NT.

Grandson of the late Frederick Nassau Molesworth, 2nd son of John Molesworth
(*b.* 1818) (ante):—
Issue of the late Major John Davenport Newall Molesworth, M.C., Roy. Corps of Signals
(TA), *b.* 1884, *d.* 1952: *m.* 1st, 1909, Mary (who *d.* 1970, having obtained a divorce 1927),
da. of A. Blake Norman, of Oakham, Rutland; 2ndly, 19—:—.
(By 1st m.) John Henry Nassau, *DSO, DFC, AFC* (Little Orchard, Snow End, Anstey, Buntingford,
Herts.), *b.* 1913; 1939-45 War (wounded, despatches, DFC, AFC, DSO); DSO 1945: *m.* 1946,
Pamela Joan, da. of the late Frederick William Guildford, of Ramsgate, Kent, and has issue living,
Peter John Norman, *b.* 1956.

Granddaughter of the late John Molesworth (*b.* 1818) (ante):—
Issue of the late Lawrence Teesdale Molesworth, *b.* 1864, *d.* 1941: *m.* 1893, Anneline
Wallace, who *d.* 1933, dau. of G. S. Bournes, of Rossport, Belmullet, co. Mayo:—
Elizabeth Wallace (of The Court House, S. Petherton, Somerset), *b.* 1894 : *m.* 1918, the Rev. Edward
Noel Mellish, V.C., M.C. D.L., who *d.* 1962, Chap. to the Forces (T.A.), and has issue living, Patrick
Molesworth, *b.* 1921,—Richard Wallace Paul (1421, Spear St., South Burlington, Vermont, USA),
b. 1923: *m.* 1956, Finetta Veronica Angell, da. of Lt.-Col. Charles Edward Kirwan Bagot, MC, of
Greengates, Painswick, Glos., and has issue living, Martin Christopher Bagot *b.* 1957, Nicholas
Charles *b.* 1961, Fiona Molesworth *b.* 1964,—Robin Hugh (Stone Lodge, South St., Wilton, Salis-
bury), *b.* 1924: *m.* 1954, Leonie Maria, da. of the late Henry Knibbeler, of Pieterpauwer Straat,
Amsterdam, Holland, and has issue living, Nicholas Noel *b.* 1960, Elizabeth Leonie Anne *b.* 1956,—
Margaret Elizabeth Claire, *b.* 1935. *Residence.*—The Court House, South Petherton, Somerset.—
Margaret Patricia Newall (Greensleeves, S. Petherton, Somerset), *b.* 1904: *m.* 1st, 1928, Theophilus
Rhys Jones, who *d.* 1959; 2ndly 1965, Howard John Bettany, and has issue living, (by 1st m.)
Theophilus Molesworth Rhys (Ash Cottage, Upper Framilode, Glos.), *b.* 1929: *m.* 1964, Jyllian, da. of
John de Vic Carey, of The Old School House, Frampton on Severn, and has issue living, Cressida
Helen *b.* 1971,—Christopher Bournes Rhys (Homestead Farmhouse, Palmers Green Lane, Brenchley,
Kent), *b.* 1931; ed. at King's Sch., Bruton: *m.* 1961, Mary, da. of the late C. T. O'Sullivan, and has
issue living, David Bournes Rhys *b.* 1963, Sophie Helen Rhys *b.* 1965.

Grandson of the late Com. George Mill Frederick Molesworth, son of the late
Rev. John Edward Nassau Molesworth, D.D. (ante) :—
Issue of the late Reginald Balfour Molesworth, *b.* 1852, *d.* 1895 : *m.* 1883, Marian, who
d. 1921, dau. of the late Edmund Thomson :—
Rev. Gilbert Edmund Nassau, *b.* 1895 ; ed. at Camb. Univ. (B.A. 1922, M.A. 1925) ; Capt. (retired),
Indian Army ; was V. of All Saints', Bradford 1927-31, V. of Bournville, Birmingham 1933-43, and
V. of Rochdale, Lancashire 1943-52, and V. of Castle Cary, Somerset 1952-7 since when Area Director
of S.W. Industrial Church Fellowship : *m.* 1923, Florence Edith Mary, dau. of the late Rev. Thomas
Fisher Maddrell, V. of Gulval, Penzance, Hon. Canon of Truro, and Examining Chap. to Bishop of
Truro, and has issue living, Michael Nassau, *b.* 1924 ; ed. at King Edward VIth School, Birmingham,
and at Sidney Sussex Coll., Camb. (BA 1948, MA 1951); is Sub.-Lt. R.N.V.R.: *m.* 1951, Heather,
who *d.* 1965, da. of the late Adm. Sir Henry Daniel Pridham-Wippell, KCB, CVO, and has issue
living, a son *b.* 1957,—John Edmund Nassau (c/o Lloyds Bank, Okehampton, Devon), *b.* 1926 ;
ed. at King's School, Bruton, at Sidney Sussex Coll., Camb., at London Univ., at Middle East
Centre of Arab Studies, and at St. Luke's Coll., Exeter; Flight-Lt. R.A.F. (ret.): *m.* 1952, Pamela
Anne, da. of Harold Richard Summers MacMullen, and has issue living, David Reginald Nassau
b. 1953, Carol Anne *b.* 1956, Elizabeth Stephanie *b.* 1958, Hilary *b.* 1964,—Richard Mark Nassau,
b. 1930 ; is 2nd Lieut. E. Lancashire Regt.,—Elizabeth Raphael, *b.* 1934. *Residence,*—Berrimans,
Northam, Bideford, N. Devon.

Granddaughter of the late Sir Guildford Lindsey Molesworth, K.C.I.E., 6th son of the
late Rev. John Edward Nassau Molesworth, D.D. (ante) :—
Issue of the late Henry Bridges Molesworth, *b.* 1855, *d.* 1954 : *m.* 1889, Jessie Fitzgerald,
who *d.* 1928, dau. of the late Com. George Mill Frederick Molesworth, R.N. (ante) :—
Mary Newall, *b.* 1896. *Residence,*—64, Vale Av., Findon, Worthing, Sussex.

Granddaughter of the late Major Edward Nassau Molesworth, son of the late Major
Edward Molesworth, eldest son of the late Robert Molesworth, 2nd son of the
late Major the Hon. Edward Molesworth (ante) :—
Issue of the late William John Molesworth, *b.* 1856, *d.* 1937 : *m.* 1892, Anne Brunette,
who *d.* 1948, dau. of the late Robert Boyd, M.D., of 1, Bolton Row, Mayfair, W. :—
Mary Nassau, *b.* 1897: *m.* 1924, Maj. Alfred Charles Stuart Smith, RA (ret.), who *d.* 1973, and has issue
living, Anthony Molesworth Stuart (87, South Promenade, St. Anne's-on-Sea, Lancs), *b.* 1928:
m. 1952, Dorothy Bennett, and has issue living, Christopher John Stuart *b.* 1953, Peter Martin
Stuart *b.* 1954, Gillian Eleanor Mary Stuart *b.* 1958,—Bridget Mary Stuart, *b.* 1927: *m.* 1952, the
Rev. Maurice Arthur Reily Collins, R. of Ockley, Dorking, Surrey, and has issue living, Jonathan
Stuart Reily *b.* 1955, Edward Charles Reily *b.* 1957. *Residence,*—Meadow House, West Meon,
Hants.

Branch from el. son of 7th son of 1st Viscount.

Grandchildren of the late Arthur Nepean Molesworth (*b.* 1856), el. son of Arthur
Molesworth (*b.* 1821), el. son of Arthur Nepean Molesworth (*b.* 1799), son of Maj.
Arthur Molesworth, el. son of the Hon. Bysse Molesworth:—
Issue of the late Arthur William Bysse Nepean Molesworth, *b.* 1902, *d.* 1958: *m.* 1922, Ruth
Patricia (5095 Sax Av., Apt. 303, Town of Mount Royal 9, Quebec, Canada), da. of the
late Thomas Gracey, of Moy, co. Armagh:—
Guilford Nepean, *b.* 1923.——John Robert, *b.* 1930: *m.* 1954, Mary, da. of Alexander Rodgers, of
Montreal, and has issue living, Deborah, *b.* 1957,—Kathryn, *b.* 1962,—Sandra, *b.* 1964.——Kathleen
Violet, *b.* 1927.——Ann, *b.* 1928: *m.* 1961, Dr. Herman Gelber, Scarborough Centenary Hosp.,
Scarborough, Ont., and has issue living, Sean Roderick, *b.* 1963.

Grandchildren of the late Thomas Nepean Molesworth, 2nd son of Arthur Nepean
Molesworth (b. 1799), (ante):—
**Issue of the late Balfour Nepean Molesworth, b. 1853, d. 1896: m. 1882, Louisa Agnes,
who d. 1938, dau. of H. H. Thompson, of Penetanguishene, Ontario, Canada :—**
Herbert Nepean, b. 1888 : m. 1912, Marjorie Kittredge, dau. of the late W. M. Thompson, of Pene-
tanguishene, Ontario, Canada, and has issue living, William Herbert (of 1850, des Cheneaux Street,
Three Rivers, Quebec, Canada), b. 1915 : m. 1938, Joan Anne, dau. of the late Charles Percival
Rudman, of Grand-Mere, Quebec, and has issue living, Michael Herbert b. 1944, Patricia Anne
b. 1942: m. 1964, Clifford Hastings Laurence, of 185, Ringuet St., Trois-Rivières, Quebec, Canada
(and has issue living, William Hastings b. 1966, Kelly Anne b. 1965,—Robert Nepean (1212, Powell
Av., Prince George, BC, Canada), b. 1923: m. 1943, Cecily Elizabeth, da. of the late Lt.-Cdr. Cecil
Alexander Wade, RN (ret.), of Edgeley,Whitchurch, Shropshire, and has issue living, Robert Alex-
ander b. 1946, Gregory Daniel b. 1951, Susan Elizabeth b. 1944: m. 1965, Robert J. Black,—Marjorie
Julia Kittredge, b. 1919: m. 1948, John MacLeod Ellis, of 99, Chester Avenue, Valois, Province of
Quebec, Canada, and has issue living, Marnie MacLeod b. 1951. Residence,—2180, Laviolette Avenue,
Three Rivers, Province of Quebec, Canada,——Lucy Darling, b. 1885. Residence,—41, Charles Street,
Georgetown, Ontario, Canada.——Muriel Agnes, b. 1891: m. 1926, Dighton Wynans Baxter, who
d. 1949. Residence,—41, Charles Street, Georgetown, Ontario, Canada.——Violet Maud, b. 1894.
Residence,—41, Charles Street, Georgetown, Ontario, Canada.

Grandchildren of the late William Ponsonby Molesworth, yst. son of Thomas Nepean
Molesworth (ante):—
**Issue of the late Major George Nepean Molesworth, Canadian Army, b. 1885, d. 1958 : m.
1916, Helen Nelles, who d. 1954, dau. of the late Sydney Bellingham Sykes, of Toronto :—**
John Sydney (74, Second St., Oakville, Ontario, Canada), b. 1919 ; Lt. RCA ; 1939-45 War: m. 1946,
Barbara Caroline, da. of Dr. Carswell Marshall, of Sawley, Clitheroe, Lancs., and has issue
living, William Marshall, b. 1949,—Hugh Carswell, b. 1952,—James Colin, b. 1959,—Helen Mary,
b. 1954. Residence,—Oakville, Ontario, Canada.——David Hugh George, b. 1927: m. 1952, Ann de
Veber, da. of the late Major Alfred Clarence Larter, of Toronto, Canada, and has issue living, Ian de
Veber, b. 1956,—Anthony Nelles, b. 1958. Residence,—156, Collier Street, Toronto, Canada.——
Margaret Jean, b. 1921. Residence,—195 William St., Oakville, Ontario, Canada.

**Grandsons of the late Rev. Thomas Molesworth, son of the late Thomas William
Ponsonby Molesworth, son of Maj. Arthur Molesworth (ante):—
Issue of the late Rev. Hugh Thomas Molesworth, b. 1860, d. 1930 : m. 1889, Alice Marian,
dau. of Edward Deshon, C.M.G., sometime Auditor-Gen. of Queensland :—**
Guilford Bysse, b. 1907: m. 1931, Catherine Maud, da. of the late Edward Charles Woodward, of
Coorparoo, Queensland, and has issue living, William Guilford Hugh (Marriott Lodge, 387, Cavendish
Rd., Coorparoo, Brisbane, Qld.) b. 1943: m. 1968, Helen, da. of John Edward McCaskie, of Coorparoo,
Brisbane, Queensland. Residence,—Cronulla, Marriott St., Coorparoo, Brisbane, Queensland.

Grandson of the late Bevil Hugh Molesworth el. son of the late Rev. Hugh Thomas
Molesworth (ante):—
Issue of the late Hugh Bevil Alec Molesworth, b. 1925, d. 1960: m. 1959, Patricia (who
m. 2ndly, 1963, Dr. Ian Martin, of 40, Carlyle Rd., E. Lindfield, NSW, 2070), da. of the late
Clive Quinton, of Wahroonga, Sydney, NSW:—
Hugh Bevil Olive, b. (posthumous) 1960.

Branch from 2nd son of 7th son of 1st Viscount.

Grandchildren of the late Maj.-Gen. Hickman Thomas Molesworth, el. son of Maj..
Gen. Arthur Molesworth, el. son of Capt. Robert Molesworth, 2nd son of the Hon-
Bysse Molesworth:—
Issue of the late Lieut.-Col. Hickman Crawford Molesworth, b. 1858, d. 1939 : m. 1st, 1883,
Margaret Amelia, who d. 1915, dau. of the late John Hopper, and widow of Surg.-Maj.
M'Lean ; 2ndly, 1920, Charlotte Anne, dau. of Alfred Thomas :—
(By 1st marriage) Arthur Crawford Valentine, b. 1885 ; formerly Lieut. 5th (Reserve) Batn. Roy.
Dublin Fusiliers, Lieut. Waterford R.G.A. (Mil.) and Lieut. Canadian Forces.——Guy Lindsay,
b. 1887 ; formerly Lieut. R.G.A.——Violet Marguerite, b. 1888.——Ivy Frederica, b. 1891 : m.
19—, David Alexander. Residence,—

Issue of the late Lieut.-Col. Robert Everard Molesworth, b. 1861, d. 1941 : m. 1st, 1889,
Catherine Isabella, who d. 1904, da. of J. Allen; 2ndly, 1908, Gladys (Westmorland Lodge,
27, Inner Park Rd., Wimbledon Common, SW19), da. of the late Louis Otto Law:—
(By 2nd m.) Robert Louis, b. 1910; formerly Lt. Indian Army.——Marianne Sheila Lindsay, b. 1914:
m. 1935, Thomas Bogue Alder, of The Flatt, Midlem, Selkirk, Roxburghshire, and has issue living,
Lucinda Ann, b. 1936,—Hermione Sarah, b. 1941.

Granddaughter of the late Rev. Thomas Charles Underwood Molesworth, 5th son
of Maj.-Gen. Hickman Thomas Molesworth (ante):—
Issue of the late Lt.-Col. Richard Cecil Molesworth, b. 1898, d. 1974: m. 1933, Susan (Orchard
Farm House, St. Catherine, Bath), da. of Harry Bazeley, of Bideford, N. Devon:—
Gillian Ann, b. 1935: m. 1959, Dr. John Dupré, of 111, Elm St., Baie d'Urpé, Montreal, Canada, and
has issue living, Matthew, b. 1961,—Luke, b. 1972,—Louisa, b. 1962.

Grandsons of the late Col. Richard Piggot Molesworth, CMG, 6th son of Maj.-Gen.
Hickman Thomas Molesworth (ante):—
Issue of the late Maj. Ralph Gerard Lindsay Molesworth, b. 1910, d. 1960: m. 1st, 1933,
Eleanor, el. da. of R. G. Rooke; 2ndly, 1948, Valerie St. Claire (10, Birch House, Limewood
Close, Bassett, Southampton), da. of Charles Francis Earle:—
(By 1st m.) Christopher Ralph, b. 1934.——Anthony John Lindsay, b. 1936.——(by 2nd m.) Richard
Charles Lindsay, b. 1950.

Granddaughter of the late Maj.-Gen. Hickman Thomas Molesworth (ante):—
**Issue of the late Col. Herbert Ellicombe Molesworth, C.M.G., D.S.O., b. 1872, d. 1941: m.
1914, Eileen Mary, who d. 1969, dau. of Col. Henry Waugh Renny-Tailyour, of Borrow-
field, co. Forfar [V. Powerscourt]:—**
Phyllis Eileen, b. 1914: m. 1956, Cyril Pickard, of 57, West End, Redruth, Cornwall.——Betty Lindsay,
b. 1919: m. 1946, Frederick A. Craswell, of Rising Sun, Boutport St., Barnstaple, Devon, and has
issue living, Lindsay, b. 1951.

**Issue of the late Brigadier Alec Lindsay Mortimer Molesworth, C.I.E., b. 1881, d. 1939 :
m. 1st, 1915, Esther Alice, who d. 1935, dau. of the late W. H. Taylor, of Buenos Aires;
2ndly, 1936, Hilda (now of 50, Courtfield Gardens, S.W.7), dau. of Alfred Henry Miles,
O.B.E., of Wellington, New Zealand :—**
(By 1st marriage) Lindsay Diana, b. 1916: m. 1940, Com. Reginald Nevill Da Costa Porter, M.B.E.,
R.N., and has issue living, Jeremy Nevill, b. 1948,—Valerie Lindsay, b. 1942. Residence,—Old
Pound Cottage, Chertsey Rd., Chobham, Surrey.

Grandchildren of Hickman Molesworth (b. 1842), el. son of Sir Robert Molesworth,
son of Hickman Blayney Molesworth, 2nd son of Capt. Robert Molesworth (ante):—
Issue of the late Surg.-Lt. Hickman Walter Lancelot Molesworth, FRCS, b. 1892, d. 1969:
   m. 1923, Caryl Margaret (De Quetteville, St. Jacques, Guernsey), da. of Stanley Hoare, of
   17, Cornwall Terr., Regent's Park, NW:—
Robert Stanley Hickman (The Cottage, Grange Rd., Widmer End, High Wycombe), b. 1934; solicitor
   1963: m. 1965, Ann, da. of A. Metcalfe-Gibson, of Greensidehead, Ravenstonedale, Westmorland,
   and has issue living, William Metcalfe, b. 1968,—Philip Hoare, b. 1970,—Catherine Jessie, b. 1966.——
   Richard Baxter, (c/o New Zealand Breweries, PO Box 3347, Wellington, NZ), b. 1939: m. 1966, Ann
   Kathleen Duncan, da. of F. N. H. Pexton, of Le Jardin Renaut, St. Saviour's, Guernsey, and has issue
   living, Edward James Hickman, b. 1967,—Rachel Jane, b. 1970,—Victoria Bridget, b. 1975.——
   Bridget Margaret, b. 1931: m. 1954, John Ormerod Heyworth, of Pucklechurch, Rockshaw Rd.,
   Merstham, Surrey, and has issue living, James Hickman Frederick, b. 1958,—Peter Lawrence
   Ormerod, b. 1963,—Caroline Margaret, b. 1956.

Granddaughter of Sir Robert Molesworth (ante):—
Issue of the late Hickman Molesworth (Judge of Court of Insolvency, Victoria), b. 1842,
   d. 1907: m. 1st, 1868, Elizabeth Emily, who d. 1881, dau. of William Rudledge ; 2ndly,
   1882, Alice Henrietta, who d. 1927, dau. of Ffloyd Minter Peck, surgeon, of Newmarket
   and Sale:—
(By 2nd m.) Œnone Florence Mary, b. 1888: m. 1st, 1911, Capt. Francis Buchanan Lefroy, who d. 1913;
   2ndly, 1921, Geoffrey H. Palmer. Residence,—24C, Brunswick Gdns., W8.

Grandchildren of the late Robert Arthur Molesworth, 2nd son of Sir Robert Moles-
   worth (ante):—
Issue of the late John Matheson Molesworth, b. 1878. d. 1942: m. 1906, Elizabeth Flora
   Frances Hill who d. 1952, dau. of the late Edwin M. James, M.R.C.S.E. :—
Richard William Edwin, b. 1908: m. 1937, Dirleen Muriel, dau. of Leslie Sprague, of Charlemont,
   Geelong, Australia, and has issue living, Michael John Leslie, b. 1941,—Simon Richard b. 1954,—
   Dirleen Corinne, b. 1949. Residence,—Cowl-Cowl, Linacre Road, Hampton, Victoria, Australia.——
   John Robert Nassau, DFC (Ballark, Morrisons, Vic., Aust.) b. 1910; Sqdn. Ldr. RAAF, and a Councillor,
   Coleraineshire, Vic., Aust.; 1939-45 War (DFC): m. 1940, Sheila Morrell, da. of Charles Armytage,
   of The Wilderness, Coleraine, Vic., Aust., and has issue living, Robert John Armytage, b. 1941,—
   John Denis Peter, b. 1944,—Morrell Frances Armytage, b. 1945: m. 1969, Michael Guy Earle [see
   Earle, Bt., colls.],—Jackalyn Armytage, b. 1949.——John Bysse, b. 1912; Private Austn. Mil. Forces;
   New Guinea 1942-44: m. 1941, Jessie Martha, da. of W. Thomas, of Chatres Towers, Qld., and has
   issue living, David John, b. 1942,—Judith Hill, b. 1946. Residence,—Abbington, Gordon, Victoria,
   Australia.——Edwin Noel Waulter, b. 1916; is a Councillor (Past Pres.), Ballanshire, Victoria,
   Australia: m. 1940, Alison Mary, da. of the late W. A. Dalrymple, of Glenluce, Gisborne, Victoria,
   Australia, and has issue living, William Anthony Hill, b. 1941,—Richard Matheson, b. 1948.
   Residence,—Emly Park, Ballan, Victoria, Australia.——Flora Roma Maroa, b. 1907: m. 1939, Frank
   Hobill Cole, and has issue living, Robert Molesworth, b. 1940,—Frank Molesworth, b. 1948,—Letitia
   Molesworth, b. 1941,—Rowena Molesworth, b. 1943.——Mary Margaret Hill, b. 1922: m. 1943,
   Richard Sladen Hope, and has issue living, Christopher Salden, b. 1947,—Roland Molesworth, b.
   1949,—Linden Kenny (son), b. 1954. Residence,—Burlendi, Coleraine, Victoria, Australia.

PREDECESSORS.—[1] ROBERT Molesworth, P.C., successively M.P. for Swords, St. Michael,
   Bodmin, and E. Retford, Ambassador to Copenhagen, and Commr. of Trade Plantations ; cr.
   Baron Philipstown, of Swords, and Viscount Molesworth (peerage of Ireland) 1716 ; d. 1725 ; s.
   by his el. son [2] JOHN, 2nd Viscount ; was successively Ambassador to Tuscany, Sardinia,
   Florence, Venice, and Turin ; d. 1726 ; s. by his brother [3] RICHARD, P.C., 3rd Viscount ; an
   eminent soldier, attained the rank of Field-Marshal ; sat as M.P. for Swords 1714 ; was A.D.C.
   to Duke of Marlborough (whose life he saved) at Ramillies, Lieut.-Gen. of the Ordnance 1739,
   and Com. in Ch. of the Forces in Ireland 1751 ; d. 1758 ; s. by his son [4] RICHARD NASSAU, 4th
   Viscount ; d. unmarried 1793, when the honours reverted to his cousin [5] ROBERT 5th Viscount,
   el. son of the Hon. William, M.P., 3rd son of 1st Viscount ; d. 1813 ; s. by his son [6] WILLIAM
   JOHN, 6th Viscount ; a Maj.-Gen. in the Army ; d. 1815 ; s. by his cousin [7] RICHARD PIGOTT,
   7th Viscount, el. son of Richard, 3rd son of the Hon. William, M.P. (ante) ; d. unmarried 1875 ;
   s. by his nephew [8] Rev. SAMUEL (son of Capt. John, R.N., 3rd son of Richard (ante), by Louisa,
   dau. of the late Rev. Dr. Tomkyns), 8th Viscount ; b. 1829 ; R. of St. Petrock Minor : m. 1st, 1862,
   Georgina Charlotte Cecil, who d. 1879, dau. of George Bagot Gosset, formerly of 4th Dragoon
   Guards ; 2ndly, 1883, Agnes, who d. 1905, dau. of the late Dugald Dove, of Nutshill, Renfrewshire,
   d. 1906 ; s. by his son [9] GEORGE BAGOT, 9th Viscount ; b. 1867 : m. 1894, Nina Alida, who d.
   1958, dau. of the late Col. H. D. Faulkner, 42nd Madras Inf. ; d. 1947 ; s. by his brother [10]
   CHARLES RICHARD, 10th Viscount ; b. 1869: m. 1906, Elizabeth Gladys who d. 1974, da. of the late
   Edward Martin Langworthy ; d. 1961 ; s. by his son [11] RICHARD GOSSETT, 11th Viscount and
   present peer ; also Baron Philipstown.

By industry and hope.

MOLSON, BARON. (Molson.) [Life Baron 1961.]

(ARTHUR) HUGH ELSDALE MOLSON,
P.C., son of the late Major John Elsdale Molson, M.P., of Goring Hall,
Worthing ; b. June 29th, 1903 ; ed. at
Lancing, and at New Coll., Oxford ;
was Parliamentary Sec., Min. of Works
1951-3, Joint Parliamentary Sec., Min.
of Transport and Civil Aviation 1953-7,
and Min. of Works 1957-9 ; a Member
of Monckton Commn. on Constitution
of Federation of Rhodesia and Nyasaland 1960 ; Chm. of Commn. of Privy
Councillors on Buganda-Bunyoro
boundary dispute 1962 ; European
War 1939-45, with 36th Searchlight
Regt., R.A., and as Staff Capt. 11th
Anti-Aircraft Div.; sat as M.P. for

Doncaster Div. of W. Riding of Yorkshire Oct. 1931 to Nov. 1935 (when he was defeated), and for High Peak Div. of Derbyshire Oct. 1939 to Jan. 1961; cr. P.C. 1956, and *Baron Molson*, of High Peak, co. Derby (Life Baron) 1961: *m.* 1949, Nancy, dau. of the late W. H. Astington, of Bramhall, Cheshire.

Arms,—Per pale azure and gules three crescents argent on a chief ermine a lion passant guardant or between two roses of the third barbed and seeded proper. **Crest,**—A crescent argent between two wings the dexter gules, the sinister azure, each charged with a maple leaf or. **Supporters,**—On either side a golden retriever dog proper gorged with a collar indented throughout or and gules lines sable.
Residences,—14, Wilton Cres., S.W.1; Cherrytrees, Kelso, Roxburghshire. *Clubs,*—Athenæum, Carlton.

MONCK, VISCOUNT. (Monck.) **Sits as BARON (U.K. 1866). [Viscount I. 1801.]**

Boldly, faithfully, successfully.

FORTITER FIDELITER FELICITER

HENRY WYNDHAM STANLEY MONCK, O.B.E., 6th Viscount ; *b.* Dec. 11th, 1905 ; *s.* 1927 ; ed. at Eton ; formerly Lieut. Coldstream Guards (Reserve) ; is a JP and a DL for Hampshire, a former Co. Dir.; and Vice-Chm. of National Asso. of Boys' Clubs since 1938; OBE (Civil) 1961: *m.* 1st, 1937 (m. diss. 1951), (Gertrude) Eva Maria, Baroness Vreto, dau. of Professor Zaunmuller-Freudenthaler, of Vienna ; 2ndly, 1951, Brenda Mildred, dau. of the late G. W. Adkins, of Bower's Close, Harpenden, Herts, and has issue by 2nd marriage.

Arms,—Gules, a chevron between three lions, heads erased argent. **Crest,**—A dragon passant wings elevated sable. **Supporters,—***Dexter*, a dragon ; *sinister*, a lion ; both argent, and holding in the fore paw a branch of laurel resting on the shoulder fructed proper.

Residence,—Hurstbourne Priors House, Whitchurch, Hants.

SONS LIVING. (*By 2nd marriage.*)
Hon. CHARLES STANLEY, *b.* April 2nd, 1953.
Hon. George Stanley, *b.* 1957.
Hon. James Stanley, *b.* 1961.

SISTERS LIVING. (*Raised to the rank of a Viscount's daughters* 1928.)
Hon. Elisabeth Noel, *b.* 1908 : *m.* 1928, William Frederic Batt, M.B.E., D.L., J.P., formerly Major Coldstream Guards, and has issue living, Simon William (The Old Rectory, Fordham, Colchester, Essex), *b.* 1931; ed. at Winchester; late Lt. Coldstream Guards: *m.* 1963, Julia Katherine, da. of R. H. M. Clayton, of 14, De Walden St., W, and has issue living, Frederick Robert *b.* 1964, Edward Alexander *b.* 1966,—Caroline Mary, *b.* 1934: *m.* 1957, Capt. Edward Brewster Taylor, of Kingole Farm, Lostwithiel, Cornwall, and has issue living, David Michael *b.* 1959, William Thomas *b.* 1961, Katharine Elizabeth *b.* 1963, Naomi Anne *b.* 1967,—Sarah Elisabeth, *b.* 1938: *m.* 1958, Capt. Peter Thomas Thistlethwayte, late Rifle Bde., of East Donyland Hall, Colchester, Essex, and has issue living, Katharine Miranda *b.* 1960, Carina Rachel *b.* 1964, Annabel Tania *b.* 1966. *Residence,*—Chaucer's Farm, Gresham, Norwich, Norfolk.
Hon. Mary Patricia, *b.* 1911 : *m.* 1935, Brigadier (Charles) Hilary Vaughan Pritchard, D.S.O., J.P., D.L. (retired), who assumed by deed poll 1956 the surname of Vaughan in lieu of his patronymic; late Roy. Welch Fusiliers and Parachute Regt., and has issue living, Susan Katharine Vaughan, *b.* 1936: *m.* 1957, David Spencer Muirhead, of Shuckburgh House, Naseby, Northants.,—Molly Cecilia Vaughan, *b.* 1941: *m.* 1962, Ian Hewitt Davies, of 12, Chalcot Sq., NW1,—Patricia Nesta Vaughan (twin), *b.* 1941,—Jane Arabella Vaughan, *b.* 1945: *m.* 1970, David Patrick M. Allen, of 87, Latymer Court, W6. *Residence,*—Maesybryner, Dolgellau, Merioneth.

PREDECESSORS.—[1] CHARLES STANLEY Monck; cr. *Baron Monck*, of Ballytrammon (peerage of Ireland) 1797, and *Viscount Monck* (peerage of Ireland) 1801; *d.* 1802; *s.* by his el. **son** [2] HENRY STANLEY, 2nd Viscount; cr. *Earl of Rathdowne* (peerage of Ireland) 1822; *d.* 1848, when the earldom expired and the barony and viscountcy devolved upon his brother [3] CHARLES JOSEPH KELLY, 3rd Viscount; *b.* 1791: *m.* 1817, Bridget, dau. of the late John Willington, Esq., of Killoskehane, co. Tipperary; *d.* 1849; *s.* by his son [4] CHARLES STANLEY, G.C.M.G., P.C., 4th Viscount, *b.* 1819; M.P. for Portsmouth 1852-7; was a Lord of the Treasury 1855-8, Gov.-Gen. of Canada 1861-7, and of Dominion of Canada 1867-8, Ch. Commr.

in Ireland 1869-81, and Lord-Lieut. of co. Dublin 1874-92; **cr.** *Baron Monck* (peerage of United Kingdom) 1866: *m.* 1844, his cousin, Lady Elizabeth Louise Mary Monck, who *d.* 1892, dau. of 1st Earl of Rathdowne (*ext.*); *d.* 1894; *s.* by his son [5] HENRY POWER CHARLES STANLEY, 5th Viscount; *b.* 1849; Vice-Lieut. co. Wicklow (High Sheriff 1887): *m.* 1874, Lady Edith Caroline Sophia Scott, who *d.* 1929, dau. of 3rd Earl of Clonmell; *d.* 1927; *s.* by his grandson [6] HENRY WYNDHAM STANLEY [son of the late Capt. the Hon. Charles Henry Stanley Monck (who *d.* killed in action 1914), el. son of 5th Viscount], 6th Viscount and present peer; also Baron Monck.

MONCKTON OF BRENCHLEY, VISCOUNT. (Monckton.) [Viscount U.K. 1957.]

To spread fame by deeds.

GILBERT WALTER RIVERS-DALE MONCKTON, *CB, OBE, MC,* 2nd Viscount; *b.* Nov. 3rd, 1915; *s.* 1965; ed. at Harrow, and Trin. Coll., Camb (MA); Maj.-Gen. (ret.), late 12th R. Lancers, formerly 5th R. Inniskilling Dragoon Gds; Col. 9th/12th R. Lancers 1967-73; Hon. Col. Kent and Sharp-shooters Yeo. 1974; Dairy Farmer; Chm. of Monckton and Partners, Ltd.; a Dir. of Anglo Portuguese Bank, United & General Trust, and Ransome Hoffmann Pollard, Ltd; Comdg. RAC, 3rd Div. 1958-63, Dep. Dir. of Personnel Admin. 1962, Dir. of Public Relations, War Office 1960-65, and Ch. of Staff, HQ, BAOR 1965-67; Pres. Kent Assocn. of Boys' Clubs and Inst. of Heraldic and Genealogical Studies 1965, of Kent Archaeological Assocn. and of Medway Productivity Assocn. since 1968, County Vice-Chm. of Scout Assocn.
(Kent) 1968-74; a DL of Kent; Pres. of British Assocn. Order of Malta since 1974; Pres. of Anglo-Belgian Union 1974; 1939-45 War (MC); Korea 1951-52; a Liveryman of Broderers' Co., Bailiff Grand Cross of Obedience Sovereign Mil. Order of Malta, and KStJ (Chm. of Council of Order of St. John for Kent 1969-75); Cdr. of Order of the Crown of Belgium; OBE (Mil) 1956, CB (Mil) 1966: *m.* 1950, Marianna Laetitia, da. of Cdr. Robert Tatton Bower, RN [By. Strickland], and has issue.

Arms.—Quarterly; 1st and 4th, sable, on a chevron between three martlets or, as many mullets of the field, *Monckton*; 2nd and 3rd, or a chevron gules a chief vair (*St. Quintin*). **Crest.**—On a wreath sable and or a martlet or. **Supporters.**—On either side a horse argent crined and unguled or gorged with a chain gold pendent therefrom an escutcheon sable charged with a rose also argent barbed and seeded proper.
Residence.—Runhams Farm, Runham Lane, Harrietsham, Maidstone, Kent, ME17 1NJ. *Clubs.*—Brooks's, Cavalry, MCC, Casino Maltese (Valetta).

SONS LIVING.
Hon. CHRISTOPHER WALTER, *b.* Feb. 14th, 1952; ed. at Harrow, and Churchill Coll., Camb. (BA); OStJ, Kt. of Honour and Devotion Sovereign Mil. Order of Malta; a Liveryman of Broderers' Co.; a journalist Yorkshire Post Newspapers, Ltd., Leeds.
Hon. Timothy David Robert, *b.* 1955; ed. at Harrow, and Roy. Agric. Coll., Cirencester.
Hon. Jonathan Riversdale St. Quintin (twin), *b.* 1955; ed. at Worth.
Hon. Anthony Leopold Colyer, *b.* 1960; ed. a Harrow.

DAUGHTER LIVING.
Hon. Rosamond Mary, *b.* 1953.

SISTER LIVING.
Hon. Valerie Hamilton (*Hon. Lady Goulding*), *b.* 1918; Hon. LLD, National Univ. of Ireland; late Subaltern WRAC (Reserve); Chm. and Man. Dir. Central Remedial Clinic, Dublin; Dame of Honour and Devotion, Sovereign Mil. Order of Malta: *m.* 1939, Wing Com. Sir William Basil Goulding, 3rd Bt. *Residences,*—Ballyrusheen, co. Cork; Dargle Cottage, Enniskerry, co. Wicklow.

WIDOW LIVING OF FIRST VISCOUNT.
BRIDGET HELEN RUTHVEN, CBE (*Dowager Viscountess Monckton of Brenchley*) (113, Eaton Sq., SW1), Lady Ruthven of Freeland (in her own right), da. of Walter Patrick Hore-Ruthven, CB, CMG, DSO, 9th Lord Ruthven of Freeland, and formerly wife of 11th Earl of Carlisle [see Ruthven of Freeland, Lady]: *m.* 1947, as his 2nd wife, the 1st Viscount Monckton of Brenchley, GCVO, KCMG, MC, PO, QC, who *d.* 1965.

PREDECESSOR.—[1] *Rt. Hon. Sir* WALTER TURNER Monckton, *GCVO, KCMG, MC, PC, QC,* son of Frank William Monckton, of Ightham Warren, Kent; *b.* 1891; Attorney-Gen. to Duchy of Cornwall 1932-47 and 1948-51, Dir.-Gen. of Min. of Information, and an Additional Dep. Under-Sec. of State for Foreign Affairs 1940, Head of Information Sers. Cairo 1941-42, Solicitor Gen. 1945, Min. of Labour and Nat. Ser. 1951-55, Min. of Defence 1955-56, and Paymaster-Gen. 1956-57; MP for Bristol West (*C*) 1951-57; cr. *Viscount Monckton of Brenchley,* of Brenchley, co. Kent (peerage of UK) 1947: *m.* 1st, 1914, Mary Adelaide Somes (who *d.* 1964, having obtained a divorce 1957), da. of Sir Thomas Colyer Colyer-Ferguson, 3rd Bt.; 2ndly, 1947, Bridget Helen, Lady Ruthven of Freeland (in her own right); *d.* 1965; *s.* by his only son [2] GILBERT WALTER RIVERSDALE, *CB, OBE, MC,* 2nd Viscount and present peer.

MONCREIFF, BARON. (Moncreiff.) [Baron U.K. 1873, Bt. S. 1626 and U.K. 1871.]

On nope.

HARRY ROBERT WELLWOOD MONCREIFF, 5th Baron and 15th Baronet of Moncreiff, and 5th of Tulliebole; *b.* Feb. 4th, 1915; *s.* 1942; ed. at Fettes Coll. ; Major (retired) R.A.S.C. Burma 1939-45 (despatches) : *m.* 1952, Enid Marion Watson, only dau. of Major Henry Watson Locke, of Belmont, Dollar, and has issue.

Arms,—Quarterly : 1st and 4th **argent, a lion rampant** gules, armed and langued azure, a chief ermine; 2nd and 3rd **argent, an oak tree** issuing out of a well in base proper, Crest,—A demi-lion rampant, as in the arms. Supporters,—Two men armed cap-a-pie, holding in the exterior hand a spear resting on the shoulder all proper, the breastplate charged with a crescent gules.

Seat,—Tulliebole Castle, Kinross-shire.

SON LIVING.
Hon. RHODERICK HARRY WELLWOOD, *b.* March 22nd, 1954.

BROTHERS LIVING.
Hon. Donald Graham Fitz-Herbert, *b.* 1919 ; sometime Capt. Argyll and Sutherland Highlanders : *m.* 1955, Catriona Sheila MacDonald, and has issue living, Ranald Patrick MacDonald, *b.* 1965,—Barbara Jane, *b.* 1957,—Frances Catriona FitzHerbert *b.* 1959,—Theresa Madeleine FitzHerbert, *b.* 1961.

Residence,—Glenleacnamuidhe, Ballachulish, Argyll. *Club,*—New (Edinburgh).

Hon. Robert Frederick Arthur (c/o Royal Hotel, Stow, Midlothian), *b.* 1924: *m.* 1951, Aileen Margaret Marr, da. of Robert Marr Meldrum, LDS, PhD, and has issue living, Richard Gerard Arthur, *b.* 1964, —Gillian Nicola Ann, *b.* 1954.

SISTERS LIVING.
Hon. Lilian Vida Lechmere, *b.* 1912 : *m.* 1942, David Robert Young, and has issue living, Robert Arthur Moncreiff, *b.* 1944,—Caroline Vida Rosemary, *b.* 1951. *Residence,*—Tanworth, Fossoway, Kinross-shire.

Hon. Nicola Gladys, *b.* 1917 : *m.* 1st, 1940, Capt. Frederick W. Gifford, R.A., who *d.* (killed in action) 1943; 2ndly, 1946, Charles John Derek Renny, who *d.* 1970, late Lt. RNVR, and had isssue living, (by 1st m.) James Alexander Moncreiff, *b.* 1942,—(by 2nd m.) Nicholas Charles Moncreiff, *b.* 1954,—Susan Miranda Fitzherbert, *b.* 1950: *m.* 1972, Anthony John O'Donnell, MB, BS, of 31, Church Vale, E. Finchley, N2,—Prudence Jane Fitzherbert, *b.* 1952. *Residence,*—The Hermitage, St. Martin's, Guernsey.

Hon. Pamela Anne, *b.* 1927; MB, ChB Edinburgh 1949: *m.* 1951, Edward James White, and has issue living, a son, *b.* 19—,—a son, *b.* 19—,—a da., *b.* 19—, a da., *b.* 19—.

COLLATERAL BRANCHES LIVING.

Granddaughter of the late Hon. James William Moncreiff (infra):—
Issue of the late Edwin Robert Moncreiff, *b.* 1877, *d.* 1962: *m.* 1904, Mary, who *d.* 1953, dau. of the late Matthew Montgomerie Bell, W.S., of Edinburgh:—
Mary Eileen, *b.* 1909: *m.* 1st, 1929, Maj. John Roy Oakley, Roy. Scots, who *d.* (killed in action in Palestine) 1939; 2ndly, 1939, Capt. Charles Philip McLaughlan, Architect, and has issue living, (by 2nd m.) Ian Wellwood, *b.* 1940; Maj. Scots Guards,—Ann Wellwood, *b.* 1944: *m.* 1965, David Godfrey-Faussett and has issue living, Katherine Sarah *b.* 1971.

Issue of the late Hon. James William Moncreiff, 3rd son of 1st Baron, *b.* 1845, *d.* 1920: *m.* 1872, Mary Lillias, who *d.* 1910, dau. of George Mitchell-Innes, of Bangour, N.B.:—
William Francis, *b.* 1882. Resides in British Columbia.

Grandchildren of the late Hon. Francis Jeffrey Moncreiff, 5th son of 1st Baron:—
Issue of the late James Hamilton Moncreiff, *b.* 1872, *d.* 1923 : *m.* 1905, Elizabeth Lilian, who *d.* 1950, dau. of Charles Harvey :—
Rt. Rev. Francis Hamilton (19, Eglinton Cres., Edinburgh, EH11 5BY), *b.* 1906; ed. at St. John's Coll., Camb. (MA); Hon. D.D. Glasgow, R. of St. Salvador's Church, Edinburgh 1947-50, and Canon of St. Mary's Cathedral, Edinburgh 1950-52; Bishop of Glasgow and Galloway 1952-73; Primus of Episcopal Church in Scotland since 1962.——Frederick Henry Wellwood, *b.* 1909; ed. at Pembroke Coll., Camb. (MA); is Flt. Lt. RAF: *m.* 1939, Gwendolen Alma, da. of P. Gifford, and has issue living, Andrew Malcolm (23, Cadogan Gdns., SW3), *b.* 1944; ed. at Pembroke Coll., Camb. (MA): *m.* 1971, Jennifer Margaret, dau. of John Chapman, of Johannesburg, and has issue living, Michael Patrick *b.* 1974,—Patricia Jane (17, Whiteheads Grove, SW3), *b.* 1941. *Residence,*—Sinoia, Rhodesia.

Issue of the late Major **Norman Halliday** Moncreiff, *b.* 1886, *d.* (of wounds in action during European War) 1916: *m.* 1912, Lucy Anna (who *d.* 1964, having *m.* 2ndly, 1921, Maj. Guy Fletcher Luther, late Sherwood Foresters, who *d.* 1953), da. of the Rev. Edward William Collinson, formerly of Casa Sicna, Freshford, Bath:—
Margaret Mildred, *b.* 1913. *Residence,*—85, Iverna Court, W8.——Elizabeth Cleather, *b.* 1915. *Residence,*—Sithean, Gilmerton, by Crieff, Perthshire.

PREDECESSORS.—[1] JOHN Moncreiff, *M.P.*, cr. a *Baronet* 1626 (of Moncreiff) with remainder to heirs male whatsoever; *d.* 1650; *s.* by his el. son [2] JOHN, 2nd Bt., who in 1663 sold the Moncreiff estates to his cousin Thomas Moncreiff, who in 1685 was cr. a *Baronet*; *d.* 1675; *s.* by his brother [3] DAVID, 3rd Bt.; *s.* by his brother [4] JAMES, 4th Bt., at whose decease the direct line of the 1st Bt. expired and the baronetcy reverted to the son of Hugh Moncreiff, youngest brother of the 1st Bt. [5] JOHN, 5th Bt.; was an eminent Physician; *d.* 1710; *s.* by his son [6] HUGH, 6th Bt.; *d.* 1744; *s.* by his kinsman, a descendant of Archibald Moncreiff, uncle of 1st Bt. [7] *Rev.* WILLIAM, 7th Bt.; *d.* 1767; *s.* by his son [8] *Rev.* HENRY, *D.D.*; was an eminent Divine of the Church of Scotland; assumed the additional surname of Wellwood; *d.* 1827; *s.* by his son [9] JAMES WELLWOOD, 9th Bt.; *b.* 1776; was a Lord of Session and Justiciary of Scotland 1829-51: *m.* 1808, Ann, who *d.* 1843, dau. of Capt. George Robertson, R.N.; *d.* 1851: *s.* by his son [10] *Rev.* HENRY WELLWOOD, *D.D.*, 10th Bt.; was an eminent Divine of the Free Church of Scotland; *d.s.p.* 1883; *s.* by his brother [11] JAMES, *P.C.*, *LL.D.*, 11th Bt., who had previously been cr. a *Baronet* (of Tulliebole) 1871, and *Baron Moncreiff*, of Tulliebole, co. Kinross (peerage of United Kingdom) 1873; *b.* 1811; M.P. for Leith Dist. (*L*) 1851-9, for Edinburgh 1859-68, and for Glasgow and Aberdeen Univs. 1868-9; was Dean of Faculty of Advocates for Scotland 1858-69, Solicitor-Gen. for Scotland 1850-51, Lord Advocate 1851, 1852-8, 1859-66, and 1868-9, and Lord Justice-Clerk 1869-88: *m.* 1834, Isabella, who *d.* 1881, dau. of Robert Bell, Sheriff of Berwick and Haddington; *d.* 1895; *s.* by his el. son [12] HENRY JAMES, 2nd Baron; *b.* 1840; Sheriff of Renfrew and Bute 1881-8, and a Judge of Court of Session, Scotland (with title of *Lord Wellwood*) 1888-1905: *m.* 1st, 1866, Susan Wilhelmine, who *d.* 1869, 3rd dau. of Sir William H. Dick-Cunyngham, 8th Bt.; 2ndly, 1873, Millicent Julia, who *d.* 1881, dau. of the late Col. Fryer, of Moulton Paddocks, Newmarket; *d.* 1909; *s.* by his brother [13] *Rev.* ROBERT CHICHESTER, 3rd Baron; *b.* 1843, V. of Tanworth 1885-1913: *m.* 1871, Florence Kate, who *d.* 1926, dau. of the late Lieut.-Col. Richard Henry FitzHerbert: *d.* 1913; *s.* by his son [14] JAMES ARTHUR FITZHERBERT, 4th Baron; *b.* 1872: *m.* 1906, Lucy Vida, who *d.* 1973, da. of David Lechmere Anderson LRCP, of Doncaster; *d.* 1942; *s.* by his el. son [15] HARRY ROBERT WELLWOOD, 5th Baron and present peer.

MONK BRETTON, BARON. (Dodson.) [Baron U.K. 1884.]

Successful by favour of Providence.

JOHN CHARLES DODSON, 3rd Baron; *b.* July 17th, 1924; *s.* 1933; ed. at Westminster, and at New Coll., Oxford: *m.* 1958, Zoë Diana, da. of Ian Douglas Murray Scott, and has issue.

Arms,—Argent, on a fesse raguly plain cotised between six fleurs-de-lis all gules, a sword fesseways point to the dexter proper, pommel and hilt or. Crest,—Two lion's jambs erased and in saltire gules, entwined by a serpent, head to the dexter proper. Supporters,—On either side a female figure proper, vested argent, mantle azure, each resting the exterior hand on an antique shield also azure, adorned gold, that on the *dexter* charged with a balance suspended, and that on the *sinister*, with a staff erect entwined by a serpent all or.

Residence,—Shelley's Folly, Cooksbridge, nr. Lewes.　*Club,*—Brooks's.

SONS LIVING.

Hon. CHRISTOPHER MARK, *b.* Aug. 2nd, 1958.
Hon. Henry, *b.* 1960.

SISTER LIVING.

Hon. Priscilla (Lower Stoneham, Lewes), *b.* 1914: *m.* 1935, Maj. Claude Thorburn Knight, late Coldstream Guards, and has issue living, Christopher William, *b.* 1943: *m.* 1969, Sylvia Caroline, da. of Jonkheer Emile van Lennep, of 34, van der Burchlaan, The Hague,—Caroline Jane, *b.* 1935: *m.* 1956, Maj. Jerome Otway Fane De Salis, Welsh Guards, of Littlecroft, Eton Rd., Datchet, Slough, SL3 9AY, and has issue living, Nicholas Charles *b.* 1957, Rodolph William *b.* 1970, Henrietta Jane *b.* 1960,—Patricia Susan *b.* 1938: *m.* 1962, Timothy Lewis Achilles Daunt, c/o Foreign Office, SW1, and has issue living, Achilles James *b.* 1963, Eleanor *b.* 1965, Alice Louise *b.* 1969,—Sarah Georgiana Ann, *b.* 1945: *m.* 1970, Cdr. Timothy Michael Bevan, RN, and has issue living, Thomas Loraine *b.* 1972.

PREDECESSORS.—[1] *Rt. Hon.* JOHN GEORGE Dodson, *C.B.*, only son of the late Rt. Hon. Sir John Dodson, *LL.D.*, M.P. for Rye 1819-23; *b.* 1825; Dep. Speaker and Chm. of Committees of House of Commons 1865-72, Financial Sec. to the Treasury 1873-4, Pres. of Local Govt. Board 1880-82, and Chancellor of the Duchy of Lancaster 1882-4; M.P. for Sussex E. (*L*) 1857-74, for Chester 1874-80, and for Scarborough 1880-84; cr. *Baron Monk Bretton*, of Conyboro and Hurstpierpoint, co. Sussex (peerage of United Kingdom) 1884: *m.* 1856, Florence, dau. of W. J. Campion, of Danny, Sussex: *d.* 1897; *s.* by his son [2] JOHN WILLIAM, *C.B.*, 2nd Baron; *b.* 1869; a J.P. and D.L. for E. Sussex; Private Sec. to Sec. of State for Colonies 1900-1903; Chm. of London County Council 1929-30: *m.* 1911, Ruth, who *d.* 1967, da. of the late Hon. Charles Brand; *d.* 1933; *s.* by his son [3] JOHN CHARLES, 3rd Baron and present peer.

MONKSWELL, BARONY OF.   (Collier.) [Baron U.K. 1885, disclaimed 1964.]

WILLIAM ADRIAN LARRY COLLIER, *MB, BCh, DPH, b.* Nov. 25th, 1913; *s.* as 4th Baron Monkswell Jan 14th, 1964; disclaimed his peerage for life April 7th, 1964; ed. at Edinburgh Univ. (MB and BCh), DPH London; adopted the additional name of Larry 1932; Member of Halstead U.D.C. since 1954; 1939-45 War with R.A.M.C., in N.-W. Europe and Middle East; *m.* 1st, 1939 (marriage dissolved 1945), Erika, da. of Dr. E. Kellner; 2ndly, 1945 (marriage dissolved 1950), Helen, da. of James Dunbar, of Edinburgh; 3rdly, 1951, Nora Selby, and has issue by 2nd and 3rd marriages.

&rms,—Argent, on a chevron azure, between in chief two demi-unicornscourant and in base an elephant's head erased gules, three oak branches slipped, leaved and fructed or. Crest,—A demi-man affrontee proper, holding in the dexter hand an oak branch slipped and leaved proper, fructed or, and resting the sinister hand on an escutcheon azure, charged with two keys saltirewise or, Supporters,—(borne by Barons Monkswell) Two Druids vested argent, wreathed about the temples with laurel leaves vert, each resting the exterior hand on an escutcheon azure, charged with a balance suspended or.

Residence,—30, Chapel St., Halstead, Essex.

SONS LIVING. (*By 2nd marriage.*)
GERARD (of Curator's House, Royal Botanic Gdns., Edinburgh), *b.* Jan. 28th, 1947; ed. at George Heriot's Sch., Edinburgh.
Neill Adrian José (of Curator's House, Royal Botanic Gdns., Edinburgh), *b.* 1948.
(*By 3rd marriage.*)
Benjamino, *b.* 1958.

DAUGHTER LIVING. (*By 3rd marriage.*)
Tiaré Penelope Katherine, *b.* 1952.

BROTHERS LIVING.
Perceval Gerard (22, Courtland Drive, Chigwell, Essex), *b.* 1915: *m.* 1st, 1940 (m. diss. 1947), Loraine Walker; 2ndly, 1949, Sheila (DOE) Macpherson, and has issue living, (by 1st m.) Anthony Gerard, *b.* 1942,—(by 2nd m.) Gavin, *b.* 1951,—Jill Tessa, *b.* 1950.
John Bernard (52, Butt Rd., Colchester), *b.* 1920: *m.* 1947, Elsie Dunbar, and has issue living, Anna Lee, *b.* 1948,—Sarah, *b.* 1950.

SISTER LIVING.
Anna Evangeline, *b.* 1918: *m.* 1940, Elvin Thorgerson, of 19, Earl St., Cambridge, and has issue living, Storm Elvin, *b.* 1944.

DAUGHTER LIVING OF THIRD BARON.
Hon. Lorna Evelyn (23, Eastbury Av., Northwood, Middlesex), *b.* 1915.

WIDOW LIVING OF SON OF SECOND BARON.
Lena Victoria (Queenie) (Corscombe, Dorchester, Dorset), da. of the late James Kennedy, of Forfar. *m.* 1953, as his 2nd wife, the Hon. Eric (Cecil Frederick) Collier, who *d.* 1968.

WIDOW LIVING OF THIRD BARON.
KATHARINE EDITH (*Baroness Monkswell*) (49, Novello St., SW6), da. of William Shaw Harriss Gastrell, of Rockbeare Grange, nr. Exeter: *m.* 1925, as his 2nd wife, the 3rd Baron, who *d.* 1964.

COLLATERAL BRANCHES LIVING.
Issue of the late Hon. John Collier, O.B.E., 2nd son of 1st Baron, *b.* 1850, *d.* 1934: *m.* 1st, 1879, Marian, who *d.* 1887, 2nd dau. of the late Rt. Hon. Thomas Henry Huxley, LL.D., F.R.S.; 2ndly, 1889, his deceased wife's sister, Ethel Gladys, who *d.* 1941, 5th dau. of the late Rt. Hon. Thomas Henry Huxley, LL.D., F.R.S.:—
(By 2nd marriage) *Sir* Laurence, *K.C.M.G., b.* 1890 ; ed. at Bedales Sch., and at Balliol Coll., Oxford ; was Envoy Extraor, and Min. Plen. to Norwegian Govt. in London 1941-2, Ambassador Extraor. and Plen. to Govt. in London 1942-5, and at Oslo, 1945-51 ; C.M.G. 1934, K.C.M.G. 1944 : *m.* 1917, Eleanor Emma Antoinette, who *d.* 1975, only da. of the late William Luther Watson, S. Lancs. Regt., and has issue living, William Oswald (34, Berwyn Rd., Richmond, Surrey), *b.* 1919; ed. at Bradfield Coll., and at Balliol Coll., Oxford; FSA; FRHistS; *m.* 1st, 1947 (m. diss. 1957) the Hon. Muriel Joan Lowry Lamb, da. of 1st Baron Rochester; 2ndly, 1958, Ina Mary Grace, da. of C. Crowne, of Little-hampton, Sussex, and has issue living, (by 1st m.) Sylvia Antoinette *b.* 1952,—(by 2nd m.) Jonathan Charles Laurence *b.* 1959, Lucy Eleanor Mary *b.* 1961, Stella Catherine Juliet, *b.* 1965. *Residence,*—Monkswell Gate, 37, Granville Rd., Limpsfield, Surrey. *Club,*—Athenæum.——Joan, *b.* 1893: *m.* 1911, Brig.-Gen. Frank Anstie Buzzard, DSO, formerly RFA, who *d.* 1950, and has issue living, John Huxley (of Haxted House, Edenbridge, Kent), *b.* 1912; ed. at Wellington Coll., and at New Coll, Oxford; Bar. Inner Temple 1937, Bencher 1966; Recorder of Dover 1968; Circuit Judge of Central Criminal Court 1974: *m.* 1946, Hilary Ann Courtney, da. of H. A. Antrobus, of Buttle's Steps, Crockham Hill, and has issue living, Christopher John Huxley *b.* 1948, Thomas Courtney *b.* 1951, Jane Phyllida *b.* 1953,—Richard Bethane (of 80, Carlton Hill, NW8), *b.* 1915; ed. at Wellington Coll., and at Magdalen Coll., Oxford; appointed Dir., National Institute of Industrial Psychology 1968: *m.* 1948, the Hon. Ann Sophia Madeline Whitfield, da. of 1st Baron Kenswood, and has issue living, Nicholas John *b.* 1952, Jacqueline Frances *b.* 1950, Jennifer Ann *b.* 1954, Angela Caroline *b.* 1956,—Pamela Lois, *b.* 1917: *m.* 1941, E. Leo Cohen, of 1, Northcote House, Heath St., NW3, and has issue living, Jonathan Frank *b.* 1946, Joan Rosalind *b.* 1943: *m.* 1965, Clive Coates, of The Stone House, Lower Basildon, Reading (and has issue living, Ben Jonathan *b.* 1968, Emma Jane *b.* 1966)" Leonie Katharine *b.* 1950. *Residence,*—Haxted Cottage, Edenbridge, Kent.

PREDECESSORS—[1] *Rt. Hon. Sir* ROBERT PORRETT COLLIER ; was Solicitor-Gen. 1863-6, and Attorney-Gen. 1868-71; M.P. for Plymouth (*L*) 1852-71, and a Judge of Judicial Committee of Privy Council 1871-86; cr. *Baron Monkswell,* of Monkswell, co. Devon (peerage of United Kingdom), 1885 ; *b.* 1817: *m.* 1844, Isabella, who *d.* 1886, el. dau. of William Rose Rose, of Wolston Heath, Coventry ; *d.* Oct. 27th, 1886 ; *s.* by his el. son [2] ROBERT, 2nd Baron ; *b.* 1845 ; a Lord-in-Waiting to Queen Victoria 1892-5, and Under-Sec. of State for War 1895:

m. 1873, Mary Josephine, who *d.* 1930, dau. of the late Joseph Alfred Hardcastle, M.P.; *d.* 1909; *s.* by his el. son [3] ROBERT ALFRED HARDCASTLE, 3rd Baron, *b.* 1875; 2nd Sec. Foreign office 1905-10: *m.* 1908, Ursula Mary, who *d.* 1915, da. of Col. Hugh Gurney Barclay, MVO, of Colney Hall, Norwich [B. Magheramorne]; 2ndly, 1925, Katharine Edith, da. of William Shaw Harriss Gastrell, of Rockbeare Grange, nr. Exeter; *d.* 1964; *s.* by his nephew [4] WILLIAM ADRIAN LARRY (son of the late Hon. Gerard Collier, 2nd son of 2nd Baron), 4th Baron, until he disclaimed his peerage 1964.

MONSELL, VISCOUNT. (Eyres Monsell.) [Viscount U.K. 1935.]

HENRY BOLTON GRAHAM EYRES MONSELL, 2nd Viscount; *b.* Nov. 21st, 1905; *s.* 1969; ed. at Eton; Lt.-Col. Intelligence Corps; 1939-45 War (despatches); has Medal of Freedom with bronze palm of USA.

Arms,—1st and 4th argent, on a chevron between three mullets sable a trefoil slipped or, *Monsell;* 2nd sable, on a chevron nebuly plain cottised between three cinquefoils or as many woolpacks proper, and for distinction a canton argent, *Eyres;* 3rd per fesse argent and or a fess chequey gules and of the first in chief a lion rampant between two crosses patée, of the third, and for distinction a canton sable, *Kettleworth.* Crests,—1st a lion rampant proper holding between the paws a mullet sable, *Monsell;* 2nd upon a mount vert a human leg couped at the thigh, in armour quarterlys able and or, the spur gold, on either side three cinquefoils slipped vert—the leg charged for distinction with a cross crosslet argent, *Eyres.* Supporters,—On either side a sea lion per chevron argent and sable semée of mullets countercharged.

Residence,—The Mill House, Dumbleton, Evesham, Worcs.

SISTERS LIVING.

Hon. Diana Sybil, *b.* 1907: *m.* 1935, Lieut.-Col. Alan Stuart Casey, Roy. Dragoons, who *d.* 1958, and has issue living, Michael Alan Eyres (Eastington Manor, Northleach, Glos.), *b.* 1943: *m.* 1968, Gillian Jamesina, da. of the late Cdr. G. B. Herbert-Jones, RNR,—Bridget Sarah, *b.* 1938: *m.* 1959, Kenneth Hamilton Muir Jack, of Abbey Cottage, Pipewell, Kettering [see Inglefield-Watson, Bt., colls.],—Susan Diana, *b.* 1940. *Residence,*—Nutmeadow House, Dumbleton, Evesham, Worcs.
Hon. Joan Elizabeth, *b.* 1912: *m.* 1st, 1939 (m. diss. 1947), William John Rayner, O.B.E.; 2ndly, 1968, Patrick Michael Leigh Fermor, DSO, OBE. *Residence.*—Kardamyli, Messenia, Greece.

WIDOW LIVING OF FIRST VISCOUNT.

ESSEX LEILA HILARY, (*Viscountess Monsell*), da. of the late Lt.-Col. the Hon. (Edward) Gerald Fleming French, DSO [see E. Ypres, colls.], and formerly wife of Vyvyan Drury: *m.* 1950, as his 2nd wife the 1st Viscount, who *d.* 1969.

PREDECESSOR,—[1] Rt. Hon. *Sir* BOLTON MEREDITH Eyres Monsell, GBE, son of Lt.-Col. Bolton James Alfred Monsell [Ogle, Bt.]; assumed the surname of Eyres Monsell 1904; First Lord of the Admiralty 1931-36; MP for S. Evesham (*C*) 1910-35; cr. *Viscount Monsell,* of Evesham, co. Worcester (peerage of UK) 1935; *b.* 1881: *m.* 1st, 1904 (m. diss. 1950), Caroline Mary Sybil, who *d.* 1959, da. of Henry William Eyres, of Dumbleton Hall, Worcester; 2ndly, 1950, Essex Leila Hilary, da. of Lt.-Col. the Hon. (Edward) Gerald Fleming French, DSO [E. Ypres], and formerly wife of Vyvyan Drury; *d.* 1969; *s.* by his only son [2] HENRY BOLTON GRAHAM, 2nd Viscount, and present peer.

MONSLOW, BARONY OF. (Monslow.) [Extinct 1966.]

DAUGHTER LIVING OF LIFE BARON (*By 1st marriage.*)

Hon. Rosemary, *b.* 1921: *m.* 1948, William Harold Sparks, of 41, Trinity St., Rhostyllen, Wrexham, Denbighshire.

WIDOW LIVING OF LIFE BARON.

JEAN BAIRD (*Baroness Monslow*) (30, Clarence Drive, Glasgow), da. of the Rev. Angus, Macdonald: *m.* 1960, as his 2nd wife, Baron Monslow (Life Peer), who *d.* 1966.

MONSON, BARON. (Monson.) [Baron G.B. 1728, Bt. E. 1611.]
[Name and Title pronounced "Munson."]

Ready for my country.

JOHN MONSON, 11th Baron,
and 15th Baronet ; *b.* May 3rd,
1932 ; *s.* 1958 ; ed. at Eton, and
at Trin. Coll., Camb. (B.A.
1954) : *m.* 1955, Emma, dau. of
the late Anthony Devas, A.R.A.,
and has issue.

Arms,—Or, two chevronels gules.
Crest,—A lion rampant proper, supporting
a column or. *Supporters*,—*Dexter*, a lion
or ; *sinister*, a griffin wings elevated
argent, beaked and membered azure ;
each gorged with a plain collar azure,
charged with three crescents or, and having
a line reflexed over the back blue.
Residence,—The Manor House, South
Carlton, Lincoln.

SONS LIVING.
Hon. NICHOLAS JOHN, *b.* Oct. 19th,
1955; ed. at Eton.
Hon. Andrew Anthony John, *b.* 1959.
Hon. Stephen Alexander John, *b.* 1961.

BROTHERS LIVING.
Hon. Jeremy David Alfonso John, *b.*
1934; ed. at Eton; Maj. Grenadier
Guards : *m.* 1958, Patricia Mary, dau.
of the late Major George Barker, of
Scarlett's Farm, Twyford, Berks, and has issue living, John Guy Elmhirst, *b.* 1962,—Antonia
Debonnaire, *b.* 1959. *Residence*,—Southlake House, Shurlock Row, Twyford, Berks.
Hon. Anthony John, *b.* 1944.

SISTER LIVING.
Hon. Sandra Debonnaire (The Old Vicarage, Aston Rowant, Oxon.), *b.* 1937: *m.* 1958 (m. diss. 1971),
Maj. William Garry Patterson, Life Guards, and has issue living, James William John, *b.* 1970,—
Debonnaire Jane, *b.* 1959,—Juliet Mary, *b.* 1963,—Annabel Kate, *b.* 1965.

WIDOW LIVING OF TENTH BARON.
BETTIE NORTHRUP, dau. of the late Lieut.-Col. E. Alexander Powell, of Riverain, Falls Village,
Connecticut, U.S.A.; *m.* 1st, 1931, the 10th Baron, who *d.* 1958; 2ndly, 1962, Capt. James Arnold
Phillips. *Residences*,—Mermaid Beach, Warwick, Bermuda; The Great House, Round Hill,
Hopewell P.O., Jamaica.

COLLATERAL BRANCHES LIVING.
See Monson, Bt.
Granddaughter of the late Rev. the Hon. Evelyn John Monson, 6th son of 6th
Baron :—
Issue of the late Capt. Charles Evelyn John Monson, *b.* 1878, *d.* 1953 : *m.* 1924, Mabel Ger-
trude (now of Orotara, 123, Yarborough Road, Lincoln), dau. of Edwin Benjamin Pritchard,
of Lincoln :—
Rachel Anne, *b.* 1926.

Grandchildren of the late Alfred John Monson (infra):—
Issue of the late Philip Evelyn John Monson, DD, First Bt., *b.* 1887, *d.* 1964: *m.* 1st, 1920,
Doris Murray, who *d.* 1942; 2ndly, 1956, Catherine A.—:—
By 1st marriage) Philip John, *b.* 1928.——Margaret Enid, *b.* 1922.

Grandchildren of the late Rev. Thomas John Monson, son of the Rev. the Hon.
Thomas Monson, 5th son of 2nd Baron:—
Issue of the late Alfred John Monson, *b.* 1860, *d.* 19—: *m.* 1881, Agnes Maud, who *d.* 1942,
da. of William Day, of Eversley Garth:—
Violet Theodosia (Fonthill Nurses' Memorial Home, Reigate Rd., Reigate, Surrey), *b.* 1891.——Constance Lilian (712, Beechley Drive, Fairwater, Cardiff): *m.* 1st, 19—, Rupert Worrell, who *d.* 19—;
2ndly, 1941, George Reeves, who *d.* 1941.

Issue of the late Henry John Monson, *b.* 1862, *d.* 1930 : *m.* 1901, Theodosia Anne Emily, who
d. 1951, dau. of the Rev. George Howard-Wright, R. of Offord D'Arcy, Hunts [B. Den-
man]:—
Thomas Debonnaire John (c/o Lawn Hospital, Union Rd., Lincoln), *b.* 1905; ed. at Haileybury:
m. 1934 (m. diss. 1956) Anna Phillipe Boies Clements.

Descendants of the late Hon. Lewis Monson (2nd son of 1st Baron) who was cr.
Baron Sondes 1760 [see E. Sondes].

PREDECESSORS.—[1] *Sir* THOMAS Monson, M.P. for co. Lincoln 1597-8, for Castle Rising 1604-11,
and for Cricklade 1614 ; Master of Armoury and Master Falconer to James 1. ; *cr. Baronet* 1611;
d. 1641; *s.* by his son [2] *Sir* JOHN *K.B.*, 2nd Bt.; M.P. for Lincon City 1660 and 1664-78; *d.* 1683;
s. by his grandson [3] *Sir* HENRY, 3rd Bt.; M.P. for Lincoln City 1679-80 ; *d.s.p.* 1718 ; *s.* by
his brother [4] *Sir* WILLIAM, *P.C.*, 4th Bt.; *d.* 1727; *s.* by his nephew [5] *Sir* JOHN, 5th Bt.;
M.P. for Lincoln City 1722-8; *cr. Baron Monson*, of Burton, co. Lincoln (peerage of Great
Britain); was Capt. of Band of Gentlemen Pensioners 1733, and First Commr. of Trade and
Plantations 1737; *d.* 1748; *s.* by his son [6] JOHN, 2nd Baron ; *d.* 1774; *s.* by his son [7] JOHN,
3rd Baron ; *d.* 1806; *s.* by his son [8] JOHN GEORGE, 4th Baron ; *b.* 1785, *d.* 1809 ; *s.* by his son
[9] FREDERICK JOHN, 5th Baron ; *d.s.p.* 1841; *s.* by his cousin [10] WILLIAM JOHN, 6th Baron ;
b. 1796: *m.* 1828, Eliza, who *d.* 1863, dau. of the late Edmund Larken, of Bedford Square,
London ; *d.* 1862; *s.* by his son [11] WILLIAM JOHN, *P.C.*, 7th Baron ; *b.* 1829; M.P. for Reigate
(*L*) 1858-62, Treasurer of H.M. Queen Victoria's Household 1874, Capt, of H.M.'s Yeomen of
the Guard 1880-85 and 1886, Master of the Horse 1892-4, and Militia A.D.C. to H.M. 1886-96;
cr. Viscount Oxenbridge, of Burton, co. Lincoln (peerage of Great Britain) 1886: *m.* 1869, the
Hon. Maria Adelaide, who *d.* 1897, dau. of 1st Earl de Montalt, and widow of 2nd Earl of
Yarborough; *d.* 1898, when the Viscountcy became ext., and he was *s.* in the Barony by his
brother [12] DEBONNAIRE JOHN, *C.V.O.*, 8th Baron, *b.* 1830: Sergeant-at-Arms to H.M.
Queen Victoria's Household, and Equerry, Comptroller, and Treasurer to H.R.H. the Duke of
Saxe-Coburg and Gotha(Duke of Edinburgh): *m.* 1861, Augusta Louisa Caroline, who *d.* 1936,
dau. of the late Lieut.-Col. the Hon. Augustus Ellis: *d.* 1900 ; *s.* by his son [13] AUGUSTUS
DEBONNAIRE JOHN, 9th Baron, *b.* 1868 : *m.* 1903, Romaine Madeleine, who *d.* 1943, dau. of the
late Gen. Roy Stone, of Meadham, New Jersey, U.S.A., and widow of Lawrence Turnure, of
New York, *d.* 1940 ; *s.* by his son [14] JOHN ROSEBERY, 10th Baron ; *b.* 1907 : Bar. Inner Temple
1931: *m.* 1931, Bettie Northrup (who *m.* 2ndly, 1962, Capt. James Arnold Phillips), dau. of Lieut.-
Col. E. Alexander Powell, of Journey's End, Chevy Chase, Maryland, U.S.A.; *d.* 1958: *s.* by his el.
son [15] JOHN, 11th Baron and present peer.

MONTAGU OF BEAULIEU, BARON. (Douglas-Scott-Montagu.)
[Baron U.K. 1885.]
[Title pronounced "Montagu of Bewly."]

'SPECTEMUR AGENDO'

Let us be judged by our actions.

EDWARD JOHN BARRINGTON DOUGLAS-SCOTT-MONTAGU, 3rd Baron; *b. Oct.* 20th, 1926; *s.* 1929; ed. at Eton, and at New Coll., Oxford; Lt. Gren. Gds. 1945-48; founder of the Montagu Motor Museum at Beaulieu 1952 (Nat. Motor Museum 1972); Pres. of Historic Houses Assocn.; Founder and Publisher of *The Veteran and Vintage* Magazine, and author of books on Motoring History, and Historic Houses: *m.* 1st, 1959 (m. diss. 1974), (Elizabeth) Belinda, only da. of the late Capt. the Hon. John de Bathe Crossley [see B. Somerleyton, colls.]; 2ndly, 1974, Fiona Margaret, da. of Richard Herbert, and has issue by 1st m.

Arms—Quarterly of four: 1st and 4th grand quarter, 1st and 4th argent, three lozenges conjoined in fesse gules, within a bordure sable, *Montagu;* 2nd and 3rd or, an eagle displayed vert, beaked and membered gules, *Monthermer;* 2nd grand quarter argent on a bend azure, an estoile or, between two crescents azure, *Scott;* 3rd grand quarter quarterly, 1st and 4th argent, a human heart gules imperially crowned or, on a chief azure three mullets of the field, *Douglas;* 2nd and 3rd azure, a bend between six crosses crosslet fitchée, the whole within a bordure or, charged with a double tressure flory counterflory, *Mar.* **Crests**,—1st, a griffin's head, couped at the neck or, winged and beaked sable; 2nd, a stag trippant proper; 3rd, a human heart gules, imperially crowned or, between two wings of the second. **Supporters**,—Two griffins or, winged and beaked sable, each charged on the shoulder with a cap of maintenance azure.

Seat,—Palace House, Beaulieu, Hants.   *Town Residence,*—Flat 11, Wyndham House, 24, Bryanston Sq., W1.

SON LIVING. *(By 1st m.)*
Hon. RALPH, *b.* March 13th, 1961.

DAUGHTER LIVING. *(By 1st m.)*
Hon. Mary Rachel, *b.* 1964.

SISTERS LIVING.

Hon. Anne Rachel Pearl (*Hon. Lady Chichester*), *b.* 1921 : *m.* 1st, 1946, Major Howel Joseph Moore-Gwyn, Welsh Guards, who *d.* 1947 ; 2ndly, 1950, Sir (Edward) John Chichester, 11th Bt., and has issue living, (by 1st m.) David John Howel, *b.* 1947: *m.* 1974, Alison Francis, yr. da. of Clifford G. White, of Woodrow Farm, Wigginton, Tring, Herts.,—(by 2nd m.) [see Colchester, Bt.]. *Residence,*—Battramsley Lodge, Boldre, nr. Lymington, Hants.

Hon. Caroline Cecily, *b.* 1925 : *m.* 1950 (George) Grainger Weston, and has issue living, Galvin, *b.* 1951, —Gregg, *b.* 1964,—Sarah, *b.* 1953. *Residences,*—Santa Clara Ranch, Marion, Texas, USA ; 301, Wiltshire, San Antonio, Texas, USA.

Hon. Mary Clare (7, Phillimore Terr., Allen St., W8), *b.* 1928: *m.* 1953 (m. diss. 1968), Viscount Garnock, el. son of 14th Earl of Lindsay.

HALF-SISTER LIVING.

Hon. Elizabeth Susan, *b.* 1909: *m.* 1962, Col. Arthur Noel Claude Varley, C.B.E. *Residence,*— By the Mill, Beaulieu, Hants.

WIDOW LIVING OF SECOND BARON.

ALICE PEARL (*Hon. Mrs. Edward Pleydell-Bouverie*), dau. of the late Major Barrington Crake, Rifle Brig.: *m.* 1st, 1920, as his second wife, the 2nd Baron, who *d.* 1929 ; 2ndly, 1936, Capt. the Hon. Edward Pleydell-Bouverie, M.V.O., R.N., who *d.* 1951 [see E. Radnor]. *Residence,*—The Lodge, Beaulieu, Hants.

PREDECESSORS.— [1] HENRY JOHN Douglas-Scott-Montagu, 2nd son of 5th Duke of Buccleuch; *b.* 1832; M.P. for Selkirkshire (*C*) 1861-8, and for S. Hampshire 1868-84 ; sometime Official Verderer of the New Forest ; cr. *Baron Montagu of Beaulieu* (peerage of United Kingdom) 1886 : *m.* 1865, the Hon. Cecily Susan Stuart-Wortley, who *d.* 1915, sister of 1st Earl of Wharncliffe; *d.* 1905 ; *s.* by his el. son [2] JOHN WALTER EDWARD, K.C.I.E., C.S.I., 2nd Baron ; *b.* 1866; Founder of *The Car* (sometime Editor), and other publications ; a Member of Road Board ; acted as a Member of War Aircraft Committee March to April 1916, and was Adviser on Mechanical Transport Ser. to Govt. of India during European War (Hon. Brig.-Gen.); a Member of Mechanical Warfare Board ; M.P. for Hants, New Forest Div. (*C*) 1892-1905 ; C.S.I. 1916, K.C.I.E. 1919 : *m.* 1st, 1889, Lady Cecil Victoria Constance, who *d.* 1919, el. dau. of 9th Marquess of Lothian ; 2ndly, 1920, Alice Pearl (who *m.* 2ndly, 1936, Capt. the Hon. Edward Pleydell-Bouverie, M.V.O., R.N., who *d.* 1951), da. of the late Major Barrington Crake, Rifle Brig.; *d.* 1929 ; *s.* by his son [3] EDWARD JOHN BARRINGTON, 3rd Baron and present peer.

MONTEAGLE OF BRANDON, BARON. (Spring Rice.) [Baron U.K. 1839.]

Faith does not fear.

GERALD SPRING RICE, 6th Baron; *b.* July 5th, 1926; *s.* 1946; ed. at Harrow; Capt. (retired) Irish Guards: *m.* 1949, Anne, dau. of the late Col. Guy James Brownlow, D.S.O., D.L., Rifle Brig., of Ballywhite, Portaferry, co. Down, and has issue.

Arms,—Quarterly; 1st and 4th, quarterly 1st and 4th, per pale indented argent and gules, 2nd and 3rd, azure, a lion rampant or; 2nd, or, on a chevron sable, between three mascles, as many mullets argent, ; 3rd, paly of six argent and azure, a bend sable. Crest,—A leopard's head affrontée, ducally crowned or. Supporters,—Not on record.

Residence,—Brick House, Wicken Bonhunt, Saffron Walden, Essex. *Clubs,*—Guards', Pratt's, Kildare Street.

SON LIVING.

Hon. CHARLES JAMES, *b.* Feb. 24th, 1953.

DAUGHTERS LIVING.

Hon. Elinor, *b.* 1950: *m.* 1974, Myles Clare Elliott.
Hon. Angela (twin), *b.* 1950: *m.* 1973, Christopher Richard Seton Sheppard.
Hon. Fiona, *b.* 1957.

BROTHER LIVING.

Hon. Michael, *b.* 1935 ; ed. at Harrow ; late Lieut. Irish Guards: *m.* 1959, Fiona, younger dau. of James Edward Kenneth Sprot, P.O. Box 114, Gillitts, Natal, and has issue living, Jonathan, *b.* 1964,—Kerry (da.), *b.* 1962. *Residence,*—Holly Hall, Chelwood Gate, Sussex. *Clubs,*—Boodle's, and Royal Norfolk and Suffolk Yacht.

SISTER LIVING.

Hon. Joan, *b.* 1928: *m.* 1953, Michael Shears Payne, MC [Harvey, Bt. (cr. 1868) ext.], of The Old Farm House, Cockpole Green, Wargrave, Berks., and has issue living, Ashley Desmond, *b.* 1956,—Karina, *b.* 1954.

WIDOW LIVING OF FIFTH BARON.

EMILIE DE KOSENKO, da. of the late Mrs. Edward Brooks, of New York, USA: *m.* 1st, 1925, the 5th Baron, who *d.* 1946; 2ndly, 1954, Col. Courtenay Fergus Ochoncar Grey Forbes, late Coldm. Gds., who *d.* 1971 [see L. Forbes, colls.]. *Residence,*—Remenham Piece, Henley on Thames, Oxon.

COLLATERAL BRANCHES LIVING.

Grandchildren of the late Stephen Edward Spring Rice, CB, el. son of the late Hon. Thomas William Spring Rice (infra):—

Issue of the late Edward Dominick Spring Rice, *b.* 1891, *d.* 1940: *m.* 1st, 1919, Margaret Lois (who *d.* 1970, having obtained a divorce 1936), da. of the late Samuel Garrett, JP, of Gower House, Aldeburgh, Suffolk, and widow of Capt. Charles Edward Coursolles Jones, Warwicks Regt.; 2ndly, 1936, Margaret Angela, *MRCS, LRCP* (who *m.* 2ndly, 1957, Prof. Hugh Owen Meredith, of Larkbeare, 85, Cumnor Hill, Oxford), da. of the late Gerald Ritchie, BCS:—

(By 1st marriage) Theodosia Cecil, *b.* 1921 : *m.* 1942, Professor Charles Martin Robertson, and has issue living, Stephen Edward (72, Lyndhurst Grove, SE15) *b.* 1946: *m.* 1966, Judith Anne, da. of the late Edwin Donald Kirk, of Sheffield,—Matthew Nicholas, *b.* 1949,—Dominick Henry (The Fosse, Sheepstead, Abingdon, OX13 6QG), *b.* 1952: *m.* 1973, Dorothy Joan, da. of William Francis Gregson, of Abingdon, Oxon.,—Thomas Morgan, *b.* 1958,—Lucy Petica, *b.* 1943: *m.* 1973, Andrew Garth Pollard, of 50, Cranley Gdns., N10,—Catherine Julie, *b.* 1950. *Residence,*—The Clock House, Sheepstead, Abingdon, Berks., OX13 6Q8.

Issue of the late Mary Honora Spring Rice, *b.* 1896, *d.* 1972: *m.* 1919, Charles Zachary Macaulay Booth, who *d.* 1968:—

James Charles Macaulay (Lower Warnicombe, Tiverton, Devon), *b.* 1921; ed. at Eton, and Trin. Coll., Camb.; Lt. RN (ret.); 1939-45 War (despatches twice, Croix de Guerre): *m.* 1951, Berry, da. of Thomas Evans, of Mydrailyn, Cardiganshire, and has issue living, Charles Robert Macaulay, *b.* 1953,—Stephen Richard Macaulay, *b.* 1958,—Antonia Mary, *b.* 1956,—Victoria Anne, *b.* 1961.——Cecilia Frances, *b.* 1924; formerly FANY: *m.* 1959, George Harold Champion, of 6, Ashcroft Court, Oaklands Rd., Bromley, Kent, and has issue living, Sara Jane, *b.* 1960,—Mary Ann, *b.* 1963.

Granddaughter of the late Hon. Thomas William Spring Rice, 2nd son of 1st Baron :—

Issue of the late Rt. Hon. Sir Cecil Arthur Spring Rice, G.C.M.G., G.C.V.O., *b.* 1859, *d.* 1918: *m.* 1904, Florence Caroline, who *d.* 1961, dau. of the late Rt. Hon. Sir Frank Cavendish Lascelles, G.C.B., G.C.M.G., G.C.V.O. [E. Harewood, colls.]:—

Mary Elizabeth (*Lady Arthur*), *M.B.E.*, *b.* 1906 : is a Serving Sister of St. John ; M.B.E. (Civil) 1950: *m.* 1935, Sir (Oswald) Raynor Arthur, KCMG, CVO, who *d.* 1973, [see Arthur, Bt., colls.]. *Residences,*—36, Argyll Rd., W8.

PREDECESSORS.—[1] Rt. *Hon.* THOMAS Spring Rice; *b.* 1790; MP for Limerick 1820-32, Cambridge 1832-9, Under-Sec. for Home Depart. 1827, Sec. of Treasury 1830-4, Sec. of State for War and Colonies 1834, Chancellor of the Exchequer 1835-9, and Comptroller Gen. of the Exchequer 1885-65 ; cr. *Baron Monteagle of Brandon,* co. Kerry (peerage of United Kingdom) 1839 ; *d.* 1866; *s.* by his grandson [2] THOMAS (el. son of the late Hon. Stephen Edmond Spring Rice, el. son of 1st Baron, by Ellen Mary, da. of the late Mr. Serjeant William Frere), 2nd Baron; *b.* 1849: *m.* 1875, Elizabeth, who *d.* 1908, da. of the late Most Rev. the Rt. Hon. Samuel Butcher, DD, 90th Lord Bishop of Meath; *d.* 1926; *s.* by his son [3] THOMAS AUBREY, *CMG, MVO,* 3rd Baron, *b.* 1886; in Diplo. Ser.; *d.* 1934; *s.* by his uncle [4] FRANCIS [younger son of the late Hon. Stephen Edmund Spring Rice (ante)]; *b.* 1852; Cdr. (ret.) RN: *m.* 1st, 1882, Elizabeth Ann, who *d.* 1922, da. of Sir Peter Fitzgerald, 1st Bt. (19th Knight of Kerry); 2ndly, 1935, Julia Emma Isabella, who *d.* 1936, da. of Sir Peter George FitzGerald, 1st Bt. (ante), and widow of Stephen Edward Spring Rice, CB; *d.* 1937; *s.* by his son [5] CHARLES, 5th Baron, *b.* 1887: *m.* 1925, Emilie de Kosenko, (who *m.* 2ndly, 1954, Col. Courtenay Fergus Ochoncar Grey Forbes, late Coldstream Guards), da. of Mrs. Edward Brooks, of New York, USA; *d.* 1946; *s.* by his son [6] GERALD, 6th Baron and present peer.

Montgomerie, Lord, son of Earl of Eglinton and Winton.

Montgomery, Earl of, see Earl of Pembroke and Montgomery.

MONTGOMERY OF ALAMEIN, VISCOUNT. (Montgomery.) [Viscount U.K. 1946.]

BERNARD LAW MONTGOMERY, K.G.,
G.C.B., D.S.O., 1st Viscount, son of the
late Rt. Rev. Henry Hutchinson Mont-
gomery, K.C.M.G., D.D., Preb. of St.
Paul's and Prelate of Order of St.
Michael and St. George, of New Park,
Moville, co. Donegal; b. Nov. 17th, 1887;
ed. at St. Paul's Sch.; Hon. LL.D.
Queen's Univ., Belfast and St. Andrews
1945, Camb., Toronto, McGill, and
Glasgow 1946, and British Columbia
Univ. 1960 ; Hon. D.C.L. Oxford
1945, Edinburgh and Dalhousie 1946,
and Newfoundland 1968; Hon.
DSc Louvain and Liège 1946; Field-
Marshal late R. Warwickshire Regt.;
1914-18 War on Staff (severely wounded,
despatches six times, D.S.O., Brevet-
Major, French Croix de Guerre with
palm, 1914 star, two medals), Palestine 1939 (despatches, medal),
1939-45 War in France, Middle East, Sicily, Italy, and N.-W. Europe
(despatches thrice, C.B., K.C.B., G.C.B., cr. Viscount, Ch. Com. of American
Legion of Merit, American D.S.M., American Ser. medal with five stars,
Orders of Suvorov and Victory of Russia, Grand Cross of Legion of Honour,
and of Orders of St. Olav of Norway, and Oak Leaf Crown of Luxembourg,
Mil. Medal of Luxembourg, Grand Cordon of Order of Leopold of Belgium,
Belgian and French Croix de Guerre, Grand Cross of Order of Lion of the
Netherlands, 1st class Order of Elephant of Denmark, Grand Cross of Order of
White Lion of Czechoslovakia, Czechoslovakian War Cross, Czechoslovakian
Star of Victory, Orders of Mil. Valour of Poland, and of George I. of Greece,
Gold Medal for Valour of Greece, 1st class Order of Ouissam Alouite of Morocco
and of Nicham-Iftikhar of Tunisia, Grand Cordon of Order of Seal of Solomon of
Ethiopia, 1939-45 star, Africa star with 8th Army clasp, Italy star, France and
Germany star. 1939-45 War medal); GSO2 at Staff Coll. 1926-29,
Senior Instructor, Staff Coll., Quetta 1934-37, Com. 9th Inf. Brig. 1937-38,
8th Div. 1938-39, 3rd Div. 1939-40, 5th Corps 1940-41, and 12th Corps 1941,
Gen. Officer Comdg.-in-Ch. S.-E. Command 1941-42, Gen. Officer Comdg.-in-Ch.
8th Army 1942-43, Gen. Officer Comdg. Allied Armies in United Kingdom
1944, and 21st Army Group 1944-45, Com.-in-Ch. of British Occupation Forces
in Germany, Mil. Gov. of British Zone of Germany, and British Member of
Allied Control Council in Germany 1945-46, Chief of Imperial Gen. Staff 1946-
48, Permanent Mil. Chm. of Coms.-in-Ch. Committee, Western European
Defence Organization 1948-51, and Dep. Supreme Com., Allied Powers in
Europe 1951-58; Col. Army Physical Training Corps. 1946-61; Col. Roy.
Warwickshire Regt. 1947-63; Pres. of Portsmouth Football Club, Roy. Surgical
Aid Soc., Preparatory Schs. Rifle Assocn., Chevrons Club, Irish Rifle Club,
Bisley, and Vice-Pres. of Gordon Boys' Sch., Boys' Brig., National Assocn. of
Girls' Clubs and Mixed Clubs, British and Foreign Bible Soc., Old Pauline Club
(St. Paul's Sch.), Roy. Armoured Corps Club, Pegasus Club, Ulster Assocn. in
London, National Assocn. of Boys' Clubs, British Legion (Portsmouth Branch),
Football Assocn., Bolton Lads Club, and National Small-Bore Rifle Assocn.,
Patron of Hampshire Co. Cricket Club, of Victory (Ex-Services) Assocn. and
Club, Sir Beachcroft Towse Ex-Service Fund for Blind, Airborne Forces
Security Fund, Old Comrades Assocn. of Army Commandos, Diocese of Can-
terbury Appeal, Warwickshire National Assocn. of Boys' Clubs, and Army Art
Soc., Vice-Patron of Army Benevolent Fund, ATS Benevolent Fund,
Hon. Patron of 36th Ulster Div. Old Comrades Assocn., and Hon.
Warden, Guild of Air Pilots and Air Navigators of British Empire;
Hon. Vice-Pres. of Boys' Bde. 1945, and a Gov. of St. Paul's Sch., 1948;
a Freeman of Mercers' Co., Fletchers' Co., Carpenters' Co., and Bonnet-
makers and Dyers Co. (Glasgow), and an Hon. Member of Institution of
Municipal and County Engineers, London Assocn. of Engineers, United Sers.
Institute of Tasmania, Old Contemptibles Assocn., Australian Paratroopers'
Assocn., National War Memorial Health Foundation, and S. African Legion
of British Empire Ser. League; an Hon. Freeman of City of London, Edinburgh, Canterbury, Blackpool, Swansea, Bolton, Hammersmith, Portsmouth,
Dover, Hastings, Brussels, Antwerp, Liège, Mons, and Tournai (Belgium),

Douglas (Isle of Man), Belfast, Newport (Monmouthshire), Chiswick and Brentford, Londonderry, Lambeth, Manchester, Huddersfield, Maidenhead, Warwick, Carlisle, Wakefield, Leamington Spa, Durham, Falaise, Vernon and Arromanches (France), Athens, Ottawa, Toronto, Vancouver, Salisbury, Chamonix, Durban, Pietermaritzburg, Ostend (Belgium), Namur (Belgium), Diest (Belgium), and Ciscar y Carde Altea (Spain); a DL of Hants; author of "The Memoirs of Field Marshal Montgomery", and "A History of Warfare", Silver Jubilee (1935) and Coronation (1937 and 1953) medals, and Médaille Militaire of France (1958); cr. DSO 1914, CB (Mil.) 1940, KCB (Mil.) 1942, GCB (Mil.) 1945, and *Viscount Montgomery of Alamein*, of Hindhead, co. Surrey (peerage of United Kingdom) and KG 1946: *m.* 1927, Elizabeth, who *d.* 1937, da. of the late Robert Thompson Hobart, ICS, and widow of Capt; Oswald Armitage Carver, and has issue.

Arms,—Azure, two lions passant guardant between three fleurs-de-lys, two in chief and one in base, and two trefoils in fesse all or. **Crest.**—Issuant from a crescent argent an arm embowed in armour, the hand grasping a broken tilting spear in bend sinister, the head pendent proper. **Supporters,**—*Dexter*, a Knight in chain armour and surcoat resting his exterior hand on his sword; *sinister*, a soldier in battle dress all proper.
Residence.—Isington Mill, Alton, Hants.   *Clubs,*—Athenæum, Savage, Naval and Military (Hon.), United Service (Hon.), Bath (Hon.), Cavalry (Hon.), MCC, I. Zingari.

SON LIVING.

Hon. DAVID BERNARD, *CBE, b.* Aug. 18th, 1928: ed. at Winchester, and at Trin. Coll., Camb.; late Lt. RTR; a Councillor Roy. Borough of Kensington and Chelsea since 1974; Chm. of Economic Affairs Cttee., Canning House 1973-74; a Dir., Yardley International, Ltd., Saracen Industrial Design, Ltd., Hill Samuel Project Finance, Ltd., Associated British Machine Tool Makers, Ltd., Editorial Advisory Board of "Vision", and Terimar Sers., Ltd.; CBE (Civil) 1975: *m.* 1st, 1953 (m. diss. 1967), Mary Raymond, yr. da. of the late Sir Charles Connell; 2ndly, 1970, Tessa, da. of the late Lt.-Gen. Sir Frederick Arthur Montague Browning, GCVO, KBE, CB, DSO, and formerly wife of Capt. Peter P. J. de Zulueta, Welsh Gds., and has issue living (by 1st m.) Henry David, *b.* 1954,—Arabella Clare, *b.* 1956. *Residence,*—61, Abbotsbury Close, W14.   *Clubs,*—Bath; Royal Fowey Yacht.

MONTROSE, DUKE OF. (Graham.)
[Duke S. 1707, Bt. S. 1625.]

Forget not.

JAMES ANGUS GRAHAM, 7th Duke, and 11th Baronet; *b.* May 2nd, 1907; *s.* 1954; ed. at Eton, and at Ch. Ch., Oxford; Hereditary Sheriff of Co. Dunbarton: Min. of Agric., Lands and Natural Resources, S. Rhodesia 1962-65, Min. of Agric., Rhodesia 1964-65, and Min. of External Affairs and Defence, Rhodesia 1966-68; 1939-45 War as Lt.-Com. RNVR; *m.* 1st, 1930, Isobel Veronica (who obtained a divorce 1950), da. of the late Lt.-Col. Thomas Byrne Sellar, CMG, DSO; 2ndly, 1952, Susan Mary Jocelyn, da. of Dr. John Mervyn Semple, of Gilgil, Kenya, and widow of Michael Raleigh Gibbs, and has issue by 1st and 2nd m.

Arms.—Quarterly: 1st and 4th or, on a chief sable three escallops of the field, *Graham*; 2nd and 3rd argent, three roses gules, barbed and seeded proper, *Montrose*. **Crest.**—An eagle, wings hovering or, preying on a stork on its back proper. **Supporters.** —Two storks argent, beaked and membered gules.
Seat.—Auchmar, Drymen, Glasgow. *Residence,*—Derry Farm, P.B. 309B, Salisbury, Rhodesia. *Clubs,* —Puffin's, Salisbury.

SONS LIVING. (By 1st marriage.)
JAMES (*Marquess of Graham*) (Auchmar, Drymen, Glasgow), *b.* April 6th, 1935; ed. at Loretto: *m.* 1970, Catherine Elizabeth MacDonnell, yst. da. of the late Capt. N. A. T. Young, Queen's Own Cameron Highlanders of Canada, and has issue.
  SON LIVING—James Alexander Norman (*Lord Fintrie*), *b.* Aug. 16th, 1973.

(By 2nd marriage.)
Lord Donald Alasdair, *b.* 1956.   Lord Calum Ian, *b.* 1958.

DAUGHTERS LIVING. (by 1st marriage.)
Lady Fiona Mary, *b.* 1932: *m.* 1966, Peter Alexander O'Brien Hannon (PO Box 10144, Johannseburg, S. Africa), and has issue living, Catherine Mary, *b.* 1968,—Veronica Maeve, *b.* 1971.

(By 2nd marriage.)
Lady Cairistiona Anne, *b.* 1955.
Lady Lilias Catriona Maighearad, *b.* 1960.

BROTHER LIVING.
Lord Ronald Malise Hamilton, *b.* 1912; ed. at Stowe, and at Trin. Coll., Camb.; sometime Lieut.-Com. RNVR; a Serving Brother of Order of St. John of Jerusalem: *m.* 1938, Nancy Edith (RYDER), da. of E. M. Baker, late Federated Malay States Civil Ser. *Residences,*—Sans Souci, Ocho Rios, Jamaica; Achavoulin, Blackwaterfoot, Isle of Arran.

SISTERS LIVING.
Lady Mary Helen Alma, *b.* 1909: *m.* 1931, Major John Perceval Townshend Boscawen, M.B.E., Gren. Gds., who *d.* 1972. [see V. Falmouth, colls.]. *Residences,*—The Old Rectory, West Clandon near Guildford, Surrey; Dubhgharadh Lodge, Isle of Arran.
Lady Jean Sybil Violet, *b.* 1920: *m.* 1947 (marriage dissolved 1957), Col. John Patrick Ilbert Fforde, and has issue living, Charles John Graham, *b.* 1948. *Residence,*—Strabane, Brodick, Isle of Arran.

UNCLE LIVING. (*Son of 5th Duke.*)

Lord Alastair Mungo, *R.N.*, *b.* 1886; became Com. 1918 (retired), and Capt. 1942; **served in** Dardanelles 1915 (wounded): *m.* 1st, 1916, Lady Meriel Olivia Bathurst, who *d.* 1936, dau. of 7th Earl Bathurst ; 2ndly, 1944, Sheelah Violet Edgeworth, dau. of the late Essex Edgeworth **Reade** [B. Templemore, colls.], and has issue living, (by 1st marriage) Ian James, *b.* 1923 ; ed. at Winchester, and at Trin. Coll., Dublin 1951; Research Fellow, Peabody Museum, Harvard Univ., Camb., Mass., USA,—Robin Angus, *b.* 1926,—Lilias Violet, *b.* 1917,—Margaret Christina, *b.* 1919: *m.* 1960, Thomas Colin Ernest Campbell-Preston, MC, TD, of Freshfield Rd., Formby, Liverpool, L37 7BG. *Residence,*—Chantry Farm, Campsea Ash, Woodbridge, Suffolk.

AUNT LIVING. (*Daughter of 5th Duke.*)

Lady Hermione Emily, *b.* 1882 : *m.* 1906, Col. Sir Donald Walter Cameron of Lochiel, K.T., C.M.G., LLD [D. Buccleuch], who *d.* 1951, and has issue living, Sir Donald Hamish, *KT, CVO, TD,* of Achnacarry, Spean Bridge, Inverness-shire. *Clubs,*—Boodle's, Pratt's, New, Puffin's], *b.* 1910; ed. at Harrow, and at Balliol Coll., Oxford (BA); Lord-Lt. for Inverness-shire since 1971; a Chartered Accountant, Part Time Member of Scottish Railways Board, and a Gov. of Harrow Sch.; Lt.-Col. Comdg. Cameron Highlanders 1955-57; Hon. Col. 4th/5th Bn., 1958-67, since when Hon. Col. 3rd (T) Bn. Queens Own Highlanders; Hon. Col. 2nd Bn. 51st Highland Volunteers 1970-75; 1939-45 War as Lt.-Col. Comdg. Lovat Scouts (TA) (despatches); CVO 1970, KT 1973: *m.* 1939, Margaret Doris, da. of the late Lt.-Col. the Hon. Nigel Charles Gathorne-Hardy, DSO [see E. Cranbrook, colls.], and has issue living, Donald Angus of Lochiel, yr., *b.* 1946: *m.* 1974, Lady Cecil Nennella Therese Kerr, da. of 12th Marquess of Lothian, and has issue living, Catherine Mary *b.* 1975, John Alastair Nigel *b.* 1954, Margaret Anne *b.* 1942: *m.* 1968, Timothy E. Nott-Bowyer, of 1, Glentham Gdns., SW13, son of the late Sir John Reginald Hornby Nott-Bower, KCVO (and has issue living, John William *b.* 1972, Katherine Margot *b.* 1970), Caroline Marion *b.* 1943: *m.* 1967, Blaise Noel Anthony Hardman, of Holly House, Micheldever, Hants., son of Air Ch. Marshal Sir (James) Donald (Innes) Hardman, GBE, KCB, DFC,—Allan, John (of Allangrange, Munlochy, Ross-shire), *b.* 1917; ed. at Harrow; is Maj. (ret.) Queen's Own Cameron Highlanders, a JP and DL for Ross-shire; 1939-45 War in Middle East (prisoner): *m.* 1945, Mary Elizabeth, el. da. of the late Col. A. V. H. Vaughan-Lee, Roy. Horse Gds., of Dillington Park, Som., and has issue living, Ewen James Hanning *b.* 1949, Archibald Keith *b.* 1955, Christina Marion *b.* 1948, Bridie Donalda Elspeth *b.* 1956,—Charles Alexander, *MC, TD* (The Cottage, Ardersier, Inverness-shire), *b.* 1920; ed. at Loretto Sch.; Lt.-Col. Comdg. Queen's Own Cameron Highlanders (TA) 1957-60; a DL for Inverness-shire; 1939-45 War in Egypt and Italy (wounded, MC): *m.* 1953, Felicia Margaret Wytchy, el. da. of the late Col. Kenneth L. Macdonald, of Tote, Skeabost Bridge, Isle of Skye, and has issue living, Kenneth Charles *b.* 1958, Johanna Margaret *b.* 1956,—Violet Hermione, *b.* 1907: *m.* 1930, John Alexander MacLaren Stewart, late Maj. 6th Batn. Black Watch (TA), of Ardvorlich, Lochearnhead, Perthshire, and has issue living, Alexander Donald (Ardvorlich, Lochearnhead, Perthshire) *b.* 1933; ed. at Wellington Coll., at Trin. Coll., Oxford (BA), and Edinburgh Univ. (LLB); a W.S.: *m.* 1970, Virginia, da. of Peter Washington, Pine Farm, Wokingham (and has issue living, Sophie Henrietta *b.* 1972), Mary Hermione *b.* 1931: *m.* 1954, Joseph Burnett-Stuart (and has issue living, George Clement *b.* 1955, Alexander James *b.* 1958, John Phillip Thomas *b.* 1963, Joanna Hermione *b.* 1960),—Marion Hester (*Lady Orr Ewing*), *b.* 1914: *m.* 1938, Maj. Sir Ronald Archibald Orr Ewing, 5th Bt., late Scots Gds. *Residence,*—4, Crown Rd. North, Glasgow, W2.

WIDOW LIVING OF SON OF 5TH DUKE.

Hon. RACHAEL MARY HOLLAND (*Lady Malise Graham*) (Througham Place, Beaulieu, Brockenhurst, Hants.), da. of 2nd Viscount Knutsford: *m.* 1919, Brig. Lord (Douglas) Malise Graham, who *d.* 1974, and has issue living [see colls., infra].

COLLATERAL BRANCH LIVING.

Issue of the late Brig. Lord (Douglas) Malise Graham, 2nd son of 5th Duke, *b.* 1883, *d.* 1974: *m.* 1919, the Hon. Rachael Mary Holland (ante), da. of 2nd Viscount Knutsford:—

Ivar Malise (The Glen, Coombe Kea, Truro, Cornwall), *b.* 1920; ed. at Eton, and Trin. Coll., Camb. (MA); Archives Dip. (London): *m.* 1958 (m. diss. 1973), Isabel Mary (CARPENTER), da. of the late C. B. Ewart, of Limpsfield, Surrey, and has issue living, Alastair David, *b.* 1959,—Lucy Helen, *b.* 1963.——Euan Douglas, *b.* 1924; ed. at Eton and Ch. Ch., Oxford (MA): *m.* 1954, Pauline Laetitia (PITT-RIVERS), da. of the late Hon-David Francis Tennant [see B. Glenconner, Colls.].

PREDECESSORS.—[1] PATRICK Graham, one of the Lords of the Regency during the minority of James II., was cr. *Lord Graham* (peerage of Scotland) 1445; *d.* about 1465; *s.* by his son [2] **WILLIAM, 2nd Lord** ; *d.* 1472 ; *s.* by his son [3] **WILLIAM, 3rd Lord** ; **fought with gallantry** at the battle of Sauchyburn 1488; cr. *Earl of Montrose* 1505; fell at Flodden 1513; *s.* by his son [4] WILLIAM, 2nd Earl; *d.* 15~1; *s.* by his grandson [5] JOHN, 3rd Earl; was Chancellor of Scotland 1599-1604, and Viceroy of Scotland 1604-8; *d.* 1608, having *m.* 1563, the Hon. Jean Drummond, and had three sons of whom the 2nd, William, was cr. a *Baronet* 1625, of Braco while to the Earldom *s.* the el. son [6] JOHN, 4th Earl ; was Pres. of the Council in Scotland 1626 ; *s.* by his son [7] JAMES, 5th Earl ; having served with the Covenanters 1638-40, espoused the royal cause, and was in 1644 cr. *Marquess of Montrose* (peerage of Scotland), and appointed Capt.-Gen. and Com.-in-Ch. of all the forces to be raised in Scotland for the King's service; having gained a number of brilliant victories over the Parliamentarians, he was surprised and totally defeated at Philiphaugh Sept. 13th, 1645; he then left Scotland, and after the execution of the King joined Charles II. at the Hague, from whence in 1650 he returned, and having raised a small force was defeated at Strachan April 17th, 1650, and being afterwards taken prisoner was on May 20th following sentenced by the Scottish Parliament to be hanged, &c., which sentence was carried out on the following day and his quartered remains after being exposed were interred beneath the gallows, from whence however they were removed at the Restoration and buried in state in the aisle of the Cathedral church of St. Giles, May 14th, 1661: *s.* by his son [8] JAMES, *P.C.*, 2nd Marquess, who was immediately after the return of Charles II. restored to his honours and estates; appointed an Extraordinary Lord of Session 1668 ; *s.* by his son [9] JAMES, 3rd Marquess; was Pres. of the Guards and Pres. of the Council; *d.* 1684; *s.* by his son [10] JAMES, *K.G., P.C.*, 4th Marquess; Lord Pres. of the Council in Scotland 1706, a Representative Peer 1707-27, Keeper of the Privy Seal 1709-13, Principal Sec. of State to George I., and Keeper of the Great Seal of Scotland 1716-33; resigned the patent of Marquessate of Montrose, and had a new charter granted 1706 with various limitations, cr. *Lord Aberuthven, Mugdock and Fintrie, Viscount Dundaff, Earl of Kincardine, Marquess of Graham and Buchanan and Duke of Montrose* (peerage of Scotland) 1707: *d.* 1742 ; *s.* by his son [11] WILLIAM, 2nd Duke, who had in 1731 *s.* his brother David who had in 1722 been cr. *Baron Graham* and *Earl Graham* (peerage of Great Britain), with remainder to his brothers; *d.* 1790 ; *s.* by his son [12] JAMES, *K.G., K.T., P.C.*, 3rd Duke; was successively M.P. for Richmond and Great Bedwin, a Lord of the Treasury, Paymaster of the Forces, Master of the Horse, Lord Justice Gen. of Scotland, Lord-Lieut. of cos. Stirling and Dunbarton, Pres. of Board of Trade, and Joint Postmaster Gen.: *d.* 1836; *s.* by his son [13] JAMES, *K.T.*, 4th Duke; *b.* 1799; sat as M.P. for Cambridge 1826-30, Lord Steward of the Household 1852, Chancellor of the Duchy of Lancaster 1858-9, and Postmaster-Gen. 1866: *m.* 1836, the Hon. Caroline Agnes Beresford, who *d.* 1894 (having *m.* 2ndly, 1876, William Stuart Stirling-Crawfurd, who *d.* 1883; 3rdly, 1888, Marcus Henry Milner), dau. of 2nd Baron Decies; *d.* 1874; *s.* by his son [14] DOUGLAS BERESFORD MALISE RONALD, *K.T.*, 5th Duke; *b.* 1852; Hon. Brig.-Gen. and Lord-Lieut. of co. Stirling; Lord Clerk Register of Scotland 1890-1925, and Chancellor of the Order of the Thistle 1917-25 ; High Commr. for Gen. Assembly of Church of Scotland 1916 : *m.* 1876 *Dame* Violet Hermione, *G.B.E.*, *LL.D.*, who *d.* 1940, dau. of Sir Frederick Ulrick Graham, 3rd Bt., of Netherby, Cumberland; *d.* 1925 ; *s.* by his el. son [15] JAMES, *K.T.*, *C.B.*, *C.V.O.*, *V.D.*, *LL.D.*, 6th Duke; *b.* 1878 ; S. Africa 1901, attached to Naval Brig., European War 1914-19 with Auxiliary

Naval Patrol; Lord-Lieut. of co. Bute 1920-53; sometime Assist. Private Sec. (unpaid) to Chancellor of the Exchequer (Rt. Hon. J. Austen Chamberlain, M.P.); Lord High Commr. to Gen. Assembly of Church of Scotland 1942 and 1943: *m.* 1906, Lady Mary Louise Douglas-Hamilton, *O.B.E.*, who *d.* 1957, dau. of 12th Duke of Hamilton; *d.* 1954; *s.* by his el. son [16] JAMES ANGUS, 7th Duke and present peer; also Marquess of Montrose, Marquess of Graham and Buchanan, Earl of Montrose, Earl of Kincardine, Earl Graham, Viscount Dundaff, Lord Graham, and Lord Aberuthven, Mugdock and Fintrie.

Moore, Viscount, son of Earl of Drogheda.

MORAN, BARON. (Wilson.) [Baron U.K. 1943.]

CHARLES McMORAN WILSON, *M.C., M.D., F.R.C.P.*, 1st Baron, son of the late John Forsythe Wilson, M.D.; *b.* Nov. 10th, 1882; M.B. and B.S. London 1908, M.D. gold medal 1913; M.R.C.S. England and L.R.C.P. London 1908, MRCP 1913, FRCP London 1921 (Pres. 1941-50); Consulting Physician to St. Mary's Hospital; formerly Chm. of Advisory Cttee. on Distinction Awards for Consultants, a Member of Senate of London Univ., Examiner in Medicine to Camb. and Birmingham Univs., Hon. Sec. of Faculty of Med., London Univ., Consultant Adviser to Min. of Health, a Member of Asso. of Physicians, and of Med. So. of London and of Harveian So., and a Fellow of Roy. So. of Med. ; Dean of St. Mary's Hospital Med. Sch. 1920-45; appointed a Member of Gen. Med. Council 1944; European War 1914-18 with Roy. Fusiliers and as Major R.A.M.C. (despatches twice, M.C., Italian Silver Medal for Mil. Valour); cr. Knt. 1938, and *Baron Moran*, of Manton, co. Wilts (peerage of United Kingdom) 1943: *m.* 1919, Dorothy, *M.B.E.*, dau. of the late Samuel Felix Dufton, D.Sc., and has issue.

Residences,—25, Bryanston Square, W.1; Marshall's Manor, Maresfield, Sussex.

SONS LIVING.

Hon. RICHARD JOHN McMORAN, *CMG, b.* Sept. 22nd, 1924; ed. at Eton, and at King's Coll., Camb.; 1943-45 War as Sub-Lt. RNVR; Ambassador to Hungary since 1973; CMG 1970: *m.* 1948, Shirley Rowntree, da. of G. J. Harris, of Bossall Hall, York, and has issue living, James McMoran, *b.* 1952,—William Edward Alexander, *b.* 1956,—Juliet (*Hon. Mrs. Jeffrey R. de C. Evans*), *b.* 1950: *m.* 1972, the Hon. Jeffrey Richard de Corban Evans, of 14, Quick St., N1 [see B. Mountevans]. *Residences,*—26, Church Row, Hamstead, NW3; Llewellyn House, Aberedw, Powys.

Hon. Geoffrey Hazlitt, *b.* 1929; ed. at Eton, and at King's Coll., Camb. (BA); FCA; late Roy. Horse Guards; Financial Dir. of Delta Metal Co., Ltd., a Member of Council of Inst. of Cost and Management Accountants: *m.* 1955, (Barbara) Jane, only da. of W. E. H. Hebblethwaite, of Itchen Stoke, Alresford, Hants., and has issue living, Nicholas Charles Hazlitt, *b.* 1957,—Hugo William Hazlitt, *b.* 1963. *Residences,*—The Manor House, Newton Valence, nr. Alton, Hants.; Cliff Lodge, Nefyn, Caerns.

MORAY, EARL OF. (Stuart.). [Earl S. 1562.]

[Title pronounced "Murry."]

Salvation through Christ the Redeemer.

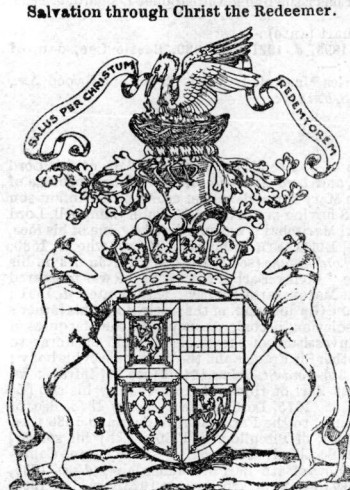

DOUGLAS JOHN MORAY STUART, 20th Earl; *b.* Feb. 13th, 1928; *s.* 1974; ed. at Trin. Coll., Camb. (BA); a JP of Perthshire: *m.* 1964, Lady Malvina Dorothea Murray, el. da. of 7th Earl Mansfield and Mansfield, and has issue.

Arms,—Quarterly: 1st and 4th the royal arms of Scotland (a lion rampant within a double tressure flory counterflory gules) surrounded with a bordure componée argent and azure, *Moray*; 2nd or, a fesse checky azure and argent, *Stewart of Doune*; 3rd or, three cushions within a double tressure flory counterflory gules, *Randolph, Earl of Moray.* Crest,—A pelican in her piety, proper. Supporters,—Two greyhounds argent, collared gules.

Residences,—Doune Park, Doune, Perthshire; Darnaway Castle, Forres, Morayshire. *Club,*—New (Edinburgh).

SON LIVING.

JOHN DOUGLAS (*Lord Doune*), *b.* Aug. 29th, 1966.

DAUGHTER LIVING.

Lady Louisa Helena, *b.* 1968.

BROTHERS LIVING.

Hon. Charles Rodney Stanford (PO Box 900, Beirut, Lebanon), *b.* 1933; ed. at Stowe, and at McGill Univ., Montreal (B.Com. 1958); late 2nd Lt. The Queen's Bays: *m.* 1961, Sasha A., el. da. of Lt.-Col. R. G. Lewis, of Stow on the Wold, and has issue living, James Benjamin, *b.* 1962,—Justin Nicholas Moray, *b.* 1964,—Duncan Douglas, *b.* 1967.

Hon. James Wallace Wilson (twin), *b.* 1933; ed. at Stowe, and at McGill Univ., Montreal (B.A. 1958), late 2nd Lieut. 13/18th Hussars: *m.* 1958, Jane-Scott, only dau. of Group Capt. Henry Gordon Richards, of Kentucky, USA, and Edmonton, Alberta, Canada, and has issue living, Elizabeth May, *b.* 1967. *Residence,*—17, Tyrawley Rd., SW6. *Club,*—Atlantic Cavalry (Montreal).

AUNT LIVING. (*Daughter of 17th Earl.*)

Lady Hermione Moray, *b.* 1899 ; *m.* 1919, Adm. Sir Henry Tritton Buller, G.C.V.O., C.B., who *d.* 1960, and has issue living, Peter Henry (of Tanyards Farm, Palmers Cross, Bramley, Surrey), *b.* 1926 ; ed. at Eton ; late R.N.V.R. : *m.* 1956, Elizabeth, dau. of W. H. P. Landon, and has issue living, Charles Peter William *b.* 1959, Alexandra Clare *b.* 1957, Susannah Louise *b.* 1960,—Patricia Moray (*Lady Ashmore*), *b.* 1929 : *m.* 1952, Vice-Adm. Sir Peter William Beckwith Ashmore, KCB, MVO, DSC (c/o Westminster Bank, 26, Haymarket, SW1), and has issue living, John Peter *b.* 1964, Jane Kyra *b.* 1957, Alison Elizabeth *b.* 1958, Catherine Patricia *b.* 1960. *Residence,*—Netherwood, Southwater, Horsham, Sussex.

DAUGHTERS LIVING OF EIGHTEENTH EARL.

Lady Mary Anne, *b.* 1926: *m.* 1st, 1945 (marriage dissolved 1960), Leonard Byng, late Lt. Gren. Gds., who *d.* 1974; 2ndly, 1961, Col. John Bovill Denham, OBE, late Scots Gds., only son of the late Sir Edward Brandis Denham, GCMG, KBE, and has issue living, (by 1st m.) Rupert Wingfield, *b.* 1946,—Francis John Stuart, *b.* 1956,—Charlotte Victoria, *b.* 1947,—Elizabeth, *b.* 1949,—Lucy Anne, *b.* 1954,—(by 2nd m.), Charles Edward, *b.* 1966,—Harriet, *b.* 1963. *Residence,*—1, Terrace Villas, Hammersmith Terr., W6.

Lady Sarah Gray (*Baroness Hillingdon*), *b.* 1928 : *m.* 1947, the 4th Baron Hillingdon. *Residence,*—Messing Park, Kelvedon, Essex.

Lady Arabella, *b.* 1934: *m.* 1956, Charles Mark Edward Boxer, and has issue living, Charles Stephen, *b.* 1961,—Henrietta Sophia, *b.* 1958. *Residence,*—54, Holland Villas Road, W14.

WIDOW LIVING OF EIGHTEENTH EARL.

BARBARA (*Dowager Countess of Moray*), dau. of J. Archibald Murray, of New York : *m.* 1924, the 18th Earl, who *d.* 1943. *Residence,*—174, Ebury Street, S.W.1.

COLLATERAL BRANCHES LIVING.

Issue of the late Hon. James Gray Stuart, CH, MVO, MC, PC (3rd son of 17th Earl) who was cr. Viscount Stuart of Findhorn 1959 [see that title].

Grandchildren of the late Charles Stuart, son of the late John Alexander Stuart, of Carnock, great-great-grandson of the late Archibald Stuart, 3rd son of 4th Earl:—

Issue of the late John Alexander Erskine Stuart, *b.* 1855, *d.* 1927: *m.* 1881, Margaret Maude Marion, who *d.* 1932, dau. of William Blackburn:—

Marjorie Violet (47, Wynford Av., Leeds, 16), *b.* 1900: *m.* 1930, the Rev. John Edmund Simpson, who *d.* 1970. and has issue living, John Stuart (29, Homesdale Av., E. Sheen, SW14) *b.* 1942; ed. at Jesus Coll., Camb. (MB; FRCS): *m.* 1968, Judith, el. da. of J. S. Rogers, of W. Horsley, Surrey, and has issue living, Rachel Jane *b.* 1972, Nicola *b.* 1974.

Issue of the late Edgar Francis Stuart, *b.* 1864, *d.* 1940 : *m.* 1885, Margaret Jones, who *d.* 1935 :—

Herbert (Prestwick, Manchester), *b.* 1893.——Francis Gerald, *b.* 1896.——Alan Bruce, *b.* 1897.—— Three daus.

Issue of the late James Stuart, *b.* 1866, *d.* 1929 : *m.* 1900, Elizabeth (now of Gilroy, California, U.S.A.), dau. of Peter Duff of Macduff :—

Charles Edward (RR3, Hewlett Rd., Kelowna, BC), *b.* 1902: *m.* 1931, Blanche Wilma Bouvette, who *d.* 1965, and has issue living, James Henry, *b.* 1934: *m.* 1955, Anna Frances Ebl, and has issue living, Charles Allan *b.* 1964, Heather Marie *b.* 1961, Sheila Christine *b.* 1962.

Issue of the late Archibald Stuart, *b.* 1868, *d.* 1937: *m.* 1896, Josephine, dau. of Robert Woolev:—

Sylvia Georgina (Box 2082, Uptown Station, San Bernardino, Cal., USA), *b.* 1905.

Issue of the late Richard Edgar Stuart, *b.* 1869, *d.* 1942: *m.* 1892, Mary, who *d.* 1939, dau. of William Evans, of St. Cruz, California, U.S.A. :—

Evelyn Edgar (1396, So Sespe, Fillmore, Cal., USA), *b.* 1899: *m.* 1931, Claude Smithwick, who *d.* 1954, and has issue living, Stuart Dawson, *b.* 1936,—Evelyn Lois, *b.* 1935: *m.* 1962, Richard Leonard Quici, of 245, Rhodes Court, Fillmore, Cal., USA, and has issue living, Christopher Leonard, *b.* 1963.

Granddaughter of Richard Edgar Stuart (ante) :—

Issue of the late Charles William Stuart, *b.* 1895, *d.* 1921: *m.* 1920, Bessie Lee, dau. of Walter W. Cook, of Milford, Utah, U.S.A. :—

Maxine Charles, *b.* (posthumous) 1922: *m.* 1944, Charles Maxwell Letz, of 12063, Smallwood Av., Downey, Cal., USA., and has issue living, Vicki Diane, *b.* 1947.

PREDECESSORS.—[1] JAMES Stuart, natural son of James V. by Margaret, dau. of 5th Lord Erskine (*de jure* 17th Earl of Mar), cr. *Earl of Moray*, and *Lord Abernethy and Strathearn* (peerage of Scotland) 1562 ; was Regent of Scotland when Queen Mary surrendered her crown to her infant son James VI. : *m.* 1562, Lady Agnes Keith (who *d.* 1588 having *m.* 2ndly 1572, Colin Campbell, Lord Lorne, afterwards 6th Earl of Argyll), dau. of 3rd Earl Marischal ; was murdered by one of his foes, Hamilton of Bothwellhaugh 1570 ; *s.* by his dau. [2] ELIZABETH *Countess of Moray*, who *m.* 1580, Sir James Stuart, who, in 1590 *s.* his father as 2nd *Lord Doune* [see *⁎⁎⁎* infra] ; Sir James on his marriage assumed the earldom, and was known as the "Bonny Earl of Moray" ; he was murdered in 1592 by the followers of the 6th Earl (afterwards 1st Marquess) of Huntly ; the Countess *d.* 1591 ; *s.* by their son [3] JAMES, 3rd Earl : *m.* 1607, Lady Anne Gordon, dau. of the instigator of his father's murder, he having previously, through the King's mediation, become reconciled to the Marquess of Huntly, obtained in 1611 from James VI. a new investiture of the whole earldom of Moray to himself and his heirs male, and failing which to his brother Sir Francis and the heirs male of his body ; *d.* 1638 ; *s.* by his son [4] JAMES, 4th Earl, who *s.* as 3rd *Lord St. Colme* 1642/3 [see †‡† infra] : *m.* 1627, Lady Margaret Home, who *d.* 1683, dau. of 1st Earl of Home, *d.* 1653 ; *s.* by his son [5] ALEXANDER, K.T., 5th Earl, *b.* 1634 ; was Justice Gen. 1675, Lord of the Treasury 1678, Sec. of State and an Extraor. Lord of Session 1680, and Commr. to the Parliament of Scotland 1686 : *m.* 1658, Emilia, who *d.* 1683, dau. of Sir William Balfour, of Pitcullo ; *d.* 1700 ; *s.* by his son [6] CHARLES, K.T., 6th Earl, *b.* circa 1660 ; cr. a *Baronet* (Scotland) 1681 : *m.* 16—, Lady Anne Campbell, who *d.* 1734, dau. of 9th Earl of Argyll, and widow of 4th Earl of Lauderdale ; *d.s.p.* 1735, when the baronetcy became ext. ; *s.* by his brother [7] FRANCIS, 7th Earl, *b.* 1673 : *m.* 1st, 1698, Elizabeth, dau. of Sir John Murray of Drumcairn ; 2ndly, 1700, the Hon. Jean Elphinstone, who *d.* 1739, dau. of 4th Lord Balmerinoch ; *d.* 1739 ; *s.* by his son [8] JAMES, K.T., 8th Earl, *b.* 1708 : *m.* 1st, 1734, Grace, who *d.* 1738, dau. of George Lockhart of Carnwath, and widow of 3rd Earl of Aboyne ; 2ndly, 1740, Lady Margaret Wemyss, who *d.* 1779, dau. of 4th Earl of Wemyss ; *d.* 1767 : *s.* by his son [9] FRANCIS, 9th Earl, *b.* 1737 ; a Representative Peer 1784-96 : cr. *Baron Stuart of Castle Stuart* (peerage of Great Britain) 1796 : *m.* 1763, the Hon. Jane, who *d.* 1786, el. dau. of John, 12th Lord Gray ; *d.* 1810 ; *s.* by his son [10] FRANCIS, K.T., 10th Earl, *b.* 1771 ; was Lord Lieut. of Elgin : *m.* 1st, 1795, Lucy, who *d.* 1798, dau. of Gen. John Scott, of Balcomie, co. Fife ; 2ndly, 1801, Margaret Jane, dau. of Sir Philip Ainslie, Knt., of Pilton, co. Edinburgh ; *d.* 1848 ; *s.* by his el. son [11] FRANCIS, 11th Earl : *d.* unmarried 1859 ; *s.* by his brother [12] JOHN, 12th Earl ; a Capt. in the Army ; *d.* unmarried 1867 ; *s.* by his half-brother [13] ARCHIBALD GEORGE, 13th Earl ; a Lt.-Col. in the Army ; *d.* 1872 ; *s.* by his brother [14] GEORGE PHILIP, 14th Earl, *b.* 1816 ; *s.* to the *Lordship of Gray* (cr. 1444-5) under special remainder 1878 ; *d.* 1895, when the Lordship of Gray (see that title) was adjudged by the Committee for Privileges of the House of Lords to Eveleen, who *d.* 1918, wife of the late James Maclaren Smith (who received Roy. Licence 1897, to assume for himself and wife the additional surname and arms of Gray), and dau. of the late Lady Jane Pounden (ante), and the peerages of 1561, 1581, 1611, and 1796 devolved on his cousin [15] EDMUND ARCHIBALD, 15th Earl ; *b.* 1840 ; assumed in 1878 the additional surname and arms of Gray, on succeeding to the estates of Margaret, Lady Gray, which he discontinued on his succession to the Earldom : *m.* 1877, Anna Mary, who *d.* 1915, dau. of the late Rev. George J. Collinson, of Clapham ; *d.* 1901 ; *s.* by his brother [16] FRANCIS JAMES, 16th Earl, *b.* 1842 ; assumed in 1895, the additional surname and arms of Gray, which he discontinued in succeeding to the Earldom : *m.* 1879, Gertrude Floyer, who *d.* 1928, dau. of the late Rev. Francis Smith ; *d.* 1909 ; *s.* by his brother [17] MORTON GARY, 17th Earl ; assumed the additional surname and arms of Gray on succeeding to the Gray and Kinfauns estates 1901 (relinquished on succession to the title) : *m.* 1890, Edith Douglas, who *d.* 1945, dau. of Rear-Adm. George Palmer ; *d.* 1930 ; *s.* by his son [18] FRANCIS DOUGLAS, *M.C.*, 18th Earl ; *b.* 1892 ; Lord-Lieut. of Morayshire 1935-43 ; European War 1914-18 as Capt. Scottish Horse (wounded, M.C.) : *m.* 1924, Barbara, dau. of J. Archibald Murray, of New York ; *d.* 1943 ; *s.* by his brother [19] (ARCHIBALD) JOHN MORTON, 19th Earl : *m.* 1922, Mabel Helen Maud, who *d.* 1968, da. of Ben Wilson, of Battlefields, Rhodesia ; *d.* 1974 ; *s.* by his el. son [20] DOUGLAS JOHN MORAY, 20th Earl and present peer : also Lord Abernethy and Strathearn, Lord Doune, Lord St. Colme, and Baron Stuart of Castle Stuart.

⁂ Sir JAMES Stuart, of Doune, co. Perth, was cr. *Lord Doune* (peerage of Scotland) 1581, with remainder to his heirs male whatsoever (a charter in confirmation 1588 gave a novodamus of the same with remainder to heirs male whatsoever bearing the name and arms of Stuart) ; Extraor. Lord of Sessions, Scotland 1584-6 : *m.* 1564, Lady Margaret Campbell, who *d.* 1592, dau. of 4th Earl of Argyll : *d.* 1590 ; *s.* by his son [2] JAMES, 2nd Lord, but styled by courtesy Earl of Moray in right of his wife (see ante).

†‡† HENRY Stuart, younger son of 1st Lord Doune (ante) was cr. *Lord St. Colme* (peerage of Scotland) 1611 with remainder to his heirs male and assigns whatsoever : *m.* 1603, Lady Jean Stuart, (who *d.* 1623, having *m.* 2ndly, 16—, Nichol Bellenden), dau. and co-heir of 5th Earl of Atholl ; *d.* 1612 ; *s.* by his son [2] JAMES, *b.* 16— ; Col. in Swedish Ser. ; *d.* 1642/3 ; *s.* by his kinsman [3] JAMES, 4th Earl of Moray (see ante).

Moreton, Lord, son of Earl of Ducie.

MORLEY, EARL OF. (Parker.) [Earl U.K. 1815.]

Reward is sure to the faithful.

JOHN ST. AUBYN PARKER, 6th Earl; *b.* May 29th, 1923; ed. at Eton; *s.* 1962; Lt.-Col. (ret.) R. Fus.; NW Europe 1944-45, and Palestine 1945-46, with KRRC; transferred R. Fus. 1947, Korea 1952-53, Middle East 1953-55, and 56; Comdg. 1st Bn. R. Fus. 1965-67; a JP for Plymouth, and a DL for Devon; Pres. of Plymouth Incorporated Chamber of Trade and Commerce, since 1970, of West Country Tourist Board since 1971, and of Fedn. of Chamber of Commerce and Traders Assocns., Cornwall since 1972, Chm. of Farm Industries Ltd., Truro since 1970, Regional Dir. of Devon and Cornwall Regional Board of Lloyds Bank since 1971 (Chm. 1974), a Member of Devon and Cornwall Cttee. of National Trust since 1969; a Gov. of Seale-Hayne Agric. Coll.: *m.* 1955, Johanna Katherine, da. of Sir John Molesworth-St. Aubyn, 14th Bt., and has issue.

Arms,—Sable, a buck's head cabossed, between two flaunches, argent. Crest,—A cubit arm couped below the elbow, the sleeve azure, cuffed and slashed argent, the hand grasping a stag's attire gules. Supporters—*Dexter,* a stag argent, collared or, pendant from the collar a shield vert, charged with a horse's head, couped argent, bridled or, *sinister,* a greyhound sable, collared or, pendent from the collar a shield gules, charged with a ducal coronet or.

Seat,—Saltram, Plympton, Devon. *Residence,*—Pound House, Yelverton, S. Devon.

SON LIVING.
MARK LIONEL (*Viscount Boringdon*), *b.* Aug. 22nd, 1956; ed. at Eton.

DAUGHTER LIVING.
Lady Venetia Katherine, *b.* 1960.

BROTHERS LIVING (*Raised to the rank of an Earl's sons* 1963.)
Hon. Robin Michael (Saltram, Plympton, Devon), *b.* 1925; ed. at Eton; Col. KRRC; Palestine 1946-48 (despatches) comdg. 2nd Bn. R. Green Jackets 1967-69.——*Hon.* Nigel Geoffrey, *b.* 1931; ed. at Eton, and at Trin. Coll., Camb.; late Grenadier Guards; with Shell Petroleum Co., Ltd.: *m.* 1965, Georgina Jane, el. da. of Sir Thomas Gordon Devitt, 2nd Bt. (cr. 1916), and has issue living, Edward Geoffrey, *b.* 1967,—Theresa Hilaria, *b.* 1966. *Residence,*—Combe Lane Farm, Wormley, Godalming, Surrey.

MOTHER LIVING.

Hon. Marjory Katharine Elizabeth Alexandra St. Aubyn, dau. of 2nd Baron St. Levan: *m.* 1919, the Hon. John Holford Parker, who *d.* 1955. *Residence,*—Saltram, Plympton, Plymouth.

PREDECESSORS.—[1] JOHN Parker, *M.P.* for Devonshire 1762-84; cr. *Baron Boringdon,* of Boringdon, co. Devon (peerage of Great Britain) 1784; *d.* 1784; *s.* by his son [2] JOHN, 2nd Baron; cr. *Viscount Boringdon* and *Earl of Morley* (peerage of United Kingdom) 1815; *d.* 1840; *s.* by his son [3] EDMUND, 2nd Earl; *b.* 1810: *m.* 1842, Harriet Sophia, who *d.* 1897, dau. of Montagu Edmund Parker, of Whiteway, Devon, and widow of William Coryton, of Pentillie Castle, Cornwall; *d.* 1864; *s.* by his son [4] ALBERT EDMUND, *P.C.,* 3rd Earl; *b.* 1843; a Lord-in-Waiting to H.M. Queen Victoria 1868-74, Under-Sec. for War 1880-85, First Commr. of Works 1886, and Chm. of Committees and Dep. Speaker of House of Lords 1889-1905: *m.* 1876, Margaret, who *d.* 1908, dau. of the late Robert S. Holford [Lindsay, Bt.] of Westonbirt, Gloucestershire; *d.* 1905; *s.* by his son [5] EDMUND ROBERT, 4th Earl; *b.* 1877; sometime Capt. T.F.; *d.* 1951; *s.* by his brother [6] MONTAGU BROWNLOW, 5th Earl; *b.* 1878; Capt. Grenadier Guards; *d.* 1962; *s.* by his nephew [7] JOHN ST. AUBYN (el. son of the late Hon. John Holford Parker, yst. son of 3rd Earl), 6th Earl and present peer; also Viscount and Baron Boringdon.

Morpeth, Viscount, son of Earl of Carlisle.

MORRIS, BARON. (Morris.) [Baron U.K. 1918.]

Always faithful.

MICHAEL DAVID MORRIS, 3rd Baron; *b.* Dec. 9th, 1937; *s.* 1975; ed. at Downside: *m.* 1st, 1959 (m. diss. 1962), Denise Eleanor, only da. of Morley Richards; 2ndly, 1962 (m. diss. 1969), Jennifer, only da. of Sq.-Ldr. Tristram Gilbert, and has issue by 2nd m.

Arms,—Barry wavy of eight argent and azure, two codfish naiant proper, on a chief of the second, a two-masted schooner in full sail, also proper. *Crest,*—A caribou's head couped at the neck proper, charged on the neck with a trefoil or. *Supporters.*—On either side a caribou charged on the shoulder with a trefoil or.

Residence,—

DAUGHTERS LIVING. (*By 2nd. m.*)

Hon. Anna Maria, *b.* 1962.
Non. Michaela Mary, *b.* 1965.

BROTHER LIVING.

Hon. EDWARD PATRICK (twin) (Highfield House, North Frodingham, Driffield, E. Yorks), *b.* Dec. 9th, 1937; ed. at Downside: *m.* 1963, Mary Beryl, el. da. of Lt.-Col. D. H. G. Thrush, of Virginia Cottage, Petham, Kent, and has issue living, Edward Patrick, *b.* 1965,—Elizabeth Mary, *b.* 1968.

SISTERS LIVING.

Hon. Aislinn Mary Katharine, *b.* 1934: *m.* 1954, Capt. Angus Jeremy Christopher Hildyard, RA (retired), and has issue living, Nicholas Alexander Cyril, *b.* 1954,—Charlotte, *b.* 1958. *Residence,*—The White Hall, Winestead, nr. Patrington, E. Yorks.

Hon. Clodagh Mary, *b.* 1936: *m.* 1964, Lt.-Col. Thomas Hugh Francis Farrell, DL, TD, of 20, New Walk, Beverley, Yorks, and has issue living, James Thomas Hugh, *b.* 1966,—Sophia Mary, *b.* 1965.

MOTHER LIVING.

Jean Beatrice (*Baroness Salmon*), (1, Melina Place, NW8; The Old Drum, Sandwich, Kent), el. da. of the late Lt.-Col. David Edward Maitland-Makgill-Crichton [see E. Lauderdale, colls.]: *m.* 1st, 1933 (m. diss. 1946), The 2nd Baron Morris, who *d.* 1975; 2ndly, 1946, Baron Salmon (Life Peer).

WIDOW LIVING OF SECOND BARON.

MARY (*Mary, Baroness Morris*), (The Old Farmhouse, Lower Denford, Hungerford, Berks.), da. of the late Rev. Alexander Reginald Langhorne, and formerly wife of Anthony Robert Agate, MRCS, LRCP: *m.* 1960, as his 2nd wife, the 2nd Baron, who *d.* 1975.

PREDECESSORS—[1] *Rt. Hon.* Sir EDWARD PATRICK Morris, *KCMG,* son of Edward Morris, of St. John's, Newfoundland; *b.* 1858; Solicitor, Newfoundland 1884; Bar. Newfoundland 1885, and a Q.C. 1896; sat for St. John's in Newfoundland Parliament 1885-1919; was a Member of Whiteway Cabinet 1889-97, Acting Attorney-Gen. 1890-95, Attorney-Gen. and Min. of Justice of Newfoundland 1902-07, Prime Min. of Newfoundland 1909-18, and a Member of British War Cabinet Feb. 1916 to Jan. 1918; a Member of Imperial Defence Cttee. 1909-18; cr. *Baron Morris,* of St. John's, in the Dominion of Newfoundland, and of the City of Waterford (peerage of United Kingdom) 1918: *m.* 1901, Isabel Langrishe, who *d.* 1934, da. of the late Rev. William Legallais; *d.* 1935; *s.* by his son [2] MICHAEL WILLIAM, 2nd Baron; *b.* 1903; Bar. Inner Temple 1925 (disbarred at own request); Solicitor 1931: *m.* 1st, 1933 (m. diss. 1946), Jean Beatrice, el. da. of the late Lt.-Col. David Edward Maitland-Makgill-Crichton [E. Lauderdale, colls.]; 2ndly, 1960, Mary, da. of the late Rev. Alexander Reginald Langhorne, and formerly wife of Anthony Robert Agate, MRCS, LRCP; *d.* 1975; *s.* by his el. son [3] MICHAEL DAVID, 3rd Baron and present peer.

MORRIS OF BORTH-Y-GEST, BARON. (Morris.) [Life Baron 1960.]

JOHN WILLIAM MORRIS, *CH, CBE, MC, PC*, son of Daniel Morris, of Liverpool; *b.* Sept. 11th, 1896; ed. at Liverpool Institute High Sch., at Trin. Hall, Camb. (BA and LLB 1920), and at Harvard Law Sch., USA; Hon. LLD Wales, British Columbia, Liverpool and Camb.; Hon Member of Canadian and American Bar Assocns.; Bar. Inner Temple 1921, a KC 1935, a Bencher 1943, and Treasurer 1967; Judge of Appeal, Isle of Man 1938-45, a Judge of High Court of Justice (King's Bench Div.) 1945-51, a Lord Justice of Appeal 1951-60, and a Lord of Appeal in Ordinary 1960-75; Pres. of London Welsh Asso. 1951-53; Pro-Chancellor of Univ. of Wales 1956-74; a DL for Caernarvonshire; Chm. of Caernarvonshire Quarter Sessions 1943-69; 1914-18 War in France with Roy. Welch Fusiliers (MC); cr. CBE (Civil) Knt. 1945, PC 1951, *Baron Morris of Borth-y-Gest,* of Borth-y-Gest, co. Caernarvonshire (Life Baron) 1960 and CH 1975.

Arms.—Vert three eagles displayed or on a chief argent a liver bird between two daffodils slipped and leaved proper. **Crest.**—On water barry wavy proper a lymphad gules in full sail argent, in front of a castle of two towers set upon a rock proper. **Supporters.**—*Dexter,* a dragon gules gorged with a collar gobony argent and vert pendent therefrom a crescent ermine; *Sinister,* a pegasus argent gorged with a collar, pendent therefrom a pair of scales or.

Addresses,—c/o House of Lords, SW1; Bryn Gauallt, Portmadoc, Gwynedd. *Clubs,*—Athenaeum Reform, Pilgrims, MCC.

MORRIS OF GRASMERE, BARON. (Morris.) [Life Baron 1967.]

CHARLES RICHARD MORRIS, *KCMG*, son of the late Meshach Charles Morris, of Hildenborough, Kent; *b.* Jan. 25th, 1898; ed. at Tonbridge Sch., and Trin. Coll., Oxford (MA); Hon. DLitt Sydney; Hon. LLD Manchester, Aberdeen, Leeds, Malta, Hull and Lancaster; Fellow and Tutor of Balliol Coll., Oxford 1922-43; Min. of Supply 1939-42, and Under-Sec. Min. of Production 1942-43; Head Master of King Edward's Sch., Birmingham 1943-48, Vice-Chancellor of Univ. of Leeds 1948-63, and Chm. of Inter-Univ. Council for Higher Education Overseas 1957-64; Chm. of Council for Training of Health Visitors and Council for Training of Social Work 1963-71, and Pro-Chancellor of Bradford Univ. 1966-70; Chm. Local Govt. Training Board 1967-75; 1914-18 War as Lt. RGA in France and Belgium; *cr.* Knt. 1953, KCMG 1963, and *Baron Morris of Grasmere,* of Grasmere, co. Westmorland (Life Peerage) 1967: *m.* 1923, Mary, OBE, da. of the late Prof. Ernest de Selincourt, of Birmingham, and has issue.

Residence,—Ladywood, White Moss, Ambleside, LA22 9SF, Cumbria. *Club,*—Athenaeum.

SON LIVING.

Hon. Charles Christopher (170, Station Rd., Wylde Green, Sutton Coldfield, Warwickshire), *b.* 1929: *m.* 1951, Cynthia Prudence, da. of the late Sir (Alfred) Alan Lethbridge Parsons, KCIE, and has issue.

DAUGHTER LIVING.

Hon. Heather Mary, *b.* 1925: *m.* 1st, 1946 (m. diss. 1972) Tom Berry Caldwell; 2ndly, 1972, Alfred G. Davey, of Coach House, Kirk Hammerton, York., and has issue (by 1st m.).

MORRIS OF KENWOOD, BARON. (Morris.) [Baron U.K. 1950.]

PHILIP GEOFFREY MORRIS, 2nd Baron; *b.* June 18th, 1928; *s.* 1954; ed. at Loughborough Coll.; late Flying Officer RAF; a JP for Inner London: *m.* 1958, The Hon. Ruth Joan Gertrude Rahle Janner, da. of Baron Janner (Life Peer), and has issue.

Residence,—Lawn Cottage, Orchard Rise, Kingston upon Thames, Surrey.

SON LIVING.

Hon. JONATHAN DAVID, *b.* Aug. 5th, 1968.

DAUGHTERS LIVING.

Hon. Diane Susan, *b.* 1960.   *Hon.* Caroline Harriet, *b.* 1961.   *Hon.* Linda Jane, *b.* 1965.

SISTER LIVING.

Hon. Hilary Zara, *b.* 1932.

WIDOW LIVING OF FIRST BARON.

FLORENCE (*Florence, Baroness Morris of Kenwood*), dau. of Henry Isaacs, of Leeds : *m.* 1924, **the 1st** Baron, who *d.* 1954.   *Residence,*—21, Wendover Court, N.W.2.

PREDECESSOR.—[1] HARRY Morris, son of the late Jacob Morris; *b.* 1893 ; was M.P. for Central Div. of Sheffield (*Lab.*) 1945-50, and for Neepsend Div. of Sheffield Feb. to March 1950 ; cr. *Baron Morris of Kenwood*, of Kenwood, City of Sheffield (peerage of United Kingdom) 1950 : *m.* 1924, Florence, dau. of Henry Isaacs, of Leeds ; *d.* 1954 ; *s.* by his only son [2] PHILIP GEOFFREY, 2nd Baron and present peer.

MORRISON, BARON. (Morrison.) [Baron U.K. 1945.]

DENNIS GLOSSOP MORRISON, 2nd Baron ; *b.* June, 21st, 1914 ; *s.* 1953 ; ed. at Tottenham Co. Sch. : *m.* 1st, 1940 (marriage dissolved 1958), Florence Alice Helena, dau. of the late Augustus Hennes, of Tottenham, N.15 ; 2ndly, 1959, Joan Eleanor, dau. of the late William R. Meech, of Acton, W.3.

Residence,—7, Ullswater Av., Felixstowe, Suffolk.

WIDOW LIVING OF FIRST BARON.

GRACE (*Grace, Baroness Morrison*), dau. of the late Thomas Glossop : *m.* 1910, the 1st Baron, who *d.* 1953. *Residence,*—7, Ullswater Av., Felixstowe, Suffolk.

PREDECESSOR.—[1] *Rt. Hon.* ROBERT CRAIGMYLE Morrison, son of the late James Morrison ; *b.* 1881 ; was a Town Councillor for Wood Green 1914-19, a co. Councillor for Middlesex 1919-24, an Alderman of Tottenham 1935-53, a Member of Metropolitan Water Board 1938-47, Chm. of Waste Food Board, Min. of Supply 1940-49, a Lord-in-Waiting to H.M. 1947-8, and Parliamentary Sec. to Min. of Works 1948-51 ; sat as M.P. for N. Div. of Tottenham (*Lab.*) 1922-31 and 1935-45 ; cr. *Baron Morrison*, of Tottenham, co. Middlesex (peerage of United Kingdom) 1945 : *m.* 1910, Grace, dau. of the late Thomas Glossop ; *d.* 1953 ; *s.* by his son [2] DENNIS GLOSSOP, 2nd Baron and present peer.

MORRISON OF LAMBETH, BARONY OF. (Morrison). [Extinct 1965.]

DAUGHTER LIVING OF LIFE PEER. (*By 1st marriage.*)

Hon. Mary Joyce, *b.* 1921 : *m.* 1st, 1941 (marriage dissolved 1948), Horace Williams (afterwards the Hon. Horace Williams), son of Baron Williams of Barnburgh (Life Peer) ; 2ndly, 1948, George Mandelson. *Residence,*—12, Bigwood Road, N.W.11.

WIDOW LIVING OF LIFE PEER.

EDITH (*Baroness Morrison of Lambeth*) (5, St. Albans St., Rochdale, Lancs.), da. of the late John Meadowcroft, of Rochdale: *m.* 1955, as his 2nd wife, Baron Morrison of Lambeth (Life Peer), who *d.* 1965.

MORTON, EARL OF. (Douglas.) [Earl S. 1458.]

Held fast.

SHOLTO CHARLES JOHN HAY DOUGLAS, 20th Earl ; *b.* April 12th, 1907 ; *s.* 1935 ; ed. at Magdalen Coll., Oxford (MA); a Fellow of the Linnæan So.; Victoria Medal of Honour, Roy. Hort. Soc.; 1939-45 War as Fl. Lt. RAFVR.

Arms.—Quarterly: 1st and 4th argent, a man's heart gules, ensigned with an imperial crown or, on a chief azure, three mullets of the field, *Douglas*; 2nd and 3rd argent, three piles issuing from the chief gules, and in chief two mullets of the field, *Douglas of Lochleven.* Crest.—A wild boar proper sticking in the cleft of an oak tree, fructed vert, with a lock holding the clefts of the tree together azure. Supporters,—Two savages, wreathed round the temples and waist, and holding in the exterior hand a club reversed, all proper.

Residence,—The Hatch, Churt, Surrey.

WIDOWS LIVING OF SONS OF NINETEENTH EARL.

Florence, dau. of the late Major Henry Thomas Timson, of Tatchbury, and of Stydd House, Lyndhurst: *m.* 1926, as his second wife, the Hon. Charles William Sholto Douglas, who *d.* 1960, and has issue, living [see colls., infra]. *Residence,*—Backbridge, Malmesbury, Wilts.

Hon. Ethel Georgiana Frances Somerset, dau. of 3rd Baron Raglan: *m.* 1914, the Hon. William Sholton Douglas, who *d.* 1932, and has issue living [see colls., infra]. *Residence,*—43, Cadogan Pl., SW1.

COLLATERAL BRANCHES LIVING.

Issue of the late Hon. Charles William Sholto Douglas, 2nd son of 19th Earl, *b.* 1881, *d.* 1960 : *m.* 1st, 1920, Alice Agnes, who *d.* 1924, dau. of Lieut.-Col. William Augustus Lane Fox-Pitt, of Presaddfed, Anglesey ; 2ndly, 1926, Florence (ante), dau. of the late Major Henry Thomas Timson, of Tatchbury, and of Stydd House, Lyndhurst :—

(By 2nd m.) JOHN CHARLES SHOLTO, *b.* March 19th, 1927: *m.* 1949, Sheila Mary, da. of the late Rev. Canon John Stanley Gibbs, M.C., of Didmarton House, Badminton, Gloucestershire, and has issue living, John Stewart Sholto, *b.* 1952,—Charles James Sholto, *b.* 1954,—Mary Pamela, *b.* 1950: *m.* 1973, Richard Callander, of Closeghyll Cottage, Hallbankgate, Brampton, Cumbria. *Residence,*—Hatton Mains, Kirknewton, Midlothian.——(By 1st m.) Helen Alice (*Baroness de Mauley* *b.* 1921: *m.* 1st, 1947, Lieut.-Col. Brian Leslie Abdy Collins, OBE, MC, RE, who *d.* 1952, of Malmule Farm, Aberdour, Fife; 2ndly, 1954, the 6th Baron de Mauley, and has issue living, (by 1st m.) Thomas Abdy, *b.* 1948,—Brian James Douglas, *b.* 1952. *Residence,*—Langford, Little Farington, Lechdale, Glos.

Issue of the late Hon. (Archibald) Roderick Sholto Douglas, 3rd son of 19th Earl, *b.* 1883, *d.* 1971: *m.* 1907, Winona Constance De Maraisville, who *d.* 1951, da. of Col. Walter Ancell Peake, DSO, of Burrough-on-the-Hill, Leics. :—

Roderick Walter Sholto (Buckstone, Banket, Rhodesia), *b.* 1908; late Maj. RAC (TA): *m.* 1st, 1935 (m. diss. 1949), Elizabeth Margaret, el. da. of the late Stephen Clement Paston Cooper [see Cooper, Bt., colls., cr. 1821]; 2ndly, 1950, Margaret, da. of the late J. M. Tennent, of Troon, Ayrshire, and has issue living, (by 1st m.) Alastair Sholto, *b.* 1949,—Anna Winona, *b.* 1936: *m.* 1965, Thomas Charles Bushby, of 53a, Bannister Rd., Braeside, Salisbury, Rhodesia, and has issue living, Lucinda Irene *b.* 1966,—Juliet Elizabeth, *b.* 1941,—(by 2nd m.) Bruce Sholto, *b.* 1951.——Patrick Sholto, *MC* (Thurston Cottage, Thurston, Bury St. Edmunds), *b.* 1912; Brig. late Black Watch, and Member of Queen's Body Guard for Scotland (R. Co. of Archers); 1939-45 War in Middle East, Sicily, Italy and France (despatches, MC and Bar): *m.* 1940 (m. diss. 1959), Maude Carol Hermione, da. of George Orr, of Kilduff House, Drem, E. Lothian; 2ndly, 1963, Alexa Granger, da. of the late Adm. John Ewen Cameron, CB, MVO, and widow of George Howard Usher Crookshank, and has issue living, (by 1st m.) Katharine Diana, *b.* 1942: *m.* 1969, Peter Robin Campbell Hendricks, of 32, Adrienne Av., Glenashley, N. Coast, Natal.——Peter Frederic Sholto, *DSO* (Giwonde, Private Bag 540, Umvukwes, Rhodesia; United Ser. and R. Aero Club), *b.* 1916; ed. at Uppingham; late Maj. A & SH; 1939-45 War (despatches, DSO, King Haakon VII of Norway's Freedom Cross, American Cert. of Merit); DSO 1941: *m.* 1942, Ursula, da. of the late Henry Somers Rivers, of Sawbridge-worth, Herts., and has issue living, (Roderick) Gavin Sholto, *b.* 1944,—Sara, *b.* 1947.——Rosemary (40, Westham Dr., Pevensey Bay, Sussex; 25, Studdridge St., SW6): *m.* 1943, Capt. William Curtis, RM, who *d.* 1960, and has issue living, Winona Penelope, *b.* 1951.

Issue of the late Hon. William Sholto Douglas, 4th son of 19th Earl, *b.* 1886, *d.* 1932 : *m.* 1914, the Hon. Ethel Georgiana Frances Somerset (ante), dau. of 3rd Baron Raglan :—

Ian Fitzroy Sholto, *b.* 1916: *m.* 1946, Heather Joan, JP, da. of the late Lt.-Col. Alexander John Hew Maclean of Ardgour [B. Inverclyde], and has issue living, William Hew Sholto, *b.* 1947; Capt. 1st Bn. Argyll Sutherland Highlanders,—Peter James, *b.* 1952,—Elizabeth Heather Winifred, *b.* 1948, *m.* 1971, Edward Inman,—Jane Charlotte Georgiana, *b.* 1950. *Residence,*—Balmaclellan House, by Castle Douglas, Kirkcudbrightshire; New (Edinburgh), Puffins (Edinburgh) Clubs.——Ronald George Sholto, *b.* 1926: *m.* 1st, 1952 (m. diss. 1957), Margaret Jean Gal Elliott-Drake, only da. of Ivor Herbert McClure, of Sutton, Province of Quebec, Canada; 2ndly, 1960, Valerie, yr. da. of William Quarterman, of 104, Cliff Rock Rd., Rubery, Birmingham, and has issue living, (by 1st m.) Roderick Olaf William Sholto, *b.* 1953,—Malcolm David Sholto, *b.* 1955,—Fiona Anne Georgiana, *b.* 1956,—(by 2nd m.) Shona Fay, *b.* 1962.——Jean Georgiana Ethel, *b.* 1922: *m.* 1949, Capt. Peter Edward Findlay Heneage, son of Lt.-Col. Sir Arthur Pelham Heneage, DSO, and has issue living, Thomas Peter William, *b.* 1950,—Charles Arthur, *b.* 1952,—Robert John, *b.* 1956,—Julia Katherine, *b.* 1960. *Residence,*—North Carlton Old Hall, Lincoln.

Issue of the late Lt. the Hon. Ronald John Sholto Douglas, OBE, RNVR, 5th son of 19th Earl, *b.* 1890, *d.* 1922: *m.* 1920, Alexandra Albertha Jean, who *d.* 1974, da. of the late Adm. Sir Frederick Tower Hamilton, GCVO, KCB [L. Belhaven, cols.] :—

Victoria Maria, *b.* 1921: *m.* 1956, as his 2nd wife, Lt.-Col. Gillachrist Campbell, RA, of Mendham Lodge, Harleston, Norfolk [V. Hawarden, colls.], and has issue living, Maria, *b.* 1956,—Sophia Frances, *b.* 1958,—Catherine, *b.* 1959

Grandchildren of the late Adm. the Hon. George Henry Douglas, 2nd son of 17th Earl:—

Issue of the late Capt. George Sholto Douglas, *b.* 1858, *d.* 1916: *m.* 1889, Lady Laura Mary Wentworth-Fitzwilliam, who *d.* 1936, dau. of the late Viscount Milton [E. Fitzwilliam] :—

Archibald Sholto George, *C.B.E.*, *b.* 1896; ed. at Eton; is Brigadier late Rifle Brig. (Prince Consort's Own); European War 1914-19 (despatches, O.B.E.), European War 1939-45 in Egypt, N. Africa, Eritrea, Persia and Iraq (CBE, 2nd class Order of Kutuzov of Russia); OBE (Mil) 1919, CBE (Mil) 1943: *m.* 1928, Patricia, da. of the late Arthur Pearson Davison, of 18, Alexander Sq., SW3, and has issue living, Colin Sholto Archibald, *b.* 1932; ed. at Eton: *m.* 1st, 1958 (m. diss. 1971), Jean. da. of the late Brig. George Streynsham Rawstorne, CBE, MC; 2ndly, 1972, Sally Anne, only da. of David Charles Humphrey Townsend, of Grindon, co. Durham, and has issue living (by 1st m.), Malcolm Sholto Colon *b.* 1966, Laura Jean *b.* 1968, (by 2nd m.) Archie Sholto James *b.* 1972, Euan Sholto David *b.* 1975,—James Sholto Arthur (Tawthorn House, By Kilmarnock, Ayrshire; Cavalry Club), *b.* 1935; ed. at Eton; Capt. 15th/19th Hussars: *m.* 1966, Tedda Ann, da. of Albert Charles Webber, of Litton Cheney, Dorchester, Dorset, and has issue living, Harry Sholto Gavin *b.* 1974,—Gavin Sholto George, *b.* 1945; ed. at Gordonstoun,—Joanna Patricia Margaret, *b.* 1948: *m.* 1972, Roger D. Day, of Newcotts Farm, Bridgwater, Som., and has issue living, Gregory Laramy *b.* 1973, Lorna Elizabeth *b.* 1974. *Residence,*—Shroton Cottage, Iwerne Courtney, nr. Blandford, Dorset. *Club,*—Army and Navy.——David Sholto William, *b.* 1899; ed. at Eton; Capt. Rifle Bde.; 1939-45 War attached King's African Rifles in Kenya and Ethiopia: *m.* 1940, Elizabeth Sarah Ione, only da. of the late Maj. George Edward Capel Cure, of Blake Hall, Ongar, Essex, and has issue living, Sheena Elizabeth, *b.* 1948. *Residence,*—Holbrook House, Heathfield, Sussex. *Club,*—Naval and Military.——Katharine Charlotte (*Lady Houldsworth*) *b.* 1898: *m.* 1921, Brig. Sir Henry Walter Houldsworth, KBE, DSO, MC, TD, late Seaforth Highlanders, who *d.* 1963, and has issue living, Rosemary Katharine, *b.* 1925: *m.* 1946, John Paul Seabrooke Daniell, Sudan Political Ser. (ret.) of Seabrooke House, Hillesden, Buckingham, and has issue living, James George Malcolm Seabrooke *b.* 1950, Sarah Katharine *b.* 1954,—Diana Mary (*Hon. Mrs. George D. Leslie Melville*), *b.* 1929: *m.* 1955, the Hon. George David Leslie Melville, of Kirkton House, Skene, Aberdeenshire [see E. Leven and Melville]. *Residence,*—Sandwood, Nairn

Grandsons of the late Capt. George Sholto Douglas (ante) :—

Issue of the late Lieut.-Col. John Sholto Henry Douglas, O.B.E., *b.* 1903, *d.* 1960: *m.* 1955, Celia (Ravensheugh, Selkirk), only da. of the late Maj. J. H. McInnes Skinner, of The Manor Lodge, E. Carleton, Norfolk, and widow of Roderick Christopher Musgrave:—
Robin Sholto John, *b.* 1956.——John Sholto James, *b.* 1959.

Grandchildren of the late Right Rev. the Hon. Arthur Gascoigne Douglas, D.D., D.C.L., Bishop of Aberdeen and Orkney, 5th son of 17th Earl:—

Issue of the late Sholto James Douglas, b. 1866, d. 1950: m. 1909, Grace Elizabeth, who d. 1968, da. of Sir James Henry Gibson-Craig, 3rd Bt. [Gibson-Craig-Carmichael, Bt.]:—

Rev. Archibald Sholto, *T.D.*, b. 1914: is V. of Siddington, and 3rd class Chap. to Forces, Cheshire Regt. (T.A.); formerly Major King's Own Scottish Borderers (T.A.); appointed Chap. to High Sheriff of Cheshire 1960. *Residence,*—Fanshawe, Siddington, near Macclesfield, Cheshire.——Hugh Alastair, b. 1915 ; formerly Conservator of Forests, Ghana : m. 1955, Elisabeth, dau. of the late Col. John Meredith Hulton, C.B.E., D.S.O., of Larges Orchard, Bracknell, and has issue living, Angela Elizabeth, b. 1956,—Coleena Jane, b. 1958. *Residence,*—Broadlands House, Brockenhurst, Hants.

Issue of the late Rev. Canon Archibald William Douglas, b. 1870, d. 1955: m. 1902, Ursula Helen, who d. 1962, second dau. of the late Capt. Robert Watts Davies, R.N., of Bloxham, Oxon:—

Joanna Katharine, b. 1912: m. 1937, James Utten Todd, of Glebe Cottage, Redgrave, nr. Diss, Norfolk, and has issue living, James Donald Utten (PO Box 4201, Beirut, Lebanon), b. 1939: m. 1962, Susan Mary Briscoe, and has issue living, Robert Alastair Utten b. 1966,—Kate Elizabeth Utten b. 1971:— William, Utten (PO Box 53, Nhulumbuy, NT 5797, Aust.), b. 1947,—Helen Patricia Utten, b. 1941: m. 1962 David Brian Wentworth (RD2, Danville, Penn., USA), and has issue living, Shaun David b. 1963, James Douglas b. 1968, Richard Benning b. 1974, Jennifer Louise b. 1965.

Descendants of the late Hon. Edward Gordon Douglas-Pennant, (brother of 17th Earl), who was cr. *Baron Penrhyn* 1866 [see that title].

PREDECESSORS.—[1] JAMES Douglas, 4th Feudal Lord of Dalkeith: m. 1459, Joanna, third dau. of King James I. of Scotland ; cr. *Earl of Morton* (peerage of Scotland) 1458 ; s. by his son, [2] JOHN, 2nd Earl, b. 1466 : m. 14—, Janet, dau. of Patrick Crichton, of Cranstoun Riddell ; d. 1513, s. by his son [3] JAMES, 3rd Earl; not having male issue made an entail of his estate and honours upon James Douglas, husband of his 3rd dau. Elizabeth: m. 1507, Katherine Stewart, natural dau. of King James IV. of Scotland; d. 1548, s. by his son-in-law [4] JAMES (ante), 4th Earl, b. 1516; not having male issue he entailed the earldom upon his nephew Archibald Douglas, 8th Earl of Angus, and his heirs male, failing which to William Douglas, of Lochleven ; was twice Chancellor and sometime High Adm. and also Regent of Scotland : m. 1543, Elizabeth, dau. of 3rd Earl (ante) ; tried for being accessory to the murder of Lord Darnley, and, being found guilty, was publicly executed at the Market Cross, Edinburgh, June 2nd, 1581, by "The Maiden," a machine he had himself introduced into Scotland ; after his execution and forfeiture the crown conferred the Earldom of Morton upon JOHN, Lord Maxwell, son of Beatrix, 2nd dau. of the 3rd Earl (ante), by her marriage with Robert, Lord Maxwell ; the grant of this honour was, however, revoked on the passing of the Act of Indemnity in 1585 to the heir of entail, and in recompense he was cr. Earl of Nithsdale, while the Earldom of Morton passed to his nephew [5] ARCHIBALD Douglas, 5th Earl (ante) [also 8th Earl of Angus], b. 1555 : m. 1st, 1573, Mary, who d. 1575, dau. of John, Earl of Mar; 2ndly 1575, Margaret (from whom he obtained a divorce), da. of 4th Earl of Rothes; 3rdly, 1587, Jean, dau. of 8th Lord Glamis. d. 1588 ; s. by his kinsman [6] Sir WILLIAM, 6th Earl (a descendant of Sir Harry Douglas, of Lugton and Lochleven, 4th son of Sir John Douglas, of Dalkeith), b. 1539-40 : m. 1554, Agnes, dau. of 4th Earl of Rothes; d. 1606 ; s. by his grandson [7] *Rt. Hon.* Sir WILLIAM, K.G. (son of Robert Douglas the younger of Lochleven, el. son of 6th Earl), 7th Earl, b. 1582 ; was a Gentleman of the Bedchamber to James VI. and Charles I., High Treasurer for Scotland 1630-35, Capt. of the Yeomen of the Guard, and in 1641 High Chancellor ; sold Dalkeith and other estates, and received in return the Islands of Orkney and Zetland, with their whole jurisdiction and royalties redeemable on payment by the crown of £30,000 ; in 1638 Aberdour was erected into a burgh of Barony, and his title was altered to *Earl of Morton* and *Lord Aberdour*: m. 1604, Lady Ann Keith, dau. of 5th Earl Marischal, d. 1648 ; s. by his son [8] ROBERT, 8th Earl : m. 16—, Elizabeth, who d. 1654, dau. of Sir Edward Villiers of Brokesby ; d. 1649 ; s. by his son [9] WILLIAM, 9th Earl ; procured a new grant of the Islands of Orkney and Zetland, but the original grant being contested those islands were annexed to the Crown by Act of Parliament 1669 : m. 1662, Lady Grizel Middleton, who d. 1666, dau. of 1st Earl of Middleton; d. 1681 ; s. by his uncle, [10] *Rt. Hon.* JAMES, 10th Earl: m. 16—, Ann, who d. 1700, dau. and co. heir of Sir James Hay, 3rd Bt. of Smithfield, d. 1686 ; s. by his son, [11] JAMES, 11th Earl ; a strenuous supporter of the Union ; d. unmarried 1715; s. by his brother, [12] ROBERT, 12th Earl ; d. unmarried 1730 ; s. by his brother, [13] GEORGE, 13th Earl, b. 1662 ; M.P. for Orkney and Sutherlandshire, 1722-30 : m. 1st, 16—, a dau. of Alexander Muirhead, of Linhouse, co. Edinburgh ; 2ndly, 17—, Frances, dau. of William Adderley, of Halstow, Kent ; d. 1738 ; s. by his son, [14] JAMES, *K.T.*, 14th Earl ; was a Lord of the Bedchamber 1739, and a Representative Peer 1739-68 ; in 1742 the Earldom of Orkney and Lordship of Zetland were by Act of Parliament disannexed from the Crown, and vested irredeemably in him, a right which he sold to Sir Laurence Dundas, 1st Baron Dundas [M. Zetland] : m. 1st, 17—, Agatha, who d. 1748, dau. of James Halyburton, of Pitcur ; 2ndly, 1755, Bridget, who d. 1805, dau. of Sir John Heathcote, 2nd Bt.; d. 1768 ; s. by his son [15] SHOLTO CHARLES, 15th Earl; b. 1732 ; a Lord of Police : m. 1758, Katherine, who d. 1823, dau. of the Hon. John Hamilton, 2nd son of 6th Earl of Haddington ; d. 1774 ; s. by his son, [16] GEORGE, *K.T.*, 16th Earl, b. 1761 ; a Representative Peer 1784-91, Chamberlain of the Queen's Household, and Lord-Lieut. of co. Fife ; cr. *Baron Douglas*, of Lochleven (peerage of Great Britain) 1791 ; d.s.p., when the Barony of Douglas became ext., and the Scottish peerages devolved upon his cousin, [17] GEORGE SHOLTO, 17th Earl (son of the Hon. John Douglas, 2nd son of 14th Earl); b. 1789; was a Representative Peer : m. 1817, Frances Theodora, who d. 1879, dau. of the Rt. Hon. Sir George Henry Rose, G.C.H. ; d. 1858 ; s. by his son, [18] SHOLTO JOHN, 18th Earl; b. 1818, was a Representative Peer : m. 1st, 1844, Helen, who d. 1850, dau. of James Watson, of Saughton, Midlothian; 2ndly, 1853, Lady Alice Anne Caroline Lambton, who d. 1907, dau. of 1st Earl of Durham ; d. Dec. 1884 ; s. by his son [19] SHOLTO GEORGE WATSON, 19th Earl, b. 1844; a Representative Peer for Scotland : m. 1877, the Hon. Helen Geraldine Maria, who d. 1949, dau. of 2nd Baron de Mauley ; d. 1935 ; s. by his grandson, [20] SHOLTO CHARLES JOHN HAY (son of the late Sholto Charles Watson, Lord Aberdour), 20th Earl and present peer ; also Lord Aberdour.

MORTON OF HENRYTON, BARONY OF. (Morton.) [Extinct 1973.]

DAUGHTER LIVING OF LIFE BARON.

Hon. Anne Margaret, b. 1926: m. 1947, Peter Andrew Hopwood Viney, D.F.C. [B. Southborough], and has issue living, Nicholas Morton, b. 1948,—Alison Margaret, b. 1951,—Elizabeth Frances, b. 1956. *Residences,*—4, Lansdowne Rd., W11; Worth House, Worth Matravers, Dorset.

WIDOW LIVING OF LIFE BARON.

MARGARET GREENLEES (*Baroness Morton of Henryton*, (78, Melton Court, SW7), da. of the late James Begg: m. 1914, Baron Morton of Henryton (Life Peer), who d. 1973.

MOSTYN, BARON. (Lloyd Mostyn.) [Baron U.K. 1831, Bt. G.B. 1778.]

ROGER EDWARD LLOYD LLOYD MOSTYN, *MC*, 5th Baron, and 6th Baronet; *b.* April 17th, 1920; *s.* 1965; ed. at Eton, Capt. 9th Queen's R. Lancers; 1939-45 War in Middle East (wounded, despatches, MC): *m.* 1st, 1943, Yvonne Margaret (who obtained a divorce 1957), da. of A. Stuart Johnson, of Henshall Hall, Congleton, Cheshire; 2ndly, 1957, Sheila Edmondson (SHAW), da. of Maj. Reginald Fairweather, of Stockwell Manor, Silverton, Devon, and has issue by 1st marriage.

My help is from the Lord.

Arms,—Quarterly: 1st and 4th, per bend sinister, ermine and ermines, a lion rampant or, *Mostyn;* 2nd and 3rd gules, a Saracen's head affrontée, erased at the neck proper, wreathed about the temples argent and sable, *Lloyd.* Crests,—1st, on a mount vert, a lion rampant or; 2nd, a Saracen's head, as in the arms; 3rd a stag trippant proper, attired or, charged on the shoulder with an escutcheon of the second, thereon a chevron of the first, between three men's heads in profile, couped at the neck, also proper. Supporters,—*Dexter,* a stag proper, attired or, charged on the shoulder with an escutcheon gules, thereon a chevron argent, between three men's heads couped in profile proper; *sinister,* a lion or, charged on the shoulder with an escutcheon argent, thereon a cross engrailed and fleurettée sable, between four Cornish choughs proper.

Seat,—Mostyn Hall, Mostyn, Flintshire. *Club,*—Royal Automobile.

SON LIVING. *(By 1st marriage.)*
Hon. LLEWELLYN ROGER LLOYD (9, Sloane Av., SW3), *b.* Sept. 26th, 1948; ed. at Eton; late Capt. Army Legal Sers.; Bar. Middle Temple 1973; in chambers Gray's Inn: *m.* 1974, Denise Suzanne, da. of Roger Duvarel, and has issue living, Alexandra Stefanie, *b.* 1975.

DAUGHTER LIVING. *(By 1st marriage.)*
Hon. Virginia Yvonne Lloyd, *b.* 1946: *m.* 1973, John Robert Hodgkinson.

SISTER LIVING.
Hon. Elizabeth Mary Gwenllian Lloyd, *b.* 1929: *m.* 1st, 1950, David Nicholas Goldsmith Duckham, from whom she obtained a divorce (Jan.) 1957; 2ndly, (May) 1957, John Henry Russell, and has issue living (by 1st marriage), Kiloran Mary, *b.* 1953. *Residence,*—8, The Vale, Chelsea, SW3.

WIDOW LIVING OF FOURTH BARON.
CONSTANCE MARY (*Mary, Baroness Mostyn*) (66, Cranmer Court, SW3), only child of the late W. E. Reynolds, of Aldeburgh, Suffolk: *m.* 1918, the 4th Baron, who *d.* 1965.

COLLATERAL BRANCHES LIVING. [*The males are in special remainder to Baronetcy.*]
Issue of the late Maj.-Gen. the Hon. Sir Savage Lloyd-Mostyn, K.C.B., 3rd son of 2nd Baron, *b.* 1835, *d.* 1914: *m.* 1891, Emily, who *d.* 1956, and dau. of the Rev. George Earle-Welby [Welby, Bt., colls.]:—
Rhona Felicia Bridget, *b.* 1893: *m.* 1929, Lieut.-Col. Edward Percy Aymer des Graz, Rifle Brig., who *d.* (killed in action) 1942 [B. Oranmore and Browne], and has issue living, Bridget Mary Rhona, *b.* 1931: *m.* 1968, Geoffrey Avenel Treherne [see Adair, Bt.]. *Residence,*—Whiteway House, Axford, Marlborough, Wilts.

Grandchildren of the late Edward Hugh Lloyd Mostyn, el. so n of the late Rev. Canon the Hon. Hugh Wynne Lloyd Mostyn, 4th son of 2nd Baron:—
Issue of the late Hugh Wynne Lloyd Mostyn, *b.* 1903, *d.* 1975: *m.* 1933, Eileen Grace (Christmas Cottage, Gundleton, Alresford, Hants.), da. of Arthur Walsh Titherley, DSc, PhD, FRIC, of Itchen Abbas Manor, Winchester:—
Roger Hugh Lloyd (7, Margesson Drive, Barnt Green, Birmingham, B45 8LR), *b.* 1941; ed. at Lancing; MB, BS London; MRCS England, MRCP London: *m.* 1967, Mary Frances, da. of Capt. Edward Fothergill Elderton, AFRaeS, AOGI, of Ryde, and has issue living, Christopher Edward, *b.* 1968,— James William, *b.* 1970.——Rosemary Eleanor Lloyd, *b.* 1933.——Jean Grant Lloyd, *b.* 1935: *m.* 1956, John Harold Matthews, of 6, Eridge Rd., W4, and has issue living, N icholas Stuart, *b.* 1958, —Sarah Jo., *b.* 1964.

Grandchildren of the late Rev. Canon the Hon. Hugh Wynne Lloyd-Mostyn, 5th son of 2nd Baron:—
Issue of the late Lt.-Col. James Pryce Lloyd Mostyn, *b.* 1879, *d.* 1968: *m.* 1915, Alix Doreen, who *d.* 1956, da. of the late Maj.-Gen. Inigo Richmund Jones, CVO, CB:—
Edwyn Inigo Lloyd, *MC* (Hill Farm House, Guilden Sutton, Chester), *b.* 1921; ed. at St. Edward's Sch., Oxford; Maj. (ret.) Scots Guards; 1939-45 War in Italy and Malaya (despatches, MC): *m.* 1st, 1942 (m. diss. 1964), Avice Louise Trevor, da. of Cdr. Sir Hugh Trevor Dawson, 2nd Bt., CBE, RN (ret.); 2ndly, 1964, Janet Hope (RUTHERFORD), da. of Eric Cecil Barnes, CMG, of Polmear, Frogham, nr. Fordingbridge; 3rdly, 1975, Mrs. Angela Leyland, and has issue living, (by 1st. m) James Michael Lloyd, *b.* 1952: *m.* 1974, Susan Hough,—Caroline Anne Lloyd, *b.* 1954,—Louise Avice Lloyd, *b.* 1956,—Annabel Alix Lloyd, *b.* 1957.——David Henry Lloyd, *b.* 1923; 1939-45 War as Rifleman Rifle Bde., and with Queen's R. Regt. (invalided): *m.* 1956, Betty, da. of the late James Francis O'Connor, of Applecross, W. Australia.——Sydna Alix Lloyd, *b.* 1917; late Jun. Com. ATS.

Not in Remainder to Barony.
Grandson of the late George Llewellyn Lloyd, 2nd son of the late William Lloyd (infra):—
Issue of the late Llewellyn Bateson Lloyd, *b.* 1887, *d.* 1952: *m.* 1910, Mabel Ellen, da. of William French :—
George Llewellyn, *b.* 1911. *Residence,*—

Grandchildren of the late William Lloyd (*b.* 1824), yr. son of Edward Bell Lloyd, el. son of Bell Lloyd, next brother of 2nd Bt and 1st Baron:—
Issue of the late Edward Bell Lloyd, *b.* 1863, *d.* 1922: *m.* 1888, Alice Maud Mary Awbery :—
Clarice Audrey, *b.* 1897. *Residence,*—Basement Flat, 31, Brittany Rd., St. Leonards, Sussex.

Grandchildren of the late Ven. William Henry Cynric Lloyd, yr. son of the late Bell Lloyd (ante):—
Issue of the late Alfred Norman Mostyn Lloyd, *b.* 1868, *d.* 1941: *m.* 1st, 1895, Harriet, who *d.* 1904, dau. of the late Canon Crompton, of Breightmet, Pinetown Estate, Natal; 2ndly, 1910, Alice Rivière, who *d.* 1944, dau. of Henry Ainsworth Condron:—
(By 1st marriage) Theodore Cynric Lloyd, *b.* 1901; B.Sc. S. Africa, M.Sc. London, and Ph.D. Columbia Univ., New York : *m.* 1937, Stella Patience, dau. of the late Alfred William McLaren.

Residence,—55, Stralenburg Flats, Box 95, Margate, Natal.——(By 2nd m.) Norman Mostyn, *RD* (Paddock Close, Hinton St. Michael, Christchurch, Hants) *b.* 1911; Com. RNR (ret.): *m.* 1941, Ethel Kathleen, da. of the late Edward Crouch, and has issue living, Edward Mostyn, *b.* 1943,—Margaret Gwynedd, *b.* 1944: *m.* 1966, Douglas Havers (Svanen, Soren Larsen & Sonners, Nykobing Mors, Denmark).——Alfred Anson, *b.* 1914: *m.* 1941, Elaine, da. of the late Horace Burdon, and has issue living, Patricia Burdon, *b.* 1943,—Barbara Ann, *b.* 1948: *m.* 1971, Robert John Kendall Slater, of 24, Tibouchina Cres., Glen Hills, Durban, S. Africa, and has issue living, Kendall Lloyd *b.* 1972, Stuart James *b.* 1974. *Address,*—PO Box 3330, Durban, Natal, S. Africa.——(By 1st m.) Gwynedd (Bahati, Winterskloof, Natal), *b.* 1899: *m.* 1934, Victor Holmes McNaghten Barrett, who *d.* 1966, and has issue living, David McNaghten (10, Zion Rd., Claremont, Cape Province, S. Africa), *b.* 1937; BSc (Chemical Technology) S. Africa 1959: *m.* 1961, Barbara Leone, da. of the late Benjamin van der Hoven, and has issue living, James McNaghten *b.* 1962, Guy McNaghten *b.* 1965.

Granddaughter of the late Charles Banastre Lloyd, son of Maj.-Gen. Banastre Pryce Lloyd, son of Llewelyn Lloyd, yst. brother of 2nd Bt. and 1st Baron:—
Issue of the late Llewelyn Lloyd, *b.* 1883, *d.* 1960: *m.* 1920, Jessie Elizabeth (of Buxton House, 132, Long Market St., Pietermaritzburg, Natal), dau. of James Thomas Forrester:—
Daphne Ellen Kate, *b.* 1921: *m.* 19—(marriage dissolved 1949), — Read, of Johannesburg, and has issue living, Arland Everard, *b.* 1944,—Susan, *b.* 1946.

PREDECESSORS.—[1] EDWARD Lloyd, Secretary of War, *d.* 1795, having in 1778 been cr. a *Baronet,* with remainder to his nephew [2] *Sir* EDWARD PRYCE Lloyd, 2nd Bt.; M.P. for Flint Borough 1806-07 and 1812-32; *b.* 1768; cr. *Baron Mostyn,* of Mostyn, co. Flint (peerage of United Kingdom) 1831; *d.* 1854; *s.* by his son [3] EDWARD, 2nd Baron; sat as M.P. for Flintshire (*LC*) 1831-37, 1841-42, and 1847-54, and for Lichfield 1846-47; was Lord-Lieut. of Merionethshire; assumed in 1831 by Roy. licence the additional surname of Mostyn; *d.* 1884; *s.* by his grandson [4] LLEWELYN NEVILLE VAUGHAN (son of the late Hon. Thomas Edward Mostyn Lloyd-Mostyn, 3rd Baron); *b.* 1856; High Sheriff of Flint 1928, and Vice-Adm. of N. Wales and Carmarthen 1898-1929; bore Royal Standard of the Principality of Wales at Coronation of King George V 1911: *m.* 1879, Lady Mary Florence Edith Clements, O.B.E., who *d.* 1933, sister of 4th Earl of Leitrim; *d.* 1929; *s.* by his son [5] EDWARD LLEWELYN ROGER, 4th Baron, *b.* 1885; High Sheriff of Flintshire 1928: *m.* 1918, Constance Mary, only child of the late W. H. Reynolds, of Aldeburgh; *d.* 1965; *s.* by his el. son [6] ROGER EDWARD LLOYD, MC, 5th Baron and present peer.

MOTTISTONE, BARON. (Seely.) [Baron U.K. 1933.]

DAVID PETER SEELY, 4th Baron, *b.* Dec. 16th, 1920; *s.* 1966; Capt. RN (ret.); FIERE; Special Assist. to Ch. of Allied Staff, Malta, 1956-58, in Command HMS *Cossack,* Far E. Fleet 1958-59; Capt. 1960, Dep. Dir. of Signals, Admiralty 1961-63, in Command of HMS *Ajax* and 24th Escort Sqdn. Far E. Fleet (despatches) 1964-65, and Naval Adviser to UK High Comnr. in Canada 1965-66; Dir. of Distributive Industry Training Board since 1969: *m.* 1944, Anthea Christine, da. of Victor McMullan, and has issue.

Arms,—Azure, three ears of wheat banded or between two martlets in pale, and as many wreaths of roses in fesse argent. **Crest,**—In front of three ears of wheat banded or, the trunk of a tree fessewise eradicated and sprouting to the dexter proper. **Supporters,**—On either side a sea-horse (hippocampus) azure, gorged with a mural crown and charged on the shoulder with a maple leaf or.
Residence,—Salterswell House, Tarporley, Cheshire. *Clubs,*—Royal Cruising, Island Sailing, Royal Commonwealth Society (Fellow), RN Sailing Association.

I hope in God.

SONS LIVING.
Hon. PETER JOHN PHILIP, *b.* Oct. 29th, 1949: *m.* 1972, Joyce, da. of Mrs. Ellen Cairns, of St. Ninians, Stirling, and has issue living, Christopher David Peter, *b.* Oct. 1st, 1974.
Hon. Patrick Michael, *b*, 1960.

DAUGHTERS LIVING
Hon. Diana Mary, *b.* 1954.
Hon. Victoria Anne, *b.* 1957.

HALF-SISTERS LIVING.
Hon. Emily Grace, *b.* 1898; Co. Councillor for Isle of Wight 1956-67: *m.* 1937, as his 2nd wife, Lt.-Col. Archibald Ogilvie Lyttelton Kindersley, CMG, DL, who *d.* 1955. *Residence,*—Rose Cottage, Mottistone, Isle of Wight.
Hon. Irene Florence, *b.* 1902: *m.* 1924, Capt. Mason Hogarth Scott, RN (ret.), who *d.* 1971 [see Scott Bt., cr. 1907, colls.]. *Residence,*—Buckland Wood House, Broadway, Worcs.
Hon. Kathleen Mary, *b.* 1907: *m.* 1946, (Clement) Maxwell Winton Haydon. *Residence,*—Paddock Hill, Lymington, Hants.
Hon. Louisa Mary Sylvia, *b.* 1913: *m.* 1941, Charles Montagu Fletcher, O.B.E., M.D., F.R.C.P., only son of the late Sir Walter Morley Fletcher, K.B.E., C.B., M.D., Sc.D., F.R.S., and has issue living, Mark Walter (13, St. Saviours' Rd., SW2), *b.* 1942: *m.* 1968, Amelia Henrietta Rose, yr. da. of Richard Tyler, of Meesden Hall, Buntingford, Herts.,—Susanna Mary, *b.* 1945: *m.* 1967, Nicholas Walter Lyell, of 72, Stockwell Park Rd., SW9, son of Sir Maurice Legat Lyell,—Caroline Anne, *b.* 1949: *m.* 1974, Christopher Simon Courtenay Stephenson Clarke, of 95, Cadogan Gdns., SW3. *Residence,*—20, Drayton Gdns., SW10.

WIDOW LIVING OF FIRST BARON.

EVELYN IZME (*Dowager Baroness Mottistone*), da. of 1st Viscount Elibank, and widow of Capt. George Crosfield Norris Nicholson, R.F.C. [see Nicholson, Bt., cr. 1912]; a J.P. for Isle of Wight: *m.* 1917, as second wife, the 1st Baron, who *d.* 1947. *Residence,*—The Dower House, Mottistone Manor, Isle of Wight.

PREDECESSORS.—[1] *Rt. Hon.* JOHN EDWARD BERNARD Seely, *CB, CMG, DSO, TD,* 4th son of Sir Charles Seely, 1st Bt.; *b,* 1868; Lord Lt. for Hants, Lt.-Col. and Hon. Col. 72nd (Hampshires Anti-Aircraft Bde. RA (TA), and 7th Hussars (Canadian Mil), Maj.-Gen. in the Army; S. Africa 1900-1901, with 4th Bn. Imperial Yeo. (DSO), 1914-18 War; Under-Sec. of State for the Colonies 1908-11, Under-Sec. of State for War 1911-12, Sec. of State for War and Pres. of Army Council 1912-14, Warfare Member of Munitions Council 1918, Parliamentary Under-Sec. to Min. of Munitions, and Dep. Min. of Munitions 1918, and Under-Sec. of State for Air 1919; MP for I of W (*C*) 1900-1906, for Liverpool, Abercromby Div. 1906-10, for Ilkeston Div. of Derbyshire 1910-22, for I of W (*L*) 1923-24; *cr. Baron Mottistone,* of Mottistone, co. Southampton (peerage of UK) 1933: *m.* 1st, 1895, Emily Florence, who *d.* 1913, da. of the Hon. Sir Henry George Louis Crichton [E. Erne]; 2ndly, 1917, the Hon. Evelyn Izme, *JP,* da. of 1st Viscount Elibank, and widow of Capt. George Crosfield Norris Nicholson, RFC; *d.* 1947, *s.* by his el. surviving son [2] (HENRY) JOHN ALEXANDER, *OBE, AEA,* 2nd Baron, *b.* 1899; Surveyor of Fabric, St. Paul's Cathedral, Architect to St. George's Chapel, Windsor; Capt. 72nd Hampshire Anti-Aircraft Bde. RA (TA); 1914-18 War with RFA in Italy; 1939-45 War as Fl. Lt., Aux.AF; *d.* 1963; *s.* by his brother [3] (ARTHUR) PATRICK WILLIAM, *TD,* 3rd Baron, *b.* 1905; Lt.-Col. Anti-Aircraft Regt. RA (TA): *m.* 1939, Wilhelmina Josephine Philippa (from whom he obtained a divorce 1949), da. of Jonkheer Frans I. Van Haeften [Brocklehurst, Bt.]; *d.* 1966: *s.* by his half-brother [4] DAVID PETER, 4th Baron and present peer.

MOULTON, BARONY OF. (Moulton.) [Extinct 1921.]

[Name pronounced "Mole-ton."]

DAUGHTER LIVING OF LIFE PEER.

Hon. Sylvia May Fletcher, *C.B.E.,* b. 1902; ed. at Girton (B.A. 1926); Bar. Middle Temple 1929; is a J.P. for E. Sussex; sometime Regional Administrator for Women's Vol. Sers. for Civil Defence, Midland Region; O.B.E. (Civil) 1942, C.B.E. (Civil) 1960. *Residence,*—Court House, Barcombe, Sussex.

WIDOW LIVING OF SON OF LIFE PEER.

Marie Josephine, dau. of the late Sebastian Bergaentzle: *m.* 1937, as his 2nd wife, the Hon. Hugh Fletcher Moulton, M.C., who *d.* 1962. *Residence,*—16, Argyll Rd., W.8.

MOUNTBATTEN OF BURMA, EARL. (Mountbatten.) [Earl U.K. 1947.]

LOUIS (FRANCIS ALBERT VICTOR NICHOLAS) MOUNTBATTEN, *KG, GCB, OM, GCSI, GCIE, GCVO, DSO, PC, FRS,*✫ 1st Earl, 2nd son of 1st Marquess of Milford Haven; *b.* June 25th, 1900; ed. at Osborne and Dartmouth, and at Christ's Coll., Camb. (Hon. Fellow 1946); Hon. LL.D. Camb. 1946; Hon. D.C.L. Oxford 1946; Hon. D.Sc. Delhi and Patna 1948; Hon. D.C.L. Leeds 1950; Hon. LL.D. Edinburgh 1954, Southampton 1955, London 1960, and Sussex 1963; entered R.N. 1913; rated Midshipman 1916; promoted Sub-Lt. 1918, Lt. 1920, Lt.-Cdr. 1928, Cdr. 1932, Capt. 1937, Commodore (1st class) 1941, Rear-Adm. 1946, Vice-Adm. 1949, Adm. 1953, and Adm. of the Fleet 1956; acting Vice-Adm., Hon. Lt.-Gen. in the army and Air Marshal R.A.F. 1942; acting Adm. 1943; became a Chartered Electrical Engineer 1927; appointed Wireless and Signal Officer, Reserve Fleet 1926, Assist. Fleet Wireless Officer, Mediterranean 1927, Flotilla Signal and Wireless Officer, 2nd Destroyer Flotilla 1928, Senior Instructor in Wireless at H.M. Signal Sch. 1929, Fleet Wireless Officer, Mediterranean 1931, to command H.M.S. *Daring* 1934 and H.M.S. *Wishart* 1935, to Naval Air Div. at Admiralty 1936, to command H.M.S. *Kelly,* and 5th Destroyer Flotilla 1939, and H.M.S. *Illustrious* 1941, Commodore Combined Operations 1941, Ch. of Combined Operations and a Member of Ch. of Staff's Cttee. 1942, Supreme Allied Cdr. S.-E. Asia 1943, and Viceroy of India March 1947; Gov.-Gen. of India 1947-48, Flag Officer Comdg. First Cruiser Squadron 1948-50, Fourth Sea Lord 1950-52, C.-in-C. Mediterranean 1952-54, and C.-in-C. Allied Forces, Mediterranean 1953-54, First Sea Lord 1955-59, and Ch. of Defence Staff, and Chm. of Chs. of Staff Cttee. 1959-65; Col., Life Guards, and Col. Comdt. of RM since 1965; Personal Naval A.D.C. to H.M. King Edward VIII 1936 and to H.M. King George VI 1937, and Personal A.D.C. to H.M. Queen Elizabeth II 1953; Gov., Capt., and Steward of Isle

---

✫ Discontinued by Roy. Warrant 1917 the style of "H.S.H." and "Prince" and the appellation of "Battenberg," and became known as Lord Louis Mountbatten in lieu of H.S.H. Prince Louis Francis of Battenberg.

of Wight since 1965, and Lord-Lieut. since 1974; a FRS, a MIEE, and Assocn. of Inst. of Naval Architects, Grand Pres. of British Commonwealth Ex-Services League, and of Roy. Over Seas League, Pres. of Royal Naval Film Corpn., of King George's Fund for Sailors, of Roy. Naval Saddle Club, of Sailors' Home and Red Ensign Club, of Gordon Smith Inst., Liverpool, of Soldiers', Sailors', and Airmen's Families Assocn., of Roy. Automobile Club, Member and Past Pres. of Inst. of Electronic and Radio Engineers, Chm. and Founder of National Electronics Research Council, an Elder Brother of Trinity House, Hon. Col. of Calcutta Light Horse, and 289th Parachute Light Regt. RHA (TA), Commodore of Roy. Thames Yacht Club, and of Sea Scouts, Past Prime Warden of Shipwrights' Co., an Hon. Member of Master Mariners' Co., a Member of Mercers', Vintners' and Grocers' Cos., and a KStJ; 1914-18 War, 1939-45 War in Far East (despatches twice, DSO, CB, KCB, cr. Viscount, Mil. Cross of Greece, Grand Cross of Order of George I of Greece, American Legion of Merit, American DSM Special Grand Cordon of Order of Cloud and Banner of China, Grand Cross of Legion of Honour, French Croix de Guerre, Grand Cross of Order of Star of Nepal, Grand Cross of Order of White Elephant of Siam, Grand Cross of Order of Lion of the Netherlands); on Staff of HRH the Prince of Wales during Australian and New Zealand Tour 1920 (MVO), and Indian Tour as Naval ADC 1921-22; High Steward of Romsey 1940; received Freedom of City of London (with Sword of Honour) and Romsey 1946, and of Edinburgh 1954; a Knight Grand Cross of Order of Dannebrog of Denmark, Knight of Order of Seraphim of Sweden, and a Highest Comd. of Order of Thiri Thudhamma of Burma; has Grand Cross of Orders of Crown and of Star of Roumania, of Isabel the Catholic of Spain, and of Order of Seal of Solomon of Ethiopia and of Mil. Order of Aviz of Porgugal, and 4th class Order of the Nile; cr. MVO. (5th class) 1920, KCVO 1922, GCVO 1937, DSP 1941, CB (Mil.) 1943, K.C.B. (Mil.) 1945, *Viscount Mountbatten of Burma*, of Romsey, co. Southampton (peerage of United Kingdom), with remainder to heirs male of his body, and in default of such issue to his elder daughter, Patricia Edwina Victoria, and the heirs male of her body; and in default of such issue to every other daughter successively in order of seniority of age and priority of birth, and to the heirs male of their bodies, and K.G. 1946, and G.C.S.I., G.C.I.E., P.C. and *Baron Romsey*, of Romsey, co. Southampton, and *Earl Mountbatten of Burma* (peerage of United Kingdom) with similar special remainders to the above mentioned 1947, G.C.B. (Mil.) 1955, O.M. 1965: *m.* 1922, the Hon. Dame Edwina Cynthia Annette Ashley, *C.I., G.B.E., D.C.V.O., LL.D.*, who *d.* 1960 (in N. Borneo on a tour on behalf of St. John Ambulance Bde.), el. da. of 1st Baron Mount Temple (ext.), and has issue.

Arms.—Quarterly: 1st and 4th, azure, a lion rampant double queued barry of ten, argent and gules, armed and langued of the last, crowned or, within a bordure compony of the 2nd and 3rd; 2nd and 3rd, argent, two pallets sable charged on the honour point with an escutcheon of the arms of the late Princess Alice (namely, the Royal Arms differenced with a label of three points argent, on the centre point charged with a rose gules barbed vert, and each of the other points with an ermine spot sable). **Crests,**—1st, out of a coronet or, two horns barry of ten, argent and gules, issuing from each three linden leaves vert, and from the outer side of each horn four branches barwise, having three like leaves pendant therefrom of the last, *Hesse*; 2nd, out of a coronet or, a plume of four ostrich feathers alternately argent and sable, *Battenberg.* **Supporters,**—On either side a lion double queued and crowned all or.

Residences,—Broadlands, Romsey, Hants.; 2, Kinnerton St., SW1; Classiebawn Castle, Cliffoney, co. Sligo. *Clubs,*—United Service, Naval and Military, R.A.F., Devonshire, Savage, Albany, Buck's, and Royal Yacht Squadron.

DAUGHTERS LIVING.

Lady PATRICIA EDWINA VICTORIA (*Baroness Brabourne*), *b.* Feb. 14th, 1924; Col-in-Ch. of Princess Patricia's Canadian Li.; a JP and DL for Kent; 1939-45 War in WRNS in S-E Asia: *m.* 1946, the 7th Baron Brabourne, and has issue living, *Hon.* Norton Louis Philip, *b.* 1947.—*Hon.* Michael John Ulick, *b.* 1950,—*Hon.* Philip Wyndham Ashley, *b.* 1961,—*Hon.* Nicholas Timothy Charles, *b.* 1964,—*Hon.* Timothy Nicholas Sean, (twin), *b.* 1964,—*Hon.* Joanna Edwina Doreen, *b.* 1955,—*Hon.* Amanda Patricia Victoria, *b.* 1957. *Residences,*—Newhouse, Mersham, Ashford, Kent; 39, Montpelier Walk, SW7.

Lady Pamela Carmen Louise, *b.* 1929 ; Lady-in-Waiting to H.M. the Queen on her tour to Australia and New Zealand 1953-54: *m.* 1960, David Nightingale Hicks, and has issue living, Ashley Louis David, *b.* 1963,—Edwina Victoria Louise, *b.* 1961,—India Amanda Caroline, *b.* 1967. *Residences,*— 2, Paulton House, SW3; Britwell Salome, Watlington, Oxon.; 5, Les Residences du Port, St. Jean Cap Ferrat, O6, France.

Mount Charles, Earl of, son of Marquess Conyngham.

MOUNT EDGCUMBE, EARL OF. (Edgcumbe.) [Earl G.B. 1789.]

At the disposal of God.

EDWARD PIERS EDGCUMBE, 7th Earl;
b. July 13th, 1903; *s.* 1965: *m.* 1944,
Victoria Effie, yst. da. of Robert
Campbell, of Lisburn, N. Ireland and
NZ, and widow of John Warbrick.

Arms,—Gules, on a bend ermines, cottised or,
three boars' heads argent. Crest,—A boar statant
argent, gorged with a wreath of oak vert, fructed or.
Supporters,—Two greyhounds argent, guttee de
poix, and gorged with a collar, dovetailed gules.

Seat,—Mount Edgcumbe, Plymouth.

BROTHER LIVING.

GEORGE AUBREY VALLETORT (77, Arapiki
Rd., Stoke, Nelson, New Zealand), *b.* Sept. 15th,
1907; BE, New Zealand; a Member of New
Zealand Inst. of Engineers, Indian Sers. of
Engineers (ret.): *m.* 1st, 1935 (m. diss. 1943),
Meta, da. of the late Charles Robert Lhoyer, of
Nancy, France; 2ndly, 1944, Una Pamela, da. of
the late Edward Lewis George, of Perth, W.
Australia, and has issue living, (by 1st marriage)
Robert Charles, *b.* 1939,—(by 2nd marriage)
Piers Valletort, *b.* 1946,—Christopher George
Mortimer, *b.* 1960.

SISTERS LIVING.

Erina Shelley, *b.* 1898: *m.* 1930, John Richard Sutton, MICE, of 16, Awatea Rd., Parnell, Auckland,
NZ, and has issue living, Gillian Mary Edgcumbe, *b.* 1941.
Ernestine Cecelia, *b.* 1899: *m.* 1929, Edwin Clay of Woodbrook Av., Windsor Gdns., Adelaide, S. Aust.,
and has issue living, Howard Edgcumbe (Lesley Cres., Crafers, S. Aust.), *b.* 1931: *m.* 1961, Helen
Muriel Jenner, of Adelaide, and has issue living, Simon Edgcumbe *b.* 1964, Sarah Georgina *b.* 1966,
Rebecca Jane *b.* 1969,—Roger Edgcumbe, *b.* 1939; PhD; BAg. Sc.,—Geraldine Ann, *b.* 1935: *m.* 1959,
Emlyn Donald Jones, of Fernbank Terr., Stonyfell, Adelaide, and has issue living, Richard Edwin
Lewis *b.* 1964, Catherine Louise *b.* 1966, Joanna Elizabeth *b.* 1972.
Francis Huia, *b.* 1901: *m.* 1920, Harold Stott, of 191, Mount Albert Rd., Mount Roskill, Auckland,
N. Zealand, and has issue living, Frank Ernest, *b.* 1921,—Georgina Amy, *b.* 1923.

DAUGHTERS LIVING OF SIXTH EARL.

Lady Hilaria Agnes, *b.* 1908: *m.* 1933, Lt.-Col. Denis Lucius Alban Gibbs, DSO, Queen's R. Regt.
(ret.), and has issue living, Jillianne Bridget, *b.* 1935: *m.* 1st, 1959 (m. diss. 1973), Maj. Martin John
Minter-Kemp, RWF (ret.); 2ndly, 1974, Anthony Alan Russell Cobbold, of the Old Vicarage,
Eccleshall, Staffs., and has issue living (by 1st m.), Robin John Edgcumbe *b.* 1963, Emma Hilaria,
b. 1960, Penelope Claire (twin) *b.* 1963,—Margaret Hilaria, *b.* 1937: *m.* 1961, the Rev. Mark Lyon,
Thornewill, RN (ret.) (c/o Coutts & Co., 440, Strand, WC2), and has issue living, John-Mark Judah
b. 1961, Luke Thomas (twin) *b.* 1961, Christopher Shane Kenelm *b.* 1968, Jeremy Lyon *b.* 1970,
Joanna Lilian *b.* 1965,—Rosamund Lucia, *b.* 1941: *m.* 1963, Lt. Cdr. Robert Nathaniel Woodard,
RN, of Browns Cottage, Toller Porcorum, Dorset, and has issue living, Rupert Piers Nathaniel
b. 1964, Jolyon Robert Alban *b.* 1969, Melissa Lucia *b.* 1967,—Penelope Mary, *b.* 1949: *m.* 1970,
Douglas Arthur Dale. *Residence,*—Aldenham, Down Rd., Tavistock, Devon.
Lady Katherine Lilian, *b.* 1910: *m.* 1st, 1936, Gp.-Capt. Francis Campbell de la Poer Beresford-Peirse,
RAF (ret.), from whom she obtained a divorce 1957 [see Beresford-Peirse, Bt., colls.]; 2ndly, 19—,
Cdr. R. Gabbett Mulhallen, CBE, RN, of 9, St. Michael's Terr., Stoke, Plymouth.
Lady Margaret Louisa, *b.* 1912: *m.* 1932, Lt.-Col. Conolly Robert McCausland, MC, DL, JP, Irish
Guards, who *d.* 1968, only son of the late Rt. Hon. Maurice Marcus McCausland (HM's Lt.), of
Drenagh, Limavady, co. Londonderry, and has issue living, Antony Richard (Drumaul House,
Randalstown, co. Antrim), *b.* 1941: *m.* 1964, Priscilla Cornwallis, el. da. of E. S. Vernon-Jones, of
Millstream House, Stadhampton, Oxford, and has issue living, Richard Cornwallis *b.* 1969, Henrietta
Elisabeth *b.* 1965,—Piers Conolly, *b.* 1949: *m.* 1970, Elizabeth, da. of Dr. James Duff, of Hampstead
Hall, Derry, and has issue living, Cuillean Benjamin *b.* 1972,—Mary Fania, *b.* 1936: *m.* 1958,
Capt. Denis Mahony, Irish Gds., of Bessborough, Balrath, co. Meath. and has issue living, Edmond
Conolly *b.* 1960, Dominick Denis Martin, *b.* 1962, Maria Louisa Siobhan *b.* 1968,—Caroline Anne,
b. 1944: *m.* 1964, Simon Maxwell Weatherby, of The Old Rectory, Sutton-under-Brailes, Banbury,
Oxon. [see V. Bangor]. *Residence,*—Streeve, Limavady, co. Londonderry.

COLLATERAL BRANCHES LIVING.

Grandchildren of the late Edward Mortimer Edgcumbe, son of the late Hon.
George Edgcumbe, yst. son of 2nd Earl:—
Issue of the late Ernest Athole Edgcumbe, *b.* 1870, *d.* 1937: *m.* 1896, Louisa Charlotte, who
d. 1949, dau. of William Martin, of Auckland, New Zealand:—
Florence Maye, *b.* 1900: *m.* 1925, Charles Richard Howard, who *d.* 1972.——Jessie Hilaria, *b.* 1911:
m. 1934, Leslie Reeves, of 37, The Mall, Mt. Mauganui, Bay of Plenty, NZ, and has issue living,
Gaynor Hilaria Ann, *b.* 1936: *m.* 1957, Arthur Herbert Lidington, of 173, Dey St., Hamilton, NZ,
and has issue living, Brett Arthur *b.* 1961, Janie Lesley *b.* 1959.

Issue of the late Gerald Richard Valletort Edgcumbe, *b.* 1871, *d.* 1908: *m.* 1900, Sarah Ann,
who *d.* 1964, da. of Maj. Broughton:—
Edward Mortimer, *b.* 1904: *m.* 1941, Mary McArthur Stone, and has issue living, Richard John, *b.*
1946,—Margaret Ann, *b.* 1942. *Residence,*—27, Tuhaere Street, Orakei, Auckland, New Zealand.
——Constance Joyce, *b.* 1901: *m.* 1922, Cecil Vincent Haysom, of 14, Newhaven Terr., Mairangi Bay,
Auckland 10, NZ, and has issue living, Bevan Valletort (47, College Rd., Northcote, N4, Auckland,
NZ), *b.* 1923: *m.* 1949, Rae Florence, da. of Leopold Valentine Landman of Hamilton, Waikato, NZ,
and has issue living, David Valletort *b.* 1951, Elizabeth Jane *b.* 1952, Sally Ann *b.* 1955.——Caroline
Vivienne, *b.* 1902. *Residence,*—21, Balfour Rd., Auckland, NZ.

PREDECESSORS.—[1] *Rt. Hon.* RICHARD Edgcumbe, *P.C.*, many years M.P. for Cornwall, St.
Germans, and Plympton, was successively a Lord of the Treasury, Joint Vice-Treasurer,
Receiver-Gen., Treasurer of War, Paymaster-Gen. for Ireland, Chancellor of the Duchy of
Lancaster, and Lord-Lieut. of Cornwall, &c.; cr. *Baron Edgcumbe,* of Mount Edgcumbe, co. Devon
(peerage of Great Britain) 1742; *d.* 1758; *s.* by his el. son [2] RICHARD, *P.C.,* 2nd Baron; M.P. for
Plympton 1747-54, and for Penryn 1754-8; was Lord-Lieut. of Cornwall, and successively a Lord
Commr. of the Admiralty, and Comptroller of the Household, &c.; *d.* unmarried 1766; *s.* by his
brother [3] GEORGE, 3rd Baron; an Adm. of the Blue; M.P. for Plympton 1754-61, and Lord-Lieut.
of Cornwall; cr. *Viscount Mount Edgcumbe and Valletort* (peerage of Great Britain) 1781, and *Earl of
Mount Edgcumbe* (peerage of Great Britain) 1789; *d.* 1795; *s.* by his son [4] RICHARD, 2nd Earl; was
Lord-Lieut. of Cornwall; *d.* 1839; *s.* by his son [5] ERNEST AUGUSTUS, 3rd Earl; *b.* 1797: *m.* 1831,
Caroline Augusta, dau. of Rear-Adm. Charles Feilding; *d.* 1861; *s.* by his son [6] WILLIAM HENRY,

G.C.V.O., P.C., 4th Earl; sat as M.P. for Plymouth (*C*) 1859-61; was Lord-Lieut. of Cornwall 1877-1917, Lord Chamberlain of H.M. Queen Victoria's Household 1879-80, Lord High Steward of H.M. Queen Victoria's Household June 1885 to Jan. 1886, and July 1886 to Aug. 1892, and A.D.C. to H.M. Queen Victoria 1887-97; a Member of Council to H.R.H. the Prince of Wales 1901-17, and Keeper of the Seal of the Duchy of Cornwall 1907-17: *m.* 1st, 1858, Lady Katharine Elizabeth Hamilton, who *d.* 1874, dau. of the 1st Duke of Abercorn, K.G.; 2ndly, 1906, his cousin, Caroline Cecilia, who *d.* 1909, dau. of the late Hon. George Edgcumbe, and widow of the 3rd Earl of Ravensworth; *d.* 1917; *s.* by his only son, [7] PIERS ALEXANDER HAMILTON, 5th Earl; *b.* 1865; Dep. Warden of the Stanneries 1913-44: *m.* 1911, Lady Edith Villiers, who *d.* 1935, dau. of 5th Earl of Clarendon; *d.* 1944; *s.* by his kinsman [8] KENELM WILLIAM EDWARD, *TD* (only son of Richard John Frederick Edgcumbe, MVO, el. son of the Hon. George Edgcumbe, yst. son of 2nd Earl), 6th Earl, *b.* 1873: *m.* 1906, Lilian Agnes, who *d.* 1964, da. of Col. Arthur Chandos Arkwright, of Hatfield Place, Witham, Essex; *d.* 1965; *s.* by his kinsman [9] EDWARD PIERS (el. son of George Valletort Edgcumbe, el. son of Edward Mortimer Edgcumbe, 2nd son of Hon. George Edgcumbe, yst. of 2nd Earl), 7th Earl and present peer; also Viscount Mount Edgcumbe and Valletort, and Baron Edgcumbe.

MOUNTEVANS, BARON. (Evans.) [Baron U.K. 1945.]

(EDWARD PATRICK) BROKE EVANS, 3rd Baron; *b.* Feb. 1st, 1943; *s.* 1974; ed. at Rugby, and Trin. Coll., Oxford: *m.* 1974, Johanna Keyzer, of The Hague.

Arms,—Argent two bars wavy azure between three boar's heads erased sable. **Crest,**—Between two cross crosslets fichee sable a demi lion erased reguardant or holding between the paws a boar's head erased also sable. **Supporters,**—On either side a king penguin proper.

Address,—c/o British Tourist Authority, Stockholm, Sweden.

Liberty.

BROTHER LIVING.

Hon. JEFFREY RICHARD DE CORBAN (14, Quick St., N1), *b.* May 13th, 1948; ed. at Nautical Coll., Pangbourne, and Pembroke Coll., Camb.: *m.* 1972, Juliet, da. of the Hon. Richard John McMoran Wilson [see B. Moran].

SISTER LIVING.

Hon. Lucinda Mary Deirdre, *b.* 1951.

UNCLE LIVING (*son of 1st Baron.*)

Hon. Edward Broke, *VRD*, *b.* 1924; ed. at Wellington Coll.; Cdr. (E) RNR (ret.); and on Stan of ICI, Ltd.: *m.* 1947, Elaine Elizabeth, da. of Capt. (*S*) W. W. Cove, RN, and has issue living, Julian Phillip Broke, *b.* 1956,—William Garth, *b.* 1959,—Rosemary, *b.* 1948. *Residence,*—

WIDOW LIVING OF SECOND BARON.

DEIRDRE GRACE (*Deirdre, Baroness Mountevans*) (5, Campden House Court, 42, Gloucester Walk, W8 4HU), da. of John O'Connell, of Buxton House, Buxton Hill, Co. Cork: *m.* 1940, the 2nd Baron, who *d.* 1974.

PREDECESSORS.—[1] *Adm.* Sir EDWARD RATCLIFFE GARTH RUSSELL Evans, *KCB, DSC*, second son of the late Frank Evans, Bar.-at-law, of 5, New Square, Lincoln's Inn, WC; *b.* 1881; served as Second Officer of relief ship *Morning* during National Antarctic Expedition 1902-4, and made two voyages to Polar regions to relief of *Discovery*; was Second in Command of British Antarctic Expedition 1910, succeeding Capt. Scott in command 1912-13; European War 1914-19 with Dover Patrol in command of *Broke* and as Senior Officer, Ostend; Rear-Adm. Comdg. Roy. Australian Navy 1929-31, Com.-in-Ch., Africa Station 1933-5, and at The Nore 1935-9; Rector of Aberdeen Univ. 1936-42; Regional Commr. for London Defence Area 1939-45; *cr. Baron Mountevans*, of Chelsea, co. London (peerage of United Kingdom) 1945: *m.* 1st, 1904, Hilda Beatrice who *d.* 1913, da. of the late Thomas Gregory Russell, Bar.-at-law, of Christchurch, New Zealand; 2ndly, 1916, Elsa, who *d.* 1963, da. of the late Richard Andvord, of Oslo, Norway; *d.* 1957; *s.* by his el. son [2] RICHARD ANDVORD, 2nd Baron; *b.* 1918; Chm. of Norwegian Export Centre and Auto-Swedish Parl. Group; late Lt. RNVR: *m.* 1940, Deirdre Grace, da. of John O'Connell, of Buxton House, Buxton Hill, Co. Cork.; *b.* 1974; *s.* by his el. son [3] (EDWARD Patrick) Broke, 3rd Baron and present peer.

Mountgarret, Baron, title of Viscount Mountgarret on Roll of H. L.

MOUNTGARRET, VISCOUNT.　(Butler.)　Sits as BARON (Baron U.K. 1911.)
[Viscount I. 1550.]

I was humbled: I am exalted.

DEPRESSVS EXTOLLOR

RICHARD HENRY PIERS BUTLER, 17th Viscount; *b.* Nov. 8th, 1936; *s.* 1966; *h.p.* to Earldoms of Ormonde and Ossory [see M. Ormonde]; ed. at Eton and RMA, late Capt. Irish Guards: *m.* 1st, 1960 (m. diss. 1969), Gillian Margaret, only da. of Cyril Francis Stuart Buckley, of 41, St. Leonard's Ter., SW3; 2ndly, 1970, Mrs. Jennifer Susan Melville Fattorini, da. of Capt. D. M. Wills, of Barley Wood, Wrington, Som., and has issue by 1st m.

Arms,—Quarterly, 1st and 4th, per fesse sable and azure, a quadrangular castle with four towers between three martlets all argent, *Rawson;* 2nd and 3rd, or, a chief indented azure, a crescent for difference, *Butler.* Crests,—1st, An eagle's head per fesse sable and azure, goutté d'or holding in the beak two annulets interlaced paleways or, *Rawson* Out of a ducal coronet or, a plume of five ostrich feathers argent, therefrom a falcon rising of the last *Butler.* Supporters,— *Dexter,* a falcon wings inverted argent, armed, membered, and belled or; *sinister,* a male griffin argent, armed, collared, and chained or.

Residences,—Stanley House, S. Stanley, Harrogate; Wyvis, Evanton, Ross-shire. *Clubs,*—White's, Pratt's.

SONS LIVING. *(By 1st m.)*
Hon. PIERS JAMES RICHARD, *b.* April 15th, 1961.
Hon. Edmund Henry Richard, *b.* 1962.

DAUGHTER LIVING. *(By 1st m.)*
Hon. Henrietta Elizabeth Alexandra, *b.* 1964.

SISTER LIVING.
Hon. Sarah Elizabeth Ann, *b.* 1932 : *m.* 1955, Geoffrey Kenneth Raynar, and has issue living, Rupert James Geoffrey, *b.* 1957,—James Augustine, *b.* 1962. *Residence,*—Bilton Hall, York.

MOTHER LIVING.
(Eglantine Marie) Elizabeth (The Dolphins, Sandwich, Kent), da. of the late William Lorenzo Christie, of Jervaulx Abbey, Middleham, Yorks.: *m.* 1931, the 16th Viscount, who *d.* 1966, having obtained a divorce 1941; 2ndly, 1956, Rear Adm. Patrick Vivian McLaughlin, CB, DSO, who *d.* 1969.

PREDECESSORS.—[1] *Hon.* RICHARD Butler, 2nd son of 8th Earl of Ormonde; cr. *Viscount Mountgarret* (peerage of Ireland) 1550; *d.* 1571; *s.* by his son [2] EDMUND, 2nd Viscount; *d.* 1602; *s.* by his son [3] RICHARD, 3rd Viscount; sat as M.P. in several Parliaments; joined O'Neile, Earl of Tyrone, in his rebellion against Queen Elizabeth; was appointed Gen. of the Irish Forces 1642, and having been outlawed was in 1652, after his death, excepted from pardon; *s.* by his son [4] EDMUND, 4th Viscount, who in 1660 received a pardon for all treasons, rebellions, etc., and was restored to his estates, &c.; *d.* 1679; *s.* by his son [5] RICHARD, 5th Viscount; led the forlorn hope against the City of Londonderry, and being taken prisoner was afterwards outlawed, and his estates forfeited ; in 1692 claimed his seat in Parliament and took the oath of fidelity, and in 1715 the outlawry was reversed; *d.* 1706; *s.* by his son [6] EDMUND, 6th Viscount; *d.* 1735; *s.* by his el. son [7] RICHARD, 7th Viscount; *d.s.p.* 1736; *s.* by his brother [8] JAMES, 8th Viscount; *d.s.p.* 1743; *s.* by his brother [9] EDMUND, 9th Viscount; *d.* 1750; *s.* by his son [10] EDMUND, 10th Viscount; *d.* 1779; *s.* by his son [11] EDMUND, 11th Viscount; *d.* 1793; *s.* by his son [12] EDMUND, 12th Viscount; cr. *Earl of Kilkenny* (peerage of Ireland) 1793; *d.* 1846, when the earldom expired, and the minor honours devolved upon his nephew [13] HENRY EDMUND, 13th Viscount, son of the Hon. Henry, 3rd son of 11th Viscount, by Anne, dau. of John Harrison, Esq., of Newton House, co. York: *m.* 1844, Frances Penelope, who *d.* 1886. only child of Thomas Rawson, of Nidd Hall, Knaresboro': *d.* 1900: *s.* by his son [14] HENRY EDMUND, 14th Viscount; *b.* 1844; assumed by R. Lic. 1891 the surname of Rawson-Butler, and the additional arms of Rawson, but in 1902 by R. Lic. resumed the surname of Butler only; cr. *Baron Mountgarret,* of Nidd, W. Riding of York (peerage of UK) 1911: *m.* 1st, 1868, Mary Eleanor, who *d.* 1900, da. of the late St. John Chiverton Charlton, of Apley Castle, Shropshire; 2ndly, 1902, Robinia Marion, who *d.* 1944, el. da. of Col. Edward Hanning Hanning-Lee, JP (formerly Comdg. 2nd Life Guards), of The Old Manor House, Bighton, Alresford, Hants; *d.* 1912; *s.* by his son [15] EDMUND SOMERSET, 15th Viscount, *b.* 1875: *m.* 1897, Cecily, who *d.* 1961, (having *m.* 2ndly, 1919, as his second wife, Lieut.-Col. Charles Hervey Hoare, DSO, who assumed by Roy. Licence 1927 the surname of Grey in lieu of his patronymic), da. of the late Arthur Grey; *d.* 1918; *s.* by his half-brother [16] PIERS HENRY AUGUSTINE, 16th Viscount; *b.* 1903: *m.* 1st, 1931 (m. diss. 1941) Eglantine Marie Elizabeth, da. of William Lorenzo Christie, of Jervaulx Abbey, Yorks.; 2ndly, 1941, (Elise) Margarita, who *d.* 1968, da. of Sir John Nicholson Barran, 2nd Bt.; *d.* 1966; *s.* by his only son [17] RICHARD HENRY PIERS, 17th Viscount and present peer; also Baron Mountgarret.

MOUNTMORRES, VISCOUNTCY OF. (de Montmorency.) [Extinct 1951.]
DAUGHTERS LIVING OF SEVENTH VISCOUNT.
Hon. Sheila Marguerite Evelyn, *b.* 1918; is a Princess Christian Nurse; 1939-45 War as London Ambulance Driver: *m.* 1950, Robert Vernon Smith, and has issue living, Alastair Vernon Bouchard de Montmorency, *b.* 1951,—Robert Herve William de Montmorency, *b.* 1953,—*Residence,*—Combe House, Backwell, Som.
Hon. Carolie Madge Warrand, *b.* 1920; is a Physiotherapist; 1939-45 War in WAAF: *m.* 1947, Douglas Morris, and has issue living, Andrew John, *b.* 1957,—Diana Pauline, *b.* 1954. *Residence,*—Danebury Hill, Lilliput, Poole, Dorset.

MOUNT TEMPLE, BARONY OF. (Ashley.) [Extinct 1939.]

DAUGHTER LIVING OF FIRST BARON. (By 1st marriage.)

Hon. (Ruth) Mary Clarisse, b. 1906; resumed by deed poll, March 1938, her maiden name of Ashley in lieu of that of Cunningham-Reid: m. 1st, 1927, Capt. Alec Stratford Cunningham-Reid, D.F.C. who obtained a divorce 1940; 2ndly, 1940, (marriage dissolved 1943) Capt. Ernest Laurie Gardner only son of the late Sir Ernest Gardner; 3rdly, 1944, as his second wife, the 4th Baron Delamee, from whom she obtained a divorce 1955, and has issue living, (by 1st m.) Michael Duncan Alec (PO Box 24930, Nairobi, Kenya), b. 1928: m. 1st, 1954, Mary Bilyard-Leake; 2ndly, 1964, Dorothea Helen, yst. da. of A. W. Welton, of 1, Bassett Close, Sutton, Surrey, and has issue living, (by 1st m.) Duncan b. 1958, Fiona b. 1956,—(by 2nd m.), James Beaumont b. 1965,—Noel Robert (18, Porchester Terr., W2; Underwood Hall, Westley Waterless), b. 1930; late Lt. Welsh Gds.; a Co. Dir.: m. 1960, Tessa Milne, da. of Denis Moore, of Croydon, Surrey, and has issue living, Mark James b. 1962, Charles Ashley b. 1968, Jane Mary b. 1964. Residence,—The Hall, Six Mile Bottom, nr. Newmarket, Suffolk.

MOWBRAY, SEGRAVE and STOURTON, BARON. (Stourton.) [Baron E. 1283; Baron E. 1295; Baron E. 1448.]

[Title pronounced " Mo-bray, Seagrave and Sturton."]

LOYAL JE SERAI DURANT MA VIE.

I will be loyal during my life.

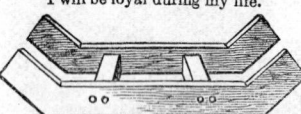

Badge of the Barons Stourton.

CHARLES EDWARD STOURTON, ★ 26th Baron Mowbray (Premier Baron of England), 27th Baron Segrave, and 23rd Baron Stourton; b. March 11th, 1923; s. 1965; ed. at Ampleforth Coll., and at Ch. Ch., Oxford; Opposition Whip, House of Lords 1967-70; a Lord-in-Waiting to HM 1970-74; Knt. of Sovereign Mil Order of Malta; 1939-45 War in NW Europe as Lt. Grenadier Guards (wounded): m. 1952, the Hon. Jane Faith de Yarburgh Bateson, only da. of 5th Baron Deramore, and has issue.

Arms,—Quarterly of six; 1st sable, a bend or between six fountains, Stourton; 2nd gules, on a bend between six crosses crosslet argent, an escutcheon or, charged with a demi-lion rampant, pierced through the mouth by an arrow, within a double treasure flory counterflory of the first, Howard; 3rd gules, a lion rampant argent, Mowbray; 4th sable, a lion rampant argent, ducally crowned or, Segrave; 5th gules, three lions passant guardant or, a label of three points argent, Plantagenet; 6th gules, a lion, rampant, within a bordure engrailed or, Talbot. Crest,—A demi monk proper, habited in russet, his girdle or and wielding in his dexter hand a scourge also or, thereon five knotted lashes. Supporters,—Dexter, a lion rampant argent, ducally crowned or; sinister, a sea-dog sable, scaled and finned or. Badge,—A drag or sledge.

Residences,—23, Warwick Sq., SW1; Marcus, by Forfar, Angus. Clubs,—Pratt's, Turf, White's.

SONS LIVING.

Hon. EDWARD WILLIAM STEPHEN, b. April 17th, 1953; ed. at Ampleforth.
Hon. James Alastair, b. 1956; ed. at Ampleforth.

SISTER LIVING.

Hon. Patricia Winifred Mary, b. 1924; sometime in Foreign Office: m. 1948, Frederick Petre Crowder, QC, MP [see B. Petre, colls.). Residence,—Charlestown, St. Austell, Cornwall.

UNCLE LIVING. (Son of 24th Baron.)

Hon. John Joseph, T.D., b. 1899; formerly Lt. 18th Hussars (Special Reserve), Yorkshire Hussars (Yeo.), and 10th Roy. Hussars, and Maj. (ret.) Roy. Norfolk Regt. (T.A.); N. Russia Relief Force 1919, 1939-45 War; sat as M.P. for S. Div. of Salford (U) Oct. 1931 to June 1945: m. 1st, 1923, Kathleen Alice (who obtained a divorce 1933), dau. of the late Robert Louis George Gunther, of 8, Prince's Gdns., S.W., and Park Wood, Englefield Green, Surrey; 2ndly, 1934, Gladys Leila (who obtained a divorce 1947), dau. of Col. Sir William James Waldron, of Ascot Cottage, Winkfield, Berks, and 77, Cromwell Rd., S.W.7, and has issue living, (by 1st marriage) Michael Godwin Plantagenet (The Old Rectory, Gt. Rollright, Chipping Norton), b. 1926; ed. at Eton; Maj. (ret.) Grenadier Guards; FRICS, QALAS; ADC to Comdt. RMA Sandhurst 1951-52, Adj. 1st Bn. Grenadier Guards 1953-55, and Staff Capt. HQ, London Dist. 1955-57; Land Agent to HRH Duke of Gloucester, Barnwell Manor Estate 1966-71, a partner, Curtis & Henson 1966-68, since when Savills: m. 1955, Lady Joanna Lambart, da. of 10th Earl of Cavan, and has issue living, Thomas Michael John b. 1965,—Henry Matthew b. 1971, Julia b. 1958, Clare Elizabeth b. 1962,—John Ralph (The Court House, Withington, Glos.), b. 1930; ed. at Eton, and at Magdalene Coll., Camb. (MA); late Lt. Gren. Gds. (Reserve): m. 1st, 1958, Virginia, da. of Basil Hordern, of The Old Rectory, Fernhurst, Sussex; 2ndly, 1967, Caroline Honor, da. of Col. J. C. O'Dwyer, of Magheracross, Ballinamallard, co. Fermanagh, and has issue living, (by 1st m.) Lucilla Mary b. 1959, (by 2nd m.) Georgina Caroline b. 1969, Jemima Nicola b. 1971,—Mary (Countess of Gainsborough), b. 1925: m. 1947, the 5th Earl of Gainsborough,—Monica Kathleen, b. 1928: m. 1955, Henry Louis Carron Greig, OVO (Gentleman Usher to HM), of Brook House, Fleet, Hants., son of the late Group Capt. Sir Louis Greig, KBE, OVO, and has issue living, Louis Stourton b. 1956; ed. at Eton; a Page of Honour to HM 1970-73, Jonathan b. 1958, George Carron b. 1960, Laura Monica (twin) b. 1960. Residence,—Miniature Hall, Wadhurst, Sussex.

AUNT LIVING. (Daughter of 24th Baron.)

Hon. Charlotte Mary, b. 1904. Residence,—Manor House, Otley, Yorkshire.

GREAT-AUNT LIVING. (Daughter of 20th Baron Stourton.)

Hon. Matilda Margaret Mary Josephine, b. 1884: m. 1910, Lieut.-Col. Baron Herbert Alexander von Metzsch-Reichenbach, who d. 1932. Residence,—Hotel Pelletier, Harcourt Street, Dublin.

★ Baron Mowbray, although Premier Baron of England, is not the holder of the Premier Barony, which at present is vested in Baroness de Ros.

WIDOW LIVING OF SON OF TWENTIETH BARON.

BEATRICE CICELY (*Hon. Mrs. Edward P. J. Corbally Stourton*) (The Garden House, Hullavington, Chippenham, Wilts.), da. of the late H. E. Page, of Wragby, Lincs., and Titchwell, Norfolk: *m.* 1934, the Hon. Edward Plantagenet Joseph CORBALLY STOURTON, who *d.* 1966, having assumed in 1927, the additional name of Corbally, and has issue [see colls., infra].

COLLATERAL BRANCHES LIVING. (*All of whom are in remainder to Baronies of Mowbray, Segrave and Stourton.*)

Issue of the late the Hon. Edward Plantagenet Joseph CORBALLY STOURTON, DSO, 4th son of 20th Baron Stourton, *b.* 1880, *d.* 1966, having assumed in 1927 the additional name of Corbally: *m.* 1934, Beatrice Cicely, da. of H. E. Page (ante):—
Nigel Edward (Oak Farm, Braydon, Swindon, Wilts., SN5 0AG), *b.* 1937; late Capt. Grenadier Guards; with IBM: *m.* 1960 (m. diss. 1975), Frances Deirdre Morton, da. of Patrick Lancaster, of Wapsbourne Manor, Sheffield Park, Sussex, and has issue living, Edward Richard, *b.* 1961,—Nicholas Simon, *b.* 1963,—Patrick Henry, *b.* 1965.——Vanessa Mary, *b.* 1935.

Grandson of the late Capt. the Hon. Everard Joseph Stourton, 5th son of 19th Baron Stourton:—
Issue of the late Everard Joseph Stourton, *b.* 1864, *d.* 1932: *m.* 1903, Ethel Maude, who *d.* 1964, da. of the late Lt.-Col. James Swinburne [see Swinburne, Bt., colls.]:—
Everard Botolph, *b.* 1905; ed. at Beaumont Coll. *Residence,—*

Granddaughter of the late Auberon Joseph Stourton, el. son of the late Hon. Albert Joseph Stourton (infra):—
Issue of the late Eudo Philip Joseph Stourton, *b.* 1900, *d.* 1975: *m.* 1927, Cicely Frances (La Grande Maison, St. John, Jersey), da. of the late Henry Hyman Haldin, KC, of 17, Montagu Sq., W1 [Leon, Bt.]:—
Veronica Philippa, *b.* 1929: *m.* 1954, Philip Biden Derwent Ashbrooke, of Seymour House, 3, Montpelier Row, Twickenham, Middx., and has issue living, Auberon Francis Biden, *b.* 1956,—Sophia Mary Veronica, *b.* 1959.

Grandchildren of the late Hon. Albert Joseph Stourton, 6th son of 19th Baron Stourton:—
Issue of the late Capt. Herbert Marmaduke Joseph Stourton, O.B.E., *b.* 1873, *d.* 1932: *m.* 1898, the Hon. Frances Mary Winefride, who *d.* 1950, dau. of 4th Viscount Southwell:—
Sir Ivo Herbert Evelyn Joseph, *CMG, OBE, KPM, b.* 1901; ed. at Stonyhurst; entered Colonial Police 1921; served in Mauritius 1921-33; was Commnr. of Police, Bermuda 1933-39, Aden 1940-45, Uganda 1945-50, and Nigeria 1950-53, and Dep. Inspector-Gen. of Colonial Police 1953-57, Inspector-Gen. 1957-66; King's Police Medal; Knt. Sovereign Mil. Order of Malta; OBE (Civil) 1939, CMG 1951, Knt. 1961: *m.* 1st, 1926, Lilian Margaret, who *d.* (result of enemy action during 1939-45 War) 1942, da. of George Dickson; 2ndly, 1945, Virginia, da. of Sir Horace James Seymour, GCMG, CVO [see M. Hertford, colls.], and has issue living, (by 1st m.) Nigel John Ivo (Westfield, Munstead, Godalming, Surrey), *b.* 1929: *m.* 1956, Rosemary Jennifer Rushworth, da. of the Hon. Mr. Justice (Sir Myles John) Abbott, Ch. Justice of Bermuda, and has issue living, Edward John Ivo *b.* 1957, Julian Nicolas *b.* 1959, Christopher Nigel Paul *b.* 1965, Lavinia Margaret Grace *b.* 1962,—Simon Nicholas (13, Selwood Terr., SW7), *b.* 1932: *m.* 1975, Pamela, da. of Charles James Baker, and widow of Alexander J. Scratchley,—Felicity Magdalen, *b.* 1927,—(by 2nd m.) Barbara Jane, *b.* 1947: *m.* 1974, Major (Archibald) Graham Buchanan-Dunlop. *Residence,—*The Old Bakery, Kimpton, Andover.——Magdalen Mary Charlotte, *b.* 1899: *m.* 1st, 1925, Archibald Ashworth Baille Hay, DSO, MC, from whom she obtained a divorce 1936; 2ndly, 1936, Robert Ducas, from whom she obtained a divorce in USA 1943; 3rdly 1947, William Brian Buchel, and has issue living, (by 2nd m.) Robert Ivo (Flat 10, 24, Lowdnes St., SW1 9JE), *b.* 1937: *m.* 1963, Patricia Provataroff,—Magda June (*Hon. Mrs. James D. D. Ogilvy*), *b.* 1938: *m.* 1959, the Hon. James Donald Diarmid Ogilvy, of Canal House, 23, Blomfield Rd., W9 [see E. Airlie). *Residence,—*Flat 10, 24, Lowdnes St., SW1X 9JE.——Barbara Bertha Mary (The Dower House, Stonor, Henley-on-Thames) *b.* 1900: *m.* 1st, 1924, Capt. Eric Charlton Tunnicliffe, Roy. Welch Fusiliers, who *d.* 1954 and from whom she had obtained a divorce 1929; 2ndly, 1929, Capt. Frank Ashton Bellville, who *d.* 1937; 3rdly, 1946, Capt. Steuart Harrison-Wallace, DSO, RN, who *d.* 1963, and has issue living, (by 1st m.) Nigel Arthur (of Mount Lodge, Portchester, Hants.), *b.* 1928; Capt. (ret.) Grenadier Guards; is with Vosper, Ltd., shipbuilders: *m.* 1957, Diana Edith (CUBITT), da. of Cdr. Peter DuCane, OBE, RN [see Pole, Bt., cr. 1628], and has issue living, Brigid Serena *b.* 1963,—Elizabeth Anne, *b.* 1926: *m.* 1947, William Alexander Mackenzie, of Barratts Park, Old Heathfield, Sussex, and has issue living, Michael Alexander Edward *b.* 1949, Margaret Anne *b.* 1955,—(by 2nd m.) Patricia Barbara, *b.* 1931: *m.* 1965, Alfred Charles Gladitz, of 18, Tregunter Rd., SW10.——Gytha Mary (The College, Froxfield, Marlborough, Wilts., SN8 3LA), *b.* 1904: *m.* 1934, Frederick Ramon de Bertrodano, 8th Marques del Moral (Spain), who *d.* 1955, and has issue living, Alfonso Michael George (Ferraz 73, Madrid 8) *b.* 1937: *m.* 1968, Carolina Garcia de la Riva, and has issue living, Miguel Ramon Marcus *b.* 1969, Ignacio José Roberto *b.* 1970, Gonzalo Alberto *b.* 1974,—Ignacio Roberto *b.* 1970,—Helen Gytha Mary, *b.* 1935: *m.* 1957, Jean le Goaëc, of Mas de Brocéliande, 83, Lorgues, Var, France, and has issue living, Yann Charles Ramon *b.* 1959, Michel Patrick Roland *b.* 1962, Annik Marie Nicole *b.* 1958, Katarina Marie Gytha *b.* 1960, Sophie *b.* 1971, Isabelle *b.* 1974.——Mary Jeanne (*Baroness Camoys*), *b.* 1913: *m.* 1938, the 6th Baron Camoys. *Residence,—*Stonor Park, Henley-on-Thames, Oxfordshire.

Issue of the late Bertha Mary Philippa Stourton, *b.* 1872, *d.* 1958: *m.* 1894, Major Frederick Bartholomew Stapleton-Bretherton, who *d.* 1938 [B. Petre]:—
Mary Henrietta STAPLETON-BRETHERTON (Woodland House, Northleigh Lane, Colehill, Wimborne Minster, Dorset, BH21 2PL), *b.* 1906; resumed the surname of Stapleton-Bretherton by deed poll 1960: *m.* 1940 (m. diss. 1953), Col. John Pell Archer-Shee, MC, late 10th Hussars, son of the late Lt.-Col. Sir Martin Archer-Shee, CMG, DSO, and has issue living, Mary Pauline Daphne Therese, *b.* 1941.

BRANCHES FROM YR. SONS OF 17TH BARON STOURTON.

Descendants of the late Hon. Edward Marmaduke Joseph VAVASOUR (3rd son of 17th Baron Stourton), who was cr. a *Baronet* 1828:—
See Vavasour, Bt., cr. 1828.

Grandchildren of the late Charles Joseph LANGDALE, son of the late Hon. Charles Joseph LANGDALE, M.P., 4th son of 17th Baron Stourton:—
Issue of the late Lieut.-Col. Philip Joseph LANGDALE, O.B.E., *b.* 1863, *d.* 1950: *m.* 1895, Gertrude, who *d.* 1939, dau. of the late Adm. Samuel Hoskins Derriman, C.B., of Uplands, Sussex, and 52, Queen's Gate, S.W.:—
Joyce Elizabeth Mary (*Countess Fitzwilliam*). *b.* 1898: *m.* 1st, 1922 (marriage dissolved 1955), the 2nd Viscount Fitz Alan of Derwent, who *d.* 1962; 2ndly, 1956, the 10th Earl Fitzwilliam. *Residences,—*Milton Peterborough; Wentworth Woodhouse, Rotherham, Yorkshire.——Alethea Alice Mary Pauline, *b.* 1902: *m.* 1923, the 2nd Baron Manton, who *d.* 1968, and from whom she obtained a divorce 1936. *Residence,—*4, Belgrave Sq., SW1.

Grandsons of the late Lt.-Col. Philip Joseph Langdale, OBE (ante):—
Issue of the late Ursula Dorothy Mary Langdale, *b.* 1903, *d.* 1969: *m.* 1931, Lt.-Col. Norman Birch, who *d.* 1960:—
Michael Edward Stafford (Walkington Park, Beverley, E. Yorks.), *b.* 1933.——Timothy Malcolm Stafford, *b.* 1937.

Grandchildren of the late Henry Joseph Stourton, son of the late Hon. Philip Henry
Joseph Stourton, 6th son of 17th Baron Stourton :—
Issue of the late Violet Mary Annette Stourton, O.B.E., *b.* 1873, *d.* 1961: *m.* 1893, Francis
Joseph Siltzer, who *d.* 1924 :—
Derek Henry (8B, Longwood, Darling Point, Sydney, NSW), *b.* 1897; ed. at Oratory Sch.: *m.* 1938,
Merlyn Seaforth, da. of William Densham, of Melbourne, Aust., and widow of Keith Poulton.——
Enid Mary, *b.* 1895: *m.* 1920, Baron Raymond Snoy d'Oppuers, who *d.* 1960, and has issue living.
Residence,—Capouillet, 1023, Chaussée d'Alsemberg, Braine l'Alleud, Belgium.

Issue of the late Amy Mary Josephine, *b.* 1874, *d.* 1954 : *m.* 1896, Frederic Dundas Harford,
C.V.O., who *d.* 1931 :—
Joan Mary (*Joan, Lady Bannerman*), *b.* 1897 : *m.* 1920, Lieut.-Col. Sir Alexander Bannerman, 11th
Bt., who *d.* 1934.   *Residence,*—28, Melton Court, S.W.7.

PREDECESSORS.—[1] Sir JOHN Stourton, Knt., was Sheriff of Wilts 1434, and of co.
Gloucester 1438, and Treasurer of the Household 1445 ; served in the Wars of France and
Normandy ; cr. *Baron Stourton*, of Stourton, co. Wilts (peerage of England) 1448 ; *d.* 1462;
s. by his son [2] WILLIAM, 2nd Baron ; *d.* 1478-9 ; *s.* by his el. son [3] JOHN, 3rd Baron; *s.*
by his son [4] FRANCIS, 4th Baron ; *d.* (young) 1486-7 ; *s.* by his uncle [5] WILLIAM, 5th Baron ;
d.s.p. 1522; *s.* by his brother [6] EDWARD, 6th Baron; appointed by Act of Parliament a
Justice of the Peace for assessing and collecting £163,000 by a poll-tax; *d.* 1535; *s.* by his son
[7] WILLIAM, 7th Baron; *d.* 1548; *s.* by his son [8] CHARLES, 8th Baron; was executed March
16th, 1557, at Salisbury, in a halter of silk, for murdering two men named Hartgill; *s.* by his
el. son [9] JOHN, 9th Baron; restored in blood by Act of Parliament 1575, and inherited the
barony ; was one of the peers on the trial of Queen Mary of Scotland ; *s.* by his brother [10]
EDWARD, 10th Baron ; *d.* 1632; *s.* by his son [11] WILLIAM, 11th Baron ; *s.* by his grandson
[12] WILLIAM, 12th Baron ; *s.* by his el. son [13] EDWARD, 13th Baron ; *d.s.p.* 1720 ; *s.* by his
brother [14] THOMAS, 14th Baron ; *d.s.p.* 1743 ; *s.* by his nephew [15] CHARLES, 15th Baron,
son of Charles, 3rd son of 12th Baron ; *d.* 1753-4; *s.* by his brother [16] WILLIAM, 16th Baron:
m. 1749, el. dau. and in her issue co-heir of Philip Howard, of Buckenham, Norfolk, and in her issue
co-heiress of her uncles, the 8th and 9th Dukes of Norfolk, to the Baronies of Mowbray and of
Segrave (see *.* infra) and of Howard, Greystock, Ferrers of Wemme, Furnival, Strange of Blackmere, Giffard of Brimmesfield, and Braose of Gower, &c.; *d.* 1781; *s.* by his son [17] CHARLES
PHILIP, 17th Baron ; *d.* 1816; *s.* by his son [18] WILLIAM JOSEPH, 18th Baron ; *d.* 1846; *s.* by
his son [19] CHARLES, 19th Baron ; *b.* 1802 : *m.* 1825, the Hon. Mary Lucy, dau. of 6th Baron
Clifford ; *d.* 1872; *s.* by his el. surviving son [20] ALFRED JOSEPH, 20th Baron, in whose
favour the abeyances of the Baronies of *Mowbray* and *Segrave* (see *.* infra) were terminated.

. [1] ROGER de Mowbray was summoned to the Parliament of England as *Baron Mowbray*
1283; having previously been summoned by Simon de Montfort, when in rebellion *temp.* Henry
III., such summons was declared void by Act of Parliament; *d.* 1298; *s.* by his son [2] JOHN,
2nd Baron; summoned to Parliament in two reigns: *m.* Alice, dau. and co-heir of William,
Baron de Braose; was executed at York 1322 for his connection with the rising of the Northern
Earls against the Despencers; his estates were forfeited, but an attainder did not follow; *s.* by
his son [3] JOHN, 3rd Baron; served in the wars of Scotland and France, and was summoned
to Parliament *temp.* Edward III.; *d.* 1361; *s.* by his son [4] JOHN, 4th Baron; summoned to
Parliament *temp.* Edward III.: *m.* Elizabeth, dau. and heir of John, 3rd Baron Segrave (see
†‡† infra), by which marriage the Segrave estates and the dignity of Lord Segrave vested in
him; slain near Constantinople 1368; *s.* by his el. son [5] JOHN, 5th Baron; cr. *Earl of Nottingham* (peerage of England) 1337 ; *d.* unmarried 1382, when the earldom expired ; *s.* by his brother
[6] THOMAS, K.G., 6th Baron; summoned as *Earl of Nottingham* (peerage of England) 1383-86 ;
and cr. Earl Marshal 1386, and *Duke of Norfolk* (peerage of England) 1397: *m.* 1st, Elizabeth,
dau. and heir of John, Lord Strange, of Blackmere; and 2ndly, Elizabeth, dau. and co-heir of
Richard FitzAlan, Earl of Arundel and Surrey ; by the latter he left two sons Thomas and
John, and two daus. Margaret, wife of Sir Robert Howard, and Isabel, wife of James, 6th Lord
Berkeley ; *d.* 1399; *s.* by his el. son [7] THOMAS, 2nd Earl, the Dukedom of Norfolk being
erroneously withheld from him. joined the rebellion of the nobles against Henry IV. 1405, and
being arrested, was beheaded at York without a trial: *d.s.p.*; *s.* by his brother [8] JOHN, 3rd
Duke ; in 1425 declared by Parliament to be entitled to the dukedom; *s.* by his son [9] JOHN,
4th Duke; obtained a confirmation of the dukedom: went as Ambassador to negotiate peace
between England and France: *m.* Eleanor, dau. of William, Baron Bourchier; *s.* by his son [10]
JOHN, 5th Duke; cr. *Earl of Warren and Surrey* (peerage of England); *d.* 1475, when the
Dukedom of Norfolk, and Earldoms of Nottingham, Warren, and Surrey expired, while the
Baronies of Mowbray and Segrave devolved upon his dau. [11] ANNE, who in infancy
was affianced to Richard, Duke of York, 2nd son of Edward IV.; he was murdered with
his brother in the Tower 1483, and the Duchess *d.s.p.*, when the baronies became abeyant
between the sons of Sir Robert Howard and Lord Berkeley (see 6th Baron Mowbray), and
remained so until the abeyance was terminated in favour of [12—22] JOHN Howard;
cr. *Baron Howard* (peerage of England) 1470, and *Duke of Norfolk* (peerage of England)
1483, with which peerages the Baronies of Mowbray and Segrave were merged until 1777,
when they again became abeyant and remained so until 1877, when the abeyances were terminated in favour of [23] ALFRED JOSEPH Stourton, 20th Baron Stourton (ante), as senior
co-heir of Margaret, wife of Sir Robert Howard (see 6th Baron Mowbray); *b.* 1829: *m.* 1865,
Mary Margaret, who *d.* 1925, dau. of the late Matthew Corbally, M.P.; *d.* 1893; *s.* by his
el. son [24] CHARLES BOTOLPH JOSEPH, 24th Baron Mowbray, 25th Baron Segrave, and 21st
Baron Stourton ; *b.* 1867 : claimed as Lord Mowbray to be placed Premier Baron of England :
m. 1893, Mary, who *d.* 1961, only child of the late Thomas Angus Constable, of Manor House, Otley,
d. 1936; *s.* by his el. son [25] WILLIAM MARMADUKE, MC, 25th Baron Mowbray, 26th Baron
Segrave, 22nd Baron Stourton, *b.* 1895; Capt. Grenadier Guards: *m.* 1921, Sheila, who *d.* 1975, da.
of the late Hon. Edward Walford Karslake Gully, CB [V. Selby, colls.]; *d.* 1965; *s.* by his only son,
[26] CHARLES EDWARD, 26th Baron Mowbray, 27th Baron Segrave, 23rd Baron Stourton and
present peer.

†‡† [1] NICHOLAS de Segrave, one of the most active leaders of the Barons *temp.* Henry III., was
summoned to Parliament of England in the King's name as *Baron Segrave* 1295; *d.* 1295; *s.*
by his son [2] JOHN, 2nd Baron; summoned to Parliament 1296-1325; was Constable of the
English Army in Scotland; taken prisoner at the battle of Bannockburn, and imprisoned
by the Scots for a year; *d.* 1325; *s.* by his grandson [3] JOHN, 3rd Baron: *m.* Margaret, sole
heiress of Thomas de Brotherton, Earl of Norfolk, 5th son of Edward I.; *d.* 1353; *s.* by his dau.
[4] ELIZABETH, wife of John, 4th Baron Mowbray (see *.* ante).

MOYLE, BARONY. (Moyle.) [Extinct 1974.]

SON LIVING OF LIFE BARON. (By 1st m.)
Hon. Roland Dunstan, *MP* (c/o House of Commons, SW1), *b.* 1928; ed. at Univ. of Wales, Aberystwyth,
and at Trin. Hall, Camb.; MP for N. Lewisham (*Lab.*) 1966-74 and for E. Lewisham since 1974;
Min. of State for NI since 1974: *m.* 1956, Shelagh Patricia, da. of Bernard Hogan, of Cardiff, and
has issue.

WIDOW LIVING OF LIFE BARON.

LENA (*Baroness Moyle*), (Hafod, Grassy Lane, Sevenoaks, Kent), da. of William Henry Bassett, of Frant, Tunbridge Wells: *m.* 1951, as his 2nd wife, Baron Moyle (Life Baron) who *d.* 1974.

MOYNE, BARON. (Guinness.) [Baron U.K. 1932.]

BRYAN WALTER GUINNESS, 2nd Baron; *b.* Oct. 27th, 1905; *s.* 1944; ed. at Eton, and at Ch. Ch., Oxford (MA); Hon. LLD Dublin 1958; Hon. LLD National Univ. of Ireland 1961; Bar. Inner Temple 1930; formerly Maj. Roy. Sussex Regt.; is a Poet and Novelist, and a Member of Irish Academy of Letters; FRSL; a Gov. of Nat. Gallery of Ireland since 1955: *m.* 1929, the Hon. Diana Freeman Mitford (who obtained a divorce 1934), da. of 2nd Baron Redesdale; 2ndly, 1936, Elisabeth, da. of the late Thomas Nelson, and has issue living by 1st and 2nd marriages.

Arms,—Per saltire gules and azure, a lion rampant or ; on a chief ermine two ducal coronets each enfiling as many arrows in saltire of the third. **Crest,**—A boar passant quarterly or and gules charged with a mullet counterchanged. **Supporters,**—On either side a Cingalese macaque sejant proper.

Judge not.

Residences,—Biddesden House, Andover, Hants.; Knockmaroon, Castleknock, co. Dublin.

SONS LIVING. (By 1st marriage.)

Hon. JONATHAN BRYAN, *b.* March 16th, 1930 ; ed. at Eton (King's Scholar), and at Trin. Coll., Oxford: *m.* 1st, 1951 (marriage dissolved 1963), Ingrid Olivia Georgia, dau. of the late Maj. Guy Richard Charles Wyndham, MC [see B. Egremont, colls.]; 2ndly, 1964, Mrs. Suzanne Phillips, da. of H. W. D. Lisney, of Cadaques, Gerona, Spain, and has issue living, (by 1st marriage) Jasper Jonathan Richard, *b.* 1954,—Valentine Guy Bryan, *b.* 1959,—Catherine Ingrid, *b.* 1952,—(by 2nd marriage) Sebastian Walter Denis, *b.* 1964,—Daphne Suzannah Diana Joan, *b.* 1967. *Residences,*—17, Kensington Sq., W8; Osbaston Hall, Market Bosworth, Nuneaton; Ermita de San Sebastian, Cadaques, Gerona, Spain.

Hon. Desmond Walter, *b.* 1931; ed. at Gordonstoun, and at Ch. Ch. Oxford (MA): *m.* 1954, H.S.H. Princess Marie-Gabrielle Sophie Joti Elisabeth Albertine Almeria, el. da. of H.S.H. Prince Albrecht Eberhard Karl Gero-Maria von Urach, Count of Württemberg, and has issue living, Patrick Desmond Karl Alexander, *b.* 1956,—Marina, *b.* 1957. *Residence,*—Leixlip Castle, co. Kildare.

(By 2nd marriage.)

Hon. Diarmid Edward (9, St. Albans Grove, W8; Crawlboys Farm, Ludgershall, nr. Andover), *b.* 1938; ed. at Winchester, and at St. Catharine's Coll., Camb. (MA); late Lt. Queen's Own Hussars; a Brewer; a Dir. of Guinness Overseas, Ltd.): *m.* 1962, Felicity, only da. of Andrew Hunter Carnwath, of The Old Vicarage, Ugley, Bishop's Stortford, Herts., and has issue living, Ewan Diarmid, *b.* 1965,—Camilla, *b.* 1963,—Lorna, *b.* 1967,—Harriet, *b.* 1970.

Hon. Finn Benjamin, *b.* 1945; ed. at Winchester, and Ch. Ch., Oxford (BA); with Depart. of Genetics, Edinburgh Univ. (PhD).

Hon. Kieran Arthur, *b.* 1949; ed. at Winchester, and Ch. Ch., Oxford (BA); Botanist.

Hon. Erskine Stuart Richard, *b,* 1953; ed. at Winchester, and Edinburgh Univ.

DAUGHTERS LIVING. (By 2nd m.)

Hon. Rosaleen Elisabeth, *b.* 1937; ed. at St. Anne's Coll., Oxford (MA): *m.* 1965, Sudhir Mulji, and has issue living, Sachin Sudhir, *b.* 1967,—Kabir Jayantilal Bryan, *b.* 1970,—Sangita Rosaleen, *b.* 1966.

Hon. Thomasin Margaret, *b.* 1947; ed. at Cranborne Chase, and Farnham Coll. of Art; Potter and Painter.

Hon. Catriona Rose, *b.* 1950; ed. at Cranborne Chase, and Winchester Co. High Sch.; LMH Oxford.

Hon. Fiona Evelyn, *b.* 1940; ed. at Cranborne Chase, and Magill Univ., Canada; a Zoologist.

Hon. Mirabel Jane, *b.* 1956; ed. at Cranborne Chase.

BROTHER LIVING.

Hon. Murtogh David, *b.* 1913 : *m.* 1949 Nancy Vivian Laura, only dau. of the late Cyril Edward Tarbolton, of Hampstead, N.W. *Residence,*—Porter's House, St. James, Barbados.

SISTER LIVING.

Hon. Grania Mève Rosaura (*Marchioness of Normanby*), *b.* 1920; Hon. LLD Dublin; a JP for North Yorks.; formerly Section Officer WAAF: *m.* 1951, the 4th Marquess of Normanby. *Residences,*—Mulgrave Castle, Whitby; Argyll House, 211, King's Rd., SW3.

PREDECESSOR.—[1] *Rt. Hon.* WALTER EDWARD GUINNESS, *D.S.O., T.D.,* 3rd son of 1st Earl of Iveagh; *b.* 1880; Lt.-Col. late Loyal Suffolk Hussars; S. Africa 1900-1901 (despatches), 1914-18 War (D.S.O. and Bar); was a County Councillor for London 1907-10, Under-Sec. of State for War 1922-23, Financial Sec. to Treasury 1923-24 and 1924-25, Min. of Agriculture and Fisheries 1925-29, Joint Parliamentary Sec. to Min. of Agriculture and Fisheries 1940-41, Sec. of State for the Colonies and Leader of the House of Lords 1941-42, Dep. Min. of State in Middle East 1942-44, and Min. Resident for United Kingdom in Middle East Jan. to Nov. 1944; cr. *Baron Moyne* of Bury St. Edmunds, co. Suffolk (peerage of United Kingdom) 1932: *m.* 1903, Lady Evelyn Hilda Stuart Erskine, who *d.* 1939, dau. of 14th Earl of Buchan; *d.* (assassinated in Cairo) 1944; *s.* by his son [2] BRYAN WALTER, 2nd Baron and present peer.

MOYNIHAN, BARON. (Moynihan.) [Baron U.K. 1929, Bt. 1922.]

ANTONY PATRICK ANDREW CAIRNES BERKELEY MOYNIHAN, 3rd Baron, and 3rd Baronet; *b.* Feb. 2nd, 1936; *s.* 1965; ed. at Stowe; late Lt. Coldstream Gds.: *m.* 1st, 1955, Ann, who obtained a divorce 1958, da. of Reuben Stanley Herbert, of Greenfield Cottage, Therfield, Royston; 2ndly, 1958 (m. diss. 1967), Shirin Roshan Berry, da. of the late Ahmed Quereshi; 3rdly, 1968, Luthgarda Maria Beltran Dela Roza, da. of Alfonzo Fernandez, of 160, P. Gomez, Caloocan City, Philippines, and has issue by 2nd and 3rd m.

Arms,—Azure, a chevron between in chief three mullets argent and in base a rose also argent barbed and seeded proper. Crest,—A demi-knight in armour affrontee, resting the sinister hand on the hip proper, and supporting with the dexter hand a spear also proper, flowing therefrom a forked pennon argent, charged with a Maltese cross sable. Supporters,—On either side an owl argent gorged with a Baron's coronet or.

Residence,—

DAUGHTERS LIVING. (*By 2nd m.*)
Hon. Miranda Dorne Ierne, *b.* 1959.

(*By 3rd m.*)
Hon. Antonita Maria Carmen Fernandez, *b.* 1969.
Hon. Aurora Luzon Maria Dolores, *b.* 1971.
Hon. Kathleen Maynila Helen Imogen Juliet, *b.* 1974.

HALF-BROTHER LIVING.
Hon. COLIN BERKELEY, *b.* Sept. 13th, 1955.

SISTERS LIVING.
Hon. Imogen Anne Ierne, *b.* 1932: *m.* 1st 1953 (m. diss. 1965), Michael Edward Peter Williams; 2ndly, 1965, Charles Ivan Vance, of Quince Cottage, Bilsington, Ashford, Kent, and has issue living (by 2nd m.), Jacqueline Belinda Ierne *b.* 1963.
Hon. Juliet Jane Margaretta, *b.* 1934: *m.* 1958, Thomas Edwin Bidwell Abraham, of Uplands, Bonnington, W. Ashford, Kent, and has issue living, James Bidwell, *b.* 1959,—John Richard, *b.* 1960.

HALF-SISTER LIVING.
Hon. Melanie June, *b.* 1957.

AUNTS LIVING. (*Daughters of 1st Baron.*)
Hon. Dorothy Wellesley (Carr Cottage, 42, Warwick Rd., Beaconsfield), *b.* 1897.
Hon. Shelagh Berkeley (48, Gregories Rd., Beaconsfield, Bucks.), *b.* 1902: *m.* 1923, Henry Wynn Parry (Knt. 1946), who *d.* 1964, and from whom she obtained a divorce 1929, and has issue living, Christopher Berkeley (4, Pembroke Villas, W8), *b.* 1924: *m.* 1953, Lamorna Cathleen, da. of A. G. W. Sawyer, of Clavering, Essex.

MOTHER LIVING.
IERNE HELEN (*Ierne, Baroness Moynihan*) (81, Sussex Sq., W2), el. da. of the late Cairnes Derrick Carrington Candy: *m.* 1931, the 2nd Baron, from whom she obtained a divorce 1952, and who *d.* 1965.

WIDOW LIVING OF SECOND BARON.
JUNE ELIZABETH, da. of Arthur Stanley Hopkins: *m.* 1st, 1952, as his 2nd wife, the 2nd Baron, who *d.* 1965; 2ndly, 1967, Neville Barton Hayman, of Burstowe, Shirley Av., Cheam, Surrey.

PREDECESSORS.—[1] *Sir* BERKELEY GEORGE ANDREW Moynihan, *K.C.M.G., C.B.,* son of the late Capt. Andrew Moynihan, V.C., 8th King's Regt.; *b.* 1865; an eminent Surg.; Pres. of Roy. Coll. of Surgs. of England 1926-32; cr. a *Baronet* 1922, and *Baron Moynihan,* of Leeds, co. York (peerage of United Kingdom) 1929: *m.* 1895, Isabella Wellesley, who *d.* 1936, dau. of Thomas Richard Jessop, FRCS, JP; *d.* 1936; *s.* by his son [2] PATRICK BERKELEY, *OBE, TD,* 2nd Baron, *b.* 1906; Chm. Exec. Cttee., Liberal Party 1947-50, and Chm. of N.-W. Metropolitan Regional Hosp. Board 1960-65: *m.* 1st, 1931, Ierne Helen (who obtained a divorce 1952), el. da. of the late Cairnes Derrick Carrington Candy; 2ndly, 1952, June Elizabeth, who *m.* 2ndly, 1967, Neville Barton Hayman), yr. da. of Arthur Stanley Hopkins, *d.* 1965; *s.* by his el. son [3] ANTONY PATRICK ANDREW CAIRNES BERKELEY, 3rd Baron and present peer.

MOYOLA, BARON. (Chichester-Clark.) [Life Baron 1971.]

JAMES DAWSON CHICHESTER-CLARK, *PC,* son of the late Capt. James Jackson Lenox-Conyngham Chichester-Clark, DSO, RN, [see M. Donegall, colls.]; *b.* Feb. 12th, 1923; ed. at Eton; Maj. (ret.) Irish Gds.; 1939-45 War (wounded); a DL of co. Derry; a Member of House of Commons of N. Ireland 1960-71, Ch. Whip 1963-66, Leader 1966-67, Min. of Agric. 1967-69 and Prime Min. 1969-71; cr. PC 1967, and *Baron Moyola,* of Castledawson, co. Londonderry (Life Baron) 1971: *m.* 1959, Moyra Maud, da. of Brig.

Arthur de Burgh Morris, CBE, DSO, and widow of Capt. T. G. Haughton, and has issue.

Arms,—Quarterly, 1st, gules three swords erect in pale proper, hilts and pommels or, a canton argent, charged with a trefoil vert, *Clark*; 2nd, chequy or and gules, a chief vair, *Chichester*; 3rd, azure fretty argent *Etchingham*; 4th, azure on a bend or three daws gules, *Dawson.* *Crest,*—Out of a mural crown an arm embowed in armour, the hand holding a dagger, all proper, charged with a trefoil vert. *Supporters,*—Not exemplified at time of going to press.

Residence,—Moyola Park, Castledawson, co. Derry.

DAUGHTERS LIVING.

Hon. Fiona, *b.* 1960.
Hon. Tara Olivia, *b.* 1962.

MUIRSHIEL, VISCOUNT. (Maclay.) [Viscount U.K. 1963.]

Trust in God

IN DEO FIDES

John Scott Maclay, *KT, CH, CMG, PC,* 1st Viscount, 5th son of 1st Baron Maclay; *b.* Oct. 26th, 1905; ed. at Winchester, and Trin Coll., Camb.; Hon. LLD Edinburgh, Strathclyde, and Glasgow; late Lt. RA (TA); Member of British Merchant Shipping Mission, Washington; Parl. Sec. to Min. of Production, May to July 1945, Chm. of National Liberal Parl. Party 1947-50, Min. of Transport and Civil Aviation 1951-52, Pres. of Assembly of Western European Union 1955-56, Min. of State for Colonial Affairs 1956-57, and Sec. of State for Scotland 1957-62; Chm., Joint Exchequer Board (NI) 1965-73; appointed Lord-Lieut. of Renfrewshire 1967; MP for Montrose (*NL*) 1940-50, and for W. Div. of Renfrewshire (*C and L*) 1950-64; *cr.* CMG 1944, PC 1952, CH 1962, *Viscount Muirshiel,* of Kilmacolm, co. Renfrewshire (peerage of UK) 1964 and KT 1973: *m.* 1930, Betty L'Estrange, who *d.* 1974, da. of the late Maj. Delaval Graham L'Estrange Astley, CB [B. Hastings, colls.].

Arms,—Or, a lion rampant azure, armed and langued gules, resting his sinister paw upon an anchor sable, all within an orle of the second, a cinque foil in dexter chief ermine. *Crest,*—A lymphad sails furled sable, flagged gules. *Supporters,*—Two muirfowl their wings close proper.

Residence,—Knapps, Kilmacolm, Renfrewshire. *Club,*—Turf; Royal Yacht Squadron.

MUNSTER, EARL OF. (Fitz-Clarence.) [Earl U.K. 1831.]

Nec Temere Nec Timide.

Neither rashly nor arfefully.

Geoffrey William Richard Hugh Fitz-Clarence, *K.B.E., P.C.,* 5th Earl; *b.* Feb. 17th, 1906; *s.* 1928; ed. at Charterhouse; formerly Capt. R.A.S.C. (T.A.); 2nd Lieut. and temporary Major Grenadier Guards; Lord-Lieut. of Surrey 1957-73; 1939-41 War (despatches); was a County Councillor for London, N. Paddington Div. 1931-7; appointed a Lord-in-Waiting to H.M. 1932, and Paymaster-Gen. 1938; was Under-Sec. of State for War and Vice-Pres. of Army Council Jan. to Sept. 1939, Parliamentary Under-Sec. of State for India and Burma Jan. 1943 to Oct. 1944, Under-Sec. of State for Home Affairs Oct. 1944 to July 1945, Parliamentary Under-Sec. of State for Colonies Oct. 1951 to Oct. 1954, and Min. without Portfolio Oct. 1954 to June 1957, and Chm., Uganda Relationshops Commn. 1960-61; elected Dep. Chm. Commonwealth Parliamentary Asso. 1955; a K.St.J.; P.C. 1954, K.B.E. (Civil) 1957: *m.* 1928, Hilary, only child of E. Kenneth Wilson, of Cannizaro, Wimbledon, S.W. [The 5th Earl *d.* Aug. 27th, 1975].

Arms.—The arms of King William IV, (without the escutcheon of the arch-treasurer of the H. R. empire, and without the crown of Hanover), debruised by a baton sinister azure, charged with three anchors or. **Crest.**—On a chapeau, gules, doubled up ermine, a lion statant guardant crowned with a ducal coronet or, and gorged with a collar azure, charged with three anchors or. **Supporters.**—*Dexter*, a lion guardant, ducally crowned or ; *sinister*, a horse argent ; each gorged with a collar azure, charged with three anchors or.

Residence,—Sandhills, Bletchingley, Surrey. *Club,*—Turf.

SISTER LIVING. *(Raised to the rank of an Earl's daughter* 1928.)

Lady (Wilhelmina) Joan Mary, *b.* 1904 : *m.* 1st, 1928, Oliver Birkbeck, who *d.* 1952 [M. Hertford, colls.]: 2ndly, 1961, Lt.-Col. Henry John Cator, MC, who *d.* 1965, and has issue living, (by 1st *m.*) Edward Harold (Kinmount, Annan, Dumfries-shire), *b.* 1929; ed. at Eton: *m.* 1958, Sarah Anne, da. of Capt. Edward William Brook [B. Gretton], and has issue living, George Charles Edward, *b.* 1964, Elizabeth Mary *b.* 1960, Nicola Susan *b.* 1962,—John Oliver (Litcham Hall, King's Lynn; Turf Club), *b.* 1936; ed. at Gordonstoun: *m.* 1964, Hermione Anne, da. of the late Maj. D'Arcy Dawes, of Leacon Hall, Warehorne, Ashford, Kent [see Thompson, Bt., colls., *cr.* 1890], and has issue living, Oliver Benjamin *b.* 1973, Lucy Claire *b.* 1966, Roseanna *b.* 1974,—Mary Joan, *b.* 1931. *Residence,*—Little Massingham House, King's Lynn, Norfolk.

COLLATERAL BRANCHES LIVING.

Issue of the late Hon. William George Fitz-Clarence, 6th son of 2nd Earl, *b.* 1864, *d.* 1899: *m.* 1887, Charlotte Elizabeth Aline, who *d.* 1902, dau. of Richard Williams:—

Wilhelmina Violet Eileen, *b.* 1895 : *m.* 1918, Major Cecil John Cokayne Maunsell, J.P., formerly R.A., who *d.* 1948 [B. Waterpark, colls.], and has issue living, Cecilia Violet Cokayne, *b.* 1919 : *m.* 1940 (marriage dissolved 1958), Lieut.-Col. George Arnold Ford Kennard, late 4th Hussars [now 3rd Bt.]. *Residence,*—

Grandchildren of the late Capt. the Hon. George Fitz-Clarence, 3rd son of 1st Earl:—

Issue of the late Brig.-Gen. Charles Fitz-Clarence, V.C., Irish Guards, *b.* 1865, *d.* (killed in action) 1914: *m.* 1898, Violet, who *d.* 1941, dau. of the late Lord Alfred Spencer-Churchill [D. Marlborough, colls.]:—

EDWARD CHARLES, *b.* Oct. 3rd, 1899 ; ed. at Eton; Capt. (retired) Irish Guards, and a Serving Brother of Order of St. John of Jerusalem : *m.* 1st, 1925, Monica Shiela Harrington, who *d.* 1958 (having obtained a divorce 1930), dau. of Sir Henry Mullenoux Grayson, K.B.E., 1st Bt.; 2ndly, 1939, Mrs. Vivian Schofield, dau. of the late Benjamin Schofield, J.P., and has issue living, (by 1st marriage) Anthony Charles (10, Brondesbury Park Mansions, Salusbury Rd., NW6), *b.* 1926: *m.* 1st, 1949 (m. diss. 1966), Louise Marguerite Diana Delvigne; 2ndly, 1966, Mrs. Pamela Margaret Hyde, and has issue living (by 1st marriage), Tara Francesca *b.* 1952, Finola Dominique *b.* 1953,—Mary-Jill, *b.* 1928: resumed the surname of Fitz-Clarence 1959: *m.* 1st, 1953 (m. annulled in New York 1960), Melvin Flyer; 2ndly, 1968, as his 2nd wife, John Walter (Brooks's Club). *Residence,*—99, Whitelands House, SW3. *Club,* Guards'.

Issue of the late Lionel Ashley Arthur Fitz-Clarence, *b.* 1870, *d.* 1936: *m.* 1913, Theodora Frances Maclean, who *d.* 1948, dau. of the late Evan A. Jack, of 1, The Grove, Boltons, S. Kensington, S.W. :—

Mary Theodora Annette, *b.* 1914: *m.* 1948, Adam Gluszkiewicz, and has issue living, Anna Judita, *b.* 1949. *Residence,*—22, Kenilworth Court, Putney, SW15.

PREDECESSORS.—[1] *Rt. Hon.* GEORGE Fitz-Clarence, F.R.S., el. natural son of King William IV by the great comic actress known as Mrs. Jordan; *b.* 1794 : Maj.-Gen. in the Army, Lieut. of the Tower, and Gov. of Windsor Castle: cr. *Baron Tewkesbury, Viscount Fitz-Clarence* and *Earl of Munster* (peerage of United Kingdom) 1831, with remainder to his brothers, Frederick, Adolphus and Augustus primogeniturely : *m.* 1819, Mary Wyndham, who *d.* 1842, natural dau. of George, 3rd Earl of Egremont; *d.* 1842; *s.* by his son [2] WILLIAM GEORGE, 2nd Earl, *b.* 1824 ; Capt. late 1st Life Guards: *m.* 1855, Wilhelmina, who *d.* 1906, dau. of the late Hon. John Kennedy-Erskine; *d.* 1901; *s.* by his el. son [3] GEOFFREY GEORGE GORDON, D.S.O., 3rd Earl, *b.* 1859 ; Major Lothian Regt.; Afghan War 1879-80, S. Africa 1881, S. Africa 1899-1902 (D.S.O.) ; *d.* 1902 ; *s.* by his brother [4] AUBREY, 4th Earl, *b.* 1862 ; a Gentleman Usher to Queen Victoria and to King Edward VII. 1885-1902 ; *d.* 1928 ; *s.* by his nephew [5] GEOFFREY WILLIAM RICHARD HUGH (son of the late Major the Hon. Harold Edward Fitz-Clarence, M.C., 7th son of 2nd Earl), 5th Earl and present peer ; also Viscount Fitz-Clarence, and Baron Tewkesbury.

MURRAY OF NEWHAVEN, BARON. (Murray.) [Life Baron 1964.]

KEITH ANDERSON HOPE MURRAY, *KCB*, son of the late Rt. Hon. Lord Murray, CMG, LLD, Judge of Court of Session, Scotland; *b.* July 28th, 1903; ed. at Edinburgh Acad., and at Edinburgh (BSc, Hon. LLD), Cornell (PhD), and Oxford (BLitt, MA, Hon. DCL) Univs., an Hon. Fellow of Downing Coll., Camb., Oriel and Lincoln Colls., Oxford, and Birkbeck Coll., London; Hon. LLD, Bristol, Camb., Hull, Southampton, Liverpool, Leicester, W. Aust., California, Strathclyde and London; Hon. DLitt, Keele; Hon. D. Univ. Stirling; Hon. DU Essex; Hon. FDS RCS, and Hon Fellow, UMIST; Fellow and Bursar of Lincoln Coll., Oxford 1937-44, and Rector and Bursar 1944-53; Chm. of Univ. Grants Cttee. 1953-63; Chancellor of Southampton Univ. 1964-74, Dir. of

Leverhulme Trust Fund 1965-72, and Visitor Loughborough Univ. of Tech. since 1968; 1939-45 War as Fl.-Lt. RAFVR; Dir. of Food and Agric., Middle East Supply Centre 1942-45; *cr.* Knt. 1955. KCB (Civil) 1963, and *Baron Murray of Newhaven*, of Newhaven, co. and City of Edinburgh (Life Baron) 1964.

Arms,—Azure, on a fess wavy argent between three mullets, two in chief and one pierced on the field in base, and in centre chief issuant from the fess a three-masted ship under full sail of the second, a bar wavy of the first; a bordure argent for difference. **Crest,**—A demi-savage proper, wreathed about the temples with juniper, holding in his dexter hand, the arm extended, an open book proper, binding and fore edges gules, and holding in his sinister hand a key azure. **Supporters,**—*Dexter*, a Newhaven fishwife, her creel on her back, basket or with fish argent, supported by a band sable about her forehead, her corsage and over-kirtle of azure pinned up, her first under-petticoat striped argent and azure, her second under-petticoat striped brown and primrose, both pinned up, her third petticoat striped white and gules, hose argent and shoe buckled argent; *sinister*, a stag proper, attired sable, gorged of a collar embattled argent, masoned sable.

Residence,—224, Ashley Gdns., SW1. *Club,*—United Oxford and Cambridge University.

MUSKERRY, BARON. (Deane.) [Baron I. 1781, Bt. I. 1710.]

ON HONOUR ET VIRTUE

FORTI ET FIDELI · NIHIL DIFFICILI

Nothing is difficult to the strong and faithful.

HASTINGS FITZMAURICE TILSON DEANE, 8th Baron, and 13th Baronet; *b.* March 12th, 1907; *s.* 1966; ed. at Dublin Univ. (MA, MB, BCh, BAO); DMR London; Radiologist to Regional Hosps., Limerick Health Authority; 1939-45 War as Capt. S. African Med. Corps, in W. Desert, Italy and Greece: *m.* 1944, Betty Fairbridge, el. da. of George Wilfred Reckless Palmer, of Glenstone, Grahamstown, S. Africa, and has issue.

Arms,—Argent, two bars gules. **Crest,**—Out of a ducal coronet or, a demi sea-otter proper. **Supporters,**—Two angels habited azure, holding in their exterior hands medallions proper.

Residence,—Springfield Castle, Drumcollogher, co. Limerick.

SON LIVING.

Hon. ROBERT FITZMAURICE, *b.* March 26th, 1948; ed. at Sandford Park Sch., Dublin, and Trin. Coll., Dublin.

DAUGHTER LIVING.

Hon. Betty Charlotte, *b.* 1951.

SISTER LIVING.

Hon. Marjorie Maria Fitzmaurice, *b.* 1900: *m.* 1955, Anthony V. Deane. *Residence,*—205, Gloucester Terr., W.2.

WIDOW LIVING OF SON OF SEVENTH BARON.

Dorothy, da. of the late Charles George Cook, of Liverpool: *m.* 1st, 1936, the Hon. Matthew Fitzmaurice Tilson Deane, who *d.* 1956; 2ndly, 1968, James Edward Anderton, of 24, Elm Rd., Windsor, Berks.

WIDOW LIVING OF SEVENTH BARON.

MURIEL DOREEN SELLARS (*Muriel Baroness Muskerry*) (44, Woodlands Rd., Liverpool 17; Cowdray, and Irish Clubs), da. of the late Arthur Gibson Simpson, of Carlisle: *m.* 1964, as his 2nd wife, the 7th Baron, who *d.* 1966.

COLLATERAL BRANCH LIVING.

Issue of the late Hon. Hamilton Robert Tilson Grogan Fitzmaurice DEANE-MORGAN, el. son of 4th Baron, *b.* 1873, *d.* 1907: *m.* 1904, Eva, who *d.* 1958 (having *m.* 2ndly, 1911, Godfrey William Edward Massy), el. dau. of William Bolton, of The Island, co. Wexford:—

Eileen (posthumous), *b.* 1907. *Residence,*—

PREDECESSORS.—[1] *Sir* MATTHEW Deane, Knt.; *cr.* a *Baronet* 1710; *d.* 1710; *s.* by his son [2] *Sir* ROBERT, 2nd Bt.; *d.* 1714; *s.* by his son [3] *Sir* MATTHEW, 3rd Bt.; M.P. for co. Cork; *d.* 1747; *s.* by his el. son [4] *Sir* MATTHEW, 4th Bt.; M.P. for Cork City; *s.* by his son [5] *Sir* ROBERT, P.C., 5th Bt.; M.P. for Tallagh; *d.* 1770; *s.* by his son [6] *Sir* ROBERT TILSON, 6th Bt.; M.P. for co. Cork; *cr. Baron Muskerry* (peerage of Ireland) 1781; *d.* 1818; *s.* by his el. son [7] JOHN THOMAS FITZMAURICE, C.B., 2nd Baron; *d.s.p.* 1824; *s.* by his brother [8] MATTHEW FITZMAURICE, 3rd Baron; *d.* 1868; *s.* by his grandson [9] HAMILTON MATTHEW TILSON FITZMAURICE, 4th Baron (son of the Hon. Robert Tilson Fitzmaurice Deane, 2nd son of TILSON FITZMAURICE, 4th Baron (son of the Hon. Robert Tilson Fitzmaurice, 2nd son of 3rd Baron, by Elizabeth Geraldine, who *d.* 19—, dau. and co-heir of Hamilton Knox Grogan-Morgan, M.P., of Johnstown Castle, co. Wexford), *b.* 1854; a Representative Peer for Ireland: *m.* 1st, 1872, Flora Georgina, who *d.* 1902, dau. of the late Hon. Chichester Thomas Foster-Skeffington; 2ndly, 1905, Lydia, who *d.* 1915, only dau. of J. L. Booth; 3rdly, 1916, Adeline, who *d.* 1950, dau. of the late P. Ryan, of The Turrets, Charleville, Ireland; *d.* 1929; *s.* by his son [10] ROBERT MATTHEW FITZMAURICE, 5th Baron; *b.* 1874: *m.* 1906, Charlotte, who *d.* 1960, dau. of John

William Henry Irvine, of Mervyn, Rosslare, co. Wexford; *d.* 1952; *s.* by his brother, [11] MATTHEW CHICHESTER CECIL FITZMAURICE, 6th Baron; *b.* 1875: *m.* 1915, Helen Henrietta Blennerhassett, who *d.* 1952, dau. of the late Brig.-Surg. Lieut.-Col. Rodolph Harman, Army Med. Ser.; *d.* 1954; *s.* by his kinsman, [12] MATHEW FITZMAURICE TILSON (son of the late Hon. Matthew James Hastings Fitzmaurice Deane, 3rd son of 3rd Baron), 7th Baron; *b.* 1874: *m.* 1st, 1897, Mabel Kathleen Vivienne, who *d.* 1954, da. of the late Charles Henry Robinson, MD, FRCSI; 2ndly, 1964, Muriel Doreen Sellars, da. of the late Arthur Gibson Simpson, of Carlisle; *d.* 1966; *s.* by his yst. son [13] HASTINGS FITZMAURICE TILSON, *MB*, *ChB*, 8th Baron and present peer.

Naas, Lord, son of Earl of Mayo.

NAIRNE, LADY. (Bigham.) [Lordship S. 1681.]

KATHERINE EVELYN CONSTANCE BIGHAM (*Viscountess Mersey*), *b.* June 22nd, 1912; *s.* 1944: *m.* 1933, the 3rd Viscount Mersey, and has issue.

Arms,—Quarterly, 1st grand quarter, parted per pale sable and argent, on a chaplet four quatrefoils counterchanged, *Nairne*; 2nd grand quarter, counterquartered, 1st and 4th or, on a fesse gules between three crosses pattee of the second in chief, and a mullet azure in base, three bezants, *Mercer*; 2nd and 3rd argent, a chevron sable between three boars' heads erased gules, *Elphinstone*; 3rd grand quarter, counterquartered, 1st and 4th paly of six, or and sable, 2nd or, a fesse chequy azure and argent, 3rd azure, three mullets argent, with a double tressure flowered and counterflowered of fleur de lis or, *Atholl*; 4th grand quarter argent, three martlets sable on a comble azure a cross or, a frane quartier (the mark of distinction of a Military Count of the French Empire) of the 3rd, charged with a sword palewise of the field, hilted and pommelled of the fourth, *Flahault*. Supporters,—*Dexter*, a pegasus ermine, bridled crined winged and unguled or, charged on the shoulder with a fleur de lis azure; *sinister*, a ratch hound proper.

Residence,—Bignor Park, Pulborough, Sussex.

SONS LIVING.

Hon. RICHARD MAURICE CLIVE (*Master of Nairne*), *b.* July 8th, 1934; ed. at Eton, and at Balliol Coll., Oxford; late 2nd Lieut. Irish Guards: *m.* 1961, Joanna, el. dau. of John Grey Murray, of Cannon Lodge, Cannon Place, NW3, and has issue living, Edward John Hallam, *b.* 1966. *Residence,* —1, Rosmead Rd., W.11.
Hon. David Edward Hugh (24, Argyll Rd., W8), *b.* 1938; ed. at Eton; late Cornet Roy. Horse Guards: *m.* (Jan.) 1965, Anthea Rosemary, el. da. of Capt. Leopold Richard Richard Seymour [see M. Hertford, colls.], and has issue living, Charles Richard Petty, *b.* 1967,—Lucinda Emma, *b.* (Nov.) 1965.
Hon. Andrew Charles, *b.* 1941; ed. at Eton, and at Worcester Coll., Oxford; 2nd Lt. Irish Guards.

SISTER LIVING.

Lady Elizabeth Mary FITZMAURICE, *b.* 1927: *m.* 1950, Major Charles William Lambton, Coldstream Guards (retired) [see E. Durham, colls.]. *Residence,*—Mortimer Hill, Mortimer, Berks.

COLLATERAL BRANCHES LIVING.

Issue of the late Major Lord Charles George Francis MERCER-NAIRNE, M.V.O., 2nd son of 9th Lord, and 5th Marquess of Lansdowne, *b.* 1874, *d.* (killed in action during European War) 1914: *m.* 1909, Lady Violet Mary Elliot-Murray-Kynynmound (who *m.* 2ndly, 1916, Col. the Hon. John Jacob Astor [see V. Astor]), dau. of 4th Earl of Minto [see M. Lansdowne].
Issue of the late Lady Emily Louisa Anne (only dau. of Emily, Lady Nairne, by the 4th Marquess of Lansdowne), *b.* 1855, *d.* 1939: *m.* 1886, Col. the Hon Everard Charles Digby, Grenadier Guards, who *d.* 1915 [see B. Digby, colls.].

PREDECESSORS.—[1] *Sir* ROBERT Nairne, Knt., a Scottish advocate and a zealous partisan of the house of Stuart; was imprisoned in the Tower of London 1651-61; appointed a Lord of Session 1661, and a Lord of Justiciary 1671; cr. *Lord Nairne* (peerage of Scotland) 1681, with remainder to the husband of his da. Margaret and the heirs of their bodies; *d.* 1683; *s.* by his son-in-law (ante) [2] *Lord* WILLIAM Murray, 2nd Lord, 4th son of 1st Marquess of Atholl; refused to take the oaths of allegiance or his seat in Parliament until after the Revolution; took part in the rebellion of 1715, was taken prisoner at Preston, and after being confined in the Tower was in 1716 attainted of high-treason and sentenced to be executed, which sentence was however respited; *d.* 1725; *s.* by his son [3] JOHN, who had previously been attainted for his connection with the rising of 1715: by Act of Parliament 1738, he was enabled to inherit property and to carry on law-suits; engaged in the insurrection of 1745, and was again attainted, having previously been cr. by the Pretender Viscount Stanley and Earl of Nairne; *d.* 1770; *s.* by his son [4] JOHN, 4th Lord, a Lieut.-Col. in the Army; *d.* 1782; *s.* by his son [5] WILLIAM MURRAY, 5th Lord, who was restored to the family honours by Act of Parliament 1824; *d.* 1830; *s.* by his son [6] WILLIAM, 6th Lord; *d.* unmarried 1837; *s.* by his kinswoman [7] MARGARET, who had in 1823 *s.* her father in the Barony of Keith (peerage of Ireland, cr. 1803); *b.* 1788: *m.* 1817, Auguste Charles Joseph, Comte de Flahault-de-la-Billarderie; *d.* 1867, when the Barony of Keith expired, and the Lordship of Nairne devolved upon her el. dau. [8] EMILY JANE, *b.* 1819; established her claim to the title 1874: *m.* 1843, Henry, el. son of Henry Charles Keith, 3rd Marquess of Lansdowne, who *d.* 1866; she *d.* 1895; *s.* by her el. son [9-11] HENRY CHARLES KEITH, 5th Marquess of Lansdowne, the Lordship being merged in the Marquessate until 1945, when, on the death of the 7th Marquess, it devolved upon his sister [12] KATHERINE EVELYN CONSTANCE, present peeress.

NAPIER and ETTRICK, LORD. (Napier.) [Lord S. 1627, Baron U.K. 1872, Bt. S. 1666.]

FRANCIS NIGEL NAPIER, 14th Lord Napier (of Merchistoun), 5th Baron Ettrick, and 11th Baronet; *b.* Dec. 5th, 1930: *s.* 1954; ed. at Eton; Maj. Scots Guards (Reserve), a DL for Ettrick and Lauderdale, a Member of Queen's Body Guard for Scotland (Roy. Co. of Archers), a Freeman of City of London, and Liveryman of Grocers' Co.; Hon. Treas. of People's Dispensary for Sick Animals; Conservative Whip, House of Lords 1970, and since 1971; Malaya 1950-51; Adjt 1st Bn. Scots Gds. 1955-57; Equerry to HRH the late Duke of Gloucester 1958-60, and Private Sec., Comptroller and Equerry to HRH the Princess Margaret, Countess of Snowdon 1973-75, since when Private Sec. and Comptroller; Dep. Ceremonial and Protocol Sec., Commonwealth Relations Office 1962-66; Pres. of St. John Ambulance of co. of London: *m.* 1958, Delia Mary, yr. da. of Archibald D. B. Pearson, of Upper Sattenham, Milford, Surrey, and has issue.

Arms,—Quarterly: 1st and 4th argent, a saltire engrailed cantoned of four roses gules, barbed vert, *Napier*; 2nd and 3rd or, on a bend azure, a mullet pierced between two crescents of the field, within a double tressure flory-counterflory of the second, *Scott of Thirlestane*; below the shield on a compartment, the top of an embattled tower argent, masoned sable, issuant there from six lances disposed saltirewise proper, three and three, with pennons azure, *Scott*. **Crest,**—A dexter arm erect couped below the elbow proper, grasping a crescent argent, *Napier*. **Supporters—***Dexter*, an eagle, wings expanded proper; *sinister*, a chevalier in coat of mail and steel cap, all proper, holding in the exterior hand a lance with a pennon azure.

Seat,—Laidlawstiel Clovenfords, Selkirkshire. **Clubs,**—Brooks's, Pratt's.

SONS LIVING.

Hon. FRANCIS DAVID CHARLES (*Master of Napier*), *b.* Nov. 3rd, 1962.
Hon. Nicholas Alexander John, *b.* 1971.

DAUGHTERS LIVING.

Hon. Louisa Mary Constance, *b.* 1961. *Hon.* Georgina Helena Katherine, *b.* 1969.

BROTHERS LIVING.

Hon. (Charles) Malcolm (Bardmony House, Alyth, Perthshire; Hanover Place, 314, Rhodes Av., Salisbury, Rhodesia; Cavalry, Turf, Civil Service (Cape Town) Clubs), *b.* 1933; ed. at Canford; late Lt. 1st R. Dragoons, and late Lt. Lothians and Border Yeo (TA); served Middle East 1952-53; a Member of Queen's Body Guard for Scotland (Roy. Co. of Archers); a Dir. of Cos., and a Founder Member of Council of Anglo Rhodesian Soc.; *m.* 1969, Lady Mariota Cecilia Murray, da. of 7th Earl of Mansfield and Mansfield, and has issue living, Eloise Dorothea, *b.* 1970,—Maryel Cecilia, *b.* 1973.
Hon. (John) Greville (Underhill, Treyford, Midhurst, Sussex; Bath Club) *b.* 1939; ed. at Fettes; Assist. Manager Antiques, H. W. Keil Ltd., Midhurst 1959-67, and Manager 1967-68, since when Man. Dir., Napier Antiques Ltd.: *m.* 1968, Juliet Elizabeth Hargreaves, only da. of Alexander Charles Durie, CBE, of Redwood House, Windlesham, Surrey, and has issue living, Lucilla Fleur Scott, *b.* 1969,—Araminta Elizabeth Muir, *b.* 1972.
Hon. (Hugh) Lenox, *b.* 1943.

UNCLE LIVING. (*Son of 12th Lord*).

Hon. Alastair John George Malcolm, *T.D.*, *b.* 1909; ed. at Merchiston, and at Sherborne; late Maj. RE (TA); Kenya Min. of Works (formerly Public Works Dept.) 1950-65; Treasurer Kenya National Museum 1966; 1939-45 War (1939-45 star, Africa star): *m.* 1933, Geraldine, da. of the late James Dunlop, of The Bield, Ayr, and has issue living, Diana Elizabeth, SRN, *b.* 1939: *m.* 1967, Maj. Robin Edward Doveton Harris, MBE, MC, late 14th/20th King's Hussars, of Bahati, Ganges Close, Mylor Harbour, Falmouth, Cornwall, and has issue living, Serita Catherine *b.* 1968, Meralynn Elizabeth *b.* 1970, Chania Rozanthe *b.* 1973. *Address,*—PO Box 14222, Kenya.

WIDOW LIVING OF SON OF TWELFTH LORD.

Helen Catherine (Kippilaw, St. Boswells, Roxburghshire), yr. da. of the late J. M. Sanderson, of Linthill, Melrose: *m.* 1967, as his 2nd wife, Cdr. the Hon. Neville Archibald John Watson Ettrick Napier, RN, who *d.* 1970.

WIDOW LIVING OF THIRTEENTH LORD.

VIOLET) MUIR (*Dowager Lady Napier and Ettrick*), el. dau. of Sir Percy Wilson Newson, 1st Bt. (ext.); is National Pres. of Young Women's Christian Assocn. of Scotland: *m.* 1928, the 13th Baron, who *d.* 1954. *Residence,*—Glen farg House, Dron, Perthshire

COLLATERAL BRANCHES LIVING.

Branch from da. of 12th Lord.

Issue of the late Hon. Augusta Caroline Georgina Harriet Mary Napier, only da.
of 12th Lord, *b.* 1901, *d.* 1962: *m.* 1922, Lieut.-Col. James Hebblethwaite Martin
Frobisher, O.B.E., M.B., B.Ch., R.A.M.C. (retired):—
Elizabeth Georgina Napier, *b.* 1924: *m.* 1946, Maj. Frank Haselar Waters, MC, late Roy. Hants. Regt.,
of the Oast Cottage, Uckfield, Sussex, and has issue living, Charles Frobisher Haselar (Hillyard
House, Danehill, Sussex), *b.* 1947; ed. at Pangbourne; ARICS: *m.* 1971, Rosemary Carter, and
has issue living, James Gordon Frobisher *b.* 1973, Katharine Jane *b.* 1974,—David Frobisher (Lange-
line, Empire Av., Hout Bay, Cape Town), *b.* 1949; ed. at King's Sch., Canterbury: ACA, AT II,
CA (SA): *m.* 1971, Charlotte Harrocks, and has issue living, Marcus Damian Napier *b.* 1973,—Susan
Frobisher, *b.* 1954,—Jane Frobisher, *b.* 1956.——Pamela Mary Napier, *b.* 1925; 1939-45 War with
WRNS: *m.* 1957, Wing-Cdr. George Hugh Nichols Gibson, DFC, AFC, of Medlars, Old Heathfield,
Sussex.——Rosemary, *LRAM*, *b.* 1929: *m.* 1952, John Derek Howard Whittome, MA, of Sessele,
Hawkhurst, Kent, and has issue living, Philipps Rosemary, *b.* 1954,—Caroline Gay, *b.* 1 956,—Anne
Katherine, *b.* 1958.

Branch from 3rd son of 11th Lord

Issue of the late Com. the Hon. Archibald Lenox Colquhoun William John George
Napier, R.N. (retired), 3rd son of 11th Lord, *b.* 1889, *d.* 1951: *m.* 1st, 1924,
Barbara Fountayne, who *d.* 1926, dau. of the Rev. Reginald William Wilberforce
(who in 1924 assumed by deed poll the surname of Puleston in lieu of his patro-
nymic), of Bittering Hall, East Dereham [B. Denman]; 2ndly, 1928, Marianne
Irene Russell, who *d.* 1958, youngest dau. of the late John Russell Cox, J.P., Lord
of the Manor of Beaminster, Dorset :—
(By 1st marriage) William Puleston Scott, *b.* 1925 ; ed. at Eton ; European War 1942-45 with Roy.
Norfolk Regt.: *m.* 1949, Rosemary Heather, da. of the late Capt. R. H. A. MacLaren, of Uphall,
Ashill, Norfolk, and has issue living, Lenox Scott, *b.* 1953; ed. at Rugby. *Residence,*—

Branch from yr. sons of 10th Lord.

Granddaughter of the late Col. the Hon. John Scott Napier, CMG, 2nd son of 10th
Lord; *b.* 1848, *d.* 1938: *m.* 1st, 1876, Isabella, who *d.* (Nov.) 1928, dau. of
Thomas Shaw, of Ditton, Lancashire, and widow of Major James Leith, V.C.;
2ndly (Dec.), 1928, Eva Ingledew, who *d.* 1946, el. dau. of Charles Selby
Davidson, formerly of Newcastle-upon-Tyne :—
Issue of the late Lilias Dorothea Scott Napier, *b.* 1884, *d.* 1973: *m.* 1913, Reginald Evan
Wynne-Roberts, late Coldm. Gds.:—
Elizabeth Mary Joan, *b.* 1914: *m.* 1935, Alan Wardale, MD, FRCS, late Sqdn. Ldr., RAF, and has
issue living, Terence Alan *b.* 1937, Beverley Joan *b.* 1939: *m.* 1972, Brian Vine. *Residence,*—
Gardners Green, Honey Hill, Wokingham, Berks.

Grandchildren of the late Hon. Mark Francis Napier, 4th son of 10th Lord:—
Issue of the late Major Claude Inverness Napier, *b.* 1880; *d.* 1946: *m.* 1917, Lillian, who *d.*
1972, el. da. of Lt.-Com. Alfred Francey, RN:—
Mark Francis, *b.* 1925: *m.* 1951, Mary Frances, da. of Prof. A. W. Ling, MSC, and has issue living,
Charles Algernon, *b.* 1953,—Robert Bruce, *b.* 1959,—Claudia Frances, *b.* 1962.——Margaret Emily,
b. 1919: *m.* 1945, Peter Hincks. *Residence,*—Wellington College, Crowthorne, Berks.——Eleanor
Rosemary Jean, *b.* 1921: *m.* 1942, Capt. Frank Wilson. *Residence,*—Heatherdown Nurseries,
Wokingham, Berks.

Issue of the late Philip Henry Napier, *b.* 1884; *d.* 1965: *m.* 1909, Gabrielle Jean, who *d.* 1936,
da. of Sir Charles Harvey, 2nd Bt. (cr. 1868):—
Nigel Claude Oliver (Highfield House, Fordcombe, Kent), *b.* 1913; ed. at Trin. Coll., Camb.; late
Maj. R.A. (T.A.); 1939-45 War (despatches): *m.* 1945, Lucy Margaret, da. of Capt. Arthur Walter
Brown, MBE, JP, who *d.* 1949, and has issue living, Alastair Denis, *b.* 1946.

Branch from 2nd son of 9th Lord.

Grandchildren of the late Maj. Francis Horatio Napier, OBE, LLD, FRCS, el. son of
the late Hon. William Napier, 2nd son of 9th Lord:—
Issue of the late Maj. Archibald John Robert Napier, *b.* 1894, *d.* 1967: *m.* 1926, Lilian Gray
Delphin (Meadow Bank, 7, Zetland Rd., Malvern), da. of Christopher Delphin Petersen,
of Oslo:—
William Francis Andrew (44, Wisbey St., Bunbury, W. Australia), *b.* 1927: *m.* 1954, Rosemary, da.
of the late Charles William Jacobs, BEM, and has issue living, Stephen Charles Edward, *b.* 1955,—
Anne-Marie, *b.* 1956.——Robert Anthony Peter (Meadow Bank, 7, Zetland Rd., Malvern), *b.* 1940.
——Charlotte Esmé Mary-Rose, *b.* 1930: *m.* 1956, Richard Harry Rose, of 12, Haines Hill, Taunton,
and has issue living, Nicholas Henry, *b.* 1957,—Alistair Donald, *b.* 1964,—Yvonne Charlotte, *b.* 1958,
—Mary Eleanor, *b.* 1961.

Issue of the late Cdr. Laurence Egerton Scott Napier, DSO, RN, *b.* 1896; *d.* 1969: *m.* 1st,
1921 (m. diss. 19—), Nora Creina, da. of Owen Christian, of Port Elizabeth, S. Africa;
2ndly, 1930 (m. diss. 19—), Florence Sylvia Jack, who *m.* 2ndly, 19—,   Tizzard, of
Flat 1, Galros Buildings, Roscommon Rd., Heathfield, Cape Town:—
(By 2nd m.) Patricia, *b.* 1931: *m.* 1952, Robert Louis Moseley, of 1, De Klerks Drive, De Klerkshof,
Edenvale, Transvaal.

Granddaughter of the late Maj.-Gen. William John Napier, CB, CMG, 3rd son of the
late Hon. William Napier (ante):—
Issue of the late Brig. Arthur Francis Scott Napier, *b.* 1890, *d.* 1971: *m.* 1915, Phyllis Grace
(Hatherley, Newland, Sherborne, Dorset), da. of the late Edward Fleming:—
Margaret Esmé Scott (Northgate, North Rd., Sherborne, Dorset), *b.* 1920: *m.* 1st, 1942, Capt. Ephraim
Stewart Cook Spence, A & SH, who obtained a divorce 1946: 2ndly, 1946, her cousin, Maj. Alex-
ander Napier, Indian Army (ret.), who *d.* 1954 (infra); 3rdly, 1957, John Whittingdale, FRCS,
who *d.* 1974, and has issue living (by 3rd m.) John Flasby Lawrance, *b.* 1959; ed. at Winchester.

Grandsons of the late Archibald Scott Napier, yst. son of the late Hon. William
Napier (ante):—
Issue of the late Maj.-Gen. Charles Scott Napier, C.B., C.B.E., *b.* 1899 ; *d.* 1946 : *m.* 1927,
Ada Kathleen (46, Markham St., Chelsea, S.W.3), da. of V. N. Douétil:—
Rev. Michael Scott, *b.* 1929; ed. at Wellington Coll., and at Trin. Coll, Camb. (MA 1955); is in Holy
Orders of Church of Rome. *Residence,*—The Oratory, S.W.7.

Issue of the late Major Alexander Napier, Indian Army, *b.* 1904, *d.* 1954 ; *m.* 1946, his cousin,
Margaret Esmé Scott (SPENCE) (who *m.* 3rdly, 1957, John Whittingdale, of Northgate,
North Road, Sherborne, Dorset), da. of the late Brig. Arthur Francis Scott Napier (ante):—
Charles Scott, *b.* 1947; ed. at Wellington, and Exeter Univ. (BA).

Branch from 2nd son of 8th Lord.

Granddaughters living of the late Col. Charles Warren Napier-Clavering, el. son of the late Rev. John Warren Napier-Clavering, 3rd son of Maj. the Hon. Charles Napier, 2nd son of 8th Lord:—
Issue of the late Helene Margaret Napier-Clavering, b. 1900, d. 1974: m. 1927, Maj.-Gen. Christopher Michael Maltby, CB, MC, DL:—
Ann Margaret (2, Green Hey, Much Hoole, Preston, Lancs.), b. 1928; ed. at Camb. Univ. (BA): m. 1958 (m. diss. 1972), John Hallam.——Barbara Helen Jessie, b. 1931: m. 1954, Brian Wilfred Hastilow, of Fairwater, Taunton School, Taunton, and has issue living, Alexander Michael, b. 1955,—David Napier, b. 1959.

Granddaughters of the late Francis Napier-Clavering, 2nd son of the late Rev. John Warren Napier-Clavering (ante):—
Issue of the late Maj.-Gen. Noel Warren Napier-Clavering, CB, CBE, DSO, b. 1888, d. 1964: m. 1921, Margaret (Tundry House, Dogmersfield, nr. Basingstoke), da. of T. W. Vigers, of Montville, St. Peter Port, Guernsey:—
Diana Margaret, b. 1926: m. 1950, John Evelyn Gray Todd, Lt. RN (ret.) ,of Glaston Hill House, Eversley, Hants., and has issue living, Michael John Clavering, b. 1951,—David Matthew, b. 1953,—Philip Napier, b. 1956,—Brian William, b. 1958.
Issue of the late Maj. Francis Donald Napier-Clavering, MC, b. 1892, d. 1969: m. 1920, Dorothy Avison (Branxholm, Start Hill, Bishop's Stortford), da. of V. A. Holroyd, of Leamington:—
Jean Margaret Avison, b. 1922; a JP for Leics.: m. 1943, Capt. James Gordon Hartridge, RA, of The White House, Groby, Leics., and has issue living, David, b. 1944: m. 1968, Deborah Jane Robson, of Markfield, Leics.,—Susan Margaret Anne, b. 1950; MCSP.——Anne Katherine, b. 1924: m. 1948, Eric G. Wood-Hill, of Binixica, San Clemente Estate, Mahon, Menorca, Baleares, Spain, and has issue living, Geoffrey Napier, b. 1951,—Heather Anne, b. 1953.—Francis Alison Eve, b. 1929: m. 1951, Maj. Richard Mansel Colville, RGJ, of Church Corner House, Michelmersh, Romsey, Hants., and has issue living, Julia Francis b. 1955,—Philippa Katherine, b. 1957,—Joanna Caroline, b. 1959,—Fiona Patricia, b. 1966.

Grandchildren of the late Capt. Arthur Lenox NAPIER, OBE, 4th son of the late Rev. John Warren Napier-Clavering (ante):—
Issue of the late Brig. John Lenox Clavering Napier, CBE, b. 1898, d. 1966: m. 1925, Grace Edythe Muriel (Puddicombe House, Drewsteignton, Exeter), da. of the late Col. Charles Augustus Young, CB, CMG [V. Guillamore, colls.]:—
Rev. Charles John Lenox (The Rectory, Warkleigh, Umberleigh, Devon, EX37 9DG), b. 1929; ed. at Radley, and at Univ. Coll., Oxford (MA): m. 1964, Jane Noel, da. of the Rev. Gerard Noel Davidson, and has issue living, William John Noel, b. 1965,—Henry Lenox Charles, b. 1967,—Anna Clare, b. 1970.——Gerald William Alistair (Puddicombe House, Drewsteignton, Exeter) b. 1932; ed. at Radley, and Gonville and Caius Coll., Camb. (MA): Lt.-Col. RE: m. 1962, Marjorie Currie, da. of Robert Torrance, and has issue living, Alexander John Robert b. 1963,—Mark b. 1964,—George, b. 1967.——Jean Elizabeth Alison, b. 1931: ed. at Roedean; MCSP: m. 1970, John Alexander Seivwright, of Crispin Cottage, Cairnie, Huntly, Aberdeenshire, AB5 4UB.

Grandchildren of the late Rev. John Warren Napier-Clavering (ante):—
Issue of the late Claude Gerald Napier-Clavering, b. 1869, d. 1938: m. 1897, Millicent Mary, who d. 1932, dau. of the Rt. Hon. William Kenrick, of The Grove, Harborne, Staffordshire:—
Mark NAPIER, b. 1898; ed. at Clifton Coll.; discontinued by deed poll 1924 the use of the surname of Clavering: m. 1921 (m. diss. 1945), Elizabeth, who d. 1974, dau. of the late Sir (Samuel) Squire Sprigge; 2ndly, 1946, Frances Alice, dau. of Dr. Henry Allen Turner, of Millbrook, Ontario, and has issue living, (by 1st m.) Julyan (a da.), b. 1922: m. 1946, Cawthra F. Mulock, of Falconfield, RR2, Newmarket, Ont., Canada, and has issue living, Richard b. 1948, Julian b. 1950, Mark b. 1951, Nigel b. 1955,—Ruth, b. 1923: m. 1944, Capt. Timothy A. Lumley-Smith, 17th/21st Lancers (of Lavethan, Blisland, Bodmin, Cornwall), son of Maj. Sir Thomas Gabriel Lumley Lumley-Smith, D.S.O., and has issue living, Elizabeth b. 1947, Sarah b. 1949, Jane b. 1951. Address,—R.R.2, Newmarket, Ontario, Canada.——Alan NAPIER, b. 1903 ; ed. at Clifton Coll.; discontinued the use of the christian name of William and the surname of Clavering on being naturalised an American Citizen: m. 1st, 1930 (m. diss. 1944), Nancy Bevill, who d. 1970, da. of Frank Pethybridge; 2ndly, 1944, Aileen Dickens Bourchier, who d. 1961, dau. of the late Ernest Bourchier Hawksley, and has issue living, (by 1st marriage) Jennifer Mary, b. 1931 : m. 1950, Robert E. Nichols, of California, U.S.A., and has issue living, David b. 1954, Christie Catherine b. 1952. Residence,—17919, Porto Marina Way, Pacific Palisades, California, U.S.A.——Mary Helen, b. 1900 ; B.A. Oxford 1925. Residence,—10, St Mary's Close, Sixpenny Handley, Salisbury, Wilts.

Granddaughters of the late Col. Edward Napier, 4th son of Maj. the Hon. Charles Napier (ante):—
Issue of the late Major Egbert Napier, b. 1867, d. (killed in action during European War, 1916: m. 1901, Evangeline, who d. 1936, da. of J. G. Dreyer, of Copenhagen, Denmark, and Valschrivierdrift, Orange River Colony:—
Evangeline Mary, b. 1904: m. 1925, Percy Henry Vincent Fosbery, and has issue living, Napier, b. 1926,—Anthony Vincent (T. H. Ranch (Est. 1879), Chilcotin Valley, BC, Canada), b. 1929.—— Esmé Georgina (c/o The Nedbank, St. George's St., Capetown, S. Africa), b. 1905: m. 1931, her cousin, Stephen Napier Bax, late Colonial Ser. Tanganyika and E. Africa High Comm. who d. 1973, and has issue living, Stephen Egbert Napier (c/o Westminster Bank, 121, High St., Oxford), b. 1932: ed. at Prince of Wales Sch., Nairobi, and St. Edmund Hall, Oxford; late Colonial Admin. Ser; with Save the Children Fund, and Consultant on Middle East: m. 1959, Jane Christine, da. of the late H. P. J. Clark, of Ratcliffs, Black Notley, Essex, and has issue living, Stephen Charles Napier b. 1962, Deborah Jane b. 1960, Kathryn Victoria b. 1964,—Peter Lawrence Napier, b. 1935; ed. at Prince of Wales Sch., Nairobi, and at Exeter Coll., Oxford (MA); formerly Colonial Ser.. Kenya: m. 1963, Andrée, el. da. of A. G. Shoyer, of Mombasa, Kenya, and has issue living, Paul Lawrence Napier b. 1964, Hayley Anne b. 1970,—Alastair Arthur Napier (Brisbane, Aust.), b. 1937; ed. at Prince of Wales Sch., Nairobi; late E. Africa High Comm: m. 1963, Valerie, da. of W. H. Wheeler, late Govt. Ser., Nairobi, and has issue living, Julia Ann b. 1967.

Grandchildren of the late Maj. the Hon. Charles Napier (ante):—
Issue of the late Col. Edward Napier, b. 1841, d. 1922: m. 1866, Marthe Louise, who d. 1918, dau. of the late William Barber Buddicom, of Penbedw Hall, Flintshire:—
Jane Rosamond (Lady Lawrence) (Westbrook Old Manor, Boxford, Newbury), b. 1878: m. 1914, as his second wife, Sir Henry Stavely Lawrence, KCSI, ICS, who d. 1949, and has issue living, John Owen Napier (Westbrook Old Manor, Boxford, Newbury), b. 1916; ed. at Haileybury: m. 1st, 1942, Prudence Helen, who d. 1943, da. of Hubert Edgar Wyatt, Civil Ser.; 2ndly, 1945, Bettine, only da. of James Walmsley, of Berwyn, Westbourne Av., Burnley, and has issue living, (by 2nd m.) John Michael Walmsley b. 1946: m. 1969, Alison Mary, da. of the late R. H. Black, (and has issue living, Peter Napier b. 1972),—Rosamond Mary b. 1949: m. 1972, Lindsey Scott McNaught.

Granddaughter of the late William Archibald Napier (infra):—
Issue of the late Clarence Napier, b. 1880, d. 1930 : m. 1909, Lillie, who d. 1961, dau. of J. Mills, of Frome, Somerset :—
Marcelle (24, Cottenham Park Rd., Wimbledon, SW20, and 14, Rue Lesueur, Paris, XVI, France), b. 1910.

Granddaughter of the late Maj. the Hon. Charles Napier (ante):—
Issue of the late William Archibald Napier, *b.* 1845, *d.* 1901: *m.* 1879, Mabel, who *d.*
1943, dau. of the late William Edward Royds, of Greenhill, Rochdale:—
Esmé, *b.* 1884 : *m.* 1905, Frank Douglas Montgomerie, formerly Lieut. The Buffs, who *d.* 1951,
and has issue living, Mollie (*Baroness Butler of Saffron Walden*), *b.* 1907: *m.* 1st, 1932, Augustine
Courtauld, DL, JP, late Lt. R.N.V.R., of Spencers, Great Yeldham, Essex, who *d.* 1959; 2ndly, 1959,
Baron Butler of Saffron Walden, CH (Life Peer), and has issue living, (by 1st marriage) Augustine
Christopher Caradoc *b.* 1934, Julien (Spencers Gt. Yeldham, Essex), *b.* 1938: *m.* 1964, Theresa Caroline,
el. da. of Sir Charles Edward Mott-Radclyffe, MP, of Baringham Hall, Norwich (and has issue living,
Thomas Julian Radclyffe *b.* 1969, Diana Catherine *b.* 1967), Stephen Napier *b.* 1940, William Mont-
gomerie (8, Elm Place, SW7) *b.* 1943: *m.* 1966, Caroline Patricia, da. of Maj. J. W. Buckley (and has
issue living, Toby Augustine, *b.* 1968, Flora Jemima, *b.* 1970), Perina *b.* 1932: *m.* 1956, Christopher
Jeremy King Fordham, of Odsey Grange, Ashwell, Herts. (and has issue living, Christopher Henry
Courtauld *b.* 1960, Louisa *b.* 1958, Arabella Napier *b.* 1962), Susanna Ruth *b.* 1950,—Pamela, *b.* 1909:
m. 1936, Sven Havsteen-Mikkelsen, of Ulvemarken, Bregninge, Aeró, Denmark, and has issue living,
Leif Alan (Gammelgaard, Bregninge, Aeró, Denmark), *b.* 1938; MA Copenhagen: *m.* 1969, Collette
Lavinia, da. of Maj. Charles Arthur Boycott, MBE, of Ludlow, Salop (and has issue living, Eleanor
Kristen *b.* 1973), Olaf Ejnar (c/o FAO, Terme di Caracalla 00100, Rome), *b.* 1941; BSc Agri: *m.* 1975,
Susanna Henrietta, da. of John Stanley Townsend, MIMC, of Springfield House, The Spinning Walk,
Shere, Surrey, Estrid *b.* 1943: *m.* 1st, 1967 (m. diss. 1974), Tom Harsem; 2ndly, 1974, Dr. Flemm-
ing Brandrup, of Priorengade 4,5600, Faaborg, Fyn, Denmark (and has issue living (by 1st m.),
Lars Olaf Havstëen, *b.* 1969). *Residence,*—Copsford Place, Marks Tey, Colchester, Essex.

Grandson of the late Adm. William Rawdon Napier, C.B., C.M.G., D.S.O. (infra):—
Issue of the late Lieut.-Com. Mark Napier, R.N., *b.* 1911, *d.* 1962: *m.* 1945, the Hon. Jean
Astley (Compass House, West Meon, Hants.), da. of 21st Baron Hastings:—
Brian Mark Lenox, *b.* 1946: *m.* 1970, Melinda, el. da. of James Prideaux, of 110, East End Rd.,
Finchley, and has issue living, Mark Anthony Rawdon, *b.* 1975,—a da., *b.* 1972.

Granddaughters of the late Com. Lenox Napier, RN, 6th son of the late Maj. the Hon.
Charles Napier (ante):—
Issue of the late Adm. William Rawdon Napier, C.B., C.M.G., D.S.O., *b.* 1877, *d.* 1951:
m. 1902, Florence Marie, who *d.* 1965, da. of the late James O'Reilly Nugent [Nugent, Bt.
cr. 1795]:—
Ellin Ruth Veronica, *b.* 1916. *Residence,*—The Anchorage, The Square, Wickham, Hants.

Issue of the late Patrick Ronald Napier, *b.* 1879, *d.* 1911: *m.* 1903, Kathleen Hilda Mary,
who *d.* 1948, 2nd dau. of the late James O'Reilly Nugent [Nugent, Bt., *cr.* 1795, colls.]:—
Patricia Marion Barbara, *b.* 1904; a nun. *Residence,*—La Rameé, 5902, Jauchelette, Belgium.

PREDECESSORS.—[1] *Rt. Hon. Sir* ARCHIBALD Napier, *P.C.,* son of John Napier, one of the
most eminent Philosophers of his age, and inventor of logarithms, of Merchistoun, Midlothian ; *b.* 1575; Gentleman of the Bedchamber to James VI. of Scotland ; accompanied the
King to England and was one of the Bearers of the Canopy in State Procession of 1603;
appointed Treasurer Depute of Scotland for life, and a Lord of Session 1623; Lord Justice-
Clerk and Master of Ceremonies 1623-4, and an Extraor. Lord of Session 1626; cr. a *Baronet*
1627, and *Lord Napier*, of Merchistoun (peerage of Scotland) 1627: *m.* 1619, Lady Margaret
Graham, who *d.* (circa) 1628, dau. of 4th Earl of Montrose; *d.* 1645; *s.* by his son [2]
ARCHIBALD, 2nd Lord ; a zealous Loyalist ; distinguished himself in the royal cause during
the Civil Wars : *m.* 1641, Lady Elizabeth Erskine, who *d.* 1683, dau. of 8th Earl of Mar ; *d.*
1660; *s.* by his son [3] ARCHIBALD, 3rd Lord ; obtained an extension of the patent with
limitation to his heirs female and their heirs male and female, and failing which to his
sisters without division and their heirs whatsoever, the female heir being compelled to take
the name and arms of Napier : *d.* 1683, when the Baronetcy became dormant [see Napier, Bt.,
cr. 1627] ; *s.* by his nephew [4] Sir THOMAS Nicolson (son of Jean, el. dau. of 2nd Lord by Sir Thomas
Nicolson, 3rd Bt., of Carnock), 4th Lord, *b.* 1669 ; *d.* unmarried 1686 ; *s.* by his aunt [5] MARGARET
Brisbane, 2nd dau. of 2nd Lord : *m.* 1676, John Brisbane, who *d.* 1684, Sec. to the Admiralty ;
d. 1706 ; *s.* by her grandson [6] FRANCIS (son of Elizabeth (Mistress of Napier), by her marriage with
Sir William Scott, 2nd Bt., of Thirlestane, cr. 1666), 6th Lord, *b.* 1705 ; assumed the name of Napier,
and *s.* to his father's *Baronetcy of Nova Scotia* 1725 ; was Lord of Police 1761 : *m.* 1st, 1729, Lady
Henrietta Hope, who *d.* 1745, dau. of 1st Earl of Hopetoun ; 2ndly, 1750, Henrietta Maria, who
d. 1795, dau. of Capt. George Johnston; *d.* 1773 ; *s.* by his son [7] WILLIAM, 7th Lord, *b.* 1730 ; a
Lieut.-Col. in the Army, and D.A.G. Forces in Scotland : *m.* 1754, the Hon. Mary Anne, who *d.* 1774,
dau. of 8th Lord Cathcart ; *d.* 1775 ; *s.* by his son [8] FRANCIS, *D.C.L.,* 8th Lord, *b.* 1758 ; was
Lord-Lieut. and Sheriff Principal of co. Selkirk ; a Representative Peer 1796, 1802, and 1807 ;
1st Lord High Commr. to Gen. Assembly of Church of Scotland 1802-16 : *m.* 1784, Maria Margaret,
who *d.* 1821, el. da. of Lt.-Gen. Sir John Clavering, KCB; *d.* 1823; *s.* by his son [9] WILLIAM
JOHN, 9th Lord; *b.* 1786; Capt. R.N.; served at Battle of Trafalgar; Rep. Peer 1824-32, Ambassador
to China 1833, and Lord of Bedchamber 1830-33: *m.* 1816, Elizabeth, who *d.* 1883, da.
of the Hon. James Cochrane Johnstone [E. Dundonald] ; *d.* 1834 ; *s.* by his son [10] FRANCIS,
P.C., K.T., LL.D., 10th Lord, *b.* 1819 ; Envoy Extraor. and Min. Plen. to U.S.A. 1857-9
and to The Hague 1859-61, Ambassador to Russia 1861-4 and to Prussia 1864-6, Gov. of Madras
1866-72, and Acting Viceroy of India 1872; cr. *Baron Ettrick*, of Ettrick, co. Selkirk (peerage
of United Kingdom) 1872: *m.* 1845, Anne Jane Charlotte, *C.I.,* dau. of the late Robert Manner,
Lockwood, of Dun-y-Greig, Glamorgan: *d.* 1898 ; *s.* by his el. son [11] WILLIAM JOHN GEORGE
11th Lord, *b.* 1846 ; Sec. to Legation at Stockholm 1887-8 and Tokio 1888-91: *m.* 1st, 1876,
Harriet Blake Armstrong, who *d.* 1897, dau. of the late Edward Lumb, of Wallington Lodge,
Surrey ; 2ndly, 1898, Grace, who *d.* 1928, dau. of the late James Cleland Burns; *d.* 1913 ; *s.* by
his el. son [12] FRANCIS EDWARD BASIL, 12th Lord, *b.* 1876 ; *m.* 1899, the Hon. Clarice Jessie
Evelyn Hamilton, who *d.* 1951, dau. of 9th Lord Belhaven and Stenton ; *d.* 1941 ; *s.* by his el. son
[13] WILLIAM FRANCIS CYRIL JAMES HAMILTON, *T.D.,* 13th Lord, *b.* 1900: Lieut.-Col. King's
Own Scottish Borderers; 1939-45 War Comdg. 6th Batn. of his Regt.; an AAG War Office 1943-44;
a Co. Councillor for Selkirkshire 1946-48 ; a Member of Roy. Co. of Archers (Queen's Body Guard
for Scotland): *m.* 1928, (Violet) Muir, el. da. of Sir Percy Wilson Newson, 1st Bt., and last; *d.* 1954;
s. by his el. son [14] FRANCIS NIGEL, 14th Lord and present peer; also Baron Ettrick.

The Napiers of Merchistoun are co-heirs general of the Celtic Earls of Lennox. Elizabeth, wife of
John Napier of Merchistoun, was grand-da. of Margaret (wife of Robert Menteith of Rusky), da. of
Duncan, 8th Earl of Lennox (executed 1425).

NAPIER OF MAGDALA, BARON. (Napier.) [Baron U.K. 1868.]

[Title pronounced "Napier of Magdahla."]

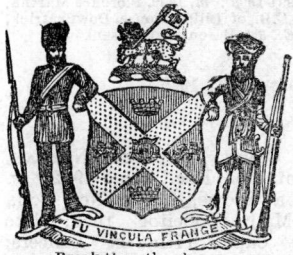

Break thou the chains.

(ROBERT) JOHN NAPIER, *O.B.E.*, 5th Baron; *b.* June 16th, 1904; *s.* 1948; ed. at Wellington Coll.; Brig. late RE; MICE; Waziristan 1936-37 (despatches), European War 1939-45 in Sicily and Italy (despatches, O.B.E.) ; O.B.E. (Mil.) 1944 : *m.* 1939, Elizabeth Marian, yst. da. of the late E. H. Hunt, FRCS, of Cheniston, Farnham, Surrey, and has issue.

Arms,—Gules, on a saltire between two mural crowns in pale, and as many lions passant in fesse or, a rose of the field. Crest,—Upon a mount vert, a lion passant or, gorged with a collar gules, therefrom a chain reflexed over the back and broken, gold, supporting with the sinister forepaw a flagstaff in bend sinister proper, flowing therefrom a banner argent, charged with a cross couped gules. Supporters,—Dexter, a soldier of the corps of Royal Engineers holding in the exterior hand a musket all proper; sinister, a Sikh Sirdar habited and holding in the exterior hand a matchlock all proper.

Residence,—8, Mortonhall Road, Edinburgh, EHa 2HW.

SONS LIVING.

Hon. ROBERT ALAN (The Rosings, 12, South Rd., Grassendale Park, Liverpool 19), *b.* Sept. 6th, 1940; ed. at Winchester, and at St. John's Coll., Camb.: *m.* 1964, Frances Clare, el. da. of A. F. Skinner, OBE, of Monks Close, Woolpit, Suffolk, and has issue living, James Robert *b.* 1966,—Frances Catherine, *b.* 1964.
Hon. Andrew Perceval, *b.* 1947.
Hon. Michael Elibank, *b.* 1953.

DAUGHTERS LIVING.

Hon. Jane Elizabeth, *b.* 1942: *m.* 1964, Christopher Thomas Butler-Cole, of The Old Manse, Carlops, Penicuik, Midlothian, and has issue living, Thomas Falcon, *b.* 1967,—Emma, *b.* 1966.
Hon. Ruth Kathleen (twin), *b.* 1947: *m.* 1972, John Arthur Self, PhD, of 70, Victoria Rd., Hawthorn East, Mel., Vic. 3123, Aust.

SISTERS LIVING.

Hon. (Marion) Kathleen, *b.* 1901 : *m.* 1930, James Robert Bargrave Armstrong, D.L., J.P., Bar.-at-law, and has issue living, Henry Napier, *b.* 1936,—John Fortescue (twin), *b.* 1936,—Kathleen Mary Percevall *b.* 1932,—Florence Margaret, *b.* 1934. *Residence,*—Fellows Hall, Killylea, co. Armagh.
Hon. (Ermine) Maude (Jack's Piece, Ogdens, Fordingbridge, Hants.), *b.* 1907.

WIDOW LIVING OF SON OF FIRST BARON.

Gladys (46, Roland Gdns., SW7), da. of the late F. M. Sir George Stuart White, VC, GCB, OM, GCSI, GCMG, GCIE, GCVO: *m.* 1917, the Hon. Sir Albert Edward Alexander Napier, KCB, KCVO, QC, who *d.* 1973, and has issue living [see colls. infra].

COLLATERAL BRANCHES LIVING.

Issue of the late Lt.-Col. the Hon. Henry Dundas Napier, C.M.G., 5th son of 1st Baron, *b.* 1864, *d.* 1941: *m.* 1897, Sybil, who *d.* 1944, el. dau. of the late John Gurney, of Sprowston Hall, Norwich:—
Arthur Henry Gurney, *OBE, b.* 1900: ed. at Wellington Coll.; formerly Col. RE; Waziristan 1922 (despatches), N-W Frontier of India 1930, 1939-42 War in Middle East (despatches, OBE); OBE (Mil) 1942: *m.* 1937, Rosemary Evelyn, da. of Charles George Lumley Cator [Blois, Bt.], and has issue living, Mary Rose, *b.* 1938,—Angela Marina, *b.* 1940,—Belinda Jane, *b.* 1946: *m.* 1968, Michael Alan Fishwick Leather, of Heath Farm House, Heath Lane, Childer-Thornton, Wirral, Cheshire, and has issue living, James Napier Fishwick *b.* 1971, Giles Napier Fishwick *b.* 1973. *Residence,*—Scutts Farm, Hartley Wintney, Hants.——Margaret Laura Evelyn, *b.* 1899: *m.* 1st, 1922, Richard Samuel Lancelot Worsley, who *d.* 1937; 2ndly, 1946, Lt.-Col. Victor Robert Jones, OBE, ED, QC, and has issue living (by 1st m.) Richard Henry Napier (Marsden Manor, Cirencester, Glos.), *b.* 1924: *m.* 1954, Juliet Anne, da. of the late Henry Herbert Nash, of Cove House, Ashton Keynes, Wilts., and has issue living, Caroline Patricia *b.* 1960, Philippa Jane *b.* 1965, Joanna Rachel *b.* 1967,—Michael Robert (Lovells Farm, Bolney, Sussex), *b.* 1926: *m.* 1964, Jane Elizabeth, yr. da. of the late Maj. Percy Alfred Love, of 48, Queen's Gate, SW7, and has issue living, Robert Napier *b.* 1966, Charles Roderick *b.* 1969, Elizabeth Frances *b.* 1965,—John Bertrand (49, Campden Hill Rd., W8), *b.* 1929: *m.* 1956, Jennifer Jane, el. da. of Sir Andrew Edmund James Clark, MBE, MC, QC, and has issue living, James Jonathan *b.* 1957, Harriet Laura *b.* 1960, Alison Margaret *b.* 1963, Victoria Mary *b.* 1966. *Residence,*—Copyhold, Cuckfield, Sussex.

Issue of the late Lt.-Col. the Hon. Charles Frederik Hamilton Napier, 7th son of 1s Baron, *b.* 1872, *d.* 1963: *m.* 1902, Helen Mary Campbell, who *d.* 1960, dau. of Col. Sir Alexander Brooke Morgan, K.C.B.:—
Charles Campbell (of Sleepy Hollow Farm, Boyertown, Pennsylvania, U.S.A.), *b.* 1903: *m.* 1931, Violet Mushla Birnie, and has issue living, Peter Charles Cornelis (1, Alexander Place, SW7), *b.* 1936: *m.* 1962, Sylvia Walker, da. of Charles Kimball-Fitts, of Lincoln, Mass., USA, and has issue living, Arianne Campbell *b.* 1962, Tanya Kimball *b.* 1968.——Helen Margaret TUCKER, 37, Coxheath Rd., Church Crookham, Hants.); reverted to the surname of Tucker 1964: *m.* 1st, 1938, Charles Richard Tucker, Capt. York and Lancaster Regt., who *d.* (of wounds received in action) 1941; 2ndly, 1944, (m. annulled 1958) Maj. Geoffrey Charles Reid, S. Staffordshire Regt., and has issue living, (by 1st m.) Rosalind Helen Morgan, *b.* 1939: *m.* 1970, Daniel Jacques Guinard, of La Belgique, 33, Le Taillan, Médoc, France.

Issue of the late Hon. Sir Albert Edward Alexander Napier, KCB, KCVO, QC, yst. son of 1st Baron; *b.* 1881, *d.* 1973: *m.* 1917, Gladys (ante), dau. of the late F. M. Sir George Stuart White, VC, GCB, OM, GCSI, GCMG, GCIE, GCVO:—
Patricia Mary Stuart, *b.* 1918: *m.* 1948, Philip E. R. English, of 14, Milborne Grove, SW10.

PREDECESSORS.—[1] *Sir* ROBERT CORNELIS Napier, *G.C.B., G.C.S.I.,* son of Major Charles Frederick Napier, R.A.; *b.* 1810; a distinguished Field-Marshal in British Army, who commanded Abyssinian Expedition 1868, and captured the fortress of Magdala; Com.-in-Ch. of Indian Forces 1870-76, and Gov. of Gibraltar 1876-82; cr. *Baron Napier of Magdala,* in Abyssinia, and of Caryngton, co. Chester (peerage of United Kingdom), 1868: *m.* 1st, 1840, Anne Sarah, who *d.* 1849, dau. of George Pearse, D.L.; 2ndly, 1861, Mary Cecilia, *C.I.,* who *d.*1930, dau. of Maj.-Gen. Edward William Smyth Scott, R.A.; *d.* 1890; *s.* by his el. son [2] ROBERT WILLIAM, 2nd Baron, *b.* 1845 ; A.D.C. to Com.-in-Ch. in India 1870-76, and to Gov. of Gibraltar 1876-81, and Assist. Mil. Sec. 1881-82: *m.* 1885, the Hon. Eva Maria Louisa, who *d.* 1930, dau. of 4th Baron Macdonald, and widow of Capt. Algernon Langham, Grenadier Guards; *d.* 1921 ; *s.* by his brother [3] JAMES PEARSE, 3rd Baron, *b.* 1849 ; Col. (retired) ;

Afghanistan 1878-9 (medal); *m.* 1876, Mabel Ellen, who *d.* 1907, dau. of the late Lieut.-Col. Windsor Parker, of Clopton Hall, Rattlesden; *d.* **1935**; *s.* by his half-brother [4] EDWARD HERBERT SCOTT, 4th Baron, *b.* 1861; formerly Lieut. 1st Vol. Batn. Princess Charlotte of Wales's (Berkshire Regt.); in Indian State Railways 1884-1909 : *m.* 1900, Florence Martha, who *d.* 1946, dau. of the late Gen. John Maxwell Perceval, C.B., of Dillon House, Downpatrick, co. Down ; *d.* 1948 ; *s.* by his son [5] (ROBERT) JOHN, *O.B.E.*, 5th Baron, and present peer.

NATHAN, BARON. (Nathan.) [Baron U.K. 1940.]

ROGER CAROL MICHAEL NATHAN, 2nd Baron; *b.* Dec. 5th, 1922; *s.* 1963; ed. at Stowe, and at New Coll., Oxford (MA); Solicitor 1950; late temporary Capt. 17th/21st Lancers; Pres. of Jewish Welfare Board 1967-71; Chm. Central British Fund for Jewish Relief and Rehabilitation, and Chm. of Exec. Cttee. Cancer Research Campaigns, FSA, FRSA, FRGS, and an Assoc. Member of Bar Assocn. of City of New York; Master of Gardeners' Co. 1963-64; 1939-45 War, as Capt. 17th/21st Lancers (twice wounded, despatches): *m.* 1950, Philippa Gertrude, da. of Maj. J. B. Solomon, MC, of Sutton, Sussex, and has issue.

Labour ennobleth.

Arms,—Or, a fesse cottised sable over all a sword erect gules, on a canton of the second a roll of parchment proper. **Crest,**—A kiln enflamed proper. **Supporters,**—*Dexter*, a lion; *sinister*, a hind argent ; each charged on the shoulder with a grenade sable fired proper.
Residence,—Collyers Farm, Lickfold, Petworth, Sussex. *Clubs,*—Athenæum, Cavalry, Gresham.

SON LIVING.
Hon. RUPERT HARRY BERNARD, *b.* May 26th, 1957.

DAUGHTERS LIVING.
Hon. Jennifer Ruth, *b.* 1952.
Hon. Nicola Janet Eleanor, *b.* 1954.

SISTER LIVING.
Hon. Joyce Constance Ina (*Hon. Lady Waley-Cohen*), *b.* 1920; ed. at St. Felix Sch., and at Girton Coll., Camb. (MA); a JP for Somerset; a Gov. of St. Felix Sch. since 1945; a Member of Exec. of Gov. Bodies of Girls Schs. Assocn.: *m.* 1943, Sir Bernard Nathaniel Waley-Cohen, 1st Bt. *Residences,*—11, Little St. James's St., SW1; Honeymead, Simonsbath, Minehead, Som.

PREDECESSOR.—[1] HARRY LOUIS Nathan, *TD, PC*, son of the late Michael Henry Nathan, JP; *b.* 1889; Under-Sec. of State for War and Vice-Pres. of Army Council 1945-46, and Min. of Civil Aviation 1946-48; MP for NE Div. of Bethnal Green (*L*) 1929-35, and for Central Div. of Wandsworth 1937-40; 1914-18 War as Maj. and temporary Lt.-Col. London Regt. (severely wounded); cr. *Baron Nathan*, of Churt, co. Surrey (peerage of UK) 1940, and a PC 1946: *m.* 1919, Eleanor Joan Clara, MA, JP, who *d.* 1972, da. of the late Carl Stettauer: *d.* 1963; *s.* by his only son [2] ROGER CAROL MICHAEL, 2nd Baron, and present peer.

Neidpath, Lord, son of Earl Wemyss and March.

NELSON, EARL. [Nelson.] [Earl U.K. 1805.]

Palmam qui meruit ferat

Let him wear the palm who has deserved it.

GEORGE JOSEPH HORATIO NELSON, 8th Earl; *b.* April 20th, 1905; *s.* 1972; ed. at Ampleforth: *m.* 1945, Mary Winifred, da. of W. Bevan, of Swansea, and has issue.

Arms,—Or, a cross patonce sable surmounted by a bend gules, thereon another bend engrailed of the field, charged with three handgrenades of the second, fired proper; a chief of augmentation wavy argent, thereon waves of the sea, from which issuant in the centre a palm tree, between a disabled ship on the dexter and a battery in ruins on the sinister, all proper. **Crests,**—1st, over a naval crown or, the chelenk or diamond plume of triumph, presented to the 1st Lord Nelson, by the Grand Signor, Sultan Selim III; 2nd, the stern of the San Joseph, Spanish man-of-war, floating in waves of the sea proper. **Supporters,**—*Dexter*, a sailor habited and armed with a cutlass, with a pair of pistols in his belt proper, his right hand supporting a pike also proper, thereon hoisted a commodore's flag gules, and his left holding a palm branch; *sinister*, a lion reguardant in his mouth two broken staffs, and flowing from the one the Spanish, and from the other the French ensigns, and in the dexter forepaw a palm branch all proper.
Residence,—27, Rabling Rd., Swanage, Dorset.

DAUGHTER LIVING.
Lady Sarah Josephine Mary, *b.* 1947.

SISTERS LIVING.
Lady Edith Mary Josephine (3, Blake Hill Cres., Parkstone, Poole, Dorset) *b.* 1897: *m.* 1921, Capt. Henry Charles Coulston, King's Own Roy. Regt. Reserve, who *d.* (on active ser.) 1940, and has issue living, John Alban Horatio Nelson (3, Blake Hill Cres., Parkstone, Poole, Dorset), *b.* 1927; Merchant Navy 1944-50: *m.* 1st, 1956 (m. diss. 1966), Sheelagh Alston Gartlan; 2ndly, 1966, Patricia Rose Neville, and has issue living, (by 1st m.) Jonathan Charles Nelson, *b.* 1957, (by 2nd m.) Andrew Peter James *b.* 1971, Catherine Mary Anne *b.* 1966, Helen Christina *b.* 1967.
Lady Mary Winefride, *b.* 1899. *Residence,*—Richmond House, 27, Rabling Rd., Swanage, Dorset.
Lady Geraldine Mary Diana, *b.* 1900; 1939-45 War with RAF Nursing Ser. *Residence,*—Richmond House, 27, Rabling Rd., Swanage, Dorset.

WIDOWS LIVING OF SONS OF FIFTH EARL.
Kathleen Cook (29, Rowans Park, Lymington, Hants.): *m.* 1916, Lt.-Col. the Hon. Charles Sebastian Joseph Horatio Nelson, who *d.* 1964, and has issue living [see colls. infra].
Kathleen Mary (27, Rabling Rd., Swanage), da. of William Burr, of Torquay: *m.* 1941, Capt. the Hon. John Marie Joseph Horatio Nelson, who *d.* 1970, and has issue living [see colls., infra].

COLLATERAL BRANCHES LIVING. (*The heirs male are in remainder to Earldom.*)
Issue of the late Lt.-Col. the Hon. Charles Sebastian Joseph Horatio Nelson, 3rd son of 5th Earl, *b.* 1896, *d.* 1964: *m.* 1916, Kathleen Cook (ante):—
Mary Teresa Muriel, *b.* 1917; 1939-45 War with S. African Air Force: *m.* 1946, Cornelius Johannes Erasmus, of 29, Rowans Park, Lymington, Hants., and has issue living, Anthony Charles, *b.* 1953, —Martina Kathleen, *b.* 1947.

Issue of the late Capt. John Marie Joseph Horatio Nelson, yst. son of 5th Earl, *b.* 1908, *d.* 1970: *m.* 1941, Kathleen Mary (ante), da. of William Burr, of Torquay:—
PETER JOHN HORATIO (136, Welbeck Rd., W. Harrow), *b.* Oct. 9th, 1941: *m.* 1969, Maureen Diana, da. of Edward Patrick Quinn, of Kilkenny and has issue living, Simon John Horatio, *b.* 1971,— Deborah Jane Mary, *b.* 1974.——Francis Edward Horatio, *b.* 1947.——Jane Priscilla, *b.* 1944: *m.* 1968, Roy Hannant, of 25, St. Margaret's Mansions, Corner of High Level and St. John's Rd., Sea Point, Cape Town, and has issue living, David John Charles, *b.* 1972,—Richard Roy, *b.* 1974,— Sally Kathleen (twin), *b.* 1974.

Grandchildren of the late Rear-Adm. the Hon. Maurice Horatio Nelson, 3rd son of 2nd Earl:—
Issue of the late Charles Burrard Nelson, *b.* 1868, *d.* 1931: *m.* 1904, Geraldine, who *d.* 1969, da. of the Rev. Ernest Henry Glencross, V. of Morval, Cornwall:—
John Charles Horatio, *b.* 1905; Com. (ret.) RN: *m.* 1934, Alice Helen, da. of the late Col. Robert Maximilian Rainey-Robinson, CB, CMG, and has issue living, Antony Burrard Horatio, *b.* 1935: *m.* 1960, Judith Constance, da. of the late Brig. Thomas Farquharson Ker Howard, DSO, of Golden-hayes, Woodlands, Southampton, and has issue living, Thomas Antony Horatio *b.* 1963, Edward Maximilian *b.* 1971, Teresa Helen *b.* 1962, Rebecca Anne *b.* 1975,—Joanna Elizabeth, *b.* 1940: *m.* 1962, Henry Bruce Milne, of Dowerfield, Long Bredy, Dorchester, and has issue living, Robert Henry *b.* 1968, Emma Alice *b.* 1970, Sarah Elizabeth *b.* 1973. *Residence,*—Forrestgate, Landford, Salisbury.——Emily Geraldine Morval, *b.* 1906: *m.* 1st, 1928, Jocelyn Panizzi Preston (who *d.* 1970, and from she obtained a divorce, 1945), son of the late Sir Frederick George Panizzi Preston, KBE; 2ndly, 1946, Cdr. Rowland Kirby, OBE, RNR, who *d.* 1971, and has issue living (by 1st m.) Simon Douglas Nelson (Badsell Park Farm, Matfield, Tonbridge, Kent), *b.* 1933: *m.* 1962, Celia Mary, da. of the late Francis Bodenham Thornely, and has issue living, Rupert Robin Nelson *b.* 1963, Adam Bodenham Nelson *b.* 1965,—(by 2nd m.) Ben Martin, *b.* 1948: *m.* 1970, Katherine Alice Mary Jackson, and has issue living, Henry Rowland *b.* 1974, Samantha Jane Alice *b.* 1972. *Residence,*—Bishops Quay, St. Martin, Helston, Cornwall.

Grandchildren of the late William Eyre Eyre-Matcham, grandson of the late Catherine Matcham, sister of 1st Baron:—
Issue of the late Capt. George Henry Eyre EYRE-MATCHAM, *b.* 1862, *d.* 1939: *m.* 1889, Constance Gertrude, who *d.* 1933, da. of the late Hon. St. Leger Richard; Glyn [B. Wolverton, colls.]:—
John St. Leger, *b.* 1890; ed. at Charterhouse, and at Corpus Christi Coll., Oxford: *m.* 1949, Norah Olivia Alice, widow of John Spencer Spear, of Imperial Airways, Athens, Greece. *Residence,*— Newhouse, Redlynch, nr. Salisbury, Wilts.——Constance Valentine, *b.* 1897: *m.* 1923, Cdr. Edmund Valentine Jeffreys, RN, and has issue living, George William Eyre (Lower Pensworth Farm, Red-lynch, nr. Salisbury, Wilts.), *b.* 1931; ed. at Radley: *m.* 1960, June, da. of Alexander Bennett, of Godshill Wood, Hants., and has issue living, Sarah Kezia Eyre *b.* 1963, Elizabeth Jemima Eyre *b.* 1964, Rachel Jane Eyre *b.* 1968,—Catharine Elizabeth Eyre, *b.* 1933: *m.* 1953, Anthony William Lane, of Over Silton Manor, Over Stilton, nr. Thirsk, N. Yorks., and has issue living, Harriet Eliza-beth *b.* 1954, Caroline Mary *b.* 1956, Georgina Margaret *b.* 1959, Victoria Anne Michell *b.* 1962, Florence Sophia *b.* 1967. *Residence,*—Loosehanger Park, Redlynch, nr. Salisbury, Wilts.

PREDECESSORS.—[1] *Sir* HORATIO NELSON, *KB,* 5th son of the late Rev. Edmund Nelson, R. of Hillborough and of Burnham Thorpe, Norfolk, *b.* 1758; one of the most eminent Naval Commanders of any age, having gained the celebrated victory of the Nile on Aug. 1, 1798, was in Nov. of the same year cr. *Baron Nelson,* of the Nile, and of Burnham Thorpe, co. Norfolk (peerage of GB), and in 1799 was cr. *Duke of Bronté,* in the kingdom of Sicily, which title he was afterwards permitted to use by royal sanction; on April 2, 1802, he completely defeated the Danish fleet off Copenhagen, and on May 22 following was cr. *Viscount Nelson of the Nile* and *of Burnham Thorpe,* co. Norfolk (peerage of UK), and on Aug. 18 of the same year was cr. *Baron Nelson of the Nile* and *of Hillborough,* co. Norfolk, with remainder to his father and the heirs male of his body, and failing them to the heirs male of the body severally and successively of his sisters Mrs. Susannah Bolton and Mrs. Catherine Matcham; on Oct. 21, 1805, having gained the ever memorable victory of Trafalgar he was mortally wounded, his remains being honoured with a public funeral in St. Paul's Cathedral on Jan. 9 ,1806: *m.* 1787. Frances Herbert, da. of William Woodward, Sen. Judge of Nevis, WI, and widow of Josiah Nisbet, MD; the barony of 1798 and the viscountcy became extinct, and the barony of 1801 and the Dukedom of Bronté devolved upon his brother [2] WILLIAM, *DD,* 2nd Baron; cr. *Viscount Merton of Trafalgar* and *of Merton,* co. Surrey, and *Earl Nelson,* of Trafalgar and of Merton, co. Surrey (peerage of UK) 1805, with a similar remainder to that of the Barony (cr. 1801); *d.* 1835; *s.* by his nephew [3] THOMAS Bolton, 2nd Earl, el. son of Susannah Bolton (ante), who in accordance with the Act of Settlement 46 Geo. III, cap. 3, assumed the surname of Nelson: *b.* 1786: *m.* 1821, Frances Elizabeth, da. and heir of John Maurice Eyre, of Landford and Brickworth, co. Wilts: *d.* 1835, when the Duchy of Bronté reverted to Charlotte Mary, only da. of the 1st Earl, and wife of Samuel, 2nd Baron Bridport, and the Earldom devolved upon his son [4] HORATIO, 3rd Earl, *b.* 1823: *m.* 1845, Lady Mary Jane Diana Agar, who *d.* 1904, da. of 2nd Earl of Normanton; *d.* 1913: *s.* by his el. son [5] THOMAS HORATIO, 4th Earl; *b.* 1857, *d.* 1947; *s.* by his brother [6] EDWARD AGAR HORATIO, 5th Earl; *b.* 1860: *m.* 1889, Geraldine, who *d.* 1936, da. of the late Henry H. Cave, of Horton Crescent, Rugby; *d.* 1951; *s.* by his el. son [7] ALBERT FRANCIS JOSEPH HORATIO, 6th Earl; *b.* 1890; a lecturer in Astronomy and Anthropology; 1914-19 War with Aust. Imperial Force, 1939-44 War as Major: *m.* 1st, 1924, Amelia, who *d.* 1937 (having obtained a divorce 1925), widow of John O. Scott; 2ndly, 1927 (in Scotland) and 1942 (in England) Marguerite Helen, who *d.* 1969, da. of Capt. J. M. O'Sullivan, of Tipperary; *d.* 1957; *s.* by his brother [8] HENRY EDWARD JOSEPH

HORATIO, 7th Earl; *b.* 1894; *d.* 1972; *s.* by his brother [9] GEORGE JOSEPH HORATIO, 7th Earl and present peer; also Viscount Merton of Trafalgar, and Baron Nelson of the Nile and of Hillborough.

NELSON OF STAFFORD, BARON.   (Nelson.)   [Baron U.K. 1960, Bt. U.K. 1955.]

HENRY GEORGE NELSON, 2nd Baron and 2nd Baronet; *b.* Jan. 2nd, 1917; *s.* 1962; ed. at Oundle, and at King's Coll., Camb. (MA); FICE, Hon.FIMechE, FIEE (Pres. 1970), FRAeS; Hon. DSc Aston, Keele and Cranfield; Hon. LLD Strathclyde; Fellow of Imperial Coll. of Science & Tech.; Chm. Gen. Elec. Co., Ltd. (Dep. Man. Dir. English Elec. Co., Ltd. 1949-56, Man. Dir. 1956-62, and Chm. and Ch. Exec. 1962-68), Joint Dep. Chm. of British Aircraft Corpn. and a Dir. of Bank of England, of Nat. Bank of Australasia, Ltd. (London Board of Advice); a Member of Advisory Cttee., of Internat. Nickel Co. (Canada), Ltd., a Member of Gov. Advisory Council on Scientific Policy 1955-58, of Advisory Council on Middle East Trade 1958-63 (Industrial Leader and Vice-Chm. 1959-63), of Advisory Council of Technology 1964-70, of Engineering Advisory Council since 1958, and of Exec. Cttee. of British Nat. Cttee World Energy Conference since 1957 (Chm. 1971-74); Chm. Defence Industries Council since 1971, Pres. of Sino-British Trade Council since 1973, a Repres. of Conference of Electronics Industry on Nat. Electronics Research Council since 1963 and a Trustee of Civil Trust 1962-72; Pres. of Electrical Research Assocn. 1963-64, of Orgalime (Organisme de Liaison des Industries Métallique Européennes) 1966-70, of British Electrical & Allied Manufacturers Assocn. 1966-67, of Locomotive & Allied Manufacturers Assocn. 1964-66, and of British Electric Power Convention 1967, and of Soc. of British Aircraft Constructors Ltd. 1961-62; Vice-Pres. of British-Nepal Soc., and of Middle East Assocn. since 1962, of Engineering Employers' Fedn. since 1963 (Gen. Council and Management Board since 1956); 1st Chancellor of Univ. of Aston, Birmingham since 1966, and a Gov. of Commonwealth Inst. since 1972; Lord High Steward of Stafford 1966-71; Hon. Member of City & Guilds of London Inst.; a Liveryman of Goldsmiths' Co. (a Member of Court 1974), and Coachmakers and Coach Harness Makers' Co. (Assist. to Court 1959-62); Benjamin Franklin Medal, Roy. Soc. of Arts: *m.* 1940, Pamela Roy, yr. da. of the late Ernest Roy Bird, MP, of New House Farm, Robertsbridge, Sussex, and has issue.

Arms,—Argent, a cross flory sable, a chief gules thereon between a Stafford knot and a rose of the first, barbed and seeded proper, a pale also of the first, charged with a sword erect of the third.   **Crest,** —An arm embowed resting on the elbow in armour proper, the gauntlet grasping a cross flory fitchée sable between two roses gules, barbed and seeded also proper.   **Supporters,**—*Dexter*, a lion guardant or charged on the shoulder with a thunderbolt azure ; *Sinister*, a grey horse proper gorged with a coronet composed of four fleur-de-lys with chains affixed thereto and reflexed over the back also or and charged on the shoulder with a Stafford knot gold.

Residences,—19, Acacia Rd., NW8 6AN; Wincote Farm, Eccleshall, Staffs.   *Clubs,*—Carlton, and Hurlingham.

SONS LIVING.

Hon. HENRY ROY GEORGE (Ackworth Grove, Pontefract Rd., High Ackworth, Pontefract, Yorks.), *b.* Oct. 26th, 1943; ed. at Ampleforth, and at Kings Coll., Camb.: *m.* 1968, Dorothy, da. of Leslie Caley, of Tibthorpe Manor, Driffield, E. Yorks., and has issue living, Alistair William Henry, *b.* 1973.
Hon. James Jonathan, *b.* 1947; ed. at Ampleforth, and McGill Univ., Canada.

DAUGHTERS LIVING.

Hon. Caroline Jane, *b.* 1942: *m.* 1964, Michael John Henry Ford, of Buckerell Old Rectory, Buckerell, Honiton, Devon, and has issue living, James Mortimer Henry, *b.* 1965,—Andrew Michael Felix, *b.* 1967,—Annabel Emma Jane, *b.* 1972.
Hon. Sally Louise, *b.* 1955: *m.* 1975, Peter Robert Jolliffe Tritton.

SISTER LIVING.

Hon. Margaret Joan, *b.* 1915 ; is a J.P. for Warwickshire: *m.* 1941, Edward Michael Price, and has issue living, Elizabeth Joan, *b.* 1943,—Susan Jane, *b.* 1944,—Anne Waldegrave, *b.* 1947.   *Residence,* —Frankton Manor, Frankton, Warwickshire.

PREDECESSOR.—[1] *Sir* GEORGE (HORATIO) Nelson, son of the late George Nelson, of 66, Muswell Hill Rd., N.; *b.* 1887; Chm. of The English Electric Co. Ltd., and other Cos.; cr. a Bt. 1955, and Baron *Nelson of Stafford*, of Hilcote Hall, co. Stafford (peerage of United Kingdom) 1960: *m.* 1913, Florence Mabel, who *d.* 1962, only dau. of the late Henry Howe, J.P., of Leics.; *d.* 1962; *s.* by his only son [2] HENRY GEORGE, 2nd Baron and present peer.

NETHERTHORPE, BARON. (Turner.) [Baron U.K. 1959.]

JAMES TURNER, 1st Baron, son of the late A. E. M. Turner, of Anston, Sheffield ; *b.* Jan. 6th, 1908 ; ed. at Knaresborough, and at Leeds Univ. (BSc (Agriculture), Hon. LLD; Hon. LLD Birmingham; Chm. of Fisons, Ltd.; Dep. Chm. of Richard Costain, Ltd. 1960-72; a Dir. of Fisons, Ltd. (Chm. 1962-73), of Lloyds Bank, of Steetley Co., Ltd., of Unigate, Ltd., of Abbey National Building Soc., and J. H. Fenner & Co. (Holdings), Ltd., and a Liveryman of Painter-Stainers' Co., and of Farmers' Co.; Pres. of NFU 1945-60, Roy. Assocn. of British Dairy Farmers 1964, and Roy. Agric. Soc. 1965; cr. Knt. 1949, and *Baron Netherthorpe,* of Anston, W. Riding of Yorkshire (peerage of United Kingdom) 1959: *m.* 1935, Margaret Lucy, da. of James Arthur Mattock, and has issue.

Work itself is pleasing.

Arms,—Argent on a Cross gules between four garbs vert five millrinds erect or a chief of stone masonry proper. Crest,—A lion passant guardant gules gorged with a collar sable charged with bezants, supporting with the dexter paw a cornucopia inverted or the fruit proper. Supporters,—*Dexter,* a bull; *sinister,* a ram, both argent horned and unguled or and gorged with a collar sable charged with bezants.

Residence,—Hadley Hurst, Hadley Common, Herts. *Clubs,*—Boodle's, City Livery, Farmers'.

SONS LIVING.

Hon. JAMES ANDREW (Boothby Hall, Boothby Pagnell, Grantham, Lincs.), *b.* July 23rd, 1936; ed. at Rugby, and at Pembroke Coll., Camb.; Vice-Chm. of Dalgety, Ltd., a Dir. Lazard Brothers & Co., Ltd., Babcock & Wilcox, Ltd., and Commercial Bank of Aust., Ltd. (London Board): *m.* 1960, Belinda, da. of F. Hedley Nicholson, of Friars Gate, Firbeck, Worksop, and has issue living, James Frederick, *b.* 1964,—Patrick Andrew, *b.* 1971,—Anna Elizabeth, *b.* 1961,—Kate Belinda, *b.* 1967.

Hon. Edward Neil (The Limes, S. Anston, Sheffield), *b.* 1941; ed. at Rugby, at Roy. Agricultural Coll., Cirencester, and London Univ.; ARICS; ALAS; Chm. of Edward Turner Cos.; a Member of Yorks. and Humberside Regional Economic Planning Council since 1975; a Freeman of Co. of Cutters in Hallamshire: *m.* 1963, Gillian Mary, el. da. of the late C. J. King, and has issue living, Charles James, *b.* 1966,—Sarah Jane, *b.* 1971.

Hon. (Philip Noel) Nigel (4, Charles St., Barnes, SW13 0NZ), *b.* 1949; ed. at Rugby, and Worcester Coll., Oxford: *m.* 1973, Anne, da. of R. Brown, of Dovecote Farm, Somerton, Oxon,

NEWALL, BARON. (Newall.) [Baron U.K. 1946.]

FRANCIS STORER EATON NEWALL, 2nd Baron; *b.* June 23rd, 1930; *s.* 1963; ed. at Eton; Capt. (ret.) 11th Hussars; Adjt. Roy. Gloucestershire Hussars 1956-58: *m.* 1956, Pamela Elizabeth, el. da. of Edward Hugh Lee Rowcliffe, TD [see Farrington, Bt.], and has issue.

Arms,—Per pale azure and gules two lions passant guardant in pale or on a chief ermine a rose of the second barbed and seeded between a lotus flower and a sprig of New Zealand fern all proper. Crest,—Issuant from an astral crown or an eagle wings elevated sable breathing flames proper. Supporters,—On either side a pegasus gorged with an astral crown or.

DEO JUVANTE

Pleasing to God.

Residence,—Wotton Underwood, Aylesbury, Bucks. *Club,*—Cavalry.

SONS LIVING.

Hon. RICHARD HUGH EATON, *b.* Feb. 19th ,1961.
Hon. David William Norton, *b.* 1963.

DAUGHTER LIVING.

Hon. Miranda Jane, *b.* 1959.

SISTERS LIVING.
Hon. Georgiana (Catridge Farm, Lacock, Chippenham, Wilts.), *b.* 1926.
Hon. Diana Olive (Tower House, Reybridge, Chippenham, Wilts.), *b.* 1927: *m.* 1956 (m. diss. 1967), John Leonard Joly, and has issue living, Harriet Diana, *b.* 1960.

WIDOW LIVING OF FIRST BARON.
OLIVE TENNYSON FOSTER (*Olivia Baroness Newall*) (c/o Coutts & Co., 1, Old Park Lane, W.1; Oriental, Cercle Interallié (Paris), and Women's City of Boston (USA) Clubs), only da. of Mrs. Francis Storer Eaton, of Boston, USA; a DStJ: *m.* 1925, as his 2nd wife, the 1st Baron, who *d.* 1963.

PREDECESSOR.—[1] *Marshal of R.A.F. Sir* CYRIL LOUIS NORTON Newall, *G.C.B., O.M., G.C.M.G.,* *C.B.E., A.M.,* son of the late Lt.-Col. William Potter Newall, Indian Army; *b.* 1886; entered Roy. Warwickshire Regt. 1905, transferred to Indian Army 1909, to R.F.C. 1914 and to R.A.F. 1919; Dir. of Operations and Intelligence, Air Min. and Dep. Ch. of Air Staff 1926-31, Comdg. Wessex Area, Air Defence 1931, and A.O.C. Middle East 1931-35, Ch. of Air Staff 1937-40, and Gov.-Gen. of New Zealand 1941-46; *cr.* 1946, *Baron Newall*, of Clifton-upon-Dunsmoor, Co. Warwick (peerage of UK) 1946: *m.* 1st, 1922, Mary Dulcie Weddell, who *d.* 1924; 2ndly, 1925, Olive Tennyson Foster, only da. of Mrs. Francis Storer Eaton, of Boston, USA; *d.* 1963; *s.* by his only son [2] FRANCIS STORER EATON, 2nd Baron, and present peer.

NEWBOROUGH, BARON. (Wynn.) [Baron I. 1776, Bt. G.B. 1742.]

ROBERT CHARLES MICHAEL VAUGHAN WYNN, *DSC*, 7th Baron, and 9th Baronet; *b.* April 24th, 1917; *s.* 1965; ed. at Oundle; late 2nd Lt. 9th Lancers SR and Lt. 16/5th Lancers; High Sheriff of Merioneth 1963; 1939-45 War as Lt. RNVR in command of MTB 74, St. Nazaire (wounded, despatches, DSC, prisoner, escaped): *m.* 1st, 1945 (m. diss. 1971), Rosamund Lavington, da. of the late Maj. Robert Barbour; 2ndly, 1971, Jennifer Caroline Acland, yst. da. of the late Capt. Cecil C. A. Allen, RN, and has issue by 1st m.

Arms.,—Sable, three fleurs-de-lis-argent. Crest,,—A dexter cubit arm erect, holding in the hand a fleur-de-lis or. Supporters,—Two lions gules, the *dexter* gorged with a plain collar charged with three fleurs-de-lis or, the *sinister* gorged with a plain collar argent charged with three crosses patée gules.

Residences,—Rhug, Corwen, Merioneth; Belan Fort, Llandwrog, Caernarvon. *Clubs,*—Naval and Military, Bembridge Sailing.

Gentle in manner, vigorous in action.

SON LIVING (By 1st m.).
Hon. ROBERT VAUGHAN, *b.* Aug. 11th, 1949; ed. at Milton Abbey.

DAUGHTERS LIVING (By 1st m.).
Hon. (Anne) Patricia Rosamund, *b.* 1947: *m.* 1970, Anthony George Budgen, of Icknield Place, Aston Rowant, Oxford, and has issue living, Mark George, *b.* 1972,—Nadine Patricia Mary, *b.* 1975.
Hon. Diana Heather Marion, *b.* 1951.

BROTHER LIVING.
Hon. Charles Henry Romer, *b.* 1923; Lt.-Com. RN (ret.): *m.* 1947, the Hon. Angela Hermione Ida Willoughby, da. of the late 11th Baron Middleton, and has issue living, Anthony Charles Vaughan, *b.* 1949; ed. at Eton, and Balliol Coll., Oxford: *m.* 1973, Jane Slane Sloan, el. da. of the Rev. William Thompson, of Oxnam Manse, Jedburgh, Roxburghshire,—Andrew Guy, *b.* 1950; ed. at Eton, and Gonville and Caius Coll., Camb.; Lt. RN. *Residence,*—Bunkersland, Withleigh, Tiverton, Devon.

UNCLE LIVING. (Raised to the rank of a Baron's son, 1958.)
Hon. Rowland Tempest Beresford, *CBE*, *b.* 1898; ed. at Uppingham, and at Trin. Hall, Camb. (MA), FIEE; Head of Engineering Information Dept., B.B.C. 1926-34, Senior Sup. Engineer 1934-43; Assist. and Dep. Ch. Engineer 1943-52, and Ch. Engineer 1952-60; 1916-18 War with R.F.C. and R.A.F.; OBE (Civil) 1949; *m.* 1943, Eleanor Mary Tydfil, da. of the late Arthur Edmund Smith-Thomas. *Residence,*—Sunningdale, The Heights, Worthing.

DAUGHTERS LIVING OF FIFTH BARON. (By 1st marriage.)
Hon. Stella Maria Glyn, *b.* 1908 : *m.* 1st, 1932, Charles Vivian Jackson, who *d.* 1936, son of Sir Charles Jackson; 2ndly, 1942, Lieut.-Col. Richard Derek Cardiff, Scots Guards, and has issue living (by 1st marriage). *Residence,*—Armscote House, Stratford-on-Avon.

(By 2nd marriage.)
Hon. Juno Odette Denisa Palma, *b.* 1940: *m.* 1963, Philip Wolfe-Parry, LDS, RCS, of 54, Hans Place, Knightsbridge, SW1, and has issue living, Edward Thomas Wilton, *b.* 1972.

WIDOW LIVING OF BROTHER OF SIXTH BARON.
Gladys Catherine, da. of the late Richard Hanbury Joseph Gurney [Buxton, Bt.]: *m.* 1915, the Hon. Arthur Romer Wynn, who *d.* 1964, and has issue living [see colls., infra].

WIDOW LIVING OF FIFTH BARON.
KATHERINE RUDKIN (*Katherine, Baroness Newborough*), dau. of Henry Stephen Murray, of Melbourne, Australia: *m.* 1947, as his third wife, the 5th Baron, who *d.* 1957. *Residence,*—Four Winds, Caernarvon.

COLLATERAL BRANCH LIVING.
Issue of the late Hon. Arthur Romer Wynn, brother of 6th Baron, *b.* 1885, *d.* 1964: *m.* 1915, Gladys Catherine (ante), da. of the late Richard Hanbury Joseph Gurney [Buxton, Bt.]:—
John Christopher Watkin Wynn (c/o Barclays Bank, D.C.O., Bulawayo, Rhodesia), *b.* 1917; 1939-45 War as Capt. R.A. in India and Burma: *m.* 1946, Cynthia Maureen, da. of the late William Dodwell

and has issue living, Nicholas Romer, *b.* 1952,—Gareth Rowland, *b.* 1958,—Ann Richenda Dodwell, *b.* 1947: *m.* 1973, Thomas William Everett (c/o Wankie National Park, Rhodesia).——Dennis Gurney Wynn, *b.* 1922: *m.* 1950, Joan Edith, da. of A. P. Bentley, of King's Lynn, Norfolk, and has issue living, Simon Charles, *b.* 1952,—Mark Gurney, *b.* 1957,—Sarah Frances, *b.* 1954,—Rebecca Helen, *b.* 1966.——Rosemary Vera Georgina WYNN, *b.* 1919; has assumed surname of Wynn: *m.* 1st, 1941 (m. diss. 1966) John Richard Boydell; 2ndly, 1966 (m. diss. 1969) John Leicester Goldsmith.

PREDECESSORS.—[1] THOMAS Wynn, Equerry to George II., Clerk to Board of Green Cloth, and M.P. for Carnarvon 1713-47; cr. a *Baronet* 1742; *s.* by his son [2] *Sir* JOHN, **2nd Bt.**, M.P. for co. Carnarvon 1754-61; *s.* by his son [3] *Sir* THOMAS, 3rd Bt.; M.P. for co. Carnarvon 1761-74, Lord-Lieut. of Carnarvonshire, and Col. of Carnarvon Militia; cr. *Baron Newborough* (peerage of Ireland) 1776: *m.* 2ndly, Maria Stella Patronilla Chiappini; *d.* 1807; *s.* by his el. son [4] THOMAS JOHN, 2nd Baron; M.P. for Carnarvonshire 1826-31; *d.* unmarried 1832: *s* by his brother [5] SPENCER BULKELEY, 3rd Baron, *b.* 1803; High Sheriff of Anglesey 1847: *m.* 1834, Frances Maria, who *d.* 1857, el. dau. of the late Rev. Walter de Winton, of Hay Castle, Brecon; *d.* 1888; *s.* by his grandson [6] WILLIAM CHARLES (son of the late Hon. Thomas John Wynn), 4th Baron; *b.* 1873; Lieut. Welsh Guards: *m.* 1900, Grace Bruce, who *d.* 1930, dau. of the late Col. Henry Montgomerie Carr; *d.* (result of active ser. during Russian War) 1916; *s.* by his brother [7] THOMAS JOHN, 5th Baron; *b.* 1878; formerly Lieut. R.N.R.: *m.* 1st, Vera Evelyn Mary (who *d.* 1940, having obtained a divorce 1938), dau. of the late Capt. Philip Montagu, 12th Lancers, of Down Hall, Dorset, and widow of Henry L. Winch; 2ndly, 1939, Denisa Josephine (who obtained a divorce 1947), dau. of the late Lazar Braun, of Subotica, Yugoslavia; 3rdly, 1947, Katherine Rudkin, dau. of Henry Stephen Murray, of Victoria. Australia; *d.* 1957; *s.* by his cousin [8] ROBERT VAUGHAN, *OBE* (son of the late Hon. Charles Henry Wynn, 3rd son of 3rd Baron), 6th Baron, *b.* 1877; S. Africa 1899-1902 (despatches twice); 1914-18 War with 9th Lancers (despatches four times, Brevet Lt.-Col.): *m.* 1913, Ruby Irene, who *d.* 1960, da. of the late Edmund Wigley Severne; *d.* 1965; *s.* by his son [9] ROBERT CHARLES MICHAEL VAUGHAN, *DSC*, 7th Baron and present peer.

NEWBURGH, COUNTESS OF. (Gravina.) [**Earl S. 1660.**]

[Title pronounced "**Newborough.**"]

MARIA SOFIA GIUSEPPINA GRAVINA DI RAMACCA, *Countess of Newburgh*; *b.* May 4th, 1889; *s.* 1941; Princess Giustiniani-Bandini, and Marchesa Bandini, and Duchess of Mondragone: *m.* 1922, Count Manfredi Gravina di Ramacca, High Commr., Danzig, who *d.* 1932.

Arms,—Quarterly: 1st bendy of six argent and gules, on a chief of the last a cross of the first, *Bandini;* 2nd gules, a tower proper, on a chief or an eagle displayed sable, *Giustiniani;* 3rd or, a lion rampant sable, *Mahony;* 4th checky or and azure, a fesse gules, *Clifford;* 5th argent, on a bend between three gilliflowers gules, an anchor of the first, all within a double tressure vert, *Leningston:* 6th, gules, on a bend argent, a grasshopper proper, *Mondragone.* Supporters — *Dexter,* a savage proper wreathed about the head and middle vert; *sinister,* a horse argent, furnished gules.

Residence,—5, Via Virginio Orsini, Rome, 00192.

COLLATERAL BRANCHES LIVING.

Grandchildren of the late Lady Elena Maria Concetta Isabella Gioacchina Giuseppa Giustiniani-Bandini (*Princess Camillo Rospigliosi*) 3rd da. of 8th Earl):—
Issue of the late Prince Giambattista Pio Sigismondo Francesco Rospigliosi, *b.* 1877, *d.* 1956: *m.* 1st, 1903, Ethel Julia, who *d.* 1924, dau. of Isaac Bronson, of New York, U.S.A.; 2ndly, 1926, Princess Flaminia, who *d.* 1948, dau. of the late Prince (Baldassare) Odescalchi:—
(**By 1st marriage**) *Prince* GIULIO CESARE TADDEO COSIMO (*Prince Rospigliosi*), *b.* Oct. 26th, 1907; is 13th Prince of Castiglione, 10th Prince of Holy Roman Empire, 10th Duke of Zagarolo, Marquis of Giuliana, Count of Chiusa, Baron of La Miraglia and Valcorrente, Lord of Aidone, Burgio, Contessa and Trappeto, and Conscribed Roman Noble, Patrician of Venice, Genoa and Pistoia: *m.* 1940, Donna Giulia, dau. of Don Guido Carlo dei Duchi Visconti di Modrone, Count of Lonate Pozzolo, and has issue living, *Prince* Filippo, *b.* 1942: *m.* 1972, Baronessa Donna Luisa Caccia Dominioni, da. of Count Annibale Caccia Dominioni, and has issue living, *Princess* Benedetta Francesca Marian *b.* 1974,—*Prince* Francesco, *b.* 1947: *m.* 1974, Clothilde, da. of Count Henri Rival de Rouville. *Residence,*—Via Corridoni, 3, Milan, Italy.——*Princess* Margherita Maria Francesca, *b.* 1909.——*Princess* Giovanna Ethel, *b.* 1911: *m.* 1937, Baron Umberto Duranti Valentini. *Residence,*—

Grandchildren of the late Prince Giambattista Pio Sigismondo Francesco Rospigliosi (ante):—
Issue of the late Princess Elena Rospigliosi (*Duchessa Antonio Lante della Rovere*), *b.* 1904, *d.* 1974: *m.* 1926, Duke Antonio Lante Montefeltro della Rovere, who *d.* 1954:—
Don Pietro (*Duke Lante Montefeltro della Rovere*), (Los Angeles, Chile), *b.* 1928; a Roman Noble, and Noble of Foligno: *m.* 1953, Marianne La Fourcalde Ithuralde, and has issue living, *Don* Marcantonio Maria Francesco, *b.* 1957,—*Donna* Angela Maria, *b.* 1956,—*Donna* Patrizia, *b.* 1959,—*Donna* Livia Francesca, *b.* 1963.——*Don* Ludovico, *b.* 1931: *m.* 1958, Lya Mendez Marquez, and has issue living, *Don* Frederico Maria, *b.* 1959,—*Donna* Alessandra, *b.* 1963,—*Donna* Elena, *b.* 1965.——*Don* Francesco, *b.* 1933: *m.* 1957, Carla dei Marchesi Spinola di Pasturana, and has issue living, *Don* Antonio *b.* 1962,—*Donna* Silvia, *b.* 1965.——*Don* Alessandro, *b.* 1936: *m.* 1964, Marina Punturieri, and has issue living, *Don* Francesco, *b.* 1966.——*Donna* Anna Vittoria (Carmelo delle Tre Madonne, Rome, Italy), *b.* 1927; a Carmelite Nun "Sister Maria Carmela del Bambin Gesu ".——*Donna* Angela, *b.* 1930: *m.* 1950, Massimo Igliori, engineer, of 28, Viale Bruno Buozzi, Rome, Italy, and has issue living, Alessandro, *b.* 1963,—Ulisse Maria, *b.* 1961,—Paola, *b.* 1952,—Benedetta, *b.* 1954,—Maria Gaia, *b.* 1959.

Grandchildren of the late Lady Elena Maria Concetta Isabella Gioacchina Giuseppa Giustiniani-Bandini (ante):—

Issue of the late Prince Francesco Luigi Giuseppe Rospigliosi, *b.* 1880;   *d.* 1943:   *m.* **1914**, Laura Macdonald Stallo, who *d.* 1972:—

Princess Francesca, *b.* 1921:   *m.* 1949, Alexander Clausen Schmidt, who *d.* 1972, and has issue living, William Francis, *b.* 1950,—Camillo Alexander, *b.* 1953,—Laura Maria, *b.* 1952.   *Residence,*—115, East 86th St., NY, 28, USA.——*Princess* Camilla, *b.* 1922:   *m.* 1st, 1945 (*m.* diss. 1964), John Eden Grace; 2ndly, 1965, Sam Fry, Jr., of 40, East 78 St., New York, NY 10021, USA.

Issue of the late Prince Ludovico Guardino Carlo Francesco Rospigliosi, *b.* 1881, *d.* **1917:**   *m.* 1904, Mildred, who *d.* 1946, dau. of William Stanley Haseltine:—

Prince Guglielmo Camillo Carlo, *b.* 1908:   *m.* 1933, (*m.* diss. 1958) the Hon. Helen Lyon-Dalberg Acton, da. of 2nd Baron Acton, and has issue living, *Prince* Ludovico Giulio Francesco Maria (62, Via Panama, Rome), *b.* 1934; Knt. of Honour and Devotion of Sovereign Mil. Order of Malta, and Knt. of Justice of Constantinian Order of St. George: *m.* 1960, Giovanna Sallier de la Tour, da. of 8th Marquis of Cordon, and has issue living, *Prince* Camillo Carlo Felice Francesco Maria *b.* 1969, *Princess* Maria Lucrezia Elena Carolina Magherita Vittoria *b.* 1966,—*Prince* Guardino Riccardo Carlo Francesco Maria, *b.* 1938; Knt. of Justice of Constantinian Order of St. George: *m.* 1961, Veronica, da. of Lt.-Col. Wilfred Price, of Devauden, Chepstow, and has issue living, *Prince* Pericles Stephen Guardino Francesco Maria *b.* 1961,—*Prince* Saladin *b.* 1964,—*Princess* Giovanna Maria Carolina Annuziata, *b.* 1935:   *m.* 1961, Giles Frere Wordsworth, of 49/51, Carnaby St., W1, and 15, Custom House Quay, Weymouth, Dorset, and has issue living, Andrew Guardino Theodore *b.* 1962, Catherine Columbine Maria Annunziata *b.* 1964, Anne Lucy Susannah *b.* 1966.

Grandchildren of the late Princess (Maria) Maddalena Clementina Rospigliosi (*Countess Ardicino della Porta*) (infra):—
Issue of the late Count Giovanni Ubaldo della Porta, *b.* 1914, *d.* 1967:   *m.* 19—, Emma Brugliese (Frontone, nr. Pesaro, Italy):—
Count Ferdinando, *b.* 1951.——*Count* Carlo, *b.* 1956.——*Countess* Giuliana, *b.* 1947.

Grandchildren of the late Lady Elena Marie Concetta Isabella Gioacchina Giuseppa Giustiniani-Bandini (*Princess Camillo Rospigliosi*) (ante):—
Issue of the late Princess Ottavia Rospigliosi, *b.* 1878, *d.* 1968: *m.* 1898, Roberto Vimercati Saneverino, Count of Castel Palazzo, who *d.* 1945:—
Count Lionello, *b.* 1911: *m.* 1936, Oretta dei Conti Ceriana Mayneri, and has issue living, Count Ludovico, *b.* 1940: *m.* 1964, Donna Agnese Tosti dei Duchi di Valminuta, and has issue living, *Count* Ottaviano *b.* 1966, *Count* Girolamo *b.* 19—,—*Countess* Roberta, *b.* 1942.——*Countess* Francesca, *b.* 1917: *m.* 1939, Enrico Budini Gattai, and has issue living, Antonello, *b.* 1940,—Leopoldo, *b.* 1942,—Roberto, *b.* 1946,—Federico, *b.* 1948,—Francesco, *b.* 1949,—Ferdinando, *b.* 1951,—Ruggero, *b.* 1955,—Rodolfo, *b.* 1957,—Giulia, *b.* 1938—Maria Vittoria, *b.* 1944,—Nicoletta, *b.* 1953,—Cristina, *b.* 1957.——*Countess* Laura, *b.* 1923: *m.* 1945, Don Livio Calenda dei Baroni di Tavani, Sqdn.-Ldr. Italian Air Force, and has issue living, *Don* Landolfo, *b.* 1946,—*Don* Michelangelo, *b.* 1953,—*Donna* Maria Nuvola, *b.* 1947,—*Donna* Maria Gloria, *b.* 1951,—*Donna* Maria Luce (twin), *b.* 1951,—*Donna* Benedetta, *b.* 1955,—*Donna* Candida, *b.* 1962.

Issue of the late Princess (Maria) Maddalena Clementina Rospigliosi, *b.* 1889, *d.* 1966: *m.* 1909, Ardicino della Porta, Count of Carpine, Biscina and Frontone:—
Count Carlo (of Le Carpini, Montone, Perugia, Italy), *b.* 1920: *m.* 1949, Laura Pignatti Morano, Countess of Custoza, and has issue living, *Count* Giammaria, *b.* 1950,—*Count* Roberto, *b.* 1955,—*Count* Giulio, *b.* 1956,—*Countess* Anna Barbara, *b.* 1952,—*Countess* Maria-Camilla, *b.* 1962,—*Countess* Maria-Veronica, *b.* 1964.—— *Count* Enzo Maria *b.* 1922.——*Countess* Laura, *b.* 1911: *m.* 1951, Lorenzo Scotti Douglas, Count of Vigoleno, who *d.* 1965.——*Countess* Lucia, *b.* 1912: *m.* 1938, Professor Gaetano Gentile (via Repetti 11, Florence, Italy), and has issue living, Fortunato, *b.* 1945,—Giovanni, *b.* 1939: *m.* 1964, Giovanna Ferragamo,—Maddalena, *b.* 1940: *m.* 1966, Giuseppe Passetti,—Ludovica, *b.* 1943.——*Countess* Maria, *b.* 1917: *m.* 1940, Count Josef Forni, and has issue living, *Count* Carlo Francesco Giuseppe Gaetano Ardicino Salvatore, *b.* 1941,—*Count* Giulio Maria Giuseppe Pietro Canisio Gaetano Anastasio, *b.* 1946,—*Countess* Anna Maria Maddalena d'Pazzi Giulia Francesca de'Paolo Giuseppina Antonia Gaetana, *b.* 1942,—*Countess* Tecdolinda Maria Assunta Laura Antonia Giuseppina Giocchina, *b.* 1943,—*Countess* Maria Cristina Beatrice Paola Giuseppina Antonia Gaetana, *b.* 1944,—*Countess* Elena Maria Teresa, *b.* 1949.

Grandchildren of Lady Nicoletta Maria Nazarena Gioacchina Margherita Giustiniani-Bandini, 4th dau. of 8th Earl, *b.* 1863, *d.* 1938 : *m.* 1881, Mario, Duke Grazioli, who *d.* 1936 :—
Issue of the late Pio, Duke G azioli, *b.* 1886, *d.* 1954: *m.* 1st, 1908, Donna Rufina Lancellotti, who *d.* 1942, da. of Don Filippo Massimo, 1st Prince Lancellotti; 2ndly, 1943, Cleo Conversi (*Duchess Grazioli* , of Casal de Pazzi, Rome, Italy:—
(By 1st marriage) Mario (*Duke Grazioli*), *b.* 1908; is Baron of Castel Porziano, and a Roman Noble. *Residence,*—Palazzo Grazioli, 102, Via del Plebiscito, Rome, Italy ——*Dcn* Massimiliano *b.* 1911: *m.* 1942, Isabella Perrone, and has issue living, *Dcn* Giulio, *b.* 1943 ——(By 2nd m.), *Don* Riccardo *b.* 1943. *Residence,*—292, Via Casal de Pazzi, Rome, Italy.——(By 1st m.), *Dcnna* Caterina, *b.* 1913: *m.* 1940, Count Gabriele Emo-Capodilsta, and has issue living, *Count* Giorgio, *b.* 1941,—*Count* Giovanni, *b.* 1944. *Residence,*—102, Via del Plebiscito, Rome, Italy.——*Donna* Anna, *b.* 1916: *m.* 1942, Don Francesco, Marquis of Caravita, Prince of Sirignano, and has issue living, *Don* Giuseppe, *b.* 1944,—Don Alvaro Pietro, *b.* 1945,—*Donna* Nila, *b.* 1951. *Residences,*—Palazzo Grazioli, 102, Via del Plebiscito, Rome, Italy; Villa Castello, Capri, Naples, Italy.

Issue of Lady (Maria) Isabella Giovanna Teresa Gioacchina Giustiniani-Bandini, 6th da. of 8th Earl, *b.* 1867, *d.* 1963: *m.* 1898, the 1st Baron Howard of Penrith, who *d.* 1939 [see that title].

PREDECESSORS.—[1] *Sir* JAMES Levingston, a zealous royalist; was cr. *Viscount Newburgh* (peerage of Scotland) 1647, and *Lord Levingston,* of Flacraig, *Viscount Kynnaird* and *Earl of Newburgh* (peerage of Scotland) 1660, with remainder to his heirs whatsoever; *d.* 1670; *s.* by his son [2] CHARLES, 2nd Earl; *d.* 1694, when the viscountcy of 1647 expired, and the peerages of 1660 devolved upon his dau. [3] CHARLOTTE MARIA, who *m.* 1st, Thomas, el. son of 2nd Baron Clifford, and 2ndly, 1724, the Hon. Charles Radcliffe, brother of the beheaded 3rd Earl of Derwentwater, who in 1731, on the death of his nephew, assumed the title of 5th Earl of Derwentwater. [Charles Radcliffe was attainted 1716 and imprisoned in Newgate, whence he escaped, but being engaged in the rising of 1745 was taken prisoner and summarily executed on his former attainder]: the Countess *d.* 1755; *s.* by her son [4] JAMES BARTHOLOMEW, 4th Earl; unsuccessfully claimed the Derwentwater estates; *d.* 1786; *s.* by his son [5] ANTHONY JAMES, 5th Earl; in 1788, by Act of Parliament, the Derwentwater estates were charged with £2,500 a year to the Earl and the heirs male of his body; *d.s.p.* 1814; *s.* by his kinsman [6] VINCENT, 6th Earl, and 6th *Prince Giustiniani* (cr. 1644) of the Papal States, son of Cecilia Mahony, only child of Anne Clifford, dau. of Charlotte Maria, Countess of Newburgh (ante), by Benedict, 5th Prince Giustiniani; he did not take proceedings to establish his claim to the earldom ; *d.* 1826 ; *s.* by his only dau. [7] MARIA CECILIA AGATHA ANNA JOSEPHA LAURENTIA DONATA MELCHIORA BALTHASSARA GASPARA, Princess Giustiniani, who *s.* her grandfather as Duchess of Mondragone; naturalized by Act of Parliament 1857, and her claims to peerages were allowed 1858 : *m.* 1815, Charles Bandini, 4th Marquis of Lanciano and Rustano (cr. 1753) in the Papal States ; *d.* 1877 ; *s.* by her son [8] SIGISMUND NICHOLAS VENANTIUS GAETANO FRANCIS, 8th Earl, *b.* 1818 ; cr. *Prince Giustiniani-Bandini* by Pope Pius IX. (with the precedence held by his ancestors the Princes Giustiniani) 1863 ; *s.* as *Duke of Mondragone* (Kingdom of Naples) 1878 ; assumed in 1850 the additional surname of Giustiniani, as adopted heir to his uncle, James, Cardinal Giustiniani, Bishop of Albano ; naturalized by Act of Parliament 1857 (20th and 21st Vic. chap. 7): *m.* 1848, Maria Sophia Angelica, who *d.* 1898, dau. of the Cavaliere Giuseppe Maria Massani; *d.* 1908; *s.* by his only son [9] CHARLES, 9th Earl' *b.* 1862: *m.* 1885, Donna Maria Lanza di Trabia, who *d.* 1949, dau. of the Prince of Trabia and Butera, of Palermo; *d.* 1941; *s.* by his dau. and only surviving child [10] MARIA SOFIA GIUSEPPINA, Countess of Newburgh and present peeress; also Viscountess Kynnaird, and Lady Levingston.

NEWCASTLE, DUKE OF. (Pelham-Clinton-Hope.) [Duke G.B. 1756.]

But hope is undaunted.

AT·SPES·INFRACTA

LOYAULTE   N'A HONTE

Loyalty knows not shame.

HENRY EDWARD HUGH PELHAM-CLINTON-HOPE, *O.B.E.*, 9th Duke; *b.* April 8th, 1907; *s.* 1941; ed. at Eton, and at Magdalene Coll., Camb.; is Squadron-Leader and acting Wing-Com. Auxiliary Air Force; O.B.E. (Mil.) 1945 : *m.* 1st, 1931, Eugenia Van Voorhees (from whom he obtained a divorce 1940), adopted dau. of David Banks, of Park Avenue, New York, U.S.A.; 2ndly, 1946, Lady (Mary) Diana Montagu - Stuart - Wortley - Mackenzie, who obtained a divorce 1959, dau. of 3rd Earl of Wharncliffe; 3rdly, 1959, Mrs. Sally Ann Wemyss Hope (JAMAL), dau. of Brigadier John Henry Antice, D.S.O., and has issue by 2nd marriage.

Arms,—Quarterly: 1st and 4th azure, on a chevron or between three bezants as many laurel leaves slipped vert, all within a bordure wavy argent, *Hope*; 2nd argent, six cross-crosslets fitchée sable, three, two, and one, on a chief azure, two mullets or, pierced gules, *Clinton*; 3rd quarterly, 1st and 4th azure three pelicans argent, vulning themselves proper; 2nd and 3rd gules, two demi-belts with buckles argent erect, the buckles in chief as an honorary augmentation (in memory of Sir John Pelham taking John, King of France, prisoner), *Pelham*. Crests,—1st (central), a broken terrestrial globe charged with a laurel leaf slipped and surmounted by a rainbow in arch all proper, the whole debruised by a bendlet sinister wavy ermine, *Hope*; 2nd (dexter), out of a ducal coronet gules, a plume of five ostrich feathers argent, banded with a line laid chevronways azure, *Clinton*; 3rd (sinister), a peacock in pride proper, *Pelham*. Supporters,—Two greyhounds argent collared and lined gules.

Residence,—5, Quay Hill, Lymington, Hants. SO4 9AR.

DAUGHTERS LIVING. (By 2nd marriage.)

Lady Patricia, *b.* 1949; assumed surname of Pelham-Clinton-Pariser 1971: *m.* 1971, Alan Pariser, of 2366, Stanley Hills Drive, Los Angeles, Cal., USA, 90046.
Lady Kathleen Marie Gabrielle, *b.* 1951: *m.* 1970, Edward Reynolds.

SISTER LIVING.

Lady Mary, *b.* 1910: *m.* 1st, 1930 (marriage annulled on her petition 1933), Charles Kenneth Horne [B. Cozens-Hardy]; 2ndly, (in Switzerland) 1939 (marriage dissolved in Switzerland 1946), Romain Alphonse Stemmer; 3rdly, 1947 (marriage dissolved 19—), William Serge Belaieff, who *d.* 1964. *Residence,*—Clumber Cottage, Sutton Veny, Warminster, Wilts.

COLLATERAL BRANCHES LIVING.

Grandchildren of the late Henry William Pelham-Clinton, 2nd son of Lord Charles Pelham-Clinton (infra):—
Issue of the late Henry Charles Frederick Pelham-Clinton, *b.* 1892, *d.* 1968: *m.* 1920, Dorothy Charlotte Middleton, who *d.* 1969, da. of the late Capt. J. Carlon, R. Canadian Regt.:—
Ethne Mary, *b.* 1923: *m.* 1951, Jasper Picton Hubbard [see B. Addington, colls.].

Issue of the late Capt. Guy Edward Pelham-Clinton, M.C., *b.* 1894, *d.* 1934: *m.* 1918, Hermione Edith Agnes (Owls Combe, Porlock Weir, Somerset), da. of the late Arthur Frederick Churchill Tollemache [see Os. Dysart, colls.]:—
EDWARD CHARLES, *b.* Aug. 18th, 1920; ed. at Eton and at Camb. Univ.; Assist. Keeper, Roy. Scottish Museum, Edinburgh; 1939-45 as Capt. RA. *Residence.*—Gillerhill, Winchburgh, West Lothian.

Granddaughter of the late Lord Charles Pelham-Clinton, 2nd son of 4th Duke:—
Issue of the late Hubert Edward Pelham-Clinton, *b.* 1862, *d.* 1913 : *m.* 1st, 1893, Louisa Brooks, who *d.* 1911, dau. of the late E. Macaulay Arnaud, of Bath, and widow of Henry Fitzwilliam Browne; 2ndly, 1911, Helen, who *d.* 1963, da. of James Halcrow, of Burton-on-Trent:—
(By 2nd marriage) Georgiana Elizabeth May, *b.* 1913; legally adopted 1916, by her aunt, Elizabeth, who *d.* 1946, widow of Charles Stapleton Pelham-Clinton : *m.* 1951, John Stuart Bordewich, M.V.O., and has issue living, John Peter Pelham, *b.* 1955. *Residence,*—L'Eperon, Crans, Valais, Switzerland.

(In remainder to Earldom of Lincoln.)

Grandsons of the late Charles Edward Fiennes-Clinton, son of the late Rev. Henry Fiennes-Clinton (infra):—
Issue of the late Edward Henry Fiennes-Clinton, *b.* 1886, *d.* (killed in action during 1914-18 War) 1916: *m.* 1912, Edith Annie (who *d.* 1965, having *m.* 2ndly, 1923, Robert Johnston Lynn, who *d.* 1970), da. of the late Capt. Horace Far East Guest:—
(By 1st marriage) Edward Horace, *b.* 1913: *m.* 1st, 1940, Leila Ruth Millen, who *d.* 1947; 2ndly, 1953, Linda Alice O'Brien, of Kalgoorlie, W. Australia, and has issue living, (by 1st marriage) Edward Gordon, *b.* 1943,—Patricia Ruth (Rosedale Rd., Chidlow, W. Aust. 6556), *b.* 1941: *m.* 1959 (m. diss. 1970), Alexander George Stuart Elrick, and has issue living, Nicholas James *b.* 1959, David Wayne *b.* 1961, Warren Stuart *b.* 1962. *Residence,*—73, Picton Rd., Bunbury, W. Aust.——Gilbert Henry, *b.* 1914. *Residence,*—62, Ferguson St., Maylands, W. Aust.

Grandson of the late Clement Walter Fiennes-Clinton (infra):—
Issue of the late Henry Fiennes-Clinton, *b.* 1885, *d.* 1972: *m.* 1924, Catherine (5775, Yonge St., Apt. 427, Willowdale, Ont., Canada), da. of the late Rev. Edmund Thomason:—

Henry Bernard (312, Patricia Av., Willowdale, 443, Ont., Canada), b. 1929: m. 1961, Carol Priscilla, da. of James Greig, of Toronto, and has issue living, Gregory Edward, b. 1970,—Richard James, b. 1972.

Granddaughter of the late Rev. Henry FIENNES-CLINTON, son of the late Clinton James Fynes-Clinton, M.P., 2nd son of the late Rev. Charles Fynes-Clinton (infra):—
Issue of the late Clement Walter Fiennes-Clinton, b. 1856, d. 1919: m. 1885. Lucy Eleanor, who d. 1944, dau. of the late H. J. Hassall :—
Lucy Eleanor Clement, b. 1886. Residence,—404, Aberdeen Av., Hamilton, Ont., Canada.

Granddaughters of the late Rev. Charles John Fynes-Clinton, 3rd son of the late Rev. Charles Fynes-Clinton, lineal representative of the late Hon. Sir Henry Fynes-Clinton, 3rd son of 2nd Earl of Lincoln :—
Issue (by 2nd marriage) of the late Rev. Charles Henry Fynes-Clinton, b. 1835, d. 1915: m. 1st, 1863, Ellen Græme, who d. 1871, dau. of the late P. R. Falkner, of Upton Hall, Notts ; 2ndly, 1873, Thomasina Gordon, who d. 1929, dau. of the late James Shaw, of Ballyoran, co. Down:—
Ida Norah Katharine, b. 1882: m. 1st, 1903, William Arthur Bedford Brennand ; 2ndly, 1916, the Rev. William Kilbride Gallagher, who d. 1967, and has issue living, (by 1st m.) Arthur Fynes, b. 1904: m. 1933, June Mary Suzanne Pienne, and has issue living, Sean Pelham, b. 1934; Lt.-Cdr. RN: m. 1956 (m. diss. 1968), Anne Christine Harding (and has issue living, Katharine Anne b. 1963), Timothy Pienne (c/o Bataatse International Petroleum Maatschappij, 30, Carli van Bylandtlaan, The Hague, Holland), b. 1935; PhD: m. 1962, Susan Marion St. John Brooks (and has issue living, Anthony Fynes b. 1969, Tessa Marion b. 1964, Nualla June b. 1966), Anna Judith b. 1937: m. 1960, Maj. Martin Leonard Scicluna, RA (c/o Barclays Bank, DCO, 1, Cockspur St., SW1),—(by 2nd m.) Gordon Charles Kilbride, DFC (of Fieldings, Harefield Rd., Middleton-on-Sea, Sussex), b. 1924: formerly Flying Officer RAF: m. 1951, Mary Rose Blockley, and has issue living, Caroline Mary b. 1953, Rosanne Elizabeth b. 1955, Katharine Mary b. 1962,—Eileen Norah Gordon Kilbride, b. 1917. Residence,—Littlecolt, Church Lane, Owermoigne, Dorchester, Dorset.

Grandchildren of the late Rev. Osbert Fynes-Clinton, 3rd son of the late Rev. Charles John Fynes-Clinton (ante):—
Issue of the late Rev. Charles Edward Fynes-Clinton, b. 1868, d. 1955 : m. 1902, Quenilda, Mary, who d. 1917, dau. of the late James Begg Shaw, of Didsbury :—
Charles John (5, Bournehall Lane, Bushey, Herts.), b. 1909; B.Sc., London; an Asso. of Roy. Sch. of Mines: m. 1943, Martha, da. of the late Samuel Mannes, of Aue, Saxony.——Hugh Arthur (Waldorf School, Constantia, Cape), b. 1913; ed. at St. John's Coll., Camb. (MA); formerly Headmaster of St. Chad's Coll., Ladysmith, Natal, and Inspector of African Education, S. Rhodesia: m. 1945, Pauline Ruth Ashton Dold, and has issue living, Oliver John, b. 1948,—Rozanne Jean, b. 1946.——Quenilda Margaret (83, de Freville Av., Cambridge), b. 1905; formerly Matron of Evelyn Nursing Home, Cambridge.——Eleanor Lloyd (83, de Freville Av., Cambridge), b. 1907.

Issue of the late Osbert Henry Fynes-Clinton, b. 1869, d. 1941: m. 1907, Gwaldys Mabel, who d. 1973, da. of the late Rev. William Hughes, V. of Llanuwchllyn, Merionethshire, and Rural Dean:—
David Osbert (32, Route de Soral, 1232, Confignon, Geneva), b. 1909; ed. at Clifton Coll., and at St. John's Coll., Oxford; entered Consular Ser. 1931; formerly HM's Consul-Gen., Zagreb, Yugoslavia: m. 1st, 1933 (m. diss. 1947) Laure Léoncie Mathilde Reyne, only da. of the late Pierre Félix Suguet; 2ndly, 1947, Betty Annie, da. of the late Arthur C. Lawrence, formerly of Iquique, Chile, and has issue living (by 2nd m.), Michael Peter (63, Riversdale Rd., Highbury, N5), b. 1949: m. 1973, Paula Valerie Neuss.

Issue of the late Robert Fynes-Clinton, b. 1879, d. 1962: m. 1907, Margaret Emma, who d. 1949, younger dau. of the late Rev. Stephen Phillips, D.D., of Heacham, Norfolk:—
Pelham (20, Eddisbury Rd., West Kirby, Wirral), b. 1910; ed. at Radley: m. 1937, Joan Elizabeth, da. of Alfred Chaplin, of West Kirby, and has issue living, Margaret Julia, b. 1949.

Granddaughters of the late Rev. Charles John Fynes-Clinton (ante) :—
Issue of the late Eustace Fynes-Clinton, b. 1845, d. 1928: m. 1879, Louisa Richenda, who d. 1933, dau. of the Rev. Francis Macaulay Cunningham, of Brightwell, Wallingford :—
e anor Mabel b. 1882. Residence,—The Garden Cottage, 32, Eldon Terr., Reading.——Katharine, b . 1888. Residence,—New Way, Frensham, Surrey.——Rosalind Mary, MBE, b. 1890; MA Oxford; MBE (Civil) 1946. Residence,—The Garden Cottage, 32, Eldon Terr., Reading.

Issue of the late Rev. Geoffrey Fynes-Clinton, b. 1847, d. 1934: m. 1873, Fanny, who d. 1888, dau. of the late Henry Searle:—
Maud Marion, b. 1880.——Mabel Fanny (35, Maltby Av., Timaru, NZ), b. 1881: m. 1905, Alfred Hillier Newton.——Irene (Clumber, 15, Newbury St., Opawa, Christchurch, NZ), b. 1887: m. 1911, Herbert Charles Stevens, who d. 1957, and has issue living, Charles Clinton (4, Kowhai Terr., Christchurch, NZ), b. 1912; Commodore RNZN (ret.); 1939-45 War: m. 1st, 1939 (m. diss. 1965) Kathleen Mary McQuilken; 2ndly, 1966, Eileen Marguerite Gafflikin, da. of the late Jock Bruce Tailyour Renny, and has issue living, (by 1st m.) Geoffrey Fynes-Clinton b. 1940: Lt. RNZN (ret.): m. 1966, Elizabeth Georgina, el. da. of Maj. Herbert Johnes Lloyd-Johnes, TD, of Fosse Hill, Coates, Cirencester, Glos.,—Nora Pelham (216, Riverlaw Terr., Christchurch 2, NZ), b. 1915: m. 1939, Rupert Garland, who d. 1969, and has issue living, Peter Rupert Fynes-Clinton (Hilldale Place, Hillsborough, Ch. Ch., NZ), b. 1941: m. 1969, Rita Maureen Matthews, (and has issue living, Kelly John b. 1970, Robin Matthew b. 1972), Timothy Heathcote Fynes (156, Wilton St., Rosedale, Invercargill, NZ), b. 1944: m. 1971, Diana Annette Wall (and has issue living, David John b. 1972, Joanna Mary b. 1974, Richard Pelham (Lockwood Rd., RD5, Palmerston North, NZ) b. 1946: m. 1970, Helene Patricia Richards, Stephen Pelham b. 1955, Rachel Fynes b. 1948: m. 1969, David James Green, of 10, Fernhill Terr., Wadestown, Wellington, NZ, (and has issue living, Andrew Rupert Pelham b. 1972, Simon James b. 1973).

Grandsons of the late Rev. Geoffrey Fynes-Clinton (ante):—
Issue of the late Geoffrey De Berdt Granger Fynes-Clinton, b. 1878, d. 1922: m. 1903, Maybelle, dau. of the late John Finamore Edwardes:—
Geoffrey Noel (5, Noble St., Wilston, Queensland), b. 1903.——Philip Nevill (105, Mein St., Hendra, Queensland), b. 1908: m. 1934, Isobel Maud Wilks, and has issue living, Geoffrey William Norreys (90, Kitchener Rd., Ascot, Queensland), b. 1932; ed. Queensland Univ. (BA, LLB): m. 1957, Joyce Kathleen Lynch, and has issue living, Stephen Philip b. 1960, Matthew James b. 1963, Timothy Pelham b. 1965,—Arthur Nevill (Fourth Av., Toowoomba, Queensland), b. 1934: ed. at Queensland Univ. (BA): m. 1956, Jacqueline Baker, and has issue living, Jamie b. 1957, Alan b. 1960, Neil b. 1963.——Pelham Osbert Granger, b. 1912.

PREDECESSORS.—[1] EDWARD, K.G., P.C., 9th Baron Clinton (see B. Clinton), successively Lord High Adm., Gov. of Boulogne, a Lord of the Bedchamber, Gov. of the Tower, and Com. in Ch. of the fleet and forces sent against France and Scotland; was cr. Earl of Lincoln (peerage of England) 1572; d. 1585; s. by his son [2] HENRY K.B., P.C., 2nd Earl; d. 1616; s. by his son [3] THOMAS, 3rd Earl; d. 1619; s. by his son [4] THEOPHILUS, K.B., 4th Earl; was a staunch Royalist, and performed the office of Carver at the Coronation of Charles II.; d. 1667; s. by his grandson [5] EDWARD, 5th Earl; d.s.p. 1692, when the Barony of Clinton became abeyant (see B. Clinton), and the earldom reverted to his cousin [6] FRANCIS FIENNES, K.B.

6th Earl, grandson of Sir Edward, 2nd son of 2nd Earl; *d.* 1693; *s.* by his son [7] HENRY, *K.G.*, 7th Earl, *b.* 1684; was successively a Gentleman of the Bedchamber to Prince George of Denmark, Master of the Horse to Prince of Wales, Paymaster-Gen., Constable of the Tower, and Cofferer of the Household: *m.* 1717, Lucy, who *d.* 1736, dau. of 1st Baron Pelham, and sister of Thomas, 1st Duke of Newcastle; *d.* 1728; *s.* by his el. son [8] GEORGE, 8th Earl, *b.* 1717; *d.* 1730; *s.* by his brother [9] HENRY FYNES, *K.G., P.C.*, 9th Earl, *b.* 1720; was a Gentleman of the Bedchamber, Lord-Lieut. of Cambridge, High Steward of Westminster, and Comptroller of the Customs of Port of London: *m.* 1744, his cousin, Catherine, who *d.* 1760, dau. and heiress of the Right Hon. Henry Pelham, and in 1768, inherited the Dukedom of Newcastle, on the death of his maternal, and the countess's paternal uncle, Thomas Pelham Holles, who in 1756 had been cr. *Duke of Newcastle-under-Lyme* (peerage of Great Britain), with special remainder to Henry, 9th Earl of Lincoln; assumed the additional surname of Pelham by Roy. licence; *d.* 1794; *s.* by his son [10] THOMAS, 3rd Duke, *b.* 1752; Maj.-Gen. in the Army and Col. 17th Light Dragoons: *m.* 1782, Lady Anna Maria Stanhope, who *d.* 1834 (having *m.* 2ndly, 1800, Gen. Sir Charles Gregan Craufurd, G.C.B., who *d.* 1821); *d.* 1795; *s.* by his son [11] HENRY PELHAM, *K.G.*, 4th Duke, *b.* 1785; Lord-Lieut. of co. Nottingham; *m.* 1807, Georgiana Elizabeth, dau. of Edward Miller Mundy, of Shipley, Derbyshire; *d.* 1851; *s.* by his son [12] HENRY PELHAM, *K.G.*, 5th Duke, *b.* 1811; was Sec. of State for the Colonies 1852-4 and 1859-64, Ch. Sec. for Ireland, Sec. of State for War, Lord Warden of the Stanneries, and successively M.P. for S. Notts., and the Falkirk Burghs: *m.* 1832 (marriage dissolved 1850), Lady Susan Harriet Catherine Hamilton Douglas-Hamilton, who *d.* 1889 (having *m.* 2ndly, 1860, M. Opdebeck, of Brussels); *d.* 1864; *s.* by his son [13] HENRY PELHAM ALEXANDER, 6th Duke; *b.* 1834: *m.* 1861, Henrietta Adela, who *d.* 1913, dau. of the late Henry Thomas Hope; *d.* 1879; *s.* by his son [14] HENRY PELHAM ARCHIBALD DOUGLAS, 7th Duke, *b.* 1864: *m.* 1889, Kathleen Florence May, O.B.E., who *d.* 1955, dau. of the late Major Henry Augustus Candy; *d.* 1928; *s.* by his brother [15] HENRY FRANCIS HOPE, 8th Duke; *b.* 1866; assumed by Roy. licence 1887 the additional surname of Hope: *m.* 1894, Mary Augusta (an actress), who *d.* 1938 (from whom he had obtained a divorce 1902), dau. of William Yohe; 2ndly, 1904, Olive Muriel, who *d.* 1912, dau. of the late George Horatio Thompson, banker, of Melbourne, and formerly wife of Richard Owen; *d.* 1941; *s.* by his son [16] HENRY EDWARD HUGH, 9th Duke and present peer; also Earl of Lincoln.

NEWCASTLE, LORD BISHOP OF. (Bowlby.)

Right Rev. RONALD OLIVER BOWLBY, son of the late Oliver Gerard Bowlby; *b.* 1926; ed. at Eton, Trin. Coll., Oxford (MA) and Westcott Ho. Theol. Coll., Camb.; Curate of St. Luke, Pallion, Sunderland, 1952-56, and St. Cuthbert, Billingham, co. Durham 1956-57, Curate in Charge, St. Aidan, Billingham 1957-59, Min. 1959-60, and Perpetual Curate 1960-66; V. of Croydon 1966-72; consecrated 9th Bishop of Newcastle 1973: *m.* 1956, Elizabeth Trevelyan, da. of the late Rev. Robert Elliott Monro [see Trevelyan Bt., cr. 1662].

Patron of the Archdeaconries of Northumberland and Lindisfarne, four Residentiary Canonries, the Hon. Canonries, and seventy-five livings.

The see of Newcastle was founded May, 1882.

Episcopal Signature,—"Ronald Newcastle."

ARMS OF THE SEE,—Gules, a cross between four lions rampant or, on chief of the last three triple towered castles of the field.

Residence,—The Bishop's House, Moor Road South, Gosforth, Newcastle-upon-Tyne, NE3 IPA.

NEWTON, BARON. (Legh.) [Baron U.K. 1892.]

[Name pronounced "**Lee.**"]

On God is my reliance.

PETER RICHARD LEGH, 4th Baron; *b.* April 6th, 1915 ; *s.* 1960 ; ed. at Eton and at Ch. Ch., Oxford (B.A. 1937, M.A. 1947); a Co. Councillor for Hants 1949-52 and 1954-55; is a J.P. for Hants; P.P.S. to Financial Sec. to the Treasury 1952-53, an Assist. Govt. Whip 1953-55, a Lord Commr. of the Treasury 1955-57, Vice-Chamberlain of H.M.'s Household 1957-59, Treasurer thereof 1959-60, Capt., Yeomen of the Guard, and Assist. Ch Whip, House of Lords 1960-62, Joint Parl. Sec., Min. of Health 1962-64, and Min. of State for Education and Science April to Oct. 1964; 1939-45 War as Maj. Grenadier Guards; sat as MP for Petersfield Div. of Hants (*C*) 1951-60: *m.* 1948, Priscilla, da. of the late Capt. John Egerton-Warburton [see Grey-Egerton, Bt., colls.], and widow of Maj. (William Matthew) Viscount Wolmer, el. son of 3rd Earl of Selborne, and has issue.

Arms,—Gules, a cross engrailed argent, in the chief point, on an inescutcheon sable, semée of estoiles, an arm in armour embowed of the second, the hand proper holding a pennon silver, all within a bordure wavy or. **Crest,**—Issuant out of a ducal coronet or, a ram's head argent, armed or, in the mouth a laurel slip vert ; the whole debruised by a pallet wavy azure. **Supporters,**—Two mastiffs proper, collared sable.

Residence,—Vernon Hill House, Bishop's Waltham, Hants.

SONS LIVING.

Hon. RICHARD THOMAS (101, Eton Rise, Eton College Rd., NW3), *b.* Jan. 11th, 1950: ed. at Eton, and Ch. Ch., Oxford.

Hon. David Piers Carlis (The Round House, Poulton, Cirencester, Glos.), *b.* 1951; ed. at Eton, and Roy. Agric. Coll., Cirencester: *m.* 1974, Jane Mary, da. of John Roy Wynter Bee, of Heather Hills, West End, Woking, Surrey.

BROTHER LIVING.

Hon. Sir Francis Michael, *KCVO, b.* 1919; ed. at Eton, Maj. (ret.) Grenadier Guards; was Assist. Private Sec. to HM Queen Elizabeth the Queen Mother 1959-59, and Equerry since 1956; Private Sec. to HRH Princess Margaret 1959-71, and Treasurer since 1971; Italy 1943-45 (despatches); MVO (4th class) 1964; CVO 1967; KCVO 1968: *m.* 1948, Ruadh Daphne, who *d.* 1973, da. of the late Alan Holmes-Watson, and has issue living, Nicholas Charles, *b.* 1951; ed. at Eton,—Laura Helen, *b.* 1954. *Residence,*—13, The Boltons, SW10. *Clubs,*—Pratt's, St. James', Brooks's, White's.

AUNT LIVING. (*Daughter of 2nd Baron.*)

Hon. Phyllis Elinor, *b.* 1895: *m.* 1918, Henry Gerard Walter Sandeman, formerly Lt. Grenadier Guards, who *d.* 1953, and has issue living, Geraldine Susan, *b.* 1923: assumed the Christian name of Geraldine 1960; *m.* 1st, 1944, Rene Jules Schutz, who *d.* 1953, R. Netherlands Army; 2ndly, 1956, Maj. Iain Douglas Usher, RE, from whom she obtained a divorce 1965,—Chloe, *b.* 1928: *m.* 1st, 1948 (m. diss. 1965), the Hon. Basil Frederick de la Pole Kenworthy [see B. Strabolgi]; 2ndly, 1975, Ian Anthony Hemensley-Beattie. *Residence,*—The Mill House, Melton, Woodbridge, Suffolk.

COLLATERAL BRANCH LIVING.

Issue of the late Lieut.-Col. the Hon. Sir Piers Walter Legh, G.C.V.O., K.C.B., C.M.G., C.I.E., O.B.E., younger son of 2nd Baron, *b.* 1890, *d.* 1955 : *m.* 1920, Sarah Polk, who *d.* 1955, dau. of the late Judge James C. Bradford, of Nashville, Tennessee, U.S.A., and widow of Capt. the Hon. Alfred Thomas Shaughnessy [see B. Shaughnessy]:—

Diana Evelyn, *b.* 1924 : *m.* 1st, 1945, the 4th Earl of Kimberley, from whom she obtained a divorce 1948 ; 2ndly, 1951, Norman Robert Colville, M.C., and has issue living, (by 2nd marriage) James Charles David, *b.* 1952; a Page of Honour to HM 1966-68. *Residences,*—Penheale Manor, Launceston, Cornwall; 11, Kensington Sq., W8.

PREDECESSORS.—[1] WILLIAM JOHN Legh, son of the late William Legh ; *b.* 1828 ; M.P. for S. Lancashire (*C*) 1859-65 and for Cheshire 1868-85 ; cr. *Baron Newton*, of Newton-in-Makerfield, co. Lancaster (peerage of United Kingdom) 1892 : *m.* 1856, Emily Jane, who *d.* 1901, dau. of the late Ven. Charles Nourse Wodehouse, Archdeacon of Norwich; *d.* 1898; *s.* by his el. son [2] THOMAS WODEHOUSE, *P.C.*, 2nd Baron; *b.*1857 ; Paymaster-Gen. 1915-16, and Assist. Under-Sec. of State for Foreign Affairs 1916; sat as M.P. for Lancashire S.W., Newton Div. (*C*) 1886-1898: *m.* 1880, Evelyn, who *d.* 1932, dau. of the late William Henry Bromley-Davenport, M.P., of Capesthorne, Cheshire ; *d.* 1942 ; *s.* by his son [3] RICHARD WILLIAM DAVENPORT, *T.D.,* 3rd Baron ; *b.* 1888 ; Capt. Yeo ; Hon. Attaché at Vienna and Constantinople 1912-14 ; Hon. Col. 7th Batn. Cheshire Regt. (T.A.) 1939-50 : *m.* 1914, the Hon. Helen Winifred Meysey-Thompson, who *d.* 1958, dau. of 1st Baron Knaresborough ; *d.* 1960 ; *s.* by his el. son [4] PETER RICHARD, 4th Baron and present peer.

NOEL-BUXTON, BARON. (Buxton.) [Baron U.K. 1930.]

RUFUS ALEXANDER BUXTON, 2nd Baron; *b.* Jan. 13th, 1917; *s.* 1948; ed. at Harrow, and at Balliol Coll., Oxford (B.A. 1938); assumed by deed poll 1944 the names of Rufus Alexander Buxton in lieu of those of Noel Alexander Noel-Buxton; was Research Assist., Agricultural Economics Institute, Oxford 1940-43, Lecturer to H.M. Forces 1942-45, Producer N. American Ser., British Broadcasting Corporation 1946-48, and with *Farmers' Weekly* 1950-52; European War 1939-40 with Artists' Rifles (invalided): *m.* 1st, 1939 (marriage dissolved 1947), Nancy, who *d.* 1949, younger dau. of the late Col. Kenneth Hugh Munro Connal, C.B., O.B.E., T.D., D.L.; 2ndly, 1948, Margaret Elizabeth, dau. of Stephanus Abraham Cloete, of Pretoria, S. Africa, and has issue by 1st and 2nd marriages.

Arms,—Argent, a lion rampant tail elevated and turned over the head sable, between two mullets of the second. Crest,—A buck's head couped gules, attired or, gorged with a collar of the last, therefrom pendent an escutcheon argent, charged with an African's head sable.
Residence,—

SONS LIVING. (*By 1st marriage.*)
Hon. MARTIN CONNAL (24, Denmark Rd., Kingston upon Thames), *b.* Dec. 8th, 1940; ed. at Bryanston, and at Balliol Coll., Oxford; assumed by deed poll 1964, the surname of NOEL-BUXTON: *m.* 1st, 1964, (m. diss. 1968) Miranda Mary, el. da. of H. A. Chisenhale-Marsh, of Gaynes Park, Epping, Essex; 2ndly, 1972, Sarah Margaret Surridge, only da. of Neil Charles Wolseley Barrett, of Twickenham Rd., Teddington, and has issue living (by 2nd m.), Charles Connal, *b.* April 17th, 1975.
Hon. Simon Campden, *b.* 1943; ed. at Bryanston, and Balliol Coll., Oxford.

(*By 2nd marriage.*)
Hon. Richard Christopher, *b.* 1950; ed. at Bryanston.

DAUGHTER LIVING. (*By 2nd marriage.*)
Hon. Clare Elizabeth Anne, *b.* 1954.

BROTHER LIVING.
Hon. Michael Barnett Noel NOEL-BUXTON, *b.* 1920; ed. at Harrow, and at Balliol Coll., Oxford; European War 1940-45 with R.A.; was in Colonial Ser. Gold Coast (now Ghana) 1947-59. *Residence,*—Stretchney, Diptford, Totnes, S. Devon. *Club,*—Flyfishers'.

SISTERS LIVING.
Hon. Jane Elizabeth Noel, *b.* 1925; relinquished surname of Noel by Public Declaration, 1957. *Residence,*—27, Redington Rd., Hampstead, N.W.3.
Hon. Sarah Edith Noel NOEL-BUXTON, *b.* 1928 : *m.* 1955, John Goldsborough Hogg, and has issue living, Sarah Jane, *b.* 1956,—Joanna Wynfreda, *b.* 1960. *Residence,*—Old Broad Oak, Brenchley, Kent.

PREDECESSOR.—[1] NOEL EDWARD Noel-Buxton, *P.C.*, 2nd son of Sir Thomas Fowell Buxton G.C.M.G., 3rd Bt.; *b.* 1869; Min. of Agriculture and Fisheries Jan. to Nov. 1924, and June 1929 to June 1930; sat as M.P. for Whitby Div. of N. Riding of Yorkshire (*L*) 1905-6, and for Norfolk, N. Div. 1910-18, and (*Lab.*) 1922-30; assumed by deed poll (enrolled at College of Arms) 1930 the additional surname of Noel before that of Buxton; *cr. Baron Noel-Buxton*, of Aylsham, Norfolk (peerage of United Kingdom) 1930 : *m.* 1914, Lucy Edith, who *d.* 1960, dau. of the late Major Henry Pelham Burn; *d.* 1948; *s.* by his son [2] RUFUS ALEXANDER Buxton, 2nd Baron and present peer.

NORBURY, EARL OF. (Graham-Toler.) [Earl I. 1827.]

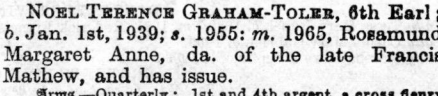

NOEL TERENCE GRAHAM-TOLER, 6th Earl; *b.* Jan. 1st, 1939; *s.* 1955: *m.* 1965, Rosamund Margaret Anne, da. of the late Francis Mathew, and has issue.

Arms,—Quarterly: 1st and 4th argent, a cross fleury gules charged with a plain cross couped of the field between four leaves vert, a crescent for difference, *Toler*; 2nd and 3rd argent, a trefoil slipped vert, on a chief sable three escallops or, *Graham*. Crest,—On a ducal coronet a fleur-de-lis or. Supporters.—*Dexter*, a horse or, bridled gules; *sinister*, a fawn proper.
Address,—c/o London Stock Exchange, EC2.

SON LIVING.
RICHARD JAMES (*Viscount Glandine*), *b.* March 5th, 1967.
DAUGHTER LIVING.
Lady Patricia Margaret, *b.* 1970.

Faithful to my king and country.

WIDOW LIVING OF FIFTH EARL.
MARGARET (*Margaret, Countess of Norbury*), da. of John Kevan Greenhalgh, of Hoylake, Cheshire: *m.* 1933, as his second wife, the 5th Earl, who *d.* 1955. *Residence,*—Barn Cottage, The Pound, Cookham, Berks.

PREDECESSORS.—[1] JOHN Toler, *K.C.*, 3rd son of the late Daniel Toler, of Beechwood, co. Tipperary; *b.* 1745; Solicitor-Gen. for Ireland 1789-98, Attorney-Gen. 1798-99, and Ch. Justice of Common Pleas 1800-27; M.P. for Tralee 1776-83, for Philipstown 1783-90, and for Newborough 1790-99; cr. *Baron Norbury*, of Ballycrenode, co. Tipperary (peerage of Ireland) 1800, and *Viscount Glandine* and *Earl of Norbury*, of Glandine, Kings Co. (peerage of Ireland) 1827, with special remainder to his second son, Hector John: *m.* 1778, Grace, who *d.* 1822 [having been cr. *Baroness Norwood*, of Knockalton, co. Tipperary (peerage of Ireland) 1797], dau. of the late Hector Graham: *d.* 1831; *s.* by his son [2] HECTOR JOHN, 2nd Earl, *b.* 1781, assumed, by Roy. licence 1825, the additional surname and arms of Graham; *s.* his el. brother in his mother's Barony of Norwood and his father's Barony of Norbury 1832: *m.* 1808, Elizabeth, who *d.* 1859, only child of the late William Brabazon; was murdered 1839; *s.* by his son [3] HECTOR JOHN, 3rd Earl; *b.* 1810: *m.* 1848, Lady Steuart Lindsay, who *d.* 1904, sister of 7th Earl of Lindsay; *d.* 1873: *s.* by his son [4] WILLIAM BRABAZON LINDSAY, 4th Earl; *b.* 1862: *m.* 1908, Lucy Henrietta Katharine, who *d.* 1966, da. of the late Rev. the Hon. William Charles Ellis [B. Howard de Walden]; *d.* 1943; *s.* by his kinsman [5] RONALD IAN MONTAGU (son of the late Lt.-Col. James Otway Graham-Toler, son of the late Hon. Otway Fortescue Graham-Toler, 2nd son of 2nd Earl), 5th Earl, *b.* 1893; formerly Capt. Roy. Inniskilling Fusiliers: *m.* 1st, 1919, Simonne Evangeline Julie Caroline (who obtained a divorce 1933), da. of Hans Apeness, of 22, Rue de Thermes, Calais; 2ndly, 1933, Margaret, da. of John Kevan Greenhalgh, of Hoylake, Cheshire; *d.* 1955; *s.* by his son [6] NOEL TERENCE, 7th Earl and present peer: also Viscount Glandine, Baron Norbury, and Baron Norwood.

NORFOLK, DUKE OF. (Fitzalan Howard.) [Duke E. 1514 with precedency of 1397.]

SOLA·VIRTUS·INVICTA

Virtue alone is unconquerable.

MILES FRANCIS FITZALAN HOWARD, *CB*, *CBE*. *MC*, 17th Duke, and Premier Duke and Earl of England; *b.* July 21st, 1915; *s.* as 12th Baron Beaumont 1971, 4th Baron Howard of Glossop 1972, and 17th Duke of Norfolk, Earl Marshal and Hereditary Marshal of England 1975; ed. at Ampleforth, and Ch. Ch. Oxford (MA); Maj.-Gen. (ret.) late Gren. Gds.; Knt. of Sovereign Order of Malta; Head of British Mil. Mission to Russian Forces in Germany 1957-59, Comdg. 70th Bde., King's African Rifles 1961-63, and GOC 1st Div. 1963-65, Dir. of Management and Support Intelligence, Min. of Defence 1965-66, and Dir. of Ser. Intelligence, Min. of Defence 1966-67; a Dir. of Robert Fleming & Co., Ltd. since 1969; 1939-45 War in France, N. Africa, Sicily, Italy, and NW Europe (despatches, MC); CBE (Mil.) 1960, CB (Mil.) 1966: *m.* 1949, Anne Mary Teresa, da. of the late Wing-Cdr. Gerald Joseph Constable-Maxwell, MC, DFC, AFC [see L. Herries of Terregles, colls.], and has issue.

Arms.—Quarterly: 1st gules, a bend between six cross-crosslets fitchée argent; on the bend an escutcheon or, charged with a demi-lion rampant, pierced through the mouth by an arrow, within a double tressure flory counterflory of the first, *Howard*; 2nd gules, three lions passant guardant in pale or, in chief a label of three points argent, *Thomas of Brotherton*; 3rd checky or and azure, *Warren*; 4th gules, a lion rampant or, *Fitzalan*; behind the shield two gold batons in saltire, enamelled at the ends sable (as *Earl Marshal*). **Crest.**—1st, issuant from a ducal coronet or, a pair of wings gules each charged with a bend between six cross-crosslets fitchée argent; 2nd, on a chapeau gules, turned up ermine, a lion statant guardant with tail extended or, ducally gorged argent, *Thomas of Brotherton*: 3rd, on a mount vert a horse passant argent, holding in the mouth a slip of oak fructed proper. **Supporters.**—*Dexter*, a lion argent; *sinister*, a horse argent, holding in his mouth a slip of oak vert, fructed proper.

Seat.—Arundel Castle, Sussex. *Residences.*—Carlton Towers, Goole, Humberside; Bacres, Hambledean, Henley-on-Thames, Oxon; Burpham Lodge, Burpham, Arundel, Sussex.

SONS LIVING.

EDWARD WILLIAM (*Earl of Arundel*), *b.* Dec. 2nd, 1956.
Lord Gerald Bernard, *b.* 1962.

DAUGHTERS LIVING.

Lady Tessa Mary Isabel, *b.* 1950: *m.* 1971, Roderick Francis Arthur Balfour [see E. Balfour, colls.].
Lady Carina Mary Gabriel, *b.* 1952.
Lady Marsha Mary Josephine, *b.* 1953.

BROTHERS LIVING.
(Raised to the rank of a Duke's sons, 1955)

Lord Michael, *KCVO*, *CB*, *CBE*, *MC*, *b.* 1916; ed. at Ampleforth, and Trin. Coll., Camb. (BA); Maj.-Gen. late Scots Gds., and Knight of Sovereign Order of Malta; a DL for Wilts.; Ch. of Staff London Dist. 1958-61, Comdg. 4th Guards Bde. Group 1961-64, Cdr. Allied Command, Europe Mobile Forces (Land Component) 1964-66, Ch. of Staff, S. Command 1967-68, and GOC London Dist. and Maj.-Gen. Comdg. the Household Div. 1968-71, since when Marshal of Diplo. Corps.; Col. Queen's Lancs. Regt. since 1970 and Hon. Col. Camb. Univ. OTC 1968-71; 1939-45 War in N.-W. Europe (despatches, MC), Palestine 1945-46, Malaya 1948-49 (MBE); MBE (Mil.) 1949, MVO (4th class) 1952, CBE (Mil.) 1962, CB (Mil.) 1968, KCVO 1971: *m.* 1st, 1946, Jean Marion, who *d.* 1947, da. of Sir Hew Clifford Hamilton-Dalrymple, 9th Bt.; 2ndly, 1950, Jane Margaret, da. of the late Capt. W. P. Meade Newman, and has issue living, (by 1st m.) Jean Mary, *b.* 1947,—(by 2nd m.) Thomas Michael, *b.* 1952; Lt. Scots Gds.,—Richard Andrew *b.* 1953,—Henry Julian Nicholas, *b.* 1954,—Alexander Rupert, *b.* 1964,—Isabel Margaret, *b.* 1951: *m.* 1975, Peter C. Bickmore. *Residence,*—Fovant House, Fovant, Salisbury, Wilts.
Lord Martin, *b.* 1922; ed. at Ampleforth, and at Trin. Coll., Camb.; late Capt. Gren. Gds.; JP of Yorks; 1939-45 War (wounded), Palestine 1945-46: *m.* 1948, Bridget Anne, da. of the late Lt.-Col. Arnold Ramsay Keppel [see E. Albemarle, colls.], and has issue living, Philip Arnold Bernard Richard, *b.* 1963,—Clare Launa, *b.* 1949: *m.* 1970, Simon Richard Browne Wood,—Sarah Anne, *b.* 1951,—Amanda Josephine Margaret, *b.* 1953,—Rose Bridget, *b.* 1957. *Residence,*—Brockfield Hall, York.

Lord Mark, *b.* 1934; ed. at Ampleforth Coll.; late Coldstream Gds.: *m.* 1961, Jacynth Rosemary, da. of Sir Martin Alexander Lindsay of Dowhill, 1st Bt., CBE, DSO, and has issue living, Amelia, *b.* 1963,—Eliza, *b.* 1964. *Residence,*—13, Campden Hill Sq., W8.

SISTERS LIVING.
(Raised to the rank of a Duke's daughters, 1975)

Lady Mariegold Magdalene, *b.* 1919: *m.* 1957, Gerald James Auldjo Jamieson, son of Sir Archibald Auldjo Jamieson, KBE, MC, and has issue living, Simon David Auldjo, *b.* 1959,—James Gerard, *b.* 1963. *Residences,*—17, Elvaston Place, SW7; Yarrow House, Elmham, Norfolk.

Lady Miriam, *b.* 1924: *m.* 1952, Lieut.-Com. Theodore Bernard Peregrine Hubbard, RN [see E. Lindsey, colls.]. *Residence.*—Morton Hall, Bury St. Edmunds, Suffolk.

Lady Miranda Mary, *b.* 1927: *m.* 1947, the Hon. Christopher Anthony Robert Emmet, JP, of Sorrels House, Fittleworth, Sussex, and 18, Tournay Rd., SW6, el son of Baroness Emmet of Amberley (Life Baroness).

Lady Mirabel Magdalene, *b.* 1931: *m.* 1952, Bernard Kelly, el. son of the late Sir David Victor Kelly, GCMG, MC, and has issue living, Dominic Noel Miles Charles David, *b.* 1953,—Anthony Noël Francis, *b.* 1955,—Crispin Bernard Noël, *b.* 1956,—David Mark Noël, *b.* 1959,—Benedict Bernard Noël d'Arenberg, *b.* 1960,—Sebastian Charles Noël, *b.* 1972,—Justin Ghislain Ostavius Noël, *b.* 1974.— Anne-Louise Marie-Noële Miranda Josephine, *b.* 1962. *Residences,*—28, Carlyle Sq., SW3; Yonder Tara, Inch, co. Wexford; Romden Castle, Smarden, Kent.

DAUGHTERS LIVING OF SIXTEENTH DUKE.
Lady Anne Elizabeth (*Lady Herries of Terregles*), *b.* 1938; see that title.

Lady Mary Katharine, *MVO*, *b.* 1940; *h.p.* to Lordship of Herries of Terregles: Lady-in-Waiting to HRH Princess Alexandra, the Hon. Mrs. Angus Ogilvy, since 1964; MVO (4th Class) 1974.

Lady Sarah Margaret, *b.* 1941.

Lady Teresa Jane (*Countess of Ancram*), *b.* 1945: *m.* 1975, Michael Andrew Foster Jude, Earl of Ancram (6, Ainslie Place, Edinburgh), el. son of 12th Marquess of Lothian.

DAUGHTERS LIVING OF FIFTEENTH DUKE.
Lady (Mary) Rachel, *DCVO*, *b.* 1905; Lady-in-Waiting to HRH Princess Marina, the Duchess of Kent 1943-68; has Order of Mercy; CVO 1954, DCVO 1968: *m.* 1st, 1939, Lt.-Col. Colin Keppel Davidson, CIE, OBE, RA, who *d.* (killed in action) 1943 [E. Albemarle]; 2ndly, 1961, Brig. Anthony Hilton Pepys, DSO, late R. Dragoons, who *d.* 1967, and has issue living, (by 1st m.) Duncan (Lilburn Tower, Alnwick), *b.* 1941; ed. at Ampleforth; a Page of Honour to HM 1955-57; R. Scots Greys 1959-63: *m.* 1965, Sarah, da. of the late Maj. Robin Filmer Wilson, and has issue living, Camilla Mary *b.* 1968, Natasha Anne *b.* 1969,—Harriet Mary, *b.* 1942: *m.* 1968, Michael Richard Sefi (Grove House, High Drive, Woldingham, Surrey), and has issue living, Charles Anthony *b.* 1974, Clare Louise *b.* 1970, Laura Mary *b.* 1972. *Residences,*—Highfield House, Crossbush, Arundel, Sussex; 24 Kylestrome House, Cundy St., Elbury St., SW1.

Lady Katherine Mary, *b.* 1912; has Order of Mercy: *m.* 1940, Lieut.-Col. Joseph Anthony Moore Phillips, DSO, MBE, DL, late King's Dragoon Guards, and has issue living, Anthony Bernard Moore, *b.* 1953. *Residence,*—Lund House, Lund, Driffield, Yorks.

Lady Winefride Alice, *b.* 1914; a JP of Suffolk: *m.* 1943, Lt.-Col. John Edward Broke Freeman, late Oxfordshire and Buckinghamshire L.I., son of the late Sir Philip Horace Freeman, KCVO, KBE, and has issue living, Charles Philip Broke, *b.* 1947,—Mary Gwendoline, *b.* 1945: *m.* 1967, Martin Richard de Laszlo, of 57, Criger Rd., SW6,—Virginia Phyllis Theresa, *b.* 1949. *Residence,*—Buxhall Vale, Stowmarket, Suffolk.

WIDOW LIVING OF SIXTEENTH DUKE.
LAVINIA MARY, *CBE* (*Lavinia, Duchess of Norfolk*), (Arundel Park, Sussex), da. of 3rd Baron Belper; bore the Queen's Canopy at Coronation of King George VI; Lord Lieut. of W. Sussex since 1975; CBE (Civil) 1971: *m.* 1937, the 16th Duke, who *d.* 1975.

COLLATERAL BRANCHES LIVING.

Descendants of the late Rt. Hon. Lord Edmund Bernard Fitzalan-Howard, KG, GCVO, DSO (3rd son of 14th Duke), who was cr. *Viscount Fitz Alan of Derwent* 1921 :—

See V. Fitz Alan of Derwent (ext.).

Granddaughter of the 2nd Baron Howard of Glossop, 2nd son of the Rt. Hon. Lord Edward George Fitzalan-Howard (who was cr. *Baron Howard of Glossop* 1869), 2nd son of 13th Duke:—

Issue of the late Hon. Philip Granville James Fitzalan Howard, Lt. W. G, *b.* 1895, *d.* (wounds in action) 1918: *m.* 1916, Gladys Cecily Clara, [who *d.* 1966, having *m.* 2ndly, 1920, Capt. Henry James Fosbery Mills, formerly KRRCR (who obtained a divorce 1931), son of Sir James Mills, KCMG; 3rdly, 1931, Maj. P. G. Riviere], da. of the late Lieut.-Col. Charles Edward Norton, CMG:—

Phillipa Gwendolen Mary (posthumous), *b.* 1918: *m.* 1940, Major Edward Guy Tyler, MC, Irish Guards, and has issue living, Peter Edward, *b.* 1944,—Virginia Anne, *b.* 1941: *m.* 1965, Carlos de Mejia, of 26, Mallord St., SW1, and has issue living, Carlos-Felipe *b.* 1967, Mariana Luisa *b.* 1971. *Residences,* —Upper Hedsor Farm, Wooburn Green, Bucks.; 17, Lennox Gdns., SW1.

Granddaughter of the late Sir (Edward) Stafford Howard, KCB (infra):—

Issue of the late Maj. Sir Algar Henry Stafford Howard, KCB, KCVO, MC, TD, *b.* 1880, *d.* 1970: *m.* 1921, the Hon. Violet Ethel Meysey-Thompson, who *d.* 1960, da. of 1st Baron Knaresborough (ext.), and widow of Capt. Alexander Moore Vandeleur:—

Anne Violet, *b.* 1923: *m.* 1952, John Cahill, of Doneen, Casteisland, co. Kerry, and has issue living, John Anthony, *b.* 1956,—Colin Algar, *b.* 1958,—Peter Francis, *b.* 1960,—Elizabeth Mary, *b.* 1953,— Alice, *b.* 1962,—Angela, *b.* 1964,—Rosemary, *b.* 1967.——Elizabeth Helen, *b.* 1924: *m.* 1958, Harold William Norman Suckling, of Roos Hall, Beccles, Suffolk, and has issue living, Penelope Anne, *b.* 1959.

Grandson of the late Henry Howard, MP, son of the late Lord Henry Thomas Howard-Molyneux-Howard, M.P., brother of 12th Duke:—

Issue of the late Sir (Edward) Stafford Howard, K.C.B., *b.* 1851, *d.* 1916: *m.* 1st, 1876, Lady Rachel Anne Georgiana Campbell, who *d.* 1906, dau. of 2nd Earl Cawdor; 2ndly, 1911, Catharine Meriel (*Lady Howard-Stepney*), *M.B.E.*, who *d.* 1952 (having assumed by Roy. licence for herself and issue 1922, the additional surname and arms of Stepney), dau. of Sir Emile Algernon Arthur Keppel Cowell-Stepney, 2nd Bt. (ext.):—

(By 2nd m.) Stafford Vaughan Stepney HOWARD, *b.* 1915; ed. at Eton, and Magdalen Coll., Oxford; Capt. Coldstream Gds. (Reserve); 1939-45 War in N. Africa, Italy, and Burma (despatches); relinquished by deed poll 1950, the additional surname of Stepney: *m.* 1st, 1936, Ursula Priscilla (who obtained a divorce 1940), da. of Lt.-Col. Sir James Nockells Horlick, 4th Bt., OBE, MC; 2ndly, 1940, Mary Gracia, da. of the late George Wilder Neville of Portsmouth, Virginia, USA, and has issue living (by 1st m.), Nicholas Stafford (Johnby Hall, Penrith, Cumbria), *b.* 1937; ed. at Eton, Magdalen Coll., Oxford, and Churchill Coll., Camb.: *m.* 1966, Phyllis Bethan, da. of Lewis Duckett, of Essex House, Dursley, Glos., and has issue living, Henry James Stafford *b.* 1972, Cecilia Charlotte *b.* 1968,—(by 2nd m.) Murray Bernard Neville Cyprian (Arianwen Cottage, St. Mary's Hill, S. Ascot, Berks.), *b.* 1942; ed. at Eton, and RMA Sandhurst; Maj. Coldstream Gds.: *m.* 1969, Lavinia Zaria, da. of the late Lt.-Col. Philip Lewis [see E. Dartmouth, colls.], and has issue living, Alexander Philip Wilder *b.* 1971, Catherine Anne Cardwell *b.* 1972,—Amanda Arianwen, *b.* 1941: *m.* 1967, Michael Noel Francis Cottrell, of Laurenden Forstal, Challock Lees, Canterbury, son of Sir Edward Baglietto Cottrell, and has issue living, Edward Stafford Cyprian *b.* 1969, Philip Howard Edward *b.* 1971, Camilla Mary Josephine *b.* 1973,—Arianwen Catharine Cardwell (twin), *b.* 1942: *m.* 1968, Christopher

Neville Neve, of Coggers, Benenden, Kent, and has issue living, Thomas Wilder Neville *b.* 1971, Eleanor Marged Deborah *b.* 1972. *Residence,*—Greystoke Castle, Penrith, Cumberland. *Club,*—Brook's.

Grandchildren of the late Robert Mowbray Howard, son of the late Henry Howard, M.P. (ante) :—
Issue of the late Major Henry Ralph Mowbray HOWARD-SNEYD, O.B.E., *b.* 1883, *d.* 1950, having assumed by Roy. Licence 1950 the additional surname and arms of Sneyd: *m.* 1st, 1911, Helen Millicent (who *d.* 1967, having obtained a divorce 1931), da. of the late William Dodge James CVO [Forbes, Bt., cr. 1823]; 2ndly, 1931, Janet Emma Jameson (HIBBERT), only da. of the late John Duthie, of Cults House, Aberdeenshire:—
(By 2nd m.) Nicholas Bryan John, *RD, b.* 1909; ed. at Christ's Hospital, and HMS Conway; Lt.-Cdr. nithwaite, Leyburn, Yorks; Brook's Club), *b.* 1940: *m.* 1963, Serena Patience, yr. da. of Thomas Lumley, of Ashcombe House, Lewes, and has issue living, Henry Lyulph, *b.* 1965,—Justin Andrew, *b.* 1966,—Antonia Caroline, *b.* 1969.——(By 1st m.) Diana Katherine, *b.* 1913: *m.* 1938, Richard Marcus Beresford, who *d.* 1968, and has issue living, Christopher Charles Howard (43, Verwood Rd., Headstone Lane, Harrow, Middx.), *b.* 1946: *m.* 1973, Philippa Susan Yates,—Patricia Mary, *b.* 1941: *m.* 1964, Christopher Arthur Roljo Wells, of Oaklands, Newport Rd., Woburn Sands, Bletchley, Bucks., and has issue living, Gavin Marcus *b.* 1965, Amanda Clare *b.* 1967,—Katherine Anne, *b.* 1943: *m.* 1st, 1965 (m. diss. 1969), Robert Neol Hutchings; 2ndly, 1969, Jeffrey Osman Streater, of 32, Eaton Place, SW1, and has issue living, Olivia Katherine Nermin *b.* 1974. *Residence,*—Walnut House, Benefield Rd., Oundle, Peterborough.——Pamela Evelyn, *b.* 1914: *m.* 1939, Ian Reginald Gilfrid Karslake, and has issue living, David Ian Howard, *b.* 1944,—Sarah Virien, *b.* 1941,—Elizabeth Ann, *b.* 1948. *Residence,*—Brookhurst Lodge, Ewhurst, Surrey.——Audrey Elizabeth, *b.* 1916: *m.* 1940, Ronald John Henry Kaulback, and has issue living, Peter John, *b.* 1948,—Bryan Henry (twin), *b.* 1948,—Sonia Elizabeth, *b.* 1941: *m.* 1967, Robin Erskine Waddell, of 453, Earlham Rd., Norwich,—Susan Georgina, *b.* 1942. *Residence,*—Ardnagashel House, Bantry, co. Cork.——Rosemary Millicent, *b.* 1917: *m.* 1st, 1939, Guy Michael Craigie Anderson, who *d.* (killed in action during 1939-45 War) 1944; 2ndly, 1946, Michael Frederick Lilly. *Residence,*—Frog Grove House, Worplesdon, Surrey.——Joan Margery, *b.* 1921: *m.* 1945, Hubert Murray Sturges, and has issue living, William Henry (The Lodge, Ravenswood Court, Kingston Hill, Kingston upon Thames), *b.* 1949: *m.* 1973, Virginia Mary, da. of Cdr. R. FitzGerald, RN, of Petworth, Sussex,—Rosemary Jane, *b.* 1946: *m.* 1971, Alastair William MacDonald. *Residence,*—Studdridge Farm, Stokenchurch, Bucks.

Grandsons of the late Henry Howard, M.P. (ante) :—
Issue of the late Rt. Hon. Sir Esme William Howard, G.C.B., G.C.M.G., C.V.O., who was cr. *Baron Howard of Penrith* 1930 [see that title].
Descendants of the late Rt. Hon. Charles Howard, (son of the late Sir William Howard, son of the late Sir Philip Howard, el. son of the late Lord William Howard, 2nd son of 4th Duke), who was cr. *Earl of Carlisle* 1661 [see that title].

Descendants of the late Col. Sir Francis Howard, 2nd son of the late Lord William Howard (ante):—

Grandchildren of the late George Howard, son of the late Sir Henry Howard, G.C.M.G., K.C.B., son of the late Sir Henry Francis Howard, G.C.B. (infra) :—
Issue of the late Capt. Henry Howard, Quarter-Master Corps, U.S. Army, *b.* 1907, *d.* 1955; *m.* 1st, 1928, Vara (from whom he obtained a divorce 1930), dau. of William Doherty; 2ndly, 1941, Natalie Bayard (who *m.* 2ndly, 1956, Kenneth Douglas Robertson, of Mer-rillton, Newport, Rhode Island, U.S.A.), dau. of the late Rev. Grenville Merrill, of Merrillton, Newport, Rhode Island, U.S.A.:—
(By 2nd marriage) George, *b.* 1944.——Natalie Bayard, *b.* 1942: *m.* 1967, Peter Alan Gordon, of Apart. 7A, 25, East 83 St., New York, NY, USA.——Mary Mowbray, *b.* 1948.

Grandchildren of the late Sir Henry Howard, G.C.M.G., K.C.B., son of Sir Henry Francis Howard, G.C.B. (infra) :—
Issue of the late Com. Henry Mowbray Howard, O.B.E., *b.* 1873, *d.* 1953: *m.* 1917, Norah Florence Annie (now of 60, Coleherne Court, S.W.7), dau. of Major John Dunlop Watson:—
Henry Edmund, *D.S.C., R.N., b.* 1923 ; is Com. ; European War 1939-45 (D.S.C.) : *m.* 1945, Sheila, younger dau. of Colin McNab Brown, of Paisley, and has issue living, Henry Colin Francis, *b.* 1947,—Catherine Jane, *b.* 1950.——Joan Cecilia, *b.* 1917: *m.* 1942, Capt. Brent Elworthy Hutton-Williams, MBE, Intelligence Corps, attached Phantom, and has issue living, Christopher Brent, *b.* 1948,—Charlotte Fiona Janet, *b.* 1944: *m.* 1969, David Fennell, of 155, Sandycombe Rd., Kew, and has issue living, Benedict Nicholas *b.* 1971. *Residence,*—4, Lansdowne House, Lansdowne Rd., W11.

Granddaughter of the late Sir Henry Francis Howard, GCB, son of the late Henry Howard, 4th in descent from Col. Sir Francis Howard (ante):—
Issue of the late Maj.-Gen. Sir Frances Howard, KCB, KCMG, *b.* 1848, *d.* 1930: *m.* 1895, Gertrude, who *d.* 1953, da. of the late Hugh Conyngham Boyd, of Ballycastle, co. Down:—
Marjorie (17, Holland Park Av., W11; Knapp Orchard, Painswick, Glos.), *b.* 1903: *m.* 1931, George John Theodore Hyde Villiers, who *d.* 1942 [E. Clarendon, colls.].

(In remainder to Barony of Beaumont only)
Issue of the late Hon. Ivy Mary Stapleton, yr. da. of 10th Baron Beaumont, *b.* (posthumous) 1895; *d.* 1967: *m.* 1929, Richard Gerald Micklethwait, of Ardsley, Barnsley, Yorks.:—
Richard Miles (Preston Hall, Uppingham), *b.* 1934; ed. at Ampleforth, and Ch. Ch., Oxford; late Capt. Grenadier Guards: *m.* 1961, Jane Evelyn, da. of the late William Melville Codrington, CMG, MC [see Codrington, Bt. (cr. 1721), colls.], and has issue living, Richard John, *b.* 1962,—William James, *b.* 1964.——Imogen Mary, *b.* 1931: *m.* 1961, Maj. John Lachlan Macdonald of Tote, of Tote House, Isle of Skye, and 50, Chelsea Park Gdns., SW3, and has issue living, Charles Lachlan, *b.* 1964,—Andrew Kenneth, *b.* 1965,—Lisabel Mary, *b.* 1969.

Grandchildren of the late Rev. John Stapleton, brother of 8th Baron Beaumont:—
Issue of the late Rev. Gilbert Stapleton, *b.* 1862, *d.* 1949 : *m.* 1st, 1891, Anna Mary Katharine, who *d.* 1891, dau. of the late Rev. Thomas Langshaw, R. of Silchester, Hants ; 2ndly, 1894, Eleanor Sarah, who *d.* 1947, dau. of the late Rev. Gibbes Jordan, R. of Tunworth, Hants:—
(By 2nd marriage) Katharine Anna, *b.* 1895. *Residence,*—Yateley Hill, Yateley, Hants.
Issue of the late Bryan Stapleton, *b.* 1871, *d.* 1941 : *m.* 1st, 1912, Geraldine Emma, who *d.* 1916, dau. of the late Col. John Henry Crowdy, R.E. ; 2ndly, 1918, Ruth Jane, who *d.* 1954, dau. of the late Richard James Friel, of Waterford :—
(By 2nd m.) Thomas, *b.* 1920; ed. at Univ. Coll., Oxford (BM and BCh, MA, DM); FRCP London; late Capt. RAMC. *Residence,*—The Foundry Cottage, Lane End, High Wycombe, Bucks.——(By 1st m.) Anne Dunscombe, *b.* 1914: *m.* 1940, David Edwyn Clark, of 215, Milner Road South, Clare-mont, Cape Town, S. Africa, and has issue living, Anthony Miles Stapleton (50, Georges Vanier St., Roxboro, Quebec, H8Y-2S3, Canada), *b.* 1941; PhD Memorial Univ., Nova Scotia: *m.* 1970, Ruth Christine, dau. of the Rev. Frederick Guy Harrison, of Appleton Roebuck, Yorks., and has issue living, Natasha Alexandra *b.* 1971,—Bryan Stapleton (1, Tottering Towers, Virginia Lane, Borrowdale, Salisbury, Rhodesia), *b.* 1944: *m.* 1971, Nicolien, da. of Leslie Lulofs, of 14, Beaumont Rd., Oak-lands, Johannesburg, and has issue living Bronwyn *b.* 1972,—Geraldine Anne, *b.* 1947.

Issue of the late Louis Henry Stapleton, *b.* 1874, *d.* 1949: *m.* 1908, Annetta Lima Smith, who *d.* 1956, dau. of the late A. Perossi:—

Diana Enid Violet Dorothea, *b.* 1911: *m.* 1939, Dr. Allan William Vaughan Eley, late Major R.A.M.C., who *d.* 1965, and has issue living, Ian Miles Stanley Vaughan, *b.* 1944; ed. at Oratory Sch., Woodcote,—Nigel Louis Allan, *b.* 1949; ed. at Oratory Sch., Woodcote. *Residence,*—The Cottage, Sonning Common, Oxon.

Grandchildren of the late Bryan John Stapleton, half-brother of 8th Baron Beaumont :—
Issue of the late Major Nicholas Stapleton, Canadian Army, *b.* 1861, *d.* (on active service during European War) 1918: *m.* 1st, 1887, Mary Magdelene, who *d.* 1946, dau. of the late Lieut.-Col. A. A. Douglas, R.M.A.; 2ndly, 1906, Mary Jane, who *d.* 1939, el. dau. of Augustus John Abraham :—
(By 2nd m.) Nicholas Bryan John, *RD*, *b.* 1909; ed. at Christ's Hospital, and HMS Conway; Lt.-Cdr. RNR (ret.), a Liveryman of Hon. Co. of Master Mariners, a Freeman of City of London; Senior Master (ret.), Roy. Fleet Auxiliary Ser.: *m.* 1940, Laetitia Frances Mary, da. of the late Col. Charles a'Court Repington, CMG. *Residence,*—38, Wilbury Cres., Hove, Sussex.——(By 1st marriage) Gwendoline Lavinia, *b.* 1888: *m.* 1923, G. Francis S. Mann, who *d.* 1931. *Residence,*—155, Henry St., Brooklyn, New York, USA.——Ruth Madelina, *b.* 1889: *m.* 1914, Stanley Yates, who *d.* 1955, and has issue living, Joan Madelaine Dampier, *b.* 1920: *m.* 1965, Jack Trill, of Little Jarrets, 61, Fulmer Drive, Gerrards Cross, Bucks. *Residence,*—Little Jarrets, 61 Fulmer Drive, Gerrards Cross, Bucks.

Issue of the late Com. Gregory Stapleton, R.N., *b.* 1864, *d.* 1938: *m.* 1904, Marie Marcella, who *d.* 1947, el. dau. of Anthony MacDermott, R.M., J.P. :—
Gregory Joseph Kenneth (Langton Herring, nr. Weymouth, Dorset), *b.* 1908; ed. at Ampleforth Coll.; Maj. Indian Army (ret.); formerly Assist. Comdt. Burma Frontier Force; has King's Police medal: *m.* 1945, Margarita, only da. of Henry Fitzroy Chamberlayne, of Stonythorpe, Warwick, and has issue living, Miles Gregory Rowland (121, Rusper Rd., Ifield, Crawley, Sussex), *b.* 1949: *m.* 1973, Delia Felicity Mary, da. of Maj. Benjamin Harold Dunkey, of 190, Cooden Drive, Bexhill-on-Sea.—— Marie Josephine, *b.* 1905: *m.* 1928, Joseph Gregory Littledale, and has issue living, Gregory Bruno (Devonia, 15, Wellington Rd., Taunton, Som.), *b.* 1932; ed. at Beaumont Coll., Old Windsor; late R. Fus.; Fellow Inst. of Data Processing; Member of British Computor Soc.: *m.* 1st, 1957, (m. diss. 1966), Patricia Jane Howard; 2ndly, 1969, Naomi Abigail, da. of G. F. A. Martin, of Dover, and has issue living (by 2nd m.) Joanne Kerra *b.* 1973. *Residence,*—40, St. Mary's Terr., Hastings.—— Elizabeth Charlotte Josephine, *b.* 1907: *m.* 1st, 1941, as his second wife, Maj. Francis John Angus Skeet, late Roy. Dublin Fusiliers; 2ndly, 1945, Maj. Casimir Paul Francis Rowland William Blennerhassett [see Blennerhassett, Bt., colls.]. *Residence,*—17, Campden Hill Rd., Kensington, W8.—— Anne Penrodas Mary Helen, *b.* 1914: *m.* 1946, Xavier Philip Mary Spruyt de Bay, and has issue living, Philip Michael, *b.* 1950,—Helen Mary, *b.* 1947: *m.* 1971, Jeremy Charles Stuart Fulford Smithies (25, Saumarez St., St. Peter Port, Guernsey); and has issue living Roland Jeremy Xavier *b.* 1973. *Residence,*—19, St. Catherines Close, Bathwick Hill, Bath.

Grandchildren of the late Cdr. Gregory Stapleton, RN (ante):—
Issue of the late Joseph Mark Hugh Stapleton, *b.* 1909; *d.* 1967: *m.* 1948, Elizabeth (28, Cavendish Rd., Woking, Surrey), da. of Sidney M. Vanheems:—
Elizabeth Mary, *b.* 1949.——Anne Mary, *b.* 1951.——Monica Mary, *b.* 1953.

Grandchildren of the late Bryan John Stapleton (ante):—
Issue of the late Antonia Marianne Angela Winefrede Stapleton, *b.* 1911, *d.* 1969: *m.* 1939, Guy George Morris Pritchett, solicitor, of 7, Flower Walk, Guildford (who m. 2ndly, 1972, Katherine Mary Elfrida, da. of Capt. John Alick Woodhouse, CBE, RN):—
Malcolm Morris (Kwetu, Send Marsh Rd., Ripley, Surrey), *b.* 1941; ed. at Beaumont and Imperial Coll., London; AIMM: *m.* 1963, Lamorna Jill, da. of David Bayly Pike, of Clandon, Surrey, and has issue living, Clare Marion, *b.* 1965,—Karen Fiona, *b.* 1967,—Sally Antonia, *b.* 1970.——Roger Morris (Wedgewood Cottage, Shamley Green, Guildford, Surrey), *b.* 1943; ed. at Beaumont Coll.: *m.* 1969, Vivien, da. of Francis Brothers, of Guildford, and has issue living, Rupert Francis Morris, *b.* 1974.—— Helen Monica, *b.* 1945: *m.* 1969, Ian Strickland, ARICS, of 2, Kings Rd., Walton-on-Thames, Surrey, and has issue living, Alexander Peter, *b.* 1967,—Matthew Douglas, *b.* 1968,—Natasha Jane, *b.* 1970.——Antonia Mary, *b.* 1947: *m.* 1971, Philip Roger Wellesley-Davies, of Elmlea, The Common, Dunsfold, Surrey, and has issue living, William George, *b.* 1971.

Issue of the late Christopher Robert Stapleton, Ph.D., *b.* 1870, *d.* 1929: *m.* 1908, Alice Cicely, who *d.* 1950, dau. of J. J. Sepple:—
Gwendoline Filumena (515, Helen Rd., Mineola, Long Island, New York USA), *b.* 1910 : *m.* 1942, Edward Joseph Battell, who *d.* 1964.——Alice Veronica Enid, *b.* 1912: *m.* 1930, John Tyler Walls, of 8, Pinebrook Av., Lakeview, W. Hempstead, Long Island, USA, and has issue living, John Tyler, *b.* 1931,—Christopher Stapleton, *b.* 1933,—Julian Davis, *b.* 1934,—Alice Enid Stapleton, *b.* 1941,— Naomi Anne, *b.* 1947,—Collette Aurora, *b.* 1948.

Issue of the late Helen Stapleton, *b.* 1862, *d.* 1958 : *m.* 1893, Wilfrid Wilberforce, who *d.* 1910 :—
Arthur Richard Anthony, *b.* 1899 : *m.* 1st, 1925, Monica Mary Hannah Bishop, who *d.* 1935 ; 2ndly, 1939, Olive Mary, dau. of Edward Charles Riddell, of Hermeston Hall, Worksop, and has issue living, (by 1st marriage) Christopher Basil Antony, *b.* 1930,—Anne Monica Mary Helen Teresa, *b.* 1928 : *m.* 1955, Charles Patrick Currey, of Diocesan College, Rondebosch, Cape Province, S. Africa, and has issue living, Michael Anthony *b.* 1957, David Charles *b.* 1958, Peter James *b.* 1960, Elizabeth Anne *b.* 1963,—(by 2nd m.) Wilfrid Gerard, *b.* 1947,—Margaret Grace Helen, *b.* 1941: *m.* 1965, George Lironi Taylor Hunt, of Barton House, Parklands, Scruton, Northallerton, N. Yorks., DL7 0QT, and has issue living, Robin George Andrew, *b.* 1968, Dominic Christopher *b.* 1971. *Residence,*— Purse Caundle, Dorset.——Everilda Helen Mary Bertrand, *b.* 1903. *Residence,*—

PREDECESSORS.—[1] *Sir* **JOHN** Howard, *K.G.*, an eminent Yorkist, distinguished himself in the French Wars of Henry VI., and in 1468 was appointed Treasurer of the King's Household; summoned to Parliament of England as *Baron Howard* 1470-83, and 1483 was cr. *Earl Marshal of England*, and *Duke of Norfolk* (peerage of England), his son and heir being at the same time cr. *Earl of Surrey* (peerage of England) ; as Earl Marshal he was authorized to bear either in the king's presence or absence a golden staff tipped at each end with black, the upper part thereof to be adorned with the royal arms, and the lower with those of his own family, and to support the dignity a grant was made of £20 a year for ever ; was subsequently constituted High Steward of England, and Lord Adm. of England, Ireland, and Aquitaine for life ; killed at Bosworth Field 1485, and was attainted the same year ; *s.* by his son [2] THOMAS, *K.G.*, 2nd Duke ; having been taken prisoner at Bosworth his Earldom was attainted and he suffered imprisonment three years in the Tower ; was restored 1489 ; appointed Lord Treasurer 1501, and in 1513 commanded the English Army at Flodden Field, when the Scots were routed and James IV. slain ; cr. *Earl Marshal of England* (for life) 1510, and *Duke of Norfolk* (peerage of England) 1514 ; *d.* 1524 ; *s.* by his son [3] THOMAS, *K.G.*, 3rd Duke ; cr. *Earl of Surrey* by patent (peerage of England) 1514 ; was High Admiral 1513, Lord Dep. of Ireland 1520, Treasurer of England 1522, Earl Marshal by patent 1533 ; attainted 1546, imprisoned in the Tower seven years, and restored 1553 ; *d.* 1554 ; *s.* by his grandson [4] THOMAS, *K.G.*, 4th Duke (son of Henry, *K.G.*, Earl of Surrey, a distinguished statesman, orator, and poet, who was accused of treason and executed during his father's lifetime 1547) ; restored in blood 1554 : being found guilty of high treason for communicating with Mary, Queen of Scots, he was beheaded 1572, when all his honours were forfeited ; *s.* by his son [5] PHILIP, who in right of his mother (Mary, da. and heir of Henry Fitzalan, Earl of Arundel) as owner of Arundel Castle became (according to the admission of Parliament 1433) 13th *Earl of Arundel* (a feudal honour-peerage of England), and *Baron Maltravers* (peerage of England) 1330 [see † infra] ; restored in blood 1581 ; attainted of high treason 1589 and *d.* a prisoner in the Tower 1595 ; *s.* by his son [6] THOMAS, 14th Earl, who during the reign of Elizabeth only bore the courtesy title of Lord Maltravers; restored by Act of Parliament 1604 to all the honours and precedence of his father; in 1627 the titles of *Baron FitzAlan, Baron Clun*, and *Baron Oswaldestre* (peerage of England), were annexed by Act of Parliament to the Earldom of Arundel, which peerages were entailed to descend to the heirs male of his body, with remainder to his heirs male, failing which to his heirs general; constituted Earl Marshal 1621, and *cr. Earl of Norfolk* 1644; *m.* 1606, Alethea, dau. of 7th Earl of Shrewsbury, becoming in her own right *Baroness Furnivall, Strange of Blackmere and Talbot*; *d.* 1646; *s.* by his son [7] HENRY FREDERICK, 15th Earl of Arundel, who had in 1631 been summoned to Parliament of England as Baron Mowbray; *d.* 1652; *s.* by his el. son [8] THOMAS, 16th Earl of Arundel; restored by Act of Parliament 1660 to Dukedom of Norfolk, with precedence of 1st Duke, and in 1661 obtained an Act confirming the same, with remainder to the male issue of his grandfather, and to other collateral branches; *d.* unmarried 1677; *s.* by his brother [9] HENRY, 6th Duke, who in 1669 had been created *Baron Howard, of Castle Rising*, and in 1672 *Earl of Norwich* (peerage of England), with remainder to various collateral branches, and hereditary *Earl Marshal* of England; was Lord-Lieut. of cos. Berks and Surrey; *d.* 1684; *s.* by his son [10] HENRY, K.G., 7th Duke; Constable and Gov. of Windsor Castle; *d.s.p.* 1701; *s.* by his nephew [11] THOMAS, 8th Duke; *d.s.p.* 1732; *s.* by his brother [12] EDWARD, 9th Duke; *d.s.p.* 1777, when the Earldom of Norwich and Barony of Howard of Castle Rising expired, the Baronies of Mowbray and Segrave [see B. Mowbray], and the Baronies of Howard, Braose of Gower, Greystock, Ferrers of Wemme, Talbot, Strange of Blackmere, Furnivall, and Giffard of Brimmesfield fell into abeyance, and the dukedom devolved upon his kinsman [13] CHARLES, 10th Duke, son of Charles, 4th son of 15th Earl of Arundel; *d.* 1786; *s.* by his son [14] CHARLES, *P.C.*, 11th Duke; *d.* 1815; *s.* by his cousin [15] BERNARD EDWARD, 12th Duke grandson of Charles Bernard, 8th son of 15th Earl of Arundel; by Act of Parliament the office of Earl Marshal and Hereditary Marshal of England were empowered to be executed by Roman Catholics; *d.* 1842; *s.* by his son [16] HENRY CHARLES, K.G., 13th Duke; *d.* 1856; *s.* by his son [17] HENRY GRANVILLE, 14th Duke; *b.* 1815; M.P. for Limerick 1851-2; assumed by Roy. licence 1842 the additional surname of FitzAlan: *m.* 1839, Augusta Mary Minna Catherine, who *d.* 1886, dau. of 1st Baron Lyons; *d.* 1860; *s.* by his son [18] HENRY, K.G., P.C., G.C.V.O., 15th Duke, *b.* 1847; was Postmaster-Gen. Aug. 1895 to March 1900, and Lord-Lieut. of Sussex 1905-17; received Roy. Victorian Chain 1911: *m.* 1st, 1877, Lady Flora Paulyna Hetty Barbara Abney-Hastings, who *d.* 1887, dau. of the late Countess of Loudoun, and of the 1st Baron Donington; 2ndly, 1904, the Hon. Gwendolen Mary Constable-Maxwell (*Lady Herries of Terregles* in her own right), who *d.* 1945, el. dau. of 11th Lord Herries of Terreglea; *d.* 1917; *s.* by his only surviving son (by 2nd m.) [19] BERNARD MARMADUKE KG, GCVO, GBE, TD, PC, 16th Duke; *b.* 1908; Joint Parl. Sec. Min. of Agric. 1941-45; KG 1937, received Roy. Victoria Chain 1953: *m.* 1937, the Hon. Lavinia Mary Strutt, CBE, da. of 3rd Baron Belper; *d.* 1975; *s.* by his Kinsman [20] MILES FRANCIS, CB, CBE, MC, 17th Duke and present peer: also Earl of Arundel [see † infra], Earl of Surrey, Earl of Norfolk, Baron Maltravers, Baron FitzAlan, Baron Clun, Baron Oswalsestre, Baron Beaumont [see ** infra], and Baron Howard of Glossop [†‡,† infra].

†According to the claim of John FitzAlan in 1433, which was upheld by the Crown, the Earldom of Arundel was held by tenure of Arundel Castle, however. William de Albini, of Buckenham, Norfolk, acquired Arundel in 1138 on his marriage to Queen Adeliza of Louvain, widow of Henry I, and was recognized from 1139 variously as Earl of Sussex, Chichester, or (more usually) Arundel [1] RICHARD FitzAlan, Lord of Clun and Oswestry, Salop (8th Earl, according to Admission of 1433), grandson of John FitzAlan by Isabel, da. of William de Albini, 5th Earl of Arundel and sister and co-heir of Hugh, 6th Earl of Arundel; was summoned to Parliament 1292 as *Earl of Arundel;* served at Carlaverock 1300: *m.* before 1285, Alasia di Saluzzo, da. of Thomas, Marquis of Saluzzo; *d.* 1302; *s.* by his son [2] EDMUND, 2nd (or 9th) Earl, *b.* 1285: *m.* 1305, Alice, da. of William de Warenne, and sister and heir of John Earl of Surrey; executed and attainted 1326, when the Castle and Honour of Arundel was granted to Edmund, Earl of Kent, son of Edward I, but in 1331, his son [3] RICHARD, 3rd Earl, was restored in blood; assumed the Earldom of Surrey 1361: *m.* 1st, 1321 (annulled 1344) Isabel, da. of Sir Hugh le Despencer; 2ndly, 1345, Lady Eleanor, da. of Henry, Earl of Lancaster, and widow of John de Beaumont; *d.* 1376; *s.* by [4] RICHARD, KG, 4th Earl, *b.* 1346: *m.* 1359, Elizabeth de Bohun, da. of William, Earl of Northampton; 2ndly, 1390, Phillipa Mortimer, da. of Edmund, Earl of March and widow of John Hastings; attainted and executed 1397 when Arundel was granted to John Holand, Duke of Exeter, but in 1400, his son [5] THOMAS, KG, 5th Earl, *b.* 1381, was restored to the Earldoms of Arundel and Surrey: *m.* 1405, Beatrice, da. of John I, King of Portugal; *d.* 1415, when representation of the Warennes Earls of Surrey passed to his sister and co-heir, of whom the descendants of the eldest, Elizabeth, Duchess of Norfolk, opposed the claim of the heir male to the Earldom of Arundel; however in 1415 [6] JOHN, *de jure* 6th Earl and Lord Maltravers [§ infra] (grandson of John, 1st Lord Arundel, brother of 4th Earl) *s.* to the Castle and Honour of Arundel and said to have been summoned to Parliament as *Earl of Arundel* 1416 but not afterwards: *m.* before 1407, Eleanor, da. of Sir John Berkeley of Beverstone, Glos.; *d.* 1421; *s.* by his son [7] JOHN, KG, 7th Earl; *b.* 1408; Capt. of Rouen 1432; his petition to be considered as Earl of Arundel by tenure of Arundel was allowed 1433; *cr. Duke of Touraine* (France) 1434; *m.* 1st, Constance Cornwall, da. of John Lord Fanhope; 2ndly, before 1429, Maud, da. of Robert Lovell and widow of Sir Richard Stafford; *d.* from wounds at Beauvais 1435; *s.* by his son [8] HUMPHREY, 8th Earl; *b.* 1429, *d.* 1438; *s.* by his uncle [9] WILLIAM, KG, 9th Earl, *b.* 1417; Warden of Cinque Ports and Constable of Dover Castle: *m.* 1438, Joan, da. of Richard Nevill, Earl of Salisbury and sister of the Kingmaker; *d.* 1487, *s.* by his son [10] THOMAS, KG, KB, 10th Earl, *b.* 1450; *m.* 1464, Margaret Woodville, da. of Richard, 1st Earl Rivers; *d.* 1524; *s.* by his son [11] WILLIAM, KG, KB, 11th Earl, *b. c.* 1476: *m.* 1st, Elizabeth Willoughby, da. of Lord Willoughby de Broke; 2ndly, 1511, Anne Percy, da. of 4th Earl of Northumberland; *d.* 1534; *s.* by his son [12] HENRY, KG, PC, 12th Earl, *b.* 1512; distinguished at taking of Boulogne; Lord Chamberlain 1546-50, High Constable at Coronations of Edward VI and Mary I: *m.* 1st, Catherine Grey, who *d.* 1532, da. of 2nd Marquess of Dorset; 2ndly, 1545, Mary, da. of Sir John Arundell of Lanherne, and widow of Robert Radclyffe, Earl of Sussex; *d.* 1580; *s.* by his grandson [13] PHILIP Howard, 13th Earl (ante).

§[1] JOHN Maltravers, *b.* about 1290; taken prisoner at Bannockburn 1314; Steward of Household to Edward III 1328; summoned to Parliament 1330, by which he is held to be 1st Lord Maltravers; Keeper of Channel Islands 1348: *m.* 1st, Millicent, da. of Maurice Lord Berkeley; 2ndly, Agnes, da. of William de Bereford of Burton, Leics., and widow of (I) Sir John d'Argentine and (ii) Sir John de Nerford; *d.* 1364, when the Barony is held to have fallen into abeyance between the two das. of his son John who *d.* 1349; on the death s.p. of the elder about 1397, the surviving [2] ELEANOR *s.: m.* 1st, John, son of Richard FitzAlan, 3rd Earl of Arundel; 2ndly, 1384, Reynold, 2nd Baron Cobham of Sterborough; *d.* 1405; *s.* by her son [3] JOHN, 3rd Baron, *b.* 1364; not summoned to Parliament: *m.* Elizabeth, da. of Edward, Baron Le Despencer; *d.* 1390; *s.* by his son [4] JOHN Lord Arundel and Maltravers, who *s.* as 6th Earl of Arundel (ante).

** [1] HENRY de Beaumont, younger son of Louis de Brienne and grandson of John de Brienne, King of Jerusalem, came to England *temp.* Edward I. and having secured the favour of that monarch obtained high employment from the crown, was rewarded with large territorial grants and made King of the Isle of Man for life; on Mar. 4, 1309 he was sworn of the Privy Council and summoned to Parliament as a *Baron of England*: he *m.* Alice, da. and heiress of Alexander Comyn, Earl of Buchan, in whose right he became Constable of Scotland and was summoned to Parliament (in right of his wife) 1334; *s.* by his son [2] JOHN, 2nd Baron; summoned to Parliament as a Baron Feb. 25, 1342; *d.* 1342, *s.* by his son [3] HENRY, 3rd Baron; *d.* 1368: *s.* by his son [4] JOHN, *K.G.*, 4th Baron; summoned to Parliament 1383-93; *d.* 1396; *s.* by his son [5] HENRY, 5th Baron; *d.* 1413; *s.* by his son [6] JOHN, *K.G.*, 6th Baron; cr. *Viscount Beaumont* 1440, being the first person honoured with the title of Viscount in England; was Lord High Chamberlain of England; *s.* by his son [7] WILLIAM, 2nd Viscount; *d.* 1507, when the Viscountcy expired and the Barony became abeyant between the descendants of his sister Joane and so continued until 1840, when the abeyance was terminated in favour of [8] MILES THOMAS Stapleton, of Carlton, co. York, 8th Baron; *b.* 1805: *m.* 1844, Isabella Anne, who *d.* 1916, dau. of 3rd Baron Kilmaine; *d.* Aug. 16, 1854; *s.* by his son [9] HENRY, 9th Baron, *b.* 1848; present at battle of Ulundi 1879: *m.* 1888, Violet, *O.B.E.*, who *d.* 1949, only dau. of Frederick Wootton Isaacson, M.P., of 18, Upper Grosvenor Street, W.; *d.* 1892; *s.* by his brother [10] MILES, 10th Baron, *b.* 1850; Lieut.-Col, Comdg. 20th Hussars: *m.* 1893, Ethel Mary, who *d.* 1937, dau. of Sir Charles Henry Tempest. 1st Bt. (*ext.*), of Heaton, Lancashire; *d.* 1895, when the title remained in abeyance between his two daus. until 1896, when it was determined in favour of the el. dau. [11] MONA JOSEPHINE TEMPEST, *OBE*, *b.* 1894: *m.* 1914, the 3rd Baron Howard of Glossop [*,* infra], who *d.* 1972; *d.* 1971; *s.* by her el. son [12] MILES FRANCIS, *CB*, *CBE*, *MC*, 12th Baron, and present peer (also 17th Duke of Norfolk).

†‡† [1] *Lord* EDWARD GEORGE Fitzalan-Howard, *PC*, 2nd son of 13th Duke of Norfolk; *b.* 1818; Vice Chamberlain of HM Household 1846-52, and Dep. Earl Marshal 1861-3; MP for Horsham (*L*) 1848-52, and Arundel 1852-68; cr. *Baron Howard of Glossop* (peerage of UK) 1869: *m.* 1st, 1851, Augusta, who *d.* 1862, only da. and heiress of the Hon. George Henry Talbot [E. Shrewsbury]; 2ndly, 1863, Winifred Mary, who *d.* 1909, da. of Ambrose de Lisle, of Garendon Park, Leics.; *d.* 1883: *s.* by his son [2] FRANCIS EDWARD, 2nd Baron, *b.* 1859: *m.* 1st, 1883, Clara Louisa, who *d.* 1887, da. of the late John Greenwood MP, of Swarcliffe Hall, Ripley, Yorks.; 2ndly, 1891, Hyacinthe, who *d.* 1930, da. of the late William Scott-Kerr, of Chatto and Sunlaws, Roxburghshire; *d.* 1924; *s.* by his son [3] BERNARD EDWARD, *MBE*, 3rd Baron, *b.* 1885: *m.* 1914, Mona Josephine Tempest, *Baroness Beaumont* in her own right, who *d.* 1971 (ante); *d.* 1972; *s.* by his el. son [4] MILES FRANCIS, *CB*, *CBE*, *MC*, 4th Baron and present peer (also 17th Duke of Norfolk).

NORMAN, BARONY OF. (Norman.) [Extinct 1950.]
WIDOW LIVING OF FIRST BARON.
PRISCILLA CECILIA MARIA (WORSTHORNE) (*Baroness Norman*), *C.B.E.*, dau. of the late Maj. Robert Reyntiens, Belgian Artillery [see E. Lindsey and Abingdon, colls.]; is a J.P.: *m.* 1933, the 1st Baron, who *d.* 1950, when the title became ext.; O.B.E. (Civil) 1963. *Residence,*—Aubrey Lodge, Aubrey Rd., W.8.

NORMANBROOK, BARONY OF. (Brook.) [Extinct 1967.]
WIDOW LIVING OF FIRST BARON.
IDA MARY (*Baroness Normanbrook*), (11, The Vale, Chelsea, SW3), da. of Edwyn Alfred Goshawk: *m.* 1929, the 1st Baron, who *d.* 1967, when the title became ext.

NORMANBY, MARQUESS OF. (Phipps.) [Marquess U.K. 1838.]

Rest in virtue.

OSWALD CONSTANTINE JOHN PHIPPS, *CBE*, 4th Marquess; *b.* July 29th, 1912; *s.* 1932; ed. at Eton, and at Ch. Ch., Oxford; late Lt. 5th Bn. Green Howards; Lord-Lt., and Custos Rotulorum of N. Riding of Yorks., 1965-74, since when of N. Yorks. and a K.St.J.; P.P.S. to Sec. of State for Dominion Affairs 1944-45, and to Lord Pres. of the Council June 1945, and a Lord-in-Waiting to H.M. 1945; Hon. LL.D. Durham; 1939-45 War in France (wounded, prisoner, MBE, MBE (Mil) 1943. CBE (Civil) 1974: *m.* 1951, the Hon. Grania Méve Rosaura Guiness, JP, LLD, da. of 1st Baron Moyne, and has issue.

Arms—Quarterly: 1st and 4th sable, a trefoil slipped within an orle of eight mullets argent *Phipps*; 2nd, paly of six argent and azure, a bend gules, *Annesley*; 3rd, the arms of King James II within a border compony ermine and azure (granted to Lady Catherine Darnley). **Crest.**—A bear's paw erased and armed gules, holding a trefoil as in the arms. **Supporters,**—*Dexter*, an unicorn ermine, armed, unguled, crined, and tufted or, and gorged with a chaplet of roses; *Sinister*, a goat ermine, armed and unguled azure, gorged at the dexter.

Seat,—Mulgrave Castle, Whitby, Yorkshire. *Town Residence,*—Argyll House, 211, King's Rd., SW3.

SONS LIVING.
CONSTANTINE EDMUND WALTER (*Earl of Mulgrave*), *b.* Feb. 24th, 1954; ed. at Eton. *Lord* Justin Charles, *b.* 1958.

DAUGHTERS LIVING.
Lady Lepel Sophia, *b.* 1952: *m.* 1975, Richard Kornicki. *Lady* Evelyn Rose, *b.* 1955. *Lady* Peronel Katharine, *b.* 1959. *Lady* Henrietta Laura, *b.* 1962. *Lady* Anne Elizabeth Grania, *b.* 1965.

SISTERS LIVING.
Katharine Mary, *b.* 1905 (does not use courtesy title): *m.* 1949, Roy Amon Harding, who *d.* 1960. *Address,*—c/o Lloyds Bank, 16, St. James's St., S.W.1. *Lady* (Gertrude) Elizabeth, *b.* 1908: *m.* 1934, Adm. Sir William Wellclose Davis, G.C.B., D.S.O., and has issue living, John Henry William (Pen-y-Bang-Ysaf, Nantgaredig, Carmarthen), *b.* 1938: *m.* 1967, Susan Mary, da. of Arthur Hopkins Jones, of Llansannor Court, Cowbridge, Glam., and has issue living, Walter William *b.* 1969,—Hugh Ross, *b.* 1946,—Georgina Elizabeth Laetitia, *b.* 1935: *m.* 1958, Cdr. Leslie Michael Macdonald Saunders Watson, RN, of Rockingham Castle, Market Harborough, Leics. (Culme-Seymour, Bt.), and has issue living, James Michael Ross *b.* 1961, David William Wentworth *b.* 1968, Fiona Jane Liebe *b.* 1965,—Anne Sophia, *b.* 1942: *m.* 1967, Charles David Forgan, of 9, Heath Hurst Rd., NW3, and has issue living, Richard Charles *b.* 1971, Janey Elizabeth *b.* 1973. *Residence,*—Coglan House, Longhope, Glos.

COLLATERAL BRANCHES LIVING.

Grandchildren of the late Lord Henry George Russell Phipps (infra):—
Issue of the late Vivian Louis Augustus Phipps, *b.* 1884, *d.* 1971: *m.* 1921, Marie Elaine, who
d. 1974, da. of G. E. Elliott, of the Logan, Qld.:—
Vivian Henry Blakeney, *b.* 1923: *m.* 1944, Elizabeth Blundell, and has issue living, Hervey Owen
b. 1925: *m.* 1947, Eda Margaret McNab, and has issue living.——Maurine Elaine, *b.* 1921:
m. 1943, James Fitz-Gibbon Hunter, of 43, Lutzow St., Wellers Hill, 4121, Brisbane, Qld.,
and has issue living, Kenneth James, *b.* 1955,—Ross Vivian, *b.* 1961,—Helen Maurine, *b.* 1945:
m. 1966, Anthony Beresford Lewis, AASA, ACIA, and has issue living, Georgia Helen *b.* 1969,
Nicholas Anthony Hunter *b.* 1971,—Barbara Elaine, *b.* 1948: *m.* 1969, Richard Wilfred Armstrong,
BEcon.,—Julie Margaret, *b.* 1952.——Daphne Margaret, *b.* 1929: *m.* 1948, Barry E. Valttila, of 3,
Michele Place, Turramurra, NSW 2074, and has issue living, Christopher Tony, *b.* 1953,—Jan Linda,
b. 1955,—Gaye Helen, *b.* 1964.

Issue of the late Lord Henry George Russell Phipps, 3rd son of 2nd Marquess,
b. 1851, *d.* 1905 : *m.* 1878, Norma, who *d.* 1935, dau. of the late James Leith Hay :—
Laura Elizabeth Minnie (Pacific Sound, 1/17, The Boulevard, Broadbeach, Qld. 4211, Aust.), *b.* 1879:
m. 1897, Arthur Walker, who *d.* 1944, and has issue living, Arthur Henry Tutin (of Logan, Beaudesert,
Queensland), *b.* 1902: *m.* 1927, Maureen Lahey, and has issue living, Laurence Tutin *b.* 1928,
Grahame Tutin *b.* 1932, Keith Tutin *b.* 1934, Fay Maureen *b.* 1939,—Robin Vivian, *b.* 1905: *m.* 1937,
Jessie Isobel Munro,—William Tutin (of Townsvale, Veresdale, Beaudesert, Queensland), *b.* 1913:
m. 1940, Windeyer St. Leger Hayes, and has issue living, William Tutin *b.* 1941, Janet Beatrice
Lucy *b.* 1942,—Russell John Munro (of Merriton, 526, Sandgate Rd., Nundah, Brisbane, Queensland),
b. 1915: *m.* 1948, Eileen May Kenyon, and has issue living, Philip John Russell *b.* 1953, Annette
Leith Hay *b.* 1949,—Colin (11, McLean St., Brighton, Qld., 4017, Aust.), *b.* 1921: *m.* 1st 1949
(m. diss. 1952), Gloria Nightingale Dohring; 2ndly, 1962, Esme Dorothy Nimmo, and has issue living,
(by 1st m.) Christine *b.* 1951, (by 2nd m.) Pauline Dorothy Laura *b.* 1966, Jan Esme Jane *b.* 1968,—
Laura Elizabeth Minnie, *b.* 1898: *m.* 1925, Colin Force Henderson, of Jumboomba, Logan, Queens-
land, and has issue living, Malcolm James *b.* 1927, Elizabeth Ann *b.* 1931, Duncan Lindsay *b.* 1934,—
Ina Mabel Egerton, *b.* 1900: *m.* 1924, Roy Burguez, and has issue living, Noel Dudley (42, Kumbari
Cres., Michelton Heights, Brisbane, Aust. 4053), *b.* 1925: *m.* 19—, Richard Arthur (of 7, Penshurst
St., Willoughby, Sydney, Aust.) *b.* 1928,—Florence Isabel, *b.* 1904: *m.* 1935, Robert Kirke, of
Woollahra, Glen Eagle, Upper Logan, via Beaudesert, Qld., and has issue living, Judith Alice Laura
b. 1936,—Eileen Violet, *b.* 1906: *m.* 1947, Edgar Vincent Brennan.——Norma Cicely Gray, *b.* 1887:
m. 1916, Henry Clement Davidson, who *d.* 1943, and has issue living, Robert Henry, *b.* 1917,—
Alastair Hastings, *b.* 1929,—Donald Geoffrey, *b.* 1931.——Mora, *b.* 1895.——Beatrice Louisa,
b. 1897: *m.* 1919, Raymond Nelson Vaughan Ralfe, and has issue living, Ian Douglas Vaughan,
b. 1921,—Elizabeth Mary Vaughan, *b.* 1923,—Gwenyth Vaughan, *b.* 1926,—Judith Vaughan, *b.* 1929.
Residence,—

(In remainder to the Earldom of Mulgrave).
Grandchildren of the late Maj. Charles Edmund Phipps, son of the late Col. the
Hon. Sir Charles Beaumont Phipps, KCB, 2nd son of 1st Earl of Mulgrave:—
Issue of the late Charles Stewart Phipps, *b.* 1871, *d.* (killed in action during European
War) 1917 : *m.* 1902, Edith Annie Webber, who *d.* 1946, dau. of the late Capt. Francis
Douglas :—
Charles Francis Douglas, *b.* 1905 : *m.* 1935, Kathleen Louise Conlan, and has issue living, John
Douglas Stewart (1109, London St., New Westminster, British Columbia), *b.* 1936: *m.* 1963, Kathleen
May Moore, and has issue living, Karleen Louise *b.* 1964, Kimberly Ann *b.* 1966, Kelly Patricia *b.*
1968. *Residence,—*112, Fifth Av., New Westminster, British Columbia.——Katherine Frances
Harriet, *b.* 1903: *m.* 1930, Alexander Herbert Garvin, who *d.* 1957, and has issue living, Alexander
Geddes (11107-127th St., Edmonton, Alberta, Canada), *b.* 1940: *m.* 1st, 1963 (m. diss. 1970), Marilynn
Hillman; 2ndly, 1971, Katherine Marion Hare, and has issue living (by 2nd m.),—Scott Andrew *b.*
1974, Karen Marie *b.* 1973,—Francis Alexandra, *b.* 1936: *m.* 1956, La Verne Young, of 9312, 114th
St., North Surrey, British Columbia, and has issue living, James Allan *b.* 1958, Susan Leslie *b.* 1960.
*Residence,—*Apart. 205, 6822, Arcola St., Burnaby, BC, Canada.——Sheila Edythe Mary, *b.* 1907:
m. 1933, Ronald E. Kirby Gordon, who *d.* 1973, and has issue living, Charles Douglas, *b.* 1939 (855
Heritage Blvd., N. Vancouver, BC): *m.* 1965, Sheila Carolyn Armstrong, and has issue living, Donald
Stewart, *b.* 1945. *Residence,—*518, W. 24th Av., N. Vancouver, BC.——Emma Doreen Stewart,
b. 1914: *m.* 1st, 1936 (m. diss. 1961), Alvah Robert Hager; 2ndly, 1964, Ian Hugh Doughty
McDiarmid, of 3770, East Blvd., Vancouver, BC, Canada, and has issue living, (by 1st m.) Robert
Stewart, *b.* 1937: *m.* 1961, Judith Frances, da. of Alvin R. Brown, of Vancouver, BC, and has
issue living, Leslie Frances *b.* 1965, Shelley Bronwyn *b.* 1967,—Rosemary Douglas, *b.* 1941:
m. 1966, Roger Phillip Thomas, of Manhattan Beach, Cal., USA, and has issue living, Lisa
Michelle *b.* 1967, Victoria Mary *b.* 1970.

Issue of the late Albert Edmund Phipps, *b.* 1873, *d.* 1945: *m.* 1899, Sydney Florence,
who *d.* 1951, dau. of Washington Boultbee, of Ancaster, Ontario:—
Stewart Beaumont (564, St. Patrick St., Vic., BC, V8S 4X3, Canada), *b.* 1900: *m.* 1st, 1921, Frances
Peacey Brown-Constable, who *d.* 1951; 2ndly, 1952, Edith Patricia Allison, da. of the late Dr.
Allison Smith, and has issue living, (by 2nd m.) Barbara Phyllis, *b.* 1923: *m.* 1946, Thomas H.
Gordon,—Diana Averill, *b.* 1937: *m.* 1958, Willem Otto Jan Groeneveld Meijer (PO Box 634,
Tuxedo Park, NY, USA),—(by 2nd m.) Geoffrey Allison, (1982, Haultain St., Vic., BC, V8R 2L5,
Canada), *b.* 1953: *m.* 1973, Leslie Elizabeth, da. of Douglas D. Clarke, of Vic., BC.——Norman
Ernest, QC (717, Eglinton Av. West, Toronto M5N 1C9, Ont.); *b.* 1907: *m.* 1944, Dorothy, da. of the
late Albert Edward Kendal-Quarry, and has issue living, David, *b.* 1945, Penelope *b.* 1948: *m.* 1972,
Barry E. Tobias.——Phyllis Lepel, *b.* 1902: *m.* 1925, David Eric Cumberland, who *d.* 1964, and has
issue living, David Keith *b.* 1930: *m.* 19—, Mary Fenn.——Ruth Audrey, *b.* 1910. *Residence,—*

Issue of the late Augustus Henry Constantine Phipps, *b.* 1882, *d.* 1946: *m.* 1909, Agnes
Fraser who *d.* 1971, da. of the late Murdoch Maclachlan, of Kilmun, Scotland:—
Charles Norman (of 405, Russell Hill Rd., Toronto, 7, Ontario), *b.* 1912: *m.* 1940, Margaret Patricia,
da. of George F. Saunders, of W. Vancouver, British Columbia.——Harriet Patricia, *b.* 1914: *m.*
1942, William Henry Brown, who *d.* 1971, and has issue living, John Arthur, *b.* 1943,—Margaret
Evelyn, *b.* 1945: *m.* 1965, Michael Barclay John Shannon, and has issue living, Michael William
b. 1965.

Grandchildren of the late Sir Constantine Edmund Henry Phipps, K.C.M,G;;
C.B., son of the late Hon. Edmund Phipps, 3rd son of 1st Earl of Mulgrave:—
Issue of the late Rt. Hon. Sir Eric Clare Edmund Phipps, G.C.B., G.C.M.G., G.C.V.O., *b.* 1875,
d. 1945: *m.* 1st, 1907, Yvonne, who *d.* 1909, dau. of the late Comte de Louvencourt, of 94,
Rue de Courcelles, Paris; 2ndly, 1911, Frances (*Lady Phipps*), (Yew Tree Cottage, Wilcot,
Pewsey, Wilts.), da. of the late Herbert Ward:—
(By 2nd m.) Mervyn Constantine Sanford (10, rue Casimir Périer, Fontainebleau, France; Cavalry
Club), *b.* 1912; ed. at Harrow and New Coll., Oxford (BA); Hon. Lt.-Col. late 7th Queen's Own
Hussars; 1939-45 War (Croix de Guerre with Palm); Mil. Attaché to Mexico and Central America
1946: *m.* 1941, Joyce Kathleen, da. of the late John Patrick Goode, and has issue living, Magdalene
Frances, *b.* 1942: *m.* 1970, Fergus Rogers,—Caroline Mary, *b.* 1943: *m.* 1965, Josep Vives i López, of
40, Maria Christina, Tarragona, and has issue living, Alexandre Constantine *b.* 1968, Catalina Rosa
b. 1965, Lucieta *b.* 1967, Marina *b.* 1974,—Elizabeth Helen, *b.* 1945,—Dorothy Charlotte, *b.* 1950,—
Mary Ann, *b.* 1953: *m.* 1973, Nicholas Fforde, and has issue living, Emily Frances *b.* 1973, Soph
Veronica *b.* 1974.——John Francis, *b.* 1933: *m.* 1956, Charm Alys, yr. da. of Eric Quick, of Londo
and has issue living, Jonathan Eric, *b.* 1957,—Anna-Rose, *b.* 1959,—Isabel Emma, *b.* 1961.—
William Anthony Dominic (31, Chepstow Villas, W11), *b.* 1936; late Able Seaman, RCN: *m.* 19
Henrietta Frances, da. of the late Henry Taylor Lamb, MC, RA [see E. Longford], and has issue livi

Frederick Fabian Aeneas, *b.* 1961,—Samuel Cornelius Dominic, *b.* 1964,—Lucian Percy Denis, *b.* 1966,—Theresa Pansy Frances, *b.* 1963.——Mary, *b.* 1923: *m.* 1949, Bonar Sykes, son of the late Maj.-Gen. the Rt. Hon. Sir Frederick Hugh Sykes, GCSI, GCIE, GBE, KCB, CMG, and has issue living, Hugh Bonar, *b.* 1950,—David Eric, *b.* 1953,—James Richard, *b.* 1956,—Alan Geoffrey, *b.* 1960. *Residence,*—Conock Manor, nr. Devizes, Wilts.——Margaret Ann, *b.* 1925: *m.* 1949, George Anthony Cary, who *d.* 1953; 2ndly, 1956, Donald Struan Robertson, Emeritus Professor of Greek, Camb. Univ., who *d.* 1961, and has issue living, (by 1st m.) Christopher Alexander George, *b.* 1950; ed. at Westminster, and Trin. Coll., Camb.: *m.* 1973, Joanna Buczkowska. *Residence,*—37, Madingley Rd., Cambridge.

Grandchildren of the late Rt. Hon. Sir Eric Clare Edmund Phipps, G.C.B., G.C.M.G., G.C.V.O. (ante):—

Issue of the late Lieut. Alan Phipps, R.N., *b.* 1915, *d.* (killed in action at Leros) 1943: *m.* 1940, the Hon. Veronica Nell Fraser (*Hon. Lady Maclean*) [who *m.* 2ndly, 1946, Sir Fitzroy Hew Royle Maclean, CBE, 1st Bt. (cr. 1957)], da. of 15th Lord Lovat:—
Jeremy Julian Joseph, *b.* 1942: *m.* 1974, Susan, da. of Lt.-Cdr. Wilfrid Crawford, RN, of Huntington, Haddington, E. Lothian.——Susan Rose, *b.* 1941: *m.* 1st, 1959, Richard St. Clair de la Mare; 2ndly, 1968, Derek Marlowe, of 71, Victoria Rd., W8, and has issue living (by 1st m.) Caspar James, *b.* 1962,—Adam John, *b.* 1964,—Laura Frances Albinia, *b.* 1960,—Selina-Rose, *b.* 1963.

PREDECESSORS.—[1] CONSTANTINE Phipps; cr. *Baron Mulgrave,* of New Ross, co. Wexford (peerage of Ireland) 1767; *d.* 1775; *s.* by his el. son [2] CONSTANTINE JOHN, *P.C.,* 2nd Baron; Capt. R.N.; went a voyage with a view to discover a N.E. passage; sat as M.P. for Newark; was Joint Paymaster of the Forces, and Lord of Trade Commn. for Indian Affairs; cr. *Baron Mulgrave,* of Mulgrave, co. York (peerage of Great Britain) 1790; *d.* without male issue 1792, when the English barony became extinct, and the Irish peerage devolved upon his brother [3] HENRY, *G.C.B.,* 3rd Baron; was a Gen. in the Army, Col. 31st Foot, and Lord-Lieut. of E. Riding of York, Chancellor of Duchy of Lancaster, Sec. of State for Foreign Affairs, and First Lord of the Admiralty; cr. *Baron Mulgrave,* of Mulgrave, co. York (peerage of Great Britain) 1794, and *Viscount Normanby* and *Earl of Mulgrave* (peerage of United Kingdom) 1812; *d.* 1831; *s.* by his son [4] CONSTANTINE HENRY, *K.G., G.C.B.,* 2nd Earl; *b.* 1797; a distinguished statesman and diplomatist; was Gov.-Gen. of Jamaica 1832-4, Lord Privy Seal 1834, Lord-Lieut. of Ireland 1835-9, Sec. of State for the Colonies 1839, and for the Home Depart. 1839-41, and Ambassador to France 1846-52, and to Court of Tuscany 1854-8; cr. *Marquess of Normanby* (peerage of United Kingdom) 1838: *m.* 1818, the Hon. Maria Liddell, dau. of 1st Baron Ravensworth; *d.* 1863; *s.* by his son [5] GEORGE AUGUSTUS CONSTANTINE, *P.C., G.C.B., G.C.M.G.,* 2nd Marquess, *b.* 1819; sat as M.P. for Scarborough (*L*) 1847-51, and 1852-8; was successively Gov. of Nova Scotia, Queensland, New Zealand, and Victoria: *m.* 1844, Laura, who *d.* 1885, dau. of the late Capt. Robert Russell, R.N.; *d.* 1890; *s.* by his el. son [6] *Rev.* CONSTANTINE CHARLES HENRY, 3rd Marquess; *b.* 1846; V. of St. Mark's, Worsley, 1872-90, and Canon of St. George's Chapel, Windsor 1891-1907: *m.* 1903, Gertrude Stansfeld, *O.B.E.,* who *d.* 1948, younger dau. and co-heiress of the late Johnston J. Foster, of Moor Park, Ludlow; *d.* 1932; *s.* by his son [7] OSWALD CONSTANTINE JOHN, 4th Marquess and present peer; also Earl of Mulgrave, Viscount Normanby, and Baron Mulgrave.
The Annesley and Darnley quarterings came to this family by the marriage of William Phipps to Lady Catherine Annesley, da. and heir of 3rd Earl of Anglesey, by his wife, Lady Catherine Darnley (Duchess of Buckingham), nat. da. of James II by Catherine Sedley, Countess of Dorchester. William and Lady Catherine Phipps were the parents of 1st Baron Mulgrave.

NORMAND, BARONY OF. (Normand.) [Extinct 1962.]

DAUGHTER LIVING OF LIFE PEER. (*By 1st marriage.*)

Hon. Patricia Drake, *b.* 1917: *m.* 1948, Douglas William Gourlay, and has issue. *Residence,*—Craigmuie, Moniaive, Thornhill, Dumfriesshire.

WIDOW LIVING OF SON OF LIFE PEER.

Elizabeth Ann (*Hon. Mrs. William Normand*), (38, Westminster Gdns., SW1), da. of James Cumming, of Deneholm, Biggar, Lanarkshire: *m.* 1945, the Hon. William Normand, who *d.* 1967, and has issue.

NORMANTON, EARL OF. (Agar.) Sits as BARON SOMERTON (U.K. 1873.) [Earl I. 1806.]

The beaten path is the safe path.

SHAUN JAMES CHRISTIAN WELBORE ELLIS AGAR, 6th Earl of Normanton, and 9th Baron Mendip; *b.* Aug. 21st, 1945; *s.* 1967; ed. at Eton, Capt. Blues and Royals; patron of three livings: *m.* 1970, Victoria Susan, only da. of John H. C. Beard, of Hookswood, Farnham, Wimborne, Dorset.

&rms,—Azure, a lion rampant or. Crest,—A demi-lion rampant or. Supporters,—Two lions, the *dexter* per bend, and the *sinister* per bend sinister, or and azure, both plain collared and chained gules, each charged on the shoulder with a crescent.

Seat,—Somerley, Ringwood, Hampshire. *Residence,*—41, Sussex Sq., W2.

BROTHER LIVING.

Hon. MARK SIDNEY ANDREW (30, Cheyne Court, Flood St., SW3 5TR), *b.* Sept. 2nd, 1948; ed. at Gordonstoun; Lt. Blues & Royals: *m.* 1973, Rosemary, da. of Maj. Philip Marnham.

AUNTS LIVING. (*Daughters of 4th Earl.*)

Lady Caroline Amy Cora, *b.* 1899. *Residence,*—Little Park, Ibsley, Ringwood, Hants., BH24 3PP.
Lady Mary Karen, *b.* 1901: *m.* 1925, Lieut.-Com. Herbert Ernest Pretyman, R.N. (retired), from whom she obtained a divorce 1945 [E. Bradford], and has issue living, John Ernest, *b.* 1929,—Anthea Karen, *b.* 1927. *Residence,*—2231, California Street, N.W., Washington, D.C., U.S.A.
Lady Amy Louise (*Amy, Baroness Biddulph*), *b.* 1905; is a CStJ: *m.* 1925, the 3rd Baron Biddulph, who *d.* 1972. *Residence,*—Under Down, Ledbury, Herefordshire.
Lady Rosemary Beatrice, *b.* 1908: *m.* 1931, Capt. Christopher John Darell Jeffreys, M.V.O., Grenadier Guards, who *d.* (killed in action during European War) 1940, only son of 1st Baron Jeffreys. *Residence,*—Chapel Cottage, Bentworth, Alton, Hants.

WIDOW LIVING OF FIFTH EARL.

Lady FIONA (*Fiona, Countess of Normanton*), (North End Park, Harbridge, Ringwood, Hants.), da. of 4th Marquess Camden: *m.* 1st, 1931, Maj. Sir (John) Gerard Henry Fleetwood Fuller, 2nd Bt., from whom she obtained a divorce 1944; 2ndly, 1944, the 5th Earl, who *d.* 1967.

COLLATERAL BRANCH LIVING.

Issue of the late Hon. **Francis William Arthur Agar, 4th son of 3rd Earl,** *b.* **1873,** *d.* **1936 :** *m.* **1897, Laura Astley, who** *d.* **1960, dau. of the late Henry Kennard, of** Shopwyke House, Chichester :—

Muriel Violet Frances, *b.* 1899: *m.* 1921, Rear-Adm. William Scott Chalmers, CBE, DSC, who *d.* 1971, and has issue living, David Quinton, *b.* 1922; 1942-45 War as Fl. Lt. RAF,—Roderick Francis, *RN*, *b.* 1928; is Lt.-Com. *Residence,*—Guessens, 7, Coach Hill, Titchfield, Hants.

PREDECESSORS.—[1] CHARLES Agar, *D.D.,* 3rd son of Henry Agar, M.P., and younger brother of James, 1st Viscount Clifden, was successively Dean of Kilmore, Bishop of Cloyne, Archbishop of Cashel, and Archbishop of Dublin and Primate of Ireland; cr. *Baron Somerton* (peerage of Ireland) 1795, *Viscount Somerton* 1800, and *Earl of Normanton* (peerage of Ireland) **1806;** *d.* **1809;** *s.* by his son [2] WELBORE ELLIS, 2nd Earl; *b.* 1778: *m.* 1816, Diana, dau. of 11th Earl of Pembroke; *d.* 1868; *s.* by his son [3] JAMES CHARLES HERBERT WELBORE ELLIS, **3rd Earl,** *b.* 1818 ; M.P. for Wilton 1841-52: *m.* 1856, the Hon. Caroline Susan Augusta, who *d.* 1915, dau. of 6th Viscount Barrington; *d.* 1896 ; *s.* by his el. surviving son [4] SIDNEY JAMES, **4th Earl ;** *b.* 1865 : *m.* 1894, Lady Amy Frederica Alice Byng, who *d.* 1961, dau. of 4th Earl of Strafford ; *d.* 1933 ; *s.* by his only son [5] EDWARD JOHN SIDNEY CHRISTIAN WELBORE ELLIS **5th Earl;** *b.* 1910: *m.* 1st, 1937, the Hon. Barbara Mary (PRIOR-PALMER), from whom he obtained a divorce 1943; 2ndly, 1944, Lady Fiona, da. of 4th Marquess of Camden, and formerly wife of Maj. Sir (John) Gerard Henry Fleetwood Fuller, 2nd Bt.; *d.* 1967; *s.* by his son [6] SHAUN JAMES CHRISTIAN WELBORE ELLIS, 6th Earl and present peer; also Viscount and Baron Somerton, and Baron Mendip [see *⁎* infra].

⁎ [1] *Rt. Hon.* WELBORE Ellis, *FRS, MP,* only surv. son of the Most Rev. Welbore Ellis, Bishop of Meath, was Sec. at War 1762-65, Treas. of the Navy 1777-82, and Sec. of State for America and the Colonies 1782; cr. 1794, *Baron Mendip,* of Mendip, Somerset (peerage of Great Britain) with re- mainder to the three el. sons of his sister Anne by her husband, Henry Agar, of Gowran: *m.* 1st, 1747, Elizabeth, who *d.* 1761, da. and heir of the Hon. Sir William Stanhope, KB; 2ndly, 1765, Anne, who *d.* 1803, sister and heir of the Rt. Hon. Hans Stanley; *d.* 1802; *s.* by his gt.-nephew [2] HENRY WELBORE Agar-Ellis 2nd Viscount Clifden, whose father, James Agar, MP, son of Anne (ante) was Postmaster Gen. of Ireland, and was cr. *Baron Clifden,* of Gowran, co. Kilkenny (peerage of Ireland) 1776, and *Viscount Clifden,* of Gowran (peerage of Ireland) 1781; *b.* 1761; MP for co. Kilkenny 1783-89; assumed the surname of Ellis by Roy. licence 1804: *m.* 1792, Lady Caroline Spencer, who *d.* 1813, da. of 4th Duke of Marlborough; his only son, George James Welbore Agar-Ellis, FRS, MP, was cr. *Baron Dover* (peerage of UK) 1831: *m.* 1822, Lady Georgina Howard, who *d.* 1860, da. of 6th Earl of Carlisle; predeceased him in 1833; *d.* 1836; *s.* by his grandson [3] HENRY, 3rd Viscount, *b.* 1825, who had *s.* his father in 1833 as 2nd Baron Dover; Gentleman of the Privy Chamber to the Prince Consort: *m.* 1861, Eliza Horatia Frederica, *VA* (Lady of the Bedchamber to Queen Victoria), who *d.* 1896, da. of Frederick Charles William Seymour; *d.* 1866; *s.* by his only son [4] HENRY GEORGE, 4th Viscount; *b.* 1863; *d.* unm. 1895; *s.* by his uncle [5] LEOPOLD GEORGE FREDERICK, 5th Viscount, *b.* 1829; MP for Kilkenny (L) 1857-74: *m.* 1864, the Hon. Harriet Stonor, who *d.* 1914, da. of 3rd Baron Camoys; *d.* 1899, when the Barony of Dover became ext., and the other honours passed to his kinsman [6] THOMAS CHARLES Agar-Robartes, 2nd Baron Robartes [son and heir of Thomas James Agar-Robartes, who was cr. *Baron Robartes,* of Lanhydrock and Truro, Cornwall 1869, son of the Hon. Charles Bagenal-Agar (who *m.* 1804, Anna Maria Hunt, heiress of Lanhydrock, great-niece of Henry Robartes 3rd Earl of Radnor, Viscount Bodmin, and Baron Robartes of Truro, all of which titles became ext. 1757) yst. son of 1st Viscount Clifden], 6th Viscount, *b.* 1844; Lord- Lieut. of Cambs. 1906-15, and MP for Cornwall, E. (L) 1880-82: *m.* 1878, Mary, who *d.* 1921, da. of the late Francis Henry Dickinson, of Kingweston, Som.; *d.* 1930; *s.* by his 2nd son [7] FRANCIS GERALD, *KCVO,* 7th Viscount, *b.* 1883; Counsellor of Embassy, Madrid 1926-27, a Member of Council, Duchy of Cornwall 1939-52, and a Lord-in-Waiting to HM 1940-45; *d.* 1966; *s.* by his brother [8] ARTHUR VICTOR, *MC,* 8th Viscount, *b.* 1887; Lt. Gren. Gds.; acting Maj. Gds. Machine Gun Regt. in 1914-18 War: *m.* 1st, 1920 (m. diss. 1945), Patience Mary, who *d.* 1956, da. of Arthur Francis Basset [Salusbury-Trelawny, Bt.]; 2ndly, 1948, Margaret, da. of Ray Carter of St. Louis, USA, formerly wife of John Harvey Thursky, and widow of John Eaton Monins; *d.* 1974, when the Viscountcy and Barony of Clifden, and the Barony of Robartes became ext., and the Barony of Mendip devolved upon [9] SHAUN JAMES CHRISTIAN WELBORE ELLIS Agar, 6th Earl of Normanton (ante).

Norreys of Rycote, Lord, son of Earl of Lindsey and Abingdon.

NORRIE, BARON. (Norrie.) [Baron U.K. 957.]

(CHARLES) WILLOUGHBY (MOKE) NORRIE, *G.C.M.G., G.C.V.O., C.B., D.S.O., M.C.,* 1st Baron, son of the late Major George Edward Moke Norrie ; *b.* Sept. 26th, 1893; ed. at Eton; Lt. Gen. late 11th Hussars, and 10th R. Hussars, and Hon. Col. 10th Inf. Btn. (The Adelaide Rifles); Member of Nat. Hunt Cttee. since 1935, and Jockey Club 1969; 1914-18 War with Cav., Inf., and Tank Corps (four times wounded, des- patches twice, MC and Bar, DSO), 1939-42 War in Middle East (CB); commanded 10th R. Hussars 1930-34, 1st Armoured Div. 1940, and 30th Corps 1941-42; Gov. of S. Australia 1944-52, and Gov.-Gen. and Com.in-Ch. of New Zealand 1952-57, Pres. of Com-

God provides for us.

bined Cavalry " Old Comrades " 1959-68, and Chancellor of Order of St. Michael and St. George 1960-68; a KStJ, and a Fellow of Roy. So. of Arts; *cr.* DSO 1919, CB (Mil.) 1942, KCMG 1944, GCMG 1952, GCVO 1954, and *Baron Norrie,* of Wellington, NZ, and of Upton, co. Gloucester (peerage of United Kingdom) 1957: *m.* 1st, 1921, Jocelyn Helen, who *d.* 1938, da. of the late Richard Henry Gosling [Dyer, Bt.]; 2ndly, 1938, Patricia Merryweather (a DStJ), da. of the late Emerson Bainbridge, MP, and has issue by 1st and 2nd marriages.

Arms.—Quarterly : 1st and 4th, ermine on a pale gules three helmets argent *Norris*; 2nd and 3rd, or on a chevron azure between two poplar trees eradicated in chief proper and a mullet of six points in base of the second a key the ward downwards of the first *Moke*. **Crests,**—An elephant's head erased sable tusked argent supporting with the trunk a garb or ; 2nd, a stag's head couped holding in the mouth a branch of poplar proper between the attires a key as in the arms pendent from a chain or. **Supporters,**—On either side a dark bay racehorse supporting between the forelegs a frond of New Zealand fern proper.
Residence,—The Ham, Wantage, Oxon. *Club,*—Cavalry.

SONS LIVING. (By 1st marriage.)

Hon. GEORGE WILLOUGHBY MOKE, *b.* April 27th, 1936; ed. at Eton; Maj. (ret.) R. Hussars; ADC to C.-in-C. Middle East Command 1961-62; GSO3 (Int.) 4th Guards Bde. 1967-69; Partner Fairfield Nurseries, Hermitage, Newbury: *m.* 1964, Celia Marguerite, da. of Maj. John Pelham Mann, MC [see Mann, Bt., Colls.], and has issue living, Mark Willoughby John, *b.* 1972,—Clare Marguerite, *b.* 1966,—Julia Jocelyn, *b.* 1968. *Residence,*—Henwick Old Farm, Newbury, Berks. *Clubs,*—Cavalry, MCC.

(By 2nd marriage.)

Hon. Guy Bainbridge (21, Radipole Rd., SW6 5DN; Cavalry Club), *b.* 1940; ed. at Eton; Maj. R. Hussars; GSO 3 HQ 1st Br. Corps 1966-67; Adjt. 10th R. Hussars 1967-69; GSO 3 HQ Far East Command 1969-71, RN Staff Coll. 1971; GSO 2 Min. of Defence (Directorate of Army Training) 1973-74: *m.* 1968, Sarah Georgina, da. of Maj. George Rudolph Hanbury Fielding, DSO [see E. Denbigh, colls.], and has issue living, Andrew Guy, *b.* 1970,—James Adam George, *b.* 1973.

DAUGHTERS LIVING. (By 1st marriage.)

Hon. Rosemary, *b.* 1926: *m.* 1959, Capt. Francis Humphrey Maurice FitzRoy Newdegate [see V. Daventry]. *Residence,*—Temple House, Arbury, Nuneaton, Warwickshire.

(By 2nd marriage.)

Hon. Sarah Merryweather, *b.* 1943; GGSM: *m.* 1974, Charles Lyon Stephenson, TD, of The Cottage, Great Longstone, Bakewell, Derbys. [see Stephenson, Bt., colls.].
Hon, Annabel Mary Adelaide (124, Swan Court, Chelsea Manor St., SW3), *b.* 1945.

North Lord, son of Earl of Guilford

NORTH, BARONY OF. (North.) [Baron E. 1554.] [Abeyant 1942.]

JOHN DUDLEY NORTH, 13th Baron ; Lieut. R.N.; *d.* (killed in action during European War) 1941, when the Barony fell into abeyance [see infra].

SISTERS LIVING OF THIRTEENTH BARON. (Co-heiresses to the Barony; raised to the rank of a Baron's daughters 1947.)

Hon. DOROTHY ANNE, *b.* May 4th, 1915 : *m.* 1st, 1937 (marriage dissolved 1950), William Robert Alexander Clive Graham, Lieut. Sherwood Foresters; 2ndly, 1950, Major John Edward Richard Bowlby, 1st Roy. Dragoons [see V. Valentia], and has issue living, (by 1st marriage) Penelope Virginia, *b.* 1940,—(by 2nd m.) [see V. Valentia]. *Residence,*—38, Burnsall St., SW3.
Hon. SUSAN SILENCE, *b.* Jan. 19th, 1920; assumed by deed poll 1943 the additional surname of Beauchamp : *m.* 1944, Frederick Guy Beauchamp, M.D., M.R.C.S., and has issue living, Susan Donne, *b.* 1944: *m.* 1965 (m. diss. 1969), the Hon. Nicholas Charles Cavendish, el. son of 5th Baron Chesham,—Sally North, *b.* 1945: *m.* 1966, Michael Robert Parkin, of 2, Charles St., W1,—Elizabeth Silence, *b.* 1950. *Residence,*—119, Harley St., W1.

MOTHER LIVING OF THIRTEENTH BARON.

Dorothy Catherine, dau. of the late Capt. J. P. Donne, 6th Dragoon Guards : *m.* 1914, the Hon. Dudley William John North, MC, who *d.* 1936. *Residence,*—

WIDOW LIVING OF THIRTEENTH BARON.

MARGARET, dau. of R. W. H. Glennie, of Cape Province, S. Africa : *m.* 1st, 1940, the 13th Baron, who *d.* (killed in action during European War) 1941; 2ndly, 1943, Lieut. Weldon Bernard James, U.S. Marine Corps. *Resides* in U.S.A.

COLLATERAL BRANCHES LIVING.

Issue of the late Hon. Roger Archibald Percy North, 2nd son of 11th Baron, *b.* 1863, *d.* 1907: *m.* 1896, Robina Ramsay Walker, who *d.* 1937, dau. of the late Edwin Barton, of Wallerawang, N.S. Wales :—
Roger Edward Francis Guilford, *b.* 1897: ed. at Harrow ; Lieut.-Col., late King's Roy. Rifle Corps, Indian Army, and Pakistan Army; European War 1914-18, Waziristan 1922, Waziristan 1937-39, European War 1939-45 : *m.* 1st, 1927 Audrey Edith Durani (who *d.* 1957, having obtained a divorce 1937), dau. of the late Mr. Justice (Alfred Edward) Martineau ; 2ndly, 1939, Isabel Floyd-Jones Carpender Burn, dau. of the late Noel Lispenard Carpender, of Long Island, U.S.A., and has issue living, (by 1st m.) Roger Robin, *b.* 1929; ed. at King's Sch., Canterbury, late Lt. RASC and King's African Rifles: *m.* 1961, Gillian Mary, yr. da. of the late Lt.-Col. William Augustus Putnam,—Desmond Peter (twin) (The Orchard, Hale St., East Peckham, Tonbridge), *b.* 1929; ed. at King's Sch., Canterbury; late Lt. RASC; with Colonial Admin. Ser., N. Nigeria 1951-55: *m.* 1960, Amanda Mary, yr. da. of P. H. B. Legge, and has issue living, Rupert Caspar Guilford, *b.* 1964, Jason Edward Guilford *b.* 1967, Emma Sophie *b.* 1962,—Neil Dermot (*Resides* in USA), *b.* 1932; ed. at King's Sch., Canterbury; an Antique Dealer,—(by 2nd m.) Edward John, *b.* 1940; ed. at Fettes Coll.: *m.* 1967, Margreth Ekstrom, of Spanga, Sweden, and has issue living, Tom Nicholas *b.* 1971, Peter James *b.* 1974. *Residence,*—The Cottage, Manor Farm, Hilton, Blandford, Dorset, DT11 0DE.——William Frederic George, *b.* 1898; Cdr. (ret.) RN; 1914-19 War; 1939-45 War: *m.* 1st, 1924, the Hon. Dorothy Hennessy (who *d.* 1961, and from whom he had obtained a divorce 1949), da. of 1st Baron Windlesham; 2ndly, 1949, Joan Mabel, da. of the late Henry Reginald Fussell, of Southey Hall, Great Bookham, Surrey, and widow of Wing-Cdr. Richard Griffith Shaw, of Littlecot, Bartley, Hants., and has issue living, (by 1st m.) Moylena Robin, *b.* 1925,—Diana Bridget, *b.* 1928: *m.* 1954, Lt.-Col. Michel Edward Ovans, MC, from whom sge obtained a divorce 1958,—(by 2nd m.) William Simon Giles, *b.* 1950,—Jeremy Frederic George, *b.* 1952. *Residence,*—Luzborough House, Romsey, Hants.

Grandsons of the late Hon. Mina Susan Georgina North (infra) :—
Issue of the late Dudley Francis North FitzGerald, *b.* 1891, *d.* 1960 : *m.* 1921, Hermine, who *d.* 1955, dau. of the late George Kiely, of Toronto :—

Michael Francis, *b.* 1921; ed. at Dartmouth Coll.; Lt.-Cdr. RN; 1939-45 War: *m.* 1943, Anne Lise, da. of the late Einar Winther, of Copenhagen, and has issue living, Robin Michael (33, Haverfield Gdns., Kew, Richmond, Surrey), *b.* 1944; ed. at Downside: *m.* 1969, Alessandra Lyn, da. of Cecil Davis, of Richmond, Surrey, and has issue living, James Dudley *b.* 1972, Sarah Emily *b.* 1974,—Christopher Francis (24, Bernard Gdns., SW19), *b.* 1945; ed. at Downside, and Lincoln Coll., Oxford (MA): *m.* 1968, Jennifer Georgina, da. of George S. Willis, of Yeovil, Som. and has issue living, Matthew Francis *b.* 1973,—Mary Anne Lise, *b.* 1961,—Emma Theresa *b.* 1967. *Residence,*—13, The Park, Yeovil, Som.——Gerald Dudley (167, Nolan House, Queens Park, Stockton-on-Tees, Cleveland), *b.* 1922; ed. at Dartmouth Coll.; 1939-45 War in RN and as Pilot RAF: *m.* 1956, Doreen, who *d.* 1969, da. of the late Alexander Spence Muter, of Middlesbrough, and has issue living, Susan Hermine, *b.* 1957.

Issue of the late Hon. Mina Susan Georgina North, el. dau. of 11th Baron, *b.* 1865, *d.* 1930, having *m.* 1889, Francis John FitzGerald, C.B.E., LL.B., Bar.-at-law, who *d.* 1939:—

John Sidney North, *C.V.O.*, *M.B.E.*, *M.C.*, *b.* 1893; ed. at Eton; Col. late Comdg. Irish Guards; Gentleman Usher to HM 1953-67, since when an Extra Gentleman Usher; 1914-18 War (despatches, MC), Russia 1919-20 (MBE), 1939-45 War; MBE (Mil.) 1919, CVO 1963: *m.* 1933, Joyce Mary (from whom he obtained a divorce 1948), da. of the late Dr. Edward Williams Hedley, MBE, of 18, St. Leonards Terr., SW3, and widow of Thomas Cecil Barber [see Barber, Bt., colls.], and has issue living, Georgiana Mary, *b.* 1935: *m.* 1956, John Kenneth Humphrey Pettit, of Stepstones, Scotlands Close, Haslemere, Surrey, and has issue living, Timothy John *b.* 1959, Richard Kenneth *b.* 1963, Nicola Susan Mary *b.* 1957. *Residence,*—24, Chelsea Sq., SW3. *Club,*—Guards'.—Winifrede Marie, *b.* 1890.

Grandchildren of the late Hon. Christina Philippa Agnes Spence, O.B.E. (formerly Benyon) (infra):—
Issue of the late Capt. Thomas Yates Benyon, *b.* (posthumous) 1893, *d.* 1958 : *m.* 1st, 1918, Louise (from whom he obtained a divorce 1928), dau. of J. J. Wicht, of Cape Town ; 2ndly, 1934, Joan Ida Bishop (of Wroxton House, 6, Gillsland Road, Edinburgh, 10), dau. of John Bayley Walters :—
(By 1st m.) John Wicht (9, Avenue Alexandra, Sea Point, Cape Town), *b.* 1921 (MA, BSoc Sc): *m.* 1966, Joan, da. of E. Robertson, of Little Brak, S. Africa, and has issue living, Kendal, *b.* 1968.——
(by 2nd m.) Thomas Yates (The Old Rectory, Adstock, Winslow, Bucks., MK18 2HY; Guards' Club), *b.* 1942; ed. at Wellington Sch., and RMA; late Lt. Scots Gds. ; a banker: *m.* 1968, Olivia Jane, yr. da. of Humphrey Scott-Plummer, of Mainhouse, Kelso, and has issue living, Thomas Yates, *b.* 1975,—Clare Julia Yates, *b.* 1969,—Camilla Lucinda Joan Yates, *b.* 1972.——Sarah Joan Yates, *b.* 1935: *m.* 1st 1956 (m. diss. 1967), Roy Ramsey; 2ndly, 1967, Andrew Harrison, and has issue living, (by 1st m.) David Andrew, *b.* 1969,—Deborah Jacqueline, *b.* 1958,—(by 2nd m.) Rachel Sarah, *b.* 1970.——Belinda Jane Yates, *b.* 1939: *m.* 1966, John Douglas Lennie, of 57, Merchiston Cres., Edinburgh, 10, and has issue living, Joanna Yates, *b.* 1966,—Rosalind Benson *b.* 1969.

Issue of the late Hon. Christina Phillipa Agnes North, O.B.E., youngest dau. of 11th Baron, *b.* 1869, *d.* 1950 : *m.* 1st, 1890, Capt. Thomas Yates Benyon, formerly 4th Hussars, who *d.* 1893 ; 2ndly, 1903, Col. Alexander Heirom Ogilvy Spence, C.I.E., C.B.E., formerly Indian Army, who *d.* 1936 :—
(By 2nd m.) Christa Marie Margaret Ogilvy, *b.* 1907: *m.* 1928, Col. Noel Stanley Alington, MC, late Indian Army, and Foreign and Political Dept., India, and has issue living, James Giles Roger (46, Atholl Rd., Camps Bay, Cape Province, S. Africa), *b.* 1929: *m.* 1960, Jean Vosloo, da. of Thomas Bell, of Salisbury, Rhodesia, and has issue living, Julian Giles *b.* 1963. *Residence,*—La Gratitude, de Villiers Rd., Somerset West, Cape Province, S. Africa.

Grandson of the late Charles North, el. son of the late Frederick North, grandson of the late Fountain North, grandson of the late Hon. Roger North, youngest son of 4th Baron North:—
Issue of the late Frederick Keppel North, *b.* 1860; *d.* 1948: *m.* 1898, Grace, who *d.* 1946, dau. of the late Gen. the Hon. Sir Percy Robert Basil Feilding, K.C.B. [B. Denbigh, colls.]:—
Roger, *b.* 1901; ed. at Eton, and at Trin. Coll., Camb. (LLB, MA); Bar. Inner Temple 1925; is a JP (formerly Chm. of Norfolk Quarter Sessions; a Recorder of the Crown Court since 1972): *m.* 1934, Pamela Susan, da. of the Rev. Henry William Leycester O'Rorke, of The Manor House, N. Litchfield, Hants., and has issue living, Thomas Frederick, *b.* 1942: *m.* 1974, Sally Catherine, da. of the late Lt.-Col. G. M. Strover, of Leigh Delamere House, Leigh Delamere, Chippenham, Wilts.,—Valerie Susan, *b.* 1937: *m.* 1967, John Ralph Sidney Guinness, of 9, Hereford Sq., SW7, and has issue living, Rupert Edward Roger *b.* 1971, Peter John Charles *b.* 1974, Lucy Arabella *b.* 1970,—Christine, *b.* 1938: *m.* 1963, Alan Blakemore, of Hatchford Park Nurseries, Cobham, Surrey, and has issue living, Emily Jasmine Alice *b.* 1964, Flora Marianne Sophie *b.* 1966, Lily Isabella Katherine Bonnie *b.* 1968, Jessica Mary Cassandra *b.* 1972,—Grace Elizabeth, *b.* 1946: BA, MB, BChir. *Residence,*—Rougham Hall, Rougham, King's Lynn.

Granddaughters of the late Frederick Keppel North (ante):—
Issue of the late Charles Percy Frederick North, *b.* 1906, *d.* 1971: *m.* 1937, Judith (Small Dean Farm, Wendover, Bucks.), da. of Harry Leon Hamlin, of Stoneyhill Farm, Amaguarett, Long Island, USA:—
Mary Grace (30, Sutton Place, New York City, USA), *b.* 1939: *m.* 1969, William Ellsworth Clow, who *d.* 1970.——Melissa Judith, *b.* 1944.

Granddaughter of the late Charles North (ante):—
Issue of the late Marjoribanks Keppel North, *b.* 1865, *d.* 1949: *m.* 1905, Edith Beatrice, J.P., who *d.* 1973, only da. of Sir George John Armytage, 6th Bt.:—
Arabella, *b.* 1909; 1939-45 War as Ch. Com. A.T.S.: *m.* 1950, Louis Euan Babington Morgan, of Lords House, Hooe, nr. Battle, Sussex.

Granddaughter of the late Marjoribanks Keppel North (ante):—
Issue of the late George Montagu North, *b.* 1906, *d.* 1953: *m.* 1940, June Margaret (who *m.* 2ndly, 1956, Robert Burton Kenward, of Stocks House and Perryfield, Udimore, Sussex), da. of the late Francis Edward Harrison, OBE, of York:—
Lavinia Keppel, *b.* 1940: *m.* 1970, Peter Jocelyn Jeffries, of Old School House, Ide Hill, Sevenoaks, Kent, and has issue living, Charles Jocelyn, *b.* 1974,—Alexandra Keppel, *b.* 1971.

Granddaughter of the late Frederick North, 5th in descent from the late Hon. Roger North, yst. son of 4th Baron North:—
Issue of the late Charles North, *b.* 1828, *d.* 1906 : *m.* 1859, Augusta, who *d.* 1917, dau. of the late Rev. the Hon. Thomas Robert Keppel [E. Albemarle, colls.] :—
Louisa Augusta, *b.* 1878; served with British Red Cross in Italy, and with Scottish Women Hospital Unit in Serbia during 1914-19 War (British and Serbian medals). *Residence,*—Small Dean, Wendover, Bucks.

PREDECESSORS—[1—9] Georgе Augustus North, 9th *Baron North*, of Kirtling, co. Camb. (by writ of summons 1554) and 3rd Earl of Guilford (see E. Guilford), *b.* 1757; *d.* 1802, when the Earldom of Guilford devolved upon his brother, and the Barony of North became abeyant, and remained so until 1841, when it was terminated in favour of his 2nd dau. [10] Susan; *b.* 1797: *m.* 1835, Col. John Sidney Doyle, M.P. (who in 1838 assumed the surname of North); *d.* 1884: *s.* by her son [11] William Henry John, 11th Baron, *b.* 1836; Bailiff Grand Cross of Sovereign Order of Malta, Pres. of that Sovereign Order in Great

Britain, and Hon. Pres. of Committee of Privileges of Maltese Nobility; *m.* 1858, Frederica, who *d.* 1915, dau. of Com. R. Howe Cockerell, R.N.; *d.* 1932; *s.* by his son [12] WILLIAM FREDERICK JOHN, 12th Baron, *b.* 1860: *m.* 1855, Arabella Valeria Keppel, who *d.* 1965, da. of the late Charles North [E. Guilford, colls.]; *d.* 1938; *s.* by his grandson [13] JOHN DUDLEY (son of the late Hon. Dudley William John North, MC, only son of 12th Baron), 13th Baron, *b.* 1917; Lt. R.N.: *m.* 1940, Margaret (who *m.* 2ndly, 1943, Lieut. Weldon Bernard James, U.S. Marine Corps), dau. of R. W. H. Glennie, of Cape Province, S. Africa; *d.* (killed in action during European War) 1941, when the Barony again fell into abeyance [see ante].

NORTHAMPTON, MARQUESS OF. (Compton.) [Marquess U.K. 1812.]
[Name pronounced "Cumpton."]

I seek but one.

WILLIAM BINGHAM COMPTON, D.S.O., 6th Marquess; *b.* Aug. 6th, 1885; *s.* 1913; ed. at Eton, and at Balliol Coll., Oxford (B.A. 1906); formerly Major Roy. Horse Guards; is a D.L. for Northants, patron of nine livings, Lieut.-Col. (retired) late Comdg. Warwickshire Yeo. a Com. of Order of Leopold II of Belgium, and a C.St.J.; European War 1914-18 (wounded, D.S.O.); D.S.O. 1919: *m.* 1st, 1921, Lady Emma Marjory Thynne, *O.B.E.* (who obtained a divorce 1942), dau. of the 5th Marquess of Bath; 2ndly, 1942, Virginia Lucie (from whom he obtained a divorce 1958), dau. of Capt. David Rimington Heaton, D.S.O., of Brookfield, Crownhill, S. Devon; 3rdly, 1958, Elspeth Grace, el. dau. of the late William Ingham Whitaker, DL [V. Melville], and formerly wife of the 19th Baron Teynham, who *d.* 1972, and has issue by 2nd m.

Arms,—Sable, a lion passant guardant or, between three esquires' helmets argent. **Crest,**—On a mount a beacon fired proper, behind it a ribbon inscribed with the words, *Nisi Dominus.* **Supporters,**—*Dexter,* a dragon ermine, ducally gorged and chained or; *sinister,* an unicorn argent, horned, maned, hoofed, and tufted sable.

Seats,— Castle Ashby, Northampton; Compton Wynyates, Tysoe, Warwick. *Town Residence,*—5, Pelham Place, SW7.

SONS LIVING. *(By 2nd marriage.)*
SPENCER DOUGLAS DAVID (*Earl Compton*) (10, Netherton Grove, SW10), *b.* April 2nd, 1946; ed. at Eton: *m.* 1st, 1967 (m. diss. 1973), Henriette Luisa Maria Bentinck, only da. of the late Baron Bentinck, and Netherlands Ambassador to France; 2ndly, 1974, Annette Marie, da. of Charles Anthony Russell Smallwood, and has issue:—
    SON LIVING (*By 1st. m*) Daniel Bingham (*Lord Wilmington*), *b.* Jan. 16th, 1973.
    DAUGHTER LIVING (*By 1st m.*) *Lady* Lara Katrina, *b.* 1968.
Lord William James Bingham, *b.* 1947; ed at Bryanston: *m.* 1973, Marlene, da . of the late Franci Hosie, and has issue living, James William, *b.* 1974.

DAUGHTERS LIVING. *(By 2nd marriage.)*
Lady Judith, *b.* 1943: *m.* 1970, Adrian Christopher Swire, of 14, Phillimore Place, W8, and has issue living, Merlin Bingham *b.* 1973,—Martha Virginia, *b.* 1972.
Lady Elizabeth, *b.* 1944: *m.* 1968, Ian Hamish Leslie Melville, of 61, Hartington Rd., Chiswick, W4 [see E. Leven and Melville, colls.].

COLLATERAL BRANCH LIVING.
Issue of the late Lord Alwyne Frederick Compton, D.S.O., 3rd son of 4th Marquess, *b.* 1855, *d.* 1911: *m.* 1886, Mary Evelyn, who *d.* 1957, dau. of the late Robert Charles de Grey Vyner [see B. Lucas, colls.]:—
Edward Robert Francis, *b.* Dec. 14th, 1891 ; ed. at Eton ; is a D.L. for W. Riding of Yorks, and for City and co. of York ; formerly Capt. 2nd Dragoons (Roy. Scots Greys) ; European War 1914-18 (wounded): *m.* 1st, 1918, Sylvia, who *d.* 1950, dau. of the late Lieut.-Col. Alexander Haldame Farquharson [Ross, Bt., cr. 1672, colls.] ; 2ndly, 1952, Mrs. Mary Elizabeth Allan Wilson, who *d.* 1957 ; 3rdly, 1958, Sallie Whitney, dau. of Dr. Leonard Sanford, of New York, U.S.A., and widow of 2nd Baron Sysonby, and has issue living, (by 1st marriage) Alwyne Arthur Compton FARQUHARSON OF INVERCAULD, *M.C.* (of Invercauld, Braemar, Aberdeenshire), *b.* 1919; ed. at Eton ; Capt. Roy. Scots Greys ; European War 1939-45 (wounded, M.C.) ; officially recognized in the surname of Farquharson of Invercauld, and as Chief of Clan Farquharson by warrant of Lord Lyon 1949, and uses his former surname as a third christian name : *m.* 1949, Frances Strickland Lovell (GORDON), dau. of the late Robert Pollard Oldham, of Seattle, Washington, U.S.A., and widow of Capt. the Hon. James Henry Bertie Rodney, M.C. [see B. Rodney],—Robert Edward John (Copt Hewick Hall, Ripon, Yorks.), *b.* 1922; ed. at Eton; late Capt. Coldstream Guards: *m.* 1952, Ursula Jane (AITKEN), da. of the late Maj. Robert Orlando Kenyon-Slaney [see B. Kenyon, colls.], and has issue living, James Alwyne *b.* 1953, Richard Clephane *b.* 1957,—Mary (twin), *b.* 1919: *m.* 1st, 1939, Bernard Harry Richard van Cutsem; 2ndly, 1947, Maj. W. D. Henderson, of Ballygown, Ulva Ferry, Mull, and has issue living, (by 1st m.) Hugh Bernard Edward *b.* 1941: *m.* 1971, Jonkvrouwe Emilie, da. of Jonkheer Pieter Quarles van Ufford, of De Dumdoorn, Aerdenhout, Holland, Geoffrey Neil *b.* 1944: *m.* 1969, Sally, only da. of Alastair McCorquodale, of Stoke Rochford, Gran-

tham, Lincs., and has issue living, Sophie b. 1975,—(by 2nd m.) Alexander William, b. 1948,—Mary Clare, b. 1951. *Residence,*—Newby Hall, Ripon. *Clubs,*—Bath, New (Edinburgh).——Clare George VYNER, b. 1894; Lt.-Cdr. (ret.) RN; is a DL for W. Riding of Yorkshire, and for City and co. of York; assumed by Roy. licence the surname of Vyner in lieu of his patronymic and the arms of Vyner quarterly, 1912: m. 1923, Lady Doris Hilda Gordon-Lennox, da. of 8th Duke of Richmond, and has issue living, Henry, b. 1932: m. 1958, Margaret (PHILIPPS), da. of Capt. Heathcote, DSO, RN, and has issue living, Harriet de Grey, b. 1959, Violet Elizabeth, b. 1962. *Residence,*—Keanchulish, Ullapool, Ross-shire.

PREDECESSORS.—[1] *Sir* HENRY Compton, Knt., **was summoned to Parliament as** *Baron Compton,* of Compton, co. Warwick (peerage of England) 1566; in 1587 was on the trial of the Queen of Scots, and was one of the principal commanders of the forces that besieged the Earl of Essex; *d.* 1589; *s.* by his son [2] WILLIAM, *K.G.,* 2nd Baron; Lord Pres. of the Marches and dominion of Wales, and Lord-Lieut. of Warwickshire; *cr. Earl of Northampton* (peerage of England) 1618; *d.* 1630; *s.* by his son [3] SPENCER, *K.B.,* 2nd Earl; was Master of the Robes to Charles, Prince of Wales, and a zealous partisan of James I.; killed at battle of Hopton Heath 1642; *s.* by his son [4] JAMES, 3rd Earl; an earnest Royalist; sat as M.P. for Warwickshire 1640-2; was Lord-Lieut. of co. Warwick, Constable of the Tower of London and Recorder of Coventry, Tamworth, and Northampton; commanded the Cavalry at first battle of Newbury 1643, and raised the siege of Banbury 1644, &c.; *d.* 1681; *s.* by his son [5] GEORGE, *P.C.,* 4th Earl; Constable of the Tower of London, and Lord-Lieut. of Warwickshire: bore the King's sceptre and cross at Coronation of William and Mary; *d.* 1727; *s.* by his el. son [6] JAMES, 5th Earl; M.P. for co. Warwick 1710-11, when he was summoned to House of peers in his father's barony of Compton: *m.* Elizabeth, in her own right Baroness Ferrers of Chartley, sister and heir of Robert Shirley, Viscount Tamworth; *d.* without male issue 1754, when the Barony of Compton devolved upon his dau. Charlotte (wife of 1st Marquess of Townshend, who also in 1770 inherited from her mother the Baronies of Ferrers of Chartley, Bourchier, Lovaine, and Basset of Drayton), and the Earldom devolved upon his brother [7] GEORGE, 6th Earl; was a Lord of the Treasury 1742; sat as M.P. for Tamworth 1726-7, and for Northampton 1727-54; *d.s.p.* 1758; *s.* by his nephew [8] CHARLES, 7th Earl, son of the Hon. Charles, M.P., 3rd son of 4th Earl; *d.s.p.* 1763; *s.* by his brother [9] SPENCER, 8th Earl; sat as M.P. for Northampton 1761-3; was Lord-Lieut. of Northamptonshire, Recorder of Northampton, and a Groom of the Bedchamber; *d.* 1796; *s.* by his son [10] CHARLES, 9th Earl, *cr. Baron Wilmington,* of Wilmington, co. Sussex, *Earl Compton,* and *Marquess of Northampton* (peerage of United Kingdom) 1812; *d.* 1828; *s.* by his son [11] SPENCER JOSHUA ALWYNE, 2nd Marquess; *b.* 1790; was Pres. of Royal So.: *m.* 1815, Margaret, dau. of Maj.-Gen. Douglas Maclean Clephane; *d.* 1851; *s.* by his son [12] CHARLES, 3rd Marquess; assumed in 1831 by Roy. licence the additional and principal surname of Douglas; *d.s.p.* 1877; *s.* by his brother [13] WILLIAM. *K.G.,* 4th Marquess, *b.* 1818; Adm. in the Navy; assumed 1851 the additional surname of Maclean, and in 1878 that of Douglas: *m.* 1844, Eliza, who *d.* 1877, dau. of the late Adm. the Hon. Sir George Elliot, K.C.B.; *d.* 1897; *s.* by his el. surviving son [14] WILLIAM GEORGE SPENCER SCOTT, *K.G., b.* 1851; Private Sec. to Lord-Lieut. of Ireland 1880-82 and Lord-Lieut. of Warwickshire 1912-13; Special Envoy to Foreign Courts to announce Accession of King George V.; M.P. for Warwickshire, S.-W., or Stratford-on-Avon, Div. 1885-6, and for Yorkshire, W. Riding, S. Part, Barnsley Div. (*L*) March 1889 to Sept. 1897: *m.* 1884, the Hon. Mary Florence Baring, who *d.* 1902, dau. of 2nd Baron Ashburton; *d.* 1913; *s.* by his el. son [15] WILLIAM BINGHAM, 6th Marquess and present peer; also Earl of Northampton, Earl Compton, and Baron Wilmington.

NORTHBOURNE, BARON. (James.) [Baron U.K. 1884, Bt. G.B. 1791.]

J'AYME·A·JAMAIS

I love for ever.

WALTER ERNEST CHRISTOPHER JAMES, 4th Baron, and 5th Baronet; *b.* Jan. 18th, 1896; *s.* 1932; ed. at Eton, and at Magdalen Coll., Oxford; late Lieut. 4th Northumberland Fusiliers; patron of two livings: *m.* 1925, Katherine, *J.P.,* dau. of the late George A. Nickerson of Boston, Mass., U.S.A., and has issue.

Arms,—Gules, a dolphin embowed or. **Crest,** —An ostrich argent, beaked and legged or. **Supporters,**—Two eagles argent, collared gules; each having pendant from the collar a shield charged with the arms.

Seat,—Northbourne Court, Deal, Kent.

SON LIVING.

Hon. CHRISTOPHER GEORGE WALTER, *b.* Feb. 18th, 1926: ed. at Eton, and at Magdalen Coll., Oxford (MA), FRICS, FLAS, FAI: *m.* 1959, Marie Sygne, el. da. of Henri Claudel, of Chatou sur Seine, and has issue living, Charles Walter Henri, *b.* 1960, —Anthony Christopher Walter Paul, *b.* 1963,— Sebastian Richard Edward Cuthbert, *b.* 1966,— Ophelia Mary Katherine Christine Aliki, *b.* 1969. *Residences,* Coldharbour, Northbourne, Kent; 81, Bedford Gdns., W8; Evistones, Otterburn, Northumberland. *Club,*—Brooks's.

DAUGHTERS LIVING.

Hon. Gwenllian Ellen, *b.* 1929: *m.* 1st, 1952 (marriage annulled 1960), Michael Hugh Rose (infra); 2ndly, 1960, Thomas Jeffrey Hemsley, of 10, Denewood Rd., Highgate, N6, and has issue living, (by 2nd marriage) William Thomas James, *b.* 1962,—Matthew Walter David, *b* 1963,—Michael Richard, *b.* 1965.

Hon. Elizabeth Sarah, *b.* 1933: *m.* 1960, Michael Edward Willis-Fleming, and has issue living, John, Michael, *b.* 1961,—Penelope Katherine, *b.* 1965. *Residence,*—2, Trafalgar Rd., Twickenham, Middlesex.

Hon. Susan Jane, *b.* 1936: *m.* 1961, Michael Hugh Rose, of Le Sirondole, Panzano-in-Chianti (Florence), Italy, son of the late Rt. Rev. Alfred Carey Wollaston Rose, formerly Bishop of Dover, and has issue living, Michael Justin, *b.* 1966,—Nell Susanna, *b.* 1961,—Emma Katherine, *b.* 1963,— Sophy Elizabeth, *b.* 1969.

Hon. Katherine Viola, *b.* 1940: *m.* 1963, John Wharton Hersey, of Coomblands Farm, Coneyhurst, Sussex, and has issue living, Robert Alexander, *b.* 1964,—John Paul, *b.* 1966,—Daniel Anthony James, *b.* 1971.

SISTER LIVING.

Hon. Mary Beatrix, *b.* 1902 : *m.* 1926, Nicholas Llewelyn Davies, and has issue living, Laura, *b.* 1928: *m.* 1951, David Leslie Duguid. *Residence,* Eythorne House, Eythorne, Dover.

WIDOW LIVING OF SON OF SECOND BARON.

Lady Serena Mary Barbara Lumley, dau. of 10th Earl of Scarbrough : *m.* 1923, as his second wife, the Hon. Robert James, who *d.* 1960, and has issue living [see colls., infra]. *Residence,*—St. Nicholas, Richmond, Yorkshire.

COLLATERAL BRANCHES LIVING.

Issue of the late Lieut.-Col. the Hon. Cuthbert James, C.B.E., M.P., 2nd son of 2nd Baron, *b.* 1872, *d.* 1930 : *m.* 1905, Florence Marion, who *d.* 1933, dau. of the late Hussey Packe [E. Kimberley]:—

Thomas, *b.* 1906 ; ed. at Eton, and at Magdalen Coll., Oxford ; European War 1939-45 ; in R.A.S.C.: *m.* 1st, 1932, Lady Germaine Elizabeth Olive (who obtained a divorce 1940), dau. of 8th Earl of St. Germans; 2ndly, 1940, Julia Mary, who *d.* 1974, having obtained a divorce 1953, da. of the late Charles Solomon, of 36, Queen's Grove, St. John's Wood, NW; 3rdly, 1953, Rosemary Heartsease Beare, da. of the late Maj. George Frederick Crisp Molineux-Montgomerie [see D. Beaufort, colls.], and widow of Capt. Reginald Dilworth Howard, RN, and has issue living (by 2nd m.), Anthony Nigel (77, Wellesley Rd., Chiswick, N4), *b.* 1944: *m.* 1973, Therese Macormack, of Mel., Aust., and has issue living, Alexander Robert *b.* 1974,—Georgina Mary, *b.* 1948: *m.* 1972, Christopher Watts; of 45, Woodley Lane, Romsey, Hants., and has issue living, Ian Charles *b.* 1973. *Residence,*—Handen Farm, Aldington, nr. Ashford, Kent.——Olivia Mary, *b.* 1909; *m.* 1934, Stephen Francis Villiers Smith, MBE [E. Clarendon, colls.], and has issue living, Timothy Francis (Cavalry Club), *b.* 1935: *m.* 1st, 1961 (m. diss. 1969), Cicely Susan Esther, da. of Brig. Charles Edward Tyron-Wilson, CBE, DSO; 2ndly, 1973, Mrs Caroline Sarah Thorpe Richardson, da. of Jack Perry, and has issue living (by 1st m.), Charles Francis *b.* 1965, Rupert Timothy *b.* 1967, Amy Louise *b.* 1963,—Clarissa Mary (*Lady Palmer*) *b.* 1938: *m.* 1957, Sir Geoffrey Christofer John Palmer, 12th Bt.,—Serena Olivia, *b.* 1940: *m.* 1963, Anthony Morden, of Hunters Lodge, Woldingham, Surrey, and has issue living, Amanda Serena *b.* 1965, Lucinda Antonia *b.* 1967. *Residence,*—Holly Cottage, Knockholt, Kent. ——Joan Rosamund, *b.* 1917: *m.* 1949, Maj. Launcelot James Francis Brydon, and has issue living, Robert Alexander, *b.* 1954,—Nadia Mary, *b* 1952. *Residence,*—The Village House, Brasted, Kent.

Issue of the late Hon. Robert James, 3rd son of 2nd Baron, *b.* 1873, *d.* 1960: *m.* 1st, 1900, Lady Evelyn Kathleen Wellesley, who *d.* 1922, da. of 4th Duke of Wellington; 2ndly, 1923, Lady Serena Mary Barbara Lumley (ante), da. of 10th Earl of Scarbrough:—

(By 1st marriage) Arthur Walter, *b.* 1904 : *m.* 1st, 1929, Zita Mary (who obtained a divorce 1932), dau. of Nico Jungman ; 2ndly, 1932, Mary Gibbs, dau. of A. H. Charlesworth, and has issue living (by 2nd m.) Lucinda Evelyn, *b.* 1933: *m.* 1st, 1953 (m. diss. 1967), Andrew Duff Tennant [see B. Glenconner, colls.]; 2ndly, 1967, Rupert Oliver Steel, of Winterbourne Holt, Newbury, and has issue living (by 1st m.) [see B. Glenconner, colls.], (by 2nd m.) James Oliver *b.* 1971, Emily Jane *b.* 1970. *Residence,*—Updown, Eastry, Kent.——(By 2nd m.) Ursula Mary-Rose (*Baroness Westbury*), *b.* 1924: *m.* 1947, the 5th Baron Westbury. *Residence,*—Barton Cottage, Malton, Yorks.——Serena Fay, *b.* 1929: *m.* 1955 (m. diss. 1963), Colin Griffith Campion. *Residence,*—St. Nicholas Garden Cottage, Richmond, Yorks.

Issue of the late Hon. Wilfrid James, 4th son of 2nd Baron, *b.* 1874, *d.* 1908 : *m.* 1900, Margaret Anne, who *d.* 1957, dau. of John Stogdon :—

Henry Norman, *b.* 1903: *m.* 1st, 1933, Constance Margaret (from whom he obtained a divorce 1946), only dau. of Capt. J. D. Macdonald, of Bucklebury Place, Woolhampton, Berks; 2ndly, 1946, Kathleen Mary, who *d.* 1959, da. of the late Charles William Hewtson; 3rdly, 1967, Marjorie, da. of the late Charles William Hewtson, and has issue living, (by 2nd marriage) John Henry, *b.* 1947,—Margaret Anne, *b.* 1950. *Residence,*—Woodlands, Adisham, nr. Canterbury, Kent.

PREDECESSORS.—[1] *Sir* WALTER JAMES Head, 2nd son of Sir Thomas Head (Knt.), of Langley Hall, Berks; was sometime Warden of the Mint; assumed in 1778 by Act of Parliament the surname of James only, and in 1791 was cr. a *Baronet*; *d.* 1829: *s.* by his grandson [2] *Sir* WALTER CHARLES, 2nd Baronet (son of the late John James, Minister Plenipotentiary to the Netherlands); *b.* 1816; M.P. for Hull (C) 1837-47: cr. *Baron Northbourne,* of Betteshanger, co. Kent (peerage of United Kingdom) 1884 : *m.* 1841, Sarah Caroline, who *d.* 1896, dau. of Cuthbert Ellison, of Hebburn Hall, Durham; *d.* 1893; *s.* by his son [3] WALTER HENRY, 2nd Baron; *b.* 1846 ; M.P. for Gateshead (L) 1874-93: *m.* 1868, Edith Emmeline Mary, who *d.* 1929, dau. of the late John Newton Lane, of King's Bromley Manor, Lichfield ; *d.* 1923 ; *s.* by his son [4] WALTER JOHN, 3rd Baron, *b.* 1869 : *m.* 1894, Laura Gwenllian, who *d.* 1952 (having *m.* 2ndly, 1935, William Curtis Green, R.A.), dau. of the late Adm. Sir Ernest Rice, K.C.B., of Sibertswold Place, Kent; *d.* 1932; *s.* by his son [5] WALTER ERNEST CHRISTOPHER, 4th Baron and present peer.

By uprightness and labour.

NORTHBROOK, BARON. (Baring.) [Baron 1866, Bt. G.B. 1793.]

[Name pronounced "Bearing."]

FRANCIS JOHN BARING, 5th Baron, and 7th Baronet; *b.* May 31st, 1915; *s.* 1947; ed. at Winchester, and at Trin. Coll., Oxford (B.A. 1937): *m.* 1951, **Rowena Margaret,** dau. of the late Brig.-Gen. Sir William Henry Manning, G.C.M.G., K.B.E., C.B., and has issue.

Arms.—1st and 4th, azure, a fesse or, in chief a bear's head proper, muzzled and ringed of the second differenced by a portcullis azure. *Baring*; 2nd and 3rd, gules, a cross patée fitchée or between three fish hauriant argent within an orle of eight cross-crosslets of the second, *Herring.* Crest,—A mullet erminois, two of the points resting on the pinions of a pair of wings conjoined and elevated argent. Supporters,—On either side a bear proper, muzzled and charged on the shoulder with a portcullis or. *Residence,*—East Stratton Farm, East Stratton, Micheldever, Hants.

SON LIVING.

Hon. FRANCIS THOMAS, *b.* Feb. 21st, 1954; ed. at Winchester.

DAUGHTERS LIVING.

Hon. Laura Anne, *b.* 1952.
Hon. Alexandra Grace, *b.* 1957
Hon. Catherine Margaret, *b.* 1965.

SISTER LIVING.
Hon. Anne (Woodlands Farm, Bramdean, Alresford, Hants.), *b.* 1917.

WIDOW LIVING OF FOURTH BARON.

CONSTANCE MAUD GRIFFIN (*Dowager Baroness Northbrook*), dau. of the late Frank Griffin, of Kew Gardens, Surrey: *m.* 1941, as his second wife, the 4th Baron, who *d.* 1947. *Residence,*—11, Broomfield Road, Kew Gardens, Richmond, Surrey.

COLLATERAL BRANCHES LIVING. (*In remainder to Baronetcy only.*)
Grandchildren of the late Thomas Charles Baring, MP, el. son of the Rt. Rev. Charles Baring, DD, Bishop of Durham, 4th son of 2nd baronet:—
Issue of the late Godfrey Nigel Everard Baring, *b.* 1870, *d.* 1934: *m.* 1908, the Hon. Ada Sybil Roche, who *d.* 1944, dau. of 2nd Baron Fermoy:—
Desmond Charles Nigel, (Ardington House, Wantage, Berks.) *b.* 1914; ed. at Eton; formerly Lieut. 3rd Carabiniers: *m.* 1938, Mary Eileen, *JP,* dau. of B. W. Warner, and has issue living, Peter (Ardington House, Wantage, Oxon.) *b.* 1939: *m.* 1973, Rose, da. of George Nigel Adams, of Fernham Manor, Faringdon, Oxon.,—Nigel (31, Dovehouse St., SW3), *b.* 1940: *m.* 1968, Jane Finola, el. da. of Francis Byrne, of 76, Rivermead Court, Hurlingham, SW6, and has issue living, Lorne Benjamin Nigel *b.* 1970,—Edward Francis Desmond, *b.* 1972,—Margaret Anne *b.* 1944.——Cynthia Cecil, *b.* 1909: *m.* 1st, 1932 (m. diss. 1947), Brig. John Theodore de Horne Vaizey, CBE, RA; 2ndly, 1947, Forest Warren, who *d.* 1963, and has issue living, (by 1st m.) John Nigel de Horne, *b.* 1935,—Anne Gillian de Horne, *b.* 1933: *m.* 1956, Simon Cooke, of Deers, Clavering, Saffron Walden, Essex, and has issue living, Jonathan Simon *b.* 1959, Adam Nicholas *b.* 1960, Matthew William *b.* 1964,—Georgina Cynthia, *b.* 1940: *m.* 1962, David Drummond Alexander, and has issue living, Gregory David *b.* 1963,—Tristram Daniel *b.* 1966,—Carola Baring, *b.* 1943: *m.* 1963, Peter Hanbury Bell, and has issue living, Geoffrey De Witt, *b.* 1963, Simon Hanbury *b.* 1965,—(by 2nd m.) Celia Manuella Sybil, *b.* 1949. *Residence,*—The Birches, 2, The Dingle, Coombe Dingle, Bristol.

Granddaughters of the late Right Rev. Charles Baring, D.D. (ante):—
Issue (by 2nd marriage) of the late Rev. Francis Henry Baring, *b.* 1848, *d.* 1914: *m.* 1st, 1881, Margaret Ann Borthwick, who *d.* 1882, widow of William Elmslie, F.R.C.S., and dau. of the late Rev. William Wallace Duncan, of Peebles; 2ndly, 1886, Amy, who *d.* 1935, dau. of the late Rev. John Alexander Stamper, of Monaline House, Newtown-mountkennedy. co. Wicklow:—
Dorothy Olive, *b.* 1890. *Residence,*—Winchester House, Overton, Hants.——Amy Rose, *b.* 1894: *m.* 1947, Edwin Daniel Doncaster, who *d.* 1950. *Residence,*—Calluna, Merdon Av., Chandler's Ford, Hants.

Descendants of the late Rt. Hon. Alexander Baring, D.C.L. (2nd son of 1st Baronet), who was cr. *Baron Ashburton* 1835 [see that title].

Grandchildren of the late Lieut.-Gen. Charles Baring, son of the late Henry Bingham Baring, M.P., el. son of the late Henry Baring, M.P., 3rd son of Sir Francis Baring, 1st Bt. :—
See Baring Bt. (cr. 1911).
Descendants of the late Edward Charles Baring [5th son of the late Henry Baring, M.P. (ante)], who was cr. *Baron Revelstoke* 1885 [see that title].

Granddaughter of the late Thomas Baring (infra):—
Issue of the late Richard Baring, *b.* 1902, *d.* 1940: *m.* 1st, (Jan.) 1922, Violetta Archer, who *d.* 1931; 2ndly, 1932, Margaret, who *d.* 1974, da. of Henry Thomas Sutton, of Zanesville, Ohio, USA:—
(By 1st m.) Cecilia Maureen Anne (105, Canfield Gdns., NW6 3DY), *b.* (Oct.) 1922.

Grandchildren of the late Henry Baring, M.P. (ante) :—
Issue of the late Thomas Baring, *b.* 1839, *d.* 1923 : *m.* 1901, Constance, who *d.* 1948, dau. of William Barron:—
Edward Thomas, *b.* 1903 ; ed. at Eton, and at Ch. Ch., Oxford ; late Major : *m.* 1st, 1926 (marriage dissolved 19—), Virginia, dau. of John Ryan ; 2ndly, 1950, Pauline Alison (BODEN), dau. of the late Frank Fawcett Copland, of Sydney, and has issue living, (by 1st m.) Thomas Michael, *TD* (Brewham House, nr. Bruton, Som.), *b.* 1927 ; Lt.-Col. Derbyshire Yeo.; Comdg. Leics. and Derbys. Yeo: *m.* 1st, 1953 (m. diss. 1965), the Hon. Sarah Katherine Elinor Norton, da. of 6th Baron Grantley, and formerly wife of 3rd Viscount Astor; 2ndly, 1966, Mrs. Gillian A. R. Graham, of Silton, Dorset, and has issue living, (by 2nd m.) Constance Nina, *b.* 1970,—(Edward) Patrick (7, Umbria St., Roehampton, SW15), *b.* 1932: *m.* 1960, Antonia Miriam, da. of the late Anthony Wentworth Guinness, of Stoke House, Stoke Albany, Market Harborough, Leics., and has issue living, Anthony Shawn *b.* 1961, Jonathan Patrick Fortune *b.* 1965, Sonya Hermione *b.* 1963, Lucita Catherine Marianne *b.* 1968,—Christopher John, *b.* 1939. *Residence,*—Heronry House Farm, Beckley, E. Sussex.

Issue of the late Rt. Hon. Sir Evelyn Baring, G.C.B., O.M., G.C.M.G., K.C.S.I., C.I.E., who was cr. *Earl of Cromer* 1901 [see that title].

Grandsons of the late Maj. Francis Charles Baring, son of the late William Henry Baring, son of the late William Baring, MP, 4th son of the late Sir Francis Baring, 1st Bt.:—
Issue of the late Major Thomas Esmé Baring, O.B.E., *b.* 1882, *d.* 1957 : *m.* 1913, Deirdré Mary Hughes, who *d.* 1973, da. of Hughes Martin, JP, formerly of Tullaghreine, Carrigtwohill, co. Cork:—
Maurice Bingham, *T.D.*, *b.* 1916; ed. at Eton, and at Magdalene Coll., Camb. (B.A. 1939, M.A. 1949); is Capt .Rifle Bde. (TA): *m.* 1941, Loveday Anne Monica, da. of the late Capt. John Tillie Coryton [V. St. Vincent, colls.], and has issue living, Lynda Anne (16, Cambridge St., SW1), *b.* 1944: *m.* 1967, Clive Edward Theo Corke, and has issue living, Shauna Bingham *b.* 1972, Anthea Lynda *b.* 1973,—Shirley Bingham, *b.* 1948. *Residence,*—Culmer House, Wormley, nr. Godalming, Surrey.——Hugo Charles, *MBE*, *MC*, *b.* 1919; ed. at Eton, and at Magdalene Coll., Camb.; formerly Maj. Rifle Bde.; 1939-45 War in Middle East and Italy (despatches, MC, MBE); MBE (Mil) 1945: *m.* 1946, Elisabeth Price, only da. of the late Maj. John Price Wylie, DSO, Sherwood Foresters, and has issue living, Anthony Hugo, *b.* 1947,—Michael William, *b.* 1950. *Residence,*—The Old Vicarage, Ramsdell, Basingstoke, Hants.

Issue of the late Arthur Francis Charles Baring, *b.* 1887, *d.* 1964: *m.* 1906, Margaret McIntyre, da. of the late George Moore, of Adelaide, S. Australia:—
Arthur Reginald, *b.* 1909.——Ian Douglas, *b.* 1915.——Robert Stanley, *b.* 1918.

Issue of the late Major Dudley William Baring, Hampshire Regt., and R.A.S.C., *b.* 1892, *d.* 1952: *m.* 1919, Cecilia Mary, who *d.* 1971, da. of the late Col. Michael Rowan Gray Buchanan, OBE, of Ettrickdale, Isle of Bute [M. Bute, colls.]:—
Francis William, *VRD*, *b.* 1920; ed. at Bradfield Coll.; Cdr. RNR; 1939-45 War: *m.* 1967, Elsie Violet, only da. of William Charles Redding. *Residence,*—72, Clarence Gate Gdns., NW1 6QR.

Grandchildren of the late Major Dudley William Baring (ante):—
Issue of the late Lieut.-Com. Michael John Baring, R.N., *b.* 1921, *d.* 1955: *m.* 1946, Pamela Anne (who *m.* 2ndly, 1959, Capt. John Ridgway Berridge Longden, RN (ret), of Rookley Manor, Kings Somborne, Hants.), da. of the late Col. Frederick Adolphus Fleming Barnardo, CIE, CBE, BSc, MD, MRCP, FRCS:—
Jeremy Michael Stuart, *b.* 1948.——Angela Jane, *b.* 1946: *m.* 1969, William George Stirling Home Drummond Moray [see D. Buccleuch, colls.]

PREDECESSORS.—[1] FRANCIS Baring, *M.P.* for Grampound 1784-90, for Calne 1796-1802, and for Chipping Wycombe 1802-6 ; was an eminent London merchant, and a Director of the H.E.I.C. 1779-92, and Chairman thereof 1792-3 ; *cr.* a *Baronet* 1793 : *m.* 1767, Harriet, dau. and co-heiress of William Herring, of Croydon, cousin and a co-heiress of Thomas Herring, Archbishop of Canterbury ; *d.* 1810 ; *s.* by his son [2] *Sir* THOMAS, 2nd Bt. ; sat as M.P. for Chipping Wycombe 1806-31 ; *d.* 1848 ; *s.* by his son [3] *Sir* FRANCIS THORNHILL, 3rd Bt. ; *b.* 1796; sat as M.P. for Portsmouth 1826-65 ; was Chancellor of the Exchequer 1839-41, and First Lord of the Admiralty 1849-52 ; *cr. Baron Northbrook*, of Stratton, co. Hants (peerage of United Kingdom) 1866 : *m.* 1st, 1825, Jane, who *d.* 1838, dau. of the Hon. Sir George Grey, 1st Bt. ; 2ndly, 1841, Lady Arabella Howard, who *d.* 1884, dau. of 1st Earl of Effingham ; *d.* 1866 ; *s.* by his son [4] *Rt. Hon.* THOMAS GEORGE, *G.C.S.I.*, *D.C.L.*, *LL.D.*; *b.* 1826 ; *cr. Viscount Baring* and *Earl of Northbrook* (peerage of United Kingdom) 1876 ; a Lord of the Admiralty 1857-58, Under-Sec. for War 1861, for India 1861-64, and for Home Depart. 1864-66, Sec. to Admiralty 1866, Under-Sec. for War 1868-72, Gov.-Gen. of India 1872-6, and First Lord of the Admiralty 1880-85 ; Lord-Lieut. of Hampshire ; M.P. for Penryn and Falmouth (*L*) 1857-66: *m.* 1848, Elizabeth Harriet, who *d.* 1867, dau. of the late Henry Charles Sturt, of Crichel House Dorset ; *d.* 1904 ; *s.* by his son [5] FRANCIS GEORGE, 2nd Earl, *b.* 1850 ; M.P. for Winchester (*L*) 1880-85, and for N., or Biggleswade, Div. of Bedfordshire (*LU*) 1886-92 ; A.D.C. to his father when Gov.-Gen. of India 1873-6 ; High Steward of Winchester and Freeman of that City : *m.* 1st, 1894, Ada Ethel Sophie, who *d.* 1894, dau. of Col. C. Davidson, C.B.; 2ndly, 1899, Florence Anita Eyre, *C.B.E.*, who *d.* 1946, dau. of the late Eyre Coote, of West Park, Hants, and widow of Sir Robert John Abercromby, 7th Bt. ; *d.* 1929, when the Earldom and Viscountcy became ext., and the Barony of Northbrook devolved upon his cousin [6] FRANCIS ARTHUR (son of the late Hon. Francis Henry Baring, 3rd son of 1st Baron), 4th Baron ; *b.* 1882: *m.* 1st, 1914, Evelyn Gladys Isabelle, who *d.* 1919, dau. of the late John George Charles, of 39, St. George's Road, S.W.1; 2ndly, 1941, Constance Maud, dau. of the late Frank Griffin, of Kew Gardens, Surrey; *d.* 1947; *s.* by his son [7] FRANCIS JOHN, 5th Baron and present peer.

NORTHCHURCH, BARONESS. (Davidson) [Life Baroness 1963.]

FRANCES JOAN DAVIDSON, *DBE* (*Viscountess Davidson*), da. of 1st Baron Dickinson; *b.* May 29th, 1894; MP for Hemel Hempstead Div. of Herts. (*U*) 1937-59; *cr.* OBE (Civil) 1920, DBE (Civil) 1952, and *Baroness Northchurch*, of Chiswick, co. Middlesex (Life Baroness) 1963: *m.* 1919, the 1st Viscount Davidson, who *d.* 1970, and has issue [see V. Davidson].

Arms.—Two coats per pale ; *Dexter*, argent, on a fesse sable between in chief two pheons azure and in base a boar's head erased of the second a portcullis chained or, *Davidson* ; *Sinister*, Or, a bend cottised between two lions passant gules, *Dickinson*. **Supporters,**—*dexter*, a horse argent charged on the shoulder with a rose gules barbed and seeded proper; *sinister* a falcon proper belled collared and lined or.

Residence,—16, Lord North St., Westminster, SW1P 3LD.

NORTHESK, EARL OF. (Carnegie.) [Earl S. 1647.]

[Name pronounced "Carneggie."]

Spot without stain.

ROBERT ANDREW CARNEGIE, 13th Earl; *b.* June 24th, 1926; *s.* 1975; ed. at Nautical Coll., Pangbourne: *m.* 1949, Jean Margaret, yr. da. of Capt. John Duncan George MacRae [see M. Bristol], and has issue.

Arms.—Quarterly; 1st and 4th, or, an eagle displayed azure, armed, beaked and membered sable and (*as an Honourable Augmentation*) charged on the breast with a naval crown of the field; 2nd and 3rd, argent, a pale gules (*Earldom of Northesk*). **Crests,**—1st, the stem of a battleship of the line with three lanthorns all proper, inflamed gules; 2nd, issuant from a naval crown or a demi-leopard proper holding a rose argent, barbed and seeded vert. **Supporters,**—two leopards reguardant proper gorged of three (visible) roses argent, barbed and seeded vert, and each leopard sustaining a banner of Saint George. **Mottoes,**—(over the first crest) "Trafalgar "; (over the second crest) " Britannia Victrix "; (below the compartment) " Tache Sans Tache ".

Residence,—Springwaters, Ballamodwa, Isle of Man.

SON LIVING.

DAVID JOHN (*Lord Rosehill*), *b.* Nov. 3rd, 1954; ed. at Eton.

DAUGHTERS LIVING.

Lady Karen Jean, *b.* 1951.
Lady Mary Barbara, *b.* 1953.

SISTERS LIVING.

Lady Mary Elizabeth (50, Riverview Gdns., Barnes, SW13), *b.* 1921: *m.* 1942 (m. diss. 1954), Maj. Donald Arthur Knights, and has issue living, Diana Elizabeth, *b.* 1943.
Lady Susan Jean, *b.* 1930: *m.* 1955, David Blackall Connell, MB, BS, of Blackwick, Devenish Rd., Ascot, Berks., and has issue living, Timothy Robert, *b.* 1956,—Alistair Douglas, *b.* 1960,—Caroline Lisa, *b.* 1958.

WIDOW LIVING OF ELEVENTH EARL.

ELIZABETH (*Betty, Countess of Northesk*) (Bear Farm, Binfield, Bracknell, Berks; Glenley Farmhouse, Glenogil, by Forfar, Angus), da. of the late Anthony A. Vlasto, formerly of Binfield Park, Bracknell, Berks.: *m.* 1929, as his 2nd wife, the 11th Earl, who *d.* 1963.

COLLATERAL BRANCHES LIVING.

Granddaughters of the late Isabella Eliza Butter CARNEGY OF LOUR, da. of the late Patrick Carnegy, CIE, son of the late Maj.-Gen. Alexander Carnegy, CB, 2nd son of the late Patrick Carnegy of Lour (*b.* 1757), great-grandson of the Hon. Patrick Carnegie of Lour, 3rd son of 2nd Earl:—
Issue of the late Lt.-Col. Ughtred Elliott Carnegy CARNEGY OF LOUR, DSO, MC, *b.* 1886, *d.* 1973: *m.* 1919, Violet, MBE, who *d.* 1965, da. of the late Henry William Henderson, of West Woodhay House, Newbury, Berks.:—
Elizabeth Patricia CARNEGY OF LOUR (Lour, co. Angus), *b.* 1925.——Christian Margaret, *b.* 1927: *m.* 1952, John Lindsay Eric Smith, CBE, FRIBA, of Shottesbrooke Park, White Waltham, Berks., and the issue living, Adam Carnegy Eric, *b.* 1953,—Bartholomew Evan Eric, *b.* 1955,—Emma Victoria Eric, *b.* 1956,—Serena Mary, *b.* 1959,—Clare Elizabeth Dido, *b.* 1962.

Grandchildren of Col. Charles Gilbert Carnegy, MVO, el. son of Gen. Alexander Carnegy, CB (infra):—
Issue of the late Rev. Canon Patrick Charles Alexander Carnegy, *b.* 1893, *d.* 1969: *m.* 1928, Joyce Eleanor (Harrington House, Moulton, Spalding, Lincs.), da. of the late W. Percy Townsley, of Roundhay, Leeds:—
Patrick Charles, *b.* 1940; ed. at Rugby, and Trin. Hall, Camb. (MA).——Colin David, *b.* 1942; ed. at Rugby, and Jesus Coll., Oxford (MA).——Daphne Joyce, *b.* 1947; ed. at Nottingham Univ. (BA).

Grandchildren of the late Gen. Alexander Carnegy, C.B., son of the late Maj. Gen. Alexander Carnegy, C.B. (ante):—
Issue of the late Rev. Preb. Frederick William Carnegy, *b.* 1865, *d.* 1939: *m.* 1898, Mildred Constance, who *d.* 1952, dau. of the late Lieut.-Col. Robert Bourne, formerly of Cowarne Court, Much Cowarne, Herefordshire:—
Hector David, *M.A., L.R.A.M.*, *b.* 1913; ed. at Oxford Univ. (B.A. 1934, M.A. 1950): *m.* 1942, Pamela Alice Burnell, dau. of Henry Stafford Burnell Tubbs, of Winteradeen, Browning Avenue, Boscombe, Hants, and has issue living, Alison Sandra Christabel, *b.* 1944. *Residence,*—9, Browning Avenue, Boscombe, Hants.——Rachel Alexandra, *b.* 1912; has Order of Mercy: *m.* 1939, Cyril Herbert Knight, F.R.C.O., A.R.C.M. (Hon.), and has issue living, Virginia, *b.* 1941,—Celia Claire, *b.* 1945. *Residence,*—44, Strouden Avenue, Bournemouth.
Issue of the late Major Harry George Carnegy (twin), *b.* 1865, *d.* 1905: *m.* 1891, Rose Marion, who *d.* 1948. dau. of the late Major James Lancaster Bell, R.A.:—
Eileen Augusta, *b.* 1898: *m.* 1924, Philip Vaughan Roberts, from whom she obtained a divorce 1936, and has issue living, Eileen Patricia, *b.* 1925,—Susan Katharine, *b.* 1926. *Residence,*—

Grandson of the late James Souter Carnegy (infra):—
Issue of the late Colin Charles Macpherson Carnegy, *b.* 1885. *d.* 1931: *m.* 1922, Mary Teresa, dau. of Michael Diaz Infante, of Léon, Mexico:—
Charles William, *b.* 1923. *Residence,*—Guadalajara, Mexico.

Grandchildren of the late Charles Carnegy, yst. son of Patrick Carnegy of Lour, *b.* 1757 (ante):—
Issue of the late James Souter Carnegy, *b.* 1847, *d.* 1915: *m.* 1877, Jean Joyce, who *d.* 1923, dau. of the late Hon. Charles Macpherson, of New Brunswick:—
James William Macpherson, *b.* 1893.——Marguerite Sophia Macpherson: *m.* 1910, James Henry Nelson, who *d.* 19—. *Residence,*—Guadalajara, Mexico.

Issue of the late Robert Bower Carnegy, *b.* 1849, *d.* 1936: *m.* 1896, Fanny Jane, who *d.* 1949, dau. of T. A. H. Dodd, formerly of Newcastle-upon-Tyne:—
Francis Anthony Roberts, *b.* 1900; *m.* 1925, Valentine, who *d.* 1969, da. of Theodore Taupmann, and has issue living, Derek Francis (Chase Cottage, Ropley, Hants.), *b.* 1928; Lt.-Cdr. RN; *m.* 1961, Judith, only da. of the late David C. Herbert, and has issue living, Miles Bower, *b.* 1962, Angus *b.* 1964,—Julian Roy (of 66, Cromford Way, New Malden, Surrey), *b.* 1931: *m.* 1957, Vivien, da. of Stewart Kay-Menzies, and has issue living, Christopher Roy *b.* 1961, Diana Elizabeth *b.* 1959. *Residence,*—Greathed Manor, Lingfield, Surrey.

PREDECESSORS.—[1] *Sir* JOHN Carnegie, Knt., Sheriff of Forfarshire, was cr. *Lord Lour* 1639, and *Earl of Ethie* 1647, which titles after the Restoration he exchanged for those of *Lord Rosehill and Inglismaldie*, of Rosehill, and *Earl of Northesk* (peerage of Scotland), with precedence in 1639 and 1647 respectively, and with remainder to heirs male and of entail in his estate; *d.* 1667; *s.* by his son [2] DAVID, 2nd Earl; *d.* 1677; *s.* by his son [3] DAVID, 3rd Earl; *d.* 1688: *s.* by his son [4] DAVID, P.C., 4th Earl; a Representative Peer, Lord of Police, and Sheriff of co. Forfar; *d.* 1729; *s.* by his el. son [5] DAVID, 5th Earl; *d.* unmarried 1741; *s.* by his brother [6] GEORGE, 6th Earl; an Adm. of the White; *d.* 1792; *s.* by his son [7] WILLIAM, GCB, 7th Earl; a distinguished Adm., who was 3rd in command at the memorable battle of Trafalgar; *d.* 1831; *s.* by his son [8] WILLIAM HOPETOUN, 8th Earl; *b.* 1794; *m.* 1843, Georgina Maria, dau. of the late Adm. the Hon. Sir George Elliot, K.C.B. [E. Minto]; *d.* 1878; *s.* by his son [9] GEORGE JOHN, 9th Earl, *b.* 1843; a Representative Peer for Scotland: *m.* 1865, Elizabeth, who *d.* 1933, dau. of the late Adm. Sir George Elliot, K.C.B.; *d.* 1891; *s.* by his el. son [10] DAVID JOHN, 10th Earl, *b.* 1865; a Representative Peer for Scotland: *m.* 1894, Elizabeth Boyle, who *d.* 1950, dau. of the late Maj.-Gen. George Skene Hallowes: *d.* 1921; *s.* by his son [11] DAVID LUDOVIC GEORGE HOPETOUN, 11th Earl, *b.* 1901; a Representative Peer for Scotland 1959-63: *m.* 1st, 1923, Jessica (who obtained a divorce 1928), dau. of the late F. A. Brown, of U.S.A.; 2ndly, 1929, Elizabeth, dau. of the late Anthony A. Vlasto, formerly of Binfield Park, Bracknell, Berks., *d.* 1963; *s.* by his kinsman [12] JOHN DOUGLAS (son of the late Lt.-Col. the Hon. Douglas George Carnegie, 2nd son of 9th Earl), 12th Earl; *b.* 1895; 1914-18 War as Maj. RFA (despatches): *m.* 1920, Dorothy Mary, who *d.* 1967, da. of Col. Sir William Robert Campion, KCMG, FSO [B. Byron]; *d.* 1975; *s.* by his yr. son [13] ROBERT ANDREW, 13th Earl.

Northington, Baron, title of Baron Henley on Roll of H. L.

NORTHUMBERLAND, DUKE OF. (Percy.) [Duke G.B. 1766, Bt. E. 1660.]

ESPERANCE · EN · DIEU
Hope in God.

HUGH ALGERNON PERCY, *KG, TD, PC*, 10th Duke, and 13th Baronet; *b.* April 6th, 1914: *s.* to the Dukedom and subsidiary titles 1940, and to Barony of Percy [cr. England (by writ) 1723] 1957 ; ed. at Eton, and Ch. Ch., Oxford; FRS; Hon. DCL, Durham; Hon. ARCVS; Lord-in-Waiting to HM May to July 1940; Lord Steward of HM Household since 1973; Pres. N. Area, British Legion, Hon. Treas. Roy. Nat. Life-Boat Institution, a JP and a KStJ; Co. Councillor of Northumberland 1944-55, Alderman 1955-57; a Member of Hill Farming Advisory Cttee. for England and Wales 1946-60, of Co. Agric. Exec. Cttee. 1948-59, and Nat. Forestry Cttee. for England and Wales 1954-60; Pres. of British Horse So. 1950, Hunters Improvement and Light Horse Breeding So. 1954, Roy. Agricultural So. of England 1956 and 1962, and British Show Jumping Assocn. 1959; Chm. of Departmental Cttee., Slaughter of Horses 1952, of Court of Durham Univ. 1956-63, of Departmental Cttee. for Recruitment of Vet. Surgs. 1964, of Agric. Research Council 1958-68, and of Ind. Cttee. of Inquiry on Foot-and-Mouth Disease 1968-69; Master of Percy Foxhounds since 1940, Pres. of Northumberland Assocn. of Boys' Clubs since 1942, of Northumberland Scout Assocn. since 1946, of N. England Shipowners' Assocn. since 1952, and of Medical Research Council since 1969, Lord-Lt. of Northumberland since 1956, and Chancellor Univ. of Newcastle upon Tyne since 1964; Chm. Agric. Econ. Development Cttee. since 1971; late Capt. Northumberland Hussars (TARO 1949-64); 1939-45 War as Capt. RA; Dep. Hon. Col., Northumbrian Vols. TAVR 1971-75; Chm. T and AFA Northumberland 1950-56 and Pres. 1965-58; Pres. TAVR Assocn. for N. England 1968-71; bore Curtana at Coronation of Queen Elizabeth II; KG 1959, PC 1973: *m.* 1946, Lady Elizabeth Diana Montagu-Douglas-Scott, da. of 8th Duke of Buccleuch, and has issue.

Arms.—Quarterly : 1st and 4th grand quarters, 1st and 4th counterquartered 1st and 4th or, a lion rampant azure ; 2nd and 3rd gules, three lucies hauriant argent, *Lucy* ; 2nd and 3rd azure, five fusils conjoined in fesse or, *Percy* ; 2nd and 3rd grand quarters quarterly 1st and 4th or, three bars wavy gules, *Drummond*; 2nd and 3rd or, a lion's head erased within a double treasure flory counterflory gules, *Drummond, coat of augmentation.* **Crest.**—On a chapeau gules, turned up ermine, a lion statant, the tail extended, azure. **Supporters.**—*Dexter,* a lion rampant azure; *sinister,* a lion rampant guardant or, ducally crowned of the last, gorged with a collar compony argent and azure.

Seats.—Alnwick Castle, Northumberland; Syon House, Brentford. *Clubs,*—Boodle's, Turf, Northern Counties.

SONS LIVING.

HENRY ALAN WALTER RICHARD (*Earl Percy*), *b.* July 1st, 1953; ed. at Eton.

Lord Ralph George Algernon, *b.* 1956.
Lord James William Eustace, *b.* 1965.

DAUGHTERS LIVING.

Lady Caroline Mary, *b.* 1947: *m.* 1947, Count Pierre de Cabarrus, and has issue living, Chiara Thérèse Cecilia, *b.* 1974.
Lady Victoria Lucy Diana, *b.* 1949.
Lady Julia Helen, *b.* 1950.

BROTHERS LIVING.

Lord Richard Charles, *b.* 1921; ed. at Eton, and at Oxford and Durham (BSc 1950) Univs.; Lecturer in Zoology, Univ. of Newcastle-upon-Tyne, Lt.-Col. (Comdg. 1959-61) Northumberland Hussars (TA), and a DL of Northumberland; 1941-45 War in France and Germany as Capt. Grenadier Guards: *m.* 1966, Sarah Jane Elizabeth, da. of Petre Norton, of The Manor House, Whalton, Northumberland, and has issue living, Algernon Alan, *b.* 1969,—Josceline Richard, *b.* 1971. *Residence,*—58, Woodsford Sq., W14. *Address,*—University of Newcastle upon Tyne. *Clubs,*—Northern Counties, Turf.
Lord Geoffrey William, *b.* 1925 ; ed. at Eton ; European War 1943-44 as 2nd Lieut. Grenadier Guards : *m.* 1955, Mary Elizabeth, da. of Ralph Lea, and has issue living, Diana Ruth, *b.* 1956. *Residence,*—Embla Vean, Towednack, St. Ives, Cornwall.

SISTERS LIVING.

Lady Elizabeth Ivy (*Elizabeth Duchess of Hamilton and Brandon*), *b.* 1916; was a Train Bearer to the Queen at Coronation of King George VI.: *m.* 1937, 14th Duke of Hamilton and Brandon, who *d.* 1973.—*Residence,*—Lennoxlove, Haddington, E. Lothian.
Lady Diana Evelyn (*Duchess of Sutherland*), *b.* 1917: *m.* 1939, the 6th Duke of Sutherland. *Residence,*—Mertoun, St. Boswell's.

WIDOWS LIVING OF SONS OF SEVENTH DUKE.

Mary (of Horstead House, Norwich), dau. of the late Capt. George Sitwell Campbell Swinton: *m.* 1922, Col. Lord William Richard Percy, C.B.E., D.S.O., who *d.* 1963, and has issue living [see colls., infra].

Stella Katherine (*Baroness Percy of Newcastle*), da. of the late Maj.-Gen. Laurence George Drummond, CB, CBE, MVO [see E. Perth, colls.]: *m.* 1918, the 1st Baron Percy of Newcastle, who *d.* 1958, when the title became ext. *Residence,*—Glebe Orchard, Etchingham, Sussex.

COLLATERAL BRANCHES LIVING.

Issue of the late Col. Lord William Richard Percy, C.B.E., D.S.O., 5th son of 7th Duke, *b.* 1882, *d.* 1963: *m.* 1922, Mary (ante), dau. of the late Capt. George Sitwell Campbell Swinton (ante):—

Henry Edward (of The Manor Farm, Rackheath, Norwich, NOR 02Z), *b.* 1925: *m.* 1952, Eileen Ruth Morley, dau. of Lt.-Col. Wilmot Smyth Caulfeild, M.C. [see V. Charlemont, colls.], and has issue living, George Robert, *b.* 1953,—James Edward Caulfeild, *b.* 1958,—Lavinia Mary, *b.* 1955,—Susan Clare, *b.* 1961.——Gerald (c/o Lonrho Ltd., Cheapside House, EC2), *b.* 1928: *m.* 1954, Jennifer, dau. of J. B. Home-Rigg, and has issue living, Richard John, *b.* 1957,—Andrew Alan, *b.* 1963,—Katherine Susan, *b.* 1955,—Diana Mary, *b.* 1965.

Issue of the late Rt. Hon. Lord Eustace Sutherland Campbell Percy (7th son of 7th Duke), who was cr. *Baron Percy of Newcastle* 1952 [see that title].

Grandchildren of the late Algernon Hugh HEBER-PERCY (infra):—
Issue of the late Brigadier Algernon George William Heber-Percy, D.S.O., *b.* 1904, *d.* 1961: *m.* 1939, Daphne Wilma Kenyon (from whom he obtained a divorce 1950), dau. of the late Eustace Bowles [see B. Macclesfield, colls.]:—
Algernon Eustace Hugh (of Hodnet Hall, Hodnet, Market Drayton, Salop; Guards' Club), *b.* 1944: ed. at Harrow; late Lt., Grenadier Guards: *m.* 1966, the Hon. Margaret Jane Lever, yst. da. of 3rd Viscount Leverhulme, and has issue living, Emily Jane, *b.* 1969,—Lucy Ann, *b.* 1970.——Zara Mary *b.* 1940: *m.* 1961, Gavin Nicholas Tait, of 49, Caithness Rd., W14, and has issue living, Lucinda Clare *b.* 1962,—Arabella Kate Louise, *b.* 1965.——Jane Maude, *b.* 1942: *m.* 1965, Maj. Harold Antony McArthur Pyman, Life Gds., of Chitterwell, Sampford Arundel, Som., son of the late Gen. Sir Harold English Pyman, GBE, KCB, DSO, and has issue living, Richard Anthony, *b.* 1968,—Victoria Clare, *b.* 1966.

Grandchildren of the late Algernon HEBER-PERCY, el. son of the late Algernon Charles HEBER-PERCY (infra):—
Issue of the late Algernon Hugh HEBER-PERCY, *b.* 1869, *d.* 1941: *m.* 1903, Gladys May, *M.B.E.,* who *d.* 1956, dau. of William Edward Montagu Hulton-Harrop, of Lythwood Hall, Shrewsbury:—
Cyril Hugh Reginald, *D.S.O., M.C.*, *b.* 1905; ed. at Harrow; is Lieut.-Col. Welsh Guards; European War 1939-45 in France (wounded, M.C., D.S.O.); D.S.O. 1945: *m.* 1st, 1933, Anne youngest dau. of the late Charles T. Garland, of Moreton Morrell, Warwickshire; 2ndly, 1944, Diana, dau. of the late Raymond Radclyffe; 3rdly, 1959, Mrs. Pamela Fairhurst, and has issue living, (by 1st marriage) Alan Cyril, *b.* 1935: *m.* 1962, Susan Mary, only da. of Michael Charles St. John Hornby [see E. Dudley, colls.], and formerly wife of John George Vanderbilt Henry, Marquess of Blandford [see D. Marlborough], and has issue living, Larisia Anne, *b.* 1968,—William David, *MBE, b.* 1939; late Assist. Adviser, Aden; MBE (Civil) 1966: *m.* 1969, Christine, da. of Terence Horatio Gates, and has issue living, Peter Hugh *b.* 1971, Robin Virginia *b.* 1969,—(by 2nd m.) Cyril Raymond, *b.* 1945: *m.* 1971, Mrs. Heather Joan Miller, and has issue living, Tamara Joan *b.* 1972. *Residence,*—Pophleys, Radnage, Bucks.——Robert Vernon, *b.* 1911; ed. at Stowe; formerly Lt. King's Dragoon Gds. Reserve: *m.* 1942, Ann Jennifer Evelyn Elizabeth (who obtained a divorce 1947), only child of Sir Geoffrey Storrs Fry, KCB, CVO, 1st Bt., and has issue living, Victoria Gala, *b.* 1943: *m.* 1960, Peter Zinovieff, 49, Deodar Rd., SW15, and has issue living, Leo *b.* 1963, Nicholas *b.* 1966, Sofka *b.* 1961. *Residence,*—Faringdon House, Faringdon, Berks.

Grandchildren of the late Josceline Reginald Heber-Percy (infra):—
Issue of the late Cdr. David Josceline Algernon Heber-Percy, DSC, RN, *b.* 1909, *d.* 1971: *m.* 1942, Olivia Mary (Twysden, Kilndown, Cranbrook, Kent), yr. da. of the late R. W. O'Brien, of Drogheda:—
Michael David (Beechenwood Farm, Hillside, Odiham, Hants.), *b.* 1943; AADip. Hons.; ARIBA: *m.* 1965, Sarah, yr. da. of Alastair Gilmour, and has issue living, Colin Michael, *b.* 1968,—Paul David, *b.* 1970.——Carol Margaret Katherine, *b.* 1947: *m.* 1st, 1970 (m. diss. 1974), Robert Ward Woolner; 2ndly, 1974, Richard Edward Warcup Ashby, of C. 136, Lamberts Lane, Midhurst, Sussex, and has issue living (by 2nd m.), Daisy Katharine, *b.* 1974.——Angela Mary, *b.* 1949: *m.* 1970, Henry Boileau Fawcett, of Colliers Green Farm, Cranbrook, Kent, and has issue living, Emily, *b.* 1972,—Kate, *b.* 1975.

Granddaughters of the late Algernon HEBER-PERCY (ante):—
Issue of the late Josceline Reginald Heber-Percy, *b.* 1880, *d.* 1964: *m.* 1904, Katharine Lousia Victoria, who *d.* 1964, da. of the late Lord Algernon Malcolm Arthur Percy:—
Mary Katherine Victoria, *b.* 1906: *m.* 1930, Gerald Wellington Williams, JP, of Crockham Hse., Westerham, Kent, and has issue living, John Gerald Robertson (53, Porchester Terr., W2), *b.* 1937: *m.* 1962, Carola Zara Lennox, el. da. of Capt. Roger Edward Lennox Harvey [see Mainwaring, Bt., ext.], and has issue living, Algernon Guy Mainwaring *b.* 1966, Fergus John *b.* 1969,—Claire Priscilla *b.* 1972,—Brioni Katharine, *b.* 1933: *m.* 1956, Maurice John Reginald Armytage [see Armytage, Bt.],—Annette Mary Helena, *b.* 1934: *m.* 1957, Andrew Philip Watson [see B. Manton, colls.].——Dorothy Elizabeth (*Lady Walker-Okeover*) *b.* 1913: *m.* 1938, Col. Sir Ian Peter Andrew Munro Walker-Okeover, DSO, TD, JP, 3rd Bt.

Grandchildren of the late Algernon Charles HEBER-PERCY, son of the late Rt. Rev. the Hon. Hugh Percy, Bishop of Carlisle, 3rd son of 1st Earl of Beverley:—
Issue of the late Rev. Henry Vernon HEBER-PERCY, *b.* 1858, *d.* 1934: *m.* 1886, Judith Elizabeth, who *d.* 1948, dau. of Sir Vincent Rowland Corbet, 3rd Bt.:—
Aleen Judith, *b.* 1889: *m.* 1918, Maj. Oliver George Graham Villiers, DSO [see E. Clarendon, colls.]. *Residence,*—53, Brockhill Rd., Hythe, Kent.——Rachel Joan (11, Chelsea Close, Manor Rd., Bexhill-on-Sea), *b.* 1893: *m.* 1918, Capt. Gerald Berkeley Villiers, OBE, RN (ret.), who *d.* 1959 [see E. Clarendon, colls.].

Issue of the late Alan William HEBER-PERCY, *b.* 1865, *d.* 1946: *m.* 1st, 1893, the Hon. Susan Alice, who *d.* 1933, dau. of 2nd Viscount Portman; 2ndly, 1936, Mabel, who *d.* 1953, dau. of the late Sir William Darracott. and widow of E. Herbert Hinds:—
(By 1st marriage) Hugh Alan, *OBE* (Dorset Farm, Box 42, White River, Transvaal), *b.* 1897; ed. at Charterhouse; Capt. (ret.) 15th/19th Hussars, and Lt.-Col. (ret.) S. African Forces: 1914-18 War (wounded), 1939-45 War in E. Africa as Staff Maj. S. African Forces and in Middle East as Lt.-Col. on Staff (despatches, OBE); OBE (Mil.) 1946: *m.* 1926, Monica Violet, da. of the late Edmond Waterton Coningsby Erskine [see E. Mar and Kellie, colls.], and widow of Lt.-Col. G. D. Maynard, and has issue living, Robin Erskine (of Louvain, White River, E. Transvaal, S. Africa), *b.* 1927; ed. at Hilton Coll., Natal; European War 1945 with S. African Engineer Corps.: *m.* 1953, Ann, da. of John Gaw,—Philip Reginald (36, Chiral Drive, Westville, Durban, Natal), *b.* 1929; ed. at Hilton Coll., Natal; is a Chartered Accountant: *m.* 1952, Cherie, da. of Johannes van Wyk, and has issue

living, Robyn (da.) *b.* 1954, Julia *b.* 1956,—John Kellie (Albury, 40, High Rd., Bramley, Johannesburg, S. Africa), *b.* 1935; ed. at Hilton Coll., Natal: *m.* 1961, Rosalind Marion, da. of the late W. H. Gathercole, and has issue living, Gillian Dorothy *b.* 1965, Helen Marjorie *b.* 1968.——Bryan, *b.* 1903; formerly Capt. RA: *m.* 1936, Etelka, da. of Istvan Kuiti, of Hungary. *Address.*—P.O. Box 38, Somerset West, Capt. Province, S. Africa.——Peter, OBE, *b.* 1908; ed. at Wellington Coll.; is Lt.Col. 55th Anti-Aircraft Regt. RA (TA); 1939-45 War in Middle East and Italy (OBE), OBE, (Mil) 1945: *m.* 1st, 1930 (divorce 1947), Josephine Sylvia, el. da. of the late Brig.-Gen. Cyril Randall Crofton, CBE, of Trobridge, Crediton; 2ndly, 1947, Elsa Maria, da. of the late Giamcomo Nission, of Pisa, Italy, and has issue living, (by 1st m.) Sylvia Venetia, *b.* 1932: *m.* 1953, David Gerald Stern, son of the late Lt.-Col. Sir Albert Gerald Stern, KBE, CMG [Orr-Lewis, Bt.], and has issue living, Mark David Robin *b.* 1955, Sylvia Louise *b.* 1957,—Susan Deirdre, *b.* 1938: *m.* 1958, Anthony Benedict Xavier Fenwick [see V. Lilford, colls.],—(by 2nd m.) Sandra Caroline, *b.* 19—. *Residence*,—Il Poggiolino, Montenero, Leghorn, Italy.——John (2, Barnhill Park, Dalkey, co. Dublin), *b.* 1910; ed. at Wellington Coll.; Group-Capt. (ret.) RAF; 1939-45 War (despatches); appointed an ADC to High Commr. for Egypt and Sudan 1936, and Air Attaché, British Embassy, The Hague 1947: *m.* 1st, 1940 (m. diss. 1949), Eve Robertson; 2ndly, 1950, Marie Elise Teixeira de Mattos, and has issue living, (by 1st m.) Christopher John (10, Butt Hill Av., Prestwich, Manchester, M25 8PN), *b.* 1941: *m.* 1964, Lyndis Elizabeth, yst. da. of the Rt. Rev. John Henry Lawrence Phillips, Lord Bishop of Portsmouth, and has issue living, William John *b.* 1965, Thomas Henry *b.* 1967, Anna *b.* 1970,—Susan Elizabeth, *b.* 1943: *m.* 1965, Earl John Sabbagh, of 76, Sheen Park, Richmond, Surrey, and has issue living, Isabella Mary *b.* 1972,—Josceline Mary, *b.* 1946: *m.* 1969, Richard Newell, of 1, Victor Close, Heavitree, Exeter, and has issue living, Adam Richard Eric *b.* 1971, Benjamin Rhodri, *b.* 1972, a da. *b.* 1975.

Grandchildren of the late Rev. Henry Percy, son of the late Rt. Rev. the Hon. Hugh Percy, Bishop of Carlisle (ante):—
Issue of the late Alfred Percy, *b.* 1850, *d.* 1907: *m.* 1st, 1878, Ada Elizabeth, who *d.* 1898, dau. of the late Rev. Daniel Packard; 2ndly, 1899, Mary Hyland:—
(By 2nd marriage) Henry, *b.* 1901: *m.* 1934, Mary Lavinia Mervyn Percy, of Fremantle, W. Australia.
——Mary (Unit 2, Waterman Terr., Mitchell Park, 5043, S. Aust.), *b.* 1903: *m.* 1930, Hugh Bernard Doherty, who *d.* 1974.

Grandchildren of the late Josceline Hugh Percy (infra):—
Issue of the late Josceline Richard Percy, *b.* 1894, *d.* 1971: *m.* 1929, Mary, who *d.* 1964, da. of Harold Nicholson, of Oak House, Farnworth, Bolton:—
Hugh Edward, *b.* 1938.——Eleanor Mary, *b.* 1940: *m.* 1962, James Rolf Adams, of 117, Keeler Av., Berkeley, Cal., USA.

Granddaughter of the late Rev. Henry Percy (ante):—
Issue of the late Josceline Hugh Percy, *b.* 1856, *d.* 1910 : *m.* 1892, Grace Anne, who *d.* 1960, el. dau. of the late Edward Percy Thompson :—
Margaret (of Buckfield, Woodbury Salterton, Exeter), *b.* 1898.

PREDECESSORS.—[1] ALGERNON Seymour, 7th Duke of Somerset (see † infra), was cr. *Baron Warkworth*, of Warkworth Castle, co. Northumberland and *Earl of Northumberland* (peerage of Great Britain) 1749, with remainder to Sir Hugh Smithson, 4th Bt. (see *₀* infra), who in 1740 *m.* Lady Elizabeth, the Duke's only surviving child; *d.* 1750; *s.* by his son-in-law [2] *Sir* HUGH Smithson, *K.G.*, 2nd Earl; assumed by Act of Parliament 1750 the surname of Percy, in lieu of his patronymic; cr. *Earl Percy* and *Duke of Northumberland* (peerage of Great Britain) 1766, and *Lord Lovaine, Baron of Alnwick* (peerage of Great Britain) 1784, with remainder to his 2nd son Algernon; *d.* 1786; *s.* by his el. son [3] HUGH, *K.G.*, 2nd Duke; *d.* 1817; *s.* by his el. son [4] HUGH, *K.G.*, 3rd Duke; was Viceroy of Ireland, Lord-Lieut. and Vice Adm. of Northumberland, and Chancellor of Univ. of Cambridge, &c.; *d.s.p.* 1847; *s.* by his brother [5] ALGERNON, *K.G.*, *P.C.*, 4th Duke; a distinguished Adm.; cr. *Baron Prudhoe*, of Prudhoe Castle, co. Northumberland (peerage of United Kingdom) 1816; was First Lord of the Admiralty 1852; *d.* 1865, when the Barony of Prudhoe became extinct, the Barony of Percy devolved upon the 7th Duke of Atholl, and the Baronetcy, the Earldom of Percy, and Dukedom reverted to his kinsman [6] GEORGE, *P.C.*, 5th Duke, el. son of Algernon, 2nd Baron Lovaine (ante) who had in 1790 been cr. *Earl of Beverley* (peerage of Great Britain); *b.* 1778; sat as M.P. for Beeralston 1808-30; was a Lord of the Treasury 1804-6, and Capt. of Yeomen of the Guard 1842-6 : *m.* 1801, Louisa Harcourt, dau. of the Hon. James Archibald Stuart-Wortley (E. Wharncliffe); *d.* 1867; *s.* by his son [7] ALGERNON GEORGE, *K.G.*, *P.C.*, 6th Duke, *b.* 1810; was a Lord of the Admiralty 1858, Vice-Pres. of Board of Trade 1859, and Lord-Privy Seal 1878-80; M.P. for Beeralston (C) 1831-2 and for N. Northumberland 1852-65; Lord-Lieut. of Northumberland, and of co. and city of Newcastle-on-Tyne: *m.* 1845, Louisa, who *d.* 1890, dau. of the late Henry Drummond, of Albury Park, Surrey; *d.* 1899; *s.* by his el. son [8] HENRY GEORGE (who in 1887 had in his father's lifetime been called to the House of Lords in the Barony of Lovaine), 7th Duke, *b.* 1846: *m.* 1868, Lady Edith Campbell, who *d.* 1913, dau. of 8th Duke of Argyll, K.G., K.T.; *d.* 1918; *s.* by his el. surviving son [9] ALAN IAN, *K.G.*, *C.B.E.*, *M.V.O.*, 8th Duke, *b.* 1880; Pres. of Roy. Institution : Lord-Lieut. of Northumberland 1918-30: *m.* 1911, Lady Helen Magdalen Gordon-Lennox, *GCVO*, *CBE*, *JP*, who *d.* 1965, da. of 7th Duke of Richmond; *d.* 1930; *s.* by his el. son [10] HENRY GEORGE ALAN, 9th Duke, *b.* 1912; Lieut. Grenadier Guards; *d.* (killed in action during European War) 1940; *s.* by his brother [11] HUGH ALGERNON, 10th Duke and present peer; also Earl of Northumberland, Earl Percy, Earl of Beverley, Baron Percy, Baron Warkworth, and Lord Lovaine, Baron of Alnwick.

† [1] ALGERNON Seymour, Earl of Hertford (afterwards 7th Duke of Somerset); summoned to Parliament 1722 by writ on death of his mother, Lady Elizabeth Percy, dau. and heir of 5th Earl of Northumberland in the erroneous belief that he had inherited the Barony of Percy (cr. 1299), which was attainted in 1406, and by sitting in 1723 a barony of writ was thereby created, and he became *Baron Percy* (cr. 1723); *s.* by his dau. [2-5] *Lady* ELIZABETH, who *m.* the 1st Duke of Northumberland (ante), the Barony being merged in the Dukedom until the death of 4th Duke in 1865, when it devolved upon his grand-nephew [6-10] JOHN JAMES HUGH HENRY Stewart-Murray, 7th Duke of Atholl (grandson of Lady Emily Frances Percy, sister of 5th Duke of Northumberland who *m.* the 1st Baron Glenlyon); *d,* 1917, when the Barony became merged in the Dukedom of Atholl until the death of the 9th Duke 1957, when it passed to [11] the 10th Duke of Northumberland (ante).

₀ [1] HUGH Smithson, a zealous royalist, cr. *Baronet* 1660; *d.* 1670; *s.* by his son [2] *Sir* JEROME, 2nd Bt.; *d.* 1684; *s.* by his son [3] *Sir* HUGH, 3rd Bt.; conformed to doctrine of the Church of England, he having been born a Roman Catholic; *d.* 1729; *s.* by his son [4] HUGH, 4th Bt., who was cr. *Duke of Northumberland* (ante).

NORTON, BARON. (Adderley.) [Baron U.K. 1878.]

It is an honour to add justice to law.

JOHN ARDEN ADDERLEY, *OBE*, 7th Baron; *b.* Nov. 24th, 1915; *s.* 1961; ed. at Radley, and at Magdalen Coll., Oxford (B.A. 1938); formerly Assist. Master at Oundle Sch. ; European War 1939-45 in N. Africa, Sicily and Italy as Major R.E. (despatches); OBE (Civil) 1964: *m.* 1946, Betty Margaret, only da. of the late James McKee Hannah, and has issue.

Arms.—Argent, on a bend azure, three mascles of the field. Crest,—On a chapeau azure, turned up ermine, a stork argent. Supporters,—On either side a stork argent, gorged with a chain or, pendent therefrom an escocheon azure, charged with a mascle also argent.

Residence,—Fillongley Hall, Coventry.

SONS LIVING.

Hon. JAMES NIGEL ARDEN (50, Adam and Eve Mews, Kensington High St., W8), *b.* June 2nd, 1947; *m.* 1971, Jacqueline Julie, el. da. of Guy W. Willett, of Trevarno, Danes Hill, Woking, Surrey.
Hon. Nigel John, *b.* 1950; Lt. Life Gds.

BROTHER LIVING.

Hon. Michael Charles, *OBE, AFC* (23, Welham Rd., Norton, Malton, Yorks.; RAF Club), *b.* 1917; ed. at Radley, and at Sidney Sussex Coll., Camb.; Wing Com. RAF (ret.); 1939-45 War (AFC and Bar), Malaya 1949-51 (King's Commendation), Korea 1951-52 (American DFC, Bronze Star and Air Medal); OBE (Mil) 1960: *m.* 1953, Margrethe Ann, *MRCVS,* only da. of Karl Gerhardt Ornbo, and has issue living, Charles Henry, *b.* 1954,—Anthony John, *b.* 1955,—David Michael, *b.* 1962,—Jane Margrethe, *b.* 1957.

SISTERS LIVING.

Hon. Rosemary Etheldreda, *b.* 1913: *m.* 1949, the Rev John Paul Drake, and has issue living, Simon Francis, *b.* 1956,—Catherine Elizabeth, *b.* 1950: *m.* 1974, John William Grace. *Residence,*—Stewkley Vicarage, Leighton Buzzard.

Hon. Elisabeth Joan, *b.* 1919: *m.* 1943, Professor (Alexander) Colin Patton Campbell, MB, ChB, MSc, FRCP(Edin.), FRCPath., and has issue living, Andrew Colin, *b.* 1943,—Richard Hubert Alexander, *b.* 1946,—Rosamund Elizabeth *b.* 1950. *Residence,*—The Priory House, Ascott-under-Wychwood, Oxon.

Hon. Mary, *b.* 1922: European War 1939-45 as 3rd Officer W.R.N.S.: *m.* 1950, Hugh Montgomery Campbell, son of the Rt. Rev. and Rt. Hon. Bishop Henry Colville Montgomery Campbell, K.C.V.O., M.C., P.C., D.D., formerly Lord Bishop of London, and has issue living, Philip Henry, *b.* 1951,—Elisabeth Mary, *b.* 1954,—Veronica, *b.* 1958. *Residence,*—16, Ashworth Rd., W.9.

AUNTS LIVING. (*Daughters of 5th Baron.*)

Hon. Joan (*Hon. Lady Hunter*), *b.* 1889: *m.* 1913, Maj.-Gen. Sir Alan John Hunter, K.C.V.O., C.B., C.M.G., D.S.O., M.C., who *d.* 1942, and has issue living, John Antony, *D.S.O., O.B.E., MC* (36, Ethelburt Av., Swaythling, Southampton), *b.* 1914; Brig. (ret.) late KRRC; 1939-45 War in N. Africa, Sicily, and N.-W. Europe; MBE (Mil) 1944, DSO 1945, OBE (Mil) 1955: *m.* 1st, (m. diss. 1971), Dauphine Laetitia Janet Colquhoun, da. of the late Nicolas Conynghame Symonds Bosanquet; 2ndly, 1971, Carole, el. da. of David Reid Milligan, MB, ChB, and has issue living, (by 1st m.), Antony Nicolas *b.* 1945, Sarah Dauphine *b.* 1947,—John Roland (of Green Farm, Geldeston, Beccles), *b.* 1918; Lt.-Col. (ret.) RA; 1939-45 War in France, N. Africa, and Italy: *m.* 1947, Jennifer Mary Roose, da. of Lt.-Col. Walter Alexander Paton, MC, and has issue living, Charles John *b.* 1951, Susan Joan *b.* 1949, Elizabeth Marian *b.* 1958, Julia Mary *b.* 1960,—Mary Arden, *b.* 1924: *m.* 1949, Brian Charles MacDermot, OBE, MVO, of The Old Rectory, St. James, Shaftesbury, Dorset, and has issue living, Alan David *b.* 1950, Mark Bernard *b.* 1951, Denis Benedict *b.* 1952, Dominic Charles *b.* 1955, Henry Simon *b.* 1958, Paul Hilary *b.* 1961, Francis Celestine *b.* 1962, Lucy Ann *b.* 1963, Jacinta Mary *b.* 1966,—Ann Eanswythe, *b.* 1925; ARCM. *Residence,*—The Bell House, Little Tew, Oxfordshire.

Hon. Lettice Mary, *b.* 1894: *m.* 1918, Squadron-Leader Charles Phillimore Lewton Firth, D.L., R.A.F., formerly Capt. Worcestershire Regt., who *d.* 1955. *Residence,*—The Dower House, Compton Durville, South Petherton, Somerset.

PREDECESSORS.—[1] Rt. Hon. Sir CHARLES BOWYER Adderley, *K.C.M.G.,* el. son of the late Charles Clement Adderley, of Hams Hall, Warwickshire, and Norton, co. Stafford; *b.* 1814; Pres. of Board of Health, and Vice-Pres. of Committee of Privy Council for Education 1858-9, Under-Sec. of State for Colonies 1866-8, and Pres. of Board of Trade 1874-8; M.P. for N. Staffordshire (C) 1841-78; cr. *Baron Norton,* of Norton-on-the-Moors, co. Stafford (peerage of United Kingdom) 1878: *m.* 1842, the Hon. Julia Anne Eliza, who *d.* 1887, dau. of 1st Baron Leigh; *d.* 1905; *s.* by his son [2] CHARLES LEIGH, 2nd Baron; *b.* 1846: *m.* 1870, Caroline, who *d.* 1922, dau. of Sir Alexander Dixie, 10th Bt.; *d.* 1926; *s.* by his el. son [3] RALPH BOWYER, 3rd Baron, *b.* 1872: *m.* 1899, Mary Louisa, who *d.* 1939, dau. of Robert Watson, formerly of Ballydarton, co. Carlow, and widow of Inglis Brady: *d.* 1933; *s.* by his brother [4] RONALD WOLSTAN FLEETWOOD, 4th Baron, *b.* 1885: *m.* 1931, Hylda, who *d.* 1950, dau. of the late Robert William Tovey, of Cheltenham, and widow of Hilary George Dunbar, of Glasgow; *d.* 1944; *s.* by his uncle [5] HENRY ARDEN (2nd son of 1st Baron), 5th Baron; *b.* 1854: *m.* 1881, Grace, who *d.* 1944, dau. of the late William Bruce Stopford-Sackville, of Drayton House, Thrapston; *d.* 1945; *s.* by his only son [6] HUBERT BOWYER ARDEN, 6th Baron; *b.* 1886; a Lay Guardian of the Sanctuary of Our Lady of Walsingham, Norfolk: *m.* 1912, Elizabeth, who *d.* 1952, dau. of the late William John Birkbeck, of Stratton Strawless Hall, Norfolk; *d.* 1961; *s.* by his el. son [7] JOHN ARDEN, 7th Baron, and present peer.

NORWICH, LORD BISHOP OF. (Wood.)

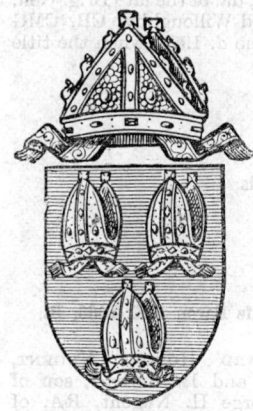

Rt. Rev. MAURICE ARTHUR PONSONBY WOOD, DSC, only son of Arthur S. Wood; b. Aug. 26th, 1916; ed. at Monkton Combe Sch., Queens' Coll., Camb. (MA), and Ridley Hall, Camb.; Chap. RNVR 1943-47 (DSC); R. of St. Ebbe, Oxon. 1947-52, V. and Rural Dean of Islington 1952-61; Proctor in Convocation, London 1955-71; Commissary Sydney 1961-71; Prin. Oak Hill Theological Coll. 1961-71; Examining Chap. to Bishop of Norwich 1962-71; consecrated 69th Bishop of Norwich (and 110th of the See) 1971; author of "Like a Mighty Army" 1956, "Your Suffering" 1959, "Christian Stability" 1968: m. 1st, 1947, S. Marjorie Pennell, who d. 1954; 2ndly, 1955, M. Margaret, da. of the late Rev. E. J. Sandford, MC, MA.

Patron of some eighty-one livings, alternately of three, and of one every third turn; also of the Archdeaconries of Norwich, Norfolk, and Lynn; Titular Abbot of St. Benet's.

The Diocese of Norwich was established in 1088, by Herbert de Lozinga, Bishop of Thetford, of the more ancient See, founded at Dunwich by Felix of Burgundy in 630.

Episcopal Signature,—"Maurice Norvic:"
ARMS OF THE SEE,—Azure, three mitres two and one labelled or.
Residence,—The Bishop's House, Norwich, NR3 1SB.

NORWICH, VISCOUNT. (Cooper.) [Viscount U.K. 1952.]

I hate and I love.

JOHN JULIUS COOPER, 2nd Viscount b. Sept. 15th, 1929; s. 1954; ed. at Eton, and at New Coll., Oxford (B.A. honours 1952); late RN; HM Foreign Ser. 1952-64; m. 1952, Anne Frances May, el. da. of the late Hon. Sir Bede Edmund Hugh Clifford, GCMG, CB, MVO [see B. Clifford of Chudleigh, colls.], and has issue.

Arms,—Or three lions rampant gules on a chief azure a portcullis chained between two fleur de lys of the first. Crest,—On the battlements of a tower argent a bull passant sable armed and unguled or. Supporters,—On either side a unicorn argent gorged with a collar with chain reflexed over the back or pendent from the collar of the dexter a portcullis chained and from that of the sinister a fleur de lys both gold.

Residence,—24, Blomfield Road, W.9.
Clubs,—Buck's, Beefsteak, RAC.

SON LIVING.
Hon. JASON CHARLES DUFF BEDE, b. Oct. 27th, 1959.

DAUGHTER LIVING.
Hon. Alice Clare Antonia Opportune (Artemis), b. 1953.

WIDOW LIVING OF FIRST VISCOUNT.
Lady DIANA OLIVIA WINIFRED MAUD MANNERS (Dowager Viscountess Norwich, known as Lady Diana Cooper), dau. of 8th Duke of Rutland: m. 1919, the 1st Viscount, who d. 1954. Residence,—10, Warwick Avenue, W.2.

PREDECESSOR.—[1] Rt. Hon. Sir ALFRED DUFF COOPER, G.C.M.G., D.S.O., P.C., son of the late Sir Alfred Cooper, F.R.C.S. [D. Fife]; b. 1890; appointed Private Sec. to Parliamentary Under-Sec. of State for Foreign Affairs, 1922; was Financial Sec., War Office 1928-29, and again (in National Govt.) 1931-33, Financial Sec. to Treasury 1934-35, Sec. of State for War 1935-37, First Lord of the Admiralty 1937-38, Min. of Information 1940-41, Chancellor of Duchy of Lancaster 1941-43, British Envoy to French National Committee in N. Africa 1943-44, and Ambassador Extraor. and Plen. to France 1944-47; European War 1914-19 as Lieut. Grenadier Guards (despatches, D.S.O.); sat as M.P. for Oldham (C) 1924-29, and for St. George's Div. of Westminster 1931-45; cr. Viscount Norwich, of Aldwick, co. Sussex (peerage of United Kingdom) 1952: m. 1919, Lady Diana Olivia Winifred Maud Manners, dau. of 8th Duke of Rutland d. 1954; s. by his only son [2] JOHN JULIUS, 2nd Viscount and present peer.

Nottingham, Earl of, see Earl of Winchilsea and Nottingham.

NUGENT, BARONY OF. (Nugent.) [Extinct 1973.]

WIDOW LIVING OF FIRST BARON

ROSALIE (*Baroness Nugent*) (40, Bramerton St., SW3), da. of the late Brig.-Gen. the Hon. Charles Strathavon Heathcote-Drummond-Willoughby, CB, CMG [see E. Ancaster, colls.]: *m.* 1935, the 1st Baron, who *d.* 1973, when the title became ext.

Nugent Baron (Austria), see Earl of Westmeath colls.

NUGENT OF GUILDFORD, BARON. (Nugent.) (Life Baron U.K. 1966, Bt. U.K. 1960.)

I have resolved.

GEORGE RICHARD HODGES NUGENT, PC; *Life Baron,* and 1*st Baronet,* son of the late Col. George H. Nugent, RA, of Churt, Surrey; *b.* June 6th, 1907; ed. at Imperial Ser. Coll. and RMA; a JP; Co. Alderman of Surrey 1951-52; Parl. Sec. Min. of Agriculture, Fisheries and Food 1951-57, and to Min. of Transport and Civil Aviation 1957-59, and Chm. of Select Cttee. on Nationalised Industries 1961-64; Chm. of Thames Conservancy Board 1960-74, of Agric. Marketing Development Exec. Cttee. 1962-68 and of Standing Conference on London Regional Planning since 1962, and of Animal Virus Research Inst. since 1964, and Pres. of Assocn. of River Authorities 1965-74; Chm. National Water Council since 1973; a Member of Guildford Diocesan Synod since 1970; Vice-Pres. of RAC; a Dep. Speaker, House of Lords; Hon. D.Univ. Surrey; FRSA; MP for Guildford Div. of Surrey (*C*) 1950-66; *cr.* PC 1962, a *Baronet* 1960, and *Baron Nugent of Guildford,* of Dunsfold, co. Surrey (Life Baron) 1966: *m.* 1937, Ruth, da. of the late Hugh G. Stafford, of Tilford, Surrey.

Arms,—Ermine, two bars gules, a canton of the last.   Crest,—A cockatrice with wings expanded vert charged with a rose argent barbed and seeded proper.   Supporters,—*Dexter,* a cockatrice wings addorsed vert beaked combed and wattled gules; *sinister,* a swan wings addorsed argent, each gorged with a collar or charged with three crescents sable.
Residence,—Blacknest Farm, Dunsfold, Godalming, Surrey.   *Clubs,*—Junior Carlton, RAC.

NUNBURNHOLME, BARON. (Wilson.) [Baron U.K. 1906.]

For laws and kings.

BEN CHARLES WILSON, 4th Baron; *b.* July 16th, 1928; *s.* 1974; ed. at Eton; Maj. (ret.) R. Horse Gds.: *m.* 1958, Ines, da. of Gerard Walravens, of Brussels, and has issue.

Arms,—Or, an ancient ship sable, on a chief azure three ducal coronets of the first.   Crest,—Between two ducal coronets or a demi-wolf sable, holding between the paws a like coronet.   Supporters,—On either side a Benedictine nun, holding in the anterior hand a rosary, all proper.

Residence,—Shillinglee Park, Chiddingfold, Surrey.

DAUGHTERS LIVING.
Hon. Lorraine Mary Charmiane Nicole, *b.* 1959.
Hon. Tatiana, *b.* 1960.
Hon. Ysabelle, *b.* 1962.
Hon. Ines (twin), *b.* 1962.

BROTHER LIVING.
Hon. CHARLES THOMAS, (Grassthorpe Mill, Sutton-on-Trent, Newark, Notts.), *b.* May 27th, 1935; ed. at Eton; was a Page of Honour to HM King George VI 1950-52: *m.* 1969, Linda Kay, da. of O. J. Stephens, of Woodlands, Challock Lees, Kent, and has issue living, Stephen Charles, *b.* 1973,—Nathalia Ellen, *b.* 1971.

HALF-BROTHER LIVING.

Hon. David Mark, *b.* 1954.

SISTER LIVING.

Hon. Charmiane Elizabeth Violet Cecilia, *b.* 1930: *m.* 1957, William Rippon Bissill, and has issue living, John James Rippon, *b.* 1957,—William Henry, *b.* 1960,—Kathleen Mary Florence, *b.* 1966. *Residence,*—Cranmer House, Aslockton, Notts.

WIDOW LIVING OF SON OF FIRST BARON.

Avery, dau. of the late Col. the Hon. Guy Greville Wilson, C.M.G., D.S.O., T.D., who *d.* 1943, and has issue living [see colls., infra]. *Residence,*—29, Campden Hill Gate, W8.

WIDOW LIVING OF THIRD BARON.

ALEX (Priory Lands, Appledore, Kent), only da. of Capt. Douglas Hockly, of 10, Eastgate, Tenterden, Kent: *m.* 1st, 1953, as his 2nd wife, the 3rd Baron, who *d.* 1974; 2ndly 1975, H. O. J. C. Jonas.

COLLATERAL BRANCH LIVING.

Issue of the late Hon. Guy Greville Wilson, C.M.G., D.S.O., T.D., 2nd son of 1st Baron, *b.* 1877, *d.* 1943: *m.* 1st, 1904, Lady Isabel Innes-Ker, who *d.* 1905, dau. of 7th Duke of Roxburghe; 2ndly, 1911, Avery (ante), dau. of the late Geoffrey Fowell Buxton, C.B. [see Buxton, Bt., colls.] :—

(By 2nd m.) Jeremy Charles, *DFC, b.* 1923; F/Lt. RAF (ret.): *m.* 1944, June Patricia, da. of the late Thomas Townsend Bucknill, and has issue living, Peter Richard, *b.* 1945,—Thomas Charles, *b.* 1946. *Residence,*—Fulmer Cottage, Fulmer, Bucks.——Malise Joy, *b.* 1913: *m.* 1942, Lieut.-Col. Archibald William Antony Smith, DSO., Coldstream Guards, and has issue living, Antony Luke, *b.* 1943,—Rupert Malise, *b.* 1944. *Residence,* Wymondham House, Melton Mowbray.——Alison Ann, *b.* 1914: *m.* 1938, Brig. John Edmund Swetenham, DSO, late 5th Dragoon Guards, and R. Scots Greys, and has issue living, John Foster (Pound Farmhouse, Rayne, Braintree, Essex), *b.* 1939; Capt. R. Scots Greys (ret.): *m.* 1964, Marion, yr. da. of G. A. Parker, of Bayways, Great Bookham, Surrey, and has issue living, Jeremy Edmund *b.* 1967, Charlotte *b.* 1966. *Residence,*—Green Farm, Brompton by Sawdon, Scarborough, Yorks.

PREDECESSORS.—[1] CHARLES HENRY Wilson, son of the late Thomas Wilson (*b.* 1792), of Cottingham and Hull, Yorkshire, by Susannah West (*b.* 1796); *b.* 1833; Chm. of the Hull Seamen's Orphan Asylum; M.P. for Kingston-upon-Hull (*L*) 1874-85, and for W. Div. of Kingston-upon-Hull 1885-1905; cr. *Baron Nunburnholme,* of the City of Kingston-upon-Hull (peerage of United Kingdom) 1906 : *m.* 1871, Florence Jane Helen, *O.B.E.,* who *d.* 1932, dau. of the late Col. William Henry Charles Wellesley, formerly 7th Fusiliers; *d.* 1907; *s.* by his el. son [2] CHARLES HENRY WELLESLEY, *C.B., D.S.O.,* 2nd Baron; *b.* 1875; S. African War 1899-1902, European War 1914-19, Sheriff of Hull 1899-1901, and Lord-Lieut. of E. Riding of Yorkshire 1908-24 : M.P. for Hull, W. Div. (*L*) Jan. 1906 to Oct. 1907: *m.* 1901, Lady Marjorie Cecilia, who *d.* 1968, dau. of 1st Marquess of Lincolnshire; *d.* 1924; *s.* by his el. son [3] CHARLES JOHN, 3rd Baron; *b.* 1904: *m.* 1st, 1927 (m. diss. 1947) Lady Mary Beatrice Thynne, who *d.* 1974, da. of 5th Marquess of Bath; 2ndly, 1953, Alex (who *m.* 2ndly 1975, H. O. J. C. Jonas), only da. of Capt. Douglas Hockly, of 10, Eastgate, Tenterden, Kent; *d.* 1974; *s.* by his el. son [4] BEN CHARLES, 4th Baron and present peer.

OAKSEY, BARON TREVETHIN AND (Lawrence.) [Baron UK 1921 and 1947.]

JOHN GEOFFREY TRISTRAM LAWRENCE (*Baron Oaksey*), 4th Baron Trevethin and 2nd Baron Oaksey; *b.* March 21st, 1929; *s.* 1971; ed. at Eton, New Coll., Oxford, and Yale Univ.; late P/O RAFVR and Lt. 9th Lancers: *m.* 1959, Victoria Mary, el. da. of Maj. John Dennistoun, MBE, of Antwick, Stud House, Letcombe Regis, Berks., and has issue.

Arms,—Per chevron argent and gules, two crosses raguly in chief of the last, and a lamb in base holding with the dexter foreleg a banner and staff, all of the first, the banner charged with a cross couped azure. **Crest,**—A dragon's head erased sable between two bugle horns counter-embowed or. **Supporters,**—*Dexter,* a Guernsey bull; *sinister,* a hart both proper.

Residence,—Hill Farm, Wilts. *Club,*—Brooks's.

SON LIVING.

Hon. PATRICK JOHN TRISTRAM, *b.* June 29th, 1960.

DAUGHTER LIVING.

Hon. Sara Victoria, *b.* 1961.

SISTERS LIVING.

Hon. (Mary) Elizabeth (*Hon. Lady Adams*), *b.* 1922: *m.* 1954, Sir Philip George Doyne Adams, KCMG, HM Foreign Ser., and has issue living, Geoffrey Doyne, *b.* 1957,—Justin Alexander, *b.* 1961,—Lucy Victoria, *b.* 1955,—Harriet Mary, *b.* 1959. *Residence,*—68, Sussex Sq., W2.

Hon. (Enid) Rosamond, *b.* 1924: *m.* 1950, Group Capt. Hugh Spencer Lisle Dundas, DSO, DFC, RAF (ret.), of The Schoolroom, Dockenfield, Farnham, Surrey, and 83, Iverna Court, W8, [see M. Zetland, colls.].

Hon. (Anne) Jennifer, *b.* 1926: *m.* 1951, Lieut.-Col. Frederick John Burnaby-Atkins, The Black Watch, and has issue living, John Charles Graham *b.* 1961,—Charlotte Elizabeth Cecily, *b.* 1952,— Catherine Rose, *b.* 1954,—Rosamond Louise, *b.* 1957. *Residence,*—14, Woodsfords Sq., W14; 3, The Street, Oaksey, Wilts.

WIDOW LIVING OF THIRD BARON TREVETHIN AND FIRST BARON OAKSEY.

Marjorie, OBE, TD, da. of the late Cdr. Charles Napier Robinson, RN; *d.* 1971; *s.* by his son [4] ATS; a JP for Wilts; OBE (Mil.) 1941; da. of the late Cdr. Charles Napier Robinson, RN (ret.): *m.* 1921, the 3rd Baron Trevethin and 1st Baron Oaksey, who *d.* 1971.

COLLATERAL BRANCH LIVING.

Issue of the late Hon. Alfred Clive Lawrence, CBE, el. son of 1st Baron Trevethin, *b.* 1876, *d.* 1926: *m.* 1924, Mildred Margaret (*Mildred, Viscountess Hailsham*), who *d.* 1964, having *m.* 2ndly, 1929, th3 1st Viscount Hailsham, who *d.* 1950, da. of the late Rev. Edward Parker Dew, of Breamore, Hants:—
Domini Margaret, *b.* 1925. *Residence,*—

PREDECESSORS.—[1] *Rt. Hon.* ALFRED TRISTRAM Lawrence, PC, son of David Lawrence, surg. of Pontypool, Monmouthshire, *b.* 1843; a Judge of High Court of Justice (King's Bench Div.) 1904-21, and Lord Ch. Justice of England 1921-2; *cr. Baron Trevethin,* of Blaengawney, co. Monmouth (peerage of United Kingdom) 1921: *m.* 1875, Jessie Elizabeth, who *d.* 1931, da. of George Lawrence, JP, *d.* 1936; *s.* by his second son [2] CHARLES TREVOR, 2nd Baron *b.* 1879; Lt.-Col. late RHA and RFA; *d.* 1959; *s.* by his brother [3] *Rt. Hon.* Sir GEOFFREY, 3rd Baron, DSO, TD, *b.* 1880; Judge of High Court of Justice (King's Bench Div.) 1932-44, Lord Justice of Appeal 1944-47, and Lord of Appeal in Ordinary 1947-57; *cr. Baron Oaksey,* of Oaksey, co. Wilts. (Peerage of UK) 1947: *m.* 1921, Majorie, OBE, TD, da. of the late Cdr. Charles Napier Robinson, RN; *d.* 1971; *s.* by his son [4] JOHN GEOFFREY TRISTRAM, 4th Baron Trevethin, 2nd Baron Oaksey and present peer.

OAKSHOTT, BARON. (Oakshott.)　[Extinct 1975.]
SONS LIVING OF LIFE BARON.

Hon. Sir ANTHONY HENDRIE OAKSHOTT, 2nd Bt., who *s.* to baronetcy (cr. 1959) 1975 [see Oakshott, Bt.].

Hon. Michael Arthur John Oakshott [see Oakshott, Bt.]

WIDOW LIVING OF LIFE BARON.

JOAN (*Joan, Baroness Oakshott*) (The Mount, Broxton, Cheshire; Flat D; 42, Eaton Sq., SW1), da. of Marsden Withington, of London and Buenos Aires: *m.* 1928, the 1st Baron and 1st Baronet, who *d.* 1975, when the peerage became ext.

O'BRIEN OF LOTHBURY. BARON. (O'Brien.)　[Life Baron 1973.]

LESLIE KENNETH O'BRIEN, *GBE, PC,* son of the late Charles John Grimes O'Brien; *b.* Feb. 8th, 1908; ed. at Wandsworth Sch.; Hon. DSc. City Univ.; entered Bank of England 1927; Ch. Cashier 1955-62, Exec. Dir. 1962-64, Dep. Gov. 1964-66, and Gov. 1963-73; a Liveryman of Mercers' Co., Hon. Liveryman of Leathersellers' Co., and a Freeman of City of London; an Advisory Dir. of Unilever Ltd., since 1973; *cr.* GBE (Civil) 1967, PC, 1970, and *Baron O'Brien of Lothbury,* of City of London (Life Baron) 1973: *m.* 1932, Isabelle Gertrude, da. of Francis John Pickett, MBE, and has issue.

Arms,—Gules bezanty, three lions passant gardant in pale, each per pale or and argent. Crest,— In front of two keys in saltire azure, a needle point downwards proper threaded gules. Supporters,— On either side a lion gardant per fess or and argent, in the mouth a key or, standing upon a heap of coins or and argent.

Clubs,—Boodle's, MCC, All England Lawn Tennis.

SON LIVING.

Hon. Michael John, (The Lodge Thursley, nr. Godalming, Surrey) *b.* 1933: *m.* 1964, Marion Sarah, da. of the late Walter Graham Blackie.

Offaly, Earl of,　grandson of Duke of Leinster.

Ogilvy Lord,　son of Earl of Airlie.

OGMORE, BARON. (Rees-Williams.) [Baron U.K. 1950.]

Faithful unto Death.

DAVID REES REES-WILLIAMS, T.D., P.C., 1st Baron, son of the late William Rees Williams, F.R.C.V.S., of Garth Celyn, Bridgend, Glamorgan ; b. Nov. 22nd, 1903 ; ed. at Mill Hill Sch., and at Univ. of Wales ; admitted a Solicitor (Honours) 1929 ; Advocate and Solicitor Straits Settlements 1930 ; Bar. Nigeria 1956; Chm. of Property Owners' Building Soc.; Dir. of Leo Laboratories, Ltd., Patron of Bridgend Rugby Football Club, Pres. of Liberal Party 1963-64, and of Bridgend YMCA; a Member of Standing Group of Privy Councillors on Peacetime Histories, and of Investiture Cttee. for Investiture of HRH the Prince of Wales; carried the Coronet at Investiture of HRH the Prince of Wales 1969; a Member of Govt. Mission to Sarawak 1946; Chm. of Burma Frontiers Area Ctte. of Enquiry 1947; was Parl. Under-Sec. of State of Colonies 1947-50, Parl. Under-Sec. of State for Commonwealth Relations 1950-51 and Min. of Civil Aviation June to Oct. 1951; a Member of UK Delegation to UN Assembly 1950, Leader of UK Delegation to, and Chm. of, African Defence Facilities Conference 1951; a Member of Departmental Cttee. on Section 2 of Official Secrets Act 1911 1971-72; 1939-45 War as Lt.-Col. RA, and with Mil. Govt., Germany; MP for S. Div. of Croydon (Lab.) 1945-50; Order of Agga Maha Thray Sithu of Burma and of Pangkuan Negara of Malaya; cr. Baron Ogmore, of Bridgend, co. Glamorgan (peerage of United Kingdom) 1950, and PC 1951: m. 1930, Alice Alexandra Constance, JP, da. of W. R. Wills (Lord Mayor of Cardiff 1945-46), and has issue.

Arms,—Azure two bars wavy argent on a chief arched of the second between as many hurts, each charged with a quatrefoil or a hurt thereon a sun in splendour of the third. Crest,—A tiger's head couped proper charged on the neck with three chevronels couped gules. Supporters,—Dexter, a tiger proper charged on the shoulder with three chevronels couped gules ; sinister, a horse argent.

Residence,—48, Cheyne Court, Royal Hospital Rd., SW3. Club,—National Liberal.

SONS LIVING.

Hon. GWILYM REES (4, Foster Rd., Chiswick, W4), b. May 5th, 1931; ed. at Mill Hill Sch., and at St. Luke's Coll., Exeter; in Dept of Environment: m. 1967, Gillian Mavis, da. of M. K. Slack, of Hindley, Lancs., and has issue living, Christine Ann, b. 1968,—Jennet Elizabeth, b. 1970.

Hon. Morgan, b. 1937; ed. at Mill Hill Sch.: Lt. R. Regt. of Wales (TA): m. 1964 (m. diss. 1970), Patricia, only da. of C. Paris Jones, of Harcourt, Constantine Bay, Padstow. Residence,—98, Elm Park Gdns., SW10.

DAUGHTER LIVING.

Hon. (Joan) Elizabeth, b. 1936; ed. at Croham Hurst Sch., and at Mont Olivet, Lausanne: m. 1st, 1957 (m. diss. 1969), Richard St. John Harris, actor; 2ndly, 1971, Rex Carey Harrison, actor, and has issue living, (by 1st m.), Damian David, b. 1958,—Jared Francis, b. 1961,—Jamie St. John, b. 1963. Residence,—Villa San Genesio, Portofino, Italy.

O'HAGAN, BARON. (Strachey.) [Baron U.K. 1870.]

Buas no bar.
Tenez le vraye.
Victory or death.
Keep the truth.

Mihi res non me rebus.

CHARLES TOWNELEY STRACHEY, 4th Baron ; b. Sept. 6th, 1945 ; s. 1961 ; a Page of Honour to H.M. 1959-62; ed. at Eton, and at New Coll., Oxford (MA); a Member of European Parl. since 1973: m. 1967, HSH Princess Tamara, el. da. of HSH Prince Michael Imeretinsky, of La Colla, Route de Castellar, Menton, France, and has issue.

Arms,—Quarterly : 1st and 4th ermine, a bend and on a chief azure a fleur de lis or, O'Hagan ; 2nd and 3rd argent, a fesse and in chief three mullets sable, Towneley. Crests,—1st, upon a fasces fessewise proper, a cubit arm vested gules, cuffed ermine, the hand holding a dagger erect, both also proper, O'Hagan ; 2nd, upon a perch or, a hawk close proper, beaked and belled gold ; round the perch a ribbon gules, Towneley. Supporters,—On either side a lion or, collared gemel sable, pendant therefrom an escutcheon argent, charged with a dexter hand couped gules. Seat,—Sutton Court, Pensford, Somerset. Residence,—Lion Gate House, Lion Gate Gdns., Richmond, Surrey.

DAUGHTER LIVING.

Hon. Nino Natalia O'Hagan, b. 1968.

BROTHER LIVING. (*Raised to the rank of Baron's son 1963.*)
Hon. RICHARD TOWNELEY, *b.* Dec. 29th, 1950; ed. at Eton.

SISTERS LIVING. (*Raised to the rank of a Baron's daughters* 1963.
Hon. Frances Towneley, *b.* 1948: *m.* 1967, the Hon. Hugh Marcus Thornely Gibson, of the Fold
Parwich, Ashbourne, Derbys. [see B. Gibson].
Hon. Jane Towneley, *b.* 1953: *m.* 1972, William Stone.

AUNT LIVING. (*Daughter of 3rd Baron.*)
Hon. Helen Frances Alice, *b.* 1912; late VAD: *m.* 1940, Capt. Ian Desmond Curry, RA, who *d.* 1969,
having assumed by deed poll 1942 the surname of Curry-Towneley-O'Hagan, and has issue living,
Padriac Desmond (13, Arlington Av., N1), *b.* 1946: *m.* 1971, Judith Patricia, only da. of the Hon.
Robin Sandbach Borwick [see B. Borwick, and has issue living, Fiann James, *b.* 1974]. *Residence,—*
24, Burgh St., Islington, N1.

MOTHER LIVING.
Lady Mary Sophia Palmer, dau. of 3rd Earl of Selborne; Lady-in-Waiting to H.M. when H.R.H.
Princess Elizabeth 1944-7, and Extra Lady-in-Waiting 1947-9: *m.* 1944, the Hon. (Thomas) Anthony
Edward Towneley Strachey, who *d.* 1955 (having assumed by deed poll 1938, the additional Christian
name of Towneley, and his mother's maiden name of Strachey in lieu of his patronymic), only son
of 3rd Baron. *Residence,—*8, Pembroke Sq., W8.

PREDECESSORS.—[1] *Rt. Hon. Sir* THOMAS O'Hagan, *K.P.*, only son of the late Edward
O'Hagan; *b.* 1812; was Solicitor-Gen. for Ireland 1860-1, Attorney-Gen. 1861-5, a Justice
of the Common Pleas in Ireland 1865-8, and Lord Chancellor of Ireland 1868-74 and 1880-1;
sat as M.P. for Tralee (*L*) 1863-5; *cr. Baron O'Hagan,* of Tullaghogue, co. Tyrone (peerage
of United Kingdom) 1870: *m.* 1st, 1836, Mary, who *d.* 1868, dau. of Charles Hamilton Teeling,
of Belfast; 2ndly, 1871, Alice Mary, who *d.* 1921, dau. and co-heiress of Col. Charles
Towneley, of Towneley, Lancashire: *d.* 1885; *s.* by his son [2] THOMAS TOWNELEY, 2nd
Baron. *b.* 1878: Lieut. Grenadier Guards: *d.* (in S. Africa) 1900: *s.* by his brother [3]
MAURICE HERBERT TOWNELEY, 3rd Baron; *b.* 1882; Hon. Major R.H.A. (T.A.) and Hon. Col.
4th (Cadet) Batn. Essex Regt. and 6th Batn. Essex Regt. (T.A.), Assist. Private Sec. (unpaid) to
First Lord of Admiralty 1906-7, a Lord-in-Waiting to King Edward VII 1907-10, and Dep. Speaker
and Dep. Chm., House of Lords 1950-61; assumed by Roy. licence 1909, the additional surname
and arms of Towneley: *m.* 1st, 1911, the Hon. Frances Constance Maddalena Strachey, who *d.*
1931, only da. of 1st Baron Strachie; 2ndly, 1937, Evelyn Violet, who *d.* 1965, da. of Harry Thornton
Ross, and widow of Lt.-Col. Henry Osbert Samuel Cadogan, R. Welch Fusiliers; *d.* 1961,; *s.* by his
grandson [4] CHARLES TOWNELEY Strachey (son of the late Hon. (Thomas) Anthony Edward
Towneley Strachey, who assumed by deed poll 1938, the additional Christian name of Towneley,
and his mother's maiden name of Strachey in lieu of his patronymic), 4th Baron and present peer.

OLIVIER, BARON. (Olivier.) [Life Baron 1970.]

I rejoice in the House of the Lord
even as the olive tree flourishes

LAURENCE KERR OLIVIER, son of the late
Rev. Gerard Kerr Olivier, of Dorking, Surrey;
b. May 22nd, 1907; ed. at St. Edward's
Sch., Oxford; Hon. MA Tufts, Mass., Hon.
DLitt. Oxford, Manchester, and London,
Hon. LLD Edinburgh; Actor, Stage and Film
Producer and Dir.; Dir. of National Theatre
of GB 1962-73; a Member of South Bank
Theatre Board since 1967; Freeman of
City of London, Cdr. Order of Dannebrog
of Denmark, Officer of Legion of Honour,
and Grand Officer Order of Merit of Italy;
1939-45 War as Lt. (A) RNVR; *cr.* Knt.
1947, and *Baron Olivier,* of Brighton, co.
Sussex (Life Baron) 1970: *m.* 1st, 1930,
Jill, da. of H. V. Esmond (actress), who
obtained a divorce 1940; 2ndly, 1940 (m.
diss. 1960), Mrs. Vivien Mary Holman (the
actress Vivien Leigh), who *d.* 1967, da. of
Ernest Hartley; 3rdly, 1961, Joan, CBE (the
actress Joan Plowright), who was *cr.* CBE
(Civil) 1970), da. of William Ernest Plowright, and formerly wife of Roger
Gage, and has issue by 1st and 3rd m.

Arms,—Argent, on a mount in base vert charged with a plough or, an olive tree fructed proper
over all two bars gemel in fess, each engrailed on the upper and invected on the lower edge azure.
Crest,—A swan rousant argent membered or, gorged with a baron's coronet proper, affixed thereto a
chain reflexed over the back, the terminal ring encircling the sinister leg or and holding in the beak an
olive branch leaved fructed proper.

*Address,—*33/34, Chancery Lane, WC2. *Clubs,—*Garrick, MCC, RAC.

SONS LIVING. (*By* 1st *m.*)
Hon. (Simon) Tarquin (31, Queensdale Rd., Holland Park, W11), *b.* 1936: *m.* 1965, Riddelle, yr. da. of
Patrick Boyce Riddell Gibson, and has issue.

(*By* 3rd *m.*)
Hon. Richard, *b.* 1961.

DAUGHTERS LIVING.   (*By 3rd m.*)
Hon. Tamsin, *b.* 1963.
Hon. Julie Kate, *b.* 1966.

Baron Olivier's uncle, the Rt. Hon. Sir Sydney Haldane Olivier, KCMG, CBE, was *cr. Baron Olivier*, of Ramsden, co. Oxford, 1924, and *d.* 1943, when the title became ext.

O'NEILL, BARON.   (O'Neill.)   [Baron U.K. 1868.]

Honours follow us without seeking.

The Red Hand of Ireland.

RAYMOND ARTHUR CLANABOY O'NEILL, 4th Baron; *b.* Sept. 1st, 1933; *s.* 1944; ed. at Eton; Maj. N. Irish Horse (AVR IIA); Lt.-Col. (RARO); a DL for co. Antrim: *m.* 1963, Georgina Mary, da. of Lord George Francis John Montagu Douglas-Scott [see D. Buccleuch], and has issue.

Arms.—Quarterly: 1st and 4th per fesse wavy, the chief argent, and the base representing waves of the sea, in chief a dexter hand couped at the wrist gules, in base a salmon naiant proper, *O'Neill*; 2nd and 3rd checky, or and gules, a chief vair, *Chichester.* **Crests,**—1st, an arm embowed in armour, the hand grasping a sword, all proper; 2nd, a stork rising, with a snake in its beak, all proper. **Supporters,**—On either side a lion gules, gorged with an antique crown argent, pendant therefrom an escutcheon; the *dexter* charged with the arms of O'Neill, and the *sinister* with those of Chichester.

Seat,—Shane's Castle, Antrim.   *Clubs,*—Turf, Ulster.

SONS LIVING.
Hon. SHANE SEBASTIAN CLANABOY, *b.* July 25th, 1965.
Hon. Tyrone Alexander, *b.* 1966.
Hon. Rory St. John, *b.* 1968.

SISTER LIVING.
Hon. Fionn Frances Bride, *b.* 1936; ed. at Heathfield, and at St. Anne's Coll., Oxford: *m.* 1961, John Albert Leigh Morgan, Dip. Ser., of 182, Ebury St., SW1, and has issue living, John Edward Rustand, *b.* 1964,—Mary Ann Frances, *b.* 1962,—Catherine Martha Annabel, *b.* 1966.

UNCLE LIVING.
Rt. Hon. Terence Marne, *b.* 1914; *cr. Baron O'Neill of the Maine* (Life Peerage) 1970 [see that title].

AUNT LIVING.   (*Raised to the rank of a Baron's daughter* 1930.)
Hon. Mary Louisa Hermione, *b.* 1905 : *m.* 1934, Lieut.-Col. (Derick) Ernest Frederick Orby Gascoigne, who *d.* 1972, son of Brig.-Gen. Sir (Ernest) Frederick (Orby) Gascoigne, KCVO, CMG, DSO, and has issue living, Arthur Bamber (1, St. Helena Terr, Richmond, Surrey) *b.* 1935; ed. at Eton, and Magdalene Coll., Camb.: *m.* 1965, Christina Mary, da. of the late Alfred Henry Ditchburn, CBE,—Brian Alvery, *b.* 1943; ed. at Eton,—Veronica Mary (*Hon. Mrs. William J. L. Plowden*), *b.* 1938: *m.* 1960, the Hon. William Julis Lowthian Plowden, el. son of Baron Plowden (Life Peer).   *Residence,*—162, Cranmer Court Whiteheads Grove, SW3.

GREAT-UNCLE LIVING.   (*Son of 2nd Baron.*)
Rt. Hon. (Robert William) Hugh (*Baron Rathcavan*), *b.* 1883; *cr.* a *Baronet* 1929, and *Baron Rathcavan* 1953 [*see* that title].

GREAT-AUNTS LIVING.   (*Daughters of 2nd Baron.*)
Hon. Rose Anne Mary, *b.* 1884 : *m.* 1920, Vice-Adm. John William Leopold McClintock, C.B., D.S.O., who *d.* 1929, and has issue living, John O'Neill, *b.* 1925 : *m.* 1953, Evelyn Monica, younger dau. of T. T. Blyth of Tunbridge Wells, Kent,—Annette Rose, *b.* 1921 : *m.* 1950, Raymond H. F. Firth, who *d.* 1967.   *Residence,*—Brewhouse, Red Hall, Ballycarry, co. Antrim.
Hon. Alice Esmeralda, *b.* 1886 : *m.* 1909, John Randal Parsons, who *d.* 1967 [E. Rosse, colls.].   *Residence,*—Little Gillions, Croxley Green, Herts.

WIDOW LIVING OF THIRD BARON.
ANN GERALDINE MARY, dau. of the Hon. Guy Lawrence Charteris [see E. Wemyss] : *m.* 1st, 1932, the 3rd Baron, who *d.* (killed in action in Italy) 1944 ; 2ndly, 1945, the 2nd Viscount Rothermere, who obtained a divorce 1952; 3rdly, 1952, Ian Lancaster Fleming, who *d.* 1964 [Rose, Bt., *cr.* 1874, colls.] *Residence,*—Sevenhampton Place, Wilts.

PREDECESSORS.—[1] *Rev.* WILLIAM Chichester, el. son of the Rev. Edward Chichester, a descendant of John Chichester, younger brother of 2nd Earl of Donegall [see M. Donegall, colls.] in 1855 succeeded to the estates of his cousin Earl O'Neill (extinct), and in that year assumed by Roy. licence the surname of O'Neill; *b.* 1813; *cr. Baron O'Neill*, of Shanes Castle, co. Antrim (peerage of United Kingdom) 1868: *m.* 1st, 1839, Henrietta, who *d.* 1857, dau. of the late Hon. Robert Torrens, a Judge of the Common Pleas in Ireland; 2ndly, 1858, Elizabeth Grace, who *d.* 1905, dau. of the Ven. John Torrens, D.D., Archdeacon of Dublin ; *d.* 1883 ; *s.* by his son [2] EDWARD, 2nd Baron, *b.* 1839; M.P. for co. Antrim (*C*) 1863-80 : *m.* 1873, Lady Louisa Katherine Emma Cochrane, who *d.* 1942, dau. of 11th Earl of Dundonald; *d.* 1928 ; *s.* by his grandson [3] SHANE EDWARD ROBERT [el. son of the late Capt. the Hon. Arthur Edward Bruce O'Neill, M.P., Household Cav., who *d.* (killed in action during European War) 1914, el. son of 2nd Baron], 3rd Baron; *b.* 1907 ; Lieut.-Col. N. Irish Horse: *m.* 1932, Anne Geraldine Mary, dau. of the Hon. Guy Lawrence Charteris [E. Wemyss] ; *d.* (killed in action in Italy) 1944 ; *s.* by his son [4] RAYMOND ARTHUR CLANABOY, 4th Baron and present peer.

O'NEILL OF THE MAINE, BARON. (O'Neill.) [Life Baron 1970.]

Honours follow us without seeking.

The Red Hand of Ireland

TERENCE MARNE O'NEILL, *PC*, yst. son of the late Capt. the Hon. Arthur Edward Bruce O'Neill, of Shane's Castle, MP for co. Antrim, and brother of 3rd Baron O'Neill; *b.* Sept. 10th, 1914; raised to the rank of a Baron's son 1930; ed. at Eton; late Capt. Irish Guards; DL of co. Antrim; 1939-45 War (wounded); a Member of House of Commons, N. Ireland 1946-70 (Dep. Speaker 1953-55), Parl. Sec. Min. of Health, N. Ireland 1948-53, Min. of Home Affairs 1956-57, Min. of Finance 1957-63, and Prime Min. 1963-69; *cr.* PC (N. Ireland) 1956, and *Baron O'Neill of the Maine,* of Ahoghill, co. Antrim (Life Baron) 1970: *m.* 1944, Katharine Jean, da. of the late William Ingham Whitaker, DL, of Pylewell Park, Lymington, Hants. [V. Melville], and has issue.

Arms,—Quarterly: 1st and 4th per fess wavy, the chief argent, and the base representing waves of the sea, in chief a dexter hand couped at the wrist gules, in base a salmon naiant proper. O'*Neill;* 2nd and 3rd checky, or and gules, a chief vair, *Chichester.* **Crest,**—1st, an arm embowed in armour, the hand grasping a sword, all proper; 2nd, a stork rising, with a snake in its beak, all proper. **Mottoes,**— Invitum sequitur honos (Honours follow us without seeking), and Lamh dearg E'rin (*The Red Hand of Ireland*). **Supporters,**—*Dexter,* a lion gules gorged with an Eastern Crown argent, pendent therefrom by a chain gold an escutcheon charged with the arms of O'Neill, namely per fess argent and on waves of the sea a fish naiant proper in chief a dexter hand appaumy couped gules; sinister, a horse argent collared gemel resting the interior hind foot on a mascle azure.

Residence,—Lisle Court, Lymington, Hants.

SON LIVING.

Hon. Patrick Arthur Ingham, *b.* 1945; ed. at Eton; Lt. QRI Hussars.

DAUGHTER LIVING.

Hon. Penelope Anne, *b.* 1947: *m.* 1970, Christopher William Kerr Devas, of Bridge Cottage, N. Fambridge, Chelmsford, Essex, [see M. Lothian, colls.].

ONSLOW, EARL OF. (Onslow.) [Earl U.K. 1801, Bt. E. 1674 (with precedence of 1660).]

Quick without impetuosity.

MICHAEL WILLIAM COPLESTONE DILLON ONSLOW, 7th Earl, and 11th Baronet (of 2nd creation); *b.* Feb. 28th, 1938; *s.* 1971; ed. at Eton, and Sorbonne; Insurance Broker: *m.* 1964, Robin Lindsay, only da. of Maj. Robert Lee Bullard III, of Atlanta, Georgia, USA, and has issue.

Arms,—Argent, a fesse gules, between six Cornish choughs proper. **Crest,**—An eagle sable, preying on a partridge or. **Supporters,**— Two falcons close proper, belled or.

Residence,—Temple Court, Clandon Park, Guildford. *Club,*—Beefsteak.

SON LIVING.
RUPERT CHARLES WILLIAM BULLARD (*Viscount Cranley*), *b.* June 16th, 1967.
DAUGHTER LIVING.
Lady Arabella Ann Teresa, *b.* 1970.
SISTER LIVING.
Lady Teresa Lorraine, *b.* 1940: *m.* 1961, Auberon Alexander Waugh of Combe Florey House, Taunton, Somerset [E. Carnarvon, colls.], and has issue living, Alexander Evelyn Michael, *b.* 1963, —Nathanial Thomas Biafra, *b.* 1968,—Margaret, Sophia Laura, *b.* 1962,—Daisy Louisa Dominica, *b.* 1967.
GREAT-AUNT LIVING. (*Daughter of 4th Earl.*)
Lady Dorothy Evelyn Augusta (*Dowager Countess of Halifax*), *CI*, *DCVO*, *LLD*, *b.* 1885; Hon. LLD Leeds 1939; is a DStJ, and a JP for E. and W. Riding of Yorkshire; appointed a Lady-in-Waiting to HM the Queen 1937, and an Extra Lady-in-Waiting 1946; CI 1926, DCVO 1953: *m.* 1909, the 1st Earl of Halifax, who *d.* 1959. *Residence,*—Bugthorpe, York.

MOTHER LIVING.
Hon. Pamela Louisa Eleanor Dillon, (12, Callcott St., W8), only da. of 19th Viscount Dillon: *m.* 1936 (m. diss. 1962) the 6th Earl, who *d.* 1971.

WIDOW LIVING OF SIXTH EARL.
NINA, *MBE* (*Jo, Countess of Onslow*) (Sturdee's, Freeland, Oxford), yr. da. of Thomas Sturdee; MBE (Civil) 1953: *m.* 1962, as his 2nd wife, the 6th Earl, who *d.* 1971.

COLLATERAL BRANCHES LIVING.

Branch from 2nd son of 2nd Earl.

Grandchildren of the late Lieut.-Col. Arthur Edward Mainwaring-Ellerker-Onslow, son of the late Col. the Hon. Thomas Cranley Onslow, M.P., 2nd son of 2nd Earl :—
Issue of the late Charles Vere Townshend MAINWARING-ELLERKER-ONSLOW, b. 1848, d. 1927, having assumed by Roy. licence 1898 the additional surnames and arms of Mainwaring-Ellerker: m. 1876, Amelia, who d. 1941, dau. of the late Frederick Roger Carter :—
Arabella Vere Gwendolen, b. 1885; is Sister Mary Vere, Community of St. Katharine. Residence,— St. Katharine's Convent, Parmoor, Henley-on-Thames.——Minnie Margaret Matilda, b. 1892, m. 1914, Sidney Victor Webb Perkins, who d. 1961, and has issue living, Barbara Opal Onslow, b. 1915: m. 1939, George Edward Twine, MA, LL.B (Cantab.), of Kolkinnon House, Up Nately, Basingstoke, Hants., and has issue living, George Nicholas, b. 1941,—Julian Edward, b. 1942. Residence,—Merry Close, Burley, Hants.
Issue of the late Arthur Edward ONSLOW, b. 1852, d. 1927: m. 1888, Emma Elizabeth Barnacote :—
Vivian Isidore. b. 1888 : m. 1st, 1912, Lily, who d. 1918, el. dau. of Charles Edward Henson, of Hope House, The Vineyard, Richmond, Surrey ; 2ndly, 1919, Annie Dorothea Rose, el. dau. of Frank Charles Davis, of Evercreech, near Bath, and has issue living, (by 2nd marriage) Arthur Charles Vivian, b. 1920,—Denzil Isidore Charles, b. 1924,—Constance Vivienne, b. 1934. Residence,—Ellerker House, Evercreech, Somerset.

Branch from 2nd son of 1st Earl.

Granddaughter of the late Frederick Horace Onslow, son of the late Capt. Arthur Onslow, son of 2nd son of 1st Earl :—
Issue of the late Arthur Onslow, b. 1871, d. 1937: m. 1893, Emily, who d. 1952, dau. of W. A. Howe, and has issue living :—
Valentine Charlotte, b. 1900. Residence,—Addison House, Niagara-on-the-Lake, Ontario, Canada.
[Male line in remainder to the Barony and Baronetcy.]

Branch from 1st son of 1st son of 2nd son of brother of 1st Baron.

Grandchildren of the late William Cleveland Onslow, son of the late Major Pitcairn Onslow, son of Rev. George Walton Onslow, el. son of George Onslow, M.P. (b. 1731), el. son of the late Lt.-Gen. Richard Onslow, nephew of 1st Baron Onslow, and uncle of 1st Earl:—
Issue of the late Guy Cleveland Onslow, b. 1884, d. 1952: m. 1916, Angela Mary, who d. 1974, da. of Robert Pearce, of Ripley Court, Surrey:—
Guildford Arthur Richard, b. 1921; ed. at Camb. Univ. (BA 19—): m. 1945, Ilse, only da. of Julius Sahm.——Rose Saltern, b. 1918.——Juliana Mary, b. 1922: m. 1952, Andrew Spalding Mackintosh, and has issue living, Robert Andrew Nicholas, b. 1954,—James Athole Guy, b. 1958,—Fiona Margaret, b. 1956,—Ruth Alison, b. 1960. Residence,—Scarp, 211B, Old Dover Road, Canterbury, Kent.

Granddaughter of the late Major Pitcairn Onslow (ante) :—
Issue of the late Maj.-Gen. George Thorp Onslow, C.B., b. 1858, d. 1921 : m. 1887, Ethel Paul, who d. 1934, dau. of the late Rev. David Kitcat, formerly R. of Weetonbirt, Gloucestershire :—
Adelaide Ethel Saltren, b. 1896 ; is a Nun.

Branch from 2nd son of 1st son of 2nd son of brothers of 1st Baron.

Grandchildren of the late Maj.-Gen. James William MACARTHUR-ONSLOW, VD (infra):—
Issue of the late James Arthur MACARTHUR-ONSLOW, b. 1898, d. 1959: m. 1923, Constance Faith, who d. 1962, da. of George Herbert of Sydney:—
James William Macleay (19, Noreen St., Chapple Hill, Brisbane, Qld., Aust.), b. 1932; ed. at Knox Gram. Sch., Wahroonga, NSW: m. 1964, Margaret Alice, da. of Colin Basil Peter Bell, of Kenmore, Brisbane, Aust., and has issue living, James Stuart Macleay, b. 1966,—Julienne Elizabeth, b. 1969. ——Susan Helen, b. 1935: m. 1962, Lt.-Col. Ian Henry Hayman, Austn. Staff Corps, of 3, Moten St., Campbell, ACT, Aust., and has issue living, Rosemary Susan, b. 1963,—Charlotte Elizabeth b. 1966.——Sandra Ruth (Unit 24, 386 Mowbray Rd., Chatswood, NSW 2067), b. 1936.

Grandchildren of the late Capt. Alexander Walton Onslow, RN, el. son of Arthur Pooley Onslow, el. son of the Rev. Arthur Onslow, 2nd son of George Onslow, MP (ante):—
Issue of the late Maj.-Gen. James William MACARTHUR-ONSLOW, V.D., b. 1867, d. 1946: m. 1897, Enid Emma, who d. 1952, da. of Arthur H. Macarthur, of N.S. Wales:—
Elizabeth Enid, b. 1903: m. 1935, Fredrik Ludwig Rothe. Residence,—15, Wyuna Rd., Point Piper, Sydney, NSW.

Issue of the late Arthur John MACARTHUR-ONSLOW, b. 1873, d. 1954, having assumed the additional surname of Macarthur: m. 1902, Christian Leslie, who d. 1949, da. of the late R. Bell, of Golf Hill, Victoria, Australia:—
Richard Walton, b. 1904; is Lt.-Col. Australian Light Horse: m. 1928, Lois Ruth, da. of H. B. Greene, of Barncleuth Sq., Sydney, NSW, and has issue living, Richard Bowring (Mooramong, Walcha Rd., NSW), b. 1934: m. 1960, Christina Helen Huntly Gordon, da. of Ronald Arthur McWilliam, of Vaucluse, Sydney, NSW, and has issue living, Richard Matthew b. 1962, Rohan James b. 1964, Lachlan Robert Hugh b. 1973,—John Walton, b. 1943,—William Robert, b. 1945.——Rosalind Sibella, b. 1917: m. 1944, John Carter, and has issue living, Charles John, b. 1950,—Prudence Mary Leslie, b. 1945: m. 1970, Hugh Geoffrey O'Neil, of Yamminga, Forges, NSW, and has issue living, Sophie Christobel Robina b. 1973. Residence,—Kikiamah, Young, NSW.

Issue of the late Brig.-Gen. George Macleay MACARTHUR-ONSLOW, CMG, DSO, VD, b. 1875, d. 1931: m. 1907, Violet Marguerite (c/o The Queen's Club, Elizabeth St., Sydney, N.S. Wales), da. of the late W. F. Gordon, of Manar, near Braidwood, N.S. Wales:—
Faith MacLeay, b. 1910: m. 1941, Ivan Lloyd Phillips, CBE, Malayan Civil Ser. (ret.), of Cranmer, Cottage, Dorchester-on-Thames, Oxon., and has issue living, Hugh Gerard Lloyd, (36 B, Cecil St., Gordon, NSW, 2072, Aust.), b. 1946: m. 1972, Rosalind, da. of H. B. Mackenzie-Wood, of Sunninghill, Mt. Ousley, NSW, and has issue living, Clare Elizabeth b. 1974.

Issue of the late Francis Arthur MACARTHUR-ONSLOW, b. 1879, d. 1938: m. 1903, Sylvia Raymond, who d. 1950, da. of the late Andrew Chisholm, of Goulburn, N.S. Wales:—
Sir Denzil, CBE, DSO, ED, b. 1904: Maj.-Gen. (ret.); GOC 2nd Div., Australian Mil. Forces 1954, and Hon. Col. 1st Bn. City of Sydney Regt. and Citizen Forces Member of Australian Mil. Board 1958; 1939-45 War in Middle East and New Guinea (despatches thrice, DSO); DSO 1941, CBE (Mil) 1951, Knt. 1964: m. 1st, 1927, Elinor Margaret, from whom he obtained a divorce 1950, da. of the late Gordon Caldwell, formerly of 4, Albert Hall Mansions, S.W.7; 2ndly, 1950, Dorothy Wolseley, MB, BS, only child of W. D. Scott, of Bellevue Hill, N.S. Wales, and has issue living, (by 1st marriage) Denzil Ion (of 2a, Holt St., Double Bay, N.S. Wales), b. 1928; Lt. (ret.) Roy. N.S. Wales Lancers: m. 1957, Jenifer Marie, da. of James Crooks, CVO, FROS, of 46, Harley St., W.1, and has issue living, Rupert Gordon b. 1962, Sophie Rose b. (Nov.) 1957, Verena Marie b. 1960,— Neil Gordon, ED, (21, Carlotta Rd., Double Bay, NSW), b. 1930; Lt.-Col. Comdg. 1/15 Armd. Regt., Royal NSW Lancers: m. 1964, Regina de Tessier, da. of the late Reginald de Tessier Prevost, of Bellevue Hill, NSW, and has issue living, Duncan Reginald b. 1966,—Euan (of East Tinwald, Loch-

maben, Dumfriesshire), *b.* 1934,—Diana Florence, *b.* 1931: *m.* 1952, Geoffrey Brian Kewley, from whom she obtained a divorce 1968, and has issue living, Robin Geoffrey *b.* 1953, Martin William *b.* 1959,—(by 2nd m.) Lee *b.* 1952,—Katrina, *b.* 1953. *Residence,*—Mount Gilead, Campbelltown, NSW.——Edward, *DSO, ED, b.* 1909; is Lt.-Col. Aust. Imperial Force; 1939-45 War in Middle East and New Guinea (despatches, DSO); DSO 1943: *m.* 1932, Winifred Hall, da. of the late William Hall Owen, of Wollongong, NSW, and has issue living, Annette Rosemary, *b.* 1933,—Pamela Jane, *b.* 1935: *m.* 1st, 1958, Paterson James Saunders, from whom she obtained a divorce 1968; 2ndly, 1971, Arthur Leslie Harrison, of Darling Point, Sydney, NSW, and has issue living (by 1st m.), Kirkland Robert Macarthur *b.* 1961, Christopher Philip *b.* 1962,—Phoebe, *b.* 1939: *m.* 1963, Hugh Geddies Atkinson, of Church Point, NSW, and has issue living, Jason Hugh *b.* 1959, Rachael Ann *b.* 1963. *Residence,*—Macquarie Grove, Camden, NSW.——Margaret Elizabeth, *MBE, b.* 1905; MBE (Civil) 1974: *m.* 1st, 1930, Lt.-Col. Reginald George Michael King, Indian Army, from whom she obtained a divorce 1955; 2ndly, 1960, John Sydney Davenport, of London, and has issue living (by 1st m.), Peter Michael, *b.* 1934: *m.* 1st, 1960 (m. diss. 1971), Diana Susan Alexander, of Toogoolawah, Qld.; 2ndly, 1972, Julia Marion Moufarrige, of Medgee, NSW, and has issue living (by 1st m.), Andrew Alister *b.* 1962, Georgina Susan *b.* 1964,—Susan Patricia, *b.* 1931: *m.* 1953, James Russell, of Carngham, Victoria 3351, Australia, and has issue living, Philip Michael *b.* 1956, Katrina Louise *b.* 1958. *Residence,*—5, Ocean Av., Double Bay, NSW.

Grandchildren of the late Arthur Loftus Onslow, el. son of the late Douglas Arthur Onslow, CE (infra):—
Issue of the late Douglas Arthur George Onslow, *b.* 1901, *d.* 1966: *m.* 1925, Margaret (Molo, Kenya), da. of Maj. John Merrick Rayner, AMIME, of Maji Chemka, Thomson's Falls, Kenya:—
Richard Douglas Loftus (PO Box 41, Knysna 6570, S. Africa), *b.* 1928; ed. at Michaelhouse, Balgowan, S. Africa, and Natal Univ.; Kenya 1952-53 with KAR: *m.* 1st, 1964 (m. diss. 1968) Mrs. Elizabeth Frances Bateman, da. of J. Gordon Elsworthy; 2ndly, 1968, Countess Ethel Elisabeth Olga Maria von Rietberg, da. of HSH Prince Ferdinand Andreas Joseph Maria of Liechtenstein [see Brunner, Bt., colls.].——Desmond Merrick, *b.* 1929; ed. at Michaelhouse, Balgowan, S. Africa, and Natal Univ. (BSc): *m.* 1954, Sylvia Patricia Melody Wiggins, of Durban, S. Africa, and has issue living, Roger, *b.* 1955,—Debra Susan, *b.* 1955,—Vanessa Mary, *b.* 1960.——Patricia Margaret Daisy, *b.* 1941.——Prudence Katherine Barbara, *b.* 1946: *m.* 1970, Robin Timothy Keigwin, of The Old Vicarage, West Anstey, S. Molton, Devon, and has issue living, Michael Douglas, *b.* 1975.

Grandsons of the late Douglas Arthur Onslow, CE, el. son of the late Lt.-Col. William Campbell Onslow, 2nd son of the Rev. Arthur Onslow (ante):—
Issue of the late Francis Robert Douglas Onslow, *b.* 1878, *d.* 1938: *m.* 1925, Mabel, who *d.* 1974, da. of William Strachan, of Edinburgh:—
Cranley Gordon Douglas, *MP, b.* 1926; ed. at Harrow, and at Oriel Coll., Oxford (MA); late Lt. 7th Queen's Own Hussars; a Co. Councillor for Kent 1961-64; served in H.M. Foreign Ser. 1951-60; M.P. for Woking Div. of Surrey (C) since 1964: *m.* 1955, Lady June Ann Hay, da. of 14th Earl of Kinnoull, and has issue living, Richard Alan Douglas, *b.* 1956,—Sandra Dorothy, *b.* 1958,—Caroline Diana, *b.* 1959,—Katharine Denise, *b.* 1961. *Residence,*—Chobham Park House, Chobham, Surrey.——Ian Denzil, *b.* 1929; ed. at Harrow, and at Grenoble Univ., France: *m.* 1954, Marjorie, da. of Albert Domville, of Stockton Heath, and has issue living, Christopher Denzil, *b.* 1956, —Mark Loftus Domville, *b.* 1958,—Michael Piers David, *b.* 1963,—Robert Douglas, *b.* 1965,—Victoria Penelope Diana (twin) *b.* 1965. *Residence,*—Durlston Court, Barton-on-Sea, Hants.

Granddaughters of the late Maj. Arthur Hughes-Onslow, el. son of the late Henry John Hughes-Onslow, 5th son of the late Rev. Arthur Onslow (ante):—
Issue of the late Cdr. Sir Geoffrey Henry Hughes-Onslow, KBE, DSC, RN, *b.* 1893, *d.* 1971: *m.* 1918, the Hon. Eileen Mabel Lowther Crofton, who *d.* 1972, da. of 4th Baron Crofton:—
Auriole Kathleen, *b.* 1919: *m.* 1945, the Rev. Simon Charles David Fergusson, [see Fergusson Bt.].—— Judith Eileen, *b.* 1923: *m.* 1945, Lt. John Thornton Lorimer, DSO, RNVR, of Pierhill, Annbank, Ayr, and has issue living, Patrick James, *b.* 1946,—Bridget Katharine Eileen, *b.* 1948.——Mary, *b.* 1929: *m.* 1952, Lt. George S. Wright, RNVR, of Castlecreavie, Kirkcudbright.

Grandchildren of the late Maj. Denzil Hughes-Onslow, 2nd son of Henry John Hughes-Onslow (ante):—
Issue of the late Capt. Oliver Hughes-Onslow, *b.* 1893, *d.* 1972: *m.* 1916, Helen Ruth (Craig, Turnberry, Ayrshire), da. of the late Rev. George Dods, BD, Min. of Barr, Ayrshire:—
Andrew George (Acton Lodge, Ascot, Berks.), *b.* 1920; ed. at at Eton, and Oxford Univ.; Capt. (ret.) Black Watch; a Member of Queen's Body Guard for Scotland (R. Co. of Archers); 1939-45 War (thrice wounded): *m.* 1944, Betty, da. of Col. M. G. Lee, of Christchurch, NZ, and has issue living, James Andrew, *b.* 1945,—Elizabeth Mary, *b.* 1949,—Sarah Jane, *b.* 1954.——Timothy Neil (Benrig, St. Boswells, Roxburghshire, and 32, Godfrey St., SW3; White's, Beefsteak, and Brooks's Clubs), *b.* 1924; ed. at Eton; Capt. (ret.); a Member of Queen's Body Guard for Scotland (R. Co. of Archers); 1939-45 War: *m.* 1950, Susan, da. of Sir William Francis Stratford Dugdale, 1st Bt. (cr. 1936), and has issue living, Archibald Edward Neil, *b.* 1954,—Richard Luke, *b.* 1958,—Henrietta, *b.* 1951.—— Fergus Erskine (Lower Norsebury, Stoke Charity, Winchester), *b.* 1929; ed. at Eton; Capt. (ret.) Rifle Bde.; a Member of Queen's Body Guard for Scotland (R. Co. of Archers): *m.* 1955, Rose Ariel, da. of Anthony Ewart Ledger Hill, OBE, of Hockley House, Twyford, Hants., and has issue living, Anthony Charles, *b.* 1957,—Olivia, *b.* 1960, Belinda Marion, *b.* 1962.——Virginia Ruth Primrose, *b.* 1917: *m.* 1st, 1942, Maj. Robert Boothby How, Black Watch, from whom she obtained a divorce 1953; 2ndly, 1969, Maurice Oliver Pease, of Eldon House, Heighington, Darlington, co. Durham, and has issue living (by 1st m.), Denzil Robert Onslow, *b.* 1944,—Primrose Jean Onslow, *b.* 1947,— Carolyn Jane Onslow, *b.* 1950.

Grandson of the late Maj. Denzil Hughes-Onslow (ante):—
Issue of the late Lt.-Com. Reginald Hughes-Onslow, RN (ret.), *b.* 1895, *d.* 1947: *m.* 1934, Daphne Helen Anne (from whom he obtained a divorce 1946; she *m.* 2ndly, 1946, Maj. John Edward Mountague Bradish-Ellames, and 3rdly, 1970, the Hon. Robert Francis Hubert Preston [see V. Gormanston]), da. of the late Col. Robert Hanbury Brudenell Bruce, DSO [see M. Ailesbury, colls.]:—
Denzil Jamie (The Old Bake House, Culworth, nr. Banbury, Oxon.), *b.* 1939; late 2nd Lt. R. Armoured Corps.: *m.* 1973, Chloé Elizabeth, da. of M.I. de Vic, of St. Cloud, Paris, and has issue living, Sophie Anne Rose, *b.* 1974.

Branch from 2nd son of 2nd son of brother of 1st Baron.

Descendants of the late Adm. Sir Richard Onslow, GCB, who was cr. a Bt. 1797, 2nd son of the late Lt.-Gen. Richard Onslow (infra):—
See **Onslow, Bt.**

Branch from 1st son of 3rd son of 2nd son of brother of 1st Baron.

Grandchildren of the late Capt. Andrew George Onslow, son of the late Richard Foley Onslow, el. son of the late Ven. Richard Francis Onslow, el. son of the Very Rev. Arthur Onslow, D.D., Dean of Worcester, yst. son of Lt.-Gen. Richard Onslow, 2nd son of Foot Onslow, brother of 1st Baron:—
Issue of the late William Onslow, *b.* 1874, *d.* 1921: *m.* 1902, Andrewina Buchanan (of Malvern, Worcs.), da. of Andrew Buchanan Torrance, of Kensington, W.:—
Robert William, *b.* 1904. *Residence,*—Lambs Barn, Oxenhall, Newent, Gloucestershire.

Issue of the late Major George Arthur Onslow, *b.* 1876, *d.* 1956: *m.* 1st, 1902, Charlotte Riou, who *d.* 1932, youngest dau. of the late Rev. Riou George Benson; 2ndly, 1933, Maud Elliot (of 5, Hillstone Court, Castle Hill Av., Folkestone, Kent), younger dau. of the late George Steele Travers Harris:—

(By 1st marriage) *Sir* Richard George, K.C.B., D.S.O., b.1904; Adm. (retired); Flag Officer (Flotillas)
Home Fleet 1954-6 ; was Com.-in-Ch., Plymouth 1958-60 ; European War 1939-44 (despatches
twice, D.S.O. and three Bars) ; D.S.O. and two Bars 1942, 3rd Bar 1944, C.B. (Mil.) 1954, K.C.B.
(Mil.) 1958: *m.* 1932, Kathleen Meriel, el. da. of Edmund C. Taylor, of Longnor Bank House, Shrews-
bury, and has issue living, Richard Edmund (Preston Bagot House, Preston Bagot, Henley-in-
Arden), *b.* 1933; Cdr. RN: *m.* 1961, Mary-Jean. el. da. of Brig. Kenneth James Garner-Smith,
OBE, of Aird House, by Inverness, and has issue living, Richard James *b.* 1962, Robert Denzil
b. 1965,—Denzil John, *b.* 1939: *m.* 1967, Susan, da. of the late B. Leach, and has issue living, Andrew
John *b.* 1968, James Denzil *b.* 1970. *Residence,*—Ryton Grove, Dorrington, Shrewsbury——John
b. 1906; Maj. (ret.) Duke of Cornwall's LI: *m.* 1956, Susan, da. of the late R. Neville Towle, and has
issue living, Andrew George, *b.* 1957,—Simon John, *b.* 1960,—Jane Elizabeth, *b.* 1958,—Sarah
Margaret, *b.* 1962,—Rachel Evelyn Mary, *b.* 1967. *Residence,*—Hurst Farm, Loxwood, Sussex.—
Mary (Troutbeck Cottage, How Mill, Carlisle, CA4 9J4), *b.* 1903: *m.* 1930, the Very Rev. William
Cyril Mayne, Dean of Carlisle, who *d.* 1962.——Hope (PO Silton, Sask., Canada), *b.* 1908: *m.* 1946,
Robert Symons, who *d.* 1973, and has issue living, Marygold, *b.* 1947.——Kathleen Theodosia,
b. 1914: *m.* 1945, Edward Godfrey Purvis Sherwood, of Applegarth, Hayton, Carlisle, CA4 9NT,
and has issue living, Edward Patrick Charles, *b.* 1946,—Andrew Godfrey Purvis, *b.* 1950: *m.* 1974,
Mary Helen, da. of the Hon. Francis Michael Hepburne-Scott [see L. Polworth],—Thomas James
Mulso, *b.* 1951,—Charlotte Claire, *b.* 1947.——Denzil Octavia, *b.* 1919.

Grandson of the late Maj. George Arthur Onslow (ante):—
Issue of the late Maj. Charles Edward Onslow, MC, *b.* 1912, *d.* 1969: *m.* 1955, Margaret Mary
Lee (Rongai, Kenya), da. of the Rev. William Marsh Lee Evans, R. of Saxby, Brigg,
Lincs.:—
John Edward, *b.* 1956.

Grandchildren of the late Augustus Paul Lumsden Onslow (infra):—
Issue of the late Augustus Charles Albert Foley George, *b.* 1888, *d.* 1965: *m.* 1914, Winifred
May, who *d.* 1971, da. of the late W. R. Williams, of Thornton Heath, Surrey:—
Winston Hillier Gopal (9, Elm Drive, Hove, Sussex), *b.* 1915: *m.* 1939, Kathleen Edis, and has issue
living, Veronica Vivien, *b.* 1943: *m.* 1969, Alan Roy Wood, Surveyor, of 9, Elm Grove, Hove, Sussex.
——Lewis Lumsden William, *b.* 1924; Journalist.——Patricia Doreen, *b.* 1927: *m.* 1956, Ronald
George Coombs, of 1, Airey Houses, Scocles Rd., Minister, Isle of Sheppey, Kent., and has issue
living, Anne Patricia, *b.* 1957.

Issue of the late Frederick Hewitt Lumsden Onslow, *b.* 1897, *d.* 1969: *m.* 1939, Olive Eveline
(The Cordylines, Delling Lane, Old Bosham, Sussex), da. of Ernest Spicer:—
Frederick Winston Lumsden (Little Clandon, 37, Fairmile Park Rd., Cobham, Surrey), *b.* 1940: *m.* 1964,
Elizabeth Maude, da. of Frank Berenger Benger, and has issue living, Robert Frederick, *b.* 1970,—
Gillian Elizabeth, *b.* 1966,—Vivien Gail, *b.* 1967.

Granddaughter of the late Rev. Arthur Andrew Onslow, 2nd son of the late Ven.
Richard Francis Onslow (ante):—
Issue of the late Augustus Paul Lumsden Onslow, *b.* 1853, *d.* 19—: *m.* 1886, Alice Maud, who
d. 1951, dau. of the late William Francis Stevenight:—
Maud Sarah Louisa, *b.* 1894: *m.* 1921, Ernest Augustus Tellam, of The Swiss Bungalow, 21, Old Lodge
Lane, Purley, Surrey, and has issue living, John Frederick Augustus Onslow, *b.* 1922: *m.* 1941,
Olive, da. of Fraser Smith, and has issue living, Michael Frederick *b.* 1943, Pauline Glynnis *b.* 1948,
Pamela Alice *b.* 1950,—Richard Glyn Onslow, *b.* 1925—Derek Lumsden Onslow, *b.* 1927: *m.* 19—,
Patricia Wells, and has issue living, Elaine *b.* 1952, Paula *b.* 1958.

Branch from 2nd son of 3rd son of 2nd son of brother of 1st Baron.

Granddaughter of the late Rev. Thomas George Onslow, *b.* 1826, *d.* 1911, son of
the Rev. Arthur Cyril Onslow, 2nd son of the Very Rev. Arthur Onslow, D.D.
(ante):—
Issue of the late Maj.-Gen. Sir William Henry Onslow, K.C.M.G., C.B., *b.* 1868, *d.* 1929:
m. 1899, Margaret Beatrice, who *d.* 1954, dau. of the late Thomas Bates, of Aydon and
Heddon, Northumberland :—
Margaret Isobel *b.* 1901: *m.* 1923, Cdr. Reginald Foster Pitt Maton, OBE, RN (ret.), who *d.* 1965.
Residence,—Harston, Chapel Row, Bucklebury, Berks.

Branch from 3rd son of 3rd son of 2nd son of brother of 1st Baron.

Grandchildren of the late Rev. Phipps Onslow, son of the late Phipps Vansittart
Onslow, yst. son of the Very Rev. Arthur Onslow, D.D. (ante):—
Issue of the late Henry Phipps Onslow, *b.* 1869, *d.* 1945: *m.* 1898, Maisie, who *d.* 1959,
da. of the Hon. T. Playford, of Drysdale, Norton's Summit, S. Australia:—
Thomas Phipps, *b.* 1907: *m.* 1945, Pauline (CALVERT), who *d.* 1970, da. of Kenneth L. Shoobridge
of Coniston, Glenora, Tasmania, and has issue living, William Phipps, *b.* 1947,—Jane Elizabeth,
b. 1945: *m.* 1969, Christopher Goodwin Morley, of Bacchus Creek, Kojonup, W. Aust., and has issue
living, Emma Patricia *b.* 1970, Georgina Joan *b.* 1972. *Residence,*—Cluan, Plenty, Tasmania.——
Helen May Jane (Cluan, Plenty, Tasmania), *b.* 1902.——Margaret Louise, *b.* 1921: *m.* 1946, Charles
Edward Rollins, and has issue living, Phillip Charles, *b.* 1947: *m.* 1970, Suzanne Mary Martin, of
Montrose, Tasmania,—Susan Louise, *b.* 1951. *Residence,*—37, Pioneer Av., Church Hill, New
Norfolk, Tasmania.

PREDECESSORS.—[1] *Sir* THOMAS Foote, Knt., Lord Mayor of London 1649; was cr. a
Baronet 1660; *d.* 1687; his son-in-law [2] ARTHUR Onslow (husband of his dau. Mary),
successively M.P. for Bramber, Sussex, Surrey, and Guildford; was cr. a *Baronet* 1674 (with precedency
of 1660); *d.* 1688; *s.* by his son [3] *Sir* RICHARD, P.C., 2nd Bt.; was successively M.P. for
Guildford, Surrey, and St. Mawes; was a Lord of the Admiralty, Speaker of House of
Commons, High Steward of Guildford, Gov. of the Levant Co., a Lord of the Treasury, Chancellor and Under-Treasurer of the Exchequer, and a Teller of the Exchequer for life; cr.
Baron Onslow, of Onslow, co. Salop, and of Clandon, co. Surrey (peerage of Great Britain)
1716, with remainder to his uncle, Denzil Onslow, and afterwards to the heirs male of his
father; *d.* 1717; *s.* by his son [4] THOMAS, 2nd Baron; *d.* 1740; *s.* by his son [5] RICHARD,
3rd Baron; *d.s.p.* Oct. 1776; *s.* by the heir male of his grandfather [6] GEORGE, P.C. (son of
Arthur Onslow, P.C., M.P., who was Speaker of the House of Commons 1727-61), 4th Baron
who in May of the same year had been cr. *Baron Cranley,* of Imber Court (peerage of Great
Britain); was successively M.P. for Rye and Surrey, Out-Ranger of Windsor Forest, a Lord of
the Treasury, Lord-Lieut. of Surrey, Treasurer of the Household and a Lord of the Bedchamber; cr. *Viscount Cranley* and *Earl of Onslow* (peerage of United Kingdom) 1801; *d.* 1814;
s. by his son [7] THOMAS, 2nd Earl; sat as M.P. for Guildford 1784-1807; *d.* 1827; *s.* by his son
[8] ARTHUR GEORGE, 3rd Earl; *d.* 1870, without surviving male issue; *s.* by his grandnephew
[9] WILLIAM HILLIER, G.C.M.G. P.C., (son of George Augustus Cranley (son of the Hon.
Thomas Cranley, 2nd son of 2nd Earl, by Mary Harriet Ann, dau. of Lieut.-Gen. William
F. B. Loftus)], 4th Earl; *b.* 1853 ; a Lord-in-Waiting to Queen Victoria 1880 and 1886-7, Under-
Sec. of State for Colonies Feb. 1887 to Feb. 1888, Parliamentary Sec. to Board of Trade Feb.
to Nov. 1888, Gov. and Com.-in-Chief of New Zealand 1888-92, Under-Sec. of State for India
July 1895 to Nov. 1900, Under-Sec. of State for the Colonies 1900-1903, Pres. of Board of
Agriculture 1903-5, and Dep. Speaker and Chm. of Committees of House of Lords 1905-11 : *m.*
1875, the Hon. Florence Coulstoun, who *d.* 1934, dau. of 3rd Baron Gardner ; *d.* 1911; *s.* by his el.
son [10] RICHARD WILLIAM ALAN, 5th Earl; *b.* 1876; High Steward of Guildford; entered
Diplo. Ser. 1901; was Assist. Private Sec. to Sec. of State for Foreign Affairs 1909-11 and
Private Sec. to Permanent Under-Sec. of State for Foreign Affairs (Rt. Hon. Sir Arthur

Nicolson, Bt., G.C.B.) 1911-15; European War 1915-19 (O.B.E., Legion of Honour); appointed a Lord-in-Waiting to H.M. 1919, Civil Lord of the Admiralty 1920, Parliamentary Sec. to Min. of Agriculture 1921, to Min. of Health 1921 and 1922, and to Board of Education 1923 (resigned Jan. 1924), Under-Sec. of State for War 1924, and Paymaster-Gen. 1928 (resigned 1929); Chm. of Committees and Dep. Speaker in House of Lords 1931-44; became Hon. Col. 30th (Surrey) Anti-Aircraft Btn., R.E. (T.A.) 1927: *m.* 1906, the Hon. Violet Marcia Catherine Bampfylde, *C.B.E., A.R.R.C.,* who *d.* 1954, dau. of 3rd Baron Poltimore; *d.* 1945; *s.* by his son [11] WILLIAM ARTHUR BAMPFYLDE, *KBE, MC, TD,* 6th Earl, *b.* 1913; Col. late RAC, High Steward of Guildford 1947-71, Capt. of the Yeoman of the Guard 1951-60: *m.* 1st, 1936 (m. diss. 1962) the Hon. Pamela Louisa Eleanor Dillon, only da. of 19th Viscount Dillon: 2ndly, 1962, Nina, MBE, da. of Thomas Sturdee; *d.* 1971; *s.* by his son [12], MICHAEL WILLIAM COPLESTONE DILLON, 7th Earl and present peer; also Viscount and Baron Cranley, and Baron Onslow.

ORANMORE AND BROWNE, BARON. Sits as BARON MEREWORTH [U.K. 1926]. (Browne.) [Baron I. 1836.]

[Mereworth title pronounced "**Merryworth.**"]

Boldly and faithfully.

DOMINICK GEOFFREY EDWARD BROWNE, 4th Baron; *b.* Oct. 21st, 1901; *s.* 1927; ed. at Eton, and at Ch. Ch., Oxford; sometime 2nd Lt. Grenadier Guards: *m.* 1st, 1925, Mildred Helen (who obtained a divorce 1936), dau. of the late Hon. Thomas Henry Frederick Egerton [see D. Sutherland, colls.]; 2ndly, 1936, Oonagh (Kindersley) (who obtained a divorce 1950), da. of the late the Hon. Arthur Ernest Guiness [see E. Iveagh colls.]; 3rdly, 1951, Constance Vera (the film actress "Sally Gray"), dau. of the late Charles Edward Stevens, and has issue by 1st and 2nd marriages.

Arms—Argent, an eagle displayed with two heads sable, langued gules. Crest,—A gryphon's head erased argent. Supporters—Dexter, a knight in ancient armour belted azure, garnished or, holding in his right hand a battle-axe chained proper, charged on the blade with a cross pattee or, on his left an ancient pointed shield gules, charged with two lioncels or, supported by a band from the right shoulder gules, studded and garnished or; sinister, a knight, also in chain armour, with a circuit of blue silk, belted gules, leaning his left hand on an ancient two-handed sword, thereon a shield argent, charged with an eagle displayed with two heads sable, langued gules. Motto—"Fortiter et fideliter."

Residence,—52, Eaton Place, SW1.

SONS LIVING. (By 1st *marriage.*)

Hon. DOMINICK GEOFFREY THOMAS, *b.* July 1st, 1929: *m.* 1957 (m. diss. 1974), Sara Margaret, da. of the late Dr. Herbert Wright, of 59, Merrion Sq., Dublin. *Residence,*—Leckenagh, Burton Port, Letterkenny, co. Donegal.

Hon. Martin Michael Dominick, *b.* 1931; ed. at Eton: *m.* 1958, Alison Margaret, only dau. of John Bradford, of Redlands, Witley, Surrey, and has issue living, Shaun Dominick, *b.* 1964,—Cara Margaret, *b.* 1961. *Residence,*—11, Campden Grove, W.8.

(By 2nd marriage.)

Hon. Garech Domnagh, *b.* 1939; ed. at Le Rosey. *Residences,*—Woodtown Manor, Rathfarnham, Dublin 14; Luggala, Roundwood, co. Wicklow.

DAUGHTERS LIVING. (By 1st *marriage.*)

Hon. Patricia Helen, *b.* 1926 : *m.* 1952, the Hon. (Michael) Anthony Rathborne Cayzer [see B. Rotherwick]. *Seat,*—Great Westwood, Kings Langley, Herts. *Residence,*—29, Hamilton House, Vicarage Gate, W8.

Hon. Judith, *b.* 1934: *m.* 1958 (Ralph) Michael Haslam, [E. Bessborough, colls.], and has issue living, Christopher William Dominick, *b.* 1960,—David Oliver Myles, *b.* 1962,—Carina Judith, *b.* 1965, *Seat,*—Cairngill, Dalbeattie, Kirkcudbrightshire. *Residence,*—22B, Elm Tree Rd., NW8.

BROTHER LIVING.

Hon. Geoffrey Charles Myles Browne, *b.* 1912; ed. at Eton, and at Corpus Christi Coll., Camb.: *m.* 1946, Kathleen Mary (who obtained a divorce 1958), dau. of the late Arland Ussher, of Eastwell, co. Galway, and widow of Capt. Joseph Fitzgerald, MC, Roy. Ulster Rifles. *Residence,*—72, Fellows Rd., NW3.

SISTER LIVING.

Hon. Kathleen Marcia, *b.* 1903: *m.* 1936. Cotterell Boughton Mordaunt-Smith, late Lieut. Welsh Guards and Warwickshire Yeo., who *d.* 1956, and has issue living, Michael Cotterell Geoffrey David (Southleigh, Hundon, Suffolk), *b.* 1937; ed. at Lancing; late Lt. The Black Watch; Middle East 1945-47 (War medal and Palestine stars): *m.* 1st 1959 (m. diss. 1971), Diana Katherine, da. of Joseph John Edward Potter, of Cheshunt Great House, Cheshunt, Herts.; 2ndly, 1972 Alexandra Sarah, da. of Arthur Hugh Alexander Cardew, of Woodlands, Copthorne, Sussex, and has issue living (by 1st m.), Michael Joseph Cotterell Nicholas *b.* 1962, Damian Kirwan Seton Towers *b.* 1968,—Olwen Marcia Blanche, *b.* 1928: *m.* 1st, 1952, Wayne Ewing Harriss, who *d.* 1958; 2ndly, 1960, Hugh Dearman Janson, of The Boat House, Queens Rd., Cowes, I. of Wight. *Residence,*—73, Onslow Sq., SW7.

WIDOW LIVING OF SON OF FOURTH BARON.

Noreen Anne (19, Eaton Row, SW1), da. of Sean MacSherry, of co. Down: *m.* 1963, the Hon. Tara Browne, who *d.* 1966, and has issue living [see colls. infra).

COLLATERAL BRANCH LIVING.
Issue of the late Hon. Tara Browne, yst. son of 4th Baron, *b.* 1945, *d.* 1966: *m.* 1963, Noreen Anne (ante), da. of Sean MacSherry of co. Down:—
Dorian Clifford, *b.* 1963.——Julian Dominick, *b.* 1965.

PREDECESSORS.—[1] DOMINICK Browne, *P.C.*, M.P. for and Lord-Lieut. of co. Mayo, was cr. *Baron Oranmore and Browne* (peerage of Ireland) 1836; *b.* 1787: *m.* 1811, Catherine Anne, el. dau. and co.-heir of Henry Monck; *d.* 1860; *s.* by his son [2] GEOFFREY DOMINICK AUGUSTUS FREDERICK, 2nd Baron, *b.* 1819; was Representative Peer for Ireland; assumed *vitâ patris* the additional surname of Guthrie on his marriage: *m.* 1859, Christina, who *d.* 1887, only child and heiress of the late Alexander Guthrie, of The Mount, Ayrshire; *d.* 1900; *s.* by his only son [3] GEOFFREY HENRY BROWNE, *K.P.*, *P.C.*, 3rd Baron; *b.* 1861; a Representative Peer for Ireland, and a Senator for S. Ireland; cr. *Baron Mereworth*, of Mereworth Castle, Kent (peerage of United Kingdom) 1926 : *m.* 1901, Lady Olwen Verena Ponsonby, who *d.* 1927, dau. of 8th Earl of Bessborough, K.P.; *d.* 1927; *s.* by his son [4] DOMINICK GEOFFREY EDWARD BROWNE, 4th Baron and present peer; also Baron Mereworth.

Orford, Earldom of, see Baron Walpole.

Oriel, Baron, title of Viscount Massereene and Ferrard on Roll of H. L.

ORKNEY, EARL OF. (Fitz-Maurice.) [Earl S. 1696.]

CECIL O'BRYEN FITZ-MAURICE, 8th Earl; *b.* July 3rd, 1919; *s.* 1951 (succession approved by Lyon Court 1955); late Driver R.A.S.C.; European War 1939-45, Korea 1950-51: *m.* 1953, Rose Katherine Durk, dau. of the late J. W. D. Silley, of Brixham, S. Devon.

Arms,—Quarterly, grand-quartered; 1st and 4th grand-quarters; argent, on a saltire gules a lymphad sails furled or, a chief ermine *Fitz-Maurice*; 2nd grand-quarter, counter-quartered; 1st and 4th, gules, three cinquefoils ermine *Hamilton*; 2nd, argent, a lymphad sails furled sable *Arran*; 3rd argent, a heart gules imperially crowned or, on a chief azure three mullets of the first *Douglas*; over all at the fess point an escallop or for difference *Lord George Hamilton, 1st Earl of Orkney*; 3rd grand-quarter, counter-quartered; 1st and 4th, gules three lions passant guardant per pale or and argent *O'Bryen*; 2nd, argent, three piles meeting in the point issuing from the chief gules; 3rd a pheon azure. Crests,—1st, a Sagittarius passant proper; 2nd, an ancient boat or, flagged azure, and issuant therefrom an oak-tree fructed and penetrated by a frame-saw proper, the frame or. Supporters,—*Dexter*, an antelope azure, armed and ducally gorged with chain reflexed across the back or; *sinister*, a stag proper attired and ducally gorged with chain reflexed across the back or, each charged upon the shoulder with a cinquefoil ermine.

Residence,—66, Dorset Av., Ferndown, Dorset.

MOTHER LIVING.
Dorothy Jeanette, dau. of the late Capt. Robert Dickie, R.N.: *m.* 1st, 1916, Douglas Frederick Harold Fitz-Maurice, who *d.* 1937; 2ndly, 1939, Com. Eric Templer Wiggins, D.S.O., R.N. *Residence,*—Lantern Hatch, Itchingfield, Sussex.

COLLATERAL BRANCHES LIVING.
Issue of the late Isabella Annie Fitz-Maurice da. of Capt. the Hon. James Terence Fitz-Maurice, 5th son of 5th Earl, *b.* 1864, *d.* 1948: : *m.* 1882, Sir Frederick Robert St. John, KCMG, *d.* 1923:—
[See V. Bolingbroke, colls.] of whom Lt.-Col. FREDERICK OLIVER ST. JOHN, *DSO*, *MC*, is *hp* to Earldom of Orkney.

Grandchildren of the late Cecil Henry Fitz-Maurice, son of Lt.-Col. William Edward Fitz-Maurice (son of John, Viscount Kirkwall, el. son of Mary, in her own right Countess of Orkney), brother of 5th Earl:—
Issue of the late Cecil Edward Arthur Fitz-Maurice, *b.* 1871, *d.* 1964: *m.* 1900, Maude Elizabeth Mary, who *d.* 1970, da. of the late T. G. Waller:—
Cecil George (7, Greyfriars, Eastgate St., Winchester), *b.* 1901.——Mildred Lillian (45, Painters Field; St. Cross, Winchester), *b.* 1902: *m.* 1938, Capt. John Major Leslie Bostock, 11th Lancers, who *d.* 1959, and has issue living, Christopher John (12, Granton Rd., Edinburgh, EH5 3QH), *b.* 1942, *m.* 1963, Yvonne Kendrick, and has issue living, Jason Guy *b.* 1969, Joanna Clare *b.* 1963, Camilla Jane *b.* 1967,—Josephine Mary, *b.* 1939: *m.* 1964, Geoffrey Stonehouse, (c/o Lloyds Bank, Guildford, and has issue living, Nicholas John *b.* 1965, Rachel Ann *b.* 1967, Stephanie Jane *b.* 1969.

PREDECESSORS.—[1] Lord GEORGE Hamilton, *K.T.*, *P.C.*, 5th son of Lord William Douglas (cr. Duke of Hamilton for life), by Anne, Duchess of Hamilton, was cr. *Lord Dechmont, Viscount Kirkwall*, and *Earl of Orkney* (peerage of Scotland) 1696, with remainder to the heirs whatsoever of his body; was a Field-Marshal in the Army, Gov. of Edinburgh Castle, Lord-Lieut. of Lanarkshire, a Lord of the Bedchamber, Gov. of Virginia, and a Representative Peer; *d.* 1737; *s.* by his dau. [2] ANNE, wife of William, 4th Earl of Inchiquin; *d.* 1756; *s.* by her dau. [3] MARY, 2nd Countess, wife of Murrough, 1st Marquess of Thomond; *d.* 1790; *s.* by her da. [4] MARY, 3rd Countess, wife of Hon. Thomas Fitzmaurice, 2nd son of John, Earl of Shelburne, and brother of 1st Marquess of Lansdowne; *d.* 1831; *s.* by her grandson [5] THOMAS JOHN HAMILTON, 5th Earl; *b.* 1803; a Representative Peer: *m.* 1826, the Hon. Charlotte Isabella, who *d.* 1883, dau. of 3rd Baron Boston; *d.* 1877; *s.* by his son [6] GEORGE WILLIAM HAMILTON, *K.C.M.G.*, 6th Earl, *b.* 1827; a Representative Peer: *m.* 1872, Amelia, widow of the Baron de Samuel, a peer of Portugal; *d.* 1889; *s.* by his nephew [7] EDMOND WALTER (son of the late Hon. Henry Warrender Fitzmaurice, 2nd son of 5th Earl), 7th Earl, *b.* 1867; Lieut.-Col. 3rd Batn. Oxfordshire L.I.: *m.* 1892, Constance Macdonald, who *d.* 1946, dau. of the late David Gilchrist; *d.* 1951; *s.* by his kinsman [8] CECIL O'BRYEN (younger son of the late Douglas Frederick Harold Fitz-Maurice, son of the late Major Douglas Commerell Menzies Fitz-Maurice, el. son of the late Com. the Hon. Frederick O'Bryen Fitz-Maurice, R.N., 3rd son of 5th Earl), 8th Earl and present peer, also Viscount Kirkwall, and Lord Dechmont.

ORMATHWAITE, BARON.   (Walsh.)   [Baron U.K. 1868, Bt. U.K. 1804.]

VERITAS · ET · VIRTUS · VINCUNT

Truth and virtue must prevail.

JOHN ARTHUR CHARLES WALSH, 6th Baron, and 7th Baronet; *b.* Dec. 25th, 1912; *s.* 1944; ed. at Eton, and at Trin. Coll., Camb.

Arms,—Argent, a fesse sable, cotised wavy gules, between six martlets of the second. **Crest,**—A griffin's head erased per fesse wavy argent and ermine, beak and ears or. **Supporters,**—On either side a griffin ermine, gorged with a collar vair, and pendent therefrom an escutcheon argent, charged with a martlet sable.

Residence,—Pen-y-bont Hall, Llandrindod Wells, Radnorshire.

SISTERS LIVING.

Hon. Jane Emily Mary (13, Mount St., W1), *b.* 1910; appointed a Lady-in-Waiting to HRH the Duchess of Gloucester 1969.

Hon. Anne Elizabeth, *b.* 1911: *m.* 1948, as his second wife, Peter Edward Bromley-Martin, who *d.* 1968 [Rouse-Boughton, Bt., colls.]. *Residence,*—The Pheasantry, Builth Wells, Powys, LD2 3NP.

COLLATERAL BRANCH LIVING.

Issue of the late Hon. Nigel Christopher Walsh, 6th son of 2nd Baron, *b.* 1867, *d.* 1931: *m.* 1904, Pauline, who *d.* 1956, youngest da. of the late Henry Francis Makins, of 180, Queen's Gate, SW:—

Emily Barbara, *b.* 1905: *m.* 1st, 1940, Peter Clifford Campbell-Martin, MC, RAF Vol. Reserve, who *d.* (killed in action) 1941; 2ndly, 1947, Robert Lewis Paton, of Gt. Orchard, Bignor, Pulborough, Sussex, and has issue living, (by 2nd m.) Hermione Ruth, *b.* 1948,—Diana Elizabeth, *b.* 1950.—— Geraldine Lettice, *b.* 1909.

PREDECESSORS.—[1] JOHN BENN, assumed in 1795 by Roy. licence the surname of Walsh and was cr. *Baronet* 1804; *s.* by his son [2] *Sir* JOHN, 2nd Bt.; *b.* 1798; sat as MP for Sudbury (*C*) 1830-4, and 1838-40, and for Radnor 1840-68; was Lord Lieut. of Radnorshire 1842-75; cr. *Baron Ormathwaite,* of Ormathwaite, co. Cumberland (peerage of United Kingdom) 1868: *m.* 1825, Lady Jane Grey, who *d.* 1877, da. of 6th Earl of Stamford and Warrington: *d.* 1881; *s.* by his son [3] ARTHUR, 2nd Baron, *b.* 1827; Lord-Lieut. for Radnorshire 1875-95: MP for Leominster (*C*) 1865-8, and for Radnorshire 1868-80: *m.* 1858, Lady Katherine Emily Mary Somerset, who *d.* 1914, da. of 7th Duke of Beaufort, KG; *d.* 1920; *s.* by his el. son [4] ARTHUR HENRY JOHN, *GCVO,* 3rd Baron; *b.* 1859; Lord-Lieut. for Radnor 1918-22; appointed an Equerry-in-Waiting to HRH the late Duke of Clarence and Avondale 1892, a Gentleman Usher to King Edward VII 1902, a Groom-in-Waiting to HM 1900, and Master of the Ceremonies 1907 (retired 1920); sat as MP for Radnorshire (*C*) 1885-92: *m.* 1890, Lady Clementine Frances Anne Pratt, who *d.* 1921, da. of 3rd Marquess Camden; *d.* 1937; *s.* by his brother [5] GEORGE HARRY WILLIAM, *MVO,* 4th Baron; *b.* 1863; *d.* 1943; *s.* by his brother [6] REGINALD, *MVO,* 5th Baron; *b.* 1868; HM's Consul at Piraeus 1897-1906, and HM Consul at Dunkirk 1906-07, and at New York 1907-10: *m.* 1908, Lady Margaret Jane Douglas-Home, who *d.* 1955, da. of 12th Earl of Home; *d.* 1944; *s.* by his son [7] JOHN ARTHUR CHARLES, 6th Baron and present peer.

Ormonde, Baron, title of Marquess of Ormonde on Roll of H. L.

ORMONDE, MARQUESS OF. (Butler.) [Marquess I. 1825.]

As I find.

Butler for ever

JAMES HUBERT THEOBALD CHARLES BUTLER, *MBE*, 7th Marquess, *b.* April 19th, 1899; *s.* 1971; ed. at Haileybury, and RMC; late Lt. KRRC; 1914-18 War (wounded); 31st Hereditary Chief Butler of Ireland; MBE (Mil.) 1921: *m.* 1935, Nan., who *d.* 1973, da. of Garth Gilpin, of USA, and has issue.

Arms,—Quarterly: 1st or, a chief indented azure *Walter*; 2nd gules, three covered cups or, *Butler*; 3rd argent, a lion rampant gules, on a chief of the second a swan close argent, between two annulets or, *Carrick*; 4th ermine, a saltire gules. Crest,—Out of a ducal coronet or, a plume of ostrich feathers, issuant therefrom a falcon rising, all argent. Supporters,—*Dexter*, a falcon argent, legged and beaked or; *sinister*, a male griffin argent, beaked, rayed, collared, and chained or

Residence,—5838, S. Washington, Hinsdale, Ill., USA. *Club*,—Naval and Military.

DAUGHTERS LIVING

Lady Constance Ann, *b.* 1940: *m.* 1965, Henry Lea Soukup, of 618, North Washington, Hinsdale, Ill., USA, and has issue living, Andrew Butler, *b.* 1969,—Meghan Ormonde, *b.* 1971.

Lady Violet Cynthia Lilah, *b.* 1946: *m.* 1971, Donald Leroy Robb, of 3300, Lake Shore Drive, Chicago, Ill., USA.

DAUGHTERS LIVING OF SIXTH MARQUESS.

Lady Jane, *b.* 1925; *m.* 1945; Lieut. Peter Heaton, R.N.V.R. from whom she obtained a divorce 1952, and has issue living, Mark Stuart Arthur, *b.* 1948. *Residence*,—La Chapelle St. Jean, La Garde Freinet, Var, France.

Lady Martha, *b.* 1926: *m.* 1950, Capt. Ashley Charles Gibbs Ponsonby, MC, late Coldm. Gds. of Grim's Dyke Farm, Woodleys, Woodstock, Oxon., el. son of Col. Sir Charles Ponsonby, TD, 1st Bt.

DAUGHTER LIVING OF FOURTH MARQUESS.

Lady Evelyn Frances (St. George's Retreat, PO Box 1, Burgess Hill, Sussex), *b.* 1887; sometime Ch. Officer WRNS: *m.* 1910, Vice-Adm. the Hon. Edmund Rupert Drummond, CB, MVO, who *d.* 1965 [see E. Perth].

COLLATERAL BRANCH LIVING

(*In remainder to the Earldoms of Ormonde and Ossory only.*)

Descendants of the late Hon. Richard Butler, (younger son of the 8th Earl), who was cr. *Viscount Mountgarret* 1550, of whom the 17th Viscount is *h.p.* to Earldoms of Ormonde and Ossory [see V. Mountgarret].

PREDECESSORS.—[1] THEOBALD FitzWalter, who accompanied Henry II. into Ireland, was cr. *Chief Butler of Ireland* 1177; *d.* about 1206; *s.* by his son [2] THEOBALD, 2nd Butler, who in 1221 assumed the surname of Le Botiler or Butler; *d.* 1230; *s.* by his son [3] THEOBALD, 3rd Butler; *d.* 1248; *s.* by his son [4] THEOBALD, 4th Butler; sat as a Baron in the Parliament of Ireland; granted the Prisage of Wines; *d.* 1285; *s.* by his el. son [5] THEOBALD, 5th Butler; sat in Parliament of Ireland as a Baron; *s.* by his brother [6] *Sir* EDMOND, Knt., 6th Butler; was Lord Dep. of Ireland 1312, and Ch. Gov. of Ireland with title of Lord Justice 1314: received the feodum of Karrik, Macgriffyn, and Roscrea 1315, and sometimes styled Earl of Karryk (Carrick); *d.* 1321; *s.* by his son [7] JAMES, cr. *Earl of Ormonde* (peerage of Ireland) 1328; had a renewed grant of the Prisage of Wines, and grant of the Regalities, &c., of co. Tipperary, with the rights of a Palatine in that co. for life; *d.* 1382; *s.* by his son [8] JAMES, 2nd Earl, was Lord Justice of Ireland; *d.* 1382; *s.* by his son [9] JAMES, 3rd Earl; erected the Castle of Gowran, and was usually known as Earl of Gowran, and afterwards purchased the Castle of Kilkenny; was Lord Justice of Ireland; *d* 1405; *s.* by his son [10] JAMES, 4th Earl; prevailed upon Henry V. to create a King of Arms in Ireland, by the title of Ireland King of Arms (altered by Edward VI. to Ulster King of Arms) and he gave lands for ever to the College of Arms, London; was Lord Dep. of Ireland 1405, and Lord-Lieut. of Ireland 1420, 1425, and 1442; *d.* 1452; *s.* by his son [11] JAMES, K.G., 5th Earl, who had in 1449 been cr. *Earl of Wiltshire* (peerage of England); was Lord Dep. of Ireland 1451; constituted Lord High Treasurer of England 1459; fell into the hands of the Yorkists at Towton, and was beheaded at Newcastle 1461, when both Earldoms were forfeited; *s.* by his son [12] JOHN, who having been at Towton was attainted; he was afterwards restored in blood, and became 6th Earl of Ormonde; was ambassador to the principal courts of Europe: *d.* unmarried 1478; *s.* by his brother [13] THOMAS, P.C., who having been attainted was restored by Act of Parliament became 7th Earl; *d.* 1515; *s.* by his kinsman [14] PIERCE, great-grandson of the 3rd Earl; he assumed the Earldom, but was compelled to relinquish it to Sir Thomas Boleyn (father of Queen Anne, Consort of Henry VIII.), who in 1525, was cr. Viscount Rochford, and in 1529 Earl of Wiltshire, in peerage of England, and in 1527 Earl of Ormonde, in peerage of Ireland; as a recompense for this abandonment he was in 1527 cr. *Earl of Ossory* (peerage of Ireland), and in the same year, on the death of Thomas Boleyn, Earl of Ormonde (ante) without surviving male issue, he was restored to the original Earldom, and became 8th Earl of Ormonde; *d.* 1539; *s.* by his son [15] JAMES, 9th Earl, who in 1536 had been cr. *Viscount Thurles*; in 1541 was confirmed by Act of Parliament in Earldom of Ormonde; *d.* 1546; *s.* by his son [16] THOMAS, K.G., 10th Earl; was Lord High Treasurer of Ireland; *d.* without surviving male issue; *s.* by his kinsman [17] WALTER, 11th Earl, son of John, 3rd son of 9th Earl; *d.* 1632; *s.* by his grandson [18] JAMES, K.G., P.C., 12th Earl; was six times Lord-Lieut. of Ireland; cr. *Marquess of Ormonde* (peerage of Ireland), 1642, *Baron Butler*, of Llanthony, and *Earl of Brecknock* (peerage of England) 1660, *Duke of Ormonde* (peerage of Ireland) 1661, and *Duke of Ormonde* (peerage of England) 1682: *m.* Elizabeth Preston, in her own right *Lady Dingwall; d.* 1688; *s.* by his grandson [19] JAMES, K.G., 2nd Duke, who in 1680 had *s.* his father as *Baron Butler*, of Moore Park (peerage of England, cr. 1666), and in 1684 his grandmother as *Lord Dingwall* (peerage of Scotland, cr. 1609); was Lord High Constable o,

England at Coronation of William and Mary, Capt. Gen. and Com. in Ch. of the Land Forces, Warden of the Cinque Ports, and Constable of Dover Castle; in 1715 was attainted of high treason, all his English honours were forfeited, and an Act was passed to annul the regalities and liberties of the co. Palatine of Tipperary; *d.* in exile 1745; *s.* by his brother [20] CHARLES, who in 1683 had been cr. *Baron Butler,* of Weston (peerage of England), and in 1693 *Baron Cloughgrenan, Viscount Tullogh,* and *Earl of Arran* (peerage of Ireland); this nobleman assumed the style of 14th Earl of Ormonde, and did not assume the Irish Dukedom or Marquessate, which had been confirmed upon his father, although the proceedings of the English legislature did not affect the Irish dignities; *d.* 1758, when his own honours and the Marquessate and Dukedom of Ormonde became extinct, the Lordship of Dingwall and the Barony of Butler, of Moore Park, reverted to the heir gen. (see Bs. Lucas of Crudwell and Dingwall), and the Earldoms of Ormonde and Ossory and the Viscountcy of Thurles became vested in his kinsman [21] JOHN, great-grandson of Richard, younger brother of the 12th Earl; he did not however assume the titles; *d.* 1766; *s.* by his cousin [22] WALTER, who did not assume the titles; *d.* 1783; *s.* by his son [23] JOHN, 17th Earl of Ormonde by decision of House of Lords 1791; *d.* 1795; *s.* by his el. son [24] WALTER, K.P., 18th Earl; cr. *Baron Butler,* of Llanthony, Mon. (peerage of UK) 1801, and *Marquess of Ormonde* (peerage of Ireland) 1816; disposed of the grant of the Prisage of Wines (see Theobald, 4th Butler) to the crown for £216,000; *d.* 1820, when the Marquessate of Ormonde and the Barony of Butler, of Llanthony, became extinct, and the other honours reverted to his brother [25] JAMES, K.P., 19th Earl; cr. *Baron Ormonde,* of Llanthony, co. Monmouth (peerage of United Kingdom) 1821, and *Marquess of Ormonde* (peerage of Ireland) 1825; was Lord-Lieut. of co. Kilkenny; *d.* 1838; *s.* by his son [26] JOHN, K.P., 2nd Marquess, *b.* 1808: *m.* 1843, Frances Jane, dau. of Gen. the Hon. Sir Edward Paget, G.C.B. (M. Anglesey), *d.* 1854; *s.* by his son [27] JAMES EDWARD WILLIAM THEOBALD, P.C., K.P., 3rd Marquess, *b.* 1844; Commodore Roy. Yacht Squadron: *m.* 1876, Lady Elizabeth Harriett Grosvenor, who *d.* 1928, dau. of 1st Duke of Westminster; *d.* 1919; *s.* by his brother [28] JAMES ARTHUR WELLINGTON FOLEY, 4th Marquess; *b.* 1849: *m.* 1887, Ellen, who *d.* 1951, dau. of the late Gen. Anson Stager, U.S.A.; *d.* 1943; *s.* by his son [5] JAMES GEORGE ANSON, 5th Marquess, *b.* 1890; Major late Life Guards: *m.* 1915, the Hon. Sybil Inna Mildred Fellowes, who *d.* 1948, dau. of 2nd Baron de Ramsey; *d.* 1949; *s.* by his brother [6] (JAMES) ARTHUR NORMAN, *CVO, MC,* 6th Marquess *b.* 1893: *m.* 1924, Jessie Carlos, who *d.* 1969, da. of the late Charles Carlos Clarke; *d.* 1971; *s.* by his cousin [7] JAMES HUBERT THEOBALD CHARLES, *MBE,* 7th Marquess and present peer; also Earl of Ormonde, Earl of Ossory, Viscount Thurles, and Baron Ormonde.

ORR-EWING, BARON.   (Orr-Ewing.)   [Life Baron 1971. Bt. U.K. 1963.]

(CHARLES) IAN ORR-EWING, *OBE*; *Life Baron,* and 1st *Baronet,* son of the late Archibald Ian Orr-Ewing [see Orr Ewing, Bt., colls., cr. 1886]; *b.* Feb. 10th, 1912; ed. at Harrow, and Trin. Coll., Oxford (MA); late Wing-Cdr. RAFVR; CEng.; PPS to Min. of Labour 1952-55, Parl. Under-Sec. Air Min. 1957-59, Parl. and Financial Sec. to Admiralty 1959, and Civil Lord of Admiralty 1959-63; Joint Vice-Chm. of 1922 Cttee. 1966-70; Chm. Metrication Board since 1972; 1939-45 War in N. Africa, Italy and NW Europe (despatches, OBE); MP for Hendon (*C*) 1950-70; cr. OBE (Mil) 1945, a *Baronet* (UK, of Hendon) 1963, and *Baron Orr-Ewing,* of Little Berkhamsted, co. Hertford (Life Baron) 1971: *m.* 1939, Joan Helen, only da. of Gordon McMinnies, of Farm House Hotel, Lower Swell, Stow-on-the-Wold, Glos., and has issue.

Arms—Argent, on a chevron ensigned with a banner between in chief two mullets and in base a representation of the path of two electrons rotating round a nucleus gules a pair of wings conjoined in lure between two lymphads sails furled penons and flags flying or. Crest,—A demi-lion rampant gules holding in the dexter paw a mullet azure and nesting the sinister paw on a portcullis chained or.
Residence,—Old Manor, Little Berkhamsted, Hertford.

(*In remainder to Baronetcy only.*)

SONS LIVING.

Hon. ALISTAIR SIMON (44, Paultons Sq., SW3), *b.* June 10th 1940; ed. at Harrow, and Trin. Coll., Oxford, ARICS; *h.a.* to Baronetcy: *m.* 1968, Victoria, da. of Keith Cameron, of Fifield House, Milton-under-Wychwood, Oxon., and has issue living, Archie Cameron, *b.* 1969,—James Alexander, *b.* 1971,—Georgina Victoria, *b.* 1974.

Hon. Ian Collin (19, Moreton Place, SW1), *b.* 1942; ed. at Harrow, and Trin. Coll., Oxford: *m.* 1973, Deirdre, el. da. of Lance Japhet, of Sandhurst, Johannesburg, and has issue living, Francis Ian Lance, *b.* 1975.

Hon. Malcolm Archie (Hampton Cottage, Down Ampney, Circencester, Glos.), *b.* 1946; ed. at Harrow, and Munich: *m.* 1973, Clare Mary, da. of Brig. George Robert Flood, *MC,* of Hawkeswell House, Little Cheverell, Devizes, Wilts., and has issue living, Harriet Kate, *b.* 1975.

Hon. Robert James, *b.* 1953; ed. at Harrow.

Orrery, Earl of, see Earl of Cork and Orrery

Ossulston, Lord, son of Earl of Tankerville.

OXFORD, LORD BISHOP OF. (Woollcombe.)

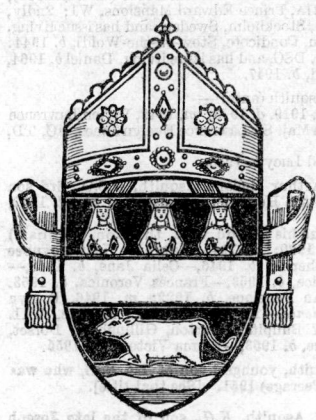

Rt. Rev. KENNETH JOHN WOOLLCOMBE, son of the Rev. Edward Percy Woollcombe, OBE, of Bradley Green, Worcs.; *b.* Jan. 2nd, 1924; ed. at Haileybury, and St. Johns Coll., Oxford (MA); 1939-45 War as Sub-Lt. RNVR; Fellow Chap. and Lecturer of St. Johns Coll., Oxford, and Licensed to Officiate Diocese, Oxford 1953-60; Tutor 1956-60; Exam. Chap. to Bishops of Worcester and Wakefield 1957-60, and to Bishop of Oxford 1958-60; Prof. of Dogmatic Theo., Gen. Theo. Seminary, NY, 1960-63, and Prin. of Edniburgh Theo. Coll. 1963-71; Canon of Edinburgh 1963-71; consecrated 39th Bishop of Oxford 1971: *m.* 1950, Gwendoline Rhona Vyvien, only child of the late Sir Reginald John Hodges, of Waverley House, Edgeworth, Stroud, Glos.

Patron of more than one hundred and sixteen livings, and of the Archdeaconries of Oxford, Buckingham, and Berkshire.

This Diocese was erected into a Bishopric by Henry VIII, 1542, out of the lands of dissolved monasteries, but in the reign of Elizabeth it was deprived of a considerable portion of the emoluments conferred by her father.

Episcopal Signature,—" Kenneth Oxon."

ARMS OF THE SEE,—Sable: a fesse argent, in chief three demi-ladies couped at the waist, heads affrontée proper, crowned or, arrayed and veiled of the second; in base an ox of the last, horned and hoofed or, passing a ford, barry wavy of four azure and argent.

Residence,—Bishop's House, Cuddesdon, Oxford.

OXFORD AND ASQUITH, EARL OF. (Asquith.) [Earl U.K. 1925.]

JULIAN EDWARD GEORGE ASQUITH, KCMG, 2nd Earl; *b.* April 22nd, 1916; *s.* 1928; ed. at Ampleforth Coll., and at Balliol Coll., Oxford (Scholar, M.A.); formerly Lt. R.E.; appointed Assist. Dist. Commr. Palestine 1942, Dep. Ch. Sec., Tripolitania 1949, Adviser to Prime Min. of Libya 1951, Administrative Sec., Zanzibar 1955, and Administrator, St. Lucia 1958; Gov. and Com.-in-Ch. of Seychelles 1962-67, and Commr. for British Indian Ocean Territory 1965-67; Constitutional Commr. Cayman Is. 1971, and Turks and Caicos Islands 1973-74; CMG 1961, KCMG 1964: *m.* 1947, Anne Mary Celestine, da. of the late Sir (Charles) Michael Palairet, KCMG, and has issue.

Arms,—Sable, on a fesse between three cross crosslets argent a portcullis of the field. Crest,— Issuant out of clouds proper, a mascle gules. Supporters,—On either side a lion purpure, charged on the shoulder with an open book argent, edged or.

Residence,—The Manor House, Mells, Frome.

SONS LIVING.

RAYMOND BENEDICT BARTHOLOMEW MICHAEL (*Viscount Asquith*), *b.* Aug. 24th, 1952
Hon. Dominic Anthony Gerard, *b.* 1957.

DAUGHTERS LIVING.

Lady Mary Annunziata, *b.* 1948.
Lady Katharine Rose Celestine, *b.* 1949: *m.* 1970, Adam Nicholas Ridley, of 52, Novello St., SW6 [see V. Ridley, colls.].
Lady Clare Perpetua Frances, *b.* 1955.

SISTERS LIVING. (*Raised to the rank of an Earl's daughters* 1928.)

Lady Helen Frances, *OBE* (Tynts Hill, Mells, Frome, Som.), *b.* 1908; BA Somerville Coll., Oxford, 1930; OBE (Civil) 1965.
Lady Perdita Rose Mary (*Perdita, Baroness Hylton*), *b.* 1910: *m.* 1931, the 4th Baron Hylton, who *d.* 1967. *Residence,*—Ammerdown, Radstock, Bath.

MOTHER LIVING.

Katharine Frances, dau. of the late Sir John (Francis Fortescue) Horner, K.C.V.O., of The Manor House, Mells, Frome: *m.* 1907, Raymond Asquith, Bar.-at-law, and Grenadier Guards, who *d.* (killed in action during European War) 1916. *Residence,*—Tynts Hill, Mells, Frome.

COLLATERAL BRANCHES LIVING.

Issue of the late Hon. Herbert Asquith, 2nd son of 1st Earl, *b.* 1881, *d.* 1947: *m.* 1910, Lady Cynthia Charteris, who *d.* 1960, dau. of 11th Earl of Wemyss and March :—

Michael Henry (The Barns, Condicote, Stow-on-the-Wold, Glos.), *b.* 1914; ed. at Winchester, and Balliol Coll., Oxford (BA); served with Friend's Ambulance Unit 1940-5: *m.* 1st, 1938 (m. diss. 1952), Diana, da. of the late Lieut.-Col. P. L. M. Battye, MC, of 21A, Prince Edward Mansions, W1; 2ndly, 1953, Helga, da. of Dr. Walther Ritter, of 5, Pokalvaegen, Stockholm, Sweden, and has issue living, (by 1st m.) Stephen Andrew Romily Michael (Manor Farm, Condicote, Stow-on-the-Wold), *b.* 1944: *m.* 1963 Nicola, da. of Lt.-Cdr. Peter Markham Scott, CBE, DSC, and has issue living, Daniel *b.* 1964, Emily Rachel *b.* 1965, Lucy Kate *b.* 1967,—Peter Edward, *b.* 1947.

Grandchildren of the late Hon. Herbert Asquith (ante):—
Issue of the late Simon Anthony Roland Asquith, *b.* 1919, *d.* 1973: *m.* 1942, Vivien Lawrence (15, Castello Av., Putney, SW15), da. of the late Maj. Sir Lawrence Evelyn Jones, MC, TD, 5th Bt. (cr. 1831):—
Conrad Robin, *b.* 1945.——Ivon Shaun, *b.* 1946.——Rosalind Lucy *b.* 1948.

Issue of the late Brig.-Gen. the Hon. **Arthur Melland** Asquith, D.S.O., 3rd son of 1st Earl, *b.* 1883, *d.* 1939: *m.* 1918, the Hon. Betty Constance, who *d.* 1962, dau. of 3rd Baron Manners:—
April Mary (*Hon. Mrs. W. Keith Rous*), *b.* 1919: *m.* 1943, as his second wife, the Hon. (William) Keith Rous [see E. Stradbroke].——Jean Constance, *b.* 1920: *m.* 1945, Lawrence Leif Toynbee [E. Carlisle, colls.], and has issue living, Rosalind Catherine, *b.* 1946,—Celia Jane, *b.* 1948,— Clare Anne, *b.* 1949,—Rachel Mary, *b.* 1950,—Sarah Alice, *b.* 1953,—Frances Veronica, *b.* 1958. *Residence,*—Ganthorpe Hall, Terrington, York.——Susan Penelope, *b.* 1922: *m.* 1946, Evelyn Basil Boothby, CMG [see Boothby, Bt., colls.]. *Residence,*—23, Holland Park Avenue, W11. ——Christine, *b.* 1926: *m.* 1952, John Hatch Clark, of Bullpits, Bourton, Gillingham, Dorset, and has issue living, John Jasper, *b.* 1958,—Lucy Caroline, *b.* 1953,—Emma Victoria, *b.* 1955.

Issue of the late Rt. Hon. Sir Cyril Asquith, youngest son of 1st Earl, who was cr. *Baron Asquith of Bishopstone* (Life Peerage) 1951. [See that title].

PREDECESSOR.—[1] *Rt. Hon. Sir* **HERBERT HENRY** Asquith, *K.G.*, son of the late Joseph Dixon Asquith, of Croft House, Morley, Yorkshire, *b.* 1852 ; a K.C., High Steward of Oxford, and an Elder Brother of the Trinity House ; M.P. for Fifeshire, E. Div. (*L*) 1886 to Nov. 1918, and for Paisley Feb. 1920 to Oct. 1924; Sec. of State for Home Depart. Aug. 1892 to June 1895, Chancellor of the Exchequer Dec. 1905 to April 1908, Prime Min. and First Lord of the Treasury April 1908 to Dec. 1916 (also Sec. of State for War and Pres. of Army Council March to Aug. 1914, and Chm. of Cabinet War Committee Nov. 1915 to Dec. 1916), and Leader of Liberal Party 1908-26 ; cr. *Earl of Oxford and Asquith* (peerage of United Kingdom) and *Viscount Asquith*, of Morley, W. Riding, of co. York, Feb. 1925 : *m.* 1st, 1877, Helen Kelsall, who *d.* 1891, el. dau. of the late Dr. Frederick Melland, of Rusholme, Manchester ; 2ndly, 1894, Emma Alice Margaret (Margot), who *d.* 1945, dau. of Sir Charles Tennant, 1st Bt. : *d.* 1928 ; *s.* by his grandson [2] JULIAN (son of the late Raymond Asquith (el. son of 1st Earl), who *d.* killed in action during European War 1916), 2nd Earl and present peer : also Viscount Asquith.

Oxmantown, Lord, son of Earl of Rosse.

PAGET OF NORTHAMPTON, BARON. (Paget.) [Life Baron 1974.]

REGINALD THOMAS GUY DES VOEUX PAGET, *QC*, son of the late Maj. Thomas Guy Frederick Paget, of Sulby Hall, Northants. [Des Voeux, Bt.]; *b.* Sept. 2nd, 1908; ed. at Eton, and Trin. Coll., Camb. (BA); Bar. Gray's Inn, and Inner Temple 1934; KC 1948; 1939-45 War as Lt. RNVR (invalided) ; MP for Northampton (*Lab.*) 1945-74; cr. *Baron Paget of Northampton*, of Lubenham, Leicestershire (Life Baron) 1974: *m.* 1931, Sybil Helen, da. of the late Sills Clifford Gibbons, widow of Sir John Bridger Shiffner, 6th Bt., and formerly wife of Sir Victor Basil John Seely, 4th Bt.

Arms,—Sable a cross engrailed between in the 1st and 4th quarters an escallop argent. Crest,—A lion rampant sable, collared or, supporting an antique shield argent, charged with an escallop sable. Supporters—Not exemplified at time of going to press.
Residences,—Lubenham Lodge, Market Harborough, Leics.; 9, Grosvenor Cottages, SW1.

Pakenham, Baron, title of Earl of Longford, on Roll of H.L.

PALMER, BARON. (Palmer.) [Baron U.K. 1933, Bt. U.K. 1916.]

Through the cross to the palm.

RAYMOND CECIL PALMER, *OBE*, 3rd Baron and 3rd Baronet; *b.* June 24th, 1916; *s.* 1950; ed. at Harrow, and at Univ. Coll., Oxford; Dir. of Assoc. Biscuit Manufacturers, Ltd., Chm. of Huntley & Palmers, Ltd., Biscuit Manufacturers, of Reading, and of Huntley, Boorne & Stevens, Ltd., Tin Box Manufacturers, of Reading; part time Member of Southern Electricity Board, Pres. of Thames Valley Trustee Savings Bank, and Chm. of National Savings Southern Industrial Advisory Cttee.; sometime Lt. Grenadier Guards (invalided); OBE (Civil) 1968: *m.* 1941, Victoria Ellen, only da. of the late Capt. J. A. R. Weston-Stevens, of Woolley Cottage, The Thicket, Maidenhead, and has issue.

Arms,—Per saltire azure and gules two palmers' staves in saltire between four escallops or. Crest,—Upon a mount vert in front of a palm tree proper three escallops fesseways or. Supporters,—On either side a palmer, supporting with the exterior hand a palmer's staff proper.

Residence,—Farley Hill House, Farley Hill, Reading. *Club.*—Guards'.

DAUGHTERS LIVING.

Hon. Carol Lylie (*Lady Wodehouse*), *b.* 1951: *m.* 1973, John Armine, Lord Wodehouse, son of 4th Earl of Kimberley.

Hon. Vanessa Marguerite, *b.* 1954.

BROTHER LIVING.

Hon. GORDON WILLIAM NOTTAGE, *OBE, TD, b.* July 18th, 1918; ed. at Eton and at Ch. Ch., Oxford; FRCM; Col. (ret.) Berkshire Yeo.; formerly local Lt.-Col. RA, on Staff; Hon. Col. of R. Yeo. (Volunteers) TAVR 1971-75, and HQ Sqdn. R. Yeo, since 1967; a JP and a DL of Berks.; High Sheriff 1965; Chm. and Man. Dir. of Associated Biscuits, Ltd.; Pres. of Reading Univ.; 1939-45 War (MBE, American Bronze Star); MBE (Mil.) 1944, OBE (Mil.) 1957: *m.* 1950, Lorna Eveline Hope, da. of Maj. Charles William Hugh Bailie, of Manderston, Berwickshire, and has issue living, Adrian Bailie Nottage, *b.* 1951,—Mark Hugh Gordon, *b.* 1954. *Residences,*—Foudry House, Mortimer, Berks.; Eldrom Newton, Duns., Berwicks. *Club.,*—Cavalry.

SISTER LIVING.

Hon. Marjorie Elizabeth, *b.* 1910: *m.* 1945, Frederick Richard Brown, M.B.E., late Capt. R.A.S.C., and has issue living, Christopher Frederick, *b.* 1946: *m.* 1972, Suzanne Ryder,—Ian Cecil Roger, *b.* 1948.—Richard Philip, *b.* 1952,—Jennifer Elizabeth, *b.* 1953: *m.* 1975, Brian Shephard. *Residence,*—4, New Park Rd., Newgate St., Hertford, Herts.

COLLATERAL BRANCH LIVING.

Issue of the late Hon. Arnold Nottage Palmer, FRCM, yr. son of 1st Baron, *b.* 1886, *d.* 1973: *m.* 1911, Marjorie, who *d.* 1966, da. of the late Alexander Freeland, of Lingfield, Surrey:—

Susan Helen (Fir Tree Farm, Hampstead Norris, Berks.), *b.* 1912.——Felicity Amy (Coombe Farm, Frilsham, Hermitage, Newbury, Berks.), *b.* 1913.——Rachel Joan, *b.* 1916: *m.* 1957, Guivi Malville. ——Nancy Gillian, *b.* 1918: *m.* 1943, David Charles Bethune Pilkington, OBE, of Appledown Frilsham, Hermitage [see Bethune Bt.].

PREDECESSORS.—[1] SAMUEL ERNEST Palmer, el. son of the late Samuel Palmer, of Northcourt, Hampstead, NW; *b.* 1858; was a Director of Huntley & Palmers, Ltd., biscuit manufacturers, of Reading, and founder of Roy. Coll. of Music Patrons' Fund, the Berkshire Scholarship, and Ernest Palmer Fund for Opera Study, also two Scholarships at Guildhall; cr. a *Baronet* 1916, and *Baron Palmer* of Reading, co. Berks (pee rage of United Kingdom) 1933: *m.* 1881, Amy Christiana, who *d.* 1947, only da. of the late Alde rman George Swan Nottage, Lord Mayor of London; *d.* 1948; *s.* by his son [2] (ERNEST) CECIL NOTTAGE, 2nd Baron: *b.* 1882; Dep. Chm. of Huntley & Palmers Ltd., biscuit manufacturers of R eading: *m.* 1909, Marguerite, who *d.* 1959, da. of the late William McKinley Osborne, of USA; *d.* 1950; *s.* by his son [3] RAYMOND CECIL, 3rd Baron and present peer.

PANNELL, BARON. (Pannell.). [Life Barron 1974.]

(THOMAS) CHARLES PANNELL, *PC*, son of the late James William Pannell; *b*, Sept. 10th, 1902; a Borough Councillor of Walthamstow 1929-34, and of Erith 1938-55 (Alderman 1944-55, Mayor 1945-46), Chm. of N-W Kent Div. Exec. for Education 1944-55, Member and Dep. Leader of Kent Co. Council Labour Group 1946-49, Parl. Delegations, Inter-Parliamentary Union in Berne 1951, and Belgium 1952; Sec. Trade Union Gp., Parl. Labour Party 1953-64; a Member of NATO Conference of Parliamentarians 1955-57, Poland 1958, and W. Germany 1960, a Delegate at Atlantic Congress 1957-58, a Member of Select Cttee. on Procedure 1958, of Joint Select Cttee. Lords and Commons, on House of Lords Reform 1962, and of Select Cttee. on Law of Privilege 1966-67; Min. of Public Building and Works 1964-66; Leader of Delegation to Singapore, and a Member of UK Delegation, Commonwealth Parl. Assocn. Conference, Ottawa 1966, Commonwealth Parl. Assocn. Delegation to NZ 1971, and of Cttee. on Privileges 1967-74; Leader Parl. Delegation to United Arab Republic 1973; Vice-Pres. of Assocn. of Municipal Corpns.; MP for W. Div. of Leeds (*Lab.*) 1949-74; cr. PC 1964, and *Baron Pannell*, of City of Leeds (Life Baron) 1974: *m.* 1929, Lilian Maud, da. of Edward William Francis Frailing, of Islington, and has issue.

Residence,—159, Glenview, Abbey Wood, SE2.

DAUGHTER LIVING.

Hon. Hilary, *b.* 1940.

PARGITER, BARON. (Pargiter.) [Life Baron 1966.]

GEORGE ALBERT PARGITER, *CBE*, son of the late William Russell Pargiter, of Green's Norton, Northants; *b.* March 16th, 1897; ed. at Towcester Gram. Sch.; an Engineer, and a DL of Greater London; Mayor of Southall 1938-40, and Ch. of Middlesex Co. Council 1959-60; Vice-Chm. of Co. Councils Assocn. 1960-63, and Chm. 1963-65, since when Vice-Pres.; MP for Spelthorne Div. of Middlesex (*Lab.*) 1945-50 and for Southall 1950-66; 1914-18 War, Gallipoli (wounded); *cr.* CBE (Civil) 1960, and *Baron Pargiter*, of Southall, London Borough of Ealing (Life Baron) 1966: *m.* 1919, Dorothy Maud, da. of Roger Woods, and has issue.

SONS LIVING.

Hon. Donald (68, Tonbridge Rd., Maidstone), *b.* 1921: *m.* 1947.
Hon. Russell Ashby (262, Macquarie St., Hobart, Tasmania), *b.* 1924; MB, BS London; a Fellow of Australian and NZ Coll. of Psychiatrists; DPM England; FRC Psych.; Snr. Hon. Psychiatrist, Roy. Hobart Hosp.: *m.* 1954, Elizabeth Edwina, da. of John George Jamieson Coghill.

DAUGHTER LIVING.

Hon. Isobel, *b.* 1931; Pharmaceutical Chemist: *m.* 1964, Ernest Cooper-Heyman, of 34, Van Dyke Close, Redhill, Surrey, RH1 2DS.

Parker, Viscount, son of Earl of Macclesfield.

PARKER OF WADDINGTON, BARONY OF. (cr. 1913.) (Parker.) [Extinct 1918]

DAUGHTER LIVING OF LIFE BARON.

Hon. Gwendolen (*Hon. Lady Schuster*), *b.* 1888 : *m.* 1908, Sir George Ernest Schuster, K.C.S.I. KCMG, CBE, MC, and has issue. *Residence,*—Nether Worton House, Middle Barton, Oxon.

[WIDOWS LIVING OF SONS OF LIFE BARON.

Mary Margaret Carmichael (c/o Standard Bank Ltd., Kingsway Branch, Baker Av., Salisbury, Rhodesia), da. of the late R. H. Mackay: *m.* 1945, as his 2nd wife, the Hon. John Stanley Parker, who *d.* 1962.——Loryn (*Baroness Parker of Waddington*), da. of Oscar Tilton Bowser of Kentucky, USA: *m.* 1924, the Hon. Sir Herbert Lister Parker, PC, who was cr. *Baron Parker of Waddington* (Life Baron) 1958, and who *d.* 1972 [see that title].

PARKER OF WADDINGTON, BARONY OF. (cr. 1958.) [Parker.] [Extinct 1972.]

WIDOW LIVING OF LIFE BARON.

LORYN (*Baroness Parker of Waddington*), (20, Dunraven St., W1), da. of Oscar Tilton-Bowser, of Kentucky, USA: *m.* 1924, Baron Parker of Waddington (Life Peer cr. 1958), who *d.* 1972, when the title became ext.

PARMOOR, BARON. (Cripps.) [Baron U.K. 1914.]

Do not trust in appearances.

ALFRED HENRY SEDDON CRIPPS, 2nd Baron; *b.* Aug. 27th, 1882; *s.* 1941; ed. at Winchester, and at New Coll., Oxford (B.A. 1907, M.A. 1929); Bar. Middle Temple 1907; was Bursar of Queen's Coll., Oxford 1928-45 (Fellow 1929).

Arms,—Chequy ermines and argent, on a chevron vert five horseshoes or. Crest,—An ostrich's head couped argent, gorged with a coronet of fleurs-de-lis, and holding in the beak a horseshoe or. Supporters,—On either side a seahorse proper, supporting a pennon ermines charged with a swan rousant argent, beaked and legged gules, ducally gorged and lined or.

Residence,—44, Admirals Walk, Bournemouth, Hants. *Club,*—Brooks's.

BROTHER LIVING.

Hon. FREDERICK HEYWORTH, *D.S.O., T.D.* (of Southridge, Wash Common, Newbury), *b.* July 4th, 1885; ed. at Winchester; is a D.L. for Bucks; formerly Lt.-Col. Bucks Yeo.; 1914-18 War in Dardanelles, Palestine, and France (wounded, D.S.O. with Bar, Belgian Croix de Guerre), 1939-45 War as temp. Lt.-Cdr. RNVR; DSO (and Bar) 1918: *m.* 1927 (marriage dissolved 1951), Violet Mary Geraldine, da. of Sir William Nelson, 1st Bt., and has issue living, Frederick Alfred Milo, *b.* 1929. *Club,*—White's.

SISTER LIVING.

Hon. Ruth Julia (*Hon. Lady Egerton*), *b.* 1884 : *m.* 1912, Sir Alfred Charles Glyn Egerton, D.Sc., FRS [B. Harlech], who *d.* 1959. *Residence,*—13, Kingston House North, Princes Gate, SW7.

WIDOW LIVING OF SON OF FIRST BARON.

Hon. Dame Isobel, *GBE*, da. of the late Cdr. Harold William Swithinbank, DL, of Denham Court, Denham, Bucks; FRSA; 1st class Order of the Briliant Star of China; GBE (Civil) 1946: *m.* 1911, the Rt. Hon. Sir (Richard) Stafford Cripps, C.H., Q.C., F.R.S., who *d.* 1952, and has issue living [see colls., infra]. *Residence,*—Greyholme, Minchinhampton, Stroud, Glos., GL6 9HA.

COLLATERAL BRANCHES LIVING.

Issue of the late Major the Hon. Leonard Harrison Cripps, C.B.E., 3rd son of 1st Baron, *b.* 1887, *d.* 1959 : *m.* 1913, Miriam Barbara, who *d.* 1960, dau. of the late Rt. Hon. Sir Matthew Ingle Joyce :—

(Matthew) Arthur Leonard, *CBE, DSO, TD, QC, b.* 1913; ed. at Eton and Ch. Ch., Oxford (MA); Bar. Middle Temple 1938, Inner Temple 1961, QC 1958, and Bencher 1965; Recorder of Nottingham 1961-71; Recorder of Crown Court since 1972; a Member of Senate of four Inns of Court 1967-71; Chm. of Disciplinary Cttee. of Milk Marketing Board since 1956, and of Home Sec.'s Advisory Cttee. on Ser. Candidates since 1966 (Dep. Chm. 1965-66); a Member of Bar Council 1967-69, and 1970-74, and of Min. of Agric's. Cttee. of Inquiry into Foot and Mouth Disease 1968-69, Chm. Reigate Cons. Assocn. 1961-64, of Research Cttee., Soc. of Cons. Lawyers 1963-67 and of Cons. Party Research Cttee. of Inquiry into Discrimination against Women in Law and Admin. 1968-69; a Member of Exec. Cttee. of Nat. Union of Cons. Assocns. 1964-72, Judge of Canterbury Court of Arches since 1969; Chm. of National Panel of Approved Coal Merchants Scheme since 1972, and of Billbrook Finance, Ltd.; author of " The Agricultural Holdings Act, 1948 ", and Editor of " Cripps on Compulsory Acquisition of Land; Powers, Procedure and Compensation"; 1939-45 War in Norway, North Africa (DSO), and Italy; DSO 1943, CBE (Civil) 1971: *m.* 1941, Margaret, da. of the late G. Johnson-Scott, of Hill House, Ashby-de-la-Zouch, and has issue living, Michael Leonard Seddon, *b.* 1942; Bar. Middle Temple 1965, and Lincoln's Inn 1969: *m.* 1971, Anne, da. of Maj. Millward-Shennan, of Moorside, Caldy-in-Wirral, and has issue living, Stephanie Margaret Julia *b.* 1974,— Jeremy George Anthony, *b.* 1943; ed. at Eton, and Case Western Reserve Univ., Cleveland, Ohio (MA); ACA; Certified Public Accountant, Ohio, USA: *m.* 1972, Mary Elizabeth, only da. of Walter Howe, of Golf Manor, Cincinatti, Ohio, USA,—Richard James Nigel, *b.* 1956. *Residence,*—Alton House, Felbridge, E. Grinstead, Sussex.——Charles Thomas Joyce, *b.* 1916; ed. at Eton, and at Ch. Ch., Oxford; formerly Capt. Roy. Tank Regt.; is a Member of London Stock Exchange: *m.* 1941, Noreen, da. of the late Dr. Hugh Pierce, of 24, Upper Duke St., Liverpool, and has issue living, Charles Hugh *b.* 1946,—Paul Alfred *b.* 1950. *Residence,*—41, Somerset Rd., Wimbledon, SW19.

Issue of the late Rt. Hon. Sir (Richard) Stafford Cripps, O.H., Q.C., F.R.S., *b.* 1889, *d.* 1952, youngest son of 1st Baron : *m.* 1911, Dame Isobel, *G.B.E.* (ante), dau. of the late Com. Harold William Swithinbank, D.L., of Denham Court, Denham, Bucks :—

John Stafford, *CBE, b.* 1912; ed. at Winchester and Balliol Coll., Oxford; President of *The Countryman,* 1947-71; Chm. of RDC Assocn. 1967-70, of Rural Cttee. of National Council of Social Ser. since 1962, and of Countryside Commn. since 1970, a Member of SE Economic Planning Council since 1966, of Cttee. on Footpaths 1967-68, of Inland Waterways Amenity Advisory Cttee. since 1968, of Nature Conservancy since 1970 and of Defence Lands Review Cttee. since 1971; CBE (Civil) 1968: *m.* 1st, 1936, Ursula, da. of the late Arthur Cedric Davy, of Whirlow Court, Sheffield; 2ndly, 1971, Ann Elizabeth, da. of Edwin G. K. Farwell, and has issue living (by 1st m.), David Stafford, *b.* 1940; ed at Bryanston, and Reading Univ.,—Timothy Francis, *b.* 1943; ed. at Eton, and Trin. Coll., Camb.,— Christopher John, *b.* 1947; ed. at Bryanston, and King's Coll., Camb.,—Richard Andrew, *b.* 1953; ed. at Bryanston, and Southampton Univ.,—Judith Ursula (PO Box 47678, 19, Hatheru Rd., Nairobi), *b.* 1938; ed. at Somerville Coll., Oxford: *m.* 1964, Sarjit Heyer, who *d.* 1974, and has issue living, Jasdev Philip *b.* 1968, Daleep Andrew *b.* 1971, Amrik Frances *b.* 1967,—Rachel Theresa, *b.* 1945; ed. at ,Univ. of Sussex: *m.* 1969 (James Oriel) Bernard Rosedale, MB, BS, of Thornsend, Kingsbury Hill Marlborough, Wilts., and has issue living, Nicholas Oriel Rupert *b.* 1972, Lawrence Andrew *b.* 1974. *Residence,*—Filkins, Lechlade, Glos. *Club,*—Farmers.——Isobel Diana CRIPPS, *b.* 1913; resumed the surname of Cripps 19—: *m.* 1938 (m. annulled on her petition 1941), Lawrence Purcell Weaver. *Residence,*—Greyholme, Minchinhampton, Glos.——Anne Theresa (*Lady Ricketts*), *b.* 1919: *m.* 1945, Capt. Sir Robert Cornwallis Gerald St. Leger Ricketts, 7th Bt., late Devonshire Regt. *Residence,*—Forwood House, Minchinhampton, Glos.——Enid Margaret (PO Box 829, Kumasi, Ashanti, Ghana), *b.* 1921: *m.* 1953, Joseph E. Appiah, and has issue living, (Kwame) Anthony Akromaampin Kusi, *b.* 1954,—Isobel Takyiwah, *b.* 1955,—Amy Adowa, *b.* 1959,—Theresa Jane, *b.* 1962.

PREDECESSOR.— [1] *Rt. Hon. Sir* CHARLES ALFRED Cripps, *K.C.V.O., K.C.,* son of the late Henry William Cripps, Q.C., of Beechwood, Marlow ; *b.* 1852; appointed Attorney-Gen. to successive Princes of Wales 1895, 1901, and 1910 (also a Member of Council), Chancellor and Vicar-Gen. to Diocese of York 1900, Chm. of Canterbury House of Laymen and a Member of its Committee 1910, a Member of Judicial Committee of Privy Council 1914, British Representative on Council of League of Nations Jan. 1924, and Ch. British Representative to League of Nations Assembly Sept. 1924 ; was Vicar-Gen. of Province of Canterbury 1902-24, First Chm. of House of Laity in National Church Assembly 1920-24, Lord Pres. of the Council Jan. to Nov. 1924, and June 1929 to Aug. 1931, and Leader of Labour Party in House of Lords Oct. 1928 to Aug. 1931 ; sat as M.P. for Mid, or Stroud, Div. of Gloucestershire (C) 1895-1900, for Stretford Div. of Lancashire (S.-E.) 1901-6, and for Bucks, S. or Wycombe Div. Jan. 1910 to Jan. 1914 ; cr. *Baron Parmoor,* of Frieth, co. Bucks (peerage of United Kingdom) 1914 : *m.* 1st, 1881, Theresa, who *d.* 1893, sixth dau. of Richard Potter, of Rusland Hall, Lancashire ; 2ndly, 1919, Marian Emily, who *d.* 1952, dau. of the late Rt. Hon. John E. Ellis, of Wrea Head, Scalby, Yorkshire ; *d.* 1941; *s.* by his son [2] ALFRED HENRY SEDDON, 2nd Baron and present peer.

PEARCE, BARON. (Pearce.) [Life Baron 1962.]

EDWARD HOLROYD PEARCE, *P.C.,* son of the late John William Ernest Pearce, of Hampstead, N.W.; *b.* Feb. 9th, 1901; ed. at Charterhouse, and at Corpus Christi Coll., Oxford (Hon. Fellow 1950); Bar. Lincoln's Inn and Middle Temple 1925, a K.C. 1945, a Bencher of Lincoln's Inn 1948, and Treasurer 1966; a Gov. of Tonbridge Sch.; Judge of High Court of Justice, Probate, Divorce and Admiralty Div. 1948-54, and Queen's Bench Div. 1954-57, a Lord Justice of Appeal 1957-62, and a Lord of Appeal in Ordinary 1962-69; Indep. Chm. of Press Council 1969-74; cr. Knt. 1948, PC 1957, and *Baron Pearce,* of Sweethaws, co. Sussex (Life Baron) 1962: *m.* 1927, Erica, da. of Bertram Priestman, RA, and has issue.

Nothing concerning man is indifferent to me

Arms,—Gules a pile ermine a chief vair. **Crest,**—Two arrows points upwards in saltire sable surmounted by a fleur de lys or. **Supporters,**—On either side, a cat ermined collared gules.

Residence,—Sweethaws, Crowborough, Sussex.

SONS LIVING.

Hon. Richard Bruce Holroyd *QC b.* 1930; ed. at Charterhouse, and at Corpus Christi Coll., Oxford;
Bar Lincoln's Inn 1955, QC 1969; Recorder of S.E. Circuit since 1971: *m.* 1958, Dornie Mary, da. of
G. J. Smith-Pert, and has issue. *Residence,*—Adams Cottage, Sweethaws, Crowborough, Sussex.
Club,—Athenaeum.
Hon. James Edward Holroyd (Turf Lodge, Slaugham Ghyll, Crowborough, Sussex ;Athenaeum and
RAC) *b.* 1934; ed. at Charterhouse, and at Corpus Christi Coll., Oxford; Bar, Middle Temple 1960:
m. 1969, Julia, yr. da. of C. D. Hill, of Tyrrellswood, Leatherhead, Surrey, and has issue.

PEARSON, BARON. (Pearson.) [Life Baron 1965.]

COLIN HARGREAVES PEARSON, *CBE, PC*,
son of Ernest William Pearson, of Minnedosa,
Manitoba, and 66, Brook Green, W6; *b.*
July 28th, 1899; ed. at St. Paul's Sch., and
at Balliol Coll., Oxford (MA, Hon. Fellow
1963, Visitor 1965-74); Bar. Inner Temple
1924, a KC 1949, a Bencher 1951, and
Treasurer 1973; Temporary Assist. Solicitor,
Office of HM Procurator-General and
Treasury Solicitor 1939-45; Recorder of
Hythe 1937-51, a Judge of High Court of
Justice (Queen's Bench Div., 1951-61, a
Lord Justice of Appeal 1961-65, and a Lord
of Appeal in Ordinary, 1965-74; a Member of
Supreme Court Rule Cttee. 1957-65, and
Chm. of Cttee. on Funds in Court 1958; Chm.
of Law Reform Cttee. 1963-72, of Court of
Inquiry into a dispute in Electricity Industry
1964, and into certain matters of Shipping
Industry 1966, and into a dispute between
BOAC and British Airline Pilots Assocn. 1967-68; Chm. of Roy. Commn. on
Civil Liability and Compensation for Personal Injury since 1973; 1914-18 War
as 2nd Lt., Guards Machine Gun Regt.; *cr.* CBE (Civil) 1946, Knt. 1951, PC
1961 and *Baron Pearson*, of Minnedosa, Canada, and Roy. Borough of Kensington (Life Baron) 1965: *m.* 1931, Sophie Grace Hermann, da. of Arthur
Hermann Thomas, MC, LLD, of Worthing, and has issue.

Arms,—Per pale azure and gules, a sun in splendour between three pears or, a chief ermine.
Crest,—Within a crown rayonée or a stag trippant proper winged argent attired and unguled or,
supporting between the forelegs a pear branch proper fructed or. **Supporters,**—On either side a
bison proper armed or pendent from the jaws three annulets interlaced sable.

Residence,—2, Crown Office Row, Temple EC4. *Clubs,*—Garrick, Roehampton.

SON LIVING.

Hon. Graham Thomas (Manor House, Manor Lane, Old Basing, Basingstoke), *b.* 1935: *m.* 1963,
Diana, da. of Vice-Adm. Sir Maxwell Richmond, KBE, CB, DSO, of 20, Parkside St., Auckland,
New Zealand, and has issue.

DAUGHTER LIVING.

Hon. Lois Jean, *b.* 1938: *m.* 1961, the Rev. Robin Jonathan Norman Smith, of St. Mary's Vicarage,
Chesham, Bucks., and has issue.

PEDDIE, BARON. (Peddie.) [Life Baron 1961.]

JAMES MORTIMER PEDDIE, *M.B.E.*, son of Crofton Peddie, of Hull and
Stirling ; *b.* April 4th, 1906 ; ed. at St. Paul's Church Sch., Hull, and at
London Sch. of Economics; Hon. LLD Manchester; JP for Cheshire; a
Dir. of Co-operative Wholesale Soc. Ltd., and of Co-operative Insurance Soc.
Ltd. 1945-65, and of Co-operative Permanent Building Soc. 1946-65, Chm. of
Co-operative Party 1958-65, and Pres. of Co-operative Congress 1958, Gov.
British Film Inst. 1949-53 (acted as Arbitrator in Film Industry), a Member
of Nat. Council of Labour 1957-65, Vice-Chm. of Reith Commn. on Advertising
1964, and Leader of Joint Parl. Deputation to Sweden 1966; a Dir. of Enalon
Plastics, Ltd. 1973; Chm. Technical Laboratory Sers., Ltd., 1972; Chm. of
Agrément Board appointed by Min. of Public Building and Works, of Advisory
Cttee. to Minister of Overseas Development; a Dir. of Trade Union Unit
Trust, Mid-Kent Water Co., Stevenson Jordan & Harrison, Ltd., Management
Consultants (Chm., 1971), and Education Sciences, Ltd., and a Trustee and
Founder Member of North West Civic Trust; a Trustee of Attlee Memorial Trust;
a Gov. of Manchester Coll. of Commerce since 1960, and a Member of Nat.
Board for Prices and Incomes since 1965 (Dep. Chmn. 1968, Chm. 1970-71), and
Advertising Standards Authority since 1972; Leader of Joint Parl. Delegation
to Finland 1968; Chm. of Post Office Users' National Council since 1969;
a Member of Council of Europe, and Assembly of Western European Union
since 1974; a Freeman of City of London; Hon. Citizen of Fort Worth, USA;
cr. Baron Peddie, of City and Co. of Kingston upon Hull (Life Baron) 1961;
MBE (Civil) 1944: *m.* 1931, Hilda Mary Alice, da. of Henry James Ernest
Bull, of Lowestoft, and Hull, and has issue.

Residence,—20, The Ridings, Epsom, Surrey. *Club,*—RAC, Europe House (Whitehall).

SON LIVING.

Hon. Ian James Crofton (4, Townsend Court, St. Johns Wood, NW8), *b.* 1945; ed. at Gordonstoun, and Univ. Coll., London (LLB); Bar. Inner Temple 1971.

DAUGHTER LIVING.

Hon. Hilary Aileen, *b.* 1938: *m.* 1959, Christopher Geoffrey Rudd, of 31, Nonsuch Court Av. Ewell, Surrey.

PEEL, EARL. (Peel.) [Earl U.K. 1929, Bt. G.B. 1800.]

WILLIAM JAMES ROBERT PEEL, 3rd Earl and 8th Baronet; *b.* Oct. 3rd, 1947; *s.* 1969; ed. at Ampleforth, Tours Univ., France, and Roy. Agric. Coll., Cirencester: *m.* 1973, Veronica Naomi Livingston, da. of Maj. John Alastair Livingston Timpson, MC, Scots Gds. [see Houstoun-Boswall, Bt.].

Arms,—Argent, three sheaves of as many arrows proper two and one, banded gules, on a chief azure a bee volant or. **Crest,**—A demi-lion rampant argent, gorged with a collar azure charged with three bezants and holding between the paws a shuttle or. **Supporters,**—*Dexter,* a lion reguardant argent, gorged with a chain or, pendant therefrom an escutcheon azure, thereon a representation of the Speaker's mace erect of the second; *sinister,* a griffin reguardant or, gorged with a gold chain, pendant therefrom an escutcheon azure, charged with a representation of the Speaker's mace of the first. *Residence,*—Gunnerside Lodge, Richmond, Yorks. *Club,*—Turf.

BROTHER LIVING.

Hon. ROBERT MICHAEL ARTHUR, *b.* Feb. 5th, 1950; ed. at Eton, and Hertford Coll., Oxford: *m.* 1973, Fiona Natalie, da. of Charles Davidson, of Dunhampstead House, Droitwich, Worcs.

AUNT LIVING. (*Daughter of 1st Earl*).

Lady Doris, *b.* 1900; a JP for Sussex, and an Alderman for Hants. Co. Council: *m.* 1927. Lieut-Col. Latham Valentine Stewart Blacker, OBE, TD, who *d.* 1964, and has issue living, David Stewart Wellesley (Molecomb, Goodwood, Chichester) *b.* 1927; ed. at Eton, and at Trin. Coll., Oxford: *m.* 1960, Mary-Rose, only da. of the Hon. Phelim Robert Hugh O'Neill [see B. Rathcavan],— Brian Latham Peel (twin) (Coldhayes, Liss, Hants.), *b.* 1927; ed. at Eton, and at Trin. Coll., Oxford: late RA; a CC for Hampshire: *m.* 1954, Jillian Ann, only da. of David Henry Stacey, of Elm Park Gdns., SW10, and has issue living, Catherine Jane *b.* 1955, Charlotte Jane *b.* 1957, Amelia *b.* 1959, Louise *b.* 1960,—Brigid Alice, *b.* 1931: *m.* 1954, Nicholas Kendall Crace, of 93, Highgate West Hill, N6, son of the late Adm. Sir John Gregory Crace, KBE, CB,—Diana Mary, *b.* 1934: *m.* 1957, Capt. Robin Francis Cavendish, MBE, late KRRC, of Furlongs, Drayton St. Leonard, Oxford [see D. Devonshire, colls.]. *Residence,*—Little Coldhayes, Liss, Hants.

WIDOW LIVING OF SON OF FIRST VISCOUNT.

Lady (Adelaide Margaret) Delia Spencer, *D.C.V.O.,* dau. of 6th Earl Spencer; was a Woman of the Bedchamber to H.M. Queen Elizabeth the Queen Mother 1939-50, since when an Extra Woman of the Bedchamber; *C.V.O.* 1947, *D.C.V.O.* 1950: *m.* 1914, the Hon. Sir Sidney Cornwallis Peel, 1st Bt., C.B., D.S.O., T.D., who *d.* 1938, when the Baronetcy became ext. *Residence,*—Barton Turf, Norwich, NR1Z 8AU.

WIDOW LIVING OF FIFTH BARONET.

BEATRICE GLADYS (*Lady Peel*), dau. of the late John Lillie: *m.* 1920, Sir Robert Peel, 5th baronet, who *d.* 1934. *Address,*—c/o Barclays Bank, 415, Strand, W.C.2.

COLLATERAL BRANCHES LIVING. (*In remainder to Viscountcy and Baronetcy only.*)

Issue of the late Major the Hon. (Arthur) George Villiers Peel, 2nd son of 1st Viscount, *b.* 1868, *d.* 1956 : *m.* 1906, Lady Agnes Lygon, who *d.* 1960, dau. of 6th Earl Beauchamp :— George Frederick, *b.* 1921; ed. at Harrow, and at New Coll., Oxford; Personal Assist. to Custodian at Pusey Memorial Library, Oxford 1950-52, Assist. Custodian thereof 1952-4, and Assist., Faculty of Theology Library, Oxford Univ. 1953-4; a Hospital Librarian, Order of St. John and British Red Cross So. since 1955, an Asst. Archivist USPG 1967-69, since when an Assist. Librarian Education Depart., Reading Univ.; a Life Gov. of Corpn. of Sons of the Clergy; 1939-45 War with R. Berks Regt. (invalided); subsequently with Air Min. (Flying Training Command): *m.* 1960, Elizabeth Mary, only da. of the late J. V. Coker, of Ruscombe, Berks. *Residence,*—Spring Cottage, Cold Harbour, Goring Heath, nr. Reading. *Clubs,*—Brooks's, English-Speaking Union.—— Juliet Agnes, *b.* 1919: *m.* 1942, Maj. George Thorne, MC, DL, late Grenadier Guards [B. Penrhyn], of Blount's Farm, Sonning Common, Reading, and has issue living, Robert George, *b.* 1943; ed. at Eton, and R. Agric. Coll., Cirencester; with Barclays Bank,—Ian David Peel, *b.* 1944; ed. at Eton, RMA, and Trin. Coll., Oxford; Capt. Grenadier Guards,—Viola Georgina Juliet, *b.* 1948.

Grandchildren of the late Rev. the Hon. Maurice Berkeley Peel, M.C., 4th son of 1st Viscount:—

Issue of the late Major David Arthur Peel, M.C., Irish Guards, *b.* 1910, *d.* (killed in action in N.-W. Europe) 1944: *m.* 1936, the Hon. Sara Carola Vanneck (Huntingfield Hall, Halesworth, Suffolk, 1P 19OQA), da. of 5th Baron Huntingfield:— Jonathan Sidney, *MC* (Barton Hall, Barton Turf, Norwich, NR1Z 8AU), *b.* 1937; ed. at Norwich Sch., at Eton, and St. Johns Coll., Camb. (MA); Capt. Rifle Bde. (ret.); a Page of Honour to HM 1951-53; a Dir. Norwich Union Insurance Gp.; Malaya 1957 (MC); Congo 1960-61: *m.* 1965, Jean Fulton, da. of Air Ch. Marshal Sir Denis Hensley Fulton Barnett, GCB, CBE, DFC, and has issue living, Ruth Miranda, *b.* 1966,—Emily Sara, *b.* 1967,—Anne Louise, *b.* 1970,—Delia Mary, *b.* 1974.—— Charles David, *b.* 1940; ed. at Eton, and at Norwich Sch.; ARIBA: *m.* 1973, Catherine Anne, da. of Duncan Mackintosh, of Woodfolds, Oaksey, Wilts., and has issue living, Thomas *b.* 1975.—— Julia Victoria Mary, *b.* 1939: *m.* 1970, Nicholas Longe, of Oak House, Hasketon, Woodbridge, Suffolk, and has issue living, William Martin Peel, *b.* 1972.

(In remainder to Baronetcy only.)

Grandchildren of the late Lawrence Moore Peel, 3rd son of Capt. Robert Moore Peel, el. son of the late Rt. Hon. William Yates Peel, MP, 2nd son of 1st baronet:—

Issue of the late Lionel Victor Moore Peel, *b.* 1901, *d.* 1937: *m.* 1924, Muriel Mildred (9295, McNaught Rd., Chilliwack, BC, Canada), da. of M. A. Murphy, of Chilliwack, BC):—

Robert John (50769, Yale Rd. East, RR1, Rosedale, BC, Canada), *b.* 1927: *m.* 1949, Mona Jean, yst. da. of A. A. E. Batchelor, and has issue living, Robert Lionel, *b.* 1952: *m.* 1972, Sheila, 6th da. of Austin Byrnes, of Chilliwack, BC,—Rodney Robin, *b.* 1955,—Darcy Edward, *b.* 1965,—Susan Holly, *b.* 1958.——Lionel Brian (6975, Centennial Drive, RR2, Sardis, BC, Canada), *b.* 1931: *m.* 1952, Beverly Ann, only da. of Harvey G. Cook, of Cultus Lake, BC, Canada, and has issue living, Brian Gregory, *b.* 1954: *m.* 1973, Sylvia, da. of Clarence Hala, of Chilliwack, BC,—Kathryn Patricia, *b.* 1964,—Kimberley Ann, *b.* 1965.——Iris Patricia, *b.* 1929: *m.* 1952, Lorne Albert Gehman (58, Broadway St., Chilliwark, BC, Canada), and has issue living, Blair Lee *b.* 1957,—Lane Peel, *b.* 1958,—Dane Robert, *b.* 1959,—Christie Robin, *b.* 1962,—Regan Corey Gehman, *b.* 1965,—Shannon Dee, *b.* 1954.

Grandchildren of the late Rev. Frederick Peel, 3rd son of the late Rt. Hon. William Yates Peel, M.P. (ante):—

Issue of the late William Charles Peel, *b.* 1863, *d.* 1930: *m.* 1st, 1889, Marion Georgiana Frances, who *d.* 1897, da. of Libert Chandler, of USA; 2ndly, 1900, Leonie Rose, da. of Constant Hallu, of Nampeel, France:—

By 2nd m.) Frederick William (P.O. Box 292, Paris, Tennessee, USA), *b.* 1900; Engineer; admitted to British nationality 1936; assumed the Christian name of William in lieu of his second Christian name of de Layney: *m.* 1924, Martha Grace, da. of William Young, of Memphis, Tennessee, USA, and has issue living, Frederick William, *b.* 1925; Lt.-Col. USAF (ret.): *m.* 1st, 1945, Clareleen Popham, of Carothersville, USA; 2ndly, 1954, Clara Elizabeth, da. of F. B. Hoover, of Enid, Oklahoma, and has issue living, (by 1st m.) Frederick William *b.* 1947, Martha Frances *b.* 1949,—(by 2nd m.) John Hoover *b.* 1962, Traci de Layney *b.* 1955,—Robert Dudley, *b.* 1937; Capt. USAAF: *m.* 1963, Mary Elizabeth, da. of Lawrence J. Macdonald, and has issue living, Elizabeth Anne *b.* 1964, Mart Martha *b.* 1966,—Robert de Layney, *b.* 1939.——Charles William, *b.* 1940: *m.* 1929, Catherine Veronica, da. of S. A. Puskac, of Hamilton, Ohio, USA.——Jack John, *b.* 1908.——Joseph, *b.* 1909; has assumed the name of Joseph in lieu of his Christian names of Lincoln Henry Tracy: *m.* (March) 1946, Hazel Pearl Gener, and has issue living, Kevin John, *b.* (Dec.) 1946. *Residence,*—8, Leichardt St., Victoria Park, W. Aust.——Laurence Tracy, *b.* 1917: *m.* 19—.——Estelle Frances: *m.* 1st, 19—, T. S. Patterson; 2ndly, 19—.——Dorothy Leonie.——Xzavia Séréna.

Grandchildren of the late Capt. Francis Peel, 4th son of the late Rt. Hon. William Yates Peel, M.P. (ante):—

Issue of the late Col. Robert Francis Peel, C.M.G., *b.* 1874, *d.* 1924 : *m.* 1903, Alice Maude, who *d.* 1957, dau. of Sir Thomas Meyrick, K.C.B., 1st Bt. :—

Chiverton Robert, *b.* 1908 ; Major (retired) Coldstream Guards ; European War 1939-41 in France : *m.* 1959, Bridget Honoria, da. of the late Edward Hornby Beckwith [Chichester, Bt.]. *Residence,*—The Hill, Weare Gifford, near Bideford, N. Devon. *Club,*—Brooks's.——Hermione Mary, *b.* 1912: *m.* 1939, Lt. Robert Ormsby Oliver, RNVR, who *d.* 1973, and has issue living, Lyon Robert, *b.* 1949. *Residence,*—Ditton Farm, St. Owen's Cross, Hereford.

Grandson of the late Col. Frederick Peel, 2nd son of the late Lt.-Col. Edmund Yates Peel, 2nd son of Lt.-Gen. the Rt. Hon. Jonathan Peel, MP, 5th son of 1st baronet:—

Issue of the late Archibald Peel, *b.* 1878, *d.* 1932 : *m.* 1908, Mary, dau. of the late Henry Whiteley, of Wakefield, Yorkshire, and adopted dau. of Reuben Thomas Saunders, formerly of Raskelf, 215, Capstone Road, Bournemouth :—

Maurice (31, Seves St., Altona, Melbourne, Australia) *b.* 1910: *m.* (March) 1935, Louisa Myrtle, da. of the late John Newby Carter, and has issue living, Maurice Newby, *b.* (Dec.) 1935,—Alfred George, *b.* 1940,—Stanley Charles, *b.* 1946,—Cyril Ronald, *b.* 1952,—Violet Ethel, *b.* 1937: *m.* 1959, Kevin George Anderson, of 59, Bladin St., Melbourne, Australia, and has issue living, Kevin John *b.* 1960, Brett Lewin *b.* 1961, Steven Maurice *b.* 1963,—Lorraine Ruth, *b.* 1945.

Grandchildren of the late Archibald Peel, *b.* 1828 (ante):—

Issue of the late Brig.-Gen. Edward John Russell Peel, C.M.G., D.S.O., *b.* 1869, *d.* 1939 : *m.* 1901, Mary Louisa, who *d.* 1959, dau. of the late Edgar Atheling Drummond, of Cadland [E. Perth, colls.] :—

Peter, *M.C., b* 1908 ; is Major Rifle Brig.; European War 1939-40 at Defence of Calais (wounded, M.C., prisoner): *m.* 1936, Valerie, only dau. of Major Gervys Charles Nevile, D.S.O., of The Manor House, Bury St. Edmunds. *Residence,*—The Manor House, Freckenham, Bury St. Edmunds.——Rosemary, *b.* 1903: *m.* 1950, John V. Morris, of 19, Selwood Terr., SW7 3QG, and Ingoldisthorpe Hall, King's Lynn, Norfolk.

Issue of the late Alfred Michael John Russell Peel, *b.* 1873, *d.* 1907: *m.* 1906, Kathleen, who *d.* 1968, having *m.* 2ndly, 1926, Ernest Charles Pulbrook, who *d.* 1940, da. of J. J. de C. Walsh, of Gwelo, Rhodesia :—

Archibald John Russell, *b.* 1907: *m.* 1946, Patricia Virtue, only dau. of Col. Baldwin Millard, of 61, Fitzjohn's Avenue, N.W.3, and has issue living, Jeremy Robert, *b.* 1946,—Michael John Russell, *b.* 1952,—Caroline Georgiana, *b.* 1948,—Elizabeth Francesca, *b.* 1950. *Residence,*—Fisher's Gate, Route des Laveurs, L'Etacq, Jersey.

Grandchildren of the late Sir Charles Lennox Peel, G.C.B., son of the late Laurence Peel, 6th son of 1st baronet :—

Issue of the late Horace Peel, *b.* 1857, *d.* 1940 : *m.* 1899, Violet, who *d.* 1948, dau. of the late Ralph Dalyell, C.B. E. Warwick, colls.]:—

Charles Algernon, *b.* 1906; ed. at Eton; is Lieut.-Col. (retired) 3rd Hussars: *m.* 1933, Katherine Louise, dau. of the late Rt. Hon. Ernest George Pretyman [E. Bradford]. and has issue living, Jeremy Charles, *b.* 1934: *m.* 1960 (m. diss. 1971), Sheila Mary Rose, da. of Capt. Charles Elphinstone Fordyce [see B. Windlesham], and has issue living, Robert Frederick Charles *b.* 1962, James Arthur Lennox *b.* 1964. *Residence,*—Invercroskie, Enochdu, by Blairgowrie, Perthshire.——Marjorie Violet, *b.* 1902: *m.* 1921, Maj. Evelyn Ronald Moncrieff Fryer, MC, Grenadier Guards, who *d.* 1967, and has issue living, Frederick Charles Horace (of Foxhill, Elstead, Surrey), *b.* 1922; ed. at Eton; Capt. late Grenadier Guards: *m.* 1952, Joan, da. of J. Kinsey, and has issue living, Rupert Frederick Daniel *b.* 1960,—Jennifer Ruth, *b.* 1925; formerly in WRNS; is a JP for Norfolk: *m.* 1946, Brian Thomas Borthwick, late Lt. RNVR [see Borthwick, Bt., colls.],—Jane Marjorie, *b.* 1936: *m.* 1st, 1957 (m. diss. 1961), John Ralph Lubbock [see B. Avebury, colls.]; 2ndly, 1962, Rupert Guy Turner Bridger, of Nine Acres, Selborne, Alton, Hants,—Belinda Mary (twin), *b.* 1936: *m.* 1974, David Anthony De La Bere Pritchett, of 77a, Queens Gate, SW7. *Residence,*—Nine Acres, Selborne, Hants.

PREDECESSORS.—[1] *Rt. Hon.* ARTHUR WELLESLEY Peel, 5th son of the late Rt. Hon. Sir Robert Peel, 2nd Bt., of Drayton Manor, Staffordshire ; *b.* 1829 ; Parliamentary Sec. to Poor Law Board 1868-71, and to Board of Trade 1871-3, Patronage Sec. to Treasury 1873-4, Under-Sec. for Home Depart. April to Dec. 1880, and Speaker (four times elected to House of Commons Feb. 1884 to April 1895; M.P. for Warwick (*L*) 1865-85, and for Warwick and Leamington 1886-95; cr. *Viscount Peel*, of Sandy, co. Bedford (peerage of United Kingdom) 1895 : *m.* 1862, Adelaide, who *d.* 1890, dau. of William Stratford Dugdale, of Merevale, Warwickshire ; *d.* 1912 ; *s.* by his el. son

[2] *Rt. Hon.* WILLIAM ROBERT WELLESLEY, *G.C.S.I.*, *G.B.E.*, 2nd Viscount; *b.* 1867; M.P. for Manchester (S. Div.) 1900-1906 ,and for Taunton 1906-12 ; appointed Joint Parliamentary Sec. (unpaid), National Ser. Depart. 1917, Under-Sec. of State for War 1919, and Chancellor of Duchy of Lancaster 1921 (also Min. of Transport (unpaid) 1921) ; was Sec. of State for India 1922-4, and again 1928-9, and Lord Privy Seal Sept. to Nov. 1931; cr. *Viscount Clanfield*, of Clanfield, co. Southampton, and *Earl Peel* (peerage of United Kingdom) 1929 : *m.* 1899, the Hon. Eleanor (Ella) Williamson, who *d.* 1949, dau. of 1st Baron Ashton (ext.); *d.* 1937 ; *s.* by his son [3] ARTHUR WILLIAM ASHTON, 2nd Earl *b.* 1901; Lord Lt. of Lancs. 1948-50: *m.* 1946, Kathleen, who *d.* 1972, da. of Michael McGrath, of Ballycullane, co. Cork; *d.* 1969; *s.* by his son [4] WILLIAM JAMES ROBERT, 3rd Earl and present peer; also Viscount Peel, and Viscount Clanfield.

₊ [1] ROBERT Peel, 3rd son of the late Robert Peel, of Peele Fold, Lancashire; *b.* 1750 ; was an eminent Cotton Spinner, M.P. for Tamworth 1790-1818, and contributed £10,000 towards promoting the war with France ; cr. a *Baronet* 1800 : *m.* 1st, 1783, Ellen, dau. of William Yates, of Spring Side, near Bury ; 2ndly, 1805, Susanna, who *d.* 1824, dau. of the late Francis Clerke ; *d.* 1830 ; *s.* by his el. son [2] *Rt. Hon.* ROBERT, 2nd Bt.; *b.* 1788 ; sometime M.P. for Oxford Univ., and subsequently for Tamworth (*C*); appointed Under-Sec. of State for the Colonies 1810, Ch. Sec. for Ireland 1812, and Sec. of State for Home Depart. 1828 ; was First Lord of the Treasury and Prime Minister 1834-5 and 1841-6 : *m.* 1820, Julia, who *d.* 1859, youngest dau. of Gen. Sir John Floyd, 1st Bt.; *d.* 1850 ; *s.* by his el. son [3] *Rt. Hon.* Sir ROBERT, *G.C.B.*, 3rd Bt.; *b.* 1822 ; sat as M.P. for Tamworth (*LC*) 1850-80, for Huntingdon (*C*) 1884-5, and for Blackburn 1885-6 ; was a Lord of the Admiralty 1852-7, and Ch. Sec. for Ireland 1861-5 : *m.* 1856, Lady Emily Hay, who *d.* 1924, dau. of 8th Marquess of Tweeddale ; *d.* 1895 ; *s.* by his only son [4] ROBERT, 4th Bt.; *b.* 1867: *m.* 1897, Mercedes, dau. of Baron de Graffenried, formerly of Thun, Switzerland ; *d.* 1925 ; *s.* by his only son [5] ROBERT, 5th Bt.; *b.* 1898: *m.* 1920, Beatrice Gladys, dau. of the late John Lillie ; *d.* 1934; *s.* by his only son [6] ROBERT, 6th Bt.; *b.* 1920 ; Ordinary Seaman R.N. ; *d.* (killed in action) 1942; *s.* by his kinsman [7] ARTHUR WILLIAM ASHTON (ante).

PEMBROKE and MONTGOMERY, EARL OF. (Herbert.) [Earl E. 1551 and 1605.]

HENRY GEORGE CHARLES ALEXANDER HERBERT, 17th Earl; *b.* May 19th, 1939; *s.* 1969; ed. at Eton, and Oxford Univ.; late RHG; Hereditary Visitor of Jesus Coll., Oxford: *m.* 1966, Claire Rose, da. of Douglas Gurney Pelly [see Pelly Bt., colls.], and has issue.

Arms,—Per pale azure and gules, three lions rampant argent. Crest,—A wyvern wings elevated vert, holding in the mouth a sinister hand couped at the wrist gules. Supporters,—*Dexter*, a panther guardant argent, incensed, spotted or, vert, sable azure, and gules, alternately, ducally collared azure; *sinister*, a lion argent, ducally collared or.

Seat,—Wilton House, Salisbury.

UNG JE SERVIRAY

One I will serve.

DAUGHTERS LIVING.

Lady Sophia Elizabeth, *b.* 1966.
Lady Emma Louise, *b.* 1969.
Lady Flora Katinka, *b.* 1970.

SISTER LIVING.

Lady Diana Mary, *b.* 1937.

UNCLE LIVING. (*Son of 15th Earl*)

Hon. DAVID ALEXANDER REGINALD, *b.* Oct. 3rd 1908; ed. at Eton; 1939-45 War as Lt. RNVR, *Address*,—Box 2304, Tangier (Socco).

AUNT LIVING. (*Daughter of 15th Earl*)

Lady Patricia (*Dowager Viscountess Hambleden*), *DCVO*, *b.* (Nov.) 1904; a Lady-in-Waiting to HM the Queen (now H.M. Queen Elizabeth the Queen Mother) since 1937; DCVO 1953: *m.* 1928, the 3rd Viscount Hambleden, who *d.* 1948. *Residence*,—Old Rectory, Ewelme, Oxon.

WIDOW LIVING OF SIXTEENTH EARL.

Lady MARY DOROTHEA HOPE, CVO (*Mary, Countess of Pembroke and Montgomery*), (The Old Rectory, Wilton, Salisbury) Hon. 1st Officer WRNS; a Lady-in-Waiting to HRH the Duchess of Kent 1934-49 and an Extra Lady-in-Waiting 1949-68; CVO 1947; da. of 1st Marquess of Linlithgow: *m.* 1936, the 16th Earl, who *d.* 1969.

COLLATERAL BRANCHES LIVING.

Descendants of the late Henry Herbert (el. son of the late Maj.-Gen. the Hon. William Herbert, 5th son of 8th Earl), who was cr. *Earl of Carnarvon* 1793 [see that title.].

PREDECESSORS.—[1] Sir WILLIAM Herbert, *K.G.*, *K.B.*, was Ch. Gentleman of the Privy Chamber, Master of the Horse 1549, twice Gov. of the Forces sent into Picardy, twice Gov. of Calais, and Capt. Gen. of the Army beyond the Seas, &c.; cr. *Baron Herbert*, of Cardiff, and *Earl of Pembroke* (peerage of England) 1551 ; *d.* 1570 ; *s.* by his el. son [2] HENRY, *K.G.*, 2nd Earl; *d.* 1601; *s.* by his son [3] WILLIAM, *K.G.*, 3rd Earl; was Lord Chamberlain of the Household; *d.* 1630; *s.* by his brother [4] PHILIP, *K.G.*, 4th Earl, who in 1605 had been cr. *Baron Herbert*, of Shurland, Isle of Sheppey, co. Kent, and *Earl of Montgomery* (peerage of England) ; was Lord Chamberlain to the Household, and Chancellor of Oxford Univ. ; *d.* 1655; *s.* by his son [5] PHILIP, 5th Earl; *d.* 1669; *s.* by his el. son [6] WILLIAM, 6th Earl; *d.* unmarried 1674 ; *s.* by his half-brother [7] PHILIP, 7th Earl; *d.* without male issue 1683 ; *s.* by his brother [8] THOMAS, *K.G.*, *P.C.*, 8th Earl; was Ambassador to States Gen. 1689, Lord Privy Seal 1700, seven times one of the Lord Justices, Lord High Adm. of England 1702 and 1708-9, and Lord Pres. of the Council 1702; at the Coronation of George I. carried the sword styled "Curtana"; *d.* 1733; *s.* by his son [9] HENRY, 9th Earl; a Lieut.-Gen. in the Army; *d.* 1750; *s.* by his son [10] HENRY, 10th Earl; was a Lieut.-Gen. in the Army, and Col. 1st Dragoons;

d. 1794; *s.* by his son [11] GEORGE AUGUSTUS, K.G., 11th Earl; *d.* 1827; *s.* by his son [12] ROBERT HENRY, 12th Earl; *d.* 1862; *s.* by his nephew [13] GEORGE ROBERT CHARLES, 13th Earl of Pembroke, and 10th Earl of Montgomery, who had already in 1861 *s.* as 2nd Baron Herbert of Lea [son of the Hon. Sidney Herbert—2nd son of 11th Earl—an eminent statesman, who *m.* 1846, Elizabeth, dau. of Lieut.-Gen. Charles Ashe A'Court; and *d.* Aug. 1861, having in Jan. of that year been cr. *Baron Herbert of Lea* (peerage of United Kingdom)], *b.* 1850: *m.* 1874, Lady Gertrude Frances Talbot, who *d.* 1906, dau. of 18th Earl of Shrewsbury; *d.* 1895; *s.* by his brother [14] SIDNEY, *G.C.V.O., P.C.,* 14th Earl; *b.* 1853; a Lord of the Treasury 1885-6 and July 1886 to Aug. 1892, and Lord Steward of the Household to Queen Victoria July 1895 to Jan. 1901, and to King Edward VII. 1901-5; M.P. for Wilton (C) 1877-85, and for Croydon 1886-95: *m.* 1877, Lady Beatrix Louisa Lambton, who *d.* 1944, dau. of 2nd Earl of Durham; *d.* 1913; *s.* by his el. son [15] REGINALD, *M.V.O.,* 15th Earl; *b.* 1880; Lieut.-Col. Roy. Horse Guards; Mayor of Wilton 1932-34, 1942-45, and 1954-55: *m.* 1904, Lady Beatrice Eleanor, *CBE,* who *d.* 1973, da. of the late Lord Alexander Victor Paget [M. Anglesey]; *d.* 1960; *s.* by his el. son [16] SIDNEY CHARLES, *CVO,* 16th Earl; *b.* 1906; Equerry to HRH The Duke of Kent 1935-42; Private Sec. and Comptroller to HRH the Duchess of Kent 1942-48; Lord Lieut. of Wilts. 1954-69: *m.* 1936, Lady Mary Dorothea Hope, *CVO,* da. of 1st Marquess of Linlithgow; *d.* 1969; *s.* by his son [17] HENRY GEORGE CHARLES ALEXANDER, 17th Earl and present pree; also Baron Herbert of Cardiff, Baron Herbert of Shurland, and Baron Herbert of Lea.

PENDER, BARON. (Denison-Pender.) [Baron U.K. 1937.]

JOHN WILLOUGHBY DENISON-PENDER, 3rd Baron; *b.* May 6th, 1933; ed. at Eton; late Capt. City of London Yeo. (TA); late Lt. 10th Hussars: *m.* 1962, Julia, da. of Richard Nevill Cannon, OBE, of Coombe Place, Lewes, and has issue.

Arms,—Quarterly: 1st and 4th gules, on a bend nebuly argent two lions' heads serscd of the first, *Pender*; 2nd and 3rd per bend sable and argent two bendlets between a unicorn's head erased in chief and three cross-crosslets in base all counterchanged, *Denison*; **Crests,**—1st, a demi-lion or resting the sinister paw upon a terrestrial globe, and grasping in the dexter paw a seax proper, pomel and hilt gold, *Pender*; 2nd, in front of a sun rising in splendour a dexter arm in bend proper, vested gules gutte-d'eau, cuff erminois, the fore-finger pointing to an estoile or. *Denison.* **Supporters,**—On either side a figure of Hermes standing on a cable-grapnel, the dexter holding in the exterior hand a Caduceus and the sinister a flash of lightning all proper.

I persevere.

Residences,—18, Hyde Park Gate, SW7; Seaway, Sandwich Bay, Kent.　*Clubs,*—White's, Pratt's.

SON LIVING.
Hon. HENRY JOHN RICHARD, *b.* March 19th, 1968.

DAUGHTERS LIVING.
Hon. Emma Charlotte, *b.* 1964.
Hon. Mary Anne Louise, *b.* 1965.

BROTHER LIVING.
Hon. Robin Charles (Jessups, Mark Beech, Edenbridge, Kent; Cavalry and White's Clubs), *b.* 1935; ed. at Eton; late Lt. 11th Hussars: *m.* 1966, Clare Nell, da. of Lt.-Col. James Currie Thomson, MBE, TD, of Aston Dene, Stevenage [see Borthwick, Bt., colls.], and has issue living, Jocelyn Andrew, *b.* 1967,—Peter Robin, *b.* 1972,—Sacha Louise, *b.* 1969.

SISTER LIVING.
Hon. Ann Camilla, *b.* 1931: *m.* 1952, Robin John Dent, of 28, Montpelier Sq., SW7, and has issue living, Annabel Jane, *b.* 1954,—Jennifer Ann, *b.* 1957.

UNCLE LIVING. (Son of 1st Baron.)
Hon. Richard Ernest, *TD* (Great Eastern, North Rd., Sandwich Bay, Kent, CT13 9PJ), *b.* 1914; ed. at Eton; a Member of Stock Exchange; Chm. Moore Park Rd. Area Residents Assocn. 1967 (Pres. 1971), and Sandwich Bay Residents Assocn. 1973; an Auxiliary Coastguard, a Member of Council of Sandwich and Dist. Community Assocn. 1973, Treas. Sandwich Parochial Church Council 1974, Pres. Sandwich and Dist. Roy. British Legion 1974; late Maj. R. Signals (TA Reserve); 1939-45 War (wounded, despatches, American Bronze Star): *m.* 1939, Louise, who *d.* 1973, only da. of the late Henry Gilbey Riviere, and has issue living, James Henry (Denton Foot, Brampton, Cumbria), *b.* 1942: *m.* 1971, Gillian, yst. da. of John C. Barnett, of Threepwood Hall, Haydon Bridge, Northumberland, and has issue living, Jamie Alexander *b.* 1973, Nicholas John *b.* 1974,—Michael Richard (twin) (26, Lennox Gdns., SW1, and Middle West Cottage, Sandwich Bay, Kent), *b.* 1942: *m.* 1972, Nadine, yr. da. of the late Henri Villiger, of Aigle, Switzerland, and has issue living, Dominic Michael *b.* 1975,—Linda Louise, *b.* 1948: *m.* 1973, John Edward Bayman, of Toby Cottages, Shrubbs Hill Lane, Sunningdale, Berks., and Middle West Cottage, Sandwich Bay, Kent, and has issue living.

WIDOW LIVING OF SECOND BARON.
CAMILLA LETHBRIDGE (*Camilla, Baroness Pender*), (169, Cranmer Court, SW3), da. of the late Willoughby Arthur Pemberton [Lethbridge, Bt., colls.]: *m.* 1930, the 2nd Baron, who *d.* 1965.

PREDECESSORS.—[1] JOHN CUTHBERT DENISON Denison-Pender, el. son of the late Sir John Denison-Pender, G.B.E., K.C.M.G.; *b.* 1882; sometime Capt. in the Army; a County Councillor for London 1910-19; European War 1914-18 in France and Belgium; M.P. for E., or Newmarket Div., of Cambridgeshire (C) 1913-18, and for Balham and Tooting Div. of Wandsworth 1918-22; cr. *Baron Pender,* of Porthcurnow, co. Cornwall (peerage of United Kingdom) 1937: *m.* 1906, Irene, who *d.* 1943, dau. of the late Sir Ernest de la Rue, K.C.V.O., of 26, Belgrave Square, S.W.; *d.* 1949; *s.* by his son [2] JOHN JOCELYN, *CBE,* 2nd Baron, *b.* 1907: *m.* 1930, Camilla Lethbridge, da. of the late Willoughby Arthur Pemberton [Lethbridge, Bt., colls.]; *d.* 1965; *s.* by his el. son [3] JOHN WILLOUGHBY, 3rd Baron and present peer.

PENNEY, BARON. (Penney.) [Life Baron 1967.]

WILLIAM GEORGE PENNEY, *OM, KBE, FRS*, son of William Alfred Penney, of Sheerness, Kent; *b.* June 24th, 1909; ed. at Tech. Sch., Sheerness, and Imperial Coll. of Science, London; PhD London and Camb., DSc London, MA Wisconsin; Hon. LLD Melbourne; Hon. DSc Durham, Oxford and Bath; Assist. Prof. of Mathematics Imperial Coll. of Science 1936-45, Prin. Scientific Officer, Dept. of Scientific and Industrial Research, Los Alamos Laboratory, New Mexico 1944-45, Ch. Supt. of Armament Research, Min. of Supply 1946-52, Dir. of Atomic Weapons Research Establishment 1953-59, a Member for Weapons Research and Development UK Atomic Energy Authority 1954-59, a Member for Scientific Research 1959-61, Dep. Chm. UK Atomic Energy Authority 1961-64, Chm. 1964-67, and R. of Imperial Coll. of Science and Technology 1967-73; Treasurer of Roy. Soc. 1956-60, and Vice-Pres. 1957-60; *cr.* OBE (Civil) 1946, KBE (Civil) 1952, *Baron Penney*, of East Hendred, in Roy. co. of Berks. (Life Baron) 1967, and OM 1969: *m.* 1st, 1935, Adele Minnie, who *d.* 1944, da. of Percy Elms, of Queenborough, Kent; 2ndly, 1945, Eleanor Joan, da. of George Quennell, of Brentwood, Essex, and has issue by 1st marriage.

Arms,—On a fess invected the upper edge embattled vert between three representations of the symbol Paramagnetic Electron, those in chief being in the orbit of the third and that in base of the second harmonic azure. **Crest,**—a semi pantheon gules semy of mullets of six points unguled, and about the neck a crown palisado or resting the dexter hoof on a pile sable. **Supporters**—on either side a horse argent unguled gules, gorged with a collar invected the upper edge embattled, vert, the interior hoof resting on a pile sable.

Residence,—Orchard House, E. Hendred, Wantage, Berks. *Club,*—Athenæum.

SONS LIVING. (*By 1st marriage.*)

Hon. Martin Charles (Ellesmere College, Ellesmere, Salop), *b.* 1938; ed. at Cranleigh, and Gonville and Caius Coll., Camb.: *m.* 1961, Margaret Heather, da. of Sqdn.-Ldr. H. Almond, DSO, DFC, of Basingstoke, and has issue.
Hon. Christopher Charles (22, Pymers Mead, Croxted Rd., Dulwich, SE21), *b.* 1941; ed. at Cranleigh, Gonville and Caius Coll., Camb., and Guy's Hosp.: *m.* 1968, Margaret, da. of Henry Bell Fairley, of Stockport, and has issue.

PENRHYN, BARON. (Douglas-Pennant.) [Baron U.K. 1866.]

[Title pronounced " Penrin."]

MALCOLM FRANK DOUGLAS PENNANT, *DSO, MBE*, 6th Baron; *b.* July 11th, 1908; *s.* 1967; ed. at Eton; Col. (ret.) late KRRC; 1939-45 in N. Africa and N.-W. Europe; MBE (Mil.) 1943, DSO 1946: *m.* 1954, Elisabeth Rosemary, da. of the late Brig. Sir Percy Robert Laurie, KCVO, CBE, DSO, and has issue.

Arms,—Quarterly: 1st and 4th per bend sinister ermine and ermines, a lion rampant or, *Pennant;* 2nd and 3rd grand quarters quarterly, 1st and 4th argent, a man's heart gules, ensigned with an Imperial crown proper, on a chief azure, three mullets of the field; 2nd and 3rd argent, three piles gules, on the two outer ones a mullet of the field, *Douglas.* **Crests,**—1st, Out of a ducal coronet an antelope's head argent, maned and tufted or, charged on the neck with a cross crosslet sable, for distinction; 2nd, a sanglier, statant, between two clefts of an oak tree with a chain and lock holding them together all proper,

With an even mind.

and above it the motto "*Lock sicker*,"—(Be secure). Supporters.—On either side an antelope proper, collared and chain reflexed over the back or, and pendant from the collar of the dexter supporter an escutcheon gules, charged with the bust of a man's head affrontée proper.

Residence,—Dean Farm, Bishop's Waltham, Hants. *Club*,—Naval and Military.

DAUGHTERS LIVING.

Hon. Gillian Francis, *b.* 1955.
Hon. Rosemary, *b.* 1957.

BROTHER LIVING.

Hon. NIGEL (Woodfield Cedars, Ombersley, Worcs.), *b.* Dec. 22nd, 1909; ed. at Eton, and at Clare Coll., Camb. (BA 1931); formerly Maj. RM: *m.* 1st, 1935, Margaret Dorothy, who *d.* 1938, da. of T. G. Kirkham, of Westholm, Jordanhill, Glasgow; 2ndly, 1940, Eleanor Stewart, da. of the late Very Rev. H. N. Craig, Dean of Kildare, and has issue living, (by 1st m.) Simon (Sunnyside School, Thorneloe, Worcester), *b.* 1938; ed. at Eton, and at Clare Coll., Camb. (BA): *m.* 1963, Josephine Maxwell, yr. da. of the late Robert Upcott, and has issue living, Edward Sholto *b.* 1966, Hugo Charles *b.* 1969, Sophie Margaret *b.* 1964,—Harriet Josephine *b.* 1972,—(by 2nd m.) Philip Morton, *b.* 1947; ed. at Eton,—Brigid Elizabeth, *b.* 1943: *m.* 1972, Richard H. Peat, of Hockwood Hall, Thetford, Norfolk, and has issue living, Harry Mark Richard *b.* 1974.

HALF-SISTERS LIVING

Hon. Bridget Violet (Old Rectory, Badingham, Woodbridge, Suffolk), *b.* 1899: *m.* 1923, Maj.-Gen. Charles Harvey Miller, CB, CBE, DSO, who *d.* 1974, and has issue living, Elspeth Bridget, *b.* 1925: *m.* 1948, Maj. John Hood Bowman, late Coldm. Gds., of The Old Rectory, Winterbourne Bassett, Swindon, Wilts., and has issue living, Sarah Elizabeth *b.* 1949: *m.* 1969, Kornel Jerzy Krzeczunowicz (and has issue living, Stefan Alexander Leon *b.* 1973), Juliet Alexandra *b.* 1950.
Hon. Eileen Maud, *b.* 1901.

SISTER LIVING.

Hon. Susan Victoria, *b.* 1918.

WIDOW LIVING OF SON OF FIFTH BARON.

Sheila (*Lady Warmington*), da. of the late Stanley Brotherhood, JP, of Thornhaugh Hall, Peterborough: *m.* 1st, 1937, as his second wife, Adm. the Hon. Sir Cyril Eustace Douglas-Pennant, KCB, CBE, DSO, DSC, who *d.* 1961; 2ndly 1972, as his 3rd wife, Sir Marshall George Clitheroe Warmington, 3rd Bt., of Itchen Abbas Lodge, Winchester, Hants.

COLLATERAL BRANCHES LIVING.

Issue of the late Adm. the Hon. Sir Cyril Eustace Douglas-Pennant, K.C.B., O.B.E., D.S.O., D.S.C., el. son of 5th Baron, *b.* 1894, *d.* 1961 : *m.* 1st, 1917, Phyllis Constance (who obtained a divorce 1936), dau. of the late Col. Oswald Mosley-Leigh, J.P., T.D., of Belmont Hall, Northwich, Cheshire; 2ndly, 1937, Sheila (ante), (who *m.* 2ndly, 1972, as his 3rd wife, Sir Marshall George Clitheroe Warmington, 3rd Bt.), da. of the late Stanley Brotherhood, J.P., of Thornhaugh Hall, Peterborough:—
(By 1st marriage) Sheila Florence, *b.* 1918 : *m.* 1st, 1946 (marriage dissolved 1950), Anthony Brine ; 2ndly, 1951, Ronald Arthur Cobb, and has issue living, (by 1st marriage). *Residence*,—197, Park West, Marble Arch, W.2.

Grandchildren of the late Lieut.-Col. the Hon. Archibald Charles Henry Douglas-Pennant, 2nd son of 1st Baron :—
Issue of the late Claud Douglas-Pennant, *b.* 1867, *d.* 1955 : *m.* 1922, Christian Eleanor Margaret (who *d.* 1968), da. of Sir Harry (William Henry Neville) Goschen, 1st Bt., KBE:—
Henry (of Little Laver Hall, Harlow, Essex; Bath and Buck's Clubs), *b.* 1925; B.A. 1946: *m.* 1957, Pamela, da. of Alfred Gaspard Le Marchant [see Le Marchant, Bt.], and has issue living, Rupert Henry, *b.* 1963,—Andrew Claud, *b.* 1967,—Edward Alfred (twin), *b.* 1967,—Venetia, *b.* 1960.—— Margaret, *b.* 1923: *m.* 1956, Patrick John Lloyd, of Yew Tree Farm, Stebbing, Essex, and has issue living, John Philip, *b.* 1960,—Phyllida Christian, *b.* 1957.——Ann, *b.* 1930: *m.* 1960, Michael Wilson, of Platts Cottage, Ecchinswell, Newbury, and has issue living, Fiona Margaret, *b.* 1962,—Sara Nicola, *b.* 1964.

Issue of the late Archibald Douglas-Pennant, *b.* 1881, *d.* 1971: *m.* 1st, 1905, Gwendoline, who *d.* 1965, da. of Alexander Fraser, JP, of Westerfield, Suffolk; 2ndly, 1967, Jean, who *d.* 1974, da. of the late Alexander Maclean, of Nairn:—
(By 1st m.) Rodney Archibald (Skirmers, Aston Tirrold, Berks.), *b.* 1913; ed. at Radley; Lt. KRRC, and temp. Maj. King's African Rifles: *m.* 1st, 1945, Rosemary Jane Delap, who *d.* 1946; 2ndly, 1947, Agnes Nydia Brailey, and has issue living (by 2nd m) Hugh Archibald, *b.* 1951,—Anthea Rose, *b.* 1948.

Granddaughter of the late Archibald Douglas-Pennant (ante):—
Issue of the late Ian Douglas-Pennant, *b.* 1906, *d.* 1941: *m.* 1931, Mary (Lower Cadleigh, Ivybridge, S. Devon), da. of the late Maj. John Williams, of Scorrier House, Scorrier, Cornwall:—
Daphne Mary, *b.* 1932: *m.* 1st, 1953, Capt. Maurice Douglas Evans, RM; 2ndly, 1965, Francis Seymour Hurndall-Waldron, Linscott, Moretonhampstead, Newton Abbot, Devon, and has issue living, (by 1st m.) Jeremy Douglas, *b.* 1958,—Claire Douglas, *b.* 1954,—Rosemary Douglas, *b.* 1956.

PREDECESSORS.—[1] *Hon.* EDWARD GORDON Douglas-Pennant, brother of 17th Earl of Morton ; *b.* 1800; assumed in 1841 by Roy. licence the additional surname of Pennant ; sat as M.P. for Carnarvonshire (*C*) 1841-66 ; was Lord-Lieut. of co. Carnarvon ; cr. *Baron Penrhyn*, of Llandegai, co. Carnarvon (peerage of United Kingdom) 1866 : *m.* 1st, 1833, Juliana Isabella Mary, who *d.* 1842, el. dau. and co-heiress of George Hay Dawkins Pennant, of Penrhyn Castle ; 2ndly, 1846, Lady Maria Louisa FitzRoy, who *d.* 1912, 2nd dau. of 5th Duke of Grafton ; *d.* 1886 ; *s.* by his son [2] GEORGE SHOLTO GORDON, 2nd Baron ; *b.* 1836 ; M.P. for Carnarvonshire (*C*) 1866-8 and 1874-80 : *m.* 1st, 1860, Pamela Blanche Rushout, who *d.* 1869, dau. of Sir Charles Rushout Rushout, 2nd Bt.; 2ndly, 1875, Gertrude Jessy, who *d.* 1940, dau. of the late Rev. Henry Glynne ; *d.* 1907 ; *s.* by his el. son [3] EDWARD SHOLTO, 3rd Baron ; *b.* 1864 ; M.P. for Northamptonshire, S. Div. (*C*) 1895-1900: *m.* 1887, the Hon. Blanche Georgiana FitzRoy, who *d.* 1944, dau. of 3rd Baron Southampton ; *d.* 1927; *s.* by his son [4] HUGH NAPIER, 4th Baron ; *b.* 1894; Hon. Col. 6th Batn. Roy. Welch Fusiliers; Lord-Lieut. of Caernarvonshire 1933-41 : *m.* 1922, the Hon. Sybil Mary Hardinge (who obtained a divorce 1941), dau. of 3rd Viscount Hardinge ; *d.* 1949; *s.* by his kinsman [5] FRANK (el. son of the late Lieut.-Col. the Hon. Archibald Charles Henry Douglas-Pennant, 2nd son of 1st Baron), 5th Baron ; *b.* 1865; Lt.-Col. KRRC: *m.* 1st, 1892 (m. diss. 1903) Maud Eleanora, who *d.* 1936, da. of the late Col. John Hardy, 9th Lancers; 2ndly, 1905, Alice Nellie, who *d.* 1965, da. of Sir William Charles Cooper, 3rd Bt., *d.* 1967; *s.* by his son [6] MALCOLM FRANK, DSO, MBE, 6th Baron and present peer.

PENTLAND, BARON. (Sinclair.) [Baron U.K. 1909.]

Fidelity.

HENRY JOHN SINCLAIR, 2nd Baron; *b.* June 6th, 1907; *s.* 1925; ed. at Wellington Coll., and at Trin. Coll., Camb. (B.A. 1929): *m.* 1941, Lucy Elisabeth Babington, dau. of the late Sir Henry Babington Smith, G.B.E., C.H., K.C.B., C.S.I. [E. Elgin], and has issue.

Arms,—Quarterly: 1st, azure, a ship at anchor, oars in saltire or, flagged gules, within a double tressure counter-flory of the second; 2nd and 3rd, or, a lion rampant gules, armed and langued azure; 4th, azure, a ship under sail or, sails argent and flags gules; over all, dividing the four quarters, a cross engrailed sable, thereon a mullet for difference, *Sinclair;* the whole within a bordure parted per pale, the dexter side indented gules, the sinister ermine. *Crest,*—A cock proper. *Supporters,* —On either side a Scotch deerhound proper, each supporting a banner azure, that to the dexter inscribed with the word "Help," and that to the sinister with the word "Hold."

Residence,—4670, Independence Av., New York City, 10471, USA.

DAUGHTER LIVING.
Hon. Mary (435 East 87th St., New York City, USA), *b.* 1942; BA Mount Holyoke, USA, 1964.

SISTER LIVING.
Hon. Margaret Ishbel, *b.* 1905; B.A. Camb. 1927. *Residence,*—2, Green Lane, West Clandon, Guildford, Surrey.

PREDECESSOR.—[1] *Rt. Hon.* JOHN Sinclair, *G.C.S.I., G.C.I.E.,* son of the late Capt. George Sinclair, 3rd son of Sir John Sinclair, 6th Bt., of Dunbeath; *b.* 1860; Sec. for Scotland and Keeper of Great Seal of Scotland 1905-12, and Gov. of Madras 1912-19; M.P. for Dunbartonshire (*L*) 1892-5, and for Forfarshire 1897-1909; cr. *Baron Pentland,* of Lyth, co. Caithness (peerage of UK) 1909: *m.* 1904, Lady Marjorie Adeline Gordon, *DBE,* who *d.* 1970, da. of 1st Marquess of Aberdeen and Temair; *d.* 1925; *s.* by his son [2] HENRY JOHN, 2nd Baron and present peer.

Perceval, Viscount, son of Earl of Egmont.

Percy, Earl, son of Duke of Northumberland.

PERCY OF NEWCASTLE, BARONY OF. (Percy.) [Extinct 1958.]
DAUGHTERS LIVING OF FIRST BARON.
Hon. Mary Edith, *b.* 1919; ed. at Bristol Univ. *Residence,*—Glebe Orchard, Etchingham, Sussex.
Hon. Dorothy Anne, *b.* 1926; ed. at Durham Univ. (M.B. and B.S. 1949): *m.* 1957, Major Thomas Robert Hales Eustace, Roy. Irish Fusiliers, and has issue living, James Maurice Percy, *b.* 1960,— Alicia Mary, *b.* 1958,—Katharine Anne, *b.* 1965. *Residence,*—Glebe House, Boughton Aluph, Ashford, Kent.

WIDOW LIVING OF FIRST BARON.
STELLA KATHERINE (*Baroness Percy of Newcastle*), dau. of the late Maj.-Gen. Laurence George Drummond, C.B., C.B.E., M.V.O. [see E. Perth, colls.]: *m.* 1918, the 1st Baron, who *d.* 1958, when the title became ext. *Residence,*—The Glebe Orchard, Etchingham, Sussex.

PERTH, EARL OF. (Drummond.) [Earl S. 1605, Viscount S. 1686.]

Honour crowns virtue

JOHN DAVID DRUMMOND, P.C·, 17th Earl of Perth and 11th (13th but for the attainder) Viscount Strathallan; b. May 13th, 1907; s. 1951; ed. at Downside, and at Camb. Univ.; a Representative Peer for Scotland 1952-63; Hereditary Thane of Lennox and Hereditary Steward of Menteith and Strathearn; late Lt. Intelligence Corps; seconded to War Cabinet Offices 1942-43, and to Min. of Production 1944-45; Min. of State for Colonial Affairs 1957-62; First Crown Estate Commr. since 1962; a Dir. of Roy. Bank of Scotland, of Schroder Ltd., Tate & Lyle, and other cos.; PC 1957: m. 1934, Nancy Seymour, da. of Reginald Fincke, of New York City, USA, and has issue.

Arms,—Or, three bars wavy gules. Crest,—A falcon rising proper. Supporters,— Two wild men wreathed about the temples and loins with oak, and each holding a club resting on his exterior shoulder, proper.

Residences,—2, Hyde Park Gardens, W.2 Stobhall by Perth. Clubs,—White's, Puffin's

SONS LIVING.

JOHN ERIC (Viscount Strathallan), (8, Melbury Rd., W14), b. July 7th, 1935; ed. at Downside and at Trin. Coll., Camb.: m. 1963, Margaret Ann, da. of the late Robin Gordon, and has issue living:—

SONS LIVING. Hon. James David, b. Oct. 24th, 1965.
Hon. Robert Eric, b. 1967.

Hon. James Reginald, b. 1938 ; ed. at Downside, and at Trin. Coll., Camb. : m. 1961, Marybelle, da. of the late Capt. Charles Gordon.

SISTERS LIVING.

Lady Margaret Gwendolen Mary, b. 1905: m. 1937, John Walker, of 2806, N. St., Washington, DC, USA, and has issue living, Gillian Elizabeth Mary, b. 1940,—John Anthony, b. 1942.
Lady Angela Alice Maryel, b. 1912 : m. 1st, 1937 (marriage dissolved 1959), Count Alessandro Augusto Giovanni Giacinto Barnaba Manassei di Collestatte, who d. 1962 [Lyle, Bt.]; 2ndly, 1960, Viggo de Wichfeld, and has issue living, (by 1st m.) John Paul James Alessandro Camillo (The Old Rectory, Drinkstone, Bury St. Edmunds), b. 1937: m. 1965, Susan Barbara, da. of the Hon. John Tonge Anthony Pellew Addington [see V. Sidmouth], and has issue living, Hugo Alexander b. 1969, Marina Catherine b. 1971,—Michael David (1, Lecky St., SW7) b. 1947,—Alessandra Mary, b. 1939: m. 1959, Francesco Montesi Righetti. Residence,—Engestofte, Maribo, Lolland, Denmark.
Lady Gillian Mary, b. 1920: m. 1946, John Murray Anderson, MC, late Capt. Seaforth Highlanders and has issue living, James Ian, b. 1952,—Sarah Mary, b. 1947,—Elisabeth Jane, b 1949,—Camilla Gillian, b. 1957. Residence,—Wilderwick House, E. Grinstead.

WIDOW LIVING OF SON OF TENTH VISCOUNT STRATHALLAN.

Lady Evelyn Frances Butler (St. George's Retreat, PO Box 1, Burgess Hill, Sussex), da. of 4th Marquess of Ormonde: m. 1910 Vice-Adm. the Hon. Edmund Rupert Drummond, CB, CVO, who d. 1965 and has issue living [see colls., infra].

COLLATERAL BRANCHES LIVING.

Issue of the late Col. the Hon. Sir Maurice Charles Andrew Drummond, K.B.E. C.M.G., D.S.O., Black Watch, 3rd son of 10th Viscount Strathallan, b. 1877, d. 1957: m. 1904, Ida Mary, who d. 1966, da. of the late George James, Drummond [see colls., infra]:—
Maurice James David, b. 1907; ed. at Eton; Bar. Lincoln's Inn 1952 ; Hon. Lieut.-Col. (retired) Seaforth Highlanders, and a Member of Queen's Body Guard for Scotland (Roy. Co. of Archers).——Myra, b. 1905: m. 1935, Martin Roland Soames [Astley, Bt.], of Glenmore, Crossmolina, co. Mayo, and has issue living, Richard Martin Francis (102, Cheyne Walk, SW10), b. 1936: m. 1964, Marilyn Mayer,—Gillian Elfrida Astley (of 35B, Blomfield Rd., W9), b. 1937: m. 1957 (m. diss. 1962), the 6th Baron Ebury.——Monica Katharine (11, Donovan Court, Drayton Gdns., SW10 9ES), b. 1916: m. 1940 (m. diss. 1954), Francis Brian Sylvester Grimston [see E. Verulam, colls.].

Issue of the late Vice-Adm. the Hon. Edmund Rupert Drummond, CB, CVO, 4th son of 10th Viscount Strathallan, b. 1884, d. 1965: m. 1910, Lady Evelyn Frances Butler (ante), da. of 4th Marquess of Ormonde:—
Anne (Beeches Farm, Tunstead, Norwich), b. 1911: m. 1st, 1930, Charles Michael Stratton [Style, Bt., colls.]: 2ndly, 1941, Capt. Lawrence N. Bickmore, R. Norfolk Regt.; 3rdly, 1947 (m. diss. 1957), Iain Arthur Murray, DSO [see E. Dunmore, colls.]; 4thly, 1961, Brig. James Charles Windsor Lewis, DSO, MC, who d. 1964, and has issue living, (by 1st marriage) John Mark (Witton Old Rectory, Norwich), b. 1931: m. 1961, Diana Miranda Martin, da. of the late Eric Martin Smith, MP, and has issue living, James Michael b. 1963, Andrew Eric Mark b. 1968, Kate Miranda b. 1965,—Margaret Anne (Viscountess Ebrington) b. 1933: m. 1961, Richard Archibald, Archibald, Viscount Ebrington [see E. Fortescue],—(by 2nd marriage) Peter Christopher, b. 1943.——Jean Constance (Paines Place, Blackboys, nr. Uckfield, Sussex), b. 1914; formerly Senior Cdr. ATS: m. 1947, Walter George Finney, TD, late Lt.-Col. RA (TA), who d. 1973, and has issue living, Sarah Anne, b. 1948: m. 1971, Giles Philip Curtis [see Curtis, Bt., colls.]—Rachel Mary, b. 1950,—Elizabeth Jean, b. 1952.

Granddaughter of the late Maj.-Gen. Lawrence George Drummond, C.B., C.B.E. M.V.O. (infra):—
Issue of the late Lindsay Drummond, b. 1891, d. 1951: m. 1924, Susan Cynthia Frances (now of Sissinghurst Place, Sissinghurst, Cranbrook, Kent), dau. of the late Alick William Cradock-Hartopp [see Cradock-Hartopp, Bt.]:—

Olivia Joan, *b.* 1929: *m.* 1957, Maj. James Stuart Perry, Special Air Service Regt., and has issue living, Marcus Lindsay, *b.* 1957,—Oliver James, *b.* 1958. *Residence,*—Upper Scullsgate Cottage, Benenden, Cranbrook, Kent.

Grandchildren of the late Adm. the Hon. Sir James Robert Drummond, G.C.B.,
2nd son of 6th Viscount Strathallan :—
Issue of the late Maj.-Gen. Laurence George Drummond, C.B., C.B.E., M.V.O., *b.* 1861; *d.* 1946 : *m.* 1886, Katherine Mary, who *d.* 1947, dau. of the late Hugh Lindsay Antrobus [Antrobus, Bt., colls.]:—
James Arthur Laurence (Rectory House, Ogbourne St. George, Wilts.), *b.* 1905; is Com. RN (ret.); sometime temporary Flying Officer RAF: *m.* 1936, Patricia, da. of Col. Sir Edward Scott Worthington, KCVO, CB, CMG, CIE.——Stella Katherine (*Baroness Percy of Newcastle*), *b.* 1895: *m.* 1918, the 1st Baron Percy of Newcastle, who *d.* 1958. *Residence,*—The Glebe Orchard, Etchingham, Sussex.

Granddaughter of the late Hon. Sir Edmund Drummond, K.C.I.E., 3rd son of 6th Viscount :—
Issue of the late Adm. Edmund Charles Drummond, *b.* 1841, *d.* 1911: *m.* 1872, Dora, who *d.* 1878, dau. of John Naylor, of Leighton Hall, Montgomery :—
Constance Dora (of Onslow Court Hotel, SW7), *b.* 1878: *m.* 1912, Adm. Edward Francis Bruen, CB, who *d.* 1952, and has issue living, Francis, *MVO, DSC* (of 54, Lincoln House, Basil St., SW3), *b.* 1918; Capt. RN; 1939-45 War at evacuation of Dunkirk (DSC.); MVO (4th class) 1957,—Anne, *b.* 1914; 1939-45 War in First Aid Nursing Yeo.: *m.* 1949, Oswald Frank Baker Baker, of The Court House, Atch Lench, Evesham, Worcs. [Middleton, Bt. colls.], and has issue living, William George *b.* 1955, Katherine Anne *b.* 1950, Juliet Constance *b.* 1951: *m.* 1975, Christopher Frank Spencer-Nairn [see Spencer-Nairn, Bt.].

Grandchildren of the late Edgar Atheling Drummond, son of the late Andrew Robert Drummond, grandson of the Hon. Robert Drummond, 3rd son of 4th Viscount Strathallan :—
Issue of the late Major Cyril Augustus Drummond, *b.* 1873 ; *d.* 1945 : *m.* 1st, 1897, Edith Belle, who *d.* 1917, dau. of L. I. Wilkins ; 2ndly, 1930, Mildred Joan (Harrington), (who *m.* 3rdly, 1948, Air Commodore John Charles Quinnell, C.B., D.F.C., of Cadland, Fawley, Southampton), dau. of the late Horace Humphrys :—
(By 2nd marriage) Maldwin Andrew Cyril, *b.* 1932: ed. at Eton; a JP for Hampshire: *m.* 1955, Susan Dorothy Maria Gabrielle, da. of Sir Kenelm Henry Ernest Cayley, 10th Bt., and has issue living, Frederica Elizabeth *b.* 1957,—Annabella Virginia, *b.* 1959. *Residence,*—Cadland, Fawley, Southampton. *Clubs*—Turf, Royal Yacht Squadron.——Robert Edgar Atheling, *b.* 1933; ed. at Eton: *m.* 1958 (m. diss. 1967), Mrs. Phyllis Field Samper, da. of Marshall Field of New York City, USA, and has issue living, Maldwin Marshall, *b.* 1959,—Fiona Mary, *b.* 1960, Bettina, *b.* 1963. *Residence,*—Stanswood Mews, Fawley, Southampton.——Annabella Frances Serena, *b.* 1938: *m.* 1st, 1957 (m. diss. 1961), David Arthur Talbot Rice [see B. Dynevor, colls.]; 2ndly, 1961 (m. diss. 1972), Gerardo Hochschild; 3rdly, 1973, John Philip Pochna, of 6, Eaton Sq., SW1, and Caherass, Croom, co. Limerick, and has issue living (by 2nd m.) Maurice Leo Robert, *b.* 1962,— Fabrizio Gerald Arturo, *b.* 1963,—Agustin Emil, *b.* 1965.

Grandson of the late Capt. Cecil George Assheton Drummond (infra):—
Issue of the late Capt. Eric Roderick Brook Drummond, late Rifle Brig., *b.* 1884, *d.* 1954 : *m.* 1905, Frederica Lillian Norey, who *d.* 1964, dau. of J. Norey Norris:—
Geoffrey Brook, *b.* (Oct.) 1905: *m.* 1939, Mary Barbara, dau. of James Arthur Unitt, M.R.C.S., L.R.C.P., of Quorn, Leicestershire, and has issue living, Frederick Brook, *b.* 1946,—Cherry Barbara, *b.* 1940: *m.* 1959, Derek C. Gibbs, of 102, Hunters Forstal Rd., Herne Bay, Kent, and has issue living, Nicholas Cary *b.* 1960, Alistair Corin *b.* 1972, Scarlett Kathryn *b.* 1961. *Residence,*—The Spinneys, Kirby Muxloe, Leicestershire.

Granddaughter of the late Andrew Robert Drummond (ante):—
Issue of the late Capt. Cecil George Assheton Drummond, *b.* 1839, *d.* 1903: *m.* 1871, Charlotte Amelia, who *d.* 1924, dau. of William Leigh Brook, of Meltham Hall, Huddersfield :—
Grace Janet, *b.* 1877: *m.* 1918, John Cecil Openshaw Bradbury, who *d.* 1955. *Residence,*—Smeeth Cottage, Smeeth, Ashford, Kent.

Grandchildren of the late Lt.-Col. Arthur Berkeley Drummond, el. son of the late Rev. Arthur Hislop Drummond (infra):—
Issue of the late Capt. Eric Arthur Drummond, RN, *b.* 1900, *d.* 1970: *m.* 1st, 1924, Molly Beryl (who obtained a divorce 1938), da. of Hugh William Croft, of Ledbury, Herefordshire; 2ndly, 1938, Elnah Raymond Russell (from whom he obtained a divorce 1947), da. of H. R. Wilding, of London; 3rdly, 1954, Mrs. Barbara Clarke (11, Bell Lane, Ludlow, Salop.), el. da. of the late Wilfred Bernard Faraday, Recorder of Barnstaple and Bideford:—
(By 1st m.) Ronald Nigel, *b.* 1925: *m.* 1st, 1948 (m. diss. 19—), Josephine Marie, da. of Jules Pourbaise, Comte de Bey; 2ndly, 1960,   , and has issue living, (by 1st m.) Iain Stewart, *b.* 1950.——John Berwick Lindsay (Priest Bridge House, Bradley Green, nr. Redditch, Worcs.), *b.* 1927: *m.* 1953, Daphne Mary, el. da. of the Rev. Edward Percy Woollcombe, OBE, late R. of Sutton, Surrey, and has issue living, Richard John, *b.* 1963,—Penelope Anne, *b.* 1954,—Sarah Jane, *b.* 1958,—Catriona Caroline, *b.* 1961.——Charles Iain (Lochranza, Monument Lane, Chalfont St. Peter, Bucks.), *b.* 1932: ed. at St. Edmund Hall, Oxford (BA): *m.* 1962, Christine Mary, only da. of Eric Stevenson Browne, of Greenleas Rd., Wallasey, Ches., and has issue living, Clare Elizabeth, *b.* 1967.——(by 2nd m.) Fiona Elnah Russell, *b.* 1940: *m.* 1st, 1963 (m. diss. 1967), Julian Patrick Selby Ormond; 2ndly, 1967, Robert Adrian Cowell, of 9, Kensington Park Gdns., W11, and has issue living, (by 2nd m.) John Maximilian Arthur *b.* 1972,—Sophia Russell Lilian *b.* 1969.——Deirdre Georgina, *b.* 1944: *m.* 1969, Nigel Builder (Rochester Univ., USA).

Grandchildren of the late Rev. Arthur Hislop Drummond, 2nd son of the late Rev. Arthur Drummond, son of the late Charles Drummond (*b.* 1759), son of the late Hon. Robert Drummond (ante) :—
Issue of the late Malcolm Cyril Drummond, *b.* 1880; *d.* 1945: *m.* 1st, 1906, Zina Lilias, who *d.* 1931, dau. of George Macartney Ogilvie, formerly I.C.S.; 2ndly, 1934, Margaret Triquet (8, Ashton Close, Pangbourne, Berks.), da. of the late Rev. Arthur Browning, of Pangbourne Rectory, Berks:—
(By 1st m.) (Arthur Malcolm) James (Woodside, Lumsden, nr. Huntly, Aberdeenshire), *b.* 1911; late Capt. R. Berks. Regt.: *m.* 1st, 1938 (m. diss. 19—), Moyra Blanche, da. of the late Frederick Barnard Elliott, CBE [B. Emly], 2ndly, 19—, Patricia, da. of the late Guy Cave, and has issue living (by 1st m.), Hamish Guy (Georgetown, Grand Cayman, BWI), *b.* 1939,—(by 2nd m.), David James, *b.* 1960,—Nicola Gesina, *b.* 1956,—Alexina Mary, *b.* 1959.——Elspeth Mary, *b.* 1907: *m.* 1935, John Franc Finch McIntyre, and has issue living, John Malcolm Drummond, *b.* 1938: *m.* 1964, Elisabeth Anne, da. of the late Douglas James Lionel Routh, MRCS, LRCP, of Torquay, and has issue living, James Amand Routh *b.* 1967, Catriona Elspeth *b.* 1964, Kirsty Elisabeth *b.* 1970,—Archibald Duncan Ogilvie (c/o Lloyds Bank, 6, Pall Mall, SW1), *b.* 1940: *m.* 1962, Dilys Mary, da. of Leslie Stuart Matthews, and has issue living, Duncan James Callum *b.* 1964, Alasdair Donald Robert *b.* 1970, Fiona Mary Elspeth *b.* 1963,—Andrew Turnbull, *b.* 1943: *m.* 1970, Susan Anne, da. of Brian Blenner-hasset, of Dublin, and has issue living, Timothy John *b.* 1971,—Christian Margaret Lilias, *b.* 1937: *m.* 1959, Michael Henry Charles Petre, of Knocksinna House, Knocksinna, Foxrock, co. Dublin [see B. Petre, colls.], Janet Marian, *b.* 1947: *m.* 1970, James Donald Roberts, of Liverpool and Toronto. ——Anna Mary (Woodside, Lumsden, Aberdeenshire), *b.* 1909; is a Carmelite nun.

Grandson of the late Robert Drummond, son of the late Charles Drummond
(b. 1790), son of the late Charles Drummond (b. 1759) (ante) :—
Issue of the late Charles Drummond, b. 1855, d. 1932 : m. 1892, Lady Caroline Elizabeth
Boyle, who d. 1958, el. dau. of the late Col. Gerald Edmund Boyle [E. Cork and Orrery] :—
Angus Julian, b. 1910 ; European War 1939-45 as Lieut. (S.) R.N.V.R. : m. 1961, the Hon. Theodosia
Beatrix Catherine Mary Meade, dau. of the late Richard Charles, Lord Gillford [see E. Clanwilliam.]
Residence,—62, Ashley Gdns., S.W.1. Club,—Travellers'.

Grandchildren of the late Rev. Morton Drummond, son of the late Charles
Drummond (b. 1790) (ante):—
Issue of the late Edmund Traherne Drummond, b. 1864, d. 1935 : m. 1892, Isabel Henrietta,
who d. 1955, dau. of the late William Knights :—
Edith Charlotte (of Little Braxted, Abbotsham, Bideford, N. Devon), b. 1893: m. 1915, the Rev.
Edmund Arthur Du Cane, formerly V. of Abbotsham, Devon, who d. 1950.

Issue of the late Gerald Morton Drummond, b. 1866, d. 1941 : m. 1896. Alice Edith, who
d. 1946, dau. of the late Col. William Julius Marshall, Suffolk Regt.:—
Edward Morton, b. 1898 ; formerly Lieut. Black Watch ; Group-Capt.(retired) R.A.F.; European War
1914-18, European War 1939-45 : m. 1922, Edith Daphne Eunice, dau. of the late Wilfred Doneraile
Stanhope Taylor [M. Headfort, colls.], and has issue living, David James Morton, (of Blacklands,
Meshaw, South Molton, Devon) b. 1925; European War 1943-45 as Lieut. Black Watch: m. 1st,
1949 (m. diss.), Cecily Winifred Jillian, only da. of Cdr. A. D. Bruford, RN (ret.), of Hailsham;
2ndly, Diana Mary, only child of the late Frederick Turner, of Barnstaple, and has issue living, (by
2nd m.) James Edward Morton b. 1966, Lilias b. 1962, Amanda b. 1963,—Charmian Eunice, b. 1923;
1939-45 War in WAAF; m. 1951, George Geoffrey Gundry-White, of 5, Elms Rd., SW4, and has
issue living, Timothy b. 1955, Patrick b. 1957, Alexander (twin) b. 1957, Jasper b. 1959, Henry
Simon b. 1960, Katherine Jane Louis b. 1952, Madeleine Anne b. 1954, Laura (twin) b. 1955,—Jean,
b. 1927: m. 1948, Gerald Charles Grenfell Robins, of Wawcott House, Kintbury, Newbury, and
has issue living, Charles David Anthony b. 1953, Angela b. 1955, Marion b. 1960. Residence,—
Pleasant, The Ridge, Cold Ash, Newbury, Berks.——Charles Morton (of Le Petit Courtil, Frie Bâton
St. Saviours, Guernsey), b. 1903; Lt.-Col. RE; 1939-45 War with E. African Engineers: m. 1937
Violet Emily Agnes, da. of the late William Andrew Pitcairn, of Edinburgh.——Andrew Morton
b. 1904; 1939-45 War as Lt. Gordon Highlanders. Residence.—10, Mornington Rd., Radlett, Herts

Grandchildren of the late George James Drummond, son of George Drummond,
el. son of George Harley Drummond, el. son of George Drummond (b. 1758),
grandson of Andrew Drummond, next brother of 4th Viscount Strathhallan:—
Issue of the late George Henry Drummond, b. 1883, d. 1963: m. 1st, 1917, Helena Kathleen,
who d. 1933, da. of T. Grattan Holt; 2ndly, 1940, Honora Myrtle Gladys (Buckden, St.
Joseph, Barbados), da. of the late Lt.-Col. Duncan Wilfrid Lambart Spiller, DSO:—
By 2nd m.) George Albert Harley, b. 1943: m. 1971 (m. diss. 1974), Rachel, da. of Michael Manley,
and has issue living, George Manley Deuere, b. 1971.——(By 1st m.) Eve, b. 1918: m. 1951, as his
second wife, Raymond Vincent de Trafford who d. 1971 [de Trafford, Bt.].——Rosemary Lucia,
b. 1919: m. 1945, Lt.-Col. Neil Phipps Foster, late Life Gds., of Whittlebury Cottage, Towcester,
Northants, and has issue living, Alexander Neil, b. 1945,—Rosanne Madeleine, b. 1947.——Edwina
Gillian, b. 1920: m. 1952, Comdt. Eric R. Miville, late French Foreign Legion, of Moyglare Stud
Farm, Maynooth, co. Kildare.——Diana Kathleen (Hon. Mrs. John Astor), b. 1926: m. 1950,
the Hon. John Astor, of Kirby House, Inkpen, Berks. [see B. Astor of Hever].——(By 2nd m.)
Annabella Elizabeth, b. 1941.——Omega Margaret (Sheepscombe House, nr. Stroud, Glos.), b. 1944:
m. 1961, Robert A. Y. Pouget, and has issue living,—Antoine Xavier, b. 1962,—Robert Harley,
b. 1965,—Alexandre, b. 1967.——Isubel Camilla, b. 1945.

Issue of the late David Robert Drummond, Lt. Scots Guards, b. 1884, d. (killed in action)
1914: m. 1907, Hilda Margaret (who d. 1972, having m. 2ndly, 1936, Maj. John Elgee
Gunning, JP, who d. 1950), da. of the late Alfred Hellver Harris, of Donnington, Chichester:—
Joan Cécile, b. 1909: m. 1st, 1933, Maurice James Newcomb, from whom she obtained a divorce 1939,
2ndly, 1942 (m. diss. 1949), Maj. Charles St. John Colthurst, RA; 3rdly, 1950, Arthur Raywid, from
whom she obtained a divorce 1970; 4thly, 1971, Alan James Fuller Eberle, MBE, BM, BCh (PO Box
38, Knysna, Cape Province, S. Africa), and has issue living, (by 1st m.) Nicholas James, b. 1935,—
(by 2nd m.) Joanna, b. 1948.——Violet Hilda, b. 1911: m. 1st, 1933, Maj. John Peter Pardoe,
late KRRC, from whom she obtained a divorce 1945; 2ndly, 1948, Maj. Anthony Swetenham,
late KRRC, and has issue living, (by 1st m.) Julian Hugh, b. 1935. Residence,—24, Norfolk Rd.,
St. John's Wood, NW8.——Winifred Pansy, b. 1914: m. 1947, Daniel F. Aitken, of Taylor's Cottage,
Mountfield, Robertsbridge, Sussex, and has issue living, David Jame s, b. 1948,—Elizabeth Ann,
b. 1949.

Issue of the late Capt. Alexander Victor Drummond, b. 1888; d. 1937: m. 1914, Ellen Pauline
Matthew (the actress, " Miss Pauline Chase "), who d. 1962, dau. of Ellis Bliss, of Washing-
ton, U.S.A.:—
Alexander Peter, b. 1927: m. 1954, Anne Audrey Ruth, dau. of Frank Seamer, of Leigh, Kent, and
has issue living, Harrie Malcolm, b. 1962,—Alexandra Elspeth, b. 1957 —Marina Jane, b. 1959.
——Jane, b. 1925: m. 1946, Irving Howbert, late Lt. US Naval Reserve, and has issue living, William
Irving, b. 1948,—Anne Noel, b. 1950,—Janet Scott, b. 1953. Residence,—33, Warnborough Rd.,
Oxford.

Granddaughter of the late Capt. Mortimer Percy Drummond, only son of the late
Andrew Drummond, 2nd son of the late George Drummond (b. 1758) (ante) :—
Issue of the late Capt. Mortimer Percy George Douglas Drummond, b. 1860; d. 1936: m.
1890, Alice Lydia, who d. 1938, dau. of the late William C. Ward, formerly of Harborne House, Tenterden:—
Sybilla Euphemia (Effie) (Christmas Hill House, 4076, North Quadra St., Victoria, BC), b. 1902:
m. 1925, Montague Arthur Weaver-Bridgman, who d. 1952, and has issue living, Hamish Drummond,
b. 1929, late Lt. RCN,—Rosemary Maude, b. 1927: m. 1951, Michael William Penn.

Grandchildren of the late Capt. Algernon Heneage Drummond (infra).
Issue of the late Algernon Cecil Heneage Drummond, b. 1880, d. 1975: m. 1917, Janetta,
who d. 1958, da. of the late Col. John Ormsby Vandeleur, CB [D St. Albans, colls.]:—
Spencer Heneage, DSC (High Orchard, Sheet, Petersfield, Hants.), b. 1922; Commodore RN; 1939-45
War (DSC): m. 1949, Patricia Pauline, da. of the late Lt.-Col. Michael Keane, OBE, RAMC, and
has issue living, Crispin Heneage, b. 1955,—Hereward John Heneage, b. 1959,—Deirdre Mary,
b. 1953,—Ianthe Mary, b. 1960,—Helena Mhairi, b. 1963.——John Vandeleur Heneage (9, Upper
Wheelan St., Newlands, Cape 7700, S. Africa), b. 1924; late Pilot, E. African Rlys. and Harbour;
Harbour Ser., S. African Rlys. since 1962: m. 1951, Annette, da. of D: Alan William Sichel, of Cape
Town, and has issue living, Anthony Christopher Heneage, b. 1954,—Richard Stuart Heneage, b.
1962,—Hugo Alistair Heneage, b. 1965.——Amanda Elizabeth, b. 1956.——Margaret Frederica, b.
1926: m. 1949, John Ironside Money, of Sabi, Midhurst Way, Constantia, Capetown, S. Africa, and
has issue living, Paul, b. 1950,—Brian, b. 1953,—Colin, b. 1956,—Olivia Margaret, b. 1959.

Issue of the late Lieut.-Com. Geoffrey Heneage Drummond, V.C., R.N.V.R., b. 1886, d.
(on active ser. during European War) 1941: m. 1918, Maude Aylmer Tindal, who d. 1967,
da. of the late Lt.-Col. Bernard Tindal Bosanquet, of Claysmore, Enfield:—
Geoffrey Mortimer Heneage, R.N., b. 1920 ; ed. at Eton ; is Lieut.-Com. ; European War 1939-45 : m.
1956, Sarah Madeline, dau. of Richard Walter Spencer, of Warsash, Southampton, and has issue
living, John Richard Geoffrey, b. 1957; ed. at Eton,—Charles Mortimer Geoffrey, b. 1958,—Caroline

Jane, *b.* 1963. *Residence,*—Faringdon, Haven Cres., Hillhead, Hants. *Club,*—Royal Naval.——
Aylmer Merelina, *b.* 1919; is a State Registered Nurse.——Iris Mary Elizabeth, *b.* 1926; 1939-45
War in WRNS: *m.* 1947, Lt.-Cdr. John Munro Crosland Fenton, DSC, RN, of Hollins, Balmaclellan,
by Castle Douglas, Kirkcudbright, and has issue living, Jeremy John Crosland, *b.* 1949; ed. at Glenalmond, and Magdalene Coll., Camb. (MA),—James Heneage Crosland, *b.* 1952; ed. at Glenalmond,
and Durham Univ. (BSc),—Geoffrey Eric Crosland, *b.* 1954; ed. at Glenalmond, and St. John's
Coll., Oxford.

Grandchildren of the late Rev. Heneage Drummond, yst. son of John Drummond
(*b.* 1766) yr. brother of George Drummond (*b.* 1758) (ante):—
Issue of the late Capt. Algernon Heneage Drummond, *b.* 1844, *d.* 1932: *m.* 1879, Margaret
Elizabeth, who *d.* 1941, dau. of William Benson, of Langtons, Alresford. Hants :—
Josceline Heneage, *OBE, DSC, b.* 1888; ed. at Eton; Cdr. RN (ret.); Assist. Sec. Forces Help Soc.,
and Lord Roberts' Workshops 1937-53; 1914-18 War (despatches, DSC); OBE (Civil) 1946: *m.* 1944,
Gwendolen Theresa, who *d.* 1975, da. of the late James Laing, of Barscobe, Balmaclellan. *Resi-
dence,*—Faire-na-Vrackie, Moulin, Pitlochry, Perthshire.——Isobel, *b.* 1887: *m.* 1906, Neville
Leckonby Phipps, who *d.* 1968. *Residence,*—78, Berrow Rd., Burnham-on-Sea, Som.

Grandchildren of the late Capt. Algernon Heneage Drummond (ante):—
Issue of the late Maurice John Heneage Drummond, *b.* 1894, *d.* 1975: *m.* 1922, Celia, who
d. 1964, da. of the late Rev. John Vaughan, Canon of Winchester:—
Rev. Christopher John Vaughan (The Rectory, Gt. Linford, Milton Keynes, Bucks., MK14 5BD),
b. 1926; ed. at Winchester, Magdalen Coll., Oxford (MA) and Ridley Hall, Camb.: *m.* 1960, Gwyneth
May, da. of George Timmis, of Hanchurch, Staffs., and has issue living, Peter John Vaughan, *b.* 1963,
—Gillian Clare *b.* 1961.——Rev. Josceline Maurice Vaughan (St. Catherine's Vicarage, Fairlop Rd.,
Leytonstone, E11), *b.* 1929; ed. at London Univ. (Dip Th., BD) and Wycliffe Hall, Oxford; late Lt.
RN: *m.* 1962, Christine Mary, BSc, da. of Alfred George Read, of 187, Lower Dale Rd., Derby, and
has issue living, Andrew Paul Graham, *b.* 1970,—Lydia Rosalind, *b.* 1964.——Rosalind Margaret
Vaughan, *b.* 1924; BA, PhD: *m.* 1st, 1947 (m. diss. 1955), Mark Arthur Monson Roberts, MA;
2ndly, 1965, Spencer Depas, of 227, Cumberland St., Brooklyn, New York, NY 11205, USA, and has
issue living (by 1st m.), Julian Francis; ed. at Winchester,—(by 2nd m.), Sophie Margaret, *b.* 1967.

PREDECESSORS.—[1] *Hon.* JAMES Drummond, 2nd son of 2nd Lord Drummond [†↓† infra];
was cr. **Lord Maderty** (peerage of Scotland) 1609 ; *d.* 1632 ; *s.* by his son [2] JOHN, **2nd Lord** ;
joined Montrose after the battle of Kilsyth and was imprisoned ; *s.* by his son [3] DAVID, **3rd
Lord** ; resigned his honours 1664, and obtained a new grant with remainder to his heirs male,
and failing whom to his nominee and his heirs ; *d.* 1684 ; *s.* by his brother [4] WILLIAM, **4th
Lord** ; held a high command in the army raised in 1648 to rescue Charles I. ; was taken prisoner
at battle of Worcester, but effecting his escape went to Russia, in which country he attained the
rank of Lieut.-Gen.; after the Restoration became Maj.-Gen. of the Forces in Scotland, Gen.
of the Ordnance, and a Lord of the Treasury ; cr. **Lord Drummond of Cromliz, and Viscount
Strathallan** (peerage of Scotland) 1686, with remainder to the heirs male of his body, which failing,
to heirs male whatsoever ; *d.* 1688 ; *s.* by his son [5] WILLIAM, **2nd Viscount** ; *d.* 1702 ; *s.* by his
son 6] WILLIAM, **3rd Viscount** ; *d.s.p.* 1711 ; *s.* by his cousin [7] WILLIAM, **4th Viscount,** son of
the Hon. Sir James, 2nd son of 1st Lord Maderty ; having espoused the cause of the Chevalier in
1745, he was slain at Culloden 1746, and the names of himself and eldest son were included in the
bill of attainder of that year ; *s.* by his son [8] JAMES, **5th Viscount,** who was not attainted until
after he had *s.* to title ; *d.* 1766 ; *s.* by his el. son [9] JAMES ; *d.* 1775 ; *s.* by his brother [10] ANDREW
JOHN, a Gen. in the Army ; petitioned unsuccessfully in 1787 for a restoration of the honours ; *d.*
unmarried 1817 ; *s.* in representation of his family by his cousin [11] JAMES ANDREW JOHN LAURENCE
CHARLES, 2nd son of the Hon. William, 2nd son of 4th Viscount; sat as M.P. for Perthshire
1812-24; was restored to his ancestral honours by Act of Parliament 1824, and was afterwards
a Representative Peer; *d.* 1851 ; *s.* by his son [12] WILLIAM HENRY, **7th Viscount** ; *b.* 1810 ;
was a Representative Peer and a Lord-in-Waiting to H.M. Queen Victoria: *m.* 1833, Christina
Maria Hersey, who *d.* 1867, dau. of Robert Baird, of Newbyth ; *d.* Jan. 23rd, 1886; *s.* by
his son [13] JAMES DAVID, **8th Viscount,** *b.* 1839; a retired Lieut.-Col. and a Representative
Peer for Scotland: *m.* 1st, 1868, Ellen, who *d.* 1873, dau. of the late Cudbert B. Thornhill,
C.I.E.; 2ndly, 1875, Margaret, who *d.* 1920, dau. of the late W. Smythe, of Methven Castle,
Perthshire; *d.* 1893 ; *s.* by his el. son [14] WILLIAM HUNTLY, **9th Viscount** ; *b* 1871; *s.* as 15th
Earl of Perth 1902 [see infra]: *m.* 1911, Anna, who *d.* 1967, da. of Jakob Strauss, of Prague, Czechoslovakia; *d.* 1937; *s.* by his half-brother [15] **Rt. Hon.** (JAMES) ERIC, *GCMG, CB,* **16th Earl,** and
10th Viscount Strathallan; *b.* 1876; a PC (cr. 1933); was Private Sec. to Under-Sec. of State for
Foreign Affairs 1906-12, and to Prime Min. 1912-15, and to Sec. of State for Foreign Affairs 1915-19;
first Sec.-Gen. of League of Nations 1919-33 ; Ambassador Extraor. and Plen. to Rome 1933-39 ;
sometime Dep. Leader of Liberal Party in House of Lords : *m.* 1904, the Hon. Angela Mary Constable-
Maxwell, who *d.* 1965, yst. da. of 11th Lord Herries of Terregles; *d.* 1951; *s.* by his son [16] JOHN
DAVID, **17th Earl, 11th Viscount Strathallan,** and present peer; also Lord Drummond. Lord
Maderty, and Lord Drummond of Cromlix.

⁎ [1] *Hon.* JOHN Drummond, *K.T.,* 2nd son of 3rd Earl of Perth, having held several high
offices of State, was in 1684 cr. **Lord Drummond of Gilstoun, and Viscount Melfort** (peerage of Scotland) 1685, and **Lord Drummond of Riccarton, Castlemaine and Gilstoun, Viscount Forth and Earl of
Melfort** (peerage of Scotland) 1686, with remainder to the heirs male of his body by his second
wife, and failing which to the heirs male of his body by his first wife, which Earldom he
resigned into the King's hands 1688, when it is said the lands and honours were created
into a new Earldom in favour of his wife for life with remainder to John, Viscount Forth,
Lord of the Regality of Forth, and the heirs male of his body, whom failing to the heirs female
of his body, whom failing to his heirs whatsoever ; on the revolution he joined James II. in
France, and was by him in 1692 cr. **Marquess of Forth and Duke of Melfort** ; and in 1701, Louis
XIV. accepted the Earl as Duke of Melfort, in the peerage of France ; title attainted by Act of
Parliament 1695, which **attainder,** however, did not affect the issue of his first marriage; *d.*
1714; *s.* by his el. son, by 2nd wife [2] JOHN, 2nd Earl and Duke of Melfort; *d.* 1754; *s.* by
his son [3] JAMES, 3rd Earl and Duke; *d.* 1766; *s.* by his el. son [4] JAMES LEWIS, 4th Earl
and Duke, who became, on the death of the 12th Earl of Perth (cr. 1605), heir male to that
peerage; *d.s.p.* 1800; *s.* by his brother [5] CHARLES EDWARD, 5th Earl and Duke of Melfort,
and 13th Earl of Perth; a Roman Catholic Prelate; *d.* 1840 ; *s.* by his nephew [6] GEORGE,
6th Earl and Duke, and 14th Earl of Perth, who, in 1853, was restored in blood by Act of
Parliament to the dignities of **Earl of Perth** (cr. 1605), **Viscount Forth, Lord Drummond, and
Lord Drummond of Riccartoun, Castlemains and Gilstoun,** he having in 1841 established his
right to the French honours; *d.* 1902, when the Earldom of Melfort became dormant, and
the Lordship of Drummond (cr. 1487) devolved upon his kinsman [7] WILLIAM HUNTLY, **9th
Viscount Strathallan (ante), also 15th Earl of Perth** (cr. 1605) [see †↓† infra].

†↓†[1] *Sir* JOHN Drummond of Cargill and Stobhall, *P.C.,* Ambassador to England 1483, was in 1487
cr. **Lord Drummond** (peerage of Scotland) ; defeated the Earl of Lennox at Tillymoss 1489 ; and
suppressed the rebellion ; was Constable of Stirling Castle and Justiciary of Scotland,
d. 1519 ; *s.* by his great-grandson [2] DAVID, 2nd Lord ; joined the Association on behalf of
Queen Mary at Hamilton 1568 ; *s.* by his son [3] PATRICK, 3rd Lord ; embraced the reformed
religion ; *s.* by his el. son [4] JAMES, 4th Baron ; was a distinguished courtier *temp.* James VI. ;
cr. **Earl of Perth** (peerage of Scotland) 1605, it is said with remainder to his heirs male
whatsoever, but the patent is not in existence ; *s.* by his brother [5] JOHN, 2nd Earl, as, it is
said, "heirs of tailzie" ; joined the Association on behalf of Charles I. 1641 ; *s.* by his
son [6] JAMES, 3rd Earl ; joined Montrose 1645, and was taken prisoner at Philiphaugh ; *d.*
1675 ; *s.* by his son [7] JAMES, *K.T.,* 4th Earl ; was Chancellor of Scotland ; said to

have had a regrant of his honours after resignation; cr. *Earl of Perth, Lord Drummond, Baron Stobhall and Montifex* 1686; in 1693 James II., after his deposition, cr. him Marquess of Drummond and Duke of Perth (titles acknowledged and confirmed in 1701 by Louis XIV. of France), and conferred upon him numerous high offices; *d.* 1716; *s.* by his son [8] JAMES, who was styled "2nd Duke of Perth," and who, having been attainted in 1715, could not succeed to the Earldom of Perth; *s.* by his el. son [9] JAMES, "3rd Duke"; wounded at Culloden; attainted 1746; *s.* by his brother [10] JOHN, "4th Duke"; attainted 1746; *d.s.p.* 1747; *s.* by his uncle [11] JOHN, "5th Duke" *d.* 1757; *s.* by his brother [12] EDWARD, "6th Duke"; *d.s.p.* 1760; *s.* by his second cousin [13] JAMES Lundin, grandson of John, 2nd son of 3rd Earl (see *⁎* ante), who assumed the name of Drummond, and also the style of Earl of Perth; *s.* by his son [14] JAMES, who assumed the Earldom; cr. *Lord Perth, Baron Drummond of Stobhall* (peerage of Great Britain) 1797; *d.* 1800, when the Lordship of Perth, Baron Drummond of Stobhall became extinct, and the next heir male to the earldom was [15] JAMES LEWIS, 4th Duke of Melfort (see *⁎* ante); *d.* 1800; *s.* by his brother [16] CHARLES EDWARD, 5th Duke of Melfort; *d.* 1840; *s.* by his nephew [17] GEORGE, 6th Duke of Melfort; in 1841, established his right to the Dukedoms of Melfort and Perth, and to be Comte de Lussan and Baron de Valrose, &c., in France; obtained a reversal of all attainders by Act of Parliament 1853: *m.* 1st, 1831, the Baroness Albertine von Rotberg Rheinweiler, who *d.* 1842, and widow of Gen. Comte Rapp; 2ndly, 1847, Susan Harriet, who *d.* 1886, dau. of Thomas Henry Bermingham Daly Sewell, of Athenry, and widow of Col. Burrowes, of Dangan Castle, Meath: *d.* 1902, when the French Dukedom became ext.; and the Earldom of Melfort, the Viscountcy of Forth, and the Lordship of Drummond of Riccartoun, Castlemaine and Gilstoun became extinct or dormant, while the Lordship of Drummond and the Earldom of Perth passed to his kinsman [18] WILLIAM HUNTLY, 9th Viscount Strathallan (ante).

Pestell, see Baron Wells Pestell.

PETERBOROUGH, LORD BISHOP OF. (Feaver.)

Rt. Rev. DOUGLAS RUSSELL FEAVER, son of the late Ernest Henry Feaver; *b.* 1914; ed. at Keble Coll., Oxford (MA), and Well, Theo. Coll.; 1939-45 War as Chap. RAFs Curate of Abbey Ch., St. Albans 1938-42; Canon and Sub-Dean of St. Albans Cathedral 1945-58; Exam. Chap. to Bishop of St. Albans 1948-58, and to Bishop of Portsmouth 1958-72; Proc. in Conv. St. Albans 1951-58, and Southwell 1970-72; V. and Rural Dean of Nottingham, and Hon. Canon of Southwell 1958-72; consecrated 35th Bishop of Peterborough 1972: *m.* 1939, Katherine Muriel Rose, da. of the late Rev. Wilfrid Thomas Stubbs.

Patron of 101 livings, the Chancellorship, the Archdeaconries of Northampton and Oakham, and the Canonries of his Cathedral.

This Bishopric was founded by Henry VIII in 1541 from the dissolved lands of the Abbey of St. Peter's founded by Saxulf, a thane of Mercia, n 653. John Chambers, the last Abbot was the first Bishop of Peterborough, 1541.

Episcopal Signature,—" Douglas Petriburg : "

ARMS OF THE SEE,—Gules, two keys in saltire endorsed between four cross-crosslet fitchée or.

Residence,—The Palace, Peterborough.

Petersham, Viscount, son of Earl of Harrington.

PETRE, BARON. (Petre.) [Baron E. 1603.]

[Name pronounced "Peter."]

Nothing without God

JOSEPH WILLIAM LIONEL PETRE, 17th Baron; *b.* June 5th, 1914; *s.* 1915; ed. at Eton ; is Capt. Essex Regt., and patron of three livings (but being a Roman Catholic cannot present): *m.* 1941, Marguerite Eileen, dau. of the late Ion Wentworth Hamilton, and has issue.

Arms,—Gules, a bend or between two escallops argent. **Crest,**—Two lions' heads erased and addorsed; the dexter or, collared azure; the sinister azure, collared or. **Supporters,**—Two lions reguardant; the *dexter* or, collared azure; the *sinister* azure, collared or.

Seats,—Ingatestone Hall, Essex; Writtle Park, Essex.

SON LIVING.

Hon. JOHN PATRICK LIONEL (Writtle Park, Essex), *b.* Aug. 4th, 1942; ed. at Eton, and Trin. Coll., Oxford: *m.* 1965, Marcia Gwendolyn, da. of Alfred Plumpton, and has issue living, Dominic William, *b.* 1966,—Mark Julian, *b.* 1969,—Clare Helen, *b.* 1973.

SISTER LIVING.

Hon. Elisabeth Mary Lionel Margaret, *b.* (posthumous) 1915: *m.* 1935, Robert Peter Healing, and has issue vi ng, Julian Robert Peter, *b.* 1939: *m.* 1971, Sabine Marie Louise Françoise, da. of Christian de Sorbier de Pougnadoresse, of Magescq, France,—Susan Elisabeth, *b.* 1945: *m.* 1966, Edward Reymond Carbutt, of Mount Hall, Gt. Horkesley, Colchester [see de Montmorency, Bt., colls.],—Carolyn Margaret (twin), *b.* 1945: *m.* 1972, Christopher Sands Clayton, son of Archibald Sands Clayton [see By. Goddard]. *Residences,*—The Priory, Kemerton, Glos.: 9, Yeomans Row, SW3.

DAUGHTER LIVING OF FOURTEENTH BARON.

Mary Frances Katherine (*Baroness Furnivall* in her own right), *b.* 1900 [see that title].

WIDOW LIVING OF SIXTEENTH BARON.

CATHERINE MARGARET (*Catherine Lady Rasch*) (of 9, Trevor St., S.W.7), dau. of the late Hon. John Boscawen [see V. Falmouth, colls.]; is a J.P. for Essex: *m.* 1st, 1913, the 16th Baron, Capt. Coldstream Guards, who *d.* (of wounds in action) 1915; 2ndly, 1921, Col. Sir Frederic Carne Rasch, 2nd Bt., who *d.* 1963.

COLLATERAL BRANCHES LIVING.

Grandchildren of the late Francis William Petre (infra):—
Issue of the late Bernard Francis Petre, *b.* 1884, *d.* 1942: *m.* 1922, Constance (now of 77, Bedford Street, St. Clair, Dunedin, New Zealand), youngest dau. of the late Capt. F. J. Easther, R.N., of Dunedin, New Zealand:—
Francis John, *b.* 1923 ; Italy 1943-5 with New Zealand Forces: *m.* 1947, Patricia Josephine, dau. of Walter Corcoran, of Dunedin. New Zealand, and has issue living, John Bernard, *b.* 1949,—David Christopher, *b.* 1954,—Gerard Michael, *b.* 1959,—Frances Mary, *b.* 1948,—Philippa Josephine, *b.* 1951.——Robert Cargill, *b.* 1925: *m.* 1954, Emily Waiwaha Kohere, and has issue living, Robert Bernard, *b.* 1961,—Christopher Andrew, *b.* 1962,—Mary Ellen, *b.* 1955,—Raewyn Kura, *b.* 1957,—Jennifer Anne, *b.* 1965.——William Bernard (of 77, Bedford St., St. Clair, Dunedin, NZ), *b.* 1927.——Constance Elizabeth Mary, *b.* 1931: *m.* 1955, Lambertus Snellaert.

Issue of the late Joseph Austin Petre, *b.* 1893, *d.* 1972: *m.* 1st, 1921, Eleanor Irene, who *d.* 1935, da. of the late H. H. Norton, of Auckland, NZ; 2ndly, 1940, Leonora Agnes, who *d.* 1941, da. of the late Robert M. Sunley, of Christchurch, NZ:—
(By 2nd m.) Anthony John (3, Paulus Terr, Cashmere, Christchurch, NZ), *b.* 1941: *m.* 1967, Barbara Ann, da. of the late Charles Armstrong, of Geraldine, NZ, and has issue living, Robert Joseph, *b.* 1973,—Ruth Leonora, *b.* 1968,—Adrienne Joanne, *b.* 1970.

Grandchildren of the late Hon. Henry William Petre, 2nd son of 11th Baron :—
Issue of the late Francis William Petre, *b.* 1847, *d.* 1918 : *m.* (March) 1881, Margaret, who *d.* 1933, el. dau. of the late Edward Bowes Cargill, of Dunedin, New Zealand:—
Henry William, *b.* 1899; 1940-44 War with NZ Forces in Middle East: *m.* 1931, Ciceley Beresford, da. of the late Anthony Francis FitzHerbert [see Fitz Herbert, Bt., colls.]. *Address,*—R.D1, Motueka, South Island, NZ.——Monica Helen Mary, *b.* 1897: *m.* 1930, Capt. John Niall Fox, MC, late RE, and has issue living, Francis Bernard Niall, *b.* 1938.——Margaret Elisabeth Mary (35, Winchester St., Merrivale, Christchurch, NZ), *b.* 1905.

Issue of the late Sebastian Henry Petre, *b.* 1856, *d.* 1934 : *m.* 1881, Catherine Elise, who *d.* 1946, dau. of the late W. Edmund Sibeth, of Rowney Abbey, Herts:—
Bernard Francis, *b.* 1891 ; formerly Capt. R.A.S.C.; European War 1914-18 (despatches): *m.* 1926, Mary Lucy, dau. of Archibald Dominic Smith-Sligo, of Inzievar, Oakley, Fife, and has issue living, Michael Henry Charles (Knocksinna House, Knocksinna, Foxrock, co. Dublin), *b.* 1930: *m.* 1959, Christian Margaret Lilias, da. of John Franc. Finch McIntyre [see E. Perth, colls.], and has issue living, Benedict Francis Joseph *b.* 1967, Duncan Michael Joseph *b.* 1969, Tanya Mairi *b.* 1961, Helena Mary Alathea *b.* 1964, Katharine Maria *b.* 1965, Elspeth Moira *b.* 1972. *Residence,*—Ferwood Lea, Oakley, Fife.

Issue of the late Robert George Petre, *b.* 1861, *d.* 1922 : *m.* 1891, Elizabeth Grace, who *d.* 1937, dau. of the late Robert Ferguson :—
Francis William, *b.* 1902 : *m.* 1932, Gertrude Féy, dau. of Philip Lowry Wright, of Bicton, Napier, New Zealand, and has issue living, John Lowry, *b.* 1934.——Sybil Mary, *b.* 1896 : *m.* 1926, the Hon. Vincent Aubrey Ward, C.B.E., who *d.* 1946 [Ward, Bt., cr. 1911]. *Residence,*—

Granddaughters of the late Sebastian Henry Petre (ante) :—
Issue of the late William Petre, *b.* 1888, *d.* 1955: *m.* 1925, Margaret Gwladys (Courts Cottage 55, Petworth Rd., Haslemere, Surrey), da. of Archibald Dacres Bruce [Smythe, Bt.]:—

Ann Mary Margaret, *b.* 1926: *m.* 1955, John Edward Turner Hales-Tooke, and has issue living, Jonathan Petre Turner Paul, *b.* 1957,—Hugh Benedict Milton, *b.* 1959,—Giles Anthony Raphael *b.* 1964. *Residence,*—20, Maids Causeway, Cambridge.——Mary Elise, *b.* 1929: *m.* 1951, Leonard Pardoe and has issue living, Sebastian William Joseph, *b.* 1956,—Matthew James Wentworth, *b.* 1960,— Louise Mary Anne, *b.* 1952. *Residence,*—7, Hereford Sq., SW7.——Helen Elizabeth, *b.* 1939: *m.* 1967, Peter Gordon Halsted.

Grandchildren of the late Capt. the Hon. Frederick Charles Edmund Petre, 3rd son of 11th Baron:—

Issue of the late Reginald William Petre, *b.* 1851, *d.* 19—: *m.* 1889, Caroline, dau. of J. Alexander Preston, of Baltimore, U.S.A.:—
Alexander, *b.* 1894: *m.* 1935, Stuart, dau. of Stuart Oliver, of Baltimore, U.S.A. *Residence,*— Baltimore, U.S.A.——Constance Achsah Ridgeley, *b.* 1897: *m.* 1921, William Carrington Stettinius, and has issue living. *Residence,*—

Granddaughter of the late Hon. Arthur Charles Augustus Petre 4th son of 11th Baron:—

Issue of the late Lawrence Joseph Petre, *b.* 1864, *d.* 1944: *m.* 1890, Jennie, who *d.* 1945, dau. of A. Williams, of Cincinnati, Ohio, U.S.A.:—
Mildred Mary, *b.* 1895; a F.R.G.S., and a Racing Motorist; holder of several World's Records; has Orders of Million Elephants and White Umbrella of Indo-China: *m.* 1926 (marriage dissolved 1941), the Hon. Victor Austin Bruce [see B. Aberdare]. *Residences,*—Priory Steps, Bradford-on-Avon, Wilts ; 18, Cumberland Terrace, Regents Park, N.W.1.

Grandchildren of the late Francis Loraine Petre, OBE (infra):—

Issue of the late Maj.-Gen. Roderic Loraine Petre, CB, DSO, MC, late Dorset Regt., *b.* 1887, *d.* 1971: *m.* 1972, Katharine Sophia, who *d.* 1973, da. of Herbert W. Bryans, of The Priory, Bradford-on-Avon, Wilts.
Francis Herbert Loraine (Colneford House, Earls Colne, Colchester, Essex), *b.* 1927; ed. at Downside and at Clare Coll., Camb. (BA); Bar. Lincoln's Inn 1952; Dep. Chm. E. Suffolk Quarter Sessions 1970; a Circuit Judge since 1972: *m.* 1958, Mary Jane, da. of Everard C. X. White, of Netherhale, Matahiwi, Masterton, NZ, and has issue living, Jonathan Charles Loraine, *b.* 1959,—William Francis, *b.* 1963,—Hugh Robert Edward, *b.* 1970, Harriett Mary, *b.* 1961.——Mary Colletta Rosamond, *b.* 1928: *m.* 1960, David Reginald Whatley, of the Down House, Lamberhurst, Kent and has issue living, Roderic Joseph *b.* 1962,—Francis Richard, *b.* 1966,—Alice Katharine Mary, *b.* 1964.

Granddaughter of the late Hon. Edmund George Petre, 5th son of 11th Baron:—

Issue of the late Francis Loraine Petre, O.B.E., *b.* 1852, *d.* 1925: *m.* 1887, Maud Ellen, who *d.* 1945, dau. of the late Rev. W. C. Rawlinson, R. of Chedburgh, Suffolk :—
Elaine Maud, *b.* 1894: *m.* 1921, Cdr. Reginald Dudley Rowe, DSC, RN (ret.), and has issue living, Barry Loraine Dudley, *DSC, RN, b.* 1922; is Lt.; 1939-45 War (DSC and Bar): *m.* 1948, Mary, da. of Robert E. Lynch, of Washington, DC, USA, and has issue living, Annette Lorraine *b.* 1949. *Address,*—c/o Westminster Bank, 1, Stratford Place, W1.

Grandchildren of the late Sir George Glynn Petre, K.C.M.G., C.B., son of the late Henry William Petre, son of 2nd son of 9th Baron :—

Issue of the late Alfred William Ralph Petre, *b.* 1866, *d.* 1959 : *m.* 1892, Gertrude Briggs, who *d.* 1938 :—
Charles, *b.* 1895.——Alfred Ralph, *b.* 1896.——Florence Gertrude (*Lady Crowder*), *b.* 1893 : *m.* 1918, Sir John (Frederick) Ellenborough Crowder, J.P., who *d.* 1961, and has issue living, Frederick Petre, *QC, MP* (Charlestown, St. Austell, Cornwall), *b.* 1919; ed. at Eton, and at Ch. Ch., Oxford; Bar. Inner Temple 1948, QC 1964; PPS to Attorney-Gen. 1954-62, Recorder of Gravesend 1960-67, since when of Colchester, and Chm., Herts. Quarter Sessions since 1963; 1939-45 War as Maj. Cold-stream Guards in N. Africa, Italy and Burma; MP for Ruislip and Northwood (C) since 1950: *m.* 1948, the Hon. Patricia Winifred Mary Stourton, da. of 25th Baron Mowbray, and has issue living, Richard John *b.* 1950; ed. at Eton: *m.* 1973, Belinda Jane, el. da. of Capt. Matthew Page-Wood [see Page-Wood, Bt.], John George *b.* 1954; ed. at Eton,—Ann Katherine Louisa, *b.* 19—: *m.* 1953, George William Smyth-Osbourne, MC, Maj. late RHA, of The Grange, Puddington, Devon,—Rosemary Dorothy Marion (*Hon. Mrs. Ronald J. Eden*), *b.* 1928: *m.* 1957, the Hon. Ronald John Eden, of Cromlix, Dunblane, Perthshire. [see B. Auckland]. *Residence,*—Charlestown, St. Austell, Cornwall.

Issue of the late Capt. Charles Bernard Petre, formerly King's Roy. Rifle Corps, *b.* 1870 *d.* 1949 : *m.* (Feb.) 1903, Muriel Rosalind, who *d.* 1961, dau. of the late W. D. Anderson :—
Robert Charles, *b.* 1912; ed. at Harrow; Maj. (ret.) Scots Guards; 1939-45 War in Norway and Italy, *m.* 1934, Mary Delphine, el. da. of the late Maj. Claude Chichester, of Tunworth Down, Basingstoke. and has issue living, Charles Henry (Tunworth Down House, Basingstoke, Hants.; White's Club), *b.* 1936: *m.* 1963, Melanie Beatrix, da. of Henry Peregrine Hoare [see E. Cadogan], and has issue living, Robert Henry *b.* 1968, Fenella Delphine *b.* 1967,—Robert Bernard (54, Westcroft Sq., W6), *b.* 1938: *m.* 1970, Caroline, da. of Lt.-Col. Peter Jackson, of Wappenham, Towcester, and has issue living, Georgina Sarah *b.* 1974,—Claudia Mary Delphine, *b.* 1943: *m.* 1971, Ambrose Patrick Eustace Scott-Moncrieff. *Residences,*—26, Holland Villas Rd., W14; Henfield, Dunkenhaigh, Clayton le Moors, Lancs. *Clubs,*—Guards, White's.——Elsie Glynn, *b.* 1905: *m.* 1st, 1926, Capt. Alwyne Malcolm Fawcett, MC, RA, who *d.* 1933; 2ndly, 1944, Francis George Hurt, who *d.* 1952; 3rdly, 1955 (m. diss. 1959), Lt.-Col. Michael Wallington, MC; 4thly, 1959, Alex James Nelms, and has issue living, (by 1st m.) Daphne *b.* 1927: *m.* 1958, Arthur James Champion, who *d.* 1968, and has issue living, Angela Kate *b.* 1968,—Susan, *b.* 1929: *m.* 1968, Basil John Fawcett-Gandy, of Melin Llan House, Penllergaer, Swansea,—(by 2nd m.) Elizabeth Glynn, *b.* 1945: *m.* 1970, Rupert Charles Wyndham (Bath Club), and has issue living, Katharine Helena *b.* 1971, Nicola Glynn *b.* 1974. *Residence,*—Northfield House, Odiham, Hants.——Christine Marjorie, *b.* 1910: *m.* 1st, 1931 (m. diss. 1943), Jerrard Ross Williamson; 2ndly, 1943, Carson Alan Edward Kossatz, and has issue living, (by 1st m.) Charles Antony (28, Burgh St., N1), *b.* 1933; Lt.-Cdr. RNR: *m.* 1967, Phillippa Marie-Theresa, da. of Lt.-Col. M. R. Braithwaite, and has issue living, Robert Jerrard *b.* 1969, Lucy Charlotte *b.* 1968,—Timothy Jerrard *b.* 1937: *m.* 1970, Christina, da. of Sir Robert Mark, QPM, Commr. of Metropolitan Police, and has issue living, Marcus *b.* 1974, Rachell *b.* 1971,—Theresa June, *b.* 1935: *m.* 1961, John Chester, of 85, Warwick Rd., Bishop's Stortford, Herts., and has issue living, Anthony James *b.* 1965,—(by 2nd m.) Robin Martin Anthony, *b.* 1949. *Residence,*—The Coachman's Cottage, Odiham, Hants.

Issue of the late Rear-Adm. Walter Reginald Glynn Petre, D.S.O., *b.* 1873, *d.* 1942: *m.* (Jan.) 1906, Agnes Marie, who *d.* 1963, yst. dau. of Capt. Eugene Cadic, of Rennes, France:—
Walter George Glynn (L'Enclos, Rue Lucas, Sark, Channel Isles), *b.* (Oct.) 1906; ed. at Oratory Sch.; Sqdn.-Ldr. RAF: *m.* 1939, Myra Millicent, only da. of the late Arthur Willows, of Rushton Manor, near Kettering, and has issue living, Michael Bernard, *b.* 1946,—Geraldine Marie, *b.* 1944: *m.* 1967, David Robin Petre-Mears, of 23, The Glebe, Hawley, Camberley, Surrey, and has issue living, Edward Petre *b.* 1968, Justine *b.* 1972,—Anne Rosalie, *b.* 1949.——Henry Edward, *b.* 1907: ed. at Oratory Sch.; is Lt.-Cdr. RNR: *m.* 1939,—Rosemary Sonia, da. of the late Benjamin Gottschalk, of 26, Ulster Place, NW1, and has issue living, Cecilia Marie, *b.* 1940: *m.* 1964, Douglas Milton Wiggins, MBE, of Sydenham House, Adderbury, Oxon, and has issue living, Nicholas James Petre *b.* 1974, Emma Jane *b.* 1966, Katherine Blanche *b.* 1968, Henrietta Clare, *b.* 1969,—Teresa Jane Glynn, *b.* 1944,—Sonia Rosemary, *b.* 1946: *m.* 1966, Dr. Robert Hancock, of 8, Daisy Lane, Horling-

ham, SW6, and has issue living, Benjamin Charles Petre b.1971,Toby Charles Petre b. 1974. *Residence,—* Underwood House, Binfield, Berks.——Edward Joseph Algernon (Down Farm, Tunworth, nr. Basingstoke), b. 1911; ed. at Nautical Coll., Pangbourne; late Capt. Black Watch and Essex Regt.; 1939-45 War (wounded): m. 1st, 1938, Diana Perry, of Weybridge; 2ndly, 1948 (m. diss. 1968) Helen Beresford, da. of Richard Cornelius, and formerly wife of Capt. Kenyon Goode.——Mary Katherine Gabrielle, b. 1909.——Marie Madeleine Ethel, b. 1913: m. 1944, Maj.-Gen. Desmond Alexander Bruce Clarke, CB, CBE, late RA of Vine Ridge, Hannington, Basingstoke, Hants., and has issue living, Desmond Walter Robert, b. 1945; Capt. RA: m. 1970, Fiona, da. of John Harrison, of The Barn Cottage, Wilmington, Sussex, and has issue living, Duncan Robert Petre b. 1971, Philippa Kate b. 1975,—Dominic Michael Bernard, b. 1949,—Damian Anthony John, b. 1958,—Antoinette Marie Edwina, b. 1947,—Amice Mary Bernadette, b. 1950: m. 1972, David Heath Thompson, of Northside, Aylsham, Norfolk, and has issue living, Joseph Andrew b. 1975.——Monica, b. 1919.

Grandson of the late Rear-Adm. Walter Reginald Glynn Petre, D.S.O. (ante):—

Issue of the late Major Gerard Malcolm Mary Laurence Petre, Essex Regt., b. 1916; d. (killed in action in France) 1944: m. r941, Pamela Marian (who m. 2ndly, 1946, Major Desmond John H. Bannister, M.C., Devonshire Regt.), dau. of Capt. G. B. Pratt, R.A. (retired):—

Andrew Charles Malcolm Glynn, b. 1944   ed. at Downside.

Grandchildren of the late Edward Henry Petre, 3rd son of the late Henry William Petre (ante):—

Issue of the late Lieut.-Col. Oswald Henry Philip TURVILLE-PETRE, b. 1862, d. 1941 (having assumed for himself and issue by Roy. licence 1907, the additional surname and arms of Turville): m. 1899, Margaret, who d. 1954, dau. of the late Laurence Trent Cave, of Ditcham Park, Petersfield, and 13, Lowndes Square, S.W.:—

Edward Oswald Gabriel, b. 1908; ed. at Ch. Ch., Oxford (B.Litt. and MA, Student 1964); Reader in Ancient Icelandic Literature 1941-53, since when Professor; is a Cdr. of Order of the Falcon of Iceland: m. 1943, Joan Elizabeth, dau. of S. Blomfield, of Colchester, and has issue living, Thorlac Francis Samuel (c/o Department of English University of Nottingham), b. 1944; ed. at Magdalen Coll. Sch., Oxford, and Jesus Coll., Oxford (MA, B.Litt.): m. 1967, Ingrid Elizabeth, da. of Rudolf Zimmerlund, of Stockholm, and has issue living, Francis Gustaf b. 1971, Crispin Gabriel, b. 1974,—Merlin Oswald, b. 1946: m. 1973, Christine Margaret, da. of Ivor Lee-Smith, of Newbury, Berks.,—Brendan Arthur Auberon, b. 1948.   *Residence,*—The Court, Old Headington, Oxford.—— Gwendeline Etheldreda, b. 1902: m. 1938, Lt.-Col. Roland Greenwood, late Highland LI, who d. 1949. *Residence,*—The Old Parsonage, Ropley, Hants.——Mary Alethea Elizabeth Evelyn, b. 1904: m. 1940, Major David Turville-Constable-Maxwell, TD, Anti-Aircraft Regt., RA [see L. Herries, colls.]. *Residence,*—Bosworth Hall, Husband's Bosworth, near Rugby.——Marion Margaret Josephine, b. 1906: m. 1934, Daniel Adrian Francis Cave [see M. Lothian, colls.].   *Residences,*— Sherwood, Newton St. Cyres, Devon; Beacon House, Inkpen, Newbury.

Grandsons of Bertram Edward Petre, yr. son of Edward Henry Petre (ante):—

Issue of the late Major Myles Seymour Edward Petre, Duke of Cornwall's L.I., b. 1913, d. (killed in action) 1942: m. 1938, Audrey Catherine (Annesley Park, Nottingham), da. of Col. John Nevile Chaworth-Musters, DSO, OBE, TD, of Annesley Park, Nottingham:—

Martin Anthony Chaworth (38, Edith Grove, SW10), b. 1940; ed. at Ampleforth: m. 1968, Selina Frances Gladstone, da. of Brig. Philip William Gladstone Pope, DSO, MC, of Cross House, Henstridge, Som., and has issue living, Edward Myles Chaworth, b. 1971,—Henrietta Claire Gladstone, b. 1969,—Mary Hartshorne, b. 1973.——Robin David Oswald (Flaxbourne, Blenheim, NZ), b. 1942; ed. at Ampleforth, and RMAS; Maj. (ret.) 17th/21st Lancers: m. 1968, Cecily Constance, el. da. of Simon Scrope, of Flaxbourne House, Gt. Ouseburn, Yorks., and has issue living, Diana Audrey Constance, b. 1969,—Nicola Mary Catherine, b. 1971.

Grandchildren of the late Louis William Henry Petre, son of Philip William Petre younger son of the late Hon. George William Petre, 2nd son of 9th Baron:—

Issue of the late Edward Philip William Petre, b. 1869, d. 1923 : m. 1890, Zoila Rosa del Carmen Larenas, who d. 1953:—

Luis Enrique, b. 1898; is a Bank Director: m. 19—, Else Newman Etienne, and has issue living, Agnes Petre Newman, b. 1924: m. 1945 (marriage dissolved 1952), Fernando Zilleruedo Vargas, Lieut. Chilean Air Force, and has issue living, Fernando b. 1951, Marie-Agnes b. 1946, Marie-Luz b 1948.——Anna Lucie, b. 1894: m. 1923, Col. Aquiles Vergara Vicuña, Bolivian Army.   *Residence,*— Casilla 956, La Paz, Bolivia.

PREDECESSORS.—[1] *Sir* JOHN Petre, Knt., only son of Sir William Petre, a Sec. of State to Henry VIII and Edward VI; MP for Essex 1584-87; cr. *Baron Petre*, of Writtle, co. Essex (peerage of England) 1603; d. 1613; s. by his son [2] WILLIAM, 2nd Baron; MP for Essex 1597-1601; d. 1637; s. by his son [3] ROBERT, 3rd Baron; d. 1638; s. by his el. son [4] WILLIAM, 4th Baron; d. a prisoner in the Tower 1683; s. by his brother [5] JOHN, 5th Baron; d. unmarried; s. by his brother [6] THOMAS, 6th Baron; Lord-Lt. of Essex; d. 1707; s. by his son [7] ROBERT, 7th Baron; d. 1713, s. by his son [8] ROBERT JAMES, 8th Baron; d. 1742; s. by his son [9] ROBERT EDWARD 9th Baron: m. Anne Howard, niece of Edward, 9th Duke of Norfolk, and who became at his death a co-heir to the Baronies of Howard, Furnivall, Strange of Blackmere, Talbot, Braose of Gower, Dacre of Gillesland, Greystock, Ferrers of Wemme, Gifford of Brimsfield and Verdon; d. 1801; s. by his son [10] ROBERT EDWARD, 10th Baron; d. 1809; s. by his son [11] WILLIAM HENRY FRANCIS, 11th Baron; d. 1850; s. by his el. son [12] WILLIAM BERNARD, 12th Baron; b. 1817: m. 1843, Mary Teresa, el. da. of the Hon. Charles Thomas Clifford; d. July 4th, 1884; s. by his el. son [13] *Right Rev.* WILLIAM JOSEPH, 13th Baron, b. 1847; Domestic Prelate at the Court of the Vatican; d. 1893; s. by his brother [14] BERNARD HENRY PHILP, 14th Baron, b. 1858: m. 1899 (Etheldreda Mary) Audrey, who d. 1959, da. of the Rev. William Robinson Clark, MA, DD, LLD, DCL, FRS (Canada), formerly V. of Taunton, Preb. of Wells, and Professor of Philosophy in Trin. Coll., Toronto; d. 1908; s. by his brother [15] PHILIP BENEDICT JOSEPH, 15th Baron; b. 1864: m. 1888, Julia Mary, who d. 1931, el. da. of the late George Cavendish Taylor, of 42, Elvaston Place, SW; d. 1908; s. by his son [16] LIONEL GEORGE CARROLL, 16th Baron; b. 1890; Capt. Coldstream Guards: m. 1913, Catherine Margaret, da. of the Hon. John Boscawen; d. (wounds in action) 1915; s. by his only son [17] JOSEPH WILLIAM LIONEL, 17th Baron, and present peer.

PHILLIMORE, BARON. (Phillimore.) [Baron U.K. 1918, Bt. U.K. 1881.]

Pray for a brave soul.

ROBERT GODFREY PHILLIMORE, 3rd Baron, and 4th Baronet; *b.* Sept. 24th, 1939; *s.* 1947; ed. at Winchester; late 2nd Lt. 9th/12th Roy. Lancers.

Arms.—Sable, three bars indented erminois, in chief an anchor between two cinquefoils or. **Crest.**—In front of a tower argent, thereon a falcon volant proper holding in the beak a lure gold, three cinquefoils fessewise or. **Supporters,** —On either side an owl proper, each charged with an anchor or.

Seat,—Coppid Hall, Henley-on-Thames.

SISTER LIVING. (*Raised to the rank of a Baron's daughter* 1949.)
Hon. Frances Phœbe, *b.* 1938 : *m.* 1961, Colin John Francis Lindsay-MacDougall of Lunga, of Lunga, Ardfern, Lochgilphead, Argyll [see E. Crawford, colls.].

UNCLES LIVING. (*Sons of 2nd Baron.*)
Hon. CLAUD STEPHEN, *b.* Jan. 15th, 1911; ed. at Winchester, and at Trin. Coll., Camb. (B.A. 1933) ; is Capt. and Acting Major 11th (City of London Yeo.) Light Anti-Aircraft Brig. R.A. (T.A.): *m.* 1944, Anne Elizabeth, dau. of the late Major Arthur Algernon Dorrien-Smith, D.S.O., of Tresco Abbey, Isles of Scilly, and has issue living, Francis Stephen, *b.* 1944: *m.* 1971 Nathalie Pequin.—Marion Miranda, *b.* 1946: *m.* 1973, Thomas Walter Montagu-Douglas-Scott [see D. Buccleuch, colls.]. *Residences,*— 42, Lowndes St., SW1; Raymans Tower, Apuldram, Chichester.
Hon. Robert George Hugh, O.B.E., *b.* 1913; ed. at Winchester, and at Trin. Coll., Camb. (B.A. 1936); Col. R.E. (ret.); a J.P. for Oxon.; European War 1939-45 in Middle East (despatches, M.B.E., O.B.E., Bronze star, Croix de Guerre); M.B.E. (Mil.) 1941, O.B.E. (Mil.) 1945: *m.* 1944, Sheila Bruce, dau. of John Farquhar MacLeod, J.P., M.B., Ch.B., of Peterculter, Aberdeenshire, and has issue living, Annabel Margaret, *b.* 1947,—Lindsay Mary MacLeod, *b.* 1951,—Sheila Leigh, *b.* 1952,— Elizabeth Anne Haig, *b.* 1955. *Residence,*—The Mill House, Shiplake, Oxon.

AUNT LIVING. (*Daughter of 2nd Baron.*)
Hon. Phœbe Margaret Dorothy (*Hon. Lady Rose*), *b.* 1912: *m.* 1937, Sir Charles Henry Rose, 3rd Bt. (cr. 1909), who *d.* 1966. *Residence,*—Hardwick Hall, Whitchurch, Oxon.

MOTHER LIVING.
Anne Julia, dau. of Maj.-Gen. Sir Cecil Edward Pereira, K.C.B., C.M.G.: *m.* 1934, Capt. the Hon. Anthony Francis Phillimore, who *d.* (killed in action during European War) 1940. *Residence,*—Coppid Hall, Henley-on-Thames.

WIDOW LIVING OF SON OF SECOND BARON.
Margaret (264, Glenwood Rd., Wheeling, W. Virginia, USA), da. of the late Gibson Lamb Caldwell, of Kenwood Place, Wheeling, W. Virginia: *m.* 1946, the Hon. Miles Godfrey Walter Phillimore, who *d.* 1972, and has issue [see colls. infra].

COLLATERAL BRANCH LIVING.
Issue of the late Hon. Miles Godfrey Walter Phillimore, yst. son of 2nd Baron, *b.* 1915, *d.* 1972: *m.* 1946, Margaret (ante), da. of the late Gibson Lamb Caldwell, of Kenwood Place, Wheeling, W. Virginia:—
Dorothy Eleanor Barbara, *b.* 1940: *m.* 1973, Rubert William Drumm.

PREDECESSORS.—[1] Rt. Hon. *Sir* ROBERT JOSEPH Phillimore, D.C.L.; *b.* 1810; cr. a *Baronet* 1881; M.P. for Tavistock (*LC*) 1855-7, and Judge of the High Court of Admiralty 1867-83, and of Court of Arches 1867-75: *m.* 1844, Charlotte Anne, who *d.* 1892, dau. of the late John Denison, M.P., of Ossington, Newark, and sister of 1st Viscount Ossington ; *d.* 1885 ; *s.* by his el. son [2] Rt. Hon. WALTER GEORGE FRANK, *G.B.E., D.C.L., LL.D.,* 2nd Bt. ; *b.* 1845; was a Judge of the High Court of Justice 1897-1913, and a Lord Justice of Appeal 1913-16; Pres. English Church Union 1919-20 ; Chm. of Naval Prize Tribunal 1918-28 ; cr. *Baron Phillimore* of Shiplake, Oxfordshire (peerage of United Kingdom) 1918 : *m.* 1870, Agnes, who *d.* 1929, el. dau. of the late Charles Manners Lushington, M.P. for Canterbury [E. Iddesleigh] ; *d.* 1929 ; *s.* by his son [3] GODFREY WALTER, *M.C.*, 2nd Baron; *b.* 1879; Capt. late Highland L.I. ; European War 1914-16 (M.C.): *m.* 1st, 1905, Dorothy Barbara, who *d.* 1915, el. dau. of Lieut.-Col. Arthur Balfour Haig, C.V.O., C.M.G. ; 2ndly, 1923, Marion (BRYCE), who *d.* 1950, dau. of the late Maj.-Gen. Cecil Robert St. John Ives ; *d.* 1947; *s.* by his grandson [4] ROBERT GODFREY (son of the late Capt. the Hon. Anthony Francis Phillimore (el. son of 2nd Baron), who *d.* (killed in action during European War) 1940), 3rd Baron and present peer.

PHILLIPS, BARONESS. (Phillips.) [Life Baroness 1964.]

NORAH PHILLIPS, only da. of William Lusher, of Fulham, SW; *b.* 1910; ed. at Marist Convent, and at Hampton Coll.; a J.P. co. of London; Gen.-Sec. of National Assocn. of Women's Clubs since 1958; a Baroness in Waiting (Govt. Whip) 1965-70; *cr. Baroness Phillips,* of Fulham, co. London (Life Baroness) 1964: *m.* 1930, Morgan Walter Phillips, who *d.* 1963, and has issue.

Address,—115, Rannoch Rd., W6.

SON LIVING.
Hon. Morgan David, *b.* 1939; ed. at St. Paul's Sch., and at Downing Coll., Camb. (BA); PGCE, Univ. of London.

DAUGHTER LIVING.
Hon. Gwyneth Patricia, *MP* (113, Cromwell Tower, EC2), *b.* 1930; ed. at Fulham Co. Secondary Sch., and Convent of Nôtre Dame, Battersea; MP for Exeter (*Lab.*) 1966-70, and for Crewe since 1974: Parl. Sec. to Board of Trade 1967-70; a Dir. of Film Production Assocn. of Gt. Britain: *m.* 1954, John Elliott Orr Dunwoody, MB, BS, who *d.* 1975, and has issue.

PIERCY, BARON. (Piercy.) [Baron U.K. 1945.]

NICHOLAS PELHAM PIERCY, 2nd Baron; *b.*
June 23rd, 1918 ; *s.* 1966; ed. at Eton, and
at King's Coll., Camb. (MA); 1939-45 War as
Lt. (A) RNVR: *m.* 1944, Oonagh Lavinia, JP,
da. of the late Maj. Edward John Lake Baylay,
DSO, and has issue.

Arms,—Per fesse indented gules and argent in chief
three pierced mullets of the last and in base a lion rampant
guardant sable. Crest,—Issuant from a bezant in front of
two spears in saltire points upwards proper a demi lion
guardant sable charged on the shoulder with a pierced mullet
argent. Supporters,—Not recorded at time of going to press.

Residence,—The Old Rectory, Elford, Tamworth, Staffs.

SONS LIVING.
Hon. JAMES WILLIAM, *b.* Jan. 19th, 1946; ed. at Shrews-
bury, and Edinburgh Univ. (BSc).
Hon. Mark Edward Pelham, *b.* 1953; ed. at Shrewsbury, and
New Coll., Oxford.

DAUGHTERS LIVING.
Hon. Charlotte Mary, *b.* 1947; ed. at Badminton Sch.:
m. 1966, Paolo Emilio Taddei, of 70, Via Lorenzo il Mag-
nifico, Florence, and has issue living, Guido, *b.* 1970,—
Caroline Rachel, *b.* 1967.
Hon. Lavinia Caroline (twin), *b.* 1947; ed. at Badminton
Sch., and St. Hugh's Coll., Oxford (MA): *m.* 1971, Nicholas
John Elliot Sealy, Rifle Bde., of Timber Hill, Chobham,
Surrey [see E. Chichester, colls.].
Hon. Henrietta Jane, *b.* 1951; ed. at Badminton Sch., and
St. Andrew's Univ.

SISTERS LIVING.
Hon. Penelope Katharine, *CBE* (Mawarden Court, Stratford-sub-Castle, Salisbury), *b.* 1916; ed. at
St. Paul's, and at Somerville Coll., Oxford; CBE (Civil) 1968.
Hon. Joanna Elizabeth (The Old Rectory, Wem, Salop.), *b.* 1923; ed. at St. Paul's, and at Somerville
Coll., Oxford; a JP, Inner London Juvenile Courts Panel: *m.* 1968, James Francis Turner.
Hon. Priscilla Jane, *b.* 1926 , ed. at Downe House, and at London Sch. of Economics: *m.* 1950, the
Rev. Thomas Fish Taylor, and has issue living, Francis Nicholas, *b.* 1954,—Ann Clemency, *b.* 1952,—
Helen Mary, *b.* 1957,—Bridget Jane, *b.* 1961. *Residence,*—The Old Rectory, Fifehead, Magdalen
Gillingham, Dorset.

WIDOW LIVING OF FIRST BARON.
VERONICA (*Veronica, Baroness Piercy*), (7, Milborne Grove, SW10), da. of the late John Hordley
Warham: *m.* 1964, as his 2nd wife, the 1st Baron, who *d.* 1966.

PREDECESSOR.—[1] WILLIAM Piercy, *CBE*, son of the late' Augustus) Edward Piercy; *b.* 1886;
Economist and Financier; Chm of Industrial & Commercial Finance Corporation Ltd. 1945-64,
a Dir. of Bank of England 1946-56, and Chm. Wellcome Trust 1960-65; *cr. Baron Piercy*, of Burford
co. Oxford (peerage of U.K.) 1945: *m.* 1st, 1915, Mary Louisa, *OBE*, who *d.* 1953, da. of the'
late Hon. Thomas Henry William Pelham, *OB* [E. Chichester, colls.]; 2ndly, 1964, Veronica, da.
of John Hordley Warham; *d.* 1966; *s.* by his son [2] NICHOLAS PELHAM, 2nd Baron and
present peer.

PIKE, BARONESS. (Pike.) [Life Baroness 1974.]

MERVYN PIKE, da. of Ivan Samuel Pike, of Okehampton, Devonshire;
b. Sept. 16th, 1918; ed. at Hunmanby Hall, E. Yorks., and Reading Univ.
(BA); 1939-45 War with WAAF; MP for Melton Div. of Leics. (*C*) 1956-74;
Assist. Postmaster-Gen. 1959-63, and Joint Parl. Under-Sec. of State, Home
Office 1963-64; a co. Councillor, W. Riding of Yorks. since 1955, and a Dir. of
Watts, Blake and Bearne since 1964; *cr. Baroness Pike*, of Melton, co. Leices-
tershire (Life Baroness) 1974.

Residences,—West Eaton House, West Eaton Place, SW1; Cold Overton, Oakham, Rutland.

PILKINGTON, BARON. (Pilkington.) [Life Baron 1968.]

WILLAM HENRY PILKINGTON, son of the
late Richard Austin Pilkington, of St.
Helens, Lancs. [B. Cozens-Hardy]; *b.* April
19th, 1905; ed. at Rugby, and Magdalene
Coll., Camb. (MA); Hon. LLD Manchester
and Liverpool; Hon. DSc. Loughborough;
Hon. DCL Kent; a Glass Manufacturer,
Chm. of Pilkington Brothers Ltd. 1949-73;
a JP for St. Helens, Lancs., Vice Lord-Lieut.
for co. Merseyside, and a Freeman of St.
Helens; Chancellor of Loughborough Univ.
since 1966; *cr.* Knt. 1953, and *Baron Pilking-
ton*, of St. Helens, co. Palatine of Lancaster
(Life Baron) 1968: *m.* 1st, 1930, Rosamond
Margaret, who *d.* 1953, da. of Col. Henry
Davis Rowan, late RAMC, of Rathmore,
Greystones, co. Wicklow; 2ndly, 1961,
Mrs. Mavis Joy Doreen Wilding, da. of
Gilbert Caffrey, of Woodleigh, Lostock
Park, Bolton, and has issue by 1st m.

Arms,—Argent a cross flory gules, voided of the field between five roses in saltire of the second barbed and seeded proper. **Crest,**—Upon a mount and between two tufts of grass vert, a mower habited per pale argent and gules, holding a scythe proper. **Supporters,**—On either side a representation of a mediaeval glass blower habited in a cap and smock of bleached cotton proper the stockings striped red and white holding in the exterior hand a blowing iron erect with a cylinder of broad glass at the lower end proper.

SON LIVING.

Rev. the Hon. John Rowan (Newhaven Rectory, Newhaven, Sussex), *b.* 1932; ed. at Rugby, and Magdalene Coll., Camb. (MA); R. of Newhaven since 1965: *m.* 1964, Celia Collison, and has issue.

DAUGHTER LIVING.

Hon. Jennifer Margaret, *b.* 1933: *m.* 1958, Dennis Jones, of Swallow Cottage, Burbage, Leics. and has issue.

PITT OF HAMPSTEAD, BARON. (Pitt.) [Life Baron 1975.]

DAVID THOMAS PITT, *MB, ChB,* son of Cyril S. L. Pitt, of St. David's, Grenada, WI; *b.* Oct. 3rd, 1913; ed. at St. David's R.C. Sch., Grenada, Grenada Boys' Secondary Sch., and Edinburgh Univ. (MB, ChB), First Jr. Pres. Student Rep. Council Edinburgh Univ. 1936-37; DCH London; JP of Greater London; Dist. Med. Officer, St. Vincent, WI 1938-39, House Phys. San Fernando Hosp., Trinidad 1939-41, Gen. Practitioner San Fernando 1941-47, and London since 1947; Dep. Mayor San Fernando 1946-47; Pres. W. Indian Nat. Party (Trinidad) 1943-47; a Member of London Co. Council 1961-65, and of GLC since 1964 (Dep. Chm. 1969-70, Chm. 1974-75); a Member of Nat. Cttee. for Commonwealth Immigrants 1965-67, and Chm. of Campaign Against Racial Discrimination 1965; a Dep. Chm. of Community Relations Commn. since 1968; cr. *Baron Pitt of Hampstead,* of Hampstead, Greater London, and Hampstead Grenada (Life Baron) 1975: *m.* 1943, Dorothy Elaine, da. of Aubrey Alleyne, and has issue.

Arms,— Not exemplified at time of going to press.

Residence,—6, Heath Drive, NW3. *Clubs,*—Royal Commonwealth Society (W. Indian), MCC.

SON LIVING.

Hon. Bruce Michael David, *b.* 19—.

DAUGHTERS LIVING.

Hon. Phyllis Leonora, *b.* 19—.
Hon. Amanda, *b.* 19—'

PLATT, BARON. (Platt.) [Life Baron 1967, Bt. U.K. 1959.]

ROBERT PLATT, *MSc, MD, FRCP, Life Baron* and 1st Baronet, son of William Platt, schoolmaster, of London and Grindleford, Derbys.; *b.* April 16th, 1900; ed. at Grindleford, and Sheffield Univ. (ChB, MD); MRCP London, FRCP; Hon. MSc Manchester; Hon. LLD Sheffield, Belfast and Manchester; Hon. MD Bristol; Hon. Member of Assocn. of American Physicians; Hon. FACP; FRACP; Hon. Fellow of Roy. Coll. of Gen. Practitioners; Hon. FRC Psych.; Hon. FRSM; Membre d'honneur de la Société de Pathologie Rénale; Physician Roy. Infirmary, Sheffield 1831–46, and Roy. Infirmary Manchester 1946-65, Editor, *Quarterley Journal of Medicine* 1948-55, Pres. of Roy. Coll. of Physicians, London 1957-62, and Chm. of Clinical Research Board, Med. Research Council 1964-67; 1939-45 War as Brig. RAMC; *cr.* a *Baronet* 1959, and *Baron Platt,* of Grindleford, co. Derby (Life Baron) 1967: *m.* 1st, 1922 (m. diss. 1974), Margaret Irene, MB, DPH, da. of Arthur Charles Cannon, schoolmaster, of Sheffield; 2ndly, 1974, Sylvia Jean, ARCM, da. of the late Sydney Charles Caveley, and formerly wife of John Alfred Haggard, and has issue by 1st m.

Arms,—Or fretty sable platée on a pale gules a rod of aesculapius gold. **Crest,**—In front of a demi plate a nightingale in full song proper. **Supporters,**—*Dexter,* a unicorn, and *Sinister,* a hart argent, each gorged with a chain or, pendant therefrom a bezant fimbriated sable.

Residence,—53, Heathside, Hinchley Wood, Esher, Surrey.

SON LIVING. (*By 1st m.*)

Hon. PETER (1, Ellison Place, Pymble, NSW 2073), *b.* July 6th, 1924; *h.a.* to Baronetcy; Prof. of Music, Sydney Univ., Aust.; 1939-45 War with RNVR (despatches): *m.* 1948, Jean Halliday, da. of Dr. Charles Philip Brentnall, and has issue living, Martin Philip (c/o Computer Sers. Univ. of Papua and New Guinea), *b.* 1952: *m.* 1971, Frances Corinne Moana, da. of Trevor Samuel Conley, and has issue living, Philip Stephen *b.* 1972, Suzanne *b.* 1971,—Margaret, *b.* 1949: *m.* 1969, Anthony Pratt Kaye,—Katherine, *b.* 1956.

DAUGHTERS LIVING. (*By 1st m.*)

Hon. Joan Elizabeth, *b.* 1927: *m.* 1952, John Bunting Allen, of Maxstoke House, Highfield Rd., Torkington, Hazel Grove, Cheshire, and has issue living, Jonathan Robert, *b.* 1953,—Paul Bunting, *b.* 1956,—Mark Benedict, *b.* 1965.
Hon. Helen Margaret, *b.* 1933: *m.* 1954, Cecil Henry Stowasser, of 1, Bird St., Herston, Queensland, Australia, and has issue living, Peter, *b.* 1955,—Robert, *b.* 1956,—Michael, *b.* 1960.

PLOWDEN, BARON. (Plowden.) [Life Baron 1959.]

EDWIN NOEL PLOWDEN, *K.C.B.*, *K.B.E.*, son of the late Roger H. Plowden, of Strachur Park, Argyll ; *b.* Jan. 6th, 1907 ; ed. in Switzerland, and at Pembroke Coll., Camb. (Hon. Fellow); Hon. DSc. Pennsylvania State Univ., and Aston Univ.; Visiting Fellow of Nuffield Coll., Oxford 1956-64; in Min. of Economic Warfare 1939-40, in Min. of Aircraft Production 1940-46 (Ch. Executive and a Member of Aircraft Supply Council 1945-46); Ch. Planning Officer and Chm. of Economic Planning Board 1947-53, Vice-Chm. Temporary Council Cttee. of N.A.T.O. 1951-52, Adviser on Atomic Energy Organisation 1953-54, and Chm. UK Atomic Energy Authority 1954-59, of Cttee. on Control of Public Expenditure 1959-61, of Cttee. of Enquiry into Organisation of Representational Sers. Overseas 1962-63, of Cttee. of Enquiry into future of UK Aircraft Industry 1964-65, and of Cttee. of Enquiry into Structure of Electricity Supply Industry 1974, Chm. of Gov. Body of Council, London Graduate Sch. of Business Studies, and of Tube Investments, Ltd.. and a Dir. of Commercial Union Assurance Co., Ltd., and of National Westminster Bank, Ltd.; cr. KBE (Civil) 1946, KCB (Civil) 1951, and *Baron Plowden,* of Plowden, co. Salop (Life Baron) 1959: *m.* 1933, Dame Bridget Horatia, DBE, JP, da. of the late Adm. Sir Herbert William Richmond, KCB [Bell, Bt., cr. 1885], and has issue.

Arms,—Azure a fesse dancettee, the upper points terminating in fleurs-de-lys or. Crest,—A buck passant sable, attired or.

Residences,—Martels Manor, Dunmow, Essex ; 7, Cottesmore Gardens, W.8. *Club,*—Brooks's.

SONS LIVING.

Hon. William Julius Lowthian (c/o Midland Bank, 69, Pall Mall, SW1), *b.* 1935; ed. at Eton, at King's Coll., Camb., and at California Univ.: *m.* 1960, Veronica Mary, only da. of Lieut.-Col. Derek Ernest Frederick Orby Gascoigne [see B. O'Neill], and has issue living, Benedict Edmund, *b.* 1963,—Luke Piers, *b.* 1967,—Frances Helen, *b.* 1965,—Eleanor Mary, *b.* 1969.
Hon. Francis John, *b.* 1945; ed. at Eton, and at Trin. Coll., Camb.

DAUGHTERS LIVING.

Hon. Anna Bridget, *b.* 1938; ed. at Newhall, Chelmsford, and at Institute of Archæology, London Univ.
Hon. Penelope Christina, *b.* 1941; ed. at St. Mary's Convent, Ascot, and at New Hall, Camb.: *m.* 1965, Christopher Roper, of 43, Lansdowne Gdns., SW8.

PLUMER, VISCOUNTCY OF. (Plumer.) [Extinct 1944.]

DAUGHTERS LIVING OF SECOND VISCOUNT.

Hon. Anne Cynthia Veronica Tempest, *b.* 1921: *m.* 1952, John Frederick Martyn Leapman, and has issue living, Joanna Mary Martyn, *b.* 1953,—Emma Hilda Martyn, *b.* 1956. *Residence,*—67, Addison Road, W.14.
Hon. Rosemary Diana Lavinia, *b.* 1929: *m.* 1949, Frederick Henry Lowry-Corry [see E. Belmore, colls.]. *Residence,*—15, Smith Street, Chelsea, S.W.3.

PLUNKET, BARON. (Plunket.) [Baron U.K. 1827]

FESTINA·LENTE
Quick, without impetuosity.

ROBIN RATHMORE PLUNKET, 8th Baron, *b.* Dec. 3rd, 1925; *s.* 1975; ed. at Eton; late Capt. Rifle Bde.: *m.* 1951, Jennifer Bailey, da. of Bailey Southwell, of Crocodile Leap Farm, Olivenhoutpoort, S. Africa.

Arms,—Sable, a bend between in sinister chief a tower and in dexter base a portcullis, all or. Crest,—A horse passant argent, charged on the side with a portcullis sable. Supporters,—*Dexter,* an antelope or; *sinister,* a horse argent; each gorged with a collar, and pendent therefrom by a chain a portcullis sable.
Residence,—Rathmore, Melsetter, Rhodesia.

BROTHER LIVING.

Hon.] SHAUN ALBERT FREDERICK SHERIDAN (Hollonds, Langton Green, Tunbridge Wells. *Club,*—White's), *b.* April 5th, 1931; ed. at Eton and L'Institut de Touraine; formerly Lt. Irish Gds., and Dist. Comdt., Kenya Police (Reserve); a Member of Institute of Directors: *m.* 1961, Judith Ann, el. da. of the late Gerard Patrick Power, of Lapworth, Warwickshire, and has issue living, Tyrone Shaun Terence, *b.* 1966, —Loelia Dorothé Alexandra *b.* 1963.

AUNT LIVING. (*Daughter of 5th Baron.*)

Hon. Moira Violet Maria, *b.* 1897: *m.* 1st, 1923, Lieut.-Col. Herbert Frederick Edgar Smith, D.S.O. (H.M.'s Body Guard), late King's Roy. Rifle Corps, who *d.* (on active ser. during European War) 1940 ; 2ndly, 1944 (marriage dissolved 1952), Capt. Ian Reddie Hamilton Black, O.B.E., R.N., and has issue living, (by 1st marriage) Fiona Priscilla, *b.* 1923 : *m.* 1955, Gilbert Marcus McNeill-Moss [By. Cushendun], of 15, Wellington Sq., SW3, and has issue living, Nigel Geoffrey *b.* 1956, Desmond Rupert *b.* 1959. *Residence,*—Flat 4, Colette Court, 126, Sloane St., SW1.

WIDOW LIVING OF SON OF FIFTH BARON.

Pamela Mary, da. of the late James Watherston, of Christchurch, NZ: *m.* 1962, the Hon (Denis) Kiwa Plunket, who *d.* 1970.

COLLATERAL BRANCHES LIVING.

Issue of the late Flight-Lieut. the Hon. Brinsley Sheridan Bushe Plunket, R.A.F. Vol. Reserve, 2nd son of 5th Baron, *b.* 1903, *d.* (on active ser. during European War) 1941: *m.* 1927, Aileen Sibell Mary (Luttrellstown Castle, Clonsilla, co. Dublin), who obtained a divorce 1940 (she *m.* 2ndly, 1956, Valerian Stux-Rybar), dau. of the late Hon. Arthur Ernest Guinness [see E. Iveagh, colls.] :—

Neelia Clotilde, *b.* 1929 : *m.* 1st, 1950 (marriage dissolved 1956), Capt. Bazil Christopher de Las Casas, 8th King's Roy. Irish Hussars; 2ndly, 1956, Michael Francis Maclean; 3rdly, 1962, Stewart Macpherson Reynolds, late Maj. Welsh Guards, of Field House, Hawkhurst, Kent, and has issue living, (by 1st marriage) Michael Brinsley, *b.* 1951,—Kevin, *b.* 1952.——Doon Aileen (*Countess Granville*), 1931: *m.* 1958, the 5th Earl Granville. *Residences*—49, Lyall Mews, SW1; Callernish, N. Uist, Inverness-shire.

Grandchildren of the late David Pierce Conyngham Plunket, (infra):—
Issue of the late Simon Patrick Conyngham Plunket, Lt. 12th Lancers, *b.* 1932, *d.* 1968: *m.* 1955, Susan Diana PLUNKET (The Old Rectory, Tichborne, Alresford, Hants.) (who m. 2ndly, 1972, Martin John Faber Morrison), da. of the late R. V. Fairney, of Hartley End House, Hartley Wintney, Hants.:—
Piers Robert Conyngham, *b.* 1959.——Sarah Doon, *b.* 1957.

Grandson of the late Most Rev. the Hon. Benjamin John Plunket, DD, Bishop of Meath (infra):—
Issue of the late David Pierce Conyngham Plunket, *b.* 1908, *d.* 1956: *m.* 1930, Sybil Marjorie (Trillick, Whichford, Shipston-on-Stour, Warwicks.), yr. da. of the late Alfred German Archer, of Seaford, Sussex:—
David Archer Lee (The Corner House, Tur Langton, Leics.; Cavalry Club), *b.* 1936; ed. at St. Colomba's Coll., Dublin: *m.* 1964, Philippa Susan, yr. da. of the late Capt. Brian St. George Daly, Lancashire Fus., of Templeogue House, co. Dublin, and has issue living, Emma Elizabeth Lee, *b.* 1966,—Arabella Susan, *b.* 1969.

Issue of the late Most Rev. the Hon. Benjamin John Plunket, D.D., Bishop of Meath 1919-25, 2nd son of 4th Baron, *b.* 1870, *d.* 1947 : *m.* 1904, Dorothea Hester, who *d.* 1936, dau. of Sir Thomas Pierce Butler, 10th Bt. (cr. 1628):—
Benjamin William Alan, MVO (Drominigle, Kilquade, co. Wicklow), *b.* 1912; ed. at Harrow, and at Camb. Univ.; formerly Hon. Attaché, British Embassy, Washington; MVO (4th class) 1939: *m.* 1943, Pamela, da. of Charles Whatley, of Burderop, Swindon, and has issue living, Charles Patrick Benjamin, *b.* 1947,—Elizabeth Lee, *b.* 1946.——Hester Elizabeth Lee (Bay View, The Harbour, Greystones, co. Wicklow), *b.* 1905: *m.* 1936, Richard Sinclair Connell, who *d.* 1969.——Olive Dorothea (*Olive, Countess Fitzwilliam*), *b.* 1911; is an OStJ: *m.* 1933, the 8th Earl Fitzwilliam, who *d.* 1948. *Residence,*—Coollattin, Shillelagh, co. Wicklow.

Grandchildren of the late Hon. Charles Bushe Plunket, 2nd son of 3rd Baron :—
Issue of the late David Darley Donnybrook Plunket, *b.* 1869, *d.* 1956 : *m.* 1900, Helen Rosanna, who *d.* 1951, dau. of the late Thomas Greene, of 49, St. Stephen's Green, Dublin :—
Brian Thomas, *b.* 1903. *Residence,*—Russetts, Town Row, Rotherfield, Sussex.——Nancy Emmeline, *b.* 1901: *m.* 1927, Colin Kingsley Stringer, of Downsview, 1, Manor Close, Willingdon, Eastbourne, Sussex, and has issue living, Hugh Conyngham, *b.* 1928: *m.* 1954, Kathleen Stevens,—Richard Darley (Riverside, Abbey View, Duton Hill, Dunmow, Essex), *b.* 1933: *m.* 1st, 1957 (m. diss. 1969), Gaye Fellowes; 2ndly, 1974, Audrey Bell, and has issue living (by 1st m.), Susan Gail *b.* 1963,—Hermione Anne, *b.* 1929——.Rosamond Sylvia, *b.* 1908: *m.* 1939, Sir Commodore Henry Sam Francis Temple Jerrard, CBE, RAF, who *d.* 1961, and has issue living, David Grattan (Hillside, Newcourt Av., Bray, co. Wicklow), *b.* 1944: *m.* 1969, Noreen, da. of Alphonsus Reginald Timothy Nolan of Alvenor, Meath Rd., Bray, co. Wicklow,—Helen Frances, *b.* 1941: *m.* 1962, John Patrick Roe, of Borrowdale, Knochnashee, Dundrum, co. Dublin. *Residence,*—Hillside, Newcourt Av., Bray, co. Wicklow.

Grandchildren of the late Hon. Arthur Cecil Crampton Plunket, 4th son of 3rd Baron:—

Issue of the late Henry Coote Lifford Plunket, *b.* 1875, *d.* 1955 : *m.* 1912, Emily Evelyn Marjorie, who *d.* 1968, da. of the late Severne Rowlands, of Ipswich, Queensland :—
Arthur Robert Lifford, *b.* 1914: *m.* 1938. Elies. dau. of Hugo Krieger, of Prague. *Residence,*—130, Sevenoaks Rd., Borkwood Park, Orpington, Kent.
   Issue of the late Archibald John Lifford Plunket, *b.* 1877, *d.* **1940**: *m.* 1909, Mary Calvert, who *d.* **1937**, dau. of the late Henry Frederick Swan, C.B., of Prudhoe Hall, Northumberland :—
Norah Mary Lifford, *b.* 1912: *m.* 1939, Hugh Honner Sancroft Baker, late Capt. R.E., of 198, Middle Drive, Darras Hall, Ponteland, Newcastle-upon-Tyne, and has issue living, Terence Sancroft, *b.* 1941.

Granddaughter of the late Hon. Patrick Plunket, 5th son of 1st Baron:—
   Issue of the late Cedric John Charles Plunket, *b.* 1854, *d.* 1898 : *m.* 1881, Alice, who *d.* 1925, dau. of the late Francis Philip Cupiss, F.R.C.S., of St. Servan, France :—
Mabel Cecilia, *b.* 1897: *m.* 1925, Rodney Colvill Jones, who *d.* 1953, and has issue living, David Stewart (Luzuriaga 1733, Hurlingham, Buenos Aires, Argentina), *b.* 1932: *m.* 1962, Pauline June *b.* 1964, Heather Ann *b.* 1969,—Ann, *b.* 1927: *m.* 1952, John A. Everard, and has issue living, Rodney *b.* 1953, Martin Kenneth *b.* 1955, Ian Patrick *b.* 1961, Susan Winifred *b.* 1957. *Residence,*—Callao 1158, 2c, Buenos Aires, Argentina.

PREDECESSORS.—[1] WILLIAM CONYNGHAM Plunket, *M.P.* for Charlemont in Irish Parliament 1798-1800, and for Dublin Univ. 1812-27, Ch. Justice of the Common Pleas in Ireland 1827-30, and Lord Chancellor of Ireland 1830-34 and 1835-41; *cr.* **Baron Plunket, of Newtown,** co. Cork (peerage of United Kingdom) 1827; *d.* 1854; *s.* by his el. son [2] THOMAS SPAN, *D.D.,* 2nd Baron; was Lord Bishop of Tuam, Killala and Achonry 1839-66; *s.* by his brother [3] JOHN, *Q.C.,* 3rd Baron; *b.* 1793: *m.* 1824, Charlotte, who *d.* 1886, dau. of the Rt. Hon. Charles Kendal Bushe, Lord Ch. Justice of Ireland; *d.* 1871; *s.* by his son [4] *Most Rev.* WILLIAM CONYNGHAM, *D.D.,* 4th Baron, *b.* 1828; Bishop of Meath 1876-84 and Archbishop of Dublin 1884-97: *m.* 1863, Anne Lee, who *d.* 1889, dau. of Sir Benjamin Lee Guinness, 1st Bt., and sister of 1st Barons Ardilaun and Iveagh; *d.* 1897; *s.* by his el. son [5] WILLIAM LEE, *G.C.M.G.,K.C.V.O.,K.B.E.,* 5th Baron, *b.* 1864; Gov. of New Zealand 1904-10; bore Standard of the Dominion of New Zealand at Coronation of King George V. 1911: *m.* 1894, Lady Victoria Alexandrina Hamilton-Temple-Blackwood, who *d.* 1968, da. of 1st Marquess of Dufferin and Ava; *d.* 1920; *s.* by his el. son [6] TERENCE CONYNGHAM, 6th Baron; *b.* 1899; Lt. Rifle Brig. (Reserve); European War 1918: *m.* 1922, Dorothé Mabel, who *d.* 1938, dau. of the late Joseph Lewis, and widow of Capt. Jack Barnato, R.A.F.: *d.* **1938**: *s.* by his el. son [7] PATRICK TERENCE WILLIAM SPAN, *KCVO*; 7th Baron; Lt.-Col. Irish Gds.; Equerry to King George VI 1948-52 and to Queen 1952-75; Dep. Master of the Household 1954-75; *d.* 1975; *s.* by his brother ROBIN RATHMORE, 8th Baron and present peer.

PLURENDEN, BARON. (Sternberg.) [Life Baron 1975.]

RUDY STERNBERG, son of George Sternberg; *b.* April 17th, 1917; ed. at Johann's Gymnasium, Germany; Chm. and Man. Dir. Sterling Gp. of Cos., and Chm. British Agric. Export Council; a Freeman of City of London, and Liveryman of Farmers' and Horners' Cos.; *cr.* Knt. 1970, and *Baron Plurenden,* of Plurenden Manor, co. Kent (Life Baron) 1975: *m.* 1951, Dorothée Monica, da. of Maj. Robert Bateman Prust, OBE, of Vancouver, BC, Canada, and has issue.

Arms,—not exemplified at time of going to press.
Residences,—Plurenden Manor, High Halden, Kent; 79B, Elizabeth St., SW1. *Club,*—City Livery.

DAUGHTERS LIVING.
Hon. Rosanne Monica Michelle, *b.* 1960.
Hon. Francesca Nicola, *b.* 1962.

PLYMOUTH, EARL OF. (Windsor-Clive.) [Baron E. 1529, Earl U.K. 1905.]

OTHER ROBERT IVOR WINDSOR-CLIVE, 3rd Earl; *b.* Oct. 9th, 1923; *s.* 1943; ed. at Eton, and at Trin. Coll. Camb.; late Capt. Coldstream Guards; is a K.St.J., a D.L. for Salop, and a F.R.S.A.: *m.* 1950, Caroline Helen, only dau. of Edward Rice, of Dane Court, Eastry, Kent, and has issue.

Arms,—Quarterly: 1st and 4th argent, on a fesse sable, three mullets or, *Clive*; 2nd and 3rd gules, a saltire argent, between twelve cross crosslets or, *Windsor.* Crests,—1st, a griffin statant argent, gorged with a ducal crown gules; 2nd, a stag's head at gaze, couped at the neck argent, attired or. Supporters,—On either side an unicorn argent, horned, maned, and hoofed or.
Residences,—Oakly Park, Ludlow; 48, Burton Court, SW3.

I trust in God.

SONS LIVING.
IVOR EDWARD OTHER (*Viscount Windsor*), *b.* Nov. 19th, 1951; ed. at Harrow.
Hon. Simon Percy, *b.* 1956.
Hon. David Justin, *b.* 1960.

DAUGHTER LIVING.
Lady Emma, *b.* 1954: *m.* 1975, Robert Arthur Smith-Dorrien-Smith, of Tresco Abbey, Isles of Scilly.

BROTHER LIVING.
Hon. Richard Archer Alan, *b.* 1928; ed. at Eton, and at Trin. Coll., Camb.; late Lieut. R.A.; *m.* 1st 1955 (m. diss. 1968) Joanna Mary, el. da. of Edward Corbet Woodall, OBE [Crawley-Boevey, Bt. colls.]; 2ndly, 1968, the Hon. (Mary) Alice Chancellor, da. of 4th Baron Hylton, and has issue living, (by 1st m.) Stephen Miles, *b.* 1956,—Cathryn Harriet, *b.* 1958,—Nell, *b.* 1974. *Residence,*—Combe, Nettlecombe, Taunton.

SISTERS LIVING.

Lady Clarissa, *b.* 1931: *m.* 1953, Major Keith Maclean Forbes Egleston, late Rifle Bde., of The Old Rectory, Weston Patrick, Basingstoke, Hants., and has issue living, Hugo Vivyan, *b.* 1955,—Sarah Caroline, *b.* 1956,—Harriet Gilian, *b.* 1962.

Lady Rosula Caroline, *b.* 1935: *m.* 1962, Dr. Alan Glyn, ERD, MP, late Capt. RHG, of 17, Cadogan Pl., SW1, and has issue living, Mary Caroline, *b.* 1963,—Anne Serena, *b.* 1964.

AUNT LIVING. (*Daughter of* 1*st Earl.*)

Lady Phyllis, *b.* 1886: *m.* 1924, Major Hugh Gordon Benton, Indian Cav. (retired), who *d.* 1931 and has issue living, Caroline Rose Melissa, *b.* 1928. *Residence,*—81, Iverna Court, Kensington, W.8.,

WIDOW LIVING OF SECOND EARL.

IRENE CORONA (*Dowager Countess of Plymouth*), dau. of 7th Earl of Wemyss; formerly Senior Comdt. ATS; is a DStJ: *m.* 1921, the 2nd Earl, who *d.* 1943. *Residence,*—12, Kings Gdns., Hove, 3.

COLLATERAL BRANCHES LIVING. (*In remainder to Barony of Windsor only.*)

Issue of the late Lady Gillian Mary Windsor-Olive, dau. of 2nd Earl, *b.* 1922, *d.* 1961: *m.* 1st, 1941 (marriage dissolved 1947), Wilfred Wooller, Lieut. R.A.; 2ndly, 1947, Lieut. Albertus Jacobus de Haan, Roy. Netherlands Navy, of The Manor Farm, Drayton, Abingdon, Berks.:—

(By 2nd marriage), Julian Jan Ivor, *b.* 1948.——Archer Anthony, *b.* 1950.——Andrew David, *b.* 1954. ——Valentine Nicholas, *b.* 1956.

Grandchildren of the late Lt.-Col. the Hon. George Herbert Windsor Windsor-Clive, son of the late Harriet, Baroness Windsor:—

Issue of the late Lt.-Col. George Windsor-Clive, CMG, *b.* 1878, *d.* 1968: *m.* 1912, Sidney Guendolen, who *d.* 1935, da. of Charles Carmichael Lacaita, of Selham, Sussex [Doyle, Bt.]:—

Robert Charles (Ashford Court, Ludlow, Salop), *b.* 1919; ed. at Eton, and RMC; Brig. (ret.), late Coldm. Gds.; 1939-45 War (wounded, despatches): *m.* 1949, Olive Mary, yr. da. of Lt.-Col. Francis Longueville, DSO, MC, and has issue living, George Francis, *b.* 1954; ed. at Eton; 2nd Lt. Coldm. Gds.,—Annabel Mary, *b.* 1951.——Francis Archer (Bury Court, Redmarley, Glos), *b.* 1922; ed. at Eton; late Capt. Coldm. Gds.; 1939-45 War (wounded, despatches): *m.* 1945, Anne Gertrude, el. da. of the late Lt.-Col. Francis Longueville, DSO, MC, and has issue living, Edward Archer, *b.* 1946; ed. at Ampleforth; Capt. Coldm. Gds.,—Robert Ivor, *b.* 1950,—Other John, *b.* 1958,—William Henry, *b.* 1960,—Frances Anne, *b.* 1948: *m.* 1972, Capt. Andrew Stow, and has issue living, Catherine Mary *b.* 1974.——Everard Ivor (69, Eccleston Sq., SW1), *b.* 1925; ed. at Eton; Col. Coldm. Gds.; 1939-45 War.——Mary Phyllis, *b.* 1921.

PREDECESSORS.—[1] *Sir* ANDREWS Windsor, K.B., distinguished himself in the French wars of Henry VIII., and was made a Knight Banneret at the battle of the Spurs 1513; summoned to Parliament of England as *Baron Windsor*, of Stanwell, co. Bucks 1529; *d.* 1543; *s.* by his son [2] WILLIAM, K.B., 2nd Baron; *d.* 1558; *s.* by his son [3] EDWARD, 3rd Baron; distinguished himself at St. Quentin, and in 1566 entertained Queen Elizabeth at his seat at Bradenham; *d.* 1574; *s.* by his el. son [4] FREDERICK, 4th Baron; *d.* unmarried 1585; *s.* by his brother [5] HENRY, 5th Baron; *d.* 1605; *s.* by his son [6] THOMAS, K.B., 6th Baron; was a Rear-Adm.: *d.s.p.* 1642; *s.* by his nephew [7] THOMAS Windsor-Hickman, P.C., 7th Baron, son of the Hon. Elizabeth Windsor by her marriage with Dixie Hickman, of Kew; assumed the additional surname of Windsor; commanded a Regt. of Horse at Naseby 1646; was Lord-Lieut. of Worcestershire, and Gov. of Jamaica 1661-2; cr. *Earl of Plymouth* (peerage of England) 1682; *d.* 1687; *s.* by his grandson [8] OTHER, 2nd Earl; *d.* 1727; *s.* by his son [9] OTHER, 3rd Earl; *d.* 1732; *s.* by his son [10] OTHER LEWIS, 4th Earl; was Custos Rotulorum of cos. Flint, Glamorgan, and Cheshire; *d.* 1777; *s.* by his son [11] OTHER HICKMAN, 5th Earl; *d.* 1799; *s.* by his son [12] OTHER ARCHER, 6th Earl; *d.s.p.* 1833, when the Barony of Windsor became abeyant between his sisters Maria, wife of 2nd Marquess of Downshire, and Harriet, wife of the Hon. Robert Henry Clive, and the earldom reverted to his uncle [13] ANDREWS, 7th Earl; *d.* unmarried 1837; *s.* by his brother [14] HENRY, 8th Earl; *d.s.p.* 1843, when the earldom became extinct. In 1855 the abeyance of the Barony of Windsor was terminated in favour of [15] HARRIET Clive (ante); *b.* 1797; assumed in 1855 by Roy. licence the additional surname of Windsor: *m.* 1819, the Hon. Robert Henry Clive, M.P., 2nd son of 1st Earl of Powis; *d.* 1869; *s.* by her grandson [16] ROBERT GEORGE Windsor-Olive, G.B.E., C.B., P.C., 1st Earl, only son of the Hon. Robert, M.P., by Lady Mary Selina Louisa Bridgeman, dau. of 2nd Earl of Bradford; *b.* 1857; Lord-Lieut. of Glamorganshire 1890-1923; Paymaster-Gen. 1891-2, and 1st Commr. of Works 1902-5; cr. *Viscount Windsor*, of St. Fagans, co. Glamorgan, and *Earl of Plymouth* (peerage of United Kingdom) 1905: *m.* 1883, Alberta Victoria Sarah Caroline, who *d.* 1944, dau. of the late Rt. Hon. Sir Augustus Berkeley Paget, P.C., G.C.B.; *d.* 1923; *s.* by his son [17] IVOR MILES, P.C., 2nd Earl; *b.* 1889; was Parliamentary Private Sec. (unpaid) to Sec. of State for Home Depart. (Rt. Hon. W. C. Bridgeman, M.P.) 1922, and Under-Sec. of State for Dominion Affairs Jan. to June 1929; became Parliamentary Sec. to Min. of Transport (in National Govt.) Nov. 1931, and Parliamentary Under-Sec., Colonial Office Sept. 1932; Parliamentary Under-Sec., Foreign Office July 1936 to May 1939; Hon. Freeman of Cardiff 1936; elected Pro-Chancellor of Univ. of Wales 1941; bore Standard of Wales at Coronation of King George VI.; sat as M.P. for Shropshire, Ludlow Div. (C) Jan. 1922 to March 1923: *m.* 1921, Lady Irene Corona Charteris, dau. of 7th Earl of Wemyss; *d.* 1943; *s.* by his son [18] OTHER ROBERT IVOR, 3rd Earl and present peer; also Baron Windsor, and Viscount Windsor.

Pollington, Viscount, son of Earl of Mexborough.

POLTIMORE BARON. (Bampfylde.) [Baron U.K. 1831, Bt. E. 1641.]

HUGH DE BURGH WARWICK BAMPFYLDE, 6th Baron, and 11th Baronet; *b.* March 25th, 1888; *s.* 1967; ed. at Winchester, and New Coll., Oxford (MA); 1914-18 War as Maj., King's African Rifles: *m.* 1918, Margaret Mary, da. of 4th Marquis de la Pasture (*cr.* France 1768), and has issue.

Arms,—Or, on a bend gules, three mullets argent. Crest,—A lion's head erased sable ducally crowned or. Supporters,—Two lions reguardant, sable, ducally crowned gules, gorged with a collar gemelle or, and pendant therefrom an escutcheon of the arms of Bampfylde.

Residence,—The Ancient House, Peasenhall, Saxmundham, Suffolk.

To rejoice in the Lord.

SON LIVING.
Hon. David Cecil Warwick (Coombe Lea, Malmesbury, Wilts.), *b.* 1924; ed. at Eton; late Capt.
KRRC; 1939-45 War (wounded): *m.* 1950, Jean Margaret, da. of the late Lt.-Col. Patrick Kinloch
Campbell, and has issue living, Michael Hugh Warwick, *b.* 1951,—Richard Ian David, *b.* 1953,—
John Spencer Warwick, *b.* 1960.

DAUGHTERS LIVING OF FOURTH BARON. (*By 1st marriage.*)
Hon. Sheila Margaret Warwick (*Hon. Lady Stucley*) (Hartland Abbey, N. Devon; Court House,
N. Molton, N. Devon), *b.* 1912; Patron of two livings: *m.* 1932, Maj. Sir Dennis Frederic Bankes
Stucley, 5th Bt., R. Devon Yeo.

WIDOW LIVING OF SON OF SIXTH BARON.
Brita Yvonne, (Boyton House, Woodbridge, Suffolk), da. of the late Baron (Rudolph) Cederstrom
[B. De Ramsey]: *m.* 1st, 1947, Capt. the Hon. Anthony Gerard Hugh Bampfylde, who *d.* 1969; 2ndly
1975, Guy Elmes, and has issue by 1st m. [see colls., infra].

COLLATERAL BRANCHES LIVING.
Issue of the late Capt. the Hon. Anthony Gerard Hugh Bampfylde, el. son of 6th
Baron, *b.* 1920, *d.* 1969: *m.* 1947, Brita Yvonne, (ante) who *m.* 2ndly, 1975, Guy
Elmes), da. of the late Baron (Rudolph) Cederstrom [B. De Ramsey]:—
MARK COPLESTONE, *b.* June 8th, 1957.——Christine Margaret Hermione, *b.* 1948: *m.* 1970, Peter
William Denby Roberts, of The Old Rectory, Whittington, via Carnforth, Lancs. [see Roberts, Bt.
colls., cr. 1909].

Issue of the late Hon. Charles Warwick Bampfylde, 2nd son of 2nd Baron, *b.*
1867, *d.* 1931 : *m.* 1891, Edith Anne, who *d.* 1959, dau. of Edward Browne :—
Marcia Warwick (2776, Cadboro Bay Rd., Victoria, BC), *b.* 1893: *m.* 1917, Dugald McFarlan McCaul,
who *d.* 1961, and has issue living, Ian Bampfylde, *b.* 1918: *m.* 1st, 1941, Mary Burgess (m. diss.
1974); 2ndly 1974, Jean Barnard,—Eric McFarlan, *b.* 1919: *m.* 1954, Janet Macgregor,—Norah
Elizabeth Joan, *b.* 1922: *m.* 3rdly, 1959, William G. Pearson, who *d.* 1967; 4thly, 1974, Edward H.
Cabeldu, of 3375, Upper Terr., Vic., BC, Canada,—Marcia Barbara, *b.* 1932.——Edith Warwick
(Dunroamin, Barbon, Kirkby Lonsdale, Westmorland), *b.* 1895.——Barbara Warwick, *b.* 1898: *m.*
1921, George Priddy-Smith, and has issue living, Nigel Derek, *b.* 1922,—Philippa, *b.* 1924,—June
Denzilla Haidee, *b.* 1927: *m.* 19—,——Thomas. *Residence,*—Bridge House, 3, Broad Oak Rd.,
Weston-super-Mare.

Issue of the late Hon. Francis Warwick Bampfylde, 3rd son of 2nd Baron, *b.*
1885, *d.* 1931: *m.* 1911, Margaret Harriet, who *d.* 1968, da. of the late Robert
Martin, of Belfast:—
Caroline Warwick, *b.* 1920: *m.* 1st, 1942 (m. diss. 1951), Wing-Cdr. Dean Lenthal Swift, Roy. Australian Air Force; 2ndly, 1951, Edward James, CMG, OBE, HM Foreign Ser., and has issue living,
(by 2nd m.) David Peter, *b.* 1954,—Susan Alexandra Caroline, *b.* 1952,—Penelope Sarah (twin), *b.*
1954. *Residence,*—Springfield House, W. Clandon, Surrey.

PREDECESSORS.—[1] JOHN Bampfylde; *M.P.* for Penryn 1640; cr. a *Baronet* 1641; *s.* by his
son [2] Sir COPLESTONE, 2nd Bt.; *d.* 1691; *s.* by his grandson [3] Sir COPLESTONE WARWICK,
3rd Bt.; M.P. for Exeter and Devon; *d.* 1727; *s.* by his son [4] Sir RICHARD WARWICK,
4th Bt.; M.P. for Devon; *d.* 1776; *s.* by his son [5] Sir CHARLES WARWICK, D.C.L., 5th
Bt.; M.P. for Exeter; was assassinated 1823; *s.* by his son [6] Sir GEORGE, 6th Bt.; *b.* 1786;
was Vice-Lieut. of Devon, and a Lord-in-Waiting to Queen Victoria; cr. *Baron Poltimore*
of Poltimore, co. Devon (peerage of United Kingdom) 1831: *m.* 2ndly, 1836, Caroline, dau.
of Gen. Frederick William Buller; *d.* 1858; *s.* by his son [7] AUGUSTUS FREDERICK GEORGE
WARWICK, P.C., 2nd Baron; *b.* 1837; Treasurer of Queen Victoria's Household 1872-4: *m.*
1858, Florence Sara Wilhelmine, who *d.* 1909, dau. of the late Richard Brinsley Sheridan, of
Frampton Court, Dorset; *d.* 1908; *s.* by his son [8] COPLESTONE RICHARD GEORGE WARWICK,
3rd Baron; *b.* 1859: *m.* 1881, the Hon. Margaret Harriet Beaumont, who *d.* 1931, dau. of
1st Baron Allendale; *d.* 1918: *s.* by his el. son [9] GEORGE WENTWORTH WARWICK, 4th
Baron, *b.* 1882: *m.* 1st, 1910, Cynthia Rachel, who *d.* 1961, da. of the late Hon. Gerald William
Lascelles [E. Harewood, colls.]; 2ndly, 1962, Barbara Pitcairn (WALKER), who *d.* 1969, da. of
Peter Nicol, of Kirkintilloch; *d.* 1965, *s.* by his brother [10] ARTHUR BLACKETT WARWICK, 5th
Baron, *b.* 1883: *m.* 1st, 1916, Catharine Frances Graham, who *d.* 1938, da. of the late Gen. the Hon.
Sir David Macdowell Fraser, GCB [L. Saltoun, colls.]; 2ndly 1939 (m. diss. 1948), Mrs. Mabel
Violet Blanche Meyrick, da. of the late Col. Arthur Hill Sandys Montgomerie, of Grey Abbey, col
Down; *d.* 1967, *s.* by his brother [11] HUGH DE BURGH WARWICK, 6th Baron and present peer.

POLWARTH, LORD. (Hepburne-Scott.) [Lord S. 1690.]
[Name pronounced "Hebburn-Scott."]

The moon will
replenish her
horns.

FIDES·PROBATA·CORONAT

Approved faith crowns.

HENRY ALEXANDER HEPBURNE-
SCOTT, *T.D.*, 10th Lord; *b.* Nov.
17th, 1916; *s.* 1944; ed. at Eton,
and at King's Coll., Camb. (M.A.);
Hon. LLD, St. Andrews, Aberdeen,
and Heriot Watt; D. Univ. Stirling;
FRSE; a Representative Peer for
Scotland 1945-63; a Member of
Queen's Body Guard for Scotland
(Roy. Co. of Archers), Vice-Lord Lt.
Borders Region (Roxburgh, Ettrick
and Landerdale); a partner in the
firm of Chiene & Tait, chartered
accountants 1950-68; Chm. Scottish
Council (Development & Industry)
1956-66 (Pres. 1966), and General
Accident Insurance Gp. 1968-72;
Min. of State Scottish Office 1972-74;
Chancellor Aberdeen Univ. 1966; a
Dir. of Bank of Scotland since 1974
(Gov. 1968-72) and of ICI Ltd. 1969-
72 and since 1974; 1939-45 War
as Capt. Lothians and Border Horse:
m. 1st, 1943 (m. diss. 1969), Caroline
Margaret, da. of the late Capt.
Robert Athole Hay [see Hay, Bt.,
colls., cr. 1635]; 2ndly, 1969, Jean,
da. of Adm. Sir Angus Edward
Malise Bontine Cunninghame Graham of Gartmore and of Ardoch, KBE,
CB, and formerly wife of Charles Eliot Jauncey, QC, and has issue by 1st m.

Arms,—Quarterly, 1st and 4th grand quarters quartered; 1st, vert, a lion rampant argent *Hume*; 2nd, argent, three papingoes vert *Pepdie*; 3rd, gules; three piles engrailed argent *Polwarth*; 4th, argent, a cross engrailed azure *St. Clair of Herdmanston*, over all on an escutcheon azure, an orange with the stalk erect, slipped proper, and over it an Imperial Crown; 2nd grand quarter or, two mullets and a crescent in base azure *Scott of Harden*; 3rd grand quarter quartered; 1st and 4th gules, on a chevron argent a rose between two lioncels combatant of the first *Hepburne of Humbie*; 2nd and 3rd argent, three dock leaves vert *Foulis*. **Crest,**—1st, a lady richly attired holding in her dexter hand the sun and in her sinister a half-moon all proper *Scott of Harden*; 2nd issuing out of a man's heart, or, an arm from the elbow proper, brandishing a scimitar of steel, with cross and pommel of gold, *Polwarth*; 3rd an oak tree proper, and a horse passant argent, saddled and bridled gules *Hepburne of Humble.* **Supporters,**—*Dexter*, a lion rampant reguardant argent, langued gules; *sinister*, a mermaid—holding in her sinister hand and resting on her shoulder a mirror all proper.

Residences,—Harden, Hawick, Roxburghshire; 42, Carlton Terr. Lane, Edinburgh, 7. *Clubs,*—Brooks's, Caledonian, New (Edinburgh).

SON LIVING. (By 1st m.)

Hon. ANDREW WALTER (*Master of Polwarth*), (Harden, Hawick, Roxburghshire), *b.* Nov. 30th, 1947; ed. at Eton, and Trin. Hall, Camb.: *m.* 1971, Isabel Anna, da. of Maj. John Freville Henry Surtees, MC, and has issue living, William Henry, *b.* 1973,—Robert Mungo, *b.* 1974.

DAUGHTERS LIVING. (By 1st m.)

Hon. Sarah Margaret, *b.* 1944.
Hon. Diana Mary, *b.* 1946.
Hon. Mary Jane, *b.* 1955.

BROTHER LIVING. (Raised to the rank of a Baron's son 1945.)

Hon. Francis Michael, *MC, b.* 1920; ed. at Eton, and at King's Coll., Camb.; a FRICS; sometime Maj. Lothians and Border Horse; a Consultant Smiths Gore, Chartered Surveyors; 1939-45 War (MC): *m.* 1946, Marjorie Hamilton, da. of Horatio John Ross [see Lighton, Bt.], and has issue living, James Patrick (c/o Barclays Bank, 8, High St., Eton, Windsor, Berks.), *b.* 1947; ed. at Eton; Capt. The Black Watch: *m.* 1972, Christian Diana, da. of Maj. John Freville Henry Surtees, MC, of Waterside House, Drayton St. Leonard, and has issue living, Walter Robert *b.* 1974,—Michael Francis, *b.* 1959, —Mary Helen, *b.* 1949: *m.* 1974, Andrew Godfrey Purvis Sherwood [see E. Onslow, colls.]. *Residence,*—Lessudden Bank, St. Boswells, Roxburghshire.

UNCLE LIVING. (Son of 9th Lord.)

Hon. Patrick John (13, Castle Rise, Belmesthorpe, Stamford, Lincs.), *b.* 1899; ed. at Trin. Coll., Camb. (BA 1921, MA 1925); formerly Lt. 5th Batn. Roy Scots, sometime R. of Kirkley: *m.* 1st, 1925, Cona, who *d.* 1961, da. of the late O. Fielding Smith, of Dublin; 2ndly, 1963, Margaret Mary, dau. of the late A. G. Riddle, of Harrow, Middlesex, and has issue living, (by 1st marriage) Patricia Mary, *b.* 1926: *m.* 1966, Peter Rudolph Ramm, of 44, Alexandra Rd., Lowestoft,—Ann Harriet, *b.* 1929: *m.* 1963, Colin Andrew Baxter, of Beaconsfield, Broomieknowe, Lasswade, Midlothian, and has issue living, Patrick Ian *b.* 1968.

AUNTS LIVING. (Daughters of 9th Lord.)

Hon. Helen Victoria, *b.* 1891 : *m.* 1919, George Freeland Barbour, D.Ph., who *d.* 1946 [Fowler, Bt., cr. 1885, ext.], and has issue, Robert Alexander Stewart, *M.C., b.* 1921; late Major Scottish Horse: *m.* 1950, Margaret Isobel, dau. of Lieut.-Col. H. Pigot, of Bishop's Stortford, and has issue living, George Freeland *b.* 1951, David Stewart *b.* 1954, Andrew James Stewart *b.* 1959, Alison Margaret *b.* 1956,—Alec Walter, *b.* 1925 : *m.* 1950, Hazel, dau. of William Brown, and has issue living, John Alexander *b.* 1951, Alastair William Stewart *b.* 1953, Walter Hugh *b.* 1956, Jean Edith *b.* 1958, Helen Christian (twin) *b.* 1958,—Edith Rachel, *b.* 1923,—Katherine Margaret, *b.* 1928,—Caroline Victoria, *b.* 1930: *m.* 1959, Julian Arthur Charles Haviland [Fergusson, Bt.], of 39, Cator Rd., SE26, and has issue living, Peter Leonard *b.* 1961, Charles Freeland *b.* 1964, Richard Francis *b.* 1967. *Residence,*—Fincastle, Pitlochry.

Hon. Margaret Mary, *b.* 1895: *m.* 1928, Douglas Benzies, who *d.* 1948. *Address,*—c/o Hon. Mrs. Barbour, Fincastle, Pitlochry.

Hon. Edith Christian, *b.* 1901: *m.* 1926, Lt.-Col. George Theodore Herbert Capron, RE, who *d.* 1970, and has issue living, George Christopher, *b.* 1935: *m.* 1958, Edna Naomi, yr. da. of C. Goldrei, of Garden House, Napier Pl., W14, and has issue living, George David *b.* 1961, Naomi Louise *b.* 1962,—Rachel Edith, *b.* 1927: *m.* 1954, Thomas Randall Cubitt, of 97, Hampstead Way, NW11 [Pelly, Bt., colls.] and has issue living, Geoffrey Thomas *b.* 1957, William George *b.* 1959, Robin Patrick *b.* 1961,—Elizabeth Victoria, *b.* 1929: *m.* 1950, David Craven Lunn-Rockliffe, of 22, Cottenham Park Rd., SW20, and has issue living, Caroline Mary, *b.* 1951, Susan Edith, *b.* 1953, Claire Elizab eth *b.* 1956, Victoria Anne *b.* 1960, Nicola Jane *b.* 1964,—Bridget Katherine, *b.* 1931. *Residence,* —Southwick Hall, Oundle, Peterborough.

COLLATERAL BRANCHES LIVING.

Issue of the late Major the Hon. Charles Francis Hepburne-Scott, youngest son of 8th Lord, *b.* 1874, *d.* 1956: *m.* 1905, Elma, who *d.* 1973, da. of the late Johnson Driver, of Maryton, Forfarshire:—
Elma Katherine, *b.* 1905. *Residence,*—24a, Rectory Close, Newbury.

Grandsons of the late Hon. Henry Robert Hepburne-Scott, 2nd son of 7th Lord :—
Issue of the late James Cospatrick Hepburne-Scott, *b.* 1882, *d.* 1942: *m.* 1907, Lady Isobel Alice Adelaide Kerr (now of 13, Seafield Road, Southbourne, Bournemouth) dau. of 9th Marquess of Lothian:—
Michael Henry (13, Hamlet Court, W6), *b.* 1909; Maj. late 16th/5th Lancers; late Dep. Assist. Dir of Army Legal Sers., War Office: *m.* 1st, 1931 (m. diss. 1949), Frances Elizabeth, da. of the late Rev. George Victor Collier, of Sotwell, Wallingford, Berks.; 2ndly, 1949, Mrs. Rohilla Ada May Petz, da. of —— Smith, and has issue living, (by 1st m.) David Michael Cospatrick (Westminster School, SW1), *b.* 1935; ed. at Eton and King's Coll., Camb. (MA); Assist. Master, Westminster Sch.,—Walter Francis (Pantiles, Beeches Rd., Farnham Common, Bucks.), *b.* 1944; ed. at Eton; MB, BS: *m.* 1968, Fiona Mary, da. of Frey Richard Ellis, MD, of 27, Links Rd., Epsom, Surrey, and has issue living, Henry Walter *b.* 1970, George Walter *b.* 1971, Edward Walter *b.* 1974,—(by 2nd m.), Angela Susan, *b.* 1949.——Walter Schomberg, *b.* 1910; is an ARIBA, and Capt. late RE: *m.* 1945, Deborah, only child of the late Tudor Ralph Castle, Lt. Queen's Roy. Regt. [D. Norfolk, colls.], and has issue living, James Ralph Schomberg, *b.* 1947,—Lyulph Mark Esmé, *b.* 1949. *Residence,*—Northfield, Prestonpans, E. Lothian.——Francis William, *b.* 1915; 1939-45 War as Maj. RASC. *Residence,*—13, Seafield Rd., Southbourne, Bournemouth.

PREDECESSORS.—[1] *Rt. Hon. Sir* PATRICK Hume, *P.C.*, an Extraor. Lord of Session 1693, Lord High Chancellor of Scotland 1696, and First Lord of the Treasury and of the Admiralty, &c., was cr. *Lord Polwarth*, of Polwarth, co. Berwick (peerage of Scotland) 1690, and *Earl of Marchmont, Viscount Blasonberry*, and *Lord Polwarth*, of Polwarth, Redbraes and Greenlaw (peerage of Scotland) 1697 : *d.* 1724 ; *s.* by his son [2] ALEXANDER, *K.T., P.C.*, 2nd Earl; was a Senator of the College of Justice, and Ambassador to Denmark and Prussia ; *d.* 1740 ; *s.* by his son [3] HUGH, 3rd Earl; was First Lord of Police in Scotland ; *d.* 1793, when the earldom, viscountcy and lordship of 1697 became extinct, and the lordship of 1690 became vested in the granddau. of the 3rd Earl of Marchmont [4] ANNE, *de jure* Lady Polwarth (dau. of Sir John Paterson, 3rd Bt., who *m.* Anne, el. dau. of the 3rd Earl of Marchmont; she *d.* 1822, before any decision regarding her claim to the Lordship had been reached ; her aunt [5] DIANA (youngest dau. of 3rd Earl of Marchmont) , became *de jure* Lady Polwarth : *m.* 1754, Walter Scott, M.P., of Harden, co. Roxburgh, Chieftain of the Scotts of Sinton, *d.* 1827; her only son and heir [6] HUGH Scott, was MP for Berwick 1780-4; assumed the additional surname of Hepburne; in 1835 he claimed and was allowed the peerage becoming 6th Lord; *d.* 1841; *s.* by his son [7] HENRY FRANCIS, 7th Lord; was a Representative Peer, Lord-Lieut. of Selkirkshire, and a Lord-in-Waiting to Queen Victoria; *d.* 1867; *s.* by his son [8] WALTER HUGH, 8th Lord, *b.* 1838; Capt. Roy. Co. of Archers (King's Body Guard for Scotland); Lord-Lieut. of co. Selkirk 1878-1919: *m.* 1st, 1863, Lady Mary Hamilton-Gordon, who *d.* 1914, da. of 5th Earl of Aberdeen; 2ndly, 1915, Katherine Grisell, who *d.* 1938, da. of the late Rev. the Hon. John Baillie; *d.* 1920; *s.* by his el. son [9] WALTER GEORGE, 9th Lord; *b.* 1864; *m.* 1888, Edith Frances, who *d.* 1930, da. of Sir Thomas Fowell Buxton, 3rd Bt.; *d.* 1944; *s.* by his grandson [10] HENRY ALEXANDER (son of the late Capt. the Hon. Walter Thomas Hepburne-Scott), 10th Lord and present peer.

PONSONBY OF SHULBREDE, BARON. (Ponsonby.) [Baron U.K. 1930.]

PRO·REGE GREGE LEGE

For the king, the law, and the people.

MATTHEW HENRY HUBERT PONSONBY, 2nd Baron ; *b.* July 28th, 1904; *s.* 1946; ed. at Balliol Coll., Oxford ; is a J.P. for W. Sussex : *m.* 1929, the Hon. Elizabeth Mary Bigham, dau. 2nd Viscount Mersey, and has issue.

Arms,—Gules, a chevron between three combs argent. *Crest,*—Out of a ducal coronet azure three arrows, points downwards, one in pale and two in saltire, entwined at the intersection by a snake proper.

Residences,—Shulbrede Priory, Linchmere, Haslemere, Surrey ; 17, South End, Kensington Square, W.8.

SON LIVING.

Hon. THOMAS ARTHUR (53, Lancaster Grove, NW3), *b.* Oct. 23rd, 1930; ed. at Bryanston, and at Hertford Coll., Oxford; Gen. Sec. of Fabian Soc., a Councillor of R. Borough of Kensington 1956-65; an Alderman of R. Borough of Kensington and Chelsea 1964-74; an Alderman GLC since 1970 (Chm. Covent Gdn. Cttee. 1973-75, and of Central Area Board since 1973); Chm. Charity Law Reform Cttee. since 1973, a Gov. of London Sch. of Econs. since 1970: *m.* 1st, 1956 (*m.* diss. 1973), Ursula Mary, yr. da. of Com. Thomas Stanley Lane Fox-Pitt, OBE, RN (ret.) [Lowther, Bt., cr. 1824]; 2ndly, 1973, Maureen Estelle, da. of Alfred William Windsor, and has issue living (by 1st m.), Frederick Matthew Thomas, *b.* 1958,—Julia Mary, *b.* 1960,— Charlotte, *b.* 1961,—Rachael Elizabeth Emma, *b.* 1964.

DAUGHTERS LIVING.

Hon. Laura Mary, *b.* 1935.
Hon. Rose Magdalen, *b.* 1940: *m.* 1966, Brian David Owen-Smith, MB, MRCP, D. Phys. Med., of 9, Lansdown Place East, Bath, and has issue living, Timothy Clive Owen, *b.* 1968,—Emma Elizabeth Jane, *b.* 1971.
Hon. Catherine Virginia, *b.* 1944: *m.* 1972, Ian Macdonald Affeck Russell.

PREDECESSOR.—[1] ARTHUR AUGUSTUS WILLIAM HARRY Ponsonby, son of the late Gen. the Rt. Hon. Sir Henry Frederick Ponsonby, G.C.B., P.C. [E. Bessborough, colls.]; *b.* 1871; in Diplo. Ser. 1894-1903, Private Sec. to Prime Min. (Rt. Hon. Sir Henry Campbell-Bannerman G.C.B., M.P.) 1905-08, Under-Sec. of State for Foreign Affairs Jan. to Nov. 1924, and leader of the Opposition in House of Lords Sept. 1931 to Sept. 1935 ; appointed Under-Sec. of State for Dominion Affairs June 1929, Parliamentary Sec to Min. of Transport Nov. 1929, and Chancellor of Duchy of Lancaster March 1931 (resigned Aug. 1931); sat as MP for Stirling Dist. (*L*) May 1908 to Nov. 1918, and for Sheffield, Brightside Div. (*Lab.*) Nov. 1922 to Jan. 1930 ; cr. *Baron Ponsonby of Shulbrede,* of Shulbrede, Sussex (peerage of United Kingdom) 1930: *m.* 1898, Dorothea, who *d.* 1963, dau. of the late Sir Charles Hubert Hastings Parry, 1st Bt. (ext.); *d.* 1946; *s.* by his only son [2] MATTHEW HENRY HUBERT, 2nd Baron and present peer.

POOLE, BARON. (Poole.) [Baron U.K. 1958.]

STRIVE·FOR·THE·RIGHT

OLIVER BRIAN SANDERSON POOLE, *C.B.E., T.D., P.C.,* 1st Baron, son of the late Donald Louis Poole, of Lloyd's; *b.* Aug. 11th, 1911; ed. at Eton, and Ch. Ch., Oxford; Hon. DSc. City Univ.; an Underwriting Member of Lloyd's, Chm. of Lazard Bros. & Co. 1965-73; Chm. of S. Pearson & Sons, Ltd., and of Whitehall Securities, Ltd.; Joint Hon. Treasurer of Conservative Party 1952-55, Chm. 1955-57, Dep. Chm. 1957-59, Joint Chm. May to Oct. 1963, and Vice-Chm. 1963-64; 1939-45 War in Palestine, Syria, Iraq, Libya, N. Africa, Sicily, and N.-W. Europe as Col. (despatches thrice, MBE, OBE, CBE, American Legion of Merit, Knight Cdr. of Order of Orange Nassau of the Netherlands with Swords); sat as M.P. for Oswestry Div. of Shropshire (*C*) July 1945 to Feb 1950; MBE (Mil) and OBE (Mil) 1943, CBE (Mil) 1945, *Baron Poole,* of Aldgate, City of London (peerage of United Kingdom) 1958

and PC 1963: *m.* 1st, 1933 (m. diss. 1951), Betty Margaret, da. of the late Capt·
Dugald Stewart Gilkison, Cameronians [B. Vernon, colls.]; 2ndly, 1952 (m·
diss. 1965), Daphne Wilma Kenyon (HEBER-PERCY), da. of the late Eustace
Bowles [see E. Macclesfield, colls.]; 3rdly, 1966, Barbara Ann, only da. of E.
A. Taylor, and has issue by 1st m.

Arms.—Per saltire or and barry undy argent and azure, in chief and in base a portcullis chained
also azure. **Crest.**—A lion's gamb erased or, enfiled by a crown composed of four trident heads set upon
a rim azure. **Supporters,**—On either side a crane proper about the neck a purse azure garnished gold.
Residence,—12, Egerton Terr., SW3.   *Clubs,*—Buck's, MCC, Royal Yacht Squadron.

SON LIVING. (*By 1st marriage.*)

Hon. DAVID CHARLES (30, Avenue D'Elyau, Paris 75116, France), *b.* Jan. 6th, 1945: *m.* 1st, 1967,
Fiona, da. of John Donald, of 69, Rivermead Court, SW6; 2ndly, 1975, Philippa, da. of Mark
Reeve, of Lower Brook House, King's Somborne, Hants., and has issue living (by 1st m.), Oliver
John, *b.* 1972.

DAUGHTERS LIVING. (*By 1st marriage.*)

Hon. Caroline, *b.* 1934 : *m.* 1955, Hugh John Lucas-Tooth, only son of Sir Hugh Vere Huntly Duff
Munro-Lucas-Tooth, 1st Bt. *Residences,*—44, Queens Gate Gdns., SW7; Parsonage Farm, East
Hagbourne, Didcot, Berks.
Hon. Alison Victoria, *b.* 1936: *m.* 1961, Dr. Fritz Zankel, of 2, Thunhofgasse 3/3, Vienna XII,
Austria, and has issue living, Michael Rudolph, *b.* 1962,—Thomas Joseph, *b.* 1964.
Hon. Sheila Marian, *b.* 1940: *m.* 1966, Cob Stenham, of 12, Hyde Park Gate, SW7.

POPPLEWELL, BARON. (Popplewell.) [Life Baron 1966.]

ERNEST POPPLEWELL, *CBE*, son of John William Popplewell, of Selby;
b. Dec. 10th, 1899; ed. at Sherburn-in-Elmet Elementary Sch.; a JP of
W. Riding of Yorks.; Vice-Chamberlain of H.M.'s Household 1947-51,
Dep. Ch. Opposition Whip 1955-59, and Chm. of Labour Parl. Transport
Group 1959-65; 1914-18 War with RMA (Belgian Croix de Guerre); MP
for W. Div. of Newcastle-on-Tyne (*Lab.*) 1945-66; *cr.* CBE (Civil) 1951, and
Baron Popplewell, of Sherburn-in-Elmet, W. Riding of co. York (Life Baron)
1966: *m.* 1922, Lavinia, da. of Samuel Rainbow, of Sherburn-in-Elmet, and
has issue.

Residence,—North View, Moor Lane, Sherburn-in-Elmet, Leeds.

SON LIVING.

(*Hon.*) John Arnold (Cricklade Rd., Highworth, Swindon), *b.* 1928: *m.* 1951.

Porchester, Lord, son of Earl of Carnarvon.

PORRITT, BARON. (Porritt.) [Life Baron 1973. Bt. UK 1963.]

ARTHUR (ESPIE) PORRITT, *GCMG, GCVO,
CBE*; *Life Baron,* and 1st *Baronet*
son of the late Ernest Edward Porritt, VD
MD, FRCS, of Wanganui, NZ; *b.* Aug. 10th
1900; ed. at Wanganui Collegiate Sch.
Otago Univ., and Magdalen Coll., Oxford
(MB, MCh, MA, Hon. Fellow Magdalen Coll.,
Hon. DSc); FRCS England, Hon. FRCS
Glasgow, Canada and Ireland, Hon. FRACS,
Hon. Fellow American Coll. of Surgs., and
S. African Coll. of Surgs.; LRCP London,
Hon. FRCP, Hon. FRACP, Hon. FRCOG.;
Hon. MD Bristol; Hon. LLD St. Andrew,
Birmingham, NZ, and Otago; late Brig.
RAMC; Consulting Surg., Hon. Surg. to St.
Mary's Hosp., and to Roy. Masonic Hosp.,
London, to King Edward VII Hosp. for
Officers, and to Hosp. of St. John and Eliza-
beth, a Member of Internat. Olympic Cttee.,
and of Med. Advisory Cttee. to War Office,
Vice-Pres. of British Empire Games Fedn., NZ Red Cross Commr. in Great
Britain and a KStJ (Prior of NZ); Pres. BMA 1960-61, of Roy. Coll. of Surgs.
1960-63, and of Roy. Soc. of Medicine 1966-67; Master of Apothecaries'
Co. 1964-66; Chm. of Civil Consulting Staff of King Edward VII Convalescent
Home for Officers, Osborne 1949-67 and Consulting Surg. to the Army 1954-67,
and Consultant Emeritus to the Army since 1971; Chm. of African Medical
and Research Foundation since 1973; Surg. to HM's Household 1936-46,
Surg. to HM King George VI 1946-52, and Sjt.-Surg. to HM The Queen
1952-67; Gov.-Gen. of NZ 1967-72; 1939-45 War in France and Middle East
(CBE); an Officer of American Legion of Merit; CBE (Mil.) 1945, KCMG 1950,
KCVO 1957, a Baronet (UK of Hampstead, co. London) 1963, GCMG 1967,
GCVO 1970, and *Baron Porritt,* of Wanganui, NZ, and of Hampstead, Greater
London (Life Baron) 1973: *m.* 1st, 1926, Mary Frances Wynne, da. of William
Bond; 2ndly, 1946, Kathleen Mary, da. of the late Alfred Sidney Peck, of
Spalding, Lincs., and has issue by 2nd m.

Arms,—Or, a serpent in bend vert between two lions heads erased gules, on a chief of the last two swords points upwards in saltire of the first, between as many roses argent both surmounted by another gules barbed and seeded proper. **Crest**,—On a wreath or and gules, a demi heraldic antelope gules armed azure collared or, holding a torch of the last enflamed proper between two fern fronds vert. **Supporters**, —*Dexter*, an eagle and *sinister* a tui bird, both proper.

Residence,—57, Hamilton Terr., NW8. *Clubs*,—Athenaeum, Buck's.

(In remainder to Baronetcy only.)

SONS LIVING. *(By 2nd m.)*

Hon. JONATHON ESPIE, *b.* July 6th, 1950; ed. at Eton, and Magdalen Coll., Oxford.
Hon. Jeremy Charles, *b.* 1953; ed. at Eton.

DAUGHTER LIVING. *(By 2nd m.)*

Hon. Joanna Mary, *b.* 1948: *m.* 1969, Simon Patrick Meredith Hardy, of 41, Bangalore St., SW15 and has issue.

PORTAL OF HUNGERFORD, BARONESS. (Portal.) [Baron U.K. 1945.]

ROSEMARY ANN PORTAL, *Baroness Portal of Hungerford*; *b.* May 12th, 1923; *s.* 1971; late Section Officer WAAF.

Arms,—Argent, a lion rampant sable between a fleur de lys azure and a rose gules barbed and seeded proper, on a chief of the third an astral crown or. **Crest**,—Issuant from an astral crown or a portal between two towers proper. **Supporters**,—*Dexter*, a pilot of the Royal Air Force; *sinister*, a mechanic of the Royal Air Force, both in service dress proper.

Residence,—West Ashling House, near Chichester.

SISTER LIVING

Hon. MAVIS ELIZABETH ALOUETTE, *b.* June 13th, 1926.

WIDOW LIVING OF FIRST VISCOUNT

JOAN MARGARET (*Viscountess Portal of Hungerford*), (West Ashling House, nr. Chichester), da. of Sir Charles Glynne, Earle Welby, OB, 5th Bt.: *m.* 1919, the 1st Viscount, who *d.* 1971, when the Viscountcy became ext.

PREDECESSOR.—[1] *Marshal of the RAF Sir* CHARLES FREDERICK ALGERNON Portal, KG, GCB, OM, DSO, MC, son of the late Edward Robert Portal, JP, of Sulham, Pangbourne; *b.* 1893; Marshal of the RAF 1944; AOC-in-C, Bomber Command March to Oct. 1940; Ch. of Air Staff 1940-45; Chm. of BAC 1960-68; bore Sceptre with the Cross at Coronation of Queen Elizabeth II; cr. *Baron Portal of Hungerford*, of Hungerford, co. Berks. (peerage of UK) 1945, with remainder to heirs male of his body, and in default of such issue to his el. da., Rosemary Ann and the heirs male of her body; and in default of such issue to every other da. successively in order of seniority of age and priority of birth, and to the heirs male of their bodies, and *Viscount Portal of Hungerford*, of Hungerford, co. Berks. (peerage of UK) 1946: *m.* 1919, Joan Margaret, da. of Sir Charles Glynne Earle Welby, OB, 5th Bt.; *d.* 1971, when the Viscountcy of Portal of Hungerford (peerage of UK) became ext., and the Barony of Portal of Hungerford devolved on his el. da. [2] ROSEMARY ANN, Baroness Portal of Hungerford and present peeress.

PORTARLINGTON, EARL OF. (Dawson-Damer.) [Earl I. 1785.]

Virtue is the way of life.

GEORGE LIONEL YUILL SEYMOUR DAWSON-DAMER, 7th Earl; *b.* Aug. 10th, 1938; *s.* 1959; ed. at Eton; a patron of two livings; a Page of Honour to HM 1953-55; a Dir. G. S. Yuill & Co. Pty. Ltd., of Sydney, Cold Storage Holdings Ltd., of London, Austn. Stock Breeders Co. Ltd., Brisbane, Queensland Trading & Holding Co. Ltd., Brisbane, and other Cos.; Pres. of Aust. Malaysia Singapore Assocn.: *m.* 1961, Davina, el. da. of the late Sir Edward Henry Windley, KCMG, KCVO [see V. Brookeborough, colls.], and has issue.

Arms,—Azure, a chevron ermine, between three arrows points downwards, or, barbed and flighted proper; on a chief argent three martlets sable, and on a canton gules a mullet or. **Crest**,—A cat's head erased at the neck, and affrontée, of a tabby colour, holding in the mouth a rat sable. **Supporters**,—Two heraldic tigers proper.

Residence,—55, Victoria Rd., Bellevue Hill, Sydney, NSW, 2023.

SONS LIVING.

CHARLES GEORGE YUILL SEYMOUR (*Viscount Carlow*), *b.* Oct. 6th, 1965.
Hon. Edward Lionel Seymour, *b.* 1967.
Hon. Henry Lionel Seymour, *b.* 1971.

DAUGHTER LIVING.

Lady Marina Davina, *b.* 1969.

BROTHER LIVING.

Hon. Lionel John Charles Seymour (Oran Park, Narellan, NSW), *b.* 1940; ed. at Eton: *m.* 1965, Rosemary, da. of P. G. M. Hancock, of Trenowth, Grampound Rd., Truro.

PREDECESSORS.—[1] WILLIAM HENRY Dawson, *M.P.* for Portarlington and for Queen's Co.; cr. *Baron Dawson*, of Dawson's Court, Queen's Co. (peerage of Ireland) 1770, and *Viscount Carlow* (peerage of Ireland) 1776; *d.* 1779; *s.* by his son [2] JOHN, 2nd Viscount; cr. *Earl of Portarlington* (peerage of Ireland) 1785; sat as M.P. for Portarlington; *d.* 1798; *s.* by his son [3] JOHN, 2nd Earl; was Col. 23rd Dragoons; present at numerous battles in the Peninsula, and at Waterloo; in 1808 *s.* to the estates of George Damer, 2nd and last Earl of Dorchester;

d. unmarried 1845; *s.* by his nephew [4] HENRY JOHN REUBEN, *K.P.*, 3rd Earl, son of Capt. the Hon. Henry Dawson (who assumed by sign manual the additional surname of Damer), by Eliza, dau. of Capt. Edmund Joshua Moriarty, R.N., and granddau. of 1st Earl of Carhampton, *b.* 1822; was a Representative Peer: *m.* 1847, Lady Alexandrina Octavia Maria Vane, who *d.* 1874, dau. of 3rd Marquess of Londonderry: *d.* 1889; *s.* by his cousin [5] LIONEL SEYMOUR WILLIAM (son of the late Col. the Rt. Hon. George Lionel Dawson-Damer, 3rd son of 1st Earl), 4th Earl, *b.* 1832; M.P. for Portarlington (*C*) 1857-65: *m.* 1855, the Hon. Harriet Lydia Montagu, dau. of 6th Baron Rokeby (*ext.*); *d.* 1892; *s.* by his el. son [6] GEORGE LIONEL HENRY SEYMOUR, 5th Earl; *b.* 1858: *m.* 1881, Emma Andalusia Frere, who *d.* 1929, dau. of the late Lord Nigel Kennedy; *d.* 1900; *s.* by his son [6] LIONEL ARTHUR HENRY SEYMOUR, 6th Earl; *b.* 1883; formerly Lt. Irish Gds.: *m.* 1907, Winnafreda, who *d.* 1975, only child of the late George Skelton Yuill, of 37 Chesham Place, SW; *d.* 1959; *s.* by his grandson [7] GEORGE LIONEL YUILL SEYMOUR (el. son of the late Air Commodore George Lionel Seymour, Viscount Carlow, only son of 6th Earl)7th Earl and present peer ; also Viscount Carlow, and Baron Dawson.

PORTLAND, DUKE OF. (Cavendish-Bentinck.) [Duke G.B. 1716.]

Fear disgrace.

WILLIAM ARTHUR HENRY CAVENDISH-BENTINCK, *K.G.*, 7th Duke ; *b.* March 16th, 1893; *s.* 1943; ed. at Eton ; Capt. Roy. Horse Guards (Reserve), Lieut.-Col. (retired) late Comdg., and Hon. Col. Notts (Sherwood Rangers) Yeo., Hon. Col. Robin Hood (Motor) Batn., and Hon. Air Commodore No. 616 (S. Yorkshire) Auxiliary Squadron R.A.F., Lord-Lieut. of Notts, and a D.L. for Caithness-shire ; European War 1914-16 ; was a Junior Lord of the Treasury Nov. 1927 to June 1929, and (in National Govt.) Sept. to Nov. 1931 ; has been Pres. of Notts T.A. Asso. since 1939 ; appointed Chancellor of Nottingham Univ. 1954 ; sat as M.P. for Notts, Newark Div. (*U*) Nov. 1922 to April 1943 ; K.G. 1948 : *m.* 1915, the Hon. Ivy, *D.B.E.* (formerly a Maid of Honour to Queen Alexandra), dau. of the late Lord Algernon Charles Gordon-Lennox [see D. Richmond, colls.], and has issue.

Arms,—Quarterly, 1st and 4th azure, a cross-moline argent, *Bentinck* ; 2nd and 3rd sable, three stags' heads embossed argent, a crescent for difference, *Cavendish*. **Crests,**—1st, out of a ducal coronet proper, two arms counter-embowed, vested gules, on the hands gloves, or, each holding an ostrich feather argent, *Bentinck;* 2nd, a snake nowed proper, *Cavendish*. **Supporters,**—Two lions double queued, the *dexter* or ; the *sinister* sable.

Seats,—Welbeck Abbey, Worksop; Langwell, Berriedale, Caithness: Bothal Castle, Northumberland. *Residence,*—Welbeck Woodhouse, Worksop, Notts.

DAUGHTER LIVING.

Lady Alexandra Margaret Anne, *b.* 1916 ; is a C.St.J.

SISTER LIVING.

Lady Victoria Alexandrina Violet, *C.V.O.*, *b.* 1890 ; appointed an Extra Woman of the Bedchamber to H.M. Queen Elizabeth the Queen Mother 1937 ; C.V.O. 1953 : *m.* 1918, Capt. Michael John Wemyss, late Household Cav. [see E. Wemyss, colls.]. *Residence,*—Wemyss Castle, East Wemyss, Fife.

COLLATERAL BRANCHES LIVING.

Issue of the late Lord Charles Cavendish-Bentinck, D.S.O., half-brother of 6th Duke, *b.* 1868, *d.* 1956 : *m.* 1897, Cicely Mary, who *d.* 1936, dau. of the late Charles Seymour Grenfell, of Elibank House, Taplow :—

Elizabeth Eileen *b.* 1901 : *m.* 1925 (marriage dissolved 1954), Major Roger Henry Wethered. *Residence,*—43, Phillimore Gardens, W.8.——Alice, *b.* 1904 : *m.* 1930, Major Terence Andrew Alfred Watt, Life Guards, who *d.* (killed on active ser. during European War) 1942, and has issue living Michael Andrew (of Greens Park, Towcester, Northants), *b.* 1933; ed. at Eton; 2nd Lt., Life Guards: *m.* 1959, Susan Myrtle, da. of Maj. Leith Ingham Tomkins Whitaker, DL, late Rifle Bde. [see V. Powerscourt], and has issue living, Charles Andrew *b.* 1964, David Alexander *b.* 1968, Sarah Alice *b.* 1962, Polly-Anna *b.* 1971. *Residence,*—West Park Farm, Ickburgh, Norfolk.

Granddaughter of the late Rt. Hon. George Augustus Frederick Cavendish Bentinck, M.P. (infra) :—

Issue of the late William George Cavendish-Bentinck, *b.* 1854, *d.* 1909 : *m.* 1880, Elizabeth, who *d.* 1943, dau. of Maturin Livingston of Staatsburg, New York :—

Ruth Evelyn, *b.* 1883 : *m.* 1907, Walter Spencer Morgan Burns, who *d.* 1929, and has issue living, *Maj.-Gen. Sir* (Walter Arthur) George KCVO, *CB, DSO, OBE, MC* (North Mymms Park, Hatfield, Herts.; Guards, Jockey, White's and Pratt's Clubs), *b.* 1911; Maj.-Gen. (ret.) Coldm. Gds.; Lord-Lt. of Herts. since 1961; 1939-45 War in Italy (despatches, DSO, MC); DSO 1941, OBE (mil.) 1953, CB (Mil.) 1961, KCVO 1962,—Cynthia Mary, *OBE* (*Lady Carew Pole*), *b.* 1908; an Alderman for Cornwall 1958-67; Chm. S-W Electricity Consultative Council 1952-73; County Organiser WRVS 1947-73; a Member of Council of English Guernsey Cattle Soc. since 1971 (Pres. 1970-71); Pres. Cornwall Branch of S-W Guernsey Cattle Breeders Assocn. 1965-69, and of Roy. Cornwall Agric. Assocn. since 1959; OBE (Civil) 1959: *m.* 1928, Col. Sir John Gawen Carew Pole, DSO, 12th Bt. (cr. 1628), of Antony House, Torpoint, Cornwall. *Residence,*—North Mymms Park, Hatfield.

Grandchildren of the late Rt. Hon. George Augustus Frederick Cavendish-Bentinck, M.P., son of the late Maj.-Gen. Lord Frederick Cavendish-Bentinck, C.B., M.P., 4th son of 3rd Duke:—

Issue of the late (William George) Frederick Cavendish-Bentinck, *b.* 1856, *d.* 1948 : *m.* 1887, Ruth Mary St. Maur, who *d.* 1953 :—

Hon. Sir FERDINAND WILLIAM, *K.B.E., C.M.G., M.C., b.* July 4th, 1888 ; ed. at Eton ; formerly Major King's Roy. Rifle Corps ; Founder of Kenya Asso. (Chm. 1932), and a Member of E. African Production and Supply Council, of E. African Advisory Council on Agriculture, Animal Industry, and Forestry, and of E. African Agricultural Forestry and Vet. Research Organisations Committee ; Chm. of Tanganyika League, and African Defence Federation 1938, and of Agricultural Production and Settlement Board, Kenya 1939-45 ; Timber Controller for E. Africa 1940-45 ; a Member of E. African Civil Defence and Supply Council 1940-45 ; European War 1914-18 (severely wounded, despatches) ; Private Sec. to Gov. of Uganda 1925-27 ; is an Officer of Order of Crown of Belgium ; was a M.L.C. and M.E.C. Kenya 1938-60, and Speaker of Legislative Council 1955-60 ; unsuccessfully contested S. Div. of Kensington (*L*) Nov. 1922 ; C.M.G. 1941, K.B.E. (Civil) 1956 : *m.* 1st, 1912, Wentworth Frances (who *d.* 1964, having obtained a divorce 1950), da. of the late William James Hope-Johnstone [M. Linlithgow, colls.]; 2ndly, 1950, Gwyneth Ethel, MBE, widow of Col. D. A. J. Bowie, RA. *Address,*—c/o Box 825, Nairobi, Kenya. *Clubs,*—Conservative, Turf, Beefsteak, Muthaiga (Nairobi).——Victor Frederick William, *CMG, b.* 1897; ed. at Wellington Coll.; sometime 2nd Lieut. Gren. Gds.; entered Diplo. Ser. 1919; became 1st Sec. 1929, and Counsellor 1942; was Chm., Joint Intelligence Sub-committee of Chiefs of Staff 1939-45, Foreign Office Adviser to Dir. of Plans 1942-45, and Ambassador Extraor. and Min. Plen to Poland 1945-47; CMG 1942: *m.* 1st, 1924, Clothilde Bruce (from whom he obtained **a** divorce 1948), da. of the late James Bruce Quigley, of Dallas Texas, USA ; 2ndly, 1948, Kathleen Elsie (TILLOTSON), da. of Arthur Barry, of Montreal, Canada, and has issue living, (by 1st m.) Mary Jane, *b.* 1929: *m.* 1963, Alexander Constantine Georgiades, of Pilton, Oundle, and has issue living, William James *b.* 1967, David Constantine *b.* 1969. *Residence,*—21, Carlyle Sq., SW3. *Clubs,*—Turf, Beeksteak.——Venetia Barbara (140, Chiltern Court, NW1), *b.* 1902.

(*In remainder to Earldom only*).—
Descendants of the late Hon. William Bentinck (or. Count of the Holy Roman Empire by Charles VI. of Austria 1732 for himself and his descendants), 2nd son of 1st Earl of Portland (infra). [In 1845 by decree of the German Diet the Counts Bentinck obtained recognition of their right to the dignities and privileges of the Mediatised Houses (Reichsunmittelbar) of Germany with style of " Erlaucht"] :—

Grandchildren of the late Lieut.-Col. Count Henry Charles Adolphus Frederick William Aldenburg-Bentinck (infra) :—
Issue of the late Capt. Count Robert Charles Aldenburg-Bentinck (*a Mediatised Count of the Holy Roman Empire*), *b.* 1875, *d.* 1932: *m.* 1915, Lady Norah Ida Emily Noel, who *d.* 1959, dau. of 3rd Earl of Gainsborough:—
Count Henry Noel (Thornbank, Potten End, Berkhamsted, Herts.), *b.* 1919; ed. at Harrow; a Mediatised Count of the Holy Roman Empire; formerly Lt. Coldstream Guards; 1939-45 War (twice wounded); *m.* 1st, 1940, Pauline Ursula, who *d.* 1967, da. of Frederick William Mellowes, of Penn House, Reynolds Close, Hampstead, NW; 2ndly, 1974, Jenifer, only da. of the late Reginald Hopkins, of 91, Kingsley Way, N2, and has issue living (by 1st m.), Timothy Robert Charles Noel, *b.* 1953; a Mediatised Count of the Holy Roman Empire,—Sorrel Deirdre, *b.* 1942: *m.* 1972, John Phillip Lister Lister-Kaye, only son of Sir John Christopher Lister Lister-Kaye, 7th Bt.,—Anna Cecilia, *b.* 1947: *m.* 1965 (m. diss. 1974), Jasper Hamilton Holmes.——*Countess* Brydgytte Blanche (Rykstraatweg, 242, Haren, Groningen, Holland), *b.* 1916: *m.* 1937, Jonkheer Adrian Hendrik Sibble van der Wyck, Capt. R. Netherlands Horse Artillery (Reserve), and Attorney to the Queen of the Netherlands, who *d.* 1973, and has issue living, Evert Rein Robert Henry, *b.* 1945,—Douglas Roderick Arthur Duncan *b.* 1955,—Caroline Norah Frédérique Adrienne, *b.* 1938: *m.* 1961, K. J. A. Baron Callot d'Escury, Estate Agent of Crown Property, Zeeland, of Kloosterzande, Zeeuws Vlaanderen, Netherlands, and has issue living, Guyon Adolf André *b.* 1962, Robert Willem Frederick *b.* 1970, Juliette Brydgytte Blanche *b.* 1963, Marina Caroline Norah *b.* 1965,—Brydgytte Agnes Dawn, *b.* 1940: *m.* 1968, Paul H. M. D. Vermeer, of Dorpstraat 41, Almen, Gelderland, Holland, and has issue living, Robert Paul Adrian Henry Simon *b.* 1968, Fiona Victoria Regina Brydgytte *b.* 1970, Nadia Norah Noël *b.* 1971,—Reïna Jeanne Woltera, *b.* 1942; a nurse: *m.* 1973, H. W. van Harrenveld, advocate, of 144, Van Hoey Laan, The Hague, and has issue living, Hugo Johannes Hendrick *b.* 1974. [See below (under 6th Count) regarding style of *Count and Countess*.]

Granddaughter of the late Lieut.-Gen. Charles Anthony Ferdinand Aldenburg-Bentinck, 4th Count Bentinck, great-grandson of the late Hon. William Bentinck, 1st Count Bentinck (ante) :—
Issue of the late Lieut.-Col. Count Henry Charles Adolphus Frederick William Aldenburg-Bentinck (Coldstream Guards), 5th Count Bentinck [who in 1874 resigned his rights as head of the family and the title of Count Bentinck to his younger brother, William Charles Philip Otho (infra)], *b.* 1846, *d.* 1903 : *m.* 1874, Henrietta Eliza Cathcart, who *d.* 1934, dau. of the late Robert McKerrell (a grandson of 8th Laird of Hillhouse), and sister of 13th Laird of Hillhouse, Ayrshire :—
Countess Ursula Victoria Henrietta, *b.* 1884; European War 1914-19 in England and France with V.A.D., European War 1939-45 as Censor at Liverpool and in London Auxiliary Ambulance Ser.; served with British Red Cross Relief in Holland and Germany 1945. *Address,*—c/o Williams Deacon's Bank, 9, Pall Mall, S.W.1.

Granddaughters of the late William Charles Philip Otho Aldenburg-Bentinck, 6th Count Bentinck (infra) :—
Issue of the late William Frederick Charles Henry Aldenburg-Bentinck, 7th Count Bentinck; *b.* 1880, *d.* 1959 : *m.* 1923, Adrienne (LABOUCHERE), dau. of the late Philip Ernst Vegelin van Claerbergen, of The Hague :—
Countess Sophie Mechtild Marie, *b.* 1924 : *m.* 1950, Count Enrico Gaetani dell' Aquila d'Aragona, and has issue living, *Donna* Benedetta Rita Maria, *b.* 1953,—*Donna* Jacobella Immacolata Scolastica, *b.* 1956,—*Donna* Giovannella Maria, *b.* 1961. *Residence,*—43, Pizzofalcone, Naples, Italy.—*Countess* Isabelle Adrienne, *b.* 1925: *m.* 1951, Count Aurel Ladislaus Franz Heinrich Ernst zu Ortenburg, and has issue living, *Count* Franz Wilhelm Friedrich Ladislaus, *b.* 1953,—*Count* Philip Wilhelm, *b.* 1955,—*Countess* Nadine Marie Elisabeth Johanna, *b.* 1957. *Residence,*—Birkenfeld, Hassfurt, Unterfranken, Germany.

Granddaughters of the late Lt.-Gen. Charles Anthony Ferdinand Aldenburg, Bentinck, 4th Count Bentinck (ante) :—
Issue of the late William Charles Philip Otho Aldenburg-Bentinck, 6th Count Bentinck, and a Count of the Holy Roman Empire, *b.* 1848, *d.* 1912, having received in 1886 Roy. licence to bear in England the title of Count of the Holy Roman Empire, with permission *for all other descendants (both male and female) of his father to bear the title of Count or Countess before their Christian names*, and assumed by patent in 1889 the title of Count of Waldeck-Limpurg : *m.* 1877, Baroness Mary Cornelia, who *d.* 1912, dau. of Charles, Baron de Heeckeren de Wassenaer, of Twickel :—
Countess Isabella Antoinette Mary Clementina, *b.* 1889 : *m.* 1914, Count William Solms-Sonnenwalde, formerly Capt. Prussian Hussars of the Guard, and has issue living, *Count* Alfred Otto Friedrich, *b.* 1932,—*Countess* Marie Helene Luise Clementine, *b.* 1917 : *m.* 1951, Günther von Bünau, of Mettmann Rhineland, Germany, and has issue living, Rudolf *b.* 1953. *Residence,*—Weldam, Goor, Holland.

Issue of the late Capt. Count Charles Reginald Adelbert Aldenburg-Bentinck (a Count of the Holy Roman Empire), *b.* 1853 ; *d.* 1934 : *m.* 1878 (marriage dissolved 1885), the

Countess Helena Agnes Alexandrina Amelia Caroline, who *d.* 1942, dau. of Adelbert, Count of Waldeck and Pyrmont:—
Countess Mary Amelia Mechtild Agnes, *b.* 1879: *m.* 1922, Rudolf Frederick, Baron de Heeckeren de Wassenaer. who *d.* 1936. *Residence,*—Twickel, Delden, Holland.

Granddaughter of the late Count Godard John George Charles Aldenburg-Bentinck, yst. son of Lt.-Gen. Charles Anthony Ferdinand Aldenburg Bentinck, 4th Count Bentinck (ante):—
Godard Adrian Henry Jules (9th Count Bentinck, and Baron Aldenburgh), *b.* 1887, *d.* 1972: *m.* 1st, 1921, Jacoba, who *d.* 1949, da. of the late Jacobus Johannes van den Heuvel; 2ndly, 1961, Alida (22, Saxen Weimarlaan, Amsterdam, Holland), da. of the late Frits Vlieger:—
Countess Louise Adrienne Jacoba, *b.* 1923: *m.* 1954, George Léon Alex de Brauwere dit de Steelant, of Delft, and Amerongen Castle, Amerongen, Holland, and has issue living, Alain George Francois, *b.* 1961,—Jemima Sophie Adrienne, *b.* 1958.

PREDECESSORS.—[1] HANS WILLIAM Bentinck, *K.G.*, *P.C.* (whose el. brother Eusebius Borchard was Baron Bentinck of Diepenheim and Schoonheten in the Netherlands), having first served William, Prince of Orange, as a Page of Honour, eventually became his confidential adviser, and after that Prince's accession to the British throne, was appointed Groom of the Stole and First Gentleman of the Bedchamber; commanded a Dutch Regt. of Horse Guards, and as a Lieut.-Gen. took a distinguished part at the battle of the Boyne 1690; cr. *Baron Cirencester, Viscount Woodstock,* and *Earl of Portland* (peerage of Great Britain) 1689; *d.* 1709; *s.* by his son [2] HENRY, 2nd Earl; was Gov. and Capt. Gen. of Jamaica, and sometime M.P. for Southampton; cr. *Marquess of Titchfield* and *Duke of Portland* (peerage of Great Britain) 1716: *m.* 1704, Elizabeth dau. of the 2nd Earl of Gainsborough (cr. 1682); *d.* 1726; *s.* by his son [3] WILLIAM, *K.G.*, 2nd Duke; *d.* 1762; *s.* by his son [4] WILLIAM HENRY CAVENDISH, *K.G.*, 3rd Duke; was M.P. for Weobley 176 1-2, Viceroy of Ireland 1782, First Lord of the Treasury 1783 and 1807, Sec. of State for HomeDepart. 1794, Pres. of the Council 1801, Chancellor of Oxford Univ., High Steward of Bristol, and Lord Lieut. of Notts; assumed the additional surname of Cavendish by Roy. licence 1801; *d.* 1809; *s.* by his son [5] WILLIAM HENRY, *P.C.*, *D.C.L.*, *F.R.S.*, 4th Duke; was Lord-Lieut. of Middlesex; Roy. licence in 1795 the additional surname of Scott; *d.* 1854; *s.* by his son [6] WILLIAM JOHN Cavendish-Bentinck-Scott, 5th Duke, *b.* 1800; sat as M.P. for Lynn 1824-6; *d.* 1879; *s.* by his kinsman [7] WILLIAM JOHN ARTHUR CHARLES JAMES, *K.G.*, *G.C.V.O.*, *T.D.*, *P.C.* (el. son of the late Lieut.-Gen. Arthur Cavendish-Bentinck, 2nd son of Lord William Charles Augustus Cavendish-Bentinck, 3rd son of 3rd Duke), 6th Duke; *b.* 1857; Hon. Col. 4th and 7th Batns. Sherwood Foresters; sometime Lord-Lieut. of Notts; Master of the Horse 1886-92 and 1895-1905, and Chancellor of Order of the Garter 1937-43; received Roy. Victorian Chain 1933; *m.* 1889, Dame Winifred, *D.B.E.*, who *d.* 1954, only dau. of the late Thomas Yorke Dallas-Yorke, of Walmsgate, Louth; *d.* 1943; *s.* by his el. son [8] WILLIAM ARTHUR HENRY, 7th Duke and present peer; also Marquess of Titchfield, Earl of Portland, Viscount Woodstock, Baron Cirencester, and Baron Bolsover.

∗∗∗ [1] AUGUSTA MARY ELIZABETH Cavendish-Bentinck, *b.* 1834; cr. *Baroness Bolsover,* of Bolsover Castle, co. Derby (peerage of United Kingdom) 1880, with remainder to the issue male of her husband by his 1st marriage: *m.* 1862, as his 2nd wife, Lieut.-Gen. Arthur Cavendish-Bentinck, who *d.* 1877, 2nd son of Lord William Charles Augustus Cavendish-Bentinck (ante), 3rd son of 3rd Duke of Portland; *d.* 1893; *s.* by her step-son [2] WILLIAM JOHN ARTHUR CHARLES JAMES, *K.G.*, *G.C.V.O.*, *T.D.*, *P.C.*, 2nd Baron and 6th Duke of Portland (ante).

PORTMAN, VISCOUNT. (Portman.) [Viscount U.K. 1873.]

EDWARD HENRY BERKELEY PORTMAN, 9th Viscount; *b.* April 22nd, 1934; *s.* 1967; ed. at Canford, and Roy. Agric. Coll., Cirencester: *m.* 1st, 1956 (m. diss. 1966), Rosemary Joy, el. da. of Charles Farris, of Coombe Bissett, Wilts.; 2ndly, 1966, Penelope Anne Hassard, yr. da. of Trevor Allin, of N. Moreton, Berks., and has issue by 1st and 2nd marriages.

Arms—Quarterly: 1st and 4th or, a fleur-de-lis azure, *Portman;* 2nd and 3rd gules, a chevron ermine, between ten crosses patée argent, six in chief and four in base, *Berkeley.* Crests.—1st, a talbot sejeant or; 2nd, a unicorn passant gules, armed and crined or. Supporters.—*Dexter,* a savage, wreathed about the head and waist with ivy, in his dexter hand a club resting on the shoulder, proper; *sinister,* a talbot or.

Residence,—Clock Mill, Clifford, Herefordshire. *Club,*—White's.

SONS LIVING. (*By 1st marriage.*)
Hon. CHRISTOPHER EDWARD BERKELEY, *b.* July 30th, 1958.

(*By 2nd marriage.*)
Hon. Alexander Michael Berkeley, *b.* 1967.
Hon. Justin Trevor Berkeley, *b.* 1969.
Hon. Piers Richard Berkeley, *b.* 1971.
Hon. Matthew Gerald Berkeley, *b.* 1973.

DAUGHTER LIVING. (*By 1st marriage.*)
Hon. Claire Elizabeth, *b.* 1959.

HALF-BROTHER LIVING.
Michael William Berkeley, *b.* 1943; ed. at Winchester.

HALF-SISTER LIVING.
Suna (Synove Isobel), *b.* 1939: *m.* 1st, 1968, (m. annulled 1970), Martin George Anthony Wilkinson; 2ndly, 1970, Simon Thomas Paul Boyle, of Waterton House, Ampney Circus. Cirencester Glos., and has issue living (by 1st m.), Heron Berkeley BOYLE, *b.* 1968,—(by 2nd m.) Kestrel Berkeley, *b.* 1970.

AUNT LIVING. (*Daughter of Seventh Viscount.*)
Hon. Penelope Isobel, *b.* 1913: *m.* 1st, 1934 (marriage dissolved 1949), Brig. Archer Francis Lawrence Olive, D.S.O., M.C., Grenadier Guards [Buxton, Bt. colls.]; 2ndly, 1949, David Arthur Salvin Bowlby, and has issue living, (by 1st m.) Henry Archer (13, Edwardes Sq., W8 6HE), *b.* 1934: *m.* 1st, 1957 (m. diss. 1963), Sonia Anne, only da. of William Rees, of Athens, Greece; 2ndly, 1964, Julia, 2nd da. of the late Fergus Boundy, of Sydney, Aust.,—Annsybella Sarah Penelope, *b.* 1936: *m.* 1st, 1955 (m. diss. 1965), Euan McCorquodale; 2ndly, 1965, Capt. Charles Patrick Hazlehurst, of Broomy Court, Wormelow, Herefordshire. *Residences,*—Inverinate, Kyle of Lochalsh, Ross-shire; The Manor, Healing, Grimsby.

DAUGHTERS LIVING OF FOURTH VISCOUNT.
Hon. Sylvia Grace, *b.* 1900: *m.* 1932, Major Thomas Gerard du Buisson, M.B.E., M.C., late R.A. *Residence,*—Reydon Lodge, Bury Rd., Newmarket, Suffolk.

Hon. Jocelyne, *b.* 1903: *m.* 1923, Capt. James Albert Garland Emmet, L.G. (ret.), and has issue living, James Edward Robert (Altidore Castle, Kilpedder, Greystones, co. Wicklow), *b.* 1926: *m.* 1956, Maud Clemency, second da. of the late Col. Noel Craig, of Washington, DC, USA, and has issue living, Philip *b.* 1960, Amanda *b.* 1958,—Patrick Simon (Old Carton, Maynooth, co. Kildare), *b.* 1932: Lt.-Cdr. RN (ret.); *m.* 1973, Anthea Moira Enid, da. of Maj. Errold Ashworth Sydney Cosby, of Stradbally, co. Leix, and has issue living, Rosalind Elizabeth *b.* 1974,—Catherine Mary, *b.* 1925: *m.* 1950, James Jerningham Corballis [B. Stafford, colls.], of Gorteen Delgany, co. Wicklow, and has issue living, Seamus Brian Jerningham *b.* 1951, Timothy Thomas *b.* 1956, Belinda Mary *b.* 1954, Sara Jane *b.* 1957. *Residences,*—Golf Cottage, Allée des Amazones, Le Touquet, France: Le Sommet, Route de Valtonne, O6, Le Cannet, France, AM.

DAUGHTERS LIVING OF FIFTH VISCOUNT.
Hon. Sheila Constance, *b.* 1927 : *m.* 1951, Michael Holland-Hibbert [see V. Knutsford, colls.]. *Residence,*—Broadclyst House, Exeter.

Hon. Rosemary, *b.* 1931: *m.* 1951, Derrick Allix Pease [see Pease, Bt., cr. 1920]. *Residences,*— 2, Britten St., SW3; Upper Woodcott, Whitchurch, Hants.

WIDOW LIVING OF SON OF SEVENTH VISCOUNT.
Marjorie Karr, dau. of the late Frederick William Harris : *m.* 1938, as his second wife, the Hon. Michael Berkeley Portman, who *d.* 1959, and has issue living [see ante]. *Residence,*—Portman Lodge, Durweston, Blandford, Dorset.

WIDOW LIVING OF EIGHTH VISCOUNT.
NANCY MAUREEN (*Nancy, Viscountess Portman*), (Sutton Waldron House, Blandford, Dorset), da. of Capt. Percy Herbert Franklin, RN (ret.): *m.* 1946, as his 2nd wife, the 8th Viscount, who *d.* 1967.

COLLATERAL BRANCHES LIVING.

Grandson of the late Berkeley Portman, el. son of the late Hon. Maurice Berkeley Portman (infra) :—
Issue of the late Com. Maurice Percy Berkeley Portman, R.N., *b.* 1884, *d.* 1928: *m.* 1918, Joan Wycliffe, who *d.* 1971, da. of the late Maj.-Gen. Charles William Thompson, CB, DSO:—
Berkeley Charles Berkeley, *b.* 1919; ed. at Wellington Coll.; late Lt. RN; is an Underwriting Member of Lloyd's: *m.* 1944, Sheila Margaret Penelope, da. of the late Capt. F. D. Mowat, RN, and has issue living, Rodney John Berkeley, *b.* 1947,—Celia Rose Berkeley, *b.* 1946: *m.* 1972, Anthony William Charlton Edwards, of 26, Lamont Rd., SW10 0JE, and has issue living, Marcella Louise Charlton *b.* 1973, Celia *b.* 1975,—Lucy Joan Berkeley, *b.* 1953,—Edwina Penelope Berkeley, *b.* 1956, —Rachel Mary Berkeley, *b.* 1961. *Residence,*—Danley Hill, Linchmere, nr. Haslemere, Surrey. *Club,*—Army and Navy.

Grandchildren of the late Com. Maurice William Portman, 2nd son of the late Hon. Maurice Berkeley Portman (infra) :—
Issue of the late Brigadier Guy Maurice Berkeley Portman, C.B., T.D., *b.* 1890, *d.* 1961; *m.* 1922, Miriam Katharine, who *d.* 1975, da. of George William Taylor [E. Wilton]:—
Anthony Seymour Berkeley, *b.* 1928 ; ed. at Eton ; late Lieut. Dorset Regt.: *m.* 1961, Penelope Helen Kathleen, da. of Derrick Warner Candy, of Kingston Warren, Wantage, Oxon., and has issue living, Michael Henry Berkeley, *b.* 1962,—Jonathan Guy Berkeley, *b.* 1965. *Residence,*—Rushmore Farm, Upton, Andover, Hants. *Club,*—Boodle's.——Lusia Edwina, *b.* 1931: *m.* 1952, Christopher David Howard, of Ryton Corner, Ryton, Shrewsbury, and has issue living, Davinia Elizabeth, *b.* 1953,—Belinda Jane, *b.* 1956.

Granddaughter of the late Hon. Maurice Berkeley Portman, 3rd son of 1st Viscount :—
Issue of the late Cecil Berkeley Portman, *b.* 1869, *d.* 1915: *m.* 1902, Florence Wyndham, who *d.* 1967, da. of the late Maj. Lachlan Forbes:—
Marigold Florence Lavinia, *b.* 1903: *m.* 1929, Raymond Patterson, and has issue living, Alan Noel (c/o Clay & Co., 750, Courtney St., Victoria, BC, Canada), *b.* 1936: *m.* 1965, Mary Elizabeth Ann, da. of Jefferey Boys, of Vancouver, and has issue living, Jeremy Patrick *b.* 1967,—Robert George (1137, Hollypark Rd., RR1 Brentwood Bay, BC), *b.* 1944: *m.* 1974, Susan Veronica Mary, da. of Henry Martyn, of Falmouth, Cornwall,—Janet Murray, *b.* 1930: *m.* 1949, David Blanchet, of 1230, Gladwin Drive, North Vancouver, British Columbia, and has issue living, Julia Claire Janet, *b.* 1949. *Address,*—2685, Queenswood Drive, Victoria, British Columbia.

Grandson of the late Montagu Berkeley Portman, youngest son of the late Hon. Maurice Berkeley Portman (ante) :—
Issue of the late Lieut.-Col. Gerald Berkeley Portman, R.A., *b.* 1903, *d.* 1954: *m.* 1st, 1928 (divorce 1945), Joan, dau. of the late Col. G. Turner ; 2ndly, 1945 (divorce 1950), Cicely Falkener, dau. of Godfrey Oliver, of Port Hill, Northam, Devon ; 3rdly 1950, Maj Elisabeth da. of Samuel Wohlin, of Lidingo, Brevik, Sweden:—
(By 2nd m.) Michael Berkeley (Port Hill, Northam, Devon), *b.* 1947; ed. at Wellington and RMA; Capt. 15/19H.

PREDECESSORS.—[1] EDWARD BERKELEY Portman, son of Edward Berkeley Portman, of Bryanston; *b.* 1799; sat as M.P. for Dorsetshire (*L*) 1823-32, and for Marylebone 1833 ; was cr. *Baron Portman,* of Orchard Portman, co. Somerset, 1837, and *Viscount Portman* (peerage of United Kingdom) 1873 : *m.* 1827, Lady Emma Lascelles, who *d.* 1865, dau. of 2nd Earl of Harewood; *d.* 1888; *s.* by his el. son [2] WILLIAM HENRY BERKELEY, *G.C.V.O.,* 2nd Viscount, *b.* 1829 ; M.P. for Shaftesbury 1852-7, and Dorsetshire (*L*) 1857-85 : *m.* 1st, 1855, the Hon Mary Selina Charlotte Wentworth-Fitzwilliam, who *d.* 1899, dau. of the late Viscount Milton, son of 5th Earl Fitzwilliam ; 2ndly, 1908, Frances Maxwell, who *d.* 1939, dau. of the late Boyd Alexan-

der Cuninghame, R.N., of Craigends, co. Renfrew, and widow of A.J. Livingstone Learmouth; *d.*
1919; *s.* by his el. son [3] HENRY BERKELEY, 3rd Viscount, *b.* 1860: *m.* 1901, Emma Andalusia
Frere, who *d.* 1929, dau. of the late Lord Nigel Kennedy, and widow of the 4th Earl of
Portarlington; *d.* 1923; *s.* by his brother [4] CLAUD BERKELEY, 4th Viscount, *b.* 1864: *m.*
1st, 1888, Mary Ada, who *d.* 1900 (having obtained a divorce 1897), dau. of the late Major
Francis Hastings Toone Gordon-Cumming [Gordon-Cumming, Bt., colls.]; 2ndly, 1898,
Harriette Mary, who *d.* 1939, dau. of the late William Stevenson; *d.* 1929; *s.* by his son
[5] EDWARD CLAUD BERKELEY, 5th Viscount, *b.* 1898; Capt. Life Guards: *m.* 1926, the Hon.
Sybil Mary Douglas-Pennant, who *d.* 1975, da. of 3rd Baron Penrhyn; *d.* 1942; *s.* by his uncle [6]
SEYMOUR BERKELEY (5th son of 2nd Viscount), 6th Viscount; *b.* 1868; *d.* 1946; *s.* by his brother
[7] GERALD BERKELEY, 7th Viscount, *b.* 1875: *m.* 1902, Dorothy Marie Isolde, who *d.* 1964, da. of Sir
Robert Sheffield, 5th Bt.; *d.* 1948; *s.* by his el. son [8] GERALD WILLIAM BERKELEY, 8th
Viscount, *b.* 1903: *m.* 1st, 1926 (m. diss. 1946), Marjorie Josephine Wernham Bentley, da. of George
Bentley Gerrard, of Montreal; 2ndly, 1946, Nancy Maureen, da. of Capt. Percy Herbert Franklin,
RN (ret.); *d.* 1967; *s.* by his nephew [9] EDWARD HENRY BERKELEY (el. son of the late Hon.
Michael Berkeley Portman, yr. son of 7th Viscount), 9th Viscount and present peer; also Baron
Portman,

PORTSMOUTH, EARL OF. (Wallop.) [Earl G.B. 1743.]

GERARD VERNON WALLOP, 9th
Earl; *b.* May 16th, 1898: *s.* 1943;
ed. at Winchester, and at Balliol
Coll., Oxford; is a Farmer;
was a Member of Milk Marketing
Board 1933-34, and an Alderman
of Hants. co Council, and Chm.
Country Landowners' Asso. 1947-
49; elected Vice-Pres., European
Electors' Union, Kenya 1952, and
Pres. 1953; a M.L.C. Kenya
1957-61; has been Chm., Forest
Advisory Committee Kenya since
1954, a Member of Research
Council, E. Africa High Commn.
since 1958, and Vice-Chm., E.
Africa, Natural Resources Re-
search Council since 1963; author
of works on Agriculture and
Sociology; 1914-18 War as Lt.
2nd Life Guards and Guards
Machine Gun Regt.; sat as M.P.
for Basingstoke Div. of Hampshire
(*C*) May 1929 to Feb. 1934: *m.*

: In following the truth.

1st, 1920, Mary Lawrence (who
obtained a divorce 1936), da. of Waldron Kintzing Post, of Bayport, Long
Island, U.S.A.; 2ndly, 1936, Bridget Cory (an O.St.J.), only da. of the late
Capt. Patrick Bermingham Crohan, R.N. (ret.), of Owlpen Old Manor, Uley,
Glos., and has issue by 1st and 2nd marriages.

Arms,—Argent, a bend wavy sable. **Crest,**—A mermaid holding in the dexter hand a mirror,
in the other a comb, all proper. **Supporters,**—Two chamois or wild goats sable. [These arms were
resumed (but without Roy. licence) by the 5th Earl, together with the family surname of Wallop].

Addresses,—c/o Estate Office, Farleigh Wallop, Basingstoke, Hants; c/o Muthaiga Country Club,
PO Box 30181, Nairobi, Kenya. *Club,*—Buck's.

SONS LIVING. *(By 1st marriage.)*

OLIVER KINTZING (*Viscount Lymington*), *b.* Jan. 14th, 1923; ed. at Eton; late Lieut. R.N.V.R.:
m. 1st, 1952, Maureen (who obtained a divorce 1954), only dau. of Lieut.-Col. Kenneth B. Stanley,
of 58, Kingston House, Princes Gate, SW7; 2ndly, 1954, Ruth Violet, who obtained a divorce 1974,
yr. da. of the late Brig.-Gen. Gerald Carew Sladen, CB, CMG, DSO, MC [Ewing, Bt.]; 3rdly 1974,
Julia, only da. of W. Graeme Ogden, DSC, of The Old Manor, Rudge, Frome, Som., and formerly
wife of Peter Robin Kirwan-Taylor, and has issue living (by 2nd m.):—
  SON LIVING (*By 2nd marriage*),—*Hon.* Quentin Gerard Carew, *b.* 1954.
  DAUGHTERS LIVING (*By 2nd marriage*),—*Hon.* Lucinda Ruth, *b.* 1956.
      Hon. Emma Geraldine Anne, *b.* 1958.
Residence,—The Old Rectory, Aldon Lane, Offham, Maidstone, Kent. *Clubs,*—Bucks, RAC.
                  (*By 2nd marriage.*)
Hon. Nicholas Valoynes Bermingham (15, Tregunter Rd., SW10; Tuft Club), *b.* 1946; ed. at Stowe: *m.*
1969, Lavinia, only da. of David Karmel, CBE, QC, of 108, Eaton Place, SW1, and has issue living,
Henry Robert Newton, *b.* 1974,—Victoria Urania Sophia, *b.* 1972.

DAUGHTERS LIVING. *(By 1st marriage.)*

Lady Anne Camilla Eveline, *b.* 1925: *m.* 1944, Capt. Lord Rupert Charles Montacute Nevill, Life Gds.
[see M. Abergavenny]. *Residences,*—Horsted Place, Uckfield, Sussex; 20A, Stanhope Gdns.,
SW7.

                  (*By 2nd marriage.*)
Lady Philippa Dorothy Bluett (*Viscountess Chelsea*), *b.* 1937: *m.* 1963, Charles Gerald John, Vis-
count Chelsea (of 51, Chelsea Sq., S.W.3), only son of 7th Earl Cadogan.
Lady Jane Alianora Borlase, *b.* 1939.

BROTHER LIVING.

Hon. Oliver Malcolm, *b.* 1905; a Rancher; served with US Army Air Corps 1942: *m.* 1st, 1929,
Jean, who *d.* 1943, dau. of Edward Small Moore, of New York; 2ndly, 1944 (marriage dissolved
1954), Mrs. Alberta J. Hines; 3rdly, 1954, Mrs. Carolyn Towle Russell, of Glenbrook, Nevada,
USA, who *d.* 1972, and has issue living, (by 1st m.) Edward John (Canyon Ranch, Big Horn, Wyoming, USA), *b.* 1930: *m.* 1st, 1952 (m. dissolved 1959), Carrol Robertson; 2ndly, 1962, Victoria

Neison, da. of H. Lyman Stebbins, of New York, USA, and has issue living, (by 1st m.) John Michael b. 1955, (by 2nd m.) Andrew Gerard b. 1965, Sam Huntington b. 1972, Harriet Walker b . 1968, Alexandra Marcina b. 1969,—Malcolm, b. 1933: m. 1st, 1955 (m. diss. 1966), Josephine Vail Stebbins; 2ndly, 1967, Judith Warren, and has issue living (by 1st m.) Malcolm Moncreiffe b. 1957, Oliver Mathew b. 1960, Paul Stebbins b. 1963, Amy Vail b. 1962,—Jean Margaret (Lady Porchester), b. 1934: m. 1956, Lord Porchester, only son of 6th Earl of Carnarvon,—Carolyn Walker, b. 1939: m. 1963, Irving Newman Alderson, of Bones Brothers Ranch, Birney, Montana, USA, and has issue living, Natalie Moore b. 1963, Jean b. 1965, Mary Roberts b. 1968. Residence,—Canyon Ranch, Big Horn, Sheridan co., Wyoming, USA.

COLLATERAL BRANCHES LIVING.

Grandchildren of the late Maj. Barton Newton Wallop William-Powlett (infra):—
Issue of the late Capt. Newton James Wallop William-Powlett, D.S.C., R.N., b. 1896, d. 1963: m. 1929, Barbara Patience (Lady William Powlett), who m. 2ndly, 1966, Vice-Adm.
Sir Peveril Barton Reibey Wallop William-Powlett, KCB, KCMG, CBE, DSO (infra), da. of Sir Bernard Eyre Greenwell, MBE, 2nd Bt.:—
Oliver Newton Wallop, b. 1933; Lt. RNR.——Ann Patience Wallop, b. 1930: m. 1953, Lt.-Col. Thomas Noel Thistlethwayte, late 60th Rifles, of Horns Farm House, Eversley, Hants., and has issue living, Rupert Thomas Newton, b. 1955,—Jane Camilla, b. 1957.——Sara Elisabeth Wallop (Hon. Mrs. Edward D. Bruce), b. 1936: m. 1960, the Hon. Edward David Bruce, of Blairhill, Rumbling Bridge, Kinross [see E. Elgin].

Grandsons of the late William Barton Powlett Wallop William-Powlett, son of the Rev. Barton Wallop, brother of 2nd Earl:—
Issue of the late Major Barton Newton Wallop William-Powlett, late Roy. Fusiliers (City of London Regt.), b. 1871, d. 1953 : m. 1895, Emily Charlotte Tyndall, who d. 1954, dau. of the late James Reibey :—
Sir Peveril Barton Reibey Wallop, KCB, KCMG, CBE, DSO (Cadhay, Ottery St. Mary, Devon; 80, Old Church St., SW3), b. 1898; Vice-Adm. (ret.); Gov. of S. Rhodesia 1954-59; a DL for Devon (High Sheriff 1972); a KStJ; 1914-18 War, 1939-45 War operations off Crete (CBE, DSO, 3rd class Order of Restitution of Poland); DSO 1942, CBE (Mil) 1945, CB (Mil) 1949, KCB (Mil) 1953, KCMG 1959: m. 1st, 1923, Helen Constance, who d. 1965, da. of the late J. Forbes Crombie, of Aberdeen; 2ndly, 1966, Barbara Patience, da. of Sir Bernard Eyre Greenwell, MBE, 2nd Bt., and widow of Capt. Newton James Wallop William-Powlett, DSC, RN (ante), and has issue living, (by 1st m.) Olivia Pansy Wallop, b. 1925: m. 1950, Lt.-Col. John Clairmont Wood, of Coombe Down, Beaminster, Dorset, and has issue living, Giles Powlett Clairmont b. 1954, Charlotte Knollys Olivia b. 1953, Louisa Ella Delamotte b. 1959,—Helen Vernon Wallop, b. 1927: m. 1951, Lt.-Cdr. Henry Victor Bruce, RN, of Barley Down House, Ovington Down, Alresford, Hants., and Sallachy, Lairg, Sutherland [see E. Elgin, Colls.],—Judith Jean Wallop (Lady Colman), of Malshanger, Basingstoke, Hants., b. 1936: m. 1955, Sir Michael Jeremiah Colman, 3rd Bt.——Peter de Barton Vernon Wallop, MC (22, St. Leonards Terr, SW3), b. 1903; Maj. 3rd Hussars (Reserve); 1939-44 War in Middle East (MC, prisoner): m. 1935, the Hon. Katherine Elizabeth Keyes, da. of 1st Baron Keyes, and has issue living, Barton Roger Wallop (Piercewebbs, Clavering, Saffron Walden), b. 1938: m. 1962, Judith, el. da. of Colin Silk, of 13, Highdown Rd., Lewes, and has issue living, Patrick Henry Wallop b. 1964, Thomas Wallop b. 1968, Katherine Wallop b. 1965,—Mary Wallop, b. 1936: m. 1957, Jonathan Janson, Lt. RNVR, of 6, Edwardes Sq., W8, and has issue living, Nicola Claire Wallop b. 1959, Lucinda Catrina b. 1961, Sara Arabella b. 1965.

PREDECESSORS.—[1] John Wallop, M.P. for Hants 1714-20; was a Lord of the Treasury 1747, Lord-Lieut. of Hants, Lord Warden and Keeper of the New Forest, Vice-Adm. of Hants, and Vice-Adm. and Gov. of the Isle of Wight; cr. Baron Wallop, of Farley Wallop, co. Southampton, and Viscount Lymington (peerage of Great Britain) 1720, and Earl of Portsmouth (peerage of Great Britain) 1743 ; d. 1762: s. by his grandson [2] John, 2nd Earl ; d. 1797; s. by his el. son [3] John Charles 3rd Earl ; d.s.p. 1853 ; s. by his brother [4] Newton, 4th Earl ; b. 1772; assumed by Roy. licence in 1794 for himself and issue the surname and arms of Fellowes only : m. 2ndly, 1820, Lady Catherine, dau. of 1st Earl Fortescue ; d. 1854; s. by his son [5] Isaac Newton, 5th Earl, b. 1825; resumed (but without Roy. licence) the family surname and arms of Wallop : m. 1855, Lady Eveline Alicia Juliana Herbert, who d. 1906, el. dau. of the Earl of Carnarvon; d. 1891 ; s. by his el. son [6] Newton, 6th Earl, b. 1856, M.P. for Barnstaple (L) 1880-85, and for Devon, N., or S. Molton, Div. 1885-91: m. 1885; Beatrice Mary, who d. 1935, only child of the late Edward Pease, of Summer House, Bewdley, and Greencroft West, Darlington; d. 1917; s. by his brother [7] John Fellowes, 7th Earl, b. 1859 ; d. 1925; s. by his brother [8] Oliver Henry, 8th Earl ; b. 1861: m. 1897, Marguerite, who d. 1938, dau. of the late S. J. Walker, of Frankfort, Kentucky, and Chicago, Illinois, USA; d. 1943; s. by his son [9] Gerard Vernon, 9th Earl and present peer; also Viscount Lymington, and Baron Wallop.

PORTSMOUTH, LORD BISHOP OF. (Gordon.)

Right Rev. (Archibald) Ronald McDonald Gordon, son of the late Sir Archibald McDonald Gordon, CMG, of Bridge House, Gerrards Cross, Bucks.; b. March 19th, 1927; ed. at Rugby, Balliol Coll., Oxford (MA), and Cuddesdon Coll.; a Fellow of St. Cross Coll., Oxford 1975; Chap. Cuddesdon Coll., 1955-59, V. of St. Peter, Birmingham 1959-67, a Member of Church Assembly and Proctor in Convocation 1965-71, Canon Residentiary of Birmingham 1967-71, and V. of St. Mary the Virgin (Univ. Church) with St. Cross and St. Peter in the East, Oxford 1971-75; consecrated 6th Bishop of Portsmouth 1975: m.

Patron of the Provostship of Portsmouth Cathedral, of ten Hon. Canonries, of 14 lay Canonries, of 4 Residentiary Canonries, of the Assist. Bishop, of the Archdeaconries of the Isle of Wight and Portsmouth, of the Chancellorship, Registrarship, and of 123 livings.

This See was founded May 1927.

Episcopal Signature.—" Ronald Portsmouth."
ARMS OF THE SEE.—Per fesse or and gules, in chief upon waves of the sea proper a lymphad sable, and in base two keys conjoined, wards outwards in bend the uppermost or the other argent, a sword interposed between them in bend sinister also argent, pommel and hilt gold.
Residence,—Bishopswood, Fareham, Hants.

POULETT, EARLDOM OF. (Poulett.) [Extinct 1973] (Barony of Poulett of Hinton St. George, E. 1627, Extinct or Dormant 1973).

DAUGHTER LIVING OF SEVENTH EARL.
Lady Bridgett Elizabeth Felicia Henrietta Augusta, *b.* 1912: *m.* 1948, Luis Robledo. *Residence,*—Edificio Angel, Calle 19, No. 6.44, Apto 407, Bogata 1, Colombia.

WIDOW LIVING OF EIGHTH EARL.
MARGARET CHRISTINE (*Countess Poulett*), (Lille Hus, Gorey Jersey), da. of Wilfred John Peter Ball of Reading: *m.* 1968, as his 3rd wife, the 8th Earl, who *d.* 1973, when the Earldom became ext. and the Barony became ext. or dormant.

Powell, see Baron Baden-Powell.

Powerscourt, Baron,   title of Viscount Powerscourt on Roll of H.L.

POWERSCOURT, VISCOUNT. (Wingfield.) Sits as BARON POWERSCOURT (U.K. 1885). [Viscount I. 1743.]

[Name pronounced "Poërscourt."]

Fidelity is of God.

MERVYN NIALL WINGFIELD, 10th Viscount; *b.* Sept. 3rd, 1935; *s.* 1973; ed. at Stowe; late Lt. Irish Gds.: *m.* 1962, (m. diss. 1974), Wendy Ann Pauline, da. of Ralph C. G. Slazenger, of Powerscourt, Enniskerry, co. Wicklow, and has issue.

𝕬rms,—Argent, on a bend gules, three pairs of wings conjoined in lure of the field. 𝕮rest,—A demi-eagle wings displayed argent, gazing on the sun proper. 𝕾upporters,—Two pegasi argent, maned, hoofed, and wings addorsed or.

Residence,—189, Koundouriston, Passalimani, Piraeus, Greece.

SON LIVING.
Hon. MERVYN ANTHONY, *b.* Aug. 21st, 1963.

DAUGHTER LIVING.
Hon. Julia, *b.* 1965.

BROTHER LIVING.
Hon. Guy Claude Patrick (3045, Jackson St., Apt. 103, San Francisco, Cal., USA), *b.* 1940; ed. at Millfield.

SISTER LIVING.
Hon. Grania Sybil Enid (*Hon. Lady Langrishe*), *b.* 1934: *m.* 1955, Sir Hercules Ralph Hume Langrishe, 7th Bt., of Knocktopher Abbey, co. Kilkenny, and Ringlestown House, Kilmessan, co. Meath.

AUNT LIVING. (*Daughter of 8th Viscount.*)
Hon. Doreen Julia, *b.* 1904: *m.* 1928, FitzHerbert Wright, formerly 15th/19th Hussars, and has issue living, Bryan Henry FitzHerbert, *b.* 1934; ed. at Eton; Maj. The Blues and Royals,—Brigid Louise, *b.* (Nov.) 1928: *m.* 1950, Julian John William Salmond, of Maidford, Norton, Malmesbury, Wilts., son of the late Marshal of the RAF Sir John Maitland Salmond, GCB, GVO, DSO [see B. Lucas of Crudwell],—Davina Julia (*Lady Boughey*), *b.* 1931: *m.* 1950, Sir Richard James Boughey, 10th Bt.,—Susan Mary, *b.* 1937: *m.* 1956, Ronald Ivor Ferguson, Life Gds., of Dummer Down, Dummer, Basingstoke, Hants. [see V, Hampden, colls.]. *Residence,*—Pudding Lane, Bright Walton, Newbury, Berks.

GREAT AUNTS LIVING. (*Daughters of 7th Viscount.*)
Hon. Olive Elizabeth, *b.* 1884: *m.* 1908, Major William John Bates Van de Weyer, M.V.O. [E. Craven], who *d.* 1946, and has issue living, Sylvain Victor Bates (of 88, Frognal, Hampstead, NW3), *b.* 1917; late Capt. RA; is a partner in the firm of Cluttons, chartered surveyors, of 5, Great College Street, SW1; has Order of Leopold of Belgium: *m.* 1941, Mary Jane, da. of Sir Valentine Holmes, QC, and has issue living, Mark Sylvain Bates *b.* 1948: *m.* 1970, Catherine Candler, Andrew Valentine Bates *b.* 1949: *m.* 1974, Margaret Lane, Robert William Bates *b.* 1950: *m.* 1971, Sarah Brett Spooner,—Myrtle Clare (Land of Nod, Headley, Bordon, Hants.), *b.* 1910: *m.* 1934, Maj.Leith Ingham Tomkins Whitaker, DL, late Rifle Bde., who *d.* 1971, and has issue living, Jeremy Ingham (Land of Nod, Headley, Bordon, Hants.) *b.* 1934; ed. at Eton; Maj. Coldstream Gds. (ret.): *m.* 1974, Philippa van Straubenzee, Timothy Michael *b.* 1936; ed. at Eton, Susan Myrtle *b.* 1939: *m.* 1959, Michael Andrew Watt, of Greens Park, Towcester [see D. Portland, colls.].—Daphne Joan (Blanchory Cottage, Hinton St. George, Som.) *b.* 1911; *m.* 1st, 1939, Sqdn.-Ldr. Charles Richard John Pink, RAF, who *d.* (on active ser.) 1941; 2ndly, 1943, Capt. Edwin Pearson Delmar Cavendish, RCA, who *d.* 1970 [see D. Devonshire, colls.], and has issue living, (by 1st m.) Richard Charles John *b.* 1941, (by 2nd m.) [see D. Devonshire, colls.]. *Residence,*—The Grey House, Clarence Rd., Dorchester, Dorset.
Hon. Lilah Katharine Julia (*Hon. Lady Morrison-Bell*), *b.* 1888: *m.* 1912, Major Sir Arthur Clive Morrison-Bell, 1st Bt. (cr 1923), who *d.* 1956. *Residence,*—11, Cumberland Mansions, W.1.

WIDOW LIVING OF NINTH VISCOUNT.
SHEILA CLAUDE, (*Sheila, Viscountess Powerscourt*), (Palma au Lac, Locarno, Switzerland), da. of the late Lt.-Col. Claude Beddington, of 33, Grosvenor St., W1: *m.* 1932, the 9th Viscount, *d.* 1973.

COLLATERAL BRANCHES LIVING.

Issue of the late Maj.-Gen. the Hon. Maurice Anthony Wingfield, C.M.G., C.V.O., DSO, yst. son of 7th Viscount, *b.* 1883, *d.* 1956: *m.* 1906, Sybil Frances, who *d.* 1967, only da. of F. D. Leyland, formerly of The Vyne, Basingstoke:—
Anthony Desmond Rex, *D.S.O., M.C., b.* 1908; ed. at Eton; Brigadier (retired) late 10th Hussars; sometime Com., 22nd Armoured Bde.; Assist. Racing and Stud Manager to H.M. 1957-63, and Stud Manager 1963; 1939-45 War in Middle East and N.W. Europe (wounded M.C., D.S.O., Order of Leopold of Belgium, Belgian Croix de Guerre; D.S.O. 1943: *m.* 1935, Juliet Constance, da. of the late William Burroughs Stanley, D.L. of Coolamber Manor, Westmeath, and Lillybrook, Budleigh Salterton, and has issue living, Deirdre Jocelyn, *b.* 1936: *m.* 1969, Basil Tiernay Pegg (BP59, Dakar, Senegal, W. Africa), and has issue living, Jonathan Mark *b.* 1973, Camilla Louise *b.* 1971. *Residence,*—Brownstown Park, Navan, co. Meath.—Jocelyn Sybil Julia, *b.* 1913: *m.* 1st, 1940, Lt.-Col. Clifford Willoughby (Peter) Hordern, who *d.* 1966; 2ndly, 1970, Ralph Hamilton Cobbold, of Broom House, Sudbourne, Woodbridge, Suffolk, and 8, Pont St., SW1.

Granddaughter of the late Richard William Wingfield (infra):—
Issue of the late Richard Mervyn Wingfield, M.C., *b.* 1894, *d.* 1951: *m.* 1918, **Lynette Agnes**, dau. of the late Major Sydney Cowper, C.M.G., J.P., of Wynberg, Cape Province, S. Africa:—

Elizabeth Sonia, *b.* 1925: *m.* 1st, 1944 (divorce 1945), Basil Wilson, Lt., S. African Air Force, 2ndly, 194–, Fl. Lt. M. J. Dunne, and has issue living, (by 1st marriage) Sandra Lynn Wingfield, *b.* 1945.— (by 2nd m.) Richard Matthew Wingfield, *b.* 1948,—Lesley Clare Wingfield, *b.* 1952,—Robin Elizabeth Wingfield, *b.* 1954. *Residence,*—8, Hazelwell Court, Sinclair St., Germiston, Transvaal, S. Africa.

Grandchildren of the late Richard Robert Wingfield, el. son of the late Rev. the Hon. Edward Wingfield, 3rd son of 4th Viscount:—
Issue of the late Richard William Wingfield, *b.* 1849, *d.* 1918: *m.* 1889, **Jessie Emily** (who *d.* 1936, having *m.* 2ndly, 1920, Thomas Edward Broster, who *d.* 1941), dau. of Benjamin Mitchell Kennedy:—

Noel Sparks, *b.* 1907; ed. at Prince Edward Sch., Salisbury; is a Farmer; formerly a Member of S. Rhodesian Parliament: *m.* 1933 .Mary Joan .dau. of R .H .Wood, and has issue living, Patrick Noel (of Belvedere North, PO Goromonzi, Rhodesia), *b.* 1934: *m.* 1st, 1960 (m. diss. 1971), Jean, da. of David Morris Williams, of Blantyre, Nyasaland; 2ndly, 1972, Margaret, da. of J. H. McKenzie Finch, of Canterbury, Kent, and has issue living (by 1st m.), Richard David Noel *b.* 1966, Sandra Joan *b.* 1963, (by 2nd m.) Jeremy James *b.* 1953,—Jenepher Cynthia, *b.* 1937: *m.* 1961, Guy Cclin Hensman, of 44, Cambridge Rd., Avondale, Salisbury, Rhodesia, and has issue living, David Guy *b.* 1965, Bridget Ann *b.* 1963. *Residence,*—Rochester, PO Goromonzi, Rhodesia.——Clare Mary Sophia (Hilton College, PO Hilton, Natal), *b.* 1904: *m.* 1926, Sydney William Hall Kennard, who *d.* 1970, 4nd has issue living, David George, *b.* 1929,—Desmond Richard, *b.* 1935.

Issue of the late Maurice de Vesci Wingfield, *b.* 1866, *d.* 1940: *m.* 1908, Ethel Grey Sharpe who *d.* 1964:—
Robert George, *b.* 1910 ; Lieut.-Col. R.E.M.E. (retired) ; was Com. R.E.M.E. Gibraltar 1948-51, and R.E.M.E. 21 (Northern) Corps Troops, T.A. 1951-4 ; European War 1939-45 in France, Burma and Addu Atoll : *m.* 1947, Mary Maud Rolfe. *Address,*—c/o Lloyds Bank, Bognor Regis, Sussex.

Grandchildren of the late Capt. Anthony Edward Foulis Wingfield (infra):
Issue of the late Gervase Christopher Brinsmade Wingfield, *b.* 1931, *d.* 1964: *m.* 1958 **Mary Margaret** (Hackney Lodge, Melton, Woodbridge, Suffolk) (who *m.* 2ndly, 1973, Dennis Henry Bagshaw Neal), da. of Dennis McGuinn, of Haverford, Penn., U.S.A.:—
Andrew Nicholas Brinsmade, *b.* 1959.——Nicola Caroline McGuinn, *b.* 1961.——Philippa Susan, *b.* 1962.

Granddaughter of the late Sir Anthony Henry Wingfield, el. son of George John Wingfield, 2nd son of Richard Robert Wingfield (ante):—
Issue of the late Capt. Anthony Edward Foulis Wingfield, Roy. Corps of Signals (T.A. Reserve), *b.* 1892, *d.* 1946: *m.* 1927, **Margaret Brinsmade** (now of The Old Rectory, Henstead, near Beccles, Suffolk), dau. of the late Professor Douglas Adam:—
Eileen Patricia Brinsmade, *b.* 1928: *m.* 1966, Prince Dmitri Galitzine, HM Dip. Ser., of 36, Charlwood Rd., SW15, and has issue living, Marina, *b.* 1968.

Grandchildren of the late Edward Rhys Wingfield, el. son of the late Capt. Edward Ffolliott Wingfield (infra):—
Issue of the late Lieut.-Col. Mervyn Edward George Rhys Wingfield, Gloucestershire Regt., *b.* 1872, *d.* 1952: *m.* 1919, **Florence Marguerite Erle** (Fayre Court, Fairford, Glos.), da. of the late Col. Richard Erle Benson, E. Yorkshire Regt.:—

Charles Talbot Rhys, *b.* 1924; ed. at Eton, and at Ch. Ch., Oxford; late Lieut. Coldstream Guards; a D .L of Glos., and High Sheriff 1962; France 1944 (wounded): *m.* 1954, the Hon. Cynthia Meriel Hill, da. of 6th Baron Sandys, and has issue living, Richard Mervyn Rhys, *b.* 1967,—Venetia Blanche, *b.* 1956,—Olivia Patricia, *b.* 1958,—Diana Mary, *b.* 1961. *Residence,*—Barrington Park, Burford, Oxon. *Club,*—Guards'.——David de Cardonnel Ffolliott Rhys (134, Finsborough Rd., SW10), *b.* 1933; ed. at Bradfield Coll.——Jonathan Fitzuryan Rhys (Edifico Mediterraneo, Fuengirola, Malaga, Spain), *b.* 1935; ed. at Eton: *m.* 1970, Judith, da. of Albert George James Gibbins, of Mount] Pleasant, Stocklane, Langford, Bristol, and widow of the Hon. Philip John Inman [see B. Inman, and has issue living, Annabel Lucy, *b.* 1973.——Mary Florence Eleanor, *b.* 1920: *m.* 1945, Sqdn.-Ldr. Neville Thomas Cole, RAF, and has issue living, Michael Duncan Mervyn, *b.* 1946,— Edward Charles Ffolliott George, *b.* 1954,—Rachel Elizabeth Rosemary, *b.* 1948. *Residence,*— Windrush Lodge, Nazeing, Essex.——Elizabeth Marguerite, *b.* 1926.

Issue of the late Major William Jocelyn Rhys Wingfield, 19th Hussars, *b.* 1873, *d.* 1942 : *m.* 1902, Sybil Annesley Giana, who *d.* 1960, dau. of the late Lieut.-Col. W. T. Markham, of Becca Hall, Yorkshire :—
William Thomas Rhys, *TD*, *b.* 1907; ed. at Bedford Sch.; is Maj. Northamptonshire Yeo. (TA), and Major Roy. Armoured Corps: *m.* 1936, Patricia, only child of the late Maj.-Gen. Sir William James Norman Cooke-Collis, K B.E.,C.B., C.M.G., D.S.O., and has issue living, Jocelyn James Rhys (Holly Tree Farm, Walpole, Halesworth, Suffolk), *b.* 1937; ed. at Eton; Maj. LI: *m.* 1968, Sara Elizabeth, only da. of Sir (Edward John) Patrick Boschetti ffolkes, 6th Bt., and has issue living, Serena Geraldine Rhys *b.* 1969, Camilla Patricia Rhys *b.* 1971,—Robert Talbot Rhys (Anchor Cottage, Anchor Yard, Knaresborough, Yorks.; Roy. Ocean Racing, Roy. Irish Yacht, and Irish Cruising Clubs), *b.* 1940; ed. at Stowe, and at Trin. Coll., Dublin (PhD): *m.* 1969, Anne Mary, da. of Lt.-Col. T. W. Hamilton, of Nunholm House, Dumfries, and has issue living, James Hamilton Rhys, *b.* 1971, Charles Timothy Rhys, *b.* 1974,—George Anthony Rhys (Hearne House, North Wootton, Shepton Mallet, Som.), *b.* 1942; ed. at Eton, and Trin. Coll., Dublin: *m.* 1968, Gloria, only da. of Bernard Bolingbroke-Kent, of Cerne Easter, Westerham, Kent, and has issue living, Rupert Bolingbroke Rhys, *b.* 1972. *Residence,*—Angel House, Elton, nr. Peterborough.

Issue of the late Sir Charles John Fitzroy Rhys Wingfield, K.C.M.G., *b.* 1877, *d.* 1960 : *m.* 1905, Lucy Evelyn (of 11, Wellington Court, Knightsbridge, S.W.1), dau. of the late Sir Edmund Douglas Veitch Fane, K.C.M.G., of Boyton Manor, Wilts :—
Diana Evelyn, *b.* 1907 : *m.* 1935, Baron Alessandro Corsi di Turri, and has issue living, Raimondo, *b.* 1937: *m.* 1964, Donna Maria Francesca di Lorenzo, and has issue living, Carlo Alessandro, *b.* 1965, Diana Lucrezia *b.* 1970,—Antonio Giuliano, *b.* 1941: *m.* 1967, Maria Grazia Barbiani, and has issue living, Flavio Alessandro *b.* 1968. *Residence,*—1, Via Masaccio, Rome, Italy.

Issue of the late Capt. Maurice Ffolliott Rhys Wingfield, *b.* 1879, *d.* 1941: *m.* 1st, 1904, Lydia Agnes (who *d.* 1963, having obtained a divorce 1911), da. of Henry Budge; 2ndly, 1916, Stephanie Agnes, who *d.* 1918, da. of the late Sir Alfred Cooper, F.R.C.S., and widow of Arthur Francis Levita, D. Fife; 3rdly, 1928, Jessie Muriel (MOLYNEUX) who *d.* 1959, having *m.* 3rdly, 1944, Maj. Frederick Graham St. Clair-Keith), dau. of the late Hon. James Dunsmuir, of Hatley Park Victoria, British Columbia:—
(By 1st m.) Muriel Violet, *b.* 1905: *m.* 1933, Lieut.-Col. Alister Cecil Maynard, MBE, Seaforth Highlanders (ret.), and has issue living, Venetia Caroline, *b.* 1936: *m.* 1st, 1957 (m. diss. 1971), John Howard Cordle, MP; 2ndly, 1971, Harry John Crawley Ross Skinner, of Warnwell House, Warmwell, Dorchester, Dorset, and has issue living (by 1st m.), Rupert Alister Peter John *b.* 1959, Sophie Jane *b.* 1958, Marina Rose *b.* 1960, Rachel Venetia *b.* 1963,—Sandra Elizabeth (Elm Tree Farm, Durley, Hants.) *b.* 1939: *m.* 1958 (m. diss. 1966) Michael John MacKinlay MacLeod, and has issue living, Torquil John MacKinlay *b.* 1959, Jocelyn Maurice Edward MacKinlay *b.* 1961, Caspar Charles MacKinlay *b.* 1963. *Residence,*—12, Victoria Grove, W8.

Issue of the late Capt. Cecil John Talbot Rhys Wingfield, *b.* 1881, *d.* (of wounds in action) 1915: *m.* 1904, Lady Violet Nita Poulett, who *d.* 1966, da. of 6th Earl Poulett.—

Edward William Rhys, *b.* 1905; ed. at Eton, and RMC; Maj. late KRRC: *m.* 1935, Lady Norah Beryl Cayzer Jellicoe, da. of 1st Earl Jellicoe, and has issue living, Philip John, *b.* 1938: *m.* 1971, Susan Johanna, da. of Maj.-Gen. Ronald Edward Coaker. CBE, MC, of Seaton Old Rectory, Uppingham, and has issue living, Edward Mervyn *b.* 1973, Venetia *b.* 1975,—Jacqueline, *b.* 1936: *m.* 1967, Maj. Anthony Chester Vivian, RWF,—Elizabeth Jane, *b.* 1941. *Residence,*—Salterbridge, Cappoquin, co. Waterford.

Granddaughters of the late Major Charles George Lewis Wingfield, 2nd son of the late Capt. Edward Ffolliott Wingfield (infra):—
Issue of the late Charles Trevor Wingfield, *b.* 1889, *d.* 1924: *m.* 1914, Liliane Laure Agnes (of Le Manoir de Camblong, Castetnau-Camblong, Basses Pyrénées, France), only child of the late Vladimir Czerny, of Petrograd, Russia:—
Tatiana Elianore Lucile Beatrice, *b.* 1916 : *m.* 1947, Brigadier Alan Godfrey Drake-Brockman, O.B.E., of The Splatts, Spaxton, Bridgwater, and has issue living, Trevor Vivian *b.* 1950.——Yvonne Angéle Primrose Czerny (61, Prévost Martin, Geneva, Switzerland), *b.* 1917.

Granddaughter of the late Capt. Edward Ffolliot Wingfield, 3rd son of the late Rev. the Hon. Edward Wingfield (ante):—
Issue of the late Capt. George Talbot Wingfield, R.N., *b.* 1854, *d.* 1936 : *m.* 1882, Maud who *d.* 1945, dau. of Rear-Adm. Joseph Edward Maitland Wilson, of Weston Peverel Plymouth :—
Elianore Maud Rhys, *b.* 1887. *Residence,*—The Dutch House, 40, The Strand, Topsham, nr. Exeter.

Grandchildren of the late Capt. Richard Thomas Wingfield, el. son of the late Rev. the Hon. William Wingfield, 4th son of 4th Viscount:—
Issue of the late Lieut.-Col. the Rev. William Edward Wingfield, D.S.O., *b.* 1867, *d.* 1927: *m.* 1896, Elizabeth Mary, who *d.* 1939, dau. of the late George Frederic Trench [B. Ashtown, colls.]:—
John Anthony David (65, Paradise Drive, Knysna, Cape Province) *b.* 1905; ed. at Marlborough Coll.; a Mining Engineer (ret.); formerly a MInstMM, S. Africa, MIMM, and Manager of Western Holdings Ltd., and of Witwatersr and Nigel Mine: *m.* 1934, Eileen Earle Leslie, da. of the late Hugh Melville, of Durban, S. Africa, and has issue living, Anthony Richard Melville, *b.* 1941; ed. at St. Andrews, Grahamstown,—John Mervyn (35, Cranswick Rd., Willowild, Sandton, Transvaal), *b.* 1944; ed. at St. Andrews, Grahamstown, Rand Univ. (BSc), and Trin. Coll., Camb. (BA): *m.* 1970, Diana Kay, da. of F. C. Harris, of Newlands, Cape Town, and has issue living, Richard John *b.* 1972, David Mervyn *b.* 1975,—Robert Edward Melville, *b.* 1950; ed. at St. Andrews, Grahamstown, and Rand Univ. (BSc): Civil Eng.,—Elizabeth Melville, *b.* 1936; BSc honours Rand; MSc London: *m.* 1963, Hugh Vincent Williams, MSc, of 04, Glen St., Kenmare, Krugersdorp, Transvaal, and has issue living, Katharine Elizabeth *b.* 1965, Julia Margaret Frances *b.* 1969, Susan Eileen Isabella *b.* 1970,—Rosemary Patricia, *b.* 1938.——Mervyn Robert George, *DSO, DSC, b.* 1911; Capt. RN (ret.); an ADC to HM 1962-67; formerly Naval Attaché, British Embassy, Athens, and Dir. of Underwater Weapons at Admiralty; 1939-45 War (DSO, DSC and Bar, despatches); DSO 1942: *m.* 1936, Sheila Mary, da. of the late Maj. J. H. P. Leschallas, formerly of Lynchmere House, Lynchmere, Sussex, and has issue living, Richard Mervyn (St. George's Wood, Haslemere, Surrey), *b.* 1942; ed. at Wellington and Pembroke Coll., Camb (MA); MICE: *m.* 1969, Diana, da. of P. M. Longhurst, of Haslemere, Surrey and has issue living, James Richard *b.* 1973,—William Peter, *b.* 1948; ed. at Wellington,—Cicely (2, Spencer Rd., S. Croydon), *b.* 1940: *m.* 1964, David Barry Knowles, Lt.-Cdr. RN, who *d.* 1967, and has issue living, Alastair David *b.* (Nov.) 1964,—Melanie Kathleen *b.* 1966. *Residence,*—Fair Winds, Liphook, Hants.——Charlotte Elfreda, *b.* 1898: *m.* 1923, Capt. Hugh May Stollery Mundy, DSC, RN (ret.), who *d.* 1967, and has issue living, Timothy Richard Wingfield, *b.* 1930; Lt.-Cdr. RN (ret.): *m.* 1967, Jill, da. of Joseph Dagleish, of Greenock, and has issue living, Annabelle Rosemary Wingfield *b.* 1968, Nicola Jill Wingfield *b.* 1970,—Pauline Elizabeth, *b.* 1927: *m.* 1958, Thomas Daly, of 60, Haling Park Rd., S. Croydon, Surrey, and has issue living, Hugh Thomas Patrick *b.* 1968, Deirdre May Elizabeth *b.* 1959, Joanna Charlotte Alice *b.* 1963.——Rosalie Emma Ruth, *b.* 1908: *m.* 1933, Ronald Holms Procter, of 5, St. George's Sq., SW1.

Granddaughter of the late Brig.-Gen. Cecil Vernon Wingfield-Stratford, CB, CMG (infra):—
Issue of the late Esmé Cecil Wingfield-Stratford, DSc, *b.* 1882, *d.* 1971: *m.* 1915, Barbara Elizabeth (The Oaks, Berkhamsted, Herts.), da. of the late Lt.-Col. Francis Henry Lancelot Errington [B. Congleton]:—
Roshnara Barbara WINGFIELD-STRATFORD-JOHNSTONE, *b.* 1916; assumed by deed poll 1970, for herself and her issue by 2nd m. the surnames of Wingfield-Stratford-Johnstone: *m.* 1st, 1941, Maj. Richard John Wrottesley, MC (now 5th Baron Wrottesley), from whom she obtained a divorce 1949; 2ndly, 1950, Lt.-Col. Norman David Melville Johnstone, MBE, Gren. Gds., of Park House, Gaddesby, Leics., and has issue living, (by 1st m.) [see B. Wrottesley],—(by 2nd m.) Esmé Edward Melville (16, Chiswick Staithe, W4 3TP), *b.* 1950: *m.* 1972, Sarah, da. of Maj. Richard Francis Birch Reynardson, and has issue living, Rupert Leo Esmé *b.* 1975,—Victoria Rose Charlotte, *b.* 1954.

Grandchildren of the late John Wingfield-Stratford, son of the late Hon. John Wingfield-Stratford, 2nd son of 3rd Viscount :—
Issue of the late Brig.-Gen. Cecil Vernon Wingfield-Stratford, C.B., C.M.G., *b.* 1853, *d.* 1939 : *m.* 1881, Rosalind Isabel, *M.B.E.,* who *d.* 1953, dau. of the late Rev. the Hon. Edward Vesey Bligh [E. Darnley]:—
Rosalind Frances Cecily, *b.* 1893: *m.* 1st, 1915, Cecil Ireland Blackburne, who *d.* 1963, having obtained a divorce 1929; 2ndly, 1929, as his second wife, Lt.-Col. Lawrence Francis Garratt, D.S.O., M.C., RA (ret.), who *d.* 1967, and has issue living, (by 1st m.) Denys Ireland (25, Preston Point Rd., Fremantle, W Australia), *b.* 1917: *m.* 1944, Pamela Mary Stephenson, and has issue living, Geoffrey Denys Ireland *b.* 1948, Judith Elizabeth *b.* 1945,—Mona Evelyn *b.* 1916: *m.* 1938, Brig. George Edwin Cotter Sikes, DSO, of Broughton House, Broughton, Malton, Yorks. [Cotter Bt., colls.], and has issue living, John Edwin George *b.* 1943, Jane Evelyn *b.* 1940. *Residence,*—Reed House, Plaxtol, Sevenoaks.

Issue of the late Richard Nevill Wingfield-Stratford, *b.* 1861, *d.* 1942: *m.* 1891, Grace Dorothea, who *d.* 1956, dau. of the late Capt. Alexander Nixon Montgomery :—
Georgina Grace Ida, *b.* 1899 : *m.* 1st, 1926, William Jannion Elliott, who *d.* 1929 ; 2ndly, 1933, Wilfrid Cole, MBE, of 3, Stanton Drive, Fleet, Hants.

Issue of the late Francis Mervyn Wingfield-Stratford, *b.* 1864, *d.* 1932 : *m.* 1906, Nora, who *d.* 1953, dau. of the late George Matthey, F.R.S., of Cheyne House, Chelsea, S.W.; and Rosemount, Eastbourne :—
Mervyn Verner, *b.* 1907; ed. at Cheltenham Coll.; formerly Lieut. Scots Guards: *m.* 1935, Anne, Helen, dau. of the late Douglas Charles Stewart-Sandeman, of Martins Heron, Bracknell, Berks, and has issue living (Mervyn) Peter Douglas (28, Lansdowne Rd., Holland Park, W11) *b.* 1936; LIM Citizen and Goldsmith of London: *m.* 1969, Jane, da. of the late Dr. Edward Worsley Burstal, of Lutterworth, and has issue living, James Richard Mervyn *b.* 1973, Annabel Jane *b.* 1971,—Georgina Isabel, *b.* 1939: *m.* 1962, J. L. M. Modley, Lt. R. E., and has issue living, Drummond *b.* 1963, Alexander *b.* 1965. *Residence,*—Heath Cottage, Heckfield, Basingstoke, Hants.

PREDECESSORS.—**[1]** RICHARD Wingfield, *M.P.* for Boyle; cr. *Baron Wingfield,* of Wingfield, co. Wexford, and *Viscount Powerscourt* (peerage of Ireland) 1743; *d.* 1751; *s.* by his el. son **[2]** EDWARD, 2nd Viscount; M.P. for Stockbridge 1756-61; *d.* unmarried; *s.* by his brother **[3]** RICHARD, 3rd Viscount; *d.* 1788; *s.* by his son **[4]** RICHARD, 4th Viscount; *d.* 1809; *s.* by his son **[5]** RICHARD, 5th Viscount; *d.* 1823: *s.* by his son **[6]** RICHARD, 6th Viscount, *b.* 1815; many years M.P. for Bath: *m.* 1836, Lady Elizabeth Frances Charlotte Jocelyn,

who d. 1884, dau. of 3rd Earl of Roden; d. 1844; s. by his son [7] MERVYN, K.P., P.C., 7th
Viscount, b. 1836; was a Representative Peer; cr. Baron Powerscourt, of Powerscourt, co.
Wicklow (peerage of United Kingdom) 1885: m. 1864, Lady Julia Coke, who d. 1931, el. dau.
of 2nd Earl of Leicester; d. 1904; s. by his son [8] MERVYN RICHARD, K.P., M.V.O., 8th
Viscount, b. 1880; was Comptroller of the Household to Lord-Lieut. of Ireland 1906-7; ap-
pointed Lieut. of co. Wicklow 1901; elected a Member of Senate of S. Ireland 1921: m. 1903,
Sybil, who d. 1946, dau. of the late Walter Pleydell-Bouverie; d. 1947; s. by his son [9]
MERVYN PATRICK, 9th Viscount, b. 1905: m. 1932, Sheila Claude, da. of the late Lt.-Col. Claude
Beddington, of 33, Grosvenor St., W1; d. 1973; s. by his el. son [10] MERVYN NIALL, 10th Viscount
and present peer; also Baron Wingfield, and Baron Powerscourt.

POWIS, EARL OF. (Herbert.) [Earl U.K. 1804.]
[Title pronounced "Po-is."]

Ung je serviray.
One will I serve.

CHRISTIAN VICTOR CHARLES HERBERT, 6th
Earl; b. May 28th, 1904; s. 1974; ed. at
Oundle, Trin. Coll., Camb. (BA), and Univ.
Coll., London; late Maj. RAOC; Bar Inner
Temple 1932; Private Sec. to Gov. and
C-in-C British Honduras 1947-55, and to
Gov. of British Guiana 1955-64; patron of
twelve livings.

Arms,—Per pale azure and gules, three lions rampant
argent. Crest,—A wyvern wings elevated addorsed vert,
gorged with a ducal coronet or, holding in the mouth a
sinister hand couped at the wrist gules. Supporters,—
Dexter, an elephant argent; sinister, a griffin, wings elevated,
argent, ducally gorged gules, and charged with five mullets
in saltire sable.
Seat,—Powis Castle, Welshpool, Powys. Clubs,—
Brooks's, MCC.

DAUGHTER LIVING OF FOURTH EARL.
Lady Hermione Gwladys, b. 1900: m. 1924, Conte Roberto Lucchesi Palli, 11th Duca della Grazia,
and 13th Principe di Campofranco, and has issue living, Violet Maria Carolina Sidonie, b. 1930.
Residence,—Le Point de Vue, Chemin des Oisillons, 1012, Lausanne, Switzerland.

WIDOW LIVING OF SON OF FOURTH EARL.
VIDA, only dau. of the late Capt. James Harold Cuthbert, D.S.O., Scots Guards; is an O.St.J.;
appointed a Lady-in-Waiting to H.R.H. the Duchess of Gloucester 1944: m 1st, 1934, Squadron-
Leader Viscount Clive, R.A.F. (17th Baron Darcy de Knayth) who d. (killed on active ser.)
1943 .only surviving son of 4th Earl, 2ndly, 1945, Brig. Derek Schuldham Schreiber, MVO, who d.
1972 [B. Faringdon], and has issue living, (by 1st m.) [see colls., infra]. Residences,—Fir Hill,
Overford, Hants.; 59, Cadogan Place, SW1.

WIDOW LIVING OF FIFTH EARL.
ELLA MARY (Countess of Powis), (The Garden House, Powis Castle, Welshpool; 4, Green St., W1), da.
of the late Col. William Hans Rathborne: m. 1932, the 5th Earl, who d. 1974.

COLLATERAL BRANCHES LIVING.
Issue of the late Squadron-Leader Mervyn Horatio Herbert, R.A.F. (Viscount
Clive) (only surviving son of 4th Earl), who s. his mother as 17th Baron Darcy
de Knayth 1929 [see that title].

Grandchildren of the late Maj.-Gen. the Hon. William Henry Herbert, 5th son of
2nd Earl:—
Issue of the late Rt. Rev. Percy Mark Herbert, KCVO, DD, b. 1885, d. 1968: m. 1922, the
Hon. Elaine Letitia Algitha Orde-Powlett (Smithy House, Chirbury, Powys), da. of 5th
Baron Bolton:—
GEORGE WILLIAM (Marrington Hall, Chirbury, Powys), b. June 4th, 1925; ed. at Eton, and at Trin.
Coll., Camb. (BA); FRICS: m. 1949, the Hon. Katherine Odeyne de Grey, da. of 8th Baron Walsing-
ham, and has issue living, John George, b. 1952,—Michael Clive, b. 1954,—Peter James, b. 1955,—
Edward David, b. 1958.——David Mark (65, Belsize Lane, Hampstead, NW3; Garrick Club),
b. 1927; ed. at Rugby, and at Trin. Coll., Camb. (MA); formerly an Assist. Master at Christ's Hosp.;
a Publisher: m. 1955, Monica Brenda, da. of L. E. Swann.——Andrew Clive, b. 1933; late Capt. R.
Norfolk Regt.; Film Dir.: m. 1963, Carol Mae, from whom he obtained a divorce 1971, yst. da. of
the late John Charlton, and has issue living, Nicholas Mark, b. 1963,—Hugo Clive, b. 1965.——
Elizabeth Barbarina, b. 1928: m. 1948, Maj. Hubert Robert Holden, MC, late R. Norfolk Regt., of
Sibdon Castle, Craven Arms, Salop, and has issue living, Robert David, b. 1956,—Caroline Elizabeth,
b. 1950: m. 1971, Richard Matthew Pieckielon-Slowick, of Holmleigh Cottage, Chirbury, Powys, and
has issue living, Daniel b. 1973,—Sarah Barbarina, b. 1953: m. 1974, Alan Hodgson, of Hope Cottage,
Whitburn, Tyne and Wear,—Jane Amanda, b. 1954.

Descendants of the late Hon. Robert Henry Clive (2nd son of 1st Earl) who
m. 1819 Harriet, Baroness Windsor in her own right [see E. Plymouth].,

PREDECESSORS.—[1] ROBERT Clive (el. son of Richard Clive of Styche, Salop), having served
three years in the Civil Service of the H.E.I.C., he entered that Co.'s Military Ser. and subsequently
became one of its most distinguished Generals, and to him England owed, to a very substantial
extent, the establishment of her dominion in India. He avenged the outrage of the "Black Hole of
Calcutta" by completely routing, in the Grove of Plassey, the forces of Surajah Dowlah amounting
to 70,000, and by dethroning the Surajah, events which gave rapid ascendency to the British power.
When Gov. of Calcutta he defeated the Dutch by sea and land and obtained from them a beneficial
treaty for the E. India Co. He was subsequently Pres. of Bengal, and sat as M.P. for Shrewsbury
1760-74; cr. Baron Clive, of Plassey, co. Clare (peerage of Ireland) 1762; K.B. 1764; d. 1774; s.
by his son [2] EDWARD, 2nd Baron; was Lord-Lieut. of cos. Salop and Montgomery; cr. Baron
Clive, of Walcot, co. Salop (peerage of Great Britain) 1794, and Baron Powis, of Powis Castle, co.
Montgomery, Baron Herbert of Chirbury, co. Salop, and Viscount Clive and Earl of Powis (peerage
of United Kingdom) 1804; d. 1839; s. by his son [3] EDWARD, K.G., 2nd Earl, b. 1785; assumed
the surname and arms of Herbert by Roy. licence 1807; was Lord-Lieut. of co. Montgomery: m.
1818, Lady Lucy Graham, dau. of 3rd Duke of Montrose; d. 1848; s. by his son [4] EDWARD JAMES
3rd Earl, b. 1818; M.P. for N. Shropshire (C) 1843-8; Lord-Lieut. of Montgomeryshire; d. 1891;
s. by his nephew [5] GEORGE CHARLES (son of the late Lt.-Gen. the Rt. Hon. Sir Percy Egerton
Herbert, K.C.B., M.P., 2nd son of 2nd Earl), 4th Earl; b. 1862; Hon. Col. 4th Battn., S. Wales
Borderers, a G.C.St.J.; sometime Prior for Wales, Order of St. John; was Lord-Lieut. for Salop
1896-1951: m. 1890, the Hon. Violet Ida Eveline Lane-Fox (Baroness Darcy de Knayth in her own
right), who d. 1929, dau. and co-heiress of 12th Baron Conyers; d. 1952; s. by his kinsman [6]
EDWARD ROBERT HENRY, CBE, TD (son of the late Col. Edward William Herbert, CB, son of the
late Hon. Robert Charles Herbert, 4th son of 2nd Earl), 5th Earl, b. 1889: m. 1932, Ella Mary, da.
of the late Col. William Hans Rathborne; d. 1974; s. by his brother [7] CHRISTIAN VICTOR CHARLES,
6th Earl and present peer; also Viscount Clive, Baron Herbert of Chirbury, Baron Powis, and Baron
Clive.

Prestwood, Viscount, son of Earl Attlee.

PRITCHARD, BARON. (Pritchard.) [Life Baron 1975.]

DEREK WILBRAHAM PRITCHARD, son of Frank Wheelton Pritchard, of Didsbury, Lancs.; *b.* June 8th, 1910; ed. at Clifton Coll.; 1939-45 War; late Col. RA (TA) in Far East, and Dir. of Radar Procurement Combined Chs. of Staff, Washington; Chm. of BNEC 1966-68 (Dep. Chm. 1965-66), of Allied Breweries Ltd. 1968-70, and of Carreras Ltd., 1970-72; Chm. of Rothman Internat. since 1972; Pres. of Inst. of Dirs. 1968-74; a Dir. of Midland Bank, Samuel Montague & Co. Ltd., and other cos.; cr. Knt. 1968, and *Baron Pritchard*, of West Haddon, Northants. (Life Baron) 1975: *m.* 1941, Denise Arfor, da. of Frank Huntbach, and has issue.

Arms,—Not exemplified at time of going to press.

Residences,—Flat 47, South St., W1; West Haddon Hall, West Haddon, Northampton, NN6 7AU

DAUGHTERS LIVING.
Hon. Rosemary Gail, *b.* 1946: *m.* 1967, Ernest Raymond Anthony Travis, of 48, Waterford Rd., SW6.
Hon. Diana Gilliam Amanda, *b.* 1948: *m.* 1969, David Huntingdon Williams, of 4118, Woodbine St., Chevy Chase, Maryland, 20015, USA.

QUEENBOROUGH, BARONY OF. (Paget.) [Extinct 1949.]

DAUGHTERS LIVING OF FIRST BARON. (*By 2nd marriage.*)

Hon. Audrey Elizabeth, *b.* 1922: *m.* 1st, (Jan.) 1945, Commandant Christian Martell, D.F.C., French Air Force, who *d.* (Aug.) 1945; 2ndly, 1946, Ronan Nelson; 3rdly 1956, Lieut.-Com. Claud Peter Harcourt Lucy, RN, from whom she obtained a divorce 1974, and has issue living, (by 2nd m.) Thomas Lorne, *b.* 1947,—Audrey Caroline, *b.* 1949,—Elizabeth Christian, *b.* 1950.
Hon. Enid Louise PAGET, *b.* 1923; resumed the surname of Paget 19—: *m.* 1947 (marriage dissolved 19—), Count (Roland) de la Poype, and has issue living, Isabelle Victorie, *b.* 1951. *Residence*,—15, Place de Temple, 1227, Carrouge, Geneva.
Hon. Cicili Carol, *b.* 1928 : *m.* 1949, Capt. Robert Victor John Evans, and has issue living, John Almeric, *b.* 1950,—Michael Hugh, *b.* 1956,—Patricia Antoinetta, *b.* 1959. *Residence*,—Squerryes Lodge, Westerham, Kent.

Queensberry, Duke of, title borne by Duke of Buccleuch.

QUEENSBERRY, MARQUESS OF. (Douglas.) [Marquess S. 1682, Bt. S. 1668.]

DAVID HARRINGTON ANGUS DOUGLAS, 12th Marquess, and 11th Baronet; *b.* Dec. 19th, 1929; *s.* 1954; ed. at Eton; late 2nd Lieut. Roy. Horse Guards; Prof. of Ceramics, Roy. Coll. of Art since 1959: *m.* 1st, 1956, Ann (m. diss. 1969), da. of Maurice Sinnett Jones, and formerly wife of George Arthur Radford; 2ndly, 1969, Alexandra Mary Clare Wyndham, da. of Guy Wyndham Sich, and has issue by 1st and 2nd wives.

Arms,—Quarterly : 1st and 4th argent, a King's heart crowned gules, on a chief azure, three stars of The first, *Douglas* : 2nd and 3rd azure, a bend between six cross crosslets fitchée or, *Mar* : the whole within a bordure or, charged with the double tressure flory-counter gules. Crest,—A heart gules, crowned and winged. Supporters,—Two flying horses argent winged or.

Residence,—

SON LIVING. (*By 2nd wife*)
SHOLTO FRANCIS GUY (*Viscount Drumlanrig*), *b.* June 1st, 1967.

DAUGHTERS LIVING. (*By 1st wife*
Lady Emma Cathleen, *b.* 1956.   Lady Alice, *b.* 1965.

(*By 2nd wife*)
Lady Kate Cordelia Sasha, *b.* 1969.

HALF-BROTHER LIVING.
Lord Gawain Archibald Francis (Shilley Aalin, Lhergydhoo, Peel, Isle of Man), *b.* 1948; LRAM: *m.* 1971, Nicolette, yr. da. of Col. Frank Alfred Eustace, OBE, RM, of Hong Kong, and has issue living, Dalziel Frances, *b.* 1971,—Elizabeth Meriel, *b.* 1974.

SISTER LIVING.
Lady Jane Katherine, *b.* 1926: *m.* 1949, David Arthur Cory-Wright [see Cory-Wright, Bt.]. *Residence,*—Jarmins Orchard, Barton St. David, Somerton, Somerset.

HALF-SISTER LIVING.
Lady Patricia Sybil DOUGLAS, *b.* 1918: *m.* 1938 (m. diss. 1950), Capt. Count John Gerard de Bendern, co. London Yeo. [B. Gerard]; 2ndly, 1952 (m. diss. 1960), Herman Hornak, and has issue living, (by 1st m.) Simon Frederick, *b.* 1946,—Caroline June, *b.* 1940,—Emma Magdalen, *b.* 1950: *m.* 1971, Nigel R. P. Dempster,—(by 2nd m.) Leo Alexander, *b.* 1953,—Francis Benedict, *b.* 1958. *Residences,* —5, Fawcett St., SW10; Butler's Farm, Herstmonceux, Hailsham, Sussex.

UNCLE LIVING. (*Son of* 10*th Marquess.*)
Lord Cecil Charles, *b.* 1898; ed. at Lancing Coll., and at R.M.C.; sometime Lieut. King's Own Scottish Borderers, and R.F.C.; European War 1914-18 (wounded): *m.* 1927, Ruby (KIRKLEY), da. of George de Vere Fenn, and has issue living, Susan Jean, *b.* 1939: *m.* 1965, Baron Joachim Botho von Bose. *Clubs,*—White's, St. James', Puffins (Edinburgh).

AUNT LIVING. (*Daughter of* 10*th Marquess.*)
Lady Dorothy Madeline, *b.* 1894; ed. at St. Paul's Girls' Sch.; 1914-18 War with British Red Cross So. in France: *m.* 1924, Capt. Esmond Brasnell Palmer, late Roy. Scots, who *d.* 1953. *Residence,*— Barn Cottage, Oakley Green, Windsor.

WIDOW LIVING OF ELEVENTH MARQUESS.
MURIEL BEATRICE MARGARET (CHUNN) (*Dowager Marchioness of Queensberry*), dau. of the late Arthur John Rowe Thornett: *m.* 1947, as his third wife, the 11th Marquess, who *d.* 1954. *Residence,*— Shilley Aalin, Lhergydhoo, Peel, Isle of Man.

COLLATERAL BRANCHES LIVING.

Grandchildren of the late Lord Sholto George Douglas, 4th son of 9th Marquess:— Issue of the late Sholto Augustus Douglas, *b.* 1900 (became a French citizen 1938), *d.* 1949: *m.* 1925, Isabelle, da. of the late François Raymon:— Douglas Bruce Georges, *b.* 1926.——Alfred, *b.* 1928.——Robert (Quartier Dandon, La Roquette, sur Siagne, France), *b.* 1933: *m.* 1964, Nicole Bourgeois, and has issue living, Marie Cristine *b.* 1965.——Georges, *b.* 1938.——Noel (son) *b.* 1939.——Elisabeth Georgette, *b.* 1927: *m.* 1952, Jean Masoin, artist, and has issue living, Sybil Elisabeth, *b.* 1953.——Sybil, *b.* 1931: *m.* 1966, Nigel Paul Mitchell-Carruthers, of 21, Rue Vernier, Nice, AM, France, and has issue living, Bruce Nigel Lawrence, *b.* 1968.——Marguerite Jeannette, *b.* 1941: *m.* 1969, Jean Demol, and has issue living Ysabelle *b.* 1965.——Jeanne (c/o National Westminster Bank, 10, Victoria Rd., Surbiton, Surrey), *b.* 1944: *m.* 19—, Horace Warren Hastings Hodgkins, who *d.* 1972, and has issue living, Warren Sholto Oliver, *b.* 1966,—Julian Percy Herbert, *b.* 1967,—Alister John Hugh, *b.* 1970.

Grandchildren of the late Arthur Henry Johnstone-Douglas (infra):— Issue of the late Robert Sholto Johnstone-Douglas, *b.* 1871, *d.* 1958: *m.* 1913, Bettina, who *d.* 1961, dau. of the late Harman Grisewood :— Robert Arthur, *b.* 1914.——Elizabeth Gwendolen Teresa, *b.* 1916: *m.* 1st, 1954, as his second wife, the 6th Earl of Craven, who *d.* 1965; 2ndly, 1966, Kenneth Harmood Banner, of Peelings Manor, Pevensey, Sussex. *Residence,*—The Dower House, Hamstead Marshall, Newbury, Berks.

Granddaughter of the late Robert Johnstone-Douglas, son of the late Henry Alexander Douglas, brother of 6th and 7th Marquesses:— Issue of the late Arthur Henry Johnstone-Douglas, *b.* 1846, *d.* 1923: *m.* 1869, Jane Maitland, who *d.* 1930, dau. of the late Stair Hathorn Stewart, of Physgill, and Glasserton, co. Wigtown:— Olive Christian, *b.* 1878: *m.* 1905, Col. Francis John Carruthers of Dormont, CB, who *d.* 1945, and has issue living, William Nigel, *b.* 1908; ed. at Wellington Coll.: *m.* 1947, Constance Margaret, yst. da. of the late Lt.-Col. Cyril Jarrett, DSO, TD, of Redlands, Gerrards Cross, Bucks,—Simon Francis (of The Leuchold, South Queensferry, West Lothian), *b.* 1911; ed. at Wellington Coll.: *m.* 1st, 1946, Pamela Elizabeth, who *d.* 1955, el. da. of the late W. Melville Foster, of Hillside, Box, Glos.; 2ndly, 1957, Rosemary Elizabeth, el. da. of the late Geoffrey H. Gilbey, MC, of Manor House, Wooburn Green, Bucks., and has issue living, (by 1st m.) James Andrew *b.* 1947: *m.* 1968, Elizabeth Pauline Downie (and has issue living, Anthony *b.* 1972, Susan *b.* 1968), Francis Melville *b.* 1953, Marianne Caroline *b.* 1948: *m.* 1972, Roger Stonier Worthy, (by 2nd m.) Elizabeth Jane *b.* 1959,—Michael George, *MC* (c/o Bron-y-Garth, Alverdiscott, Bideford, N. Devon), *b.* 1913; ed. at Wellington Coll.: *m.* 1946, Maureen Dorothea Booker, and has issue living, Ian Robert *b.* 1947: *m.* 1970, Junko Maetani, David Noel *b.* 1949: *m.* 1972, Ellen McCann (and has issue living, James Stuart *b.* 1973), Peter Michael *b.* 1952, Richard George *b.* 1959, Ann Elizabeth *b.* 1955,—Hew Douglas (Ardallie, Luss, Dunbartonshire), *b.* 1944; ed. at Wellington Coll.; formerly Sqdn.-Ldr. RAF: *m.* 1st, 1939 (m. diss. 1954), Pamela, only da. of the late Lt.-Col. T. G. J. Torrie, 2nd Life Gds.; 2ndly, 1954, Julia Kathleen, only da. of T. Gorst, and has issue living, (by 1st m.) Christopher Hew *b.* 1940, John Anthony *b.* 1941, (by 2nd m.) Gavin Michael *b.* 1956, Emma Lucy *b.* 1959,—Oliver (Nelsie Dene, Upper Shillong, Shillong 5, Assam), *b.* 1920; ed. at Trin. Coll., Glenalmond. *Residence,*—Millstone Rig, Lockerbie, Dumfriesshire.

Granddaughters of the late Arthur Henry Johnstone-Douglas (ante):— Issue of the late Nina Johnstone-Douglas, OBE, *b.* 1881, *d.* 1964: *m.* 1919, Stair Agnew Gillon, of Wallhouse and Abbey St. Bathans, who *d.* 1954:— Isabella Agnew (Abbey St. Bathans, Duns, Berwickshire) *b.* 1920.——Helen Douglas, *b.* 1928; ed. at Edinburgh Univ. (MA): *m.* 1954, John Jardine Dobie, MA, FLAS, of Ferneycastle, Reston, Berwicks., and has issue living, William Stair Jardine, *b.* 1955,—Douglas Jardine, *b.* 1956,—James Alexander Jardine, *b* 1958,—Andrew Gillon Jardine, *b.* 1962.

Grandchildren of the late Right Rev. Henry Alexander Douglas, Bishop of Bombay, son of the late Henry Alexander Douglas (ante):— Issue of the late Archibald Charles Douglas, *b.* 1861, *d.* 1939 : *m.* 1896, Betty, who *d.* 1960, dau. of Andrew S. McClelland, C.A. :— Archibald Andrew Henry (Ashley, Shalbourne, Marlborough, Wilts.; Savile Club), *b.* 1902; ed. at Clifton, and Glasgow Univ. (BSc): *m.* 1935, Marjorie Gordon, el. da. of the late Dr. Grey Brown, and has issue living, Archibald Sholto Gordon (Flat 8, 83, Ladbroke Grove, W11) *b.* 1937,—Ian Andrew McClelland (RAF Kinloss, Forres, Morayshire), *b.* 1939; Sqdn. Ldr. RAF: *m.* 1967, Jennifer Merrett, of Plymouth, and has issue living, Kirsten Lucy *b.* 1969,—Katherine Veronica, *b.* 1943: *m.* 1963, Richard Ninian Barwick Clegg, of Greenfield Farm, Antrobus, Northwich, Ches., only son of Sir Cuthbert Barwick Clegg, TD, and has issue living, Aidan Charles Barwick *b.* 1966, Sebastian James Barwick *b.* 1969, Flavia Mary Rosabel *b.* 1968,—Ursula Rosemary (twin), *b.* 1943: *m.* 1968, William Harvey Righter, Prof. of Comparative Literature, Hong Kong Univ.——James Sholto, *TD* (PO Box 296, Bulawayo, Rhodesia; Bulawapo Club), *b.* 1905; ed. at Repton; late Lt.-Col. 51st (Westmorland and Cumberland) Field Regt. RA (TA); 1939-45 War (wounded).——Marjorie Charlotte, *b.* 1900: *m.* 1927, David Gordon Cochran, woh *d.* 1972, and has issue living, Hugh Douglas (Balfour, Aboyne, Aberdeenshire), *b.* 1932: *m.* 1st, 1958, Joan, who *d.* 1961, da. of John Fleming, of Colt Hill, Bieldside, Aberdeen; 2ndly, 1962, Maria-Luisa, only da. o °¹arco Minio-Paluello, of Mira Taglio, Venice, and has issue living, (by 1st m.) David Alexar   ᴄ.1958, Joanna Mary Isabella *b.* 1960, (by 2nd m.) Marco Gordon *b.* 1963, Adam Michelangelo *b.* 1967,—Francis Gordon (Beech-wood, Pitfodels, Aberdeen), *b.* 1934: *m.* 1963, Ann Jill, el. da. of the late Leslie Reynolds, and has issue living, Neil Reynolds *b.* 1965, Jeremy Douglas *b.* 1969, Michael John *b.* 1972, Nicola Vivien *b.* 1967,—Diana Marjorie, *b.* 1928: *m.* 1950 (m. diss. 1965) the Rev. Alan Robson, and has issue living, Mark Bennet *b.* 1956, Simon Patrick *b.* 1961, Lucy Diana *b.* 1954.   *Residence,*—Balfour, Aboyne, Aberdeenshire.——Lucy Elizabeth (15, Seafield Court, Seafield Rd., Aberdeen), *b.* 1907.

Grandchildren of the late (Hon.) John Douglas, C.M.G. (infra):—

Issue of the late (Hon.) Edward Archibald Douglas, |*b.* 1877, *d.* 1947 : *m.* 1907, Annette Eileen, who *d.* 1966, 2nd da. of the Hon. Mr. Justice Virgil Power (a Puisne Judge of Supreme Court, Queensland), of Rockhampton, Queensland:—
Edward Sholto, *b.* 1909 ; ed at St. Ignatius Coll., Sydney ; European War 1939-45 as Major Australian Imperial Force : *m.* 1939, Mary Constance, dau. of the late C. M. Curr, of Buckie, N.S. Wales.   *Residence,*—81, Markwell Street, Hamilton, Brisbane, Queensland.——*Rev.* Francis Hugh, *b.* 1914 ; ed. at St. Ignatius Coll., Sydney.——*Rev.* Kenneth Maxwell, *b.* 1921 ; ed. at Downlands Coll., Toowoomba ; is Missionary of the Sacred Heart.——Gavin James, *b.* 1926 ; ed. at Downlands Coll., Toowoomba, and at Queensland Univ. (M.B. and B.S. 1948) ; F.R.A.C.S. 1955 : *m.* 1951, Clare, dau. of J. H. McHugh, of Townsville, Queensland, and has issue living, Edward John, *b.* 1952,—Andrew Benedict, *b.* 1957,—Gavin Gerard, *b.* 1958,—Christopher James *b.* 1962,—Margot Anne, *b.* 1953,—Helen Penny, *b.* 1955,—Annette Josepa *b.* 1960,—Mary Patrice *b.* 1964.   *Residence,*—107, Stanley St., North Ward, Townsville, Queensland.——Andrew Brice, *b.* 1931; ed. at Downlands Coll., Toowoomba: *m.* 1957, Lorraine, da. of R. J. Lawson, of Brisbane, and has issue living, Sholto Francis, *b.* 1958,—David James, *b.* 1960,—Maxwell Richard, *b.* 1966,—Andrew Brice Christopher, *b.* 1968.   *Residence,*—17, Sutherland Av., Ascot, Brisbane, Queensland.——Evelyn Clare Mary, *b.* 1911.

Issue of the late Henry Alexander Cecil Douglas, *b.* 1879, *d.* 1952 : *m.* 1st, 1910, Flora Isabel, who *d.* 1910, dau. of Charles Hugh Macdonald, formerly of Kilcoy, Queensland ; 2ndly, 1914, Catherine Cecilia (of 11, Inverness Street, Ascot, Brisbane, Queensland), dau. of the late T. C. Beirne, M.L.C., of Queensland :—
(By 2nd marriage) Alexander Michael, *b.* 1926 ; ed. at Downlands Coll., Queensland : *m.* 1954, Morna Therese, dau. of Michael Patrick O'Rourke, of Brisbane, Queensland, and has issue living, Henry Alexander Michael, *b.* 1955,—Richard John, *b.* 1957,—Alexander Rodney, *b.* 1958,—Andrew Beirne, *b.* 1960,—James Patrick, *b.* 1965.   *Residence,*—17, Palm Av., Ascot, Brisbane, Qld.——Mary Beirne, *b.* 1915: *m.* 1938, John Peter Fihelly, and has issue living, John Douglas (8, Palm Av., Ascot, Brisbane, Qld.), *b.* 1948: *m.* 1969, Margaret Lynne Hunter, and has issue living, Jon Hunter *b.* 1969—Mary Carolyn, *b.* 1939: *m.* 1961, Hugh Francis Molloy, MRCS, LRCP, DObstRCOG, DDM, FACD, of 2, Futuna Lane, Hunter's Hill, Sydney, NSW 2110, and has issue living, Hugh Dominic *b.* 1962, John Henry Francis *b.* 1970, Mary Kathleen *b.* 1965,—Sue Catherine, *b.* 1944.   *Residence,*—14, Sword St., Ascot, Brisbane, Qld.——Sybil Catharine *b.* 1918: *m.* 1943, Lt.-Cdr. Alan B. Bryan, R. Aust. Navy, and has issue living, Alan Douglas, *b.* 1944—Henry Beirne, *b.* 1947,—Edward Alan, *b.* 1954,—Neil Beirne, *b.* 1961,—Mary Christine, *b.* 1949.   *Residence,*—14, Inverness St., Ascot, Brisbane, Qld.

Issue of the late Hugh Maxwell Douglas, Lieut. Australian Forces, *b.* 1881, *d.* (of wounds in action during European War) 1918 : *m.* 1904, Hannah Elizabeth, second dau. of E. L. Thornton, formerly of Warwick, Queensland :—
Henry Alexander (37, Ormond St., Ascot, Brisbane, Queensland), *b.* 1908: *m.* 1938, Ethel Audrey, da. of the late Dr. A. E. Malaher, and has issue living, Henry John, *b.* 1942: *m.* 1966, Susan, da. of E. Clark, of Balgowlah Heights, Sydney, and has issue living, Elizabeth Jane *b.* 1967,—Kathrine, *b.* 1938: *m.* 1961, John Francis Douglas, of Springfield, Mitchell, Qld., and has issue living, Andrew *b.* 1963, Grahame *b.* 1965, James *b.* 1968.——Edward Octavius *b.* 1913.   *Residence,*—Rupert Terr., Ascot, Brisbane, Qld.

Grandson of the late Henry Alexander Douglas, 3rd son of Sir William Douglas, 4th Bt., and brother of 6th and 7th Marquesses :—

Issue (by 2nd marriage) of the late (Hon.) John Douglas, C.M.G., *b.* 1828, *d.* 1904 : *m.* 1st, 1860, Mary, who *d.* 18—, dau. of the Rev. J. Simpson, and widow of William Howe, of Sydney, N.S.W. ; 2ndly, 1877, Sarah, dau. of Michael Hickey, of Ballimorris, co. Clare :—
Hon. Robert Johnstone, *b.* 1883 ; ed. at Sydney Univ. (B.A. 1904) ; Bar. Queensland 1906 ; was a Puisne Judge of Supreme Court, Queensland (Northern) 1923 ; is a Knight Com. of Order of St. Gregory the Great : *m.* 1912, Alice Mary, dau. of the late Andrew Ball, of Townsville, Queensland, and has issue living, Robert Andrew (of 24, Lawson Street, Mysterton, Townsville, Queensland), *b.* 1915 ; ed. at St. Joseph's Coll., Nudgee, and at Melbourne Univ. (M.B. and B.S. 1939); FRACP 1967; MRCP London 1952; formerly Maj. Australian Army Med. Corps. Middle East, New Guinea and Tarakan 1940-45 : *m.* 1949, Barbara, dau. of the late Rev. John Shaw, of Adelaide, S. Australia, and widow of Harry Buzolich, of Melbourne, Australia, and has issue living, Robert John *b.* 1950, Sholto James Shaw *b.* 1960, Catriona *b.* 1952, Barbara Selina *b.* 1953, Sarah *b.* 1955,—James Archibald (of Greyleaves, Morgan St., Albion Heights, Brisbane, Queensland), *b.* 1917; ed. at St. Joseph's Coll., Nudgee; Bar. Queensland 1946, QC 1966; Maj. Australian Inf. (ret.); Puisne Judge of Supreme Court of Queensland since 1965; Middle East, New Guinea, and Russia 1940-45: *m.* 1943, Marjorie Mary, dau. of the late James Campbell Ramsay, of Brisbane, Queensland, and has issue living, Robert Ramsay (18, Towers St., Albion Heights, Brisbane, Qld.) *b.* 1944; ed. at Villanova Coll., Coorparoo, and Qld. Univ. (LLB); Bar. Qld. 1968; Sqdn.-Ldr. RAAF Reserve: *m.* 1970, Jennifer Farmar, da. of Frank Wilmot Horton, of Blenheim, NZ (and has issue living, Robert Horton *b.* 1970, John Archibald *b.* 1975, Charlotte Mary *b.* 1972), Francis Maxwell (Selborne Chambers, Phillip St., Sydney, NSW), *b.* 1946; ed. at Villanova Coll., Coorparoo, Qld. Univ. (BA, LLB) and Camb. Univ. (LLB); Bar. Qld. 1969; Bar. NSW 1975: *m.* 1972, Sigrun Balvinsdottir, da. of Baldvin Einarsson, of Rekjavik, Iceland (and has issue living, James Baldvin *b.* 1974), James Sholto *b.* 1950; ed. at Villanova Coll., Coorparoo, Qld. Univ. (BA, LLB); Bar Qld. 1973, Catherine Alice Mary *b.* 1948: *m.* 1974, Roger John Stredwick,—Hugh Maxwell *b.* 1920; ed. at St. Joseph's Coll., Nudgee; Capt. Australian Army; Middle East, New Guinea, and Borneo 1940-45: *m.* 1947, Jean Duncan, only da. of the late E. L. Love, of Adelaide, S. Australia, and has issue living, John Duncan *b.* 1949,—Beatrice Rose Mary, *b.* 1919: *m.* 1947, Cornelius James Howard, of 984, Burke Rd., Deepdene, Melbourne, Australia, and has issue living, Catherine Mary *b.* 1952, Elizabeth Anne *b.* 1953,—Alice Mary, *b.* 1922: *m.* 1949, Thomas William Capell, MB, BS, FRACS, MRCOG, of 2, Plam Grove, Balwyn E8, Melbourne, Australia, and has issue living, William Douglas *b.* 1951, Andrew Thomas *b.* 1954, Jane Marie *b.* 1950.   *Residence,*—Rosebank, Pimlico, Townsville, Queensland.

Grandson of the late Walter Douglas-Irvine, 3rd son of the late Lord William Robert Keith Douglas, MP (infra):—

Issue of the late Rev. Henry Archibald DOUGLAS (who reverted to that surname only 1919)' *b.* 1883, *d.* 1962: *m.* 1913, Beatrice Alice (Fosbrooke House, Clifton Drive, Lytham, Lancs.); da. of Thomas William Gratrix, of Liverpool:—
Walter Francis Edward (of 32, St. Leonard's St., Stamford, Lincs.), *b.* 1917; ed. at Exeter Coll., Oxford (B.A. 1938, M.A. 1950): *m.* 1944, Eugenie Nellie, yst. da. of Gustave Chaudoir, of Highgate, N., and has issue living, Francis Gustave, *b.* 1946,—Mark Gavin, *b.* 1958,—Ruth Mary, *b.* 1947; DipAD(Fashion): *m.* 1971, William Francis Wright of 14, Alma St., Taunton, Som.,—Josephine Eugenie, *b.* 1950: *m.* 1973, Alan Michael Locker,—Rachel Margaret, *b.* 1954: *m.* 1974, Richard Palmer.

Grandchildren of the late Charles Irvine Douglas, 4th son of the late Lord William
Robert Keith Douglas, MP (who was raised to the rank of a Marquess's yr. son
1837), 4th son of Sir William Douglas, 4th Bt., and brother of 6th and 7th Mar-
quesses:—
Issue of the late Robert Keith Douglas, *b.* 1874, *d.* 1917: *m.* 1902, Louisa Mary (who m. 2ndly,
1924, Major Hugh Fraser, late Rifle Brig.), youngest dau. of the late Rev. Horace
Charles Ripley, sometime V. of Minster-Lovell, Witney, Oxon:—
Archibald William (La Cohue, Hérupe, St. John, Jersey), *b.* 1907; ed. at Malvern, and Brasenose Coll.
Oxford (MA); late Maj. Int. Corps.; 1939-45 War: *m.* 1934, Barbara Middlemost, who *d.* 1970,
yr. da. of the late Herbert Pratt Bairstow, and has issue living, Janet Valerie, *b.* 1937: *m.* 1959,
John Percival Harris, of Tudor Court, Fairmile Park Rd., Cobham, Surrey, and has issue living,
Steven Oliver *b.* 1965, Juliet *b.* 1961, Charlotte *b.* 1963,—Alison Rosemary, *b.* 1939: *m.* 1967, Brian
Woodcock, of Thorncroft, Ribchester, Preston, Lancs., and has issue living, Sara Jane *b.* 1969, James
William *b.* 1970.

Issue of the late John Campbell Douglas, *b.* 1876, *d.* 1960: *m.* 1910, Violet Douglas, who
d. 1972, da. of the late C. J. Daniell, of Cuyim, Punta del Este, Uruguay:—
Charles Sholto, *b.* 1915 ; European War 1939-45 as Major King's Own Scottish Borderers : *m.* 1941,
Christian F., dau. of the late Maj.-Gen. Francis James Marshall, C.B., C.M.G., D.S.O., and has
issue living, Helen Frances, *b.* 1942: *m.* 1971, Clive Eden Walker, (PO Box MP76, Mount Pleasant,
Salisbury, Rhodesia), and has issue living, Alice Megan *b.* 1973,—Katharine Anne, *b.* 1943: *m.* 1969,
Timothy MacDermot-Roe, of Seapoint House, Bray, co. Wicklow, and has issue living, Charles
Alexander *b.* 1974, Katherine Emma *b.* 1972,—Margaret Jean, *b.* 1945. *Residence,*—King's Lodge,
Cookham Dean, Berks.——Violet Katherine, *b.* 1910: *m.* 1935, John Griffith O'Donoghue, and has
issue living, Susan, *b.* 1936: *m.* 1956, A. L. K. Liddle, and has issue living, Nocholas John Kestell
b. 1958, Alan Digby Simon *b.* 1959, Juliet Susan *b.* 1965,—Margaret Ann (Peggy), *b.* 1938: *m.* 1960,
Christopher James Waller, Queen's Roy. Irish Hussars (*Club*,—Cavalry), and has issue living, Sarah
Louise *b.* 1961, Celia Katherine *b.* 1963. *Residence,*—Drumcowie, Malin, co. Donegal.——Margaret
Elizabeth, *b.* 1918: *m.* 1945, Craig Cooper, and has issue living. *Residence,*—Cherryhill Farm,
RRI, Freelton, Ontario, Canada.

Grandchildren of the late Edward Douglas, son of the late Gen. Sir James Dawes
Douglas, son of the late Major James Sholto Douglas, grandson of Sir John
Douglas, 3rd Bt.:—
Issue of the late Lieut.-Col. Montagu William Douglas, C.S.I., C.I.E., *b.* 1863, *d.* 1957 : *m.*
1891, Helen Mary Isabelle, *O.B.E.*, who *d.* 1943, dau. of the late Ven. G. W. Downer
Archdeacon of Kingston, Jamaica :—
Edward Montagu, *b.* 1891: LDSRCS, England 1928; Capt. (ret.) Welch Regt.; 1914-15 War, 1939-45
War: *m.* 1937, Lavinia Rose, da. of Arthur Edgar Wood. *Residence,*—54, New Rd., Chatham.——
Helen Elisabeth Margaret Mary, *b.* 1893; is an Author and Novelist, a FRGS, and a LLCM, 15 years
Lecturer in English at Osmania Univ. Coll. for Women Hyderabad, Deccan; assumed the additional
Christian names of Margaret Mary on being received into the Roman Catholic Church 1944; has
Kaisar-i-Hind silver medal, and Bronze medal for Art: *m.* 1920, Geoffrey Bernard Douglas-Pulleyne,
Indian Police, who *d.* 1956. *Residence,*—Rosa Mystica, 98, Central Avenue, Salisbury, Rhodesia.

Granddaughters of the late Sir John Douglas K.C.M.G. (ante):—
Issue of the late Francis William Douglas ; *b.* 1874, *d.* 1953 ; *m.* 1908, Violet Eleanor Jane,
who *d.* 1956, dau. of the late John More O'Faral :—
Joan Margaret, *b.* 1909: *m.* 1928, Peter Maurice Jacques Koch de Gooreynd, who *d.* 1973, and has issue
living, Timothy William Jacques Leopold (Quinta Duffnotti, Funchal, Lagos, Algarve, Portugal),
b. 1930; late Lt. Scots Guards: *m.* 1953, Maunagh Jean, da. of the late Maj. the Hon. Frederick
Francis George Hennessy, MBE, Grenadier Guards [see B. Windlesham colls.], and has issue living,
Peter Frederick Leopold *b.* 1958, Alexander Francis William *b.* 1969, Stella Antoinette Jeanne *b.* 1954,
Manuela Enriqueta Maria *b.* 1957, Annabel Maria Therese *b.* 1963,—Simon Philip Julian Guy, *b.* 1936;
late Lt. Irish Guards:—Enriqueta Mary Jeanne (*Hon. Mrs. John M. Lindesay-Bethune*), *b.* 1933:
m. 1953, the Hon. John Martin Lindesay-Bethune, of King's Cottage, Kew Green, Richmond, Surrey
[see E. Lindsay].——Helen Sholto, *b.* 1910: *m.* 1st, 1932, Edward William Eric Mann, who *d.* (killed
in action during European War) 1943; 2ndly, 1950, Wilfred Harry Levita. *Residence,*—41, Eaton
Place, SW1X 8BX.

PREDECESSORS.—[1] *Sir* WILLIAM Douglas, 9th Feudal Baron of Drumlanrig; entertained
James VI. at his mansion : cr. *Lord Douglas of Hawick and Tibbers,* and *Viscount Drum-
lanrig* (peerage of Scotland) 1628, and *Earl of Queensberry* (peerage of Scotland) 1633, with
remainder to his heirs male bearing the surname and arms of Douglas; *d.* 1640 ; *s.* by his son
[2] JAMES, 2nd Earl ; a zealous Royalist; *d.* 1671 ; *s.* by his son [3] WILLIAM, *P.C.*, 3rd Earl ;
Justice-Gen. of Scotland 1680-2, Extraordinary Lord of Session 1681, and High Treasurer of
Scotland and Constable and Gov. of Edinburgh Castle 1682 ; cr. *Lord Douglas of Kinmont,
Middlebie and Dornoch, Viscount Nith, Torthorwald and Ross, Earl of Drumlanrig and Sanquhar,*
and *Marquess of Queensberry* (peerage of Scotland) 1682, with remainder to his heirs male
whatsoever, and *Marquess of Dumfriesshire,* and *Duke of Queensberry* (peerage of Scotland) 1683,
with remainder to heirs male ; *d.* 1695 ; *s.* by his el. son [4] JAMES, *K.G.*, 2nd Duke ; Lord High
Treasurer of Scotland, Sec. of State and Lord High Commr., and First Commr. on the part of Scotland
to discuss the measure of the Union ; in 1706 surrendered the Marquessate of Dumfriesshire and the
Dukedom of Queensberry, and in the same year received a new grant of those honours extending the
remainder to the heirs of entail descended from William, 1st Earl of Queensberry ; cr. *Baron Ripon,
Marquess of Beverley* and *Duke of Dover* (peerage of Great Britain) 1708 with special remainder to
his 2nd son Charles and younger sons in tail male ; *d.* 1711 ; *s.* (according to decision of House of
Lords 1812) by his el. surviving son in the Marquessate and Earldom of Queensberry, the Viscountcy
of Drumlanrig, and the Lordship of Douglas of Hawick and Tibbers, these not being mentioned in
the resignation and regrant of 1706, were not affected by it and descended according to the original
limitation, and in the Dukedom and other titles (by his nomination) by his second surviving
son, Charles (infra) [5] JAMES, 3rd Marquess ; an idiot, probably from birth, who never used the
titles ; *d.* 1715 ; *s.* by his brother [6] CHARLES, 3rd Duke, who had in 1706 been cr. *Viscount Tibbers*
and *Earl of Solway* (peerage of Scotland), with remainder to the heirs of his father not in succession
to the Dukedom of Queensberry ; *d.* without surviving issue 1778, when the English honours expired
and the Scottish peerage devolved upon [7] WILLIAM, *K.T.,* (only son of William, 2nd Earl of March,
el. son of William, 1st Earl of March, 2nd son of 1st Duke, who had been cr. *Earl of March, Viscount
Peebles, and Lord Douglas of Neidpath, Lyne and Munard* (peerage of Scotland) 1697, with remainder
to heirs male of his body, failing which to heirs of ent: il of the Lordships and lands of Neidpath), 4th
Duke, who in 1731 had *s.* his father as 3rd Earl of March (ante), and in 1748 his mother as 4th *Earl of
Ruglen* (peerage of Scotland, cr. 1665) ; cr. *Baron Douglas of Amesbury* (peerage of Great Britain)
1768 ; *d.* 1810, when the Barony of Douglas of Amesbury and the Earldom of Ruglen became ext., and
the Earldom of March and inferior dignities (cr. 1697) passed to the 8th Earl of Wemyss (grandson
of Lady Anne Douglas, daughter of 1st Duke of Queensberry and sister of 1st Earl of March, on whom
the lordships and lands of Neidpath were entailed), the Dukedom of Queensberry, Marquessate of
Dumfriesshire, Earldom of Drumlanrig and Sanquhar, Viscountcy of Nith, Torthorwald and Ross,
and Lordship of Douglas of Kinmont, Middlebie and Dornoch reverted to the 3rd Duke of Buccleuch
(grandson of Lady Jane Douglas, el. dau. of 2nd Duke of Queensberry), and the Marquessate and
Earldom of Queensberry, Viscountcy of Drumlanrig, and Lordship of Douglas of Hawick and
Tibbers devolved upon his kinsman and heir male [8] *Sir* CHARLES Douglas, 5th Bt. of Kelhead (4th
in descent from Sir James Douglas of Kelhead, who was created a baronet of Nova Scotia 1668 with
remainder to heirs of his body, el. surviving son of Col. Sir William Douglas of Kelhead, 2nd son of

1st Earl of Queensberry), who became the 6th Marquess of Queensberry) ; cr. *Baron Solway*, of Kin-mount, co. Dumfries (peerage of United Kingdom) 1833; *d.s.p.* 1837, when the Barony of Solway became ext., and he was *s.* in the Scottish honours by his brother [9] JOHN, 7th Marquess ; *d.* 1856 ; *s.* by his son [10] ARCHIBALD WILLIAM, *P.C.*, 8th Marquess ; *b.* 1818 : *m.* 1840, Caroline Margaret, who *d.* 1904, dau. of Gen. Sir William Robert Clayton, 5th Bt. ; was M.P. for Dumfriesshire (*LC*) 1847-56, and Comptroller of the Household 1853-6 ; *d.* 1858 : *s.* by his son [11] JOHN SHOLTO, 9th Marquess, *b.* 1844 : *m.* 1st, 1866, Sibyl, who *d.* 1935, having obtained a divorce 1887, dau. of the late Alfred Montgomery ; 2ndly, 1893 (marriage annulled 1894), Ethel, dau. of Edward Charles Weeden, of Eastbourne ; *d.* 1900 ; *s.* by his el. surviving son [12] PERCY SHOLTO, 10th Marquess, *b.* 1868: *m.* 1st, 1893, Anna Maria, who *d.* 1917, dau. of the late Rev. Thomas Walters, V. of Boyton, Cornwall ; 2ndly, 1918, Mary Louise, who *d.* 1956, dau. of the late Richard Bickel, of Cardiff, and widow of Ernest Morgan ; *d.* 1920 ; *s.* by his el. son [13] FRANCIS ARCHIBALD KELHEAD, 11th Marquess, *b.* 1896 ; Capt. Black Watch (Roy. Highlanders) ; European War 1914-19 (twice wounded) ; sometime a representative Peer for Scotland : *m.* 1st, 1917, Irene Clarice (from whom he obtained a divorce 1925), dau. of H. W. Richards, of Regent's Park, N.W. ; 2ndly, 1926, Kathleen Sabine (who *d.* 1959, having obtained a divorce 1946), dau. of the late Harrington Mann ; 3rdly, 1947, Muriel Beatrice Margaret (CHUNN), dau. of the late Arthur John Rowe Thornett ; *d.* 1954 ; *s.* his by el. son [14] DAVID HARRINGTON ANGUS, 12th Marquess and present peer ; also Earl of Queensberry, Viscount Drumlanrig, and Lord Douglas of Hawick and Tibbers.

Quenington, Viscount, son of Earl St. Aldwyn.

QUIBELL, BARONY OF. (Quibell.) [Extinct 1962.]

DAUGHTER LIVING OF FIRST BARON. (By 1st marriage.)

Hon. Edith Ellen, *b.* 1904: is Pres. of Roy. So. for Prevention of Cruelty to Animals, Scunthorpe, a Dir. of Quibell & Hardy Ltd., builders and contractors, and a J.P. for Parts of Lindsey, Lincoln-shire; was Mayoress of Scunthorpe 1953-4: *m.* 1954, Eric Bennard Cuthbert, who assumed by deed poll 1962 the surname of Bennard in lieu of his patronymic. *Residence,*—Spring House, Winteringham, Lincolnshire.

WIDOW LIVING OF FIRST BARON.

CATHERINE CAMERON RAE (*Baroness Quibell*), of Beccles, Suffolk; Pres. of Scunthorpe and Dist. Spastic So.: *m.* 1954, as his 2nd wife, the 1st Baron, who *d.* 1962, when the title became ext. *Residence,*—38, Exeter Rd., Scunthorpe, Lincs.

RADCLIFFE, VISCOUNT. (Radcliffe.) [Viscount U.K. 1962.]

CYRIL JOHN RADCLIFFE, *G.B.E.*, *P.C.*, son of Capt. Alfred Ernest Radcliffe, of North Court, Finchamp-stead, Berks; *b.* March 30th, 1899; ed. at Haileybury, and at New Coll., Oxford (B.A. 1921, M.A. 1926); Bar. Inner Temple 1924, a K.C. 1935, and a Bencher 1943; Fellow of All Souls Coll., Oxford 1922-36; Hon. D.C.L., Oxford 1961; Hon. LL.D. Univ. of Wales, St. Andrews, N.-W. Univ., Illinois, USA, Sussex, and Man-chester; Hon. DLitt Warwick; chm. of Board of Govs., Sch. of Oriental and African Studies; a Trustee of Shakespeare Birthplace Inst., and of Sir John Soane's Museum, an Hon. Member of Institution of Civil Engineers, and an Hon. Fellow of Institute of Bankers; Ch. Press

Ever Faithful.

Censor, Min. of Information 1940-41, and Director-Gen. there 1941-45, Chm., Punjab and Bengal Boundary Commns. 1947, Vice-Chm. of Gen. Council of the Bar 1946-49, and Chm. of Roy. Commission on Income Tax 1952-55, Chm. of Gen. Advisory Council BBC 1953-55, Constitutional Commr. for Cyprus 1956, and Chm. of Cttee. of Inquiry into Monetary and Credit System 1957-59, into Security Procedures and Practices 1962, of Tribunal of Inquiry into Vassal Case 1962-63, and of Privy Council Cttee. of Inquiry into "D" Notices, 1967, and Lord of Appeal in Ordinary 1949-64; a Trustee of British Museum 1958-67 (Chm. 1963-66), and of British Museum (Natural History) 1963-69; First Chancellor of Warwick Univ. since 1965; 1914-18 War in France as 2nd Lt. Labour Corps; *cr.* KBE (Civil) 1944, GBE (Civil) 1948, a PC and *Baron Radcliffe,* of Werneth, co. Lancaster (Life Baron) 1949, and *Viscount Radcliffe,* of Hampton Lucy, co. Warwick (peerage of UK) 1962: *m.* 1939, the Hon. Antonia Mary Roby (TENNANT), da. of 1st Baron Charnwood.

Arms,—Ermine four bendlets engrailed sable. Crest,—On a wreath argent and sable issuant from a tower or, a bull's head ermines. Supporters,—On either side a black Labrador retriever proper.

Residences,—5, Campden Hill Gate, Duchess of Bedford Walk, W.8; Hampton Lucy House, Warwick.

RADNOR, EARL OF. (Pleydell-Bouverie.) [Earl G.B. 1765, Bt. G.B. 1714.]
[Name pronounced "Pleddel-Booverie."]

My country is dear; liberty is dearer.

JACOB PLEYDELL-BOUVERIE, 8th Earl, and 11th Baronet; *b.* Nov. 10th, 1927; *s.* 1968; ed. at Harrow, and Trin. Coll., Camb.; patron of one living: *m.* 1st, 1953 (m. diss. 1962), Anne Garden Farquharson, da. of Donald Farquharson Seth-Smith, MC; 2ndly, 1963, Margaret, da. of the late Robin Fleming, of Catter House, Drymen, and has issue by 1st and 2nd marriages.

Arms,—Quarterly: 1st and 4th, per fesse or and argent, an eagle displayed, with two heads sable, on the breast an escutcheon gules, charged with a bend vair, *Bouverie* 2nd and 3rd, argent a bend gules, guttée d'eau between two ravens sable, a chief checky, or and sable, *Pleydell.* Crest, —A demi-eagle with two heads displayed sable, ducally gorged or, and charged on the breast with a cross crosslet argent. Supporters,—Two eagles reguardant, wing. elevated sable, ducally gorged or, each charged on the breast with a cross crosslet argent.

Residence,—Longford Castle, Salisbury, SP5 4EF.

SONS LIVING. (*By 1st marriage.*)
WILLIAM (*Viscount Folkestone*), *b.* Jan. 5th, 1955.
Hon Peter John, *b.* 1958.

DAUGHTERS LIVING. (*By 2nd marriage.*)
Lady Lucy, *b.* 1964.
Lady Martha (twin), *b.* 1964.
Lady Belinda, *b.* 1966.
Lady Frances, *b.* 1973.

BROTHER LIVING.
Hon. Reuben (The Dower House, Slindon, Arundel, Sussex), *b.* 1930; ed. at Harrow; late 2nd Lt. Roy. Scots Greys: *m.* 1956, Bridget Jane, el. da. of the late John Fowell Buxton [see Buxton, Bt., colls.], and has issue living, Edward, *b.* 1957,—Jasper John, *b.* 1964,—Rosalind Mary, *b.* 1960.

HALF-BROTHER LIVING.
Hon. Richard Oakley (Lawrence End, Peters Green, Luton, Beds.), *b.* 1947; ed. at Harrow, and Roy. Agric. Coll., Cirencester.

SISTERS LIVING.
Lady Jane, *b.* 1923: *m.* 1945, Richard Anthony Bethell, of Rise Park, Hull [Cotterell, Bt.], and has issue living, Hugh Adrian, *b.* 1952,—William Anthony, *b.* 1957,—Camilla, *b.* 1946: *m.* 1966, Peter Charles Freeman Gregory-Hood [see V. Hood, colls.],—Sarah, *b.* 1948: *m.* 1969, David Ratcliffe Brotherton, of Wold Dyke Farm, Middleton-on-the-Wolds, Driffield, Yorks.

Lady Phœbe (The Bothy, Longford Park, Salisbury), *b.* 1932: *m.* 1955 (m. diss. 1963), Hubert Beaumont Phipps, and has issue living, Hubert Grace, *b.* 1958,—Melissa Adeane, *b.* 1955.

Lady Harriot, *b.* 1935: *m.* 1965, Mark Iain Tennant, of 30, Abbey Gdns., NW8, and Balfluig Castle, by Alford, Aberdeenshire [see B. Glenconner, colls.].

UNCLE LIVING. (*Son of 6th Earl.*)
Hon. Peter, *b.* 1909; ed. at Harrow, and at Trin. Coll., Camb.; Maj. KRRC: *m.* 1st, 1938, Audrey Evelyn (FIELD) (who *d.* 1968, having obtained a divorce 1946), da. of the late William Dodge James, CVO [Forbes, Bt.]; 2ndly, 1947, Audrey (BELLVILLE), da. of the late Capt. Glen Kidston, and has issue living, (by 2nd m.) James, *b.* 1950. *Residences,*—Landford Lodge, Salisbury, Wilts. *Club,*— White's.

AUNTS LIVING. (*Daughters of 6th Earl.,*)
Lady Jeane, *b.* 1892 ; Ch. Comdt. A.T.S. (retired): *m.* 1914, George Gerald Petherick, who *d.* 1946, el. son of the late G. T. Petherick, of Porthpean House, St. Austell, Cornwall, and has issue living, George David (Dipple Lodge, Wooburn Common, High Wycombe, Bucks.), *b.* 1917; ed. at Harrow, and at Trin. Coll., Camb. (BA): Bar. Inner Temple 1948; late Maj. 3rd King's Own Hussars (Regular Army Reserve); C.C. for Wilts. 1967-69; 1939-45 War (despatches twice): *m.* 1940, Evelyn Nancy (from whom he obtained a divorce 1946, whom he re-married 1961, and divorced 1971), da. of the late Maj. (William) Bertram Bell [B. Barrymore, ext.], and has issue living, George Robin (Dean's Farm House, Stratford-sub-Castle, Salisbury, Wilts.) *b.* 1941; ed. at Harrow; Capt. The Life Guards (Regular Army Reserve): *m.* 1968, Christine Elizabeth Clark, (and has issue living, Andrew William *b.* 1970, Sarah Jane *b.* 1972),—Christopher (83, Addison Rd., W14; Tredeague, Porthpean, St. Austell, Cornwall), *b.* 1922; ed. at Harrow; late Capt. Life Gds.; 1939-45 War: *m.* 1951, Countess Charlotte, da. of the late Count Raben-Levetzau, and has issue living, Martin Gerald Siegfried *b.* 1957, Thomas Henry *b.* 1962, Catherine Anastazia *b.* 1952: *m.* 1974, John Randal Timothy Collins [see B. Bicester], Harriet Louise *b.* 1953,—Julian (*Hon. Mrs. A. John P. H. M. Ashley-Cooper*), *b.* 1915; formerly Junior Com. ATS: *m.* 1946, Major the Hon. (Anthony) John Percy Hugh Michael Ashley-Cooper, Life Guards (Reserve), of Tregonwell Lodge, Cranborne, Wimborne, Dorset [see E. Shaftesbury],—Anne (*Baroness Burnham*), *b.* 1919; formerly Senior Com. ATS: *m.* 1942, the 5th Baron Burnham, of Hall Barn, Beaconsfield, Bucks.,—Jenefer Mary, *b.* 1927: *m.* 1953, Percy Basil Browne, of Torr House, Westleigh, Bideford, N. Devon, and has issue living, Benjamin James *b.* 1954, William Toby *b.* 1955, Mary Alice *b.* 1959. *Residence,*—The West Flat, Hall Barn, Beaconsfield, Bucks.

Lady Elizabeth, *b.* 1897. *Residence,*—Ducarts, Stanford Dingley, Berks.

Lady Margaret, *b.* 1903 : *m.* 1923, Lieut.-Col. Gerald Barry, M.C. [see Barry, Bt., colls.]. *Residence,*— Lake House, Great Witchingham, Norwich, NR1 5SJ.

Lady Helen, *O.B.E., b.* 1908 ; O.B.E. (Civil) 1946 : *m.* 1931, Major the Hon. David John Smith, CBE [see V. Hambleden]. *Residence,*—King's Copse House, Bucklebury, Berks.

WIDOWS LIVING OF SONS OF SIXTH EARL.
Alice Pearl, dau. of the late Major Barrington Crake, Rifle Brig., and widow of 2nd Baron Montagu of Beaulieu : *m.* 1936, Capt. the Hon. Edward Pleydell-Bouverie, M.V.O., R.N., who *d.* 1951, and has issue living [see colls., infra]. *Residence,*—The Lodge, Beaulieu, Hants.

Mrs. Katharine Bradley Martin (Syosset, Long Island, NY, USA), da. of the late Robert E. Tod, of New York: *m.* 1949, as his 2nd wife, the Hon. Bartholomew Pleydell-Bouverie, OBE, who *d.* 1965 [see colls. infra].

MOTHER LIVING.

Helena Olivia (The Beacon, Mundersley, Norfolk), da. of the late Charles Robert Whorwood Adeane, CB, of Babraham Hall, Cambridge [B. Leconfield, colls.]: *m.* 1st, 1922 (m. diss. 1942), the 7th Earl of Radnor, who *d.* 1968; 2ndly, 1943, Brig. Montacute William Worrell Selby-Lowndes, DSO, who *d.* 1972.

WIDOW LIVING OF SEVENTH EARL.

ANNE ISOBEL GRAHAM, *OBE*, *(Dowager Countess of Radnor)*, (Avonturn, Alderbury, Salisbury), da. of Lt.-Col. Richard Oakley, DSO, and widow of Richard Thomas Reynolds Sowerby: *m.* 1943, as his 2nd wife, the 7th Earl, who *d.* 1968.

COLLATERAL BRANCHES LIVING.

Issue of the late Capt. the Hon. Edward Pleydell-Bouverie, M.V.O., R.N., 2nd son of 6th Earl, *b.* 1899, *d.* 1951: *m.* 1936, Alice Pearl (ante), dau. of the late Major Barrington Crake, Rifle Brig., and widow of 2nd Baron Montagu of Beaulieu:—
Robin (28, Brechin Place, SW7), *b.* 1937: *m.* 1960, Anne-Louise, da. of Bruce Durham.

Issue of the late Hon. Bartholomew Pleydell-Bouverie, 3rd son of 6th Earl, *b.* 1902, *d.* 1965: *m.* 1st, 1927, Lady Doreen Clare Hely-Hutchinson, who *d.* 1942, da. of 6th Earl of Donoughmore; 2ndly, 1949, Mrs. Katharine Bradley Martin (ante), da. of the late Robert E. Tod, of New York:—
(By 1st marriage) Simon (The Castle House, Deddington, Oxon.), *b.* 1928; ed. at Harrow; late 2nd Lt. Life Guards: *m.* 1961, Vivien Eleanor, only da. of Sir Richard Michael Keane, 6th Bt., and has issue living, David Archie, *b.* 1964,—Grania Clare *b.* 1962,—Juliet Rose, *b.* 1968,—Alice Susan, *b.* 1970.——Penelope Jane, *b.* 1932: *m.* 1955, Michael Francis Meredith-Hardy, of Radwell Mill, Baldock, Herts., and has issue living, Richard, *b.* 1957,—Luke, *b.* 1959,—John Octavian, *b.* 1962,—Paul Bartholomew, *b.* 1966.

Granddaughter of the late Col. the Hon. Stuart Pleydell-Bouverie, D.S.O., O.B.E., T.D. (infra):—
Issue of the late Christopher Pleydell-Bouverie, *b.* 1901, *d.* 1949: *m.* 1930, Kathleen Adele (who obtained a divorce 1939), dau. of the late William Henry Carpenter Gelshenen, of New York, and 7, Cadogan Gardens, S.W.:—
Anne Patricia, *b.* 1933: *m.* 1953, Peter James Grant, Lieut. Queen's Own Cameron Highlanders (T.A. Reserve), and has issue living, Charles Ludovic, *b.* 1956,—Laura Marguerite, *b.* 1959. *Residence,—*

Issue of the late Col. the Hon. Stuart Pleydell-Bouverie, D.S.O., O.B.E., T.D., 2nd son of 5th Earl, *b.* 1877, *d.* 1947: *m.* 1900, Edith Dorothy, who *d.* 1949, dau. of the late Albert Vickers, of 14, Cadogan Square, S.W.:—
David, *b.* 1911; ed. at Charterhouse: *m.* 1946, Mrs. Alice Astor Harding, who *d.* 1956 having obtained a divorce 1952, da. of the late Col. John Jacob Astor. *Residence,—*The Valley of The Moon, Glen Ellen, California, USA.

Issue of the late Hon. Duncombe Pleydell-Bouverie, 2nd son of 4th Earl, *b.* 1842, *d.* 1909: *m.* 1883, Maria Eleanor, who *d.* 1936, dau. of Sir Edward Hulse, 5th Bt.:—
Katharine Harriot Duncombe, *b.* 1895. *Residence,—*Kilmington Manor, Warminster, Wilts.

Issue of the late Hon. Kenelm Pleydell-Bouverie, 6th son of 4th Earl, *b.* 1852, *d.* 1921: *m.* 1905, Evelyn Bertie Charlotte, who *d.* 1936, dau. of the late David Maitland Makgill-Crichton [E. Lauderdale, colls.]:—
Ralph Kenelm (of 44, Bloomfield Terr., SW1), *b.* 1910; ed. at Harrow.——Bertrand Eric (Blue Bridge House, Halstead, Essex), *b.* 1914; ed. at Trin. Coll., Camb. (BA 1939); 1939-45 War (despatches): *m.* 1950, Pamela, adopted da. of the late Lt.-Col. Roderick William Macdonald, CIE, DSO, and has issue living, Rupert William, *b.* (Dec.) 1950; ed. at Harrow,—Nigel Justin, *b.* 1955,—Prunella Sarah, *b.* 1952.——Doris, *b.* 1909; is a JP for W. Suffolk, and a co. Alderman. *Residence,—*Pump Lane House, Pump Lane, Bury St. Edmunds, Suffolk.

Granddaughter of the late Walter Pleydell-Bouverie, only son of the late Rt. Hon. Edward Pleydell-Bouverie, 2nd son of 3rd Earl:—
Issue of the late Major Humphrey Pleydell-Bouverie, M.B.E., *b.* 1883, *d.* 1958: *m.* 1922, Margaret Elfrida (of Patio, Westward Ho!, N. Devon), dau. of R. H. Holden, formerly of Talton House, Stratford-on-Avon:—
Ann, *b.* 1923: *m.* 1st, 1943 (marriage dissolved 1953), Lieut.-Col. Eric Charles Twelves-Wilson, V.C., late E. Surrey Regt., Colonial Administration, Tanganyika ; 2ndly, 1953, John Kennett Walker, who *d.* 1954, and has issue living, (by 1st marriage) Michael Charles Bouverie, *b.* 1947,—Anthony, *b.* 1949, (by 2nd marriage) Diana, *b.* 1954. *Residence,—*Chorley, Lancashire.

Grandchildren of the late Adm. Frederick William Pleydell-Bouverie, el. son of the late Rev. the Hon. Frederick Pleydell-Bouverie, 4th son of 2nd Earl:—
Issue of the late Wilfred Pleydell-Bouverie, *b.* 1856, *d.* 1922: *m.* 1888, Rachel, who *d.* 1922, dau. of George Murray Perry:—
Hugh Wyndham (Hancock St., Harding, Natal) *b.* 1900: *m.* 1926, Viola Elizabeth, da. of Walter Holloway Usher, and has issue living, Robin Wyndham (Longford (Private Bag), Harding, Natal) *b.* 1935: *m.* 1960, Jean Elizabeth Vermaak, and has issue living, Kim Wyndham *b.* 1965, Penelope Ann *b.* 1961, Carolyn *b.* 1963, Lynn Michelle *b.* 1968,—Peter Hugh, *b.* 1943,—Joy, *b.* 1927: *m.* 1950, Neville Ramsey Barrett, 1, Springfield Rd., Winterton, Natal, and has issue living, Roger Hugh *b.* 1950, Maureen *b.* 1953, Judy *b.* 1959, Monica Viola, *b.* 1937: *m.* 1959,—Norman Herring, of Chertney, Cederville, E G, S. Africa.——Ellen Georgina Kathleen, *b.* 1892: *m.* 1915, William Barclay Leslie Lowth [Barclay, Bt.], and has issue living, Peter Leslie Bouverie, *b.* 1915,—Peggy Kathleen Leslie Bouverie, *b.* 1917,—Daphne Frances Leslie, *b.* 1921,—Betty Leslie Frances, *b.* 1924. *Residence,—*14, Sherwood Drive, Meyrick Park, Salisbury, Rhodesia.

Grandchildren of the late Seymour Pleydell-Bouverie, 2nd son of Philip Pleydell-Bouverie, son of the hon. Philip Pleydell-Bouverie, MP, 5th son of 2nd Earl:—
Issue of the late Lieut.-Com. Philip Hales Pleydell-Bouverie, R.N.V.R., *b.* 1900, *d.* 1951: *m.* 1st, 1923, Alice Margaret (who obtained a divorce 1927), dau. of William Alfred Ingram, of 5, Highbury Grove, N.; 2ndly, 1927, Beth Olivia (GAGE), adopted dau. of the late Brig.-Gen. Ronald Maclachlan, Rifle Brig.; 3rdly, 1945, Kathleen, dau. of J. T. Fell, of Bristol:—
(By 1st marriage) Patricia, *b.* 1924: *m.* 1949, John Marshall, Solicitor, and has issue living, Roland, *b.* 1950,—Richard James, *b.* 1954.—Sheila Ann, *b.* 1953. *Residence,—*Hill House, Andover Road, Newbury.——(By 2nd m.) Lois, *b.* 1928: *m.* 1950, Gunther Wolff (RR1, Huron Line, Windsor, Ontario), and has issue living, Adrian, *b.* 1957.——Xenia, *b.* 1929: *m.* 1964, Alec Ronald Ayliffe, of RDI Waiuku, NZ, and has issue living, Gillian Xenia, *b.* 1966.

PREDECESSORS.—[1] WILLIAM Des Bouveries, an eminent Turkey merchant; cr. a *Baronet*, 1714; *d.* 1717; *s.* by his el. son [2] *Sir* EDWARD, 2nd Bt.; *d.* 1736; *s.* by his brother [3] *Sir* JACOB, 3rd Bt.; was M.P. for and Recorder of New Sarum; cr. *Lord Longford*, Baron of Longford, and *Viscount Folkestone* (peerage of Great Britain) 1747; *d.* 1761; *s.* by his son [4]

WILLIAM, 2nd Viscount; cr. *Baron Pleydell-Bouverie*, of Coleshill, co. Berks, and *Earl of Radnor* (peerage of Great Britain) 1765, with remainder to the earldom in default of male issue to the male descendants of his father; *d.* 1776; *s.* by his son [5] JACOB, 2nd Earl; *d.* 1828; *s.* by his son [6] WILLIAM, 3rd Earl; *b.* 1779; sat as M.P. for Salisbury 1802-28: *m.* 2ndly, Anne Judith, dau. of Sir Henry Paulet St. John Mildmay, 3rd Bt.; *d.* 1869; *s.* by his son [7] JACOB, 4th Earl, *b.* 1815; was Lord-Lieut. of Wilts: *m.* 1840, Lady Mary Augusta Frederica Grimston, who *d.* 1879, dau. of 1st Earl of Verulam; *d.* 1889; *s.* by his el. son [8] WILLIAM, 5th Earl, *b.* 1841; was Treasurer of the Household 1885-6 and 1886; sat as M.P. for Wiltshire S. (*C*) 1874-85, and for Enfield Div. of Middlesex 1885-9: *m.* 1866, Helen Matilda, who *d.* 1929, dau. of the late Rev. Henry Chaplin, of Blankney, Lincoln; *d.* 1900; *s.* by his el. son [9] JACOB, *C.I.E.*, *C.B.E.*, 6th Earl, *b.* 1868; M.P. for Wilts, S., or Wilton, Div. (*C*) 1892-1900, and Lord-Lieut. for Wilts 1925-30: *m.* 1891, Julian Eleanor Adelaide, who *d.* 1946, dau. of the late Charles Balfour, of Newton Don; *d.* 1930; *s.* by his son [10] WILLIAM, *KG*, *KCVO*, 7th Earl, *b.* 1895; Chm. of Rothamsted Experimental Station 1938-64, and Forestry Commn. 1952-63; Officia. Verderer of New Forest 1964-66, and Lord Warden of the Stanneries 1933-65: *m.* 1st, 1922 (m. diss. 1942), Helena Olivia (who *m.* 2ndly, 1943, Brig. Montacute William Worrell Selby-Lowndes, DSO), da. of the late Charles Robert Whorwood Adeane, CB, [B. Leconfield, colls.]; 2ndly, 1943, Anne Isobel Graham, OBE, da. of Lt.-Col. Richard Oakley, DSO, and widow of Richard Thomas Reynolds Sowerby; *d.* 1968; *s.* by his son [11] JACOB, 8th Earl and present peer; also Viscount Folkestone, Baron Longford (peerage of GB), and Baron Pleydell-Bouverie.

RADSTOCK, BARONY OF, (Waldegrave.) [Extinct 1953.]

DAUGHTER LIVING OF FIFTH BARON.

Hon. Elizabeth Alexandra Sophia, *b.* 1902: *m.* 1941, as his second wife, Baron Friedrich (Fritz) von Bültzingslöwen, who *d.* 1943. *Residence,*—Planken, Liechtenstein.

WIDOW LIVING OF SON OF FIFTH BARON.

Lady Hersey Margaret Boyle, dau. of 8th Earl of Glasgow: *m.* 1st, 1940, Com. the Hon. John Montagu Granville Waldegrave, D.S.C.. R.N., who *d.* (killed on active ser. during European War) 1944; 2ndly, 1947, John Goring, CBE, TD [see Goring, Bt., colls.], and has issue living (by 1st marriage) [see colls., infra]. *Residence,*—Findon Park House, Findon, Sussex.

COLLATERAL BRANCH LIVING.

Issue of the late Com. the Hon. John Montagu Granville Waldegrave, D.S.C., R.N., only son of 5th Baron, *b.* 1905, *d.* (killed in action during European War) 1944: *m.* 1940, Lady Hersey Margaret Boyle [(ante) who *m.* 2ndly, 1947, John Goring (see Goring, Bt., colls.)], dau. of 8th Earl of Glasgow :—
Horatia Marion, *b.* 1941: *m.* 1970, Oliver John Diggle.——Griselda Hyacinthe, *b.* 1943: *m.* 1967, Charles D. S. Drace-Francis (c/o FCO, King Charles St., SW1), and has issue living, James, *b.* 1969,—Alexander John, *b.* 1971.

RAGLAN, BARON. (Somerset.) [Baron U.K. 1852.]

MUTARE·VEL·TIMERE·SPERNO

I scorn to change or fear.

FITZROY JOHN SOMERSET, 5th Baron; *b.* Nov. 8th, 1927; *s.* 1964; ed. at Westminster, and at Magdalen Coll., Oxford; Capt. Welsh Guards (Reserve of Officers); JP, and a DL for Mon.; Chm. of Cwmbran New Town Development Corpn.; a Crown Estate Commr. since 1970: *m.* 1973, Alice, yr. da. of Peter Baily, of Great Whittington, Northumberland.

Arms,—Quarterly : 1st and 4th azure, three fleurs-de-lis or, *France;* 2nd and 3rd gules, three lions passant guardant in pale or, *England;* the whole within a bordure compony argent and azure. Crest,—A portcullis or, nailed azure, with chains pendant therefrom gold. Supporters, —*Dexter*, a panther argent, spotted of various colours, fire issuant from the mouth and ears proper, gorged with a plain collar and chained or; *sinister*, a wyvern, wings endorsed, vert, holding in the mouth a sinister hand, couped at the wrist, gules.

Seat,—Cefntilla Court, Usk, Monmouthshire.

BROTHER LIVING.

Hon. GEOFFREY, *b.* Aug. 29th, 1932; ed. at Westminster, and at Roy. Agricultural Coll.; is Lt. Grenadier Guards (Reserve); a co. Councillor of Berks. since 1966: *m.* 1956, Caroline Rachel, da. of Col. Edward Roderick Hill, DSO, JP [see E. St. Aldwyn, colls.], and has issue living, Arthur Geoffrey, *b.* 1960,—Belinda Caroline, *b.* 1958,—Lucy Ann, *b.* 1963. *Residence,*—The Old Malt House, Upper Lambourn, Berks.

SISTERS LIVING.

Hon. Janetta, *b.* 1925; ed. at St. Hugh's Coll., Oxford (BA 1945, MA 1951): *m.* 1956, Prof. Joseph Vincent Ridgely, of 4819, Keswick Rd., Baltimore, Maryland 21210, USA, and has issue living, Julia Frances Somerset, *b.* 1963.

Hon. Cecily, *b.* 1938: *m.* 1961, Jonkheer Jan T. P. Steengracht van Moyland, Capt. late Irish Guards, of 14, Addison Av., W11, and Lanwecha, Llandenny, Usk, Mon., and has issue living, Jonkheer Henry Jan Berrington, *b.* 1963,—Jonkvrowe Suzanna Cecily, *b.* 1968.

UNCLE LIVING. (*Son of 3rd Baron.*)

Hon. Nigel FitzRoy, *C.B.E., D.S.O., M.C., b.* 1893; ed. at King William's Coll., Isle of Man; Brigadier (retired) late Gloucestershire Regt.; sometime Assist. Mil. Sec., S. Command, India and A.D.C. to Gov. of S. Australia; European War 1914-18 with his Regt., and with Machine Gun Corps (twice wounded, despatches thrice, Brevet Major, M.C., D.S.O.), Afghan War 1919, European War 1939-45 Comdg. 145th Inf. Brig. in France (despatches, prisoner, C.B.E.); D.S.O. 1919, C.B.E. (Mil.) 1945: *m.* 1922, Phyllis Marion Offley, dau. of the late Dr. Henry O. Irwin, of Boulder, W. Australia, and has issue living, David Henry FitzRoy (of White Wickets, Boars Head, Crowborough, Sussex), *b.* 1930; ed. at Wellington Coll., and at Peterhouse, Camb. (B.A. 1952, M.A. 1956): *m.* 1955, Ruth Ivy, dau. of Wilfred Robert Wildbur, of King's Lynn, and has issue living, Henry Robert FitzRoy *b.* 1961, Louise Charlotte *b.* 1956,—Susan Mary, *b.* 1923: *m.* 1953, Patrick William Mackenzie Dean, of Eastmere House, Lincoln, and has issue living, James FitzRoy *b.* 1954, Julia Mary Mackenzie, *b.* 1956, Veronica Jane Somerset *b.* 1958, Rosemary Elizabeth *b.* 1964. *Residence,*—18, St. Anne's Cres., Lewes, Sussex.

AUNTS LIVING. (*Daughters of 3rd Baron.*)

Hon. Ethel Georgiana Frances, *b.* 1889: *m.* 1914, the Hon. William Sholto Douglas, who *d.* 1932 [see E. Morton]. *Residence,*—43, Cadogan Pl., SW1.
Hon. Ivy Felicia, *b.* 1897: *m.* 1947, as his second wife, Raymond Marwood-Elton Carey, F.R.I.B.A. *Residence,*—26, Drayton Gardens, S.W.10.

COLLATERAL BRANCH LIVING.

Issue of the late Maj. the Hon. Wellesley FitzRoy Somerset, 2nd son of 3rd Baron, *b.* 1887, *d.* 1969: *m.* 1917, Lesley, who *d.* 1969, da. of the late F. G. Vivian, of St. Fagan, Glam.:—
Mary Felicia, *b.* 1923: *m.* 1945, Thomas Copland Studdert, MD, FRCP, of Crinkle Hill, Newby West, Carlisle, and has issue living, Christopher John, *b.* 1947,—Peter Wellesley, *b.* 1949,—Mark Jeremy, *b.* 1953.

Issue of the late Capt. the Hon. Arthur Charles Edward Somerset, 2nd son of 2nd Baron, *b.* 1859, *d.* 1948: *m.* 1893, Louisa Eliza, who *d.* 1940, dau. of the late John Grant Hodgson:—
Victoria Mary Blanche, *b.* 1905; is a J.P. for Berks: *m.* 1926, Capt. Thomas Leopold McClintock Lonsdale, late Grenadier Guards, and has issue living, Norman John McClintock (of 41, Chelsea Square, S.W.3), *b.* 1926: *m.* 1957, Fiona Bentley, and has issue living, James Leopold Somerset *b.* 1958, Joanna Mary *b.* 1957, Emma Jane Blanche *b.* 1962. *Residences,*—Kingstone Lisle Park, Wantage; Flat 9, 17, Cadogan Sq., S.W.

PREDECESSORS.—[1] *Field-Marshal Lord* FitzRoy James Henry Somerset, *G.C.B.*, son of the 5th Duke of Beaufort; *b.* 1788; distinguished himself in the Peninsula, and lost an arm at Waterloo; was many years Mil. Sec. to Duke of Wellington, and Master-Gen. of the Ordnance 1854; commanded the English troops in the Crimea 1854-5, and gained the victories of the Alma, Inkerman, and Balaclava; cr. *Baron Raglan,* of Raglan, co. Monmouth (peerage of United Kingdom) 1852: *m.* 1814, Lady Emily Harriet, dau. of 3rd Earl of Mornington; *d.* June 28th, 1855, whilst commanding the troops before Sebastopol; *s.* by his son [2] Richard Henry FitzRoy, 2nd Baron, *b.* 1817: *m.* 1st, 1856, Lady Georgiana Lygon, who *d.* 1865, dau. of 4th Earl Beauchamp; 2ndly, 1871, Mary Blanche, who *d.* 1916, dau. of Sir Walter Rockliff Farquhar, 3rd Bt.; *d.* May 3rd, 1884; *s.* by his son [3] George FitzRoy Henry, *G.B.E., C.B.*, 3rd Baron, *b.* 1857; Under-Sec. of State for War Nov. 1900 to Aug. 1902, and Lieut.-Gov. of the Isle of Man 1902-19: *m.* 1883, Lady Ethel Jemima Ponsonby, who *d.* 1940, dau. of the 7th Earl of Bessborough; *d.* 1921; *s.* by his el. son [4] FitzRoy Richard, 4th Baron, *b.* 1885; Maj. Grenadier Guards; Lt.-Col. and Brevet Col. Monmouthshire Militia 1930-35, Lord-Lieut. of Monmouthshire 1942-64, and Pres., National Museum of Wales 1957-62: *m.* 1923, the Hon. Julia Hamilton, who *d.* 1971, da. of 11th Lord Belhaven and Stenton; *d.* 1964; *s.* by his 2nd son [5] FitzRoy John, 5th Baron, and present peer.

Ramsay, Lord, son of Earl of Dalhousie.

RAMSEY OF CANTERBURY, BARON. (Ramsey.) [Life Baron 1974.]

Rt. Rev. and *Rt. Hon.* (Arthur) Michael Ramsey, *PC, DD*, son of the late Arthur Stanley Ramsey, Fellow of Magdalene Coll., Camb.; *b.* Nov. 14th, 1904; ed. at Repton, and Magdalene Coll., Camb. (MA, DD); Hon. DD. Durham, Camb., Leeds, Edinburgh, Hull, Manchester, London, Trin. Coll., Toronto, Huron Coll., Virginia Theol. Seminary, Univ. of King's Coll., Halifax, Nova Scotia, Pacific Lutheran Univ. Camb., Mass., and Episcopal Theo. Sch., Camb., Mass.; Hon. DCL Oxon., Kent, and Nashotah House (USA); Hon. LLD Canterbury NZ, and Occidental Coll., Los Angeles; Hon. Dr. of Sacred Theol., Columbia, Gen. Theol. Seminary, NY, and Woodstock Coll., NY; Hon. DLitt. Keele, and Newfoundland; Hon. Dir. Theol. Inst. and Catholique of Paris; Curate at Liverpool Parish Church 1928-30, Sub-Warden of Lincoln Theol. Coll. 1930-36, Lect. of Boston Parish Church 1936-38, V. of St. Benedict, Camb. 1939-40, Canon of Durham Cathedral, and Van Mildert Prof. of Divinity, Durham Univ. 1940-50, Regius Prof. of Divinity, Camb. Univ. 1950-52, and Canon and Preb. of Lincoln Cathedral 1951-52; 88th Bishop of Durham 1952-56, 92nd Archbishop of York, Primate of England and Metropolitan 1956-61, and 100th Archbishop of Canterbury and Primate of All England

and Metropolitan 1961-74; PC 1956, and *Baron Ramsey of Canterbury*, of Canterbury, co. of Kent (Life Baron) 1974; received Roy. Victorian Chain 1974: *m*. 1942, Joan Alice Chetwode, da. of the late Lt.-Col. Francis Alexander Chetwode Hamilton, MC, The Cameronians (Scottish Rifles).

Residence,—The Old Vicarage, Cuddesdon, Oxon.

Ranfurly, Baron, title borne by Earl of Ranfurly on Roll of H. L.

RANFURLY, EARL OF. (Knox.) Sits as BARON RANFURLY.
(U.K. 1826). [Earl I. 1831.]

I move and prosper.

THOMAS DANIEL KNOX, K.C.M.G., 6th Earl; *b*. May 29th, 1913; *s*. 1933; ed. at Eton, and at Trin. Coll., Camb. (B.A. 1935); a K.St.J.; an A.D.C. to Gov.-Gen. and Com.-in-Ch. of Commonwealth of Australia 1936-38; Gov. and Com.-in-Ch. of the Bahamas 1953-56; Chm. Colonial Mutual Life Assurance Soc. (London Branch), of Madame Tussaud's, of Bain Dawes Gp., Ltd., and of the London Clinic; a Dir. Inchcape & Co., Ltd.; Pres. Shaftesbury Homes, and Arethusa; Ch. Scouts Commnr. Greater London; 1939-45 War (prisoner); KCMG 1955: *m*. 1939, Hermione, OBE, CStJ), da. of G. R. P. Llewellyn, and has issue.

Arms,—Gules, a falcon volant or, within an orle, wavy on the outer, and engrailed on the inner edge, argent. **Crest,**—A falcon close, standing on a perch proper. **Supporters,**—Two falcons, wings inverted proper, beaked, membered, belled, ducally collared and lined, or.

Residence,—Great Pednor, Chesham, Bucks.

DAUGHTER LIVING.
Lady Caroline, *b*. 1948: *m*. 1975, John Edward Simmonds.

MOTHER LIVING.
Hilda Susan Ellen, dau. of Sir Daniel Cooper, 2nd Bt. (cr. 1863): *m*. 1st, 1912, Thomas Uchter Caulfeild, Viscount Northland, Capt. Coldstream Guards, who *d*. (killed in action) 1915; 2ndly, 1917, as his second wife, Com. the Hon. Geoffrey Edward Mills, R.N.V.R., who *d*. 1917 [see B. Hillingdon]; 3rdly, 1918, Capt. Michael Wardell, late 10th Hussars, from whom she obtained a divorce 1929; 4thly, 1929, Julien Joseph Lezard, Bar.-at-Law, and has issue living, (by 1st marriage) [see ante]. *Residence,*— The Mill House, Great Missenden, Bucks.

COLLATERAL BRANCHES LIVING.
Issue of the late Lady Constance Harriet Stuart Knox, DCVO, 2nd da. of 5th Earl; *b*. 1885, *d*. 1964: *m*. 1905, Maj. Evelyn Milnes-Gaskell, JP, DL, who *d*. 1931 [E. Portsmouth]:—

Mary Juliana, *b*. 1906: *m*. 1934, Lewis Motley, of Cronkhill, Crosshouses, Shrewsbury, and has issue living, Christopher Stephen (Wenlock Abbey, Much Wenlock, Salop), *b*. 1935: *m*. 1961, Miranda Frances, da. of the late Sir Anthony Joseph Henry Doughty Doughty-Tichborne, 14th Bt., (ext.), and has issue living, William Michael, *b*. 1962, Mark Charles *b*. 1966, Samantha Antonia Clare *b*. 1964, Abigail Anne Louise *b*. 1970.

Grandsons of the late Edward Knox, OBE, el. son of Capt. Henry Needham Knox, 2nd son of Hon. John Henry Knox, MP, 3rd son of 1st Earl:—
Issue of the late Capt. John Needham Knox, RN, *b*. 1890, *d*. 1967: *m*. 1926, Monica (Brett Vale, Chelsworth, Ipswich), da. of the late Maj.-Gen. Sir Gerald Charles Kitson, KCVO, CB, CMG:—

GERALD FRANCOYS NEEDHAM (Maltings Chase, Nayland, Colchester), *b*. Jan. 4th, 1929; ed. at Wellington Coll.; Lt.-Cdr. (ret.) RN: *m*. 1955, Rosemary, only da. of the late Air Vice-Marshal Felton Vesey Holt, CMG, DSO, and has issue living, Edward John, *b*. 1957,—Rupert Stephen, *b*. 1963,—Elizabeth Marianne, *b*. 1959,—Frances Christina, *b*. 1961.——*Rev.* Thomas Anthony (Long Marston Vicarage, Herts.), *b*. 1931; ed. at Wellington Coll., and at Durham Univ. (BA): *m*. 1959, Susan Phoebe, da. of Arthur Pollard Matthews, of 182, Aileen Way, Grass Valley, Cal., USA, and has issue living, James Michael, *b*. 1962,—David Andrew, *b*. 1965,—Anne Margaret, *b*. 1960.

Grandchildren of the late Octavius Newry Knox, 3rd son of the Hon. John Henry Knox, MP (ante):—
Issue of the late Leonard Needham Knox, *b*. 1879, *d*. 1956: *m*. 1924, Berthe Heléne (60, Castlebar Road, Ealing, W5), da. of the late Henri Joseph Brel:—
John Leonard, *b*. 1925 ; ed. at Radley, at Worcester Coll., Oxford (B.A. 1951, M.A. 1958), and at Paris Univ.; Bar. Lincoln's Inn 1953 ; late Lieut. R.A.: *m*. 1953, Anne Jacqueline, dau. of Herbert Mackintosh, of Frensham, Surrey, and has issue living, Thomas Francis Needham, *b*. 1964,—Diana Jane, *b*. 1957,—Catherine Mary, *b*. 1959,—Margaret Lucy, *b*. 1960. *Residence,*—60, Castlebar Rd, Ealing, W.5.——Lucy Mary, *b*. 1927: *m*. 1960, Peter James Denholm, and has issue living, William Leonard, *b*. 1962,—John Peter, *b*. 1964,—Eva Mary, *b*. 1969. *Address,*—Lot 5, Phillips Rd., Byford, W. Aust. 6201.

(In remainder to Viscountcy of Northland.)

Grandchildren of the late Vesey Edmond Knox, el. son of the Rev. Francis Edmond Knox, 2nd son of the Hon. Vesey Knox, 3rd son of 1st Viscount Northland:—
Issue (by 1st m.) of the late Edmond Francis Vesey Knox, KC, *b.* 1865, *d.* 1921: *m.* 1st, 1891, Annie Elizabeth, who *d.* 1907, dau. of the late William Lloyd, of Llanmaes, Glam.; 2ndly, 1917, Agnes Mary, who *d.* 1949, dau. of Julius Beerbohm, and widow of R. Nevill:—

Columb Thomas, *b.* 1897; ed. at Rugby, and at R.M.C. is an Author and Journalist (" Collie Knox "); Capt. Reserve of Officers, late The Queen's Roy. Regt. and R.F.C., and late Bimbash, (Lt.-Col.) Sudan Defence Force; sometime ADC to Govs. of Bombay and Uganda, and to Gov.-Gen. of Sudan and Sirdar of Egypt; 1914-18 War as Pilot RFC (wounded, medal): *m.* 1944 (m. diss. 1948), Gwendoline Frances Mary, da. of the late E. Davidson Mitchell. *Residence,—*10E, Sussex Heights, Brighton, BN1 2FQ.——Dilys Myfanwy, *b.* 1899: *m.* 1st, 1923 (m. diss. 1933), Maj. David Charles Gilbert Dickinson, The Queen's Roy. Regt., who *d.* 1942; 2ndly, 1934, Lt.-Col. Arthur Sullivan, The Queen's Roy. Regt. (ret.) (having had issue (by 2nd m.) Christopher Knox *b.* 1934, *d.* 1958). *Residence,—*48 Sussex Sq., Brighton.

Issue of the late Charles Thomas Gisborne Knox, *b.* 1868, *d.* 1957 : *m.* 1893, Ethel Flora, who *d.* 1935, dau. of Surg.-Gen. Archibald Henry Fraser :—
Ethel Eileen, *b.* 1894: *m.* 1941, Benjamin Joseph Redding. *Residence,—*Apt. 4, 1958 York Av., Vancouver, 9, BC, Canada.

Issue of the late Gen. Sir Harry Hugh Sidney Knox, KCB, DSO, *b.* 1873, *d.* 1971: *m.* 1904, Grace Una, who *d.* 1954, da. of the late Rev. Robert Augustine Storres, R. of Shanklin, Isle of Wight:—
Una Sheila Colleen (*Lady Nye*), (Fallowfield, Hightown Hill, Ringwood, Hants.), *b.* 1905; Kaisar-i-Hind Gold Medal: *m.* 1st, 1924, (m. diss. 1939), Lt-Gen. Noel David Stevenson, 1st Bn. Black Watch (R. Highlanders); 2ndly, 1939, Lt-Gen. Sir Archibald Edward Nye, GCSI, GCMG, GCIE, KCB, KBE, MC, who *d.* 1967, and has issue living (by 1st m.) Terence Carew Stevenson KNOX (328, Canford Lane, Bristol), *b.* 1926; ed. at Marlborough Coll.; Maj. (ret.) R. Anglian Regt.; assumed by deed poll 1956 the names of Terence Carew Stevenson Knox in lieu of Terrence Knox Carew Stevenson; Industrial Training Officer Steels Garages Ltd.: *m.* 1959, Elizabeth Angela, da. of Brig. Derrick John Burton Houchin, DSO, MC, and has issue living, Robert Arthur *b.* 1961, Philippa Karen *b.* 1963,——Sheila Noelle, *b.* 1929: *m.* 1955, Francis Anthony Kitchener Harrison, of Lea Farms, Bramley, Surrey, and has issue living, Richard Anthony *b.* 1956, Michael David Knox *b.* 1960, Nicholas Francis *b.* 1965, Patricia Sheila *b.* 1957,—(by 2nd m.) Harriet Mary Sheila, *b.* 1945: *m.* 1st, 1965 (m. diss. 1970), Michael FitzGerald Heathcoat-Amory [see V. Amory, colls.]; 2ndly, 1974, Robin A. Stormonth-Darling, of Balvarran, by Bridge of Cally, Blairgowrie, Perthshire.

Grandchildren of the late Rev. Charles Beresford Knox, son of the late Rev. James Spencer Knox, son of the late Rt. Rev. the Hon. William Knox, D.D., Bishop of Derry, 4th son of 1st Viscount Northland :—
Issue of the late Rev. Charles Edward Leslie Beresford Knox, *b.* 1864, *d.* 1956 : *m.* 1903, Ethel Margaret, who *d.* 1952, dau. of the late Rev. Francis John Dickson, of Ribchester, Lancashire : —
Charles Francis Beresford (5, Dukes Meadow, Stapleford, Cambridge), *b.* 1917; ed. at Tonbridge, and at Keble Coll., Oxford (BA 1939); late Capt. RA: *m.* 1941, Margaret Eugenie Morgan, and has issue living, Richard Charles, *b.* 1944: *m.* 1967, Doris Frey,—John Edward, *b.* 1949.——Margaret Leslie (2, Quarry Close, Hansford Sq., Bath, BA2 5LP), *b.* 1904.——Christina Kathleen Mary (38, Pinehurst Rd., Westmoors, Wimborne, Dorset, BH22 0AP), *b.* 1910.

Grandchildren of the late Clara Elizabeth Knox [dau. of the late Rev. James Spencer Knox (ante)], *d.* 1860 : *m.* 1847, John Madden, J.P., D.L., late Lieut. 41st Regt., who *d.* 1903, of Roslea Manor, co. Fermanagh, and Aghafin House, Clones, co. Monaghan:—
Issue of the late Walter Wilmot Madden, late Lieut. R.N., *b.* 1853, *d.* 1943 : *m.* 1886, Eleanor, who *d.* 1925, dau. of Charles Ferdinand Bischoff, of Woodlands Estate, Waiuku, New Zealand :—
Charles Beresford (of Rosslea, 15, Belvedere St., Epsom, Auckland, 3, NZ), *b.* 1898; formerly an Officer in Union Steamship Co.; late New Zealand Civil Ser.; served with New Zealand Forces 1918-19: *m.* 1926, Elsie Madge, da. of John Masefield, of Dilston, Great South Rd., Remuera, Auckland, NZ, and has issue living, Ian Beresford (Rosslea, 15, Belvedere St., Epsom, Auckland, 3, NZ), *b.* 1931; ed. at Auckland Univ. (MA), Otago Univ. (LLB), Auckland Teachers' Training Coll., and Law Sch., Auckland Univ.; Bar. and Solicitor, Dunedin 1971; late Legal Officer, New Zealand Civil Service. ——Dora Christina (84, Hutton St., Otahuhu, Auckland, NZ), *b.* 1889: *m.* 1913, R. D. P. Woods, who *d.* 1918.

Granddaughter of the late Walter Wilmot Madden, late Lt. R.N. (ante):—
Issue of the late Eva Kathleen Madden, *b.* 1886, *d.* 1969: *m.* 1911, John Francis Wilson, of 84B, Hutton St., Otahuhu, Auckland, NZ:—
Kathleen Frances (Otahuhu, NZ), *b.* 1925: *m.* 1949, Vincent George Harrison, of 84, Hutton St., Otahuhu, Auckland 6, NZ, and has issue living, David James, *b.* 1960,—Robin Gay, *b.* 1950: *m.* 1971, Terence Charles Pawson, of Auckland, NZ,—Lynley Joy, *b.* 1956.

Granddaughter of Dora Christina Woods (ante):—
Issue of the late Isabel Ruth, *b.* 19—, *d.* 1948: *m.* 1946, Owen Leonard Hooker, late Lt. R.N., of Auckland, New Zealand:—
Christina, *b.* 1947; SRN, NZ: *m.* 1971, Svend Auge Jensen, of Svensongade 12, S.T.V. 9000, Aalborg, Denmark, and has issue living, Jenson, *b.* 1973.

Grandson of the late Andrew Ferguson Knox, son of the late Rt. Rev. the Hon. William Knox, D.D. (ante):—
Issue of the late Lieut.-Col. Robert Ferguson Knox, *b.* 1868, *d.* 1935: *m.* 1896, Edith Mary, who *d.* 1960, dau. of T. W. D. Humphreys, of Donoughmore House, Castlefin, co. Donegal:—
William Humphreys (Thanet Lodge, Crow Hill, Broadstairs) *b.* 1897; ed. at Haileybury; Lieut.-Col. (ret.) RE; 1914-18 War in France and Belgium (two medals), N.-W. Frontier of India 1919. Iraq 1920, Waziristan 1937: *m.* 1929, Nell Barbara, da. of the late T. Hone Jones.

Grandson of the late Rev. Thomas Knox, son of the late Ven. the Hon. Charles Knox, 6th son of 1st Viscount Northland:—
Issue of the late Com. Vesey Knox, R.N., *b.* 1847, *d.* 18—: *m.* 1885, Helen, dau of the late Benjamin William Leigh, of Manchester and Valparaiso:—
Albert Vesey Bent, *b.* 1887. *Residence,—*

PREDECESSORS.—[1] THOMAS KNOX, *M.P.* for Dungannon; cr. *Baron Welles,* of Dungannon, co. Tyrone (peerage of Ireland) 1781, and *Viscount Northland* (peerage of Ireland) 1791; *d.* 1818: *s.* by his son [2] THOMAS, 2nd Viscount: cr. *Baron Ranfurly* (peerage of United Kingdom) 1826, and *Earl of Ranfurly* (peerage of Ireland) 1831 ; *d.* 1840; *s.* by his son [3] THOMAS, 2nd Earl; *d.* 1858; *s.* by his son [4] THOMAS, 3rd Earl; *b.* 1816: *m.* 1848, Harriet, who *d.* 1891, dau. of James Rimington, Esq., of Broomhead Hall, co. York; *d.* 1858: *s.* by his el. son [5] THOMAS GRANVILLE HENRY STUART, 4th Earl; *d.* 1875 ; *s.* by his brother [6] UCHTER JOHN MARK, *G.C.M.G., P.C.,* 5th Earl, *b.* 1856 ; a Lord-in-Waiting to Queen Victoria 1895-7, and Gov. of New Zealand 1897-1904 : *m.* 1880, the Hon. Constance Caulfeild, who *d.* 1932, dau. of 7th Viscount Charlemont; *d.* 1933 ; *s.* by his grandson [7] THOMAS DANIEL (son of the late Capt. Thomas Uchter Caulfeild, Viscount Northland, only son of 5th Earl), 6th Earl and present peer ; also Viscount Northland, Baron Welles, and Baron Ranfurly.

RANK, BARONY OF. (Rank.) [Extinct 1972.]
DAUGHTERS LIVING OF FIRST BARON.

Hon. Ursula Helen, *b.* 1919: *m.* 1952, Lance Robert Newton, who *d.* 1969, and has issue living, Joseph Robert, *b.* 1956,—Carol, *b.* 1953,—Nicol Jane, *b.* 1960. *Residence,*—Church Farm, Saltby, Melton Mowbray, Leics.

Hon. Shelagh Mary, *b.* 1923 : *m.* 1st, **1945** (divorce 1955), Fred M. Packard, late Lieut. Signal Corps, U.S. Army ; 2ndly, 1957, Major Rosslyn Fairfax Huxley Cowen, M.B.E., and has issue living, (by 1st marriage) Frederick Arthur Rank, *b.* 1949,—Susan Mary, *b.* 1947,—(by 2nd marriage) Andrew Edward, *b.* 1958,—Stuart Huxley, *b.* 1960. *Residence,*—Pipers Hill, Sutton Scotney, Winchester, Hants.

RANKEILLOUR, BARON. (Hope.) [Baron U.K. 1932.]

But hope is unbroken.

PETER ST. THOMAS MORE HENRY HOPE, 4th Baron; *b.* May 29th, 1935; *s.* 1967; ed. at Ampleforth.

Arms,—Azure, on a chevron or between three bezants, a bay leaf slipped vert, a bordure ermine. *Crest,*—A broken globe surmounted of a rainbow proper. *Supporters,*—Not rematriculated at Lyon Court at time of going to press.

Residence,—Achaderry House, Roy Bridge, Inverness-shire.

SISTER LIVING.

Hon. Anne Mary, *b.* 1936: *m.* 1958, John Stephen Dobson, and has issue living, Dominic Stephen Christopher Charles, *b.* 1959,—Philippa Mary, *b.* 1961,—Catherine Teresa, *b.* 1962. *Residence,*—Papplewick Lodge, Nottinghamshire.

DAUGHTERS LIVING OF SECOND BARON.

Hon. Bridget, *b.* 1920: *m.* 1942, Lt.-Col. George Henry Hugh Coles, Prince of Wales Own Regt., of 39, Parish St., Zebbug, Mosta, Malta, GC, and has issue living, Caroline Mary, *b.* 1942: *m.* 1965, Maj. Rodney Gilbert Stapleton Cotton, RA, of 10, Upper Gordon Rd., Camberley, Surrey, and has issue living, Nicholas Henry Stapleton *b.* 1968, Martha Louise *b.* 1966,—Elizabeth Anne, *b.* 1944: *m.* 1967, Capt. Hugh Rollo Gillespie, Queens R. Irish Hussars, of 8, Hunt's Common, Hartley Wintney, Hants., and has issue living, Simon Rollo *b.* 1970, James Hugh *b.* 1973,—Mary Jane, *b.* 1948.

Hon. Jean Margaret (*Hon. Lady Wilson*), *b.* 1923: *m.* 1st, 1942, Capt. Anthony Paul, from whom she obtained a divorce 1955; 2ndly, 1955, Lt.-Gen. Sir Alexander James Wilson, KBE, MC, of Goldhill Farm House, Edingley, Newark, Notts. [see Starkey, Bt.], and has issue living, (by 1st m.) Anthony Hugh, *b.* 1951,—Sarah Margaret, *b.* 1943: *m.* 1965, Nigel John Kington Blair-Oliphant and has issue living, Richard Mark *b.* 1967, David Iain *b.* 1969,—Susan Caroline, *b.* 1949,—(by 2nd m.) [see Starkey, Bt.].

Hon. Alison Mary MERIVALE-AUSTIN (7, Cheyne Court, SW3), *b.* 1927: *m.* 1st, 1945, Maj. Bruce Gardiner Merivale-Austin, late Black Watch, from whom she obtained a divorce 1959; 2ndly, 1960 (m. declared null and void 1963), Maj. C. E. Stearns, who *d.* 1968, and has issue living, (by 1st m.) Griselda Mary, *b.* 1946: *m.* 1972, Ali Jazayeri Arab,—Deborah Deirdre Ann, *b.* 1948: *m.* 1972, Paul Thornton Calvert.

Hon. Barbara Mary, *b.* 1930 : *m.* 1954, William Edward Peter Louis Drummond-Murray [E. Perth, colls.], and has issue living, Andrew Philip, *b.* 1958,—James, *b.* 1959,—Robert, *b.* 1965,—Walter David, *b.* 1973,—Isabel Mary, *b.* 1966. *Residence,*—Old Hadlow House, Hadlow Down, Uckfield, Sussex.

MARY SIBYL (*Baroness Rankeillour*), (Little Orchard, Liphook, Hants), da. of the late Lt-Col. Wilfred, Ricardo, DSO, of Hook Hall, Surrey: *m.* 1933, the 3rd Baron, who *d.* 1967.

COLLATERAL BRANCH LIVING.

Issue of the late Hon. Richard Frederick Hope, OBE, yst. son of 1st Baron, *b.* 1901, *d.* 1964:— *m.* 1938, Helen Sybil Mary, who *d.* 1971, da. of the late Alfred Charlemagne Lambart [E. Cavan, colls.]:—

MICHAEL RICHARD (Barningham Hall, Bury St. Edmunds), *b.* Oct. 21st, 1940; ed. at Downside: *m.* 1964, Elizabeth Rosemary, el. da. of Col. Francis H. Fuller, of Wakelins, Genesis Green, Wickhambrook, Newmarket, Suffolk, and has issue living, James Francis, *b.* 1968,—Henrietta Mary, *b.* 1965,—Louisa Mary, *b.* 1966.——Simon James (103, Frescade Cres., Basingstoke, Hants.), *b.* 1941; ed. at Downside.——Margaret Mary, *b.* 1945: *m.* 1966, Neil Arnold Slater, of Marshborough House, Woodnesborough, Sandwich, Kent, and has issue living, Richard Benjamin Arnold, *b.* 1968,—Katherine Helen, *b.* 1970.

PREDECESSORS.—[1] *Rt. Hon.* JAMES FITZALAN Hope, son of the late James Robert Hope-Scott, Q.C. [see M. Linlithgow, colls.]; *b.* 1870; was Parliamentary Private Sec. (unpaid) to successive Postmaster-Gens. (Duke of Norfolk and Marquess of Londonderry) 1896-1901, to Pres. of Board of Trade (Rt. Hon. G. W. Balfour, M.P.) 1901, and to Colonial Sec. (Rt. Hon. A. Lyttelton, M.P.) 1904-5, Treasurer of H.M.'s Household 1915-16, a Junior Lord of the Treasury 1916-18, Financial Sec. to Min. of Munitions 1919-21, and Chm. of Committees and Dep. Speaker in House of Commons 1921-4 and 1924-9; sat as M.P. for Sheffield, Brightside Div. (*C*) 1900-1906, and for Sheffield, Central Div. 1908-29; *cr.* *Baron Rankeillour*, of Buxted, co. Sussex (peerage of UK) 1932: *m.* 1st

1892, Mabel Helen, *OBE*, who *d*. 1938, da. of Francis Riddell, of Cheeseburn Grange, Northumberland; 2ndly, 1941, Lady Beatrice Minnie Ponsonby Moore, who *d*. 1966, da. of 9th Earl of Drogheda, and widow of Capt. Struan Robertson Kerr-Clark, Seaforth Highlanders; *d*. 1949; *s*. by his son [2] ARTHUR OSWALD JAMES, *G.C.I.E.*, *M.C.*, 2nd Baron; *b*. 1897; was Parliamentary Private Sec. (unpaid) to Min. of Mines 1924-9, a Junior Lord of the Treasury 1935-7, Treasurer of H.M's. Household 1937-9, Gov. of Madras 1940-46, and M.P. for Warwickshire, Nuneaton Div. (*C*) 1924-29, and for Birmingham, Aston Div. 1931-9 ; European War 1914-18 as Capt. Coldstream Guards (MC): *m*. 1919, Grizel, who *d*. 1975, da. of Brig.-Gen. Sir Robert Gordon Gilmour, 1st Bt., CB, CVO, DSO; *d*. 1958; *s*. by his brother [3] HENRY JOHN, 3rd Baron; *b*. 1899; Lt.-Col. Scots Guards: *m*. 1933, Mary Sibyl, da. of the late Lt.-Col. Wilfrid Ricardo, DSO, of Hook Hall, Surrey; *d*. 1967; *s*. by his only son [4] PETER ST. THOMAS MORE HENRY, 4th Baron and present peer.

RATHCAVAN, BARON. (O'Neill.) [Baron U.K. 1953, Bt. U.K. 1929.]

(ROBERT WILLIAM) HUGH O'NEILL, *P.C.*, 1st Baron and 1st Baronet, 3rd son of 2nd Baron O'Neill; *b*. June 8th, 1883; ed. at Eton, and at New Coll., Oxford (B.A. 1905); Hon. LL.D. Belfast 1923; Bar. Inner Temple 1909 ; Major late Roy. Irish Rifles (formerly Lieut. North of Ireland Imperial Yeo.); was H.M.'s Lieut. for co. Antrim 1948-59; European War 1915-17 in Roy. Irish Rifles, and on Staff, Palestine 1918, as Dep. Judge Advocate-Gen.; was Chm. of Conservative Private Members 1922 Cttee. in House of Commons 1935-39, and Under-Sec. of State for India and Burma 1939-40; became Pro-Chancellor, Queen's Univ., Belfast 1922; a C.St.J.; unsuccessfully contested Stockport (*C*) Jan. 1906; sat as M.P. for Antrim Co., Mid Antrim Div. (*U*) Feb. 1915 to Oct. 1922, for Antrim Co. Nov. 1922 to Feb. 1950, and for N. Div. of Antrim Feb. 1950 to Oct. 1952; sat for Antrim Co. (Parliament of N. Ireland) May 1921 to April 1929 (was first Speaker of that Parliament June 1921 to May 1929) ; cr. P.C. (Ireland) 1921, (N. Ireland) 1922, and (Great Britain) 1937, a *Baronet* 1929, and *Baron Rathcavan*, of The Braid, co. Antrim (peerage of United Kingdom) 1953 : *m*. 1909, Sylvia, who *d*. 1972, da. of Walter A. Sandeman, of Morden House, Royston, and has issue.

Arms,—Quarterly : 1st and 4th per fesse wavy, the chief argent, and the base representing waves of the sea, in chief a dexter hand couped at the wrist gules, in base a salmon naiant proper. *O'Neill*; 2nd and 3rd checky, or and gules, a chief vair, *Chichester* ; a mullet for difference. **Crests,**—1st, an arm embowed in armour, the hand grasping a sword, all proper ; 2nd, a stork rising, with a snake in its beak, all proper. **Mottos,**—Invitum sequitur honos (Honours follow us without seeking), and Lamh dearg E'rin (*The Red hand of Ireland*). **Supporters,**—On either side a heron proper standing on a billet fessewise wavy argent charged with a bar wavy azure.

Residences,—Cleggan Lodge, Ballymena, co. Antrim ; 28, Queen's Gate Gardens, S.W.7. *Clubs,*—Carlton, Ulster.

SONS LIVING.

Rt. Hon. PHELIM ROBERT HUGH (Lizard Manor, Aghadowey, co. Londonderry; Brooks's Club), *b*. Nov. 2nd, 1909; ed. at Eton; late Maj. RA; MP (*UU*) for N. Antrim (UK Parl.) 1952-59, and in Parl. of NI 1959-73 (*U* and later *Alliance*) (Parl. suspended March 1972); Min. of Education 1969 and Agric. 1969-71; PC (NI) 1969: *m*. 1st, 1934, Clare Désirée (who *d*. 1956, and from whom he had obtained a divorce 1944), da. of Detmar Blow [B. Tollemache, colls.]; 2ndly, 1953, Bridget Doreen (EDWARDS-MOSS), da. of the late Maj. the Hon. Richard Coke [see E. Leicester, colls.], and has issue living, (by 1st m.) Hugh Detmar Torrens, *b*. 1939; ed. at Eton,—Mary-Rose, *b*. 1935: *m*. 1960, David Stewart Wellesley Blacker [see E. Peel],—(by 2nd m.) Rosetta Anne, *b*. 1954,—Moira Louisa, *b*. 1961,—Grania Elizabeth, *b*. 1963.

Hon. Sir Con Douglas Walter, *G.C.M.G.*, *b*. 1912; ed. at Eton, and at Balliol Coll., Oxford; Bar. Inner Temple 1936; formerly a Fellow of All Souls' Coll., Oxford; formerly H.M.'s Chargé d'Affaires at Peking; sometime an Assist. Under Sec., Foreign Office; H.M.'s Ambassador to Finland 1960-63, Ambassador to European Communities in Brussels 1963-65, and Dep. Under-Sec. in charge of Economic Affairs, Foreign Office 1965-68; Dep. Under-Sec. Foreign Office 1969-72; 1939-45 War; CMG 1953, KCMG 1962, GCMG 1972: *m*. 1st, 1940 (m. diss. 1954), Rosemary Margaret, only da. of the late Harold Pritchard, FRCP; 2ndly, 1954, Baroness Carola Hertha Adolfine Emma Harriet Luise (Mady), who *d*. 1960, da. of the late Baron Max von Holzing-Berstett, and widow of Baron Wilhelm Pleikart Marschall von Bieberstein; 3rdly, 1961, Mrs. Anne-Marie Lindberg, of Helsinki, Finland, and has issue living, (by 1st m.) Rowan Peter Hugh, *b*. 1944,—Onora Sylvia, *b*. 1947: *m*. 1963, Edward Nell, of 173, Warren St., Brooklyn, NY, USA. *Residence,*—37, Flood St., SW3. *Club,*—Travellers'.

Hon. Nial Arthur Ramleh, *b*. 1918; ed. at Eton; formerly Major Irish Guards; 1939-45 War (despatches): *m*. 1966, Virginia Lois, da. of the late John Douglas Legge, MC [see E. Dartmouth, colls.]. *Residence,*—Mill of Syde, Kennethmont, Huntly, Aberdeenshire.

RATHCREEDAN, BARON. (Norton.) [Baron U.K. 1916.]

CHARLES PATRICK NORTON, *T.D.*, 2nd Baron ; *b.* Nov. 26th, 1905 ; *s.* 1930 ; ed. at Wellington Coll., and at Lincoln Coll., Oxford (B.A. 1928, M.A. 1935) ; Bar. Inner Temple 1931 ; admitted a Solicitor 1936 ; late Major 4th Batn. Oxford and Bucks L.I. (T.A.) ; European War 1939-45 (prisoner) : *m.* 1946, Ann Pauline, dau. of the late Surg.-Capt. William Bastian, R.N., and has issue.

Arms,—Per fesse or and azure, in chief a lion passant sable and in base a maunch ermine. Crest,—A tiger's head couped at the neck, holding in the mouth a broken spear in bend proper. Supporters,—On either side a tiger reguardant proper, collared and chained argent, the collar of that on the dexter side charged with three roses gules, and that on the sinister side with three trefoils vert.

Seat,—Bellehatch Park, Oxon.

You may break but shall not bend me.

SONS LIVING.
Hon. CHRISTOPHER JOHN, *b.* June 3rd, 1949 ; ed. at Wellington.
Hon. Adam Gregory, *b.* 1952.

DAUGHTER LIVING.
Hon. Elizabeth Ann, *b.* 1954.

BROTHER LIVING.
Hon. Michael Adrian, *b.* 1907 ; ed. at Wellington Coll., and at Trin. Coll., Camb. (B.A. 1929). *Residence,*—44, Roebuck House, Palace St., S.W.1. *Club,*—Reform.

SISTER LIVING.
Hon. Sylvia Beatrice ; ed. at Somerville Coll., Oxford (MA) : *m.* 1933, Wing-Com. Rowland David George, DSO, OBE, R. Auxiliary Air Force, and has issue living, Kester William Norton (Harpsden Wood Lodge, Harpsden, Henley-on-Thames), *b.* 1934 : *m.* 1963, Philippa Jane, da. of the late Maj. P. W. Morley, R. Warwickshire Regt., and has issue living, Lawrence Sebastian Norton *b.* 1965, Philip Zachary Norton *b.* 1969, Isobel Rosalind Norton *b.* 1967,—Ryan Cecil Norton (Haugh Potticks House, Winsley, Bradford on Avon), *b.* 1936 : *m.* 1966, Jacqueline Maria Margaret, da. of John Trethowan, of The Close, Salisbury, and has issue living, Alexander Rowland Norton *b.* 1967, Lucinda Claire Norton *b.* 1970,—Eiluned Mary Norton, *b.* 1940 : *m.* 1964, Patrick Alan Crozier-Cole, of Hillside House, Farley, Salisbury, Wilts., SP5 1AB, and has issue living, Jeremy Acheson *b.* 1967, Timothy John *b.* 1972, Zoë Louise *b.* 1965, Lucilla Mary *b.* 1969. *Residence,*—Sycamore House, Bathford, nr. Bath.

PREDECESSOR.—[1] CECIL WILLIAM Norton, son of the late William Norton, R. of Baltinglass, Ireland ; *b.* 1850 ; a Junior Lord of the Treasury 1905-10, Assist. Postmaster-Gen. 1910-16, and Assist. Parliamentary Sec. (unpaid), Min. of Munitions and Supply in the House of Lords 1919-21 ; M.P. for W. Div. of Newington July 1892 to Jan. 1916 ; *cr. Baron Rathcreedan,* of Bellehatch Park, Oxon (peerage of United Kingdom) 1916 : *m.* 1st, 1880, Cecilia Lafayette, who *d.* 1898, dau. of James Kennedy, of The Limes, co. Down, and widow of William Thomas Cavendish, of Thornton Hall, Bucks, and Crakemarsh Hall, Stafford ; 2ndly, 1903, Marguerite Cecil, who *d.* 1955, dau. of Sir Charles Philip Huntington, 1st Bt.; *d.* 1930 ; *s.* by his son [2] CHARLES PATRICK, 2nd Baron and present peer.

RATHDONNELL, BARON. (McClintock-Bunbury.) [Baron I. 1868.]

THOMAS BENJAMIN McCLINTOCK-BUNBURY, 5th Baron ; *b.* Sept. 17th, 1938 ; *s.* 1959 ; ed. at Charterhouse ; Lt. RN : *m.* 1965, Jessica Harriet, da. of George Gilbert Butler, [see B. Dunboyne, colls.] and has issue.

Arms,—Quarterly : 1st and 4th argent, on a bend sable, three chess-rooks of the field ; 2nd and 3rd per pale gules and azure, a chevron ermine, between three escallops argent. Crests,—1st, two swords in saltire argent, hilted or, pierced through a leopard's face of the last ; 2nd, a lion passant proper. Supporters,—Dexter, a lion ; sinister, a leopard ; both proper, each gorged with a collar ermine, and charged on the shoulder with an escallop argent.

Seat,—Lisnavagh, Rathvilly, co. Carlow.

Power is stronger by unity.

SONS LIVING.

Hon. WILLIAM LEOPOLD, *b.* July 6th, 1966.
Hon. George Andrew Kane, *b.* 1968.
Hon. James Alexander Hugh, *b.* 1972.

SISTERS LIVING.

Hon. Katharine Alexandra, *b.* 1940: *m.* 1960, James Joseph Doyle, of Tobinstown, Tullow, co. Carlow.
Hon. Hermione Jane, *b.* 1943.
Hon. Pamela Rosemary, *b.* 1948.

WIDOW LIVING OF FOURTH BARON.

Pamela, el. dau. of the late John Malcolm Drew, of Eversley, near Milnthorpe, Westmorland ; late
3rd Officer WRNS; is an Artist (Pamela Drew), a Member of Roy. Soc. of Marine Artists, and Kronfeld
Club, and a part-time official Artist to RAF: *m.* 1st, 1937, the 4th Baron, who *d.* 1959; 2ndly,
1961, Maj. Hugh Caruthers Massy [see B. Massy, colls.]. *Residence,*—The Studio, Ballinatray,
Youghal, co. Cork.

PREDECESSORS.—[1] JOHN M'CLINTOCK, *M.P.* for co. Louth 1857-9; *b.* 1798; was Lord-Lieut.
of co. Louth and Col. Louth Militia; *cr. Baron Rathdonnell,* of Rathdonnell, co. Donegal
(peerage of Ireland) 1868, with remainder to the issue male of his deceased brother, Capt.
William Bunbury McClintock-Bunbury, R.N., M.P.; *d.* 1879; *s.* by his nephew [2] THOMAS
KANE (son of the late Capt. M'Clintock-Bunbury, R.N., M.P. *ante*), by Pauline Caroline
Diana Mary, dau. of Sir James Stronge, 2nd Bt.), 2nd Baron, *b.* 1848 ; was H.M.'s Lieut. for co.
Carlow 1890-1929 (High Sheriff 1876), and a Representative Peer: *m.* 1874, Katherine Anne,
who *d.* 1925, dau. of the Right Hon. Henry Bruen, P.C., of Oak Park, co. Carlow ; *d.* 1929; *s.*
by his son [3] THOMAS LEOPOLD, *M.B.E.*, 3rd Baron, *b.* 1881; High Sheriff of Carlow 1908-9 ;
m. 1912, Ethel Synge, who *d.* 1922, dau. of the late Robert Wilson Ievers, C.M.G.; *d.* 1937 ;
s. by his son [4] WILLIAM ROBERT, 4th Baron ; *b.* 1914; Major 15th/19th Hussars : *m.* 1937,
Pamela (who *m.* 2ndly, 1961, Major Hugh Caruthers Massy), el. dau. of the late John Malcolm
Drew, of Eversley, near Milnthorpe, Westmorland ; *d.* 1959 ; *s.* by his son [5] THOMAS BENJAMIN,
5th Baron and present peer.

RAVENSDALE, BARON. (Mosley.) [Baron U.K. 1911.]

NICHOLAS MOSLEY, *MC,* 3rd Baron; *b.*
June 25th, 1923; *s.* 1966; *h.a.* to Baronetcy
of Mosley; ed. at Eton, and Balliol Coll.,
Oxford; 1939-45 War in Italy (MC) as Capt.,
Rifle Bde.: *m.* 1st, 1947 (m. diss. 1974),
Rosemary Laura, da. of the late Marshal of
the RAF Sir John Maitland Salmond, GCB,
CMG, CVO, DSO [see B. Lucas of Crudwell];
2ndly, 1974, Verity Elizabeth, 2nd da. of
John Raymond, of Winslade House, Basing-
stoke, Hants., and formerly wife of John
Adrian Bailey, and has issue by 1st m.

Arms,—Quarterly, 1st and 4th, sable, a chevron
between three pickaxes argent, *Mosley;* 2nd and 3rd
argent, on a bend sable, three popinjays or, collared gules,
Curzon. Crest,—An eagle displayed ermine.
Supporters,—*Dexter,* a raven proper; *sinister, a*
popinjay proper collared gules.
Residence,—9 Church Row, NW3.

Custom rules the law.

SONS LIVING (*By* 1*st m.*)

Hon. SHAUN NICHOLAS, *b.* Aug. 5th, 1949.
Hon. Ivo Adam Rex, *b.* 1951.
Hon. Robert, *b.* 1955.

DAUGHTER LIVING. (*By* 1*st m.*)

Hon. Clare, *b.* 1959.

BROTHER LIVING. (*Raised to the rank of a son of a Baroness* 1967.)
Hon. Michael (Durham Cottage, Christchurch St., Chelsea, SW3), *b.* 1932; ed. at Eton, and London
Sch. of Economics.

SISTER LIVING. (*Raised to the rank of a daughter of a Baroness* 1967.)
Hon. Vivien Elisabeth (11, Mulberry Walk, Chelsea, SW3); *b.* 1921: *m.* 1949, Desmond Francis Forbes
Adam, who *d.* 1958 [see Adam, Bt. colls., *cr.* 1917].

AUNT LIVING. (*Daughter of* 1*st Baron Ravensdale and* 1*st Marquess Curzon of Kedleston.*) (*In
special remainder.*)

Lady Alexandra Naldera, *CBE* (65, Eaton Place, SW1), *b.* 1904; a CStJ; Order of Merit (4th Class) of
Italy, Order of Merit of Italian Republic (4th Class), and Cross of Merit (1st Class) of Sovereign Mil.
Order of Malta; CBE (Civil) 1975: *m.* 1925 (m. diss. 1955), Maj. Edward Dudley Metcalfe, MVO,
MC, Indian Army (ret.), who *d.* 1957, and has issue living, David Patrick (7, Chelsea Sq., SW3.
Clubs,—White's, Buck's), *b.* 1927; ed. at Eton; late Lt. Irish Guards; a Dir. of Steward Smith &
Co. Ltd., and a Member of Lloyd's: *m.* 1st, 1957 (m. diss. 1964), Alexandra Irene, who *d.* 1966, da. of
Michael Boycun, of Fort William, Ontario, and widow of Sir Alexander Korda; 2ndly, 1968, the
Countess de Chauvigny de Blot, and has issue living, (by 1st m.) Julian Edward *b.* 1959, Charles
Michael *b.* 1962, Zara Naldera *b.* 1957 (by 2nd m.) Edward George Anthony *b.* 1970,—Davina Naldera,
b. 1930: *m.* 1966, John Hugo Eastwood,—Linda Mary (twin), *b.* 1930: *m.* 1965, Henry Tilford
Mortimer, of Woodstock, Tuxedo Par, New York, USA.

PREDECESSORS.—[1] GEORGE NATHANIEL Curzon, *KG, GCSI, GCIE, PC, FRS*, el. son of 4th Baron Scarsdale; *b.* 1859; Under-Sec. of State for India 1891-92, Under-Sec. of State for Foreign Affairs 1895-8, Viceroy and Gov.-Gen. of India 1898-1904 and again 1904-5, Lord Privy Seal 1915-16, Lord Pres. of the Council and Leader of the House of Lords, and Sec. of State for Foreign Affairs 1919-24 (also Leader of House of Lords), and again Lord Pres. of the Council and Leader of the House of Lords 1924-52; *cr. Baron Curzon of Kedleston*, co. Derby (peerage of Ireland) 1898, and *Baron Ravensdale*, of Ravensdale, co. Derby, with special remainder, in default of issue male, to his el. da. and the heirs male of her body, failing whom to his other daus. in like manner in order of primogeniture, *Viscount Scarsdale*, of Scarsdale, co. Derby, with special remainder in default of issue male, to his father (the 4th Baron Scarsdale, whom he succeeded in the Barony) and the heirs male of his body, *Earl Curzon of Kedleston*, co. Derby (all in peerage of U.K.) 1911, and *Earl of Kedleston*, co. Derby, and *Marquess Curzon of Kedleston* (peerage of U.K.) 1921; *s.* as 5th Baron Scarsdale and 9th Baronet (both of Scotland and England) 1916: *m.* 1st, 1895, Mary Victoria, *C.I.*, who *d.* 1906, el. da. of the late Levi Zeigler Leiter, of Washington, USA; 2ndly, 1917, *Dame* Grace Elvina Trilla, *GBE*, who *d.* 1958, da. of the late J. Monroe Hinds, of Alabama, USA, and widow of Alfred Duggan, of Buenos Aires; *d.* 1925, when the Irish Barony of 1898, the Earldom of 1911, and the Marquessate of 1921, became ext., while the Barony (cr. 1761) and the Viscountcy of Scarsdale, together with the two Baronetcies, passed to his nephew, Richard Nathaniel Curzon [see that title], and the Barony of Ravensdale devolved by special remainder upon his el. da. [2] MARY IRENE; *b.* 1896; Treasurer of Musicians' Benevolent Fund; *cr. Baroness Ravensdale of Kedleston*, of Kedleston, co. Derby (Life Baroness) 1958; *d.* 1966, when the Barony of Ravensdale (cr. 1911) devolved on her nephew [3] NICHOLAS Mosley, *MC* [el. son of Lady Cynthia Blanche Mosley (2nd da. of 1st Marquess Curzon of Kedleston and 1st Baron Ravensdale), who *d.* 1933, having *m.* 1920, as his 1st wife, Sir Oswald Ernald Mosley, 6th Bt.], 3rd Baron, and present peer.

RAVENSWORTH, BARON. (Liddell.) [Baron U.K. 1821, Bt. E. 1642.]

ARTHUR WALLER LIDDELL, 8th Baron, and 13th Baronet; *b.* July 25th, 1924; *s.* 1950; ed. at Harrow; formerly Radio Engineer, British Broadcasting Corporation: *m.* 1950, Wendy, adopted dau. of J. Stuart Bell, of Studio House, Cookham, Berks, and has issue.

Arms,—Argent, fretty gules, on a chief of the second three leopards' faces or. **Crest,**—A lion rampant sable, semée of billets or, and crowned with an Eastern coronet gold. **Supporters,**—On either side a leopard or, semée of golps, gorged with a mural crown purpose.

Seat,—Eslington Park, Whittingham, Northumberland.

———

SON LIVING.
Hon. THOMAS ARTHUR HAMISH, *b.* Oct. 27th, **1954.**

DAUGHTER LIVING.
Hon. Jane Alice, *b.* 1952.

One and the same.

SISTER LIVING.
(*Raised to the rank of a Baron's daughter* 1951.)
Hon. Sophie Harriet, *b.* 1927; ed. at Central High Sch., Newcastle-on-Tyne, and at King's Coll., Durham Univ.

SISTER LIVING OF SEVENTH BARON.
Hon. Beatrice Sophie, *b.* 1906: *m.* 1931, Edward Richard Speyer, and has issue living, Jocelyne Isolda, *b.* 1933: *m.* 1958, Alan Richard Tait, of 1430, Avenida Marechal Gomes da Costa, Oporto, Portugal, and has issue living, Matthew Edward *b.* 1960,—Valentine Antonia, *b.* 1938: *m.* 1974, Nicholas John Windsor Gaffney, of Flat 1, 13, South Hill Park Gdns., Hampstead, NW3. *Residence*,—39, Rivermead Court, Ranelagh Gdns., SW6.

COLLATERAL BRANCHES LIVING.

Grandchildren of the late Capt. Augustus Frederick Liddell, C.V.O., son of the late Col. the Hon. George Augustus Liddell, 6th son of 1st Baron:—
Issue of the late Guy Maynard Liddell, C.B., C.B.E., M.C., *b.* 1892, *d.* 1958: *m.* 1926 (marriage dissolved 1943), the Hon. Calypso Baring, who *d.* 1974, da. of 3rd Baron Revelstoke:—
Peter Lorillard (Burnside Farm, Church Rd., Paddock Wood, Kent), *b.* 1927: *m.* 1st, 1951 (m. diss. 1966), Anne Jamieson, da. of Capt. F. M. Cannon, US Naval Res. Med. Corps, of San Rafael, California, USA; 2ndly, 1970, Joan Hopkinson, and has issue living, (by 1st m.) Peter Guy, *b.* 1952,—David John, *b.* 1954,—Thomas Andrew, *b.* 1960,—Alice, *b.* 1958.——Elizabeth Gay, *b.* 1928: *m.* 1946 (m. diss. 19—), Carl Paulson, and has issue living, Jay, *b.* 1950, Mark, *b.* 1957,—Sandra, *b.* 1947.—— Anne Jennifer, *b.* 1931: *m.* 1951, Joseph Enzensperger, of 2430, Hillcrest, Medford, Oregon, USA, and has issue living, Joseph, *b.* 1952,—Janet, *b.* 1957,—Ann, *b.* 1959.

[*The male line is in remainder to Baronetcy.*]

Grandchildren of the late Edward Henry Liddell, son of the late Very Rev. Henry George Liddell, D.D., son of the late Rev. Henry George Liddell, 2nd son of 5th Bt.:—
Issue of the late Lieut.-Col. Geoffrey William Liddell, D.S.O., *b.* 1884, *d.* 1955: *m.* 1915, his 2nd cousin, Mary Sophia (of Old Farm House, Cottonworth, Fullerton, Andover, Hants), dau. of the late Charles Lyon Liddell (infra):—

Charles Henry, *MC*, *b.* 1917; ed. at Eton; Maj. (ret.) Rifle Bde., and a JP for Hants. (High Sheriff 1975); 1939-45 War (wounded, MC): *m.* 1944, Pamela Mary, da. of the late Maj. Antony Hubert Gibbs, JP, of Pytte, Clyst St. George, and has issue living, James Edward Cory (Cottonworth House, Fullerton, Andover, Hants.), *b.* 1947; ed. at Eton, and R. Agric. Coll., Cirencester: *m.* 1970, Rachel Anne, yr. da. of Maj. George De Pree, late 60th Rifles, KRRC, of Little Knelle Farm, Beckley, Rye, Sussex [see E. Galloway, colls.], and has issue living, a da. *b.* 1975,—(Mary) Susan, *b.* 1944: *m.* 1964, Antony Michael Ansell, of Glebe House, Shurlock Row, Reading [Fuller, Bt.], and has issue living, Michael James Kirkpatrick *b.* 1970, Harriet Mary *b.* 1966, Alexandra Jane *b.* 1968,—Alice Margaret, *b.* 1950: *m.* 1973, Christopher Nicholas Allen. *Residence,*—Fullerton Grange, Andover, Hants.—— Thomas Lyon, *b.* 1920; ed. at Radley, and at Worcester Coll., Oxford; 1939-45 War as Capt. Rifle Bde: *m.* 1951, Susan Mary, da. of the late C. R. V. Coutts, of the Court Lodge, Chelsfield, Kent, and has issue living, Edward Henry, *b.* 1953; ed. at Eton, and Magdalene Coll., Camb.,—Roderick William, *b.* 1955; ed. at Eton, and Worcester Coll., Oxford,—David Lyon, *b.* 1959; ed. at Eton,— Emma Mary (twin), *b.* 1955; ed. at Wycombe Abbey, and St. Hilda's Coll., Oxford. *Residence,*— Dorman's Corner, Lingfield, Surrey.——William Adrian (Westover, Goodworth Clatford, Andover, Hants.), *b.* 1924; ed. at Radley, and at Magdalene Coll., Camb. (BA 19—, MA 19—); late Lt. RNVR; 1939-45 War (despatches): *m.* 1956, Anne Primrose, da. of the late Group Capt. R. W. G. Lywood, of Bay Cottage, Scilly, Kinsale, co. Cork, and has issue living, William George, *b.* 1958; ed. at Eton,—Mary Clare, *b.* 1960,—Caroline Sophia, *b.* 1962.——Geoffrey Andrew (Flat 2, 50, Sloane St., SW1X 9SN), *b.* 1926; ed. at Radley; late RN; 1939-45 War: *m.* 1958, Jillian Mary (CLIFTON-BROWNE), da. of David Walkinshaw, of The Lodge, Highfield, Haslemere, Surrey, and has issue living, Charles David Andrew, *b.* 1960; ed. at Marlborough.

Grandchildren of the late Very Rev. Henry George Liddell, D.D. (ante):—
Issue of the late Sir Frederick Francis Liddell, K.C.B., K.C., *b.* 1865, *d.* 1950: **m.** 1901, Mabel Alice, who *d.* 1959, dan. of the late Arthur Magniac :—
Henry George Magniac (204, Ranch Arcade, Hendrick Verwoerd Drive, Randburg, 2001, Johannesburg, S. Africa), *b.* 1902; ed. at Winchester; 1939-45 War with Rhodesian Forces: *m.* 1932, Amelia Lydia, da. of William Albert Walker, of Gadzema, Rhodesia, and has issue living, Eric Henry George (3691, Stirling Rd., Bryanston, Transvaal, S. Africa), *b.* 1935: *m.* 1958, Jane-Anne, da. of the late Maj Walter John Hoskins, RA, of Elston, Shrewton, Wilts., and has issue living, Karen Anne *b.* 1961, Jacqueline Toni *b.* 1962, Bridget Alice *b.* 1964.——Maurice Arthur *OBE, b.* 1905; ed. at Marlborough Coll., and at Ch. Ch., Oxford (BA); Bar. Lincoln's Inn 1930; is a Partner in Dyson, Bell & Co., parliamentary agents, of 15, Great College St., Westminster, SW1; 1939-45 War as Fl. Lt. RAFVR (invalided), OBE (Civil) 1969: *m.* 1937, Alix, OBE, da. of the late Adm. Mark Edward Frederick Kerr, CB, MVO [see M. Lothian, colls.], and has issue living, Virginia Sarah Alix, *b.* 1941: *m.* 1962, Simon Claude Ashton, of 27, Newton Rd., W2, and has issue living, Guy Julian Claude *b.* 1964, Melanie Isabel *b.* 1967, Jessica Alix *b.* 1970,—Judith Rose *b.* 1944: *m.* 1968, David Mark Jackson, BA, BM, BCh, FFARCS, of 27, Grafton Sq., SW4 (c/o Princess Margaret Hospital, Okur Rd., Swindon, Wilts.), and has issue living, Luke Hadley *b.* 1970, Felix Mark *b.* 1973. *Residence,*—Flat F, 3, West Eaton Place, SW1.——Bridget Elvira, *b.* 1908: *m.* 1st, 1931, Peter Lockwood Smith-Dorrien, from whom she obtained a divorce 1937; 2ndly, 1939, Lewis Civval, who *d.* 1973, and has issue living, (by 2nd *m.*) Martha Bridget Liddell, *b.* 1941: *m.* 1966, George Patrick Francis Ennor, of Lyfield House, Ewhurst, Cranleigh, Surrey, and has issue living, Julian George *b.* 1970, Daniel Lewis *b.* 1974, Charlotte Annabella *b.* 1968,—Julia Jane, *b.* 1942: *m.* 1974, Oliver James Malim Case, of 35, Fabian Rd., SW6,—Camila Frances, *b.* 1946: *m.* 1974, Philip Lee Malin Case, of 17, Kelmscott Rd., SW11. *Residences,*—Woodards Farm, Oakley, Surrey; 24, Eaton Pl., SW1.

Issue of the late Lionel Charles Liddell, M.V.O., *b.* 1868, *d.* 1942: *m.* 1902, Florence Ella, who *d.* 1942, dau. of the late Arthur Magniac, of The Hermitage, Ascot :—
Lionel Arthur, *O.B.E., T.D., b.* 1903; ed. at Winchester, and at Ch. Ch., Oxford; is Lieut.-Col. R.A.; European War 1939-45 (despatches); O.B.E. (Mil.) 1953: *m.* 1923, Beatrice, dau. of the late T. S. Hillas-Drake.——Philip, *b.* 1904; ed. at Winchester; Headmaster of St. Andrew's Sch., East-bourne 1946-69: *m.* 1944, Elizabeth Jane Boret, da. of the late Colledge Leader, of Newmarket, and has issue living, Susan Jane, *b.* 1946: *m.* 1970, Anthony Gatehouse Hide, of 57020 Bolgheri, Livorno, Italy, and has issue living, Philip Edward *b.* 1973, Lucinda Jane *b.* 1971. *Residence,*—Meadow Farm, Stretham, Ely, Cambs.

Granddaughters of the late Charles Liddell, son of the late Rev. Henry George Liddell (ante):—
Issue of the late Charles Lyon Liddell, *b.* 1861, *d.* 1911: *m.* 1891, Margaret Emily Gresham, who *d.* 1948, dau. of the late Granville William Gresham Leveson-Gower [D. Sutherland, colls.]:—
Mary Sophia, *b.* 1893: *m.* 1915, her 2nd cousin, Lt.-Col. Geoffrey William Liddell, DSO, who *d.* 1955 (ante). *Residence,*—Old Farm House, Cottonworth, Fullerton, Andover, Hants. ——Christabel Etrenne, *b.* 1897: *m.* 1922, Capt. Robert Millington Synge, who *d.* 1964 [see Synge, Bt., colls.] *Residence,*—Butts Gate, Wisborough Green, Sussex.——Joan Elizabeth, *b.* 1899: *m.* 1934, Richard Walter Dundonald Cave [see Cave, Bt., colls.]. *Residence,*—Overwey, Tilford, Farnham, Surrey.

PREDECESSORS.—[1] THOMAS Liddell, a zealous supporter of Charles I.; cr. *Barone*[t] 1642; *d.* 1650; *s.* by his son [2] *Sir* THOMAS, 2nd Bt.; *d.* 1697; *s.* by his son [3] *Sir* HENRY' 3rd Bt.; *d.* 1723; *s.* by his grandson [4] *Sir* HENRY, 4th Bt.; M.P.; cr. *Baron Ravensworth,* of Ravensworth Castle (peerage of Great Britain) 1747; *d.* 1784, when the barony became extinct, and the baronetcy devolved upon his nephew [5] *Sir* HENRY GEORGE, 5th Bt.; *d.* 1791; *s.* by his son [6] *Sir* THOMAS HENRY, 6th Bt.; cr. *Baron Ravensworth* (peerage of United Kingdom) 1821; *d.* 1855; *s.* by his son [7] HENRY THOMAS, 2nd Baron; *b.* 1797; M.P. for Northumberland (C) 1826-30, for N. Durham 1837-47, and for Liverpool 1853-5; cr. *Baron Eslington*, of Eslington Park, co. Northumberland, and *Earl of Ravensworth* (peerage of United Kingdom) 1874: *m.* 1820, Isabella Horatia, dau. of the late Lord George Seymour (M. Hertford); *d.* 1878; *s.* by his son [8] HENRY GEORGE, 2nd Earl, *b.* 1821; M.P. for Northumberland S. (C) 1852-78: *m.* 1st, 1852, Diana, who *d.* 1890, dau. of the late Orlando Gunning-Sutton, R.N.; 2ndly, 1892, Emma Sophia Georgiana, who *d.* 1939 (having *m.* 3rdly, 1904, James William Wadsworth), dau. of the late Hon. Richard Denman, and widow of Capt. Oswin Cumming Baker Cresswell; *d.* 1903; *s.* by his brother [9] ATHOLE CHARLES, 3rd Earl, *b.* 1833: *m.* 1866, Caroline Cecilia (who *d.* 1909, having *m.* 2ndly, 1906, as his second wife, her cousin, the 4th Earl of Mount Edgcumbe), dau. of the late Hon. George Edgcumbe; *d.* 1904, when the Earl-dom became ext., but the Barony of Ravensworth passed to his cousin [10] ARTHUR THOMAS (son of the late Rev. the Hon. Robert Liddell, 5th son of 1st Baron), 5th Baron, *b.* 1837: *m.* 1866, Sophia Harriett, who *d.* 1918, dau. of Sir Thomas Walker, 2nd Bt.; *d.* 1919; *s.* by his el. son [11] GERALD WELLESLEY, 6th Baron, *b.* 1869: *m.* 1899, Isolda Blanche, who *d.* 1938, dau. of Charles Glyn Prideaux Brune, of Prideaux Place, Cornwall; *d.* 1932; *s.* by his son [12] ROBERT ARTHUR, *E.D.,* 7th Baron, *b.* 1902; Major R.A. (T.A.); *d.* 1950; *s.* by his cousin [13] ARTHUR WALLER (son of the late Hon. Cyril Arthur Liddell, 2nd son of 5th Baron), 8th Baron and present peer.

RAYLEIGH, BARON. (Strutt.) [Baron U.K. 1821.]

Tenax propositi.
Tenacious of purpose.

JOHN ARTHUR STRUTT, 5th Baron; *b.* April 12th, 1908; *s.* 1947; ed. at Eton, and at Trin. Coll., Camb. (B.A. 1929, M.A. 1935): *m.* 1934, Ursula Mary, dau. of the late Lt.-Col. Richard Hugh Royds Brocklebank, DSO, of 18, Hyde Park Sq., W.

Arms,—Azure, on a chevron argent, between three cross-crosslets fitchée or, as many leopards' faces proper. Crest,—A demi-lion azure, gorged with a mural crown, holding in the dexter paw a cross-crosslet fitchée or, and resting the sinister on a shield sable, charged with a chevron argent, between three cross-crosslets fitchée also or. Supporters,—*Dexter*, a reindeer or, collared and attired sable *sinister*, a monkey proper, banded round the loins and chained, chain reflexed over the back or.

Seat,—Terling Place, Chelmsford, Essex. *Residence,*—18, Hyde Park Square, W.2.

BROTHERS LIVING.

Hon. CHARLES RICHARD, *b.* May 25th, 1910; ed. at Eton, and at Trin. Coll., Camb. (B.A. 1931, M.A. 1934); Capt. (retired) R.A.: *m.* 1952, the Hon. Jean Elizabeth Davidson, dau. of 1st Viscount Davidson, and has issue living, John Gerald, *b.* 1960,—Anne Caroline, *b.* 1955, Mary Jean, *b.* 1957. *Residence,*—Berwick Place, Hatfield Peverel, Chelmsford, Essex. *Club,*—Brooks's.

Hon. Hedley Vicars, *b.* 1915; ed. at Eton, and at Trin. Coll., Camb.; Capt. (retired) Scots Guards. *Residence,*—Mulroy, co. Donegal. *Club,*—Brooks's.

HALF-BROTHER LIVING.

Hon. Guy Robert. *b.* 1921; ed. at Eton, and at Trin. Coll., Camb. (B.A. 1943). *Residence,*—47, Winchester St., SW1.

SISTER LIVING.

Hon. Daphne (*Baroness Acton*), *b.* 1911: *m.* 1931, the 3rd Baron Acton, Ca-na Rosalinda, Pollensa, Mallorca.

WIDOW LIVING OF FOURTH BARON.

KATHLEEN ALICE (*Dowager Baroness Rayleigh*), O.B.E., dau. of the late John Coppin-Straker, of Stagshaw House, Northumberland, and widow of Capt. James Harold Cuthbert, D.S.O., Scots Guards; O.B.E. (Civil) 1918 : *m.* 1920, as his second wife, the 4th Baron, who *d.* 1947. *Residence,*—Longwood, Liss, Hants.

COLLATERAL BRANCHES LIVING.

Grandson of the late Hon. Richard Strutt, 3rd son of 2nd Baron:—
Issue of the late Capt. Geoffrey St. John Strutt, CBE, *b.* 1888, *d.* 1971: *m.* 1912, Sybil Eyre, who *d.* 1975, da. of Sir Walpole Lloyd Greenwell, 1st Bt.:—
Antony Geoffrey, OBE (St. Catherine's Court, Bath), *b.* 1913; ed. at Winchester; Wing Cdr. RAF; OBE (Mil.) 1952; *m.* 1st, 1939, Ebba Lunderbye, from whom he obtained a divorce 1951; 2ndly, 1951, Molly Waters, and has issue living, (by 1st m.) Vivienne Ebba, *b.* 1941,—(by 2nd m.) Stephen Nigel, *b.* 1952,—Michael Geoffrey, *b.* 1958,—Ian, *b.* 1965,—Denise Olivia, *b.* 1955,—Pamela, *b.* 1957.

Grandchildren of the late Capt. Geoffrey St. John Strutt, CBE (ante):—
Issue of the late Lt. Stephen Alistair Strutt, RNVR, *b.* 1918, *d.* 1949: *m.* 1941, Felicity Anne (Logierait House, Ballinluig, Perthshire) (who *m.* 2ndly, 1959, Brig. David Campbell Mullen, CBE, who *d.* 1968), da. of Mervyn Sorley MacDonnell:—
Paul Alistair, *b.* 1944.——Stephen Mark Alistair, *b.* 1948.——Lucinda Alistaire, *b.* 1942.

Grandchildren of the late Hon. Edward Gerald Strutt, CH, 5th son of 2nd Baron:—
Issue of the late Gerald Murray Strutt, *b.* 1880, *d.* 1955: *m.* 1910, Rhoda, *OBE*, who *d.* 1968, 2nd da. of the late Collingwood Hope, CBE, KC, formerly Recorder of Bolton, of Crix, Hatfield, Peverel:—
Pamela, *b.* 1911: *m.* 1935, Richard Gatty, JP, yr. son of the late Sir Stephen Herbert Gatty, KC, and has issue living, Jonathan (Carrington House, Lawn Rd., Milford-on-Sea, Hants), *b.* 1937: *m.* 1962, Valerie Cynthia, da. of Alfred H. Adcock, and has issue living, Fiona Katherine Adelaide *b.* 1963, Philippa Margaret *b.* 1965,—Jessica Margaret, *b.* 1938,—Rhoda Pamela, *b.* 1943: *m.* 1964, John David Bucknill, of The Grange, Grateley, Andover, and has issue living, Stephen *b.* 1965, Gemma Martha *b.* 1967, Charlotte *b.* 1969. *Residence,*—Pepper Arden, Northallerton, Yorks.——Ursula Joyce, *b.* 1917; 1939-45 War in WRNS: *m.* 1948, Maj. James Richard Edwards Harden, DSO, MC, and has issue living, David James, *b.* 1954, Thérèse Annabella, *b.* 1949,—Carolyn Emily, *b.* 1952. *Residence,*—Nanhoran, Pwllheli, Caernarvonshire.

Issue of the late John James Strutt, *b.* 1881, *d.* 1968: *m.* 1914, the Hon. Agnes Roger Dewar, who *d.* 1919, da. of 1st Baron Forteviot:—
Edward Alexander (Garlieston House, Garlieston, Wigtownshire), *b.* 1914; a DL for Wigtownshire; 1939-45 War with RAF: *m.* 1975, Mrs. Janet Roper-Caldbeck.——Joan Eleanor (31, Ennismore Gdns., SW7), *b.* 1916.

Issue of the late Capt. Edward Jolliffe Strutt, *b.* 1884, *d.* 1964: *m.* 1912, Amélie, who *d.* 1954, da. of the late Frederic Devas:—
Mark Frederic, *MC, TD* (Crix, Hatfield Peverel, Essex), *b.* 1913; ed. at Winchester; F.R.I.C.S.; Lt.-Col. RA (TA), and a DL for Essex (High Sheriff 1970); 1939-45 War in Middle East (MC): *m.* 1946, Estelle Elaine, da. of Capt. Sir Thomas Reedham Berney, MC, 10th Bt., and widow of Maj. Kenneth William Bols, Indian Army [Strickland-Constable, Bt., colls.], and has issue living, Charlotte Olivia, *b.* 1947: *m.* 1969, Bruce Dudley Ryder, of Crix, Hatfield Peverel, Essex [see E. Harrowby, colls.].——Sir Nigel Edward, TD (Sparrows, Terling, Chelmsford, Brooks's and Farmers' Clubs), *b.* 1916; ed. at Winchester, and Wye Coll. (Fellow 1970); Maj. Essex Yeo. (ret.); a DL for Essex; High Sheriff 1966; Chm. and Man. Dir. Strutt & Parker (Farms) Ltd.. and Man. Dir. of Lord Rayleigh's Farms Inc.; Chm. Agric. Advisory Council since 1969, Hon. Fellow of Roy. Agric. Soc. of England 1971 and Pres. Essex Agric. Soc. 1972; 1939-45 War as Capt. 104th (Essex) Yeo. RHA

(TA); Middle East 1939-45 (wounded, prisoner); Knt. 1972.——Gillian Leonora, *b.* 1918: *m.* 1st. 1941 (m. diss. 1959), the Rt. Hon. Harold Anthony Nutting [now 3rd Bt.]; 2ndly, 1961, Brig. Oliver George Brooke, CBE, DSO, of The Manor House, Gt. Cheverell, Devizes [see V. Brooke-borough, colls.].

Issue of the late Hon. Hedley Vicars Strutt, 6th son of 2nd Baron, *b.* 1864, *d.* 1891: *m.* 1885, Elizabeth, who *d.* 1888, dau. of the late John Knight:—

Hilda Elizabeth, *b.* 1886: *m.* 1912, Major Francis Deverell, MC, who *d.* 1941, late London Regt., and has issue living, Pamela Clare, *b.* 1913: *m.* 1938, Almon Chamberlin Greenman, of Daphné I (bat 3), 49 (bis) Av. St. Jerome, Aix en Provence, 13100, France, and has issue living, Michael Almon (Davenport, Iowa, USA), *b.* 1943: *m.* 1st, 1964 (m. diss. 1971), Danielle Carol (AVEILLAN), da. of Mme. Jean H. Daza, of Cadiz; 2ndly, 1973, Donna Jean, da. of Stanley Henricks, of 6133, N. Fair-lawn, Peoria, Illinois, USA (and has issue living (by 1st m.) Alexandra Natasha *b.* 1968), John Francis (1801 E. 4th St., Duluth, Minnesota, USA), *b.* 1946: *m.* 1973, Katherine Kellogg, da. of George Milroy Marshall, of 1116, Weed St., New Canaan, Connecticut, 06840, USA, Elizabeth Clare *b.* 1939: *m.* 1st, 1960 (m. diss. 1969), Donald Eric Tingle; 2ndly, 1970, Richard Burbank Parker (Maritime Trading Co., PO Box 652, Camden, Maine 04843, USA) (and has issue living (by 1st m.) Jennifer Clare *b.* 1961, Penelope Jones *b.* 1963, (by 2nd m.) Eleanor Elizabeth *b.* 1972),—Diana Lorette, *b.* 1916: *m.* 1944, Roger Peter Plowden-Wardlaw, Maj. 16th Light Cavalry, Indian Army (ret.), of 46, Malvern Court, Onslow Sq., SW7, and has issue living, Amanda Jane *b.* 1954. *Residence,*—48, Malvern Court, Onslow Sq., SW7.

PREDECESSORS.—[1] *Lady* CHARLOTTE MARY GERTRUDE FITZGERALD, dau. of James, 1st Duke of Leinster, and wife of Col. Joseph Holden Strutt, M.P. for Maldon 1790-1827, was cr. *Baroness Rayleigh,* of Terling Place, co. Essex (peerage of United Kingdom) 1821 ; *s.* by her son [2] JOHN JAMES, 2nd Baron ; *b.* 1796 : *m.* 1842, Clara Elizabeth Latouche, who *d.* 1900, dau. of the late Capt. Richard Vicars, R.E. ; *d.* 1873 ; *s.* by his son [3] JOHN WILLIAM, *O.M., P.C., D.C.L., LL.D., D.Sc., F.R.S.,* 3rd Baron, *b.* 1842 ; sometime Lord-Lieut. of Essex ; the eminent scientist ; Nobel Prize-man, Chancellor of Camb. Univ., Hon. Professor of Natural Philosophy at Roy. Institution, and Scientific Adviser to the Trinity House ; four years Professor of Experimental Physics in Camb. Univ. : *m.* 1871, Evelyn Georgiana Mary, who *d.* 1934, dau. of the late James Maitland Balfour, of Whittingehame, Prestonkirk ; *d.* 1919 ; *s.* by his el. son [4] ROBERT JOHN, 4th Baron ; *b.* 1875 ; a F.R.S. ; Pres. of British Asso. 1938, and of Roy. Institution 1945 : *m.* 1st, 1905, Lady Mary Hilda Clements, who *d.* 1919, dau. of 4th Earl of Leitrim ; 2ndly, 1920, Kathleen Alice, *O.B.E.,* dau. of the late John Coppin-Straker, of Stagshaw House, Northumberland, and widow of Capt. James Harold Cuthbert, D.S.O., Scots Guards ; *d.* 1947 ; *s.* by his son [5] JOHN ARTHUR, 5th Baron and present peer.

Raynham, Viscount, son of Marquess Townshend.

REA, BARON. (Rea.) [Baron U.K. 1937, Bt. U.K. 1935.]

[Name pronounced " Rea."]

Ready for everything.

PHILIP RUSSELL REA, *O.B.E., P.C.,* 2nd Baron and 2nd Baronet, *b.* Feb. 7th, 1900; *s.* 1948; ed. at Westminster at Ch. Ch., Oxford (MA), and at Grenoble Univ.; is a Merchant Banker, an Underwriter at Lloyds, a Co. Director, a Gov. of Westminster Sch., JP and DL of Greater London; in Foreign Office 1945-50, Ch. Liberal Whip in House of Lords, and Dep. Lord Chm. of Cttees. 1950-55, and Liberal Leader in House of Lords 1955-67; a Member of BBC Gen. Advisory Council 1957-62; Leader of Parliamentary Delegation to Burma and Indonesia 1954; Pres. of Liberal Party 1955; a Member of UK Delegation to Council of Europe 1957, and of Parlia-mentary Delegations to USA and Hong Kong 1958; a Dep. Speaker House of Lords since 1950, and a Member of Political Honours Scrutiny Cttee. since 1962; a Member of Lord Chancellor's Advisory Cttee. on Justices of the Peace for Inner London; served in Grenadier Guards 1918-19; 1939-45 War as Lt.-Col. KRCC attached Special Forces (despatches); an Officer of Order of Crown of Belgium, and a Chevalier of Legion of Honour; French Croix de Guerre with Palm; Grand Commander of Nat. Order of Merit of France; OBE (Civil) 1946; PC 1962: *m.* 1922, Lorna, da. of the late Lewis O. Smith, of Glasgow, and has issue.

Arms,—Or, on a fesse wavy azure between three stags courant gules, a lymphad sails furled of the field. *Crest,*—A stag at gaze gules, resting the dexter foreleg on an anchor or. *Supporters,*—On either side a stag gules, charged on the shoulder with a bezant, thereon an anchor azure.

Residence,—30, Smith Sq., SW1. *Clubs,*—Garrick, Grillons, National Liberal (Pres.), Special Forces (Pres.).

DAUGHTER LIVING.

Hon. Ann Felicity, *b.* 1923; European War 1941-5 as 3rd Officer W.R.N.S.: *m.* 1945, Malcolm Grane Ludovic Martin Munthe, M.C., Gordon Highlanders (son of the late Dr. Axel Munthe), and has issue living, Adam John, *b.* 1946,—Guy Sebastian, *b.* 1948,—Philippa Periwinkle, *b.* 1955. *Resi-dences,*—Southside House, Wimbledon Common, S.W.; Much Marcle, Herefordshire.

BROTHER LIVING.

Hon. Findlay Russell, *b.* 1907; ed. at Westminster, and at New Coll., Oxford; formerly Lt., Intelli-gence Corps; a Member of Chelsea Borough Council 1945-49; Member of St. Marylebone Borough

Council 1960-62: *m.* 1st, 1932 (m. diss. 1944), Margaret Hermione, el. da. of the late Col. Kenneth, Hope Bruce, DSO; 2ndly, 1947 (m. diss. 1959), Eileen Clemence; 3rdly, 1959, Helen Margaret, da. of the late B. H. Richardson, of Edinburgh, and has issue living, (by 1st m.) Benjamin Russell (26, Mostyn Rd., SW19), *b.* 1936: *m.* 1st, 1964 (m. diss. 1972), Angela, only da. of A. J. Bradley; 2ndly, 1973, Dorinda Anne, da. of S. Cutting, of Bath, Avon, and has issue living (by 1st m.), Susannah *b.* 1968, (by 2nd m.) James Russell *b.* 1973, Thomas Russell *b.* 1975,—Joanna, *b.* 1934: *m.* 1957, Robert Cecil Seeckts, of Clock House, Groombridge, Sussex, and has issue living, Richard Philip *b.* 1966, Rosemary Anne *b.* 1958, Sarah Elizabeth *b.* 1960, Katherine Mary *b.* 1963. *Residence,*—Weald Cottage, Weald, Sevenoaks, Kent.

SISTERS LIVING.

Hon. Isabella Russell, *b.* 1897 ; ed. at Newnham Coll., Camb.; *m.* 1922, His Honour Judge Jesse Basil Herbert, MC, QC, who *d.* 1972, son of the late Sir Jesse Herbert, and has issue living, Carola (*Lady Beevor*), *b.* 1930: *m.* 1966, as his 2nd wife, Sir Thomas Agnew Beevor, 7th Bt.—Phoebe, *b.* 1932; a JP of Birmingham: *m.* 1955, Richard Mark Van Oss, of Old House Farm, Hanbury, Bromsgrove, Worcs., and has issue living, Thomas Richard *b.* 1957, Celia Catherine *b.* 1959. *Residence,*—Swallowfield Park, nr. Reading, Berks.
Hon. Elisabeth Russell (*Hon. Lady Clapham*), *b.* 1911; ed. at Newnham Coll., Camb. (MA); a JP of London: *m.* 1935, Sir Michael John Sinclair Clapham, KBE, son of the late Sir John Harold Clapham, CBE, Litt.D, FBA, and has issue living, Adam John, *b.* 1940,—Charles Marcus, *b.* 1942: *m.* 1971, Margaret Golledge,—Giles Sinclair, *b.* 1946,—Antonia, *b.* 1938: *m.* 1966, Barry Till, MA, of 44, Canonbury Sq., N1, and has issue living, Lucy Rose Victoria *b.* 1969, Emily Carolyn Rose *b.* 1971. *Residence,*—26, Hill St., W1X 7FU.

COLLATERAL BRANCH LIVING.

Issue of the late Hon. James Russell Rea, 2nd son of 1st Baron, *b.* 1902, *d.* 1954: *m.* 1st, 1926, Betty Marion, who *d.* 1965, da. of Arthur Bevan, MD; 2ndly, 1942, Isobel Mary (SHEPLEY), who *d.* 1965, da. of Robert William Pringle, of Edinburgh:—
(By 1st m.) (JOHN) NICOLAS, *MD* (15, Tanza Rd., NW3), *b.* June 6th, 1928; ed. at Christ's Coll., Camb. (MA, MD); DPH, DCH, D.Obst.: *m.* 1951, Elizabeth Anne, da. of the late William Hensman Robinson, and has issue living, Matthew James, *b.* 1956,—Daniel William, *b.* 1958,—Quentin Thomas, *b.* 1961,—John Silas Nathaniel, *b.* 1965.——Charles Julian (62, Dukes Av., N10), *b.* 1931: *m.* 1st, 1951 (m. diss. 1964), Bridget, da. of the late Montagu Slater; 2ndly, 1964, Anne, da. of William Robson, and has issue living, (by 1st m.) Steven, *b.* 1956,—Julia, *b.* 1952, (by 2nd m.) William, *b.* 1965,—James, *b.* 1968,—Lucy, *b.* 1966,—Kate, *b.* 1972.

PREDECESSOR.—[1] WALTER RUSSELL REA, son of the late Rt. Hon. Russell Rea, *M.P.* of Tanhurst, Dorking, Surrey, and Dean Stanley Street, SW1; *b.* 1873; a Merchant Banker, and Pres. of Free Trade Union ; was Comptroller of H.M.'s Household 1931-2 ; sat as M.P. for Scarborough (*L*) 1906-18, for N. Div. of Bradford 1923-4, and for Dewsbury 1931-5 ; *cr.* a *Baronet* 1935, and *Baron Rea,* of Eskdale, co. Cumberland (peerage of United Kingdom) 1937: *m.* 1st, 1896, Evelyn, who *d.* 1930, dau. of J. J. Muirhead, J.P., of Edinburgh; 2ndly, 1931, Jemima, who *d.* 1964 dau. of the Rev. Alexander Ewing; *d.* 1948; *s.* by his el. son [2] PHILIP RUSSELL, 2nd Baron and present peer.

READING, MARQUESS OF. (Isaacs.) [Marquess U.K. 1926.]

MICHAEL ALFRED RUFUS ISAACS, *M.B.E., M.C.,* 3rd Marquess; *b.* March 8th, 1916 ; *s.* 1960 ; ed. at Eton and at Balliol Coll., Oxford; a Member of The Stock Exchange; 1939-45 War as Major Queen's Bays and on Staff (MC; MBE (Mil.)) 1945: *m.* 1941, Margot Irene, yr. da. of the late Percival Angustus Duke, OBE, of Watts Close, Tadworth, Surrey, and has issue.

Arms,—Sable, a bend between two leopards' faces or, on a chief argent a fasces fessewise proper. **Crest,**—In front of a leopard's head couped sable, a faces as in the arms. **Supporters,**—On either side a leopard proper, round the neck a collar or, pendent therefrom an escutcheon argent charged with a human head affrontée proper, erased at the neck, ducally crowned or.

Residences,— Staplefield Grange, Haywards Heath, Sussex; 30, Cadogan Place, SW1. *Club,*— City of London.

Either do not attempt or complete.

SONS LIVING.

SIMON CHARLES HENRY RUFUS (*Viscount Erleigh*) (3, Charlwood Pl., SW1; Cavalry Club), *b.* May 18th, 1942; ed. at Eton, and Tours Univ., France; Lt. 1st The Queen's Dragoon Gds. 1961-64; a Member of London Stock Exchange.
Lord Anthony Michael Rufus, *b.* 1943; ed. at Gordonstoun: *m.* 1972, Anne Puglsey.
Lord Alexander Gerald Rufus, *b.* 1957.

DAUGHTER LIVING.

Lady Jacqueline Rosemary Margot Rufus, *b.* 1946.

SISTERS LIVING.

Lady Joan Alice Violet Rufus (*Baroness Zuckerman*), *b.* 1918; is a JP: *m.* 1939, Baron Zuckerman, OM, KCB, FRS [Life Baron]. *Residence,*—The Shooting Box, Burnham Thorpe, King's Lynn, Norfolk.

Lady Elizabeth Anne Mary (Rufus) (Holberry Cottage, Bishops Sutton, Hants.), *b.* 1921: formerly Junior Com. ATS: *m.* 1945, Maj. Derek Francis Hornsby, KRRC, who *d.* 1971 [B. Belper], and has issue living, Richard Gerald, *b.* 1948,—David Julian, *b.* 1953.

PREDECESSORS.—[1] *Sir* RUFUS DANIEL Isaacs, *G.C.B., G.C.S.I., G.C.I.E., G.C.V.O., P.C.,* son of the late Joseph Michael Isaacs, merchant and shipbroker, of London ; *b.* 1860 ; sat as M.P. for Reading (*L*) 1904-13 ; appointed Solicitor-Gen. March 1910, Attorney-Gen. Oct. 1910 (with a seat in the Cabinet from June 1912), and Lord Chief Justice of England 1913-21; Pres. Anglo-French Mission to USA 1915, Special British Representative to USA 1917, High Commr. in USA, and Ambassador Extraor. and Plen. on Special Mission 1918-19, Viceroy of India 1921-6, and Sec. of State for Foreign Affairs (in National Government) Aug. to Nov. 1931, became Capt. of Deal Castle 1926, and Lord Warden of the Cinque Ports 1934 ; cr. *Baron Reading*, of Erleigh, Berks (peerage of United Kingdom) 1914, *Viscount Reading*, of Erleigh, Berks (peerage of United Kingdom) 1916, *Viscount Erleigh*, of Erleigh, Berks, and *Earl of Reading* (peerage of United Kingdom) Nov. 1917, and *Marquess of Reading* (peerage of United Kingdom) 1926 : *m.* 1st, 1887, *Dame* Alice Edith, *G.B.E., C.I.,* who *d.* 1930, dau. of Albert Cohen, merchant, of London; 2ndly, 1931, *Dame* Stella, GBE, (*Baroness Swanborough*), who *d.* 1971, da. of the late Charles Charnaud; *d.* 1935; *s.* by his son [2] GERALD RUFUS, GCMG, CBE, MC, TD, PC, QC, 2nd Marquess ; *b.,* 1889 ; a Bencher and Treasurer of Middle Temple ; was Joint Parliamentary Under-Sec. of State for Foreign Affairs 1951-53, and Joint Min. of State for Foreign Affairs 1953-7 : Hon. Col. Inns of Court Regt. (TA) 1947-59: *m.* 1914, the Hon. Eva Violet Mond, CBE, JP, who *d.* 1973, da. of 1st Baron Melchett; *d.* 1960; *s.* by his son [3] MICHAEL ALFRED RUFUS, 3rd Marquess and present peer, also Earl of Reading, Viscount Reading, Viscount Erleigh, and Baron Reading.

REAY, LORD. (Mackay.) [Lord S. 1628, Bt. S. 1627.]
[Title pronounced "Ray."]

HUGH WILLIAM MACKAY, 14th Lord and 14th Baronet; *b.* July 19th, 1937; *s.* 1963; ed. at Eton, and Ch. Ch., Oxford; is Chief of the Clan Mackay, and Baron Mackay van Ophemert in the Netherlands; Member of European Parl., Strasbourg, since 1973: *m.* 1964, the Hon. Annabel Térèse Fraser, da. of 15th Lord Lovat, and has issue.

ARMS,—Azure, on a chevron argent, between three bears'-heads couped argent, muzzled gules, a roebuck's head erased, between two hands grasping daggers, the points turned towards the buck's head, all proper. Crest,—A dexter arm erect couped at the elbow, the hand grasping a dagger also erect proper. Supporters—*Dexter,* a pikeman armed at all points ; *sinister,* a musketeer, both proper.
Residences,—Ophemert in Gelderland, Holland, 11, Wilton Cres., S.W.1.   *Clubs,*—St. James', Turf; Beefsteak, Puffin's.

SON LIVING.
Hon. ÆNEAS SIMON (*Master of Reay*), *b.* March 20th, 1965.

DAUGHTER LIVING.
Hon. Laura Elizabeth, *b.* 1966.

SISTERS LIVING.
Hon. Elizabeth Mary, 1938: *m.* 1962, Nicholas Hardwick Fairbairn, QC, MP, of Fordell Castle, by Dunfermline, Fife, and has issue living, Charlotte Elizabeth, *b.* 1963,—Anna-Karina, *b.* 1966,— Francesca Katharine Nichola, *b.* 1969.

Hon. Margaret Anne (Upper Huntlywood, Earlston, Berwickshire), *b.* 1941.

UNCLE LIVING. (*Son of 12th Lord.*)
Baron (and *Hon.*) Alexander Willem Rynhard (of De Lindenlaan, 76, Schapendrift, Blaricum, N.H., Holland), *b.* 1907.

AUNT LIVING. (*Daughter of 12th Lord.*)
Baroness (and *Hon.*) Maria Christina Elisabeth (De Eeckwal, Dalfsen (O), Netherlands), *b.* 1904.

WIDOW LIVING OF THIRTEENTH LORD.
CHARLOTTE MARY (*Charlotte, Lady Reay*) (Hoebridge, Melrose, Roxburghshire), da. of the late William Younger, of Ravenswood, Melrose: *m.* 1936, the 13th Lord, who *d.* 1963.

COLLATERAL BRANCHES LIVING.

Granddaughters of the late Baron Theodoor Philip Mackay, 2nd son of Johan François Hendrik Jacob Ernestus Mackay, brother of 11th Lord:—
Issue of the late Baron Constantyn Willem Ferdinand Mackay, *b.* 1870, *d.* 1955 : *m.* 1st, 1898, Jonkvrouw Petronella Adamina Hoeufft, who *d.* 1933; 2ndly, 1937, Dr. C. Frida Katz, who *d.* 1963:—
(By 1st marriage) *Baroness* Jacqueline Jeanette, *b.* 1899 : *m.* 1946, Jonkheer Dr. Johan Fredrik Theodoor Van Valkenburg. *Residence,*—41, Stadionkade, Amsterdam, Holland.——*Baroness* Adelaide Cornelie, *b.* 1902 : *m.* 1927, Gustaaf Carel Ferdinand Schoch. *Residence,*—Pittsburgh, USA.——*Baroness* Henriette Margaretha (Parallelweg 96, Oosterbeek, Holland), *b.* 1904.——*Baroness* Margaretha Clara Françoise, *b.* 1909: *m.* 1937, the Rev. Henri Jean Louis André Couvée, who *d.* 1969. *Residence,*—61, Joh. Bildersstraat, The Hague.

Grandsons of the late Baron Æneas Mackay (infra):—
Issue of the late Lt.-Col. Baron Daniel Mackay, *b.* 1900, *d.* 1969: *m.* 1927, Henriette Constance Adèle (van Moersselestraat 21, The Hague), da. of Dr. Alfred Joan Labouchere, of Zeist, Holland:—
Baron Donald (269, Irislaan, Oegstgeest, Holland), *b.* 1928 ; Lt.-Col. RNAF: *m.* 1968, Danielle Christine, da. of Dr. Hendrik Gerrit Beins.——*Baron* Alfred Alexander (248, Parkweg, Voorburg, Holland), *b.* 1930: *m.* 1965, Diana Margaret, da. of Sydney Jesty Elwin, of Strathfield, NSW, and has issue living, *Baron* Andrew Robert, *b.* 1967,—*Baroness* Caroline Jane, *b.* 1969.——*Baron* Hugo Carel Æneas (84, Soesterbergsestraat, Soest, Netherlands), *b.* 1936: *m.* 1967, Gwendoleen, who *d.* 1973, da. of Elbert Waller.——*Baron* Eric Joan Maurits (25, Wilhelminalaan, Haren, Groningen, Holland), *b.* 1938: *m.* 1963, Susan Jane, da. of Francis McNeill, and has issue living, *Baron* Patrick Joan, *b.* 1967,—*Baroness* Alexandra, *b.* 1966,—*Baroness* Helen Danielle, *b.* 1969,—*Baroness* Madeline, *b.* 1971.

Grandchildren of the late Baron Theodoor Philip Mackay (ante):—

Issue of the late Baron Æneas Mackay, b. 1872, d. 1932: m. 1899, Jonkvrouwe Hermina Olasina, who d. 1945, dau. of Lieut.-Gen. Jonkheer J. C. C. den Beer Poortugael, Min. of War, and Privy Councillor:—

Baron Reinhard Alexander (Flat 15, 81, Schouwweg, Wassenaar, nr. Hague), b. 1903; is a Knight of St. John (Netherlands branch); 1939-45 War as Liaison Officer in Unified Command in Java, 1942, and as ADC to Gen. Sir Archibald Wavell: m. 1930, Greta Ernestina, da. of Jan Adriaan Smits, of The Hague, Holland, and has issue living, Baroness Sonja Gratia, b. 1931: m. 1953, Hendrik Willem Balthasar Croiset van Uchelen, of The Round, 42, Dene Rd., Northwood, Middx., and has issue living, Eric Alexander b. 1958, Helen Astrid b. 1955.——Baron Theodoor Philip (Twello, Gelderland, Holland), b. 1911; Burgomaster: m. 1941, Zsófia Friderika Emma, da. of Dr. Andor Henrik Ráthonyi Reusz, of Budapest, Hungary, and has issue living, Baron Æneas, b. 1942: m. 1975, Yvonne Marie-Blanche, da. of Frans Wyers,—Baroness Marguerite Louise, b. 1943: m. 1964, Dr. Bernard Rudolf Grüninger, of La Chaux de Fonds, Rue de la Prairie 76, Switzerland, and has issue living, Daniel Robert b. 1966, Marie-Anne b. 1968,—Baroness Lilian Mary, b. 1945: m. 1970, Jan Willem Stuart, of The Hague,—Baroness Zsófia Alexandra, b. 1951.——Baroness Louisa Wilhelmina Elizabeth Amarantha, b. 1906.——Baroness Erica, b. 1916: m. 1974, Jonkheer Gerard Beelaerts van Blokland, of 35, van Montfoortlaan, The Hague.

Issue of the late Baron Edward Mackay, b. 1873, d. 1950: m. 1902, Ina Petronella Lycklamà à Nyeholt, who d. 1903:—

Baroness Catherina Margaretha Elisabeth, b. 1903: m. 1923, Ernest Johannes Désandré, of 444, Saratoga Av., Apt. 24-H, Santa Clara, Cal. 95050, USA, and has issue living, Edward Ernest, b. 1929,—Ina Catherina Elisabeth, b. 1932.

Issue of the late Baron Dirk Rynhard Johan Mackay, b. 1876, d. 1960: m. 1st, 1906, Johanna Elisabeth Blaauw, who d. 1920; 2ndly, 1927 (divorce 1937), Violet, dau. of Edward Egerts; 3rdly, 1939, Helena Esme Egerts (of 44, Willemstraat, The Hague, Holland):—

(By 1st m.) Baron Johan Jacob (120, Harbor View Lane, Harbor Bluffs, Largo, Fa., USA), b. 1909: m. 1936, Elizabeth E., da. of William Holman, and has issue living, Baron Derrick Philip (Casilla 116, Talca, Chile), b. 1937: m. 1964, Juanita Carminia Hederra Sepulveda, da. of Agusto Hederra Silva, and has issue living, Baron Christian Andrés b. 1965, Baron Alejandro Andrés b. 1967, Baron John Hugo (Casilla 116, Talca, Chile), b. 1941: m, 1971, Sylvia Bravo Perucca, da. of Ladislao Bravo,—Baroness Johanna Elizabeth, b. 1939: m. 1970, German del Rio, and has issue living, German Andrés b. 1971,—Baroness Marie Louise, b. 1952.——Baron Johan Hugo, b. 1914, Commodore, RNN (ret.): m. 1945, Margaret Pearse Herbert, and has issue living, Baron Alexander Rijnhard, b. 1950,—Baron Donald Johan, b. 1964,—Baroness Carol Huguette, b. 1954.——Baron Eric Rynhard Alexander, b. 1917: m. 1943, Gertrud Brückman, and has issue living, Baron Æneas, b. 1944,—Baron Paul, b. 1946,—Baron Eric, b. 1953.——Baroness Helene Gérardine, b. 1907: m. 1926, Rodney Frederick Jarrett Sterwin, and has issue living, Peter Philip, b. 1930,—Angela Helen, b. 1929.—Baroness Anna Maria, b. 1913: m. 1st, 1933 (m. diss. 1948), George Eschauzier, of The Hague, Holland; 2ndly, 1949, Herman B. Baruch, former American Ambassador to Holland, who d. 1953; 3rdly, 1958, Rolf Robert, of 120, Harbor View Lane, Largo, Florida, USA, and has issue living, (by 1st m.) Pierre George, b. 1940,—Hilda Susan, b. 1934,—Johanna Elisabeth, b. 1936.——(By 2nd m.) Baroness Patricia, b. 1928: m. 1951 (m. diss. 1959), Leonard Johannes Mens, and has issue living, Edward Maarten, b. 1955.

Issue of the late Baron Daniel Mackay, b. 1878, d. 1962: m. 1st, 1906 (divorce 1921), Helene Hommel; 2ndly, 1921, Marie Françoise, who d. 1959, dau. of Hugo François Lamaison; 3rdly, 1960, Anna Minke (De Reigers Hof, 15, Kieftweg, Hierden, Holland), da. of Johannes Weyer:—

(By 1st m.) Baron Donald Theodore (c/o National Westminster Bank, High St., Barnstaple, N. Devon), b. 1910; Lt.-Cdr. (ret.) R. Netherlands Navy; 1939-45 War with RN (Submarines): LRCP, LRCS Ed, LRFP & S Glas.; m. 1945, Kathleen, da. of P. S. Pearce, and has issue living, Baron Niall, b. 1956,—Baroness Moira, b. 1952.——Baroness Maria Christine Jeanette, b. 1907.——(By 2nd m.) Baroness Maria Constantia (Voorsterweg 153, Tonden, post Voorst, Gelderland, Holland), b. 1922: m. 1947, (m. diss. 1961) Johan Barthold Frans Bosch Ridder van Rosenthal, and has issue living, Lodewijk Hendrik Nicolaas, b. 1948,—Roelina Gijsbertha Gerardina, b. 1951,—Nicolette, b. 1953.——Baroness Juliana Anna (Houtlaan 50, Leiden, Holland) b. 1925: m. 1950 (m. diss. 1960), Count Rutger Jan Moritz Albert Schimmelpenninck, and has issue living, Count Gerrit Marius, b. 1951,—Countess Marie Danielle, b. 1952.

Granddaughters of the late Baron Willem Karel Mackay, yst. son of the late Johan François Hendrik Jacob Ernestus Mackay (ante):—

Issue of the late Baron Barthold Mackay, b. 1871, d. 1945: m. 1898, Jonkvrouwe Alpheda Louise, who d. 1935, dau. of Jonkheer Cornelis Charles van der Wyck :—

Baroness Justine Cornelia, b.1898: m.1925, Marie Jacob Hendrik de Bruyn van Melis-en-Mariekerke, late Sec. of Supreme Council of Nobility, who d. 1964, and has issue living, Alpheda Louisa, b. 1926,—Gertrude Emma Marie, b. 1929. Residence,—Ruychrocklaan 187, The Hague, Holland.—— Baroness Catharina Wilhelmina Adrienne, b. 1905: m. 1927 (marriage dissolved 1940), Lambertus Hendrik Slotemaker.——Baroness Johanna Elisabeth, b. 1907: m. 1st, 1936, Capt. Patrick Alexander Agnew, Seaforth Highlanders (T.A.), who d. (killed in action during European War) 1943 [see Agnew, Bt. cr. 1629, colls.]; 2ndly, 1944 (m. diss. 1965), Lt.-Col. William Stanley Baird. Residence,—56, Lexham Gdns., W8.

PREDECESSORS.—(1) Sir DONALD Mackay, Knt., el. son of Hulstean Du of Farr, and Strathnaver; b. 1590; a distinguished royalist soldier, was cr. a Baronet 1627, and Lord Reay (peerage of Scotland, 1628, with remainder to his heirs male for ever bearing the name and arms of Mackay: m. 1st, 1610, Barbara Mackenzie, sister of 1st Earl of Seaforth; 2ndly before 1631, (marriage annulled) Rachel Winterfield or Harrison; 3rdly, Elizabeth, dau. of Robert Thomson, of Greenwich; 4thly, Marjorie, dau. of Francis Sinclair of Stirkoke; d. 1649; s. by his son [2] JOHN, 2nd Lord, who espoused the royal cause: m. 1st, 1636, Isabel Sinclair; 2ndly, Barbara, dau. of Col. Hugh Mackay of Scourie; d. about 1681; s. by his grandson [3] GEORGE, F.R.S. (son of the late Donald Mackay, Master of Reay), 3rd Lord: m. 1st, 1702, Margaret, dau. of Lt.-Gen. Hugh Mackay of Scourie; 2ndly, Janet, dau. of John Sinclair of Ulbster and widow of Benjamin Dunbar, younger, of Hempriggs; 3rdly, 1713, Mary, dau. of John Doull of Thuster, W.S.; d. 1748; s. by his son [4] DONALD, 4th Lord: m. 1st, 1732, Marion, who d. 1740, dau. of Sir Robert Dalrymple; 2ndly, 1741, Christian, who d. 1763, dau. of James Sutherland, of Pronsie; d. 1761; s. by his el. son [5] GEORGE, 5th Lord: m. 1st, 1758, his cousin, Marion, who d. 1759, dau. of the late Col. the Hon. Hugh Mackay; 2ndly, 1760, Elizabeth, who d. 1780, dau. of the late John Fairlie, Collector of Customs at Ayr; d. 1768; s. by his half-brother [6] HUGH, 6th Lord; d. unmarried 1797; s. by his cousin [7] ERIC (son of the late Hon. George Mackay, 3rd son of 3rd Lord), 7th Lord; b. 1773; d. 1847; s. by his brother [8] ALEXANDER, 8th Lord; b. 1775: m. 1809, Marion, who d. 1865, dau. of Col. Gall, and widow of David Ross; d. 1863; s. by his son [9] ERIC, 9th Lord; d. unmarried 1875; s. by his kinsman [10] ÆNEAS (son of Barthould John Christian Mackay [who was cr. Baron Mackay d'Ophemert, of the Netherlands], great-grandson of the Hon. Æneas Mackay, Brig.-Gen. in Dutch Ser., 2nd son of 2nd Lord), 10th Lord; b. 1806; was Min. of State, and Vice-Pres. of Privy Council of the Netherlands: m. 1837, Mary Catherine Anne Jacoba, who d. 1886, dau. of Baron Fagel, Privy Councillor of the Netherlands; d. 1876; s. by his son [11] DONALD JAMES, K.T., G.C.S.I., G.C.I.E., P.C., 11th Lord; b. 1839; naturalized by Act of Parliament 1877, and cr. Baron Reay, of Durness (peerage of United Kingdom) 1881; Lord-Lieut. of co. Roxburgh 1892, Gov. of Bombay 1885-90, Under-Sec. of State for India 1894-5, and first Pres. of British Acad. 1902-7: m. 1877, Fanny Georgiana Jane, C.I., who d. 1917, dau. of the late Richard Hasler, of Aldingbourne, Sussex, and widow of Capt. Alexander Mitchell, M.P., of Stow; d. (Aug.) 1921, when the United Kingdom Barony (cr. 1881) became ext., and he was s. in the Scottish titles by his cousin [12] Baron ERIC (only son of the late Baron Æneas Mackay, son of Johan François Hendrik Jakob Ernestus Mackay, brother of 10th Lord), 12th Lord, b. 1870: m. 1901, Baroness Maria Johanna Bertha Christina Van Dedem, who d. 1932; d. (Nov.) 1921; s. by his el. son [13] ÆNEAS ALEXANDER, 13th Lord; b. 1905; naturalized a British subject 1938; in Foreign Office 1939-47; a Representative Peer 1955-9: m. 1936, Charlotte Mary, dau. of the late William Younger, of Ravenswood, Melrose; d. 1963; s. by his only son [14] HUGH WILLIAM, 14th Lord and present peer.

REDCLIFFE-MAUD, BARON. (Redcliffe-Maud.) [Life Baron 1967.]

JOHN PRIMATT REDCLIFFE REDCLIFFE-MAUD, GCB, CBE, yr. son of the late Rt. Rev. John Primatt Maud, Bishop of Kensington; b. Feb. 3rd, 1906; assumed by deed poll and enrolled at Coll. of Arms 1967, the surname of Redcliffe-Maud; ed. at Eton. and New Coll., Oxford (Hon. Fellow); Hon. LLD Witwatersrand, Natal, Leeds, and Nottingham; Hon. DSocSc Birmingham; Fellow and Dean of Univ. Coll., Oxford 1929-39, Hon. Fellow 1956, Master of Birkbeck Coll., London Univ. 1939-43, Sec. Min. of Reconstruction 1944-45, and Permanent Sec. Min. of Education 1945-52, Min. of Fuel and Power 1952-56, Min. of Power 1956-58, High Commr. for UK in S. Africa 1959-61, Ambassador 1961-63, and UK High Commr. for Basutoland, Bechuanaland Protectorate and Swaziland 1959-63; Chm. of Exec. Board of UNESCO 1949, and a Member of Economic Planning Board 1952-58; Chm. of Roy. Commn. on Local Govt. in England 1966-69; Master of Univ. Coll., Oxford 1963-76; High Bailiff of Westminster and Searcher of the Sanctuary since 1967; cr. CBE (Civil) 1942, KCB (Civil) 1946, GCB (Civil) 1955, and Baron Redcliffe-Maud, of City and co. of Bristol (Life Baron) 1967: m. 1932, Jean, yr. da. of John B. Hamilton, of Melrose, and has issue.

Address,—c/o Master's Lodgings, University College, Oxford.

SON LIVING.
Hon. Humphrey John Hamilton MAUD, b. 1934.

DAUGHTERS LIVING.
Hon. Caroline Mary Stewart, b. 1939: m. 1967, the Rev. Joel Pugh, of 115, East Fairfax St., Falls Church, Virginia, 22046 USA.
Hon. Virginia Jean Furse, b. 1943: m. 1970, Roger Frank Nicholls.

REDESDALE, BARON. (Mitford.) [Baron U.K. 1902.]

CLEMENT NAPIER BERTRAM MITFORD, 5th Baron; b. Oct. 28th, 1932; s. 1963; ed. at Eton: m. 1958, Sarah Georgina Cranstoun, yr. da. of Brig. Alston Cranstoun Todd, OBE, of Bramblehurst, Limes Lane, Buxted, Sussex, and has issue.

Arms,—Quarterly; 1st and 4th argent, a fesse between three moles sable, Mitford; 2nd and 3rd azure, three lozenges conjoined in fesse or, a canton ermine, Freeman. Crests,—1st, two hands couped at the wrist proper, grasping a sword erect piercing a boar's head erased sable, Mitford; 2nd, a demi-wolf argent, charged on the shoulder with a fesse dancettée gules, and

God careth for us.

holding between the paws a lozenge or, Freeman. Supporters.—On either side an eagle wings expanded sable, beaked and membered or, charged on the breast with a lozenge also or, and gorged with a wreath of shamrock vert.

Residences,—2, St. Mark's Sq., N.W.1; The School House, Rochester, Newcastle upon Tyne.

SON LIVING.
Hon. RUPERT BERTRAM, b. July 18th, 1967.
DAUGHTERS LIVING.
Hon. Emma, b. 1959.
Hon. Tessa, b. 1960.
Hon. Georgina Kathryn Mercia, b. 1961.
Hon. Victoria-Louise, b. 1962.
Hon. Henrietta Jane, b. 1965.
Hon. Georgina Clementine, b. 1968.

AUNTS LIVING. (Daughters of 1st Baron.)
Hon. Joan, b. 1887: m. 1907, Capt. Denis Herbert Farrer, who d. 1945, sometime Northamptonshire Regt., and has issue living, Michael Edgar (Brayfield House, Olney, Bucks.), b. 1920; ed. at Stowe, and at New Coll., Oxford; Burma 1944-45 as temporary Maj. Gordon Highlanders, attached to Scots Fusiliers: m. 1949, Constance Morgenstern, who obtained a divorce 1964, and has issue living, Ruth Carol b. 1950: m. 1971, George Christopher Hartigan,—Ralph Paul, MC (Wayshill, Stogumber, Taunton), b. 1922; ed. at Stowe, and at New Coll., Oxford; 1944-45 War as temporary Capt. Welsh Guards (MC): m. 1950, Ann Grace, da. of Lt.-Col. John Robert Hutchison, DSO, of Wayshill, Stogumber, Taunton, and has issue living, Patricia Ann b. 1951, Julia b. 1954, Rosemary b. 1956,—Joan (Brayfield Lodge, Olney, Bucks.), b. 1913: m. 1st, 1936, Guillermo Enrique de Udy, who d. 1941; 2ndly, 1949, Col. Paul Rodzianko, CMG, who d. 1965,—Ann (5A, North Gate, Prince Albert Rd., NW8), b. 1916: m. 1941, David Edgar Alderson Horne, who d. 1970, and has issue living, Ann Clare b. 1944. Residence,—Brayfield House, Olney, Bucks.
Hon. Daphne (twin) (Dowager Baroness Denham), b. 1895: m. 1919, the 1st Baron Denham, who d. 1948. Residence,—10, West St., Olney, Bucks.

DAUGHTERS LIVING OF SECOND BARON.
Hon. Pamela, b. 1907: m. 1936, Wing-Com. Derek Ainslie Jackson, O.B.E., D.F.C., A.F.C., D.Sc., F.R.S., R.A.F. Vol. Reserve, from whom she obtained a divorce 1951. Residence,—Woodfield House, Caudle Green, nr. Cheltenham, Glos. GL53 9PR.

Hon. Diana (*Hon. Lady Mosley*), *b.* 1910 : *m.* 1st, 1929, the Hon. Bryan Walter Guinness (from whom she obtained a divorce 1934)—afterwards 2nd Baron Moyne ; 2ndly, 1936, as his second wife, Sir Oswald Ernald Mosley, 6th Bt. *Residence,*—1, Rue des Lacs, Orsay, 91, Essonne, France.
Hon. Jessica Lucy, *b.* 1917 : *m.* 1st, 1937, Esmond Marcus David Romilly, Pilot Officer Roy. Canadian Air Force, who *d.* (killed in action during European War) 1942 : 2ndly, 1943, Robert Edward Treuhaft, of New York, U.S.A., and has issue living (by 2nd marriage) Benjamin, *b.* 1947,—(by 1st marriage) Anne Constancia, *b.* 1941. *Residence,*—6411, Regent St., Oakland, California, U.S.A.
Hon. Deborah Vivien (*Duchess of Devonshire*), *b.* 1920 : *m.* 1941, the 11th Duke of Devonshire. *Residences,*—Chatsworth, Bakewell, Derbyshire ; Bolton Abbey, Yorkshire ; Lismore Castle, co. Waterford ; 4, Chesterfield Street, W.1.

MOTHER LIVING.

Flora, dau. of the late Cdr. Gerard Talbot-Napier, R.N., and widow of Henry Lane Eno: *m.* 1931, the Hon. (Ernest) Rupert Bertram Ogilvy Freeman-Mitford, 5th son of 1st Baron, who *d.* 1939. *Residence,*—7, Rue Michel-Chauvet, Geneva, Switzerland.

COLLATERAL BRANCH LIVING.

Issue of the late Major the Hon. Clement Bertram Ogilvy Freeman-Mitford, D.S.O., el. son of 1st Baron, *b.* 1876, *d.* (killed in action) 1915 : *m.* 1909, Lady Helen Alice Willington Ogilvy, [who *d.* 1973, having *m.* 2ndly, 1918, Capt. Henry Courtney Brocklehurst, who *d.* (killed in action) 1942, and from whom she had obtained a divorce 1931 [Brocklehurst, Bt.]; 3rdly, 1933, Lt.-Col. Harold Bligh Nutting], da. of 11th Earl of Airlie:—
Rosemary Ann, *b.* 1911: *m.* 1932, Cdr. Richard James Bailey, OBE, RN, who *d.* 1969, and has issue living, Richard Lee Clement (49, Lawrence Gdns, Mill Hill, NW7), *b.* 1933; ed. at Charterhouse: *m.* 1959, Barbara Joyce, el. da. of S. G. Ede, of Fowey, Cornwall, and has issue living, Samantha Kate *b.* 1967,—Michael Lee George, *b.* 1934; ed. at Charterhouse: *m.* 1964, Diana Jane, da. of the late Maj. Laurence Deacon, and has issue living, Anthony Michael George *b.* 1966, Clementine Jane *b.* 1969,—Ann Clementine, *b.* 1936: *m.* 1964, Peter Calver, Hockley House Stud, Cheriton, Alresford, Hants., only son of the late Sir Robert Henry Sherwood Calver, QC,—Diana Penelope, *b.* 1940: *m.* 1960, William Henry Gordon Leaf, of Midcot, The Hill, Burford, Oxon, and has issue living, James-William Richard Tyrrell *b.* 1963, Jessica Frances Rosemary *b.* 1961,—Lavinia Jessica Iris, *b.* 1944: *m.* 1st, 1965 (m. diss. 1974), Antony Carlson; 2ndly, 1975, Hugh Brewis Bailey, MRCS, LRCP, of Hillcrest, 214, Newmarket Rd., Norwich, NR4 7LA, and has issue living (by 1st m.), Sarah Rosemary Iris *b.* 1967, Lucy *b.* 1969,—Annabel Lee Christine, *b.* 1945: *m.* 1974, Malcolm Valentine (Tendaho Plantation Share Co., Box 3389, Addis Ababa, Ethiopia). *Residence,*—Mitford Cottage, Westwell, Burford, Oxon.——Clementine Mabell Kitty (*Lady Beit*), *b.* (posthumous) 1915: *m.* 1939, Sir Alfred Lane Beit, 2nd Bt. *Residences,*—Russborough, Blessington, co. Wicklow; 137, Beach Rd., Gordon's Bay, Cape Province, S. Africa; 2, Little Boltons, SW10.

PREDECESSORS.—This family descends from John Mitford of London, merchant (*d.* 1720), 3rd son of Robert Mitford of Mitford Castle, Northumberland. John Mitford, Speaker of House of Commons and Lord Chancellor of Ireland; was cr. Baron Redesdale 1802. His son was cr. Earl of Redesdale 1877, both titles becoming ext. 1886. The latter devised his estates to his cousin Algernon Bertram Mitford. [1] *Sir* ALGERNON BERTRAM Freeman-Mitford, G.C.V.O., K.C.B., son of Henry Reveley Mitford, of Exbury House, Hants; *b.* 1837; Sec. to H.M.'s Commrs. of Public Works and Buildings 1874-6; M.P. for Stratford-on-Avon (*C*) 1892-5; assumed by Roy. licence 1886 the additional surname and arms of Freeman; cr. *Baron Redesdale*, of Redesdale, co. Northumberland (peerage of U.K.) 1902: *m.* 1874, Lady Clementine Gertrude Helen Ogilvy, who *d.* 1932, dau. of 7th Earl of Airlie; *d.* 1916; *s.* by his el. surviving son [2] DAVID BERTRAM OGILVY, 2nd Baron; *b.* 1878; Capt. late Northumberland Fusiliers; a Member of Select Committee of Peerages in abeyance 1925: *m.* 1904, Sydney, who *d.* 1963, dau. of the late Thomas Gibson Bowles (sometime M.P. for King's Lynn), of 25, Lowndes Sq., S.W.; *d.* 1958; *s.* by his brother [3] BERTRAM THOMAS CARLYLE OGILVY, D.S.O., 3rd Baron; *b.* 1880; Capt. R.N.; High Sheriff of Oxon 1935: *m.* 1925, Mary Margaret, who *d.* 1967, da. of the late Thomas Cordes, JP, DL; *d.* 1962; *s.* by his brother [4], JOHN POWER BERTRAM OGILVY, 4th Baron, *b.* 1885: *m.* 1914 (marriage annulled in Germany on her petition 1914), Marie Anne, da. of Friedrich Viktor von Friedlander-Fuld, of Berlin; *d.* 1963; *s.* by his nephew [5] CLEMENT NAPIER BERTRAM (son of the Hon. (Ernest) Rupert Bertram Ogilvy Freeman-Mitford, 5th son of 1st Baron), 5th Baron and present peer.

REDMAYNE, BARON. (Redmayne.) [Life Baron 1966, Bt. U.K. 1964.]

Without blood no victory

MARTIN REDMAYNE, *DSO, TD, PC; Life Baron* and 1st *Baronet,* son of Leonard Redmayne; *b.* Nov. 16th, 1910; ed. at Radley; a DL for Notts.; a JP of Nottingham 1948-66, a Lord Commr. of the Treasury 1953-59, Dep. Ch. Govt. Whip 1955-59, and Parl. Sec. to the Treasury and Ch. Govt. Whip 1959-64; MP for Rushcliffe Div. of Notts. (*C.*) 1950-66; 1939-45 War as Brig. late Sherwood Foresters in Italy, Comd. 66th Inf. Bde.; *cr.* DSO 1944, PC 1959, a *Baronet* 1964, and *Baron Redmayne,* of Rushcliffe, co. Nottingham (Life Baron) 1966: *m.* 1933, Anne, da. of John Griffiths, and has issue.

Arms.—Gules two chevronels between three cushions ermine tasselled or, a bordure engrailed argent. **Crest,**—In front of a cushion as in the arms fessewise, a horse's head argent maned gules. **Supporters,**—*Dexter,* a Herdwick ram proper, poll gules; *sinister,* a lion or, maned gules.

Residence,—27, Hans Place, SW1.

SON LIVING.

Hon. NICHOLAS JOHN (Walcote Lodge, Walcote, Lutterworth, Leics.), *b.* Feb. 1st, 1938; *h.a.* to Baronetcy: *m.* 1963, Ann, da. of Frank Birch Saunders, of The Mews, Kineton, Warwicks., and has issue living, Giles Martin, *b.* 1968,—Camilla Jane, *b.* 1966.

REID, BARONY OF. (Reid.) [Extinct 1975.]

WIDOW LIVING OF LIFE BARON.

ESTHER MAY (*Baroness 'Reid*) (Danefold, W. Grinstead, Sussex), da. of the late C. B. Nelson, and widow of Gerald Frank Brierley: *m.* 1933, Baron Reid (Life Baron), who *d.* 1975.

Reidhaven, Viscount, son of Earl of Seafield.

REIGATE, BARON. (Vaughan-Morgan.) [Life Baron 1970, Bt. U.K. 1960.]

JOHN KENYON VAUGHAN-MORGAN, PC; *Life Baron* and 1st *Baronet*, son of the late Sir Kenyon Pascoe Vaughan-Morgan, OBE, MP; *b.* Feb. 2nd, 1905; ed. at Eton, and Ch. Ch., Oxford, (MA); Chm. of Board of Govs. of Westminster Hosp. 1963-74; a Member of Court of Assistants of Merchant Taylors' Co. (Master 1970); a Dir. of Morgan Crucible Co. Ltd.; Hon. Freeman of Reigate; Parl. Sec., Min. of Health Jan. to Sept. 1957, and Min. of State Board of Trade 1957-59; MP for Reigate (C) 1950-70; Dep. Chm. S. Westminster Magistrates Bench 1966-74; 1939-45 War as Lt.-Col. Welsh Gds., and GSOI, HQ, 21st Army Group (despatches); *cr.* PC 1961, a *Baronet* 1960, and *Baron Reigate*, of Outwood, co. Surrey (Life Baron) 1970: *m.* 1940, Emily Redmond, da. of the late William Redmond Cross, of New York City, USA, and has issue.

Arms,—Quarterly; 1st and 4th, or, five lozenges conjoined in fesse gules between three lymphads, sails furled sable colours flying of the second, *Morgan;* 2nd and 3rd, sable on a chevron or, between three boys' heads couped at the shoulders proper crined or enwrapped about the neck with a snake as many spear heads embrued proper, *Vaughan.* **Crests,**—1st, argent and sable a cock gules resting the dexter claw on a bundle of twigs banded proper; 2nd, in front of a boy's head, as in the Arms, two spears saltirewise proper. **Supporters,**—*Dexter,* a dragon gules; *sinister,* a camel or, with one hump. *Residence,*—36, Eaton Sq., SW1. *Club,*—Brooks's.

DAUGHTERS LIVING.

Hon. Julia Redmond, *b.* 1943; BA London: *m.* 1962, Henry Walter Wiggin, of Brainge, Putley, Ledbury, and 33, Ladbroke Gdns., W11 2PX [see Wiggin, Bt. colls.].
Hon. Deborah Mary, *b.* 1944: *m.* 1966, Michael Whitfield, of 8, Scarsdale Villas, W8 [see E. Howe, colls.].

REITH, BARONY OF. (Reith.) [Baron UK 1940, disclaimed 1972.]

Whatsoever.

CHRISTOPHER JOHN REITH, *b.* May 27th, 1928; *s.* as 2nd Baron June 16th, 1971, disclaimed his peerage for life April 21st, 1972; ed. at Eton, and Worcester Coll., Oxford (MA); late RN: *m.* 1969, Penelope Margaret Ann, el. da. of the late Henry Rowland Morris, of Beeston, Notts., and has issue.

Arms,—Or, a cross engrailed sable between four mullets gules, on a chief of the last a lion passant of the field. **Crest,**—An eagle rising reguardant proper. **Supporters,**—(borne by Barons Reith) Two eagles, wings addorsed proper.

Residence,—Whitebank Farm, Methven, Perthshire.

SON LIVING
Hon. JAMES HARRY JOHN, *b.* June 2nd, 1971.

DAUGHTER LIVING
Hon. Julie Katharine, *b.* 1972.

SISTER LIVING
Hon. Marista Muriel, *b.* 1932; ed. at St. George's, Ascot, and at St. Andrews Univ. (MA); a Member of Staff of National Trust for Scotland: *m.* 1960, the Rev. Robert Murray Leishman, MA, Chap. Roy. Edinburgh (Psychiatric) Hosp.; Lecturer New Coll., Edinburgh; and has issue living, Mark Murray, *b.* 1962,—Iona Marista, *b.* 1963,—Martha Katharine, *b.* 1965,—Kirsty Jane, *b.* 1969. *Residence,*—50, Caiystane Av., Edinburgh, EH10 6SH.

WIDOW LIVING OF FIRST BARON
MURIEL KATHARINE (*Baroness Reith*) (Parkhill House, Rattray, Blairgowrie, Perthshire), yr. da. of the late John Lynch Odhams, of Southwick, Sussex: *m.* 1921, the 1st Baron, who *d.* 1971.

PREDECESSOR.—[1] Rt. Hon. Sir JOHN CHARLES WALSHAM REITH, KT, GCVO, GBE, CB, TD, DCL, LLD, 5th son of the late Very Rev. George Reith, DD, of Aberdeen, and Glasgow; *b.* 1889; first Gen. Man. and Man. Dir. of British Broadcasting Co. Ltd. 1922-26, Dir. Gen. of BBC 1926-38; Min. of Information, Jan. to May 1940; Min. of Transport, May to Oct. 1940; Min. of Works and Bldgs., and 1st Commr. of Works 1940-42; *cr.* Baron Reith, of Stonehaven, co. Kincardine (peerage of UK) 1940: *m.* 1921, Muriel Katharine, yr. da. of the late John Lynch Odhams, of Southwick, Sussex; *d.* 1971; *s.* by his only son [2] CHRISTOPHER JOHN, 2nd Baron, until he disclaimed his peerage 1972.

REMNANT, BARON. (Remnant.) [Baron U.K. 1928, Bt. U.K. 1917.]

JAMES WOGAN REMNANT, 3rd Baron, and 3rd Baronet; *b.* Oct. 23rd, 1930; *s.* 1967; ed. at Eton; Lt. Coldstream Guards (Reserve); FCA: *m.* 1953, Serena Jane, only da. of Cdr. Sir Clive Loehnis, KCMG, RN (ret.) [see E. Harrowby, colls.], and has issue.

Arms,—Sable, a bend vair between two shel-drakes proper all within two flaunches argent and charged with a cinquefoil gules. **Crest,**—Between rushes a sheldrake proper, holding in the beak a rose gules, barbed, seeded, leaved and slipped proper. **Supporters,**—On either side a dolphin proper charged with a cinquefoil gules.

Residence,—Bear Place, Hare Hatch, Reading, Berks. *Club,*—City of London.

Let him who has deserved the palm bear it.

SONS LIVING.
Hon. PHILIP JOHN, *b.* Dec. 20th, 1954; ed. at Eton.
Hon. Robert James, *b.* 1956; ed. at Eton.
Hon. Hugo Charles, *b.* 1959.

DAUGHTER LIVING.
Hon. Melissa Clare, *b.* 1963.

SISTER LIVING.
Hon. Susan Frances, *b.* 1938: *m.* 1967, Alan Tyser, of 11, Pelham Cres., SW7, and has issue living, Harry, *b.* 1968.

WIDOW LIVING OF SECOND BARON.
NORAH SUSAN (*Dowager Lady Remnant*) (Bear Ash, Hare Hatch, Reading, Berks.), da. of the late Lt.-Col. Alexander John Wogan-Browne, India Cav.: *m.* 1924, the 2nd Baron, who *d.* 1967.

COLLATERAL BRANCH LIVING.
Issue of the late Hon. Peter Farquharson Remnant, yr. son of 1st Baron, *b.* 1897, *d.* 1968: *m.* 1923, Betty, who *d.* 1965, da. of the late William George Tanner, of Frenchay, Glos.:—
Dawn, *b.* 1927: *m.* 1951, Antony Stewart Hooper, of Brook House, Doynton, Bristol, and has issue living, Susan Jane, *b.* 1952,—Mary Sandra, *b.* 1953,—Carol Ann, *b.* 1956.——Merrial (27, The Boltons, SW10, and Ipsden House, Ipsden, Oxon.), *b.* 1934: *m.* 1st, 1954 (m. diss. 1960), Arthur James Wesley-Smith; 2ndly, 1962, Henry James Stockley who *d.* 1967; 3rdly, 1958, Ivor John Crosthwaite, DSO, and has issue living, (by 1st m.) Shane, *b.* 1955,—Linda, *b.* 1957,—(by 2nd m.) Marian Julia, *b.* 1963.

PREDECESSORS—[1] JAMES FARQUHARSON Remnant, *C.B.E.*, son of the late Frederick William Remnant, of Southwold, Suffolk ; *b.* 1863 ; a Member of Select Committee on Taxation of Land Values (Scotland) 1904, of Roy. Commn. on Canals and Inland Navigation 1906-10, of Select Committee on Police Day of Rest 1908-9, of Home Office Committee on Conditions and Pay of Police 1919, and of Rating Machinery Committee 1924 ; M.P. for Holborn Div. of Fins-bury (*C*) March 1900 to Nov. 1918, and for Holborn (*U*) Dec. 1918 to June 1928 ; cr. a *Baronet* 1917, and *Baron Remnant*, of Wenhaston, co. Suffolk (peerage of United Kingdom) 1928 : *m.* 1892, Frances Emily, who *d.* 1944, da. of the late Robert Gosling, of Hassobury, Essex; *d.* 1933; *s.* by his el. son [2] ROBERT JOHN FARQUHARSON, *MBE*, 2nd Baron, *b.* 1895: *m.* 1924, Norah Susan, da. of the late Lt.-Col. Alexander John Wogan-Browne; *d.* 1967; *s.* by his only son [3] JAMES WOGAN, 3rd Baron and present peer.

RENDLESHAM, BARON. (Thellusson.) [Baron I. 1806.]
[Name pronounced "Tellusson."]

CHARLES ANTHONY HUGH THELLUS-SON, 8th Baron; *b.* March 15th, 1915; *s.* 1943; ed. at Eton; late Capt. R. Signals: *m.* 1st, 1940, Margaret Eliza-beth (who obtained a divorce 1947), da. of Lt., Col. Robin Rome; 2ndly, 1947, Clare, da. of the late Lt.-Col. D. H. G. McCririck, and has issue by 1st and 2nd marriages.

Arms,—Quarterly, wavy or and argent: in the 1st and 4th quarters, two wings barwise in pale and expanded towards the dexter sable, each charged with a trefoil slipped in fesse, the point towards the sinister or; in the 2nd and 3rd quarters, an oak tree eradicated vert, thereon an escutcheon placed bendwise gules, and charged with three guttés argent. **Crest,**—A demi-greyhound salient argent, collared sable, between two wings elevated and expanded sable, each charged with a trefoil slipped or. **Supporters,**—Two greyhounds reguardant argent, plain collared sable.

Residence,—9, Pelham Place, S.W.7.

By labour and honesty.

SON LIVING. (*By 2nd marriage*)
Hon. CHARLES WILLIAM BROOKE, *b.* Jan. 10th, 1954; ed. at Eton.

DAUGHTERS LIVING. (*By 1st marriage.*)
Hon. Caroline (*Hon. Lady Goring*), *b.* 1941 : *m.* 1960, Sir William Burton Nigel Goring, 13th Bt. *Residence,*—89, Cornwall Gdns., S.W.7.
(*By 2nd marriage.*)
Hon. Sarah Ann, *b.* 1949.
Hon. Antonia, *b.* 1956.
Hon. Jaqumine, *b.* 1960.

BROTHER LIVING (*Raised to the rank of a Baron's son* 1945).

Hon. Peter Robert, *b.* 1920; ed. at Eton; is Capt KRRC: *m.* 1st, 1947 (divorce 1950), Pamela (TUFNELL), who *d.* 1968, da. of the late Oliver Ivan Parker [E. Macclesfield, colls.]; 2ndly, 1952, Celia, da. of James Walsh, and has issue living, (by 2nd m.) James Hugh, *b.* 1961,—Peter Richard, *b.* 1962.

[SISTER LIVING (*Raised to the rank of a Baron's daughter* 1945).
Hon. Cynthia Adeline Elizabeth, *b.* 1916.

MOTHER LIVING.
Gwynnydd, dau. of Sir Robert Augustus William Colleton, C.B., 9th Bt. (ext.): *m.* 1914, Lieut. Col. the Hon. Hugh Edmund Thellusson, D.S.O., who *d.* 1926. *Club,*—Hamilton.

PREDECESSORS.—[1] PETER ISAAC THELLUSSON, son of Peter Thellusson, M.P. for Malmesbury 1796-7, a wealthy London merchant, and the descendant of a French Protestant nobleman; *cr.* Baron Rendlesham (peerage of Ireland) 1806 ; *d.* 1808 ; *s.* by his el. son [2] JOHN, 2nd Baron ; *d.* 1832 ; *s.* by his brother [3] WILLIAM, 3rd Baron ; was in Holy Orders ; *d.* 1839 ; *s.* by his brother [4] FREDERICK, 4th Baron ; *b.* 1798 : *m.* 1838, Eliza Charlotte, dau. of Sir George Beeston Prescott, 2nd Bt., and widow of James Duff, *d.* 1852 ; *s.* by his son [5] FREDERICK WILLIAM BROOK, 5th Baron, *b.* 1840 ; M.P. for Suffolk E. (C) 1874-85 : *m.* 1861, Lady Egidia Montgomerie, who *d.* 1880, dau. of 18th Earl of Eglinton, K.T. ; *d.* 1911 ; *s.* by his el. son [6] FREDERICK ARCHIBALD CHARLES, *b.* 1868 : *m.* 1st, 18—, Lilian, who *d.* 1931, dau. of the late J. Manly, J.P., of Kingston, Jamaica ; 2ndly, 1931, Dolores Olga, who *d.* 1959, dau. of Sir William Lewis Salusbury-Trelawny, 10th Bt., and widow of Henry Harcourt Williams ; *d.* 1938 ; *s.* by his brother [7] PERCY EDWARD, 7th Baron ; *b.* 1874: *m.* 1922, Gladys Dunlop, O.B.E., who *d.* 1933, dau. of Andrew Vans Dunlop Best; *d.* 1943 ; *s.* by his nephew [8] CHARLES ANTHONY HUGH (son of the late Lieut.-Col. the Hon. Hugh Edmund Thellusson, D.S.O., 3rd son of 5th Baron), 8th Baron and present peer.

Renfrew, Baron of, title borne by Prince of Wales.

RENNELL, BARON.   (Rodd.)   [Baron U.K. 1933.]

FRANCIS JAMES RENNELL RODD, K.B.E., C.B., 2nd Baron, *b.* Oct. 25th, 1895 ; *s.* 1941; ed. at Eton, and at Balliol Coll., Oxford (MA); Hon. LLD. Manchester 1962; is a Dir. of Morgan, Grenfell & Co., a Member of Council of British Assocn., Vice-Lieut. and a J.P. for Herefordshire, Hon. Vice-Pres. and Hon. Life Member of Roy. Geographical Soc. (Pres. 1945-48), and a Trustee of British Sch. of Rome; formerly Visiting Fellow of Nuffield Coll., Oxford; 1914-18 War as Capt. RFA in France, Egypt, Italy, and Palestine (despatches, Order of St. Maurice and St. Lazarus of Italy), 1939-45 War in W., E., and N. Africa, and in Sicily and Italy as Maj.-Gen. and Ch. Political Officer (despatches, C.B., K.B.E.); sometime a 2nd Sec. in Diplo. Ser.; C.B. (Mil.) 1943, K.B.E. (Mil.) 1944: *m.* 1928, the Hon. Mary Constance Vivian Smith, da. of 1st Baron Bicester, and has issue.

Recte omnia duce Deo.
With God for guide, all is right.

Arms,—Argent, two trefoils slipped sable on a chief of the second, three crescents of the first. *Crest,*—A representation of the Colossus of Rhodes, over the shoulder a bow, in the dexter hand an arrow and in the sinister a cup, all proper. *Supporters,*—On either side a Cornish chough, wings elevated and addorsed proper. charged on the breast with a trefoil slipped argent.
Residence,—The Rodd, near Presteigne, Radnorshire. *Club,*—Beefsteak.

DAUGHTERS LIVING.
Hon. Joanna Phoebe, *b.* 1929: *m.* 1966, Comte Gérard de Renusson d'Hauteville, of 7, rue A Coutureau St. Cloud, Hauts de Seine, France.
Hon. Juliet Honor, *b.* 1930: *m.* 1957, Brian Boobbyer, and has issue living, Philip Christopher, *b.* 1963,—Mark Tremayne, *b.* 1967. *Residence,*—4, Victoria Rd., Oxford.
Hon. Mary Elizabeth Jill, *b.* 1932 : *m.* 1954, Michael William Langan Dunne, and has issue living, John Francis Jeremy, *b.* 1957,—Stephen Michael Damian, *b.* 1961,—Mary Jemima, *b.* 1955,—Teresa Mary Claire, *b.* 1962,—Miranda Mary, *b.* 1966. *Residences,*—7, Elvaston Mews, SW7; Ashley Farm, Stansbatch, Pembridge, Herefordshire.
Hon. Rachel Georgiana, *b.* 1935: *m.* 1964, Richard Douglas Blythe, of Kordabup, Denmark, W. Aust., and has issue living, Joseph Matthew Gerard, *b.* 1968,—Matthew Francis, *b.* 1970.

SISTER LIVING.
Hon. Evelyn Violet Elizabeth (*Baroness Emmet of Amberley*), *b.* 1899; *cr. Baroness Emmet of Amberley* (Life Baroness) 1964 [see that title].

COLLATERAL BRANCHES LIVING
Issue of the late Cdr. the Hon. Gustaf Guthrie Rennell Rodd, OBE, RN, yr. son of 1st Baron, *b.* 1905, *d.* 1974: *m.* 1st, 1932, Yvonne Mary, who obtained a divorce 1948, da. of the late Sir Charles Murray Marling, GCMG, CB [see Marling, Bt.]; 2ndly, 1948 (m. diss. 1966), Claude Rosemary (CALVERT), da. of Archibald W. D. Dove, of Kingston Hill, Surrey:—

(By 1st m.) (John Adrian) Tremayne (89, Antill Rd., N3), b. 1935; ed. at Downside and RNC, Dartmouth; Lt. RN.

PREDECESSOR.—[1] Rt. Hon. Sir (James) Rennell Rodd, G.C.B., G.C.M.G., G.C.V.O., son of the late Major James Rennell Rodd; b. 1858; was Envoy Extraor. and Min. Plen. to Stockholm 1904-8, and Ambassador Extraor. and Min. Plen. to Italy 1908-19; sat as M.P. for St. Marylebone 1928-32 (C); cr. Baron Rennell, of Rodd, co. Hereford (peerage of United Kingdom) 1933: m. 1894, Lilias Georgina, who d. 1951, dau. of the late James Alexander Guthrie, of Craigie, Forfar; d. 1941; s. by his el. son [2] FRANCIS JAMES RENNELL, 2nd Baron and present peer.

RENWICK, BARON. (Renwick.) [Baron U.K. 1964, Bt. U.K. 1927.]

To work is to pray.

HARRY ANDREW RENWICK, 2nd Baron and 3rd Baronet; b. Oct. 10th, 1935; s. 1973; ed. at Eton; partner in W. Greenwell & Co., Stockbrokers, of London and Edinburgh: m. 1965, Susan Jane, da. of the late Capt. Kenneth Stephen B. Lucking, Cheshire Regt., and has issue.

Arms,—Argent, a husbandman in the act of sowing proper, on a chief azure a thunderbolt between two bulls, heads caboshed or. Crest,—a thunderbolt or. Supporters, —Dexter, a black poodle proper; sinister, a tabby cat proper.
Residence,—8, Lyall St., SW1.

SONS LIVING.

Hon. ROBERT JAMES, b. Aug. 19th, 1966.
Hon. Michael David, b. 1968.

SISTERS LIVING.

Hon. Susan Mary, b. 1930; a JP for Hants.: m. 1955, the Hon. John Francis Harcourt Baring, of Stratton Park, Micheldever, Winchester, el. son of 6th Baron Ashburton.
Hon. Jennifer, b. 1932: m. 1st, 1954 (m. diss. 1967), Anthony Duncan Rowe; 2ndly, 1973, Roy Philip Arthur, of Le Bel Royale, Bel Royale, Jersey, and has issue living (by 1st m.), Giles Robert Timothy, b. 1956,—Antonia Tanya, b. 1959.
Hon. Belinda Anne, b. 1934: m. 1959, John Horatio Gordon Shephard, of The Old School House, Winkfield, Berks., and has issue living, William, b. 1962,—Sarah, b. 1959.

AUNT LIVING.

Agnes Mary: m. 1926, Julius Ernst Guthe, of Kepwick Hall, Thirsk, and has issue living, Digby Julius Ernest, b. 1927,—Ann Mary, b. 1929,—Elizabeth Penelope, b. 1932,—Margaret Renwick, b. 1936.

MOTHER LIVING.

Dorothy Mary, da. of the late Maj. Harold Parkes, of the Dial House, Alveston, Stratford-on-Avon: m. 1st, 1929 (m. diss. 1953), Sir Robert Burnham Renwick, KBE, 2nd Bt. (subsequently 1st Baron Renwick); 2ndly, 1953, John FitzAdam Ormiston, of Miserden House, Miserden, Glos.

WIDOW LIVING OF FIRST BARON.

(Edith) Joan (Joan, Baroness Renwick), (Herne's Cottage, Windsor Forest, Berks.), only da. of the late Sir Reginald Clarke, CIE, and widow of Maj. John Ogilvy Spencer, WG: m. 1953, as his 2nd wife, the 1st Baron, who d. 1973.

PREDECESSOR.—[1] HARRY (BENEDETTO) RENWICK, KBE, son of Andrew Renwick, of Windsor, b. 1861; cr. a Baronet 1927: m. 1897, Frederica Louisa, da. of Robert Laing, of Stirling; d. 1932; s. by his only son [2] Sir ROBERT BURNHAM RENWICK, KBE, 2nd Bt. b. 1904; Industrialist; Chm. of Airbourne Forces, 1943-45; Controller of Communications Air Min. and Communications Equipment, Min. of Aircraft Production 1942-45; Chm. Asso. TV 1961; cr. Baron Renwick, of Coombe, co. Surrey (peerage of UK) 1964: m. 1st, 1929 (m. diss. 1953), Dorothy Mary, da. of the late Maj. Harold Parkes, of the Dial House, Alverston, Stratford-on-Avon; 2ndly, 1953, Edith Joan, only da. of the late Sir Reginald Clarke, CIE; and widow of Maj. John Ogilvie Spencer, WG; d. 1973; s. by his el. son [3] HARRY ANDREW, 2nd Baron and present peer.

REVELSTOKE, BARON. (Baring.) [Baron U.K. 1885.]

By uprightness and labour.

RUPERT BARING, 4th Baron; b. Feb. 8th, 1911; s. 1934; ed. at Eton; formerly 2nd Lt. Roy. Armoured Corps (T.A.): m. 1934, the Hon. Florence (Flora) Fermor-Hesketh (who d. 1971, having obtained a divorce 1944), da. of 1st Baron Hesketh, and has issue.

Arms,—Azure, a fesse or, in chief a bear's head proper, ringed or, differenced by a hurt, thereon a mullet erminois. Crest,—A mullet erminois, between two wings argent. Supporters,—Dexter, a bull argent; sinister, a bear proper, muzzled or, each charged on the shoulder with a mullet erminois.

Residence,—Lambay and, co. Dublin.

SONS LIVING.

Hon. JOHN, b. Dec. 2nd, 1934; ed. at Eton.
Hon. James Cecil, b. 1938; ed. at Eton: m. 1968, Aneta, yr. da. of the late Erskine A. H. Fisher, and has issue living, Alexander Rupert, b. 1970,—Thomas James, b. 1971.

SISTER LIVING.

Hon. Daphne, b. 1904: m. 1926, Arthur Joseph Laurence Pollen, who d. 1968 [see Pollen, Bt., colls.].
Residence,—Oray Cottage, Harpsden, Henley-on-Thames.

COLLATERAL BRANCHES LIVING.

Issue of the late Brig.-Gen. the Hon. Everard Baring, C.V.O., C.B.E., 4th son of 1st Baron, *b*. 1865, *d*. 1932 : *m*. 1904, Lady Ulrica Duncombe, who *d*. 1935, dau. of 1st Earl of Feversham :—

Helen, *b*. 1906 : *m*. 1939, as his second wife, Maj. Gordon Bentley Foster. *Residence,*—Leysthorpe, Oswaldkirk, Yorks.——Audrey, *b*. 1909: *m*. 1st, 1933, Lt.-Col. Sir Charles Frederick Richmond Brown, 4th Bt., Comdg. 7th Batn. Green Howards (TA), who obtained a divorce 1948 ; 2ndly, 19—, Lt.-Col. Campbell K. Finlay, of West Ardhu, Dervaig, Isle of Mull.——Elizabeth, *b*. 1915. *Residence,*—

Grandchildren of the late Hon. Hugo Baring, O.B.E., youngest son of 1st Baron :—

Issue of the late Francis Anthony Baring, *b*. 1909, *d*. (killed in action during European War) 1940: *m*. 1933, Lady Rose Gwendolen Louisa McDonnell, DCVO (43, Pembroke Sq., W8), da. of 7th Earl of Antrim :—

Nicholas Hugo (2, Kildare Terr., W2, and The Grange, Shalbourne, nr. Marlborough, Wilts.), *b*. 1934; ed. at Eton, and at Magdalene Coll., Camb.; late Lieut. Coldstream Gds.: *m*. 1972, Diana, da. of the late Lt.-Col. Charles Crawfurd, and has issue living, Francis Charles, *b*. 1973.——Peter, (13, Chalcot Cres., NW1, and Inglewood Lodge, Kintbury, Berks.) *b*. 1935; ed. at Eton, and at Magdalene Coll., Camb.: *m*. 1960, Teresa Anne, da. of the Hon. Maurice Richard Bridgeman, CBE [see V. Bridgeman], and has issue living, Guy Francis, *b*. 1965, Max Maurice, *b*. 1967,—Hugo John, *b*. 1970.—— Susan Violet, *b*. 1938: *m*. 1962, Henry Joseph Rogaly, of 43, Laurier Rd., NW5, and has issue living, Benjamin Nelson, *b*. 1963,—Sarah Rose, *b*. 1965,—Rachel Frances, *b*. 1968,—Jessica Hilary, *b*. 1971.

PREDECESSORS.—[1] EDWARD CHARLES Baring, son of the late Henry Baring, M.P. (see B. Northbrook, colls.] ; *b*. 1828 ; was head of the mercantile firm of Baring Brothers and Co., Bishopsgate Street, E.C. ; cr. *Baron Revelstoke,* of Membland, co. Devon (peerage of United Kingdom) 1885 : *m*. 1861, Louisa Emily Charlotte, who *d*. 1892, dau. of John Crocker Bulteel, of Flete, Devon ; *d*. 1897 ; *s*. by his son [2] *Rt. Hon.* JOHN, 2nd Baron, *G.C.V.O., b*. 1863 : a partner in the firm of Baring Bros. and Co. (Limited), and a Director of Bank of England ; a Member of Council of H.R.H. the Prince of Wales 1907-29, Receiver-Gen. of Duchy of Cornwall 1908-29, and Lord-Lieut. for Middlesex 1926-9 ; *d*. 1929 ; *s*. by his brother [3] CECIL, 3rd Baron ; *b*. 1864 : *m*. 1902, Maude, who *d*. 1922, dau. of the late Pierre Lorillard ; *d*. 1934 ; *s*. by his son [4] RUPERT, 4th Baron and present peer.

RHODES, BARON. (Rhodes.) [Life Baron 1964].

Come on!

HERVEY RHODES, *KG, DFC, PC,* son of John Eastwood Rhodes, of Greenfield, Oldham; *b*. Aug. 12th, 1895; ed. at St. Mary's Elementary Sch., Greenfield, and Huddersfield Tech. Coll.; Hon. Dr. Tech. Bradford; Hon. LLD Manchester; a KStJ; a Freeman of Ashton-under-Lyne; Founder of H. Rhodes & Bros., Woollen Manufacturers, of Delph, Oldham 1921 (Chm. 1921-61), Chm. of Saddleworth UDC 1944-45, PPS to Min. of Pensions 1948, Parl. Sec. to Board of Trade 1950-51, Vice-Chm. of Parl. and Scientific Cttee. 1962-64, and Chm. of Lancs. and Cheshire Group of Lab. MPs 1964; again Parl. Sec. Board of Trade 1964-66; a DL of co. Lancaster since 1971 (Lord Lieut. 1968-71); 1914-18 War with King's Own Roy. Lancs. Regt., commissioned Yorks Regt., and seconded to RFC in France (wounded, DFC and Bar); MP for Ashton-under-Lyne (*Lab.*) 1945-64; cr. *Baron Rhodes,* of Saddleworth, W. Riding of Yorks. (Life Baron) 1964, PC 1969, and KG 1972: *m*. 1925, Ann, da. of John Henry Bradbury, of Greenfield, Oldham, and has issue.

Arms,—Vert, semy of acorns or two trumpets in saltire argent, the mouth pieces downward, on a chief or two Lancashire child's clogs, toes inward sable, the caps and studs or. Crest,—A cotton plant fructed proper between, to the dexter, a rose argent, and to the sinister a rose gules, both barbed and seeded, stalked and leaved proper. Supporters,—*Dexter*, a lion or; sinister, a ram proper.

Residence,—Cribbstones, Delph, Oldham.

DAUGHTERS LIVING.

Hon. Pamela, *b*. 1927: *m*. 1953, Walter L. Hemphill, of 4237, Osage Av., Philadelphia 4, Pa, U.S.A., and has issue.
Hon. Helen, *b*. 1929: *m*. 1954, John Sutcliffe, JP, of Lower Carr, Diggle, Dobcross, nr. Oldham, Lancs. and has issue.

RHYL, BARON. (Birch.) [Life Baron 1970.]

LIBERTAS

(EVELYN) NIGEL CHETWODE BIRCH, *OBE, PC,* son of the late Gen. Sir (James Frederick) Noel Birch, GBE, KCB, KCMG, [Chetwode, Bt.]; *b*. Nov. 18th, 1906; ed. at Eton; Parl. Under-Sec. of State for Air 1951-52, Parl. Sec., Min. of Defence 1952-54, Min. of Works 1954-55, Sec. of State for Air 1955-56, and Economic Sec. to Treasury 1956-58; Pres. of Johnson Soc., Lichfield 1966; MP for Flintshire (*C*) 1945-50, and for W. Flintshire 1950-70; 1939-45 War as Lt.-Col. KRRC; cr. OBE (Mil) 1945, PC 1955, and *Baron Rhyl,* of Holywell in the parish of Swanmore, co. Southampton (Life Baron) 1970: *m*. 1950, the Hon. Esme Consuelo Helen Glyn, OBE, da. of 4th Baron Wolverton.

Arms,—Quarterly per fess wavy argent and azure, in the first and fourth quarters a mullet sable, and in the second and third a cross crosslet fitche or, in the fess point a rose gules barbed, seeded, slipped and leaved proper. **Crest,**—Issuant from a fish weir sable, staked gules, a demi eagle displayed sable, beaked or, langued gules. **Supporters,** on either side a sea dragon or, langued azure, semy of roses gules, barbed and seeded proper and gorged with a fish weir sable, staked gules.

Residences,—Holywell House, Swanmore, Hants.; 73, Ashley Gdns., SW1. *Clubs,*—White's, Pratt's.

RIBBLESDALE, BARONY OF. (Lister.) [Extinct 1925.]

DAUGHTER LIVING OF FOURTH BARON.

Hon. Diana (*Diana, Countess of Westmorland*), *b.* 1893 : *m.* 1st, 1913, Percy Lyulph Wyndham, Lieut. Coldstream Guards, who *d.* (killed in action) 1914 [B. Leconfield, colls.]; 2ndly, 1918, Capt. Arthur Edward Capel, C.B.E., who *d.* 1919; 3rdly, 1923, the 14th Earl of Westmorland, who *d.* 1948, and has issue living, (by 2nd marriage) Ann Diana France Ayesha, *b.* 1919; *m.* 1st, 1940, the Rt. Hon. George Reginald Ward, M.P. (now Viscount Ward of Witley), who obtained a divorce 1951 [see E. Dudley]; 2ndly, 1951, (m. diss. 1966) (Richard) Thurstan Holland-Martin, of Conderton who *d.* 1968, and has issue living, (by 1st m.) [see V. Ward of Witley], (by 2nd m.), Barnaby Robert *b.* 1952, Giles Thurstan *b.* 1955,—June (*posthumous*), *b.* 1920: *m.* 1948, Franz Osborn. *Residence,*—Lyegrove, Badminton, Gloucestershire.

RICHMOND and GORDON, DUKE OF. (Gordon-Lennox.) [Duke (Richmond) E. 1675, Duke (Lennox) S. 1675, Duke (Gordon) U.K. 1876.]

FREDERICK CHARLES GORDON-LENNOX, 9th Duke of Richmond and Lennox, and 4th Duke of Gordon; also Duke of Aubigny in France; *b.* Feb. 5th, 1904; *s.* 1935; ed. at Eton, and at Ch. Ch., Oxford; Hereditary Constable of Inverness Castle, patron of five livings; late Lieut R. Tank Corps (TA); 1939-45 as Fl. Lt. RAF; bore Sceptre with the Dove at Coronations of King George VI and Queen Elizabeth II; *m.* 1927, Elizabeth Grace, da. of the late Rev. Thomas William Hudson, formerly V. of Wendover, Bucks, and has issue.

Arms,—Quarterly: 1st and 4th grand quarters, the Royal arms of Charles II (viz. quarterly; 1st and 4th, France and England quarterly; 2nd, Scotland; 3rd, Ireland), the whole within a bordure company argent and gules charged with eight roses of the second, barbed and seeded proper, *Lennox,* over all an inescutcheon gules, three buckles or, *Aubigny*; 2nd and 3rd grand quarters quarterly, 1st azure, three boars' heads couped or, *Gordon*; 2nd or, three lions, heads erased gules, *Badenoch*; 3rd or, three crescents within a double tressure counterflory gules, *Seton*; 4th azure, three cinquefoils argent, *Fraser*. **Crests,**—1st, a bull's head erased sable horned or, *Lennox*; 2nd, on a chapeau gules, turned up ermine, a lion statant guardant or, ducally crowned gules, and gorged with a collar compony of four pieces, argent and gules, charged with eight roses of the last, *Richmond*; 3rd, out of ducal coronet, a stag's head affrontée proper, attired with ten tynes or. **Supporters,**—*Dexter,* a unicorn argent, armed, crined and unguled, or; *sinister,* an antelope argent, also armed, crined, and unguled, or, and each supporter gorged with a collar compony as the crest.

Seat,—Goodwood, Chichester, Sussex. *Residences,*—Carne's Seat, Goodwood, Chichester, Sussex; Trevaney, Constantine Bay, Padstow, Cornwall; 29, Hyde Park St., W2. *Club,*—Bath.

SONS LIVING.

CHARLES HENRY (*Earl of March and Kinrara*), *b.* Sept. 19th, 1929 ; ed. at Eton, and at William Temple Coll., Rugby; late 2nd Lt. KRRC; a Chartered Accountant, a Member of House of Laity of General Synod for Diocese of Chichester, and of Central and Exec. Cttee. of World Council of Churches and Chm. of Board for Mission and Unity of General Synod since 1972; a Church Commr.: *m.* 1951, Susan Monica, da. of Col. Cecil Everard Montague Grenville-Grey, CBE [see Morrison Bell, Bt. (cr. 1905), colls.], and has issue:—

> SON LIVING,—CHARLES HENRY (*Lord Settrington*), *b.* Jan. 8th, 1955.
>
> DAUGHTERS LIVING,—*Lady* Ellinor Caroline, *b.* 1952.
> *Lady* Louisa Elizabeth, *b.* 1967.

Residence,—Goodwood House, Chichester.

Lord Nicholas Charles, *MVO, b.* 1931; ed. at Eton, and at Worcester Coll., Oxford; Head of News Depart. FCO since 1973; late 2nd Lt. RRRC; MVO (4th class) 1957: *m.* 1958, Mary, only da. of the late Brig. Hudleston Noel Hedworth Williamson, DSO, MC [see Williamson, Bt., colls.], and has issue living, Anthony Charles, *b.* 1969,—Sarah Caroline, *b.* 1960,—Henrietta Mary, *b.* 1962,—Lucy Elizabeth, *b.* 1965. *Address,*—c/o FCO, SW1.

SISTER LIVING.

Lady Doris Hilda, *b.* 1896 : *m.* 1923, Lieut.-Com. Clare George Vyner, R.N. [see M. Northampton, colls.]. *Residence,*—Fountains Hall, Ripon.

COLLATERAL BRANCHES LIVING.

Grandchildren of the late Brig.-Gen. Lord Esmé Charles Gordon-Lennox, KCVO, CMG, DSO (infra):—

Issue of the late Capt. Reginald Arthur Charles Gordon-Lennox, OBE, *b.* 1910, *d.* 1965: *m.* 1942, Pamela Cicely (4, Woodley Rd., Plumstead, CP, S. Africa), da. of Capt. Christopher Digby Leyland, Life Gds. [Cotterell, Bt.]:—

James David Charles (1A, Lawrence Rd., W5), *b.* 1944: *m.* 1973, Sally Cooper, da. of John Roger Cooper Brain.——Clare Evelyn, *b.* 1946: *m.* 1967, Edmund Clive Lardner-Burke, of 4, Woodley Rd., Plumstead, CP, S. Africa.

Issue of the late Brig.-Gen. Lord Esmé Charles Gordon-Lennox, K.C.V.O., **C.M.G., D.S.O., 2nd son of 7th Duke,** *b.* 1875, *d.* 1949 : *m.* 1st, 1909, the Hon. Hermione Frances Caroline Fellowes, who *d.* 1971, having obtained a divorce, 1923 [she *m.* 2ndly, 1923, as his second wife, Baron (Rudolph) Cederstrom, who *d.* 1947], da. of 2nd Baron De Ramsey; 2ndly, 1923, Rosamond Lorys, who *d.* 1961, da. of the late Vice-Adm. Norman Craig Palmer, CVO:—

(By 2nd marriage) Sara Carolyn, *b.* 1933: *m.* 1st, 1956, Sir William Andrew Malcolm Martin Oliphant Montgomery Cuninghame, 11th Bt., who *d.* 1959; 2ndly, 1959, Ewen Alastair John Fergusson, son of Sir Ewen Macgregor Field Fergusson, and has issue living, (by 2nd m.) Ewen Alexander Nicholas, *b.* 1965,—Anna Rosamund Harriot, *b.* 1961,—Iona Frances, *b.* 1967. *Residence,*—1, Putney Park Av., SW15.

Issue of the late Major Lord Bernard Charles Gordon Lennox, 3rd son of 7th **Duke,** *b.* 1878, *d.* (killed in action) 1914 : *m.* 1907, the Hon. Evelyn, who *d.* (result of enemy action) 1944, dau. of 1st Baron Loch :—

Sir George Charles, *KBE, CB, CVO, DSO, b.* 1908; ed. at Eton; Lt.-Gen. late Grenadier Guards; a Page of Honour to H.M. 1921-24; G.O.C. 3rd Div. 1957-59, Comdt., Roy. Mil Acad., Sandhurst 1959-63; Dir.-Gen. of Mil. Training, War Office 1963-64 and G.O.C.-in-C. Scottish Command 1964-66; Col. The Gordon Highlanders 1965; appointed King of Arms of Order of British Empire 1968; 1939-45 War in N. Africa and Italy (wounded, despatches, DSO); DSO 1943, CVO 1952; CB (Mil.) 1959, KBE (Mil.)1964: *m.*1931, Nancy Brenda, da. of Maj. Sir Lionel Edward Hamilton Marmaduke Darell, DSO, 6th Bt., and has issue living, Bernard Charles, *MBE* (Hill House, Eversley, Hants.), *b.* 1932; ed. at Eton; Lt.-Col. Grenadier Guards; a Page of Honour to HM 1946-49; MBE (Mil.) 1968: *m.* 1958, Sally-Rose, only da. of J. W. Warner, of The Old Rectory, Stanton, nr. Broadway, Worcs., and has issue living, Edward Charles *b.* 1961; appointed a Page of Honour to HM 1974, Angus Charles *b.* 1964, Charles Bernard *b.* 1970,—David Henry Charles, *b.* 1935; ed. at Eton; Lt.-Col. Gren. Gds. *Residence,*—Gordon Castle, Fochabers, Morayshire.——*Sir* Alexander Henry Charles, *KCVO, CB, DSO, b.* 1911; Rear-Adm. (ret.); Pres. of RN Coll., Greenwich 1961-62, since when Serjeant at Arms, House of Commons; 1939-45 War with N. Russia Convoys (despatches, DSO); DSO 1942, CB (Mil) 1962: *m.* 1936, Barbara, da. of the late Maj.-Gen. Julian Steele, and has issue living, Michael Charles, *b.* 1938; ed. at Eton; Lt.-Cdr. RN: *m.* 1974, Jennifer Susan, da. of the late Capt. the Hon. Vicary Paul Gibbs [see B. Aldenham, colls.],—Andrew Charles, *b.* 1948; Lt. RN: *m.* 1973, Julia Jane Neill, da. of the late Dr. J. Neill Morrison. *Residences,*—Farm Cottage, The Quag, Midhurst, Sussex; Culkein Lodge, Drumbeg, by Lairg, Sutherland.

Issue of the late Col. Lord Algernon Charles Gordon-Lennox, 2nd son of 6th **Duke,** *b.* 1847, *d.* 1921 : *m.* 1886, *Dame* Blanche, *D.B.E.,* who *d.* 1945, dau. of the late Col. the Hon. Charles Henry Maynard [V. Maynard, ext.]:—

Hon. Ivy (*Duchess of Portland*), *D.B.E.,* *b.* 1887 ; was a Maid of Honour to Queen Alexandra 1912-15 ; Chm. of Council of National Asso. for Prevention of Tuberculosis; D.B.E. (Civil) 1958 : *m.* 1915, the 7th Duke of Portland. *Residences,*—Welbeck Woodhouse, Worksop, Notts; Langwell, Berriedale, Caithness.

Grandson of the late Rt. Hon. Lord Walter Charles Gordon-Lennox, 4th son of 6th Duke:—

Issue of the late Capt. Victor Charles Hugh Gordon-Lennox, *b.* 1897, *d.* 1968: *m.* 1st, 1923 (m. diss. 1928), Mrs. Anne Dorothy Bridge, who *d.* 1963, da. of the late Edward Cazalet Browne; 2ndly, 1932 (m. diss. 1940), da. of the late Adm. Sir Charles Edmund Kingsmill, of Ballybeg, Ottawa; 3rdly, 1958, Norah Julia Wensley (Pear Tree Cottage, Sinnington, York), da. of Edward Guy Schofield, of Leeds:—

(By 2nd m.) Henry George Charles (Villa L'Enclos, Chemin Ormond, Troinex, Geneva), *b.* 1934: *m.* 1958, Odile Steinmann, of Grenoble, France, and has issue living, Ian Charles, *b.* 1959, Philip George Hugh, *b.* 1962,—Geneviève Ann, *b.* 1961.

PREDECESSORS.—[1] CHARLES Lennox, *K.G.,* illegitimate son of King Charles II., by Louise Renée de Penancoet de Keroualle, (who was cr. by H.M. *Baroness Petersfield, Countess of Fareham, and Duchess of Portsmouth* for life, and by Louis XIV. of France Duchess d'Aubigny) ; *b.* 1672; cr. *Baron of Settrington,* of Settrington, co. York, *Earl of March, Duke of Richmond* (peerage of England) 1675, and *Lord of Torboulton,* of Torboulton, *Earl of Darnley* and *Duke of Lennox* (peerage of Scotland) 1675 ; *d.* 1723; *s.* by his son [2] CHARLES, *K.G., K.B., P.C.,* 2nd Duke, *b.* 1701; was High Constable of England at coronation of George II., Master of the Horse and on four occasions a Lord Justice to administer the government during the absence of the king; in 1734, on the death of his grandmother, he became *Duke d'Aubigny* (cr. 1684) in France; *d.* 1750; *s.* by his son [3] CHARLES, *K.G.,* 3rd Duke, *b.* 1735 ; carried the sceptre at the Coronation of George III.; was Ambassador to France 1765, Principal Sec. of State 1766, and Master-Gen. of the Ordnance 1782 ; *d.s.p.* 1806 ; *s.* by his nephew [4] CHARLES, *K.G.,* 4th Duke, *b.* 1764 ; a Gen. in the Army ; M.P. for Sussex 1790-1806 ; was Lord-Lieut. of Ireland 1807-13, and Gov.-Gen. of Canada 1818-19 : *m.* Charlotte. dau. of Alexander, 4th Duke of Gordon; *d.* 1819; *s.* by his son [5] CHARLES, *K.G., P.C.,* 5th Duke; *b.* 1791; was Lord-Lieut. of Sussex; assumed in 1836 by patent the additional surname of Gordon; the title of Duke D'Aubigny was confirmed to him and registered by Parliament of France 1777, and re-confirmed 1816 by Louis XVIII.; *m.* 1817, Lady Carolin, Paget, dau. of 1st Marquess of Anglesey ; *d.* 1860 ; *s.* by his son [6] CHARLES HENRY, *K.G., P.C., D.C.L., LL.D.,* 6th Duke of Richmond and Lennox; *b.* 1818 ; Lord-Lieut. of co. Banff, and an Elder Brother of Trinity House ; M.P. for W. Sussex (C) 1841-60; A.D.C. to Com.-in-Ch. (Duke of Wellington and Viscount Hardinge) 1842-54, Pres. of Poor Law Board 1859, and of Board of Trade 1867-8 and 1885, Lord Pres. of Council 1874-80, *ex officio* Keeper of the Great Seal of Scotland, Sec. for Scotland and Vice-Pres. of Committee of Council on Education in Scotland 1885-6; cr. *Earl of Kinrara,* and *Duke of Gordon* (peerage of United Kingdom) 1876 : *m.* 1843, Frances Harriet, who *d.* 1887, el. dau. of the late Algernon Frederic Greville ; *d.* 1903; *s.* by his son [7] CHARLES HENRY, *K.G., G.C.V.O., C.B.,* 7th Duke; *b.* 1845 ; sat as M.P. for W. Sussex (C) 1869-85, and for S.W., or Chichester, Div. of Sussex 1885-8 ; Hereditary Constable of Inverness Castle, an A.D.C. to Queen Victoria, King Edward VII., and King George V. 1896-1920, Lord-Lieut. and Custos Rotulorum of cos. Elgin and Banff 1903-28, and Chancellor of Aberdeen Univ. 1917-28; bore Sceptre with Dove at Coronation of King George V. 1911: *m.* 1st, 1868, Amy Mary, who *d.* 1879, el. dau. of the late Percy Ricardo, of Bramley Park, Guildford ; 2ndly, 1882, Isabel Sophie, who *d.* 1887, dau. of William George Craven; *d.* 1928 ; *s.* by his son [8] CHARLES HENRY, *D.S.O., M.V.O.,* 8th Duke ; *b.* 1870 ; Lieut.-Col. Reserve of Officers ; S. Africa 1900 (despatches, D.S.O.) ; accompanied Special Mission to Foreign Courts to announce Accession of King George V. 1910 ; appointed Lord Lt. of co. Elgin 1928 : *m.* 1893, Hilda Madaleine, DBE, who *d.* 1971, el. da. of Henry A. Brassey, of Preston Hall, Aylesford; *d.* 1935; *s.* by his son [9] FREDERICK CHARLES, 9th Duke and present peer; also Earl of March, Earl of Darnley, Earl of Kinrara, Baron of Settrington, and Lord of Torboulton.

RIDLEY, VISCOUNT. (Ridley.) [Viscount U.K. 1900, Bt. G.B. 1756.]

Constant in loyalty.

MATTHEW WHITE RIDLEY, *TD*, 4th Viscount, and 8th Baronet; *b.* July 29th, 1925; *s.* 1964; ed. at Eton, and at Balliol Coll., Oxford; Brevet-Col. Northumberland Hussars (TA); a DL, and Alderman for Northumberland, and Chm. of Northumberland Co. Council; ADC to Gov. of Kenya 1952-53: *m.* 1953, Lady Anne Katherine Lumley, da. of 11th Earl of Scarbrough, and has issue.

Arms,—Gules, on a chevron argent between three falcons proper, as many pellets. *Crest,*—A bull passant the tail turned over the back gules. *Supporters,*—Two bulls gules, each gorged with a collar gemelle or and charged on the shoulder with three mullets, pierced argent.

Seat,—Blagdon, Seaton Burn, Northumberland.

SON LIVING.

Hon. MATTHEW WHITE, *b.* Feb. 7th, 1958.

DAUGHTERS LIVING.

Hon. Cecilia Anne, *b.* 1953.
Hon. Rose Emily, *b.* 1956.
Hon. Mary Victoria, *b.* 1962.

BROTHER LIVING.

Hon. Nicholas, *MP*, *b.* 1929; ed. at Eton, and at Balliol Coll., Oxford; late Capt. Northumberland Hussars (TA); an AMICE; Joint Parl. Sec., Min. of Tech. 1970, and under-Sec. of State, Dept. of Trade and Industry 1970-72; MP for Cirencester and Tewkesbury (*C*) since 1959: *m.* 1950 (m. diss. 1974), the Hon. Clayre Campbell, da. of 4th Baron Stratheden and Campbell, and has issue living, Jane, *b.* 1953,—Susanna, *b.* 1955,—Jessica Clayre, *b.* 1957. *Residence,*—The Old Rectory, Naunton, Cheltenham.

AUNTS LIVING. (*Daughters of 2nd Viscount.*)

Hon. Gwladys Marjorie, *b.* 1900: *m.* 1920, Capt. Cecil Gordon-Ives, Scots Guards, who *d.* 1928. *Residence,*—Rock House, Annestown, Waterford.
Hon. Vivien Catherine Evelyn, *b.* 1906; re-admitted to British Nationality 1940: *m.* 1934, Baron Hans Karg von Bebenburg, and has issue living, Margaret, *b.* 1937. *Residence,*—10, Hapsburgergasse, Vienna, I, Austria.

COLLATERAL BRANCHES LIVING.

Grandson of the late Major the Hon. Sir Jasper Nicholas Ridley, K.C.V.O., O.B.E. (*infra*):—
Issue of the late Jasper Alexander Maurice Ridley, Lieut. King's Roy. Rifle Corps, *b.* 1913, *d.* (on active ser. in Italy) 1943: *m.* 1939, the Hon. Helen Laura Cressida Bonham Carter (Pinchards, Stockton, Warminster, Wilts), da. of Baroness Asquith of Yarnbury (Life By. ext.):—
Adam Nicholas (52, Novello St., SW6), *b.* 1942: *m.* 1970, Lady Katherine Rose Celestine Asquith, da. of the 2nd Earl of Oxford and Asquith.

Issue of the late Maj. the Hon Sir Jasper Nicholas Ridley, K.C.V.O., O.B.E. 2nd son of 1st Viscount, *b.* 1887, *d.* 1951: *m.* 1911, Countess Nathalie, who *d.* 1968, da. of H. E. the late Count Benckendorff, Russian Ambassador in London:—
Oliver John, *b.* 1918; ed. at Eton, and at Balliol Coll., Oxford.——Katharine Sophy, *b.* 1912: *m.* 1941, Eugene Lampert, and has issue living, Alexander (348, Woodstock Rd., Oxford), *b.* 1943: *m.* 1965, Sally Box, and has issue living, Gregory *b.* 1965, Christopher *b.* 1967,—Nicholas (26, Lonsdale Rd., Harborne, Birmingham, 17), *b.* 1945: *m.* 1969, the Hon. Jill Mary Joan Lyon-Dalberg-Acton, da. of the 3rd Baron Acton, and has issue living, Katherine *b.* 1969, Frances *b.* 1971. *Residence,*—10, Canterbury Rd., Oxford.

(*In remainder to the Baronetcy only.*)

Grandson of the late Henry Colborne Maunoir Ridley, only son of the late Rev. William Henry Ridley, el. son of the late Rev. Henry Colborne Ridley, 3rd son of 2nd baronet:—
Issue of the late Capt. William Henry Wake Ridley, OBE, RN, *b.* 1887, *d.* 1955: *m.* 1913, Vera, who *d.* 1965, da. of Charles Walker, formerly of Launceston, Tasmania, and widow of Gerald Stuart Eardley-Wilmot [Eardley-Wilmot, Bt., colls.]:—
William Terence Colborne, *CB, OBE, b.* 1915; Rear-Adm.; Port Adm. HM Naval Base, Rosyth, 1971-72; 1939-45 War in S.W. Pacific (despatches twice); OBE (Mil.) 1954, CB (Mil.) 1968: *m.* 1938, Barbara, da. of R. L. Allen, of Hartford, Cheshire, and has issue living, Peter William Wake (c/o National Westminster Bank, The Hard, Portsmouth), *b.* 1939; Lt.-Cdr. RN: *m.* 1965, Jenifer, da. of Capt. W. J. M. Teale, RN, and has issue living, Timothy Jaspar William *b.* 1967, Nicolas Henry Sumner *b.* 1971. *Residence,*—The Green, Brompton Ralph, Taunton.

Granddaughter of the late Arthur William Ridley, 3rd son of the Rev. Nicholas James Ridley, 2nd son of the Rev. Henry Colborne Ridley (ante):—
Issue of the late Mervyn Adrian Toucher Ridley, *b.* 1886, *d.* 1951: *m.* 1920, Sybil Henrietta who *d.* 1966. dau. of the late Capt. Charles Robert Kennet Fergusson. late Cameron Highlanders [Fergusson, Bt., colls.], and widow of Capt. Malcolm Cosmo Bonsor [Bonsor, Bt.].
Susan Frances, *b.* 1921: *m.* 1949, Major Richard Mark Chaplin, Coldstream Guards, and has issue living, David Frank, *b.* 1951,—Mervyn Henry, *b.* 1958,—Serena Jane, *b.* 1954. *Residence,*—Stoke Albany House, Market Harborough.

Grandchildren of the late Rev. Oliver Matthew Ridley, 3rd son of the late Rev. Henry Colborne Ridley (ante):—
Issue of the late Major Edward Keane Ridley, *b.* 1861, *d.* 1947: *m.* 1903, Ethel Janet, who *d.* 1962, dau. of the late Alexander Forbes Tweedie:—
Edward Alexander Keane, *CB* (c/o Coutts & Co., 440 Strand, WC2), *b.* 1904; ed. at Wellington, and at Keble Coll., Oxford (B.A. 1925, M.A. 1955); Solicitor 1928; Principal Assist. Treasury Solicitor 1956-69; ret. 1969; CB (Civil) 1963.——Audrey Janet, *b.* 1916: *m.* 1941, Robert Ian Sworder, and has issue living, Robert Guy, *b.* 1953,—Rachael Helen, *b.* 1943,—Christina Elizabeth, *b.* 1946: *m.* 1974, Anthony J. A. Thompson. *Residence,*—Little Dudswell, Northchurch, Berkhampsted, Herts.

Issue of the late **Frank Colborne Ridley**, *b.* 1864, *d.* 1940: *m.* 1896, Eva Mary, who *d.* 1964, da. of Henry Houseman, of 23, Craven Hill Gdns., W.:—

Keith Vivian Colborne (Cherry Orchard, Rosemary Lane, Tidenham Chase, Chepstow, MP6 7OX, Gwent), *b.* 1904: *m.* 1933, Joan Madeline Marling, da. of the late Rev. E. Marling Roberts, and has issue living, Richard Nicholas (The Bell, Burleigh, Stroud, Glos.), *b.* 1939: *m.* 1st, 1963 (m. diss. 1973), Susan Gwynne Hadingham; 2ndly, 1974, Penelope Anne Brewer, and has issue living (by 1st m.), Caroline Lois *b.* 1964, Jacqueline Claire *b.* 1966,—Henry Colborne, *b.* 1944: *m.* 1969, Mary Randall Acierto, of Chicago, USA, and has issue living, Emily Marling *b.* 1971,—Gillian Elizabeth, *b.* 1937: *m.* 1960, John Hunt, and has issue living, Graham *b.* 1961, Natalie *b.* 1962.——Majorie Frances, *b.* 1901: *m.* 1st, 1921, Leonard Treise Morshead, RE, who *d.* 1931; 2ndly, 1931, Col. Sydney Keith Pembroke, Manchester Regt. (ret.), who *d.* 1950, and has issue living, (by 1st m.) *Rev.* Ivo Francis Trelawny (9, Thornton Rd., SW19), *b.* 1927: *m.* 1969, Anne Elizabeth, da. of Alfred Durham Eric Dunning, and has issue living, Timothy Francis *b.* 1969, Elizabeth Trelawny *b.* 1971, Sarah Anne (twin) *b.* 1971,—Lavender Evelyn Trelawny, *b.* 1922: *m.* 1950, Cecil Philip Creswell Martin, of 7, Clock House, Mead, Oxshott, Surrey, and has issue living, Claire Frances *b.* 1951, Virginia Rose *b.* 1953, Selina Mary *b.* 1957. *Residence*,—Clevelands, Steel's Lane, Oxshott, Surrey.

Issue of the late **Clarence Oliver Ridley**, O.B.E., *b.* 1869, *d.* 1951: *m.* 1st, 1896, Anne Arabella who *d.* 1898, dau. of Gregory William Eccles, formerly of 6, Melrose Road, Southfields, S.W.; 2ndly, 1900, Gertrude Henrietta, who *d.* 1951, second dau. of Henry Houseman (ante):—

(By 2nd marriage) Barbara Frances, *b.* 1907: *m.* 1937, Thomas C. S. Bullick, and has issue living, Timothy John (Athelings, Milton Abbas), *b.* 1938: *m.* 1965, Tessa Mary Garstang, and has issue living, Claire Elizabeth *b.* 1966, Judith *b.* 1969,—Caroline Bridget, *b.* 1941: *m.* 1965, Anthony Townsend Parker, of 9, Holton Rd., Buckingham, and has issue living, Rachel *b.* 1966, Alison *b.* 1968, Jessica *b.* 1971,—Sheila Mary, *b.* 1945: *m.* 1969, Geoffrey Scott Clark, RN, and has issue living, Jeremy Scott *b.* 1971. *Residence*,—The Leys, Tarrant Keynston, Blandford, Dorset.

Granddaughter of the late Col. John Henry Ellis Ridley, son of the late Rev. Henry John Ridley, son of the late Rev. Henry Ridley, D.D., brother of 2nd baronet.:—

Issue of the late **Brig.-Gen. Charles Parker Ridley**, C.B., *b.* 1855, *d.* 1937: *m.* 1879, Edyth Hamilton, dau. of the late George Beauchamp Cole, of Heatham House, Twickenham:—

Iris Brooke: *m.* 1911, Geoffrey Lowndes Wright, and has issue living, a son, *b.* 19—,—a son, *b.* 19—.

PREDECESSORS.—[1] Matthew White, only surviving son of, Matthew White; Sheriff of Northumberland 1756; *cr.* a *Baronet* 1756, with remainder to the heirs-male of his sister, Elizabeth, wife of Matthew Ridley, of Heaton; *d.* 1763; *s.* by his nephew [2] Sir Matthew White Ridley, 2nd Bt.; *b.* 1745: M.P., for Newcastle-upon-Tyne: *m.* 1777, Sarah, dau. of Benjamin Colborne, of Bath; *d.* 1813; *s.* by his el. son [3], Sir Matthew White, 3rd Bt.; *b.* 1778; M.P. for Newcastle-upon-Tyne: *m.* 1803, Laura, dau. of George Hawkins; *d.* 1836; *s.* by his el. son [4] Sir Matthew White, 4th Bt.; *b.* 1807; M.P. for Northumberland N. (*C*) 1859-60: *m.* 1841, Cecilia Anne, dau. of Sir James Parke (who became subsequently Lord Wensleydale); *d.* 1877; *s.* by his el. son [5] Sir Matthew White, 5th Bt.; *b.* 1842; *cr.* Viscount Ridley and Baron Wensleydale, of Blagdon and Blyth, co. Northumberland (peerage of United Kingdom) 1900; M.P. for Northumberland N. (*C*) 1868-85, and for Blackpool Div. of Lancashire N. Aug. 1886 to Dec. 1900; Under Sec. of State for Home Depart. 1878-80, Financial Sec. to Treasury 1885-6, and Sec. of State for Home Depart. 1895-1900: *m.* 1873, the Hon. Mary Georgina Marjoribanks, who *d.* 1899, dau. of 1st Baron Tweedmouth; *d.* 1904; *s.* by his son [6] Matthew White, 2nd Viscount; *b.* 1874; M.P. for Stalybridge (*C*) 1900-1904: *m.* 1899, the Hon. Rosamond Cornelia Gladys Guest, who *d.* 1947, dau. of 1st Baron Wimborne; *d.* 1916; *s.* by his el. son [7] Matthew White, *CBE*, 3rd Viscount; *b.* 1902; Chm. of Northumberland Co. Council 1940-46 and 1949-52, and Regional Controller, N. Region, Min. of Production 1942-49; Hon. Col. Northumberland Hussars (TA) 1962-64: *m.* 1924, Ursula, *OBE*, who *d.* 1967, da. of Sir Edwin Landseer Lutyens, OB, KCIE, PRA, LLB [E. Lytton]; *d.* 1964; *s.* by his el son [8] Matthew White, 4th Viscount and present peer; also Baron Wensleydale.

RIPON, LORD BISHOP OF. (Moorman.)

Right Rev. John Richard Humpidge Moorman, *DD*, DLitt, son of the late Prof. Frederic William Moorman, of Leeds; *b.* June 4th, 1905; ed. at Gresham's Sch., Holt, and at Emmanuel Coll., Camb. (MA, DD, Hon. Fellow 1959); Hon. Litt.D. Leeds, and St. Bonadventure, USA; R. of Fallowfield, Manchester 1935-42; V. of Lanercost, Cumberland 1945-46, Principal of Chichester Theological Coll., and Chancellor of Chichester Cathedral 1946-56, and Preb. of Heathfield in Chichester Cathedral 1956-59; consecrated 9th Bishop of Ripon 1959; *m.* 1930, Mary Caroline, DLitt, only da. of the late Prof. George Macaulay Trevelyan, OM, CBE [see Trevelyan Bt., (cr. 1874) colls.].

Patron of forty-seven livings, and of eight alternately with others, all the Canonries in his Cathedral, and of the Archdeaconries of Richmond and Leeds, and the Chancellorship of the Diocese.

The See of Ripon was founded in 678, but was afterwards merged in the See of York and reconstituted a separate diocese in 1836.

Episcopal Signature,—"John Ripon."

Arms of the See,—Argent, on a saltire gules, two keys in saltire, wards upwards or, on chief of the second a holy lamb proper.

Residence,—Bishop Mount, Ripon, Yorks. HG4 5DP.

RITCHIE-CALDER. BARON, (Calder.) [Life Baron 1966.]

PETER RITCHIE CALDER, *CBE*, son of David Lindsay Calder, of Forfar; *b.* July 1st, 1906; ed. at Forfar Acad.; MA Edinburgh; Author and Journalist; Montague Burton Prof. of International Relations, Edinburgh Univ. 1961-67; in Foreign Office 1941-45; Chm. of Metrication Board 1969-72; Privy Council Member of Gen. Council of Open Univ. since 1969; Senior Fellow Center for Study of Democratic Insts., Santa Barbara, Cal. since 1972; *cr.* CBE (Civil) 1945 and *Baron Ritchie-Calder, of Balmashannar, Royal Burgh of Forfar (Life Baron) 1966: *m.* 1927, Mabel Jane Forbes, da. of Dr. David McKail, of Glasgow, and has issue.

Residence,—1, Randolph Place, Edinburgh 3. *Clubs,*—Savile, University Staff, Press (Edinburgh), Scottish Arts, Century (New York).

SONS LIVING.
Hon. Nigel David Ritchie (8, The Chase, Furnace Green, Crawley, Sussex), *b.* 1931; ed. at Merchant Taylors' Sch., and at Sidney Sussex Coll., Camb. (MA); author and television script writer; Editor of *New Scientist* 1962-66: *m.* 1954, Elisabeth, da. of Alfred James Palmer and has issue.
Hon. Angus Lindsay Ritchie (6 Buckingham Terr., Edinburgh, 4), *b.* 1942; ed. at Wallington Co. Sch., King's Coll., Camb. (MA), and Univ. of Sussex (D.Phil); an Author: *m.* 1963, Jennifer, da. of Prof. David Daiches, and has issue.
Hon. Allan Graham Ritchie (10, Denny Crescent, SE11 4UY), *b.* 1944; ed. at New Sherwood Sch., Ewell Tech. Coll., and London Univ. (BSc, PhD); Lecturer in Mathematics, London Univ.: *m.* 1967, Anne Margaret, da. of Robert A. Wood, and has issue.

DAUGHTERS LIVING.
Hon. Fiona Catherine Ritchie, *b.* 1929; ed. at Rosebery Co. Sch., Epsom, London Sch. of Economics (BSc. Econ.), and Univ. of Essex: *m.* 1949, Dr. Ernest Rudd, of 51, High St., Brightlingsea, Essex, CO7 0AQ, and has issue.
Hon. Isla Elizabeth Ritchie, *b.* 1947; ed. at Nonsuch Co. Sch., Cheam, St. George's, Edinburgh, and Froebel Inst. of Education, Roehampton: *m.* 1971, Alan Evans, of 56, Bedford Court Mansions, Bedford Av., WC1.

RITCHIE OF DUNDEE, BARON. (Ritchie.) [Baron U.K. 1905.]

JOHN KENNETH RITCHIE, *PC*, 3rd Baron; *b.* Sept. 22nd, 1902; *s.* 1948; ed. at Winchester, and at Magdalen Coll., Oxford; a Stockbroker, Partner in the firm of Capel-Cure Myers, and a Director of Hutchinsons, Ltd.; Mayor of Winchelsea 1934; Dep. Chm. of Stock Exchange 1954-59, and 1965-72, Chm. 1959-1965; 1939-45 War as Capt. King's R. Rifle Corps; PC 1965: *m.* 1945, Joan Beatrice, who *d.* 1963, da. of the late Rev. Henry Charles Lenox Tindall, of Peasmarsh, Sussex. [The 3rd Baron *d.* Oct. 20th, 1975.]

Arms,—Argent, an anchor sable, on a chief of the last three lions' heads erased of the first. Crest,—Out of an Eastern crown or a unicorn's head argent, armed of the first and charged on the neck with an anchor sable. Supporters,—On either side an unicorn gules, gorged with an Eastern crown or, the *dexter* charged on the shoulder with a purse or, the *sinister* with a balance, also or.

Honour is acquired by virtue.

Residences,—Lower Bosney, Iden, Sussex ; 40 Thurloe Sq., S.W.7.

BROTHERS LIVING.
Hon. COLIN NEVILLE OWER, *b.* July 9th, 1908; ed. at Trin. Coll., Oxford (BA 1929): *m.* 1943, Anne Petronill (HUNTLEY), da. of H. C. Burra, of Rye, Sussex. *Residence,*—5, Fairmeadow, Rye Hill, Rye, Sussex.
Hon. Harold Malcolm, *b.* 1919; ed. at Stowe, and at Trin. Coll., Oxford (MA); 1940-45 War as Capt. KRRC: *m.* 1948, Anne, da. of the late Col. C. G. Johnstone, MC, of Durban, S. Africa, and has issue living, Charles Rupert Rendall, *b.* 1958,—Philippa Jane *b.* 1954. *Residence,*—The Poplars, Beckley, Rye, Sussex.

SISTER LIVING.
Hon. Margaret Ruth, *b.* 1913 : *m.* 1943, Major (William Arthur) Martin Chippindale, Worcestershire Regt. (ret.) [B. Sandys], and has issue living, Philip John, *b.* 1949,—Jean Margaret, *b.* 1945. *Residence,*—Wintons, Peasmarsh, Rye, Sussex.

COLLATERAL BRANCH LIVING.
Issue of the late Lieut.-Col. the Hon. Harold Ritchie, D.S.O. (with Bar), The Cameronians (Scottish Rifles), younger son of 1st Baron, *b.* 1876, *d.* (of wounds in action during European War) 1918 : *m.* 1907, Ella, who *d.* 1956 [she *m.* 2ndly, 1922, Surg.-Lieut.-Col. Evelyn John Hansler Luxmoore, M.C., Life Guards, who *d.* 1955], dau. of the late Robert Chambers Priestley, of Terriers House, High Wycombe, Bucks :—

Ian Charles (Highway House, Hog's Back, Seale, Farnham, Surrey) *b.* 1908: *m.* 1st, 1931 (m. diss. 1946), Ann Dundas, da. of the late Gen. Sir Robert Dundas Whigham, GCB, KCMG, DSO; 2ndly, 1946, Pamela Eveleen Elizabeth (WHITE), da. of Reginald Vickers, of Broomwood, Kettlewell Hill, Woking, and has issue living, (by 1st m.) Harold Bruce, *b.* 1933.—Fiona, *b.* 1934.——William Nigel, *b.* 1914; is Flt.-Lt. RAF Vol. Res.: *m.* 1939, Baroness Sibylla, da. of the late Baron von Hirschberg of Murnau, Bavaria, and has issue living, James Antony Gregor, *b.* 1945,—Andrew William, *b.* 1947,—Caroline Elisabeth (*Hon. Mrs. Hugh Gathorne-Hardy*) *b.* 1943: *m.* 1971, the Hon. Hugh Gathorne-Hardy [see E. Cranbrook]. *Residence,*—Mariners, Bradfield, Berks.——Jean, *b.* 1910: *m.* 1932, Capt. John Buller Edward Hall, RN, who *d.* (killed in action during European War) 1940, and has issue living, Joanna Mary, *b.* 1934: *m.* 1st, 1958 (m. diss. 1966), David Kenneth Poland: 2ndly, 1967, Arthur Gordon Fairley, of 9, The Avenue, Petersfield, Hants., and has issue living, (by 1st m.) Kevin John *b.* 1959, Jeremy David *b.* 1961,—Penelope Jane, *b.* 1937: *m.* 1963, Richard Peter Ellis, of Appletrees, Brenchley, Kent, and has issue living, Thomas *b.* 1964, Robert John *b.* 1965, Katherine Mary *b.* 1967, Lucy Jane *b.* 1969. *Residence,*—Restgarth, Streatley-on-Thames, Berks.——Pamela Helen, *b.* 1915: *m.* 1939, James Dunbar Whatman. MC, late Maj. Gren. Gds. [Child, Bt. (cr. 1919)], and has issue living, Elizabeth Jean, *b.* 1942,—Ann Mary (twin), *b.* 1942,—Rosemary Pamela, *b.* 1946. *Residence,*—Northcote Hill, Shamley Green, Guildford, Surrey.

PREDECESSORS—[1] *Rt. Hon.* CHARLES THOMSON Ritchie, *P.C.* (whose el. brother was cr. a Baronet 1903), son of the late William Ritchie, of Rockhill, Broughty Ferry, *b.* 1838 ; M.P. for Tower Hamlets (*C*) Feb. 1874 to Nov. 1885, for Tower Hamlets, St. George Div. 1885 to 1892, and for Croydon May 1895 to Dec. 1905 ; Sec. to the Admiralty June 1885 to Jan. 1886, Pres. of Local Govt. Board Aug. 1886 to Aug. 1892 (with a seat in the Cabinet from April 1887), Pres. of Board of Trade (with a seat in the Cabinet) June 1895 to Oct. 1900, Sec. of State for Home Depart. Oct. 1900 to Aug. 1902, and Chancellor of the Exchequer Aug. 1902 to Sept. 1903 ; cr. *Baron Ritchie of Dundee,* of Welders, Chalfont St. Giles, co. Buckingham (peerage of United Kingdom) Dec. 1905 : *m.* 1858, Margaret, who *d.* 1905, dau. of the late Thomas Ower, of Perth ; *d.* Jan. 1906 ; *s.* by his el. surviving son [2] CHARLES, 2nd Baron ; *b.* 1866 ; was Chm. of Port of London Authority 1925-41, and Pres. of Dock and Harbour Authorities Asso. 1938-41 : *m.* 1898, Sarah Ruth, who *d.* 1950, dau. of the late Louis Jennings M.P. ; *d* 1948 ; *s.* by his el. surviving son [3] JOHN KENNETH, 3rd baron and present peer.

RIVERDALE, BARON. (Balfour.) [Baron U.K. 1935, Bt. U.K. 1929.]

IN ·ARDUIS·FIDELIS

Faithful in difficulties.

ROBERT ARTHUR BALFOUR, 2nd Baron, and 2nd Baronet ; *b.* Sept. 1st, 1901 ; *s.* 1957 ; ed. at Aysgarth, and at Oundle ; late Lt. Cdr. RNVR; Pres. of Balfour & Darwins, Ltd., and a Dir. of subsidiary Cos. of the Group, Patron of Sheffield Savings Bank (Gov. 1948-58), Town Trustee of Sheffield Town Trust, a DL of S. Yorks. county; elected Master of Cutlers' Co. of Sheffield 1946; appointed Consul for Belgium for Sheffield area 1945; Pres. of Milling Cutter and Reamer Trade Assocn. 1936-54 (Vice-Pres. 1954-57, Hon. Vice-Pres. 1958), of Twist Drill Traders' Assocn. 1946-55, and of National Federation of Engineers' Tool Manufacturers 1951-57 (Hon. Vice-Pres. since 1957), and Chm. of British Council of Australian Assocn. of British Manufacturers 1954-57; Pres. of Sheffield Chamber of Commerce 1950 (Joint Hon. Sec. since 1957), and a Member of British National Cttee., International Chamber of Commerce, of National Production Advisory Cttee., and of W. Hemisphere Exports Council (formerly Dollar Exports Council) 1957-61; a Member of Management Cttee. of High Speed Steel Assocn. 1947-65, of Executive Council of Assocn. of British Chambers of Commerce since 1950 (Vice-Pres. 1952-54, Chm. of Overseas Cttee. 1953-57, Dep. Pres. 1954-57, Pres. 1957-58), of Crucible and High Speed Steel Conference, Standing Cttee. since 1951, and Guardian of Standard of Wrought Plate within City of Sheffield since 1948; Commodore of Roy. Cruising Club 1961-66; 1939-45 War as Lt.-Cdr. RNVR; a Chevalier of Order of the Crown of Belgium, Officer of Order of Leopold II of Belgium, and Medaille Civique de Première Classe of Belgium: *m.* 1st 1926, Nancy Marguerite, who *d.* 1928, da. of the late Engineer Rear-Adm. Mark Rundle, DSO; 2ndly, 1933, Christian Mary, da. of the late Maj. Arthur Rowland Hill [see V. Hill, colls.], and has issue by 1st and 2nd marriages.

Arms,—Per chevron argent and sable, in chief two crosses pattée of the second and in base a sun in splendour per pale or and of the first. Crest,—In front of a dragon's head sable a sun as in the arms. Supporters,—On either side a dragon sable, each charged on the wing, the dexter with a garb. and the sinister with a cross pattée or.
Residence,—Ropes, Grindleford, near Sheffield. Clubs—Bath, Royal Cruising, Sheffield.

SONS LIVING. (By 1st marriage.)

Hon. MARK ROBIN, *b.* July 16th, 1927; ed. at Aysgarth Sch., Yorks., and at Trin. Coll. Sch., Port Hope, Canada; Exec. Chm. Balfour Darwins, Ltd., Eagle & Globe Steel Co., Ltd., Eagle & Globe Pty., Ltd., and Arthur Balfour, Ltd., a Member of Exec. Cttee. of BISPA (former Chm. of Tool Steel Product Gp., BISPA); Pres. of National Fedn. of Engineers' Tool Manufacturers; Chm. of Right Trades House, Ltd., Chm. of Sheffield Rolling Mills, Ltd. 1969-74; a Vice-Consil for Finland, a Freeman of Blacksmiths Co., Master of Cutlers' Co., Sheffield 1959: *m.* 1959, Susan Ann, el. da. of R. P. Phillips, of Gartmore, 390, Sandygate Rd., Sheffield, and has issue living, Anthony Robert, *b.* 1960,—Nancy Ann, *b.* 1963,—Kate Frances, *b.* 1967. *Residence,*—The White House, Hollow Meadows, Sheffield. *Club,*—Royal Automobile, Sheffield.

(By 2nd marriage,)
Hon. David Rowland, *b.* 1938 ; ed. at Harrow, and at Queens' Coll., Camb.

DAUGHTER LIVING. *(By 2nd marriage.)*
Hon. Frances Christian, *b.* 1946.

BROTHER LIVING.
Hon. Francis Henry, *TD, b.* 1905; ed. at Oundle; late Maj. RA (TA); Knt. of Order of Dannebrog of Denmark; Vice-Consul for Denmark 1947-60: *m.* 1st, 1932, Muriel Anne, who *d.* 1970, da. of the late Eng. Rear-Adm. Ralph Berry; 2ndly, 1971, Daphne Cecelia, da. of A. C. Moss, of Rochfort, Bathampton, Bath, and has issue living, (by 1st m.) Arthur Michael (The Winnats, 120, Valley Rd., Chorleywood, Herts.), *b.* 1938; ed. at Oundle, and at Bristol Univ. (BSc 1960); a GIMechE: *m.* 1962, Rita Ann, el. da. of L. C. Fance, of 21, Ashley Close, Charlton Kings, Cheltenham, and has issue living, Edward Francis *b.* 1965, James Henry *b.* 1966, Anna Louise *b.* 1971,—Jeremy Ralph, *b.* 1948: *m.* 1974, Wendy, da. of W. H. Seal, of 153, Southdown Rd., Bath,—Bridget Anne, *b.* 1933: *m.* 1957, Ewan Peter Graham, of, 8, Shrimpton Close, Knotty Green, Beaconsfield, Bucks., and has issue living, Philip James *b.* 1959, Stephen Paul *b.* 1960, Adam Timothy *b.* 1964,—Frances Elizabeth, *b.* 1934: *m.* 1958, Charles David Plows, MB, of Tanglewood, 7, Moor Hall Drive, Four Oaks, Sutton Coldfield, and has issue living, Ian Julian *b.* 1960, Christopher Mark *b.* 1962. *Residence,*—Garden Cottage, Bathampton, Bath.

SISTERS LIVING.
Hon. Mary Josephine (*Hon. Lady Fooks*), *b.* 1900; ARCM: *m.* 1st, 1931, Ernest Henry Bruce, Indian Police (ret.), who *d.* 1948; 2ndly, 1954, as his third wife, Sir Raymond Hatherell Fooks, CBE, KPM. *Residence,*—Broom Hill Copse, Boar's Hill, Oxford.
Hon. Primrose Keighley, *b.* 1913: *m.* 1933, Oliver Grahame Hall, who *d.* 1974, having assumed by deed poll 1945 the christian name of Claude in lieu of Oliver, and the surname of Muncaster in lieu of his patronymic and has issue living, Martin Grahame Muncaster (Clouds Hill, Lynchmere, Haslemere), *b.* 1934: *m.* 1959, Iona Gilbert, and has issue living, Timothy Grahame MacGeoch *b.* 1960, Oliver Martin Keighley *b.* 1964, Miranda Jane *b.* 1962,—Clive Muncaster (The Manor Stables, Gt. Haseley, Oxford), *b.* 1936: *m.* 1959, Ursula Mary, el. da. of the late Capt. Edward Brotherton-Ratcliffe, and has issue living, Maximilian Nicholas Clive *b.* 1960, Peregrine Luke *b.* 1962, Crispin Claude *b.* 1965, Caspar Amadeus *b.* 1967, Quentin Augustine *b.* 1971. *Residence,*—Whitelocks, Sutton, Pulborough, Sussex.

PREDECESSOR.—[1] ARTHUR Balfour, *G.B.E.*, son of the late Herbert Balfour ; *b.* 1873 ; a Steel Manufacturer, Chm. of Arthur Balfour & Co., Ltd., and of C. Meadows & Co., Ltd., of Sheffield, Chm. of Advisory Council for Scientific and Industrial Research 1937-57, Vice-Consul for Denmark 1899-1947, Master Cutler of Sheffield 1911-12, Pres. of Asso. of British Chambers of Commerce 1923-4, and of British Council 1947-50 ; *cr.* K.B.E. (Civil) 1923, a *Baronet* 1929, Baron *Riverdale,* of Sheffield, co. York (peerage of United Kingdom) 1935, and G.B.E. (Civil) 1942 : *m.* 1899, Frances Josephine Keighley (a C.St.J.), who *d.* 1960, dau. of the late Charles Henry Bingham ; *d.* 1957 : *s.* by his el. son [2] ROBERT ARTHUR, 2nd Baron and present peer.

ROBBINS, BARON. (Robbins.) [Life Baron 1959.]

LIONEL CHARLES ROBBINS, *CH, CB,* son of the late Rowland Richard Robbins, CBE, of Hollycroft, Sipson, Middlesex; *b.* Nov. 22nd, 1898; ed. at Southall County Sch., at Univ. Coll., London, and at London Sch. of Economics (BSc Economics; Hon. Fellow); MA Oxford; Dr. in Science, Economics and Finance, Technical Univ. of Lisbon; LLD Strasbourg, Camb., Leicester, and California; LHD Columbia; DLitt Durham, Exeter, Strathclyde, Sheffield, and Heriot Watt; DSc (Econ.) London; a Fellow and Lecturer of New Coll., Oxford 1927-29; Hon. Fellow, Univ. Coll., London, Manchester Coll. of Tech. and London Graduate Sch. of Business Studies; Dr. of York Univ; Hon. DUniv. Stirling; Hon. LLD, Council of Nat. Acad. Awards; a Dir. of Roy. Opera House since 1956; Prof. of Economics, London Univ. 1929-61, Dir. of Economic Section of War Cabinet Secretariat 1941-45, a Member of Board of Trustees of National Gallery 1952-59 (Chm. 1954-59, and 1962-67), again 1960-67, and 1967-74, and a Member of Board of Trustees of Tate Gallery 1953-59, and 1962-67; Chm. of *Financial Times* 1961-70; a FBA, a Member of Accademia del Lincei, Rome, American Philosophical Soc., and American Acad. of Arts and Sciences, and an Associate Fellow of National Acad. of Education, America, and author of " An Essay on the Nature and Significance of Economic Science," " The Theory of Economic Policy in English Classical Political Economy," " Autobiography of an Economist," and other works; Pres. of Roy. Economic Soc. 1954-56, and of British Acad. 1963-67; Chancellor of Univ. of Stirling since 1968, and Chm. of Court of Govs. London Sch. of Economics 1969-73; 1914-18 War with RFA; *cr.* CB (Civil) 1944, and *Baron Robbins,* of Clare Market, City of Westminster (Life Baron) 1959, and CH 1968; *m.* 1924, Iris Elizabeth, da. of A. G. Gardiner, of The Spinney, Whiteleaf, Bucks., and has issue.

Residence,—10, Meadway Close, NW11. *Club,*—Reform.

SON LIVING.
Hon. Richard, *b.* 1927; ed. at Dauntsey's Sch., and at New Coll., Oxford: *m.* 1st, 1952 (m. diss. 1961); 2ndly, 1961, Mrs. Brenda Dorothy Rooker Roberts, da. of Douglas E. Clark, and has issue by 1st marriage. *Residence,*—50, Highbury Hill, N5.

DAUGHTER LIVING.
Hon. Anne, *b.* 1925; ed. at N. London Collegiate Sch., and at Univ. Coll., London: *m.* 1958, Christopher Johnson, of 39, Wood Lane, N6, and has issue.

ROBENS OF WOLDINGHAM, BARON. (Robens.) [Life Baron 1961.]

ALFRED ROBENS, *PC*, son of the late George Robens, of Manchester; *b.* Dec. 18, 1910; Hon. DCL Newcastle; Hon. LLD Leicester, and Manchester; Hon. MIMin.E; a Fellow of Manchester Coll. of Science and Tech.; a Member of Manchester City Council 1942-45, PPS to Min. of Transport 1945-47, Parl. Sec. to Min. of Fuel and Power 1947-51, Min. of Labour and National Ser. April to Oct. 1951, and Dep. Chm. of National Coal Board Oct. 1960 to Feb. 1961, and Chm. 1961-71; a Member of Roy. Commn. on Trade Unions and Employers' Assocns. 1965-68; a Gov. of Queen Elizabeth Training Coll. for Disabled since 1951, and of London Sch. of Economics since 1965, Chm. of Board of Govs., Guy's Hosp. since 1965, a Dir. of Bank of England, and of Times Newspapers since 1966; Pres. of Advertising Assocn. 1963-67; Chm. of Joint Steering Cttee. for Malta 1967; Chancellor of Univ. of Surrey since 1966. Chm. of Council of Manchester Business Sch. since 1964, a member of NEDC 1962-72, Dep. Chm. of Foundation on Automation and Human Development since 1962, Chm. of Special Cttee. of Enquiry into Health and Safety of Persons in Employment, of Vickers Ltd., and of Johnson Matthey Ltd.; MP for Wansbeck Div. of Northumberland (*Lab.*) 1945-50, and for Blyth 1950-60; cr. PC 1951, and *Baron Robens of Woldingham*, of Woldingham, co. Surrey (Life Baron) 1961: *m.* 1936, Eva, da. of Frederick Powell, of Manchester.

Residence,—Walton Manor, Walton on the Hill, Surrey.

ROBERTHALL, BARON. (Roberthall.) [Life Baron 1969.]

ROBERT LOWE ROBERTHALL, *KCMG*, *CB*, son of the late Edgar Hall, of Silverspur, Queensland; *b.* March 6th, 1901; assumed by deed poll 1969 (enrolled in Coll. of Arms) the surname of Roberthall; ed. at Qld. Univ. (B.Eng.), and Magdalen Coll., Oxford (MA); Fellow of Trin. Coll., Oxford 1927-50; Dir. of Economic Section, Cabinet Office 1947-53, and Economic Adviser to Govt. 1953-61; Prin. of Hertford Coll., Oxford 1964-67; cr. CB (Civil) 1950, KCMG 1954, and *Baron Roberthall*, of Silverspur, Queensland, and of Trenance, co. Cornwall: *m.* 1st, 1932, (m. diss. 1968), Laura Margaret, da. of the late George Edward Linfoot; 2ndly, 1968, Perilla Thyme, da. of the late Sir Richard Vynne Southwell, and formerly wife of Patrick Horace Nowell-Smith, and has issue by 1st m.

Residence,—34, Maunsel St., SW1.   *Club,*—Travellers'.

DAUGHTERS LIVING. (*By 1st m.*)

Hon. Felicity Margaret, *b.* 1936; ed. at Oxford High Sch. for Girls, and Lady Margaret Hall, Oxford; Research Assist., Mass. Inst. of Tech. 1957-66, Editor, Inst. for Research on Poverty (Univ. of Wisconsin) 1966-67, since when Assist. to Dir.: *m.* 1957, Thomas Skidmore, of 2025, Chadbourne Av., Madison, Wisconsin, USA, 53705, and has issue.

Hon. Anthea Mary, *b.* 1939; ed. at Oxford High Sch. for Girls, and Lady Margaret Hall, Oxford; Journalist: *m.* 1966, David Max Wilkinson, of 112, Hemingford Rd., N1, and has issue.

Roberts, see Baron Goronwy-Roberts.

ROBERTSON OF OAKRIDGE, BARON. (Robertson.)
[Baron U.K. 1961, Bt. U.K. 1919.]

WILLIAM RONALD ROBERTSON, 2nd Baron, and 3rd Baronet; *b.* Dec. 8th, 1930; *s.* 1974; ed. at Charterhouse; Maj. (ret.) R. Scots Greys: *m.* 1972, Celia Jane, yr. da. of William Elworthy, of the Manor House, Winterborne Monkton, Dorchester, Dorset.

Arms,—Gules, two swords in saltire argent, hilted and pommelled gold, the points downwards, between in chief a sun in splendour, in base a fleur-de-lis or, and in fesse two wolves' heads erased of the second. Crest,—Issuant from a coronet of fleur-de-lis or, a demi-wolf argent, gorged with an Eastern crown gold, supporting with the dexter paw a lance proper thereon a pennon per fesse gules and argent. Supporters.—Dexter, a grey charger in review order; sinister, a springbok proper.
Residence,—259, Dover House Rd., SW15.

SISTERS LIVING.

Hon. Christine Veronica Helen, *b.* 1927: *m.* 1949, Lt.-Col. Robert Hugh Cuming, MBE, JP, and has issue living, Brian Hugh Douglas, *b.* 1950; Lt. RN,—Alastair Nicholas, *b.* 1958,—Frances Mary Christine, *b.* 1952. *Residence,*—Hill Farm, Bragenham, Leighton Buzzard, Beds.

Hon. (Catharine) Fiona, *b.* 1939: *m.* 1965, Allan Claude Chapman, of Sillwood, Aspley Guise, Milton Keynes, Bucks., and has issue living, Caroline Fiona, *b.* 1968,—Katharine Jean (twin), *b.* 1968.

AUNT LIVING.

Helen Millicent (*Lady Vincent*), *b.* 1905: *m.* 1938, Sir Lacey Eric Vincent, d Bt. (*cr.* 1936), who *d.* 1963. *Residence,*—17, Bresby House, Rutland Gate, S.W.7.

WIDOW LIVING OF FIRST BARON.
EDITH CHRISTINA (*Edith, Baroness Robertson of Oakridge*); (Iles Green, Far Oakridge, Glos.); an OStJ; da. of James Black Macindoe, of 10, Park Circus, Glasgow: *m.* 1926, the 1st Baron, who *d.* 1974.

PREDECESSORS.—[1] *Field-Marshal Sir* WILLIAM ROBERT Robertson, *GCB, GCMG, GCVO, D.S.O.*, son of the late Thomas Charles Robertson ; *b.* 1860 ; enlisted in 16th Lancers 1877; commissioned as 2nd Lieut. 3rd Dragoon Guards 1888 ; Chitral Relief Force 1895 (severely wounded-D.S.O.), S. Africa 1900 as D.A.A.G., Army Head Quarters, European War 1914-19, becoming Ch. of Imperial Gen. Staff (Legion of Honour, K.C.B., Lieut.-Gen., Croix de Guerre, Orders of Crown of Italy, of White Eagle of Serbia with Swords, of Chia Ho of China, of St. Alexander Nevsky of Russia, and of Rising Sun of Japan, G.C.M.G., thanked by Parliament, *cr.* Baronet, granted £10,000) ; *cr.* a *Baronet* 1919 : *m.* 1894, Mildred Adelaide, who *d.* 1942, dau. of the late Lieut.-Gen. T. C. Palin, Indian Army, *d.* 1933; *s.* by his son [2] BRIAN HUBERT, *GCB, GBE, KCMG, KCVO, DSO, MC,* 2nd Bt., *b.* 1896; mil. Gov. of British Zone, Germany 1947-49, UK High Commr. for Germany 1949-50, C-in-C, MELF 1950-53, Chm. of British Transport Comman. 1953-61; Col. Comdr. RE 1950-60, and REME 1951-61; *cr. Baron Robertson of Oakridge,* of Oakridge, Glos. (peerage of UK) 1961: *m.* 1926, Edith Christina, OStJ, da. of James Black Macindoe, of Glasgow; *d.* 1974; *s.* by his son [3] WILLIAM RONALD, 2nd Baron and present peer.

ROBINS, BARONY OF. (Robins.) [Extinct 1962.]
DAUGHTERS LIVING OF FIRST BARON.
Hon. Diana Mary Wroughton, *b.* 1920: *m.* 1940, Col. John Offley Crewe-Read, OBE, of Croft House, Aston Tirrold, nr. Didcot, Oxon., and has issue living, David Offley, *b.* 1944,—Christohper Thomas Malcolm, *b.* 1951,—Joanna Christina (11, Gledhow Gdns., SW5), *b.* 1941: *m.* 1st 1962 (m. diss. 1969), Capt. John Anthony Frank Morton, late RHA; 2ndly, 1974, Alasdair James Hew Saunders, [see Culme-Seymour Bt., colls.].
Hon. Philippa Mary Ellis, *b.* 1923: *m.* 1946, Col. Patrick Danvers McCraith, MC, TD, DL, and has issue living, Michael Ellis, *b.* 1949,—Sally Victoria, *b.* 1947: *m.* 1971, Patrick George Francis Lort-Phillips, Capt. 9th/12th Lancers. [V. Cobham, colls.]. *Residence,*—Cranfield House, Southwell, Notts.

ROBINSON, BARONY OF. (Lister Robinson.) [Extinct 1952.]
DAUGHTER LIVING OF FIRST BARON.
Hon. Mary Teresa, *b.* 1914 : *m.* 1939 (marriage dissolved 1951), Paul Henry Mills Richey, D.F.C. and has issue living, Peter Michael, *b.* 1945,—Simon Anthony, *b.* 1947,—Ann Mary Teresa, *b.* 1941: *m.* 1960, Alistair Norris Cowin, of 24, Ilchester Mansions, Abingdon Rd., W.8, and has issue living, Amanda Mary Theresa *b.* 1961, Emma Teresa *b.* 1963,—Pauline Mary, *b.* 1943: *m.* 1967, Antony Michael Lawson-Smith, of 1, Willow Court, Willow Pl., SW1, and has issue living, Dominic *b.* 19—, Michael Charles *b.* 1971. *Residence,*—57, Sloane Gdns., SW1.

ROBOROUGH, BARON. (Lopes.) [Baron U.K. 1938, Bt. U.K. 1805.]

MASSEY HENRY EDGCUMBE LOPES, 2nd Baron, and 5th Baronet; *b.* Oct. 4th, 1903; *s.* 1938; ed. at Eton, and Ch. Ch., Oxford (BA); Hon. LLD Exeter; a DL 1946, Vice-Lt. 1951-58, Lord-Lt. since 1958, a JP of Devon County; Co. Alderman for Devon 1956-74; High Steward of Barnstaple; Chm. of SW Devon Divisional Education Exec. 1952-74, of Dartmoor National Park 1965-74, and of Devon Outward Bound Sch.; a Member of Duchy of Cornwall Council 1958-68; Maj. (ret.) R. Scots Greys; Hon. Col., Devon Army Cadet Force since 1967; 1939-45 War with Roy. Armoured Corps (wounded); ADC to Gov.-Gen. of S. Africa 1936; a KStJ: *m.* 1936, Helen, only da. of the late Lt.-Col. E. A. F. Dawson, Rifle Bde., and has issue.

Do to another as you would be done by.

Arms,—Quarterly: 1st and 4th, azure, a chevron or charged with three bars gemells; gules between three eagles rising of the seconed on a chief of the second five lozenges of the first; 2nd and 3rd, in a landscape field a fountain proper, thereout issuing a palm-tree also proper. *Crests,*—1st, a lion sejant erminois gorged with a collar gemelle gules, the dexter forepaw resting on a lozenge azure ; 2nd, a dexter arm couped and embowed, habited purpure, purfled and diapered or, cuffed argent, holding in the hand proper a palm-branch vert. *Supporters,—Dexter,* a lion proper gorged with a collar gemel and charged on the shoulder with a lozenge azure ; *sinister,* a bull also proper, charged on the shoulder with a like lozenge.
Seat,—Maristow, Roborough, S. Devon. *Residence,*—Bickham, Roborough, S. Devon.

SONS LIVING.
Hon. HENRY MASSEY (Bickham House, Roborough, Plymouth), *b.* Feb. 2nd, 1940; ed. at Eton; late Lt. Coldstream Guards: *m.* 1968, Robyn, el. da. of John Bromwich, of Stamford Hill, Bacchus Marsh, Vic., Aust., and has issue living, Massey John Henry, *b.* 1969,—Andrew James, *b.* 1971.
Hon. George Edward, *b.* 1945: *m.* 1975, the Hon. Sarah Violet Astor, da. of 2nd Baron Astor of Hever.

DAUGHTER LIVING.
Hon. Myra Bertha Ernestine, *b.* 1937.

SISTERS LIVING.

Hon. Margaret Beatrix, *b.* 1898: *m.* 1927, Maj. Henry Archibald Roger Graham, who *d.* 1970, [E. Pee, colls.], and has issue living, Roger Henry William GRAHAM-PALMER, *b.* 1941; assumed by deed poll 1968 the additional surname of Palmer: *m.* 1969, Vanessa Audrey, da. of Walter Neville Dru Drury, and has issue living, Archibald Roger *b.* 1970, Annabelle Rae *b.* 1971,—Gillian Mary Millicent (*Lady Wagner*), *b.* 1927; Licence ès Sciences Morales (Geneva) 1950: *m.* 1953, Sir Anthony Richard Wagner, KCVO, DLitt, FSA, Garter Principal King of Arms, of 68, Chelsea Sq., SW3, Wyndham Cottage, Aldeburgh, Suffolk, and has issue living, Roger Henry Melchior *b.* 1957, Mark Anthony *b.* 1958, Lucy Elizabeth Millicent *b.* 1954: *m.* 1974, Robert Anthony Page, of 46, Sholebroke Av., Leeds, 7,— Fiona Margaret GRAHAM (336, Central Park West, New York 25, USA), *b.* 1929; MB and BS London 1956; MRCS England and LRCP London 1956, Diplo. in Psychiatry, American Board of Psychiatry and Neurology 1964; resumed her maiden name 1962: *m.* 1958 (m. diss. 1962), Jawad Idriss, MC,— Mavis Ellen, *b.* 1933: *m.* 1st, 1960, (m. diss. 1970) Anthony Brian Simmonds; 2ndly, 1971, Edwin Frederick Sharp, of Budleigh, Oalfield Rd., Ashtead, Surrey, and has issue living (by 1st m.) Keith Antony Scot *b.* 1961, Graham Richard Scot (twin) *b.* 1961,—Alison Helen Constance *b.* 1963; MA: *m.* 1961, Geoffrey William Heath, MA, of Longacre, Horsley's Green, Stokenchurch, Bucks., and has issue living, Simon Geoffrey *b.* 1969, Nicola Jane *b.* 1965, Miranda Gillian *b.* 1967. *Residences,*— 12, Hans Cres., SW1; Old Mill Cottage, Micheldever, Winchester.

Hon. Constance Elizabeth (*Hon. Lady Cheke*) (The Rock Hotel, Yelverton, S. Devon), *b.* 1901: *m.* 1939, Sir Marcus John Cheke, KCVO, CMG, who *d.* 1960.

PREDECESSORS.—[1] MANASSEH MASSEY Lopes, son of the late Mordecai-Rodrigues Lopes, of Clapham, S.W.; *b.* 1755; was successively M.P. for Evesham, South Devon, Barnstaple, and Westbury; cr. a *Baronet* 1805 with special remainder to his nephew, Ralph Franco, son of his younger sister, Esther, wife of Abraham Franco, of London: *m.* 1795, Charlotte, who *d.* 1833, dau. of the late John Yeates, of Monmouthshire; *d.* 1831; *s.* by his nephew [2] RALPH (ante), 2nd Bt.; *b.* 1788; assumed by Roy. licence 1831 the surname of Lopes in lieu of his patronymic and the arms of Lopes quarterly with those of Franco; sat as M.P. for Westbury (*C*) 1832-7 and 1841-7, and for South Devonshire (*C*) 1849-54: *m.* 1817, Susan Gibbs, who *d.* 1870, el. dau. of the late A. Ludlow, of Heywood House, Wilts.; *d.* 1854; *s.* by his el. son [3] (LOPES) MASSEY, *P.C.*, 3rd Bt.; *b.* 1818; sat as M.P. for Westbury (*C*) 1857-68, and Devonshire, S. Div. 1868-85, and was a Civil Lord of the Admiralty 1874-80: *m.* 1st, 1854, the Hon. Bertha Yarde-Buller, who *d.* 1872, dau. of 1st Baron Churston; 2ndly, 1874, Louisa, who *d.* April 1908, dau. of Sir Robert William Newman, 1st Bt. (cr. 1836); *d.* Jan. 1908; *s.* by his only son [4] HENRY YARDE BULLER, 4th Bt.; *b.* 1859; sat as M.P. for Grantham (*C*) 1892-1900; cr. *Baron Roborough*, of Maristow, co. Devon (peerage of United Kingdom) Jan. 1938: *m.* 1891, Lady Albertha Louisa Florence Edgcumbe who *d.* 1941, dau. of 4th Earl of Mount Edgcumbe; *d.* April 1938; *s.* by his only son [5] MASSEY HENRY EDGCUMBE, 2nd Baron and present peer.

ROBSON, BARONY OF. (Robson.) [Extinct 1918.]

WIDOW LIVING OF SON OF LIFE BARON

Iris Emmeline (*Hon. Mrs. Harold B. Robson*) (Pinewood Hill, Wormley, Surrey), da. of the late Reginald Abel Smith [V. Knutsford]: *m.* 1922, as his 2nd wife, Col. the Hon. Harold Burge Robson, only son of Baron Robson (Life Peer), who *d.* 1964.

ROBSON OF KIDDINGTON, BARONESS. (Robson.) [Life Baroness 1974.]

INGA-STINA ROBSON, da. of Erik R. Arvidsson, of Stockholm; *b.* Aug. 20th, 1919; Pres. Women's Liberal Fedn. 1968-69 and 1969-70; Pres. Liberal Party Organisation 1970-71; Chm. of Liberal Party Environment Panel since 1971; Chm. Board of Govs., Queen Charlotte's and Chelsea Hosps., and of S-W Thames Regional Health Authority; cr. *Baroness Robson of Kiddington*, of Kiddington in Oxfordshire (Life Baroness) 1974: *m.* 1940, Lawrence William Robson, FCS, FCMA, JDipMA, and has issue.

Arms,—Not exemplified at time of going to press.
Residence,—Kiddington Hall, Woodstock, Oxon.

SON LIVING.

Hon. Erik Maurice William (The Old Rectory, Nether Kiddington, Woodstock, Oxon.), *b.* 1943.

DAUGHTERS LIVING.

Hon. Kristina Elizabeth, *b.* 1946: *m.* 1967, Iain McLaren Mason, of The Dower House, Kiddington, Woodstock, Oxon.

Hon. Vanessa Jane, *b.* 1949: *m.* 1973, Jonathan Martin Potter, of Wood Farm House, Woodleys, Woodstock, Oxon.

ROCHDALE, VISCOUNT. (Kemp.) [Baron U.K. 1913, Viscount U.K. 1960.]

I hope for light.

JOHN DURIVAL KEMP, O.B.E., T.D., 1st Viscount; b. June 5th, 1906; s. as 2nd Baron 1945; cr. Viscount Rochdale, of Rochdale, co. Palatine of Lancaster (peerage of U.K.) 1960; ed. at Eton, and at Trin. Coll., Camb. (BA); Col. late RA (TA), Hon. Brig., a DL for Cumbria; Chm. of Kelsall & Kemp, Ltd., of Rochdale 1950-71; Dep. Chm. of W. Riding Worsted & Woollen Co., Ltd. 1969-72, and of Williams & Glyn's Bank Ltd.; Upper Bailiff of Weavers' Co. 1949-50, and 1956-57; Hon. Col. 851st (Westmorland and Cumberland, Yeo.) Field Battery RA (TA) 1959-67 a Member of Central Transport Consultative Committees 1952-57, Pres. of National Union of Manufacturers 1953-56, and a Member of Dollar Export Council (later W. Hemisphere Export Council) 1953-64, a Gov. of BBC 1954-59, Pres. of N.-W. Area British Legion 1955-61, and Chm. of Cotton Board 1957-62, of Cttee. of Enquiry into Major Ports of Great Britain 1961-62, and of National Ports Council 1964-67; Chm. of Cttee. of Inquiry into Shipping Industry 1967-70; Chm. of Harland & Wolff Ltd., Belfast since 1971, and a Dir. of Nat. & Commercial Banking Group Ltd., since 1971; Pres. of N-W Industrial Development Assocn. since 1974; 1939-45 War as temporary Brig. (despatches); OBE (Mil.) 1945: m. 1931, Elinor Dorothea, CBE, JP, da. of the late Ernest H. Pease, of Mowden, Darlington, and has issue.

Arms,—Argent, a chevron engrailed gules between two estoiles in chief azure, and a rose of the second in base barbed and seeded proper. Crest,—A cubit arm erect, vested argent, cuffed azure, the hand proper grasping a chaplet vert encircling a rose as in the arms. Supporters,—On either side a ram or, charged on the shoulder with a rose gules, slipped and leaved proper.

Seat,—Lingholm, Keswick. Club,—Lansdowne.

SON LIVING.

Hon. ST. JOHN DURIVAL, b. Jan. 15th, 1938: m. 1960, Serena Jane, da. of the late Michael Clark-Hall, of Wissenden, Bethersden, Kent, and has issue living, Jonathan Hugo Durival, b. 1961, —Christopher George, b. 1969,—Joanna Victoria, b. 1964,—Susanna Jane b. 1965.

SISTER LIVING.

Hon. Diana Helen (Hon. Lady Barlow). b. 1904: m. 1928, Sir John Denman Barlow, 2nd Bt. (cr. 1907). Residence,—Bradwell Manor, Sandbach, Cheshire.

PREDECESSOR.—[1] GEORGE Kemp, C.B., son of the late George Tawke Kemp, of Beechwood, Rochdale; b. 1866; Chm. of Kelsall & Kemp, Ltd., woollen manufacturers, and Lord-Lieut. of Middlesex; S. Africa 1900-1902 with Imperial Yeo. (despatches), 1914-19 War in Gallipoli and Egypt as Brig.-Gen.; M.P. for Heywood Div. of Lancashire (L) 1895-1906, and for N.-W. Div. of Manchester 1910-12; cr. Baron Rochdale, of Rochdale, co. Palatine of Lancaster (peerage of United Kingdom) 1913: m. 1896, Lady Beatrice Mary Egerton, MBE, who d. 1966, da. of 3rd Earl of Ellesmere; d. 1945; s. by his son [2] JOHN DURIVAL, 1st Viscount and present peer; also Baron Rochdale.

ROCHE, BARONY OF. (Roche.) [Extinct 1956.]

SONS LIVING OF LIFE PEER.

Hon. John Fenwick Adair, b. 1903; ed. at Rugby, and at Wadham Coll., Oxford (B.A. 1924, M.A., 19—): m. 1928, Ethel Meverell, dau. of the late Kennett Champain Bayley [see Laurie, Bt., colls.], and has issue. Residence,—Hospital Rd., Moreton-in-Marsh, Glos.

Hon. Thomas Gabriel, Q.C., b. 1909; ed. at Rugby, and at Wadham Coll.. Oxford; Bar. Inner Temple 1932, and a Q.C.1955; appointed Recorder of Worcester 1959, and a Church Commr. for England 1961; European War 1939-45 as Lieut.-Col. R.A. (despatches). Residence,—Chadlington, Oxford. Chambers,—Queen Elizabeth Building, Temple, E.C.4. Club,—United University.

DAUGHTER LIVING OF LIFE PEER.

Hon. Helen Patricia, b. 1906: m. 1931, Squadron-Leader Edward Garmondsway Waldy, RAFVR, and has issue. Residence,—Chadlington, Oxford.

ROCHESTER, BARON. (Lamb.) [Baron U.K. 1931.]

FOSTER CHARLES LOWRY LAMB, 2nd Baron; b. June 7th, 1916; s. 1955; ed. at Mill Hill, and at Jesus Coll., Camb. (MA); formerly Capt. 23rd Hussars; Employment Adviser, Mond Div. ICI, Ltd. since 1965: m. 1942, Mary Carlisle, BA, da. of Thomas Benjamin Wheeler, CBE, of 8, Abbey Lane, Hartford, Ches., and has issue.

Residence,—The Hollies, Hartford, Cheshire.

SONS LIVING.

Hon. DAVID CHARLES, *b.* Sept. 8th, 1944; ed. at Shrewsbury and Sussex Univ.: *m.* 1969, Jacqueline, da. of John Alfred Stamp, of Torquay.

Hon. Timothy Michael, *b.* 1953; ed. at Shrewsbury, and Queen's Coll., Oxford.

DAUGHTER LIVING.

Hon. Elizabeth Mary, *b.* 1951: *m.* 1974, Thomas Meredith McIlroy.

BROTHERS LIVING.

Rev. the Hon. Roland Hurst Lowry, *b.* 1917; ed. at Mill Hill, and at Jesus Coll., Camb., (BA 1938, MA 1942); sometime Chap. RAF; Gen. Sec. of British Evangelical Council: *m.* 1943, Vera Alicia, da. of the late A. H. Morse, and has issue living, Andrew Michael, *b.* 1951: *m.* 1974, Helen, da. of Eric Mitchell, of 30, Fisher Av., Rugby,—Rosemary Elizabeth, *b.* 1947: *m.* 1969, David Pike, of 3, Laburnham Rd., Weston-super-Mare, and has issue living, Sarah Louise *b.* 1971,— Hilary Jennifer, *b.* 1949: *m.* 1972, Howard Jackson, of 27, Grayfield Av., Moseley, Birmingham,— Valerie Judith, *b.* 1955. *Residence,*—21, Woodstock Rd. N, St. Albans, Herts.

Hon. Kenneth Henry Lowry, *b.* 1923;ed. at Harrow, and at Trin. Coll., Oxford (B.A. 1944, M.A., 1949); formerly Instructor-Lt. RN; Head of Religious Broadcasting, BBC 1963-66; Sec. of BBC 1967-68; Dir. Public Affairs BBC since 1969; Commonwealth Fund Fellow, Harvard Univ., USA, 1953-55: *m.* 1952, Elizabeth Anne Saul, and has issue living, Stephen Ernest Henry, *b.* 1957,— Sarah Elizabeth Hurst, *b.* 1955,—Caroline Mary Anne, *b.* 1966. *Residence,*—25, South Terr., SW7.

SISTERS LIVING.

Hon. Mary Pleasant Lowry, *b.* 1919; L.R.A.M. 1939: *m.* 1941, the Rev. Desmond William Adair Stride. *Residence,*—Chaplain's House, Heathfield, Ascot, Berks.

Hon. Muriel Joan Lowry, *b.* 1921; ed. at Oxford Univ. (BA 1943, MA 1957); Senior Lecturer in Education, Loughborough Coll. of Education; formerly 3rd Sec., British Embassy, Oslo: *m.* 1947 (m. diss. 1957), William Oswald Collier [see B. Monkswell, colls.]. *Residence,*—64, Outwood Drive, Loughborough.

WIDOW LIVING OF FIRST BARON.

ROSA DOROTHEA (*Dorothy, Baroness Rochester*), younger dau. of the late William John Hurst, J.P., of Drumaness, Ballynahinch, co. Down: *m.* 1913, the 1st Baron, who *d.* 1955. *Residence,*—Upfield Chase, Croydon, Surrey.

PREDECESSOR.—[1] ERNEST HENRY Lamb, *C.M.G.,* el. son of the late Benjamin Lamb, of Thorn-down, Windlesham, Surrey, and Shorne, Rochester, Kent, *b.* 1876; a retired Transport Contractor; was Paymaster-Gen. (in National Govt.) 1931-35; represented Min. of Labour in House of Lords 1931-5; Vice-Pres. of Methodist Church 1941-2, and of British Council of Churches 1942-4; sat as M.P. for Rochester (*L*) 1906-10, and 1910-18; *cr. Baron Rochester,* of Rochester, co. Kent (peerage of United Kingdom) 1931: *m.* 1913, Rosa Dorothea, younger dau. of the late William John Hurst, J.P., of Drumaness, Ballynahinch, co. Down: *d.* 1955; *s.* by his el. son [2] FOSTER CHARLES LOWRY, 2nd Baron and present peer.

ROCHESTER, LORD BISHOP OF. (Say.)

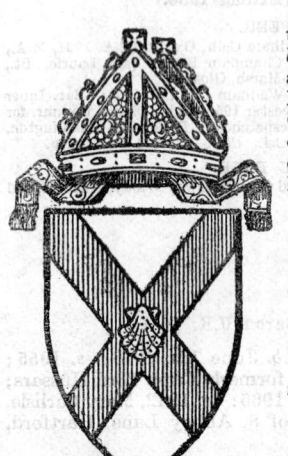

Rt. Rev. (RICHARD) DAVID SAY, *D.D.,* son of the late Com. Richard Say, O.B.E., R.N.V.R.; *b.* Oct. 4th, 1914; ed. at Univ. Coll. Sch., and at Christ's Coll., Camb. (B.A. 1938, M.A. 1941); D.D. Lambeth 1961; is Sub-Prelate and Chap. Order of St. John of Jerusalem; was Gen. Sec. of British Council of Churches 1947-55, and R. of Bishop's Hatfield and Domestic Chap. to Marquess of Salisbury 1955-61; consecrated 104th Bishop of Rochester 1961; Chap. to Pilgrims of Great Britain since 1968; appointed High Almoner to the Queen 1970: *m.* 1943, Irene, *J.P.,* el. dau. of the late Seaburne Rayner, of Exeter.

Patron of seventy-six livings, of the Archdeaconries of Rochester, Tonbridge, and Bromley, two Residentiary Canonries, and of all the Honorary Canonries.

Rochester is one of the most ancient Bishoprics. It was founded by Augustine. Justus was Bishop in 604.

Episcopal Signature,—" David Roffen : "

ARMS OF THE SEE,—Argent, on a saltire gules, an escallop or.

Residence,—Bishopscourt, Rochester, ME1 1TS. *Club,*— United Oxford and Cambridge University.

ROCKLEY BARON. (Cecil.) [Baron U.K. 1934.]

Late, but in earnest.

ROBERT WILLIAM EVELYN CECIL, 2nd Baron; *b.* Feb. 28th, 1901; *s.* 1941; ed. at Eton, at Ch. Ch., Oxford, and at Yale Univ., USA; Brig. (ret.) RA, and an Engineer: *m.* 1933, Anne Margaret, da. of the late Adm. the Hon. Sir Herbert Meade-Featherstonhaugh, G.C.V.O., C.B., D.S.O. [see E. Clanwilliam, colls.] and has issue.

Arms,—Barry of ten argent and azure, over all six escutcheons, three, two, and one, sable, each charged with a lion rampant of the first, and for difference a crescent gules charged with another crescent or, a crescent gules for difference. Crest,—Six arrows in saltire or, barbed and flighted argent, girt together with a belt gules, buckled and garnished gold, over the arrows a morion cap proper. Supporters,—On either side a lion ermine, gorged with a collar or pendent therefrom an escutcheon, the dexter sable a lion argent, and the sinister gules, three tilting spears erect or, headed argent.
Residences,—Lytchett Heath, Poole, Dorset; 10, Clive House, 5, Connaught Place, W.2.

SONS LIVING.

Hon. JAMES HUGH, *b.* April 5th, 1934; ed. at Eton, and at New Coll., Oxford: *m.* 1958, Lady Sarah Primrose Beatrix Cadogan, el. da. of 7th Earl Cadogan, and has issue living, Anthony Robert, *b.* 1961, —Caroline Anne, *b.* 1960,—Camilla Sarah, *b.* 1965. *Residence,*—6, Manresa Rd., SW3.

Hon. Charles Evelyn, (Wilcote House, Charlbury, Oxon.), *b.* 1936; ed. at Eton: *m.* 1965, Jennifer Anne, da. of Duncan Mackinnon, of Swinbrook House, Burford, Oxon., and has issue living, David *b.* 1971,—Arabella Elizabeth, *b.* 1967,—Lucinda, *b.* 1970.

DAUGHTER LIVING.

Hon. Elizabeth Anne, *b.* 1939 : *m.* 1961, Capt. Andrew Arnold Lyon Wills, late Life Guards [see Wills, Bt. (cr. 1904), colls.]. *Residence,*—Middleton House, Longparish, Andover, Hants.

SISTER LIVING.

Hon. Maud Katharine Alicia, *b.* 1904 : *m.* 1927, Col. Richard Greville Acton Steel, T.D., R.A. (from whom she obtained a divorce 1955), and has issue living, Juliet Maud, *b.* 1928,—Oriel Hermione, *b.* 1930 : *m.* 1958, Basil William Robinson, of 41, Redcliffe Gardens, S.W.10, and has issue living, William James *b.* 1959, Alicia Frances *b.* 1962. *Residence,*—8, Cranley Place, S.W.7.

PREDECESSOR.—[1] *Rt. Hon. Sir* EVELYN Cecil, *G.B.E.,* el. son of the late Lieut.-Col. Lord Eustace Brownlow Henry Gascoyne Cecil [M. Salisbury, colls.]; *b.* 1865; M.P. for Herts. E., or Hertford Div. (C) 1898-1900, for Aston Manor 1900-1918, and for Aston Div. of Birmingham 1918-29; cr. *Baron Rockley*, of Lytchett Heath, co. Dorset (peerage of United Kingdom) 1934: *m.* 1898, the Hon. Alicia Margaret Amherst, *C.B.E.*, who *d.* 1941, dau. of 1st Baron Amherst of Hackney ; *d.* 1941 ; *s.* by his son [2] ROBERT WILLIAM EVELYN, 2nd Baron and present peer.

Rocksavage, Earl of, son of Marquess of Cholmondeley.

RODEN, EARL OF. (Jocelyn.) [Earl I. 1771, Bt. E. 1665.]

To do my duty.

ROBERT WILLIAM JOCELYN, 9th Earl and 13th Baronet ; *b.* Dec. 4th, 1909 ; *s.* 1956 ; became Capt. R.N. 1951 ; European War 1939-45 (despatches thrice) : *m.* 1937, Clodagh Rose (an Officer Sister of Order of St. John), da. of the late Edward Robert Kennedy [see Kennedy, Bt., colls.], and has issue.

Arms,—Azure, a circular wreath or torse argent and sable, with four hawks' bells conjoined thereto in quadrangle or. Crest,—A falcon's leg erased at the thigh proper, belled or. Supporters—Two falcons proper, wings inverted belled or.
Residence—Bryansford, co. Down.

SONS LIVING.

ROBERT JOHN (*Viscount Jocelyn*) (The White House, Chaddleworth, Newbury, Berks.); *b.* Aug. 25th, 1938: *m.* 1970, Sara Cecilia, da. of Brig. Andrew Dunlop, of Que Que, Rhodesia.

Hon. Thomas Alan, *b.* 1941; Lt. RN: *m.* 1966, Fiona Alice da. of Capt. R. D. Cairns, DSO, RN, of Taghmon, co. Wexford, and has issue living, Moira Anne, *b.* 1969.

Hon. James Michael, *b.* 1943.

SISTERS LIVING.

Lady Elizabeth (Teviot, Firgrove, Cape Prov., S. Africa), *b.* 1907: *m.* 1st, 1927, Gerald Francis Annesley, from whom she obtained a divorce 1940 [E. Annesley]; 2ndly, 1940, the Hon. Charles Dudley Anthony Ross, from whom she obtained a divorce, 1949 [see Bs. de Ros]; 3rdly, 1954, Com. Warden Sydney Learmouth Gilchrist, RN (ret.), who *d.* 1958; 4thly, 1967, Brig. Edward Maxwell Tyler, DSO, MC, late RA, who *d.* 1974, and has issue living, (by 1st m.) Margaret Elizabeth, *b.* 1929: *m.* 1957, Douglas Farquhar Ogilvie, of House of Pitmuies, by Forfar, Angus, and has issue living, Douglas Ruaraidh *b.* 1958, Grania Marquerite *b.* 1961, Carey Valentia *b.* 1966,—Patricia Mabel, (9, Ravencourt Sq., W6), *b.* 1933: *m.* 1954, Peter Saunders, from whom she obtained a divorce 1974, and has issue living, John Justin *b.* 1956, Will *b.* 1960, Emma Elizabeth *b.* 1955, Tabitha *b.* 1962,—(by 2nd m.) [see Bs. de Ros].

Lady Mabel Kathleen, *b.* 1915 : *m.* 1st, 1937, Richard Neville Brooke, late Lieut. Scots Guards (from whom she obtained a divorce 1959), only son of Sir Richard Christopher Brooke, 9th Bt. (cr. 1662); 2ndly, 1960, Sir Nicolas John Alexander Cheetham, KCMG, of 50, Cadogan Sq., SW1X 0JW.

PREDECESSORS.—[1] ROBERT Jocelyn, successively Solicitor-Gen., Attorney-Gen., and Lord High Chancellor of Ireland, and twelve times a Lord Justice in the absence of the Viceroy, was cr. *Baron Newport*, of Newport (peerage of Ireland) 1743, and *Viscount Jocelyn* (peerage of Ireland) 1755; *d.* 1756; *s.* by his son [2] ROBERT, 2nd Viscount; was M.P. for Old Leighlin 1743, and Auditor-Gen. of Ireland 1750; *s.* his kinsman as 5th Bt. 1770 (see *₊* infra); cr. *Earl of Roden*, of High Roding, co. Tipperary (peerage of Ireland) 1771; *d.* 1797; *s.* by his son [3] ROBERT, *K.P.*, 2nd Earl; was M.P. for Dundalk, and joint Auditor-Gen. for Ireland; *d.* 1820; *s.* by his son [4] ROBERT, *K.P.*, *P.C.*, 3rd Earl, *b.* 1788; was M.P. for Dundalk, Auditor-Gen. of the Exchequer in Ireland, and Custos Rotulorum of co. Louth; cr. *Baron Clanbrassil*, of Hyde Hall, co. Herts (peerage of United Kingdom) 1821; *s.* by his grandson [5] ROBERT, 4th Earl; was a Lord-in-Waiting to H.M. 1874-80; *d.* unmarried 1880; *s.* by his uncle [6] JOHN STRANGE, 5th Earl (2nd son of 3rd Earl), *b.* 1823: *m.* 1851, the Hon. Sophia Hobhouse, who *d.* 1916, 2nd dau. of 1st Baron Broughton; *d.* 1897, when the Barony of Clanbrassil became ext. and he was *s.* in the other honours by his kinsman [7] WILLIAM HENRY (son of the late Hon. John Jocelyn, 4th son of 2nd Earl), 6th Earl, *b.* 1842; *d.* 1910; *s.* by his brother [8] ROBERT JULIAN, 7th Earl, *b.* 1845; Lieut.-Col. in the Army: *m.* 1882, Ada Maria, who *d.* 1931, dau. of the late Col. Soame Gambier Jenyns, C.B.; *d.* 1915; *s.* by his son [9] ROBERT SOAME, 8th Earl; *b.* 1883; Capt. (ret.) N. Irish Horse, and a Representative Peer: *m.* 1905, Elinor Jessie, who *d.* 1962, dau. of the late Joseph Charlton Parr; *d.* 1956; *s.* by his son [10] ROBERT WILLIAM, 9th Earl and prese t peer; also Viscount Jocelyn and Baron Newport.

₊ [1] ROBERT Jocelyn, of Hyde Hall; cr. a *Baronet* 1665; *d.* 1712; *s.* by his son [2] *Sir* STRANGE 2nd Bt.; *d.* 1734; *s.* by his el. son [3] *Sir* JOHN, 3rd Bt.; *d.* unmarried 1741; *s.* by his brother [4] *Sir* CONVERS, *M.D.*, 4th Bt.; Sheriff of Hertford 1745; *d.* unmarried 1770; *s.* by his kinsman [5] ROBERT, 2nd Viscount Jocelyn (see ante) grandson of Thomas, 3rd son of 1st Bt.

RODNEY, BARON. (Rodney.) [Baron G.B. 1782, Bt. G.B. 1764.]

NON·GENERANT·AQUIL Æ·COLUMBAS

Eagles do not bring forth doves.

JOHN FRANCIS RODNEY, 9th Baron, and 9th Baronet; *b.* June 28th, 1920; *s.* 1973; ed. at Stowe, and McGill Univ., Canada; 1939-45 War as Lt. Commandos (despatches); a Dir. of Vacuumati Ltd., of 129, Kingsway, WC2: *m.* 1951, Régine Elisabeth Lucienne Jeanne Thérèse Marie Ghislaine, yr. da. of the late Chevalier Rogert Egide Marie Ghislain Pangaert d'Opdorp, of Château Rullingfen, Looz, Belgium, and has issue.

Arms.—Or : three eagles displayed with wings inverted purpure. Crest,—On a ducal coronet or, an eagle, wings displayed and inverted purpure. Supporters,—Two eagles, wings inverted purpure, beaked and membered or, each sustaining with the interior claw a banner of St. George, the staves proper, each enfiled with a naval coronet gold.

Residence,—38, Pembroke Rd., W8. *Club*,—White's.

SON LIVING.
Hon. GEORGE BRYDGES, *b.* Jan. 3, 1953; ed. at Eton.

DAUGHTER LIVING.
Hon. Anne, *b.* 1955.

BROTHER LIVING.

Hon. Michael Christopher (11683-72 Av., Edmonton, Alberta, Canada), *b.* 1926; ed. at Upper Canada Coll., and McGill Univ., Canada (BA 1948); Bar Canada 1950; 1939-45 War with RCN: *m.* 1st, 1953 (m. diss. 1973), Anne, da. of David Yuile, of Montreal, Canada; 2ndly, 1974, Penelope Jane, da. of Eric Gaener, of Edmonton, Alberta, Canada, and has issue living (by 1st m.), Patricia, *b.* 1955,—Jocelyn, *b.* 1959,—Jennifer, *b.* 1962.

SISTERS LIVING.

Hon. Diana Rosemary (9745-110 St., Edmonton, Alberta, Canada), *b.* 1924; ed. at McGill Univ., Canada (BA 1949); 1939-45 War with WRCNS.
Hon. Sylvia Corisande, *b.* 1930; ed. at McGill Univ., Canada (B.A 1952): *m.* 1962, Eric de Bellaigue, of 7, Blomfield Rd., W9, and has issue living, Nicholas Charles Rodney, *b.* 1966,—Justin Christopher George Lowther, *b.* 1971.

UNCLE LIVING (*Son of 7th Baron.*)

Hon. (Charles Christian) Simon, *b.* 1895 ; ed. at Repton ; formerly Lieut. 7th Batn. Hampshire Regt.; sometime a partner in the firm of Rowe & Pitman, Stockbrokers, of 43, Bishopgate, E.C.2 ; European War 1914-18 as Capt. The King's (Liverpool Regt.) and Lieut. Grenadier Guards (prisoner), European War 1939-45 as Major Grenadier Guards : *m.* 1922, Gladys, who *d.* 1966, dau. of the late John Hamar Greenwood, Bar.-at-law, of Whitby, Canada. *Residence,*—Brizes Park, Kelvedon Hatch, Essex.

WIDOW LIVING OF SON OF SEVENTH BARON.

Frances Strickland Lovell, dau. of the late Robert Pollard Oldham, of Seattle, Washington, U.S.A.: *m.* 1st, 1928, as his second wife, Capt. the Hon. James Henry Bertie Rodney, M.C., who *d.* 1933; 2ndly, 1938 (marriage dissolved 1948), Charles Gordon ; 3rdly, 1949, Capt. Alwyne Arthur Compton. M.C., Roy. Scots Greys, who was officially recognized in the surname of Farquharson of Inver-cauld, and as Chief of Clan Farquharson by warrant of Lord Lyon 1949, and who uses his former surname as a third christian name [see M. Northampton, colls.]. *Residence,*—Invercauld, Braemar, Aberdeenshire.

COLLATERAL BRANCHES LIVING.

Grandchildren of the late Hon. Robert William Henry Rodney, 2nd son of 6th Baron:—
Issue of the late Lt.-Cdr. Mervyn Harley Rodney, *b.* 1890, *d.* 1964: *m.* 1st, 1915, Dorothy, who *d.* 1917, da. of the late Rev. Benjamin Norton Thompson, of 30, Victoria St., Tenby; 2ndly, 1921 (marriage dissolved 1956), Louise, da. of the late Prof. Armand Halleux:—
(By 1st marriage) Nigel Robert Harley (Springfield Farm, Sidbury, Devon), *b.* 1917; Cdr. R.N.; 1939-45 War (despatches four times): *m.* 1946, Patricia Ann Merlyn, da. of the late Lt.-Col. Harley Wentworth Ashburner, DSO, and has issue living, Nicholas Simon Harley (24, rue Albert-Joly, 78000 Versailles, France), *b.* 1947: *m.* 1973, Maïté Bernadette Edith, da. of Henri Pinet des Ecots, of Chateau de Curty, Imphy, 58 Nièvre, France,—Christopher Lossie Charles, *b.* 1957,—Julia Diana, *b.* 1951,—Emma Gabrielle, *b.* 1952.——(by 2nd m.) John Armand, *MC* (The Well House, Great Amwell, Herts.), *b.* 1921; ed. at Uppingham, and at Magdalen Coll., Oxford; formerly Capt. Cold-stream Guards; 1939-45 War (MC): *m.* 1951, Gertrude Evelyn, da. of the late Capt. Simon John James, and has issue living, Peter Miles, *b.* 1953,—David James, *b.* 1965.

Issue of the late Group-Capt. Ivor Morgan Rodney, O.B.E., R.A.F. (retired), *b.* 1896, *d.* 1954: *m.* 1931, Althea Caroline Winifred (Glen Hill, Walmer, Kent), el. da. of the late Sir Gerald Woods Wollaston, KCB, KCVO, FSA, late Garter Principal King of Arms:—
Sarah Patience, *b.* 1933: *m.* 1959, Brian Woodard, of 69, Bernham Rd., Hellesdon, Norwich, and has issue living, Anthony John, *b.* 1960,—Paris Morgan, *b.* 1962,—Craig Charles, *b.* 1963,—Helen Mary *b.* 1961.——Prudence Jane, *b.* 1936: *m.* 1960, Keith Hyde Wollaston, of Gower House, Barton-under-Needwood, Staffs., and has issue living, Andrew James Rodney, *b.* 1961,—Rachel Althea Rodney, *b.* 1963,—Frances Jane Rodney, *b.* 1964,—Catherine Mary Rodney (twin), *b.* 1964.——Alicia Henrietta Althea, *b.* 1937: *m.* 1960, David John Pentin, of Ashley House, Brewery Lane, Bridge, Canterbury, and has issue living, John Mark, *b.* 1964,—Richard Harley, *b.* 1969,—Caroline Louise, *b.* 1962,—Edward Michael, *b.* 1971.

Grandson of the late Frederick James Rodney, son of the late Hon. Mortimer Rodney, 7th son of 2nd Baron :—
Issue of the late Reginald George Rodney, *b.* 1873, *d.* 1933: *m.* 1916, Patricia Lissette du Châtel, who *d.* 1964, da. of the late William James MacGrath, of co. Tipperary :—
Philip Harley Brydges (Yerrel Cottage, 96, Sherford Rd., Elburton, Plymouth), *b.* 1917: *m.* 1951, Janet Barker, and has issue living, Julie Rose Patricia, *b.* 1954,—Faye Jessica Frances Corisande, *b.* 1958.

PREDECESSORS.—[1] *Adm.* Sir GEORGE BRYDGES Rodney, (son of Henry Rodney, great-grandson of Sir John Rodney, by Jane (cousin german to Edward VI.), dau. of Sir Henry Seymour, brother of 1st Duke of Somerset and Queen Jane Seymour), an eminent Naval Commander, who, having gained numerous victories, eventually in 1782 defeated the French fleet under the Comte de Grasse, whom he took prisoner, the result of this success was the peace of Versailles Jan. 20th, 1783; cr. *Baronet* 1764, and *Baron Rodney*, of Rodney Stoke, co. Somerset (peerage of Great Britain) 1782; granted by Parliament a pension of £2,000 a-year to himself and his successors (commuted 1924); successively M.P. for Saltash, Okehampton, Penrhyn, and Northampton; *d.* 1792; *s.* by his son [2] GEORGE, 2nd Baron; sat as M.P. for Northampton; *d.* 1802; *s.* by his el. son [3] GEORGE, 3rd Baron; was Lord-Lieut. of Radnor; *d.* 1842; *s.* by his brother [4] THOMAS JAMES, 4th Baron; assumed the additional surname and arms of Harley by Roy. licence 1805; *d.* unmarried 1843; *s.* by his brother [5] SPENCER, 5th Baron; was Rector of Elmley, Kent; *d.* unmarried 1846; *s.* by his nephew [6] ROBERT DENNETT, 6th Baron, son of Capt. the Hon. Robert, R.N., 4th son of 2nd Baron; *b.* 1820 : *m.* 1850, Sarah, who *d.* 1882, dau. of the late John Singleton; *d.* 1864: *s.* by his son [7] GEORGE BRIDGES HARLEY DENNETT, 7th Baron : *b.* 1857 : *m.* 1st, 1891, the Hon. Corisande Evelyn Vere Guest, who *d.* 1943 (having obtained a divorce 1902), dau. of 1st Baron Wimborne ; 2ndly, 1903, Charlotte Eugenia, who *d.* 1939, dau. of the late Edmund Probyn, of Longhope and Huntley, Gloucestershire : *d.* 1909 ; *s.* by his el. son [8] GEORGE BRIDGES HARLEY GUEST, 8th Baron; *b.* 1891: *m.* 1917, Lady Marjorie Lowther, who *d.* 1968, da. of 6th Earl of Lonsdale; *d.* 1973; *s.* by his 2nd son [9] JOHN FRANCIS, 9th Baron and present peer.

ROLLO, LORD. (Rollo.) [Lord S. 1651, and Baron U.K. 1869.]

ERIC JOHN STAPYLTON ROLLO, 13th Lord ; *b.* Dec. 3rd, 1915 ; *s.* 1947 ; ed. at Eton ; Capt. late Grenadier Guards ; a JP of Perthshire; 1939-45 War: *m.* 1938, Suzanne, da. of W. H. B. Hatton, of Broome House, Clent, Worcs., and has issue.

Fortune makes way through everything.

Arms—Or, a chevron between three boars, heads erased azure, armed proper langued gules. Crest,—A stag's head couped at the neck proper Supporters.—Two stags proper.
Residence.—Pitcairns, Dunning, Perthshire.
Club,—Guards'.

SONS LIVING.

Hon. DAVID ERIC HOWARD (*Master of Rollo*), (20, Draycott Av., SW3), *b.* March 31st, 1943; ed. at Eton; Capt. Gren. Gds.: *m.* 1971, Felicity Anne Christian, only da. of Lt.-Cdr. John Bruce Lamb, RN, of Burrow House, Tywardreath, Cornwall, and has issue living, James David William, by 1972,—Thomas Stapylton, *b.* 1975.
Hon. James Malcolm (Corwar House, Barrhill, Girvan, Ayrshire), *b.* 1946; ed. at Eton, and Ch. Ch., Oxford (BA): *m.* 1968, Henrietta Elizabeth Flora, da. of Maj. Alasdair David Forbes Boyle [see E. Glasgow, colls.].

DAUGHTER LIVING.

Hon. Erica Helen Susan (78, Elm Park Rd., S.W.3), *b.* 1939.

BROTHER LIVING.

Hon. David Ian, *M.B.E., M.C., b.* 1921: late Capt. Grenadier Guards; European War 1939-45 in N. Africa and Italy (wounded, M.B.E., M.C.); M.B.E. (Mil.) 1944 : *m.* 1948, Bridget Mary, da. of Brigadier James Erskine Stirling, D.S.O. [see D. Devonshire, colls.], and has issue living, Norman Hamish, *b.* 1955,—Joanna Mary, *b.* 1949,—Carolyn Louise, *b.* 1952,—Harriet Clarissa Jane, *b.* 1960. *Address,—*

HALF-BROTHERS LIVING.

Hon. John Dunning, *b.* 1931.
Hon. Simon David Paul (Biffens Boatyard, Staines, Middx.), *b.* 1939; ed. at Eton: *m.* 1964, Valerie, yr. da. of R. W. G. Willis, MA, of 8, Links View, Newton Green, Sudbury, Suffolk, and has issue living, Michelle Leila, *b.* 1971.

SISTER LIVING.

Hon. Jean Helen, *b.* 1926: *m.* 1952, Lt.-Col. Robert Henry Heywood-Lonsdale, MBE, MC, Grenadier Guards, of Bapton Manor, Warminster, Wilts. [V. Valentia], and has issue living, Thomas Norman, *b.* 1953,—Helen Jane, *b.* 1957,—Clare Jane, *b.* 1961,—Emma Lucinda, *b.* 1962.

AUNTS LIVING. (*Raised to the rank of a Baron's daughters* 1946.)

Hon. Torfrida Henrietta Louisa, *b.* 1891 ; late Dep. Matron, Birmingham Gen. Hospital ; European War 1939-45 with First Aid Nursing Yeo. *Residence,—*Lochearnhead, Perthshire.
Hon. Gylla Constance Susan (*Hon. Lady MacGregor of MacGregor*), *O.B.E., b.* 1899 ; has 1st class Order of Vasa of Sweden ; O.B.E. (Civil) 1948 : *m.* 1925, Capt. Sir Malcolm MacGregor of MacGregor, C.B., C.M.G., R.N., 5th Bt. (cr. 1795), who *d.* 1958. *Residence,—*Craggan House, Lochearnhead, Perthshire.

WIDOW LIVING OF BROTHER OF TWELFTH LORD.

Diana Joan (Barley Thorpe, Oakham, Rutland), da. of the late Edward Castell Wrey [see Wrey Bt.]: *m.* 1st 1932 (m. diss. 1946) Jocelyn Abel Smith, who *d.* 1966; 2ndly, 1946, as his 2nd wife, the Hon. William Hereward Charles Rollo, MC (who was raised to the rank of a Baron's son 1946), who *d.* 1962.

WIDOW LIVING OF TWELFTH LORD.

LILY MARIE (COCKSHUT), dau. of Max Seiflow, of Hatch End, Middlesex: *m.* 1st, 1937, as his third wife, the 12th Baron, who *d.* 1947 ; 3rdly, 1949, Richard Andrew Perceval Leach. *Residence,—*Coupar Grange, Coupar Angus, Perthshire.

COLLATERAL BRANCHES LIVING.

Issue of the late Hon. William Hereward Charles Rollo, M.C. (who was raised to the rank of a Baron's son 1946), younger brother of 12th Lord, *b.* 1890, *d.* 1962: *m.* 1st, 1917, Lady Kathleen Nina Hill, who *d.* 1960 (having obtained a divorce for desertion 1946), da. of 6th Marquess of Downshire; 2ndly, 1946, Mrs. Diana Joan Abel Smith (ante), da. of the late Edward Castell Wrey [see Wrey, Bt.]:—
(By 1st marriage) Peter Andrew, *MBE* (7, Herbert Cres., SW1), *b.* 1919, Lieut. RN (ret.); Far East 1945; MBE (Mil.) 1946: *m.* 1953, Patricia Mary, da. of the late Capt. Charles Cairn Best, and has issue living, William Raoul, *b.* 1955,—Susan Mary, *b.* 1957.

Grandson of the late Hon. Gilbert de Ste. Croix Rollo (infra):—
Issue of the late Alexander David Rollo, *b.* 1909: *m.* 1st, 1934 (m. diss. 19—), Maud Mary Venn; 2ndly, 1952, Margaret Valmai, who *d.* 1961, only da. of William Slaney Wilmot:—
(By 2nd m.) Calum John Slaney, *b.* 1953.

Issue of the late Hon. Gilbert de Ste. Croix Rollo, youngest son of 10th Lord, *b.* 1872, *d.* 1932 : *m.* 1904, Margaret Freda Evelyn, who *d.* 1959, dau. of the late Robert Crawford Antrobus, JP [Antrobus, Bt.]:—
Robert Duncan, *b.* 1911; late Maj. Suffolk Regt.; 1939-45 War: *m.* 1936, Violet Augustine, da. of the late Russell Charles Stanhope [see E. Harrington, colls.] and has issue living, Gilbert Mark, *b.* 1937: *m.* 1968, Paulette Beatrice, da. of Lt.-Col. Aubrey Charles Stanhope, USAF (ret.) [see E. Harrington, colls.], and has issue living, Catherine Anne *b.* 1969,—Charles, *b.* 1950,—Mary Rose, *b.* 1938.——Glory Evelyn, *b.* 1905: *m.* 1934, Capt. Bernard Henry Esme Howard, MC, who *d.* 1949 [D. Norfolk, colls.]. *Residence,—*Johnby Hall, Greystoke, Penrith, Cumberland.

PREDECESSORS.—[1] Sir ANDREW Rollo; cr. *Lord Rollo,* of Duncrub (peerage of Scotland) 1651, with remainder to his heirs male whatsoever; *s.* by his son [2] JAMES

2nd Lord; d. 1669; s. by his son [3] ANDREW, 3rd Lord; d. 1700; s. by his son [4] ROBERT, 4th Lord; was implicated in the rising of 1715, but having surrendered he obtained the benefit of the Act of Grace 1716; d. 1758; s. by his el. son [5] ANDREW, 5th Lord; served as Brig.-Gen. in the first American War; d. without surviving issue 1765; s. by his brother [6] JOHN 6th Lord; d. 1783; s. by his son [7] JAMES, 7th Lord; d. 1784; s. by his son [8] JOHN 8th Lord; served with the Guards in Flanders 1793-5; d. 1846; s. by his son [9] WILLIAM 9th Lord; b. 1809; m. 1834, Elizabeth, dau. of John Rogerson; d. 1852; s. by his son [10] JOHN ROGERSON, 10th Lord; b. 1835; was a Representative Peer for Scotland 1860-68; cr. Baron Dunning (peerage of UK) 1869: m. 1857, Agnes Bruce, who d. 1906, el. da. of Lt.-Col. Trotter, of Ballindean House, co. Perth; d. 1916; s. by his el. son [11] WILLIAM CHARLES WORDSWORTH, CB, 11th Lord; b. 1860; formerly Lt.-Col. and Hon. Col. 3rd Batn. Black Watch (Roy. Highlanders): m. 1882, Mary Eleanor, who d. 1929, da. of the late Beaumont Williams Hotham; d. 1946; s. by his nephew [12] JOHN ERIC HENRY (son of the late Hon. Eric Norman Rollo, 2nd son of 10th Lord), 12th Lord; b. 1889: m. 1st, 1915, Helen Maud, who d. 1928, dau. of Frederick Chetwynd-Stapylton; 2ndly, 1930, Phyllis Carina (who obtained a divorce 1936), only dau. of the late Bernard Sanderson; 3rdly, 1937, Mrs. Lily Marie Cockshut, dau. of Max Seiflow, of Hatch End, Middlesex; d. 1947; s. by his el. son [13] ERIC JOHN STAPYLTON, 13th Lord and present peer; also Baron Dunning.

ROMER, BARONY OF. (Romer.) [Extinct 1944.]

WIDOW LIVING OF SON OF LIFE PEER.

Frances Evelyn Lebeau (Hon. Lady Romer) (Orchard House, Littlestone, Kent), da. of the late Alfred Kemp of Epping: m. 1925, as his 2nd wife, the Rt. Hon. Sir Charles Robert Ritchie Romer, OBE, who d. 1969, and has issue.

ROMILLY, BARON. (Romilly.) [Baron U.K. 1866.]

[Name and Title pronounced "Rom-illy."]

WILLIAM GASPARD GUY ROMILLY, 4th Baron; b. March 8th, 1899; s. 1905: ed. at Eton, and at R.M.C.; Hon. M.A. Oxford 1943; Major (retired) late Coldstream Guards; a Member of Marlborough cum Ramsbury Rural Dist. Council 1940-74 (Chm. 1964-67); 1918 War in France and Belgium (two medals), European War 1939-45; was a Train Bearer at Coronation of King George V. 1911: m. 1st, 1929, the Hon. Diana Joan Sackville-West (who d. 1975, having obtained a divorce 1944), da. of 4th Baron Sackville; 2ndly, 1944, Dora Sybil, who d. 1960, da. of the late Reginald Morris, of Holly Lodge, Seymour Walk, Chelsea, SW; 3rdly, 1966, Marion Elizabeth Jessie, da. of the late Charles M. Clover, of Blewbury, Berks and widow of Capt. Lionel Cecil [M. Salisbury].

Arms,—Argent, in base a rock with nine points, issuant from each of which a lily all proper; on a chief azure, a crescent between two mullets of the first. Crest,—Upon a rock proper, a crescent argent. Supporters,—On either side a greyhound argent, gorged with a collar flory counterflory azure, and charged on the shoulder with a lily slipped proper.
Residence,—Bridge House, Chilton Foliat, Hungerford, Berks.

PREDECESSORS.—[1] Rt. Hon. Sir JOHN Romilly, M.P. for Bridport 1832-5, and for Devonport (L) 1847-52; was Solicitor-Gen. 1848-50, Attorney-Gen. 1850-1, and Master of the Rolls 1851-73; cr. Baron Romilly, of Barry, co. Glamorgan (peerage of United Kingdom) 1866; b. 1802: m. 1833, Caroline Charlotte, dau. of the Rt. Rev. William Otter, D.D., Lord Bishop of Chichester: d. 1874; s. by his son [2] WILLIAM, 2nd Baron, b. 1835; Clerk of Enrolments in Chancery: m. 1st, 1865, Emily Idonea Sophia, who d. 1866, dau. of Lieut.-Gen. Sir John Gaspard Le Marchant; 2ndly, 1872, Helen, who d. 1889, dau. of the late Edward Hanson Denison; d. 1891; s. by his only son [3] JOHN GASPARD LE MARCHANT, 3rd Baron; b. 1866: m. 1897, Violet Edith Grey, who d. 1906, dau. of Sir Philip Le Belward Grey Egerton, 11th Bt.; d. 1905; s. by his only son [4] WILLIAM GASPARD GUY, 4th Baron, and present peer.

ROMNEY, EARL OF. (Marsham.) [Earl U.K. 1801, Bt. E. 1663.]

CHARLES MARSHAM, 6th Earl, and 12th Baronet; b. July 9th, 1892; s. 1933: ed. at Eton, Lieut.-Col. (retired) Coldstream Guards, a J.P., a D.L. for Norfolk and Norwich; patron of one living; formerly Pres. of National Council of Young Men's Christian Assos. of England, Wales and Ireland; 1914-18 War in France and Belgium (wounded, 1914 star, two medals), 1939-45 War: m. 1918, Marie Henrietta Margaret, da. of Sir Colin Richard Keppel, GCVO, KCIE, CB, DSO [see E. Albemarle, colls.]. [The 6th Earl d. Sept. 6th, 1975].

Arms,—Argent, a lion passant in bend gules, between two bendlets azure. Crest,—A lion's head erased gules. Supporters,—Two lions azure, semée of cross crosslets and each gorged with a naval coronet or.

Seat,—Gayton Hall, King's Lynn.

Not for himself, but for his country.

COLLATERAL BRANCHES LIVING.

Issue of the late Lieut.-Col. the Hon. Reginald Hastings Marsham, O.B.E., 2nd
son of 4th Earl, *b.* 1865, *d.* 1922 : *m.* 1908, Dora Hermione, who *d.* 1923, dau. of
the late Charles North [E. Guilford, colls.] :—
MICHAEL HENRY (Wensum Farm, West Rudham, King's Lynn), *b.* Nov. 22nd, 1910; ed. at Sherborne; formerly Maj. RA : *m.* 1939, Frances Aileen, da. of the late Maj. J. R. Landale, Indian Army.
——Anne Rhoda (P.O. Box 27, Gilgil, Kenya), *b.* 1909; 1939-45 War as Section Officer, WAAF;
Kenya Police Reserve 1952-60.

Grandchildren of the late Hon. Sydney Edward Marsham, yst. son of 4th Earl:—
Issue of the late Col. Peter William Marsham, MBE, *b.* 1913, *d.* 1970: *m.* 1946, Hersey (Crow-
field House, Crowfield, Ipswich), da. of the late Maj. the Hon. Richard Coke [see E. Leicester,
colls.]:—
Julian Charles, *b.* 1948.——Lavinia, *b.* 1950: *m.* 1973, Simon James Macdonald Lockhart, of 40,
Reporton Rd., SW6 7JR.——Sarah, *b.* 1954.

Grandchildren of the late Rev. the Hon. John Marsham, 2nd son of 3rd Earl:—
Issue of the late Walter John Marsham, *b.* 1869, *d.* 1945: *m.* 1908, **Frances Leonora**,
who *d.* 1956, dau. of the late Edward Philip Monckton [V. Galway, colls.] :—
John Edward (16, Barchester Rd., Langley, Bucks.), *b.* 1910: *m.* 1st, 1937 (m. diss. 1970), Jean Frances,
da. of the late Reginald Cambden Clare Hayward: *m.* 2ndly, 1970, Mrs. Evelyn Moore, da. of Lesley,
George Rush and has issue living (by 1st m.), Richard John, *b.* 1946: *m.* 1964, Janet Anne Wilson,
and has issue living, Gary Frederick *b.* 1964, Stephen John *b.* 1967,—Gillian Dawn (1, Belmont Vale,
Maidenhead, Berks.), *b.* 1938: *m.* 1st, 1956, Donald James Griffin, who *d.* 1959; 2ndly, 1961 (m. diss.
1964), Alan Henry Craig; 3rdly, 1968, Abdul Hanif Rashid, who *d.* 1971, 4thly, Thomas William
McConnell, and has issue living (by 1st m.) Pauline Elizabeth *b.* 1956, Celaine Margaret *b.* 1959 (by
3rd m.), Aftab Hanif *b.* 1970.——Violet Lenora, *b.* 1913: *m.* 1940, George Anthony Batterbury,
and has issue living, Adrian William George, *b.* 1944,—Mark Richard George, *b.* 1947,—Edward
Anthony George, *b.* 1949,—Susan, *b.* 1942. *Residence*,—1324, St. David St., Victoria, BC.

Issue of the late Capt. Cyril Montagu Charles Marsham, D.C.M., *b.* 1871 ; *d.* 1943 : *m.*
1911, Gladys Helen, who *d.* 1965, da. of the late Douglas Kingsford, Bar.-at-law:—
Peter, *b.* 1912: *m.* 1938, Margaret, dau. of Benjamin Harral, of Cawthorne, Barnsley, Yorkshire,
and has issue living, John Kingsford, *b.* 1942; Maj. LI,—Robert Harral, *b.* 1946,—Marion Caroline,
b. 1939: *m.* 1961, Richard Naylor, and has issue living, Charles Gray Marsham *b.* 1962, Margaret
Kingsford *b.* 1964. *Residence*,—King's Acre, Coddington, Ledbury.——Richard Douglas Hollins-
head, *b.* 1913: Maj. (ret.) Worcester Regt.: *m.* 1947, Shirley, da. of John Hannah, of The Mill House,
Mathon, Malvern, Worcestershire, and has issue living, Richard Charles Hannay, *b.* 1948,—David
John Hollinshead, *b.* 1954,—Catherine Elizabeth, *b.* 1952. *Residence*,—Llwynbedw, Cwn Cych,
Newcastle Emlyn, Carmarthenshire.

Issue of the late Lieut.-Col. Hubert Wheler Marsham, *b.* 1876, *d.* 1952. *m.* 1904, Blanche
Mary Frederica" who *d.* 1963, el. dau. of the late Charles Joseph Stonor [B. Camoys,
colls.]:—
Hubert Anthony Lucius, *O.B.E.*, *b.* 1905; Com. (retired) R.N.; European War 1939-42 (O.B.E.);
O.B.E. (Mil.) 1942 : *m.* 1953, Margaret Mary, younger dau. of the late Ambrose Joseph Devas.
Residence,—Bacons, Fordingbridge, Hants.——Sylvia Mary Blanche, *b.* 1910. *Residence*,—
Cox's Quarter, East Lulworth, Dorset.

Granddaughters of the late Hugh Sydney Marsham-Townshend, el. son of the late
Hon. Robert Marsham-Townshend, 2nd son of 2nd Earl:—
Issue of the late Capt. Thomas Marsham-Townshend, Scots Guards, *b.* 1915, *d.* (of
wounds received in action during European War)1944 : *m.* 1940, Averil Innes (who *m.*
2ndly, 1945, Col. John Robert Stephenson Clarke, O.B.E., M.C., Scots Guards, of Pickwell,
Bolney, Sussex), dau. of the late Major Lewis Frederic Innes Loyd:—
June, *b.* 1942: *m.* 1962, Bryan Montagu Norman, of 31, Redcliffe Rd., SW10.——Susan (posthumous),
b. 1944: *m.* 1972, Dr. Piero Studiati Berni, of Molina di Quosa, Pisa, Italy, and has issue living,
Cesare Studiati, *b.* 1972.

(In remainder to Barony of Romney and Baronetcy).

Grandchildren of the late Robert Henry Bullock-Marsham, 2nd son of the late
Robert Bullock-Marsham, el. son of the late Rev. the Hon. Jacob Marsham,
DD, 3rd son of 2nd Baron:—
Issue of the late Major Charles George FIELD-MARSHAM, *b.* 1872, *d.* 1956 ; assumed by deed
poll 1920 the surnames of Field-Marsham in lieu of his patronymic : *m.* 1904, Mary
Dorothea, who *d.* 1970, only child of Edward Knight, of Keswick Old Hall, Norfolk:—
Robert Edward, *b.* 1905 ; ed. at Eton; Major The Bays: *m.* 1st, 1936, Geraldine Hamilton, from
whom he obtained a divorce 1950 ; 2ndly, 1950, Joan Helen, dau. of the late Percy Llewellyn
Nevill [see M. Abergavenny, colls.]. and widow of Charles Austen Field-Marsham (infra). *Residence*,
—Tophill Farm, Langton Green, Kent.——Mary Elizabeth, *MBE* (Tender Meads, Fordcambe, Tun-
bridge Wells), *b.* 1907; MBE (Civil) 1964.

Grandson of Major Charles George FIELD-MARSHAM (ante):—
Issue of the late Charles Austen FIELD-MARSHAM, Lieut. Life Guards, *b.* 1910, *d.*
(on active ser. during European War) 1941 : *m.* 1935, Joan Helen [who *m.* 2ndly, 1950,
as his second wife, Major Robert Edward Field-Marsham, The Bays (ante)], dau. of the
late Percy Llewellyn Nevill [see Abergavenny, colls.] :—
Rupert Charles Edward (29, Roxborough St. West, Toronto, Canada), *b.* 1938; ed. at Eton, and at
McGill Univ.; 2nd Lt. R. Armoured Corps: *m.* 1st, 1963 (m. diss. 1973), Marilyn, da. of Dr. G. B.
Maugham, of Westmount, Montreal; 2ndly, 1973, Lindsay, da. of Robert Dale-Harris, of Uxbridge,
Ont., and has issue living (by 1st m.), Robert Scott, *b.* 1964,—Rupert Charles, *b.* 1968,—(by 2nd m.),
George Robert, *b.* 1975.

Grandsons of the late Robert Anstruther MORRIS-MARSHAM (infra):—
Issue of the late Richard Henry Austruther Morris-Marsham, *b.* 1905, *d.* 1975: *m.* 1st, 1929,
(m. diss. 1951) Iris Rose Sophia, da. of Capt. Dennis Larking, CMG, RN; 2ndly, 1951,
Eileen Reba (Spilfeathers, Ingatestone, Essex), only da. of the late Victor di Halfalla
Nahum, of Italy, and formerly wife of Neville Blond, CMG, OBE:—
(By 1st m.) David Charles Robert, *b.* 1930; ed. at Eton, and Merton Coll., Oxford.——Jack Richard
(The Old Rectory, White Roding, Dunmow, Essex, CM6 1RJ), *b.* 1936; ed. at Eton: *m.* 1963,
Agnes Margaret (Molly), da. of Maj.-Gen. Walter Rutherfoord Goodman, CB, DSO, MC, and has
issue living, James Jonathan, *b.* 1964,—Dominic Rutherfoord, *b.* 1967,—Tiffany Jane, *b.* 1969.

Grandson of the late Robert Henry Bullock-Marsham (ante):—
Issue of the late Robert Anstruther MORRIS-MARSHAM, *b.* 1875; *d.* 1946; assumed by
Roy. licence 1924 the surname and arms of Morris in addition to and before that of
Marsham : *m.* 1904, Jessie Dorothy, who *d.* 1931, el. dau. of Andrew Richard Motion,
formerly of Upton House, near Banbury :—
Antony Cuthbert, *b.* 1909: *m.* 1935, Camilla, da. of the late Charles Humphrey Style [see Style, Bt.,
colls.], and has issue living, Jacqueline, *b.* 1939: *m.* 1969, Michael Raymond Coulman, of 126,
Kensington Park Rd., W11. *Residence*,—Leybourne Lodge, West Malling, Kent.

Grandchildren of the late Rev. Cloudesley Dewar Bullock-Marsham, 3rd son of Robert Bullock-Marsham (ante):—

Issue of the late Cloudesley Henry Bullock-Marsham, *b.* 1879, *d.* 1928 : *m.* 1911, Algitha, who *d.* 1972, da. of the late Rev. the Hon. Algernon Robert Parker [E. Macclesfield, colls.]:—

Cloudesley George, *b.* 1917; ed. at Eton; Maj. 297th (Kent Yeo.) Light Anti-Aircraft Regt. RA (TA); 1939-45 War (prisoner): *m.* 1941, Suzanne, da. of Dudley Holloway. *Residence,*—The Forge, Hamptons, Tonbridge, Kent.——Algernon James (The Old Rectory, Great Langton, Northallerton), 1919; ed. at Eton, and at Ch. Ch., Oxford,; Capt. KRRC: 1939-45 War (prisoner): *m.* 1948, Elizabeth, da. of Air Vice-Marshal Malcolm Henderson, CB, CIE, DSO, and has issue living, Charles James Lessels, *b.* 1950.——Vere Frances, *b.* 1913: *m.* 1932, George Ronald Pigé Leschallas, and has issue living, Anthony George, *b.* 1933,—James Ronald Percy, *b.* 1943,—Lavinia Frances, *b.* 1934,—Suzanne Vere, *b.* 1939. *Residence,*—Little Canon, Wateringbury, Kent.

PREDECESSORS.—[1] *Sir* JOHN **Marsham,** *M.P.*, one of the six Clerks of the Court of Chancery 1638-44 and 1660-80 : cr. a *Baronet* 1663 ; *d.* 1685 ; *s.* by his son [2] *Sir* JOHN, 2nd Bt. ; *d.* 1692 ; *s.* by his son [3] *Sir* JOHN, 3rd Bt. ; *d.* unmarried 1696 ; *s.* by his uncle [4] *Sir* ROBERT, Knt., 4th Bt. ; was one of the six clerks in Chancery 1680-95 ; sat as M.P. for Maidstone 1698-1703; *d.* 1703; *s.* by his son [5] *Sir* ROBERT, 5th Bt.; was Gov. of Dover Castle; sat as M.P. for Maidstone 1708-16 ; cr. *Baron of Romney,* of Romney, co. Kent (peerage of Great Britain) 1716 ; *d.* 1724 ; *s.* by his son [6] ROBERT, *D.C.L., F.R.S.,* 2nd Baron ; *d.* 1793; *s.* by his son [7] CHARLES, 3rd Baron, successively M.P. for Maidstone and Kent; in 1799 entertained George III. at the Mote, when H.M. reviewed about 6,000 of the Kentish Volunteers; was Lord-Lieut. of Kent; cr. *Viscount Marsham* and *Earl of Romney* (peerage of U.K.) 1801; *d.* 1811; *s.* by his son [8] CHARLES, 2nd Earl; was successively M.P. for Hythe and Downton; *d.* 1845; *s.* by his son [9] CHARLES, 3rd Earl ; *b.* 1808; sat as M.P.for W. Kent (*C*) 1841-5 : *m.* 1832, Lady Margaret Harriet Montagu-Douglas-Scott, who *d.* 1846, da. of 4th Duke of Buccleuch; *d.* 1874; *s.* by his son [10] CHARLES, 4th Earl; *b.* 1841 : was a Lord-in-Waiting to H.M. Queen Victoria 1889-92 : *m.* 1863, Lady Frances Augusta Constance Muir-Campbell-Rawdon-Hastings, who *d.* 1910, dau. of 2nd Marquess of Hastings ; *d.* 1905 ; *s.* by his el. son [11] CHARLES, 5th Earl ; *b.* 1864 ; Hon. Lieut.-Col. (retired) 4th Batn. Bedfordshire Regt., and Pres. of Marine So.: *m.* 1890, Anne Louisa, who *d.* 1936, dau. of Sir Edward Henry Scott, 5th Bt. (cr. 1821); *d.* 1933 ; *s.* by his son [12] CHARLES, 6th Earl and present peer ; also Viscount Marsham, and Baron Romney.

Ronaldshay, Earl of, son of Marquess of Zetland.

ROOTES, BARON. (Rootes.) [Baron U.K. 1959.]

Forwards into the Future

(WILLIAM) GEOFFREY ROOTES, 2nd Baron, *b.* June 14th, 1917; *s.* 1964; ed. at Harrow, and at Ch. Ch. Oxford; FBIM; FRSA; Chm. of Chrysler UK Ltd. (formerly Rootes Motors Ltd.) 1967-73, a Member of National Economic Development Cttee. for Motor Manufacturing Industry 1968-73, Chm. of Exec. Cttee. of Motor Manufacturers and Traders, Ltd. 1972-73 (Pres. 1960-61), a Member of Council of Confedn. of British Industry 1967-74, of Council of Inst. of Dirs., and of Council of Warwick Univ. 1956-74 (Chm. of Careers Advisory Board); Pres. of Motor & Cycle Trades Benevolent Trust Fund 1968-70, and of Motor Industry Research Assocn. 1970-71; a Member of Europe Cttee. since 1972, Pres., Inst. of Motor Industry since 1973, a Dir. of Ranks Hovis McDougall and of Joseph Lucas Industries since 1973, and Chm. of Game Conservancy since 1975; 1939-45 War as Capt. and temporary Maj. RASC: *m.* 1946, Marian, da. of the late Lt.-Col. Herbert Roche Hayter, DSO, and widow of Wing-Cdr. J. H. Slater, AFC, and has issue.

Arms,—Ermine within an orle azure a bugle horn sable garnished or stringed gules. **Crest,**—On a wreath argent and vert a cubit arm bendwise in armour or the hand proper grasping a spear in bend also proper flying therefrom a forked pennon barry argent and azure semée of plates and bezants. **Supporters,**—On either side a horse argent gorged with a chain pendent therefrom a wheel or.

Residences,—North Standen House, nr. Hungerford, Berks.; Glenalmond House, Glenalmond, Perthshire. *Clubs,*—Buck's, St. James'.

SON LIVING.
Hon. NICHOLAS GEOFFREY, *b.* July 12th, 1951; ed. at Harrow.

DAUGHTER LIVING.
Hon. Sally Hayter, *b.* 1947: *m.* 1968, Andrew Beauchamp St. John, of Cul-na-Cloich, Glenalmond, Perthshire [see B. St. John of Bletso, colls.].

WIDOW LIVING OF SON OF FIRST BARON.
Elizabeth Margaret (Dallick House, Glenalmond, Perthshire), da. of the late Rev. Humphrey Gordon Barclay, OVO, MC, and widow of Lt. Norman Lewis Philips [E. Ducie, colls.]: *m.* 1944, the Hon. Brian Gordon Rootes, who *d.* 1971, and has issue [see colls. infra].

COLLATERAL BRANCH LIVING.
    Issue of the late Hon. Brian Gordon Rootes, yr. son of 1st Baron, b. 1919, d. 1971:
    m. 1944, Elizabeth Margaret (ante), da. of the late Rev. Humphrey Gordon
    Barclay, CVO, MC, and widow of Lt. Norman Lewis Philips [E. Ducie, colls.]:—
William Brian (Dallick House, Glenalmond, Perthshire), b. 1944: m. 1969, Alicia Graham, yst. da. of
    F. Graham Roberts, of East Farm House, Piddlehinton, Dorset, and has issue living, Talitha Alice
    Louisa, b. 1973.

PREDECESSOR.—[1] Sir William Edward Rootes, GBE, son of the late William Rootes, of Hawk-
    hurst, Kent; b. 1894; Chm. of Rootes, Ltd.; Chm. of Dollar Exports Council 1951-60, and of
    successor body, W. Hemisphere Exports Council 1961-64: m. 1st, 1916 (marriage dissolved 1951),
    Nora, who d. 1964, da. of Horace Press; 2ndly, 1951, Ruby Joy (Ann), who d. 1968, da. of Capt.
    Gordon Duff, widow of Sir Charles Thomas Hewitt Mappin, 4th Bt., and formerly wife of Sir Francis
    Henry Grenville Peek, 4th Bt.; d. 1964; s. by his el. son [2] (WILLIAM) GEOFFREY, 2nd Baron
    and present peer.

ROSEBERY, EARL OF.   (Primrose.)   [Earl S. 1703.   Bt. S. 1651.]

By faith and trust.

NEIL ARCHIBALD PRIMROSE, 7th Earl,
and 9th Baronet; b. Feb. 11th, 1929; s.
1974; ed. at Stowe, and New Coll., Oxford;
patron of three livings; a DL for Midlothian: m. 1955, Alison Mary Deirdre, da.
of the late Ronald William Reid, MS, FRCS
[see Chaytor, Bt., colls.], and has issue.

Arms,—Quarterly: 1st and 4th vert. three primroses within
a double tressure flory counterflory or Primrose; 2nd and
3rd argent, a lion rampant, double queued sable Cressy.
Crest,—A demilion gules holding in the dexter paw a
primrose or. Supporters,—Two lions or.
    Seats,—Dalmeny House, South Queensferry, W.
Lothian; Mentmore, Leighton Buzzard; Cleveland House,
Newmarket.

SON LIVING.
HARRY RONALD NEIL (Lord Dalmeny), b. Nov. 20th, 1967.

DAUGHTERS LIVING.
Lady Lucy Catherine Mary, b. 1955.
Lady Jane Margaret Helen, b. 1960.
Lady Emma Elizabeth Anne, b. 1962.
Lady Caroline Sara Frances, b. 1964.

HALF-SISTER LIVING.
Lady Helen Dorothy, b. 1913: m. 1933, the Hon. Hugh Adeane Vivian Smith [see B. Bicester.]. Resi-
    dence,—Souldern Manor, Bicester, Oxon.

WIDOW LIVING OF SIXTH EARL.
Hon. Dame EVA ISABEL MARIAN Strutt, DBE, LLD, JP (Eva, Countess of Rosebery), (Mentmore,
    Leighton Buzzard; Cleveland House, Newmarket), da. of 2nd Baron Aberdare, and formerly wife
    of 3rd Baron Belper, who d. 1956; a JP for Bucks., and a Chevalier of Legion of Honour; DBE
    (Civil) 1955: m. 1924, as his 2nd wife, the 6th Earl, who d. 1974.

COLLATERAL BRANCHES LIVING.
    Issue of the late Capt. the Right Hon. Neil James Archibald Primrose,
    MC, MP, Yeo., 2nd son of 5th Earl, b. (Dec.) 1882; d. (killed in action during
    European War) 1917: m. 1915, Lady Victoria Alice Louise Stanley [who d.
    1927, having m. 2ndly, 1919, Capt. Sir (Harold) Malcolm Bullock, MBE, late
    Scots Guards (cr. Bt. 1954, ext. 1966)], da. of 17th Earl of Derby:—
Ruth Alice Hannah Mary (Countess of Halifax), b. 1916 : m. 1936, the 2nd Earl of Halifax. Residences,
    —Garrowby, York; Swynford Paddock, Six Mile Bottom, Cambridgeshire.

        Granddaughter of the late Hon. Bouverie Francis Primrose, CB, son of 4th Earl:
    Issue of the late Francis Archibald Primrose, b. 1843, d. 1922 : m. 1872, Jane, who
    d. 1921, dau. of George King, of Sydney, N.S.W.
Gwendolen Gertrude Maude (Fir Trees, Kingwood Firs, Grayshott, Hindhead, Surrey).

        (Not in remainder to United Kingdom Earldom.)
    Grandsons of the late Edward Montagu Primrose, son of the late Hon. Francis
    Ward Primrose, M.P., 2nd son of 3rd Earl :—
    Issue of the late Ralph Gore Primrose, b. 1875, d. 1921 : m. 1913, Agatha Vera (of Suite 310,
    1009, West 10th Avenue, Vancouver, British Columbia), dau. of David Moss Coulter :—
Gerald Edward David, b. 1914 : m. 1950, Anne Loletta, dau. of James Ranney Broughton, of Atwood,
    Ontario, and has issue living, James Ralph, b. 1952. Residence,—350, La Prenda, Millbrae, Cali-
    fornia, U.S.A.——Neil, b. 1918: BA, BEd: m. 1944, Margaret Verna, da. of the late Henry James
    Francis, of Portsmouth, and has issue living, David Neil (2278, Midas St., Abbotsford, BC, Canada),
    b. 1945: m. 1966, Anna Joyce, da. of F. C. Walters, of White Rock, BC, and has issue living, David
    Francis Neil b. 1966, Douglas James Baird b. 1970,—Margaret Jane Elizabeth b. 1948,—Deirdre
    Katherine, b. 1951,—Anne Jennifer, b. 1954. Residence,—14210, Wheatley Av., White Rock,
    British Columbia.

PREDECESSORS.—[1] ARCHIBALD Primrose, Clerk of the Privy Council, cr. a Baronet (N.S.) by
    Charles II, 1651, and after the Restoration (1661) was appointed a Lord of Session and Lord Clerk
    Register with the title of Lord Carrington; d. 1679; s. by his son [2] Sir WILLIAM, 2nd Bt.; was
    Clerk of the Notaries: d. 1687; s. by his son [3] Sir JAMES, 3rd Bt.; MP for Edinburghshire
    1702-3; cr. Lord Primrose and Castlefield, and Viscount Primrose (peerage of Scotland)
    1703, with remainder to the heirs male of his father: d. 1706; s. by his el. son [4] ARCHI-
    BALD, 2nd Viscount; d. unmarried 1716; s. by his brother [5] HUGH, 3rd Viscount; a
    Lieut.-Col. in the Army ; d.s.p. 1741, when the peerages expired, and the baronetcy devolved upon

his kinsman [6] JAMES, 6th Bt., who had in 1723 *s.* his father as 2nd *Earl of Rosebery* (see *₊* infra) ; *d.* 1755 ; *s.* by his son [7] NEIL, *K.T.*, 3rd Earl ; a Representative Peer 1768-84 ; *d.* 1814 ; *s.* by his son [8] ARCHIBALD JOHN, *K.T., P.C.*, 4th Earl, *b.* 1783 ; was unsuccessively M.P. for Helston and Cashel, and Lord-Lieut. of Linlithgowshire ; cr. *Baron Rosebery*, of Rosebery, co. Edinburgh (peerage of United Kingdom) 1828 : *m.* 1st, 1808, Harriet, dau. of the Hon. Bartholomew Bouverie [E. Radnor] ; *d.* 1868 ; *s.* by his grandson [9] ARCHIBALD PHILIP, *K.G., K.T., P.C.* (el. son of Archibald, Lord Dalmeny, M.P., by Lady Catherine Lucy Wilhelmine Stanhope, dau. of 4th Earl Stanhope), 5th Earl ; *b.* 1847 ; Lord-Lieut. of cos. Linlithgow 1873-1929, and Edinburgh 1884-1929, an Elder Brother of Trinity House, Lord Rector of Aberdeen Univ. 1878-81, Under-Sec. of State for Home Depart. 1881-3, Lord Rector of Edinburgh 1882-5, Lord Privy Seal and First Commr. of Works and Public Buildings Feb. to June 1885, temporary Keeper of the Great Seal of Scotland 1885, Sec. of State for Foreign Affairs 1886 and Aug. 1892 to March 1894, and Premier, First Lord of the Treasury, and Lord Pres. of the Council March 1894 to June 1895, and Lord Rector of Glasgow 1899-1902 ; Special Envoy to Court of Vienna to announce Accession of King George V. 1910 ; held Canopy at Coronations of Kings Edward VII and George V : cr. KG 1892, KT 1895, *Baron Epsom*, of Epsom, co. Surrey, and *Viscount Mentmore*, of Mentmore, and *Earl of Midlothian* (peerage of United Kingdom) 1911 ; received Victorian Chain 1917 : *m.* 1878, Hannah, who *d.* 1890, dau. and heiress of the late Baron Meyer de Rothschild ; *d.* 1929 ; *s.* by his son [10] ALBERT EDWARD HARRY MAYER ARCHIBALD, *KT, DSO, MC, PC*, 6th Earl ; *b.* 1882 ; doyen of British Turf as racehorse owner, and breeder ; Steward of Jockey Club 1929-32, and 1945-48 ; MP for Midlothian (*L*) 1906-10 ; Regional Commr. for Scotland 1941-45 ; Sec. of State for Scotland 1945 ; Chm. of Nat. Liberal Party 1945-47 : *m.* 1st, 1909 (m. diss. 1919), Lady Dorothy Alice Margaret Augusta Grosvenor, who *d.* 1966, sister of 3rd Duke of Westminster ; 2ndly, 1924, the Hon. Dame Eva Isabel Marian Strutt, DBE, LLD, JP, da. of 2nd Baron Aberdare, and formerly wife of 3rd Baron Belper ; *d.* 1974, *s.* by his yr. son [11] NEIL ARCHIBALD, 7th Earl and present peer ; also Earl of Midlothian, Viscount Rosebery, Viscount Inverkeithing, Viscount Mentmore, Lord Primrose and Dalmeny, Lord Dalmeny and Primrose, Baron Rosebery, and Baron Epsom.

₊[1] ARCHIBALD Primrose, 4th son of Sir Archibald Primrose, 1st Bt. (ante), M.P. for Edinburgh 1695, Gentleman of the Bedchamber to Prince George of Denmark, and a Commr. for the Treaty of the Union, was cr. *Lord Primrose and Dalmeny* and *Viscount of Rosebery* (peerage of Scotland) 1700, with remainder to his issue male and female successively, and in default thereof to the heirs of entail in the lands of Rosebery ; and *Lord Dalmeny and Primrose, Viscount Inverkeithing*, and *Earl of Rosebery* (peerage of Scotland) 1703, with remainder to his issue male and female successively ; was a Representative Peer 1708-14 ; *d.* 1723 ; *s.* by his son [2] JAMES, 2nd Earl, *b.* 1741 ; *s.* as 6th Bt. (see ante).

ROSSE, EARL OF. (Parsons.) [Earl I. 1806, Bt. I. 1677.]

For God and the king.

LAURENCE MICHAEL HARVEY PARSONS, *KBE*, 6th Earl and 9th Baronet ; *b.* Sept. 28th, 1906 ; *s.* 1918 ; ed. at Eton, and at Ch. Ch., Oxford (MA) ; Hon. LLD Dublin 1950 and Belfast 1964 ; is Capt. Irish Guards, Chm. of Standing Commission on Museums and Galleries, a F.S.A. (London, and Ireland), a F.R.A.S., a F.R.S.A., an Hon. F.R.I.B.A., and a M.R.I.A. ; Pro-Chancellor of Dublin Univ. since 1965 (Vice-Chancellor 1949-64) ; Pres., Georgian Group (Chm. 1947-68) ; Dep. Chm. of National Trust ; NW Europe 1944-45 (M.B.E.) ; M.B.E. (Mil.) 1945, KBE (Civil) 1974 : *m.* 1935, Anne (ARMSTRONG-JONES), only da. of the late Lieut.-Col. Leonard Messel, OBE, of Nymans, Staplefield, Sussex, and has issue.

Arms,—Gules, three leopards' faces argent. **Crest,**—A cubit arm proper, grasping a poleaxe gules. **Supporters,**—Two ounces argent, spotted sable, and gorged with a plain collar gules, charged with four bezants.

Seats,—Birr Castle, co. Offaly ; Womersley Park, Doncaster. *Residence,*—18, Stafford Terr., W.8. *Clubs,*—Brooks's, Royal Automobile, Kildare Street (Dublin).

SONS LIVING.

WILLIAM BRENDAN (*Lord Oxmantown*) (Birr Castle, co Offaly), *b.* Oct. 21st, 1936 ; ed. at Eton, Grenoble Univ. and Ch. Ch., Oxford (MA) ; late 2nd Lt. Irish Guards ; Admin. Officer UN Tech. Assistance Board, Ghana, 1963-65 ; Assist. Resident Representative, UN Development Programme, Dahomey 1965-68 and Area Officer for Mid-West Africa 1968-70, since when Assist. Resident Representative, Iran : *m.* 1966, Alison Margaret, el. da. of Maj. John Davey Cooke-Hurle, of Startforth Hall, Barnard Castle, co. Durham, and has issue:—
SON LIVING. *Hon.* Laurence Patrick, *b.* March 31st, 1969.
DAUGHTER LIVING. *Hon.* Alicia Siobhan Margaret Nasreen, *b.* 1971.

Hon. Desmond Oliver Martin (Birr Castle, co. Offaly), *b.* 1938 ; ed. at Eton : *m.* 1965, Aline, da. of George Alexander Macdonald, MB, of Gable End, Priors Marston, Rugby, and has issue living, Rupert Alexander Michael, *b.* 1966,—Desmond Edward Richard, *b.* 1968.

WIDOW LIVING OF FIFTH EARL.

FRANCES LOIS (*Lois, Viscountess de Vesci*), dau. of Sir Cecil Edmund Lister-Kaye, 4th Bt. : *m.* 1st, 1905, the 5th Earl, who *d.* (of wounds in action during European War) 1918 ; 2ndly, 1920, the 5th Viscount de Vesci, who *d.* 1958. *Residence,*—Womersley Park, Doncaster.

COLLATERAL BRANCHES LIVING.

Grandchildren of the late Hon. Richard Clere Parsons, 5th son of 3rd Earl:—
Issue of the late Lieut.-Col. William Frederic Parsons, D.S.O., *b.* 1879, *d.* 1956 : *m.* 1915, Clara Helena, da. of the late Hon. Edward Gerald Strutt [B. Rayleigh, colls.]:—
Desmond Richard, *b.* 1916.——Nancy Olivia, *b.* 1919.

Issue of the late Arthur David Clere Parsons, *b.* 1881, *d.* 1955 : *m.* 1914, Doris, who *d.* 1970, da. of the late Norman C. Cookson, of Oakwood, Wylam, Northumberland:—

Arthur Christopher (of Hatchwood House, Odiham, Hants; Army and Navy, and City of London Clubs), b. 1919: 1939-45 War as Maj. RA: m. 1945, Veronica Rosetta de Courcy, el. da. of Maj.-Gen. Sir Guy de Courcy Glover, KBE, CB, DSO, MC [B. Kingsale, colls.], and has issue living, John Christopher, b. 1946,—Rosemary Anne, b. 1948: m. 1975, John B. Burke, of Town Farm House, Earls Green, Stowmarket, Suffolk,—Daphne Phoebe, b. 1951: m. 1971, Capt. Hugh Richard Oliver-Bellasis [see Bates, Bt. cr. 1880, colls.].——Norman Charles, b. 1925: m. 1953, Katharine Alison, second da. of Col. H. H. Gardiner, MC, late RA, and has issue living, Giles Randal, b. 1957,—Deborah Anne, b. 1954,—Clare Elizabeth, b. 1959,—Katharine Mary, b. 1963. Residence,—East House, Middle Brunton, Newcastle upon Tyne, 3.——Theodora Phoebe, b. 1915: m. 1939, Lt.-Cdr. James Bertram Everard Wainwright, DSO, OBE, RN, who d. (on active ser.) 1943, and has issue living, Andrew, b. 1943,—Susan, b. 1941: m. 1967, Richard Edward Dawson. Residence,—Brackenwood, Blackheath, Guildford.——Phyllis Rosemary, b. 1918: m. 1st, 1945, as his second wife, Capt. Ian Stanley Akers-Douglas, Berks. Yeo., who d. 1952 [see V. Chilston, colls.]; 2ndly, 1955, John Anthony Cobham Shaw, of The Old Rectory, Upper Stondon, Henlow, Beds. [see By. of Cobham].

    Issue of the late Rev. Canon Laurence Edmund Parsons, b. 1883, d. 1972: m. 1911, Lydia Dorothy, who d. 1964, da. of the late Frederic Foster Le Trobe-Bateman:—
Mary Alice, b. 1912.
    Issue of the late Rev. Canon Richard Edward Parsons, b. 1888, d. 1971: m. 1917, Hester Katherine, who d. 1954, da. of the late Maj. John William Ainslie Drummond [E. Perth, colls.]:—
Rev. Desmond John (All Saints Vicarage, Rosendale Rd., W. Dulwich, SE21), b. 1925; ed. at Eton; Late Lt. Irish Gds.; Organising Sec. and Dep. Warden, Moor Park Coll. for Adult Education 1950-61, and a Gov. 1961: m. 1968, Althea Hermione, da. of Charles Anthony Stanley Prowse [see Millais, Bt.], and has issue living, Benedict Desmond Drummond, b. 1969,—Francesca Catherine, b. 1972.——Agnes Mary, b. 1918: m. 1941, Maj. Cosmo Rex Ivor Russell [see B. Ampthill, colls.].——Hester Clere, b. 1920: m. 1940, David Hastings Gerald Russell, late Lt RNVR [see B. Ampthill, colls.].——Elizabeth Frances, b. 1923.——Rachel Anne, b. 1927.

    Grandchildren of the late Hon. Lawrence Parsons, son of 2nd Earl:—
    Issue of the late Rev. Randolph Cecil Parsons, b. 1852, d. 1941: m. 1901, Florence, Emily, who d. 1946, dau. of William Ashton :—
John Cecil Lawrence (12, Addicott Rd., Weston-super-Mare), b. 1905: m. 1940, and has issue living, Michael Charles, b. 1950,—Cynthia, b. 1948.——Joan Mary (12, Addicott Rd., Weston-super-Mare), b. 1906.

PREDECESSORS.—[1] LAWRENCE Parsons; cr. a Baronet 1677; was attainted by King James's Parliament 1689, and sentenced to death; d. 1698; s. by his son [2] Sir WILLIAM, 2nd Bt.; d. 1740; s. by his grandson [3] Sir LAWRENCE, 3rd Bt.; was M.P. for King's Co. 1741; d. 1749; s. by his son [4] Sir WILLIAM, 4th Bt.; was M.P. for King's Co.; d. 1791; s. by his son [5] Sir LAWRENCE, 5th Bt.; successively M.P. for Dublin University and King's Co.; in 1807 s. his father's half-brother as 2nd Earl of Rosse (see *,* infra); was a Representative Peer, and last Joint Postmaster-Gen. for Ireland; d. 1841; s. by his son [6] WILLIAM, K.P., 3rd Earl; b. 1800; sat as M.P. for King's Co. (L) 1821-34; was a Representative Peer, Pres. of Royal So., Chancellor of Dublin Univ.; erected upon his estate at Parsonstown between the years 1828 and 1845 an enormous telescope at the cost of more than £20,000: m. 1836, Mary, who d. 1885, dau. and el. co-heir of John Wilmer Field, of Heaton Hall, co. York; d. 1867; s. his by his son [7] LAWRENCE, K.P., D.C.L., F.R.S., 4th Earl; b. 1840: a Representative Peer and Chancellor of Dublin Univ.; Lieut. and Custos Rotulorum of King's Co. (High Sheriff 1867): m. 1870, (Frances) Cassandra, who d. 1921, dau. of 4th Baron Hawke; d. 1908: s. by his son [8] WILLIAM EDWARD, 5th Earl, b. 1873; a Representative Peer, and Lieut. and Custos Rotulorum of King's co.; Major Irish Guards: m. 1905, Frances Lois, dau. of Sir Cecil Edmund Lister-Kaye, 4th Bt.; d. (of wounds received in action during European War) 1918; s. by his son [9] LAURENCE MICHAEL HARVEY, 6th Earl and present peer; also Baron Oxmantown.

, [1] LAWRENCE Parsons, 2nd son of Sir Lawrence, 3rd Bt. (ante), was cr. Baron Oxmantown (peerage of Ireland) 1792, with remainder to his nephew Sir Lawrence Parsons, 5th Bt. (ante), Viscount Oxmantown (peerage of Ireland) 1795, without the special remainder, and Earl of Rosse (peerage of Ireland) 1806, with remainder to his nephew aforesaid; d. 1807, when the Viscountcy became ext., and he was s. in the other honours by his nephew [2] Sir LAWRENCE, 2nd Earl and 5th Bt. (ante).

ROSSLYN, EARL OF. (St. Clair-Erskine.) [Earl U.K. 1801, Bt. S. 1666.]

ANTHONY HUGH FRANCIS HARRY ST. CLAIR-ERSKINE, 6th Earl, and 10th Baronet; b. May 18th, 1917; s. 1939; ed. at Eton, and at Magdalen Coll., Oxford; Capt. (retired) King's Roy. Rifle Corps; Member of Lloyd's, and a Director of R. F. Kershaw, Ltd.; N.-W. Europe 1944-5 with Canadian Army (despatches): m. 1955 (marriage dissolved 1962), Athenaïs de Mortemart, only dau. of the late Louis Victor, Duc de Vivonne, and has issue.

    Arms.—Quarterly: 1st argent, a cross engrailed sable, St. Clair; 2nd argent, a pale sable, Erskine; 3rd azure, a bend between six cross crosslets fitchée or, Mar; 4th argent, on a chevron between three roses gules, a fleur-de-lis of the field, Wedderburn. Crest.—A demi-phœnix in flames, wings expanded and elevated proper. Supporters.—Dexter, an eagle, wings inverted proper, gorged with a plain collar argent, thereon a rose gules; sinister, a griffin, wings elevated proper, beaked and membered or.

    Residence,—Stonerwood Park, Petersfield, Hants. Clubs —White's, Royal Automobile, New Edinburgh), Travellers' (Paris), MCC, Royal and Ancient.

SON LIVING.
PETER (Lord Loughborough), b. March 31st, 1958.

DAUGHTER LIVING.
Lady Caroline, b. 1956.

UNCLE LIVING. (Son of 5th Earl.)
Hon. David Simon, b. 1917; ed. at Ampleforth Coll., and at Merton Coll., Oxford (Scholar, MA); Maj. R. Scots; N.-W. Europe 1944-45 (despatches): m. 1948, Antonia Mary (who d. 1965, having obtained a divorce 1959), dau. of the late Adm. of the Fleet Sir John Donald Kelly, G.C.B., G.C.V.O., and has issue living, Jonathan Harry, b. 1949. Residences,—3, Culford Gdns., S.W.3; St. Fride-wide's Cottage, Knighton, Swindon.

AUNT LIVING. (*Daughter of 5th Earl.*)
Lady Mary Sybil (Stowell Park, Pewsey, Marlborough, Wilts.), *b.* 1912: *m.* 1st, 1933, Philip Gordon
Dunn (afterwards 2nd Bt.), from whom she obtained a divorce 1944; 2ndly, 1946, as his second wife,
Robin Francis Campbell, DSO, from whom she obtained a divorce 1959, late Capt. Gen. List, only
son of the Rt. Hon. Sir Ronald Hugh Campbell, GCMG; 3rdly, 1962, Charles R. McCabe from whom
she obtained a divorce 1969; 4thly, 1969, Sir Philip Gordon Dunn, 2nd Bt., (ante).

PREDECESSORS.—[1] *Rt. Hon.* ALEXANDER Wedderburn, *PC*, MP for the Ayr Burghs 1761-8,
for Castle Rising 1774, for Okehampton 1774-8, and for Bishops Castle 1778-80, having been
Solicitor-Gen., and Attorney-Gen. was in 1780 cr. *Baron Loughborough*, of Loughborough, co. Leicester
(peerage of Great Britain); was Lord High Chancellor of Great Britain 1793-1801; cr. *Baron Loughborough*, of Loughborough, co Surrey (peerage of Great Britain) 1795, with remainder to his nephew
Sir James Erskine, 6th Bt. (see *** infra) and *Earl of Rosslyn* (peerage of United Kingdom) 1801,
with similar remainders; *d.s.p.* 1805; *s.* by his nephew [2] JAMES, *GCB*, *PC*, 2nd Earl; assumed
the additional surname of St. Clair by Roy. licence 1805; sat as MP for Castle Rising 1782-84, for
Morpeth 1784-90 and for Kirkcaldy 1796-1805; was Director-Gen. of Chancery in Scotland 1785-1837,
a Lieut.-Gen. in the Army, Lord-Lieut. of Fifeshire, and Lord Pres. of the Council 1834-5; *d.* 1837;
s. by his son [3] JAMES ALEXANDER, *PC*, 3rd Earl; *b.* 1802; was a Gen. in the Army, Col. 7th
Hussars, Master of the Buckhounds 1841-6, and Under-Sec. of State for War 1859: *m.* 1826, Frances,
da. of Lieut.-Gen. William Wemyss; *d.* 1866; *s.* by his son [4] FRANCIS ROBERT, *PC*, 4th Earl;
b. 1833; High Commr. to Gen. Assembly of Church of Scotland 1874, 1878, 1879, and 1880, and Capt.
of Corps of Gentlemen-at-Arms 1886-90; *d.* 1890: *m.* 1866, Blanche Adeliza, who *d.* 1933, da. of
Henry FitzRoy, and widow of Col. the Hon. Charles Henry Maynard; *s.* by his el. son [5] JAMES
FRANCIS HARRY, 5th Earl, *b.* 1869: *m.* 1st, 1890, Violet Aline, who *d.* 1945 (from whom he had
obtained a divorce in Scotland 1902), da. of the late Robert Charles de Grey Vyner [B. Lucas, colls.];
2ndly, 1905, Georgeiana, then a member of the dramatic profession, who *d.* 1917 (having obtained
a divorce 1907), younger da. of George Robinson, of Minneapolis, USA; 3rdly 1908, Vera Mary,
who *d.* 1975, da. of the late Eric Edward Bayley, formerly Lt. 17th Lancers; *d.* 1939; *s.* by his
grandson [6] ANTHONY HUGH FRANCIS HARRY (son of the late Francis Edward Scudamore, Lord
Loughborough, el. son of 5th Earl), 6th Earl and present peer; also Baron Loughborough.

* [1] CHARLES Erskine, successively M.P. for cos. Clackmannan and Stirling; cr. a *Baronet*
1666; *s.* by his el. son [2] *Sir* JAMES, 2nd Bt.; killed at battle of Landen 1693, unmarried;
s. by his brother [3] *Sir* JOHN, 3rd Bt.; M.P. for Clackmannan; *d.* 1739; *s.* by his el. son
[4] *Sir* CHARLES, 4th Bt.; killed at the battle of Laffeldt 1747, unmarried; *s.* by his brother
[5] *Sir* HENRY, 5th Bt.; a Lieut.-Gen. in the Army; sat as M.P. for Ayr and for Anstruther:
m. Janet, dau. of Peter Wedderburn (Lord Chesterhall), a Lord of Session; *s.* by his son [6]
Sir JAMES, 6th Bt., who *s.* his uncle as 2nd Earl of Rosslyn (ante).

ROSSMORE, BARON. (Westenra.) [Baron I. 1796 and U.K. 1838.]

After battles, rewards.

WILLIAM WARNER WESTENRA, 7th
Baron; *b.* Feb. 14th, 1931; *s.* 1958;
ed. at Eton, and at Trin. Coll., Camb.
(B.A. 1957); is 2nd Lieut. Somerset
L.I.

ᴁrms,—Quarterly: 1st and 4th per bend or
and argent, in chief a tree eradicated vert, and
in base waves of the sea, therein a sea-horse
naiant, reguardant, all proper, *Westenra;* 2nd
and 3rd quarterly, 1st and 4th azure, three mullets
argent, *Murray;* 2nd and 3rd gules, three martlets
within a bordure or, *Cairnes.* Crest,—A lion rampant proper. Supporters,—*Dexter*, a trooper of the
5th Dragoons in uniform, and holding in his right
hand a sword, point downwards; *sinister*, a black
charger of the same regiment, caparisoned proper.

Residence,—Rossmore, co. Monaghan.

SISTER LIVING.

Hon. Brigid Mary WESTENRA (Pratolino, Radda-in-
Chianti, Siena, Italy), *b.* 1928; reverted to her
maiden name: *m.* 1956 (m. diss. 1969), the Hon.
Jonathan Alan Howard [see B. Strathcona and
Mount Royal].

WIDOW LIVING OF SON OF FIFTH BARON.

Margaret Cecilia Sulivan (HOPE), dau. of the Rev.
George Sullivan Edgcombe: *m.* 1936, as his
second wife, the Hon. Richard Westenra, who
d. 1944. *Residence,*—West Lodge, Sheringham,
Norfolk.

WIDOW LIVING OF SIXTH BARON.

DOLORES CECIL (LEE) (*Dowager Baroness Rossmore*), dau. of the late Lieut.-Col. James Alban Wilson,
D.S.O., Indian Army, of West Burton, Yorks.: *m.* 1927, the 6th Baron, who *d.* 1958. *Residence,*—
The Keepers Cottage, Rossmore, co. Monaghan.

COLLATERAL BRANCHES LIVING.

Grandson of Maj. the Hon. Peter Craven Westenra, 4th son of 3rd Baron:—
Issue of the late Petronella Mary Kathleen Westenra, *b.* 1897, *d.* 1966: *m.* 1920, Capt.
Edward Theobald Walsh Church, RN, who *d.* 1948:—
John Arthur (Yarde, Stoke Gabriel, Totnes, Devon), *b.* 1921: *m.* 1948, Gillian Favell Yorke, da. of
the late Geoffrey Sankey, of Laburnum Cottage, Winchelsea, Sussex, and has issue living, Timothy
John Edward, *b.* 1955,—Josephine Arabella, *b.* 1954,—Anthea Mary Charlotte, *b.* 1958.

Issue of the late Hon. Richard Westenra, 2nd son of 5th Baron, *b.* 1893, *d.*
1944: *m.* 1st, 1919, Alice Florence (who *d.* 1975, having obtained a divorce 1936), da. of
Maxwell Vandeleur Blacker-Douglass, of Seafield, Millbrooke, Jersey, Channel
Islands; 2ndly, 1936, Mrs. Margaret Cecilia Sulivan (HOPE) (ante), dau. of the
Rev. George Sullivan Edgcombe:—
(By 1st marriage) Cynthia, *b.* 1920: *m.* 1947, Eric Miles, and has issue living, Richard Christopher,
b. 1955,—Caroline Rose, *b.* 1948,—Sylvia Claire, *b.* 1950. *Residence,*—Seafield House, Millbrook,
Jersey.

PREDECESSORS.—[1] ROBERT Cuninghame, son of the late Col. David Cunninghame; b. 17—; a Gen. in the Army, and Col. 5th Dragoons; M.P. for Tulske 1751-60, for Armagh 1761-8, for Monaghan 1769-96. and for E. Grinstead 1788-9; cr. *Baron Rossmore*, of Monaghan, co. Monaghan (peerage of Ireland) 1796, with remainder to his wife's nephews, Henry Alexander Jones (who *d.s.p.*) and Warner William and Henry Westenra: *m.* 1754, Elizabeth, who *d.* 1824, second dau. and co-heiress of the late Col. John Murray; *d.* 1801; *s.* by his nephew [2] WARNER WILLIAM Westenra, 2nd Baron; *b.* 1765; M.P. for co. Monaghan 1800-1801; cr. *Baron Rossmore*, of co. Monaghan (peerage of United Kingdom) 1838: *m.* 1st, 1791, Marianne, who *d.* 1807, dau. of the late Charles Walsh, of Walsh Park, co. Tipperary; 2ndly, 1819, Lady Augusta Charteris, who *d.* 1840, dau. of Francis, Lord Elcho; *d.* 1842; *s.* by his el. son [3] HENRY ROBERT, 3rd Baron; *b.* 1792; was M.P. for co. Monaghan 1818-32 and 1834-42, and afterwards Lord-Lieut. thereof: *m.* 1st, 1820, Anne Douglas Hamilton, who *d.* 1844; 2ndly, 1846, his cousin, Julia Ellen Josephine, who *d.* 1912, dau. of Henry Lloyd, of Farinrory, co. Tipperary; *d.* 1860; *s.* by his el. son [4] HENRY CAIRNES, 4th Baron; Cornet 1st Life Guards; *d.* 1874; *s.* by his brother [5] DERRICK WARNER WILLIAM, 5th Baron, *b.* 1853; Lieut. of co. Monaghan: *m.* 1882, Mittie, O.B.E., who *d.* 1953, dau. of Christopher Richard Naylor, of Hooton Hall, Cheshire; *d.* 1921; *s.* by his el. son [6] WILLIAM, 6th Baron; *b.* 1892; European War 1914-18, European War 1939-45 as Lieut. R.N.V.R.: *m.* 1927, Dolores Cecil (LEE), dau. of the late Lieut.-Col. James Alban Wilson, D.S.O., Indian Army, of West Barton, Yorkshire; *d.* 1958; *s.* by his only son [7] WILLIAM WARNER, 7th Baron, and present peer.

ROTHERMERE, VISCOUNT. (Harmsworth.) [Viscount U.K. 1919, Bt. U.K. 1910.]

He who acts diligently acts well.

ESMOND CECIL HARMSWORTH, 2nd Viscount, and 2nd Baronet; *b.* May 29th, 1898; *s.* 1940; ed. at Chatham House, Ramsgate, and at Eton; Chm. of Associated Newspapers, Ltd. 1937-71, since when Pres., and Dir. of Group Finance; a Trustee of Reuter's Trust; sometime Capt. RMA; an ADC to Prime Min. at Peace Conference, Paris 1919, Chm. of Newspaper Proprietors' Asso. 1935-61, Pres. of Newspaper Press Fund 1935-37, and Chancellor of Newfoundland Memorial Univ. 1952-61; MP for Isle of Thanet Div. of Kent (*U*) 1919-29: *m.* 1st (Jan.) 1920, Margaret Hunam (from whom he obtained a divorce 1938), da. of the late William Redhead; 2ndly, 1945, Ann Geraldine Mary (from whom he obtained a divorce 1952), da. of the Hon. Guy Lawrence Charteris [see E. Wemyss] and widow of 3rd Baron O'Neill: *m.* 3rdly, 1966, Mrs. Mary Ohrstrom, da. of Kenneth Murchison, of Dallas, Texas, and has issue by 1st and 3rd m.

Arms,—Azure, two rolls of paper in saltire or, banded in the centre gules, between four bees volant of the second. **Crest,**—Between two ostrich feathers or a cubit arm erect proper, the hand grasping a roll of paper or. **Supporters,**—On either side a gladiator fully habited and accoutred, the dexter holding in the exterior hand a sword, and the sinister holding on the exterior arm a shield all proper, each charged on the breast with a fountain.

Residences,—Warwick House, Stable Yard, St. James's Palace, S.W.1; Daylesford House, Moreton-in-Marsh, Glos. *Clubs,*—Buck's, Beefsteak, White's.

SONS LIVING. (By 1st marriage.)
Hon. VERE HAROLD ESMOND (86, Eaton Sq., SW1; Boodle's Club, Roy. Yacht Sqdn.), *b.* Aug. 27th, 1925; ed. at Eton, and at Kent Sch., Conn., USA; Dir. of Reuters since 1970, and Chm. of Asso. Newspapers, Ltd. since 1971; launched new *Daily Mail* May 3rd, 1971, and new *Evening News* Sept. 16th, 1974; Chm. of Newsvendors' Benevolent Inst. Festival Appeal 1963, Pres. of National Advertising Benevolent Soc. 1964, Festival Pres. Newspaper Press Fund 1966, Vice-Pres. Newspaper Press Fund 1967; Cdr. Order of Merit of Republic of Italy: *m.* 1957, Patricia Evelyn Beverley, da. of John William Matthews, FRCS, and formerly wife of Capt. Christopher John Brooks [see B. Crawshaw], and has issue living, Harold Jonathan Esmond Vere, *b.* 1967,—Geraldine, *b.* 1957,—Camilla Patricia Caroline, *b.* 1964.

(By 3rd marriage.)
Hon. Esmond Vyvyan, *b.* 1967.

DAUGHTERS LIVING. (By 1st marriage.)
Hon. Lorna Peggy Vyvyan (*Hon. Lady Cooper-Key*), *b.* (Oct.) 1920 : *m.* 1941, Sir (Edmund Mc) Nell Cooper-Key, of The Grange, Ramsden, Oxford [Wigram, Bt., colls.], and has issue living (Kevin) Esmond (Peter) (8, Stanhope Place, W2), *b.* 1943: *m.* 1971, Lady Mary Gaye Georgiana Lorna Curzon, da. of 6th Earl Howe, and has issue living, Pandora Lorna Mary *b.* 1973,—Emma Charlotte, *b.* 1958.

Hon. Esmé Mary Gabrielle (*Countess of Cromer*), *b.* 1922; a Lady of the Bedchamber to HM 1867-71, and an Extra Lady of the Bedchamber to HM since 1974: *m.* 1942, the 3rd Earl of Cromer. *Residence,* —French Street Farm, Westerham, Kent.

PREDECESSOR.—[1] *Rt. Hon.* HAROLD SIDNEY Harmsworth, 2nd son of the late Alfred Harmsworth, Bar.-at-Law; *b.* 1868; sometime Ch. Proprietor of the *Daily Mail, Evening News,* etc., Chm. of Associated Newspapers, Ltd., and a Director of the Amalgamated Press, Ltd.; was Director-Gen. of Roy. Army Clothing Depart. 1916, and Pres. of Air Council 1917-18; cr. a *Baronet,* 1910, *Baron Rothermere,* of Hemsted, co. Kent (peerage of UK) 1914, and *Viscount Rothermere,* of Hemsted, co. Kent (peerage of UK) 1919: *m.* 1893, Mary Lilian, who *d.* 1937, dau. of George Wade Share, of Forest Hill, SE.; *d.* 1940; *s.* by his third but only surviving son [2] ESMOND CECIL, 2nd Viscount and present peer; also Baron Rothermere.

ROTHERWICK, BARON. (Cayzer.) [Baron U.K. 1939, Bt. U.K. 1924.]

(HERBERT) ROBIN CAYZER, 2nd Baron, and 2nd Baronet; *b.* Dec. 5th, 1912; *s.* 1958; ed. at Eton, and at Ch. Ch. Oxford (B.A. 1935); formerly Major The Greys (Supplementary Reserve); is Dep. Chm. of British & Commonwealth Shipping Co. Ltd., and of Associated cos.; Middle East 1939-45: *m.* 1952, Sarah Jane, only dau. of Sir Michael Nial Slade, 6th Bt., and has issue.

Arms,—Per chevron azure and argent, two estoiles or and an ancient ship with three masts, sails furled sable, pinions flying gules; a chief invected of the third charged with a rose gules barbed and seeded proper between two fleurs-de-lis of the first. **Crest,**—A sea-lion erect proper, gorged with a naval crown and holding in his dexter paw an estoile gold. **Supporters,**—*Dexter*, a lion; and *sinister*, a Bengal tiger proper; each gorged with a naval crown or, and grasping a flagpole also proper, flying therefrom a banner gules, thereon a lozenge argent charged with a lion rampant, also gules.

Seats,—Cornbury Park, Charlbury, Oxon.; Lanfine, Newmilns, Ayrshire. *Residence,*—51, Eaton Sq., SW1. *Clubs,*—Turf, White's.

SONS LIVING.
Hon. HERBERT ROBIN, *b.* March 12th, 1954.
Hon. Charles William, *b.* 1957.
Hon. Avon Arthur, *b.* 1968.

DAUGHTER LIVING.
Hon. Robina Jane, *b.* 1953.

BROTHER LIVING.
Hon. (Michael) Anthony (Rathborne), *b.* 1920; ed. at Eton, and RMC; Lt. (ret.) The Greys; Chm. of Liverpool Steamship Owners Assoc. 1956-57; Pres. of Inst. of Shipping & Forwarding Agents 1963 and 1964, of Chamber of Shipping 1967-68, and of Herts. Agric. Soc. 1974; a Dep. Chm. of British & Commonwealth Shipping Co. Ltd., and a Trustee of National Maritime Museum; 1939-45 War in Middle East (wounded, despatches): *m.* 1952, the Hon. Patricia Helen Browne, da. of 4th Baron Oranmore and Browne, and has issue living, Linda Kinvara, *b.* 1953,—Rosanne, *b.* 1956,—Verena Brigid, *b.* 1961. *Seat,*—Great Westwood, Kings Langley, Herts. *Residence,*—29, Hamilton House, Vicarage Gate, W8. *Clubs,*—Boodle's, and Royal Yacht Squadron.

SISTERS LIVING.
Hon. Pamela Penelope, *b.* (Jan.) 1912: *m.* 1939, Brigadier the Hon. Richard Gustavus Hamilton-Russell, DSO, DL, late 17th/21st Lancers [see V. Boyne]. *Residences,*—Smeaton Manor, Northallerton, Yorkshire; 42, Cranmer Court, Sloane Av., SW3.
Hon. Molly Angela, *b.* 1917: *m.* 1944, Maj.-Gen. Francis Brian Wyldbore Wyldbore-Smith, CB, DSO, OBE [see Smith-Marriott, Bt., colls.]. *Residences,*—34, Cleveland Sq., W2; Grantham House, Grantham.

PREDECESSOR.—[1] HERBERT ROBIN Cayzer, 5th son of Sir Charles (William) Cayzer, 1st Bt. (cr. 1904), of Gartmore, Perthshire; *b.* 1881; Chm. British & Commonwealth Steamship Co. Ltd., Clan Line Steamers Ltd., Union Castle Mail Steamship Co. Ltd., and other cos.; M.P. for S. Div. of Portsmouth (*C*) 1918-22, and 1923-39; cr. a Baronet 1924, and Baron *Rotherwick*, of Tylney, co. Southampton (peerage of United Kingdom) 1939: *m.* 1911, Freda Penelope, who *d.* 1961, dau. of the late Col. William Hans Rathbone, formerly of Scripplestown and of Kilcogy, co. Cavan; *d.* 1958; *s.* by his el. son [2] (HERBERT) ROBIN, 2nd Baron and present peer.

ROTHES, EARL OF. (Leslie.) [Earl S. before 1457.]
[Title pronounced "Roth-ez."]

IAN LIONEL MALCOLM LESLIE, 21st Earl; *b.* May 10th, 1932, *s.* 1975; ed. at Eton; late Sub-Lieut. RNVR: *m.* 1955, Marigold Evans, only da. of the late Sir David Martyn Evans-Bevan, 1st Bt., and has issue.

Arms,—Quarterly: 1st and 4th argent, on a bend azure three buckles or, *Leslie*; 2nd and 3rd or, a lion rampant, gules, debruised by a ribbon sable, *Abernethy.* **Crest,**—A demi-griffin proper. **Supporters,**—Two griffins, wings elevated, proper.

Residence,—Tanglewood, W. Tytherley, Salisbury, Wilts.

SONS LIVING.
JAMES MALCOLM DAVID (*Lord Leslie*), *b.* June 4th, 1958.
Hon. Alexander John, *b.* 1962.

SISTERS LIVING.
Lady Jean, *b.* 1927: *m.* 1949, Roderick Robin Mackenzie [Troubridge, Bt.]. *Residence,*—Kingfisher House, Ampfield, Hants.
Lady Evelyn, *b.* 1929: *m.* 1949, Gerard William Mackworth Mackworth-Young [see Young, Bt. cr. 1813, colls.]. *Residences,*—21, St. Petersburgh Place, W2 4LA; Barrs Lodge, Taynuilt, Argyll.

UNCLE LIVING (Son of 19th Earl.)
Hon. John Wayland, *b.* 1909; ed. at Stowe, and at Corpus Christi Coll., Camb.; European War 1939-43 as Flight-Lieut. RAF Vol. Reserve (invalided); is a Member of Queen's Body Guard for Scotland (Roy. Co. of Archers); *m.* 1932, Coral Angela, da. of the late George Henry Pinckard, JP, of Combe Court, Chiddingfold, Surrey, and 9, Chesterfield

St., W1, and has issue living, Alastair Pinckard, *TD* (Grays House, Bramley, Basingstoke). *Clubs,*—Carlton, Pratt's), *b.* 1934; ed. at Eton; formerly Capt. RHF (TA); a Member of Queen's Body Guard for Scotland (Roy. Co. of Archers): *m.* 1963, Rosemary, da. of Cdr. Hubert Wyndham Barry, RN, of Hill House, Broughton, Hants. [see Barry, Bt., colls.], and has issue living, David John *b.* 1967, Fiona Jane *b.* 1965, Ann Mary *b.* 1973,—Amber Elizabeth, *b.* 1939: *m.* 1964, Beresford Robert Winder White, of Midsummer House, Littlebury, Saffron Walden, and has issue living, Rupert Beresford *b.* 1936, Alexander Richard Beresford *b.* 1968. *Residence,*—East Kintrockat, Brechin, Angus. *Club,*—New (Edinburgh).

WIDOW LIVING OF TWENTIETH EARL.

BERYL VIOLET (*Beryl, Countess of Rothes*) (Strawberry House, Chiswick Mall, Chiswick, W4), only da. of James Lionel Dugdale, of Crathorne, Yorks.: *m.* 1926, the 20th Earl, who *d.* 1975.

COLLATERAL BRANCH LIVING.

Issue of the late Hon. Edward Courtenay Haworth-Leslie, 2nd son of Mary Elizabeth, Countess of Rothes, *b.* 1840, *d.* 1911: *m.* 1890, Caroline Edith, who *d.* 1948, dau. of Thomas Tregenna Biddulph, of The Earee, Shoalhaven, N.S. Wales :—

Edward Biddulph, *b.* 1895; 1914-18 War as Cpl. AIF in France.——Martin Tregenna (29, Calvert Av., Killara, NSW), *b.* 1896; Lt. Australian Reserve of Officers; 1914-18 War in Egypt, Gallipoli, and France (wounded): *m.* 1st, 1928, Nettie Margaret, who *d.* 1943, da. of William Harper, of Napier, NZ; 2ndly, 1945, Joyce Enid, da. of the Rev. Alfred James Gardner, of Chatswood, NSW, and widow of the Rev. L. M. Dunstan, and has issue living, (by 1st m.), Mary Haworth, *b.* 1936.——Norman Evelyn, *b.* 1898: *m.* 1944, Helen Thomson, da. of James Thomson Robertson.

PREDECESSORS.—[1] GEORGE Leslie, *cr. Lord Leslie* (peerage of Scotland 1445), and *Earl of Rothes* (peerage of Scotland) before 1457 ; *d.* 488 *s.* by his grandson [2] GEORGE, 2nd Earl ; *s.* by his brother [3] William, 3rd Earl; killed at Flodden 1513 ; *s.* by his son [4] GEORGE, 4th Earl, Lord of Session; *d.* 1558; *s.* by his son [5] ANDREW, 5th Earl; *s.* by his son [6] JOHN, 6th Earl; *d.* 1641; *s.* by his son [7] JOHN, 7th Earl; carried the Sword of State at the Coronation of Charles II at Scone 1651; was taken a prisoner at battle of Worcester, his estates were forfeited, and he was kept in confinement 1651-8; on the Restoration he was constituted Pres. of the Council, and an Extraordinary Lord of Session, and was in 1663 High Commr. to the Parliament at Edinburgh, and in 1664 Keeper of the Privy Seal; obtained in 1663 a charter conferring the *Earldom of Rothes,* and the Lordship of Leslie, regranted as *Leslie and Ballenbreich* in default of male issue upon his el. dau. and her descendants male and female, with the stipulation that the Earldoms of Rothes and Haddington should not be united, and in 1680 was cr. *Lord Auchmuty and Caskieberry, Viscount Lugtown, Earl of Leslie, Marquess of Ballenbreich,* and *Duke of Rothes* (peerage of Scotland) ; *d.* without male issue 1681, when the peerages of 1680 expired, and the Earldom of Rothes and inferior honours devolved upon his el. dau. [8] MARGARET, wife of Charles, 5th Earl of Haddington; *d.* 1700; *s.* by her el. son [9] JOHN Hamilton, 9th Earl ; assumed the surname of Leslie; was Vice-Adm. of Scotland 1714 ; *d.* 1722 ; *s.* by his son [10] JOHN, *K.T.,* 10th Earl; a Lieut.-Gen. in the Army, and Com.-in-Ch. of the Forces in Ireland ; *d.* 1767; *s.* by his son [11] JOHN, 11th Earl; *d.s.p.* 1773; *s.* by his el. sister [12] JANE ELIZABETH, wife of George Raymond Evelyn; *d.* 1810; *s.* by her son [13] GEORGE WILLIAM, 13th Earl; assumed the surname of Leslie; *d.* 1817; *s.* by his dau. [14] HENRIETTA ANNE, wife of George Gwyther; assumed the name of Leslie: *d.* 1819; *s.* by her son [15] GEORGE WILLIAM EVELYN, 15th Earl: *b.* 1809; *m.* 1831, Louisa, who *d.* 1886, dau. of Col. Anderson Morshead, R.E.; *d.* 1841; *s.* by his son [16] GEORGE WILLIAM EVELYN, 16th Earl; *d.* unmarried 1859 ; *s.* by his sister [17] HENRIETTA ANDERSON MORSHEAD : *m.* 1861, the Hon. George Waldegrave-Leslie, son of 8th Earl Waldegrave; *d.s.p.* Feb. 10th, 1886; *s.* by her aunt [18] MARY ELIZABETH (2nd dau. of Henrietta Anne [ante No. 14]), *b.* 1811: *m.* 1835, Martin E. Haworth, who *d.* Nov. 1886, having in March of that year assumed (for himself and family) by Roy. licence the additional surname of Leslie; *d.* 1893; *s.* by her grandson [19] NORMAN EVELYN (son of the late Martin Leslie Leslie, who *d.* before his mother *s.* to the Earldom), 19th Earl ; *b.* 1877 ; sometime a Representative Peer for Scotland : *m.* 1900, Lucy Noël Martha (who *d.* 1956, having *m.* 2ndly, 1927, Col. Claud Macfie, DSO), only child of the late Thomas Dyer-Edwardes, of Prinknash Park, Gloucester, and Charmandean, Broadwater, Sussex; *d.* 1927; *s.* by his son [20] MALCOLM GEORGE DYER EDWARDES, 20th Earl *b.* 1902; Representative Peer for Scotland 1931-59; Maj. Gen. List: *m.* 1926, Beryl Violet, only da. of James Lionel Dugdale, of Crathorne Hall, Yorks.; *d.* 1975; *s.* by his son [21] IAN LIONEL MALCOLM, 21st Earl and present peer; also Lord Leslie and Ballenbreich.

Rothesay, Duke of, title borne by Prince of Wales.

ROTHSCHILD, BARON. (Rothschild.)   [Baron U.K. 1885, Bt. U.K. 1847.]

Concord, integrity, industry.

NATHANIEL MAYER VICTOR ROTHSCHILD, *GBE, GM,* 3rd Baron, and 4th Baronet; *b.* Oct. 31st, 1910; *s.* 1937; ed. at Harrow, and at Trin. Coll., Camb (PhD, MA and ScD; Fellow 1935-39, Hon. Fellow 1961); Hon. Fellow of Weizmann Inst. of Science, Rehovoth, of Univ. Coll., Camb., and of Bellairs Res. Inst. of McGill Univ., Barbados, and Inst. of Biology and Hon. DSc. Newcastle upon Tyne, Manchester, and Technion, Haifa; Hon. PhD Tel Aviv Univ.; an Admin, Assist, War Office 1940-45 (despatches). Chm. of Agricultural Research Council 1948-58, Vice-Chm. of Shell Research Ltd., 1961-63, Chm. 1963-70, and Research Co-ordinator, Roy. Dutch Shell Group 1965-70; an FRS, and an Asso. KStJ; Dir. Gen., Central Policy Review Staff, Cabinet Office 1970-74; American Legion of Merit and Bronze Star; GBE (Civil) 1975: *m.* 1st, 1933, Barbara (from whom he obtained a divorce 1946), da. of the late St. John Hutchinson, KC, Bar.-at-law, Recorder of Hastings; 2ndly, 1946, Teresa Georgina, MBE, MA, da. of the late Robert John Grote Mayor, CB, of 26, Addison Av., W11, and has issue by 1st and 2nd m.

Arms.—Quarterly: 1st or, an eagle displayed sable langued gules; 2nd and 3rd azure, issuing from the dexter and sinister sides of the shield, an arm embowed proper, grasping five arrows points to the base argent; 4th or, a lion rampant proper, langued gules, over all an escutcheon gules, thereon

a target, the point to the dexter proper. Crest,—1st (centre), issuant from a ducal coronet or, an eagle displayed sable; 2nd (dexter), out of a ducal coronet or, between open buffalo horns per fesse or and sable, a mullet of six points or; 3rd (sinister), out of a ducal coronet or, three ostrich feathers, the centre one argent, the exterior ones azure. Supporters, (of the Austrian Barony),—Dexter, a lion rampant or; sinister, an unicorn argent.
Residence,—

SONS LIVING. (By 1st marriage.)

Hon. NATHANIEL CHARLES JACOB, *b.* April 29th, 1936; ed. at Eton, and at Ch. Ch., Oxford: *m.* 1961. Serena Mary, dau. of Sir Philip Gordon Dunn, 2nd Bt. (cr. 1921) and has issue living, Nathaniel Philip Victor James, *b.* 1971,—Hannah Mary, *b.* 1962,—Beth Matilda, *b.* 1964,—Emily Magda, *b.* 1967. *Residences,—*28, Warwick Av., W9; Doves House, Ham, Wilts.

(By 2nd marriage.)
Hon. Amschel Mayor James, *b.* 1955.

DAUGHTERS LIVING. (By 1st marriage.)

Hon. Sarah, *b.* 1934; ed. at St. Hilda's Coll., Oxford.　　*Hon.* Miranda, *b.* 1940.

(By 2nd marriage.)
Hon. Emma Georgina, *b.* 1948.　　　　　　　　*Hon.* Victoria Katherine, *b.* 1953.

SISTERS LIVING. (Raised to the rank of a Baron's daughters 1938.)

Hon. Miriam Louisa, *b.* 1908; DSc; Prof. Roy. Free Hosp., and a Trustee of British Museum: *m.* 1943, George Lane, MC, and has issue living, Charles Daniel, *b.* 1948,—Mary Rozsika, *b.* 1945,—Charlotte Theresa, *b.* 1951,—Johanna Miriam, *b.* 1951. *Residence,—*Ashton Wold, Oundle.
Hon. Elizabeth Charlotte, *b.* 1909.
Hon. Kathleen Annie Pannonica, *b.* 1913; is Representative for Members of American Federation of Musicians: *m.* 1935, Baron Jules de Koenigswarter, French Ambassador Extraor. and Plen., who obtained a divorce 1955, and has issue living, Patrick, *b.* 1936; MA 1963,—Shaun, *b.* 1948,— Janka, *b.* 1938,—Berit, *b.* 1946,—Kari, *b.* 1950. *Residence,—*63, Kingswood Road, Weehawken, New Jersey, U.S.A.

COLLATERAL BRANCHES LIVING.

(In remainder to Baronetcy only.)
Grandchildren of the late Leopold DE ROTHSCHILD, C.V.O., son of the late Baron Lionel Nathan Rothschild, el. brother of 1st baronet :—
Issue of the late Major Lionel Nathan DE ROTHSCHILD, O.B.E., *b.* 1882, *d.* 1942: *m.* 1912, Marie-Louise Eugenie, who *d.* 1975, da. of the late Edmond Beer, of Paris:—
Edmund Leopold, *TD, b.* 1916; ed. at Harrow, and at Trin. Coll., Camb. (MA); Hon. LLD Memorial Univ. of Newfoundland 1961; Order (1st Class) of the Sacred Treasure of Japan; Major RA (TA); Chm. of N. M. Rothschild & Sons Ltd.; 1939-45 War (wounded): *m.* 1948, Elizabeth Edith, da. of the late Marcell Lentner, of Vienna, Austria, and has issue living, Nicholas David, *b.* 1951,—David Lionel, *b.* 1955,—Katherine Juliette, *b.* 1949: *m.* 1971, Marcus Ambrose Paul Agius, of 7, South Terr., SW7,—Charlotte Henrietta (twin), *b.* 1955. *Residence,—*Inchmery House, Exbury, South-ampton.——Leopold David, *b.* 1927.——Rosemary Leonora, *b.* 1913: *m.* 1st, 1934, Maj. the Hon. Denis Gomer Berry, TD, late Gren. Gds who obtained a divorce 1942 [see V Kemsley]; 2ndly, 1942, John Antony Seys, of Venn Farm, Morchard Bishop, nr. Crediton, Devon, and has issue living, (by 1st m.) [see V. Kemsley],— (by 2nd m.) David Godfrey Antony, *b.* 1947.——Naomi Louisa Nina, *b.* 1920: *m.* 1st, 1941, Jean Pierre Reinach, who *d.* (killed in action during 1939-45 War) 1942; 2ndly, 1947, Bertrand Goldschmidt, and has issue living, (by 1st m.) Jocelyne Marguerite Marie Louise, *b.* 1942: *m.* 1965, Claude Brice, of Paris,—(by 2nd m.) Paul Lionel, *b.* 1952,—Emma Louise, *b.* 1955. *Residence,—*11, Boulevard Flandrin, Paris, XVI.
Issue of the late Anthony Gustav DE ROTHSCHILD, *b.* 1887, *d.* 1961 : *m.* 1926, Yvonne (of Ascott Cottage, Wing, Leighton Buzzard, Bedfordshire), da. of the late Robert Cahen d'Anvers, of Paris:—
Evelyn Robert Adrian (Ascott, Wing, Leighton Buzzard, Beds.), *b.* 1931: *m.* 1st, 1966 (m. diss 1971), Jeanette, da. of the late Ernest Bishop; 2ndly 1973, Victoria, da. of Lewis Schott, and has issue living, (by 2nd m.) Jessica, *b.* 1974.——Renée Louis Marie, *b.* 1927: *m.* 1955, Peter David Robeson. *Residence,—*Fences Farm, Tyringham, Newport Pagnell, Bucks.

PREDECESSORS.—[1] ANTHONY de Rothschild, second son of Nathan Mayer Rothschild, of Frankfort-on-Main, who was cr. a Baron of the Austrian Empire 1822; *b.* 1810; a merchant and banker in London; cr. a *Baronet* 1847 with remainder to the issue of the sons of his elder brother, Lionel: *m.* 1840, Louisa, who *d.* 1910, dau. of the late Abraham Montefiore, of Stamford Hill, Middlesex; *d.* 1876; *s.* by his nephew [2] NATHANIEL MAYER, *G.C.V.O., P.C.* (el. son of the late Baron Lionel Nathan de Rothschild, M.P., the first Member of the Jewish persuasion to enter Parliament), 2nd baronet; *s.* by special remainder, his uncle, *Sir* ANTHONY, as 2nd Baronet 1876, and cr. *Baron Rothschild,* of Tring, co. Hertford (peerage of United Kingdom) 1885; Lord-Lieut. of Bucks 1887-1915; M.P. for Aylesbury (L) 1865-85: *m.* 1867, Emma Louisa, who *d.* 1935, dau. of Baron Charles de Rothschild, of Frankfort-on-the-Main; *d.* 1915; *s.* by his el. son [3] LIONEL WALTER, 2nd Baron, *b.* 1868; M.P. for Bucks, Mid, or Aylesbury Div. (LU) 1899-1910; *d.* 1937; *s.* by his nephew [4] NATHANIEL MAYER VICTOR (only son of the Hon. (Nathaniel) Charles Rothschild, 2nd son of 1st Baron), 3rd Baron and present peer.

ROWALLAN, BARON. (Corbett.) [Baron U.K. 1911.]

God feeds the ravens.

THOMAS GODFREY POLSON CORBETT, *K.T., K.B.E., M.C., T.D.,* 2nd Baron; *b.* Dec. 19th, 1895; *s.* 1933; ed. at Eton; Hon. LL.D. McGill Univ., Montreal 1948, Glasgow Univ. 1952, and Birmingham 1957; Lieut.-Col. Roy. Scots Fusiliers, and a D.L. for Ayrshire; is a K.St.J.; European War 1914-18 in Gallipoli, Egypt, Palestine, France and Belgium with Ayrshire Yeo., and Grenadier Guards (wounded M.C., 1914-15 star, two medals), France 1940; Ch. Scout of British Commonwealth and Empire 1945-59; Gov. of Tasmania 1959-63, and Hon. Col. Roy. Tasmanian Regt. 1960-63; is an Hon. Freeman of Edinburgh; K.B.E. (Civil) 1951, K.T. 1957: *m.* 1918, Gwyn Mervyn (a CStJ), who *d.* 1971, da. of J. B. Grimond, of Abbotsford Cres., St. Andrews, and has issue.

Arms,—Quarterly, 1st and 4th argent, a key fesse. wise, wards downwards between two ravens sable *Corbett;* 2nd and 3rd, azure, a chevron or between two bears' heads couped argent muzzled gules in chief, and in base a cross moline of the third, *Polson*. **Crest,**—A branch of an oak proper, thereon a raven sable. *Supporters,*—*Dexter*, a salmon proper holding in its mouth a jewelled ring or; *sinister*, a seal also proper.

Residence,—Rowallan, Kilmarnock.

SONS LIVING.

Hon. ARTHUR CAMERON, *b.* Dec. 17th, 1919; ed. at Eton, and at Oxford Univ.; is Capt. Ayrshire Yeo.; 1939-45 War (despatches, Croix de Guerre): *m.* 1945 (m. diss 1962), Eleanor Mary, da. of the late George Frederic Boyle [see E. Glasgow, colls.], and has issue living, John Polson Cameron (Tour, Kilmaurs, Ayrshire), *b.* 1947; ed. at Eton: *m.* 1970, Susan Jane Dianne Green, and has issue living, Jason William Polson Cameron *b.* 1972, Joanna Gwyn Alice Cameron *b.* 1974,—Sarah Elizabeth Cameron, *b.* 1949: *m.* 1968, Roderick Maclean, of 7, Rumbold Rd., SW6, and has issue living, Iona Charlotte *b.* 1969, Sophy Emma *b.* 1972,—Anne Mary Cameron, *b.* 1953: *m.* 1972, Rodney Turner and has issue living, Nicola Anne Maria *b.* 1974,—Rosalind Eleanor Cameron, *b.* 1958.

Hon. Thomas Anthony, *MC, b.* 1921; ed. at Eton; is Capt. Grenadier Guards; 1939-45 War (twice wounded, despatches, MC). *Residence,*—La Grange, Newmarket. *Club,*—Guards'.

Hon. Joseph Mervyn, *b.* 1929; ed. at Corpus Christi Coll., Camb. (B.A. 1953); is 2nd Lieut. Roy, Scots Fusiliers: *m.* 1960, the Hon. Catherine Lyon-Dalberg-Acton, dau. of 3rd Baron Acton, and has issue living, Sebastian, *b.* 1963,—Victoria, *b.* 1961. *Residence,*—Chittlegrove, Rendcomb, nr. Cirencester, Gloucestershire.

Hon. Robert Cameron, *b.* 1940 ; ed. at Eton, and at Oxford Univ.

DAUGHTER LIVING.

Hon. Fiona Elizabeth Cameron, *b.* 1942: *m.* 1st, 1966 (m. diss. 1972), David Richard Amherst Cecil [see B. Amherst of Hackney, colls.]; 2ndly, 1974, W. G. Patterson, of 43, Holland Villas Rd., W14.

SISTER LIVING.

Hon. Elsie Cameron; a JP for Oxfordshire; has Serbian Samaritan Cross. *Residence,*—Spelsbury House, Spelsbury, Oxon.

PREDECESSOR.—[1] ARCHIBALD CAMERON Corbett, son of the late Thomas Corbett, J.P., of South Park, Cove, Dunbartonshire; *b.* 1856; sat as M.P. for Tradeston Div. of Glasgow (*L*) 1885-1911; *cr. Baron Rowallan*, of Rowallan, co. Ayr (peerage of United Kingdom) 1911: *m.* 1887, Alice Mary, who *d.* 1902, only dau. of John Polson, of Castle Levan, by Gourock; *d.* 1933; *s.* by his son [2] THOMAS GODFREY POLSON, *M.C.*, 2nd Baron and present peer.

ROWLEY, BARONY OF. (Henderson.)　[Extinct 1968.]

WIDOW LIVING OF LIFE BARON.

MARY ELIZABETH (*Baroness Rowley*), (P.O.B. 5, Miami Shores, Florida 33153, USA), da. of Ernest Verrall Barnes, of Finchley, N., and widow of Harold Gliksten, of London: *m.* 1958, Baron Rowley (Life Peer), who *d.* 1968.

ROXBURGHE, DUKE OF. (Innes-Ker.)　[Duke S. 1707, Bt. S. 1625.]
[Title pronounced "**Roxborough.**" Name pronounced "**Innez-Carr.**"]

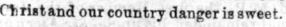
Christ and our country danger is sweet.

GUY DAVID INNES-KER, 10th Duke, 11th Baronet, and Premier Baronet of Scotland or Nova Scotia; *b.* Nov. 18th, 1954; *s.* 1974; ed. at Eton, and RMA; 2nd Lt. Blues and Royals (RHG and 1st Dragoons);

Arms,—Quarterly : 1st and 4th grand quarters counter quartered, 1st and 4th, vert on a chevron between three unicorns' heads erased argent, armed and maned or, as many mullets sable ; 2nd and 3rd, gules, three mascles or, 2nd and 3rd grand quarters, argent three mullets of six points azure. **Crests,**—1st, a unicorn's head erased argent, armed and maned or ; 2nd, a boar's head erased proper, langued gules. **Supporters,**—Two savages wreathed about the head and middle with laurel, and holding in their exterior hands a club resting on the shoulder all proper. *Seat,*—Floors Castle, Kelso, Roxburghshire.

BROTHER LIVING.

Lord ROBERT ANTHONY, *b.* May 28th, 1959.

WIDOW LIVING OF NINTH DUKE.

MARGARET ELIZABETH (*Duchess of Roxburghe*), (Floors Castle, Kelso, Roxburghshire), da. of the late Capt. Frederick Bradshaw McConnel, Gordon Highlanders, of Knockdalian, Colmonell, Ayrshire, and formerly wife of Lt.-Col. James Cunningham Church, MC, late Argyll and Sutherland Highlanders: *m.* 1954, as his 2nd wife, the 9th Duke, who *d.* 1974.

COLLATERAL BRANCHES LIVING.

Granddaughter of the late Lieut.-Col. Lord Alastair Robert Innes-Ker, C.V.O., D.S.O. (infra):—
Issue of the late Major David Charles Innes-Ker, R.A., *b.* 1910, *d.* 1957 : *m.* 1939, Christa Irene Valentine (who obtained a divorce 1948), dau. of Lieut.-Col. Chandos de Paravacini, OBE, of Birkholme Manor, Corby, Lincolnshire :—
Mary Ann, *b.* 1941. *Residence,*—

Issue of the late Lieut.-Col. Lord Alastair Robert Innes-Ker, C.V.O., D.S.O., 2nd son of 7th Duke, *b.* 1880, *d.* 1936 : *m.* 1907, Anne, who *d.* 1959, dau. of the late William Lawrence Breese, of New York :—
(Eloise) Jean Horatia, *b.* 1915: *m.* 1940, Reginald Baron Black, late Sqdn.-Ldr. RAFVR, and has issue living, Nicola Jean-Anne, *b.* 1943: *m.* 1972, Archibald Donald Orr Ewing, of Camilty Mill, Harburn, West Calder, Midlothian [see Orr Ewing, Bt.]. *Residence,*—Creagh Castle, Doneraile, co. Cork.

Descendants of Thomas Ker, of Ferniehirst, brother of Walter Ker, great-great-grandfather of 1st Earl of Roxburghe :—

See M. Lothian.

(*In remainder to Baronetcy only.*)
Descendants of Alexander Innes, younger brother of James Innes, of Cromey, great-grandfather of 1st baronet :—

Grandchildren of the late Arthur Charles Innes-Cross (who assumed the additional surname of Cross by Roy. Licence 1888), son of Arthur Innes, of Dromantinell co. Down, 8th in descent from Alexander Innes:—
Issue of the late Arthur Charles Wolseley Innes, M.C., Irish Guards, who relinquished the additional surname of Cross 19—; *b.* 1888, *d.* 1940: *m.* 1915, Etta Maud, who *d.* 1971, da. of William Bradshaw, of Ordley Hill:—
Arthur Charles Sydney, *b.* 1922 ; in R.A.F. ; *d.* (killed in action) 1943.——William Anthony Wolseley, *b.* 1935; ed. at Eton.——Anne, *b.* 1929: *m.* 1959, Cdr. R. I. C. Ryland, RN, of 5, Hillgate Place, W8.

PREDECESSORS.—[1] *Sir* ROBERT Ker, Knt.; cr. *Lord Roxburghe* (peerage of Scotland, before March 31st, 1600, *Lord Ker of Cessford and Cavertoun,*and *Earl of Roxburghe* (peerage of Scotland) 1616, which honours in 1648 were by charter confirmed in remainder to his grand-son the Hon. William Drummond, who was 4th son of his dau. Jean by her marriage with the 2nd Earl of Perth, and after him upon the three sons successively of his grand-dau. Jean, by her marriage with the 3rd Earl of Wigton, with the express stipulation that whoever should succeed should marry Jean, the dau. of his deceased son Harry, and failing her the next eldest dau. Anne, and failing her the next dau. Margaret, and a final remainder to heirs male whatsoever ; was Keeper of the Privy Seal 1637 ; *d.* 1650 ; *s.* by his grandson (ante) [2] WILLIAM Drummond, 2nd Earl ; assumed the surname of Ker, and *m.* his cousin Jean, according to the stipulation of the remainder; *d.* 1675 ; *s.* by his son [3] *Rt. Hon.* ROBERT, 3rd Earl ; *d.* 1682 ; *s.* by his el. son [4] ROBERT, 4th Earl ; *d.* unmarried 1693 ; *s.* by his brother [5] JOHN, K.G.; was Sec. of State 1704 ; cr. *Viscount Broxmouth, Earl of Kelso, Marquess of Bowmont and Cessford,* and *Duke of Roxburghe* (peerage of Scotland) 1707, with remainder to the heirs who should inherit the Earldom of Roxburghe ; *d.* 1741 ; *s.* by his son [6] ROBERT, 2nd Duke, who in 1722 had been cr. *Baron Ker,* of Wakefield, co. York, and *Earl Ker* (peerage of Great Britain); *d.* 1755 ; *s.* by his son [7] JOHN, K.G., K.T., 3rd Duke ; *d.* unmarried 1804 when the peerages of Great Britain (cr. 1722) expired, and the Scottish honours devolved upon his kinsman [8] WILLIAM, 4th Duke, who in 1797 had *s.* as 7th *Lord Bellenden of Broughton,* peerage of Scotland, cr. 1661 ; *d.s.p.* 1805, when the Lord-ship of Bellenden of Broughton became extinct and the Scottish peerages remained dormant until 1812, when they were successfully claimed by [9] JAMES Innes, great-grandson of Lady Margaret (ante), 3rd grand-dau. of the 1st Earl, by her marriage with Sir James Innes, 3rd Bt. (see †↓† infra), assumed in 1767 by Roy. licence the additional surname of Norcliffe, and relinquished it in 1807 on the death of his first wife ; *d.* 1823 ; *s.* by his only son by his 2nd marriage [10] JAMES HENRY ROBERT, K.T., 6th Duke ; *b.* 1816 ; cr. *Earl Innes* (peerage of United Kingdom) 1837 ; was Lord-Lieut. of Berwickshire, and a Lieut.-Gen. of Royal Co. of Archers : *m.* 1836, Susanna Stephania, dau. of Lieut.-Gen. Sir James Charles Dalbiac, K.C.H., *d.* 1879 ; *s.* by his son [11] JAMES HENRY ROBERT, 7th Duke, *b.* 1839 ; M.P. for Roxburghshire (*L*) 1870-74 ; Lord-Lieut. of co. Roxburgh, and one of H.M. Queen Victoria's Body Guard of Scotland : *m.* 1874, Lady Emily Anne Spencer-Churchill, O.B.E., V.A., who *d.* 1923, dau. of 6th Duke of Marlborough ; *d.* 1892 ; *s.* by his el. son [12] HENRY JOHN, K.T., M.V.O., 8th Duke, *b.* 1876 ; bore Queen Consort's Crown at Coronation of King Edward VII. 1902, and St. Edward's Staff at Coronation of King George V. 1911 ; was Chancellor of the Order of the Thistle : *m.* 1903, Mary, who *d.* 1937, dau. of the late Ogden Goelet, of Newport, USA; *d.* 1932; *s.* by his only son [13] GEORGE VICTOR ROBERT JOHN, 9th Duke, *b.* 1913: *m.* 1st, 1935 (m. diss. 1953), Lady Mary Evelyn Hungerford Crewe-Milnes, da. of 1st Marquess of Crewe (ext.); 2ndly, 1954, Margaret Elisabeth, da. of the late Capt. Frederick Bradshaw McConnel, Gordon Highlanders, of Knockdalian, Colmonell, Ayrshire, and formerly wife of Lt.-Col. James Cunningham Church, MC; *d.* 1974; *s.* by his el. son [14] GUY DAVID, 10th Duke, and present peer; also Marquess of Bowmont and Cessford, Earl of Roxburghe, Earl of Kelso, Earl Innes, Viscount Broxmouth, Lord Roxburghe, and Lord Ker of Cessford and Cavertoun.

†↓† [1] *Rt. Hon. Sir* ROBERT Innes, (19th Baron of Innes, co. Moray, from 1160); M.P. for Elgin and Forres-shire 1639-41 ; cr. a *Baronet* with remainder to heirs male whatsoever 1625 ; *d.* 1658 ; *s.* by his son [2] *Sir* ROBERT, 2nd Bt. ; M.P. for Moray 1661-78 ; *s.* by his son [3] *Sir* JAMES, 3rd Bt. : *m.* Lady Margaret Ker (ante), dau. of Harry, son of 1st Earl of Roxburghe ; *s.* by his son [4] *Sir* HARRY, 4th Bt. ; M.P. for Moray in Union Parliament 1707 ; *d.* 1721 ; *s.* by his son [5] *Sir* HARRY, 5th Bt. ; *d.* 1762 ; *s.* by his son [6] *Sir* JAMES, 6th Bt., who *s.* as 5th Duke of Roxburghe(ante).

ROYLE, BARON. (Royle.) [Life Baron 1964.]

CHARLES ROYLE, son of the late Charles Royle, of Abbeville, Mile End Lane, Stockport; *b.* Jan. 23rd, 1896; ed. at Stockport Gram. Sch.; a JP of Brighton; Pres. of Manchester and Salford Meat Trades Assocn. 1942-43, Meat Agent to Min. of Food 1939-45, Pres. of Stockport Labour Party 1934-38, a JP of Stockport 1937-59, and Lord Commr. of the Treasury 1950-51; Dep. Chm. Council of Magistrates Assocn. 1954-67; Chm. of Alliance Building Soc.; 1914-18 War with RE; MP for West Salford (*Lab.*) 1945-64; cr. *Baron Royle,* of Pendleton, City of Salford (Life Baron) 1964: *m.* 1919, Florence da. of Henry Smith, of Stockport, and has issue. [Baron Royle *d.* Sept. 30th, 1975].

Residence,—Abbotswell, Frogham, Fordingbridge, Hants.

DAUGHTER LIVING.
Hon. Joan Mary ROBERTS (Springfield Cottage, Southampton Rd., Fordingbridge, Hants.), *b.* 1920; assumed surname of Roberts by deed poll 19—.

Royston, Viscountess, see Earl of Hardwicke.

RUFFSIDE, VISCOUNTCY OF. (Brown.) [Extinct 1958.]

DAUGHTER LIVING OF FIRST VISCOUNT.

Hon. Audrey Pellew, *b.* 1908; cr. *Baroness Hylton-Foster* (Life Baroness) 1965 [see that title].

RUGBY, BARON. (Maffey.) [Baron U.K. 1947.]

ALAN LOADER MAFFEY, 2nd Baron; *b.* April 16th, 1913; *s.* 1969; ed. at Stowe; 1939-45 War as Fl. Lt. RAF: *m.* 1947, Margaret, da. of Harold Bindley, of Burton-on-Trent, and has issue.

Arms,—Ermine, a fort with two towers proper, issuant from the base a pile reversed sable, a chief dancette or, surmounted by a pile azure, charged with an increscent argent. Crest, —A gauntlet fessewise grasping a lantern proper. Supporters,—On either side an Afghan hound proper gorged with a collar with chain reflexed over the back or.

Residence,—Grove Farm, Frankton, Rugby.

PASS FRIEND

SONS LIVING.

Hon. JOHN RICHARD, *b.* Aug. 28th, 1949; ed. at Harrow.
Hon. Robert Charles, *b.* 1951: *m.* 1974, Anne Penelope, yr. da. of David Hale, of Somerden, Chiddingstone, Kent, and has issue living, Timothy James Howard, *b.* 1975.
Hon. Christopher Alan, *b.* 1955.
Hon. Mark Andrew, *b.* 1956.

DAUGHTERS LIVING.

Hon. Selina Penelope, *b.* 1952.
Hon. Alicia Dorothy, *b.* 1960.

BROTHER LIVING.

Hon. Simon Chelmsford Loader (Mount Isa, Qld., Aust.), *b.* 1919; ed. at Rugby; formerly Lt. Coldstream Guards; 1939-45 War in France (wounded): *m.* 1949 (m. diss. 1962), Andrée Norma, da. of George Middleton, of London, and has issue living, Penelope Ann, *b.* 1950: *m.* 1973, Richard Patrick James Lacy, of Flat 10, 231, Sussex Gdns., W2 [see Tyrwhitt, Bt.].

SISTER LIVING.

Hon. Penelope Loader (*Hon.* Lady Aitken), *MBE* (47, Phillimore Gdns., W8), *b.* 1910; MBE Civil), 1955: *m.* 1938, Sir William Traven Aitken, KBE, MP, who *d.* 1964; and has issue living, Jonathan William Patrick, *MP*, *b.* 1942; ed. at Eton, and Ch. Ch., Oxford (MA); MP for Thanet East (*C*) since 1974,—Maria Penelope Katharine, *b.* 1945: *m.* 1st, 1968, Mark Richard Durden-Smith; 2ndly, 1972, Nigel Davenport.

PREDECESSOR—[1] *Sir* JOHN LOADER Maffey, *GCMG, KCB, KCVO, CSI, CIE*, son of the late Thomas Maffey, of Rugby; *b.* 1877; Gov.-Gen. of the Sudan 1926-33; Permanent Under-Sec. of State for the Colonies 1933-37; UK Rep res. in Eire 1939-49; cr. *Baron Rugby*, of Rugby, co. Warwick (peerage of UK) 1947: *m.* 1907, Dorothy Gladys, OBE, who *d.* 1973, da. of the late Charles Lang Huggins, JP, of Hadlow Grange, Buxted; *d.* 1969; *s.* by his el. son [2] ALAN LOADER, 2nd Baron, and present peer.

RUNCIMAN OF DOXFORD, VISCOUNT. (Runciman.) [Viscount U.K. 1937. Bt. U.K. 1906.]

WALTER LESLIE RUNCIMAN, *O.B.E.*, *A.F.C.*, 2nd Viscount, and 3rd Baronet; *b.* Aug. 26th, 1900 ; *s.* 1949 ; ed. at Eton, and at Trin. Coll., Camb. (BA 1922, MA 1928); Hon. DCL Durham 1937; is Chm. of Walter Runciman & Co. Ltd., a DL for Northumberland, an Elder Brother of Trinity House, and an Hon. Air Commodore: Chm. of Council of Armstrong Coll., Univ. of Durham 1935-37, Director-Gen. of British Overseas Airways Corporation 1940-43, Air Attaché, British Embassy, Teheran 1943-46, and Pres. of Roy. Institution of Naval Architects 1951-61; Chm. of Gen. Council of British Shipping, and Pres. of Chamber of Shipping of United Kingdom 1952; Chm. of Trustees of Nat. Maritime Museum 1961-72; Chm. of British Hallmarking Council since 1974; OBE (Civil) 1946: *m.* 1st, 1923, Rosamond Nina (from whom he obtained a divorce 1928), da. of the late Rudolph Chambers Lehmann, of Fieldhead, Bourne End, Bucks; 2ndly, 1932, Katharine Schuyler, da. of the late William R. Garrison, of New York, and has issue by 2nd marriage.

Arms,—Per fesse or and azure a lymphad oars in action, the sail charged with a thistle leaved and slipped proper, flags flying to the dexter gules. Crest,—A seahorse erect gules, holding in the fore fins a thistle as in the arms. Supporters,—On either side a seahorse or gorged with a chain pendent therefrom a grappling iron azure.

Seat,—Doxford, Chathill, Northumberland. *Residence,*—46, Abbey Lodge, Park Rd., NW8 9AT.
Clubs,—Brooks's, Royal Yacht Squadron (Commodore).

SON LIVING. (*By 2nd marriage.*)

Hon. WALTER GARRISON (36, Carlton Hill, NW8; Brooks's Club), *b.* Nov. 10th, 1934; ed. at Eton, and at Trin. Coll., Camb. (Fellow 1959-63, and since 1971): *m.* 1963, Ruth, da. of the late Joseph Hellman of Johannesburg, and has issue living, David Walter, *b.* 1967,—Lisa, *b.* 1965,—Catherine, *b.* 1969.

BROTHER LIVING.

Hon. Sir Steven (James Cochran Stevenson), *b.* 1903; ed. at Eton, and at Trin. Coll., Camb. (MA, Fellow); Hon. LittD, Oxford, and Camb.; Hon. LL.D. Glasgow; Hon. DLitt. Durham, London and St. Andrews; Hon. DPh Salonika 1951; Hon. DD, Wabash, Indiana, Hon. DHL Chicago, an Author (" Steven Runciman "), a FBA, and a Knight Cdr. of Order of Phoenix of Greece; Prof. of Byzantine Act and History at Istanbul Univ. 1942-45; Prepresentative of Britsh Council in Greece 1945-47; Knt. 1958. *Residence,*—Elshieshields, Lockerbie, Dumfriesshire.

SISTER LIVING.

Hon. Katharine (*Hon. Lady Lyell*), *b.* 1909: *m.* 1st, 1931, the 4th Baron Farrer, who *d.* 1954; 2ndly, 1955, Sir Maurice Legat Lyell, who *d.* 1975. *Residence,*—Puddephats Farm, Markyate, Herts.

PREDECESSORS.—[1] WALTER Runciman, son of the late Walter Runciman, of Dunbar; *b.* 1847; head of the firm of Walter Runciman & Co., Ltd., shipowners, of Newcastle, London, etc., Chm. of Anchor Line, Ltd., Glasgow, and a Member and Chm. of various other shipping organizations; M.P. for Hartlepool (L) 1914-18; cr. a *Baronet* 1906, and *Baron Runciman,* of Shoreston, co. Northumberland (peerage of United Kingdom) 1933 : *m.* 1868, Ann Margaret, who *d.* 1933, elder dau. of the late John Lawson, of Blakemoor Northumberland; *d.* Aug. 1937; *s.* by his only son [2] WALTER, 2nd Baron; *b.* 1870: Chm. of United Kingdom Provident Institution 1920-31; Pres. of Chamber of Shipping of United Kingdom 1926; was Parliamentary Sec. to Local Govt. Board 1905-07, Financial Sec. to the Treasury 1907-08, Pres. of Board of Education 1908-11, Pres. of Board of Agriculture and Fisheries, and Commr. of H.M. Woods, Forests, and Land Revenues 1911-14, Pres. of Board of Trade 1914-16, again Pres. of Board of Trade (in National Govt.) 1931-7, and Lord Pres. of the Council 1938-9; Head of Mission to Czechoslovakia 1938; sat as M.P. (L) for Oldham 1899-1900, for Dewsbury 1902-18, for Swansea, W. Div. 1924-9, and for St. Ives Div. of Cornwall 1929-37; cr. *Viscount Runciman, of Doxford,* of Doxford, co. Northumberland (peerage of United Kingdom) June 1937 : *m.* 1898, Hilda (M.P. for Cornwall, St. Ives Div. (L) 1928-9), who *d.* 1956, dau. of the late James Cochran Stevenson (sometime M.P. for South Shields), of Westhoe, South Shields : *d.* 1949 ; *s.* by his el. son [3] WALTER LESLIE, 2nd Viscount and present peer ; also Baron Runciman.

RUNCORN, BARONY OF. (Vosper.) [Extinct 1968.]

WIDOW LIVING OF LIFE BARON.

HELEN NORAH (*Baroness Runcorn*) (102, Drayton Gdns., SW10), da. of the late Sir (Joseph) Crosland Graham, of Plas-yn-Rhos, Ruthin, Denbighshire; a JP for Middlesex, a Member of Merton, Sutton and Wandsworth Area Health Authority (Teaching) and of Westminster Hosp. Special Trustee since 1974; Chm. of Westminster Hosp. Research Trust Advisory Panel, and a Gov. of Westminster Hosp. Teaching Group 1972-74: *m.* 1966, as his 2nd wife, Baron Runcorn (Life Peer), who *d.* 1968.

RUSHCLIFFE, BARONY OF. (Betterton.) [Extinct 1949.]

DAUGHTERS LIVING OF FIRST BARON. (*By 1st marriage.*)

Hon. Averil Diana, *b.* 1914: *m.* 1st, 1939, Major Richard Wyndham-Quin Going, KOSB, who *d.* (killed in action in Normandy) 1944; 2ndly, 1946, Col. Charles Walter Philipps Richardson, DSO, KOSB, [Foley-Philipps, Bt.], and has issue living, (by 1st m.) Christopher Wyndham, *b.* 1944: *m.* 1975, Elizabeth Susan, da. of James Christy Brownlow, of Ballydugan House, co. Down,—Penelope Clare, *b.* 1942: *m.* 1965, Capt. Arthur David Bentley Brooks, The Queen's R. Irish Hussars, and has issue living, Jonathan Wyndham *b.* 1970, Emma Frances *b.* 1968,—(by 2nd m.) Mark Rushcliffe, *b.* 1947: *m.* 1973, Cherry Victoria, yst. da. of Sidney Smart, of Home Farm, Cokethorpe Park, Witney, and has issue living,—Melanie Claire *b.* 1974. *Residence,*—Ashe Warren House, Overton, Hants.
Hon. Claudia Violet, *b.* 1917: *m.* 1937, Maj. Derek Swithin Allhusen, 9th Lancers, and has issue living, Timothy Frederick, (Windsor House, St. Lawrence, Jersey), *b.* 1942: *m.* 1965, Annabel Victoria, only da. of the late John Creighton Morris, and has issue living, Nicolas Christian *b.* 1970, Alexia Suzanne *b.* 1966, Lara Victoria *b.* 1968,—Rosemary Claudia, *b.* 1944: *m.* 1973, Capt. Jeremy Grimble Groves, 17th/21st Lancers. *Residences,*—The Manor House, Claxton, Norwich; Flat 1, 22, St. James's Sq., SW1.

RUSHOLME, BARON. (Palmer.) [Baron U.K. 1945.]

ROBERT ALEXANDER PALMER, 1st Baron, son of William Palmer ; *b.* Nov. 29th, 1890; ed. at St. Mary's Sch., Ashton-on-Mersey; a JP for Manchester; Fellow of Chartered Inst. of Transport; Pres. International Co-operative Alliance 1939-49, Pres. of Co-operative Congress 1945, a Member of British Transport Commn. 1947-59, and Chm. of Board of Survey, Inland Waterways, and of Coastal Shipping Advisory Cttee. 1947-56, and of London Midland Board of British Transport Commn. 1950-61, and a Dir. of Thomas Cook & Son, Ltd., and Asso. Cos. 1950-67; Pres. of Inst. of Travel Agents since 1963; 1914-18 War in Egypt, France and Belgium with Manchester Regt.; cr. *Baron Rusholme,* of Rusholme, City of Manchester (peerage of UK) 1945.

The world my province.

Arms,—Per chevron gules and argent in chief two escallops of the second and in base a palmer's purse sable. Crest,—In front of rushes a heron proper resting the dexter claw upon an escallop sable. Supporters,—On either side a heron holding in the beak two bullrushes slipped and leaved all proper.

MUNDUS MEA PROVINCIA

Residence,—Rusholme Gdns., Manchester, M14 5LR.

RUSSELL, EARL. (Russell.) [Earl U.K. 1861.]

JOHN CONRAD RUSSELL, 4th Earl;
b. Nov. 16th, 1921; s. 1970; ed. at
Dartington Hall Sch., and California and Harvard Univs.; late
RNVR; Admin. Asst. HM Treasury
1947-49: m. 1946, Susan Doniphan
(from whom he obtained a divorce
1955), da. of the late Nicholas
Vachel Lindsay, American Poet, and
has issue.

Arms,—Argent, a lion rampant gules, on a
chief sable, three escallops of the field, over the
centre escallop a mullet. Crest,—A goat
stantant argent, armed and unguled or.
Supporters,—Dexter, a lion gules; sinister, an
heraldic antelope gules, armed, unguled, tufted,
ducally gorged and chained, the chain reflexed
over the back or; each supporter charged on the
shoulder with a mullet argent.

Residence, — Carn Voel, Porthcurno,
Penzance.

What will be, will be.

DAUGHTER LIVING.
Lady Sarah Elizabeth, b. 1946.

HALF-BROTHER LIVING.
Hon. CONRAD SEBASTIAN ROBERT (29, Hamilton Rd., SW19), b. April 15th, 1937; ed. at Eton, and
at Merton Coll., Oxford; Reader in History, Bedford Coll., London Univ.: m. 1962, Elizabeth, da.
of Horace Sanders, of 9, Victoria Rd., Harborne, Birmingham, and has issue living, Nicholas Lyulph,
b. 1968,—John Francis, b. 1971.

SISTER LIVING.
Lady Katharine Jane, b. 1923: m. 1948, the Rev. Charles William Stuart Tait, of Falls Village, Conn.
06 031, USA, and has issue living, David Alexander, b. 1951,—Jonathan Francis, b. 1955,—Andrew
Michael Philip, b. 1961,—Benjamin Peter, b. 1965,—Anne Elizabeth, b. 1953.

MOTHER LIVING.
Dora Winifred, MBE, da. of the late Sir Frederick William Black, KCB: m. 1st, 1921, as his second
wife, the 3rd Earl, who d. 1970, and from whom she obtained a divorce 1935; 2ndly, 1940, Gordon
Grace.

WIDOW LIVING OF THIRD EARL.
EDITH (Countess Russell) (Plas Penrhyn, Penrhyndeudraeth, Merionethshire), da. of Edward Bronson
Finch, of New York: m. 1952, as his 4th wife, the 3rd Earl, who d. 1970.

COLLATERAL BRANCH LIVING.
Issue of the late Hon. Francis Albert Rollo Russell, 3rd son of 1st Earl, b. 1849,
d. 1914: m. 1st, 1885, Alice Sophia, who d. 1886, dau. of the late Thomas
Spragging Godfrey, of Balderton Hall, Notts; 2ndly, 1891, Gertrude Ellen
Cornelia, who d. 1942, dau. of the late Henry Joachim, of 13, Airlie Gardens,
W.8:—

By 2nd m.) Margaret Frances, b. 1894: m. 1918, Edward Mayow Hastings Lloyd, CB, CMG, who d.
1968, and has issue living, John Russell (5, Belle Vue Gdns., Brighton BN2 2AA), b. 1923,—Robert
Edward (14, The Holdings, Hatfield, Herts), b. 1925: m. 1952, Marion Margaret, el. da. of Norman
Capener, FRCS, of Exeter, and has issue living, Michael Norman Hastings b. 1955, Nicholas Edward
b. 1958, David Russell b. 1963, Anna Frances b. 1953, Mary Jennifer b. 1961,—Frances Eleanor,
b. 1920: m. 1st, 1941 (marriage dissolved 1947), Michael Barratt Brown; 2ndly, 1953, Dougal
McLean Ronald, of 20, Ailsa Rd., Twickenham, Middlesex, and has issue living, (by 1st marriage)
Christopher John b. 1945, Richard Rollo b. 1947, (by 2nd marriage) Ian McKenzie Lloyd b. 1961,
Katharine Margaret b. 1955. Residence,—Tillingbourne Hey, 43, Gravel Lane, Hemel Hempstead.

PREDECESSORS.—[1] Lord JOHN Russell, K.G., 3rd son of 6th Duke of Bedford; b. 1792; sat
as M.P. for Tavistock (L) 1813-17, 1818-19, and 1830-2, for Huntingdonshire 1820-6, for Bandon
1826-30, for S. Devonshire 1832-5, for Stroud 1835-41, and for London 1841-61; was Sec. for Home
Depart. 1835-9, for the Colonies 1839-41 and 1855, Sec. for Foreign Affairs 1852-3 and 1859-65,
Premier and First Lord of the Treasury 1846-52 and 1865-6, and Lord Pres. of the Council
1854-5; cr. Viscount Amberley and Earl Russell (peerage of United Kingdom) 1861: m. 1st,
1835, Adelaide, who d. 1838, dau. of Thomas Lister, of Armitage Park, and widow of 2nd
Baron Ribblesdale; 2ndly, 1841, Lady Frances Anna Maria Elliot, dau. of 2nd Earl of Minto,
G.C.B.; d. 1878; s. by his grandson [2] JOHN FRANCIS STANLEY (son of John, Viscount
Amberley, M.P., by the Hon. Katherine Louisa, dau. of 2nd Baron Stanley of Alderley),
2nd Earl, b. 1865; tried by his Peers at Westminster 1901 (free pardon granted by His
Majesty and recorded in proceedings of House of Lords July 1911); Parliamentary Sec. to
Min. of Transport June 1929, and Under-Sec. of State for India Dec. 1929-31: m. 1st, 1890,
Mabel Edith, who d. 1908 (having obtained a divorce 1901), dau. of Sir Claude Edward Scott,
4th Bt. (cr. 1821); 2ndly, 1901, Mollie (who obtained a divorce 1915), dau. of George Cooke;
3rdly, 1916, Mary Annette (an authoress), who d. 1941, dau. of H. Herron Beauchamp, and widow
of Count (Henning August) Von Arnim; d. 1931; s. by his brother [3] BERTRAND ARTHUR
WILLIAM O M, 3rd Earl, b. 1872; Philosopher and Mathematician: m. 1st, 1894, Alys Whitall (who
d. 1951, having obtained a divorce 1921), da. of Robert Pearsall Smith; 2ndly, 1921, Dora Winifred,
MBE (who obtained a divorce 1935), da. of the late Sir Frederick William Black, KCB; 3rdly,
1936, Patricia Helen (who obtained a divorce 1952), da. of Henry Evelyn Spence; 4thly, 1952,
Edith, da. of the late Edward Bronson Finch, of New York; d. 1970; s. by his son [4] JOHN CONRAD,
4th Earl and present peer; also Viscount Amberley.

RUSSELL OF KILLOWEN, BARONY OF. (cr. 1929.) (Russell.) [Extinct 1946.]

SON LIVING OF LIFE BARON.
Rt. Hon. Sir Charles Ritchie (*Baron Russell of Killowen*), b. 1908 [see that title].

DAUGHTER LIVING OF LIFE BARON.
Hon. Margaret Mary, b. 1905: m. 1941, Milan Bratza Yovanovitch, who d. 1964, and has issue [see Russell, Bt., cr. 1916].
Residence,—Lane End, Walton-on-the-Hill, Tadworth, Surrey.

RUSSELL OF KILLOWEN, BARON. (Russell.) [Life Baron 1975.]

CHARLES RITCHIE RUSSELL, *PC*, son of the late Francis Xavier, Baron Russell of Killowen, PC (Life Baron cr. 1929); b. Jan. 12th, 1908; ed. at Beaumont and Oriel Coll., Oxford (MA, Hon. Fellow 1962); Bar. Lincoln's Inn 1931, KC 1948, Bencher 1952, Treas. 1972; Attorney-Gen. Duchy of Cornwall 1951-60, Judge of High Court of Justice (Chancery Div.) 1960-62, and Lord Justice of Appeal 1962-75, since when Lord of Appeal in Ordinary; Pres. Restrictive Practices Court 1961-62; 1939-45 War with RA (Airborne) in N-W Europe (wounded, despatches, French Croix de Guerre with Star); cr. Knt. 1960, PC 1962, and *Baron Russell of Killowen*, of Killowen, co. Down, (Life Baron) 1975: m. 1933, Joan Elizabeth, only child of the late James Aubrey Torrens, MD, FRCP, of 46, Wimpole St., W1, and has issue.

Arms,—Argent, a lion rampant gules on a chief sable three escallops of the first, the whole within a bordure engrailed vert. **Crest,**—A goat passant argent armed or, charged on the body fessewise with three trefoils slipped vert.
Residence,—Orchard House, Sheepdown, Petworth, W. Sussex, GU28 0BN. *Clubs,*—Garrick, Beefsteak.

SONS LIVING (*In special remainder to Baronetcy cr. 1916, only.*)
Hon. Valentine Francis Xavier Michael, b. 1938; ed. at Beaumont, and Oriel Coll., Oxford.
Hon. (Francis) Damian, b. 1947; ed. at Beaumont, and Trin. Coll., Dublin.

DAUGHTER LIVING.
Hon. Julian Mary, b. 1935: m. 1955, Anthony Rodney Allfrey, of 6, Culford Gdns., SW3, see Fox, Bt., (ext.).

RUSSELL OF LIVERPOOL, BARON. (Russell.) [Baron U.K. 1919.]

EDWARD FREDERICK LANGLEY RUSSELL, *C.B.E., M.C.*, 2nd Baron; b. April 10th, 1895; s. 1920; ed. at Liverpool Coll., and at St. John's Coll., Oxford; Bar. Gray's Inn 1931; Brigadier (ret.) late The King's Regt. (Liverpool) and 20th Lancers (Indian Army); Assist. Judge Advocate Gen. British Expeditionary Force 1939-40, Dep. Judge Advocate Gen. at 1st Army Headquarters 1942-43, at Allied Force Headquarters 1943-45, to Middle East Forces 1945-46, and to British Army of the Rhine 1946-51, and Assist. Judge Advocate Gen. 1951-4; is author of 'The Scourge of the Swastika', 'Though The Heavens Fall', 'The Knights of Bushido', 'That Reminds Me', 'If I Forget Thee', 'The Royal Conscience', 'The Trial of Adolf Eichmann', 'The Tragedy of the Congo', 'South Africa—Today and Tomorrow', 'Knight of the Sword', 'Deadman's Hill, Was Hanratty Guilty', 'Caroline The Unhappy Queen', and 'The Return of the Swastika': 1914-18 War (wounded, despatches, MC with two bars), 1939-45 in France, N. Africa and Italy (despatches, OBE, CBE); OBE (Mil) 1943, CBE (Mil) 1945: m. 1st, 1920 (m. diss. 1933) Constance Claudine, yr. da. of the late Col. Philip Cecil Harcourt Gordon, CMG, RAMC; 2ndly, 1933 (m. diss. 1946), Joan Betty, da. of the late David Ewart, OBE, MD, FRCS, of Chichester; 3rdly, 1946, Alix, who d. 1971, only da. of the late Marquis de Brévaire d'Alaincourt, and widow of Comte de Richard d'Ivry; 4thly, 1972, Selma, da. of   , and widow of A. W. Brayley, and has issue by 1st and 2nd marriages.

Arms,—Per saltire sable and or, in chief an estoile argent, two roses in fesse gules, barbed and seeded proper, and in base a thistle leaved and slipped of the second.   **Crest,**—An owl wings expanded argent, beaked and legged or, resting the dexter claw on an estoile azure.   **Supporters,**— On either side an owl argent, beaked and legged or, gorged with a chaplet of roses gules, leaved vert *Club,*—Authors'.

SON LIVING. *(By 1st marriage.)*

Hon. LANGLEY GORDON HASLINGDEN, *M.C., b.* Sept. 14th, 1922; ed. at Charterhouse; 1940-45 War as Capt. Grenadier Guards (M.C.): *m.* 1951, Kiloran Margaret, dau. of the late Hon. Sir Arthur Jared Palmer Howard, KBE, CVO [see B. Strathcona and Mount Royal, colls.], and has issue living, Simon, *b.* 1952,—Adam, *b.* 1957,—Daniel, *b.* 1962,—Emma, *b.* 1955,—Annabel, *b.* 1959,—Lucy, *b.* 1968.   *Residence,*—Ash Farm, Stourpaine, Blandford, Dorset. [The Hon. Langley G. H. Russell *d.* Sept. 16th, 1975].

DAUGHTERS LIVING. *(By 1st marriage.)*

Hon. Anne Philippa (1450, McTavish Rd., Sidney, RR2, Vancouver Island, Canada), *b.* 1924: *m.* 1947, Gershom Radcliffe Layton Warren, late Maj. Canadian Army.

(By 2nd marriage.)

Hon. Crystal, *b.* 1936 : *m.* 1955, John Mark Essington-Boulton, and has issue living, James Clive, *b.* 1958,—Nicolette, *b.* 1956.   *Residence,*—

PREDECESSOR.—[1] *Sir* EDWARD RICHARD Russell, son of the late Edward Haslingden Russell, of London; *b.* 1834; editor of *Liverpool Daily Post and Mercury*; M.P. for Glasgow, Bridgeton Div. (L) 1885-7; cr. *Baron Russell of Liverpool,* of Liverpool, co. Palatine of Lancaster (peerage of United Kingdom) 1919: *m.* 1st, 1858, Eliza Sophia, who *d.* 1901, dau. of Stephen Bradley, of Bridge, Canterbury; 2ndly, 1902, Jean Stewart, who *d.* 1927, dau. of the late Alexander Macdonald, of Campbeltown, Argyllshire, and widow of Joseph McFarlane; *d.* 1920; *s.* by his grandson [2] EDWARD FREDERICK LANGLEY, *M.C.* (son of the late Richard Henry Langley Russell, 2nd son of 1st Baron), 2nd Baron and present peer.

Ruthven of Canberra, Viscount, son of Earl of Gowrie.

RUTHVEN OF FREELAND, LADY. (Ruthven.) [Lordship S. 1651.]

[Title pronounced "Rivven."]

BRIDGET HELEN RUTHVEN, *CBE (Dowager Viscountess Monckton of Brenchley), b.* July 27th, 1896; *s.* 1956 (her petition as heir of line and heir of tailzie of 1st Lord allowed in Lyon Court 1967, and her succession to the Peerage recognized), (formerly Senior Controller ATS and Dir. of Women's Auxiliary Corps (India); CBE (Mil.) 1947: *m.* 1st, 1918, the 11th Earl of Carlisle, who *d.* 1963, having obtained a divorce 1947; 2ndly, 1947, as his second wife, the 1st Viscount Monckton of Brenchley, who *d.* 1965, and has issue by 1st m.

Arms,—Paly of six argent and gules, a bordure ermine (as bordure for difference from the paternal coat of the spouse, Moncreiffe, of the founder of the House of Ruthven of Freeland).   **Crest,**—A goat's head coupled argent attired or.   **Supporters,**—Two goats argent, attired, maned and unguled or, gorged of collars gules.   *Residence,*—113, Eaton Sq., SW1.

SON LIVING. *(By 1st marriage.)*

CHARLES JAMES RUTHVEN HOWARD, *M.C. (Earl of Carlisle), b.* Feb. 21st, 1923; ed. at Eton 1939-45 War as Lt. Rifle Bde. (severely wounded, M.C.): *m.* 1945, the Hon. Ela Hilda Aline Beaumont, only dau. of 2nd Viscount Allendale, and has issue:—

SONS LIVING,—George William Beaumont (*Viscount Morpeth*), *b.* Feb. 15th, 1949. Hon. Philip Charles Wentworth, *b.* 1963.
DAUGHTERS LIVING,—*Lady* Jane Annabelle, *b.* 1947: *m.* 1968, John David Vaughan Seth-Smith, of 34, Epirus Rd., SW6, and has issue living, Gemma Bridget Annabel, *b.* 1972.
Lady Emma Bridget, *b.* 1952: *m.* 1974, John Langton-Lockton.

Residence,—Naworth Castle, Brampton, Cumberland.

DAUGHTER LIVING. *(By 1st marriage.)*

Lady Carolyn Bridget Dacre HOWARD, *b.* 1919; formerly Subaltern, ATS.

WIDOW LIVING OF SON OF EIGHTH LORD.

Lydia Gladys, dau. of the late Henry Adams, of Cannon Hill, Maidenhead: *m.* 1st, 1905, the Hon. Philip James Leslie Hore-Ruthven, who *d.* 1908; 2ndly, 1912, Maj.-Gen. Hugh Wharton Myddelton Watson, C.B., C.M.G., D.S.O., who *d.* 1938.   *Residence,*—

WIDOW LIVING OF NINTH LORD.

JUDITH GORDON (Digbigh, Foreland Rd., Bembridge, Isle of Wight), yr. da. of the late Bertie E. Bell, of Guernsey: *m.* 1st, 1953, as his second wife, the 9th Lord, who *d.* 1956; 2ndly, 1965, Maj. Digby R. Peel, late RA, who *d.* 1971.

COLLATERAL BRANCHES LIVING.

Grandson of the late Rt. Hon. Sir Alexander Gore Arkwright Hore-Ruthven, V.C., G.C.M.G., C.B., D.S.O., P.C. (2nd son of 8th Lord) who was cr. *Earl of Gowrie* 1945 [see that title].

(Also in remainder to Barony of Ruthven of Gowrie.)

Issue of the late Col. the Hon. Christian Malise Hore-Ruthven, 3rd son of 8th Lord, *b.* 1880, *d.* 1969: *m.* 1925, the Hon. Angela Margaret Manners ,RRC, who *d.* 1970, da. of 3rd Baron Manners:—

James John Malise (42, Westminster Gdns., Marsham St., SW1P 4JD), b. 1935; ed. at Eton: m. 1965, Helen Dron, el. da. of John S. Craig, of Woodridge, Milngavie, Glasgow, and has issue living, Alexander Malise, b. 1972.——Nancy Margaret, b. 1927.——Sarah Constance Anne, b. 1930: m. 1962, James Baynard-Smith, of 8, Hernes Rd., Oxford, and has issue living, Peter James, b. 1966,—Christopher Ruthven, b. 1972.

Granddaughters of the late Hon. Charles Edward Stewart Hore-Ruthven, O.B.E., brother of 8th Lord:—
Issue of the late Charles Hore-Ruthven, b. 1876, d. 1963: m. 1910, Elyned Rhona, who d. 1965, da. of the late Thomas Wood [B. Tollemache]:—
Elcha Cecilia (Knoll House, Aylsham, Norfolk), b. 1912: m. 1934 (m. diss. 1968), William Herbert Harrison, and has issue living, Rhona Moya, b. 1936: m. 1958, Edward Luddington [E. Leicester], and has issue living, Nicholas Edward b. 1960, Christopher Mark b. 1963, Andrew William b. 1965,—Zara Carolyn b. 1938: m. 1962, Alastair Neil Campbell Harris, of Gatehampton Manor, Goring-on-Thames, and has issue living, James Neil b. 1966, Clare Louise b. 1966, Lucinda Zara b. 1968,—Susan Juliet, b. 1945: m. 1967, Charles Bannatyne Watson, of Margrie House, Borgue, Kirkcudbrightshire, and has issue living, Adam Bannatyne b. 1971, Sara Cecilia b. 1969,—Susannah, b. 1946.——Elyned Barbara, MBE, b. 1915; MBE (Mil) 1946: m. 1940, John Allan Legh Barratt, of Upgate House, Swannington, nr. Norwich, and has issue living, David John, b. 1947,—Charles William Legh, b. 1949.

PREDECESSORS.—[1] Sir THOMAS Ruthven (great-grandson of William, 2nd Lord Ruthven, cr. 1487-8, who was grandfather of 1st Earl of Gowrie), Col. of a Regt., a Commr. for the Treaty of Ripon 1641, and a Commr. of Exchequer 1649, was cr. Lord Ruthven of Freeland (peerage of Scotland) 1651; the patent is stated to have been burnt with the house of Freeland in 1750, and the limitations are not accurately known, nevertheless as the dignity was retained (together with many extinct titles) on the Union Roll, it has been presumed that the honour was to heirs-general; d. 1673; s. by his son [2] DAVID, 2nd Lord; was a Lord of the Treasury in Scotland; d. unmarried 1701, when the estates devolved by entail upon his youngest sister [3] Jean, and at her death in April 1722 they passed to her nephew Sir William Cunningham, Bt. (only son of her elder sister Anne, and also heir of line), who d. in Oct. 1722, having assumed the surname of Ruthven upon the death of the 2nd Lord, but (living only six months after his accession to the estates) without ever having assumed the title; his cousin, however, [4] ISABELLA [dau. of the Hon. Elizabeth (2nd dau. and heir of line of 1st Lord) by her marriage with Sir Francis Ruthven, Knt.], was summoned as a Lady to the Coronation of George II., and recognized in the Lordship of Ruthven of Freeland: m. Col. James Johnson, who assumed the name of Ruthven; d. 1730; s. by her son [5] JAMES, 5th Lord; d. 1783; s. by his son [6] JAMES, 6th Lord; d. 1789; s. by his son [7] JAMES, 7th Lord; d.s.p. 1853; s. by his sister [8] MARY ELIZABETH THORNTON: m. 1806, Walter Hore, who assumed the additional surname of Ruthven; d. 1864; s. by her grandson [9] WALTER JAMES, 8th Lord Ruthven of Freeland (b. 1838), who, like his predecessors, voted at the Election of Representative Peers for Scotland, and was cr. Baron Ruthven of Gowrie (peerage of United Kingdom) 1919 : m. 1869, Lady Caroline Annesley Gore, who d. 1914, dau. of 4th Earl of Arran; d. 1921; s. by his el. son [10] WALTER PATRICK, C.B., C.M.G., D.S.O., 9th Lord; b. 1870; Maj.-Gen. late Scots Guards; commanded Bangalore Brig. 1920-24, and London Dist. 1924-8, and was Lieut.-Gov. of Guernsey 1929-34 : m. 1st, 1895, Jean Leslie, who d. 1952, dau. of the late Norman George Lampson [Lampson Bt., colls.]; 2ndly, 1953, Judith Gordon (who m. 2ndly, 1965, Maj. Digby R. Peel), da. of the late Bertie E. Bell, of Guernsey; d. 1956; s. in the Barony of Ruthven of Gowrie (peerage of United Kingdom) by his great-nephew the 2nd Earl of Gowrie, and in the Lordship of Ruthven of Freeland by his el. da. [11] BRIDGET HELEN, Lady Ruthven of Freeland and present peeress.

RUTLAND, DUKE OF. (Manners.) [Duke E. 1703.]

POUR·Y·PARVENIR.

In order to accomplish.

CHARLES JOHN ROBERT MANNERS, C.B.E., 10th Duke of Rutland; b. May 28th, 1919; s. 1940; ed. at Eton, and at Trin. Coll., Camb. (BA); Capt. Gren. Gds., and patron of eleven livings; Chm. of E. Midlands Economic Planning Council since 1971; CBE (Civil) 1962: m. 1st, 1946, Anne Bairstow (from whom he obtained a divorce 1956), da. of the late Major William Cumming Bell, of Binham House, Edgerton, Huddersfield; 2ndly, 1958, Frances Helen, da. of Charles Sweeny, of 70, South Audley St., W1, and has issue by 1st and 2nd marriages.

Arms,—Or, two bars azure, a chief quarterly, azure and gules; in 1st and 4th quarters two fleurs-de-lis, and in the 2nd and 3rd a lion passant guardant, all or. Crest,—On a chapeau gules, turned up ermine, a peacock in pride proper. Supporters, —Two unicorns, armed, unguled, maned and tufted, or.

Seats,—Haddon Hall, Bakewell, Derby ; Belvoir Castle, Grantham.

SONS LIVING. (By 2nd marriage.)
DAVID CHARLES ROBERT (Marquess of Granby), b. May 8th, 1959.
Lord Edward John Francis, b. 1965.

DAUGHTERS LIVING. (By 1st marriage.)
Lady Charlotte Louisa, b. 1947.
(By 2nd marriage.)
Lady Helen Teresa Margaret, b. 1962.

BROTHERS LIVING.
Lord John, b. 1922; ed. at Eton, and at New Coll., Oxford; formerly Capt. Life Guards, and 2nd Special Air Ser. Regt. : m. 1957, Mary Diana, youngest dau. of the late Lieut.-Col. Lancelot Geoffrey Moore, D.S.O., and has issue living, Richard John Peveril, b. 1963,—Elizabeth Diana, b. 1959,—Lucy Rachel, b. 1961. Residences,—Reservoir Cottage, Knipton, Grantham, Lincolnshire; Haddon Hall, Bakewell, Derbyshire.

Lord Roger David (Belcombe Court, Bradford-on-Avon), *b.* 1925 ; ed. at Eton; formerly 2nd Lt. Grenadier Guards: *m.* 1965, Finola St. Lawrence, only da. of T. E. Daubeney, and has issue living, Moira Violet Joanna, *b.* 1966,—Phœbe Constance Adeliza, *b.* 1968.

SISTERS LIVING.

Lady Ursula, *b.* 1916: was a Train Bearer to the Queen at Coronation of King George VI. : *m.* 1st, 1943, Anthony Freire Marreco, late Lieut. R.N.V.R., who obtained a divorce 1948; 2ndly, 1951, Robert Erland Nicolai d'Abo, who *d.* 1970, and has issue living, (by 2nd m.) John Henry Erland, *b.* 1953,—Richard Winston Mark, *b.* 1956,—Louisa Jane, *b.* 1955. *Residences,*—West Wratting Park, Cambs.; 29, Kensington Sq., W8.

Lady Isabel Violet Kathleen, *b.* 1917: *m.* 1st, 1936, as his second wife (marriage dissolved 1951), Group Capt. Thomas Loel Evelyn Bulkeley Guinness, O.B.E., Auxiliary Air Force (Reserve); 2ndly, 1953, Sir Robert George Maxwell Throckmorton, 11th Bt., and has issue living, (by 1st marriage) William Loel Seymour, *b.* 1939: *m.* 1971, Agnes Elizabeth Lynn, only da. of I. T. M. Day, and has issue living, Sheridan William *b.* 1972, Thomas Seymour *b.* 1973,—Serena Belinda Rosemary (*Marchioness of Dufferin and Ava*) *m.* 1941: *m.* 1964, the 5th Marquess of Dufferin and Ava, of 4, Holland Villas Rd., W14 and Clandeboye, Bangor, co. Down. *Residences,*—Coughton Court, Alcester, Warwickshire; Molland, South Molton, N. Devon.

AUNT LIVING. (*Daughter of 8th Duke.*)

Lady Diana Olivia Winifred Maud (*Lady Diana Cooper*), *b.* 1892 : *m.* 1919, the 1st Viscount Norwich, who *d.* 1954. *Residence,*—10, Warwick Avenue, W.2.

WIDOW LIVING OF NINTH DUKE.

KATHLEEN (*Dowager Duchess of Rutland*), dau. of the late Francis John Tennant [see B. Glenconner, colls.]; is a J.P.; bore the Queen's Canopy at Coronation of King George VI.: *m.* 1916, the 9th Duke, who *d.* 1940. *Residence,*—21, Wilton Street, S.W.1.

COLLATERAL BRANCHES LIVING.

Issue of the late Lieut.-Col. Lord Robert William Orlando Manners, C.M.G., D.S.O., King's Roy. Rifle Corps, and attached to Northumberland Fusiliers, 4th son of 7th Duke, *b.* 1870, *d.* (killed in action during European War) 1917: *m.* 1902, Mildred Mary, O.B.E., who *d.* 1934, dau. of the late Rev. Charles P. Buckworth, and widow of Major Henry Edward Buchanan-Riddell, King's Roy. Rifle Corps [Riddell, Bt.] :—

Elizabeth Katharine Joan, *b.* 1904: *m.* 1932, Lieut.-Col. John Norman Pulteney Lascelles, Coldstream Guards [see E. Harewood, colls.], who *d.* (on active service during European War) 1939. *Residence,*—Saywell Farm, Bedmonton, Sittingbourne, Kent.

Grandchildren of the late Rev. William Manners-Sutton, 2nd son of the late Frederick Manners-Sutton, 3rd son of the late Capt. John Manners-Sutton, M.P., 2nd son of the late Lord George Manners-Sutton, 3rd son of 3rd Duke :—
Issue of the late Frederick William Manners-Sutton, *b.* 1865, *d.* 1946: *m.* 1902, Winifred Grace Richardson, who *d.* 1970:—

John Lumley, *b.* 1914 : *m.* 1949, Elizabeth Mary Gylda Eliot, dau. of A. N. G. Irving, of Lesmurdie, W. Australia, and has issue living, John Frederick, *b.* 1955,—Elizabeth Marjorie Inez (33, Springfield Rd., NW8), *b.* 1950.——Melanie Grace, *b.* 1952. *Residence,*—2, Garland Road, Dalkeith, W. Australia. ——Dorothy Joyce, *b.* 1904: *m.* 1926, John Bouverie Primrose, and has issue living, John Robert Manners, *b.* 1927,—Roger Bouverie Manners, *b.* 1934,—Edwin Neil Manners, *b.* 1942,—Diana Marjorie Manners, *b.* 1938. *Residence,*—Wallington, via Geelong, Victoria, Australia.——Freda Grace, *b.* 1905 : *m.* 1925, Keith Lee Roberts, who *d.* 1949, and has issue living, Christopher Manners, *b.* 1932,—Antony John, *b.* 1938,—Joanna Margaret, *b.* 1935. *Residences,*—Bendon, 19, Fernhurst Grove, Kew, E4, Melbourne, Australia; Longford, Clyde, Victoria, Australia.——Evelyn Mabel (119, The Terrace, Ocean Grove, Vic., Aust.), *b.* 1909: *m.* 1928, John Kenneth Finlay, MBE, who *d.* 1970, and has issue living, Chester Manners, *b.* 1932,—Warwick Henry, *b.* 1934,—John Lexton, *b.* 1936.

Descendants of the late Rt. Hon. Thomas Manners-Sutton [5th son of the late Lord George Manners-Sutton (ante)], who was cr. *Baron Manners* 1807 [see that title].

PREDECESSORS.—[1] *Sir* THOMAS Manners, *K.G.*, 13th Baron de Ros (see Bs. de Ros), was cr. *Earl of Rutland* (peerage of England) 1525; *d.* 1543; *s.* by his son [2] HENRY, *K.G.*, 2nd Earl; was Constable of Nottingham Castle, and Pres. of the North; he completed the re-building of Belvoir Castle; *d.* 1563; *s.* by his son [3] EDWARD, *K.G.*, 3rd Earl; *d.* 1587 without male issue, when the Barony of de Ros reverted to his dau. Elizabeth, wife of Lord Burleigh (see M. Exeter), and the earldom devolved upon his brother [4] JOHN, 4th Earl; *d.* 1588; *s.* by his el. son [5] ROGER, 5th Earl; *d.s.p.* 1612; *s.* by his brother [6] FRANCIS, *K.G.*, 6th Earl; who in 1616 had been cr. *Baron Roos*, of Hamlake (peerage of England); in 1618 *s.* his cousin, son of Elizabeth, Baroness de Ros (ante), as 17th Baron de Ros; *d.* 1632, when the Barony of Roos of Hamlake expired, and the other honours devolved upon his brother [7] GEORGE, 7th Earl; *d.s.p.* 1641, when the Barony of de Ros reverted to Katherine, wife of George Villiers, 1st Duke of Buckingham (cr. 1623), and the earldom devolved upon his cousin [8] JOHN, 8th Earl; *d.* Sept., 1679; *s.* by his son [9] JOHN, 9th Earl, who in April, 1679, had been summoned to Parliament as *Baron Manners of Haddon*, co. Derby (peerage of England); was Lord-Lieut. of Leicestershire; cr. *Marquess of Granby* and *Duke of Rutland* (peerage of England) 1703; *d.* 1711; *s.* by his son [10] JOHN, *K.G.*, 2nd Duke; *b.* 1676; successively M.P. for Derbyshire, Leicestershire, and Grantham, and Lord-Lieut. of Leicestershire: *m.* 1st, 1693, Catharine Russell, who *d.* 1711, dau. of William, Lord Russell, 2nd son of 1st Duke of Bedford; 2ndly, 1713, the Hon. Lucy Sherard, who *d.* 1751, dau. of 2nd Baron Sherard; *d.* 1721; *s.* by his son [11] JOHN, *K.G.*, *P.C.*, 3rd Duke; *b.* 1696; was Lord-Lieut. of co. Leicester 1721-79, Chancellor of Duchy of Lancaster 1727-36, Lord Steward of the Household 1755-61, and Master of the Horse 1761-66: *m.* 1717, the Hon. Bridget Sutton, who *d.* 1734, dau. of 2nd Baron Lexinton; *d.* 1779; *s.* by his grandson [12] CHARLES, *K.G.*, *P.C.* (son of the late John, Marquess of Granby, el. son of 3rd Duke), 4th Duke; was M.P. for Camb. Univ. 1774-9, and Viceroy of Ireland 1784-7: *m.* 1775, Lady Mary Isabella Somerset, who *d.* 1831, dau. of 4th Duke of Beaufort; *d.* 1787; *s.* by his son [13] JOHN HENRY, *K.G.*, 5th Duke; *b.* 1778; was Lord-Lieut. of co. Leicester, Recorder of Grantham, Cambridge, and Scarborough, and Col. Leicestershire Militia: *m.* 1799, Lady Elizabeth Howard, dau. of 5th Earl of Carlisle, K.G. ; *d.* 1857; *s.* by his son [14] CHARLES JOHN CECIL, *K.G.*, 6th Duke; *b.* 1815; sat as M.P. for Stamford (*C*) 1837-52, and for N. Leicestershire 1852-7; *d.* 1888; *s.* by his brother [15] JOHN JAMES ROBERT, *K.G.*, *G.C.B.*, *P.C.*, *D.C.L.*, *LL.D.*, 7th Duke, First Commr. of Works (with a seat in the Cabinet) 1852, 1858-9 and 1866-7, Postmaster-Gen. 1874-80 and 1885-6, and Chancellor of Duchy of Lancaster July 1886 to Aug. 1892; sat as M.P. for Newark (*C*) 1841-7, for Colchester 1850-57, for Leicestershire N. 1857-85, and for E., or Melton, Div. of Leicestershire 1885-8 ; cr. *Baron Roos of Belvoir*, co. Leicester (peerage of United Kingdom) 1896 : *m.* 1st, 1851, Catherine Louisa, who *d.* 1854, dau. of the late Col. George Marlay, C.B.; 2ndly, 1862, Janetta, who *d.* 1899, dau. of Thomas Hughan, of Airds ;

d. 1906; *s.* by his son [16] HENRY JOHN BRINSLEY, *K.G.* (who had been called to the House of Lords in his father's Barony of Manners of Haddon 1896, and *s.* as 8th Duke of Rutland and 2nd Baron Roos of Belvoir 1906), 8th Duke; *b.* 1852; Principal Private Sec. to Marquess of Salisbury June 1885 to Jan. 1886, and Aug. 1886 to March 1888; Lord-Lieut. of Leicestershire 1900-25; M.P. for E., or Melton, Div. of Leicestershire (*C*) 1888-95: *m.* 1882, Marion Margaret Violet, who *d.* 1937, dau. of the late Col. the Hon. Charles Hugh Lindsay, C.B.; *d.* 1925; *s.* by his younger son, [17] JOHN HENRY MONTAGU, 9th Duke; *b.* 1886: *m.* 1916, Kathleen, dau. of Francis John Tennant [B. Glenconner, colls.] *d.* 1940; *s.* by his el. son [18] CHARLES JOHN ROBERT, 10th Duke and present peer; also Marquess of Granby, Earl of Rutland, Baron Manners of Haddon, and Baron Roos of Belvoir.

RYDER OF EATON HASTINGS, BARON. (Ryder.) [Life Baron 1975.]

SYDNEY THOMAS (DON) RYDER, son of John Ryder; *b.* Sept. 16th, 1916; ed. at Ealing County Gram. Sch.; Editor of *Stock Exchange Gazette* 1950-60; Joint Man. Dir. Kelly Iliffe Holdings, and Associated Iliffe Press, Ltd. 1961-63, Man. Dir. 1961-63, Dir. IPC 1963-70, Man. Dir. Reed Paper Gp. 1963-68 and Chm. and Ch. Exec. Reed Internat., Ltd. (formerly Reed Gp., Ltd.) 1968-75; Pres. of Nat. Materials Handling Centre 1970-75; Vice-Pres. of Roy. Soc. of Prevention of Accidents 1973-75, Dir. of Metropolitan Estate and Property Corpn., Ltd. 1972-75, Member of Council BIM 1970-75, of British Gas Board, and Reserve Pension Board 1973-75, of UK S. Africa Trade Assocn. 1974-75; Govt. Ch. Industrial Adviser since 1975; cr. Knt. 1972, and *Baron Ryder of Eaton Hastings,* of Eaton Hastings, Oxon (Life Baron) 1975: *m.* 1950, Eileen, da. of William Dodds, and has issue.

Arms,—Not exemplified at time of going to press.
Residence,—The Penthouse, Century Court, NW8 9LD.

SON LIVING.

Hon. Michael John, *b.* 1953.

DAUGHTER LIVING.

Hon. Jill Patricia, *b.* 1950.

SACKVILLE, BARON. (Sackville-West.) [Baron U.K. 1876.]

LIONEL BERTRAND SACKVILLE-WEST, 6th Baron; *b.* May 30th, 1913; *s.* 1965; ed. at Winchester, and Magdalen Coll., Oxford (BA); late Capt. Coldm. Guards, and a Member of Lloyd's; patron of eleven livings; 1939-45 War (prisoner): *m.* 1st, 1953, Jacobine Napier, who *d.* 1971, da. of J. R. Menzies-Wilson, of Fotheringhay Lodge, Nassington, Peterborough, and widow of Capt. John Hichens, RA; 2ndly, 1974, Arlie Roebuck, da. of Charles Woodhead, of Romany Rye, Brisbane, Aust., widow of Maj. Hugh Dalzell Stewart, W. Yorks. Regt., and formerly wife of Maj.-Gen. Sir Francis Wilfred de Guingand, KBE, CB, DSO, and has issue by 1st m.

Arms,—Quarterly: 1st and 4th argent, a fesse dancettee sable, *West;* 2nd and 3rd or and gules, a bend vair, *Sackville.* **Crests,**—1st, out of a ducal coronet or, a griffin's head azure, beaked and eared gold; 2nd out of a coronet composed of a fleur-de-lis or, an estoile argent. **Supporters,**—On either side a griffin azure, beaked and eared or, ducally gorged gold, therefrom pendent an escutcheon, that on the dexter charged with the arms of West, and that on the sinister with the arms of Sackville.

JOUR·DE·MA·VIE

The day of my life.

Residence,—Knole, Sevenoaks, Kent. *Club,* —Brooks's.

DAUGHTERS LIVING. (By 1st m.)

Hon. Teresa, *b.* 1954.
Hon. Catherine Jacobine, *b.* 1956.
Hon. Sophia Anne, *b.* 1957.
Hon. Victoria Mary, *b.* 1959.
Hon. Sarah Elizabeth, *b.* 1960.

BROTHER LIVING.

HUGH ROSSLYN INIGO, *MC* (Knole, Sevenoaks, Kent); Brooks's, and United Service Clubs), *b.*
Feb. 1st, 1919; ed. at Winchester, and at Magdalen Coll., Oxford (MA); late Capt. R Tank Regt.;
ARICS; Admin. Officer, N. Nigeria 1946-59; 1939-45 War (wounded, MC, French Croix de Guerre):
m. 1957, Bridget Eleanor, da. of Capt. Robert Lionel Brooke Cunliffe, CBE, RN [see Cunliffe,
Bt., colls.], and has issue living, Robert Bertrand, *b.* 1958,—William Lionel, *b.* 1967,—Mary Cecilie,
b. 1960,—Elizabeth Anne, *b.* 1962,—Jane Eleanor, *b.* 1964.

SISTER LIVING.

Elizabeth Margaret (21, Whiteheads Grove, SW3), *b.* 1911: *m.* 1943, Thomas Bradwall Barlow [see
Barlow. Bt., cr. 1901].

PREDECESSORS. — [1] *Hon.* MORTIMER Sackville-West (4th son of 5th Earl De La Warr);
b. 1820; held several high appointments in Royal Household, and was cr. *Baron Sackville,* of
Knole, co. Kent (peerage of United Kingdom), 1876, with special remainder, failing heirs male
of his body, to his brothers Lionel and William Edward respectively in like manner [see E.
De La Warr, colls.]: *m.* 1st, 1847, Fanny Charlotte, dau. of the late Maj.-Gen. William Dickson,
C.B. ; 2ndly, 1873, Elizabeth, dau. of the late Charles William Faber, Esq., of Northaw House,
Barnet ; *d.* 1888; *s.* by his brother [2] LIONEL SACKVILLE, *G.C.M.G.,* 2nd Baron ; *b.* 1827; was
Min. to Argentine Republic 1872-8, to Madrid 1878-81, and to Washington 1881-8 ; *d.* 1908, when
a suit was brought by Henri Ernest Jean Baptist Sackville-West under the Declaration of
Legitimacy Act, claiming to be el. legitimate son of the 2nd Baron by Josephine Duran de
Ortega (" Pepita"), but in 1910 the petition was dismissed, and there *s.* to the Barony under the
special remainder the 2nd Baron's nephew [3] LIONEL EDWARD (el. son of the late Lieut.-Col.
the Hon. William Edward Sackville-West), 3rd Baron, *b.* 1867 ; a Director of Bank of Liverpool
and Martins: *m.* 1890, his cousin, Victoria Sackville-West, who *d.* 1936 ; *d.* 1928 ; *s.* by his
brother [4] CHARLES JOHN, *K.B.E., C.B., C.M.G.,* 4th Baron, *b.* 1870; Maj.-Gen., late King's Roy.
Rifle Corps; British Representative at Supreme War Council, Versailles 1918 and 1919, Mil. Attaché
at Paris 1920-4, and Lieut.-Gov. of Guernsey 1925-9: *m.* 1st, 1897, Maud Cecila, who *d.* 1920, dau.
of the late Matthew John Bell, of Bourne Park, Kent [B. St. Leonards]; 2ndly, 1924, Anne (BIGE-
LOW), who *d.* 1961, dau. of the late William Meredith, of New York; *d.* 1962; *s.* by his son [5]
EDWARD CHARLES, 5th Baron, *b.* 1901, *d.* 1965; *s.* by his cousin [6] LIONEL BERTRAND (el. son of
the Hon. Bertrand George Sackville-West, yst. brother of 4th Baron),6th Baron and present peer.

SAINSBURY, BARON. (Sainsbury.) [Life Baron 1962.]

ALAN JOHN SAINSBURY, el. son of the late John Benjamin Sainsbury; *b.*
Aug. 13th, 1902; ed. at Haileybury; Hon. Fellow of Inst. of Food Science and
Techn.; Pres. of J. Sainsbury, Ltd., Grocery and Provision Merchants;
Vice-Pres. of Roy. Soc. for Encouragement of Arts, Manufactures and Com-
merce 1962-66, and Pres. of Multiple Shops Federation 1963-65, of Grocers'
Inst. 1963-66, and of Internat. Assocn. of Chain Stores 1965-68, and Chm. of
Min. of Health Cttee. of Inquiry into relationship of Pharmaceutical Industry
with Nat. Health Ser. 1965-67, a Member of EDC for Distributive Trades
1964-68, Pres. of Roy. Inst. of Public Health and Hygiene 1965-70, and a
Gov. of City Literary Inst. 1967-69; Chm. of Uganda Asian Relief Trust
1972-74; Pres. of Pestalozzi Children's Village Trust since 1963, Member of
Food Research Advisory Cttee. 1960-70 (Chm. 1965-70), Vice-Pres. of Assocn.
of Agric. since 1965, a Member of Court of Univ. of Essex since 1966, and Chm.
of Trustees Overseas Students Advisory Bureau since 1969; Pres. Distributive
Trades Education and Training Council since 1975; a Member of Exec. Cttee.
of PEP; cr. *Baron Sainsbury,* of Drury Lane, Borough of Holborn (peerage
of UK) 1962; Hon. Sec. Labour Friends of Israel: *m.* 1st, 1925 (m. diss. 1939),
Doreen Davan, da. of Leonard Adams: *m.* 2ndly, 1944, Anne Elizabeth, da.
of Paul Lewy, and has issue by 1st and 2nd marriages.

Residence,—Flat 8, 34, Bryanston Sq., W.1.

SONS LIVING. (By 1st marriage.)

Hon. John Davan (Stamford House, Stamford St., SE1; Garrick Club), *b.* 1927; a Dir. of J. Sainsbury,
Ltd. since 1958, and Chm. since 1969: *m.* 1963, Mrs. Anya Linden Tamarin, da. of G. C. Eltenton,
and has issue.
Hon. Simon David Davan, *b.* 1930; Vice-Chm. and a Director of J. Sainsbury, Ltd.
Hon. Timothy Alan Davan, *MP* (c/o House of Commons, SW1A 0AA; Boodle's Club), *b.* 1932; is a
Dir. of J. Sainsbury, Ltd.; MP for Hove (C) since 1973: *m.* 1961, Susan Mary, da. of Brig. James
Alastair Harry Mitchell, OBE, DSO, and has issue.

DAUGHTER LIVING. (By 2nd marriage.)

Hon. Paulette Ann, *b.* 1946: *m.* 1970, James Anderson, and has issue.

ST. ALBANS, DUKE OF. (Beauclerk.) [Duke E. 1684.]
[Name pronounced "Bo-clare."]

AUSPICIUM MELIORIS ÆVI

A pledge of better times.

CHARLES FREDERIC AUBREY DE VERE BEAUCLERK, *OBE*, 13th Duke; *b.* Aug. 16th, 1915; *s.* 1964; ed. at Eton, and at Magdalene Coll., Camb. (MA); late Col. Intelligence Corps, and Dir. Films Div., Central Office of Information; patron of two livings, Hereditary Grand Falconer, and Hereditary Registrar of Court of Chancery; 1939-45 War in Mediterranean (OBE); OBE (Mil) 1945: *m.* 1st, 1938 (marriage dissolved 1947), Nathalie Chatham, da. of the late Percival Field Walker, of Rythe Court, Thames Ditton, Surrey; 2ndly, 1947, Suzanne Marie Adèle, da. of the late Emile William Fesq, of Mas Mistral, Vence, France, AM, and has issue by 1st and 2nd marriages.

Arms,—Quarterly: 1st and 4th grand quarters the royal arms of King Charles II., 1st and 4th France and England, quarterly; 2nd Scotland; 3rd Ireland; the whole debruised by a baton sinister gules, charged with three roses argent, *Beauclerk;* 2nd and 3rd grand quarters quarterly gules and or, in the 1st quarter a mullet argent *de Vere.*

Crest,—On a chapeau gules, turned up ermine, a lion statant guardant or, ducally crowned per pale argent and gules, and gorged with a plain collar gules, charged with three roses argent. **Supporters**—*Dexter,* an antelope argent, armed and unguled or; *sinister,* a greyhound argent, each collared as the crest.

Residence,—St. Albans, 30, Cheyne Gardens, SW3 5HH.   *Clubs,*—Brooks's, St. James', Beefsteak.

SONS LIVING. (*By 1st marriage.*)
MURRAY DE VERE (*Earl of Burford*) (3, St. George's Court, Gloucester Rd., SW7; MCC, and Hurlingham Club), *b.* Jan. 19th, 1939; ed. at Tonbridge; a Chartered Accountant; a Freeman of City of London, and a Liveryman of Drapers' Co.: *m.* 1st, 1963 (m. diss. 1974), Rosemary Frances, only da. of Dr. Francis Harold Scoones, JP, of Rosecourt, Greenford, Middlesex; 2ndly, 1974, Cynthia Theresa Mary, da. of the late Lt.-Col. William James Holdsworth Howard, DSO, and formerly wife of Sir Anthony Robin Maurice Hooper, 2nd Bt., and has issue by 1st m.:—
    SON LIVING,—Charles Francis Topham de Vere (*Lord Vere of Hanworth*), *b.* Feb. 22nd, 1965.
    DAUGHTER LIVING,—*Lady* Emma Caroline de Vere, *b.* 1963; ed. at Roedean.

(*By 2nd marriage.*)
Lord Peter Charles de Vere (Beauclerk Ranch, Evans Ridge Rd., Anapolis, Calif. 95412), *b.* 1948; ed. at Eton: *m.* 1972, Beverley June, da. of the late Alva Edwin Bailey, of Calif., USA, and has issue living, Angela Grace de Vere, *b.* 1974.
Lord James Charles Fesq de Vere, *b.* 1949; ed. at Eton.
Lord John William Aubrey de Vere (399, Blas Cerdena, Lima, 27, Peru), *b.* 1950; ed. at Eton.

DAUGHTER LIVING. (*By 2nd marriage.*)
Lady Caroline Anne de Vere, *b.* 1951; ed. at Fritham House, and Queen's Gate Sch.: *m.* 1970, Neil St. John ffrench Blake, of Barn House, Midgham, Woolhampton, Reading, Berks., and has issue living, Clare Eleanor de Vere, *b.* 1972.

COLLATERAL BRANCHES LIVING.

Granddaughter of the late William Nelthorpe Beauclerk (infra):—
Issue of the late Major Aubrey Nelthorpe Beauclerk, *b.* 1879, *d.* 1916: *m.* 1911, Vera Eileen May, who *d.* 1975, having *m.* 2ndly, 1919, Capt. Gerald Andrew Greig, late R. Scots Fusiliers, who *d.* 1950), da. of the late Capt. W. H. Francis, formerly 28th Regt.:—
Daphne Diana de Vere, *b.* 1911: *m.* 1933, Count Claude Chauvin de Précourt, who *d.* 1971, and has issue living, François Charles Christian (Le Courtil, Saint Ideuc, 35, Paramé, France), *b.* 1936: *m.* 1962, Sabine, da. of the Comte de Vautibault, of Laval, Mayenne, France and has issue living, Claude Henri Aubrey *b.* 1963, Rémy François Xavier *b.* 1972, Ghislaine *b.* 1967,—Philippe Etienne (27, Rue Borjuis-Desbordes, Versailles, 78, France), *b.* 1938: *m.* 1961, Marie-Noelle, da. of René Gasquet, of Neuilly-sur-Seine, France, and has issue living, Aude Emilie *b.* 1962, Laure Sabine Pierrette *b.* 1963, Clarisse Agnes *b.* 1966, Marguerite *b.* 1972,—Jean Yves (Le Bouscater, Bouchet de la Lauze, Ponteils par Génolac, 30, France), *b.* 1943: *m.* 1970, Nathalie, da. of Dr. Dubel, of France, and has issue living, Penelope *b.* 1971,—Ann Victoria, *b.* 1944.   *Residence,*—Kennards, Amberley, Sussex.

Grandchildren of the late Maj. Aubrey Nelthorpe Beauclerk (ante):—
Issue of the late Hermione de Vere Beauclerk, *b.* 1915, *d.* 1969: *m.* 1939, James Dewar, MBE, GM, FCA, of 6, Hyde Park Gardens, W2 2LT.—
Peter de Vere BEAUCLERK-DEWAR (45, Airedale Av., Chiswick, W4 2NW; New (Edinburgh), and Puffins Clubs), *b.* 1943; recognised in the surname and arms of Beauclerk-Dewar by Lyon Court 1965; ed. at Ampleforth; Lt. RNR; FSA Scot.; Falkland Pursuivant Extraor. since 1975; co-author of "The House of Nell Gwyn" 1974; a Liveryman of Haberdashers' Co.; Knt. of Sovereign Mil. Order of Malta: *m.* 1967, Sarah Ann Sweet Verge, el. da. of Maj. Lionel John Verge Rudder, late DCLI, of the Old Dairy Barn, Bibury, Glos., and has issue living, James William Aubrey de Vere, *b.* 1970,—Alexandra Hermione Sarah, *b.* 1972,—Emma Diana Peta, *b.* 1973.——Gillian de Vere, *b.* 1944: *m.* 1964, Peter Jonh Lawrence Silley, MIMarE, of Park House, Eynsford, Kent, and has issue living, Natasha Margaret, *b.* 1965,—Tanya Anne, *b.* 1967.

Granddaughter of the late Capt. Lord Frederick Charles Peter Beauclerk, R.N., 2nd sur. son of 8th Duke:—
Issue of the late William Nelthorpe Beauclerk, *b.* 1849, *d.* 1908: *m.* 1st, 1878, Jane Isabella,

who *d*. 1888, dau. of the late Rev. James Rathborne, R. of W. Tytherley, Dean, Salisbury; 2ndly, 1892, Evelyn Amy, who *d*. 1933, dau. of Sir Robert Hart, 1st Bt., G.C.M.G. :—
(By 1st marriage) Florence Frederika de Vere, *b*. 1885 : *m*. 1912, Lieut.-Col. Reginald Joseph Bentinck, late 30th Lancers, Indian Army, who *d*. 1937, and has issue living, George Walter Zeno, *b*. 1913,—Gwynella de Vere, *b*. 1915,—Moyra de Vere, *b*. 1917: *m*. 1947, Dominic Mintoff, Prime Min. of Malta, of The Olives, Tarxien, Malta, and has issue living, Anne *b*. 1949: *m*. 1971, Bernard McKenna, Joan *b*. 1951,—Primrose de Vere, *b*. 1921: *m*. 1951, Surg.-Capt. Richard Howard Cowling, RN (ret.), of 50, Cliffe Way, Warwick, and has issue living, Charles Richard Bentinck *b*. 1952; ed. at Haileybury: *m*. 1974, Mary Duffy, Peter John *b*. 1954; ed. at Haileybury. *Residence*,—Flat 9, Hatherley House, Lansdown Rd., Cheltenham, Glos.

Granddaughter of Thomas Wentworth Sydney Beauclerk, 2nd son of Lord Charles Beauclerk, 5th son of 8th Duke:—
Issue of the late Wentworth Preston Beauclerk, *b*. 1875, *d*. 1921: *m*. 1894, Jennie Mabel Hayward, who *d*. 1959:—
Barbara, *b*. 1913: *m*. 1940, Joseph John Betz, of 2505, NE 7th Place, Fort Lauderdale, Florida, 53304, USA, and has issue living, Robert George, (1334, E Capital St., Washington, DC, USA), *b*. 1942; Capt. (ret.) US Army: *m*. 1973, Emilie Jeanne, da. of Lt.-Col. Francis Scellato, of Falls Church, Virginia, USA,—Sydney Wentworth, *b*. 1941: *m*. 1971, Charles Barnhill, of Milton, Florida, USA,—Doreen, *b*. 1948; ed. at Alabama Univ. (BA), and Tennessee Univ. (MA).

Grandchildren of the late Isabella Julia Beauclerk (who *d*. 1930, having *m*. 1867, the Chevalier Surg.-Maj. George Albert Palatiano, MD), yr. da. of Aubrey William de Vere Beauclerk, MP. el. son of Charles George Beauclerk (infra):—
Issue of the late Constantine Beauclerk Palatiano, *b*. 1868, *d*. 1943: *m*. 1901, Euphroinas, who *d*. 1957, da. of Miltiades Rhally, of Athens:—
Anthony (124, Capodistria St., Corfu, Greece; Corkyra Club), *b*. 1902; lawyer: *m*. 1937, Elly da. of Pericles Lascari, of Corfu, and has issue living, George Albert, *b*. 1940; Lt. Roy. Hellenic Navy.—
Frederik, *b*. 1906.——Katherine, *b*. 1912: *m*. 1935, Count Spiridion de Bulgaris, lawyer, of 32, St. Spiridions Rd., Corfu, Greece (Corkya Club), and has issue living, Octavius, *b*. 1936,—George Miltiades Sergius, *b*. 1942; engineer.

Grandchildren of the late Charles Robert Beauclerk, son of the late Charles George Beauclerk, grandson of the late Lord Sydney Beauclerk, 5th son of 1st Duke:—
Issue of the late William Topham Sidney Beauclerk, *b*. 1864, *d*. 1950: *m*. 1910, Lola de Penalver, who *d*. 1972, da. of Enrique, Conde de Penalver y Marqués de Arcos in Spain:—
Rafael Charles, *MBE* (31, Marryat Rd., Wimbledon, SW19), *b*. 1917; 1939-45 War as Capt. Intelligence Corps. (MBE, French Croix de Guerre); MBE (Mil) 1945: *m*. 1957, Noirine Mary, el. da. of J. Bowen, of Bowen's Cross, co. Cork, and has issue living, William Rafael, *b*. 1961,—Dolores Mary, *b*. 1958.——Diana Mary, *b*. 1924. *Residences*,—Villa Etchè Biskiak, Av. des Chênes Biarritz, France; 31, Marryatt Rd., Wimbledon, SW19.

PREDECESSORS.—[1] *Sir* CHARLES Beauclerk, *KG*, natural son of Charles II, by Eleanor Gwynn; *b*. 1670; cr. *Baron Heddington*, co. Oxford, and *Earl of Burford* (peerage of England) 1676, and *Duke of St. Albans* (peerage of England) 1684; Hereditary Registrar of the Court of Chancery, Hereditary Grand Falconer of England and Capt. of Band of Gentlemen Pensioners: *m*. 1694, Lady Diana de Vere, who *d*. 1742, el. da. and heir of 20th and last Earl of Oxford; *d*. 1726; *s*. by his son [2] CHARLES, *KG*, *KB*, 2nd Duke; *b*. 1696, Lord Warden of the Forests, Master Falconer of England, and a Lord of the Bedchamber: *m*. 1722, Lucy, who *d*. 1752, da. of Sir John Werden, 2nd Bt.; *d*. 1751; *s*. by his son [3] GEORGE, 3rd Duke; *b*. 1730: *m*. 1752, Jane who *d*. 1778, da. and heir of Sir Walter Roberts, 6th Bt.; *d.s.p.* 1786; *s*. by his kinsman [4] GEORGE (grandson of Lord William, 2nd son of 1st Duke), 4th Duke; *b*. 1758, *d*. unm. 1787; *s*. by his cousin [5] AUBREY, [son of Vere, Lord Vere of Hanworth. 3rd son of 1st Duke, who *d*. 1781, having in 1750 been cr., *Baron Vere of Hanworth* (peerage of G.B.)], 5th Duke; *b*. 1740: *m*. 1763, Lady Catherine Ponsonby, who *d*. 1789, da. of 2nd Earl of Bessborough; *d*. 1802; *s*. by his son [6] AUBREY, 6th Duke; *b*. 1765; Lt.-Col. Foot Guards: *m*. 1st, 1788, Jane, who *d*. 1800, da. of John Moses of Hull; 2ndly, 1802, Grace Louisa, who *d*. 1816, da. of John Manners of Grantham Grange, Lincs., by Lady Louisa Manners (later Tollemache) Countess of Dysart; *d*. 1815; *s*. by his son [7] AUBREY, 7th Duke; *b*. 1815; *d*. 1816; *s*. by his uncle [8] WILLIAM, 8th Duke; *b*. 1766: *m*. 1st, 1791, Charlotte, who *d*. 1797, da. of the Rev. Robert Carter Thewall; 2ndly, 1799, Maria Janetta, who *d*. 1822, da. of John Nelthorpe, of Little Grimsby Hall, Lincs.; *d*. 1825; *s*. by his son [9] WILLIAM AUBREY DE VERE, 9th Duke; *b*. 1801: *m*. 1st, 1827, Harriet (actress), da. of Matthew Mellon, and widow of Thomas Coutts, banker of London ; 2ndly, 1839, Elizabeth Catherine, who *d*. 1893, da. of Gen. Joseph Gubbins, of Kilfrush, co. Limerick; *d*. 1849 ; *s*. by his son [10] WILLIAM AMELIUS AUBREY DE VERE, PC, 10th Duke; *b*. 1840; Capt. of HM's Yeoman of the Guard 1873-74: *m*. 1st, 1867, Sybil, who *d*. 1871, da. of the Hon. Charles Grey; 2nd, 1874, Grace, who *d*. 1926, da. of Ralph Bernal Osborne, MP, of Newtown Anner, co. Tipperary; *d*. 1898; *s*. by his el. son [11] CHARLES VICTOR ALBERT AUBREY DE VERE, 11th Duke; *b*. 1870; *d*. 1934; *s*. by his half-brother [12] OSBORNE DE VERE, *TD*, 12th Duke; *b*. 1874; Capt. 17th Lancers and Maj. S. Notts. Hussars: *m*. 1918, Lady Beatrix Frances, *GBE*, who *d*. 1953, da. of the 5th Marquess of Lansdowne, and widow of 6th Marquess of Waterford; *d*. 1964; *s*. by his kinsman [13] CHARLES FREDERIC AUBREY DE VERE (only son of Aubrey Topham Beauclerk, 3rd son of Lord Charles Beauclerk, 4th son of 8th Duke), 13th Duke, and present peer; also Earl of Burford, Baron Hedington, and Baron Vere of Hanworth.

ST. ALBANS, LORD BISHOP OF. (Runcie.)

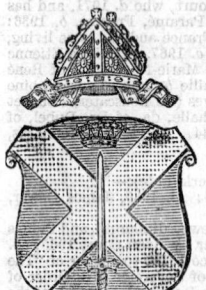

Rt. Rev. ROBERT ALEXANDER KENNEDY RUNCIE, *MC*, son of Robert Dalziel Runcie; *b*. Oct. 2nd, 1921; ed. at Merchant Taylors' Sch., Crosby, Brasenose Coll., Oxford, and Westcott House, Camb. (BA); MA Oxford; Curate, All Saints, Gosforth 1950-52, Chap., Westcott House, Camb. 1953-54, and Vice-Prin. 1954-56; Fellow, Dean and Assist. Tutor, Trin. Hall, Camb. 1956-60; Select Preacher, Camb. 1957 and Oxford 1959, and V. of Cuddesdon and Prin. of Cuddesdon Coll. 1960-69; Consecrated 7th Bishop of St. Albans 1970; 1939-45 War with Scots Guards (MC): *m*. 1957, Angela Rosalind, da. of J. W. Cecil Turner.

Patron of sixty-four livings, and alternately of six, the Archdeaconries of St. Albans and Bedford, and twenty-four Honorary Canonries.
The See of St. Albans was founded May 4th, 1877.
Episcopal Signature,—" Robert St. Albans."
ARMS OF THE SEE,—Azure, a saltire or; over all a sword in pale point upwards, pomme and hilt gold, surmounted by a celestial crown of the second.
Residence,—Abbey Gate House, St. Albans.

ST. ALDWYN, EARL. (Hicks Beach.) [Earl U.K. 1915, and Bt. E. 1619.]

MICHAEL JOHN HICKS BEACH, *KBE*, *TD*, *PC*, 2nd Earl, and 10th Baronet; *b.* Oct. 9th, 1912; *s.* 1916; ed. at Eton; late Maj. 1st Roy. Gloucestershire Hussars; appointed Joint Parliamentary Sec., Min. of Agriculture and Fisheries 1954, Min. of Agriculture, Fisheries and Food 1955-64; Ch. Whip, House of Lords and Capt. of the Hon. Corps of Gentlemen-at-Arms 1958-64, and again 1970-74; Opposition Ch. Whip, House of Lords 1964-70, and since 1974; is a JP and DL for Gloucestershire, and a KStJ (Vice-Chancellor since 1969); PC 1959; KBE (Civil) 1964: *m.* 1948, Diana Mary Christian (SMYLY), da. of the late Henry Christian George Mills [see B. Hillingdon, colls.], and has issue.

Arms,—Quarterly: 1st and 4th, vaire, argent and gules, a canton azure charged with a pile or. *Beach;* 2nd and 3rd, gules, a fesse wavy between three fleurs-de-lis or, a crescent for difference, *Hicks.* **Crest,**—A demi-lion rampant argent, ducally gorged or, and holding in the paws an escutcheon azure, charged with a pile or. **Supporters,**—*Dexter,* a knight armed cap-à-pie in the middle of the fourteenth century, his jupon charged with the arms of *Beach,* namely, vaire argent and gules, on a canton azure a pile or ; *sinister,* a knight similarly vested, his jupon charged with the arms of *Hicks,* namely, gules a fesse wavy between three fleur-de-lis, or, a crescent argent for difference.

IOVT · EN · BONNE · HEVRE.

All in good time.

Residences,—Williamstrip Park, Cirencester, Gloucestershire; 13, Upper Belgrave St., SW1. *Clubs,*—Pratt's, Royal Yacht Squadron.

SONS LIVING.
MICHAEL HENRY (*Viscount Quenington*), *b.* Feb. 7th, 1950.
Hon. Peter Hugh, *b.* 1952.
Hon. David Seymour, *b.* 1955; a Page of Honour to HM 1969-71.

SISTER LIVING. (*Raised to the rank of an Earl's daughter 1920.*)
Lady Delia Mary, *b.* 1910 : *m.* 1934, Brigadier Sir Charles Michael Dillwyn-Venables-Llewelyn, **3rd** Bt., M.V.O. *Residence,*—Llysdinam, Newbridge-on-Wye, Radnorshire.

COLLATERAL BRANCHES LIVING. (*In remainder to the Baronetcy only.*)

Grandsons of the late William Frederick Hicks Beach, 2nd son of 8th Bt.:—
Issue of the late Michael Hicks Beach, *b.* 1872, *d.* 1953 : *m.* 1907, Helène, who *d.* 1941, dau. of Arthur Des Fosses, formerly of Montreal :—
Michael, *b.* 1909: *m.* 1st, 1932, Dorothy, da. of the late Robert Stratton, formerly of Nottingham; 2ndly, 1944, Eunice, who *d.* 1973, da. of the late Rudolph J. Thanisch, of Boston, Mass., USA; 3rdly, 1974, Grace Vera, da. of the late Henry Moos, Sr., of Union City, NJ, USA, and widow of Charles Arthur Rankin, and has issue living (by 1st m.), Heather Diane HICKS BEACH, *b.* 1935; has reverted to maiden name of Hicks Beach: *m.* 1957 (m. diss. 1970), Edward Lionel Peck and has issue living, Brian Michael *b.* 1960, Heather Anne *b.* 1959. *Residence,*—917, Gardenia St., Amarillo, Texas, USA.——John Hugh (of 55, Clinton Rd., Bedford Hills, New York, USA), *b.* 1915: *m.* 1945, Jeanne Potter, da. of Herbert McGuhy, of Bedford Hills, and has issue living, John Hugh, *b.* 1960,— Lucinda, *b.* 1948,—Priscilla, *b.* 1950.

Granddaughter of the late Michael Hicks Beach (ante):—
Issue of the late Frederick Edward Hicks Beach, *b.* 1911, *d.* 1972: *m.* 1st, 1933 (m. diss. 1947), Harriet Green (who m. 2ndly, 1947, Oren Clark Burt); 2ndly, 1947, Lois (5230, 101st St., Jacksonville, Florida, 32210, USA), da. of John W. Lainhart, of Washington, DC, USA :—
(By 1st m.) Frances Helene Burt (934, East 40th St., Brooklyn, N.Y. 11210), *b.* 1942.

Grandchildren of the late Ellis Hicks Beach (infra):—
Issue of the late Maj. William Whitehead Hicks Beach, TD, DL, *b.* 1907, *d.* 1975: *m.* 1939, Diana (Witcombe Park, Gloucester), da. of Christopher Gurney Hoare:—
Mark William (Pond Farm, Worminghall, Bucks.), *b.* 1943: *m.* 1966, Cecilia Ruth, ed. da. of Douglas Allan Wright, of Gannymede, Ashford, Kent, and has issue living, Andrew William, *b.* 1970,—Lucinda Jane, *b.* 1975.——Elizabeth Anne *b.* 1940: *m.* 1962, Simon Erne St. Houlston Clarke, of Pennybridge Farm, Mayfield, Sussex, and has issue living, Martin, *b.* 1963,—Timothy, *b.* 1965.——Rosemary Gillian *b.* 1944: *m.* 1965, Maj. David Murray Naylor, Scots Gds. [see Holt, Bt., cr. 1935, ext.]

Grandchildren of the late William Frederick Hicks Beach (ante):—
Issue of the late Ellis Hicks Beach, *b.* 1874, *d.* 1943: *m.* 1903, Nancy, who *d.* 1942, dau. of Spencer Whitehead, sometime a Master of Supreme Court :—
Rachel, *b.* 1904: *m.* 1934, Col. Edward Roderick Hill, DSO, JP, Coldstream Guards, and has issue living, Michael Roderick *b.* 1939,—Caroline Rachel (*Hon. Mrs. Geoffrey Somerset*), *b.* 1936: *m.* 1956, the Hon. Geoffrey Somerset [see B. Raglan]. *Residence,*—St. Arvan's Court, Chepstow, Mon.——Anne (*Baroness Leigh*), *b.* 1908: *m.* 1931, the 4th Baron Leigh. *Residence,*—Adelstrop House, Moreton-in-Marsh, Glos.——Letitia, *b.* 1909: *m.* 1st, 1931, Horace Alfred Townsend, from whom she obtained a divorce 1939; 2ndly, 1947, George Miles, from whom she obtained a divorce 1960; 3rdly, 1960, John Messent Grover, sol., of Garden Cottage, Rookery Rd., Downe, Kent, and has issue living, (by 1st m.) John (23, Aldersmead Rd., Beckenham, Kent), *b.* 1934: *m.* 1957, Andrina Hume,—Tomazin, *b.* 1933: *m.* 1953, Stanley John Geller, of 71, Bemerton Gdns., Kirby Cross, Frinton-on-Sea,—(by 2nd m.) George Rufus, *b.* 1948,—Richard Josef, *b.* 1951.

Issue of the late Edward Howe Hicks Beach, *b.* 1875, *d.* 1967: *m.* 1903, Alberta Louise, who *d.* 1946, da. of William Penn Jaynes, of Vancouver:—
Edward Adryan, *b.* 1915: *m.* 1st, 1936, Evelyn (from whom he obtained a divorce 1940), da. of Clarence Dale, of Los Angeles, Cal., USA; 2ndly, 1940, Linnea Maria, da. of the late Andrew Holst, of Los Angeles, Cal., USA, and has issue living, (by 1st m.) Edward Erick, *b.* 1941,—Frederick Howe, *b.* 1944.——Clara Violet Louise, *b.* 1905: *m.* 1954, Ralph Elmer Wilson, of 4181, Lincoln Av., Culver City, Cal. 90230, USA.——Doris Margaret, *b.* 1910: *m.* 1934, Harry Roderic Theodore Marble, of 2107, Marine St., Santa Monica, Cal. 90405, USA, and has issue living, Harry Arthur, *b.* 1936: *m.* 1966, Marilyn Francis, da. of Francis A. Schneider, of Oxford, Iowa, USA, and has issue living, Daniel Edward *b.* 1966, Timothy John *b.* 1968, Karen Margaret *b.* 1971,—William Edward

b. 1947,—Michael Stephen (twin), *b.* 1947,—Linnea Louise, *b.* 1940: *m.* 1959, Charles Bartl Adams, and has issue living, Gregory Walter *b.* 1962, Brian Roderic *b.* 1965, Steven Edward *b.* 1968.

Grandsons of the late Maj. Archibald William Hicks Beach, son of the late Rt. Hon. William Wither Bramston Beach, MP, son of the late William Beach, MP, son of 2nd son of 6th Bt.:—

Issue of the late William Guy Hicks Beach, *b.* 1891, *d.* 1953 : *m.* 1st, 1914, Fanny Muriel (who obtained a divorce 1932), dau. of Ninian B. Stewart, of Dunloe, Wemyss Bay, and 14, Park Circus, Glasgow; 2ndly, 1932, Beatrice Mary Uniacke, who *d.* 1975, da. of Arthur Johnstone, formerly Indian Police:—
(By 1st marriage) Michael William Bramston, *D.S.C.*, *b.* 1919 ; ed. at Eton, and at Pembroke Coll., Camb.; Lieut. R.N.V.R.; European War 1939-45 (D.S.C.) : *m.* 1940, Kathleen Edyth Doreen Augusta, dau. of Sir Brodrick Cecil Denham Arkwright Hartwell, 4th Bt., and has issue living, Michael Brodrick, *b.* 1942: *m.* 1970, Carolyn Anne, only da. of Sir Richard Ashton Beaumont, KCMG, OBE. *Residence,*—40, Burton Court, SW3.——Peter Stewart, *OBE* (Boscobel, Hammer Lane, Grayshott, Hindhead, Surrey), *b.* 1924; Cdr. RN; 1939-45 War (despatches); OBE (Mil.) 1968: *m.* 1950, Victoria Margaret, da. of R. V. Nelson, and has issue living, Sally Elizabeth, *b.* 1953.——Geoffrey Robert Wither, *b.* 1925: *m.* 1952, Rosemary Wendy Wolseley-Charles, and has issue living, Nicholas Charles, *b.* 1960,—Fiona Susan, *b.* 1955. *Residence,*—Regency House, Abbey Rd., Bourne End, Bucks.

PREDECESSORS. –[1] WILLIAM Hicks of Beverston Castle, co. Gloucester, only son of Sir Michael Hicks, descended from Robert Hicks of Bristol, a merchant in London, and father of the famous Sir Baptist Hicks, created (1628) Viscount Campden, from whom spring the Noels, Earls of Gainsborough ; *b.* 1596 ; cr. a *Baronet* 1619 ; *d.* 1680 ; *s.* by his son [2] WILLIAM, 2nd Bt.; *d .703* ; *s.* by his son [3] HENRY, 3rd Bt.; twice *m.*; *d.* 1755 ; *s.* by his only son [4] ROBERT, 4th Bt.; *d.* 1768 ; *s.* by his cousin [5] JOHN BAPTIST (son of Charles Hicks), 5th Bt. ; *d.* 1792 : *s.* by his cousin [6] HOWE (son of Howe Hicks, of Witcombe, Gloucestershire, 6th Bt.; *b.* 1722: *m.* 1739 ; *d.* 1801 ; *s.* by his son [7] WILLIAM, 7th Bt.; *b.* 1754: *m.* 1st, 1785, Judith, who *d.* 1787, dau. of Edward Witcombe ; 2ndly, 1793, Anne Rachael, dau. of T. L. Chute, who *d.* 1839; *d.* 1834 ; *s.* by his great nephew [8] MICHAEL (son of Michael Hicks-Beach, of Netheravon, Wilts, whose father assumed the additional surname of Beach), 8th Bt. ; M.P. for E. Gloucestershire 1854 : *m.* 1832, Harriet Victoria, who *d.* 1900, dau. of John Stratton, of Farthinghoe Lodge ; *d.* 1854 ; *s.* by his son [9] MICHAEL EDWARD, *P.C.*, *D.C.L.*, *b.* 1837 ; M.P. for E. Gloucestershire (C) 1864-85, and for W. Div. of Bristol 1885-1906 ; Parliamentary Sec. to Poor Law Board March to Aug. 1868, Under-Sec. for Home Office Aug. to Dec. 1868, Ch. Sec. for Ireland 1874-8, Sec. of State for the Colonies 1878-80, a Member of Committee of Council on Education in Scotland and Chancellor of the Exchequer 1885-6, again Ch. Sec. for Ireland July 1886 to March 1887, Pres. of Board of Trade Feb. 1888 to Aug. 1892, a Church Estates Commr. 1892-5, and again Chancellor of the Exchequer 1895-1902 ; *s.* to the Baronetcy 1854, and was cr. *Viscount St. Aldwyn,* of Coln St. Aldwyn, co. Gloucester (peerage of the United Kingdom) 1906, and *Viscount Quenington,* of Quenington, co. Gloucester, and *Earl St. Aldwyn,* of Coln St. Aldwyn, co. Gloucester (peerage of United Kingdom) 1915 : *m.* 1st, 1864, Caroline Susan, who *d.* 1865, dau. of the late John Henry Elwes, of Colesborne Park, Cheltenham [Bromley-Wilson, Bt.]; 2ndly, 1874, Lady Lucy Catherine. who *d.* 1940, dau. of 3rd Earl Fortescue; *d.* 1916 ; *s.* by his grandson [10] MICHAEL JOHN, 2nd Earl and present peer (son of the late Capt. Michael Hugh Hicks-Beach, M.P., Gloucestershire Hussars Yeo., Viscount Quenington, son of 1st Earl, who *d.* (killed in action during European War) 1916, by Marjorie, who *d.* 1916, dau. of the late Henry Dent Brocklehurst, of Sudeley Castle, Winchcombe); also Viscount St. Aldwyn, and Viscount Quenington.

St. Andrews, Earl of, son of Duke of Kent.

ST. AUDRIES, BARONY OF. (Fuller-Acland Hood.) [Extinct 1971.]
[See also Fuller-Acland Hood, Bt.]
DAUGHTERS LIVING OF FIRST BARON.
Hon. Audrey Mildred (Fairfield, Stogursey, Bridgwater, Som.), *b.* 1889.
Hon. Maud Isabel (Fairfield, Stogursey, Bridgwater, Som.), *b.* 1892.

WIDOW LIVING OF SON OF FIRST BARON.
Phyllis Lily Frances (Wootton House, nr. Glastonbury, Somerset), da. of Dr. Denys B. I. Hallett, of 47, Sheen Common Drive, Richmond, Surrey: *m.* 1939, the Hon (Arthur) John Palmer Fuller-Acland-Hood, who *d.* 1964, and has issue living [see colls., infra].

COLLATERAL BRANCH LIVING.
Issue of the late Hon. (Arthur) John Palmer Fuller-Acland-Hood, yr. son of 1st Baron, *b.* 1906, *d.* 1964: *m.* 1939, Phyllis Lily Frances (ante), da. of Dr. Denys B. I. Hallett, of 47, Sheen Common Drive, Richmond, Surrey:—
Elizabeth Periam (*Lady Gass*) *b.* 1940: *m.* 1975, Sir Michael David Irving Gass, KCMG, of Broadway, Butleigh Wooton, Som.——Mary Mildred (Wootton House, Glastonbury), *b.* 1941: *m.* 1961, Timothy Stephen (Toby) Hodder-Williams, who *d.* 1969.——Sylvia (Wootton House, nr. Glastonbury, Som.), *b.* 1944.

St. Cyres, Viscount, son of Earl of Iddesleigh.

ST. DAVIDS, VISCOUNT. (Philipps.) [Viscount U.K. 1918, Bt. E. 1621.]

Patriotism my motive.

JESTYN REGINALD AUSTEN PLANTAGENET PHILIPPS, 2nd Viscount, and 14th Baronet; b. Feb. 19th, 1917; s. 1938 to Viscountcy of St. Davids, and 1974 to Baronies of Strange of Knokin, Hungerford and de Moleyns; ed. at Eton; Lieut. RNVR: m. 1st, 1938, Doreen Guinness (who d. 1956, having obtained a divorce 1954), only da. of Capt. Arthur Jowett, of Toorak, Melbourne, Australia; 2ndly, 1954, Elisabeth Joyce (who obtained a divorce 1959), el. da. of Dr. E. A. Woolf, of Hove, Sussex; 3rdly, 1959, Evelyn Marjorie, only da. of the late Dr. John Edmund Guy Harris, of The Heritage, Bray-on-Thames, Berks, and has issue by 1st m.

Arms,—Argent, a lion rampant sable, ducally gorged and chained or. Crest,—A lion as in the arms. Supporters,—Dexter, a knight vested in chain armour, the jupon charged with the arms of Philipps and resting his exterior hand upon the hilt of his sword; sinister, a knight vested in plate armour, his jupon charged with arms of Wogan (or, on a chief sable, three martlets of the field) and resting the exterior hand upon the hilt of the sword; both standing upon a battlemented wall, all proper.

Residence,—15, St. Mark's Cres., Regents Park, NW1.

SON LIVING. (By 1st marriage.)

Hon. COLWYN JESTYN JOHN (14A, Alwyne Place, N1), b. Jan. 30th, 1939; ed. at Sevenoaks Sch.; late 2nd Lt. Welsh Guards: m. 1965, Augusta Victoria Correa Larrain, da. of the late Don Estantislao Correa Ugarte, of Santiago, Chile, and has issue living, Rhodri Colwyn, b. 1966,—Roland Augusto Jestyn Estanislao, b. 1970.

DAUGHTERS LIVING. (By 1st marriage.)

Hon. Rowena Frances, b. 1940: m. 1959, David Elford, of Cheviot House, View Rd., The Patch, Vic., Aust., and has issue living, Richard, b. 1962,—Wendy, b. 1960,—Suzanne, b. 1964,—Leonie, b. 1965.
Hon. Myfanwy Ann (23, Pyrland Rd., Islington, N5), b. 1944: m. 1968, Anthony John Frederick Smith, and has issue living, Tobias Peter John, b. 1971,—Benjamin Crosby, b. 1973.
Hon. Rhiannon Elisabeth, b. 1946: m. 1974, Donald Hudson Chapman, of Austen House, New Inn Rd., Barley, Southampton.
Hon. Eiddwen Sara (Roch Cottage, 15, Newton Toney, nr. Salisbury, Wilts.), b. 1948.

SISTER LIVING.

Hon. Lelgarde de Clare Elizabeth, b. 1918: m. 1950, Colin Charles Evans, and has issue living, Roland Anthony Christopher, b. 1951,—William Harold Sandford, b. 1953,—Lorna Susan (twin), b. 1953. Residence,—Kilmartin House, Mulhuddart, co. Dublin.

COLLATERAL BRANCHES LIVING.
(Male line in remainder to Baronetcy).

Issue of the late Maj.-Gen. Sir Ivor Philipps, K.C.B., D.S.O., 2nd son of 12th Baronet, b. 1861, d. 1940: m. 1891, Marian Isobel, O.B.E., who d. 1945, dau. of the late James Buchanan Mirrlees, of Redlands, Glasgow :—

Marjorie Elise, b. 1892: m. 1925, Lieut.-Col. (Vincent) Basil Ramsden, D.S.O., M.C., who d. 1936, and has issue living, Ivor Basil, MBE (Cosheston Hall, Pembroke Dock), b. 1929; late Maj. Welsh Gds.; MBE (Mil) 1959: m. 1955, Carola Bird, and has issue living, David Ivor b. 1957, Richard Gerald b. 1962, Clarissa Elizabeth b. 1959, Victoria Gillian b. 1964,—Philippa Elizabeth, b. 1927: m. 1952, Robert Morier Sheffield Neave, MC, MRCVS [see Neave, Bt., colls.]. Residence,—Costyn, Cosheston, Pembroke Dock.

Issue of the late Owen Crosby Philipps (who was cr. Baron Kylsant 1923), 3rd son of 12th Baronet, b. 1863, d. 1937, when the Barony became ext. [see that title].

Issue of the late Laurence Richard Philipps (who was cr. Baron Milford 1939), 6th son of 12th Baronet, b. 1874, d. 1962 [see that title].

PREDECESSORS.—This family is of great antiquity in South Wales. Among its ancestors was Sir Aaron ap Rhys, who attended Richard I. into the Holy Land 1190, where he behaved so gallantly against the Saracens, that he is said to have received from Richard the Knighthood of the Sepulchre of Our Saviour, his arms of a lion rampant sable, and the addition of a " Crown and Chain ". Sir Thomas Philipps, Knt., of Picton Castle, accompanied Henry VIII twice to France. His descendant [1] Sir JOHN Philipps, Knt., of Picton, co. Pembroke; MP for Pembroke 1597-8 and Oct.-Dec. 1601 ; cr. a Baronet 1621 : m. Anne, dau. of Sir John Perrott, of Haroldston ; d. 1629 ; s. by his el. son [2] RICHARD, 2nd Bt. : m. Elizabeth, dau. of Sir Erasmus Dryden, Bt.; d. 16— ; s. by his son [3] ERASMUS Philipps, 3rd Bt. : M.P. for Pembroke 1654-5 and Jan.-April, 1659 : m. 1st, Cicely, dau. of Thomas, Earl of Winchilsea ; 2ndly, Katharine, el. dau. and co-heir of Edward D'Arcy, of Newhall, co. Derby ; d. 1697 ; s. by his second son [4] JOHN, 4th Bt. ; M.P. for Pembroke 1695-1702, and for Haverfordwest 1718-1722 : m. 1697, Mary, dau. of Anthony Smith ; d. 1736 ; s. by his el. son [5] Erasmus, 5th Bt. ; M.P. for Haverfordwest 1726-43 ; d. 1743 ; s. by his brother [6] JOHN, 6th Bt. ; M.P. for Carmarthen 1741-7, for Petersfield 1754-61, and for co. Pembroke 1761-4 : m. Elizabeth, dau. of Henry Shepperd ; d. 1764 ; s. by his only son [7] RICHARD, 7th Bt. ; M.P. for co. Pembroke 1765-70 and 1786-1812, Lord-Lieut. of co. Pembroke 1786 ; cr. Baron Milford 1776 : m. 1764, Mary, dau. of James Philipps, of Penty Park ; d. 1823, when the Barony of Milford became ext. and the Baronetcy passed to his kinsman [8] ROWLAND HENRY Philipps-Laugharne-Philipps (descendant of Hugh Philipps, third son of 1st Bt.), 8th Bt. : m. 1812, Elizabeth, who d. 1834, dau. of James Frampton ; d. 1882 ; s. by his brother [9] WILLIAM, 9th Bt. ; b. 1794 : m. 1829, Elizabeth, who d. 1865, dau. of George White ; d. 1850 ; s. by his only son [10] GODWYN, 10th Bt. ; b. 1840 ; d. 1857 ; s. by his kinsman [11] Rev. Sir JAMES EVANS Philipps, 11th Bt. ; b. 1793 : m. 1822, Mary Anne, who d. 1833, dau. of Benjamin Bickley ; d. 1873 ; s. by son [12] Rev. Sir JAMES ERASMUS, 12th Bt. ; b. 1824 ; V. of Warminster 1859-1897, and Canon of Salisbury : m. 1859, the Hon. Mary Margaret, who d. 1913, dau. of the late Rev. the Hon. Samuel Best ; d. 1912 ; s. by his el. son [13] JOHN WYNFORD, 13th Bt. ; b. 1860 ; cr. Baron St. Davids, of Roch Castle, co. Pembroke (peerage of United Kingdom) 1908, and Viscount St. Davids, of Lydstep Haven, co. Pembroke (peerage of United Kingdom) 1918: m. 1st, 1888, Nora, who d. 1915, dau. of the late I. Gestenberg, of Stockleigh House, Regent's Park, N.W.; 2ndly, 1916, Lady Elizabeth Frances (Baroness Strange of Knokin, Hungerford, and de Moleyns in her own right), who d. 1974 [see † infra] da. of the late Major the Hon. Paulyn

Francis Cuthbert Rawdon-Hastings; *d.* 1938; *s.* by his 3rd but only surviving son [14] JESTYN REGINALD AUSTEN PLANTAGENET, 2nd Viscount and present peer: also Baron Strange of Knokin, Hungerford, de Moleyns, St. Davids.

†—[1] *Sir* WALTER Hungerford, *KG*; served with distinction in France; was Steward of the Household to Henry VI; summoned to Parliament of England as *Baron Hungerford* 1426-49; *d.* 1449; *s.* by his son [2] ROBERT, 2nd Baron; summoned to Parliament 1450-5: *m.* Margaret, only da. of William, *Baron Botreaux* (peerage of England, cr. 1386); *d.* 1458; *s.* by his son [3] ROBERT, 3rd Baron, who had previously 1445-52 been summoned to Parliament of England as *Baron de Moleyns* (or *Molines*); was never summoned as Baron Hungerford; joined the Lancastrian interests, and being made prisoner at the battle of Hexham his honours and estates were attained, and he was beheaded at Newcastle 1463; *s.* by his son [4] THOMAS, who espoused the cause of Edward IV, but subsequently exerted his influence for the restoration of Henry IV, he was seized and beheaded as a traitor 1479: he left issue by his first marriage [5] MARY, who obtained the reversal of her father's and grandfather's attainders, and was styled Baroness Hungerford, Botreaux, and Molines (or de Moleyns); she *m.* Edward Hastings, son and heir of William, 1st *Baron Hastings* (peerage of England, cr. 1461); *s.* by her son [6—15] GEORGE, 6th Baron; cr. *Earl of Huntingdon* 1529; in which peerage the Baronies of Hungerford, Botreaux, de Moleyns (or Molines) and Hastings were merged until 1789, when the 10th Earl *d.s.p.*, and was *s.* by his sister [16] ELIZABETH, wife of John Rawdon, 1st *Earl of Moira* (peerage of Ireland, cr. 1762): *d.* 1808; *s.* by her son [17] FRANCIS, *KG*, *GCB*, who in 1793 had *s.* his father as 2nd Earl of Moira; a Gen. in the Army, Lord-Lieut. of the Tower Hamlets, Constable of the Tower of London, and successively Gov.-Gen. of India and Gov. and Com.-in-Ch. of Malta; assumed the name of Hastings in addition to that of Rawdon; cr. *Baron Rawdon*, of Rawdon, co. York (peerage of Great Britain) 1783, and *Viscount Loudoun, Earl of Rawdon*, and *Marquess of Hastings* (peerage of United Kingdom) 1816: *m.* Flora Mure-Campbell, *Countess of Loudoun*, in her own right; *d.* 1826; *s.* by his son [18] GEORGE AUGUSTUS FRANCIS, 2nd Marquess, who in 1840 *s.* his mother as 7th Earl of Loudoun: *m.* 1831, Barbara, *Baroness Grey de Ruthyn* (peerage of England, cr. 1324); he *d.* 1844; *s.* by his el. son [19] PAULYN REGINALD SERLO, 3rd Marquess; *d.* unmarried 1851; *s.* by his brother [20] HENRY WEYSFORD CHARLES PLANTAGENET, 4th Marquess, who in 1858 *s.* to his mother's Barony of Grey de Ruthyn; *d.* 1868, when the Barony of Rawdon, the Viscountcy of Loudoun, the Earldoms of Moira and Rawdon, and the Marquessate of Hastings became extinct and the Baronies of Grey de Ruthyn, Hastings, Hungerford, Botreaux, and de Moleyns (or Molines) became abeyant between his sisters, and the Earldom of Loudoun and minor Scottish honours devolved upon his el. sister [21] EDITH MAUD Abney-Hastings, in whose favour in 1871, the abeyance of the Baronies of Hastings, Hungerford, Botreaux and de Moleyns (or Molines) was terminated; *b.* 1833: *m.* Charles Frederick Clifton, who in 1859 assumed the names of Abney-Hastings, and in 1880 was cr. *Baron Donington*, of Donington Park, co. Leicester (peerage of United Kingdom); she *d.* 1874; *s.* by his son [22] CHARLES EDWARD HASTINGS, 11th Earl of Loudoun, *b.* 1855; an Hereditary Bearer of one of the Golden Spurs: *m.* 1880, the Hon. Alice Mary Elizabeth Fitzalan-Howard, who *d.* 1915, da. of 1st Baron Howard of Glossop; *d.* 1920, when the Barony of Donington devolved upon his brother Gilbert Theophilus Clifton Clifton-Hastings-Campbell, and the Earldom of Loudoun upon his niece, Edith Maud, el. da. of the late Major the Hon. Paulyn Francis Cuthbert Rawdon-Hastings, while the Baronies of Botreaux, de Moleyns (or Molines), Hungerford, and Hastings fell into abeyance between the daus. of the late Major the Hon. Paulyn Francis Cuthbert Rawdon-Hastings, brother of 11th Earl of Loudoun, the abeyance in the Baronies of Hungerford and de Moleyns, as well as in the Barony of Strange of Knokin (cr. by writ 1299) [see *⁎⁎* infra] being shortly afterwards in Feb. 1921 terminated in favour of the el. [23] ELIZABETH FRANCES, Viscountess St. Davids (ante).

⁎⁎ [1] JOHN le Strange, son of John le Strange, of Knokin, co. Salop, was summoned by writ to Parliament 1299 and 1308-9 as *Lord Strange de Knokin*; *d.* 1309; *s.* by his son [2] JOHN; summoned to Parliament 1311; *d.* 1311; *s.* by his son [3] JOHN; summoned to Parliament 1312-13; *d.* 1323; *s.* by his brother [4] ROGER; summoned to Parliament 1341-47; *d.* 1349; *s.* by his son [5] ROGER; summoned to Parliament 1355-82; *d.* 1382; *s.* by his son [6] JOHN; summoned to Parliament 1383-97; *m.* Maud, da. and co-heir of John, Lord Mohun of Dunster (cr. 1299); *d.* 1387; *s.* by his son [7] RICHARD, *b.* 1381; in 1431 became (through his mother) *Lord Mohun de Dunster*; *d.* 1449; *s.* by his son [8] JOHN; summoned to Parliament 1446-72; *d.* 1477; *s.* by his only da. [9] JOAN: *m.* 1482, George, Lord Stanley, *KG*, son of the 1st Earl of Derby, who in right of his wife was summoned to Parliament as *Lord Strange de Knokin* 1482-96; *d.* 1513; *s.* by her el. son [10] THOMAS, *b.* 1485, who in 1504 had *s.* as 2nd Earl of Derby, as well as to the Barony of Stanley (cr. 1456); *d.* 1521; *s.* by his son [11] EDWARD, 3rd Earl, *b.* 1509; *d.* 1572; *s.* by his son [12] HENRY, 4th Earl, *b.* 1521; summoned to Parliament in his father's Barony of Strange of Knokin 1558-75; *d.* 1593; *s.* by his son [13] FERDINANDO, 5th Earl, *b.* 1559; summoned to Parliament in his father's Barony of Strange de Knokin 1588-92; *d.* 1594; when the Earldom of Derby devolved upon his brother, and the Baronies of Strange de Knokin, Mohun de Dunster, and Stanley fell into abeyance between his daughters and co-heirs, until in 1921 the abeyance in the Barony of Strange de Knokin was determined in favour of [14] ELIZABETH FRANCES, Viscountess St. Davids (ante).

ST. EDMUNDSBURY AND IPSWICH, LORD BISHOP OF. (Brown.)

Right Rev. LESLIE WILFRID BROWN, *CBE*, *DD*, son of the late Harry Brown, of Cuffley, Herts., *b.* June 10th, 1912; ed. at Enfield Gram. Sch., and London Coll. of Divinity, London Univ. (MTh); Hon. MA Camb.; Hon. Fellow, Downing Coll., Camb.; DD 1957; CMS Missionary to Cambridge Nicholson Inst., Kottayam, Travancore (Vice-Prin. 1938-40), and Chap. to Bishop of Travancore 1938-43; Fellow Commoner and Chap., Downing Coll., Camb. 1943-44; Prin. of Kerala United Theological Seminary, Trivandrum 1946-50; Church of S. India 1947-52; Chap. of Jesus Coll., Camb. 1950-51; consecrated Bishop of Uganda 1953; Archbishop of Uganda, Rwanda and Burundi 1961-65; translated 6th Bishop of St. Edmundsbury and Ipswich 1966; Chap. and Sub-Prelate of Order of St. John since 1968; CBE (Civil) 1965: *m.* 1939, Annie Winifred, da. of the Hon. R. D. Megaw, of Belfast.

Patron of sixty-one livings, three Archdeaconries, and twenty-four Honorary Canonries. This See was founded 1914.

Episcopal Signature,——Leslie St. Edm. & Ipswich.
ARMS OF THE SEE,—Per pale gules and azure between three ducal coronets a demi-lion passant guardant conjoined to the demi-hulk of an ancient ship or.
Residence,—Bishop's House, 14, Park Rd., Ipswich, IP1 3ST.

ST. GERMANS, EARL OF. (Eliot.) [Earl U.K. 1815.]

Press close upon those who take the lead.

NICHOLAS RICHARD MICHAEL ELIOT, 9th Earl ; *b.* Jan. 26th, 1914 ; *s.* 1960 ; ed. at Eton ; is Capt. Duke of Cornwall's L.I. (attached Roy. Armoured Corps), and patron of three livings ; European War 1939-45 : *m.* 1st, 1939, Helen Mary (who *d.* 1951, having obtained a divorce 1947), dau. of the late Lieut.-Col. Charles Walter Villiers, C.B.E., D.S.O. [E. Clarendon, colls.] ; 2ndly, 1948, Margaret Eleanor (EYSTON) (from whom he obtained a divorce 1959), dau. of the late Lieut.-Col. William Francis George Wyndham, M.V.O., of Heathfield Lodge, Midhurst; 3rdly, 1965, Mrs. Mary Bridget Lotinga, da. of the late Sir Thomas Shenton Whitelegge Thomas, GCMG, OBE, and has issue by 1st marriage.

Arms,—Argent, a fesse gules, between double cottises wavy azure. **Crest,**—An elephant's head argent, plain collared gules. **Supporters,**—Two eagles reguardant, wings displayed and inverted proper, each charged on the breast with an ermine spot sable.

Residence,—Les Arcs, Chemin du Signal, 1807, Blonay, Vaud, Switzerland.

SON LIVING. (*By* 1*st marriage.*)

PEREGRINE NICHOLAS (*Lord Eliot*) (of Port Eliot, St. German's, Cornwall), *b.* Jan. 2nd, 1941; ed. at Eton: *m.* 1964, the Hon. Jacquetta Jean Frederica Lampson, da. of the 1st Baron Killearn, and has issue.

SONS LIVING,—*Hon.* Jago Nicholas Aldo, *b.* March 24th, 1966.
 Hon. Louis Robert, *b.* 1968.
 Hon. Francis Michael, *b.* 1971.

DAUGHTER LIVING. (*By* 1*st marriage.*)

Lady Frances Helen Mary (*Countess of Shelburne*), *b.* 1943: *m.* 1965, the Earl of Shelburne, el. son of 8th Marquess of Lansdowne. *Residences,*—Bowood, Calne, Wilts.; 19, Walton St., SW3.

BROTHER LIVING.

Hon. (Montagu) Robert (Vere), *b.* 1923; ed. at Eton, and at Ch. Ch., Oxford; is Hon. Capt. Grenadier Guards; a Page of Honour to H.M. 1937-40; a Councillor of City of Westminster 1953-62; a Train Bearer at Coronation of King George VI; has Coronation medal (1937); 1944-45 War (wounded), Palestine 1945 (medal). *Residence,*—Lux Cross House, Pengover Rd., Liskeard, Cornwall, PL14 3EQ.

SISTER LIVING.

Lady (Germaine) Elizabeth Olive, *b.* 1911 : *m.* 1st, 1932, Thomas James, from whom she obtained a divorce 1940 [see B. Northbourne, colls.]; 2ndly, 1950 (marriage dissolved 1963), the Hon. (Kenneth) George Kinnaird, who *d.* 1973 [L. Kinnaird]. *Resides* in New York.

DAUGHTER LIVING OF SIXTH EARL.

Lady Cathleen Blanche Lily, *b.* 1921; a co-heir presumptive to Baronies of Botetourt and Herbert (cr. 1461) [see D. Beaufort, colls.]: *m.* 1st, 1946, Capt. John Seyfried, Roy. Horse Guards, who obtained a divorce 1956 ; 2ndly, 1957, Havelock Henry Trevor Hudson, and has issue living, (by 1st marriage) David John, *b.* 1952,—Sarah Diana, *b.* 1949,—(by 2nd marriage) Michael Guy Havelock, *b.* 1962,—Louise Deborah, *b.* 1958. *Residence,*—The Old Rectory, Stanford Dingley, Berks.

WIDOW LIVING OF BROTHER OF EIGHTH EARL.

Eleanor Whyte Hughes, dau. of James Andrew Brownlee: *m.* 1933, as his fourth wife, Capt. the Hon. Arthur Ernest Henry Eliot, who *d.* 1936. *Residence,*—

COLLATERAL BRANCHES LIVING.

Issue of the late Lieut.-Col. the Hon. Christian Edward Cornwallis Eliot, O.B.E., brother of 7th and 8th Earls, *b.* 1872, *d.* 1940: *m.* 1st, 1897, Laura Grey, who *d.* 1938, dau. of Lieut.-Col. Sir George Chetwode, 6th Bt. ; 2ndly, 1938, Daisy Blossom Roberts, who *d.* 1965, da. of the late Alexander Elkan:—
(Frederica) Betty Cornwallis (*Betty, Lady Markham*), (P.O. Box 583, Mbabane, Swaziland), *b.* 1900: *m.* 1923, Capt. Robert Wigram Crawford, formerly King's R. Rifle Corps, from whom she obtained a divorce 1929; 2ndly, 1942 as his third wife, Sir Charles Markham, 2nd Bt., who *d.* 1952.

Issue of the late Hon. Edward Granville Eliot, brother of 7th and 8th Earls, *b.* 1878, *d.* 1950 : *m.* 1907, Clare Louisa, who *d.* 1927, dau. of the late William Robert Phelips [E. Bessborough, colls.] :—

The Ven. Peter Charles, *MBE, TD, b.* 1910; ed. at Wellington Coll., and at Magdalene Coll., Camb., (B.A. 1931, M.A. 1935) ; admitted a Solicitor 1934 ; late Lieut.-Col. 297th (Kent Yeo.) Light Anti-Aircraft Regt., RA (TA); Assist. Curate of St. Martin-in-the-Fields, WC2, 1954-57, and V. of Cockermouth 1957-61, Rural Dean of Cockermouth and Workington 1960-61, and V. of Cropthorne with Charlton 1961-65, Archdeacon of Worcester since 1961 and Residentiary Canon of Worcester since 1965 ; MBE (Mil) 1945 : *m.* 1934, Lady Alethea Constance Dorothy Sydney, da. of 1st Earl Buxton (ext.). *Residence,*—12, College Green, Worcester.——Margaret Augusta, *b.* 1914: *m.* 1943, Richard Alan John Asher, MD, FRCP, who *d.* 1969, and has issue living, Peter, *b.* 1944: *m.* 19—,—Jane, *b.* 1946,—Clare, *b.* 1948. *Residence,*—32A, Abbey Rd., NW8.——Susan, *b.* 1921: *m.* 1943, Thomas George Horsey Asher, who *d.* 1966, and has issue living, John, *b.* 1945,— Charles, *b.* 1948,—James *b.* 1950,—Anne, *b.* 1945. *Residence,*—112, Ifield Rd., SW10.

PREDECESSORS.—[1] EDWARD Eliot, *M.P.* for Cornwall, and Receiver Gen. of Duchy of Cornwall; cr. *Baron Eliot,* of St. Germans, Cornwall (peerage of Great Britain) 1784; assumed the additional surname of Craggs by Roy. licence 1789; *d.* 1804; *s.* by his son [2] JOHN, 2nd Baron; cr. *Earl of St. Germans* (peerage of United Kingdom) 1815, with remainder to his brother ; *d.s.p.* 1823 ; *s.* by his brother [3] WILLIAM, 2nd Earl; was successively Ambassador to the States Gen. and to Munich, M.P. for Liskeard, and a Lord of the Treasury; *d.* 1845; *s.* by his son [4] EDWARD GRANVILLE, *G.C.B., P.C.,* 3rd Earl; *b.* 1798; sat as M.P. for Liskeard 1824-32, and for Cornwall, E. (*C*) 1837-45; was a Lord of the Treasury 1827-32, Envoy to Spain 1835, Ch. Sec. for Ireland 1841-5, Postmaster-Gen. 1845, Lord-Lieut. of Ireland 1852-5, Lord Steward of the Household 1857-8 and 1859-66, and Special Dep. Warden of Stannaries 1852-77: *m.* 1824, Lady Jemima Cornwallis, dau. and co-heiress of 2nd and last Marquess Cornwallis; *d.* 1877; *s.* by his son [5] WILLIAM GORDON CORNWALLIS, 4th Earl; sat as M.P. for Devonport (*L*) 1866-8; called to the Upper House in his father's Barony of Eliot 1870; *d.* unmarried 1881; *s.* by his brother [6] HENRY CORNWALLIS, 5th Earl, *b.* 1835 ; in R.N. 1848-53 and Foreign Office 1855-81 : *m.* 1881, the Hon. Emily Harriet Labouchere, who *d.* 1933, dau. of 1st Baron Taunton (ext.); *d.* 1911; *s.* by his yr. son [7] JOHN GRANVILLE CORNWALLIS, 6th Earl, *b.* 1890 ; Capt. R. Scots Greys: *m.* 1918, Lady Blanche Linnie Somerset, who *d.* 1968, da. of 9th Duke of Beaufort, *d.* 1922; *s.* by his cousin [8] GRANVILLE JOHN (el. son of Col. the Hon. Charles George Cornwallis Eliot, C.V.O., 6th son of 3rd Earl), 7th Earl ; *b.* 1867: *d.* 1942 ; *s.* by his brother [9] MONTAGUE CHARLES, K.C.V.O., ⊙.B.E., 8th Earl ; *b.* 1870 ; a Gentleman Usher to King Edward VII. 1901-8, and a Groom in Waiting 1908-10, a Gentleman Usher to King George V. 1911-36, Groom of the Robes 1920-36, and an Extra Groom in Waiting 1924-36, and 1937-60 ; European War 1914-19 as Lieut.-Com. R.N.V.R.: *m.* 1910, Helen Agnes, who *d.* 1962, dau. of the late Arthur Post, of New York; *d.* 1960; *s.* by his el. son [10] NICHOLAS RICHARD MICHAEL, 9th Earl and present peer; also Baron Eliot.

ST. HELENS, BARON. (Hughes-Young.) [Baron U.K. 1964.]

MICHAEL HENRY COLIN HUGHES-YOUNG, *MC*, 1st Baron, son of the late Brig.-Gen. Henry George Young, CIE, DSO, of Skeffington Lodge, Antrim; *b.* Oct. 28th, 1912; ed. at Harrow; Lt.-Col. (ret.) The Black Watch; attached to French Army 1934, and seconded to King's African Rifles 1935; Conservative Central Office 1948-55, PPS to Min. of State, Board of Trade, and Assist. Whip (unpaid) 1956-58, a Lord Commnr. of Treasury 1958-62, Dep. Govt. Ch. Whip 1959-64, and Treasurer to H.M. Household 1962-64; 1939-45 War; MP for Central Div. of Wandsworth (*C*) 1955-64: *cr. Baron St. Helens,* of St. Helens, co. Palatine of Lancaster (peerage of UK) 1964: *m.* 1939, Elizabeth Agnes, who *d.* 1956, yst. da. of the late Capt. Richard Blakiston-Houston [Blakiston Bt.], and has issue.

Arms—Or three piles sable each charged with a fountain. **Crest**—A dexter cubit arm proper charged with a fountain a hand grasping an arrow fesswise proper. **Supporters**—*Dexter*, a wolf gules; *sinister*, a griffin sable; each charged on the shoulder with a portcullis or. *Residence,*—Marchfield, Binfield, Berks. *Club,*—Carlton.

SON LIVING.

Hon. RICHARD FRANCIS, *b.* Nov. 4th, 1945; ed. at Nautical Coll., Pangbourne.

DAUGHTERS LIVING.

Hon. Henrietta Maria, *b.* 1940: *m.* 1970, Brian Turnbull Julius Stevens.
Hon. Selina Lillian, *b.* 1944: *m.* 1969, Jonathan Basil Morton Peto [see Peto, Bt., colls., cr. 1927].
Hon. Louisa Nina, *b.* 1949: *m.* 1974, Maj. James Frances Arbuthnott, Black Watch [see V. Arbuthnott, colls.]

ST. JOHN OF BLETSO, BARON. (St. John.) [Baron E. 1559, Bt. E. 1660.]
[Title pronounced "Sinjun of Bletso."]

JOHN MOUBRAY RUSSELL ST. JOHN,
19th Baron, and 16th Baronet; *b.* Aug.
3rd, 1917 ; *s.* 1934.

Arms,—Argent, on a chief gules, two mullet,
or. **Crest,**—On a mount vert, a falcon rising
or, belled of the last, ducally gorged gules.
Supporters,—Two monkeys proper.

DATA FATA SECUTUS

Following his allotted fate.

SISTERS LIVING.
Hon. Helen Evelyn (c/o Balfour & Manson, SSC,
58, Frederick St., Edinburgh, EH2 1LS), *b.*
1906.
Hon. Katherine Barbara, *b.* 1907 ; is Section
Officer W.A.A.F.: *m.* 1945, George William
Uttley, MA, BSc, late Fl.-Lt. RAF (c/o The Lord
Weymouth School, Warminster, Wilts.), and has
issue living, Alathea, St. John, *b.* 1947.
Hon. Margaret Beaufort, *b.* 1909: *m.* 1934, Charles
Somerville Carmichael, and has issue living,
Margaret Mary, *b.* 1940. *Residence,*—Old Mill
House, Newton Blossomville, Bedford.
Hon. Sybilla Laura Russell, *b.* 1915: *m.* 1943,
Howard Ernest Churchill Fey, and has issue
living, Margaret Angela *b.* 1945: *m.* 1971, Anthony
Norman Carter, BSc (c/o Lloyds Bank, Uttoxeter,
Staffords.).—Deborah Susan, *b.* 1947: *m.* 1969,
William Ronald Nicholson, 348, Ware Rd.,
Hailey, Herts. *Residence,*—Delfryn, Old Road,
Minera, near Wrexham, North Wales.
AUNT LIVING. (*Daughter of 16th Baron.*)
Hon. Margaret, *b.* 1887; is a Member of a Religious
Community (Anglican).

WIDOW LIVING OF SON OF SIXTEENTH BARON.
Noreen Mary Hay, dau. of the late Major Robert Francis Ladeveze Napier [see Napier, Bt., cr. 1627,
colls.]: *m.* 1914, the Hon. Charles Paulet St. John, who *d.* 1945. *Residence,*—Beach Lodge, North
Berwick.

WIDOW LIVING OF EIGHTEENTH BARON.
ELIZABETH MAY (*Baroness St. John of Bletso*), dau. of the late Lloyd Griffith, of Hurst Court, Ore
Hastings, and widow of Col. Edward Charles Ayshford Sanford, C.M.G., of Nynehead Court, Somer-
set: *m.* 1923, as his second wife, the 18th Baron, who *d.* 1934. *Residences,*—Chipley Park,
Wellington, Somerset ; 8, Lennox Gardens, S.W.1. *Club,*—Guards'.

COLLATERAL BRANCHES LIVING.
Granddaughters of the late Lt. Col. the Hon. Rowland Tudor St. John, Durham LI
(infra):—
Issue of the late Rev. Oliver John Frank Lockwood St. John, DSC, *b.* 1914, *d.* 1972: *m.* 1938,
Elva Rosemary (29, Bay Rd., Alverstoke, Hants.), da. of Alfred John Skinn, MB, ChB,
of Hong Kong:—
Vyvian Elaine, *b.* 1940: *m.* 1972, Patrick Nelson Maudsley, of 18, Tudor Way, Wellingborough,
Northants., and has issue living, Ruth Claire, *b.* 1973.——Juliet Rosemary, *b.* 1943; SRN: *m.* 1967,
Brian William Ellis Johnson, ARIBA, of 18, Danbury St., Islington, N1, and has issue living, George
St. John, *b.* 1969.——Katherine Alice (twin), *b.* 1969.——Diana Hazel Susan, *b.* 1946; BA: *m.* 1970,
Ewart John Holmes, ARIBA, MRTPI, of 57, Sussex Way, N7, and has issue living, Rowland St.
John, *b.* 1973,—Oliver John, *b.* 1975.——Margaret Vanessa Lucy *b.* 1948: *m.* 1969, George Marlay
Spencer, BA (c/o Williams & Glyn's Bank, Holt's Branch, Whitehall, SW1), and has issue living,
Rachel Marlay, *b.* 1972,—Abigail, *b.* 1974.

Issue of the late Lt.-Col. the Hon Rowland Tudor St. John, Durham LI, 3rd so n of
16th Baron, *b.* 1882, *d.* 1948 : *m.* 1912, Katharine Madge, who *d.* 1954, dau. of the
late Sir Frank Lockwood, Q.C., M.P. :—
ANDREW BEAUCHAMP, *TD*, *b.* Aug. 23rd, 1918; ed. at Wellington Coll.; is Lt.-Col. RA (TA Reserve):
m. 1955, Katharine, da. of the late A. G. Berg, and has issue living, Anthony Tudor, *b.* 1957. *Residence,*—Rosetta, Forest Rd., Oranjezicht, Cape Town, S. Africa.——Elaine Barbara Julia, *b.* 1921:
m. 1939, Lt.-Col. John Francis Whidborne (ret.) RA, and has issue living Richard St. John, *MBE*
(c/o Glyn, Mills & Co., Kirkland House, Whitehall, SW1), *b.* 1942: Maj. AAC, MBE (Mil.) 1973:
m. 1965, Linda Beverley, da. of Cyril Trevor Sherwood, of Child Oakeford, Dorset, and has issue
living, Nicholas St. John, *b.* 1969, James Oliver St. John *b.* 1973,—Julia Lauretta, *b.* 1943. *Residence,*—Hannaford Old House, nr. Ashburton, S. Devon.

Grandchildren of the late Rev. the Hon. Edmund Tudor St. John, 3rd son of 14th
Baron:—
Issue of the late Col. Edmund Farquhar St. John, C.M.G., D.S.O., *b.* 1879, *d.* 1945 : *m.* 1921,
Henrietta Frances (now of 30, Royal Circus, Edinburgh), dau. of the late Col. James
Alexander Dalmahoy, M.V.O., W.S. :—
Edmund Oliver, *W.S.*, *b.* 1927 ; ed. at Trin. Coll., Glenalmond ; W.S. 1953 : *m.* 1959, Elizabeth
Frances, only dau. of Lieut.-Col. H. R. Nicholl, of Lipwood Hall, Haydon Bridge, Northumberland,
and has issue living, Charles Henry Oliver, *b.* 1963,—Nicola Rosemary, *b.* 1960,—Emma Harriet,
b. 1968. *Residence,*—Lynedale House, West Linton, Peebles-shire.——Frances Dalmahoy, *b.* 1931.
Residence,—30, Royal Circus, Edinburgh.

Issue of the late Maj. Beauchamp Tudor St. John, *b.* 1880, *d.* 1965: *m.* 1910, Madeleine
Ethel (Craigveigh, Aboyne, Aberdeenshire), da. of the late J. Ellis Goodbody, of
Thornville, Limerick:—
Roger Ellis Tudor, *CB*, *MC* (Harelaw, Virginia Water, Surrey), *b.* 1911; ed. at Wellington Coll.;
Maj.-Gen. (ret.); Dep. Col. (Northumberland) R. Regt. of Fusiliers 1968-69 ; Comd., British Army
Staff and Mil. Attaché Washington 1933-65, and Pres. of Regular Commns. Board 1965-67; 1939-45
War (despatches, MC), Kenya 1955 (despatches); CB (Mil.) 1965: *m.* 1943, Rosemary Jean Douglas,
da. of the late Ronald Vickers, and has issue living, Henry Edward Tudor, *b.* 1949,— Angela Lucy,
b. 1944: *m.* 1970, Capt. Christopher Rohan Delacombe, R. Scots., only son of Maj.-Gen. Sir Rohan

Delacombe, KCMG, KCVO, KBE, CB, DSO, and has issue living, Caroline May *b.* 1971, Sophie
Clare *b.* 1973,—Jane Margaret, *b.* 1946,—Alice Rosemary, *b.* 1950: *m.* 1974, Hugh Martyn Williams.
——Michael Beauchamp, *DSC* (of Bepton Lodge, Midhurst, Sussex), *b.* 1915; Cdr. (ret.) RN; 1939-
45 War with Submarines (DSC): *m.* 1944, Pamela Patience, da. of the late Sir Arthur Rundell
Guinness, KCMG, and has issue living, Andrew Beauchamp (Cul-na-Cloich, Glenalmond, Perthshire),
b. 1945: *m.* 1968, the Hon. Sally Hayter Rootes, da. of 2nd Baron Rootes,—Clare Pamela, *b.* 1947:
m. 1968, David Waldorf Astor, of Bruern Grange, Milton-under-Wychwood, Oxon. [see V. Astor],—
Hermione Patience, *b.* 1951 : *m.* 1973, William Stanhope Owen, and has issue living, Georgina
Hermione, *b.* 1974.
　　　Issue of the late Cdr. Richard St. John, RN, *b.* 1883, *d.* 1967: *m.* 1st, 1909, Edith Meriel (who
　　　d. 1971, having obtained a divorce 1913), da. of the late Lt.-Col. Neil Benjamin Edmonstone
　　　Edmonstone, Bt., colls.]; 2ndly, 1913, Margaret Louise Causton, who *d.* 1957:—

(By 2nd m.) John Richard (40, Arkwright Rd., NW3), *b.* 1917; ed. at Wellington Coll.; Capt. (ret.,
RM: *m.* 1st, 1943, Helen Mary, da. of the late H. O. Coleman; 2ndly, 1952, Diana Elwell, yst. da.
of Col. E. S. Sinnott, and has issue living, (by 1st m.) Tudor Richard, *b.* 1946,—Lucinda Jill, *b.*
1944: *m.* 1968, Andrew Jon Cameron Beaumont, ARICS, of Tideford Farmhouse, Tideford, Cornwall, and has issue living, Richard Peregrine *b.* 1973, Charlotte Lucinda *b.* 1971,—(by 2nd m.) Clare
Sylvia, *b.* 1955,—Katharine Elinor Margaret, *b.* 1957.

　　　Grandchildren of Richard Fleming St. Andrew St. John, son of Henry St. Andrew
　　　St. John, son of Rev. John Francis Seymour St. John, 2nd son of the Very
　　　Rev. the Hon. St. Andrew St. John, DD, 2nd son of 10th Baron:—
　Issue of the late Winstan St. Andrew St. John, M.R.C.S., L.R.C.P., *b.* 1872, *d.* 1962: *m.*
　　　1909, Violet Julia Louisa, dau. of the late Henderson James Twigg, of Petane Grange,
　　　Petane, Hawks Bay, New Zealand:—
Orford Henderson St. Andrew, *b.* 1910; ed. at Wellington Coll., and at Hertford Coll., Oxford (B.A.
1932); 1939-45 War as Capt. Gen. List (Movement Control, attached Intelligence).
　　　Issue of the late Major Edward Churchill St. John, *b.* 1878, *d.* 1956 : *m.* 1906, Irene, who *d.*
　　　1956, dau. of Col. Charles Edward Shepherd, formerly Indian Army:—
Edward Richard Gordon, *b.* 1911 ; Lieut.-Col. (retired) R.A. : *m.* 1943, Mary Aderyn Jones-Davies,
and has issue living, Catherine Aderyn, *b.* 1944,—Margaret Joan, *b.* 1949. *Residence,*—The Dial
House, Rockbourne, near Fordingbridge, Hants.——Catherine Margaret, *b.* 1907. *Residence,*—
22, Greenway, Crediton, Devon.

　　　Issue of the late Lieut.-Com. Arthur Beauchamp St. John, R.N. (retired), *b.* 1884, *d.* 1948: *m.*
　　　1914, Lucinda Mary Stanly, dau. of the late Hon. John French, of Miramar, Queenstown,
　　　Ireland, and Rotra House, Frenchpark, co. Roscommon:—
Œnone Mary, *b.* 1917.——Deirdre Mary, *b.* 1919.

　　　Granddaughters of the late George Beauchamp Fleming St. John, son of the Rev.
　　　George St. John, son of the Rev. John Francis Seymour St. John (ante):—
　Issue of the late Harry Beauchamp St. John, *b.* 1886, *d.* 1957: *m.* 1919, Mary Katherine,
　　　who *d.* 1947, da. of the late Moreton Hyde Fitzhardinge, of Sydney, NSW:—
Barbara Margaret (27, Centennial Av., Lane Cove, Sydney, NSW), *b.* 1920.——Gladys, *b.* 1922; 1939-45
War in AWAS: *m.* 1945, Norman Wycliffe Fairfax, 65, Bantry Bay Rd., French's Forest, NSW 2086,
and has issue living, John Beauchamp, *b.* 1949,—Helen Margaret, *b.* 1947.

　　　Grandchildren of the late Rev. Harris Fleming St. John (infra):—
　Issue of the late Oliver Stukeley Fleming St. John, *b.* 1881, *d.* 1955 : *m.* 1st, 1913, Agnes
　　　Jane, who *d.* 1916, dau. of Arthur Jenkins, of Pencombe, Herefordshire; 2ndly, 1924,
　　　Elizabeth Sarah Ross, who *d.* 1933:—
(By 2nd marriage) Paul Fleming, *b.* 1928: *m.* 1953, Lesley Patricia, yst. da. of Albert Edwin Marsh, of
Perth, W. Australia, and has issue living, Brian Fleming, *b.* 1954,—Peter Michael, *b.* 1957,—Nola
Margaret, *b.* 1955,—Pauline Maree Teresa, *b.* 1960,—Julie Frances, *b.* 1964. *Residence,*—Mallee
E. Yuna, W. Australia.——Oliver Peter (Aquinas College, Manning, W. Aust.), *b.* 1929.——Michael
Fleming, *b.* 1932: *m.* 1958, Teresa Josephine, da. of Thomas W. Murphy, of Finchley, N3, and has
issue living, Nicholas Fleming, *b.* 1961,—Andrew Thomas *b.* 1963,—Philip Ambrose, *b.* 1965,—
Robert Oliver, *b.* 1968. *Residence,*—23, Holmwood Gdns., Finchley, N3.——Joan Fleming, *b.* 1925:
m. 1947, Stanley John Simpson, and has issue living, Christopher John, *b.* 1950,—Peter James,
b. 1952,—John Andrew, *b.* 1957,—Richard Stephen Francis, *b.* 1960,—Pauline Mary, *b.* 1948:
m. 1968, Kenneth Gerald Glasgow (c/o B. P. Australia, Port-Hedland, W. Aust.),—Catherine Anne,
b. 1966.——(By 1s m.) Evelyn Mary Fleming (31, Mayfield Rd., Crouch End, N8), *b.* 1915: *m.* 1943,
Daniel Reidy, who *d.* 1969, and has issue living, Richard Daniel Kenneth, *b.* 1944.

　　　Grandson of the late Fleming St. John, son of the late Rev. John Francis Seymour
　　　St. John (ante):—
　Issue of the late Rev. Harris Fleming St. John, *b.* 1833, *d.* 1903 : *m.* 1878, Gertrude
　　　Margaret, who *d.* 1923, dau. of the late Charles E. Ward, of Clifton :—
Rev. St. Andrew Fleming, *b.* 1887 ; ed. at Haileybury, and at Keble Coll., Oxford (B.A. 1909);
formerly Chap. to Community of St. John the Divine Pietermaritzburg, and R. of Peakirk and
Glinton. *Residence,*—Two Chimneys, Westhope, Hereford.

　　　Grandson of the late Col. Sir Oliver Beauchamp Coventry St. John, K.C.S.I. (infra):—
　Issue of the late Lieut.-Col. Sir Henry Beauchamp St. John. K.C.I.E., C.B.E., Indian Army,
　　　b. 1874, *d.* 1954: *m.* 1907, Olive Amy, who *d.* 1963, dau. of the late Lt.-Col. Charles Herbert,
　　　C.S.I.:—
Oliver Charles Beauchamp, *C.M.G.*, *b.* (Oct.) 1907; ed. at Charterhouse; Lt.-Col. (ret.) Indian Army
(Foreign and Political Ser.); C.M.G. 1963: *m.* 1st, 1935, Elizabeth Mary, who *d.* 1957, da. of Philip
Lambton; 2ndly, 1966, Mary, da. of John Greenway, and widow of John Gillum Maxwell-Gumbleton
and has issue living, (by 1st m.) Simon Lambton Beauchamp (3030, Whitehurst Way, Marietta,
Georgia, 30062, USA), *b.* 1940: *m.* 1971, Margaret Lee, step-da. of Perry Leslie Owen, of Tampa
Florida, USA, and has issue living, Ryan Christopher Beauchamp *b.* 1972,—Sarah Mary, *b.* 1937:
m. 1957, Michael Geoffrey Morvaren Mayhew, of Lone Pine, 51, Petts Wood Rd., Petts Wood, Kent,
and has issue living, Nicholas Morvaren *b.* 1959, Charles Geoffrey *b.* 1966, Hamish St. John *b.* 1968,
Amanda Elizabeth *b.* 1962,—Victoria Anne, *b.* 1942,—Vanessa Margaret, *b.* 1944: *m.* 1964, Nicholas
John Connolly, of Monks Gate Cottage, Monks Gate, Horsham, and has issue living, Rupert St.
John *b.* 1965, Philippa Joan, *b.* 1964, Victoria Maria *b.* 1967. *Residence,*—Curtle Cottage, Beaulieu,
Hants.   *Club,*—Naval and Military.

　　　Grandson of the late Lt.-Col. Oliver Henry Beauchamp St. John (infra):—
　Issue of the late Robert St. John, *b.* 1884, *d.* 1968: *m.* 1st, 1912, Dorothy Mary, who *d.* 1958,
　　　da. of the late Daniel Willink; 2ndly, 1959, Dorothy Kathleen (7, Cunningham House,
　　　Park Av., Bexhill-on-Sea), da. of the late A. L. Beardsley, of Bognor Regis:—
(By 1st m.) Oliver Moubray (Blaenwern, 95A, High St., Harston, Cambridge), *b.* 1921: *m.* 1968, Mar-
garet Elunid Corbett, da. of William John Jones, of Ilchester, Pont-Newynydd, Mon.
　　　Granddaughter of the late Lt.-Gen. Robert St. John, 3rd son of the late Thomas
　　　St. John (*b.* 1765), 3rd son of the Very Rev. The Hon. St. Andrew St. John, DD
　　　(ante):—
　Issue of the late Lieut.-Col. Oliver Henry Beauchamp St. John, *b.* 1847, *d.* 1917 : *m.* 1880,
　　　Bertha Frederica, who *d.* 1936, dau. of the late Col. John Scriven, J.P.:—
Selina Barbara Clara, *b.* 1888: *m.* 1913, John Felix Fielding (Lieut. 1st Batn. Suffolk Regt. during
1914-18 War). *Residence,*—6, Grove End Rd., St. John's Wood, NW8.

Grandson of the late Lieut.-Col. Oliver Henry Beauchamp St. John (ante):—
Issue of the late Philip George St. John, *b.* 1890, *d.* 1942: *m.* 1920, Lois Irene, *MBE*, who
d. 1965, da. of the Rev. Robert Peel Willock, R. of Warmington, and Canon of Coventry:—
Anthony Philip, *b.* 1925: *m.* 1st, 1947 (m. diss. 1951), Elizabeth Dawes; 2ndly, 1959, Shelagh Marie
James, and has issue living, (by 1st m.) David Warren, *b.* 1950,—(by 2nd m.) Oliver Philip, *b.* 1959,—
Trudie Sophia, *b.* 1961,—Katherine Emma, *b.* 1963.

Grandchildren of the late Com. Thomas Charles St. Andrew St. John (infra):—
Issue of the late Robert Henry Beauchamp St. John, *b.* 1878, *d.* 1956: *m.* 1st, 1901, Agnes
Mary Sybil, who *d.* 1915, dau. of the late Capt. Frederick Shelton, Argyll and Sutherland
Highlanders; 2ndly, 1916, Edith Mary, dau. of the late Capt. Cape Hutton, of Iver,
Bucks :—
(By 1st m.) Dorothy Mary Beaufort, *b.* 1902: *m.* 1962, Magnus Karl Olof Friman, of 24, Sheepfold
Lane, Amersham, Bucks.——(By 2nd m.) Margaret Mary (Princess Christian Ward, National Hospital,
Queen Sq., WC2), *b.* 1919: *m.* 1940, Wing-Cdr. David Vere George Mawhood, OBE, RAF (ret.)
and has issue living, Martin David St. John *b.* 1945,—Simon St. John, *b.* 1947.
Issue of the late St. John St. Andrew Newell St. John, *b.* 1884, *d.* 1962: *m.* 1910 Mary
Audrey, who *d.* 1957, dau. of C. E. Hicks, of North Battlefold, Saskatchewan, Canada:—
Andrew Charles, *b.* 1927: *m.* 1952, Cecile Marie, dau. of W. J. Calnan, of Vancouver, British Columbia
and has issue living, Marie Patricia, *b.* 19—,— Janet Mary, *b.* 1956.——Mary Cecilia, *b.* 1912: *m.* 1932,
Walter Davidson.——Ella Monica, *b.* 1917: *m.* 1942, W. H. Davis, Pilot Officer Roy. Canadian Air
Force.——Hilda Margaret, *b.* 1925: *m.* 1949, Victor Leon Charbonneau, of 4104, Prince Albert Rd.,
Vancouver, 10, British Columbia, and has issue living, Susan Hilda, *b.* 1951.

Granddaughter of the late Lieut.-Gen. Robert St. John (ante):—
Issue of the late Com. Thomas Charles St. Andrew St. John, *b.* 1853, *d.* 1920 ; *m.* 1877,
Cecilia, who *d.* 1950, dau. of the late Major Henry Lavie (Bombay Army):—
Helen Cecilia Mary, *b.* 1880: *m.* 1905, Henry Halley, who *d.* 1939, and has issue living, Cecilia Helen
b. 1906: *m.* 1929, John Knox,—Margaret, *b.* 1907: *m.* 1946, Travis Warren. *Residence,—*

Grandchildren of the late Henry St. John (*b.* 1852) (infra):—
Issue of the late Rev. Canon Frederick de Port St. John, *b.* 1879, *d.* 1963 : *m.* 1908, Hannah
Phœbe Mabel, who *d.* 1950, dau. of the late Samuel Lucas Charles Pyrke, J.P., of Tam-
worth, N.S. Wales:—
Oliver Beauchamp (Mowll Memorial Village, 284, Castle Hill Rd., Castle Hill, NSW 2154), *b.* 1909.——
Roland Tyrwhitt, *MBE* (6, Shirley St., Indooroopilly, Qld. 4068); *b.* 1914; ed. at Sydney Univ.
(BEcon); BA Qld.; late Lt. AIF; an Assoc. of Aust. Soc. of Accountants; Registrar of Diocese
of Brisbane, and Province of Qld 1946-74; Capt. Aust. Citizen Mil. Forces 1952-63; a Member of
Standing Cttee. of Gen. Synod of Ch. of England in Aust. 1960-74, of Anglican Consultative Council
of Anglican Communion, and of National Council of Independent Schs. of Aust. 1970-74; MBE (Civil)
1968: *m.* 1949, Margaret, who *d.* 1972, da. of the late Ven. Archdeacon Reginald Beatty Massey,
Home Mission Sec. of Diocese of Brisbane, Qld., and has issue living, David Henry, *b.* 1951; ed. at
Qld. Univ. (BSc),—Paul Michael, *b.* 1953; ed. at Qld. Univ. (BSc),—Nigel Alexander, *b.* 1958,—
Julian Andrew, *b.* 1963,—Philippa Robin, *b.* 1955.——Edward Henry, *QC* (28, Morella Rd., Clifton
Gdns., NSW 2088; Mt. Elliott, Holgate, NSW), *b.* 1916; ed. at Sydney Univ. (BA, LLB); Bar.-
at-law 1940, and a QC 1956; sometime Capt. AIF; Austn. Parl. as Member for Warringah 1966-69;
Pres., International Comm. of Jurists, Austn. Section since 1961; a Member of Intern. Comm.
of Jurists, Geneva 1966; Pres. of S. Africa Defence and Aid Fund in Aust. since 1963; Vice-Pres.
Intern. Law Assocn., Aust. Branch since 1961; Austn. delegate to Commonwealth and Empire
Law Conference, London, 1955, and to Congresses of Intern. Comm. of Jurists, New Delhi 1959,
Rio de Janeiro 1962, and Bangkok 1965, official observer at S. African Treason Trials on behalf
of British Section of Intern. Comm. of Jurists 1959, and Member of Malta Constitutional Commn.
1960; 1939-45 War in Middle East, and New Guinea: *m.* 1st, 1940, Sylvette, who *d.* 1954, da. of Jean
Meer Gugenheim, of Alsace; 2ndly, 1955, Valerie Erskine, da. of Henry John Winslow, late of London,
and has issue living, (by 1st m.) Madeleine, *b.* 1941; ed. at Univ. of Sydney (BA): *m.* 1965, Christopher Roger Tillam, BA—Colette, *b.* 1944,—(by 2nd m.) Oliver Winslow, *b.* 1956,—Edward Erskine,
b. 1960,—Patrick Graeme, *b.* 1963.——Margery Patricia, *b.* 1910: *m.* 1952, Maj. Maitland Buckeridge,
The Buffs (ret.), of 36, The Battlement, Castlecraig, NSW 2068.——Marion (33, Moncur St., Woollahra, NSW, 2025), *b.* 1911: *m.* 1936, the Rev. Harold William Baker, who *d.* 1966, late Asst. Master
and Chap. of King's Sch., Parramatta, NSW, and has issue living, Richard St. John (27, Dalton Rd.,
St. Ives, NSW 2075), *b.* 1937: *m.* 1964, Virginia Dale, da. of Eric D. Craig, of Warawee, NSW, and
has issue living, Andrew William St. John *b.* 1967, Miranda Alice *b.* 1969, Camilla Lucy *b.* 1972,—
Felicity Ruth (37, Nevern Sq., SW5) *b.* 1940; ed. at Sydney Univ. (BA); lecturer, Univ. Coll.,
London,—Priscilla Marion, *b.* 1948; ed. at Univ. of NSW (BA Hons.): *m.* 1971, David Maxwell,
of 31, Bradford St., Balmain, NSW 2041.——Margaret, *b.* 1919: *m.* 1940, Edward John Minchin,
former Assist. Crown Solicitor for NSW, of 2, The Bastion, Castlecrag, NSW 2068 ; 26, Warri Cres.,
MacMasters Beach, NSW, and has issue living, Antony St. John (13, Duigan Pl., Scullin, ACT, 2614),
b. 1942; ed. at Univ. of NSW (BCom), and Aust. National Univ. (MEc): *m.* 1970, Elizabeth Hume,
BA, da. of Armand Francis Gunner, Metrop. Manager, Rural Bank of NSW, Sydney, and has issue
living, Thomas Edward *b.* 1972,—Mary Annabel, *b.* 1948: *m.* 1972, Michael William Ritchie, of 1,
Sunnyside Cres., Castlecrag, NSW 2068, and has issue living, Angela Margaret *b.* 1974.——Florence
Anne, *b.* 1924; ed. at Sydney Univ.; formerly in WRANS: *m.* 1955, Frank Heller, BSc, PhD, of 84,
Wood Vale, N10, and has issue living, Michael Guy St. John, *b.* 1957,—Juliet Margarethe, *b.* 1961,—
Clare Andrea, *b.* 1964.——Pamela Mary ST JOHN (30, Birdwood St., Balwyn, Vic. 3103, Aust.),
b. 1925; Dip. Adv. Studies in Ed.-Cert. KTC (Adelaide): assumed the name of St. John 1972;
lecturer at Melbourne Kindergarten Teachers' Coll. since 1957: *m.* 1946 (m. diss. 1959) Ronald Fry,
late RN, who *d.* 1971, and has issue living, Jeremy William St. John ST. JOHN, *b.* 1952; ed. at Mel-
bourne Univ. (LLB); Bar. and Solicitor Aust. 1975,—Jennifer Jane, *b.* 1949; TITC (Melbourne);
TTCTD (Melbourne),—Catherine Mary ST. JOHN, *b.* 1957.
Issue of the late Ambrose St. John, *b.* 1896, *d.* 1968: *m.* 1925, Mary Kathleen (49, Gordon
St., Port Macquarie, NSW 2444), da. of Peter Gaffney, of Sydney, NSW:—
Kevin Joseph, *b.* 1926.——Desmond Henry, *b.* 1932: *m.* 19—, Mavis Duncan, of Rockhampton, Qld.,
and has issue living, Lorelle *b.* 19—,—Deborah, *b.* 19—,—Sandra, *b.* 1963.——Marlene Illina, *b.*
1936: *m.* 1962, David Steuart, Rawdon Island, Hastings River, NSW, and has issue living, Nicolle,
b. 1963.

Granddaughters of the late Frederick St. John, son of the late Henry St. John, 5th
son of the late Very Rev. the Hon. St. Andrew St. John (ante):—
Issue of the late Henry St. John, *b.* 1852, *d.* 1939 : *m.* 1877, Jessie, who *d.* 19—, dau. of Donald
Macdonald, of Port Macquarie, N.S.W. :—
Maud Charlotte, *b.* 1878: *m.* 1907, Roger Williamson Wilson, who *d.* 1948, and has issue living, Roger
Williamson (of Canberra, Australia), *b.* 1908: *m.* 19—, and has issue living,—Donald St. John
(of Port Macquarie, NSW), *b.* 1912: *m.* 19—, Phyllis Clump, and has issue living, Desmond *b.* 19—,
Una *b.* 19—, Verna *b.* 19—, Ena Maude, *b.* 1910,—Marjorie, *b.* 1919. *Residence,*—17, Queen St.,
Port Macquarie, NSW.——Violet Jessie, *b.* 1883. *Residence,*—98 William St., Port Macquarie,
NSW.

Granddaughters of the late Oliver St. John (infra):—
Issue of the late Oliver Beauchamp St. John, *b.* 1895, *d.* 1970: *m.* 1st, 1921 (m. diss. 19—)
Winifred Lyndall Fox, of Hastings, Sussex; 2ndly, 1944, Josephine Lorna, who *d.* 1969,
da. of W. Kurtze, of Saskatoon, Canada:—
(By 1st m.) Patricia Jocelyn, *b.* 1922: *m.* 1941, Prof. John Alexander McCarter, PhD, FRSC, of 472,
Lawson Rd., London, Ont., Canada, N6G 1X8, and has issue living, David Graham (511, Hibiscus
Av., London, Ont., Canada), *b.* 1946: *m.* 1968, Janice Evelyn, da. of R. E. Yates, of Walkerton, Ont.,

Canada, and has issue living, Robert Alexander *b.* 1974,—Robert Malcolm (c/o Dept. of Zoology, University of British Columbia, Vancouver, BC, Canada), *b.* 1948: *m.* 1971, Bonnie Gail, da. of Lorne E. Davis, of London, Ont.,—William Alexander, *b.* 1955,—Patricia Lyndall, *b.* 1953.——Josephine Lyndall (5448, Halifax St., Burnaby 2, BC, Canada), *b.* 1925: *m.* 1947 (m. diss. 1974), and has issue living, Rodney William, *b.* 1949: *m.* 19—, Leonora Marie Dixon,—Donald MacKenzie, *b.* 1953,— Richard Michael, *b.* 1957,—Diane Louise, *b.* 1962.

Granddaughters of the late Frederick St. John (ante):—
Issue of the late Oliver St. John, *b.* 1857, *d.* 19— : *m.* 1891, Alice, dau. of the late Samuel Richardson, of Ingatestone, Essex :—
Olive Alice, *b.* 1892: *m.* 1913, Gordon Thomson, of 302, Island Lodge, Ottawa, Ont., Canada, and has issue living, Jack, *b.* 1916: *m.* and has issue,—David, *b.* 1920: *m.* and has issue,—Margaret, *b.* 1915: *m.* 1934, A. Ambridge, of Ottawa, Ont., and has issue,—Ruth, *b.* 1918: *m.* and has issue,—Beth, *b.* 1922: *m.* and has issue.——Constance Muriel, *b.* 1893: *m.* 1914, Bernard Freeman, of 5077, Orchard Av., Bethal Park, Pa. 15102, USA, and has issue living, Jack *b.* 1952, Richard *b.* 1955,—Bernard Keith, (Santa Barbara, Cal. ,USA): *m.* 1st, 1939, (m. diss. 1971), Florence Pozzi; 2ndly, 1971, Mildred Stockton, and has issue living (by 1st m.) Ronald Keith *b.* 1942: *m.*, and has issue,—Oliver Franklin (437, Princeton Av., Ventura, Cal., USA), *b.* 1922: *m.* 1946, Marjorie Smith, and has issue living, Kim Donna *b.* 1954, Cindy *b.* 1955,—Constance Mary, *b.* 1924: *m.* 1948, John A. Pusateri (5077, Orchard Av., Bethel Park, Pa., USA), and has issue living, John Freeman *b.* 1952, Keith David *b.* 1957, Marilyn *b.* 1949: *m.* and has issue, Kathleen Alice *b.* 1950: *m.* Jill Anne *b.* 1964, Lisa Mary *b.* 1966.

PREDECESSORS.—[1] OLIVER St. John (descended from John St. John, el. son of Sir Oliver St. John of Bletso, who *m.* Margaret, great-granddaughter of Roger de Beauchamp, who was summoned to Parliament of England as *Baron Beauchamp of Bletshoe* 1363-79, since when that title has not been assumed), cr. *Baron St. John of Bletso,* co. Beds (peerage of England) 1559; *d.* 1592; *s.* by his el. son [2] JOHN, 2nd Baron ; was one of the peers who sat on the trial of Mary, Queen of Scots ; *d.* without male issue 1596, when the Barony of Beauchamp devolved upon his dau. Anne, wife of William, Lord Howard, el. son of the 1st Earl of Nottingham, and the Barony of St. John devolved upon his brother [3] OLIVER, 3rd Baron ; *d.* 1618 ; *s.* by his el. son [4] OLIVER, 4th Baron ; cr. *Earl of Bolingbroke* (peerage of England) 1624 ; *d.* 1646 ; *s.* by his grandson [5] OLIVER, 2nd Earl ; *d.* 1688 ; *s.* by his brother [6] PAULET, 3rd Earl ; *d.* unmarried 1711, when the earldom became extinct and the barony devolved upon his kinsman [7] PAULET ST. ANDREW, 7th Baron, who had previously *s.* his father as 4th Bt. (see *⚬⚬* infra) ; *d.* 1714 ; *s.* by his uncle [8] WILLIAM, 8th Baron ; *d.* unmarried 1720 ; *s.* by his brother [9] ROWLAND, 9th Baron ; *d.* unmarried 1722 ; *s.* by his brother [10] JOHN, 10th Baron ; *d.* 1757 ; *s.* by his son [11] JOHN, 11th Baron ; *d.* 1767 ; *s.* by his el. son [12] HENRY BEAU-CHAMP, 12th Baron ; *d.* 1805 ; *s.* by his brother [13] ST. ANDREW, 13th Baron ; *d.* 1817 ; *s.* by his son [14] ST. ANDREW BEAUCHAMP, 14th Baron ; *b.* 1811: *m.* 1838, Eleanor, who *d.* 1899, dau. of the late Vice-Adm. Sir Richard Hussey-Hussey, *G.C.M.G., K.C.B.* ; *d.* 1874 ; *s.* by his son [15] ST. ANDREW, 15th Baron, *b.* 1840 : *m.* 1868, Ellen Georgiana, who *d.* 1890, dau. of the late Edward Senior, Poor Law Commr., Ireland ; *d.* 1887 ; *s.* by his brother [16] BEAUCHAMP MOUBRAY, 16th Baron ; *b.* 1844 ; Lord-Lieut. of Bedfordshire : *m.* 1st, 1869, Helen Charlotte, who *d.* 1909, 2nd dau. of the late Harry Thornton, of Kempston Grange, Beds ; 2ndly, 1911, Ethel Susan, who *d.* 1945, dau. of the late John Habington Barneby Lutley, of Brockhampton, Herefordshire ; *d.* 1912 ; *s.* by his son [17] HENRY BEAUCHAMP OLIVER, 17th Baron ; *b.* 1876 ; *d.* 1920 ; *s.* by his brother [18] MOUBRAY ST. ANDREW THORNTON, 18th Baron ; *b.* 1877 : *m.* 1st, 1905, Evelyn Geraldine, who *d.* 1918, youngest dau. of the late Capt. Andrew Hamilton Russell (formerly 58th Regt.), of The Heath House, Petersfield, Hants ; 2ndly, 1923, Elizabeth May, dau. of Lloyd Griffith, of Hurst Court, Ore, Hastings, and widow of Col. Edward Charles Ayshford Sanford, C.M.G., of Nynehead Court, Somerset ; *d.* 1934 ; *s.* by his only son [19] JOHN MOUBRAY RUSSELL, 19th Baron and present peer.
*⚬*The Hon. Sir Rowland St. John, 4th son of the 3rd Baron St. John of Bletso (see ante), had, with other issue [1] OLIVER, cr. a *Baronet* 1660 ; *d.* 1661 ; *s.* by his son [2] *Sir* ANDREW, 2nd Bt. ; *d.* 1708 ; *s.* by his son [3] *Sir* ST. ANDREW, 3rd Bt. ; *s.* by his son [4] *Sir* PAULET ST. ANDREW, 4th Bt., who succeeded as 7th Baron St. John of Bletso (see ante).

ST. JUST, BARON.   (Grenfell.)   [Baron U.K. 1935.]

Honest duty.

PETER GEORGE GRENFELL, 2nd Baron ; *b.* July 22nd, 1922; *s.* 1941; ed. at Harrow ; is Hon. Lieut. King's Roy. Rifle Corps ; N.-W. Europe 1944-5 : *m.* 1st, 1949 (marriage dissolved 1955), Leslie, dau. of the late Condé Nast, of New York, U.S.A. ; 2ndly, 1956, Maria Britneva, and has issue by 1st and 2nd marriages.

Arms,—Gules, on a fesse between three organ rests or, a mural crown of the field. Crest,—On a mural crown gules, a gryphon passant or, holding in the beak a sprig of laurel proper. Supporters,—*Dexter,* a Gate Porter of the Bank of England supporting in the exterior hand his staff of office ; *sinister,* a sailor of the Mercantile Marine, all proper.

Residences,—Wilbury Park, Newton Tony, Salisbury; 9 Gerald Rd., SW1. Club,—White's.

DAUGHTERS LIVING.   (*By 1st marriage.*)
Hon. Laura Claire, *b.* 1950.

(*By 2nd marriage.*)
Hon. Catherine, *b.* 1957.
Hon. Natasha Jeannine Mary, *b.* 1959.

PREDECESSOR.—[1] EDWARD CHARLES GRENFELL, son of the late Henry Riversdale Grenfell, M.P., of Bacres, Henley-on-Thames ; *b.* 1870 ; sat as M.P. for City of London (*C*) 1922-35 ; cr. *Baron St. Just,* of St. Just in Penwith, co. Cornwall (peerage of United Kingdom) 1935 : *m.* 1913, Florence Emily, who *d.* 1971, el. dau. of George William Henderson, of 17, Chesham Place, S.W.. ; *d.* 1941; *s.* by his only son [2] PETER GEORGE, 2nd Baron and present peer.

ST. LEONARDS, BARON. (Sugden.) [Baron U.K. 1852.]

Thou shalt conquer by toil.

JOHN GERARD SUGDEN, 4th Baron;
b. Feb. 3rd, 1950; *s.* 1972.

Arms,—Azure, on a fesse or between two
maidens' heads couped and crined in chief
proper, and a leopard's head erased in base of
the second, an annulet. Crest,—A leopard's
head erased sable, gorged with a baron's coronet or. Supporters,—On either side a leopard
or, pelletty, and gorged with a baron's coronet
lined azure.

Residence,—17, Craigford Drive, Artane,
Dublin, 5.

BROTHERS LIVING.
Arthur Herbert (1, Abbey Park, Killester,
Dublin, 5), *b.* 1942: *m.* 1967, Phyllis Muldoon,
d has iliving, Arthur John, *b.* 1968.
Philip Hugh (237, Buttercup Park, Barndale,
Dublin, 5), *b.* 1944: *m.* 1965, Roseanna Mary
da. of Michael Hill, and has issue living,
Philip Hugh, *b.* 1966, —Mark Antony, *b.* 1974,
—Rebecca Julie, *b.* 1969.
Hugh David, *b.* 1947.

UNCLE LIVING.
EDWARD CHARLES, MB, BCh, (4, Half Moon St.,
Wl), *b.* July 24th, 1902; MRCS England;
LRCP London; MRCOG; late Maj. RAMC.

MOTHER LIVING.
Julia Sheila (17, Craigford Drive, Artane,
Dublin), da. of the late Philip Wyatt, of
Curragh, co. Kildare: *m.* 1949, Arthur Herbert
Sugden, who *d.* 1958.

SISTER LIVING OF THIRD BARON. (*Raised to the rank of a Baron's daughter* 1912.)

Hon. Margery Edith, *b.* 1885: *m.* 1918, Maj. Robert Jocelyn Rowan Waller, DSO, who *d.* 1968, and has
issue living, Beryl, *b.* 1919; ed. at Camb. Univ. (BA 1943): *m.* 1950, Christopher Spencer Bayley, of
Durham Ox, Old Town, Kirkby Lonsdale, Westmorland [see D. Marlborough, colls.],—Joyce Edith,
b. 1923: *m.* 1947, Robert Crescent Holford Risley, and has issue living, Simon Crescent *b.* 1950,
Susan Hope *b.* 1953. *Residence,*—Ickford House, Little Ickford, nr. Aylesbury, Bucks.

COLLATERAL BRANCH LIVING.
Issue of the late Hon. Emma Frances Mary Sugden, sister of 2nd Baron, *b.* 1852,
d. 1930: *m.* 1888, George Reid, who *d.* 1939:—
Emma Frances Mary Sugden (1237, Glenn Av., San José, Cal., 95125, USA), *b.* 1891.——Marianne
Blanche Geraldine (1237, Glenn Av., San José, Cal. USA), *b.* 1893: *m.* 1924, Bruce Shafter Bothwell,
who *d.* 1969, and has issue living, Gordon Reid (2621, Canous Rd., San José, Cal., USA), *b.* 1929:
m. 1949, Jeanette Keebaugh, and has issue living, Gordon Reid *b.* 1952, Glenn Allen *b.* 1953, Judith
Ann *b.* 1955,—Winifred Sugden, *b.* 1927: *m.* 1946, Robert Hamilton Light, of 169, Ely Place, Palo
Alto, Cal., USA, and has issue living, Douglas Mason (169, Ely Place, Pato Alto, Calif. 94306, USA),
b. 1950: *m.* 1974, Wendy Seppi; Kenneth George *b.* 1952, Russell Wellington *b.* 1964, Claudia
Jeanne *b.* 1947: *m.* 1968, Lee Russell Ahlstrom, of 141, Shasta Av., McCloud, Cal., USA (and has
issue living, Christina *b.* 1970, Caroline *b.* 1974).

PREDECESSORS.—[1] *Sir* EDWARD Sugden *K.B.*, *D.C.L.*, M.P. for Weymouth 1826-30, for
St. Mawes 1831-2, and for Ripon (C) 1837-41; was Solicitor-Gen. 1829-30, Lord Chancellor of
Ireland 1834-5 and 1841-6, and Lord High Chancellor of England 1852: *m.* 1808, Winifred, who *d.* 1861,
only child of John Knapp; *d.* 1875; *s.* by his grandson [2] EDWARD BURTENSHAW (son of the
Hon. Henry Sugden, el. son of 1st Baron, by Marianne, dau. of Lieut.-Col. Cookson, of
Neasham Hall, Durham), 2nd Baron; *b.* 1847; *d.* 1908: *m.* 1876, Marianne Caroline, who *d.*
1947, dau. of the late Capt. George Astley Charles Dashwood; *s.* by his nephew [3] FRANK
EDWARD (son of the late Hon. Henry Frank Sugden, next brother of 2nd Baron), 3rd Baron; *b.* 1908;
d. 1972; *s.* by his kinsman [4] JOHN GERARD (son of Arthur Herbert Sugden, el. son of Arthur Henry
Sugden, only son of the Rev. the Hon. Arthur Sugden, 3rd son of 1st Baron), 4th Baron and present
peer.

ST. LEVAN, BARON. (St. Aubyn.) [Baron U.K. 1887, Bt. U.K. 1866.]

IN · SE · TERES ·
Exact in himself.

FRANCIS CECIL ST. AUBYN, 3rd Baron, and
4th Baronet ; *b.* April 18th, 1895 ; *s.* 1940 ;
ed. at Eton ; is patron of one living, and a
JP and a DL for Cornwall; late Maj. Gren.
Gds.; one of HM Body Guard of Hon. Corps
of Gentlemen-at-Arms since 1973; 1914-18
War (twice wounded), 1939-45 War: *m.* 1916,
the Hon. Clementina Gwendolen Catharine
Nicolson, *JP*, da. of 1st Baron Carnock, and
has issue.

Arms,—Ermine, on a cross gules, five bezants, all
within a bordure wavy of the second. Crest,—A rock
proper, therefrom a Cornish chough rising sable, the
whole debruised with a bendlet sinister wavy ermine.
Supporters,—Two lions or, each gorged with a chain
proper and pendant therefrom an escutcheon, that of the
dexter, per fesse azure and argent, in chief a naval
crown between two laurel branches saltirewise or, in base
the frame of a vessel proper; that of the sinister, sable,
charged with five bezants.

Residence,—Avallon, Green Lane, Marazion, Cornwall. *Club,*—Army and Navy.

SONS LIVING.

Hon. JOHN FRANCIS ARTHUR, *D.S.C., b.* Feb. 23rd, 1919; ed at Eton, and at Trin. Coll., Camb. (BA); Fellow of Roy. Soc. for Encouragement of Arts; admitted a Solicitor 1948; sometime Lt. RNVR; High Sheriff of Cornwall 1974: *m.* 1970, Susan, yr. da. of the late Maj.-Gen. Sir John Noble Kennedy, GCMG, KCVO, KBE, CB, MC. *Residence,*—21, Ennismore Gdns., SW7. *Club,*—Brooks's.

Hon. (Oliver) Piers, *M.C. b.* 1920 ; ed. at Wellington Coll, and at St. James's Sch., Maryland, U.S.A.; European War 1939-45 as Capt. 60th Rifles and Parachute Regt. (despatches, M.C.): *m.* 1948; Mary Bailey, dau. of Bailey Southwell, of Crocodile Leap Farm, Olievenhoutpoort, S. Africa, and has issue living, James Piers Southwell, *b.* 1950,—Nicholas Francis, *b.* 1955,—Fiona Mary, *b.* 1952. *Residences,*—Lodge Farm House, Ringmer, Sussex ; Flat 2, 22, Elvaston Place, S.W.7. *Club,*—Brooks's.

Hon. Giles Rowan, *b.* 1925 ; ed. at Wellington Coll., at Glasgow Univ., and at Trin. Coll., Oxford ; FRSL; 1939-45 War as Ordinary Seaman RN (invalided). *Residences,*—Baldwins' Bec, Eton Coll., Windsor; St. Cloud, Callow End, Worcester. *Clubs,*—Brooks's, Beefsteak.

DAUGHTERS LIVING.

Hon. Jessica Gwendolen, *b.* 1918: *m.* 1939, John Patrick Koppel, late Major Welsh Guards, and has issue living, Patrick Anthony (Flat 6, 27, Egerton Gdns., SW7), *b.* 1944: *m.* 1st, 1967 (m. diss. 1971), Jacqueline Ann, da. of J. N. Fairrie; 2ndly, 1974, Jenny, da. of Cecil White,—Lamorna Jessica, *b.* 1940: *m.* 1964, Ian Clinton Elliot, of 28, Bloomfield Terr., SW3, and has issue living, Patrick Ian *b.* 1965, Shane Robert *b.* 1970,—Susan Katherine Dorothy, *b.* 1942: *m.* 1963, Richard Noël Dobbs, of 58, Ridgeway Pl., Wimbledon, SW19, and has issue living, Richard Francis Conway *b.* 1966, Alexander Noel *b.* 1967, Jessica Katherine Ann *b.* 1971. *Residence,*—Stainforth House, Settle, Yorks.

Hon. Philippa Catherine, *b.* 1922: *m.* 1948, Evelyn Charles Lacy Hulbert-Powell, late Lieut. Queen's Roy. Regt., and has issue living, Charles George Lacy, *b.* 1952,—Francis Peter Lacy, *b.* 1961,—Elizabeth Catherine Lacy, *b.* 1950,—Veronica Mary Lacy, *b.* 1954,—Teresa Philippa Lacy, *b.* 1956. *Residence,*—Old Place Farm, Mayfield, Sussex.

DAUGHTERS LIVING OF SECOND BARON.

Hon. Marjory Katharine Elizabeth Alexandra, *b.* 1893 : *m.* 1919, the Hon. John Holford Parker, who *d.* 1955 [see E. Morley]. *Residence,*—Saltram, Plympton, Plymouth.

Hon. Hilaria Lily, *b.* 1894. *Residence,*—11, Lancaster Court, Seymour St., W2.

COLLATERAL BRANCHES LIVING.

Grandchildren of the Hon. Lionel Michael St. Aubyn, MVO (infra):—
Issue of the late Lt.-Cdr. Geoffrey Piers St. Aubyn *b.* 1922, *d.* 1964: *m.* 1958, Valerie Elizabeth, who *d.* 1964, only da. of the late Wing-Cdr. B. W. T. Hare, of Curtisknowie, Totnes:—
Michael Piers, *b.* 1959.——Rupert Trelawny, *b.* 1963.——Camilla Elizabeth, *b.* 1961.
Issue of the late Capt. the Hon. Lionel Michael St. Aubyn, MVO, 1st son of 1st Baron, *b.* 1878, *d.* 1965: *m.* 1915, Lady Mary Theresa Parker, who *d.* 1932, da. of the 3rd Earl of Morley:—
Thomas Edward (Tangier House, Wootton St. Lawrence, Basingstoke), *b.* 1923; late Maj. 60th Rifles: *m.* 1953, Henrietta Mary, only da. of Sir Henry Grey Studholme, CVO, MP, 1st Bt., and has issue living, Sarah Elizabeth, *b.* 1955,—Caroline Mary, *b.* 1957,—Judith Clare, *b.* 1962.

(In remainder to the Baronetcy only.)

Grandchildren of the late Col. Edward St. Aubyn (infra):—
Issue of the late Lieut.-Col. Guy Stewart St. Aubyn, O.B.E., *b.* 1870, *d.* 1924 : *m.* 1899, Florita, who *d.* 1925, dau. of the late Pascoe du Pre Grenfell, of Wilton Park, Bucks:—
Barbara Edith, *b.* 1904 : *m.* 1924, Major Donald Victor Charles McBarnet, Scots Guards (Reserve), who *d.* (killed in action during European War) 1944 [E. Mar and Kellie, colls.], and has issue living, Jean Florita, *b.* 1926 : *m.* 1948, William H. Beale, son of Sir Samuel Richard Beale, K.B.E. — Gillian Isabella, *b.* 1932: *m.* 1955, Bernard Cribbins, of Hedgerow, Hamm Court, Weybridge, Surrey. *Residence,*—Kilmeny, Ballantrae, by Girvan, Ayrshire.——Juliet Mary, *b.* 1905: *m.* 1925, William Eustace Pitt Miller, Maj. Grenadier Guards (Reserve) [Quilter, Bt.], and has issue living, Robin Pitt Miller (7, Ripplevale Grove, N1), *b.* 1928; ed. at Eton,—Timothy Hugh Pitt (Albany, W1), *b.* 1937; ed. at Eton. *Residence,*—Foxborough Hall, Melton, nr. Woodbridge, Suffolk.— Violet Susan May, *b.* 1909: *m.* 1929, Raymond Lort-Phillips, Capt. Scots Guards (ret.), and has issue living, Guy Stewart (408, Barkers Rd., Hawthorn, Melbourne, Australia), *b.* 1930; ed. at Eton; late Capt. Welsh Guards: *m.* 1956, Norah Eugenie, da. of Hans Rodolphe de Jenner, of Château de Müri, Berne, Switzerland, and has issue living, Piers Wickham *b.* 1957, Giles Raymond *b.* 1958, Edward St. Aubyn *b.* 1966,—Peregrine Edward Grenfell, *b.* 1937; ed. at Charterhouse, and at Trin. Coll., Camb. (BA Hons); Solicitor 1962: *m.* 1963, Carolyn Diana, only da. of George A. B. Docker, of The Garden Cot, Warborough, Oxon., and has issue living, Penelope Samantha, *b.* 1964, Venetia Nike *b.* 1968,—Anthony Frederick FitzRoy, *b.* 1944; ed. at Eton; late Capt. Gren. Gds.: *m.* 1971, Saranne, da. of J. H. Alexander, of co. Dublin, and formerly wife of 10th Baron Calthorpe. *Residence,*—La Colline, Gorey, Jersey.

Issue of the late Col. Edward Geoffrey St. Aubyn, DSO, *b.* 1880, *d.* 1960: *m.* 1905, Beatrice Rosa Andalusia, who *d.* 1968, da. of J. Audley Harvey, formerly of Ickwell-Bury, Bedfordshire:—
Roger (Domaine de Balthazar, Chemin du Gros Cerveau, 83, Ollioules), *b.* 1906; ed. at Eton, and at London Univ.; formerly Lt. 4th Hussars; MRCS England and LRCP London 1946: *m.* 1st, 1939 (m. diss. 1957), Baroness Sophie Helene, da. of Baron Heinrich von Puthon; 2ndly, 1957 (m. diss. 1968), Lorna, el. da. of Capt. Alastair Mackintosh, and has issue living. (by 1st m.) Lamorna, *b.* 1944: *m.* 1965, David Julian Cotton, Capt. RGJ, TAVR, of 50, Bowerdean St., SW6, and has issue living, Caroline Mary Sophie *b.* 1966,—Diana, *b.* 1945: *m.* 1970, Daniel Romer-Lee, of 8, Stokenchurch St., SW6, and has issue living, Christopher Daniel *b.* 1972, Serena, Isabel Hilaria *b.* 1974,—(by 2nd m) Edward, *b.* 1960,—Alexandra, *b.* 1958.

Issue of the late Col. Edward St. Aubyn, 4th son of 1st baronet, *b.* 1837, *d.* 1914, *m.* 1st, 1866, Edith, who *d.* 1875, dau. of the late Adm. the Hon. Keith Stewart, C.B., son of 8th Earl of Galloway; 2ndly, 1879, Eugenia Susannah, who *d.* 1886, dau. of David Barclay Chapman, of Downshire House, Roehampton, and widow of George Henry FitzRoy; 3rdly, 1891, Ada Mary, who *d.* 1948, dau. of the late Col. Sir Robert Thomas White-Thomson, K.C.B. [Ferguson-Davie, Bt.]:—
(By 3rd m.) Hildegarde Ada, *b.* 1894. —— Bridget Catherine, *b.* 1901: *m.* 1st, 1922, the Rev. Preb. Arthur Gerald Sayer, who *d.* 1971; 2ndly, 1974, Arthur Henry Odell, of Swallowfield House, Dormansland, Lingfield, Surrey, and has issue living (by 1st m.), Julian Honywood ST. AUBYN-SAYER (of Carminow House, Links Rd., Winchester), *b.* 1926; Capt RN; assumed by deed poll 1947 the additional surname of St. Aubyn: *m.* 1953, Hazel Mary, da. of Hope Charles Phipps Tiarks, of Galatura Estate, Ceylon, and has issue living, David Anthony *b.* 1954, Paul Richard *b.* 1956, Mark Julian *b.* 1961, Catherine Mary *b.* 1957,—Madryn Bridget, *b.* 1924: *m.* 1949, Frank Waldron, of 43, Harvey Rd., Croxley Green, Herts., and has issue living, Geoffrey Michael *b.* 1952, John Edward Gerald *b.* 1957, Charles Robert Frank *b.* 1962, Mary Frances Madryn *b.* 1953, Johanna Catherine *b.* 1966.

PREDECESSORS.—[1] EDWARD ST. AUBYN, *b.* 1799; cr. *Baronet* 1866: *m.* 1828, Emma, who *d.* 1887, dau. of Gen. Knollys; *d.* 1872; *s.* by his son [2] JOHN, 2nd Bt.; *b.* 1829; M.P. for Cornwall W. (*L*) 1858-85, and for W., or St. Ives, Div. of Cornwall (*LU*) 1885-7; Mayor of Devonport 1890 and 1891; cr. *Baron St. Levan*, of St. Michael's Mount, Cornwall (peerage of United King-

dom) 1887: *m.* 1856, Lady Elizabeth Clementina Townshend, who *d.* 1910, dau. of 4th Marquess
Townshend: *d.* 1908; *s.* by his son [3] JOHN TOWNSHEND, *C.B.*, *C.V.O.*, 2nd Baron, *b.* 1857; Col.
and Hon. Brig.-Gen. late Grenadier Guards, and Dep. Warden of the Stannaries of Cornwall and
Devon: *m.* 1st, 1892, Lady Edith Hilaria Edgcumbe, who *d.* 1931, da. of 4th Earl of Mount Edgcumbe; 2ndly, 1933, Julia Georgiana Sarah, who *d.* 1938, dau. of Sir George Orby Wombwell, 4th
Bt., and widow of 2nd Earl of Dartrey; *d.* 1940; *s.* by his nephew [4] FRANCIS CECIL (son of the
late Hon. Arthur James Dudley Stuart St. Aubyn, 4th son of 1st Baron), 3rd Baron and present
peer.

ST. OSWALD, BARON. (Winn.) [Baron U.K. 1885.]

All for God and my country.

ROWLAND DENYS GUY WINN, *M.C.*, 4th
Baron; *b.* Sept. 19th, 1916; *s.* 1957; ed. at
Stowe; Capt. and acting Maj. 8th King's R.
Irish Hussars and a DL of W. Riding of Yorks.,
and of York; Hon. Col. 150 (Northumbrian)
Regt. RCT (V), a Lord in Waiting to HM
1959-62, and Joint Parliamentary Sec., Min. of
Agric., Fisheries and Food 1962-64, elected
Pres. of So. of Yorkshiremen in London and
Yorks. So. 1960; Pres. of Yorks Area Young
Conservatives since 1965; Pres. Yorks. Agric.
Soc. 1968, and W. Riding of Yorks. Playing
Fields Assocn. since 1970; Vice-Pres. Anglo-
Polish Soc. since 1969; Pres. Yorks. Region Nat. Soc. for Mentally Handi-
capped Children; Member of European Parl., Strasbourg since 1973; Middle
East 1940-44, SE Asia 1945 (wounded, despatches), Korea 1950-52 (MC
Chevalier of Order of Leopold of Belgium with palm, Croix de Guerre with
palm): *m.* 1st, 1952, Laurian (from whom he obtained a divorce 1955), da. of
Sir (George) Roderick Jones, KBE; 2ndly, 1955, Marie Wanda, yr. da. of the
late Sigismund Jaxa-Chamiec, of Filtrowa, Warsaw, Poland.

Arms.—Ermine, on a fesse vert, three eagles displayed or. Crest,—A demi-eagle or, collared
ermine. Supporters—Two dragons reguardant vert, each gorged with a cord or, and pendant therefrom an escutcheon gules, each charged with a rose argent.

Residences,—Nostell Priory, Wakefield, Yorks.; White Lodge, 12, Gilston Rd., S.W.10.
Clubs,—Cavalry, Garrick, Beefsteak, Pratt's, Press, Special Forces.

BROTHER LIVING.

Hon. DEREK EDWARD ANTHONY, *b.* July 9th, 1919; ed. at Stowe; formerly Lieut. King's
Roy. Rifle Corps (Supplementary Reserve); is Capt. Army Air Corps (Regular Army Reserve);
European War 1939-45 in Middle East and N. Africa (wounded): *m.* 1954, Charlotte Denise Eileen,
only dau. of Wilfrid Haig Loyd [see Oakeley, Bt.], and has issue living, Charles Rowland Andrew,
b. 1959,—Geva Charlotte Caroline, *b.* 1955. *Residence,*—White Lodge, 12, Gilston Rd., SW10.
Clubs,—Lansdowne, White's, Airborne.

UNCLE LIVING. (*Son of 2nd Baron.*)

Hon. Reginald Henry, *b.* 1899; ed. at Eton, and at Ch. Ch., Oxford; formerly Major Grenadier
Guards: *m.* 1924, Alice, dau. of late Moncure Perkins, of Virginia, U.S.A., and has issue
living, Elizabeth Susan, *b.* **1925,—Anne (***Hon. Mrs. Mark H. Wyndham***),** *b.* **1926:** *m* **1947,** Capt.
the Hon. Mark Hugh Wyndham, MC, 12th Roy. Lancers, of Yew Tree Farm, Ascott, Shipston on
Stour, Warwicks. [see B. Egremont]. *Residence,*—Stuart House, Delp St., Sandwich, Kent. *Clubs,*—
White's, Buck's.

WIDOW LIVING OF THIRD BARON.

EVE CAREW (*Eve, Baroness St. Oswald*), dau. of Charles Greene: *m.* 1915, the 3rd Baron, who *d.* 1957.
Residence,—White Lodge, 12, Gilston Road, S.W.10.

WIDOW LIVING OF SON OF SECOND BARON.

Mrs. Theodora Thorpe Dixon, (P.O. Box 1184, Southampton, NY. 11968, USA), da. of Warren Thorpe,
of New York, USA: *m.* 1938, the Hon. Charles John Frederic Winn, who *d.* 1968.

COLLATERAL BRANCH LIVING.

Issue of the late Hon. Charles John Frederic Winn, *b.* 1896, *d.* 1968: *m.* 1st 1919,
the Hon. Olive Cecilia Paget (who *d.* 1974, having obtained a divorce 1925), da. of
1st Baron Queensborough; 2ndly, 1929, Katherine (who obtained a divorce
1938), da. of Henry Van Hevkelom; 3rdly, 1938, Mrs. Theodora Thorpe Dixon
(ante):—
(By 1st m.) Pauline Katharine (2 East 67th St., New York, NY 10021, USA), *b.* 1920: *m.* 1st, 1940 (m.
diss 1947), Group Capt. the Hon. Edward Frederick Ward, RAF [see E. Dudley]; 2ndly, 1948 (m.
diss 1958), Norman Frank Butler; 3rdly, 1960 (m. diss. 1970), Boyd de Brossard; 4thly, 1974,
Edward Lee Cave, and has issue living, (by 2nd m.) Sandra Pauline Whitney, *b.* 1949: *m.* 1972,
Timothy Heise,—Paget, *b.* 1953: *m.* 1970, Baron Ernst von Wedel, and has issue living.——Susan
Mary Sheila, *b.* 1923: *m.* 1st, 1946 (m. diss. 1971), Capt. the Hon. Geoffrey Denis Erskine Russell, late
Irish Guards, now 4th Baron Ampthill; 2ndly, 1972, Lt.-Col. Edward Remington-Hobbs, DSO,
OBE, of 109, Westbourne Terr., W2 6QT,——(by 2nd m.) Michael Peter Anthony (301, East 69th
St., New York, 10021, NY., USA), *b.* 1933: *m.* 1963, Caroline Knowlton Lipscomb, of New York,
and Southport, Conn., USA, and has issue living, Charles Michael Anthony, *b.* 1967.
Issue of the late Hon. Cecil Henry Winn, 5th son of 1st Baron, *b.* 1866, *d.* 1934 :
m. 1913, Alice Marjorie Iris, who *d.* 1964, da. of the late Henry Darley, of
Aldby Park, York:—
Henry John, DSO, MC (Manor House, Aiskew, Bedale, Yorks.), *b.* 1914; Maj. (ret.) R. Northumberland
Fus.; 1939-45 War in Egypt, N. Africa, and Italy (twice wounded, MC), Korea 1950-51 (wounded,
despatches, DSO), Kenya 1954 (despatches); DSO 1951: *m.* 1960, Pamela Sylvia, only da. of Ernest
Charles de Rougemont, C.B.E., and has issue living, Martin John, *b.* 1961, Fiona Jane, *b.* 1962.
Residence,—Home Farm, Habrough, Lincolnshire.——Geoffrey Mark Victor, *b.* 1918; late Capt.
R.E.; European War 1940-45 in N.-W. Europe and S.-E. Asia: *m.* 1958, Alice Alexandra, dau.
of the late Peter Haig Haig-Thomas [E. Normanton], and has issue living, Geoffrey George, *b.*
1966,—Alice Rosemary *b.* 1960,—Iris Alexandra, *b.* 1964. *Residence,*—Aldby Park, Stamford
Bridge, York.

PREDECESSORS.—[1] ROWLAND WINN (el. son of the late Charles Winn, of Nostell Priory,
Yorkshire, and Appleby Hall, Lincolnshire); *b.* 1820; M.P. for N. Lincolnshire (*C*) 1868-85; a
Lord of the Treasury 1874-85; was cr. Baron St. Oswald, of Nostell, co. York (peerage of United
Kingdom) 1885: *m.* 1854, Harriet Maria Amelia, who *d.* 1926, dau. of the late Col. Henry
Dumaresq; *d.* 1893; *s.* by his el. son [2] ROWLAND, 2nd Baron ; *b.* 1857; sat as M.P. for
Pontefract (*C*) 1885-93: *m.* 1892, Mabel Susan, who *d.* 1919, dau. of Sir Charles Forbes, 4th Bt., of
Newe, Aberdeenshire; *d.* **1919;** *s.* **by his son** [3] **ROWLAND GEORGE, 3rd Baron ;** *b.* **1893 ;** Capt.
Coldstream Guards; *m.* **1915, Eve Carew, dan. of Charles Greene:** *d.* **1957 ;** *s.* **by his el. son** [4]
ROWLAND DENYS GUY, 4th Baron, and present peer.

ST. VINCENT, VISCOUNT. (Jervis.) [Viscount U.K. 1801.]

RONALD GEORGE JAMES JERVIS, 7th Viscount; *b.* May 3rd, 1905; *s.* 1940; ed. at Sherborne; is patron of one living; 1939-45 War as acting Lt.-Cdr. R.N.V.R.: *m.* 1945, Constance Phillida Anne, only dau. of the late Lieut.-Col. Robert Hector Logan, O.B.E., late Loyal Regt., and has issue.

Arms,—Sable, a chevron ermine, between three martlets argent. Crest,—Out of a naval coronet or, encircled round the rim by a wreath of laurel vert, a demi-pegasus argent, wings elevated azure, thereon a fleur-de-lis gold. Supporters,—*Dexter*, an eagle, wings elevated, grasping in the left claw a thunderbolt, all proper; *sinister*, a pegasus argent, wings elevated azure, thereon a fleur-de-lis or.

Residence,—Les Charrienes, St. Ouen, Jersey.

SONS LIVING.
Hon. EDWARD ROBERT JAMES, *b.* May 12th, 1951
Hon. Ronald Nigel John, *b.* 1954.

DAUGHTER LIVING.
Hon. Cassandra Phillida Anne, *b.* 1949.

SISTER LIVING.
Hon. Ivy Lorna, *b.* 1895 : *m.* 1920, W. Laurence Whittemore, M.C., and has issue living, a son, *b.* 1928; —a da., *b.* 1926. *Residence,*—St. James, Long Island, Harbour House, NY, USA.

COLLATERAL BRANCHES LIVING.
Issue of the late Col. the Hon. St. Leger Henry Jervis, D.S.O., 5th son of 3rd Viscount, *b.* 1863, *d.* 1952 : *m.* 1905, Hilda Maud, who *d.* 1942, only dau. of the late Thomas Collier :—
Crystal Guina Lucy, *b.* 1906 : *m.* 1st, 1927, Brigadier Thomas James Bolle Bosvile, C.B.E., D.S.O., M.C., Rifle Brig., who *d.* 1945; 2ndly 1946, A. H. MacNab, and has issue living, (by 1st marriage) Thomas Jervis Bolle, *b.* 1932. *Residence,*—Pitminster Lodge, Taunton.——Hilda Violet Ursula, *b.* 1909: *m.* 1934, Lieut.-Col. John Alexander Goschen, OBE, Grenadier Guards (afterwards 3rd Viscount Goschen), who obtained a divorce 1949. *Residence,*—Pitminster Lodge, Taunton, Som.
  Granddaughter of the late Edward John Parker-Jervis, son of the late Hon. Edward Swynfen Parker-Jervis (infra) :—
Issue of the late Edward St. Vincent Parker-Jervis, *b.* 1863; *d.* 1941 : *m.* 1889, Winifred Maria, who *d.* 1915 (having obtained a judicial separation 1898), dau. of Walter Reynolds :—
Grace Winifred, *b.* 1892: *m.* 1947, Gilbert Efward George Devonshire.
  Grandsons of Edward St. Vincent Parker-Jervis (ante) :—
Issue of the late Lieut. St. Vincent John Parker-Jervis, R.N.V.R., *b.* 1891, *d.* 1931 : *m.* 1917, Marianita (of 1869, South Marine Drive, Vancouver 14, British Columbia; she *m.* 2ndly, 19—, John Frederick Harker), younger dau. of the late C. T. Roller, of Burnham, Bucks :—
Antony St. Vincent, *b.* 1919; ed. at Ampleforth Coll.; Capt. Roy. Canadian Horse Artillery: *m.* 1942, Doris Beauchamp, dau. of the late George Beauchamp Taverner, of Winryl, East Close, Middleton-on-Sea, Sussex, and Midhurst, Longwood Drive, Roehampton, S.W., and has issue living, Nicholas St. Vincent (3310, West 8th Av., Vancouver, BC, Canada), *b.* 1943; ed at Univ. of BC (BA) and Oxford (Dip. Ed.): *m.* 1967, Patsy K., da. of Masao Hayashi, of Steveston, BC, Canada, —Antony Leigh, *b.* 1947,—Hilary Anne, *b.* 1950.——Noel John, *b.* 1920: ed. at Ampleforth Coll.; late Lance-Bombadier, Roy. Canadian Artillery: *m.* 1st, 1950 (m. diss. 1954), Jean Mary Columbus; 2ndly, 1956, Betty, third da. of the late Jasper Rutherford, and has issue living, (by 2nd marriage) Jonathan Rutherford, *b.* 1962. *Residence,*—11026, 83rd Av., Edmonton, Alberta.
  Granddaughters of the late Maj. Edward Mainwaring Parker-Jervis, MC, (infra):—
Issue of the late Robert St. Vincent Parker-Jervis, *b.* 1908, *d.* 1973: *m.* 1st, 1936 (m. diss. 1946), Lucy, who *d.* 1966, only da. of Maj. William Edward Burrill, of the Green, Masham, Ripon; 2ndly, 1946, Pamela Violet (Cherrington House, Shipston-on-Stour, Warwicks), da. of the late Capt. Alexander Moore Vandeleur, Life Gds. [By Knaresborough], and formerly wife of Lt.-Col. Lennox John Livingstone-Learmonth, DSO, MC:—
(By 1st m.) Diana Elizabeth, *b.* 1937: *m.* 1958, Roger Parker-Jervis (infra).——(by 2nd m.) Linda, *b.* 1946: *m.* 1970, Capt. Michael Lord, of Dunley Lodge, Odiham, Hants., and has issue living, Simon James Austin, *b.* 1972,—Guy Robert Thomas, *b.* 1974.——Sally Anne, *b.* 1947.——Angela, *b.* 1949.
  Granddaughter of the late William Robert Parker Jervis, 3rd son of the late Hon. Edward Swynfen Parker-Jervis, yst. son of 2nd Viscount:—
Issue of the late Major Edward Mainwaring Parker-Jervis, M.C., *b.* 1880, *d.* 1935: *m.* 1906, Eleanor Dora, who *d.* 1955, dau. of Alfred Charles Lyon, formerly of Albrighton Hall, Albrighton, Salop :—
Rosemary Eleanor, *b.* 1914: *m.* 1940, Brig. Francis Peter Barclay, DSO, MC, late R. Norfolk Regt., and has issue living, Christopher Thomas, *b.* 1946; ed. at Harrow. *Residence,*—Little Dunham Lodge, King's Lynn, Norfolk.
  Grandsons of the late Thomas Swynfen Parker-Jervis, 7th son of the late Hon. Edward Swynfen Parker-Jervis (ante):—
Issue of the late Humphrey Parker-Jervis, *b.* 1889, *d.* 1948: *m.* 1922, Helen Frances (of Brook Cottage, Uley, Dursley, Gloucestershire), dau. of Sir John Ralph Starkey, 1st Bt. :—
John Humphrey (Martens Hall Farm, Longworth, Abingdon, Oxon.), *b.* 1923; ed. at Radley: 1939-45 War as Capt. RE: *m.* 1956, Elizabeth Margaret, da. of Richard Durrant Trotter, of Brin House, Flichity, Inverness, and has issue living, Simon Humphrey, *b.* 1961,—Fiona Mary, *b.* 1965,—Mary Clare, *b.* 1966.——Christopher Thomas (c/o Barclays Bank, 18, Southgate St., Gloucester), *b.* 1929; ed. at Radley; Lt.-Cdr. RN: *m.* 1959, Gillian Bowden, and has issue living, Edward Christopher, *b.* 1960,—William Thomas, *b.* 1965,—Sarah Belinda, *b.* 1967.
  Issue of the late George Parker-Jervis, *b.* 1895, *d.* 1973: *m.* 1924, Ruth Alice (20, Great Hampden, Great Missenden, Bucks.), da. of the late Charles Edward Farmer:—
James (Orchard Hey, Runcton, Chichester, Sussex), *b.* 1926; ed. at Eton; Lt.-Cdr. RN (ret.): *m.* 1956, Sybil Anne, da. of Thomas Prain Douglas Murray, MBE, TD, JP, of Templewood, Brechin, Angus, and widow of the Hon. John Michael Inigo Cross [see V. Cross], and has issue living, Andrew Swynfen, *b.* 1959,—Harriet Anne, *b.* 1957.——Nicholas (The Manor House, South Littleton, Evesham, Worcs.), *b.* 1927; ed. at Eton, and at Magdalene Coll., Camb.: *m.* 1960, Elisabeth Henley, da. of J. T. Morgan, of Llaneinydd, St. Nicholas, Glam., and has issue living, George Rhidian, *b.* 1961,—Thomas Fabyan, *b.* 1974,—Catherine Elizabeth, *b.* 1964.——Roger (Cherington House, Shipston-on-Stour, Warks.), *b.* 1931; ed. at Eton, and Magdalene Coll., Camb.: *m.* 1958, Diana Elizabeth, da. of the late Robert St. Vincent Parker-Jervis (ante), and has issue living, Edward Swynfen, *b.* 1959,—Guy, *b.* 1960,— Lucy Alice, *b.* 1966.

PREDECESSORS.—[1] *Adm. the Rt. Hon. Sir* JOHN Jervis, *G.C.B.*, 2nd son of the late Swynfen Jervis, of Meaford, Staffordshire; *b.* 1734; a celebrated Naval Commander, who in 1797 obtained a splendid victory over the Spanish Fleet at Cape St. Vincent; First Lord of the Admiralty 1801-4; M.P. for Launceston 1783-4, for Great Yarmouth 1784-90, and for Chipping Wycombe 1790-94: *m.* 1783, his cousin, Martha, who *d.* 1816, dau. of the late Rt. Hon. Sir Thomas Parker, Lord Ch. Baron of the Exchequer; *cr. Baron Jervis*, of Meaford, co. Stafford, and *Earl of St. Vincent* (peerage of Great Britain) 1797, and *Viscount St. Vincent*, of Meaford, co. Stafford (peerage of United Kingdom) 1801, with remainder to his nephews, William Henry Ricketts and Edward Jervis Ricketts successively, and after them to his niece Mary, wife of the 7th Earl of Northesk, and her heirs male; *d.* 1823, when the barony and earldom became extinct and the viscountcy devolved upon his surviving nephew [2] EDWARD JERVIS Ricketts, 2nd Viscount; *b.* 1767; assumed by Roy. licence 1823 the surname of Jervis only; *d.* 1859; *s.* by his grandson [3] CARNEGIE ROBERT JOHN, 3rd Viscount; *b.* 1825: *m.* 1848, Lucy Charlotte, who *d.* 1900, dau. of John Baskervyle Glegg, of Withington Hall, Cheshire; *d.* 1879; *s.* by his son [4] JOHN EDWARD LEVESON, 4th Viscount; *b.* 1850; *d.* from wounds received at battle of Abu Klea Jan. 1885; *s.* by his brother [5] CARNEGIE PARKER, 5th Viscount; *b.* 1855: *m.* 1885, Rebecca May (from whom he obtained a divorce 1896), dau. of the late James Baston, of Barrow-in-Furness; *d.* 1908; *s.* by his brother [6] RONALD CLARGES, 6th Viscount; *b.* 1859: *m.* 1894, Marion Annie, who *d.* 1911, dau. of the late James Brown, of Orchard, Carluke, and Petit Menage, Jersey; *d.* 1940; *s.* by his son [7] RONALD GEORGE JAMES, 7th Viscount and present peer.

SALISBURY, LORD BISHOP OF.

Right Rev. GEORGE EDMUND REINDORP, *DD*, son of the late Rev. Hector William Reindorp; *b.* Dec. 19th, 1911; ed. at Felsted, and at Trin. Coll., Camb. (MA); DD Lambeth 1961; D.Univ. Surrey 1970; author of " What About You " 1956, " No Common Task " 1957, " Putting it over—ten points for Preachers " 1961, and " Over to You " 1963; Curate of St. Mary Abbots, Kensington 1937-46, Chap. RNVR 1938-48, V. of St. Stephen's, Rochester Row, with St. Mary, Vincent Square, Westminster 1946-50, St. Andrew's, Ashley Place, Westminster 1948-53, and of St. Stephen's with St. John's, Westminster 1950-57, Commissary, Natal 1948-61, New Guinea 1956, and Cape Town 1958-61, and Provost of Southwark Cathedral, and V. of St. Saviour with All Hallows, Southwark 1957-61; consecrated 5th Bishop of Guildford 1961; translated 100th Bishop of Salisbury 1973; 1939-45 War as Chap. RNVR: *m.* 1943, Alix Violet, da. of Dr. A. D. Edington, of Durban, S. Africa.

Patron of 102 livings, and 34 alternately, the Precentorship, Chancellorship, Treasurership, and Succentorship of his Cathedral, and other Canonries, and Archdeaconries of Dorset, Sarum, Wilts., and Sherborne.

The Bishopric was founded at Sherborne, 705; Wells and Exeter were separated from it in 905; in 1075, it was removed to Old Sarum, and in 1220 to Salisbury.

Episcopal Signature.—George Sarum.

ARMS OF THE SEE,—Azure, Our Lady crowned, holding in her dexter arm the Infant Jesus, and in her sinister a sceptre, all or, round both the heads circles of glory of the last.

Residence,—South Canonry, The Close, Salisbury. *Clubs,*—Ski Club of Great Britain, Kanduhar.

SALISBURY, MARQUESS OF. (Gascoyne-Cecil.) [Marquess G.B. 1789.]

Late, but seriously.

ROBERT EDWARD PETER GASCOYNE-CECIL, 6th Marquess; *b.* Oct. 24th, 1916; *s.* 1972; ed. at Eton; a DL for Dorset; patron of seven livings, Capt. Gren. Gds.; MP for W. Bournemouth (*C*) 1950-54: *m.* 1945, Marjorie Olein, da. of Capt. the Hon. Valentine Maurice Wyndham-Quin, RN [see E. Dunraven], and has issue.

Arms.—Quarterly: 1st and 4th barry of ten argent and azure, over all six escutcheons, three, two, and one, sable, each charged with a lion rampant of the first, a crescent gules for difference *Cecil;* 2nd and 3rd argent, on a pale sable, a conger's head erased and erect or, charged with an ermine spot, *Gascoyne.* **Crests,**—1st, six arrows in saltire or, barbed and feathered argent, banded gules, buckled and garnished gold, surmounted by a morion or steel cap proper; 2nd, a conger's head erased and erect or, charged with an ermine spot. **Supporters,**—On either side a lion ermine.

Seat,—Hatfield House, Hatfield. *Residence,*—Manor House, Cranborne, Dorset.

SONS LIVING.

ROBERT MICHAEL JAMES (*Viscount Cranborne*), (36, Montpelier Sq., SW7), *b.* Sept. 30th, 1946: *m.* 1970, Hannah Ann, da. of Lt.-Col. William Joseph Stirling of Keir [see Stirling-Maxwell, Bt., dormant], and has issue:—

SON LIVING,—*Hon.* Robert Edward William, *b.* 1970.
DAUGHTER LIVING,—*Hon.* Elizabeth Ann, *b.* 1972.
Lord Richard Valentine, *b.* 1948; Capt. Gren. Gds. (despatches 1973).
Lord Charles Edward Vere, *b.* 1949.
Lord Valentine William, *b.* 1952; a Page of Honour to HM Queen Elizabeth The Queen Mother 1966-67.
Lord Michael Hugh, *b.* 1960.

DAUGHTER LIVING.
Lady Rose Alice Elizabeth, *b.* 1956.

UNCLE LIVING (*Son of 4th Marquess*).
Lord (**Edward Christian**) David, *C.H.*, *b.* 1902; ed. at Eton, and at Ch. Ch., Oxford (B.A. 1924,
MA 1927); Hon. LittD Leeds, London and Glasgow; Hon. LLD St. Andrews, and Liverpool; a
Fellow of Wadham Coll., Oxford 1928-31, and of New Coll., Oxford 1938; was a Trustee of National
Portrait Gallery 1935-50; Goldsmith Professor of English Literature, Oxford Univ. 1948-
69; CH 1949: *m.* 1932, Rachel, da. of the late Sir Desmond MacCarthy, and has issue living,
Jonathan Hugh, *b.* 1939; ed. at Eton and New Coll., Oxford: *m.* 1963, Vivien Sarah Frances, el.
da. of David G. Heilbron, of 2, Clevedon Drive, Glasgow, W2,—Hugh Peniston (c/o History Dept.,
Leeds Univ.), *b.* 1941; ed. at Eton, and New Coll., Oxford (BA): *m.* 1972, Mirabel, da. of Richard
Walker of the Close, Withington, Glos., and has issue living, Conrad James Sebastian *b.* 1973, a da.
b. 1975,—Alice Laura, *b.* 1947: *m.* 1975, Angelo Hornak. *Residence,*—Red Lion House, Cranborne,
Dorset. (*Club*)—White's.

AUNTS LIVING (*Daughters of 4th Marquess*).
Lady Beatrice Edith Mildred (*Dowager Baroness Harlech*), *DCVO, b.* 1891; a Lady of the Bedchamber
to H.M. the Queen 1941-46, and an Extra Lady of the Bedchamber 1946-49; an Extra Lady of
the Bedchamber to H.M. Queen Elizabeth the Queen Mother since 1953; DVCO 1947: *m.* 1913,
the 4th Baron Harlech, who *d.* 1964. *Residence,*—14, Ladbroke Rd., W.1.
Lady Mary Alice (*Dowager Duchess of Devonshire*), *G.C.V.O., C.B.E., b.* 1895; Hon. LL.D. Leeds 1954,
and Exeter 1956; Mistress of the Robes to H.M. the Queen 1953-66; Chancellor of Exeter Univ.
1956-70; CBE (Civil) 1946, GCVO 1955: *m.* 1917, the 10th Duke of Devonshire, who *d.* 1950.
Residences,—107, Eaton Sq., SW1; Moorview, Edensor, Bakewell, Derbys.

WIDOW LIVING OF FIFTH MARQUESS.
ELIZABETH VERE (*Elizabeth, Marchioness of Salisbury*), (Hatfield House, Hatfield; Cranborne Lodge,
Cranborne, Dorset; 2, Swan Walk, SW3), da. of the late Col. the Rt. Hon. Lord Richard Frederick
Cavendish, CB, CMG [see D. Devonshire, colls.]: *m.* 1915, the 5th Marquess, who *d.* 1972.

COLLATERAL BRANCHES LIVING.
Issue of the late Rt. Rev. Lord William Rupert Ernest Gascoyne-Cecil, D.D.,
Bishop of Exeter, 2nd son of 3rd Marquess, *b.* 1863, *d.* 1936: *m.* 1887, Lady
Florence Mary Bootle-Wilbraham, who *d.* 1944, dau. of 1st Earl of Lathom:—
Victor Alexander, *b.* 1891; Maj. Hampshire Regt., and a JP and a DL for Essex 1954-68 (High Sheriff
1950); 1914-18 War (twice wounded): *m.* 1915, Stella, da. of the late Lt.-Col. Arthur Watson of
Dublin, and has issue living, Rupert Arthur Victor CECIL, *DFC* (Silverdale, Mill St., Islip,
Oxford), *b.* 1917; MA Oxon 1945, DPh 1942; Wing-Cdr. (ret.) RAFVR; relinquished by deed
poll 1955, the surname of Gascoyne; Vice-Prin. of Linacre Coll., Oxford; 1939-45 War (DFC and
Bar): *m.* 1st, 1940 (m. diss. 1970), Helen Moira Rosemary Phillips, only child of the late Col. Roland
Luker, CMG, MC; 2ndly, 1970, Anna Teresa, da. of Donald Hodson, of 10, Wood Lane, Highgate,
N6 [V. Arbuthnott], and has issue living (by 1st m.) Desmond Hugh (c/o National Westminster Bank,
121, High St., Oxford) *b.* 1941; ed. at Magdalen Coll. Sch., Queen's Coll., Oxford (MA) and Berne
Univ.; First Sec. HM Diplo. Ser. : *m.* 1964, Ruth Elizabeth, da. of Dr. Werner Sachs, of 19, Tides-
well Rd., SW15 (and has issue living, Thomas Desmond *b.* 1966, Nicholas David *b.* 1968, Andrew
Peter *b.* 1971, Sarah Ruth *b.* 1972), Timothy Rupert (c/o Nat. Westminster Bank, 121, High St.,
Oxford), *b.* 1944; ed. at Magdalen Coll. Sch., Exeter Coll., Oxford (MA), and Munich Univ., June
Elizabeth *b.* 1946: *m.* 1968, Michael Durnford Robb, of 24, Claremont Rd., Teddington, Middx. (and
has issue living, Geoffrey Edward *b.* 1972, Joanna Frances *b.* 1970) (by 2nd m.) Flora *b.* 1971, Maud *b.*
1972,—Anthony Robert (of Woodlands, Butts Green, Sandon, Chelmsford, Essex), *b.* 1921: *m.* 1st,
1944, Mary Hood (from whom he obtained a divorce 1951), only da. of the Rev. Ernest James
Simpson, of Great Burstead Vicarage, Billericay, Essex: 2ndly, 1952, Alison Julia, only da. of the
late H. C. Foster, of Little Baddow, Essex, and has issue living, (by 1st m.) Michael Anthony *b.* 1649
Jennifer Mary *b.* 1947, (by 2nd m.) Richard David *b.* 1953, Caroline Alison *b.* 1955, Rosalind Julia
b. 1962. *Residence,*—Green Hanger, Rettendon Common, Chelmsford.——Eve Alice, *b.* 1900: *m.*
1929, Vice-Adm. Richard Benyon, CB, CBE, who *d.* 1968 [see Shelley, Bt., cr. 1611, colls.].
Residence,—The Lamdens, Beenham, Reading.——Mary Edith (twin) (*Mary Baroness Manners*),
b. 1900: *m.* 1921, the 4th Baron Manners who *d.* 1972. *Residence,*—North End House, Avon,
Christchurch, Hants.

Granddaughter of the late Rt. Rev. Lord William Rupert Ernest Gascoyne-Cecil,
D.D., Bishop of Exeter (ante):—
Issue of the late Randle William Gascoyne-Cecil, *b.* 1889, *d.* (killed in action during European
War) 1917: *m.* 1st, 1914, Dorothy Janaway, who *d.* 19—, and from whom he had obtained
a divorce 1916; 2ndly, 1916, Elizabeth Claire, who *d.* 1972, da. of George Turner:—
(By 2nd marriage) Anne Mary (posthumous), *b.* 1918: European War 1939-45 as 2nd Officer W.R.N.S.:
m. 1945, David Bryce Wilson, Lieut.-Com. Roy. Canadian Naval Vol. Reserve, and in Canadian
Foreign Ser., and has issue living, Andrew David Randle, *b.* 1956,—Elizabeth Anne, *b.* 1946,—Carolyn
Susan Mary, *b.* 1948,—Jennifer Laura Eve *b.* 1951,—Deborah Rosalind Louise, *b.* 1952. *Residence,*
—371, Daly Av., Ottawa, 2, Canada.

Issue of the late Col. Lord Edward Herbert Gascoyne-Cecil, K.C.M.G., D.S.O.,
4th son of 3rd Marquess, *b.* 1867, *d.* 1918: *m.* 1894, Violet Georgina [(ante),
who *m.* 2ndly, 1921, the 1st Viscount Milner, who *d.* 1925], dau. of the late
Adm. Frederick Augustus Maxse [see Bs. Berkeley, colls.]:—
Helen Mary (*Helen, Baroness Hardinge of Penshurst*), *b.* 1901: *m.* 1921, the 2nd Baron Hardinge of
Penshurst, who *d.* 1960. *Residence,*—South Park, Penshurst, Kent.

Grandchildren of the late Lieut.-Col. Lord Eustace Brownlow Henry Gascoyne-
Cecil, 3rd son of 2nd Marquess :—
Issue of the late Rt. Hon. Evelyn Cecil, G.B.E., who was cr. Baron Rockley 1934 :—
[See that title.]

Grandchildren of the late Lord Arthur Cecil, 6th son of 2nd Marquess :—
Issue of the late Capt. Arthur William James Cecil, *b.* 1875, *d.* 1906: *m.* 1906, the Hon.
Beatrice Susan Theodosia Stuart-Wortley, who *d.* 1973, da. of 1st Baron Stuart of Wortley
(ext.):—
Robert Arthur, *b.* 1921; ed. at Winchester; formerly Capt. King's Roy. Rifle Corps. *Residence,*—
11 Duke St., W1.——Mary Elizabeth, *b.* 1908: *m.* 1935, Noel Charles Douglas Wilkey, formerly
Capt. RA, who *d.* 1970, and has issue living, Caroline Margaret, *b.* 1938: *m.* 1960, Michael Christopher
Keith Oldridge, of Sedgewell House, Sonning Common, Reading, and has issue living, Timothy
James Ross *b.* 1963, Dominic Robert John *b.* 1965, Lucy Mary *b.* 1966. *Residence,*—Crabapples,
High St., Whitchurch, Reading.

PREDECESSORS.—[1] *Rt. Hon. Sir* ROBERT Cecil, *K.G., P.C.,* younger son of William Cecil,
1st Baron Burghley [see M. Exeter]; was Sec. of State 1596-1612, Chancellor of Duchy of Lancaster 1597-9, Lord Privy Seal 1597-1612, and Lord High Treasurer 1608-12; *cr. Baron Cecil,* of

Essendon, co. Rutland (peerage of England) 1603, *Viscount Cranborne* (peerage of England, 1604, and *Earl of Salisbury* (peerage of England) 1605 ; *d.* 1612 ; *s.* by his son [2] WILLIAM, *K.G.*, 2nd Earl ; *d.* 1668 ; *s.* by his grandson [3] JAMES, *K.G.*, 3rd Earl ; *d.* 1683 ; *s.* by his son [4] JAMES, 4th Earl ; having become a convert to the Roman Catholic faith the House of Commons in 1689 resolved that he be impeached for high treason, but the prosecution was not proceeded with ; *d.* 1694 ; *s.* by his son [5] JAMES, 5th Earl ; carried King Edward's staff at the coronation of George I. ; *d.* 1728 ; *s.* by his son [6] JAMES, 6th Earl ; *d.* 1780 ; *s.* by his son [7] JAMES, *K.G.*, 7th Earl ; cr. *Marquess of Salisbury* (peerage of Great Britain) 1789 ; sat as M.P. for Bedwin ; was Lord Chamberlain of the Household 1783-1804, and Lord-Lieut. of Herts ; *d.* 1823 ; *s.* by his son [8] JAMES BROWNLOW, *K.G.*, *P.C.*, *D.C.L.*, 2nd Marquess ; *b.* 1791 ; was Lord Pres. of the Council 1858-9, and Lord-Lieut. of Middlesex ; in 1821 assumed by Roy. licence the additional surname of Gascoyne : *m.* 1st, 1821, Frances Mary, dau. and heir of the late Bamber Gascoyne ; 2ndly, 1847, Lady Mary Catherine Sackville-West, dau. of 5th Earl Delawarr ; *d.* 1868 ; *s.* by his second son [9] ROBERT ARTHUR TALBOT, *K.G.*, *G.C.V.O.*, *P.C.*, 3rd Marquess ; *b.* 1830 ; M.P. for Stamford (*C*) 1853-68 ; Sec. of State for India 1866-7 and 1874-8, and for Foreign Affairs 1878-80, Special Ambassador at Conference on Eastern Affairs held at Constantinople 1876-7, 2nd Plen. for Great Britain at Congress of Berlin 1878, Prime Minister and Sec. of State for Foreign Affairs June 1885 to Feb. 1886, Prime Minister and First Lord of the Treasury June 1886 to Jan. 1887, Prime Minister and Sec. of State for Foreign Affairs Jan. 1887 to Aug. 1892, and again Prime Minister and Sec. of State for Foreign Affairs June 1895 to Nov. 1900, and Prime Minister and Lord Privy Seal 1900-1902 : *m.* 1857, Georgina, *C.I.*, *V.A.*, who *d.* 1899, dau. of the late Hon. Sir Edward Hall Alderson, a Baron of the Court of Exchequer ; *d.* 1903 ; *s.* by his son [10] JAMES EDWARD HUBERT, *KG*, *GCVO*, *CB*, *PC*, 4th Marquess ; *b.* 1861 ; sometime High Steward of Westminster and Hertford ; served in Herts Yeo., Bedfordshire Regt. (T.A.), and R.A. (T.A.), becoming Maj.-Gen. ; S. Africa 1900 (despatches, C.B.) ; was Under-Sec. of State for Foreign Affairs 1900-1903, Lord Privy Seal 1903-5, Lord Privy Seal and Pres. of Board of Trade 1905, and Lord Pres. of the Council and Dep. Leader of the House of Lords (also temporary Chancellor of the Duchy of Lancaster) 1922-4, and again Lord Privy Seal 1924-9 (also Leader of the House of Lords 1925-9, and of Opposition 1929-31) ; appointed Lord High Steward 1937 ; bore St. Edward's Crown at Coronation of King George VI. ; sat as M.P. for Darwen Div. of N.-E. Lancashire (*C*) 1885-92 and for Rochester 1893-1903 : *m.* 1887, Lady Cicely Alice Gore, who *d.* 1955, second da. of 5th Earl of Arran ; *d.* 1947 ; *s.* by his son [11] ROBERT ARTHUR JAMES, *KG*, *PC*, 5th Marquess *b.* 1893 ; MP for S. Dorset (*C*) 1929-41 ; called to House of Lords in his father's Barony of Cecil 1941 ; Sec. of State for Dominions Affairs 1940-42, and 1943-45, for Colonies 1942 and for Commonwealth Relations 1952, Lord Privy Seal 1942-43 and 1951-52, and Lord Pres. of the Council 1952-57 ; Leader of House of Lords 1942-43 and 1951-57 ; Chancellor Liverpool Univ. 1951-71 ; Chancellor of Order of the Garter 1960-72 : *m.* 1915, Elizabeth Vere, da. of the late Col. The Rt. Hon. Lord Richmond Frederick Cavendish, CB, CMG [D. Devonshire] ; *d.* 1972 ; *s.* by his son [12] ROBERT EDWARD PETER, 6th Marquess and present peer ; also Earl of Salisbury, Viscount Cranborne, and Baron Cecil.

SALMON, BARON. (Salmon.) [Life Baron 1972.]

CYRIL BARNET SALMON, *PC*, son of the late Montagu Salmon ; *b.* Dec. 28th, 1903 ; ed. at Mill Hill Sch., and Pembroke Coll., Camb. (MA ; Hon. Fellow 1965) ; Bar Middle Temple 1925, KC 1945, Bencher 1953, and Treas. 1972 ; Recorder of Gravesend 1947-57, a Judge of High Court (Queen's Bench Div.) 1957-64, and a Lord Justice of Appeal 1964-72, since when a Lord of Appeal in Ordinary ; JP for Kent ; 1939-45 War with 8th Army in Italy ; cr. Knt., 1957, PC 1964, and *Baron Salmon,* of Sandwich, co. Kent, 1972 : *m.* 1st, 1929, Rencie, who *d.* 1942, da. of the late Sydney Gorton Vanderfelt, OBE ; 2ndly, 1946, Jean Beatrice, el. da. of the late Lt.-Col. David Edward Maitland-Makgill-Crichton [see E. Lauderdale, colls.], and formerly wife of 2nd Baron Morris, who *d.* 1975, and has issue by 1st m.

Arms—Per chevron gules and ermine, in chief two horses rampant argent, and in base a sword erect gules, hilt and pommel or a chief gold. **Crest**—A bundle of sticks proper bound by a riband pendent therefrom a hexagram interlaced or. **Supporters**—*Dexter,* a lion rampant ; *Sinister,* an Alsatian wolfdog proper ; each resting the exterior foreleg on a bundle of sticks also proper by a riband or.

Residences,—1, Melina Place, NW8 ; The Old Drum, Sandwich, Kent.   *Clubs,*—St. James', Athenaeum.

SON LIVING   (*By* 1st *m.*)

Hon. David Neville Cyril (Holne Cott., Holne, nr. Ashburton, Devon), *b.* 1935 : *m.* 1st, 1958 (m. diss. 1972), Heather Turner-Laing ; 2ndly, 1973, Sarah Harrison.

DAUGHTER LIVING   (*By* 1st *m.*)

Hon. Gai Rencie, *b.* 1933 : *m.* 1st 1955, Martin Treves, who *d.* 1970 ; 2ndly, 1974, Geoffrey Robinson of Flass Hall, Esh Winning, co. Durham.

Saltersford, Baron, title of Earl of Courtown on Roll of H.L.

SALTOUN, LORD. (Fraser.) [Lord S. 1445.]

[Title pronounced "Salton."]

ALEXANDER ARTHUR FRASER, *M.C.*, 19th Lord; *b.* March 8th, 1886; *s.* 1933; ed. at Eton; a Representative Peer for Scotland 1935-63; Capt. (ret.), Hon. Maj. Gordon Highlanders; CA Edinburgh; a Member of Roy. Co. of Archers (Queen's Body Guard for Scotland); 1914-18 War (prisoner, MC): *m.* 1920, Dorothy Geraldine, da. of Sir Charles Glynne Earle Welby, 5th Bt, CB, and has issue.

Arms,—Quarterly: 1st azure, three cinquefoils argent, *Fraser;* 2nd or, a lion rampant gules, surmounted by a bend dexter sable, *Abernethy;* 3rd gules, three lions rampant argent, *Ross;* 4th argent, three piles gules, *Wishart.* **Crest,**—An ostrich with a horseshoe in its beak, all proper. **Supporters,**—Two angels wings expanded and endorsed proper, vested in flowing white garments.

Residence,—Cross Deep, Twickenham. *Clubs,*—Athenæum, New (Edinburgh).

DAUGHTER LIVING.

Hon. FLORA MARJORY, *b.* Oct. 18th, 1930: *m.* 1956, Capt. Alexander Arthur Alphonso David Maule Ramsay of Mar, Grenadier Guards (ret.) [see E. Dalhousie, colls.], and has issue living, Katharine Ingrid Mary Isabel FRASER, *b.* 1957,—Alice Elizabeth Margaret RAMSAY, *b.* 1961,—Elizabeth Alexandra Mary RAMSAY, *b.* 1963. *Residence,*—Cairnbulg Castle, Fraserburgh, Aberdeenshire, AB4 5TH.

WIDOW LIVING OF SON OF EIGHTEENTH LORD.

Margaret Elizabeth (Lanquedoc, Firgrove, Cape Province), da. of Reginald Barnes, of St. Ermin's, Westminster: *m.* 1934, as his second wife, Rear Adm. the Hon. George Fraser, DSO, RN, who *d.* 1970, and has issue living [see colls., infra].

COLLATERAL BRANCHES LIVING.

Issue of the late Rear Adm. the Hon. George Fraser, DSO, RN, 2nd son of 18th Lord, *b.* 1887, *d.* 1970: *m.* 1st, 1920, Elizabeth FRASER SPENCER STANHOPE, da. of *d.* 1964, having assumed by Roy. licence 1945, the additional surnames of Spencer Stanhope, da. of the late John Montague Spencer-Stanhope [Milborne-Swinnerton-Pilkington, Bt., colls.]; 2ndly, 1934, Margaret Elizabeth (ante), da. of Reginald Barnes, of St. Ermin's, Westminster:—

(By 1st m.) Simon Walter (Invercreran, Appin, Argyllshire; New Club), *b.* 1924; ed. at Eton: *m.* 1st, 1950 (m. diss. 1962), Jean Madeline Frances, da. of the late Prof. John Masson Gulland, FRS, of 8, Great Stuart St., Edinburgh; 2ndly, 1962 (m. diss. 1971), Yvonne, da. of Edwin Valère Newby; 3rdly, 1971, Cheryl Mary Eleanor, da. of David McNeil Williams of Summerfield House, Cheshire, and formerly wife of Richard Charles Sheffield [see Sheffield, Bt., colls.], and has issue living (by 1st m.) Isabel Madeline, *b.* 1951,—Elspeth Caroline, *b.* 1954,—(by 2nd m.) Alistair John, *b.* 1963,—Deborah Gail, *b.* 1965,—(by 3rd m.) James David, *b.* 1971,—William Alexander, *b.* 1972.——(by 2nd m.) Robert Andrew Gerard (Stennis, Somerset West, Cape Province), *b.* 1935: *m.* 1964, Sarah Elizabeth, da. of Brig. Gerald Edward Peck, OBE, DSO, and has issue living, David Alexander George, *b.* 1966,—Fiona Elizabeth, *b.* 1965.——Patrick George (Lanquedoc, Figrove, Cape Province), *b.* 1938.

Issue of the late Brig. the Hon. William Fraser, DSO, MC, yst. son of 18th Lord, *b.* 1890, *d.* 1964: *m.* 1919, Pamela Cynthia who *d.* 1975, da. of the late Cyril Francs Maude [see V. Hawarden, colls.], and widow of Maj. William La Touche Congreve, VC, DSO, MC:—

Sir David William, *KCB, OBE* (Vallenders, Isington, Alton, Hants.; Turf and Pratt's Clubs), *b.* 1920; Lt.-Gen. late Gren. Gds.; ed. at Eton, and Ch. Ch., Oxford; 1939-45 War; Cyprus 1958, Cameroun 1961, and Borneo 1964; GOC 4th Div. 1969-71, Asst. Ch. of Defence Staff 1971-73, since when Vice-Ch. of Gen. Staff; OBE (Mil.) 1952, KCB (Mil) 1973: *m.* 1st, 1947 (m. diss. 1952), Anne, da. of the late Brig. Edward William Sturgis Balfour, CVO, DSO, OBE, MC [E. Balfour]; 2ndly, 1957, Julia Frances Oldridge, da. of the late Maj. C. James Oldridge de la Hey, and has issue living, (by 1st m.) Antonia Isabella, *b.* 1949,—(by 2nd m.) Alexander James, *b.* 1960,—Simon William David, *b.* 1963,—Arabella Katharine, *b.* 1958,—Lucy Caroline, *b.* 1965.

Issue of the late Hon. Mary Alexandra Fraser, da. of 18th Lord, *b.* 1892, *d.* 1969: *m.* 1st, 1918, Lt.-Cdr. John Robert Auber Codrington, RN, who *d.* 1918 [V. Hambleden]; 2ndly, 1928, Maj. Arthur Balcarres Wardlaw Ramsay, DL, JP [B. Magheramorne, colls.], who *d.* 1956:—

(By 2nd m.) Euphan Mary, *b.* 1931: *m.* 1955, Richard Hanbury-Tenison, of Bryngwyn Manor, Raglan, Mon., and Lough Bawn, co. Monaghan, and has issue living, John Wardlaw, *b.* 1957,—William Ayscough, *b.* 1962,—Capel Thomas, *b.* 1965,—Sarah, *b.* 1956,—Laura Mary, *b.* 1966.——Elizabeth Mary, *b.* 1934: *m.* 1955, Simon Anthony Helyar Walker-Heneage, of Coker Court, Yeovil, Som., and the Raswell, Loxhill, Godalming, Surrey, and has issue living, James, *b.* 1957,—Celia, *b.* 1956,—Arabella, *b.* 1959,—Sophie, *b.* 1962,—Sarah Phoebe, *b.* 1974.

PREDECESSORS.—[1—6] *Sir* LAURENCE Abernethy; cr. *Lord Saltoun*, of Abernethy (peerage of Scotland) 1445, and the title passed in regular succession for five generations; in 1587 the 6th Lord was *s.* by his son [7] GEORGE, 7th Lord; *s.* by his son [8] JOHN, 8th Lord; *s.* by his son [9] ALEXANDER, 9th Lord; *d.s.p.* 1668; *s.* by his cousin [10] ALEXANDER, 10th Lord, son of Margaret, dau of, 7th Lord by her marriage with Alexander Fraser, of Philorth; title confirmed by patent 1670 and ratified by Parliament; wounded at battle of Worcester; *d.* 1693; *s.* by his grandson [11] WILLIAM, 11th Lord; *d.* 1716; *s.* by his son [12] ALEXANDER, 12th Lord; *d.* 1748; *s.* by his el. son [13] ALEXANDER, 13th Lord; *d.* unmarried 1751; *s.* by his brother [14] GEORGE, 14th Lord; *d.* 1782; *s.* by his son [15] ALEXANDER, 15th Lord; *d.* 1793; *s.* by his son [16] ALEXANDER GEORGE, 16th Lord; a Lieut.-Gen. in the Army, and Representative Peer; *d.s.p.* 1853; *s.* by his nephew [17] ALEXANDER, 17th Lord, son of the Hon. William, 3rd son of 15th Lord; was a

Representative Peer : *m.* 1849, Charlotte, 2nd dau. of Thomas Browne Evans, Esq., of Dean House, Oxfordshire ; *d.* Jan. 31st, 1886 ; *s.* by his son [18] ALEXANDER WILLIAM FREDERICK, *C.M.G.*, 18th Lord : *b.* 1851 ; a Representative Peer for Scotland, and Capt. King's Body Guard for Scotland (Roy. Co. of Archers) : *m.* 1885, Mary Helena, who *d.* 1940, sister of Sir Henry Christopher Grattan-Bellew, 3rd Bt.; *d.* 1933 ; *s.* by his el. son [19] ALEXANDER ARTHUR, 19th Lord and present peer.

SAMUEL, VISCOUNT. (Samuel.) [Viscount U.K. 1937.]

EDWIN HERBERT SAMUEL, *C.M.G.*, 2nd Viscount; *b.* Sept. 11th, 1898; *s.* 1963; ed. at Westminster, and at Balliol Coll., Oxford (B.A. 1920); 1914-18 War as 2nd Lieut. R.F.A.; in Palestine Civil Ser. 1920-48; Dir. of Broadcasting, Palestine 1945-48, and visiting Prof. at Inst. for Israel and Middle East, Dropsie Coll., Philadelphia, USA 1948-49, and at Graduate Sch. of Public Affairs State Univ. of New York at Albany, 1963, visiting lecturer, Univ. of Witwatersrand 1955; Prin. of Inst. of Public Administration, Israel since 1945; Senior Lecturer in British Institutions at Hebrew Univ. 1954-69, Sen. Mellon Fellow Grad. Sch. of Public and Internat. Affairs, Pittsburgh, Univ. 1970, Dir. of *Jewish Chronicle* 1957-70, of Ellern's Investment Corpn., Tel Aviv since 1964, of Vallentine Mitchell (publishers) since 1965, and of Moller Textile Corporation, Haifa since 1965; CMG 1947: *m.* 1920, Hadassah, da. of Judah Goor, of Tel Aviv, Palestine, and has issue.

Arms.—Or, a bend between two caps of liberty gules, on a chief sable a balance of the first. **Crest,**—In front of a sun rising or a dove wings elevated and addorsed, holding in the beak an olive branch proper. **Supporters,**—On either side a lion or, the *dexter* gorged with a collar gules and resting the interior hind leg on a stump of oak eradicated and sprouting proper; the *sinister* gorged with an Eastern Crown also gules and resting the interior hind leg on a stump of olive eradicated and sprouting also proper.
Residence,—15, Rashba Rd., Jerusalem, Israel. *Address,*—c/o House of Lords, S.W.1.

SONS LIVING.

Hon. DAVID HERBERT (c/o Isotope Dept., Weizmann Institute of Science, Rehovot, Israel), *b.* July 8th, 1922; ed. at Balliol Coll., Oxford (MA); PhD Hebrew Univ., Jerusalem 1953; Sherman Prof. of Physical Chemistry, and Dean, Faculty of Chemistry Weizmann Institute, Rehovot, Israel; Research Fellow, Harvard Univ., Camb., Mass., USA 1957-58; Dep. Chm. Lawrence Radiation Laboratory Univ. of California, Berkeley 1965-66; Dep. Chm. of Scientific Council 1963-65, a member of Board, Israel Science Teaching Centre since 1967, and of Israel Centre for Psychobiology since 1971; 1939-45 War as Capt. RA (despatches): *m.* 1st, 1950 (m. diss. 1957), Esther, da. of the late J. Berelowitz, of Cape Town, S. Africa; 2ndly, 1960, Mrs. Rinna Dafni, da. of the late Meir Grossman, of Herzliyah, Israel, and has issue living, (by 1st m.) Judith, *b.* 1951,—(by 2nd m.) Naomi Rachel, *b.* 1962.

Hon. Dan Judah (39, Carlyle Sq., SW3), *b.* 1925; ed. at Rugby, and at Balliol Coll., Oxford (MA) formerly Maj. Yorkshire Hussars; with Sch. of Advanced Intern. Studies, Wash. 1950-51; Gen. Manager of Shell Co. of Thailand 1962-66, with Shell Oil Co., New York 1966-67, Pres. of Belgian Shell Co. 1967-70, Gen. Man., Regional Marketing, Shell International Chemical Co., London, 1971-72, since when Marketing Co-ordinator (Oil), and Dir. of Shell International Petroleum Co.; Chm. Board of Management SEATO Graduate Sch. of Eng., Bangkok 1963-66, and UK Trustee of Asian Inst. of Technology 1966-68, and since 1973; Cdr. of Order of Roy. Crown of Thailand; Officer Order of Crown of Belgium: *m.* 1957, Nonni (Esther), da. of the late Max Gordon, of Johannesburg, S. Africa, and has issue living, Jonathan Herbert, *b.* 1955,—Lia Miriam, *b.* 1961,—Maia Tessa, *b.* 1963.

BROTHERS LIVING.

Hon. Philip Ellis Herbert, *b.* 1900; ed. at Westminster, and at Trin. Coll., Camb.; 1939-45 War with Hong Kong Vol. Defence Corps (prisoner). *Clubs,*—Royal Institution, Royal Overseas League, Victory Ex-Services.
Hon. Godfrey Herbert, *CBE, b.* 1904; ed. at Westminster, and Balliol Coll., Oxford (B.A. 1926, M.A. 1947); Hon. Lieut.-Col. R. E., F.R.I.B.A. (ret.); an Asso. of Town Planning Inst.; Sec. of Roy. Fine Art Commn. 1948-69; 1939-45 War; CBE (Civil) 1969. *Residence,*—15, Hans Place, SW1. *Clubs,*—Athenæum, Reform.

SISTER LIVING.

Hon. Nancy Adelaide, *b.* 1906: ed. at Oxford Univ. (B.A. 1928, M.A. 1955): *m.* 1935, Arthur Gabriel Salaman, MB, BCh, MRCS, LRCP, and has issue living, John Redcliffe (25, Heol. Don, Whitchurch, Cardiff), *b.* 1937; ed. at Bedales, and at Clare Coll., Camb. (MA), MB, MChir, FRCS: *m.* 1961, Patricia Faith, da. of Edward G. Burkett,—William Herbert (41, Avenue Rd., Wimborne, Dorset), *b.* 1940; ed. at Bedales, and at Clare Coll., Camb. (BA): *m.* 1963, Alison Spears, da. of Dr. Phillippe Sidney de Quetteville Cabot,—Susan Caroline, *b.* 1936: *m.* 1960, Reginald Valentine Clery,— Juliet Miriam, *b.* 1942: *m.* 1961, Reuben Selek. *Residence,*—1, Belmont Hill, Newport, Saffron Walden, Essex.

PREDECESSOR.—[1] *Sir* HERBERT LOUIS SAMUEL, *G.C.B., O.M., G.B.E., P.C.,* son of the late Edwin Louis Samuel, of Claremont, Prince's Park, Liverpool, and 9, Kensington Gore, S.W., banker; *b.* 1870; Under-Sec. of State for Home Dept. 1905-9, Chancellor of Duchy of Lancaster, 1909-10, Postmaster Gen. 1910-14, Pres. of Local Govt. Board 1914-16, again Postmaster Gen. 1915, again Chancellor of Duchy of Lancaster 1915-16, Sec. of State for Home Dept. 1916, British Special Commr. to Belgium 1919, High Commr. for Palestine 1920-25, again Sec. of State for Home Dept. 1931-2; M.P. for Cleveland Div., N. Riding of Yorks (*L*) 1902-18, and for Darwen Div. of Lancs. 1929-35; Chm. Liberal Party Organization 1917-29, Leader of Liberal Parliamentary Party 1931-35, and Dep. Leader of Liberal Party in the House of Lords 1941-4, and Leader 1944-55; cr. *Viscount Samuel,* of Mount Carmel and of Toxteth, City of Liverpool (peerage of U.K.) 1937: *m.* 1897, Beatrice, who *d.* 1959, youngest dau. of the late Ellis Abraham Franklin; *d.* 1963; *s.* by his el. son [2] EDWIN HERBERT, and Viscount and present peer.

SAMUEL OF WYCH CROSS, BARON. (Samuel.) [Life Baron 1972.]

HAROLD SAMUEL, son of the late Vivian Samuel; *b.* April 23rd, 1912; ed. at Mill Hill, and Coll. of Estate Management; FRICS; Hon. Fellow of Magdalene Coll., Camb. since 1961, and Univ. Coll., London since 1968; Chm. of The Land Securities Investment Trust Ltd., and of The Central London Housing Trust for the Aged; a Dir. of Railway Sites, Ltd. (British Rail) 1962-65; a Vice-Pres. of British Heart Foundation; a Member of Covent Garden Market Authority 1961-74, of the Land Commn. 1967-70, of Reserve Pension Board 1974, of Court of Patrons, Roy. Coll. of Surgs., of Courts Sussex Univ., Univ. Coll., Swansea, and City Univ. of Special (Rebuilding) Cttee. of The Roy. Instn. of Chartered Surveyors, and of Crown Estate Commrs. Regent St. Cttee., and a Trustee of Mill Hill Sch.; *cr.* Knt. 1963, and *Baron Samuel of Wych Cross,* of Wych Cross, co. Sussex (Life Baron) 1972: *m.* 1936, Edna, da. of Harry Nedas, of London, and has issue.

Arms.—Argent, a bend gules masoned or, between two masons' trowels bendwise proper, on a chief vert a balance or. **Crest**—In front of a demi sun or, a house martin wings addorsed proper. **Supporters**—On either side an old man proper bearded in flowing robes argent and shod with sandals that to the dexter holding in the exterior hand a horn of ointment proper, lid and virols or, that to the sinister holding beneath the exterior arm two scrolls proper.
Residences,—75, Avenue Rd., Regent's Park, NW8; Wych Cross Place, Forest Row, Sussex. *Club,* —Devonshire.

DAUGHTERS LIVING.

Hon. Carole, *b.* 1942: *m.* 1963, Geoffrey Clive Henry Lawson, of Innisfree, Woodland Drive, East Horsley, Surrey.
Hon. Marion, *b.* 1944: *m.* 1964, Guy Anthony Naggar, of 61, Avenue Rd., NW8.

SANDERSON OF AYOT, BARONY OF. (Sanderson.) [Baron U.K. 1960, disclaimed 1971.]

ALAN LINDSAY SANDERSON, *b.* Jan. 12th, 1931; *s.* as 2nd Baron Aug. 15th, 1971, disclaimed his peerage for life Sept. 28th, 1971; ed. at Uppingham; MB, BS London; MRCP London: *m.* 1959, Gertrud, da. of Herman Bocshsler, and has issue.

Arms,—Paly of six argent and azure on a bend sable a mullet of the first between two annulets or. **Crest,**—A talbot passant argent pied and eared sable resting the dexter forepaw on an annulet or. **Supporters,**—(borne by Barons Sanderson of Ayot). On either side a talbot sejant erect argent pied and eared sable.

Residence,—2, Caroline Close, W2.

SON LIVING.

Hon. MICHAEL, *b.* Dec. 6th, 1959.

DAUGHTERS LIVING.

Hon. Evelyn, *b.* 1961.
Hon. Frances, *b.* 1963.
Hon. Andrea, *b.* 1964.
Hon. Stephanie, *b.* 1970.

BROTHER LIVING.

Hon. Murray Lee (twin) (PO Box 2253, Kitwe, Zambia), *b.* 1931; ed. at Rugby, at Trin. Coll., Oxford, and at King's Coll., Camb.; a Co. Dir.; Admin. Officer, Kenya, 1956-63: *m.* 1st, 1966 (m. diss. 1972) Muriel, da. of the late George Williams; 2ndly, 1973, Eva, da. of the Rev David Simfukwe, and has issue living, (by 2nd m.) Basil, *b.* 1974.

SISTER LIVING.

Hon. Pauline Maud, *b.* 1929; MA Oxford; Dr. de l'Université de Paris:*m.* 1952, Robert Henry Matarasso, of Church Hill Farm, Burton Dassett, Leamington Spa, and has issue living, Pascale, *b.* 1955,—Antoine, *b.* 1957,—François, *b.* 1958,—Veronique, *b.* 1964.

PREDECESSOR.—[1] BASIL Sanderson, *MC,* son of Harold Arthur Sanderson, of Jenkyn Place, Bentley, Hants.; *b.* 1894; Dir. of Shipping in Port, Min. of Shipping 1939-41, Head of Port Transit Control, Min. of War Transport 1941-45, and Man. Dir. of Shaw Sevill & Albion Co., Ltd. 1945-59, and Chm. 1947-63; *cr. Baron Sanderson of Ayot,* of Welwyn, co. Hertford (peerage of UK) 1960: *m.* 1927, Evelyn Constance, who *d.* 1940, da. of Joseph Bruce Ismay, of Costelloe, co. Galway, and London; *d.* 1971; *s.* by his el. son [2] ALAN LINDSAY, 2nd Baron, until he disclaimed his peerage, 1971.

SANDFORD, BARON. (Edmondson.) [Baron U.K. 1945.]

Rev. JOHN CYRIL EDMONDSON, *DSC*, 2nd Baron; *b.* Dec. 22nd, 1920; *s.* 1959; ed. at Eton; Cdr. RN (ret.); 1939-45 War with Eastern Med. Fleet, Allied Landings in N. Africa, Sicily and Normandy (DSC); on Staff of C-in-C. Far East 1951-53, and Cdr. Home Fleet Flagships 1955-56; Curate of St. Nicholas, Harpenden, 1958-63; Exec. Chap. to Bishop of St. Albans 1965-68; Conservative Whip, House of Lords 1966-68; a Parl. Sec., Min. of Housing and Local Govt. June to Oct. 1970, and a Parl. Under-Sec. of State Dept. of Environment 1970-73, and of Dept. of Education and Science 1973-74; Chm. of Herts. Council of Social Ser. 1966-69, of Westminster Council of Social Ser. 1969-70, and of Church Army Board 1969-70: *m.* 1947, Catharine Mary, da. of the Rev. Oswald Andrew Hunt, and has issue.

Arms,—Azure, a cross couped and pointed between, in chief two lions combatant, and in base as many swans, wings elevated and addorsed respectant, all or. Crest,—In front of a portcullis or a dexter arm embowed in armour fessewise, the hand clenched proper. Supporters,—On either side a pikeman of Honourable Artillery Company armed and accoutred supporting with the exterior hand a pike erect proper, the dexter charged with a portcullis chained or, and the sinister with an oak tree eradicated and fructed also proper, the trunk pierced by three arrows or flighted azure (the badge of the Edmondson family).

Residence,—6, Smith Sq., SW1. *Club,*—Ski Club of Great Britain.

SONS LIVING.
Hon. JAMES JOHN MOWBRAY (103, North Warwick Av., Burnaby, BC, Canada), *b.* July 1st, 1949; ed. at Eton, and York Univ.; school teacher: *m.* 1973, Ellen Sarah, da. of Jack Shapiro, of Toronto.
Hon. Nicholas Mark, *b.* 1956; ed. at Eton.

DAUGHTERS LIVING.
Hon. Margaret Catharine, *b.* 1947; ed. at Downe House Sch., and Trin. Coll., Dublin; social worker.
Hon. Frances Mary, *b.* 1953; ed. at Downe House Sch., and Bristol Univ.

BROTHER LIVING.
Hon. Anthony James Kinghorn (Upton Manor, East Knoyle, Salisbury, Wilts.), *b.* 1924; ed. at Eton and Harvard Univ.; Capt. (ret.) Grenadier Guards: *m.* 1st, 1947 (m. diss. 1959), Olivia Charlotte, yst. da. of the late Rev. Oswald Andrew Hunt; 2ndly, 1969, Hilary Pauline, da. of Lt.-Col. Edward Shirley Trusler, OBE, and has issue living (by 1st m.), Charles Anthony, *b.* 1949,—Simon Andrew, *b.* 1955,—Anthony James, *b.* 1957,—Elizabeth Anne, b. 1951,—(by 2nd m.), Rupert James Kinghorn, *b.* 1972.

PREDECESSOR.—[1] *Sir* ALBERT JAMES Edmondson, son of the late James Edmondson, of Weston, Herts.; *b.*1886 ; Major Hon. Artillery Co.; Parliamentary Private Sec. to Min. of Pensions 1924-29 and 1931-34, an Assist. Govt. Whip 1937, a Junior Lord of the Treasury 1939, Vice-Chamberlain of H.M.'s Household 1939, Treasurer of H.M.'s Household 1942-5, Dep. Ch. Whip 1942-5, and High Steward of Banbury 1947 ; sat as M.P. for Banbury Div. of Oxfordshire (*C*) 1922-45 ; cr. *Baron Sandford,* of Banbury, co. Oxford (peerage of United Kingdom) 1945 : *m.* 1911, Edith Elizabeth, who *d.* 1946, dau. of George James Freeman ; *d.* 1959 ; *s.* by his el. son [2] *Rev.* JOHN CYRIL, 2nd Baron and present peer.

SANDHURST, BARON. (Mansfield.) [Baron U.K. 1871.]

JOHN EDWARD TERENCE MANSFIELD, *DFC*, 5th Baron; *b.* Sept. 4th, 1920; *s.* 1964; ed. at Harrow; Managing Dir. of Leslie Rankin, Ltd.; 1939-45 War as Flight-Lt., R.A.F.V.R. Bomber Command (DFC): *m.* 1st, 1942, Priscilla Ann (who *d.* 1970, and from whom he obtained a divorce 1946), da. of the late J. Fielder Johnson; 2ndly, 1947, Janet Mary, el. da. of the late John Edward Lloyd, of Long Island, New York, USA, and has issue by 2nd marriage.

Arms,—Argent, on a chevron embattled azure, between three maunches sable an Eastern crown or; on a chief enrailed of the third a lion of the fourth combatant with a tiger cowed proper. Crest,—Out of an Eastern crown argent, a griffin's head sable beaked or, between two branches of laurel proper. Supporters,—*Dexter,* A horse argent mane and tail sable, charged on the shoulder with a rose gules barbed and seeded proper, holding in the mouth a branch of laurel vert; *sinister,* a tiger cowed proper, gorged with a collar therefrom a chain reflexed over the back sable.

Residence,—Les Sapins, St. Mary, Jersey. *Clubs,*—Pathfinder, United (Jersey), MCC.

SON LIVING. *(By 2nd marriage.)*
Hon. GUY RHYS JOHN (1, Crown Office Row, WC2; Leander Club, MCC), *b.* March 3rd, 1949; ed.
at Harrow, and Oriel Coll., Oxford (BA); Bar. Middle Temple 1972.

DAUGHTER LIVING. *(By 2nd marriage.)*
Hon. Victoria Elizabeth, *b.* 1957; ed. at Benenden, and Univ. of Bordeaux.

BROTHER LIVING.
Hon. Ralph Geoffrey Knyvet, *b.* 1926; ed. at Haileybury; OStJ; Managing Dir. of Hatch Mans-
field & Co., Ltd., of 64/65, Cowcross St., EC1M 6JT; County Dir. for Oxon. of St. John Ambulance
Assocn. 1970-72; 1939-45 War with Fleet Air Arm: *m.* 1st, 1952, Hélène Gertrude (who *d.* 1975, and
from whom he obtained a divorce 1960), only da. of the late James Montague Coutts Duffus of
Dalclaverhouse, of The Mansion House, Claverhouse, by Dundee, Angus; 2ndly, 1961, Evelyn
Cecil, yr. da. of the late Sir Ronald Barry Keefe, and has issue living, (by 1st m.) Penelope Sara
Hélène, *b.* 1953,—Trudé Charlotte Victoria, *b.* 1955,—Tessa Emily¸Henrietta, *b.* 1959,—(by 2nd m.)
Morley Rafael Kate, *b.* 1965. *Residence,*—Millington House, Thorpe Green, Thorp-le-Soken, Essex
CO16 0AB. *Clubs,*—Carlton, Pratt's.

SISTER LIVING.
Hon. Valerie (*Viscountess Parker*), *b.* 1918: *m.* 1938, Viscount Parker, el. son of 7th Earl of
Macclesfield. *Residence,*—Shirburn Castle, Watlington, Oxfordshire.

COLLATERAL BRANCH LIVING.
Issue of the late Hon. Henry William Mansfield, 3rd son of 1st Baron, *b.* 1860,
d. 1933: *m.* 1885, Katharine Rachel, who *d.* 1928, dau. of James Charles, J.P.,
of Kennet House, Harrow:—
Katharine Rose, *b.* 1886: *m.* 1919, Capt. Joseph Herbert Mayne, late Bedfordshire and Hertfordshire
Regt., who *d.* 1950, and has issue living, Shelagh Rose, *b.* 1922: *m.* 1950, John Bryett Watson, of
7026, Blenheim St., Vancouver, BC, Canada,—Maureen Heriot (P.O. Konza, Kenya), *b.* 1927:
m. 1961, James Alexander Sands. *Residence,*—2176, West 40th Avenue, Vancouver, 13, British
Columbia.

PREDECESSORS.—[1] *Gen. the Rt. Hon. Sir* WILLIAM ROSE Mansfield, *G.C.B., G.C.S.I., P.C.,
D.C.L.*; *b.* 1819; Col. 35th Foot; served in Sutlej Campaign 1845-6, commanded 53rd Regt.
in the Punjab 1848-9; employed in Peshawur operations 1851-2; appointed responsible military
adviser to ambassador at Constantinople 1855, and accompanied Lord Stratford de Redcliffe to
the Crimea; was Ch. of Staff during Indian Mutiny Campaign 1857-9, Com.-in-Ch. in India
1865-70, and Com. of Forces in Ireland 1870-5; cr. *Baron Sandhurst,* of Sandhurst, co. Berks
(peerage of United Kingdom) 1871: *m.* 1854, Margaret, dau. of Robert Fellowes, of
Shotesham Park, Norfolk; *d.* 1876; *s.* by his son [2] WILLIAM, *G.C.S.I., G.C.I.E., G.C.V.O.,
P.C.,* 2nd Baron, *b.* 1855; a Lord-in-Waiting to H.M. Queen Victoria 1880-85, Under-Sec. of
State for War 1886 and 1892-5, and Gov. of Bombay 1895-1900; appointed Lord Chamberlain
of the Household 1912, a Member of Govt. Committee for Employment of Disabled Soldiers and
Sailors 1915, and again Lord Chamberlain of the Household 1916 and Jan. 1919; Treasurer of
St. Bartholomew's Hospital 1908-21; cr. *Viscount Sandhurst,* of Sandhurst, Berks (peerage of
United Kingdom) 1917: *m.* 1st, 1881, Lady Victoria Alexandrina Spencer, *C.I.,* who *d.* 1906,
dau. of 4th Earl Spencer; 2ndly, 1909, Eleanor Mary Caroline, *O.B.E.,* who *d.* 1934, dau. of the late
Matthew Arnold, and widow of the Hon. Armine Wodehouse, C.B., M.P.; *d.* 1921, when
the Viscountcy became ext., and he was *s.* in the Barony by his brother [3] JOHN WILLIAM,
3rd Baron, *b.* 1857: *m.* 1888, Edith Mary, who *d.* 1939, dau. of the late John Higson, J.P., of
Oakmere Hall, Hartford, Cheshire; *d.* 1933; *s.* by his son [4] RALPH SHELDON, *O.B.E.,* 4th
Baron, *b.* 1892: *m.* 1917, Victoria Morley, who *d.* 1961, da. of Edward Berners Upcher, formerly
of Kirby Cane, Sheringham; *d.* 1964; *s.* by his el. son [5] JOHN EDWARD TERENCE, 5th Baron
and present peer.

Sandon, Viscount, son of Earl of Harrowby.

SANDWICH, EARLDOM OF. (Montagu.) [Earl E. 1660, disclaimed 1964.]

ALEXANDER VICTOR EDWARD PAULTE
MONTAGU, *b.* May 22nd, 1906; *s.* as 10th
Earl June 15th, 1962, disclaimed his peerages
for life, July 24th, 1964; ed. at Eton, and at
Trin. Coll., Camb. (BA 1928, MA 1941);
1939-45 War with 5th (Hunts.) Bn. North-
amptonshire Regt. in France, and as Maj.,
Gen. Staff, Home Forces; Private Sec. to Rt.
Hon. Stanley Baldwin, MP, 1932-34, Treas-
urer, Junior Imperial League 1934-35, Chm. of
Tory Reform Cttee., House of Commons 1943,
MP for S. Div. of Dorset (*C*) 1941-62; Pres.
Anti-Common Market League since 1962;
Chm. Conservative Trident Gp. 1973: *m.* 1st,
1934 (marriage dissolved 1958), (Maud)
Rosemary, da. of the late Maj. Ralph
Harding Peto [see Peto, Bt., *cr.* 1855, colls.];
2ndly, 1962 (m. annulled 1965), Lady Anne,
MBE, yst. da. of 9th Duke of Devonshire,
and widow of Christopher John Holland-
Martin, MP, and has issue by 1st marriage.

Arms,—Quarterly: 1st and 4th argent three fusils,
conjoined in fesse gules within a bordure sable,
Montagu; 2nd and 3rd or, an eagle displayed vert, beaked
and membered gules, *Monthermer.* **Crest,**—A griffin's head
couped at the neck or, wings elevated sable. **Supporters,**

(borne by Earls of Sandwich)—*Dexter*, a triton proper, crowned with an Eastern crown or, and holding in his right hand a trident sable; *sinister*, an eagle with wings expanded vert, beaked and membered gules.

Residence,—Mapperton, Beaminster, Dorset. *Clubs*,—Brooks's, Carlton.

SONS LIVING. (*By 1st marriage.*)

JOHN EDWARD HOLLISTER (has not used courtesy title of Viscount Hinchingbrooke since 1970) (69, Albert Bridge Rd., SW11), *b.* April 11th, 1943; ed. at Eton, and at Trin. Coll., Camb. (BA): *m.* 1968, (Susan) Caroline, da. of the Rev. Perceval Ecroyd Cobham Hayman, of Rogate Vicarage, Petersfield, and has issue living, Luke Timothy Charles, *b.* 1969,—Orlando William, *b.* 1971,— Jemima Mary, *b.* 1973.

Hon. (George Charles) Robert (49, Lower Chiswick Staithe, Hartington Rd., W4), *b.* 1949; ed. at Eton: *m.* 1970, Donna Marzia, da. of ¦Conte Brigante Colonna, and has issue living, Oliver Drogo, *b.* 1974,—Fiamma Fleur, *b.* 1971,—Bona Frances, *b.* 1972.

DAUGHTERS LIVING. (*By 1st marriage.*)

Sarah Jane Helen, of 21, Sudeley St., N1, *b.* 1935: *m.* 1959, Alessandro Ballarin, and has issue living' Katerina Teresa, *b.* 1960,—Antonia Barbara, *b.* 1964.

Elizabeth Anne, *b.* 1937: *m.* 1961, Torquil Patrick Alexander Norman [see Norman, Bt., cr. 1915].

Lady Katharine Victoria, *b.* 1945; ed. at Cranborne Chase Sch., and London Univ. (BA Hons.): *m.* 1965, Nicholas Victor Hunloke, of 52, Walham Grove, Fulham, SW6 [see D. Devonshire].

Lady Julia Frances, *b.* 1947.

SISTERS LIVING.

Lady (Mary) Faith, *b.* 1911: *m.* 1st, 1938, Philip Booth Nesbitt, **from whom she obtained a** divorce in U.S.A. 1941; 2ndly, 1948, Com. Sir Michael Culme-Seymour, 5th Bt., R.N. (retired), and has issue living, (by 1st m.) Caroline Gemma, *b.* 1939: *m.* 1964, Andrew Best, of 12, Woodstock Rd., Bedford Park, W4, and has issue living, Matthew Thomas *b.* 1966,—Anna Josephine *b.* 1965. *Residence*,—Wytherston, Powerstock, Bridport, Dorset.

Lady Elizabeth, *b.* 1917. *Residence*,—La Respelido, Mougins, France, A.M.

WIDOW LIVING OF SON OF NINTH EARL.

Hon. Janet Gladys (CAMPBELL), dau. of 1st Baron Beaverbrook: *m.* 2ndly, 1935, **as his second** wife, the Hon. (William) Drogo Sturges Montagu, Flying Officer Auxiliary Air Force, who *d.* (on active service during European War) 1940 ; 3rdly, 1942, Major (Thomas) Edward Dealtry Kidd, M.B.E., Roy. Canadian Artillery, and has issue living, (by 1st marriage) [see D. Argyll, colls.],—(by 2nd m.) [see colls., infra]. *Residence*,—Slythehurst, Ewhurst, Surrey.

WIDOW LIVING OF NINTH EARL.

ELLA LILIAN (AMIYA) (*Dowager Countess of Sandwich*), dau. of the late George Sully, of N. Petherton, Som.): *m.* 1952, as his second wife, the 9th Earl, who *d.* 1962. *Residence*,—24, Monckton Court, Addison Rd., W14.

COLLATERAL BRANCH LIVING.

Issue of the late Hon. (William) Drogo Sturges Montagu, Flying Officer Auxiliary Air Force, 2nd son of 9th Earl, *b.* 1908, *d.* (on active ser. during European War) 1940 : *m.* 1st, 1931, Tanis Eva Bulkeley (who obtained a divorce 1935), dau. of Benjamin Seymour Guinness; 2ndly, 1935, the Hon. Janet Gladys (CAMPBELL) (ante) [she *m.* 3rdly, 1942, Major Thomas Edward Dealtry Kidd, M.B.E., Roy. Canadian Artillery], dau. of 1st Baron Beaverbrook :—

(By 1st m.) John Dru (Domaine de Migron, Biarritz, France), *b.* 1932; is Lt. RNR: *m.* 1958, Sari Palacio, and has issue living, Sophie, *b.* 1959,—Bridget Doon, *b.* 1961,—Sarah Tanis, *b.* 1965.——(By 2nd m.) William Drogo (Sunset Lodge Drive, Gibbes, St. Peter, Barbados), *b.* 1936.

PREDECESSORS.—[1] *Rt. Hon. Sir* EDWARD Montagu, *K.G., P.C.*, son of the late Sir Sidney Montagu, youngest brother of 1st Earl of Manchester; *b.* 1625; a distinguished Parliamentary Gen., and afterwards Lord High Adm. of England ; M.P. for Huntingdonshire 1644-7 ; cr. *Baron Montagu*, of St. Neots, Hunts, *Viscount Hinchingbrooke* and *Earl of Sandwich* (peerage of England) 1660: *m.* 1642, the Hon. Jemima Crewe, who *d.* 1674, dau. of 1st Baron Crewe; *d.* (killed in action in the great sea-fight with the Dutch, off Southwold Bay) 1672; *s.* by his son [2] EDWARD, 2nd Earl ; *b.* 16—; was Ambassador at Lisbon 1678: *m.* 1668, the Hon. Mary Boyle, who *d.* 1671, dau. of 2nd Earl of Cork ; *d.* 1689; *s.* by his son [3] EDWARD, 3rd Earl; *b.* 1670; was Lord-Lieut. of co. Huntington: *m.* 1689, the Hon. Elizabeth Wilmot, who *d.* 1757, dau. of 2nd Earl of Rochester; *d.* 1729; *s.* by his grandson [4] JOHN, 4th Earl; *b.* 1718; was successively a Sec. of State and First Lord of the Admiralty; *d.* 1792; *s.* by his son [5] JOHN, 5th Earl; *d.* 1814; *s.* by his son [6] GEORGE JOHN, 6th Earl; *b.* 1773; *d.* 1818; *s.* by his son [7] JOHN WILLIAM, *P.C.*, 7th Earl; *b.* 1811; was Master of the Buckhounds, 1858-9, and Lord-Lieut. of Huntingdonshire: *m.* 1st, 1838, Lady Mary Paget, who *d.* 1859, dau. of 1st Marquess of Anglesey, K.G.; 2ndly, 1865, Lady Blanche Egerton, dau. of 1st Earl of Ellesmere; *d.* 1884; *s.* by his son [8] EDWARD GEORGE HENRY, *K.C.V.O.*, 8th Earl, *b.* 1839; Lord-Lieut. of Hunts 1891-1916; M.P. for Huntingdon (*C*) 1876-84; *d.* 1916; *s.* by his nephew [9] GEORGE CHARLES (son of the late Rear-Adm. the Hon. Victor Alexander Montagu, C.B., 2nd son of 7th Earl), 9th Earl; *b.* 1874; Assist. Private Sec. to Pres. of Board of Agriculture 1898-1900; M.P. for S. Div. of Hunts (*C*) 1900-6: *m.* 1st, 1905, Alberta, who *d.* 1951, dau. of the late William Sturges, of New York; 2ndly, 1952, Ella Lilian (Amiya), dau. of the late George Sully, of N. Petherton, Somerset; *d.* 1962; *s.* by his elder son [10] ALEXANDER VICTOR EDWARD PAULET, 10th Earl, also Viscount Hinchingbrooke, and Baron Montagu, until he disclaimed his peerages 1964.

SANDYS, BARON.   (Hill.)   [Baron U.K. 1802.]

[Title pronounced " Sands."]

RICHARD MICHAEL OLIVER HILL, 7th Baron ; *b.* July 21st, 1931 ; *s.* 1961 ; late Lieut. R. Scots Greys ; a DL of Worcs.; FRGS; patron of one living; a Lord-in-Waiting to HM Jan. to March 1974: *m.* 1961, Patricia Simpson, da. of the late Capt. Lionel Hall, MC, of Park-gate, Lower Beeding, Sussex.

Arms.— Quarterly : 1st and 4th or, a fesse dancettée, between three cross crosslets fitchée gules, *Sandys*; 2nd and 3rd sable, on a fesse argent, between three leopards passant guardant or, spotted of the field, as many escallops gules, *Hill*. **Crests,**— 1st, a griffin segreant per fesse or and gules, *Sandys*; 2nd, a reindeer's head couped at the neck gules, attired and plain collared or, *Hill*. **Supporters,**—Two griffins, with wings elevated per fesse, or and gules, each gorged with a collar dancettée, of the last.

Seat,—Ombersley Court, Droitwich, Worcester-shire. *Club,*—Cavalry.

Probum non pœnitet.
The honest man has not to repent

SISTER LIVING.

Hon. Cynthia Meriel, *b.* 1929: *m.* 1954, Charles Talbot Rhys Wingfield [see V. Powerscourt, colls.]. *Residence,*—Barrington Park, Burford, Oxon.

WIDOW LIVING OF BROTHER OF SIXTH BARON.

Hon. Patricia Ierne Wilmot Tufton (c/o Lloyds Bank, 6, Pall Mall, S.W.1), dau. of 2nd Baron Hoth-field: *m.* 1921, Lt.-Col. the Hon. George Chenevix Hill, who *d.* 1963, having been raised to the rank of a Baron's son 1950, and has issue living [see colls., infra].

WIDOW LIVING OF SIXTH BARON.

CYNTHIA MARY (*Cynthia*, *Baroness Sandys*), dau. of the late Col. Frederic Richard Thomas Trench-Gascoigne, D.S.O. [see B. Ashtown, colls.] : *m.* 1924, the 6th Baron, who *d.* 1961. *Residence,*— Himbleton Manor, near Droitwich, Worcester.

COLLATERAL BRANCH LIVING.

Issue of the late Lt.-Col. the Hon. George Chenevix Hill, yst. brother of 6th Baron, *b.* 1887, *d.* 1963: *m.* 1921, the Hon. Patricia Ierne Wilmot Tufton (ante), dau. of 2nd Baron Hothfield:—

MARCUS TUFTON (Flat 13, Regina Court, Molyneux Park Rd., Tunbridge Wells), *b.* March 15th, 1931; ed. at Eton, and at St. John's Coll., Camb.; late RAF.

PREDECESSORS.—[1] MARY, wife of 2nd Marquess of Downshire, inherited the estates of her uncle, Edwin, 2nd and last Baron Sandys, cr. 1743, and was cr. *Baroness Sandys*, of Ombersley, co. Worcester (peerage of United Kingdom) 1802, with remainder to her sons Arthur Moyses William, Arthur Marcus Cecil, Arthur Augustus Edwin, and George Augustus successively, and failing them to her el. son Arthur Blundell; *d.* 1836; *s.* by her 2nd son [2] ARTHUR MOYSES WILLIAM, 2nd Baron; a Lieut.-Gen. in the Army; *d.* unmarried 1860; *s.* by his brother [3] ARTHUR MARCUS CECIL, P.C., 3rd Baron; assumed in 1861 by Roy. licence the surname of Sandys, in lieu of Hill: *m.* 1837, Louisa, who *d.* 1886, dau. of Joseph Blake, *d.* 1863; *s.* by his son [4] AUGUSTUS FREDERICK ARTHUR, 4th Baron, *b.* 1840: *m.* 1872, Augusta, who *d.* 1903, dau. of Sir Charles Des Vœux, 2nd Bt; *d.* 1904; *s.* by his brother [5] MICHAEL EDWIN MARCUS, 5th Baron, *b.* 1855: *m.* 1886, Marjorie Clara Pentreath, who *d.* 1929, dau. of the late John Morgan, of Brighton; *d.* 1948; *s.* by his kinsman [6] ARTHUR FITZGERALD SANDYS *HILL* (son of the late Arthur Blundell George Sandys Hill, el. son of the late Lord George Augustus Hill, M.P., 5th son of Mary, Baroness Sandys), 6th Baron; *b.* 1876; Lieut.-Col. R.E.: *m.* 1924, Cynthia Mary, dau. of the late Col. Frederic Richard Thomas Trench-Gascoigne, D.S.O.; *d.* 1961; *s.* by his son [7] RICHARD MICHAEL OLIVER, 7th Baron and present peer.

SAVILE, BARON.   (Lumley-Savile.)   [Baron U.K. 1888.]

GEORGE HALIFAX LUMLEY-SAVILE, 3rd Baron; *b.* Jan. 24th, 1919; *s.* 1931; ed. at Eton; a DL for W. Yorks. and for City of York, a JP for Dewsbury and patron of two livings; OStJ; formerly Capt. Duke of Wellington's Regt.; Burma 1943-44 attached Lincolnshire Regt.

Arms,— Argent, on a bend sable, three owls affrontée of the first, within a bordure wavy of the second. **Crest,**—An owl affrontée argent, debruised by a bendlet sinister wavy sable. **Supporters,**—Two talbots ermine, each gorged with a collar wavy sable, pendent therefrom an escutcheon or charged with a popinjay vert, collared gules.

Seats,—Gryce Hall, Shelley, via Huddersfield; Walshaw, Hebden Bridge. *Clubs,*—St. James', Brooks'.

BEE ☙ FAST

BROTHER LIVING.

Hon. HENRY LEOLINE THORNHILL, (38 Carlyle Sq., SW3. *Clubs,* White's, Guards'); *b.* Oct. 2nd, 1923; ed. at Eton; late Lieut. Grenadier Guards; European War 1939-45 (wounded): *m.* 1st, 1946, Presiley June (*m.* diss.

1951), only da. of Major G. H. E. Inchbald, of 28/2 Porchester Gdns., W2; 2ndly, 1961, Caroline Jeffie who *d.* 1970, da. of Peter Julian Clive, of Biarritz, France [By. Muir-Mackenzie]; 3rdly, 1972, Margaret Ann, ARCM, da. of Edward Matthew Phillips, of Vancouver, BC, and widow of Peter Alexander Bruce [E.|Elgin and Kincardine], and has issue living, (by 1st m.) John Anthony Thornhill, *b.* 1947,— (by 3rd m.), James George Augustus, *b.* 1975, — Peter Edward Henry (triplet), *b.* 1975,—Robin William Matthew (triplet), *b.* 1975.

SISTER LIVING.

Hon. Deirdre Barbara Elland, *b.* 1928: *m.* 1948, Col. Kent Kane Parrot, U.S. Air Force (ret.), and has issue living, Jonathan Kent, *b.* 1950,—Richard Halifax, *b.* 1952,—Barbara Elland, *b.* 1959. *Residence,*—5506, Grove St., Chevy Chase, Maryland, USA.

PREDECESSORS.—[1] JOHN Savile, *G.C.B., P.C.*, natural son of 8th Earl of Scarbrough, *b.* 1818; Envoy Extraor. and Min. Plen. to Saxony 1866-67, to Swiss Confederation 1867-68, and to Brussels 1868-83, and Ambassador Extraor. and Min. Plen. to Italy 1883-88; assumed by Roy. licence 1887 the surname of Savile in lieu of Lumley; cr. *Baron Savile,* of Rufford, Notts (peerage of United Kingdom) 1888, with remainder, in default of male issue, to his nephew, John Savile Lumley, only son of the late Rev. Frederick Savile Lumley; *d.* 1896; *s.* under the special remainder by his nephew [2] JOHN, KCVO, 2nd Baron, *b.* 1855; served in Foreign Office and Diplo Ser.; assumed by Roy, licence 1898 the surname of Savile after that of Lumley, and the arms of Savile only: *m.* 1st, 1894, Gertrude Violet, who *d.* 1912, da. of the late Charles Francis Webster-Wedderburn, and widow of Horace Augustus Helyar, of Coker Court, Somersetshire; 2ndly, 1916, Esmé Grace Virginia, who *d.* 1958, only da. of the late John Hyem Wolton, and formerly wife of Capt. Claude Levita (from whom she obtained a divorce 1914); *d.* 1931; *s.* by his el. son [3] GEORGE HALIFAX, 3rd Baron and present peer.

SAYE and SELE, BARON. (Fiennes.) [Baron E. 1447 and 1603.]

[Name pronounced "Fines."]

Ask for a brave spirit.

NATHANIEL THOMAS ALLEN FIENNES, 21st Baron; *b.* Sept. 22nd, 1920; *s.* 1968; ed. at Eton, and New Coll., Oxford; relinquished by deed poll 1965 the additional surnames of Twisleton and Wykeham; 1939-45 War in Rifle Bde. (despatches twice): *m.* 1958, Mariette Helena, only da. of Maj.-Gen. Sir (Arthur) Guy Salisbury-Jones, GCVO, CMG, CBE, MC [see de Bunsen, Bt., ext.], and has issue.

Arms,—Quarterly: 1st and 4th azure, three lions rampant or, *Fiennes* ; 2nd and 3rd argent, a chevron between three moles sable, *Twisleton.* Crests,—1st, a wolf sejant proper, gorged with a spiked collar, the line therefrom reflexed over the back or, *Fiennes* ; 2nd, an arm embowed, vested sable, cuffed argent, holding in the hand proper a mole spade or, headed and armed of the second, *Twisleton.* Supporters,—Two wolves argent, gorged and lined as the crest. *Seat,*—Broughton Castle, Banbury.

SONS LIVING.
Hon. RICHARD INGEL, *b.* Aug. 19th, 1959.
Hon. Martin Guy, *b.* 1961.
Hon. William John, *b.* 1970.

DAUGHTER LIVING.
Hon. Susannah Hersey (twin), *b.* 1961.

BROTHER LIVING.
Very Rev. the Hon. Oliver William TWISLETON-WYKEHAM-FIENNES (The Deanery, Lincoln), *b.* 1926; ed. at Eton, and New Coll., Oxford (MA); late Lt. Rifle Bde.; Chap. St. J.; Dean of Lincoln since 1968: *m.* 1956, Juliet, yr. da. of the late Dr. Trevor Heaton, of 3, St. Martins Sq., Chichester, and has issue living, Adam Hugh, *b.* 1961,—James William, *b.* 1964,—Celia Ruth, *b.* 1957,—Laura Charlotte, *b.* 1959.

AUNT LIVING. *(Daughter of 18th Baron.)*
Hon. Cecily Marion Violet Joan, *b.* 1900 : *m.* 1928, John William Dunne, F.R.Ae.S., who *d.* 1949, formerly Lieut. Wiltshire Regt., and has issue living, John Geoffrey Christopher, *b.* 1929,—Rosemary Elizabeth Cecily, *b.* 1931. *Residence,*—Green End, Chadlington, Oxon.

COLLATERAL BRANCHES LIVING.
Grandchildren of the late Hon. Eustace Edward Twisleton-Wykeham-**Fiennes** (2nd son of 17th Baron), who was cr. a Baronet 1916:—
See Twisleton-Wykeham-Fiennes, Bt.
Issue of the late Hon. Beatrice Emmeline Augusta Twisleton-Wykeham-Fiennes, dau. of 17th Baron, *b.* 1857, *d.* 1929: *m.* 1881, Capt. Moubray Allfrey, 15th Hussars:—
Arthur Moubray St. Crispin, *b.* 1881 ; ed. at Eton, and New Coll., Oxford : *m.* 1st, 1909, Joan Louisa, who *d.* 1946, dau. of the late Edmund Henry Clutterbuck, of Hardenhuish Park Chippenham, 2ndly, 1948, Cecilia Muriel, dau. of Lieut.-Col. Trevor Chichele Plowden, and has issue living, (by 1st marriage) Moubray Antony Arthur, *b.* 1909. *Residence,*—Hillside, Sunningdale, Berks.

Grandchildren of the late Col. the Hon. Ivo de Vesci Edward Twisleton-Wykeham-Fiennes, C.B., 3rd son of 16th Baron:—
Issue of the late Maj. Nathaniel Ivo Edward Twisleton-Wykeham-Fiennes, DSO, *b.* 1876, *d.* 1963: *m.* 1901, Elsie, who *d.* 1968, da. of Col. Frederick Jacob Ponsonby Hill, R. Scots.:—
Rev. Geoffrey Ivo Frederick (E. Worldham Manor, Alton, Hants.), *b.* 1906; ed. at Winchester, and at Trin. Coll., Oxford (MA); Universities Mission to Central Africa 1932-64; Canon Emeritus of Lusaka.——Elizabeth Margaret, *b.* 1916: *m.* 1950, John Ley Greaves, MD, FRCP, of The Manor House, Headbourne Worthy, Winchester, and has issue living, Francis Fiennes Ley, *b.* 1952; ed. at Repton,—Peter Fiennes Ley, *b.* 1955, ed. at Repton,—Elizabeth Anne Fiennes, *b.* 1951: *m.* 1974, Timothy Somerset Charrington, of The Croft, Farrington, nr. Alton, Hants.,—Jane Katherine Fiennes (twin), *b.* 1955.

Grandchildren of the late Rev. the Hon. Wingfield Stratford Twisleton-Wykeham-Fiennes, 4th son of 16th Baron:—
Issue of the late Gerard Yorke Twisleton-Wykeham-Fiennes, C.B.E., *b.* 1864, *d.* 1926: *m.* 1905, Gwendolen, who *d.* 1968, da. of the late Francis Gisborne of Holme Hall, Bakewell:—
Gerard Francis Gisborne, *OBE, b.* 1906; ed. at Winchester, and at Hertford Coll., Oxford (MA), Chm. of E. Railway Board, and Gen. Manager of E. Region, British Railways 1965-68; OBE (Civil) 1957: *m.* 1st, 1934, Norah, who *d.* 1960, el. da. of Thomas Davies, of Llangollen; 2ndly, 1962, Jean (Kerridge). da. of James Valentine, of Dovercourt, and has issue living, (by 1st marriage)

Jeremy (21, Wentworth Mansions, Keats Rd., NW3), *b.* 1937: *m.* 1962, Else Brekke, da. of Niels Larsen, of Knuthenborg Park, Bandholm, Denmark, and has issue living, Sine *b.* 1962, Nicole Juana *b.* 1968,—Michael Wynn (12, Housman Rd., Street, Som.), *b.* 1941: *m.* 1966, Rosalie, da. of Stanley Sheppard, of Street, Som., and has issue living, Rupert Yorke *b.* 1969, Hugo Barnabas *b.* 1971, Joshua Gisborne *b.* 1974,—Gerard Ivor, *b.* 1946: *m.* 1973, Jane, da. of Neil Digney, of Wimbledon,— Joslin Mary, *b.* 1939: *m.* 1963, Pierre Michael Landell-Mills, of 3212, 38th St. MW, Washington, DC 20016, USA, and has issue living, Julius Paul *b.* 1965, Nicholas *b.* 1967, Natasha *b.* 1972,—Bronwen Margaret *b.* 1944: *m.* 1967, Oliver Addis, of Pound Cottage, Benington, Herts., and has issue living, Thomas Oliver *b.* 1970, Helen Mary *b.* 1968, Harriet Jane *b.* 1972.——Richard Nathaniel, *MRCVS*, *b.* 1909; ed. at Winchester, and at Magdalene Coll., Camb. (BA 1925); late Uganda Vet. Ser.; *m.* 1st, 1941, Mary Morwenna Daphne (who obtained a divorce 1948), da. of the late Rev. James Rashleigh Hale, sometime V. of Yalding, Maidstone; 2ndly, 1948, Alice Tremlett, da. of the late William Cowie, of Singapore, and has issue living, (by 2nd m.) Richard George, *b.* 1950,—Frances Elizabeth, *b.* 1947: *m.* 1969, Maj. Michael P. K. Beatty, TD RE (TAVR), of The Moor House, Milford, Stafford, and has issue living, Geraldine Alice Martindale *b.* 1971, Rosanna Mary Gisborne *b.* 1973. *Address,*—c/o Zoological Society, Regents Park, NW1.——*Sir* John Saye Wingfield, *KCB, QC, b.* 1911; ed. at Winchester, and Balliol Coll., Oxford (BA); Bar Middle Temple 1936; Bencher 1969; QC 1972; First Parl. Counsel 1968-72; CB (Civil) 1953; KCB (Civil) 1970: *m.* 1937, Sylvia Beatrice, da. of the late Rev. Charles Robert Loraine McDowall [Burdett, Bt., cr. 1665], and has issue living, Nicholas John *b.* 1940; ed. at Winchester, and Merton Coll., Oxford: *m.* 1969, Vicki Karen, da. of W. Alan Thomas, of Stourbridge, Worcs., and has issue living, Alexander William *b.* 1971, John Edward *b.* 1973, Katherine *b.* 1974,—William Gerard, *b.* 1946,—Judith Mary, *b.* 1938. *Residence,*—Mill House, Preston, Sudbury, Suffolk. *Club,*—Athenaeum.——Michael Yorke, *b.* 1912; ed. at Winchester, and at New Coll., Oxford; 1939-45 War as Capt. RA: *m.* 1957, Jacqueline, da. of the Rev. Edward Montmorency Guildford, and has issue living, Toby Jonathan, *b.* 1961.—Peter Guilford, *b.* 1963. *Residence,*—Little Park, Wadhurst, Sussex. *Club,*—Junior Carlton.——David Eustace Matindale, *CBE, b.* 1916; ed. at Winchester, and at New Coll., Oxford (MA): 1939-45 War as Lt. Malayan RNVR (wounded); CBE (Civil) 1964. *Address,*—21, Alexander Sq., SW3.

Issue of the late Alberic Arthur Twisleton-Wykeham-Fiennes, *b.* 1865, *d.* 1919: *m.* 1895, Gertrude Theodosia, who *d.* 1934, da. of the late Henry Fitz-George Colley [see V. Harberton, colls.]:—

Sir Maurice Alberic (90, Eaton Sq., SW1; Gowers Close, Sibford Gower, Banbury, Oxon.), *b.* 1907; ed. at Repton; OEng, MIMechE; Knt. 1965: *m.* 1st, 1932 (m. diss. 1964), Sylvia, da. of Maj. David Finlay, late 7th Dragoon Gds.; 2ndly, 1967, Erika Hueller, da. of Dr. Herbert Hueller von Huellen-ried, of Vienna, and has issue living, (by 1st m.) Mark (8, William St., Kilkenny, co. Kilkenny), *b.* 1933; ed. at Eton: *m.* 1962, Jennifer Anne Mary Alleyne, da. of Brig. Henry Alleyne Lash, Indian Army (ret.), of Bridge End, Churt, Surrey, and has issue living, Ralph Nathaniel *b.* 1962, Magnus Hubert *b.* 1955, Jacob Mark *b.* 1970, Joseph Alberic (twin) *b.* 1970, Martha Maria *b.* 1964, Sophia Victoria *b.* 1967,—Alberic George, *b.* 1947; ed. at Lyceum Alpinum, Zuoz,—Elizabeth *b.* 1935; BSc. Econ. London: *m.* 1965, Lt.-Col. Richard James Heslop Randall, MA (Oxon), and has issue living, William Basil *b.* 1966, Michael Matthew Shaun *b.* 1968, Roland Patrick James *b.* 1970,—Antonia Susan Maria, *b.* 1939: *m.* 1970, John Houlton Ewing Mocatta, of The Old Rectory, Bradfield St. George, Bury St. Edmunds, Suffolk, and has issue living, Antonia Irena Maria *b.* 1971 Marie-Gabrielle *b.* 1974,—Henrietta Celia, *b.* 1943.——Winifred Joan (8, Banbury Lane, Byfield, Daventry, Northants.), *b.* 1897: *m.* 1928, Capt. Maurice Charles Prendergast Vereker, MC, who *d.* 1963 [see V. Gort, colls.].——Audrey Gertrude, *b.* 1899. *Residence,*—15, Wilson Court, Speen, Newbury.——Celia Mary, *b.* 1902: *m.* 1932, Noel Rooke, who *d.* 1953. *Residence,*—The Green, Culworth, Banbury, Oxon.

Issue of the late Caryl Wentworth Twisleton-Wykeham-Fiennes, *b.* 1869; *d.* 1948: *m.* 1897, Kathleen Isabella, who *d.* 1961, dau. of the late James Staples Hawkins, J.P. [Brooke, Bt., cr. 1822, colls.]:—
Marjorie Alice (91, Philbeach Gdns, SW5), *b.* 1899.

Grandchildren of the late Caryl Wentworth Twistleton-Wykeham-Fiennes (ante):—
Issue of the late Maj. Cecil Wingfield Twistleton-Wykeham-Fiennes, RMLI, *b.* 1897, *d.* 1972: *m.* 1st, 1920, Margaret Annie, who *d.* 1921, da. of Philip Robinson, of Egginton, Derby; 2ndly, 1923 (m. diss. 1936), Jessie Mary Goddard, da. of Nicholas Goddard Jackson, of Duddington, Northants; 3rdly, 1940, Elizabeth Stockton, who *d.* 1961, da. of George Perry Fiske, of New York:—
(By 2nd m.) Anthony Patrick (c/o ABC, Box 487, GPO Sydney, NSW), *b.* 1927: *m.* 1966, Prudence June, da. of Edward Woodward Pearce, of Perth, W. Aust., and has issue living, Nicholas Mark, *b.* 1969,—Nathaniel Woodward, *b.* 1973.——(Kathleen) Patricia, *b.* 1925: *m.* 1958, Richard Graham Shedden, MC, of Bowers Barn, Blandford Forum, Dorset, and has issue living, Simon Rory Lindesay, *b.* 1963,—Emma Lavinia, *b.* 1959.

Granddaughter of the late Rev. the Hon. Wingfield Stratford Twisleton-Wykeham-Fiennes, (ante):—
Issue of the late Lt.-Col. John Temple Twisleton-Wykeham-Fiennes, *b.* 1877; *d.* 1970: *m.* 1929, Constance Astbury, who *d.* 1939, da. of the late David Ross, of Holywood, co. Down:—
Bridget Susan Winifred, *b.* 1935: *m.* 1956, Melvin Marriott, and has issue living, Crispin John Fiennes, *b.* 1966,—Josephine Susan, *b.* 1957,—Esmeralda Jane, *b.* 1959,—Prudence Ann, *b.* 1964,—Samantha Sara, *b.* 1968.

PREDECESSORS.—[1] *Sir* JAMES Fiennes, Constable of Dover, Warden of the Cinque Ports and Lord Treasurer of England; summoned to Parliament 1446-7-9, and said to have been cr. *Lord Saye and Sele* by patent 1447; was imprisoned in the Tower as a partisan of the Duke of Suffolk, and in 1451 was beheaded by Jack Cade's mob at the Standard in Cheapside; *s.* by his son [2] WILLIAM, 2nd Lord; was Constable of Porchester and Pevensey Castles, and Vice-Adm. of England; summoned to Parliament 1451-69; killed at the Battle of Barnet 1471; *s.* by his son [3] HENRY, 3rd Lord; bore the title of Lord Saye but was not summoned to Parliament; *d.* 1476: *s.* by his son [4] RICHARD. *de jure* 4th Lord; was not summoned to Parliament; *s.* by his son [5] EDWARD, *de jure* 5th Lord; did not assume the title; *s.* by his son [6] RICHARD, *de jure* 6th Lord, who did not assume the title; *d.* 1573; *s.*, by his son [7] RICHARD, *K.B.*; obtained confirmatory recognition of his claim to the Barony, and in 1603 was cr. by letters patent *Baron Saye and Sele* (peerage of England), with re-mainder to his heirs-gen. with precedence of that date; *d.* 1613; *s.* by his son [8] WILLIAM, 8th Baron; was a Commr. of the Public Safety, and a distinguished leader in the contest between the Parliament and Charles I., and at his residence at Broughton the secret dis-cussions of resistance to the Court took place; cr. *Viscount Saye and Sele* (peerage of England) 1624; *d.* 1662; *s.* by his el. son [9] JAMES, 2nd Viscount; *d.* 1674 without sur-viving male issue, when the barony became abeyant between his daus., Elizabeth, wife of John Twisleton, and Frances, wife of Andrew Ellis, and the viscountcy devolved upon his nephew [10] WILLIAM, 3rd Viscount, son of Col. the Hon. Nathaniel Fiennes, Speaker of Cromwell's Upper House, who was 2nd son of the 8th Baron; *d.* 1696; *s.* by his son [11] NATHANIEL, 4th Viscount; *d.* unmarried 1710; *s.* by his cousin [12] LAWRENCE, 5th Viscount (son of Col. the Hon. John, one of Cromwell's Lords, who was 3rd son of 8th Baron); *d.s.p.* 1742; *s.* by his cousin [13] RICHARD, 6th Viscount (son of the Rev. Richard Fiennes); *d.* 1781, when the viscountcy expired, and the abeyance of the barony of Saye and Sele, which owing to the death of one of the two co-heirs had belonged de jure since 1715 to [14] CECIL, *de jure* Baroness Saye and Sele (dau. of John Twisleton, of Barley Hall, ante), then to her son [15] FIENNES, *de jure* 11th Baron Saye and Sele, and subsequently to his son [16] JOHN, *de jure* 12th Baron Saye and Sele was terminated in favour of the latter's son [17] THOMAS Twisleton, 13th Baron, great-great-grandson of Elizabeth, da. of 2nd Viscount (ante); Gen. in the Army and Col. 9th Foot; *d.* 1788; *s.* by his son [18] GREGORY WILLIAM, 14th Baron; assumed in 1825 the additional surnames of Fiennes and Eardley; *d.* 1844; *s.* by his son [19] WILLIAM THOMAS, 15th Baron; *d.* unmarried 1847; *s.* by his cousin [20] FREDERICK, *D.C.L.*, 16th Baron, 3rd son of the Ven. the Hon. Thomas James Twisleton, D.D., by Anne, dau. and co-heir of Benjamin Ashe: *b.* 1799; assumed by Roy. licence 1849 the additional surnames of Wykeham-Fiennes: *m.* 1st, 1827, the Hon. Emily Wingfield, who *d.* 1837, dau. of the 4th Viscount Powerscourt; 2ndly, 1857, the Hon. Caroline Leigh, dau. of the 1st Baron Leigh; *d.* 1887; *s.* by his el. son [21] JOHN FIENNES, 17th Baron, *b.* 1830: *m.* 1856, Lady Augusta Sophia Hay, who *d.* 1915, dau. of 10th Earl of Kinnoull; *d.* 1907; *s.* by his el. son [22] GEOFFREY CECIL, 18th Baron; *b.* 1858; was Comptroller of H.M.'s Household 1912-15: *m.* 1884, Marion Ruperta Murray, who *d.* 1946, dau. of the late Major Robert Bartholomew Lawes, of Old Park, Dover; *d.* 1937; *s.* by his el. son [23] GEOFFREY RUPERT CECIL, 19th Baron: *b.* 1884; Bar. Inner Temple 1911; *d.* 1949; *s.* by his brother [24] IVO MURRAY, *OBE, MC*, 20th Baron; *b.* 1885; Lt.-Col. RA; High Steward of Banbury 1959-68: *m.* 1919, Hersey Cecilia Hester, who *d.* 1968, da. of the late Capt. Sir Thomas Dacres Butler, KCVO [E. Minto, colls.]; *d.* 1968; *s.* by his el. son [25], NATHANIEL THOMAS ALLEN, 21st Baron and present peer.

SCARBROUGH, EARL OF. (Lumley.) [Earl E. 1690.]

RICHARD ALDRED LUMLEY, 12th Earl; *b.* Dec. 5th, 1932; *s.* 1969; ed. at Eton, and Magdalen Coll., Oxford; late Lt. Queen's Own Yorks. Dragoons, and 2nd Lt. 11th Hussars: *m.* 1970, Lady Elizabeth Ramsay, da. of the 16th Earl of Dalhousie.

Arms,—Argent, a fesse gules, between three parrots vert, collared of the second. **Crest,**—A pelican in her piety, proper. **Supporters,**—Two parrots, wings expanded, vert, beaked and membered gules.

A sound conscience is a wall of brass.

Residence,—Sandbeck Park, Rotherham. *Clubs,*—White's, Pratt's.

SISTERS LIVING.

Lady Mary Constance, *OBE*, *b.* 1923; a DStJ; OBE (Civil) 1974: *m.* 1952, col. Roger Fleetwood Hesket, OBE, TD, DL, who relinquished by deed poll 1956 the additional surname of Fleetwood, and has issue living, Robert Fleetwood, *b.* 1956,—Laura, *b.* 1953,—Sarah Frances, *b.* 1954. *Residence,*—Meols Hall, Southport, Lancs.

Lady Elizabeth (*Baroness Grimthorpe*), *b.* 1925: *m.* 1954, the 4th Baron Grimthorpe; appointed a Lady of the Bedchamber to HM Queen Elizabeth, The Queen Mother 1973. *Residence,*—Westow Hall, York.

Lady Anne Katharine (*Viscountess Ridley*), *b.* 1928: *m.* 1953, the 4th Viscount Ridley. *Residence,*—Blagdon, Seaton Burn, Northumberland.

Lady Jane Lily Serena, *b.* 1935: *m.* 1963, Hugh Wiley of Oak Hill, Palmyra, Virginia, USA, and has issue living, Justin, *b.* 1964,—Marcus Thomas, *b.* 1966,—Peter Alexander, *b.* 1971.

AUNT LIVING. (Raised to the rank of an Earl's daughter 1945.)

Lady Lilian Mary Theodora, *b.* 1900: *m.* 1927, Lt.-Col. Clive Grantham Austin, RHA, JP, DL, who *d.* 1974, and has issue living, Anne Constantia (*Lady Scott*), *b.* 1929: *m.* 1951, Lt.-Col. Sir James Walter Scott, 2nd Bt. cr. 1962,—Marygold Ellinor Gabrielle, *b.* 1931: *m.* 1956, John Alexander Noble Graham, CMG, only son of Sir John (Reginald) Noble Graham, VC, OBE, 3rd Bt. (cr. 1906),—Phyllida Mary Katharine (*Hon. Mrs. Richard M. O. Stanley*), *b.* 1934: *m.* 1956, *Hon.* Richard Morgan Oliver Stanley, of 13, Cromwell Cres., SW5 [see B. Stanley of Alderley],—Susan Primrose, *b.* 1936,—Rosemary Dorothea, *b.* 1929: *m.* 1967, Charles Edward Ifan Wynne Finch, of Cefnamlwch, Tudweiliog, Pwllheli, Caerns. [see E. Aylesford, colls.]. *Residence,*—Roundwood, Micheldever, Hants.

DAUGHTER LIVING OF TENTH EARL.

Lady Serena Mary Barbara, *b.* 1901; is a D.St.J., and a J.P. for Richmond: *m.* 1923, the Hon. Robert James, who *d.* 1960 [see B. Northbourne, colls.]. *Residence,*—St. Nicholas, Richmond, Yorkshire.

WIDOW LIVING OF ELEVENTH EARL.

KATHARINE ISABEL, *DCVO, (Dowager Countess of Scarbrough)*, (Lumley Park House, Chester-le-Street, co. Durham); Lady of the Bedchamber to HM Queen Elizabeth the Queen Mother 1947-53, since when Extra Lady of the Bedchamber; a DStJ; Kaisar-i-Hind gold medal; DCVO 1962; da. of the late Robert Finnie McEwen, of Bardrochat, Ayrshire, and Marchmont, Berwickshire [B. Napier of Magdala]: *m.* 1922, the 11th Earl, who *d.* 1969.

PREDECESSORS.—[1] *Sir* RICHARD Lumley, Knt., garrisoned Lumley Castle on behalf of the Royal cause, and was a principal commander under Prince Rupert; cr. *Viscount Lumley* (peerage of Ireland) 1628; *s.* by his grandson [2] RICHARD, *P.C.*, 2nd Viscount; commanded a regt. of Horse at Battle of Sedgemoor 1685; was a Gentleman of the Bedchamber to Prince of Orange, Lieut.-Gen. of Forces in Flanders, Lord-Lieut. of Durham and Northumberland, and Chancellor of the Duchy of Lancaster, &c.; cr. *Baron Lumley*, of Lumley Castle, co. Durham (peerage of England) 1681, and *Viscount Lumley* and *Earl of Scarbrough* (peerage of England) 1690; *d.* 1721; *s.* by his el. son [3] RICHARD, *K.G.*, 2nd Earl; *d.* unmarried 1740; *s.* by his brother [4] THOMAS, 3rd Earl; assumed the surname of Saunderson by Roy. licence 1723; *d.* 1752; *s.* by his son [5] RICHARD, *P.C.*, 4th Earl; was Cofferer of the Household, Dep. Earl Marshal of England, and Joint Vice-Treasurer of Ireland; *d.* 1782; *s.* by his el. son [6] GEORGE AUGUSTUS, 5th Earl; *d.* unmarried 1807; *s.* by his brother [7] RICHARD, 6th Earl; sat as M.P. for Lincoln city; *d.* 1832; *s.* by his brother [8] JOHN, 7th Earl; assumed the surname of Savile by Act of Parliament; was Preb. of York and Rector of Winteringham; *d.* 1835; *s.* by his son [9] JOHN, 8th Earl; assumed by Roy. licence 1836 the additional and principal surname of Savile; was Lord-Lieut. of Nottinghamshire; *d.* unmarried 1856; *s.* by his cousin [10] RICHARD Lumley, 9th Earl, son of Frederick Lumley-Savile, son of the Hon. Frederick Lumley (5th son of 4th Earl); *b.* 1813: *m.* 1846, Frederica Mary Adeliza, who *d.* 1907, dau. of the late Andrew Robert Drummond; *d.* 1884; *s.* by his son [11] ALDRED FREDERICK GEORGE BERESFORD, *K.G., G.B.E., K.C.B., T.D.*, 10th Earl, *b.* 1857; late Hon. Col. (sometime Comdg.) Yorkshire Dragoons (Yeo.), and Bailiff of Egle and Bailiff Grand Cross of Order of St. John of Jerusalem (Sub-Prior thereof 1923-43); Lord-Lieut. of W. Riding of Yorkshire 1892-1904; S. Africa 1900 with Imperial Yeo.; Director-Gen. of Territorial and

Vol. Forces 1917-21 with rank of Maj.-Gen.: *m.* 1899, Lucy Cecilia, who *d.* 1931, el. dau. of Cecil Dunn Gardner, and widow of Robert Ashton; *d.* 1945; *s.* by his nephew [11] (LAWRENCE) ROGER, *KG, GCSI, GCIE, GCVO, TD, PC* (son of the late Brig.-Gen. the Hon. Osbert Victor George Atheling Lumley, CMG, 3rd son of 9th Earl), 11th Earl, *b.* 1896; Gov. of Bombay 1937-43; Lord Chamberlain 1952-63; Grand Master of United Grand Lodge of English Freemasons 1951-67, and Pro Grand Master 1967-69, and a Permanent Lord-in-Waiting to HM 1963-69: *m.* 1922, Katharine Isabel, DCVO, da. of the late Robert Finnie McEwen, of Bardrochat, Ayrshire, and Marchmont, Berwickshire [B. Napier of Magdala]; *d.* 1969; *s.* by his only son [12] RICHARD ALDRED, 12th Earl and present peer; also Viscount and Baron Lumley.

SCARSDALE, VISCOUNT. (Curzon.) [Baron G.B. 1761, Viscount U.K. 1911, Bt. (S.) 1636 and (E.) 1641.]

Justly and mildly.

RICHARD NATHANIEL CURZON, *T.D.*, 2nd Viscount, 6th Baron, and 10th Baronet; *b.* July 3rd, 1898; *s.* 1925; ed. at Eton; formerly Lieut. 2nd Dragoons (Roy. Scots Greys); sometime Hon. Attaché in Diplo. Ser.; is Major and Hon. Col. R.A. (T.A.), a Director of Arthur Woollacotts Ltd., of Blackfriars House, E.C., a Mil. Member of Derbyshire T.A. Assoc., patron of four livings, Vice-Pres. British Boxing Board of Control, a K.St.J., and Co. Director, Derby St. John Ambulance Assocn.; 1914-18 War, with R. Scots Greys in France and Belgium; 1939-45 War, as Maj. R.A. in Middle East: *m.* 1st, 1923 (m. diss. 1946), Mildred Carson, who *d.* 1969, da. of the late William Roland Dunbar, of Huyton, Lancs.; 2ndly, 1946, Mrs. Ottilie Margarete Julie Harris (formerly, Ensign First Aid Nursing Yeo.), da. of the late Charles Pretzlik, of 155, Sloane St., SW1, and has issue by 1st marriage.

Arms.—Argent, on a bend sable, three popinjays or, collared gules. *Crest.*—A popinjay rising, wings displayed and inverted or, collared gules. *Supporters.*—Two female figures, the *dexter* representing Prudence, habited argent, mantled azure, holding in her sinister hand a javelin, entwined by a remora proper; the *sinister* representing Liberality, habited argent mantled purpure, and holding in both hands a cornucopia proper. *Mottoes*—Let Curzon holde what Curzon helde; Recte et suaviter.

Seat,—Kedleston, Derby. *Clubs,*—Buck's, Royal Automobile.

DAUGHTERS LIVING. (*By 1st marriage.*)

Hon. Anne Mildred (Hill Farm, Garsdale, Sedbergh, Cumbria), *b.* 1923; 1942-44 War in ATS: *m.* 1942 (marriage dissolved 1960), Maj. Walter James Latimer Willson, DSO, Grenadier Guards, son of Sir Walter Stuart James Willson, and has issue living, Simon James Curzon (Apt. 61, Garrucha, Almeria, Spain), *b.* 1942: *m.* 1968, Sarah, el. da. of Douglas Ferris Hewat Jaboor, MB, of La Maison De la Fontaine, Mont Perrine, St. Lawrence, Jersey, [see Aykroyd, Bt., cr. 1920] and has issue living, Alexander James Alfred Curzon *b.* 1969,—Benjamin William Curzon *b.* 1971,—Nicholas William, *b.* 1951,—Jacqueline Anne Curzon, *b.* 1945: *m.* 1957, Anthony Julian Bavin.
Hon. Gloria Mary, *b.* 1927: *m.* 1951, John Garland Bearman, and has issue living, Christopher Charles *b.* 1952,—Anthony Richard, *b.* 1955. *Residence,*—La Maison du Marais, St. Ouen, Jersey.
Hon. Juliana Eveline (The Sail Inn, Dromineer, Nenagh, co. Tipperary), *b.* 1928: *m.* 1st, 1948, George Derek Stanley Smith, who *d.* 1963, and from whom she obtained a divorce 1952; 2ndly, 1953 (m. diss. 1956), Frederick Nettlefold; 3rdly, 1956, as his 2nd wife (m. diss. 1962), Sir Dudley Herbert Cunliffe-Owen, 2nd Bt.; 4thly, 1962 (m. diss. 1972), as his 2nd wife, John Roberts [see Roberts, Bt., colls., cr. 1909], and has issue living, (by 1st m.) Charles Peregrine, *b.* 1952, Venetia Mary, *b.* 1950,—(by 2nd m.) Caroline Anne *b.* 1954,—(by 3rd m.) [see Cunliffe-Owen, Bt.],—(by 4th m.) [see Roberts, Bt., cr. 1999].
Hon. Diana Geraline (Cruz 47, Atico, Barcelona, Spain), *b.* 1934.

SISTERS LIVING. (*Raised to the rank of a Viscount's daughters 1939.*)
Hon. Rosamond Mary (*Hon. Lady Cary*), *b.* 1893: *m.* 1924, Sir Robert Archibald Cary, M.P., 1st Bt. *Residence,*—Wrotham Water, Wrotham, Kent.

DAUGHTER LIVING OF FIRST VISCOUNT SCARSDALE AND FIRST MARQUESS CURZON OF KEDLESTON.
See under B. Ravensdale.

COLLATERAL BRANCHES LIVING. (*In remainder to Viscountcy of Scarsdale, cr. 1911, Barony of Scarsdale. cr. 1761, and the Baronetcies.*)
Issue of the late Hon. Francis Nathaniel Curzon. 3rd son of 4th Baron, *b.* 1865; *d.* 1941: *m.* 1922, Winifred Phyllis, who *d.* 1961, dau. of the late Capt. Christian Combe, of Strathconan, Ross-shire, [M. Conyngham]:—

FRANCIS JOHN NATHANIEL (Weston Lodge, Kedleston, Derby; County Club, Derby), *b.* July 28th, 1924; ed. at Eton; late Capt. Scots Gds.: *m.* 1st, 1948, Solange Yvonne Palmyre Ghislaine, who *d.* 1974, and from whom he obtained a divorce 1967, da. of the late Oscar Hanse, of Belgium; 2ndly, 1968, Helene Gladys Frances, only da. of the late Maj. William Ferguson Thomson, of Kinellar, Aberdeenshire, and has issue living, (by 1st m.) Peter Ghislain Nathaniel, *b.* 1949; ed. at Ampleforth,—David James Nathaniel, *b.* 1958; ed. at Stowe,—Annette Yvonne, *b.* 1953,—(by 2nd m.) Richard Francis Nathaniel, *b.* 1959,—James Fergus Nathaniel, *b.* 1970.——Christian Avril (6, Montpelier St., SW7), *b.* 1923.

Issue of the late Hon. Assheton Nathaniel Curzon, 4th son of 4th Baron, b. 1867.
d. 1950: m. 1897, Mercy Lilian, who d. 1936, dau. of the late Haughton Charles
Okeover [B. Waterpark]:—
Rhona Lilian (Dove Cottage, Mayfield, Ashbourne, Derbys.), b. 1900: m. 1930, Lt.-Col. Patrick
Richard Butler, DSO, who d. 1967, and has issue living, William Richard Rupert (11, Neville St.,
SW7), b. 1933: m. 1958, Anthea, da. of Lt.-Col. William Fawdington Dundas, DSO, and has issue
living, Piers William Patrick Richard Nathaniel b. 1966, Annabelle Francesca b. 1961, Nigheann
Elizabeth Anthea, b. 1963, Laura Rhona Victoria Fleur b. 1970.——Vera Lillian (twin), b. 1900.
Residence,—Dove Cottage, Mayfield, Ashbourne, Derbys.

(In remainder to Baronetcies only.)
Descendants of the late Assheton Curzon (2nd son of 4th baronet), who was cr.
Viscount Curzon 1802 [see E. Howe].

PREDECESSORS.—From the muniments at Kedleston this family can trace descent from Robert
de Courson, Seigneur of Courson, nr. Lisieux, Normandy, who was granted Fishead, Oxon, W.
Lockinge, Berks., etc. by William I. His grandson, Richard de Courson, was granted Knights' fees
of Croxall, Kedleston, Edinghall and Twyford, cos. Derby and Stafford. Richard's 2nd son Stephen
(who m. Elfrica, da. of Olav King of Man) held Fauld, Staffs. The senior line terminated in Mary,
da. and heir of Sir George Curzon of Croxall, who m. c. 1612, Edward Sackville, 4th Earl of Dorset,
KG, the second line being Curzon of Kedleston, and the third, Curzon of Waterperry (Bts. ext. 1750);
[1] JOHN Curzon (cr. a Baronet of Scotland 1636 and of England 1641), el. son of John Curzon of
Kedleston, MP for Derbys; d. 1686; s. by his son [2] Sir NATHANIEL, 2nd Bt.; d. 1718; s. by
his son [3] Sir JOHN, 3rd Bt.; sat as MP for Derbyshire 1702-27; d. unmarried 1727; s. by his
brother [4] Sir NATHANIEL, 4th Bt.; sat as MP for Derbyshire 1727-58; his 2nd son was cr. Viscount
Curzon (see E. Howe); d. 1758; s. by his el. son [5] Sir NATHANIEL, 5th Bt.; cr. Baron Scarsdale,
of Scarsdale, co. Derby (peerage of Great Britain) 1761; was Chm. of Cttee. for Privileges of House of
Lords; d. 1804; s. by his son [6] NATHANIEL, 2nd Baron; d. 1837; s. by his son [7] NATHANIEL,
3rd Baron; d. unmarried 1856; s. by his nephew [8] Rev. ALFRED NATHANIEL HOLDEN, 4th Baron
(2nd son of the Rev. the Hon. Alfred Curzon, 2nd son of 2nd Baron), b. 1831; R. of Kedleston:
m. 1856, Blanche, who d. 1875, da. of the late Joseph Pocklington Senhouse, of Netherhall, Cumberland; d. 1916; s. by his el. son [9] GEORGE NATHANIEL, KG, GCSI, GCIE, PC, FRS, 5th Baron,
1st Earl and 1st Marquess Curzon of Kedleston; b. 1859; Under-Sec. of State for India Nov. 1891
to Aug. 1892, Under-Sec. of State for Foreign Affairs 1895-98, Viceroy and Gov.-Gen. of India
1898-1904, and again 1904-5, Lord Warden of the Cinque Ports and Constable of Dover Castle
1904-5, Lord Privy Seal 1915-16, Pres. of first Air Board May to Dec. 1916 (also became a Member of
Cabinet War Council July 1916), Lord Pres. of the Council and Leader of the House of Lords (with a
seat in the War Cabinet) Dec. 1916 to Nov. 1919, and Sec. of State for Foreign Affairs Nov. 1919 to
Jan. 1924 (also Leader of the House of Lords), and again Lord Pres. of the Council and Leader of the
House of Lords Nov. 1924 to March 1925; sat as MP for SW Lancashire, Southport Div. (C)
1886-98; bore Standard of Empire of India at Coronation of King George V 1911; cr. Baron Curzon
of Kedleston, co. Derby (peerage of Ireland) 1898, and Baron Ravensdale, of Ravensdale, co. Derby,
with special remainder in default of issue male to his el. da. and the heirs male of her body, failing
whom to his other das. in like manner in order of primogeniture, Viscount Scarsdale, of Scarsdale,
co. Derby, with special remainder in default of issue male, to his father (the 4th Baron Scarsdale,
whom he succeeded in the Barony) and the heirs male of his body, Earl Curzon of Kedleston, co.
Derby (all in peerage of UK) 1911, KG 1916, and Earl of Kedleston, co. Derby and Marquess Curzon of
Kedleston (peerage of UK) 1921; s. as 5th Baron Scarsdale and as 9th Baronet (both of Scotland and
England) 1916; received Roy. Victorian Chain 1903: m. 1st, 1895, Mary Victoria, CI, who d. 1906
(had Kaisar-i-Hind gold medal), el. da. of the late Levi Zeigler Leiter, of Dupont Circle, Wash., USA;
2ndly, 1917, Dame Grace Elvina Trilla, GBE, who d. 1958, da. of the late J. Monroe Hinds, of Ala-
bama, USA, widow of Alfred Duggan, [M. Curzon of Kedleston (ext.)]; d. 1925, when the Irish
Barony of 1898, the Earldom of 1911, the Marquessate and Earldom of 1921 became ext., and the
Barony of Ravensdale devolved by special remainder upon his el. da. Mary Irene, and the Barony
(cr. 1761) and Viscountcy of Scarsdale, together with the two Baronetcies, passed to his nephew [10]
RICHARD NATHANIEL (son of the late Col. the Hon. Alfred Nathaniel Curzon, 2nd son of 4th Baron
Scarsdale), 2nd Viscount and present peer, also Baron Scarsdale.

SCHUSTER, BARONY OF. (Schuster.) [Extinct 1956.]

DAUGHTER LIVING OF FIRST BARON.

Hon. Elizabeth Alice, b. 1902: m. 1925, Theodore Francis Turner, QC, from whom she obtained a
divorce 1949, and has issue living, Christopher Gilbert (Dean Close House, Lansdown Rd., Chelten-
ham, and Meadow House, Rhossili, Swansea), b. 1929; Headmaster of Dean Close Sch.: m. 1961,
Lucia, yr. da. of the late Prof. S. R. K. Glanville, and has issue living, Matthew Dominic Stephen b.
1964, Rosalie Frances b. 1962, Catherine Mary b. 1967,—Michael John (30, Shrewsbury House,
Cheyne Walk, SW3; Orchard House, Maidford, Towcester, Northants), b. 1931; BA Camb.; Bar.
Inner Temple 1955; QC 1974: m. 1st, 1956 (m. diss. 1965), the Hon. Susan Margaret Nevill Money-
Coutts, da. of 7th Baron Latymer; 2ndly, 1965, Frances Deborah, da. of the Hon. Mr. Justice (Sir
David Powell) Croom-Johnson, of 28, Rutland St., SW7, and has issue living, (by 1st m.) Mark
Christopher b. 1959, Louise Margaret Ruth b. 1960, (by 2nd m.) James Christopher b. 1957, David
Benjamin b. 1968,—Jennifer Frances Elizabeth, b. 1927: m. 1st, 1948 (m. diss. 1961), James Ashley
Nasmyth [V. Hawarden, colls.]; 2ndly, 1961 His Honour Judge (William Henry) Hughes, of Old
Wardour House, Tisbury, Wilts., and has issue living, (by 1st m.) Kim Ashley b. 1952, Luke Alex-
ander b. 1957, Jessica Anne b. 1954, (by 2nd m.) Polly Anne Helena b. 1952. Residence,—The
Grange, North Cadbury, nr. Yeovil, Som.

Scrymgeour, Lord, son of Earl of Dundee.

SEAFIELD, EARL OF. (Ogilvie-Grant) [Earl S. 1701.]

IAN DEREK FRANCIS OGILVIE-GRANT, *b.* Mar. 20th, 1939; *s.* 1969; ed. at Eton; recognised in the surname of Ogilvie - Grant by warrant of Lord Lyon 1971: *m.* 1st, 1960 (m. diss. 1971), Mary Dawn Mackenzie, el. da. of Henry Illingworth, of 35, Gloucester Sq., W2; 2ndly, 1971, Leila, da. of Mahmoud Refaat, of Cairo, and has issue by 1st m.

Arms,—Quarterly; 1st and 4th grand quarters, quarterly, 1st and 4th, argent, a lion passant guardant gules, crowned with an imperial crown or, and 2nd and 3rd, argent, a cross engrailed sable, *Ogilvie*; 2nd and 3rd grand quarters, gules, three antique crowns or, *Grant*. Crests,—*Dexter*, a lady richly attired from the waist upwards proper wearing a pointed fifteenth century head-dress argent, *Ogilvie*; *sinister*, a burning hill between two Scots Pine saplings proper, *Grant*. Supporters,—*Dexter*, a lion rampant guardant or, armed gules: *sinister*, a savage or naked man bearing upon his shoulder a club proper and wreathed about the head and middle with a laurel vert. *Seats*,—Cullen House, Cullen , Banffshire; Castle Grant, Grantown-on-Spey, Morayshire; Kinveachy Forest, Boat of Garten, Inverness-shire.

SONS LIVING. (*By 1st m.*)

Hon. JAMES ANDREW (*Viscount Reidhaven and Master of Seafield*), *b.* Nov. 30th, 1963.
Hon. Alexander Derek Henry, *b.* 1966.

SISTER LIVING.

Lady Pauline Anne STUDLEY-HERBERT, *b.* 1944; resumed surnames of Studley-Herbert: *m.* 1964, (m. diss. 1970), James Henry Harcourt Illingworth.

COLLATERAL BRANCHES LIVING. *In remainder to the Earldom, the Barony of Strathspey, and the Baronetcy* (cr. 1625) [see B. Strathspey].

Issue of the late Trevor Ogilvie Grant (2nd son of 10th Earl), who *s.* as 4th Baron Strathspey 1915 [see that title].
Grandchildren of the late William Robert Ogilvie-Grant, son of the late Capt. the Hon. George Henry Essex Ogilvie-Grant, 6th son of 6th Earl:—
Issue of the late Eleanora Ogilvie-Grant, *b.* 1892, *d.* 1956: *m.* 1st, 1913, Lt.-Com. Reginald William Blake, RN (ret.), who *d.* 1927, and from whom she obtained a divorce 1926; 2ndly, 1926, Lt.-Com. Sir Roger Thomas Twysden, 10th Bt., who *d.* 1934:—
(By 1st m.) Pamela Rosemary, *b.* 1916: *m.* 1937, Col. Leslie Brindley Bream Beuttler, OBE, Duke of Welington's Regt., and has issue living, Michael Simon Brindley Bream, *b.* 1940,—Nicholas Randolph Kerr, *b.* 1943,—Caroline Jane (*Hon. Mrs. Alan K. M. Clark*) *b.* 1942: *m.* 1958, the Hon. Alan Kenneth McKenzie Clark (Saltwood Castle, Kent) [see B. Clark], and has issue living, James Alasdair Kenneth *b.* 1960, Andrew McKenzie, *b.* 1962. *Residence,*—Finca Villordo, Benalmàdena, Malaga, Spain.——Lavinia Elizabeth, *b.* 1921: *m.* 1954, Lt.-Col. Charles Edward Morton, TD, City of London Yeo. (TA) [Durrant, RE], of Printstile, Bidborough, Tunbridge Wells, and has issue living, Roger Thomas, *b.* 1957,—Louise Jean, *b.* 1955.
Issue of the late Marjorie Elspeth Ogilvie-Grant, *b.* 1894, *d.* 1967: *m.* 1921, Capt. Ronald Fitzhardinge Speir, formerly RE [B. Gifford]:—
(John Hugh) Anthony (Japan Air Lines Co., Ltd., Box 3427, Johannesburg, S. Africa), *b.* 1925; Capt. S. African Inf. Corps: *m.* 1st, 1946 (m. diss. 1952), Isobel, da. of James Snart, of Leicester; 2ndly, 1974, Joan Margaret, da. of A. Valentine, of Krugersdorp, S. Africa, and has issue living (by 1st m.), Helen Joanna, *b.* 1948: *m.* 1969, David George Thomson, of 1, Xyloid, Lords Av., Windsor, Randburgh, S. Africa, and has issue living, Iain James Speir *b.* 1973,—Fiona Margaret, *b.* 1951: *m.* 1973, Michael John Haughey, of 11, Berrymede Rd., W4 5JE, and has issue living, Barnaby Michael Fitzhardinge Speir *b.* 1975, Rachel Mary Speir *b.* 1974.——Elizabeth Jean (Flat 5, 13, Upper Phillimore Gdns., W8), *b.* 1922.——Diana Marigold (6, Abbotsford Place, St. Andrews, Fife), *b.* 1932.
Issue of the late Alison Jean Ogilvie-Grant, *b.* 1896, *d.* 1970: *m.* 1923, Capt. Reginald Cornwallis Hargreaves, MVO, MC, formerly Rifle Vde, who *d.* 1974:—
Basil John Alexander (26, Cadogan Place, SW1), *b.* 1925: *m.* 1960, (m. diss. 1972), Anne Mary Beatrice Stacey, and has issue living, Charles John Cornwallis, *b.* 1966.——Alison June (Swallowfield, Enton Green, Godalming, Surrey), *b.* 1928.

PREDECESSORS.—[1] *Sir* WALTER Ogilvie, Knt., was cr. *Lord Ogilvie of Deskford* (peerage of Scotland) 1616; *s.* by his son [2] JAMES, 2nd Lord; cr. *Earl of Findlater* (peerage of Scotland) 1638, and obtained in 1641 a new patent with remainder to his daughter Elizabeth and her husband Sir Patrick Ogilvy, who at his death became [3] PATRICK and ELIZABETH, Earl and Countess of Findlater; the Earl *d.* 1658; *s.* by his son [4] JAMES, 3rd Earl, *d.* 1711; *s.* by his son [5] JAMES, 4th Earl, who had in 1698 been cr. *Lord Ogilvy of Cullen* and *Viscount Seafield* (peerage of Scotland), with remainder, failing heirs male of the body, to heirs of entail, and in 1701 *Lord Ogilvy of Deskford*, and *Cullen, Viscount Reidhaven*, and *Earl of Seafield* (peerage of Scotland), with the same special remainder; was an eminent lawyer, and held successively the offices of Solicitor Gen. and Sec. of State for Scotland, Lord Chief Baron of the Exchequer, High Commr. to the Gen. Assembly of the Church, Keeper of the Great Seal in Scotland, and Pres. of the Court of Session; *d.* 1730; *s.* by his son [6] JAMES, 5th Earl of Findlater and 2nd Earl of Seafield; *d.* 1764; *s.* by his son [7] JAMES, 6th Earl of Findlater and 3rd Earl of Seafield; *d.* 1770; *s.* by his son [8] JAMES, 7th Earl of Findlater and 4th Earl of Seafield; *d.* 1811, when the Earldom of Findlater expired, and the peerages of 1698 and 1701 reverted to his heir-general [9] *Sir* LEWIS ALEXANDER Grant of Grant, 9th Bt., who became 5th Earl of Seafield; assumed 1811 the additional surname of Ogilvie; MP for Elginshire 1790-96; *d.* unmarried 1840; *s.* by his brother [10] FRANCIS WILLIAM, 6th Earl of Seafield; MP for various Scottish constituencies 1802-40; was Lord-Lt. of co. Inverness, and a Representative Peer; *d.* 1853; *s.* by his son [11] JOHN CHARLES, *KT*, 7th Earl, *b.* 1815; having been a Representative Peer, was cr. *Baron Strathspey*, of Strathspey, cos. Inverness and Moray (peerage of UK) 1858: *m.* 1850, the Hon. Caroline Henrietta Stuart, who *d.* 1911 (having succeeded in 1884 to the Grant and Seafield estates, and having devised them in trust for the 11th Earl and his successors in title), da. of 11th Lord Blantyre; *d.* 1881; *s.* by his son [12] IAN CHARLES, 8th Earl, *b.* 1851; *d.s.p.* 1884, when the Barony of Strathspey became ext. *s.* in Scottish peerages of 1658 and 1701 by his uncle [13] JAMES, 9th Earl, 4th son of 6th Earl, by Mary Anne, da. of John Charles Dunn, of St. Helena and Higham House; *b.* 1817; sat as MP for Elgin and Nairnshire (C) 1868-74; cr. *Baron Strathspey* (peerage of

UK) 1884: *m.* 1st, 1841, Caroline Louisa, who *d.* 1850, da. of the late Eyre Evans, of Ash Hill Towers, Limerick; 2ndly, 1853, Constance Helena, who *d.* 1872, da. of Sir Robert Abercromby, 5th Bt.; 3rdly, 1875, Georgiana Adelaide, da. of the late Gen. Frederick Nathaniel Walker, KCH, of Manor House, Bushey, and widow of William Stuart, of Aldenham Abbey, Herts.; *d.* 1888; *s.* by his el. son [14] FRANCIS WILLIAM, 10th Earl, *b.* 1847: *m.* 1874, Ann (" Nina ") Trevor Corry, who *d.* 1935, da. of the late Maj. George Thomas Evans, of Ash Hill Towers, co. Limerick, and Clooneavin, Otago, NZ; *d.* 1888; *s.* by his el. son [15] JAMES, 11th Earl, *b.* 1876; 30th Chief of the Clan Grant; Capt. Queen's Own Cameron Highlanders: *m.* 1898, Mary Elizabeth Nina, who *d.* 1962, da. of the late Joseph Henry Townend, MD, JP, of Christchurch, NZ; *d.* (of wounds in action) Nov. 1915, when the Barony of Strathspey and the Baronetcy devolved upon his brother, but in the Scottish Peerages he was *s.* by his only child [16] NINA CAROLINE, Countess of Seafield, *b.* 1906: *m.* 1930, Derek Studley-Herbert (who *d.* 1960, having assumed by deed poll 1939, the additional surnames of Ogilvie-Grant, and from whom she obtained a divorce 1957), F/O RAFVR, and late Gren. Gds.; *d.* 1969; *s.* by her only son [17] IAN DEREK FRANCIS, 13th Earl, and present peer; also Viscount Seafield, Viscount Reidhaven, Lord Ogilvie of Cullen, and Lord Ogilvie of Deskford and Cullen.

Seaford, Baron, see Baron Howard de Walden and Seaford.

SEEAR, BARONESS. (Seear.) [Life Baroness 1971.]

BEATRICE NANCY SEEAR, da. of the late Herbert Charles Seear, of Croydon; *b.* Aug. 7th, 1913; ed. at Croydon High Sch., Newnham Coll., Camb., and LSE; Pres. of Liberal Party Organisation 1965-66; Reader in Personnel Management, London Sch. of Economics, 1970; *cr. Baroness Seear*, of Paddington, City of Westminster (Life Baroness) 1971.
Residence,—The Garden Flat, 44, Blomfield Rd., W9.

SEEBOHM, BARON. Seebohm). [Life Baron 1972.]

FREDERIC SEEBOHM, *TD*, son of Hugh Exton Seebohm; *b.* Jan. 18th, 1909; ed. at Leighton Park, Reading, and Trin. Coll., Camb.; Hon. LLD Nottingham; High Sheriff Herts. 1970-71; a Dir. of Barclays Bank (Dep. Chm. 1968-74), of Barclays Bank Internat. Ltd. (formerly Barclays Bank DCO) (Chm. 1965-72), of Friends Provident Group (Chm. 1962-68), of Gillett Bros. Discount Co., Ltd., of Industrial Commercial Finance Corpn., of Barclays Bank SA (Vice-Chm. 1971-73), and of Société Financière Européenee (Chm. since 1974); Chm. Govt. Cttee. Local Authority and Allied Personal Social Sers. 1965-68; Chm. of Finance for Industry, Industrial and Commercial Finance Corpn. and Finance Corpn. for Industry since 1974; 1939-45 War as Lt.-Col. RA: Assist. Ch. Ops. Section Air Defence Div. SHAEF (despatches); *cr.* Knt. 1970, and *Baron Seebohm*, of Hertford, co. Hertford (Life Baron) 1972: *m.* 1932, Evangeline, da. of His Honour the late Sir Gerald Berkeley Hurst, QC, and has issue.

Arms,—Or a balance sable on a chief azure three bezants. **Crests,**—On front of a sword erect point upwards proper sheathed sable between two roses argent barbed, seeded slipped and leaved proper, a skein of wool fesswise argent. **Supporters,**—On the dexter side a hart and the sinister side a ram, both guardant proper and collared or.
Residences,—5, Lowndes Lodge, Cadogan Place, SW1; Brook House, Dedham, Essex, CO7 6AB.
Clubs,—Brooks's, Carlton.

SON LIVING.

Hon. Richard Hugh (Bradfield End, Manningtree, Essex), *b.* 1933: *m.* 1966, Margaret Evelyne Hok.

DAUGHTERS LIVING.

Hon. Victoria, *b.* 1927: *m.* 1958, Oliver Nigel Valentine Glendinning, of 84, Muswell Hill Rd., N10.
Hon. Caroline, *b.* 1940: *m.* 1st, 1962 (m. diss. 1967), Roger John Smith; 2ndly, 1974, Walter H. Lippincott, of 315, East York, NY 10022, USA.

SEFTON, EARLDOM OF. (Molyneux.) [Extinct 1972.]
WIDOW LIVING OF SEVENTH EARL.

JOSEPHINE (*Countess of Sefton*), (Croxteth Hall, Liverpool; Abbeystead, Lancaster); OStJ; da. of the late George Nathan Armstrong, of Glenns, Va., USA, and formerly wife of Erskine Gwynne: *m.* 1941, the 7th Earl, who *d.* 1972, when the title became extinct.

SEGAL, BARON. (Segal.) [Life Baron 1964.]

SAMUEL SEGAL, *MRCS, LRCP*, son of the late Prof. H. Segal; *b.* April 2nd, 1902; ed. at Roy. Gram. Sch., Newcastle upon Tyne, at Jesus Coll., Oxford (MA, Hon. Fellow), and at Westminster Hospital (MRCS, LRCP); Casualty Surg. and House Physician, Westminster Hosp., and Sen. Clinical Assist., Gt. Ormond St. Children's Hosp. 1927-29, Senior Med. Officer, RAF Naval Co-operation Group, Middle East 1942-43, Regional Med. Officer, Min. of Health 1951-62; a Member of Parl. Delegation to Austria and Egypt 1946, Nigeria,

Cameroons, Gold Coast, Sierra Leone, and Gambia 1947, Hungary 1965, and Hong Kong and Singapore 1968, and Foreign Office Mission to Persia 1947 and Viet-Nam 1968, and Leader of Parl. Delegation to Malawi 1966; Chm. of Nat. Soc. for Mentally Handicapped Children since 1975, and a Member of Council, Oxford Soc.; Visitor, Manchester Coll., Oxford 1972; Hon. Trea. Anglo-Iranian Parly. Group since 1970; Leader of Parly. Delegation to W. Indies, UK Delegate to IPU Conference, Tokyo, and a Member of Parly. Delegation to S. Korea 1974; Vice-Pres. Music Therapy Charity, Ltd., since 1972, a Dep. Speaker and Dep. Chm. of Cttees., House of Lords since 1973, Chm of British Assocn. for the Retarded since 1974; 1939-45 War as Sqd.-Ldr. RAF Med. Ser. in Aden, Western Desert and Syria, and HQ, RAF Middle East, and Med. Staff, Air Min.; MP for Preston (*Lab.*) 1945-50; *cr. Baron Segal*, of Wytham, Roy. Co. of Berkshire (Life Baron) 1964: *m.* 1934, Molly, da. of Robert J. Rolo, OBE, of Alexandria, Egypt, and has issue.

    Residence,—Wytham Abbey, Oxford; 803, Hawkins House, Dolphin Sq., SW1.   *Clubs,*—RAF, Oxford and Cambridge United University.

DAUGHTERS LIVING.

Hon. Maureen, *b.* 1935: *m.* 1956, Jeremy Hadfield, of 19, Christchurch Hill, N.W.3, and has issue.
Hon. Valerie, *b.* 1943: *m.* 1967, Paul Nicholas David Pelham, of 24, Frognal Lane, NW3, and Creaseys Farm, Hutton, Essex, and has issue.

SELBORNE, EARL OF. (Palmer.) [Earl U.K. 1882.]

The palm is for virtue.

JOHN ROUNDELL PALMER, 4th Earl; *b.* March 24th, 1940, ed. at Eton and Ch. Ch., Oxford; a JP for Hants.; Vice Chm. of The Apple and Pear Development Council 1971-73 Tres. of Bridewell R. Hosp. (King Edward's Sch. Witley) since 1972, and Vice-Chm. Hops Marketing Board since 1973: *m.* 1969, Joanna Van Antwerp, yr. da. of Evan James, of Upwood Park, Abingdon, Berks., and has issue.

    Arms,—Argent, two bars sable, charged with three trefoils slipped of the field; in chief a greyhound courant of the second, collared or. **Crest,**—A mount vert, thereon a greyhound sejant sable, collared or, charged on the shoulder with a trefoil slipped argent. **Supporters,**—On either side a greyhound sable, collared or, and charged on the shoulder with a trefoil slipped argent.

    Residence,—Temple Manor, Selborne, Alton, Hants.; *Club,*—Brooks's.

SONS LIVING.

WILLIAM LEWIS, (*Viscount Wolmer*), *b.* Sept. 1st, 1971.
Hon. George Horsley, *b.* 1974.
Hon. Luke James (twin), *b.* 1974.

BROTHER LIVING.

Hon. Henry William (10, Crescent Grove, SW4), *b.* 1941; ed. at Eton, and at Ch. Ch., Oxford: *m.* 1968, Minette, el. da. of Sir Patrick William Donner, of Hurstbourne Park, Whitchurch, Hants., and has issue living, Benjamin Matthew, *b.* 1970,—Robert Henry, *b.* 1972.

SISTER LIVING.

Hon. Katherine Elizabeth, *b.* 1938: *m.* 1958, the Hon. David Laurence Robert Nall-Cain, of Carton, Maynooth, co. Kildare [see B. Brocket].

UNCLE LIVING. (*Son of 3rd Earl.*)

Hon. Robert Jocelyn, *M.C., b.* 1919: ed. at Winchester, and at Balliol Coll., Oxford; is a J.P. for Hants; has been a Co. Councillor for Hants since 1954; late Major Coldstream Guards; European War 1939-45 in Italy (despatches, M.C.): *m.* 1950, Anne Rosemary, Baroness Lucas of Crudwell, and Dingwall (in her own right), and has issue living, *Hon.* Ralph Matthew, *b.* 1951,—*Hon.* Timothy John, *b.* 1953,—*Hon.* Anthea Amabel, *b.* 1956; assumed by deed poll 1963 the additional christian name of Amabel. *Residence,*—The Old House, Wonston, Winchester, Hants. *Club,*—Brooks's.

AUNTS LIVING. (*Daughters of 3rd Earl.*)

Lady Anne Beatrice Mary, *b.* 1911: ed. at Somerville Coll., Oxford (B.A. 1934): *m.* 1935, the Rev. John Salusbury Brewis, who *d,* 1972 [Duckworth-King, Bt., colls.], and has issue living, Thomas William, *b.* 1927; ed. at Eton; Master, Sydney C. of E. Gram. Sch., NSW,—Robert Salusbury (19, Crescent Grove, SW4), *b.* 1939; ed. at Eton: *m.* 1955, Irena, el. da. of the late Wiktor Grubert,—Mary Elizabeth Maud, *b.* 1947: *m.* 1970, David A. O. Tweedie, of 27, Rutland Gate, SW7,—Susan Amy, *b.* 1949; ed. at King's Coll., London: *m.* 1975, Edward Crispin Akers Martineau. *Residence,*—Benham's House, Benham's Lane, Vlackmoor, Liss, Hants.
Lady Laura Mary, *b.* 1915; Lambeth Diploma in Theology 1944; was Chaplain's Assist. to A.T.S. 1942-6; Sec. to Women's Land Army (Hampshire) 1940-42: *m.* 1948, the Rt. Rev. Cyril Eastaugh, MC, 34th Bishop of Peterborough, 1961-72, and has issue living, Andrew Nathaniel, *b.* 1954,—Laura Jane Catherine, *b.* 1949: *m.* 1972, William McDonell Eddis,—Elisabeth Mary, *b.* 1951. *Residence,*—Blackmoor, Hants.
Lady Mary Sophia, *b.* 1920; Lady-in-Waiting to H.M. when H.R.H. Princess Elizabeth 1944-7, and Extra Lady-in-Waiting 1947-9: *m.* 1944, Maj. the Hon. (Thomas) Anthony Edward Towneley Strachey, who *d.* 1955, only son of 3rd Baron O'Hagan. *Residence,*—8, Pembroke Sq., W.8.

MOTHER LIVING.

Priscilla (*Baroness Newton*), dau. of the late John Egerton-Warburton [see Grey-Egerton, Bt., colls.]: *m.* 1st, 1936, William Matthew, Maj. Viscount Wolmer, who *d,* (on active ser.) 1942; 2ndly, 1948, the 4th Baron Newton. *Residence,*—Vernon Hill House, Bishop's Waltham, Hants.

WIDOW LIVING OF SON OF 3RD EARL.

Joanna Constance (3, Holland Park, W11); a JP for Inner London; el. da. of Sir Edmund Castel Bacon, KG, KBE, TD, 14th Bt.: *m.* 1974, the Hon. Edward Roundell Palmer, who *d.* 1974, and has issue [see colls., infra.].

WIDOW LIVING OF SON OF SECOND EARL.

Hon. Dorothy Cecily Sybil Loder (Saint Michel, Rue à l'Or, St. Saviours, Guernsey), da. of 1st Baron Wakehurst: *m.* 1922, the Hon. (William Jocelyn) Lewis Palmer, who *d.* 1971, and has issue [see colls. infra.].

COLLATERAL BRANCHES LIVING.

Issue of the late Hon. Edward Roundell Palmer, yst. son of 3rd Earl, *b.* 1926, *d.* 1974: *m.* 1957, Joanna Constance (ante), el. da. of Sir Edmund Castell Bacon, KG, KBE, TD, 14th Bt.:— Francis Mark Bacon, *b.* 1958.——Matthew Roundell, *b.* 1955.——Henrietta Cecilia, *b.* 1960.—— Lucinda Beatrice, *b.* 1962.

Issue of the late Hon. (William Jocelyn) Lewis Palmer, yst. son of 2nd Earl, *b.* 1894, *d.* 1971: *m.* 1922, the Hon. Dorothy Cecily Sybil Loder (ante), da. of 1st Baron Wakehurst:—

Rev. Stephen Roundell (The Croft, Croft Av., Penrith, Cumberland), *b.* 1923; ed. at Eton and Ch. Ch., Oxford (MA); 1939-45 War as Capt. RE: *m.* 1952, Joyce, da. of the Rev. Walter Darling Topping, and has issue living, William Jocelyn, *b.* 1953,—Andrew Nicholas, *q.* 1955.——Penelope Jane, *b.* 1925: *m.* 1965, David George Jamison, BM (Medical Sch., Cambridge Univ., Cambridge; The Old Mill House, Balsham, Cambs.).

PREDECESSORS.—[1] *Rt. Hon. Sir* ROUNDELL Palmer, *P.C., b.* 1812; M.P. for Plymouth (*L*) 1847 52 and 1853-7, and for Richmond 1861-72; was Solicitor-Gen. 1861-3, Attorney-Gen. 1863-6, and **Lord High Chancellor 1872-4, and 1880-85; cr. Baron Selborne, of Selborne, co. Southampton (peerage of United Kingdom) 1872, and Viscount Wolmer and Earl of Selborne (peerage of United Kingdom)** 1882: *m.* 1848, Lady Laura Waldegrave, who *d.* 1885, 3rd dau. of 8th Earl Waldegrave; *d.* 1895; *s.* by his only son [2] WILLIAM WALDEGRAVE, *K.G., P.C., G.C.M.G.,* 2nd Earl, *b.* 1859; was Under-Sec. of State for Colonies 1895-1900, First Lord of the Admiralty 1900-05, High Commr. for S. Africa and Gov. of Transvaal 1905-10, and Pres. of Board of Agriculture and Fisheries 1915-16; sat as M.P. for E. or Petersfield Div. of Hampshire (*LU*) 1885-92, and for W. Div. of Edinburgh 1892-5: *m.* 1883, Lady Beatrix Maud Cecil, who *d.* 1950, dau. of 3rd Marquess of Salisbury; *d.* 1942; *s.* by his el. son [3] ROUNDELL CECIL, *CH, PC,* 3rd Earl, *b.* 1887; Asst. Postmaster-Gen. 1924-29; Min. of Economic Warfare 1942-45; MP for Newton Div., S.W. Lancs (*LU*) 1910-18, and Aldershot (*C*) 1918-40; called to House of Lords in his father's Barony of Selborne 1941: *m.* 1st, 1910, the Hon, Grace Ridley, who *d.* 1959, da. of 1st Viscount Ridley; 2ndly, 1966, Mrs. Valerie Irene Josephine Margaret de Thomka Bevan, who *d.* 1968, da. of the late J. A. N. de Thomka de Thomka haza, Sec. of State for Hungary; *d.* 1971; *s.* by his grandson [4] JOHN ROUNDELL (el. son of the late William Matthew, Maj. Viscount Wolmer, el. son of 3rd Earl), 4th Earl and present peer; also Viscount Wolmer, and Baron Selborne.

SELBY, VISCOUNT. (Gully.) [Viscount U.K. 1905.]

MICHAEL GUY JOHN GULLY, 4th Viscount; *b.* Aug. 15th, 1942; *s.* 1959; ed. at Harrow; ACA; ATII: *m.* 1965, Mary Theresa, da. of Capt. Thomas F. Powell, of 10, Pelham Cres., SW7, and has issue.

Arms.—Argent, a lion rampant sable between four escallops gules, on a chief of the last as many escallops or. *Crest.*—Between two wings erect or, an arm vested sable, cuffed argent, the hand grasping a sword erect proper. *Supporters,*— *Dexter,* an owl sable, charged with a balance or; *sinister,* an eagle sable, charged with a portcullis or.

Seat,— Shuna Castle, Island of Shuna, Argyll. *Residence,*—Ardfern House, by Lochgilphead, Argyll.

SON LIVING.

Hon. EDWARD THOMAS WILLIAM, *b.* Sept. 21st, 1967.

DAUGHTER LIVING.

Hon. Catherine Mary Albinia, *b.* 1971.

BROTHER LIVING.

Hon. James Edward Hugh Grey, *b* 1945; ed. at King's Sch., Canterbury: *m.* 1971, Fiona Margaret, only da. of Ian S. Mackenzie, of Iona.

Nec temere nec tarde.
Neither rashly nor slowly.

SISTERS LIVING.

Hon. (Helen) Alexandra Briscoe (Boulters Lock Island, Maidenhead, Berks), *b.* 1934: *m.* 1st 1952 (m. diss. 1965), Roger Moreton Frewen, who *d.* 1972; 2ndly, 1971, David O'Grady Roche, el. son of Lt.-Cdr. Sir Standish O'Grady Roche, DSO, RN, 4th Bt., and has issue living (by 1st m.), Jonathan Briscoe Moreton, *b.* 1953,—Robert Edward Jerome, *b.* 1957,—Charles Grey Justin, *b.* 1959. —(by 2nd m.) [see Roche Bt.].

Hon. Audrey Lucille Veronica, *b.* 1936: *m.* 1955, Henry William Edward Briscoe, of Rocketdale, P.O. Mount Prospect, Natal, and has issue living, Charles Hylton William, *b.* 1960,—Robert England Michael, *b.* 1962,—Adam, *b.* 1971,—Catherine Sarah Susan, *b.* 1956,—Elizabeth Judith Audrey, *b.* 1958,—Joy Joanna, *b.* 1965.

AUNTS LIVING. (*Daughters of 2nd Viscount.*)

Hon. Signe Evelyn, *b.* 1909: *m.* 1938, MaxBrandenstein, who assumed the name of Mark Leslie, Brandon, and has issue living, Lionel Roderick Evelyn, *b.* 1939,—Vanessa Maxine, *b.* 1947. *Residence,*—2, Tyrawley Rd., SW6.

Hon. Helen Janice Patricia, *b.* 1915. *Residence,*—Derwent Lodge, Lansdowne Road, Tunbridge Wells.

Hon. Elizabeth Millicent (Box 43148, Nairobi, Kenya), *b.* 1917: *m.* 1948, Clarence Henry Quentin McConnell, who *d.* 1972, and has issue living, Quentin Grey, *b.* 1953,—Janet Elizabeth, *b.* 1949: *m.* 1970, and has issue living a da. *b.* 1971,—Jacqueline Bridget, *b.* 1952.

WIDOW LIVING OF THIRD VISCOUNT.

VERONICA CATHERINE BRISCOE (*Dowager Viscountess Selby*), da. of the late J. George: *m.* 1933, the 3rd Viscount, who *d.* 1959. *Residence,*—The Dower House, Island of Shuna, Argyll.

PREDECESSORS.—[1] *Rt. Hon.* WILLIAM COURT Gully, son of the late James Manby Gully, M.D., of The Priory, Great Malvern, *b.* 1835; Recorder of Wigan 1886-95, and Speaker of the House of Commons 1895-1905; M.P. for Carlisle (*L*) 1886-1905: cr. *Viscount Selby,* of the City of Carlisle (peerage of United Kingdom) 1905: *m.* 1865, Elizabeth Anne Walford, who *d.* 1906, el. dau. of the late Thomas Selby, of Whitley and Wimbish, Essex; *d.* 1909; *s.* by his el. son [2] JAMES WILLIAM HERSCHELL, 2nd Viscount; *b.* 1867: *m.* 1st, 1893, Ada Isabel, who *d.* 1931 (having obtained a divorce 1909), dau. of the late Alexander George Pirie, of Stoney-wood House, Aberdeen; 2ndly, 1909, Dorothy Evelyn, who *d.* 1951, dau. of the late Sir William Grey, K.C.S.I.; *d.* 1923; *s.* by his son [3] THOMAS SUTTON EVELYN, 3rd Viscount; *b.* 1911; Paymaster Lieut.-Com. R.N.R. (retired): *m.* 1933, Veronica Catherine Briscoe-George, dau. of the late J. George; *d.* 1959; *s.* by his son [4] MICHAEL GUY JOHN, 4th Viscount and present peer.

SELKIRK, EARL OF. (Douglas-Hamilton.) [Earl S. 1646.]

GEORGE NIGEL DOUGLAS-HAMILTON, *G.C.M.G.*, *G.B.E.*, *A.F.C.*, *P.C.*, *Q.C.*, 10th Earl; *b.* Jan. 4th, 1906; *s.* 1940; ed. at Eton, at Balliol Coll., Oxford (B.A. and M.A. 1933), and at Paris, Bonn, Vienna, and Edinburgh (LL.B. 1933) Univs.; a Scottish Representative Peer 1945-63; Advocate, Scotland 1934, and a Q.C. 1959; Group-Capt. late Auxiliary Air Force, a Member of Queen's Body Guard for Scotland (Roy. Co. of Archers), Dep. Keeper of the Palace of Holyrood House 1937-72, and a Freeman of Hamilton; was a Member of Edinburgh Town Council 1935-40, a Commr. (unpaid) of Gen. Board of Control for Scotland 1936-39, Commr. for Special Areas in Scotland 1937-39 a, Lord-in-Waiting to HM Nov. 1951 to Nov. 1953, and Paymaster-Gen. 1953 to Dec. 1955, Chancellor of Duchy of Lancaster Dec. 1955 to Jan. 1957, First Lord of the Admiralty Jan. 1957 to Oct. 1959, and UK Commr. for Singapore and Commr.-Gen. S.-E. Asia 1959-63; Chm. of Conservative Commonwealth Council 1965-72; Pres. of Building Socs. Assocn. since 1965, of Roy. Central Asian Soc. since 1966, and of Nat. Ski Fedn. of Great Britain 1965-68; Chm. of Victoria League since 1971; Hon. Chief, Salteaux Indians 1967; 1939-45 War (despatches, OBE), OBE (Mil) 1941, PC 1955, GCMG 1960, GBE 1963: *m.* 1949, Audrey Durell, da. of the late Maurice Drummond-Sale-Barker.

Arms,—Quarterly: 1st and 4th grand quarters, argent, a heart gules imperially crowned proper, on a chief azure three mullets argent, *Douglas* ; 2nd grand quarter, counter-quartered, 1st azure a lion rampant argent, crowned or, *Galloway* ; 2nd or a lion rampant gules, surmounted of a ribband sable, *Abernethy* ; 3rd argent three piles gules, *Jedforest* ; 4th or, a fess chequy azure and argent surmounted of a bend gules charged with three buckles or, *Stewart* ; 3rd grand quarter, counter-quartered, 1st and 4th gules, three cinquefoils ermine, *Hamilton* ; 2nd and 3rd argent, a lymphad, sails furled, sable flagged gules, *Arran* ; over the grand quarters at the fesspoint a crescent sable. **Crest,**—On a chapeau gules furred ermine a salamander in flames, proper. **Supporters,**—*Dexter*, a savage wreathed about the head and middle with laurel, holding in his exterior hand a club, resting in a brandished posture on his shoulder, all proper ; *sinister*, an antelope argent, armed and unguled or, gorged with an earl's coronet proper and having a chain reflexed over the back, also or.

Residences,—Rose Lawn Coppice, Wimborne, Dorset; 60, Eaton Place, S.W.1.

COLLATERAL BRANCH LIVING.
      Issue of the late Lord Malcolm Avondale Douglas-Hamilton, OBE, DFC, next brother of 10th Earl, and 3rd son of 13th Duke of Hamilton, *b.* 1909, *d.* 1964: *m.* 1st, 1931 (m. diss. 1952), (Clodagh) Pamela, only child of the late Lt.-Col. the Hon. Malcolm Bowes-Lyon, CBE [see E. Strathmore, colls.]; 2ndly, 1953, Natalie, CBE, da. of Maj. Nathaniel Braditt Wales, of New York, and Boston, USA, and widow of Edward Bragg Paine, of New York:—(By 1st marriage) [see D. Hamilton, colls.] of whom ALASDAIR MALCOLM (*Master of Selkirk*), *b.* Sept. 10th, 1939, is *h.p.* to the Earldom.

PREDECESSORS.—[1] Lord WILLIAM Douglas, K.G., P.C., 4th son of 1st Marquess of Douglas; *b.* 1634; a Commr. of Treasury 1686-89 and an Extraor. Lord of Session 1686-89 and 1689-94 ; cr. *Lord Daer and Shortcleuch* and *Earl of Selkirk* (peerage of Scotland) 1646, and *Duke of Hamilton; Marquess of Clydesdale, Earl of Arran, Lanark and Selkirk, Lord Aven, Machansire, Polmont and Daer* (peerage of Scotland) 1660 for life only; having resigned his Lordships and Earldom into the King's hands, who in 1688 re-conferred them, with the precedence of 1646, upon his 3rd son, Charles, and his younger sons primogeniturely (provided that, if the said son Charles, or any of his brothers or the heirs male of their bodies succeeded to the Dukedom of Hamilton, cr. 1643, the Earldom should pass to the then Duke's next brother), and with further remainder to his Grace's other heirs male; in conformity with the new patent the 3rd son [2] CHARLES, P.C., *b.* 1662, became 2nd Earl; was Lord Clerk Register 1696 and 1733, a Lord of the Bedchamber and a Representative Peer; *d.* 1739; *s.* by his brother [3] JOHN, 3rd Earl, *b.* 1664, who in 1697 had been cr. *Lord Hilhouse, Viscount Riccartoun,* and *Earl of Ruglen* (peerage of Scotland), with remainder to heirs of his body whatsoever; *d.* 1744; *s.* in Earldom of Ruglen, and in peerages of 1697 by his dau. Anne, while the honours of 1646 reverted to his grand-nephew [4] DUNBAR Hamilton (grandson of Lord Basil, 6th son of 1st Earl), 4th Earl, *b.* 1722; resumed the paternal surname of Douglas, was a Representative Peer: *m.* 1758, Helen, who *d.* 1802, dau. of the late Hon. John Hamilton; *d.* 1799; *s.* by his 7th son [5] THOMAS, 5th Earl, *b.* 1771; a Representative Peer: *m.* 1807, Isabella, who *d.* 1871, dau. of Andrew Blackburn; *d.* 1820; *s.* by his son [6-9] DUNBAR JAMES, 6th Earl; *d.* 1886; *s.* by his kinsman the 12th Duke of Hamilton, the Earldom being merged in the Dukedom until 1940, when it devolved under the terms of special destination upon [10] (GEORGE) NIGEL (2nd son of 13th Duke of Hamilton) 10th Earl and present peer; also Lord Daer and Shortcleuch.

SELSDON, BARON. (Mitchell-Thomson.) [Baron U.K. 1932, Bt. U.K. 1900.]

God will provide.

MALCOLM McEACHARN MITCHELL-THOMSON, 3rd Baron, and 4th Baronet; *b.* Oct. 27th, 1937; *s.* 1963; ed. at Winchester: *m.* 1965, Patricia Anne, da. of Donald Smith, and has issue.

Arms.—Per pale argent and gules between three mascles a stag's head cabossed all counter-changed. Crest,—A dexter hand couped at the wrist proper grasping a cross-crosslet fitchée in bend sinister gules. Supporters, —Two sea-horses proper, crined sable, finned or.
Residence,—33, Cadogan Lane, SW1.

SON LIVING.
Hon. CALLUM MALCOLM McEACHARN, *b.* Nov. 7th, 1969.

SISTER LIVING.
Hon. Mary Gail, *b.* 1939: *m.* 1963, Patrick John O'Kelly, MB, BCh, of 10, Parkview Place, Staten Island, New York, 10310, USA, and has issue living, Sebastian Patrick Sean, *b.* 1964,—Shane, *b.* 1968,—Niall, *b.* 1970.

HALF-SISTER LIVING.
Hon. Petrina Frances Anne, *b.* 1945: *m.* 1967, James Geoffrey Lennox Pugh, late Gren. Gds., of Heath House, Milton-under-Wychwood, Oxon., and has issue living, Henry William Geoffrey, *b.* 1974,—Emma Louise, *b.* 1969.

MOTHER LIVING.
Phoebette (of 57A, Tufton St., S.W.1), da. of the late Crossley Swithinbank, of Donnington Grove, Newbury: *m.* 1st, 1936 (m. diss. 1944), the 2nd Baron, who *d.* 1963; 2ndly, 1949 (m. diss. 1966), Simon Talbot Sitwell, DFC.

WIDOW LIVING OF SECOND BARON.
DOROTHY (99, Dovehouse St., Chelsea, SW3), da. of the late Frederick John Greenish, of Honnington Hall, London: *m.* 1st, 1944, as his 2nd wife, the 2nd Baron, who *d.* 1963; 2ndly, 1972, Charles Larking.

PREDECESSORS.—[1] *Sir* MITCHELL Thomson, 4th son of the late Andrew Thomson, of Seafield, Alloa, by Janet, dau. of William Mitchell, *b.* 1846; was Lord Provost of Edinburgh 1897-1900; assumed by Roy. licence 1900 the additional surname of Mitchell; cr. a *Baronet* 1900: *m.* 1st, 1876, Eliza Flowerdew, who *d.* 1877, dau. of the late William Lowson, of Balthayock, Perthshire; 2ndly, 1880, Eliza Lamb, who *d.* 1926, dau. of the late Robert Cook, shipowner, of Leith; *d.* 1918; *s.* by his son [2] *Rt. Hon.* Sir WILLIAM LOWSON, *K.B.E.,* 2nd Bt., *b.* 1877; was Parliamentary Sec. to Min. of Food 1920-21, and to Board of Trade 1921-2, and Postmaster-Gen. 1924-9; M.P. for N.-W. Div. of Lanarkshire (*U*) 1906-10, for N. Down Div. of co. Down 1910-18, for Maryhill Div. of Glasgow 1918-22, and for S. Div. of Croydon 1923-32; cr. *Baron Selsdon,* of Croydon, co. Surrey (peerage of United Kingdom) 1932: *m.* 1st, 1909, Anne Madeleine (who *d.* 1946, having obtained a divorce for desertion in the Scottish Courts 1932), dau. of the late Sir Malcolm Donald McEacharn, of Galloway House, Garlieston, and Goathland, Melbourne; 2ndly, 1933, Effie Lilian Loder, who *d.* 1956, dau. of the late Lieut.-Col. Charles Brennan, of Mullingar; *d.* 1938; *s.* by his son [3] PATRICK, 2nd Baron *b.* 1913: *m.* 1st. 1936 (marriage dissolved 1944), Phoebette, da. of Crossley Swithinbank, of Donnington Grove, Newbury; 2ndly, 1944, Dorothy (who m. 2ndly 1972, Charles Larking), da. of the late Frederick John Greenish, of Honnington Hall, Lincoln; *d.* 1963; *s.* by his only son [4] MALCOLM McEACHARN, 2rd Baron and present peer.

SEMPILL, LADY. (Sempill.) [Lordship S. 1489.]

ANN MOIRA SEMPILL, *b.* March 19th, 1920; *s.* 1965; late Petty Officer WRNS: *m.* 1st, 1941 (m. diss. 1945), Capt. Eric Holt, Manchester Regt.; 2ndly, 1948, Lt.-Col. Stuart Whitemore Chant-Sempill, OBE, MC, late Gordon Highlanders (who assumed by decree of Lyon Court 1966 the additional name of Sempill) and has issue by 1st and 2nd marriages.

Arms,—Argent, a chevron checky gules and of the field, between three hunting horns sable, garnished and stringed of the second. Crest,—A stag's head argent, attired with ten tines azure, collared with a Prince's crown or. Supporters,—Two greyhounds argent collared gules.

Residences,—Druminnor Castle, Rhynie, Aberdeenshire. 18A, Chatsworth Court, W8.

SONS LIVING. (*By 2nd marriage.*)
Hon. JAMES WILLIAM STUART WHITEMORE *SEMPILL* (*Master of Sempill*), *b.* Feb. 25th, 1949; ed. at Oratory Sch., St. Clare's Hall, Oxford (BA), and Hertford Coll., Oxford.
Hon. Ian David Whitemore CHANT-SEMPILL, *b.* 1951; ed. at Oratory Sch.; Lt. Gordon Highlander.

DAUGHTER LIVING. (*By 1st marriage.*)
Hon. Frances Marian CHANT-SEMPILL, *b.* 1942.

HALF SISTERS LIVING.
Hon. Janet Cecilia FORBES-SEMPILL, *b.* 1942.
Hon. Kirstine Elizabeth FORBES-SEMPILL, *b.* 1944: *m.* 1968, John Michael Forbes-Cable (who assumed by deed poll 1968 the additional surname of Forbes).
Hon. Brigid Gabriel FORBES-SEMPILL, *b.* 1945.

UNCLE LIVING. (*Son of 18th Lord.*)
Hon. Sir Ewan FORBES OF BRUX, 11th baronet [see Forbes, Bt., cr. 1630].

WIDOW LIVING OF NINETEENTH LORD.

CECILIA ALICE (*Cecilia, Lady Sempill*) (Sloane Cottage, Long Melford, Suffolk; Craigievar Castle, Lumphanan, Aberdeenshire), da. of the late B. E. Dunbar-Kilburn, of Ledwell, Sandford St. Martin, Oxon: *m.* 1941, as his 2nd wife, the 19th Lord, who *d.* 1965.

COLLATERAL BRANCHES LIVING.

Issue of the late Rear-Adm. the Hon Arthur Lionel Ochoncar Forbes-Sempill, yst. son of 17th Lord, *b.* 1877, *d.* 1962: *m.* 1st, 1903, Muriel Emily (who *d.* 1954, having obtained a divorce 1914), dau. of the Rev. Walter Spencer, formerly of Fownhope Court, Hereford; 2ndly, 1919, Helen Mabel, who *d.* 1921, dau. of the late Major John Allen, of Brackley House, Brackley, Northants; 3rdly, 1926, Mary Cutting Holland, who *d.* 1940, dau. of the late Arthur J. Cumnock, of 521, Park Av., New York:—

(By 3rd m.) John Alexander Cumnock (Little Auchendon, Newton Stewart, Wigtownshire; Naval and Military Club), *b.* 1927; late Capt. Seaforth Highlanders; a Producer/Dir.: *m.* 1st, 1958 (m. diss. 1964), Penelope Margaret Ann, da. of Arthur Gordon Grey-Pennington; 2ndly, 1966, Jane Carolyn, only da. of C. Gordon Evans, of Morar, Portpatrick, Wigtownshire.——(by 2nd m.) Janet, *b.* 1920; formerly Sergeant ATS: *m.* 1958, Norman Walker, of Harrietsfield House, Ancrum, Jedburgh, Roxburghshire, who assumed 1958, by deed poll the additional surname of Forbes before his patrony-mic, and has issue living, Ian, *b.* 1960.

Issue of the late Hon. Evelyn Courtenay Forbes-Sempill, dau. of 17th Lord, *b.* 1868, *d.* 1934: *m.* 1894, Lieut.-Col. Duncan Vernon Pirie, OBE, JP, DL, a Member of King's Body Guard for Scotland (Roy. Co. of Archers), who *d.* 1931:—
Alexander William, *b.* 1899; sometime Lt. Seaforth Highlanders; 1914-18 War: *m.* 1935, Annet Richardson, and has issue living, Ridley Gordon (15A, Kingsgate St., Winchester), *b.* 1936; ed. at Winchester, and at King's Coll., Camb. (BA): *m.* 1962, Eva Maria Lenel, and has issue living, Edward Duncan *b.* 1968, Fernanda *b.* 1964. *Residence,*—Bourton Orchard, Pen Selwood, Wincanton, Som.——Douglas Gordon, *b.* 1910; ed. at Winchester; is a Member of Queen's Body Guard for Scotland (Roy. Co. of Archers); was Private Sec. and ADC to Gov. of Mauritius 1937-40, Private Sec. to Gov. of Kenya 1946-47, in Colonial Office 1947-50, and in HM Foreign Ser. 1950-53; 1939-45 War as Lt.-Col. Coldstream Guards (despatches, Legion of Honour): *m.* 1954, Jean Frances Caroline Alicia Dorothea Grant, yst. da. of the late Evelyn George Massey Carmichael of Carmichael, OBE, JP, FSA [Colquhoun, Bt.], and has issue living, Douglas Alastair Carmichael *b.* 1957. *Residences,*—The Old House, Milland, Liphook, Hants.; 12, Culford Gdns., SW3. *Club,*—Boodle's.——Evelyn Jean-Gordon, *b.* 1895: *m.* 1926, Col. Owen Evelyn Wynne, OBE, late RE, who *d.* 1974, son of Gen. Sir Arthur Singleton Wynne, GCB, and has issue living, Robert Owen, *b.* 1930,—Evelyn Valérie, *b.* 1928; ed. at St. Andrews Univ. (MA 1950): *m.* 1957, Thomas Syme Drew, of Welton, Coupar Angus, Perth-shire, son of the late Maj.-Gen. Sir James Syme Drew, KBE, CB, DSO, MC, and has issue living, Rachel Jean *b.* 1961. *Residence,*—Court Wood, Sandle Heath, Fordingbridge, Hants.——Valentine Grizel, *b.* 1900. *Residence,*—Paddock Cottage, Hurstpierpoint, Sussex.——Valerie Marguerite (Old Rectory House, Coombe Bissett, Salisbury, Wilts.), *b.* 1906: *m.* 1962, Henry Ernest Spry, OBE, who *d.* 1967.

Grandsons of the late Hon. James Ochoncar Forbes, brother of 17th Lord:—
Issue of the late Lieut.-Col. James Ochoncar Forbes, *b.* 1867; *d.* 1945: *m.* 1912, Nora Maude, who *d.* 1958, dau. of the late Douglas Charles Abercromby [Abercromby, Bt., colls.]:—
Patrick Walter, OBE, *b.* 1914; Lt.-Col. Gordon Highlanders (Reserve); a DL for Aberdeenshire; OBE (Mil.) 1959: *m.* 1939, Margaret Hawthorne, da. of C. H. Lydall, of Brightling, Sussex, and has issue living, Andrew Iain Ochoncar, *b.* 1945,—Mhairi Margaret, *b.* 1942,—Shelagh Anne, *b.* 1948. *Residence,*—Corse, Lumphanan, Aberdeenshire.——David Ochoncar, *b.* 1917. *Residence,*—Loanhead, Corse, Lumphanan, Aberdeenshire.

Grandchildren of the late Hon. Elizabeth Forbes, el. sister of 17th Lord, who *d.* 1890, having *m.* 1854, Robert Grant, who *d.* 1894:—

Issue of the late Charlotte Elizabeth Henrietta Grant, who *d.* 1934, having *m.* 1886, Philip Alexander Holland, who *d.* 1914, having assumed the surname of Grant:—
Alexander Philip Fullerton HOLLAND, *b.* 1887.——Helen Charlotte Elizabeth, *b.* 1890: *m.* 1922, Robert Addie, who *d.* 1934. *Residence,*—West Lodge, Druminnor, Rhynie, Huntly, Aberdeenshire. *Club,*—V.A.D. Ladies'.

Grandchildren of the late Alexander Mansfield Forbes (infra):—
Issue of the late Duncan Alexander Forbes, *b.* 1888, *d.* 1964: *m.* 1918, Sybil Dorothy, who *d.* 1948, da. of the late John Mitchell, of Ceylon:—
Duncan, MC (39, Gilbert Rd., Cambridge), *b.* 1922; Lecturer in History, Camb. Univ., and a Fellow of Clare Coll., Camb.: *m.* 1947, Sheila, da. of the Rev. Clement John Morton, and has issue living, Duncan Alastair, *b.* 1949: *m.* 1971, Angela, da. of Francis Ralph Sargent, and has issue living, Joy Mary, *b.* 1972,—Ian (twin), *b.* 1949: *m.* 1973, Pamela, da. of Dr. Douglas Bailey, and has issue living, Nicholas Ian *b.* 1973,—Helen Morag, *b.* 1954.——Jean Mhari, *b.* 1919.——Katherine Ann (Inveroy, Roy Bridge, Inverness-shire), *b.* 1926: *m.* 1947, Albert Cook, from whom she obtained a divorce 1956, and has issue living, Rosemary Ann, *b.* 1948,—Valerie, *b.* 1952.

Granddaughter of the late Hon. Sarah Forbes, 2nd sister of 17th Lord, who *d.* 1891, having *m.* 1852, Duncan Forbes, who *d.* 1894 [infra]:—
Issue of the late Alexander Mansfield Forbes, *b.* 1858, *d.* 1932: *m.* 1887, Mary Antoinette, who *d.* 1960, dau. of the late Alexander Forbes, of Galleries, Aberdeen:—
Mhari Margaret, *b.* 1891: *m.* 1st, 1918, Arthur Hadyn Parry, who *d.* 1944, and from whom she had obtained a divorce 1935 ; 2ndly, 1935, Major Stuart Frederick Maxwell Ferguson, M.C., formerly R.A., and has issue living, (by 1st marriage) Mhari Elisabeth Forbes, *b.* 1921. *Residence,*—Broad-mead Copse, Wanborough, Guildford, Surrey.

Granddaughters of the late Hon. Caroline Anne Forbes, youngest sister of 17th Lord, who *d.* 1896, having *m.* 1862, the Rev. Frederick Walter Robberds, R. of Salford, Bristol, who *d.* 1898 :—

Issue of the late Most Rev. Walter John Forbes Robberds, D.D., *b.* 1863, *d.* 1944 : *m.* 1896 Mary Ethel Fox, who *d.* 1962, dau. of the late S. G. James, formerly of Pinhoe, Devon:—
Jean Fitzroy, *b.* 1899: *m.* 1926, Gilbert S. James. *Residence,*—Sheepwood, The Ridgeway, Westbury-on-Trym, Bristol.——Ethel Margaret, *b.* 1901: *m.* 1938, John Whitehead, and has issue living, Janet Margaret, *b.* 1929; ed. at St. Andrews Univ. (MA): *m.* 1968, Peter John Low, of 21, Corbar Rd., Buxton, Derbys., and has issue living, Caroline Margaret *b.* 1969, Elizabeth Hilary *b.* 1971, Polly Alexandra *b.* 1973. *Residence,*—6, Calverley Park, Tunbridge Wells, Kent.——Katharine Frances, *b.* 1904: *m.* 1924, Francis David Jefferson Bruist, and has issue living, Mary (Beechwood, Glen Rd., Dunblane, Perthshire), *b.* 1926: *m.* 1st, 1945 (m. diss. 1966), Roland Sydney Hill, who *d.* 1972; 2ndly, 1967, William James Drysdale, and has issue living, (by 1st m.), Andrew Forbes *b.* 1955, David Jefferson *b.* 1957, Susan Frances *b.* 1946: *m.* 1969, Donald Drysdale, CA, of 98, Red-ford Loan, Colinton, Edinburgh, EH13 0AT (and has issue living, Michael Christopher *b.* 1972, Alastair Nicholas *b.* 1974), Alison Margaret *b.* 1949; MA Edinburgh: *m.* 1971, Iain Taylor Carruthers, of 36, Coltbridge Av., Murrayfield, Edinburgh, EH12 AH8, and has issue living, Catherine Lucy Forbes *b.* 1974),—Margaret Brora, *b.* 1930: *m.* 1954, Charles Richard Butterworth, of Wayside, Shoreham, Kent, and has issue living, Emma Mary *b.* 1955,—Charlotte Clunes, *b.* 1958. *Residence,*—Fairney-know, by Arbroath, Angus.

PREDECESSORS.—[1] *Sir* JOHN Sempill, Knt., cr. *Lord Sempill* (peerage of Scotland) **about**
1489; killed at Flodden 1513; *s.* by his son [2] WILLIAM, 2nd Lord; *d.* about 1550; *s.* by his
son [3] ROBERT, 3rd Lord, known as "The Great Lord Sempill"; *s.* by his grandson [4] ROBERT,
4th Lord; was Ambassador from James VI. to Spain 1596; *s.* by his son [5] HUGH, 5th Lord;
d. 1639; *s.* by his el. son [6] FRANCIS, 6th Lord; *d.s.p.* 1644; *s.* by his brother [7] ROBERT, 7th
Lord; *d.* 1675; *s.* by his son [8] FRANCIS, 8th Lord; *d.s.p.* 1684; *s.* by his sister [9] ANNE, **wife**
of Robert Abercromby, who in 1685 was cr. *Lord Glassford* for life; obtained in 1688 a new charter
settling the Lordship of Sempill, in default of male issue, upon her daughters without division by
her then or any future husband; *d.* 1695; *s.* by her el. son [10] FRANCIS, 10th Lord; *d.* unmarried;
s. by his brother [11] JOHN, 11th Lord; *d.* unmarried 1716; *s.* by his brother [12] HUGH, 12th Lord;
commanded left wing of Govt. Army at Culloden 1746; *d.* 1746; *s.* by his son [13] JOHN, 13th
Lord; *d.* 1782; *s.* by his son [14] HUGH, 14th Lord; *b.* 1758; *m.* 1787, Maria, dau. of Charles
Mellish, of Ragnal, Notts: *d.* 1830; *s.* by his son [15] SELKIRK, 15th Lord; *d.* unm. 1835; *s.* by
his sister [16] MARIA JANET: *m.* 1836, Edward Candler, who were both allowed by Roy. Licence
1853 to assume the name and arms Sempill only; *d.s.p.* 1884; *s.* by her kinsman [17] *Sir* WILLIAM
Forbes, 8th Bt. of Craigievar, grandson of the Hon. Sarah, el. da. of 13th Lord, *b.* 1836; assumed in
1885, the additional and principal surname of Sempill: *m.* 1st, 1858, Caroline Louisa, who *d.* 1872
and whom he divorced 1861, da. of Sir Charles Forbes, 3rd Bt., of Newe; 2ndly, 1862, Frances Emily,
who *d.* 1887, da. of Sir Robert Abercromby, 5th Bt.; 3rdly, 1890, Mary Beresford, who *d.* 1930,
da. of the late Henry Sherbrooke, of Oxton, Notts.; *d.* 1905; *s.* by his son [18] JOHN, 17th Lord,
b. 1863; Hon. Col. 5th Bn. Gordon Highlanders (T.A.), a Representative Peer for Scotland:
m. 1892, Gwendolen, who *d.* 1944, da. of the late Herbert Prodgers, of Hington St. Michael,
Chippenham, Wilts; *d.* 1934; *s.* by his son [19] WILLIAM FRANCIS, *AFC*, 19th Lord, *b.* 1893;
a Representative Peer for Scotland, Wing-Cdr. RNAS and Col. RAF, a pioneer in aviation: *m.* 1st,
1919, Eileen Marion, who *d.* 1935, da. of Sir John Lavery, RA; 2ndly, 1941, Cecilia Alice, da. of
B. E. Dunbar-Kilburn, of Ledwell, Sandford St. Martin, Oxon; *d.* 1965; *s.* in the baronetcy of
Forbes of Craigievar by his brother Sir Ewan Forbes of Brux, 11th Bt. [see Forbes, Bt.], and in
the Lordship by his el. da. [20] ANN MOIRA, Lady Sempill and present peeress.

SEROTA, BARONESS. (Serota.) [Life Baroness 1967.]

BEATRICE SEROTA. da. of Alexander Katz; *b.* Oct. 15th, 1919; ed. at
London Sch. of Economics (BSc Econ); a JP of Inner London; a Member of
LCC 1954-65 (Chm. of Children's Cttee. 1958-65) and of GLC (Lambeth)
1964-67; a Member of Advisory Council in Child Care and Central Training
Council in Child Care 1958-68, of Advisory Council on Penal System 1966-68;
Chm. of Health Education Council 1967-69, a Baroness in Waiting to HM
1968-69, and Min. of State, Dept. of Health and Social Security 1969-70; Pres.
of National Council for Unmarried Mother and Her Child since 1971; a Member
of Community Relations Comm. 1971; cr. *Baroness Serota,* of Hampstead in
Greater London (Life Baroness) 1967: *m.* 1942, Stanley Serota, FICE, and has
issue.

Residence,—78, Fitzjohn's Av., NW3.

SON LIVING.

Hon. Nicholas Andrew, *b.* 1946; ed. at Camb. Univ.

DAUGHTER LIVING.

Hon. Judith Alexandra Anne, *b.* 1948; ed. at Roy. Coll. of Music, Manchester.

Settrington, Lord, grandson of Duke of Richmond.

Seymour, Lord, son of Duke of Somerset.

SHACKLETON, BARON. (Shackleton.) [Life Baron 1958.]

EDWARD ARTHUR ALEXANDER SHACKLETON,
KG, OBE, PC, son of the late Maj. Sir Ernest
Henry Shackleton, CVO, OBE, Antarctic
explorer; *b.* July 15th, 1911; ed. at Radley,
and at Magdalen Coll., Oxford (MA); Hon.
LLD Newfoundland; an Author, Lecturer and
Broadcaster; accompanied Expeditions to
Borneo and Sarawak, 1932, and to Ellesmere
Land 1934-35, a Dir. of John Lewis Partner-
ship 1958-64, Pres. Arctic Club 1960, and Pres-
of R. Geographical Soc. 1971-74 (Vice-Pres.
1962-67, and 1969-71); Chm. of RTZ Develop-
ment Enterprises, Ltd., and Dir. of Corpn. of
RTZ Development Enterprises, Ltd.; Min. of
Defence for RAF 1964-67, Min. without
Portfolio, and Dep. Leader House of Lords
1967-68, Lord Privy Seal Jan. to April 1968,
Paymaster-Gen. April to Nov. 1968, and again
Lord Privy Seal 1968-70; Leader of House of
Lords 1968-70, and Leader of the Opposition,
House of Lords 1970-74; Min. in Charge of
Civil Ser. Dept. 1968-70; Cuthbert Peek
Award (RGS) 1933; Ludwig Medallist (Munich
Geog. Soc.) 1938; 1939-45 War as Wing-Cdr.

By endurance we conquer. RAFVR in Intelligence Branch (despatches
twice, OBE); MP for Preston (*Lab.*) 1946-50,
and for Preston S. Div. 1950-55; cr. OBE (Mil.) 1945, *Baron Shackleton,* of
Burley, co. Southampton (Life Baron) 1958, PC 1966, and KG 1974: *m.* 1938,
Betty Muriel Marguerite, da. of the late Capt. Charles E. Homan, Elder
Brother of Trinity House, and has issue.

Arms,—Or, on a fesse gules, three lozengy buckles tongues palewise gold, on a canton of the second a cross humettée of the third. Crest,—A poplar tree proper, charged with a buckle as in the arms.
Residence,—Long Coppice, Canford Magna, Wimborne, Dorset. *Clubs,*—Bath, Savile.

SON LIVING.
Hon. Charles Edward Ernest (10, Canonbury Grove, N1), *b.* 1942; ed. at Radley, and at Magdalen Coll., Oxford: *m.* 1970, Lady Caroline Harriet Hastings, da. of the 15th Earl of Huntingdon.

DAUGHTER LIVING.
Hon. Alexandra Mary Swinford. *b.* 1940; ed. at Trin. Coll., Dublin: *m.* 1969, Richard Charles Bergel, MB, BS, of Dolphin House, Cricket Hill, Yateley, Camberley, Surrey.

SHAFTESBURY, EARL OF. (Ashley-Cooper.) [Earl E. 1672, Bt. E. 1622.]

ANTHONY ASHLEY-COOPER, 10th Earl, and 11th Baronet ; *b.* May 22nd, 1938 ; *s.* 1961 ; ed. at Eton, and at Ch. Ch., Oxford; late Lt. 10th Hussars; Hon. Citizen S. Carolina, USA; Chm. London Philharmonic Orchestra Council; patron of eight livings: *m.* 1966, Mrs. Bianca Maria Le Vien, da. of the late Gino de Paolis.

Arms,—Quarterly : 1st and 4th argent, three bulls passant sable, armed and unguled or. *Ashley* ; 2nd and 3rd gules, a bend engrailed between six lions rampant or, *Cooper.* Crest,—On a chapeau gules, turned up ermine, a bull statant sable, armed, unguled and ducally gorged or. Supporters,—*Dexter,* a bull sable, armed, unguled, ducally gorged and chain reflexed over the back or ; *sinister,* a talbot azure, ducally gorged or.

Residence,—St. Giles's House, Wimborne, Dorset. *Club,*—Turf.

SISTER LIVING. (*Raised to the rank of an Earl's daughter* 1962.)
Lady Frances Mary Elizabeth, *b.* 1940.

UNCLE LIVING. (*Son of 9th Earl.*)
Hon. (ANTHONY) JOHN PERCY HUGH MICHAEL, *b.* Oct. 5th, 1915 ; ed. at Eton, and at Trin. Coll., Oxford ; is Major Life Guards (Reserve), and a C.St.J. ; European War 1939-45 : *m.* 1946, Julian, dau. of the late Capt. George Gerald Petherick [see E. Radnor], and has issue living, Susan Mary Jeane, *b.* 1946,—Caroline Sibell, *b.* 1948,—Elizabeth Julian, *b.* 1950,—Mary Patricia, *b.* 1953. *Residence,*—Tregonwell Lodge, Cranborne, Wimborne, Dorset.

AUNTS LIVING. (*Daughters of 9th Earl.*)
Lady Dorothea Louise (*Viscountess Head*), *b.* 1907 ; is an O.St.J. : *m.* 1935, the 1st Viscount Head. *Residence,*—Throope Manor, Bishopstone, Salisbury.
Lady Lettice Mildred Mary, *b.* 1911 ; is an O.St.J.; late Flight Officer W.A.A.F.; European War 1939-45 (despatches). *Residence,*—Butts Close, Wimborne St. Giles, Dorset.

MOTHER LIVING.
Françoise, dau. of George Souilier : *m.* 1st, 1937, as his second wife, Lord Ashley, who *d.* 1947, el. son of 9th Earl; 2ndly, 1947, Col. François Goussault, French Air Force. *Residence,*—53, Blvd. Victor Hugo, Neuilly-sur-Seine 92, France.

COLLATERAL BRANCH LIVING.
Granddaughter of the late Rt. Hon. (Anthony) Evelyn Melbourne ASHLEY, 4th son of 7th Earl:—
Issue of the late Rt. Hon. Wilfred William ASHLEY, who was cr. *Baron Mount Temple* 1932 [see that title].

PREDECESSORS.—[1] *Sir* JOHN Cooper, sometime M.P. for Poole; cr. *Baronet* 1622; *d.* 1631; *s.* by his son [2] *Sir* ANTHONY ASHLEY, *P.C.,* an able and prominent statesman, who having originally espoused the royal cause, afterwards joined the Parliamentarians, and eventually assisted to restore the monarchy; cr. *Baron Ashley,* of Wimborne St. Giles, co. Dorset (peerage of England) 1661, and *Baron Cooper,* of Paulett, co. Somerset, and *Earl of Shaftesbury* (peerage of England) 1672; was Lord-Lieut. of Dorset, Chancellor of the Exchequer 1667-72, Lord High Chancellor of England 1672-3, and Lord Pres. of the Council 1679; *d.* 1683; *s.* by his son [3] ANTHONY ASHLEY, 2nd Earl; *d.* 1699; *s.* by his son [4] ANTHONY, 3rd Earl; designated by Voltaire as the boldest English philosopher; *d.* 1713; *s.* by his son [5] ANTHONY, 4th Earl; *d.* 1771; *s.* by his el. son [6] ANTHONY ASHLEY, 5th Earl; *d.* 1811; *s.* by his brother [7] CROPLEY ASHLEY, 6th Earl ; *b.* 1768; was Chm. of Committees in House of Lords ; *d.* 1851; *s.* by his son [8] ANTHONY Ashley-Cooper, K.G., P.C., 7th Earl ; was Lord-Lieut. of Dorsetshire; sat as M.P. for Woodstock (*C*) 1826-30, for Dorchester 1830, for Dorsetshire 1831-46 and for Bath 1847-51; *d.* Oct. 1st, 1885 ; *s.* by his son [9] ANTHONY, 8th Earl ; *b.* 1831; sat as M.P. for Hull (*L.C.*) 1857-9, and for Cricklade 1859-65 : *m.* 1857, Lady Harriet Augusta Anne Seymourina Chichester, who *d.* 1898, only dau. of 3rd Marquess of Donegall; *d.* 1886; *s.* by his son [10] ANTHONY, K.P., G.C.V.O., C.B.E., P.C., 9th Earl ; *b.* 1869 ; Capt. 10th Hussars ; Lieut.-Col. and Hon. Col. Comdg. N. Irish Horse 1902-12, and H.M.'s Lieut. 1903-11, Commr. of Congested Dists. Board for Ireland 1902-14, Chamberlain to Queen Mary (when Princess of Wales) 1901-10, Lord Chamberlain to Queen Mary 1910-22, Chm. of National Advisory Council for Juvenile Employment (England and Wales) 1928-31, and Lord Steward of H.M.'s Household 1922-36 ; Chancellor of Belfast Univ. 1910-23 ; Lord-Lieut. for Dorset 1916-52 ; European War 1914-18 ; Chm. of Dorset Co. Council 1924-46 : *m.* 1899, Lady Constance Sibell Grosvenor (a D.J.St.J.), who *d.* 1957, dau. of the late Earl Grosvenor ; *d.* 1961 ; *s.* by his grandson [11] ANTHONY (son of the late Anthony, Lord Ashley, el. son of 9th Earl), 10th Earl and present Peer ; also Baron Ashley, and Baron Cooper.

SHANNON, EARL OF. (Boyle.) **Sits as BARON CARLETON (G.B. 1786).**
[Earl I. 1756.]

Virtue outlives the grave.

POST FUNERA
VIVIT
VIRTUS

SPECTEMUR·AGENDO

Let us be judged by our actions.

RICHARD BENTINCK BOYLE, 9th Earl;
b. Oct. 23rd, 1924; *s.* 1963; late Capt.
Irish Guards: *m.* 1st, 1947 (marriage
dissolved 1955), Donna Catherine Irene
Helen, da. of the Marchese Demetrio
Imperiali di Francavilla; 2ndly, 1957,
Susan Margaret, da. of the late John
Russell Hogg [M. Lothian], and has issue
by 2nd marriage.

Arms,—Per bend embattled argent and gules,
a crescent for difference. **Crest,**—Out of a ducal
coronet or a lion's head per pale embattled argent
and gules, and charged with a crescent for
difference. **Supporters,**—Two lions, the *dexter* per
pale embattled gules and argent, the *sinister* per
pale embattled argent and gules, each charged
with a crescent for difference.

Residence,—Old Loose Court, Loose, Maidstone,
Kent. *Club,*—White's.

SON LIVING. (*By 2nd marriage.*)
RICHARD HENRY JOHN (*Viscount Boyle*),
b. Jan. 19th, 1960.

DAUGHTERS LIVING. (*By 2nd marriage.*)
Lady Georgina Susan, *b.* 1961.
Lady Caroline Mary Victoria, *b.* 1965.

AUNT LIVING. (*Daughter of Sixth Earl.*)
Lady Helen (of 43, Cadogan Place, S.W.1), *b.* 1898; late Sec. of Army and Navy Club: *m.* 1922,
Maj. Cyril Bourchier Barlow, Indian Army, from whom she obtained a divorce 1933, and has issue
living, Michael Roderick, *b.* 1929; ed. at Rugby, and at Trin. Coll., Camb.

WIDOW LIVING OF EIGHTH EARL.
MARJORIE (*Dowager Countess of Shannon*), da. of S. A. Walker of Ootacamund, India: *m.* 1923, the
8th Earl, who *d.* 1963.

COLLATERAL BRANCHES LIVING.
Grandchildren of the late Vice-Adm. the Hon. Robert Francis Boyle, MVO, 3rd son
of 5th Earl:—
Issue of the late Cdr. Vivian Francis Boyle, R.N., *b.* 1902, *d.* 1962: *m.* 1929, Margaret Ruth
Howard, da. of Charles Howard Tripp, of Timaru, New Zealand:—
Robert Francis (McDowell St., Rotorua, NZ), *b.* 1930; a Ranger, NZ Forest Ser.: *m.* 1956, Janet
Eleanor Ashley, da. of Selwyn Ashley Cooper, of Rotorua, NZ, and has issue living, David
de Crespigny, *b.* 1959,—Robert Andrew, *b.* 1961,—Judith Eleanor, *b.* 1957.——Moyra Anne, *b.* 1936:
m. 1960, William Francis Leonard, of 4, Gifford St., St. Heliers, Auckland, NZ, and has issue living,
Mark Francis, *b.* 1961,—Phillippa Jane, *b.* 1962,—Virginia Anne, *b.* 1965.
Issue of the late Hon. Walter John Harry Boyle, C.B.E., 4th son of 5th Earl, *b.*
1869, *d.* 1939: *m.* 1900, Ethel Horatia, who *d.* 1949, dau. of the late Edward
R. Fisher-Rowe [B. Ravensworth]:—
Walter Julian Algernon (of Upton Farm, Ockham, Surrey), *b.* 1918; ed. at Westminster Sch.; is
Lt. R.N.V.R.: *m.* 1941, Anita Diana, dau. of the late W. H. Greenhow, of Rowmore, Cobham.—
Helena Diana Victoria, *b.* 1907: *m.* 1932 (m. diss. 1961), Edward Locker Delmar-Morgan, AMIEE,
and has issue living, John Oliver Julian (41, High St., Saltford, Bristol, BS18 3EJ), *b.* 1934, ed. at
Eton: *m.* 1962, Penelope Jane, da. of E. E. Eaton Woodhouse [Crofton, Bt., cr. 1801, colls.], and
has issue living, Susannah Clare, *b.* 1963, Rebecca Jane, *b.* 1965,—Patricia Jane, *b.* 1941: *m.* 1966,
Peter George Edmund Fowler, of 1788, Herd Rd., Duncan, Vancouver Island, BC, Canada, and has
issue living, Patricck Michael Thomas *b.* 1968, Charles Richard *b.* 1971. *Residence,*—10, Pine Court,
Chew Magna, Bristol.
Issue of the late Capt. the Hon. Edward Spencer Harry Boyle, R.N., 5th son of
5th Earl, *b.* 1870, *d.* 1937: *m.* 1904, Lily, who *d.* 1953, dau. of the late W. Beaumont Gardner, of Palermo, Sicily:—
Patric] Spencer, *b.* 1905; is Lt.-Cdr. R.N.V.R.: *m.* 1st, 1932, Vera Maude Radcliffe Agnew, who
d. (Feb.) 1940, dau. of Daniel Radcliffe, J.P., LL.D., of Pen-y-Lan, Cardiff; 2ndly, (Aug.) 1940,
Rita, dau. of the late Cecil Berens ,J.P., and has issue living, (by 1st marriage) Michael Patrick
Radcliffe (of Ashe Park, Basingstoke, Hants.), *b.* 1934; ed. at Eton; Capt. (ret.), Irish Guards;
co. Councillor of Hants. since 1970: *m.* 1962, Lady Nell Carleton Harris, da. of 6th Earl of Malmesbury, and has issue living, Robert Algernon Radcliffe *b.* 1963, Rupert *b.* 1968, Maria *b.* 1964,—(by
2nd m.) David Spencer, *b.* 1942. *Residence,*—Ashe, P.O. Balgowan, Natal.

PREDECESSORS.—[1] HENRY Boyle, *P.C., M.P.* for co. Cork 1715–56, Speaker of the Irish House
of Commons, fifteen times Lord Justice of Ireland, and Chancellor of the Exchequer and Commr.
of the Treasury; cr. *Baron Castle Martyr, Viscount Boyle,* and *Earl of Shannon* (peerage of Ireland)
1756; *d.* 1764; *s.* by his son [2] RICHARD, K.P., P.C., 2nd Earl; was successively M.P. for Dungarvan and for co. Cork, Master-Gen. of the Ordnance 1766–70, and Vice-Treasurer of Ireland 1781,
&c.; cr. *Baron Carleton,* of Carleton, co. York (peerage of Great Britain) 1786; *d.* 1807; *s.* by his
son [3] HENRY, K.P., 3rd Earl; was Custos Rotulorum of co. Cork, and Clerk of the Pells in Ireland;
d. 1842; *s.* by his son [4] RICHARD, 4th Earl; *b.* 1809: *m.* 1832, Emily Henrietta, dau. of Lord
George Seymour (M. Hertford); *d.* 1868; *s.* by his son [5] HENRY BENTINCK, 5th Earl, *b.* 1833:
m. 1st, 1859, Lady Blanche Emma Lascelles, who *d.* 1863, dau. of 3rd Earl of Harewood; 2ndly,
1868, Julia Charlotte, who *d.* 1921, dau. of Sir William Edmund Cradock-Hartopp, 3rd Bt.; *d.*
1890; *s.* by his el. son [6] RICHARD HENRY, 6th Earl, *b.* 1860: *m.* 1895, Nellie, who *d.* 1910, dau.
of the late Charles Thompson, of 14, Park Sq., N.W.; *d.* 1906; *s.* by his el. son [7] RICHARD BER-
NARD, 7th Earl, *b.* 1897; Lt. Roy. Fusiliers; *d.* (killed in action during European War) 1917; *s.* by
his brother [8] ROBERT HENRY, 8th Earl: *b.* 1900; Capt. Indian Army; A.D.C. to Gov. of Madras
1923: *m.* 1923, Marjorie, dau. of S. A. Walker of Ootacamund, India; *d.* 1963; *s.* by his only son
[9] RICHARD BENTINCK, 9th Earl and present peer; also Viscount Boyle, Baron Castle Martyr,
and Baron Carleton. [*Note,* this title derived from Shannon Park, co. Cork and *not* the River
Shannon.]

SHARP, BARONESS. (Sharp.) [Life Baroness 1966.]

EVELYN ADELAIDE SHARP, *GBE*, da. of the late Rev. Charles James Sharp, V. of Ealing, W5; *b.* May 25th, 1903; ed. at St. Paul's Girls' Sch., and at Somerville Coll., Oxford (BA, Hon. Fellow, Hon. DCL); Hon. LLD Camb.; Hon. DCL Manchester; Permanent Sec. Min. of Housing and Local Govt. 1955-66; a Member of Board of ITA 1966-73; *cr.* DBE (Civil) 1948, GBE (Civil) 1961, and *Baroness Sharp*, of Hornsey in Greater London (Life Baroness) 1966.

Residence,—The Small House, Dinton, Salisbury.

SHARPLES, BARONESS. (Sharples.) [Life Baroness 1973.]

PAMELA SHARPLES, da. of Keith William Newall; *b.* Feb. 11th, 1923; ed. at Southover Manor, Lewes; 1939-45 War as LACW with WRAF; *cr. Baroness Sharples*, of Chawton, in Hampshire (Life Baroness 1973): *m.* 1946, Sir Richard Christopher Sharples, KCMG, OBE, MC, Gov. of Bermuda, who *d.* (assassinated in Bermuda) 1973, and has issue.

Arms,—Argent, a chevron vert between in chief two copper beech trees eradicated, and in base a white tailed tropicbird (Phaethon Lepturus), a volant proper, for *Sharples*, on an escutcheon of pretence the Arms of *Newall*, Per saltire argent and gules, a crozier in fesse or between three bustards, wings elevated and addorsed, counterchanged.

Supporters,—On either side a Great Dane dog, resting the interior hind foot proper on a portcullis or.

Residence,—Southfield Farm, Chawton, Alton, Hants.

SONS LIVING.

Hon. Christopher John, *b.* 1947: *m.* 1975, Sharon, el. da. of Robert Sweeny, of Montague Sq., W1.
Hon. David Richard, *b.* 1955.

DAUGHTERS LIVING.

Hon. Fiona, *b.* 1949.
Hon. Miranda, *b.* 1951.

SHAUGHNESSY, BARON. (Shaughnessy.) [Baron U.K. 1916.]

With a strong hand.

WILLIAM GRAHAM SHAUGHNESSY, 3rd Baron; *b.* March 28th, 1922; *s.* 1938; ed. at Bishop's Coll. Sch., and at Bishop's Univ., Lennoxville, Canada; Major (retired) Canadian Army; Executive Assist. to Canadian Min. of Finance 1949-51; elected Pres. of Commonwealth So., Canada 1959: *m.* 1944, Mary, only dau. of the late John Whitley, of Letchworth, and has issue.

Arms,—Per fesse gules and azure, in chief two mill-rinds, and in base an ancient harp or, within a bordure engrailed ermine. **Crest,**—Issuing from an antique crown or, a dexter cubit arm in armour and gauntleted, grasping a two-headed battle-axe, all proper. **Supporters,**—*Dexter*, an Irish wolfhound proper, gorged with a collar argent charged with three trefoils vert; *sinister*, a beaver proper, gorged with a collar argent charged with three maple leaves gules.

Address,—1227, Sherbrook St. West, Montreal, Canada.

SONS LIVING.

Hon. PATRICK JOHN, *b* Oct. 23rd, 1944.
Hon. Michael James, *b.* 1946.

DAUGHTERS LIVING.

Hon. Brigid Mary, *b.* 1948.   *Hon.* Marion Kathleen, *b.* 1951.

SISTERS LIVING.

Hon. Hazel Marion, *b.* 1914: *m.* 1938, James R. Ballantyne, who *d.* 1970, and has issue living, William James, *b.* 1945,—Marion Graham, *b.* 1942. *Residence,*—2, Ballantyne Terr., Dorval, Quebec, Canada.
Hon. Bridget Ann (235, Heath St. East, Toronto, Ont., Canada), *b.* 1916.

COLLATERAL BRANCH LIVING.

Issue of the late Capt. the Hon. Alfred Thomas Shaughnessy, Canadian Expeditionary Force, younger son of 1st Baron, *b.* 1887, *d.* (killed in action during European War) 1916: *m.* 1912, Sarah Polk, who *d.* 1955 (having *m.* 2ndly, 1920, Lieut.-Col. the Hon. Sir Piers Walter Legh, G.C.V.O., C.M.G., C.I.E., O.B.E., who *d.* 1955 [see B. Newton, colls.]), dau. of the late Judge James O. Bradford, formerly of Nashville, Tennessee, U.S.A. :—

Thomas Bradford (21, Upper Trafalgar Place, Montreal, Canada), *b.* 1915; Bar. Montreal 1947; is Capt. Welsh Gds. (Reserve): *m.* 1949, Margot, da. of the late William D. Chambers, of Montreal, and has issue living, Amanda Marguerite Polk, *b.* 1951,—Roxane Elizabeth, *b.* 1952,—Tara Evelyn, *b.* 1954.——Alfred James (*posthumous*) (Ringwold House, Middle Wallop, Hants.), *b.* 1916; is Capt, Gren. Gds. (Reserve): *m.* 1948, Jean Margaret, da. of the late George Lodge, of Kirkella, Yorks. and has issue living, Charles George Patrick, *b.* 1955,—David James Bradford, *b.* 1957.——Elizabeth Sarah Polk, *b.* 1913: *m.* 1st, 1932 (m. diss. 1946), the 2nd Baron Grenfell; 2ndly, 1946, Maj. Berkeley Buckingham Howard Stafford, KRRC, who *d.* 1966; 3rdly, 1969 Trevor Walton (Rex) King, of 40, Bramham Gdns., SW5, and has issue living, (by 1st m.), [see B. Grenfell].

PREDECESSORS.—[1] THOMAS GEORGE Shaughnessy, *K.C.V.O.*, son of Thomas Shaughnessy, of Limerick; *b.* 1853; was Pres. Canadian Pacific Railway 1899-1918 (Chm. of Board of Directors); also a Director of all this Co.'s allied lines; cr. *Baron Shaughnessy*, of City of Montreal, Dominion of Canada, and of Ashford, co. Limerick (peerage of United Kingdom) 1916: *m.* 1880, Elizabeth Bridget, who *d.* 1937, dau. of N. Nagle, of Milwaukee, U.S.A.; *d.* 1923; *s.* by his son [2] WILLIAM JAMES, *K.C.*, 2nd Baron; *b.* 1883; K.C. Canada; a Director of Canadian Pacific Railway Co., of Canadian Bank of Commerce, and other Cos.: *m.* 1911, Marion Laura, who *d.* 1936, dau. of the late Robert Kilgour Graham, of Montreal, Canada; *d.* 1938; *s.* by his only son [3] WILLIAM GRAHAM, 3rd Baron and present peer.

SHAWCROSS, BARON. (Shawcross.) [Life Baron 1959.]

HARTLEY WILLIAM SHAWCROSS, *GBE, PC, QC*, son of the late John Shawcross, MA; *b.* Feb. 4th, 1902; ed. at Dulwich Coll., and Geneva; Hon. LLM Liverpool; Hon. LLD Columbia (USA), Bristol, Michigan, Lehigh (USA), Sussex, and Liverpool; Hon. DCL New Brunswick, and Hull; Bar. Gray's Inn 1925, Bencher 1939, KC 1939, and Treasurer 1955; a Member of Bar Council (Chm. 1952-57), Hon. Fellow of American Bar Foundation, and Hon. Member of American and New York Bars; Recorder of Salford 1941-45, and Kingston upon Thames 1946-54; Attorney-Gen. 1945-51 and Pres. of Board of Trade April to Oct. 1951; a Prin. Delegate for UK to Assemblies of UN 1945-49, Ch. Prosecutor for UK before Internat. Mil. Tribunal Nuremberg 1945-46, and UK Member of Permanent Court of Arbitration, The Hague 1950, Chm. Royal Commn. on the Press 1961-62, Med. Research Council 1961-65, Sussex Discharged Prisoners' Aid Soc. 1962-66, and City Panel on Take-Overs and Mergers 1968; a JP for Sussex; a Dir. of EMI, Ltd., Ranks Hovis Macdougall, Ltd., Caffyns Motors, Ltd., Morgan et Cie Internat. SA, Upjohns (UK), Ltd., Morgan et Cie SA, Hawker Siddeley Group, Ltd., and Times Newspapers, Ltd., Chm. of Morgan Guaranty Trust Co.'s Internat. Advisory Council, and Upjohns UK, Ltd.; Pres. of Rainer Foundation (formerly London Police Court Mission), and of British Hotels and Restaurants Assocn.; a Member of Exec. of Internat. Commn. of Jurists, and of Council of Internat. Chamber of Commerce; Chm. of Friends of Atlantic Union, Internat. Law Section, British Inst. of Internat. & Comparative Law, and " Justice " (British Branch Internat. Commn. of Jurists); a Member of Court, London Univ.; Chancellor of Sussex Univ. since 1965; Indep. Chm. of Press Council since 1974; MP for St. Helens (*Lab.*) 1945-58; cr. Knt. 1945, PC 1946, *Baron Shawcross*, of Friston, co. Sussex (Life Baron) 1959, and GBE (Civil) 1974: *m.* 1st, 1924, Rosita Alberta, who *d.* 1943, da. of William Shyvers, of Upminister Lodge, Essex; 2ndly, 1944, Joan Winifred, who *d.* 1974, da. of Hume Mather, of Carlton Lodge, Tunbridge Wells, and has issue by 2nd m.

Arms,—Per pale azure and gules on a saltire between four annulets argent an ermine spot sable. **Crest,**—Upon the battlements of a tower proper a martlet gules holding in the beak a cross paty fitchy or. **Supporters,**—*Dexter*, a lion argent gorged with a chain sable pendant therefrom an escutcheon also sable charged with a balance or ; *sinister*, a griffin sable armed and langued azure gorged with a chain, pendent therefrom a portcullis or.

Residences,—Friston Place, Sussex; 12, Grays Inn Sq., WC1. *Address,*—33, Lombard St., EC3. *Clubs,*—Bucks., White's, Royal Automobile, Royal Cornwall Yacht, Royal Yacht Squadron, New York Yacht, and Travellers' (Paris).

SONS LIVING. (*By 2nd marriage.*)

Hon. William Hartley Hume (40, Estelle Rd., NW3), *b.* 1946; ed. at Eton and Univ. Coll., Oxford: *m.* 1972, Marina Warner.
Hon. Hume, *b.* 1953; ed. at Eton.

DAUGHTER LIVING. (*By 2nd marriage.*
Hon. Joanna, *b.* 1948; ed. at Benenden, and London Univ.

Sheffield and Stanley of Alderley, Baron (see Stanley of Alderley).

SHEFFIELD, LORD BISHOP OF. (Fallows.)

Rt. Rev. (WILLIAM) GORDON FALLOWS, son of William Fallows; *b.* June 21st, 1913; ed. at Barrow Gram. Sch., St. Edmund Hall, Oxford (MA), and Ripon Hall, Oxford; V. of Styvechale, Coventry 1939-45, Rural Dean of Preston 1946-55, Proctor in Convocation 1950-55, Archdeacon of Lancaster 1955-59, V. of Preston 1945-59, Prin. of Ripon Hall, Oxford 1959-68, Chap. to HM 1953-68, Examining Chap. to Bishop of Wakefield 1968-71, and Bishop Suffragan of Pontefract 1968-71; appointed 4th Bishop of Sheffield 1971; OCF 1941-44: *m.* 1940, Edna Mary, da. of the late Frederick Blakeman.

Patron of seventy livings, and the Rural Deaneries of Attercliffe, Doncaster, Ecclesfield, Ecclesall, Hallam, Laughton, Rotherham, Tankersley, Wath, and Snaith.
This See was founded 1914.
𝕰𝖕𝖎𝖘𝖈𝖔𝖕𝖆𝖑 𝕾𝖎𝖌𝖓𝖆𝖙𝖚𝖗𝖊—"Gordon Sheffield."

ARMS OF THE SEE,—Azure, a crosier in pale ensigned by a fleur-de-lys vert between in fesse a key surmounted by a sword in saltire to the dexter, and to the sinister eight arrows interlaced and banded saltirewise, all or.

Residence,—Bishopscroft, Snaithing Lane, Sheffield, S10 3LG.

Shelburne, Earl of, son of Marquess of Lansdowne.

SHEPHERD, BARON. (Shepherd.) [Baron U.K. 1946.]

MALCOLM NEWTON SHEPHERD, *PC,* 2nd Baron; *b.* Sept. 27th, 1918; *s.* 1954: Capt. of HM Body Guard of Hon. Corps of Gentlemen-at-Arms 1964-67; Dep. Speaker and Ch. Whip, House of Lords 1964-67; a Min. of State Commonwealth Office 1967-70, and Dep. Leader House of Lords 1968-70; Lord Privy Seal and Leader of the House of Lords since 1974; 1939-45 War as Lt. RASC in N. Africa, Sicily, and Italy; PC 1965: *m.* 1941, Allison, da. of Patrick Redmond, of 56, Carrick Knowe, Parkway, Edinburgh, and has issue.
Residence,—29, Kennington Palace Court, Sancroft St., SE11.

SONS LIVING.

Hon. GRAEME GEORGE, *b.* Jan. 6th, 1949.
Hon. Douglas Newton, *b.* 1952.

SISTER LIVING.

Hon. Margaret Eleanor, *b.* 1922 : *m.* 1949, Theodore Leonard Bates, and has issue living, Andrew Michael, *b.* 1952,—Suzanne Katherine Michele, *b.* 1960. *Residence,*—45, Whyteleafe Hill, Whyteleafe, Surrey.

PREDECESSOR.—[1] *Rt. Hon.* GEORGE ROBERT Shepherd, *P.C.,* son of the late George Robert Shepherd, of Spalding, Lincolnshire, *b.* 1881 ; Ch. Opposition Whip, and a Dep.-Speaker, House of Lords and a Member of Parliamentary Committee of Labour Party ; National Agent of Labour Party 1928-46 ; was a Lord-in-Waiting to H.M. Oct. 1948 to July 1949 ; Capt. of Yeomen of the Guard July to Oct. 1949, and Capt. of Gentlemen-at-Arms and Ch. Govt. Whip in House of Lords Oct. 1949 to Oct. 1951; cr. *Baron Shepherd,* of Spalding, co. Lincoln (peerage of United Kingdom) 1946: *m.* 1915, Ada, who *d.* 1975, da. of the late Alfred Newton, of Halstead, Essex; *d.* 1954; *s.* by his son [2] MALCOLM NEWTON, 2nd Baron and present peer.

SHERBORNE, BARON.   (Dutton.)   [Baron G.B. 1784.]

CHARLES DUTTON, 7th Baron; *b.* May 13th, 1911; *s.* 1949; ed. at Stowe; is patron of two livings: *m.* 1943, Joan Molesworth, dau. of Sir James Hamet Dunn, 1st Bt. (cr. 1921), and widow of John Antony Jenkinson [Jenkinson, Bt., colls.].

Arms,—Quarterly, argent and gules; in the 2nd and 3rd quarters a fret or.   Crest,—A plume of five ostrich feathers argent, azure, or, vert, and gules.   Supporters,—Two wolves argent, each gorged with a plain collar azure, charged with three garbs or.
Seat,—Lodge Park, Aldsworth, Cheltenham.

SERVABO   FIDEM
I will keep my word.

BROTHER LIVING.

Hon. GEORGE EDWARD, *b.* Sept. 23rd, 1912; ed. at Stowe: *m.* 1st, 1945, Joan (from whom he obtained a divorce 1957), dau. of the late Capt. Harold Thomas Bennett East, Hon. Artillery Co.; 2ndly, 1959, Mrs. Pauline Stewart Shephard, dau. of the late Major Stewart Robinson. *Residence,*—Sherborne, Cheltenham, Gloucestershire.

SISTER LIVING.

Hon. Juliet Elizabeth (Windrush Manor, Windrush, Oxford), *b.* 1915.

COLLATERAL BRANCHES LIVING.

Issue of the late Vice-Adm. the Hon. Arthur Brandreth Scott Dutton, C.B., C.M.G. (raised to rank of a Baron's son 1920), brother of 6th Baron, *b.* 1876, *d.* 1932: *m.* 1914, Doriel, who *d.* 1941, dau. of Sir John Adam Hay, 9th Bt. (cr. 1635):—
Julia Meliora, *b.* 1914: *m.* 1939, Bertram Salisbury Butler, formerly Sqdn.-Ldr. RAFVR, and has issue living, Doriel Julia Primrose, *b.* 1941: *m.* 1964, Gavin Fleming Crawford, of 7, Woodsford Sq., Addison Rd., W14, and has issue living, Charles William Norrie *b.* 1970, Caroline Doriel *b.* 1966, Sarah Elizabeth *b.* 1968. *Residence,*—Burton Manor, Pulborough, Sussex.——Doriel Rowena, *b.* 1916: *m.* 1940, Ian Norman Bayles, DFC, Wing-Cdr. RAFVR, of Chatsworth Park, Tabilk, Vic., Aust., and has issue living, Alastair Ian (Gilgai, Nagambie, Vic., Aust.) *b.* 1941: *m.* 1967, Judith Alison, el. da. of Geoffrey Ryan, of Willowmavin, Vic., Aust., and has issue living, Emma Rowena *b.* 1970, Fiona Alison *b.* 1973,—Archibald James Norman, *b.* 1948,—Aprilla Rowena, *b.* 1946: *m.* 1968, John Beaufort Somerset, of 1, Trafalgar Rd., Camberwell, Vic., Aust., and has issue living, Sarah Penelope *b.* 1970, Catherine Rowena *b.* 1971,—Amanda Mary, *b.* 1951,—Ayliffe Julia (twin), *b.* 1951. *Residence,*—Chatsworth Park, Tabilk, Vic., Aust.

Grandchildren of the late Hon. John Thomas Dutton, 2nd son of 2nd Baron:—
Issue of the late Henry John Dutton, *b.* 1847, *d.* 1935: *m.* 1888, Blanche Eleanor, who *d.* 1946, dau. of the late Laurence Cave, of Ditcham Park, Petersfield:—
Ralph Stawell, *b.* 1898; ed. at Eton, and at Ch. Ch., Oxford; was High Sheriff of Hampshire 1944; is a F.S.A. *Residences,*—Hinton Ampner House, Alresford, Hants; 95N, Eaton Square, S.W.1.——Blanche Mary Stukeley, *b.* 1894. *Residence,*—13, Moore Street, S.W.3.——Ursula Mary Lavinia, *b.* 1896. *Residence,*—Joan's Acre, Hinton Ampner, Alresford, Hants.——Joane Mary Sherborne, *b.* 1902. *Residence,*—Brick Kiln Farm, W. Meon, Hants.

PREDECESSORS.—[1] JAMES Dutton, *M.P.* for Gloucestershire (descendant of Thomas Dutton, who purchased the manor of Sherborne in the 16th century), was cr. *Baron Sherborne,* of Sherborne, co. Gloucester (peerage of Great Britain) 1784; *d.* 1820; *s.* by his son [2] JOHN, 2nd Baron; *b.* 1779; *m.* 1803, the Hon. Mary Stawell Bilson-Legge, dau. and heiress of 2nd and last Baron Stawell [E. Dartmouth]; *d.* 1862; *s.* by his son [3] JAMES HENRY LEGGE, 3rd Baron; *b.* 1804: *m.* 1st, 1826, Lady Elizabeth Howard, who *d.* 1845, dau. of 16th Earl of Suffolk; 2ndly, 1857, Susan Elizabeth, who *d.* 1907, dau. of the late James Block, of Charlton, Wilts; *d.* 1883; *s.* by his son [4] EDWARD LENOX, 4th Baron; *b.* 1831; *m.* 1894, Emily Theresa, who *d.* 1905, dau. of the late Baron de Stern; *d.* 1919; *s.* by his brother [5] *Rev.* FREDERICK GEORGE, 5th Baron, *b.* 1840, *d.* 1920; *s.* by his nephew [6] JAMES HUNTLY, D.S.O. (el. son of the late Col. the Hon. Charles Dutton, 5th son of 3rd Baron), 6th Baron; *b.* 1873; S. Africa 1899-1902, European War 1914-19 as Major Roy. Scots (D.S.O.): *m.* 1908 Ethel Mary; who *d.* 1969, el. da. of the late William Baird, of Elie, Fife, and Cambusdoon, Ayrshire; *d.* 1949; s. by his el. son [7] CHARLES, 7th Baron, and present peer.

SHERFIELD, BARON.   (Makins.)   [Baron U.K. 1964.]

ROGER MELLOR MAKINS, *GCB, GCMG,* 1st Baron, son of the late Brig.-Gen. Sir Ernest Makins, KBE, CB, DSO; *b.* Feb. 3rd, 1904; ed. at Winchester, and at Ch. Ch., Oxford; Hon. DCL Oxford, Hon. LLD Sheffield, Hon. FICE, Fellow of All Souls' Coll., Oxford, and of Winchester Coll., Hon. Student Ch. Ch. Oxford, and Hon. DLitt Reading; Bar. Inner Temple 1927; Min. at Washington 1945-47, Assist. Under-Sec. of State, Foreign Office 1947-48, Dep. Under-Sec. of State 1948-52, Ambassador to USA 1952-56, Joint Permanent Sec. to The Treasury 1956-60, and Chm. of UK Atomic Energy Authority 1960-64; Chm. Board of Govs., Imperial Coll. of Science and Technology 1962-74, of Industrial and Commercial Finance Corporation 1964-74, of Hill Samuel & Co., Ltd., 1966-70, of A. C. Cossor since 1968, and of Wells-Fargo, Ltd. since 1972 and other cos.; Pres. of Parliamentary and Scientific Cttee. 1969-72, and of

British Standards Instn. 1970-72; Chancellor of Reading Univ. since 1970; Warden of Winchester Coll. since 1974; *cr.* CMG 1944, KCMG 1949, KCB (Civil) 1953, GCMG 1955, GCB (Civil) 1960 and *Baron Sherfield,* of Sherfield-on-Loddon, co. Southampton (Peerage of UK) 1964: *m.* 1934, Alice Brooks, el. da. of the late Hon. Dwight F. Davis, and has issue.

Arms,—Argent or a fesse embattled counter embattled gules between in chief two falcons proper belled or, and in base a lion's face of the second, an annulet or between two besants. **Crest,—** A dexter arm embowed in armour proper encircled by an annulet or and holding a flagstaff, therefrom flowing a banner argent charged with a lion's face gules. **Supporters,—***Dexter,* a lion sable pendent from a chain about the neck or a bezant charged with a model representing an atom of lithium 6 Sable, *Sinister,* a bald headed eagle rising proper adorned likewise about the neck the bezant charged with a lawn tennis racquet erect gules.

*Residences,—*Sherfield Court, nr. Basingstoke; 8, Southwick Place, W.2.

*Clubs,—*Boodle's, Pratt's, MCC.

SONS LIVING.

Hon. CHRISTOPHER JAMES, *b.* July 23rd, 1942; ed. at Winchester and New Coll., Oxford; Fellow of All Souls Coll., Oxford; HM Foreign Ser.

Hon. Dwight William, *b.* 1951; ed. at Winchester, and Ch. Ch., Oxford.

DAUGHTERS LIVING.

Hon. Mary, *b.* 1935: *m.* 1959, as his 2nd wife, the Hon. Hugo John Laurence Philipps, of 16, Tregunter Rd., S.W.10, only son of the 2nd Baron Milford.

Hon. Cynthia (twin), *b.* 1935: *m.* 1967, Oliver James Colman, of 35, Greville Rd., NW6 [see Colman, Bt., *cr.* 1907].

Hon. Virginia, *b.* 1939; ed. at Lady Margaret Hall, Oxford: *m.* 1972, David Michael Shapiro, of 14, Woodstock Rd., W4, and has issue.

Hon. Patricia, *b.* 1946: *m.* 1966, Michael Ordway Miller (Box 255, Star Route, Sausalito, Cal., USA).

SHINWELL, BARON. (Shinwell.) [Life Baron 1970].

EMANUEL SHINWELL, *CH, PC,* son of the late Samuel Shinwell, of Glasgow; *b.* Oct. 18th, 1884; formerly National Organiser Marine Workers' Union; Pres. of Glasgow Trades Council 1912 and 1916-19; Parl. Sec. to Dept. of Mines Jan. to Nov. 1924, Parl. and Financial Sec., War Dept. 1929-30, and Min. of Fuel and Power 1945-47, Sec. of State for War 1947-50, Min. of Defence 1950-51, and Chm. of Parl. Labour Party 1964-67; MP for Linlithgowshire (*Lab.*) 1922-24 and 1928-31, for Seaham Div. of Durham 1935-50, and for Easington Div. of Durham 1950-70; *cr.* PC 1945, CH 1965, and *Baron Shinwell,* of Easington, co. Durham (Life Baron) 1970: *m.* 1st, 1903, Fay Freeman, who *d.* 1954; 2ndly, 1956, Dinah, who *d.* 1971, da. of the late Carl Ludwig Meyer, of Denmark; 3rdly, 1972, Sarah, da. of Solomon Stungo, and formerly wife of Alfred Hurst, and has issue by 1st m., 3 sons and a da.

*Residence,—*Oslo Court, St. John's Wood, NW8.

SHREWSBURY AND WATERFORD, EARL OF. (Chetwynd-Talbot.) [Earl E. 1442, I. 1446, and G.B. 1784.]

Ready to accomplish.

attired or, *Chetwynd.* **Supporters,—**Two talbots argent. **Badge,—**A talbot passant argent.

JOHN GEORGE CHARLES HENRY ALTON ALEXANDER CHETWYND CHETWYND-TALBOT, 21st Earl, and Premier Earl (on the Roll) in peerages both of England and Ireland; *b.* Dec. 1st, 1914; *s.* 1921; ed. at Eton; is Hereditary Lord High Steward of Ireland, late Capt. R.A., and patron of eleven livings; formerly a Co. Councillor for Staffordshire; was Staff-Lt. to H.R.H. the Duke of Gloucester 1940-42, and Pres. of Asso. of Agriculture 1949-56; Middle East and Italy 1942-44: *m.* 1st, 1936 (marriage dissolved 1963), Nadine, yr. dau. of the late Brig.-Gen. Cyril Randel Crofton, C.B.E., of Trobridge, Crediton, Devon; 2ndly, 1963, Aileen Mortlock, and has issue by 1st marriage.

Arms,—Quarterly, 1st and 4th, gules, a lion rampant, within a bordure engrailed or, *Talbot;* 2nd and 3rd azure, a chevron between three mullets or, *Chetwynd.* **Crests,—**1st, on a chapeau gules, turned up ermine, a lion statant, with the tail extended or, *Talbot;* 2nd, a goat's head erased argent,

*Residence,—*Sentier De Priolaz 8, 1802, Corseaux, Vaud, Switzerland. *Club,—*Royal Yacht Squadron.

SONS LIVING. (*By 1st marriage.*)

CHARLES HENRY JOHN BENEDICT CROFTON CHETWYND (*Viscount Ingestre*) (Ivy House Farm, Drointon, Stowe-by-Chartley, nr. Stafford), *b.* Dec. 18th, 1952; ed. at Harrow: *m.* 1974, Deborah Jane, only da. of Noel Staughton Hutchinson, of Ellerton House, Sambrook, Salop, and has issue.

DAUGHTER LIVING—*Hon.* Victoria Jane, *b.* 1975.

Hon. Paul Alexander Anthony Bueno, *b.* 1957.

DAUGHTERS LIVING. (*By 1st marriage.*)

Lady Charlotte Sarah Alexandra, *b.* 1938: *m.* 1965, Camillo Cavazza dei Conti Cavazza, of S. Felice del Benaco, Brescia, Italy, and has issue living, Sigmar, *b.* 1966,—Eric, *b.* 1969,—Livia, *b.* 1967.

Lady Josephine Sylvia Rose, *b.* 1940: *m.* 1965, Stafford Antony Saint, The Woodman, Sandridge, St. Albans, and has issue living, Stafford Alexander Antony Talbot, *b.* 1970,—Helen Elizabeth Charlotte, *b.* 1966,—Victoria Nadine Mary, *b.* 1968.

Lady Catharine Laura, *b.* 1945: *m.* 1966, Richard Sebastian Endicott Chamberlain, of Blanchards, Barnes Lane, Milford-on-Sea, Hants., and has issue living, Thomas Endicott, *b.* 1973,—Sophie Anne Zacyntha *b.* 1968,—Caroline Amy, *b.* 1971.

Lady Marguerite Mary, *b.* 1950: *m.* 1970, Guy William Brisbane, of 228, Meadville Rd., Ealing, W5.

SISTER LIVING. *(Raised to the rank of an Earl's daughter* 1921.*)*

Lady Victoria Audrey Beatrice, *b.* 1910 : *m.* 1st, 1932, the 6th Baron Sheffield, from whom she obtained a divorce 1936; 2ndly, 1945, His Honour Judge (Gwyn Rhyse Francis) Morris, QC. *Residences,*—Carpmael Building, Temple, EC4; Penylan Hall, Llechryd, Cardiganshire.

COLLATERAL BRANCHES LIVING.

Grandson of the late Brig.-Gen. Arthur Hervey Talbot, son of the late Charles Arthur Talbot, son of the late Rev. the Hon. Arthur Chetwynd-Talbot, 3rd son of 2nd Earl Talbot:—

Issue of the late Lieut.-Col. Douglas Hervey Talbot, D.S.O., M.C., *b.* 1882, *d.* 1927: *m.* 1914, Dorothy Helen Roylance, dau. of the late William Roylance Court, J.P. [Walker, Bt., cr. 1886]:—

Bryan Hervey (Aston Lodge, Aston, Runcorn, Cheshire), *b.* 1916; ed. at Marlborough Coll.; 1940-46 War as F/L RAFVR: *m.* 1940, Katherine, da. of R. J. Hughes, of Llandudno, and has issue living, Andrew Hervey, *b.* 1946: *m.* 1972, Hilda Margaret Priscilla Williams, SRN,—Howard Douglas (Oak Cottage, Picton Gorse, Chester), *b.* 1948: *m.* 1972, Christine Anne, da. of W. A. A. Dutton, of Hoole Bank, Chester,—Marie Luize, *b.* 1942: *m.* 1966, John Bernard Haycraft, of New House Farm, Dorsington, Stratford-upon-Avon, and has issue living, Alexander Richard *b.* 1969, Oliver Talbot *b.* 1972, Simon Hervey *b.* 1973,—Wendy Robina Roylance, *b.* 1949: *m.* 1973, Rodger Price.

Granddaughter of the late Charles Arthur Talbot (ante):—

Issue of the late Gwendolen Mary Talbot, *b.* 1861, *d.* 1948 : *m.* 1880, Harry Wyndham Jefferson, who *d.* 1918 :—

Guendolen: *m.* 1925, Cecil John Rhodes, and has issue living, (Cecil) John *b.* 1926; ed. at Stowe; served in R.N. 1943-7: *m.* 1954, Maud Elin Margareta, dau. of Capt. Folke Lindesvard, of Stockholm, Sweden, and has issue living, Peter John Anders *b.* 1957, David Cecil *b.* 1959, Andrew Christopher *b.* 1962,—Rosemary Ursula Guendolen *b.* 1931. *Residences,*—Pinegrove, Stoke Park, Stokes Poges, Bucks: 4, Elm Park Lane, Chelsea, SW3.

Grandchildren of the late Rev. the Hon. Arthur Chetwynd-Talbot (ante):—

Issue of the late Col. Hervey Talbot, *b.* 1838, *d.* 1884: *m.* 1874, Eva Julietta, who *d.* 1888 [having *m.* 2ndly, 1887, Capt George Capel Ralph Curzon Fenwick, who *d.* 1909, of Plâs Ffron, Wrexham (see Phillipps, Bt.)], dau. of Henry Crawshay, of Oaklands Park, Newnham, Gloucestershire:—

Muriel Marguerita, *b.* 1875 : *m.* 19—, Percy Logan. *Residence,*—

Issue of the late Rev. Arthur Henry Chetwynd-Talbot, *b.* 1855 ; *d.* 1927: *m.* 1903, Eveline Mary who *d.* 1952, el. dau. of the late Col. C. J. Ashton, of Little Onn Hall, Staffordshire, and Newton, Hyde, Cheshire:—

John Arthur, *AFC* (84, Loudoun Rd., NW8 0ND), *b.* 1905; ed. at Harrow, and at Sidney Sussex Coll., Camb. (BA); 1939-45 War, as Sq. Ldr. RAFVR (AFC): *m.* 1st, 1929 (m. diss. 1963) Helen Mary, who *d.* 1969, el. da. of Adm. Cyril Samuel Townsend, CB; 2ndly, 1963, Betty Verral, yr. da. of the Rev. Augustus George Allton, and has issue living, (by 1st m.) John Edward (Rookery Cottage, Monk Sherborne, Basingstoke, Hants., RG26 5HL), *b.* 1934: *m.* 1st, 1959 (m. diss. 1964), Sonja Ann, da. of the late Roger Walker, of South Corner, Duncton, Sussex; 2ndly, 1967, Belinda Bess, yr. da. of Maj. Euan Gilchrist, of Monk Sherborne Hse., Monk Sherborne, Hants., and has issue living, (by 1st m.) Jane Sonja *b.* 1960, Sarah Ann *b.* 1962, (by 2nd m.) Edward John *b.* 1969, Mary Rowena *b.* 1968, Prudence Ankaret (twin) *b.* 1969,—Susan Mary, *b.* 1930: *m.* 1954, William Byars Thomson, of The Mill House, Rowfant, Crawley, Sussex, and has issue living, Geoffrey Charles Byars *b.* 1958, Richard William Byars *b.* 1960, Mary Rose Byars *b.* 1962,—Ankaret Helen, *b.* 1932: *m.* 1955, John Orcheston Dean, of 31, Second St., Oakville, Ont., Canada, and has issue living, John Anthony *b.* 1962, Joanna Elizabeth *b.* 1956, Philippa Ankaret *b.* 1958, Louise Helen *b.* 1960.——*Rev.* Arthur Charles Ashton (Flat 2, Park Lodge, 2, Blackwater Rd., Eastbourne, BN21 4JE), *b.* 1907; ed. at Harrow, and at Ch. Ch., Oxford (MA); Curate of St. John the Divine, Kennington, SW, 1933-37; a Member of Univs.' Mission to Central Africa, Nyasaland 1937-40, Curate of St. Peter's, Edgmond, Newport, Salop, 1940-43, Assist. Priest of All Saints', Margaret St., W1, 1943-45, R. of Wrington, Som., 1945-53, V. of Wantage, Berks., 1953-60, and R. of Catsfield, 1960-73: *m.* 1945, Pamela Mountjoy, da. of H. J. Say, of Dartford, Kent, and has issue living, Clare Eveline, *b.* 1946: *m.* 1968, Malcolm Garfield Green, of 2, Garden Cottages, Friars-Matfield, Tonbridge, Kent, and has issue living, Timothy Ashton Garfield *b.* 1969, Caroline Anne *b.* 1971.——*His Honour Judge* Richard Michael Arthur (42, The Lindens, Newbridge Cres., Tettenhall Rd., Wolverhampton, and 7, St. Leonard's Close, Bridgnorth, Salop), *b.* 1911; ed. at Harrow, and at Magdalene Coll., Camb. (MA); Bar. Middle Temple 1936, and Bencher 1962; a Member of Bar Council 1956-61; Chm. of Quarter Sessions, co. Salop 1967-71 (Dep. Chm. 1950-67), and Recorder of Banbury 1955-71; Hon. Recorder since 1972; Circuit Judge since 1972: 1939-45 War as Maj. KSLI.——Mary Eveline (*Lady Goodbody*), *b.* 1906: *m.* 1929, Gen. Sir Richard Wakefield Goodbody, GCB, KBE, DSO, and has issue living, Jeremy Richard Arthur (Hartfoot, Ansty, Dorchester, Dorset), *b.* 1932; ed. at Shrewsbury: *m.* 1963, Sarah, yr. da. of Rex Lovelace, of Piddlehinton, Dorchester, and has issue living, Richard Jeremy, *b.* 1965, Lucy Jane *b.* 1969,—Patrick Robert Gerald (c/o Lloyds Bank, 15, Cheapside, EC2), *b.* 1935; ed. at Shrewsbury, and at Wadham Coll., Oxford (BA): *m.* 1971, Ruth, yr. da. of W. D. Conolly, and has issue living, Mary Rose Victoria *b.* 1972, Emily Jane Daisy *b.* 1974,—Robert Marcus, *b.* 1939; ed. at St. Edward's Sch., Oxford, and at Trin. Coll., Dublin (BA); Lt. RA,—Lydia Janet, *b.* 1930. *Residence,*—Broadlea Farm, Sutton Waldron, Blandford, Dorset.——Anne Elizabeth (7, St. Leonard's Close, Bridgnorth, Salop), *b.* 1910; ed. at Oxford Univ. (BA 1932); 1939-45 War in WRNS.

Grandson of the late Col. Hervey Talbot (ante):—

Issue of the late Arthur Aston Talbot, *b.* 1881, *d.* 1918: *m.* 1912, Mary Winifred, who *d.* 1964, da. of the late A. Battiscombe, of Hinton Court Hereford:—

Patrick Edward Aston (1941, Arrowhead Drive, St. Petersburg, Florida 33703, USA), *b.* 1913; sometime in R. Aircraft Establishment: *m.* 1936, Gwyneth, yr. da. of the late Lt.-Col. Herbert Gaussen Sargeaunt, RA, and has issue living, David Nugent Aston (Quebec, Canada), *b.* 1939: *m.* 1962, Carole, da. of Oakley Pawson, of Ontario, and has issue living, John Oakley Aston *b.* 1964, Jeanne Davida *b.* 1962, Rachel Millicent *b.* 1966, —Maryan Gwyneth (Beau Coin Lodge, La Haule, Jersey), *b.* 1938.

Grandchildren of the late Rt. Hon. John Gilbert Talbot, el. son of the late Hon. John Chetwynd-Talbot, QC, 4th son of 2nd Earl Talbot:—

Issue of the late Rt. Hon., Sir George John Talbot, *b.* 1861, *d.* 1938: *m.* 1897, Gertrude Harriot, who *d.* 1941, da. of the late Albemarle Cator of Woodbastwick Hall, Norfolk:—

Thomas George, *C.B.*, *Q.C.*, *b.* 1904; Bar. Inner Temple 1929, a Q.C. 1954 and a Bencher 1960; has been Counsel to Chm. of Committees, House of Lords since 1953; 1939-45 War as Capt. Scots Guards; C.B. (Civil) 1960: *m.* 1933, the Hon. Cynthia Edith Guest, dau. of 1st Viscount Wimborne, and has issue living, Charles John, *b.* 1947,—Meriel Cornelia, *b.* 1935: *m.* 1966, Robert David Hugh Boyd, MB, MRCP, of 9, Torriano Cottages, NW5, and has issue living, Thomas Dixon *b.* 1957, Diana Charlotte *b.* 1969, Lucy Madeleine *b.* 1974,—Joanna, *b.* 1938: *m.* 1964, Alan Malcolm Smith, of Edells, Markbeech, Edenbridge, Kent, and has issue living, Bertram Thomas, *b.* 1967, Emily Mary *b.* 1965, Flora *b.* 1971,—Mary Gertrude, *b.* 1942. *Residence,*—Falconhurst, Edenbridge, Kent.

Issue of the late John Edward Talbot, *b.* 1870, *d.* 1937: *m.* 1898, Mabel, who *d.* 1949, dau. of Archibald Balfour, of 65, Pont Street, S.W.:—
Evan Arthur Christopher, *M.B.E.*, *b.* 1903; ed. at Eton; Lieut.-Col. (retired) Grenadier Guards; European War 1939-45 (M.B.E.); M.B.E. (Mil.) 1945: *m.* 1926, Félicité Annette Cynthia, dau. of Lt.-Col. William Edward Long, and has issue living, Christopher Michael Edward, (The Old Vicarage, Tilford, Farnham, Surrey), *b.* 1928; late Lt. RN: *m.* 1962, Suzanne Barbara, el. da. of the late Arthur Dulley, and has issue living, Sarah Josephine *b.* 1964, Miranda Meriel *b.* 1966, Alice Elizabeth *b.* 1969,—Catherine, *b.* 1930: *m.* 1958, Clement Francis Kelly, of Lion House, Kingston Blount, Oxon, and has issue living, Anthea Jane, *b.* 1959, Felicity Ankaret *b.* 1962. *Residence,*—Old Brewhouse, Kingston Blount, Oxon.——Richard Eustace, *b.* 1907; ed. at Eton: *m.* 1933, Sheila Katherine, da. of the late Lt.-Col. Frank Evelyn Seely [see Seely, Bt., colls.]. *Residence,*—Fyning Manor, Rogate, Sussex.——Anne Meriel, *b.* 1899.——Joan Ankaret, *b.* 1901: *m.* 1928, Capt. Eric Hyde Villiers, DSO, who *d.* 1964 [see E. Clarendon, colls.]. *Residence,*—Ulcombe Pl., Maidstone.

Granddaughter of the late Rt. Rev. Edward Stuart Talbot, D.D., Lord Bishop of Winchester, son of the late Hon. John Chetwynd-Talbot, Q.C. (ante):—
Issue of the late Rt. Rev. Neville Stuart Talbot, M.C., D.D., Bishop of Pretoria 1920-32, *b.* 1879, *d.* 1943: *m.* 1918, Cecil Mary, who *d.* 1921, dau. of William Seymour Eastwood, of West Stoke House, Chichester:—
Elizabeth, *b.* 1919; late Flight Officer W.A.A.F.; is a J.P.: *m.* 1946, Ronald Arthur Chalk, and has issue living, Gilbert John, *b.* 1947,—Sarah Elizabeth, *b.* 1950. *Residence,*—Flat 5, 12, Loudwater House, Rickmansworth, Herts.

Granddaughter of the late George Canning Talbot, son of the late Rev. the Hon. George Gustavus Chetwynd-Talbot (infra):—
Issue of the late Major John Arthur William Talbot, *b.* 1876, *d.* 1918: *m.* 1906, Barbara Grace, who *d.* 1938, el. dau. of the late Rowland Ticehurst, of Crickley, Witcombe, Gloucestershire:—
Lettice Mary, *b.* (Dec.) 1907: *m.* 1934, George Butt Miller, who *d.* 1958, and has issue living, Thomas Butt (La Planque, Torteval, Guernsey), *b.* 1935; ed. at Eton, and New Coll., Oxford (MA); Solicitor 1966: *m.* 1965, Jane Mary, da. of C. C. Roberts, of Bepton Old Rectory, Midhurst,—Robert Cottrell Butt (20, Clarendon St., SW1), *b.* 1947; ed. at Worksop Coll., Trin. Coll., Dublin (BA), and Edinburgh Univ. (M.Litt.): *m.* 1971, Patricia Georgina, da. of Dr. G. MacBrian, of Bath, and has issue living, George Talbot *b.* 1974,—John Richard Butt, *b.* 1950; ed. at Stanbridge Sch., and Duke Univ., N. Carolina,—Barbara Blanche, *b.* 1938,—Mary Ruth, *b.* 1939. *Residence,*—Donhead Lodge, Shaftesbury, Dorset.

Granddaughter of the late Gustavus Arthur Talbot, MP, yr. son of the late Rev. the Hon. George Gustavus Chetwynd-Talbot, 5th son of 2nd Earl Talbot:—
Issue of the late Com. Reginald George Talbot, C.B.E., *b.* 1881, *d.* 1939: *m.* 1909, Mary Helen Charlotte, who *d.* 1922, dau. of the late Hon. Henry Robert Hepburne-Scott [B. Polwarth, colls.]:—
Alethea Cecil (*Alethea, Lady Mackeson*), *b.* 1913: *m.* 1940, Brig. Sir Harry Ripley Mackeson, 1st Bt., who *d.* 1964. *Residences,*—2 Orchard Court, Portman Sq., W.1.; The Old Rectory, Great Mongeham, Deal; Eton House, Docking, Norfolk.

Granddaughters of the late Lieut.-Col. Gerald Francis Chetwynd-Talbot, 3rd son of the late Rev. the Hon. William Whitworth Chetwynd-Talbot, 6th son of 2nd Earl Talbot:—
Issue of the late Stafford Cecil Chetwynd-Talbot, *b.* 1880, *d.* 1950: *m.* 1905, Ethel Lilian Caroline Leslie, who *d.* 1963, dau. of the late Robert Leslie Gault, of Montreal:—
Charlotte Henrietta Dorwin, *b.* 1908: *m.* 1935, Richard Charles Powys-Smith, late Lieut.-Cdr. R.N.R. and has issue living, Richard Talbot, *b.* 1941: *m.* 1970, Lavinia Susan Sanderson, and has issue living, James Robert Talbot *b.* 1972. *Residence,*—Lower Broomborough, Totnes, S. Devon.
Issue of the late Sir Gerald Francis Chetwynd-Talbot, K.C.V.O., C.M.G., O.B.E., *b.* 1881, *d.* 1945: *m.* 1920, Hélène, who *d.* 1975, da. of S. Jarislowsky, of Paris, and widow of Capt. Charles Labouchere, French Army:—
Isobel Helen Henrietta, *b.* 1923: *m.* 1942, Antony Mackenzie Smith, OBE, MC, British Council, late Capt. Gordon Highlanders, and has issue living, Peter (British Council, Cairo) *b.* 1946: *m.* 1973, Sandra Gay-French, and has issue living, Helen Sarah *b.* 1974,—Duncan John Gerald, *b.* 1951,—Jane Elizabeth, *b.* 1947: *m.* 1972, Robin Martin, of 16, Jocelyn Rd., Richmond, Surrey, and has issue living, James Benedict *b.* 1973,—Catherine Isobel, *b.* 1957. *Residence,*—Backfields End, Winchelsea, Sussex.

Grandsons of the late Col. the Hon. Sir Wellington Patrick Manvers Chetwynd-Talbot, K.C.B., 8th son of 2nd Earl Talbot:—
Issue of the late Gilbert Edward Chetwynd-Talbot, *b.* 1876, *d.* 1950: *m.* 1905, Geraldine Mary, who *d.* 1953, dau. of the late Rev. Frederick William Murray, R. of Stone, and Canon of Rochester [D. Atholl, colls.]:—
Patrick Gilbert Murray, *b.* 1905; ed. at Haileybury; late Major R.A. (T.A.): *m.* 1928, Audrey, dau. of the late Julius Ernst Guthe, J.P., of Kepwick Hall, Thirsk, and has issue living, Humphrey John Patrick (33, Beaumont Av., St. Albans), *b.* 1930; ed. at Winchester, and at Univ. Coll. Oxford (MA): *m.* 1953, Anne, twin da. of the late Capt. Edward Glyn de Styrap Jukes-Hughes, OBE, RN (ret.), of Stourbridge House, Milton-on-Stour, Gillingham, Dorset, and has issue living, Kathryn Helen Anne *b.* 1957, Jennifer Mary *b.* 1958, Annabel Jean *b.* 1961,—Michael Gilbert (Willow Cottage, S. Newton, Salisbury, Wilts.), *b.* 1931; ed. at Eton: *m.* 1956, Bridget Adèle, da. of the late Sidney Terence Evelyn Pook Ennion, and has issue living, Rupert Edward Terence Gilbert, *b.* 1962, Tobias, *b.* 1963, Juliet Emma Serena *b.* 1958,—Janet Ivory Audrey, *b.* 1932: *m.* 1954, Donald Craufurd Robertson, of 45, Park Rd., Chiswick, W4, and has issue living, James Craufurd, *b.* 1958, William Alexander *b.* 1959, David Kenneth Craufurd *b.* 1964. *Residence,*—Malt House, Easton, Winchester.——Edward Hugh Frederick, *MBE* (of Fyfield House, Pewsey, Wilts.), *b.* 1909; ed. at Haileybury; is Capt. late RA; 1939-45 War (MBE), MBE (Mil) 1945: *m.* 1935, Cynthia Phœbe Duncan, da. of the late Noel McGrigor Phillips, of Stoke d'Abernon Manor, Cobham, and has issue living, Mark Patrick (Scencliffe Grange, Coxwold, York 1), *b.* 1941; Maj. late Coldm. Gds.; *m.* 1970, Elizabeth Ann, da. of Sacheverel O. F. Bateman, of Alton Hall, Holbrook, Suffolk, and has issue living, Nicholas John *b.* 1971, Lara Katherine, *b.* 1973,—Anthea, *b.* 1939: *m.* 1963, Philip Simon Antill, of Scofton Farm House, Worksop, Notts., and has issue living, Vanessa Cicely *b.* 1964, Juliet Willa *b.* 1966, Helen Meriel *b.* 1969, Jemima Louise *b.* 1971,—Meriel, *b.* 1944: *m.* 1964, Mark Alexander Wyndham Baker, of Jubilee Cottage, Newtown Common, Newbury [see Macnaghten, Bt., colls.].

Grandchildren of the late Charles Alexander Price Chetwynd-Talbot, son of the Hon. Gerald Chetwynd-Talbot, 9th son of 2nd Earl Talbot:—
Issue of the late Charles Fleming Chetwynd Chetwynd-Talbot, *b.* 1879, *d.* 1933: *m.* 1906, Margaret Dorothy, who *d.* 1969, da. of Lt.-Col. Dunbar Fraser Huyshe, formerly RHA:—
Charles John Huyshe Chetwynd, *b.* 1910; ed. at Eton; Reuter's Ch. Correspondent for Ethiopia;

1st British War Correspondent accredited to Marshal Tito in Yugoslavia 1944 (prisoner): *m.* 1933, Jane (VAUGHAN), el. da. of the late David Wheldon Jones, of Blaenddol, Festiniog, N. Wales, and has issue living, John Vaughan Chetwynd, *b.* 1941; ed. at Eton; was Page to Earl of Shrewsbury at Coronation of Queen Elizabeth II,—Frances Elizabeth, *b.* 1947: *m.* 1974, Peter Henry Mayes. *Residence,*—Plas Blaenddol, Festiniog, Merioneth. *Club,*—Travellers'——Gilbert Alexander Lucius Chetwynd, *b.* 1918; ed at Eton: Lt.-Col. (ret.) late Comdg. 14th/20th King's Hussars; formerly Assist. Mil. Sec. to C.-in-C., Middle East; Sec., Albany, Piccadilly, since 1967; 1939-45 War in Iraq, Syria, Persia (despatches), and Italy. *Residences,*—L 1, Albany, Piccadilly,W1; Pleasant Cottage, Brightwell-cum-Sotwell, Wallingford, Oxon. *Club,*—Cavalry.——Geraldine Cecil Barbara, *b.* 1907; formerly Subaltern First Aid Nursing Yeo. *Residences,*—Mansion Basement, Albany, Piccadilly, W1; Pleasant Cottage, Brightwell-cum-Sotwell, Wallingford, Oxon.

Issue of the late Gilbert Patrick Chetwynd-Talbot, *b.* 1887, *d.* 1958: *m.* 1921, Alice Alethea (from whom he obtained a divorce 1929), dau. of C. H. Christopher Moller, of Lindsey House, Cheyne Walk, Chelsea, S.W.:—
Christopher Patrick Chetwynd, *RD* (The Old Parsonage, Cranbourne, Winkfield, Windsor), *b.* 1922; ed. at Harrow, and at Corpus Christi Coll., Camb.; 1939-45 War as Lieut. RNVR: *m.* 1955, Rosalind Mary, da. of Air Vice-Marshal Christopher Neil Hope Bilney, CB, CBE.——Barbara Maud Mary, *b.* 1924: *m.* 1949, Douglas Scott. *Residence,*—Nigg Mains, Nigg, Ross-shire.

Grandchildren of the late Maj. Henry Charles Talbot, son of the Rev. Henry George Talbot, el. son of the Very Rev. Charles Talbot, son of 3rd son of 1st Baron:—
Issue of the late Capt. Henry Fitzroy George Talbot, D.S.O., R.N., *b.* 1874, *d.* 1920: *m.* 1904, Susan Blair Athol, who *d.* 1951, only dau. of the late William Allison:—
Sir Arthur Allison Fitzroy, *KBE, CB, DSO, b.* 1909; Vice-Adm. (ret.); formerly Naval Attaché, Moscow; Commodore RN Barracks, Portsmouth 1957-59; Flag Officer, Arabian Seas and Persian Gulf 1960-62, C.-in-C., Atlantic, and S. American Station 1962-65, and of Plymouth Command 1965-67; 1939-45 War, operations off Norway and Dieppe (wounded); DSO 1940 (Bar 1944), CB (Mil.) 1961, KBE (Mil.) 1964: *m.* 1940, Joyce Gertrude, el. da. of the late Frank Edward Linley, of 28, Lower Sloane St., SW1, and Fowey, Cornwall, and has issue living, Anthea Jane, *b.* 1944: *m.* 1969, James A. H. Charrington, of Cherry Orchard, Shaftesbury, Dorset, and has issue living, Melissa Clare *b.* 1970, Lucinda Rose *b.* 1973,—Elizabeth, *b.* 1945: *m.* 1969, Michael Shuttleworth, RM, of 31, Holland Rd., W14, and has issue living, Ashton Fitzroy *b.* 1972, Henry Ashton *b.* 1974. *Residence,*—Thickthorn Manor, nr. Ilminster, Som. *Club,*—United Service.——Nesta Cecil, *b.* 1905: *m.* 1929, Capt. John Hext Lewes, OBE, RN (ret.), Lieut. of Dyfed since 1974, of Llanllyr, nr. Lampeter, Cardiganshire, and has issue living, John William Talbot, *RN* (Y Fron, Maesycrugiau, Pencader, Carmarthenshire. *Club,*—United Service), *b.* 1931; is Lt.-Cdr.; Korea 1950-51; *m.* 1st, 1954 (m. diss. 1963), Mary Georgiana, da. of the late Pascoe Anthony George Glyn [see B. Wolverton, colls.]; 2ndly, 1967, Margaret Jane, da. of Owen Fenner Clayton, of Hurst House, Langharne, Carmarthenshire, and has issue living, (by 1st m.) John Pascoe *b.* 1955, James Glyn *b.* 1959, Alice Mary Rhiannon *b.* 1957, (by 2nd m.) Owain Vaughan *b.* 1967, Angharad Hope *b.* 1972,—Loveday Elisabeth Talbot, *b.* 1932: *m.* 1956, Robert George Gee, of Village Farm, Barby, Rugby, and has issue living, Matthew George Cooper *b.* 1960, Patrick Robert Cooper *b.* 1963, Emma Louise Moya *b.* 1962,—Gwenllian Anne Talbot, *b.* 1934: *m.* 1955, Capt. John Franklin Kidd, RN, of Whitbourne Springs, Corsley, Winchester, and has issue living, John Christopher William *b.* 1957, Elisabeth Ceridwen *b.* 1958.

Grandsons of the late Maj. Edward Frederick Talbot-Ponsonby (infra):—
Issue of the late Lt.-Col. John Arthur Talbot-Ponsonby, *b.* 1907, *d.* 1969: *m.* 1st, 1931 (m. diss. 1956), Frances Elizabeth, only da. of the late Douglas H. Fraser; 2ndly, 1957, Daphne TALBOT-PONSONBY (Newberry House, Todenham, Moreton-in-Marsh, Glos.) (who *m.* 2ndly, 1972, Capt. Thomas Hanbury), el. da. of the late Percival Augustus Duke, OBE, and formerly wife of Capt. Jack Brittain-Jones, OBE:—
(By 1st m.) Michael Clement (10, Westmoreland Pl., SW1), *b.* 1932: *m.* 1956, Judith Katharine Gibson, and has issue living, Caroline Frances, *b.* 1958,—Charlotte Jane, *b.* 1963,—Lucy Elizabeth, *b.* 1965,—Katherine Louisa, *b.* 1967.——Peter William, *b.* 1938: *m.* 1962, Sarah Vansittart, da. of the late Sir Eric Vansittart Bowater, of Dene Pl., Surrey, and has issue living, Nina, *b.* 1964,—Jessica, *b.* 1965,—Eila, *b.* 1972.

Grandchildren of the late Charles William TALBOT-PONSONBY (who assumed by Roy. Licence 1866, the additional surname of Ponsonby), el. son of the late Adm. Sir Charles Talbot, KCB, 2nd son of the late Very Rev. Charles Talbot (ante):—
Issue of the late Major Edward Frederick TALBOT-PONSONBY, *b.* 1872, *d.* 1946: *m.* 1899. Marion Theodora, who *d.* 1969, da. of William Nicholson, of Basing Park, Alton, Hants., and 2, South Audley St., W:—
Marion Constance, *b.* 1904: *m.* 1923, Col. Ernest Elliot Buckland Mackintosh, DSO, late RE, who *d.* 1957, and has issue living, Jill, *b.* 1925: 1939-45 War in WRNS: *m.* 1949, Kenneth Holloway, of Cherrywood, Mannings Heath, Horsham, Sussex, and has issue living, Simon Jeremy *b.* 1953, Sarah Amanda *b.* 1955. *Residence,*—Hinton Woodlands, Bramdean, Alresford, Hants.

Issue of the late Charles George Talbot-Ponsonby, *b.* 1874, *d.* 1937: *m.* 1914, Violet Mary, who *d.* 1945, dau. of Capt. Raymond Parr [B. Dunsany]:—
Edward FitzRoy, *b.* 1916; ed. at Harrow: *m.* 1st, 1938, Bertha Marie Louise Muriel (from whom he obtained a divorce 1960), da. of H. C. Barber, of Trinity Hill, Jersey; 2ndly, 1960 (m. diss, 1967), Shirley Rhona Mearns; 3rdly, 1967, Anja Edith Boudewijn, of Cowes, and has issue living, (by 1st m.), Nigel Edward Charles, *b.* 1946,—Suzanne Molly, *b.* 1939: *m.* 1957 (m. diss. 19—), Lt. James Granville Lucas, RN [see Lucas, Bt., colls.]. *Residence,*—Langrish House, Langrish, nr. Petersfield, Hants.

Issue of the late Com. Frederick William Talbot-Ponsonby, R.N., *b.* 1879, *d.* 1930: *m.* 1913, Hannah, who *d.* 1952, dau. of the late John Ritchie Findlay, of Aberlour, Banff-shire:—
Evelyn John, *b.* 1915; ed. at Harrow, and at Trin. Coll., Camb. (MA): formerly Lieut. R.N.V.R.: *m.* 1943, Hilary, dau. of T. Kingsley Curtis, of 82, Highgate West Hill, N6, and has issue living, *Rev.* Andrew (Acton Burnell Rectory, Shrewsbury, Salop, SY5 7PE), *b.* 1944; ed. at Harrow: *m.* 1968, Alice Margaret, da. of Raymond Whittier Baldwin, of Alderley Edge, Ches. [see Barlow, Bt., cr. 1902, colls.], and has issue living, Daniel Frederick *b.* 1971, Thomas Martin *b.* 1973,—Christopher, *b.* 1950,—Simon *b.* 1952,—Elizabeth Hannah, *b.* 1945: *m.* 1969, Dr. John Michael Beck, of 4, St. Mary's Av., Harrogate, and has issue living, Mark Thomas Coulton *b.* 1972, Tess Adwoa Margaret Nora *b.* 1970,—Celia, *b.* 1947: *m.* 1971, David McTeer, F/L RAF, and has issue living, Stuart *b.* 1973. *Residence,*—Edgeworth House, Berkhamsted, Herts.——Felicity Philippa (*Lady Scott*), *b.* 1918: *m.* 1951, Lt.-Cdr. Sir Peter Markham Scott, CBE, DSC, late RNVR [Bruce, Bt., cr. 1804, colls.], and has issue living, Richard Falcon, *b.* 1954,—Dafila Kathleen, *b.* 1952. *Residence,*—The New Grounds, Slimbridge, Gloucestershire.

Issue of the late Major Arthur Hugh Brabazon Talbot-Ponsonby, formerly Hampshire Regt., *b.* 1885, *d.* 1952: *m.* 1913, Alianore Rachel, who *d.* 1974, da. of the late Sir (Edward) Stafford Howard, KCB [D. Norfolk, colls.]:—
Alathea Rachel Constance, *b.* 1914: *m.* 1935, Major Guy Richard Tufnell Gillett, R.A., who *d.* (killed on active service during European War) 1942; 2ndly, 1944, Peter Delmé-Radcliffe, of Punsholt Farm, W. Tisted, Alresford, Hants, and has issue living, (by 1st marriage) Aurea June *b.* 1936: *m.* 1964, Timothy Edward Pritchard Thornycroft, of High Wyck, Sleepers Hill, Winchester, and has issue living, John FitzRoy *b.* 1965,—Benjamin Delmé *b.* 1968,—Julia Geraldine (26, Parchment St., Winchester, Hants.) *b.* 1939: *m.* 1964 (m. diss. 1970), Ivor Russell.

Grandchildren of the late Maj. Francis Arthur Bouverie Talbot, 2nd son of the late Adm. Sir Charles Talbot, KCB, (ante):—

Issue of the late Major Edward Charles Talbot, *b.* 1881, *d.* (of wounds in action) 1915 :   *m.* 1908, Dorothy Maynard, who *d.* 1947, dau. of the late Sir William Gibbons, K.C.B. [Gibbons, Bt., cr. 1752, colls.]:—

Patricia Mary, *b.* 1909: *m.* 1937, Brig. Denys Edward Osbert Thackwell, C.B.E., late R.E., and has issue living, William Talbot Roche, *b.* 1947; ed. at Sherborne, and RMA; Lt. RE,—Sara Charlotte, *b.* 1938: *m.* 1959, John Grey Turnbull, of Castle View, Horton, Wimborne, Dorset, [see E. Stamford], Catherine Patricia, *b.* 1939: *m.* 1965, Gerald Anthony Delaney, of Witherenden Hill, Burwash, Sussex, and has issue living Rachel Ann *b.* 1965,—Alexandra Ruth *b.* 1967. *Residence,*—Perrymead, Partridge Rd., Brockenhurst, Hants.

Issue of the late Vice-Adm. Sir Cecil Ponsonby Talbot, KCB, KBE, DSO, *b.* 1884, *d.* 1970, *m.* 1912, Bridget, who *d.* 1960, da. of the late R. B. D. Bradshaw, of Fairfield, Barrow-in-Furness:—

John (c/o Midland Bank, Woking, Surrey), *b.* 1925; ed. at Radley; Lt.-Col. RA; Defence Attaché, Vienna: *m.* 1954, Janet Wyndham, da. of Lt.-Gen. Sir William Wyndham Green, KBE, CB, DSO, MC, and has issue living, David John, *b.* 1960,—Anthony Francis Wyndham, *b.* 1961,—Peter Charles, *b.* 1964.—Barbara Bridget, *b.* 1919: *m.* 1940, Cdr. Richard Molyneux Favell, DSC, RN, of Penberth, St. Buryan, Cornwall, and has issue living, Frances Barbara Molyneux, *b.* 1943: *m.* 1965, John Michael Middlecott Banham, and has issue living, Mark Richard Middlecott *b.* 1968, Serena Frances Tamsin *b.* 1970, Morwenna Bridget Favell *b.* 1972,—Bridget Alathea, *b.* 1946: *m.* 1970, David Llewelyn Hugh-Jones, and has issue living, Tristan Llewelyn *b.* 1973, Demelza Alice *b.* 1971,—Julia Alice, *b.* 1949.

Granddaughter of the late George Ponsonby Talbot (infra) :—
Issue of the late Vice-Adm. Arthur George Talbot, C.B., D.S.O., *b.* 1892, *d.* 1960 : *m.* 1918, Doris, who *d.* 1972, da. of the late Charles Fremantle Branson:—

Diana Maud Ponsonby, *b.* 1921 : *m.* 1942, Major Leslie Alban Harris, O.B.E., D.S.C., R.M. (Fleet Air Arm) (ret.), and has issue living, Nicholas Graham Talbot, *b.* 1947; ed. at Sherborne; Lt. RN (Fleet Air Arm): *m.* 1971, Jennifer Jane Stuart, da. of Capt. Justin Mallinson, of Bredy, Burton Bradstock, Dorset. *Residence,*—39, South St., W1.

Granddaughter of the late Adm. Sir Charles Talbot, K.C.B. (ante) :—
Issue of the late George Ponsonby Talbot, *b.* 1853, *d.* 1924 : *m.* 1887, Blanche, who *d.* 1922, dau. of the late Adm. the Hon. George Henry Douglas [E. Morton, colls.]:—
Hylda Alice, *b.* 1889. *Residence,*—Wentworth, Rotherham.

Grandchildren of the late Maj.-Gen. FitzRoy Somerset Talbot, son of the late Col. George Talbot, yst. son of the late Very Rev. Charles Talbot (ante):—
Issue of the late Col. George Reginald Fitzroy Talbot, *b.* 1870, *d.* 1931 : *m.* 1902, Eleanor Morwenna, who *d.* 1949, only dau. of the late Rev. Roger Granville, M.A., Sub-dean of Exeter, of Pilton House, Pinhoe, near Exeter:—

Granville FitzRoy (Lapworth Cottage, Elstead, Surrey), *b.* 1908; is Col. late R. Tank Regt.: *m.* 1938, Kathleen Betty, only da. of Gerald Townend, of Woking, and has issue living, John FitzRoy (c/o Williams & Glyn's Bank, Kirkland House, Whitehall, SW1), *b.* 1945; MB, BS, MRCS, LRCP: *m.* 1972, Esmé, yst. da. of Dr. R. de Brath Ashworth, of Holdfast Hall, Warfield.——Gwendoline Betty Alice, *b.* 1905.

PREDECESSORS.—[1] *Sir* GILBERT Talbot, Lord Chamberlain to Edward III., was summoned to Parliament of England 1331; *d.* 1346; *s.* by his son [2] RICHARD, 2nd Baron, and a Knight Banneret; was summoned to Parliament 1331-55; *d.* 1356, possessed of immense estates; *s.* by his son [3] GILBERT, 3rd Baron; summoned to Parliament 1362-86; *d.* 1387; *s.* by his son [4] RICHARD, 4th Baron; summoned to Parliament as Ricardo *Talbot de Blackmere* in his father's lifetime 1387: *m.* Ankaret, dau. and heiress of John, 5th Baron *Strange of Blackmere*; *d.* 1396; *s.* by his son [5] GILBERT, 5th Baron ; *d.* 1419 ; *s.* by his dau. [6] ANKARET : *d.* unmarried 1431 ; *s.* by her uncle [7] JOHN, *K.G.*, 7th Baron, who having *m.* 1408, Maud (*suo jure* Baroness Furnivall), dau. of Thomas (Nevill) Lord Furnivall, in 1409 had been summoned to Parliament as " Johann, *Talbot de Furnyvall* " ; became Lord Justice of Ireland 1412, and was Lord-Lieut. thereof 1414-21 ; was a celebrated warrior and gloriously sustained the cause of Henry VI. throughout his French realm ; his successes were, however, in 1429, checked by the Maid of Orleans at Patay, when his army was routed and himself taken prisoner : he was soon exchanged, and again pursued a career of victory ; cr. *Earl of Shrewsbury* (peerage of England) 1442, and *Earl of Waterford* (peerage of Ireland) 1446 ; was Ambassador to France 1443 : appointed Lieut. of the Duchy of Aquitaine 1453, and on July 20th of that year was killed at the battle of Chastillon ; *s.* by his son [8] JOHN, K.G., K.B., 2nd Earl ; was Lord Chancellor of Ireland 1446, and Lord High Treasurer of England 1457 ; killed, at battle of Northampton 1460, while fighting for the Red Rose; *s.* by his son [9] JOHN, 3rd Earl; *d.* 1473; *s.* by his son [10] GEORGE, K.G., 4th Earl ; served with distinction at the battle of Stoke; *d.* 1528; *s.* by his son [11] FRANCIS, K.G., P.C., 5th Earl ; summoned to Parliament in lifetime of his father ; was one of the few public men who, having served Queen Mary; was admitted to the Privy Council of Elizabeth; *d.* 1560; *s.* by his son [12] GEORGE, K.G., 6th Earl; had the charge of Mary, Queen of Scots, for many years, and assisted at her execution; appointed Lord High Steward of England at the arraignment of the Duke of Norfolk, and Earl Marshal after the Duke's execution; *d.* 1590; *s.* by his son [13] GILBERT, K.G., 7th Earl ; *d.* without male issue, when the Baronies of Talbot, Furnivall, and Strange of Blackmere became abeyant between his three daughters, eventually devolving upon the last surviving Alathea, wife of Thomas, 14th Earl of Arundel ; *s.* in the earldom by his brother [14] EDWARD, 8th Earl; *d.* 1617; *s.* by his kinsman [15] GEORGE, 9th Earl, descendant in the 4th generation of Sir Gilbert, 3rd son of 2nd Earl; *d.* 1630; *s.* by his nephew [16] JOHN, 10th Earl; *d.* 1653; *s.* by his son [17] FRANCIS, 11th Earl; killed in a duel with George Villiers, 2nd Duke of Buckingham, 1667; *s.* by his son [18] CHARLES, K.G., 12th Earl; held some of the most important offices in the state, and was a prominent statesman *temp.* William and Mary, Anne, and George I.; conformed to the Protestant cause 1679; cr. *Marquess of Alton* and *Duke of Shrewsbury* 1694 ; *d.s.p.* 1717, when the marquessate and dukedom expired. and the earldom reverted to his cousin [19] GILBERT, 13th Earl, son of the Hon. Gilbert, 2nd son of 10th Earl; was in Holy Orders of Church of Rome ; *d.* 1743; *s.* by his nephew [20] GEORGE, 14th Earl; *d.s.p.* 1787; *s.* by his nephew [21] CHARLES, 15th Earl; *d.s.p.* 1827 ; *s.* by his nephew [22] JOHN, 16th Earl; *d.* 1852; *s.* by his cousin [23] BERTRAM ARTHUR, 17th Earl; *d.* 1856 ; *s.* by his kinsman [24] HENRY JOHN Chetwynd-Talbot (infra), C.B., P.C., 18th Earl; who, in 1849, had *s.* as 3rd *Earl Talbot* and 5th *Baron Talbot* (see *⁎⁎* infra) ; was an Adm. and Capt. of Corps of Gentlemen-at-Arms, &c.; *d.* 1868; *s.* by his son [25] CHARLES JOHN, 19th Earl; *b.* 1830; sat as M.P. for N. Staffordshire 1859-65, and for Stamford 1868 ; was Capt. of Hon. Corps of Gentlemen-at-Arms 1874-7 : *m.* 1855, Anne Theresa, who *d.* 1912, dau. of Com. Richard Howe Cockerell, R.N.; *d.* 1877; *s.* by his son [26] CHARLES HENRY JOHN, K.C.V.O., 20th Earl; *b.* 1860; was Lord High Steward of Ireland : *m.* June 18th, 1882. Ellen Mary, who *d.* 1940, dau. of the late Charles Rowland Palmer-Morewood [B. Byron], and the divorced wife of Alfred Edward Miller Mundy, of Shipley Hall, Derby ; *d.* 1921 ; *s.* by his grandson [27] JOHN GEORGE CHARLES HENRY ALTON ALEXANDER CHETWYND (son of the late Charles John Alton Chetwynd, Viscount Ingestre, M.V.O., who *d.* 1915), 21st Earl and present peer ; also Earl of Waterford, Earl Talbot, Viscount Ingestre, and Baron Talbot.

⁎⁎[1] CHARLES Talbot, P.C., eighth in descent from the Hon. Sir Gilbert Talbot, 3rd son of 2nd Earl of Shrewsbury; sat successively as M.P. for Tregony and Durham; was an eminent lawyer, and in 1723 attained the summit of his profession on being constituted Lord High Chancellor of England; cr. *Baron Talbot,* of Hensol, co. Glamorgan (peerage of Great Britain)

1723; *d.* 1737 ; *s.* by his son [2] WILLIAM, *P.C.*, 2nd Baron; was Lord Steward of the Household; cr. *Earl Talbot* (peerage of Great Britain), 1761, and *Baron Dinevor*, of Dynevor, co. Carmarthen (peerage of Great Britain), 1780, with remainder *to his dau. Cecil, wife of George Rice, M.P., and her issue male; *d.* 1782, when the earldom expired, the barony of Dinevor passed to his dau. (ante), and the Barony of Talbot reverted to his nephew [3] JOHN CHETWYND, 3rd Baron; sat as M.P. for Castle Rising; cr. *Viscount Ingestre* and *Earl Talbot* (peerage of Great Britain) 1784, and assumed by Roy. licence the additional surname and arms of Chetwynd; *d.* 1793; *s.* by his son [4] CHARLES, *K.G.*, 2nd Earl; was Viceroy of Ireland, and Lord-Lieut. of Staffordshire; *d.* 1849; *s.* by his son [5] HENRY JOHN (ante), 3rd Earl, who in 1856 *s.* as 18th Earl of Shrewsbury.

Shute, Baron, title borne by Viscount Barrington on Roll of H. L.

SHUTTLEWORTH, BARON. (Kay-Shuttleworth.) [Baron U.K. 1902, Bt. U.K. 1850.]

CHARLES UGHTRED JOHN KAY-SHUTTLEWORTH, *M.C.*, 4th Baron, and 5th Baronet ; *b.* June 24th, 1917 ; *s.* 1942 ; ed. at Eton. and at Magdalene Coll., Camb. (B.A. 1938, M.A. 1952) ; Capt. (retired) R.H.A., and a J.P. and a D.L. for Lancaster ; European War 1939-42 in France, Belgium, and Middle East (twice wounded, M.C.) : *m.* 1947, Anne Elizabeth, da. of the late Col. Geoffrey Francis Phillips, CBE, DSO [V. Ridley, colls.], and has issue. [The 4th Baron *d.* Oct. 6th, 1975.]

Kind kin when known keep.

Arms,—Quarterly : 1st and 4th, **argent, three** shuttles sable, tipped and threaded or ; 2nd and 3rd, argent, two bendlets sable between as many crescents azure, between the bendlets three ermine spots. **Crests,—**1st, a cubit arm in armour proper, grasping in the gauntlet a shuttle as in the arms, *Shuttleworth* ; 2nd, on a crescent azure a goldfinch proper, *Kay*. **Supporters,—***Dexter*, a weaver habited in cap and apron proper, holding in the exterior hand a shuttle as in the arms ; *sinister*, a seaman holding in his exterior hand a ship's lamp, all proper.

Residences,—Leck Hall, Carnforth, Lancashire; 73, Cranmer Court, SW3.

SONS LIVING.

Hon. CHARLES GEOFFREY NICHOLAS, *b.* Aug. 2nd, 1948: *m.* 1975, Mrs. Ann Mary Barclay, da. of James Whatman, of Northcote Hill, Shamley Green, Surrey.

Hon. Robert James, *b.* 1954.

Hon. Edward Roger Noël, *b.* 1962.

DAUGHTER LIVING.

Hon. Sarah Rachel Jane, *b.* 1950: *m.* 1970, Richard Francis Foster, of 29, Bedford Gdns., W8 [see M. Ailesbury, colls.].

SISTER LIVING OF SECOND AND THIRD BARONS.
(*Raised to the rank of a Baron's daughter* 1940.)

Hon. Rosemary Florence Angela, *b.* 1915. *Residence,*—Fir Tree Cottage, Stedham, near Midhurst, Sussex.

MOTHER LIVING OF SECOND AND THIRD BARONS.

Selina Adine KAY-SHUTTLEWORTH, dau. of the late Brig.-Gen. the Hon. Francis Charles Bridgeman [see E. Bradford, colls.] ; assumed by deed poll 1920 the additional surname of Shuttleworth, and resumed by deed poll 1935, the surname of Kay-Shuttleworth in lieu of that of Shuttleworth-King : *m.* 1st, 1913, Capt. the Hon. Lawrence Ughtred Kay-Shuttleworth, R.F.A., who *d.* (killed in action during European War) 1917 (despatches) ; 2ndly, 1920, as his second wife, Maj.-Gen. William Birchall Macaulay King, C.M.G., D.S.O., V.D., who *d.* 1950, and has issue living, (by 1st marriage) [see ante]. *Residence,*—House of the Sons of God, Clareville Grove, S.W.7.

MOTHER LIVING.

Sibell Eleanor Maud, dau. of the late Charles Robert Whorwood Adeane, C.B., of Babraham, Cambridge [B. Leconfield, colls.] : *m.* 1st, 1914, Capt. the Hon. Edward James Kay-Shuttleworth, Rifle Brig., who *d.* (accidentally killed during European War) 1917 (despatches) ; 2ndly, 1920, Rev. the Hon. Charles Frederick Lyttelton, M.C., who *d.* 1931 [see V. Cobham] ; 3rdly, 1937, Roger Thomas Baldwin Fulford, CVO, and has issue living, (by 1st m.) [see ante],—(by 2nd m.) [see V. Cobham, colls.]. *Residence,*—Barbon Manor, Carnforth, Lancs.

COLLATERAL BRANCH LIVING.

Issue of the late Robert Kay-Shuttleworth, 2nd son of 1st Baronet, *b.* 1847, *d.* 1934: *m.* 1896, Ethel Clementina, who *d.* 1962, dau. of the late Alfred J. Freeman, M.D., of Villa delle Palme, San Remo, Italy:—

Helen Victoria (Whitefolds, 28, Dorset Rd. South, Bexhill-on-Sea), *b.* 1905: *m.* 1936, Major Wynyard Montagu Hall, late W. Yorkshire Regt., who *d.* 1949.

PREDECESSORS.—[1] *Sir* JAMES PHILLIPS Kay-Shuttleworth, el. son of the late Robert Kay, of Brookshaw, Bury, Lancashire ; *b.* 1804 ; was Sec. to the Committee of the Privy Council on Education 1839-49 ; cr. a *Baronet* 1850 : *m.* 1842, Janet, who *d.* 1872, only child and heiress of Robert Shuttleworth, of Gawthorpe Hall, whose surname he assumed by Roy. licence in addition to his patronymic ; *d.* 1877 ; *s.* by his el. son [2] *Sir* UGHTRED JAMES, *P.C.*, 2nd Bt., *b.* 1844 ; Under-Sec. of State for India Feb. to April 1886, Chancellor of Duchy of Lancaster April to Aug. 1886, Parliamentary Sec. to Admiralty 1892-5, and Lord-Lieut. and Custos Rotulorum of Lancashire 1908-28 ; M.P. for Hastings (*L.*) 1869-80, and for Clitheroe Div. of N.-E. Lancashire 1885-1902 ; cr. *Baron Shuttleworth*, of Gawthorpe, co. Palatine of Lancaster (peerage of United Kingdom) 1902 : *m.* 1871, Blanche Marion, who *d.* 1924, dau. of the late Sir Woodbine Parish, K.C.H. ; *d.* 1939 ; *s.* by his grandson [3] RICHARD UGHTRED PAUL (son of the late Capt. the Hon. Lawrence Ughtred Kay-Shuttleworth, R.F.A. (el. son of 1st Baron), who *d.* killed in action during European War 1917), 2nd Baron, *b.* 1913 ; Flying Officer R.A.F. Vol. Reserve, and a J.P. and Co. Councillor for Lancashire ; *d.* (killed in action during Battle of Britain) 1940 ; *s.* by his brother [4] RONALD ORLANDO LAWRENCE, 3rd Baron, *b.* (posthumous), 1917 ; Capt. R.A. (T.A.) ; *d.* (killed in action in N. Africa) 1942 ; *s.* by his cousin [5] CHARLES UGHTRED JOHN (son of the late Capt. the Hon. Edward James Kay-Shuttleworth (2nd son of 1st Baron), who *d.* (accidentally killed during European War 1917), 4th Baron and present peer.

SIDMOUTH, VISCOUNT. (Addington.) [Viscount U.K. 1805.]

RAYMOND ANTHONY ADDINGTON, 6th Viscount; b. Jan. 24th, 1887; s. 1953; ed. at Cheltenham Coll., and at R.M.C.; Major (ret.) 26th Light Cav., Indian Army; 1914-18 War in France and Belgium (three medals), S. Persia 1918-19 (medal with clasp), Waziristan 1919-20 (medal with clasp): m. 1913, Gladys Mary Dever, dau. of the late Thomas Francis Hughes, Commr. of Imperial Chinese Customs, and has issue.

Liberty under a pious king.

Arms,—Per pale ermine and ermines, a chevron charged with five lozenges counter-changed, between three fleurs-de-lis or. Crest,—A cat-a-mountain sejant guardant proper, bezantée, the dexter forepaw resting on an escutcheon azure, charged with a mace erect, surmounted with a regal crown or, within a bordure engrailed argent. Supporters,—Two stags, the dexter ermines, the sinister ermine, both attired and gorged with a chain, pendent therefrom a key, all or.

Residence,—Highway Manor, Calne, Wilts.

SONS LIVING.

Hon. JOHN TONGE ANTHONY PELLEW, b. Oct. 3rd, 1914; ed. at Downside, and at Brasenose Coll., Oxford; Colonial Ser.. Kenya (retired): m. 1940, Barbara Mary Angela, dau. of Bernard Rochford, OBE, of 7, Prince's Gate, SW7, and has issue living, Christopher John, b. 1941; ed. at Downside, and Brasenose Coll., Oxford: m. 1963, Clio Mona, only da. of John Peristiany, of 15, Karneadon St., Athens,—Jeremy Francis, b. 1947; ed. at Ampleforth: m. 1970, Grete Henningsen,—Veronica Mary, b. 1944,—Susan Barbara, b. 1945: m. 1965, Count John Paul James Alessandro Camillo Manassei di Collestatte [see E. Perth],—Janet Teresa, b. 1949,—Pauline Rosemary, b. 1951,—Mary Margaret, b. 1956. Residence,—Stivers, Nightingales Lane, Chalfont St. Giles, Bucks. Clubs, —Carlton, Nairobi (Kenya).
Hon. Hiley William Dever, b. 1917; Lt.-Cdr. RN (ret.), MIMechE; 1939-45 War: m. 1942, Brenda Swanney, da. of the late Robert Charles Wallace, CMG, PhD, DSc, Principal of Queen's Univ., Kingston, Canada, and has issue, Robert Hiley, b. 1944,—Charles Haviland, b. 1949,—Frances Clare, b. 1947. Residence,—578, Hollywood Place, Sarnia, Ontario, Canada.
Hon. Thomas Raymond Casamajor, M.C., b. 1919; ed. at Downside; Major (retired) R.H.A. 1939-45 War with Commandos (MiD): m. 1947, Veronique, who d. 1970, da. of Emile Wirtz, of Antwerp, Belgium, and has issue living, Peter John Gerald, b. 1948,—Donald Emile, b. 1949,—Francis Henry, b. 1955,—Lucy Anne, b. 1952,—Carol Jacqueline, b. 1953,—Tonia Veronica, b. 1956, —Edwina, b. 1960. Residence,—Highway Farm, near Calne, Wilts.
Hon. Gurth Louis Francis, b. 1920; ed. at Downside, and at Brasenose Coll., Oxford (MA); 1939-45 War with RAF (Air Crew): m. 1950, Patience Gillian, da. of the late Col. L. E. Travers, RE, and has issue living, Martin Gerald Francis, b. 1952,—David Anthony Brian, b. 1955,—Mark Nicholas Guy, b. 1957,—Mary Clare, b. 1951,—Catherine Dorothy, b. 1953,—Deirdre Anne (twin), b. 1955,—Monica Jane (twin), b. 1957,—Barbara Mary, b. 1961,—Jane Margaret, b. 1964. Address,—47, Clarence St., Devonport, Auckland, NZ.
Hon. Leslie Richard Bagnall, DFC; b. 1923; ed. at Downside; Lt.-Col. (ret.) late RA; Comdg. Essex Yeo. 1965-66; Malaya 1948, Korea 1951-52 (DFC): m. 1955, Anne,el. da. of Capt. Trevor Hume [Lacy, Bt.], and has issue living, William Leslie Hume, b. 1956,—Richard Charles Raymond, b. 1958,—Sarah Anne Clare, b. 1961,—Alice Mary Cynthia, b. 1964. Residence,—Polebridge, Sutton Veny, Warminster, Wilts. Club,—Army and Navy.
Rev. the Hon. Raleigh Hugh Leonard, b. 1926; ed. at Downside, and at Pembroke Coll., Camb.; European War 1939-45 as Lieut. Rifle Bde. Residence,—The Oratory, Brompton Road, S.W.7.

DAUGHTERS LIVING.

Hon. Prudence Mary, b. 1916: m. 1939, Lieut.-Com. Hugo Edward Forbes Tweedie, D.S.C., R.N., son of the late Adm. Sir Hugh Justin Tweedie, K.C.B., and has issue living, Alexander Hugh Carmichael (PO Box 478, Gabarone, Botswana), b. 1942: m. 1966, Wendy, da. of Basil Henry Francis Templer, and has issue living, Michael Hugh Quarter b. 1970, Lisa Ann b. 1967, Jessica Margret b. 1968,—Dominic James Drumelzier, b. 1945,—Julian Michael Forbes (The Cottage, High Trees, 23, Clayton Av., Hassocks, Sussex), b. 1947: m. 1970, Shirley Mousley,—Stephen John Oliver, b. 1952,—Teresa Frances, b. 1940: m. 1964, Nicolas Alexander Victor Garratt Carp (c/o Hongkong & Shanghai Banking Corpn., 1, Queens Rd. Central, Hong Kong), and has issue living, Sarah Frances b. 1965, Juliet Anne b. 1967, Victoria Teresa b. 1970, Lucy Beatrice b. 1973,—Monica Mary, b. 1954,—Prudence Margaret, b. 1956. Address,—PO Box 8245, Nairobi, Kenya.
Hon. Mary Octavia, b. 1927 :, m. 1st, 1953, David Christopher Leeming; 2ndly, 1959, David Tilling Wroth, and has issue living, (by 1st marriage) Toby, b. 1955. Residence,—Morleigh Cottage, Savernake Forest, Marlborough, Wilts.
Hon. Elizabeth Clare, b. 1928. Residence,—Highway Manor, Calne, Wilts.

SISTER LIVING.

Hon. Marjorie Ruth, b. 1889: m. 1910, Col. Oscar Mark Harris, DSO, R.H.A., who d. 1965, and has issue living, Diana Elena, b. 1911: m. 1935, Com. John Quicke, RN, of Ashbrittle, Wellington, Som., and 45, Ladbroke Rd., W11, and has issue living, Andrew Charles Addington b. 1936, Edward Francis John b. 1939, Mary Penelope Susan b. 1946. Residence,—70, Magdalen Rd., Exeter.

WIDOW LIVING OF FIFTH VISCOUNT.

MARY (MURDOCH) (Mary, Viscountess Sidmouth), dau. of the late Sir Donald Campbell Johnstone, formerly Ch. Judge of Ch. Court, Punjab: m. 1915, the 5th Viscount, who d. 1953. Residence,—Lodes, Kingston St. Mary, Taunton, Somerset.

COLLATERAL BRANCHES LIVING.

Grandchildren of the late Col. the Hon. Leonard Allen Addington, 3rd son of 2nd Viscount:—
Issue of the late Major William Leonard Addington, b. 1856, d. 1919: m. 1890, Augusta, who d. 1942, dau. of the late Rev. H. G. Hayter-Hames, of Chagford, Devon:—
Leonard George, DSC (Ryefield House, Conon Bridge, Ross-shire), b. 1892; Cdr. (ret.) RN: m. 1939, Sheena, da. of the late Hector Forbes, 13th Laird of Culloden.——Stella Lætitia (29B, Lexham Gdns., W8 5JR), b. 1904.

Issue of the late Major Hiley Reginald Addington, *b.* 1861, *d.* 1940 : *m.* 1893, Nelly, who *d.* 1956, dau. of the late Osmond de Lancey Priaulx, of The Mount, Guernsey :—
Rupert Hiley Priaulx, *b.* 1898 ; Major R.A. (retired) ; European War 1916-18 in France and Belgium (twice wounded, two medals); European War 1939-45, (despatches twice), present at Evacuation from Dunkirk (wounded, four medals): *m.* 1935, Margaret Penrose, dau. of Lieut.-Col. William Lambert Penrose Mark-Wardlaw. *Residence,*—Green Bushes, 3, Fountain Hill, Budleigh Salterton, Devon. *Club,*—Army and Navy.

PREDECESSORS.—[1] *Rt. Hon.* HENRY Addington, ; M.P. for Devizes 1784-1805, **Speaker** of the House of Commons 1789-1801, First Lord of the Treasury and Chancellor of **the** Exchequer 1801-4, Pres. of the Council 1805-6, Lord Privy Seal 1806, Home Sec. 1812-22, **High** Steward of Westminster and Reading, Gov. of the Charterhouse, and Dep. Ranger of Richmond Park, &c.; cr. *Viscount Sidmouth* (peerage of United Kingdom) 1805; *d.* 1844; *s.* by his **son [2]** WILLIAM LEONARD, 2nd Viscount; *b.* 1794; was in Holy Orders: *m.* 1820, Mary, who *d.* 1894, el. dau. of the Rev. John Young, Rector of Thorpe Malsor, co. Northampton; *d.* 1864; *s.* by his son **[3]** WILLIAM WELLS, 3rd Viscount, *b.* 1824; M.P. for Devizes 1863-4 : *m.* 1848, Georgiana Susan, who *d.* 1896, dau. of the late Very Rev. the Hon. George Pellew, D.D. ; *d.* 1913; *s.* by his el. son **[4]** GERALD ANTHONY PELLEW BAGNALL, 4th Viscount, *b.* 1854 : *m.* 1881. Ethel Mary, who *d.* 1954, only dau. of the late Capt. Louis Charles Henry Tonge, R.N. ; *d.* 1915 ; *s.* by his el. son **[5]** GERALD WILLIAM, 5th Viscount, *b.* 1882 ; Capt. Devonshire Regt. and Chm. of Honiton Rural Dist. Council; European War 1914-18 in India, Mesopotamia, Aden and Salonika; *m.* 1915, Mary Murdoch, dau. of the late Sir Donald Campbell Johnstone, formerly Ch. Judge of Ch. Court, Punjab ; *d.* 1953 ; *s.* by his brother, **[6]** RAYMOND ANTHONY, 6th Viscount and present peer.

SIEFF, BARONY OF. (Sieff.) [Extinct 1972.]

SONS LIVING OF LIFE BARON.

Hon. Michael David *CBE* (Michael House, Baker St., W1), *b.* 1911; ed. at Manchester Gram. Sch.; Asst. Managing Dir. of Marks and Spencer, Ltd., 1965-71, and Joint Managing Dir. 1971-72, since when a Vice-Chm.; and Joint Managing Dir.; Hon. Col. late RAOC (TA); 1939-45 War as Col. RAOC; OBE (Civil) 1975: *m.* 1st, 1932 (m. diss. 1975), Daphne Madge Kerin, da. of Cyril Aaron Michael; 2ndly, 1975, Elizabeth Pitt, and has issue (by 1st m.).
Hon. Sir Marcus Joseph, *OBE* (Michael House, Baker St., W1), *b.* 1913; ed. at Manchester Gram. Sch., at St. Paul's, and at Corpus Christi Coll., Camb. (BA); Col. late RA (TA); an Assist. Managing Dir. of Marks and Spencer, Ltd., 1963-65, Vice-Chm., an Assist. Managing Dir. 1965-67, Vice-Chm. and Joint Managing Dir. 1967-71, and Dep. Chm. and Joint Managing Dir 1971-72, since when Chm., and Joint Managing Dir.; a Member of BNEC 1965-71; Chm. of Export Cttee. for Israel 1965-68; Vice-Pres. of Joint Palestine Appeal; 1939-45 War; OBE (Mil) 1944, Knt. 1971: *m.* 1st, 1937 (m. diss. 1947), Rosalie Fromson; 2ndly, 1951 (m. diss. 1953), Elsie Florence Gosen; 3rdly, 1956 (m. diss. 1962), Brenda Mary Beith; 4thly, 1963, Mrs. Pauline Lily Moretzki, da. of Friedrich Spatz, and has issue by 1st, 3rd and 4th m.

DAUGHTER LIVING OF LIFE BARON.

Hon. Judith Hannah, *b.* 1921: *m.* 1st, 1941 (*m.* diss. 1947) Konrad Steiner; 2ndly, 1947 (*m.* diss. 1962), Philip Giaquinto; 3rdly, 1962, Abraham Shechterman, of 20, Dubnow St., Tel Aviv, Israel, and has issue by 1st and 2nd marriages.

Silchester, Baron, title of Earl of Longford on Roll of H. L.

SILKIN, BARONY OF. (Silkin.) [Baron U.K. 1950, disclaimed 1972.]

ARTHUR SILKIN, *b.* Oct. 20th, 1916; *s.* as 2nd Baron May 11th, 1972, disclaimed his peerage for life May 18th, 1972; ed. at Dulwich Coll., and Peterhouse, Camb. (BA honours); with Civil Ser. Coll.; 1939-45 War as F/O RAF: *m.* 1969, Audrey, da. of the late Thomas Bennett.

Residence,—33, Woodnook Rd., SW16.

BROTHERS LIVING.

Rt. Hon. SAMUEL CHARLES, *QC, MP*, *b.* March 6th, 1918; ed. at Dulwich Coll., and at Trin. Hall, Camb. (BA honours 1939); Bar. Middle Temple 1941, a QC 1963, and Bencher 1970; Vice-Pres. of Labour Lawyers' Soc. since 1971 (Chm. 1964-71), of Parl. Labour Party's European Affairs and Common Market Group 1966-70, of Legal Cttee. of Council of Europe 1967-70, and of Select Cttee. on Parl. Privilege 1967-68; a Member of Roy. Comm. on Penal System 1965-66, and Recorder of Bedford 1966-72, Member of Assembly of Council of Europe and Assembly of W. European Union 1966-70, and Leader of British Delegation 1968-70; Opposition Solicitor Gen. 1970-74, since when Attorney-Gen.; a Gov. of Maudsley and Bethlem Hosps. 1969-70, and MP for Dulwich Div. of Camberwell (*Lab.*) 1964-74, since when of Southwark (Dulwich); 1939-45 War as Lt.-Col. RA (despatches); PC 1974: *m.* 1941, Elaine Violet, da. of the late Arthur Stamp, of London, and has issue living, Christopher Lewis, *b.* 1947; LLB London,—Peter David Arthur, *b.* 1952: *m.* 1974, Frances Kemp,— Charlotte Ann, *b.* 1944; BEd. Oxford: *m.* 1965, Francis Josephs, MA, of 49, Randolph St., Oxford, and has issue living, Thomas Daniel *b.* 1972,—Patricia Jane (twin), *b.* 1947; BA Sussex: *m.* 1970, Michael Johnson, BA. *Address,*—c/o Lambs Building, Temple, EC4.

Rt. Hon. John Ernest, *MP*, *b.* 1923; ed. at Dulwich Coll., and at Trin. Hall, Camb. (MA, LLB); Solicitor 1950; 1939-45 War as Lt. RNVR; Councillor of St. Marylebone 1962-64; MP for Deptford (*Lab.*) 1963-74, since when of Lewisham (Deptford); a Lord Commr. of Treasury (Govt. Whip) 1964-66, and Treasurer to HM Household (Dep. Ch. Whip) April to July 1966, Parl. Sec. to Treasury (Govt. Ch. Whip) 1966-70 and Min. of Public Building and Works 1969-70; Min. of State of Planning and Local Govt. since 1974; PC 1966: *m.* 1950, Rosamund John (LLOYD) (actress), da. of F. Jones, and has issue living, Rory Lewis, *b.* 1954. *Residence,*—Vine House, Staplehurst, Kent; 7, Storeys Gate, SW1.

WIDOW LIVING OF FIRST BARON.

MARGUERITE SCHLAGETER (*Baroness Silkin*), (24, Victoria Rd., W8; Green Shadows, Chase Lane, Haslemere, Surrey): *m.* 1964, as his 3rd wife, the 1st Baron, who *d.* 1972.

PREDECESSOR.—[1] *Rt. Hon.* LEWIS Silkin, CH; *b.* 1889; Min. of Town and Country Planning 1945-50, Dep. Leader of Labour Party, House of Lords 1955, and MP for Peckham Div. of Camberwell (*Lab.*) 1966-50; cr. *Baron Silkin,* of Dulwich, co. London (peerage of UK) 1950: *m.* 1st, 1915, Rosa Neft, who *d.* 1947; 2ndly, 1948, Frieda M., who *d.* 1963, da. of the late Rev. Canon Pilling, of Norwich, and widow of J. F. F. Johnson; 3rdly, 1964, Marguerite Schlageter; *d.* 1972; *s.* by his el. son. **[2]** ARTHUR, 2nd Baron, until he disclaimed his peerage 1972.

SILSOE, BARON. (Eve.) [Baron U.K. 1963, Bt. U.K. 1943.]

(ARTHUR) MALCOLM TRUSTRAM EVE, *G.B.E., M.C., T.D., Q.C.,* 1st Baron, and 1st Baronet, son of the late Sir Herbert Trustram Eve, K.B.E., *b.* April 8th, 1894; ed. at Winchester, and at Ch. Ch., Oxford (MA); Bar. Inner Temple 1919, K.C. 1935, Bencher 1942, Reader 1965 and Treasurer 1966; late Col. and temp. Brig. R. Welch Fusiliers (T.A.); an Hon. Member of Roy. Institution of Chartered Surveyors and of Chartered Auctioneers' and Estate Agents' Institute, Hon. Vice-Pres. of Town Planning Institute, and an Hon. Fellow of Institute of Municipal Treasurers and Accountants, and Institute of Builders; Chm. of Air Transport Licensing Authority 1938-39, of War Damage Commn. 1941-49, of Building Apprenticeship and Training Council 1943-47, of War Works Commn., and of Local Govt. Boundary Commn. 1945-49, of Central Land Board 1947-49, of Burnham Cttees. on Teachers' Salaries 1950-53, and of Police Council on Police Salaries 1951, a Dir. Yorks. Insur. Co. Ltd. 1951-66, a Member of Church Assembly 1952-57, Chm. of St. George's Hosp. 1952-54 (Chm. of Med. Sch. 1948-54), and of Road Haul. Disposal Board 1953-56; Pres. of Ski Club of GB 1950-54; Chm. of Lord Mayor's Nat. Flood and Tempest Distress Fund 1953, Member of Gen. Council of King Edward's Hospital Fund for London 1953, Chm. of Prime Min's Cttee. on Administration of Crown Lands 1954, of Electoral Boundaries Commn., Mauritius 1957, and of Fiji Sugar Inquiry Commn. 1961, First Crown Estate Commr. 1954-62, First Church Estates Commr. 1954-69 (Third Commr. 1952-54), and Gov. of Peabody Trust 1957-65; Independent Chm. of Cement Makers' Federation 1951-70, Pres. of Cembureau (International) Cement Makers' Assocn. 1952-70, Pres. of Kandahar Ski Club 1965-69 and Hon. Treasurer of Roy. Coll. of Nursing 1964-70 (Vice-Pres. since 1969); Gentleman Usher of the Purple Rod, Order of British Empire 1960-69; Coconut Industry Survey, Fiji 1963; 1914-18 War as Capt. R. Welch Fusiliers, GSO3, 53rd Div. and Bde. Maj. 159th Inf. Bde. in Gallipoli, Egypt and Palestine (MC); 1939-45 War as AA & QMG, 53rd Div. and Comdg. 158th (R. Welch) Inf. Bde.; *cr.* GBE (Civil) 1950, and *Baron Silsoe,* of Silsoe, co. Bedford (Peerage of UK 1963): *m.* 1st, 1927, Marguerite, who *d.* 1945, da. of the late Sir Augustus Meredith Nanton; 2ndly, 1946, Margaret Elizabeth, da. of the late Henry Wallace Robertson, Ayton, Berwicks., and has issue by 1st m.

Arms,—Sable, two swords, points upwards, in saltire argent pommels and hilts or, on a chief of the second a closed book gules, garnished of the third, between two torteaux. **Crest,—**Issuant from a mural crown or, an apple tree fructed, the trunk entwined by a serpent proper. **Supporters,—**On either side a Kashmir goat argent horned winged and gorged with a mural crown or.

*Residence,—*Lower Ballacottier, Kirk Onchan, Isle of Man.

SONS LIVING. *(By 1st m.).*

Hon. DAVID MALCOLM TRUSTRAM, *QC* (Neals Farm, Wyfold, Reading, Berks., RG4 9JB; Oxford and Cambridge Univ. Club), *b.* May 2nd, 1930; ed. at Winchester, at Ch. Ch., Oxford (MA), and at Columbia Univ., New York; Bar. Inner Temple 1955; Bar Auditor Inner Temple 1965-70; Bencher 1970; QC 1972; late 2nd Lt. RWF, and Lt., Queen Victoria's Rifles (TA): *m.* 1963, Bridget Min, da. of Sir Rupert Charles Hart-Davis, of The Old Rectory, Marske-in-Swaledale, Richmond, Yorks., and has issue living, Simon Rupert, *b.* 1966,—Amy Janet, *b.* 1964.

Hon. Peter Nanton Trustram (twin) (Priory Court, Duns Tew, Oxon.; Ski Club of Great Britain), *b.* 1930; ed. at Winchester, and at Ch. Ch., Oxford (MA); Lt.-Col. R. Green Jackets; late 2nd Lt. R. Welch Fus., and Queen Victoria's Rifles (TA); student US Armed Forces Staff Coll. 1972, and British Army Staff, Washington 1972-73, since when Cmdg. Officer Oxford Univ. Officers Training Corps.: *m.* 1961, Petronilla Letiere Sheldon, da. of the late Jannion Steele Elliott, of Dowles Manor, Bewdley, Worcs., and has issue living, Richard Malcolm Jannion, *b.* 1963,—Nicholas Dominic Peter, *b.* 1965.

SIMEY, BARONY OF. (Simey.) [Extinct 1969.]

SON LIVING OF LIFE PEER.

Hon. Thomas Iliff (Modyn, Eversley Park, Chester, CH2 2AJ), *b.* 1938; ed. at St. Christopher's Sch., Letchworth; Chartered Architect 1965; a tree conservationist; a Member of Simey Reardon Partnership: *m.* 1963, Fiona, da. of A. G. Porteous, of Menstrie, Clackmannanshire, and has issue.

WIDOW LIVING OF LIFE PEER.

MARGARET BAYNE (*Baroness Simey*), (3, Blackburne Terr., Blackburne Pl., Liverpool 8), da. of John Aiton Todd: *m.* 1935, Baron Simey (Life Peer), who *d.* 1969.

SIMON, VISCOUNT. (Simon.) [Viscount U.K. 1940.]

JOHN GILBERT SIMON, *C.M.G.*, 2nd Viscount, *b.* Sept. 2nd, 1902 ; *s.* 1954 ; ed. at Winchester (Scholar), and at Balliol Coll., Oxford (Scholar); CMG 1947: *m.* 1930, James Christie, da. of William Stanley Hunt, and has issue.

Arms,—Gules three lotus flowers in pale proper between two flaunches or each charged with a lion rampant of the field. Crest,—Upon a well proper an eagle rising or. Supporters,—Dexter, a guillemot ; sinister, a monal proper.

Residence,—New Park, Buckfastleigh, Devon.

SON LIVING.

Hon. JAN DAVID (Nairn Cottage, Dog Kennel Lane, The Common, Chorleywood, Herts.), *b.* July 20th, 1940; ed. at Westminster: *m.* 1969, Mary Elizabeth, da. of John Joseph Burns, of Sydney, NSW, and has issue living, Fiona Elizabeth Christie, *b.* 1971.

DAUGHTER LIVING.

Hon. Gemma Louise, *b.* 1934: *m.* 1956, Brian Hunter, and has issue living, Ian, *b.* 1957,—Alan, *b.* 1958. Residence,—66, Westfields Avenue, S.W.13.

J'AI AINSI MON NOM

Such is my name.

SISTER LIVING.

Hon. Joan Angel Allsebrook, *b.* 1901 ; is a J.P. for Hants : *m.* 1924, Capt. John Allan Bickford-Smith, RN (ret.), who *d.* 1970, and has issue living, Hilary John, *b.* 1926, Lt.-Cdr. RN (ret.): *m.* 1st 1951, Anne Marie, da. of T. O. Kawe, of Nasby, Sweden; 2ndly, 1974, Mrs. Susan G. Marshall, of Petersfield, Hants., and has issue living (by 1st m.), Christopher John *b.* 1956, Susan Anne, *b.* 1952, Karin Elizabeth *b.* 1953,—Margaret Angel, *b.* 1924: *m.* 1951, John Gilbert McAllan, of 16, Knoll Rd., Sidcup, Kent, and has issue living, Ian *b.* 1951, Gordon *b.* 1953, Andrew Douglas *b.* 1958, Sheila Joan *b.* 1956, Catherine Margaret *b.* 1959,—Caroline Mary (25, Broomfield Rd., Bexleyheath, Kent), *b.* 1926: *m.* 1950, Dr. Norman Kennedy, who *d.* 1965, and has issue living, Tessa Frances *b.* 1951, Valerie Sarah *b.* 1955, Elizabeth Jane *b.* 1957. Residence,—Younghouse, Liss, Hants.

PREDECESSOR.—[1] Rt. Hon. Sir JOHN ALLSEBROOK SIMON, *GCSI, GCVO, OBE, PC, QC,* only son of the late Rev. Edwin Simon, a Congregational Min.; *b.* 1873; was Solicitor-Gen. 1910-13, Attorney-Gen. (with a seat in the Cabinet) 1913-15, Sec. of State for Home Depart. 1915-16, Sessional Chm. and Dep. Leader of Ind. Liberal Party in House of Commons 1922-4, and Chm. of Indian Statutory Commn. 1927-30, R101 Airship Inquiry 1930, and Roy. Commn. on Population 1943-6 ; appointed Sec. of State for Foreign Affairs (in National Govt.) 1931, Sec. of State for Home Affairs and Dep. Leader of House of Commons 1935, and Chancellor of the Exchequer 1937 (also Member of War Cabinet 1939) ; Lord High Chancellor 1940-45 ; sometime Leader of Liberal National Party; High Steward of Oxford Univ., European War 1917-18 as Major R.A.F. (despatches) ; sat as M.P. for S.W., or Walthamstow, Div. of Essex (L) 1906-18 ; and for Yorkshire W. Riding, Spen Valley Div. 1922-40 ; cr. *Viscount Simon,* of Stackpole Elidor, co. Pembroke (peerage of United Kingdom) 1940 : *m.* 1st, 1899, Ethel Mary, who *d.* 1902, dan. of Gilbert Venables ; 2ndly, 1917, Kathleen *D.B.E.,* who *d.* 1955, dau. of Francis Eugene Harvey, of Wexford, and widow of T. Manning, M.D., *d.* 1954; *s.* by his only son [2] JOHN GILBERT, *CMG,* 2nd Viscount and present peer.

SIMON OF GLAISDALE, BARON. (Simon.) [Life Baron 1971.]

JOCELYN EDWARD SALIS SIMON, *PC,* son of the late Frank Cecil Simon, of 51, Belsize Park, NW3; *b.* Jan. 15th, 1911; ed. at Gresham's Sch., Holt, and Trin. Hall, Camb.; Bar. Middle Temple 1954, KC 1951, and Bencher 1958; Joint Parl. Under-Sec. of State, Home Office 1957-58, Financial Sec. to the Treasury 1958-59, Solicitor-Gen. 1959-62, and Pres. of Probate, Divorce and Admiralty Div. of High Court 1962-71, when a Lord of Appeal in Ordinary; 1939-45 War as Maj. RTR, and Lt.-Col. Staff; MP for W. Middlesbrough (*C*) 1951-62; *cr.* Knt. 1959, PC 1961, and *Baron Simon of Glaisdale,* of Glaisdale, in N. Riding, co. York. (Life Baron) 1971: *m.* 1st, 1934, Gwendolen Helen, who *d.* 1937, da. of E. J. Evans; 2ndly, 1948, Fay Elizabeth Leicester, JP, da. of Brig. H. Guy A. Pearson, of Jersey, and has issue by 2nd m.

Arms,—Not exemplified at time of going to press.
Residence,—Midge Hall, Glaisdale, Whitby, Yorks. Town Address,—Carpmael Buildings, Temple, EC4.

SONS LIVING. (By 2nd m.)

Hon. Peregrine Charles Hugo, *b.* 1950.
Hon. Benedict Mark Leycester, *b.* 1953.
Hon. Dominic Crispin Adam, *b.* 1958.

SIMON OF WYTHENSHAWE, BARON. (Simon.) [Baron U.K. 1947.]

ROGER SIMON, 2nd Baron, *b.* Oct. 16th, 1913 ; *s.* 1960 (but does not use the title) ; ed. at Gresham's Sch., Holt, and at Gonville and Caius Coll., Camb. ; European War 1940-45 : *m.* 1951 (Anthea) Daphne, dau. of Sidney George William May, and has issue.

    Residence,—Oakhill, Chester Avenue, Richmond, Surrey.

SON LIVING.
Hon. MATTHEW, *b.* April 10th, 1955; ed. at St. Paul's Sch.

DAUGHTER LIVING.
Hon. Margaret, *b.* 1953.

BROTHER LIVING.
Hon. Brian, *b.* 1915 ; ed. at Gresham's Sch., Holt, and at Trin. Coll., Camb.; European War 1940-45: *m.* 1941, Joan Home, dau. of the late Capt. Home Peel, D.S.O., M.C. [By. Emmott], and has issue living, Alan, *b.* 1943,—Martin, *b.* 1944.   *Residence,*—11, Pendene Rd., Leicester.

PREDECESSOR—[1] ERNEST DARWIN Simon, son of the late Henry Simon, of Lawnhurst, Didsbury ; *b.* 1879 ; an Engineer and Contractor, and Pres. of Simon Carves, Ltd., and of Henry Simon, Ltd. ; Lord Mayor of Manchester 1921-2 ; Parliamentary Sec. to Min. of Health (in National Govt.) Sept. to Oct. 1931 ; was Chm. of British Broadcasting Corporation 1947-52 ; sat as M.P. for Withington Div. of Manchester (*L*) 1923-4 and 1929-31 ; cr. *Baron Simon of Wythenshawe,* of Didsbury, City of Manchester (peerage of United Kingdom) 1947: *m.* 1912, Shena Dorothy, who *d.* 1972, da. of John Wilson Potter, of Westminster, SW1, *d.* 1960; *s.* by his el. son [2] ROGER, 2nd Baron and present peer.

SINCLAIR, LORD. (St. Clair.) [Lord S. about 1449, confirmed 1488-9.]
[Title pronounced "Sinclair," and name pronounced "St. Clair."]

CHARLES MURRAY KENNEDY ST. CLAIR, *M.V.O.,* 17th Lord; *b.* June 21st, 1914; *s.* 1957; ed. at Eton, and at Magdalene Coll., Camb.; a Representative Peer for Scotland 1959-63; Major late Coldstream Guards ; is a Member of Queen's Body Guard for Scotland (Roy. Co. of Archers); Portcullis Pursuivant of Arms 1949-57, and York Herald 1957-68; Hon. Genealogist to Roy. Victorian Order 1960-68; an Extra Equerry to H.M. Queen Elizabeth the Queen Mother since 1953; Palestine 1939 (despatches), 1939-45 War (wounded); MVO (4th class) 1953: *m.* 1968, Anne Lettice, yr. da. of Sir Richard Charles Geers Cotterell, CBE, TD, 5th Bt., and has issue.

    Arms,—Quarterly: 1st and 4th, azure, a lymphad sails furled and oars in saltire within a double tressure, flory counterflory or, *Orkney*; 2nd and 3rd, azure, a ship under sail or, *Caithness*; over all an escutcheon of pretence argent, charged with a cross engrailed azure *Sinclair.* **Crest,**—A swan, wings elevated argent, ducally collared and chain or. **Supporters,**—Two griffins proper, beaked and membered or.
    Residence,—Knocknalling, Dalry, Kirkcudbrightshire.

SON LIVING.
Hon. MATTHEW MURRAY KENNEDY (*Master of Sinclair*), *b.* Dec. 9th, 1968.

DAUGHTERS LIVING.
Hon. Laura Anne, *b.* 1972.
Hon. Annabel Lettice, *b.* 1973.

SISTER LIVING.
Hon. Patricia Mary, *b.* 1912: *m.* 1940, Lieut.-Col. Charles Archibald Richard Coghill, O.B.E., Scots Guards (ret.), of Brette House, Brancaster, King's Lynn, and has issue living, Hugh Murray Charles, *b.* 1950: *m.* 1973, Elisabeth Ann Edwina, yr. da. of the Rev. Mark Wynn-Eyton,—Sarah, *b.* 1948: *m.* 1972, Peter Grosvenor Hopkins, of 21, Kieldon Rd., SW11.—Patricia Jane, *b.* 1949: *m.* 1970, Graham Merrison, of Starlock House, Playden, Rye, Sussex.

COLLATERAL BRANCHES LIVING.

    Grandchildren of the late Hon. Lockhart Matthew St. Clair, CIE, CBE, 4th son of 14th Lord:—
    Issue of the late Maj.-Gen. George James Paul St. Clair. C.B., C.B.E., D.S.O., *b.* 1885, *d.* 1955 : *m.* 1911, Charlotte Theresa Orme, who *d.* 1961, dau. of the late Major Archibald Cosmo Little [E. Shrewsbury]:—

Malcolm Archibald James, *TD*, *b.* 1927; ed. at Eton; is a Farmer; MP for S.-E. Div. of Bristol (*C.* 1961-63; Lt.-Col. Comdg. R. Glos. Hussars (TA) 1967-69: *m.* 1955, Mary-Jean, only da. of Wing-Cdr. Caryl Liddell Hargreaves, of Broadwood House, Sunningdale, Berks. [B. Ravensworth, colls.], and has issue living, Hugh Alan Charles, *b.* 1957,—Andrew David Paul, *b.* 1960,—Vannessa Alice Rosabel, *b.* 1971. *Residences,*—Upton House, Tetbury, Glos.; 23, Sloane Gdns., SW1. *Clubs,*—White's, Cavalry. ——Helen Mary Orme, *b.* 1918: *m.* 1951, George Bradshaw Emslie, MBE, and has issue living, Martin George St. Clair, *b.* 1952,—Philip James Guy, *b.* 1953,—Nigel Paul St. Clair, *b.* 1955. *Residences,*— Lusaka, Zambia; Old Manor House, Ditchling, Sussex.—Rosabelle Evelyn Teresa, *b.* 1919.—— Guendolen Helen Charlotte, *b.* 1920: *m.* 1966, Maurice Owen Griffith Cleaver, of Upton Lodge, Tetbury, Glos.

Issue of the late Lockhart Frederick Charles St. Clair, *b.* 1896, *d.* 1960 : *m.* 1919, Evelyn Mary Josephine (who *d.* 1957, having obtained a divorce 1933), dau. of the late Nicholas J. Synnott [V. Furness, Naas, co. Kildare [V. Netterville] ; 2ndly, 1934, Sylvia Violet Francina, dau. of Major Marwood Elton Lane, of Haloowella, Norwood, Ceylon :—
(By 1st m.) Jean Margaret Alice, *b.* 1920: *m.* 1st, 1941, Cecil Geoffrey Monson; 2ndly, 1952 (m. diss. 1969), Jack Mervyn Frank Baer.

Grandchildren of the late Adm. William Home Chisholme St. Clair, el. son of the late Com. the Hon. Charles St. Clair (infra):—
Issue of the late Capt. Frederic Cathcart Guy St. Clair, R.N., *b.* 1878, *d.* 1931: *m.* 1913, Maude Sophie Childers, who *d.* 1962, yr. da. of Capt. S. H. Childers Thompson, R.N. (ret.), formerly of Taplow, Bucks:—
Derek Charles ST. CLAIR-STANNARD, *M.B.E.*, *b.* 1919 ; formerly in H.M. Foreign Ser. ; is Public Relations Officer to Roy. Agricultural So. of England ; 1939-45 War as Lt. R.N.V.R. (M.B.E.) ; assumed by deed poll 1939, the additional surname of Stannard ; M.B.E. (Mil.) 1945 : *m.* 1953, Elizabeth Ann, dau. of Douglas Charles Baskett, and has issue living, Matthew Peter, *b.* 1954,— Lucie, *b.* 1955,—Sophie Alexandra, *b.* 1958,—Josephine Camilla, *b.* 1965. *Residence,*—Wildfields Farm, Wood St., Guildford.——Enid Joyce (1792, Westbrook Cres., Vancouver, BC, Canada) *b.* 1913: *m.* 1943, Prof. James Fischer-Sobell, MA, PhD, FRSC, late Wing-Com. RAF, who *d.* 1973, having assumed by deed poll 1945, the surname of St. Clair-Sobell in lieu of that of Fischer-Sobell, and has issue living, Guy James (1792, Westbrook Cres., Vancouver, BC, Canada), *b.* 1944; BA.

Grandsons of the late Matthew John St. Clair (infra):—
Issue of the late Eva Pringle St. Clair, *b.* 1873, *d.* 1964: *m.* 1905, John Conyngham Mc-Causland, who *d.* 1953:—
John Conyngham (4/65, Muston St., Mosman, NSW 2088), *b.* 1906; BSc; an Asso. of Sydney Tech. Coll. (Chem.): *m.* 1934, Laura, da. of George Daniel Baker, and has issue living, Michael John Conyngham (Trewern, Craig-y-Don Rd., Bangor, Caernarvonshire, N. Wales), *b.* 1945; ed. at New England Univ., Australia (BSc), and Univ. of Wales (BA): *m.* 1966, Prudence Louise, BA, da. of Rolland Earl Graham, and has issue living, John Conyngham *b.* 1971,—Margot Caroline, *b.* 1938: *m.* 1962, Prof. Robert Garth Nettheim, LLB, of 12, Union St., Mosman, NSW 2088, and has issue living, Daniel Garth *b.* 1966, Matthew John *b.* 1969, Anna Laura *b.* 1968.——Charles Pringle (184, Jersey Rd., Woollahra, NSW 2025), *b.* 1910; MA Sydney: *m.* 1952 (m. diss. 1966), Astrid Anna, da. of Aage Madsen, and has issue living, Bruce Charles Madsen, *b.* 1954,—Malcolm Montgomery, *b.* 1957,—Sigrid Kristina; ed. at Aust. Nat. Univ. (BA), *b.* 1953,—Viveca Tonny Ingrid, *b.* 1959.

Granddaughter of the late Com. the Hon. Charles St. Clair, 3rd son of 13th Lord:—
Issue of the late Matthew John St. Clair, *b.* 1845, *d.* 1926 : *m.* 1869, Charlotte Fraser, who *d.* 1921, dau. of D. M. Sinclair, Police Magistrate, of Warwick, Queensland:—
Beatrice Cerise (5A, Dettman Av., Longueville, 2066, NSW), *b.* 1890: *m.* 1914, Ralph Bernard Bolitho Snowdon, who *d.* 1936, and has issue living, Marion, *b.* 1914: *m.* 1st, 1937, Percy Clarence Harris, who *d.* 1966; 2ndly, 1970, Clement John Ollett, of 5A, Dettman Av., Longueville 2066, NSW, and has issue living (by 1st m.), John *b.* 1938; ed. at Gore Hill Tech. Coll. (Dip. of Wool Classing): *m.* 1963, Barbara McFarland (and has issue living, Scott St. Clair *b.* 1964), David *b.* 1940; ed. at Hawkesbury Agric. Coll. (Dip. Agric.), and Univ. of New England: *m.* 1967, Javelle Middleton (and has issue living, Stuart *b.* 1969), Rodney *b.* 1942; ed. at Gore Hill Tech. Coll.: *m.* 1969, Rhonya Moore, Douglas *b.* 1944; ed. at Gore Hill Tech. Coll.: *m.* 1966, Marie Byrne (and has issue living, Paul St. Clair *b.* 1967), Ian *b.* 1951, Violet Cerise *b.* 1939: *m.* 19—, Rodney Atfield, FIA, Isobel Joan, *b.* 1946: *m.* 1962, Giuseppi Schelero (and has issue living, Mark *b.* 1963), Diana *b.* 1948,—Joan St. Clair, *b.* 1917: *m.* 1st, 1940 (m. diss. 1953), Alleyn Mearns; 2ndly, 1955, Raymond Francis, of 2, Baldry St., Chatswood, NSW, and has issue living, (by 2nd m.) Raymond *b.* 1956, Ronald *b.* 1958,—Anna, *b.* 1921: *m.* 1st, 1936 (divorce 1944), Bruce McEwan; 2ndly, 1947, Murray Stevens, of 8251, President Court Blvd. 26, Apart. 11, Kansas City, Missouri, USA 64131, and has issue living, (by 2nd m.) Murray Carl *b.* 1948, (by 1st m.) Valerie *b.* 1941, Pamela *b.* 1943.

Grandchildren of the late Percival James St. Clair, el. son of James Andrew St. Clair (infra):—
Issue of the late Rodney Samuel St. Clair, *b.* 1919, *d.* 1964: *m.* 1942, Beatrice Wyatt Walker (Trefusis, Boomi, N.S. Wales):—
Malcolm Clive, *b.* 1943: *m.* 1971, Julie Murphy, and has issue living, Rodney James, *b.* 1973.—— Rosslyn Violet, *b.* 1947: *m.* 1971, Iain Couper.——Linda Helen, *b.* 1953.

Granddaughters of the late James Andrew St. Clair, 5th son of the Hon. Charles St. Clair (ante):—
Issue of the late Charles Archibald St. Clair, *b.* 1878, *d.* 1917 : *m.* 1913, Madeline Smith:— Joan Madeline, *b.* 1914. *Residence,*—

Issue of the late Christopher Fenwick St. Clair, *b.* 1882, *d.* (killed in action in France) 1918: *m.* 1914, Ethel Maud Cheesbrough :—
Erica Webster, *b.* 1916: *m.* 1940, Duncan Cannon McConnel, and has issue living, Christopher David, *b.* 1951,—Rosemary Robina St. Clair, *b.* 1941,—Diana Rose, *b.* 1946: *m.* 1968, Arthur Edmund de Norbury Rogus, and has issue living, Andrew de Norbury *b.* 1970, Scott McConnel *b.* 1972, James McConnel *b.* 1974. *Residence,*—Cressbrook, Toogoolawah, Queensland.

PREDECESSORS.—[1] WILLIAM Sinclair, 3rd Earl of Orkney (cr. 1379) ; a Lord of Parliament as *Lord Sinclair* about 1449; cr. *Earl of Caithness* 1455; resigned the Earldom of Orkney to the Crown 1470 and the Earldom of Caithness later ; *s.* by his son [2] WILLIAM ; *s.* by his son [3] HENRY, who in 1488 was confirmed as a Peer of Parliament as *Lord Sinclair* (peerage of Scotland ; killed at Flodden Field 1513 ; *s.* by his son [4] WILLIAM, 4th Lord ; *d.* 1570 ; *s.* by his son [5] HENRY, 5th Lord ; *d.* 1601 ; *s.* by his grandson [6] HENRY, 6th Lord ; *d.* 1602 ; *s.* by his brother [7] JAMES, 7th Lord ; *d.* 1607 ; *s.* by his brother [8] PATRICK, 8th Lord ; *d.* 1617 ; *s.* by his son [9] JOHN, 9th Lord ; *d.* 1676 ; *s.* by his grandson [10] HENRY (son of John St. Clair by Catherine, Mistress of Sinclair, dau. of 9th Lord Sinclair), 10th Lord ; obtained a charter under the Great Seal 1677 confirming all the honours, precedence, and dignities, &c., enjoyed by his precedessors, with remainders respectively to his brother Henry and his father's brothers Robert, George, and Matthew, and tailing them to his own heirs male whatsoever; *d.* 1723, his el. son [11] JOHN, having been engaged in the Rebellion of 1715 was attainted, and never assumed the title ; *d.s.p.* 1750; his brother [12] JAMES also did not assume the title ; a Gen. in the Army and a distinguished diplomatist ; *d.* 1762, when the Lordship became dormant and remained so until 1782, when through [13] CHARLES [son of Matthew (ante)], *de jure* 11th Lord ; *s.* by his son [14] ANDREW, *de jure* 12th Lord, the House of Lords confirmed the claim of his son [15] CHARLES, who thus became 13th Lord, and the first of his line who held the title without descent from the original Lords; was a Representative Peer, *d.* 1863 ; *s.* by his son [16] JAMES, 14th Lord ; *b.* 1803 ; a Representative Peer: *m.* 1830, Jane, dau. of Archibald Little, Esq., of Shabden Park, Surrey ; *d.* 1880; *s.*

by his son [17] CHARLES WILLIAM, 15th Lord, *b.* 1831; a Representative Peer; Col. in Army; Crimean Campaign 1854-55: *m.* 1870, Margaret Jane, who *d.* 1935, dau. of James Murray, of 16, Bryanston Square, W.; *d.* 1922; *s.* by his son [18] ARCHIBALD JAMES MURRAY, *M.V.O.*, 16th Lord; *b.* 1875; Extra Equerry to H.R.H. Prince Arthur of Connaught 1914-38; a Representative Peer for Scotland: *m.* 1906, Violet Frances, who *d.* 1953, dau. of the late Col. John Murray Kennedy, M.V.O., of Knocknalling, Dalry, Galloway; *d.* 1957; *s.* by his only son [19] CHARLES MURRAY KENNEDY, 17th Lord and present peer.

SINCLAIR OF CLEEVE, BARON. (Sinclair.) [Baron U.K. 1957.]

ROBERT JOHN SINCLAIR, *K.C.B., K.B.E.*, 1st Baron, son of the late Robert Henry Sinclair; *b.* July 29th, 1893; ed. at Glasgow Acad., and at Oriel Coll., Oxford (B.A. 1914, M.A. 1918, Hon. Fellow 1959); Hon. LLD Bristol 1959; Chm. of Imperial Tobacco Co., Ltd., 1947-59, and Pres. 1959-67, and Chm. of Finance Corpn. for Industry Ltd. 1960-64 and of Bristol Waterworks Co. 1960-71; a Dir. of Gen. Accident Fire and Life Assurance Corporation, Ltd. and of Debenture Corpn. Ltd.; Pro-Chancellor of Bristol Univ. 1946-70; a Member of Standing Security Comm. since 1966; Dep. Dir. of Inspection of Munitions 1917-19; a Member of Prime Min.'s Advisory Panel of Industrialists 1939; Director-Gen. of Army Requirements, War Office 1939-42, a Member of Supply Council 1939-42, and a Member of Army Council 1940-42; Dep. for Min. of Production on Combined Production and Resources Board, Washington 1942-43; Ch. Executive, Min. of Production 1943-45; Pres. of Fedn. of British Industries 1949-51; High Sheriff of Somerset 1951-52; 1914-18 War in Gallipoli as Lt. King's Own Scottish Borderers (wounded, despatches, MBE, 1914-15 star, two medals); received American medal of Freedom with gold palm 1947; cr. MBE (Mil.) 1919, KBE (Civil) 1941, KCB (Civil) 1946, and *Baron Sinclair of Cleeve,* of Cleeve, co. Somerset (peerage of United Kingdom) 1957: *m.* 1917, Mary Shearer, da. of the late Robert Shearer Barclay, and has issue.

𝕬rms,— Or a cross engrailed sable in the first quarter a sword erect proper on a chief also sable three martlets gold. 𝕮rest,—In front of a saltire argent a dove proper beaked and legged gules in the beak an olive branch also proper. 𝕾upporters,—*Dexter,* a griffin sable; *sinister,* a unicorn argent. Each gorged with a chaplet of white may leaved and flowered proper.

Residence,—Cleeve Court, nr. Bristol. *Clubs,*—Athenaeum, United Oxford and Cambridge University, Army and Navy.

SON LIVING.

Hon. JOHN ROBERT KILGOUR, *OBE,* *b.* Nov. 3rd, 1919; ed. at Winchester; Lt.-Col. (ret.) Queen's Own Highlanders; Mil. Attaché, Leopoldville 1960-63; with SHAPE 1964-66, and Min. of Defence 1967-69; 1939-45 War (despatches); MBE (Mil) 1954; OBE (Mil) 1963: *m.* 1950, Patricia, da. of Lawrence Hellyer, of The Hewke, Lockerbie, Dumfriesshire, and has issue living, John Lawrence Robert, *b.* 1953,—Juliet, *b.* 1951,—Jane, *b.* 1955. *Address,*—c/o Williams & Glyn's Bank, Holt's Branch, Kirkland Hse, Whitehall, SW1. *Club,*—United Service.

SINHA, BARON. (Sinha.) [Baron U.K. 1919.]

SUHDINDRO PROSANNO SINHA, 3rd Baron; *b.* Oct. 29th, 1920; *s.* 1967; ed. at Bryanston Sch.; Chm. and Managing Dir. of Mcneill and Barry, Ltd., Calcutta: *m.* 1945, Madhabi, da. of the late Monoranjan Chatterjee, of Calcutta, and has issue.

𝕬rms,—Argent, on a chevron ermine between in chief two lotus flowers and in base an Adjutant bird, three fountains all proper. 𝕮rest,—A demi-tiger supporting a fasces erect proper. 𝕾upporters,—On either side an Adjutant bird proper, collared or.

Residence,—7, Lord Sinha Road, Calcutta, India.

SON LIVING.
Hon. SUSHANTO, *b.* 1953.

DAUGHTERS LIVING.
Hon. Manjula, *b.* 1947.
Hon. Anjana, *b.* 1950.

BROTHER LIVING.
Hon. A.K., *b.* May 18th, 1930.

HALF SISTERS LIVING.
Hon. Bina, *b.* 1917.
Hon. Gita, *b.* 1918.

SISTER LIVING.
Hon. Sheila, *b.* 1923.

UNCLE LIVING. (*Son of 1st Baron.*)
Hon. Tarun, *b.* 1899; ed. a Hertford Coll., Oxford (BA).

AUNTS LIVING. (*Daughters of 1st Baron.*)

Hon. Kamala, *b.* 1892 : *m.* 1st, 1910 (divorce 1943), Ashoke Chandra Gupta, O.B.E., Accountant-Gen. (retired), Central Revenue, India ; 2ndly, 1943, J. Burnier, and has issue living, (by 1st marriage) Anil Kumar, *b.* 1918. *Address,—*Paris.

Hon. Bijoli, *b.* 1900 : *m.* 1918, Runge Lall Dutt, and has issue living, Brinda, *b.* 1919 : *m.* 1938, Lieut. David Leslie Gordon, R.N.,—Anjali, *b.* 1924. *Residence,—*

WIDOW LIVING OF SECOND BARON.

NIRUPAMA (*Nirupama, Baroness Sinha*), (7, Lord Sinha Rd., Calcutta, India), yr. da. of Rai Bahadur Lalit Mohan Chatterjee: *m.* 1919, as his 2nd wife, the 2nd Baron, who *d.* 1967.

COLLATERAL BRANCHES LIVING.

Issue of the late Hon. Sisir Sinha, 2nd son of 1st Baron, *b.* 1890, *d.* 1950: *m.* 1917, (Lord Sinha Rd., Calcutta, India), da. of :—
Indrajit (7/1, Lord Sinha Rd., Calcutta, India), *b.* 1918: *m.* 1951, Sunanda, da. of the late S. Seu, of Calcutta, and has issue living, Premola, *b.* 1954.——Anita, *b.* 1921.

Issue of the late Hon. Sushil Kumar Sinha, 3rd son of 1st Baron, *b.* 1895, *d.* 1968: *m.* 1st (Oct.) 1919, a da. (who *d.* Dec. 1919), of the late Sir Atul Chandra Chatterjee, GCIE, KCSI, ICS; 2ndly, 1921, Romola (Alipore, Calcutta, India), da. of D. S. K. Mullick:—
(By 2nd m.) Arun, *b.* 1939.——Leila, *b.* 1937.

PREDECESSORS. —[1] *Rt. Hon. Sir* SATYENDRA PRASANNA Sinha, *K.C.S.I., P.C., K.C.* (the first Indian to be created a peer), son of Siti Kantha Sinha, of Raipur, Birbhum, Bengal, *b.* 1864 ; was a Member of Viceroy's Council 1909-10, Advocate-Gen. and a M.L.C., Bengal 1916-19 ; Under-Sec. of State for India Jan. 1919 to Nov. 1920, and Gov. of Bihar and Orissa Nov. 1920 to Nov. 1921 ; represented India at Special War Conference 1917 and 1918 ; appointed a Member of Judicial Committee of Privy Council 1926 ; *cr. Baron Sinha,* of Raipur, Presidency of Bengal (peerage of United Kingdom) 1919 : *m.* 1880, Gobindo Mohini, who *d.* 1938, dau. of Krislo Chunder Mitter, Zemindar of Maheta, District Burdwan, India; *d.* 1928; *s.* by his son [2] AROON KUMAR, 2nd Baron; *b.* 1887; writ of summons to House of Lords granted 1939: *m.* 1st, 1916, Pryatama (Rani), who *d.* 1919, el. da. of Rai Bahadur Lalit Mohan Chatterjee; 2ndly, 1919, Nirpuama, yr. da. of Rai Bahadur Lalit Mohan Chatterjee (ante); *d.* 1967; *s.* by his son [3] SUDHINDRO PROSANNO, 3rd Baron and present peer.

SKELMERSDALE, BARON. (Bootle-Wilbraham.) [Baron U.K. 1828.]

In the haven there is rest.

ROGER BOOTLE-WILBRAHAM, 7th Baron; *b.* April 2nd, 1945; *s.* 1973; ed. at Eton, Lord Wandsworth Coll., Basingstoke; Proprietor of Broadleigh Gdns. 1972, Man. Dir. Broadleigh Nurseries, Ltd. 1973: *m.* 1972, Christine Joan, only da. of Phillip Roy Morgan, of 2, Hollins Lane, Hampsthwaite, Harrogate, and has issue.

Arms,—Quarterly: 1st and 4th argent, three bendlets wavy azure, *Wilbraham;* 2nd and 3rd gules, on a chevron engrailed, between three combs argent, as many crosses partée fitchée, of the field. *Bootle.* Crest,—1st, a wolf's head erased argent; 2nd, a demi-lion reguardant proper, holding in the paws an escutcheon gules, charged with a cross flory argent. Supporters,— *Dexter,* a wolf argent; gorged with a plain collar azure, and pendent therefrom an escutcheon charged with the ancient arms of Wilbraham, viz. azure, two bars argent, and a canton sable, thereon a wolf's head erased argent; *sinister,* a wolf proper, collared or, and from the collar pendent an escutcheon as the dexter.

*Residence,—*Barr House, Bishops Hull, Taunton, Somerset.

DAUGHTER LIVING.

Hon. Carolyn Ann, *b.* 1964.

SISTERS LIVING.

Hon. Lavinia, *b.* 1937: *m.* 1969, Robert Brian Noel Massey, of Melbury, Kingston Hill, Kingston upon Thames, Surrey.

Hon. Olivia, *b.* 1938: *m.* 1961, Anthony John Hoole-Lowsley-Williams, of The Chalet, Hollington, Woolton Hill, Newbury, Berks., [Makins, Bt.], and has issue living, Richard Edward, *b.* 1962,—Hugh Sebastian, *b.* 1964,—Benjamin Christopher, *b.* 1968.

Hon. Daphne (Latchmoor Cottage, Ogdens, Fordingbridge), *b.* 1946.

AUNT LIVING.

Yvonne (Latchmoor Cottage, Ogdens, Fordingbridge, Hants), *b.* 1898.

PREDECESSORS.—[1] EDWARD Bootle-Wilbraham; *b.* 1771; M.P. for Westbury 1795-6, for Newcastle-under-Lyme 1796-1812, and for Dover 1818-28 ; *cr. Baron Skelmersdale* (peerage of United Kingdom) 1828 ; *d.* 1853 ; *s.* by his grandson [2] EDWARD, *G.C.B., P.C.* (son of the Hon. Richard Bootle-Wilbraham, M.P.), 2nd Baron ; *b.* 1837 ; Lord-in-Waiting to H.M. Queen Victoria 1866-8, Capt. of Yeomen of the Guard 1874-80, and Lord Chamberlain of H.M.'s Household 1885-6, 1886-92, and 1895-8 ; *cr. Earl of Lathom* (peerage of United Kingdom) 1880 : *m.,* 1860, Lady Alice Villiers, who *d.* 1897, 2nd dau. of 4th Earl of Clarendon ; *d.* 1898; *s.* by his el. son [3] EDWARD GEORGE, 2nd Earl, *b.* 1864 : *m.* 1889, Lady Wilma Pleydell-Bouverie, who *d.* 1931, only surviving dau. of 5th Earl of Radnor ; *d.* 1910 ; *s.* by his only son [4] EDWARD WILLIAM, 3rd Earl; *b.* 1895: *m.* 1927, Marie Xenia, who *d.* 1974, da. of E. W. de Tunzelman, of Singapore (formerly wife of Ronald William Morrison, from whom she obtained a divorce 1921); *d.* 1930, when the Earldom of Lathom became ext., and the Barony of Skelmersdale devolved upon his kinsman [5] ARTHUR GEORGE, *MC,* (el. son of the late Col. Arthur Bootle-Wilbraham, a grandson of 1st Baron), 5th Baron; *b.* 1876; *d.* 1969; *s.* by his cousin [6] LIONEL, *DSO, MC* (only son of Lionel Bootle-Wilbraham, grandson of 1st Baron), 6th Baron, *b.* 1896; Lt.-Col. Coldm. Gds.: *m.* 1936, Ann, who *d.* 1974, da. of the late Percy Cuthbert Quilter [Quilter, Bt., colls.]; *d.* 1973; *s.* by his son [7] ROGER, 7th Baron and present peer.

Slane, Viscount, grandson of **Marquess Conyngham.**

SLATER, BARON. (Slater.) [Life Baron 1970.]

JOSEPH SLATER, *BEM,* son of William Slater; *b.* June 13th, 1904; ed. at Chilton Lane Elementary Sch.; Miner; Lodge Official of Miners' Union 1929-50; a Parish Councillor 1930-33, a Dist. Councillor 1937-44, and a Co. Councillor, Durham 1944-50; a Member of Durham Miners Exec. Cttee. 1944-47, and of Hosp. Management Cttees. 1944-50; PPS to Leader of the Opposition 1960-64; Assist. Postmaster-Gen. 1964-70; MP for Sedgefield Div. of Durham (*Lab.*) 1950-70; *cr.* Baron Slater, of Ferryhill, co. Durham (Life Baron) 1970: *m.* 1928, Hilda, da. of Gilbert James Clement, and has issue.

Residence,—5, Witton Rd., Ferryhill, co. Durham.

SON LIVING.

Hon. Brian, *b.* 1948.

DAUGHTER LIVING.

Hon. Elizabeth, *b.* 1934: *m.* 1955, Frank Davison, of 1, Seymour Grove, Eaglescliffe, co. Durham.

SLIGO, MARQUESS OF. (Browne.) [Marquess I. 1800.] Sits as BARON MONTEAGLE (U.K. 1806).

Follow the right.

DENIS EDWARD BROWNE, 10th Marquess; *b.* Dec. 13th, 1908; *s.* 1952; ed. at Eton: *m.* 1930, José Gauche, and has issue.

Arms,—Sable, three lions passant in bend between four bendlets argent. Crest,—An eagle displayed vert. Supporters,—*Dexter,* a talbot proper, gorged with a baron's coronet; *sinister,* a horse argent.

Seat,—Westport House, Westport, co. Mayo. *Club,*—Kildare Street.

SON LIVING.

JEREMY ULICK (*Earl of Altamont*), *b.* June 4th, 1939: *m.* 1961, Jennifer June, dau. of Major Derek Cooper, M.C., of Dunlewey, co. Donegal, and has issue:—
　DAUGHTERS LIVING,—*Lady* Sheelyn Felicity, *b.* 1963.
　Lady Karen Lavinia, *b.* 1964.
　Lady Lucinda Jane, *b.* 1969.

BROTHER LIVING

(*Raised to the rank of a Marquess's son* 1953)

Lord Ulick, *b.* 1915; ed. at Eton; European War 1939-45 as Capt. R.A. in Italy and Middle East: *m.* 1st, 1942, Mrs. Elma (WARREN), who *d.* 1959, dau. of Capt. Andrew Burmanoff; 2ndly, 1962, Fiona Glenn, and has issue living, (by 2nd marriage) Sebastian Ulick *b.* 1964,—Ulicia Catherine *b.* 1962. *Residence,*—32, The Little Boltons, SW10.

SISTERS LIVING.

(*Raised to the rank of a Marquess's daughters* 1953)

Lady Sheelah Annette (twin), *b.* 1908: *m.* 1930, John Dalrymple Winn Treherne, who *d.* 1972, and has issue living, Roland Dalrymple, *b.* 1935; ed. at Eton,—Oona Cicely, *b.* 1930: *m.* 1950, Christopher Paul Mansel Campbell Methuen-Campbell [see B. Methuen, colls.]. *Residence,*—The New House, Otley, Ipswich.

Lady Noreen, *b.* 1910: *m.* 1931, Clive Ali Chimmo Branson, who *d.* (killed in action in Far East) 1944, and has issue living, Rosa (46, Southwood Av., Highgate, N6), *b.* 1933: *m.* 1st, 1954 (m. diss. 1966), Alan Hopkins; 2ndly, 1971, Henry Joseph Harper, and has issue living, (by 1st m.) Michael Stephen *b.* 1958, Peggy Ann *b.* 1955. *Residence,*—46, Southwood Av., N6.

DAUGHTER LIVING OF SIXTH MARQUESS.

Lady Doreen Geraldine (*Dowager Baroness Brabourne*), *C.I.,* *b.* 1896; is a D.St.J.; was Dep. Vice-Chm. of Overseas League 1953-56; C.I. 1937: *m.* 1919, the 5th Baron Brabourne, who *d.* 1939. *Residence,*—64, Kingston House North, Knightsbridge, SW7.

COLLATERAL BRANCHES LIVING.

Granddaughters of the late Lord Richard Howe Browne, 6th son of 2nd Marquess:—
　Issue of the late Major Percy Howe Browne, *b.* 1868, *d.* 1940: *m.* 1897, Alice Tremlett, dau. of the late Capt. Charles Henry Marillier:—
Margaret Kathleen (Eastview Mill, Chalford, Stroud, Glos.), *b.* 1898: *m.* 1924, Almeric Hugh Seymour, O.B.E., who *d.* 1950, and has issue living, Timothy Hugh, *b.* 1928: *m.* 1958, Elisabeth Valerie, dau. of Dr. Rayner Thrower, and has issue living, Meryl Penelope Jane *b.* 1959, Elizabeth Anne Peronel *b.* 1961, Catherine Fiona Margaret *b.* 1964, Joanna Melanie Ruth (twin) *b.* 1964,—Elizabeth Jennifer Jane (Valley House, Chalford, Stroud, Glos.), *b.* 1934: *m.* 1957 (m. diss. 1969), Capt. Rhoderick Stewart Cochrane-Dyet, 9th/12th Roy. Lancers, and has issue living, Charles Nicholas *b.* 1958, Christopher John Richard *b.* 1963, Amanda Jane *b.* 1961.

Issue of the late Cyril Edward Browne, O.B.E., *b.* 1873, *d.* 1960: *m.* 1902, Alice Christina, who *d.* 1962, dau. of Frederick Thomas Lewin, D.L., of Castlegrove, near Tuam, co. Galway, and Cloghans, co. Mayo:—

Phyllis Marion Alice, *b*. 1913; ed. at Trin. Coll., Dublin (Mod. BA): *m*. 1941, Harold Hugh Brodei Ind, of Delphi Lodge, Kilcoole, co. Wicklow, and has issue living, Peter Lewin Brodie, *b*. 1944; ed. at Eton and Trin. Coll., Dublin (BA),—Christina Isabel Mary, *b*. 1942; ed. at Trin. Coll., Dublin (BA): *m*. 1970, Sqdn. Ldr. Robin Worthington Scott, of Pepys, Blounce, S. Warnborough, nr. Basingstoke, and has issue living, Gervase Roderick John *b*. 1971, Nicholas Hugo Howe *b*. 1972,—Miranda Eleanor Phyllis (2515, Overlook Rd., Cleveland, Ohio 44106, USA), *b*. 1946: *m*. 1971, John Morris O'Connor, Assist. Prof. of Philosophy, Case Western Reserve Univ., Cleveland, and has issue living, Amanda Evelyn Alice *b*. 1974.——Marjory Maud, *b*. 1916: *m*. 1954, Charles Hastings Doyne, and has issue living, Charles Philip, *b*. 1955. *Residence*,—The Priory, Ballymore, co. Cork.

Grandsons of the late Major Percy Howe Browne

Issue of the late Lieut.-Com. Anthony Howe Browne, R.N., *b*. 1905, *d*. (killed in action during European War) 1940: *m*. 1931, Joyce Mary Le Roy (who *m*. 2ndly, 1946, Squadron Leader Graham Doody, A.C.A.), dau. of John Collin, of Trumpington, Cambridge :—

Patrick Ulick Anthony Howe (27, Lanhill Rd., W9), *b*. 1935; ed. at Eton; and Magdalene Coll., Camb.: *m*. 1962, Gerd, da. of Anders Hamer, of Norway, and has issue living, Patrick Alexander Howe, *b*. 1965,—Anthony Howe, *b*. 1967,—Cecile, *b*. 1963.——Michael John Le Roy (29, Lanhill Rd., W9), *b*. 1936: *m*. 1959 (m. diss. 1969), Sarah Ruth, da. of James Edward Kenneth Sprot, of Natal, and has issue living, Richard Howe, *b*. 1962,—Jeremy Ulick, *b*. 1963.

(In remainder to Earldom of Altamont, Viscountcy of Westport, and Barony of Mount Eagle only.)

Grandchildren of the late William Denis Browne, yr. son of the Very Rev. Denis Browne, Dean of Emly, 3rd son of the Rt. Hon. Denis Browne, MP, 2nd son of 2nd Earl of Altamont:—

Issue of the late Louisa Muriel Browne, *b*. 1882, *d*. 1956: *m*. 1906, Edward Mansel, FRIBA, who *d*. 1941:—

Rev. Canon James Seymour Denis, *MVO* (Marlborough Gate, St. James's Palace, SW1), *b*. 1907; Sub Dean of HM Chapels Poyal, Dep. Clerk of The Closet, Sub Almoner, and Domestic Chap. to HM; MVO 1972: *m*. 1942, Ann Monica, who *d*. 1974, da. of Amyas T. Waterhouse, MD, of Oxford, and has issue living, Elizabeth Alison, *b*. 1947.——Rowan Muriel Nona, *b*. 1909: *m*. 1971, Maurice James Waterhouse, of 3A, Brookside, Headington, Oxford.——Eleanor Mary, *b*. 1911: *m*. 1937, the Rev. William Blyth Sells, of The Vicarage, Curdridge, Southampton, and has issue living.——Bridget Alicia Persis (20, Lorne Rd., Southsea, Hants.), *b*. 1913: *m*. 1932, F. Noël Lucas, and has issue living.

Grandchildren of the late Capt. Perceval Altamont Browne (infra):—

Issue of the late Percy Frederick Browne, *b*. 1872, *d*. 1959 : *m*. 1904, Ruth Reynolds, who *d*. 1957, dau. of John Reynolds Warren, of Berea, Durban, S. Africa.:—

Nancye Maud (8, Mandalay, 233, High Level Rd., Sea Point, Cape Town, S. Africa), *b*. 1905: *m*. 1945, Maj. Aubrey James Rous, and has issue living, Patrick James *b*. 1947,——Moya Lennox, *b*. 1917: *m*. 1944, Richard Read Birtwistle, of Crooked Field, Chaigley, Clitheroe, Lancs., and has issue living, Susan Lennox, *b*. 1947: *m*. 1972, Capt. D. C. Koch, of Salisbury, Rhodesia.

Grandchildren of the late Percy Frederick Browne (ante):—

Issue of the late Patrick Warren Browne, *b*. 1908, *d*. 1944 : *m*. 1936, Ada Elizabeth Minnie Barnes, who *m*. 2ndly, 1946 (m. diss. 1954) Charles Edward Halton Duprez, and has resumed the surname of Browne:—

Michael Lewis, *b*. 1940.——Phillip Anthony (45, Clifton Court, NW8), *b*. 1941.——Patricia Ruth, *b*. 1937.

Granddaughter of the late John Denis Browne, son of the late Rt. Hon. Denis Browne, M.P. (ante):—

Issue of the late Capt. Perceval Altamont Browne, *b*. 1841, *d*. 1919 : *m*. 1871, Caroline Maude, who *d*. 1937, dau. of James Hunt, of Brighton :—

Muriel, *b*. 1886: *m*. 1918, Horace Muir Lyster. *Residence*,—Montreal, Canada.

Grandchildren of the late George Robert Browne, son of the Rev. George Browne, (infra) :—

Issue of the late George Denis Gun Browne, *b*. 1874, *d*. 1946: *m*. 1901, Gertrude Bessie, who *d*. 1953, youngest dau. of John Robert Sutton Hudson :—

Denis George Robert Anthony Gun (Calais, Dal Josaphat, nr. Paarl, Cape Province, S. Africa), *b*. 1907: *m*. 1960, Violet Ailsa, dau. of Charles Henry Stewart-Fess, of Wallasey, Cheshire.——Gertrude Frances Hester, *b*. 1905: *m*. 1st, 1931, George Ryder Runton, who *d*. 1935; 2ndly, 1945, Roger Sydney McCulloch (Private Bag, 703, Enkeldoorn, Rhodesia), and has issue living, (by 1st m.) Aileen Frances, *b*. 1932: *m*. 1950, John Geoffrey Harrison, of Mocambique, PEA, and has issue living Michael John *b*. 1952, Rosemary Ann *b*. 1954,—(by 2nd m.) Jane Ann Louise, *b*. 1946: *m*. 1968, Marie Denis Guiot-Pascau, of Salsibury, Rhodesia.

Grandchildren of the late Rev. Robert Browne, son of the late Rev. George Browne, 5th son of the late Rt. Hon. Denis Browne, M.P. (ante) :—

Issue of the late Robert Denis Browne, *b*. 1867, *d*. 1937 : *m*. 1905, Beatrice, who *d*. 1957, dau. of the late H. J. Batson, of Hampstead, N.W.:—

Robert John Denis, *b*. 1907 ; M.R.C.S., L.R.C.P.; European War 1939-45 as Surg.-Lieut. R.N.V.R.: *m*. 1949, Norah Mary, dau. of David Haywood, of Burton-on-Trent, and has issue living, Stephen Denis, *b*. 1950,—Anthony David, *b*. 1958,—Margaret, *b*. 1952. *Residence*,—1536, Pershore Road, Birmingham, 30.——Terence Francis Denis, *b*. 1910 ; European War 1939-45 with Roy. Tank Regt. in Middle East, and W. Desert : *m*. 1947, Avril Honor, dau. of William T. Thompson, of Rustington, Sussex, and has issue living, Peter Malyon Denis, *b*. 1953,—Ian Anthony Denis, *b*. 1956. *Residence*, —The Mount, 20, Woodfield Lane, Ashtead, Surrey.

Issue of the late Rev. Cyril George Denis Browne, *b*. 1873, *d*. 1952 : *m*. 1906, Sarah H. J. dau. of Charles Crooks Higby :—

Rev. Cyril Theodore Martin (The Rectory, Inveresk Rd., Tilston, Malpas, Cheshire), *b*. 1912; R. of Tilston and Shocklach.——Muriel Eunice Myra, *b*, 1907. *Residence*,—

Issue of the late Ambrose George Denis Browne, *b*. 1875, *d*. 1954: *m*. 1st, 1915, Alice Winifred who *d*. 1938, dau. of the late Sir William Henry White, K.C.B.; 2ndly, 1941, Gertrude Mariana, who *d*. 1973, yr. da. of the late Rev. John Kipling Quarterman, MA, of Blackheath, SE3:—

(By 1st marriage) William Robert Anthony Denis, *b*. 1924 ; is a F.R.I.C.S. : *m*. 1949, Eileen Beatrice Louise, dau. of Horace Hugh Percival Hunt, of High Ham, Somerset, and has issue living, James Anthony Ulick Denis, *b*. 1956,—Caroline Elizabeth Anne Denis, *b*. 1952. *Residence*,—19, Hughenden Rd., Clifton, Bristol 8.——Winifred Anne Denis, *b*. 1921: *m*. 1950, John Henry Bateman, MA, of The Orchard, 18A, Chapel Lane, Wilmslow, Ches.

Grandchildren of the late Henry Browne, 2nd son of the late George Browne, 3rd son of the late Maj. John Browne, el. son of Col. the Rt. Hon. Arthur Browne, MP, 2nd son of 1st Earl of Altamont:—

Issue of the late Ernest Henry Browne, *b*. 1863, *d*. 1928: *m*. 19—, Beatrice Brownrigg, who *d*. 1964:—

Ernest Henry (126, Ohiro Bay Parade, Wellington, S2, NZ), *b*. 1913.——Beatrice Mary (92, Cabra Park, Phibsborough, Dublin), *b*. 1911.

Granddaughter of the late Rev. John Denis Browne, son of the late George Townshend Browne, son of the late Col. the Rt. Hon. Arthur Browne, M.P. (ante) :—

Issue of the late Rev. Valentine John Augustus (altered by deed poll 1897 to " Valentine, Denis "), *b*. 1843, *d*. 1933: *m*. 1884, Frances Elizabeth, dau. of the late William Rose, Bar.-at-law:—

Rosalind Frances, *b*. 1885. *Residence*,—

PREDECESSORS.—[1] JOHN Browne, son of Peter Browne of Westport, grandson of Sir John Browne, 1st Bt. (cr. 1636) [see B. Kilmaine], was M.P. for Castlebar 1749-60 ; cr. *Baron Mount Eagle of Westport,* co. Mayo (peerage of Ireland) 1760, *Viscount Westport* (peerage of Ireland) 1768, and *Earl of Altamont* (peerage of Ireland) 1771 ; *d.* 1776 ; *s.* by his son [2] PETER, 2nd Earl, sat as M.P. for co. Mayo ; *d.* 1780, *s.* by his son [3] JOHN DENIS, *K.P., P.C.,* 3rd Earl ; sat as M.P. for co. Mayo ; cr. *Marquess of Sligo* (peerage of Ireland) 1800, and *Baron Monteagle,* of Westport, co. Mayo (peerage of United Kingdom) 1806 ; *d.* 1809 ; *s.* by his son [4] HOWE PETER, *K.P., P.C.,* 2nd Marquess ; *b.* 1788 : *m.* 1816, Hester Catherine, el. dau. of 13th Earl of Clanricarde ; *d.* 1845 ; *s.* by his son [5] GEORGE JOHN, 3rd Marquess, *b.* 1820 : *m.* 1st, 1847, Louisa Ellen Frances Augusta Smythe, who *d.* 1852, dau. of 6th Viscount Strangford ; 2ndly, 1858, Julia Catherine Anne Nugent, who *d.* 1859, el. dau. of 9th Earl of Westmeath ; 3rdly, 1878, Isabelle, who *d.* 1927, dau. of the late Vicomte de Peyronnet ; *d.* 1896 ; *s.* by his brother [6] JOHN THOMAS, 4th Marquess ; *b.* 1824 ; sat as M.P. for co. Mayo 1857-68 ; *d.* 1903 ; *s.* by his brother [7] HENRY ULICK, 5th Marquess ; *b.* 1831 : *m.* 1855, Catharine Henrietta, who *d.* 1914, dau. of the late William Stephens Dicken, Dep. Inspector-Gen. Indian Med. Ser. ; *d.* 1913 ; *s.* by his el. son [8] GEORGE ULICK, 6th Marquess ; *b.* 1856 ; in 1916 *s.* to *Earldom of Clanricarde* (cr. 1800) [see *⁎⁎* infra] ; appointed Lieut. and Custos Rotulorum for co. Mayo 1914 : *m.* 1887, Agatha Stewart, who *d.* 1965, dau. of the late J. Stewart Hodgson, of Haslemere ; *d.* 1935; *s.* by his only son [9] ULICK DE BURGH, *M.C.,* 7th Marquess ; *b.* 1898 ; Capt. (retired) The Greys ; European War 1914-19 (M.C.) ; *d.* 1941 ; *s.* by his uncle [8] ARTHUR HOWE, *K.B.E., C.B.* (3rd son of 5th Marquess), 8th Marquess ; *b.* 1867 ; Col. late S. Staffordshire Regt. and Roy. Munster Fusiliers ; on Gen. Staff, Special Intelligence Directorate, War Office 1914-19 (K.B.E.) ; Principal Assist. Sec., Imperial War Graves Commn. 1919-30 : *m.* 1919, Lilian Whiteside, who *d.* 1953, dau. of Charles Chapman, and widow of Major A. F. Mann ; *d.* 1951 ; *s.* by his brother [9] TERENCE MORRIS, 9th Marquess ; *b.* 1873 ; was Sup., Bengal Police 1894-1907, *d.* 1952 ; *s.* by his nephew [10] DENIS EDWARD (el. son of the late Lieut.-Col. Lord Alfred Eden Browne, *D.S.O.,* 5th son of 5th Marquess), 10th Marquess, and present peer : also Earl of Altamont, Earl of Clanricarde, Viscount Westport, Baron Mount Eagle, and Baron Monteagle.

⁎⁎ [1] ULICK BURKE or de Burgh, great grandson of Ulick de Bourke, MacWilliam Eighter, feudal Lord of Clanricarde, collateral heir male of Earls of Ulster; Gov. of Connaught; cr. *Baron of Dunkellin,* and *Earl of Clanricarde* (peerage of Ireland) 1543; *d.* 1544 ; *s.* by his son [2] RICHARD, 2nd Earl; was Lord-Lieut. or Ireland; *d.* 1582; *s.* by his son [3] ULICK, 3rd Earl; his 4th son, John, was cr. *Viscount Burke,* of Clanmories, co. Mayo (peerage of Ireland) 1629, with remainder to the issue male of his father, which title, on the death of the 2nd Viscount, merged into the Earldom; *d.* 1601; *s.* by his son [4] RICHARD, 4th Earl; cr. *Baron Somerhill* and *Viscount Tunbridge* (peerage of England) 1624, and *Earl of St. Albans* (peerage of England) 1628; *d.* 1635; *s.* by his son [5] ULICK, 5th Earl; cr. *Marquess of Clanricarde* (peerage of Ireland) 1646; *d.* without male issue 1658, when the English peerages and the Marquessate became extinct, and the Irish Earldom devolved upon his cousin [6] RICHARD, 6th Earl, el. son of Sir William Burke, 3rd son of 3rd Earl; *d.* 1666; *s.* by his brother [7] WILLIAM, 7th Earl; *d.* 1687; *s.* by his son [8] RICHARD, 8th Earl: *s.* by his brother [9] JOHN, 9th Earl, Col. of a regiment of foot in the army of James II; being taken prisoner at the battle of Aghrim 1691, was outlawed and attainted, and his estates were forfeited ; his children however claimed their several remainders prior to the sale of the forfeitures and recovered the same ; in 1701 the Earl was, by Act of Parliament, acquitted of his treasons and attainder ; and restored to his estates, *d.* 1722 ; *s.* by his son [10] MICHAEL, 10th Earl; *d.* 1726 ; *s.* by his son [11] JOHN SMITH, 11th Earl; resumed by sign manual the ancient surname of De Burgh, *d.* 1782 ; *s.* by his son [12] HENRY, *K.P., P.C.,* 12th Earl; Gov. of co. Galway ; cr. *Marquess of Clanricarde* (peerage of Ireland) 1789 ; *d.s.p.* 1795, when the Marquessate became extinct ; *s.* in Earldom by his brother [13] JOHN THOMAS, 13th Earl; a Gen. in the Army and Gov. of co. Galway ; cr. *Earl of Clanricarde* (peerage of Ireland) 1800, with remainder to his two daughters and their issue male according to priority of birth ; *d.* 1808 ; *s.* by his son [14] ULICK JOHN, *K.P., P.C.,* 14th Earl ; *b.* 1802 ; was Under-Sec. for Foreign Affairs 1826-7, Ambassador at St. Petersburg 1838-40, Postmaster-Gen. 1846-52, Lord Privy Seal 1858, and Lord-Lieut. of co. Galway, &c. ; cr. *Marquess of Clanricarde* (peerage of Ireland) 1825, and *Baron Somerhill,* of Somerhill, co. Kent (peerage of United Kingdom) 1826 : *m.* 1825, the Hon. Harriet, who *d.* 1876, dau. of the Rt. Hon. George Canning and of his wife Viscountess Canning in her own right ; *d.* 1874 ; *s.* by his son [15] HUBERT, 2nd Marquess ; *b.* 1832 ; assumed in 1862 the additional surname of Canning, by Roy. licence, as heir of his maternal uncle, the 1st Earl Canning ; M.P. for co. Galway (*L*) 1867-71 ; *d.* 1916, when the Marquessate of Clanricarde and the Barony of Somerhill became ext., and the Barony of Dunkellin, and Earldom of Clanricarde (cr. 1543), and the Viscountcy of Bourke became ext., while the Earldom of Clanricarde (cr. 1800) devolved under special remainder upon his cousin [16] GEORGE ULICK, 6th Marquess of Sligo (ante).

SLIM, VISCOUNT. (Slim.) [Viscount U.K. 1960.]

A recompense is fairer from a depth.

JOHN DOUGLAS SLIM, *OBE,* 2nd Viscount ; *b.* July 20th, 1927 ; *s.* 1970 ; Lt.-Col. (ret.) A & SH and Special Air Ser. Regt. ; *cr.* OBE (Mil) 1973 : *m.* 1958, Elisabeth, da. of Arthur Rawdon Spinney, CBE, and has issue.

Arms,—Gules semée of swords erect argent a lion rampant ; or, on a canton quarterly azure and also argent a mullet of seven points gold. Crest,—Out of a Crown Vallary or a peacock in its pride proper gorged with a collar and with line reflexed over the back gold. Supporters,—*Dexter,* a British soldier in jungle-green battle dress with web equipment the exterior hand supporting a rifle with bayonet affixed; *Sinister,* a Gurkha rifleman in North-West Frontier dress with web equipment the exterior hand supporting a rifle all proper.

Address,—c/o Lloyds Bank, 6, Pall Mall, SW1. *Club,*—Special Forces.

SONS LIVING.

Hon. MARK WILLIAM RAWDON, *b.* Feb. 13th, 1960.
Hon. Hugo John Robertson, *b.* 1961.

DAUGHTER LIVING.

Hon. Mary Ann, *b.* 1964.

SISTER LIVING.

Hon. Una Mary, *b.* 1930: *m.* 1953, Maj. Peter Nigel Stewart Frazer, Grenadier Guards, of Puddington Lodge, Tiverton, Devon, and has issue living, Sarah Juliet, *b.* 1953,—Jennifer Jane, *b.* 1956,—Emma Mary, *b.* 1965.

WIDOW LIVING OF 1st VISCOUNT.

AILEEN (*Aileen, Viscountess Slim*) (6, Eaton Mansions, SW1), da. of the Rev. J. A. Robertson, of Edinburgh; DStJ; has Kaisar-I-Hind Medal: *m.* 1926, the 1st Viscount, who *d.* 1970.

PREDECESSOR.—[1] *Sir* WILLIAM JOSEPH SLIM, *KG, GCB, GCMG, GCVO, GBE, DSO, MC*, son of the late John Slim of Bristol; *b.* 1891; Field Marshal; GOC 14th Army 1943-45, Allied Land Forces, SE Asia 1945-46, Dep. Chm. Rly. Exec. 1948, CIGS. 1948-53, Gov.-Gen. of Aust. 1953-60, and Gov. and Constable Windsor Castle 1964-70; *cr. Viscount Slim*, of Yarralumla, ACT, and of Bishopston, City and Co. of Bristol (peerage of UK) 1960: *m.* 1926, Aileen, da. of the Rev. J. A. Robertson, of Edinburgh; *d.* 1970; *s.* by his son [2] JOHN DOUGLAS, 2nd Viscount and present peer.

SNOW, BARON. (Snow.) [Life Baron 1964.]

CHARLES PERCY SNOW, *CBE*, son of William Edward Snow, FRCO, of Leicester; *b.* Oct. 15th, 1905; ed. at Christ's Coll., Camb. (PhD and Fellow 1930); Hon. LL.D. Leicester, Liverpool, St. Andrews, Brooklyn Polytechnic Inst., Univ. of Bridgeport, Conn., and York Univ., Toronto; Hon. Fellow Founders Coll., York Univ., Toronto; Hon. DLitt Dartmouth, Temple, Syracuse, Pittsburgh, Bard, Ithaca, Westminister Colls., USA, W. Ontario, and Memorial Newfoundland; Hon. DHL Washington, Michigan, Kenyon, and Hebrew Union Coll.; Hon. DPhilSc, Rostov Univ.; Extraor. Fellow of Churchill Coll., Camb., and Fellow Morse Coll., Yale; Hon. DSc Pennsylvania Mil. Coll., and Alfred Univ.; an Author; Foreign Hon. Member of American Acad. of Arts and Sciences, and Hon. Member of American Acad. Inst.; Tutor of Christ's Coll., Camb. 1935-42, and 1944-45, and a Civil Ser. Commr. 1945-60; Pres. of Library Assocn. 1961; Rector of St. Andrew's Univ. 1961-64; Parl. Sec. to Min. of Technology 1964-66; Diamond Jubilee Medal Catholic Univ. of America 1964; Centennial Eng. Medal, Pennsylvania Mil. Coll.; and Resolution of Esteem, Congressional Cttee. on Science and Astronautics 1966; *cr.* CBE (Civil) 1943, Knt. 1957, and *Baron Snow*, of City of Leicester (Life Baron) 1964: *m.* 1950, Pamela Hansford, CBE (Civil 1975), da. of Reginald Kenneth Johnson, and has issue.

Ārms,—Azure, semy of snow crystals proper. Crest,—A telescope fesswise between two pens in saltire proper. Supporters,—On either side a Siamese Cat proper.

Residence,—85, Eaton Terr, SW1. *Clubs,*—Savile, Garrick, MCC, Century (New York).

SON LIVING.

Hon. Philip Charles Hansford, *b.* 1952; ed. at Eton, and Balliol Coll., Oxford.

SNOWDON, EARL OF (Armstrong-Jones.) [Earl U.K. 1961.]

ANTONY CHARLES ROBERT ARMSTRONG-JONES, *GCVO*, 1st Earl, son of the late Ronald Owen Lloyd Armstrong-Jones, MBE, QC, of Plas Dinas, Caernarvonshire; *b.* Mar. 7th, 1930; ed. at Eton, and at Jesus Coll., Camb.; Constable of Caernarvon Castle since 1963; *cr. Viscount Linley,* of Nymans, co. Sussex, and *Earl of Snowdon* (peerage of UK) 1961; GCVO 1969: *m.* May 6th, 1960, HRH The Princess Margaret Rose, da. of HM the late King George VI, and has issue.

Ārms,—Sable on a chevron argent, between in chief two fleurs de lis, and in base an eagle displayed or, four pallets gules. Crest,—A stag statant gules attired collared and unguled or between two arms embowed in armour the hands proper each grasping a fleur de lis gold. Supporters,—*Dexter,* a griffin, and *sinister,* an eagle, each with wings elevated and addorsed or, and has issue.

What God wills will be.

Residence,—Kensington Palace, W.8. *Clubs,* —Buck's, Leander, Hawkes.

SON LIVING.

DAVID ALBERT CHARLES (*Viscount Linley*), *b.* Nov. 3rd, 1961; ed. at Bedales.

DAUGHTER LIVING.

Lady Sarah Frances Elizabeth, *b.* 1964.

SODOR AND MAN, LORD BISHOP OF. (Nicholls.)

Right Rev. VERNON SAMPSON NICHOLLS, son of Ernest C. Nicholls, of Truro, Cornwall; *b.* Sept. 3rd, 1917; ed. at Truro Sch., Univ. of Durham, and Clifton Theo. Coll., Bristol (LTh); Chap. to Forces 1944-46; V. of Meopham 1946-56, Rural Dean of Cobham 1953-56, V. and Rural Dean of Walsall, and Chap. to Walsall Gen. Hosp. 1956-67, Preb. of Curborough, Lichfield Cathedral 1964-67, and Archdeacon of Birmingham 1967-74; consecrated 77th Bishop of Sodor and Man 1974: *m.* 1943, Phyllis, da. of Edwin Potter, of Stratford-on-Avon.

The original See was founded by Germanus in 447. [Sodor is an abbreviation of Sodorenses, the Hebrides and Western Islands of Scotland, now called "The Isles" in the Episcopal Church of Scotland, which were formerly under this Bishop's jurisdiction.] The Bishop has neither seat nor vote in the House of Lords, as he legislates in the Isle of Man, where there is a separate form of government.

𝕰piscopal Signature,—"Vernon Sodor and Man."
ARMS OF THE SEE,—Argent, upon a pedestal the Virgin Mary with arms extended between two coronetted pillars, in her dexter hand a church proper and in base, upon an escutcheon, the arms of Man—viz., gules, three legs in armour conjoined at the thigh, and flexed at the knee, the escutcheon being surmounted by a mitre.
Palace,—Bishop's Court, Isle of Man.

SOMERLEYTON, BARON. (Crossley.) [Baron U.K. 1916, Bt. U.K. 1863.]

SAVILE WILLIAM FRANCIS CROSSLEY, 3rd Baron and 4th Baronet; *b.* Sept. 17th, 1928; *s.* 1959; ed. at Eton; Capt. (retired) Coldstream Guards; a co. Councillor and a DL of Suffolk, and a Dir. of E. Anglian Water Co.; is Patron of one living: *m.* 1963, Belinda Maris, da. of Vivian Loyd, of Kingsmoor, Ascot, and has issue.

𝕬rms—Gules, a chevron indented ermine between two cross-crosslets in chief, and a saltire coupled in base or Crest,—A demi-hind erased proper, charged with two bars holding between the feet a cross-crosslet or. Supporters,— On either side a hind proper, semée of cross-crosslets or.
Seat,—Somerleyton Hall, Lowestoft. *Club,*—Guards'.

OMNE·BONVM   AB·ALTO

All good is from above.

SON LIVING
Hon. HUGH FRANCIS SAVILE, *b.* Sept. 27th, 1971.

DAUGHTERS LIVING.
Hon. Isabel Alicia Claire, *b.* 1964.
Hon. Camilla Mary Lara, *b.* 1967.
Hon. Alicia Phyllis Belinda, *b.* 1969.
Hon. Louisa Bridget Vivien, *b.* 1974.

BROTHER LIVING.
Hon. Richard Nicholas, *TD* (Westfield Farm, Settrington, Malton, York. *Clubs,*—Cavalry, Yorkshire); *b.* 1932; ed. at Eton and RMA; Lt.-Col. 9th Queen's R. Lancers (ret.); Maj. Queens Own Yeo. (TA): *m.* 1958, Alexandra Anne Maitland, only da. of Charles Donald Graham Welch, of Perrot Farm, Graffham, Sussex, and has issue living, John Dickon Francis, *b.* 1966,—Amanda Carolyn, *b.* 1960,—Lucinda Mary, *b.* 1962.

SISTER LIVING.
Hon. Mary, *b.* 1926; a J.P. of Huntingdon and Peterborough: *m.* 1950, Maj. William Birkbeck, Coldstream Guards (ret.), of Bainton House, Stamford, Lincs., and has issue living, Anthony William Savile, *b.* 1956,—Victoria Mary, *b.* 1951,—Priscilla Bridget, *b.* 1952,—Rosetta Sybil, *b.* 1958.

AUNTS LIVING. (*Daughters of 1st Baron.*)
Hon. Phyllis Patty, *M.B.E., b.* 1890; sometime Subaltern and Temporary Junior Com. A.T.S.; is a J.P. for Norfolk; *M.B.E.* (Mil.) 1942: *m.* 1917, Capt. Evelyn Hugh Barclay, formerly Scots Guards, who *d.* 1956, and has issue living, Ione Jean, *b.* 1918: *m.* 1940 (m. diss.1963), Capt. Harold Felix Cassel, RA [now 3rd Bt.],—Ursula Evelyn, *b.* 1921; is temporary Jun. Cdr. ATS; 1939-45 War (despatches): *m.* 1947, Maj.-Gen. David Lanyon Lloyd Owen, DSO, OBE, MC, Queen's Roy. Regt., and has issue living, Michael David Hugo *b.* 1948, Piers Savile Charles *b.* 1950, Christopher Barclay Anthony *b.* 1952. *Residence,*—Herringfleet Hall, Lowestoft.

Hon. Monica Victoria (*Hon. Lady Smith*), *b.* 1897: *m.* 1918, Lieut.-Gen. Sir Arthur Francis Smith, KCB, KBE, DSO, MC, late Coldstream Gds., of Greathed Manor, Lingfield, Surrey [see E. Kintore, colls.].

WIDOW LIVING OF SECOND BARON.

BRIDGET (*Bridget, Baroness Somerleyton*), *MBE,* da. of William Douro Hoare, CBE, of Guessons, Welwyn, Herts.; is a Gov. of National Corporation for Care of Old People, and a JP for Suffolk; MBE (Civil) 1946: *m.* 1924, the 2nd Baron, who *d.* 1959. *Residence,*—White House, Somerleyton, Lowestoft.

COLLATERAL BRANCH LIVING.

Issue of the late Capt. the Hon. John de Bathe Crossley, 2nd son of 1st Baron, *b.* 1893, *d.* 1935: *m.* 1st, 1918, Dorothy Frances (who *d.* 1955, having obtained a divorce 1930), dau. of Capt. Sir George Everard Cayley, 9th Bt.; 2ndly, 1930, Sybelle Winifred, who *d.* 1963, dau. of Cyril Augustus Drummond [E. Perth, colls.]:—

(By 1st m.) Anthony Everard Savile (Milima, PO Woolooga, Qld. 4570, Aust.), *b.* 1920: *m.* 1956, Jean Margaret Gillian, el. da. of D. O. Russell, of Kipkarren River, Kenya and has issue living, John de Bathe, *b.* 1958,—Timothy Elgon Savile, *b.* 1963,—Marguerite, *b.* 1957,—Julia, *b.* 1960.——Charles John (Linda Cruises, Cosgrove Lock, Milton Keynes, Bucks., MK19 7JR; *Club,*—International Sportsmen's), *b.* 1921: *m.* 1957, Catherine Adelaide Anne (FANE), da. of Gabriel Noel Dyer [Legard, Bt., colls.].——(By 2nd m.) (Elizabeth) Belinda (Kings Rew, Blackfield, Southampton), *b.* 1932: *m.* 1959 (m. diss. 1974), the 3rd Baron Montagu of Beaulieu.

PREDECESSORS.—[1] FRANCIS Crossley, son of John Crossley, of Halifax, *b.* 1817; M.P. for Halifax (*L*) 1852-9, and for the North-West Riding of Yorkshire 1859-72; cr. a *Baronet* 1863: *m.* 1845, Martha Eliza, who *d.* 1891, dau. of Henry Brinton; *d.* 1872; *s.* by his only son [2] *Sir* SAVILE BRINTON, *G.C.V.O., P.C.,* 2nd Bt.; *b.* 1857; M.P. for N., or Lowestoft, Div. of Suffolk (*LU*) 1885-92, and for Halifax 1900-1906; Paymaster-Gen. 1902-5, and a Lord-in-Waiting to H.M. 1918-24; cr. *Baron Somerleyton,* of Somerleyton, co. Suffolk (peerage of United Kingdom) 1916: *m.* 1887, Phyllis, *C.B.E.,* youngest dau. of Gen. Sir Henry Percival de Bathe, K.C.B., 4th Bt.; *d.* 1935; *s.* by his el. son [3] FRANCIS SAVILE, *M.C.,* 2nd Baron; *b.* 1889; Major late 9th Lancers and a Director of John Crossley & Sons, Ltd., of Halifax: *m.* 1924, Bridget, *M.B.E.,* dau. of William Douro Hoare, C.B.E., of Guessons, Welwyn, Herts; *d.* 1959; *s.* by his el. son [4] SAVILE WILLIAM FRANCIS, 3rd Baron and present peer.

SOMERS, BARON. (Cocks.) [Baron G.B. 1784, Bt. G.B. 1772.]

[Title pronounced "**Summers.**"]

To be useful, rather than conspicuous.

JOHN PATRICK SOMERS COCKS, 8th Baron, and 8th Baronet; *b.* April 30th, 1907; *s.* 1953; BMus; ARCM; Prof. Roy. Coll. of Music; Dir. of Music, Epsom Coll., 1949-53: *m.* 1st, 1935, Barbara Marianne, who *d.* 1959, da. of Charles Henry Southall, of Norwich; 2ndly, 1961, Dora Helen, da. of the late John Mountfort.

Arms,—Quarterly; 1st and 4th sable, a chevron between three stags' attires argent, *Cocks;* 2nd and 3rd vert, a fesse dancettée ermine, *Somers.* Crest—On a mount vert, a stag lodged and reguardant argent, attired and hoofed sable. Supporters,—Two lions, each gorged with a collar dancettée vert.

Residence,—35, Links Road, Epsom, Surrey.

SISTER LIVING.

Hon. Helen Judith, *b.* 1901: *m.* 1st, 1949, T. Everett Malen, who *d.* 1961; 2ndly, 1965, Earl G. Henry, of 810, Lighthouse Av., Apt. 307, Pacific Grove, Calif. 93950, USA.

DAUGHTER LIVING OF SIXTH BARON.

Hon. (Violet) Elizabeth Virginia, *b.* 1922: formerly 3rd Officer in W.R.N.S.: *m.* 1947, Major Benjamin Alexander Frederick Hervey-Bathurst, Grenadier Guards [see Hervey-Bathurst, Bt.]. *Seat,*—Eastnor Castle, Ledbury, Herefordshire.

WIDOW LIVING OF SIXTH BARON.

(DAISY) FINOLA (*Dowager Baroness Somers*), *C.B.E.,* dau. of the late Capt. Bertram Meeking; formerly Ch. Commr., Girl Guides' Asso.; C.B.E. (Civil) 1950: *m.* 1921, the 6th Baron, who *d.* 1944. *Residence,*—Garden Cottage, Eastnor Castle, Ledbury.

COLLATERAL BRANCHES LIVING.

Grandchildren of the late Philip Alphonso Somers Cocks, CMG, son of the late Hon. John James Thomas Somers Cocks, brother of the 5th Baron:—
Issue of the late John Sebastian Somers Cocks, OVO, OBE, *b.* 1907, *d.* 1964: *m.* 1946, Marjorie Olive (19, Kempson Rd., SW6), da. of the late Arthur Julius Weller:—

PHILIP SEBASTIAN SOMERS, *b.* Jan. 4th, 1948.——Anne Gwenllian Somers, *b.* 1950: *m.* 1971, Martin Alan Walker.——Frances Mary Somers, *b.* 1953.

    Grandchildren of the late Rev. Philip John Cocks (infra):—
    Issue of the late Henry Bromley Cocks, *b.* 1896, *d.* 1967: *m.* 1922, Edith Hazel (69, Peverel St., Riccarton, Christchurch, 4, NZ), da. of the late F. H. Melville Walker, of Christchurch, NZ:—
Alan Bromley (55, La Trobe St., Pakuranga, Auckland, NZ), *b.* 1930: *m.* 1955, Pamela Fay, da. of A. H. Gourlay, of Christchurch, NZ, and has issue living, Martin Bromley, *b.* 1957,—Lynette Marguerite, *b.* 1960,—Gillian Fay, *b.* 1962,—Judith Grace Somers *b.* 1973——Pamela Somers, *b.* 1927; ed. at Canterbury Coll., NZ (MA): *m.* 1968, Allan John Hall, LLB, of 6, Ann St., Gisborne, NZ, and has issue living, Veronica Ann, *b.* 1970,—Rosemary Meagan, *b.* 1972.
    Issue of the late John Reginald Cocks, *b.* 1898, *d.* 1973: *m.* 1920, Mary Dillworth, da. of the late Charles Dillworth Fox, of Christchurch, NZ:—
John Alexander (RD Turua, NZ), *b.* 1921.——Timothy Charles (Somersdale, RD3, Kaukapakapa, NZ), *b.* 1923: *m.* 1949, June Alice Fantham, and has issue living, Ross Basil (18A, Walton St., Remuera, Auckland, NZ), *b.* 1951: *m.* 1972, Janice Evelyn, yst. da. of Pat Russell, of Silverdale,—Barry John, *b.* 1954,—Helen Julie, *b.* 1958.——Kathleen Mary, *b.* 1922: *m.* 1946, Archibald Stewart Gray, of Parapara Rd. Tiran Waikato, NZ, and has issue living, Peter Stewart, *b.* 1946,—Sidney Charles, *b.* 1948,—Mary Kathleen, *b.* 1949,—Barbara Elizabeth, *b.* 1951.——Phoebe Somers, *b.* 1925: *m.* 1949, Roland Hunter, of Bermur Rd., Belmont, Lower Hutt, NZ, and has issue living, James Reginald *b.* 1953,—Roger Paul, *b.* 1956,—Ann Helen, *b.* 1950,—Janel Clair, *b.* 1951,—Peggy Jane, *b.* 1958.
    Issue of the late Ven. Hubert Maurice Cocks, BD, *b.* 1901: *m.* 1928, Mary (13, Jackson's Rd., Christchurch, NZ), da. of O. D. Matson, of Fendalton, Christchurch, NZ:—
Rev. Michael Dearden Somers (St. Nicholas Vicarage, Christchurch, NZ), *b.* 1928; ed. at Canterbury Coll., NZ and at Oxford (MA); V. of St. Nicholas, Christchurch, NZ: *m.* 1958, Barbara Phyllis, el. da. of Hector Frank Allan, of Nelson, NZ, and has issue living, Richard Martin, *b.* 1966,—Charlotte Elizabeth, *b.* 1959,—Andrea Jane, *b.* 1961,—Stephanie Anne, *b.* 1963.——Jonathan Somers (67, East Belt, Lincoln, Canterbury, NZ), *b.* 1933: *m.* 1962, Audrey Geraldine, da. of Aubrey William Scott, of Burnham, NZ, and has issue living, Jeremy Andrew Somers, *b.* 1964,—Jennifer Mary, *b.* 1963.

    Granddaughter of the late Rev. Henry Bromley Cocks, son of Rev. Henry Somers Cocks, son of the Hon. Reginald Cocks, 4th son of 1st Baron:—
    Issue of the late Rev. Philip John Cocks, *b.* 1866; *d.* 1938: *m.* 1895, Mary, who *d.* 1952, dau. of the late John Gebbie:—
Edith May Somers, *b.* 1905; late Nursing Sister NZF; 1939-45 War in Middle East. *Residence,*— Greystone, Baltonsborough, Glastonbury, Som.

    Grandchildren of the late Rev. Henry Bromley Cocks (ante):—
    Issue of the late Frederic Armine Cocks, *b.* 1871, *d.* 1966: *m.* 1900, Mary Louisa, who *d.* 1951, da. of the late Capt. — Parsons, of Rangiora, NZ:—
Douglas Edgar West (12, Conway St., Christchurch, NZ), *b.* 1901: *m.* 1925, Olive May, da. of the late Joseph Messines, and has issue living, Peter Douglas, *b.* 1937,—Patricia Somers, *b.* 1927,— Helen Marion, *b.* 1930——Armine Christopher Somers (113, Cranford St., Christchurch 1, NZ), *b.* 1903: *m.* 1936, Ella, da. of L. Buryan, and has issue living, Robin Fraser (Brookside Rd., Rolleston, 5RD, Christchurch, NZ) *b.* 1944: *m.* 1969, Anita Josephine, da. of K. A. J. Smith, of Christchurch, NZ, and has issue living, Rodney Somers *b.* 1969, Calvin James *b.* 1972,—Dennis Somers (c/o Southland Boys' High School, Invercargill, NZ), *b.* 1947: *m.* 1971, Allison Elspeth, da. of W. H. Cook, of Dacre, Southland, NZ,—Diane Beverley, *b.* 1939: *m.* 1962, Douglas Bernard Charles Williams, of 85, Breezes Rd., Christchurch, NZ, and has issue living, Shane Douglas *b.* 1962, Brent Charles *b.* 1965,—Juliet Elizabeth, *b.* 1940: *m.* 1964, Donald Martin Stirton, and has issue living Rachel *b.* 1972.——Charles John Somers (80, Harakeke St., Riccarton, Christchurch, NZ), *b.* 1904: *m.* 1932, Hazel, da. of William Steel, of Christchurch, NZ, and has issue living, Geoffrey Somers (37, Holmwood Rd., Christchurch, NZ), *b.* 1934: *m.* 1959, Madeline Mary, da. of R. J. Coulter, of Ashburton, NZ, and has issue living, Richard Somers *b.* 1962, Mark Somers *b.* 1967, Elizabeth Mary *b.* 1968, Charlotte Ann *b.* 1972,—Ian Somers (45, Fendallton Rd., Christchurch, NZ), *b.* 1940; APANZ: *m.* 1961, Beverley Claire, da. of G. W. Kearney, of Christchurch, NZ, and has issue living, Tracey Jane *b.* 1962, Sarah Hilary *b.* 1964,—Sandra Christine, *b.* 1944; ed. at Canterbury Univ., NZ (BA): *m.* 1970, Thomas Desmond Keenan, MD, ChB, of 7, St. Andrews Sq., Christchurch, NZ, and has issue living, Timothy James *b.* 1969.——Patrick Somers (26, Waimairi Rd., Upper Riccarton, Christchurch, NZ), *b.* 1905: *m.* 1943, Evelyn May, da. of Lealand Bertram Iles, and has issue living, Barbara Mary, *b.* 1944,—Yvonne Dawn, *b.* 1946,—Cynthia Joan, *b.* 1950,—Marion Elizabeth, *b.* 1952.

    Issue of the late Charles Richard Cocks, *b.* 1877, *d.* 1944: *m.* 1926, Fanny (of 71, Garden Road, Fendalton, Christchurch, New Zealand), dau. of S. E. Hubbard, of Dunedin, New Zealand:—
Charles Bromley, *b.* 1928: ed. at Canterbury Coll., New Zealand (LL.B. 1956).
    Issue of the late Frances Mercy Cocks, *b.* 1864, *d.* 1927: *m.* 1894, Walter Septimus Fisher:— Heathcote Walter, *b.* 1902.——Felix Malenne, *b.* 1907.——Harriet Mercy, *b.* 1896: *m.* 1922, Robert Sharpe Alford, and has issue living, Robert James, *b.* 1922,—Margaret Elizabeth, *b.* 1925.——Margaret Agatha, *b.* 1899.——Barbara Elizabeth (of Dummer Clump, nr. Basingstoke, Hants), *b.* 1900: *m.* 1925, Capt. Robert Bradshaw Wilmot Sitwell, C.B.E., R.N. (ret.), who *d.* 1946, and has issue living, Peter Sacheverell, *b.* 1935: *m.* 1960, Claire Veronica, dau. of Ralph Cobbold, and has issue living, Alexander Sacheverell *b.* 1961,—Christopher Robert *b.* 1963,—Mary Frances *b.* 1927, *m.* 1946, Andrew John Craig Harvey, late Lt. 5th Inniskilling Dragoon Guards, of Lainston House, Sparsholt, Hants, and has issue living, Nicholas Robert *b.* 1952, Charles Andrew Craig *b.* 1963, Juliet Elizabeth *b.* 1947, Lucinda Mary *b.* 1955,—(Violet) Joan *b.* 1932: *m.* 1956, Comte François de Pourtalès, of La Verrerie, Lombach, Bas Rhin, France, and has issue living, Jérôme Alexander *b.* 1960, Claire Mélanie *b.* 1958.

PREDECESSORS.—[1] CHARLES Cocks, *M.P.* for Reigate; cr. a *Baronet* 1772; and *Baron Somers,* of Evesham, co. Worcester (peerage of Great Britain) 1784; *d.* 1806; *s.* by his son [2] JOHN SOMERS, 2nd Baron; M.P. for Grampound, Lord-Lieut. of Herefordshire, and Recorder of Gloucester; cr. *Viscount Eastnor* and *Earl Somers* (peerage of United Kingdom) 1821; *d.* 1841; *s.* by his son [3] JOHN SOMERS, 2nd Earl; *b.* 1788; was Lord-Lieut. of Herefordshire, and Col. Hereford Militia; assumed the additional surname of Somers by Roy. licence *1841*; *d.* 1852; *s.* by his son [4] CHARLES SOMERS, 3rd Earl; *b.* 1819; sat as M.P. for Reigate (*C*) 1852-7: *m.* 1850, Virginia, who *d.* 1910, dau. of the late James Pattle, B.C.S.; *d.* 1883, when the viscountcy and earldom became extinct and the barony devolved upon his kinsman [5] PHILIP REGINALD Cocks, 5th Baron (son of the late Lieut.-Col. the Hon. Philip James Cocks, M.P., 3rd son of 1st Baron), *b.* 1815: *m.* 1859, Camilla, who *d.* 1904, dau. of the late Rev. William Newton, V. of Old Cleeve, Somerset; *d.* 1899; *s.* by his grand-nephew [6] ARTHUR HERBERT TENNYSON, *K.C.M.G.,* *D.S.O.,* *M.C.* (son of the late Herbert Haldane Somers Cocks, a descendant of 3rd son of 1st Baron), 6th Baron; *b.* 1887; Lieut.-Col. late 1st Life Guards; was a Lord-in-Waiting to H.M. King George V. 1924-6, and Gov. of Victoria, Australia 1926-31; Ch. Scout of United Kingdom and the British Commonwealth 1941-4; European War 1914-19 (M.C., D.S.O.): *m.* 1921, (Daisy) Finola, *C.B.E.,* dau. of the late Capt. Bertram Meeking; *d.* 1944; *s.* by his uncle [7] ARTHUR PERCY SOMERS (4th son of the late Arthur Herbert Cocks, C.B., brother of 5th Baron), 7th Baron; *b.* 1864; European War 1915-17 with Canadian Forces: *m.* 1896, Benita, who *d.* 1950, dau. of the late Major Luther Sabin, of U.S.A.; *d.* 1953; *s.* by his son [8] JOHN PATRICK SOMERS, 8th Baron and present peer.

***John Somers, Lord Chancellor 1697-1700, was cr. *Baron Somers,* of Evesham 1697, and *d.* 1716, when his title became ext. His sister and co-heir, Mary, *m.* Charles Cocks, of Worcester, by whom she was mother of John Cocks, father of 1st Baron, of second creation (ante).

SOMERSET, DUKE OF. (Seymour.) [Duke E. 1547, Bt. E. 1611.]

FOY·POVR·DEVOIR·

Faith for duty.

PERCY HAMILTON SEYMOUR, 18th Duke, and 16th Baronet; *b.* Sept. 27th, 1910; *s.* 1954; ed. at Blundell's Sch., Tiverton, and at Clare Coll., Camb. (B.A. 1933); Major (retired) Wilts. Regt., patron of two livings, a D.L. and Pres. of British Legion for Wilts.: *m.* 1951, Gwendoline Collette (Jane), da. of the late Maj. J. C. C. Thomas, N. Staffordshire Regt., of Burn Cottage, Bude, Cornwall, and has issue.

Arms,—Quarterly: 1st and 4th or, on a pile gules, between six fleurs-de-lis azure, three lions of England; 2nd and 3rd gules, two wings conjoined in lure or, *Seymour.* Crest,—Out of a ducal coronet or, a demi-phœnix in flames proper. Supporters,—*Dexter*, a unicorn argent, armed, unguled, and crined, or, gorged with a ducal coronet, per pale azure and gold, and chained of the last; *sinister*, a bull azure, armed, unguled, ducally gorged and chained, or.

Seats,—Maiden Bradley, Warminster, Wilts; Berry Pomeroy, Totnes, S. Devon.

SONS LIVING.

JOHN MICHAEL EDWARD (*Lord Seymour*), *b.* Dec. 30th, 1952.
Lord Francis Charles Edward, *b.* 1956.

DAUGHTER LIVING.
Lady Anne Frances Mary, *b.* 1954.

SISTER LIVING.
Lady Susan Mary, *b.* 1913; late Divisional Pres. British Red Cross So., Warminster. *Residence,*—Sunnyside, Maiden Bradley, Wilts.

COLLATERAL BRANCHES LIVING.
Issue of the late Major Lord Percy St. Maur, 2nd son of 14th Duke, *b.* 1847, *d.* 1907: *m.* 1899, the Hon. Violet White, who *d.* 1927, dau. of 2nd Baron Annaly :—
Lettice (*Lady McCreery*), *b.* 1902: *m.* 1928, Gen. Sir Richard Loudon McCreery, GCB, KBE, DSO, MBE, MC, late 12th Roy. Lancers, who *d.* 1967, and has issue living, Robert James, *b.* 1930: *m.* 1959, Jeanette, yr. da. of Keith Wright, of The Rookery, Fenstanton, Hunts,—Henry Jonathan, *b.* 1934; ed. at Eton,—Charles Anthony Selby, *b.* 1942,—Sarah Virginia, *b.* 1940: *m.* 1961, Capt. Hugo Ivo Meynell, 9/12th Roy. Lancers. *Residence,*—Stowell Hill, Templecombe, Som.

Grandson of the late Rev. Henry Seymour, son of the late Henry John Hyde Seymour, grandson of the late Very Rev. Lord Francis Seymour, Dean of Wells, 4th son of 8th Duke:—
Issue of the late Henry Sydney Seymour, *b.* 1855, *d.* 1930 : *m.* 1896, the Hon. Helen, who *d.* 1944, dau. of the late Rt. Hon. William Henry Smith, M.P. [V. Hambleden]:—
Edward William, *b.* 1897; ed. at Eton, and at New Coll., Oxford; is a J.P. and D.L. for Dorset; was High Sheriff of Dorset 1957; European War 1915-19 in France as Lieut. Grenadier Guards Special Reserve, European War 1939-45 as Lieut.-Col. R.A. (Devon Yeo.): *m.* 1925, Barbara Judith, dau. of the late Lieut.-Col. George Reginald Lascelles, C.V.O., O.B.E. [see E. Harewood, colls.]. *Residence,*—Tarrant Abbey, Blandford, Dorset.

Descendants of the late Rt. Hon. Francis Seymour-Conway, (4th son of the Rt. Hon. Sir Edward Seymour, 4th Bt., grandfather of 8th Duke), who was cr. *Baron Conway of Ragley* 1703 [see M. Hertford].

PREDECESSORS.—[1] Sir EDWARD Seymour, *KG., KB, PC,* el. surv. son of Sir John Seymour of Wolf Hall, Wilts. (by Marjorie, da. of Sir Henry Wentworth, KB, of Nettlestead, Suffolk, a descendant of Edward III) and brother of Queen Jane Seymour; *b.* c. 1500: *m.* 1st, c. 1527, Katherine, (whom he repudiated and who probably *d.* before 1535), da. and co-heir of Sir William Fillol of Woodlands, Dorset; 2ndly, c. 1535, Anne (who *d.* 1582, having *m.* 2ndly Francis Newdegate) da. of Sir Edward Stanhope of Rampton, Notts; cr. *Viscount Beauchamp* (peerage of England), with remainder to heirs male of his body *hereafter* to be begotten, 1536, and *Earl of Hertford* (peerage of England) with remainder to his issue male by his present or any future wife 1537, *Baron Seymour* and *Duke of Somerset* (peerage of England) with a special remainder to his issue male by his 2nd wife, failing which to his male descendants by his 1st and any other wife 1547; Protector of the Realm to his nephew Edward VI 1547-1549; found guilty of felony Dec. 1st, 1551, and executed on Tower Hill, Jan. 22nd 1552; attainted April 12th, 1552, by Act of Parliament, and all his honours forfeited. His el. surv. son, by his 2nd wife [2] Sir EDWARD, *KB; b.* 1539; cr. *Baron Beauchamp* and *Earl of Hertford* (peerage of England) 1559; Ambassador to Brussels 1605: *m.* 1st (secretly) 1560, Lady Katherine (sister of Lady Jane Grey), da. of Henry Grey, 1st Duke of Suffolk; on discovery of this marriage he was fined £15,000 (later remitted to £3,000) "for seducing a virgin of the blood royal" and he and his wife imprisoned in the Tower; the m. was pronounced invalid 1561, but validity was established in 1606; she *d.* 1568 in captivity at Cockfield Hall, Suffolk; he *m.* 2ndly c. 1595, Frances Howard, who *d.* 1598, da. of 1st Lord Howard of Effingham; 3rdly, 1601, Frances Howard (who *d.* 1639 having *m.* 2ndly Ludovic Stuart, 1st Duke of Richmond), da. of 1st Viscount Howard of Bindon, and widow of Henry Pranell; *d.* 1621; *s.* by his grandson [3] WILLIAM, KG, KB, PC (2nd but eventually el. son and heir of Edward Lord Beauchamp, who *d.* 1612, el. son of 1st Earl by 1st wife) 2nd Earl; *b.* 1587; bore King Edward's staff at Coronation of Charles I 1626; Gov. of Prince of Wales (Charles II) 1641-43; Royalist Lt.-Gen. of South-West and S. Wales 1642-43; restored to Barony of Seymour and Dukedom of Somerset 1660: *m.* 1st (secretly) 1610, Lady Arabella Stuart, da. and heir of 5th Earl of Lennox and 1st cousin of James I, for which they were both imprisoned in the Tower, where she *d. s.p.* 1615; 2ndly, 1617, Lady Frances Devereux, who *d.* 1674, sister and co-heir of 3rd Earl of Essex; *d.* 1660: *s.* by his grandson [4] WILLIAM, 3rd Duke (son and heir of Henry, Lord Beauchamp); *b.* 1652; *d. unm.* 1671; *s.* by his uncle [5] JOHN, 4th Duke, *b.* 1629; *m.* 1661, Sarah (who *d.* 1692, having *m.* 3rdly, 1682, the 2nd Baron Coleraine) da. and co-heir of Sir Edward Alston, MD, and widow of George Grimston; *d.* 1675, when the Marquessate of Hertford became ext. and his estates passed to his niece Elizabeth (sister of 3rd Duke) who *m.* 1676 the 2nd Earl of Ailesbury; *s.* by his kinsman [6] FRANCIS (3rd Baron Seymour of Trowbridge) 5th Duke (son of Charles 2nd Baron, son of Francis 1st Baron (cr. 1641), yr. brother of 2nd Duke) *b.* 1658; *d.* 1678, having been shot at the door of his inn at Lerice, Italy, by Horatio

Botti, a Genoese nobleman, who alleged his wife had been insulted by the Duke's companions; *s.* by his brother [7] CHARLES, *KG*, 6th Duke (" The Proud Duke ") *b.* 1662; Master of the Horse 1702-12 and 1714-15: *m.* 1st, 1682 Lady Elizabeth Percy (Mistress of the Robes to Queen Anne), who *d.* 1722, da. and heir of 11th Earl of Northumberland and widow of Henry Cavendish Earl of Ogle and Thomas Thynne of Longleat; 2ndly, 1726, Lady Charlotte Finch, who *d.* 1773, da. of 7th Earl of Winchilsea and 2nd Earl of Nottingham; *d.* 1748; *s.* by his son [8] ALGERNON, 7th Duke; *b.* 1684; summoned to Parliament as *Lord Percy* 1722 under the erroneous belief that this Barony had been vested in his mother, and took his seat, by which the Barony of Percy was cr. by writ; cr. *Baron Warkworth*, of Warkworth Castle, co. Northumberland, and *Earl of Northumberland* (peerage of Great Britain) 1749, with remainder to his son-in-law, Sir Hugh Smithson, and *Baron Cockermouth*, of Cockermouth Castle, and *Earl of Egremont*, with remainder to his nephews, Sir Charles Wyndham, Bt., and Percy O'Brien (who was afterwards cr. Earl of Thomond); *m.* 1715, Frances, who *d.* 1754, da. of the Hon. Henry Thynne, son of 1st Viscount Weymouth; *d.* 1750, when the Earldom of Hertford, and the Baronies of Beauchamp and Seymour of Trowbridge expired, the Barony of Warkworth and Earldom of Northumberland devolved upon his son-in-law Sir Hugh Smithson, the Barony of Cockermouth and Earldom of Egremont reverted to his nephew Sir Charles Wyndham, the Barony of Percy (cr. 1722), passed to his dau. Lady Elizabeth, wife of Sir Hugh Smithson (ante), and the Barony of Seymour and Dukedom of Somerset descended to the heir male of the 1st Duke by his 1st m. [9] EDWARD, 8th Duke, who had previously *s.* as 6th Bt. (see * infra); *b.* 1695; MP for Salisbury 1741; *m.* 1717, Mary, who *d.* 1768, da. and heir of Daniel Webb of Melksham, Wilts.; *d.* 1757; *s.* by his el. son [10] EDWARD, 9th Duke; *b.* 1718, *d.* unm. 1792; *s.* by his brother [11] WEBB, 10th Duke; *b.* 1718: *m.* 1769, Anna Maria, who *d.* 1802, da. and heir of John Bonnell; *d.* 1793; *s.* by his son [12] EDWARD ADOLPHUS, 11th Duke; *b.* 1775: *m.* 1800, Lady Charlotte Douglas-Hamilton, dau. of 9th Duke of Hamilton and Brandon; *d.* 1855: *s.* by his son [13] EDWARD ADOLPHUS, *KG*, 12th Duke, *b.* 1804; MP for Totnes; *b.* 1775: *m.* 1800, Lady Admiralty 1859-66; cr. *Earl of St. Maur* (peerage of UK) 1863; *d.* 1885, when the Earldom of St. Maur became extinct, and the Dukedom of Somerset and Barony of Seymour passed to his brother [14] ARCHIBALD HENRY ALGERNON, 13th Duke, *b.* 1810; *d.* 1891; *s.* by his brother [15] ALGERNON PERCY BANKS, 14th Duke, *b.* 1813: *m.* 1845, Horatia Isabella Harriet, who *d.* 1915, dau. of the late John Philip Morier, HM Min. at Dresden; *d.* 1894; *s.* by his el. son [16] ALGERNON, 15th Duke *b.* 1846; bore Orb at Coronations of King Edward VII and King George V: *m.* 1877, Susan Margaret who *d.* 1936, yr. dau. of the late Charles Mackinnon; *d.* 1923; *s.* by his cousin [17] EDWARD HAMILTON, *KBE*, *CB*, *CMG* (son of the late Rev. Francis Payne Seymour), 16th Duke, *b.* 1860; Brig.-Gen.; in March 1925 he established before the Cttee. for Privileges of the House of Lords his right to the Dukedom as grandson of Capt. Francis Edward Seymour, RN, el. son of Col. Francis Compton Seymour (grandson of 8th Duke), who *m.* 1787, Leonora, widow of John Hudson (who *d.* 1786 in Calcutta): *m.* 1881, Rowena, who *d.* 1950, dau. of the late George Wall, of Colombo; *d.* 1931; *s.* by his son [18] EVELYN FRANCIS EDWARD, *DSO*, *OBE*, 17th Duke, *b.* 1882; Lt.-Col. (ret.) R. Dublin Fusiliers and Devonshire Regt., Col. Gen. Staff, and Lord-Lieut. for Wilts.; S. Africa 1901-02 (Queen's medal with five clasps), 1914-18 War (despatches, DSO, OBE); bore Sceptre at Coronation of King George VI: *m.* 1906, Edith Mary, who *d.* 1962, only child of the late W. Parker, JP, of Whittington Hall, Derbyshire; *d.* 1954; *s.* by his only son [19] PERCY HAMILTON, 18th Duke and present peer; also Baron Seymour.

* [1] EDWARD Seymour, M.P. for Devon (el. son of Sir Edward Seymour, who was el. son of 1st Duke of Somerset by his 1st marriage) ; cr. a *Baronet* 1611 ; *d.* 1613; *s.* by his son [2] *Sir* EDWARD, *K.B.*, 2nd Bt.; was M.P. for Devon; *d.* 1659; *s.* by his son [3] EDWARD-3rd Bt.; sat as M.P. for Devon; *d.* 1688; *s.* by his son [4] *Sir* EDWARD, *P.C.*; promoted the impeachment of Lord Clarendon, and was Speaker of the Long Parliament, *d.* 1708 ; *s.* by his son [5] *Sir* EDWARD, 5th Bt.; *d.* 1741; *s.* by his son [6] *Sir* EDWARD, 6th Bt., who *s.* as 8th Duke of Somerset (ante).

Somerton, Baron, title of Earl of Normanton on Roll H. L.

SONDES, EARL. (Milles-Lade.) [Earl U.K. 1880.]

Be what you seem to be.

HENRY GEORGE HERBERT MILLES-LADE, 5th Earl; *b.* May 1st, 1940; *s.* 1970; ed. at Eton: *m.* 1968 (m. diss. 1969), Primrose Anne, da. of the late Lawrence Stopford Llewellyn Cotter [see Cotter, Bt., colls.], and formerly wife of Richard Hugh Nicholas Creswell.

Arms—Ermine, a fer de moulin between two martlet in pale sable; on a chief engrailed azure, two marlion's wings conjoined or. Crest,—A lion rampant erminois, holding between the paws a fer de moulin, as in the arms. Supporters,—*Dexter*, a griffin wings elevated argent, gorged with a marquess' coronet or; *sinister*, a bear proper, gorged with a belt argent, rimmed, buckled and charged with two crescents, or.

Residence,—Lees Court, Faversham, Kent.

AUNTS LIVING. (*Raised to the rank of an Earl's daughters* 1942.)

Lady Angela, *b.* 1913.   Lady Diana, *b.* 1919.

Lady Isabel (*Countess of Derby*), *b.* 1920; appointed Hon. Col. 319th (E. Lancashire) Batn. W.R.A.C. (T.A.) 1956 : *m.* 1948, the 18th Earl of Derby. *Residences*,—Knowsley, Prescot; Stanley House, Newmarket.

COLLATERAL BRANCH LIVING.

Granddaughters of the late Hon. Richard Watson, M.P., 4th son of 2nd
Baron :—
Issue of the late Edward Spencer Watson, b. 1843, d. 1889: m. 1871, Mary Blanche, who
d. 1910, dau. of the late George Hall, M.D.:—
Margaret Isabella, b. 1877. *Residence,*—Ewelme Manor, Ewelme, Oxford.——Evelyn Horatia, b.
1884. *Residence,*—Ewelme Manor, Ewelme, Oxford.——Cicely Eleanor, b. 1887.——Gwendolen
Olivia, b. 1888. *Residence,*—Ewelme Manor, Ewelme, Oxford.

PREDECESSORS.—[1] *Hon.* LEWIS MONSON, 2nd son of 1st Baron Monson, assumed the
surname of Watson on succeeding to the estates of his cousin Thomas, 3rd and last Earl of
Rockingham; cr. *Baron Sondes,* of Lees Court, co. Kent (peerage of Great Britain), 1760; d.
1795; s. by his son [2] LEWIS THOMAS Watson, 2nd Baron; d. 1806; s. by his son [3] LEWIS
RICHARD, 3rd Baron; d. unmarried 1836; s. by his brother [4] GEORGE JOHN, 4th Baron; b.
1794; in 1820 assumed by Roy. licence the surname of Milles only: m. 1823, Eleanor, who
d. 1883, dau. of Sir Edward Knatchbull, 8th Bt.; d. 1874; s. by his son [5] GEORGE WATSON
Milles, 5th Baron, b. 1824; M.P. for E. Kent (C) 1866-74; cr. *Viscount Throwley,* of co. Kent,
and *Earl Sondes,* of Lees Court, co. Kent (peerage of United Kingdom) 1880: m. 1859,
Charlotte, who d. 1927, dau. of Sir Henry Stracey, 5th Bt.; d. 1894, s. by his el. son [6] GEORGE
EDWARD, 2nd Earl, b. 1861; d. 1907; s. by his brother [7] LEWIS ARTHUR, 3rd Earl, b. 1866:
m. 1913, Emma Beatrice, who d. 1935, dau. of the late Percy Hale-Wallace, and widow of
James Meakin, of Westwood Manor, Staffordshire :d. 1941; s. by his nephew [8] GEORGE HENRY
(only son of the late Hon. Augustus Milles-Lade, 4th son of 1st Earl), 4th Earl; b. 1914: m.
1939, Pamela, who d. 1967, da. of Lt.-Col. Herbert McDougall, of Cawston Manor, Norfolk, and 23,
Wilton Cres., Belgrave Sq., SW1; d. 1970; s. by his son [9], HENRY GEORGE HERBERT, 5th Earl and
present peer; also Viscount Throwley, and Baron Sondes.

SOPER, BARON. (Soper.) [Life Baron 1965.]

Rev. DONALD OLIVER SOPER, son of Ernest Frankham Soper, of Wandsworth, SW; b. Jan. 31st, 1903; ed. at Aske's Sch., Hatcham, at St. Catharine's
Coll., Camb. (MA), at Wesley House, Camb., and at London Sch. of Economics
(PhD); Min. of South London Mission 1926-29 and of Central London Mission
1929-36 since when Supt.; Min. of W. London Mission; Chm. of Shelter since
1974; cr. *Baron Soper,* of Kingsway, London Borough of Camden (Life
Peerage) 1965: m. 1929, Marie Gertrude, da. of Arthur Dean, of Norbury,
and has issue.

Residence,—Kingsway Hall, Kingsway, WC2.

DAUGHTERS LIVING.

Hon. Ann Loveday Dean, b. 1931: m. 1952, Gabriel Horn, MD, of King's College, Cambridge.
Hon. Bridget Mary Dean, b. 1933: m. 1956, Owen H. Kemmis, MA, of 92, Wildwood Rd., NW11.
Hon. Judith Catharine Dean, b. 1942: m. 1970, Alan Jenkins, of 33, Midholm, NW11.
Hon. Caroline Susan Dean, b. 1946: m. 1975, Terence Blacker, el. son of Gen. Sir Cecil Hugh Blacker,
KCB, OBE, MC [see Buxton, Bt., colls.].

SORENSEN, BARONY OF. (Sorensen.) [Extinct 1971.]

SON LIVING OF LIFE BARON.

Hon. MICHAEL MALCOLM REGINALD (37, Nassington Rd., NW3), b. 1919: m. 1960, Jennifer,
da. of William Adams, of Stockbridge, Newcastle upon Tyne, and has issue.

DAUGHTER LIVING OF LIFE BARON.

Hon. Moira Muriel, b. 1917: m. 1951, Derek Gerald Clark, of 15, Crossing Rd., Epping, and has issue.

WIDOW LIVING OF LIFE BARON.

MURIEL (*Baroness Sorensen*), (38, Woodside Park Av., Walthamstow, E17 3NP); JP of Essex; da. of
the late Rev. W. Harvey Smith, of Long Sutton, Lincs.: m. 1915, Baron Sorensen (Life Baron),
who d. 1971.

SOULBURY, VISCOUNT. (Ramsbotham.) [Viscount U.K. 1954.]

NON VI SED VIRTUTE

JAMES HERWALD RAMSBOTHAM, 2nd Viscount; b. March 21st, 1915; s. 1971; ed. at
Eton, and Magdalen Coll., Oxford: m. 1949,
Anthea Margaret, who d. 1950, da. of the
ate David Wilton.

𝔄rms,—Sable on a chevron or between three plates
each charged with a cross pattée gules a ram's head
erased of the field. 𝔠rest,—A plate charged with a
ram's head erased per pale gules and sable. 𝔖upporters,—
On either side a raven proper charged with a plate thereon
a cross pattée gules.

Address,—c/o Godden Holme & Co., 5, Upper Belgrave
St., SW1.

Not by force but by virtue.

BROTHER LIVING.

Hon. Sir PETER EDWARD, KCMG, b. Oct. 8th, 1919; ed. at Eton, and at Magdalen Coll., Oxford; NW
Europe 1944-45 as Lt.-Col. Intelligence Corps (despatches, Croix de Guerre with palm); a Member of
HM Diplo. Ser.; British High Commr. in Cyprus 1969-71, and Ambassador to Iran 1971-73, since
Ambassador to USA; CMG 1964, KCMG 1972: m. 1941, Frances Marie, da. of Hugh Massie Blom-
field, and has issue living, Oliver Peter (5, The Green, Marlborough, Wilts.), b. 1943: m. 1965,

Meredith Anne, only da. of Brian Jones, of The White House, Easton Royal, Pewsey, Wilts., and has issue living, Edward Herwald b. 1966, Benedict b. 1967, Alexander b. 1969,—Simon, b. 1949,—Mary Frances, b. 1945. *Residences,*—British Embassy, Wash. DC, USA; East Lane, Ovington, Alresford, Hants.

SISTER LIVING.

Hon. Joan Eleanor, b. 1917 : m. 1950, Major Robert Hardress Standish O'Grady, M.C., Irish Guards, and has issue living, Jeremy Robert, b. 1953,—Jane Elizabeth, b. 1952,—Selina Joan b. 1956. *Residences,*—32, Addison Av., Holland Park, W11; Redlap House, Dartmouth, Devon.

PREDECESSOR—[1] *Rt. Hon. Sir* HERWALD Ramsbotham, *GCMG, GCVO, OBE, MC,* son of Herwald Ramsbotham, JP, of London; b. 1887; Min. of Pensions 1936-39, 1st Commr. of Works 1939-40, Pres. of Board of Education 1940-41, Chm. of Assistance Board 1941-48, and Gov.-Gen. of Ceylon 1949-54; MP for Lancaster (C) 1929-41; *cr. Baron Soulbury,* of Soulbury, co. Buckingham (peerage of UK) 1941, and *Viscount Soulbury,* of Soulbury, co. Buckingham (peerage of UK) 1954; *m.* 1st, 1911, Doris Violet, OStJ, who d. 1954, da. of Sinauer de Stein; 2ndly, 1962, Ursula, who d. 1964, da. of the late Amand Jerome, and widow of Frederick Wakeham; d. 1971; *s.* by his el. son [2] JAMES HERWALD, 2nd Viscount and present peer; also Baron Soulbury.

SOUTHAMPTON, BARONY OF. (FitzRoy.) [Baron G.B. 1780, disclaimed 1964.]

CHARLES FITZROY, b. Jan. 3rd, 1904; *s.* as 5th Baron Southampton, Dec. 7th, 1958; disclaimed his peerage for life, March 16th, 1964; ed. at Harrow; late Lt. Roy. Horse Guards: *m.* 1st, 1927, Margaret, who d. 1931, da. of the Rev. Prebendary Herbert Mackworth Drake, V. of Berry Pomeroy, Devon; 2ndly, 1940, Mrs. Phyllis Joan Leslie, who obtained a divorce 1944; 3rdly, 1951, Rachel Christine, da. of Charles Zaman, of Lille, France, and has issue by 1st marriage.

Arms,—Quarterly: 1st and 4th, France and England quarterly; 2nd, Scotland; 3rd, Ireland; the whole debruised by a baton sinister compony argent and azure, and with a crescent for difference. **Crest,**—On a chapeau gules, turned up ermine, a lion statant guardant or, ducally crowned azure, and gorged with a collar counter compony argent and azure. The ornament and recompense of virtue **Supporters,**—(borne by Barons Southampton) *Dexter,* a lion guardant or, ducally crowned azure, gorged with a collar compony argent and blue; *sinister,* a greyhound argent gorged as the dexter.

Address,—Preluna Hotel, Sliema, Malta.

SON LIVING. (By 1st marriage.)

Hon. CHARLES JAMES (Garden Cottage, Slogarie, Mossdale, by Castle Douglas, Kirkcudbright-shire), b. Aug. 12th, 1928: m. 1951, Pamela Anne, da. of Edward Percy Henniker, of Clematis, Yelverton, S. Devon, and has issue living, Edward Charles, b. 1955,—Geraldine Anne, b. 1951.

SISTERS LIVING.

Hon. Victoria Alexandrina Sibell, b. 1898: m. 1925, Major William Vandeleur Beatty, who d. 1953 and from whom she had obtained a divorce 1941. *Residence,*—Tedfold Stud Farm, Okehurst Rd. Billingshurst, Sussex, RH14 9HU.

Hon. Ismay Hilda Margaret, b. 1908: m. 1928, Brigadier Walter Morley Sale, C.V.O., O.B.E., late R. Horse Guards, and has issue living, Charles Richard Walter (Charlcot, Ripon, Yorks.; Turf Club), b. (Nov.) 1928; late Capt. R. Horse Guards: m. 1958, Marian Eleanor, da. of Maj. John Darling Young, of Thornton Hall, Bletchley, Bucks, and has issue living, Nigel Richard b. 1962, Lucinda Marian b. 1965,—Caroline Ismay Maud, b. 1934. *Residence,*—Heveningham House, Halesworth, Suffolk.

COLLATERAL BRANCHES LIVING.

Issue of the late Capt. the Rt. Hon. Edward Algernon FitzRoy, M.P. (Speaker of House of Commons 1928-43), 2nd son of 3rd Baron, b. 1869, d. 1943 : m. 1891, Muriel, C.B.E. [dau. of the late Lieut.-Col. the Hon. Archibald Charles Henry Douglas-Pennant (see B. Penrhyn, colls.)], who was cr. *Viscountess Daventry* 1943 [see that title].

Grandson of the late Maj.-Gen. William FitzRoy, el. son of the late William Simon Haughton FitzRoy, el. son of the late Lieut.-Gen. the Hon. William FitzRoy (infra):—

Issue of the late Capt. Frederick Henry FitzRoy, R.D., R.N.R., b. 1872, d. 1937: m. 1904, Eleanor, who d. 1969, da. of the late William Allan, of Avondale, Gosforth:—

William Wentworth STEWART-FITZROY (Nordhvall, Dornoch, Sutherland), b. 1907; Capt. RN (ret.); late Commodore Supt., H.M. Dockyard, Singapore, and H.M.'s Naval Attaché at Belgrade; appointed Naval ADC to HM 1961; Admiralty Regional Officer, Scotland, 1962-72; Hon. Sheriff for Sutherland 1974; he and his issue assumed by deed poll 1958 the additional surname of Stewart before their patronymic: m. 1934, Margaret Patricia, da. of the late Douglas Stewart Grant, of New York, USA, and has issue living, Allan Wentworth (12, St. Georges Av., Warblington, Havant, Portsmouth), b. 1935; Cdr. RN: m. 1960, Susan, da. of Capt. Horace Gerald Southwood, OBE, DSC, RN, and has issue living, Louise b. 1962, Jane b. 1964, Helen b. 1967,—Douglas James Fitzflaad, b. 1943,—Roderick Charles, b. 1947: m. 1972, Susan, da. of H. O. Ruse, of Arbroath, and has issue living, James b. 1973,—Anne Patricia (RD1, South Starksboro, Vermont 05487, USA), b. 1936.

Grandsons of the late Capt. George Dartmouth FitzRoy, 2nd son of the late William Simon Haughton FitzRoy (ante):—

Issue of the late Gordon Duncan Seymour FitzRoy, *b.* 1868, *d.* 1936: *m.* 1st, 1891, **Marie** E., who *d.* 1894, widow of Howell Turner, M.D., of Norwich; 2ndly, 189-, N. Adalia Leasure, of Arkansas City, Kansas, U.S.A. :—
(By 2nd marriage) Albert Loring, *b.* 1900.——Francis George, *b.* 1903.

Granddaughters of the late Rev. Frederick Thomas William Coke FitzRoy, son of the late Lieut.-Gen. the Hon. William FitzRoy, 7th son of 1st Baron:—
Issue of the late Cecil Augustus Fitzroy, *b.* 1844, *d.* 19—: *m.* 1873, Susannah, dau. of William Beetham, formerly of Taita, Wellington, New Zealand :—
Maud le Strange, *b.* 18—.——Gwendoline le Strange, *b.* 18—: *m.* 1918, Ronald W. Williams. *Residence,*—Napier, New Zealand.

PREDECESSORS.—[1] *Lieut.-Gen.* CHARLES FitzRoy, 2nd son of Lord Augustus **FitzRoy** [D. Grafton]; cr. *Baron Southampton,* of Southampton, co. Hants (peerage of **Great** Britain) 1780; *d.* 1797; *s.* by his son [2] GEORGE FERDINAND, 2nd Baron, was a Lieut.-Gen. in the Army and Col. 34th Regt.; *d.* 1810; *s.* by his son [3] CHARLES, 3rd Baron; *b.* 1804; was Lord-Lieut. of Northampton: *m.* 1st, 1826, Harriet, who *d.* 1860, dau. of the late Hon. Henry FitzRoy Stanhope; 2ndly, 1862, Ismania Catherine, *V.A.,* who *d.* 1918, dau. of the late Walter Nugent, a Baron of the Austrian Empire; *d.* 1872: *s.* by his son [4] CHARLES HENRY, *O.B.E.,* 4th Baron, *b.* 1867; Capt. 10th Hussars, and Lieut.-Col. Yorkshire Regt.: *m.* 1892, Lady Hilda Mary Dundas, who *d.* 1957, dau. of 1st Marquess of Zetland; *d.* 1958; *s.* by his son [5] CHARLES, 5th Baron, until he disclaimed his peerage 1964.

SOUTHBOROUGH, BARON. (Hopwood.) [Baron U.K. 1917.]

FRANCIS JOHN HOPWOOD, 3rd Baron ; *b.* March 7th, 1897 ; *s.* 1960; ed. at Westminster, and at Ch. Ch., Oxford; Managing Dir. of Shell Transport & Trading Co. Ltd. 1951-70 (Dir. 1946-51), and of Shell Petroleum Co. Ltd. and of Shell Petroleum NV 1946-57 (Dir. 1957-70); a Com. of Order of Orange Nassau of the Netherlands; 1914-18 War as Sub-Lieut. RNVR; seconded to staff of Irish convention, and Sec. to War Trade Advisory Cttee.; Knt. 1953; *m.* 1918, Audrey Evelyn Dorothy, da. of the late Edgar George Money, and has issue.

Arms,—Paly of six ermine and vert a bend raguly or, charged with three escallops gules. *Crest,*—On a mount vert, a saltire raguly gules surmounted by an escallop argent.
Supporters,—On either side a squirrel sejant proper.
Residence,—Bingham's Melcombe, Dorset.   *Club,*—Brooks's.

SON LIVING.

Hon. FRANCIS MICHAEL *,b.* May 3rd .1922 ; ed. at Wellington Coll., and at Ch. Ch., Oxford ; is an Underwriting Member of Lloyd's and a Director of Glanvill, Enthoven & Co., Ltd.; 1939-45 War as Lt. Rifle Bde.: *m.* 1945, Moyna Kemp, da. of Robert J. K. Chattey. *Residence,*—50A Eaton Square, SW1. *Club,*—Brooks's.

DAUGHTER LIVING.

Hon. Moira, *b.* 1919 : *m.* 1st, 1940, Peter Anthony Stanley Woodwark, Acting Pilot Officer, R.A.F. Vol. Reserve, who *d.* (killed in action during European War) 1943, son of the late Col. Sir (Arthur) Stanley Woodwark, C.M.G., O.B.E., M.D. .F.R.C.P. : 2ndly, 1946, Joseph McArthur Rank, and has issue living, (by 2nd marriage) Colin Rowland Hopwood, *b.* 1948: *m.* 1972, Lavinia Ruth Phillips, and has issue living, James Benjamin *b.* 1974,—(by 1st marriage) Caroline Nicola, *b.* 1943: *m.* 1966, Richard Hugh Payne, and has issue living, Alexander Richard *b.* 1971, Samantha *b.* 1969,—(by 2nd m.) Camilla Moira, *b.* 1953: *m.* 1971, Jeremy Allan Jennings. *Residence,*—Landhurst, Hartfield, Sussex.

HALF-SISTER LIVING.

Hon. Gladys Mary Neill, *b.* 1886: *m.* 1911, Brigadier Alfred Henry Hopwood, C.B., D.S.O., late Roy. Lincolnshire Regt., who *d.* 1956, and has issue living, Neill (of 77, Hallam Court, 35, Hallam St., W1), *b.* 1916: *m.* 1962, Josephine Vivien, who *d.* 1967, da. of Maj. Roger Tweedy. *Residence,*—77, Hallam Court, 35, Hallam St., W1.

PREDECESSORS.—[1]*Rt. Hon. Sir* FRANCIS JOHN STEPHENS Hopwood, *G.C.B., G.C.M.G.,G.C.V.O., K.C.S.I., P.C.,* son of the late James Thomas Hopwood, Bar.-at-Law ; *b.* 1860 ; was Permanent Sec. to Board of Trade 1901-7, Permanent Under-Sec. of State for the Colonies 1907-11 (also Registrar of Order of St. Michael and St. George 1907-9, and Sec. thereof 1909-11), Vice-Chm. of Development Commn. 1911-12, and an Additional Civil Lord of the Admiralty 1912-17 ; cr. *Baron Southborough,* of Southborough, Kent (peerage of United Kingdom) 1917 : *m.* 1st, 1884, Alice, who *d.* 1889, dau. of the late Capt. William James Smith-Neill, R.A., J.P., of Swindridgemuir, Ayrshire ; 2ndly, 1892, Florence Emily, who *d.* 1940, dau. of the late Lieut.-Gen. Samuel Black, C.S.I., C.I.E. ; *d.* 1947 ; *s.* by his el. son [2] (JAMES) SPENCER NEILL, 2nd Baron ; *b.* 1889 ; sometime with Board of Trade and Min. of Labour ; lent to War Trade Intelligence Depart., and War Trade Depart.; European War 1915-16 as 2nd Lieut. Queen's Own Roy. W. Kent Regt.: *m.* 1923, Dorothy Stewart, who *d.* 1972, da. of the late Col. Archibald Young Leslie, DL, JP, 14th Laird of Kininvie, Banffshire: *d.* 1960; *s.* by his half-brother [3] *Sir* FRANCIS JOHN, 3rd Baron and present peer.

SOUTHESK, EARL OF. (Carnegie.)   [Earl S. 1633, Bt. S. 1663.]

CHARLES ALEXANDER CARNEGIE, K.C.V.O., 11th Earl, and 8th Baronet; b. Sept. 23rd, 1893; s. 1941; ed. at Eton; Major (retired) Scots Guards, and a D.L. for Kincardineshire and Angus; K.C.V.O. 1926: m. 1st, Nov. 12th, 1923, H.H. Princess Alexandra Victoria Georgina Bertha Maud, who d. 1945, younger dau. of H.R.H. the late Princess Royal and the 1st Duke of Fife [see "ROYAL FAMILY," and D. Fife]; 2ndly, 1952, Evelyn Julia, el. dau. of Lieut.-Col. Arthur Peere Williams-Freeman, D.S.O., O.B.E., and widow of Major Ion Edward FitzGerald Campbell, Duke of Cornwall's L.I., [see Campbell, Bt., cr. 1815, colls.], and has issue by 1st marriage.

Arms,—Argent, an eagle displayed azure, armed, beaked, and membered gules, on its breast an antique covered cup or. Crest, —A thunderbolt proper, winged or. Supporters, —Two talbots argent collared gules.
  Residence,—Kinnaird Castle, Brechin, Angus. Club,—Guards.

DREAD GOD

SON LIVING. (By 1st marriage.)
JAMES GEORGE ALEXANDER BANNERMAN (Duke of Fife), b. Sept. 23rd, 1929 ; s. his aunt as 3rd Duke of Fife 1959 [see that title]: m. 1956, the Hon. Caroline Cecily Dewar, from whom he obtained a divorce 1966, el. da. of 3rd Baron Forteviot, and has issue:—
  SON LIVING,—David Charles (Earl of Macduff), b. March 3rd, 1961.
  DAUGHTER LIVING,—Lady Alexandra Clare, b. 1959.
  Residence,—Elsick House, Stonehaven, Kincardineshire. Clubs,—Turf, Pratt's, Royal Northern (Aberdeen).

BROTHERS LIVING.
Hon. Alexander Bannerman, b. 1894; Cdr. (ret.) RN: m. 1st, 1919, Susan Ottilia, who d. 1968, da. of the late Maj. Ernest Rodakowski; 2ndly, 1969, Mrs. Cynthia Averil Gurney, el. da. of the late Brig. Harold Vincent Spencer Charrington, DSO, MC, and has issue living (by 1st m.); Raymond Alexander (Crimonmogate, Lonmay, Aberdeenshire), b. 1920; Maj. late Scots Guards; 1939-45 War (thrice wounded, despatches): m. 1st, 1943, Patricia Elinor Trevor (who obtained a divorce 1953), da. of Cdr. Sir Hugh Trevor Dawson, RN (ret.), 2nd Bt. (cr. 1920); 2ndly, 1964, Diana Denyse Hay, Countess of Erroll, and has issue living, (by 1st m.) Alexandra Susan Anne b. 1944: m. 1969, John Sherman, of Apt. 16K, 400, East 77th St., New York, 10021, USA (and has issue living, Charles Alexander Hoyt b. 1970), Susan Katharine Maud b. 1946: m. 1968, Dudley Gordon de Chair, 5th R. Inniskilling Dragoon Gds. (and has issue living, Oliver Dudley Raikes b. 1970), (by 2nd m.) Jocelyn Jacek Alexander Bannerman b. 1966. Residence,—Vann Farm, Hawkley, Hants.
Hon. James Duthac, T.D., b. 1910; ed. at Eton, and at Trin. Coll., Camb. (B.A. 19—); is Major 4/5th Batn. Black Watch (T.A.): m. 1935, Claudia Katharine Angela, da. of the late Hon. Lord Blackburn [E. Strathmore], and has issue living, Robin Andrew Duthac, b. 1937; ed. at Eton; late Capt., Queen's Dragoon Gds.: m. 1st, 1962, Hon. (Selina) Polly Dawson Eccles, da. of 1st Baron Eccles; 2ndly, 1970, Mrs. Jennifer Louise Puxley, da. of G. H. Robins, MBE, and has issue living, (by 1st m.), Andrew James b. 1963, (by 2nd m.) Simon Duthac b. 1971, Tessa b. 1972. Residence,—Balloch, Alyth, Perths.

SISTERS LIVING.
Lady Katherine Ethel, b. 1892: m. 1917, Major Arthur Rivers Bosanquet, M.C., King's Own Roy. Regt., from whom she obtained a divorce 1940, and has issue living, David Francis Rivers (of Pednor Croft, Little Pednor, Chesham, Bucks.), b. 1918; Capt. R.A.: m. 1st, 1941, June (from whom he obtained a divorce 1947), only child of Bertram Park, O.B.E., of The Old Shooting Box, Eastcote, Pinner ; 2ndly, 1947, Patience Margery, dau. of the late R. S. Hooper, of Polefields, Cowden, Kent, and has issue living, (by 2nd marriage) Simon Rivers b. 1948, Michael John b. 1953, —Annette Katherine Jeanne, b. 1920,—Maud Mariota, b. 1923. Residence,—High St. House, Watlington, Oxon.
Lady Mary Elisabeth. b. 1899 : m. 1932, Vice-Adm. Sir (Edward Michael) Conolly Abel Smith, G.C.V.O., C.B, and has issue living, Michael James Abel, b. 1939: m. 1972, Karen, yr. da. of Iain Malcolmson, of Icomb Place, Stow-on-the-Wold,—Rosemary Jane, b. 1936: m. 1956, Capt. Robert Wolrige Gordon, late Grenadier Guards, of Esslemont, Ellon, Aberdeenshire, and has issue living, Charles Iain Robert b. 1961, Henrietta Anne b. 1959. Residence,—Ashiestiel, Galasheils, Selkirkshire.

WIDOW LIVING OF SON OF NINTH EARL.
Violet Mabel, dau. of the late Philip Affleck Fraser, of Reelig, Inverness-shire: m. 1913, Major the Hon. Robert Francis Carnegie, who d. 1947, and has issue living [see colls., infra]. Residence,—

COLLATERAL BRANCHES LIVING.
  Issue of the late Rt. Hon. Sir Lancelot Douglas Carnegie, G.C.V.O., K.C.M.G., 2nd son of de jure 9th Earl, b. 1861, d. 1933 : m. 1890, Marion Alice de Gournay, who d. 1961, dau. of the late Henry Ford Barclay, of Monkhams, Woodford, Essex :—
James Murray, b. 1909 ; ed. at Eton, and at Ch. Ch., Oxford ; European War 1939-45 as Capt. R.A.: m. 1939, Diana Winifred Mary, dau. of the late Arthur H. Renshaw [E. Leitrim], and has issue living, Susan Diana, b. 1943,—Charlotte Marion, b. 1954,—Sophie Winifred (twin), b. 1954. Residence,—Polefields, Cowden, Kent.——Mariota Susan (Lady Gurney), b. 1892: m. 1911, Sir Hugh Gurney, KCMG, MVO, who d. 1968, and has issue living, Ronald Hugh, b. 1931; ed. at Eton, and at Trin. Coll., Oxford; late 2nd Lt. Black Watch,—Priscilla Laura, b. 1912: m. 1948, Lt.-Col. Anthony Duncan Hunter, DSO, RE,—Isabel Marion (Lady John A. C. Kerr), b. 1924: m. 1949, Lord John Andrew Christopher Kerr, late Capt. Scots Gds. [see M. Lothian],—Susan Richenda, b. 1937. Residence,—1, Sloane Gdns., SW1.——Dorothea Helena (Dorothy, Countess of Mansfield), b. 1906: m. 1928, the 7th Earl of Mansfield, who d. 1971.
  Issue of the late Major the Hon. Robert Francis Carnegie, 3rd son of de jure 9th Earl b. 1869, d. 1947 : m. 1913, Violet Mabel (ante), dau. of the late Philip Affleck Fraser, of Reelig, Inverness-shire:—
David James, b 1915; ed. at Lancing Coll.; Somaliland, Abyssinia, and Madagascar 1939-42

with Armoured Cars and as Lieut. King's African Rifles (despatches): *m.* 1949, Stella Theresa, dau. of the late James John Cleveland. of Blackheath, Kent, and widow of Peter James Moseley Leigh of Belmont Hall, Cheshire. *Clubs.*—Naval and Military, Muthaiga Country (Nairobi).——John Fraser, *D.F.C.*, *b.* 1922; ed. at Prince of Wales Sch., Nairobi; formerly Flight-Lieut. R.A.F.; European War 1941-5 (D.F.C.): *m.* 1955, Gunhild Aline Avalon, dau. of Com. Arthur Avalon Mackinnon of Mackinnon, O.B.E., R.N. (retired), 36th Ch. of Clan Fingon, and has issue living James Robert, *b.* 1956,—Susan Mary, *b.* 1957. *Address,*—Carnegie, Ngobit Estate Ltd., Private Bag P.O. Naro Moru, Kenya.

Grandsons of the late Major the Hon. Robert Francis Carnegie (ante):—
Issue of the late Robert Murray Carnegie, *b.* 1917, *d.* 1954: *m.* 1949, Pauline Frances, who *d.* 1954, dau. of Capt. F. H. Farmer:—
Ian Francis, *b.* 1949.——Alastair Robert, *b.* 1951.

Grandson of the late George David Howard Fullerton-Carnegie (infra):—
Issue of the late Maj. George Travers Fullerton-Carnegie, *b.* 1921, *d.* 1975: *m.* 1945, Frances May, who *d.* 1974, da. of the late Lt.-Col. Alexander Sydney Duggan, MBE:—
George Christopher Howard, (11 Av. Avant Poste, 1003, Lausanne, Switzerland), *b.* 1946; ed. at La Cleirière, Switzerland, and Lausanne Univ.

Grandson of the late Edward Hugo Wakefield FULLERTON-CARNEGIE, OBE, son of the late Maj.-Gen. George FULLERTON-CARNEGIE, son of the late George FULLERTON-CARNEGIE, el. son of the late John Fullerton-Carnegie, el. son of the late George Carnegie, brother of 3rd Bt. and *de jure* 6th Earl:—
Issue of the late George David Howard FULLERTON-CARNEGIE, M.C., *b.* 1894, *d.* 1937: *m.* 1920, Marian Margery (who *m.* 2ndly, 1946, Staffan John Söderblom), dau. of the late Rev. R. L. Lacey, of Castlepark House, Exmouth:—
David Howard, *b.* 1926. *Residence,*—

PREDECESSORS.—[1] *Rt. Hon Sir* DAVID Carnegie, an Extraordinary Lord of Session and High Sheriff of co. Forfar, was cr. *Lord Carnegie,* of Kinnaird (peerage of Scotland) 1616, and *Earl of Southesk* and *Lord Carnegie,* of Kinnaird and Leuchars (peerage of Scotland) 1633, with remainder to heirs male; *d.* 1658; *s.* by his son [2] JAMES, 2nd Earl; High Sheriff of co. Forfar; one of the Commrs. chosen to sit in the Parliament of England 1652; *d.* 1669; *s.* by his son [3] ROBERT, 3rd Earl; High Sheriff of co. Forfar; *d.* 1688; *s.* by his son [4] CHARLES, 4th Earl; High Sheriff of co. Forfar; did not go to Court or Parliament after the Revolution; *d.* 1699; *s.* by his son [5] JAMES, 5th Earl; engaged in the Rebellion of 1715 (honours attainted by Act of Parliament and estates forfeited); *d.* 1729: *s.* in representation of family by [6] *Sir* JAMES Carnegie, *M.P.,* 3rd Bt. (see *⁎⁎* infra); *s.* by his son [7] *Sir* DAVID, *M.P.,* 4th Bt.; *d.* 1805; *s.* by his son [8] *Sir* JAMES, M.P., 5th Bt.; *b.* 1799: *m.* 1825, Charlotte, dau. of the Rev. Daniel Lysons, of Hempsted Court, Gloucester; *d.* 1849; *s.* by his son [9] *Sir* JAMES, 6th Bt.; *b.* 1827; confirmed in Earldom as 9th Earl (together with the minor honours) and attainder reversed 1855, and cr. *Baron Balinhard,* of Farnell, co. Forfar (peerage of United Kingdom) 1869; Lord-Lieut. of Kincardineshire 1849-56: *m.* 1st, 1849, Lady Catherine Hamilton Noel, who *d.* 1855, dau. of 1st Earl of Gainsborough; 2ndly, 1860, Lady Susan Catherine Mary Murray, who *d.* 1915, el. dau. of 6th Earl of Dunmore; *d.* 1905; *s.* by his el. son [10] CHARLES NOEL, 10th Earl; *b.* 1854: *m.* 1891, Ethel Mary Elizabeth, who *d.* 1947, only dau. of Sir Alexander Bannerman, 9th Bt.; *d.* 1941; *s.* by his el. son [11] Charles Alexander, 11th Earl and present peer; also Lord Carnegie, and Baron Balinhard.

⁎⁎ [1] *Hon.* ALEXANDER Carnegie, 4th son of 1st Earl of Southesk, *s.* by his son [2] DAVID, cr. a *Baronet* 1663; *s.* by his son [3] JOHN, 2nd Bt.; *d.* 1729; *s.* by his son [4] *Sir* JAMES, 3rd Bt., who *s.* the 5th Earl as head of the family (see ante).

SOUTHWARK, LORD BISHOP OF. (Stockwood.)

Right Rev. (ARTHUR) MERVYN STOCKWOOD, *DD,* son of the late John Arthur Stockwood; *b.* May 27th, 1913; ed. at Kelly Coll., Tavistock, and at Christ's Coll., Camb. (MA); DD Lambeth; HonDLitt Sussex; Blundell's Sch. Missioner, and Curate of St. Matthew, Moorfields, Bristol 1936-41, and V. thereof 1941-55, Hon. Canon of Bristol 1953-55, and V. of St. Mary the Great, Univ. Church of Camb. 1955-59; consecrated 6th Lord Bishop of Southwark 1959; was a member of Bristol City Council 1946-55, and of Camb. City Council 1956-8.

Patron of one hundred and twenty-three livings, of the Archdeaconries of Southwark, Kingston, Lewisham, and Wandsworth, and of Provostship and six Residentiary Canonries in Southwark Cathedral.

This See was founded by Act of Parliament 1905.
Episcopal Signature.—Mervyn Southwark.
Arms of the See.—Argent, eleven fusils in cross conjoined, seven in pale fessewise, four in fesse palewise, and in the dexter chief a mitre, all gules.

Office,—Bishop's House, 38, Tooting Bec Gardens, SW16 1QZ.

SOUTHWELL, LORD BISHOP OF. (Wakeling.)
[See pronounced "**Suthell.**"]

Rt. Rev. JOHN DENIS WAKELING, *MC,* son of the Rev. John Lucas Wakeling; *b.* Dec. 12th, 1918; *ed.* at Dean Close Sch., Cheltenham, and St. Catharine's Coll., Camb. (MA); 1939-45 War as Maj. RM (MC); Assist. Curate Barwell, Leics. 1947; Chap. of Clare Coll., Camb., and Chap. to Cambridge Pastorate 1950-51, V. of Emmanuel, Plymouth 1952-59, Preb. of Exeter Cathedral, 1957, and Preb. Emeritus 1959; V. of Barking 1959-65, and Archdeacon of West Ham 1965-70; consecrated 7th Bishop of Southwell 1970: *m.* 1941, Josephine Margaret, da. of Benjamin Charles Broomhall, FRCS, LRCP.

Patron of ninety-seven livings, and of five alternately with the Crown, and the Archdeaconries of Newark and Nottingham.

The See of Southwell was founded Feb. 2nd, 1884.

𝕰piscopal 𝕾ignature—"**Denis Southwell.**"

𝕬rms of the 𝕾ee,—Sable, three fountains proper, a chief or, thereon a pale azure, charged with a representation of the Virgin Mary seated, bearing the Infant Christ or, between, on the dexter side a stag lodged proper, and on the sinister two staves raguly crossed vert.

Residence,—Bishop's Manor, Southwell, Notts.

SOUTHWELL, VISCOUNT. (Southwell.) [Viscount I. 1776, Bt. I. 1662.]
[Title pronounced "**Suthell.**"]

Not an unknown knight.

PYERS ANTHONY JOSEPH SOUTHWELL, 7th Viscount, and 10th Baronet; *b.* Sept. 14th, 1930 ; *s.* 1960 ; Capt. (retired) 8th Hussars : *m.* 1955, Barbara Jacqueline, dau. of A. Raynes, and has issue.

𝕬rms,—Argent, three cinquefoils pierced gules, charged on each leaf with an annulet of the field. 𝕮rest,—A demi-Indian goat argent, armed and eared gules, ducally gorged or, and charged on the body with three annulets in bend also gules. 𝕾upporters, —Two Indian goats argent. ducally collared, chained, and charged on the body with three annulets gules.

Residence,—4, Rosebery Av., Harpenden, Herts.

SONS LIVING.

Hon. RICHARD ANDREW PYERS, *b.* June 15th, 1956.

Hon. Charles Anthony John, *b.* 1962.

SISTERS LIVING.

Evelyn Mary Elizabeth, *b.* 1926 : *m.* 1952, Harold Hope, and has issue living, Carol, *b.* 1953,—Valerie, *b.* 1956. *Residence,*—19, Mortlake Street, Islington, Christchurch, New Zealand.——Barbara Frances Magdalene, *b.* 1928 : *m.* 1949, Peter Fowler, and has issue living, Vivienne Anne, *b.* 1951,—Gillian Clare, *b.* 1953. *Residence,*—Beech Tree House, Market Drayton, Salop.

DAUGHTER LIVING OF SIXTH VISCOUNT.

Hon. Susan Mary, *b.* 1926: *m.* 1951, Keith Francis MacRae, of 27, Dennis Rd., Slacks Creek, via Brisbane, Queensland, and has issue living, John Francis, *b.* 1952,—Paul Finlay, *b.* 1955.

DAUGHTERS LIVING OF FIFTH VISCOUNT.

Hon. Elizabeth Katherine Mary, *b.* 1904 : *m.* 1930, Col. Donald Robert Grant Cameron, M.B.E., The Roy. Scots (ret.), who *d.* 1961, and has issue living, Angus Duncan John (Shamrock Farm, Assington, Colchester, Essex), *b.* 1932: *m.* 1960, Gillian Jane, yr. da. of F. Basil Tomkins, of Wimborne, Dorset, and has issue living, Edward Richard Pyers, *b.* 1963,—Catriona Louise *b.* 1961, — Iain Donald Robert (22, The Driveway, Canvey Island, Essex), *b.* 1937: *m.* 1963, Victoria Margaret Williams, and has issue living, James *b.* 1965, John (twin) *b.* 1965, Susan Fiona *b.* 1964, Elizabeth *b.* 1966. *Residence,*—5, Osborne Mansions, Luxborough St., W1.

Hon. Joan Evelyn Mary, *b.* 1909. *Residence,*—Orchard Way, Pitminster, Taunton.

WIDOW LIVING OF SON OF FIFTH VISCOUNT.

Daphne Lewin, dau. of Sir Geoffrey Lewin Watson, 3rd Bt. (cr. 1918, ext.) : *m.* 1932, Lieut. Com. the Hon. John Michael Southwell, R.N., who *d.* (killed on active ser. during European War) 1944. *Residence,*—Buckclose, Longparish, Andover, Hants.

MOTHER LIVING.

Agnes Mary Annette, dau. of the late Charles William Clifford [see Clifford, Bt., cr. 1887]: *m.* 1924, the Hon. Francis Joseph Southwell, who *d.* 1953. *Residence,*—Beech Tree House, Market Drayton, Salop.

COLLATERAL BRANCHES LIVING.

Grandchildren of the late Charles Josiah Southwell, el. son of the late Josiah South- well, 2nd son of the late Thomas Southwell, son of the Hon. John Southwell, 4th son of 1st Baron:—
Issue of the late Walter Stedman Southwell, *b.* 1853, *d.* 1939 : *m.* 1881, Janet, who *d.* 1951, dau. of the late William Renton:—
Bertie Charles Sydney Stedman (7, Kooyong Koot Rd., Hawthorn, Vic., Aust.), *b.* 1882; late Capt. 59th Bn. AIF: *m.* 1921, Elsie Annie, da. of the late J. S. Wenden, and has issue living, Evelyn John Stedman (2, Terry St., Balwyn, Vic., Aust.), *b.* 1923; late 2nd Commando Squad. 2/AIF: *m.* 1951, Shirley Jean, da. of Robert Ingram Kennison, of 94, Prospect Rd., Geelong, and has issue living, Robert John *b.* 1953, Anne Heather *b.* 1952,—Alec James *QC*, (17, Parslow St., Malvern, Victoria 3144, Aust.), *b.* 1926; late RANR; Judge, Co. Court, Vic.: *m.* 1957, Margot Rose, da. of Frank Tracy, of Mount Eliza, Vic., Aust., and has issue living, Peter James *b.* 1961, Kay Tracy *b.* 1962,— Lorna Wendy, *b.* 1921: *m.* 1945, William Chilton Brooks, MBE, VRD, late Cdr. RNVR, and has issue living, Anthony Dennis Chilton, *b.* 1946, Richard James Chilton *b.* 1953, Jonathan Peter Chilton *b.* 1955,—Mary Joy, *b.* 1924: *m.* 1949, Edward Russell Wilmoth, MC, late Lt.-Col. Aust. Imperial Force, of 16, Haverbrack Av., Malvern, Vic., Aust., and has issue living, Stephen Guy Russell *b.* 1952, Peter Charles Russell *b.* 1960, Wendy Anne *b.* 1950, Rosemary Susan *b.* 1954, Jennifer Mary *b.* 1959, Sarah Jane *b.* 1962.——Maida Lyttelton, *b.* 1898: *m.* 1932, Baden McIntyre, and has issue living, John Southwell (1, Keating St., Black Rock, Melbourne, Vic., Aust.), *b.* 1936: *m.* 1st, 1959 (m. diss. 1966), Patricia Agnes, da. of Francis Carney; 2ndly, 1967, Margaret Ruth, da. of John Moore Wilson, of 76, Hall St., Ormond, Mel., Aust., and has issue living, (by 1st m.) Colin John Southwell *b.* 1960, Lynn Rebecca *b.* 1963, (by 2nd m.) Stephen David *b.* 1971,—Mary Ursula, *b.* 1933: *m.* 1954, the Rev. William Booth Gill, of 19, Clan Brae Av., Burwood, Vic., Aust., and has issue living, Andrew William Booth *b.* 1964, Shirley Elizabeth *b.* 1955, Barbara Marie *b.* 1958, Teresa Margaret *b.* 1960, Jennifer Rose *b.* 1961, Dulcie Robyn (twin) *b.* 1961, Christine Anne *b.* 1962, Nicole Joy *b.* 1966, Angelique Faith *b.* 1969. *Residence,*—4/210, Warrigal Rd., Burnwood, Melbourne, Vic., Aust., 3125.

Issue of the late Sydney Martin Southwell, *b.* 1858, *d.* 1941 : *m.* 1893, Lillie, who *d.* 1956, dau. of the late Nathaniel Grew, of Belmont Park, Lee, Kent, and Sevenoaks, Kent :—
Freeman Grew, *b.* 1901. *Residence,*—Stonecoombe, 39, Kempshott Road, SW16.

Grandchildren of the late Thomas Martin Southwell, J.P., 2nd son of the late Josiah Southwell, (ante):—
Issue of the late Frank Marven Southwell, *b.* 1859, *d.* 1935 : *m.* 1887, Florence Isabel, who *d.* 1930, dau. of the late Rev. Henry James Cotton. [V. Combermere, colls.]:—
Gladys Florence, *b.* 1888. *Residence,*—26, St. Leonard's Close, Bridgnorth, Salop.——Margaret Majendie, *b.* 1898. *Residence,*—26, St. Leonard's Close, Bridgnorth, Salop.
Issue of the late Rt. Rev. Henry Kemble Southwell, C.M.G., D.D., formerly Bishop Suffragan of Lewes, *b.* 1860, *d.* 1937 : *m.* 1888, Charlotte Edith, who *d.* 1958, dau. of the late Henry Freer Radford, of Broughton Astley, Leicestershire :—
Eileen Augusta Baden, (*Lady Stirling-Hamilton*) *b.* 1905 : *m.* 1930, Capt. Sir Robert William Stirling-Hamilton, 12th Bt. *Residence,*—Puriton Lodge, Hambrook, near Chichester, Sussex.
Issue of the late Rev. Lionel Jenner Southwell, V. of Halford, Salop, *b.* 1869, *d.* 1905 : *m.* 1900, Hannah Stewart, who *d.* 1954, dau. of the late Col. S. Stitt, of Holmfield, Oxton, Wirral, Cheshire :—
Rev. Canon Eric Medder Baden, *b.* 1902; ed. at Lancing, and at St. Catharine's Coll., Camb. (MA); R. of Nantwich since 1951, and Hon. Canon of Chester Cathedral since 1963. *Residence,*—The Rectory, Nantwich, Cheshire.

PREDECESSORS.—[1] *Sir* THOMAS Southwell, Knt.; cr. *Baronet* 1662; *s.* by his grandson [2] *Sir* THOMAS, P.C., 2nd Bt.; sat as M.P. for co. Limerick 1702-17; cr. *Baron Southwell,* of Castle Mattress (peerage of Ireland) 1717; *d.* 1720; *s.* by his son [3] *Sir* THOMAS, 2nd Baron; *d.* 1766; *s.* by his son [4] THOMAS GEORGE, 3rd Baron; sat as M.P. for Enniscorthy; cr. *Viscount Southwell* (peerage of Ireland) 1776; *d.* 1780; *s.* by his son [5] THOMAS ARTHUR, 2nd Viscount; *d.* 1796; *s.* by his son [6] THOMAS ANTHONY, K.P., 3rd Viscount; *d.* 1860; *s.* by his nephew [7] THOMAS ARTHUR JOSEPH, K.P., 4th Viscount; *b.* 1836; was Lord-Lieut. of co. Leitrim: *m.* 1871, Charlotte Mary Barbara, who *d.* 1929, dau. of Sir Pyers Mostyn, 8th Bt.; *d.* 1878: *s.* by his son [8] ARTHUR ROBERT PYERS JOSEPH MARY, 5th Viscount; *b.* 1872: *m.* 1897, the Hon. Dorothy Katharine Walrond who *d.* 1952, dau. of 1st Baron Waleran; *d.* 1944; *s.* by his son [9] ROBERT ARTHUR WILLIAM JOSEPH, 6th Viscount; *b.* 1898; late R.N.: *m.* 1st, 1926, Violet Mary Weldon (who obtained a divorce 1931), dau. of Paymaster-Com. Francis Weldon Walshe, MVO, OBE, RN (ret.); 2ndly, 1943, Josephine, who *d.* 1973, da. of Denis Joseph de la Mole, and formerly wife of Capt. Henry Noel Marryat Hardy, DSO, RN; *d.* 1960; *s.* by his nephew [10] (PYERS) ANTHONY Joseph (son of the Hon. Francis Joseph Southwell, 2nd son of 5th Viscount), 7th Viscount and present peer ; also Baron Southwell.

SPENCER, EARL. (Spencer.) [Earl G.B. 1765, Viscount U.K. 1905.]

God defend the right.

EDWARD JOHN SPENCER, *MVO*, 8th Earl; *b.* Jan. 24th, 1924; *s.* 1975; ed. at Eton; late Capt. R. Scots Greys; DL and Co. Councillor for Northants; High Sheriff Northants. 1959; Patron of twelve livings; a temp. Equerry to HM King George VI 1950-52, and to HM the Queen 1952-54; 1939-45 War (despatches); ADC to Gov. of S. Aust. 1947-50; Dep. Hon. Col., The R. Anglian Regt. (Northants) TAVR since 1972; Chm. Nat. Assocn. of Boys' Clubs, Pres. Northants Assocn. of Boys' Clubs, a Trustee of King George's Jubilee Trust, and of Nene Foundation; MVO (4th class) 1954: *m.* 1954 (m. diss. 1969), the Hon. Frances Ruth Burke Roche, da. of 4th Baron Fermoy, and has issue.

Arms,—Quarterly argent and gules, in the 2nd and 3rd quarters a fret or, over all on a bend sable three escallops of the first. **Crest,**—Out of a ducal coronet or, a griffin's head argent, gorged with a collar gemelle gules, between two wings expanded and elevated, also argent. **Supporters,—** *Dexter*, a griffin wings elevated per fesse ermine and erminois; *sinister*, a wyvern wings elevated ermine; each chained and gorged with a collar sable, flory and counterflory, charged with three escallops, argent.

Residences,—Althorp, Northampton; Park House, Sandringham, Norfolk. *Clubs,*—Turf, Brooks's, MCC.

SON LIVING.

CHARLES EDWARD MAURICE (*Viscount Althorp*—pronounced Altrup), *b.* May 20th, 1964.

DAUGHTERS LIVING.

Lady Elizabeth Sarah Lavinia, *b.* 1955.
Lady Cynthia Jane, *b.* 1957.
Lady Diana Frances, *b.* 1961.

SISTER LIVING.

Lady Anne, *b.* 1920; sometime 3rd Officer WRNS: *m.* 1944, Capt. Christopher Baldwin Hughes Wake-Walker, RN [see Walker, Bt., cr. 1856, colls.]. *Residence,*—East Bergholt Lodge, Suffolk.

UNCLE LIVING (*Son of 6th Earl.*)

Hon. George Charles (2, Parliament Sq., Castletown, I. of Man; Travellers' Club) *b.* 1903; ed. at RNCs, Osborne and Dartmouth; 1939-45 War as Capt. RA (TA): *m.* 1st, 1931 (m. diss. 1962) Barbara C., da. of Benjamin Blumenthal, of Paris; 2ndly, 1966, Mrs. Sheila Stuart-French, who *d.* 1968, and has issue living, (by 1st m.) George Cecil Robert Maurice, *b.* 1932; ed. at Eton; formerly Lt. 11th Hussars,—Maud Catherine Hélène, *b.* 1934: *m.* 1958, Gerald Weiler, of Briarhill, Briarcliff Manor, NY 10510, USA.

AUNTS LIVING (*Daughters of 6th Earl.*)

Lady (Adelaide Margaret) Delia, *D.C.V.O.,* *b.* 1889 ; Hon. F.R.C.M. 1955 ; was a Woman of the Bedchamber to H.M. Queen Elizabeth the Queen Mother 1939-50, since when an Extra Woman of the Bedchamber ; C.V.O. 1947, D.C.V.O. 1950 : *m.* 1914, Col. the Hon. Sir Sidney Cornwallis Peel, 1st Bt., C.B., D.S.O., T.D., who *d.* 1938, when the title became ext. *Residence,*—Barton Turf, Norwich, NRIZ 8AU.

Lady (Alexandra) Margaret Elizabeth, *b.* 1906: *m.* 1931, the Hon. Henry Montagu Douglas-Home, MBE [see B. Home of the Hirsel], from whom she obtained a divorce 1947. *Residence,*—Trimmers, Burnham Market, Norfolk.

PREDECESSORS.—The Hon. John Spencer, M.P., 3rd son of 3rd Earl of Sunderland (D. Marlborough), had issue [1] JOHN, sometime M.P. for Warwick; cr. *Baron Spencer*, of Althorp, co. Northampton, and *Viscount Spencer* (peerage of Great Britain) 1761, and *Viscount Althorp* and *Earl Spencer* (peerage of Great Britain) 1765 ; *d.* 1783; *s.* by his son [2] GEORGE JOHN, K.G., 2nd Earl; was First Lord of the Admiralty 1794-1801, and Sec. of State for Home Depart. 1806-7; *d.* 1834; *s.* by his el. son [3] JOHN CHARLES, M.P. for Northamptonshire S., and Chancellor of the Exchequer 1830-4; *d.* 1845; *s.* by his brother [4] FREDERICK, K.G., C.B., 4th Earl; *b.* 1798; Rear-Adm. ; Lord Chamberlain 1846-8, and Lord Steward of the Household 1854-7 : *m.* 1st, 1830, Elizabeth Georgina, dau. of William Stephen Poyntz, M.P., of Cowdray, Sussex; 2ndly, 1854, Adelaide Horatia Elizabeth, dau. of Sir Horace Beauchamp Seymour [M. Hertford]; *d.* 1857; *s.* by his son [5] JOHN POYNTZ, K.G., P.C., D.C.L., LL.D., 5th Earl, *b.* 1835; Groom of the Stole to the Prince Consort 1859-61, and to King Edward VII. when Prince of Wales 1862-6, Lord-Lieut. of Ireland 1868-74 and 1882-5, and of Northamptonshire 1872-1908, Lord Pres. of Council 1880-83 and 1886, and First Lord of Admiralty 1892-95; M.P. for S. Northamptonshire (*L*) 1857; Member of Council of Prince of Wales 1898-1910, and Member of Council of Duchy of Cornwall and Keeper of its Privy Seal 1901-7 : *m.* 1858, Charlotte Frances Frederica, *V.A.,* who *d.* 1903, 4th dau. of Frederick Charles William Seymour [M. Hertford, colls.]; *d.* 1910; *s.* by his half-brother [6] CHARLES ROBERT, K.G., G.C.V.O., P.C., *b.* 1857 (who had been cr. *Viscount Althorp,* of Great Brington, co. Northampton, peerage of United Kingdom 1905), 6th Earl ; was Parliamentary Groom-in-Waiting to Queen Victoria Jan. to July 1886, Vice-Chamberlain to the Household Aug. 1892 to June 1895, Lord Chamberlain of the Household 1905-12, and Lord-Lieut. of Northants 1908-22 ; M.P. for N. Northamptonshire (*L*) April 1880 to Nov. 1885, and for Mid Div. of Northamptonshire 1885-95 , and Oct. 1900 to Dec. 1905 : *m.* 1887, the Hon. Margaret Baring, who *d.* 1906, dau. of 1st Baron Revelstoke; *d.* 1922; *s.* by his el. son [7] ALBERT EDWARD JOHN, *TD, D.Litt,* 7th Earl; *b.* 1892; Capt. 1st Life Gds.; Lord Lieut. of Northants. 1952-67; Chm. Advisory Council, Victoria & Albert Museum 1961-69: *m.* 1919, Lady Cynthia Ellinor Beatrix Hamilton, DCVO, OBE (Lady of the Bedchamber to HM Queen Elizabeth the Queen Mother), who *d.* 1972, da. of 3rd Duke of Abercorn; *d.*1975; *s.* by his only son [8] EDWARD JOHN, 8th Earl and present peer; also Viscount Althorp, and Viscount and Baron Spencer.

SPENCER-CHURCHILL, BARONESS. (Spencer-Churchill.) [Life Baroness 1965.]

CLEMENTINE OGILVY SPENCER-CHURCHILL, *GBE*, da. of the late Col. Sir Henry Montagu Hozier, KCB [E. Airlie] ; *b.* April 1st, 1885 ; ed. at Berkhamsted Girls' Sch., and at Sorbonne, Paris; Hon. LL.D. Glasgow; Hon. DCL Oxford; a Freeman of Wanstead and Woodford, and a C.St.J.; organised Canteens for munitions workers, YMCA in N.E. Metropolitan Area 1914-18 (CBE), Chm. of Red Cross Aid to Russia Fund 1939-46, of Fulmer Chase Maternity Hosp. for Wives of Junior Officers 1940-46, and of National Hostels Cttee. of YWCA 1948-51; *cr.* CBE (Civil) 1918, GBE (Civil) 1946, and *Baroness Spencer-Churchill*, of Chartwell, co. Kent (Life Baroness) 1965: *m.* 1908, Rt. Hon. Sir Winston Leonard Spencer-Churchill, KG, OM, CH, TD, who *d.* 1965 and has issue [see D. Marlborough, colls.].

Arms.—*Spencer-Churchill* [see D. Marlborough], over all an inescutcheon vair on a chevron gules three bezants a chief gyronny or and sable, *Hozier.*

Residence,—Flat 26, 7, Princes Gate, SW7.

SPENS, BARON. (Spens.) [Baron U.K. 1959.]

WILLIAM GEORGE MICHAEL SPENS, 2nd Baron; *b.* Sept. 18th, 1914; *s.* 1973; ed. at Rugby, and New Coll., Oxford (MA); Bar. Inner Temple 1945; late Maj. RA: *m.* 1941, Joan Elizabeth, da. of the late Reginald Goodall, and has issue.

Arms,—Quarterly, 1st and 4th, or, a lion rampant gules within a bordure of the last charged with eight roses argent, *Spens of Lathallan,* in the dexter chief point a heart ensigned with an Imperial crown, both proper; 2nd and 3rd, gyronny of eight, or and sable, charged of a quarter in dexter chief per bend argent and azure, *Campbell of Glendouglas;* over all on an inescutcheon or, a lion rampant gules surmounted by a bend sable charged with three mascles argent, which inescutcheon is ensigned with the circlet of a Lord-Baron's coronet, *Spens.* Crest,— A hart's head erased proper. Supporters,—*Dexter,* an elephant; *Sinister,* a mallard wings close, both proper.

Residence,—Lambden, Pluckley, nr. Ashford, Kent.

SONS LIVING.

Hon. PATRICK MICHAEL REX (Gould, Frittenden, Kent), *b.* July 22nd, 1942; ed. at Rugby and Corpus Christi Coll., Camb. (BA; ACA); a Dir. of Morgan Grenfell & Co., Ltd.: *m.* 1966, Barbara Janet Lindsay, da. of Rear Adm Ralph Lindsay Fisher, CB, DSO, OBE, DSC, and has issue living, Patrick Nathaniel George, *b.* 1968,—Sarah Helen, *b.* 1970.

Hon. William David Ralph (Marsh Mills Cottage, Over Stowey, Som.), *b.* 1943; ed. at Rugby, and Corpus Christi Coll., Camb. (MA); Bar. Inner Temple 1972: *m.* 1967, Gillian Mary, only da. of Albert Edwin Jowett, OBE, MD, FRCS, of the Old Rectory, Over Stowey, and has issue living, James Michael William, *b.* 1969,—Tamsin Caroline, *b.* 1971.

DAUGHTER LIVING.

Hon. Mallowry Ann (Lambden, Pluckley, Ashford, Kent), *b.* 1949.

SISTERS LIVING.

Hon. Patricia Mary, *b.* 1919: *m.* 1946, Anthony MacGregor Grier, CMG, late Overseas Civil Ser. of Callow Hill House, Callow Hill, Redditch, and has issue living, Anthony Richard MacGregor, *b.* 1948,—Francis John Roy, *b.* 1955,—Lynda Mary, *b.* 1947.

Hon. Emily Susan, *MBE b.* 1924; MBE (Civil) 1970.

WIDOW LIVING OF FIRST BARON.

KATHLEEN ANNIE FEDDEN (*Dowager Baroness Spens*), (Beacon Cottage, Blenenden, Kent), da. of the late Roger Dodds, of Bath, and Northumberland: *m.* 1963, as his 2nd wife, the 1st Baron, who *d.* 1973.

COLLATERAL BRANCH LIVING.

Issue of the late Capt. Robert Richard Patrick Spens, M.C., Roy. Norfolk Yeo., younger son of 1st Baron, *b.* 1917, *d.* (killed on active ser.) 1942: *m.* 1939, Elisabeth Clare, (who m. 2ndly, 1955, Francis David Corbin, TD, of Mayfield House, Wootton Rivers, Marlborough, Wilts.) da. of George Catterall Leach:—

Helen Charmian, *b.* 1940: *m.* 1960, William Thomas Scott, of Balfunning, Balfron, Stirlingshire, and has issue living, Thomas Robert George, *b.* 1973,—Elisabeth Charlotte, *b.* 1962,—Alexandra Mary, *b.* 1965.

PREDECESSOR.—*Rt. Hon. Sir* (WILLIAM) PATRICK Spens, *KBE,* son of the late Nathaniel Spens, of 1, St. Mary Abbot's Court, Kensington, W.; *b.* 1885, Bar. Inner Temple; Commr. of Imperial War Graves Commn. 1931-43 and 1949-65; Ch. Justice of India 1943-47; Chm. of Arbitral Tribunal for India and Pakistan 1947-48; MP for Ashford, Kent (*C*) 1933-43, and S. Kensington 1950-59; *cr. Baron Spens,* of Blairsanquhar, co. Fife (peerage of UK) 1959: *m.* 1st, Hilda Mary, who *d.* 1962, da. of Lt.-Col. Wentworth Grenville Bowyer [B. Denham, colls.]; 2ndly, 1963, Kathleen Annie Fedden, da. of Roger Dodds, of Bath and Northumberland; *d.* 1973; *s.* by his el. son [2] WILLIAM GEORGE MICHAEL, *MBE,* 2nd Baron and present peer.

STAFFORD, BARON. (Fitzherbert.) [Baron E. 1640.]

BASIL FRANCIS NICHOLAS FITZ-
HERBERT, 14th Baron; b. April 7th,
1926 ; s. 1941; ed. at Ampleforth Coll. ;
is patron of one living (but being a
Roman Catholic cannot present) ;
formerly Lieut. Scots Guards : m.
1952, Morag Nada, yr. dau. of the late
Lieut.-Col. Alastair Campbell, of
Altries, Milltimber, Aberdeenshire,
and has issue.

Arms,—Argent, a chief vairée or and gules,
over all a bend sable, Fitzherbert. Crest,—A
dexter cubit arm in armour erect, the hand
appearing clenched within the gauntlet.
Supporters,—Dexter, a lion argent; sinister, a
swan, wings inverted argent, gorged with a
ducal coronet per pale gules and sable.
Seat,—Swynnerton Park, Stone, Staffordshire.

One I will serve.

SONS LIVING.

Hon. FRANCIS MELFORT WILLIAM,
March 13th, 1954.
Hon. Thomas Alastair, b. 1955.
Hon. Philip Basil, b. 1962.

DAUGHTERS LIVING.

Hon. Aileen Mary, b. 1953.
Hon. Caroline Fiona, b. 1956.
Hon. Wendy Helen, b. 1961.

COLLATERAL BRANCHES LIVING.

Issue of the late Hon. Mary Beatrice Theresa Fitzherbert, el. sister of 12th and 13th
Barons, b. 1862, d. 1949 : m. 1895, as his second wife, Sir Trevor John Chichele
Chichele Plowden, K.C.S.I., who d. 1905 :—
Wilhelmina Marjorie, b. 1901.——Hester Mary Beatrice, b. 1902: m. 1922, Com. Kenneth Gordon
Poland, RNVR, who d. 1970, and has issue living, Trevor Peter Gordon, b. 1923; Lt.-Cdr. RN (ret.):
m. 1944, June Mary, who d. 1969, da. of Henry Bowlby, of 100, Elm Park Gdns., SW [V. Combermere,
colls.], and has issue living, Peter Kenneth b. 1945, Jill b. 1948,—John Michael (of Merrymead, Pet-
worth Rd., Haslemere, Surrey), b. 1925; ed. at Downside and at Trin. Coll., Camb.: m. 1952, Diana
Mary Angela Forbes, da. of the late Leo Forbes O'Connor [see B. Byron], and has issue living, Simon
John Joseph b. 1957. Jonathan David b. 1958, Matthew John b. 1963, Sara Daphne Mary b. 1954, Lucy
Mary b. 1959,—David Kenneth, b. 1929; ed. at Downside: m. 1st, 1958 (m. diss. 1967), Joanna Mary,
el. da. of the late Capt. J. B. Hall, RN; 2ndly, 1967, Isie Suzetli, only da. of the late Maj. Louis
Esselen, of S Africa, and has issue living, (by 1st m.) Kevin John b. 1959, Jeremy David b. 1961, (by
2nd m.) Caroline Mary b. 1969,—Michael Desmond (Bridgefott, Stedham, Midhurst), b. 1937; ed.
at Downside: m. 1969, Elizabeth, da. of Philip Asprey, of Perry, Worplesdon, Surrey, and has issue
living, Lara Hester Mary b. 1969,—Daphne Elizabeth Beatrice, b. 1933: m. 1960, Edward Kendall
Thorneycroft, MBE, TD, of Silver Leys, Wormley, Surrey, and has issue living, Tom Edward b. 1962,
Mary Louise b. 1961. Residence,—Downlands, Liphook, Hants.
      Grandchildren of the late Hon. Alice Mary Wilhelmina Trappes-Lomax (infra):—
Issue of the late Brig. Basil Charles Trappes-Lomax, M.C., b. 1896, d. 1963: m. 1929, Diana
Mary (121, Southgate St., Bury St. Edmunds), da. of the late Cdr. A. E. Silvertop, R.N.
David Edward (Great Hockham Hall, Thetford), b. 1930; ed. at Downside; Maj. Scots Guards.——
John Michael, b. 1947; ed. at Downside, and Gonville and Caius Coll., Camb.——Alice Mary, b. 1938:
m. 1959, John Edward Benedict Wells, of Creaber, Gidleigh, Newton Abbot, Devon, and has issue
living, Benedict Swithin, b. 1960,—Thomas Edward, b. 1962,—Katherine Mary Horatia, b. 1959.
      Issue of the late Nicholas Hugh Trappes-Lomax, b. 1911, d. 1969: m. 1938, Gertrude Maisie
(Croft Cottage, Checkendon, Reading), da. of the late Lt.-Col. Hugh Charles Stockwell,
OBE:—
Hugh Richard Nicholas, b, 1943.——Mark Clement, b. 1946.——Tessa Margaret, b. 1941.——Nicola
Frances, b. 1944: m. 1964, Anthony Miles Trevor Eastwood, of Haighton House, Grimsargh, nr.
Preston, Lancs., and has issue living, Anthony Charles, b. 1965,—Benjamin Miles, b. 1966,—Carl
Hugh, b. 1968.
      Issue of the late Hon. Alice Mary Wilhelmina Fitzherbert, 3rd sister of 12th and
13th Barons, b. 1873, d. 1955: m. 1894, Richard Trappes-Lomax, J.P., Major
Yeo., of Allsprings, Great Harwood, Lancashire, who d. 1936:—
Stephen Richard (MC, TD (The Old Vicarage, Tunstead, Norwich NR12 8HT; Naval and Military
Club), b. 1913; ed. at Stonyhurst, and at New Coll., Oxford; Maj. late London Rifle Bde.; 1939-45
War in Middle East (wounded, MC): m. 1952, Alison Marjorie Gundrede, only da. of G. A. Perkins,
of Bure House, Lamas, Norwich, and has issue living, Francis George, b. 1955,—Richard Nicholas
Henry, b. 1960,—Mary Alison Catherine, b. 1953,—Clare Gundrede, b. 1957.——Anthony Fitzherbert,
b. 1915; ed. at Stonyhurst, and at Corpus Christi Coll., Oxford; formerly Nigerian Forest Dept.:
m. 1960, Patricia Margaret, da. of the late Ronald Haswell Taylor, of Oak Lodge, Barton-on-Sea,
Hants. Residence,—Tudun Wada, San Pawl Tat-Targa, Nazzar, Malta, GC.

PREDECESSORS.—[1] Sir WILLIAM Howard, K.B. (3rd son of Thomas Howard, cr. Earl of
Norfolk 1644): m. Mary, only sister of Henry, 5th (or but for attainder 14th) Baron de
Stafford; in 1640 he and his wife were cr. Baron and Baroness Stafford (peerage of England),
with remainder, in default of heirs male of the body, to the heirsof their bodies, and Viscount
Stafford (peerage of England), with remainder to his issue male; subsequently tried for
complicity in Titus Oates plot, attainted 1678 and executed 1680; his wife was cr. Countess
of Stafford 1688 for life; she d. 1693 ; s. by her son [2] HENRY STAFFORD, de jure 2nd
Baron ; cr. Earl of Stafford (peerage of England) 1688, with remainder to his brothers John
and Francis ; d.s.p. 1719 ; s. by his nephew [3] WILLIAM, 2nd Earl, and de jure 3rd Baron
Stafford, el. son of the Hon. John (ante) ; s. by his son [4] WILLIAM MATTHIAS, 3rd Earl,
and de jure 4th Baron Stafford; d.s.p. 1750 ; s. by his uncle [5] JOHN PAUL STAFFORD, 4th
Earl, and de jure 5th Baron Stafford ; d.s.p. 1762, when the earldom expired, and the barony
vested in [6—7] Mary, wife of Sir George Jerningham, 5th Bt., only child of Mary Plowden,
sister of 4th Earl; attainder of the 1st Viscount was reversed 1824, and on July 6th, 1825,
the House of Lords resolved that [8] Sir GEORGE WILLIAM Jerningham, 7th Bt. (cr. 1621),
had made out his claim to be 8th Baron Stafford; unsuccessfully claimed the Barony of
Stafford, cr. 1299; assumed 1826 by Roy. licence additional surname and arms of Stafford ;
d. 1851 ; s. by his son [9] HENRY VALENTINE, 9th Baron ; b. 1802; d. Nov. 30th, 1884 ; s. by

his nephew [10] AUGUSTUS FREDERICK FITZHERBERT, son of the Hon. Edward (2nd son of 8th Baron), 10th Baron, *b.* 1830; *d.* 1892; *s.* by his brother [11] FITZHERBERT EDWARD, 11th Baron, *b.* 1832; *d.* 1913; *s.* by his nephew [12] FRANCIS EDWARD Fitzherbert-Stafford, *D.S.O.* (son of the late Basil Thomas Fitzherbert, of Swynnerton Park, Stone [who *m.* 2ndly, 1887, Emma Eliza, Baroness Stafford, who *d.* 1912], by Emily Charlotte, who *d.* 1881, sister of 10th and 11th Barons), 12th Baron, *b.* 1859; was Lord High Steward of Stafford; assumed by Roy. licence 1913 for himself and issue the additional surname of Stafford: *m.* 1903, Dorothy Hilda, who *d.* 1958, 3rd dau. of the late Albert Octavius Worthington, J.P., D.L., of Maple Hayes, Lichfield; *d.* 1932; *s.* by his brother [13] EDWARD STAFFORD JOSEPH Fitzherbert, *K.C.B.*, 13th Baron; *b.* 1864; Adm.; Com.-in-Chief African Station 1918-20; *d.* 1941; *s.* by his nephew [14] BASIL FRANCIS NICHOLAS (son of the late Capt. the Hon. Thomas Charles Fitzherbert, A.M., brother of 13th Baron), 14th Baron and present peer.

STAIR, EARL OF. (Dalrymple.) [Earl S. 1703, Bt. S. 1664 and 1698.]

JOHN AYMER DALRYMPLE, *CVO MBE*, 13th Earl, and 14th Baronet of Stair and 10th of Killock; *b.* Oct. 9th, 1906; *s.* 1961; ed. at Eton; is Col. late Scots Guards, Capt. Gen. Queen's Body Guard for Scotland (Roy. Co. of Archers), Gold Stick for Scotland, and Lord-Lt. of Wigtownshire; 1939-45 War in Middle East and Central Mediterranean (despatches, MBE); MBE (Mil) 1941, CVO 1964: *m.* 1960, Davina Katharine, da. of the late Hon. Sir David Bowes-Lyon, KCVO [see E. Strathmore colls.], and has issue.

Arms,—Quarterly: 1st, or, on a saltire azure nine lozenges of the field, *Dalrymple*; 2nd or, a chevron chequy sable and argent between three water bougets of the second, *Ross*; 3rd grand quarter, quarterly, 1st and 4th counterquartered, 1st and 4th gules, three cinquefoils ermine, 2nd and 3rd, argent, a galley sails furled sable, the whole within a border compony argent and azure, the first charged with hearts gules, and the second with gules, on a fesse between three crescents or, as mullets argent, *Hamilton of Bargany*; 2nd and 3rd, many mullets azure, *de Franquetot*; 4th grand quarter, quarterly, 1st and 4th gules, on a chevron between three cinquefoils argent, as many round buckles azure, *Hamilton of Fala*; 2nd and 3rd gules, three martlets argent, *Makgill*. **Crest.**—A rock proper. **Supporters.**—Two storks holding in their beaks, a fish, all proper.

Seat,—Lochinch Castle, Stranraer, Wigtownshire. *Clubs,*—Guards', Turf.

SONS LIVING.

JOHN DAVID JAMES (*Viscount Dalrymple*), *b.* Sept. 4th 1961.
Hon. David Hew, *b.* 1963.
Hon. Michael Colin, *b.* 1965.

BROTHERS LIVING.

Hon. Hew North, *T.D.*, *b.* 1910; ed. at Eton; formerly Capt. 2nd Batn. Black Watch (T.A.); is a Member of Queen's Body Guard for Scotland (Roy. Co. of Archers), and a D.L. for Ayrshire; N. Africa and Burma 1943-5 (twice wounded): *m.* 1938, Mildred Helen, dau. of the late Hon. Thomas Henry Frederick Egerton [see D. Sutherland, colls.], and has issue living, Robert Hew, *b.* 1946 *Residence,*—Castlehill, Ballantrae, Ayrshire.

Hon. Colin James, *b.* 1920; ed. at Eton, and at Trin. Coll., Camb. (B.A. 1941); Major (retired) Scots Guards, a Member of Queen's Body Guard for Scotland (Roy. Co. of Archers), and a D.L. for Midlothian; Italy 1944-5: *m.* 1st, 1945 (marriage dissolved 1954), Pamela Mary, only dau. of Major Lamplugh Wickham, C.V.O.; 2ndly, 1956, Fiona Jane, only dau. of the late Adm. Sir Ralph Alan Bevan Edwards .K.C.B., C.B.E., and has issue living, (by 2nd marriage) Andrew David, *b.* 1959,—(by 1st m.) Caroline Mary, *b.* 1946: *m.* 1973, Michael Scott, of Troloss, Elvanfoot, Lanarkshire,—(by 2nd m.) Serena Jane, *b.* 1957,—Rose Joanna, *b.* 1962. *Residence,*—Oxenfoord Mains, Dalkeith, Midlothian. *Clubs,*—Guard's, New (Edinburgh).

SISTERS LIVING.

Lady Jean Margaret, *DCVO*, *b.* 1905; appointed a Woman of the Bedchamber to HM Queen Elizabeth the Queen Mother 1947; CVO 1957, DCVO 1969: *m.* 1931, Lt.-Col. (Arthur) Niall Talbot Rankin, Scots Guards, who *d.* 1965 [see Rankin, Bt., colls. cr. 1898]. *Residences,*—House of Treshnish, Calgary, Isle of Mull; 3, Catherine Wheel Yard, St. James's St., SW1.
Lady Marion Violet, *b.* 1908; a JP of Pembrokeshire; has Order of Mercy: *m.* 1930, Major the Hon. Richard Hanning Philipps, MBE, Welsh Guards [see B. Milford]. *Residences,*—Picton Castle, Haverfordwest, Pembrokeshire; 5, Connaught Place, W2.

COLLATERAL BRANCHES LIVING. (*In special remainder to Earldom.*)

Grandchildren of the late Col. the Hon. North de Coigny DALRYMPLE-HAMILTON, MVO, 2nd son of 10th Earl:—
Issue of the late Adm. Sir Frederick Hew George Dalrymple-Hamilton of Bargany, KOB; *b.* 1890; *d.* 1974: *m.* 1918, Gwendolen, who *d.* 1974, da. of Sir Cuthbert Edgar Peek, 2nd Bt.:—
North Edward Frederick, *CVO*, *MBE*, *DSC* (Lovestone House, Girvan, Ayrshire. *Clubs,*—United Service, Pratt's, New (Edinburgh)), *b.* 1922; ed. at Eton; Capt. RN (ret.) and Brig. of Queen's Body Guard for Scotland (Roy. Co. of Archers); a DL for Ayr; 1940-45 War (DSC), Korea 1952-53 (MBE); MBE (Mil) 1953, MVO (4th class) 1954, CVO 1961: *m.* 1949, the Hon. Mary Helen Colville, el. da. of 1st Baron Clydesmuir, and has issue living, North John Frederick, *b.* 1950; a Page of

Honour to HM Queen Elizabeth The Queen Mother 1964-66,—James Hew Ronald, *b.* 1955.——
Christian Margaret *b.* 1919.——Graeme Elizabeth, *b.* 1926: *m.* 1948, Alexander Grant Laing, MC,
of Logie House, Logie, Morayshire [Grant, Bt., cr. 1924], and has issue living, Alasdair North Grant
b. 1949; ed. at Eton; Lt. Scots Guards, Fergus Hew Grant *b.* 1951; ed. at Gordonstoun, Carolyn
Margaret Grant *b.* 1952, Fiona Mary Grant *b.* 1954.

        Granddaughter of the late George North Dalrymple, el. son of the Hon. George Grey
        Dalrymple, 2nd son, of 9th Earl:—
Issue of the late Maj. Walter Grey North Hamilton-Dalrymple, *b.* 1896, *d.* 1969: *m.* 1929
  (m. diss. 1946), Melisande Germaine Violet Craigie Hunter:—
Dawn Mary Kathleen, *b.* 1930: *m.* 1956, Peter Humphrey Methuen, of Elliston, St. Boswells, Roxburghshire, and has issue living, Piers Harry North Dalrymple, *b.* 1966.

        Grandson of the Hon. George Grey Dalrymple (ante):—
Issue of the late Walter Francis Dalrymple, *b.* 1857, *d.* 1892: *m.* (Jan.) 1886, Agnes,
  Raney, dau. of the late William Charles Owen, of Penrhoe, Pembrokeshire:—
Basil Walter (c/o Lloyds Bank, 6, Pall Mall, S.W.1), *b.* 1891; 1914-18 War; 1939-45 War as Adjt.
R.A.F.: *m.* 1st, (Jan.) 1920 (marriage dissolved in Scottish Courts 1925), Aileen Eugenie, only da. of
the late Major Charles May Hayes-Newington, late King's and Cheshire Regts.; 2ndly, 1930, Erica
Isolde, dau. of Lt.-Col. P. N. G. Reade, R.A., and has issue living, (by 1st marriage) Elizabeth Mary
Wetherell, *b.* (Oct.) 1920; late Com. ATS: *m.* 1945 (m. diss. 1954), Anthony Edward Home Phillips,
Sub-Lt. RNVR, only son of the late Sir Herbert Phillips, KCMG, OBE, and has issue living, Anthony
Jeremy Herbert Home *b.* 1947.

        Descendants of the late Hon. Sir Hew Dalrymple, M.P. (3rd son of 1st Viscount
        Stair), who was cr. a *Baronet* 1698 :—
See Hamilton-Dalrymple, Bt.
        Descendants of the late Robert Dalrymple-Horn-Elphinstone [2nd son of the
        late Robert Dalrymple-Horn-Elphinstone, el. son of the late Hew Dalrymple,
        2nd son of the late Hon. Sir Hew Dalrymple (ante)], who was cr. a *Baronet*,
        1828 :—
See Elphinstone-Dalrymple, Bt.

PREDECESSORS.—[1] James Dalrymple, a Lord of Session as Lord Stair, was cr. a *Baronet*
(of Stair) 1664; appointed Pres. of Court of Session 1671; removed from that office 1681, and re-
appointed in 1688, after the revolution; cr. *Lord Glenluce and Stranraer* and *Viscount Stair*
(peerage of Scotland) 1690; *d.* 1695; *s.* by his son [2] John, 2nd Viscount; was Lord Justice
Clerk, Lord Advocate for Scotland, and a Principal Sec. of State, which latter office he resigned
in consequence of the part he took in the massacre of Glencoe; cr. *Lord Newliston, Glenluce*
and *Stranraer, Viscount Dalrymple* and *Earl of Stair* (peerage of Scotland) 1703, with remainder
to the heirs male of his father; *d.* 1707; *s.* by his son [3] John, K.T., 2nd Earl; an eminent
military commander; attained the rank of Field Marshal, and was sometime ambassador to
France; his brother the Hon. William (heir presumptive), having *m.* the Countess of Dumfries,
a peeress in her own right, he in 1707 surrendered all his honours to the Crown, and obtained
a new charter empowering him to name as his successor any male descendant of the 1st
Viscount, and in virtue of this authority he in 1747, shortly before his death, nominated by deed
his nephew John, 2nd son of his 2nd brother George; this nomination was contested, and the
House of Lords decided in favour of the 2nd son of the Hon. William and the Countess of
Dumfries (ante) viz. [4] James, 3rd Earl: *d.s.p.* 1760: *s.* by his el. brother [5] William, 4th
Earl, who had previously *s.* as 4th *Earl of Dumfries*; *d.s.p.* 1768, when the Earldom of Dumfries devolved upon his nephew Patrick Macdowal, Esq., and the Earldom of Stair passed to his
cousin [6] John, 5th Earl, who had been nominated for the title by the 2nd Earl; *d.* 1789; *s.*
by his son [7] John, 6th Earl; a Representative Peer, and sometime Ambassador to Prussia,
d.s.p. 1821; *s.* by his cousin [8] John William Henry, 7th Earl, son of Gen. William Dalrymple, Lieut.-Gov. of Chelsea Hospital; *d.s.p.* 1840; *s.* by his kinsman [9] John Hamilton,
K.T., 8th Earl, who had previously *s.* as 5th Bt. (see *•*•* infra); was a Gen. in the Army; cr.
Baron Oxenfoord, of Cousland, co. Edinburgh (peerage of United Kingdom) 1841, with remainder
to his brother; *d.* 1853; *s.* by his brother [10] North Hamilton, 9th Earl; *b.* 1776: *m.* 1st, 1817,
Margaret, dau. of J. Penny, of Arrad; *d.* 1864; *s.* by his son [11] John Hamilton, K.T.,
10th Earl, *b.* 1819; sat as M.P. for Wigtownshire 1841-56; was Lord High Commr. to Gen. Assembly
of Church of Scotland 1869-71; many years Lord-Lieut. of Ayrshire and Lord-Lieut. of co. Wigtown:
m. 1846, Louisa Jane Henrietta Emily, who *d.* 1896, dau. of the Duc de Coigny; *d.* 1903; *s.* by his
son [12] John Hew North Gustave Henry, 11th Earl, *b.* 1848; Provost of Stranraer 1900-
1909, and Lord High Commr. to Gen. Assembly of Church of Scotland 1910: *m.* 1878, Susan
Harriet (who *d.* 1946, and from whom he had obtained a divorce 1905), dau. of Sir James
Grant-Suttie, 6th Bt.; *d.* 1914; *s.* by his son [13] John James, K.T., D.S.O., 12th Earl; *b.* 1879;
formerly Lieut.-Col. Scots Guards; M.P. for Wigtownshire (C) 1906-14; Lord High Commr. to
Church of Scotland 1927 and 1928, and Lord-Lieut. of Wigtownshire 1935-61; European War 1914-
19 (DSO): *m.* 1904, Violet Evelyn, JP, who *d.* 1968, da. of Col. Frederick Henry Harford; *d.* 1961;
s. by his son [14] John Aymer, 13th Earl and present peer; also Viscount Stair, Viscount Dalrymple, Lord Glenluce and Stranraer, Lord Newliston, and Baron Oxenfoord.

••* [1] *Hon.* James Dalrymple, 2nd son of 1st Viscount; cr. a *Baronet* (of Killock) 1698; *s.* by
his son [2] *Sir* John, 2nd Bt.: *d.* 1740; *s.* by his son [3] *Sir* William, 3rd Bt.; *d.* 1771;
s. by his son [4] *Sir* John, 4th Bt.; was a Baron of the Court of Exchequer in Scotland:
m. his cousin Elizabeth Macgill, the heir and representative of the Viscount Oxenford, and
assumed the surnames of Hamilton and Macgill; *d.* 1810; *s.* by his son [5] *Sir* John
Hamilton Dalrymple, 5th Bt., who *s.* as 8th Earl of Stair (ante).

STALBRIDGE, BARONY OF. (Grosvenor.) [Extinct 1949.]
DAUGHTER LIVING OF FIRST BARON.
Hon. Eleanor Lilian, *b.* 1885: *m.* 1906, Major Josceline Charles Henry Grant, 3rd Roy. Scots, who *d.*
1947, and has issue living, Elspeth Josceline, CBE (Green End, Oaksey, Malmesbury, Wilts.)
b. 1907; Member of Gen. Advisory Counc il BBC 1952-59, and UK Ind. Member of Monkton Advisory
Comn. on Central Africa 1959; CBE (Civil) 1962: *m.* 1931, Gervas, Huxley, CMG, MC, who *d.* 1971.
Residence,—Quinta dos Passarinhos, Sargucal, Lagos, Algarve, Portugal.

STAMFORD, EARL OF. (Grey.) [Earl E. 1628.]

According to my power.

ROGER GREY, 10th Earl, and 11th
Baron Grey of Groby; *b.* Oct. 27th, 1896;
s. 1910; ed. at Eton, and at New Coll.,
Oxford ; sometime 2nd Lieut. Territorial
Force Reserve; a JP for Cheshire
(DL 1937-74); Charter Mayor of
Altrincham 1937 and Mayor 1937-8;
was Parliamentary Private Sec. (un-
paid) to Sec. of State for India March
to Aug. 1922.

Arms,—Barry of six argent and azure.
Crest.—A unicorn passant ermine, armed, and
unguled or, in front of the sun in splendour.
Supporters.—Two unicorns ermine, armed, unguled, tufted, and maned or.

Residence.—Dunham Massey Hall, Altrincham. *Club,*—Travellers'.

SISTER LIVING.

Lady Jane, *b.* 1899: *m.* 1927, the Rev. Peveril
Hayes Turnbull, who *d.* 1972, and has issue
living, John Grey, (Castle View, Horton,
Wimborne, Dorset), *b.* 1928; Capt. RA (ret.):
m. 1959, Sara Charlotte, el. da. of Brig. Denys
Edward Osbert Thackwell, CBE [see E. Shrewsbury, colls.], and has issue living, Mark Robert
b. 1961, Christopher John *b.* 1963, Anthony Lawrence *b.* 1965, Elizabeth Frances *b.* 1960, Alison
Jane *b.* 1967,—Oliver (High Wells, Natland, Kendal, Cumbria), *b.* 1933: *m.* 1963, Vivian Helen,
yr. twin da. of Sir Herbert Ingram, 3rd baronet, and has issue living, Harry *b.* 1971, Jane Lucy
b. 1965, Clare Catherine *b.* 1966, Sarah *b.* 1968,—Marjorie, *b.* 1932: *m.* 1958, David John Wykeham
Williams, of 10, St. George's Cres., Carlisle. *Residence,*—The Cottage, Brandeston, Woodbridge,
Suffolk.

PREDECESSORS.—[1] *Sir* HENRY Grey, Knt., son of Lord John Grey, of Pirgo, Essex, and
nephew of Henry Grey, K.G., 1st Duke of Suffolk, who was executed and attainted 1554, was
cr. *Baron Grey of Groby,* co. Leicester (peerage of England) 1603; *d.* 1614; *s.* by his grandson
[2] HENRY, 2nd Baron; cr. *Earl of Stamford* (peerage of England) 1628; was Lord-Lieut. of
Leicestershire 1641-2; commanded the Parliamentary Forces in W. of England 1642; his el. son
Lord Grey, who predeceased him, was one of the judges upon the trial of Charles I., and one of
those who signed the warrant for the king's execution; *d.* 1673; *s.* by his grandson [3] THOMAS,
2nd Earl; *d.s.p.* 1720; *s.* by his cousin [4] HARRY, 3rd Earl; *d.* 1739; *s.* by his son [5] HARRY,
4th Earl, *b.* 1715; was sometime M.P. for Leicestershire: *m.* Lady Mary Booth, dau. and heiress
of George, 2nd Earl of Warrington and 3rd Baron Delamer; *d.* 1768; *s.* by his son [6] GEORGE
HARRY, 5th Earl, *b.* 1737; cr. *Baron Delamer* and *Earl of Warrington* (peerage of Great Britain)
1796; *d.* 1819; *s.* by his son [7] GEORGE HARRY, 6th Earl; was Lord-Lieut. of co. Chester; *d.*
1845; *s.* by his grandson [8] GEORGE HARRY, 7th Earl, son of George Harry, Lord Grey (who in
1832 had been summoned to Parliament in his father's Barony of Grey of Groby); *s.* his
father in Barony of Grey of Groby 1835; was a great patron of the Turf: *m.* 1st, 1848, Elizabeth,
who *d.* 1854, da. of John Billage, of Wincanton, Somerset; 2ndly, 1855, Catherine, who
d. 1905, da. of the late Henry Cocks; *d.* Jan. 2, 1883, when the Barony of Delamer,
and the Earldom of Warrington became extinct, and the Earldom of Stamford and Barony of
Grey of Groby devolved upon his kinsman [9] *Rev.* HARRY (grandson of the Hon. John, 3rd
son of 4th Earl of Stamford, and son of the Rev. Harry Grey), 8th Earl, *b.* 1812: *m.* 1st, 1844,
Susan Gaydon, who *d.* 1870; 2ndly, 1873, Anne Macnamara, who *d.* 1874; 3rdly, 1880, Martha
Solomon, who *d.* 1916, having re-*m.* 1892, Pieter Pieterse, of Wellington, Cape Colony; *d.*
1890; *s.* by his nephew [10] WILLIAM, 9th Earl; *b.* 1850; adjudged 9th Earl of Stamford and
10th Baron Grey of Groby, by Committee for Privileges of House of Lords 1892: *m.* 1895,
Elizabeth Louisa Penelope, O.B.E., who *d.* 1959, dau. of the Rev. Charles Theobald, R. of Lasham,
Hants, Rural Dean of Alton, and Hon. Canon of Winchester; *d.* 1910; *s.* by his only son [11]
ROGER, 10th Earl and present peer; also Baron Grey of Groby.

STAMFORDHAM, BARONY OF. (Bigge.) [Extinct 1931.]

DAUGHTER LIVING OF FIRST BARON.

Hon. Margaret, *b.* 1885. *Residence,*—25, Connaught Square, W.2.

STAMP, BARON. (Stamp.) [Baron U.K. 1938.]

FIDEI·COMMISSA·TENEO

I hold in trust that which is trusted to me.

TREVOR CHARLES STAMP, 3rd Baron; *b.* Feb. 13th, 1907; *s.* 1941; ed. at Leys Sch., and at Gonville and Caius Coll., Camb. (M.A., M.D.); M.R.C.S. England and L.R.C.P. London: FRCPath.; Fellow of Post-graduate Med. Sch.; Prof. Emeritus of Bacteriology, London Univ.; American Medal of Freedom with Silver Palm: *m.* 1932, Frances Dawes, da. of the late Charles Henry Bosworth, of Evanston, Illinois, U.S.A., and has issue.

Arms,—Gules between two garbs or three bezants in bend each charged with a horse passant sable. **Crest,**—Issuant from a mount vert bezantee a demi-horse argent. **Supporters,**—On either side a horse argent resting the interior hind leg on a bezant.

Residences,—Middle House, 7, Hyde Park St., W.2 ; Pennyroyal, Hedgerley, Bucks. *Club,*—Athenaeum.

SONS LIVING.

Hon. TREVOR CHARLES BOSWORTH (Flat 6, 20, Bolton Gdns., SW5), *b.* Sept. 18th, 1935; ed. at Leys Sch., and at Gonville and Caius Coll., Camb. (MD); MSc Yale; MRCP London, and MRCPE: *m.* 1963, Anne Carolynn, from whom he obtained a divorce 1971, da. of John Kenneth Churchill, of Tunbridge Wells, and has issue living, Catherine Anne Louise, *b.* 1963,—Emma Caroline, *b.* 1968.

Hon. Josiah Richard (27, Maida Av., W2), *b.* 1943; ed. at Winchester, and at Queen's Coll., Camb. (BA)

BROTHERS LIVING.

Hon. Arthur Maxwell, *b.* 1915 ; ed. at Leys Sch., and at Clare Coll , Camb. (B.A. 1937, M.A. 1941) ; Bar. Inner Temple 1939; is Lt.-Col. Intelligence Corps, Chm. of Maxwell Stamp Associates Ltd., and a Dir. of Hill Samuel & Co. Ltd., Triplex Holdings Ltd. and De la Rue Co., Ltd.: *m.* 1st, 1938, Janet Tyler (from whom he obtained a divorce 1943), da. of B. Tyler Bryan, of Beaumont, Texas, USA. 2ndly, 1944, Mary Hagon, and has issue living, (by 2nd m.), Anthony Philip Josiah, *b.* 1947: *m.* 1970, Rosemary Ann, only da. of Hume Boggis-Rolfe, CB, CBE, of 22, Victoria Sq., SW1,—Marian Ellina, *b.* 1945; ed. at Somerville Coll., Oxford (BA, DPhil): *m.* 1967, Clinton Richard Dawkins,—Alison Mary *b.* 1950; ed. at Somerville Coll., Oxford. *Residences,*—Ebbs House, Combs., Stowmarket, Suffolk; 19, Clarence Gate Gdns., Glentworth St., NW1. *Club,*—Athenaeum.

Hon. Jos Colin, *b.* 1917; ed. at Leys Sch., and at Queens' Coll., Camb. (MA); late Lt. RNVR; Dir. of Marketing Sers. for Europe. of American Express Internat.: *m.* 1st, 1940, Althea (from whom he obtained a divorce 1956), da. of the late Mrs. William Dawes, of Evanston, Illinois, USA; 2ndly, 1958, Gillian Penelope, da. of the late Guy St. J. Tatham, of Johannesburg, SA, and has issue living, (by 1st m.) Olive Judith *b.* 1941; ed. at Wellesley Coll., Mass., USA (BA): *m.* 1963, Eugene Humphrey, of 720, West Huron, Ann Arbor, Michigan, USA, and has issue living, Alison Dudley *b.* 1968,—Althea Patricia Dawes, *b.* 1943; ed. at Wellesley Coll., Mass., USA (BA),—Ann Jocelyn, *b.* 1945, Rowena Jane, *b.* 1953, (by 2nd m.) Robert Colin, *b.* 1960,—Jonathan Guy, *b.* 1963. *Residence,*—12, Ullswater Rd., SW13. *Clubs,*—East India, Sports and Public Schools, and Little Ship.

DAUGHTERS LIVING OF SECOND BARON.

Hon. Nancy Elizabeth (11, Harpes Rd., Summertown Oxford), *b.* 1931 ; ed. at St. Andrews Univ. (MA 1953).

Hon. Veronica, *b.* 1934; MRCS, and LRCP 1960: *m.* 1961, Richard Alfred Hugh McWatters, of The Grove, Dundry, Bristol, son of the late Sir Arthur Cecil McWatters, CIE, and has issue living, Rupert Charles, *b.* 1967,—Philippa Mary, *b.* 1964,—Bridget Penelope, *b.* 1965.

Hon. Jessica Catherine, *b.* 1936; ed. at London Univ. (BA 1958): *m.* 1961, John Edward Chalmers Dow, and has issue living, Charlotte Mary, *b.* 1963,—Juliette Elizabeth Chalmers, *b.* 1966. *Residence,*—72, Freelands Rd., Bromley, Kent, BR1 3HY.

WIDOW LIVING OF SECOND BARON.

KATHARINE MARY (*Katharine,* Baroness *Stamp*), dau. of Tom Wickett, of Redruth : *m.* 1929, the 2nd Baron, who *d.* (result of enemy action during 1939-45 War) 1941. *Residence,*—23, Portland Rd., E. Grinstead, Sussex.

PREDECESSORS.—[1] *Sir* JOSIAH CHARLES Stamp, *G.C.B., G.B.E., D.Sc.,* son of the late Charles Stamp, of Yomah, Bexley; *b.* 1880; was Assist. Sec. to Board of Inland Revenue 1916-19, Sec. and Director Nobel Industries, Ltd. 1919-26, and a Director of Imperial Chemical Industries, Ltd. 1927-8; appointed a Member of Roy. Comm. on Income Tax 1919, British Member of Reparations Expert ("Dawes") Committee 1924, a Member of Coal Mines Enquiry Court 1925, a Reparation Expert for Great Britain 1929, and Chm. Canadian Grain Futures Enquiry 1931 ; Chm. and Pres. of Executive of London, Midland and Scottish Railway, a Director of Bank of England, Adviser on Economic Co-ordination, Past Pres. Roy. Statistical So., and Pres. National Institute of Economic Research and of So. of Genealogists, Col. Comdg. Engineer and Railway Staff Corps (T.A.), and Hon. Col. Transportation, R.E. (Supplementary Reserve) ; Charter Mayor of Beckenham 1935, and Pres. British Asso. for Advancement of Science 1936: *m.* 1903, Olive Jessie, who *d.* (result of enemy action during European War) 1941, dau. of Alfred Marsh; cr. *Baron Stamp,* of Shortlands, co. Kent (peerage of United Kingdom) 1938 ; *d.* (result of enemy action during European War) April 16th, 1941; *s.* by his el. son (by decision of House of Lords 10th Sept. 1941, and approved by H.M. King George VI., the decision being analogous to the Law of Property Act 1925, which provides that where two persons have died in circumstances rendering it uncertain which of them survived the other, such deaths should be presumed to have occurred in order of seniority)[2] WILFRID CARLYLE, 2nd Baron, *b.* 1904 : *m.* 1929, Katharine Mary, dau. of Tom Wickett, of Redruth; *d.* (result of enemy action during European War) April 16th, 1941; *s.* by his brother [3] TREVOR CHARLES, 3rd Baron and present peer.

Stanhope, Earldom of, see Chesterfield and Stanhope.

STANLEY OF ALDERLEY, BARON SHEFFIELD AND OF. (Stanley)
[Baron I. 1783, U.K. 1839 and 1848, and Bt. E. 1660.]

THOMAS HENRY OLIVER STANLEY. (*Baron Stanley of Alderley*), 8th Baron Sheffield, 8th Baron Stanley of Alderley, and 14th Baronet; *b.* Sept. 28th, 1927; *s.* 1971; ed. at Wellington; Capt. (ret.), Coldm. Gds.: *m.* 1955, Jane Barrett, da. of the late Ernest George Hartley, of Lower Farm, Milton-under-Wychwood, Oxon., and has issue.

Arms,—Argent, on a bend azure, three bucks' heads cabossed or; a crescent for difference. **Crest,**—On a chapeau gules, turned up ermine, an eagle with wings expanded or, preying upon an infant proper, swaddled gules, banded argent. **Supporters** (appertaining to the Barony of Stanley of Alderley)—*Dexter,* a stag or, gorged with a ducal crown, line reflexed over the back, and charged on the shoulder with a mullet azure; *sinister,* a lion reguardant proper, gorged with a plain collar argent charged with three escallops gules.

Residences,—Rectory Farm, Stanton St. John, Oxford; Trysglwyn Fawr, Rhos y Bol, Amlwch, Anglesey.

Without changing.

SONS LIVING.
Hon. RICHARD OLIVER, *b.* April 24th, 1956; ed. at St. Edward's Sch., Oxford.
Hon. Charles Ernest, *b.* 1960.
Hon. Harry John, *b.* 1963.

DAUGHTER LIVING.
Hon. Lucinda Maria, *b.* 1958.

BROTHER LIVING. (*Raised to the rank of a Baron's son* 1973.)
Hon. Richard Morgan Oliver (13, Cromwell Cres., SW5), *b.* 1931; ed. at Winchester and New Coll., Oxford: *m.* 1956, Phyllida Mary Katharine, da. of Lt.-Col. Clive Grantham Austin, RHA, JP, DL [see E. Scarbrough], and has issue living, Martin Thomas Oliver, *b.* 1957,—Oliver Hugh, *b.* 1959,—Serena Emma Rose, *b.* 1961,—Laura Sylvia Kathleen, *b.* 1968.

DAUGHTER LIVING OF SIXTH BARON.
Hon. Edwina Maureen, *b.* 1933: *m.* 1st, 1953 (m. diss. 1966), John Dawnay Innes, who *d.* 1966 [V. Downe, colls.]; 2ndly, 1968, J. Philip Epstein, and has issue living, (by 1st m.) Thomas John Stanley, *b.* 1954,—Richard James, *b.* 1955,—Mary Clementine Adelaide, *b.* 1960. *Residence,*—22, Stevenage Rd., SW6.

DAUGHTERS LIVING OF FIFTH BARON.
Hon. Mary Katharine Adelaide. *b.* 1906 : *m.* 1926, the Hon. Maurice Fox Pitt Lubbock, who *d.* 1957 [see B. Avebury]. *Residence,*—High Elms House, Downe, Orpington, Kent.
Hon. Pamela Margaret (*Hon. Lady Cunynghame*), *b.* 1909; Actress: *m.* 1941, Squadron-Leader Sir (Henry) David St. Leger Brooke Selwyn Cunynghame, 11th Bt., R.A.F. Vol. Reserve. *Residence,*—15, Madeline Rd., SE20.
Hon. Victoria Venetia, *b,* 1917: *m.* 1942, Lt.-Cdr. James Douglas Woods, Roy. Canadian Naval VR, and has issue living, Virginia Louise, *b.* 1943,—Teresa Clare, *b.* 1946. *Residence,*—31, Boswell Av. Toronto 180, Ont., Canada.

AUNT LIVING. (*Daughter of 4th Baron.*)
Hon. Sylvia Laura, *O.B.E.,* *b.* 1882; O.B.E. (Civil) 1962: *m.* 1906, Brig.-Gen. the Hon. Anthony Morton Henley, C.M.G., D.S.O., who *d.* 1925 [see B. Henley]. *Residence,*—39, Melton Court, S.W.7.

MOTHER LIVING.
Lady (Alice) Kathleen Violet Thynne, el. dau. of 5th Marquess of Bath: *m.* 1919, Lieut.-Col. the Hon. Oliver Hugh Stanley, DSO, who *d.* 1952. *Residence,*—East Woodlands Vicarage, Frome, Somerset.

WIDOW LIVING OF SIXTH BARON.
KATHLEEN MARGARET (*Baroness Stanley of Alderley*) (Villa Pax, Grouville, Jersey), da. of the late Cecil Murray Wright, of Malden, Surrey, and widow of Sir Edmund Frank Crane: *m.* 1961, as his 4th wife, the 6th Baron, who *d.* 1971.

PREDECESSORS.—[1] Rt. Hon. JOHN Holroyd, *M.P.* for Coventry; cr. *Baron Sheffield,* of Dunnamore, co. Meath (peerage of Ireland) 1781, *Baron Sheffield,* of Roscommon (peerage of Ireland) 1783 with remainder to the daus. of his 1st marriage and their heirs male, *Baron Sheffield,* of Sheffield, co. York (peerage of United Kingdom) 1802, and *Viscount Pevensey* and *Earl of Sheffield* (peerage of Ireland) 1816 ; Pres. of Board of Agriculture 1803, and Lord of Board of Trade, &c. ; *d.* 1821 ; *s.* by his son [2] GEORGE AUGUSTUS FREDERICK CHARLES, 2nd Earl ; *b.* 1802 ; a Lord-in-Waiting to H.M. Queen Victoria 1858-9 : *m.* 1825, Harriet, dau. of 2nd Earl of Harewood ; *d.* 1870 ; *s.* by his son [3] HENRY NORTH, 3rd Earl ; *b.* 1832 ; M.P. for Sussex E. (*C*) 1857-65 ; *d.* 1909, when the Irish Barony (cr. 1781), the United Kingdom Barony (cr. 1802), and the Earldom (cr. 1816) became *ext.* ; *s.* in the Irish Barony (cr. 1783) under the special remainder by his kinsman [4] EDWARD LYULPH, *P.C.,* 4th Baron Stanley of Alderley (grandson of Lady Maria Josepha Holroyd, dau. of 1st Earl of Sheffield) [see *⁎⁎* infra]; *b.* 1839 ; in 1909 *s.* to Barony of *Sheffield* (cr. 1783); M.P. for Oldham (*L*) 1880-85 : *m.* 1873, Mary Katharine, *C.B.E.,* who *d.* 1929, dau. of the late Sir (Isaac) Lowthian Bell, 1st Bt. ; *d.* 1925 ; *s.* by his son [5] ARTHUR LYULPH, *K.C.M.G.,* 5th Baron ; *b.* 1875 ; was Director of National Bank of Australasia and of Australian Mercantile, Land, and Finance Co. (Limited) ; formerly a Member of Woods and Forests Committee ; sometime Parliamentary Private Sec. (unpaid) to Postmaster-Gen. (Rt. Hon. S. C. Buxton, M.P.), Private

Sec. (unpaid) Office of Woods and Forests, and a Member of Select Committee on Peerages in abeyance ; Gov. of Victoria 1914-20 : M.P. for Cheshire, Eddisbury Div. (*L*) Jan. 1906 to Jan. 1910 ; *m.* 1905, Margaret Evelyn, who *d.* 1964, da. of Henry Evans Gordon, of 59, Cadogan Gdns., S.W.; *d.* 1931; *s.* by his son [6] EDWARD JOHN, 6th Baron; *b.* 1907: *m.* 1st, 1932, Lady Victoria Audrey Beatrice Chetwynd-Talbot (who obtained a divorce 1936), da. of the late Charles John Alton Chetwynd, Viscount Ingestre, MVO [E. Shrewsbury]; 2ndly. 1944 (m. diss. 1948), Louise Sylvia, da. of Arthur Hawkes, and widow of Douglas Fairbanks; 3rdly, 1951, Thérèse, who obtained a divorce 1957, da. of Gen. Husson, of Toulon, France; 4thly, 1961, Kathleen Margaret, da. of the late Cecil Murray Wright, and widow of Sir Edmund Frank Crane; *d.* March 3rd, 1971, *s.* by his brother [7], LYULPH HENRY VICTOR OWEN, 7th Baron *b.* 1915, *d.* June 23rd, 1971; *s.* by his cousin [8] THOMAS HENRY (3rd son of Lt.-Col. the Hon Oliver Hugh Stanley, DSO, yst. son of 4th Baron), 8th Baron and present peer; also Baron Stanley of Alderley, and Baron Eddisbury.

•ₒ• [1] THOMAS Stanley, Bar.-at-law, descended from the Hon. Sir John Stanley, 3rd son of 1st Baron Stanley [see E. Derby] ; cr. a *Baronet* 1660 ; *s.* by his son [2] *Sir* PETER, 2nd Bt. ; was High Sheriff of Cheshire 1678 ; *d.* 1701 ; *s.* by his son [3] *Sir* THOMAS, 3rd Bt. ; *d.* 1721 ; *s.* by his eldest son [4] *Sir* JAMES, 4th Bt. ; *d.* 1746 ; *s.* by his brother [5] *Sir* EDWARD, 5th Bt. ; *d.* 1755 ; *s.* by his son [6] *Sir* JOHN THOMAS, 6th Bt.; was a Gentleman of the Privy Chamber and Clerk of the Cheque to the Yeomen of the Guard ; *d.* 1807 ; *s.* by his son [7] *Sir* JOHN THOMAS, 7th Bt. ; cr. *Baron Stanley of Alderley* (peerage of United Kingdom) 1839 : *m.* Lady Maria Josepha Holroyd, dau. of 1st Earl of Sheffield; *d.* 1850 ; *s.* by his son [8] EDWARD JOHN, *P.C.*, 2nd Baron, who in 1848 had been cr. *Baron Eddisbury*, of Winnington (peerage of United Kingdom); *b.* 1802; sat as M.P. for Hendon 1831, and for N. Cheshire 1832-41, and 1847-8 ; was Under-Sec. of Home Depart. 1834, Sec. to Treasury 1835-41, Under-Sec. for Foreign Affairs 1846-52, Vice-Pres. of Board of Trade 1852, Pres. of Board of Trade 1855-8, and Postmaster-Gen. 1859-66 : *m.* 1826, the Hon. Henrietta Maria, who *d.* 1895, dau. of 13th Viscount Dillon ; *d.* 1869 ; *s.* by his son [9] HENRY EDWARD JOHN, 3rd Baron ; *b.* 1827 ; Sec. of Legation at Athens 1854-9 : *d.s.p.* 1903 ; *s.* by his brother [10] EDWARD LYULPH, *P.C.*, 4th Baron, who *s.* as 4th Baron Sheffield 1909 (ante).

STANSGATE, VISCOUNTCY OF.   (Benn.)   [Viscount U.K. 1942, disclaimed 1963.]

Rt. Hon. ANTHONY (NEIL) WEDGWOOD BENN, *M.P.*; *b.* April 3rd, 1925; *s.* as 2nd Viscount Nov. 17th, 1960, but made it known that he did not wish to claim the Viscountcy; disclaimed his peerage for life July 31st, 1963, having unsuccessfully attempted to renounce his right of succession 1955 and 1960; ed. at Westminster, and at New Coll., Oxford (MA); CIEE; FRSA; Hon. LLD Strathclyde; Hon. DTech Bradford; Hon. DSc. Aston; late PO RAFVR, and Sub-Lt. Fleet Air Arm; 1939-45 War; Postmaster-Gen. 1964-66, and Min. of Tech. 1966-70; Chm. of Labour Party 1971-2; Sec. of State for Industry, and Min. of Posts and Telecommunications 1974-75, since when Sec. of State for Energy; MP for SE Div. of Bristol (*Lab.*) 1950-60; re-elected May 1961, but debarred from sitting by judgment of Election Court 1961; MP for SE Div. of Bristol since 1963, PC 1964: *m.* 1949, Caroline Middleton, MA, da. of the late James Milton De Camp, of Handasyde Court, Cincinnati, USA, and has issue.

Arms,—see Benn, Bt. (cr. 1914), not used.

Residence,—12, Holland Park Av., W.11.

_____

SONS LIVING.

STEPHEN MICHAEL WEDGWOOD, *b.* Aug. 21st, 1951.
Hilary James Wedgwood, *b.* 1953.
Joshua William Wedgwood, *b.* 1958.

DAUGHTER LIVING.

Melissa Anne Wedgwood, *b.* 1957.

BROTHER LIVING.

Hon. David Julian Wedgwood, *b.* 1928; ed. at Balliol Coll., Oxford (B.A. honours 1951): *m.* 1959, June Mary, M.A., el. da. of the late Ernest Charles Barraclough, and has issue living, Piers Michael Wedgwood, *b.* 1962,—Cordelia Frances Margaret Wedgwood, *b.* 1964. *Residences,*—4, Liskeard Gdns., Blackheath, SE3; Stansgate, Southminster, Essex.

WIDOW LIVING OF FIRST VISCOUNT.

MARGARET EADIE (*Viscountess Stansgate*); First Pres. of Congregational Fedn. of England 1972-73, since when Pres. Emeritus; da. of the late Daniel Turner Holmes, formerly MP for Govan Div. of Lanarkshire: *m.* 1920, the 1st Viscount, who *d.* 1960. *Residences,*—10, North Court, Great Peter St., SW1; Stansgate Abbey House, nr. Southminster, Essex.

PREDECESSOR.—[1] (WILLIAM) WEDGWOOD Benn, *D.S.O.*, *D.F.C.*, *P.C.*, 2nd son of Sir John William Benn, 1st Bt. (cr. 1914); *b.* 1877; Sec. of State for India 1929-31, and Sec. of State for Air 1945-46; sat as M.P. for St. George's Div. of Tower Hamlets (L) 1906-18, for Leith 1918-27, for Aberdeen, N. Div. (Lab.) 1928-31, and Gorton Div. of Manchester 1937-41; cr. *Viscount Stansgate*, of Stansgate, co. Essex (peerage of United Kingdom) 1942: *m.* 1920, Margaret Eadie, dau. of the late Daniel Turner Holmes, formerly M.P. for Govan Div. of Lanarkshire; *d.* 1960: *s.* by his 2nd son [2] ANTHONY (NEIL) WEDGWOOD, 2nd Viscount, until he disclaimed his Peerage 1963.

STEDMAN, BARONESS.   (Stedman.)   [Life Baroness 1974.]

PHYLLIS STEDMAN, *OBE*, da. of Percy Adams; *b.* July 14th, 1916; ed. at County Gram. Sch., Peterborough; a Member of Board of Peterborough Development Corpn. since 1972, and Vice-Chm. of Cambs. County Council since 1973; cr. OBE (Civil) 1965, and *Baroness Stedman*, of Longthorpe, in City of Peterborough (Life Baroness) 1974: *m.* 1941, Henry William Stedman.

Residence,—Green Pastures, Grove Lane, Longthorpe, Peterborough, Northants.

STEWART OF ALVECHURCH, BARONESS. (Stewart.) [Life Baroness 1974.]

MARY ELIZABETH STEWART, da. of Herbert Birkinshaw, of Barnt Green, Worcs.; *b.* ; ed. at King Edward VI High Sch., Birmingham, and Bedford Coll., London Univ.; 1939-45 War with WRAF; a JP for co. of London; tutor, Workers Educ. Assocn. 1945-64; Member of Fabian Soc. Exec. Cttee. since 1950 (Chm. 1963); Chm. of Board of Govs. Charing Cross Hosp. 1966-74; Chm. of Board of Govs., of Fulham Gilliatt Comprehensive Sch. since 1974; cr. *Baroness Stewart of Alvechurch,* of Fulham, Greater London (Life Baroness) 1974: *m.* 1941, the Rt. Hon. (Robert) Michael (Maitland) Stewart, CH, MP [see PRIVY COUNCIL].
Residence,—11, Felden St., SW6.

STOCKS, BARONESS. (Stocks.) [Life Baroness 1966.]
SON LIVING OF LIFE BARONESS.
Hon. John Rendel (Flat 1, 10, The Paragon .Blackheath, SE3), *b.* 1918; ed. at Rugby and Liverpool Univ. (BSc); 1939-45 War with RN: *m.* 1946, Beryl, da. of Edward Bolton, and has issue.
DAUGHTERS LIVING OF LIFE BARONESS.
Hon. Mary Ann, *b.* 1915: *m.* 1942, Arthur Patterson, CMG of 42, Campden Hill Sq., W3 and has issue.
Hon. Helen Jane, *b.* 1920.

STOKES, BARON. (Stokes.) [Life Baron 1969.]

DONALD GRESHAM STOKES, *TD,* son of Harry Potts Stokes, of Rock Towers Hotel, Looe; *b.* March 22nd 1914; ed. at Blundell's Sch., and Harris Inst. of Technology, Preston; C. Eng.; FIMechE; MSAE; FIMI; FCIT; Hon. LLD Lancaster; Hon. DTech. Loughborough; Hon. DSc. Southampton, and Salford; late Lt.-Col. REME; DL for Lancs.; Gen. Sales Manager Leyland Motors Ltd., 1950, Dir. 1954, Chm. and Managing Dir. Leyland Motor Corpn., 1967, and of British Leyland Motor Corpn. Ltd. since 1968, Ch. Exec. since 1973, a Member of NW Economic Planning Council 1965-70; Chm. NEDC for Electronics Industry 1966-68; a Dir. of National Westminster Bank, Vice-Pres. of Employers' Eng. Fedn., a Member of Council CBI, a Member of Soc. of Motor Manufacturers & Traders, of EDC for Motor Manufacturing Industry; and of National Advisory Council for Motor Manufacturing Industry; Liveryman of Carmen Co.; Officer of Order of Crown of Belgium; Cdr. of the Order of Leopold II of Belgium; cr. Knt. 1965, and *Baron Stokes,* of Leyland, co. Palatine of Lancaster (Life Baron) 1969: *m.* 1939, Laura Elizabeth Courteney, da. of Frederick C. Lamb, and has issue.

Arms,—Gyronny of eight or and sable, a lion rampant double queued ermine, on a chief or an estoc erect between two speedwell flowers stalked and leaved proper. **Crest,**—A demi lion double queued ermine, holding between the paws a piston with connecting rod argent, the crown inflamed proper. **Supporters,**—*Dexter,* a lion reguardant double queued ermine; *sinister,* a horse argent, crined and unguled sable.
Residence,—25, St. James's Pl., SW1. *Clubs,*—RAC, Royal Western Yacht.

SON LIVING.
Hon. Michael Donald Gresham, *b.* 1947; ed. at Southampton Univ. (BSc): *m.* 1970, Inger Anita, yr. da. of Douglas Percy, of Hotspur House, Hythe, Hants.

STONHAM, BARONY OF. (Collins.) [Extinct 1971.]
SON LIVING OF LIFE BARON.
Hon. Ian Grenville Victor (40, Paul St., Islington, N1), *b.* 1941; ed. at Queen's Coll., Taunton, and at Kingston Gram. Sch.: *m.* 1968, Sandra Felicity Bell, and has issue.
WIDOW LIVING OF LIFE BARON.
VIOLET MARY (*Baroness Stonham*), (96, Waterfall Rd., N14), da. of Thomas E. Savage, of Crouch End, N.: *m.* 1929, Baron Stonham [Life Peer], who *d.* 1971.

STOPFORD OF FALLOWFIELD, BARONY OF. (Stopford.) [Extinct 1961.]
SON LIVING OF LIFE PEER.
Hon. Thomas, *b.* 1921; ed. at Manchester Gram. Sch., and at Manchester Univ.; European War 1939-45 as Capt. RA: *m.* 1943, Mary Howard, da. of the late Alfred James Small, of Manchester, and has issue. *Residence,*—85, Higher Woolbrook Park, Sidmouth, Devon.
WIDOW LIVING OF LIFE PEER.
LILY (*Baroness Stopford of Fallowfield*), dau. of the late John Allan, of Blackburn : *m.* 1916, Baron Stopford of Fallowfield (Life Baron), who *d.* 1961. *Residence,*—3, Stevens Lane, Woolbrook, Sidmouth, Devon, EX10 9UL.

Stormont, Viscount, son of Earl of Mansfield and Mansfield.

Stourton, Baron, see Baron Mowbray, Segrave and Stourton.

STOW HILL, BARON. (Soskice.) [Life Baron 1966.]

FRANK SOSKICE, PC, QC, son of David Soskice of London; b. July 23rd, 1902; ed. at St. Paul's Sch., and at Balliol Coll., Oxford (BA); Bar. Inner Temple 1926, and a KC and Bencher 1945; Solicitor-Gen. 1945-51, Attorney-Gen. April to Oct. 1951, Home Sec. 1964-65, and Lord Privy Seal 1965-66; 1939-45 War as Maj. Oxford and Bucks L.I. in E. Africa and Middle East; MP for E. Div. of Birkenhead (Lab.) 1945-50, for Neepsend Div. of Sheffield 1950-55, and for Newport, Mon. 1956-66; cr. Knt. 1945, PC 1948, and Baron Stow Hill, of Newport, co. Monmouth (Life Baron) 1966: m. 1940, Susan Isabella Cloudesley, da. of William Auchterlony Hunter, of Spean Bridge, Inverness-shire, and issue.

Arms,—Argent, perched on a triple mount in base vert, charged with a portcullis chained or, a dove wings expanded and in the beak a ship of olive proper in chief two portcullises chained gules. Crest,—Between two wings addorsed azure a paint brush and a quill pen in saltire proper, both tipped gules. Supporters,—On either side a pegasus azure pendent from a chain about the neck a portcullis or.

Address,—c/o House of Lords, SW1. Clubs,—Garrick, London Rowing, Special Forces, Royal Commonwealth Society.

SONS LIVING
Hon. David William, b. 1941; ed. at Winchester, and Trin Coll., Oxford: m. 1966, Alison, da. of Walter Black, of Nately Scures House, Hook, Hants.
Hon. Oliver Cloudesley Hunter, b. 1947: ed. at Winchester, and Trin. Hall, Camb.

Strabane, Viscount, grandson of Duke of Abercorn.

STRABOLGI, BARON. (Kenworthy.) [E. 1318.]
[Title pronounced "Strabogie."]

DAVID MONTAGUE DE BURGH KENWORTHY, 11th Baron; b. Nov. 1st, 1914; s. 1953; ed. at Gresham's Sch., Holt; a co-heir to the Barony of Cobham; 1939-45 War in France and Middle East as Maj. and acting Lt.-Col. RAOC; PPS to Leader of House of Lords and Lord Privy Seal 1969-70; Assist. Opposition Whip, House of Lords 1970-74, since when Dept. Ch. Whip; Capt. of Queen's Bodyguard of Yeomen of the Guard since 1974; Pres. AEGIS since 1965: m. 1st 1939 (m. diss. 1946), Denise, yr. da. of Jocelyn William Godefroi, MVO; 2ndly, 1947 (m. diss. 1951), Angela, only child of George Street, of Barton Lawn, nr. Elstree, Herts; 3rdly, 1955 (m. diss. 1961), Myra Sheila Litewka; 4th, 1961, Doreen, el. da. of the late Alexander Morgan, of Ashton-under-Lyne, Lancs.

Arms,—Argent, an eagle displayed gules surmounted by a bend vert, thereon three fleur-de-lis or. Crest,—An eagle displayed argent, collared gules, holding in either claw a fleur-de-lis gold.
Without noise.   Address,—c/o House of Lords, S.W.1.

BROTHERS LIVING.

Rev. the Hon. JONATHAN MALCOLM ATHOLL (The Vicarage, 234, Anerley Rd., Penge, SE20), *b.* Sept. 16th, 1916; ed. at Oundle, at Pembroke Coll., and at Ridley Hall, Camb. (MA); Curate of St. Mary's, Hornsey Rise, N. 1941-43, and a Chap. to Forces 1943-47, R. of St. Clements, Oxford 1947-54, V. of Hoddesdon 1954-63, and of All Saints, Burton-on-Trent 1963-65, Chap. of St. John's, Bangalore, and V. of Christ Church, Penge, since 1966: *m.* 1st, 1943, Joan Marion, who *d.* 1963, da. of the late Claude Gilbert Gaster, of Tunbridge Wells; 2ndly, 1963, Victoria Hewitt, and has issue living, (by 1st m.) Elizabeth Joan, *b.* 1944: *m.* 1964, Geoffrey Greetham, of The Gables, 92, Station Rd., Willingham, Cambs., and has issue living, Jonathan *b.* 1967, Matthew *b.* 1968, Alexander *b.* 1971,—Brenda Marion, *b.* 1946: *m.* 1974, Geoffrey Collins,—(by 2nd m.) Andrew David Whitley, *b.* 1967,—James Atholl, *b.* 1971,—Penelope Ruth, *b.* 1964.

Hon. Basil Frederick de la Pole (149, Gloucester Rd., SW7; Hurlingham, Istanbul and Oxford Carlton, Devonshire Clubs, Anglo-Turkish Society, *b.* 1920; ed. at Oundle, and at Lincoln Coll., Oxford (MA); FInstPet; MInstT; Capt. RA (TA Reserve); 1939-45 War in Norway, Greece, Crete, Middle East, India and Germany (prisoner): a Member of Turco-British Assocn., and of Lincoln Soc.: *m.* 1948, Chloë,from whom he obtained a divorce 1965, da. of the late Henry Gerard Walter Sandeman [see B. Newton], and has issue living, Forflissa Viola, *b.* 1949: *m.* 1970, William John Healey, of Mount Pleasant, Higher Eastwood, Todmorden, Yorks.,—Nicolette Elizabeth, *b.* 1950: *m.* 1972, Prof. John Russell Vincent, of 14, Berkley House, Charlotte St., Bristol 1,—Emma Iseult, *b.* 1958.

SISTER LIVING.

Hon. Ferelith Rosemary Florence (*Hon. Lady Hood*), *b.* 1918: *m.* 1946, Sir Harold Joseph Hood, T.D., 2nd Bt. *Residence,*—31, Avenue Rd., St. John's Wood, N.W.8.

WIDOW LIVING OF SON OF NINTH BARON.

Amy Catherine, da. of the late Frederick Evitt, of Rook Hall, Maldon, Essex: *m.* 1913, the Rev. the Hon. Cuthbert Reginald Leatham Kenworthy, who *d.* 1963, and has issue living [see colls., infra].

MOTHER LIVING.

Doris Whitley (*Doris, Lady Strabolgi*), only child of the late Sir Frederick Whitley Whitley-Thomson JP, MP: *m.* 1913, the 10th Baron, who *d.* 1953, and from whom she had obtained a divorce 1941 *Residence,*—137, Gloucester Rd., SW7.

COLLATERAL BRANCH LIVING.

Issue of the late Rev. the Hon. Cuthbert Reginald Leatham Kenworthy, 2nd son of 9th Baron, *b.* 1889, *d.* 1963: *m.* 1913, Amy Catherine (ante), dau. of the late Frederick Evitt, of Rook Hall, Maldon, Essex:—

Cuthbert Reginald D'Isney (St. Medden's, Fintray, Dyce, Aberdeen; Army and Navy Club), *b.* 1914; Maj. Gordon Highlanders; 1939-45 War: *m.* 1st, 1947, Joan Mary, da. of Lt.-Col. R. A. G. Stewart, RM (ret.), of Winthorpe House, Newark; 2ndly, 1960, Mrs. Peggy Owtram, and has issue living, (by 1st m.) Duncan Alexander D'Isney, *b.* 1950,—Sheena Mary, *b.* 1948.

PREDECESSORS.—[1] MADACH, 1st Earl of Atholl (cr. S., *circa* 1122), was nephew of Malcolm III. and Duncan I., Kings of Scotland ; *s.* by his son [2] MALCOLM, 2nd Earl ; *s.* by his son [3] HENRY, 3rd Earl ; *s.* by his dau. [4] ISABELLA, Countess of Atholl : m. Thomas of Galloway (*jure uxoris* Earl of Atholl) ; *s.* by her son [5] PATRICK, 5th Earl ; murdered 1242 ; *s.* by his aunt [6] FERELITH, Countess of Atholl, younger dau. of 3rd Earl : m. David Hastings (*jure uxoris* Earl of Atholl) ; one of the Guarantors of the Treaty of Peace with Henry III. 1244 ; *s.* by her dau. [7] ADA, Countess of Atholl : m. John of Strabolgi (or Strathbogie), son of David of Strabolgi, and grandson of Duncan, Earl of Fife, who granted the lands of Strathbogie to the above-mentioned David ; *s.* by her son [8] DAVID, 8th Earl ; joined the 7th Crusade under Louis IX. of France ; *d.* of the plague at Carthage 1270 ; *s.* by his son [9] JOHN, 9th Earl ; taken prisoner by the English at Battle of Methven 1306, and subsequently executed in London : m. Margory, dau. of Donald, Earl of Mar, and sister of Isabel, wife of Robert Bruce, King of Scotland ; *s.* by his son [10] DAVID (de Strabolgi), 10th Earl ; summoned to Parliament as Lord Strabolgi 1318 ; *d.* 1326 ; *s.* by his el. son [11] DAVID, 11th Earl of Atholl, and 2nd Lord Strabolgi ; summoned to Parliament as Lord Strabolgi 1329-34 ; a famous soldier ; accompanied his kinsman, Lord Balliol, in invasion of Scotland, when a much larger force of their opponents was defeated at battle of Dupplin Moor (tactics employed became model for English armies, and also affected military procedure on the Continent) ; killed at battle of Kilblane 1335 ; *s.* by his only son [12] DAVID, 12th Earl of Atholl and 3rd Lord Strabolgi ; summoned to Parliament as Lord Strabolgi 1335-1369 ; went to the wars in France with the Black Prince in 1355: *m.* Catherine, da. of 2nd Lord Ferrers of Groby ; *d.s.p.* 1369, when the Scottish Earldom of Atholl (cr. *circa* 1122) ceased to be borne in England, and the English Barony of Strabolgi fell into abeyance between his das. and co-heirs, and so remained until 1496, when it is held to have passed to the sole surviving representative of the co-heirs [13] Sir EDWARD Burgh, *de jure* 4th Baron (son of Thomas Burgh temp. 1431-95); MP for co. Lincoln: *m.* 1477, Anne, da. of Sir Thomas Cobham of Sterborough Castle, and widow of 2nd Baron Mountjoy; *d.* 1528; *s.* by his son [14] THOMAS, *de jure* 5th Baron; summoned to Parliament as Lord Burgh 1529: *m.* 1st, 1497, Agnes, da. of Sir William Tyrwhitt; 2ndly, 15—, Alice, da. of William London, and widow (i) of Sir Thomas Bedingfield and (ii) of Sir Edmund Rokewood; *d.* 1550; *s.* by his el. surviving son [15] WILLIAM, 2nd Baron Burgh, and *de jure* 6th Baron Strabolgi; summoned to Parliament as Lord Burgh 1551-80 : *m.* 15—, Catherine, dau. of Edward, Earl of Lincoln ; *d.* 1584 ; *s.* by his el. surviving son [16] THOMAS, *K.G.*, 3rd Baron Burgh, and *de jure* 7th Baron Strabolgi ; summoned to Parliament as Lord Burgh 1584-97 ; Ambassador to Scotland 1593, and Lord Dep. of Ireland 1597 : *m.* 15—, Frances, dau. of John Vaughan, of Sutton-on-Derwent ; *d.* 1597 ; *s.* by his el. surviving son [17] ROBERT, 4th Baron Burgh, and *de jure* 8th Baron Strabolgi ; *d.s.p.* (about) 1600, when the Baronies fell into abeyance between his four sisters, among whose descendants they so remained until the abeyances were determined in 1916, the Barony of Strabolgi being called out of abeyance in favour of [18] CUTHBERT MATTHIAS Kenworthy (only surviving son of the late Rev. Joseph Kenworthy, R. of Acworth, co. York, by Harriet Elizabeth, dau. of Capt. William Henry Cockerell Leatham, of Kirkham Abbey, Carleton, Yorkshire, and a co-heiress to the Barony), 9th Baron Strabolgi, *b.* 1853 ; established his claim as a co-heir to the Baronies of Burgh and Cobham 1912 : *m.* 1884, Elizabeth Florence, who *d.* 1951, dau. of George Buchanan Cooper, of Sacramento, California, U.S.A. ; *d.* 1934 ; *s.* by his el. son [19] JOSEPH MONTAGUE, *R.N.*, 10th Baron Strabolgi: *b.* 1886 ; Lieut.-Com. (retired) ; with Grand Fleet, on Admiralty War Staff, and Assist. Chief of Staff, Gibraltar during European War 1914-18 ; was Ch. Opposition Whip in House of Lords 1937-45 ; sat as M.P. for Kingston-upon-Hull, Central Div. (*L* afterwards *Lab.*) 1919-29 : *m.* 1st, 1913, Doris Whitley (who obtained a divorce 1941), only child of the late Sir Frederick Whitley Whitley-Thomson, J.P., M.P.; 2ndly, 1941, Mrs. Geraldine Mary (HAMILTON), who *d.* 1970, da. of the late Maurice Francis; *d.* 1953; *s.* by his el. son [20] DAVID MONTAGUE DE BURGH, 11th Baron Strabolgi and present peer.

[The title of Strabolgi is derived from the Aberdeenshire district of Strathbogie, being the valley of the river Bogie, which flows into the Deveron; and Strathbogie Castle was the seat of the Earls of Atholl.]

STRADBROKE, EARL OF. (Rous.) [Earl U.K. 1821, Bt. E. 1660.]

JOHN ANTHONY ALEXANDER ROUS, 4th Earl, and 9th Baronet; *b.* April 1st, 1903; *s.* 1947; ed. at RNCs. Osborne and Dartmouth, and Ch. Ch., Oxford (Hon. MA); FRSA; Cdr. RN (ret.); late Hon. Col. 660th Heavy Anti-Aircraft Regt. RA (TA); Lord-Lt. of Suffolk since 1948; Agriculturalist and Forester; a JP for Suffolk, a KStJ, Vice-Pres. of R. British Legion, and Pres. Eastern Area of R. British Legion, Vice-Pres. of Assocn. of Drainage Authorities; a Dir. of Daejan Holdings, Ltd., and Vice-Pres. of TA & VR (A) for E. Anglia; a County Councillor for E. Suffolk 1931-45, and an Alderman 1953-64: *m.* 1929, Barbara, yr. da. of the late Lord Arthur Hugh Grosvenor [see D. Westminster, colls.], and has issue.

Arms,—Sable, a fesse dancettée or, between three crescents argent. Crest,—A pyramid of bay leaves, in the form of a cone, vert. Supporters,—Dexter, a lion, gorged with a wreath of olive proper; *sinister*, a seahorse, gorged with a wreath of olive proper, the tail resting on an anchor azure.

Residence,—Henham, Wangford, Beccles, Suffolk. Clubs,—Travellers', Jockey (New Rooms), Royal Norfolk and Suffolk Yacht.

DAUGHTERS LIVING.

Lady Marye Violet Isolde, *b.* 1930.

Lady Penelope Anne, *b.* 1932 : *m.* 1st, 1950, Com. Ian Dudley Stewart Forbes, D.S.C., R.N., from whom she obtained a divorce 1960 [see Forbes, Bt., colls., cr. 1823]; 2ndly, 1961, (m. diss. 1969), John Cator [Cayley Bt.]. Residence,—26, Cambridge St., SW1.

BROTHERS LIVING.

Hon. (WILLIAM) KEITH, *b.* Mar. 10th, 1907; ed. at Geelong Gram. Sch.; Lt. (E) RN (ret.), and Lt. RNVR; 1939-45 War: *m.* 1st, 1935, Pamela Catherine Mabell (who *d.* 1972 having obtained a divorce 1941), da. of the late Capt. the Hon. Edward James Kay-Shuttleworth [B. Shuttleworth, colls.]; 2ndly, 1943, April Mary, da. of the late Brig. Gen. the Hon. Arthur Melland Asquith, DSO [see E. Oxford and Asquith, colls.], and has issue living, (by 1st m.) Robert Keith (58-60, Fernleigh Rd., Caringbah, NSW 2229), *b.* 1937; ed. at Harrow: *m.* 1960, Dawn Antoinette, da. of Thomas Edward Beverley, of Brisbane, and has issue living, Robert Keith *b.* 1961, Wesley Alexander *b.* 1972, Ingrid Arnel *b.* 1963, Sophia Rayner *b.* 1964, Heidi Simone *b.* 1966, Pamela Keri *b.* 1968, Brigitte Aylena *b.* 1970,—William Edward (RHQ Coldstream Guards, Wellington Barracks, SW1), *b.* 1939; ed. at Harrow, and at RMA, Sandhurst; Maj. Coldstream Gds.: *m.* 1970, Judith Rosemary, da. of the late Maj. Jocelyn Arthur Persse, Rifle Bde., and has issue living, James Anthony Edward, *b.* 1972,— (by 2nd m.) John ,*b.* 1950.—Christine Caroline Catherine, *b.* 1946,—Henrietta Elizabeth, *b.* 1947,— Virginia, *b.* 1954: *m.* 1974, Antony William Hew Gibbs [see Hamilton Dalrymple Bt.]. Residence, Clovelly Court, Bideford, N. Devon. Clubs,—Hurlingham, and Royal Yacht Squadron.

Hon. George Nathaniel, *b.* 1911; ed. at Harrow, at Geelong Gram. Sch., and at Trin. Coll., Camb. (BA), Maj. (ret.) The Life Guards; a co. Councillor for E. Suffolk; served with Trans-Jordan Frontier Force 1938-42 ; Palestine 1936-39 (despatches) : 1939-45 War (Africa star, France and Germany star): *m.* 1949, Joyce, yst. da. of the late Col. Charles Harpur, OBE, and has issue living, Robert Charles, *b.* 1953; ed. at Harrow,—Georgina Alice, *b.* 1951: *m.* 1935, Charles H. W. Holloway,— Veronica Rose, *b.* 1958,—Frances Diana, *b.* 1961. Residence,—Dennington Hall, nr. Woodbridge, Suffolk.

Hon. Peter James Mowbray (Priors Mead, Quality St., Merstham, Surrey, GH1 3BB), *b.* 1914; ed. at Harrow and at Melbourne Gram. Sch.; Major (ret.) 16th/5th Lancers; 1939-45 War (Italy Star) *m.* 1942, Elizabeth Alice Mary, who *d.* 1968, da. of the late Maj. the Hon. Alastair Thomas Joseph Fraser, DSO [L. Lovat, colls.], and has issue living, Michael James Mowbray, *b.* 1945,—Simon Roderick, *b.* 1950,—John Sebastian, *b.* 1953,—Edmund Felix, *b.* 1954,—Peter Joseph, *b.* 1956,— Christopher Hugh, *b.* 1958,—Petronilla, *b.* 1943: *m.* 1966, T. Peter J. Cockin, 46, Grove Hill Rd., Tunbridge Wells, and has issue living, James Francis John *b.* 1968, John Joseph *b.* 1970, Charles Hereward John *b.* 1974, Antonia Patricia Mary *b.* 1967,—Helena Sibyl, *b.* 1947,—Elizabeth Anne, *b.* 1951,—Philippa Mary Katharine, *b.* 1960.

SISTERS LIVING.

Lady Pleasance Elizabeth, *b.* 1899: *m.* 1923, Owen McKenna, and has issue living, Wilfrid Patrick John (of 149, Melrose Av., Chateauguay, Prov. of Quebec, Canada) *b.* 1924: *m.* 1951, Moira, only dau. of Hugh McFadden, and has issue living, Vivyan John (known as Ian), *b.* 1952, Sara Elizabeth Anne *b.* 1954, Marye Patricia *b.* 1956, Philippa Jane *b.* 1959, Adrienne Claire *b.* 1965,—Maureen Sophia *b.* 1927. Residence,—56, St. James's Gdns., Holland Park, W11.

Lady Catherine Charlotte, OBE (55, Seckford St., Woodbridge, Suffolk), *b.* 1900; Ex-Services War Disabled Help Depart. in Suffolk; OBE (Civil) 1972.

PREDECESSORS.—This family descends from Sir Peter Rous of Dennington, near Stradbroke, Suffolk, *temp.* early 14th century. Henham became the principal seat in 1544. [1] JOHN ROUS, M.P. for Dunwich; cr. a Baronet 1660; *s.* by his son [2] *Sir* JOHN, 2nd Bt.; High Sheriff of Suffolk *d.* 1730; *s.* by his son [3] *Sir* JOHN, 3rd Bt.; *d.* unmarried; *s.* by his half-brother [4] *Sir* ROBERT, 4th Bt.; *s.* by his son [5] *Sir* JOHN, 5th Bt.; was M.P. for Suffolk; *d.* 1771; *s.* by his son [6] *Sir* JOHN, 6th Bt.; sat as M.P. for Suffolk 1780-96; cr. *Baron Rous*, of Dennington, co. Suffolk (peerage of Great Britain) 1796, and *Viscount Dunwich* and *Earl of Stradbroke* (peerage of United Kingdom) 1821: *m.* 2ndly, 1792, Charlotte Maria, dau. of Abraham Whittaker; *d.* 1827; *s.* by his son [7] JOHN EDWARD CORNWALLIS, 2nd Earl; *b.* 1794; was Lord-Lieut. of Suffolk; served in Peninsular War (medal with five clasps) and in Belgian Campaign 1815: *m.* 1857, Augusta, dau. of the Rev. Sir Christopher John Musgrave, 9th Bt., and widow of Col. Bonham; *d.* Jan. 27th, 1886; *s.* by his son [8] GEORGE EDWARD JOHN MOWBRAY, K.C.M.G., C.B., C.V.O., C.B.E., 3rd Earl; *b.* 1862; Lord-Lieut. and Vice-Adm. of Suffolk; Gov. of Victoria, Australia 1920-26, and Parliamentary Sec. to Min. of Agriculture and Fisheries 1928-9; European War 1914-19 (C.B.E.): *m.* 1898, Dame Helena Violet Alice, D.B.E., who *d.* 1949, dau. of the late Lieut.-Gen. James Keith Fraser, C.M.G.; *d.* 1947; *s.* by his son [9] JOHN ANTHONY ALEXANDER, 4th Earl and present peer; also Viscount Dunwich, and Baron Rous.

STRAFFORD, EARL OF. (Byng.) [Earl U.K. 1847.]

ROBERT CECIL BYNG, 7th Earl; *b.*
July 29th, 1904; *s.* 1951: *m.* 1st,
1934 (marriage dissolved 1947), Maria
Magdalena Elizabeth, dau. of the late
Henry Cloete, C.M.G., of Alphen, S.
Africa; 2ndly, 1948, Clara Evelyn,
dau. of the late Sir Nusserwanjee
Nowrosjee Wadia, K.B.E., C.I.E.,
and has issue by 1st marriage.

Arms,—Quarterly: sable and argent, in
the first quarter a lion rampant of the
second; over all in bend sinister, a representation of the Regimental Colour of the
31st Regt. of Foot. **Crests,**—1st, out of a
mural crown or, an arm, embowed gules,
cuffed azure, grasping the Regimental Colour
of the said Regt., and pendent from the
wrist by a crimson riband, the gold cross
awarded to the 1st Lord Strafford, and on an
escroll, the word "Mouguerre"; 2nd, an
heraldic antelope statant ermine, attired and
crined or. **Supporters,**—*Dexter,* an heraldic
antelope ermine, attired and crined or;
sinister, a lion or.

Residence,—98, Cheyne Walk, S.W.10.

I will defend.

SONS LIVING. *(By 1st marriage.)*
THOMAS EDMUND *(Viscount Enfield),* *b.* Sept. 26th, 1936; ed. at Eton, and at Clare Coll., Camb.:
m. 1963, Jennifer Mary Denise, el. dau. of the late Rt. Hon. William Morrison May, M.P., of Mertoun
Hall, Holywood, co. Down, and has issue living. *Residences,*—Abbots Worthy House, Abbots
Worthy, Winchester; 23, Lamont Rd., SW10.

SONS LIVING.—*Hon.* William Robert, *b.* 1964.
Hon. James Edmund, *b.* 1969.

DAUGHTERS LIVING,—*Hon.* Georgia Mary Caroline, *b.* 1965.
Hon. Harriet Clare Tara, *b.* 1967.

Hon. Julian Francis (98, Cheyne Walk, SW10), *b.* 1938; ed. at Eton; Capt. Queen's R. Rifles (TA):
m. 1966, Ingela Brita, da. of Axel Berglund, of Stockholm, and has issue living, Francis Gustaf,
b. 1968,—George Michael Alexander, *b.* 1973.

DAUGHTERS LIVING OF SIXTH EARL.
Lady (Florence) Elizabeth Alice BYNG, *b.* 1897; resumed the surname of Byng in lieu of that of
Lafone by deed poll (enrolled at College of Arms), 1952: *m.* 1928, Michael William M. Lafone,
from whom she obtained a divorce 1931, and has issue living, Julian Michael Edmund BYNG (of
5, St. James's Sq., S.W.1), *b.* (Oct.) 1928; assumed the surname of Byng in lieu of his patronymic
by deed poll (enrolled at College of Arms) 1952; ed. at Eton, at Lausanne Univ., and at King's
Coll., Camb.; Bar. Inner Temple 1954: *m.* 1960, Eve Finola, only da. of Capt. Michael Wellesley-
Wesley, of Tahilla, co. Kerry, and has issue living, Robert Michael Julian Wentworth *b.* 1962,
Thomas Francis Edmund Wentworth, *b.* 1970, Georgiana Margaret Elizabeth *b.* 1964. *Residence,*—
Wrotham Park, Barnet, Herts.
Lady Mary Millicent Rachel, *b.* 1899: *m.* 1927, Maj.-Gen. (Robert) Francis Brydges Naylor, C.B.,
CBE, DSO, MC, late R. Signals, who *d.* 1971, and has issue living, Christopher Charles Francis,
b. 1929; late Capt. 12th Lancers: *m.* 1959, Helen Lovelock, da. of Thomas Crimmins Burke,
of Tuxedo Park, New York, USA,—Edmund John Robert (Elm House, Bentley Heath, Barnet,
Herts.), *b.* 1930; ed. at Eton, and at King's Coll., Camb.: *m.* 1956, Margaret Anne St. Aubyn,
el. da. of Col. Charles Carmichael, of The Stone House, Finmere, near Buckingham, and has issue
living, Charles Edmund Francis *b.* 1956, Katharine Elizabeth Jane *b.* 1960, Juliet Ginevra Anne
b. 1961, Rosalind Margaret Mary *b.* 1964,—Mary Elizabeth Katharine, *b.* 1933: *m.* 1966, Colin
Middleton Campbell. *Residence,*—Dancer's Hill House, Barnet, Herts.

AUNT LIVING. *(Daughter of 5th Earl.)*
Lady Hester Joan *(Joan, Countess of Cavan),* D.B.E., *b.* 1888; was Lady-in-Waiting to H.R.H.
Princess Mary 1918-22, and to H.M. the Queen (when Duchess of York) during tour of Australia and
New Zealand 1927; an Extra Lady-in-Waiting to The Princess Royal 1932-66; DBE (Civil) 1927: *m.*
1st, 1913, Capt. the Hon. Andrew Edward Somerset Mulholland, Irish Guards, who *d.* (killed
in action) 1914 [see B. Dunleath]; 2ndly, 1922, as his second wife, the 10th Earl of Cavan,
who *d.* 1946. *Residence,*—39, Knightsbridge Court, Sloane St., SW1.

COLLATERAL BRANCHES LIVING.
Issue of the late Lieut.-Col. the Hon. Antony Schomberg Byng, D.S.O., 5th son
of 5th Earl, *b.* 1876, *d.* 1934: *m.* 1902, Lucy Margaret, who *d.* 1940, youngest
dau. of Edward Howorth Greenly, of Titley Court, Herefordshire:—
William Humphrey Schomberg, *b.* 1906; ed. at Radley; European War 1939-43 as Major Intelligence
Corps in Middle East (despatches): *m.* 1935, Mona, who *d.* 1964, da. of the late Capt. Oswald
Charles Merriman Barry, DSO, RN. *Residence,*—Mangertonbeck, W. Milton, Bridport, Dorset.
Club,—White's.

Issue of the late Major the Hon. Lionel Frances George Byng, 6th son of 2nd Earl,
b. 1858, *d.* 1915: *m.* 1902, Lady Eleanor Mabel Howard, who *d.* 1945 (having *m.*
2ndly, 1922, Henry Ernest Atkinson, who *d.* 1926), dau. of 18th Earl of Suffolk
and Berkshire:—
Eleanor Myrtle Howard, *b.* 1908. *Residence,*—Manton Lodge Farm, Manton, Oakham, Rutland,
LE15 8SS.

Grandson of the late Violet Byng (who m. 1883, Edmund Distin Maddick), da. of
Capt. the Hon. William Frederick Byng, 2nd son of 1st Earl:—
Issue of the late Maj. Edmund Cecil Strafford Byng Maddick, *b.* 1884, *d.* 1965: *m.* 1918,
Onoria Doris (Weavers Cottage, Headcorn, Kent), da. of Cecil Heywood, of Heywood,
Lancs.:—
Cecil Distin Byng, *MBE* (Richmond Farm, Hawkenbury, Staplehurst, Kent), *b.* 1919; ed. at Canford;
Lord of the Manors of Wellingborough Hatton, Wellingborough Crowland and Irithlingborough,
Northants., and Patron of living of Wellingborough; 1939-45 War, as Maj., Parachute Regt. and
DAA and QMG 1st Parachute Bde.; MBE (Mil) 1946: *m.* 1942, Myra Joan, da. of Richard Fryer,
of Maidenhead, and has issue living, Antony Strafford (Richmond Cottage, Hawkenbury, Kent),
b. 1943: *m.* 1967, Meridith Caroline Chamberlain, of Melbourne, Aust., and has issue living, Nicholas

Charles Strafford, *b.* 1970,—Christopher Richard, *b.* 1945,—Susan Patricia MADDICK (124, Lexham Gdns., W8), *b.* 1950, assumed by deed poll 1975 her maiden name of Maddick: *m.* 1970 (m. diss. 1975), Jozef Ludwicki.

PREDECESSORS.—[1] *Sir* JOHN BYNG, *G.C.B.*, *G.C.H.* *P.C.*, (great-grandson of the 1st Viscount Torrington, and of Thomas Wentworth, 1st Earl of Strafford of 2nd creation 1711) was one of the most distinguished military commanders during the Peninsular War ; *b.* 1772 ; cr. *Baron Strafford* (peerage of United Kingdom) 1835, and *Viscount Enfield* and *Earl of Strafford* (peerage of United Kingdom) 1847: *m.* 1st, 1804, Mary Stevens, who *d.* 1806, da. of Peter Mackenzie, of Grove House, Middlesex; 2ndly, 1808, Marianne, who *d.* 1845, da. of Sir Walter James James (formerly Head) 1st Bt.; *d.* 1860; *s.* by his son [2] GEORGE STEVENS, *PC*, *FRS*, 2nd Earl; *b.* 1806; sat as MP for Milborne Port (*L*) 1831, for Poole 1835-7, and for Chatham 1837-52; was a Lord of the Treasury 1834, Comptroller and Treasurer of HM Queen Victoria's Household 1841, and Sec. of Board of Control 1846-7: *m.* 1st, 1829, Lady Agnes Paget, who *d.* 1845, da. of 1st Marquess of Anglesey, KG ; 2ndly, 1848, the Hon. Harriet Elizabeth Cavendish, da. of 1st Baron Chesham; *d.* Oct. 1886; *s.* by his son [3] GEORGE HENRY CHARLES, 3rd Earl, *b.* 1830; called to the House of Lords in his father's Barony of Strafford 1874; Parliamentary Sec. to Poor Law Board 1865-6, Under-Sec. of State for Foreign Affairs 1870-74, a Lord-in-Waiting to HM Queen Victoria 1880, Under-Sec. of State for India 1880-83, and First Civil Ser. Commr. (unpaid) 1880-88; Lord-Lieut. of Middlesex: *m.* 1854, Lady Alice Harriet Frederica Egerton, who *d.* 1928, da. of 1st Earl of Ellesmere, KG ; *d.* 1898; *s.* by his brother [4] HENRY WILLIAM JOHN, *K.C.V.O.*, *C.B.*, 4th Earl, *b.* 1831 ; Page of Honour to H.M. Queen Victoria 1840-47, Groom-in-Waiting 1872-4, and Equerry 1874-99 : *m.* 1st, 1863, the Countess Henrietta Daneskiold Samsoe, who *d.* 1880 ; 2ndly, 1898, Cora, who *d.* 1932, widow of S. Colgate, of U.S.A. ; *d.* 1899 ; *s.* by his brother [5] FRANCIS EDMUND CECIL, 5th Earl, *b.* 1835 ; V. of St. Peter's, S. Kensington 1867-89, and Chap. to Speaker of House of Commons 1874-89 : *m.* 1st, 1859, Florence Louisa, who *d.* 1862, dau. of Sir William Miles, 1st Bt. ; 2ndly, 1866, Emily Georgina, who *d.* 1929, el. dau. of the late Adm. Lord Frederick Herbert Kerr ; *d.* 1918 ; *s.* by his son [6] EDMUND HENRY, 6th Earl; *b.* 1862; a Co. Alderman for Middlesex and Herts : *m.* 1894, Mary Elizabeth, who *d.* 1951, dau. of Sir Thomas Edward Colebrooke, 4th Bt. ; *d.* 1951; *s.* by his nephew [7] ROBERT CECIL (son of the late Hon. Ivo Francis Byng, 4th son of 5th Earl), 7th Earl and present peer ; also Viscount Enfield, and Baron Strafford.

STRANG, BARON. (Strang.) [Baron U.K. 1954.]

WILLIAM STRANG, *G.C.B.*, *G.C.M.G.*, *M.B.E.*, 1st Baron, son of the late James Strang, of Englefield, Berks ; *b.* Jan. 2nd, 1893 ; ed. at Palmer's Sch., at Univ. Coll., London (B.A. 1912, Fellow 1946), and at the Sorbonne, Paris ; Hon. LL.D. London 1954 ; European War 1914-19 with 4th Batn. Worcestershire Regt. and Headquarters 29th Div. (M.B.E.) ; was Sec., H.M.'s Legation, Belgrade 1919-22, employed in Foreign Office 1923-30, Counsellor at H.M.'s Embassy, Moscow 1930-33, Counsellor in Foreign Office 1933-39, Assist. Under-Sec. of State, Foreign Office 1939-43, British Representative on European Advisory Commn. with rank of Ambassador 1943-45, Political Adviser to Com.-in-Ch., British Forces in Germany 1945-47, Permanent Under-Sec. of State, Foreign Office (German Section) 1947-49, Permanent Under-Sec. of State, Foreign Office 1949-53, Chm. of National Parks Commn. 1954-66, of Food Hygiene Advisory Council 1955-71. of Roy. Inst. of International Affairs 1958-66, and of Coll. Cttee., Univ. Coll., London 1963-71; a Dep. Speaker of House of Lords since 1962; cr. MBE (Mil) 1918, CMG 1932 CB (Civil) 1939, KCMG 1943, KCB (Civil) 1948. GCMG 1950. GCB (Civil) 1953, and *Baron Strang*, of Stonesfield, co. Oxford (peerage of UK) 1954: *m.* 1920, Elsie Wynne, who *d.* 1974, da. of the late J. E. Jones, of Addiscombe, and has issue.

Residence,—14, Graham Park Rd., Gosforth, Newcastle-upon-Tyne, NE3 4BH.

SON LIVING.

Hon. COLIN, *b.* June 12th, 1922; ed. at Merchant Taylors' Sch. and at St. John's Coll., Oxford (M.A., B.Phil.): *m.* 1st, 1948, Patricia Marie, da. of Meiert O. Avis, of Johannesburg, S. Africa; 2ndly, 1955, Barbara Mary Hope, dau. of Frederick Albert Carr, of Wimbledon, S.W., and has issue living, (by 2nd m.) Caroline Jane, *b.* 1957. *Residence,*—14, Graham Park Rd., Gosforth, Newcastle-ppon-Tyne, NE3 4BH.

DAUGHTER LIVING.

Hon. Jean, *b.* 1921.

STRANGE, BARON. (Drummond of Megginch.) [Baron E. 1628.]

JOHN DRUMMOND OF MEGGINCH, 15th Baron; *b.* May 6th, 1900; *s.* (on termination of abeyance) 1964; 10th of Megginch; ed. at Eton; late Lt. Grenadier Guards; author (as John Drummond) of ten books of fact and fiction: *m.* 1928, Violet Margaret Florence (PEEL), who *d.* 1975, da. of Sir Robert William Buchanan-Jardine, 2nd Bt., and has issue.

Arms,—Per fesse wavy, or and gules. Crest,—Two arms drawing an arrow to the head proper in a bow or. Supporters, *Dexter,* a naked savage wreathed about the head and middle with oak leaves, holding over his dexter shoulder a club all proper; *sinister,* a knight armed at all points, vizor of his helmet up, a spear resting on his sinister arm also proper.

Seat,—Megginch Castle, Errol, Perthshire. *Residence,*—Tholt E Will, Isle of Man. *Clubs,*—Bath, M.C.C.

DAUGHTERS LIVING. *(Co-heirs presumptive.)*

Hon. (JEAN) CHERRY, *b.* Dec. 17th, 1928; *ed.* at St. Andrew's (MA), and Camb. Univs.: *m.* 1952, Capt. Humphrey ap Evans, MC, of Megginch Castle, Errol, Perthshire, who assumed the name of Drummond of Megginch by decree of Lyon Court 1966, and has issue living, Adam Humphrey, *b.* 1953; *ed.* at Eton and RMA; Lt. Gren. Gds.,—Humphrey John Jardine, *b.* 1961; *ed.* at Eton,— John Humphrey Hugo, *b.* 1966,—Charlotte Cherry, *b.* 1955; *ed.* at Heathfield,—Amelie Margaret Mary, *b.* 1963; *ed.* at Heathfield,—Catherine Star Violetta, *b.* 1967.

Hon. HEATHER MARY, *b.* Nov. 9th, 1931: *m.* 1954, Lt.-Cdr. Andrew Christian Currey, R.N., of White Lodge, Portchester, Hants., and has issue living, Robert James Drummond, *b.* 1955,— John Andrew Fairbridge, *b.* 1959,—Arabella Mary Christian, *b.* 1958.

Hon. MARGARET APRIL IRENE, *b.* April 3rd, 1939: *m.* 1963, Quentin Charles Somerville Agnew-Somerville, of Somerville, Navan, co. Meath, el. son of Sir Peter Garnett Agnew, 1st Bt. (cr. 1957).

PREDECESSORS [1] JAMES Stanley, later 7th Earl of Derby, was summoned to Parliament by writ 1628 as *Baron Strange.* The Barony followed succession of the Earldom [2-3] until the death of 9th Earl of Derby 1702, when it fell into abeyance between his two daughters, Lady Henrietta and Lady Elizabeth Stanley. On the death of Lady Henrietta in 1714, the Barony devolved on her sister [4] *Lady* ELIZABETH, *b.* 16—: *m.* 1st, 1706, the 4th Earl of Anglesey, who *d.* 1710; 2ndly, 1714, the 1st Earl of Ashburnham, who *d.* 1737, *d.* 1718; *s.* by her da. (by 2nd m.) [5] *Lady* HENRIETTA BRIDGET Ashburnham, *b.* 17—, *d.* unm. 1732; *s.* by her Gt. Uncle [6] JAMES Stanley, 10th Earl of Derby, and 6th Baron Strange, who *d.s.p.* 1736; *s.* as Baron Strange and in the sovereignty of the Isle of Man by his kinsman [7] JAMES Murray, 2nd Duke of Atholl, K.T., and 7th Baron Strange, (grandson of Lady Amelia Ann Sophie Stanley, da. of 7th Earl of Derby and 1st Baron Strange, who *m.* 1659, John Murray, 1st Marquess of Atholl); *d.* 1764; *s.* in the Barony of Strange and in the sovereignty of the Isle of Man by his da. [8] *Lady* CHARLOTTE, *b.* 1731: *m.* 1753, her cousin, John Murray, 3rd Duke of Atholl; *d.* 1805; disposed of the sovereignty of the Isle of Man to British Gov. in 1765 for £70,000; *s.* by her el. son [9] JOHN, 4th Duke of Atholl, and 9th Baron Strange, from whom it followed succession of the Dukedom [10-14] to JAMES THOMAS, 9th Duke and 14th Baron Strange, *d.* unm. 1957, when the Barony of Strange fell into abeyance between the representatives of the three daughters of the 4th Duke, (i) Lady Charlotte Murray, who *m.* 1st, 1797, Sir John Menzies 4th Bt., who *d.* 1800; 2ndly, 1801, Adm. Sir Adam Drummond of Megginch, KCH, (ii) Lady Amelia Sophia Murray, who *m.* 1809, the 6th Viscount Strathallan [E. Perth], and (iii), Lady Elizabeth Murray, who *m.* 1808, Maj.-Gen. Sir Evan John Murray MacGregor, 2nd Bt., and so continued until 1964, when the abeyance was terminated (after petition to H.M. the Queen) in favour of [15] JOHN Drummond of Megginch (only son of Capt. Malcolm Drummond, JP, DL, 9th of Megginch, and great grandson of Lady Charlotte Drummond), 15th Baron and present peer.

Strange of Knokin, Hungerford, and de Moleyns, Baron, see Viscount St. Davids.

Strathallan, Viscount, son of Earl of Perth.

STRATHALMOND, BARON. (Fraser.) [Baron U.K. 1955.]

WILLIAM FRASER, *CMG, OBE, TD,* 2nd Baron; *b.* May 8th, 1916; *s.* 1970; *ed.* at Loretto, and Clare Coll., Camb. (MA); Bar. Inner Temple and Lincoln's Inn 1946; KStJ; Man. Dir. of Kuwait Oil Co. 1959-62, and Dir. of British Petroleum Co., Ltd. 1962-74; 1939-45 War as Lt.-Col. RASC in NW Europe (OBE, American Bronze Star; OBE (Mil) 1944, CMG 1967): *m.* 1945, Letitia, da. of the late Walter Martin Krementz, of Morristown, New Jersey, USA, and has issue.

Arms,—Tierce in pairle azure gules and sable three cinquefoils or. **Crest,**—In front of a bezant gutté d'huile a stag's head erased proper. **Supporters**—*Dexter,* a pheasant; *sinister,* a grouse proper.

Residence,—Hillfields Farm, Lower Basildon, Berks.

SON LIVING.

Hon. WILLIAM ROBERTON, *b.* July 22nd, 1947; *ed.* at Loretto: *m.* 1973, Amanda Rose, yr. da. of the Rev. Gordon Clifford Taylor, of St. Giles-in-the-Fields Rectory, Gower St., SW1.

DAUGHTERS LIVING.

Hon. Cordelia, *b.* 1949.
Hon. Christina, *b.* 1954.

SISTER LIVING.

Hon. Mary Joan, *b.* 1922: *m.* 1945, Neil Gowanloch Westbrook, and has issue living, Fraser Gowanloch, *b.* 1946,—Mary Joan, *b.* 1950: *m.* 1974, Robert Michael John Keene. *Residence,*—White Gables, Prestbury, Cheshire.

PREDECESSOR.—[1] WILLIAM Fraser, *CBE,* son of the late William Fraser, of Glasgow; *b.* 1888; Chm. of British Petroleum Co., Ltd. 1941-56; *cr. Baron Strathalmond,* of Pumpherston, co. Midlothian (peerage of UK) 1955: *m.* 1913, Mary Roberton, who *d.* 1963, da. of the late Thomson McLintock, of Glasgow; *d.* 1970; *s.* by his son [2] WILLIAM, *CMG, OBE, TD,* 2nd Baron and present peer.

Strathavon and Glenlivet, Lord, grandson of Marquess of Huntly.

STRATHCARRON, BARON   (Macpherson.)   [Baron U.K. 1936, Bt. U.K. 1933.]

DAVID WILLIAM ANTHONY BLYTH MACPHERSON, 2nd Baron, and 2nd Baronet; *b.* Jan. 23rd, 1924; *s.* 1937; ed. at Eton, and at Jesus Coll., Camb.; formerly Fl.-Lt. RAFVR; motoring correspondent of *The Field;* a Partner in the firm of Strathcarron & Co., a Dir. of Kirchoffs (London) Ltd., Kirchoffs (E. Africa) Ltd., of Seabourne Shipping Co., Ltd., and of Dorada Holdings Ltd.; Pres. of Guild of Motoring Writers; author of *Motoring for Pleasure*: *m.* 1st (Feb.), 1947 (m. annulled on his petition Sept. 1947), Valerie Cole; 2ndly, 1948, Diana Hawtry, who *d,* 1973, da. of the late Cdr. R. H. Deane, of Cooden, Sussex, and formerly wife of J.N.O. Curle; 3rdly, 1974, Mary Eve, da. of the late John Comyn Higgins, CIE, and formerly wife of the Hon. Anthony Gerald Samuel [see V. Bearsted], and has issue by 2nd marriage.

Arms,—Per fesse or and azure a galley of the first, masts, oars, and tackling proper, flagged gules, in the dexter chief point a hand couped fesseways holding a dagger paleways, and in the sinister a cross-crosslet fitchée of the last; over all a fesse chequy of the second and argent. Crest,—A cat-a-mountain sejant guardant, and having its dexter paw raised proper. Supporters—*Dexter*, a private soldier of the Cameron Highlanders in field service dress of the period 1916-18; *sinister*, a Macpherson clansman of the period 1745.

Residences,—55, Cumberland Terr., Regents Park, N.W.1; Otterwood, Beaulieu, Hants.

SONS LIVING.   (*By 2nd m.*)
Hon. IAN DAVID PATRICK, *b.* March 31st, 1949.
Hon. Andrew Charles James, *b.* 1959.

SISTERS LIVING.

Hon. Fiona (*Hon. Lady Runge*), *b.* 1917: *m.* 1935, Sir Peter Francis Runge, who *d.* 1970, and has issue living, Anthony Peter, *b.* 1937; ed. at Eton, and Trin. Coll., Oxford: *m.* 1970, Mrs. Susan Grievson. da. of Denis Cooil, of Struan, Balla Salla, I. of Man,—Charles David (45, Merthyr Terr., Barnes), *b.* 1944; ed. at Eton, and Ch. Ch., Oxford: *m.* 1967, Harriet, da. of John Bradshaw, of Withers, Inkpen, Berks.,—Michael Robert, *b.* 1947,—Julia Norah (Little Finings, Lane End, High Wycombe), *b.* 1939: *m.* 1958 ,Michael D'Arcy Stephens ,[B. McGowan] and has issue living, D'Arcy Mark, *b.* 1965, Katherine Alison *b.* 1960. *Residence,*—The Brick House, Cadmore Common, High Wycombe, Bucks., HP14 3PS.

Hon. Ann Patricia (*Hon. Lady Lowson*) (Carmurie, Elie, Fife; Oratory Cottage, 33, Ennismore Gdns. Mews, SW7 1H2) *b.* 1919; is an OStJ: *m.* 1936, Sir Denys Colquhoun Flowerdew Lowson, 1st Bt., who *d.* 1975.

PREDECESSOR.—[1] *Rt. Hon.* (JAMES) IAN Macpherson, *P.C., K.C.,* son of James Macpherson J.P., of Inverness; *b.* 1880; M.P. for Ross and Cromarty (*L*) 1911-18, and for Inverness-shire Ross-shire and Cromarty, Ross and Cromarty Div. 1918-35; successively Parliamentary Under Sec. of State for War, Dep. Sec. of State and Vice-Pres. of Army Council, Ch. Sec. for Ireland, and Min. of Pensions; cr. a *Baronet* 1933, and *Baron Strathcarron*, of Banchor, co. Inverness (peerage of United Kingdom) 1936 : *m.* 1915, Jill, who *d.* 1956, dau. of Sir George Wood Rhodes, J.P., 1st Bt.; *d.* 1937; *s.* by his only son [2] DAVID WILLIAM ANTHONY BLYTH, 2nd Baron and present peer.

STRATHCLYDE, BARON. (Galbraith.) [Baron U.K. 1955.]

THOMAS DUNLOP GALBRAITH, *P.C.*, 1st Baron, son of the late William Brodie Galbraith, J.P., of Overton, Kilmacolm, Renfrewshire ; *b.* March 20th, 1891 ; Hon. F.R.C.P. Edinburgh 1960, and Hon. Fellow, Roy. Coll. of Physicians and Surgeons, Glasgow 1961 ; Com. R.N. (retired), a Chartered Accountant, and an Hon. Gov. of Glasgow Acad. ; was a Member of Glasgow Corporation 1933-40, and Magistrate 1938-40, Joint Parliamentary Under-Sec. of State for Scotland May to Aug. 1945, and again Nov. 1951 to April 1955, and Min. of State, Scottish Office April 1955 to Oct. 1958 ; a Gov. of Wellington Coll. 1947-61; Chm. of North of Scotland Hydro-Electric Board 1959-67; European War 1914-18, European War 1939-45 on Staff of Com.-in-Ch., Coast of Scotland, and as Dep. British Admiralty Supply Representative in USA; MP for Pollock Div. of Glasgow (*U*) 1940-55; a Freeman of Dingwall and Aberdeen; cr. PC 1953 and *Baron Strathclyde*, of Barskimming, co. Ayr (peerage of United Kingdom) 1955: *m.* 1915, Ida Jean, da. of the late Thomas Galloway, JP, of Auchendrane, Ayrshire, and has issue.

Ârms,—Gules, three bears' heads erased argent, muzzled azure, within a bordure indented or charged with three mullets of the third, a crescent of the second for difference. Crest,—A bear's head erased gules, muzzled argent. Supporters,—Two bears gules, muzzled argent.
Residence,—Barskimming, Mauchline, Ayrshire. *Clubs*,—United Service, Carlton, New (Edinburgh), Western (Glasgow), Conservative (Glasgow).

SONS LIVING.

Hon. THOMAS GALLOWAY DUNLOP, *MP*, *b.* March 10th, 1917; ed. at Wellington, and Ch. Ch., Oxford (MA), and at Glasgow Univ. (LLB); is a Gov. of Wellington Coll., and a Member of Queen's Body Guard for Scotland (Roy. Co. of Archers); 1939-45 War as Lt. RNVR; Assist. Conservative Whip March to Nov. 1950, and Scottish Unionist Whip 1951-54, a Lord Commr. of the Treasury 1951-54, Comptroller of HM Household 1954-55, Treasurer of HM Household 1955-57, Civil Lord of the Admiralty, and Chm. of Cttee. on Nuclear Propulsion for Merchant Ships 1957-59, Joint Parl. Under-Sec. of State for Scotland 1959-62 and Joint Parl. Sec., Min. of Transport 1963-64; MP for Hillhead Div. of Glasgow (*U*) since 1948: *m.* 1956 (m. diss. 1974), Simone Clothilde Fernande Marie Ghislaine, el. da. of the late Jean du Roy de Blicquy, of Belgium, and has issue living, Thomas Galloway Dunlop du Roy de Blicquy, *b.* 1960,—Charles William du Roy de Blicquy, *b.* 1962,—Anne Marie Ghislaine du Roy, *b.* 1957. *Residence*,—Barskimming, Mauchline, Ayrshire. *Clubs*,—Carlton, New (Edinburgh), Conservative (Glasgow).
Hon. James Muir Galloway, *b.* 1920; ed. at RN Coll., Dartmouth, Ch. Ch., Oxford (MA): Lt. RN; 1939-42 War (wounded, invalided): *m.* 1945, Anne, el. da. of Maj. Kenneth Paget, of Old Rectory House, Itchen Abbas, Hants., and has issue living, Brodie Thomas Paget, *b.* 1948,—James Muir Paget, *b.* 1955,—John Kenneth Paget, *b.* 1956,—Sara Caroline Paget, *b.* 1950. *Residence*,—Carterhaugh, Selkirk.
Hon. Norman Dunlop Galloway, *b.* 1925; ed. at Wellington Coll.; a Dir. of Ben Line Steamers Ltd. since 1968; 1939-45 War as Sub-Lieut. RNVR: *m.* 1950, Susan Patricia, el. da. of Com. J. H. F. Kent, of La Coupe, St. Martin, Jersey, Channel Islands, and has issue living, Norman Thomas Galloway, *b.* 1955,—Patricia Jane, *b.* 1951,—Diana Susan, *b.* 1954. *Residence*,—Pilmuir, Haddington, E. Lothian.
Hon. David Muir Galloway, *b.* 1928; ed. at Wellington Coll., and at Roy. Agricultural Coll., Cirencester: *m.* 1967, Marion Bingham, da. of Maj. Bruce Bingham Kennedy, TD, of Doonholm, Ayr, and has issue living, William James Kennedy *b.* 1970,—Fiona Jane Kennedy, *b.* 1968,—Mary Ida Galloway, *b.* 1973. *Residence*,—Burnbrae Lodge, Mauchline, Ayrshire.

DAUGHTERS LIVING.

Hon. Ida Jean Galloway, *b.* 1922; 1939-45 War as 3rd Officer WRNS.
Hon. Heather Margaret Anne Galloway, *b.* 1930.

STRATHCONA AND MOUNT ROYAL, BARON. (Howard.) [Baron U.K. 1900.]

DONALD EUAN PALMER HOWARD, 4th Baron ; *b.* Nov. 26th, 1923 ; *s.* 1959 ; ed. at Eton, at Trin. Coll., Camb., and at McGill Univ., Montreal; late Lt. RNVR; a DL for Angus; a Lord in Waiting to HM, and a Govt. Whip 1973-74, and Parl. Under-Sec. of State for RAF Jan. to March 1974: *m.* 1954, Lady Jane Mary Waldegrave, da. of 12th Earl Waldegrave, and has issue.

Ârms,—Quarterly, 1st and 4th argent, on a bend indented between four cross-crosslets gules, three maple leaves or ; 2nd and 3rd gules, on a fess argent, between a demi-lion rampant or in chief, and a canoe of the last with four men rowing proper, in the stern a flag of the second flowing towards the dexter inscribed with the letters N.W. sable, in base a hammer surmounted of a nail in saltire of the last. Crest,—On a mount vert a beaver eating into a maple tree proper. Supporters,—*Dexter*, a trooper of the Regiment of Strathcona's Horse proper ; *sinister*, a navvy standing on a railway sleeper, chaired and railed all proper.
Seat,—Isle of Colonsay, Argyll, 89, Barkston Gdns. SW5 0EU. *Club*,—Brooks's.

A leader of men.

SONS LIVING.
Hon. DONALD ALEXANDER SMITH, *b.* June 24th, 1961.
Hon. Andrew Barnaby, *b.* 1963.

DAUGHTERS LIVING.
Hon. Jane Elisabeth Stirling, *b.* 1955.
Hon. Katharine Mary, *b,* 1956: *m.* 1975, Gavin M. J. Strachan.
Hon. Caroline Anne, *b.* 1959.
Hon. Emma Laura Louise (twin), *b.* 1963.

BROTHERS LIVING.
Hon. Barnaby John, *b.* 1925; ed. at Eton, and at Trin. Coll., Camb. (B.A. Law 1948, M.A. 1954); appointed Commr., S. Rhodesian Forestry Commn. 1957; European War 1943-45 as Sub-Lt. RNVR (Air Branch): *m.* 1st, 1952 (m. diss. 1967), Elizabeth, da. of Frank M. Mayfield, of 300, McKnight Rd., St. Louis, Missouri, USA; 2ndly, 1970, Mrs. F. N. H. Bishop, da. of the late Ambrose Chambers, and has issue living, (by 1st m.) Alan Sterling, *b.* 1956,—Elizabeth Kiloran, *b.* 1957,—Sarah Ann Catriona, *b.* 1962. *Addresses,*—Beaverdam Farm, PO Box 238, Umtali, Rhodesia; PO Box 246, Pine Brook Rd., Bedford, NY, USA 10506; Stann's Bay, PO Englishtown, Nova Scotia, Canada. *Club,*—Royal Aero.
Hon. Jonathan Alan (Sporrvaegen 8, Jakobsberg, Sweden) *b.* 1933; ed. at Eton, Trin. Coll., Camb., R. Inst. of Tech., Stockholm, and Stockholm Univ.; late 2nd Lt. Coldstream Guards, and Argyll & Sutherland Highlanders (TA): *m.* 1st 1956 (m. diss. 1969), the Hon. Brigid Mary Westenra, da. of 6th Baron Rossmore; 2ndly, 1970, Cecilia Philipson, and has issue living (by 1st m.), Nicola Charlotte, *b.* 1958,—Kiloran Emma, *b.* 1959,—(by 2nd m.) Olof Philipson, *b.* 1970.

SISTER LIVING
Hon. Diana Catriona, *b.* 1935: *m.* 1956, Michael Leslie Ogilvy Faber of The Mill, Bawburgh, Norwich, NOR 46X, and has issue living, Rory Valdemar, *b.* 1956,—Guy Donald George, *b.* 1959,—Laura Diana, *b.* 1958,—Charlotte Victoria (twin), *b.* 1958.

AUNT LIVING. (*Daughter of Margaret Charlotte, Baroness Strathcona and Mount Royal.*)
Hon. Edith Mary Palmer CONGLETON, *M.B.E.*, *b.* 1895; formerly Assist. Co. Organiser for S. Hampshire Women's Vol. Sers. ; formerly County Councillor for Hants; assumed by deed poll 1951, the surname of Congleton in lieu of that of Aldridge ; has Order of Mercy with Bar ; M.B.E. (Civil) 1941 : *m.* 1st, 1918, the 6th Baron Congleton, who *d.* 1932 ; 2ndly, 1946, Flight-Lieut. Alfred Eric Rowland Aldridge, who *d.* 1950. *Residences,*—61, Furzecroft, George Street, W.1; Ulva House, Isle of Ulva, by Mull, Argyll.

WIDOW LIVING OF SON OF MARGARET CHARLOTTE, BARONESS STRATHCONA AND MOUNT ROYAL.
Lady Leonora Stanley Baldwin (Wappingthorn, Steyning, Sussex; 6, Chesterfield SY, W1), da. of 1st Earl Baldwin of Bewdley: *m.* 1922, Capt. the Hon. Sir Arthur Jared Palmer Howard, KBE, CVO, who *d.* 1971, and has issue [see colls. infra.].

WIDOW LIVING OF THIRD BARON.
Hon. DIANA EVELYN LODER (*Diana, Baroness Strathcona and Mount Royal*), dau. of 1st Baron Wakehurst: *m.* 1922, the 3rd Baron, who *d.* 1959. *Residence,*—Headbourne Worthy Grange, Winchester.

COLLATERAL BRANCH LIVING.
Issue of the late Capt. the Hon. Sir Arthur Jared Palmer Howard, KBE, CVO, yst. son of Margaret Charlotte, Baroness Strathcona and Mount Royal, *b.* 1896, *d.* 1971: *m.* 1922, Lady Leonora Stanley Baldwin, (ante), da. of 1st Earl Baldwin of Bewdley:—

Robin Jared Stanley, *b.* 1924; ed. at Eton, and Trin. Coll., Camb. (MA); 1939-45 War with Scot Gds.——Alexander (Wappingthorn, Steyning, Sussex), *b.* 1930; ed. at Eton, and Trin. Coll. Camb. (MA): *m.* 1959, Penelope Joanna, da. of Gershom Radcliffe Layton Warren, of Saanichton BC, Canada, and has issue living, Shamus Alexander, *b.* 1962,—Harry Alexander, *b.* 1967,—Rory Jared, *b.* 1973.——Kiloran Margaret (*Hon. Mrs. Langley G. H. Russell*), *b.* 1926: *m.* 1951, the Hon. Langley Gordon Haslingden Russell, MC, who *d.* 1975 [see B. Russell of Liverpool].——Jill, *b.* 1934: *m.* 1958, Peter James Scott Lumsden, of 24, Holland Villas Rd., W14, and has issue living, James Herbert, *b.* 1962,—Alice Margaret, *b.* 1961,—Susanna Helen, *b.* 1965.

PREDECESSORS.—[1] *Sir* DONALD ALEXANDER Smith, *G.C.M.G., G.C.V.O., D.C.L., LL.D., F.R.S.*, son of the late Alexander Smith, of Archieston, Scotland , *b.* 1820 ; entered Hudson Bay Co.'s Ser. at an early age, and was last Resident Gov. of that Corporation as a governing body ; was Special Commr. during 1st Riel Rebellion in Red River Settlements 1869-70 (thanked by Gov.-Gen. in Council) ; appointed a M.E.C. (first) of N.W. Territory 1870 ; represented Winnipeg and St. John's in Manitoba Legislature 1871-84 ; elected M.P. for Selkirk in Canadian House of Commons 1871, 1872, 1874, and 1878, and for Montreal West 1887 and 1891, which constituency he represented until 1896 ; sworn P.C. Canada 1896, and was appointed High Commr. in Great Britain for the Dominion 1896 ; raised a body of mounted troops—Strathcona's Horse—for service in S. Africa 1900 ; cr. G.C.M.G. 1896, G.C.V.O. 1908, *Baron Strathcona and Mount Royal*, of Glencoe, co. Argyll, and Mount Royal, Quebec, Canada (peerage ot United Kingdom) 1897, and *Baron Strathcona and Mount Royal*, of Mount Royal, Quebec, Canada, and Glencoe, co. Argyll (peerage of UK) 1900, with special remainder in default of male issue to his only da. Margaret Charlotte, and her heirs male: *m.* 1853, Isabella Sophia, who *d.* 1913, dau. of the late Richard Hardisty, of Canada ; *d.* 1914, when the Barony (cr. 1897) became ext., while in that of 1900 he was *s.* under the special remainder by his only dau. [2] MARGARET CHARLOTTE Howard, *b.* 1854 : *m.* 1888, Robert Jared Bliss Howard, O.B.E., F.R.C.S., who *d.* 1921 ; *d.* 1926 ; *s.* by her son [3] DONALD STIRLING PALMER Howard, 3rd Baron ; *b.* 1891 ; Major London Scottish (T.A.) ; was M.P. for Cumberland, N. Div. (*U*) 1922-26, Parliamentary Private Sec. (unpaid) to Parliamentary Sec. to Min. of Labour 1923-4, Parliamentary Private Sec. to First Lord of the Admiralty 1925-7, and Under-Sec. of State for War and Vice-Pres. of Army Council 1934-39 ; appointed Capt. of Yeomen of the Guard 1931 ; *m.* 1922 the Hon. Diana Evelyn Loder, dau. of 1st Baron Wakehurst ; *d.* 1959 ; *s.* by his son [4] DONALD EUAN PALMER, 4th Baron and present peer.

STRATHEDEN AND CAMPBELL, BARON. (Campbell.) [Baron U.K. 1836.]

ALASTAIR CAMPBELL, *CBE*, 4th Baron; *b.*
Nov. 21st, 1899; *s.* 1918; ed. at Eton; Hon.
LL.D. Edinburgh Univ.; Brig. (ret.) late
Coldstream Guards (Col. Comdg. 1945-6), and
Ensign, Queen's Body Guard for Scotland
(Roy. Co. of Archers); Staff Officer, Local
Forces Kenya and Uganda 1936-9, Comdg.
32nd Guards Bde. and 4th Inf. Bde. 1946-9,
and Dep. Dir. of Personal Sers., War Office
1949-50; Chm. of Edinburgh and E. of Scot-
land Coll. of Agriculture 1956-70, and of
Roxburgh, Berwick and Selkirk, Territorial
and Auxiliary Forces Assocn. 1958-63, and
Hill Farming Research Organization 1958-69,
Convener, Roxburgh Co. Council 1960-68,
Vice-Lieut. of Roxburghshire since 1962,
and Pres. of Assocn. of Co. Councils in Scot-

AUDACTER ET APERTE

Boldly and openly.

land 1966-68; Chm., Historic Buildings
Council for Scotland since 1969; 1939-45 War (wounded, despatches); CBE
(Civil) 1964: *m.* 1st, 1923, Jean Helen St. Clair, *CBE*, who *d.* 1956, da. of
Col. William Anstruther-Gray [Anstruther, Bt. colls.]; 2ndly, 1964, Mrs. Noël
Christabel Vincent, da. of the late Capt. Conrad Viner, and has issue by 1st m.

Arms,—Gyronny of eight or and sable, within a bordure engrailed quarterly, or and azure
charged with eight buckles counterchanged. *Crest,*—A boar's head erased, gyronny of eight, of
and sable. *Supporters,*—(*Barony of Stratheden*) On either side a buck argent, attired and hoofed
or, that on the dexter gorged with a collar counter-compony gules and of the second, therefrom
pendent an escutcheon gyronny of eight or and sable and that on the sinister gorged with a collar or,
therefrom pendent an escutcheon gold, charged with three chaplets of laurel two and one proper.—
(*Barony of Campbell*) On either side a lion guardant gules, that on the *dexter* gorged with a collar or,
pendant therefrom an escutcheon azure, charged with a saltire argent, and that on the *sinister*
gorged with a wreath of shamrocks proper, therefrom an escutcheon checky or and gules.

Seat—Hunthill, Jedburgh. *Clubs,*—Guards', New (Edinburgh).

DAUGHTERS LIVING. (*By 1st marriage.*)

Hon. Moyra Jean, *b.* 1924.
Hon. Clayre (212, Lambeth Rd., SE1), *b.* 1927: *m.* 1950 (m. diss. 1974), the Hon. Nicholas Ridley, MP
[see V. Ridley].
Hon. Fiona, *b.* 1932.

BROTHER LIVING. (*Raised to the rank of a Baron's son* 1921.)

Hon. GAVIN, *b.* Aug. 28th, 1901 ; ed. at Eton ; is Major (retired) King's Roy. Rifle Corps and
Lieut.-Col. 19th (Kenya) Batn. King's African Rifles; European War 1939-45 in Abyssinia and
Madagascar: *m.* 1933, Evelyn Mary Austen, dau. of the late Col. Herbert Austen Smith, C.I.E., and
has issue living, Donald (Lara, Ballinger Rd., Buderim, Qld. 5446, Aust.), *b.* 1934: *m.* 1957, Hilary
Ann Holland, da. of Lt.-Col. W. D. Turner, of Simonstown, S. Africa, and has issue living, David
Anthony *b.* 1963, Tania Ann *b.* 1960, Wendy Meriel *b.* 1969, Joyce Margaret *b.* 1971. *Address,*—
16, Kings Park Av., Crawley, W. Aust. 6009. *Club,*—Lansdowne.

COLLATERAL BRANCH LIVING.

Issue of the late Hon. Kenneth Hallyburton Campbell, 3rd son of 3rd baron, *b.*
1871, *d.* 1947 : *m.* 1905, Rosalinda Emily, who *d.* 1960, dau. of the late Henry
Maurice William Oppenheim [B. Dunboyne, colls.] :—

Ian George Hallyburton, *QC, b.* 1909: ed. at Charterhouse, and at Trin. Coll., Camb. (MA); Bar-at-law
Inner Temple and Lincoln's Inn 1932, and a QC 1957; Hon. Col. Rifle Bde.; 1939-45 War in
France and N. Africa: served with Allied Commn. Italy and Allied Mil. Govt. Austria; Lord
Chancellor's Legal Visitor 1963: *m.* 1949, Betty Yolande, da. of the late Somerset Maclean, and
widow of Lt.-Col. (Hugh) Allan Bruno, MBE. *Residence,*—Greywalls, Liphook, Hants. *Clubs,*—
Boodle's, Brooks's.

PREDECESSORS.—[1] JOHN Campbell, *PC*; *b.* 1779; a distinguished lawyer, judge, and bio-
graphical writer; sat successively as MP for Stafford, Dudley, and Edinburgh (*L*), and
having held for many years the offices of Solicitor-Gen. and Attorney-Gen., was in 1841 appointed Lord Chancellor of Ireland, and cr. *Baron Campbell,* of St. Andrews, co. Fife (peerage of
United Kingdom); was Chancellor of the Duchy of Lancaster 1846, Lord Ch. Justice of England
1850-9, and Lord High Chancellor of Great Britain 1859-61: *m.* 1821, the Hon. Mary Elizabeth
Scarlett (dau. of 1st Baron Abinger), who in 1836 was cr. in her own right *Baroness Stratheden,* of
Cupar, co. Fife (peerage of United Kingdom); *d.* 1861; *s.* by his son [2] WILLIAM FREDERICK,
2nd Baron, who in 1860 had *s.* his mother as 2nd Baron Stratheden, *b.* 1824; M.P. for Cambridge
(*L*) 1847-52, and for Harwich 1859-60; *d.* 1893; *s.* by his brother [3] HALLYBURTON GEORGE,
3rd Baron, *b.* 1829 : *m.* 1865, Louisa Mary, who *d.* 1923, el. dau. of the late Rt. Hon. Alexander
James Beresford Beresford-Hope, M.P.; *d.* 1918; *s.* by his grandson [4] ALASTAIR (son of the late
Capt. the Hon. John Beresford Campbell, D.S.O., son of 3rd Baron), 4th Baron and present peer;
also Baron Campbell.

STRATHMORE AND KINGHORNE, EARL OF. (Bowes Lyon.) [Earl S. 1606 and 1677, Earl U.K. 1937.]

In Thee, O Lord, have I put my trust.

FERGUS MICHAEL CLAUDE BOWES LYON, 17th Earl; *b.* Dec. 31st, 1928; *s.* 1972; formerly Capt. Scots Gds.: *m.* 1956, Mary Pamela, yr. da. of Brig. Norman Duncan McCorquodale, MC, and has issue.

Arms,—Quarterly: 1st and 4th argent, a lion rampant azure, armed and langued gules, within a double tressure flory counterflory of the second, *Lyon;* 2nd and 3rd ermine, three bows, strings palewise proper, *Bowes.* Royal Augmentation (granted to the holder of the Earldom only)—An inescutcheon en surtout azure, thereon a rose argent, barbed vert, seeded or, ensigned with an Imperial Crown proper, within a double tressure flory-counterflory of the second, the said inescutcheon ensigned with an Earl's coronet proper. Crest,—Between two slips of laurel, a lady to the girdle, habited, and holding in her right hand a thistle all proper. Supporters,—*Dexter,* a unicorn argent, armed, unguled, maned, and tufted or; *sinister,* a lion per fesse or and gules.

Seat,—Glamis Castle, co. Angus. *Residence,*—Holwick Hall, Middleton-in-Teesdale, co. Durham.

SON LIVING.

MICHAEL FERGUS, (*Lord Glamis*), *b.* June 7th, 1957; a Page of Honour to HM Queen Elizabeth The Queen Mother 1971-73.

DAUGHTERS LIVING.

Lady Elizabeth Mary Cecilia, *b.* 1959.
Lady Diana Evelyn, *b.* 1966.

BROTHER LIVING. (*Raised to the rank of an Earl's son 1974.*)
Hon. Michael Albemarle, *b.* 1940; ed. at Eton.

SISTERS LIVING. (*Raised to the rank of an Earl's daughters 1974.*)
Lady Mary Cecilia, *b.* 1932; appointed an Extra Lady-in-Waiting to HRH Princess Alexandra, the Hon. Mrs. Angus Ogilvy, 1970: *m.* 1951, Timothy James Alan Colman, late Lt. RN, of Bixley Manor, Norwich, NOR 04W, and has issue living, James Russell, *b.* 1962,—Matthew Geoffrey, *b.* 1966,—Sarah Rose, *b.* 1953,—Sabrina Mary, *b.* 1955,—Emma Elizabeth, *b.* 1958.
Lady Patricia Maud (twin) (Abbey Lodge, Wymondham, Norfolk), *b.* 1932: *m.* 1964 (m. diss. 1970), Oliver Robin Tetley, and has issue living, Alexander, *b.* 1965.

AUNT LIVING. (*Daughter of 14th Earl.*)
Lady Elizabeth Angela Marguerite (*H.M. Queen Elizabeth The Queen Mother*), *b.* 1900 [see " ROYAL FAMILY "]: *m.* April 26th, 1923, H.M. King George VI., who *d.* Feb. 6th, 1952. *Residences,*—Clarence House, S.W.1; Royal Lodge, Windsor Great Park, Berkshire; Castle of Mey, Caithness.

WIDOW LIVING OF SON OF FOURTEENTH EARL
Rachel Pauline (*Hon. Lady Bowes-Lyon*), dau. of the late Col. the Rt. Hon. Herbert Spender-Clay, C.M.G., M.C., M.P. [V. Astor]: *m.* 1929, the Hon. Sir David Bowes-Lyon, K.C.V.O., who *d.*1961, and has issue living [see colls., infra]. *Residence,*—St. Pauls Walden Bury, Hitchin, Herts.

COLLATERAL BRANCHES LIVING. (*Not in remainder to United Kingdom Earldom.*)
Issue of the late Hon. John Herbert Bowes-Lyon, 2nd son of 14th Earl, *b.* 1886, *d.* 1930: *m.* 1914, the Hon. Fenella Hepburn-Stuart-Forbes-Trefusis, who *d.* 1966 dau. of 21st Baron Clinton :—
Anne Ferelith (*H.H. Princess Anne of Denmark*) (of 81, Carlisle Mansions, Carlisle Place, S.W.1), *b.* 1917: *m.* 1938, Lt.-Col. Viscount Anson, late Grenadier Gds. (who *d.* 1958, and from whom she had obtained a divorce 1948), el. son of 4th Earl of Lichfield; 2ndly, 1950, H.H. Prince Georg of Denmark, CVO.——Diana Cinderella, *b.* 1923: *m.* 1960, Peter Gordon Somervell, son of the late Sir Arnold Colin Somervell, OBE, DL. *Residence,*—Fettercairn House, Fettercairn, Kincardineshire.

Issue of the late Capt. the Hon. Fergus Bowes-Lyon, Black Watch (Roy. Highlanders), 4th son of 14th Earl, *b.* 1889, *d.* (killed in action during European War) 1915: *m.* 1914, Lady Christian Norah Dawson-Damer (ante) (who *d.* 1959, having *m.* 2ndly, 1919, Capt. William F. Martin, who *d.* 1947), dau. of 6th Earl of Portarlington :—
Rosemary Lusia, *b.* 1915: *m.* 1945, Edward Wilfrid George Joicey-Cecil [see M. Exeter, colls.]. *Residence,*—Braddocks, Solefields, Sevenoaks, Kent.

Issue of the late Hon. Sir David Bowes-Lyon, K.C.V.O., youngest son of 14th Earl, *b.* 1902, *d.* 1961 : *m.* 1929, Rachel Pauline (ante), dau. of the late Col. the Rt. Hon. Herbert Spender-Clay, C.M.G., M.C., M.P. [V. Astor] :—
Simon Alexander (Bury Farm, St. Pauls Walden, Hitchin, Herts); *b.* 1932: *m.* 1966, Caroline, da. of the Rt. Rev. Victor Joseph Pike, Bishop Suffragan of Sherborne, and has issue living, Fergus Alexander, *b.* 1970,—David Victor, *b.* 1973,—Rosemary Pema, *b.* 1968.——Davina Katharine (*Countess of Stair*), *b.* 1930: *m.* 1960, the 13th Earl of Stair. *Residence,*—Lochinch Castle, Stranraer, Wigtowshire.

Grandchildren of the late Hon. Francis Bowes-Lyon, 2nd son of 13th Earl:—
Issue of the late Capt. Geoffrey Frances Bowes-Lyon, Black Watch (Roy. Highlanders), *b.* 1886, *d.* 1951: *m.* 1914, Edith Katharine, who *d.* 1971, da. of Sir Lewis Amherst Selby-Bigge, KCB, 1st Bt.:—
r Francis James Cecil, *KCVO, CB, OBE, MC* (Highfield House, Slindon, Arundel, Sussex; White's Club), *b.* 1917; ed. at Eton; Maj.-Gen. (ret.) late Gren. Gds.; GOC 52 (Lowland) Div. Dist. 1966-68, GOC Comdg. Berlin (British Sector) 1968-70, and GOC London Dist. and Maj.-Gen. Co mdg. The Household Div. 1971-73; a Gentleman Usher to HM since 1974; NW Europe 1944-45 (MC and Bar), OBE (Mil) 1962, CB (Mil) 1970, KCVO 1973: *m.* 1941, Mary, da. of the late Sir Humphrey Edmund de Trafford, MC, 4th Bt., and has issue living, John Francis, *b.* 1942,—David James, *b.* 1947,—Fiona Ann, *b.* 1944: *m.* 1966, Joseph Henry Goodhart, of Ellerker House, Everingham, York.——Anne Caroline Lindsay, *b.* 1916: *m.* 1939, Lewellyn Ross Llewellyn, and has issue living, Charles Llewellyn, *b.* 1943,—Simon Lindsay, *b.* 1945.——Susannah Sarah, *b.* 1920: *m.* 1940, Peter Hugh Dudley Ryder, MBE, Hon. Lt.-Col. late R. Armoured Corps TA Reserve; [see E. Harrowby, cols.]. *Residence,*—The Spanish House, Wardija, Malta, GC.

Grandchildren of the late Hon. Ernest Bowes-Lyon (infra):—
Issue of the late Hubert Ernest Bowes-Lyon, *b.* 1883, *d.* 1959 : *m.* 1st, (Jan.) 1905, Mary
Agnes, who *d.* 1914, da. of James Hay Smeaton; 2ndly, 1919, Margaret, who *d.* 1966, da. of
Frank Nuttall, of Belfast, and widow of J. Graham:—

By 1st m.) Hubert Ernest Malcolm, *b.* 1907; Flight-Lt. RAF Reserve: *m.* 1943 (m. diss. 1964),
Fanny Rose Jacobs, who *d.* 1969, and has issue living, Jennifer Merrill, *b.* 1944.——Douglas Ian
Gordon, *b.* 1912.——Constance Mary (Mbombura House, PO Box 1137, Blantyre, Malawi), *b.* (Dec.)
1904; obtained a decree of legitimation by Court of Session, Edinburgh, June 1924: *m.* 1933, George
Clark Dow, who *d.* 1967.——(By 2nd m.) Sonia Gabrielle, *b.* 1922: *m.* 1948, Lt.-Col. Stephen Otteran
Murphy MBE, of Higher Polgrain, St. Wenn, Bodmin.

Issue of the late Hon. Ernest Bowes-Lyon, 3rd son of 13th Earl, *b.* 1858, *d.* 1891
m. 1882, Issobel Hester, who *d.* 1945, dau. of the late Harvey Drummond
[E. Perth, colls.]:—
Marjorie Effie (*Lady Winter*) (Cherry Leaf Cottage, Langport Rd., Somerton, Som.), *b.* 1889: *m.* 1st,
1909, Capt. Douglas Walkden Roberts, RA, who *d.* 1920; 2ndly, 1924, Richmond Campbell Pinder,
who *d.* 1926; 3rdly, 1927, Brig.-Gen. Sir Ormonde de l'Epée Winter, KCB, CB, CMG, DSO, who
d. 1962, and has issue living, (by 1st marriage) Daphne Ernestine, *b.* 1915.——Ernestine Hester
Maud, *b.* 1891: *m.* 1st, 1910, Francis Winstone Scott; 2ndly, 1918, Ronald Charles Grant, 10th
Baron de Longueüil (cr. France 1700), who *d.* 1959, and has issue living, (by 1st marriage) Anthony
Leonard, *b.* 1911,—Patrick Drummond, *b.* 1913,—(by 2nd marriage) Raymond David, *b.* 1921; 11th
Baron de Longueüil: *m.* 1946, Anne Patricia, da. of the late Patrick Brough Maltby, and has issue
living, Michael Charles *b.* 1947. *Residence,*—Navarreux, France, BP.

Issue of the late Hon. Patrick Bowes-Lyon, 5th son of 13th Earl, *b.* 1863, *d.* 1946 :
m. 1893, Alice Wiltshire, who *d.* 1953, ward of the late Capt. Arthur Lister-Kaye,
of Manor House, Stretton-on-Dunsmore:—
Margaret Anne, *b.* 1907 : *m.* 1945, Lieut.-Col. Francis Arthur D'Abreu, E.R.D., Ch.M., F.R.C.S.,
late RAMC, and has issue living, Anthony Patrick John, *b.* 1946: *m.* 1967, Rachel Green, and has
issue,—Francesca Ann, *b.* 1948: *m.* 1970, Kieran Fogarty,—Anna Teresa, *b.* 1950. *Residences,*—
36, Cumberland Terr., Regents Park, NW1; Thatch Cottage, Hambleden, Henley-on-Thames.

Issue of the late Lieut.-Col. the Hon. Malcolm Bowes-Lyon, C.B.E., youngest son
of 13th Earl; *b.* 1874, *d.* 1957 : *m.* 1907, Winifred, who *d.* 1957, dau. of Hector
John Gurdon-Rebow, J.P., formerly of Wyvenhoe Park, Essex:—
Clodagh Pamela (*Pamela, Lady Lever*) (Lessudden, St. Boswells, Roxburghshire), *b.* 1908: *m.* 1st, 1931
(m. diss. 1952), Lord Malcolm Avondale Douglas-Hamilton, OBE, DFC, RAF, who *d.* 1964 [see D.
Hamilton and Brandon]; 2ndly, 1962, Sir Tresham Joseph Philip Lever, 2nd Bt., who *d.* 1975.

PREDECESSORS.—[1] PATRICK Lyon, P.C., grandson of Sir John Lyon, of Forteviot, and
afterwards of Glamis, co. Forfar (who *m.* Jean, dau. of King Robert II. of Scotland) ; was one
of the hostages to the English 1424-7 for the ransom of King James I.; cr. *Lord Glamis* 1445,
and appointed Master of the Household 1452 ; *d.* 1459 ; *s.* by his son [2] ALEXANDER, 2nd Lord,
d.s.p. 1485; *s.* by his brother [3] JOHN, P.C., 3rd Lord ; was Justice Gen. of Scotland ; *d.* 1497;
s. by his son [4] JOHN, 4th Lord ; *d.* 1500; *s.* by his el. son [5] GEORGE, 5th Lord ; *d.* 1505;
s. by his brother [6] JOHN, 6th Lord ; *d.* 1528 ; his son Lord Glamis, his widow, a kinsman,
and an old priest were indicted for designs against the life of James V. by poison or witchcraft;
Lady Glamis was condemned to the flames and suffered on the Castle Hill at Edinburgh, July
17th, 1537, Lord Glamis was sentenced to be executed and his estates forfeited, but was respited
until he attained his majority; the accuser, however, having confessed that the whole story
was a fabrication his lordship was released, and in 1543 was restored by Act of Parliament to
his honours and estates, and *s.* as [7] JOHN, 7th Lord ; *d.* 1558 ; *s.* by his son [8] JOHN, 8th
Lord ; was Lord Chancellor of Scotland 1575 ; *d.* 1578 ; *s.* by his son [9] PATRICK, P.C., 9th
Lord ; was Capt. of the Guard ; cr. *Earl of Kinghorne* (peerage of Scotland) 1606 ; *d.* 1615 ; *s.*
by his son [10] JOHN, 2nd Earl ; *d.* 1647; *s.* by his son [11] PATRICK, P.C., 3rd Earl ; was a
Lord of the Treasury, an Extraordinary Lord of Session ; obtained in 1672 a new charter
extending the remainder to his heirs and assigns whatsoever, and in 1677 another charter
providing that he and each successive inheritor of the title should be styled *Lord Glamis,
Tannadyce, Sidlaw and Strathdichtie, Viscount Lyon,* and *Earl of Strathmore and Kinghorne ;*
d. 1695 ; *s.* by his son [12] JOHN, 4th Earl ; *d.* 1712 ; *s.* by his el. son [13] JOHN, 5th Earl,
was slain in the rebellion of 1715 at battle of Sheriffmuir; *s.* by his brother [14] CHARLES,
6th Earl ; *b.* 17—: *m.* 1725 ; *d.* 1728 ; *s.* by his brother [15] JAMES, 7th Earl ; *b.* 1702 : *m.*
(May) 1731, Mary, who *d.* (Sept.) 1731, dau. of Dr. Charles Oliphant ; *d.* 1735 ; *s.* by his brother
[16] THOMAS, 8th Earl ; *b.* 1704 : *m.* 1736, Jean, who *d.* 1778, dau. of James Nicholson, of West
Rainton, co. Durham ; *d.* 1753 : *s.* by his son [17] JOHN, 9th Earl ; assumed by Act of Parliament
1767 the surname of Bowes : *m.* 1767, Mary Eleanor, who *d.* 1800, dau. and heir of George Bowes of
Streatlam Castle, co. Durham ; *d.* 1776 ; *s.* by his el. son [18] JOHN, 10th Earl ; cr. *Baron Bowes,* of
Streatlam Castle (peerage of United Kingdom) 1815 ; *d.* 1820 ; *s.* by his brother [19] THOMAS, 11th
Earl ; resumed the surname of Lyon before that of Bowes : *m.* 1800, MaryElizabeth Louisa Rodney,
who *d.* 1811, dau. and heir of George Carpenter, of Redbourn, Herts, *d.* 1846 ; *s.* by his grandson
[20] THOMAS GEORGE, 12th Earl, son of George, Lord Glamis, by Charlotte, dau. of Joseph Valentine
Grimstead ; was a Representative Peer ; *d.* 1865 ; *s.* by his brother [21] CLAUDE, 13th Earl ; *b.*
1824 ; Lord-Lieut. of co. Forfar ; a Representative Peer 1870-87 ; assumed the surname of Bowes-
Lyon in lieu of Lyon-Bowes ; cr. *Baron Bowes,* of Streatlam Castle (peerage of United Kingdom)
1887 : *m.* 1852, Frances Dora, who *d.* 1922, dau. of Oswald Smith, of Blendon Hall, Kent ; *d.* 1904 ;
s. by his son [22] CLAUDE GEORGE, K.G., K.T., G.C.V.O., 14th Earl ; *b.* 1855 ; 32 years Lord
Lieut, of co. Angus ; cr. *Earl of Strathmore and Kinghorne* (peerage of United Kingdom) 1937 ;
m. 1881, Cecilia Nina, G.C.V.O., who *d.* 1938, dau. of the late Rev. Charles William Cavendish-
Bentinck [D. Portland, colls.]; *d.* 1944; *s.* by his son [23] PATRICK, 15th Earl, *b.* 1884:
m. 1908, Lady Dorothy Beatrix Osborne, who *d.* 1946, dau. of 10th Duke of Leeds; *d.*
1949; *s.* by his son [24] TIMOTHY PATRICK, 16th Earl, *b.* 1918: *m.* 1958, Mary Bridget, who *d.* 1967,
da. of Peter Brennan, of Clonasee, co. Leix; *d.* 1972; *s.* by his cousin [25] FERGUS MICHAEL CLAUDE
(el. son of the Hon. Michael Claude Hamilton Bowes-Lyon, 5th son of 14th Earl), 17th Earl and
present peer; also Earl of Strathmore and Kinghorne (cr. UK 1937), Viscount Lyon, Lord Glamis,
Tannadyce, Sidlaw and Strathdichtie, and Baron Bowes.

STRATHSPEY, BARON. (Grant of Grant.) [Baron U.K. 1884, Bt. N.S. 1625.]

[Title pronounced "Strathspay."]

DONALD PATRICK TREVOR GRANT OF GRANT, 5th Baron, and 17th Baronet ; *b.* March 18th, 1912 ; *s.* 1948 ; ed. at Stowe Sch. ; is 32nd Chief of the Clan Grant, and late Lieut.-Col. Gen. List ; recognised in the surname of Grant of Grant by decree of Lord Lyon 1950 : Assist. Ch. Land Agent Defence Lands Sers.: *m.* 1st, 1938, Alice, only child of the late Francis Bowe, of Timaru, New Zealand; 2ndly, 1951, Olive, only dau. of the late Wallace Henry Grant, of Norwich, and has issue by 1st and 2nd marriages.

Arms,—Gules, three antique crowns or. Crest,—A burning hill proper. Supporters.—Two savages or naked men wreathed about the head and middle with laurel, each bearing on his exterior shoulder a club, proper. *Residence,*—111, Elmsride, W. Wittering, Sussex.

SONS LIVING. (*By 1st marriage.*)

Hon. JAMES PATRICK, *b.* Sept. 9th, 1943: *m.* 1966, Linda, da. of David Piggott, of Forfar, and has issue living, Carolyn Anne Maclean, *b.* 1967.

(*By 2nd marriage.*)

Hon. Michael Patrick Francis, *b.* 1953; ed. at Harrow.

DAUGHTERS LIVING. (*By 1st marriage.*)

Hon. Geraldine Janet, GRANT OF GRANT (24, Denbigh Rd., W11 2SN), *b.* 1940; resumed surname of Grant of Grant 1972: *m.* 1963 (m. diss. 1972), Neil Hamish Cantlie, yr. son of the late Adm. Sir Colin Cantlie, KBE, CB, DSO.

Hon. Jacqueline Patricia, *b.* 1942: *m.* 1966, Malcolm Usheen Lingen Hutton, of Kinsley, Banchory, Kincardineshire.

(*By 2nd marriage.*)

Hon. Amanda Caroline, *b.* 1955.

SISTER LIVING.

Hon. Lena Barbara Joan, *b.* 1907: *m.* 1934, Herbert Frank Onslow, who *d.* 1970 [see Onslow, Bt., colls.]. *Residence,*—17, Damask Close, Weston, nr. Hitchin, Herts.

COLLATERAL BRANCHES LIVING. (*In remainder to Baronetcy only.*)

See E. Seafield, colls.

PREDECESSORS.—[1—5] Sir HUMPHREY Colquhoun, 5th Bt., of Luss (cr. 1625), obtained 1704 a new patent with original precedence giving remainder to his son-in-law, James Grant ; *d.* 1718 ; *s.* by his son-in-law [6] Sir JAMES, 6th Bt. ; *d.* 1747 ; *s.* by his son [7] Sir LUDOVICK, 7th Bt. ; sat as M.P. for co. Moray 1741-61 : *m.* 2ndly, Lady Margaret Ogilvie, dau. of Earl of Find-later ; *d.* 1773 ; *s.* by his son [8] Sir JAMES, 8th Bt. ; sat as M.P. for Elgin and Forres 1761-8, and was Lord-Lieut. of Inverness-shire ; *d.* Feb. 1811 ; *s.* by his son [9] Sir LEWIS ALEXANDER Grant of Grant, 9th Bt., who in Oct. 1811 *s.* as 5th Earl of Seafield ; assumed in 1811 the additional surname of Ogilvie ; M.P. for Elginshire 1790-96 ; *d.* unmarried 1840 ; *s.* by his brother [10] FRANCIS WILLIAM, 6th Earl ; M.P. for various Scottish constituencies 1802-40 ; Lord-Lieut. of co. Inverness, and a Representative Peer ; *d.* 1853 ; *s.* by his son [11] JOHN CHARLES, *K.T.*, 7th Earl, *b.* 1815 ; a Representative Peer ; cr. *Baron Strathspey,* of Strathspey, cos. Inverness and Moray (peerage of United Kingdom) 1858 : *m.* 1850, the Hon. Caroline Hen-rietta Stuart, who *d.* 1911, dau. of 11th Baron Blantyre ; *d.* 1881 ; *s.* by his son [12] IAN CHARLES, 8th Earl, *b.* 1851 ; *d.s.p.* 1884, when the Barony of Strathspey became ext. ; *s.* in Scotch peerages of 1698 and 1701 by his uncle [13] JAMES, 9th Earl (3rd son of 6th Earl, by Mary Anne, dau. of John Charles Dunn, of St. Helena and Higham House), *b.* 1817 ; M.P. for Elgin and Nairnshire (*C*) 1868-74 ; cr. *Baron Strathspey* (peerage of United Kingdom) 1884 : *m.* 1st, 1841, Caroline Louisa, who *d.* 1850, dau. of the late Eyre Evans, of Ash Hill Towers, Limerick ; 2ndly, 1853, Constance Helena, who *d.* 1872, dau. of Sir Robert Abercromby, 5th Bt. ; 3rdly, 1875, Georgiana Adelaide, dau. of the late Gen. Frederick Nathaniel Walker, K.C.H., of Manor House, Bushey, and widow of William Stuart, of Aldenham Abbey, Herts ; *d.* 1888 ; *s.* by his el. son [14] FRANCIS WILLIAM, 10th Earl, *b.* 1847 : *m.* 1874, Ann ("Nina") Trevor Corry, dau. of Major George Thomas Evans, of Clooneavin, Otago, New Zealand ; *d.* 1888 ; *s.* by his el. son [15] JAMES, 11th Earl, *b.* 1876 ; Capt. Queen's Own Cameron Highlanders : *m.* 1898, Mary Elizabeth Nina, dau. of the late Joseph Henry Townend, M.D., J.P., of Christchurch, New Zealand ; *d.* (of wounds in action) Nov. 1915, when the Earldom of Seafield devolved upon his only dau., and he was *s.* in the Barony of Strathspey and the Baronetcy by his brother [16] TREVOR, 4th Baron, *b.* 1879 : *m.* 1st, 1905, Alice Louisa, who *d.* 1945, dau. of the late Thomas Masterman Hardy Johnston, M.I.C.E., of London, and subsequently Christchurch, New Zealand ; 2ndly, 1947 Elfrida Minnie Fass, who *d.* 1949, da. of the late Gordon William Alexander Cloete, J P, of Cape Prov., S, Africa, and widow of Lt.-Col. George Capron, York and Lancaster Regt.; *d.* 1948 ; *s.* by his son DONALD (PATRICK), 5th Baron and present peer.

STRICKLAND, BARONY OF. (Strickland.) [Extinct 1940.]

DAUGHTERS LIVING OF FIRST BARON. (*By 1st marriage.*)

Hon. Cecilia, *b.* 1897 ; was a M.L.A., Malta 1950-53 : *m.* 1927, Capt. Hubert Edmund Francis de Trafford, formerly 1st Dragoons, who *d.* 1974 [see de Trafford, Bt., colls.]. *Residence,*—Xlendi, Gozo, Malta, GO.

Hon .Mabel, *O.B.E.*, *b.* 1899; attached to Naval Headquarters, Malta 1917-18; Assist. Sec., Con-stitutional Party, Malta 1921-45, and Vice-Chm. thereof 1950-52; Editor of *Times of Malta* 1935-50. and of *Sunday Times of Malta* 1935-56, Chm. Xara Palace Hotel Co. Ltd., Malta 1949-62, and again since 1966; a Dir. of Allied Malta Newspapers Co., Ltd. 1938-55, and of Progress Press Co. Ltd.,

1957-62; Hon. Corresponding Sec. of Roy. Commonwealth Soc. since 1943, Leader of Progressive Constitutional Party since 1953, and Chm. of Allied Malta Newspapers Ltd. since 1966; a MLA Malta 1950-53 and again 1962-64, and an MP of Malta 1964-66; a CStJ; has Coronation (1953, medal, and Astor Award; OBE (Civil) 1944. *Residence,*—Villa Parisio, Malta, GC. *Clubs,*— Lansdowne, Malta Union, and Royal Commonwealth Society.

Constance (c/o Poste Restante, The Post Office, Port Swettenham, Malaysia) *b.* 1912; does not use courtesy style of Hon.; Licentiate of Apothecaries' Hall of Ireland 1953; Ship's Surg., Alfred Holt & Co. 1955-56; Med. Officer, Depart. of Aborigine Affairs, Malaya 1957-60; Chest Physician, Singapore Anti-TB Assocn. 1960-65; Ship's Surg., Malaysian Armed Forces since 1970.

Stuart, Viscount, son of Earl Castle Stewart.

STUART OF FINDHORN, VISCOUNT. (Stuart.) [Viscount U.K. 1959.]

DAVID RANDOLPH MORAY STUART, 2nd Viscount; *b.* June 20th, 1924; *s.* 1971; ed. at Eton; late Lt. KRRC; Maj. 6/7th R. Welch Fus. (TA); FRICS; Page of Honour to HM 1938-40; DL of Caerns. 1963-68: *m.* 1st, 1945, Grizel Mary Wilfreda, who *d.* 1948, da. of the late Theodore Fyfe, and widow of Michael Gillilan; 2ndly, 1951, Marian, da. of the late Gerald Wilson, of Kintbury, Berks., and has issue by 1st and 2nd m.

Arms,—Quarterly : 1st, or, a lion rampant within a double tressure flory counterflory gules, all within a bordure compony azure and argent, *Stuart;* 2nd, or, a fess chequy azure and argent, *Stewart of Doune* ; 3rd, or, three cushions within a double tressure flory counterflory gules, *Randolph;* 4th, gules, a lion rampant within a bordure engrailed argent, *Gray* ; all within a bordure or for difference. Crest,—In a nest vert a pelican feeding her young or, about her neck a collar engrailed gules. Supporters,—Two capercailzie proper, their wings closed.

Residences,—Flat 6, 6-7, Collingham Gdns., SW5; Butts Cottage, Kintbury, Berks. *Clubs,*— Buck's, Bath, White's.

SONS LIVING. (By 1st m.)
Hon. (JAMES) DOMINIC, *b.* 1948; ed. at Eton.

(By 2nd m.)
Hon. Andrew Moray, *b.* 1957.

DAUGHTERS LIVING. (By 2nd m.)
Hon. Chloe Anne-Marie, *b.* 1952.
Hon. Rosalie Jane, *b.* 1954.
Hon. Vanessa Mary, *b.* 1960.

BROTHER LIVING.
Hon. John Douglas (White's Club), *b.* 1925; Lt. (ret.) RN: *m.* 1st, 1957 (m. diss. 1958), Mrs. Cecile Margaret Tonge, da. of G. H. Barr; 2ndly, 1969 (m. diss. 1972), Lady Caroline Child-Villiers, da. of the 9th Earl of Jersey and formerly wife of Gilbert Edward George Lariston, Viscount Melgund [see E. Minto].

SISTER LIVING.
Hon. Jean Davina, *b.* 1932: *m.* 1st, 1951, John Reedham Erskine Berney, Lt. Roy. Norfolk Regt., who *d.* (killed in action in Korea), 1952, son of Major Sir Thomas Reedham Berney, MC, 10th Bt.; 2ndly, 1954, Percy William Jesson, and has issue living, (by 1st marriage) [see Berney, Bt.], (by 2nd marriage) Rayner Charles Percy, *b.* 1956,—James Gray, *b.* 1959,—Arabella Clare Lucy, *b.* 1962. *Residence,*—Finchingfield, Braintree, Essex.

WIDOW LIVING OF FIRST VISCOUNT.
Lady RACHEL CAVENDISH, *OBE* (*Dowager Viscountess Stuart of Findhorn*), (Elm Cottage, Finching field, nr. Braintree, Essex, CM7 4LD); OBE (Civil) 1946, da. of the 9th Duke of Devonshire: *m.* 1923 the 1st Viscount, who *d.* 1971.

PREDECESSOR.—[1] *Rt. Hon.* JAMES GRAY Stuart, *CH, MVO, MC,* 3rd son of 17th Earl of Moray; *b.* 1897; Ch. Conservative Whip 1941-48, Sec. of State for Scotland 1951-57, Chm. of Unionist Party in Scotland 1950-62, and MP for Moray and Nairn 1923-59; *cr. Viscount Stuart of Findhorn,* of Findhorn, co. Moray (peerage of UK) 1959: *m.* 1923, Lady Rachel Cavendish, da. of 9th Duke of Devonshire; *d.* 1971; *s.* by his el. son [2] DAVID RANDOLPH MORAY, 2nd Viscount and present peer.

SUDELEY, BARON.   (Hanbury-Tracy.)   [Baron U.K. 1838.]

MEMORIA · PII · ÆTERNA

The pious are held in everlasting remembrance.

Badge of the Barons Sudeley.

MERLYN CHARLES SAINTHILL HANBURY-TRACY, 7th Baron; *b.* June 17th, 1939: *s.* 1941; ed. at Eton, and at Worcester Coll., Oxford (BA).

Arms.—Quarterly: 1st and 4th or, an escallop in the chief point sable, between two bendlets gules, *Tracy;* 2nd and 3rd or, a bend engrailed vert plain cotised sable, *Hanbury.* **Crests.**—1st, on a chapeau gules, turned up ermine, an escallop sable, between two wings or; 2nd, out of a mural coronet sable, a demi-lion rampant or, holding in the paws a battle-axe sable, helved gold. **Supporters.**—On either side a falcon, wings elevated proper, beaked and belled or. **Badge.**—A fire beacon, and in front thereof and chained thereto a panther ducally gorged, the tail nowed.

Address,—c/o Williams & Glyn's Bank, 19 and 21 Grosvenor Gdns., SW1.   *Club,*—Brooks's.

SISTER LIVING OF SIXTH BARON. (*Raised to the rank of a Baron's daughter* 1933.)
Hon. Ursula Katharine, *b.* 1909: *m.* 1st, 1935, Brig. Claude Nicholson, CB, late 16th/5th R. Lancers, who *d.* (whilst a prisoner) 1943; 2ndly, 1946, Group Capt. Archibald Hugh Herbert MacDonald, DFC, who *d.* 1947, and has issue living, (by 1st m.) Richard Hugh, (Woodcott House, Whitchurch, Hants.) *b.* 1936; late Capt. 16th/5th Queen's R. Lancers: *m.* 1960, Margaret Jane, yr. da. of Lt.-Col. Henry Charles Minshull Stockdale [see B. Faringdon], and has issue living, James Alexander *b.* 1965, Camilla *b.* 1962,—Sylvia Mary Victoria (The Old Rectory, Orlingbury, Northants), *b.* 1939: *m.* 1965, Christopher Minshull Stockdale, who *d.* 1970, [B. Faringdon], and has issue living, Mary Violet *b.* 1968. *Residence,*—Great Eastwards, Binley, Andover.

MOTHER LIVING OF SEVENTH BARON.
Colline Ammabel, da. of the late Lt.-Col. Collis George Herbert St. Hill [Maryon-Wilson, Bt. and widow of Lt.-Col. Frank King, DSO, OBE, 4th Hussars (Reserve): *m.* 1937, Capt. (Michael) David Charles Hanbury-Tracy, who *d.* (of wounds received in action during European War) 1940. *Residence,*—The Red House, N. Cadbury, Yeovil.

WIDOW LIVING OF SIXTH BARON.
ELIZABETH MARY, da. of Rear-Adm. Sir Arthur Bromley, KCMG, CVO, 8th Bt.: *m.* 1st, 1940, the 6th Baron, who *d.* (on active ser.) 1941: 2ndly, 1965, Maj. Arthur James Robert Collins, CVO, of 38, Clarence Terr., Regent's Park, NW1 4RD; and Kirkman Bank, Knaresborough, Yorks.

COLLATERAL BRANCHES LIVING.

Granddaughter of the late Hon. Felix Charles Hubert Hanbury Tracy, 3rd son of 4th Baron:—
Issue of the late Ninian John Frederick Hanbury Tracy, *b.* 1910, *d.* 1971: *m.* 1st, 1935 (m. diss. 1954), the Hon. Blanche Mary Arundell, da. of 15th Baron Arundell of Wardour; 2ndly, 1954, Daphne Mary Christian (The Red House, Lacock, Wilts.), da. of the late Lt.-Col. Vivian Henry, CB [Milbank, Bt.], and widow of Maj. Charles Scott:—
(By 1st m.) Jennifer Avril, *b.* 1941: *m.* 1964, Martin Robert Morland, c/o FCO, SW1, el. son of Sir Oscar Charles Morland, GBE, KCMG, and has issue living, William, *b.* 1965,—Anthony, *b.* 1967,—Catherine Mary, *b.* 1966.

Grandson of the late Lieut.-Col. the Hon. Frederick Stephen Archibald Hanbury Tracy, 5th son of 2nd Baron:—
Issue of the late Major Eric Thomas Henry Hanbury-Tracy, O.B.E., *b.* 1871, *d.* 1953: *m.* 1902, Dorothy Louisa, who *d.* 1951, dau. of the late Sir Edward Harris Greathed, K.C.B., of Uddens, Dorset [Osborn, Bt.]:—
CLAUD EDWARD FREDERICK HANBURY-TRACY-DOMVILE, *TD, b.* Jan. 11th, 1904; ed. at Eton, and at Trin. Coll., Camb. (BA); Maj. RA (TA); assumed by deed poll 1961, the additional surname of Domvile: *m.* 1st, 1927 (m. diss. 1948), Veronica May, da. of the late Cyril Grant Cunard [see Cunard, Bt., colls.]; 2ndly, 1954, Marcella Elizabeth, da. of the late Canon J. Willis-Price, and has issue living (by 1st m.), Desmond Andrew John HANBURY-TRACY (York House, Easebourne, Midhurst), *b.* 1928; ed. at Sherborne: *m.* 1st, 1957 (m. diss. 1966), Jennifer Lynn, da. of Dr. R. C. Hodges, of Elizabethan House, Warwick; 2ndly, 1967, Lillian, da. of Nathaniel Laurie, and has issue living, (by 1st m.) Nicholas *b.* 1959; (by 2nd m.), Timothy Christopher Claud, *b.* 1968,—Charles William Justin HANBURY-TRACY (1, Belitha Villas, Islington, N1), *b.* 1933; ed. at Sherborne: *m.* 1969, Sarah Jane, da. of the late Lt.-Col. G. Ashley and has issue living, Justin *b.* 1971, Emily *b.* 1970,—Mary Claudia Elizabeth, *b.* 1931: *m.* 1953, Robert Singlehurst Cross, of Foxbury Meadow, Godalming, Surrey, and has issue living, Edward Robert *b.* 1956, Lucy Cunard *b.* 1954, Sylvia Mary *b.* 1961, Anna Elizabeth *b.* 1964. *Residence,*—Bedborough, Uddens, Wimborne, Dorset.

PREDECESSORS.—[1] CHARLES Hanbury, 3rd son of the late John Hanbury, of Pontypool Park, Mon. (deriving from the same source as the Barons Bateman); *b.* 1777; MP for Tewkesbury; Chm.

of Commn. to Judge Designs for new Houses of Parliament 1835; cr. *Baron Sudeley* of Toddington, co. Gloucester (peerage of UK) 1838: *m.* 1798, the Hon. Henrietta Susanna, who *d.* 1839, only child and heir of Henry, 8th and last Viscount Tracy, who in the same year took by sign manual the surname and arms of Tracy in lieu of his patronymic, and assumed the surname of Hanbury-Tracy; *d.* 1858; *s.* by his son [2] THOMAS CHARLES, 2nd Baron; *b.* 1801; assumed by Roy. licence the surname of Leigh 1806, which name in 1839 he discontinued by Roy. licence, and again assumed the surname of Hanbury: *m.* 1831, Emma Eliza Alicia, who *d.* 1888, da. of the late George Hay Dawkins-Pennant, of Penrhyn Castle, co. Caernarvon; *d.* 1863; *s.* by his el. son [3] SUDELEY CHARLES GEORGE, 3rd Baron; *d.* 1877; *s.* by his brother [4] CHARLES DOUGLAS RICHARD, PC, FRS, 4th Baron; *b.* 1840; MP for Montgomery Dist. (*L*) 1863-77; a Lord-in-Waiting to Queen Victoria 1880-85, and Capt. Hon. Corps of Gentlemen-at-Arms 1886: *m.* 1868, Ada Maria Katherine, who *d.* 1928, da. of the late Hon. Frederick James Tollemache [Os. Dysart]; *d.* 1922; *s.* by his el. son [5] WILLIAM CHARLES FREDERICK, 5th Baron, *b.* 1870: *m.* 1905, Edith Celandine who *d.* 1975, and from whom he obtained a divorce 1922), da. of the late Lieut. Lord Frances Horace Pierrepont Cecil, RN [M. Exeter]; *d.* 1932; *s.* by his nephew [6] RICHARD ALGERNON FREDERICK (son of the late Major the Hon. Algernon Henry Charles Hanbury-Tracy, CMG, 2nd son of 4th Baron), 6th Baron; *b.* 1911; Major Roy. Horse Guards: *m.* 1940, Elizabeth Mary, da. of Rear-Adm. Sir Arthur Bromley, KCMG, CVO: *d.* (on active ser. during European War) 1941; *s.* by his kinsman [7] MERLYN CHARLES SAINTHILL (son of the late Capt. (Michael) David Charles Hanbury Tracy, grandson of 4th Baron), 7th Baron and present peer.

Sudley, Baron, title of Earl of Arran on Roll of H. L.

    „   **Viscount,**   son of Earl of Arran.

SUFFIELD, BARON. (Harbord-Hamond.) **[Baron G.B. 1786, Bt. G.B. 1745.]**

ANTHONY PHILIP HARBORD-HAMOND, *M.C.*, 11th Baron, and 12th Baronet ; *b.* June 19th, 1922 ; *s.* 1951; ed. at Eton; Maj. Coldm. Gds. (ret.); appointed one of HM Body Guard of Hon. Corps of Gentlemen-at-Arms 1973; an Officer of Order of Orange Nassau of the Netherlands with swords; 1941-45 War in N. Africa and Italy; Malaya 1948-50 (MC): *m.* 1952, Elizabeth Eve, el. da. of the late Judge (Samuel Richard) Edgedale, QC, of Field Lodge, Crowthorne, Berks, and has issue.

ᴬrms,—Quarterly: 1st and 4th quarterly, azure and gules, four lions rampant argent, and in the entre an imperial crown or, *Harbord*; 2nd and 3rd argent, a fleur-de-lis gules, *Morden*. Crest,—On a chapeau gules turned up ermine, a lion couchant argent. Supporters,—*Dexter*, a lion or, charged on the shoulder with a fleur-de-lis gules, and gorged with a crown flory, chain reflexed over the back, azure; *sinister*, a leopard guardant proper, gorged with a similar coronet and chain or.

Residence,—Langham Lodge, Holt, Norfolk. *Club,*—Guards'.

ÆQUANIMITER

Even mindedly.

SONS LIVING.
Hon. CHARLES ANTHONY ASSHETON, *b.* Dec. 3rd, 1953.
Hon. John Edward Richard, *b.* 1956.
Hon. Robert Philip Morden, *b.* 1964.

DAUGHTER LIVING.
Hon. Caroline Mary Elaine, *b.* 1960.

SISTERS LIVING.
Hon. Penelope Mary, *b.* 1915.
Hon. Charity Patricia, *b.* 1917.

DAUGHTERS LIVING OF SIXTH BARON.
Hon. Doris Cecilia HARBORD, *b.* 1900. *Residence,*—Gunton Park, Norwich.
Hon. Lettice Evelyn HARBORD, *b.* 1904. *Residence,*—Harbord House, Cromer, Norfolk.

COLLATERAL BRANCHES LIVING.
Issue of the late Ralph Assheton Harbord, brother of 10th Baron, *b.* 1859, *d.* 1913 : *m.* 1889, Mary Ada, who *d.* 1900, dau. of the late Major Francis Hastings Toone Gordon-Cumming [Gordon-Cumming, Bt.] :—
Judith Mary, *b.* 1900. *Residence,*—St. John's Guest House for Blind Ladies, 1, Shakespeare Road, Worthing.

Issue of the late Lionel Anthony Harbord, R.A.F., brother of 10th Baron, *b.* 1870, *d.* 1919 : *m.* 1893, Sophy Mary Theresa, who *d.* 1956, dau. of the late Henry Sydenham Singleton, of Hazely, Winchfield, and 8, Prince's Gate, S.W. [Lamb, Bt] :—
Phyllis Mary, *b.* 1895 : *m.* 1919, George Henry Pryce, who *d.* 1950, and has issue living, Richard Anthony Mostyn, *b.* 1921; Maj. Indian Army (ret.),—Mary Rosamond, *b.* 1924. *Residence,* Sandys, Burley, nr. Ringwood, Hants.——Sophie Almina (Anchor House, Stuntney, Ely), *b.* 1902: *m.* 1921 (m. diss. 1938), Gerald Howard Wilson, and has issue living, Gillian Mary (Hilbre School, Holway Rd., Sheringham, Norfolk), *b.* 1923,—April Geraldine (61, Ashdown Way, Ipswich), *b.* 1925.
Issue of the late Maurice Assheton Harbord, youngest brother of 10th Baron, *b.* 1874, *d.* 1954 : *m.* 1st, 1905, Isabel Jessie Lowth (from whom he obtained a divorce 1918), 4th dau. of Baron Frederick von Wurzburg Schade, and widow of Richard Hedley Robinson, of Kirkby Mallory Hall, Leicestershire; 2ndly, 1929, Ethel Florence, dau. of George William Goldsmith, of Hastings, and widow of Francis Tugwell Cowley:—
(By 2nd marriage) Patrick Rupert Shirley, *b.* 1930 : *m.* 1955, Jean Shirley, dau. of Reginald George Webb, of Pebsham Farm Cottage, Bexhill-on-Sea, and has issue living, Alan Anthony, *b.* 1956, —Shirley Ann, *b.* 1958. *Residence,*—16, Clarence Road, Bohemia, St. Leonards-on-Sea.——Ralph Assheton Edward, *b.* 1932 : *m.* 1959, Angela, only dau. of S. D'Eath, of 5, Conqueror Road, St. Leonards, Sussex, and has issue living, Richard, *b.* 1964. *Residence,*—77, Park View, Hastings.

Grandchildren of the late Hon. Ralph Harbord, 6th son of 3rd Baron:—

Issue of the late Capt. Edward Ralph Harbord, D.S.O., M.C., *b.* 1870, *d.* 1950: *m.* **1906**, Annie Evelyn (of 21, High Bond End, Knaresborough, Yorkshire), dau. of Henry Herbert Riley-Smith, of Toulston, Tadcaster, Yorkshire:—

William Edward, *b.* 1908 ; ed. at Eton, and at Worcester Coll., Oxford : *m.* 1st, 1938, Vivien Sylvia (from whom he obtained a divorce 1949), dau. of the late Lieut.-Col. Foster Newton Thorne ; 2ndly, 1950, Christine Winifred (from whom he obtained a divorce 1959), dau. of Alan Higham, and has issue living, (by 1st m.) Charles Francis (29, Holmead Rd., SW6; Buck's Club), *b.* 1943; ed. at Harrow: *m.* 1973, Honor Lois, da. of Tom Saul, of Seacroft, Lincs.,—(by 2nd m.) Christopher Evelyn, *b.* 1953, Gay Diana, *b.* 1951. *Residence,*—11, Granby Rd., Harrogate. *Clubs,* Buck's, MCC.——Ralph Evelyn, *b.* 1915; ed. at Eton: European War 1939-45 as Lt. RNVR (sometime Flag Lt. to Com-in-Ch., Plymouth): *m.* 1950, Madeline Betty Kezia, da. of the late Robert Finlay-Greig, and has issue living, Robert Ralph, *b.* 1950; 2nd Lt. The R. Green Jackets,—Jeremy Julian, *b.* 1953. *Residence,*—Heathcroft, S. Ascot, Berks.——Bridget, *b.* 1907: *m.* 1931, Noel F. Nickols, who *d.* 1966. *Residence,* —49, Rutland Drive, Harrogate.——Elizabeth Mary, *b.* 1912; 1939-45 War as Ch. Officer WRNS, a CStJ: *m.* 1946, Capt. John Michael Hodges, DSO, RN, of Black Bear, Kirdford, Billingshurst, Sussex, son of the late Sir Michael Henry Hodges, KCB, CMG, MVO, and has issue living, Patrick Michael (Forge Cottage, Tintern, Gwent), *b.* 1948; ed. at Eton: *m.* 1974, Alison Mary, da. of Wing-Cdr. Roy Dossetter, RAF, of Pen-y-bryn, Upper Clatford, Hants.— Judith Evelyn, *b.* 1952; ed. at Roedean.——Dorothy Primrose, *b.* 1919: *m.* 1939, Maj. Edward d'Abo KOYLI (Reserve), and has issue living, Philip Edward (77, Park Walk SW10), *b.* 1941; ed. at Harrow: *m.* 1972, Fay Mary St. Claire, da. of the late William Barbour, and has issue living, Camilla Sophie Louise *b.* 1973,—Michael David (16, Albion St., W2), *b.* 1944; ed. at Harrow: *m.* 1966, Margaret Evelyn, da. of George Lyndon, of Chelmsford, and has issue living, Benjamin Byron *b.* 1967, Olivia Jane *b.* 1969,—Andrew Gerard Noel, *b.* 1948: ed. at Harrow,—Penelope Carol (twin), *b.* 1948: *m.* 1970, Nicholas Brian Baker, of 3, Leinster Sq., W2. *Residence,*—The Grange, Bexhill-on-Sea, Sussex.——Molly (Peppers Farm, Burton Lazars, Melton Mowbray), *b.* 1921: *m.* 1st, 1941, Roy Laird-Macgregor, Lt. RA from whom she obtained a divorce 1946; 2ndly, 1953, John Cecil Atkinson Clark, who *d.* 1960 [Meyrick, Bt.], and has issue living (by 2nd m.), George Evelyn, *b.* 1960.

PREDECESSORS.—[1] Sir **William** Morden, *K.B.*, was cr. a *Baronet* 1745; assumed by Roy. licence the surname of Harbord in lieu of his patronymic; *d.* 1770 ; *s.* by his son [2] Sir **Harbord** Harbord, 2nd Bt.; was M.P. for Norwich; cr. **Baron Suffield**, co. Norfolk (peerage of Great Britain) 1786; *d.* 1810; *s.* by his el. son [3] **William Assheton**, 2nd Baron ; *d.* 1821 ; *s.* by his brother [4] **Edward**, 3rd Baron; *b.* 1781: *m.* 1st, 1809, the Hon. Georgiana, dau. and heiress of George, 2nd Baron Vernon; 2ndly, 1826, Emily Harriet, dau. of Evelyn Shirley, of Ettington Park, Warwickshire; *d.* 1835; *s.* by his son [5] **Edward Vernon**, 4th Baron ; *d.s.p.* 1853; *s.* by his half-brother [6] **Charles**, G.C.V.O., K.C.B., P.C., 5th Baron ; *b.* 1830; Lord-in-Waiting to Queen Victoria 1868-72, Lord of Bedchamber to Prince of Wales 1872-1901, and Permanent Lord-in-Waiting to King Edward VII. 1901-10 : *m.* 1st, 1854, Cecilia Annetta, who *d.* 1911, dau. of the late Henry Baring; 2ndly, 1911, Frances Amelia Jessie, who *d.* 1934, only dau. of the late Major Robert Poole Gabbatt, R.A., and widow of Col. Charles C. Rich, R.H.A.; *d.* 1914; *s.* by his el. son [6] **Charles**, C.B., M.V.O., 6th Baron, *b.* 1855 ; a Groom-in-Waiting to H.M. Queen Victoria 1895-1901: *m.* 1896, Evelyn Louisa, J.P. who *d.* 1951, dau. of the late Capt. Eustace John Wilson-Patten [see B. Winnarleigh]; *d.* 1924 ; *s.* by his el. son [7] **Victor Alexander Charles**, 7th Baron ; *b.* 1897 : *m.* 1925, the Hon. Olwen Gwynne Philipps (from whom he obtained a divorce 1937), dau. of 1st Baron Kylsant (ext.) ; *d.* 1943 ; *s.* by his brother [8] **John**, 8th Baron; *b.* 1907; *d.* 1945 ; *s.* by his kinsman [9] **Geoffrey Walter** (3rd son of the late Hon. William Harbord, 4th son of 3rd Baron), 9th Baron; *b.* 1861: *m.* 1902, Eliza Jane, who *d.* 1933, dau. of John Mills, and widow of A. R. Beaumont, 16th Lancers; *d.* 1946, *s.* by his cousin [10] **Richard Morden** (son of the late Rev. the Hon. John Harbord, 5th son of 3rd Baron), 10th Baron; *b.* 1865; Adm.; Egyptian War 1882, European War 1914-19; assumed by Roy. Licence 1917 the additional surname of Hamond: *m.* 1913, Nina Annette Mary Crawfuird, who *d.* 1955, el. dau. of John William Hutchison of Laurieston Hall, and Edingham, Kirkcudbright; *d.* 1951; *s.* by his only son [11] **Anthony Philip**, 11th Baron and present peer.

SUFFOLK and BERKSHIRE, EARL OF. (Howard.) [Earl Suffolk E. 1603 and Berkshire E. 1626.]

NOUS MAINTIENDRONS

We will maintain.

Michael John James George Robert Howard, 21st Earl of Suffolk and 14th Earl of Berkshire : *b.* March 27th, 1935 ; *s.* 1941 ; ed. at Winchester: *m.* 1st, 1960 (m. diss. 1967), Mme. Simone Paulmier, da. of Georges Litman, of Paris; 2ndly, 1973, Anita Robsahm, yr. da. of Robin Fuglesang, of Cuckfield, Sussex, and has issue living by 2nd m.

Arms.—Quarterly : 1st gules, a bend between six cross-crosslets fitchée argent, on the bend an escutcheon or, charged with a demi-lion rampant, pierced through the mouth with an arrow, and within a doubletressure flory-counterflory gules, *Howard*; 2nd gules, three lions passant guardant in pale or, and a label of three points argent, *Thomas of Brotherton*: 3rd, checky or and azure, *Warren*; 4th gules, a lion rampant argent, *Mowbray*: in the centre of the four quarterings a crescent for difference. **Crest,**— On a chapeau gules, turned up ermine, a lion statant guardant tail extended or, gorged with a ducal coronet argent, and charged on the body with a crescent for difference. **Supporters,**— Two lions argent, each charged on the shoulder with a crescent sable.

Seat,—Charlton Park, Malmesbury.

SON LIVING.

Alexander Charles Michael Winston **Robsahm** (*Viscount Andover*), *b.* Sept. 17th, 1974.

BROTHERS LIVING.

Hon. Maurice David Henry (3, Walpole St., SW3), *b.* 1936; ed. at Eton; served with RN (Suez) 1955-57.

Hon. Patrick Greville (Garsdon Mill, Malmesbury, Wilts.), *b.* 1940; ed. at Eton , at Grenoble (France) and Heidelberg Univs., and at Peterhouse Camb .(BA); Lt. R. Wiltshire Yeo: *m.* 1966, Mary Elizabeth, da. of Dr. Clarence Laverne Johnson, of 140, Park Lane, W1 [see Royden, Bt.], and has issue living, Jason Patrick, *b.* 1968,—Rory Alexander, *b.* 1970,—Timothy Charles, *b.* 1973,—Charles Edward, *b.* 1974.

UNCLES LIVING. (*Sons of 19th Earl.*)

Hon. Cecil John Arthur, *b.* 1908 ; ed. at Eton: *m.* 1939, Frances Drake. *Residence,*—1511, Summit Ridge Drive, Beverly Hills, California, U.S.A.

Hon. Greville Reginald, *b.* 1909; ed. at Eton; formerly Lieut. King's Shropshire LI; is Lt.-Cdr.; RNR; 1939-45 War with Destroyers; was a Councillor of City of Westminster 1937-50 (Mayor 1946-47); MP for St. Ives Div. of Cornwall (*National L* and *C*) 1950-66: *m.* 1945, Mary, da. of the late W. S. Ridehalgh, and has issue living, Caroline Margaret, *b.* 1947: *m.* 1965, Nigel Stacey. *Residence,*—Redlynch, Brouch nr. Mersch, Luxembourg. *Clubs,*—Royal Cornwall Yacht, RNVR, White's.

WIDOW LIVING OF SON OF EIGHTEENTH EARL.

Nancy Induna Frances Caroline (The Red House, Tydehams, Newbury), el. da. of the late Edgar Lubbock, LLB [see B. Avebury], *m.* 1925, the Hon. James Knyvett Estcourt Howard, who *d.* 1964, and has issue living [see colls., infra].

COLLATERAL BRANCHES LIVING.

Issue of the late Hon. James Knyvett Estcourt Howard, 2nd son of 18th Earl, *b.* 1886, *d.* 1964: *m.* 1925, Nancy Induna Frances Caroline, ante, el. da. of the late Edgar Lubbock, LLB [see B. Avebury, colls.]:—
Virginia Mary Eloise, *b.* 1926: *m.* 1948, Capt. David John Richard Ker, MC, DL, late Coldstream Guards, of Portavo, Donaghadee, Co. Down, and has issue living, David Peter James, *b.* 1951,—Caroline Moira, *b.* 1949: *m.* 1968 (m. diss. 1972), Thomas William Fellowes [see V. Hampden, colls.]—Camilla Rosanna Gian, *b.* 1959.——Priscilla Margaret, *b.* 1930: *m.* 1954, Jeremy Porter, of Dalchully, Laggan, Newtownmore, Inverness-shire.

Grandson of the late Hon. Greville Theophilus Howard, 2nd son of 17th Earl :—
Issue of the late Brigadier Sir Charles Alfred Howard, G.C.V.O., D.S.O., *b.* 1878, *d.* 1958: *m.* 1908, Miriam Eleanore, who *d.* 1969, dau. of the late Lieut.-Col. Edward Mashiter Dansey, O.B.E. [B. Gifford] :—
Henry Redvers Greville, *b.* 1911 ; Lieut.-Col. (retired) King's Roy. Rifle Corps : *m.* 1st, 1940, Patience (from whom he obtained a divorce, 1946), dau. of Lieut.-Col. C. R. Nicholl, of 52, Queen's Gate, S.W.7 ; 2ndly, 1948, Odette, dau. of Henry Clark, of Ventnor, Isle of Wight, and widow of Flight-Lt. Gordon-Crosby, RAF, and has issue living, (by 1st m.) Greville Patrick Charles (36, Brompton Sq., SW3), *b.* 1941: *m.* 1968, Zoë, yr. da. of Douglas Walker, of 65, Pont St., SW1, and Paris,—Amanda Susan Diana (Castle Rising, King's Lynn, Norfolk), *b.* 1943: *m.* 1968, Alexander Simon James Montague Burton, who *d.* 1972, and has issue living, Michael Alexander Greville James *b.* 1971, Sophie Amelia Sarah *b.* 1970,—(by 2nd m.) Katherine Venetia, *b.* 1948. *Residence,*—Castle Rising, nr. King's Lynn, Norfolk.

PREDECESSOF S.—[1] *Lord* THOMAS Howard, *K.G., P.C.*, 2nd son of Thomas, 4th Duke of Norfolk, was summoned to Parliament in right of his mother as *Baron Howard de Walden* (peerage of England) 1597, and in 1603 was cr. *Earl of Suffolk* (peerage of England) ; was a Commr. for executing the office of Earl Marshal of England, in which capacity he was mainly instrumental in discovering the Gunpowder Plot ; elected Chancellor of Cambridge University 1613 ; was Lord High Treasurer of England 1613-18 ; *d.* 1626 ; *s.* by his son [2] THEOPHILUS, *K.G., P.C.*, 2nd Earl; summoned to Parliament in his father's Barony of Howard de Walden; was Lord Warden of the Cinque Ports, Constable of Dover Castle, and Capt. of the Band of Gentlemen Pensioners; *d.* 1640; *s.* by his el. son [3] JAMES, *K.B.*, 3rd Earl; *d.* 1689 without male issue, when the Barony of Howard de Walden went into abeyance between his daughters, and the Earldom devolved upon his brother [4] GEORGE, 4th Earl, who *d.s.p.* 1691; *s.* by his next brother [5] HENRY, 5th Earl; *d.* 1709; *s.* by his son [6] HENRY, 6th Earl, who in 1706 had been cr. *Baron Chesterford*, Co. Essex and *Earl of Bindon*, Co. Dorset (peerage of GB); was sometime Dep. Earl Marshal, in which capacity in 1707 he held a Court of Chivalry; *d.* 1718; *s.* by his son [7] CHARLES WILLIAM, 7th Earl; *d.s.p.* 1722, when the Barony of Chesterford and the Earldom of Bindon expired, and the Earldom of Suffolk devolved upon his uncle [8] EDWARD, 8th Earl ; *d.* unmarried 1731; *s.* by his brother [9] CHARLES, 9th Earl; *d.* 1733; *s.* by his son [10] HENRY, 10th Earl; *d.s.p.* 1745; *s.* by his kinsman [11] HENRY BOWES, *PC*, 11th Earl, who had previously *s.* as 4th *Earl of Berkshire* (see *⁎⁎* infra); appointed Dep. Earl Marshal of England 1708; *d.* 1757; *s.* by his grandson [12] HENRY, 12th Earl; *d.* 1779; *s.* by his son [13] HENRY, 13th Earl; *d.* 1779; *s.* by his great-uncle [14] THOMAS, 14th Earl, 3rd son of 11th Earl; *d.s.p.* 1783; *s.* by his kinsman [15] JOHN, 15th Earl, great-grandson of the Hon. Philip, 7th son of 11st Earl of Berks.; was a Gen. in the Army; *d.* 1820; *s.* by his son [16] THOMAS, 16th Earl; *d.* 1851; *s.* by his son [17] CHARLES JOHN, 17th Earl; *b.* 1804; sat as M.P. for Malmesbury (*L*) 1832-41 : *m.* 1829, Isabella, who *d.* 1891, dau. of Lord Henry Howard and niece of 12th Duke of Norfolk; *d.* 1876; *s.* by his son [18] HENRY CHARLES, 18th Earl of Suffolk and 11th Earl of Berkshire, *b.* 1833; M.P. for Malmesbury (*L*) 1859-68: *m.* 1868, Mary Eleanor Lauderdale, who *d.* 1928, dau. of the late Hon. Henry Amelius Coventry; *d.* 1898 : *s.* by his el. son [19] HENRY MOLYNEUX PAGET, 19th Earl of Suffolk and 12th Earl of Berkshire, *b.* 1877; Maj. RFA: *m.* 1904, Marguerite Hyde, who *d.* 1968, da. of the late Levi Zeigler Leiter, of Dupont Circle, Washington, USA ; *d.* (killed in action) 1917; *s.* by his el. son [20] CHARLES HENRY GEORGE, *GC*, 20th Earl of Suffolk and 13th Earl of Berkshire; *b.* 1906: *m.* 1934, Mimi, who *d.* 1966, da. of the late Alfred George Forde-Pigott; *d.* (on active ser.) 1941; *s.* by his el. son [21] MICHAEL JOHN JAMES GEORGE ROBERT, 21st Earl of Suffolk, and 14th Earl of Berkshire and present peer; also Viscount Andover, and Baron Howard of Charlton.

⁎⁎ [1] *Hon.* THOMAS Howard, *KG*, 2nd son of the 1st Earl of Suffolk was cr. *Baron Howard of Charlton*, co. Wilts, and *Viscount Andover* (peerage of England) 1625, and *Earl of Berkshire* (peerage of England) 1626; *d.* 1660; *s.* by his son [2] CHARLES, 2nd Earl; was summoned to Parliament in his father's Barony of Howard; *d.* 1679; *s.* by his brother [3] THOMAS, 3rd Earl; *d.* 1706; *s.* by his great-nephew [4] HENRY BOWES, 4th Earl (grandson of the Hon. William, 4th son of 1st Earl), who *s.* as 11th Earl of Suffolk (ante).

SUMMERSKILL, BARONESS. (Summerskill.) [Life Baroness 1961.]

EDITH CLARA SUMMERSKILL, *CH, PC*, da. of the late Dr. William Summerskill, of Blackheath, SE3; *b.* April 19th, 1901; ed. at King's Coll., London; MRCS England, and LRCP London; Hon. LLD Newfoundland; a Co. Councillor for Middlesex 1933-38, Parl. Sec. to Min. of Food 1945-50, Min. of National Insurance 1950-51, and Chm. of British Labour Party 1954-55; MP for W. Div. of Fulham (*Lab.*) 1938-55, and for Warrington 1955-61; cr. PC 1949, *Baroness Summerskill,* of Ken Wood, co. London (Life Baroness) 1961, and CH, 1966: *m.* 1925, Edward Jeffrey Samuel, MB, BS, of Llanelly, Carmarthenshire.

Residence,—Pond House, Millfield Lane, Highgate, N.6.

SON LIVING.

Hon. Michael Brynmor SUMMERSKILL (40, Cadogan Sq., SW1), *b.* 1927; ed. St. Paul's Sch., and at Oxford Univ. (BCL, MA); Bar. Middle Temple 1952: *m.* 1st, 1951, Florence, da. of Sydney Elliott; 2ndly, 19—, Audrey Alexandra Brônté Blemings, and has issue by 1st m.

DAUGHTER LIVING.

Hon. Shirley SUMMERSKILL, *MP* (c/o House of Commons, SW1), *b.* 1931; ed. at Oxford Univ. (BM, BCh and MA); MP for Halifax (*Lab*) since 1964; an Under-Sec. of State Home Office since 1974: *m.* 1957, John Ryman, Bar.-at-law.

SUTHERLAND, COUNTESS OF. (Sutherland.) [Earl S. about 1235.]

ELIZABETH MILLICENT SUTHERLAND (*Countess of Sutherland*), *b.* March 30th, 1921; *s.* 1963; adopted the surname of Sutherland under Scots Law 1963: *m.* 1946, Charles Noel Janson, DL, late Welsh Guards, and has issue.

Arms.—Gules, three mullets Or (as the ancient Arms of Sutherland of that Ilk), on a bordure of the second a double tressure flory-counterflory of the first (as an Honourable Augmentation). **Crest.**—A Cat-a-mountain sejant rampant proper. **Supporters.**—Dexter, a savage man wreathed about the head and loins with laurel proper, holding in his exterior hand a iub Gules resting upon his shoulder, sinister, another like savage sustaining in his sinister hand and against his shoulder, upon a staff ensigned by the coronet of an Earl, a bannerette Gules, charged of three mullets Or.

Seat,—Dunrobin Castle, Golspie, Sutherland. *Residences,*—39, Edwardes Sq., W8; House of Tongue, by Lairg, Sutherland; Uppat House, Brora, Sutherland.

SONS LIVING.

ALISTAIR CHARLES ST. CLAIR *SUTHERLAND* (*Lord Strathnaver*)(Uppat House, Brora, Sutherland), *b.* Jan. 7th, 1947; ed. at Eton and Ch. Ch., Oxford; Detective Constable, CID Metropolitan Police: *m.* 1968, Eileen Elizabeth, only da. of Richard W. Baker, of Princeton, USA, and has issue.

DAUGHTERS LIVING, *Hon.* Rachel Elizabeth, *b.* 1970.
Hon. Rosemary Millicent, *b.* 1972.

Hon. Martin Dearman SUTHERLAND-JANSON (twin), *b.* 1947; ed. at Eton: *m.* 1974, the Hon. Mary Ann Balfour, da. of 1st Baron Balfour of Inchrye.

DAUGHTER LIVING.

Lady Annabel Elizabeth Hélène SUTHERLAND, *b.* 1952.

COLLATERAL BRANCHES LIVING.

Issue of the late Lady Rosemary Millicent Sutherland-Leveson-Gower, R.R.C., younger dau. of 4th Duke, *b.* 1893, *d.* 1930: *m.* 1919, Viscount Ednam, afterwards 3rd Earl of Dudley [see that title].

Grandchildren of the late Lord Francis Leveson-Gower (2nd son of 3rd Duke), who *s.* his mother as 2nd Earl of Cromartie [see that title].

Grandchildren of the late Lady Florence Leveson-Gower, el. dau. of 3rd Duke, *b.* 1855, *d.* 1881: *m.* 1876, the Rt. Hon. Henry Chaplin, afterwards 1st Viscount Chaplin, who *d.* 1923:—
Issue of the late Eric, 2nd Viscount Chaplin [see that title].
Issue of the late Hon. Edith Helen Chaplin, *D.B.E., b.* 1879, *d.* 1959: *m.* the 7th Marquess of Londonderry, who *d.* 1949 [see that title].
Issue of the late Hon. Florence Chaplin, *b.* 1881, *d.* 1949: *m.* 1920, Charles Richard Hoare, who *d.* 1933:—
Henry Richard (of Wardley House, Wardley, Uppingham, Rutland), *b.* 1922; ed. at Eton; late Life Guards; High Sheriff of Rutland 1961.——Charles Hugh (High Farm, Alexton, Uppingham, Rutland), *b.* 1923; ed. at Eton; High Sheriff of Rutland 1969; 1939-45 War as Lt. RNVR: *m.* 1949, Gillian Lieth, da. of Samuel Ernest Chesterman, and has issue living, a son, *b.* 1955,—a son, *b.* 1959,—a da., *b.* 1952.——Helen (of Wardley, Uppingham, Rutland), *b.* 1921.

Descendants of the late Lady Elizabeth Georgiana Leveson-Gower, V.A., C.I., el. dau. of 2nd Duke, *b.* 1824, *d.* 1878: *m.* 1844, the 8th Duke of Argyll, who *d.* 1900 [see that title].

Granddaughter of the late Lady Evelyn Leveson-Gower, 2nd dau. of 2nd Duke, *b.* 1825, *d.* 1869: *m.* 1843, the 12th Lord Blantyre, who *d.* 1900 [see Gladstone Bt., colls.].

Descendants of the late Lady Caroline Leveson-Gower, 3rd dau. of 2nd Duke, *b.* 1827, *d.* 1887: *m.* 1847, the 4th Duke of Leinster, who *d.* 1887 [see that title].

Descendants of the late Lady Constance Gertrude Leveson-Gower, yst. dau. of 2nd Duke, *b.* 1834, *d.* 1880: *m.* 1852, the 1st Duke of Westminster [see that title].

Descendants of the late Lord Francis Leveson-Gower (cr. *Earl of Ellesmere*], 3rd son of Elizabeth, Countess of Sutherland and 1st Duke [see D. Sutherland].

Descendants of the late Lady Charlotte Sophia Leveson-Gower, el. dau. of Elizabeth, Countess of Sutherland and 1st Duke, *b.* 1788, *d.* 1870: *m.* 1814, the 13th Duke of Norfolk [see that title]. Descendants of the late Lady Elizabeth Mary Leveson-Gower, younger dau. of Elizabeth, Countess of Sutherland and 1st Duke, *b.* 1797, *d.* 1891 : *m.* 1819, the 2nd Marquess of Westminster, who *d.* 1869 [see D. Westminster].

PREDECESSORS.—[1] WILLIAM of Murray (Moray, the vast northern province of which his family were the leading barons at end of 12th century) afterwards called William of Sutherland, el. son of Hugh Freskin or de Moray, Lord of Duffus in Moray; *s.* his father as Lord of Sutherland before 1222; *cr.* Earl of Sutherland after 1232; *d.* 1248; *s.* by his son [2] WILLIAM Sutherland, 2nd Earl; defeated Norse invaders of Sutherland 1263; *d.* 1306/7; *s.* by his el. son [3] WILLIAM, 3rd Earl, attended Parliament at St. Andrews 1308/9 as an adherent of King Robert Bruce; *d.* 1330; *s.* by his brother [4] KENNETH, 4th Earl: *m.* (according to Sir Robert Gordon) Mary, dau. of Donald, Earl of Mar; killed at Halidon Hill 1333; *s.* by his el. son [5] WILLIAM, 5th Earl; taken prisoner at Nevill's Cross 1346; had a blood feud with the Mackays of Strathnaver that lasted three centuries: *m.* 1st, 1342, Margaret, who *d.* 1346, dau. of King Robert I; 2ndly, 1347, Joan, dau. of Sir John Menteith of Rusky, and widow of Malise, 7th Earl of Strathearn, of John Campbell, Earl of Atholl, and of Maurice Moray, Earl of Strathearn; *d.* about 1371; *s.* by his el. surv. son (by 2nd wife) [6] ROBERT, 6th Earl, after whom his castle of Dunrobin ("Robert's Castle") was named; mentioned by Froissart as a leader of invasion of England 1388; *m.* 1389, Margaret Stewart, nat. dau. of Alexander, Earl of Buchan, "the Wolf of Badenoch", 4th son of King Robert II; *d.* about 1427; *s.* by his el. son [7] JOHN, 7th Earl; knighted on battlefield near Liège 1408; resigned Earldom to his son John, Master of Sutherland 1456: *m.* Margaret, who *d.* 1509/10, dau. of Sir William Baillie of Lamington; *d.* about 1460; his el. surv. son [8] JOHN, 8th Earl; *s.* 1456; became an idiot 1494: *m.* 1st, (according to Sir Robert Gordon) dau. of Alexander Macdonald, Lord of the Isles and Earl of Ross; 2ndly, Fingole, said to have been dau. of William, Thane of Cawdor, and widow of Sir John Munro, 11th of Foulis; 3rdly, Catherine; *d.* about 1508; *s.* by his son, by his first wife [9] JOHN, *de jure* 9th Earl; also became mentally incapable, so was ward of the Crown, his estates being administered by High Treasurer; his service as heir was opposed by his half-brother Alexander (son of 2nd marriage), who in 1509 resigned his claim; *d.* 1514; *s.* by his sister [10] ELIZABETH, Countess of Sutherland: *m.* about 1500 Adam Gordon of Aboyne (who *d.* 1538), *jure uxoris* 10th Earl of Sutherland, 2nd son of 2nd Earl of Huntly; constantly at war with her half-brother, who seized Dunrobin Castle; she resigned Earldom, with consent of her husband in favour of her son Alexander 1527, who was infeft in reversion: *d.* 1535; *s.* by their grandson [11] JOHN Gordon (el. son of Alexander Gordon, Master of Sutherland, who *m.* Lady Janet Stewart, dau. of 2nd Earl of Atholl, and *d.* 1529/30) 11th Earl; *b* 1525; accompanied Queen Dowager to France 1550, and *cr.* Knt. of St. Michael there; involved in Earl of Huntly's revolt, and dignities and titles forfeited 1563, when he fled to Flanders; restored by Parliament in 1567; assisted at Queen Mary's marriage to Bothwell: *m.* 1st, 1545/46, Lady Elizabeth Campbell, who *d.s.p.* about 1548, dau. of 3rd Earl of Argyll, and widow of James, Earl of Moray, nat. son of James IV; 2ndly, 1548, Lady Helen Stuart, who *d.* 1564, dau. of 12th Earl of Lennox and widow of 6th Earl of Erroll; 3rdly. Marion Seton, who *d.* (poisoned) 1567, dau. of 4th Lord Seton, and widow of 4th Earl of Menteith; *d.* (poisoned) at Dunrobin 1567; *s.* by his only surviving son [12] ALEXANDER, 12th Earl, *b.* 1552; Hereditary Sheriff of Inverness; acquired Lordship of Strathnaver from Earl of Huntly in exchange for Aboyne; made peace treaties with his ancestral enemies the Mackay chief and Earl of Caithness: *m.* 1st, 1567 (marriage dissolved 1572) Lady Barbara Sinclair, el. dau. of 4th Earl of Caithness; 2ndly, 1573, Lady Jean Gordon (who *m.* 3rdly 1599 Alexander Ogilvie of Boyne, and *d.* 1629), dau. of 4th Earl of Huntly, and formerly wife of 4th Earl of Bothwell (afterwards husband of Mary, Queen of Scots); *d.* 1594; *s.* by his el. son [13] JOHN, 13th Earl, *b.* 1576, bore the Sword of State before the King at Rising of Parliament 1597, which he claimed as his hereditary right; encouraged industry in Sutherland, opening coalpits at Brora; obtained 1601 a novodamus of Earldom, which was erected into a Regality, with grant of Hereditary Shrievalty of Sutherland (his territories being specially erected into a sheriffdom), in favour, failing heirs male of his body, of his brothers and their issue male, whom all failing, to Adam Gordon, 3rd son of 1st Marquess of Huntly and his heirs male whatsoever: *m.* 1600, the Hon. Agnes Elphinstone, who *d.* 1617, el. dau. of 4th Lord Elphinstone; *d.* 1615; *s.* by his 4th but el. surv. son [14] JOHN, 14th Earl, *b.* 1609; was the first man to sign the National Covenant 1638; active Covenanter during Civil War (Commr. for Sutherland); Col. of Horse and Foot, Sutherland; Lord Privy Seal (for Cromwell) 1656-58; bore the Sceptre at opening of 1st Parliament of Charles II 1661; obtained 1662 a novodamus of Earldom in favour of his son George, Lord Strathnaver; *m.* 1st, 1632, Lady Jean Drummond, who *d.* 1637, dau. of 1st Earl of Perth; 2ndly, 1639, Hon. Anne Fraser, who *d.s.p.* 1658, dau. of 7th Lord Lovat: *d.* 1679; *s.* by his only surv. son [15] GEORGE, 15th Earl, *b.* 1633; Commr. of Great Seal (for William III) 1689; obtained 1681 a novodamus of Earldom in favour of his el. son and their heirs male of the body, whom failing, to Lord Strathnaver's el. dau. and other heirs named: *m.* 1659, Lady Jean Wemyss, who *d.* 1715; dau. and heir of line of 2nd Earl of Wemyss, and widow of Archibald, Earl of Angus, son of 1st Marquess of Douglas; *d.* 1703; *s.* by his son [16] JOHN Gordon, (later Sutherland) *K.T., P.C.*, 16th Earl, *b.* 1661; secured Inverness for William III; raised his own Regt. of Foot, which he commanded in Flanders campaign 1694; later Lt.-Gen.; Commr. for the Union 1706; was elected one of the first 16 Representative Peers; as Lord-Lt. of all the six northern counties, he held them for George I against Jacobite Rising 1715; resumed ancient surname of Sutherland about 1670; obtained 1706 a novodamus of Earldom in favour of his son Lord Strathnaver and himself, and their heirs male of the body, whom failing the heirs female of the body of Lord Strathnaver without division, and their issue male, whom failing the Earl's heirs female: *m.* 1st, 1680, Helen Cochrane, who *d.* 1690, dau. of William Lord Cochrane [E. Dundonald]; 2ndly, Lady Katherine Tollemache, who *d.* about 1705, dau. of Countess of Dysart (Duchess of Lauderdale) and widow of James, Lord Doune [E. Moray]; 3rdly, 1727, Frances, who *d.* 1732, dau. of Sir James Hodgson of Bramwith Hall, Yorks, and widow of Sir Thomas Travell; *d.* 1733; *s.* by his grandson [17] WILLIAM, 17th Earl (son of William, Lord Strathnaver, by Katherine, dau. of William Morison of Prestongrange, E. Lothian); *b.* 1708; a Representative Peer; supported Govt. 1745-46, present at Culloden; received £1,000 in compensation for abolition of Hereditary Shrievalty of Sutherland 1747: *m.* 1734, Lady Elizabeth Wemyss, who *d.* 1747, dau. of 3rd Earl of Wemyss; *d.* 1750; *s.* by his only son [18] WILLIAM, 18th Earl *b.* 1735; Lt.-Col. Comdt. of a Bde. of Highlanders; a Representative Peer: *m.* 1761, Mary, who *d.* 1766, dau. and co-heir of William Maxwell, of Preston, Kirkcudbright; *d.* 1766; *s.* by his only surv. dau. [19] ELIZABETH, Countess of Sutherland, *b.* 1765; her right to the Peerage, which was opposed by Sir Robert Gordon, descendant of 2nd son of 12th Earl, as heir male of body of Adam Gordon, Earl of Sutherland, husband of Elizabeth Countess of Sutherland [20 ante], and by George Gordon of Forse, as heir male of 1st Earl, was confirmed by House of Lords 1771; raised Sutherland Fencibles 1779 and 1793: *m.* 1785, the 1st Duke of Sutherland; *d.* 1839 [20–23]; succession followed the Dukedom of Sutherland until the death of 5th Duke 1963; he was *s.* in the Earldom by his niece [24] ELIZABETH MILLICENT (only da. of the late Lord Alistair St. Clair Sutherland-Leveson-Gower, M.C., 2nd son of 4th Duke), Countess of Sutherland and present peeress; also Lady Strathnaver.

SUTHERLAND, DUKE OF. (Egerton.) [Duke U.K. 1833, Bt. E. 1620.]

JOHN SUTHERLAND EGERTON,
6th Duke; *b.* May 10, 1915; *s.*
as 5th Earl of Ellesmere 1944,
and as 6th Duke of Sutherland
1963; ed. at Eton, and at Trin.
Coll., Camb.; late Capt. Roy.
Armoured Corps (TA), and a DL
for Berwickshire; 1939-45 War
(prisoner): *m.* 1939, Lady Diana
Evelyn Percy, dau. of 8th Duke
of Northumberland.

Arms,—Argent, a lion rampant gules
between three pheons sable. **Crest.**—On a
chapeau gules, turned up ermine, a lion
rampant of the first, supporting an arrow
or, feathered and headed argent. **Supporters,**—*Dexter,* a horse argent, ducally
gorged or; *sinister,* a griffin or, ducally gorged
azure.

Seats,—Mertoun, St. Boswell's, Roxburghshire; Stetchworth Park, Newmarket,
Suffolk. *Clubs,*—Jockey, White's, Turf.

SISTERS LIVING.

Lady Jane Mary, *b.* 1909: *m.* 1934, Capt. Richard Ladislas Scrope, Coldstream Guards, and has issue
living, Simon Egerton (6, Blomfield Rd., W9 1AH), *b.* 1934; late 2nd Lt. Coldm. Gds.: *m.* 1970,
Jane, da. of Sir Kenneth Wade Parkinson [see By. Bingley, ext.], and has issue living, Simon Henry
Richard *b.* 1974, Emily Katharine *b.* 1972,—Elizabeth Jane, *b.* 1937. *Residence,*—Danby House,
Middleham Leyburn, Yorks.
Lady Mary, *b.* 1911: *m.* 1945, Lieut.-Col. Conyers Stephen Scrope, M.C., Green Howards, and has
issue living, Annabel Margaret Diana, *b.* 1945,—Rosemary, *b.* 1947,—Diana Therese Violet, *b.*
1951. *Residence,*—Denton Lodge, Harleston, Norfolk.
Lady Susan Alice, *b.* 1913: *m.* 1933 (m. diss. 1966), Maj. John Marjoribanks Askew, Grenadier Guards,
and has issue living, Henry John, *b.* 1940; ed. at Eton,—Sarah Caroline, *b.* 1936: *m.* 1959, Charles
Michael Henderson, of Barnsley Park, Cirencester, and 30, Phillimore Gdns., W.8 [see B. Faringdon,
colls.]. *Residence,*—Stone House, Sprouston, Kelso, Roxburghshire.
Lady Margaret, *b.* 1918; sometime Junior Com. A.T.S.; was a Lady-in-Waiting to H.R.H. Princess
Elizabeth 1946-9: *m.* 1948, Sir John Rupert Colville, CB, CVO [see V. Colville of Culross, colls.].
Residences,—32 Hyde Park Sq., W.2; The Old Rectory Stratfield Saye Reading
Lady Alice, C.V.O., *b.* 1923; appointed a Lady-in-Waiting to H.M. the Queen when H.R.H. Princess
Elizabeth 1949, and a Woman of the Bedchamber to H.M. the Queen 1953; C.V.O. 1957. *Resi-
dences,*—26, Hans Crescent, S.W.1; Stetchworth Park, Newmarket.

WIDOW LIVING OF FIFTH DUKE.

CLARE JOSEPHINE (DUNKERLEY) (*Clare, Duchess of Sutherland*) (14, Hyde Park Gdns., W2; ES
Carregedur, Capdedera, Mallorca, Spain), da. of the late Herbert O'Brien, of Calcutta: *m.* 1944, as his
2nd wife, the 5th Duke, who *d.* 1963.

WIDOW LIVING OF FOURTH EARL OF ELLESMERE.

VIOLET (*Countess of Ellesmere*) (of Stetchworth Park, Newmarket, Suffolk, and 26, Hans Cres., S.W.1)
dau. of 4th Earl of Durham; a D.G.St.J.: *m.* 1905, the 4th Earl, who *d.* 1944.

COLLATERAL BRANCHES LIVING.

Issue of the late Capt. Lord Alistair St. Clair Sutherland-Leveson-Gower, M.C.,
2nd son of 4th Duke, *b.* 1890, *d.* 1921: *m.* 1918, Elizabeth Hélène, who *d.* 1931
(having *m.* 2ndly, 1931, Col. Baron George Osten Driesen), dau. of Warren
Gardener Demarest, of New York City:—
Elizabeth Millicent (*Countess of Sutherland*); *s.* as Countess of Sutherland 1963 [see that title].
Issue of the late Hon. Francis William George Egerton, 2nd son of 3rd Earl of
Ellesmere, *b.* 1874, *d.* 1948: *m.* 1897, Hilda Margaret, who *d.* 1958, dau. of the late
Canon Curteis:—
CYRIL REGINALD, *b.* Sept. 7th, 1905; ed. at Lancing, and at Trin. Coll., Camb.; European War
1939-45 as Capt. Hampshire Regt.; was Prime Warden of Dyers' Co., 1954: *m.* 1st, 1934, Mary,
who *d.* 1949, dau. of the Rt. Hon. Sir Ronald Hugh Campbell, G.C.M.G.; 2ndly, 1954, Mary Truda,
only dau. of the late Sir (Thomas) Sydney Lea, 2nd Bt., and has issue living, (by 1st marriage)
Francis Ronald, *b.* 1940,—Lucy Helen, *b.* 1937: *m.* 1958, Michael A. Pelham, JP, of 41, Yeoman's
Row, SW3, and has issue living, Charles Peregrine *b.* 1959, Laura Mary *b.* 1962,—Katharine Mary, *b.*
1942,—Alice Marion, *b.* 1946: *m.* 1971, Thomas David Fremantle [see B. Cottesloe, colls.]. *Residence,*
—Hall Farm, Newmarket, Suffolk.——Phyllis Mary (5, y Llys, Landbedr Hall, Ruthin, Clwyd),
b. 1900: *m.* 1st, 1920, Guy Coltman Rogers, from whom she obtained a divorce 1933; 2ndly, 1934,
Anthony Richards, from whom she obtained a divorce 1946, and has issue living, (by 1st m.) Helen
Coltman (4, Townland Close, Biddenden, Kent), *b.* 1920,—Penelope Elizabeth, *b.* 1922: *m.* 1947,
Lt.-Cdr. Charles St. Clair Cameron, RN, of Beechwood, Corfton, nr. Craven Arms, Salop, and has
issue living, Belinda Jane *b.* 1948: *m.* 1971, Andrew James Murcott, of The Ridge Farm, Linley,
Bishop's Castle, Salop, Stella Mary *b.* 1954, Penelope Anne (twin) *b.* 1954,—Gillian Margaret, *b.* 1927:
m. 1st, 1954 Francesco Aprea, from whom she obtained a divorce 1969; 2ndly, 1970, Sidney Alfred
Lewitt, of Longwater, Llanbedr, Ruthin, Clwyd, and has issue living, (by 1st m.) Elizabeth Ann
b. 1964.
Issue of the late Hon. Thomas Henry Frederick Egerton, 3rd son of 3rd Earl of
Ellesmere, *b.* 1876, *d.* 1953: *m.* 1902, Lady Bertha Anson, who *d.* 1959, dau. of
3rd Earl of Lichfield:—
Mildred Helen (*Hon. Mrs. Hew N. Dalrymple*), *b.* 1903: *m.* 1st, 1925, the 4th Baron Oranmore and
Browne, from whom she obtained a divorce 1936; 2ndly, 1938, Capt the Hon. Hew North Dalrymple,
T.D., late Black Watch (T.A.) [see E. Stair]. *Residence,*—Castlehill, Ballantrae, Ayrshire.——
Pamela Katharine, *b.* 1918: *m.* 1940, Lieut.-Col. Ralph Capel Stockley, Roy. Northumberland
Fusiliers, who *d.* (killed in action during European War) 1944, and has issue living, Jane Margaret,
b. 1942: *m.* 1974, Gerard Balfour Chichester, of Llangoed, Llyswen, Brecon, Powys,—Sally Elizabeth,
b. 1944. *Residence,*—Wren Cottage, Tit *e*Hill, Englefield Green, Surrey.
Grandsons of the late William Francis Egerton, son of the late Adm. the Hon.
Francis Egerton, 2nd son of 1st Earl of Ellesmere:—

Issue of the late Capt. Francis Egerton, *b.* 1896, *d.* 1935: *m.* 1921, the Hon. Doris Mary
Pottinger Meysey-Thompson [who *d.* 1953, having *m.* 2ndly, 1938, Major John Humphrey
Allison Seed, T.D., D.L., J.P., Yorkshire Hussars (Yeo.)], dau. of 1st Baron Knaresborough:—
Anthony Francis, *b.* 1921; ed. at Eton; formerly Lieut. 60th Rifles, and Flight Lieut. R.A.F.: *m.*
1946, Pauline Clodagh, dau. of Trevor Toulmin Seaton Leadam, of Colebrook, Watersfield, Sussex,
and has issue living, Simon Francis Cavendish, *b.* 1949,—Fulke Charles Granville, *b.* 1952. *Resi-*
dence,—Passfield Manor, Liphook, Hants. *Club,*—Brooks's.——Michael Godolphin, *b.* 1924; ed·
at Eton; formerly Lieut. 17th/21st Lancers: *m.* 1st, 1951, Nicolette, younger dau. of Guilio Giorgio
de Gardiol, of La Fontana, Lusana, San Giovanni, Italy; 2ndly, 1957, Elizabeth Anne Bowring,
only dau. of Leslie Bowring Wimble, of Romany Ridge, North Chailey, Lewes, Sussex, and has issue
living, (by 2nd m.) Mark William Godolphin, *b.* 1958,—Robin Michael Bowring, *b.* 1962,—Nicholas
b. 1967.——David William, *b.* 1930; ed. at Stowe; Capt. (ret.) 17th/21st Lancers: *m.* 1956, Patricia
Mar y Treharne, da. of the late Archibald Alan Treharne Thomas, formerly wife of William Rippon
Bissill, and has issue living, Francis David, *b.* 1959. *Residence,*—Priory Farm, Kington St.
Michael, Chippenham, Wilts. *Club,*—Cavalry.

Grandson of the late Lieut.-Col. the Hon. Arthur Frederick Egerton, 4th son of
1st Earl of Ellesmere:—
Issue of the late Claude Francis Arthur Egerton, *b.* 1864, *d.* 1957: *m.* 1900, Alexandra, who
d. 1938, dau. of the late H. N. Ritchie, of Thorpe, Surrey, and widow of Charles Bellairs:—
Scrope Arthur Francis Sutherland, *b.* 1902; Lieut.-Col. (ret.) Highland L.I.: *m.* 1933, Marjorie,
dau. of the late Hugh Morrison, M.P. [E. Granville], and has issue living, Sarah Jane Mary, *b.* 1934,—
Susan Alexandra, *b.* 1936: *m.* 1957, David John Yorke [see B. Clitheroe],—Katharine Rose, *b.*
1946. *Residence,*—Pertwood Manor, Hindon, Salisbury, Wilts.

(In remainder to Marquessate of Stafford)
Descendants of the late Rt. Hon. Lord Granville Leveson-Gower, G.C.B.
(youngest son of 1st Marquess of Stafford), who was cr. *Earl Granville* 1833 [see
that title].

(In remainder to Earldom of Gower)
Granddaughter of the late John Leveson-Gower, great-grandson of 1st Earl
Gower :—
Issue (by 2nd marriage) of the late Capt. John Edward Leveson-Gower, *b.* 1826, *d.* 1892:
m. 1st, 1850, Harriet Jane, who *d.* 1878, dau. of the late Capt. John Hunter; 2ndly,
1879, Katherine Elizabeth, who *d.* 1928, dau. of Basil Edward Arthur Cochrane [E. Dun-
donald, colls.]:—
Idonea Gertrude, *b.* 1883 : *m.* 1907, Henry Michael Hodgson, O.B.E., and has issue living, Peter
Charles (Shirburn Lodge, Watlington, Oxford, OX9 5HU), *b.* 1910; ed. at Wellington Coll., and
Corpus Christi Coll., Camb.: *m.* 1939, Cicell Alicia King, of Arley Rectory, Warwickshire, and
has issue living, Charles Christopher *b.* 1945: *m.* 1969, Catherine Rose, da. of Arthur Roy Collins
of The Gate House, Hunsdon, Ware (and has issue living, Henry Charles *b.* 1971, Alice Catherine
b. 1973), Arnold Henry *b.* 1949, Judith Gertrude *b.* 1941, Helen Grizel Alicia, *b.* 1947: *m.* 1972,
Lt.-Cdr. John Glasson, RN,—Henry Edward (of Astley Abbots, Bridgnorth, Salop), *b.* 1912: *m.* 1938,
Natalie Beatrice, da. of Duncan Davidson, of Priory Row, Coventry,—Elizabeth Katharine (Calle
Mijas 30, Pueblo Lopez, Fuengirola, Malaga, Spain), *b.* 1909: *m.* 1939, Richard Townsend, who
d. 1957. *Residence,*—Astley Abbots, Bridgnorth, Salop.

Grandchildren of the late Col. Charles Camerton Leveson-Gower, CMG, OBE, el.
son of the late Capt. Hugh Broke Boscawen Leveson-Gower, 2nd son of John
Leveson-Gower (ante):—
Issue of the late Lt.-Col. Harold Boscawen Leveson-Gower, *b.* 1905, *d.* 1973: *m.* 1930, Kath
leen Mary (The Green, Cotherstone, Barnard Castle, co. Durham), da. of the late Sir Murrough
John Wilson, KBE [B. Inchiquin, colls.]:—
Charles Murrough (Sleningford Grange, Ripon, Yorks.), *b.* 1933; ed. at Eton; Maj. Yorks. Yeo. (TA):
m. 1960, Rosemary Ann, da. of the late Maj. Charles John Frederick Platt, 3rd Hussars, of Muir-
houselaw, St. Boswells, Roxburghshire, and has issue living, Mark Broke, *b.* 1961,—Henry Boscawen, *b.* 1962,—Alice Victoria, *b.* 1966.——Anastasia, *b.* 1931: *m.* 1958, Capt. Robert Kynaston
Studd, of Manor Farm, Rockbourne, Fordingbridge, Hants., el. son of Sir Eric Studd, OBE, 2nd Bt.

Issue of the late Brig-Gen. Philip Leveson-Gower, CMG, DSO, DL, *b.* 1871, *d.* 1939: *m.* 1899,
Eleanor Marcia, who *d.* 1975, da. of Christopher R. Nugent, JP, formerly of The Hall,
Pinner, Middx.
Hugh Nugent, *b.* 1900; ed. at Haileybury; Brigadier late R.A.; sometime Lieut. R.F.A.,
and Capt. and A.D.C. to Gen. Officer Comdg.-in-Ch., Allied Armies, Constantinople: *m.* 1st,
1934 (marriage dissolved 1948), Avril Joy, dau. of the late Sir John Ashley Mullens, and formerly
wife of Prince George Imeretinsky ; 2ndly, 1949, Rachel Wilkins, dau. of Major H. H. Grotrian,
of Claridge House, Davies Street, W.1, and has issue living, (by 1st marriage) Lucinda Gaye,
b. 1935: *m.* 1955, Spencer Le Marchant, MP [see Le Marchant, Bt.]. *Residence,*—Charleshill Court,
Tilford, Surrey.——Elizabeth Ellen, *b.* 1915: *m.* 1945, Mark William Harford, who *d.* 1969, and has
issue living, Philip Hugh, *b.* 1946,—Gerald Mark, *b.* 1948. *Residence,*—Little Sodbury Manor,
Chipping Sodbury, Gloucestershire.

Grandchildren of the late Granville William Gresham Leveson-Gower, son of the
late William Leveson-Gower (*b.* 1806) (infra):—
Issue of the late Granville Charles Gresham Leveson-Gower, *b.* 1865, *d.* 1948 : *m.* 1894,
Evelyn Mildred, who *d.* 1957, dau. of the late Henry A. Brassey, of Preston Hall,
Aylesford :—
Richard Henry Gresham (of Titsey Place, Oxted, Surrey), *b.* 1894; ed. at Eton; 1914-19 War in France;
as Lt. Grenadier Guards (Special Reserve); 1939-45 War as Maj. Special List (T.A. Reserve),
D.A.Q.M.G. (Movements), London Dist. 1944-47.——Thomas Christopher Gresham (of Titsey Place,
Oxted, Surrey), *b.* 1903; ed. at Eton, and at Trin. Coll., Camb.

Issue of the late Rev. Frederick Archibald Gresham Leveson-Gower, *b.* 1871, *d.* 1946 : *m.*
1st, 1897, Cecil Eyre, who *d.* 1939, dau. of Sir Walpole Lloyd Greenwell, 1st Bt.; 2ndly,
1940, Elizabeth, who *d.* 1964, da. of the late George Dodds, of Newcastle-on-Tyne:—
(By 1st marriage) Humphrey Leigh Gresham, *b.* 1908 : *m.* 1929, Tracy, dau. of the late R. Hughes.
——Judeth Elyn Gresham, *b.* 1905 : *m.* 1st, 1928, Malcolm Septimus Vaughan ; 2ndly, 1939, Errol
Reginald Thorold Holmes, who *d.* 1960, and has issue living, (by 1st marriage) Gresham Neilus, *b.*
1934,—Jennifer Audrey, *b.* 1930,—Sarah Elyn, *b.* 1932,—(by 2nd marriage) Lavinia, *b.* 1940,—
Theresa, *b.* 1942. *Residence,*—Tudor Cottage, Long Crendon, Aylesbury.

Issue of the late Evelyn Marmaduke Gresham Leveson-Gower, *b.* 1872, *d.* 1938 : *m.* 1906,
Elo Janet Catherine, who *d.* 1963, dau. of the late Lieut.-Col. James Ross Farquharson
[Ross, Bt., cr. 1672, colls.]:—
Alastair Marmaduke Gresham, *b.* 1907 : *m.* 1st, 1934, Marjorie Blackburn, who *d.* 1936, dau. of the
late Herbert Cawtheray ; 2ndly, 1939, Barbara, dau. of William George Higgins, and has issue living,
(by 1st marriage) Anthony Gresham, *b.* 1934,—(by 2nd marriage) Robert Alastair, *b.* 1946. *Resi-*
dence,—5, Rosehill Av., Horsell, Woking, Surrey.——Rupert Evelyn Gresham (of Manor Farm,
Standlake, Withey, Oxon.), *b.* 1911: Capt. King's Own Roy. Regt.: *m.* 1956, May, dau. of William
Clinkard, and has issue living, Charles William Gresham, *b.* 1959,—Catherine Anne Gresham,
b. 1957.

Issue of the late Capt. Cecil Octavius Gresham Leveson-Gower, M.B.E., *b.* 1875, *d.* 1937:
m. 1899, Emma Mary, who *d.* 1964, dau. of the late Philip de Clermont, of Ivy
House, Godstone :—

Constance Violet Gresham, b. 1913. *Residence,*—Ridge End Cottage, Oxted, Surrey.

Granddaughter of the late William Leveson-Gower (b. 1806), son of the late William Leveson-Gower (b. 1779), 3rd son of the late Adm. the Hon. John Leveson-Gower, 6th son of 1st Earl Gower :—
Issue of the late Arthur Francis Gresham Leveson-Gower, b. 1851, d. 1922: m. 1881, Caroline Frederica, who d. 1895, youngest dau. of the late George Savile Foljambe, of Osberton, Notts, and of the late Selina, Viscountess Milton [E. Liverpool, *ext.*] :—
Victoria Sibell Ermyntrude Gresham, b. 1887; assisted Soldiers' and Sailors' Families Assocn. during 1914-18 War ; has Health Visitors' Certificate Central Midwives Board, and Diploma of Institute of Hygiene. *Address.*—207, Scar Lane, Milnsbridge, Huddersfield.

PREDECESSORS.—[1] *Sir* THOMAS Gower, Knt. ; cr. a *Baronet* 1620 ; s. by his son [2] *Sir* THOMAS, 2nd Bt. ; a zealous partisan of Charles I. ; s. by his grandson [3] *Sir* THOMAS, 3rd Bt. ; a Col. of Foot ; d. unmarried 1689 ; s. by his uncle [4] *Sir* WILLIAM Leveson-Gower, 4th Bt. ; sat for many years as M.P. for Newcastle-under-Lyme ; d. 1691 ; s. by his son [5] *Sir* JOHN, 5th Bt. ; was Chancellor of the Duchy of Lancaster cr. *Baron Gower*, of Stittenham, co. York (peerage of Great Britain) 1703 ; d. 1709 ; s. by his son [6] JOHN, *P.C.*, 2nd Baron ; was Lord Privy Seal, twice one of the Lords Justice during the King's absence, and Custos Rotulorum of Staffordshire ; cr *Viscount Trentham* and *Earl Gower* (peerage of Great Britain) 1746 ; d. 1754 ; s. by his son [7] GRANVILLE, *K.G.*, 2nd Earl ; sat successively as M.P. for Bishop's Castle, Westminster, and Lichfield ; was a Lord of the Admiralty 1749, Lord-Lieut. of Staffordshire, Lord Privy Seal 1755-7, Master of the Horse 1757, Keeper of the Great Wardrobe 1760, Lord Chamberlain 1763-5, and Pres. of the Council 1768-79 and 1783-94 ; cr. *Marquess of Stafford* (peerage of Great Britain) 1786 ; d. 1803 ; s. by his son [8] GEORGE GRANVILLE, *K.G.*, *P.C.*, 2nd Marquess: was summoned to Parliament in his father's Barony of Gower 1799; was Ambassador to Paris 1790-2 : m. 1785, Elizabeth, in her own right *Lady Strathnaver* and *Countess of Sutherland* (peerage of Scotland, see Css. Sutherland, ante); cr. *Duke of Sutherland* (peerage of United Kingdom) 1833; d. 1833; s. by his son [9] GEORGE GRANVILLE, *K.G.*, 2nd Duke; summoned to Parliament in his father's Barony of Gower 1826, and in 1839 s. his mother as Baron Strathnaver and Earl of Sutherland; b. 1786; sat as M.P. for St. Mawes 1808; was Lord-Lieut. of co. Sutherland, and Custos Rotulorum of Staffordshire: m. 1823, Harriet Elizabeth Georgiana, *V.A.*, dau. of 6th Earl of Carlisle; d. 1861; s. by his son [10] GEORGE GRANVILLE, *K.G.*, 3rd Duke, b. 1828; M.P. for Sutherland (*L*) 1852-61; Lord-Lieut. of Cromartie and Sutherland: m. 1st, 1849, Anne, *V.A.* [cr. *Countess of Cromartie*, *Viscountess Tarbat* of Tarbat, *Baroness Castlehaven* of Castlehaven and *Baroness Macleod* of Leod (peerage of United kingdom) 1861, with remainder to her second surviving son Francis and the heirs male of his body, to each other of her younger sons in like manner in priority of birth, to said Francis and the heirs of his body, to each other her younger sons in like manner in priority of birth, to her daughter Florence and the heirs of her body, and to each other of her daughters in like manner in priority of birth], who d. 1888 (when the Earldom of Cromartie devolved, in accordance with the special remainder upon her second surviving son, Francis), only child of John Hay Mackenzie; 2ndly, 1889, Mary Caroline, who d. 1912, dau. of the Rev. Richard Michell, D.D., and widow of Arthur Kindersley Blair, 71st Highland L.I.; d. 1892; s. by his el. son [11] CROMARTIE, *K.G.*, 4th Duke; b. 1851; Mayor of Longton 1895; M.P. for Sutherland (*L*) 1874-86; K.G. 1902: m. 1884, Lady Millicent Fanny St. Claire-Erskine, who d. 1955 (having m. 2ndly, 1914, Brig.-Gen. Percy Desmond Fitzgerald, D.S.O., 11th Hussars, from whom she obtained a divorce 1919, and 3rdly, 1919, Lieut.-Col. Geoffrey Ernest Hawes, D.S.O., M.C., Roy. Fusiliers (ret.), who d. 1945), dau. of 4th Earl of Rosslyn; d. 1913; s. by his el. son [12] GEORGE GRANVILLE SUTHERLAND, *K.T.*, *P.C.*, 5th Duke, b. 1888; Lord High Commr. to Gen. Assembly of Ch. of Scotland 1921 and 1922, Under Sec. of State for Air 1922-24, Paymaster-Gen. 1925-28, Under Sec. of State for War 1928-29, Lord Steward of H.M. Household to King Edward VIII 1936, and High Steward of Kingston upon Thames 1953-63: m. 1st, 1912, Lady Eileen Gwladys Butler, who d. 1943, dau. of 7th Earl of Lanesborough; 2ndly, 1944, Mrs. Clare Josephine Dunkerly, dau. of the late Herbert O'Brien, of Calcutta; d. 1963; s. in the Earldom of Sutherland and Lordship of Strathnaver by his niece, Elizabeth Millicent, dau. of the late Capt Lord Alistair St. Clair Sutherland-Leveson-Gower, M.C., 2nd son of 4th Duke, and wife of Charles Noel Janson [see Cs. Sutherland], and in his other honours by his kinsman [13] JOHN SUTHERLAND Egerton, 5th Earl of Ellesmere [see infra *₀*], 6th Duke, and present peer; also Marquess of Stafford, Earl Gower, Earl of Ellesmere, Viscount Trentham, Viscount Brackley, and Baron Gower.

₀[1] *Lord* FRANCIS Leveson-Gower, *K.G.*, *P.C.*, yr. surv. son of 1st Duke; M.P. for Sutherland, 1826-31 and for S. Lancashire 1835-36; a Lord of the Treasury 1827, Ch. Sec. for Ireland 1828, and Lord-Lieut. of Lancashire; assumed the name of Egerton by Roy. licence on succeeding to the estates of the 3rd and last Duke of Bridgwater; cr. *Viscount Brackley* and *Earl of Ellesmere* (peerage of U.K.) 1846; d. 1857; s. by his son [2] GEORGE GRANVILLE FRANCIS, 2nd Earl, b. 1823: m. 1846, Lady Mary Louisa Campbell, who d. 1916, dau. of 1st Earl Cawdor; d. 1862; s. by his son [3] FRANCIS CHARLES GRANVILLE, 3rd Earl, b. 1847: m. 1868, Lady Katharine Louisa Phipps, who d. 1926, dau. of 2nd Marquess of Normanby; d. 1914; s. by his el. son [4] JOHN FRANCIS GRANVILLE SCROPE, *M.V.O.*, 4th Earl, b. 1872: m. 1905, Lady Violet Lambton, dau. of 4th Earl of Durham; d. 1944; s. by his only son [5] JOHN SUTHERLAND, 5th Earl, and afterwards 6th Duke of Sutherland (ante).

SWANSEA, BARON. (Vivian.) [Baron U.K. 1893, Bt. U.K. 1882.]

JOHN HUSSEY HAMILTON VIVIAN, 4th Baron, and 4th Baronet ; b. Jan. 1st, 1925 ; s. 1934 ; ed. at Eton, and at Trin. Coll., Camb.; a DL for Powys: m. 1956 (m. diss. 1973), Miriam Antoinette, who d. 1975, da. of A. W. F. Caccia-Birch, MC, of Guernsey Lodge, Marton, New Zealand, and has issue.

Arms.—Or, on a chevron azure, between three lions' heads erased proper, as many annulets gold ; on a chief embattled gules, a wreath of oak or, between two martlets argent. **Crests.**—1st, a lion's head erased proper charged with two bezants palewise and gorged with a collar gules, thereon three annulets or, with a chain of the last ; 2nd, issuant from a bridge of one arch embattled and having at each end a tower proper, a demi-hussar, in the uniform of the 18th Reg., holding in his right hand a sabre and in his left a red pennon flying to the sinister. **Supporters.**—*Dexter*, a dragon wings elevated gules, gorged with a collar or charged with three torteaux; *sinister*, a horse argent, saddle and bridle proper, trappings gules, gorged with a collar sable charged with three bezants.

Live by the spirit of God.

Residence,—Glanyrafon, Erwood, Builth Wells, Powys.

SON LIVING.
Hon. RICHARD ANTHONY HUSSEY, b. Jan. 24th, 1957.

DAUGHTERS LIVING.

Hon. Amanda Ursula Georgina, *b.* 1958.
Hon. Louisa Caroline Sarah, *b.* 1963.

SISTERS LIVING.

Hon. Rosemary Winifred, *b.* 1927: *m.*, 1947 (m. diss. 1969) Robert John Pulleine Eden, Capt. T.A.
[see Eden, Bt., colls.], and has issue living, Sarah, *b.* 1948. *Residence,*—Mountneys, Roxwell, near
Chelmsford, Essex.
Hon. Averil, *b.* 1930; a JP for Herts.: *m.* 1953, Alexander William Houston, and has issue living, Peter
Richard Vivian, *b.* 1954,—Charles Robson Hamilton, *b.* 1959,—Claire Mary, *b.* 1956. *Residence,*—
The Little House, Datchworth, Knebworth, Herts.

COLLATERAL BRANCH LIVING. *(Not in remainder.)*

Granddaughter of Col. Sir Arthur Pendarves Vivian, KCB, brother of 1st Baron:—
Issue of the late Major Henry Wyndham Vivian, *b.* 1868, *d.* 1901: *m.* 1899, Lady Maude
Clements, who *d.* 1932 (having *m.* 2ndly, 1910, Christopher Foulis Roundell, CBE [see
Os. Dysart, colls.]), dau. of 4th Earl of Leitrim :—
Audrey (Emily), *b.* 1899: *m.* 1921, (Richard) Preston Graham-Vivian, MVO, MC, Norroy and Ulster
King of Arms (ret.) (who assumed by Roy. licence 1929 the additional surname of Vivian after
Graham) [see Graham, Bt., cr. 1783]. *Residences,*—Wealden House, Warninglid, Sussex; 26,
Clabon Mews, Cadogan Sq., SW1.

PREDECESSORS.—[1] HENRY HUSSEY Vivian, el. son of John Henry Vivian, M.P., brother
of 1st Baron Vivian ; *b.* 1821; M.P. for Truro (*L*) 1852-7, for Glamorganshire 1857-85, and for
Swansea Dist. 1885-93; cr. a *Baronet* 1882, and *Baron Swansea*, of Singleton, co. Glamorgan
(peerage of United Kingdom) 1893 : *m.* 1st, 1847, Jessie Dalrymple, who *d.* 1848, dau. of Ambrose
Goddard, M.P., of The Lawn, Swindon ; 2ndly, 1853, Caroline Elizabeth, who *d.* 1868, dau.
of Sir Montague John Cholmeley, M.P., 2nd Bt. ; 3rdly, 1870, Averil, who *d.* 1934, dau. of
Capt. Richard Beaumont, R.N. ; *d.* 1894 ; *s.* by his el. son [2] ERNEST AMBROSE, 2nd Baron ;
b. 1848; *d.* 1922; *s.* by his half-brother [3] ODO RICHARD, *D.S.O., M.V.O.*, 3rd Baron ; *b.* 1875;
European War 1914-18 as Lieut.-Col. Comdg. 14th Batn. Roy. Irish Rifles (D.S.C.) : *m.* 1906;
the Hon. Winifred Hamilton, who *d.* 1944, dau. of 1st Baron HolmPatrick ; *d.* 1934 ; *s.* by
his only son [4] JOHN HUSSEY HAMILTON, 4th Baron and present peer.

SWAYTHLING, BARON. (Montagu.) [Baron U.K. 1907, Bt. U.K. 1894.]

SWIFT · YET · SURE

STUART ALBERT SAMUEL MONTAGU, *O.B.E.,*
3rd Baron, and 3rd Baronet ; *b.* Dec. 19th, 1898;
s. 1927; ed. at Clifton Coll., at Westminster
Sch., and Trin. Coll., Camb., (MA); a JP for
co. Surrey; formerly a Dir. of Samuel
Montagu & Co., Ltd., bankers; Master of
Farmers' Co. 1962-63; Pres. of English
Guernsey Cattle Soc. 1950-51, and 1971-72,
and of Roy. Assocn. of British Dairy Farmers
1972-73 (Dep. Pres. 1970-72, and 1973-74);
Lt. Gren. Gds. 1917-20, and Reserve of
Officers 1920-30; OBE (Civil) 1947: *m.* 1st
1925, Mary Violet (from whom he obtained a
divorce 1942), el. da. of the late Maj. Walter
Henry Levy, DSO [V. Bearsted]; 2ndly, 1945,
Jean Marcia (KNOX), *CBE* (Ch. Controller
and Director of ATS 1941-43), da. of the late
G. G. Leith Marshall, and has issue by
1st marriage.

    Arms,—Or, on a mount proper, a tent argent between
on the dexter a staff proper, flowing therefrom a pennon
azure, charged with a lion rampant of the field, and on the
sinister a palm tree also proper. **Crest,**—A stag statant holding in the mouth a sprig of palm proper, in
front of a flagstaff also erect proper, therefrom flowing to the dexter a banner azure, charged with a
lion rampant or. **Supporters,**—On either side a figure representing a soldier of ancient Judea.

Seat,—Crastock Manor, Crastock, Woking. *Club,*—Bath.

SONS LIVING. *(By 1st marriage.)*

Hon. DAVID CHARLES SAMUEL, *b.* Aug. 6th, 1928; ed. at Eton, and at Trin. Coll., Camb. BA);
Chm. of Orion Bank, Ltd., 1 London Wall, EC2, and Pres. of Asso. for Jewish Youth: *m.* 1951,
Christine Francoise (Ninette), da. of Edgar Dreyfus, of 5, Rue de Chaillot, Paris, and has issue living
Charles Edgar Samuel, *b.* 1954,—Fiona Yvonne, *b.* 1952,—Nicole Mary, *b.* 1956. *Residences,*—
25, Kingston Hse S., Ennismore Gdns., SW7; The Kremlin, The Severals, Newmarket, Suffolk.
Hon. Anthony Trevor Samuel, *b.* 1931; ed. at Eton; late 2nd Lt. Queen's Regt.; Chm. of Abingworth,
Ltd., of 26, St. James's St., SW1A 1HA: *m.* 1962, Deirdre Bridget, yr. da. of Brig. Ronald Henry
Senior, DSO, TD [see B. Joicey], and has issue living, Rupert Anthony Samuel, *b.* 1965,—Damian
William Samuel, *b.* 1970,—Georgina Mary, *b.* 1963. *Residence,*—78, Chelsea Park Gdns., SW3.

DAUGHTER LIVING. *(By 1st marriage.)*

Hon. Jean Mary, *b.* 1927: *m.* 1951, Lintorn Trevor Highett, M.C., and has issue living, Paul Lintorn
b. 1958,—Clare Joanna, *b.* 1956,—Stephanie Jane, *b.* 1963. *Residence,*—2A, Gore St., SW7.

BROTHERS LIVING.

Hon. Ewen Edward Samuel, *CBE, QC, b.* 1901; ed. at Westminster Sch., Harvard Univ., USA and
Trin. Coll., Camb. (LLB, MA); Bar. Middle Temple 1924, KC 1939, Bencher 1949 and Treasurer
1968; DL for Hants; Recorder of Devizes 1944-51, and Southampton 1951-60, Dep. Chm. Hampshire
Quarter Sessions 1948-51, and Chm. 1951-60; Dep. Chm. Judge Advocate of the Fleet 1945-73;
Dep. Chm., Middlesex Quarter Sessions 1954-56, Chm. 1956-65, Chm., Greater London (Middlesex
Area) Quarter Sessions 1965-69 (Judge 1969); Chm. of Gen. Purposes Cttee. of Roy. Yachting
Assocn. 1960-68 (RYA Award 1971), and of Central Council of Magistrates Courts Cttee. 1963-71;
Pres. of United Synagogue 1954-62; 1939-45 War as Lt.-Cdr. RNVR (3rd class Order of Crown of

Yugoslavia); Hon. Capt. RNR 1973; OBE (Mil.) 1944, CBE (Civil) 1950: *m.* 1923, Iris Rachel, da. of Solomon Joseph Solomon, RA, formerly of 18, Hyde Park Gate, W, and has issue living, Jeremy Peter Samuel (of 7, Pickwick Rd., Dulwich Village, SE2 7JN), *b.* 1927: *m.* 1955, Gwen E. Ingledew, of Westhouses, Derby, and has issue living, Simon Joseph Samuel *b.* 1959, Rachel Mary *b.* 1956, Sarah Ruth *b.* 1958,—Jennifer Iris Rachel *b.* 1931. *Residences,*—24, Montrose Court, Exhibition Rd., SW7 2QQ; Warren Beach, Beaulieu, Hants. SO4 7XJ. *Club,*—Royal Ocean Racing.

Hon. Ivor Goldsmid Samuel, *b.* 1904; ed. at Westminster Sch., at Roy. Coll. of Science, **and at King's Coll., Camb. (B.A. 1924, M.A. 1930); Laureate of Lenin Peace Prize 1959; has 1st Class Order of Liberation of Bulgaria, and Order of the Pole Star of Mongolia: *m.* 1927, Eileen, da. of** Francis Anton Hellstern. *Residences,*—Old Timbers, Verdure Close, Watford, WD2 7NJ; Digro, Rousay, Orkney.

SISTER LIVING.

Hon. Joyce Ida Jessie, *b.* 1909; a JP for Wilts.: *m.* 1941, as his second wife, Capt. Oliver Harry Frost, MBE, MC, formerly Middlesex Regt. and RAF, and has issue living, Timothy Oliver (Orchard House, Ogbourne St. George, Marlborough, Wilts., SN8 1SU), *b.* 1943; ed. at Marlborough, and at King's Coll., Camb. (MA): *m.* 1968, Charlotte Birgitta Baskerville, yr. da. of T. H. B. Mynors, of Moseham House, Wadhurst, Sussex, and has issue living, Samuel Timothy Einar *b.* 1973. *Residence,*—The Manor House, Ogbourne St. George, Wilts.

COLLATERAL BRANCH LIVING.

Issue of the late Hon. Gerald Samuel Montagu, 3rd son of 1st Baron, *b.* 1880, *d.* 1956 : *m.* 1909, Florence, who *d.* 1961, dau. of Percy M. Castello, formerly of 20, Chalfont Court, Clarence Gate, N.W.1 :—
Bryan de Castro Samuel, *b.* 1916; ed. at Stowe; European War 1939-45 as Capt. R.A.: *m.* 1950, Elcie, da. of the late John Weiser, of 5 Rowan Walk, N2. *Residence,*—The Loft, 26 Groom Place, SW1.——Ina, *b.* 1913: *m.* 1937, Alexander Poliakoff, and has issue living, Martyn, *b.* 1947,—Stephen, *b.* 1952,—Lucinda Jane, *b.* 1957,—Miranda Ann, *b.* 1959. *Residences,*—13 Addison Road, W14; Ashenden, Guestling, Sussex.

PREDECESSORS.—[1] Montagu Samuel-Montagu, son of the late Louis Samuel, watchmaker of Liverpool; *b.* 1832; founder of the banking firm of Samuel Montagu and Co., of Old Broad Street, E.C.; granted Roy. licence 1894 to assume surnames of Samuel-Montagu (surname of Samuel not now used by descendants) ; M.P. for Tower Hamlets, Whitechapel Div. (*L*) 1885-1900 ; cr. a *Baronet* 1894, and *Baron Swaythling,* of Swaythling, co. Southampton (peerage of United Kingdom) 1907 : *m.* 1862, Ellen, who *d.* 1919, dau. of the late Louis Cohen, of the Stock Exchange; *d.* 1911; *s.* by his el. son [2] Louis Samuel, 2nd Baron, *b.* 1869 ; head of the banking firm of Samuel Montagu and Co., of Old Broad Street, E.C. : *m.* 1898, Gladys Helen Rachel, *OBE,* who *d.* 1965, da. of Col. Albert Edward Williamson Goldsmid, MVO; *d.* 1927; *s.* by his son [3] Stuart Albert Samuel, 3rd Baron and present peer.

SWINFEN, BARON. (Eady.) [Baron U.K. 1919.]

Through difficulties to the heights.

Charles Swinfen Eady, 2nd Baron; *b.* Feb. 2nd, 1904 ; *s.* 1919 ; ed. at Eton ; Bar. Inner Temple 1931 ; a JP for N. Yorks.; a CC for N. Riding of Yorks. 1961-74, since when of N. Yorks.: *m.* 1st, 1937, Mary (from whom he obtained a divorce 1945), da. of Col. Harold Mynors Farmar, CMG, DSO; 2ndly, 1950, Averil Kathleen Suzanne (Knowles), da. of the late Major William Marshall Hickman Humphreys, of Broomfield House, Midleton, co. Cork, and has issue by 1st m.

Arms.—Per pale argent and vert, on a chevron between three battle-axes, as many ermine spots, all counter-charged. Crest,—A demi-lion rampant vert, charged on the body with a battle-axe erect, and holding a like axe in bend argent. Supporters,— Dexter, a lion guardant vert charged with a battle-axe argent ; sinister, a lion guardant argent charged with a battle-axe vert.

Residence,—Medina House, Spanish Point, co. Clare.

Clubs,—Carlton, St. James'.

SONS LIVING. (By 1st marriage.)

Hon. Roger Mynors Swinfen (Dene House, Wingham, Canterbury, Kent), *b.* Dec. 14th, 1938; ed. at Westminster; late Lt. Roy. Scots; ARICS: *m.* 1962, Patricia Anne, only da. of the late F. D. Blackmore, of Doone, Highfield Park, Dundrum, co. Dublin, and has issue living, Charles Roger Peregrine Swinfen, *b.* March 8th, 1971,—Georgina Mary Rose Swinfen, *b.* 1964,—Katharine Anne Dorothy Swinfen, *b.* 1966,—Arabella Victoria Eleanor, *b.* 1969.

Hon. Hugh Toby Swinfen, *b.* 1941; ed. at Bryanston.

PREDECESSOR. — [1] *Rt. Hon.* Sir Charles Swinfen Eady, son of George John Eady, of Chertsey, *b.* 1851 ; a Judge of High Court of Justice 1901-13, a Lord Justice of Appeal 1913-18, and Master of the Rolls 1918-19'; cr. *Baron Swinfen,* of Chertsey, co. Surrey (peerage of United Kingdom, Nov. 1st, 1919 : *m.* 1894, Blanche Maude, who *d.* 1946, dau. of the late S. W. Lee, of Dereham, Putney Hill, S.W. ; *d.* Nov.15th, 1919 ; *s.* by his only son [2] Charles Swinfen, 2nd Baron and present peer.

SWINTON, EARL OF. (Cunliffe-Lister.) [Earl U.K. 1955.]

DAVID YARBURGH CUNLIFFE-LISTER, 2nd Earl; *b.* March 21st, 1937; *s.* 1972; ed. at Winchester, and Roy. Agric. Coll., Cirencester: *m.* 1959, Susan Lilian Primrose (*Baroness Masham of Ilton*)) (Life Peeress), yr. da. of the late Sir Ronald Norman John Charles Udny Sinclair, 8th Bt. (cr. 1704).

Arms,—Quarterly; 1st and 4th, ermine, on a fesse sable three mullets or and (for distinction) a cross crosslet of the second, *Lister*; 2nd, sable, three conies courant argent, and (for distinction) a cross crosslet of the last, *Cunliffe*; 3rd, or, two chevronels sable, on a chief of the second three escallops of the first, *Greame*. *Crests*,—1st, a stag's head proper, erased or, attired sable, charged on the neck (for distinction) with a cross crosslet sable, *Lister*; 2nd a greyhound sejant argent, collared with a ring attached sable, charged on the shoulder (for distinction) with a cross crosslet sable, *Cunliffe*; 3rd, two wings endorsed semee of escallops sable, *Greame*. *Supporters*,—On either side a stag proper, the dexter gorged with a chain or, suspended from the dexter a rose argent, barbed and seeded proper and from the sinister an escallop also argent.

Residence,—Dykes Hill House, Masham, Ripon, Yorks. HG4 4NS.

BROTHER LIVING. *(Raised to the rank of an Earl's son 1974.)*

Hon. NICHOLAS JOHN (Glebe House, Masham, Ripon, Yorks.), *b.* Sept. 4th, 1939; ed. at Winchester, and at Worcester Coll., Oxford; late Lt. WG; Solicitor 1966: *m.* 1966, Elizabeth Susan, da. of William Stephen Ian Whitelaw, CH, MC, MP, of Ennim, Penrith, Cumberland [see Hay, Bt., cr. 1635], and has issue living, Mark William Philip, *b.* 1970,—Lorna Mary, *b.* 1968.

WIDOW LIVING OF SON OF FIRST EARL.

Mary Stewart CUNLIFFE-LISTER; resumed by deed poll 1973 the surname of Cunliffe-Lister; da. of the late Robert G. Leggatt, of Hamilton, Lanarkshire, formerly wife of Robert Noel Stewart Humphries; *m.* 2ndly, 1947, as his second wife, the Hon. Philip Ingram Cunliffe-Lister, DSO, who *d.* 1956; 3rdly, 1958 (*m.* diss. 1969), Robert Alexander Pleasant Craigie, and has issue living, (by 2nd m.) [see colls., infra]. *Residence*,—Framfield Lodge, Eastbourne Rd., Uckfield, E. Sussex.

COLLATERAL BRANCH LIVING.

Issue living of the late Hon. Philip Ingram Cunliffe-Lister, D.S.O., younger son of 1st Earl, *b.* 1918, *d.* 1956: *m.* 1st, 1940 (marriage dissolved 1947), Rosina Gladys, da. of A. G. Embury, of Cambridge; 2ndly, 1947, Mary Stewart CUNLIFFE-LISTER (ante), da. of the late Robert G. Leggatt, of Hamilton, Lanarkshire:—

(By 1st marriage) Philip Algernon Guy, *b.* 1941; ed. at Stowe. *Residence*,—Les Mouettes, Albecq, Guernsey.——(By 2nd m.) Julian Michael, *b.* 1949.——(By 1st m.) Simone Philippa Judith Clare, *b.* 1943: *m.* 1965, Jack Frederick Deakin, and has issue living, Lorna-Jane, *b.* 1970,—Deborah Simone Jackeline, *b.* 1971.——(By 2nd m.) Madeline Frances Anne, *b.* 1950.

PREDECESSOR.—[1] *Rt. Hon.* Sir PHILIP Cunliffe-Lister, *GBE, CH, MC*, son of the late Lt.-Col. Yarburgh George Lloyd-Greame, of Sewerby House, Bridlington; *b.* 1884; assumed by Roy. licence 1924 the surname of Cunliffe-Lister; Pres. of Board of Trade 1922-24, 1924-29, and 1931; Sec. of State for Colonies 1931-35, and for Air 1935-38; Min. Resident in W. Africa 1942-44; Min. of Civil Aviation 1944-45; Chancellor of The Duchy of Lancaster and Min. of Materials 1951-52, and Sec. of State for Commonwealth Relations 1952-55; MP for Hendon (C.) 1918-35; *Viscount Swinton*, of Masham, co. York (peerage of UK) 1935, and *Baron Masham*, of Ellington, co. York and *Earl of Swinton* (peerage of UK) 1955: *m.* 1912, Mary Constance, who *d.* 1974, da. of the late Rev. Charles Ingram William Roynton [Boynton, Bt., colls.]; *d.* 1972; *s.* by his grandson [2] DAVID YARBURGH (son of the late Maj. the Hon. John Yarburgh Cunliffe-Lister, el. son of 1st Earl), 2nd Earl, and present peer; also Viscount Swinton and Baron Masham.

SYSONBY, BARON. (Ponsonby.) [Baron U.K. 1935.]

For the king, the law, and the people.

JOHN FREDERICK PONSONBY, 3rd Baron; *b.* Aug. 5th, 1945; *s.* 1956.

Arms,—Gules, a chevron between three combs argent. *Crest*,—Out of a ducal coronet azure three arrows, points downwards, one in pale and two in saltire, entwined at the intersection by a snake proper. *Supporters*,—On either side a lion guardant crowned with a Saxon crown or, and charged on the shoulder with a key, wards downwards and inwards azure.

Residence,—Newby Hall, Ripon, Yorks.

SISTER LIVING.

Hon. Carolyn Mary, *b.* 1938.

AUNT LIVING. *(Daughter of 1st Baron.)*

Hon. Lœlia Mary (*Hon. Lady Lindsay of Dowhill*), *b.* 1902: *m.* 1st, 1930, as his 3rd wife, the 2nd Duke of Westminster, who *d.* 1953, and from whom she had obtained a divorce 1947; 2ndly, 1969, Sir Martin Alexander Lindsay of Dowhill, CBE, DSO, 1st Bt. *Residence*,—The Old Vicarage, Send, Woking, Surrey.

WIDOW LIVING OF SECOND BARON.

SALLIE WHITNEY, dau. of Dr. Leonard Cutler Sanford, of New York, U.S.A., and formerly wife of George Edward Monkland: *m.* 2ndly, 1936, the 2nd Baron, who *d.* 1956 ; 3rdly, 1958, Major Edward Robert Francis Compton [see M. Northampton, colls.]. *Residence*,—Newby Hall, Ripon, Yorks.

PREDECESSORS.—[1] *Rt. Hon. Sir* FREDERICK EDWARD GREY *Ponsonby, G.C.B., G.C.V.O.,* son of the late Gen. the Rt. Hon. Sir Henry Frederick Ponsonby, G.C.B., G.C.V.O. [B. Bessborough, colls.]; *b.* 1867; formerly Major and Brevet Lieut.-Col. Grenadier Guards; was an Equerry-in-Ordinary to Queen Victoria 1894-1901, Assist. Keeper of the Privy Purse and Assist. Private Sec. to Queen Victoria 1897-1901, and Equerry-in-Ordinary, an Assist. Keeper of the Privy Purse, and an Assist. Private Sec. to King Edward VII. 1901-10; appointed an Equerry-in-Ordinary to H.M. King George V. 1910, Keeper of H.M.'s Privy Purse and an Extra Equerry 1914, Treasurer to the King and Keeper of the Privy Purse 1920, and Lieut.-Gov. of Windsor Castle and Constable of the Round Tower 1928; Receiver-Gen. of Duchy of Lancaster; S. Africa 1901-2, European War 1914; cr. *Baron Sysonby,* of Wonersh, co. Surrey (peerage of United Kingdom) June 1935: *m.* 1899, Victoria Lily Hegan, who *d.* 1955, dau. of the late Col. Edmund Hegan Kennard, of 25, Bruton Street, W.; *d.* Oct. 1935; *s.* by his son [2] EDWARD GASPARD, *D.S.O.,* 2nd Baron, *b.* 1903; Lieut.-Col. 5th Batn. Queen's Roy. Regt. (T.A.); European War 1939-40 (D.S.O.): *m.* 1936, Sallie Whitney (MONKLAND), dau. of Dr. Leonard Sanford, of New York, U.S.A.; *d.* 1956; *s.* by his only son [3] JOHN FREDERICK, 3rd Baron and present peer.

Talbot, Earl of, title borne by Earl of Shrewsbury.

TALBOT OF MALAHIDE, BARON (Talbot.) [Baron I. 1831.]

Strong and faithful.

JOSEPH HUBERT GEORGE TALBOT, 9th Baron; *b.* April 22nd, 1899; *s.* 1975; late Lt. Coldm. Gds.: *m.* 1st, 1924, Helene, who *d.* 1961, da. of M. Gouley, of Bessancourt, Seine-et-Oise, France; 2ndly, 1962 (m. diss. 1970), Beatrice Bros, of 20, Rue Frederic, Passy, Nice.

Arms,—Quarterly: 1st and 4th grand quarters quarterly, 1st and 4th gules, a lion rampant or within a bordure engrailed erminois; 2nd and 3rd argent, a lion rampant gules, armed and langued azure; 2nd quarter, bendy of ten argent and gules; 3rd grand quarter, argent, a lion rampant gules, armed and langued azure; a crescent sable for difference. Crests,—1st, on a chapeau, gules, doubled ermine, a lion passant erminois; 2nd, a talbot passant langued gules. Supporters,—*Dexter,* a talbot or; *sinister,* a lion gules.

Seat,—Malahide Castle, co. Dublin. *Residence,*—Oakfield, Forest Row, Sussex.

SISTER LIVING.

Cicely Mary Gertrude, *b.* 1891: *m.* 1916, Capt. Edmund Garman, late RASC, of Chestnut Bank, Nooklands, Fulwood, Preston, and has issue living, Edmund David Talbot, *b.* 1922,—Joseph Cyril Talbot, *b.* 1924,—Elizabeth Mary, *b.* 1917: *m.* 1946, Richard Stanton Kevil, of Burgh Hall, Chorley, Lancs.

DAUGHTER LIVING OF EIGHTH BARON.

Hon. Ann Cecily Mary, *b.* 1931: *m.* 1955, Col. Edward Reginald Edwards, of Malahide Cottage, West End, Hornton, Banbury, Oxon., and has issue living, Edward David, *b.* 1956,—John Llewellyn, *b.* 1958,—Richard Reginald, *b.* 1973.

SISTER LIVING OF SEVENTH BARON. (*Raised to the rank of a Baron's daughter* 1949.) *Hon.* Rose Maud (Malahide Castle, co. Dublin), *b.* 1915.

WIDOWS LIVING OF SIXTH AND EIGHTH BARONS.

JOYCE GUNNING, dau. of the late Frederick Kerr, formerly of 85, Coleherne Court, S.W.5: *m.* 1st, 1924, the 6th Baron, who *d.* 1948: 2ndly, 1951, Brigadier John Smith McCombe, *D.S.O.,* late RAMC, who *d.* 1959. *Residence,*—Danny, Hurstpierpoint, Sussex.

CECILY ELIZABETH (*Cecily, Baroness Talbot of Malahide*), (20, Hampton Rd., Redland, Bristol, BS6 6HL), da. of Maj. Garstang Hodgson, of Clevedon, Som.: *m.* 1924, the 8th Baron, who *d.* 1975.

COLLATERAL BRANCHES LIVING. (*In remainder to Irish Barony only.*)

Grandsons of the late Reginald Aloysius Talbot (infra):— Issue of the late Reginald John Arthur ARUNDELL, *b.* 1900, *d.* 1953 (having assumed by Roy. licence 1945 the surname of Arundell in lieu of his patronymic and the arms of Arundell): *m.* 1929, Winifred, who *d.* 1954, dau. of R. B. S. Castle, of Prestatyn, Flint:— REGINALD JOHN RICHARD, *b.* Jan. 9th, 1931: *m.* 1935, Laura Duff, da. of the late Group Capt. John Edward Tennant, DSO, MC [see B. Glenconner, colls.], and has issue living, Richard John Tennant, *b.* 1957,—Juliet Anne Tennant, *b.* 1959,—Catherine Mary Tennant, *b.* 1960,—Caroline Rose Tennant, *b.* 1962,—Lucy Veronica Tennant, *b.* 1965. *Residence,*—Hook Manor, Donhead St. Andrew, nr. Shaftesbury, Wilts.——Edward Renfric, (159, Woodhouse Lane, Bishop Auckland, co. Durham), *b.* 1933; ed. at Oratory Sch.; Maj. Somerset and Cornwall L.I.: *m.* 1961, Margaret Ann Honoria, da. of Brig. John Francis Macnab, CBE, DSO, and has issue living, Lucinda Margaret Beatrice, *b.* 1962,—Camilla Edwina Clare, *b.* 1965,—Nicola Marina Merry, *b.* 1967.

Grandchildren of the late John Reginald Francis George Talbot, son of the late Adm. the Hon. Sir John Talbot, GCB, 3rd son of 1st Baroness:— Issue of the late Reginald Aloysius Talbot, *b.* 1870, *d.* 1922: *m.* 1898, Mabille Mary, who *d.* 1942, dau. of the late Hon. Robert Arthur Arundell [B. Arundell of Wardour, colls.]:— Joseph Hubert Edward Pius, *b.* 1903: *m.* 1943, Mercia Cecelia Cowell, and has issue living, Clive Richard (18, Upper Belgrave Rd., Seaford, Sussex), *b.* 1943: *m.* 1965, Pamela Maureen, da. of Basil Coxwell, of Bahia, Brazil, and has issue living, Richard Paul *b.* 1966, Anthony John *b.* 1967, Nicola Louise Cecilia *b.* 1970. *Address,*—c/o A. R. Barton & Co., 20, Copthall Av., EC2.——Robert Peter Frederick Gerard, *b.* 1916: *m.* 1944, Blanche Edna Caseley.——Lucy Geraldine Mary (North Chideock, Bridport, Dorset), *b.* 1907.——(Hilda Mary) Clare (Park Lodge, East Lulworth, Wareham, Dorset), *b.* 1913: *m.* 1972, Lt.-Col. Peter Coventry Grnant, RE (ret.) who *d.* 1973, yr. son of the late Maj.-Gen. Sir Philip Gordon Grant, KCB, CMG, RE [E. Coventry, colls.].

PREDECESSORS.—Richard Talbot, of Malahide Castle, heir male of the ancient Lords of Malahide (barons by tenure): *m.* [1] MARGARET, el. dau. of James O'Reilly, Esq., of Ballinlough, co. Westmeath (of the Milesian princely house of Breffney); she was cr. 1831 *Baroness Talbot of Malahide* and *Lady Malahide of Malahide,* co. Dublin (peerage of Ireland), with remainder to her issue male by her late husband Richard Talbot; *d.* 1834; *s.* by her el. son [2] RICHARD WOGAN, 2nd Baron; cr. *Baron Furnival* (peerage of United Kingdom) 1839; *d.* 1849; without surviving male issue, when the Barony of Furnival became extinct, and the Barony of Talbot of Malahide devolved upon his brother [3] JAMES, 3rd Baron; *b.* 1767; *d.* 1850; *s.* by his son [4] JAMES, LL.D., F.R.S., 4th Baron; *b.* 1805; sat as M.P. for Athlone (*L*)

1832-5; cr. *Baron Talbot de Malahide* (peerage of United Kingdom) 1856: *m.* 1842, Maria Margaretta, who *d.* 1873, dau. of Patrick Murray, of Simprim, Forfarshire; *d.* 1883; *s.* by his son [5] RICHARD WOGAN, 5th Baron; *b.* 1846: *m.* 1st, 1873, Emily Harriet, who *d.* 1898, dau. of Sir James Boswell, 2nd Bt. (*ext.*); 2ndly, 1901, Dame Isabel Charlotte, *D.B.E.*, who *d.* 1932, dau. of the late Robert Blake Humfrey, of Wroxham House, Norwich, and widow of John Gurney, of Sprowston Hall, Norfolk; *d.* 1921; *s.* by his son [6] JAMES BOSWELL, 6th Baron; *b.* 1874: *m.* 1924, Joyce Gunning, dau. of the late Frederick Kerr, formerly of 84, Coleherne Court, S.W.5. *d.* 1948; *s.* by his cousin [7] MILO JOHN REGINALD, *CMG*, (son of the late Col. the Hon. Milo George Talbot CB, 4th son of 4th Baron), 7th Baron; *b.* 1912; Ambassador to Laos 1955-56; *d.* 1973, when the UK *Barony of Talbot de Malahide* became ext.; *s.* in the Irish peerage of *Baron Talbot of Malahide*, by his Kinsman [8] REGINALD STANISLAUS VICTOR, *MC* (2nd son of John Reginald Charles Talbot, grandson of Adm. the Hon. Sir John Talbot, GCB, 3rd son of 1st Baroness), 8th Baron; *b.* 1897: *m.* 1924, Cecily Elizabeth, da. of Maj. Garstang Hodgson, of Clevedon, Som.; *d.* 1975; *s.* by his brother [9] JOSEPH HUBERT GEORGE, 9th Baron and present peer.

Tamworth, Viscount, son of Earl Ferrers.

TANGLEY, BARONY OF. (Herbert.) [Extinct 1973.]

SON LIVING OF LIFE BARON.
Hon. Peter Meldrum (Byways, Little London, Witley, Surrey), *b.* 1936: *m.* 1961, Annabel Binnie, and has issue.

DAUGHTERS LIVING OF LIFE BARON.
Hon. Elizabeth Ann, *b.* 1933; ed. at Oxford Univ. (MA, BM, BCh): *m.* 1960, Hon. Michael Cottrell Brain, DM, of 889, Park Av., W., Burlington, Ontario, Canada [see B. Brain].
Hon. Jane Katherine, *b.* 1938; GRSM, LRAM: *m.* 1964, George Kenneth Beattie, of Big Oak, Churt, Farnham, Surrey, and has issue.
Hon. Alison Margaret, *b.* 1943; LRAM, ARCM: *m.* 1965, John Michael Bradshaw, of Cherrydale, W. Clandon, Surrey, and has issue.

WIDOW LIVING OF LIFE BARON.
GWENDOLEN HILDA (*Baroness Tangley*), (Tangley Way, Blackheath, Guildford, Surrey); da. of the late Thomas Langley Judd, CBE: *m.* 1932 Baron Tangley (Life Peer), who *d.* 1973.

TANKERVILLE, EARL OF. (Bennet.) [Earl G.B. 1714.]

CHARLES AUGUSTUS GREY BENNET; 9th Earl; *b.* July 28th, 1921; *s.* 1971; 1939-45 War as Fl. Lt. RAFVR: *m.* 1st, 1943, Virginia (from whom he obtained a divorce 1950), da. of the late Louis Diether, of Vancouver, BC; 2ndly, 1954, Georgiana Lilian Maude, da. of the late Gilbert Wilson, DD, of Regina, Sask., and has issue by 1st and 2nd m.

Arms,—Gules, three demi-lions rampant argent, in the centre point a bezant. **Crests,**—1st, out of a mural coronet or, a lion's head gules, charged on the neck with a bezant; 2nd, a scaling ladder or. **Supporters**—Two lions argent, ducally crowned or, and charged on the shoulder with a torteau.

To serve the king with good will.

Seat,—Chillingham Castle, Alnwick, Northumberland.
Residence,—139, Olympia Way, San Francisco, Cal., USA.

SON LIVING. (By 2nd m.)
PETER GREY (*Lord Ossulston*), *b.* Oct. 18th, 1956.

DAUGHTERS LIVING. (By 1st m.)
Lady Corisande Elizabeth, *b.* 1947.
(By 2nd m.)
Lady Alexandra Katherine, *b.* 1955.
Lady Anne Thérèse (twin) *b.* 1956.

BROTHER LIVING.
Rev. the Hon. George Arthur Grey (Motcombe Vicarage, Shaftesbury), *b.* 1925; ed. at Radley, and Corpus Christi Coll., Camb. (MA); V. in Shaston Team Min. since 1973; author of " Electricity and Modern Physics " 1965: *m.* 1957, Hazel (Jane) G., da. of the late Ernest W. G. Judson, of Bishopswood, Chard, Somerset, and has issue living, Adrian George, *b.* 1958,—Neil Robert, *b.* 1961,—Helen Jane, *b.* 1964.

HALF-BROTHER LIVING.
Hon. Ian (Estate House, Chillingham, Chatton, Northumberland), *b.* 1935; ed. at Radley, and Corpus Christi Coll., Camb. (MA); Lt. RNR.

HALF-SISTER LIVING.
Lady Corisande, *b.* 1938: *m.* 1963, Lt.-Cdr. Timothy Bain Smith, RN, and has issue living, James, *b.* 1964,—Charles, *b.* 1966.

UNCLE LIVING (Son of 7th Earl.)
Hon. George William, *b.* 1903; ed. at Winchester, and at Trin. Coll., Camb. (B.A. 1925, M.A. 1933); is a Fellow of British Horological Institute: *m.* 1929, Constance Clare, dau. of Cyril Wace. *Residence,*—Polwarth, Greenlaw, Berwickshire.

MOTHER LIVING.
Roberta; a JP for W. Suffolk; da. of the late Percy Mitchell: *m.* 1st, 1920, the 8th Earl, who *d.* 1971, and from whom she obtained a divorce 1930; 2ndly, 1930, John Holt Wilson, of Broomhills, Botesdale, Diss, Norfolk.

WIDOW LIVING OF EIGHTH EARL.
VIOLET, (*Violet, Countess of Tankerville*), (Chillingham Castle, Alnwick, Northumberland), da. of Erik Pallin, of Stockholm JP of Northumberland; has Order of Vasa of Sweden: *m.* 1930, as his 2nd wife, the 8th Earl, who *d.* 1971.

PREDECESSORS.—[1] *Sir* JOHN Bennet, *K.B.*, el. son of the late Sir John Bennet, of Dawley; cr. *Baron Ossulston*, of Ossulston, co. Middlesex (peerage of England) 1682; he and the heirs male of his body are in special remainder to the titles of his younger brother Henry, who was cr. *Baron Arlington*, of Arlington, co. Middlesex, *Viscount Thetford* and *Earl of Arlington* (peerage of England) 1672: *m.* 1st, 1661, Lady Elizabeth, who *d.* 167-, dau. of 1st Earl of Middlesex, and widow of 2nd Earl of Mulgrave ; 2ndly, 16—, Bridget, who *d.* 1703, dau. of the late John Howe. of Langar, Nottingham : *d.* 1682 ; *s.* by his son [2] CHARLES, *K.T.*, 2nd Baron : *m.* 1695, Lady Mary Grey, da. and heiress of 1st and last Earl of Tankerville (cr. 1695), and after the demise of his father-in-law he was cr. *Earl of Tankerville* (peerage of Great Britain); *d.* 1722 ; *s.* by his son [3] CHARLES, *K.T.*, 2nd Earl ; filled several high positions about the Court 1728-40 : *m.* 17—, Camilla, who *d.* 1775, dau. of the late Edward Colville, of Whitehouse, Durham ; *d.* 1753 ; *s.* by his son [4] CHARLES, 3rd Earl ; M.P. for Northumberland 1748-53 : *m.* 1742, Alicia, who *d.* 1775, dau. of Sir John Astley, 2nd Bt. (cr. 1662, ext.) ; *d.* 1767 ; *s.* by his son [5] CHARLES, 4th Earl : *m.* 1771, Emma, who *d.* 1836, dau. of Sir James Colebrook, Bt.; *d.* 1822 ; *s.* by his son [6] CHARLES AUGUSTUS, *P.C.*, 5th Earl ; *b.* 1776 ; Joint Postmaster-Gen. 1782-3 and 1784-6 : *m.* 1806, Corisande Armandine Sophie Leónice Helene, who *d.* 1865, dau. of Antoine, Duke de Gramont ; *d.* 1859 ; *s.* by his son [7] CHARLES, 6th Earl ; *b.* 1810 ; M.P. for N. Northumberland (*C*) 1832-59, Capt. Hon. Corps of Gentlemen-at-Arms 1866-7, and Lord Steward of the Household 1867-8 ; summoned to House of Lords in his father's Barony of Ossulston 1859 : *m.* 1850, Lady Olivia Montagu, who *d.* 1922, el. dau. of 6th Duke of Manchester ; *d.* 1899 ; *s.* by his second son [8] GEORGE MONTAGU, 7th Earl, *b.* 1852 : *m.* 1895, Leonora Sophia, who *d.* 1949, dau. of the late J. G. van Marter, sometime of New York ; *d.* 1931 ; *s.* by his el. son [9] CHARLES AUGUSTUS KER, 8th Earl, *b.* 1897 : *m.* 1st, 1920, Roberta (who obtained a divorce 1930), da. of the late Percy Mitchell; 2ndly, 1930, Violet, JP, da. of Erik Pallin, of Stockholm; *d.* 1971; *s.* by his son [10] CHARLES AUGUSTUS GREY, 9th Earl and present peer; also Baron Ossulston.

TANLAW, BARON. (Mackay.) [Life Baron 1971.]

SIMON BROOKE MACKAY, yst. son of 2nd Earl of Inchcape; *b.* March 30th, 1934; ed. at Eton, and Trin. Coll., Camb. (MA); late 2nd Lt. 12th R. Lancers; Dir. of Inchcape & Co., Ltd.; Pres. of Kensington Liberal Assocn. 1971; Dep. Chm. Scottish Liberal Party 1972; Pres. Sarawak Assocn. 1972; Chm. Building Cttee., Univ. Coll. of Buckingham; cr. *Baron Tanlaw*, of Tanlawhill, co. Dumfries (Life Baron) 1971: *m.* 1959, Joanna Susan, only da. of Maj. John Henry Hirsch, of Sungrove Lodge, Newbury, and has issue.

Arms,—Parted per chevron azure and argent, in chief two lymphads of the 2nd and in base a tiger's face affrontée proper, on a chief or a cross engrailed per cross indented azure and sable. **Crest,**—A falcon proper, hooded gules, issuant out of a five-pointed Eastern crown or. **Supporters,**—*Dexter,* a Prejevalski's mare proper; *sinister,* a roe deer also proper.

Residences,—14/16, Cockspur St., SW1Y 5BL; Tanlawhill, Eskdalemuir, Dumfries-shire.

SON LIVING.

Hon. James Brooke, *b.* 1961.

DAUGHTERS LIVING.

Hon. Iona Héloïse, *b.* 1960.
Hon. Rebecca Alexandra, *b.* 1967.

Tarbat, Viscount,   son of Earl of Cromartie.

Tavistock, Marquess of,   son of Duke of Bedford.

TAYLOR, BARON. (Taylor.) [Life Baron 1958.]

STEPHEN JAMES LAKE TAYLOR, *M.D.*, son of the late John Reginald Taylor, M.I.C.E., of Little Court, Shalbourne, Marlborough, Wilts : *b.* Dec. 30th, 1910 : ed. at Stowe and London Univ. (B.Sc. 1st Class honours BS, MD.); MRCS England and LRCP London; MRCP; FRCP; Hon. LLD St. Thomas, NB; Pres. and Vice-Chancellor Memorial Univ. of Newfoundland 1967-73, since when visiting Prof. of Medicine; formerly Med. Dir., Harlow Industrial Health Ser., Consultant in Occupational Health to Richard Costain Ltd., and a Member of Harlow New Town Corpn., Visiting Research Fellow, Nuffield Provincial Hosps. Trust, and Vice-Chm. British Film Corpn.; Dir. of Home Intelligence 1941-45, PPS to Dep. Prime Min. and Lord Pres. of Council 1948-50, and Parl. Under-Sec., Commonwealth Relations and Colonial Offices 1964-65; 1939-45 War with RNVR as Surg. Lt.-Cdr.; sat as MP (*Lab.*) for Barnet Div. of Herts. July 1945 to Feb. 1950, when he was defeated; cr. *Baron Taylor*, of Harlow, co. Essex (Life Baron) 1958: *m.* 1939, May Doris Charity, *MB, BS, MRCP, LRCP*, da. of the late Wron George Clifford, and has issue.

Residence,—Plas-y-Garth, Glyn Ceiriog, Llangollen, Clwyd.

SONS LIVING.

Hon. Jeremy Stephen (19 Ayresome Av., Leeds, LS8 1BB), *n.* 1940; ed. at Highgate; a Television Executive: *m.* 1964, Christina, yr. da. of the late John Bruce Holmes, of 37, Redington Rd., NW3 [L. Forbes, colls.], and has issue.
Hon. Charles Richard Herbert, *b.* 1950; ed. at Highgate.

DAUGHTER LIVING.

Hon. Elizabeth Trilby Charity, *b.* 1943; ed. at Univ. of Sussex: *m.* 1971, Paul Stephen Masterman, of 92, Marylebone High St., W1M 3DE.

TAYLOR OF GRYFE, BARON. (Taylor.) [Life Baron 1968.]

THOMAS JOHNSTON TAYLOR, son of John Sharp Taylor, of Glasgow; *b.* April 27th, 1912; ed. at Bellahouston Acad., Glasgow; Chm. of Forestry Commn. since 1970, and of Morgan Grenfell (Scotland), Ltd., a Member of Exec. Cttee., Scottish Council (Development and Industry) since 1964, of British Railways Board, and a Board Member of Scottish Television Ltd. since 1968, and of Friends Provident and Century Group since 1972; a Dir. Whiteways Laidlaw & Co. since 1971, and Scottish Metropolitan Property Co. Ltd. since 1972; *cr. Baron Taylor of Gryfe,* of Bridge of Weir, Renfrewshire (Life Baron) 1968: *m.* 1943, Isobel, da. of Williams Wands., and has issue.

Residence,—The Cottage, Auchenames, Kilbarchan, Renfrewshire, PA10 2PM. *Club,*—Caledonian (London).

DAUGHTERS LIVING.

Hon. Jill, *b.* 1945: *m.* 1969, Dr. Thomas Egli, of Carmenstrasse, Basle, Switzerland.
Hon. Joyce, *b.* 1948: *m.* 1969, Alan Begbie, of 51 Spiers Rd., Bearsden, Glasgow.

TAYLOR OF MANSFIELD, BARON. (Taylor.) [Life Baron 1966.]

HARRY BERNARD TAYLOR, *CBE,* son of the late Henry Taylor, of Mansfield Woodhouse, Notts.; *b.* Sept. 18th, 1895; ed. at Oxclose Lane Sch., Mansfield Woodhouse; a JP of Notts.; PPS to Min. of National Insurance 1945-50, and Parl. Sec. to Ministry of National Insurance 1950-51; MP for Mansfield Div. of Notts. (*Lab.*) 1941-66; *cr.* CBE (Civil) 1966, and *Baron Taylor of Mansfield,* of Mansfield, co. Nottingham (Life Baron) 1966: *m.* 1921, Clara Annie, da. of John Ashley, of Mansfield Woodhouse, and has issue.

Residence,—47 Shakespeare Av., Mansfield Woodhouse, Notts.

SON LIVING.

Hon. Bernard Alfred (126, Mansfield St., Sherwood, Nottingham), *b.* 1922: *m.* 1952.

TAYSIDE, BARONY OF. (Urquhart.) [Extinct. 1975.]

SONS LIVING OF LIFE BARON.

Hon. William James Lauchlan (Thorngarth, 139, Strathern Rd., Broughty Ferry, Dundee; Eastern (Dundee) Club), *b.* 1944; ed. at Fettes Coll., and Glasgow Univ. (BSc Hons); CA; Member of Inst. of Taxation; *m.* 1967, Wendy Helen Cook, and has issue.
Hon. Ronald Douglas Lauchlan (Eastern (Dundee) Club), *b.* 1948; ed. at Fettes Coll., and Edinburgh Univ. (LLB); CA.

DAUGHTER LIVING OF LIFE BARON.

Hon. Hilda Louise Lauchlan, *b.* 1950; ed. at St. Leonards Sch., St. Andrews, and Bedford Coll. of Physical Education.

WIDOW LIVING OF LIFE BARON.

HILDA GWENDOLINE, *BSc* (*Baroness Tayside*) (The Manor, Forfar, Angus), da. of John Thomson Harris, of Dundee: *m.* 1939, Baron Tayside (Life Peer), who *d.* 1975.

TEDDER, BARON. (Tedder.) [Baron U.K. 1946.]

JOHN MICHAEL TEDDER, 2nd Baron; *b.* July 4th, 1926; *s.* 1967; ed. at Dauntsey's Sch., Magdalene Coll., Camb. (ScD), and Birmingham Univ. (PhD, DSc); FRSE; FRIC; Purdie Prof. of Chemistry, Univ. of St. Andrews: *m.* 1952, Peggy Eileen, yr. da. of Samuel George Growcott, of Birmingham, and has issue.

Arms.—Not exemplified at time of going to press.

Residence,—Little Rathmore, Kennedy Gdns., St. Andrews, Fife.

SONS LIVING.

Hon. ROBIN JOHN, *b.* April 6th, 1955.
Hon. Andrew Jonathan, *b.* 1958.

DAUGHTER LIVING.

Hon. Anne Rosalinde, *b.* 1963.

HALF-BROTHER LIVING.

Hon. Richard Seton, *b.* 1946.

SISTER LIVING.

Hon. Mina Una Margaret, *b.* 1920; formerly Assist. Librarian, British Embassy, Wash., USA; BBC, TV 1954-7, and Scottish TV Glasgow 1957-65; Dist. Commr., Nat. Savings, Alnwick, Northumberland.

PREDECESSOR.—[1] *Marshal of the RAF Sir* ARTHUR WILLIAM Tedder, *GCB,* yr. son of Sir Arthur John Tedder, *CB; b.* 1890; 1914-18 War with Dorset Regt., and RFC; AOC Far East, Singapore 1936-38, Dir.-Gen. of Research and Development, Air Min. 1938-40, Dep. Air Member for Development and Production 1940, Dep. AOC in C. Middle East 1940-41, AOC in C. Middle East 1941-42, AOC in C. Mediterranean 1943, Dep. Supreme Cdr. SHAEF 1943-45, Ch. of Air Staff 1946-49, and Chm. of British Joint Sers. Mission, Washington USA 1950; Chancellor of Camb. Univ. 1950-67; *cr. Baron Tedder,* of Glenguin, co. Stirling (peerage of UK) 1946: *m.* 1st, 1915, Rosalinde, who *d.* 1943, da. of William McIntyre Maclardy, of Sydney, NSW; 2ndly, 1943, Mrs. Marie de Seton Black, who *d.* 1965, da. of Col. Sir Bruce Gordon Seton, *CB,* 9th Bt. (cr. 1663); *d.* 1967. *s.* by his 2nd son, [2] JOHN MICHAEL, 2nd Baron and present peer.

TEIGNMOUTH, BARON. (Shore.) [Baron I. 1797, Bt G.B. 1792.]

We perish by what is lawful.

FREDERICK MAXWELL AGLIONBY SHORE, *DSC*, 7th Baron, and 7th Baronet; *b.* Dec. 2nd, 1920; *s.* 1964; ed. at Wellington Coll.; Lt. R.N.V.R.; 1939-45 War (despatches twice, DSC and Bar): *m.* 1947 (marriage annulled 1952), Daphne Beryl, only da. of W. H. Freke-Evans, of Hove.

Arms,—Argent, a chevron sable, between three holly leaves vert. Crest.—A stork reguardant proper, holding in its dexter claw a stone sable. Supporters.—Two storks reguardant proper, each crowned with an Eastern crown or.

Residences,—Brownsbarn, co. Kilkenny; 50, Pont St., SW1. *Club,*—East India and Sports.

SISTER LIVING.

Hon. Elizabeth Mary, *b.* 1916: *m.* 1942, Maj. Charles John Patrick Barnwell, Somerset L.I., and has issue living, Patrick Hugh Lowry, *b.* 1948. *Residence,*—Wick Manor, Curry Rivel, Somerset.

WIDOW LIVING OF SON OF FIFTH BARON.

Fairlie, da. of Charles H. Wilkie, of Hazelbrae, Nairn: *m.* 1923, the Hon. Noel Beilby Porteus Shore, who *d.* 1934. *Residence,*—Orchard House, Tickenham, Avon.

WIDOW LIVING OF SIXTH BARON.

CAROLINE (*Baroness Teignmouth*) (Brownsbarn, co. Kilkenny), only da. of the late Col. Willoughby Digby Marsh, R.E. of Brownsbarn, co. Kilkenny: *m.* 1915, the 6th Baron, who *d.* 1964.

PREDECESSORS.—[1] *Rt. Hon.* JOHN Shore, el. son of the late Thomas Shore, of Melton, Suffolk; *b.* 1751; Member of Supreme Council Bengal 1786, Gov.-Gen. of India 1792-8, and a Commr. of Indian Affairs; cr. a *Baronet* 1792, and *Baron Teignmouth*, of Teignmouth, co. Devon (peerage of Ireland) 1797: *m.* 1786, Charlotte, dau. of James Cornish, of Teignmouth; *d.* 1834; *s.* by his son [2] CHARLES JOHN, D.C.L., LL.D.; *b.* 1796; M.P. for Marylebone (*C*) 1838-41: *m.* 1838, Caroline, dau. of the late William Browne, of Tallantire Hall, Cumberland; *d.* 1885; *s.* by his son [3] CHARLES JOHN, 3rd Baron; *b.* 1840; *m.* 1880, Alice Frances, who *d.* 1937, el. dau. of the late John Frederick Bigge, V. of Stamfordham; *d.* 1915; *s.* by his brother [4] FREDERICK WILLIAM JOHN, 4th Baron, *b.* 1844: *m.* 1894, Anne Louisa, who *d.* 1937, dau. of the late Peter Connellan; *d.* 1916; *s.* by his brother [5] HENRY NOEL, 5th Baron; *b.* 1847; a Com. R.N.: *m.* 1880, Mary Aglionby, who *d.* 1934, dau. of the Rev. Beilby Porteus, Hon; Canon of Carlisle; *d.* 1926; *s.* by his son [6] HUGH AGLIONBY, 6th Baron; *b.* 1881: *m.* 1915, Caroline, only da. of the late Col. Willoughby Digby Marsh, R.E. of Brownsbarn, co. Kilkenny; *d.* 1964, *s.* by his 2nd son [7] FREDERICK MAXWELL AGLIONBY, 7th Baron and present peer.

TEMPLE OF STOWE, EARL. (Temple-Gore-Langton.) [Earl U.K. 1822.]

RONALD STEPHEN BRYDGES TEMPLE-GORE-LANGTON, 7th Earl; *b.* Nov. 5th, 1910; *s.* 1966; patron of five livings.

Arms,—Quarterly : 1st and 4th grand quarters, quarterly sable and or, a bend argent, *Langton* : 2nd grand quarter, gules, a fesse between three cross-crosslets fitchée or, *Gore:* 3rd grand quarter, quarterly, 1st and 4th or, an eagle displayed sable; 2nd and 3rd argent, two bars sable, each charged with three marlets or, *Temple.* Crests,—1st, An eagle or and a wyvern vert, their necks entwined reguardant, *Langton;* 2nd, on a mount vert, an heraldic tiger salient argent, ducally gorged or, *Gore;* 3rd, on a ducal coronet or, a martlet gold, *Temple.* Supporters,—Dexter, a lion per fesse nebuly or and gules, gorged with a ribbon of the last, pendant therefrom an escutcheon of the arms of *Langton; sinister,* a horse argent, semée of eaglets displayed sable, gorged with a ribbon gules, pendent therefrom an escutcheon of the arms of *Gore.*

Address,—c/o National Bank of Australasia Ltd., 271, Collins St., Melbourne, Australia.

SISTER LIVING. (*Raised to the rank of an Earl's daughter* 1941.)

Lady Elizabeth Ann, *b.* 1908: *m.* 1927, Group-Capt. Peter Bathurst, RAF, who *d.* 1970 [see E. Bathurst, colls.]. *Residence,*—Tolzey Cottage, Queen Charlton, near Bristol.

WIDOW LIVING OF SIXTH EARL.

JOAN HELEN (*Countess Temple of Stowe*), (Burrow Hall, via Carnforth, Lancs.), da. of Charles Abbott, of Penn, Bucks.: *m.* 1943, as his second wife, the 6th Earl, who *d.* 1966.

COLLATERAL BRANCHES LIVING.

Issue of the late Cdr. the Hon. Evelyn Arthur Temple-Gore-Langton, DSO, RN. yst. son of 4th Earl, *b.* 1884, *d.* 1972: *m.* 1922, Irene, who *d.* 1967, da. of Brig.-Gen. Cavendish Walter Gartside-Spaight, of Derry Castle, Killaloe, co. Clare:—

(WALTER) GRENVILLE ALGERNON (The Cottage, Easton, Winchester), *b.* Oct. 2nd, 1924: *m.* 1st, 1954, Zillah Ray, who *d.* 1966, da. of James Boxall, of Tillington, Petworth, Sussex; 2ndly, 1968, Margaret Elizabeth Graham, only da. of the late Col. Henry William Scarth of Breckness, of Skaill House, Orkney, and has issue living (by 1st m.), James Grenville, *b.* 1955,—Robert Chandos, *b.* 1957, —Anna Clare, *b.* 1960.——Elspeth Dorina, *b.* 1926: *m.* 1950, Thomas Alfred Spry Carlyon, of Rialton Barton, St. Columb Minor, Newquay, Cornwall, and has issue living, William Thomas Alfred, *b.* 1951, —Nicola Elspeth, *b.* 1954.

Grandchildren of the late Col. the Hon. Henry Powell Gore-Langton, (infra):—
Issue of the later Cdr. Hubert Edwin Gore-Langton, DSO, RN, *b.* 1883, *d.* 1968: *m.* 1902, his cousin, Lady Alice Mary Temple-Gore-Langton, who *d.* 1961, da. of 4th Earl Temple of Stowe:—
Alaric Hubert St. George (Hatch Park, Hatch Beauchamp, Somerset), *b.* 1918; Lt.-Cdr. RN; 1939-45 in Med., Atlantic and S-E Asia: *m.* 1946, Margaret Edwina, el. da. of Col. D.McLeod Douglas, MC, of Sanderstead, Surrey, and has issue living, Chandos Alaric Graham, *b.* 1949,—Grenville Julian Brydges, *b.* 1954,—Clare Margaret (twin), *b.* 1954.

Grandchildren of the late Robert Lancelot Gore-Langton (infra):—
Issue of the late Montagu Grenville Gore-Langton, *b.* 1919, *d.* 1968: *m.* 1944, Wilda Handlen, who *m.* 2ndly, 1971, Geoffrey D. Smiley, of 3396, Hilton Rd., Duncan, BC, Canada:—
Robert Edward (Physiological Laboratory, Cambridge, CB2 3EG), *b.* 1950: ed. at Vic. Univ., BC (BSc).——Dixie Gillian, *b.* 1945: *m.* 1971, John Molloy, of 2835, Cedar Hill Rd., Vic., BC, Canada.

Granddaughters of the late Col. the Hon. Henry Powell Gore-Langton (infra):—
Issue of the late Robert Lancelot Gore-Langton, *b.* 1885, *d.* 1948: *m.* 1914, Winifreda Lilian Margaret (2759, Sea View Rd.), Victoria VI, BC, Canada), da. of the late Capt. Arthur G. Nixon, Rifle Bde. (Prince Consort's Own):—
Margaret Coëline, *b.* 1920: *m.* 1944, Andrew William Stewart, RCAF, of 2326, Lincoln Rd., Victoria, BC, Canada, and has issue living, Ronald David, *b.* 1961,—Heather Margaret, *b.* 1948,—Victoria Ann, *b.* 1953.——Gillian Mary, *b.* 1925: *m.* 1950, Hugo Wuerzer, Capt. 255th (W. Somerset Yeo. and Dorset Garrison) Medium Regt., RA (TA), and has issue living, Nigel John, *b.* 1955,—Robert Guy, *b.* 1959,—Wendy Margaret, *b.* 1951,—Jane Felicity, *b.* 1956. *Residence,*—Cherry Hinton, Stonegallows, Taunton, Somerset.

Issue of the late Col. the Hon. Henry Powell Gore-Langton, brother of 4th Earl, *b.* 1854, *d.* 1913: *m.* 1878, Marguerite Lucy, who *d.* 1915, dau. of the late Major R. Guthrie MacGregor:—
Richard Gerald (5421, Old West Rd., Victoria, BC, Canada), *b.* 1892: 1914-18 War as acting Maj. RHA (TA), 1939-45 War as Lt.-Cdr. RCN: *m.* 1st, 1925 (m. diss. 1936), Laura Edith Pryor, da. of the late Herbert W. Bevan; 2ndly, 1936, Doreen Audrey, da. of Aubrey H. Davies, MB, MRCS, LRCP, and has issue living (by 1st m.), Richard Eric Bevan (5465, Alderley Rd., Victoria, BC, Canada), *b.* 1933: *m.* 1957, Marjorie Joyce, da. of the late Thomas A. Boag, and has issue living, Richard Thomas *b.* 1959, Laura Gay *b.* 1961,—(by 2nd m.) Gerald Hugh, *b.* 1947,—Norman Guy, *b.* 1950,—Dorothy Veronica, *b.* 1952.

PREDECESSORS.—[1] RICHARD Temple-Nugent-Grenville, K.G., 2nd Marquess of Buckingham [see V. Cobham]; assumed 1799, by Roy. licence, the additional surnames of Brydges-Chandos; was cr. *Earl Temple of Stowe* (with remainder to his granddau. Anna Eliza Mary, afterwards wife of William Henry Powell Gore-Langton, M.P.), *Marquess of Chandos*, and *Duke of Buckingham and Chandos* (peerage of United Kingdom) 1822, [2—3] in which title the Earldom of Temple was merged until the death of the 3rd Duke of Buckingham and Chandos (*ext.*) in 1889, when it devolved upon his nephew [4] WILLIAM STEPHEN Gore-Langton [son of the late William Henry Powell Gore-Langton, M.P. (ante)], 4th Earl, *b.* 1847; M.P. for Mid Somerset (C.) 1878-85; assumed by Roy. licence 1892 the additional surname and arms of Temple: *m.* 1870, Helen Mabel, who *d.* 1919, 2nd dau. of Sir Graham Graham-Montgomery, 3rd Bt.: *d.* 1902; *s.* by his son [5] ALGERNON WILLIAM STEPHEN, 5th Earl; *b.* 1871; *m.* 1913, Agnes Florence Regina, who *d.* 1941, dau. of Charles K. de Laporte, and widow of Alred, Burrows, of Melbourne; *d.* 1940; *s.* by his nephew [6] CHANDOS GRENVILLE (son of the late Capt. the Hon. Chandos Graham Temple-Gore-Langton, 2nd son of 4th Earl); 6th Earl; *b.* 1909: *m.* 1st, 1934 (m. diss. 1940), Frances Vauriel Fenton, da. of Maj. Francis Vivian Lister, OBE, of Ashwick Grove, Oakhill, Bath; 2ndly, 1943, Joan Helen, da. of Charles Abbott, of Penn, Bucks.; *d.* 1966; *s.* by his brother [7] RONALD STEPHEN BRYDGES, 7th Earl and present peer.

VIRTUTIS·AVORUM·PRÆMIUM·

The reward of the virtue of my ancestors.

TEMPLETOWN, VISCOUNT. (Upton.) [Viscount I. 1806.]

HENRY AUGUSTUS GEORGE MOUNTJOY HENEAGE UPTON, 5th Viscount; *b.* Aug. 12th, 1894; *s.* 1939; formerly Lieut. E. Kent Mounted Rifles (T.F.); has been a Member of County Council of Stewartry of Kirkcudbright since 1929: *m.* 1st, 1916, Alleyne, who *d.* 1974, da. of the late Henry Lewes Conran, RN, formerly of Gordon Downs, Queensland; 2ndly, 1975, Margaret Violet Louisa, el. da. of the late Lt.-Col. Henry Arthur Clowes, 1st Life Guards, and widow of Col. Sir Lionel George Archer Cust, CBE [see B. Brownlow, colls.] and has issue by 1st m.

Arms.—Sable, a cross moline or. *Crest.*—On a ducal coronet or, a war-horse passant sable, bridled, saddled (without stirrups), and accoutred. *Supporters.*—*Dexter*, a war-horse sable, caparisoned as the crest; *sinister*, a knight in complete armour, his helmet adorned with a red plume, having a spear in his right hand, and on his left arm a shield, charged as the arms.

Residence,—The Holme, Balmaclellan, Castle Douglas, Kirkcudbrightshire. *Club,*—New (Edinburgh).

DAUGHTER LIVING. (*By* 1st *marriage.*)
Hon. Alleyne Evelyn Maureen Louisa, *b.* 1921; late ATS: *m.* 1947, Maj. John Hackett, late RAOC (*Club,*—Antofagasta, Chile), and has issue living, a son, *b.* 19—. *Address,*—

PREDECESSORS.—[1] CLOTWORTHY Upton, Clerk Comptroller to the Princess Dowager of Wales, was cr. *Baron Templetown*, of Templetown, co. Antrim (peerage of Ireland) 1776; *d.* 1785; *s.* by his son [2] JOHN HENRY, 2nd Baron; *b.* 1771; cr. *Viscount Templetown* (peerage of Ireland) 1806; *m.* 1796, Lady Mary Montagu, dau. of 5th Earl of Sandwich; *d.* 1846; *s.* by his el. son [3] HENRY MONTAGU, 2nd Viscount; *d.* unmarried 1863; *s.* by his brother [4] GEORGE FREDERICK, G.C.B., 3rd Viscount, *b.* 1802: a Gen. in the Army, and a Representative **Peer**; sat as M.P. for Antrim (*C*) 1859-63: *m.* 1850, Susan, who *d.* 1894, dau. of F.-M. Sir Alexander Woodford, G.C.B., G.C.M.G.; *d.* 1890; *s.* by his nephew [5] HENRY EDWARD MONTAGUE DORINGTON CLOTWORTHY (son of the late Hon. Edward John Upton, 4th son of 1st Viscount), 4th Viscount; a Representative Peer for Ireland: *m.* 1883, Lady Evelyn Georgiana Finch-Hatton, who *d.* 1932, dau. of 10th Earl of Winchilsea; *d.* 1939; *s.* by his second but only surviving son (the elder having been killed in action during European War 1915) [6] HENRY AUGUSTUS GEORGE MOUNTJOY HENEAGE, 5th Viscount and present peer; also Baron Templetown.

TENBY, VISCOUNT. (Lloyd George.) [Viscount U.K. 1957.]

YGWIR YBYD
YN ERBYN

DAVID LLOYD GEORGE, 2nd Viscount; *b.* Nov. 4th, 1922; *s.* 1967; ed. at Eastbourne Coll., and Jesus Coll., Camb. (MA honours); Bar Inner Temple 1953; 1939-45 war, as Capt. RA.

Arms,—Azure over water barry wavy in base a bridge of one arch proper, on a chief argent a portcullis sable between two daffodils stalked and leaved also proper. **Crest**—A demi-dragon gules holding between the claws a portcullis sable. **Supporters**—*Dexter,* a dragon gules; *sinister* a lion or each gorged with a collar compony argent and vert; pendent from that of the dexter an escutcheon argent charged with a martlet sable, and from that of the sinister an escutcheon gules charged with a port between two towers also argent.

BROTHER LIVING
Hon. WILLIAM (Triggs, Crondall, nr. Farnham, Surrey), *b.* Nov. 7th, 1927; ed. at Eastbourne Coll., and St. Catharine's Coll., Camb. (Exhibitioner BA honours); Capt. RWF (TA); a JP for Hants.: *m.* 1955, Ursula, yst. da. of the late Lt.-Col. Henry Edward Medlicott, DSO, and has issue living, Timothy Henry Gwilym, *b.* 1962,—Sara Gwenfron, *b.* 1957,—Clare Mair, *b.* 1961.

PREDECESSOR.—[1] GWILYM Lloyd George, TD, PC, 2nd son of 1st Earl Lloyd George of Dwyfor; *b.* 1894; MP for Pembrokeshire (*L*) 1922-24 and 1929-50, and N. Newcastle-upon-Tyne (*L and C*) 1951-57; Min. of Fuel and Power 1942-45, Min. of Food 1951-54, and Home Sec. and Min. for Welsh Affairs 1954-57; cr. *Viscount Tenby*, of Bulford, co. Pembroke (Peerage of UK) 1957: *m.* 1921, Edna Gwenfron, who *d.* 1971, da. of David Jones, of Gwnfa, Denbigh; *d.* 1967; *s.* by his el. son [2] DAVID, 2nd viscount and present peer.

TENNYSON, BARON. (Tennyson.) [Baron U.K. 1884.]

Look backward and forward.

HAROLD CHRISTOPHER TENNYSON, 4th Baron; *b.* March 25th, 1919; *s.* 1951; ed. at Eton, and at Trin. Coll., Camb. (BA); Hon. Freeman of Lincoln.

Arms,—Gules, a bend nebuly or, thereon a chaplet vert, between three leopards' heads jessant de lys of the second. **Crest,**—A dexter arm in armour, the hand in a gauntlet or, grasping a broken tilting spear enfiled with a garland of laurel. **Supporters.**—Two leopards rampant guardant gules, semée de lys and ducally crowned or.
Residence,—18, Rue Galilée, Paris, XVI. *Club,*—White's.

BROTHER LIVING.
Hon. MARK AUBREY, *DSC*, Foston Hall, Foston, Yorks.; White's Club, and Royal Yacht Squadron, *b.* March 28th, 1920; Cdr. RN; 1939-45 War (despatches, DSC): *m.* 1964, Deline Celeste Budler.

COLLATERAL BRANCHES LIVING.
Grandchildren of the late Hon. Lionel Tennyson (infra):—
　　Issue of the late Alfred Browning Stanley Tennyson, *b.* 1878, *d* 1952: *m.* 1912, the Hon. Margaret Cicely Drummond, who *d.* 1963, dau. of 10th Viscount Strathallan [E. Perth]:—
James Alfred, *D.S.C.*, *b.* 1913; Lieut.-Com. R.N. (retired); is in New Zealand Govt. Ser.; European War 1939 (despatches, D.S.C.): *m.* 1954, Beatrice Aventon, dau. of A. T. Young, of Wellington, New Zealand, and has issue living, David Harold Alexander, *b.* 1960,—Alan James Drummond, *b.* 1965. *Residence,*—222A, Karori Rd., Wellington, W5, NZ.——Aubrey Drummond (51/53, Eardley Cres., SW5) *b.* 1920; is Capt. late Essex Regt. and Sudan Defence Force; formerly attached Sudan Govt.: *m.* 1966, Mai Chin Yau, and has issue living, Davina May, *b.* 1969.——Eleanor Rachel (46, Riverside Gdns., Romsey, SO5 8HN, Hants.), *b.* 1915; is an Artist, and Art Teacher, Atherley Sch., Southampton; formerly Professor of Art, Baylor Univ., Waco, Texas, USA: *m.* 1st, 1945 (m. diss. 1954), Maj. David Rainsford Moore, Essex Regt.; 2ndly, 1967, William Charles Bigg, RAF (ret.).

Issue of the late Hon. Lionel Tennyson, 2nd son of 1st Baron, *b.* 1854, *d.* 1896: *m.* 1878, Eleanor Bertha Mary, who *d.* 1915 [having *m.* 2ndly, 1888, as his second wife, the Rt. Hon. Augustine Birrell, K.C., LL.D., who *d.* 1933], dau. (by 1st marriage) of the late Frederick Locker :—

Sir Charles Bruce Locker, *C.M.G., b.* 1879 ; ed. at Eton, and at King's Coll., Camb. (B.A. 1st class Classics 1902, Hon. Fellow 1951) ; Fellow of Bedford Coll., London 1954 ; Hon. LL.D., Camb. 1955 ; Bar. Gray's Inn 1905 ; is a F.R.C.A., and F.R.S.L., and Vice-Pres., Federation of British Industries ; appointed Junior Equity Counsel to H.M. Office of Works 1908, Legal Assist. to Colonial Office 1911, and Dep. Director, Federation of British Industries 1918 ; C.M.G. 1915, Knt. 1945 : *m.* 1909, Ivy Gladys, *O.B.E.,* who *d.* 1958, dau. of W. J. Pretious, and has issue living, (Beryl) Hallam Augustine, *b.* 1920 : *m.* 1945, Margot Wallach, and has issue living, Charles Jonathan Penrose *b.* 1955, Sita Rosalind Joanna *b.* 1950. *Residence,*—23, The Park, N.W.11.

Grandchildren of Sir Charles Bruce Locker Tennyson, C.M.G. (ante):—
Issue of the late Capt. Charles Julian Tennyson, *b.* 1915, *d.* (killed in action in Burma) 1945 : *m.* 1937, Yvonne (who *m.* 2ndly, 1947, Michael Jeans), dau. of Col. R. B. le Cornu :—
Simon, *b.* 1939. *Residence,*—Valley Farm, Walberswick, Suffolk.——Penelope (twin), *b.* 1939.

PREDECESSORS.—[1] ALFRED Tennyson, *D.C.L.,|F.R.S.,* son of the late Rev. George Clayton Tennyson, LL.D., R. of Somersby, *b.* 1809 ; Poet Laureate 1850-92 ; cr. *Baron Tennyson,* of Aldworth, Sussex, and Freshwater, Isle of Wight (peerage of United Kingdom) 1884 : *m.* 1850, Emily, who *d.* 1896, dau. of Henry Sellwood, of Berkshire ; *d.* 1892 ; *s.* by his el. son [2] HALLAM, *G.C.M.G., P.C.,* 2nd Baron, *b.* 1852 ; Gov. and Com.-in-Ch. of S. Australia 1899-1902, and Gov.-Gen. of Commonwealth of Australia 1902-4 ; appointed Dep. Gov. and Steward of the Isle of Wight 1913 : *m.* 1st, 1884, Audrey Georgiana Florence, who *d.* 1916, dau. of the late Charles John Boyle ; 2ndly, 1918, Mary Emily, who *d.* 1931, dau. of Charles Robert Prinsep, Advocate-Gen. of Calcutta, and widow of Andrew Hichens ; *d.* 1928 ; *s.* by his el. son [3] LIONEL HALLAM, 3rd Baron, *b.* 1889 ; Major Rifle Brig. (Reserve), and Hon. Col. 51st (London) Anti-Aircraft Brig. R.A. (T.A.) : *m.* 1st, 1918, the Hon. Clarissa Madeline Georgiana Felicité (who *d.* 1960, and from whom he had obtained a divorce 1928), dau. of 1st Baron Glenconner, and formerly wife of Capt. William Adrian Vincent Bethell, 2nd Life Guards ; 2ndly, 1934, Carroll (from whom he obtained a divorce 1943), dau. of Howard Elting, of Chicago, U.S.A., and widow of Joseph William Donner, of Buffalo, U.S.A. ; *d.* 1951 ; *s.* by his el. son [4] HAROLD CHRISTOPHER, 4th Baron and present peer.

TENTERDEN, BARONY OF. (Abbott.) [Extinct 1939.]

DAUGHTER LIVING OF FOURTH BARON.

Hon. Gwen Elfrida Penelope, *b.* 1908: *m.* 1941, William Fisher of 136, Norbiton Hall, Kingston upon Thames, and has issue living, Robert Anthony Abbot, *b.* 1942,—David James Abbott *b.* 1951.

TERRINGTON, BARON. (Woodhouse.) [Baron U.K. 1918.]

Labour conquers all things.

JAMES ALLEN DAVID WOODHOUSE, 4th Baron ; *b.* Dec. 30th, 1915 ; *s.* 1961 ; ed. at Winchester ; Major (retired) Roy. Norfolk Regt. and Queen's Westminster Rifles (King's Roy. Rifle Corps) T.A.; a Member of London Stock Exchange, a Dir. of S. J. Carr & Co., Ltd., Gunmakers, and a partner in the firm of Sheppards and Chase, Clements House, Gresham St., E.C.2; Vice-Chm. of London Group of Oxford Cttee. for Famine Relief, and Dep. Chm. of Wider Share Ownership Council; a Dep. Chm. of Cttees., House of Lords 1961-63; an A.D.C. to G.O.C. Madras 1940; 1939-45 War in India, N. Africa, and Middle East (wounded): *m.* 1942, Suzanne, dau. of Col. T. S. Irwin, J.P., D.L., late Roy. Dragoons, of Justice-town, Carlisle, and Mill House, Holton, Suffolk, and has issue.

Arms,—Per fesse or and azure, issuant in chief a hurst of oak trees proper, in base two bars wavy argent. **Crest,**—A demi-woodman proper issuant out of a wreath of roses argent, barbed and seeded also proper, supporting in the dexter hand an axe or. **Supporters,**—On either side an Airedale terrier proper, gorged with a ducal coronet or.
Residences,—Alward House, Alderbury, Salisbury; 8, Radnor Walk, SW3. *Clubs,*—Boodle's, Pratt's.

DAUGHTERS LIVING.
Hon. Lavinia Valerie, *b.* 1943: *m.* 1974, Nicholas George Bolton, son of Sir George Lewis French Bolton, KCMG.

Hon. Georgina Caroline, *b.* 1946.

Hon. Davina Mary, *b.* 1955; Lady in Waiting to HRH The Princess Margaret, Countess of Snowdon since 1975.

BROTHER LIVING.
Hon. CHRISTOPHER MONTAGUE, *DSO, OBE, b.* May 11th, 1917; *ed.* at Winchester and New Coll., Oxford (MA); Director-Gen. of Roy. Inst. of International Affairs 1955-59, Parl. Sec. to Min. of Aviation 1961-62 and Joint Parl. Under-Sec. of State for Home Dept. 1962-64; Dir. of Education and Training CBI 1966-70; 1939-45 War in Middle East as temporary Col. Intelligence Corps (despatches twice, DSO, OBE); has American Legion of Merit, and Order of Phoenix of Greece with Swords; M P for Oxford (*C*) 1959-66, and 1970-74; DSO 1943, OBE (Mil) 1944: *m.* 1945, Lady Davidema Katharine Cynthia Mary Millicent Bulwer-Lytton, da. of 2nd Earl of Lytton, and widow of the 5th Earl Erne, and has issue living, Christopher Richard James, *b.* 1946; MB, BS: *m.* 1975, Anna Margaret, da. of the Hon. Hugo John Laurence Philipps, el. son of 2nd Baron Milford,— Nicholas Michael John, *b.* 1949: *m.* 1973, Mary Jane Stormont, da. of D. M. Stormont Mowat, of Long Crendon, Bucks.,—Emma Davina Mary, *b.* 1954. *Residence,*—Bois Mill, Latimer, Bucks.

AUNT LIVING. (*Daughter of 1st Baron.*)
Hon. Kathleen Jessie: *m.* 1911, Eugene Monier Wason, who *d.* 1966, and has issue living, Rigby James Monier, *b.* 1912: *m.* 1943, Mildred Mons, da. of the late C. O. Thomas, of Penzance, and has issue living, Ivor Cecil Monier *b.* 1949,—Eugene Romer, *b.* 1914: *m.* 1939, Emily Margaret Elliot, who *d.* 1957, da. of the late J. P. Miller, and has issue living, John Eugene Monier *b.* 1940, David Romer *b.* 1946, Virginia Elliott *b.* 1942, Patricia Kathleen Minna *b.* 1944,—Peter Cathcart (106, Frognal, Hampstead, NW3), *b.* 1924; *ed.* at Stowe, and at New Coll., Oxford (MA), and at Univ. Coll., London(BA, PhD); a Fellow of British Psychological Soc.; a Member of Scientific Staff, Med. Research Council since 1953; Research Fellow in Cognitive Studies, Harvard Univ. 1962-63; Reader in Psycholinguistics, Univ. Coll., London, 1970; 1939-45 War as Lt. RAC: *m.* 1951, Marjorie Vera, da. of Frank James Salberg, CIE, MBE, VD, and has issue living, Armorer Janet *b.* 1956, Sarah Kathleen Romer *b.* 1958. *Residence,*—8, Cavendish Pl., Bath.

PREDECESSORS.—[1] JAMES THOMAS Woodhouse, son of James Woodhouse, of Flamborough; *b.* 1852; M.P. for Huddersfield (*L*) 1895-1906; a Railway and Canal Traffic Commr. 1906-21, and Chm. Losses under Defence of the Realm Commn. 1915-21; *cr. Baron Terrington,* of Huddersfield, co. York (peerage of United Kingdom) 1918: *m.* 1876, Jessie, who *d.* 1942, dau. of W. J. Reed, formerly of Skidby, Yorkshire; *d.* 1921; *s.* by his el. son [2] HAROLD JAMES SELBORNE, *O.B.E.,* 2nd Baron, *b.* 1877: *m.* 1st, 1918, Vera Florence Annie [M.P. for Bucks, Wycombe Div. (*L*) 1923-4] (she obtained a divorce 1926), dau. of H. G. Bousher, and widow of Guy Ivo Sebright, son of Sir Guy Thomas Saunders Sebright, 12th Bt.; 2ndly, 1927, Rena de Vere, who *d.* 1973, da. of the late Capt. William Molyneux Shapland-Swiny, 42nd Roy. Highlanders (The Black Watch), and sometime A.D.C. to H.R.H. the late Duke of Edinburgh, of Ballymurrogh and Cloghamon, co. Wexford; *d.* 1940; *s.* by his brother [3] HORACE MARTON, *K.B.E.,* 3rd Baron, *b.* 1887; Principal Assist. Sec., Min. of Labour and National Ser. 1941-4, Dep. Speaker and Dep. Chm. of Committee, House of Lords 1949 : *m.* 1st, 1914, Valerie, who *d.* 1958, dau. of the late George Allen Phillips of Leydens House, Edenbridge, Kent; 2ndly, 1959, Mrs. Phyllis Mary Haggard, who *d.* 1971, da. of the late W. W. Drew, ICS; *d.* 1961; *s.* by his son [4] JAMES ALLEN DAVID, 4th Baron and present peer.

TEVIOT, BARON. (Kerr.) [Baron U.K. 1940.]

Late, but in earnest.

CHARLES JOHN KERR, 2nd Baron; *b.* Dec. 16th, 1934; *s.* 1968; *ed.* at Eton: *m.* 1965, Patricia Mary, da. of the late Alexander Harris, and has issue.

Arms,—Quarterly: 1st and 4th gules, on a chevron argent three mullets of the field, *Kerr of Ferniehurst;* 2nd and 3rd per fess gules and vert, on a chevron argent between three mascles in chief or and a unicorn's head in base of the third, horned of the fourth, three mullets of the first. *Kerr of Cessford;* in the centre of the quarters a rose or. *Crest,*—A stag's head erased proper. *Supporters,*—Two border terriers proper.
Residence,—32, Dale Av., Hassocks, Sussex.

SON LIVING.
Hon. CHARLES ROBERT, *b.* Sept. 19th, 1971.

WIDOW LIVING OF FIRST BARON.
(FLORENCE) ANGELA (*Angela, Baroness Teviot*), (Timber Ash House, Chaddleworth, Newbury), da. of the late Lt.-Col. Charles Walter Villiers, CBE, DSO [see E. Clarendon, colls.]: *m.* 1930, as his 2nd wife, the 1st Baron who *d.* 1968.

PREDECESSOR.—[1] CHARLES IAIN Kerr, *DSO, MC,* son of Charles Wyndham Rudolph Kerr [M. Lothian, colls.]; *b.* 1874; Lt.-Col. R. Horse Guards; Junior Lord of the Treasury 1937-39 Comptroller of HM's Household 1939-40, Chm. of Liberal National Party 1940-56, Ch. Whip of Liberal National Party in House of Lords 1945; MP for Montrose (*L*) 1932-40; *cr. Baron Teviot,* of Burghclere, co. Southampton (peerage of UK) 1940: *m.* 1st, 1911, (m. diss. 1930), Muriel Constance, da. of the late William Gordon-Canning, of Hartpury, Glos.; 2ndly, 1930, Florence Angela, da. of the late Lt.-Col. Charles Walter Villiers, CBE DSO [E. Clarendon, colls.]; *d.* 1968; *s.* by his only son [2] CHARLES JOHN, 2nd Baron, and present peer.

TEYNHAM, BARON. (Roper-Curzon.) **[Baron E. 1616.]**

[Title pronounced "Tenham."]

SPES MEA IN DEO

My hope is in God.

JOHN CHRISTOPHER INGHAM ROPER-CURZON, 20th Baron; *b.* Dec. 25th, 1928; *s.* 1972; ed. at Eton; late Capt. The Buffs (TA), and 2nd Lt. Coldm. Gds.; Land Agent; OStJ; ADC to Gov. of Bermuda 1953 and 1955 to Gov. of Leeward Is. 1955-56 (Private Sec. 1956) and to Gov. of Jamaica 1962; Palestine 1948; Pres. of Inst. of Commerce: *m.* 1964, Elizabeth, yr. da. of the late Lt.-Col. the Hon. David Scrymgeour-Wedderburn, DSO, [see E. Dundee, colls.], and has issue.

Arms,—Quarterly: 1st and 4th argent, on a bend sable, three popinjays or, collared gule *Curzon*; 2nd and 3rd per fesse azure and or, a pale counterchanged, and three stags' heads eased of the second, *Roper*. **Crests,**—1st a popinjay rising, wings displayed and inverted or collared gules, *Curzon*; 2nd, a lion rampant sable, supporting on the dexter forepaw a ducal coronet or, *Roper*. **Supporters,**—*Dexter,* a buck or; *sinister,* an heraldic tiger regardant argent.

Residence,—The Severalls, Hatherop, Cirencester, Glos. **Clubs,**—Turf, House of Lords Yacht, Puffin's (Edinburgh), Ocean Cruising.

SONS LIVING.

Hon. DAVID HENRY INGHAM, *b.* Oct. 5th, 1965.
Hon. Jonathan Christopher James, *b.* 1973.

DAUGHTERS LIVING.

Hon. Emma Elizabeth, *b.* 1966.
Hon. Sophie Patricia, *b.* 1967.
Hon. Lucy Elspeth, *b.* 1969.
Hon. Hermione Marie Hilda Edith (twin) *b.* 1973.

BROTHER LIVING.

Hon. Michael Henry, *b.* 1931; Lt. (ret.) RN; an OStJ: *m.* 1964 (m. diss. 1967), Maria, only da. of the late Maj. R. V. Taylor, 16th/5th, Queen's R. Lancers. *Residence,*—75, Eccleston Square Mews SW1.

HALF SISTERS LIVING.

Hon. Henrietta Margaret Fleur, *b.* 1955.
Hon. Holly Anne-Marie, *b.* 1963.

UNCLE LIVING. (*Son of 18th Baron*).

Hon. Ralph Henry (121, Lansdowne Rd., W11; Guards' Club), *b.* 1899; ed. at Eton; Foreign Ser. 1948-56; Chargé d'Affaires Yemen 1953-55, and HM Consul at Skoplje, Yugoslavia 1955-56; 1914-18 War with the Buffs [E. Kent Regt.) (wounded); 1939-45 War as Capt. and acintg Lt.-Col. Scots Guards: *m.* 1960, Dorothy, who *d.* 1967, da. of the late William Dixon Campbell, of 35, Ladbroke Sq., W11.

MOTHER LIVING.

Elspeth Grace (*Marchioness of Northampton*) (Castle Ashby, Northampton; Compton Wynyates, Tysoe, Warwick; 5, Pelham Place, SW7), el. da. of the late William Ingham Whitaker, DL [V. Melville]: *m.* 1st, 1927 (m. diss. 1954), the 19th Baron, who *d.* 1972; 2ndly, 1958, as his 3rd wife, the 6th Marquess of Northampton.

WIDOW LIVING OF NINETEENTH BARON.

ANNE RITA (Inwood House, Sarisbury Green, Hants), da. of the late Capt. Leicester Charles Assheton St. John Curzon-Howe, MVO, RN [see E. Howe, colls.]: *m.* 1st, 1955, as his 2nd wife, the 19th Baron, who *d.* 1972; 2ndly, 1975, Dr. Ian Edwards.

COLLATERAL BRANCHES LIVING.

Granddaughter of the late Capt. Edward Dacre Roper, son of the late Capt. Philip Henry Roper, son of the late Hon. Philip Roper, 5th son of 10th Baron :—
Issue of the late Frank Dacre Roper, *b.* 1848, *d.* 1930 : *m.* 1874, Caroline Amy Louisa, who *d.* 1913, dau. of John Belgrave Guazzaroni Franklin :—
Edith Florence, *b.* 1878. *Residence,*—25, Cavendish Rd., Clapham Common, SW12.

Grandchildren of the late Blayney Tenison Roper (*b.* 1853) (infra):—
Issue of the late Lt.-Col. Richard Blayney Roper, *b.* 1897, *d.* 1964: *m.* 1930, Elmslie, who *d.* 1962, da. of the late William Forbes-Garden:—
Christopher Blayney (c/o National and Grindlays Bank, 13, St. James's Sq., S.W.1), *b.* 1932; late 2nd Lt. RE; an Asso. of Camborne Sch. of Mines: *m.* 1963, Elizabeth Garthorne, 2nd da. of the late Andrew Ian Dalglish Brown, of Johannesburg, and has issue living, Katherine Elizabeth, *b.* 1966,—Margaret Jennifer, *b.* 1967,—Philippa Garthorne, *b.* 1969.——Margaret Elizabeth, *b.* 1935: *m.* 1959, Maj. John David Cousins, (c/o Lloyds Bank, 6 Pall Mall, SW1) 10th Princess Mary's Own Gurkha Rifles, and has issue living, Terence David, *b.* 1969,—Elizabeth Mary, *b.* 1972.

Granddaughter of the late Blayney Tenison Roper (*b.* 1811), yst. son of the Very Rev. Henry Roper, DD, el. son of the Rev. the Hon. Richard Henry Roper, yst. son of 8th Baron:—
Issue of the late Blayney Tenison Roper, *b.* 1853, *d.* 1938: *m.* 1892, Emily Elizabeth, who *d.* 1937, dau. of the late J. C. Christian, of Sligo:—
Aileen Emily (Wayside, Church Rd., Greystones, co. Wicklow): *m.* 1939, Gerald Richard Butler, who *d.* 1953.

Grandson of the late Capt. Charles Cadwaladr Trevor-Roper (el. son of George Edward, 3rd son of Charles Blayney, el. son of Cadwallader Blayney TREVOR-ROPER, 2nd son of the Rev. the Hon. Richard Henry Roper, yst. son of 8th Baron):—

Issue of the late Flight-Lieut. Richard Dacre Trevor-Roper, D.F.C., D.F.M., R.A.F., b. 1915. d. (killed in action over Germany) 1944: m. 1942, Patricia Audrey Edwards, who m. 2ndly, 1949, Frank Marvin, and 3rdly, 1955, John Derick Straight, of Flat 2, Sindlesham Mill, Wokingham, Berks.:—

Charles Antony (Sindlesham Mill, Mill Lane, Sindlesham, Berks.), b. 1943; ed. at Wellington, and Reading Univ. (BSc, PhD): m. 1967, Carol Elizabeth, da. of Charles James Pape, of 4, Vauxhall Drive, Woodley, Reading, and has issue living, Dacre Gabriel, b. 1969.

Granddaughters of the late George Edward Trevor-Roper (ante):—

Issue of the late Capt. Charles Cadwaladr Trevor-Roper, Hampshire Regt., b. 1884, d. (of wounds in action during European War) 1917: m. 1913, Gertrude Alice, who d. 1962 [having m. 2ndly, 1925, Major Robert Hugh Polyntz, M.C., late The King's Shropshire L.I., who d. 1931], dau. of W. G. Clabby, Indian Police:—

Elizabeth Alice, b. 1914: m. 1935, Harry Hyde Parker [see Parker, Bt., cr. 1681]. Residence,—Peirce House, Charing, Ashford, Kent.——Anne, b. 1916: m. 1941, Josiah Maddocks, of 8, Northgate, Goosnargh, Preston, Lancs., and has issue living, Richard James (8, Lindle Close, Hutton, Preston, Lancs.), b. 1943: m. 1965, Dorothy Suzanne Pallett, and has issue living, John Charles James, b. 1967, Valerie Suzanne b. 1966,—David Hugh b. 1950.

Grandchildren of the late Arthur Messeena Trevor-Roper (infra):—

Issue of the late Richard Teynham Trevor-Roper, b. 1903, d. 1968: m. 1928, Lilian M. Prestwood (153, Leicester Rd., Thurcaston, Leics.),—

Richard Eric (14, Groby Rd., Glenfield, Leics.), b. 1928: m. 1st, 1954 (m. diss. 1959), Patricia Anne McClintock; 2ndly, 1964, Marilyn Elizabeth Fox, and has issue living (by 1st m.), Richard Patrick, b. 1955.——Kathleen Edith, b. 1931: m. 1951, Kenneth Leslie Jones, of 139, Leicester Rd., Thurcaston, Leics., and has issue living, Nigel Kenneth, b. 1952: m. 1972, Gillian Anne Hardy.

Granddaughters of Richard Henry Trevor-Roper (infra):—

Issue of the late Ernest Messeena Trevor-Roper, b. 1875, d. 1956: m. 1904, Claire, who d. 1942, da. of the late John Dodson, of Altrincham:—

Irene Dorothy, b. 1906: m. 1st, 1934 (m. annulled 1941), Clifford Frank Humphris; 2ndly, 1962, John Ernest Llewellyn Poulson, of Padiss Corner, Ogdens, Fordingbridge, Hants.

Issue of the late Arthur Messeena Trevor-Roper, b. 1876, d. 1966: m. 1902, Mary Wynifred, who d. 19—, da. of James Keel, of Froglands, Cheddar, Somerset:—

Cyril Peter (Pixholme Cottage, Pixham Lane, Dorking, Surrey), b. 1916: m. 1940, Lorna Eileen, da. of the late Harry J. Smith, of Hillside Terr., Dorchester, Dorset, and has issue living, 3 das.—— Kathleen Victoria, b. 1911: m. 1940, George Stanley White, of Fore St., Ivybridge, Devon.—— Margaret Elizabeth, b. 1923: m. 1946, Niels Peter Nielsen, of 23, Hampshire Rd., Aylestone, Leicester, LE2 8HF.

Grandchildren of the late Charles Blayney Trevor-Roper (ante):—

Issue of the late Richard Henry Trevor-Roper, b. 1834, d. 1889: m. 1864, Grace Carr (who d. 1909, having m. 2ndly, 1901, Hugh William Trevor-Roper, who d. 1903), dau. of Henry Messeena, M.D.:—

Bertie William Edward, MB, MRCS, b. 1885; ed. at Victoria Univ., Manchester (MB and ChB 1908); MRCS and LRCP London 1908: m. 1910, Kathleen Elizabeth, who d. 1964, da. of William Davison, and has issue living, Hugh Redwald (of 8, St. Aldate's, Oxford, and Chiefswood, Melrose, Roxburghshire), b. 1914; ed. at Charterhouse, and at Ch. Ch., Oxford (MA, Student 1945); late temporary Maj. Intelligence Corps (TA); author of " The Last Days of Hitler ", and other works; Regius Prof. of Modern History, Oxford, since 1957: m. 1954, Lady Alexandra Henrietta Louisa (HOWARD-JOHNSTON), da. of 1st Earl Haig,—Patrick Dacre, MB, BCh (3 Park Sq. West, NW1. Clubs,— Athenaeum, Beefsteak), b. 1916; ed. at Charterhouse, and at Clare Coll., Camb. (BA 1937, MB and BCh 1940, MA 1941); MRCS and LRCP 1940; FRCS England 1947; Ophthalmic Surg., Westminster and Moorfields Eye Hosps., and late Capt. New Zealand Med. Corps.,—Sheila Grace, b. 1912: m. 1st, 1942 (m. diss. 1972), Keith M. Price, TD; 2ndly, 1972, A. Colin Kingham, MC, of Flat 44, Grosvenor House, Park Lane, W1, and has issue living (by 1st m.), Martin Trevor b. 1946, Nicholas David b. 1948. Residence,—20, Bondgate Without, Alnwick, Northumberland.

Grandchildren of the late Dacre Trevor-Roper, 5th son of Charles Blayney Trevor-Roper (ante):—

Issue of the late Lennard Carew Trevor-Roper, b. 1876, d. 1948: m. 1st, 1898, Margaret Helen, who d. 1901, dau. of the late James Laffan, of Killarney ; 2ndly, 1909, Lisbeth Rankin, who d. 1970 da. of Alexander Knight Stein:—

(By 1st marriage) Kathleen Mary, b. 1900 : m. 1924, Major Robert Henry Bolton, M.M., T.D., Sherwood Foresters. Residence,—Wentworth, Downderry, Torpoint, Cornwall.——(By 2nd marriage) Lennard Dacre, b. 1910 : m. 1935, Constance May, dau. of John H. Barr, of Abergele, Denbighshire.——Janet Rankin, b. 1911 ; formerly 3rd Officer, W.R.N.S.: m. 1942, Major Vivian M. E. Bateson, King's(Liverpool) Regt., who d. 1959, and has issue living, Simon Vivian Ranulf, b. 1946,— Julia Janet, b. 1948: m. 1965, John Read, and has issue living, Sean b. 1965, Amber Ruth b. 1966. Residence,—8, South Close, Green Lane, Morden, Surrey.——Elsie, b. 1913, formerly in WRNS: m. 1942, Humphrey Barton Henderson, LDS, who d. 1955, and has issue living, John Trevor Howard (3, Meadow Bank, Tylers Green, High Wycombe, Bucks.), b. 1945: m. 1969, Jenifer Kinanne Mackay,— Stella Marian, b. 1947: m. 1966, Dennis James Aris of Chiltern Cottage, Edelsborough, Dunstable, and has issue living, Merryll Natasha b. 1971. Residence,—21, Green Lane, Amersham, Bucks.

Issue of the late Rev. Ranulph Dacre Trevor-Roper, b. 1893, d. 1975: m. 1916, Joan Fraser (16, Hanover Court, Fieldfare, Covingham, Swindon, SN3 5BG), da. of the late Robert Fraser Woodcock, MRCS, of Wigan:—

Robert ffarington (32, Ravenswood Rd., Bristol 6), b. 1917; ed. at Univ. Coll. Sch.; Maj. (ret.), Lancashire Fus.; N. Africa 1942-43 (wounded): m. 1941, Dorothy Davina, yst. da. of the late James MacKay, of Edinburgh.——Anthony Dacre, MC (Hillands Cottage, Melchbourne, Beds.), b. 1921; ed. at Univ. Coll. Sch.; Capt. (ret.) Indian Army and Lt. Lancashire Fus.; Burma 1943-45 (wounded), Korea 1950-51 (MC): m. 1954, Amy Frances, yst. da. of the late Capt. John Douglas Collins, of Burton Bradstock, Dorset, and has issue living, Julian Dacre, b. 1956,—Christopher Charles ffarington, b. 1964,—Mary Anne, b. 1954,—Susan Elizabeth, b. 1958.——Helen Bennetta, b. 1919: m. 1st, 1940, Richard Stoate; 2ndly, 1957, Terence H. Summers, of Greenacres, Swinderby Rd., Collingham, Newark, Notts.——Joan Everilda (4, Wetherell Pl., Bristol, B58 1AR), b. 1923: m. 1940 (m. diss. 1968), Owen John Howell, ARIBA, and has issue living, Robin John (6, Burlington Rd., Redland, Bristol, BS6 6TL), b. 1941: m. 1963, Pamela Ann, da. of Alfred Raymond Reader, of Northampton, and has issue living, Jonathan Raef b. 1964, Nicholas Dacre b. 1966, Christopher Noel b. 1969, Benjamin James b. 1970,—Trevor Owen b. 1944: m. 1965, Gillian, el. da. of Roland Poole, of Croydon,—Jennifer Eve, b. 1949: m. 1970, Anthony Stephen Duval.

Grandsons of the late William Roper (infra):—

Issue of the late Charles Roper, b. 1874, d. 1955: m. 1913, Josephine Marita, who d. 1953, dau. of the late Adam Cook Newell, R.M., of Killgorrive House, Ballinasloe:—

Richard Charles, b. 1920; 1940-42 War with N. Irish Horse: m. 1957, Therese Margaret, da. of the late Henry Lewis Norman D'Arcy, of Glenageary, co. Dublin. Residence,—40, Belvedere Rd., Westmount, Montreal, Canada.

Issue of the late William Trevor Roper, b. 1880, d. 1956 : m. 1st, 1913, Elsie Beatrice, who d. 1934, dau. of Thomas Holt, of Oxton, Cheshire ; 2ndly, 1938, Janet Pegman, of Clontarf, Dublin :—

(By 1st marriage) Trevor Holt, *b.* 1914 : *m.* 1938, Hylda Florence Marks, and has issue living, Penelope Margaret, *b.* 1944: *m.* 1968, David Allengame Proger, of Plumtree Cottage, High St., Little Milton, Oxon. OX9 7PU, and has issue living, Lizanne Margaret *b.* 1969, Philippa Jane *b.* 1972. *Residence,*— 19, Woodlawn Park, Churchtown Rd., Dublin.——Dacre Alexander, *b.* 1921; 1939-45 Wat as Lt. RNVR: *m.* 1945, Sylvia Mary, da. of Thomas H. Jameson, of Dublin, and has issue living, Lynda Susan, *b.* 1948.

Grandson of the late Hon. Sir Henry Roper, son of the late William Roper, son of the late Rev. the Hon. Richard Henry Roper (ante) :—

Issue of the late Henry Charles Roper, *b.* 1850, *d.* 1916: *m.* 1912, Hilda Kate Marguerite Collen, who *d.*1966, dau. of Alfred John Stearn, formerly of Bythe Church, Cambridge:—
Alexander John Henry, *T.D.*, *b.* 1913; ed. at King's Coll., London (B.Sc. 1934) ; is Capt. R.A.: *m.* 1947, Marjorie Edith, dau. of Henry Broom Vines, formerly of Lower Field, Bourton, Berks, and has issue living, Richard Henry, *b.* 1948,—Margaret Hilda Jane, *b.* 1950. *Residence,*—Lower Mill, Ashbury, Berks.

PREDECESSORS. — [1] *Sir* JOHN Roper, Knt., was cr. *Baron Teynham,* of Teynham, co. Kent (peerage of England) 1616; *d.* 1618; *s.* by his son [2] CHRISTOPHER, 2nd Baron ; *d.* 1622; *s.* by his son [3] JOHN *K.B.,* 3rd Baron; *d.* 1627; *s.* by his son [4] CHRISTOPHER; 4th Baron; *d.* 1673; *s.* by his son [5] CHRISTOPHER, 5th Baron ; was Lord-Lieut. of co. Kent· *d.* 1692; *s.* by his el. son [6] JOHN, 6th Baron ; *d.* unmarried ; *s.* by his brother [7] CHRIS-TOPHER, 7th Baron; *d.* unmarried ; *s.* by his brother [8] HENRY, 8th Baron ; conformed to the Established Church, and took his seat in the House of Lords 1715 ; was a Lord of the Bed-chamber to George I. ; *d.* 1722 ; *s.* by his el. son [9] PHILIP, 9th Baron ; *d.* unmarried 1727 ; *s.* by his brother [10] HENRY, 10th Baron; *d.* 1781; *s.* by his son [11] HENRY, 11th Baron ; *d.* 1786; *s.* by his el. son [12] HENRY, 12th Baron ; *d.* unmarried 1806; *s.* by his brother [13] JOHN, 13th Baron ; *d.* unmarried 1824 ; *s.* by his cousin [14] HENRY FRANCIS, 14th Baron, son of the Hon. Francis Roper, 4th son of 10th Baron ; *b.* 1768 ; assumed in 1788 by Roy. licence the surname of Curson in lieu of his patronymic, and in 1813 by Roy. licence he assumed the surnames of Roper-Curzon, in lieu of his then name : *m.* 1788, Bridget, dau. and heiress of Thomas Hawkins, of Nash Court ; *d.* 1842; *s.* by his el. son [15] HENRY, 15th Baron ; *d.s.p.* 1842 ; *s.* by his brother [16] GEORGE HENRY, 16th Baron, *b.* 1798: *m.* 1st, 1822, Miss Eliza Joynes, of Sevenoaks, who *d.* 1871 ; 2ndly, 1873, Elizabeth, dau. of the late William Jay, Lieut. R.A. ; *d.* 1889; *s.* by his son [17] HENRY GEORGE, 17th Baron, *b.* 1822: *m.* 1860, Harriet Anne Lovell, who *d.* 1916, dau. of the Rev. Thomas Heathcote ; *d.* 1892; *s.* by his el. son [18] HENRY JOHN PHILIP SYDNEY, 18th Baron, *b.* 1867: *m.* 1895, Mabel, who *d.* 1937, dau. of the late Lieut.-Col. Henry Green Wilkinson, Scots Guards ; *d.* 1936 ; *s.* by his el. son [19] CHRISTOPHER JOHN HENRY, *DSO, DSC*; 19th Baron; *b.* 1896; Capt. RN; Dep. Chm. of Cttees, House of Lords 1946-59, and Chancellor of Primrose League 1948: *m.* 1st, 1927 (m. diss. 1954), Elspeth Grace, el. da. of William Ingham Whitaker [V. Melville]; 2ndly, 1955, Anne Rita (who *m.* 2ndly, 1975, Dr. Ian Edwards), da. of Capt. Leicester Charles Assheton St. John Curzon-Howe, MVO, RN [E. Howe]; *d.* 1972; *s.* by his el. son [20], JOHN CHRISTOPHER INGHAM, 20th Baron and present peer.

THANKERTON, BARONY OF. (Watson.) [Extinct 1948.]

DAUGHTER LIVING OF LIFE PEER.
Hon. Sophia Margaret, *b.* 1907: *m.* 1936, Michael John Callow, and has issue. *Residence,*—Relf House, Rockshaw Rd., Merstham, Surrey.

WIDOW LIVING OF SON OF LIFE BARON.
Enid Agnes (1/1, Ravelston House Rd., Edinburgh 4), da. of the late Colin Balantyne, of Kirna, Walker-burn: *m.* 1934, the Hon. William Douglas Watson, TD, WS, who *d.* 1971.

THOMAS, BARON. (Thomas.) [Life Baron 1971.]

(WILLIAM) MILES (WEBSTER) THOMAS *DFC,* son of William Henry Thomas, of Ruabon; *b.* March 2nd, 1897; ed. at Broms-grove Sch., and Birmingham Univ.; an Engineer; OStJ; a Life Gov. of Birmingham Univ., and a Gov. of Stowe Sch.; joined Morris Motors 1924, Vice-Chm. and Man. Dir. Morris Motors Ltd. and Subsidiary Cos. 1940-47; Chm. of Cruiser Tank Production Gp. 1940-42, of British Tank Engine Mission to America 1942, of Public Relations, British Motor Industry 1943-46, and of BOAC 1949-56; Pres. Internat. Air Transport Assocn. 1951-52; Chm. of Council, Fedn. of Chambers of Commerce of British Empire 1945; Pres. Soc. of Motor Manufacturers and Traders 1947-48, Chm. Development Co-ordinating Commn. Govt. of S. Rhodesia 1947, and Pres., Advertising Assocn. 1942-52; Chm. Development Corpn. of Wales 1958-67, and Agricultural Central Trading Ltd. 1962-67; Pres. National Savings Cttee. 1965-72 (Chm. 1965-70); 1914-18 War with Light Armoured Motor Battery in German E. Africa, and with RFC and RAF in Middle East, India and Russia (DFC); cr. Knt. 1943, and *Baron Thomas,* of Remenham, Roy. Co. of Berks. (Life Baron) 1971: *m.* 1924, Hylda Nora, da. of the late George Church, of Littlemore, Oxon., and has issue.

Arms,—Argent, a wheel sable on a chief gules, two wings conjoined in lure or Crest,—A torch enflamed or, within a trivet sable. Supporters,—*Dexter,* a mute swan, wings addorsed proper; *sinister,* a peregrine falcon, wings addorsed, also proper.

Residence,—Remenham Court, Henley-on-Thames, Oxon. *Clubs,*—Athenaeum, Garrick, RAC, RAF.

SON LIVING.

Hon. (William) Michael Webster (27, Caroline Terr., SW1) *b.* 1926: *m.* 1952, Ann, da. of the late Col. Philip Kirby-Green, and has issue.

DAUGHTER LIVING.

Hon. Sheila, *b.* 1925: *m.* 1948, Julian von Bergen, of Ellicombe, Minehead, Som., and has issue.

THOMSON OF FLEET, BARON. (Thomson.) [Baron U.K. 1964.]

ROY HERBERT THOMSON, *GBE*, 1st Baron, son of Herbert Thomson; *b.* June 5th, 1894; ed. at Jarvis Collegiate, Toronto; FRSA; FBIM; Hon. DLitt. St. John's Memorial Univ., Newfoundland; Hon. DCL, New Brunswick; Hon. LHD, N. Michigan Univ.; Hon. LLD, Long Island; Joint Chm. of Thomson Organisation Ltd. (and subsidiaries including *The Times* and *The Sunday Times*), and of The Thomson Newspapers Ltd., Toronto, Canada, Founder of The Thomson Foundation, Vice-Pres. of Periodical Proprietors Assocn., Ltd., a Dir. of Security Trust Co., Ltd., a Trustee of Reuters, and a Liveryman of Stationers and Newspaper Makers' Co., Chancellor of Memorial Univ. of Newfoundland 1961-66; Vice-Chm. of Council of Commonwealth Press Union since 1964; a Cdr. of Roy. Order of Phoenix of Greece; *cr. Baron Thomson of Fleet*, of Northbridge, City of Edinburgh (peerage of UK) 1964, GBE (Civil) 1970: *m.* 1916, Edna Alice, who *d.* 1951, da. of John Irvine, of Drayton, Ont., and has issue.

Arms.—Argent, a stag's head cabossed proper on a chief azure between two mullets a huntinghorn of the first, stringed gules. Crest,—A beaver sejant erect proper, blowing upon a hunting-horn argent, slung over his dexter shoulder by a ribband of the Dress Tartan proper to Thomson of that Ilk and his dependers. Supporters.—Dexter, a Mississauga Indian, habited in the proper costume of his tribe, holding in his dexter hand a bow all proper; sinister, a shepherd, bearing in his sinister hand a shepherd's crook, on his head a bonnet all proper, and wearing a kilt of the usual tartan proper to Thomson of that Ilk and his dependers.

Residence,—Alderbourne Arches, Gerrards Cross, Bucks. *Clubs,*—RAC, York (Toronto), National (Toronto), Albany (Toronto), Toronto (Toronto).

SON LIVING.

Hon. KENNETH ROY (8, Kensington Palace Gdns., W8; 8, Castle Frank Rd., Toronto 5, Ont., Canada) *b.* Sept. 1st, 1923; ed. at Upper Canada Coll., and Camb. Univ.; Pres. and Chm. Thomson Newspapers Ltd., Toronto, Jt. Chm. of Thomson Organisation Ltd.; 1939-45 War with RCAF: *m.* 1956, Nora Marilyn, da. of A. V. Lavis, of Toronto, and has issue living, David Kenneth Roy, *b.* 1957,—Peter John, *b.* 1965,—Lesley Lynne, *b.* 1959.

DAUGHTER LIVING

Hon. Phyllis Audrey (c/o Thomson Organisation Ltd., PO Box 4YG, 4 Stratford Place, W1A 4YG), *b.* 1917: *m.* 1947, Clarence Elwood Campbell, and has issue living, Linda Christine *b.* 1949,—Patricia Gay, *b.* 1951,—Susan Elaine, *b.* 1954.

THORNEYCROFT, BARON, (Thorneycroft.) [Life Baron 1967.]

(GEORGE EDWARD) PETER THORNEYCROFT, *PC*, son of the late George Edward Mervyn Thorneycroft, DSO, of Dunston Hall, Stafford [Cs. Dysart, colls.]; *b.* July 26th, 1909; ed. at Eton; Parl. Sec. to Min. of War Transport May to July 1945, Pres. of Board of Trade 1951-57, Chancellor of the Exchequer Jan. 1957, resigned Jan. 1958, Min. of Aviation 1960-62, Min. of Defence 1962-64; Sec. of State for Defence, April to Oct. 1964; Chm of Trust Houses Forte since 1971; Chm. of Pirelli Ltd., of Pirelli General Cable Works Ltd., and Pye of Cambridge Ltd.; MP for Stafford (*C*) 1938-45, and for Monmouth 1945-66; *cr.* PC 1951, and *Baron Thorneycroft*, of Dunston, co. Stafford (Life Peerage) 1967: *m.* 1st, 1938 (m. diss. 1949) Sheila Wells, da. of E. W. Page, Tettenhall; 2ndly, 1949 Countess Carla Roberti, da. of the late Count Malagola Cappi, of Ravenna, Italy, and has issue by 1st and 2nd m.

ARMS,—Not exemplified at time of going to press.
Address,—House of Lords, SW1. *Club,*—Army and Navy.

SON LIVING. (*By 1st marriage.*)

Hon. John Hamo (21, St. Peters St., Islington, N1), *b.* 1940: *m.* 1971, Delia, yst. da. of William Lloyd, of Penallt, Mon., and has issue.

DAUGHTER LIVING. (*By 2nd marriage.*)

Hon. Victoria Elizabeth Anne, *b.* 1951: *m.* 1975, Richard H. Nathanson.

THURLOW, BARON. (Hovell-Thurlow-Cumming-Bruce.) [Baron G.B. 1792.]

We have been.

Faith is the sister of Justice.

Wherever fate may call.

FRANCIS EDWARD HOVELL-THURLOW CUMMING-BRUCE, KCMG, 8th Baron; b. March 9th, 1912; s. 1971; ed. at Shrewsbury Sch. and Trin. Coll., Camb. (MA); Dept. of Agric. for Scotland 1935-37; Sec. to British High Commn. in NZ 1939-44, and Canada 1944-45, Private Sec. to Sec. of State for Commonwealth Relations 1947-49, Counsellor; British High Commn. in New Delhi 1949-52; Adviser to Gov. of Cold Coast 1955, Dep. High Commr. in Ghana 1957, and in Canada 1958; High Commr. for UK in NZ 1959-63, and in Nigeria 1963-66, Dep. Sec. in Diplo. Ser. 1966-68, and Gov. of Bahamas 1968-72; KStJ; CMG 1957, KCMG 1961: m. 1949, Yvonne Diana, da. of the late Aubyn Wilson, of Westerlees, St. Andrews, Fife, and has issue.

Arms.—Quarterly: 1st or, a saltire gules, on a chief of the last in the sinister canton a mullet of the first, charged with a crescent of the second, and for distinction a cross crosslet gold, *Bruce*; 2nd azure, three garbs or, and for distinction in the centre chief point a cross crosslet of the last, *Cumming*; 3rd argent, upon a chevron between two chevronels sable, three portcullises, with chains and rings of the field, *Thurlow*; 4th or, a cross sable, *Hovell*. **Crest.**—1st, upon a cap of maintenance proper, a dexter arm in armour from the shoulder, resting on the elbow also proper, the hand holding a sceptre erect or, the arm charged for distinction with a cross crosslet gules; 2nd a lion rampant or, holding in the dexter paw a dagger proper, charged on the shoulder for distinction with a cross crosslet azure; 3rd a raven proper, with a portcullis hung round her neck argent; 4th a greyhound couchant or, collared and line reflexed over the back sable. **Supporters.**—Two greyhounds or, collared and lined sable.

Residences,—Old Vicarage, Mapledurham, Reading; 16, Warwick Av., W2. *Club,*—Travellers'.

SONS LIVING.

Hon. ROUALEYN ROBERT, b. April 13th, 1952; ed. at Milton Abbey.
Hon. Peter Torquil Francis, b. 1962.

DAUGHTERS LIVING.

Hon. Diana Miranda, b. 1954.
Hon. Aubyn Cecilia, b. 1958.

BROTHERS LIVING.

Hon. Mr. Justice (Hon. Sir James Roualeyn (twin), b. 1912; ed. at Shrewsbury Sch., and at Magdalene Coll., Camb.; Bar. Middle Temple 1937, a Bencher 1959, and Treas. 1975; was Chancellor of Diocese of Ripon 1954-57, Recorder of Doncaster 1957-59 and of York 1959-61 and Junior Counsel, Treasury (Common Law) 1959-64, a Judge of High Court of Justice (Divorce, Probate and Admiralty Div.) 1964-71, since when Presiding Judge, Wales and Chester Circuit; 1939-45 War as Lt.-Col. RA in Iraq, Syria, Egypt, N. Africa, and E. Mediterranean; Knt. 1964: m. 1955, Lady (Anne) Sarah Alethea Marjorie Savile, da. of 6th Earl of Mexborough, and has issue living, Edward Simon, b. 1958,—Richard Henry, b. 1963,—Jane Mary, b. 1956. *Residence,*—1, Mulberry Walk, SW3. *Clubs,*—Pratt's, United Universities.

Hon. Alexander Pascoe, OBE, b. 1917; ed. at Shrewsbury Sch., and at Trin. Coll., Camb. (MA); Colonial Admin. Ser. 1941-60, since when Home Civil Ser.; OBE (Civil) 1960: m. 1942, Catherine Agnes, da. of the Rev. Hamilton Blackwood, of Scalby, Yorks., and has issue living, Charles Hamilton, b. 1947,—Nicholas Christian, b. 1949,—Catherine Veronica, b. 1943: m. 1970, George Nikolaou Yannoulopoulos. *Residence,*—Little House, Dedham, Essex.

COLLATERAL BRANCHES LIVING.
(Male line were in special remainder to Barony.)

Grandchildren of the late Lt.-Col. Reginald Heber Thurlow, 5th son of the late Rev. Charles Augustus Thurlow, son of the late Rev. Edward South Thurlow, son of John Thurlow, youngest brother of 1st Baron:—
Issue of the late Vera Sydney Thurlow, b. 1884, d. 1952: m. 1911, Brig. Edward Frederick William Lees, DSO, late RE, who d. 1969:—
Matthew George, b. 1919; Major Roy. Sussex Regt.——Zoë Josephine, b. 1915: m. 1942, Lt.-Col. John Euston Bell Finlay, CB, OBE, TD, former Commr. Board of Customs and Excise, and has issue living, George Edward James, b. 1948,—Robina Zoë, b. 1944. *Residences,*—38, Sloane Court West, SW3; Bernards Gate Hse., Lavant Rd., Chichester, Sussex.

Granddaughters of the late Lt.-Col. Hugh Hovell Thurlow (twin, b. 1848), son of the Rev. Charles Augustus Thurlow (ante):—
Issue of the late Brig. (Edward) Guy (Lethbridge) Thurlow, CBE, DSO, b. 1881, d. 1966: m. 1912, Margaret Merry, who d. 1952, dau. of Lt.-Col. E. H. Vaughan:—
Nancy Katharine, b. 1914: m. 1940, Henry George Willis, of Three Acres, Brushford, Dulverton, Som., and has issue living, Nicholas Michael Thurlow, b. 1942,—Ian Henry, b. 1946.——Rosemary Margaret, b. 1919; formerly Junior Cdr. ATS; has Territorial Efficiency medal: m. 1947, Maj. Jasper John Ogilvie, MBE, Somerset LI, who d. 1974, and has issue living, Philip John, b. 1948; ACA,—David Jasper, b. 1952.

PREDECESSORS.—[1] Rt. Hon. EDWARD Thurlow, having been Solicitor-Gen. and Attorney-Gen., was in 1778 appointed Lord High Chancellor of England, and cr. *Baron Thurlow*, of Ashfield, co. Suffolk (peerage of Great Britain); held the Great Seal from June 1778 till April 1783 and from Dec. 1783 to 1792, when he was cr. *Baron Thurlow,* of Thurlow, co. Suffolk (peerage of Great Britain), with remainder to his brothers: d. unmarried 1806, when the Barony of Thurlow, of Ashfield expired, and the Barony of Thurlow, of Thurlow, devolved upon his nephew [2] EDWARD, 2nd Baron, el. son of the Rt. Rev. Thomas Thurlow, Lord Bishop of Durham;

assumed in 1814 by Roy. licence the additional surname of Hovell; d. 1829 ; s. by his son [3] EDWARD, 3rd Baron; b. 1814; m. 1836, Sarah, who d. 1840, only dau. of Peter Hodgson; d. 1857; s. by his el. son [4] EDWARD THOMAS, 4th Baron: d. 1874 ; s. by his brother [5] THOMAS JOHN, P.C., 5th Baron ; b. 1838 ; a Lord-in-Waiting to Queen Victoria 1880-85, High Commr. to Gen. Assembly of Church of Scotland 1886, and Paymaster-Gen. 1886 ; assumed in 1873 by Roy. licence the additional surname of Bruce, and in 1874 the additional surname of Cumming: m. 1864, Lady Elma Bruce, who d. 1923, dau. of 8th Earl of Elgin, K.T. ; d. 1916; s. by his son [6] Rev. CHARLES EDWARD, 6th Baron; b. 1869; V. of St. Andrew, and Rural Dean, Bishop Auckland 1913-22, Rural Dean of Liverpool N. 1926-30, and R. of Sedgefield, co. Durham 1930-39 : m. 1909, Grace Catherine, who d. 1959, dau. of the late Rev. Henry Trotter, formerly V. of Ch. Ch., Barnet, d. 1952, s. by his el. son [7] HENRY CHARLES, CB, CBE, DSO, 7th Baron, b. 1910; Maj.-Gen. late Seaforth Highlanders; GOC Troops, Malta 1962-63. d. 1971; s. by his brother [8] FRANCIS EDWARD, 8th Baron and present peer.

THURSO, VISCOUNT. (Sinclair.) [Viscount U.K. 1952, Bt. G.B. 1786.]

ROBIN MACDONALD SINCLAIR, 2nd Viscount and 5th Baronet; b. Dec. 24th, 1922; s. 1970; ed. at Eton, New Coll., Oxford, and Edinburgh Univ.; a JP for Caithness since 1959; CC for Caithness 1949-61 and 1965-73, Town Councillor Thurso 1957-61 and 1965-73, Baillie 1960 and 1969, Dean of Guild 1968, Police Judge 1971, a DL for Caithness 1952-64, Vice-Lt. 1964-73, since when Lord Lt.; 1939-45 War as Fl.-Lt. RAF: m. 1952, Margaret Beaumont, da. of the late Col. Josiah James Robertson, DSO, TD, DL, JP, of Norwood, Wick, Caithness, and widow of Lt. Guy Warwick Brokensha, DSC, RN, and has issue.

Arms,—Quarterly : 1st, azure, a ship at anchor, her oars erected in saltire, within the royal tressure or ; 2nd and 3rd or, a lion rampant gules ; 4th, azure, a ship under sail or ; over all dividing the quarters, a cross engrailed quarterly argent and sable, all within a bordure quartered or and gules, the last charged with three stars of the first. Crest,—A star of six points waved argent, rising from a cloud proper. Supporters,— Two red deer proper.

Seat,—Dalnawillan, Altnabreac, Caithness.   Residence,—Thurso East Mains, Caithness.   Clubs,— RAF, New (Edinburgh).

SONS LIVING.
Hon. JOHN ARCHIBALD, Yr. of Ulbster, b. Sept. 10th, 1953.
Hon. Patrick James, b. 1954.

DAUGHTER LIVING.
Hon. Camilla Janet, b. 1957.

BROTHER LIVING.
Hon. Angus John, b. 1925 ; ed. at Eton, and New Coll., Oxford; formerly Lt. Scots Gds.; NW Europe 1945; is with Central Office of Information; was with BBC 1950-54, and Nigerian Broadcasting Corporation 1954-58: m. 1st, 1955 (m. diss. 1967), Pamela Karen, da. of Dallas Bower; 2ndly, 1968, Judith Anne Percy, and has issue living, (by 2nd m.) Isaiah William Columba Stroma, b. 1971. Residence,—3, Ennismore Gdns., SW7 ; 3, Lambridge, Bath.   Club,—Pratt's.

SISTERS LIVING.
Hon. Catherine, b. 1919: m. 1957, Kazimierz Zielenkiewicz, and has issue living, Clementina Stewart, b. 1958.   Residence,—The Mill House, Isle Brewers, Taunton.
Hon. Elizabeth, b. 1921: m. 1942, Lt.-Col. Archibald Michael Lyle, Scottish Horse (ret.) [see Lyle, Bt.].   Residence,—Ricmore Lodge, Dunkeld, Perths.

COLLATERAL BRANCHES LIVING. (In remainder to Baronetcy only).

Issue of the late George Felix Standish Sinclair, 2nd son of 3rd baronet, b. 1861, d. 1943: m. 1884, Margaret, who d. 1932, sister of Sir John Rose George Sinclair, 7th Bt., of Dunbeath:—
Olive Margaret Camilla, (1, York House, Kensington Church St., W8), b. 1892: m. 1914, Maj. William Adam Sedgwick Rough, late Bedfordshire and Herts. Regt. and RAF, who d. 1969, and has issue living, William George Sedgwick, OBE (of Queenbury, Reed, nr. Royston, Herts), b. 1915; is Lt.-Col. Intelligence Corps (TA); formerly Capt. and temp. Maj. 14th/20th King's Hussars; OBE (Mil) 1959: m. 1940, Margaret Marion, da. of James Gibbings Tavener, of North Tawton, Devon, and has issue living, William Roger Peter b. 1951, Caroline Ann b. 1943: m. 1962, Michael Patrick Spens of Wormiston, of Wormiston Hse., by Crail, Fife, and 87, Eaton Terr., SW1 (and has issue living, Cosmo Patrick b. 1970, Claudia Catherine b. 1966, Iona Louise b. 1968), June Maribel b. 1946,—Maribel Joan Sedgwick, b. 1916: m. 1938 (m. diss. 1973), Maj.-Gen. Henry Templer Alexander, CB, CBE, DSO, late Cameronians and has issue living, David Sinclair (14, South Parade, Blossom St., York, b. 1941, Jane Maribel b. 1943: m. 1975, Jean Frederic Raoul-Duval, Catherine b. 1950,—Caroline Margaret Sedgwick, TD, b. 1921; 1939-45 War with ATS: m. 1947, Maj. Valentine O'Brien Adams, Devonshire Regt., of Whitehouse Farm, Hinton, nr. Saxmundham, Suffolk, and has issue living, Caroline b. 1948, Priscilla Anne b. 1954.

Grandson of the late Ven. John Stewart Sinclair (infra):—
Issue of the late Very Rev. Ronald Sutherland Brook Sinclair, M.C., b. 1894, d. 1953: m. 1924, Patience Penelope (of Mill-in-the-Mint, Mill Lane, Harbledown, Canterbury), dau. of Herbert Chitty, F.S.A.:—
Christopher Ronald (5, Fentiman Rd., SW8), b. 1936; ed. at King's Sch., Canterbury, and at Exeter Coll., Oxford; Journalist: m. 1969, Penelope Ann, da. of Edwin Alfred Springett, and has issue living, Sophie Letitia, b. 1971.

Grandchildren of the late Rev. William Sinclair, 5th son of 1st baronet :—
Issue of the late Ven. John Stewart Sinclair, *b.* 1853, *d.* 1919 : *m.* 1893, Clara Sophia, who *d.* 1948, dau. of J. Dearman Birchall, J.P., of Bowden Hall, Gloucestershire :—
Sir **John Alexander,** *K.C.M.G., C.B., O.B.E., b.* 1897; formerly Sub-Lieut. R.N.; Maj. Gen. (ret.) late R.A.; formerly Col. Comdt. R.A.; European War 1914-19 in R.N., European War 1939-45 (O.B.E., C.B.); O.B.E. (Mil.) 1940, C.B. (Mil.) 1945, K.C.M.G. 1953: *m.* 1927, **Esmè Beatrice,** dau. of the late Ven. Thomas Karl Sopwith, Archdeacon of Canterbury, and has issue living, Ian Alexander Charles, (36, Hillcourt Rd., SE22) *b.* 1938; ed. at Eton, and Worcester Coll., Oxford, (BA, PhD): *m.* 1969, Elma Elizabeth, da. of Charles Henry Williams, of Victoria House, 6, The Square, Braunton, Devon, and has issue living, Andrew George *b.* 1970, John Charles *b.* 1972, Elizabeth Beatrice *b.* 1974,—Roderick John, *b.* 1944: *m.* 1970, Lucinda Martin, da. of the late Eric Martin Smith, MP,—Jean Esme, *b.* 1929: *m.* 1961, Christopher Bruce Seagrim, of Hill Farm, Pulborough, Sussex, and has issue living, John Christopher *b.* 1965, Victoria Esme *b.* 1962,—Iona, *b.* 1931: *m.* 1955, Maj.-Gen. Robin Macdonald Carnegie, OBE, late Queen's Own Hussars, of Coombe Bank, Uckfield, Sussex, yr. son of the late Sir Francis Carnegie, CBE, and has issue living, Rupert Alexander *b.* 1959, Catriona Jean *b.* 1957, Rachel Clare *b.* 1962. *Residence,*—East Ashling Grange, Chichester, Sussex.——Diana Clara, *b.* 1899: *m.* 1923, Thomas Elcho Vardon Ross, who *d.* 1960, and has issue living, John Durnford Sinclair, *b.* 1927. *Residence,*—23, Little London, Chichester, Sussex.——Margaret (*Lady Chilton*), *b.* 1903: *m.* 1926, Lt.-Gen. Sir Maurice Somerville Chilton, KBE, CB, late RA, who *d.* 1956, and has issue living, Richard Thomas Sutherland (35, Perrymead St., SW6 3SN), *b.* 1931; ed. at Winchester, and at Magdalen Coll., Oxford: *m.* 1962, Ann Virginia, da. of the late Arthur Trevor Gough,—April Elizabeth, *b.* 1928,—Jane Margaret, *b.* 1934: *m.* 1957, Brig. Richard John Bishop, MBE, MC, late RA (ret.), of Little Grange, White Colne, Colchester, and has issue living, Charles Richard Maurice *b.* 1960, Katharine Margaret *b.* 1958. *Residence,*—The Grange Slindon, Sussex.

Issue of the late Col. Hugh Montgomerie Sinclair, C.B., C.M.G., C.B.E., *b.* 1855, *d.* 1924 : *m.* 1905, Rosalie Sybil, who *d.* 1969, second da. of the late Sir John Jackson, CVO, LLD, FRSE, JP, of 48, Belgrave Square, SW:—
Hugh Macdonald, *b.* 1910; ed. at Winchester, and at Oxford Univ. (BSc, BM, MA, DM, Hon. DSc); FRCP; Fellow and Tutor of Magdalen Coll., Oxford, and an Officer of Order of Orange Nassau of the Netherlands; has American Medal of Freedom with silver palm. *Residence,*—Lady Place, Sutton Courtenay, Berks. *Club,*—Athenæum.—Rosalie Helen, *b.* 1908: *m.* 1941, Capt. Royston O'Neil Haddock, late RASC, and has issue living, Rogan Shane, *b.* 1942,—Janet Rosalie (North Cottage, Stoke Rivers, Barnstaple), *b.* 1943: *m.* 1970 (m. diss. 1973), Ernest Lewis Vine,—Bridget Helen, *b.* 1948: *m.* 1968, Dennis Ivor Maddocks, of 1, Raleigh Close, South Molton, Devon, and has issue living, Robin Hugh *b.* 1970, Nicholas John *b.* 1972. *Residence,*—Higher Hannaford, Landkey, Barnstaple, Devon.

PREDECESSORS— [1] *Rt. Hon.* JOHN Sinclair, only son of the late George Sinclair; *b.* 1754; a P.Cs and Founder of the Board of Agriculture; cr. a *Baronet*, 1786, with remainder, in default of his own **male issue, to male issue of his daughters respectively :** *m.* 1st, 1776, Sarah, who *d.* 17—, dau. of, **the late Alexander Maitland, of Stoke Newington ;** 2ndly, 1788, the Hon. Diana Macdonald of **Macdonald, who** *d.* 1845, dau. of 1st Baron Macdonald ; *d.* 1835 ; *s.* by his son [2] *Sir* GEORGE, 2nd **Bt. ;** *b.* 1790 ; M.P. for Caithness-shire (L) 1811-18 and 1831-41 ; *m.* 1816, Lady Catherine Camilla **Tollemache, who** *d.* 1863, sister of 8th Earl of Dysart ; *d.* 1868 ; *s.* by his only surviving son [3] *Sir* JOHN GEORGE TOLLEMACHE, 3rd Bt.; *b.* 1824 ; sometime Page of Honour to Queen Adelaide ; **M.P.** for Caithness-shire (L) 1869-85 : *m.* 1853 (marriage dissolved 1878), Jane Isabella Harriet, **who** *d.* 1889, dau. of the late William Standish Standish, of Duxbury Park, Lancashire ; *d.* 1912; *s.* by his grandson [4] ARCHIBALD HENRY MACDONALD, KT, CMG, PC, (son of the late Clarence Granville Sinclair, el. son of 3rd baronet), 4th Bt. *b.* 1890; Sec. of State for Scotland (Nat. Govt.) 1931-32, Leader of Liberal Party in House of Commons 1935-45, Lord Rector of Glasgow Univ. 1938-45, Sec. of State for Air 1940-45, MP for Caithness and Sutherland (L) 1922-45; cr. *Viscount Thurso*, of Ulbster, co. Caithness (peerage of UK) 1952: *m.* 1918, Marigold, who *d.* 1975, da. of the late Lt.-Col. James Stewart Forbes [Forbes, Bt., colls., cr. 1823]; *d.* 1970, *s.* by his el. son [5] ROBIN MACDONALD, 2nd Viscount and present peer.

Tiverton, Viscount, son of Earl of Halsbury.

TODD, BARON. (Todd.) [Life Baron, 1962.]

ALEXANDER (ROBERTUS) TODD, *F.R.S.*, son of the late Alexander Todd, J.P., of Glasgow; *b.* Oct. 2nd, 1907; ed. at Allan Glen's Sch., at Glasgow (DSc), at Frankfurt-on-Main (PhD), and at Oxford (DPhil) Univs.; MA, Camb.; Hon. LLD Glasgow, Melbourne, Edinburgh, Manchester, and California; Hon. DSc Durham, and other Univs.; a FRS, and an Hon. Fellow of Oriel Coll., Oxford, and Churchill Coll., Camb.; Sir Samuel Hall Prof. of Chemistry, Manchester Univ. 1938-44; Chm. of Advisory Council on Scientific Policy 1952-64, and of Roy. Commn. on Med. Education 1965-68, Pres. of Chemical Soc. 1960-62, and Master of Salters' Co. 1961-62; Prof. of Organic Chemistry, Camb. Univ. 1944-71; Managing Trustee of Nuffield Foundation since 1951 (Chm. since 1973), and Master of Christ's Coll., Camb., and First Chancellor of Strathclyde Univ. since 1963; Nobel Prize for Chemistry 1957; cr. Knt. 1954, and *Baron Todd*, of Trumpington, Cambs.: *m.* 1937, Alison Sarah, el. da. of Sir Henry Hallett Dale, OM, GBE, MD, FRCP, FRS, and has issue.

Arms,—Gules a chevron between in chief two foxes' masks, and in base a serpent embowed biting the tail or. Crest,—In front of an open book proper bound or, a fox passant guardant gules. Supporters,—Dexter, an ounce, and Sinister, a fox, each sable bezanty and gorged with a Ducal Coronet, with chain reflexed over the back or, pendant from the coronet by a like chain an escutcheon blue celeste.

Residence,—The Masters' Lodge, Christ's College, Cambridge. Club,—Athenæum.

SON LIVING.

Hon. Alexander Henry (16, Windermere Drive, Alderley Edge, Cheshire), b. 1939; ed. at The Ley Sch., Camb., and at Oriel Coll., Oxford (D.Phil): m. 1967, Joan Margaret, da. of F. W. Koester of Campbell, Cal., USA.

DAUGHTERS LIVING.

Hon. Helen Jean, b. 1941; ed. at Somerville Coll., Oxford: m. 1963, Philip Edgar Brown, of 124 Edge Hill, Darras Hall, Ponteland, Newcastle upon Tyne, and has issue.
Hon. Hilary Alison, b. 1946.

TOLLEMACHE, BARON. (Tollemache.) [Baron U.K. 1876.]

[Name and Title pronounced "**Tolmash.**"]

I trust and am content.

TIMOTHY JOHN EDWARD TOLLE-MACHE, 5th Baron, b. Dec. 13th, 1939; s. 1975; ed. at Eton; late Lt. Coldm. Gds.; a Dir. of Tollemache and Cobbold Breweries, Ltd., and a patron of four livings: m. 1970, Alexandra Dorothy Jean, da. of the late Col. Hugo Meynell, MC [see E. Halifax, colls.] and has issue.

Arms,—Argent, a fret sable. Crest,—A horse's head erased gules, between two wings or, pellety. Supporters,—On either side a stag guardant proper, gorged with a collar flory counterflory or.

Seats,—Helmingham Hall, Stowmarket, Suffolk; Peckforton Castle, Tarporley, Cheshire Residence,—43, Belgrave Mews North, SW1 Clubs,—White's, Pratt's, Boodles.

DAUGHTER LIVING.

Hon. Selina Karen, b. 1973.

BROTHERS LIVING.

Hon. (JOHN) NICHOLAS LYONEL (74, Bedford Gdns., W8), b. June 13th, 1941; ed. at Eton, Trin. Coll., Camb. (MA) and Harvard Univ., USA (MBA): m. 1971, Heide Eva Marie, da. of Gunther Wiedeck, of Bonn.
Hon. Michael David Douglas (26, Argyll Rd., W8), b. 1944; ed. at Eton, and at Trin. Coll., Camb. (MA): m. 1969, Theresa, da. of Peter Bowring, of 77, Campden Court, Campden Hill Rd., W8, and has issue living, Lyonel John Peter, b. 1973,—Archibald Robert Bowring (twin), b. 1973,—Melissa Natasha, b. 1971.
Hon. Hugh John Hamilton (19, Clarendon St., SW1) b. 1946; ed. at Eton.

DAUGHTERS LIVING OF THIRD BARON.

Hon. Dorothy Ceciley, b. 1907: m. 1942, Air Commodore Reynell Henry Verney, CBE, RAF, who d. 1974 [B. Willoughby de Broke, colls.]. Residence,—Stone House, Bishop's Hill, Lighthorne, Warwick.
Hon. Frances Patricia, b. 1908: m. 1949 (m. diss. 1965), Charles Edward Lloyd-Worth. Residence,—Duntisbourne Leer, nr. Cirencester, Glos.
Hon. Sybil Diana, b. 1930: m. 1966, Harold Diehl.

WIDOW LIVING OF THIRD BARON.

LYNETTE (Lynette, Baroness Tollemache), MBE, Flat 2, Clover Cottage, South Cliff, Eastbourne, da. of the late Alfred Vincent Pawson, of Nynehead Court, Somerset; is an OStJ; MBE (Civil) 1944: m. 1928, as his second wife, the 3rd Baron, who d. 1955.

WIDOW LIVING OF FOURTH BARON.

DINAH SUSAN (Dinah, Baroness Tollemache) (The Home Farm, Peckforton, Tarporley, Cheshire), da. of the late Sir Archibald Auldjo Jamieson, KBE, MC: m. 1939, the 4th Baron, who d. 1975.

COLLATERAL BRANCHES LIVING. (All of whom are in remainder to the Earldom of Dysart.

Grandchildren of the late Hon. Hamilton James Tollemache, 4th son of 1st Baron:—
Issue of the late Henry Robert Tollemache, b. 1888, d. 1931: m. 1912, Ethel Maud, who d. 1953, dau. of the late John Irwin, of Belmont, Mullingar:—
Anthony Henry Hamilton, GC (215, Hills Rd., Cambridge), b. 1913; Squad. Ldr., R. Aux. A.F.; 1939-45 War (wounded, GC): m. 1st, 1947 (marriage dissolved 1960), Françoise, da. of Comte Jean de Hautecloque, French Ambassador to Canada; 2ndly, 19—, Celia, da. of the late Bryce Cochrane, of McLaren Rd., Edinburgh, and has issue living, (by 1st marriage) Richard Lionel, b. 1950,—Gregory Marmaduke Anthony, b. 1954,—Alexander Anthony, b. 1958,—Catherine, b. 1948: m. 1970, Malcolm Woolff,—Juliette, b. 1956.——Karine Irene Elizabeth, b. 1916: m. 1945, Cdr. William Gordon Jack, RN, and has issue living, Michael Anthony Gordon, b. 1946,—David Lionel, b. 1954,—Vanessa Bettine, b. 1948. Residence,—Redgate, Uppingham, Rutland.

Grandsons of the late Winifred Gertrude Blow (infra):—
Issue of the late Richard Purcell Blow, *b.* 1915, *d.* 1963: *m.* 1939, Diana Hermione, who *d.*
1967, da. of the late Capt. William Adrian Vincent Bethell [B. Glenconner]:—
Richard David Detmar (26, Lennox Gdns., SW1), *b.* 1942.——Adrian Simon (61A, S. Audley St., W1),
b. 1943.

Grandchildren of the late Hon. Hamilton James Tollemache (ante):—
Issue of the late Winifred Gertrude Tollemache, *b.* 1882, *d.* 1954: *m.* 1910, Detmar Blow,
J.P., F.R.I.B.A., who *d.* 1939:—
Jonathan Oliver Tollemache, *b.* 1919; ed. at Eton, and at Balliol Coll., Oxford; 1939-45 War in Middle
East and Italy as Capt. Coldstream Guards (wounded); was Personal Assist. to Director of Mil.
Govt., British Zone, Germany 1945-46: *m.* 1962, Elaine Helga, da. of E. F. L. de Silva, Ceylonese
Ambassador to France, and has issue living, Detmar Hamilton Lorenz Arthur, *b.* 1963,—Amaury
Hugh John Jellings, *b.* 1965,—Selina Jane, *b.* 1966.   *Residence,*—Hilles House, Stroud, Glos.——
Lucilla, *b.* 1923: *m.* 1948, Philip Warre-Cornish, and has issue living, Alexander Philip Hubert
Detmar, *b.* 1949,—James Damian, *b.* 1952.   *Residence,*—20, Pembroke Rd., Kensington, W8.
Issue of the late Hon. Stanhope Alfred Tollemache, 6th son of 1st Baron, *b.* 1855,
d. 1934 : *m.* 1905, Elizabeth, who *d.* 1958, dau. of W. Monks:—
Rhona Elizabeth, *b.* 1906: *m.* 1st, 1935, George Harrison, of Johannesburg, who *d.* 1935 ; 2ndly,
1944, Wlodzimierz Jan Zbrowski, late of Warsaw, Poland, who in 1950 assumed the name of John
Vladimir Moreton Monks.   *Residence,*—Bentley Cottage, St. Just-in-Roseland, Truro.——Sheila
Joyce, *b.* 1911: *m.* 1st, 1936 (m. diss. 1946), Francis William Frederick Otter-Barry, who *d.* 1967;
2ndly, 1947, as his second wife, Capt. John Claude Smiley, Middx. Yeo. (TA Reserve) [see Smiley,
Bt.].   *Residence,*—5, Cadogan St., SW3.——Ina Elaine (of Angel House, Stonham, Stowmarket,
Suffolk), *b.* 1916.

Grandchildren of the late Maj. the Hon. Douglas Alfred Tollemache (infra):—
Issue of the late Capt. Humphrey Douglas Tollemache, RN, *b.* 1893, *d.* 1970: *m.* 1924,
Elsie Violet (30, Kingston House South, Ennismore Gdns., SW7), da. of the late William
George Raphael [Goldsmid, Bt.]:—
Michael Humphrey (Tollemache Hall, Offton, Ipswich, IP8 4RT), *b.* 1930; ed. at Eton: *m.* 1968, Gay
Rosemary D. O'Grady, da. of H. E. O'Grady Thompson, of Castle Garde, co. Limerick, and has issue
living, Rosamond Sybil, *b.* 1969,—Juliet Elsie, *b.* 1974.——Jean Margherita (*Lady Grant*), (House
of Monymusk, Aberdeenshire), *b.* 1927: *m.* 1953, Sir Francis Cullen Grant, 12th Bt., who *d.* 1966.

Issue of the late Major the Hon. Douglas Alfred Tollemache, 8th son of 1st Baron,
b. 1862, *d.* 1944 : *m.* 1887, Alice Mary, who *d.* 1959, el. dau. of the late John
Head :—
Mary Cynthia (Meadowcroft, 16, Trumpington Rd., Cambridge), *b.* 1890: *m.* 1916, Lt.-Col. Guy
Rattray Dubs, MC, who *d.* 1930, formerly King's Roy. Rifle Corps.——Angela Mariota, *b.*
1900; appointed Hon. Col. 307 (N. Command) Btn. WRAC (TA) 1956: *m.* 1st, 1923, as his second
wife, the 3rd Baron Belper, who *d.* 1956; 2ndly, 1958, Norman Tollemache (formerly Wrigley).
Residence,—Bentley House, Ipswich.

Issue of the late Hon. Ranulph Carteret Tollemache, 10th son of 1st Baron, *b.* 1866,
d. 1960 : *m.* 1889, Annie Mary, who *d.* 1923, dau. of the late William Smith, of
Haverstock Hill, N.W. :—
Devereux John Rex, *b.* 1891: *m.* 1914, Gladys Victoria, who *d.* 1960, da. of John Waddington, of 19,
Brunswick Terr., Hove, Sussex, and Waddington Old Hall, Yorks.——Harold Vincent (Flat 6,
Westbourne Gdns., Folkestone) *b.* 1895; Capt. late Indian Cav.: *m.* 1937, Marjorie Violet, da. of the
late W. H. Lonsdale, of Rangoon, and has issue living, Laurence Ranulph (1, Cress Way, Faversham,
Kent), *b.* 1938: *m.* 1960, Maureen Elizabeth, da. of Harold Hex, of Taunton, Som., and has issue
living, Paul Laurence *b.* 1965, Clare Elizabeth *b.* 1968,——Elfreyda, *b.* 1900: *m.* 1938, Noel Sedgwick.
——Sybil, *b.* 1901: *m.* 1921, Henry Richard Clarke, and has issue living.   *Residence,*—

Granddaughters of the late Hon. Ranulph Carteret Tollemache, 10th son of 1st
Baron :—
Issue of the late Com. Lawrence Lionel Tollemache, R.N., *b.* 1894, *d.* 1954 : *m.* 1926, Violet
Mary (she *m.* 2ndly, 1956, Laurence Reid, of White Ash, Ngauruhoe St., Taupo, NZ), da.
of John Bayly A'Deane:—
Margaret Ngaire Yoskyl A'Deane, *b.* 1928: *m.* 1955, Antony Percy Jackson, of White Pines, Takapau,
Hawkes Bay, New Zealand, and has issue living, Peter Lawrence, *b.* 1956,—Timothy, *b.* 1959,—
Ashley, *b.* 1961,—Alison, *b.* 1958,—Ngaianne, *b.* 1962.——Anna A'Deane, *b.* 1950: *m.* 1974, Andrew
Berne Vallance, of Punawai Station, Takapau, Hawke's Bay, NZ.

PREDECESSORS.—[1] JOHN JERVIS Tollemache of Helmingham Hall, Suffolk, son of the late
Adm. John Richard Delap Tollemache (formerly Halliday), maternal grandson of 4th Earl
of Dysart, sat as M.P. for Cheshire S. (C) 1841-68, and for Cheshire W. 1868-72, and was cr.
Baron Tollemache, of Helmingham, co. Suffolk (peerage of United Kingdom) 1876; *b.* 1805: *m.*
1st, 1825, Georgiana Louisa, who *d.* 1846, dau. of Thomas Best; 2ndly, 1850, Eliza-
Georgiana, who *d.* 1918, dau. of James Duff; *d.* 1890; *s.* by his el. son [2] WILBRAHAM
FREDERIC, 2nd Baron ; *b.* 1832: M.P. for Cheshire W. (C) 1872-85: *m.* 1st, 1858, Lady Emma
Georgiana Stewart, who *d.* 1869, 2nd dau. of 9th Earl of Galloway; 2ndly, 1878, Mary, who
d. 1939, dau. of the late Right Hon. Lord Claude Hamilton [see D. Abercorn, colls.]; *d.*
1904 ; *s.* by his grandson [3] BENTLEY LYONEL JOHN (son of the late Hon. Lyonel Plantagenet
Tollemache, el. son of 2nd Baron), 3rd Baron ; *b.* 1883; Capt. 3rd Batn. Cheshire Regt., Lieut.-Com.
R.N.V.R., and Capt. R.G.A.: *m.* 1st, 1902, Wynford Rose, who *d.* 1926, only dau. of the late Gen.
Sir Arnold Burrowes Kemball, K.C.B., K.C.S.I.; 2ndly 1928, Lynette, *M.B.E.,* dau. of Alfred
Vincent Pawson, of Nynehead Court, Somerset; *d.* 1955 ; *s.* by his kinsman [4] JOHN EDWARD
HAMILTON, *M C* (only son of the late Maj.-Gen. Edward Devereux Hamilton Tollemache, DSO, MC,
el. son of the late Hon. Hamilton James Tollemache, 4th son of 1st Baron), 4th Baron; *b.* 1910;
Maj. Coldm. Gds.: *m.* 1939, Dinah Susan, da. of the late Sir Archibald Auldjo Jamieson, KBE, MC;
d. 1975; *s.* by his el. son [5] TIMOTHY JOHN EDWARD, 5th Baron and present peer.

TOMLIN, BARONY OF. (Tomlin.) [Extinct 1935.]

DAUGHTERS LIVING OF LIFE BARON.

Hon. Joan Olivia (*Hon. Lady Trower*), *b.* 1894 ; is a J.P. for Herts : *m.* 1920, Sir William Gosselin
Trower, who *d.* 1963, and has issue.   *Residence,*—Stansteadbury, Ware, Herts.
Hon. Helen Rosa, *b.* 1906: *m.* 1932, Prof. Frank Goldby, MD, FRCP, of 1, St. Mark's Court, Barton
Rd., Cambridge.

WIDOW LIVING OF SON OF LIFE BARON.

Julia Frances (17, Percy St., W1), da. of the late Oliver Strachey, CBE [see Strachey, Bt. colls.]:
m. 1st, 1927, the Hon. Stephen Tomlin, who *d.* 1937; 2ndly, 1952 (m. diss. 1967), Lawrence Burnett
Gowing, CBE.

TORPHICHEN, LORD. (Sandilands.) [Lord S. 1564.]

[Title pronounced "Tor-fikken."]

I hope for better things.

SPERO·MELIORA

JAMES ANDREW DOUGLAS SANDI-
LANDS, 15th Lord, *b.* Aug. 27th, 1946;
s. 1975.

SISTER LIVING.

Hon. Alison Mary, *b.* 1944: *m.* 1966, David
Maurice Baldwin, of 8, Pinewood Close, Longacres, St. Albans, Herts., and has issue living,
Emma Alison, *b.* 1968,—Petra Josephine, *b.*
1972.

MOTHER LIVING.

Mary Thurston, only da. of Randle Vaudrey, of
Edgbaston, Birmingham: *m.* 1943 (m. diss.
1952), the Hon. James Bruce Sandilands,
Master of Torphichen (later 14th Lord Torphichen), who *d.* 1975.

WIDOW LIVING OF THIRTEENTH LORD.

ISABEL FERNANDEZ (*Isabel*, *Lady Torphichen*)
(PO Box 61, Nanyuki, Kenya), da. of Richard Bowen Daniel, of Jacksonville, Fla., USA, and widow
of Richard Youel Phillips, of Greystones, Nanyuki, Kenya: *m.* 1950, as his 2nd wife, the 13th
Lord, who *d.* 1973.

WIDOW LIVING OF FOURTEENTH LORD.

PAMELA MARY (*Lady Torphichen*) (Calder House, Mid-Calder, Midlothian), da. of the late John Howard
Snow, and widow of Thomas Hodson-Pressinger: *m.* 1973, as his 3rd wife, the 14th Lord, who
d. 1975.

COLLATERAL BRANCHES LIVING.

Issue of the late Hon. Walter Alexander Sandilands, yst. son of 12th Lord, *b.* 1888,
d. 1966: *m.* 1918 (m. diss. 1930), Nancy Margaret, da. of Hubert Powell, of
Lewes:—
BRUCE WALTER (*Master of Torphichen*) (6, Walmer Court, Cranes Park, Surbiton, Surrey, KT5 8AQ),
OBE, *b.* July 14th, 1921; Overseas Survey Ser. ret.; Surveyor GLC; OBE (Civil) 1970.——Douglas
Robert Alexander (Peelings, Peelings Lane, Westham, Surrey), *b.* 1926: *m.* 1949, Ethel Louise
Burkitt, and has issue living, Robert Powell, *b.* 1950: *m.* 1974, Cheryl Lin Watson, of Eastbourne.
——Jean Eleanor, *b.* 1920: *m.* 1st, 1947, Edward Cecil Doudney, who *d.* 1955, and from whom she
had obtained a divorce 1950; 2ndly, 1955, Col. Greville Steel, TD, of Southrop Lodge, Lechlade,
Glos., and has issue living, (by 2nd m.) James Alexander Drummond, *b.* 1958.——Jonet Christian,
b. 1924: *m.* 1944, Capt. John Osborne Wigg, RN, and has issue living, Anthony John Osborne,
b. 1955,—Coralie Ann Osborne, *b.* 1945,—Nina Jonet Osborne, *b.* 1947.

Granddaughters of the late Hon. John Hope Sandilands (*raised to the rank of a*
Baron's son 1870), brother of 12th Lord :—
Issue of the late James Bruce Sandilands, *b.* 1883, *d.* 1951: *m.* 1909, Aline, who *d.* 1972, da.
of F. G. Taylor, of Uralla, NSW:—
Helen Lucy, *b.* 1909: *m.* 1936, Richard Riley Trevitt, of Braeside, Uralla, NSW, and has issue living,
Richard John (Sandon, Uralla, NSW), *b.* 1938: *m.* 1961, Mollie Juanita Blomfield, of Quirindi, NSW,
and has issue living, Marcus John *b.* 1964, Justin James *b.* 1966, Annette *b.* 1963,—Simon Bruce,
b. 1942: *m.* 1965, Robyn Anne Brown, of Uralla, NSW, and has issue living, Shaun Richard *b.* 1967,
Fiona Jane *b.* 1969,—Robin Ann Lucy, *b.* 1939: *m.* 1965, David Edward Moore, of Perth, and has
issue living, Richard Edward *b.* 1966, Andrew Geoffrey *b.* 1968, Amanda Gillian *b.* 1969.——Aline
Dorothy, *b.* 1920: *m.* 1st, 1941, Godfrey Rees-Jones, RAAF, who *d.* (killed in action over Germany)
1942; 2ndly, 1955, Arthur Harold Roberts, and has issue living, (by 2nd m.) Marc Bruce, *b.* 1959,—
Ian Geoffrey, *b.* 1964,—Julie Aline, *b.* 1957.   *Residence*, 36, Invercauld Rd., Goonellabah, via Lismore, NSW.

Granddaughter of the late James Bruce Sandilands (ante):—
Issue of the late Geoffrey Bruce Hope Sandilands, Roy. Australian Air Force, *b.* 1922, *d.*
(killed on active ser. during European War) 1944: *m.* 1944, Dorothy Mary (who *m.*
2ndly, 1952, Henry Myron Carlson, of 3,000, Quadra Street, Victoria, British Columbia)
dau. of — Joyce, of Victoria, British Columbia :—
Joyce Hope (posthumous), *b.* 1945: *m.* 1964, Duncan Leslie Atchison, CA, of RR1, 2375, Townend Rd.,
Duncan, BC, Canada, and has issue living, James Geoffrey, *b.* 1965,—Christine Anne, *b.* 1967.

PREDECESSORS.—[1] Sir JAMES Sandilands, 8th feudal Baron of Calder, a Knight of Malta
and Chief of that Order in Scotland, having resigned the property of the Knights of St. John to
Queen Mary, was cr. *Lord Torphichen* (peerage of Scotland) 1564, with remainder to his
heirs and assigns whatsoever ; *d.s.p.* 1579 ; *s.* by his great-nephew [2] JAMES, 2nd Lord ; *d.* 1617 ;
s. by his el. son [3] JAMES, 3rd Lord ; *d.* unmarried 1622 ; *s.* by his brother [4] JOHN, 4th Lord ;
d. 1637 ; *s.* by his el. son [5] JOHN, 5th Lord ; *d.* unmarried 1649 ; *s.* by his brother [6] WALTER,
6th Lord ; *d.* 1690 ; *s.* by his son [7] JAMES, 7th Lord ; a zealous supporter of the Scottish Union ,
was a Commr. of Police; *d.* 1753; *s.* by his son [8] WALTER, 8th Lord; *d.* 1765; *s.* by his son [9]
JAMES, 9th Lord ; was a Representative Peer; *d.s.p.* 1815 ; *s.* by his cousin [10] JAMES, 10th Lord;
el. son of the Hon. Robert, 8th son of 7th Lord ; *d.* 1862   *s.* by his son [11] ROBERT, 11th Lord ,
d. 1869 ; *s.* by his nephew [12] JAMES WALTER, 12th Lord (el. son of the Rev. the Hon. John, 2nd
son of 10th Lord, by Helen, dau. of James Hope, Clerk to the Signet), *b.* 1846 ; a Representative
Peer : *m.* 1881, Francis Ellen (whom he divorced 1890), el. dau. of the late Lieut.-Gen. Charles
Parke Gordon CB; *d.* 1915; *s.* by his second son [13] JOHN GORDON, 13th Lord; *b.* 1886: *m.* 1st,
1916, Grace Douglass, who *d.* 1948, da. of Winslow Pierce, of Bayville, Long Island, New York;
2ndly, 1950, Isabel Fernandez, da. of Richard Bowen Daniel, of Jacksonville, Fla., USA, and widow
of Richard Youel Phillips, of Greystones, Nanyuki, Kenya; *d.* 1973; *s.* by his son [14] JAMES
BRUCE, 14th Lord and present peer.

TORRINGTON, VISCOUNT. (Byng.) [Viscount G.B. 1721, Bt. G.B. 1715.]

TIMOTHY HOWARD ST. GEORGE BYNG, 11th Viscount, and 11th Baronet ; *b.* July 13th, 1943; *s.* 1961; ed. at Harrow and St. Edmund Hall, Oxford: *m.* 1973, Susan Honour, da. of Michael George Thomas Webster, of The Vale, Windsor Forest, Berks. [M. Conyngham].

᛭rms,—Quarterly, sable and argent, in the 1st quarter a lion rampant of the second. ᚳrest,—An heraldic antelope ermine. ᚢupporters,—*Dexter*, an heraldic antelope ermine, armed, unguled, maned and tufted or, standing on a ship's gun proper ; *sinister*, a sea-horse proper also on a ship's gun.

Residence,—South End House, High Ham, Langport, Somerset.

I will defend.

AUNTS LIVING. (*Daughters of 10th Viscount.*)

Hon. Honor (26, Swan Court, SW7), *b.* 1912: *m.* 1937 (m. diss. 1951), Lisle Marles Humphreys.
Hon. (Rosamond Stella) Frances, *b.* 1937: *m.* 1960, Antony B. Cobb, of Highbury, Lane End, Bembridge, Isle of Wight, and has issue living, Dorian Byng, *b.* 1965,—Michelle Pandora, *b.* 1961.

GREAT AUNT LIVING. (*Raised to the rank of a Viscount's daughter* 1945.)

Hon. Gladys Irene, *b.* 1891 : *m.* 1910, Henry Portsmouth, who *d.* 1933, and has issue living, Henry Byng, *b.* 1911: *m.* 1939, Daphne, da. of Duncan H. Grubb, of Basingstoke,—Mary Byng, *b.* 1913: *m.* 1939, Maj. Frank Gifford Rothery, Hampshire Regt., who *d.* (killed in action during European War) 1943. *Residence,*—6, The Drive, Oakley, Basingstoke, Hants.

MOTHER LIVING.

Anne Yvonne, dau. of the late Capt. R. G. P. Wood, Dragoon Guards, of Durban, Natal : *m.* 1st, 1942, Paymaster-Lieut. the Hon. George Byng, R.N., who *d.* (on active ser. during) European War) 1944, only son of 10th Viscount ; 2ndly, 1951, Howard Henry Masterton Carpenter. *Residence,*—South End House, High Ham, Langport, Somerset.

COLLATERAL BRANCHES LIVING.

Grandson of the late Lt.-Col. Alfred Molyneux Cranmer-Byng, el. son of Capt. Henry Byng, RN (infra):—
   Issue of the late Capt. Launcelot Alfred Cranmer Byng, *b.* 1872, *d.* 1945: *m.* 1st, 1894, Harriet, who *d.* 1913, da. of Isaac Hammersley; 2ndly, 1916, Daisy Elaine (Boyes Croft, Dunmow, Essex), da. of N. B. Beach, of Chelmsford:—
(By 2nd marriage) JOHN LAUNCELOT, *MC, b.* March 18th, 1919; MA 1944; Prof. of History, Toronto Univ.; formerly Lecturer in History at Univ. of Hong Kong ; 1939-45 War as Maj. Airborne Forces (MO): *m.* 1955, Margaret Ellen, da. of R. H. Hardy, of Sevenoaks, Kent, and has issue living, Colin Hugh, *b.* 1960,—Alison Caroline, *b.* 1956,—Sheila Margaret, *b.* 1962. *Residence,*—190, Glengrove Av., Toronto, Canada.

   Grandson of the late Capt. Henry Byng, RN, el. son of the late Vice-Adm. the Hon. Henry Dilkes Byng, 4th son of 5th Viscount:—
   Issue of the late Major Arthur Hervey Byng, late Leinster Regt. (formerly Lieut. R.N.), *b.* 1845, *d.* 1923 : *m.* 1869, Florence, who *d.* 1914, dau. of the late William Fuller Maitland of Stansted Hall, Bishop's Stortford :—
John Anstruther, *b.* 1877 ; S. Africa 1901 (Queen's medal), German S.-W. Africa 1914-15: *m.* 1915. Rachel Wyllie, dau. of William Hampden Brodie, of Glenbucket, Scotland, and has issue living, Arthur Maitland (Glenbucket, Box 1146, Rustenburg 0300, Transvaal), *b.* 1917: Abyssinia, N. Africa and Italy 1939-45 with S. African Artillery: *m.* 1965, Joan Stuart Marr, and has issue living, Joanne Rachel *b.* 1969, Ann Maitland *b.* 1970,—Julienne Wyllie, *b.* 1919: *m.* 1941, John Duncan, of Durban, Natal, and has issue living, Annette Jenifer *b.* 1943, Patricia Jane *b.* 1945, Julienne Rachel *b.* 1947,—Norah Cranmer, *b.* 1921: *m.* 1949, John Winnall Franklin Hampton,—Mary Maitland, *b.* 1923: *m.* 1946, Harold Hampshire Division, and has issue living, Ian Hampshire *b.* 1948. *Residence,*—

   Descendants of the late Rt. Hon. Sir John Byng, G.C.B., G.C.H. (3rd son of the late George Byng, M.P., el. son of the late Hon. Robert Byng, 3rd son of 1st Viscount), who was cr. *Earl of Strafford* 1847 [see that title].

PREDECESSORS.—[1] *Adm. Sir* GEORGE Byng, Knt., an eminent naval commander knighted 1704 ; cr. a *Baronet* 1715, and *Baron Byng*, of Southill, co. Bedford, and *Viscount Torrington* (peerage of Great Britain) 1721 : sat as M.P. for Plymouth 1705-21, and was Treasurer of the Navy 1725, and First Lord of the Admiralty 1727 ; *d.* 1733; *s.* by his el. son [2] PATTEE *P.C.*, 2nd Viscount ; sat successively as M.P. for Plymouth and Bedfordshire ; was Treasurer of the Navy 1724-7, and sometime Vice Treasurer and Paymaster-Gen. for Ireland, and Capt. of the Yeomen of the Guard; *d.* 1747; *s.* by his brother [3] GEORGE, 3rd Viscount ; a Maj.-Gen. in the Army; *d.* 1750; *s.* by his el. son [4] GEORGE, 4th Viscount ; *d.* 1812 ; *s.* by his brother [5] JOHN, 5th Viscount; *d.* 1813; *s.* by his son [6] GEORGE, 6th Viscount ; *b.* 1768; was a Vice-Adm.; *d.* 1831 ; *s.* by his son [7] GEORGE, *D.C.L.*, 7th Viscount ; *b.* 1812: was Gov. of Ceylon 1847-50, a Lord-in-Waiting to H.R.H. the Prince Consort 1853-9, and to H.M. Queen Victoria 1859-84; *d.* April 26th, 1884; *s.* by his nephew [8] GEORGE STANLEY, 8th Viscount [son of the late Major the Hon. Robert Barlow Palmer Byng, 3rd son of 6th Viscount, and Elizabeth Maria Lowther (who *m.* 2ndly, 1861, the Rev. William Winchester), dau. of Col. Gwatkin], *b.* 1841 ; a Lord-in-Waiting to H.M. Queen Victoria: *m.* 1st, 1882, Alice Arabella, who *d.* 1883, dau. of James Jameson, of Airfield, Dublin; 2ndly, 1885, Emmeline St. Maur, who *d.* 1912 ; dau. of the Rev. Henry Seymour; *d.* 1889 : *s.* by his son [9] GEORGE MASTER, 9th Viscount, *b.* 1886 ; was a Page of Honour to Queen Victoria and to King Edward VII 1899-1903 ; sometime a Railway and Canal Commr.: *m.* 1st, 1910, Eleanor, who *d.* 1931 (having obtained a divorce 1921), el. dau. of the late Edwin Souray, of Long Ditton, Surrey ; 2ndly, 1923, Norah Elizabeth Ursula (FERENS), who *d.* 1968, da. of the late Capt. Robert Wood-Pottle, 5th R. Irish Lancers; *d.* 1944; *s.* by his cousin [10] ARTHUR STANLEY (son of the late Hon. Sydney Byng, brother of 8th Viscount), 10th Viscount; *b.* 1876; Lt.-Col. RASC; S. Africa 1899-1902 (DCM), 1914-18 War (Officer of Legion of Honour): *m.* 1st, 1909 (m. diss. 1936), Louise Annette, da. of Joseph Rawlins; 2ndly, 1936 (m. diss. 1952), Rosamund Ella, da. of the late Vice-Adm. Alexander Percy Davidson, DSO; *d.* 1961; *s.* by his grandson [11] TIMOTHY HOWARD ST. GEORGE (only son of the late Paymaster-Lt. the Hon. George Byng, RN, only son of 10th Viscount), 11th Viscount and present peer; also Baron Byng.

TOWNSHEND, MARQUESS. (Townshend.) [Marquess G.B. 1787, Bt. E. 1617.]

GEORGE JOHN PATRICK DOMINIC TOWN-SHEND, 7th Marquess, and 12th Baronet; b. May 13th, 1916; s. 1921; ed. at Harrow; is patron of thirteen livings; Chm. of Anglia Television, Ltd., Anchor Enter-prises, Ltd., Raynham Farm Co., Ltd., Norfolk Agric. Station, Vice-Pres. of Norwich Union Life Insurance Soc. and a Dir. of Associated Cos.; a Dir. of London Merchant Securities, Ltd., D. E. Longe & Co., E. Coast Grain, Ltd.; a Gov. of Roy. Agric. Soc. of England, and a Trustee of E. Anglian Trustee Savings Bank; 55 (Suffolk and Norfolk Yeo.) Anti Tank Regt. 1936, ADC to GOC-in-C, E. Command 1936-39, Personal Assist. to CIGS 1939-40, Scots Guards 1940-45: m. 1st, 1939 (m. diss. 1960), Elizabeth Pamela Audrey, only da. of Maj. Thomas Luby, late Judicial Commr., ICS; 2ndly, 1960, Ann Frances, only da. of the late Arthur Pellew Darlow, and has issue by 1st and 2nd m.

Arms,—Azure, a chevron ermine, between three escallops argent. Crest,—A stag statant proper, attired and unguled or. Supporters,—Dexter, a stag sable attired and unguled or; sinister, a greyhound argent. Seat,—Raynham Hall, Norfolk. Clubs,—White's, Pratt's, Norfolk.

HÆC·GENERI·INCREMENTA·FIDES
Faith obtained these honours for our race.

SONS LIVING. (By 1st m.)
CHARLES GEORGE (Viscount Raynham), b. Sept. 26th, 1945; ed. at Eton: m. 1975, Hermione, da. of Lt.-Cdr. Robert Martin Dominic Ponsonby [see E. Bessborough, colls.]
(By 2nd m.)
Lord John Patrick, b. 1962.

DAUGHTERS LIVING. (By 1st m.)
Lady Carolyn Elizabeth Ann TOWNSHEND (46, Rue du Bois de Boulogne, 92200 Neuilly-sur-Seine, France), b 1940; has resumed the surname of Townshend: m. 1962 (m. diss. 1971), Antonio Capellini, and has issue living, Vincenzo Charles, b. 1963.
Lady Joanna Agnes, b. 1943: m. 1962 (m. diss. 1968), Jeremy George Courtenay Bradford, and has issue living, Francis James Patrick, b. 1963.
(By 2nd marriage)
Lady Katherine Ann b. 1963.

COLLATERAL BRANCHES LIVING.

Granddaughter of the late Charles Thornton Townshend, son of the late Rev. Lord George Osborne Townshend (infra):—
Issue of the late Maj.-Gen. Sir Charles Vere Ferrars Townshend, K.C.B., D.S.O., b. 1861, d. 1924: m. 1898, Alice, who d. 1965, da. of the late Count Louis Cahen d'Anvers, of Château de Champs, Seine et Marne, France, and 2, Rue de Bassano, Paris:—
Audrey Dorothy Louise, b. 1900: m. 1922 (m. diss. 1936), Count Baudouin de Borchgrave d'Altena, and has issue living, Count Arnaud (370, Park Av., New York City, NY, USA), b. 1926; ed. at King's Sch., Canterbury: m. 1st, 1950 (m. diss. 1959), Dorothy Solon; 2ndly, 1959, (m. diss. 1969), Eileen Ritschel; 3rdly, 1969, Alexandra Darielle Villard, and has issue living, (by 1st m.) Arnaud b. 1951, (by 2nd m.) Trisha Theresa b. 1961,—Countess Marina, b. 1932: m. 1955, Charles Winton Browne Rankin, MBE, of 10, Cottesmore Gdns., W8, and has issue living, Gavin Philippe Baudouin b. 1957, James Rowland Evelyn b. 1959. Residence,—78, Osborne Villas, Hove.

Grandson of the late George Ferrars Townshend (infra):—
Issue of the late Ferrars Ernest Osborne Townshend, b. 1882, d. 1953: m. 1910, Isabel Dorothy Ferrers, who d. 1971, da. of W. H. Nicholson, of Rama Rama, New Zealand:—
Henry George, b. 1911: m. 1943, Elaine Florence, dau. of T. E. Frith, of Melbourne, Australia, and has issue living, Ferrars Edwin, b. 1944,—Anthony Stuart, b. 1956. Residence,—9A, Waiake St., Torbay, Auckland 10, NZ.

Grandchildren of the late Rev. Lord George Osborne Townshend (infra):—
Issue of the late George Ferrars Townshend, b. 1854, d. 1942: m. 1st, 18—, Elizabeth Brenda Baillie, who d. 1891: 2ndly, 18—, Clara Jenkins, of Auckland, New Zealand:—
(By 1st marriage) Geoffrey Keith, b. 1888. Residence,—52, Slaney Street, Bluff, Southland, New Zealand.——Doris TOWNSHEND, b. 1886: m. 1909, Carl August Nienholdt (from whom she obtained a divorce 1928, and reverted to her maiden name), and has issue living,——(by 2nd m.) Rua Hildyard Bute, b. 1902.——Rere, b. 1904: m. 1924, Digby Felix McGarry, of 201, Victoria Av., Remuera, Auckland NZ, and has issue living, Digby Rochefort Dillon, b. 1925: m. 1954, Kathrine Mary Palmer.

Granddaughter of the late George Ferrars Townshend (ante):—
Issue of the late George Ferrars Vere Townshend, b. 1897, d. 1957: m. 1921, Fanny Elizabeth, dau. of James Matthew Brassington, of Staffordshire:—
Diana Vere, b. 1927: m. 1949, Noel Trevor Gedye, M.I.Struct.E., A.M.N.Z.I.E., and has issue living, Christopher John, b. 1950,—Stephen Warren, b. 1952,—Michael Jonathan, b. 1957. Residence,—103, Ngapuhi Road, Remuera, Auckland, New Zealand.

Grandsons of the late Ernest Edwin Townshend, 3rd son of the late Rev. Lord George Osborne Townshend, yr. brother of 4th Marquess:—
Issue of the late Clifford Edwin Townshend, b. 1884, d. 1958: m. 1915, Rose Evelyn, dau. of John Abraham Greensill, of Picton, Marlborough, New Zealand:—
John Edwin (PO Box 736, Napier, NZ), b. 1918; 1939-45 with RNZAF: m. 1943, Mary, da. of William Joseph Curran Sharp, and has issue living, Keith Edwin, b. 1948,—Margaret Ann, b. 1944: m. 1st, 1963 (m. diss. 1974), LAC Earl Dudley Gee; 2ndly, 1974, John Leslie Taylor, of 1019, Hood St., Hastings, NZ, and has issue living, (by 1st m.) Richard John Earl b. 1969, Michelle Margaret b. 1963, Lisa Ann b. 1966.——George Maling (5, Whakarine Av., Napier, NZ), b. 1921; ed. at Marlborough Coll., NZ; a JP, and a City Councillor of Napier; 1939-45 War with RNZAF: m. 1944, Alice Joyce, el. da. of Alfred Wilfred Nye, of Long Bay Rd., Coromandel, NZ, and has issue living, Colin David,

b. 1948,—Yvonne Joy, *b.* 1946.——Charles Roberts (10, Lambton Rd., Napier, NZ), *b.* 1926; ed. at Marlborough Coll., NZ: *m.* 1952, Dorothy Winifred, da. of Frederick Leo Luks, of Aukland, NZ, and has issue living, Robert Paul, *b.* 1965,—Denise Kaye, *b.* 1955.

Granddaughter of the late Augusta Mary Townshend (who m. 1865, Col. George Brooke Meares), only da. of the Rev. Lord George Osborne Townshend (ante):—
Issue of the late Lt.-Col. Cyril Frankland Meares, DSO, *b.* 1880, *d.* 1963: *m.* 1919, Mary Katharine, who *d.* 1959, da. of the late Rev. Edward Mansfield Clements, R. of Barkston, Lincs., and widow of Lt.-Col. James Cosmo Russell, DSO [D. Bedford, colls.]:—
Iris Muriel (30, Queen's Gate Gdns., SW7), *b.* 1925: *m.* 1953 (m. diss. 1966), William BertramHesmond-halgh, and has issue living, Ivo Laurence George, *b.* 1956,—Serena Katherine Beatrice, *b.* 1958.

PREDECESSORS.—[1] ROGER Townshend, *M.P.* for Norfolk 1627; cr. **a** *Baronet* 1617; *d.* 1637; *s.* by his el. son [2] *Sir* ROGER; 2nd Bt.; *s.* by his brother [3] *Sir* HORATIO, 3rd Bt. **a** zealous royalist, who rendered valuable assistance in restoring the monarchy; was sometime M.P. for Norfolk; cr. *Baron Townshend,* of Lynn Regis (peerage of England) 1661, and *Viscount Townshend,* of Rainham (peerage of England) 1682; *d.* 1687; *s.* by his son [4] CHARLES, KG, PC, 2nd Viscount; was Lord-Lt. of Norfolk, Capt. of Yeoman of the Guard 1707-11, Ambassador to the Hague 1709-10, a Lord Justice, Principal Sec. of State 1714-16 and 1721-30, and Pres. of the Council 1720; *d.* 1738; *s.* by his son [5] CHARLES, 3rd Viscount, who in 1723 had been summoned to Parliament in his father's Barony of Lynn; was a Lord of the Bedchamber, Custos Rotulorum of Norfolk, and Master of the Jewels; *d.* 1767; *s.* by his son [6] GEORGE, P.C., 4th Viscount; a Field-Marshal in the Army and a successful military commander, was cr. *Marquess Townshend* (peerage of Great Britain) 1787; sat as M.P. for Norfolk, Lt.-Gen. of the Ordnance 1763-67 and Master-Gen. 1772-82, Viceroy of Ireland 1767, Gov. of Jersey, &c., Lord-Lieut. of Norfolk, &c.: *m.* 1st, 1751, Charlotte, who *d.* 1770, in her own right (through her mother) Baroness Ferrers of Chartley, and (through her father) Baroness Compton; 2ndly. 1773, Anne, who *d.* 1819, dau. of Sir William Montgomery, 1st Bt.; *d.* 1807; *s.* by his son [7] GEORGE, 2nd Marquess, who following the death of his mother 1770, was summoned to Parliament as *Baron Ferrers de Chartley,* and in 1784 had been cr. *Earl of Leicester* (peerage of Great Britain); was Postmaster-Gen. 1794-8, and Lord Steward of the Household 1799-1802; *d.* 1811; *s.* by his son [8] GEORGE FERRERS, 3rd Marquess; *d.s.p.* 1855, when the Earldom of Leicester became extinct, the Baronies of Ferrers of Chartley, Compton, &c. became abeyant, and the Barony, Viscountcy, and Marquessate of Townshend devolved upon his cousin [9] JOHN, 4th Marquess; *b.* 1798; was a Rear-Adm.: *m.* 1825, Elizabeth Jane, who *d.* 1877, dau. of Rear Adm. Lord George Stuart, C.B. (M. Bute); *d.* 1863; *s.* by his son [10] JOHN VILLIERS STUART, 5th Marquess, *b.* 1831; M.P. for Tamworth (L) 1856-63: *m.* 1865, Lady Anne Elizabeth Clementina Duff, who *d.* 1925, dau. of the 5th Earl of Fife; *d.* 1899: *s.* by his only son [11] JOHN JAMES DUDLEY STUART, 6th Marquess, *b.* 1866: *m.* 1905, Gladys Ethel Gwendolen Eugénie (who *d.* 1959, having *m.* 2ndly, 1946, Bernard le Strange), el. dau. of the late Thomas Sutherst, Bar.-at-Law; *d.* 1921; *s.* by his son [12] GEORGE JOHN PATRICK DOMINIC, 7th Marquess and present peer; also Viscount Townshend, of Rainham and Baron Townshend, of Lynn Regis.

TRANMIRE, BARON. (Turton.) [Life Baron 1974.]

ROBIN (ROBERT) HUGH TURTON, *KBE, MC, PC,* son of the late Maj. Robert Bell Turton, of Kildale Hall, York. [Blackett, Bt.]; *b.* Aug. 8th, 1903; ed. at Eton, and Balliol Coll., Oxford (BA); Bar. Inner Temple 1926; a JP and a DL of N. Riding of Yorks.; Parl. Sec. Min. of National Insur. 1951-53, Joint Parl. Sec. Min. of Pensions and National Insur. 1953-54, Joint Parl. Under-Sec. of State for Foreign Affairs 1954-55 and Min. of Health 1955-57; MP for Thirsk and Malton (C) 1929-74; Chm. Commonwealth Industries Assocn. Ltd.; 1939-45 War as Lt.-Col. Green Howards (MC); cr. PC 1955, KBE (Civil) 1971, and *Baron Tranmire,* of Upsall, co. N. Yorks. (Life Baron 1974): *m.* 1928, Ruby Christian, da. of the late Robert Thomas Scott, of Beechmont, Sevenoaks, Kent, and has issue.

Arms,—Not exemplified at time of going to press.

Residences,—Upsall Castle, Thirsk, Yorks.; 15, Greycoat Gdns., SW1.

SONS LIVING.

Hon. Michael Andrew, *b.* 1929.
Hon. Timothy Robert Scott, *b.* 1934.
Hon. Gerald Christopher (Colt House, Feliskirk, Yorks.), *b.* 1937; a farmer: *m.* 1967, Alexandra Susan, da. of Lt.-Col. S. Oliver, of 6, Maison Dieu, Richmond, Yorks, and has issue.

DAUGHTER LIVING.

Hon. Gillian Hermione Christian, *b.* 1930: *m.* 1960, David Poulett Wells, BM, BCh, of Hilperton House, Hilperton, Trowbridge, Wilts.

TREDEGAR, BARONY OF. (Morgan.) [Extinct, 1962.]

WIDOW LIVING OF SIXTH BARON.

JOANNA (*Joanna, Baroness Wharton*) (Matacelle, Mougins, France, A.M.), only da. of Walter Henry Law-Smith, of Adelaide, S. Australia: *m.* 1st, 1938, (m. diss. 1954) Cdr. A. B. Russell, DSO, RN; 2ndly, 1954 the 6th Baron who *d.* 1962, when the title became ext.; 3rdly, 1967, the 9th Baron Wharton who *d.* 1969.

TREFGARNE, BARON. (Trefgarne.) [Baron U.K. 1947.]

DAVID GARRO TREFGARNE, 2nd Baron; *b*. March 31st, 1941; *s*. 1960; ed. at Haileybury, and at Princeton Univ., USA; awarded Roy. Aero Club Bronze Medal (jointly) for flight UK to Aust. and back in light aircraft 1963: *m*. 1968 Rosalie, da. of Peter Lane, of Holywell, Hook Heath, Woking, and has issue.

Arms,—Or, a dragon rampant gules, over all a bend azure charged with a leek of the first between two thistles stalked and leaved proper. Crest,—A palm tree, suspended therefrom by a strap proper an escutcheon or, charged with a portcullis chained gules. Supporters,—On either side is Herefordshire bull proper, charged on the shoulder with an escutcheon or, thereon a portcullis chained sable.

Address,—c/o Barclays Bank, Chobham, Surrey. Clubs,—East India, Sports and Public Schools, United Service and Royal Aero.

SONS LIVING.
Hon. GEORGE GARRO, *b*. Jan. 4th, 1970.
Hon. Justin Peter Garro, *b*. 1973.

BROTHERS LIVING.
Hon. Trevor Garro (1, Darnley Terr., W11), *b*. 1944; ed. at Cheltenham; Cranfield Sch. of Management 1968-69; a Dir. Pentos Ltd.: *m*. 1967, Diana Elizabeth, da. of the late Michael Gibb, of Forge House, Taynton, Oxon., and has issue living, Rupert Michael Garro, *b*. 1972,—Oliver Edward Garro, *b*. 1974.

Hon. Gwion George Garro, *b*. 1953.

SISTER LIVING.
Hon. Mary Elizabeth, *b*. 1946.

WIDOW LIVING OF FIRST BARON.
ELIZABETH, yst. da. of the late Charles Edward Churchill, of Ashton Keynes, Wilts.; resumed the surname of Trefgarne by deed poll 1968: *m*. 1st, 1940, the 1st Baron, who *d*. 1960; 2ndly, 1962 (m. diss. 1966), Com. Anthony Tosswill Courtney, OBE; 3rdly, 1971, Hugh Cecil Ker, of Tower of Lethendy, Meikleour, Perthshire.

PREDECESSOR.—[1] GEORGE MORGAN Trefgarne, son of the late Rev. David Garro-Jones of Milford Haven; *b*. 1894; assumed by deed poll (enrolled at College of Arms) 1954 the surname of Trefgarne in lieu of his patronymic; was Parliamentary Sec., Min. of Production 1942-5, Chm. of Television Advisory Committee 1945-9, and Founder Chm. of Colonial Development Corporation 1947-50; sat as M.P. for S. Div. of Hackney (*L*) 1924-9, and for N. Div. of Aberdeen (*Lab*.) 1935-45; cr. *Baron Trefgarne*, of Cleddau, co. Pembroke (peerage of U.K.) 1947: *m*. 1940, Elizabeth (who *m*. 2ndly, 1962 (m. diss. 1966), Com. Anthony Tosswill Courtney, OBE, and 3rdly, 1971, Hugh Cecil Ker), yst. da. of the late Charles Edward Churchill, of Ashton Keynes, Wilts.; *d*. 1960; *s*. by his el. son [2] DAVID GARRO, 2nd Baron and present peer.

TRENCHARD, VISCOUNT. (Trenchard.) [Viscount U.K. 1936, Bt. U.K. 1919.]

THOMAS TRENCHARD, *M.C.*, 2nd Viscount and 2nd Baronet; *b*. Dec. 15th, 1923; *s*. 1956: ed. at Eton; a Dir. of Unilever Ltd., and Unilever NV; 1939-45 War as Capt. KRRC (MC): *m*. 1948, Patricia S., da. of the late Adm. Sir Sidney Robert Bailey, KBE, CB, DSO, and has issue.

Arms,—Per pale argent and azure, on the first three pallets sable, all within a bordure of the last. Crest,—A cubit arm erect, vested azure, cuffed argent, holding in the hand a cinquedea sword, both proper. Supporters,—On either side an eagle close gules, each charged on the neck, the dexter with a thistle slipped and leaved and the sinister with truncheon erector.

Residence,—Abdale House, North Mimms, Herts. Club,—Brooks's.

Know thyself

SONS LIVING.
Hon. HUGH, *b*. March 12th, 1951: *m*.1975, Fiona Elizabeth, da. of the Hon. James Ian Morrison, [see B. Margadale].
Hon. John, *b*. 1953.
Hon. Thomas Henry, *b*. 1966.

PREDECESSOR.—[1] *Marshal of the R.A.F. Sir* HUGH MONTAGUE Trenchard, *GCB, OM, GCVO, DSO*, son of the late Capt. Henry Montague Trenchard; *b*. 1873; S. Africa 1900-1902 with Imperial Yeo., Bushman Corps, and Canadian Scouts (dangerously wounded), S. Nigeria 1904 in command (despatches), 1904-5 Comdg. patrol through Ibibio and Kwa country. 1905-6 in command of Bendo-Onitsha Hinterland Expedition (despatches, D.S.O.), European War 1914-18 as Gen. Officer Comdg. Mil. Wing of RFC as Ch. of Air Staff (RAF) and as GOC-in-C, Inter-Allied Indep. Air Force, thanked by Parliament, cr. a Baronet, granted £10,000; Ch. of Air Staff and Member of Air Council 1918 and 1918-30, Prin. Air ADC to HM 1921-25, and Commr. of Metro, politan Police 1931-35; bore Third Sword at Coronation of King George VI; cr. a *Baronet* 1919-*Baron Trenchard*, of Wolfeton, co. Dorset (peerage of United Kingdom) 1930, and *Viscount Trenchard*, of Wolfeton, co. Dorset (peerage of United Kingdom) 1935: *m.* 1920, Katherine Isabel Salvin, who *d.* 1960, dau. of the late Edward Salvin Bowlby, of Gilston Park, Herts, and Knoydart, Invernessshire, and widow of Capt. the Hon. James Boyle; *d.* 1956; *s.* by his younger son [2] THOMAS, 2nd Viscount and present peer; also Baron Trenchard.

TREND, BARON. (Trend.) [Life Baron 1974.]

BURKE ST. JOHN TREND, *GCB*, *CVO*, *PC*, el. son of the late Walter St. John Trend; *b.* Jan. 2nd, 1914; ed. at Whitgift, and Merton Coll. (Hon. Fellow), Oxford; Hon. DCL Oxford; entered Civil Ser. 1936; Prin. Private Sec. to Chancellor of Exchequer 1945-49, Under-Sec. HM Treas. 1949-55, Office of Lord Privy Seal 1955-56, Dep. Sec. of Cabinet 1956-59, 3rd Sec. Treas 1959, and 2nd Sec. 1960-62, and Sec. of Cabinet 1963-73, since when R. of Lincoln Coll., Oxford; cr. CVO 1953, CB (Civil) 1955, KCB (Civil) 1962, GCB (Civil) 1968, PC 1972, and *Baron Trend*, of Greenwich in Greater London (Life Baron) 1974: *m.* 1949, Patricia Charlotte, el. da. of the late Rev. Gilbert Shaw, and has issue.

Arms,—not exemplified at time of going to press.

Residence,—18, St. German's Place, SE3. *Club,*—Athenaeum.

SONS LIVING.

Hon. Michael St. John, *b.* 1952.
Hon. Patrick St. John, *b.* 1955.

DAUGHTER LIVING.

Hon. Catharine, *b.* 1950: *m.* 1966, Colin James Rawlinson.

TRENT, BARONY OF. (Boot.) [Extinct 1956.]

DAUGHTERS LIVING OF SECOND BARON.

Hon. Barbara Jacqueline (31, Milner St., SW3), *b.* 1915: *m.* 1934 (m. diss. 1973), Maj. Willoughby Rollo Norman [see Norman, Bt.].

Hon. Joceleyne Mary, *b.* 1917: *m.* 1947, Maj. Harcourt Michael Scudamore Gold, MC, of West Stratton House, nr. Winchester, Hants., and has issue living, John Angus Harcourt, *b.* 1958,—Charmian Joy, *b.* 1950: *m.* 1st, 1969 (m. diss. 1973), Frederick James Meynell [see E. Halifax, colls.]; 2ndly, 1974, James Richard Nicholson [see Nicholson Bt., cr. 1912].

Hon. Margaret Anne, **b.** 1920: *m.* 1st, 1940 (marriage dissolved 1948), Major John Edward Jocelyn Davie, Derbyshire Yeo.: 2ndly, 1949, Air Vice-Marshal Somerled Douglas Macdonald, C.B., C.B.E., DFC, and has issue living, (by 1st marriage) Simon John, *b.* 1941,—Anne Clare, *b.* 1943: *m.* 1964, Robin Gerard d'Abo, of 49, Porchester Terr., W2. *Residence,*—Ballaig, by Crieff, Perths.

Hon. Elizabeth Campbell, *b.* 1927: *m.* 1947, Major Michael Woodbine Parish, M.C., Notts Yeo., **and** has issue living, Clement Robin Woodbine, *b.* 1950,—Suzanne Woodbine, *b.* 1948,—Caroline Woodbine, *b.* 1953,—Emma Woodbine, *b.* 1957. *Residence,*—Walcot Hall, Lydbury North, Salop.

DAUGHTERS LIVING OF FIRST BARON.

Hon. Dorothy Florence, *b.* 1890: *m.* 1913, Capt. Wilfrid Montagu Bruce, C.B.E., R.D., R.N.R. (retired), who *d.* 1953 [see Bruce, Bt., cr. 1894, colls.]. *Residence,*—Les Pommiers, St. Lawrence, Jersey.

Hon. Margery Amy, *b.* 1892: *m.* 1921, Alexander McArthur Holman, and has issue living, John Francis, *OBE* (Glenton House, Rickarton, Stonehaven, Kincardineshire, and 24, Wellington Sq., SW3), *b.* 1924; OBE (Civil) 1964: *m.* 1957, Lady Diana Elizabeth Virginia Sydney Baird, da. of 12th Earl of Kintore, and has issue living, Richard Ian *b.* 1958, Edward Alexander *b.* 1960, Georgina Mary *b.* 1962, Emma Charlotte *b.* 1966,—Christopher Boot (of Foxcote, Shipston-on-Stour, Warwicks. and Acharacle, Argyllshire), *b.* 1926: *m.* 1950, the Hon. Elizabeth Winifred Ponsonby, da. of 5th Baron de Mauley, and has issue living, Sarah Charlotte *b.* 1951, Serena Jane *b.* 1952, Alice Elgiva *b.* 1956, Catherine Rose *b.* 1963,—David McArthur (6, Montpelier Place, SW7, and Killiemore House, Kilfinichen, Mull), *b.* 1928: *m.* 1st, 1952 (m. diss. 1965), Felicity, da. of the late Capt. Rickard Charlie Donovan, CBE, RN; 2ndly, 1966, Valerie, da. of the late Harold William Leslie Pryor, and has issue living (by 1st m.), Mark Rickard *b.* 1957, (by 2nd m.) Michael Jesse *b.* 1967, Andrew McArthur *b.* 1968. *Residence*—Springland, Millbrook, Jersey.

WIDOW LIVING OF SECOND BARON.

MARGARET JOYCE (*Baroness Trent*), dau. of the late Frederick Haigh Pyman, of 82, Fitzjohn's Avenue, Hampstead, N.W. : *m.* 1914, the 2nd Baron, who *d.* 1956, when the title became ext. *Residence,*—Mount Grove, St. Laurence, Jersey.

TREVELYAN, BARON. (Trevelyan.) [Life Baron 968.]

TYME·TRYETH·TROTH

HUMPHREY TREVELYAN, *KG, GCMG, CIE, OBE,* son of the late Rev. George Philip Trevelyan [see Trevelyan, Bt. colls., cr. 1662]; *b.* Nov. 27th, 1905; ed. at Lancing, and Jesus Coll., Camb. (MA, Hon. Fellow); Hon. LLD Camb., and Leeds; Hon DCL Durham; Indian Civil Ser., and Indian Political Ser. 1929-47; Foreign Ser. 1947-65; Counsellor HM Embassy, Baghdad 1948-50, Economic Adviser UK High Commr. in Germany 1951-53, HM Chargé d'Affaires, Peking 1953-55, Ambassador to Egypt 1955 56, Under-Sec. UN 1958, Ambassador to Iraq 1958-61, Dep. Under-Sec. FO 1962, and Ambassador to USSR 1962-65; ret. from Diplo. Ser. 1965; High Commr. for Aden and S. Arabia 1967; Pres. of Council of Foreign Bondholders 1965; a Trustee of British Museum since 1969 (Chm. of Trustees since 1970); Chm. of Roy. Inst. of International Affairs; a Dir. of British Petroleum Co., of Gen. Electric Co. Ltd., and of British Bank of Middle East; *cr.* OBE (Civil) 1941, CIE 1947, CMG 1951, KCMG 1955, GCMG 1965, *Baron Trevelyan,* of Saint Veep, co. Cornwall (Life Baron) 1968, and KG 1974: *m.* 1937, Violet Margaret, da. of the late Gen. Sir William Henry Bartholomew, GCB, CMG, DSO, and has issue.

Arms,—Gules, a demi-horse argent hoofed and maned Or, issuing out of water in base proper, **Crest,**—Two arms counter-embowed proper, habited Azure, holding in the hands a bezant. **Supporters,** —On either side a dolphin Azure crowned with a Baron's Coronet proper. *Residence,*—13, Wilton St., SW1. *Clubs,*—Pratt's, Beefsteak.

DAUGHTERS LIVING.

Hon. Susan Anne, *b.* 1941: *m.* 1961, Harald Busse (c/o Ministry of Foreign Affairs, Bonn, W. Germany), and has issue living, Allan George, *b.* 1962,—Jan Michael, *b.* 1963,—Nicola Andrea, *b.* 1967. *Hon.* Catherine Mary, *b.* 1943.

Trevethin and Oaksey, Baron, see Oaksey.

TREVOR, BARON. (Hill-Trevor.) [Baron U.K. 1880.]

CHARLES EDWIN HILL-TREVOR, 4th Baron; *b.* Aug. 13th, 1928 ; *s.* 1950 ; ed. at Shrewsbury; is patron of two livings, a J.P. for Denbighshire, and an OStJ: *m.* 1967, Susan Janet Elizabeth, da. of Ronald Ivor Bence, DSC, URD, BM, of 13, Bournbrook Rd., Selly Oak, Birmingham, and has issue.

Arms,—Quarterly : 1st and 4th per bend sinister ermine and ermines, a lion rampant or, *Trevor :* 2nd and 3rd sable, on a fesse argent, between three leopards passant guardant or, spotted of the field, as many escallops gules, *Hill.* **Crests,**—1st, a wyvern, wings addorsed sable, *Trevor ;* 2nd, a reindeer's head couped at the neck gules, attired and plain collared or, *Hill.* **Supporters**—*Dexter,* a lion armine, gorged with a ducal coronet and chained or, the chain reflexed over the back ; pendant from the collar a shield argent, charged with the crest of Trevor ; *sinister* a leopard or, spotted sable, gorged with a ducal coronet and chained or, the chain reflexed over the back ; pendent from the collar a shield ermines charged with the crest of Hill.

Seats,—Brynkinalt, Chirk, Wrexham ; Auch, Bridge of Orchy, Argyllshire.

SONS LIVING.
Hon. MARK CHARLES, *b.* Jan. 8th, 1970.
Hon. Iain Robert, *b.* 1971.

BROTHER LIVING.
Hon. Nevill Edward (Plas Lledrod, Llansilin, Denbighshire), *b.* 1931; Flying Officer RAF (ret.); a DL for Denbighshire (High Sheriff 1965-66); ADC to Com.-in-Ch. Fighter Command, 1958-59; ADC to Ch. of Air Staff 1960-61: *m.* 1963, Deborah, only da. of the late W. T. B. Jowitt, of Killinghall, Harrogate, and has issue living, Caroline Anne, *b.* 1965,—Diana Rosemary, *b.* 1967.

WIDOW LIVING OF SECOND BARON.
PHYLLIS (*Phyllis, Baroness Trevor*), da. of J. A. Sims, of Ings House, Kirton-in-Lindsey, Lincolnshire; is an OStJ: *m.* 1927, the 3rd Baron, who *d.* 1950. *Residence,*—The Holt, Chirk, Wrexham.

PREDECESSORS.—[1] *Lord* ARTHUR EDWIN HILL, 3rd son of 3rd Marquess of Downshire, K.P.; *b.* 1819; M.P. for co. Down (*C*) 1845-80; assumed the maternal surname of Trevor 1862, on succeeding to the estates of Viscount Dungannon; *cr.* *Baron Trevor*, of Brynkinalt, co. Denbigh (peerage of United Kingdom) 1880: *m.* 1st, 1848, Mary Emily, who *d.* 1855, el. dau. of Sir Richard Sutton, 1st Bt.; 2ndly, 1858, the Hon. Mary Catherine Curzon, who *d.* 1911, sister of 4th Baron Scarsdale; *d.* 1894; *s.* by his el. son [2] ARTHUR WILLIAM, 2nd Baron, *b.* 1852; Lieut.-Col. 1st Life Guards, and Vice-Lieut. for Denbighshire; Comdt. Denbighshire Vol. Regt. 1917-20 (Hon. Col.): *m.* 1st, 1894, the Hon. Annie Mary Eleanor Fraser, who *d.* 1895, dau. of 17th Baron Saltoun, and divorced wife of 15th Baron Zouche; 2ndly, 1897, Rosamond, *M.B.E.*, who *d.* 1942, dau. of the late Hon. Edmund George Petre [see B. Petre, colls.], and widow of 4th Earl of Bantry (*ext.*); *d.* 1923; *s.* by his half-brother [3] CHARLES EDWARD, 3rd Baron, *b.* 1863: *m.* 1927, Phyllis, dau. of J. A. Sims, of Ings House, Kirton-in-Lindsey, Lincolnshire; *d.* 1950; *s.* by his el. son [4] CHARLES EDWIN, 4th Baron and present peer.

TRIMLESTOWN, BARON. (Barnewall.) [Baron I. 1461.]

I had rather die than be disgraced.

CHARLES ALOYSIUS BARNEWALL, 19th Baron; *b.* June 2nd, 1899; *s.* 1937; ed. at Ampleforth Coll.; formerly Lieut. Irish Guards: *m.* 1st, 1926, Muriel, who *d.* 1937, dau. of Edward Oskar Schneider, of Mansfield Lodge, Whalley Range, Manchester; 2ndly, 1952, Freda Kathleen, da. of the late Alfred Watkins, of Ross-on-Wye, and has issue by 1st marriage.

Arms,—Ermine, a bordure engrailed gules. **Crest,**—A plume of five ostrich feathers or, gules, azure, vert, and argent, and issuant therefrom a demi falcon rising of the last. **Supporters,**—*Dexter,* a griffin argent; *sinister,* a lion gules.

Residence,—Tigley, Dartington, Totnes, Devon. *Clubs,*—Royal Irish Yacht (Dun Laoghaire), Royal Yacht (Cork).

SONS LIVING. (*By 1st marriage.*)
Hon. ANTHONY EDWARD (20, Swan St., Boxford, Suffolk) *b.* Feb. 2nd, 1928; ed. at Ampleforth; late Irish Guards: *m.* 1963, Lorna Margaret Marion, da. of the late Douglas Ramsay.
Hon. Raymond Charles (Tigley, Dartington, Totnes, Devon), *b.* 1930; ed. at Ampleforth.

DAUGHTER LIVING. (*By 1st marriage.*)
Hon. Diana, *b.* 1929: *m.* 1954, Anthony Gerard Astley Birtwistle, and has issue living, Caroline Muriel Mary *b.* 1955,—Emma Francis Mary, *b.* 1957,—Lucinda Jane Mary, *b.* 1960,—Sophia Louise Mary, *b.* 1964. *Residence,*—Hatch Hill House, Hindhead, Surrey.

SISTER LIVING.
Hon. Ivy Esmay Myee (c/o Barclays Bank, Rondebosch, Cape, S. Africa), *b.* 1890: *m.* 1st, 1917, John Radcliff (formerly Colonial Ser., Nigeria), who *d.* 1953; 2ndly, 1956, John Kidd, who *d.* 1958, and has issue living, (by 1st m.) John Travers (of Kildare, 4, Silverdale, Pinelands, Cape Town, S. Africa), *b.* 1924; ed. at Ampleforth Coll.: Burma 1943-45 (Pacific Star): *m.* 1952, Yvonne Mavourneene Cooke, of Cape Town, S. Africa, and has issue living, Stuart Gavin *b.* 1957, Anne Margaret *b.* 1953,—Helena Joan Ivy, *b.* 1920: *m.* 1940, Peter H. B. Blakelock, late Capt. RA, of Freezers, Partridge Green, Sussex, and has issue living, Neil Hamilton, *b.* 1946, Robina Averil *b.* 1944: *m.* 1st, 1962, John A. G. Lloyd; 2ndly, 1970, Graham Primrose, of 4537, Old William Penn Highway, Monroeville, Pa. 15146, USA, and has issue living, (by 2nd m.) Colin Graham, *b.* 1973, Craig Michael *b.* 1975),—Queenie Irene Margaret (of 5, Harrington Court, Harrington Rd., Brighton, Sussex), *b.* 1927: *m.* 1948, Capt. Ian E. Allanson, late RE, who *d.* 1954, and has issue living, Antony David *b.* 1949,—Pamela Esmay Emma, *b.* 1929: *m.* 1954, Kenneth Craig Westwood (c/o Commonwealth Savings Bank of Australia, 8, Donnington St., Vermont Gdns., Balcatta, Perth, W. Australia), and has issue living, Trevor John *b.* 1958, Susan Joan *b.* 1955.

PREDECESSORS.—[1] *Sir* ROBERT Barnewall, was *cr.* *Baron Trimlestown*, of Trimlestown, co. Meath (peerage of Ireland) 1461; *s.* by his son [2] CHRISTOPHER, 2nd Baron; *s.* by his el. son [3] JOHN, 3rd Baron; appointed Vice-Treasurer of Ireland 1522. High Treasurer 1524, and Lord High Chancellor 1534; *d.* 1538; *s.* by his son [4] PATRICK, 4th Baron; *s.* by his el. son [5] ROBERT, 5th Baron; *d.s.p.* 1573; *s.* by his brother [6] PETER 6th Baron; *d.* 1598; *s.* by his son [7] ROBERT, 7th Baron; *d.* 1639; *s.* by his grandson [8] MATTHIAS (el. son of the Hon. Christopher Barnewall, el. son of 7th Baron), 8th Baron; *d.* 1667; *s.* by his el. son [9] ROBERT, 9th Baron; *d.* 1687; *s.* by his son [10] MATTHIAS, 10th Baron; *d.s.p.* 1692; *s.* by his brother [11] JOHN, 11th Baron: *m.* 1703, Margaret, dau. and heiress of Sir John Barnewall; *s.* by his el. son [12] ROBERT, 12th Baron; *d.* 1779; *s.* by his only son [13] THOMAS, 13th Baron; a Knight of Malta; *d.s.p.* 1796; *s.* by his cousin [14] NICHOLAS (son of the Hon. Richard Barnewall, 3rd son of 11th Baron), 14th Baron; *b.* 1726; was twice *m.*; *d.* 1813; *s.* by his only son [15] JOHN THOMAS, 15th Baron, *b.* 1773: *m.* 1793, Maria Theresa, dau. of R. Kirwan; *d.* 1839; *s.* by his son [16] THOMAS, 16th Baron, *b.* 1796; *m.* 1836, Margaret Randalina, who *d.* 1872, dau. of Philip Roche; *d.* 1879, when the title became dormant until claimed in 1891 by his kinsman [17] CHRISTOPHER PATRICK MARY, *de jure*, 17th Baron, son of Charles Barnewall, of Meadstown, co. Meath, and great-grandson of Richard Barnewall, of Fyanstown (a descendant of the Hon. Patrick Barnewall, 2nd son of the 7th Baron), on whom the 14th Baron, failing his own issue male, entailed his estates: he *d.* 1891, before he had established his right to vote at the Election of Representative Peers; *s.* by his brother [18] CHARLES ALOYSIUS, 18th Baron; *b.* 1861; adjudged 18th Baron Trimlestown by Committee for

Privileges of House of Lords in 1893 : *m.* 1st, 1889, Margaret Theresa, who *d.* 1901, **dau. of**
Richard John Stephens, of Brisbane ; 2ndly, 1907, Mabel Florence, who *d.* 1914, dau. of William
Robert Shuff, of Torquay, Devon ; 3rdly, 1930, Josephine Francesca, who *d.* 1945, dau. of
Rt. Hon. Sir Christopher John Nixon, P.C., M.D., 1st Bt. ; *d.* 1937 ; *s.* by his only surviving
son [19] **CHARLES ALOYSIUS**, 19th Baron and present peer.

TRURO, LORD BISHOP OF. (Leonard.)

Right Rev. GRAHAM DOUGLAS LEONARD, *DD*, only
son of the late Rev. Douglas Leonard, MA ; *b.* May 8th,
1921 ; ed. at Monkton Combe Sch., Bath, Balliol Coll.,
Oxford (MA), and Westcott House, Camb. ; Hon.
DD Episc. Theo. Seminary, Kentucky ; 1939-45 War as
Capt. Oxford and Bucks. LI ; V. of Ardleigh, Essex
1952-55, Dir. of Religious Education, Diocese of St.
Albans 1955-58, Hon. Canon St. Albans 1955-57,
Canon Residentiary 1957-58, and Canon Emeritus
1958 ; Gen. Sec. Nat. Soc. and Sec. C. of E. Schs.
Council 1958-62 ; Archdeacon of Hampstead, Exam.
Chap. to Bishop of London, and R. of St. Andrew
Undershaft with St. Mary Axe, City of London 1962-64 ;
Preacher to Univ. of Oxford 1968 ; consecrated Bishop
of Willesden (Suffragan for Diocese of London) 1964 ;
translated as 11th Bishop of Truro 1973 ; Joint-author
of "Growing into Union " 1970, and author of " The
Gospel is for Everyone " 1971 : *m.* 1943, Vivien Priscilla,
da. of the late M. B. R. Swann, MD.

Patron of two archdeaconries, twenty-four canonries, and sixty-
three livings, of one alternately with the Crown, and of one other alternately, and three jointly.

The See of Truro was founded Dec. 9th, 1876, and comprises the old Archdeaconry of Cornwall,
which previously had formed part of the Diocese of Exeter.

Episcopal Signature,—Graham Truron :

ARMS OF THE SEE,—Argent, on a saltire gules, a sword and key in saltire or, and in base a fleur-de-
lis sable, all within a bordure of the last charged with fifteen bezants.

Residence,—Lis Escoop, Truro. *Club,*—Athenæum.

TRYON, BARON. (Tryon.) [Baron U.K. 1940.]

DO RIGHT AND FEAR NOT

CHARLES GEORGE VIVIAN TRYON, *GCVO*,
KCB, *DSO*, *PC*, 2nd Baron ; *b.* May 24th,
1906 ; *s.* 1940 ; ed. at Eton ; Brigadier (ret.)
late Grenadier Guards ; was A.D.C. to Gov.-
Gen. of Canada 1933-34, and Com., 5th
Guards Brig. 1945-47 ; Assist. Keeper of
HM's Privy Purse 1949-52, and Keeper of the
Privy Purse and Treasurer to HM the Queen
1952-71, since when a Permanent Lord-in-
Waiting to HM ; a Com. of Legion of Honour ;
N.-W. Europe 1944-45 (despatches, D.S.O.) ;
D.S.O. 1945, K.C.V.O. 1953, K.C.B. (Civil)
1962, GCVO 1969, PC 1971 : *m.* 1939,
Etheldreda Josephine, da. of Sir Merrik
Raymond Burrell, 7th Bt., CBE, and has
issue.

Arms,—Azure a fesse embattled between in chief three
estoiles and in base a portcullis chained or. *Crest,*—Issuant from a coronet composed of four roses set
upon a rim or a bear's head sable charged with seven stars in the form of the constellation ursa major
gold. *Supporters,*—*Dexter,* an army pensioner in hospital uniform ; *sinister,* a postman holding
with the exterior hand a letter sack over his shoulder proper.

Residence,—Church Farm, Great Durnford, Salisbury.

SON LIVING.

Hon. ANTHONY GEORGE MERRIK, *b.* May 26th, 1940 ; ed. at Eton ; a Page of Honour to H.M.
1954-56 ; Capt. Roy. Wilts. Yeo.: *m.* 1973, Dale Elizabeth, el. da. of Barry Harper, of Melbourne,
Vict.

DAUGHTER LIVING.

Hon. Patricia Joan Kathleen, *b.* 1942 : *m.* 1973, C. Ranald Macdonald.

BROTHER LIVING.

Hon. Aylmer Douglas (41, Dover St., W1 ; Boodle's Club), *b.* 1909 ; ed. at Eton, and at Trin. Coll.,
Camb. (BA) ; formerly Capt. Grenadier Guards.

PREDECESSOR.—[1] *Rt. Hon.* GEORGE CLEMENT Tryon, son of the late Vice-Adm.
Sir George Tryon, K.C.B., *b.* 1871 ; was Min. of Pensions Oct. 1922 to Jan. 1924, Nov. 1924
to June 1929, and Sept. 1931 to June 1935, Postmaster-Gen. June 1935 to April 1940,
Chancellor of Duchy of Lancaster April to May 1940, First Commr. of Works May to Oct.
1940, and Parliamentary Sec. to Min. of Pensions Oct. to Nov. 1940 ; sat as M.P. for Brighton
(C) 1910-40 ; cr. *Baron Tryon*, of Durnford, co. Wilts. (peerage of United Kingdom) 1940 :
m. 1905, the Hon. Averil Vivian, who *d.* 1959, dau. of 1st Baron Swansea ; *d.* 1940 ; *s.* by his son [2]
CHARLES GEORGE VIVIAN, 2nd Baron and present peer.

TUCKER, BARON. (Tucker.) [Life Baron U.K. 1950.]

FREDERICK JAMES TUCKER, *P.C.*, son of Frederick Nugent Tucker, of The Grey House, Epsom ; *b.* May 22nd, 1888 ; ed. at Winchester and at New Coll., Oxford (B.A. 1911, Hon. Fellow 1946) ; Bar. Inner Temple 1914, a K.C. 1933, a Bencher 1937, and Treasurer 1960 ; a Member of Gen. Council of Bar 1929-37, Recorder of Southampton 1936-37, a Judge of High Court of Justice (King's Bench Div.) 1937-45, a Lord Justice of Appeal 1945-50, and a Lord of Appeal in Ordinary 1950-61 ; European War 1914-19 as Lieut., Gen. List ; cr. Knt. 1937, P.C. 1945, and *Baron Tucker*, of Great Bookham, co. Surrey (Life Baron) 1950: *m.* 1918, Benedicta, who *d.* 1972, da. of the Rev. Charles P. Berryman, of Camberley. Surrey.

Arms,—Azure, on a chevron or between in-chief two lions' gambes erased, and in base a sea horse argent, a pale sable between two roses gules barbed and seeded proper. Crest,—A sea horse supporting with the dexter paw a battle axe argent hafted or. Supporters,—*Dexter*, a springbok proper charged on the shoulder with a fasces or; *sinister*, a lion guardant or charged on the shoulder with a fasces proper.

Residence,—Fairfield House, Great Bookham, Surrey.

TWEEDDALE, MARQUESS OF. (Hay.) [Marquess S. 1964.]

DAVID GEORGE MONTAGU HAY, *GC*, 12th Marquess; *b.* Oct. 25th, 1921; *s.* 1967; presumed heir to Baronetcy of Hay of Smithfield and Haystoun (cr. 1635); ed. at Eton; Lt. RNR (ret.); Hereditary Chamberlain of Dunfermline; AM 1941; Lloyd's and Roy. Life Saving Medals: *m.* 1st, 1946, the Hon. Sonia Mary Peake (who obtained a divorce 1958), da. of 1st Viscount Ingleby; 2ndly, 1959, Nella Doreen, da. of M. Dutton, and has issue by 1st and 2nd marriages.

Arms,—Quarterly: 1st and 4th, argent, three inescutcheons gules, *Hay* ; 2nd, gules, three bars ermine, *Gifford of Yester ;* 3rd, azure, three cinquefoils argent, *Fraser.* Crest,—A goat's head erased argent, horned or. Supporters,—Two bucks proper, attired or, collared azure, the collars charged with three cinquefoils argent.

Residence,—Tavool, I. of Mull.

SONS LIVING.   (*By 1st marriage.*)

EDWARD DOUGLAS JOHN (*Earl of Gifford*); (70, Campden Hill Towers, Notting Hill Gate, W11); *b.* Aug. 6th, 1947; ed. at Milton Abbey Sch., and Trin. Coll., Oxford.
Lord Charles David Montagu (twin), *b.* 1947; ed. at Milton Abbey Sch., and Trin. Coll., Oxford.
Lord Alistair James Montagu, *b.* 1955.

(*By 2nd marriage.*)

Lord Andrew Arthur George, *b.* 1959.
Lord Hamish David Montagu (twin), *b.* 1959.

SISTER LIVING.   (*Raised to the rank of a Marquess's daughter 1970*).

Lady Maryoth Christina HAY (Forbes Lodge, Gifford, E. Lothian) *b.* 1918, resumed by deed poll the surname of Hay 1971: *m.* 1st, 1940 (m. diss. 1954), Lt.-Col. George Richard Trotter, R. Scots Greys, who *d.* 1970 [E. Eglinton]; 2ndly, 1954, as his 2nd wife, Sir Gifford Wheaton Grey Fox, 2nd Bt., who *d.* 1959 when the title became extinct; 3rdly, 1963 (m. diss. 1971), Sir John Hastings James, KCVO, CB, and has issue living, (by 1st m.) Richard Reginald, *b.* 1941: *m.* 1974, Marion M., el. da. of Lt.-Col. Ralph Maxwell Campbell, of Binfield House, Binfield Heath, Henley, Oxon,—Edward George, *b.* 1943: *m.* 1973, Jemima Rachel McLay, el. da. of Niel Mills, of Upton Grey House, Hants. [see B. Hazlerigg],—Bridget Mary, *b.* 1944.

HALF-SISTER LIVING.   (*Raised to the rank of a Marquess's daughter 1970*).

Lady Caroline Susan Elizabeth, *b.* 1930: *m.* 1st, 1953 (m. diss. 1970), Richard Noel Marshall Armitage; 2ndly, 1970, Reginald Charles Tyrrell, of Capplegill, Moffat, Dumfries-shire, and has issue living, (by 1st m.) Charles Edward Marshall, *b.* 1954,—Alexander James, *b.* 1958.

DAUGHTERS LIVING OF ELEVENTH MARQUESS.

Lady Hélène Candida (*Viscountess Kemsley*) (Thorpe Lubenham Hall, Market Harborough); an OStJ, *b.* 1913: *m.* 1933, the 2nd Viscount Kemsley.
Lady (Marguerite) Georgina Christine, *b.* 1916 : *m.* 1941, Capt. Arthur Nicholas Coleridge, late Irish Guards [see B. Coleridge, colls]. *Residence*,—33, Peel Street, W.8.
Lady (Christine) Daphne, *b.* 1919 : *m.* 1st, 1939 (marriage dissolved 1947), Lieut.-Col. David Morley-Fletcher, T.D., Rifle Brig. ; 2ndly, 1957, Lieut.-Col. Francis Robert Cameron Stewart, late Indian Army, el. son of the late Sir Francis Hugh Stewart. C.I.E., and has issue living, (by 1st marriage) Hugo David Montagu, *b.* 1940: *m.* 1967, Josceline Mary, yr. da. of the Hon. Mr. Justice (Sir Henry Josceline) Phillimore, and has issue living, Gifford *b.* 1969, Hester *b.* 1972,—Victoria Catherine Margaret, *b.* 1942. *Residence*,—Middle Blainslie by Galashiels, Selkirkshire.

Lady Frances Elizabeth Ann, *b.* 1926 : *m.* 1956, Nigel Arthur Pearson, son of Sir Neville Arthur Pearson, 2nd Bt. *Residence,*—Dovecote Farm, Nutley, Sussex.

STEP-MOTHER LIVING.

Audrey Clara Lilian (*Lady Menzies*) (5, The Manor, Davies St., W1); da. of Sir Thomas Paul Latham, 1st Bt.: *m.* 1st, 1921, Henry Ralph Stanley Birkin (afterward 3rd Bt.), who *d.* 1933, and from whom she obtained a divorce 1927; 2ndly, 1928, as his second wife, Lt.-Col. Lord Edward Douglas John Hay, Gren. Gds., who *d.* (killed on active ser.) 1944; 3rdly, 1948, the Hon. Niall Greville Chaplin, yr. son of 2nd Viscount Chaplin, who *d.* 1963, and from whom she obtained a divorce 1952; 4thly, 1952, Maj.-Gen. Sir Stewart Graham Menzies, KCB, KCMG, DSO, MC, who *d.* 1968.

WIDOW LIVING OF ELEVENTH MARQUESS.

MARJORIE HELEN (*Marjorie, Marchioness of Tweeddale*), (Casa Azul, Djema el Mokra, Tangier), da. of the late Henry John Wagg, OBE, and formerly wife of Lt.-Col. Joseph Henry Nettlefold: *m.* 1945, as his 2nd wife, the 11th Marquess, who *d.* 1967.

COLLATERAL BRANCHES LIVING.

Issue of the late Capt. Lord Arthur Vincent Hay, 2nd son of 10th Marquess, *b.* 1886, *d.* (killed in action at battle of the Aisne) 1914 : *m.* 1911, Menda, who *d.* 1959 (having *m.* 2ndly, 1916, Lieut.-Col. Robert Edward Kennard Leatham, D.S.O., who *d.* 1948), dau. of the late Ambrose Ralli, of 24, Gloucester Square, Hyde Park, W. :—

Jean (*Jean, Lady Makins*), *b.* 1912: *m.* 1932, Lt.-Col. Sir William Vivian Makins, 3rd Bt., Welsh Guards, who *d.* 1969. *Residence,*—Littlehayes, Itchen Abbas, near Winchester, Hants.

Grandchildren of the late James Gordon Hay, el. son of Lt.-Gen. Lord James Hay, 2nd son of 7th Marquess:—
Issue of the late Maj. Malcolm Vivian Hay of Seaton, *b.* 1881, *d.* 1962: *m.* 1st, 1902, Florence Erlington, who *d.* 1943; 2ndly, 1956, ¡Alice Ivy (5, Belgrave Cres., Edinburgh, EH4 3HQ); a DStJ; da. of Herbert John Wigmore, of Perth, W. Australia:—

(By 1st m.) James Malcolm (Edinglassie, Huntly, Aberdeenshire), *b.* 1907; Maj. Gordon Highlanders (ret.); a DL of Aberdeenshire; 1939-45 War (wounded): *m.* 1941, Mary Eleanora Basset, da. of the late Charles Ernest Basset Lothian Curzon [see E. Howe, colls.], and has issue living, Malcolm Charles, *b.* 1956,—Elizabeth Mary, *b.* 1942,—Joanna Margaret, *b.* 1945,—Nicola Anne, *b.* 1958.——Peter Brian (Easter Ross, Comrie, Perthshire), *b.* 1918; Maj. Gordon Highlanders (ret.); 1939-45 War (despatches, prisoner): *m.* 1946, Marigold Armatrude, da. of Col. A. G. Eden, of Culver, nr. Exeter, and has issue living, Angus Malcolm, *b.* 1947; Lt. R. Scots Greys,—James Andrew, *b.* 1949: *m.* 1975, Emma, da. of (Rondle) Owen (Charles) Stable, QC, of Buckler's Hall, Much Hadham, Herts.,—Charlotte Jerardine, *b.* 1959.——Elizabeth Charlotte Sarah (*Lady Hodson*) (Myrtle Cottage, E. Ilsley, Newbury), *b.* 1904: *m.* 1928, Sir Arnold Wienholt Hodson, KCMG, who *d.* 1944, and has issue living, Jean Rosemary (Myrtle Cottage, E. Ilsley, Newbury, Berks.), *b.* 1930: *m.* 1958 (m. diss. 1972), John Wilfrid Gillams, and has issue living, Judith Elizabeth *b.* 1960, Charlotte Louise *b.* 1963,—Elisabeth Anne, *b.* 1934: *m.* 1963, Anthony Arthur Verrier, of 1, Nicosia Rd., Wandsworth, SW18, and has issue living, Charles Simpson *b.* 1966, Frances Joan *b.* 1968.——Georgina Catherine, *b.* 1910. ——Frances Mary *b.* 1914.

Issue of the late Capt. Cuthbert Joseph Hay, *b.* 1882, *d.* 1970: *m.* 1908, Letitia Griffith (Fiveways, Cookham, Berks.), da. of Frederick Heylighter Fausset, of Willsborough, co. Sligo:—

Ronald Cuthbert, *DSO, DSC* (South Mill, Amesbury, Wilts.) *b.* 1916; ed. at Ampleforth; Cdr. RN; 1939-45 War, (DSO, DSC and Bar); DSO 1945: *m.* 1945, Barbara, da. of Lt.-Col. George Rochfort Grange, of Strathblane, Stirlingshire, and has issue living, Charles Edward Ronald, *b.* 1948; ed. at Ampleforth,—James Philip Burness, *b.* 1957,—Penelope Rochfort, *b.* 1946,—Sara Elizabeth, *b.* 1951. ——John Malcolm (Mirrabooka, 56, Mugga Way, Red Hill, Canberra, ACT), *b.* 1918; ed. at Ampleforth; Lt.-Cdr. RN; 1939-45 War: *m.* 1952, Alicia Gertrude Maria, da. of Herbert Moore, of Sydney, NSW, and has issue living, Richard Malcolm, *b.* 1953: *m.* 1972, Maureen Loretta, da. of Walter Larkin, of San Francisco, Calif., USA.——Vivien Mary (Fiveways, Cookham, Berks.) *b.* 1909: *m.* 1st, 1937, M. John Ripley, who *d.* 1947; 2ndly, 1960, Samuel K. Jerome, who *d.* 1966, and has issue living, (by 1st m.) Michael, *b.* 1939.——Margaret Patricia, *b.* 1911.——Mary Charlotte, *b.* 1915.

Granddaughters of the late Capt. William Drummond Ogilvy-Hay-Newton, el. son of John Stuart Hay-Newton, grandson of Richard Hay Newton, uncle of 7th Marquess:—
Issue of the late Lieut.-Col. Stuart Hay, D.S.O., *b.* 1876, *d.* 1960: *m.* 1908, Inna Vera Evelyn, who *d.* 1971, da. of the late Hon. Louis Guy Scott [E. Clonmell, colls.]:—
Inna Veronica Adeline, *b.* 1909: *m.* 1966, Brig. Stanley Oswald Jones, OBE, MC, late RWF, of Long Hill House, Meré, Warminster, Wilts.——Vera Jean (Woodhouse Farm, Marsh, Aylesbury, Bucks.), *b.* 1910.——Evelyn Sheelagh (twin), *b.* 1910.

Grandchildren of the late William Hope Hay, el. son of Maj.-Gen. Alexander Charles Hay (infra):—
Issue of the late Lt.-Col. George Harold Hay, DSO, *b.* 1893, *d.* 1967: *m.* 1935, Patricia Mary (Duns Castle, Berwickshire), da. of Maj. Etienne Hugonin, of Edinburgh:—
Alexander Douglas (Duns Castle, Berwickshire), *b.* 1948: *m.* 1973, Aline Mary, da. of Robert Macdougall, of Edinburgh.——Philip Antony, *b.* 1950: *m.* 1975, Helena Anne, da. of F. Sim, of Alloa.—Caroline Mary, *b.* 1944: *m.* 1967, George Michael Mackinnon Thomson, of The Mill House, Kemnay, Aberdeenshire, and has issue living, George Jolyon Hay, *b.* 1970,—Mary Emma Julia (twin), *b.* 1970. ——Barbara Elizabeth, *b.* 1947.

Granddaughter of the late Maj.-Gen. Alexander Charles Hay, son of the late William Hay, grandson of the late Robert Hay (*b.* 1731), grandson of the late Hon. William Hay, 2nd son of 1st Earl:—
Issue of the late Edward George Hay, *b.* 1879, *d.* 1945: *m.* 1917, Ascelin Frances Collett, dau. of the late James Collett-Mason, J.P., of Ashurst Place, Langton Green, Kent :—
Nora Margaret (c/o Lloyds Bank, South St., Worthing, Sussex), *b.* 1922: *m.* 1942, John Robertson Campbell, and has issue living, David Michael Hay, *b.* 1944,—Christopher William John, *b.* 1949,—Stuart Calvin, *b.* 1953,—Tessa Margaret, *b.* 1946,—Lynn Nora Mary, *b.* 1952,—Sally Anne Frances, *b.* 1956.

Grandsons of the late Robert James Alexander Hay, son of Robert Hay (*b.* 1799), son of Robert Hay (*b.* 1731) (ante):—
Issue of the late Robert William Seton Hay, *b.* 1878, *d.* 1965: *m.* 19—, Maria, who *d.* 1961, da. of Antonio Baratti:—
Robert Dino James (18, Piazza dei Vespri Siciliani, Rome), *b.* 1901: *m.* 1942, Laura, da. of Gen. N. Fochetti, and has issue living, William Robert Alexander, *b.* 1947,—Patricia Caterina Maria, *b.* 1944.——Alexander Giuseppe (Colle Mattia, 00030 Colonna, Rome, Italy), *b.* 1906: *m.* 1937, Giovanna Bice, da. of Cdr. Mario Dasso, and has issue living, Andrew Alexander Mario, *b.* 1941,—Mary Grace Alexandra, *b.* 1939,—Roberta Alexandra, *b.* 1942,—Jane Alexandra, *b.* 1948,—Daniela Alexandra, *b.* 1953.

Issue of the late James William Hay, *b.* 1841, *d.* 1917: *m.* 1874, Joséphine Maria Ruth Alvarez-Molyneux, who *d.* 1886 :—
Daisy Maria Kalitza, *b.* 1875.——Madeleine Christian, *b.* 1882. *Residence,*—

Descendants of the late James Hay (4th in descent from the Hon. John Hay, 2nd son of 3rd Lord Hay of Yester), who was cr. a *Baronet* 1635 :—
See Hay, Bt., cr. 1635.

PREDECESSORS.—[1] JOHN HAY; cr. *Lord Hay of Yester* (peerage of Scotland) 1488; *s.* by his son [2] JOHN, 2nd Lord; fell at Flodden 1513; *s.* by his son [3] JOHN, 3rd Lord; *s.* by his son [4] JOHN, 4th Lord; was imprisoned for some years in the Tower of London, having been taken prisoner at the battle of Pinkie 1547; *d.* 1557; *s.* by his son [5] WILLIAM, 5th Lord; *s.* by his el. son [6] WILLIAM, 6th Lord; *s.* by his brother [7] JAMES, 7th Lord; *s.* by his son [8] JOHN, 8th Lord; commanded a Regt. in the Royal Army 1639; cr. *Earl of Tweeddale* (peerage of Scotland) 1646; *d.* 1654; *s.* by his son [9] JOHN, *P.C.*, 2nd Earl; sat as M.P. for Haddington-shire in Cromwell's Parliament; assisted at Coronation of Charles II. at Scone; having been a Commr. of the Treasury and an Extra Lord of Session was in 1692 appointed Lord Chancellor of Scotland; cr. *Viscount Walden, Earl of Gifford,* and *Marquess of Tweeddale* (peerage of Scotland) 1694, with remainder to his heirs male whatsoever; *d.* 1697; *s.* by his son [10] JOHN, *P.C.*, 2nd Marquess; was High Treasurer of Scotland 1695, High Commr. to the Scottish Parliament 1704, Lord Chancellor of Scotland 1704-5, and sometime a Representative Peer; *d.* 1713; *s.* by his son [11] CHARLES, 3rd Marquess; was Pres. of Court of Police, Lord-Lieut. of Haddingtonshire, and a Representative Peer; *d.* 1715; *s.* by his son [12] JOHN, *P.C.*, 4th Marquess; was a Representative Peer, the last person who held the office of Extraordinary Lord of Session, Sec. of State for Scotland 1742-6, Principal Keeper of the Signet, and in 1761 Justice-Gen. of Scotland; *d.* 1762; *s.* by his son [13] GEORGE, 5th Marquess; *d.* 1770; *s.* by his uncle [14] GEORGE, 6th Marquess; *d.* unmarried 1787; *s.* by his kinsman [15] GEORGE, 7th Marquess, grandson of Lord William, 3rd son of 2nd Marquess; was Lord-Lieut. of Haddington, and a Representative Peer; *d.* 1804; *s.* by his son [16] GEORGE, *K.T., G.C.B.*, 8th Marquess; *b.* 1787: a Field-Marshal; served with distinction in the Peninsular War; a Representative Peer, Gov. and Com. in Ch. at Madras 1842-48, Col. 2nd Life Guards, and Lord-Lieut. of Haddingtonshire: *m.* 1816, Lady Susan Montagu, da. of 5th Duke of Manchester; *d.* 1876; *s.* by his son [17] ARTHUR, 9th Marquess; *b.* 1824; Lieut.-Col. Grenadier Guards: *m.* 1st, 1857, Helena Eleanora Augusta, who *d.* 1871, dau. of Count de Kielmansegge; 2ndly, 1873, Julia Charlotte Sophia, who *d.* 1937 (having *m.* 2ndly, 1887, the Rt. Hon. Sir John Rose, G.C.M.G., P.C., 1st Bt., who *d.* 1888; 3rdly, 1892, Major Sir William Eden Evans-Gordon, who *d.* 1913), dau. of Keith Stewart Mackenzie; *d.* 1878; *s.* by his brother [18] WILLIAM MONTAGU, *K.T.*, 10th Marquess; *b.* 1826 : in B.C.S. 1845-62; M.P. for Taunton (*L*) 1865-8, and for Haddington Dist. 1878; Lord High Commr. for the Gen. Assembly of Church of Scotland 1889-92, 1896, and 1897; cr. *Baron Tweeddale,* of Yester, co. Haddington (peerage of United Kingdom) 1881: *m.* 1878, Candida Louise, *C.B.E.*, who *d.* 1925, dau. of Vincenzo Bartolucci. of Cantiano, Italy; *d.* 1911; *s.* by his el. son [19] WILLIAM GEORGE MONTAGU, 11th Marquess; *b.* 1884; Lord-Lt. of E. Lothian 1944-67: *m.* 1st, 1912, Marguerite Christine Ralli, who *d.* 1944, step da. of Lewis Einstein; 2ndly, 1945, Marjorie Helen, da. of the late Henry John Wagg, OBE, and formerly wife of Lt.-Col. Joseph Henry Nettleford; *d.* 1967; *s.* by his nephew [20], DAVID GEORGE MONTAGU, *GC* (son of Lt.-Col. Lord Edward Douglas John Hay (3rd son of 10th Marquess), and Violet Florence Catherine Bridget, da. of Maj. Cameron Barclay [B. Decies]), 12th Marquess and present peer; also Earl of Gifford, Earl of Tweeddale, Viscount Walden, Lord Hay of Yester, and Baron Tweeddale.

TWEEDMOUTH, BARONY OF. (Marjoribanks.) [Extinct 1935.]

DAUGHTERS LIVING OF THIRD BARON.

Hon. Moyra, *b.* 1902: *m.* 1st, 1923, Lieut.-Col. Reginald Francis Heyworth, 1st Roy. Dragoons, who *d.* (killed in action during European War) 1941; 2ndly, 1948, Major Reginald Brodrick Freeman-Thomas, King's Own Yorkshire L.I., and has issue living, (by 1st marriage) John, *b.* 1925 : *m.* 1950, Susan Elizabeth Hamersley, da. of Sir John Henry Burder, E.D.,—Anne (*Lady Pease*) *b.* 1924: *m.* 1st, 1946 (m. diss. 1955), Flight-Lieut. David Henry Lewis Wigan, RAFVR, 2ndly, 1956, Sir Richard Thorn Pease (3rd Bt. [cr. 1920]) of Hindley House, Stocksfield, Northumberland. *Residence,*— Kingswall House, nr. Malmesbury, Wilts.

Hon. (Millicent) Joan, *b.* 1906: *m.* 1935 (marriage annulled on her petition 1937), Sir Charles Michael Robert Vivian Duff-Assheton-Smith, 3rd Bt. *Residence,*—45 Westminster Gardens, S.W.1.

TWEEDSMUIR, BARON. (Buchan.) [Baron U.K. 1935.]

Not following meaner things.

JOHN NORMAN STUART BUCHAN, *CBE, CD,* 2nd Baron; *b.* Nov. 25th, 1911; *s.* 1940; ed. at Eton, and at Brasenose Coll., Oxford; Hon. LL.D. Aberdeen 1948, and Queen's, Ontario 1955; is a F.R.G.S., a F.R.S.A., and a F.Z.S.; was Assist. Dist. Officer, Uganda 1934-36, and in Hudson Bay Co.'s Ser. 1937-39; elected Rector of Aberdeen Univ. 1948; Pres. of Federation of Commonwealth and British Empire Chambers of Commerce 1955-57, and of Inst. of Export 1963-67, and a Member of Board BOAC 1955-64; a Gov. of Commonwealth Inst. since 1958; Hon. Col. Hastings and Prince Edward Regt. (Canadian Mil.) 1955-60; 1939-45 War in Sicily, and Italy as Lt.-Col. Hasting and Prince Edward Regt. (Canadian Mil.) and on Staff (wounded, despatches twice, OBE); Order of Orange Nassau of the Netherlands with Swords; OBE (Mil.) 1945; CBE (Civil) 1964: *m.* 1948, the Rt. Hon. Priscilla Jean Fortescue (*Baroness Tweedsmuir of Belhelvie, PC,* da. of Brig. Alan Fortescue Thomson, DSO, and widow of Maj. Sir Arthur Lindsay Grant, 11th Bt. (cr. 1705), and has issue.

$Arms,$—Azure, a fesse between three lions' heads erased argent. $Crest,$—A sunflower proper. $Supporters,$—*Dexter,* a stag proper, attired or, collared gules; *sinister,* a falcon proper, jessed, belled, and beaked or, armed and collared gules.

Residences,—40, Tufton Court, S.W.1; Potterton House, Balmedie, Aberdeenshire. *Clubs,*—Travellers', Carlton, Pratt's, Flyfishers'.

DAUGHTER LIVING.

Hon. Priscilla Susan (*Lady James A. Douglas-Hamilton*) *b.* 1949: *m.* 1974, Lord James Alexander Douglas-Hamilton [see D. Hamilton and Brandon].

BROTHERS LIVING.

Hon. WILLIAM DE L'AIGLE, *b.* Jan. 10th, 1916; ed. at Eton, and at New Coll., Oxford; is Sqdn.-Ldr. R.A.F. Vol. Reserve: *m.* 1st, 1939 (m. diss. 1946), Nesta, only da. of Lt.-Col. C. D. Crozier; 2ndly, 1946 (m. diss. 1960), Barbara Howard, who *d.* 1969, da. of E. N. Ensor, of 24, Chivelston Court, Wimbledon Parkside, SW; 3rdly, 1960, Sauré Cynthia Mary, da. of the late Maj. G. E. Tatchell, R. Lincs. Regt., and has issue living, (by 1st m.) Perdita Caroline, *b.* 1940: *m.* 1968, Edward Connolly, RFD 4, West Brattleboro, Vermont 0351, USA, and has issue living, Cressida *b.* 1969, —(by 2nd m.) John William Howard de l'Aigle, *b.* 1950,—Charles Walter Edward Ralph, *b.* 1951,— James Ernest *b.* 1954,—Deborah Charlotte, *b.* 1947: *m.* 1966, Bernard Harold Ian Halley Stewart, of 121, St. George's Rd., SE1, and has issue living, Henry Ernest Alexander Halley *b.* 1972, Lydia Barbara Rose Anna Phoebe *b.* 1969, Dorothy Louisa Charlotte Amabel *b.* 1970,—Laura Mary Clare, *b.* 1953,—Ursula Margaret Bridget (twin), *b.* 1953,—(by 3rd m.) Alexander Edward, *b.* 1961. *Residence,*—Maynards, Little Stampford, Saffron Walden, Essex CB10 2QP. *Club,*—Travellers'.

Hon. Alastair Francis, *CBE, b.* 1918; ed. at Eton, and at Ch. Ch., Oxford; Correspondent of *The Observer* in Washington, USA, 1951-55, Diplomatic and Defence Correspondent of *The Observer* 1955-58, and Dir. of Inst. for Strategic Studies, London 1958-69; Comdt., Roy. Coll. of Defence Studies (IDC) 1970-71; Montague Burton Prof. of International Relations, Oxford Univ. since 1972; late Maj. 14th Canadian Hussars; Dieppe Raid 1942, NW Europe 1944-45; MBE (Mil) 1945, CBE (Civil) 1968: *m.* 1942, Hope, da. of the late David Gordon Gilmour, of Ottawa, Canada, and has issue living, David John Washington, *b.* 1947: *m.* 1974, Sarah, da. of George L. Cawkwell, of 8, Moreton Rd., Oxford,—Benjamin William Alastair, *b.* 1948: *m.* 1974, Elizabeth, da. of Maj. Peter Oakleigh-Walker of the Meade, Pankridge St., Crondall, Surrey,—Anna Virginia Pauline, *b.* 1953. *Residence,*—Waterloo House, Brill, Bucks. *Clubs,*—Garrick, Beefsteak.

SISTER LIVING.

Hon. Alice Caroline Helen (*Hon. Lady Ramsay-Fairfax-Lucy*), *b.* 1908: *m.* 1933; Maj. Sir Brian Fulke Ramsay-Fairfax-Lucy, 5th Bt., who *d.* 1974. *Residences,*—The Mill, Fosse Bridge, Cheltenham; Charlecote Park, Warwick.

WIDOW LIVING OF FIRST BARON.

SUSAN CHARLOTTE (*Susan, Baroness Tweedsmuir*), dau. of the late Capt. the Hon. Norman de l'Aigle Grosvenor [see B. Ebury, colls.]: *m.* 1907, the 1st Baron, who *d.* 1940. *Residence,*—Hill House, Burford, Oxon.

PREDECESSOR.—[1] *Rt. Hon.* JOHN BUCHAN, *G.C.M.G., G.C.V.O., C.H.,* son of the late Rev. John Buchan, of Glasgow; *b.* 1875; a well-known Author; sat as M.P. for Edinburgh, St. Andrews, Glasgow and Aberdeen Univs. (C.) 1927-35; was Lord High Commr. to Gen. Assembly of Church of Scotland 1933 and 1934, and Gov.-Gen. and Com.-in-Ch. Dominion of Canada 1935-40; cr. *Baron Tweedsmuir*, of Elsfield, co. Oxford (peerage of United Kingdom) 1935: *m.* 1907, Susan Charlotte, dau. of Capt. the Hon. Norman de l'Aigle Grosvenor; *d.* 1940; *s.* by his son [2] JOHN NORMAN STUART, 2nd Baron and present peer.

TWEEDSMUIR OF BELHELVIE, BARONESS. (Thomson.) [Life Baroness 1970.]

PRISCILLA JEAN FORTESCUE THOMSON, *PC,* da. of the late Brig. Alan Fortescue Thomson, DSO, *b.* Jan. 25th, 1915; Delegate Council of Europe 1950-53, a Member of Commonwealth Parl. Delegation West Indies 1955, UK Delegate to UN Gen. Assembly 1960-61, Joint Parl. Under-Sec. of State, Scottish Office 1962-64; Min. of State, Scottish Office 1970-72, and of FCO 1972-74; MP for S. Aberdeen (C) 1946-66; cr. *Baroness Tweedsmuir of Belhelvie,* of Potterton, co. Aberdeen (Life Baroness) 1970, and PC 1974: *m.* 1st, 1934, Maj. Sir Arthur Lindsay Grant, 11th Baronet (cr. 1705), who *d.* (killed in action) 1944; 2ndly, 1948, the 2nd Baron Tweedsmuir, and has issue living by 1st and 2nd m.

Arms,—Not matriculated at Lyon Court at time of going to press.
Residences,—40, Tufton Court, SW1; Potterton House, Balmedie, Aberdeenshire.

DAUGHTERS LIVING. (By 1st m.)

Hon. Joanna Catherine, *b.* 1935: *m.* 1954 (m. diss. 1966), Dominick Jones, son of Sir (George) Roderick Jones, KBE, and has issue living, Romily Arthur, *b.* 1956.

Hon. Anne Margaret, *b.* 1937; ed. at Lady Margaret Hall, Oxford: *m.* 1965, Nicolas Mangriotis, of 57, Ypsilantou St., Athens, 140, Greece, and has issue living, Paraskevas, *b.* 1971,—Arthur, *b.* 1974.

(By 2nd m.)

See Baron Tweedsmuir.

TWINING, BARONY OF. (Twining.) [Extinct 1967.]

SONS LIVING OF LIFE PEER.

Hon. John Peter (3, The Ridgeway, Guildford; Reform Club), *b.* 1929; ed. at Charterhouse, and at Brasenose Coll., Oxford; Colonial Ser. 1953-63; an Admin. Officer, City of Guilds of London Inst.: *m.* 1954, Mary Avice, da. of Brig. Joseph Hector Denly Bennett, CBE, and has issue.

Hon. William Lawrence, *b.* 1934; ed. at Charterhouse, at Brasenose Coll., Oxford, and at Chicago Univ.; Prof. of Law, Queen's Univ., Belfast 1965-72, since when Prof. of Law Univ. of Warwick: *m.* 1957, Penelope Elizabeth, da. of Richard Wall Morris, of Dublin, and has issue. *Address,*—c/o Lloyds Bank, 222, Strand, WC2.

TYRRELL, BARONY OF. (Tyrrell.) [Extinct 1947.]

DAUGHTER LIVING OF FIRST BARON.

Hon. Harriet Anne Mary Tyrrell, *b.* 1904; assumed by deed poll 1930, the additional Christian names of Mary Tyrrell: *m.* 1st, 1930, Sir Adrian Holman, KBE, CMG, MC, who *d.* 1974, and from whom she obtained a divorce 1932 (granted dissolution of marriage by rescript of Holy Office, Rome 1933); 2ndly, 1934, Capt. Jack William Leslie Crawshay, MC, Hon. Attaché to British Embassy, Paris, who *d.* 1950 [Leslie, Bt., cr. 1876]. *Residence,*—5, Surrey Cottage, Norfolk Place, Littlehampton, Sussex.

Tyrone, Baron, title of Marquess of Waterford on Roll of H. L.

Earl of, son of Marquess of Waterford.

ULLSWATER, VISCOUNT.

Magistratum indicat Virum

The office shows the man.

(Lowther.) [Viscount U.K. 1921.]

NICHOLAS JAMES CHRISTOPHER LOW-THER, 2nd Viscount; *b*. Jan. 9th, 1942; *s*. 1949; ed. at Eton, and at Trin. Coll., Camb.; Capt. Wessex Yeo.: *m*. 1967, Susan, da. of James Howard Weatherby of Lemington Grange, Moreton-in-Marsh, [see Wake, Bt.], and has issue.

Arms,—Or, six annulets, three, two, and one, sable, a crescent for difference. Crest,—A dragon passant argent. Supporters,—On either side a horse argent, gorged with a wreath of laurel vert and charged on the shoulder with a portcullis chained or

Residence,—Knoyle Down Farm, Hindon, Salisbury.

DAUGHTERS LIVING.

Hon. Emma Mary, *b*. 1968.
Hon. Clare Priscilla, *b*. 1970.

SISTER LIVING.

(*Raised to the rank of a Viscount's Daughter* 1951.)

Hon. Kirstin Elizabeth. *b*. 1939: *m*. 1966, Capt. Caledon Alexander, late 7th Queen's Own Hussars, of Crudwell Court, Malmesbury, Wilts., and has issue living, James Caledon, *b*. 1969,—Charlotte Jane, *b*. 1968.

HALF AUNTS LIVING.

(*Raised to rank of a Viscount's Daughters* 1950.)

Hon. Rosemary, *b*. 1922: *m*. 1945, Lt. Douglas Cyril Aubrey Goolden, RNVR, and has issue living, Michael Cyril Christopher, *b*. 1947,—Alastair Richard Lowther, *b*. 1954,—Jill Priscilla, *b*. 1949. *Residence*,—Forge Cottage, Withyham, Sussex.

Hon. Jennifer, *b*. 1932 : *m*. 1st, 1954 (marriage dissolved 1962), as his second wife, the 7th Earl of Lonsdale; 2ndly, 1962, William Edward Clayfield, Ft.-Lt. RAF.

WIDOW LIVING OF SON OF FIRST VISCOUNT.

Dorothy LOWTHER, dau. of Arthur Bromley-Davenport, and formerly wife of Guy Loveridge; resumed the surname of Lowther in lieu of Cullen by deed poll 1951 : *m*. 2ndly, 1921, as his second wife, Major the Hon. Christopher William Lowther, who *d*. 1935 ; 3rdly, 1936, Capt. Hugh Ellin Davies Cullen, M.C., from whom she obtained a divorce 1951 ; 4thly, 1958, as his second wife, Charles Glennie de Rougemont. *Residence*,—Old Shalesbrook, Forest Row, Sussex.

PREDECESSOR.—[1] *Rt. Hon. Sir* JAMES WILLIAM Lowther, *G.C.B.*, son of the late Hon. William Lowther, brother of 3rd Earl of Lonsdale; *b*. 1855; Bar. Inner Temple 1879, and a Bencher 1906; was 4th (unpaid) Charity Commr. 1887-91, Under-Sec. of State for Foreign Affairs 1891-2, Chm. of Committee of Ways and Means and Dep. Speaker of House of Commons 1895-1905, and Speaker 1905-21; Chm. of Political Honours Commn. 1923-4; sat as M.P. for Rutland (*C*) 1883-5, for Mid, or Penrith, Div. of Cumberland 1886-1918, and for Cumberland, Penrith and Cockermouth Div. 1918-21; cr. *Viscount Ullswater*, of Campsea Ashe, co. Suffolk (peerage of UK) 1921: *m*. 1886, Mary Frances, who *d*. 1944, da. of the late Right Hon. Alexander James Beresford-Hope, MP, of Bedgebury Park, Cranbrook; *d*. 1949; *s*. by his great-grandson [2] NICHOLAS JAMES CHRISTOPHER (son of the late Lt. John Arthur Lowther, MVO, RNVR, son of the late Maj. the Hon. Christopher William Lowther, el. son of 1st Viscount), 2nd Viscount and present peer.

Ulster, Earl of, son of Duke of Gloucester.

UPJOHN, BARONY. (Upjohn.) [Extinct 1971.]

WIDOW LIVING OF LIFE BARON.

MARJORIE DOROTHY BERTHA (*Baroness Upjohn*), (Orpen's Hill House, Birch, Colchester), da. of the late Maj. Ernest Murray Lucas [see Lucas, Bt., colls.] *m*. 1947, the 1st Baron, who *d*. 1971, when the title became ext.

UVEDALE OF NORTH END, BARONY OF. (Woodall.) [Extinct 1974.]

WIDOW LIVING OF FIRST BARON.

JOYCE ELEANOR, *JP*, (*Baroness Uvedale of North End*), (1, The Park, North End Rd., NW11), da. of the late S. H. Holman, of Highgate, N6, and St. Margaret's Bay, Kent, and widow of the Rt. Hon. Hastings Bertrand Lees-Smith, DSc, MP: *m*. 1949, the first Baron Uvedale of North End, MD, FRCS, who *d*. 1974, when the title became ext.

Uxbridge, Earl of, son of Marquess of Anglesey.

VALENTIA, VISCOUNT.   (Annesley.)
[Viscount I. 1642, with precedence of 1622, Bt. I. 1620.]
[Name pronounced "Ansley."]

By the love of virtue.

Residence,—St. Michael's, Lea, Malmesbury, Wilts.

FRANCIS DIGHTON ANNESLEY, *M.C.*, *M.R.C.S.*, *L.R.C.P.*, 14th Viscount and Premier Baronet of Ireland ; *b.* Aug. 12th, 1888 ; *s.* 1951 (established his succession 1959) ; M.R.C.S. and L.R.C.P. 1914 ; Brig. late R.A.M.C.; late Cottonian Family Trustee of British Museum; European War 1914-18 (M.C., Belgian Croix de Guerre), Afghanistan 1919, Waziristan 1922-23, European War 1939-45 : *m.* 1925, Joan Elizabeth, dau. of the late John J. Curtis, of Sunnybrook, Sandhurst, and has issue.

Arms,—Paly of six argent and azure, over all a bend gules. **Crest,**—A Moor's head in profile couped proper, wreathed about the temples argent and azure. **Supporters,**—*Dexter,* a Roman soldier in armour or, short sleeves and apron gules, face, arms, and legs bare, the latter sandalled, argent : on his head a helmet gold, on the top three feathers of the second, holding in his exterior hand a shield, thereon a female's head ; *sinister,* a Moorish prince proper, in armour or, wreathed round the temples argent and azure, short sleeves and apron gules, boots gold, behind him a sheaf of arrows proper, fastened by a pink ribbon, in his exterior hand a bow proper.

SON LIVING.
Hon. RICHARD JOHN DIGHTON (of Shumba Farm, Sinoia, Rhodesia), *b.* Aug. 15th, 1929; ed. at Marlborough; Capt. R.A. (ret.): *m.* 1957, Anita Phyllis, dau. of W. A. Joy, of Bristol, and has issue living, Francis William Dighton, *b.* 1959,—Richard Dighton, *b.* 1962,—Peter John, *b.* 1967,—Sarah Joy, *b.* 1958.

DAUGHTERS LIVING.
Hon. Elizabeth Mary Jean, *b.* 1926: *m.* 1948, Maj. James Terence Ralph Sylvester Bradley, MA, CEng., MIERE, of Knighton Manor, Durweston, Blandford, Dorset, and has issue living, Charles Robin, *b.* 1959,—Fiona Elizabeth, *b.* 1949,—Heather Mary, *b.* 1951,—Catherine Alison, *b.* 1957.
Hon. Susan Margaret, *b.* 1931: *m.* 1954. Peter Lindsay Miln, and has issue living, Jeremy James, *b.* 1956,—Teresa Clare, *b.* 1958,—Eleanor Eve, *b.* 1961,—Jesica Rose, *b.* 1964. *Residence,*—Bosinver, St. Austell, Cornwall.
Hon. Helen Jennifer Frances, *b.* 1935 : *m.* 1957, Simon FitzRoy Casswell, and has issue living, Hugh FitzRoy, *b.* 1958,—Edward FitzRoy (twin), *b.* 1958,—Jane Elizabeth, *b.* 1962,—Karen Mary, *b.* 1969. *Residence,*—The Limes Farm, Smarden, near Ashford, Kent.

DAUGHTERS LIVING OF ELEVENTH VISCOUNT.
Hon. Lettice, *C.V.O.*, *b.* 1885 ; was a Lady-in-Waiting to H.M. Queen Elizabeth the Queen Mother when Duchess of York 1932-7, and a Woman of the Bedchamber to H.M. when Queen 1937-44, since when an Extra Woman of the Bedchamber ; an O.St.J. ; C.V.O. 1937 : *m.* 1911, Major Geoffrey Vaux Salvin Bowlby, Roy. Horse Guards, who *d.* (killed in action) 1915, and has issue living, John Edward Richard (of 38, Burnsall Street, S.W.3), *b.* 1914 ; a Major 1st Roy. Dragoons (Reserve of Officers) : *m.* 1950, the Hon. Dorothy Anne (GRAHAM), sister of 13th Baron North, and has issue living, Gina Anne *b.* 1954,—Elizabeth Mary (*Countess of Meath*), *b.* 1913 : *m.* 1940, the 14th Earl of Meath. *Residence,*—Middleton-Stoney, Bicester.
Hon. Dorothy, *b.* 1892 : *m.* 1921, Joseph Francis Vaughan Gibbs, and has issue living, Caryl Antony Vaughan (1, Lombardy Place, W.2), *b.* 1926; late Lt. Grenadier Guards: *m.* 1959, Christiana Maria Theresa (BENNIE), da. of Erich von Machanek zu Marienthal, of Vienna, and has issue living, Nicola Jane *b.* 1960, Alexandra Henrietta *b.* 1966,—Brenda Mary, *b.* 1929: *m.* 1957, Cecil Ralph Timothy Edwards, Lt. Welsh Guards (Reserve), of The Manor House, Sutton Park, Guildford, Surrey, and has issue living, Mark James Timothy *b.* 1957, Simon Martin Ralph *b.* 1959, Stephen Jonathan Hugh *b.* 1967, Jane Alexandra *b.* 1961, Katharine Mary *b.* 1963. *Residence,*—8, Lincoln House, Basil St., SW1.

WIDOW LIVING OF THIRTEENTH VISCOUNT.
GLADYS MAY KATHLEEN (*Gladys, Viscountess Valentia*), da. of the late Uriah Fowler: *m.* 1938, the 13th Viscount, who *d.* 1951. *Residence,*—Wassall House, Wincanton, Somerset.

COLLATERAL BRANCHES LIVING.
Issue of the late Philip de Vere Annesley, brother of 13th Viscount, *b.* 1879, *d.* 1949: *m.* 1907, Christabel Charlotte, *BEM*, who *d.* 1955, da. of the late John Christopher Tomson:—
Anne Christabel de Vere (*Lady Thompson*), *b.* 1909; assumed by deed poll 1941 the additional christian name of Anne: *m.* 1939, Sir Richard Hilton Marler Thompson, 1st baronet (cr. 1963), of Rhodes House, Sellindge, Ashford, Kent.

Granddaughter of the late Arthur Annesley, 2nd son of the late Rev. Arthur Annesley, son of the late Rev. Arthur Henry Annesley, D.D., great-grandson of the late Hon. Francis Annesley, 4th son of 1st Viscount :—
Issue of the late Arthur Francis Biscoe Annesley, *b.* 1849, *d.* 1915 : *m.* 1891, Kate, who *d.* 1922, dau. of the late Richard Gillespie :—
Caroline Vere, *b.* 1893 : *m.* 1st, 1917, Richard Vincent Sturt, late Lieut. R.G.A., who *d.* 1923 ; 2ndly, 1926, Arthur Cyril Wallis, and has issue living, (by 2nd marriage) Christopher Arthur Annesley (Briarfield, 34, Guildown Rd., Guildford), *b.* 1928: *m.* 1955, Jeanne Marie Brady, and has issue living, Julia Caroline Annesley *b.* 1957, Nicola Jane Annesley *b.* 1959, Anna Marie Annesley *b.* 1965,—(by 1st m.) Margaret Vere, *b.* 1918: *m.* 1946, Capt. Graham Pile, of Chalmers, Rue des Cotils, Vallée des Vaux, Jersey, and has issue living, Hugh Richard Graham *b.* 1948, Verity Katherine *b.* 1952. *Residence,*—Briarfield, 34, Guildown Rd., Guildford.

Granddaughter of the late Rev. William Annesley, 3rd son of the late Rev. Arthur Annesley (ante):—
Issue of the late Major Oliver Francis Theodore Annesley, *b.* 1842, *d.* 1905: *m.* 1885, Isabel, who *d.* 1935, dau. of the late Charles Addington Hanbury, of Belmont House, East Barnet, Herts [Mackenzie, Bt., of Gairloch, cr. 1703, colls.]:—

Isabel Myrtle (Nutbeam, Duntisbourne Leer, Cirencester), *b.* 1888: *m.* 1921, Lt.-Col. Edward Shirley Godman, OBE, late Dorset Regt., who *d.* 1951, and has issue living, Desmond Frederick Shirley (of Great Rissington Manor, Cheltenham, Glos.), *b.* 1927; formerly Capt. 1st Roy. Dragoons; a JP of Glos.: *m.* 1954, Angela Janice Mary, da. of the Rev. J. C. Rowson, and has issue living, Hugh Edward Corlett *b.* 1955, John *b.* 1963, Alice Nichola *b.* 1957, Lucy *b.* 1960,—Isabel Hope (Nutbeam Farm, Duntisbourne Leer, Cirencester, Glos.), *b.* 1923: *m.* 1955 (m. diss. 1970), Patrick Nathan Chesmore, and has issue living, Rupert Nathan *b.* 1957, Lucinda Isabel *b.* 1956.

Grandchildren of the late Lt.-Col. Reginald Carey Annesley, son of George Annesley, yst. son of the late Rev. Arthur Annesley (ante):—
Issue of the late Lt.-Col. Clifford Reginald Templeman Annesley, DSO, *b.* 1877, *d.* 1971: *m.* 1907, Clara Mabel, who *d.* 1954, el. da. of Lt.-Col. Samuel Martin Gully, Norfolk Regt.:—
Reginald Clifford Martin (c/o Barclays Bank, DCO, PO Box 702, Bulawayo, Rhodesia), *b.* 1909; ed. at Stowe; late British S. Africa Police: *m.* 1940, Ann Isabella, el. da. of John Robert Strachan, of Firthview, Tain, Ross-shire, and has issue living, Kathleen Elaine Vere, *b.* 1941: *m.* 1966, Beverley Aldington Bird (PO Box 587, Bulawayo, Rhodesia),—Sheila Rosalind, *b.* 1945: *m.* 1965, Michael Stuart Allen, B.S.A. Police (PO Box 583, Bulawayo, Rhodesia).——Vere Bessie Mabel (18, Wykeham Place, Lymington, Hants.), *b.* 1910.
Issue of the late Maj. Martin Tyndale Annesley, *b.* 1896, *d.* 1965: *m.* 1935, Marjorie Jex Blake (74, Clarendon Rd., Norwich, NOR 42F), el. da. of Lt.-Col. B. E. Winter, of Lowestoft:—
Richard Bruce (Fairbanks, 30, Amersham Rd., High Wycombe, Bucks.), *b.* 1937: *m.* 1972, Elizabeth Mary, Emily, da. of Thomas Doyle, of Armanagh, Glenbrook, co. Cork, and has issue living, Charlotte Mary, *b.* 1973,—Philippa Vere, *b.* 1975.

Descendants of the late William Annesley, M.P. (3rd son of the Hon. Francis Annesley, 4th son of 1st Viscount), who was cr. *Viscount Glerawly* 1766 [see E. Annesley].

PREDECESSORS.—[1] *Rt. Hon. Sir* FRANCIS Annesley, filled during forty years numerous high official positions in Ireland, and sat for sometime as M.P. for Armagh; cr. a *Baronet* 1620; in 1621 obtained by patent a reversionary grant to the peerage of *Viscount Valentia* (peerage of Ireland) at the decease of the then viscount; cr. *Baron Mountnorris*, of Mountnorris, co. Armagh (peerage of Ireland) 1628; in 1635 he publicly offended Lord Strafford, the Lord Deputy of Ireland, and for this offence he was tried, and found guilty, and sentenced to deprivation of military rank and to be shot or beheaded at the pleasure of the General; the capital punishment was not carried out, but he suffered a long imprisonment in Dublin Castle; *d.* 1660; *s.* by his son [2] ARTHUR, 2nd Viscount; was Treasurer of the Navy 1667, and Lord Privy Seal 1673; cr. *Baron Annesley*, of Newport Pagnel, co. Bucks, and *Earl of Anglesey* (peerage of England) 1661; *d.* 1686; *s.* by his son [3] JAMES, 2nd Earl; *d.* 1690; *s.* by his el. son [4] JAMES, 3rd Earl; *d.* 1702; *s.* by his brother [5] JOHN, 4th Earl; *d.* 1710; *s.* by his brother [6] ARTHUR, 5th Earl; *d.* 1737; *s.* by his kinsman [7] RICHARD, 6th Earl, who had previously *s.* as 5th *Baron Altham* (peerage of Ireland, cr. 1680), he being 2nd son of the 3rd Baron Altham, who was 3rd son of the 1st Earl; after the assumption of the earldom by this peer a Mr. James Annesley claimed the earldom as son of Arthur, 4th Baron Altham, and alleged that in his infancy he had been kidnapped by his uncle Richard (6th Earl), and in 1743 he commenced a suit of law to recover the property from his uncle and obtained a verdict, though he did not further pursue his claim to the earldom, and his uncle continued to be recognised as earl; *d.* 1761; *s.* by his son [8] ARTHUR, 8th Viscount, whose claims to the Baronies of Mountnorris, Altham, and the Viscountcy of Valentia were twice confirmed by the Irish Parliament, while his claim to the Barony of Annesley and Earldom of Anglesey was refused by the English Parliament; cr. *Earl of Mountnorris* (peerage of Ireland) 1793; *d.* Mountnorris expired; *s.* in the Baronetcy, Barony of Mountnorris, and Viscountcy of Valentia by his kinsman [10]ARTHUR, 10th Viscount, 5th in descent from Francis, 4th son of 1st Viscount; *d.* 1863; *s.* by his grandson [11] ARTHUR, *KCVO*, *CB*, 11th Viscount, son of the Hon. Arthur Annesley (el. son of 10th Viscount by Flora Mary, who *d.* 1884, da. of Lt.-Col. James Macdonald of Clanranald); Comptroller of the Household to Queen Victoria 1898-1901, and to King Edward VII 1901-05, and a Lord-in-Waiting to King George V 1915-24; cr. *Baron Annesley of Bletchington*, co. Oxford (peerage of UK) 1917: *m.* 1878, Laura Sarah, who *d.* 1933, da. of Daniel Hale Webb, of Wykeham Park, and widow of Sir Algernon William Payton, 4th Bt.; *d.* 1927; *s.* by his son [12] CARYL ARTHUR JAMES, *CVO*, 12th Viscount; *b.* 1883; Maj. 1st R. Dragoons; High Steward of Banbury 1932-47; Private Sec. to HRH Prince Arthur of Connaught 1922-38; *d.* unm. 1949, when the Barony of Annesley of Bletchington (peerage of UK) became ext.; *s.* in his other titles by his kinsman [13] *Rev.* WILLIAM MONCKTON, 13th Viscount (el. son of the Rev. Henry Arthur Annesley, el. son of Arthur Annesley, great grandson of the Rev. Martin Annesley, DD, grandson of the Hon. Francis Annesley, 4th son of 1st Viscount); |*b.* 1875; V. of Brewham-cum-Redlynch, Somerset, and Cottonian Family Trustee of British Museum: *m.* 1938, Gladys M. Kathleen, da. of the late Uriah Flower; *d.* 1951; *s.* by his cousin [14] FRANCIS DIGHTON (son of the late George Dighton Annesley, uncle of 13th Viscount); 14th Viscount and present peer; also Baron Mountnorris.

Vane, Earl, title of Marquess of Londonderry on Roll of H. L.

VANSITTART, BARONY OF. (Vansittart.) [Extinct 1957.]

DAUGHTER LIVING OF FIRST BARON. (*By 1st marriage.*)
Hon. Cynthia, *b.* 1922: *m.* 1st, 1942 (marriage dissolved in California, U.S.A. 1954), Frederick C. Whitman; 2ndly, 1955, Edward Hart Mackay, and has issue living, (by 1st marriage) Michael Robert Vansittart, *b.* 1944,—Jonathan Crocker, *b.* 1948,—Kevin Crocker, *b.* 1950,—Tania Vansittart, *b.* 1942,—(by 2nd marriage) Robert Vansittart, *b.* 1958,—Donald James Edward, *b.* 1961. *Residence,*—2655, Clay St., San Francisco, U.S.A.

WIDOW LIVING OF FIRST BARON.
SARITA ENRIQUETA (*Baroness Vansittart*), dau. of the late Herbert Ward, of 105, Avenue Malakoff, Paris, and widow of the Rt. Hon. Sir Colville Adrian de Rune Barclay, K.C.M.G., C.B., C.B.E., M.V.O. [see Barclay, Bt.]: *m.* 1931, as his second wife, the 1st Baron, who *d.* 1957, when the title became ext. *Residence,*—8, Hyde Park Gdns., W2.

Vaughan, Viscount, son of Earl of Lisburne.

VAUX OF HARROWDEN, BARON. (Gilbey.) [Baron E. 1523.]
[Title pronounced "Vawks of Harrowden."]

Today, not tomorrow.

Rev. PETER HUBERT GORDON GILBEY, 9th Baron ; *b.* June 28th, 1914 ; *s.* 1958 ; ed. at Ampleforth Coll., and at St. Benet's Hall, Oxford (B.A. 1939, M.A. 1943) ; is in Holy Orders of Church of Rome, and a Monk of Ampleforth Abbey.

Arms,—Quarterly, 1st and 4th gules, a fesse nebulée or, in chief a horse rampant between two estoiles and the like in base, all of the last, *Gilbey* ; 2nd and 3rd : Per bend sinister ermine and erminois a lion rampant or, *Mostyn.*—Supporters—*Dexter,* a griffin sable beaked or the forelegs gold ; *sinister,* a buck or each gorged with a torse argent and gules pendant therefrom by a ring gold an escutcheon of the Arms of Vaux (checky, or and gules ; on a chevron azure, three roses gold).

Address,—St. Mary's Priory, Buttermarket St., Warrington, Lancashire.

BROTHER LIVING.
Hon. JOHN HUGH PHILIP, *b.* Aug. 4th, 1915; ed. at Ampleforth Coll., and at Ch. Ch., Oxford (BA 1937); formerly Maj. Duke of Wellington's Regt.: *m.* 1939, Maureen, da. of Hugh Gilbey, of Shellwood Bend, Leigh, Reigate, Surrey, and has issue living, Antony William (Lascelles, Matching Green, Essex), *b.* 1940; ed. at Ampleforth: *m.* 1964, Beverley Walton, and has issue living, Richard *b.* 1965, Philip Alexander Charles *b.* 1967, Victoria Caroline *b.* 1969,—William John (Priory Cottage, Priory Way, Datchet, Bucks.), *b.* 1944: *m.* 1971 Caroline Ball, and has issue living, Thomas *b.* 1972, Charlotte *b.* 1974,—Michael Christopher (89, Archway St., Barnes, SW13), *b.* 1948: *m.* 1971, Linda, yst. da. of the late Arthur Sebastian Gilbey [see Gilbey, Bt., colls.], and has issue living Henry John *b.* 1973, Julian Sebastian *b.* 1975,—Penelope Margaret, *b.* 1942: *m.* 1965, John Charles Haynes, of Evelith Mill, Shifnal, Salop, and has issue living, Charles *b.* 1967, Alexandra *b.* 1966, Clare *b.* 1969. *Residence,*—Cholmondeley Cottage, 2, Cholomondeley Walk, Richmond, Surrey.

SISTER LIVING.
Hon. Mary Agnes Margaret, *b.* 1928.   *Residence,*—Dolphins, Gt. Harrowden, Wellingborough.

AUNTS LIVING. *(Daughters of 7th Baron.)*
Hon. Gladys Flora, *b.* 1889 : *m.* 1911, George Victor Bellasis Charlton, who *d.* 1943, and has issue living, Eleanor Margaret Mary, *b.* 1912,—Anne Mary Georgina, *b.* 1913: *m.* 1948, Hugh Dougal Fyfe Baird, and has issue living, Rosemary Gillian *b.* 1950,—Joan Mary Winifrede, *b.* 1916: *m.* 1st, 1940, Ian Johnstone, Pilot Officer RAF, who *d.* (killed in action during European War) 1941; 2ndly, 1945, Harry James Hubert Ripper, Flying Officer, RAF, of Greys Cottage, Sible Hedingham, Essex, and has issue living, (by 2nd m.) Christopher James *b.* 1946, Judith Caroline *b.* 1949: *m.* 1971, Philip William Ford, and has issue living, Samantha Anne *b.* 1973,—Dorothy Mary Amy, *b.* 1919: *m.* 1958, Digby Michael Auden, of Dolphin House, Hardingstone, Northampton, and has issue living, Penelope Clare *b.* 1960,—Frances Mary Elizabeth, *b.* 1924: *m.* 1947, Stephen Louis Dudley Ripper, of Orchard House, High Street Green, Sible Hedingham, Halstead, Essex, and has issue living, Anne Mary Frances *b.* 1948, Susan Mary Margaret *b.* 1951, Catherine Mary Alison *b.* 1955: *m.* 1974, George Hales. *Residence,*—The Manor House, Great Harrowden, near Wellingborough, Northamptonshire.
Hon. Dorothy Alice MOSTYN, *b.* 1893; ed. at Bedford Coll., London (B.A. 1922) ; is a Religious of Institute of Christian Education. *Residence,*—Farnborough Hill Convent College, Farnborough, Hants.

COLLATERAL BRANCHES LIVING.
Grandchildren of the late Hon. Harold Plantagenet Mostyn, yr. brother of 7th Baron:—
   Issue of the late George Anthony Mostyn, *b.* 1898, *d.* 1972: *m.* 1924, Catharine Sibylla (50, Cranley Mews, SW7), da. of the late Bernard Henry Holland, CB [see V. Knutsford, colls.]:—
Richard Anthony (3, Flamingo Drive, Greenside, Umtali, Rhodesia), *b.* 1927; Lt. RN (ret.): *m.* 1961, Mary, da. of J. J. Michie, of Marian Hill, Natal, and has issue living, Anthony, Damian *b.* 1964,—Christopher Francis Joseph, *b.* 1966,—Nicola Mary, *b.* 1961,—Clare Sibylla, *b.* 1963.——Valentine Francis (50, Cranley Mews, SW7), *b.* 1943; ed. at Oxford Sch. of Architecture, and Canterbury Sch. of Architecture (Dip. Arch.); ARIBA: *m.* 1974, Gay, da. of H. Field (PO Box 1167, Malibo, Calif. 90265), and has issue living, Amy Clare, *b.* 1974.——Juliet Veronica, *b.* 1925: *m.* 1952, Anthony Lightfoot, of Valley Cottage, Brundish, nr. Woodbridge, Suffolk, and has issue living, Edward Jude, *b.* 1953,—Dominic Anthony, *b.* 1955,—Paul Jerome, *b.* 1956,—Mary Victoria, *b.* 1959,—Catherine Lucy, *b.* 1966.——Joan Elizabeth Verena, *b.* 1948: *m.* 1971, Anthony John Dyson.
   Descendants of the late Barbara Maria Mostyn, sister of 6th Baron, who *m.* 1833, Sir Frederick William Slade, Q.C., 2nd Bt.:—
See Slade, Bt.

PREDECESSORS.—[1] *Sir* NICHOLAS Vaux, a distinguished soldier and statesman, was summoned to Parliament of England as *Baron Vaux of Harrowden*, 1523 ; *d.* 1523 ; *s.* by his son [2] THOMAS, 2nd Baron ; *d.* 1562 ; *s.* by his son [3] WILLIAM, 3rd Baron ; was summoned to Parliament 1563-89 ; *d.* 1595 ; *s.* by his grandson [4] EDWARD, 4th Baron; summoned to Parliament 1620 ; *d.s.p.* 1661; *s.* by his brother [5] HENRY, 5th Baron ; *d.* unmarried 1662, when the barony became abeyant between his surviving sister Joyce, and the heirs of his sisters Mary (Lady Symeon) and Catherine (Baroness Abergavenny), and remained so until 1838, when the abeyance was terminated in favour of the heir of Mary, the el. sister [6] GEORGE Mostyn, 6th Baron, son of Mary Lucinda, née Butler, by her *m.* with Charles Browne-Mostyn, 2nd son of Sir Edward Mostyn, 5th Bt. ; *d.* 1883 ; *s.* by his grandson [7] HUBERT GEORGE CHARLES (el. son of the late Major the Hon. George Charles Mostyn), 7th Baron ; *b.* 1860 ; appointed Attache in Diplo. Ser. 1884, became a 3rd Sec. 1886, and a 2nd Sec. 1891 ; retired 1899 : *m.* 1st, 1886, Eleanor Margaret, who *d.* 1896, dau. of Sir Alexander Matheson, M.P., 1st Bt. ; 2ndly, 1902, Margaret Annette Jane Chichele, who *d.* 1922, dau. of the late Sir William Chichele Plowden, K.C.S.I. [Bass, Bt.]; 3rdly, 1924, Mary Winifride Teresa (Freyda), who *d.* 1944, dau. of Sir Joseph Edward Radcliffe, 4th Bt., and widow of Capt. Thomas Cecil de Trafford, Roy. Fusiliers [de Trafford, Bt., colls.] ; *d.* 1935, when the Barony again fell into abeyance between his three daus., and so remained until July 1938, when it was terminated by Letters Patent in favour of the el. [8] GRACE MARY ELEANOR Gilbey, *b.* 1887 : *m.* 1911, William Gordon Gilbey who *d.* 1965 ; *d.* 1958 ; *s.* by her el. son [9] *Rev.* PETER HUBERT GORDON, 9th Baron and present peer.

VENTRY, BARON. (Eveleigh-de-Moleyns.) [Baron I. 1800, Bt. I. 1797.]
[Name pronounced "Eevly-demmoleens."]

ARTHUR FREDERICK DAUBENEY OLAV EVELEIGH-DE-MOLEYNS, 7th Baron and 7th Baronet; *b.* July 28th, 1898; *s.* 1936; ed. at Wellington Coll.; 1914-18 War as Lt. Irish Gds. and RAF (wounded), 1939-45 War as Fl.-Lt. RAFVR; late Hon. Air Commodore No. 902 (co. London) (Balloon) Squadron, AAF; Freedom Medal of Norway.

Arms,—Quarterly, 1st and 4th sable, on a chief ermine three fusils gules; 2nd and 3rd per pale or and sable, two chevronels between three griffins passant counterchanged. **Crests,** —1st, a savage's head couped at the shoulders and affrontée, proper; 2nd, a goat's head erased, per chevron or and sable, attired of the 2nd, in the mouth a branch of laurel proper. **Supporters,**—Two lions or, ducally collared and chained azure.

VIVERE VINCERE SAT

To conquer is to live enough.
Residence,—Lindsay Hall, Lindsay Rd., Branksome, Dorset.

WIDOW LIVING OF BROTHER OF SIXTH BARON.
Marguerite, dau. of George Edward Noon: *m.* 1899, the Hon. John Gilbert Eveleigh-de-Moleyns, who *d.* 1928, and has issue living [see colls., infra]. *Residence,*—19, Linver Rd., SW6.

WIDOW LIVING OF SON OF SIXTH BARON
Olivia Phœbe, (317, The Water Gdns., Hyde Park, W2) da. of Capt. Percy Neave Leathers, of Fayre Cottage, Robertsbridge, Sussex, and widow of Lord John Victor Albert Blosse Conyngham, son of 6th Marquess Conyngham: *m.* 1963, as his 4th wife, the Hon. Francis Alexander Innys Eveleigh-Ross-de-Moleyns, who *d.* 1964.

COLLATERAL BRANCHES LIVING.
Issue of the late Hon. Francis Alexander Innys EVELEIGH-ROSS-DE-MOLEYNS, son of 6th Baron, *b.* 1901, *d.* 1964: *m.* 1st, 1925, Norah Caroline, who *d.* 1937, da. of Robert Hudson; 2ndly, 1938, Joan (who obtained a divorce 1952), el. da. of Harold Wesley, of The Wilderness, East Molesey, Surrey, and widow of Flight-Lt. H. G. Adams; 3rdly, 1954, Dorothy Mercado, who *d.* 1957, da. of Samuel Harvey, of London, and widow of Sir Charles Henry Augustus Frederick Lockhart Ross, 9th Bt.; 4thly, 1963, Olivia Phœbe (ante), da. of Capt. Percy Neave Leathers, of Fayre Cottage, Robertsbridge, Sussex, and widow of Lord John Victor Albert Blosse Conyngham, son of 6th Marquess Conyngham:—
(By 1st marriage) Valencia, *b.* 1928: *m.* 1950, Capt. Nathaniel Duncan Spry Grant-Dalton, R.A., and has issue living, Kevin Duncan Spry, *b.* 1952,—Miranda Jane, *b.* 1955.——(by 2nd marriage) ANDREW WESLEY DAUBENY DE MOLEYNS (Burnham House, Delny, Ross-shire), *b.* May 28th, 1943; assumed by deed poll 1966 the surname of Daubeny de Moleyns: *m.* 1963, Nelly Edouard Renée, da. of Abel Chaumillon, of Loma de los Riseos, Villa Angel, Torresmolinos, Malaga, Spain, and has issue living, Francis Wesley, *b.* 1965,—Elizabeth-Anne Stuart, *b.* 1964,—Brigitte, *b.* 1967.——Sally, *b.* 1940: *m.* 1964, Robin Hart, and has issue living, Christopher *b.* 1965,—Penelope, *b.* 1966,—Caroline, *b.* 1968,—Rachel, *b.* 1970.

Grandchildren of the late Hon. John Gilbert Eveleigh-de-Moleyns (infra):—
Issue of the late John Andrew WAUCHOPE, *b.* 1900, *d.* 1956, having assumed the surname of Wauchope in lieu of his patronymic 1945: *m.* 1923, Rosemary Eve (c/o Mackenzie & Black, W. S., 28, Castle Street, Edinburgh, 2), dau. of the late Rear-Adm. John Arthur Tuke:—
Andrew Dermod (Lochtower, Yetholm, Kelso), *b.* 1932: *m.* 1957, Jennifer Siggers, and has issue living, James Andrew, *b.* 1963,—Ian Simon (twin) *b.* 1963,—Fiona Jane, *b.* 1958,—Nicola Anne, *b.* 1959.——Brian Murray Xavier, *b.* 1936.——Œnone Eileen Frances, *b.* 1931: *m.* 1952, Timothy Robert Crum Willis, The Hill, Drumaness, Ballynahinch, co. Down, and has issue living.
Issue of the late Hon. John Gilbert Eveleigh-de-Moleyns, brother of 6th Baron, *b.* 1878, *d.* 1928: *m.* 1899, Marguerite (ante), dau of George Edward Noon:—
Eileen Mildred Alice, *b.* 1912: *m.* 1939, Harold Alan Coldham, LL.B., and has issue living, Simon Frederick Russell, *b.* 1940,—Christopher Alan, *b.* 1943,—Marie Audrey (twin), *b.* 1943. *Residence,*—Anmer House, Thornbury Rd., Osterley, Middlesex.

Granddaughter of the late Rev. William Bishop de Moleyns, 2nd son of the late Major the Hon. Edward de Moleyns, 5th son of 1st Baron:—
Issue of the late Rev. Alured Bayfield de Moleyns, *b.* 1851, *d.* 1925: *m.* 1888, Mary Louisa, who *d.* 1908, el. dau. of John Lyon (retired Fleet Paymaster, R.N.):—
Alice Louisa Eveleigh, *b.* 1889. *Residence.*—

PREDECESSORS.—[1] THOMAS MULLINS; cr. a *Baronet* 1797, and *Baron Ventry*, of Ventry, co. Kerry (peerage of Ireland) 1800; *d.* 1824; *s.* by his son [2] WILLIAM TOWNSEND, 2nd Baron; *d.* 1827; *s.* by his nephew [3] THOMAS TOWNSEND AREMBERG, 3rd Baron; *b.* 1786; resumed the ancient family name of De Moleyns by Roy. licence 1841: *m.* 1821, Eliza Theodora, dau. of Sir John Blake, 10th Bt.; *d.* 1868; *s.* by his son [4] DAYROLLES BLAKENEY, 4th Baron, *b.* 1828; a Representative Peer; assumed 1874 the additional surname and arms of Eveleigh: *m.* 1860, Harriet Elizabeth Frances, who *d.* 1906, dau. of Andrew Wauchope, of Niddrie Marischal, Midlothian; *d.* 1914; *s.* by his el. son [5] FREDERICK ROSSMORE WAUCHOPE, D.S.O., 5th Baron, *b.* 1861; *d.* 1923; *s.* by his brother [6] ARTHUR WILLIAM, 6th Baron, *b.* 1864: *m.* 1897, Evelyn Muriel Stuart, who *d.* 1966, dau. of Lansdowne Daubeney, of Norton Malreward, Somerset, *d.* 1936; *s.* by his el. son [7] ARTHUR FREDERICK DAUBENEY, 7th Baron and present peer.

This family descends from Col. Frederick Mullins of Burnham, Norfolk, who settled in Ireland about 1666, and M. Jane, da. and co-heir of the Very Rev. John Eveleigh, Dean of Ross. The Mullins family claim descent from the de Moleyns, though the descent remains to be proved. They may have taken their name from Moulins la Marche, Orne, Normandy; see Complete Peerage, Vol. IX, p. 43, for a note on the origin of this family.

Vere of Hanworth, Baron, grandson of Duke of St. Albans.

VERNON, BARON. (Venables-Vernon.) [Baron G.B. 1762.]

JOHN LAWRANCE VENABLES-VERNON, 10th
Baron; *b.* Feb. 1st, 1923; *s.* 1963; ed. at
Eton, and at Magdalen Coll., Oxford; Bar.
Lincoln's Inn 1949; a JP for Derbys.;
served in Cabinet Office 1953-57, Colonial
Office, Kenya 1957-58, and Foreign Office
1958-60; 1939-45 War as Capt. Scots Gds.:
m. 1955, Sheila Jean, yr. da. of W. Marshall
Clark, *OBE,* of Johannesburg, S. Africa, and
has issue.

Arms,—Quarterly: 1st and 4th grand quarters
quarterly 1st and 4th argent, a fret sable; 2nd and 3rd or,
on a fesse azure, three garbs of the field, *Vernon;* 2nd and
3rd azure, two bars argent, *Venables.* Crests,—1st, a
boar's head erased sable, ducally gorged or, *Vernon;* 2nd,
a wyvern, with wings endorsed, standing on a fish weir or
trap, devouring a child, and pierced through with an arrow
in fesse, all proper, *Venables.* Supporters,—*Dexter,* a
lion gules, collared, and chain reflexed over the back or;
sinister, a boar sable, ducally gorged, and chain reflexed
over the back or.

or
Ver non semper viret.
Vernon always flourishes ; or
The spring does not always flourish.

Seat,—Sudbury Hall, Derby.   Club,—Boodle's.

DAUGHTERS LIVING.

Hon. Georgina Frances, *b.* 1963.
Hon. Joanna Elizabeth, *b.* 1965.

AUNT LIVING. (*Daughter of 8th Baron.*)

Hon. Fanny Lawrance, *b.* 1886: *m.* 1st, 1910, Maurice Raoul-Duval, who *d.* (killed in action
at Verdun) 1916; 2ndly, 1918, Lieut. Jean de Kermaingant, and has issue living, (by 1st marriage) Alain, *b.* 19—,—Sonia : *m.* 1st, 19— (divorce 19—), Vicomte de Contades, of Mont Geoffroy,
Maine et Loire, France; 2ndly, 19—, Marquis de la Rozière,—Eliane: *m.* 19—, Comte d'Espoons.
Residence,—

WIDOW LIVING OF NINTH BARON.

VIOLET MIRIAM (*Violet, Baroness Vernon*) (Fishers, Mayfield, Tunbridge Wells), da. of the late Lt.-Col.
Charles Herbert Clay [Nightingale, Bt.]: *m.* 1915, the 9th Baron, who *d.* 1963.

COLLATERAL BRANCHES LIVING.

Granddaughter of the late Hon. William John Borlase-Warren-Venables-Vernon,
2nd son of 5th Baron:—
Issue of the late Reginald William Borlase-Warren-Venables-Vernon, *b.* 1856 *d.* 1912:
m. 1879, Edith Georgiana, dau. of William Smith Cowper Cooper, of Toddington
Park, Harlington, Beds:—
Mabel Eveline, *b.* 1883: *m.* 1909, Frank Southby Walker. *Residence,—*
Issue of the late Lewis HARCOURT [son of the late Rt. Hon. Sir William George
Granville Venables-Vernon-Harcourt, K.C., M.P.], who was cr. *Viscount Har-
court* 1917 [see that title].
Of whom WILLIAM EDWARD HARCOURT (*Viscount Harcourt*), *b.* Oct. 5th, 1908, is *h.p.* to the Barony
of Vernon.

Granddaughter of the late Rt. Hon. Sir William George Granville Venables-
Vernon-Harcourt, K.C., M.P., 2nd son of the late Rev. William Harcourt, 4th
son of the Most Rev. the Hon. Edward Harcourt, Archbishop of York, 3rd
son of 1st Baron:—
Issue of the late Robert Venables-Vernon-Harcourt, who discontinued the use of the
surnames of Venables-Vernon, *b.* 1878, *d.* 1962: *m.* 1911, Margorie Laura (of Malwood,
Lyndhurst, Hants., and 9, Headfort Place, S.W.1), dau. of the late William Samuel
Cunard [see Cunard, Bt., colls.]:—
Mary Elizabeth, *b.* 1922: *m.* 1950, Com. Ian Rochfort Johnston, R.N., of 8, Pembroke Gardens Close,
W.8, and has issue living, Sarah Elizabeth, *b.* 1956,—Laura Catherine, *b.* 1960.

Grandchildren of the late Augustus George Vernon-Harcourt, FRS, el. son of Adm.
Frederick Edward Vernon-Harcourt (infra):—
Issue of the late Simon Evelyn Vernon-Harcourt, *b.* 1882, *d.* 1966: *m.* 1916, Dorothy
Margaret, MBE (60, Burton Court, SW3), da. of the late Sir Robert Hudson, GBE:—
Robert (Theydon Mount, Epping, Essex), *b.* 1918; ed. at Marlborough, and Ch. Ch., Oxford (MA);
1939-45 War as Capt. RTR: *m.* 1948, Sylvia Jeanette, da. of the late Lt.-Col. Charles Henry Kitch-
ing, DSO.——Anne, *b.* 1925.

Grandchildren of the late Leveson Francis Vernon-Harcourt, MICE, 2nd son of
Adm. Frederick Edward Vernon-Harcourt (infra):—
Issue of the late Leveson William Vernon-Harcourt, *b.* 1871, *d.* 1909: *m.* 1899, Rose Adelaide
(who *d.* 1959, having *m.* 2ndly, 1914, Matthew Liddell, who *d.* 1934), dau. of Frederick
Lawrence:—
William Ronald Denis, *OBE* (posthumous), *b.* 1909; ed. at Eton, and at Magdalene Coll., Camb.
(BA 1930); Col. (ret.) late S. Wales Borderers; Civil Defence Officer, S.-E. Hants. 1958-68; Burma
1941-42 (despatches); OBE (Mil.) 1947: *m.* 1937, Nancy Everil, only child of the late Lt.-Col.
Bertram Henry Leatham, DSO, and has issue living, Anthony William (Monks Farm, Debden Green,
Saffron Walden, Essex), *b.* 1939: *m.* 1966, Cherry Stanhope, da. of Thomas Corbin, of Lime Tree
House, Spaldwick, Hunts., and has issue living, Simon Anthony *b.* 1969, Edward William *b.* 1973,
Charlotte Lucy *b.* 1968,—Anne Dorothy (12, Three Acres, Denmead, Hants.), *b.* 1945: *m.* 1967
(*m.* diss. 1974), Nicholas Bloxam, and has issue living, Richard William *b.* 1971. *Residence,—*
Pipers Hill, Denmead, Hants.——(Rose Mary) Dorothy, *b.* 1900: *m.* 1st, 1922, the Hon. Frederick
Somerset Gough-Calthorpe, only son of 8th Baron Calthorpe, who *d.* 1935; 2ndly, 1949, Lt.-Col.
Guy Alexander Ingram Drury, MC, late Grenadier Guards. *Residence,—*Siggswood, Waldron,
E. Sussex.

Granddaughters of the late Adm. Frederick Edward Vernon-Harcourt, 5th son of
the late Most Rev. the Hon. Edward Harcourt (ante):—
Issue of the late Augustus George Vernon-Harcourt, F.R.S., *b.* 1834, *d.* 1919: *m.* 1872, the
Hon. Rachel Mary Bruce, who *d.* 1927, dau. of 1st Baron Aberdare:—
Winifred, Rachel *b.* 1886: *m.* 1913, Herbert John Schiele, who *d.* 1919, and has issue living, Rachel
b. 1914,—Pamela, *b.* 1918. *Residence,—*3, Brookside, Headington, Oxford.
Issue of the late Leveson Francis Vernon-Harcourt, M.I.C.E., *b.* 1839, *d.* 1907: *m.* 1870,
Alice, who *d.* 1919, dau. of the late Lieut.-Col. Henry Rowland Brandeth, R.E.:—
Violet Mary, *b.* 1883: *m.* 1911, John Pascoe Elsden, Bar.-at-law, who *d.* 1950, and has issue living

John Anthony, *b.* 1911: *m.* 1943, Patrick Carton, and has issue living, Noel Anthony *b.* 1953, Diana *b.* 1947,—Richard William Hilary (of Glimpses, Cookham, Berks) (twin), *b.* 1911: *m.* 1950, Maureen Elizabeth, da. of George Gerard Shiel, and has issue living, Sarah Amanda *b.* 1952, Susan Elizabeth *b.* 1954. *Residence,—*

Grandchildren of the late Rev. Evelyn Hardolph Harcourt-Vernon, son of the late Granville Harcourt-Vernon, son of the late Most Rev. the Hon. Edward Harcourt (ante):—

Issue (by 2nd marriage) of the late Edward Evelyn Harcourt-Vernon, *b.* 1853, *d.* 1932 : *m.* 1st, 1879, Grace, who *d.* 1881, dau. of the late Rev. Alleyne FitzHerbert [Fitz-Herbert, Bt.] ; 2ndly, 1883, Frances Theresa, who *d.* 1937, dau. of Sir William FitzHerbert, 4th Bt.:—

Egerton Gervase Edward, *MC* (of Polmood, Cranbrook, Kent), *b.* 1899; ed. at Eton; Capt. Grenadier Gds.; 1914-18 War in France (MC, two medals), 1939-45 War: *m.* 1932, Norma, da. of H. Hatherly, and has issue living, Anne Letitia, *b.* 1933,—Pamela Teresa Marygold, *b.* 1938; ed. at Bedgebury Park, Medway Coll. of Tech. (BSc London) and Newnham Coll., Camb. (MA): *m.* 1961, Antony Dawson Cox, MRCP, of 4, Court Lane Gdns., SE21, and has issue living, Simon *b.* 1962, Nicholas *b.* 1964, Hugo Francis *b.* 1967,—Rosalind Elizabeth Ida, *b.* 1942: *m.* 1966, Christopher Howell, of 22, Bencombe Rd., Marlow Bottom, Marlow-on-Thames, Bucks. and has issue living, Candida Justine *b.* 1969.

Issue of the late Rev. Algernon Hardolph Harcourt-Vernon, *b.* 1858, *d.* 1936 : *m.* 1st, 1881, Kate, who *d.* 1883, dau. of J. Caudler ; 2ndly, 1886, Georgina Marguerite, who *d.* 1951, dau. of the late John Martin :—

(By 2nd m.) Dorothy Margaret, *b.* 1887. *Residence,*—Loquats, Ficksburg, Orange Free State, S. Africa.——Marjorie Frances, *b.* 1891: *m.* 1924, Ritchie Francis Henry Moffett, Lt. S. African Air Force, who *d.* 1957. *Residence,—*

Grandchildren of the late Herbert Evelyn Harcourt-Vernon, yst. son of the late Rev. Evelyn Hardolph Harcourt-Vernon (ante):—
Issue of the late Arthur Arundel Harcourt—Vernon, *b.* 1895, *d.* 1971: *m.* 1925, Alice Margaret (137, Heddington Av., Toronto 12, Canada), da. of the late Rev. Edward Cartwright Cayley [see Cayley, Bt., colls.]:—
Granville Patrick (57, Glengowan Rd., Toronto 12, Canada), *b.* 1926: *m.* 1954, Deborah Perry Smith, and has issue living, Geoffrey William, *b.* 1958,—Catherine, *b.* 1956,—Susan Elizabeth, *b.* 1961.——Hugh (24, Dunbar Rd., Toronto 5, Ont., Canada), *b.* 1930: *m.* 1953, Elizabeth Virginia Richardson, and has issue living, Christopher Hugh, *b.* 1956,—Nancy Margaret, *b.* 1960,—Tannis Elizabeth, *b.* 1964.——John Anthony, *b.* 1938.——Joy, *b.* 1934.——Rosemary, *b.* 1935: *m.* 1960, the Rev. John Francis Moorhead (Box 284, Plaster Rock, New Brunswick, Canada), and has issue living, Margaret Patricia, *b.* 1961,—Nancy Catherine, *b.* 1967,—Cynthia Mabel, *b.* 1970.

PREDECESSORS.—[1] GEORGE Vernon, son of Henry Vernon of Sudbury, Derby, and Anne, dau. and heir of Thomas Pigott by Mary, sister and heir of Sir Peter Venables, Baron of Kinderton, Cheshire; M.P. for Lichfield; assumed in 1728 by Roy. licence the additional surname of Venables and in 1762 was cr. *Baron Vernon, Baron of Kinderton,* co. Chester (peerage of Great Britain), *d.* 1780; *s.* by his el. son [2] GEORGE, 2nd Baron; sat as M.P. for Glamorganshire 1774; *d.* 1818; *s.* by his half-brother [3] HENRY, 3rd Baron; *d.* 1829; *s.* by his son [4] GEORGE CHARLES, 4th Baron; *d.* 1838; *s.* by his son [5] GEORGE JOHN, 5th Baron; *b.* 1803; assumed in 1837 by sign manual the surname of Warren only for himself and subsequent issue; *d.* 1866; *s.* by his son [6] AUGUSTUS HENRY, 6th Baron; *b.* 1829: *m.* 1851, Lady Harriet Frances Maria Anson, who *d.* 1898, dau. of 1st Earl of Lichfield: *d.* 1883; *s.* by his son [7] GEORGE WILLIAM HENRY, *P.C.,* 7th Baron, *b.* 1854; Capt. Hon. Corps of Gentlemen-at-Arms 1892-4: *m.* 1885, Frances Margaret, who *d.* 1940, dau of Francis Lawrance, of New York; *d.* 1898; *s.* by his el. son [8] GEORGE FRANCIS AUGUSTUS, 8th Baron, *b.* 1888; *d.* (while on active service as Capt. Derbyshire Yeo. during European War) 1915; *s.* by his brother [9] FRANCIS WILLIAM LAWRANCE, 9th Baron; *b.* 1889; Lt.-Cdr. R.N.: *m.* 1915, Violet Miriam Nightingale, dau. of the late Lt.-Col. Charles Herbert Clay; *d.* 1963; *s.* by his only son [10] JOHN LAWRANCE, 10th Baron and present peer.

VERULAM, EARL OF. (Grimston.) [Earl U.K. 1815, Bt. E. 1629.]

JOHN DUNCAN GRIMSTON, 7th Earl and 14th Baronet; *b.* April 21st, 1951; *s.* 1973; ed. at Eton, and Ch. Ch., Oxford, a patron of six livings.

Arms,—Quarterly : 1st and 4th argent, on a fesse sable, three rowels of six points or pierced gules ; in the dexter chief an ermine spot sable, *Grimston ;* 2nd sable, a fesse dancettée between two leopards' faces or, *Luckyn ;* 3rd argent, three bugle horns sable, stringed gules, *Forrester.* Crest,— A stag's head erased proper, attired or. Supporters, —*Dexter,* a stag reguardant proper, attired or; *sinister,* a griffin reguardant or.

Seat,—Gorhambury, St. Albans, Herts.

SISTERS LIVING.

Lady ELISABETH HARIOT (*Elisabeth, Viscountess Pollington*), *b.* 1939; *h.p.* to Lordship of Forrester of Corstorphine: *m.* 1958, Viscount Pollington, from whom she obtained a divorce 1972, el. son of 7th Earl of Mexborough.

Lady Hermione Frances, *b.* 1941: *m.* 1st, 1965, (m. diss 1971) Richard John Perronet Thompson; 2ndly, 1971, James Darell Dickson Thompson-Schwab, of Kingfield, Penton, Carlisle, Cumberland.

Lady Romayne Bryony, *b.* 1946: *m.* 1973, John Roberts Bockstoce, of West Hartford, Connecticut, USA.

Moderate things are stable.

Lady Iona Charlotte, *b.* 1953.

MEDIOCRIA FIRMA

WIDOW LIVING OF SIXTH EARL.

MARJORIE RAY (*Countess of Verulam*), (Gorhambury, St. Albans, Herts.), da. of the late Walter Atholl Duncan: *m.* 1938, the 6th Earl, who *d.* 1973.

COLLATERAL BRANCHES LIVING.

(*In remainder to Lordship of Forrester of Corstorphine only*)
Issue of the late Lady Helen Grimston, el. da. of 3rd Earl, *b.* 1879, *d.* 1947: *m.* 1908, the Rt. Hon. Sir Felix Cassel, 1st Bt., who *d.* 1953:—
[see Cassel, Bt.]
Issue of the late Lady Hermione Grimston, 2nd da. of 3rd Earl, *b.* 1881, *d.* 1924: *m.* 1904, Cdr. Bernard Buxton, DSO, RN, who *d.* 1923:—
[see Buxton, Bt., colls.]
Issue of the late Lady Aline Grimston, 3rd da. of 3rd Earl, *b.* 1883, *d.* 1972: *m.* 1907, Maj. Geoffrey Arthur Barnett, MBE [B. Ormathwaite], who *d.* 1957:—
Peter Cedric (Prae Wood House, St. Albans), *b.* 1910; ed. at Eton, and Magdalen Coll., Oxford; late Capt.: *m.* 1941, Sylvia Kenny, OBE, and has issue living, Ulric David, *b.* 1942; ed. at Eton, and Magdalen Coll., Oxford: *m.* 1969, Marie-Jane, da. of Capt. de Frégate Jean Levasseur, and has issue living, Rory Nicholas *b.* 1971,—Patricia, *b.* 1945: *m.* 1968, Oscar Jorge Potier, of 59, Hyde Park Gate, SW7, and has issue living, Rupert Alexander *b.* 1969,—Susan, *b.* 1947: *m.* 1967, Capt. Charles Temple Blackwood, late Gren. Gds. [V. Torrington, colls.], of Brickworth Park, Whiteparish, Salisbury, and has issue living, James Temple *b.* 1969, Jonathan Charles *b.* 1971.——Yvonne Frances (*Hon. Mrs. Charles S. Vereker*), *b.* 1913: *m.* 1938, the Hon. Charles Standish Vereker, who *d.* 1941, only son of 6th Viscount Gort.

Issue of the late Lady Elizabeth Grimston, 4th da. of 3rd Earl, *b.* 1885, *d.* 1975: *m.* 1st, 1908, Maj. Hesketh Vernon Hesketh-Pritchard, DSO, MC, who *d.* 1922; 2ndly, 1927, Maj. Thomas Augustus Motion, JP, who *d.* 1942:—
(By 1st m.) Michael (Low Hall, Seathwaite, Broughton-in-Furness, Lancs.) *b.* 1909; ed. at Fettes; Maj. (ret.) RA: *m.* 1938, Venetia Alice, da. of the late Sir Frederick Daniel Green, and has issue living, Richard Michael (Steel's Farmhouse, Stock, Essex), *b.* 1939: *m.* 1965, Elizabeth Susan, da. of John Cuthbert Ottaway, MBE, TD, of Beech Bottom, St. Albans, and has issue living, James Michael *b.* 1966, Thomas Richard Edward *b.* 1969, Rebecca Sophie Venetia *b.* 1971,—Cicely Elizabeth Theodosia, *b.* 1942: *m.* 1966, Martin Charles Jacoby, MA, FLS, of Hill Cottage, Thurloxton, Taunton, and has issue living, Charles John *b.* 1967, Katherine Venetia *b.* 1970,—Venetia, *b.* 1948; ed. at Trin. Coll., Dublin (BA): *m.* 1972, David Richard Lascelles, of 29 Inkermann Rd., NW5.——(By 2nd m.), Joan Elizabeth Mary, *b.* 1929; ed. at St. Anne's Coll., Oxford; JP: *m.* 1958, Murray Stuart Smith QC, of Serge Hill, Abbots Langley, Herts., and has issue living, Jeremy Hugh, *b.* 1955; ed. at Radley,—Mark, *b.* 1958,—Thomas Richard Steven Peregrine, *b.* 1960,—Katherine, *b.* 1957,—Jane, *b.* 1961,—Elizabeth (twin), *b.* 1961.

Issue of the late Lady Sibyl Grimston, 5th da. of 3rd Earl, *b.* 1887, *d.* 1968: *m.* 1915, Maj. the Hon. Alastair Thomas Joseph Fraser, DSO, who *d.* 1949:—
[see L. Lovat, colls.]
Issue of the late Lady Vera Grimston, SRN, yst. da. of 3rd Earl, *b.* 1890, *d.* 1970: *m.* 1922, Maurice Francis Headlam, CB, CMG, who *d.* 1956:—
Anthony Francis (42, Cadogan Sq., SW1), *b.* 1923; ed. at Eton (KS), and King's Coll., Camb. (Scholar); 1939-45 War with KRRC: *m.* 1956, Jill Caroline, da. of the late Bruce R. Campbell, of Sydney, Aust., and has issue living, Hugh Francis, *b.* 1960,—Caroline Ann, *b.* 1963.——Christopher Grimston (Dallachie, Fearn, Ross-shire), *b.* 1925; ed. at Eton (KS), and King's Coll., Camb. (Scholar); 1939-45 War with RNVR: *m.* 1959, Sarah, da. of the late Sir John Richard Hobhouse, MC, and has issue living, Thomas Walter, *b.* 1962,—Catherine Sophia, *b.* 1960.——James Nicholas, *b.* 1926; ed. at Eton, and New Coll., Oxford (Scholar): *m.* 1966, Elizabeth Jane, da. of Sir Peter William Shelley Yorke Scarlett, KCMG, KCVO, and has issue living,—Anthony John Nicholas, *b.* 1969,—Fenella Jane, *b.* 1967,—Mary Amelia, *b.* 1973.

(*Male line in remainder to all peerages*).

Issue of the late Rev. Canon the Hon. Robert Grimston, 3rd son of 2nd Earl *b.* 1860, *d.* 1927; *m.* 1896, Gertrude Mary Amelia, who *d.* 1949, dau. of the late Rev. Charles Villiers, R. of Croft, Yorks.:—

Sir ROBERT VILLIERS (*Baron Grimston of Westbury*), *b.* 1897; *cr.* a Baronet 1952, and *Baron Grimston of Westbury* 1964 [see that title]; *h.p.* to Earldom of Verulam.——Violet Gwendolen, *b.* 1903: *m.* 1926, Lt.-Col. Arthur William Acland, OBE, MC, TD, Gren. Gds. [see Acland, Bt., cr., 1890, colls.]. *Residence*,—Yeoman's, 4, Queens Rd., Cowes, Isle of Wight, PO31 8BQ.

Grandson of the late George Sylvester Grimston, son of the late Rev. the Hon. Francis Sylvester Grimston, 5th son of 1st Earl:—
Issue of the late Francis Sylvester Grimston, OIE, *b.* 1876, *d.* 1969: *m.* 1907, Eleanor Vincent, who *d.* 1960, da. of the late Arthur W. L. Reddie:—
Francis Brian Sylvester (c/o National Westminster Bank, 63, Piccadilly, W1; Royal Thames & Ocean Racing Clubs), *b.* 1908; ed. Cheltenham; late S/Ldr. RAFVR: *m.* 1940 (m. diss. 1954) Monica Katherine, da. of the late Col. the Hon. Sir Maurice Charles Andrew Drummond, KBE, CMG, DSO [see E. Perth].

PREDECESSORS.—[1] WILLIAM Luckyn (*M.P.* for St. Albans), great-nephew of Sir Samuel Grimston, 3rd Bt. (*ext.*), whose surname he assumed on succeeding to the estates, was cr. *Baron Dunboyne* and *Viscount Grimston* (peerage of Ireland) 1719, and in 1736 *s.* his brother as 5th Bt. (cr. 1629); *d.* 1756; *s.* by his son [2] JAMES, 2nd Viscount; *d.* 1773; *s.* by his son [3] JAMES BUCKNALL, 3rd Viscount; *cr.* *Baron Verulam*, of Gorhambury, co. Herts (peerage of Great Britain) 1790; *d.* 1809; *s.* by his son [4] JAMES WALTER, 4th Viscount, who in 1808 had *s.* his maternal cousin Anna Maria as 10th *Lord Forrester of Corstorphine* (see *.*.* infra) ; *b.* 1775; M.P. for St. Albans 1802-8; Lord-Lieut. of co. Herts; cr. *Earl of Verulam* (peerage of United Kingdom) 1815: *m.* 1807, Lady Charlotte Jenkinson, dau. of 1st Earl of Liverpool; *d.* 1845; *s.* by his son [5] JAMES WALTER, 2nd Earl, *b.* 1809; M.P. for St. Albans (C) 1830, for Newport 1831; and for Hertfordshire 1832-45; a Lord-in-Waiting to H.M. Queen Victoria 1852 and 1858-9, sometime Lord-Lieut. of Herts : *m.* 1844, Elizabeth Joanna, who *d.* 1886, dau. of Richard Weyland, of Woodeaton, Oxford ; *d.* 1895 ; *s.* by his el. son [6] JAMES WALTER, 3rd Earl, *b.* 1852 ; M.P. for Mid., or St. Albans, Div. of Herts (C) 1885-92 : *m.* 1878, Margaret Frances, who *d.* 1927, dau. of Sir Frederic Ulric Graham, 3rd Bt., of Netherby ; *d.* 1924 ; *s.* by his son [7] JAMES WALTER, 4th Earl, *b.* 1880 : *m.* 1909, Lady Violet Constance Maitland Brabazon, who *d.* 1936, dau. of 12th Earl of Meath ; *d.* 1949 ; *s.* by his son [8] JAMES BRABAZON, 5th Earl ; *b.* 1910 ; Mayor of St. Albans 1956-7 ; *d.* 1960 ; *s.* by his brother JOHN [9] 6th Earl and present peer ; also Viscount Grimston, Baron Verulam, Baron Dunboyne, and Lord Forrester of Corstorphine.

.[1] GEORGE Forrester of Corstorphine, Midlothian, el. son of Henry Forrester of Corstorphine ; cr. *Lord Forrester of Corstorphine* (peerage of Scotland) 1633, with remainder to his heirs male whatsoever ; on the death of his only son without issue, he resigned his peerage and obtained a re-grant thereof 1651 with remainder to James Baillie, husband of his fifth dau. Joanna and their issue in tail male, remainder to William Baillie, husband of Lilias his sixth and youngest dau. and their issue in tail male, remainder to the issue of James and William by their said wives, in tail general, the el. dau. of such issue to be heir of line, with a final remainder to James Baillie and his heirs male or of entail made by him, all parties to bear the name and arms of Forrester jointly with

his own : *m.* 1606, Christian, dau. of Sir William Livingston of Kilsyth ; *d.* 1652 ; *s.* by his son-in-law [2] JAMES Baillie (afterwards Forrester), 2nd Lord ; *b.* 1629 ; was fined £2,500 under Cromwell's Act of Grace 1654 : *m.* 1st, 1649, Joanna, dau. of 1st Lord Forrester of Corstorphine (ante) ; 2ndly, 1661, Janet, 3rd dau. and co-heir of Patrick Ruthven, 1st Earl of Forth and Brentford ; *d.* 1679 ; *s.* by his brother [3] WILLIAM, *de jure* 3rd Lord ; *b.* 1632 ; did not assume the title : *m.* circa 1650 Lilias, youngest dau. of 1st Lord Forrester of Corstorphine (ante) ; *d.* 1681 ; *s.* by his son [4] WILLIAM, 4th Lord ; *b.* 16— : *m.* circa 1684, Margaret, dau. of Sir Andrew Birnie, of Saline, Judge of Court of Session ; *d.* 1705 ; *s.* by his son [5] GEORGE, 5th Lord ; *b.* 1688 ; Lt.-Col. 26th Foot (Cameronians), and Col. 30th Foot, and of Horse Grenadier Guards : *m.* circa 1724, Charlotte, who *d.* 1743, dau. of Anthony Rowe ; *d.* 1727 ; *s.* by his son [6] GEORGE, 6th Lord ; *b.* 1724 ; Capt. R.N. ; *d.* unm. 1748 ; *s.* by his cousin [7] WILLIAM (son of Capt. the Hon. John Forrester, R.N., youngest son of 4th Lord), 7th Lord ; *b.* 17— : *m.* 17—, Hannah —, who *d.* 1825 ; *d.* 1763 ; *s.* by his cousin [8] CAROLINE, el. sister of 6th Lord (who *s.* under terms of special remainder) ; *b.* 17— : *m.* 17—, Capt. George Cockburn of Ormiston, RN ; *d.* 1784 ; *s.* by her dau. [9] ANNA MARIA : *b.* 17— ; *d.* unm. 1808 ; *s.* by her cousin [10] JAMES WALTER Grimston, son of James Buckna, Grimston, 3rd Viscount Grimston, by Harriet, da. and heir of Edward Walter, and Hon. Harriol Forrester, youngest dau. of 5th Lord, who in 1809 *s.* as 4th Viscount Grimston (ante).

VESTEY, BARON. (Vestey.) [Baron U.K. 1922, Bt. U.K. 1913.]

From labour stability.

SAMUEL GEORGE ARMSTRONG VESTEY, 3rd Baron, and 3rd Baronet ; *b.* March 19th, 1941 ; *s.* 1954 ; ed. at Eton ; is Lt. Scots Gds.; patron of one living: *m.* 1970, Kathryn Mary, el. da. of John Eccles, of Moor Park, Herts., and has issue.

Arms,—Azure, in base barry wavy of four argent and of the first an iceberg issuant proper, on a chief of the second three eggs also proper. Crest.—In front of a springbok's head couped at the neck proper three mullets fessewise azure. Supporters,—Dexter, a sheep proper ; sinister, a bull argent.

Residence,—Stowell Park, Gloucestershire.

DAUGHTER LIVING
Hon. Saffron Alexandra, *b.* 1971.

BROTHER LIVING.
(*Raised to the rank of a Baron's younger son* 1955.)
Hon. MARK WILLIAM (Stowell Park, Glos.), *b.* April 16th, 1943 ; ed. at Eton ; 2nd Lt. Scots Guards: *m.* 1975, Rose Amelia, da. of Lt.-Col. Peter Thomas Clifton, DSO [see Bruce, Bt., cr. 1804].

AUNTS LIVING. (*Daughters of 2nd Baron*).
Hon. Kathleen Sarah, *b.* 1909: *m.* 1st, 1928, Maj. Philip Wilfrid Cripps, KRRC, who *d.* 1965, having obtained a divorce 1936 ; 2ndly, 1936, Capt. Maurice John Kingscote, who *d.* 1959, having obtained a divorce 1942 [B.Gifford]; 3rdly, 1942, Major Geoffrey Harbord, MC, who *d.* 1953 ; 4thly, 1955, Com. William Canning Eykyn, RN (ret.), who *d.* 1972, and has issue living, (by 1st m.) Michael William Philip (of Barn Hill, Ewhurst, near Cranleigh, Surrey), *b.* 1930; formerly Lt. RN : *m.* 1952, Belinda J., da. of the late Major Angus Arthur Ferguson, of Auchencairn, Castle Douglas, and has issue living, Giles William Michael *b.* 1956, Matthew Frederick Philip *b.* 1958, Adrian Angus *b.* 1961, Sophie Sarah *b.* 1954, Louisa Jane *b.* 1963. *Residences,*—The Long Cottage, Sandwich, Kent; 8, Ennismore Gdns., SW7 1NL.

Hon. Joan Frances, *M.B.E.*, *b.* 1914 ; sometime Lieut. First Aid Nursing Yeo.: M.B.E. (Civil) 1946 : *m.* 1st, 1934, Major John Hammon Paine, formerly King's Roy. Rifle Corps, who obtained a divorce 1944 ; 2ndly, 1954, John Lindesay Compton Shedden, and has issue living, (by 1st m.) Christopher Hammon (Dame Alice Farm, Watlington, Oxon., and Wellshead, Exford, nr. Minehead), *b.* 1935; ed. at Eton, and at Oxford Univ. (MA, BM and BCh); MRCP London; FFR England: *m.* 1959, Susan, da. of the late Dr. Martin, of Bridgwater, and has issue living, Edward Hammon *b.* 1960, Simon John Hammon *b.* 1964, Lucy Hammon *b.* 1962, Alice Sarah *b.* 1968. *Residences,*—The Manor, Fossebridge, Glos.; Greenhill Farm, Chedworth, Glos.

MOTHER LIVING. (*Raised to the rank of a Baron's Widow* 1955.)
(HELEN) PAMELA FULLERTON (MELBA) (*Pamela, Baroness Vestey*), da. of the late George Nesbitt Armstrong [see Armstrong, Bt., cr. 1841, colls.]: *m.* 1939, Capt. the Hon. William Howarth Vestey, Scots Guards, who *d.* (killed in action in Italy) 1944. *Residence,*—Coombe Cottage, Coldstream, Vic., Australia.

COLLATERAL BRANCHES LIVING.
Issue of the late Hon. George Ellis Vestey, 2nd son of 1st Baron, *b.* 1884, *d.* 1968: *m.* 1909, Florence May, who *d.* 1964, da. of Thomas Webster, of Melling, Lancs.:—
Florence Mary, *b.* 1913: *m.* 1945, Anthony Hugh Stevens, TD, late Maj. RA, of Old Place, Harpsden, Henley-on-Thames, and has issue living, Hugh Charles, *b.* 1946; ed. at Winchester, and Univ. of Michigan (BA): *m.* 1972, Nicola Priscilla, da. of John Bridgman, of Prestbury, Cheshire,—Angela Mary, *b.* 1948: *m.* 1972, Aubrey John Adams.——Norah, *b.* 1916: *m.* 1944, Maj. William Bellingham Denis Dobbs, R. Ulster Rifles (ret.), of Kilgarron, Enniskerry, co. Wicklow, and has issue living, George Denis Kildare, *b.* 1947.——Rosemary Florence, *b.* 1944: *m.* 1971, David Michael Cochrane Elsworth Steen [see Cochrane, Bt.],—Susan Norah, *b.* 1951.——Alice (Appleton House, Appleton-le-Street, Malton, N. Yorks., YO17 0PG, *b.* 1918: *m.* 1st, 1939, William Ernest Legard, F/O, RAF, who *d.* (killed in action) 1940 [see Legard, Bt., colls.]; 2ndly, 1943, Col. Basil Perry Beale, OBE, MC, DL, RASC, who *d.* 1967, and has issue living, (by 1st m.) Richard Basil William, *b.* 1944,—Stephen Dudley Norman, *b.* 1950: *m.* 1972, Elizabeth Helen, da. of Peter Green, of The Rookery, Kirkby Malham, Skipton, Yorks., and has issue living, Zoë Helen *b.* 1973,—Elizabeth Alice, *b.* 1947.

Issue of the late Hon. Leonard Vestey, 3rd son of 1st Baron, *b.* 1888, *d.* 1954: *m.* 1st, 1919, Hilda Dorothy (who *d.* 1943, having obtained a divorce 1931), da. of Thomas Thompson; 2ndly, 1931, Eleanor Margery (who *d.* 1972, having *m.* 3rdly, 1955, Dr. Richard Taylor, and 4thly, 19—, Frank Fisher), widow of Capt. F. W. H. Simpson , RA:—

(By 1st m.) Joyce (19, Elamang Av., Kirribilli, Sydney, NSW 2061), b. 1920: m. 1st, 1949 (m. diss. 1953), Henry Willis Maxwell Telling; 2ndly, 1966, Dr. Thomas Hugh Strong, and has issue living, (by 1st m.) Michael Henry Maxwell, b. 1950.——Elizabeth Anne (26, Eldon Rd., W8), b. 1923: m. 1946 (m. diss. 1962), Lt.-Cdr. Patrick Brougham, RN, and has issue living, Christopher John (129, Chiltern Court, Baker St., NW1 5ST), b. 1947; ed. at Radley, and Worcester Coll., Oxford (BA); Bar. Inner Temple 1969: m. 1974, Mary Owen, da. of Timothy Traherne Corker, of 19, Park St. East, NW1,—Nicholas Dominic Leonard, b. 1954; ed. at Radley,—Margaret Elizabeth Jane, b. 1948: m. 1970, Hugh Robert John Simpson, of 184, Bourne Vale, Hayes, Bromley, Kent, and has issue living, Antony John b. 1972, Tracey Jane b. 1975.

PREDECESSORS.—[1] WILLIAM Vestey, el. son of Samuel Vestey, of Liverpool; b. 1859; was Joint Head of Blue Star Line; cr. a *Baronet* 1913, and *Baron Vestey*, of Kingswood, co. Surrey (peerage of United Kingdom) 1922: m. 1st, 1882, Sarah, who d. 1923, dau. of George Ellis; 2ndly, 1924, Evelyn, who d. 1941, dau. of H. Brodstone, of Superior, Nebraska, U.S.A.; d. 1940; s. by his el. son [2] SAMUEL, 2nd Baron; b. 1882; High Sheriff of Gloucestershire 1933: m. 1908, Frances Sarah, who d. 1969, da. of John Richard Howarth, of Freshfield, Lancs.; d. 1954; s. by his grandson [ ] SAMUEL GEORGE ARMSTRONG (son of the late Capt. the Hon. William Howarth Vestey, only son of 2nd Baron), 3rd Baron and present peer.

VICKERS, BARONESS. (Vickers.) [Life Baroness 1974.]

JOAN HELEN VICKERS, *DBE*, da. of the late Horace Cecil Vickers; b. 1907; ed. at St. Monica's Coll., Burgh Heath, Surrey; Member of LCC 1937-45; with Colonial Office 1946-49; Chm. of Anglo-Indonesian Soc., and of Status of Women Cttee., and Pres. Internat. Bureau for Suppression of Traffic in Persons; Pres. Inst. for Qualified Private Secretaries since 1969, and Internat. Friendship League since 1972; MP for Devonport (*C*) 1955-74; BRCS in S-E Asia (MBE), Netherlands Red Cross Medal 1946, and Polish Medal 1972; cr. MBE (Civil) 1946, DBE (Civil) 1964, and *Baroness Vickers*, of Devonport, co. Devon (Life Baroness) 1974.
Residence,—6, Albermarle Villas, Devonport, Devon.

Villiers, Viscount, son of Earl of Jersey.

VIVIAN, BARON. (Vivian.) [Baron U.K. 1841, Bt. U.K. 1828.]

ANTHONY CRESPIGNY CLAUD VIVIAN, 5th Baron, and 5th Baronet; b. March 4th, 1906; s. 1940; ed. at Eton; European War 1939-40 in R.A.: m. 1930, Victoria Ruth Mary Rosamond, dau. of Capt. Henry Gerard Laurence Oliphant, D.S.O., M.V.O., R.N., and has issue.

Arms,—Or, on a chevron azure, between three lions' heads erased proper, as many annulets gold; on a chief embattled gules, a wreath of oak or, between two medals, that on the dexter representing the gold medal and clasp given to the first baron for his services in the actions of Sahagun, Benevente and Orthes; and that on the sinister the silver Waterloo medal. **Crest,**—Issuant from a bridge of one arch embattled, and having at each end a tower, a demi-hussar in the uniform of the 18th Regt. holding in his right hand a sabre, and in his left a pennon flying to the sinister gules, and inscribed with gold letters, "Croix d'Orade." **Supporters,**—*Dexter,* a grey horse caparisoned, thereon mounted a hussar of the 7th Regt. of Light Dragoons (Hussars) habited, armed and accoutred, his sword drawn proper; *sinister,* a bay horse guardant, caparisoned, thereon mounted a lancer of the 12th Regt. of Lancers, habited, armed and accoutred, supporting his lance, also proper.

Live, as one about to live hereafter.

Residence,—154, Coleherne Court, SW5.

SONS LIVING.

Hon. NICHOLAS CRESPIGNY LAURENCE (352A, Kings Rd., SW3. *Club,*—Cavalry), b. Dec. 11th, 1935; ed. at Eton and Madrid Univ.; Maj. The R. Scots Dragoon Gds. (Carabiniers and Greys): m. 1st, 1960 (m. diss. 1972), Catherine Joyce, yst. da. of James Kenneth Hope, CBE, DL; 2ndly, 1972, Carol, el. da. of F. Alan Martineau, MBE, JP, of Valley End House, Chobham, Surrey, and has issue living (by 1st m.), Charles Hussey Crespigny b. 1966,—Henrietta Mary, b. 1963,—(by 2nd m.), Natasha Sarah, b. 1973.

Hon. Victor Anthony Brabazon Ralph (Lilac Cottage, Cadley, Collingbourne Ducis, Wilts.), b. 1940; late Merchant Navy: m. 1966, Inger Johanne, yr. da. of Advokat Per Gulliksen, of Sandeford, Norway, and has issue living, Thomas Crespigny Brabazon, b. 1971,—Arabella Victoria, b. 1973.

DAUGHTER LIVING

Hon. Sally Ann Marie Gabrielle, b. 1930: m. 1st, 1954 (m. diss. 1962) (William) Robin Charles Edward Cecil Lowe; 2ndly, 1963, Charles William Munro Wilson, of 12, Wellington Sq., SW3, and has issue living (by 2nd m.), Alexander Vivian, b. 1965.

SISTER LIVING

Hon. Daphne Winifred Louise, b. 1904: m. 1st, 1926, the 6th Marquess of Bath, from whom she obtained a divorce 1953; 2ndly, 1953, Maj. Alexander Wallace Fielding, DSO. *Residence,*—Galerie des Pâtres, Uzès, Gard, France.

HALF-SISTER LIVING.

Hon. Ursula Vanda Maud (*Countess of Glasgow*), *b.* 1912: *m.* 1st, 1935 (m. diss. 1946), Maj. Philip Alexander Clement Bridgewater, 5th Roy. Inniskilling Dragoon Guards; 2ndly, 1946 (m. diss. 1960), Maj. Sir William Fane Wrixon-Becher, MC, 5th Bt.: 3rdly, 1962, the 9th Earl of Glasgow, and has issue living, (by 1st m.) Adrian Alexander (Manor Farm, Bassingbourn, Royston, Herts), *b.* 1936: *m.* 1st, 1958, Charlotte, el. da. of the Rev. Michael Ernest Christopher Pumphrey, R. of Hunsdon, Herts.; 2ndly, 1969, Lucy Mary le Breton, da. of Sir Basil Hardington Bartlett, 2nd Bt., and has issue living, (by 1st m.) Thomas George Michael *b.* 1964, Emma Mary *b.* 1960, Sophia Charlotte *b.* 1962, (by 2nd m.) Nancy le Breton *b.* 1971, Daisy Maud *b.* 1973,—Vanda Alexandra Clare, *b.* 1940: *m.* 1959, John Henry Geers Cotterell, el. son of Lt.-Col. Sir Richard Charles Geers Cotterell, CBE, TD, 5th Bt.,—(by 2nd m.) [see Wrixon-Becher, Bt.]. *Residences,*—Kelburn Fairlie, Ayrshire; 110, Cheyne Walk, SW10.

WIDOW LIVING OF SON OF FOURTH BARON.

Mary Alice (Montastery Garden, Edington, Westbury, Wilts.), da. of the late Francis John Gordon Borthwick, WS [see Ld. Borthwick, colls.]: *m.* 1943, Lt.-Cdr. the Hon. Douglas David Edward Vivian, DSC, RN, who *d.* 1973, and has issue [see colls. infra].

COLLATERAL BRANCHES LIVING.

Issue of the late Lt.-Cdr. the Hon. Douglas David Edward Vivian, DSC, RN, yr. son of 4th Baron, *b.* 1915, *d.* 1973: *m.* 1943, Mary Alice (ante), da. of the late Francis John Gordon Borthwick, WS [see Ld. Borthwick, colls.]:—
Deborah Mary, *b.* 1944: *m.* 1971, Nicholas John Hinton, of 13, Ashington Rd., SW6.——Rose Emma Margaret, *b.* 1945: *m.* 1st, 1965, (m. diss. 1973), James Collet Norman; 2ndly, 1973, Benjamin Bernard Goodden, of 22, Petersham Mews, SW7, and has issue living (by 1st m.), Rupert Montagu, *b.* 1966,—Jason Douglas, *b.* 1968,—Melissa Rose, *b.* 1970.——Eugenie Nancy, *b.* 1947: *m.* 1966, Capt. Simon N. J. Burne, 9th/12th R. Lancers, and has issue living, Lucy Caroline, *b.* 1970.——Victoria Alice (twin), *b.* 1947: *m.* 1972, Nicholas Charlton Dudley Craig, of Whittington Close, Great Whittington, Newcastle-on-Tyne.——Charlotte Claire, *b.* 1950: *m.* 1971, Charles Robert Dimpfl, of 38, Tregunter Rd., SW7.

Grandchildren of the late Hon. Claude Hamilton Vivian (infra):—
Issue of the late Lieut.-Col. Claud Esmé Vivian, M.C., *b.* 1882, *d.* 1928: *m.* 1914, Emily, dau. of the late Col. Michael Rowan Gray Buchanan, O.B.E. [M. Bute, colls.]:—
Elizabeth Frederica Amesbury, *b.* 1916: *m.* 1947, Maj. Claude Fanning-Evans, JP, DL, late Durham LI. *Residence,*—Plas Cadnant, Menair Bridge, Anglesey.——Ann (Cae Du, Dwyran, Anglesey), *b.* 1923: *m.* 1953, Desmond Brennan, MB, who *d.* 1970, and has issue living, Vincent Patrick Esme, *b.* 1958,—Claire Patricia Ann, *b.* 1956,—Hazel Mary, *b.* 1961.

Grandchildren of the late Capt. Eric Paul Vivian, RN (infra):—
Issue of the late Capt. Desmond Walter Paul Vivian, 12th R. Lancers; *b.* 1925, *d.* 1974: *m.* 1949, Rose (Langford Gate, Sydling St. Nicholas, Dorset), da. of Capt. Charles Houssemayne du Boulay, RN, of Exton House, Exton, Hants.:—
Christopher John Desmond, *b.* 1956.——Vanda Rose, *b.* 1950.——Clare Veronica, *b.* 1952.

Issue of the late Capt. Eric Paul Vivian, R.N., *b.* 1891, *d.* 1961: *m.* 1922, Evelyn Audrey (of Hook Cottage, Hambledon, Hants), el. dau. of Capt. Thomas Pryse Arthur Holford, late 10th Hussars, of Duntish Court, Buckland Newton, Dorset:—
Patrick Cyril, *b.* 1929; ed. at Camb. Univ. (BA 1950, MA 1958, MB and BCh 1953, DRCOG 1958); late Capt. RAMC: *m.* 1961. Pamela Mary, da. of Lieut.-Col. Richard Rees Davies, JP, DL, of Ceris, Bangor, Caernarvonshire, and has issue living, Simon Paul Richard, *b.* 1962,—Susan Caroline, *b.* 1964. *Residence,*—Pumney, Sutton Courtenay, nr. Abingdon, Berks.——Charles Evelyn, *b.* 1937. *Residence,*—Hook Cottage, Hambledon, Hants.

Issue of the late Hon. Claud Hamilton Vivian, 4th son of 2nd Baron, *b.* 1849, *d.* 1902: *m.* 1878, Constance Emily, who *d.* 1905, dau. of the late Capt. Jules Sartoris, of Hoppesford Hall, Warwick:—
Robert Crespigny Gwynedd (Les Landes Farm, St. Mary, Jersey (C.I.), *b.* 1898; ed. at Eton; Capt. 2nd Life Guards (ret.): *m.* 1925, Violet Clinton, da. of Clinton Holme, of Ruthin, N. Wales, and has issue living, Robin Audley Clinton (7, Moncorvo Close, Ennismore Gdns., SW7), *b.* 1936; late Lt. 12th Roy. Lancers: *m.* 1961, Alice Penelope, only da. of the late Lt. Caesar Charles Hawkins, DSC, RN [see Hawkins, Bt., colls.], and has issue living, Rupert James *b.* 1970, Claire Jennifer *b.* 1971,—Edith Evelyn, *b.* 1926: *m.* 1954, Arnold Euston More Bloomer, of 97, High St., Eton, Windsor, and has issue living, Anthony Leonard Clinton *b.* 1964, Angela Gwyneth More *b.* 1960,—Pamela Blanche Gwynedd, *b.* 1929: *m.* 1955, John Charles Mark Fullerton, of Norwood Grange, Iver, Bucks. [Palmer, Bt., cr. 1886], and has issue living, John Robert Mark *b.* 1959, David Adam Grey *b.* 1968, Carolin Jane *b.* 1956.

Granddaughter of the late Lieut.-Col. Claud Esmé Vivian, M.C. (ante):—
Issue of the late Capt. Claud Panton Vivian, R.H.A., *b.* 1920, *d.* (of wounds received in action in Normandy) 1944: *m.* 1943, Margaret Eleanor (who *m.* 2ndly, 1947, Charles Dundas Lawrie, of Plâs Gwyn, Pentraeth, Anglesey), only dau. of Alec E. Baird, O.B.E., of Hailes Brae, Colinton, Edinburgh:—
Amanda Mary Panton, *b.* 1944.

PREDECESSORS.—[1] *Sir* RICHARD HUSSEY Vivian, *G.C.B., G.C.M.G., G.C.H., P.C.,* &c.; *b.* 1775; a Lt.-Gen. in the Army, and a distinguished soldier; was Col. 1st R. Dragoons, Com. of the Forces in Ireland, M.P. for Windsor, Equerry to George IV., and Master Gen. of Ordnance 1835-41; cr. a *Baronet* 1828, and *Baron Vivian,* of Glynn, and of Truro, co. Cornwall (peerage of United Kingdom) 1841: *m.* 1st, 1804, Eliza, dau. of Philip Champion de Crespigny, of Aldborough, Suffolk; *d.* 1842; *s.* by his son [2] CHARLES CRESPIGNY, 2nd Baron; sat as M.P. for Bodmin (L) 1837-42: was Lord-Lieut. of Cornwall 1856-77: *m.* 1st, 1833, Arabella, who *d.* 1837, dau. of the Rev. John Middleton Scott, of Ballygannon, co. Wicklow; 2ndly, 1841, Mary Elizabeth, who *d.* 1907, el. dau. of Jones Panton, of Plasgwyn, Anglesey; *d.* April 24, 1886; *s.* by his son [3] HUSSEY CRESPIGNY, *G.C.M.G., C.B., P.C.,* 3rd Baron, *b.* 1834; Agent and Consul-Gen. in Moldavia and Wallachia 1874-6, and in Egypt 1876-9, Min. at Berne 1879-81, Envoy Extraor. and Min. Plen. to Swiss Confederation 1881, to Denmark 1881-4, and at Brussels 1884-9, and Ambassador Extraor. and Plen. to Rome 1891-3: *m.* 1876, Louisa Alice, who *d.* 1926, dau. of Robert George Duff, of Wellington Lodge, Ryde; *d.* 1893: *s.* by his only son [4] GEORGE CRESPIGNY BRABAZON, *D.S.O.,* 4th Baron, *b.* 1878; Col. (retired) T.A.; sometime Major 17th Lancers; S. Africa 1900-01, European War 1914-18 (D.S.O.): *m.* 1st, 1903, Barbara (from whom he obtained a divorce 1907), dau. of the late William Atmar Fanning; 2ndly, 1911, Nancy Lycett, *MBE,* who *d.* 1970, da. of Sir Edward Lycett Green, 2nd Bt. [cr. 1886], and widow of Capt. Adrian Rose, Roy. Horse Guards ; *d.* 1940; *s.* by his son [5] ANTHONY CRESPIGNY CLAUD, 5th Baron and present peer.

WADE, BARON. (Wade.) [Life Baron 1964.]

DONALD WILLIAM WADE, son of the late William Mercer Wade, of Ilkley, Yorks.; b. June 16th, 1904; ed. at Mill Hill, and at Trin. Hall, Camb. (MA, LLB); Solicitor 1929; DL N. Yorks.; Liberal Whip 1956-62, and Dep. Leader, Liberal Parl. Party 1962-64; MP, W. Div. of Huddersfield, (L.) 1950-64; cr. Baron Wade, of Huddersfield, co. Yorks. (Life Baron) 1964: m. 1932, Ellenora Beatrice, da. of F. H. Bentham, of Bradford, and has issue.

Arms,—Gules a rose argent, barbed and seeded proper, issuant from either flank a demi portcullis, chained or. Crest,—In front of a book bound gules edged or, thereon a ram's head argent armed or, a crescent ermine. Supporters,—On either side a ram argent armed and unguled or, gorged with a Baron's coronet proper, and pendant therefrom by a riband gules an escutcheon of the Arms.
Residence,—High Houses, Woth-in-Nidderdale, Pateley Bridge, N. Yorks. Clubs,—Reform and National Liberal.

SONS LIVING.

Hon. Donald William Mercer (15, Grosvenor Court, Anerley Hill, Upper Norwood, SE19), b. 1941, ed. at Silcoates Sch., and at Trin. Hall, Camb. (MA).
Hon. Robert Alexander Mercer (Leeming Stile, Thornthwaite, Harrogate, Yorks.), b. 1943; ed. at Mill Hill, and Trin. Coll., Camb. (MA, LLB); Solicitor 1968: m. 1967, Jennifer Jane, da. of Leslie Elliott, of Grantley Grange, High Grantley, Ripon.

DAUGHTERS LIVING.

Hon. Helen Mary, b. 1933: m. 1963, the Rev. Lionel Ralph Wickham, of 16, Chetwynd Drive, Southampton.
Hon. Rosalind Beatrice, b. 1937: m. 1961, Richard David Morrish, solicitor, of 34, St. Margaret's Rd., Horsforth, Leeds.

WAKEFIELD, LORD BISHOP OF. (Treacy.)

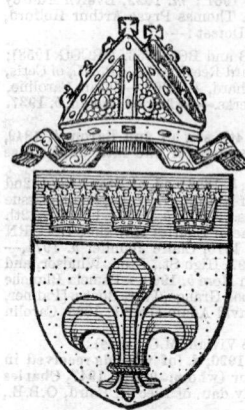

Right Rev. ERIC TREACY, MBE, son of George Treacy, of Rangoon; b. June 2nd, 1907; ed. at Haberdashers' Sch., King's Coll., London, and St. Aidan's, Birkenhead; LLD Leeds; V. of Edge Hill, Liverpool 1936-40; Chap. to HM Forces 1940-45; SCF N.-W. Europe 1944-45 (despatches, MBE); R. of Keighley 1945-49, Hon. Canon of Bradford Cathedral 1946-49 and Wakefield Cathedral 1949-55; Canon Residentiary 1955-68; Archdeacon of Halifax 1949-61, and V. of Halifax 1950-61; Bishop of Pontefract (Suffragan for Diocese of Wakefield) and Archdeacon of Pontefract 1961-68; translated 8th Bishop of Wakefield 1968; Hon. Freeman of Halifax; MBE (Mil.) 1944: m. 1932, Mary Leyland, da. of J. A. Shone, JP of Hoylake.

Patron of sixty-six livings, and of the Archdeaconries and Canonries in his Cathedral.

Episcopal Signature.—Eric Wakefield.

ARMS OF THE SEE,—Or, a fleur-de-lys azure, on a chief of the last three celestial crowns the field.

Residence,—Bishop's Lodge, Woodthorpe Lane, Wakefield.

WAKEFIELD OF KENDAL, BARON. (Wakefield.) [Baron U.K. 1963.]

(WILLIAM) WAVELL WAKEFIELD, 1st Baron, son of the late Roger William Wakefield, M.B., J.P., of Birklands, Kendal, Westmorland; b. March 10th, 1898; ed. at Sedbergh, and at Pembroke Coll., Camb. (MA); a Dir. of Portman Building Soc., and other Cos., and a Member of Council Roy. Nat. Mission to Deep Sea Fishermen, and a Vice-Pres. of Roy. Albert Hall; Pres. of Water Ski Fedn., and Metropolitan Assocn. of Building Socs.; PPS to Under-Sec. of State for Dominions 1936-38, to Sec. of Overseas Trade Dept. 1939-40, and to Under-Sec. of State for Air 1940-42, Dirl of Air Training Corps 1942-44, and Chm. of Parliamentary Scientific Cttee. 1952-55; Pres. Rugby Football Union 1950-51; 1914-18 War with RNAS and RAF (despatched, two medals), 1939-45 War as Fl.-Lt. RAF; MP for Swindon Div. of Wilts (C) 1935-45, and for St. Marylebone 1945-63; cr Knt. 1944, and Baron Wakefield of Kendal, of Kendal, co. Westmorland, 1963:

m. 1919, Rowena Doris, da. of the late Llewellyn Lewis, OBE, MD, JP, of Neath, S. Wales, and has issue.

𝕬𝖗𝖒𝖘,—Argent two barrulets sable between three owls proper. 𝕮𝖗𝖊𝖘𝖙,—A bat displayed proper charged on each wing with a crescent argent. 𝕾𝖚𝖕𝖕𝖔𝖗𝖙𝖊𝖗𝖘,—*Dexter*, a skier with skis and sticks proper; *sinister*, a figure representing a member of the England Rugby Football team with ball proper. *Residences,*—71, Park St., W1; The Old House, Kendal, Westmorland. *Clubs,*—Carlton, International Sportsmen's.

DAUGHTERS LIVING.

Hon. Joan Rosemary (6, St. James' Terr., Regents Park, NW8) *b.* 1920: *m.* 1944, Capt. Antony Edward Montague Raynsford, RN (ret.), of Milton Malsor Manor, Northampton, and has issue living, Richard Wakefield, *b.* 1945,—Julia Daphne, *b.* 1948.

Hon. Mary Sheila, *b.* 1922: *m.* 1945, Brig. Richard Frank Bradshaw Hensman, CBE, of 4, St. James's Terr. Mews, Regents Park, NW8, and has issue living, Peter Richard Wavell, *b.* 1948: *m.* 1973, Claire Theresa, da. of Peter Wallace Henderson, MC, BM,—Suzannah Mary, *b.* 1953.

Hon. Ruth Isabel, *b.* 1932: *m.* 1955, Maj. Nigel James Clarkson Webb, Buckstone House, Carnforth, Lancs., and has issue living, Edward James, *b.* 1966,—Georgina Anne, *b.* 1957,—Carolyn Mary, *b.* 1958.

WAKEHURST, BARON. (Loder.) [Baron U.K. 1934.]

A sound conscience is a wall of brass.

Residence,—53, Clabon Mews, SW1.

(JOHN) CHRISTOPHER LODER, 3rd Baron; *b.* Sept. 23rd, 1925; *s.* 1970; ed. at Eton, King's Sch., nr. Sydney, NSW, and Trin. Coll., Camb. (MA, LLB); Bar. Inner Temple 1950; a CStJ; late Sub-Lt. RANVR and RNVR; 1939-45 in W. Pacific: *m.* 1956, Ingeborg, da. of Walter Krumbholz, and has issue.

𝕬𝖗𝖒𝖘,—Quarterly; 1st and 4th grand quarters; Azure, on a fesse between in chief a portcullis chained and in base a martlet or, three stags' heads caboshed proper, *Loder*; 2nd grand quarter, quarterly, the Royal Arms of Charles II, 1st and 4th, France and England quarterly, 2nd, Scotland, 3rd, Ireland, and overall a baton sinister gules charged with three roses argent, barbed and seeded proper, *Beauclerk*; 3rd grand quarter, quarterly gules and or, in the first a mullet argent, *de Vere*. 𝕮𝖗𝖊𝖘𝖙,—A stag's head caboshed transfixed by an arrow bendwise point downwards all proper, between two escallops or. 𝕾𝖚𝖕𝖕𝖔𝖗𝖙𝖊𝖗𝖘,—*Dexter*, A Russian brown bear proper; *sinister*, a greyhound argent gorged with a collar checky of the last and azure.

SON LIVING.

Hon. TIMOTHY WALTER, *b.* March 28th, 1958.

DAUGHTER LIVING.

Hon. Christina Anne, *b.* 1959.

BROTHERS LIVING.

Hon. James David Gerald (31, Lennox Gdns., SW1), *b.* 1928; ed. at Geelong Gram Sch., Victoria, and Trin. Coll., Camb. (BA); Bar. Inner Temple 1952; OStJ; late Lt. Coldstream Guards.

Hon. Robert Beauclerk (14, Ladbroke Grove, W11), *b.* 1934; ed. at Eton, and at Trin. Coll., Camb.: *m.* 1973, Josette, da. of Josef Bromovsky, of Ottmanach, Pisheldorf, Kaernten, Austria.

SISTER LIVING.

Hon. Henrietta Marguerite Jean, *b.* 1922: *m.* 1953, John Wilmot Reader-Harris, and has issue living, Michael John, *b.* 1957,—Sarah Margaret, *b.* 1959. *Residence,*—Glenconner, Dirleton Av., N. Berwick, E. Lothian.

AUNTS LIVING. (*Daughters of 1st Baron*).

Hon. Dorothy Cecily Sybil, *b.* 1896: *m.* 1922, the Hon. (William Jocelyn) Lewis Palmer, who *d.* 1971 [see E. Selborne]. *Residence,*—Saint Michel, Rue a l'Or, St. Saviours, Guernsey.

Hon. Victoria Helen, *b.* 1899: *m.* 1928, Major Alan Rees Colman, Norfolk Yeo. and Air Transport Auxiliary, who *d.* (killed on war ser.) 1943. *Residence,*—66, Campbell Court, Queens' Gate Gdns., SW7.

Hon. Diana Evelyn (*Diana, Baroness Strathcona and Mount Royal*), *b.* (twin) 1899 : *m.* 1922, the 3rd Baron Strathcona and Mount Royal, who *d.* 1959. *Residence,*—Headbourne Worthy Grange, Winchester.

WIDOW LIVING OF SECOND BARON.

Dame MARGARET, *DBE* (*Margaret, Baroness Wakehurst*), (31, Lennox Gdns., SW1); Hon. LLD Belfast; GCStJ; DBE (Civil) 1965; da. of Sir Charles Tennant, 1st Bt. [see B. Glenconner]: *m.* 1920, the 2nd Baron, who *d.* 1970.

PREDECESSORS.—[1] GERALD WALTER ERSKINE Loder, 5th son of Sir Robert Loder, 1st Bt.; *b.* 1861; was an Assist. Private Sec. to Pres. of Local Govt. Board 1888-92, and to Sec. of State for India 1896-1901; sat as M.P. for Brighton (*C*) 1889-1905; cr. *Baron Wakehurst*, of Ardingly, co. Sussex (peerage of United Kingdom) 1934: *m.* 1890, Lady Louise de Vere Beauclerk, who *d.* 1958, el. dau. of 10th Duke of St. Albans ; *d.* 1936 ; *s.* by his only son [2] JOHN DE VERE, *KG, KCMG*, 2nd Baron, *b.* 1895; MP for E. Leicester (*C*) 1924-29, and Lewes 1931-36; Gov. of NSW 1937-46, and N. Ireland 1952-64: *m.* 1920, Dame Margaret, DBE, da. of Sir Charles Tennant, 1st Bt. [B. Glenconner]; *d.* 1970; *s.* by his el. son [3] (JOHN) CHRISTOPHER, 3rd Baron and present peer.

WALDEGRAVE, EARL. (Waldegrave.) [Earl G.B. 1729, Bt. E. 1643.]

[Name and Title pronounced "**Wallgrave**."]

Press forward.

GEOFFREY NOEL WALDEGRAVE, KG, TD, 12th Earl, and 16th Baronet ; b. Nov. 21st, 1905 ; s. 1936 ; ed. at Winchester, and at Trin. Coll., Camb.; Chm. of Agricultural Executive Cttee. for Somerset 1948-51, a Co. Alderman for Somerset 1949-58, Liaison Officer to Min. of Agriculture and Fisheries 1952-57, and Vice-Lt. for Somerset 1955-60; Joint Parliamentary Sec. to Min. of Agriculture, Fisheries and Food 1957-62; Chm. of Forestry Commn. 1963-65; a Member of Prince's Council, Duchy of Cornwall 1951-58, and since 1965, and Lord Warden of the Stanneries since 1965; 1939-45 War as Maj. RA (TA); an Officer of American Legion of Merit; cr. KG 1971: m. 1930, Mary Hermione, da. of the late Lt.-Col. Arthur Morton Grenfell, DSO [V. Cobham, colls.], and has issue.

Arms.—Per pale argent and gules. **Crest.**—Out of a ducal coronet or, a plume of five ostrich feathers, the first two argent, the third per pale argent and gules, and the last two gules. **Supporters.**—Two talbots sable, ears gold, each gorged with a mural coronet argent.

Residence,—Chewton House, Chewton Mendip, Bath.

SONS LIVING.

JAMES SHERBROOKE (*Viscount Chewton*), b. Dec. 8th, 1940; ed. at Eton, and Trin. Coll., Camb.
Hon. William Arthur, b. 1946; ed. at Eton, Corpus Christi, Oxford, and Harvard Univ.; a Fellow of All Souls, Oxford.

DAUGHTERS LIVING.

Lady Sarah Caroline, b. 1931: m. 1955, Ernest George Wright, GM, of Beaumont House, Wells, Somerset, and has issue living, Thomas Geoffrey, b. 1956,—David, b. 1957.
Lady Jane Mary (*Baroness Strathcona and Mount Royal*), b. 1934: m. 1954, the 4th Baron Strathcona, and Mount Royal. *Residences,*—Isle of Colonsay, Argyll ; 89, Barkston Gdns., SW5 0EU.
Lady Elisabeth Jeronima, b. 1936: m. 1963, the Hon. John James Evelyn Dewar, el. son of 3rd Baron Forteviot. *Residence,*—6, Holland Villas Rd., W14.
Lady Anne Hermione, b. 1937: m. 1971, John Dennis Boles, of The Old Rectory, Englefield, Theale, Reading.
Lady Susan Katharine, CVO, b. 1939; appointed a Woman of the Bedchamber to HM 1960; CVO 1971, m. 1959, Marmaduke James Hussey, and has issue living, James Arthur, b. 1961; appointed a Page of Honour to HM 1975,—Katharine Elizabeth, b. 1964. *Residence,*—86, Chelsea Park Gdns., SW3.

SISTERS LIVING.

Lady Elisabeth Katharine, b. 1897: m. 1918, the Rev. George Algernon Randolph, late R. of Charlcombe, Bath, of South Woodside, Corfe, Taunton, Somerset [B. Middleton, colls.], and has issue living, Herbert Noel Edmund, b. 1919,—Anne Elisabeth, b. 1920: m. 1950, George William Sweetnam, and has issue living, Robert William b. 1954,—Irene Mary (Woodside West, Corfe, Somerset), b. 1923: m. 1947, Maj. Peter John Browning, and has issue living, George Noel Francis b. 1949, Gregory Thomas Richard b. 1962, Katharine Mary Helen b. 1948, Sophia Anne Caroline b. 1952.
Lady (Gabrielle) Sophia Annette, b. 1908: m. 1935, Major John Stephen Schilizzi, R.A.S.C. [Rall, Bt.], and has issue living, Stephen Noel John (15, Lennox Garden Mews, SW1), b. 1937: m. 1959, Diana, only da. of Eustace Allfrey, of Chacombe Priory, near Banbury, Oxon,—Gabrielle Anne Mary, b. 1936: m. 1957, Capt. Gordon Shafto Hedley, late 17th/21st Lancers of Turweston Glebe, Brackley, Northants, and has issue living, Nicholas Edward John b. 1962, Caroline Mary b. 1957, Anne Penelope b. 1959,—Helena Margaret, b. 1939. *Residence,*—Chacombe House, near Banbury, Oxon.

COLLATERAL BRANCH LIVING.

Descendants of Adm. the Hon. Sir William Waldegrave, G.C.B. (2nd son of 3rd Earl), who was cr. *Baron Radstock* 1800 [see that title].

PREDECESSORS.—[1] *Sir* EDWARD Waldegrave, Knt., sometime M.P. for Sudbury ; when 70 years of age took up arms in the royal cause ; cr. a *Baronet* 1643 ; afterwards eminently distinguished as a military leader ; s. by his son [2] *Sir* HENRY, 2nd Bt.; d. 1658 ; s. by his son [3] *Sir* CHARLES, 3rd Bt.; s. by his son [4] *Sir* HENRY, 4th Bt.; cr. *Baron Waldegrave,* of Chewton, co. Somerset (peerage of England) 1686 ; was Comptroller of the King's Household ; d. 1689 ; s. by his son [5] JAMES, K.G., P.C., 2nd Baron ; conformed to the Church of England and took his seat in the House of Lords 1722 ; was Ambassador to Emperor of Germany 1727-37; cr. *Viscount Chewton* and *Earl Waldegrave* (peerage of Great Britain) 1729; d. 1741; s. by his el. son [6] JAMES, K.G., P.C., 2nd Earl ; was successively a Lord of the Bedchamber, Steward of the Duchy of Cornwall, Gov. to George Prince of Wales and to Prince Edward, Duke of York, and Teller of the Exchequer, &c.; d. 1763 ; s. by his brother [7] JOHN, K.G., 3rd Earl ; sat as M.P. for Oxford and Newcastle-under-Lyme ; was Master of the Horse, Gov. of Plymouth, a Groom of the Bedchamber, and Lord-Lieut. of Essex ; d. 1784 ; s. by his son [8] GEORGE, 4th Earl ; was Col. 14th Regt.; d. 1789 ; s. by his el. son [9] GEORGE, 5th Earl ; d. 1794 ; s. by his brother [10] JOHN JAMES, 6th Earl ; a Lieut.-Col. in the Army ; d. 1835 ; s. by his son [11] GEORGE EDWARD, 7th Earl ; d.s.p. 1846 ; s. by his uncle [12] WILLIAM, C.B. (4th son of 4th Earl), 8th Earl ; was a Vice-Adm.; d. 1859 ; s. by his grandson [13] WILLIAM FREDERICK, P.C. (el. son of William Frederick, Viscount Chewton, by Frances, V.A., dau. of the late Capt. John Bastard, R.N.), 9th Earl, b. 1851 ; a Lord-in-Waiting to Queen Victoria Aug. 1886 to Aug. 1892 and July 1895 to Aug. 1896, Capt. of the Yeomen of the Guard 1896-1906, and Ch. Conservative Whip in the House of Lords 1896-1911 : m. 1874, Lady Mary Dorothea Palmer, D.B.E., who d. 1933, dau. of 1st Earl of Selborne ; d. 1930 ; s. by his only son [14] WILLIAM EDWARD SEYMOUR, 10th Earl, b. 1882 ; d. 1933 ; s. by his uncle [15] HENRY NOEL (2nd son of William Frederick, Viscount Chewton), 11th Earl, b. 1854 : m. 1892, Anne Katharine, who d. 1962, dau. of the late Rev. William Pollexfen Bastard, of Buckland Court, Ashburton and Kitley, Devon ; d. 1936 ; s. by his only son [16] GEOFFREY NOEL, 12th Earl and present peer ; also Viscount Chewton, and Baron Waldegrave.

WALERAN, BARONY OF. (Walrond.) [Extinct 1966.]

WIDOW LIVING OF SECOND BARON

VALENTINE ROTHWELL (*Baroness Waleran*), (22, Launceston Place, W8), da. of the late Eric Oswald Anderson, CBE: *m.* 1954, as his third wife, the 2nd Baron, who *d.* 1966, when the title became ext.

WALES, PRINCE OF, see "Royal Family."

WALKDEN, BARONY OF. (Walkden.) [Extinct 1951.]

DAUGHTERS LIVING OF FIRST BARON,

Hon. Mary, *b.* 1907: *m.* 1924, Duncan Matheson McCowen, who *d.* 1969, and has issue living, Alexander Duncan, *b.* 1925,—Jean Mary, *b.* 1929. *Residence,*—Flat 10, Blenheim Court, 17, New Church Rd., Hove.

Hon. Margaret, *b.* 1914. *Residence,*—7, Priory Avenue, Hastings.

Walker, see Baron Gordon-Walker

WALLACE OF CAMPSIE, BARON. (Wallace.) [Life Baron 1974.]

GEORGE WALLACE, son of John Wallace; *b.* Feb. 13th, 1915; ed. at Queen's Park Secondary Sch., and Glasgow Univ.; a DL of Co. of City of Glasgow; Hon. Sheriff Substitute of Lanarkshire at Hamilton 1971; established Wallace, Cameron & Co., Ltd. 1948 (Chm. and Man. Dir. since 1948); a Dir. of Smith & Nephew Asso. Cos., Ltd. since 1973; Chm. of E. Kilbride & Stonehouse Development Corpn. since 1969, and Pres. of Glasgow Chamber of Commerce 1974; 1939-45 War as Fl. Lt. RAF; cr. *Baron Wallace of Campsie*, of Newlands, co. of City of Glasgow 1974.

Arms,—not exemplified at time of going to press.
Residence,—14, Fernleigh Rd., Glasgow G43 2UE. *Clubs,*—Royal Scottish Automobile, Caledonian.

WALLACE OF COSLANY, BARON. (Wallace.) [Life Baron 1974.]

GEORGE DOUGLAS WALLACE, son of the late George Wallace, of Cheltenham; *b.* April 18th, 1906; ed. at Cheltenham Central Sch.; 1939-45 War as Sgt. RAF; Govt. Whip 1947-50; PPS to Lord Pres. of Council 1964-66, to Sec. of State for Commonwealth Affairs 1966-67, and to Min. of State for Housing and Local Govt. 1967-68; Speaker's Panel of Chairmen 1970-74; MP for Chislehurst (*Lab.*) 1945-50, and for Norwich North 1964-74; cr. *Baron Wallace of Coslany*, of Coslany, City of Norwich, (Life Baron) 1974: *m.* 1932, Vera, da. of William Joseph Randall, of Guildford, Surrey, and has issue.
Residence,—44, Shuttle Close, Sidcup, Kent, DA15 8EP.

SON LIVING.

Hon. Michael George (35, Winchelsea Av., Bexley Heath, Kent), *b.* 1944: *m.* 1974, Susan, da. of Henry William Price.

DAUGHTER LIVING.

Hon. Elizabeth Anne, *b.* 1933.

WALPOLE, BARON. (Walpole.) [Baron G.B. 1723 and 1756.]

Let him be true to himself.

ROBERT HENRY MONTGOMERIE WALPOLE, *T.D.*, 9th Baron Walpole, and 7th Baron Walpole of Wolterton; *b.* April 25th, 1913; *s.* 1931; ed. at Eton, at South-Eastern Agricultural Coll., Wye, and at Roy. Agricultural Coll., Cirencester; is Capt. R.A., and patron of six livings: *m.* 1937, Nancy Louisa, dau. of the late Frank Harding Jones, of 21, Abingdon Court, W.8, and has issue.

Arms—Or, on a fesse, between two chevrons sable three cross-crosslets of the field. **Crest.**—A Saracen's head in profile, couped at the shoulders proper, ducally crowned or, and from the coronet flowing a red cap turned down in front, tasselled, and charged with a catherine-wheel gold. **Supporters,**—*Dexter*, an antelope argent; *sinister*, a stag argent, each gorged with a collar checky or and azure, and therefrom a chain reflexed over the back gold.
Seat, Wolterton Hall, Erpingham, Norwich, NOR. 44Y. *Clubs,*—Bath, Norfolk (Norwich).

SON LIVING.

Hon. ROBERT HORATIO (Mannington Hall, Norwich, NOR 18Y), *b.* Dec. 8th, 1938; ed. at Eton, and at King's Coll., Camb.: *m.* 1962, Judith, yr. da. of T. T. Schofield, of Harpenden, Herts., and has issue living, Jonathan Robert Hugh, *b.* 1967,—Benedict Thomas Orford, *b.* 1969,—Alice Louise, *b.* 1963—Emma Judith, *b.* 1964.

DAUGHTER LIVING.

Hon. Phillida Ann, *b.* 1950: *m.* 1973, Clive Grainger Morgan-Evans, of Keeper's Cottage, Mossymere, Mannington, Norwich, NR11 7BD, and has issue living, Edward Grainger, *b.* 1973.

SISTER LIVING. *(Raised to the rank of a Baron's daughter* 1939).

Hon. Pamela Frances, *OBE, b.* 1908; MBE (Civil) 1954, OBE (Civil) 1960. *Residence,*—Greystones, Sir Lowry's Pass, Cape Province, S. Africa.

DAUGHTER LIVING OF FIFTH EARL OF ORFORD.

Lady Anne Sophia, *b.* 1919: *m.* 1939, Col. Joseph Eric Palmer, CBE, TD, DL, and has issue living, John Robert Walpole (Dirnanean, Blairgowrie, Perthshire), *b.* 1943: *m.* 1971, Carolyn, da. of W. H. Atkinson-Clark, of Ashintully Castle, Kirkmichael, Blairgowrie,—Anthony Eric Fletcher, *b.* 1945; *m.* 1969, Nicola Mary, da. of H. Maude, of Gisborne, NZ. *Residence,*—Rosemoor, Torrington, Devon.

WIDOW LIVING OF FIFTH EARL OF ORFORD.

EMILY GLADYS (*Countess of Orford*), dau. of the late Rev. Thomas Henry Royal Oakes, formerly R. of Thurgarton, Norwich: *m.* 1917, as his second wife, the 5th Earl of Orford, who *d.* 1931, when the Earldom became ext. *Residence,*—Cockshilhay. Torrington, Devon.

COLLATERAL BRANCHES LIVING.

Grandson of the late Rt. Hon. Spencer Horatio Walpole, QC, 2nd son of the late Thomas Walpole (*b.* 1755), son of the Hon. Thomas Walpole, 2nd son of 1st Baron Walpole of Wolterton:—

Issue of the late Sir Horatio George Walpole, K.C.B., *b.* 1843, *d.* 1923 : *m.* 1870, Selina Maria. who *d.* 1925, dau. of the late John Thomas Perceval [E. Egmont, colls.]:—
Robert Spencer Hobhouse (16, The Knoll, Fairfield Rd., Framlingham, Suffolk), *b.* 1881; ed. at Wellington Coll.; formerly Major Rifle Brig. (Prince Consort's Own): *m.* 1923, Edith Winifred, da. of the late S. H. Keeling, of Parkfield, Kenilworth, and has issue living, Horace Jeremy Spencer, *RN* (Moor Farm Cottage, Oaksey, nr. Malmesbury, Wilts.), *b.* 1924; is Lieut.-Com.: *m.* 1950, Mary Elizabeth Bruce Kidman, and has issue living, Robert Charles Spencer (Buscot Farm Cottage, Buscot, Faringdon, Oxon.) *b.* 1955: *m.* 1975, Diana Bishop, Caroline Mary Bruce *b.* 1951, Elizabeth Jane Bruce *b.* 1953, Lucy Margaret Bruce (twin) *b.* 1955: *m.* 1974, Stephen Ashcroft, of 12, Caulby Lane, Stoughton, Leics., Charlotte Victoria Bruce *b.* 1960,—Selina Elizabeth, *b.* 1932: *m.* 1971, John Whipp, of 19A, Bridge St., Framlingham, Suffolk.

Granddaughter of the late Lieut.-Gen. Sir Robert Walpole, KCB, 3rd son of the late Thomas Walpole (ante):—
Issue of the late Spencer Charles Walpole, *b.* 1852, *d.* 1934: *m.* 1885, Jessie Madeline, who *d.* 1926, dau. of the late Rev. Tressilian George Nicholas, V. of W. Molesey, Kingston-on-Thames :—
Lucy Gertrude, *b.* 1893. *Residence,*—Strawberry Hill, Ufford, Woodbridge, Suffolk.

Grandchildren of the late Rev. Robert Seymour Walpole, son of the late Rev. Robert Walpole, el. son of the late Hon. Robert Walpole, 4th son of 1st Baron Walpole of Wolterton:—
Issue of the late Herbert Reginald Robert Seymour Walpole, *b.* 1853, *d.* 1928 : *m.* 1882, Jane Sophia, who *d.* 1916, dau. of W. Palmer Kent. C.E.. of Tasmania :—
Francis Seymour, *b.* 1895.——Florence Louise, *b.* 1885.——Lucy Apthorp, *b.* 1887: *m.* 1912, Robert Balcombe Beggs.——Agnes Jane, *b.* 1893: *m.* 1918, Theodore Beggs, JP, who *d.* 1940 (a MLC of Victoria, Australia 1910-28), and has issue living, Diana Charlotte, *b.* 1920: *m.* 1941, Cyril Maxwell Howell, of Glenfine, Private Bag, Ballarat, Victoria, Australia, and has issue living, Richard Maxwell Theodore *b.* 1945, Gillian Diana Beggs *b.* 1943,—Penelope Clamina, *b.* 1922: *m.* 1950, Julian Orm Smith, FRCS, of 42, Washington Street, Toorak, Victoria, and has issue living, Jeremy Orm *b.* 1952,—Theodora, *b.* 1926,—Prudence Elizabeth, *b.* 1928. *Residence,*—Eurambeen Station, Victoria, Australia.

PREDECESSORS.—[1] *Sir* ROBERT Walpole, *K.G., K.B.*, a distinguished statesman; sat as M.P. for Lyme Regis 1702-42; was successively a Lord of the Treasury, Chancellor of the Exchequer, a Lord Justice, sole Sec. of State, and Prime Minister; made a K.G. 1726, while a Commoner; cr. *Baron Walpole*, of Houghton, *Viscount Walpole* and *Earl of Orford* (peerage of Great Britain) 1742; *d.* 1745; *s.* by his son [2] ROBERT, *K.B.*, 2nd Earl, who had in 1723 been cr. *Baron Walpole*, of Walpole, co. Norfolk (with remainder to his brothers Edward and Horace, and in default thereof to the heirs male of his father, and in default thereof to the heirs male of his grandfather) : *m.* 1724, Margaret, afterwards in her own right Baroness Clinton; the Earl *d.* 1751; *s.* by his son [3] GEORGE, 3rd Earl, who in 1781 *s.* his mother as 16th *Baron Clinton* (peerage of England, cr. 1332); was a Lord of the Bedchamber and Ranger of St. James's and Hyde Parks; *d.* 1791, when the Barony of Clinton reverted to his kinsman, Robert George William Trefusis [see B. Clinton], and the Earldom devolved upon his uncle [4] HORACE, 4th Earl; sat successively as M.P. for Collington, Castle Rising, and King's Lynn, but was more distinguished for literary than political attainments; was Usher of the Receipt of the Exchequer, Comptroller of the Great Roll, and Keeper of the Foreign Receipts, having retired from public life he purchased a villa at Twickenham and transformed it into the celebrated Gothic mansion known as Strawberry Hill, where he printed his own works and many curious pieces; *d.* unmarried 1797, when all the honours expired except the Barony of Walpole of Walpole (cr. 1723) which devolved upon his first cousin [5] HORATIO, 4th Baron, who in 1757 had *s.* his father, who was brother of 1st Earl, as 2nd *Baron Walpole of Wolterton* (peerage of Great Britain, cr. 1756), sat as M.P. for Lynn Regis 1747-57; cr. *Earl of Orford* (peerage of United Kingdom) 1806; *d.* 1809; *s.* by his son [6] HORATIO, 2nd Earl; M.P. for Wigan 1780-4, and for King's Lynn 1784-1809; *d.* 1822; *s.* by his son [7] HORATIO, 3rd Earl; *b.* 1783; was High Steward of Lynn, and Col. W. Norfolk Militia: *m.* Mary, dau. of the late William Augusta Fawkener, of Brocton Hall, Salop; *d.* 1858; *s.* by his son [8] HORATIO WILLIAM, 4th Earl, *b.* 1813; M.P. for Norfolk 1835-7: *m.* 1841, Harriet Bettina Frances, who *d.* 1886, dau. of the late Hon. Sir Fleetwood Broughton Reynolds Pellew; *d.* 1894; *s.* by his nephew [9] ROBERT HORACE (son of the late Hon. Frederick Walpole, M.P., 3rd son of 3rd Earl), 5th Earl, *b.* 1854: *m.* 1888, Louise Melissa, who *d.* 1909, dau. of D. C. Corbin, of New York; 2ndly, 1917, Emily Gladys, dau. of the Rev. Thomas Henry Royal Oakes, R. of Thurgarton, Norwich; *d.* 1931, when the Earldom of Orford became ext., and the Baronies of Walpole and Walpole of Wolterton devolved upon his cousin [10] ROBERT HENRY MONTGOMERIE (son of the late Horatio Spencer Walpole, descended from the late Hon. Thomas Walpole, brother of 1st Earl of Orford, cr. 1806), 9th Baron, and present peer ; also Baron Walpole of Wolterton.

WALSINGHAM, BARON. (de Grey.) [Baron G.B. 1780.]

JOHN DE GREY, *MC*, 9th **Baron**; *b.* Feb. 21st, 1925; *s.* 1965; ed. at Wellington Coll., and at Magdalen Coll., Oxford (MA); Lt.-Col. (ret.) RA; patron of three livings; 1939-45 War, Palestine 1947, Korea 1951-52 (MC), Malaya 1954-56, Cyprus and Suez 1956, Aden 1957-58 and 1961-63, Far East (Borneo) 1963-65: *m.* 1963, Wendy Elizabeth, da. of Edward S. Hoare, of Southwick, Sussex, and has issue.

To bespirited, not inactive.

Arms.—Barry of six argent and azure, in chief three annulets gules. **Crest,**—A wyvern's head, or. **Supporters,**—Two wyverns reguardant argent, collared azure, chained or, and charged on the breast with three annulets gules.

Residence,—Merton Hall, Thetford, Norfolk. *Clubs,*—Army and Navy, Farmers', Norfolk County (Norwich).

SON LIVING.
Hon. ROBERT, *b.* June 21st, 1969.

DAUGHTERS LIVING.
Hon. Sarah Jane, *b.* 1964.
Hon. Elizabeth Anne, *b.* 1966.

SISTERS LIVING.
Hon. Lavender Hyacinth, *b.* 1923; European War 1942-45 with First Aid Nursing Yeo. in N. Africa, Italy, India and Ceylon : *m.* 1946, Major William d'Arcy Garnier, R.A. *(Club,*—United Service), and has issue living, James Hugh, *b.* 1948,—Richard Charles, *b.* 1950,—Edward Henry, *b.* 1952,—Katharine Juliet, *b.* 1958. *Address,*—c/o Lloyds Bank, 6, Pall Mall, S.W.1.

Hon. Margaret Isolda, *b.* 1926 ; European War 1944-45 in W.R.N.S. : *m.* 1950, Major Geoffrey Edward Ford North, M.C., and has issue living, David John Ford, *b.* 1959,—Amanda, *b.* 1951,—Joanna Katharine, *b.* 1953,—Belinda Jane, *b.* 1955. *Residence,*—Colleton Hall, Rackenford, Tiverton, Devon.

Hon. Katharine Odeyne, *b.* 1928 : *m.* 1949, George William Herbert [see E. Powis, colls.]. *Residence,*—Marrington Hall, Chirbury, Montgomeryshire.

UNCLE LIVING. (Son of Seventh Baron.)
Hon. Richard Patrick, *TD, b.* 1900; ed. at Eton, and at Trin. Coll., Camb. (MA); a JP of Norfolk, sometime Capt. Cambridgeshire Regt. (TA); 1939-45 War in Norway and Malaya: *m.* 1st, 1925, Cynthia Estelle, who *d.* 1967, da. of the late Thomas Hewitt Myring, of Norfolk St., Park Lane, W; 2ndly, 1969, Dorothy, da. of the late Thomas Knight, of Sidcup, Kent. *Residence,*—The Hassocks, Merton, Thetford, Norfolk.

AUNT LIVING. (Daughter of Seventh Baron.)
Hon. Margaret Henrietta, *b.* 1889 : *m.* 1st, 1912, Bethell Godefroy Bouwens, who *d.* 1942 [E. Cavan]; 2ndly, 1948, Cyril Fabian Johnston, who *d.* 1958, and has issue living, (by 1st marriage), Derek (of Old Manor House, Littleton, Shepperton, Middx.), *b.* 1913; formerly Maj. RASC: *m.* 1944, Doreen Gaskin, ATS, and has issue living, Dirk Murray *b.* 1947; ed. at King's Coll. Sch., Wimbledon: *m.* 1971, Sally Elizabeth Madoc, of Saham Toney, Norfolk, Adrian John *b.* 1948; ed. at King's Coll. Sch., Wimbledon, and RMA: *m.* 1971, Caroline Anne Beaumont, of Staines, Middx., Carel Peter *b.* 1950; ed at King's Coll. Sch., Wimbledon, and RMA: Lt. RE, Philippa Sara *b.* 1945; SRN: *m.* 1972, Robert John Fowler, MRAI, of Dublin (and has issue living, Sanna Margrethe *b.* 1974),—Anne, *b.* 1914: *m.* 1937, Osmond Janson Masterman, of Gift Howe, South Park Orcs., Gerrards Cross, Bucks., and has issue living, Diccon Lambart (c/o Barclays Bank, Gerrards Cross, Bucks.; RAF Club) *b.* 1941; ed. at St. Edward's Sch., Oxford, and Worcester Coll., Oxford (MA); Fl. Lt. RAF: *m.* 1964, Gillian Elizabeth Ferraro, of Hawkhurst, Kent, Crispin Grant *b.* 1944; ed. at St. Edward's Sch., Oxford, and Southampton Univ. (BA), Veryan Loveday Serrell, *b.* 1948q ed. at Aberdeen Univ. (BA),—Lettice, *b.* 1921. *Residence,*—Caudle Springs, Carbrooke, Thetford, Norfolk.

COLLATERAL BRANCHES LIVING.
Grandsons of the late Nigel de Grey, CMG, OBE (infra):—
Issue of the late John de Grey, *b.* 1911, *d.* 1973: *m.* 1939, Averil (Oliver House, Buckden, Hunts.), da. of the late Herman de Zoete, of Sproughton, Suffolk:—
Michael John (31, Whitmore Lane, Sunningdale, Berks.), *b.* 1942: *m.* 1966, Carolyn Althea Jane, da. of John Ernest Haldane Blackie, of The Bell House, Alconbury, Hunts., and has issue living, Rachel Emma, *b.* 1969,—Helen Sarah, *b.* 1970.—Anthony, *b.* 1948: *m.* 1975, Miranda Murdoch.

Grandchildren of the late Rev. the Hon. Arnald de Grey, 3rd son of 5th Baron :—
Issue of the late Nigel de Grey, C.M.G., O.B.E., *b.* 1886, *d.* 1951 : *m.* 1910, Florence Emily Frances, who *d.* 1963, dau. of the late Spencer William Gore [R. Arran, colls.]:—
Roger, *ARA, b.* 1918; ed. at Eton; Capt. Roy. Armoured Corps; NW Europe, 1944-45 (wounded, Bronze Star of USA); ARA 1962: *m.* 1942, Flavia Hatt, da. of the late Lt.-Col. Clinton Irwin, MC, of Silver Bridge, Chideock, Dorset, and has issue living, Spencer Thomas, *b.* 1944,—Robert Fulke, *b.* 1948: *m.* 19—,— Emilia Jane Mary, *b.* 1952. *Residence,*—5-6, Camer St., Meopham, Kent.— Barbara, *b.* 1915: *m.* 1946, Patrick Alexander Vans of Barnbarroch (formerly Vans Agnew), and has issue living, James Edward, *b.* 1950,—Margaret Olivia, *b.* 1948: *m.* 1968, John Francis Mills, of The Old Valley Inn, Chalford, Stroud, Glos., and has issue living, Oliver John *b.* 1970, Emily Anne *b.* 1972. *Residence,*—Stanfields, Kingscourt Lane, Rodborough, Stroud, Glos.

PREDECESSORS.—[1] *Sir* WILLIAM de Grey, Knt., having filled the offices of Solicitor-Gen., Attorney-Gen. and Ch. Justice of the Common Pleas, was cr. *Baron Walsingham,* of Walsingham, co. Norfolk (peerage of Great Britain) 1780; sat as M.P. for Newport, Cornwall, 1762-8, and for Cambridge University 1770; *d.* 1781; *s.* by his son [2] THOMAS, 2nd Baron; was for 20 years Chairman of Committees of House of Lords; *d.* 1818; *s.* by his el. son [3] GEORGE, 3rd Baron; he was burned to death April 26th, 1831, his wife dying the following day; *s.* by his brother [4] THOMAS, 4th Baron; was Archdeacon of Surrey, and Prebendary of Winchester, &c.; *d.* 1839; *s.* by his son [5] THOMAS, 5th Baron; *b.* 1804: *m.* 1st, Augusta Louisa, dau. of Sir Robert Frankland Russell, 7th Bt.; 2ndly, the Hon. Emily Elizabeth Julia Thellusson, dau. of 2nd Baron Rendlesham; *d.* 1870; *s.* by his son [6] THOMAS, 6th Baron, *b.* 1843; M.P. for Norfolk (C) 1865-70, and a Lord-in-Waiting to Queen Victoria 1874-5: *m.* 1st, 1877, Augusta Selina Elizabeth (Leila), who *d.* 1906, dau. of the late William Locke [see Os. Dysart, colls.], widow of Ernest, Lord Burghersh [E. Westmorland], and formerly wife of Don Luigi Caracciolo, Duke of San Teodoro; 2ndly, 1903, Marion Gwytherne-Williams, of Belvedere, St. Lawrence, Isle of Wight, who *d.* 1913, dau. of the late Thomas Rhys Withers; 3rdly, 1914, Agnes Baird, who *d.* 1926, dau. of the late Frederick Shand Hemming, and widow of Richard Dawson, of Lealands, Hellingly; *d.* 1919; *s.* by his son [7] JOHN AUGUSTUS, 7th Baron, *b.* 1849; a Metropolitan Police Magistrate 1905-19: *m.* 1st, 1883, Elizabeth Henrietta,

who d. 1927, da. of Patrick Grant, HEICS; 2ndly, 1928, Marguerite, who d. 1931, da. of the late
Walter Vernon, of Trematon Lodge, Anerley, SE, and widow of Thomas Godley, of Scarborough;
d. 1929; s. by his son [8] GEORGE, DSO, OBE, 8th Baron, b. 1884; Lt.-Col. R. Norfolk Regt.
1914-18 War (thrice wounded): m. 1919, Hyacinth Lambart, who d. 1968, da. of the late Lt.-Col.
Lambart Henry Bouwens, RHA; d. 1965; s. by his son [9] JOHN, MC, 9th Baron and present peer.

WALSTON, BARON. (Walston.) [Life Baron 1961.]

HENRY DAVID LEONARD GEORGE
WALSTON, son of the late Sir Charles
Walston; b. June 16th, 1912; ed. at
Eton, and at King's Coll., Camb.;
a JP for Cambridge; Director-Gen. of
Agriculture, British Zone of Germany,
and Agricultural Adviser for Germany,
Foreign Office 1946-47; Parl. Under-
Sec. of State, Foreign Office 1964-67,
and Parl. Sec. Board of Trade 1967;
Chm. of Inst. of Race Relations 1968-71;
a Crown Estate Comnr. since 1967;
Chm. of E. Anglia Econ. Planning
Council since 1970; a Member of UK
Delegation to the Consultative Assembly
of Council of Europe 1970; Member of
European Parl. Strasbourg since 1975; cr. Baron Walston, of Newton, co.
Cambridge (Life Baron) 1961: m. 1935, Catherine Macdonald, da. of David H.
Crompton, of Rye, New York, USA, and has issue.

Arms,—Quarterly or and azure in chief two lions combatant and in base two similar lions counter-
changed within a bordure ermine. Crest,—Upon a rock an oak tree proper between two wings azure.
Supporters,—Dexter, A farm labourer supporting by the exterior hand a sheaf of barley; sinister,
a West Indian supporting likewise a stalk of bananas all proper.
  Residences,—Town's End Springs, Thriplow, Cambridge; A14, Albany, W1; Marquis, St. Lucia,
W. Indies. Clubs,—Brooks's, County (Cambridge).

SONS LIVING.
Hon. Oliver (Thriplow Farm, Thriplow, Royston, Herts.) b, 1941: m. 1st, 1966, Leslie, da. of Milton A.
  Gordon, of New York; 2ndly, 1969, Anne Dunbar, of Washington, DC, and has issue.
Hon. William (Mortimer's Farm, Foxton, Cambs.), b. 1942: m. 1963, Hilary Blanche, da. of William
  Osselton Galbraith, and has issue.
Hon. James Patrick Francis, b. 1949.

DAUGHTERS LIVING.
Hon. Anne Sheridan, b. 1937: m. 1960, Charles Edward Brewin, of Middle Culham Farmhouse, Henley-
  on-Thames, and has issue.
Hon. Susan (twin), b. 1942

WARD OF NORTH TYNESIDE, BARONESS. (Ward.) [Life Baroness 1974.]
IRENE MARY BEWICK WARD, CH, DBE, da. of the late Alfred John Bewick
Ward, of London; b. 1895; a JP of Newcastle upon Tyne; Hon. Fellow Lucy
Cavendish Collegiate Soc., Cambridge; Hon. FRSA; MP for Wallsend (C)
1931-45, and for Tynemouth 1950-74; cr. CBE (Civil) 1929, DBE (Civil)
1955, CH 1973, and Baroness Ward of North Tyneside, of North Tyneside, co.
of Tyne and Wear (Life Baroness) 1974.
  Residence,—4, Roseworth Terr., Gosforth, Newcastle upon Tyne 3.

WARD OF WITLEY, VISCOUNT. (Ward.) [Viscount U.K. 1960.]

GEORGE REGINALD WARD, P.C., 1st Viscount, youngest son of 2nd Earl of Dudley, b. Nov. 20th, 1907; ed. at Eton, and at Ch. Ch., Oxford; Group Capt. (retired) R.A.F.; is a Freeman of City of London; was Under-Sec. of State for Air March 1952 to Dec. 1955, Parliamentary and Financial Sec. to the Admiralty Dec. 1955 to Jan. 1957, and Sec. of State for Air Jan. 1957 to Oct. 1960; European War 1939-45; sat as M.P. for Worcester (C) July 1945 to Oct. 1960: cr. P.C. 1957, and Viscount Ward of Witley, of Great Witley, co. Worcester (peerage of U.K.) 1960: m. 1st, 1940, Ann Diana France Ayesha (from whom he obtained a divorce 1951), dau. of the late Capt. Arthur Edward Capel, C.B.E. [see By. of Ribblesdale]; 2ndly, 1962, Barbara Mary Colonsay (ASTOR), dau. of the late Capt. Ronald Frank Rous McNeill, Irish Guards, and has issue by 1st marriage.

Arms,—Chequy or and azure a bend ermine. Crest,—Out of a ducal coronet or a lion's head azure. Supporters,—On either side the figure of an angel proper crined and winged or vested azure each holding in the exterior hand by the chains a portcullis gold.

Residences,—Friars Well, Aynho, Banbury, Oxon; 47, Berkeley Sq., W1X 5DB. Clubs,—White's, Pratt's.

SON LIVING. (By 1st marriage.)
Hon. ANTHONY GILES HUMBLE, b. June 10th, 1943; ed. at Eton.

DAUGHTER LIVING. (By 1st marriage.)
Hon. Georgina Anne WARD, b. 1941; reverted to her maiden name by deed poll 1971: m. 1966 (m. diss. 1971) Alastair Forbes.

WARDINGTON, BARON. (Pease.) [Baron U.K. 1936.]

Peace and hope.

Harlech. Residence,—72, Ladbroke Rd., W11.
Ocean Racing.

CHRISTOPHER HENRY BEAUMONT PEASE, 2nd Baron; b. Jan. 22nd, 1924; s. 1950; ed. at Eton; late Capt. Scots Guards; a partner in the firm of Hoare & Co., Govett, Ltd.; an Alderman of City of London 1960-63; 1939-45 War (wounded): m. 1964, Audrey (DUNFEE), da. of John White.

Arms,—Per fesse azure and gules, a fesse nebuly ermine between two lambs passant in chief argent, and in base upon a mount proper a dove rising argent, holding in the beak a pea stalk, the blossom and pods proper. Crest,—Upon the capital of an Ionic column a dove rising, holding in the beak a pea stalk as in the arms. Supporters,—On either side a fox or, charged on the shoulder with a bugle horn stringed sable.

Seat,—Wardington Manor, Banbury, Oxon.
Town Residence,—29, Moore Street, S.W.3.

BROTHER LIVING.
Hon. WILLIAM SIMON, b. Oct. 15th, 1925; ed. at Eton, and at New Coll., Oxford (MA); MB and BS London; FRCS England; late Capt. Gren. Gds.; Consultant Surg. ENT Depart., Central Middx. Hosp.: m. 1962, the Hon. Elizabeth Jane Ormsby-Gore, da. of 4th Baron Harlech. Clubs,—Pratt's, Royal Yacht Squadron, Royal Ocean Racing.

WIDOW LIVING OF FIRST BARON.
Hon. DOROTHY CHARLOTTE (Dorothy, Baroness Wardington), da. of 1st Baron Forster, and widow of Capt. the Hon. Harold Fox Pitt Lubbock, Grenadier Guards [see B. Avebury]: m. 1923, the 1st Baron, who d. 1950. Residence,—Lepe House, Exbury, Southampton.

PREDECESSOR.—[1] JOHN WILLIAM BEAUMONT Pease, 1st Baron, son of the late John William Pease, D.C.L.,of Pendower, Newcastle-upon-Tyne, and Nether Grange, Alnmouth, Northumberland; b. 1869; Chm. of Lloyds Bank 1922-45, and of Bank of London and S. America 1922-47; cr. Baron Wardington of Alnmouth, co. Northumberland (peerage of United Kingdom) 1936: m. 1923, the Hon. Dorothy Charlotte, dau. of 1st Baron Forster, and widow of Capt. the Hon. Harold Fox Pitt Lubbock, Grenadier Guards [see B. Avebury]; d. 1950; s. by his el. son, [2] CHRISTOPHER HENRY BEAUMONT, 2nd Baron and present peer.

WARING, BARONY OF. (Waring.) [Extinct 1940.]
DAUGHTER LIVING OF FIRST BARON.
Hon. Eleanor Gladys, b. 1894: m. 1923, Capt. Arthur Cunliffe Bernard Critchley-Waring, DSO, who d. 1930, and has issue living, Angus Cunliffe Bernard (Falcon House, The Mount, Esher, Surrey; Canada Club and Roy. Commonwealth Society), b. (posthumous) 1930; ed. at Charterhouse and at Harvard Univ.; late Lt. 5th Dragoon Guards, Pres., Lothian House Ltd. of Lothian House (U.K.) Ltd., and of Lothian Mews (Bloor) Ltd., and a Dir. of 100 Bloor Street West, Ltd., Toronto, and late Gov.-Gen.'s Horse Guards (Mil. Reserve Unit); a Member of National Executive, Canadian Save the Children Fund: m. 1957, Anita Elaine Harrison, and has issue living, Nicole Simone b. 1959,— Maureen Caroline, b. 1928, m. 1958 John Tinner, of The White House, Steep Lane, Findon, Sussex, and has issue living, Dominic Cornelius John b. 1962, Anna Linda b. 1958, Maria Regina b. 1960, Helen Andrea b. 1970. Residence,—Warenne Lodge, Broomers Hill Lane, Pulborough, Sussex.

WARWICK, EARL BROOKE AND OF. (Greville.) [Earl G.B. 1746.]

I scarcely call these things our own.

CHARLES GUY FULKE GREVILLE, 7th Earl : b. March 4th, 1911 ; s. 1928 ; ed. at Eton ; Lieut. Grenadier Guards (Reserve) ; is patron of two livings, a J.P., a D.L., Hon. Col. 268th Field Regt. R.A. (T.A.), and a Gov. of Birmingham Univ., of Warwick Kings Schs., of Roy. Shakespeare Theatre, and of Univ. Coll. Hospital ; has been an Alderman of Warwick since 1952 (Mayor 1951-52) ; was a Co. Councillor for Warwickshire 1934-36 : m. 1st, 1933, Rose (from whom he obtained a divorce 1938), dau. of the late David Cecil Bingham [see E. Lucan, colls.] ; 2ndly, 1942, Mary Kathleen (BELL) (from whom he obtained a divorce 1949), dau. of Percy Clifford Hopkinson; 3rdly, 1963, Mme. Janine Detry de Marès, and has issue by 1st marriage.

Arms,—Sable, on a cross, engrailed or five pellets, all within a bordure engrailed of the second or. Crests,—1st, out of a ducal coronet gules, a demi-swan, with wings expanded and elevated argent beaked of the first; 2nd, a bear sejant argent, muzzled gules, supporting a ragged staff of the first. Supporters,—Two swans, wings inverted, argent legged, beaked, and ducally gorged gules.

Club,—Royal Yacht Squadron.

SON LIVING. (By 1st marriage.)

DAVID ROBIN FRANCIS GUY (*Lord Brooke*), b. May 15th, 1934; ed. at Eton; a JP for Warwickshire, and a Gov. of Roy. Shakespeare Theatre; Warwickshire Yeo. (TA), late Life Guards: m. 1956, Sarah Anne Chester, from whom he obtained a divorce 1967, da. of Alfred Chester Beatty, of Owley, Wittersham, Kent, and has issue:—
    SON LIVING.—*Hon.* Guy David, b. Jan. 30th, 1957; ed. at Eton.
    DAUGHTER LIVING.—*Hon.* Charlotte Anne, b. 1958.
Residence,—Warwick Castle, Warwick. *Club,*—White's.

COLLATERAL BRANCHES LIVING.
Issue of the late Hon. Maynard Greville, youngest son of 5th Earl, b. 1898, d. 1960: m. 1918, Dora, who d. 1957, dau. of the late Edward Pape, of Moor Hall, Battle, and 26, Portland Place, W. :—
Felice, b. 1919 : m. 1940, Eric J. Spurrier. *Residences,*—7, Wadham Gardens, Hampstead, N.W.3; Perryfields, Easton Lodge, Dunmow, Essex.
        Issue of the late Lieut.-Col. the Hon. Alwyn Henry Fulke Greville, C.V.O., 2nd son of 4th Earl, b. 1854, d. 1929: m. 1888, Mabel Elizabeth Georgina, O.B.E., who d. 1940, dau. of the late Ernald Smith, of Selsdon Park, Croydon:—
Phyllis Dorothy Lindsay, b. 1892 : m. 1916, Brigadier Guy Elland Carne Rasch, C.V.O., D.S.O., late Gren. Gds., who d. 1955 [see Rasch, Bt.]. *Residences,*—Trelyon, Rock, Wadebridge, Cornwall; 27, Swan Court, SW3.

(In remainder to Barony of Brooke only.)
Descendants of the late Fulke Southwell Greville-Nugent [2nd son of the late Algernon Greville, great-grandson of the Hon. Algernon Greville, M.P., 2nd son of 5th Baron Brooke], who was cr. *Baron Greville* 1869 [see that title].

Grandsons of the late Brooke Southwell Greville, el. son of Maj. Southwell Greville, brother of 1st Baron Greville (infra):—
    Issue of the late Lt.-Col. Guy George Frederick Fulke Greville, DSO, b. 1884, d. 1966: m. 1911, Esther Hope, who d. 1968, da. of Henry Erskine Girard:—
Guy Eric Fulke, MC, ERD, b. 1911; Capt. R. Tank Regt. (Reserve); 1939-45 War in N. Africa, France, India and Malaya (prisoner, escaped): m. 1st, 1934, Mary Henrietta, da. of Sir Harry Waechter, 1st Bt., CMG; 2ndly, 19—,—and has issue living, (by 1st m.) Guy Jonathan Fulke, b. 1941,—René Brooke Fulke, b. 1947,—Priscilla Mary Caroline, b. 1935: m. 1957, Dr. Richard Michael Holmes, of 20, Parkside, Cambridge, and has issue living, Guy Aladar b. 1960, Michael Aristide b. 1966, Jacquetta Noël Barbara b. 1959,—Charlotte Anne, b. 1937: m. 1954, Bernard Morton-Stevens, of 58, Kew Bridge Court, Chiswick, W4,—(by 2nd m.) Peregrine, b. 19—,—,—Hugh, b. 19—.——Hugh Edward Arderne Fulke, b. 1914.

        Granddaughters of the late Maj. Southwell Greville (ante):—
    Issue of the late Brooke Southwell Greville, b. 1855, d. 1945 : m. 1879, Charlotte Priscilla, who d. 1933, dau. of the late E. B. Clough, of Pietermaritzburg, Natal:—
Charlotte Caroline Muriel, b. 1880: m. 1901, George McKechnie.——Irene Fanny Gwendoline Gertrude, b. 1888.——Cecil Violet Enid, b. 1896: m. 1927, Wing-Cdr. Edward Irvine Russell, RAF. *Residence,*—

Grandson of the late Stapleton Fulke Greville, el. son of the late Rear-Adm. Stapleton John Greville, grandson of Lt.-Col. Henry Francis Greville, yr. brother of Capt. William Fulke Greville, RN, MP (ante):—
    Issue of the late John Algernon Fulke Greville, b. 1896, d. 1968: m. 1929, Frances Alice (Old Farm Cottage, Church Lane, Hemingford Abbots, Hunts.), da. of Harry Bird Harper:—
John Brooke Fulke (314, Robin Hood Lane, Hall Green, Birmingham, 28), b. 1930: m 1958, Maureen Constance, da. of L. A. Parkhouse, and has issue living, Robert John Fulke, b. 1960.
        Granddaughters of the late Rear-Adm. Stapleton John Greville (ante):—
    Issue of the late Henry Brooke Macartney Crewe Greville, b. 1870, d. 1944 : m. 1906, Cecilia Ada, who d. 1959, dau. of Lieut.-Col. Sir Frederick Thomas Arthur Hervey-Bathurst, 4th Bt. :—
Beatrice Sheila, b. 1910 : m. 1936, Michael James Farrer, who d. 1960, and has issue living, Julia Mary Cecilia, b. 1950,—Anne Selina Lucy, b. 1953. *Residence,*—37, Cadogan Street, S.W.3.——Margaret Ishla, b. 1914. *Residence,*—Ridge Hill Cottage, Kingscote, E. Grinstead, Sussex.

PREDECESSORS.—[1] *Rt. Hon. Sir* FULKE Greville, a favourite courtier of Queen Elizabeth I, was successively keeper of the signet to the Council in the Marches of Wales, Treasurer of the Navy, and Chancellor of the Exchequer; obtained, *temp.* James I., a grant of Warwick Castle and its dependencies; cr. *Baron Brooke,* of Beauchamp's Court. co. Warwick (peerage of England) 1621, with remainder to his cousin, Robert, son of Fulke Greville, of Thorpe Latimer, co. Lincoln; *d.* unmarried 1628; *s.* by his kinsman [2] ROBERT, 2nd Baron, son of Fulke (*ante*); sat as M.P. for Warwick; was a distinguished Gen. in the Parliamentary Army during the Civil Wars; killed at the assault of Lichfield 1642; *s.* by his el. son [3] FRANCIS, 3rd Baron; *s.* by his brother [4] ROBERT, 4th Baron; was one of the Commrs. deputed to invite the return of Charles II.; *d.* 1676; *s.* by his brother [5] FULKE, 5th Baron; was Recorder of Warwick; *d.* 1710; *s.* by his grandson [6] FULKE, 6th Baron; *d.* unmarried; *s.* by his brother [7] WILLIAM, 7th Baron; was Recorder of Warwick; *d.* 1727; *s.* by his son [8] *Sir* FRANCIS, K.T., 8th Baron; was Recorder of Warwick, and Lord-Lieut. of Warwickshire; cr. *Earl Brooke* (peerage of Great Britain) 1746, and *Earl of Warwick* (peerage of Great Britain) 1759; *d.* 1773; *s.* by his son [9] GEORGE, 2nd Earl; sat as M.P. for Warwickshire; was a Lord of Trade and Recorder of Warwick; *d.* 1816; *s.* by his son [10] HENRY RICHARD, K.T., 3rd Earl; *b.* 1779; was Lord-Lieut. of Warwickshire: *m.* 1816, Sarah, widow of 3rd Baron Monson, and dau. of 2nd Earl of Mexborough; *d.* 1853; *s.* by his son [11] GEORGE GUY, 4th Earl, *b.* 1818; M.P. for S. Warwickshire (*C*) 1846-53: *m.* 1852, Lady Anne Charteris, dau. of 8th Earl of Wemyss and March; *d.* 1893; *s.* by his el. son [12] FRANCIS RICHARD CHARLES GUY, 5th Earl, *b.* 1853; M.P. for Somerset E. (*C*) 1879-85, and for Colchester 1888-92; Lord-Lieut. of Essex 1901-19 : *m.* 1881, Frances Evelyn, who *d.* 1938, dau. of the late Col. the Hon. Charles Henry Maynard [V. Maynard (*ext.*), colls]; *d.* 1924; *s.* by his el. son [13] LEOPOLD GUY FRANCIS MAYNARD, C.M.G., M.V.O., 6th Earl; *b.* 1882; Capt. 1st Life Guards; Hon. Brig.-Gen. Overseas Mil. Forces of Canada, Hon. Lieut.-Col. T.F. Reserve; S. African War 1900, European War 1914-19 as A.D.C. to Com.-in-Ch., and Comdg. 4th and 12th Canadian Inf. Brigs.; Reuter's Special Correspondent during Russo-Japanese War 1904-5 : *m.* 1909, Elfrida Marjorie, who *d.* 1943, dau. of Sir William Eden, 7th Bt.; *d.* 1928; *s.* by his el. son [14] CHARLES GUY FULKE, 7th Earl and present peer; also Baron Brooke.

Waterford, Earl of, title borne by Earl of Shewsbury

WATERFORD, MARQUESS OF. (Beresford.)   Sits as BARON TYRONE.
(G.B. 1786).   [Marquess I. 1789, Bt. I. 1665.]

No dependence but in the Cross.

JOHN HUBERT DE LA POER BERESFORD, 8th Marquess, and 12th Baronet; *b.* July 14th, 1933 ; *s.* 1934 ; ed. at Eton ; Lieut. Roy. Horse Guards Supplementary Reserve : *m.* 1957, Lady Caroline Olein Geraldine Wyndham-Quin, dau. of 6th Earl of Dunraven and Mount-Earl, and has issue.

Arms,—Quarterly: 1st and 4th argent, semée of cross crosslets fitchée and three fleurs-de-lis within a bordure engrailed sable, *Beresford*; 2nd and 3rd argent, a chief indented sable, *De la Poer*.   Crest,—A dragon's head erased azure, the neck pierced with a broken tilting spear, and holding the point broken off in the mouth.   Supporters,—Two angels, habited in white robes reaching to the ankles, hair and wings inverted or, the exterior arm extended and holding a sword erect proper, pommel and hilt gold.

Seats,—Curraghmore, Portlaw, co. Waterford ; Glenbride Lodge, Valleymount, co. Wicklow.   *Clubs,*—Turf, White's.

SONS LIVING.
HENRY NICHOLAS DE LA POER (*Earl of Tyrone*), *b.* March 23rd, 1958.
Lord Charles Richard de la Poer, *b.* 1960.
Lord James Patrick de la Poer, *b.* 1965.

DAUGHTER LIVING.
Lady Alice Rose de la Poer, *b.* 1970.

BROTHER LIVING.
Lord Patrick Tristram de la Poer, *b.* 1934; ed. at Eton; Capt. (ret.) RHG: *m.* 1964 (m. diss. 1971), Mrs. Julia Carey, da. of Col. Thomas Cromwell Williamson, DSO, and has issue living, Valentine Tristram, *b.* 1965,—Samantha Julia *b.* 1969.   *Residence,*—84, Cornwall Gdns., SW7.

AUNTS LIVING. (*Daughters of 6th Marquess.*)
Lady Katharine Nora de la Poer, *b.* 1899: *m.* 1926, Maj.-Gen. Sir David Dawnay, KCVO, CB, DSO, late 10th Roy. Hussars, who *d.* 1971 [see V. Downe, colls.].   *Residence,*—Whitfield Court, Waterford.
Lady (Beatrix) Patricia de la Poer, *b.* 1902: *m.* 1926, Lynden Roberts Miller, Bar.-at-Law, and has issue living, David, *b.* 1929; Maj. The Blues and Royals: *m.* 1955, Mariegold Winifred, da of Major Thomas John Arnott [see Arnott Bt.], and has issue living, Mark *b.* 1958, Christopher Declan *b.* 1961, Victoria Jane *b.* 1968,—Jean, *b.* 1932: *m.* 1956, Lt.-Cdr. Hugh Cecil Edmund Bulley, RN (ret.), and has issue living, Sarah *b.* 1957, Henrietta *b.* 1959, Emma *b.* 1961.   *Residence,*—Georgetown House, Kilmacthomas, co. Waterford.

WIDOW LIVING OF SON OF SIXTH MARQUESS.

Rachel (Dangan Cottage, Thomastown, co. Kilkenny), da. of George Kennett Page, of Upton Lodge, Bursledon, Hants.: *m.* 1945, Maj. Lord William Mostyn de la Poer Beresford, who *d.* 1973, and has issue [see colls. infra].

WIDOW LIVING OF SEVENTH MARQUESS.

JULIET MARY, dau. of the late Major David Balcarres Lindsay [see E. Crawford, colls.]: *m.* 1st, 1930, the 7th Marquess, who *d.* 1934; 2ndly, 1946, Lieut.-Col. John Eric Durnford Silcock. *Residence,*—Newtown Anner, Clonmel, co. Tipperary.

COLLATERAL BRANCHES LIVING.

[Branch from 2nd son of 6th Marquess of Waterford.]

Issue of the late Maj. Lord William de la Poer Beresford, 2nd son of 6th Marquess, *b.* 1905, *d.* 1973: *m.* 1945, Rachel (ante), da. of George Kennett Page, of Upton Lodge, Bursledon, Hants.:—

Meriel, *b.* 1948: *m.* 1970, Joseph Power, of Shanavaughy, Ballacolla, co. Leix, and has issue living, James Anthony, *b.* 1972,—Rosemarie Ann, *b.* 1970.—Nicola, *b.* 1950.
(*Male line in remainder to Earldom of Tyrone*).

[Branch from 2nd son of 1st Earl of Tyrone.]

Grandchildren of the late George Stuart de la Poer Beresford, 2nd son of Arthur George de la Poer Beresford, 2nd son of George William de la Poer Beresford, el. son of John Beresford (*b.* 1796), el. son of Rt. Rev. George de la Poer Beresford, 2nd son of the Rt. Hon. John de la Poer Beresford (*b.* 1738), 2nd son of 1st Earl of Tyrone:—

Issue of the late Arthur de la Poer Beresford, *b.* 1903, *d.* 1931 : *m.* 1926, Helen, who *d* dau. of the late Thomas Cull, of Perth, W. Australia :—
John de la Poer, *b.* 1927 ; Snr. Technical Officer, Commonwealth Scientific and Industrial Research Organisation : *m.* 1951, Pamela, dau. of Glen J. Sloman, of Applecross, W. Aust. and has issue living, Marcus de la Poer, *b.* 1952,—Graham de la Poer, *b.* 1954,—Simon Stuart de la Poer, *b.* 1961,—Shelley Louise, *b.* 1957. *Residence,*—Doubleview, Perth, W. Australia
——Margaret Pamela de la Poer, *b.* 1930: *m.* 1953, Lt.-Col. Eric McPhearson McCormick, and has issue living, Gordon Rory, *b.* 1954,—Peter James, *b.* 1956,—Angus Roy, *b.* 1957,—Hamish John *b.* 1961.

Issue of the late Major Brian de la Poer Beresford, M.C., Australian Forces, *b.* 1910, *d.* (killed in action in New Guinea) Dec. 1942: *m.* (April) 1942, Valmai, only dau. of Merlyn B. Jones, of Perth, W. Australia:—

Brian George de la Poer (posthumous) (3, Circe Circle, Dalkeith, W. Australia), *b.* 1943; Bar. at Law and Solicitor, Australia: *m.* 1964, Deborah Frances, only da. of Albert Francis Gamble, of Evalley, Koorda, W. Australia, and has issue living, Brian James de la Poer, *b.* 1967,—Victoria Jane, *b.* 1965.

Grandchildren of the late Arthur George de la Poer Beresford (ante):—
Issue of the late George Stuart de la Poer Beresford (twin), *b.* 1877, *d.* 1965: *m.* 1st, 1900, Margaret, who *d.* 1920, da. of the late Edward Hooper, of Melbourne, Victoria; 2ndly, 1923, Kathleen, who *d.* 1950, da. of the late Thomas Cull, of Perth, W. Australia; 3rdly, 1950, Faith (178, Coode St., Como 6152, W. Aust.), da. of the Rev. F. G. O'Halloran, of Perth, W. Australia, and widow of Sqdn. Ldr. Preston Williams, MC:—

By 1st marriage) Marjory Ellen de la Poer, *b.* 1901.——Rosemary de la Poer, *b.* 1917: *m.* (Feb.) 1948, Flight Lt. Reginald Harold Sutton, DFC, RAAF, of Must St., Portland, Victoria, Australia, and has issue living, David Beresford, *b.* 1953,—Georgia Jane, *b.* (Dec.) 1948,—Ann Rosemary, *b.* 1950.

Issue of the late Marcus John de la Poer Beresford, *b.* 1882, *d.* 1952 : *m.* 1st, 1910, Alice Janet Schmidt, who *d.* 1935, of Victoria, Australia ; 2ndly, 1936, Edith, dau. of the late Capt. George Wilkins, of Young, N.S. Wales :—
(By 1st marriage) Marcus de la Poer, *b.* 1912 : *m.* 1936, Marie Helmers, and has issue living, Marcus Edward de la Poer, *b.* 1937,—Brian de la Poer, *b.* 1942.——John de la Poer, *b.* 1913 ; S.-W. Pacific 1944-45 with Australian Imperial Force : *m.* 1936, Helen Wilson, and has issue living, John de la Poer, *b.* 1942,—Helen de la Poer, *b.* 1937,—Barbara de la Poer, *b.* 1940. *Residence,*—Turramurra, N.S. Wales.

Issue of the late Henry Mayo de la Poer Beresford, *b.* 1889, *d.* 1948: *m.* 1921, Nathalie, who *d.* 1963, da. of the late Robert Muir, of Middle Brighton, Victoria, Australia:—
Joan de la Poer, *b.* 1922: *m.* 1965, Ralph Louis Bewick, MBE, TD, R. Fusiliers (TA) (ret.), of The Holt, Outwood Lane, Kingswood, Surrey.——Judith de la Poer, *b.* 1930: *m.* 1954, Lt.-Col. Robin William Hone, R. Australian Regt., and has issue living, David Christopher, *b.* 1958,—Carolyn Louise, *b.* 1963. *Address,*—18, Orange Grove, Kensington Park, S. Aust. 5068.

Issue of the late Capt. William Russell de la Poer Beresford, M.C., *b.* 1893; *d.* 1938: *m.* 1923, Marie Isobel, who *d.* 1944, dau. of Samuel Cowper Ward. of Adelaide. S. Australia:—
Diana Mary de la Poer, *b.* 1924: *m.* 1946, Arthur John Watson, FRCP, FRACP, of 48, Barnard St., N. Adelaide, S. Aust., and has issue living, Christopher John Beresford (7, Athelney Av., St. Peters, S. Aust.), *b.* 1948: *m.* 1970, Georgiana Henry, and has issue living, Michaela, *b.* 1970,—Johanna Mary Beresford, *b.* 1950: *m.* 19—, Rolf Alexander Detmering, of 8, Ambach/Starnbergersee, Hof Luigenkam, W. Germany,—Robina Anne Beresford, *b.* 1960.——Marie Suzanne de la Poer, *b.* 1925: *m.* 1946, Murray Frew Bonnin, Solicitor, late Australian Imperial Force, and has issue living, John Frew, *b.* 1951,—David Frew, *b.* 1952. *Residence,*—Iveston, Le Fevre Terr., N. Adelaide, S. Aust.

Grandchildren of the late Richard de la Poer Beresford, 3rd son of George William de la Poer Beresford (ante):—

Issue of the late Claude Richard de la Poer Beresford, *b.* 1888, *d.* 1945, : *m.* 1915, Edith Marion (Flat 2, 47, Buxton St., N. Adelaide, S. Aust), da. of Christopher Beaven, of Adelaide, S. Australia:—

Ben Richard de la Poer, *b.* 1927; late RAN; AASA: *m.* 1955, Janet Marcia, da. of John Essington Grime, of The Pines, Green Point, NSW, and has issue living, William Richard de la Poer, *b.* 1959,—John Ben de la Poer, *b.* 1965,—Charles Patrick de la Poer, *b.* 1966,—Mary Lynne de la Poer, *b.* 1956. *Residence,*—36, Brunswick St., North Walkerville, S. Australia.——Donald Charles de la Poer (44, Regent St., E. Brighton, Victoria 3187, Aust.), *b.* 1933: *m.* 1962, Ruth Tisdall, and has issue living, Peter Mark de la Poer, *b.* 1965,—Susan Jane de la Poer, *b.* 1964.——Sydney May de la Poer, *b.* 1917: *m.* 1937, Leonard Arthur Ranson Evans, late AIF, and has issue living, Michael John de la Poer Beresford, *b.* 1941,—Elizabeth Jane, *b.* 1946.——Molly Clodagh de la Poer, *b.* 1920: *m.* 1940, Harold de Vall Amphlett, late AIF, and has issue living, John de Vall, *b.* 1949,—Margaret de Vall, *b.* 1947. *Residence,*—

Issue of the late Guy Erroll de la Poer Beresford, *b.* 1889, *d.* 1944: *m.* 1921, Dorothy Margaret (52, Walkerville Terr., Gilberton, S. Australia), da. of W. T. McCoy, of Adelaide:—
Richard de la Poer, *b.* 1922; 1939-45 War in RAAF: *m.* 1945, Elizabeth Leitch, and has issue living, Marcus Richard de la Poer, *b.* 1950,—Melaine de la Poer, *b.* 1948.——Margaret de la Poer, *b.* 1925: *m.* 1947, Jan Edgar Marr, late AIF, and has issue living.

Granddaughter of the late George William de la Poer Beresford (ante):—
Issue of the late Richard de la Poer Beresford, *b.* 1856, *d.* 1917: *m.* 1887, Sydney Julia, who
d. 1920, dau. of the late John Acraman, of Adelaide:—
Eileen May de la Poer, *M.B.E.*, *b.* 1894; has Coronation medal (1953); M.B.E. (Civil) 1942: *m.* 1915,
Harold Rischbieth, F.R.C.S., who *d.* 1943, and has issue living, John Beresford Wills, *V.R.D.* (of
12, St. Andrew's Street, Walkerville, S. Australia), *b.* 1917; European War 1939-45 as Lieut. Roy
Australian Naval Reserve: *m.* 1944, Joan, dau. of the late J. O. Stephenson, of Perth, W. Australia
and has issue living, Ian Harold *b.* 1954, Peggy Jane *b.* 1956,—Henry George, *VRD, MB, BS,*
FRACP, DCH (306, Ward St., N. Adelaide, S. Australia), *b.* 1920; 1942-45 War as Surg.-Lt. R.
Australian Naval Reserve: *m.* 1945, Nancy Fearon, da. of the late Geoffrey Henderson, of S. Australia, and has issue living, Geoffrey John *b.* 1959, Margot Henderson *b.* 1949, Judith Anne *b.* 1951,
Suzanne Joan *b.* 1955,—Richard Harold Charles, *MB, BS, MRCP, FRACP* (40 Church Terr.,
Walkerville, S. Aust.), *b.* 1927: *m.* 1957, Judith Ann, da. of the late Robert K. Wood, and has issue
living, Peter Robert *b.* 1957, Henry Mark *b.* 1958, Thomas John Hugh *b.* 1962, Anne Caroline *b.*
1960. *Residence,*—43, Barnard St., N. Adelaide, S. Australia.

Grandson of the late Col. Marcus Wylly de la Poer Beresford, 2nd son of the late
John Beresford (*b.* 1796) (ante):—
Issue (by 1st marriage) of the late Marcus Henry de la Poer Beresford, C.M.G., I.S.O.,
b. 1857, *d.* 1934: *m.* 1st, 1882, Margery Mary, who *d.* 1920, dau. of the Rev. John Connell,
formerly R. of the Grenadines, St. Vincent, W. Indies ; 2ndly, 1921, Florence Mary,
who *d.* 1922, dau. of the late Edward Mitchell, of Ranelagh, Dublin :—
Julian Walter de la Poer, *b.* 1886 ; sometime Capt. Inland Water Transport: *m.* 1921, Henriette
Josephine Amelie Geraldine (from whom he obtained a divorce 1940), dau. of Col. Comdt.
B. Bochart, of Namur, Belgium. *Residence,*—

Grandson of the late Edward Beresford, yr. son of George de la Poer Beresford,
el. son of the Rt. Hon. and Most Rev. Marcus Gervais Beresford, DD, Archbishop
of Armagh, 2nd son of the Rt. Rev. George de la Poer Beresford (ante):—
Issue of the late George Henry William de la Poer Beresford, *b.* 1904, *d.* 1961: *m.* 1926,
Mary (from whom he obtained a divorce 1949), dau. of George Richardson, of Molesley :—
John George de la Poer (4557, Sherbrooke St. W., Apart. 304, Westmount, Quebec, Canada), *b.* 1927:
m. 1960, Jeanne Frances, da. of William Steward, of London, and has issue living, Stephen de la
Poer, *b.* 1961,—Mark de la Poer, *b.* 1962,—Clare Jeanne, *b.* 1964.

Grandchildren of the late George Henry William de la Poer Beresford (ante):—
Issue of the late Timothy Edward de la Poer Beresford, *b.* 1931, *d.* 1964: *m.* 1955, Mary
Thom Leburn (Maureen) (who *m.* 2ndly, 1965, Maj. Matthew Alexander Forrester of
Harbourne Hall, High Halden, Kent), only child of the late John Waugh, of Edinburgh:—
Michael John de la Poer, *b.* 1957.——Karen Mary de la Poer, *b.* 1959.

Grandson of the late Maj. Henry Marcus Beresford, yr. son of the late Rt. Hon.
and Most Rev. Marcus Gervais Beresford, Archbishop of Armagh (ante) :—
Issue of the late Lieut.-Col. Kennedy Beresford, *b.* 1862, *d.* 1943: *m.* 1st, 1894, Grace, who
d. 1931, dau. of the late Major J. F. des Barres ; 2ndly, 1935, Rose Miriam, who *d.* 1950,
dau. of the late Lieut.-Col. Anthony Oliver Molesworth [V. Molesworth, colls.] :—
(By 1st marriage) Gervais de la Poer, *M.B.E.*, *M.C.*, *D.S.M.*, *b.* 1895; ed. at Marlborough ; is
temporary Col. R.E. ; formerly an E. Indian merchant; European War 1915-17 (despatches,
D.S.M., M.C., 2nd class Order of St. Anne of Russia with swords) ; M.B.E. (Mil.) 1942 : *m.* 1st, 1927,
Nada Celina, who *d.* 1956, dau. of Harry L. Wormald, of Bramhall, Cheshire ; 2ndly, 1957, Rosemary Helen Arnaud Gange, dau. of the late Lieut.-Col. G. H. Painter, R.E., of Epsom, Surrey,
and has issue living, (by 1st marriage) Michael Marcus Gervais de la Poer, *b.* 1928 ; ed. at Marlborough, and at Birmingham Univ. ; is Lieut. 8th Hussars (Reserve). *Address,*—c/o Westminster
Bank, Milsom Street, Bath.

Grandchildren of the late John Barré Beresford, el. son of Henry Barré Beresford,
yst. son of the Rt. Hon. John de la Poer Beresford (*b.* 1738) (ante):—
Issue of the late Col. William Randal Hamilton Beresford-Ash, *b.* 1859, *d.* 1938
(having assumed by Roy. licence 1901, the additional surname of Ash): *m.* 1886,
Lady Florence Marion Browne, who *d.* 1946, dau. of 5th Marquess of Sligo :—
Douglas, *b.* 1887 ; ed. at Eton ; Major (retired) Roy. Fusiliers (City of London Regt.), and a D.L.
for co. Londonderry ; European War 1914-19 (wounded, despatches) : *m.* 1930, Lady Betty,
Helena Joanna Rous who *d.* 1969, da. of 3rd Earl of Stradbroke, and has issue living, John Randal
b. 1938, ed. at Eton: *m.* 1968, Agnès Marie Colette, da. of Count Guy de Lamberterie, of 3, rue
Frédéric Magisson, Paris XV, and has issue living, Louisa Jane *b.* 1971. *Residence,*—Ashbrook, co.
Londonderry. *Clubs,*—United Service, Kildare Street.

Issue of the late Lieut.-Col. Marcus John Barré de la Poer Beresford, D.S.O., *b.* 1868,
d. (result of enemy action during European War) 1944: *m.* 1914, Alma, who *d.* 1963,
da. of David Methven, of Hillside, 31, Elsworthy Rd., Regent's Park, NW3:—
Patricia Douglas Methven, *b.* 1924: *m.* 19—, —Carter. *Residence,*—

Granddaughter of the late Capt. George de la Poer Beresford, yst. son of Henry
Barré Beresford (ante):—
Issue of the late Lieut. Tristram Henry Barré Beresford, R.N., *b.* 1851, *d.* 1917: *m.* 1878,
Helen Frederika Conyers, who *d.* 1935, dau. of the late Lieut.-Col. F. H. Lang :—
Maud Clara Emily, *b.* 1882 : *m.* 1917, Capt. T. Lachasse, E. African Regt., who *d.* (killed in action
during European War) 1918, and has issue living, Bettine Mary Dolores (*posthumous*), *b.* 1918:
m. 1936, Linden Crawford, and has issue living, Alan Thomas *b.* 1942, Charles Edward *b.* 1945.
Residence,—

Branch from 3rd son of 1st Earl of Tyrone.

Decendants of the late Most Rev. the Hon. William Beresford, D.D. (3rd son of
1st Earl of Tyrone), who was cr. *Baron Decies* 1812 [see that title].

PREDECESSORS.—[1] Sir TRISTRAM Beresford, *M.P.* for Londonderry, was cr. a *Baronet* 1665;
d. 1673; *s.* by his son [2] Sir RANDAL, 2nd Bt.; *s.* by his son [3] Sir TRISTRAM, 3rd Bt.;
commanded a Regt. of Foot against James II., and was attainted by Parliament; *d.* 1701; *s.*
by his son [4] Sir MARCUS, 4th Bt.: *m.* 1717, Lady Catharine Poer (*Baroness La Poer* in her
own right, cr. by writ of summons 1375 *et seq.*), dau. and heiress of James, 3rd Earl of Tyrone
and Baron La Poer; cr. *Baron Beresford*, of Beresford, co. Cavan, and *Viscount Tyrone*
(peerage of Ireland) 1720, and *Earl of Tyrone* (peerage of Ireland) 1746; *d.* 1763; *s.* by his son
[5] GEORGE DE LA POER, 2nd Earl, who in 1769 *s.* his mother in the Barony of De La Poer; cr.
Baron Tyrone, of Haverfordwest, co. Pembroke (peerage of Great Britain) 1786, and *Marquess
of Waterford* (peerage of Ireland) 1789; *d.* 1800; *s.* by his son [6] HENRY DE LA POER, *K.P.,*
P.C., 2nd Marquess was Gov. of co. Waterford and Col. of Waterford Militia; *d.* 1826; *s.* by
his el. son [7] HENRY DE LA POER, *K.P.,* 3rd Marquess; *d.* 1859; *s.* by his brother [8] JOHN
DE LA POER, 4th Marquess; *b.* 1814; was in Holy Orders, a Rural Dean, and Incumbent of
Mullaghbrack: *m.* 1843, Christiana, dau. of Charles Powell Leslie, M.P., of Glaslough,
co. Monaghan ; *d.* 1866; *s.* by his son [9] JOHN HENRY DE LA POER, *P.C.,* *K.P.,* 5th Marquess, *b.*
1844; Lord-Lieut. of co. Waterford ; M.P. for Waterford Co. (*C*) 1865-6, and Master of the Buck-
hounds 1885-6 : *m.* 1st, 1872, Florence Grosvenor, who *d.* 1873, dau. of Major George Rowley,
Bombay Army, and the divorced wife of the Hon. John C. W. Vivian; 2ndly, 1874, Lady
Blanche Elizabeth Adelaide, dau. of 8th Duke of Beaufort; *d.* 1895; *s.* by his only son [10]
HENRY DE LA POER, *K.P.,* 6th Marquess, *b.* 1875 : *m.* 1897, Lady Beatrix Frances Fitzmaurice,

G.B.E., who *d.* 1953 (having *m.* 2ndly, 1918, the 12th Duke of St. Albans), dau. of 5th Marquess of Lansdowne; *d.* 1911; *s.* by his el. son [11] JOHN CHARLES DE LA POER, 7th Marquess, *b.* 1901: *m.* 1930, Juliet Mary, dau. of Major David Balcarres Lindsay; *d.* 1934; *s.* by his el. son [12] JOHN HUBERT DE LA POER, 8th Marquess and present peer; also Earl of Tyrone, Viscount Tyrone, Baron La Poer, Baron Beresford, and Baron Tyrone.

WATERPARK, BARON. (Cavendish.) [Baron I. 1792, Bt. G.B. 1755.]

Secure by caution.

FREDERICK CARYLL PHILIP CAVENDISH, 7th Baron, and 8th Baronet; *b.* Oct. 6th, 1926; *s.* 1948; ed. at Eton; late Lieut. Grenadier Guards: *m.* 1951, Danièle Alice, dau. of Roger Guirche, of 1, Avenue Bugeaud, Paris, and has issue.

Arms,—Sable, three stags' heads cabossed argent, attired or, within a bordure of the second. Crest.—On a ducal coronet or, a serpent nowed fessewise proper. Supporters,—Dexter, a stag, per fesse indented gules and sable, attired and unguled or; sinister, a stag proper, attired and unguled or, and gorged with a chaplet of four roses argent and azure, alternately.

Residences,—22, Ovington Gdns., SW3; Bletchingdon, Oxford. *Clubs,*—Guards, Royal Aero.

SON LIVING

Hon. RODERICK ALEXANDER, *b.* Oct. 10th, 1959.

DAUGHTERS LIVING.

Hon. Caroline Laurence Patricia, *b.* 1952.
Hon. Juliet Enid, *b.* 1953.

SISTER LIVING.

Patricia Enid (Broadlands Stud, Somerset West, C.P., S. Africa), *b.* 1925: *m.* 1st, 1950 (m. diss. 19—), Frank Thomas O'Neill; 2ndly, 1958, Count Aymar de Roussy de Sales; 3rdly, 1969, Frank Thomas O'Neill (ante).

DAUGHTERS LIVING OF SIXTH BARON. (By 1st marriage.)

Hon. Cecilia Claribel, *b.* 1903: *m.* 1933, James Mitchell Anderson, M.D., Ch.B., who *d.* 1963, and has issue living, Isabel Juliet Cavendish, *b.* 1937: *m.* 1957, Clifford Anthony Broom, and has issue living, Nicholas James *b.* 1959, Christopher David *b.* 1961,—Annabel Fiona Macpherson Cavendish, *b.* 1940: *m.* 1st, 1962 (m. diss. 1970), Manfred Selfert; 2ndly, 1971, Haven Lamar Dunn, of 5442, Prince Scotty St., Las Vegas, Nevada, USA, and has issue living (by 1st m.), Jenny Elisabeth *b.* 1965. *Residence,*—Courtenay Beach, Kingsway, Hove, Sussex.

(By 2nd marriage.)

Hon. Margaret, *b.* 1907: *m.* 1934, Wallace Edward Thomas Leaver, B.Sc. who *d.* 1972, and has issue living, Diana Cavendish, *b.* 1938: *m.* 1961, Charles Peter Parnell Wiggins, of East Cross, Tenterden, Kent, and has issue living, Rupert Alexander Cavendish *b.* 1963, Philippa Cavendish *b.* 1962,—Elizabeth Cavendish, *b.* 1942. *Residence,*—St. Benets, Beech Hill, Bridge, Canterbury.

Hon. Winifred *b.* 1909: *m.* 1929. Albert Frank Tribe, Trinity House Pilot, who *d.* 1962, having assumed by deed poll 1944 the additional surname of Cavendish, and by letters patent, 1944 the Arms of Cavendish quarterly with Tribe, and has issue living, Barrie Cavendish (of Leeside, Bay Rd., Dovercourt, Essex), *b.* 1930: *m.* 1957, Jane McGeorge, only dau. of Surg. Rear-Adm. David Duncan, CB, OBE, and has issue living, Alan Cavendish *b.* 1960, Sonia Cavendish *b.* 1963. *Residence,*—Ragstone Cottage, Meadow Close, Bridge, Canterbury, Kent.

WIDOW LIVING OF SIXTH BARON.

JEANNE, (*Dowager Baroness Waterpark*), dau. of Pierre Lassalette: *m.* 1929, as his fifth wife, the 6th Baron who *d.* 1948. *Residence,*—

COLLATERAL BRANCH LIVING.

Grandsons of the late Charles Tyrell Cavendish, second son of the late Hon. Richard Cavendish, 2nd son of 2nd Baron :—

Issue of the late Tyrell William Cavendish, *b.* 1875, *d.* 1912: *m.* 1906, Julia Florence, who *d.* 1963, only child of Henry Siegel, of New York:—

Henry Siegel, *b.* 1908; ed. at Eton, and at Trin. Coll., Camb.; European War 1939-45 as Squadron-Leader Auxiliary Air Force: *m.* 1940, Diana Linda, dau. of Edward Hewish Ryle, and has issue living, William Henry Tyrell, *b.* 1940. *Residence,*—15, Cadogan Lane, SW1.——Geoffrey Manners (Bank Flat, Barclays Bank Chambers, 33, Market St., Nottingham), *b.* 1910; ed. at Stowe; CEng; MIEE; a Member of Institution of British Radio Engineers; has Diploma of Faraday House Engineering Coll.; late Air Min. Examiner in Scientific and Electrical Section of Aeronautical Inspection Directorates: *m.* 1st, 1937, Cæcilia Frances Patricia, who *d.* 1968, da. of Godfrey Pharazyn, of Waewaepa Dannevirke, Hawkes Bay, NZ; 2ndly, 1967, Mrs. Pamela Newman, and has issue living, (by 1st m.) Caroline Anne, *b.* 1938: *m.* 1964, Charles Grellan Aliaga-Kelly, BArch, ARIBA, MTPI, FRIAI, of Clare Villa, Coliemore Rd., Dalkey, co. Dublin, and has issue living, William John *b.* 1967,—Cecilia Bridget, *b.* 1941.

PREDECESSORS.—[1] *Rt. Hon.* HENRY Cavendish, P.C.; M.P. for Lismore, Teller of the Exchequer in Ireland, Collector for Cork, and a Commr. for Revenue (Ireland); cr. a *Baronet* 1755: *d.* 1776; *s.* by his son [2] *Sir* HENRY, P.C., 2nd Bt.; sat as M.P. for Lostwithiel; was Receiver-Gen. in Ireland: *m.* 1757, Sarah, dau. and heir of Richard Bradshaw, which lady was in 1792 cr. *Baroness Waterpark*, of Waterpark, co. Cork (peerage of Ireland), with remainder to her issue male by Sir Henry Cavendish; she *d.* 1807; *s.* by her son [3] RICHARD, 2nd Baron, who in 1804 had *s.* his father as 3rd Bt.; *d.* 1830; *s.* by his son [4] HENRY MANNERS, 3rd Baron; *b.* 1793; was Col. Derbyshire Militia, and a Lord-in-Waiting: *m.* 1837, the Hon. Eliza Jane, *V.A.*, who *d.* 1894, dau. of 1st Viscount Anson; *d.* 1863; *s.* by his son [5] HENRY ANSON, 4th Baron; *b.* 1839: *m.* 1873, Emily, who *d.* 1925, dau. of the late John Stenning: *d.* 1912; *s.* by his son [6] CHARLES FREDERICK, 5th Baron, *b.* 1883; *d.* 1932; *s.* by his cousin [7] HENRY SHEPPARD HART (el. son of the late William Thomas Cavendish, grandson of 2nd Baron), 6th Baron: *b.* 1876; was a hunter and explorer in Africa, Patagonia, Australia, Soloman Islands, and Canada: *m.* 1st, 1902, Isabel Emilie (an actress), who *d.* 1927 (having obtained a divorce 1906), da. of John Wimburn Jay; 2ndly, 1906, May (who *d.* 1969, having obtained a divorce 1913), da. of William Ernest Burbridge, of Bromley, Kent; 3rdly, 1913 (marriage dissolved in France 1919), Elise, dau. of Emmanuel Adolphe Herran, formerly Sec. to French Embassy in London; 4thly, 1920 (marriage dissolved in France 1929) Georgette, dau. of Ivan Zlateffmoloff Chandronnier of Bulgaria; 5thly, 1929, Jeanne, dau. of Pierre Lassalette; *d.* 1948; *s.* by his nephew [8] FREDERICK CARYLL PHILIP (only son of the late Brig.-Gen. Frederick William Laurence Sheppard Hart Cavendish, brother of 6th Baron), 7th Baron and present peer.

WATKINS, BARON. (Watkins.) [Life Baron 1972.]

TUDOR ELWYN WATKINS, el. son of the late Howell Watkins, JP, of Aber-
crave, Swansea Valley; *b.* May 9th, 1903; ed. at Harlech Coll.; Alderman
Breconshire Co. Council 1940-73; Lord Lieut. of Powys since 1975; Political
Agent for Brecon and Radnor 1928-33, MP (*Lab.*) Brecon and Radnor 1945-70,
and PPS to Sec. of State for Wales 1964-68; Gen. Sec. Breconshire Assocn. of
Friendly Socs. 1937-48; Chm. of Powys County Council since 1974; Chm.
Brecon Beacons Nat. Park Cttee. and of Powys Agric. Wages Cttee.; Hon.
Freeman Brecon Borough; *cr. Baron Watkins*, of Glyntawe, co. Brecknock,
(Life Baron) 1972: *m.* 1936, Bronwen Richards, da. of the late Thomas
Stather, of Talgarth.

Residence.—Bronafon, Penyfan Rd., Brecon.

WATKINSON, VISCOUNT. (Watkinson.) [Viscount U.K. 1964.]

HAROLD ARTHUR WATKINSON, *CH, PC*,
1st Viscount, son of Arthur G. Watkinson,
of Walton-on-Thames; *b.* Jan. 25th, 1910; ed.
at Queen's Coll., Taunton, and King's Coll.,
London; PPS to Min. of Transport and Civil
Aviation 1951-52; Parl. Sec. to Min. of
Labour and National Ser. 1952-55, Min. of
Transport and Civil Aviation 1955-59, and
Min. of Defence 1959-62, and Chm. of Cttee.
for Exports to USA 1964-67; Managing Dir.
of Schweppes Group 1963-68, Chm. Cadbury
Schweppes, Ltd., 1969-74, and of BIM 1968-70;
Pres. of Inst. of Grocery Distribution 1972-73;
a Dir. of British Insulated Callenders Cables,
Ltd., and a Dep. Chm. of Midland Bank, Ltd.;
1939–45 War as Lt.-Cdr. RNVR; MP for
Woking Div. of Surrey (*C*) 1950-64; *cr.* PC
1955, CH 1962, and *Viscount Watkinson,* of Woking, co. Surrey (peerage of
UK) 1964: *m.* 1939, Vera, da. of John Langmead of Northwood, Ford, Sussex,
and has issue.

Arms—Vert fretty and three fleeces or. **Crest.**—A ram passant proper on an antique cannon
sable garnished or. **Supporters.**—*Dexter*, a weaver holding in the exterior hand a shuttle; *sinister*
a shepherd holding with the exterior hand a crook all proper.

Residences.—Dibbles, West Clandon, Surrey; Clive House, 2, Connaught Place, W.2. *Clubs,*—
Carlton, RNVR, Royal Yacht Squadron.

DAUGHTERS LIVING.

Hon. Sarah Margaret, *b.* 1944: *m.* 1965, David Bethune Spicer, of Old Farmhouse, Church Rd., North
Waltham, nr. Basingstoke, Hants., and has issue living, Mary Bethune, *b.* 1966,—Joanna Margaret,
b. 1968,—Eliza Jane, *b.* 1970.
Hon. Rosemary Jane, *b.* 1947.

WAVELL, EARLDOM OF. (Wavell.) [Extinct 1953.]

DAUGHTERS LIVING OF FIRST EARL.

Lady Eugénie Pamela, *b.* 1918 : *m.* 1942, Arthur Francis Walter Humphrys, O.B.E., formerly Lieut.,
Col. Indian Army, only son of Lieut.-Col. Sir Francis Humphrys, G.C.M.G., G.C.V.O., K.B.E., C.I.E.,
and has issue living, Francis Wavell Harold James, *b.* 1944,—Henry Owen Rookhurst, *b.* 1946-
Eugénie Cecilia, *b.* 1950. *Residence.*—Marston Meysey Grange, near Cricklade, Wilts.
Lady Felicity Ann, *b.* 1921 : *m.* 1947, Major Peter Maitland Longmore, M.C., R.A. [Maitland, Bt.
colls.], of Rook Farm, Funtington, Chichester, and has issue living, Richard Martin Wavell, *b.* 1948,—
Andrew Nigel Murray, *b.* 1953,—Ann Christina, *b.* 1950,—Fiona Elaine, *b.* 1963.
Lady Joan Patricia Quirk *b.* 1923 : *m.* 1st, 1942, Capt. the Hon. Simon Nevill Astley, 7th Hussars,
who *d.* 1946 [see B. Hastings]; 2ndly, 1948, Maj. Harry Alastair Gordon, MC, Gordon Highlanders,
who *d.* 1965; 3rdly, 1973, Maj. Donald Struan Robertson, Scots Gds., of Winkfield Plain Farm,
Winkfield, Windsor, Berks., SL4 4QU, and has issue living, (by 1st m.) [see B. Hastings], (by 2nd m.)
Anthea Leila, *b.* 1949: *m.* 1970, Timothy Hanbury,—Patricia, *b.* 1951.

WIDOW LIVING OF FIRST EARL.

EUGÉNIE MARIE (*Countess Wavell*), *CI*, (United Service Club and Royal Over Seas League) da. of the
late Col. John Owen Quirk, CB, DSO; CI 1943: *m.* 1915, the 1st Earl, who *d.* 1950.

WAVERLEY, VISCOUNT. (Anderson.) [Viscount U.K. 1952.]

DAVID ALASTAIR PEARSON ANDERSON, 2nd Viscount; *b.* Feb. 18th, 1911; *s.* 1958; ed. at Malvern Coll., and at Camb. Univ. (B.A. 1934, M.A., M.B., and B.Chir. 1938), M.R.C.S. England and L.R.C.P. London 1936; M.R.C.P. 1946; F.R.C.P. 1957; is a Consultant Physician, Roy. Berkshire Hospital, Reading; European War 1939-45 with R.A.F. (Med. Branch): *m.* 1948, Lorna Myrtle Ann, dau. of Lieut.-Col. F. H. Ledgerwood, and has issue.

Arms,—Argent, a saltire engrailed between a mullet in chief and a lotus flower in base, and in each flank a crescent gules; on a chief sable three martlets of the field. Crest,—A demi-lion rampant or, armed and langued azure, holding in his dexter forepaw a branch of olive proper. Supporters,—Two horses argent, crined and unguled or.

Residence,—Path Hill, near Whitchurch, Oxon. *Club,*—Travellers'.

SON LIVING.
Hon. JOHN DESMOND FORBES, *b.* Oct. 31st, 1949; ed. at Malvern.

DAUGHTER LIVING.
Hon. Patricia Mairead Janet, *b.* 1955.

SISTER LIVING.
Hon. Dame Mary Mackenzie, *DBE*, *b.* 1916; Brig. WRAC; Dir. WRAC, and Hon. ADC to HM, 1967-70; MBE (Mil) 1958, DBE (Mil) 1970: *m.* 1973, Frithjof Pihl, of Engö, Tjöme, Norway.

PREDECESSOR.—[1] *Rt. Hon. Sir* JOHN ANDERSON, GOB, OM, GCSI, GCIE, FRS, son of the late David A. P. Anderson, of Westland House, Eskbank, Midlothian; *b.* 1882; entered Colonial Office 1905, became Principal Clerk National Health Insurance Commn. 1912, Sec. thereto 1913, Sec. Min. of Shipping 1917-19, Second Sec. Min. of Health 1919, Chm. and a Commr. of Board of Inland Revenue 1919, Joint Under-Sec. for Ireland 1920, and Permanent Under-Sec. of State for Home Depart. 1922; Gov. of Bengal 1932-37, Lord Privy Seal 1938-9, Sec. of State for Home Depart. and Min. of Home Security 1939-40, Lord Pres. of the Council (Member of War Cabinet) 1940-43, and Chancellor of the Exchequer 1943-45; Chm. of Port of London Authority 1946-58; sat as M.P. for Edinburgh, St. Andrews, Glasgow, and Aberdeen Univs. (*National*) 1938-50; cr. *Viscount Waverley*, of Westdean, co. Sussex (peerage of United Kingdom) 1952: *m.* 1st, 1907, Christina, who *d.* 1920, da. of the late Andrew Mackenzie, of Edinburgh; 2ndly, 1941, Ava, who *d.* 1974, da. of the late J. E. C. Bodley, and widow of Ralph Wigram, CMG; *d.* 1958; *s.* by his only son [2] DAVID ALASTAIR PEARSON, 2nd Viscount and present peer.

WEDGWOOD, BARON. (Wedgwood.) [Baron U.K. 1942.]

PIERS ANTHONY WEYMOUTH WEDGWOOD, 4th Baron, *b.* Sept. 20th, 1954; *s.* 1970.

Arms,—Gules four mullets in cross and a canton argent. Crest,—On a ducal coronet, a lion passant argent. Supporters, —On either side a lion rampant queue fourchée argent supporting a staff raguly gules.

Residence,—Drywick, Shear Hill, Petersfield, Hants.

SISTERS LIVING.
Hon. Susan Margaret, *b.* 1950.
Hon. Sarah Jane Edith, *b.* 1958.

GREAT-AUNTS LIVING.
(Daughters of 1st Baron).

Hon. Helen Bowen, *b.* 1895; ed. at Newnham Coll., Camb.; a JP for Cambs.: *m.* 1920, Michael Stewart Pease, who *d.* 1966, and has issue living, Rendel Sebastian (of The Poplars, West Ilsley, Newbury, Berks), *b.* 1922; ed. at Bedales Sch., and Camb. Univ. (MA, ScD): *m.* 1952, Susan, da. of the late

I split asunder obstacles.

Capt. (S) Sir Frank Todd Spickernell, KBE, CB, CVO, DSO, RN [Broughton, Bt.], and has issue living, Christopher Fabian Delves *b.* 1956, Michael Roland Wedgwood *b.* 1959, Rosamund Mary *b.* 1953, Sarah Frances *b.* 1955, Joanna Rowan *b.* 1963,—Roger Fabian Wedgwood (5, Belleview Rd., Holmdel, NJ, USA), *b.* 1936; ed. at Bedales Sch., and at Trin. Coll., Camb. (Fellow): *m.* 1960, Caroline Ann, el. da. of Peter R. Bowring, of Cuckfield, Sussex, and has issue living, Joseph Henry Bowring *b.* 1963, James Edward *b.* 1969, Emma Ruth *b.* 1961,—Noel Joanna, *b.* 1920; ed. at Camb. Univ. (MB 1947),—Jocelyn Richenda Gammell (*Lady Huxley*), *b.* 1925; ed. at Camb. Univ.; is a JP for Cambridgeshire: *m.* 1947, Prof. Sir Andrew Fielding Huxley, FRS, of Manor Field, Grantchester, Cambridgeshire, and has issue living, Stewart Leonard *b.* 1949, Janet Rachel *b.* 1948, Camilla Rosalind *b.* 1952, Eleanor Bruce *b.* 1959, Henrietta Catherine *b.* 1960, Clare Marjory Pease *b.* 1962,—Rosamund Dorothy Benson, *b.* 1935; ed. at Camb. Univ.; a Civil Servant. *Residence,*—1, High St., Girton, Cambridge.
Hon. Elizabeth Julia (55, Gretton Court, High St., Groton, Cambs.), *b.* 1907.

WIDOWS LIVING OF SECOND AND THIRD BARONS.

EDITH MAY (*Edith, Baroness Wedgwood*), da. of William Telfer, of Glasgow: *m.* 1920, the 2nd Baron, who *d.* 1959. *Address,*—Cattolica, 18, Hayling Rise, Worthing, Sussex.

JANE WEYMOUTH (*Baroness Wedgwood*), (Drywick, Shear Hill, Petersfield, Hants.), da. of William James Poulton, of Kenjockety, Molo, Kenya: *m.* 1949, as his 2nd wife the 3rd Baron, who *d.* 1970.

COLLATERAL BRANCH LIVING.
Issue of the late Hon. Josiah Wedgwood, yr. son of 1st Baron; *b.* 1899; *d.* 1968: *m.* 1919, Dorothy Mary, OBE, who *d.* 1974, da. of Percy James Winser, of Knutsford:—

John (91, Clifton Hill, NW8), *b.* 1919; ed. at Camb. Univ. (MA, BCh, MD); FRCP; 1939-45 War, as Surg. Lt. RNVR: *m.* 1st, 1943 (m. diss. 1971), Margaret, da. of A. S. Mason; 2ndly, 1972, Jo Alice Tamlyn, da. of the late Harold Swann Ripsher, and has issue living (by 1st m.), Antony John (70, Noel Rd., N1), *b.* 1944; ed. at Marlborough, and Trin. Coll., Camb. (MA): *m.* 1970, Angela Margaret Mary Page, and has issue living, a da. *b.* 1975,—Simon James (18, Rosary Gdns., SW7), *b.* 1949,— Nicholas Ralph, *b.* 1951,—Judith Margaret Susannah, *b.* 1946: *m.* 1966, Christopher Anthony Wingfield Tracy, of 9A, St. Mary's Rd., Wimbledon, SW19, and has issue living, Emma *b.* 1970, Victoria *b.* 1974,—Katherine Sarah, *b.* 1955.——Josiah Ralph (3717, 41st Av. NE, Seattle, Washington 98105, USA), *b.* 1924; ed. at Harvard Univ. (MD): *m.* 1943, Virginia Lloyd, da. of Edward Eyre Hunt, of Wash., DC, and has issue living, Josiah Francis, *b.* 1950,—Jeffrey Galton, *b.* 1953: *m.* 1974, Cynthia Baird,—John Ralph Christopher, *b.* 1964.——Jennifer Susan, *b.* 1927: *m.* 1945, Emil Wendel Lehmann, MSc, of 34, Knoll Drive, Princeton, New Jersey, USA, and has issue living, John Winser, *b.* 1951,—Mark Wedgwood, *b.* 1954.

PREDECESSORS.—[1] *Col. the Rt. Hon.* JOSIAH CLEMENT WEDGWOOD, *D.S.O.*, 2nd son of the late Clement Francis Wedgwood, master potter, of Barlaston, Staffordshire, *b.* 1872 ; S. Africa 1899-1902, European War 1914-19 as Col. (D.S.O.); Chancellor of Duchy of Lancaster (also Ch. Civil Commr.) Jan. to Nov. 1924 ; sat as M.P. for Newcastle-under-Lyme (*L., Lab.*, and *Ind.*) Jan. 1906 to Jan. 1942 ; cr. *Baron Wedgwood*, of Barlaston, co. Stafford (peerage of United Kingdom) 1942: *m.* 1st, 1894, the Hon. Ethel Kate, who *d.* 1952 (having obtained a divorce 1919), dau. of 1st Baron Bowen; 2ndly, 1919, Florence Ethel, who *d.* 1969, da. of the late Edward Guy Willett; *d.* 1943; *s.* by his son [2] FRANCIS CHARLES BOWEN, 2nd Baron; *b.* 1898; an Artist: *m.* 1920, Edith May, da. of William Telfer, of Glasgow; *d.* 1959; *s.* by his only son [3] HUGH EVERARD, 3rd Baron, *b.* 1921: *m.* 1st, 1945 (m. annulled 1947), Jeno Annette Heather, only child of Ralph S. Leake, of Bournemouth; 2ndly, 1949, Jane Weymouth, da. of William James Poulton, of Kenjockety, Molof Kenya; *d.* 1970; *s.* by his only son [4] PIERS ANTHONY WEYMOUTH, 4th Baron and present peer.

WEEKS, BARON. (Weeks.) [Extinct 1960.]

DAUGHTERS LIVING OF FIRST BARON.

Hon. Pamela Rose, *b.* (Nov.) 1931 : *m.* 1957, Lieut.-Com. Henry Walter Plunkett-Ernle-Erle-Drax, RN (ret.) [see B. Dunsany, colls.]. *Residence,*—Charborough Park, Wareham, Dorset.

Hon. Venetia Daphne (*Hon. Lady Troubridge*), *b.* 1933: *m.* 1954, Lt.-Cdr. Sir Peter Troubridge, RN (ret.), 6th baronet. *Residence,*—The Manor House, Elsted, Sussex.

WIDOW LIVING OF FIRST BARON.

CYNTHIA MARY (*CUMMING*), (*Baroness Weeks*) dau. of John Wood Irvine : *m.* (Feb.) 1931, as his second wife, the 1st Baron, who *d.* 1960, when the title became ext. *Residence,*—Flat 11, 46, Lowndes Sq., SW1.

WEIR, VISCOUNT. (Weir.) [Viscount U.K. 1938.]

WILLIAM KENNETH JAMES WEIR, 3rd Viscount, *b.* Nov. 9th, 1933; *s.* 1975; ed. at Eton and Trin. Coll., Camb. (BA); Chm. and Ch. Exec., The Weir Group, Ltd. since 1972; a Dir., British Steel Corpn., and Gt. Northern Investment Trust, Ltd., and a member of Court, Bank of England; a Member of Queen's Body Guard for Scotland (Roy. Co. of Archers): *m.* 1964, Diana Lucy (m. diss. 1974), da. of Peter Lewis MacDougall of Rockcliffe, Ont., Canada, and has issue.

Arms,—Azure, a cogwheel or, winged argent, in chief the sun in his splendour of the second. *Crest,*—A wing argent charged with a thistle slipped proper. *Supporters*—Two winged horses argent, armed and crined or.

Residence,—Rodinghead, Mauchline, Ayrshire. *Clubs,*—White's, Travellers' (Paris), Knickerbocker (New York).

SON LIVING.

Hon. JAMES WILLIAM HARTLAND, *b.* June 6th, 1965.

DAUGHTER LIVING.

Hon. Lorna Elizabeth, *b.* 1967.

BROTHERS LIVING.

Hon. Douglas Nigel (Creagdhubh Lodge, Newtonmore, Inverness-shire), *b.* 1935; ed. at Eton and Trin. Coll., Camb.: *m.* 1964, Penelope Anne, da. of Group Capt. John Whitehead, of Bent Mead, Waltham St. Lawrence, Berks., and has issue living, Juliet Anne, *b.* 1964,—Lucy, *b.* 1966,—Nicola Jean, *b.* 1969.

Hon. George Anthony (Fiunary House, Newton Mearns, Renfrewshire, and 20, Royal Avenue House, Royal Av., SW3), *b.* 1940; ed. at Winchester, at Trin. Coll., Camb. (BA), and at Mass. Inst. of Technology, USA (SM, PhD): *m.* 1962, Hon. Jane Caroline Anstruther-Gray, da. of Baron Kilmany (Life Peer), and has issue living, William John, *b.* 1971,—Edward Kenneth, *b.* 1972,—Belinda Jane, *b.* 1974.

Hon. James Richard Canning, *b.* 1949; ed. at Winchester.

SISTER LIVING.

Hon. Janet Sibella, *b.* 1947.

AUNT LIVING. (*Daughter of 1st Viscount.*)

Hon. Elspeth Marjory Jessie, *b.* 1912: *m.* 1st, 1933, Richard Fairfax William Cartwright, J.P., who *d.* 1954, son of the late Rt. Hon. Sir Fairfax Leighton Cartwright, GCMG, GCVO; 2ndly, 1957,

Eustace Benyon Hoare, who *d.* 1961, and has issue living (by 1st m.), Elizabeth Armine Julia, *b.* 1939. *Residences,*—9, Lansdown Cres., Bath; Flat 70, Eaton Sq., SW1.

WIDOW LIVING OF SON OF FIRST VISCOUNT.
Irene Marguerite Robertson, dau. of the late James McKechnie, J.P., of 44, Dalziel Drive, Glasgow: *m.* 1950, the Hon. John William Weir, who *d.* 1953. *Residence,*—Dunderave Castle, Inveraray, Argyll.

WIDOW LIVING OF SECOND VISCOUNT.
DOROTHY (*Dorothy, Viscountess Weir*) (Montgreenan, Kilwinning, Ayrshire; 28, Roebuck House, Palace St., Victoria, SW1), da. of the late William Yerrington Dear, and widow of Edward F. Hutton: *m.* 1973, as his 2nd wife, the 2nd Viscount who *d.* 1975.

PREDECESSORS—[1] *Rt. Hon. Sir* WILLIAM DOUGLAS Weir, *GCB,* son of the late James Weir, of Over Courance, Dumfriesshire ; *b.* 1877 ; Hon. Pres. of G. & J. Weir Holdings, Ltd., and a Director of International Nickel Co. of Canada ; was Scottish Director of Munitions 1915-16, Controller of Aeronautical Supplies ; and a Member of Air Board 1917-18, Director-Gen. of Aircraft Production, Min. of Munitions 1918, Sec. of State and Pres. of Air Council April to Dec. 1918, Director-Gen. of Explosives and Chemical Supplies, Min. of Supply 1939-41, and Chm. of Tank Board 1943 ; *cr. Baron Weir,* of Eastwood, co. Renfrew (peerage of U.K.) 1918, and *Viscount Weir,* of Eastwood, co. Renfrew (peerage of U.K.) 1938 : *m.* 1904, Alice Blanche, who *d.* 1959, dau. of the late John MacConnachie of Glasgow; *d.* 1959; *s.* by his only son [2] (JAMES) KENNETH, 2nd Viscount, *b.* 1905; Engineer; (Chm. of Weir Group, Ltd. of Glasgow, 1955-72: *m.* 1st, 1929 (Dorothy Isabel), Lucy, who *d.* 1972, only da. of James Fuidge Crowdy, MVO, Asst. Sec. to Gov. Gen. of Canada; 2ndly, 1973, Dorothy, da. of William Yerrington Dear, and widow of Edward F. Hutton; *d.* 1975; *s.* by his el. son [3] WILLIAM KENNETH JAMES, 3rd Viscount and present peer; also Baron Weir.

WELLINGTON, DUKE OF. (Wellesley.) [Duke U.K. 1814.]

Fortune is the companion of valour.

ARTHUR VALERIAN WELLESLEY, *MVO, OBE, MC,* 8th Duke, Prince of Waterloo in Netherlands (cr. 1815), Duque da Victoria and Marquez de Torres Vedras (cr. 1812) and Conde de Vimeiro (cr. 1811) in Portugal, and Duke of Ciudad Rodrigo (cr. 1812), and a Grandee (1st class) in Spain, which he became on the renunciation by his father (published in Official Gazette Madrid, 20th Feb., 1968); *b.* July 2nd 1915; *s.* 1972: ed. at Eton; patron of four livings; Brig. (ret.) late RHG; OC RHG 1954-58, Silver Stick-in-Waiting, and Lt.-Col. Comdg. Household Cav. 1959-60, and Comdg. 22nd Armd. Bde. 1960-61, CRAC, 1st British Corps 1962-64, and Defence Attaché Madrid 1964-67; Col.-in-Ch. The Duke of Wellington's Regt. since 1974; Hon. Col. 2nd Br. Wessex Regt.; Co. Councillor for Hants. 1967-73, a Dir. of Massey Ferguson Holdings, Ltd., Massey-Ferguson, Ltd., Toronto, and Motor Iberica SA (Spain); a Gov. of Wellington Coll. since 1965; 1939-45 War in Middle East, Italy, and NW Europe (MC); MVO (4th class) 1952, OBE (Mil.) 1957: *m.* 1944, Diana Ruth, only da. of the late Maj.-Gen. Douglas Fitzgerald McConnel, of Knockdolian, CB, CBE, DSO, and has issue.

Arms.—Quarterly: 1st and 4th gules, a cross argent, in each quarter five plates in saltire, *Wellesley:* 2nd and 3rd or, a lion rampant gules, ducally collared gold, *Cowley:* over all, in the centre chief point, an escutcheon of augmentation charged with the Union badge. *Crest.*—Out of a ducal coronet or, a demi-lion rampant gules, holding in the paws a forked pennon argent, flowing to the sinister, charged with the cross of St. George, the ends gules. *Supporters,*—Two lions gules, gorged with Eastern coronets, and chained or.

Seat,—Stratfield Saye House, Reading, RE7 2B2. *Residence,*—Park Corner, Heckfield, Basingstoke, Hants. *Town Residence,*—Apsley House, Piccadilly, W1V 9FA. *Clubs,*—Turf, White's, Buck's.

SONS LIVING.
ARTHUR CHARLES VALERIAN (*Marquess of Douro*), *b.* Aug. 19th, 1945; ed. at Eton, and Ch. Ch., Oxford.
Lord Richard Gerald, *b.* 1949; ed. at Eton and Roy. Agric. Coll., Cirencester: *m.* 1973, Joanna, el. da. of John Sumner, of Marston St. Lawrence, Oxon., and has issue living, a da. *b.* 1975.
Lord John Henry, *b.* 1954; ed. at Eton.
Lord James Christopher Douglas, *b.* 1964.

DAUGHTER LIVING.
Lady Caroline Jane, *b.* 1951.

SISTER LIVING.
Lady Elizabeth (Oliver's Farm, Bramley, Basingstoke, Hants.), *b.* 1918: *m.* 1939 (m. diss. 1960), Capt. Thomas Clyde, Horse Guards, and has issue living, Jeremy, *b.* 1941: *m.* 1970, Vanessa, da. of Harold Field,—William Jonathan, *b.* 1949.

DAUGHTER LIVING OF FIFTH DUKE.
Lady Anne Maud, *b.* 1910; *s.* her brother (6th Duke of Wellington) as Duchess of Ciudad Rodrigo and a Grandee (1st class) in Spain (cr. 1812) 1943, but relinquished this title in favour of her uncle the 7th Duke of Wellington 1949: *m.* 1933, (marriage dissolved 1963), Capt. the Hon. David Reginald Rhys, Welsh Guards [see B. Dynevor]. *Residence,*—

WIDOW LIVING OF SON OF FOURTH DUKE.
Jean (*Lady George Wellesley*) (Flat 5, Woodsford, 14, Melbury Rd, W14 8LS), da. of the late McGillivray, of The Braes of Glenlivet, Banffshire: *m.* 1955, as his 2nd wife, Lt.-Col. Lord George Wellesley, MC, who *d.* 1967.

COLLATERAL BRANCHES LIVING.
Issue of the late Capt. Lord Richard Wellesley, 2nd son of 4th Duke, *b.* 1879, *d.* (killed in action) 1914 : *m.* 1908, Louise Nesta Pamela, who *d.* 1946, having

m. 2ndly (in New York), 1917, his younger brother, Major Lord George **Wellesley,** M.C. (ante), dau. of Sir Maurice FitzGerald (*20th Knight of Kerry*), C.V.O., 2nd Bt. :—

Pamela (*Hon. Mrs. Denis G. Berry*), *b.* 1912 : *m.* 1st, 1933, as his second wife, Lieut Charles Robert Archibald Grant, RN (ret.), who *d.* 1972, and from whom she obtained a divorce 1943 [E. Rosebery]; 2ndly, 1947, as his second wife, Major the Hon. Denis Gomer Berry, TD, late Grenadier Guards, of Brockenhurst Park, Hants., SO4 7QP [see V. Kemsley], and has issue living, (by 1st m.) *Rev.* Antony Charles Richard, *b.* 1934; ed. at Eton and at Ch. Ch., Oxford,—(by 2nd m.) [see V. Kemsley].
——Mary (*posthumous*), *b.* 1915. *Residence,*—12, Clarence Terr., NW1 4RD.

Issue of Lt.-Col. the late Lord George Wellesley, MC, son of 4th Duke, *b.* 1889, *d.* 1967: *m.* 1st (in New York), 1917, Louise Nesta Pamela, who *d.* 1946, da. of Sir Maurice FitzGerald, CVO (*20th Knight of Kerry*), 2nd Bt., and widow of his el. brother, Capt. Lord Richard Wellesley (see ante); 2ndly, 1955, Jean (ante), da. of the late John McGillivray, of The Braes of Glenlivet, Banffshire:—

(By 1st m.) Richard, *MC* (Buckland Mead, Buckland, Faringdon, Berks), *b.* 1920; ed. at Wye Coll.; late RA (TA); a DL for Berks; High Sheriff of Berks 1955; Middle East and Med. 1940-45 (MC): *m.* 1st, 1948, (m. diss. 1970), Ruth, da. of the late Peter Haig Haig-Thomas [E. Normanton]; 2ndly 1970, Jill, da. of Gp. Capt. E. Burton, and has issue living, (by 1st m.) Charles, *b.* 1955,—John, *b.* 1962, —Nesta, *b.* 1951,—Lucy, *b.* 1953.

(*In remainder to Earldom of Mornington, Viscountcy of Wellesley and Barony of Mornington only.*)

Granddaughter of the late Col. William Henry Charles Wellesley, 2nd son of the Hon. Gerald Valerian Wellesley, D.D., 4th son of 1st Earl of Mornington :—

Issue of the late Lieut.-Col. Gerald Valerian Wellesley, *b.* 1852, *d.* 1914: *m.* 1878, Kathleen, who *d.* 1910, dau. of Edward C. Carleton, of Old Bawn, Bray, co. Dublin:—

Kathleen Geraldine Helen (Greenways, Donhead St. Mary, Shaftesbury, Dorset), *b.* 1883: *m.* 1910, Capt. Walton Mellor, Roy. Irish Regt., who *d.* (killed in action) 1914, and has issue living, Kathleen Florence Walton, *b.* 1911: *m.* 1942, Ronald Kemp (Jenkins Corner, Donhead St. Mary, Shaftesbury, Dorset), and has issue living, Jonathan Walton Manfred (Greystones Cottage, Park Rd., Crediton, Devon) *b.* 1946: *m.* 1971, Jane Mary, el. da. of the Rev. Harold Walter Budgen, of Kingswear, Dartmouth, Devon, (and has issue living, Emma Kathleen Margaret *b.* 1971).

Grandchildren of the late Lieut.-Col. Gerald Valerian Wellesley (ante):—
Issue of the late Lieut.-Col. Frederic Henry Burton Wellesley, *b.* 1880, *d.* 1955 : *m.* 1907, Helen Evelyn, who *d.* 1960, dau. of the late W. H. Cobb, of South Woods Hall, Thirsk, Yorkshire :—

Frederick Henry Valerian, *b.* 1908 ; Major Duke of Wellington's Regt. (retired) : *m.* 1938, Nancy Evelyn, dau. of Percy Saunders, and has issue living, Evelyn Angela Juliana, *b.* 1938 : *m.* 1961, John Albert Searle,—Helen Christabel Kate, *b.* 1947: *m.* 1975, Daniel Levasseur,—Rosalind Jane, *b.* 1954. *Residence,*—Church Hill, Crayke, York.——Evelyn Geraldine Ruth, *b.* 1917: *m.* 1951, John Frederick Akroyd, and has issue living, Ailsa Evelyn Margaret, *b.* 1954,—Cecilia Ruth Lorraine, *b.* 1960. X*Residence,*—5, Appleton Road, Bishopsthorpe, York.

Granddaughters of the late Col. William Henry Charles Wellesley (ante):—
Issue of the late Edmond Ernest Charles Wellesley, *b.* 1858, *d.* 1886: *m.* 1882, Florence S. Louisa, who *d.* 1937 (having *m.* 2ndly, 1890, the Rev. Arthur John Burr, M.A., of 27, Marlborough Road, Bournemouth), dau. of the late John Platt, M.P., D.L., of Oldham, and Bryn-y-neuadd, N. Wales:—

Muriel Alice, *b.* 1883: *m.* 1906, Percival William Clifford Goodchild. *Residence,*—
Issue of the late Major Cecil George Wellesley, O.B.E., *b.* 1869, *d.* 1932: *m.* 1906, Winifred Mary (who *d.* 1959, having *m.* 2ndly, 1933, Lieut.-Col. Clifford Charles Horace Twiss, D.S.O., who *d.* 1947), dau. of the late Hon. Reginald Parker [E. Macclesfield, colls.] :—

Lettice Jane Katherine, *b.* 1908: *m.* 1930, Peter Jocelyn Lambert, MC, and has issue living, Peter Miles (Old Barkfold House, Plaistow, Billingshurst, Sussex), *b.* 1931; late Maj. Gren. Gds.: *m.* 1959, Armorel Madeleine Frances Tress, da. of Maj. Sir Rupert Rodney Francis Tress Barry, 4th Bt., and has issue living, Peter Tobin *b.* 1966, Annabel Madeleine Jane *b.* 1960, Miranda Caroline Tress *b.* 1962,—April Daphne Claire, *b.* 1934: *m.* 1954, Michael Gascoigne Falcon, of Keswick Old Hall, Norwich, and has issue living, Michael *b.* 1956, Andrew *b.* 1958, Claire Isabella *b.* 1960. *Residence,*—Ash Tree Farm, Wissett, Halesworth, Suffolk.——Pamela, *b.* 1909: *m.* 1938, Maj.-Gen. Edward Noel Keith Estcourt, DSO, OBE, late RA, of The Vyne, Sherborne St. John, Basingstoke, and has issue living, Edward James (c/o Lloyds Bank, Yorktown Branch, London Rd., Camberley, Surrey), *b.* 1939; Maj. RA: *m.* 1963, Jennifer Clare McLaren, and has issue living, Edward Rory Charles *b.* 1965, Angus James *b.* 1963,—Adrian Charles (c/o Lloyds Bank, 6, Pall Mall, SW1), *b.* 1942; late Lt. Parachute Regt.: *m.* 1967, Judith Mary, da. of Col. G. W. Preston, of Beck Cottage, Mene-thorpe, Malton, Yorks., and has issue living, Suzannah Jane *b.* 1970, Charlotte Pamela *b.* 1972,—Hermione Jessica Jane, *b.* 1947: *m.* 1970, Christopher Hugh James Cousins, of 5, Bentley Court, Kensington Gdns. Sq., W2.

Grandchildren of the late Edmond Ernest Charles Wellesley (ante) :—
Issue of the late Gerald Valentine Wellesley, *b.* 1885, *d.* 1933: *m.* 1918, Christine Adelina (who *m.* 2ndly, 1937, Capt. R. Douglas Boyd, formerly Roy. Munster Fusiliers and R.A., T.A.), dau. of F. H. Jelley, of Wandsworth Common, S.W. :—

Philip Vernon Charles *b.* 1921; Senior Immigration Officer, Nairobi: *m.* 1952, Marguerite Victoria, da. of A. C. Clark, of Barnstaple, and has issue living, Barbara Victoria, *b.* 1958.——Eileen Valerie Christine, *b.* 1922.——Florence Geraldine Joan, *b.* 1924: *m.* 1948, Capt. John Gabriel Combe, and has issue living, Michael Valerian Wellesley, *b,* 1948,—Jeremy Vernon Wellesley, *b.* 1952,—Patricia Daphne Eastburn, *b.* 1950. *Residence,*—

Descendants of the late Hon. Sir Henry Wellesley (5th son of 1st Earl of Mornington), who was cr. *Baron Cowley* 1828 [see E. Cowley].

PREDECESSORS.—[1] *Rt. Hon.* Sir **ARTHUR** Wellesley, *K.G., G.C.B.,* &c., 3rd son of 1st Earl of Mornington, *b.* 1769 ; entered 73rd Regt. 1787 ; became a Gen. 1808, and a Field-Marshal 1815 ; sat as M.P. for Trim in the Irish Parliament ; cr. *Baron Douro,* of Wellesley, co. Somerset, and *Viscount Wellington of Talavera and of Wellington,* co. Somerset (peerage of United Kingdom) 1809, *Earl of Wellington,* co. Somerset (peerage of United Kingdom) 1812, *Marquess of Wellington* (peerage of United Kingdom) 1812, *Marquess Douro* and *Duke of Wellington* (peerage of United Kingdom) 1814, *Count of Vimeiro* in Portugal 1811, *Duke of Ciudad Rodrigo* (and a Grandee of the 1st class) in Spain 1812, *Duke of Vittoria* and *Marquis of Torres Vedras* in Portugal 1812, and *Prince of Waterloo,* in the Netherlands 1815; the brilliant services of the 'Great Duke" are unrivalled in military history, but they are too varied to be particularized in this volume; in recognition of these services he was awarded the highest honours that could be conferred, besides large pecuniary awards, while the Sovereigns of various European countries conferred upon him their highest titles of nobility ; was Premier 1828-30 and 1834-5, Chancellor of University of Oxford, Lord High Constable of England, Lord Warden of the Cinque Ports, Constable of the Tower and of Dover Castle, Lord-Lieut. of Hants, Chief Ranger of Hyde, St. James's and other Parks, Com. in Chief, Col. of Grenadier Guards, Col.-in-Chief of Rifle Brigade, &c.: *m.* 1806, the Hon. Catherine Sarah Dorothea Pakenham, who *d.* 1831, second dau. of 2nd Baron Longford; *d.* Sept. 14th, 1852; *s.* by his son [2] **ARTHUR RICHARD,** 2nd Duke, *b.* 1807; sat as M.P. for Aldborough (*C*) 1829-30 and 1831, and for Norwich 1837-52; was Master of the Horse 1853-8, a Lieut.-Gen. in the Army and Lord-Lieut. of Middlesex; *s.* in 1863 as 6th Earl of Mornington [see infra *⁎,⁎*]; *d.s.p.* Aug. 13th, 1884; *s.* by his nephew [3] **HENRY,** 3rd Duke, el. surviving son of Maj.-Gen. Lord Charles Wellesley,

MP (2nd son of 1st Duke), by Augusta Sophia Anne, only child of the Right Hon. Henry Manvers Pierrepont [E. Manvers], *b.* 1846 ; M.P. for Andover (C) 1874-80 : *m.* 1882, Evelyn Katrine Gwenfra, who *d.* 1939, dau. of the late Col. Thomas Peers Williams, M.P., of Temple House, Great Marlow ; *d.* 1900 ; *s.* by his brother [4] ARTHUR CHARLES, K.G., G.C.V.O., 4th Duke, *b.* 1849 ; Col. (retired) late Grenadier Guards ; bore Union Standard at Coronations of Edward VII. 1902, and George V. 1911 : *m.* 1872, Kathleen Emily Bulkeley Williams, who *d.* 1927, dau. of the late Robert Griffith Williams [Williams-Bulkeley, Bt., colls.]; *d.* 1934 ; *s.* by his el. son, [5] ARTHUR CHARLES, 5th Duke, *b.* 1876 : *m.* 1909, the Hon. Lilian Maud Glen Coats, who *d.* 1946, dau. of 1st Baron Glentanar ; *d.* 1941 ; *s.* by his only son [6] HENRY VALERIAN GEORGE, 6th Duke, *b.* 1912 ; Capt. Duke of Wellington's Regt. and Commando ; *d.* (killed in action during European War) 1943, when he was *s.* in the Dukedom of Ciudad Rodrigo and as a Grandee (1st class) in Spain (cr. 1812) by his sister, Lady Anne Maud, wife of the Hon. David Reginald Rhys, and in the British and Portuguese titles by his uncle [7] GERALD, KG, 3rd son of 4th Duke, 7th Duke, *b.* 1885 ; Lt.-Col. Gren. Gds ; Surveyor of HM's Works of Art 1936-44; Chancellor of Southampton Univ. 1951-62; Gov., Capt. and Steward of Isle of Wight 1957-65 : *m.* 1914, Dorothy, who *d.* 1956, da. of the late Robert Ashton, of Croughton, C heshire; *d.* 1972, *s.* by his son [8] ARTHUR VALERIAN, 8th Duke and present peer ; also Marquess of Wellington, Marquess Douro, Earl of Mornington, (I), Earl of Wellington, Viscount Wellesley, (I), Viscount Wellington of Talavera and Wellington, Baron Mornington (I), and Baro Douro; Prince of Waterloo in Netherlands (cr. 1815). Duke of Vittoria and Marquis of Torres Vedras (cr. 1812) and Count of Vimeiro (cr. 1811) in Portugal, and Duke of Ciudad Rodrigo and an Grandee (1st class in Spain (cr. 1812).

* [1] RICHARD, *M.P.*, son of Henry Colley, M.P., assumed in 1728 by Roy. licence the surname of Wesley ; sat as M.P. for Trim 1729-46; cr. *Baron of Mornington* (peerage of Ireland) 1746; *d.* 1758; *s.* by his son [2] GARRET, 2nd Baron ; sat as M.P. for Meath 1757-8; cr. *Viscount Wellesley* and *Earl of Mornington* (peerage of Ireland) 1760 ; *d.* 1781; *s.* by his son [3] RICHARD, K.G., K.P., 2nd Earl: sat as M.P. for Trim, 1780-1, Beeralston 1784-6, Saltash 1786-7, Windsor 1787-96 and Sarum 1796-7; was Gov.-Gen. of India 1798-1805, Ambassador to Spain 1809, Ch. Sec. of State for Foreign Affairs 1809-12, Lord-Lieut. of Ireland 1821, 1833-4; cr. *Marquess Wellesley* (peerage of Ireland) 1799 ; *d.s.p.* 1842, when the Marquessate became extinct; *s.* by his brother [4] WILLIAM, G.C.H., P.C., 3rd Earl; assumed in 1778 the surname of Wellesley-Pole : sat at M.P. for Trim 1783-90, East Looe 1790-94, and Queen's Co. 1801-21; was Postmaster-Gen. in 1835; cr. *Baron Maryborough* (peerage of U.K.) 1821; *d.* 1845; *s.* by his son [5] WILLIAM POLE, 4th Earl; assumed in 1812 the additional surnames of Tylney-Long; *d.* 1857; *s.* by his son [6] WILLIAM ARTHUR, 5th Earl; *d.* unmarried 1863, when the Barony of Maryborough became ext. and the honours of the first Earl devolved upon his cousin [7] ARTHUR RICHARD, 6th Earl, who had previously succeeded as 2nd Duke of Wellington [see ante].

WELLS-PESTELL, BARON.   (Wells-Pestell.)   [Life Baron 1965.]

REGINALD ALFRED WELLS-PESTELL, son of Robert Pestell, of Highgate, N.; *b.* Jan. 27th, 1910; ed. at Lyulph Stanley Gram. Sch., and at Univ. of London (MA, LLD); FPhS; assumed the additional surname of Wells by deed poll 19—; a JP of London, a Sociologist, and a Member of Inner London Probation Cttee.; a Member of LCC 1946-52, Councillor of Stoke Newington 1945-49 (Mayor 1947-49), and a co. Councillor of E. Suffolk 1946-67; formerly a Probation Officer in London, and a Founder Member of National Marriage Guidance Council 1938; appointed a Lord-in-Waiting to HM 1974; 1939-45 War as Capt. KRRC; cr. *Baron Wells-Pestell*, of Combs, co. Suffolk (Life Peerage) 1965: *m.* 1935, Irene, da. of the late Arthur Wells, and has issue.
Residence,—Murcott, Oxford, OX5 2RE.

SONS LIVING.

Hon. Philip (7, Woodberry Av., Winchmore Hill, N21), *b.* 1941: *m.* 1965, Holly, da. of Lorne Hopkins, of Conn., USA, and has issue.
Hon. Richard (2, Queen's Mansions, Queen's Av., Muswell Hill, N10), *b.* 1945: *m.* 1973, Claudia Marseille, step-da. of Prof. John Gerhart, of Berkeley, Calif., USA.

WEMYSS AND MARCH, EARL OF. (Charteris.) [Earl S. 1633 and 1697.]
[Title pronounced "Weems."]

This is our Charter.

FRANCIS DAVID CHARTERIS, KT, 12th Earl of Wemyss and 8th Earl of March ; *b.* Jan. 19th, 1912 ; *s.* 1937; ed. at Eton, and at Balliol Coll., Oxford (BA); Hon. LLD, St. Andrews; a JP of E. Lothian; Lord Lieut. since 1967; a Member of Queen's Body Guard for Scotland (R. Co. of Archers); Lord Clerk Register of Scotland and Keeper of HM Signet since 1974; Chm. of Roy. Commn. on Ancient and Historical Monuments of Scotland, and of Scottish Cttee. of Marie Curie Memorial Foundation; Vice-Chm. of Marie Curie Memorial Foundation, Pres. of National Trust for Scotland, and of the Thistle Foundation for Severely Disabled Scottish Ex-Servicemen, and of National Bible Soc. of Scotland; a Dir. of Scottish Television, and of Standard Life Assurance Co.; late Capt. Lovat Scouts (TA Reserve); Colonial Admin. Ser., Basutoland 1937-44, and Lord High Commr. to Gen. Assembly of Church of Scotland 1959 and 1960; Middle East 1941-

44 with Basuto Troops as Maj.: KT 1966: *m.* 1940, Mavis Lynette Gordon, BA, el. da. of the late E. E. Murray, of Hermanus, Cape Province, S. Africa, and has issue.

Arms,—Quarterly: 1st and 4th argent, a fesse azure, within a double treasure flory counterflory gules, *Charteris;* 2nd and 3rd or, a lion rampant saole, *Wemyss.* **Crest,**—A dexter hand holding up a dagger paleways proper. **Supporters,**—Two swans, wings elevated proper, gorged with earl's coronets about their necks.

Residence,—Gosford House, Longniddry, East Lothian. *Club,*—New (Edinburgh).

SON LIVING.

JAMES DONALD (*Lord Neidpath*), *b.* June 22nd, 1948; ed. at Eton, Univ. Coll., Oxford (MA); a Page of Honour to HM Queen Elizabeth the Queen Mother 1962-64.

DAUGHTER LIVING.

Lady Elizabeth Mary, *b.* 1941: *m.* 1964, David Holford Benson, of 11, Brunswick Gdns., W8, son of the late Lt.-Col. Sir Reginald (Rex) Lindsay Benson, DSO, MVO, MC, and has issue living, Matthew James, *b.* 1966,—Henrietta Katharine, *b.* 1969,—Katharine Emma, *b.* 1971.

BROTHER LIVING.

Rt. Hon. Sir Martin Michael Charles, *KCB, KCVO, OBE, b.* 1913; ed. at Eton; Lieut-Col. (ret.) KRRC; Private Sec. to HM (when HRH Princess Elizabeth) 1949-52. Assist. Private Sec. to HM 1952-72, since when Private Sec., and Keeper of the Queen's Archives; an Extra Equerry to HM 1956; Officer of Legion of Honour; 1941-45 War in Middle East; OBE (Mil) 1946, MVO (4th class) 1953, CB (Civil) 1958, KCVO 1962, PC 1972, KCB (Civil) 1972: *m.* 1944, the Hon. (Mary) Gay Hobart Margesson, da. of 1st Viscount Margesson, and has issue living, Andrew Martin, *b.* 1947,—Harold Francis, *b.* 1950,—Francesca Mary, *b.* 1945. *Residence,*—Apart 25, St. James's Palace, SW1. *Clubs,*—White's, Travellers'.

AUNTS LIVING. (*Daughters of 11th Earl.*)

Lady Mary, b. 1895: *m.* 1st, 1915, Algernon Walter Strickland, who *d.* 1938 [see Strickland-Constable, Bt., colls.]; 2ndly 1943, Major John George Lyon, R.A. *Residence,*—Apperley Court, Gloucester.
Lady Irene Corona (*Dowager Countess of Plymouth*), *b.* 1902: sometime Senior Comdt. Auxiliary Territorial Ser., and a D.St.J.: *m.* 1921, the 2nd Earl of Plymouth, who *d.* 1943. *Residence,*—6, Marine Parade, Penarth, S. Glam.

WIDOW LIVING OF SON OF ELEVENTH EARL.

Violet (The Old House, Didbrook, Winchcombe, Glos.), da. of the late Alfred Charles Masterton Porter, of Dundee: *m.* 1945, as his 2nd wife, Capt. the Hon. Guy Lawrence Charteris, who *d.* 1967.

COLLATERAL BRANCHES LIVING.

Grandchildren of the late Capt. the Hon. Guy Lawrence Charteris (infra):—
Issue of the late Capt. Hugo Francis Guy Charteris, MC, *b.* 1922, *d.* 1970: *m.* 1948, Virginia Mary Forbes (The Grange, Elvington, York), da. of Colin Gordon Forbes Adam, CSI [see Adam, Bt., cr. 1917]:—
James Hugo Desmond, *b.* 1958.——Frances Irene Anne, *b.* 1950.——Virginia Jane, *b.* 1953.——Perdita Rosemary, *b.* 1955.

Issue of the late Capt. the Hon. Guy Lawrence Charteris, 2nd son of 11th Earl, *b.* 1886, *d.* 1967: *m.* 1st, 1912, Frances Lucy, who *d.* 1925, da. of Francis John Tennant [B. Glenconner]: 2ndly, 1945, Violet (ante), da. of the late Alfred Charles Masterton Porter:—
(By 1st m.) Ann Geraldine Mary (Sevenhampton Place, Wilts.), *b.* 1913: *m.* 1st, 1932, the 3rd Baron O'Neill, who *d.* (killed in action) 1944; 2ndly, 1945, the 2nd Viscount Rothermere, who obtained a divorce 1952; 3rdly, 1952, Ian Lancaster Fleming, who *d.* 1964 [Rose Bt., cr. 1874, colls.].—Frances Laura, (*Laura, Duchess of Marlborough*) (58, Portman Towers, Georges St., W1H 5PN), *b.* 1915: *m.* 1st, 1933, the 2nd Viscount Long, who *d.* (killed in action 1944), and from whom she had obtained a divorce 1943; 2ndly, 1943, as his 2nd wife (m. diss. 1954), the 3rd Earl of Dudley; 3rdly, 1960, Michael Temple Canfield; 4thly, 1972, the 10th Duke of Marlborough, who *d.* 1972.

Grandchildren of the late Lady Lilian Harriet Charteris (who *m.* 1st, 1872, Sir Henry Carstairs Pelly, 3rd Bt., who *d.* 1877, and 2ndly, 1882, Sir Henry Francis Redhead Yorke, KCB, who *d.* 1914), 2nd dau. of 10th Earl:—
Issue of the late Maurice Francis Yorke, *b.* 1883, *d.* 1962: *m.* 1918, Maud, who *d.* 1941, only dau. of the late Adm. Sir Charles Holcombe Dare, KCMG, CB, MVO:—
Richard Maurice Redhead (of Rockville, Garelochhead, Dunbartonshire), *b.* 1920: *m.* 1951, Jean Brenchley.——Elizabeth, *b.* 1919: *m.* 1st, 1939, Ronald Henry Davidson Orr; 2ndly, 1949, Gerald Philip Hugo, of Fyning Twitten, Fyning Lane, Rogate, W. Sussex.——Susan, *b.* 1923: *m.* 1st, Alexander John Sutherland Cassavetti; 2ndly, 1959, (Prince) Nicolas Baltazzi Mavrocordato, 1, Markov Botsari, Halandri, Athens, and has issue living, (by 1st marriage) Julian Cemetrius, *b.* 1950.

Issue of the late Anne Evelyn Pelly, *d.* 1923: *m.* 1913, Capt. Thomas Henry Rivers Bulkeley, CMG, MVO, who *d.* (killed in action) 1914:—
Robert Arthur Henry (605, Mountjoy House, Barbican, EC2Y BBP; Mas des Vallettes, Tourettes sur Loup, France, AM), *b.* 1914: Maj. Scots Guards: *m.* 1st, 1937 (marriage dissolved 1949), Anne Charmain, da. of the late Maj. Henry Nevile Fane, Coldstream Guards [see B. Clinton, colls.]; 2ndly, 1951, Elisabeth Charlotte Marie, da. of Ernst Neustadtl, of Vienna, and has issue living, (by 1st marriage) Miranda Jane *b* 1938: *m.* 1963, John Goglis, of 43, Artemidis St., Glyfada, Athens, and has issue living, Dimitri *b.* 1965.

Issue of the late Constance Lilian Pelly, *d.* 1947: *m.* 1900, the 12th Earl of Crawford:—
See E. Crawford.
Issue of the late Lady Hilda Charteris, 3rd dau. of 10th Earl, *b.* 1851, *d.* 1901: *m.* 1880, the 1st Earl of Midleton [see that title].

Grandchildren of the late Capt. the Hon. Frederick William Charteris, RN, 5th son of 9th Earl:—
Issue of the late Col. Nigel Keppel Charteris, CMG, DSO, OBE, *b.* 1878, *d.* 1967: *m.* 1904, Katharine Margaret, who *d.* 1961, el. da. of Sir John Walter Buchanan Riddell, 11th Bt.:—
John Douglas (Kelly's Park Farm, P.O. Box 345, Umtali, Rhodesia), *b.* 1914; ed. at Radley; Maj. R. Scots (ret.); Palestine 1937-38; 1939-45 War (despatches): *m.* 1st, 1943, Mrs. Catherine Pitcairn Colley, who *d.* 1957, da. of the late Capt. W. P. Nunneley, Black Watch; 2ndly, 1958, Jean Haigh, of Umtali, Rhodesia, and has issue living, (by 1st m.) Sarah Keppel, *b.* 1945: *m.* 1970, Peter Brown, and has issue living, Robert *b.* 1972, Christopher (twin) *b.* 1972,—(by 2nd m.) Martin Ian, *b.* 1960,—Bridget Alison, *b.* 1958.——David Nigel (Edifici Rossell 4ex1°, La Massana, Principat D'Andorra, via Spain), *b.* 1920; ed. at Lancing: late Lt RNVR: *m.* 1952, Euphemia Mary, who *d.* 1969, da. of Maj.-Gen. Sir (John) Drummond Inglis, KBE, CB, MC, and has issue living, Nigel Drummond Keppel, *b.* 1958,—Angela Katharine Keppel, *b.* 1953,—Helen Mary Keppel, *b.* 1956.——Margaret Olive (Ashley Holt, Bentworth, Alton, Hants.), *b.* 1950: *m.* 1st, 1930, Lt.-Cdr. Michael Richard Hallam Murray, RN (ret.), who *d.* 1938; 2ndly, 1954, Maj. Eric Cecil Lewis Copner, Devon Regt., who *d.* 1968, and has issue living, (by 1st m.) Christopher Philip Hallam, *b.* 1937: *m.* 1967, Judith Mary, da. of the

late Lt.-Col. I. B. MacInnes, and has issue living, James Michael Hallam *b.* 1969, Justin Richard Hallam *b.* 1973, Harriet Alexandra Hallam *b.* 1970,—Susan Barbara, *b.* 1930: *m.* 1974, Leslie Max Pritchard,—Katharine Bridget, *b.* 1934: *m.* 1956, Lt. John Charles Brian Taite, RN, and has issue living, Roderick Michael James *b.* 1966, Clare Bridget *b.* 1959, Caroline Rachel *b.* 1960.———Anne Louisa, *b.* 1909: *m.* 1939, John Arkwright Bonham-Carter, DSO, OBE, ERD, FCIT, formerly Maj. R. Tank Regt. [Alleyne, Bt.], of Flat 16, Duchess of Bedford House, Duchess of Bedford Walk, W8, and has issue living, Richard Francis (9, Weald Rd., Sevenoaks, Kent), *b.* 1940: *m.* 1968, Josephine Ann Gallimore, and has issue living, Nicola Jane *b.* 1969, Claire Helen *b.* 1972,—Nigel John (The Old School House, Cretingham, Woodbridge, Suffolk) *b.* 1945.

　　　Grandson of the late James Hay Erskine Wemyss, MP, el. son of Lt. Gen. William Wemyss, MP, eldest son of Hon. James Wemyss, MP, 3rd son of 5th Earl:—

　Issue (by 1st marriage) of the late Randolph Gordon Erskine Wemyss, *b.* 1858, *d.* 1908: *m.* 1st, 1884, Lady Lilian Mary Paulet (who *d.* 1952, having obtained a divorce 1898), dau. of 14th Marquess of Winchester; 2ndly, 1898, Lady Eva Cecilia Wellesley, who *d.* 1948, dau. of 2nd Earl Cowley :—

Michael John WEMYSS OF THAT ILK, *b.* 1888; 1914-18 War as Capt. RHG (wounded); a DL for Fifeshire and recognised as Chief of the name of Wemyss by Lord Lyon 1910: *m.* 1918, Lady Victoria Alexandrina Violet Cavendish Bentinck, *CVO*, da. of 6th Duke of Portland, and has issue living, David (of Invermay, Forteviot, Perthshire), *b.* 1920: ed. at Eton; formerly Capt. Roy. Corps of Signals: *m.* 1945, Lady Jean Christian Bruce, da. of 10th Earl of Elgin and Kincardine, and has issue living, Michael James *b.* 1947: *m.* 1975, Charlotte Mary da. of the late Lt.-Col. Royle Bristowe, of Brookhampton Hall, Iokleton, Cambs., Charles John *b.* 1952,—Andrew Michael (Torrie House, Newmills, Dunfermline, Fife), *b.* 1925; ed. at Eton: *m.* 1967, Janet Alethea, only da. of Maj. John Swire Scott, of Eredine House, Dalmally, Argyll, and has issue living, William John *b.* 1970, Isabella Alethea *b.* 1968. *Residence,*—Wemyss Castle, East Wemyss, Fife.

　　　Grandson of the late Major James Wemyss, son of the late James Wemyss, 2nd son of the late Hon. James Wemyss, M.P. (ante) :—

　Issue of the late Maj.-Gen. Binfield Wemyss, *b.* 1844, *d.* 1904: *m.* 1876, Mildred, who *d.* 1921, dau. of Henry Unwin, B.C.S. :—

Alan Binfield, *b.* 1886; formerly Capt. Dorsetshire Regt., and Capt. Roy. Corps of Signals (T.A.): *m.* 1921, Caroline Ethel, dau. of Com. E. A. Constable (formerly R.N.), Dep. Conservator, Port of Calcutta, and has issue living, John Michael, *b.* 1924. *Residence,*—

PREDECESSORS.—[1] Rt. Hon. JOHN Wemyss, was cr. by Charles I. a *Baronet of Nova Scotia* 1625, *Lord Wemyss of Elcho* (peerage of Scotland) 1628, and *Lord Elcho and Methel* and *Earl of Wemyss* (peerage of Scotland) 1633 ; he eventually espoused the cause of the Covenant; *d.* 1649; *s.* by his son [2] DAVID, 2nd Earl; constructed at his own cost the harbour of Methil, in 1672 resigned his honours to the crown, and in the same year obtained a new patent with original precedency and extending the limitation to his dau.; *d.* 1679, when the baronetcy expired and the peerages devolved upon his dau. [3] MARGARET; *d.* 1705; *s.* by her son [4] DAVID, P.C., 4th Earl; was Lord High Adm. of Scotland, a Commr. for concluding the Treaty of Union, and a Representative Peer; *d.* 1720; *s.* by his son [5] JAMES, 5th Earl; *d.* 1756; *s.* by his el. son [6] DAVID, *de jure* 6th Earl, who having been attainted in 1746 did not succeed to the titles and they remained dormant ; *d.s.p.* 1787, when the peerages but for the attainder would have devolved upon his younger brother [7] FRANCIS, *de jure* 7th Earl ; *b.* 1725 ; assumed the surname of Charteris in lieu of that of Wemyss on being made his heir by his maternal grandfather, Col. Francis Charteris, of Amisfield, who *d.* 1732 ; enabled by Act of Parliament in 1771 to retain the surname, arms and estates of Charteris, of Amisfield, notwithstanding the devolution upon him of the Earldom of Wemyss, or any other title, which under the will of Col. Charteris had been prohibited ; assumed the Earldom of Wemyss on the death of his el. brother ; *d.* 1808; *s.* by his grandson [8] FRANCIS, 8th Earl; *b.* 1772; in 1810 on the death of the 4th Duke of Queensberry, who was also 3rd Earl of March hes. (under special remainder, being the lineal heir male of Lady Anne Douglas, sister of 1st Earl of March) (see *⁎⁎* infra), as 4th *Earl of March*, and in 1821 was cr. *Baron Wemyss*, of Wemyss, co. Fife (peerage of United Kingdom) ; obtained a reversal of the attainder in 1826 ; was Lord-Lieut. of co. Peebles, *d.* 1853 ; *s.* by his son [9] FRANCIS, 9th Earl; *b.* 1796; was Lord-Lieut. of Haddingtonshire: *m.* 1817, Lady Louisa Bingham, who *d.* 1882, dau. of 2nd Earl of Lucan; *d.* Jan. 1st, 1883 ; *s.* by his son [10] FRANCIS, G.C.V.O., LL.D., 10th Earl; *b.* 1818 ; was Scotch Lord of the Treasury 1853 5, and an A.D.C. to Queen Victoria 1881-1901, to King Edward VII. 1901-10, and to King George V. 1910-14 ; M.P. for E. Gloucestershire (*LC*) 1841-6, and for Haddingtonshire 1847-83 : *m.* 1st, 1843, Lady Anne Frederica Anson, who *d.* 1896, dau. of 1st Earl of Lichfield ; 2ndly, 1900, Grace, who *d.* 1946, dau. of the late Major Blackburn ; *d.* 1914; *s.* by his el. surviving son [11] HUGO RICHARD, 11th Earl; *b.* 1857; M.P. for Haddingtonshire (*C*) 1883-5, and for Ipswich 1886-95: *m.* 1883, Mary Constance, who *d.* 1937, dau. of the late Hon. Percy Scawen Wyndham; *d.* 1937; *s.* by his grandson [12] FRANCIS DAVID (son of the late Capt. Hugo Francis Lord Elcho, who *d.*, killed in action during European War, 1916), 12th Earl and present peer ; also Earl of March, Viscount of Peebles, Lord Elcho and Methel, Lord Douglas of Neidpath, Lyne, and Munard, and Lord Wemyss of Elcho.

⁎⁎ [1] Lord WILLIAM DOUGLAS, 2nd son of 1st Duke of Queensberry, *b.* circa 1665 ; Gov. of Edinburgh Castle 1702-4 ; received from his father on his marriage the lands of Neidpath and others in Peeblesshire ; cr. *Lord Douglas of Neidpath, Lyne, and Munard, Viscount of Peebles*, and *Earl of March* (peerage of Scotland) 1697, with remainder to heirs male of his body, failing which to his other heirs male and of tailzie ; *m.* 1693, Lady Jane Hay, who *d.* 1729, dau. of 1st Marquess of Tweeddale; *d.* 1705; *s.* by his son [2] WILLIAM, 2nd Earl; *b.* circa 1696: *m.* 17—, Lady Anne Hamilton (who *s.* her father as Countess of Ruglen 1744 and who *m.* 2ndly, 1747, Anthony Sawyer, and *d.* 1748), dau. of 3rd Earl of Selkirk and 1st Earl of Ruglen ; *d.* 1731 ; *s.* by his son [3] WILLIAM, K.T., 3rd Earl, *b.* 1725, *s.* his kinsman as 4th Duke of Queensberry 1778, and his mother as 4th Earl of Ruglen 1748 ; cr. *Baron Douglas of Amesbury*, co. Wilts (peerage of Great Britain) 1768 ; *d.* unm. 1810, when the Barony of Douglas of Amesbury and the Earldom of Ruglen became ext., the Dukedom ot Queensberry reverted to the 3rd Duke of Buccleuch, the Marquessate and Earldom of Queensberry passed to his kinsman Sir Charles Douglas, 5th Bt., of Kelhead, and the Earldom of March devolved on his kinsman [4] FRANCIS, 4th Earl (great-great-grandson of Lady Anne Douglas, wife of 4th Earl of Wemyss, and sister of 1st Earl of March), who had *s.* as 8th Earl of Wemyss 1808, but on account of his predecessor's forfeiture none of the titles was recognised by the Crown until his attainder was reversed in 1826 (ante).

WENLOCK, BARONY OF. [Extinct 1932.]

DAUGHTER LIVING OF SIXTH BARON.

Hon. Ursula Mary (*Baroness Wraxall*), *O.B.E., R.R.C., b.* 1888 ; was a Maid of Honour to H.M. Queen Mary 1912-27; Regional Representative, S-W Region, of British Red Cross Soc. 1942-46, and Pres. Somerset branch 1946-71; a Serving Sister of Order of St. John of Jerusalem : *m.* 1927, as his second wife, the 1st Baron Wraxall, who *d.* 1931. *Residence,*—Tyntesfield, Bristol.

DAUGHTER LIVING OF THIRD BARON.
Hon. Irene Constance, *b.* 1889; a Dame of Grace of Order of St. John of Jerusalem: *m.* 1920, Colin Gurdon Forbes Adam, CSI, ICS [see Adam, Bt.]. *Residence,*—The Grange, Elvington, York YO4 5AD.

West, see Baron Granville-West.

WESTBURY, BARON. (Bethell.) [Baron U.K. 1861.]

DAVID ALAN BETHELL, *M.C.*, 5th Baron ; *b.* July 16th, 1922 ; *s.* 1961 ; ed. at Harrow ; Capt. Scots Guards; a DL for N. Yorks.; Equerry to HRH the Duke of Gloucester 1947-49; 1939-45 War in N. Africa and Italy (twice wounded, despatches, MC): *m.* 1947, Ursula Mary-Rose, da. of the late Hon. Robert James [see B. Northbourne, colls.], and has issue.

Arms.—Argent, on a chevron engrailed azure between three boars' heads couped sable, an estoile or, all within a bordure of the same. **Crest**—Out of a crown vallery or, an eagle's head sable, between two wings azure, charged on the breast with an estoile as in the arms. **Supporters.**—On either side an eagle, wings addorsed azure, ducally crowned, collared, and charged on the breast with an estoile or.

Ap Ithel (the old Welsh family name).

Residence,—Barton Cottage, Malton, Yorkshire. *Club,*—Turf.

SONS LIVING.
Hon. RICHARD NICHOLAS, *b.* May 29th, 1950.

Hon. James David William, *b.* 1952: *m.* 1974, Emma, yr. da. of Malise Nicolson, of Frog Hall, Tilston, Malpas, Cheshire.

DAUGHTER LIVING.
Hon. Celia Mary, *b.* 1955.

SISTER LIVING. *(Raised to the rank of a Baron's daughter* 1930.*)*
*Hon.*Veronica Wenefryde Nefertari. *b.* 1917 : *m.* 1941, Lieut.-Col. James Innes, Coldstream Guards (retired) [see E. Lonsdale]. *Residence,*—Larkenshaw, Chobham, Surrey.

COLLATERAL BRANCHES LIVING.
Issue of the late Adm. the Hon. Sir Alexander Edward Bethell, G.C.M.G., K.C.B., 2nd son of 2nd Baron, *b.* 1855, *d.* 1932: *m.* 1890, Hilda Mary, who *d.* 1928, dau. of the late Benjamin Huntsman, of West Retford Hall, Notts:—
Agatha Hilda, *b.* 1895: European War 1914-18 as Assist. Principal W.R.N.S., European War 1939-45, as Ch. Com. A.T.S. : *m.* 1922, Com. John Bertram Aubrey Marsden-Smedley, R.N., who *d.* 1959, and has issue living, Andrew Bethell (of Glebe House, Bayton, Kidderminster, Worcestershire), *b.* 1926 ; ed. at Stowe, and at Trin. coll., Camb. (B.A. 1947): *m.* 1960, Lavinia Ann, youngest dau. of Sir Thomas Claude Harris Lea, 3rd Bt., and has issue living, Robert Andrew, *b.* 1962, William Bethell *b.* 1964,—Penelope Anne, *b.* 1930: *m.* 1962, David John Charlton Meyrick of Gt. Wedlock, Gumfreston, Tenby [see Meyrick, Bt.],—Agatha Susan, *b.* 1931, ed. at Girton Coll., Camb. (BA 1954); Bar. Middle Temple 1957. *Residence,*—31, Draycott Place, Chelsea, SW3.

Grandson of the late Hon. Slingsby Bethell, CB (infra):—
Issue of the late Slingsby Westbury Bethell, *b.* 1861, *d.* 1936 : *m.* 1890, Sophia Isabella, who *d.* 1940, dau. of the late Capt. John Hobhouse Inglis Alexander, C.B., R.N. :—
Jocelyn Slingsby, *C.B.E.*, *b.* 1897; Capt. R.N. (ret.); European War 1914-18 (despatches), European War 1939-45 (despatches, O.B.E.); O.B.E. (Mil.) 1943: *m.* 1929, Violet Monica, dau. of William George Peareth-Kincaid-Lennox [Rouse-Broughton, Bt., colls.]. *Residence,*—Easter Aberchalder, Gorthleck, Inverness-shire.

Grandchildren of the late Lionel Beresford Bethell, 3rd son of the late Hon. Slingsby Bethell, CB (infra):—
Issue of the late Maj. Vivian Lionel Slingsby Bethell, *b.* 1897, *d.* 1967: *m.* 1928, Joan Ker, da. of the late John Manwell:—
Richard Ker Slingsby, *OBE* (Imberdown, Woodlands Lane, Liss, Hants.; *Club,*—Army and Navy) *b.* 1928; Capt. RN, OBE (Mil.) 1973: *m.* 1953, Anne, da. of H. Frost, and has issue living, Helena Susan Mary, *b.* 1955,—Theresa Jane, *b.* 1956,—Jane Ker, *b.* 1959.—Deirdre Ann, *b.* 1929: *m.* 1952 (m. diss. 1964), Sir Hugo Giles Edmund Sebright, 14th Bt.

Granddaughter of the late Hon. Slingsby Bethell, CB (infra):—
Issue of the late Llwelyn Slingsby Bethell, *b.* 1889, *d.* 1971: *m.* 1914, Margery Gladys (7, Bigwood Av., Hove), da. of the late George Stanley Farnell, Prin. of Victoria Coll., Jersey:—
Margaret Eve Slingsby, *b.* 1915: *m.* 1939, Cdr. Warwick Bracegirdle, DSC, RAN, and has issue living, Simon Warwick Slingsby, *b.* 1941,—Nicolas, *b.* 1944,—Phillada Ann, *b.* 1946.

Issue of the late Hon. Slingsby Bethell, C.B., 2nd son of 1st Baron, *b.* 1831, *d.* 1896: *m.* 1st, 1855, Caroline, who *d.* 1886, dau. of the late William J. Chaplin, M.P., of Ewhurst Park, Hants; 2ndly, 1888, Laura Beatrice, who *d.* 1925, dau. of the Rev. Frederick Webster Maunsell, R. of Symondsbury, Bridport :—
(By 2nd m.) Richard Alfred Slingsby, *b.* 1892; *d.* 1975; Lt.-Cdr. 1921; ret. 1935; 1914-18 War; 1939-45 War as Cdr. RN: *m.* 1930, Frances Elizabeth, da. of the late Lt.-Col. Charles Maxwell Shurlock Henning, of Frome House, Dorchester, and has issue living, Maxwell Slingsby (Oakenclough, Higher Sutton, Macclesfield, Ches.), *b.* 1931; ed. at Wellington Coll., and at Camb. Univ. (MB and DCh, MA and DPM): *m.* 1953, Pamela Mary, da. of the late Hubert Fletcher, and has issue living, Charles Maxwell Slingsby *b.* 1957, Nicola Slingsby *b.* 1953, Juliet Slingsby *b.* 1955, Zoe Melisende Slingsby *b.* 1958,—David Slingsby (Frome House, Dorchester), *b.* 1934; ed. at Camb. Univ. (MA): *m.* 1964, Sadie Melfort, da. of Lt.-Col. &. G. M. Baldwin, of Culver House, Payhembury, Devon, and has issue living, Richard Slingsby, *b.* 1965, Christopher Maunsell Slingsby *b.* 1966, Zillah Slingsby *b.* 1968. *Residence,*—Frome House, Dorchester, Dorset.

PREDECESSORS.—[1] *Rt. Hon.* Sir RICHARD Bethell, *D.C.L.*; sat as M.P. for Aylesbury 1851-9, and for Wolverhampton 1859-61; was Solicitor-Gen. 1852-6, Attorney-Gen. 1856-8 and 1859-61, and Lord Chancellor of England 1861-5; cr. *Baron Westbury*, of Westbury (peerage of United Kingdom) 1861; *d.* 1873; *s.* by his son [2] RICHARD AUGUSTUS, 2nd Baron; *b.* 1830; was a Registrar in Bankruptcy: *m.* 1851, Mary Florence, who *d.* 1901, dau. of the Rev. Alexander Fownes-Luttrell ; *d.* 1875 ; *s.* by his son [3] RICHARD LUTTRELL PILKINGTON, 3rd Baron; *b.* 1852: *m.* 1882, Lady Agatha Manners Tollemache, who *d.* 1941, sister of 9th Earl of Dysart; *d.* 1930 ; *s.* by his grandson [4] RICHARD MORLAND TOLLEMACHE (son of the late Capt. the Hon. Richard Bethell, only son of 3rd Baron), 4th Baron ; *b.* 1914; European War 1939-45 as Major R.E.; *d.* 1961 ; *s.* by his brother [5] DAVID ALAN, 5th Baron and present peer.

D.—38

WESTER WEMYSS, BARONY OF. (Wemyss.) [Extinct 1933.]
DAUGHTER LIVING OF FIRST BARON.

Hon. Alice Elizabeth Millicent, *b.* 1906: *m.* 1953, Major Francis Henry Cunnack, RA (ret.), who *d.* 1974. *Residence,—*Saint Suliac, Ille et Villaine, France.

WESTMEATH, EARL OF. (Nugent.) [Earl I. 1621.]

I have resolved.

WILLIAM ANTHONY NUGENT, 13th Earl; *b.* Nov. 21st, 1928; *s.* 1971; ed. at Marlborough; late Capt. RA; Assist. Master, St. Andrew's Sch., Pangbourne: *m.* 1963, Susanna Margaret, only da. of His Hon. Judge (James Charles Beresford Whyte) Leonard, of Cross Trees, Sutton Courtenay, Berks., and has issue.

𝔄rms,—Ermine, two bars gules. 𝔠rest,—A cockatrice, wings elevated and displayed, vert. Supporters,—Two cockatrices, wings elevated, vert.

*Residence,—*Farthings, Rotten Row Hill, Tutts Clump, Bradfield, Berks.

SONS LIVING.
SEAN CHARLES WESTON (*Lord Delvin*), *b.* Feb. 16th, 1965.
Hon. Patrick Mark Leonard, *b.* 1966.

SISTER LIVING.
Lady Pamela Joan, *b.* 1921; sometime Section Officer W.A.A.F.: *m.* 1950, Lieut.-Col. Peter John Barbary, OBE, GM, TD, DL, FRIBA who *d.* 1969, and has issue living, Michael John Nugent, *b.* 1951—Joanna Clare Nugent, *b.* 1955. *Residence,—*Briar Rose Cottage, 17, Landeryon Gdns., Penzance, Cornwall.

COLLATERAL BRANCHES LIVING.
Granddaughters of the late Maj.-Gen. St. George Mervyn Nugent, son of the late Christopher Edmund John Nugent, a descendant of the late Oliver Nugent, brother of 13th Baron Delvin :—
Issue of the late Maj.-Gen. Sir Oliver Stewart Wood Nugent, K.C.B., D.S.O., *b.* 1860, *d.* 1926: *m.* 1899, Catherine Percy, who *d.* 1970, da. of the late Thomas Evans Lees, of Betley Hall, Ches.:—
Marian Catherine Theffania, *b.* 1903: *m.* 1927, Lt. Robert Vesey Stoney, R.N.V.R., who *d.* (on active ser. during European War) 1944, and has issue living, Robert Oliver Vesey, *R.N.* (of Rosturk Castle, Westport, co. Mayo), *b.* 1928; is Com.: *m.* 1st, 1953, the Hon. Kathleen Benita Brooke, who *d.* 1961, dau. of 1st Viscount Alanbrooke; 2ndly, 1963, Monica Ann, dau. of the late Col. Ralph Joyce, and has issue living, (by 1st m.) Robert Alanbrooke Vesey *b.* 1956, Alan Vesey *b.* 1958, Benita Theffania Vesey *b.* 1954, (by 2nd m.), Eleanor Ann Vesey *b.* 1965, Charlotte Elizabeth Vesey *b.* 1966,—Myles Samuel Vesey (of Ryevale Mill, Leixlip, co. Kildare), *b.* 1930; ed. at Harrow: *m.* 1956, Alison Marsh, of Aasleagh House, Leenane, co. Galway, and has issue living, William St. George Vesey *b.* 1959, Catherine Vesey *b.* 1957,—*Rev.* Thomas Vesey (The Rectory, Broughshane, co. Antrim), *b.* 1934; ed. at Harrow, at Oriel Coll., Oxford, and at Trin. Coll., Dublin: *m.* 1962, Caroline, da. of Anthony Reynolds, of Braam Camp, Barreiro, Portugal, and has issue living, Samuel Vesey *b.* 1963, James Anthony Vesey *b.* 1969, Anabel Fania Vesey *b.* 1966,—Colum John Vesey, *b.* 1939; ed. at Harrow,—Phoebe Catherine Vesey, *b.* 1932: *m.* 1962, Hubert John Brooke Allen, and has issue living, Roland John Stoney *b.* 1963, Myles Robert *b.* 1965, Priscilla Marion *b.* 1968,—Theffania Vesey (*posthumous*), *b.* 1944: *m.* 1965, Oliver William Everett; HM Dip Ser. (c/o British High Commn., New Delhi), and has issue living, Kathleen Louise *b.* 1966, Grania Brigid *b.* 1969. *Residence,* —Ardagh Lodge, Westport, co. Mayo.——Alison Joan Elliott, *b.* 1909: *m.* 1947, Harry Gerhard Hirschberg, LLD, of Farren-Connell, Mount Nugent, co. Cavan.

(*In remainder to Barony of Delvin.*)
Grandsons of the late Albert Llewellyn Nugent, 4th son of Walter Nugent (cr. Baron of Austria 1859, with remainder to issue male and female), 10th in decent from Andrew Nugent of Clonlost, yr. son of Andrew Nugent of Donore, brother of 11th Baron Delvin:—
Issue of the late Albert Beauchamp Nugent, 5th Baron Nugent, *b.* 1874, *d.* 1938: *m.* 1914, Frances Every Douglas, who *d.* 1950, dau. of the late Lieut. Robert Douglas Campbel R.N., of Blythswood House, Renfrew [B. Blythswood, colls.]:—
David James Douglas (*Baron Nugent*), *b.* 1917; *s.* his brother as 7th Baron Nugent 1944; ed. at Lancing: *m.* 1968, Mary Louise, JP, who *d.* 1975, el. da. of the late William Henry Wroth, of Big-bury Court, Devon, and widow of Howard Seys-Phillips. *Residences,—*Longbridge Deverill House, Wilts.; 4, Gloucester Place Mews, Portman Sq., W1.
Issue of the late Brig.-Gen. Frank Henry BURNELL-NUGENT, C.B., D.S.O., O.B.E., *b.* 1880, *d.* 1942 (having assumed the additional name of Burnell): *m.* 1905, Ellen Mary, who *d.* 1941, only dau. of Thomas Coke Burnell, of St. Cross Grange, Winchester :—
Anthony Frank, *DSC, RN*; *b.* 1906; became Cdr. 1942; retired 1945; 1939-45 War (despatches, DSO): *m.* 1941, Gian Mary, da. of the late Rear-Adm. Charles Otway Alexander, of Wilford Rise, Woodbridge, Suffolk, and has issue living, Charles Anthony, *b.* 1942,—James Michael, *b.* 1949; ed. at Stowe and Corpus Christi Coll., Camb.; Lt. RN: *m.* 1963, Henrietta Mary, yst. da. of the Rt. Rev. Robert Wilmer Woods, KCVO, Bishop of Worcester,—Mary, *b.* 1947: *m.* 1967, John Richard Con-way Lloyd of, Alone House, Stutton, Ipswich, and has issue living, John Conway *b.* 1970, Lucy Ellen *b.* 1972,—Sheila Jane, *b.* 1951. *Residence,—*Stutton Manor, Ipswich, IP9 2TB.

PREDECESSORS.—[1] RICHARD Nugent, 12th Baron of Delvin, and Lord Dep. of Ireland 1528, was summoned to Parliament of Ireland 1486, 1490, and 1493; *d.* 1538; *s.* by his grandson [2] RICHARD, 13th Baron; *d.* 1559; *s.* by his son [3] CHRISTOPHER, 14th Baron; *d.* 1602; *s.* by his son [4] RICHARD, 15th Baron; cr. *Earl of Westmeath* (peerage of Ireland) 1621; *d.* 1641; *s.* by his grandson [5] RICHARD, 2nd Earl; *d.* 1684; *s.* by his grandson [6] RICHARD, 3rd Earl; was a Capuchin Friar; *d.* 1714; *s.* by his brother [7] THOMAS, 4th Earl; having been outlawed for his adhesion to the cause of James II. the outlawry was afterwards reversed and his honours and estates restored; *d.* 1752; *s.* by his brother [8] JOHN, 5th Earl; a Major-Gen. in the Army; *d.* 1754; *s.* by his son [9] THOMAS, K.P., 6th Earl; conformed to the Established Church; *d.* 1792; *s.* by his son [10] GEORGE FREDERICK, 7th Earl; *d.* 1814; *s.* by his son [11] GEORGE THOMAS JOHN, 8th Earl; was Lord-Lieut. of co. Westmeath, and a Representative Peer; cr. *Marquess of Westmeath* (peerage of Ireland) 1822; *d.* 1871, when the marquessate became extinct, and the earldom devolved upon his kinsman [12] ANTHONY FRANCIS, 9th Earl, descendant of Thomas, 2nd son of 2nd Earl, whose father was called 4th Lord Riverston (a title that had been conferred by James II. after his deposition); *b.* 1805; established his claim to the Earldom 1871; *d.* 1879; *s.* by his son [13] WILLIAM ST. GEORGE, 10th Earl, *b.* 1832: *m.* 1866, Emily Margaret, who *d.* 1906, dau. of the late Andrew William Blake, J.P., D.L., of

Furbough, co. Galway; *d.* 1883; *s.* by his son [14] ANTHONY FRANCIS, 11th Earl, *b.* 1870; a Representative Peer for Ireland; *d.* 1933; *s.* by his brother [15] GILBERT CHARLES, 12th Earl, *b.* 1880: *m.* 1915, Doris, who *d.* 1968, da. of the late Charles Imlach, of Liverpool; *d.* 1971; *s.* by his son [16] WILLIAM ANTHONY, 13th Earl and present peer, also Baron Delvin.

WESTMINSTER, DUKE OF. (Grosvenor.) [Duke U.K. 1874, Bt. E. 1622.]

VIRTVS · NON · STEMMA

Virtue, not ancestry.

ROBERT GEORGE GROSVENOR, *TD,* 5th Duke, and 14th Baronet; *b.* April 24th, 1910; *s.* 1967; ed. at Eton; Lt.-Col. (ret.) N. Irish Horse (Hon. Col. RAC, TAVR 1971-75), a JP and a Vice-Lt. of co. Fermanagh, and a DL of Cheshire, and a CStJ; High Sheriff co. Fermanagh 1952; ADC to Gov. of N. Ireland 1953-55, and PPS to Sec. of State for Foreign Affairs 1957-59; MP for Fermanagh and S. Tyrone (*U*) 1955-64; a Senator, N. Ireland 1964-67; 1939-45 War with RA in Middle East: *m.* 1946, the Hon. Viola Maud Lyttelton, da. of the 9th Viscount Cobham, and has issue.

Arms,—Quarterly: 1st and 4th azure, a portcullis with chains pendant or, on a chief of the last, between two united roses of York and Lancaster a pale, charged with the arms of King Edward the Confessor *City of Westminster* (Augmentation); 2nd and 3rd azure, a garb or, *Grosvenor.* **Crest,**—A talbot statant or. **Supporters,** —Two talbots reguardant or, collared azure.

Residences,—Ely Lodge, Enniskillen, co. Fermanagh; Eaton, Chester.

SON LIVING
GERALD CAVENDISH (*Earl Grosvenor*), *b.* Dec. 22nd, 1951; ed. at Harrow.

DAUGHTERS LIVING
Lady Leonora Mary (*Countess of Lichfield*), *b.* 1949: *m.* 1975, the 5th Earl of Lichfield. *Residences,*—Shugborough Hall, Stafford; 22, Clarence Terr., Regents Park, NW1.
Lady Jane Meriel, *b.* 1953.

DAUGHTERS LIVING OF SECOND DUKE.
Lady Ursula Mary Olivia, *b.* 1902: *m.* 1st, 1924, William Filmer-Sankey, formerly Lieut. 1st Life Guards, who obtained a divorce 1940; 2ndly, 1940, Stephen Vernon, and has issue living, (by 1st marriage) Patrick Hugh, *b.* 1925: *m.* 1956, Josephine, only dau. of the late Ronald Griffin. *Residence,*—.
Lady Mary Constance, *b.* 1910. *Residence,*—Churton Lodge, Churton, Cheshire.

WIDOWS LIVING OF SECOND AND FOURTH DUKE
ANNE WINIFRED (*Anne, Duchess of Westminster*), only da. of the late Brig.-Gen. Edward Langford Sullivan, C.B., C.M.G., of Glanmire House, co. Cork: *m.* 1947, as his fourth wife, the 2nd Duke, who *d.* 1953. *Residences,*—Eaton Lodge, Eccleston, Chester; Lochmore, Lairg, Sutherland.
SALLY (*Sally, Duchess of Westminster*), (Hill House, Wickwar, Glos.), twin da. of the late George Perry: *m.* 1945, the 4th Duke, who *d.* 1967.

COLLATERAL BRANCHES LIVING.
Granddaughter of the late Lord Arthur Hugh Grosvenor (infra):—
Issue of the late Robert Arthur Grosvenor, M.C., *b.* 1895, *d.* 1953: *m.* 1925, Doris May, of Oak Ash Farm, Chaddleworth, Berks, dau. of the late Frederick William Wignall [Tate, Bt., colls.]:—
Robina Jill, *b.* 1930: *m.* 1st 1951 (marriage dissolved 1961), Michael Philip Forsyth-Forrest; 2ndly, 1961, R. Mills of Soloman's Court, Chalford, Glos., and has issue living, (by 1st m.) Anita, *b.* 1952,—Tessa, *b.* 1955—(by 2nd m.), Robin, *b.* 1962,—Serena Laura Rosanna, *b.* 1965.

Issue of the late Lord Arthur Hugh Grosvenor, 2nd son of the 1st Duke, *b.* 1860, *d.* 1929: *m.* 1893, Helen, who *d.* 1950, dau. of Sir Robert Sheffield, 5th Bt.:—
Constance Isolde, *b.* 1900: *m.* 1930, Major William Reginald James Alston-Roberts-West, Grenadier Guards, who *d.* (killed in action) 1940 [E. De La Warr, colls.], and has issue living, James William, *b.* 1935: *m.* 1958, Camilla Audrey, da. of Anthony Seymour Bellville, of The White House, Bembridge, I. of Wight, and has issue living,—George Arthur, *b.* 1937; ed. at Eton; Capt. Gren. Guards. *Residence,*—Lime Tree House, Asthall, Burford, Oxford.—Barbara (*Countess of Stradbroke*), *b.* 1901: *m.* 1929, the 4th Earl of Stradbroke. *Residence,*—Henham, Beccles, Suffolk.

Issue of the late Lord Edward Arthur Grosvenor, 9th son of 1st Duke, *b.* 1892, *d.* 1929: *m.* 1914, Lady Dorothy Margaret Browne [who *d.* 1961; she *m.* 2ndly, 1930, the Hon. Sir Evan Edward Charteris, KC, who *d.* 1940 (E. Wemyss and March)], da. of 5th Earl of Kenmare:—
Beatrice Elizabeth Katharine, *C.B.E.*, *b.* 1915; was Dep. Sup-in-Ch., St. John Ambulance Brig. 1953-8 (despatches); a D.St.J.; resumed her maiden name of Grosvenor by deed poll 1953; O.B.E. (Civil) 1945: *m.* 1944 (marriage annulled 1945), as his second wife, Major Richard Desiré Girouard, son of the late Col. Sir (Edouard) Percy Cranwill Girouard, K.C.M.G., D.S.O. *Residence,*—Kenmare House, Killarney, co. Kerry.

(*In remainder to the Marquessate.*)
Descendants of the late Rt. Hon. Lord Thomas Grosvenor, G.C.H., D.C.L. (2nd son of 1st Marquess), who *s.* his maternal grandfather (under special remainder) as 2nd *Earl of Wilton* 1814 [see that title].

Descendants of the late Rt. Hon. Lord Robert Grosvenor, (3rd son of 1st Marquess of Westminster), who was cr. *Baron Ebury* 1857 [see that title].

PREDECESSORS.—[1] Sir RICHARD Grosvenor, Knt., of Eaton, Cheshire, M.P. for Cheshire, was cr. a *Baronet* 1622; *d.* 1645; *s.* by his son [2] *Sir* RICHARD, 2nd Bt.; *d.* 1664; *s.* by his grandson [3] *Sir* THOMAS, 3rd Bt.; sat as M.P. for Chester; *d.* 1700; *s.* by his el. son [4] *Sir* RICHARD, 4th Bt.; was Grand Cupbearer at the coronation of George II, *d.s.p.* 1732; *s.* by his brother [5] *Sir* THOMAS, 5th Bt.; was M.P. for Chester; *d.* 1733; *s.* by his brother [6] *Sir* ROBERT, 6th Bt.; sat as

M.P. for Chester; *d.* 1755; *s.* by his son [7] *Sir* RICHARD, 7th Bt.; cr. *Baron Grosvenor,* of Eaton, co. Chester (peerage of Great Britain) 1761, and *Viscount Belgrave* and *Earl Grosvenor* (peerage of Great Britain) 1784: *m.* 1776, Henrietta (who *m.* 2ndly, 1802, the 6th Baron de Hochepied, and *d.* 1828), dau. of Henry Vernon, of Hilton Park, Staffs.; *d.* 1802; *s.* by his son [8] ROBERT, 2nd Earl; cr. *Marquess of Westminster* (peerage of United Kingdom) 1831; was Lord-Lieut. of Flintshire: *m.* 1794, Lady Eleanor Egerton, who *d.* 1846, dau. of 1st Earl of Wilton; *d.* 1845; *s.* by his son [9] RICHARD, *K.G., P.C.,* 2nd Marquess; *b.* 1795; was Lord-Lieut. of Cheshire: *m.* 1819, Elizabeth Mary, who *d.* 1891, dau. of 1st Duke of Sutherland; *d.* 1869, *s.* by his son [10] HUGH LUPUS, 3rd Marquess: *b.* 1825; Lord-Lieut. of Cheshire, and of co. London; Master of the Horse 1880-85; M.P. for Chester (*L*) 1847-69; cr. *Duke of Westminster* (peerage of United Kingdom) 1874: *m.* 1st, 1852, Lady Constance Gertrude Leveson-Gower, who *d.* 1880, dau. of 2nd Duke of Sutherland, K.G.; 2ndly, 1882, the Hon. Katharine Caroline Cavendish, C.B.E., who *d.* 1941, dau. of 2nd Baron Chesham; *d.* 1899; *s.* by his grandson [11] HUGH RICHARD ARTHUR, *G.C.V.O., D.S.O.* (only son of Victor Alexander, Earl Grosvenor), 2nd Duke; *b.* 1879; Lord-Lieut. of Cheshire 1906-20; S. Africa 1900-02, and 1914-18 War: *m.* 1st, 1901, Constance Edwina, CBE (who *d.* 1970, having obtained a divorce 1919), da. of the late Col. William Cornwallis-West [E. De La Warr]; 2ndly, 1920, Violet Mary Geraldine (who obtained a divorce 1926), da. of Sir William Nelson, 1st Bt.; 3rdly, 1930, the Hon. Lœlia Mary Ponsonby (who obtained a divorce 1947), da. of 1st Baron Sysonby; 4thly, 1947, Anne Winifred, only da. of the late Brig-Gen. Edward Langford Sullivan, OB, CMG, of Glanmire House, co. Cork; *d.* 1953; *s.* by his cousin [12] WILLIAM (son of the late Lord Henry George Grosvenor, 3rd son of the 1st Duke), 3rd Duke; *d.* 1963; *s.* by his cousin [13] GERALD HUGH, *DSO, PC,* (el. son of the late Capt. Lord Hugh William Grosvenor, 6th son of 1st Duke) 4th Duke; *b.* 1907; Lt.-Col. 9th Lancers; Col. 9th/12th Lancers 1961-67; High Sheriff of Cheshire 1959; Lord Steward of HM Household 1964-67: *m.* 1945, Sally, twin da. of the late George Perry; *d.* 1967; *s.* by his brother ROBERT GEORGE, *T.D.* [14] 5th Duke, and present peer; also Marquess of Westminster, Earl Grosvenor, Viscount Belgrave, and Baron Grosvenor.

WESTMORLAND, EARL OF.   (Fane.)   [Earl E. 1624.]

Disgrace not the altar.

DAVID ANTHONY THOMAS FANE, *KCVO*, 15th Earl; *b.* March 31st, 1924; *s.* 1948; ed. at Eton; late Capt. Roy. Horse Guards; 1939-45 War (wounded); appointed a Lord-in-Waiting to HM 1955; KCVO 1970: *m.* 1950, Barbara Jane, da. of Lieut.-Col. Sir Roland Lewis Findlay, 3rd Bt., and has issue.

Arms,—Azure, three dexter gauntlets back affrontée or. Crest,—Out of a ducal coronet or, a bull's head of a brindled colour, armed gold, and charged with a rose gules. Supporters,—*Dexter*, a griffin, per fesse argent and or, collared, and line reflexed over the back sable; *sinister*, a pied or brindled bull, collared and lined or, at the end of the line a ring and three staples of the last.

Residence,—19, South Eaton Place, SW1.

SONS LIVING.

HENRY DAVID ANTHONY FRANCIS (*Lord Burghersh*), *b.* Aug. 1st, 1951.
Hon. Harry St. Clair, *b.* 1953; Page of Honour to HM 1966-68.

DAUGHTER LIVING.

Lady Camilla Diana, *b.* 1957.

BROTHER LIVING.

Hon. Julian Charles (32, Blenheim Terr., NW8), *b.* 1927; ed. at Harrow.

SISTER LIVING.

Lady Rose, *b.* 1930: *m.* 1st, 1950 (m. diss. 1969), Capt. John Macdonald-Buchanan, MC, Scots Gds. (ret.) [see By. Woolavington]; 2ndly, 1972, John V. Bardsley, of St. Mary's House, Tormarton, Glos.

AUNT LIVING.   (*Daughter of 13th Earl.*)

Lady Gloria Sybil (57A, De Lisle Rd., Bournemouth), *b.* 1902.

WIDOW LIVING OF SON OF THIRTEENTH EARL.

AGATHA ISABEL (of The Old Rectory, Careby, Stamford), dau. of the late Lt.-Col. Arthur Acland-Hood-Reynardson [see Fuller-Acland-Hood, Bt., colls.]: *m.* 1926, Lt.-Col. the Hon. Mountjoy John Charles Wedderburn Fane, T.D., who *d.* 1963, and has issue living [see colls., infra].

WIDOW LIVING OF FOURTEENTH EARL.

Hon. DIANA (*Diana, Countess of Westmorland*), dau. of 4th Baron Ribblesdale (ext.) and widow of (1) Percy Lyulph Wyndham, Lieut. Coldstream Guards [B. Leconfield], and (2) Capt. Arthur Edward Capel, C.B.E.: *m.* 1923, the 14th Earl, who *d.* 1948. *Residence,*—Lyegrove, Badminton, Gloucestershire.

COLLATERAL BRANCHES LIVING.

Issue of the late Lt.-Col. the Hon. Mountjoy John Charles Wedderburn Fane, T.D., 2nd son of 13th Earl, *b.* 1900, *d.* 1963: *m.* 1926, Agatha Isabel (The Old Rectory, Careby, Stamford), da. of the late Lt.-Col. Arthur Acland-Hood-Reynardson [see Fuller-Acland-Hood, Bt., colls.] (ante):—

Antony Charles Reynardson (Rutherwyke House, Lyne, Chertsey, Surrey), *b.* 1927; Lt.-Cdr. RN (ret.) *m.* 1956, Caroline Mary Rokeby, dau. of the late Hugh D. Holland, of The Crossways, Englefield Green, Surrey, and has issue living, Edward Hugh Reynardson, *b.* 1957,—Olivia Mary Rokeby, *b.* 1960,—Charlotte Evelyn Langham, *b.* 1967.——Daphne Sybil, *b.* 1929.

Grandchildren of the late William Dashwood Fane, son of the late William Fane; son of the late Hon. Henry Fane, M.P., younger son of 8th Earl:—

Issue of the late Col. William (Vere Reeve) KING-FANE, *b.* 1868, *d.* 1943 (having assumed by Roy. licence 1920 the surname of King in addition to and before that of Fane): *m.* 1895, Helen Beatrice, who *d.* 1962, dau. of the late Thomas Holdsworth Newman [Newman, Bt., cr. 1836, colls.]:—

Henry William Newman, *OBE, b.* 1897; ed. at Charterhouse; Capt. (ret.) RA; 1915-18 War; 1939-45 War; OBE (Civil) 1974: *m.* 1946, Dorothy Mary, only da. of the late Alexander Findlay, of Llantarnam, Monmouthshire, and has issue living, Mary Helen, *b.* 1947. *Residence,*—Fulbeck Hall, Grantham.——Charles William (Ashmansworth Manor, Newbury), *b.* 1904; ed. at Charterhouse;

late Lt. RNVR; a Member of Lloyd's: *m.* 1st, 1931 (m. diss. 1966), Pauline Margaret, da. of the Rt. Rev. Ernest Morell Blackie, Dean of Rochester; 2ndly, 1966, Pamela Mary, da. of the late Capt. Robert Millington Synge [see Synge, Bt., colls.], and has issue living, (by 1st wife), Peter William (14, Moore Park Rd., Fulham, SW6), *b.* 1939; ed. at Eton: an underwriting Member of Lloyds: *m.* 1969, Ruth, da. of the late John Paske Yeomans,—Angela Pauline, *b.* 1936: *m.* 1964, Lt. Cdr. Kenneth Patrick Bruce-Gardyne, RN, of Nettlebed House, Droxford, Southampton, and has issue living, James Patrick *b.* 1965, Vere Alexander *b.* 1973, Victoria Sophia *b.* 1969, (by 2nd wife) Eleanor Mary, *b.* 1965,—Georgina Rachel, *b.* 1966,—Rose Christabel, *b.* 1968.——Elizabeth Christine (Church Cottage, Acol, Birchington, Kent), *b.* 1906: *m.* 1931, Col. Jeffrey Maurice Lambert, OBE, late RE, who *d.* 1967, and has issue living, John Alexander, *b.* 1932,—Janetta, *b.* 1936.

Grandchildren of the late Col. William (Vere Reeve) KING-FANE (ante):—

Issue of the late Lieut. Francis Christopher Fane, R.N., *b.* 1900, *d.* 1947: *m.* 1931, Joyce Patricia (who *m.* 2ndly, 1957, Maj. Vincent Tofts, TD, late Indian Army, of Long Farm Cottage, Scrivelsby, Horncastle, Lincs., da. of the late Rev. W. Hugh Hancock:—

Julian Francis, *b.* 1938; ed. at Marlborough and Emmanuel Coll., Camb (MA): *m.* 1965, Mary Julia, da. of Michael W. Allday, of The Shrubbery, Hartlebury, Worcs., and has issue living, Andrew Julian, *b.* 1967,—Alexandra Julia, *b.* 1969. *Residence,*—Fulbeck Manor, Grantham.——Susan Cicely, *b.* 1932: *m.* 1953, Lt.-Col. John Lindley Marmion Dymoke MBE, late R. Anglian Regt., 34th Queen's Champion of England [By. Lindley, ext.], and has issue living, Francis John Fane Marmion, *b.* 1955,—Philip Henry Marmion, *b.* 1957,—Charles Edward Marmion, *b.* 1961. *Seat,*—Scrivelsby Court, Horncastle, Lincs. *Club,*—United Service.——Rosemary Lilias, *b.* 1934: *m.* 1954, Derek Cecil Stevenson, MB, BS, MRCS, LRCP, FRCS, and has issue living, Christopher Peter, *b.* 1956,—Melody Jane, *b.* 1958,—Catherine Fane, *b.* 1960,—Mary-Louise, *b.* 1969. *Residence,*—Fulbeck, Kellerberrin, W. Aust.——Belinda Joyce (twin), *b.* 1938; *m.* 1971, Gary Douglas Phillips; AMRSH; DipPh NZ, of Cliff Grange, Greenough, PO Walkaway, Aust.

Grandchildren of the late Cecil Francis William Fane, 2nd son of the late Robert George Cecil Fane, 7th son of the late Hon. Henry Fane, M.P. (ante):—

Issue of the late John Lionel Richards Fane, *b.* 1884, *d.* 1945: *m.* 1928 Barbara Kathleen [(Quinta do Moinho, Guia, Algarve, Portugal, and 1, Camelia Court, New St. John's Rd., St. Helier, Jersey, who *m.* 3rdly, 1947, Bryan Northam Gibbs, MBE, who *d.* 1965, and 4thly, 1969, John Sidney Mason, who *d.* 1974] da. of the late Falconer Lewis Wallace, OBE, of Candacraig, Aberdeenshire [M. Anglesey, colls.], and formerly wife of the late Capt. Oliver Henry Douglas Vickers:—

Vere John Alexander (10, Goodwood Hill, Singapore, 9; White's Club), *b.* 1935; ed. at Eton, and at Trin. Coll., Camb.; late Lt. Coldm. Gds.: *m.* 1964, Tessa Helen Murray, only da. of John Murray Prain, DSO, OBE, DL, of Mugdrum, Newburgh, Fife and has issue living, Rupert John Alexander, *b.* 1967,—Miranda Helen, *b.* 1968.——Venetia Sophia Diana (Drumwhill, Mossdale, by Castle Douglas), *b.* 1930.

Grandchildren of the late Major John Augustus Fane. el. son of the late Col. John William Fane, MP, son of John Fane, MP (*b.* 1775), el. son of John Fane, MP, son of Henry Fane, yr. brother of 8th Earl:—

Issue of the late Francis Luther Fane, *b.* 1865, *d.* 1954: *m.* 1st, 1906, Mary, who *d.* 1927, da. of the late John Henry Horris of Ballarat, Victoria, Australia; 2ndly, 1929, Beatrice Jane, who *d.* 1961, el. dau. of the late Harry Coppleston, of Lostwithiel, Cornwall:—

(By 2nd m.) John Coppleston Luther (Wormsley, Watlington, Oxon.; MCC, Guards' Club), *b.* 1933; ed. at Harrow, and Emmanuel Coll., Camb.; late Lt. Welsh Guards.——Anne Isabel, *b.* 1931: *m.* 1954, Colin Irvin Richmond-Watson, and has issue living, Harry Fane, *b.* 1956,—Angus Colin John, *b.* 1958,—Elizabeth Frances Aves, *b.* 1960,—Sarah Eleanor, *b.* 1962. *Residence,*—Ingham House, Watlington, Oxon.

Issue of the late Sydney Algernon Fane, *b.* 1867, *d.* 1929: *m.* 1894, Selina Violet, who *d.* 1939, da. of the late Loftus Fitz-Wygram [Wigram, Bt., colls.]:—

Gerard William Reginald, *DSC, b.* 1898; 1915-19 War as Capt. RAF (DSC): *m.* 1st, 1919, Constance Rhoda Elizabeth, who *d.* 1969, da. of Sir Nicholas Henry Bacon, 13th Bt.; 2ndly, 1970, Phyllis Jane, da. of the late Hugh Jackson, of Chevington, and has issue living (by 1st m.), Peter Gerard Scrope (Bridge Farm, Swefling, Saxmundham, Suffolk), *b.* 1921; ed. at Eton; Lt. RNVR: *m.* 1st, 1948 (m. diss. 1955), Cecilie Christine, da. of the late Einar Walter Nansen, High Court Advocate, of Oslo, Norway; 2ndly, 1961 (m. annulled 1962), Juliet, da. of the late Brig. George Maitland-Edwards, DSO, and widow of Wing-Cdr. Trevor Owen Freeman, DSO, DFC; 3rdly, 1963, Mrs. Anne Barclay Melville-Ross, da. of the late Lt.-Col. Henry Gamble, OBE, of Instow, Devon, —Julian Raymond, *b.* 1925. *Residences,*—Feering Place, Kelvedon, Colchester; The Gate House, Dullingham, Newmarket. *Club,*—Boodles.

Granddaughter of the late Sydney Algernon Fane (ante):—

Issue of the late Cdr. Nigel Loftus Henry Fane, RNR, *b.* 1904, *d.* 1973: *m.* 1st, 1935 (m. diss. 1959), Catharine Henrietta, who *d.* 1968, da. of Henry P. Hussey, of Bricklehurst Manor, Stonegate, Sussex; 2ndly, 1960 (m. diss. 1971), Dorothy Mai, da. of John Farrington, and widow of Borras Noel Hamilton Whiteside [see L. Belhaven and Stenton]:—

(By 1st m.) Patricia Margaret, *b.* 1936: *m.* 1958, Charles Henry David Denning, of the Old Vicarage, Stonegate, Wadhurst, Sussex, yr. son of Lt.-Gen. Sir Reginald Francis Stewart Denning, KBE, CB, and has issue living, James Henry, *b.* 1959,—Guy William, *b.* 1962,—Sophia Jane, *b.* 1964,—Venetia Mary, *b.* 1966.

Grandchildren of the late Capt. Henry George Fane:—

Issue of the late Hubert William Fane, *b.* 1378, *d.* 1949: *m.* 1911, Tilda, who *d.* 1953, dau. of the late A. von Adametz:—

Robert William Augustus, *M.B.E., b.* 1913: ed. at Oundle Sch., and at Emmanuel Coll., Camb., formerly Major R.A.; is a M.I.C.E., and an A.M.I.Mech.E.; Italy 1943-45 (M.B.E.); M.B.E. (Mil.) 1945: *m.* 1940, Elinor Valerie, da. of the late Hon. William Borthwick [see Borthwick, Bt., colls.] and has issue living, Andrew William Mildmay, *b.* 1949; ed. at Radley, and Emmanuel Coll., Camb., —Peter Robert Spencer, *b.* 1956,—Priscilla Margaret, *b.* 1943,—Lavinia Anne, *b.* 1947,—Angela Elizabeth, *b.* 1954. *Residence,*—Hoo House, Hoo, Woodbridge, Suffolk. *Club,*—Junior Carlton.——Dorothy Louisa, *b.* 1917: *m.* 1st, 1938, Capt. Frederick James Colville, Gordon Highlanders, who *d.* (killed in action at Dunkirk) 1940 [V. Colville of Culross, colls.]; 2ndly, 1941 (m. diss. 1962), Lt.-Cdr. Clifford John Maddocks, RNVR, MIME; 3rdly, 1962, Lt.-Col. John Anthony Russell Freeland, late Queen's R. Regt., and has issue living (by 2nd m.) Cynthia Diana, *b.* 1944: *m.* 1967, John Charles Johnson Orchard, of Honington Glebe, Honington, nr. Shipston-on-Stour, Warwicks., and has issue living, Alaister Mildmay Heywood *b.* 1971, Alexandra Rosemary Fane *b.* 1969,—Anne Susan, *b.* 1948: *m.* 1968, Richard Fullerton Evetts, of Monks Farm, Smarden, Kent, and has issue living, Toby James Fullerton *b.* 1970. *Residence,*—18, Shirley Rd., Hove, Sussex.

Issue of the late Francis John Fane, *b.* 1885, *d.* 1963: *m.* 1915, Violet, who *d.* 1970, da. of the late G. Clifford Bower, of Newquay, Bromley, Kent:—

Peter Francis George (Wildermere, Haughurst Hill, Baughurst, Hants. *Club,*—Junior Carlton), *b.* 1917; ed. at Marlborough, and at Emmanuel Coll., Camb. (MA 1939); Capt. (ret.) RA; 1939-45 War (prisoner): *m.* 1939, Diana, only da. of the late Col. G. H. Hogkinson, and has issue living, Francis Michael George (c/o Barclays Bank, High St., Oxford), *b.* 1941; ed. at Peterhouse, Rhodesia, and Emmanuel Coll., Camb. (BA): *m.* 1967, Anne Bridget Gribble, and has issue living, Thomas Francis *b.* 1968, Suzanne *b.* 1972,—Victoria, *b.* 1947: *m.* 1966, Martin Richard Cardale, of Melbourne, Aust., and has issue living, George Martin *b.* 1970, Miranda Lucy *b.* 1968,—Sarah Lucy *b.* 1962.——Henry John, *MC* (Gay Street Farm, Pulborough, Sussex), *b.* 1919; ed. at Marlborough; Maj. RA (ret.); 1939-45 War (MC): *m.* 1945 (m. diss. 1970, Agatina, da. of Onorevole, Count Saverio d'Ayala, of Rome, and has issue living, Richard John George, *b.* 1946,—Patrick Henry, *b.* 1949.——Elizabeth Daphne (of Alderley, Pine Av., Camberley, Surrey): *m.* 1940, Lt.-Col. John David Logan Dickson, MC, RHA, who *d.* 1958, and has issue living, Jeremy David Fane (128, Somerset Rd., Wimbledon Common, SW19), *b.* 1941; ed. at Marlborough, and Emmanuel Coll., Camb. (BA): *m.* 1965, Patricia, da. of Laurence Cleveland Martin, MD, FRCP, and has issue living, James David Laurence *b.* 1970, Lucy Camilla *b.* 1971,—Sally Ann, *b.* 1942.

Grandchildren of the late Col. John William Fane, MP (ante):—

Issue of the late Cecil Fane, *b.* 1859, *d.* 1948: *m.* 1st, 1892, Alice Mary, who *d.* 1899, dau. of the Rev. Thomas Ward Goddard. formerly V. of Nazeing, Essex; 2ndly 1913, Florence Marjorie, who *d.* 1967, d. of William Ferrand [B. Bolton, colls.]:—

(By 1st marriage) Valentine Cecil, *b.* 1893. *Residence.*—Carters, Sawbridgeworth, Herts.——(By 2nd marriage) Adrian Cecil (of Riverdale, Delgany, co. Wicklow), *b.* 1916; ed. at Eton; late Lt. Gloucestershire Regt.: *m.* 1952, Elizabeth Muriel Wheeler, of Garbally, Bruff, co. Limerick, and has issue living, Henry Cecil, *b.* 1954——Gwendoline Anne, *b.* 1953.——John William (84, Addison Rd., Enfield, Middlesex), *b.* 1919: *m.* 1st, 1944, Doreen, from whom he obtained a divorce 19—, da. of A. Lawrence, of Waltham Abbey; 2ndly, 1963, Mrs. Gwen Kelly, and has issue living (by 1st marriage) Anthony John, *b.* 1948,—Sheila Rosamond, *b.* 1951.——Kathleen Marjorie, *b.* 1914: *m.* 1944, Maj. Michael Charles Selfe Langdon, of 35, Filsham Rd., St. Leonards-on-Sea, Sussex, and has issue living, Christopher Michael Fane (211, Harley Shute Rd., St. Leonards-on-Sea), *b.* 1945; ed. at St. Edward's Sch., Oxford, and Queen's Coll., Camb. (BA): late Lt. 5th (V) Bn. The Queen's Regt.; admitted a Solicitor 1970: *m.* 1967, Penelope Diana Wall, of Belvedere, Rock Lane, Guestling, Sussex, and has issue living, Rupert Christopher Fane *b.* 1971,—Patrick John (36, Gillsmans Park, St. Leonards on Sea) *b.* 1947; ed. at St. Edwards Sch., Oxford; Chartered Accountant: *m.* 1973, Hilary Peers Carter, of Fairbourne, Forewood Lane, Crowhurst, Surrey.——Winifred Anne, *b.* 1917; late Flight Officer WAAF: *m.* 1949, Philip William Dacre Stuart, of RR4, Brampton, Ont., Canada, and has issue living, Peter Robin, *b.* 1953,—Penelope Anne, *b.* 1951: *m.* 1970, Eric Douglas Honsberger, of 10. Lausanne Cres., West Hill, Ont., Canada.

Granddaughters of the late Col. Frederick John Fane, son of the late Rev. Frederick Adrian Scrope Fane, 2nd son of the late John Fane, M.P. (ante):—
Issue of the late Frederick Luther Fane, MC, *b.* 1875, *d.* 1960: *m.* 1938, Edna Mary (the Old Nursing Home, Barham, Claydon, Ipswich), da. of the late Henry James Meads, of Eastbourne:—

Elizabeth Anne, *b.* 1946.——Rosemary Enid, *b.* 1952. *Residence.*—Priors, Kelvedon Hatch, Brentwood, Essex.

PREDECESSORS.—[1] *Sir* FRANCIS Fane, was cr. *Baron Burghersh* and *Earl of Westmorland* (peerage of England) 1624, and in 1626 *s.* his mother as *Baron Le Despencer* [see V. Falmouth]; *d.* 1628 ; *s.* by his son [2] MILDMAY, K.B., 2nd Earl ; *d.* 1665 ; *s.* by his el. son [3] CHARLES, 3rd Earl ; *d.s.p.* 1691 ; *s.* by his half-brother [4] VERE, K.B., 4th Earl ; *d.* 1693; *s.* by his el. son [5] VERE, 5th Earl ; *d.* unmarried 1699 ; *s.* by his brother [6] THOMAS, 6th Earl ; *d.s.p.* 1736: *s.* by his brother [7] JOHN, 7th Earl. a Lieut.-Gen. in the Army and a distinguished military officer under the Duke of Marlborough; cr. *Baron Catherlough* (peerage of Ireland) 1733; *d.* 1762 when the Barony of Catherlough became extinct, the Barony of Le Despencer passed to Sir Frances Dashwood, Bt. [see V. Falmouth] and the Barony of Burghersh and Earldom of Westmorland devolved upon his kinsman [8] THOMAS, *M.P.*, the descendant of Sir Francis Fane, 3rd son of 1st Earl ; *d.* 1771: *s.* by his son [9] JOHN, 9th Earl ; *d.* 1774 ; *s.* by his son [10] JOHN, K.G., 10th Earl ; *d.* 1841; *s.* by his son [11] JOHN, G.C.B., G.C.H., 11th Earl; *b.* 1784; a Gen. in the Army and a distinguished military officer, was afterwards Ambassador at Berlin 1841, and at Vienna 1851, and Special Commr. at Conference at Vienna 1855 : *m.* 1811, Lady Priscilla Anne Wellesley, dau. of 3rd Earl of Mornington; *d.* 1869: *s.* by his son [12] FRANCIS WILLIAM HENRY, C.B., 12th Earl, *b.* 1825 ; Col. Coldstream Guards : *m.* 1857, Lady Adelaide Ida Curzon, 2nd dau. of 1st Earl Howe, G.C.B.; *d.* 1891 ; *s.* by his only surviving son [13] ANTHONY MILDMAY JULIAN, C.B.E., 13th Earl, *b.* 1859;Col., and an A.D.C. to H.M.; S. Africa 1902 : *m.* 1st, 1892, Lady Sybil Mary St. Clair-Erskine, who *d.* 1910, dau. of 4th Earl of Rosslyn; 2ndly, 1916, Catherine Louise, who *d.* 1973, da. of the late Rev. John S. Geale; *d.* 1922; *s.* by his el. son [14] VERE ANTHONY FRANCIS ST. CLAIR, 14th Earl, *b.* 1893; Lt. (ret.) RN: *m.* 1923, the Hon. Diana, da. of 4th Baron Ribblesdale (ext.), and widow of (1) Percy Lyulph Wyndham, Lt. Coldstream Gds. [E. Leconfield], and (2) Capt. Arthur Edward Capel, CBE; *d.* 1948; *s.* by his el. son [15] DAVID ANTHONY THOMAS, 15th Earl and present peer; also Baron Burghersh.

WESTWOOD, BARON. (Westwood.)   [Baron U.K. 1944]

DEEDS NOT WORDS

WILLIAM WESTWOOD, 2nd Baron ; *b.* Dec. 25th, 1907; *s.* 1953; FCIS; a JP for Newcastle upon Tyne: *m.* 1937, Marjorie, only child of Arthur Bonwick, of Heaton, Newcastle upon Tyne, and has issue.

Arms.—Argent, a lion rampant gules, between three lymphads sable, flags flying to the dexter of the second. Crest.—A mullet argent, charged with a thistle slipped and leaved proper. Supporters,— On either side a sea-lion argent, charged on the shoulder with two anchors in saltire sable.

Residence.—12, Westfield Drive. Gosforth, Newcastle-upon-Tyne, NE3 4XU, Northumberland.

SONS LIVING.

Hon. WILLIAM GAVIN (15, The Oval, Woolsington, Newcastle upon Tyne), *b.* Jan. 30th, 1944; ed. at Fettes; ACA: *m.* 1969, Penelope, el. da. of Charles Edgar Shafto, VRD, MB, of 67, Jesmond Park West, Newcastle upon Tyne, 7, and has issue living, William Fergus, *b.* Nov. 24th, 1972,— Alistair Cameron, *b.* 1974.

Hon. Nigel Alistair, *b.* 1950; ed. at Fettes.

BROTHER LIVING.

Hon. James Young Shaw, *b.* 1915; formerly Capt. Roy. Fleet Aux.: *m.* 1941 (m. diss. 1969), Joan, only child of Raymond Potts, and has issue living, Roger Douglas (Swallowtail Cottage, Hobbs Lane, Beckley, Rye, Sussex), *b.* 1943; ed. at Westminster, and New Coll., Oxford (MA, DipEd); P/O RAFVR.

SISTER LIVING.

Hon. **Margaret Taylor Young,** *b.* 1913; formerly 3rd Officer, W.R.N.S.: *m.* 1st, 1934, William B. Lynn; 2ndly, 1945 (m. diss. 1974), John Bruce Campbell, formerly Roy. Canadian Artillery, and has issue living, (by 2nd m.), Robert Bruce, *b.* 1948,—Helen Jean Laura, *b.* 1946. *Residence,*—7, South Park Court, Gerrards Cross, Bucks.

WIDOW LIVING OF SON OF FIRST BARON.

Mary Katherine (70, Granville Court, Newcastle upon Tyne NE2 1TR), da. of John Carter: *m.* 1939, the Hon. Douglas Wilkie Westwood, who *d.* 1968, and has issue living [see colls., infra].

COLLATERAL BRANCH LIVING.

Issue of the late Hon. Douglas Wilkie Westwood, 2nd son of 1st Baron, *b.* 1910, *d.* 1967: *m.* 1939, Mary Katherine (ante), da. of John Carter:—

Carol Margaret, *b.* 1945: *m.* 1966, Maj. (John) Stephen Ralli, Rifle Bde. (ret.), of 4, Penzance Place, Holland Park, W11, and has issue living, Charles Douglas Stephen, *b.* 1968.

PREDECESSOR.—[1] WILLIAM Westwood, *O.B.E.*, son of the late William Westwood, of Dundee; *b.* 1880; was National Supervisor of Ship Constructors' and Shipwrights' Asso. 1913-29, and Gen. Sec. thereof 1929-45, Ch. Industrial Adviser 1942-45, a Lord-in-Waiting to H.M. 1945-47, and Chm. of Mineral Development Committee under Min. of Fuel and Power 1946-49 ; *cr. Baron Westwood,* **of** Gosforth, co. Northumberland (peerage of United Kingdom) 1944: *m.* 1st, 1905, Margaret Taylor, who *d.* 1916, dau. of the late William Young, of Dundee ; 2ndly, 1918, Agnes Helen Flockhart, who *d.* 1952, dau. of the late James Downie, of Dundee ; *d.* 1953 ; *s.* by his el. son [2] WILLIAM, 2nd Baron, and present peer.

Weymouth, Viscount, son of Marquess of Bath.

WHARNCLIFFE, EARL OF. (Montagu-Stuart-Wortley-Mackenzie.)
[Earl U.K. 1876.]

ALAN JAMES MONTAGU-STUART-WORTLEY-MACKENZIE, 4th Earl ; *b.* March 23rd, 1935 ; *s.* 1953 ; ed. at Eton ; is in R.N.V.R., and patron of one living : *m.* 1957, Aline Margaret, dau. of the late Robert Fernie Dunlop Bruce, of Dyson Holmes House, Wharncliffe Side, near Sheffield, and has issue.

Arms,—Quarterly : 1st azure, a stag's head caboshed, within two branches of laurel or, *Mackenzie ;* 2nd argent, on a bend between six martlets gules three bezants, a canton or charged with a fesse checky azure and argent within a double tressure flory counterflory gules, *Wortley ;* 3rd or, a fesse checky azure and argent within a double tressure flory counterflory gules, *Stuart ;* 4th argent, three lozenges conjoined in fesse gules within a bordure sable, *Montagu.* Crest,—1st, an eagle, wings displayed and inverted, rising from a rock all proper ; 2nd, an eagle's leg erased or, issuant therefrom three ostrich feathers proper, charged on the thigh with a fesse checky azure and argent; 3rd, a lion rampant gules, and in an escrol over the motto "*Nobilis Ira*"; 4th a griffin's head couped or, wings endorsed and beak sable. Supporters.—*Dexter,* a horse argent, bridled and gorged with a collar, flory counterflory gules ; *sinister,* a stag proper gorged as the dexter.

Seat,—Wharncliffe House, Wortley, Sheffield.

He flourishes with the honour of his ancestors.

AVITO · VIRET · HONORE

DAUGHTERS LIVING.

Lady Joanna Margaret, *b.* 1959.
Lady Rowena, *b.* 1961.

SISTERS LIVING.

Lady Ann Lavinia Maud, *b.* 1919; formerly in Mechanised Transport Corps : *m.* 1939, as his 2nd wife, Cdr. Vivian Russell Salvin Bowlby, RN (ret.), who *d.* 1972, and has issue living, Michael Robin Salvin, *b.* 1947. *Residence,*—Graitney, Highfield, Eaglescliff, co. Durham.

Lady (Mary) Diana, *b.* 1920 ; 1939-45 War in Mechanised Trans. Corps. : *m.* 1946, as his second wife, the 9th Duke of Newcastle, from whom she obtained a divorce 1959. *Residence,*—Cortington Manor, Warminster, Wilts.

Lady Barbara Maureen, *b.* 1921; formerly in Women's Land Army : *m.* 1943, David Cecil Ricardo, Lieut. (retired) 8th King's Roy. Irish Hussars, and has issue living, Dorrien Harry Ralph, *b.* 1952,—Richard Michael David, *b.* 1955. *Residence,*—The Lodge, Carlton House, Wortley, Sheffield.

Lady Mary Rosemary Marie Gabrielle, *b.* 1930 : *m.* 1953, David Courtenay Mansel Lewis [see Warner, Bt.]. *Residence,*—Stradey Castle, Llanelly, Carmarthenshire.

WIDOW LIVING OF SON OF SECOND EARL.

Lucy, dau. of — Perrin : *m.* 1st, 1921, the Hon. Edward Thomas Montagu-Stuart-Wortley, who *d.* 1923; 2ndly, 1925, Frank Leslie Russell. *Residence,*—

WIDOW LIVING OF THIRD EARL.

Lady (MAUD LILIAN) ELFRIDA MARY WENTWORTH-FITZWILLIAM (*Elfrida, Countess of Wharncliffe*), dau. of 7th Earl Fitzwilliam : *m.* 1918, the 3rd Earl, who *d.* 1953. *Residence,*—Carlton House, Wortley, Sheffield.

COLLATERAL BRANCHES LIVING.

Issue of the late Maj.-Gen. the Hon. Edward James MONTAGU-STUART-WORTLEY, C.B., C.M.G., D.S.O., M.V.O., brother of 2nd Earl, *b.* 1857, *d.* 1934 : *m.* 1891, Violet, *C.B.E.*, who *d.* 1953, dau. of the late James Alexander Guthrie, of Craigie, Dundee :—

Elizabeth Valetta (*Elizabeth, Countess of Lindsey and Abingdon*), *b.* 1896; is a Chevalier of Legion of Honour : *m.* 1st, 1917, Capt. Allastair Edward George Grant, formerly 9th Lancers, who *d.* 1947, and from whom she obtained a divorce 1922; 2ndly, 1928, the 13th Earl of Lindsey and 8th Earl of Abingdon, who *d.* 1963. *Residence,*—2, Curzon Place, Park Lane, W1.

Grandchildren of the late Hon. Ralph Granville Montagu-Stuart-Wortley (infra):—
Issue of the late Ralph Montagu-Stuart-Wortley, *b.* 1897, *d.* 1961: *m.* 1924, Isabella (of 269, Center St., Bath, Maine, USA), da. of George R. Wood, of Bedford Village, New York:—

ALAN RALPH, *b.* July 27th, 1927 : *m.* 1952, Virginia Anne, dau. of W. Martin Claybaugh, and has issue living, Richard Alan Montagu, *b.* 1953,—William Ralph, *b.* 1959,—Anne Steele, *b.* 1955. *Residence,*—532 Oakridge Drive, Cheshire, Connecticut, USA.——Elizabeth Anne (9829, Belhaven Rd., Bethesda, Maryland, USA), *b.* 1925; MS, PhD: *m.* 1948 (m. diss. 1964) Chester Lyman Kingsbury, and has issue living, Chester Lyman, *b.* 1950,—Meredith Ellen, *b.* 1952,—Michelle Elizabeth, *b.* 1957.——Joan Isabella, *b.* 1928: *m.* 1951, Harry A. Bishop, of Bath, Maine, USA.

Issue of the late Hon. Ralph Granville Montagu-Stuart-Wortley, brother of 2nd Earl, *b.* 1864, *d.* 1927 : *m.* 1891, Virginia Maria, who *d.* 1941, dau. of the late Adm. Winfield Scott Schley, of U.S. Navy :—

Anne, *b.* 1908 : *m.* 1st, 1930, Davenport Plumer, Jnr., from whom she obtained a divorce 1941 ; 2ndly, 1941, Edmund R. Sawtelle, who *d.* 1964, and has issue living, (by 1st marriage) Davenport, has issue living, (by 2nd m.) Nancy Stuart-Wortley, *b.* 1944. *Residence,*—20, Bradford Court, Marblehead, Mass., USA.

Issue of the late Lieut.-Gen. the Hon. Sir (Alan) Richard MONTAGU-STUART-WORTLEY, K.C.B., K.C.M.G., D.S.O., youngest brother of 2nd Earl, *b.* 1868, *d.* 1949 : *m.* 1900, the Hon. Maud Julia Mary Winn, who *d.* 1938, dau. of 1st Baron St. Oswald :—

Henry James, *b.* 1906; ed. at Winchester. *Residence,*—PO Box 266, Nakuru, Kenya. *Clubs,*—MCC, Muthaiga Country (Kenya).——Marjorie Susan, *b.* 1901: *m.* 1929, Maj. Roger Orlando Bridgeman, who *d.* 1975, [see E. Bradford, colls.]. *Residence,*—The Lodge, Beaminster, Dorset.

Issue of the late Rt. Hon. Charles Beilby Stuart-Wortley (son of the late Rt. Hon. James Archibald Stuart-Wortley, QC, MP, youngest son of 1st Baron), who was cr. *Baron Stuart of Wortley* 1917 [see that title].

PREDECESSORS.—[1] *Rt. Hon.* JAMES ARCHIBALD Stuart-Wortley-Mackenzie (grandson of 3rd Earl of Bute, K.G.), successively M.P. for Bossiney and Yorkshire, and Lord-Lieut. of co. York ; was cr. *Baron Wharncliffe*, of Wortley, co. York (peerage of United Kingdom) 1826, was Lord Privy Seal 1834 and Lord Pres. of the Council 1841 ; *d.* 1845; *s.* by his son [2] JOHN, 2nd Baron; *b.* 1801: *m.* 1825, Lady Georgiana Elizabeth, who *d.* 1884, dau. of 1st Earl of Harrowby ; *d.* 1855; *s.* by his son [3] EDWARD MONTAGU STUART GRANVILLE, 3rd Baron, *b.* 1827 ; cr. *Viscount Carlton* and *Earl of Wharncliffe* (peerage of United Kingdom) 1876, with remainder to his brother, Francis Dudley ; assumed in 1880 by Roy. licence the additional surname of Montagu: *m.* 1855, Lady Susan Charlotte Lascelles, who *d.* 1927, dau. of 3rd Earl of Harewood ; *d.* 1899; *s.* by his nephew [4] FRANCIS JOHN (el. son of the late Hon. Francis Dudley Montagu-Stuart-Wortley), 2nd Earl, *b.* 1856: *m.* 1886, Ellen, who *d.* 1922, dau. of the late Lieut.-Gen. Sir Thomas Lionel John Gallwey, K.C.M.G. ; *d.* 1926 ; *s.* by his son [5] ARCHIBALD RALPH, 3rd Earl ; *b.* 1892 ; sometime Capt. Life Guards : *m.* 1918, Lady Maud Lilian Elfrida Mary Wentworth-Fitzwilliam, dau. of 7th Earl Fitzwilliam ; *d.* 1953 ; *s.* by his only son [6] ALAN JAMES, 4th Earl, and present peer ; also Viscount Carlton, and Baron Wharncliffe.

WHARTON, BARONY OF. (Vintcent.) [Baron E. 1544-5.] [Abeyant 1974.]

DAUGHTERS LIVING OF ELIZABETH DOROTHY VINTCENT, BARONESS WHARTON.
(*Co-heiresses to the Barony.*)

Hon. MYRTLE OLIVE FELIX, *b.* Feb. 20th, 1934: *m.* 1958, Henry MacLeod Robertson (Harry Robinson, Composer), of 9, Gipsy Lane, SW15, and has issue living, Myles Christopher David, *b.* 1964,—Christopher James, *b.* 1969,—Nicholas Charles (twin), *b.* 1969,—Patricia Lesley, *b.* 1966.
Hon. CAROLINE ELIZABETH, *b.* Aug. 28th, 1935: *m.* 1970, Lt.-Cdr. Jonathon Cecil Appleyard-List, RN, and has issue living, Zoe, *b.* 1973.

WIDOW LIVING OF 9TH BARON.

JOANNA, only da. of Walter Henry Law-Smith, widow of 6th Baron Tredegar and formerly wife of Cdr. A. B. Russell, DSO, RN: *m.* 3rdly, 1967, the 9th Baron, who *d.* 1969; 4thly, 19—, Bruce Yorke, of La Maison Blanche, 1111, Monnar VD, Switzerland.

COLLATERAL BRANCH LIVING.

Issue of the late Eustace Kemeys-Tynte, younger brother of 8th Baron, *b.* 1878, *d.* 1949 : *m.* 1902, Ann, dau. of the late John Emerson :—
Eleanor Vanessa Rosabelle (Trevaldwyn, Flat 3, Montpellier Park, Llandrindod Wells, Powys), *b.* 1904.

WHEATLEY, BARON. (Wheatley.) [Life Baron 1970.]

JOHN WHEATLEY, PC, son of Patrick Wheatley; b. Jan. 17th, 1908; ed. at St. Aloysius Coll., Glasgow, Mount St. Mary's Coll., Sheffield, and Glasgow Univ. (MA, LLD); Hon. Fellow of Educational Inst. of Scotland; Scottish Bar. 1932, Advocate-Depute 1945-47, Solicitor-Gen. for Scotland March to Oct. 1947, Lord Advocate 1947-51, and a KC 1947; Chm. of Cttee. on Teaching Profession in Scotland 1961-63, a Member of Roy. Commn. on Penal System in England and Wales 1964-66, and Chm. of Roy. Commn. on Local Govt. in Scotland 1966-69, and of Cttee. on Ground Safety at Sports Grounds 1971-72; 1939-45 War as Capt. RA and JAG's Depart.; a Lord of Session with title of *Lord Wheatley* since 1954, and Lord Justice Clerk for Scotland since 1972; MP for E. Edinburgh (*Lab.*) 1947-54; *cr.* PC 1947, and *Baron Wheatley,* of Shettleston, Co. of City of Glasgow (Life Baron) 1970: *m.* 1935, Agnes, da. of Samuel Nichol, of Tollcross, Glasgow, and has issue.

Residence,—Braemar House, 3, Whitehouse Terr., Edinburgh, EH9 2EU.

SONS LIVING.

Hon. John (12, Scotland St., Edinburgh, 3), b. 1941: *m.* 1970, Bronwin, da. of Alexander Fraser.
Hon. Patrick, b. 1943: *m.* 1968, Sheena, da. of the late Douglas James Lawrie.
Hon. Anthony, b. 1945; ed. at Fordham Univ., NY.
Hon. Michael, b. 1949: *m.* 1971, Anne, da. of Thomas Barry.

DAUGHTER LIVING.

Hon Kathleen Mary Agnes, b. 1937: *m.* 1963, Thomas (Tam) Dalyell of The Binns, MP, of the Binns, Linlithgow [see Dalyell, Bt., Dormant].

WHITBURGH, BARONY OF, (Borthwick.) [Extinct 1967.]

SISTER LIVING FIRST BARON. (*Raised to rank of a Baron's daughter Feb.* 1913.)
Hon. Sybil Mary: *m.* 1937, Lt.-Col. Vernon Whitamore, OBE, IMS, who d. 1959. *Residence,*—49, Hallam St., W1.

WIDOW LIVING OF BROTHER OF FIRST BARON.

Irene Evangeline (Fox Hills, Long Cross, Surrey, and 86, Eaton Place, SW1), da. of the late George Wise, JP, of Roslyn House, Croydon, NSW: *m.* 1912, the Hon. James Alexander Borthwick, who d. 1961, and has issue living [see Borthwick, Bt.].

WHITE, BARONESS. (White.) [Life Baroness 1970.]

EIRENE LLOYD WHITE, da. of the late Thomas Jones, CH, LLD, of Brynhir, Aberystwyth; b. Nov. 7th, 1909; ed. at St. Paul's Girls' Sch., and Somerville Coll., Oxford (Hon. Fellow 1966); Min. of Labour Officer 1933-37, and 1941-45; Political Correspondent *Manchester Evening News* 1945-49; a Member of Nat. Exec. Cttee., Labour Party 1947-53, and 1958-72 (Chm. 1968-69); Parl. Sec., Colonial Office 1964-66, Min. of State for Foreign Affairs 1966-67, and Min. of State, Welsh Office 1967-70; Dep. Chm., Metrication Board 1972; Pres. of Nat. Council of Women (Wales); MP for E. Flint (*Lab.*) 1950-70; *cr.* *Baroness White,* of Rhymney, co. Monmouth (Life Baroness) 1970: *m.* 1948, John Cameron White, who d. 1968.

Residences,—36, Westminster Gdns., Marcham St., SW1; Panteg, Ceinws, Machynlleth, Mont.

WICKLOW, EARL OF, (Forward-Howard.) [Earl I. 1793.]

WILLIAM CECIL JAMES PHILIP JOHN PAUL FORWARD-HOWARD, 8th Earl, b. Oct. 30th, 1902; s. 1946; ed. at Eton, and at Merton Coll., Oxford (B.A. 1925); European War 1939-45 as Capt. Roy. Fusiliers; is a Knight of Sovereign Order of Malta: *m.* 1959, Eleanor, dau. of Professor Rudolph Butler, of Dublin.

Arms,—1st and 4th, quarterly: 1st and 4th grand quarters gules, a bend between six cross crosslets fitchée argent on a canton azure a sun in splendour proper, *Howard,* 2nd and 3rd argent a lion rampant gules, *Forward;* 2nd and 3rd argent, a chevron gules between three bulls heads couped sable, armed or, *Boleyne.* Crest,—On a chapeau gules, turned up ermine, a lion statant guardant the tail extended or, ducally gorged of the first, holding in his mouth an arrow fessewise proper. Supporters,—Two stags proper, ducally gorged and chained or, and charged on the shoulder with a cross crosslet fitchée argent.

Residence,—Sea Grange, Sandycove, Dun Laoghaire, co. Dublin.

Serve God and rejoice.

COLLATERAL BRANCH LIVING.
Issue of the late Hon. Hugh Melville Forward-Howard, 3rd son of 6th Earl, b.
1883, d. 1919: m. 1908, Mary Emily, who d. 1941, dau. of Benjamin Aymar
Sands, of New York, and Southampton, Long Island, U.S.A. :—
CECIL AYMAR, b. Sept. 13th, 1909. Residence,—155, East 52nd Street, New York, U.S.A.——
Katharine Frances Theodosia, b. 1910. Residence,—Kiltennel House, Gorey, co. Wexford.

PREDECESSORS—[1] Rt. Hon. RALPH Howard, M.P. for co. Wicklow; was cr. Baron,
Clonmore, of Clonmore, co. Carlow (peerage of Ireland) 1776, and Viscount Wicklow (peerage of
Ireland)1785: m. 1755, Alice, dau. of William Forward, M.P. for Donegal, who in 1793 was cr.
Countess of Wicklow (peerage of Ireland); the Viscount d. 1785; s. by his el. son [2] ROBERT
2nd Viscount, who in 1807 on the death of his mother s. as 2nd Earl of Wicklow; d. unmarried
1815; s. by his brother [3] WILLIAM, 3rd Earl; assumed by Roy. licence 1780 the surname of
Forward, and in 1815 resumed by Roy. licence the paternal surname of Howard, to use in
addition to and after that of Forward; d. 1818; s. by his son [4] WILLIAM FORWARD, K.P.,
4th Earl; was a Representative Peer and Lord-Lieut. of co. Wicklow; d. 1869; s. by his
nephew [5] CHARLES FRANCIS ARNOLD, 5th Earl, son of the Rev. the Hon. Francis Howard,
2nd son of 3rd Earl, by his second wife, Sarah, who d. 1892, dau. of Charles Hamilton, of
Hamwood, co. Meath; was a Representative Peer; d. 1881; s. by his brother [6] CECIL
RALPH, b. 1842; a Representative Peer for Ireland: m. 1st, 1876, Francesca Maria, who d.
1877, dau. of Thomas Chamberlayne, of Cranbury Park, Winchester; 2ndly, 1880, Fanny
Catharine, who d. 1914, dau. of Richard Robert Wingfield, of Fairy Hill, co. Wicklow; d.
1891; s. by his el. son [7] RALPH FRANCIS, 7th Earl, b. 1877; a Representative Peer; a
Senator of Irish Free State 1922-3: m. 1st, 1902, Lady Gladys Mary Hamilton, who d. 1917,
dau. of 2nd Duke of Abercorn; 2ndly, 1942, Lady Beatrix Frances Gertrude, who d. 1957, dau. of
14th Earl of Pembroke, and widow of Major Sir Nevile Rodwell Wilkinson, K.C.V.O., F.S.A.,
A.R.E.; d. 1946; s. by his son [8] WILLIAM CECIL JAMES PHILIP JOHN PAUL, 8th Earl and present
peer; also Viscount Wicklow, and Baron Clonmore.

WIDGERY, BARON. (Widgery.) [Life Baron 1971.]

JOHN PASSMORE WIDGERY, OBE, TD, PC,
son of Samuel Widgery of S. Molton, Devon;
b. July 24th, 1911; ed. at Queen's Coll.,
Taunton; Bar. Lincoln's Inn 1946; QC 1958,
Bencher 1961; late Brig. RA TA; Recorder
of Hastings 1959-61, a Judge of High Court
of Justice (Queen's Bench Div.) 1961-68, and
a Lord Justice of Appeal 1968-71, since when
Lord Ch. Justice of England; a DL of
London; 1939-45 War as Lt.-Col. RA in NW
Europe; cr. OBE (Mil.) 1945, Knt. 1961, PC
1968 and Baron Widgery of South Molton,
Devon (Life Baron) 1971: m. 1948, Ann, da.
of the late William Edwin Kermode, of Peel,
Isle of Man.

Arms,—Vert, on water in base barry wavy proper a lymphad argent, and a chief gules charged
with a canon between two millrinds or. Crest,—rising from a rocky mount a widgeon proper, in the
beak a pair of scales or. Supporters,—Dexter, an owl guardant, and sinister a widgeon proper.

Address,—Royal Courts of Justice, WC2. Club,—Garrick.

WIGG, BARON. (Wigg.) [Life Baron 1967.]

GEORGE EDWARD CECIL WIGG, PC, son of the late Edward William Wigg;
b. Nov. 28th, 1900; ed. at Fairfields Council Sch., and Queen Mary's Gram.
Sch., Basingstoke; served in Regular Army 1919-37; Col. RAEC 1945-46;
PPS to Rt. Hon. Emmanuel Shinwell as Min. of Fuel and Power 1945-47, as
Sec. of State for War 1947-50, and as Min. of Defence 1950-51; a Member
of Racecourse Betting Control Board 1958-61, and of Totalisator Board
1961-64; MP for Dudley (Lab.) 1945-67; Paymaster Gen. 1964-67, and
Chm. of Horse Race Betting Levy Board 1967-72; 1914-18 War; 1939-45 War;
cr. PC 1964, Baron Wigg, of Borough of Dudley (Life Baron) 1967: m. 1930,
Florence M., da. of William Veal, and has issue.

Residences,—26A, Warwick Sq., SW1; 117, Newcastle Rd., Trent Vale, Stoke-on-Trent.

DAUGHTERS LIVING.
Hon. Mary Cecilia, b. 1930: m. 1958, Robert Cartlidge, of 9, Grigor Drive, Inverness.
Hon. Jean Audrey, b. 1932: m. 1955, Andrew Huggins.
Hon. Maureen Ann, b. 1934: m. 1964, Alfred John Mudge, of 6, St. Michael's Close, Weeping Cross,
Stafford.

WIGODER, BARON. (Wigoder.) [Life Baron 1974.]

BASIL THOMAS WIGODER, QC, son of Phillip I. Wigoder, LRCPI, LRCSI,
of 2, St. John St., Deansgate, Manchester 3; b. Feb. 12th, 1921; ed. at Manchester Gram. Sch., and Oriel Coll., Oxford (MA); Bar. Gray's Inn 1946,
Bencher 19— (Master of the Bench 1972); a Member of Gen. Council of the
Bar since 1970, and a Recorder of the Crown Court since 1972; Chm. Liberal
Party Exec. 1963-65, and Liberal Party Organising Cttee. 1965-66, Vice-Pres.
of Liberal Party 1966; 1939-45 War, as Lt. RA, in Middle East, Italy, and
Greece; cr. Baron Wigoder, of Cheetham, in City of Manchester (Life Baron)
1974: m. 1948, Yoland, da. of Ben Levinson, and has issue.

Residence,—29, Henstridge Place, NW8. Chambers,—3, Temple Gdns., EC4. Clubs,—Reform,
MCC.

SONS LIVING.

Hon. Justin, *b.* 1951.
Hon. Charles, *b.* 1960.
Hon. Giles, *b.* 1963.

DAUGHTER LIVING.

Hon. Carolyn (twin), *b.* 1963.

WIGRAM, BARON. (Wigram) [Baron U.K. 1935.]

Sweet is the love of one's country.

(GEORGE) NEVILLE (CLIVE) WIGRAM, MC, 2nd Baron; *b.* Aug. 2nd, 1915; *s.* 1960; ed. at Winchester, and at Magdalen Coll., Oxford; late Lt.-Col. Gren. Gds.; a JP and a DL for Glos.; a Page of Honour to HM 1925-32, and Mil. Sec. and Comptroller to Gov.-Gen. of NZ 1946-49; a Gov. of Westminster Hosp. 1967; 1939-45 War: *m.* 1941, Margaret Helen, da. of Gen. Sir Augustus Francis Andrew Nicol Thorne, KCB, CMG, DSO [B. Penrhyn], and has issue.

Arms—Argent, on a pale gules three escallops or ; over all a chevron engrailed counterchanged, and on the chief waves of the sea, thereon a ship representing an English vessel of war of the 16th century, with four masts, sails furled proper, colours flying gules. Crest—On a mount vert, a hand in armour in fesse couped at the wrist proper, charged with an escallop holding a fleur-de-lis erect or. Supporters,—On either side a Bengal Lancer holding in the exterior hand a lance proper.
Residence,—Poulton Fields, Cirencester, Gloucestershire. *Club,*—Guards'.

SON LIVING.

Hon. ANDREW FRANCIS CLIVE, *b.* March 18th, 1949; ed. at Winchester, and RMA; Capt. Gren. Gds.: *m.* 1974, Gabrielle Diana, yst. da. of the late R. D. Moore, of Wellington, NZ.

DAUGHTERS LIVING.

Hon. Margaret Cherry, *b.* 1942: *m.* 1972, Maj. Greville John Wyndham Malet, R. Hussars, of Vale House, Little Somerford, Chippenham, Wilts. [see Malet, Bt., colls.].
Hon. Anne Celia, *b.* 1945: *m.* 1973, Capt. Evelyn John Webb-Carter, Gren. Gds. [see V. Hood, colls.]

PREDECESSOR.—[1] CLIVE WIGRAM, G.C.B., G.C.V.O., C.S.I., P.C., son of the late Herbert Wigram [see Wigram, Bt., colls.], *b.* 1873 ; Lieut.-Col. and Brevet Col. (retired) Indian Army; was an Extra Equerry-in-Waiting to Prince of Wales 1906-10, an Equerry-in-Waiting and Assist. Private Sec. to King George V. 1910-31, Private Sec. and an Extra Equerry 1931-36 (also Keeper of H.M.'s Privy Purse 1935-36) and Keeper of H.M.'s Archives 1936-45 ; acted as Assist. to Ch. of Staff of the Prince of Wales during tour in India 1905-6 ; S. Africa 1900, with Kitchener's Horse ; Dep. Constable and Lieut.-Gov. of Windsor Castle 1936-45 ; Permanent Lord-in-Waiting to H.M. King George VI. 1936-52, and to H.M. Queen Elizabeth II. 1952-60 ; *cr.* Baron Wigram, of Clewer, co. Berks (peerage of United Kingdom) 1935 : *m.* 1912, Nora Mary, who *d.* 1956, dau. of the late Col. Sir Neville Francis Fitzgerald Chamberlain, K.C.B., K.C.V.O., *d.* 1960 ; *s.* by his son [2] GEORGE NEVILLE (CLIVE), 2nd Baron and present peer.

WILBERFORCE, BARON. (Wilberforce.) [Life Baron 1964.]

RICHARD ORME WILBERFORCE, *CMG, OBE, PC,* son of Samuel Wilberforce, of Lavington House, Petworth, Sussex; *b.* March 11th, 1907; ed. at Winchester, and at New Coll., Oxford; Bar. Middle Temple 1932, and QC 1954; a Judge of High Court of Justice (Chancery Div.) 1961-64, since when a Lord of Appeal in Ordinary; High Steward of Oxford Univ. since 1967; appointed Chm. of Court of Inquiry into power workers' dispute 1970; 1939-45 War as Brig. late RA in Norway and Germany (OBE); *cr.* OBE (Mil) 1944, CMG 1956, Knt. 1961, PC 1964, and Baron Wilberforce, of city and co. of Kingston-upon-Hull (Life Baron) 1964: *m.* 1947, Yvette Marie, da. of Roger Lenoan, of Paris, and has issue.

Residence,—8, Cambridge Place, W.8. *Club,*—Athenæum.

SON LIVING.

Hon. Samuel Herbert, *b.* 1951; ed. at Eton.

DAUGHTER LIVING.

Hon. Anne Catherine, *b.* 1948: *m.* 1975, Lindsay Stuart Burn.

WILLIAMS, BARONY OF. (Williams.) [Extinct 1966.]

DAUGHTER LIVING OF FIRST BARON

Hon. Gweneth Mary, *b.* 1927: *m.* 1st, 1947 (marriage dissolved 1958), Hugh Sharp Eadie, A.M.I.E.E.; 2ndly, 1961, Donald Walter Alexander Brown, M.B., Ch.B., and has issue living (by 1st marriage), Graham Edward, *b.* 1949.—Dianne Claire, *b.* 1951. *Residence,*—39, Blenheim Gdns., Aveley, S. Ockendon, Essex.

WIDOW LIVING OF FIRST BARON

LAVINIA (*Baroness Williams*) (4, The Hallgate, Blackheath Park, Blackheath, SE3), da. of Charles Northam, of Plumstead, SE18: *m.* 1921, the 1st Baron, who *d.* 1966, when the title became ext.

WILLIAMS OF BARNBURGH, BARON. (Williams.) [Extinct 1967.]

SON LIVING OF LIFE BARON.

Hon. Horace, *b.* 1914 : *m.* 1st, 1941 (marriage dissolved 1948), the Hon. Mary Joyce Morrison, dau. of Baron Morrison of Lambeth (Life Peer) ; 2ndly, 1952, Margaret Dick Chisholm, dau. of William Green. *Residence,*—11, Lombardy Drive, Berkhamsted, Herts.

DAUGHTER LIVING OF LIFE BARON.

Hon. Doris (346, Thorne Rd., Doncaster), *b.* 1916 : *m.* 1939, Robert Kesteven Lee, who *d.* 1967.

WIDOW LIVING OF LIFE BARON.

ELIZABETH ANN (*Baroness Williams of Barnburgh*), (346, Thorne Rd., Doncaster), da. of Thomas Andrews, of Mexborough: *m.* 1910, Baron Williams of Barnburgh (Life Baron), who *d.* 1967.

WILLIAMSON, BARON. (Williamson.) [Life Baron, 1962.]

THOMAS WILLIAMSON, *C.B.E.*, son of the late James Williamson, of 111, Alder Hey Rd., St. Helens, Lancs.; *b.* Sept. 2nd, 1897; ed. at Knowsley Rd. Sch., St. Helens; Hon. LL.D. Camb. 1959; a J.P. for Liverpool; a Member of Liverpool City Council 1929-35, Gen. Sec. National Union of Gen. and Municipal Workers 1946-61, a Member of Labour Party National Executive 1940-47 and a Member of Trades Union Congress Gen. Council 1947-62 (Chm. 1956-57); 1914-18 War, with R.E.; M.P. for Brigg Div. of Lincs. (*Lab.*) 1945-48; *cr.* C.B.E. (Civil) 1950, Knt. 1956, and *Baron Williamson,* of Eccleston, Borough of St. Helens, Lancs. (Life Baron) 1962: *m.* 1925, Hilda, dau. of the late John Hartley, of St. Helens, and has issue.

Arms,— Per saltire gules and sable three arms conjoined at the shoulder and flexed in a triangle, each hand proper grasping a hammer or, over all a sun in splendour gold. **Crest,**—Out of a mural crown sable masoned argent, a pelican proper supporting a Caduceus. **Supporters,**—On either side a secretarybird proper, in their beak a square buckle gules.

Residence,—Hurst Lea Court, Brook Lane, Alderley Edge, Cheshire.

DAUGHTER LIVING.

Hon. Milba Hartley, *b.* 1926: *m.* 1952, Jack Fleming Eccles, of 11, Sutton Rd., Alderley Edge, Cheshire, and has issue.

WILLINGDON, MARQUESS OF. (Freeman-Thomas.) [Marquess U.K. 1936.]

INIGO BRASSEY FREEMAN-THOMAS, 2nd Marquess ; *b.* July 25th, 1899 ; *s.* 1941 ; ed. at Eton; Capt. (retired) Indian Cav., Major (retired) 98th (Sussex Yeo.) Field Brig. R.A. (T.A.), and Squadron-Leader R.A.F. Vol. Reserve ; was a Liberal Whip in House of Lords 1948-9, and Ch. Liberal Whip 1949-50; a KStJ : *m.* 1st, 1924, Maxine Frances Mary (from whom he obtained a divorce 1932), dau. of Sir Johnston Forbes-Robertson; 2ndly, 1934, Mary (from whom he obtained a divorce 1939), dau. of Basil S. Foster ; 3rdly, 1943, Daphne, el. dau. of the late Seymour Caldwell.

Arms,—Quarterly : 1st and 4th argent, three lions rampant gules, a chief azure, *Thomas* ; 2nd and 3rd ermine, two pallets azure, over all three fusils conjoined in fesse or, *Freeman.* **Crests,**—1st, a demi-lion rampant gules charged on the shoulder with an ermine spot argent, *Thomas* ; 2nd, issuant out of an antique crown azure, a boar's head proper, *Freeman.* **Supporters,** —On either side a freeman armed cap-à-pie in English armour of the 17th century proper.

Residence,—Kilbees Farm, Winkfield, Windsor Forest, Berks.

PREDECESSOR.—[1] Rt. Hon. FREEMAN Freeman-Thomas, *G.C.S.I.*, *G.C.M.G.*, *G.C.I.E.*, *G.B.E.*, only son of the late Frederick Freeman-Thomas, J.P., of Ratton, and Yapton, Sussex; *b.* 1866 : A.D.C. to Gov. of Victoria (Baron Brassey) 1895-8, and a Junior Lord of the Treasury Dec. 1905 to Jan. 1906; appointed a Lord-in-Waiting to H.M. 1911, Gov. of Bombay 1913, Gov. of Madras 1919, and Gov.-Gen. and Com.-in-Ch., Dominion of Canada 1926 ; Viceroy and Gov.-Gen. of India 1931-6; became Lord Warden of the Cinque Ports, Constable of Dover Castle, and Chancellor of Order of St. Michael and St. George 1936 ; assumed the additional surname of Freeman 1892 ; sat as M.P. for Hastings (*L*) 1900-1906, and for S.-E., or Bodmin, Div. of Cornwall 1906-10 ; cr. *Baron Willingdon*, of Ratton, Willingdon, co. Sussex (peerage of United Kingdom) 1910, *Viscount Willingdon*, of Ratton, co. Sussex (peerage of United Kingdom) 1924, *Viscount Ratendone*, of Willingdon, co. Sussex, and *Earl of Willingdon* (peerage of United Kingdom) 1931, and *Marquess of Willingdon* (peerage of United Kingdom) 1936 : *m.* 1892, Lady Marie Adelaide, *C.I.*, *G.B.E.*, who *d.* 1960, dau. of 1st Earl Brassey ; *d.* 1941; *s.* by his only surviving son [2] INIGO BRASSEY, 2nd Marquess and present peer ; also Baron Willingdon, Viscount Willingdon, Viscount Ratendone and Earl of Willingdon.

WILLIS, BARON. (Willis.) [Life Baron 1963.]

EDWARD HENRY WILLIS, son of Alfred John Willis, of Tottenham; *b.* Jan. 13th, 1918; ed. at Downhills Central Sch., Tottenham N.; a Dramatist and Screenwriter; a Gov., Nat. Film Sch.; Pres. of Writers Guild 1965-68 (Chm. 1958-64); 1939-45 War with Roy. Fusiliers; cr. *Baron Willis*, of Chislehurst, co. Kent [Life Baron] 1963: *m.* 1944, Audrey Mary, da. of Alfred Hale, and has issue.

Arms.—Or a saltire gules on a chief vert three fountains. **Crest.**—In front of a weeping willow tree a well head proper. **Supporters.**—On either side a willet (common snipe). proper supporting with the beak a quill or.

Residence,—5, Shepherds Green, Chislehurst, Kent. *Club,*—Press.

SON LIVING.

Hon. John Edward, *b.* 1946.

DAUGHTER LIVING.

Hon. Sally Ann Hale, *b.* 1951.

WILLOUGHBY DE BROKE, BARON. (Verney.) [Baron E. 1491.]
[Title pronounced "Willoughby de Brook."]

Virtue prevails.

JOHN HENRY PEYTO VERNEY, *MC, AFC*, 20th Baron; *b.* May 21st, 1896; *s.* 1923; ed. at Eton, and RMC, Capt. (ret.) 17th/21st Lancers, Air Commodore (ret.) R. Aux. A.F.; a JP and Lord-Lieut. of Warwickshire 1939-67, a KStJ, and patron of two livings; a Member of the Jockey Club (Steward 1944-47 and 1954-56), and of National Hunt Cttee. (Steward 1942-44, 1950-53 and 1964-67), Chm., Tattersall's Cttee. 1948-53, Dir. Birmingham Racecourse Co. Ltd. 1932-65 (Chm. 1952-65), of Steeplechase Co. (Cheltenham) Ltd. 1944-71 (Chm. 1953-71), of Race Finish Recording Co. Ltd., and later Racecourse Tech. Sers. Ltd. 1947-70 (Chm. 1959-70); Dir. and Chm. of Wolverhampton Racecourse Co. Ltd. 1947-71; Pres., Hunters' Improvement So. 1957-58; Pres of Warwicks. Assocn. of Boys' Clubs, of Warwicks. Boy Scouts Assocn., and of Council of Order of St. John 1946-67; Cdr. 605 (Co. Warwick) Sqdn. AAF 1936-39 (Air Efficiency Award, AFC), Hon. Col. Queen's Own Warwicks, and Worcs. Yeo. (TA) 1942-63; 1914-18 War (wounded, MC); 1939-45 War (despatches); Dep. Dir. of Public Relations, Air Min. 1941-44, and Director 1945-46: *m.* 1933, Rachel, da. of Sir (Robert) Bourchier Sherard Wrey, 11th Bt., and has issue.

Arms.—Quarterly: 1st and 4th gules, three crosses recercellé or, a chief vair ermine and ermines ; 2nd and 3rd quarterly argent and gules, a bear sejant sable. **Crests.**—1st, a Saracen's head, affrontée, couped at the shoulders proper, ducally crowned or ; 2nd, a demi-bear sable, holding in his paws a lozenge, pierced or. **Supporters.**—Two antelopes argent, semée of torteaux, armed and unguled or.

Residences,—Fox Cottage, Kineton, Warwickshire, CV35 0LP; 2, Upper Phillimore Gdns., W8 7HA. *Clubs,*—Cavalry, White's.

SON LIVING.

Hon. LEOPOLD DAVID (Ditchford Friary, Shipston on Stour, Warwicks.), *b.* Sept. 14th, 1938; ed. at Le Rosey, and at New Coll., Oxford: *m.* 1965, Petra Daphne, 2nd da. of the late Col. Sir John Renton Aird, MVO, MC, 3rd Bt., and has issue living, Rupert Greville, *b.* 1966,—John Mark, *b.* 1967.

DAUGHTER LIVING.

Hon. Susan Geraldine, *b.* 1942: *m.* 1st, 1964 (m. diss. 1969), Jeremy James Wagg [Horlick, Bt.] resumed by deed poll 1969 her maiden name; 2ndly, 1972, Robie David C. Uniacke, and has issue living (by 2nd m.), Caspar, *b.* 1973.

COLLATERAL BRANCHES LIVING.

Issue of the late Hon. Blanche Verney, el. dau. of 18th Baron, *b.* 1872, *d.* 1947 : *m.* 1898, Capt. Michael Granville Lloyd Lloyd-Baker, Gloucestershire Yeo., who *d.* (killed in action during European War) 1916 :—
Audrey Pamela Lloyd, *b.* 1908. *Residence,*—Curlew, Gulley Lane, Brightstone, I. of Wight.

Issue of the late Hon. Patience Verney, 2nd da. of 18th Baron, *b.* 1873, *d.* 1965: *m.* 1896, Lt.-Col. Basil Hanbury, who *d.* 1933 [Mackenzie, Bt., cr. 1702, colls.]:—
Harold Greville, *QC* (Marlborough House, Falmouth), *b.* 1898; ed. at Charterhouse, and at Brasenose Coll., Oxford (DCL); Bar. Inner Temple 1922; Hon. Bencher 1951, and a QC 1960; late Lt. Warwickshire Yeo.; Vinerian Prof. Emeritus of English Law; Fellow of Lincoln Coll., Oxford 1921-49 (Hon. Fellow 1949); Fellow of All Souls Coll., Oxford 1949-64; Dean of Faculty of Law, and Visiting Prof., Univ. of Ife 1962-63, and Univ. of Nigeria 1964-66: *m.* 1927, Anna Margaret Geelmuyden, da. of the late Hannibal Dreyer (Adviser to Post & Telegraph Dept., Thailand), of Copenhagen.

Issue of the late Rev. the Hon. Walter Robert Verney, 2nd son of 17th Baron, *b.* 1846, *d.* 1912: *m.* 1879, Elizabeth Georgina, who *d.* 1941, dau. of the late Major Robert Wilberforce Bird, of Barton House, Shipston-on-Stour:—
Clare, *b.* 1887. *Residence,*—Rosemary Cottage, Lighthorne, Warwick.

Issue of the late Hon. Alice Jane Verney, 2nd dau. of 17th Baron, *b.* 1849, *d.* 1882: *m.* 1874, Edward William Tritton, who *d.* 1902:—
Claude (da.), *b.* 1881. *Residence,*—Trafalgar Cottage, Teignmouth, S. Devon.

Issue of the late Hon. Susan Emma Verney, 3rd dau. of 17th Baron, *b.* 1852, *d.* 1941: *m.* 1885, Edmund Temple Godman, who *d.* 1894:—
John, *CBE, b.* 1886, Lt.-Col. (ret.) 15th/19th Hussars; JP and DL for Glos. (High Sheriff 1942); Chm. Glos. Co. Council 1946-56; CBE (Civil) 1957. *Residence,*—Banks Fee, Loughborough, Moreton-in-Marsh, Gloucestershire. *Club,*—Cavalry.

PREDECESSORS.—[1] *Sir* ROBERT Willoughby, Knt., who took part in the victory of Bosworth, was summoned to the Parliament of England as *Lord Willoughby de Broke* 1491; was Capt. Gen. of the Forces sent to aid the Duke of Brittany against the French, *temp.* Henry VII. and subsequently Marshal of the English Army sent into France: *m. circa* 1475, Blanche, dau. and co-heir of Sir John Champernowne, of Beer Ferrers, Devon; *d.* 1502; *s.* by his son [2] ROBERT, 2nd Baron; summoned to Parliament 1511: *m.* 1st, Elizabeth, who *d.* 1503, dau. and co-heir of 2nd Baron Beauchamp of Powyk; 2ndly, Lady Dorothy Grey (who *m.* 2ndly, 15—, William Blount, 4th Baron Mountjoy, and *d.* 1553), dau. of 1st Marquess of Dorset; *d.* 1522; when the barony fell into abeyance between the three daus. of his el. son Edward Willoughby, and so remained until 1558, when the sole surviving grand-dau. (her sisters dying without issue) [3] ELIZABETH, became *de jure* Baroness: *m. circa* 1534, as his second wife, Sir Fulke Greville; *d.* 1560; *s.* by her el. son [4] *Sir* Fulke, *de jure* 4th Baron, *b.* 1535. M.P. for Warwick 1586: *m. circa* 1553, Lady Anne Nevill, dau. of 4th Earl of Westmorland: *d.* 1606; *s.* by his only son [5] *Sir* Fulke, *de jure* 5th Baron; *b. circa* 1554; cr. *Baron Brooke,* of Beauchamp's Court, co. Warwick 1621, with remainder to his cousins Robert and William Greville; *d.* 1628, when the Barony of Brooke passed to Robert Greville [see E. Warwick] and the right to the Barony of Willoughby de Broke devolved on his sister [6] MARGARET, *de jure* Baroness; *b. circa* 1561: *m.* before 1584, Sir Richard Verney, of Compton Verney, co. Warwick; *d.* 1631; *s.* by her el. son [7] *Sir* GREVILLE, *de jure* 7th Baron; *b. circa* 1587: *m.* 1618, Catherine, dau. of Sir Robert Southwell, of Woodrising, Norfolk; *d.* 1642; *s.* by his el. son [8] GREVILLE, *de jure* 8th Baron; *b. circa* 1620: *m.* 16—, the Hon. Elizabeth Wenman, who *d.* 1649, dau. of 2nd Viscount Wenman of Tuam, *d.* 1648; *s.* by his only child [9] *Sir* GREVILLE, *KB, de jure* 9th Baron, *b.* (posthumously) 1649: *m.* 1667, Lady Diana Russell (who *m.* 2ndly, 1675 the 3rd Baron Alington of Killard, and *d.* 1701), dau. of 1st Duke of Bedford; *d.* 1668; *s.* by his only child [10] WILLIAM, *de jure* 10th Baron; *b.* 1668; *d.* 1683; *s.* by his great-uncle [11] *Sir* RICHARD (3rd son of *de jure* 7th Baron), 11th *de jure* Baron; established his claim to the Barony before the House of Lords 1696: *m.* 1st, before 1658, Elizabeth, dau. and heir of George Turpin; 2ndly, *circa* 1677, Frances, dau. of Thomas Dove; *d.* 1711; *s.* by his son [12] GEORGE, 12th Baron; *b.* 1659; was Dean of Windsor: *m.* 1688, Margaret, who *d.* 1729, dau. and heir of Sir John Heath; *d.* 1728; *s.* by his son [13] RICHARD, 13th Baron; *b.* 1693: *m.* 1st, 17—, Penelope, dau. of Clifton Packe; 2ndly, 17—, Elizabeth, who *d.* 1767, dau. of Nathaniel Williams; *d.s.p.* 1752; *s.* by his nephew [14] JOHN, 14th Baron, son of the Hon. John Verney, 3rd son of 12th Baron; *b.* 1762; assumed in 1772 the additional surname of Peyto: *m.* 1761, Lady Louisa North, who *d.* 1798, dau. of 1st Earl of Guilford; *d.* 1816; *s.* by his son [15] JOHN, 15th Baron; *b.* 1762; *d. unm.* 1820; *s.* by his brother [16] HENRY, 16th Baron; *d.s.p.* 1852; *s.* by his nephew [17] ROBERT JOHN, 17th Baron, son of the Hon. Louisa, dau. of 14th Baron by her marriage with the Rev. Robert Barnard; *b.* 1809; assumed in 1852 the surname of Verney in lieu of his patronymic: *m.* 1842, Georgiana Jane, who *d.* 1889, dau. of Maj.-Gen. Thomas William Taylor, *CB,* of Ogwell. Devon; *d.* 1862; *s.* by his son [18] HENRY, 18th Baron; *b.* 1844: *m.* 1867, Geraldine, who *d.* 1894, el. dau. of the late James H. Smith-Barry, Esq., of Marbury Hall, Cheshire, and Fota Island, Cork; *d.* 1902; *s.* by his son [19] RICHARD GREVILLE, 19th Baron, *b.* 1869; M.P. for Warwickshire, S.E., or Rugby Div. (C) 1895-1900: *m.* 1895, Marie Frances Lisette, *OBE,* who *d.* 1941, dau. of the late Charles Addington Hanbury; *d.* 1923; *s.* by his son [20] JOHN HENRY PEYTO, 20th Baron and present peer.

Wilmington, Baron, grandson of Marquess of Northampton.

WILSON, BARON. (Wilson.) [Baron U.K. 1946.]

PATRICK MAITLAND WILSON, 2nd Baron; *b.* Sept. 14th, 1915; *s.* 1964; ed. at Eton, and at King's Coll., Camb.; Lt.-Col. Rifle Bde.; 1939-45 War in Greece and Middle East (despatches): *m.* 1945, Violet Storeen, da. of the late Maj. James Hamilton Douglas Campbell, OBE [B. Clarina, ext.].

Arms,—Sable, a wolf salient or, on a chief of the last a pale of the first charged with a fleur-de-lys argent between two pellets. **Crest,**—A demi wolf or, the sinister paw resting on a pellet charged with a fleur-de-lys gold. **Supporters,**—*Dexter,* a rifleman; *sinister,* a bugler, both of the Rifle Brigade, in full dress proper.

Address,—c/o Barclays Bank, Cambridge.

SISTER LIVING.

Hon. Maud Maitland, *b.* 1917. *Residence,*—Hampton Court Palace, E. Molesey, Surrey.

WIDOW LIVING OF FIRST BARON.

HESTER MARY (*Hester, Lady Wilson*) (Hampton Court Palace, E. Molesey, Surrey), da. of Philip James Digby Wykeham, late of Tythrop House, Oxon.: *m.* 1914, the 1st Baron, who died 1964.

PREDECESSOR.—[1] *Sir* HENRY MAITLAND Wilson, *GCB, GBE, DSO,* son of Arthur Maitland Wilson, OBE, of Stowlangtoft Hall, Suffolk; *b.* 1881; Field Marshal late Rifle Bde. (O.C. 1st Bn. 1927-30, and Col. Comdt. 1939-51; G.O.C.-in-C. British Troops in Egypt 1939-41, Mil. Gov. and G.O.C.-in-C. Cyrenaica, G.O.C.-in-C. British Troops in Greece, G.O.C., British Troops in Palestine and Transjordan, G.O.C., Allied Forces in Syria, and G.O.C. 9th Army 1941, G.O.C.-in-C., Persia and Iraq 1942-43, and Middle East 1943-44, Supreme Allied Comd. in Mediterranean Theatre 1944-45, and Head of British Joint Staff Mission, Washington 1945-47, Constable of H.M. Tower of London 1955-60; *cr. Baron Wilson,* of Libya and of Stowlangtoft, co. Suffolk (Peerage of U.K.) 1946: *m.* 1914, Hester Mary, da. of Philip James Digby Wykeham, late of Tythrop House, Oxon.; *d.* 1964; *s.* by his only son [2] PATRICK MAITLAND, 2nd Baron and present peer.

WILSON OF LANGSIDE, BARON. (Wilson.) [Life Baron 1967.]

HENRY STEPHEN WILSON, *PC, QC,* son of the late James Wilson of Glasgow, Solicitor; *b.* March 21st, 1916; ed. at Glasgow High Sch., and Glasgow Univ. (MA, LLB); Bar. Scotland 1946, QC 1965; Advocate Depute 1948-51, Sheriff Substitute of Greenock 1955-56, and Glasgow 1956-65, Solicitor-Gen. for Scotland 1965-67, and Lord Advocate 1967-70; Dir. Scottish Courts Admin. since 1971; 1939-45 War with HLI and RAC (Commnd. 1940, demobilized as Capt. 1946); *cr.* PC 1967, and *Baron Wilson of Langside,* of Broughton, in co. of Edinburgh (Life Baron) 1969: *m.* 1942, Jessie Forrester, da. of the late William Nisbet Waters, of Paisley.

Residence,—Dunallan, Kippen, Stirlingshire. *Club,*—RSAC (Glasgow).

WILSON OF RADCLIFFE, BARON. (Wilson.) [Life Baron 1974.]

ALFRED WILSON, son of the late William Barnes Wilson; *b.* June 10th, 1909; ed. at Newcastle upon Tyne Tech. Sch.; FCIS; FBIM; Dep. Sec. and Exec. Officer, Co-operative Wholesale Soc. 1953-65, Sec. 1965-68, and Ch. Exec. Officer 1969-74; Chm. of Co-operative Bank, Ltd. 1971-74, and of F. C. Finance, Ltd. 1969-74; Joint Dept. Chm. Spillers French (Holdings), Ltd., 1972-74, and Joint Chm. J. W. French (Milling & Banking) Holdings, Ltd. 1971-74; *cr. Baron Wilson of Radcliffe,* of Radcliffe, Lancs. (Life Baron) 1974: *m.* 1932, Elsie, da. of Arthur Hulton, and has issue.

Residence,—58, Ringley Rd., Whitefield, Manchester.

DAUGHTER LIVING.

Hon. Moyra Christine, *b.* 1943: *m.* 1964, Dr. Arthur Crowther, of 8, Delfur Rd., Bramhall, Cheshire.

WILTON, EARL OF. (Egerton.) [Earl U.K. 1801.]

SEYMOUR WILLIAM ARTHUR JOHN EGERTON, 7th Earl; *b.* May 29th, 1921; *s.* 1927; ed. at Eton; *m.* 1962, Diana Elizabeth Lea (NAYLOR-LEY-LAND), dau. of Roy Galway, of St. Ronans, Winkfield Row, Ascot, Berks.

Arms,—Argent, a lion rampant gules, between three pheons, points downwards sable. **Crest,**—Three arrows, points downwards, one in pale and two in saltire or, barbed and fledged sable, band gules, and tasseled or. **Supporters,**—*Dexter,* a wyvern, wings inverted or; *sinister,* a lion argent, ducally crowned or.

I trust to virtue, not to arms.

Residence,—47, Chester Sq., SW1. *Club,*—White's.

SISTER LIVING.

Lady Alexandra Mariota Flora (of Chimney Cottage, Gressenhall, E. Dereham, Norfolk), *b.* 1919: *m.* 1939 (m. diss. 1962), Patrick Thomas Beasley, and has issue living, Lavinia Mary, *b.* 1945: *m.* 1st, 1966 (m. diss. 1971), Confrey A. Phillips; 2ndly, 1974, (John) Richard Aykroyd, of Ivy Farm, Roecliffe, Boroughbridge, York, YO5 9LY [see Aykroyd, Bt., colls., cr. 1920], and has issue living (by 1st m.), Emma Bernadette *b.* 1968.

AUNT LIVING. (*Daughter of 5th Earl.*)

Lady Mary Cecilia, *b.* 1901: *m.* 1923, Roderick Bulteel Boyd, who *d.* 1968, and has issue living, a son *b.* 1934,—a da., *b.* 1927,—a da., *b.* 1930. *Residence,*—Nanuyki, Kenya.

WIDOW LIVING OF SON OF FIFTH EARL.

Pamela Yolanda, dau. of the late Major Henry A. C. Darley, of Aldby Park, Yorkshire: *m.* 1st, 1947, as his second wife, the Hon. George Arthur Egerton, who *d.* 1947; 2ndly, 1950, Maj. George Rowland Hill Cholmley, MC, late KOYLI [V. Hill, colls.]. *Residence,*—Grange Garth, Wintringham, Malton, Yorkshire.

COLLATERAL BRANCH LIVING. (*In special remainder.*)

Descendants of the late Lord Robert Grosvenor (3rd son of 1st Marquess of Westminster), who was *cr. Baron Ebury* 1857 [see that title]:—

Of whom FRANCIS EGERTON (*Baron Ebury*), *b.* Feb. 8th, 1934; is *h.p.* to the Earldom.

PREDECESSORS.—[1] *Sir* THOMAS Egerton, 7th Bt., of Oulton, was *cr. Baron Grey de Wilton,* of Wilton Castle, co. Hereford (peerage of Great Britain) 1784, and *Viscount Grey de Wilton* and *Earl of Wilton* (peerage of United Kingdom) 1801, with remainder to the 2nd and all the younger sons successively of his dau. Eleanor, wife of Lord Belgrave, afterwards 1st Marquess of West-minster; *d.* 1814, when the Barony of Grey de Wilton expired, the baronetcy reverted upon the lineal descendant of the 1st Bt. (see Grey-Egerton, Bt.), and the viscountcy and earldom devolved upon his grandson [2] Rt. Hon. THOMAS Grosvenor, *GCH, DCL,* 2nd Earl; *b.* 1799; was Lord Steward of the Household; assumed in 1821 by sign manual the surname of Egerton in lieu of

Grosvenor: *m.* 1st, 1821, Lady Mary Margaret Stanley, dau. of 12th Earl of Derby; 2ndly, 1863, Isabella, who *d.* 1916, dau. of the late Major Elton Smith, of Ilminster: *d.* 1882; *s.* by his el. son [3] ARTHUR EDWARD HOLLAND GREY, 3rd Earl; *b.* 1833; sat as M.P. for Weymouth (*C*) 1859-65, and for Bath 1873-4: *m.* 1858, Lady Elizabeth Charlotte Louisa Craven, who *d.* 1919, dau. of 2nd Earl of Craven; cr. *Baron Grey de Radcliffe* (peerage of United Kingdom) 1875; *d.s.p.* Jan. 19th, 1885, when the Barony of Grey de Radcliffe became extinct, and the peerage of 1801 devolved upon his brother [4] SEYMOUR JOHN GREY, 4th Earl; *b.* 1839: *m.* 1862, Laura Caroline, who *d.* 1916, da. of the late William Russell; *d.* 1898; *s.* by his son [5] ARTHUR GEORGE, 5th Earl, *b.* 1863: *m.* 1895, the Hon. Mariota Thellussou, who *d.* 1924, dau. of 5th Baron Rendlesham; *d.* 1915; *s.* by his el. son [6] SEYMOUR EDWARD FREDERICK, 6th Earl; *b.* 1896: *m.* 1917, Brenda, who *d.* 1930, dau. of the late Sir William Petersen, KBE, of Eigg, Inverness; *d.* 1927; *s.* by his son [7] SEYMOUR WILLIAM ARTHUR JOHN, 7th Earl and present peer; also Viscount Grey de Wilton.

Wiltshire, Earl of, son of Marquess of Winchester.

WIMBORNE, VISCOUNT. (Guest.) [Viscount U.K. 1918, Baron U.K. 1880 and 1910, Bt. U.K. 1838.]

By iron, not by the sword.

IVOR FOX-STRANGWAYS GUEST, 3rd Viscount, and 5th Baronet; *b.* Dec. 2nd, 1939; *s.* 1967; ed. at Eton; Chm. of Harris & Dixon, Ltd. since 1972; Joint Master Pytchley Hounds since 1968: *m.* 1966, Victoria, only da. of the late Col. Mervyn Doyne Vigors, DSO, MC, and has issue.

ᨏrms.—Azure, on a chevron or, between three swans' heads erased proper, as many crosses moline sable. ᨏrest.—A swan's head, erased proper, gorged with a collar or, and charged underneath with a cross moline as in the arms, between two ostrich feathers or. ᨏupporters.— On either side a figure habited as Vulcan, resting his exterior hand on an anvil and holding in front thereof a sledge hammer, all proper.

Residence,—Ashby St. Ledgers, Rugby.

SON LIVING.
Hon. IVOR MERVYN VIGORS, *b.* Sept. 19th, 1968.

BROTHERS LIVING.
Hon. Julian John (Shotley House, Harringworth, Corby, Northants), *b.* 1945; ed. at Stowe: *m.* 1970, Emma Jane Arlette, el. da. of Cdr. Archibald Gray, RN (ret.), of Tilbridge, Gt. Staughton, St. Neots, Hunts.

Hon. Charles James (The Cottage, Ashby St. Ledgers, Rugby), *b.* 1950; ed. at Harrow.

SISTER LIVING.
Hon. Frances Ann (420, East 86th St., New York, USA), *b.* 1942: *m.* 1971, Ernest Martin Johnson.

AUNT LIVING (*Daughter of 1st Viscount*).
Hon. Cynthia Edith, *b.* 1908 : *m.* 1933, Capt. Thomas George Talbot, C.B., Q.C.,[see E. Shrewsbury and Talbot, colls.], of Falconhurst, Edenbridge, Kent.

WIDOW LIVING OF SON OF FIRST BARON.
Kathleen Susan, dau. of the late Graham Paterson [E. Huntingdon]: *m.* 1924, Major the Hon. (Oscar) Montague Guest, who *d.* 1958, and has issue living [see colls., infra.]. *Residence,*—Cabalva House, Whitney on Wye, Hereford.

WIDOW LIVING OF SECOND VISCOUNT.
Lady MABEL EDITH FOX-STRANGWAYS (*Dowager Viscountess Wimborne*) (Rozel, Mount Durand, St. Peter Port, Guernsey), da. of 6th Earl of Ilchester: *m.* 1938, the 2nd Viscount, who *d.* 1967.

COLLATERAL BRANCHES LIVING. (*In remainder to the Barony of Wimborne and the Baronetcy only.*)

Issue of the late Lieut.-Col. the Hon. (Christian) Henry Charles Guest, 2nd son of 1st Baron, *b.* 1874, *d.* 1957 : *m.* 1911, the Hon. Frances Henrietta Lyttelton, who *d.* 1918, dau. of 8th Viscount Cobham :—

John Spencer Churchill, *b.* 1913 : *m.* 1948, Margaret Hetherington, dau. of the late Henry Craft Houck, of Schenectady, New York, U.S.A., and has issue living, Richard Lyttelton, *b.* 1954,— Cornelia Schermerhorn, *b.* 1952. *Residence,*—839, Weed St., New Canaan, Connecticut, U.S.A.

Issue of the late Capt. the Rt. Hon. Frederick Edward Guest, C.B.E., D.S.O., M.P., 3rd son of 1st Baron, *b.* 1875, *d.* 1937 : *m.* 1905, Amy, who *d.* 1959, dau. of Henry Phipps :—

Winston Frederick Churchill, *b.* 1906; is Capt. US Marines: *m.* 1st, 1934 (divorce 1944), Helena, dau. of C. E. F. Mccann, of New York; 2ndly, 1947, Lucy Douglas Cochrane, and has issue living, (by 1st m.) Winston (Berry Hill Rd., Oyster Bay, Long Island NY, USA), *b.* 1936: *m.* 1967, Helen Shields, and has issue living, Winston Frederick Churchill *b.* 1968, Helena Woolworth *b.* 1970,— Frederick Edward (Cove Neck Rd., Oyster Bay, Long Island, New York, USA), *b.* 1938: *m.* 1963, Stephanie, da. of the late Walter F. Wanger, and has issue living, Victoria Woolworth *b.* 1966, Vanessa Wanger *b.* 1973,—(by 2nd m.) Alexander Michael Dudley, *b.* 1954,—Cornelia Cochrane, *b.* 1963. *Residence,*—651, North County Rd., Palm Beach, Florida, USA.——Raymond Richard (Powhatan, Plantation King George, Va., USA), *b.* 1907: *m.* 1st, 1935, Elizabeth Sturgis, da. of Frank Lyon Polk; 2ndly, 1953 Mrs. Ellen Tuck Astor, da. of Francis Ormond French; 3rdly, 19—,

HH Princess Caroline, da. of the late HH Prince Alexandre Murat, and has issue living, (by 1st m.) Raymond Richard (Rock Hill Farm, Front Royal, Virginia, USA), b. 1939: m. 19—, Patricia Donovan, and has issue living, Mary Elizabeth b. 1964,—Elizabeth Polk, b. 1937: m. 1st 19—, Edward B. Condon; 2ndly, 1965, George C. Stevens, of 2903, North St. NW, Washington, DC, USA, and has issue living (by 1st m.) Caroline b. 1959, (by 2nd m.) Michael Murrow b. 1966,—Virginia b. 1946.—(by 3rd m.) Achille, b. 19—.—Diana, b. 1909; re-assumed the surname of Guest in lieu of that of Sevastopoulo by deed poll 1938: m. 1st, 1934 (divorce 1937), Marc Sevastopoulo; 2ndly, 1943, Count Jean de la Valdene, and has issue living, (by 1st m.) Diane Lorraine, b. 1935: m. 1955, Pierre Firmin-Didot, of 6 Av. Raphael, Paris XVI, and has issue living—(by 2nd m.) Guy Winston, b. 1944,—Lorraine Aimee, b. 1946. Residence,—Chateau St. Georges Motel, Eure, France, 15.

Issue of the late Major the Hon. (Oscar) Montague Guest. youngest son of 1st Baron, b. 1888, d. 1958: m. 1924, Kathleen Susan (ante), da. of the late Graham Paterson [E. Huntingdon]:— Bertie Warner (of The Lime House, Tilford, Surrey), b. 1925: m. 1949, Margaret Rose, dau. of Charles Lamond Henderson, Q.C., and has issue living, Jonathan Bertie, b. 1952,—Veronica Susan, b. 1953,—Harriet Clare, b. 1955,—Diana Charlotte, b. 1959.——Patrick Henry, b. 1927: m. 1951, Juliet Marian, dau. of the late H. M. James, and has issue living, Peter Hugh, b. 1952,—Matthew James, b. 1954,—David Christian, b. 1960. Residence,—14, Hobury St., S.W.10.——Cornelia Rowena, b. 1928: m. 1st, 1949 (marriage dissolved 1955), Hugh Dearman Janson; 2ndly, 1957, Peter Frederick Arthur Denman [see B. Denman, colls.], and has issue living, (by 1st marriage) Charles James, b. 1952,—Sarah, b. 1950,—(by 2nd m.) [see B. Denman, colls.]. Residence,—Duke's House, 23, Lawrence St., SW3.——Revel Sarah, b. 1931: m. 1963, Robert Alan Albert, of 9, Holland Park, W11, and has issue living, Justin Thomas b. 1965,—Corisande Charlotte, b. 1967.

(In remainder to the Baronetcy only.)

Grandchildren of the late Arthur Edward Guest, brother of 1st Baron:—
Issue of the late (Arthur) Rhuvon Guest, b. 1869, d. 1946 : m. 1901, Hilda Eugenia, who d. 1959, dau. of the late Adm. the Hon. Keith Stewart, C.B. [E. Galloway, colls.] :—
Evan Rhuvon, b. 1902 ; ed. at Eton, and at Roy. Coll. of Science, London (B.Sc. 1924) : m. 1st, 1935 (divorce 1952), Columba Mary Dolores Heathcote, M.B., B.Ch., who d. 1955, dau. of Joseph Francis O'Carroll, MD, of Lynwood, Dundrum, co. Dublin; 2ndly, 1952, Christabel (WIGGETT), da. of the late John Thomas Kelly, of the Isle of Man. Residence,—The Old Coach House, Old Hatfield, Herts.——Mary Adeline (39, Argyll Rd., W8), b. 1904: m. 1929, Capt. Henry T. W. Bousfield, late Indian Army, who d. 1967.——Pamela Margaret (Windrush Cottage, Inkpen, Berks.), b .1905.

PREDECESSORS.—[1] JOSIAH JOHN Guest, son of the late Thomas Guest, of Dowlais, Glamorgan ; b. 1785; M.P. for Honiton 1825-31, and for Merthyr Tydvil 1832-52; cr. a Baronet 1838 : m. 1st, 1817, Maria Elizabeth, who d. 1818, dau. of William Ranken; 2ndly, 1833, Lady Charlotte Elizabeth Bertie, who d. 1895 (having m. 2ndly, 1855, Charles Schreiber, M.P., who d. 1884), dau. of 9th Earl of Lindsey; d. 1852; s. by his son [2] Sir IVOR BERTIE, 2nd Bt., b. 1835; cr. Baron Wimborne, of Canford Magna, Dorset (peerage of United Kingdom) 1880 : m. 1868, Lady Cornelia Henrietta Maria Spencer-Churchill, who d. 1927, el. dau. of 7th Duke of Marlborough; d. 1914; s. by his el. son [3] IVOR CHURCHILL, P.C., 2nd Baron, b. 1873; M.P. for Plymouth (L) 1900-1906, and for Cardiff 1906-10; Paymaster-Gen. 1910-12, a Lord-in-Waiting to H.M. 1913-15, and Lord-Lieut. of Ireland 1915-18 ; cr. Baron Ashby St. Ledgers, of Ashby St. Ledgers, co. Northampton (peerage of United Kingdom) 1910, and Viscount Wimborne, of Canford Magna, Dorset (peerage of United Kingdom) 1918 : m. 1902, the Hon. Alice Katherine Sibell Grosvenor, who d. 1948, dau. of 2nd Baron Ebury; d. 1939; s. by his only son [4] IVOR GROSVENOR, OBE, 2nd Viscount, b. 1903; PPS to Under-Sec. of State for Air 1943-45; MP for Breconshire 1935-39: m. 1938, Lady Mabel Edith Fox-Strangways, da. of 6th Earl of Ilchester; d. 1967; s. by his son [5] IVOR FOX-STRANGWAYS, 3rd Viscount, and present peer; also Baron Ashby St. Ledgers, and Baron Wimborne.

WINCHESTER, LORD BISHOP OF. (Taylor.)

Rt. Rev. JOHN VERNON TAYLOR, DD, son of the late Rt. Rev. John Ralph Strickland Taylor, Bishop of Sodor and Man.; b. Sept. 11th, 1914; ed. at St. Lawrence Coll., Ramsgate, Trin. Coll., Camb. (MA), St. Catherine's Soc., Oxford, Wycliffe Hall, Oxford, and Inst. of Education, London; Hon. DD Wycliffe Coll., Toronto; Curate, All Souls, Langham Place, W1, 1938-40; Curate in Charge, St. Andrew's Church, St. Helens, Lancs. 1940-43; Warden of Bishop Tucker Coll., Mukono, Uganda 1945-54; Research Worker, Internat. Missionary Council 1955-59; Africa Sec. CMS 1959-63; Gen. Sec., CMS 1963-74; Hon. Canon of St. Paul's Cathedral, Kampala 1963-74; consecrated 94th Lord Bishop of Winchester 1974: m. 1940, Margaret, da. of Walter Stanley Wright.

Patron of 89 livings, and of 23 alternately with other Patrons, the Canonries in his Cathedral, and the Archdeaconries of Winchester and Basingstoke.

This Diocese, founded in 636, includes the larger part of Hampshire, and the Channel Islands.

Episcopal Signature,—" John Winton:"

ARMS OF THE SEE,—Gules, two keys endorsed in bend, the upper or, the lower argent between them a sword in bend sinister of the third, hilt and pommel gold.
Residence,—Wolvesey, Winchester.

WINCHESTER, MARQUESS OF. (Paulet.) [Marquess E. 1551.]

Love loyalty.

NIGEL GEORGE PAULET, 18th Marquess, and Premier Marquess of England; *b.* Dec. 22nd, 1941; *s.* 1968: *m.* 1967, Rosemary Anne, da. of Maj. Aubrey John Hilton, of Salisbury, Rhodesia, and has issue.

Arms,—Sable, three swords in pile, points downwards, proper, pommels and hilts, or. Crest.—A falcon, wings displayed or, belled of the same, and ducally collared gules. Supporters,— Two hinds purpure, semée of estoiles, and ducally gorged or.

Residence,—Lydford Cottage, 35, Whyteladies Lane, Borrowdale, Salisbury, Rhodesia.

SONS LIVING.
CHRISTOPHER JOHN HILTON (*Earl of Wiltshire*), *b.* July 30th, 1969.
Lord Richard George, *b.* 1971.

BROTHER LIVING. (*Raised to the rank of a Marquess's son* 1970).
Lord Timothy Guy, *b.* 1944.

SISTER LIVING. (*Raised to the rank of a Marquess's daughter* 1970).
Lady Jane Angela, *b.* 1939: *m.* 1972, Christopher John Fisher.

AUNT LIVING.
Violet Susan Mary (Lydford Hall, Lydford-on-Fosse, Somerton, Somerset), *b.* 1903.

SISTERS LIVING OF SEVENTEENTH MARQUESS.
(*Raised to the rank of a Marquess's daughters* 1970.)
Lady Pamela (Basing Cottage, Denham Place, Denham, Bucks.), *b.* 1909.——
Lady Eileen Cecil Theo, *b.* 1916: *m.* 19—, Joseph Fitton, of 1610E., 11th Av., Vancouver 12, BC, Canada.

MOTHER LIVING.
Hazel Margaret, da. of Maj. Danvers Wheeler, RA, of Salisbury, Rhodesia: *m.* 1st, 1937, George Cecil Paulet, who *d.* 1961; 2ndly, 1962, George Meyer.

WIDOW LIVING OF SIXTEENTH MARQUESS.
BAPSY (*Bapsy, Marchioness of Winchester*), da. of the late Most Rev. Khurshedji Pavry, High Priest of the Parsees in India; MA Columbia Univ., New York 1925; a Member of Council of World Alliance for International Peace through Religion, and Author of "Heroines of Ancient Iran" 1930; has Order of Merit of Iran: *m.* 1952, as his 3rd wife, the 16th Marquess, who *d.* 1962.

COLLATERAL BRANCH LIVING.
　　Issue of the late John Valentine Paulet, uncle of 17th Marquess, *b.* 1909, *d.* 1970: *m.* 1945, Mira Elizabeth, da. of Edmund Francis Smith, of Mossel Bay, Cape Province:—
Michael John, *b.* 1945; with British S. Africa Police, Salisbury, Rhodesia: *m.* 1967, Gail Lisbeth, yr. da. of the late John Blackwood Ward, of Bulawayo.——Pamela Elizabeth, *b.* 1947.

PREDECESSORS.—[1] *Sir* WILLIAM Paulet, *K.G.*, was cr. *Baron St. John of Basing* (peerage of England) 1539, *Earl of Wiltshire* (peerage of England) 1550, and *Marquess of Winchester* (peerage of England) 1551; was an executor to the will of Henry VIII., and Lord Treasurer of England *temp.* Edward VI. and Queens Mary I. and Elizabeth I.; *d.* 1572; *s.* by his son [2] JOHN, 2nd Marquess; summoned to Parliament in his father's barony of St. John; *d.* 1576; *s.* by his son [3] WILLIAM 3rd Marquess; summoned to Parliament in his father's barony of St. John; *d.* 1598; *s.* by his son [4] WILLIAM, 4th Marquess; entertained Queen Elizabeth with magnificence at his seat at Basing, by which and other expenses he became involved in pecuniary difficulties; *d.* 1628; *s.* by his son [5] JOHN, 5th Marquess, a zealous partisan of Charles I.; his seat at Basing was after a protracted siege by the Parliamentarians burned to the ground, when property of the value of £200,000 was destroyed; *d.* 1675; *s.* by his son [6] CHARLES, 6th Marquess; cr. *Duke of Bolton* (peerage of England) 1689; *d.* 1689; *s.* by his son [7] CHARLES, 2nd Duke; was Lord-Lieut. of Ireland 1717; *d.* 1722; *s.* by his el. son [8] CHARLES, *K.G.*, 3rd Duke; was Lord Lieut. and Constable of the Tower of London; *d.* 1754; *s.* by his brother [9] HARRY, 4th Duke; *d.* 1759; *s.* by his son [10] CHARLES, *K.B.*, 5th Duke; was Lieut. of the Tower of London, and Lord-Lieut. of Hants; *d.* unmarried 1765; *s.* by his brother [11] HARRY, 6th Duke; was an Adm. of the White; *d.* 1794, when the dukedom expired, and the barony, earldom, and marquessate devolved upon his kinsman [12] GEORGE, 12th Marquess, descendant of Lord Henry, 3rd son of 4th Marquess; *d.* 1800; *s.* by his son [13] CHARLES INGOLDSBY, 13th Marquess; *b.* 1765; assumed in 1839 the additional surname of Burroughs: *m.* 1800, Anne dau. of John Andrews, Esq., of Shotney Hall, co. Northumberland; *d.* 1843; *s.* by his son [14] JOHN, 14th Marquess, *b.* 1801: *m.* 1855, the Hon. Mary Montagu, who *d.* 1868, el. dau. of 6th Baron Rokeley (*ext.*); *d.* 1887; *s.* by his son [15] AUGUSTUS JOHN HENRY BEAUMONT, 15th Marquess: *b.* 1858; Major Coldstream Guards; killed at battle of Magersfontein in S. Africa 1899; *s.* by his brother [16] HENRY WILLIAM MONTAGU, 16th Marquess, *b.* 1862; Lord-Lieut. of Hants. 1904-17; Chm. of Hants. Co. Council 1905-9; Major Rifle Bde. in France 1914-17: *m.* 1st, 1892, Dame Charlotte Josephine, *G.B.E.*, who *d.* 1924, dau. of the late Col. John Stanley Howard, of Ballina Park, co. Wicklow, and widow of Samuel Garnett; 2ndly, 1925, Caroline, who *d.* 1949, dau. of Abraham Hoffnung, and widow of Major Claude Marks, D.S.O.; 3rdly, 1952, Bapsy Pavry, *M.A.*, dau. of the Most Rev. Khurshedji Pavry; *d.* 1962, *s.* by his kinsman [17] RICHARD CHARLES (only son of the late Major Charles Standish Paulet, *M.V.O.*, grandson of the late Rev. Lord Charles Paulet, 2nd son of 13th Marquess), 17th Marquess, *b.* 1905, *d.* 1968; *s.* by his kinsman [18] NIGEL GEORGE (el. son of George Cecil Paulet, el. son of Cecil Henry Paulet, uncle of 17th Marquess), 18th Marquess and present peer; also Earl of Wiltshire, and Baron St. John of Basing.

WINCHILSEA AND NOTTINGHAM, EARL OF. (Finch Hatton.)
[Earl E. 1628 and 1681, Bt. E. 1611 and 1660.]

Conscious of no guilt.

CHRISTOPHER DENYS STORMONT FINCH HATTON, 16th Earl of Winchilsea, 11th Earl of Nottingham, 17th Baronet of Eastwell, and 11th Baronet of Raunston; *b.* Nov. 17th, 1936; *s.* 1950; ed. at Eton, and at Gordonstoun; Hereditary Lord of Roy. Manor of Wye: *m.* 1962, Shirley, el. da. of the late Bernard Hatfield, of Wylde Green, Sutton Coldfield, and has issue.

Arms,—Argent, a chevron between three griffins passant sable. Crest,—A pagasus courant argent, wings expanded or. Supporters,—*Dexter*, a pegasus wings elevated argent, ducally gorged or; *sinister*, a griffin wings elevated sable, gorged as the dexter.

Residence,—South Cadbury House, nr. Yeovil, Somerset.

SON LIVING.

DANIEL JAMES HATFIELD (*Viscount Maidstone*), b. Oct. 7th, 1967.

DAUGHTER LIVING.

Lady Alice Nan Christiane, b. 1970.

BROTHER LIVING.

Hon. Robin Heneage (Town House Farmhouse, Clemsfold, Horsham, Sussex), b. 1939; ed. at Gordonstoun: m. 1962, Molly Iona, yr. da. of Col. Palgrave Dawson Turner Powell, of Damson Hill Cottage, Swanmore, Hants., and has issue living, Christopher Benjamyn b. 1966,—Rupert Stormont, b. 1968,—Louisa Henrietta Mari, b. 1971.

AUNTS LIVING.

(*Daughters of 14th Earl.*)

Lady Daphne Margarita, b. 1913: m. 1935, Air-Commodore Whitney Willard Straight, C.B.E., M.C., DFC, Auxiliary Air Force, and has issue living, Camilla Caroline b. 1937: m. 1960, Maj. Michael Ian Vansittart Bowater, Scots Guards, son of Lt.-Col. Sir Ian Frank Bowater, DSO, TD [see Bowater, Bt., cr. 1939],—Amanda Betsy, b. 1952. *Residence,*—The Aviary, Windmill Lane, Southall, Middlesex.

Lady (Henrietta) Diana Juanita, b. 1916: m. 1938, as his second wife, Peter Frank Tiarks, MC, who d. 1975, and has issue living, Caspar Peter Frank, b. 1948; ed. at Millfield: m. 1973, Susan, el. da. of James Maple-Brown, of Springfield, Goulburn, NSW,—Tania Henrietta, b. 1939: m. 1960, Michael Joseph Bennet Parker, of Gooderstone Manor, Gooderstone, King's Lynn, and has issue living, Stephen Favon b. 1960, Benjamin James b. 1962,—Anita Daphne, b. 1941; ed. at St. Hilda's Coll., Oxford (BA): m. 1963, Euan Malcolm Macphail, BA, of Ramillies, 6, High St., Woodstock, Oxon., and has issue living, Camilla Janet b. 1964, Madeleine Diana b. 1968. *Residence,*—Melplash Court, Bridport, Dorset.

MOTHER LIVING.

Countess Gladys, third dau. of Count László Széchényi, formerly Hungarian Min. in London: m. 1st, 1935, the 15th Earl, who d. 1950, and from whom she had obtained a divorce 1946; 2ndly, 1954, Arthur Talbot Peterson, who d. 1962. *Residence,*—Apt. 17d, 110, East 57 St., New York, N.Y., USA 10022,

COLLATERAL BRANCHES LIVING.

Granddaughters of the late Rev. William Robert Finch Hatton, son of the late Rev. the Hon. Daniel Heneage Finch Hatton, brother of 10th Earl of Winchilsea and Nottingham:—

Issue of the late Brig.-Gen. Edward Heneage Finch Hatton, C.M.G., D.S.O., late the Buffs, b. 1868, d. 1940: m. 1912, Dagmar G. (of 18, Southwood Court, Hampstead Garden Suburb, N.W.11), dau. of the late Col. Francis George Archibald Wiehe, formerly 68th Durham L.I.:—

Ann Zephine, b. 1912: m. 1943, Group-Capt. Maurice Ashdown Newnham, O.B.E., D.F.C., R.A.F. VR, and has issue living, Nicola Ann, b. 1946. *Residence,*—Hazel Cottage, Liss, Petersfield, Hants.
——Essex Dagmar FINCH HATTON, b. 1916. *Residence,*—18, Southwood Court, Hampstead Garden Suburb, NW11.

Descendants of the late Hon. Heneage Finch (2nd son of 1st Earl of Nottingham), who was cr. *Earl of Aylesford* 1714 [see that title].

PREDECESSORS.—[1] Sir MOYLE Finch, Knt., was cr. a *Baronet* 1611 (of Eastwell): m. Elizabeth, only dau. of Sir Thomas Heneage, Knt., of Copt Hall, Essex, which lady was cr. *Viscountess Maidstone* (peerage of England) 1623 and *Countess of Winchilsea* (peerage of England) 1628: Sir Moyle d. 1614; s. by his son [2] Sir THEOPHILUS, 2nd Bt., d.s.p.; s. by his brother [3] Sir THOMAS, 3rd Bt., who in 1633 s. his mother as 2nd Earl; d. 1634; s. by his son [4] HENEAGE, 3rd Earl; an earnest royalist; having rendered efficient aid in restoring the monarchy was in 1660 cr. by Charles II. *Baron FitzHerbert of Eastwell*, co. Kent (peerage of England); was Lord-Lieut. of co. Kent; d. 1689; s. by his grandson [5] CHARLES, 4th Earl; d. 1712; s. by his uncle [6] HENEAGE, 5th Earl; d.s.p. 1726; s. by his half-brother [7] JOHN, 6th Earl; d.s.p. 1729, when the Barony of FitzHerbert of Eastwell became extinct, and the baronetcy, viscountcy and earldom reverted to his kinsman [8] DANIEL, P.C., 7th Earl, who in 1682 had s. his father as 2nd Earl of Nottingham (see *⁎₈* infra); was Sec. of State 1689-94 and 1702-4, Lord Pres. of the Council 1714-16, and Lord-Lieut. of Kent; d. 1730; s. by his son [9] DANIEL, 8th Earl; d.s.p. 1769: s. by his nephew [10] GEORGE, K.G., 9th Earl, son of the Rt. Hon. William Finch, M.P., 2nd son of 7th Earl; was Lord Lieut. of co. Rutland; d. unmarried 1826; s. by his cousin [11] GEORGE WILLIAM Finch Hatton 10th Earl, grandson of the Hon. Edward, MP (5th son of 7th Earl), who assumed without Roy. licence the additional surname of Hatton; b. 1791, m. 1st, 1814, Lady Georgiana Charlotte, da. of 3rd Duke of Montrose; 2ndly, 1837, Emily Georgiana, dau. of the Rt. Hon. Sir Charles Bagot, G.C.B.; 3rdly, 1849, Fanny Margaret, who d. 1909, dau. of Edward Royd Rice, of Dane Court, Kent; d. 1858; s. by his son [12] GEORGE JAMES, 11th Earl, b. 1815; sat as M.P. for Northamptonshire (C) 1837-41; m. 1st, 1846,

Lady Constance Henrietta Paget, who *d.* 1878, dau. of 2nd Marquess of Anglesey ; 2ndly, 1882, Lady Elizabeth Georgiana, who *d.* 1904, widow of George Leopold Bryan, M.P., and dau. of 2nd Marquess of Conyngham ; *d.* 1887 ; *s.* by his half-brother [13] MURRAY EDWARD GORDON, 12th Earl, *b.* 1851 ; M.P. for Lincolnshire S. (*C*) 1884, and for Lincolnshire, Holland, or Spalding, Div. 1885-7 ; largely interested in agricultural questions: *m.* 1875, Edith, who *d.* 1944, dau. of the late Edward William Harcourt; *d.* 1898; *s.* by his brother [14] HENRY STORMONT, 13th Earl, *b.* 1852 : *m.* 1882, Anne, who *d.* 1924, dau. of the late Adm. of the Fleet Sir Henry John Codrington, K.C.B. ; *d.* 1927 ; *s.* by his son [15] GUY MONTAGU GEORGE, *O.B.E., D.S.C.,* 14th Earl, *b.* 1885 ; European War 1915-18 (D.S.C., O.B.E.) : *m.* 1910, Margaretta Armstrong, who *d.* 1952, dau. of Anthony Joseph Drexel, of Philadelphia, U.S.A.; *d.* 1939 ; *s.* by his son [16] CHRISTOPHER GUY HENEAGE, 15th Earl, *b.* 1911 ; Lieut. R.N.V.R. : *m.* 1st, 1935, Countess Gladys (who obtained a divorce 1946), third dau. of Count László Széchényi, Hungarian Min. in London; 2ndly, 1946, Agnes Mary, who *d.* 1964, da. of the late Patrick Joseph Conroy, JP, of Malvern House, Wigan; *d.* 1950; *s.* by his son [17] CHRISTOPHER DENYS STORMONT, 16th Earl and present peer; also Viscount Maidstone, and Baron Finch.

** [1] Sir HENEAGE Finch, Knt., *P.C.*, son of the Hon. Sir Heneage Finch, Speaker of the House of Commons (3rd son of Sir Moyle Finch and Elizabeth, Countess of Winchilsea), sat successively as M.P. for Canterbury, St. Michael's, and Oxford; in 1660 was appointed Solicitor-Gen., knighted, and cr. a *Baronet* (of Raunston) 1660; in 1670 became Attorney-Gen.; in 1673 was made Keeper of the Great Seal, and cr. *Baron Finch*, of Daventry, co. Northampton (peerage of England) ; in 1675 was promoted to be Lord High Chancellor of England and cr. *Earl of Nottingham* (peerage of England); was nominated 1677 Lord High Steward of England; *d.* 1682; *s.* by his son [2] DANIEL, 2nd Earl, who in 1729 *s.* as 7th Earl of Winchilsea (ante).

WINDLESHAM, BARON. (Hennessy.) [Baron U.K. 1937 Bt. U.K. 1927.]

I live by force and arms.

DAVID JAMES GEORGE HENNESSY, *PC,* 3rd Baron, and 3rd Baronet; *b.* Jan. 28th, 1932; *s.* 1962; ed. at Ampleforth, and at Trin. Coll., Oxford (MA); late Lt. Gren. Gds.; Managing Dir. of Grampian Television 1967-70; Chm. of Bow Group 1959-60 and 1962-63, and a Member of Westminster City Council 1958-62; Min. of State Home Office 1970-72, Min. of State, N. Ireland 1972-73; Lord Privy Seal, and Leader of House of Lords 1973-74, and Leader of the Opposition, House of Lords Oct. 1974; Joint Man. Dir. of ATV Network since 1974; cr. PC 1973: *m.* 1965, Prudence, yr. da. of Lt.-Col. R. T. W. Glynn, MC, of Harlesford House, Tetsworth, Oxon., and has issue.

Arms,—Gules, a boar passant proper, on a chief or a trefoil slipped vert between two roses of the field, barbed and seeded also proper. Crest,—In front of a dexter arm embowed in armour, the hand grasping a battle-axe, a trefoil slipped and a red rose stalked and leaved saltirewise, all proper. Supporters,—On either side an Officer of the Irish Brigade in the service of the King of France in the eighteenth century proper, the dexter supporting with the exterior hand a gold mounted and tasselled staff proper.

Residence,—59, Ridgway Place, SW19 4SP. *Clubs,*—Carlton, Royal and Ancient, Beefsteak.

SON LIVING.
Hon. JAMES RUPERT, *b.* Nov. 9th, 1968.

DAUGHTER LIVING
Hon. Victoria Jane, *b.* 1966.

SISTERS LIVING.
Hon. Marie-Louise (*Hon. Lady de Zulueta*), *b.* 1930: *m.* 1955, Sir Philip Francis de Zulueta, and has issue living, Francis Philip Harold, *b.* 1959,—Louise Angela Mary, *b.* 1956. *Residences*—11, Vicarage Gdns., W8; La Souco, Roquebrune, Alpes Maritimes, France.
Hon. Rosalie Ann, *b.* 1934: *m.* 1960, Peter John Gervase Elwes, of 75, Murray Rd., Wimbledon, SW19 [B. Rennell], and has issue living, Luke Andrew Cary, *b.* 1961,—Benedict James, *b.* 1963,—Marcus David, *b.* 1964,—Harriet Clare, *b.* 1968.
Hon. Annabel Jane, *b.* 1937: *m.* 1963, Ian Duncan Chisholm, MRCP, of Bourton House, Flax Bourton, Som., and has issue living, Roderick Bryan Duncan, *b.* 1964,—Daniel Hugh, *b.* 1966,—Alexander James, *b.* 1968,—John Malcolm, *b.* 1970.

AUNTS LIVING (*Daughters of 1st Baron.*)
Hon. Violet Ethel Mary, *b.* 1901: *m.* 1935, Capt. Charles Elphinstone Fordyce, late Seaforth Highlanders, and has issue living, John Stewart Elphinstone (26, Dry Mill Rd., Tonbridge, Kent), *b.* 1936; ed. at Ampleforth: *m.* 1961, Patricia Rose, da. of A. G. Noyce, of Billericay, Essex, and has issue living, Andrew John Elphinstone *b.* 1963, Nicholas Charles *b.* 1965, Dominic James *b.* 1967,—Sheila Mary Rose, *b.* 1939: *m.* 1960 (m. diss. 1971), Jeremy Charles Peel [see E. Peel, colls.]. *Residence,*—Bracken Lodge, Churt, Surrey.
Hon. Noreen Madeleine, *b.* 1910: *m.* 1931 (marriage dissolved 1948), Michael Bull, and has issue living, Michael Matthew (Manor Croft, Normandy, Guildford), *b.* 1932; ed. at Ampleforth; is Maj. Coldstream Guards: *m.* 1962, Jane, only dau. of Harry Inglis, of Lane Lodge, Stoke Green, Slough, Bucks, and has issue living, Richard Matthew Charles, *b.* 1963, Philip Henry *b.* 1969, Emma Jane, *b.* 1964,—George Jeffrey (The Old Vicarage, Arkesden, Saffron Walden), *b.* 1936; ed. at Ampleforth: *m.* 1960, Fleur-Thérèse, only da. of Patrick Freeland, of Rhodesia, and has issue living, George Sebastian Matthew *b.* 1960, Rupert Frederick Alain *b.* 1963, Justin Bartholomew Peter *b.* 1964, Cassian Michael Thomas *b.* 1968, Tamsin Emily Mary, *b.* 1972. *Residence,*—Belgravia Court, 33, Ebury St., SW1.

Hon. Kathleen Irene Mary, *b.* 1914: *m.* 1947, Wilfred Ernest Barnett, of Pullington Cottage, Benenden, Cranbrook, Kent, and has issue living, Robin George, *b.* 1951; ed. at Worth Abbey Sch.: *m.* 1973, Carolyn Steward, el. da. of Ronald E. Plummer, of Rowley, Wadhurst, Sussex,—Nicholas James, *b.* 1955; ed. at Worth Abbey Sch.

WIDOW LIVING OF SON OF FIRST BARON.

Merritt Jean (Harwood Lodge, Newbury, Berks.), da. of the late Alfred A. Longsdon: *m.* 1932, Maj. the Hon. Frederick Francis George Hennessy, MBE, who *d.* 1969, and has issue [see colls. infra.].

WIDOW LIVING OF SECOND BARON.

PAMELA (DINAN) (58, Eaton Sq., SW1), da. of Francis Kennedy: *m.* 2ndly, 1957, as his 2nd wife, the 2nd Baron, who *d.* 1962; 3rdly, 1966, William Marsden Elverston-Trickett.

COLLATERAL BRANCH LIVING.

Issue of the late Maj. the Hon. Frederick Francis George Hennessy, MBE, yr. son of 1st Baron; *b.* 1906, *d.* 1969: *m.* 1932, Merritt Jean (ante), da. of the late Alfred A. Longsdon:—

Peter Grant Auguste (Saintburyhill, Froyle, Alton, Hants.) *b.* 1944: *m.* 1968, Sally Ann, yst. da. of Dr. Clarence Laverne Johnson [see Royden, Bt.], and has issue living, James George, *b.* 1970,— Katherine Ann, *b.* 1973.——Maunagh Jean, *b.* 1933: *m.* 1953, Timothy William Jacques Leopold Koch de Gooreynd [see M. Queensberry, colls.].——Susan Jane, *b.* 1938: *m.* 1963, Charles Edward Morley-Fletcher, of Park Gate, Petersham, Surrey, and has issue living, Michael Francis, *b.* 1964,— Patrick Edward, *b.* 1966,—Frederick Maurice, *b.* 1969,—Caroline Angela Elisabeth, *b.* 1971.

PREDECESSORS—[1] GEORGE RICHARD JAMES Hennessy, *O.B.E.*, son of the late Richard Hennessy, of Bagnolet, Cognac, France; *b.* 1877; High Sheriff of Hants 1910-11; European War 1915-18 as Major King's Roy. Rifle Corps and on Staff of 5th Div.; was Parliamentary Private Sec. (unpaid) to Min. of Labour 1921-22, a Junior Lord of the Treasury 1922-24, and 1924-25, Vice-Chamberlain of H.M.'s Household 1925-28, Treasurer of H.M's Household 1928-29 and (in National Govt.) Sept. to Nov. 1931, and Vice-Chm. Conservative and Unionist Party 1931-41; sat as M.P. for Winchester Div. of Hampshire (*U*) 1918-31; cr. a *Baronet* 1927, and *Baron Windlesham*, of Windlesham, co. Surrey (peerage of United Kingdom) 1937: *m.* 1898, Ethel Mary, who *d.* 1951, dau. of the late Charles Reginald Wynter; *d.* 1953; *s.* by his el. son [2] JAMES BRYAN GEORGE, 2nd Baron; *b.* 1903; Brig. late Grenadier Guards: *m.* 1st, 1929, Angela Mary, who *d.* 1956, da. of the late Julian Duggan; 2ndly, 1957, Mrs. Pamela Dinan, who *m.* 3rdly 1966, William Marsden Elverston-Trickett, da. of Francis Kennedy; *d.* 1962;; *s.* by his son [3] DAVID JAMES GEORGE, 3rd Baron and present peer.

WINDSOR, DUKEDOM OF, see Royal Family.

WINDSOR, FAMILY AND HOUSE NAME OF THE ROYAL FAMILY.

Windsor, Viscount, son of Earl of Plymouth.

WINTERBOTTOM, BARON. (Winterbottom.) [Life Baron 1965.]

IAN WINTERBOTTOM, son of George Harold Winterbottom; *b.* April 13th, 1913; ed. at Charterhouse, and at Clare Coll., Camb.; Personal Assist. to Regional Commr., Hamburg 1946-49, and Private Sec. to Min. of Civil Aviation 1949; Under Sec. of State, Min. of Defence (RN) 1966-67, Parl. Sec., Min. of Public Building and Works 1967-68, and an Under-Sec. of State, Min. of Defence; 1939-45 War as Capt. R. Horse Guards; MP for Central Div. of Nottingham (*Lab.*) 1950-55; a Lord in Waiting to HM since 1974; cr. *Baron Winterbottom*, of Clopton, co. Northampton (Life Peerage) 1965: *m.* 19—, Irene Eva (Ira), da. of the late Dr. Walter Munk, of Mount Carmel, Haifa, and has issue.

Residence,—25, Donne Place, SW3.

SONS LIVING.

Hon. John, *b.* 1940.   *Hon.* Graham Anthony, *b.* 1948.
Hon. Dudley Walter Gordon, *b.* 1946.

DAUGHTER LIVING.

Hon. Caroline Margaret Alyson, *b.* 1950.

WINTERTON, EARL. (Turnour.) [Earl I. 1766.]
[Name pronounced "Turner."]

To be, rather than seem to be.

ROBERT CHAD TURNOUR, 7th Earl (has not yet proved his Peerage by establishing his right to vote at an election for Irish Representative Peers); *b.* Sept. 13th, 1915; *s.* 1962; ed. at Nutana Coll.; Flight-Sergeant, Roy. Canadian Air Force; with Canadian N.A.T.O. Force Sqdn., Sardinia 1957-58; 1939-45 War: *m.* 1st, 1941, Kathleen Ella, who *d.* 1969, da. of D. B. Whyte, of Saskatoon, Saskatchewan, Canada; 2ndly, 1971, Marion Eleanor, da. of the late Arthur Phillips, of Stirling, Ont., Canada.

Arms.—Ermines, on a cross quarterly, pierced argent, four fers de moline sable. *Crest.*—A lion passant guardant argent, holding in the dexter fore paw a fer de moline, sable. *Supporters.*—Two lions argent, semée of fers de moline, sable.
Residence,—1356-55th St., Delta, BC, Canada.

BROTHER LIVING.

CECIL NOEL, *DFM, CD, b.* Dec. 11th, 1919; ed. at Nutana Coll. and at Saskatchewan Univ.; late Fl.-Lt., Roy. Canadian Air Force: *m.* 1941, Evelyn Isobel, da. of J. C. A. Oulton, of Saskatoon, Saskatchewan, Canada, and has issue living, Donald David, *b.* 1943: *m.* 1968, Jill Pauline, da. of J. Esplan, of RR2, Prescott, Ont.,—Robert, *b.* 1950,—Murray John, *b.* 1951.

SISTER LIVING.

Margaret Ethel, b. 1917: m. 1939, Donald S. McGeary, of 58. St. Andrews Court Aurora, Ont., Canada, and has issue living, Donald Garth, b. 1941,—Robert Wayne, b. 1944,—Hugh Gordon, b. 1951: m. 1974, Karen Louise, da. of Walter Warms, of 56, Thatcher Drive, Winnipeg, Canada,—James Douglas, b. 1954,—Wendy Louise, b. 1948: m. 1968, Miles Stanton Cullum, of 225, Conway St., Winnipeg, Man., Canada.

COLLATERAL BRANCHES LIVING.

Grandchildren of the late Emily Isabella Turnour (who m. 1870, Capt. William George England, RN), da. of the late Hon. Heys Turnour, 2nd son of 3rd Earl:—
Issue of the late Capt. George Plunkett England, RN, b. 1877, d. 1956: m. 1904, Hilda, Dingwall, who d. 1963:—
Frances Margaret, b. 1910: m. 1935, Capt. William Alexander Dallmeyer, DSO, RN, of Ashleigh, Tavistock, Devon, and has issue living, Charles William, b. 1938: m. 1964, Charlotte Rosalind Makin, and has issue living, Rebecca Charlotte b. 1965, Louisa Jane b 1967,—Sophie Elizabeth b. 1969,—Joanna Margaret, b. 1945.——Elizabeth Ruth (Ashleigh, Tavistock, Devon), b. 1916.

Issue of the late Capt. Richard Bruce England, DSO, RN, b. 1883, d. 1959: m. 1915, Dorothea Katherine, who d. 1967, da. of the late Alexander Felix Clarke, JP, of Midgham House Berks:—
Richard Michael, TD, (Ferrises, Upper Woolhampton, Reading), b. 1918; late Maj. Berks. Yeo.: m. 1949, Diana Mary, da. of the late Olive Uzielli, MC, and has issue living, Richard Bruce Plunkett, b. 1951,—William Anthony, b. 1954.

Issue of the late Emily Isabella England (ante):—
Hugh Turnour, CB, DSO, b. 1884; Rear Adm. (ret.): m. 1918, Alice Marian, who d. 1968, da. of the late Rev. Claypon Bellingham [Bellingham, Bt., colls.], and has issue living, David Alan Claypon b. 1924; late Sub-Lt. RNVR,—Marian Joy, b. 1918: m. 1950, David Workman, and has issue living, Andrew David Hugh b. 1955, Ian William George b. 1958, Caroline Joy b. 1951, Rosemary Susan b. 1952,—Katharine Zoë, b. 1921.

Grandchildren of the late John Horatio Turnour, 5th son of the late Rev. the Hon. Adolphus Augustus Turnour, 3rd son of 2nd Earl:—
Issue of the late Keppel Arthur Turnour, b. 1856, d. 1930: m. 1878, Margaret, who d. 1901, dau. of the late C. C. Wallace, of Greenbank, Isle of Bute:—
Donald Winterton, b. 1883.——James Owen, b. 1884.——Keppel Ernest, b. 1885.——Alice, b. 1881. m. 1910, Cecil Henry Henty.——Sybil Ruth, b. 1890. Residence,—

Issue of the late Edward Edmund Hewitt Turnour, b. 1864, d. 1915: m. 1900, Mary Ann, dau. of Duncan C. Milne, of Adelaide, S. Australia:—
Marjorie Balman Winterton, b. 1906. Residence,—

PREDECESSORS.—[1] EDWARD TURNOUR Garth|assumed in 1744 by Roy. licence the surname of Turnour; cr. Baron Winterton, of Gort, co. Galway (peerage of Ireland) 1761, and Viscount Turnour and Earl Winterton (peerage of Ireland) 1766; d. 1788; s. by his son [2] EDWARD Turnour, 2nd Earl; d. 1831; s. by his son [3] EDWARD, 3rd Earl; d. 1833; s. by his son [4] EDWARD, 4th Earl; b. 1810: m. 1832, Maria, who d. 1904, dau. of Sir Peter Pole, 2nd Bt.; d. 1879; s. by his son [5] EDWARD, 5th Earl; b. 1837: m-1882, Lady Georgiana Susan Hamilton, who d. 1913, dau. of 1st Duke of Abercorn, K.G.; d. 1907; s. by his only son [6] EDWARD, T.D., P.C., 6th Earl, b. 1883; Major T.A. Reserve, Sussex Yeo.; Under-Sec. of State for India 1922-4, and 1924-29, Chancellor of Duchy of Lancaster 1937-9, Dep. Sec. of State for Air, and Vice-Pres. of Air Council 1938, Assist. to Home Sec. 1938-9, and Paymaster Gen. 1939; M.P. for Horsham Div. of Sussex (C) 1904-18, for Horsham and Worthing Div. 1918-45, and for W. Sussex 1945-51; cr. Baron Turnour (peerage of U.K.) 1952: m. 1924, the Hon. Cecilia Monica Wilson, who d. 1974, da. of 2nd Baron Nunburnholme; d. 1962, when the UK Barony (cr. 1952) became ext.; s. by his kinsman [7] ROBERT CHAD (el. son of Cecil Turnour, grandson of Charles Chad Turnour, el. son of the Rev. the Hon. Adolphus Augustus Turnour, 3rd son of 2nd Earl), 7th Earl, and present peer; also Viscount Turnour and Baron Winterton.

Winton, Earl of, title borne by Earl of Eglinton.

WISE, BARON. (Wise.) [Baron U.K. 1951.]

JOHN CLAYTON WISE, 2nd Baron; b. June 11th, 1923; s. 1968; a Farmer: m. 1946, Margaret Annie, da. of Frederick Victor Snead, of Banbury, and has issue.
    Residence,—Ramsley Farm, North Elmham, Norfolk.　Club,—Farmers'.

SONS LIVING.

Hon. CHRISTOPHER JOHN CLAYTON, b. March 19th, 1948; ed. at Norwich Sch. and Southampton Univ. (B.Sc. hons).
Hon. Martin Highfield, b. 1950; ed. at Norwich Sch. and Bristol Univ. (MB, ChB).

SISTERS LIVING.

Hon. Joan Mary, b. 1912: m. 1938, John Reginald Wood, and has issue living, Michael George, b. 1939,—David Clayton, b. 1946,—Roger John, b. 1947,—Mary Janet, b. 1941. Residence,—Ham Farm, Berrow, Burnham-on-Sea, Somerset.
Hon. Jean Phyllis, b. 1914: m. 1939, Lieut.-Col. John Patrick Turrill, O.B.E., T.D., R.A., and has issue living, John Ewen, b. 1948,—Judith Elizabeth, b. 1946,—Ruth Eleanor, b. 1947. Residence,—94, Albert Rd., Caversham, Reading.
Hon. Eileen Ellen, b. 1916: m. 1940, Sq. Ldr. Gerald Edmund Hastings, RAF, and has issue living, Tanera, b. 1943: m. 19—,—Eileen Mary, b. 1948,—Bridget Talmine, b. 1950. Residence,—

WIDOW LIVING OF FIRST BARON.

KATE ELIZABETH (Kate, Baroness Wise), (The Great Wood Cottage, N. Elmham, Norfolk), da. of the late John Michael Sturgeon, of Horringer, Bury St. Edmunds: m. 1911, the 1st Baron, who d. 1968.

PREDECESSOR.—[1] FREDERICK JOHN Wise, son of Edward Wise, of Bury St. Edmunds; b. 1887; MP for King's Lynn (Lab.) 1945-51; cr. Baron Wise, of King's Lynn, co. Norfolk (peerage of UK); 1951: m. 1911, Kate Elizabeth, da. of John Michael Sturgeon, of Horringer, Bury St. Edmunds; d. 1968; s. by his son [2] JOHN CLAYTON, 2nd Baron, and present peer.

Wodehouse, Baron, son of Earl of Kimberley.

WOLFENDEN, BARON. (Wolfenden.) [Life Baron 1974.]

JOHN FREDERICK WOLFENDEN, *CBE*, son of the late George Wolfenden, of Bournemouth; *b*. June 26th, 1902; ed. at Wakefield Sch., and Queen's Coll., Oxford (MA); Fellow and Tutor of Magdalen Coll., Oxford 1929-34, Headmaster of Uppingham Sch. 1934-44, and of Shrewsbury Sch. 1944-50; Vice-Chancellor of Reading Univ. 1950-63; Chm. of Headmaster's Conference 1945, 1946 and 1949, of Departmental Cttee. on Homosexual Offences and Prostitution 1954-57, of Board for Social Responsibility 1957-60, and of Univ. Grants Cttee. 1963-68, Dir. and Prin. Librarian British Museum 1968-73; Dir. of Pre-Entry Training, Air Min. 1941, Chm. of Board of Education of Youth Advisory Council 1942-45; cr. CBE (Civil) 1942, Knt. 1956, and *Baron Wolfenden*, of Westcott, Co. of Surrey (Life Baron) 1974: *m*. 1932, Eileen Le Messurier, 2nd da. of A. J. Spilsbury, and has issue.

Arms,—Not exemplified at time of going to press.

Residence,—The White House, Westcott, nr. Dorking, Surrey. *Club,*—Athenaeum.

SON LIVING.
Hon. Daniel Mark (44, Mortimer St., W1), *b*. 1942: *m*. 1972, Sally Frankel.
DAUGHTERS LIVING.
Hon. Priscilla, *b*. 1937: *m*. 1959, Col. F. L. Dainty, of Garderhouse, Whalsay, Shetland Isles.
Hon. Deborah, *b*. 1943: *m*. 1966, Frank Eveleigh, of 82, Rotherfield Way, Caversham, Kent, and has issue.

Wolmer, Viscount, grandson of Earl of Selborne.

WOLVERTON, BARON. (Glyn.) [Baron U.K. 1869.]

NIGEL REGINALD VICTOR GLYN, 5th Baron; *b*. June 23rd, 1904; *s*. 1932; ed. at Eton; is Capt. R.A. (T.A.) and patron of one living.

Arms.—Argent, an eagle displayed with two heads sable, guttée d'or. **Crest,**—An eagle's head, erased sable, guttée d'or; in the beak an escallop argent. **Supporters,**—On either side an eagle with wings elevated sable, guttée d'or, gorged with a collar gemel or, and holding in the beak an escallop argent.

Residence,—Queensberry House, Newmarket, Suffolk.

Firm to my trust.

SISTER LIVING.
Hon. Esmé Consuelo Helen, *OBE* (*Baroness Rhyl*), *b*. 1908; Regional Administrator, N. Midland Civil Defence Region, Women's Vol. Sers. during 1939-45 War; OBE (Civil) 1946: *m*. 1950, Baron Rhyl (Life Baron). *Residences,*—Holywell House, Swanmore, Hants.; 73, Ashley Gdns., SW1.

COLLATERAL BRANCHES LIVING.

Grandchildren of the late Maurice Carr Glyn (*infra*):—
Issue of the late Sir Francis Maurice Grosvenor Glyn, KCMG, *b*. 1901, *d*. 1969: *m*. 1st 1926, (m. diss. 1937), Jane, who *d*. 1964, da. of William Perkins, of Seattle, USA; 2ndly, 1941, Mary Elspeth, who *d*. 1966, da. of the late Tom Garnett, of Waddow Hall, Clitheroe, and formerly wife of the late Kenneth James Milln:—
(By 1st m.) JEREMY CHRISTOPHER (The Bury, Little Hadham, Herts.), *b*. Oct. 1st, 1930; ed. at Eton, and Worcester Coll., Oxford (MA): *m*. 1956, Robina Elspeth, da. of Sir George Arthur Harford, 2nd Bt., and has issue living, Lucinda Mary, *b*. 1958.——Pamela Jane (9, The Green, Green Close, Borrowdale, Salisbury, Rhodesia), *b*. 1928: *m*. 1950 (m. diss. 1972), Geoffrey Pooley, and has issue living, Alexander Pascoe, *b*. 1951,—Hilary John, *b*. 1953.

Grandchildren of the late Hon. Pascoe Charles Glyn, 6th son of 1st Baron:—
Issue of the late Maurice George Carr Glyn, *b*. 1872, *d*. 1920: *m*. 1897, the Hon. Maud Grosvenor, who *d*. 1948, dau. of 2nd Baron Ebury:—
John Patrick Riversdale, *CBE*, *b*. 1913; ed. at Eton, and at New Coll., Oxford; is Maj. Grenadier Gds.; 1939-45 War (wounded); CBE (Civil) 1974: *m*. 1937, Audrey Margaret, da. of the late Richard Stubbs, of Haseley Manor, Oxford, and has issue living, Christopher Richard (51, Kingston House North, SW7), *b*. 1938; ed. at Eton; FRICS: *m*. 1st, 1961 (m. diss. 1967), Carolyn Jane, yr. da. of Antony N. Hunter, of 33, Brompton Sq., SW7; 2ndly, 1975, Mrs. Frances S. E. Stuart Black, and has issue living (by 1st m.), Sara-Jane *b*. 1963, Amanda Camilla *b*. 1966,—Andrew John (58, Lonsdale Rd., Oxford) *b*. 1943; ed. at Eton, and New Coll., Oxford (MA); Fellow of Corpus Christi Coll., Oxford: *m*. 1965, Celia Laws, and has issue living, Miles John *b*. 1966, Lucy Abigail *b*. 1968,—Susan, *b*. 1940: *m*. 1962, Nicholas G. Mills, of Lower House, Little Barrington, Burford, Oxon., and has issue living, Charlotte Sophia *b*. 1964, Maria Louise Greenaway *b*. 1967,—Joanna Caroline, *b*. 1955. *Residence,*—The Dower House, Chute Standen, Andover.——Hilary Beaujolais, *b*. 1916; ed. at Eton; Capt. RASC; Assist. Managing Dir. of Gallaher, Ltd.: *m*. 1938, Caroline, da. of William Perkins Bull, QC, of Lorne Hall, Rosedale, Toronto, Canada, and has issue living, James Hilary (57, Lower Straithe, Hartington Rd., W4), *b*. 1939: *m*. 1964, Lucinda March, da. of Wing-Cdr. Gordon Haywood, RAF [see E. Darnley], and has issue living, Casper *b*. 1969, Marina Jane *b*. 1966,—Ann, *b*. 1941; has discontinued use of Christian name of Caroline: *m*. 1968, Padmanabh Vijai Pillai,—Sarah GLYN *b*. 1948; has resumed her maiden name of Glyn 1971: *m*. 1967 (m. diss. 1971), Richard Patrick King. *Residence,*—Oakum House, Albury, Ware, Herts.

Granddaughter of the late Maurice George Carr Glyn (ante):—

Issue of the late Pascoe Anthony George Glyn, *b.* 1911, *d.* 1935: *m.* 1934, Katharine Florita (who *m.* 2ndly, 1936, Patrick Lort-Phillips, Lieut. Grenadier Guards, of Knowles Farm, Lawrenny, Kilgetty, Pembrokeshire), dau. of the late Lieut.-Col. Arthur Morton Grenfell, DSO [V. Cobham, colls.]:—

Mary Georgiana, *b.* 1935: *m.* 1954 (marriage dissolved 1963), Lt.-Cdr. John William Talbot Lewes RN [see E. Shrewsbury, colls.]:—

Issue of the late Right Rev. the Hon. Edward Carr Glyn, D.D., 9th son of 1st Baron, *b.* 1843, *d.* 1928: *m.* 1882, Lady Mary Emma Campbell, who *d.* 1947, dau. of 8th Duke of Argyll:—

Margaret Isabel Frances (*Hon. Lady Meade-Fetherstonhaugh*) (Clive Lodge, Albury, Surrey), *b.* 1888, *m.* 1911, Adm. the Hon. Sir Herbert Meade-Fetherstonhaugh, GCVO, CB, DSO, who *d.* 1964 [see E. Clanwilliam].

PREDECESSORS.—[1] George Carr Glyn, 4th son of Sir Richard Carr Glyn, 1st Bt.; *b.* 1797; was a partner in the banking house of Glyn, Mills, Currie and Co., and Chairman of the London and North Western Railway; cr. *Baron Wolverton*, of Wolverton, co. Bucks (peerage of United Kingdom) 1869: *m.* 1823, Marianne, dau. of the late Pascoe Grenfell, of Taplow Court, Bucks; *d.* 1873; *s.* by his son [2] George Grenfell, *P.C.*, 2nd Baron, *b.* 1824; sat as M.P. for Shaftesbury (*L*) 1857-73, and was successively Joint Sec. to Treasury, Paymaster-Gen., and Postmaster-Gen.: *m.* 1848, Georgiana Maria, who *d.* 1894, dau. of the Rev. George Tufnell, of Uffington, Berks; *d.* 1887; *s.* by his nephew [3] Henry Richard, 3rd Baron, *b.* 1861: *d.s.p.* 1888: *s.* by his brother [4] Frederic, 4th Baron, *b.* 1864; a partner in the Metropolitan banking firm of Glyn, Mills and Co.; a Lord-in-Waiting to Queen Victoria 1891-3, and Vice-Chamberlain of the Household to King Edward VII. 1902-5: *m.* 1895, Lady Edith Amelia Ward, *C.B.E.*, who *d.* 1956, dau. of 1st Earl of Dudley; *d.* 1932; *s.* by his son [5] Nigel Reginald Victor, 5th Baron and present peer.

WOODBRIDGE, BARONY OF. (Churchman.) [Extinct 1949.]

DAUGHTER LIVING OF FIRST BARON.

Hon. Vera Kate, *b.* 1913: *m.* 1936, Peter William Barnett, and has issue living, Garry Charles (c/o Barclays Bank, 1, Pall Mall E., SW1) *b.* 1939; Maj. Black Watch: *m.* 1969, Margaret Jennifer, yr. da. of the late T. M. Banks of Solai, Kenya, and has issue living, Robert William *b.* 1971,—Isla Jane, *b.* 1940: *m.* 1967, Thomas Gordon R. Cook, of Home Farm, Poulton, Cirencester, Glos., and has issue living, James Thomas *b.* 1969, Andrew Charles *b.* 1972. *Residence,*—Campsie Hill, Guildtown, nr. Perth.

WOOLAVINGTON, BARONY OF. (Buchanan.) [Extinct 1935.]

DAUGHTER LIVING OF FIRST BARON.

Hon. Catherine (*Hon. Lady Macdonald-Buchanan*), *b.* 1895: OStJ: *m.* 1922, Maj. Sir Reginald Narcissus Macdonald-Buchanan, KCVO, MBE, MC (who assumed by deed poll 1922 the additional name of Buchanan), late Scots Guards, and has issue living, John, *MC* (The Stone House, Lower Swells, Stow-on-the-Wold, Glos. *Clubs,*—Bucks', Turf, Whites), *b.* 1925; ed. at Eton; Capt. (ret.) Scots Gds.; NW Europe 1944-45 (wounded) Malaya 1948-50: *m.* 1st, 1950 (m. diss. 1969) Lady Rose Fane, da. of 14th Earl of Westmorland; 2ndly, 1969, Jill Rosamonde, da. of Maj.-Gen. Cecil Benfield Fairbanks, CB, OBE, and formerly wife of Jonathan William Salusbury-Trelawny [see Salusbury, Trelawny, Bt., colls.], and has issue living, (by 1st m.) Alastair Reginald *b.* 1960, Fiona Mary *b.* 1954: *m.* 1975, Nigel Douglas Pilkington, Serena *b.* 1956, (by 2nd m.) Kate Charlotte *b.* 1970,—Lucy Rosamonde *b.* 1972,—Alexander James (Baynton House, Coulston, Westbury, Wilts.), *b.* 1931: *m.* 1960, Elizabeth Vivian, da. of the Hon. Hugh Adeane Vivian Smith, MBE [see B. Bicester], and has issue living, Hugh James *b.* 1961, James Iain *b.* 1963, Nicholas Mark *b.* 1967, Charles Alexander *b.* 1970,—Jean Catherine, *b.* (Oct.) 1922: *m.* 1947, Maj. Roger Humphreys, late Gren. Gds., of Tarrant Gunville Manor, Blandford Forum, Dorset,—Mary Cynthia Anne, *b.* 1934: *m.* 1958, Maj. Christopher R. Philipson, late Life Gds., of Lofts Hall, Saffron Walden, Essex, and has issue living, Caroline Mary *b.* 1959, Joanna Catherine *b.* 1961. *Residences,*—Cottesbrooke Hall, Northampton; Egerton House, Newmarket, Suffolk; Scatwell, Muir-of-Ord, Ross-shire.

WOOLLEY, BARON (Woolley.) [Life Baron 1967.]

Harold Woolley, *CBE,* son of William Woolley, JP, of Blackburn, Lancs.; *b.* Feb. 6th, 1905; ed. at Blackburn Gram. Sch., Woodhouse Grove Sch., Yorks., and Lancs Sch. of Agric.; DL of Cheshire; Vice-Pres. NFU of England and Wales 1948, and again 1955, Dep. Pres. 1949-50, and again 1956, Chm. of Parl. Cttee. 1948-57, of Employers' Representatives Agricultural Wages Board for England and Wales 1950-57, and of Agricultural Apprenticeship Council of England and Wales 1951-60, and President of NFU 1960-66; cr. CBE (Civil) 1958, Knt. 1964, and *Baron Woolley,* of Hatton, co. Palatine of Chester (Life Peerage) 1967: *m.* 1st, 1926,

Martha Annie, who *d.* 1936, da. of William Jeffs, of Helsby, Cheshire; 2ndly, 1937, Hazel Eileen, who *d.* 1975, da. of Thomas Archer Jones, of Chirk, Denbighshire, and has issue by 1st and 2nd m.

Residence,—Hatton House, Hatton Heath, Cheshire. *Club,*—Farmers'.

SONS LIVING. (*By 1st marriage.*)

Hon. William Graham (Hatton Hall, Hatton Heath, Cheshire), *b.* 1927: *m.* 1955, Joan, who *d.* 1974, da. of Ralph Thomas Rowlands, of Connah's Quay, Flintshire, and has issue.

Hon. Harold Ewart (1350, Laurier Av., Vancouver, BC, Canada), *b.* 1929; MD, FRCS(C): *m.* 1954, Margaret, yr. da. of Alderman T. S. Bennett, JP, of Worcester, and has issue.

Hon. David Jeffs (3050, Spencer Drive, W. Vancouver, BC, Canada), *b.* 1934; NDA: *m.* 1958, Freda Constance, da. of Alfred W. S. Walker, of Barrow-in-Furness, and has issue.

Hon. Peter Jeffs (2660, Queens Av., W. Vancouver, BC, Canada), (twin), *b.* 1934: MA, CA: *m.* 1960, Lois, da. of Edward Chanter, of Tiverton, Devon, and has issue.

DAUGHTERS LIVING. (*By 2nd marriage.*)

Hon. Hazel Eleanor, *b.* 1938: *m.* 1961, William David Harper, MB, BChir., of Queens Corner, Hoylake, Cheshire, and has issue.

Hon. Christine Maralyn, *b.* 1946: *m.* 1970, Barrie Scott Morgan, BSc, PhD, of 17, Amesbury Rd., Epping, Essex.

WOOLTON, EARL OF. (Marquis.) [Earl U.K. 1956.]

By fortitude and courage it shall be given.

SIMON FREDERICK MARQUIS, 3rd Earl, *b.* May 24th, 1958; *s.* 1969.

Arms—Sable, on a bend engrailed between two garbs or a rose gules barbed and seeded proper between two lions rampant of the field. Crest,—Suspended from and between the antlers of a stag proper a stirrup and leather. Supporters,—On either side a lion rampant or, gorged with a riband azure, pendent therefrom by a chain also or, an escutcheon azure charged with a liver bird argent.

Residences,—31, Tite St., SW3; Strone House, Bridge of Cally, Blairgowrie, Perthshire.

SISTER LIVING.

Lady Alexandra Susan, *b.* 1961.

AUNT LIVING.
(*Daughter of 1st Earl.*)

Lady Margaret Judith, *TD* (6, Egerton Terr., SW3), *b.* 1917; formerly Junior Com. ATS: *m.* 1945, Maj. John Hele Sandeman-Allen, RA, who *d.* 1958, and has issue living, Charles James, *b.* 1954,—Judith Sandeman (70, Walton St., SW3 2HH), *b.* 1947: *m.* 1947 (m. diss. 1973), George Hugh Pigot [see Pigot, Bt., colls.].—Hilary Sandeman, *b.* 1949: *m.* 1973, Donald William Robertson Boyd, and has issue living, Clare Sandeman *b.* 1974.

WIDOWS LIVING OF FIRST AND SECOND EARLS.

MARGARET ELUNED MB, ChB (*Countess of Woolton*) (The Old Vicarage, Walberton, Arundel, Sussex), only da. of Richard Thomas: *m.* 1962, as his 2nd wife, the 1st Earl, who *d.* 1964.

CECILY JOSEPHINE (Strone House, Bridge of Cally, Blairgowrie, Perthshire; 3, Tite St., SW3), da. of Maj. Sir Alexander Penrose Gordon-Cumming, MC, 5th Bt.: *m.* 1st, 1957, as his 2nd wife, the 2nd Earl, who *d.* 1969; 2ndly, 1969 (m. diss. 1974), the 3rd Baron Forres.

PREDECESSORS.—[1] *Sir* FREDERICK JAMES Marquis, *CH, PC,* son of Thomas Robert Marquis, of Liverpool; *b.* 1883; Chm. of Lewis's Investment Trust and Asso. Cos. 1936 and Hon. Pres.; Min. of Food 1940-43, Min. of Reconstruction 1943-45, Lord Pres. of Council May to July 1945, and 1951-52, and Chancellor of Duchy of Lancaster 1952-55 (and Min. of Materials 1953-54); Chm. of Conservative Party 1946-55; Chancellor of Manchester Univ. 1944-64; *cr. Baron Woolton,* of Liverpool, co. Lancaster (peerage of U.K.) 1939, *Viscount Woolton,* of Liverpool, co. Lancaster (peerage of U.K.) 1953, and *Earl of Woolton,* and *Viscount Walberton,* of Walberton, co. Sussex (peerage of U.K.) 1956: *m.* 1st, 1912, Maud, who *d.* 1961, da. of Thomas Smith of Manchester; 2ndly, 1962, Margaret Eluned, MB, ChB, only da. of Richard Thomas; *d.* 1964; *s.* by his only son [2] ROGER DAVID, 2nd Earl, *b.* 1922: *m.* 1st, 1946 (m. diss. 1953), the Hon. Lucia Edith Lawson, only da. of 4th Baron Burnham; 2ndly, 1957, Cecily Josephine, (who m. 2ndly, 1969 (m. diss. 1974) the 3rd Baron, Forres) da. of Maj. Sir Alexander Penrose Gordon-Cumming, MC, 5th Bt.; *d.* 1969; *s.* by his only son [3] SIMON FREDERICK, 3rd Earl and present peer; also Viscount Woolton, Viscount Walberton, and Baron Woolton.

WOOTTON OF ABINGER, BARONESS. (Wootton.) [Life Baroness 1958.]

BARBARA FRANCES WOOTTON, dau. of the late Dr. James Adam ; *b.* April 14th 1897; ed. at Perse High Sch. for Girls, Camb., and at Girton Coll., Camb. (MA); Hon. LHD Columbia Univ.; Hon. LLD Liverpool, Nottingham, Hull, York and Aberdeen; Hon DSc, Aston, Birmingham, and Bath; Hon. D.Soc.Sc. Southampton; Prof. of Social, Studies, Univ. of London 1948-52, a Gov. of BBC 1950-56, and Nuffield Research Fellow, Bedford Coll., London 1952-57; JP for co. London 1926-70 (Chm. of Metropolitan Juvenile Courts 1944-62); Chm. of National Parks Commn. since 1966, and Countryside Commn. 1968-69; after her second marriage continued to be known by the surname of Wootton; *cr. Baroness Wootton of Abinger,* of Abinger Common, co. Surrey (Life Baroness) 1958: *m.* 1st 1917, John Wesley Wootton, who *d.* 1917; 2ndly, 1935, George Percival Wright, who *d.* 1964.

Residence,—High Barn, Abinger Common, Dorking, Surrey.

WORCESTER, LORD BISHOP OF. (Woods.)

Rt. Rev. ROBERT WILMER WOODS, *KCVO*, son of the late Rt. Rev. Edward Sydney Woods, DD, Lord Bishop of Lichfield; *b.* Feb. 15th, 1914; ed. at Gresham's Sch., Holt, and Trin. Coll., Camb. (MA); Chap. to the Forces 1942-46 (despatches); V. of S. Wigston, Leicester 1946-51, Archdeacon of Singapore, and V. of St. Andrew's Cathedral Singapore 1951-58, Archdeacon of Sheffield and R. of Tankersley, Yorks. 1958-62, and Dean of Windsor, and Domestic Chap. to HM 1962-70; consecrated 110th Bishop of Worcester 1971; a Member of Council of Duke of Edinburgh's Award Scheme and of Public Schs. Commn. 1968; Dir. of Christian Aid 1969; Chm. of Church's Television Centre since 1969; Prelate of Order of St. Michael and St. George since 1971; KCVO 1971: *m.* 1942, Henrietta Marion, JP, da. of Kenneth Henry Wilson, OBE, JP, and has issue.

Patron of sixty-six livings, of seven alternately with others, and the Archdeaconries of Dudley and Worcester, and eighteen Hon. Canonries.

This See was founded by Ethelred, King of the Mercians, in 679.

Episcopal Signature:—" Robin Worcester."

ARMS OF THE SEE,—Argent, ten torteaux, four, three, two and one.

Residence,—The Bishop's House, Hartlebury Castle, Kidderminster, Worcs.

Worlingham, Baron, title of Earl of Gosford on Roll of H.L.

Worsley, Baron, son of Earl of Yarborough.

WRAXALL, BARON. (Gibbs.) [Baron U.K. 1928.]

GEORGE RICHARD LAWLEY GIBBS, 2nd Baron; *b.* May 16th, 1928: *s.* 1931; ed. at Eton, and RMA; late Maj. N. Somerset and Bristol Yeo., and late Lt. Coldstream Guards.

Arms,—Argent, three battle-axes erect sable within a bordure nebuly of the last. *Crest,*—A dexter arm embowed in armour, the hand in a gauntlet proper bearing a battle-axe bendwise sinister sable. *Supporters,*—On either side a St. Kilda sheep proper, each charged on the shoulder with a portcullis chained or.

Seat,—Tyntesfield, Bristol. *Clubs,*—Royal Automobile, Cavalry.

BROTHER LIVING.

Hon. EUSTACE HUBERT BEILBY (Coddenham House, Coddenham, nr. Ipswich; Pratt's and Brooks's Clubs), *b.* July 3rd, 1929; ed. at Eton, and at Ch. Ch., Oxford: *m.* 1957, Evelyn Veronica, only da. of the late S. K. Scott, of Reydon Grove Farm, Southwold, Suffolk, and has issue living, Antony Hubert, *b.* 1958,—Andrew Christopher, *b.* 1965,—Jonathan Charles William, *b.* 1969, Miranda Caroline, *b.* 1961,—Alexandra Mary Henrietta, *b.* 1971.

HALF-SISTER LIVING.

Hon. Doreen Albinia de Burgh, *b.* 1913: *m.* 1937, Charles Bathurst Norman, Bar.-at-Law, and has issue living, George Alfred Bathurst (14, Bloomfield Terr., SW1), *b.* 1939; Bar. Inner Temple 1961: *m.* 1st, 1967 (m. diss. 1967), Prudence Veronica, da. of F. H. Keenlyside, of Salisbury, Rhodesia; 2ndly, 1973, Susan Elizabeth, da. of James Ball, of 46, Park Av., Bromley, Kent,— Victoria Mary (Brundon Farm, Sudbury, Suffolk), *b.* 1940: *m.* 1961 (m. diss. 1967), Raymond Edward Barthorp, late Capt. Northamptonshire Regt., and has issue living, Nicola Vivien *b.* 1964. *Residence,*—Villa Villetri, Vallée des Vaux, Jersey.

Tenacious of purpose.

WIDOW LIVING OF FIRST BARON.

URSULA MARY (*Baroness Wraxall*), *OBE, RRC,* da. of 6th Baron Wenlock; a Maid of Honour to H.M. the Queen 1912-27; Regional Representative, S.-W. Region, of British Red Cross Soc. 1942-46; now Pres. Somerset branch; a Serving Sister of Order of St. John of Jerusalem; OBE (Civil) 1945: *m.* 1927, as his second wife, the 1st Baron, who *d.* 1931. *Residence,*—Tyntesfield, Bristol.

PREDECESSOR.—[1] *Rt. Hon.* GEORGE ABRAHAM Gibbs, el. son of the late Antony Gibbs, of Tyntesfield, Bristol, and 16, Hyde Park Gardens, W.; *b.* 1873; was Parliamentary Private Sec. to Sec. of State for the Colonies (Rt. Hon. W. H. Long, M.P.) and a Govt. Whip in House of Commons 1917-21, and Treasurer of H.M.'s Household April 1921 to Jan. 1924 and Nov. 1924 to Jan. 1928 ; M.P. for W. Div. of Bristol (*U*) Jan. 1906 to Jan. 1928 ; cr. P.C. 1923, and *Baron Wraxall*, of Clyst St. George, co. Devon (peerage of United Kingdom) 1928 : *m.* 1st, 1901, Victoria Florence de Burgh Long, *C.B.E.*, who *d.* 1920, el. dau. of the Rt. Hon. Walter Hume Long, M.P. (afterwards 1st Viscount Long of Wraxall) ; 2ndly, 1927, the Hon. Ursula Mary Lawley, *R.R.C.*, dau. of 6th Baron Wenlock ; *d.* 1931 ; *s.* by his son [2] GEORGE RICHARD LAWLEY, 2nd Baron and present peer.

WRENBURY, BARON. (Buckley.) [Baron U.K. 1915.]

JOHN BURTON BUCKLEY, 3rd Baron; *b.* June 18th, 1927; *s.* 1940; ed. at Eton, and at King's Coll., Camb. (MA); Solicitor 1952; a partner in the legal firm of Freshfields, of Grindall House, 25, Newgate St., EC1 1956-74, since when of Thomson Snell & Passmore, of 3, Lonsdale Gdns., Tunbridge Wells; Assist. Legal Adviser to National Trust 1955-56: *m.* 1st, 1956 (m. diss. 1961), Carolyn Joan Maule, da. of Col. Ian Burn-Murdoch, OBE, of Gartincaber, Doune, Perthshire; 2ndly, 1961, Penelope Sara Frances, da. of Edward Fort, of The White House, Sixpenny Handley, Dorset, and has issue by 2nd m.

Arms,—Azure, a chevron cottised between two stags' heads cabossed in chief and a garb in base all or, on a chief engrailed ermine a buckle between two crosses patée fitchée gules. *Crest,*—On a mount vert a demi-stag at gaze gules, attired and gorged with a collar, a chain attached reflexed over the back or, supporting a garb of the last. *Supporters,*—On either side a buck at gaze gules, collared, attired, and chained or.

Residence,—Oldcastle, Dallington, near Heathfield, Sussex. *Club*—Oriental.

SON LIVING. (*By 2nd marriage.*)

Hon. WILLIAM EDWARD, *b.* June 19th, 1966.

DAUGHTERS LIVING. (*By 2nd marriage.*)

Hon. Elizabeth Margaret, *b.* 1964.

Hon. Katherine Lucy, *b.* 1968.

SISTER LIVING.

Hon. Mary Graham, *b.* 1929: *m.* 1961, John Richard Seymour Homan, of 30, High St., Ticehurst, Sussex, and has issue living, Robert Seymour, *b.* 1964,—Frances Mary, *b.* 1967,—Rosalind Clare, *b.* 1969.

UNCLES LIVING. (*Sons of 1st Baron.*)

Hon. Colin Burton, *MB, BCh., b.* 1899; ed. at Eton, and at King's Coll., Camb. (BA 1922, MA, 1927, MB, BCh, 1927): *m.* 1925, Evelyn Joyce, da. of Hugh C. Webster, of Lea House, Harpenden, Herts, and has issue living, Martin Christopher Burton, (3, New Sq., Lincoln's Inn, WC2,) *b.* 1936: *m.* 1964, Victoria Gay, da. of Dr. Stanhope Furber, of Oak Cottage, Bracknell, Berks., and 14, Wimpole St., W1, and has issue living, Arthur Burton *b.* 1967, Hannah Kate *b,* 1965, Amanda Victoria *b.* 1968, Jessica Beth *b.* 1971,—Bridget Elizabeth, *b.* 1929,—Jessica Margaret, *b.* 1932,—Alison Rachel, *b.* 1933: *m.* 1959, Benjamin Fisher,—Hazel, *b.* 1934. *Residence,*—Greenstead, Windermere, Westmorland.

Rt. Hon. Lord Justice (*Sir* Denys Burton), *MBE, b.* 1906; ed. at Eton, and at Trin. Coll., Oxford (MA, Hon. Fellow); Bar. Lincoln's Inn 1928, and a Bencher 1949; Pro-Treasurer Lincoln's Inn 1967, and Treasurer 1969; Master, Merchant Taylors' Co. 1972; a CStJ; Junior Treasury Counsel 1949-60, and a Judge of High Court of Justice (Chancery Div.) 1960-70, since when a Lord Justice of Appeal; a Judge of Restrictive Practices Court 1962-70 (Pres. 1968-70), a Member of Law Reform Cttee. since 1963, and Pres. of Senate of four Inns of Court 1970-72; has American Medal of Freedom; 1939-45 War as Maj. RAOC; MBE (Mil) 1945; Knt. 1960; PO 1970: *m.* 1932, Gwendolen Jane, da. of the late Sir Robert Armstrong-Jones, CBE, MD, FRCP, FRCS, DSc, of Plas Dinas, Caerns., and has issue living, Jane Gwenllian Armstrong, *b.* 1936: *m.* 1958, Christopher John Slade, QC, of 12, Harley Gdns., SW10, and has issue living, Richard Penkivil *b.* 1963, Lucinda Jane *b.* 1959, Victoria Albinia *b.* 1962, Amelia Caroline *b.* 1966,—Catherine Elizabeth Armstrong, *b.* 1938: *m.* 1961, Charles Kenneth Roylance Nunneley, of 8, Priory Walk, SW10, and has issue living, Luke James Charles *b.* 1963, Alice Georgina *b.* 1964, Clare Sabina *b.* 1967, Frances Mary *b.* 1969,—Marion Miranda Armstrong, *b.* 1945. *Residences,*—11, Selwood Place, SW7; Plas Dinas, Caernarvonshire; Stream Farm, Dallington, Sussex. *Clubs,*—United University, Beefsteak.

AUNTS LIVING. (*Daughters of 1st Baron.*)

Hon. Joyce Burton, *b.* 1889. *Residence,*—Caldicote, Lindfield, Sussex.

Hon. Muriel Burton, *b.* 1894; *m.* 1920, Bernard Warren Williams (sometime RFA), who *d.* 1970, son of the late Hon. James Rowland Williams, of Kew Park, Westmoreland, Jamaica, and has issue living, Michael Roger (29, South Canterbury Rd., Canterbury), *b.* 1921; FRCS: *m.* 1955, Barbara Mary, da. of Hubert James Isles, and has issue living, Simon Hugh *b.* 1959, Sarah Fidelia *b.* 1957, Rachel Lucinda *b.* 1960, Serena Cicely *b.* 1962,—Anthony James, *CMG* (Jollys, Salehurst, E. Sussex), *b.* 1923; entered HM Diplo. Ser. 1945; Min. British Embassy Rome since 1973; CMG 1971: *m.* 1955, Countess Hedwig Gabrielle, da. of the late Count Erwin von Neipperg, and has issue living, James Kilian *b.* 1958, Adam Benedict *b.* 1959, Henrietta *b.* 1956, Antonia *b.* 1961,—Hugh Raby (5, Gauden Rd., SW4), *b.* 1929: *m.* 1964, Rosemary Jane, da. of the late Rev. G. T. Shetliffe, and has issue living, Edward Joseph *b.* 1968, Fidelia Elisabeth *b.* 1973. *Residence,*—Copse Mountain House, Kew Park, Bethel Town, Jamaica.

Hon. Olive Burton, *b.* 1896; ed. at Somerville Coll., Oxford (B.A. 1922, B.M. 1925, D.M. 1932), L.R.C.P. London and M.R.C.S. England 1925; M.R.C.P. 1928: *m.* 1949, the Ven. Stephen Romney Maurice Gill, Archdeacon of Mamba, Papua, who *d.* 1954. *Residence,*—Belsfield House, Bowness-on-Windermere, Cumbria.

Hon. Dame Ruth Burton, *D.B.E., b.* 1898; Bar. Lincoln's Inn 1926; is a J.P., and a co. Alderman for E. Sussex; D.B.E. (Civil) 1959. *Residence,*—Toll Wood Cottage, Netherfield, Battle, Sussex.

WIDOW LIVING OF SECOND BARON.

HELEN MALISE (*Helen, Baroness Wrenbury*), dau. of His Honour John Cameron Graham, of Ballewan-Blanefield, Stirlingshire: *m.* 1925, the 2nd Baron, who *d.* 1940. *Residence,*—Church End, Dallington, nr. Heathfield, Sussex.

PREDECESSORS.—[1] *Rt. Hon.* HENRY BURTON Buckley, son of the late Rev. John Wall Buckley, V. of St. Mary's, Paddington, W.; *b.* 1845; was a Member of the Bar Committee and of Bar Council 1882-98, a Judge of High Court of Justice 1900-1906, and a Lord Justice of Appeal 1906-15; cr. *Baron Wrenbury*, of Old Castle, Sussex (peerage of United Kingdom) 1915; *m.* 1887, Bertha Margaretta, who *d.* 1960, dau. of Charles Edward Jones, of 20, Cornwall Gardens,

S.W.; *d.*1935; *s.* by his son [2] BRYAN BURTON, 2nd Baron, *b.* 1890 : *m.* 1925, Helen Malise, dau. of His Honour John Cameron Graham, of Ballewan, Blanefield, Stirlingshire : *d.* 1940 ; *s.* by his son [3] JOHN BURTON, 3rd Baron and present peer.

WRIGHT, BARONY OF. (Wright.) [Extinct 1964.]
WIDOW LIVING OF LIFE BARON.
MARGERY AVIS (*Baroness Wright*) (of Durley House, Savernake, Marlborough), da. of the late C. F. Bullows, of Sutton Coldfield: *m.* 1923, the 1st Baron, who *d.* 1964.

WRIGHT OF ASHTON UNDER LYNE, BARONY OF. (Wright.) [Extinct 1974.]
SONS LIVING OF LIFE BARON.
Hon. Owen Mortimer (Wingthorne, Scade Rd., Newton, Swansea), *b.* 1934: *m.* 1960, Barbara, da. of Arthur Hudson, and has issue.
Hon. Glyn David (92, Old Rd., Ashton under Lyne, Lancs.), *b.* 1940: *m.* 1965, May Elizabeth, da. of George Frederick Alldridge, and has issue.
WIDOW LIVING OF LIFE BARON.
KATHLEEN (*Baroness Wright of Ashton under Lyne*) (12, Brookfield Grove, Ashton under Lyne, Lancs.), da. of Squire Firth, of Earby, Yorks.: *m.* 1933, Baron Wright of Ashton under Lyne (Life Baron), who *d.* 1974.

WROTTESLEY, BARON. (Wrottesley.) [Baron U.K. 1838, Bt. E. 1642.]

RICHARD JOHN WROTTESLEY, *M.C.*, 5th Baron and 13th Baronet; *b.* July 7th, 1918; *s.* 1962; ed. at Harrow; Maj. RHG (Reserve); O St J; patron of three livings; 1939-45 War in France and Germany (MC): *m.* 1st, 1941 (m. diss. 1949), Roshnara Barbara, only da. of the late Capt. Esmé Cecil Wingfield-Stratford, DSc [see V. Powerscourt, colls.]; 2ndly, 1949 (m. diss. 1953), Mrs. Joyce Marion Rainey, da. of the late Frederick A. Wallace; 3rdly, 1955, Mary Ada Van Echten, only dau. of Edgar Dryden Tudhope, of 25, Dennekamp, Kenilworth, Cape Province, S. Africa, and has issue by 1st, 2nd and 3rd marriages.

Arms,—Or, three piles sable and a canton ermine. Crest,—Out of a ducal coronet or a boar's head ermine, crined and tusked gold. Supporters,—On either side a unicorn argent, armed, maned, tufted, unguled, gorged with a ducal coronet, and chain reflexed over the back or pendent from the coronet an escutcheon, charged with the arms of Wrottesley.

Strength is increased by union.

Residence,—De Verdon House, Josephine Rd., Claremont, Cape, S. Africa.

GRANDSON LIVING.
Issue of the late the Hon. Richard Francis Gerard Wrottesley, 2nd son of 5th Baron, *b.* 1942, *d.* 1970: *m.* 1967 (Nevada) Georgina Anne (infra), el. da. of Lt.-Col. Peter Thomas Clifton, DSO [see Bruce, Bt., cr. 1804, colls.]:—
CLIFTON HUGH LANCELOT DE VERDON, *b.* Aug. 10th, 1968.

SONS LIVING. (*By 2nd m.*)
Hon. Mark, *b.* 1951.
(*By 3rd marriage.*)
Hon. Stephen John, *b.* 1955.
Hon. Nicholas Charles, *b.* 1963.

WIDOW LIVING OF SON OF FIFTH BARON.
Georgina Anne, el. da. of Lt.-Col. Peter Thomas Clifton, DSO [see Bruce, Bt., cr. 1804, colls.]: *m.* 1967 (Nevada), the Hon. Richard Francis Gerard Wrottesley, who *d.* 1970, and has issue [see ante].

MOTHER LIVING.
Kate May (of The Cotswolds, Kenilworth, Cape Prov., S. Africa), da. of the late Douglas Howard Harris, of Johannesburg, S. Africa: *m.* 1917 (marriage dissolved 1926), the Hon. Walter Bennet Wrottesley, who *d.* 1962, yst. son of 3rd Baron.

COLLATERAL BRANCH LIVING.
(*In remainder to Baronetcy.*)
Grandson of the late Rev. Francis John Wrottesley, son of the late Rev. Edward John Wrottesley, son of the late Com. Edward Wrottesley, R.N., 5th son of 8th baronet:—
Issue of the late Edward Algernon Wrottesley, *b.* 1879, *d.* 1957 : *m.* 1906, Mabel Letitia, who *d.* 1955, dau. of the late Francis Clowes, J.P., of Sutton Hall, Stalham, Norfolk:—
(Arthur) John Francis, *b.* 1908 ; ed. at Wellington Coll., and at Univ. Coll., Oxford (B.A. 1929, M.A. 1933) ; Bar. Inner Temple 1932 ; European War 1939-45 as Capt. Roy. Norfolk Regt.: *m.* 1936, Marjorie Mary, only dau. of the late Frank Wilde, of Moorland Road, Edgbaston, and has issue living, David John, *b.* 1940: *m.* 1969, Christine Ann, only da. of Henry Smith, of Sheffield,—Michael Francis, *b.* 1945: *m.* 1973, Francesca Jacqueline, only da. of the late Jack Miller,—Elizabeth Mavis, *b.* 1938: *m.* 1962, Capt. John Michael Parr, RAEC, and has issue living, Richard John *b.* 1964, Sarah Anne Elizabeth *b.* 1965,—Letitia Marjorie (twin), *b.* 1945: *m.* 1968, Graeme Allan Lythe, of Auckland, NZ, and has issue living, Edward Graeme *b.* 1970, James Edgar *b.* 1972. *Residence,*—48, Warrington Cres., W9 1EP. *Chambers,*—1, Hare Court, Temple, EC4.

PREDECESSORS.—[1] *Sir* WALTER Wrottesley, Knt., son of Sir Hugh Wrottesley (**High Sheriff** of co. Stafford), descended in the male line from Sir Hugh de Wrottesley, K.G. (temp. 1348), a zealous royalist, was cr. a *Baronet* 1642; *d.* 1659; *s.* by his son [2] *Sir* WALTER, 2nd Bt.; *d.* 1686; *s.* by his son [3] *Sir* WALTER, 3rd Bt.; *d.* 1712; *s.* by his son [4] *Sir* JOHN, *M.P.*, 4th Bt.; *d.* 1726; *s.* by his el. son [5] *Sir* HUGH, 5th Bt.; *d.* 1729; *s.* by his brother [6] *Sir* WALTER, 6th Bt.; *d.* 1731; *s.* by his brother [7] *Sir* RICHARD, 7th Bt.; was sometime M.P. for Tavistock, and a Principal Clerk of the Board of Green Cloth; subsequently took Holy Orders, and having been a Royal Chaplain was appointed Dean of Worcester; *d.* 1769; *s.* by his son [8] *Sir* JOHN, 8th Bt.; was a Maj.-Gen. in the Army, sometime M.P. for Staffordshire and Equerry to H.R.H. the Duke of York; *d.* 1787; *s.* by his son [9] *Sir* JOHN, 9th Bt.; having been successively M.P. for Staffordshire and Lichfield, was cr. *Baron Wrottesley*, of Wrottesley, co. Stafford (peerage of United Kingdom) 1838; *d.* 1841; *s.* by his son [10] JOHN, *D.C.L.*, *F.R.S.*, 2nd Baron; *b.* 1798; was Pres. of the Royal So., and one of the founders of the Astronomical So.; *m.* 1821, Sophia Elizabeth, dau. of the late Thomas Giffard, of Chillington, Staffordshire, *d.* 1867; *s.* by his son [11] ARTHUR, 3rd Baron; *b.* 1824; a Lord-in-Waiting to Queen Victoria 1869-74 and 1880-85, and Lord-Lieut. of Staffordshire 1871-87: *m.* 1861, the Hon. Augusta Elizabeth Denison, who *d.* 1887, dau. of 1st Baron Londesborough; *d.* 1910; *s.* by his el. son [12] VICTOR ALEXANDER, 4th Baron; *b.* 1873; *d.* 1962; *s.* by his nephew [13] RICHARD JOHN (only son of the late Hon. Walter Bennet Wrottesley, youngest son of 3rd Baron), 5th Baron and present peer.

WYFOLD, BARON. (Hermon-Hodge.) [Baron U.K. 1919, Bt. U.K. 1902.]

Glory is the reward of valour.

HERMON ROBERT FLEMING HERMON-HODGE, 3rd Baron, and 3rd Baronet; *b.* June 26th, 1915; *s.* 1942; ed. at Eton and at Le Rosey, Switzerland; is Capt. Gren. Gds. (Res.), and a Dir. of Robert Fleming Holdings, Ltd.

Arms,—Sable, a lion couchant erminois holding between the paws a bale of cotton proper. **Crest,**—An eagle, wings addorsed and inverted or, supporting with the dexter claw an increscent argent, and looking at the rays of the sun issuant from clouds proper. **Supporters,**—On either side a trooper of the Oxfordshire Yeomanry (Queen's Own Oxfordshire Hussars).

Seat,—Wyfold Lodge, Reading. *Residence,*—Sarsden House, Churchill, Oxon.

SISTERS LIVING.

Hon. Pamela Kate, *b.* 1908: *m.* 1st, 1938, Viscount Fincastle, who *d.* (killed in action during European War) 1940, only son of 8th Earl of Dunmore; 2ndly, 1944, Capt. Follett Watson Bell, R.A., and has issue living, (by 1st marriage) [see E. Dunmore],—(by 2nd marriage) Ewan Follett, *b.* 1945,—Donald, *b.* 1948: *m.* 1971, Elizabeth Browne of Montreal, Canada,—Lorna Marilyn, *b.* 1951. *Residence,*—Dalness House, Glenetive, Ballachulish, Argyllshire.

Hon. Lorna Frances, *b.* 1911: *m.* 1941, John Barkley Schuster, T.D. [Parker of Waddington, By.], and has issue living, Peter Jonathan, *b.* 1952,—Richard Douglas, *b.* 1953,—Joanna Valentine, *b.* 1950: *m.* 1971, Orme Roosevelt Clarke [see Clarke, Bt., cr. 1831]. *Residence,*—The Manor Farm, Nether Worton, Oxon.

Hon. Dorothy Charmian, *b.* 1913: *m.* 1938, Maj. Richard Evelyn Fleming, M.C., T.D., late Lovat Scouts [Rose, Bt., cr. 1874, colls.], and has issue living, James Roland, *b.* 1944: *m.* 1975, Kate, da. of the late D. A. Rooksby,—Adam Richard, *b.* 1948,—George Andrew, *b.* 1950,—Roderick John, *b.* 1954,—Fergus Hermon Robert, *b.* 1959,—Kathleen Alexandra, *b.* 1941: *m.* 1962, Capt. Simon John Loder, late Gren. Gds., of Resthill Farm, Over Worton, Middle Barton, Oxon. [see Loder, Bt., colls.],—Mary Fern, *b.* 1943: *m.* 1971, Jeremy Donnithorne Taylor, of North Aston Manor, Oxford,—Dorothy Frances, *b.* 1955. *Residences,*—Leygore Manor, Northleach, Glos.; 12, Hyde Park Sq., W2.

Hon. Valentine Kathleen, *b.* 1918.

AUNT LIVING. (*Daughter of 1st Baron.*)

Hon. Nona Carol, *b.* 1897 : *m.* 1924, Harold Montagu Worsley, M.C., who *d.* 1956, having assumed by deed poll 1924, the additional surname of Hermon. *Residence,*—Bensgrove Farm, Goring Heath, Oxfordshire.

WIDOW LIVING OF SON OF FIRST BARON.

Sybil Rika, dau. of Capt. Percy Richard Hare [see E. Listowel, colls.]: *m.* 1934, Major the Hon. Robert Edward Udny Hermon-Hodge, D.S.O., who *d.* 1937. *Residence,*—Wyfold Lodge, Reading.

WIDOW LIVING OF SECOND BARON.

DOROTHY (*Baroness Wyfold*), el. dau. of Robert Fleming, of Joyce Grove, Oxfordshire, and 27, Grosvenor Square, W.: *m.* 1906, the 2nd Baron, who *d.* 1942. *Residences,*—Sarsden House, Churchill, Oxford; Glenkinglass, by Taynuilt, Argyll.

COLLATERAL BRANCH LIVING.

Issue of the late Rear-Adm. Hon. Claude Preston Hermon-Hodge, D.S.C., R.N., 5th son of 1st Baron, *b.* 1888, *d.* 1952 : *m.* 1918, Gwendoline Rose, who *d.* 1949, dau. of J. Goulding Davis, Public Works Depart., India:—

Pauline Frances Gwendoline, *b.* 1921: *m.* 1947, Major Meyrick James Magrath, DFC, RA, of Underacre, Pythingdean, Pulborough, Sussex, RH20 1BT, and has issue living, Carol Rose, *b.* 1949.——Stella Riette, *b.* 1925: *m.* 1949, David Ashley Courtenay, of Woodcutters, Ambersham Common, Midhurst, and has issue living, David Anthony Orin, *b.* 1958,—Geraldine, *b.* 1953.

PREDECESSORS.—[1] ROBERT TROTTER Hermon-Hodge, *T.D.*, el. son of the late George William Hodge, of Newcastle-upon-Tyne; *b.* 1851 ; sat as M.P. for Accrington Div. of N.-E. Lancashire (*C*) 1886-92, for S., or Henley, Div. of Oxfordshire 1895-1906 and 1917-18, and for Croydon 1909-10; sometime Lieut.-Col. and Hon. Col. Comdg. Queen's Own Oxfordshire Hussars Yeo.; assumed by Roy. licence the additional surname of Hermon 1903 ; cr. a *Baronet* 1902, and *Baron Wyfold*, of Accrington, co. Lancaster (peerage of United Kingdom) 1919: *m.* 1877, Frances Caroline, who *d.* 1929, only dau. of Edward Hermon, of Wyfold Court, Oxon; *d.* 1937, *s.* by his son [2] ROLAND HERMON, *D.S.O.*, *M.V.O.*, 2nd Baron; *b.* 1880; Major and Brevet Lieut.-Col. late Reserve of Officers; S. Africa 1899-1902, European War 1914-18 (D.S.O.): *m.* 1906, Dorothy, el. dau. of Robert Fleming, of Joyce Grove, Oxfordshire, and 27, Grosvenor Square, W.1; *d.* 1942; *s.* by his son [3] HERMON ROBERT FLEMING, 3rd Baron and present Peer.

WYNFORD, BARON. (Best.) [Baron U.K. 1829.]

Liberty in the laws.

ROBERT SAMUEL BEST, *M.B.E.*,
8th Baron; *b.* Jan. 5th, 1917; *s.*
1943; ed. at Eton; Lieut.-Col.
(ret.) RWF; a DL of Dorset;
M.B.E. (Mil.) 1952: *m.* 1941:
Anne Daphne Mametz, dau. of the
late Maj.-Gen. John Randle
Minshull-Ford, C.B., D.S.O., M.C.
[Harmood-Banner, Bt.], and has
issue.

Arms,—Sable, a cinquefoil within an
orle of cross crosslets or; on a canton of
the last, a portcullis of the first. Crest,—
Out of a ducal coronet or, a demi-ostrich
rising argent, in its beak a cross crosslet
fitchée gold, gorged with a plain collar,
and pendent therefrom a portcullis sable.
Supporters,—Two eagles reguardant, wings
elevated, each standing on a Roman fasces,
all proper.

Seat,—Wynford House, Maiden Newton, Dorset.

SON LIVING.
Hon. JOHN PHILIP ROBERT, *b.* Nov.
23rd, 1950; ed. at Radley, and Keele
Univ.

DAUGHTERS LIVING.
Hon. Caroline Anne Sabina, *b.* 1942: *m.* 1964, Edward Patrick Gundry, of 87, Howards Lane, SW15
[see Williams, Bt., cr. 1915].
Hon. Jacqueline Dorothy Mametz, *b.* 1946: *m.* 1969, Jeremy James Richard Pope, of Field Cottage,
Compton Abbas West, Maiden Newton, Dorset.

BROTHER LIVING.
Hon. Patrick George Matthew (Meadow Court, Tockenham, Swindon, Wilts.; Boodle's Club), *b.* 1923,
ed. at Wellington Coll.; Lt. RNVR: *m.* 1947, Heather, da. of Hamilton Gardner, and has issue living;
Christopher John Patrick, *b.* 1948: *m.* 1973, Anna Marion Richmond Rowe, only da. of David Rowe,
Mitchell, of Moorey, Coleshill, Bucks.,—David Robert, *b.* 1953,—Philip Edward Fraser, *b.* 1960,—
Clare Phyllis, *b.* 1955.

SISTER LIVING.
Hon. Edith Joy Marion, *b.* 1915: *m.* 1937, Com. Walpole John Eyre, R.N. (retired), and has issue
living, Charles George Samuel, *b.* 1948: *m.* 1971, Carol Anne Spink,—Ruth Evelyn, *b.* 1938.
Residence,—Sadborow, near Chard, Somerset.

DAUGHTERS LIVING OF SIXTH BARON.
Hon. Grace Janet Mary, *b.* 1907: *m.* 1930, Edward Kenneth Macleod Hilleary, MVO, of Little Wood
cote, Upham, Hants., and has issue living, Shena Sarah, *b.* 1931: *m.* 1954, Lt.-Cdr. Harry R. Cornell
RN (ret.), of Garden House, Droxford, Hants.,—Wendy Jemina, *b.* 1933: *m.* 1954, Ian Hedderwick,
of Ellekner, Albany, W. Aust. 6329,—Gilian Marianne (5, Gedintailor, Braes, Skye), *b.* 1936.
Hon. Eva Constance Edith, *b.* 1909: *m.* 1932, Philip Valentine Mackinnon, son of the late Rt. Hon.
Sir Frank Douglas Mackinnon, Lord Justice of Appeal, and has issue living, Michael Alexander
(The Schools, Shrewsbury), *b.* 1936: *m.* 1964, Cleodie Jean Sheila, el. da. of Maj.-Gen. Harry Mac-
donald, CB, CIE, DSO. Residence,—Toller Fratrum, Maiden Newton, Dorset.
Hon. Mary Jemima, *b.* 1912: *m.* 1944, John Hendy, and has issue living, John Giles, *b.* 1948,—Peter
Gerard, *b.* 1953. Residence,—15, Ranelagh Rd., Ealing, W5.

COLLATERAL BRANCHES LIVING.
Issue of the late Adm. the Hon. Sir Matthew Robert Best, KCB, DSO, MVO, 3rd
son of 5th Baron, *b.* 1878, *d.* 1940: *m.* (Jan.) 1908, Annis, who *d.* 1971, da. of
C. F. Wood, of Lee Priory, Littlebourne, Canterbury:—

George Frederic Matthew, *b.* (Dec.) 1908; Capt. RN (ret.) Dep. Dir. of Naval Intelligence 1956-58,
and Commodore Arabian Seas & Persian Gulf 1958-60; ADC to HM 1960: Co. Councillor for Dorset
since 1962; 1939-45 War in Atlantic, W. Africa, Mediterranean and Rangoon (despatches): *m.* 1940,
Rosemary Elizabeth, da. of Maj. J. Chadwick-Brooks, OBE, of Bedford Park, W4, and has issue liv-
ing, John Vincent Matthew, *b.* 1948; ed. at Sussex Univ. (BSc): *m.* 1970, Penelope Ann, da. of John,
H. Williams, of Washington, DC, USA; and Isle of Arran, and has issue living, Tobias Graham
b. 1974, Philippa Hannah, *b.* 1972,—Annis Rosemary Georgina, *b.* 1944: *m.* 1971, Maj. Richard M.
Connaughton, RCT, and has issue, Michael Thomas George *b.* 1972, Emma Caroline Jane *b.* 1974.
Residence,—Wallhayes, Nettlecombe, Bridport, Dorset. Club,—Army and Navy.——Margaret
Annis, *b.* 1913: *m.* 1st, 1937, Com. Alexander Pollock Gibson, RN, who *d.* (killed on active serv.
during 1939-45 War) 1940; 2ndly, 1941, as his second wife, Capt. Godfrey Alexander French,
OBE, RN, and has issue living, (by 2nd m.) Matthew, *b.* 1945; Lt. RN,—David, *b.* 1947: *m.* 1974,
Sarah Anne, da. of the Rt. Rev. Henry David Halsey, Bishop of Carlisle,—Jenny Margaret, *b.* 1950.
Residence,—The Old Rectory, Stoke Abbot, Beaminster, Dorset.

Issue of the late Capt. the Hon. James William Best, O.B.E., V.D., youngest son
of 5th Baron, *b.* 1882, *d.* 1960: *m.* 1914, Florence Mary Bernarda, who *d.* 1961,
dau. of Sir Elliott Lees, 1st Bt., D.S.O.:—

Thomas William, *CB*, (Hincknowle, Melplash, Bridport; United Service and Royal Aero Club), *b.* 1915;
Rear-Adm. (ret.); Capt. Supt. of Admiralty Surface Weapons Estab., and ADC to HM 1964, and
Flag Officer, Gibraltar 1964-66; 1939-45 War, Salerno (despatches), and Normandy; Korea 1951-52
(despatches); CB (Mil) 1966: *m.* 1942, Brenda Joan, da. of the late F. A. Hellaby, MC, LIB. of
Auckland, NZ, and has issue living, Rupert Thomas (Hincknowle, Melplash, Bridport, Dorset)
b. 1943, Lt. Cdr. RN: *m.* 1971, Margaret Ludgate, da. of Maj. Alan Murray, 3rd Carabiniers (Prince
of Wales's Dragoon Gds.), and has issue living, Thomas Matthew *b.* 1973,—James Frederick, *b.* 1948;
BA Oxon,—Joanna Mavis, *b.* 1945; ed. at Durham Univ. (BA): *m.* 1970, Maj. Thomas James
Knott, RE, son of Lt.-Gen. Sir Harold Edwin Knott, KCB, OBE, MD, and has issue living, Felicity
Anne *b.* 1971, Alison Joanna *b.* 1973.——Giles Bernard (The Cottage, Little Bredy, Dorchester, Dorset; 62, Holland Park, W11), *b.* 1925; ed. at Wellington and Jesus Coll., Oxford; Bar. Inner Temple
1951; Dep. Chm. Dorset Quarter Sessions 1967-71, and Recorder of Crown Court 1972-75, since
when Circuit Judge.—Henry Nicholas, *b.* 1930: *m.* 1963, Elizabeth Rose Ursula, el. da. of Hans
Joachim Druckenbrodt, of Marburg, W. Germany, and Rittergut Minsleben, Wernigerode, E. Germany, and has issue living, Frederick Henry Achim, *b.* 1964.——Alice Mary, *b.* 1919: *m.* 1939,

Christopher Wentworth Dilke, late Lt.-Col. RA [see Dilke, Bt.]. *Residences,*—1, Campden Grove, W8; Valehouse Farm, Whitchurch Canonicorum, Bridport, Dorset.——Helen Margaret, *b.* 1923.

Grandchildren of the late Capt. the Hon. James William Best, OBE, VD (ante):—
Issue of the late Samuel James Best, *b.* 1927, *d.* 1974: *m.* 1954, Jennifer Elspeth Mary (Kings House, Powerstock, Dorset), el. da. of Max H. Heilbut:—
Crispin John, *b.* 1955.——Jane Mary, *b.* 1957.——Susannah Catherine, *b.* 1962.——Deborah Gabriel, *b.* 1966.

Grandchildren of the late Capt. the Hon. John Charles Best, 2nd son of the late Rev. the Hon. Samuel Best, 3rd son of 1st Baron :—
Issue of the late Capt. William Best, Roy. Welch Fusiliers, *b.* 1874, *d.* 1950 : *m.* 1903, Constance Adela, who *d.* 1963, dau. of the late Col. Charles Wingfield, of Onslow, Shrewsbury:—
Frank Charles, *OBE* (Vivod, Llangollen, Denbighshire), *b.* 1906; late Conservator Forestry Commn.; OBE (Civil) 1964.——John William, *MBE* (of Lawton Hall, Leominster, Herefordshire), *b.* 1912; formerly Fl.-Lt. RAF; 1939-45 War (prisoner); MBE (Mil.) 1964: *m.* 1st, 1938 (m. diss. 1959), Mary Constance, da. of Robert Charles Otter, of Royston Manor, Clayworth; 2ndly, 1959, Mary Elizabeth (CORBIN), da. of the late Dr. Edward Lancelot Bunting, of Hardwicke Manor, Worcs., and has issue living, (by 1st m.) Robert John *b.* 1946,—Antonia Mary, *b.* 1948: *m.* 1970, Christopher Duncan Steuart Wilson-Clarke, of Achareidh, Nairn.——Hilda Mary, *b.* 1909: *m.* 1935, Ranald Macdonald Brodie Macalister, formerly Capt. Roy. Indian Army Ser. Corps. and has issue living, Angus Charles, *b.* 1937,—Fiona Anne, *b.* 1947. *Residence,*—Glenbarr, Tarbert, Argyll.

Grandchildren of the late Hon. Thomas William Best, 3rd son of the late Rev. the Hon. Samuel Best, 3rd son of 1st Baron :—
Issue of the late Capt. Humphrey Willie Best, C.B.E., D.S.O., R.N., *b.* 1884, *d.* 1959 : *m.* 1914, Helen Grace, who *d.* 1975, da. of the late Mrs. James Meakin, of Weeford, Ashby-de-la-Zouch:—
Walter John, *b.* 1917: *m.* 1941, Elizabeth, yst. dau. of Kenneth M. Simpson, of Trinidad, has issue living, Anne Mackintosh, *b.* 1944: *m.* 1966, Robert Brian Massey of Stockton Heath, and 8, Gilwell Rd., Valsayn Park, Trinidad, and has issue living, Stewart John *b.* 1967,—Ian James *b.* 1972,—Fiona Elizabeth Wynford, *b.* 1949: *m.* 1972, Anthony John Cotter, of 47, Rushden Way, Farnham, Surrey. *Residence,*—4, Queen's Park West, Port of Spain, Trinidad.——Peter Anthony (c/o Lloyds Bank, Chichester, Sussex), *b.* 1922; is Flight-Lieut. RAF; 1939-45 War (prisoner): *m.* 1948, Sheelah Gillian Vernon St. John, only da. of the late Lt.-Col. D. St. J. Baxter, of Chichester, Sussex, and has issue living, Peter Kimble, *b.* 1952,—Jeremy Dean, *b.* 1954,—Hilary Jane *b.* 1949.—— Pamela Grey, *b.* 1920: *m.* 1947, Philip H. Hawkins, of Veryan, Sheafe Drive, Cranbrook, Kent, and has issue living, Jonathan Edward Spencer, *b.* 1953,—Caroline Tessa, *b.* 1948: *m.* 1971, James Harvey Bradnock, of 88, Exeter St., Salisbury, Wilts.

PREDECESSORS.—[1] *Rt. Hon.* Sir WILLIAM DRAPER Best, *D.C.L.,* 3rd son of the late Thomas Best, of Haslebury Pluckett, Somerset ; *b.* 1767; appointed Solicitor to the Prince of Wales 1813, and Attorney-Gen. 1816; sat successively as M.P. for Petersfield and Bridport; was a Judge of the Common Pleas 1819-24, and Chief Justice of that Court 1824-9; sometime Dep. Speaker of House of Lords; cr. *Baron Wynford,* of Wynford Eagle, co. Dorset (peerage of United Kingdom) 1829: *m.* 1794, Mary Anne, who *d.* 1840, dau. of the late Jerome Knapp; *d.* 1845 ; *s.* by his son [2] WILLIAM SAMUEL, 2nd Baron ; *b.* 1798: *m.* 1821, Jane, who *d.* 1895, dau. of William Thoyts, of Sulhampstead, Berks ; *d.* 1869 ; *s.* by his son [3] WILLIAM DRAPER MORTIMER, 3rd Baron, *b.* 1826: *m.* 1857, Caroline Eliza Montague, who *d.* 1913, el. dau. of Evan Baillie, of Dochfour ; *d.* 1899 ; *s.* by his brother [4] HENRY MOLYNEUX, 4th Baron, *b.* 1829 ; *d.* 1903; *s.* by his cousin [5] GEORGE (son of the late Rev. the Hon. Samuel Best, 3rd son of 1st Baron), 5th Baron, *b.* 1838: *m.* 1870, Edith Anne, who *d.* 1924, dau. of Matthew Henry Marsh, of Ramridge House, Andover; *d.* 1904; *s.* by his son [6] PHILIP GEORGE, *D.S.O.,* 6th Baron; *b.* 1871; Major (retired) R.F.A.; European War 1914-19 (DSO): *m.* 1906, the Hon. Eva Lilian Napier, who *d.* 1974, da. of 2nd Baron Napier of Magdala; *d.* 1940; *s.* by his brother [7] SAMUEL JOHN, 7th Baron, *b.* 1874: *m.* 1st, 1914, Evelyn Mary Aylmer, who *d.* 1929, da. of Maj.-Gen. Sir Edward Sinclair May, KCB, CMG; 2ndly, 1930, Marguerite, who *d.* 1966, da. of Charles Pratt, and widow of William Kenneth Allies; *d.* 1943; *s.* by his el. son [8] ROBERT SAMUEL, 8th Baron and present peer.

WYNNE-JONES, BARON. (Wynne-Jones.) [Life Baron 1964.]

WILLIAM FRANCIS KENRICK WYNNE-JONES, son of the late Rev. T. J. Jones, of Shaistaganj, India; *b.* May 8th, 1903; ed. at Monkton Combe Sch., Bath, at Univ. Coll. of Wales, and at Balliol Coll., Oxford (DSc); FRIC, FInstF; Prof. of Chemistry, Univ. Coll., Dundee, St. Andrews Univ. 1938-47, Head of Chemistry Div., Roy. Aircraft Establishment, Farnborough, 1943-45, and Prof. of Physical Chemistry, King's Coll., Durham Univ. 1947-54; Hon. Dir. of Coke Research Laboratories, Univ. of Newcastle upon Tyne 1948-68, Prof. of Chemistry and Head of Sch. of Chemistry, Univ. of Newcastle upon Tyne 1954-68 and Pro Vice-Chancellor 1965-68; Prof. Emeritus, Univ. of Newcastle upon Tyne since 1968; cr. *Baron Wynne-Jones,* of Abergele, co. Denbighshire (Life Baron) 1964: *m.* 1st, 1928, Ann, who *d.* 1969, da. of Duncan Drummond, of Auchterarder, Perthshire; 2ndly, 1972, Rusheen, da. of Neville Preston, and has issue by 1st m.

Residence,—16, Chelsea Embankment, SW3.

DAUGHTERS LIVING. *(By 1st m.).*
Hon. Kristin, *b.* 1931: *m.* 1956, Dr. Charles Joseph Gallagher, who *d.* 1964, and has issue.
Hon. Sigrid, *b.* 1935: *m.* 1962, Dr. Marvin Goldiner, of Oakland, Cal., U.S.A., and has issue.

YARBOROUGH, EARL OF. (Pelham.) [Earl U.K. 1837.]

The love of country prevails.

JOHN EDWARD PELHAM, 7th Earl; *b.* June 2nd, 1920; *s.* 1966; ed. at **Eton**, and at Trin. Coll., Camb.; **Maj.** (ret.) Gren. Gds.; Vice-Lt. of Lincs., and High Sheriff, 1964; 1939-45 War in France and NW **Europe**: *m.* 1957, Mrs. (Florence) **Ann** Petronel Duffin, da. of the late John Herbert Upton, of Ing-**mire**, Yorks.; and has issue.

ärms.—The two coats of *Pelham* quarterly, viz., 1st and 4th azure, three pelicans argent vulning themselves proper; 2nd and 3rd gules, two pieces of belt erect argent decorated with buckles and studs or. **Crest.**—A peacock in his pride argent. **Supporters.**—*Dexter*, a bay horse reguardant, charged on the body with three ancient buckles gold; *sinister*, a water spaniel dog reguardant or, charged on the body with three crosses flory sable.

Seat,—Brocklesby Park, Habrough, Lin-colnshire. *Residences*,—The Pines, Swans Lane, Bembridge, I. of Wight; Flat 6, 97, Cadogan Gdns., SW3. *Clubs*,—Guards, Boodle's, and Royal Yacht Squadron.

SON LIVING.

CHARLES JOHN (*Lord Worsley*), *b.* Nov. 5th, 1963.

DAUGHTERS LIVING.

Lady Sophia, *b.* 1958.
Lady Arabella, *b.* 1960.
Lady Vanessa Petronel, *b.* 1961.

SISTER LIVING.

Lady Janet Marcia Rose DOUGLAS PENNANT, *b.* 1923 : *m.* 1948, John Charles Harper, who assumed by Roy. licence 1950 the surname and arms of Douglas Pennant in lieu of his patronymic, son of Sir Charles Henry Harper, K.B.E., C.M.G., and has issue living, Richard Charles, *b.* 1955,—Edmond Hugh, *b.* 1960. *Residence*,—Penrhyn, Bangor, N. Wales.

DAUGHTERS LIVING OF FIFTH EARL. (*Co-heiresses to Baronies of Fauconberg and Conyers.*)

Lady Diana Mary, *b.* 1920 ; is a State Registered Nurse : *m.* 1952, Robert Miller, and has issue living, Anthea Theresa LYCETT, *b.* 1954; adopted by Michael H. L. Lycett[infra], whose surname she assumed but retains right of succession to the Baronies,—Beatrix Diana, *b.* 1955. *Address*,—c/o Rhobank Corporation Ltd., Box 2270, Salisbury, Rhodesia.

Lady (June) Wendy, *b.* 1924; late 3rd Officer WRNS: *m.* 1959, Michael Hildesley Lycett, late Major Roy. Scots Greys, of West Grange, Scots Gap, Morpeth, Northumberland.

WIDOW LIVING OF FIFTH EARL.

NANCYE (*Dowager Countess of Yarborough*), dau. of the late Alfred Brocklehurst: *m.* 1919, the 5th Earl, who *d.* 1948. *Residence*,—Harston, Grantham.

COLLATERAL BRANCH LIVING.

Issue of the late Hon. Henry Cornwallis Pelham, 3rd son of 3rd Earl, *b.* 1868, *d.* 1924(having assumed by Roy. licence 1905 the surname and arms of Pelham only): *m.* 1892, Edith Katherine, who *d.* 1966, da. of the late Col. William Arthur Roberts, formerly R.H.A., and subsequently Ch. Constable of Metropolitan Police:—

Harry Francis (All Saints Vicarage, Church Rd., Highgate, N6) *b.* 1905; ed. at Eton; formerly Flight Lt. RAFVR.——Marjorie Edith, *b.* 1897: *m.* 1919, Henry George Dacres Dixon, who *d.* 1947, and has issue living, Michael George Dacres (23, Spring Rd., Kentfield, San Francisco, Cal., USA), *b.* 1922; formerly Capt. King's Roy. Rifle Corps; 1939-45 War (wounded, invalided out): *m.* 1st, 1946 (m. diss. 1960), Evelyn Nancy, da. of Maj. (William) Bertram Bell, 12th Lancers [By. Barrymore]; 2ndly, 1960, Azneve, da. of the late Martin Takakjian, of Long Island, New York, USA, and has issue living, (by 1st m.), Henry George, *b.* 1948 Annabel Jane, *b.* 1954,—Anthony John Dacres (Wheelham House, Milltown, Newbridge, co. Kildare), *b.* 1924; Maj. 17th/21st Lancers; 1939-45 War in Italy: *m.* 1st, 1950 (m. diss. 1964), Juliet, da. of Graham Carmichael; 2ndly, 1964, Philippa Joan Lanfear, da. of Capt. Simon Ralph Fane Spicer, 12th Lancers, of Carnew Castle, co. Wicklow [E. Westmor-land], and has issue living, (by 1st m.) Caroline Louise *b.* 1953, (by 2nd m.) Charlotte Patricia *b.* 1965, Emily Henrietta, *b.* 1967,—Robin Charles Dacres (Cowsley Wood, Wadhurst, Sussex), *b.* 1926; late Lt. King's Roy. Rifle Corps: *m.* 1956, Sarah Manners Baron, and has issue living, Charles Richard *b.* 1960, Anna *b.* 1957, Sophia (twin) *b.* 1957,—Elizabeth Marjorie Dacres, *b.* 1920: *m.* 1939, Edward Butler-Henderson, of 43, Lowndes Sq., SW1 [see B. Faringdon, colls.]. *Residence*,—Winton, Austen Way, Gerrard's Cross, Bucks.

PREDECESSORS.—[1] CHARLES Anderson-Pelham, *M.P.* for Beverley 1768-74, and for Lincolnshire 1774-94, was cr. *Baron Yarborough*, of Yarborough, co. Lincoln (peerage of Great Britain) 1794; *d.* 1823; *s.* by his son [2] CHARLES, *D.C.L.*, *F.R.S.*, 2nd Baron; sat as M.P. for Great Grimsby 1803-7, and for Lincolnshire 1807-23; cr. *Baron Worsley*, of Appuldurcombe, Isle of Wight, and *Earl of Yarborough* (peerage of United Kingdom) 1837; *d.* 1846 ; *s.* by his son [3] CHARLES ANDERSON WORSLEY, 2nd Earl; sat as M.P. for Newport, Isle of Wight 1830-1, and for N. Lincolnshire 1832-47; was Lord-Lieut. of co. Lincoln: *d.* 1862; *s.* by his son [4] CHARLES ANDERSON PELHAM, 3rd Earl; *b.* 1835; sat as M.P. for Grimsby 1857-62: *m.* 1858, Lady Victoria Alexandrina, who *d.* 1927, dau. of 4th Earl of Listowel; *d.* 1875; *s.* by his son [5] *Rt. Hon.* CHARLES ALFRED WORSLEY, *K.G.*, 4th Earl; *b.* 1859 ; Vice-Adm. and Lord-Lieut. for Lincolnshire : Capt. of H.M.'s Hon. Corps of Gentlemen-at-Arms 1890-92, and Lieut.-Col. Comdg. Lincolnshire Imperial Yeo. 1901-7; assumed for himself and issue by Roy. licence 1905 the surname and arms of Pelham only: *m.* 1886, the Hon. Marcia Amelia Mary Lane-Fox (*Baroness Fauconberg and Conyers* in her own right), O.B.E., who *d.* 1926, el. dau. of 12th Baron Conyers ; *d.* 1936 ; *s.* by his son [6] SACKVILLE GEORGE, *M.C.*, 5th Earl ; *b.* 1888 ; Lieut.-Col. Comdg. Notts Yeo. (Sherwood Rangers) ; European War 1914-19 (M.C.), European War 1939-45 : *m.* 1919, Nancye, dau. of the late Alfred Brocklehurst ; *d.* 1948, when the Baronies of Fauconberg and Conyers fell into abeyance between his two daughters, and he was *s.* in the Earldom and the Baronies of Yarborough and Worsley by his brother [7] MARCUS HERBERT, 6th Earl, *b.* 1893; a DL for Lincs, 1950-66: *m.* 1919, the Hon. Pamela Douglas-Pennant, who *d.* 1968, da. of 3rd Baron Penrhyn; *d.* 1966; *s.* by his son [8], JOHN EDWARD, 7th Earl and present peer; also Baron Yarborough, and Baron Worsley.

Yarmouth, Earl of, son of Marquess of Hertford.

YORK, LORD ARCHBISHOP OF. (Blanch.)

Most Rev. and Rt. Hon. STUART YARWORTH BLANCH, *PC,* son of William Edwin Blanch; *b.* 1918; ed. at Alleyns Sch., Dulwich, and St. Catherine's Soc., and Wycliffe Hall, Oxford (MA); 1940-45 War as Navigator RAF; V. of Eynsham, Oxon. 1952-57, Vice-Prin. of Wycliffe Hall Oxford 1957-60; Oriel Canon of Rochester and Warden of Rochester Th. Coll. 1960-66; consecrated 5th Bishop of Liverpool 1966 and enthroned 94th Archbishop of York, Primate of England and Metropolitan 1975; Sub-Prelate, Order of the Hospital of St. John of Jerusalem since 1975; PC 1975: *m.* 1943, Brenda Gertrude; da. of the late William Arthur Coyte.

Patron of 129 livings, of six alternately with others, and of one conjointly, the Archdeaconries of York, Cleveland, and the East Riding, and the Canonries in his Cathedral.

The Archbishopric of York was founded A.D. 625, and the Province comprises fourteen Sees.

Archiepiscopal Signature,—" Stuart Ebor : "

ARMS OF THE SEE,—Gules, two keys in saltire argent, in chief a regal crown proper.

Residence,—Bishopthorpe, York.

YOUNG, BARONESS. (Young.) [Life Baroness 1971.]

JANET MARY YOUNG, da. of John Norman Leonard Baker; *b.* Oct. 23rd, 1926; ed. at Headington Sch., Oxford, Prospect Hill Sch., New Haven, Conn., USA, and St. Annes Coll., Oxford (MA): a Member of Oxford City Council 1957-72 (Alderman 1967-72); a Baroness-in-Waiting to HM 1972-73; Parl. Under-Sec. of State Dept. of Environment 1973-74; cr. *Baroness Young,* of Farnworth, co. Palatine of Lancaster (Life Baroness) 1971: *m.* 1950, Geoffrey Tyndale Young, and has issue.

Residence,—23, Northmoor Rd., Oxford.

DAUGHTERS LIVING

Hon. Alexandra Janet, *b.* 1951.
Hon. Rosalind Ann, *b.* 1954.
Hon. Juliet Marguerite, *b.* 1962.

YOUNGER OF LECKIE, VISCOUNT. (Younger.) [Viscount U.K. 1923, Bt. 1911.]

Swift and bold.

EDWARD GEORGE YOUNGER, *O.B.E., T.D.,* 3rd Viscount, and 3rd Baronet; *b.* Nov. 21st, 1906; *s.* 1946; ed. at Winchester, and at New Coll., Oxford (B.A. 1928); Lt.-Col. (ret.) Argyll and Sutherland Highlanders (T.A.); Lord Lt. of Stirlingshire; 1939-45 War as Col. Gen. Staff (OBE); OBE (Mil.) 1940: *m.* 1930, Evelyn Margaret, MBE, da. of the late Alexander Logan McClure, KC (Sheriff of Aberdeen, Kincardine, and Banff), of 16, Heriot Row, Edinburgh, and has issue.

Arms,—Parted per saltire or and gules, a rose counter-changed, in base a martlet sable, on a chief azure three covered cups or. *Crest,*—An armed leg couped at the thigh proper, garnished and spurred or. *Supporters,*—*Dexter,* a lion rampant sable ; *sinister,* a wolf argent ; both armed and langued gules.

Seat,—Leckie, Gargunnock, Stirlingshire.

Younger as the years go by.

D.—39

SONS LIVING.

Hon. GEORGE KENNETH HOTSON, *TD*, *MP* (Easter Leckie, Gargunnock, Stirlingshire), *b.*
Sept. 22nd, 1931; ed. at Winchester, and at New Coll. Oxford (BA); late Maj. Argyll and Sutherland
Highlanders (TA); Korea 1951; a DL for Stirlingshire; a Gov. of Roy. Scottish Acad. of Music 1962-70;
Scottish Conservative Whip 1965; Dep. Chm. of Scottish Conservative & Unionist Assocn. 1967-70,
and Joint Parl. Under-Sec. of State for Scotland for Development 1970-74, Min. of State for Defence
Jan. to March 1974; Chm. of Conservative Party in Scotland since 1974; MP for Ayr Div. of Ayr-
shire and Bute since 1964: *m.* 1954, Diana Rhona, el. da. of Capt. Gerald Seymour Tuck, DSO,
RN (ret.), of Little London, Chichester, and has issue living, James Edward George, *b.* 1955,—Charles
Gerald Alexander, *b.* 1959,—Andrew Seymour Robert, *b.* 1962,—Joanna Rosland, *b.* 1958.
Hon. Alexander James, *b.* 1933; ed. at Winchester, and at Worcester Coll., Oxford (BA 1956); late
Capt. Argyll and Sutherland Highlanders (TA); Dir. of Sir Joseph Causton & Sons, Ltd. 1963-68;
Managing Dir. of Robt. Maclehose & Co. Ltd.; Korea 1952: *m.* 1959, Annabelle Christine, da. of
the late Gerald Furnivall, of Middle Brook, Bishop's Waltham, Hants., and has issue living, Nicholas
Gerald Gilmour, *b.* 1963,—Rupert Edward Alexander, *b.* 1966,—Amanda Charlotte Frances, *b.*
1961,—Araminta Lucy, *b.* 1967. *Residence,*—Arngibbon House, Kippen, Stirlingshire.
Hon. Robert Edward Gilmour, *b.* 1940; ed. at Winchester, and at New Coll., Oxford (BA): *m.* 1972,
Helen Hayes, of Craigdhu, Barbreck, Lochgilphead, Argyll.

DAUGHTER LIVING.

Hon. Rosalind Evelyn, *b.* 1937 *m.* 1960, Thomas Ross Charles Cropper, and has issue living, Charles,
Thomas Howe, *b.* 1962,—Robert Douglas, *b.* 1969,—Jill Marion, *b.* 1961,—Annabel Rosalind, *b.*
1966. *Residence,*—Greenhills, Willow Tree, NSW.

BROTHER LIVING.

Rt. Hon. Sir Kenneth Gilmour, *KBE, b.* 1908; ed. at Winchester, and at New Coll., Oxford (MA);
Bar. Inner Temple 1932; 1939-45 War as 2nd Lieut. and acting Major Intelligence Corps; was
Parliamentary Private Sec. to Min. of State 1945-47, Parliamentary Under-Sec. of
State, Home Office 1947-50, and Min. of State, Foreign Office 1950-51; Dir. Roy. Institute of Inter-
national Affairs 1959-71; sat as MP for Grimsby (*Lab.*) July 1945 to Sept. 1959; PC 1951, KBE
(Civil) 1972: *m.* 1934, Elizabeth Kirsteen, only da. of the late W. D. Stewart, of Achara, Duror,
Argyll, and has issue living, James Samuel, *b.* 1951,—Susannah Mary, *b.* 1936,—Christina Lucy,
b. 1950. *Residence,*—3, Clareville Grove, SW7.

SISTERS LIVING.

Hon. Elizabeth Maud, *b.* 1913: *m.* 1937, Lieut.-Col. Kenneth Bulstrode Lloyd Davidson, Argyll and
Sutherland Highlanders, and has issue living, Charles Kenneth Lloyd (Sherborne Ranch, SSI Kam-
loops, BC, Canada), *b.* 1938; ed. at Haileybury; Capt. Rocky Mountain Rangers (CA Mil.); ADC
to Lt. Gov. of BC: *m.* 1961, Diana Margaret, only da. of the late H. C. Watts, of 5, Lansdown Grove
Court, Lansdown, Bath, and has issue living, Ilona Margaret *b.* 1969, Rosemary Nicole *b.* 1971,—
Andrew James Lloyd, *b.* 1944; ed. at St. Columba's and Trin. Colls., Dublin,—Claude John Lloyd,
b. 1947; ed. at St. Columba's Coll., Dublin, and RMA; Lt. R. Irish Rangers: *m.* 1971, Bridget
Jane Phyllis, yr. da. of the late Raymond Salmon, of Kenya,—Alastair Michael Lloyd, *b.* 1954;
ed. at St. Columba's Coll., Dublin,—Anne Elizabeth, *b.* 1952. *Residence,*—The Manor House,
Eglinton, co. Derry.
Hon. Anne Margaret, *b.* 1920: *m.* 1943, Capt. James Timothy Noël Price, RA (ret.), of the Moorings,
Port Lewaigue, Ramsey, Isle of Man [see O'Brien, Bt., cr. 1849].

PREDECESSORS.—[1] GEORGE Younger, el. son of the late James Younger, brewer, of Alloa,
by Janet, who *d.* 1912, dau. of the late John McEwan, of Alloa; *b.* 1851; was Chm. of George
Younger & Son, Ltd., of Alloa, and a Director of National Bank of Scotland, and of Lloyds Bank,
Ltd.; Lord-Lieut. for Stirlingshire 1926-9; M.P. for Ayr (*C*) Jan. 1906 to Oct. 1922; cr. a *Baronet*
1911, and *Viscount Younger of Leckie*, of Alloa, Clackmannanshire (peerage of United Kingdom)
1923: *m.* 1879, Lucy, who *d.* 1921, dau. of Edward Smith, M.D., F.R.S., of Heanor Fall, Derbyshire, and Harley Street, W.; *d.* 1929; *s.* by his son [2] JAMES, 2nd Viscount, *b.* 1880; Lieut.-
Col. (retired) Fife and Forfar Yeo., Vice-Lieut. for Clackmannanshire, a Director of George
Younger & Son, Ltd., of Alloa, and Ensign of Roy. Co. of Archers (King's Body Guard for
Scotland); European War 1914-19 (D.S.O.): *m.* 1906, Maud, who *d.* 1957, dau. of Sir John Gilmour,
1st Bt.; *d.* 1946: *s.* by his son [3] EDWARD GEORGE, 3rd Viscount and present peer.

YPRES, EARL OF. (French.) [Earl U.K. 1922.]

JOHN RICHARD CHARLES LAMBART
FRENCH, 3rd Earl; *b.* Dec. 30th, 1921;
s. 1958; ed. at Winchester, and at Trin.
Coll., Dublin; European War 1939-45 as
Capt. King's Roy. Rifle Corps: *m.* 1st,
1943 (m. diss. 1972), Maureen Helena,
da. of H. John Kelly, US Foreign Ser.
(ret.); 2ndly, 1972, Deborah, da. of
R. Roberts, of Liverpool, and has issue by
1st and 2nd ms.

Arms,—Ermine, a chevron sable, a crescent for
difference. **Crest,**—A dolphin embowed proper.
Supporters,—*Dexter*, a lion guardant or, supporting
a staff proper with a banner of the Union; *sinister*,
a lion or, supporting a staff proper with a banner paly
of three, sable, gold and gules.

Residence,—

I would rather die than be dishonoured.

DAUGHTERS LIVING. (*By 1st m.*)
Lady Charlene Mary Olivia, *b.* 1946: *m.* 1965, Charles
Mordaunt Milner, of Nun Appleton, P.O. Windmill,
Cape, S. Africa [see Milner, Bt.].
Lady Sarah Mary Essex, *b.* 1953.
Lady Emma Mary Helena, *b.* 1958.
(*By 2nd m.*)
Lady Lucy Kathleen, *b.* 1975.

SISTER LIVING.

Lady Patricia Mary Charlemont, *b.* 1919: *m.* 1942, Henry Edmund Roland Kingsbury [E. Bradford, colls.], and has issue living, Philip Charles Orlando (3, Bensbury Close, Putney Heath, SW15),
b. 1944; ed. at Winchester; late 2nd Lt. 15th/19th King's R. Hussars: *m.* 1971, Huberta Maria Daly,
da. of the late Maj. Jobst Heinrich von Reinhard, and has issue living, Julian Henry Orlando *b.*
1972, Francis Alexander Lowndes *b.* 1973,—Gerald Richard Charlemont, *b.* 1945; ed. at Winchester:
m. 1975, Clico, only da. of Capt. Bernard MacIntyre, RN (ret.) of Curry Mallet, Som. *Residences,*—
Wentworth Lodge, Iver Heath, Bucks.; Skiathos, Greece.

AUNT LIVING. (*Daughter of 1st Earl.*)

Lady Essex Eleonora, *O.B.E.*, *b.* 1886 ; is a Dame of Grace of Order of St. John of Jerusalem, O.B.E. (Civil) 1918. *Residence,*—The Lodge, 32, Sheldon Avenue, N.6.

COLLATERAL BRANCH LIVING.

Issue of the late Lt.-Col. the Hon. (Edward) Gerald Fleming French, DSO, 2nd son of 1st Earl; *b.* 1883, *d.* 1970: *m.* 1906, Leila, who *d.* 1959, da. of Robert King, JP, formerly of Natal, S. Africa:—

Essex Leila Hilary (*Viscountess Monsell*), *b.* 1907: *m.* 1st, 1929, Vyvyan Drury, from whom she obtained a divorce 1935; 2ndly, 1950, the 1st Viscount Monsell, and has issue living, (by 1st m.) Romayne, *b.* 1930.——Violet Valerie (*Hon. Mrs. Philip L. Kindersley*), *b.* 1909: *m.* 1st, 1931, the 4th Baron Brougham and Vaux, who *d.* 1967, and from whom she obtained a divorce 1934; 2ndly, 1936, the Hon. Philip Leyland Kindersley, of Holford Manor, North Common, Chailey, Sussex [see B. Kindersley].

PREDECESSORS.—[1] *F.-M. the Rt. Hon. Sir* JOHN DENTON PINKSTONE French, *K.P.*, *G.C.B.*, *OM, GCVO, KCMG, PC,* only son of Capt. John Tracy French, RN, of Ripple Vale, Kent; *b.* 1852; Sudan Expedition 1884-5, S. Africa 1899-1901 Comdg. Cav. Div., and subsequently Comdg. in Cape Colony (promoted Lieut.-Gen., K.C.B.); commanded British Expeditionary Force in France during European War 1914-15 (O.M., Croix de Guerre (France), Médaille Militaire (France); cr. Viscount, thanked by Parliament, granted £50,000); a Member of Imperial Defence Committee 1905, Inspector-Gen. of the Forces and Pres. of Selection Board 1907-12, Ch. of Imperial Gen. Staff 1911-14 (also 1st Mil. Member of Army Council), Com.-in-Ch. of Troops in United Kingdom 1915-18, and Lord-Lieut. of Ireland 1918-21 (with a seat in the Cabinet from Oct. 1919); Capt. of Deal Castle 1923-5; cr. *Viscount French of Ypres,* and of High Lake, co. Roscommon (peerage of United Kingdom) 1916, and *Earl of Ypres* (peerage of United Kingdom) **1922**: *m.* 1880, Eleonora Anna, who *d.* 1941, dau. of Richard William Selby-Lowndes, of Elmers, Bletchley; *d.* 1925; *s.* by his son [2] JOHN RICHARD LOWNDES, 2nd Earl; *b.* 1881; late Capt. R.A.: *m.* 1st, 1916, Olivia Mary, who *d.* 1934, dau. of the late Maj.-Gen. Thomas John; 2ndly, 1941, Violet Laird, who *d.* 1970, only da. of the late Col. James Laird Irvine, CB, RE; *d.* 1958; *s.* by his son [3] JOHN RICHARD CHARLES LAMBART, 3rd Earl and present peer; also Viscount French of Ypres.

ZETLAND, MARQUESS OF. (Dundas.) [Marquess U.K. 1892, Bt. G.B. 1762.]

LAWRENCE ALDRED MERVYN DUNDAS, 3rd Marquess, 5th Earl of Zetland, 6th Baron Dundas, and 7th Baronet; *b.* Nov. 12th, 1908; *s.* 1961; ed. at Harrow, and at Trin. Coll., Camb.; is Lieut. and temporary Major Yorkshire Yeo., a D.L. of North Riding of Yorks., and patron of one living; 1939-45 War in Middle East (despatches): *m.* 1936, Penelope, dau. of the late Col. Ebenezer John Lecky Pike, C.B.E., M.C., of Little Glebe, Fontwell, Sussex, and has issue.

Arms—Argent, a lion rampant gules, within a double tressure flory counterflory, all within a bordure azure. **Crest.**—A lion's head affrontée gules, encircled by an oak bush proper. **Supporters**—Two lions proper, each crowned with an antique crown or, and gorged with a chaplet of oak leaves vert; pendant from each chaplet an escutcheon, that on the *dexter* charged with the arms of *Bruce,* viz. argent, a saltire and chief gules, and on a canton argent, a lion rampant azure ; that on the *sinister* with the arms of *Fitzwilliam,* viz. lozengy or and gules.

Seat.—Aske, Richmond, Yorkshire. *Residence,* 59, Cadogan Place, SW1.

Try.

ESSAYEZ

SONS LIVING.

LAWRENCE MARK (*Earl of Ronaldshay*) (Hill House, Cheriton, Alresford, Hants.), *b.* Dec. 28th, 1937; ed. at Harrow, and at Camb. Univ.; late 2nd Lt. Grenadier Guards: *m.* 1964, Susan, da. of Guy Chamberlin, of Shefford House, Great Shefford, Newbury, and has issue:—

SONS LIVING—Robin Lawrence (*Lord Dundas*), *b.* March 5th, 1965.

Hon. James Edward, *b.* 1967.

DAUGHTERS LIVING—Lady Henrietta Kate, *b.* 1970.

Lady Victoria Clare, *b.* 1973.

Lord David Paul Nicholas (35, Maxwell Rd., SW6), *b.* 1945: *m.* 1971, Corinna, da. of Denys Scott, of 11, Glebe Place, SW3.

Lord (Richard) Bruce (74, Rosaville Rd., SW6), *b.* 1951: *m.* 1974, Jane Melanie, yst. da. of E. S. Wright, of 47, Montrose Place, SW1.

DAUGHTER LIVING.

Lady Serena Jane, *b.* 1940: *m.* 1964, Cdr. Nigel Ion Charles Kettlewell, RN, of The Close, Marley Common, Haslemere, Surrey, and has issue living, Robert James, *b.* 1965,—Melissa Jane, *b.* 1968,—Charlotte Rose, *b.* 1970.

SISTERS LIVING.

Lady Viola Mary (of F.11, Sloane Avenue Mansions, SW3, and Cromwell House, Speen, Newbury, Berks.) *b.* 1910.

Lady Jean Agatha, *b.* 1916: *m.* 1939, Capt. Hector Lorenzo Christie, who *d.* 1969, and has issue living, William Lawrence, *b.* 1948,—Carolyn Anne, *b.* 1947: *m.* 1st, 1966 (m. diss. 1970), John Julian Reynolds, [see Reynolds, Bt.]; 2ndly, 1974, Robert Scully, of San Francisco, USA. *Residence,*—Framland, Wantage, Oxon.

COLLATERAL BRANCHES LIVING.   (*In remainder to the Earldoms, Barony and Baronetcy.*)
        Grandchildren of the late Hon. John Charles Dundas, brother of 1st Marquess :—
    Issue of the late Charles Lawrence Dundas, *b.* 1871, *d.* 1922 : *m.* 1896, Georgina Mary, who *d.* 1950, widow of Capt. C. M. Stevens :—
Margaret, *b.* 1899: *m.* 1920, Brig. John George Smyth, VC, MC (afterwards 1st Bt.), from whom she obtained a divorce 1940. *Residence,*—39, Fitzjames Av., W.14.
        Issue of the late Frederick James Dundas, *b.* 1877, *d.* 1950 : *m.* 1913, Sylvia Mary (of Blair Drummond, Perthshire, by Stirling), el. dau. of Hugh March Phillipps, of Chapel Court, Kenn, near Exeter :—

Hugh Spencer Lisle, *DSO, DFC* (Schoolroom, Dockenfield, Farnham, Surrey, and 83, Iverna Court, W8. White's Club) *b.* 1920; ed. at Stowe: Group Capt. (ret.) RAF: commanded No. 601 (co. of London) Flying Squadron, RAAF 1947-9; 1940-45 War (despatches, DFC); DSO 1944 (Bar 1945): *m.* 1950, the Hon (Enid) Rosamond Lawrence, da. of 3rd Baron Trevethin and 1st Baron Oaksey, and has issue living, James Frederick Trevor, *b.* (Nov.) 1950;—Sarah Jane, *b.* 1953,—Amanda Rose, *b.* 1956.——Elizabeth Mary (*Lady Muir*), *b.* 1914: *m.* 1936, Sir John Harling Muir, 3rd Bt. *Residence,*—Blair Drummond Perthshire, by Stirling.——Alice, *b.* 1918: *m.* 1st, 1939 (m. diss. 1950), Patrick John Macdonald; 2ndly, 1952, Dennis Charles Drake, Surg.-Cdr. RN (ret.), and has issue living, (by 1st m.) Ann Virginia, *b.* 1940,—Mary Gillian, *b.* 1942. *Residence,*—87, South Hill Park, Hampstead, NW3——Charmian, *b.* 1931: *m.* 1955, Maurice R. Snowden, of Garden House, Tudor Hall, Banbury, Oxon., and has issue living, John Frederick Hugh, *b.* 1955,—Mark Lawrence, *b.* 1957.

        Issue of the late Hon. William Fitzwilliam James Dundas, brother of 1st Marquess, *b.* 1860, *d.* 1945 : *m.* 1892, Mary Maud, who *d.* 1945, dau. of the late Lieut.-Col. H. A. Prinsep:—
Robert Bruce, *b.* 1900: *m.* 1934, Enid Mary, el. dau. of the late Com. F. W. Roberts, R.N., and has issue living, David Lawrence, *b.* 1936; ed. at Shrewsbury, and at Balliol Coll., Oxford (Domus Exhibitioner),—Jennifer Elizabeth Mary, *b.* 1942: *m.* 1963, John Warren Williams, of 6, Swinton Close, Ipswich, Suffolk, and has issue living, Patricia Helen *b.* 1965. *Residence,*—Corrie, Broadford, Isle of Skye.——Margaret Beryl, *b.* 1893: *m.* 1920, Capt. James Chaigneau Colvill, RN (ret.), and has issue living, Susan Patricia, *b.* 1922: *m.* 1946, Capt. Francis Magan, and has issue living, Arthur Shaen *b.* 1953, Sarah Jane *b.* 1948. *Residence,*—Clogheren, Baily, co. Dublin.—— Mary Gwendolen, *b.* 1894.——Janet Elizabeth, *b.* 1911.
        Issue of the late Hon. Cospatrick Thomas Dundas, brother of 1st Marquess, *b.* 1862, *d.* 1906 : *m.* 1892, Maud [who *d.* 1949, having *m.* 2ndly, 1912, Major Sir Harry Edward Spiller Cordeaux, K.C.M.G., C.B., who *d.* 1943], dau. of the late Hon. George Wentworth-Fitzwilliam, M.P. [E. Fitzwilliam. colls.] :—
Elgiva Margaret (*Elgiva, Baroness de Mauley*), *b.* 1897: *m.* 1920, the 5th Baron de Mauley, who *d.* 1962. *Residence,*—Little Faringdon, Lechlade, Glos.——Ida Victoria Alice (11, Lanchester Court, Seymour St., W2 2JQ) *b.* 1905.

        Grandchildren of the late Hon. Cospatrick Thomas Dundas (ante):—
    Issue of the late Vice-Adm. John George Lawrence Dundas, C.B., C.B.E., *b.* 1893, *d.* 1952: *m.* 1928, Ruth (1968, Tenth Av., San Francisco, Cal. 94 116, USA), da. of Archibald Coleman:—
John Archibald Lawrence /17, Eddy St., West Newton, Mass., 02165, USA), *b.* 1942: MD: *m.* 1967, Dorothy Folk, da. of H. Bradford Washburn, of Boston, Mass., and has issue living, Michael Henry Lawrence, *b.* 1969,—Patrick George Bradford, *b.* 1973,—Jennifer Deirdre, *b.* 1971.——Elgiva Ruth, *b.* 1929: *m.* 1951, Penn Thomas Watson, of 4408, Pamlico Drive, Raleigh, N. Carolina, USA, and has issue living, Rom Purefoy, *b.* 1955,—Ruth Coleman, *b.* 1952,—Clare Thomas, *b.* 1958.——Rosemary Maud, *b.* 1933: *m.* 1954, Dr. Robert Gray Patton, of 85, Parker Av., San Francisco, Cal. 94118, USA, and has issue living, Mary Gray, *b.* 1956,—Sarah Dundas, *b.* 1959,—Susannah McCrae, *b.* 1964. ——Deirdre Clare, *b.* 1935: *m.* 1st, 1958 (m. diss. 1960), Clifford Enright; 2ndly, 1961, Dr. Walter Munro Newton of 340, Indian Trail Drive, Southern Pines, N. Carolina 28387, USA, and has issue living, (by 1st m.) Iva Margaret, *b.* 1959 (by 2nd m.) Walter Monroe, *b.* 1962,—Elisabeth Dundas, *b.* 1970.——Alexandra Mary, *b.* 1946: *m.* 1965 (m. diss. 1973), John Andrew Todd, and has issue living, John Andrew, *b.* 1970.
        (*In special remainder to Baronetcy only.*)
        Grandson of the late Thomas George Dundas (infra):—
    Issue of the late Thomas Archibald Dundas, *b.* 1880, *d.* 19—: *m.* 1903, Sybil Katherine, da. of the late F. R. Hampshire:—
Thomas Archibald David, *b.* 1904.
        Grandson of the late Joseph Dundas, son of the late Lt.-Col. Thomas Dundas, son of the late Thomas Dundas, MP, brother of 1st Bt.:—
    Issue of the late Thomas George Dundas, *b.* 1853, *d.* 1929 : *m.* 1879, Mary, who *d.* 1923, dau. of the late Lieut.-Col. Duncan Henry Caithness Reay Davidson, of Tulloch [Mackenzie, Bt., cr. 1703 (of Gairloch), colls.]:—
Ronald George, *b.* 1885: *m.* 1912, Olive Mary, da. of Robert Scott-Day, and has issue living, Eleanor Mary, *b.* 1914. *Residence,*—Los Angeles, California, USA.

PREDECESSORS.—[1] LAWRENCE Dundas, Comy.-Gen. and Contractor to the Army 1747-59; cr. a *Baronet* 1762 with remainder to his brother Thomas ; M.P. for Edinburgh 1768-81 ; *d.* 1781 ; *s.* by his son [2] *Sir* THOMAS, 2nd Bt. ; M.P. for co. Stirling 1768-9 ; Lord-Lieut. and Vice-Adm. of Orkney and Shetland ; *cr. Baron Dundas,* of Aske, co. York (peerage of Great Britain) 1794; *d.* 1820 ; *s.* by his son [3] LAWRENCE, 2nd Baron ; successively M.P. for Richmond and York. Lord-Lieut. and Vice-Adm. of Orkney and Shetland ; *cr. Earl of Zetland* (peerage of United Kingdom) 1838 ; *d.* 1839 ; *s.* by his son [4] THOMAS, *K.G.,* 2nd Earl ; M.P. for Richmond 1818-30 and 1835-9, and York 1830-32 and 1833-5; Lord-Lieut. of N. Riding of York, and Grand Master of Freemasons of England 1843-69 ; *d.* 1873 ; *s.* by his nephew [5] *Rt.* Hon. LAWRENCE, *K.T.* (el. son of the Hon. John Charles Dundas, M.P., 4th son of 1st Earl, by Margaret Matilda, who *d.* 1907, dau. of James Talbot, of Mary Ville, co. Wexford). 3rd Earl, *b.* 1844 ; M.P. for Richmond (L) 1872-3 ; Lord-in-Waiting to Queen Victoria 1880, and Lord-Lieut. of Ireland 1889-92 ; cr. K.T. 1900, and *Marquess of Zetland and Earl of Ronaldshay,* in co. of Orkney and Shetland (peerage of United Kingdom) 1892 : *m.* 1871, Lady Lilian Selina Elizabeth Lumley, who *d.* 1943, dau. of 9th Earl of Scarbrough ; *d.* 1929 ; *s.* by his el. son [6] LAWRENCE JOHN LUMLEY, *K.G., G.C.S.I., G.C.I.E., P.C.,* 2nd Marquess, *b.* 1876 ; formerly Capt. 1st N. Riding of Yorkshire Artillery, W. Div. R.A., Major 4th Batn. Green Howards, and Hon. Col. 62nd (Northumbrian) Anti-Aircraft Brig. R.A. (T.A.) ; sat as M.P. for Hornsey Div. of Middlesex 1907-16; appointed a Member of Roy. Commn. on Indian Public Ser. 1912, Gov. of Bengal 1916, and Pres. of Roy. Geographical So. 1922 (a Trustee thereof 1925-47), and of Roy. India So. 1923-50 ; Sec. of State for India 1935-40 (also for Burma 1937-40) ; Chm. of Executive Committee of National Trust 1931-45, and Lord Lieut. of N. Riding of Yorkshire 1945-51 ; bore Sword of State at Coronation of King George VI: *m.* 1907, Cicely, who *d.* 1973, da. of Col. Mervyn Archdale, formerly 12th Lancers; *d.* 1961; *s.* by his el. son [7] LAWRENCE ALDRED MERVYN, 3rd Marquess and present peer; also Earl of Zetland, Earl of Ronaldshay, and Baron Dundas.

ZOUCHE, BARON. (Frankland.) [Baron E. 1308, Bt. (E.) 1660.]
[Title pronounced "Zooch."]

JAMES ASSHETON FRANKLAND, 18th Baron and 12th Baronet; b. Feb. 23rd, 1943; s. to Baronetcy 1944, and to Barony 1965; co-heir to Baronies of St. Maur and Grey of Codnor; Capt. 15th/19th King's R. Hussars.

Arms.—Azure, a dolphin naiant embowed or, on a chief of the second two saltires gules. Crest.—A dolphin hauriant argent and entwined round an anchor erect proper.

Residence,—Courthouse, Leck, Carnforth, Lancs.

UNCLE LIVING. (*Son of Mary Cecil, Baroness Zouche.*)
Hon. ROGER NATHANIEL, *b.* April 11th, 1909; ed. at Charterhouse, and at Pembroke Coll., Camb. (BA): *m.* 1st, 1931, Elizabeth Cecil (from whom he obtained a divorce 1947), da. of Arthur Cecil Sanday; 2ndly, 1947, Olivia, da. of the late Rev. the Hon. Nigel Campbell and widow of Maj. S. J. R. Bucknell, Irish Gds. [see E. Cawdor, colls.], and has issue living, (by 1st m.) Timothy Cecil (47, Ennerdale Rd., Kew, Surrey), *b.* 1931: *m.* 1957, Lynette, da. of Ian Hope Dundas, and has issue living, Nicholas Charles *b.* 1958, Mathew Curzon *b.* 1962, Adam Christian *b.* 1965,—Frederick Mark, *b.* 1934. *Residence,*—39, Cadogan Sq., SW1.

AUNT LIVING. (*Daughter of Mary Cecil, Baroness Zouche.*)
Hon. Barbara Mary FRANKLAND, *b.* 1906 : resumed by deed poll 1958 her maiden surname of Frankland in lieu of that of Lucas: *m.* 1st, 1926 (marriage dissolved 1937), Brig. Otho Leslie Prior-Palmer, 9th Lancers (DSO 1945, Knt. 1959); 2ndly, 1937 (marriage dissolved 1943), the 5th Earl of Normanton, who *d.* 1967; 3rdly, 1943 (m. diss. 1962), Peter Lucas, and has issue living, (by 1st m.) Diana Mary Leslie, *b.* 1929: *m.* 1974, Bruno de Marco. *Residence,*—Ridge House, Stockland, Honiton, Devon.

COLLATERAL BRANCHES LIVING.
(*In remainder to the Barony only.*)
Grandchildren of the late Emily Anne Curzon (dau. of the late Hon. Edward Cecil Curzon, 2nd son of Harriet Anne, Baroness de la Zouche), who *m.* 1861, Augustus Frederick Wentworth Gore, formerly 7th Hussars:—

Issue of the late Francis Southwell Cecil Charles Gore, Lieut. Middlesex Regt., *b.* 1879, *d.* (wounds in action during European War) 1917 : *m.* 1904, Frances Rose Mary (now of 8, Grange Gardens, Eastbourne), only dau. of C. Maybrook :—

Frederick Edward Cecil, *b.* 1905. *Residence,*—8, Grange Gardens, Eastbourne.——Francis Norton Wentworth, C.B.E., *b.* 1906 ; Brigadier (retired) late R.A. ; O.B.E. (Mil.) 1947, C.B.E. (Mil.) 1960 : *m.* 1939, Else Gurli Astrid, dau. of the late Evald Christensen, of Copenhagen, Denmark, and has issue living, Peter Wentworth, *b.* 1946; Capt. Queen's Own Hussars,—Frances Jane Wentworth, *b.* 1947: *m.* 1970, Maj. Colijn Thomson-Moore, Irish Gds., of 14, Clareville Court, Clareville Grove, SW7. *Residence,*—11, Coleherne Court, The Little Boltons, SW5.

(*Not in remainder to the Barony.*)
Issue of the late Maj. Arthur Pelham Frankland, DSO, 2nd son of 9th baronet *b.* 1874, *d.* 1948: *m.* 1st, 1898, Margaret Annie Phœbe Seton, who *d.* 1953 (having obtained a divorce 1934), da. of the late Charles Compton Seton [Seton, Bt., *cr.* 1663, colls.]; 2ndly, 1934, Ethel Theresa Gerard, who *d.* 1962, da. of the late Humphrey Jeffrey Walmesley, JP, of Inglewood House, Hungerford :—

(By 1st m.) Marion Annie Margaret, *b.* 1900: *m.* 1930, Eric Stewart Grant, of 11A, Albert Court, Kensington Gore, SW7, and has issue living, Anne Margaret, *b.* 1932.——Rosalind Lucy Seton, *b.* 1904: *m.* 1928, Lt.-Col. Augustus Cameron Hancocks, MC, RA, who *d.* 1970, and has issue living, Charles Robin, *b.* 1929,—Rosemary Patricia, *b.* 1937. *Residence,*—27, Cherry Court, Cheriton Rd., Folkestone.

PREDECESSORS.—[1] WILLIAM la Zouche, Lord of Haryngworth, was summoned to Parliament of England as a Baron 1308-14; *d.* 1352; *s.* by his grandson [2] WILLIAM, 2nd Baron; summoned to Parliament during his grandfather's lifetime 1348-51, and after his grandfather's decease 1352-82; *d.* 1382: *s.* by his son [3] WILLIAM, 3rd Baron; summoned to Parliament 1383-94; *d.* 1396; *s.* by his son [4] WILLIAM, K.G., 4th Baron; summoned to Parliament 1396-1414; *d.* 1415; *s.* by his son [5] WILLIAM, 5th Baron; summoned to Parliament 1426-63; *d.* 1463; *s.* by his son [6] WILLIAM, 6th Baron, who in 1466 was summoned to Parliament in right of his mother as *Baron St. Maur; d.* 1468; *s.* by his son [7] JOHN, 7th Baron; was summoned to Parliament 1482-3; attainted 1485, and attainder reversed 1495 ; again summoned to Parliament 1509-15; *d.* 1526; *s.* by his son [8] JOHN, 8th Baron; summoned to Parliament 1529-48; *d.* 1550; *s.* by his son [9] RICHARD, 9th Baron; was summoned to Parliament 1552; *d.* 1552; *s.* by his son [10] GEORGE, 10th Baron; summoned to Parliament 1553-66; *d.* 1569; *s.* by his son [11] EDWARD, 11th Baron; was summoned to Parliament 1571-1625; was Lieut. of N. and S. Wales, and Constable of Dover and Warden of the Cinque Ports; *d.* 1625, when the Baronies of Zouche and St. Maur became abeyant between his two daus., Elizabeth and Mary, and remained so until 1815, when the abeyancy of the Barony of Zouche was terminated in favour of [12] *Sir* CECIL Bisshopp, 8th Bt., who became 12th Baron in right of his mother, she being the descendant in the 6th generation of Elizabeth, el. dau. of 11th Baron (ante) ; *d.* 1828, when the baronetcy devolved upon his cousin, and the barony became abeyant between his two daus., Harriet Anne Curzon (infra), and Katherine Annabella, wife of Sir George Richard Brooke-Pechell, 4th Bt. ; in 1829 the abeyance was terminated in favour of his el. dau. [13] HARRIET ANNE, known as Baroness de la Zouche : *m.* 1808, the Hon. Robert Curzon, M.P., son of 1st Viscount Curzon [see E. Howe]; *d.* 1870; *s.* by her son [14] ROBERT Curzon, 14th Baron; *b.* 1810;

was M.P. for Clitheroe: *m.* 1850, Emily Julia, dau. of the Rt. Hon. Sir Robert Wilmot-Horton, 3rd Bt.: *d.* 1873: *s.* by his son [15] ROBERT NATHANIEL CECIL GEORGE, 15th Baron; *b.* 1851: *m.* 1875, the Hon. Annie Mary Eleanor Fraser (from whom he obtained a divorce 1876), who *d.* 1895, 2nd dau. of 17th Baron Saltoun; *d.* 1914; *s.* by his sister [16] DAREA, *b.* 1860; *d.* 1917; *s.* by her cousin [17] MARY CECIL (da. of the late Col. George Augustus Curzon, grandson of the late Harriet Anne, Baroness de la Zouche), *b.* 1875: *m.* 1901, Sir Frederick William Francis George Frankland, 10th Bt. who *d.* 1937 [see *₊* infra]; *d.* 1965 *s.* by her grandson [18] *Sir* JAMES ASSHETON Frankland (only son of the Hon. Sir Thomas William Assheton Frankland, 11th Bt.), who *s.* as 12th Bt. 1944 (infra); 18th Baron and present peer.

₊ [1] WILLIAM, son of *Sir* Henry Frankland of Thirkelby, Yorks., *b. c.* 1640; MP for Thirsk, *cr.* a Baronet of England 1660: *m.* 1662, Arabella, who *d.* 1687, da. of the Hon. Henry Belasyse, *d.* 1697, *s.* by his el son [2] *Sir* THOMAS, 2nd Bt., *b. c.* 1665; PMG 1690-1715 and MP for Thirsk, *m.* 1683, Elizabeth, who *d.* 1733, da. of Sir John Russell, 4th Bt. (*cr.* 1629) by Frances, da. of Oliver Cromwell, Lord Protector: *d.* 1726; *s.* by his el. son [3] *Sir* THOMAS, 3rd Bt.; a Lord of Admiralty 1730-41 and MP for Harwich and Thirsk: *m.* 1st, Dinah, who *d.* 1741, da. of Francis Topham; 2ndly, 1743, Sarah Moseley, who *d.* 1783; *d.* 1747; *s.* by his nephew [4] *Sir* CHARLES HENRY, 4th Bt. (el. son of Henry Frankland, 4th son of 2nd Bt.) *b.* 1716; Collector at Boston, Mass., 1741-57 and Consul-Gen. at Lisbon 1757-67: *m.* 1756, Agnes (who *m.* 2ndly, 1781, John Drew, banker, and *d.* 1783) da. of Edward Surriage, of Marblehead, New England; *d.* 1768; *s.* by his brother [5] *Sir* THOMAS, 5th Bt., *b.* 1718; Admiral of the White and MP for Thirsk: *m.* 1743, Sarah Rhett, of S. Carolina, who *d.* 1808; *d.* 1784; *s.* by his el. surv. son [6] *Sir* THOMAS, FRS, 6th Bt., *b.* 1750; MP for Thirsk: *m.* 1773, Dorothy, who *d.* 1820, da. of William Smelt; *d.* 1831; *s.* by his only surv. son [7] *Sir* ROBERT, 7th Bt.; *b.* 1784; MP for Thirsk; assumed by Roy. Lic. 1837 the surname of Russell after Frankland on inheriting Chequers Court, Bucks. from Sir Robert Greenhill Russell, Bt.: *m.* 1815, Louisa Anne, who *d.* 1871, da. of Lord George Murray [D. Atholl]; *d.* 1849; *s.* by his cousin in the Baronetcy but not the estates [8] *Sir* FREDERICK WILLIAM, 8th Bt. (el. son of the Rev. Canon Roger Frankland, yst. son of 5th Bt.), *b.* 1793; served at Waterloo and Peninsula: *m.* 1821, Katherine Margaret, who *d.* 1871, da. of Capt. Isaac Scarth; *d.* 1878; *s.* by his el. surv. son [9] *Sir* WILLIAM ADOLPHUS, 9th Bt. *b.* 1837; Lt.-Col. R.E.: *m.* 1864, Lucy Ducarel, who *d.* 1928, da. of Francis Adams, of Clifton, Glos.; *d.* 1883; *s.* by his el. son [10] *Sir* FREDERICK WILLIAM FRANCIS GEORGE, 10th Bt., *b.* 1868; Maj. Beds. Regt. Matabele and S. African Wars: *m.* 1st, 1890, Charlotte, who *d.* 1892, da. of John Augustus di Zerega of New York; 2ndly, 1901, Mary Cecil Curzon, *Baroness Zouche*, who *d.* 1965 (ante); *d.* 1937; *s.* by his el. son [11] *Hon. Sir* THOMAS WILLIAM ASSHETON, 11th Bt., *b.* 1902; Maj. 15th/19th Hussars: *m.* 1st, 1931 (m. diss, 1941), Edna Maud, da. of Frederick Hynde Fox; 2ndly, 1942, Pamela Catherine Mabell (ROUS), da. of Capt. the Hon. Edward James Kay-Shuttleworth [B. Shuttleworth] and who *m.* 3rdly, 1946, Henry Michael Barclay; *d.* 1944; *s.* by his only son [12] *Sir* JAMES ASSHETON, 12th and present Bt., who *s.* as 18th Baron Zouche (ante) 1965.

ZUCKERMAN, BARON. (Zuckerman.) [Life Baron 1971.]

SOLLY ZUCKERMAN, *OM, KCB, FRS*, son of the late Moses Zuckerman; *b.* May 30th, 1904; ed. at Cape Town Univ.; Hon. Dr. Bordeaux; Hon. DSc Sussex, Jacksonville (USA), and Bradford; Hon. LLD Birmingham; Hon. FRCS England; FRCP London; Foreign Member American Philosophical Soc.; Hon. Sec. of Zoological Soc. of London; a Trustee, British Museum (Natural History); Scientific Adviser on Planning, Allied Expeditionary Air Forces, and Scientific Dir. RAF Bombing Analysis Unit 1939-46; Sands Cox Prof. of Anatomy Birmingham Univ. 1943-68. Dep. Chm. of Advisory Council on Scientific Policy 1948-64, a Member of Agric. Research Council 1949-59, Chm. of Natural Resources (Tech.) Cttee. 1951-64, and of Defence Research Policy Cttee. 1960-64; Ch. Scientific Adviser to Sec. of State for Defence 1960-66, and Ch. Scientific Adviser Cabinet Office 1964-71; Representative at NATO Cttee. of National Dirs. of Research and Development 1964; Prof. at Large, E. Anglia Univ. since 1969; Chevalier of Legion of Honour; American Medal of Freedom with Silver Palm *cr.* CB (Civil) 1946, Knt. 1956, KCB (Civil) 1964, OM 1968, and *Baron Zuckerman*, of Burnham Thorpe, co. Norfolk (Life Baron) 1971: *m.* 1939, Lady Joan Alice Violet Rufus Isaacs, da. of 2nd Marquess of Reading, and has issue.

Arms,—Tierced in pale each per bend bevilled Or and Gules. **Crest.**—On a cap of state Gules turned up ermine a Lion Sejeant Or supporting a book bound Azure clasped Or. **Supporters,**—*Dexter,* a great ape (Gorilla Gorilla); *Sinister,* a Tarsier (Tarsius Spectrum) both proper.

Residence,—The Shooting Box, Burnham Thorpe, King's Lynn, Norfolk.

SON LIVING.

Hon. Paul Sebastian, *b.* 1945; ed. at Rugby, and Trin. Coll., Camb.: *m.* 1972, Mrs. Janette Hampel, da. of R. R. Mather, of Stoke-by-Clare, Suffolk.

DAUGHTER LIVING.

Hon. Stella Maria, *b.* 1947.

PEERS'

Sons and Daughters, Brothers and Sisters, Widows of Sons of Peers, and Maids of Honour; also Grandchildren of Dukes, Marquesses and Earls.

(BEARING COURTESY TITLES.)

Abbey, Lady Ursula H. .. Cairns, E.
Abraham, Hon. Juliet J. M. Moynihan, B.
Acheson, Lady Isabella A... Gosford, E.
Acheson, Hon. Patrick B. V.
M. .. .. Gosford, E.
Acloque, Hon. Camilla .. .. Howard de
Walden, B.

A'Court, Hon. James
Holmes .. .. Heytesbury, B.
A'Court, Hon. Sarah C.
Holmes .. .. Heytesbury, B.
Acton, Hon. Edward D. J.
Lyon-Dalberg .. .. Acton, B,
Acton, Hon. Jane Lyon-
Dalberg- .. .. Acton, B.
Acton, Hon. Joan H. J. M.
C. Lyon-Dalberg- .. .. Acton, B.
Acton, Hon. John C. Lyon-
Dalberg- .. .. Acton, B.
Acton, Hon. Margaret M. T.
Lyon-Dalberg- .. .. Acton, B.
Acton, Hon. Peter H. Lyon-
Dalberg- .. .. .. Acton, B.
Acton, Hon. Richard G.
Lyon-Dalberg- .. .. .. Acton, B.
Acton, Hon. Robert P. Lyon-
Dalberg- .. .. Acton, B.
Adam, Hon. Irene C. .. .. Wenlock, By.
Adam, Hon. Vivien E. .. Ravensdale, B.
Adams, Hon. Eileen E. .. Castlemaine, B.
Adams, Hon. M. Elizabeth.. Trevethin and
Oaksey, B.
Adams, Hon. Marjorie H. .. Darwen, B.
Adderley, Hon. James N. A. Norton, B.
Adderley, Hon. Michael C. A. Norton, B.
Adderley, Hon. Nigel J. .. Norton, B.
Addington, Hon. Elizabeth
C. .. .. Sidmouth, V.
Addington, Hon. Gurth L. F. Sidmouth, V.
Addington, Hon. Hiley W. D. Sidmouth, V.
Addington, Hon. John T. A.
P. .. .. Sidmouth, V.
Addington, Hon. Leslie R. B. Sidmouth, V.
Addington, Hon. Raleigh H.
L. .. .. Sidmouth, V.
Addington, Hon. Thomas R.
C. .. .. Sidmouth, V.
Addison, Hon. Michael .. Addison, V.
Adeane, Hon. George E. .. Adeane, B.
Adrian, Hon. Richard H. .. Adrian, B.
Agar, Lady Caroline A. C... Normanton, E.
Agar, Hon. Mark S. A. .. Normanton, E.
Agnew, Hon. Agneta J. H. .. Campbell of
Eskan, B.
Agnew, Hon. Clare R. .. .. Glentoran, B.
Agnew, Hon. Lady (Doreen
M.) .. .. Jessel, B.
Agnew, Hon. Joyce V. .. Godber, B.
Agnew, Lady Teresa J. .. Ilchester, E.
Aikman, Hon. Pamela H. .. Glenarthur, B.
Aird, Lady Priscilla .. .. Ancaster, E.
Aird, Lady Margaret D.
Stirling- .. .. Glasgow, E.
Aitken, Hon. Laura .. .. Beaverbrook, By.
Aitken, Hon. Maxwell W. H. Beaverbrook, By.
Aitken, Hon. Lady (Penelope
L.) .. .. Rugby, B.
Alchin, Hon. Juliet A. .. Hankey, B.
Alexander, Hon. Ada K. .. Bellew B.
Alexander, Hon. Brian J. .. Alexander of
Tunis, E.
Alexander, Lady Elizabeth
J. .. .. Caledon, E.
Alexander, Hon. Kirstin E... Ullswater, V.
Alexander, Lady Mary B. .. Bath, M.
Alexander, Hon. Robert W.
P. .. .. Alexander of
Potterhill, B.
Alexander, Hon. Thomas B. Alexander of
Potterhill, B.
Allan, Hon. Alexander C. S. Allan of Kilma-
hew, B.
Allan, Hon. Jane M. .. .. Allan of Kilma-
hew, B.
Allanby, Lady Anne S. E. .. Mexborough, E.
Allen, Hon. Joan C. C. .. Allen of Hurt-
wood, By.
Allen, Hon. Joan E. .. .. Platt, B.

Allen, Hon. Lionel P. .. .. Allen of Fallow-
field, B.
Allen, Lady Margaret J.
Sandeman- .. .. .. Woolton, E.
Allenby, Hon. Claude W. H. Allenby, V.
Allenby, Hon. Michael J. H. Allenby, V.
Allfrey, Hon. Julian M. .. Russell of Kill-
owen, B.
Allhusen, Hon. Claudia V. .. Rushcliffe, By.
Allsopp, Hon. Charles H. .. Hindlip, B.
Allsopp Hon. Elizabeth T. Hindlip, B.
Allsopp, Hon. John P. .. Hindlip, B.
Allsopp, Hon. Norah H. .. Hatherton, B.
Alport, Hon. Arthur E. B... Alport, B.
Altham, Hon. Elizabeth O... McNair, B.
Aly Khan, Hon. Joan B. .. Churston, B.
Ameer Ali, Lady Eleanor C.A. Dartrey, E.
Amherst, Hon. Humphrey W. Amherst, E.
Amherst, Lady Joan G. E... Amherst, E.
Ammon, Hon. Ada M. .. Ammon, By.
Ammon, Hon. May J. .. .. Ammon, By.
Amory, Hon. Margaret I. G. Howard de Wal-
Heathcote- den, B.
Anderson, Hon. Cecilia C. .. Waterpark, B.
Anderson, Hon. Elizabeth M. Bannerman of
Kildonan, By.
Anderson, Lady Flavia J. L. Halsbury, E.
Anderson, Lady Gillian M. Perth, E.
Anderson, Hon. John D. F... Waverley, V.
Anderson, Hon. Patricia M. J. Waverley, V.
Anderson, Hon. Paulette A. Sainsbury, B.
Andrew, Hon. Gwyneth M. Aberdare, B.
Anggard, Hon. Adele B. A. Hankey, B.
Annan, Hon. Amanda L. .. Annan, B.
Annan, Hon. Juliet L. .. .. Annan, B.
Annesley, Lady Clare .. .. Annesley, E.
Annesley, Hon. Frances E... Annesley, E.
Annesley, Hon. Michael R... Annesley, E.
Annesley, Hon. Nora K. .. Annesley, E.
Annesley, Hon. Patricia C... Annesley, E.
Annesley, Hon. Philip H. .. Annesley, E.
Annesley, Hon. Richard J. D. Valentia, V.
Anstey, Lady Evelyn F. .. Devon, E.
Arbuthnott, Hon. Hugh S. .. Arbuthnott, V.
Arbuthnott, Hon. John K. O. Arbuthnott, V.
Arbuthnott, Hon. Louisa M. St. Helens, B.
Arbuthnott, Hon. Norah G. Arbuthnott, V.
Arbuthnott, Hon. Susanna M. Arbuthnott, V.
Arbuthnott, Hon. William D. Arbuthnott, V.
Archer, Hon. Ruth E. .. Daryngton, B.
Archer, Hon. Sonia G. O. .. Birdwood, B.
Armit, Hon. Serena H. C. .. Caldecote, V.
Armstrong, Hon. M. Kath- Napier of Mag-
leen dala, B.
Armstrong, Hon. Peter W... Armstrong of
Sanderstead, B.
Arthur, Hon. Janet S. .. .. Brain, B.
Arthur, Hon. Jennifer .. Renwick, B.
Arthur Hon. Matthew R. .. Glenarthur, B.
Arthur, Hon. Simon M. .. Glenarthur, B.
Arthur, Hon. Victoria .. .. Glenarthur, B.
Arthurton, Hon. Phillipa S... Mills, V.
Arundell, Hon. Charlotte A.
Monckton- .. .. .. Galway, V.
Arwyn, Hon. Arwyn H.D. .. Arwyn, B.
Ashby, Hon. Michael F. .. Ashby, B.
Ashby, Hon. Peter N. .. Ashby, B.
Ashe. Hon. Estelle E. S. .. Kingsale, B.
Ashford, Lady Winifred A. G. Dundonald, E.
Ashton, Hon. Thomas J. .. Ashton of Hyde,
B.
Askew, Lady Susan A. .. Sutherland, D.
Aspden, Hon. Judith A. .. Harmar-Nicholls,
B.
Aspinall, Lady Sarah M. .. Howe, E.
Asquith, Lady Clare P. F. .. Oxford and
Asquith, E.
Asquith, Hon. Dominic A. G. Oxford and
Asquith, E.
Asquith, Lady Helen F. .. Oxford and
Asquith, E.
Asquith, Hon. Jane .. ... Asquith of
Bishopstone,By.
Asquith, Hon. Luke .. .. Asquith of
Bishopstone,By.
Asquith, Lady Mary A. .. Oxford and
Asquith, E.

Asquith, Hon. Paul .. .. *Asquith of Bishopstone, By.*
Assheton, Hon. Nicholas .. *Clitheroe, B.*
Assheton, Hon. Ralph J. .. *Clitheroe, B.*
Astley, Hon. Delaval T. H... *Hastings, B.*
Astley, Hon. Harriet M. .. *Hastings, B.*
Astley, Hon. Justin E. .. *Hastings, B.*
Astor, Hon. Bridget M. .. *Astor of Hever, B.*
Astor, Hon. Elizabeth L. .. *Astor of Hever, B.*
Astor, Hon. Emily M... .. *Astor, V.*
Astor, Hon. Francis D. L. .. *Astor, V.*
Astor, Hon. Gavin .. .. *Astor of Hever, B.*
Astor, Hon. Hugh W. .. *Astor of Hever, B.*
Astor, Hon. Janet E. .. *Astor, V.*
Astor, Hon. John .. .. *Astor of Hever, B.*
Astor, Hon. John J. .. *Astor, V.*
Astor, Hon. John J. .. .. *Astor of Hever, B.*
Astor, Hon. Michael L. .. *Astor, V.*
Astor, Hon. Pauline M. .. *Astor, V.*
Astor, Hon. Philip D. P. .. *Astor of Hever, B.*
Astrom, Hon. Brenda .. *Cooper of Stockton Heath, B.*
Atkin Hon. William R. .. *Atkin, By.*
Atkins Hon. A. Jennifer Burnaby- .. .. .. *Trevethin and Oaksey, B.*
Atkinson, Hon. Patricia .. *Beswick, B.*
Attlee, Lady Jane E. .. *Attlee, E.*
Attlee, Hon Rosemary .. *Elton, B.*
Austin, Hon. Alison M. Merivale .. .. .. *Rankeillour, B.*
Austin, Lady Lilian M. T... *Scarbrough, E.*
Ayre, Lady Margaret I. .. *Mar, E.*
Bailey, Hon. Christopher R. *Glanusk, B.*
Bailey, Lady Daphne M. .. *Cadogan, E.*
Bailey, Hon. Irma .. .. *Cozens-Hardy, B.*
Baillie, Hon. Alexander J. . *Burton, B.*
Baillie, Hon. Mrs. Arthur M. A... .. .. .. *Burton, B.*
Baillie, Hon. Evan M. R. .. *Burton, B.*
Baillie, Hon. Fiona M. .. *Burton, B.*
Baillie, Hon. Georgina F. .. *Burton, B.*
Baillie, Hon. Peter C. .. *Burton, B.*
Baillie, Hon. Philippa U. M. *Burton, B.*
Baillieu, Hon. David C. L. *Baillieu, B.*
Baillieu, Hon. Edward L. .. *Baillieu, B.*
Baillieu, Hon. James W. L. *Baillieu, B.*
Baillieu, Hon. Robert L. .. *Baillieu, B.*
Bailward, Hon. Diana P. F. *Basing, B.*
Baily, Lady Sarah D. .. .. *Glasgow, E.*
Baird, Hon. Alexander D. .. *Kintore, E.*
Baldwin, Hon. Alison M. .. *Torphichen, L*
Baldwin, Hon. Benedict A. S. *Baldwin of Bewdley, E.*
Baldwin, Lady Esther L. .. *Baldwin of Bewdley, E.*
Balfour, Hon. Aurea V. .. *Ashburton, B.*
Balfour, Hon. David A. .. *Kinross, B.*
Balfour, Hon. David R. .. *Riverdale, B.*
Balfour, Lady Evelyn B. .. *Balfour, E.*
Balfour, Hon. Frances C. .. *Riverdale, B.*
Balfour, Hon. Francis H. .. *Riverdale, B.*
Balfour, Lady Griselda D. R. *Airlie, E.*
Balfour, Hon. Ian .. .. *Balfour of Inchrye, B.*
Balfour, Hon. Mark R. .. *Riverdale, B.*
Balfour, Lady Mary E. .. *Balfour, E.*
Balfour, Hon. Phyllis E. .. *Goschen, V.*
Balfour, Hon. Tessa M. I. .. *Beaumont, B.*
Ball, Hon. Ann M. .. .. *Gordon-Walker, B.*
Ballantyne, Hon. Hazel M. . *Shaughnessy, B.*
Balogh, Hon. Christopher T. *Balogh, B.*
Balogh, Hon. Penelope K. T. *Balogh, B.*
Balogh, Hon. Stephen B. .. *Balogh, B.*
Bampfylde, Hon. Mrs. Anthony G. H. .. .. *Poltimore, B.*
Bampfylde, Hon. David C. W. .. .. *Poltimore, B.*
Banbury, Hon. Anna J. .. *Banbury of Southam, B.*
Banbury, Hon. Carolyn .. *Banbury of Southam, B.*
Banbury, Hon. Charles W... *Banbury of Southam, B.*
Bankes, Hon. Juliet A. .. *Forres, B.*
Banks, Hon. Alistair R. H. *Banks, B.*
Banks, Hon. Graham T. H. *Banks, B.*
Bannerman, Hon. Calum R. M. *Bannerman of Kildonan, B.*
Bannerman, Hon. John W. M. *Bannerman of Kildonan, B.*
Barbary, Lady Pamela J. .. *Westmeath, E.*
Barber, Hon. Josephine J. A. *Barber, B.*
Barber, Hon. Louise P. L. .. *Barber, B.*
Barbour, Hon. Helen V. .. *Polwarth, L.*
Barclay, Hon. Phyllis P. .. *Somerleyton, B.*
Bardsley, Lady Rose .. *Westmorland, E.*

Barford, Hon. Marian W. .. *Ashfield, By.*
Baring, Hon. Alexandra G. *Northbrook, B.*
Baring, Hon. Alice O. .. *Howick of Glendale, B.*
Baring, Hon. Angela M. .. *Ashburton, B.*
Baring, Hon. Anne.. .. .. *Northbrook, B.*
Baring, Hon. Catherine M .. *Northbrook, B.*
Baring, Hon. Francis T. .. *Northbrook, B.*
Baring, Hon. James C. .. *Revelstoke, B.*
Baring, Hon. Jessica M. C. .. *Howick of Glendale, B.*
Baring, Hon. John .. .. *Revelstoke, B.*
Baring, Hon. John F. H. .. *Ashburton, B.*
Baring, Hon. Laura A. .. *Northbrook, B.*
Baring, Hon. Robin A... .. *Ashburton, B.*
Baring, Hon. Rachel M. .. *Howick of Glendale, B.*
Baring, Lady Rose G. L. .. *Antrim, E.*
Baring, Hon. Sarah K. E. .. *Grantley, B.*
Baring, Hon. Susan M. .. *Renwick, B.*
Baring, Hon. Vivian J. R. .. *Cromer, E.*
Barker, Hon. Olwen G. .. *Kylsant, By.*
Barlow, Hon. (Diana H.) Lady .. .. *Rochdale, V.*
Barlow, Hon. Dorothy .. .. *Emmott, By.*
Barlow, Lady Helen .. .. *Shannon, E.*
Barnes, Hon. E. Seymour .. *Methuen, B.*
Barnes, Hon. Janet E. .. *Maclean, B.*
Barnes, Hon. Ronald A. H. *Gorell, B.*
Barnett, Hon. Kathleen I. M. *Windlesham, B.*
Barnett, Hon. Vera K... .. *Woodbridge, B.*
Barnewall, Hon. Anthony E. *Trimlestown, B.*
Barnewall, Hon. Raymond C. *Trimlestown, B.*
Barnwell, Hon. Elizabeth M. *Teignmouth, B.*
Barrand, Hon. Jane .. .. *King-Hall, By.*
Barrington, Hon. Elizabeth F. M... .. .. .. *Delamere, B.*
Barrow, Hon. Hilary A. .. *Evans of Hungershall, B.*
Barry, Lady Margaret .. .. *Radnor, E.*
Barry, Lady Sarah S. .. *Harrington, E.*
Bartholomew, Hon. Noreen *Long, V.*
Barton, Hon. Elizabeth J. B. *Boyd-Orr, By.*
Barton, Lady Mary G... .. *Breadalbane, E.*
Barttelot, Hon. (M. A. Fiona), Lady .. .. *Forester, B.*
Barwell, Hon. Sheila M. R. *McNair, B.*
Basset, Lady Carey E. .. *Leicester, E.*
Basset, Lady Elizabeth .. *Dartmouth, E.*
Basualdo, Hon. Lucy .. *Cowdray, V.*
Bates, Hon. Margaret E. .. *Shepherd, B.*
Bateson, Hon. Ann K. de Yarburgh .. .. .. *Deramore, B.*
Bateson, Hon. Mrs. Eustace de Yarburgh- .. .. .. *Deramore, B.*
Bateson, Hon. Judith K. de Yarburgh- .. .. .. *Deramore, B.*
Bathurst, Hon. Alexander E. S. .. .. *Bathurst, E.*
Bathurst, Hon. Christopher H. L... .. .. *Bledisloe, V.*
Bathurst, Hon. David C. L. *Bledisloe, V.*
Bathurst, Lady E. Ann .. *Temple of Stowe, E.*
Bathurst, Hon. George B. .. *Bathurst, E.*
Bathurst, Lady Henrietta M. L. .. .. *Bathurst, E.*
Bathurst, Hon. V. Elizabeth V. Hervey- .. .. .. *Somers, B.*
Batt, Hon. Elisabeth N. .. *Monck, V.*
Baxendale, Lady Elizabeth J. *Fortescue, E.*
Baxter, Hon. Helen M. .. *Hawarden, V.*
Bayford, Hon. H. Elizabeth M. *Croft, B.*
Bayliss, Hon. Mary S. .. *Bridgeman, V.*
Beach, Hon. David S. Hicks *St. Aldwyn, E.*
Beach, Hon. Peter H. Hicks *St. Aldwyn, E.*
Beamish, Hon. Andrea T. .. *Chelwood, B.*
Beamish, Hon. Claudia H. .. *Chelwood, B.*
Bearman, Hon. Gloria M. *Scarsdale, V.*
Beasley, Lady Alexandra N. F. *Wilton, E.*
Beattie, Hon. Jane K. .. *Tangley, By.*
Beatty, Lady Diana A. .. *Beatty, E.*
Beatty, Lady Miranda K. *Beatty, E.*
Beatty, Hon. Nicholas D. .. *Beatty, E.*
Beatty, Hon. V. A. Sibell .. *Southampton, By.*
Beauchamp, Lady Evelyn L. A. .. .. *Carnarvon, E.*
Beauchamp, Hon. Susan S. North- .. .. *North, By.*
Beauclerk, Lady Emma C. de V. .. .. *St. Albans, D.*
Beauclerk, Lord James C. F. de V. .. .. *St. Albans, D.*
Beauclerk, Lord John W. A. de V. .. .. *St. Albans, D.*
Beauclerk, Lord Peter C. de V. .. .. *St. Albans, D.*
Beaumont, Hon. Alaric C. B. *Beaumont of Whitley, B.*
Beaumont, Hon. Ariadne G. *Beaumont of Whitley, B.*

Daniel, Lady Valerie D. .. *Lloyd George of*
    Dwyfor, E.
Danks, Hon. Serena M. .. *Gifford, B.*
Darby, Hon. Meril K. .. *Home of the*
    Hirsel, B.
D'Arcy, Lady Margaret F. G. *Kinnoull, E.*
Darling, Hon. Isabel .. .. *Darling of Hills-*
    borough, B.
Darling, Hon. Lucinda M. J. *Darling, B.*
Darling, Hon. Peter G. .. *Darling of Hills-*
    borough, B.
Darling, Hon. R. Julian .. *Darling, B.*
das Neves, Hon. Amanda
M. A. .. .. *Grey of Naunton,*
    B.
Davey, Hon. Heather M. .. *Morris of*
    Grasmere, B.
Davey, Hon. Mary .. .. *Bowden, B.*
Davidson, Hon. Alexandra F. *Davidson, V.*
Davidson, Hon. Camilla B. .. *Davidson, V.*
Davidson, Hon. Elizabeth M. *Younger of*
    Leckie, V.
Davidson, Hon. Georgina C. *Davidson, V.*
Davidson, Hon. Kristina L. *Davidson, V.*
Davidson, Hon. Malcolm W.
M. .. .. *Davidson, V.*
Davies, Hon. Annie B. .. .. *Macpherson of*
    Drumochter, B.
Davies, Hon. Arwyn H. .. *Arwyn, B.*
Davies, Hon. Catherine Joy *Darwen, B.*
Davies, Hon. David D. .. *Davies of*
    Penrhys, B.
Davies, Hon. Edward D. G. *Davies, B.*
Davies, Hon. Eldrydd J. .. *Davies, B.*
Davies, Hon. F. Ronald .. *Darwen, B.*
Davies, Hon. Gwynfor .. *Davies of*
    Penrhys, B.
Davies, Hon. Islwyn E. E. *Davies, B.*
Davies, Hon. Jonathan H... *Davies, B.*
Davies, Hon. Mary B. .. .. *Northbourne,*
    B.
Davies, Hon. Philip C. M. .. *Davies, B.*
Davies, Hon. Roger M. .. .. *Darwen, B.*
Davies, Hon. Stephen H. .. *Darwen, B.*
Davies, Hon. Thomas B. .. *Darwen, B.*
Davies, Lady Venetia C. K... *Kinnoull, E.*
Davies, Hon. Harriett L. R.
Llewelyn .. .. *Llewelyn-*
    Davies, B.
Davies, Hon. Rebecca *Llewelyn-*
Llewelyn   *Davies, B.*
Davies, Hon. Rachel M. Lloyd *Clifden, Vy.*
Davis, Lady Alison E. .. *Attlee, E.*
Davis, Hon. Beatrice M. .. *Mills, V.*
Davis, Lady G. Elizabeth .. *Normanby, M.*
Davis, Hon. Catherine R.
Lovell- .. .. *Lovell-Davis, B.*
Davis, Hon. Stephen L.
Lovell- .. .. *Lovell-Davis, B.*
Davison, Hon. Alexander .. *Broughshane, B.*
Davison, Hon. Elizabeth .. *Slater, B.*
Davison, Hon. W. Kensing-
ton .. .. *Broughshane, B.*
Dawnay, Lady Angela C. R. *Buccleuch, D.*
Dawnay, Hon. George W. ff. *Downe, V.*
Dawnay, Hon. Iris I. A. .. *Ingleby, V.*
Dawnay, Hon. James R. .. *Downe, V.*
Dawnay, Lady Katherine N.
De la P. .. .. *Waterford, M.*
Dawnay, Hon. Richard H. .. *Downe, V.*
Dawnay, Hon. Sarah F. .. *Downe, V.*
Dawson, Hon. Ivy M... .. *Auckland, B.*
Deakin, Hon. Rose A. .. *Donaldson of*
    Kingsbridge, B.
Dean, Hon. Thalia M... .. *Craigmyle, B.*
Deane, Hon. Betty C. .. .. *Muskerry, B.*
Deane, Hon. Marjorie M. F. *Muskerry, B.*
Deane, Hon. Robert F. .. *Muskerry, B.*
de Bellaigue, Hon. Sylvia C. *Rodney, B.*
Debenham, Hon. Daphne J. *Godber, B.*
de Bunsen, Hon. Alexandra .. *Carrington, B.*
de Cabarrus, Lady Caroline *Northumberland,*
M. .. .. *D.*
de Caicedo, Hon. Camilla
E. M. E. .. .. *Jessel, B.*
de Chair, Lady A. Juliet D.
M. .. .. *Fitzwilliam, E.*
de Courcy, Hon. Diana R. .. *Kingsale, B.*
Deen, Hon. L. Anne G. .. *Kinloss, Bs.*
d'Erlanger, Hon. M. Elizabeth
J. .. .. *Exmouth, V.*
de Fresnes, Lady Fiona H. *Loudoun, Cs.*
de Grey, Hon. Elizabeth A... *Walsingham, B.*
de Grey, Hon. Richard P. .. *Walsingham, B.*
de Grey, Hon. Robert .. *Walsingham, B.*
de Grey, Hon. Sarah J. .. *Walsingham, B.*
de Kermaignant, Hon.
Fanny L. .. .. .. *Vernon, B.*
de Koenigswarter, (Hon.
Kathleen A. P.) Baroness
Jules .. .. *Rothschild, B.*
Delap, Hon. Anastasia D. .. *Glenkinglas, B.*

de Laszlo, Hon. Sandra D. ... *Hacking, B.*
Delevingne, Hon. Angela M.
H. .. .. *Greenwood, V.*
de Ligne La Tremoille, H.H.
    Princess Charles (Lady
    Moira de Ligne La Tremoille) *Granard, E.*
de Lisle, Hon. Mary R. .. *Ingleby, V.*
della Grazia (Lady Hermione *Powis, E., and*
    G. Palli), Duchessa .. ..   *Darcy de*
    Knayth, Bs.
de Marffy, Hon. Pelline M... *Acton, B.*
de Moleyns, Hon. Mrs. Francis
    A. I. Eveleigh-Ross- *Ventry, B.*
de Moleyns, Hon. Mrs. John
    G. Eveleigh- *Ventry, B.*
Denham, Lady Mary A. .. *Moray, E.*
Denman, Hon. Christopher J. *Denman, B.*
Denman, Hon. James S. .. *Denman, B.*
Denman, Hon. Richard T. S. *Denman, B.*
Denmark (Anne F.), Princess
    Georg of *Strathmore, E.*
Denning, Hon. Robert G. .. *Denning, B.*
Dennys, Hon. Lavinia M. Y. *Cobham, V.*
Dent, Hon. Ann C. .. *Pender, B.*
Dent, Lady Elizabeth B. M. *Kinnoull, E.*
Dent, Hon. Rosamond .. *Furnivall, By.*
de Renusson d'Hauteville,
    Hon. Joanna P. .. .. *Rennell, B.*
de Rosnay (Hon. Stella C.)
    Baroness Joël .. .. .. *Gladwyn, B.*
de Trafford, Hon. Cecilia .. *Strickland, By.*
Devas, Hon. Penelope A. .. *O'Neill of the*
    Maine, B.
de Verteuil, Lady Dorothy
M. .. .. *Cranbrook, E.*
de Vilallonga, Hon. Essylt P. *Howard de*
    Walden, B.
de Villiers, Hon. Alexander C. *de Villiers, B.*
de Villiers, Hon. John M. .. *de Villiers, B.*
Devlin, Hon. Dominick .. *Devlin, B.*
Devlin, Hon. Gilpatrick .. *Devlin, B.*
Devlin, Hon. Matthew .. *Devlin, B.*
Devlin, Hon. Timothy .. *Devlin, B.*
Dewar, Lady Elisabeth J. *Waldegrave, E.*
Dewar, Hon. John J. E. .. *Forteviot, B.*
Dewar, Hon. Simon T. .. *Forteviot, B.*
Dewhurst, Hon. Irene M. .. *Forteviot, B.*
de Wichfeld, Lady A. A.
    Maryel .. .. *Perth, E.*
de Zulueta, Hon. Marie-
    Louise .. .. *Windlesham, B.*
Diamond, Hon. Derek .. *Diamond, B.*
Diamond, Hon. Joan. .. *Diamond, B.*
Diamond, Hon. Martin .. *Diamond, B.*
Diamond, Hon. Ruth .. *Diamond, B.*
Dickinson, Hon. Andrew .. *Dickinson, B.*
Dickinson, Hon. David C. .. *Dickinson, B.*
Dickinson, Rev. the Hon.
    Hugh G. .. .. .. *Dickinson, B.*
Dickinson, Hon. Martin H... *Dickinson, B.*
Dickinson, Hon. Peter M. de
B. .. .. *Dickinson, B.*
Dickinson, Hon. Mrs. Richard
    S. W. .. .. *Dickinson, B.*
di Montelera (Lady Moira
    M.), Countess .. .. *Granard, E.*
Diehl, Hon. Sybil D. .. .. *Tollemache, B.*
Digby, Hon. A. Elmar.. .. *Digby, B.*
Digby, Hon. Henry N. K... *Digby, B.*
Digby, Hon. Rupert S. .. *Digby, B.*
Digby, Hon. Zara J. .. *Digby, B.*
Dillon, Hon. Charles H. R. *Dillon, V.*
Dillon, Hon. Ethel L. .. *Clonbrock, By.*
Dillon, Hon. Inès M. J. .. *Dillon, V.*
Dillon, Hon. Madeleine M. .. *Dillon, V.*
Dillon, Hon. Michael E. .. *Dillon, V.*
Dillon, Hon. Patrick D. .. *Dillon, V.*
Dillon, Hon. Priscilla F. .. *Hazlerigg, B.*
Dillon, Hon. Richard A. L. *Dillon, V.*
di Montecorona (Hon.
    Beatrice), Marchesa .. *Inchiquin, B.*
Dinwiddy, Hon. Caroline L. *Franks, B.*
Dipple, Hon. Susan M. N. .. *Latymer, B.*
Dixon, Hon. Daphne C. R. *Harmsworth, B.*
Dixon, Hon. Edwina .. .. *Duncan-Sandys,*
    B.
Dixon, Hon. Peter H. .. *Glentoran, B.*
Dixon, Hon. Thomas R. V. .. *Glentoran, B.*
Dobson, Hon. Anne .. .. *Rankeillour, B.*
Dodson, Hon. Christopher .. *Monk Bretton, B*
Dodson, Hon. Henry .. .. *Monk Bretton, B.*
Doig, Lady I. Clare .. *Denbigh, E.*
Donald, Hon. Angela C. .. *McFadzean, B.*
Donaldson, Hon. Thomas H. *Donaldson of*
    Kingsbridge, B.
Donovan, Hon. Hugh D. .. *Donovan, B.*
Donovan, Hon. John .. *Donovan, B.*
Dormer, Hon. Joseph S. P... *Dormer, B.*
Dormer, Hon. Rosamund J. *Dormer, B.*
Douglas, Lady Alice .. *Queensberry, M.*
Douglas, Lord Cecil C. .. *Queensberry, M.*
Douglas, Hon. Mrs. Charles
    W. S. .. .. *Morton, E.*

Faber, Hon. Diana C..	Strathcona and Mount Royal, B.
Fabling, Hon. Fiona F. ..	Gray, L.
Facetti, Hon. Mary F. ..	Braintree, By.
Fagan, Hon. M. Isabella ..	Arundell of Wardour, By.
Fairbairn, Hon. Elizabeth M.	Reay, L.
Fairbairn, Hon. Susan.. ..	Hill of Luton, B.
Fairfax, Hon. Hugh N. T. ..	Fairfax of Cameron, L.
Fairfax, Hon. Peregrine J.W.	Fairfax of Cameron, L.
Fairfax, Hon. Rupert A. J...	Fairfax of Cameron, L.
Fairfax, Hon. Serena F. ..	Fairfax of Cameron, L.
Falkiner, Hon. Lucy A. V...	Braye, B.
Fane, Lady Camilla D. ..	Westmorland, E.
Fane, Lady Gloria S.	Westmorland, E.
Fane, Hon. Harry St. C. ..	Westmorland, E.
Fane, Hon. Julian C.	Westmorland, E.
Fane, Hon. Mrs. Mountjoy J. C. W.	Westmorland, E.
Fanshawe, Lady Beatrix L. E.	Cadogan, E.
Fanshawe, Hon. Maura C.	Carbery, B.
Faram, Hon. Felicity L. ..	Dudley, Bs.
Farrar, Lady Sidney M. C. A.	Buckinghamshire, E.
Farrell, Hon. Clodagh M. ..	Morris, B.
Farrell, Lady Katherine M. V.	Anglesey, M.
Farrer, Hon. Anne L.	Farrer, By.
Farrer, Hon. Dame Frances M.	Farrer, By.
Farrer, Hon. Joan	Redesdale, B.
Farrer, Hon. (Marjorie L.) Lady	Hanworth, V.
Feather, Hon. Harry A. ..	Feather, B.
Feilding, Hon. Mrs. Basil E.	Denbigh, E.
Feilding, Hon. Mrs. David C.	Denbigh, E.
Feilding, Hon. Henry A. ..	Denbigh, E.
Feilding, Hon. Hugh R. ..	Denbigh, E.
Feilding, Lady Louisa ..	Denbigh, E.
Feilding, Lady Samantha C. B.	Denbigh, E.
Fellowes, Hon. Andrew E. ..	De Ramsey, B.
Fellowes, Hon. Carol A. ..	Ailwyn, B.
Fellowes, Hon. J. David C.	De Ramsey, B.
Fellowes, Hon. John A. ..	De Ramsey, B.
Fellowes, Hon. Sarah	De Ramsey, B.
Fergusson, Hon. Lady (Amanda M.)	Ferrier, B.
Ferguson, Hon. George D...	Ballantrae, B.
Fermor, Hon. Joan E. ..	Monsell, V.
Ferris, Hon. Greta S. B. Grant-	Harvington, B.
Ferris, Hon. Henry M. P. Grant-	Harvington, B.
Fetherstonhaugh, Hon. Lady Meade-	Clanwilliam, E.
Fey, Hon. Sybilla L. R. ..	St. John of Bletso, B.
Fforde, Lady Jean S. V. ..	Montrose, D.
ffrench, Hon. Clare K. G. M.	ffrench, B.
ffrench, Hon. Mrs. John M.V.	ffrench, B.
ffrench, Hon. Robuck J. P. C. M.	ffrench, B.
ffrench, Hon. Rose S. I. M.	ffrench, B.
Field, Hon. Geraldine ..	Gridley, B.
Field, Hon. H. Elizabeth D.	Gisborough, B.
Fielding, Hon. Daphne W. L.	Vivian, B.
Fiennes, Hon. Martin G. ..	Saye and Sele, B.
Fiennes, Hon. Richard I. ..	Saye and Sele, B.
Fiennes, Hon. Susannah H.	Saye and Sele, B.
Fiennes, Hon. William J. ..	Saye and Sele, B.
Fiennes, Hon. Oliver W. Twistleton-Wykeham- ..	Saye and Sele, B.
Finch, Hon. Marjorie ..	Cooper of Stockton Heath, B.
Findlay, Lady Mary C. ..	Dartmouth, E.
Firth, Hon. Lettice M. ..	Norton, B.
Fisher, Hon. Benjamin V. ..	Fisher, B.
Fisher, Hon. Bridget A. ..	Fisher, B.
Fisher, Hon. Charles D. ..	Fisher of Lambeth, By.
Fisher, Hon. Frances A. ..	Fisher, B.
Fisher, Hon. Francis F. ..	Fisher of Lambeth, By.
Fisher, Hon. Geoffrey R. C...	Fisher of Lambeth, By.
Fisher, Hon. Gwen E. P. ..	Tenterden, By.
Fisher, Hon. Sir Henry A. P.	Fisher of Lambeth, By.
Fisher, Hon. Humphrey R.	Fisher of Lambeth, By.
Fisher, Lady Jane A. ..	Winchester, M.
Fisher, Hon. Patrick V. ..	Fisher, B.
Fisher, Hon. Richard T. ..	Fisher of Lambeth, By.
Fiske, Hon. Giles G.	Fiske, B.
Fitton, Lady Eileen C. T. ..	Winchester, M.
FitzGerald, Hon. Mrs. Eustace R.	FitzGerald, B.
FitzGerald, Lord John ..	Leinster, D.
FitzGerald, Lady Nesta ..	Leinster, D.
Fitzherbert, Hon. Aileen M.	Stafford, B.
Fitzherbert, Hon. Caroline F.	Stafford, B.
Fitzherbert, Hon. Francis M. W..	Stafford, B.
Fitzherbert, Hon. Philip B. ..	Stafford, B.
Fitzherbert, Hon. Thomas A.	Stafford, B.
Fitzherbert, Hon. Wendy H.	Stafford, B.
Fitzmaurice, Lady Arabella H. M. Mercer Nairne Petty-	Lansdowne, M.
Fitzmaurice, Lady Georgina E. Petty-	Lansdowne, M.
Fitzmaurice, Lady Rachel B. V. Mercer Nairne Petty-..	Lansdowne, M.
Fitzmaurice, Hon. William N. C. Mercer Nairne Petty-	Lansdowne, M.
Fitzroy, Hon. Charles J. ..	Southampton, By.
FitzRoy, Lord Charles P. H.	Grafton, D.
FitzRoy, Lady Emily C. ..	Grafton, D.
FitzRoy, Lord Edward A. C.	Grafton, D.
FitzRoy, Lady Henrietta F. D..	Grafton, D.
FitzRoy, Lady Louise H. ..	Grafton, D.
FitzRoy, Hon. Nancy J...	Daventry, V.
FitzRoy, Lady Olivia R. M.	Grafton, D.
FitzRoy, Lady Virginia M. E.	Grafton, D.
Fleming, Hon. D. Charmian	Wyfold, B.
Fleming, Lady F. G. Caroline	Gosford, E.
Fleming, Hon. Gloria L. E...	Emmet of Amberley, Bs.
Fleming, Hon. Elizabeth S. Willis-	Northbourne, B.
Fletcher, Hon. David C. M.	Fletcher, B.
Fletcher, Hon. Jonathan J. M.	Fletcher, B.
Fletcher, Hon. Louisa M. S.	Mottistone, B.
Fletcher, Lady Victoria M. D.	Denbigh, E.
Flint, Pamela M.	Lee of Newton, B.
Florey, Hon. Charles du V. ..	Florey, B.
Flower, Hon. Anthony J. W.	Ashbrook, B.
Flower, Lady Gloria R. M.	Lisburne, E.
Flower, Hon. Michael L. W.	Ashbrook, V.
Floyd, Lady Gillian M. K...	Exeter, M.
Floyd, Hon. (Kathleen F.) Lady	Gretton, B.
Focke, Lady Tana M. ..	Caledon, E.
Foley, Hon. Alexandra M. ..	Foley, B.
Foley, Hon. Mildred C. ..	Foley, B.
Foley, Hon. Thomas H. ..	Foley, B.
Foljambe, Lady Jane R. M...	Liverpool, E.
Foljambe, Hon. Ralph E. A. S.	Liverpool, E.
Fontayn, Hon. Barbara W. Cole-	Latham, B.
Fooks, Hon. (Mary J.) Lady	Riverdale, B.
Foot, Hon. Benjamin A. ..	Caradon, B.
Foot, John W.	Foot, B.
Foot, Hon. Oliver I. ..	Caradon, B.
Foot, Hon. Paul M. ..	Caradon, B.
Forbes, Hon. Mrs. Donald A.	Granard, E.
Forbes, Lady Georgina A. ..	Granard, E.
Forbes, Hon. John	Granard, E.
Forbes, Hon. Jonathan A...	Forbes, L.
Forbes, Hon. Malcolm N. ..	Forbes, L.
Forbes, Hon. Pamela S. ..	McCorquodale of Newton, By.
Ford, Hon. Caroline J. ..	Nelson of Stafford, B.
Ford, Hon. (Virginia) Lady	Brand, By.
Forde, Lady Anthea G. ..	Belmore, E.
Fordyce, Hon. Violet E. M.	Windlesham, B.
Forester, Hon. E. Catherine Weld-	Cobham, V.
Forester, Hon. G. C. Brooke Weld-	Forester, B.
Forester, Hon. Kythe P. Weld-	Forester, B.
Fortescue, Hon. Celia A. ..	Fortescue, E.
Fortescue, Hon. Charles H. R.	Fortescue, E.
Fortescue, Hon. Laura M. ..	Fortescue, E.
Fortescue, Lady Margaret ..	Fortescue, E.
Fortescue, Hon. Martin D...	Fortescue, E.
Fortescue, Hon. Sarah J. ..	Fortescue, E.
Fortescue, Hon. Seymour H.	Fortescue, E.
Forster, Hon. Valentine H. I. D. Arnold-	Mitchison, By.
Foss, Hon. Janet M. P. ..	Brecon, B.
Foster, Lady Caroline A. ..	Cadogan, E.
Foster, Hon. Gillian R. ..	Forbes, L.
Foster, Hon. Jane M. E. ..	Ashbrook, V.
Foster, Hon. Sarah R. J. ..	Shuttleworth, B.
Foster, Hon. Susan E. ..	Bridgeman, V.
Fountain, Hon. Wendy S. C.	Macpherson of Drumochter, B.
Fowler, Hon. Barbara F. M.	Southwell, V.
Fowler, Lady Jennifer E. ..	Donegall, M.
Fox, Hon. Margaret J. ..	Davidson, V.
Fox, Hon. (Myra A.) Lady	Eltisley, By.

Fox, Hon. Janet Lane- .. *Hamilton of Dalzell, B.*

Fox, Hon. Marcia A. M.
Lane- .. .. *Bingley, By.*
Foxwell, Lady Edith S. .. *Cavan, E.*
Francis, Lady Elizabeth .. *Annesley, E.*
Frankland, Hon. Barbara M. *Zouche, B.*
Frankland, Hon. Roger N... *Zouche, B.*
Franklin, Hon. Joan E. .. *Auckland, B.*
Franks, Hon. Alison E. .. *Franks, B.*
Fraser, Hon. Alexander A. M. *Fraser of Tully-
belton, B.*
Fraser, Hon. Andrew R. M. *Lovat, L.*
Fraser, Hon. Angus S. J. .. *Fraser of
Kilmorack, B.*
Fraser, Hon. Ann .. .. .. *Fraser of
Allander, By.*
Fraser, Lady Antonia .. *Longford, E.*
Fraser, Hon. Belinda A. .. *Fraser of
Allander, By.*
Fraser, Hon. Caroline E. .. *Fraser of
Allander, By.*
Fraser, Hon. Christina .. *Strathalmond, B.*
Fraser, Hon. Cordelia .. *Strathalmond, B.*
Fraser, Hon. Elizabeth P. .. *Methuen, B.*
Fraser, Hon. Fiona M.. .. *Lovat, L.*
Fraser, Hon. Mrs. George .. *Saltoun, L.*
Fraser, Hon. Hugh A. J. .. *Lovat, L.*
Fraser, Hon. Hugh C. P. J. *Lovat, L.*
Fraser, Hon. Kim M. .. .. *Lovat, L.*
Fraser, Hon. Muriel .. *Lovat, L.*
Fraser, Hon. Patricia L. .. *Fraser of
Allander, By.*
Fraser, Hon. Simon A. .. *Lovat, L.*
Fraser, Hon. Mrs. William .. *Saltoun, L.*
Fraser, Hon. William R. .. *Strathalmond, B.*
Fraser, Lady Sarah L. Neill- *Buchan, E.*
Frazer, Hon. Una M.. .. *Slim, V.*
Freeman, Lady Winefride A. *Norfolk, D.*
Freeman, Lady Jean E.
Williams- .. .. *Caithness, E.*
Freeston, Hon. Anne B. .. *Jackson, of
Burnley, B.*
Freke, Hon. John A. Evans- *Carbery, B.*
Freke, Hon. Michael P. Evans- *Carbery, B.*
Freke, Hon. Mrs. Ralfe
Evans- .. .. *Carbery, B.*
Freke, Hon. Stephan R.
Evans- .. .. *Carbery, B.*
Fremantle, Hon. Cecilia J. .. *Cottesloe, B.*
Fremantle, Hon. Christopher
E. .. .. *Cottesloe, B.*
Fremantle, Hon. Edward W. *Cottesloe, B.*
Fremantle, Hon. Flora C. .. *Cottesloe, B.*
Fremantle, Hon. John T. .. *Cottesloe, B.*
Fremantle, Hon. Katharine
D. H. .. .. *Cottesloe, B.*
French, Lady Emma M. H. *Ypres, E.*
French, Lady Essex E. .. *Ypres, E.*
French, Lady Lucy K. .. .. *Ypres, E.*
French, Hon Fulke C. A. J... *De Freyne, B.*
French, Hon. Mrs. Hubert J. *De Freyne, B.*
French, Lady Iona M. H. .. *Loudoun, Cs.*
French, Hon. Patrick F. .. *De Freyne, B.*
French, Lady Rosemary .. *Inchcape, E.*
French, Lady Sarah M. E. .. *Ypres, E.*
French, Hon. Vanessa R. B. *De Freyne, B.*
French, Hon. Mrs. William J. *De Freyne, B.*
Freyberg, Hon. Annabel P. *Freyberg, B.*
Freyberg, Hon. Christina M. G. *Freyberg, B.*
Freyberg, Hon. Valerian B. C. *Freyberg, B.*
Freyberg, Hon. Venetia R... *Freyberg, B.*
Friesen, (Lady Caroline M.)
Baroness Bernard .. .. *Cawdor, E.*
Frift, Hon. Victoria W. D. .. *Lyveden, B.*
Frost, Hon. Joyce I. J. .. *Swaythling, B.*
Frost, Hon. Lucy (Lucile) K. *Grimthorpe, B.*
Frost, Hon. Raymond.. .. *Gaitskell, Bss.*
Fullard, Hon. Glenys .. .. *Macdonald of
Gwaenysgor, B.*
Fulton, Hon. Alan .. .. *Fulton, B.*
Fulton, Hon. Charity .. *Fulton, B.*
Fulton, Hon. Duncan .. .. *Fulton, B.*
Fulton, Hon. Oliver .. .. *Fulton, B.*
Fummi, Lady C. Anne .. *Crawford, E.*
Gage, Hon. George J. St. C. *Gage, V.*
Gage, Hon. Henry N. .. .. *Gage, V.*
Gairdner, Hon. (Evelyn C.)
Lady .. .. *Castlemaine, B.*
Galbraith, Hon. David M. G. *Strathclyde, B.*
Galbraith, Hon. Heather M.
A. G. .. .. *Strathclyde, B.*
Galbraith, Hon. Ida, J. G. *Strathclyde, B.*
Galbraith, Hon. James M. G. *Strathclyde, B.*
Galbraith, Hon. Norman
D. G. .. .. *Strathclyde, B.*
Galbraith, Hon. Thomas
G. D. .. .. *Strathclyde, B.*
Gallagher, Hon. Kristin .. *Wynne-Jones, B.*
Gamester, Hon. Jane M. .. *Annesley, E.*
Ganzoni, Hon. Mary J. .. *Belstead, B.*
Gardiner, Hon. Carol .. *Gardiner, B.*

Gardiner, Hon. Susanna C. C. *Greenwood of
Rossendale, B.*
Garner, Hon. Christopher
J. S. .. .. *Garner, B.*
Garnell, Lady Caroline L. .. *Bradford, E.*
Garner, Hon. Helena G. .. *Garner, B.*
Garner, Hon. Joseph J. .. *Garner, B.*
Garnett, Hon. Anne J. E. .. *Delamere, B.*
Garnier, Hon. Lavender H. *Walsingham, B.*
Garnsworthy, Hon. Charles E. *Garnsworthy, B.*
Garrett, Hon. Valda J. .. *Lyveden, B.*
Garthwaite, Hon. Waveney M. *Mancroft, B.*
Garton, Hon. Annabel J. .. *Hudson, Vy.*
Gascoigne, Hon. E. Ann .. *Harcourt, V.*
Gascoigne, Hon. Mary L. H. *O'Neill, B.*
Gaussen, Hon. Diana B. .. *Hereford, V.*
Gaussen, Lady Mary E. .. *Amherst, E.*
Geddes, Hon. Mrs. Alexander *Geddes, B.*
Geddes, Hon. David C. .. *Geddes, B.*
Geddes, Hon. James G. N... *Geddes, B.*
Geddes, Hon. John R. C. .. *Geddes, B.*
Geddes, Hon. Margaret C. .. *Geddes, B.*
Gee, Hon. Joan M. .. .. *Hives, B.*
Gellhorn, Hon. Olive S. .. *Layton, B.*
Geoghegan, Hon. Mary C. B. *Fermoy, B.*
George, Hon. Sylvia B. .. *Rathcreedan, B.*
George, Lady Julia M. V.
Lloyd .. .. *Lloyd George of
Dwyfor, E.*
George, Hon. Robert J. D.
Lloyd .. .. *Lloyd George of
Dwyfor, E.*
George, Hon. William Lloyd *Tenby, V.*
Gerard, Hon. Heloise K. M. *Gerard, B.*
Gibbs, Hon. Antonia M. .. *Aldenham, B.*
Gibbs, Hon. Dorothy .. .. *Valentia, V.*
Gibbs, Hon. Elizabeth B. .. *Howick of
Glendale, B.*
Gibbs, Hon. Eustace H. B... *Wraxall, B.*
Gibbs, Hon. Lady .. .. *Aldenham, B.*
Gibbs, Hon. George H. P. .. *Aldenham, B.*
Gibbs, Lady Hilaria A. .. *Mount Edg-
cumbe, E.*
Gibbs, Hon. Humphrey V... *Aldenham, B.*
Gibbs, Hon. Rosalind M. .. *Aldenham, B.*
Gibbs, Lady Sarah .. .. *Lucan, E.*
Gibbs, Hon. Vicary T... .. *Aldenham, B.*
Gibson, Hon. Clive P. .. *Gibson, B.*
Gibson, Hon. Mrs. Edward
G. M. .. .. *Ashbourne, B.*
Gibson, Hon. Edward B. G. *Ashbourne, B.*
Gibson, Hon. Frances T. .. *O'Hagan, B.*
Gibson, Hon. Hugh M. T... *Gibson, B.*
Gibson, Hon. Piers N... .. *Gibson, B.*
Gibson, Hon. William D. .. *Ashbourne, B.*
Gibson, Hon. William K. .. *Gibson, B.*
Gifford, Hon. Polly A... .. *Gifford, B.*
Gifford, Hon. Thomas A. .. *Gifford, B.*
Gilbey, Hon. John H. P. .. *Vaux of Harrow-
den, Bs.*
Gilbey, Hon. Mary A. M. .. *Vaux of Har-
rowden, Bs.*
Giles, Lady Katharine P. .. *De La Warr, E.*
Gill, Hon. Olive B. .. .. *Wrenbury, B.*
Gill, Hon. Rosemary E. G... *Gorell, B.*
Gilmour, Lady Caroline M. .. *Buccleuch, D.*
Gilmour, Lady Mary C. R... *Abercorn, D.*
Gilmour, Hon. Victoria L. .. *Cadogan, E.*
Gilpin, Hon. A. Mary de B. *Allendale, V.*
Glendinning, Hon. Victoria.. *Seebohm, B.*
Glover, Lady Sarah J. .. *Craven, E.*
Glyn, Lady Rosula C. .. .. *Plymouth, E.*
Godfrey, Hon. S. Lois .. *Mitchison, By.*
Godley, Hon. Christopher J. *Kilbracken, B.*
Godley, Hon. Wynne A. H. *Kilbracken, B.*
Godsal, Lady Elizabeth C. .. *Courtown, E.*
Goff, Hon. Angela E. .. .. *Airedale, B.*
Gold, Hon. Jocelyne M. .. *Trent, By.*
Goldby, Hon. Helen R. .. *Tomlin, By.*
Goldinor, Hon. Sigrid .. *Wynne-Jones, B.*
Goodale, Hon. Pamela M. D. *Hirst, By.*
Goodhart, Hon. Celia McC. *Hemingford, B.*
Goodrich, Hon. Audrey .. *Elton, B.*
Goodwin, Hon. Gillian T. M. *Chorley, B.*
Goolden, Hon. Rosemary .. *Ullswater, V.*
Gordon, Lord Adam G. .. *Huntly, M.*
Gordon, Lord Alastair N. J... *Aberdeen and
Temair, M.*
Gordon, Lord Douglas C. A. *Huntly, M.*
Gordon, Hon. Katharine E. *Foot, B.*
Gordon, Lord Roderic A. .. *Huntly, M.*
Gore, Lady Barbara S. .. *Eglinton, E.*
Gore, Lady Janet H. .. .. *Cawdor, E.*
Gore, Hon. Philip .. .. *Arran, E.*
Gore, Hon. Alice M. S.
Ormsby- .. .. *Harlech, B.*
Gore, Hon. Francis D.
Ormsby- .. .. *Harlech, B.*
Gore, Hon. John J. Ormsby- *Harlech, B.*
Gore, Hon. Pandora B.
Ormsby- .. .. *Harlech, B.*

Goring, Hon. (Caroline) Lady	Rendlesham, B.
Goring, Lady Hersey M. ..	Glasgow, E.
Goschen, Hon. Caroline E...	Goschen, V.
Goschen, Hon. Giles J. H. ..	Goschen, V.
Gosling, Lady Caroline V. ..	Halifax, E.
Gough, Lady Hyacinth K. A.	Kilmorey, E.
Gough, Hon. Madeline E. ..	Kinnaird, L.
Goulding, Hon. (Valerie H.) Lady	Monckton of Brenchley, V.
Gourlay, Hon. Patricia D. ..	Normand, By.
Gower, Lady Marcia R. A. Leveson-	Granville, E.
Gower, Hon. Niall J. Leveson-	Granville, E.
Graham, Lord Alastair M. ..	Montrose, D.
Graham, Lady Cairistiona A.	Montrose, D.
Graham, Lord Calum I. ..	Montrose, D.
Graham, Lady D. Malise ..	Knutsford, V.
Graham, Lord Donald A. ..	Montrose, D.
Graham, Lady Lilias C. M...	Montrose, D.
Graham, Hon. Margaret B.	Roborough, B.
Graham, Lord Ronald M. H.	Montrose, D.
Grant, Hon. Eleanor L. ..	Stalbridge, By.
Grant, Lady Katherine ..	Dysart, Cs.
Grant of Grant, Hon. Amanda C.	Strathspey, B.
Grant of Grant, Hon. G. Janet	Strathspey, B.
Grant of Grant, Hon. James P.	Strathspey, B.
Grant of Grant, Hon. Michael P. F.	Strathspey, B.
Grant, Hon. Alexander D. H. Ogilvie-	Seafield, E.
Granville, Hon. Linda ..	Granville of Eye, B.
Graves, Hon. Cerise E. G. ..	Graves, B.
Gray, Hon. Andrew G. D. S. Campbell-	Gray, L.
Gray, Hon. Kathleen E. M.	Gray, L.
Gray, Hon. Cethlyn I... ..	Gray, L.
Gray, Hon. Cailain D. Campbell-	Gray, L.
Gray, Hon. Iona C. Campbell-	Gray, L.
Gray, Hon. Lucinda M. Campbell-	Gray, L.
Greaves, Lady Rosamund A.	Dysart, Cs.
Green, Hon. Jane B. R. ..	Bicester, B.
Greenacre, Lady Elizabeth M. B.	Lindsay, E.
Greenall, Hon. Edward G. ..	Daresbury, B.
Greene, Hon. Judith M. ..	Gordon-Walker, B.
Greenhill, Hon. Catherine E.	Greenhill, B.
Greenhill, Hon. Malcolm ..	Greenhill, B.
Greenhill, Hon. Nigel D. St. G.	Greenhill of Harrow, B.
Greenhill, Hon. Robin J. ..	Greenhill of Harrow, B.
Greenhill, Hon. Shelia A.	Greenhill, B.
Greenogh, Hon. Mary H. ..	Banbury of Southam, B.
Greenway, Hon. Ambrose C. D.	Greenway, B.
Greenway, Hon. Mervyn S. K.	Greenway, B.
Greenway, Hon. Nigel P. ..	Greenway, B.
Greenway, Lady Sheelah F. L.	Kingston, E.
Greenwood, Hon. Michael G. H.	Greenwood, V.
Grenfell, Hon. Aline M. ..	Grenfell, B.
Grenfell, Hon. Catherine ..	St. Just, B.
Grenfell, Hon. Julian P. F. St. I.	Grenfell, B.
Grenfell, Hon. Laura C. ..	St. Just, B.
Grenfell, Hon. Natasha J. M.	St. Just, B.
Grenville, Hon. Bevil D. S. C. Freeman-	Kinloss, Ly.
Grenville, Hon. Hester J. A. Freeman-	Kinloss, Ly.
Grenville, Hon. Teresa M. N. Freeman-	Kinloss, Ly.
Grenville, Hon. Harry N. Morgan-..	Kinloss, Ly.
Grenville, Hon. Robert W. Morgan-	Kinloss, Ly.
Gretton, Hon. Anthony D.E.	Gretton, B.
Gretton, Hon. John H. ..	Gretton, B.
Gretton, Hon. Mary A... ..	Gretton, B.
Greville, Hon. Charlotte A...	Warwick, E.
Greville, Hon. Guy D. ..	Warwick, E.
Grey, Hon. Amanda M. A. ..	Grey of Naunton, B.
Grey, Hon. Jeremy F. A. ..	Grey of Naunton, B.
Grey, Hon. Jolyon K. A. ..	Grey of Naunton, B.
Gridley, Hon. Alison E. V. ..	Gridley, B.
Gridley, Hon. Richard D. A...	Gridley, B.
Gridley, Hon. Susan L. ..	Gridley, B.
Gridley, Hon. Vivienne N. ..	Gridley, B.
Grier, Hon. Patricia M. ..	Spens, B.
Grierson, Lady Daphne O...	Cavan, E.

Griffin, Lady Jane	Lucan, E.
Grigg, Hon. Annabel D. ..	Altrincham, By.
Grigg, Hon. Anthony U. D. D.	Altrincham, By.
Grimond, Hon. Laura M. ..	Asquith of Yarnbury, By.
Grimshaw, Hon. Shelagh M. M.	Milner of Leeds, B.
Grimston, Hon. Cecil A. S. ..	Grimston of Westbury, B.
Grimston, Lady Iona C. ..	Verulam, E.
Grimston, Hon. June M. ..	de Mauley, B.
Grimston, Hon. Michael J. H.	Grimston of Westbury, B.
Grimston, Hon. Robert W. S.	Grimston of Westbury, B.
Grosvenor, Hon. Georgina L.	Ebury, B.
Grosvenor, Hon. Hugh R. ..	Ebury, B.
Grosvenor, Lady Jane M. ..	Westminster, D.
Grosvenor, Hon. Julian F. M.	Ebury, B.
Grosvenor, Lady Mary C. ..	Westminster, D.
Grosvenor, Hon. Richard A.	Ebury, B.
Grosvenor, Hon. Robert V...	Ebury, B.
Grosvenor, Hon. William W.	Ebury, B.
Guest, Hon. Andrew B. G...	Guest, B.
Guest, Hon. Charles J... ..	Wimborne, V.
Guest, Hon. Christopher J. G.	Guest, B.
Guest, Hon. David W. G. ..	Guest, B.
Guest, Hon. Ivor M. V... ..	Wimborne, V.
Guest, Hon. Julian J.	Wimborne, V.
Guest, Hon. Mrs. O. Montague	Wimborne, V.
Guest, Hon. Simon E. G. ..	Guest, B.
Guest, Hon. Hadley Haden-	Haden-Guest, B.
Guest Hon. Peter Haden- ..	Haden-Guest, B.
Gueterbock, Hon. Cynthia E.	Berkeley, By.
Guinness, Hon. Catriona R. ..	Moyne, B.
Guinness, Hon. Desmond W.	Moyne, B.
Guinness, Hon. Diarmid E.	Moyne, B.
Guinness, Lady Emma L.	Iveagh, E.
Guinness, Hon. Erskine S. R.	Moyne, B.
Guinness, Hon. Finn B. ..	Moyne, B.
Guinness, Hon. Fiona E. ..	Moyne, B.
Guinness, Lady Henrietta ..	Iveagh, E.
Guinness, Hon. Jonathan B.	Moyne, B.
Guinness, Hon. Kieran A. ..	Moyne, B.
Guinness, Lady Louisa J. ..	Iveagh, E.
Guinness, Hon. Mirabel J. ..	Moyne, B.
Guinness, Hon. Murtogh D.	Moyne, B.
Guinness, Hon. Rory M. B.	Iveagh, E.
Guinness, Hon. Thomasin M.	Moyne, B.
Gully, Hon. Catherine M. A.	Selby, V.
Gully, Hon. Edward T. W.	Selby, V.
Gully, Hon. Helen J. P. ..	Selby, V.
Gully, Hon. James E. H. Y.	Selby, V.
Gundry, Hon. Caroline A. S.	Wynford, B.
Gunston, Lady Doris G. ..	Dufferin, M.
Gurdon, Hon. Brampton C.	Cranworth, B.
Gurdon, Hon. Louisa-Jane	Cranworth, B.
Gurdon, Hon. Sacha W.,R...	Cranworth, B.
Gwinnett, Lady Doreen S. ..	Belmore, E.
Gwyn, Hon. Clare	Devlin, B.
Hackett, Hon. Alleyne E. M. L.	Templetown, V.
Hacking, Hon. Belinda A. ..	Hacking, B.
Hacking, Hon. Crrina G. ..	Hacking, B.
Hacking, Hon. Daniel R. ..	Hacking, B.
Hacking, Hon. Douglas F. ..	Hacking, B.
Hacking, Hon. Edgar B. ..	Hacking, B.
Hacking, Hon. Fiona M. ..	Ferrier, B.
Hacking, Hon. L. Bruce ..	Hacking, B.
Haddon, Hon. Teresa M. ..	Head, V.
Hadfield, Hon. Maureen ..	Segal, B.
Hadley, Lady Paulina M. L.	Cottenham, E.
Hadwen, Hon. Sibell A. J. ..	Cromartie, E.
Haig, Lady Adrienne R. ..	Haig, E.
Haig, Lady Elizabeth V. T.	Haig, E.
Haire, Hon. Christopher P. ..	Haire of White-abbey, B.
Haire, Hon. Michael J. K. ..	Haire of White-abbey, B.
Hale, Hon. Dorothy L. ..	Hale, B.
Hale, Hon. Ian W. P' ..	Hale, B.
Hall, Hon. (Diana J.) Lady ..	Sackville, B.
Hall, Hon. Georgina A. ..	Hall, V.
Hall, Hon. Jane O.	Braintree, By.
Hall, Hon. Lena M.	Hall, V.
Hall, Hon. Ann King- ..	King-Hall, By.
Hall, Hon. Susan King- ..	King-Hall, By.
Hallward, Hon. Alice H. ..	Atholstan, By.
Hamilton, Hon. Archibald G.	Hamilton of Dalzell, B.
Hamilton, Lord Claud A. ..	Abercorn, D.
Hamilton, Lady Claud D. ..	Abercorn, D.
Hamilton, Lord Claud N. ..	Abercorn, D.
Hamilton, Hon. Evelyn W. J.	Holmpatrick, B.
Hamilton, Hon. Frederick C. A.	Belhaven, L.
Hamilton, Lady Grizel W. L.	Dundonald, E.
Hamilton, Hon. Hans J. D.	Holm Patrick, B.
Hamilton, Hon. Ion H. J. ..	Holm Patrick, B.

Penney, Hon. Martin C.   ..   *Penney, B.*
Penny, Hon. Carol A.   ..   *Marchwood, V.*
Penny, Hon. David G. S.   ..   *Marchwood, V.*
Penny, Hon. Patrick G.   ..   *Marchwood, V.*
Peploe, Lady Dorothy V.   ..   *Darnley, E.*
Pepper, Hon. Elizabeth J. G.   *Guest, B.*
Pepys, Lady M. Rachel   ..   *Norfolk, D.*
Pepys, Hon. P. S. Nadine ..   *Camoys, B.*
Pepys, Lady Rose E. I.   ..   *Cottenham, E.*
Perceval, Lady Geraldine E.
U. .. ..   *Egmont, E.*
Perceval, Hon. Joanna I. L.   *Hatherton, B.*
Percy, Lord Geoffrey W.   ..   *Northumberland, D.*
Percy, Lord James W. E.   ..   *Northumberland, D.*
Percy, Lady Julia H.   ..   ..   *Northumberland, D.*
Percy, Hon. Linda D. Vane   *Ebury, B.*
Percy, Hon. Mary E.   ..   ..   *Percy of Newcastle, By.*
Percy, Lord Ralph G. A.   ..   *Northumberland, D.*
Percy, Lord Richard C.   ..   *Northumberland, D.*
Percy, Lady Victoria L. D...   *Northumberland, D.*
Percy, Lady William R.   ..   *Northumberland, D.*
Percy, Hon. M. Jane Heber-   *Leverhulme, V.*
Perowne, Hon. (Agatha V.)
Lady .. ..   *Allendale, V.*
Pery, Hon. Adrian P. ..   ..   *Limerick, E.*
Pery, Lady Alison D. ..   ..   *Limerick, E.*
Pery, Hon. Michael H. C.   *Limerick, E.*
Pestell, Hon. Philip Wells ..   *Wells-Pestell, B.*
Pestell, Hon. Richard Wells..   *Wells-Pestell, B.*
Peterken, Hon. Hyacinthe A.   *Hatherton, B.*
Petherick, Hon. Bridget F. K.   *Cornwallis, B.*
Petherick, Lady Jeane ..   ..   *Radnor, E.*
Peto, Hon. Selina L.   ..   ..   *St. Helens, B.*
Petre, Hon. John P. L.   ..   *Petre, B.*
Petsopoulos, Lady Charlotte
M. R. P.   ..   ..   ..   *Bessborough, E.*
Phelps, Hon. Helen R.   ..   *Cozens-Hardy B.*
Philipps, Hon. Colwyn J. J.   *St. Davids, V.*
Philipps, Hon. Eiddwen S...   *St. Davids, V.*
Philipps, Hon. Elizabeth J.   *Kindersley, B.*
Philipps, Hon. Gwenllian ..   *Milford, B.*
Philipps, Hon. Hugo J. L. ..   *Milford, B.*
Philipps, Hon. James P.   ..   *Milford, B.*
Philipps, Lady Jean M.   ..   *Antrim, E.*
Philipps, Lady Marion V. ..   *Stair, E.*
Philipps, Hon. Mary   ..   ..   *Sherfield, B.*
Philipps, Hon. Richard H...   *Milford, B.*
Philipps, Hon. William S. ..   *Milford, B.*
Phillimore, Hon. Mrs. An-
thony F.   ..   ..   ..   *Phillimore, B.*
Phillimore, Hon. Claud S. ..   *Phillimore, B.*
Phillimore, Hon. Mrs. Miles
G. W.   ..   ..   ..   *Phillimore, B.*
Phillimore, Hon. Robert G. H.   *Phillimore, B.*
Phillips, Lady Katherine M.   *Norfolk, D.*
Phillips, Hon. Margaret A. A.   *Harmsworth, B.*
Phillips, Hon. Morgan D.   ..   *Phillips, Bs.*
Phipps, Lady Anne E. G.   ..   *Normanby, M.*
Phipps, Lady Evelyn R.   ..   *Normanby, M.*
Phipps, Lady Henrietta L...   *Normanby, M.*
Phipps, Lord Justin C.   ..   *Normanby, M.*
Phipps, Lady Lepel S.   ..   *Normanby, M.*
Phipps, Lady Peronel K.   ..   *Normanby, M.*
Phipps, Lady Phœbe ..   ..   *Radnor, E.*
Phipps, Lady Sybil A...   ..   *Buccleuch, D.*
Pickering, Hon. Veronica M.   *Fisher of Rednal, Bs.*
Pickford, Hon. Felicity J. ..   *Mills, V.*
Pickett, Hon. Patricia M. ..   *Kershaw, B.*
Piercy, Hon. Henrietta J. ..   *Piercy, B.*
Piercy, Hon. James W.   ..   *Piercy, B.*
Piercy, Hon. Mark E. P.   ..   *Piercy, B.*
Piercy. Hon. Penelope K. ..   *Piercy, B.*
Pihl, Hon. Dame Mary M. ..   *Waverley, V.*
Pike, Lady Romayne A.   ..   *Meath, E.*
Pilkington, Hon. John R.   ..   *Pilkington, B.*
Pink, Lady Dora E.   ..   ..   *Ely, M.*
Pither, Hon. Pauline R.   ..   *Lambury, By.*
Pitman, Hon. Lady (Mar-
garet B.)   ..   ..   ..   *Luke, B.*
Pitt, Hon. Amanda   ..   ..   *Pitt of Hampstead, B.*
Pitt, Hon. Bruce M. D.   ..   *Pitt of Hampstead, B.*
Pitt, Hon. Phyllis L.   ..   *Pitt of Hampstead, B.*
Plank, Hon. Marion R.   ..   *Blyton, B.*
Platt, Hon. Pauline M.   ..   *Fisher of Rednal, Bs.*
Platt, Hon. Peter   ..   ..   *Platt, B.*
Plowden, Hon. Anna B.   ..   *Plowden, B.*
Plowden, Hon. Francis J. ..   *Plowden, B.*
Plowden, Hon. William J. L.   *Plowden, B.*
Plummer, Hon. Enid K.   ..   *Gridley, B.*

Plummer, Hon. Pamela L.
Scott-   ..   ..   *Kinross, B.*
Plumptre, Hon. Francis C...   *Fitzwalter, B.*
Plumptre, Hon. Henry B. ..   *Fitzwalter, B.*
Plumptre, Hon. Julian B. ..   *Fitzwalter, B.*
Plumptre, Hon. William E.   *Fitzwalter, B.*
Plumptre, Hon. Wyndham G.   *Fitzwalter, B.*
Plunket, Hon. Mrs. D. Kiwa   *Plunket, B.*
Plunket, Hon. Robin R.   ..   *Plunket, B.*
Plunket, Hon. Shaun A. F. S.   *Plunket, B.*
Plunkett, Hon. Beatrice M.   *Dunsany, B.*
Plunkett, Hon. Edward J. C.   *Dunsany, B.*
Plunkett, Hon. Jonathan O.   *Louth, B.*
Plunkett, Hon. Olivia J. ..   *Louth, B.*
Plunkett, Hon. Otway J. O.   *Louth, B.*
Plunkett, Hon. Mrs. Randal
P. R. O.   ..   ..   ..   *Louth, B.*
Plunkett, Hon. Stephanie P.   *Louth, B.*
Plunkett, Hon. Timothy J.O.   *Louth, B.*
Pole, Hon. Victoria M. A.
Carew   ..   ..   ..   *Leverhulme V.*
Pollen, Hon. Daphne   ..   *Revelstoke, B.*
Pollock, Hon. David S. G.   *Hanworth, V.*
Pollock, Hon. Richard C. S.   *Hanworth, V.*
Pollock, Hon. Rosemary T.   *Berners, Bs.*
Pollock, Lady Zinnia R.   ..   *Londesborough, B.*
Pomeroy, Hon. Robert W. ..   *Harberton, V.*
Pomeroy, Hon. Rosamond M.   *Harberton, V.*
Pomeroy, Hon. Thomas De V.   *Harberton, V.*
Ponsonby, Hon. Mrs. Bertie
B.   ..   ..   *Bessborough, E.*
Ponsonby, Hon. Carolyn M.   *Sysonby, B.*
Ponsonby, Hon. Laura M. ..   *Ponsonby of Shulbrede, B.*
Ponsonby, Lady Martha   ..   *Ormonde, M.*
Ponsonby, Hon. Thomas A.   *Ponsonby of Shulbrede, B.*
Ponsonby, Hon. Thomas M.   *De Mauley, B.*
Ponsonby, Hon. (Winifred
M.) Lady   ..   ..   ..   *Aldenham, B.*
Ponté, Lady Jennifer J.   ..   *Howe, E.*
Poole, Hon. Anne R. D.   ..   *Croft, B.*
Poole, Hon. David C...   ..   *Poole, B.*
Pope, Hon. Jacqueline D. M.   *Wynford, B.*
Popplewell, Hon. John A. ..   *Popplewell, B.*
Porritt, Hon. Jeremy C.   ..   *Porritt, B.*
Porritt, Hon. Jonathon E...   *Porritt, B.*
Portal, Hon. Cicely W.   ..   *Goschen, V.*
Portal, Hon. Mavis E. ..   ..   *Portal of Hungerford, V.*
Portman, Hon. Alexander
M. B.   ..   ..   ..   *Portman, V.*
Portman, Hon. Christopher
E. B.   ..   ..   ..   *Portman, V.*
Portman, Hon. Claire E.   ..   *Portman, V.*
Portman, Hon. Justin T. B.   *Portman, V.*
Portman, Hon. Matthew G.
B.   ..   ..   *Portman, V.*
Portman, Hon. Mrs. Michael
B.   ..   ..   *Portman, V.*
Portman, Hon. Piers R. B. ..   *Portman, V.*
Portsmouth, Hon. Gladys I.   *Torrington, V.*
Postan, Lady Cynthia R. ..   *Albemarle, E.*
Potter, Hon. Vanessa J.   ..   *Robson of Kiddington, Bs.*
Pover, Hon. Joan V.   ..   ..   *Brockway, B.*
Powell, Hon. Beryl   ..   ..   *Davies of Penrhys, B.*
Powell, Lady Violet G.   ..   *Longford, E.*
Powell, Hon. David M.
Baden-   ..   ..   ..   *Baden-Powell, B.*
Powell, Hon. Wendy D. L.
Baden-   ..   ..   ..   *Baden-Powell, B.*
Powell, Hon. Philippa C.
Hulbert-   ..   ..   ..   *St. Levan, B.*
Powlett, Hon. Harry A. N.
Orde-   ..   ..   ..   *Bolton, B.*
Powlett, Hon. Michael B.
Orde-   ..   ..   ..   *Bolton, B.*
Powlett, Hon. Patrick C.
Orde-   ..   ..   ..   *Bolton, B.*
Powlett, Hon. Katherine E.
William-   ..   ..   ..   *Keyes, B.*
Powys, Hon. Clare L.   ..   *Lilford, B.*
Powys, Hon. Emma-Jane ..   *Lilford, B.*
Powys, Hon. Hannah V. ..   *Lilford, B.*
Powys, Hon. Sarah M. ..   ..   *Lilford, B.*
Pratt, Hon. Jonathan   ..   *Camden, M.*
Pratt, Lord Michael J. H. ..   *Camden, M.*
Pratt, Lord Roderic A. N. ..   *Camden, M.*
Pratt, Lady Samantha C. ..   *Camden, M.*
Preston, Hon. Angela Camp-
bell-   ..   ..   ..   *Cowdray, V.*
Preston, Hon. Robert F. H.
T. ..   ..   *Gormanston, V.*
Preston, Hon. Jenico F. T...   *Gormanston, V.*
Pretyman, Hon. Camilla ..   *Cranworth, B.*
Pretyman, Lady M. Karen ..   *Normanton, M.*

Strang, Hon. Colin .. .. *Strang, B.*
Strang, Hon. Jean .. .. *Strang, B.*
Strangways, Hon. Raymond
G. Fox- .. .. .. *Ilchester, E.*
Streatfeild, Lady Moyra C... *Courtown, E.*
Strickland, Hon. Constance *Strickland, By.*
Strickland, Hon. Mabel .. *Strickland, By.*
Stride, Hon. Mary P. L. .. *Rochester, B.*
Stride, Hon. Susan .. .. *Macdonald of*
 Gwaenysgor, B.
Strutt, Hon. Charles R. .. *Rayleigh, B.*
Strutt, Hon. Desmond R. .. *Belper, B.*
Strutt, Hon. Guy R. .. .. *Rayleigh, B.*
Strutt, Hon. Hedley V. .. *Rayleigh, B.*
Strutt, Hon. Jean E. .. .. *Davidson, V.*
Strutt, Hon. Margaret .. .. *Belper, B.*
Strutt, Hon. Peter A. .. .. *Belper, B.*
Strutt, Hon. Richard H. .. *Belper, B.*
Stuart, Hon. Alicia St. G. .. *Charlemont, V.*
Stuart, Hon. Andrew M. .. *Stuart of*
 Findhorn, V.
Stuart, Lady Bridget A. .. *Castle Stewart, E*
Stuart, Lady Caroline .. *Jersey, E.*
Stuart, Hon. Charles R. S... *Moray, E.*
Stuart, Hon. Chloe A-M .. *Stuart of*
 Findhorn, V.
Stuart, Lady David .. .. *Bute, M.*
Stuart, Hon. J. Dominic .. *Stuart of*
 Findhorn, V.
Stuart, Hon. James W. W... *Moray, E.*
Stuart, Hon. John D. .. .. *Stuart of*
 Findhorn, V.
Stuart, Lady Louisa H. .. *Moray, E.*
Stuart, Hon. Rosalie J. .. *Stuart of*
 Findhorn, V.
Stuart, Hon. Simon W. E. .. *Castle Stewart, E.*
Stuart, Hon. Vanessa M. .. *Stuart of*
 Findhorn, V.
Stuart, Lord Anthony
Crichton- .. .. .. *Bute, M.*
Stuart, Lord David O.
Crichton- .. .. .. *Bute, M.*
Stuart, Lady Eileen C.
Crichton- .. .. .. *Bute, M.*
Stuart, Lord James C.
Crichton- .. .. .. *Bute, M.*
Stuart, Lady Janet E. Crich-
ton- .. .. *Eglinton, E.*
Stuart, Lady Rhidian Crich-
ton- .. .. *Bute, M.*
Stuart, Lord Robert Crichton- *Bute, M.*
Stuart, Lady Sophia A. Crich-
ton- .. .. *Bute, M.*
Stucley, Hon. (Sheila M. W.)
Lady .. .. *Poltimore, B.*
Studd, Lady Kathleen .. *Leitrim, E.*
Sturt, Hon. Penelope A. .. *Hillingdon, B.*
Summerskill, Hon. Michael
B. .. .. *Summerskill, Bs.*
Surrell, Hon. Maureen D. .. *Lyveden, B.*
Sutcliffe, Hon. D. Valerie P... *Garvagh, B.*
Sutcliffe, Hon. Helen .. *Rhodes, B.*
Sutherland, Lady Annabel
E. H. .. .. *Sutherland, Cs.*
Sutherland, Hon. Rachel E. *Sutherland, Cs.*
Sutherland, Hon. Rosemary
M. .. .. *Sutherland, Cs.*
Svejdar, Lady Honor D. M. *Iveagh, E.*
Svenningson, Hon. Daphne R. *Garvagh, B.*
Swan, Lady Hilda S. M. .. *Iddesleigh, E.*
Swann, Hon. Lydia M. .. .. *Lifford, V.*
Swire, Lady Judith .. .. *Northampton,*
 M.
Szpiganowicz, Lady Patricia A. *Clancarty, E.*
Tabor, Hon. Pamela R. .. *Glendyne, B.*
Taddei, Hon. Charlotte M. .. *Piercy, B.*
Tait, Lady Katharine J. .. *Russell, E.*
Talbot, Hon. Cynthia E. .. *Wimborne, V.*
Talbot, Hon. Rose M. .. .. *Talbot of Mala-*
 hide, B.
Talbot, Hon. Paul A. A. B.
Chetwynd- .. .. .. *Shrewsbury, E.*
Tangye, Lady Marguerite R. *Darnley, E*
Tapsell, Hon. Cecilia A. .. *Hawke, B.*
Tatum, Hon. Marguerite B. *Cadman. B.*
Taylor, Hon. Bernard A. .. *Taylor of Mans-*
 field, B.
Taylor, Hon. Charles R. H. *Taylor, B.*
Taylor, Hon. Cicely E. .. *Buckland, By.*
Taylor, Hon. Jeremy S. .. *Taylor, B.*
Taylor, Hon. L. L. Carole .. *Alport, B.*
Taylor, Hon. Marilyn R. .. *Fisher of*
 Camden, B.
Taylor, Hon. Pamela M. .. *Geddes of Epsom,*
 B.
Taylor, Hon. Priscilla J. .. *Piercy, B.*
Taylor, Hon. Sylvia M. .. *Joicey, B.*
Taylor, Lady Ursula D. .. *Ailesbury, M.*
Taylor, Hon. Kenneth B.
Suenson- .. .. .. *Grantchester, B.*
Taylour, Lady Millicent O. M. *Headfort, M.*
Taylour, Lady Olivia S. D. A. *Headfort, M.*

Taylour, Lady Rosanagh
E. A. M. .. .. .. *Headfort, M.*
Taylour, Lord William D. .. *Headfort, M.*
Tedder, Hon. Andrew J. .. *Tedder, B.*
Tedder, Hon. Anne R. .. *Tedder, B.*
Tedder, Hon. Mina U. M. .. *Tedder, B.*
Tedder, Hon. Richard S. .. *Tedder, B.*
Tedder, Hon. Robin J. .. *Tedder, B.*
Telfer, Hon. Lætitia M. .. *Balfour of*
 Burleigh, L.
Tenison, Lady Bridget H.
King- .. .. *Kingston, E.*
Tenison, Lady Maria L. King- *Kingston, E.*
Tennant, Lady Anne V. .. *Leicester, E.*
Tennant, Hon. Catherine E. *Glenconner, B.*
Tennant, Hon. Colin C. P. .. *Glenconner, B.*
Tennant, Hon. Mrs. David F. *Glenconner, B.*
Tennant, Hon. Lady Emma *Devonshire, D.*
Tennant, Lady Harriot .. *Radnor, E.*
Tennant, Hon. Irene A. .. *Gage, V.*
Tennant, Hon. James G. H. *Glenconner, B.*
Tennant, Lady Margaret H.
I. M. .. .. *Airlie, E.*
Tennant, Hon. Stephen J. N. *Glenconner, B.*
Tennant, Hon. Tobias W. .. *Glenconner, B.*
Tennyson, Hon. Mark A. .. *Tennyson, B.*
Tetley, Lady Patrica M. .. *Strathmore, E.*
Thellusson, Hon. Antonia .. *Rendlesham, B.*
Thellusson, Hon. Charles
W. B. .. .. *Rendlesham, B.*
Thellusson, Hon. Cynthia A. E. *Rendlesham, B.*
Thellusson, Hon. Mrs. Hugh
E. .. .. *Rendlesham, B.*
Thelluson, Hon. Jaqumine .. *Rendlesham, B.*
Thellusson, Hon. Peter R. .. *Rendlesham, B.*
Thellusson, Hon. Sarah A... *Rendlesham, B.*
Thesiger, Hon. Dawn L. .. *Chelmsford, V.*
Thesiger, Hon. Frederic O. P. *Chelmsford, V.*
Thesiger, Hon. Philippa M. *Chelmsford, V.*
Thesiger, Hon. Tiffany G. .. *Chelmsford, V.*
Thomas, Hon. Deborah M. *Glanusk, B.*
Thomas, Hon. Guendaline A. *Bellew, B.*
Thomas, Hon. Jacqueline .. *Cooper of*
 Stockton Heath,
 B.
Thomas, Hon. Vanessa *Gladwyn, B.*
Thomas, Hon. W. Michael W. *Thomas, B.*
Thomas, Hon. Moyra Free-
man- .. .. *Tweedmouth, By.*
Thompson, Hon. Tessa M. .. *Dacre, Bs.*
Thompson, Hon. Isabel
Vaughan- .. .. .. *Craigmyle, B.*
Thomson, Hon. Elizabeth F. *Francis-Williams,*
 By.
Thomson, Hon. Kenneth R. *Thomson of*
 Fleet, B.
Thomson, Hon. Callum
M. M. Mitchell- .. .. *Selsdon, B.*
Thorne, Lady Anne P. .. *Limerick, E.*
Thorne, Hon. (Margaret)
Lady .. .. *Penrhyn, B.*
Thornely, Hon. Muriel H. .. *Cobham, B.*
Thorneycroft, Hon. John H. *Thorneycroft, B.*
Thorold, Hon. Phyllis M. .. *Ampthill, B.*
Throckmorton, Lady Isabel
V. K. .. .. *Rutland, D.*
Thynne, Hon. Ceawlin H. L. *Bath, M.*
Thynne, Lord Christopher J. *Bath, M.*
Thynne, Hon. Lenka A. .. *Bath, M.*
Thynne, Lady Silvy C. .. *Bath, M.*
Thynne, Lord Valentine C... *Bath, M.*
Tiarks, Lady H. Diana J. .. *Winchilsea, E.*
Tidborough, Hon. Christine G. *Addison, V.*
Timpson, Lady Selina C. .. *Clanwilliam, E.*
Todd, Hon. Alexander H. .. *Todd, B.*
Todd, Hon. Hilary A. .. .. *Todd, B.*
Toler, Lady Patricia M.
Graham .. .. .. *Norbury, E.*
Tollemache, Hon. Hugh J. H. *Tollemache, B.*
Tollemache, Hon. John N. L. *Tollemache, B.*
Tollemache, Hon. Michael
D. D. .. .. *Tollemache, B.*
Tollemache, Hon. Timothy
J. E. .. .. *Tollemache, B.*
Tomlins, Hon. Angela M. .. *Carbery, B.*
Tonge, Hon. Judith F. .. *Allen of Fallow-*
 field, B.
Tooth, Hon. Caroline Lucas- *Poole, B.*
Torrado, Lady Melissa C. F.
de .. .. *Darnley, E.*
Tottenham, Lady Ann E. .. *Ely, M.*
Tottenham, Lady George R. *Ely, M.*
Tottenham, Lord Richard I. *Ely, M.*
Tottenham, Lord Timothy C. *Ely, M.*
Townsend, Lady Juliet .. *Birkenhead, E.*
Townshend, Lord John P. .. *Townshend, M.*
Townshend, Lady Katherine A. *Townshend, M.*
Tracy, Hon. Blanche M. *Arundell of*
 Hanbury- *Wardour, By.*
Travis, Hon. Rosemary G. *Pritchard, B.*
Tree, Lady Anne E. B. .. *Devonshire, D.*
Trefgarne, Hon. George G. *Trefgarne, B.*

Wilkinson, Hon. Muriel M.	De Freyne, B.	
Williams, Hon. Diana G. A.	Pritchard, B.	
Williams, **Hon. Elsie**	Macdonald of Gwaenysgor, B.	
Williams, Hon. Horace ..	Williams of Barnburgh, B.	
Williams, Hon. John M.	Francis-Williams, By.	
Williams, Lady Mary R. ..	Grafton, D.	
Williams, Hon. Muriel B. ..	Wrenbury, B.	
Williams, Hon. Ruth M. ..	Cullen of Ashbourne, B.	
Williams, Hon. U. Moyra	Avebury, B.	
Williams, Hon. Olivia, Hoole-Lowsley-	Skelmersdale, B.	
Williams, Lady C. M. Fiona Lowsley-	Bute, M.	
Williams, Hon. Gwilym Rees-	Ogmore, B.	
Williams, Hon. Morgan Rees-	Ogmore, B.	
Williams, Lady Penelope Wynn-	Jowitt, E.	
Williamson, Hon. Alastair S. G.	Forres, **B.**	
Williamson, Hon. Angus S...	Forres, B.	
Williamson, Hon. Astrid S...	Forres. B.	
Willis, Hon. John E.	Willis, B.	
Willis, Hon. Sally A. H. ..	Willis B.	
Willison, Hon. Modwena ..	Hatherton B.	
Willoughby, Hon. Mrs. Charles C. W.	Middleton, B.	
Willoughby, Hon. H. E. Christopher	Middleton, B.	
Willoughby, Hon. John H. F.	Middleton, B.	
Willougby, Hon. Lucy C. A.	De L'Isle, V.	
Willoughby, Hon. Michael O. J.	Middleton, B.	
Willoughby, Hon. Thomas H. R.	Middleton, B.	
Willoughby, Lady Nancy J. M. Heathcote-Drummond- ..	Ancaster, E.	
Wills, Hon. Edward R. H.	Dulverton, B.	
Wills, Hon. Elizabeth A. ..	Rockley, B.	
Wills, Hon. Gilbert M. H. ..	Dulverton, B.	
Wills, Hon. Jean C. ..	Elphinstone, L.	
Wills, Hon. Robert I. H. ..	Dulverton, B.	
Wills, Hon. Sarah M. H. ..	Dulverton, B.	
Wills, Hon. Victor P. H. ..	Dulverton, B.	
Willson, Hon. Anne M. ..	Scarsdale, V.	
Wilson, Hon. Charles T. ..	Nunburnholme, B.	
Wilson, Hon. David M. ..	Nunburnholme, B.	
Wilson, Hon. Geoffrey H. ..	Moran, B.	
Wilson, Hon. Mrs. Guy G...	Nunburnholme, B.	
Wilson, Hon. Ines	Nunburnholme, B.	
Wilson, Hon. Jean M. ..	Rankeillour, B.	
Wilson, Hon. Joyce M. ..	Broughshane, B.	
Wilson, Hon. Lorraine M. C. N.	Nunburnholme, B.	
Wilson, Hon. Margaret E. ..	Maybray-King, B.	
Wilson, Hon. Mary S. ..	Drumalbyn, B.	
Wilson, Hon. Maud M. ..	Wilson, B.	
Wilson, Hon. R. John M...	Moran, B.	
Wilson, Hon. Sally A. M. G.	Vivian, B.	
Wilson, Hon. Shirley C. ..	Cunliffe, B.	
Wilson, Hon. Tatiana ..	Nunburnholme, B.	
Wilson, Hon. Ysabelle ..	Nunburnholme, B.	
Wilson, Hon. Yvette L. ..	Baillieu, B.	
Winch, Hon. Jean R. V. ..	Falkland, V.	
Windsor, Lady Helen M. L.	Kent, D.	
Windsor, Lord Nicholas C. E. J.	Kent, D.	
Wingfield, Hon. Cynthia M.	Sandys, B.	
Wingfield, Hon. Guy C. P...	Powerscourt, V.	
Wingfield, Hon. Julia	Powerscourt, V.	
Wingfield, Hon. Mervyn A.	Powerscourt, V.	
Wingfield, Lady Norah B. C.	Jellicoe, E.	
Winn, Hon. Mrs. Charles J. F.	St. Oswald, B.	
Winn, Hon. Derek E. A. ..	St. Oswald, B.	
Winn, Hon. Reginald H. ..	St. Oswald, B.	
Winn, Hon. John R. Allanson-	Headley, B.	
Winn, Hon. Mrs. John V. Allanson-	Headley, B.	
Winn, Hon. Owain G. Allanson-	Headley, B.	
Winn, Hon. Susan E. Allanson-	Headley, B.	
Winnington, Lady Betty M.	Lichfield, E.	
Winterbottom, Hon. Caroline M. A.	Winterbottom, B.	
Winterbottom, Hon. Dudley W. G.	Winterbottom, B.	
Winterbottom, Hon. Graham A.	Winterbottom, B.	
Winterbottom, Hon. John ..	Winterbottom, B.	
Wise, Hon. Christopher J. C.	Wise, B.	
Wise, Hon. Martin H... ..	Wise, B.	
Wodehouse, Hon. Charles J.	Kimberley, E.	
Wodehouse, Hon. Edward A.	Kimberley, E.	
Wodehouse, Hon. Henry W.	Kimberley, E.	
Wolff, Hon. Mary Clifford ..	Clifford of Chudleigh, B.	
Wood, Hon. Joan M.	Wise, B.	
Wood, Hon. Marion E. ..	Ashton of Hyde, B.	
Wood, Hon. Richard F. ..	Halifax, E.	
Wood, Hon. (Joan L.) Lady Hill-	Hampden, V.	
Woodhouse, Hon. Christopher M.	Terrington, B.	
Woodhouse, Lady Davidema, K. C. M. M.	Lytton, E.	
Woodhouse, Hon. Davina M.	Terrington, B.	
Woodhouse, Hon. Georgina C.	Terrington, B.	
Woodruff, Hon. Marie I. A.	Acton, B.	
Woods, Hon. Victoria V. ..	Stanley of Alderley, B.	
Woolley, Hon. David J. ..	Woolley, B.	
Woolley, Hon. Harold E. ..	Woolley, B.	
Woolley, Hon. Peter J. ..	Woolley, B.	
Woolley, Hon. William G. ..	Woolley, B.	
Woolley, Hon. Elizabeth A. C. Duke-	Hylton, B.	
Wooten, Lady Jane H. H. ..	Lonsdale, E.	
Worlock, Hon. Ann	Edmund-Davies, B.	
Worsley, Hon. Bridget ..	Clitheroe, B.	
Worsley, Hon. Carolyn W ..	Hardinge, V.	
Worsley, Hon. Nona C. Hermon-	Wyfold, B.	
Worth, Hon. Frances P Lloyd-	Tollemache, B.	
Worthy, Hon. Margaret ..	Balfour of Burleigh, B.	
Wright, Hon. Doreen J. ..	Powerscourt, V.	
Wright, Hon. Glyn D... ..	Wright of Ashton under Lyne, By.	
Wright, Hon. Jane A. ..	Hatherton, B.	
Wright, Hon. Owen M. ..	Wright of Ashton under Lyne, By.	
Wright, Lady Sarah C. ..	Waldegrave, E.	
Wright, Lady Jane K. Cory-	Queensberry, M.	
Wrightson, Hon. (Rosemary M.) Lady	Dawson of Penn, V.	
Wroth, Hon. Mary O. ..	Sidmouth, V.	
Wrottesley, Hon. Mark ..	Wrottesley, B.	
Wrottesley, Hon. Nicholas C.	Wrottesley, B.	
Wrottesley, Hon. Mrs. Richard F. G.	Wrottesley, B.	
Wrottesley, Hon. Stephen J.	Wrottesley, B.	
Wyatt, Hon. Margaret A. ..	Ebbisham, B.	
Wyhowski, Hon. Oriel A. D. Luczyc	Massereene, B.	
Wyndham, Hon. Caroline E.	Egremont, B.	
Wyndham, Hon. Mrs. E. Humphrey..	Egremont, B.	
Wyndham, Hon. Harry H. P.	Egremont, B.	
Wyndham, Hon. Mark H... ..	Egremont, B.	
Wyndham, Hon. Ursula C. ..	Egremont, B.	
Wynn, Hon. Mrs. Arthur R.	Newborough, B.	
Wynn, Hon. A. Hermione I.	Middleton, B.	
Wynn, Hon. Charles H. R. ..	Newborough, B.	
Wynn, Hon. Diana H. M. ..	Newborough, B.	
Wynn, Hon. Robert V. ..	Newborough, B.	
Wynn, Hon. Rowland T. B.	Newborough, B.	
Wynne, Hon. Nancy C. ..	Henley, B.	
Yerburgh, Hon. Robert R. G.	Alvingham, B.	
Yerburgh, Hon. Susannah E.	Alvingham, B.	
Yorke, Hon. Adelaide M. ..	Biddulph, B.	
Yorke, Hon. Jemima R. ..	Hardwicke, E.	
Yorke, Lady Rose M. S. ..	Hardwicke, E.	
Yorke, Lady Victoria M. V.B.	Hardwicke, E.	
Young, Hon. Alexandra J. ..	Young, Bs.	
Young, Hon. Alice M. Z. ..	Kennet, B.	
Young, Hon. Audrey L. ..	Kennet, B.	
Young, Hon. Easter D. ..	Kennet, B.	
Young, Hon. Emily T. ..	Kennet, B.	
Young, Hon. Gillian M. ..	Colgrain, B.	
Young, Hon. Juliet M... ..	Young, Bs.	
Young, Hon. Lilian V. L... ..	Moncreiff, B.	
Young, Hon. Mopsa M. ..	Kennet, B.	
Young, Hon. Rosalind A. ..	Young, Bs.	
Young, Hon. William A. T.	Kennet, B.	
Young, Hon. Richard F. Hughes-	St. Helens, B.	
Young, Lady Evelyn Mackworth-	Rothes, E.	

Younger, Hon. Alexander J.   *Younger of Leckie, V.*
Younger, Hon. George K. H.   *Younger of Leckie, V.*
Younger, Hon. Kenneth G.   *Younger of Leckie, V.*
Younger, Hon. Robert E. G.   *Younger of Leckie, V.*

Yovanovitch, Hon. Margaret M.   *Russell of Killowen, By.* (cr. 1929)
Zankel, Hon. Alison V.   ..   *Poole, B.*
Zielenkiewicz, Hon. Catherine   *Thurso, V.*
Zuckerman, Hon. Paul S.   ..   *Zuckerma D.*
Zuckerman, Hon. Stella M. ..   *Zuckerman,*
Zvegintzov, Hon. Rachel K.   *Glanusk, B.*

SURNAMES OF PEERS AND PEERESSES, WHERE THESE DIFFER FROM PEERAGE TITLES, ARRANGED UNDER LAST SURNAME

Where the final part of a compound surname is identical with the peerage title, it has not been included.

Surname	Peerage
ACHESON	Gosford, E.
A'COURT, HOLMES	Heytesbury, B.
ADDERLEY	Norton, B.
ADDINGTON	Sidmouth, V.
AGAR	Normanton, E.
ALEXANDER	Caledon, E.
ALLSOPP	Hindlip, B.
AMAN	Marley, B.
ANDERSON	Waverley, V.
ANNESLEY	Valentia, V.
ANSON	Lichfield, E.
ARTHUR	Glenarthur, B.
ARUNDELL, MONCKTON-	Galway, V.
ASQUITH	Oxford & Asquith, E.
ASSHETON	Clitheroe, B.
ASTLEY	Hastings, B.
BAILEY	Glanusk, B.
BAILLIE	Burton, B.
BALFOUR	Kinross, B.
BALFOUR	Riverdale, B.
BAMPFYLDE	Poltimore, B.
BARING	Ashburton, B.
BARING	Cromer, E.
BARING	Howick of Glendale, B.
BARING	Northbrook, B.
BARING	Revelstoke, B.
BARNES	Gorell, B.
BARNEWALL	Trimlestown, B.
BARRIE	Abertay, By.
BATESON, DE YARBURGH-	Deramore, B.
BATHURST	Bledisloe, V.
BEACH, HICKS-	St. Aldwyn, E.
BEAMISH	Chelwood, B.
BEAUCLERK	St. Albans, D.
BEAUMONT	Allendale, V.
BEAVAN	Ardwick, B.
BECKETT	Grimthorpe, B.
BENNET	Tankerville, E.
BENTINCK, CAVENDISH-	Portland, D.
BERESFORD	Decies, B.
BERESFORD	Waterford, M.
BERNARD	Bandon, E.
BERRY	Camrose, V.
BERRY	Hartwell, B.
BERRY	Kemsley, V.
BERTIE	Lindsey & Abingdon, E.
BEST	Wynford, B.
BETHELL	Westbury, B.
BEVAN	Lee of Ashridge, Bs.
BETHUNE, LINDESAY-	Lindsay, E.
BIGHAM	Mersey, V.
BIGHAM	Nairne, L.
BINGHAM	Clanmorris, B.
BINGHAM	Lucan, E.
BIRCH	Rhyl, B.
BLACKWOOD, HAMILTON-TEMPLE-	Dufferin, M.
BLADES	Ebbisham, B.
BLIGH	Darnley, E.
BOOTH, SCLATER-	Basing, B.
BOSCAWEN	Falmouth, V.
BOURKE	Mayo, E.
BOUVERIE, PLEYDELL-	Radnor, E.
BOWDEN	Aylestone, B.
BOWYER	Denham, B.
BOYD	Kilmarnock, B.
BOYLE	Cork, E.
BOYLE	Glasgow, E.
BOYLE	Shannon, E.
BRABAZON	Meath, E.
BRAND	Hampden, V.
BRETT	Esher, V.
BRIDGEMAN	Bradford, E.
BRODRICK	Midleton, E.
BROOKE	Alanbrooke, V.
BROOKE	Brookeborough, V.
BROOKS	Crawshaw, B.
BROUGHTON	Fairhaven, B.
BROWNE	Craigton, B.
BROWNE	Kilmaine, B.
BROWNE	Oranmore & Browne, B.
BROWNE	Sligo, M.
BROWNLOW	Lurgan, B.
BRUCE, HOVELL-THURLOW-CUMMING-	Thurlow, B.
BUCHAN	Tweedsmuir, B.
BUCKLEY	Wrenbury, B.
BULLER, MANNINGHAM-	Dilhorne, B.

Surname	Peerage
BULLER, YARDE-	Churston, B.
BUNBURY, McCLINTOCK-	Rathdonnell, B.
BUTLER	Carrick, E.
BUTLER	Dunboyne, B.
BUTLER	Lanesborough, E.
BUTLER	Mountgarret, V.
BUTLER	Ormonde, M.
BUXTON	Noel-Buxton, B
BRUCE, BRUDENELL-	Ailesbury, M.
BRUCE	Aberdare, B.
BRUCE	Balfour of Burleigh, L.
BRUCE	Elgin, E.
BYNG	Strafford, E.
BYNG	Torrington, V.
CAIN, NALL-	Brocket, B.
CALDER	Ritchie-Calder, B.
CAMPBELL	Argyll, D.
CAMPBELL	Breadalbane, E.
CAMPBELL	Cawdor, E.
CAMPBELL	Colgrain, B.
CAMPBELL	Glenavy, B.
CAMPBELL	Stratheden, B.
CANNING	Garvagh, B.
CAPELL	Essex, E.
CARBERRY	Carbery, B.
CARINGTON	Carrington, B.
CARNEGIE	Fife, D.
CARNEGIE	Northesk, E.
CARNEGIE	Southesk, E.
CARY	Falkland, V.
CAULFEILD	Charlemont, V.
CAVE, VERNEY-	Braye, B.
CAVENDISH	Chesham, B.
CAVENDISH	Devonshire, D.
CAVENDISH	Waterpark, B.
CAYZER	Rotherwick, B.
CECIL	Amherst of Hackney, B.
CECIL	Exeter, M.
CECIL	Rockley, B.
CECIL, GASCOYNE-	Salisbury, M.
CHALONER	Gisborough, B.
CHARTERIS	Wemyss, E.
CHICHESTER	Donegall, M.
CHICHESTER	Templemore, B.
CHOLMONDELEY	Delamere, B.
CHUBB	Hayter, B.
CHURCHILL, SPENCER-	Marlborough, D.
CLARK, CHICHESTER-	Moyola, B.
CLIVE, WINDSOR-	Plymouth, E.
COCHRANE	Dundonald, E.
COCKS	Somers, B.
COKAYNE	Cullen of Ashbourne, B.
COKE	Leicester, E.
COLE	Enniskillen, E.
COLLINS	Stonham, B.
COLVILLE	Clydesmuir, B.
COMPTON	Northampton, M.
CONWY, ROWLEY-	Langford, B.
COOPER	Norwich, V.
COOPER, ASHLEY-	Shaftesbury, E.
COPLEY, BEWICKE-	Cromwell, B.
CORBETT	Rowallan, V.
CORRY, LOWRY-	Belmore, E.
COTTON, STAPLETON-	Combermere, V.
COURTENAY	Devon, E.
COUTTS, MONEY-	Latymer, B.
COX, ROXBEE	Kings Norton, B.
CRAIG	Craigavon, V.
CRICHTON	Erne, E.
CRIPPS	Parmoor, B.
CROSSLEY	Somerleyton, B.
CUBITT	Ashcombe, B.
CURZON	Howe, E.
CURZON	Scarsdale, V.
CURZON, ROPER-	Teynham, B.
CUST	Brownlow, B.
DALRYMPLE	Stair, E.
DAMER, DAWSON-	Portarlington, E.
DAVIDSON	Northchurch, Bs.
DAVIES	Darwen, B.
DAVISON	Broughshane, B.
DAWNAY	Downe, V.
DEANE	Muskerry, B.
DE COURCY	Kingsale, B.
DE GRAY	Walsingham, B.
DE MOLEYNS, EVELEIGH-	Ventry, B.
DENISON	Londesborough, B.
DEVEREUX	Hereford, V.
DEWAR	Forteviot, B.

Surname	Peerage
DIXON	Glentoran, B.
DODSON	Monk Bretton, B.
DOUGLAS	Morton, E.
DOUGLAS	Queensberry, M.
DOUGLAS, AKERS-	Chilston, V.
DRUMMOND	Perth, E. and Strange, B.
DUGDALE	Crathorne, B.
DUKE	Merrivale, B.
DUKES	Dukeston, By.
DUNCOMBE	Feversham, B.
DUNDAS	Melville, V.
DUNDAS	Zetland, M.
DUTTON	Sherborne, B.
EADY	Swinfen, B.
EDEN	Auckland, B.
EDEN	Avon, E.
EDEN	Henley, B.
EDGCUMBE	Mount Edgcumbe, E.
EDMONDSON	Sandford, B.
EDWARDES	Kensington, B.
EDWARDS	Chelmer, B.
EGERTON	Sutherland, D.
EGERTON	Wilton, E.
ELIOT	St. Germans, E.
ELLIOT-MURRAY-KYNYNMOUND	Minto, E.
ELLIS, SCOTT-	Howard de Walden, B.
ERSKINE	Buchan, E.
ERSKINE	Mar & Kellie, E.
ERSKINE, ST. CLAIR-	Rosslyn, E.
EVANS	Energlyn, B.
EVANS	Mountevans, B.
EVE	Silsoe, B.
FANE	Westmoreland, E.
FEILDING	Denbigh, E.
FELLOWES	Ailwyn, B.
FELLOWES	De Ramsey, B.
FERRIS, GRANT	Harvington, B
FIENNES	Saye & Sele, B.
FITZ-CLARENCE	Munster, E.
FITZGERALD	Leinster, D.
FITZHERBERT	Stafford, B.
FITZ-MAURICE	Orkney, E.
FITZMAURICE, MERCER NAIRNE PETTY-	Lansdowne, M.
FITZROY	Daventry, V.
FITZROY	Grafton, D.
FLOWER	Ashbrook, V.
FOLJAMBE	Liverpool, E.
FOOT	Caradon, B.
FORBES	Granard, E.
FRANKLAND	Zouche, B.
FRASER	Lovat, L.
FRASER	Saltoun, L.
FRASER	Strathalmond, B.
FREKE, EVANS-	Carbery, B.
FREMANTLE	Cottesloe, B.
FRENCH	de Freyne, B.
FRENCH	Ypres, E.
GALBRAITH	Strathclyde, B.
GANZONI	Belstead, B.
GEORGE, LLOYD	Tenby, V.
GIBBS	Aldenham, B.
GIBBS	Wraxall, B.
GIBSON	Ashbourne, B.
GIFFARD	Halsbury, E.
GILBEY	Vaux of Harrowden, B.
GLYN	Wolverton, B.
GODLEY	Kilbracken, B.
GORDON	Aberdeen, M.
GORDON	Huntly, M.
GORE	Arran, E.
GORE, ORMSBY-	Harlech, B.
GOWER, LEVESON-	Granville, E.
GRAHAM	Montrose, D.
GRANT OF GRANT	Strathspey, B
GRANT, OGILVIE-	Seafield E.
GRAVINA	Newburgh, C.
GRAY, ANSTRUTHER-	Kilmany, Cs.
GREAVES	Dysart, Cs.
GREENALL	Daresbury, B.
GRENFELL	St. Just B.
GRENVILLE, FREEMAN-	Kinloss, L.
GREVILLE	Warwick, E.
GREY	Stamford, E.
GRIMSTON	Verulam ,E
GROSVENOR	Ebury, B.
GROSVENOR	Westminster, D
GUEST	Wimborne, V.
GUINNESS	Iveagh, E.
GUINNESS	Moyne, B
GULLY	Selby, V.
GURDON	Cranworth, B.
HAMILTON	Abercorn, D.
HAMILTON	Belhaven, L.
HAMILTON	Holm Patrick, B.
HAMILTON, BAILLIE-	Haddington, E.
HAMILTON, DOUGLAS-	Selkirk, E.
HAMOND, HARBORD-	Suffield, B.
HAMPDEN, HOBART-	Buckinghamshire, E.

Surname	Peerage
HANDCOCK	Castlemaine, B.
HARDY, GATHORNE-	Cranbrook, E.
HARE	Blakenham, V.
HARE	Listowel, E.
HARMSWORTH	Rothermere, V.
HARRIS	Malmesbury, E.
HASTINGS	Huntingdon, E.
HASTINGS, ABNEY-	Loudoun, C.
HATTON, FINCH	Winchilsea, E.
HAY	Erroll, C.
HAY	Kinnoull, E.
HAY	Tweeddale, M.
HENDERSON	Faringdon, B.
HENDERSON	Rowley, B.
HENNESSY	Windlesham, B.
HEPBURN, BUCHAN-	Hailes, By.
HERBERT	Carnarvon, E.
HERBERT	Hemingford, B.
HERBERT	Pembroke, E.
HERBERT	Powis, E.
HERBERT	Tangley, By.
HERVEY	Bristol, M.
HEWITT	Lifford, V.
HIBBERT, HOLLAND-	Knutsford, V.
HICKS, JOYNSON-	Brentford, V.
HILL	Downshire, M.
HILL, CLEGG-	Hill, V.
HODGE, HERMON-	Wyfold, B.
HOGG	Hailsham of St. Marylebone, B.
HOOD	Bridport, V.
HOOD, FULLER-ACLAND-	St. Audries, By.
HOPE	Glendevon, B.
HOPE	Linlithgow, M.
HOPE	Rankeillour, B.
HOPE, PELHAM-CLINTON-	Newcastle, D.
HOPKINSON	Colyton, B.
HOPWOOD	Southborough, B.
HOWARD	Carlisle, E.
HOWARD	Effingham, E.
HOWARD	Strathcona, B.
HOWARD	Suffolk, E.
HOWARD, FITZALAN	Herries of Terregles, Bs.
HOWARD, FITZALAN	Norfolk, D.
HOWARD, FORWARD-	Wicklow, E.
HUBBARD	Addington, B.
HUGGINS	Malvern, V.
HUTCHINSON	Ilford, By.
HUTCHINSON, HELY-	Donoughmore, E.
INGRAMS	Darcy de Knayth, Bs.
INSKIP	Caldecote, V.
IRBY	Boston, B.
ISAACS	Reading, M.
JACKSON	Allerton, B.
JAMES	Northbourne, B.
JEBB	Gladwyn, B.
JERVIS	St. Vincent, V.
JOCELYN	Roden, E.
JOHNSTON, LAWSON-	Luke, B.
JOHNSTONE, VANDEN-BEMPDE-	Derwent, B.
JOLLIFFE	Hylton, B.
JONES	Maelor, B.
JONES, ARMSTRONG--	Snowdon, E.
JONES, GWYNNE	Chalfont, B.
KEARLEY	Devonport, V.
KEITH	Kintore, Cs.
KEMP	Rochdale, V
KENNEDY	Ailsa, M.
KENWORTHY	Strabolgi, B.
KEPPEL	Albemarle, E.
KER INNES-	Roxburghe, D.
KERR	Lothian, M.
KERR	Teviot, B.
KING	Lovelace, E.
KITSON	Airedale, B.
KNATCHBULL	Brabourne, B.
KNIGHTLEY, FINCH-	Aylesford, E.
KNOX	Ranfurly, E.
KYNYNMOUND, ELLIOT-MURRAY-	Minto, E.
LADE, MILLES-	Sondes, E.
LAMB	Rochester, B.
LAMBART	Cavan, E.
LAMPSON	Killearn, B.
LANGTON, TEMPLE-GORE-	Temple, E.
LASCELLES	Harewood, E.
LAW	Coleraine, B.
LAW	Ellenborough, B.
LAWRENCE	Trevethin, B.
LAWSON	Burnham, B.
LEGGE	Dartmouth, E.
LEGH	Newton, B.
LEITH	Burgh, B.
LENNOX, GORDON	Richmond, D.
LESLIE	Rothes, E.
LEVER	Leverhulme, V.
LEWIS	Brecon, B.

Surname	Peerage	Surname	Peerage
Lewis	Essendon, B.	Peake	Ingleby, V.
Lewis	Merthyr, B.	Pearson	Cowdray, V.
Liddell	Ravensworth, B.	Pease	Daryngton, B.
Lindsay	Crawford, E.	Pease	Gainford, B.
Lister, Cunliffe-	Swinton, E.	Pease	Wardington, B.
Littleton	Hatherton, B.	Pelham	Chichester, E.
Loder	Wakehurst, B.	Pelham	Yarborough, E.
Lopes	Roborough, B.	Pellew	Exmouth, V.
Low	Aldington, B.	Pennant, Douglas-	Penrhyn, B.
Lowther	Lonsdale, E.	Penny	Marchwood, V.
Lowther	Ullswater, V.	Pepys	Cottenham, E.
Lubbock	Avebury, B.	Perceval	Egmont, E.
Lumley	Scarbrough, E.	Percy	Northumberland, D.
Lygon	Beauchamp, E.	Pery	Limerick, E.
Lyon, Bowes	Strathmore, E.	Philipps	Milford, B.
Lysaght	Lisle, B.	Philipps	St. Davids, V.
Lyttelton	Chandos, V.	Philipps	Strange of Knokin, Bs.
Lyttelton	Cobham, V.	Phipps	Normanby, M.
McDonnell	Antrim, E.	Plumptre	FitzWalter, B.
Mackay	Inchcape, E.	Plunkett	Dunsany, B.
Mackay	Reay, L.	Plunkett	Fingall, E.
Mackay	Tanlaw, B.	Plunkett	Louth, B.
Mackenzie	Amulree, B.	Pollock	Hanworth, V.
Mackenzie	Cromartie, E.	Pomeroy	Harberton, V.
Mackenzie, Montagu-Stuart-Wortley-	Wharncliffe, E.	Ponsonby	Bessborough, E.
		Ponsonby	de Mauley, B.
McLaren	Aberconway, B.	Ponsonby	Sysonby, B.
Maclay	Muirshiel, V.	Powlett, Orde-	Bolton, B.
Macpherson	Drumalbyn, B.	Powys	Lilford, B.
Macpherson	Strathcarron, B.	Pratt	Camden, M.
Maffey	Rugby, B.	Preston	Gormanston, V.
Maitland	Lauderdale, E.	Primrose	Rosebery, E.
Major, Henniker-	Henniker, B.	Prittie	Dunalley, B.
Makins	Sherfield, B.	Quin, Wyndham-	Dunraven, E.
Manners	Rutland, D.	Ramsay	Dalhousie, E.
Mansfield	Sandhurst, B.	Ramsbotham	Soulbury, V.
Marquis	Woolton, E.	Rhys	Dynevor, B.
Marsham	Romney, E.	Rice, Spring	Monteagle of Brandon, B.
Mason	Blackford, B.	Richards	Milverton, B.
Maude	Hawarden, V.	Roberts	Clywd, B.
Maxwell	Farnham, B.	Robinson	Martonmere, B.
Maxwell	de Ros, Bs.	Roche	Fermoy, B.
Meade	Clanwilliam, E.	Rodd	Rennell, B.
Melville, Leslie	Leven, E.	Rous	Stradbroke, E.
Millar	Inchyra, B.	Russell	Ampthill, B.
Mills	Hillingdon, B.	Russell	Bedford, D.
Mitford	Redesdale, B.	Russell	de Clifford, B.
Molyneux	Sefton, E.	Russell, Hamilton-	Boyne, V.
Mond	Melchett, B.	Ruthven, Hore-	Gowrie, E.
Montagu	Manchester, D.	Ryder	Harrowby, E.
Montagu	Swaythling, B	Sackville	De La Warr, E.
Montague	Amwell, B.	St. Aubyn	St. Levan, B.
Montgomerie	Eglinton, E.	St. Clair	Sinclair, L.
Moore	Drogheda, E.	St. John	Bolingbroke, V.
Moreton	Ducie, E.	St. Leger	Doneraile, V.
Morgan, Vaughan	Reigate, B.	Samuel	Bearsted, V.
Morley, Hope-	Hollenden, B.	Sanders	Bayford, By.
Morris	Killanin, B.	Sandilands	Torphichen, L.
Morrison	Dunrossil, V.	Saumarez	de Saumarez, B.
Morrison	Margadale, B.	Savile	Mexborough, E.
Mosley	Ravensdale, B.	Scarlett	Abinger, B.
Mountbatten	Edinburgh, D.	Scott	Eldon, E.
Mountbatten	Milford Haven, M.	Scott, Hepburne-	Polwarth, L.
Muff	Calverley, B.	Scott, Montagu-Douglas-	Buccleuch, D.
Mulholland	Dunleath, B.	Seager	Leighton of St. Mellons, B.
Murray	Atholl, D.	Seely	Mottistone, B.
Murray	Dunmore, E.	Sempill	Sempill, L.
Murray	Mansfield, E.	Seymour	Somerset, D.
Murray, Erskine-	Elibank, L.	Seymour	Hertford, M.
Needham	Kilmorey, E.	Shaw	Craigmyle, B.
Nevill	Abergavenny, M.	Shaw	Kilbrandon, B.
Neville	Braybrooke, B.	Shirley	Ferrers, E.
Newton	Eltisley, By.	Shore	Teignmouth, B.
Nicolson	Carnock, B.	Siddeley	Kenilworth, B.
Nivison	Glendyne, B.	Sidney	De L'Isle, V.
Noble	Glenkinglas, B.	Silverstone	Ashdown, E.
Noel	Gainsborough, E.	Sinclair	Caithness, E.
North	Guilford, E.	Sinclair	Pentland, B.
Northcote	Iddesleigh, E.	Sinclair	Thurso, V.
Norton	Grantley, B.	Skeffington	Massereene, V.
Norton	Rathcreedan, B.	Smith	Bicester, B.
Nugent	Westmeath, E.	Smith	Birkenhead, E.
O'Brien	Inchiquin, B.	Smith	Colwyn, B.
of Mar	Mar, E.	Smith	Hambleden, V.
Ogilvy	Airlie, E.	Smith, Buchanan-	Balerno, B.
O'Neill	Rathcavan, B.	Snow	Burntwood, B.
Orr	Boyd-Orr, B.	Somerset	Beaufort, D.
Paget	Anglesey, M.	Somerset	Raglan, B.
Pakenham	Longford, E.	Soskice	Stow Hill, B.
Pakington	Hampton, B.	Souter	Audley, B.
Palmer	Lucas of Crudwell, Bs.	Spencer	Churchill, V.
Palmer	Rusholme, B.	Stanhope	Harrington, E.
Palmer	Selborne, E.	Stanley	Derby, E.
Parker	Macclesfield, E.	Stanley	Sheffield, B.
Parker	Morley, E.	Stern	Michelham, B.
Parnell	Congleton, B.	Stewart	Galloway, E.
Parsons	Rosse, E.	Stewart, Vane-Tempest-	Londonderry, M.
Paton, Noel-	Ferrier, B.	Stonor	Camoys, B.
Paulet	Winchester, M.	Stopford	Courtown, E.
		Storey	Buckton, B.
		Stourton	Mowbray, B.

Surname			Peerage
STRACHEY	..	..	O'Hagan, B.
STRACHEY	..	..	Strachie, B.
STRANGWAYS, FOX-	..		Ilchester, E.
STRAUSS	..	..	Conesford, By.
STRUTT	..	..	Belper, B.
STRUTT	..	..	Rayleigh, B.
STUART	..	..	Castle Stewart, E.
STUART	..	..	Moray, E.
STUART, CRICHTON-	..		Bute, M.
SUGDEN	..	..	St. Leonards, B.
TALBOT, CHETWYND-	..		Shrewsbury, E.
TAYLOR, SUENSON-	..		Grantchester, B.
TAYLOUR	..	..	Headfort, M.
TENISON, KING-	..		Kingston, E.
TENNANT	..	..	Glenconner, B.
THELLUSSON	..		Rendlesham, B.
THESIGER	..	..	Chelmsford, V.
THOMAS, FREEMAN-	..		Willingdon, M.
THOMSON	..	..	Tweedsmuir of Belhevie, Bs.
THOMSON, MITCHELL-	..		Selsdon, B.
THYNNE	..	..	Bath, M.
TOLER, GRAHAM-	..		Norbury, E.
TOTTENHAM	..	..	Ely, M.
TRACY, HANBURY-	..		Sudeley, B.
TREFUSIS, FANE-	..		Clinton, B.
TRENCH	..	..	Ashtown, B.
TRENCH, LE POER	..		Clancarty, E.
TUFTON	..	..	Hothfield, B.
TURNER	..	..	Netherthorpe, B.
TURNOUR	..	..	Winterton, E.
TURTON	..	..	Tranmire, B.
UPTON	..	..	Templetown, V.
URQUHART	..	..	Tayside, B.
VANE	..	..	Barnard, B.
VANE, FLETCHER-	..		Inglewood, B.
VANNECK	..	..	Huntingfield, B.
VAUGHAN	..	..	Lisburne, E.
VEREKER	..	..	Gort, V.
VERNEY	..	..	Willoughby de Broke, B.
VERNON	..	..	Lyveden, B.
VESEY	..	..	de Vesci, V.
VILLIERS	..	..	Clarendon, E.
VILLIERS, CHILD-	..		Jersey, E.
VINTCENT	..	..	Wharton, By.

Surname			Peerage
VIVIAN	..	..	Swansea, B.
WALLACE	..	..	Dudley, Bs.
WALLOP	..	..	Portsmouth, E.
WALROND	..	..	Waleran, B.
WALSH	..	..	Ormathwaite, B.
WARD	..	..	Bangor, V.
WARD	..	..	Dudley, E.
WARRENDER	..		Bruntisfield, B.
WATSON	..	..	Manton, B.
WEDDERBURN, SCRYMGEOUR-			Dundee, E.
WEIR	..	..	Inverforth, B.
WELLESLEY	..	..	Cowley, E.
WELLESLEY	..	..	Wellington, D.
WEST, SACKVILLE-	..		Sackville, B.
WESTENRA	..	..	Rossmore, B.
WHITE	..	..	Annaly, B.
WHITELEY	..	..	Marchamley, B.
WHITFIELD	..	..	Kenswood, B.
WILBRAHAM, BOOTLE-			Skelmersdale, B.
WILLEY	..	..	Barnby, B.
WILLIAMS	..	..	Berners, Bs.
WILLIAMS	..	..	Francis-Williams, By.
WILLIAMS, REES-	..		Ogmore, B.
WILLIAMSON	..	..	Forres, B.
WILLOUGHBY	..	..	Middleton, B.
WILLOUGHBY, HEATHCOTE- DRUMMOND-			Ancaster, E.
WILLS	..	..	Dulverton, B.
WILSON	..	..	Moran, B.
WILSON	..	..	Nunburnholme, B.
WINGFIELD	..	..	Powerscourt, V.
WINN	..	..	St. Oswald, B.
WINN, ALLANSON-	..		Headley, B.
WODEHOUSE	..	..	Kimberley, E.
WOOD	..	..	Halifax, E.
WOODALL	..	..	Uvedale of North End, B.
WOODHOUSE	..	..	Terrington, B.
WRIGHT	..	..	Wootton of Abinger, Bs.
WYNDHAM	..	..	Egremont, B.
WYNDHAM	..	..	Leconfield, B.
WYNN	..	..	Newborough, B.
YERBURGH	..	..	Alvingham, B.
YORKE	..	..	Hardwicke, E.
YOUNG	..	..	Kennet, B.
YOUNG, HUGHES-	..		St. Helens, B.

THE PRIVY COUNCIL
OF THE UNITED KINGDOM AND NORTHERN IRELAND.

EACH member is entitled to the prefix of *Right Honourable* to his name.
A Member of Privy Council of Northern Ireland. (It was announced in 1973 that no further appointments will be made, but existing members will retain their rank, style and obligations.)

" *cr.* 19— " signifies the date of appointment to the Council.

Lord President of the Council—*Rt. Hon.* EDWARD WATSON SHORT, M.P.

ABERDARE, *Rt. Hon. Baron*; *cr.* 1974.

ADEANE, *Lt.-Col. the Rt. Hon. Baron, GCB, GCVO; cr.* 1953.

ADEMOLA, *Rt. Hon. Sir* Adetokunbo Adegboyega, *GCON, KBE,* el. son of the late HH Ademola II, Alake of Abeokuta, KBE, CMG, *b.* 1906; ed. at King's C l.; Lagos, and at Camb. Univ. (BA honours 1931, MA 1934); Bar. Middle Temple 1934; a Magistrate Nigeria 1939-49, a Puisne Judge 1949-54, and Ch. Justice W. Nigeria 1955-58, and Ch. Justice, Federation of Nigeria (now Federal Republic) 1958-72; Chm. of National Cencus Board since 1972; *m.* 1939, Kofoworola, MBE, BA, da. of the late Eric Olawolu Moore, CBE; *cr.* Knt. 1957, PC 1963, KBE (Civil) 1963, CFR 1960, GCON 1972. 1, *The Close, Adetokunbo Ademola St., Victoria Island, Lagos, Nigeria; Island, Yoruba, and Metropolitan (Lagos) Clubs.*

ADERMANN, *Rt. Hon. Sir* Charles Frederick, *KBE,* son of the late Charles Aldermann; *b.* 1896; a JP of Queensland; Dep. Australian Representative, 15th Session UN Economic Commn. for Asia and the Far East, Queensland 1959, and Leader of Australian Delegation to Commonwealth Parl. Conference, Wellington, NZ 1965; a Member, House of Representatives, Queensland 1943-72 (Chm. of Cttees. 1950-58); Dep. Speaker Oct. to Nov. 1950, Aug. to Oct. 1955, and March to June 1956). Dep. Leader of Australian Country Party 1964-66, and Min. of State for Primary Industry 1958-67: *m.* 1926, Mildred, da. of the late S. T. Turner of Wooroolin, Queensland; *cr.* 1966, KBE (Civil) 1971. *Fisher St., Kingaroy, Queensland.*

ALDINGTON, *Rt. Hon. Baron, K.C.M.G., C.B.E., D.S.O., T.D.; cr.* 1954.

ALPORT, *Lieut.-Col. the Rt. Hon. Baron, T.D.; cr.* 1960.

AMERY, *Rt. Hon.* (Harold) Julian, MP. son of the late Rt. Hon. Leopold (Charles Maurice) Stennett Amery, C.H. ; *b.* 1919 ; ed. at Eton, and Balliol Coll., Oxford; a Delegate to Consultative Assembly of Council of Europe 1950-3 and 1956, a Member of Round Table Conference on Malta 1955, Parl. Under-Sec. of State and Financial Sec., War Office 1957-8, Parl. Under-Sec. of State, Colonial Office 1958-60, Sec. of State for Air 1960-62 and Min. of, Aviation 1962-64; Min. of Public Building and Works June to Oct. 1970, Min. for Housing and Construction 1970-72, and Min. of State Foreign and Commonwealth Office 1972-74; MP for Brighton Pavilion (C) since 1969, 1939-45 War as Fl. Sgt. RAF and as Capt. Gen. List in Egypt, Balkans and China; MP for Div. of N. Preston (C) 1950-66: *m.* 1950, Catherine, da. of the Rt. Hon. (Maurice) Harold Macmillan, [D. Devonshire]; *cr.* 1960. 112, *Eaton Sq., SW1; White's, Beefsteak, Carlton and Buck's Clubs.*

AMORY, *Rt. Hon. Viscount, KG, GCMG, T.D.; cr.* 1953.

ANDERSON, *Rt. Hon.* (Margaret) Betty HARVIE, OBE, TD, MP, da. of the late Thomas Alexander Harvie Anderson, of Quarter, by Denny; *b.* 1915; ed. at St. Leonard's Sch., St. Andrews; a DL for Stirling; Coy. Com. ATS 1938, Adjt. Reception Depot 1940, Snr. Comd. Mixed Heavy A-A Regt., RA 1942-43, Ch. Comd. Mixed Heavy A-A Regt. Bde. 1943-46; Co. Councillor for Stirlingshire 1945-49; a Member of Exec. Cttee. of 1922 Cttee. 1962-70, and since 1974, of Chm's Panel House of Commons 1966-70, and of Roy. Commn. on Local Govt. in Scotland 1966-69; Dep. Chm. of Ways and Means

1970-74; MP for E. Renfrewshire (C) since 1959: *m.* 1960, John Francis Penrose Skrimshire, MD, FRCP; *cr.* OBE (Civil) 1956, PC 1974. *Quarter, by Denny, Stirlingshire.*

§ANDREWS. *Rt. Hon.* John Lawson Ormrod, son of the late Rt. Hon. John Miller Andrews, CH; *b.* 1903; a DL for co. Down; Min. of Health and Local Govt. 1957-61, of Commerce 1961-63, and Finance 1963-64; Senator since 1964; Dep. Prime Min. 1968-72 (Parliament suspended March 1972): *m.* 1928 Marjorie Elaine Maynard, da. of Alfred Morgan James, of Newport, Mon.; *cr.* 1957. *Maxwell Court, Comber, Belfast; Ulster Reform (Belfast) Club.*

ANTHONY, *Rt. Hon.* John Douglas, MP, son of the late Hubert Lawrence Anthony; *b.* 1929; ed. at Murwillumbah High Sch., King's Sch., Parramatta, and Qld. Agric. Coll., Gatton, Qld. (QDA); MHR Aust. since 1957, and MEC since 1963; Min. for the Interior, Aust. 1964-67, Min. for Primary Industry 1967-71, and Dep. Prime Min. and Min. for Trade and Industry 1971-72; Leader of Australian Country Party since 1971: *m.* 1957, Margot MacDonald, da. of Alton Budd; *cr.* 1971. *Sunnymeadows, Murwillumbah, NSW 2484; Union (Sydney) Club.*

ARMSTRONG OF SANDERSTEAD; *Rt. Hon. Baron, GCB, MVO; cr.* 1973.

ATKINS, *Rt. Hon.* Humphrey Edward, MP, son of the late Capt. E. D. Atkins, of Nyeri, Kenya; *b.* 1922; ed. at Wellington Coll.; 1939-45 War; Lt. RN 1943-48; PPS to Civil Lord of the Admiralty 1959-62; Opposition Whip 1967-70, and Treas. to HM Household 1970-73, since when Govt. Ch. Whip; MP for Merton and Morden (C) 1955-70, since when for Spelthorne: *m.* 1944, Adela Margaret, da. of the late Maj. Sir Robert Spencer-Nairn, TD, 1st Bt.; *cr.* 1973. 3, *North Court, Great Peter St., SW1; Beech House, Bembridge, I. of Wight; Brooks's Club.*

ATKINSON, *Rt. Hon. Sir* Fenton, son of Hon. Sir Cyril Atkinson; *b.* 1906; ed. at Winchester, and at New Coll., Oxford; Bar. Lincoln's Inn 1928, a QC 1953, and a Bencher 1958; Judge of Salford Hundred Court of Record 1953-60, a Judge of High Court of Justice (Queen's Bench Div.) 1960-68, and a Lord Justice of Appeal 1968-71; 1939-45 War: *m.* 1929, Margaret Mary, da. of James E. Roy, of Radlett, Herts; *cr.* Knt. 1960, PC 1968. *Dalbeathie House, Dunkeld, Perthshire.*

AVON, *Rt. Hon. the Earl, KG, MC; cr.* 1934.

AVONSIDE, *Rt. Hon. Lord; cr.* 1962 [see "LORDS OF SESSION".]

AYLESTONE, *Rt. Hon. Baron, CBE; cr.* 1962.

AZIKIWE, *Rt. Hon.* Nnamdi, son of Obededom Chukwuemeka Azikiwe ; *b.* 1904 ; ed. at Church Missionary So. Central Sch., Onitsha, at Methodist Boys' High Sch., Lagos, at Hope Waddell Training Institute, Calabar, at Storer Coll., Harpers Ferry, U.S.A., at Howard Univ., Washington, D.C., at Lincoln Univ., Pennsylvania, at Pennsylvania Univ., and at Columbia Univ., New York; MA; MSc; LLD; DLitt; Hon. Dr. of Civil Law, Liberia, Hon. Dr. of Science, Lagos; Editor in Ch. of " African Morning Post," Accra 1934-7, and of " W. African Pilot " 1937-45, Managing Director of Zik's Press Ltd. 1937-52, and of Comet Press Ltd. 1945-43, Correspondent for Associated Negro Press 1944-47, and for Reuter's 1944-46, Chm. of African Continental Bank, Ltd. 1944-53, and of W. African Pilot Ltd. and Associated Newspapers of Nigeria Ltd., and six other Cos. 1952-53; ■

Member of Executive Committee of Mambü Party, Accra 1935-37 of Nigerian Youth Movement 1937-41, and of Lagos Broadcasting Committee 1940-45, and Chm. of Nigerian Real Estate Corporation Ltd. 1952-3, Gen. Sec. of National Council of Nigeria and the Cameroons 1944-46, and Pres. 1946-60, a M.L.C., Nigeria 1947-51, a Member of Foot Commn. for Nigerianisation of Civil Ser. 1948, Leader of Opposition, House of Assembly, W. Nigeria 1952-3, Min. E. Nigeria 1954-7, a Member of House of Assembly, E. Nigeria 1954-9, and of House of Representatives 1954 and 1960, a P.C. of E. Nigeria 1954-59, Leader of Educational Missions to Europe and U.S.A. for establishment of Nigerian Univ. 1955 and 1959, Premier of E. Nigeria 1954-59, Pres. of Senate of Federation of Nigeria, Jan. to Nov. 1960, Gov.-Gen. and C-in-C of Nigeria 1960-63, and Pres. 1963-66; Chm. of Provisional Council of Nigeria Univ. 1960-61; Chancellor Lagos Univ. since 1972, and Joint Pres. Anti-Slavery Soc. for Human Rights, London since 1970; a KStJ, a Fellow Institute of Journalists, a Life Member of British Assocn. for Advancement of Science, a Member of American Soc. of International Law, of American Anthropological Assocn., of American Political Science Soc., and of American Ethnological So., a Life Fellow of the Roy. Economic So., and of Roy. Anthropological Institute, and an Author and a Poet; Ndichie Chief Ozizanie Obi of Onitsha 1963: *m.* 1936, Flora Ogbenyeanu, da. of Chief Ogoegbunam, the Adazia of Onitsha (Ndichie Chief); *cr.* 1960. *Onuiyi Haven, PO Box 7, Nsukka, Nigeria.*

BACON, *Rt. Hon.* Baroness, *CBE; cr.* 1966.

§BAILIE, *Rt. Hon.* Robin John; *b.* 1937; ed. at Rainey Endowed Sch. and Queen's Univ. Belfast (LLB); Solicitor 1961; Member of House of Commons NI (*U*) 1969-72; Min. of Commerce 1971-72: *m.* 1961, Margaret Francis, da. of Charles Boggs; *cr.* 1971. *39A, Malone Park, Belfast, 9.*

BAKER, *Rt. Hon. Sir* George Gillespie, *OBE*; son of the late Capt. John Kilgour Baker, of Stirling: b. 1910; ed. at Strathallan Sch., Perthshire, and at Brasenose Coll., Oxford (BA, BCL Hon Fellow 1967); Bar. Middle Temple 1932, QC 1952, Bencher 1961, Dep. Treas. 1975; Recorder of Bridgnorth 1946-50, of Smethwick 1950-52, and of Wolverhampton 1952-61; a Judge of High Court of Justice (Probate, Divorce and Admiralty Div.) 1961-71, and Pres. of High Court of Justice (Probate, Divorce and Admiralty Div.) April to Oct. 1971, since when Pres. of High Court of Justice (Family Div.), and Presiding Judge Wales and Chester Circuit 1970-71; Dep. Chm. of Salop Quarter Sessions 1955-72 and Chm. Lord Chancellor's Cttee. Mechanical Recording of Court Proceedings 1965-71, and of Gen. Optical Council 1959-61; 1939-45 War as Lt.-Col. The Cameronians (Scottish Rifles) (OBE): *m.* 1935, Jessie McCall, da. of the late Thomas Scott Findlay, of Mount Vernon, Glasgow; *cr.* OBE (Mil.) 1945. Knt. 1961, PC 1971, *Camrie, Overstream, Loudwater, Rickmansworth, Herts; 2, Plowden Bldgs., Temple, EC4.*

BAKER, *Rt. Hon.* Philip John NOEL-, son of the late Joseph Allen Baker, M.P. ; *b.* 1889 ; ed. at Bootham, at Haverford Coll., U.S.A., and at King's Coll., Camb. (MA, Fellow 1915-63, since when Hon. Fellow); PPS to Sec. of State for Foreign Affairs 1931; Joint Parl. Sec. Min. of War Transport 1942-45, Min. of State, Foreign Office 1945-46, Sec. of State for Air 1946-47, Sec. of State for Commonwealth Relationships 1947-50, and Min. of Fuel and Power 1950-51; Chm. of Labour Party 1946-47; Chm., Foreign Affairs Group, Par. Labour Party 1964; Pres. Internat. Council on Sport and Physical Education (consultative status with UNESCO) 1960; awarded Nobel Peace Prize 1959; assumed by deed poll 1921 the surname of Noel-Baker, MP for Coventry (*Lab.*), 1929-31, for Derby 1936-50, and for Derby S. 1950-70: *m.* 1915, Irene, who *d.* 1956, da. of Frank Noel, of Euboea, Greece; *cr.* 1945. 16, *South Eaton Place, SW1.*

BALFOUR OF INCHRYE, *Rt. Hon.* Baron, *M.C.; cr.* 1941.

BALNIEL, *Rt. Hon.* Baron [see E. Crawford and Balcarres]; *cr.* 1972.

BARBER, *Rt. Hon.* Baron, *TD: cr.* 1963.

BARNETT, *Rt. Hon.* Joel, *MP*, son of the late Louis Barnett, of Manchester; *b.* 1923; ed. at Central High Sch., Manchester; FCCA; 1939-45 War as Sgt. RASC; Snr. partner J. C. Allen & Co., Manchester 1954-74; Chm. Parl. Labour Party Economic & Finance Gp. 1967-70; a Member of Public Accounts Cttee. 1966-71, of Public Expenditure Cttee. 1971-74, and of Select Cttee. on Tax Credits 1973; Ch. Sec. HM Treasury since 1974; MP for Heywood and Royton Div. of Lancs. (*Lab.*) since 1964: *m.* 1949, Lilian Stella, da. of Abraham Goldstone; *cr.* 1975. 10, *Park Lane, Whitefield, Lancs.; Flat 92, 24, John Islip St., Westminster, SW1.*

BARROW, *Rt. Hon.* Errol Walton, son of Reginald Grant Barrow, DD; *b.* 1920; ed. at Harrison Coll., Barbados, and LSE (BS. Econ); LLD McGill; Bar. Lincoln's Inn 1949; Private Practice at Bar. W. Indies 1950-61; Premier Barbados 1961-66, since when Prime Min.; MLA Barbados 1951-56 and since 1958; 1939-45 War as F/O RAF, in France, Holland, Belgium and Germany: *m.* 1945, Carolyn, da. of the late Rev. Dr. George Marshal Plaskett; *cr.* 1969. *Culloden Farm, Barbados; RAF Reserve, and Barbados Cruising Clubs.*

BARWICK, *Rt. Hon. Sir* Garfield Edward John, *GCMG, QC,* son of the late Jabez Edward Barwick, of Sydney, NSW, *b.* 1903; ed. at Fort St. High Sch., Sydney, and at Sydney Univ (BA, LLB); Bar. NSW 1927, and KC 1941, and KC Victoria 1945, and QC Queensland 1958; Pres. of NSW Bar. Assocn. 1950-52, and 1955-56, and of Australian Law Council 1952-54; a Member of House of Representatives, Commonwealth of Australia 1958-64; Attorney-Gen. 1958-63, and Min. for External Affairs 1961-64 since when Ch. Justice of the High Court of Australia; Leader of Australian Delegation to UN 1960, 1962, 1963 and 1964; Chancellor of Macquarie Univ., Sydney, NSW, since 1967: *m.* 1929, Norma Mountier da. of the late William H. Symons; *cr.* Knt, 1953, PC 1964, GCMG 1965. *Mundroola. George St., Careel Bay, Sydney NSW; High Court of Australia, Sydney NSW; Australian (Sydney), and Melbourne Clubs.*

BEADLE, *Rt. Hon. Sir* (Thomas) Hugh William, *CMG, OBE,* son of Arthur William Beadle, of Salisbury, Rhodesia; *b.* 1905; ed. at Diocesan Coll., Cape Town, and at Queen's Coll., Oxford (Hon. Fellow); Bar 1931, and a KC 1946; a MLA,S. Rhodesia 1939-50, Min. of Justice, of Education, of Health, and of Internal Affairs 1946-50, and a Judge of High Court 1950-61, since when Ch. Justice; has Cross of Grand Cdr. of Order of Phoenix of Greece; 1939-45 War with Roy. W. African Frontier Force, and S. Rhodesian Forces: *m.* 1954, Olive, da. of the late Maj. Staley Jackson; *cr.* OBE (Civil) 1946, CMG 1957, Knt. 1960; PC 1964. *Hillside, Bulawayo, Rhodesia; Bulawayo, and Salisbury (Rhodesia) Clubs.*

BEAUFORT, *His Grace the Duke of, K.G.,* *G.C.V.O.; cr.* 1936.

BENN, *Rt. Hon.* Anthony (Neil) Wedgwood, *MP* [see V. Stansgate], *cr.* 1964.

BESWICK, *Rt. Hon.* Baron; *cr.* 1968.

BEVINS, *Rt. Hon.* John Reginald, son of John M. Bevins, of Liverpool: *b.* 1908, ed. at Liverpool Collegiate Sch.; was P.P.S, to Min. of Housing and Local Govt. 1951-53, Parliamentary Sec., Min. of Works 1953-57, Parliamentary Sec., Min. of Housing and Local Govt. 1957-59, and Postmaster-Gen. 1959-64; Past Chm. and Man. Dir. Francis Industries Ltd.; author and journalist; 1939-45 War with RHA and as Maj. RASC; MP for Toxteth Div. of Liverpool (*C*) 1950-64: *m.* 1933, Mary Leonora, da. of J. O. Jones, of Liverpool; *cr.* 1959. 37, *Queen's Drive, Liverpool,* 18.

BLAKENHAM, *Rt. Hon. Viscount,* *O.B.E.; cr.* 1955.

§BLEAKLEY, *Rt. Hon.* David Wylie, son of John Wesley Bleakley; *b.* 1925; ed. at Ruskin Coll., Oxford and Queens Univ., Belfast; Principal of Belfast Further Education Centre 1955-58; MP (*Lab.*) for Victoria, N. Ireland 1958-65; Head of Dept. of Economics and Political Studies, Methodist Coll., Belfast 1965-67, and of Dept. of Industrial Relations, Kivukoni Coll., Dar-es-Salaam 1967-60; Min. of Community Relations, N. Ireland 1971, Member of N.I. Assembly (*N.I. Lab. Party*) 1973-74, and of

NI Convention since 1975: *m.* 1949, Winifred, da. of the late Alfred Wason; *cr.* 1971, 10, *Ardgreenan Drive, Belfast*, 4.

BOTTOMLEY, *Rt. Hon.* Arthur George, *O.B.E., M.P.,* son of George Howard Bottomley, of Tottenham, N.; *b.* 1907; was a Member of Walthamstow Borough Council 1929-49 (Mayor 1945-6), Dep. Regional Commr., S.-E. Area 1941-5, Parl. Under-Sec. of State for Dominion Affairs 1946-47, and Sec. for Overseas Trade 1947-51; Sec. of State for Commonwealth Relations 1964-66, and Min. of Overseas Development 1966-67; MP for Chatham Div. of Rochester (*Lab.*) 1945-50, and for Rochester and Chatham 1950-59; MP for Middlesbrough East 1962-74, and Teesside (Middlesbrough) since 1974: *m.* 1936, Dame Bessie Ellen, DBE, da. of Edward Wiles, of Walthamstow, E.; *cr.* OBE (Civil) 1941, PC 1951. 19, *Lichfield Rd., Woodford Green, Essex.*

BOYD OF MERTON, *Rt. Hon. Viscount, CH; cr.* 1951.

BOYD-CARPENTER, *Rt. Hon. Baron; cr.* 1954.

BOYLE OF HANDSWORTH, *Rt. Hon. Baron; cr.* 1962.

§**BRADFORD,** *Rt. Hon.* Roy Hamilton, son of Joseph Hamilton Bradford, of Rockcorry, co. Monaghan; *b.* 1920; ed. at Roy. Belfast Academical Inst., and Trin. Coll., Dublin (BA); Army Intelligence 1943-47; Producer and Writer, BBC since 1950, Dir. of Geoffrey Sharp Ltd. since 1962; Member of House of Commons N.I. (*U*) 1965-73 (Parliament suspended March 1972), Assist. Whip, Unionist Party 1966, Parl. Sec. Min. of ed. 1967, Ch. Whip 1968-69, Min. of Commerce, N. Ireland 1969-71, and Min. of Development 1971-72; Member of NI Assembly 1973-74: *m.* 1946, Hazel Elizabeth, da. of Capt. W. Lindsay, of Belfast; *cr.* 1969. *Ardkeen, Carnalea, co. Down; Ulster (Belfast) Club.*

BRECON, *Rt. Hon. Baron ; cr.* 1960.

BRIDGE, *Rt. Hon. Lord Justice (Sir Nigel Cyprian),* son of the late Cdr. Cyprian Dunscombe Charles Bridge, RN: *b.* 1917; ed. at Marlborough; Bar. Inner Temple 1947; Junior Counsel to HM Treasury in Common Law 1964-68, and a Judge of High Court of Justice (Queen's Bench Div.) 1968-75; Presiding Judge for Crown Court, Western Circuit 1972-74; Lord Justice of Appeal since 1975; 1939-45 War as Capt. KRRC in Italy, France and Germany: *m.* 1944, Margaret, da. of Leonard Heseltine Swinbank; *cr.* Knt. 1968; PC 1975. *The Old Rectory, Dowdeswell, Cheltenham. Glos.*

BROOKE OF CUMNOR, *Rt. Hon. Baron, CH; cr.* 1955.

§**BROOKEBOROUGH,** *Rt. Hon. Viscount, cr.* 1971.

BROWN, *Rt. Hon. Baron, MBE; cr.* 1970.

BROWN, [see George-Brown].

BROWNE, *Rt. Hon. Lord Justice (Sir Patrick Reginald Evelyn), OBE, TD,* son of the late Prof. Edward Granville Browne, of Cambridge: *b.* 1907; ed. at Eton and Pembroke Coll., Cambridge; Bar. Inner Temple 1931, QC 1960, Bencher 1962; Dep. Chm. Cambs. and Isle of Ely Quarter Sessions 1963-65, and Essex Quarter Sessions 1963-66; a Judge of High Court of Justice (Queen's Bench Div.) 1965-74, since when a Lord Justice of Appeal; 1939-45 War as Lt.-Col. RA (OBE): *m.* 1931, Evelyn Sophie Alexandra, who *d.* 1966, da. of the late Sir Charles Walston, of Newton Hall, Cambridge; *cr.* OBE (Mil.) 1945; Knt. 1965, PC 1974. *7, Campden Hill Sq., W8; Thriplow Bury, Thriplow, Cambs.*

BUCKLEY, *Rt. Hon. Lord Justice (Hon. Sir Denys Burton), MBE* [see B. Wrenbury]. *cr.* 1970.

BUSTAMANTE, *Rt. Hon. Sir* William Alexander, *GBE; b.* 1884; served as a Spanish soldier in Morocco, a Police Officer in Cuba, a Tramwayman in Panama, and a Dietician in New York; Founder of Bustamante Industrial Trade Union 1938, and of Jamaica Labour Party 1943; a Member of House of Representatives, Jamaica (Leader of Govt. 1944-54, Leader of Opposition 1955-62, and Prime Min. and Min. of External Affairs, Jamaica 1962-67): *m.* 1st, 19—, Mildred Edith Blanck; 2ndly, Gladys Maud Longbridge; *cr.* Knt. 1955, PC 1964, GBE (Civil) 1967. 24, *Tucker Av., Liguamea, Jamaica.*

BUTLER OF SAFFRON WALDEN, *Rt. Hon. Baron, KG, CH; cr.* 1939.

BYERS, *Rt. Hon. Baron, OBE; cr.* 1972.

CAIRNS, *Rt. Hon. Lord Justice (Sir David Arnold Scott),* son of the late Alderman David Cairns, JP, a Freeman of Sunderland; *b.* 1902; ed. at Bede Sch., Sunderland, and at Pembroke Coll., Camb. (LLB, MA); BSc London; Bar. Middle Temple 1926, KC 1947, and Bencher 1958; Chm. of Statutory Cttee. of Pharmaceutical Soc. of Great Britain 1952-60, of Monopolies and Restrictive Practices Commn. 1954-56, and of Advisory Cttee. on Rhodesian Travel Restrictions 1968-70; Recorder of Sunderland 1957-60; Commr. of Assize 1957 and again 1959; a Judge of High Court of Justice (Probate, Divorce, and Admiralty Div.) 1960-70, since when a Lord Justice of Appeal: *m.* 1932, Irene Cathery, da. of the late Augustus Phillips, of Derby; *cr.* Knt. 1955, PC 1970. *Applecroft, The Warren, Ashstead, Surrey.*

CALLAGHAN, *Rt. Hon.* (Leonard) James, *MP,* son of Ch. Petty Officer James Callaghan, of Portsmouth; *b.* 1912; ed. at Portsmouth Gram. (Northern) Sch.; Parl. Sec. to Min. of Transport 1947-50, Parl. and Financial Sec. to Admiralty 1950-51; Chancellor of the Exchequer 1964-67, and Home Sec. 1967-70; Sec. of State for Foreign and Commonwealth Affairs since 1974; MP, S. Cardiff (*Lab.*) 1945-50, since when for SE Cardiff: *m.* 1938, Audrey Elizabeth, da. of Frank Moulton, Loose, Kent; *cr.* 1964. 1, *Carlton Gdns., SW1.*

CAMPBELL, *Rt. Hon. Sir* Ronald Ian, *GCMG, CB; cr.* 1950 [see Campbell, Bt., *cr.* 1815].

CAMPBELL OF CROY, *Rt. Hon. Baron, MC; cr.* 1970.

CANTERBURY, *Most Rev. and Rt. Hon. the Lord Archbishop of, D.D.* ; *cr.* 1961.

CARADON, *Rt. Hon. Baron, GCMG, KCVO, OBE; cr.* 1968.

CARR, *Rt. Hon.* (Leonard) Robert, *M.P.,* son of Ralph Edward Carr, of The Croft, Totteridge, N.20; *b.* 1916; ed. at Westminster, and at Gonville and Caius Coll., Camb. (MA); PPS to Sir Anthony Eden, as Sec. of State for Foreign Affairs 1951-55, and as Prime Min. 1955, Parl. Sec. to Min. of Labour 1955-58; Sec. for Tech. Co-operation 1963-64; Sec. of State for Employment and Productivity June to Oct. 1970, for Employment 1970-72, Lord President of the Council and Leader of the House of Commons April to Nov. 1972, and Sec. of State for Home Affairs 1972-74; a Dir., Metal Closures Group, Ltd. 1954-63 and 1965-70 (Dep. Chm. 1958-63), and Chm. John Dale Ltd. 1958-63 and 1965 70; for Mitcham (*C*) 1950-74, and Sutton (Carshalton) since 1974: *m.* 1943, Joan Kathleen, da. of Dr. E. W. Twining; *cr.* 1963. *Monkenholt, Hadley Green, Herts.;* 14, *North Court, Great Peter St., SW1; Brooks's and Carlton Clubs.*

CARRINGTON, *Rt. Hon. Baron, K.C.M.G., M.C.* ; *cr.* 1959.

CASEY, *Rt. Hon. Baron, KG, GCMG, CH, DSO, M.C.* ; *cr.* 1939.

CASTLE, *Rt. Hon.* Barbara Anne, *MP,* da. of Frank Betts, of Nottingham; *b.* 1911; ed. at Bradford Girls' Gram. Sch., and at St. Hugh's Coll., Oxford (BA, Hon. Fellow); Hon. DTech. Loughborough, and Bradford; Assist. Editor of *Town and County Councillor* 1936-40, a Member of St. Pancras Borough Council 1937-45, a Member of Metropolitan Water Board 1940-45, Admin. Officer, Min. of Food 1941-44, Housing Correspondent and Forces Adviser, *Daily Mirror,* 1944-45, Chm. of Labour Party 1958-59 (Vice-Chm. 1957); a Member of National Executive Cttee. of Labour Party since 1950; Min. of Overseas Development 1964-65, Min. of Transport 1965-68, and First Sec. of State and Sec. of State for Employment and Productivity 1968-70; Sec. of State for Social Sers. since 1974; MP for Blackburn (*Lab.*) 1945-50, for E. Div. of Blackburn 1950-55, and for Blackburn since 1955: *m.* 1944, Edward Cyril Castle, who was *cr.* Baron Castle (Life Baron) 1974; she does not use title of Baroness; *cr.* 1964. *House of Commons, SW1.*

CHALFONT, *Rt. Hon. Baron, OBE, MC, cr.* 1964.

CHAMPION, *Rt. Hon. Baron; cr.* 1967.

CHARTERIS, *Lt.-Col. the Rt. Hon.* Sir Martin Michael Charles, *KCB, KCVO, OBE* [see E. Wemyss].

CHATAWAY, *Rt. Hon.* Christopher John, son of Denys Percival Chataway; *b.* 1931; ed. at Sherborne, and Magdalen Coll., Oxford (BA); Parl. Sec. Min. of Education 1962-64, Parl. Under-Sec. of State Dept. of Education and Science 1964, Leader Inner London Education Cttee. ILEA 1967-69; Min. of Posts and Telecommunications 1970-72, Min. for Industrial Development 1972-74; World record 5,000 metres 1954, and 3 Miles 1955; a Man. Dir. Orion Bank, Ltd., and a Dir. Fisons, Ltd., and B.E.T., Ltd.; MP for N. Lewisham (*C*) 1959-66, and for Chichester 1969-74; *m.* 1959, Anna Maria, da. of H. Lett; *cr.* 1970. *Lordington Mill, Chichester, Sussex; Carlton Club.*

CHESHAM, *Rt. Hon. Baron; cr.* 1964.

CITRINE, *Rt. Hon. Baron, G.B.E. ; cr.* 1940.

CLAYDEN, *Rt. Hon.* Sir (Henry) John, son of the late Harold William Clayden, of Johannesburg, S. Africa; *b.* 1904; ed. at Dioeesan Coll., Capetown, at Charterhouse, and at Brasenose Coll., Oxford (BA); Hon LLD Witwatersrand; Bar. Inner Temple 1926, Advocate (Johannesburg) 1927, and a KC 1945; a Judge of Supreme Court of S. Africa (Transvaal Provincial Div.) 1946-55 and 1964-65, Judge of Federal Supreme Court, Federation of Rhodesia and Nyasaland 1955-60, and Ch. Justice 1960-64; Chm. of Industrial Tribunal since 1967; 1939-45 War, with S. African Engineer Corps and S. African Staff Corps: *m.* 1948, Gwendoline Edith da. of the late J. W. Lawrance, of Johannesburg, S. Africa; *cr.* Knt. 1958, PC 1963. 8, *Walton St., SW3.*

CLITHEROE, *Rt. Hon. Baron; cr.* 1944.

COBBOLD, *Rt. Hon. Baron, KG, G.C.V.O., cr.* 1959.

COBHAM, *Rt. Hon. Viscount, KG, GCMG, GCVO, TD, cr.* 1967.

COLERAINE, *Rt. Hon. Baron ; cr.* 1943.

COLYTON, *Rt. Hon. Baron, C.M.G.; cr.* 1952.

CORFIELD, *Rt. Hon.* Sir Frederick Vernon, *QC,* son of the late Brig. Frederick Alleyne Corfield, DSO, OBE, of Chatwall Hall, Salop; *b.* 1915; ed. at Cheltenham Coll., and RMA Woolwich; Bar. Middle Temple 1945; QC 1972; commnd. 1935; 1939-45 War as Capt. RA (prisoner, despatches); ret. 1946; farmer 1946-56; MP for S. Glos. (*C*) 1955-74; Joint Parl. Sec. Min. of Housing and Local Govt. 1962-64; Min. of State, Board of Trade June to Oct. 1970, Min. of Aviation Supply 1970-71, and Min. for Aerospace 1971-72; *m.* 1945, Elizabeth Mary Ruth, yr. da. of the late Edmund Coston Taylor, of Arden, Church Stretton, Salop; *cr.* PC 1970, Knt. 1972. 9, *Randolph Mews, W9; Wordings Orchard, Sheepscombe, Stroud, Glos.; United Servicq and Royal Aero Club.*

COUSINS, *Rt. Hon.* Frank, son of Charles Fox Cousins; *b.* 1904; ed. at King Edward Sch., Doncaster; Assist. Gen. Sec., Transport and Gen. Workers Union 1955-56, and Gen. Sec. 1956-69; a Member of British Transport Joint Consult. Council 1955-63 of Min. of Labour Nat. Joint Advisory Council 1956, and of Executive Council of International Transport Workers Federation 1956-64 (Pres. 1958-60 and 1962-64), Vice-Pres. since 1968); a Member of Council of Scientific and Industrial Research 1960-64, and Min. of Technology 1964-66; a Member of Gen. Council TUC since 1956 (seconded 1964-66), and of NEDC since 1962, and Chm. Community Relations Commn. since 1968; MP for Nuneaton (*Lab.*) 1965-66: *m.* 1930, Annie Elizabeth Judd; *cr.* 1964. *Germoe, Ropers Lane, Wrington, Bristol.*

§CRAIG, *Rt. Hon.* William, son of the late John Craig; *b.* 1924; ed. at Roy. Sch., Dungannon, and at Queen's Univ., Belfast; Solicitor N. Ireland 1952; Min. of Home Affairs, Govt. of N. Ireland 1963-64, of Health and Local Govt. 1964-65, of Development 1965-66, and of Home Affairs 1966-68; a Founder Member and Pres. of Ulster Young Unionists' Council; a Member of House of Commons NI 1960-73 (Ch. Govt. Whip 1962-63) (Parliament suspended March 1972); Member of NI Assembly

(*UUUC*) 1973-74, and of NI Convention since 1975; Founder Member and Leader of Ulster Vanguard 1972: *m.* 1960, Doris Hilgendorff; *cr.* 1963. *Hilgencraigs, Annadale Av., Belfast, BT73JJ.*

CRAIGTON, *Rt. Hon., Baron, C.B.E.; cr.* 1961.

CRATHORNE, *Rt. Hon. Baron, T.D.; cr.* 1951.

CROMER, *Rt. Hon. Earl of, GCMG, MBE; cr.* 1966.

CROSLAND, *Rt. Hon.* (Charles) Anthony (Raven), *MP,* son of the late Joseph Beardsell Crosland; *b.* 1918; ed. at Highgate and at Trin. Coll., Oxford (MA); Fellow and Lecturer in Economics and Junior Dean, Trin. Coll., Oxford 1947-50; MP for S. Div. of Glos. (*Lab.*) 1950-55, and for Grimsby since 1959; Economic Sec. to Treasury 1964-65, Sec. of State for Education and Science 1965-67, Pres. of Board of Trade 1967-69, and Sec. of State for Local Govt. and Reg. Planning 1969-70; Sec. of State for the Environment since 1974; 1939-45 War with R. Welch Fusiliers, and as Capt. Parachute Regt.: *m.* 1st, 1952 (m. diss. 1957), Hilary Anne Hathaway, only da. of Henry Sarson, of Himley Lodge, Newbury; 2ndly, 1964, Mrs. Susan Catling, da. of Mark Watson, of Baltimore, USA; *cr.* 1965. 37, *Lansdowne Rd., W11.*

CROSS OF CHELSEA, *Rt. Hon. Baron. cr.* 1969.

§CURRAN, *Rt. Hon.* Sir Lancelot Ernest, son of the late Miles Curran; *b.* 1899; ed. at Roy. Belfast Academical Institution; B.A. and LL.B. Queen's Univ., Belfast ; Bar. King's Inns 1923, a Q.C. N. Ireland 1943, and a Bencher 1946 ; was a Member of House of Commons, N. Ireland 1945-9, Parliamentary Sec., Min. of Finance, and Ch. Whip 1945, Attorney Gen. 1947-49, a Judge of High Court of Justice, N. Ireland 1949-56, and a Lord Justice of Appeal, Supreme Court of Judicature, N. Ireland 1956-75; 1914-18 War with RFC and RAF, 1939-45 War as Major: *m.* 1924, Doris, da. of the late James Lee, Gov. of Malone Training Sch., Belfast; *cr.* PC 1957, Knt. 1964. *Wentworth, Deramore Park, Belfast.*

DANCKWERTS, *Rt. Hon.* Sir Harold Otto, son of William Otto Danckwerts, KC, of 2, Brechin Place, S.W.7 ; *b.* 1888 ; ed. at Winchester Coll., at Balliol Coll., Oxford M.A., and at Harvard Univ., U.S.A.; Bar. Lincoln's Inn 1913, a Bencher 1941, and Treasurer 1962; Tutor to Law So. 1914-23, and Reader to Law So. 1923-41; appointed Junior Counsel to Treasury and Board of Trade in Chancery Matters and Junior Counsel to Attorney-Gen. in Charity Matters 1941, a Judge of High Court of Justice (Chancery Div.) 1949; a Lord Justice of Appeal 1961-69; 1914-18 War as Capt. Inns of Court Squadron E. Riding of Yorks. Yeo. and Machine Gun Corps (despatches): *m.* 1st 1918, Florence, Mary, who *d.* 1969, da. of the Rev. James Pride, D.D., R. of Bridlington, 2ndly, 1969, Ella Hamilton, yr. da. of Hubert Marshall, of Glasgow; *cr.* Knt. 1949, PC 1961. 4, *Stone Buildings, Lincoln's Inn, WC2.*

DARLING OF HILLSBOROUGH, *Rt. Hon. Baron; cr.* 1966.

DAVIES, *Rt. Hon.* John Emerson Harding, *MBE, MP,* son of Arnold Thomas Davies; *b.* 1916; ed. at St. Edward's Sch. ,Oxford; Hon. Dr. Essex and Loughborough Univs.; Gen. Manager Markets, British Petroleum Co. 1956-60, a Dir. BP Trading 1960, Vice-Chm. and Man. Dir. Shell-Mex and BP 1961-65, Dir.-Gen. CBI 1965-69, and a Dir. Hill Samuel Gp. 1969-70 and Dep. Chm. since 1974; Min. of Technology July to Oct. 1970, Sec. of State for Trade and Industry, and Pres. of Board of Trade 1970-72, and Chancellor of Duchy of Lancaster 1972-74; MP for Knutsford (*C*) since 1970; a Gov. St. Edward's Sch., Oxford, and Windlesham House Sch. Trust; 1939-45 War as Maj. RASC G2 (Tech.) with Combined Ops. Experimental Estab.: *m.* 1943,Vera Georgina, da. of George William Bates; *cr.* 1970. *House of Commons, SW1; Carlton, Beefsteak, and Oriental Clubs.*

DAVIES, *Rt. Hon.* Sir [William] Arthian, son of the late Arthian Davies, of Borth, Cardiganshire; *b.* 1901; ed. at Dulwich Coll., and at Trin. Coll., Oxford; Bar. Inner Temple 1925, a KC 1947, and a Bencher 1952; was Junior Counsel to Min. of Labour and National Ser.

1934-47, Recorder of Merthyr Tydfil 1946-49, Dep. Chm. of Quarter Sessions, Cardiganshire and Recorder of Chester 1949-52, and Dep. Chm. of Quarter Sessions, Bucks. 1951-61, and Chm. 1961-71; a Judge of High Court of Justice (Probate, Divorce and Admiralty Div. 1952-9, and Queen's Bench Div. 1959-61), 1952-61, and a Lord Justice of Appeal 1961-74; Dep. Ch., Parliamentary Boundary Commn. for Wales 1959-61; a DL of Bucks. since 1967: *m.* 1933, Mary Bailey, da. of Henry Liptrot, of Aberystwyth; *cr.* Knt. 1952, PC 1961. *Ballinger Lodge, Great Missenden, Bucks; Oriental Club.*

DAVIES OF LEEK, *Rt. Hon. Baron; cr.* 1969.

DEEDES, *Rt. Hon.* William Francis, *MC,* son of Herbert William Deedes, of Galt, Hythe, Kent [B. Ashtown, colls.], *b.* 1913; ed. at Harrow; Parliamentary Sec., Min. of Housing and Local Govt. 1954-55, Joint Parliamentary Under-Sec. of State, Home Office 1955-57, and Min. without Portfolio 1962-64; Editor of *The Daily Telegraph* since 1975; 1939-45 War as Maj. KRRC (TA); a DL of Kent; MP for Ashford Div. of Kent (C) 1950-74: *m.* 1942, Evelyn Hilary, da. of Clive Branfoot, of Stonegrave, Yorks; *cr.* 1962. *New Hayters, Aldington, Kent; Junior Carlton Club.*

DE FREITAS, *Rt. Hon.* Sir Geoffrey Stanley, *KCMG, MP,* son of the late Sir Anthony de Freitas, OBE; *b.* 1913; ed. at Haileybury, at Clare Coll., Camb. (Hon. Fellow). (Pres. of Camb. Union), and at Yale Univ., USA (Mellon Fellow); Bar. Lincoln's Inn 1937; PPS to Prime Min. 1945-46, Under-Sec. of State for Air 1946-50, and for Home Affairs 1950-51; UK Delegate to UN Assembly 1949 and 1964, to Council of Europe 1951-54, and again 1965-70 (Leader of UK Delegation and Pres. of Assembly), and to NATO Parliamentarians Conference 1955-60 and 1965 (Leader of UK Delegation) and since 1969; British High Commr. in Ghana 1961-63, and First Head of Mission in Kenya, and High Commr. 1963-64; 1939-45 War with RA and RAF; MP for Central Nottingham (*Lab.*) 1945-50, for Lincoln 1950-61, and for Kettering since 1964: *m.* 1938, Helen Graham, da. of Laird Bell, KBE, of Illinois, USA; *cr.* KCMG 1961, PC 1967. *c/o House of Commons, SW1; 11, Trumpington Rd., Cambridge; Reform, and Garrick Clubs.*

DE LA WARR, *Rt. Hon. the Earl, G.B.E.; cr.* 1936.

DE L'ISLE, *Rt. Hon. Viscount, V.C., KG, GCMG, GCVO; cr.* 1951.

DELL, *Rt. Hon.* Edmund Emanuel, *MP,* son of the late Reuben Dell; *b.* 1921; ed. at Owen's Sch., London, and Queen's Coll., Oxford (MA); Lecturer, Queen's Coll., 1947-49, Exec. ICI 1949-63, and Simon Research Fellow Manchester Univ. 1963-64; Joint Parl. Sec. Min. of Technology 1966-67, Joint Parl. Under-Sec. of State Dept. of Economic Affairs 1967-68, Min. of State, Board of Trade 1968-69, Min. of State, Dept. of Employment and Productivity 1969-70; Paymaster-Gen. since 1974; Pres. Manchester and Salford Trades Council 1958-61; Chm. Public Accounts Cttee. 1972-74; MP for Birkenhead (*Lab.*) since 1964; 1939-45 War as Lt. RA in NW Europe; author of "Political Responsibility and Industry," 1973: *m.* 1963, Susanne Regina, da. of the late Henry Gottschalk; *cr.* 1970. 4 *Reynolds Close, NW11 7EA.*

DENNING, *Rt. Hon. Baron; cr.* 1948.

DEVLIN, *Rt. Hon. Baron; cr.* 1960.

DEVONSHIRE, *His Grace the Duke of, MC; cr.* 1964.

DIAMOND, *Rt. Hon. Baron; cr.* 1965.

DIEFENBAKER, *Rt. Hon.* John George, *Q.C.,* son of William Thomas Diefenbaker, of Hawkesville, Ontario, Canada; *b.* 1895; ed. at Saskatoon Collegiate Institute, and at Saskatchewan Univ. (MA, LLB, Hon. DCL); Hon. MEIC; Hon. LLD McMaster 1953, Dartmouth Coll. and McGill 1957, St. Mary's, Halifax, Wesleyan, British Columbia, New Brunswick, Laval, Delhi, and Punjab 1958, and Montreal, Michigan, Princeton, Assumption, Wayne, Ottawa, Queen's, Roy. Mil. Coll., Kingston, Toronto, and Dalhousie 1961, and Memorial Univ., St. John's, Newfoundland 1961 and Alberta; Hon. DCL Acadia 1956 and Bishop's 1958,

and W. Ontario, Saskatchewan, Mount Allison, and Depauw 1960; Hon. Dr. of Humanities Oklahoma 1960; Hon. Litt.D. Dropsie Coll. 1961; D.Litt.S., Victoria Univ., Toronto 1961; Bar. Sakatchewan 1919, Alberta 1951, Saskatchewan and Ontario 1960, British Columbia 1958, and Hon. Bar. Manitoba 1970, a KC Saskatchewan 1929, and; Q.C. Ontario 1960; Hon. Bencher, Law Soc. of Upper Canada 1960, and Hon. Master of The Bench Gray's Inn 1958; Vice-Pres. (Saskatchewan) of Canadian Bar. Assocn. 1939-42 (Hon. Life Member 1957); a Member of House of Commons, Canada since 1940, and Leader of Progressive Conservative Party of Canada 1956-67, Leader of Conservative Party in Saskatchewan 1937-40, of Federa Progressive Conservative Party 1956-57, of Opposition in House of Commons, Canada Jan. to June 1957, Prime Min. 1957-63, and Leader of HM Opposition 1963-67; Chancellor of Sask. Univ. since 1969; a PC of Canada, Hon. Col. N. Sask. Regt., and R. Canadian Inf. Corps, an Hon. FRS (Canada), an Hon. Fellow of Roy. Architectural Institute of Canada, a Member of Illustre y Nacional Colegio de Abogados (Mexico), and a Life Member of Nat. Trust for Scotland; Chm. of Ottawa Conference of Parliamentarians from British Empire and Members of United States Senate and House of Representatives 1943; a Member of Canadian Delegation to Empire Parliamentary Asso. in Bermuda and Washington 1946, to Commonwealth Parliamentary Asso. in Wellington, New Zealand, and Canberra, Australia 1950, and to 7th Session of United Nations Gen. Assembly, New York 1952; attended United Nations Organization meeting in San Francisco 1945, Commonwealth Prime Min.'s Conference, London 1957, 1960 and 1961, and N. Atlantic Treaty Organization Heads of Govt. Meeting, Paris 1957; Min. in attendance on H.M. the Queen on her visit to Washington, and Chicago, U.S.A. during Roy. Tour of 1959; Hon. Chief of Cree Indians (Chief Eagle), of Sioux Indians (Chief Walking Buffalo) and of Kainai Chieftains (Chief Many Spotted Horses); 1914-18 War as Lt. Canadian Army (invalided): *m.* 1st, 1929, Edna May Brower, who *d.* 1951; 2ndly, 1953, Olive Evangeline Palmer, LLD, DCL, da. of the late Rev. C. B. Freeman, DD; *cr.* 1957. 115, *Lansdowne Rd. South, Ottawa, Canada; 246, 19th Street West, Prince Albert, Saskatchewan, Canada; Kiwanis (Prince Albert), and Albany (Toronto) Clubs.*

DILHORNE, *Rt. Hon. Viscount, QC; cr.* 1954.

DIPLOCK, *Rt. Hon. Baron; cr.* 1961.

§DOBSON, *Rt. Hon.* John; MA; MP for West Down (U) in Parliament of N. Ireland (Parliament suspended March 1972); Leader of the N. Ireland House of Commons 1969-71; *cr.* 1969, *Belville, Lurgan Rd., Banbridge, co. Down.*

DORMAN-SMITH [see Smith].

DRUMALBYN, *Rt. Hon. Baron, KBE; cr.* 1962.

DU CANN, *Rt. Hon.* Edward Dillon Lott, *MP,* son of Charles Garfield Lott du Cann, of Gray's Inn, W.C.1; *b.* 1924; ed. at Woodbridge Sch., and St. John's Coll., Oxford (MA); Economic Sec. to Treasury 1962-63, and Min. of State, Board of Trade 1963-64; Founder of Unicorn Group of Unit Trusts 1957; Chm. of Barclays Unicorn Ltd. 1967-72, and Cannon Assurance, Ltd. 1970; Chm. Conservative Party Organization 1965-67; Chm. Select Cttee. on Public Expenditure 1971-72, since when Chm. of 1922 Cttee., and of Select Cttee. on Public Accounts; Hon. Col. 155 (Wessex) Regt. RCT (Vols.); 1939-45 War as Sub. Lt. RNVR with MTB's; MP for Taunton (C) since 1956; *m.* 1962, Sallie Innes, da. of the late James Henry Murchie, of Caldy, Cheshire; *cr.* 1964. 19, *Lord North St., SW1; Cothay Manor, Greenham, Wellington, Somerset; Carlton and Somerset County (Taunton) Clubs.*

DUNCAN-SANDYS, *Rt. Hon. Baron, CH; cr.* 1944.

DUNDEE, *Rt. Hon. the Earl of; cr.* 1959.

ECCLES, *Rt. Hon. Viscount, K.C.V.O.; cr.* 1951.

EDEN, *Rt. Hon.* Sir John Benedict, *Bt., MP.; cr.* 1972.

EDINBURGH, *H.R.H. the Duke of, K.G., KT, OM, GBE;* introduced 1951 [see " ROYAL FAMILY "].

GODBER, *Rt. Hon.* Joseph Bradshaw, *M.P.*, son of the late Isaac Godber, formerly of Willington Manor, nr. Bedford; *b.* 1914; ed. at Bedford Sch.; Assist. Govt. Whip 1955-57, Parliamentary Sec. Min. of Agriculture 1957-60, Under Sec. of State, Foreign Office 1960-61, Min. of State for Foreign Affairs 1961-63, Sec. of State for War June to Oct. 1963, and Min. of Labour 1963-64; Min. of State, Foreign and Commonwealth Office 1970-72, Min. of Agric. Fisheries and Food 1972-74; MP for Grantham Div. of Lincs. (C) 1951-74, and for Kesteven and Rutland (Grantham Div.) since 1974: *m.* 1936, Miriam, da. of Haydon Sanders; *cr.* 1963. *Willington Manor, nr. Bedford; Constitutional Club.*

GOFF, *Rt. Hon.* Lord Justice (*Sir* Reginald William), son of the late William Kingsley Goff; *b.* 1907; ed. at Sutton Co. Gram Sch., and London Univ. (LLB Hons.); Bar. Lincoln's Inn 1929, QC 1953, and Bencher 1959; a Judge of High Court of Justice (Chancery Div.) 1965-75, since when a Lord Justice of Appeal; a Fellow Univ. Coll., London 1968, and King's Coll., London 1970; 1939-45 War with AFS and as Wing Cdr. RAF (Assist. Judge Advocate Gen.): *m.* 1944, Marjorie Morwenna, da. of the late Rev. A. Garfield Curnow of Wallington; *cr.* Knt. 1966, PC 1975. *Kingsley Croft, Downs Way, Tadworth, Surrey; Royal Overseas League.*

GORDON-WALKER, *Rt. Hon. Baron, CH; cr.* 1950.

GORONWY-ROBERTS, *Rt. Hon. Baron; cr.* 1968.

GORTON, *Rt. Hon.* John Grey, *CH*, son of J. R. Gorton, of Melbourne; *b.* 1911; ed. at Geelong Gram. Sch., and Brasenose Coll., Oxford (MA); an orchardist; Senator for Victoria 1949-68, since when MHR Aust.; Min. for Navy 1958-63, Min. Assisting Min. for External Affairs 1960-63, Min. i/c of CRISO 1962-68, Min. for Works, and under PM as Min. in Charge of Commonwealth Activities in Education and Research 1963-66, Min. for Interior 1963-64, Min. for Works 1966-67, Min. for Education and Science 1966-68, Prime Min. 1968-71, and Min. for Defence March to Aug. 1971; Member of Parl. Liberal Party Exec. and Liberal Party Spokesman on Environment and Conservative and Urban and Regional Development 1973-74; 1939-45 War as Fl. Lt. RAAF (wounded): *m.* 1935, Bettina, da. of G. Brown, of Bangor, Maine, USA; *cr*, PC 1968, CH 1971. *Parliament House, Canberra, Aust.; Melbourne Club.*

GREENWOOD OF ROSSENDALE, *Rt. Hon. Baron; cr.* 1964.

GRIMOND, *Rt. Hon.* Joseph, *T.D., M.P.*, son of Joseph Bowman Grimond, of St. Andrews, Fife; *b.* 1913; ed. at Eton, and at Balliol Coll., Oxford (BA); Hon. LLD. Edinburgh; Hon. DCL Kent; Bar. Middle Temple 1937; Dir. of Personnel, European Office, UNRRA 1945-47, Sec., Nat. Trust for Scotland 1947-49, and Ch. Liberal Whip 1950; Leader of Parl. Lib. Party 1956-67; Rector of Edinburgh Univ. 1960-63, and R. Aberdeen Univ. 1969-72; Chancellor Kent Univ. since 1970; 1939-45 War as Maj. Fife and Forfar Yeo.; a Dir. of The Guardian; MP for Orkney and Shetland (L) since 1950: *m.* 1938, the Hon. Laura Miranda Bonham Carter, da. of Baroness Asquith of Yarnbury (Life Baroness); *cr.* 1961. *Old Manse of Firth, Grimbister, Orkney; 71, Kew Green, Richmond, Surrey.*

GUEST, *Rt. Hon. Baron; cr.* 1961.

GUNTER, *Rt. Hon.* Raymond Jones, son of the late Miles Gunter, of Llanhilleth, Mon.; *b.* 1909; ed. at Newbridge Secondary Sch.; Railway Clerks Assocn. Branch Officer 1929-41, Pres. of Transport Salaried Staffs Assocn. 1956-64; Chm. of Labour Party 1964-65 (Vice-Chm. 1963-64), a Member of National Executive Labour Party 1956-66, Min. of Labour 1964-68, and Min. of Power April to June 1968; Freeman of City of London; 1939-45 War; MP for SE Div. of Essex (*Lab.*) 1945-50, for Doncaster 1950-51, and for Southwark 1951-72: *m.* 1934, Elsie, who *d.* 1971, da. of James Elkins, of Nantyglo, Mon.; *cr.* 1964. 12, *Westminster Palace Gdns., SW1; Reform Club.*

HAILSHAM OF ST. MARYLEBONE, *Rt. Hon. Baron, CH, QC; cr.* 1956.

HARLECH, *Rt. Hon. Baron, KCMG; cr.* 1957.

HART, *Rt. Hon.* Judith Constance Mary, *MP*, da. of Harry Ridehalgh, of Arncliffe, Whalley, Lancs.; *b.* 1924; ed. at Clitheroe Roy. Gram. Sch., and London Sch. of Economics (BA); Joint Parl. Under-Sec., Scottish Office 1964-66, Min. of State for Commonwealth Affairs 1966-67, Min. of Social Security 1967-68, Paymaster Gen. 1968-69 and Min. for Overseas Development 1969-70, and 1974-75; MP for Lanark (*Lab.*) since 1959; author of "Aid and Liberation" 1972: *m.* 1946, Dr. Anthony Hart; *cr.* 1967. 3, *Ennerdale Rd., Kew, Richmond, Surrey.*

HARVIE ANDERSON [see Anderson.]

HARVINGTON, *Rt. Hon. Baron; cr.* 1971.

HASLUCK, *Rt. Hon. Sir* Paul Meernaa Caedwalla, *GCMG, GCVO*, son of the late E. M. C. Hasluck, of Mt. Lawley, W. Aust. *b.* 1905; ed. at Perth Mod. Sch., and W. Aust. Univ. (MA); MHR Aust. 1949-69; Min. for Territories, Aust. 1951-63, and of Defence 1963-64, and Min. for External Affairs 1964-69, Gov.-Gen. of Aust. 1969-74; KStJ: *m.* 1932, Alexandra Margaret Martin da. of J. W. Darker; *cr.* 1966, GCMG 1969, GCVO 1970. *Prudential Bldg.,* 95, *St. George's Terr., Perth, W. Aust.*

HATTERSLEY, *Rt. Hon.* Roy Sydney George, *BSc, MP*, son of Frederick Roy Hattersley, of Sheffield; *b.* 1932; ed. at Sheffield City Gram. Sch., and Hull Univ. (BSc); journalist and Health Ser. Exec. 1956-64, a Member Sheffield City Council 1957-65 (Chm. Housing Cttee. and Public Works Cttee.), PPS to Min. of Pensions and National Insurance 1964-67, Jt. Parl. Sec. Dept. of Employment and Productivity (formerly Min. of Labour) 1967-69, Min. of Defence for Admin. 1969-70; Min. of State, FCO since 1974; MP for Sparkbrook Div. of Birmingham (*Lab.*) since 1964: *m.* 1956, Molly, da. of Michael Loughran, of Consett, co. Durham; *cr.* 1975. *c/o House of Commons, SW1; Reform Club.*

HEAD, *Rt. Hon.* Viscount, *G.C.M.G., C.B.E., M.C.; cr.* 1951.

HEALD, *Rt. Hon. Sir* Lionel Frederick, *QC*, son of the late James Heald, of Parrs Wood, Didsbury, Lancashire; *b.* 1897; ed. at Charterhouse, and at Ch. Ch., Oxford (B.A. 1920); Bar. Middle Temple 1923, a K.C. 1937, and a Bencher 1946; was Junior Counsel to Board of Trade 1931-37, an Additional Member of Bar Council 1947, and Attorney-Gen. Oct. 1951 to Oct. 1954; elected Vice-Chm. of Gen. Council of the Bar. 1957; is J.P. for Surrey; European War 1914-18 with R.E., European War 1939-45 as Air Commodore R.A.F. Vol. Reserve: unsuccessfully contested S.-W. Div. of St. Pancras (C) July 1945; MP for Chertsey Div. of Surrey 1950-70: *m.* 1st, 1923, Flavia (who *d.* 1959, and from whom he had obtained a divorce 1928), da. of the late Lt.-Col. James Stewart Forbes [Forbes, Bt., colls.]; 2ndly, 1929, Daphne Constance, *OBE* (DStJ), da. of the late Montague Whittingham Price; *cr.* Knt. 1951, P.C. 1954. *Chilworth Manor, Guildford, Surrey; Queen Elizabeth Building, Temple, E.C.4.*

HEALEY, *Rt. Hon.* Denis Winston, *MBE, MP*, son of William Healey, of Keighley; *b.* 1917; ed. at Bradford Gram. Sch., and at Balliol Coll., Oxford (MA); Sec. International Dept. of Labour Party 1945-52, a Member of Parl. Cttee. of Labour Party 1959-64; Sec. of State for Defence 1964-70; Chancellor of the Exchequer since 1974; 1939-45 War as Maj. RE, in N. Africa and Italy (despatches, MBE); MP for SE Div. of Leeds (*Lab.*) 1952-55, since when of E. Div. of Leeds: *m.* 1945, Edna May, da. of Edward Edmunds, of Coleford, Glos.; *cr.* MBE (Mil.) 1945, PC 1964. 11, *Downing St., SW1.*

HEATH, *Rt. Hon.* Edward Richard George, *M.B.E., M.P.*, son of William George Heath; *b.* 1916; ed. at Chatham House Sch., Ramsgate, and Balliol Coll., Oxford (Hon. Fellow); Hon. DCL Oxford; Hon. DTech Bradford; Hon. Fellow Nuffield Coll Oxon.; Hon. FRCO; Hon. FRCM; Lord Commr. of Treasury 1951, Joint Dep. Govt. Ch. Whip 1952-53, Dep. Govt. Ch. Whip 1953-55, Parliamentary Sec. to the Treasury and Ch. Govt. Whip 1955-59, Min. of Labour 1959-60, Lord Privy Seal (with Foreign Office responsibilities) 1960-63 and Sec. of State for Industry, Trade and Regional Development, and Pres. of Board of Trade 1963-64; Leader of

HM Opposition 1965-70, Prime Minister, and First Lord of the Treasury 1970-74; Pres. Fedn. of Univ. Cons. and Unionist Assocns. since 1959, and Chm. Commonwealth Parl. Assocn. 1970-74, and again Leader of the Opposition 1974-75; VP Bach Choir since 1970; Charlemagne Prize 1963, Freiherr Von Stein Foundation Prize, Estes J. Kefauver Prize, and Stresseman Gold Medal 1971; Cyril Foster Memorial Lecture, Oxford 1965: Winner, Sydney to Hobart Ocean Race 1969; Capt. Britain's winning Admiral's Cup Team 1971; 1939-45 War as Col. RA in NW Europe (despatches, MBE); MP for Bexley (C) Feb. 1950-74, since when for Bexley (Sidcup); cr. MBE (Mil) 1946, PC 1955. c/o House of Commons, SW1; Buck's and Carlton Clubs, and Royal Yacht Squadron.

HENDERSON, Rt. Hon. Baron ; cr. 1950.

HERBISON, Rt. Hon. Margaret McCrorie, da. of the late John Herbison, of Shotts, Lanarkshire; b. 1907; ed. at Bellshill Acad. and at Glasgow Univ.; formerly a Teacher of English and History; Joint Under-Sec. of State for Scotland 1950-51, Min. of Pensions and National Insur. 1964-66, and Min. of Social Security 1966-67; Chm. of Select Cttee. on Overseas Aid 1969; Lord High Commr. to Gen. Assembly of Ch. of Scotland 1970; MP for N. Div. of Lanarkshire (Lab.) 1945-70; cr. 1964. 61, Shotts Kirk Rd., Shotts, Lanarkshire.

HILL OF LUTON, Rt. Hon. Baron; cr. 1955.

HODSON, Rt. Hon. Baron, M.C.; cr. 1951.

HOLYOAKE, Rt. Hon. Sir Keith Jacka, GCMG, CH, son of Henry Victor Holyoake, of Riwaka, Motueka, NZ; b. 1904; Hon. LLD Victoria, NZ and Korea; Dep. Prime Min. and Min. of Agric., Marketing and Scientific Research, NZ 1949-57, Prime Min., and Min. for Maori Affairs 1957, Leader of the Opposition 1957-60, Prime Min. and Min. for Foreign Affairs 1960-72; a MHR NZ 1932-38, and again since 1943; Freeman of City of London: m. 1935, Norma Janet, da. of Garden Ingram; cr. PC 1954, CH 1963, GCMG 1970. 41, Pipitea St., Wellington, NZ; Wellington, and National (Wellington), Ruahine (Dannevirke), and Pahiatua (Pahiatua, Wellington) Clubs.

HOME OF THE HIRSEL, Baron, KT, cr. 1951.

HORNSBY-SMITH, Rt. Hon. Baroness, DBE; cr. 1959.

HOUGHTON OF SOWERBY, Rt. Hon. Baron, CH; cr. 1964.

HOWE, Rt. Hon. Sir (Richard Edward) Geoffrey, QC, MP, son of the late Benjamin Edward Howe; b. 1926; ed. at Winchester, and Trin. Hall, Camb. (MA, LLB); Bar. Middle Temple 1952, QC 1965, Bencher 1969; a Member Exec. Cttee. of " Justice " 1963-70, Dep. Chm. Glamorgan Quarter Sessions 1966-70, Solicitor-Gen. 1970-72, and Min. for Trade and Consumer Affairs 1972-74; MP for Bebington (C) 1964-66, Reigate 1970-74, and Surrey (E. Div.) since 1974: m. 1953, Elspeth Rosamund Morton, da. of the late Philip Morton Shand; cr. Knt. 1970, PC 1972. c/o Barclays Bank, 4, Vere St., W1; Carlton Club.

HOY, Rt. Hon. Baron; cr. 1969.

HUGHES, Rt. Hon. Baron, CBE; cr. 1970.

HUGHES, Rt. Hon. Cledwyn, MP, son of the late Rev. Henry David Hughes; b. 1916; ed. at Holyhead Gram. Sch., and Univ. Coll. of Wales, Aberystwyth (LL.B.); Solicitor 1940; a Member, County Councils' Assocn.; Min. of State for Commonwealth Relations 1964-66, Sec. of State for Wales 1966-68, Min. and of Agric., Fisheries and Food 1968-70; MP for Anglesey (Lab.) since 1951; 1939-45 War as Fl. Lt. RAFVR: m. 1949, Jean Beatrice, JP da. of Capt. Jesse Hughes; cr. 1966. Ty Gwyn, Holyhead, Anglesey.

INMAN, Rt. Hon. Baron ; cr. 1947.

IRVINE, Rt. Hon. Sir Arthur James, QC, MP, son of the late James Mercer Irvine, KC; b. 1909; ed. at Edinburgh Acad., Edinburgh Univ. (MA), and Oriel Coll., Oxford (MA); Hon. Fellow Oriel Coll., Oxford since 1969; Bar. Middle Temple 1935, QC 1958, Master of Bench 1965; Sec. to Lord Ch. Justice of England 1935-40, Recorder of Colchester 1965-67, and Solicitor Gen. 1967-70; MP for Edge Hill Div. of Liverpool (Lab.) since 1947: m. 1937, Eleanor, da. of E. E. T. Morris, of Petersfield, Hants.; cr. Knt. 1967, PC 1970. 20, Wellington Sq., Chelsea, SW3.

IRVING, Rt. Hon. Sydney, MP, son of Sydney Irving; b. 1918; ed. at LSE (BSc(Econ) DipEd); Treasurer of HM Household, and

Dep. Ch,. Govt. Whip 1964-66, Dep. Chm. Ways and Means 1966-68, and Chm. of Ways and Means, and Dep. Speaker House of Commons 1968-70; Dep. Pro-Chancellor Kent Univ. 1968-71, Dir. of Foundation Fund, Kent Univ. 1971-74; MP for Dartford (Lab.) 1955-70, and since 1974: m. 1942, Mildred, da. of Charlton Weedy; cr. 1969. 10, Tynedale Close, Dartford, Kent.

ISAACS, Rt. Hon. George Alfred; b. 1883; Gen. Sec. of National So. of Operative Printers and Assistants 1909-49; Mayor of Southwark 1919-21 (Hon. Freeman 1957); P.P.S. to Sec. of State for the Colonies 1924, to Lord Privy Seal 1929-31, and to First Lord of the Admiralty 1942-5, Min. of Labour and National Ser. 1945-51, and Min. of Pensions Jan. to Oct. 1951; a J.P. and a D.L. for Surrey; M.P. for Gravesend Div. of Kent (Lab.) 1923-4 (when he was defeated), for N. Div. of Southwark 1929-31 (when he was defeated), and also 1939-50, and for Southwark 1950-59: m. 1905, Flora, da. of Richard Beasley, of Whipps Cross, Essex; cr. 1945. Mole Cottage, 166 Portsmouth Rd., Cobham, Surrey.

JAMES, Rt. Hon. Lord Justice (Maj. Sir Arthur Evan), son of John William James; b. 1916; ed. at Caterham Sch., and Jesus Coll., Oxford (BCL, MA); Hon. Fellow Jesus Coll., Oxford; Bar. Middle Temple 1939, QC 1960; Barstow Scholar, Council of Legal Education 1939; Recorder of Gt. Grimsby 1962-63, and Derby 1963-65; Dep. Chm. Warwicks. Quarter Sessions 1962-71; a Judge of High Court of Justice (Queen's Bench Div.) 1965-72; Presiding Judge for Crown Court, Midland and Oxford Circuit 1971-72, since when a Lord Justice of Appeal; a Member Parole Board 1967-70 (Vice-Chm. 1969-70); Chm. Vehicle & Gen. Tribunal of Enquiry 1971; Chm. Home Sec. Cttee. on Distribution of Criminal Business, since 1973; a DL of W. Midlands: m. 1993, Eileen Brenda, da. of A. G. Mills; cr. Knt. 1965, PC 1973. 2, Crown Office Row, Temple, EC4; Cartrefiago, Beech Hill Rd., Sutton Coldfield, Warwicks.

JAMES, Rt. Hon. Sir (John) Morrice Cairns, GCMG, CVO, MBE, son of the late Lewis Cairns James; b. 1916; ed. at Bradfield, and Balliol Coll., Oxford (BA); UK Dep. High Commr. at Lahore 1952-53, and at Karachi 1955-56; Assist. Under-Sec. Commonwealth Relations Office 1957-58, UK Dep. High Commr. in India 1958-61, High Commr. for UK in Pakistan 1961-66, Dep. Under-Sec. of State for Commonwealth Affairs 1966-68, Permanent Under-Sec. of State for Commonwealth Affairs 1968 and British High Commr. in India 1968-71, since when British High Commr. in Aust.; King of Arms, Order of St. Michael and St. George since 1975; 1939-45 War with RN and as Lt.-Col. RM: m. 1st, 1948, Elizabeth Margaret Roper, who d. 1966, da. of Francis Piesse: m. 2ndly, 1968, Mme. Geneviève Sarasin; cr. MBE (Mil) 1944, CMG 1957, CVO 1961, KCMG 1962, PC 1968, GCMG 1975. British High Commission, Commonwealth Av., Canberra, ACT, Aust.; Traveller's Club.

JAY, Rt. Hon. Douglas Patrick Thomas, M.P., son of the late Edward Aubrey Hastings Jay, O.B.E., of Hampstead, N.W.3; b. 1907; ed. at Winchester, and New Coll., Oxford; a Fellow of All Souls Coll. Oxford 1930-37, and since 1968; City Editor of the Daily Herald 1937-40, Assist. Sec., Min. of Supply 1940-43, Principal Assist. Sec., Board of Trade 1943-45, Personal Assist. to Prime Min. 1945-46, Economic Sec. to Treasury 1947-50, Financial Sec. to Treasury 1950-51, and Pres. of Board of Trade 1964-67; a Member of Board of Courtaulds 1967-70; a Dir. Trades Union Unit Trust, and Chm. Common Market Safeguards Campaign, and London Motorway Action Gp.; author of " Socialist Case " 1937, " Socialism in the New Society " 1962, and " After the Common Market " 1968; MP for N. Div. of Battersea (Lab.) 1946-74, and Wandsworth (Battersea North) since 1974: m. 1st, 1933, (m. diss. 1972), Margaret, da. of James Clerk Maxwell Garnett, CBE; 2ndly, 1972, Mary Lavinia Thomas; cr. 1951. House of Commons, SW1.

JELLICOE, Rt. Hon. the Earl; D.S.O., M.C.; cr. 1963.

JENKIN, Rt. Hon. Charles Patrick Fleeming, MP, son of Charles Oswald Frewin Jenkin; b. 1926; ed. at Clifton Coll., and Jesus Coll., Camb. (MA); Bar. Middle Temple

1952, Adviser the Distillers' Co. Ltd. 1957-70, Financial Sec. to the Treas. 1970-72, Ch. Sec. to HM Treas. since 1972; MP for Wanstead and Woodford (C) since 1964; 1939-45 War as Capt. Cameron Highlanders in Italy: *m.* 1952, Alison Monica, da. of Capt. (S) Philip Skelton Graham, RN; *cr.* 1973. *9, Hurst Av., Highgate, N6 5TX; W. Essex, Conservative Club.*

JENKINS, *Rt. Hon.* Roy Harris, *MP,* son of the late Arthur Jenkins, MP, of Greenlands, Pontypool; *b.* 1920; ed. at Abersychan Gram. Sch., Pontypool, and at Balliol Coll., Oxford; P.P.S. to Sec. of State for Commonwealth Relations 1940-50, Min. of Aviation 1964-65, and Home Sec. 1965-67, Chancellor of the Exchequer 1967-70; Dep. Leader of Parl. Labour Party 1970-72; Home Sec. since 1974; 1939-45 War with RA; MP for Central Div. of Southwark (*Lab.*) 1948-50, since when for Stechford Div. of Birmingham: *m.* 1945, (Mary) Jennifer, da. of Sir (George) Parker Morris; *cr.* 1964. *33, Ladbroke Sq., W11; St. Amand's House, E. Hendred, Berks.; Brooks's Club.*

JONES, *Rt. Hon.* Aubrey, son of Evan Jones of Merthyr Tydfil; *b.* 1911; ed. at Cyfarthfa Castle Sch., Merthyr Tydfil, and at London Sch. of Economics (B.Sc. Economics, Hon. Fellow, a Gov.); PPS to Min. of State for Economic Affairs 1952, and to Min. of Materials 1953-55, Gen. Director British Iron and Steel Fedn. 1955, Min. of Fuel and Power 1955-57, and Min. of Supply 1957-59; a Dir. of Staveley Industries Ltd. 1962-65 (Chm. 1964-65), of Nettlefolds Steel Co. Ltd., 1960-65, and of Courtaulds Ltd. 1960-63, and Chm. Laporte Industries (Holdings) Ltd. 1970-72; Chm. Cornhill Insurance Co., Ltd. 1972-74; Industrial Fellow Commoner, Churchill Coll., Camb. 1973-73; Leading Adviser to Nigerian Public Ser. Review Commn. 1973-74, and to Iranian Govt. on Agric. Development Plan 1974-75, and a Dir. Thomas Tilling, Ltd. since 1971, MP for Hall Green Div. of Birmingham (C) 1950-65; Chm. of National Board for Prices and Incomes 1965-70; 1939-45 War as Capt. Intelligence Corps.: *m.* 1948, Joan, da. of G. Godfrey-Isaacs, of Ridgehangar, Hillcrest Rd., Ealing, W5; *cr.* 1955. *4, Plane Tree House, Duchess of Bedford's Walk, W8 7QT; Brooks's Club.*

§JONES, *Rt. Hon. Lord Justice (Sir* Edward. Warburton), son of the late Hume Riversdale Jones, RM, of Glenwillan, Portrush, co. Antrim; *b.* 1912; ed. at Portora Roy. Sch., and at Trin. Coll., Dublin (BA, LLB); Bar. N Ireland 1936 and QC 1948; Bar. Middle Temple 1964; a Member of House of Commons, N. Ireland 1951-68, Attorney-Gen. N. Ireland 1964-68, and a Judge of the High Court of Justice, N. Ireland 1968-73, since when a Lord Justice of Appeal, Supreme Court of Judicature, N. Ireland; 1939-45 War, Lt.-Col. R. Irish Fusiliers: *m.* 1st, 1941, Margaret Anne, who *d.* 1953, 2nd da. of William Smellie, of Trearddur Bay, Anglesey; 2ndly, 1953, Ruth Buchan, 3rd da. of William Smellie, of Trearddur Bay, Anglesey; *cr.* PC 1965, Knt. 1973. *The Royal Courts of Justice, Belfast, N. Ireland; Hopefield Cottage, Kincora Av., Belfast; Craig-y-Mor, Trearddur Bay, Anglesey; Army and Navy Club.*

JOSEPH, *Rt. Hon. Sir* Keith Sinjohn, *Bt., M.P.; cr.* 1962.

§KELLY, *Rt. Hon. Mr. Justice* (John William Basil), son of the late Thomas William Kelly; *b.* 1920; ed. at Methodist Coll. Belfast, and Trin. Coll., Dublin (BA); LLB; Bar. N. Ireland, 1944, QC 1958; Sen. Crown Counsel co. Fermanagh 1965-66, and co. Tyrone 1966-67; MP (*U*) for Mid-Down, N. Ireland since 1964 (Parliament suspended March 1972); Attorney Gen. 1968-72; a Judge of the High Court of Justice, N. Ireland 1964-73 (Parliament suspended of the late Thomas Colmer Colthurst; *cr.* 1969. *St. Catherine's, Circular Road East, Cultra, co. Down; Ulster Reform (Belfast) Club.*

KILBRANDON, *Rt. Hon. Baron; cr.* 1971.

KILMANY, *Rt. Hon. Baron, MC; cr.* 1962.

KIRK, *Rt. Hon.* Herbert Victor, son of Alexander Kirk, of Antrim Rd., Belfast; *b.* 1912; ed. at Queen's Univ., Belfast (BComSc 1940); FCA; a JP of Belfast; a Member of N. Ireland Parl. (*U*) 1956-73 (Parliament suspended March 1972); Member

of NI Assembly (*U*) 1973-74; Min. of Labour and Nat. Insurance 1962-64; Min. of Education 1964-65 and Min. of Finance 1965-72: *m.* 1944, Gladys, da. of William Dunn; *cr.* 1962. *38, Massey Av., Belfast 4; Ulster and Reform (Belfast) Clubs.*

KITTO, *Rt. Hon. Sir* Frank Walters, *KBE,* son of the late James Walters Kitto, O.B.E.; *b.* 1903: ed. at N. Sydney High Sch., and at Sydney Univ. (B.A. 1924, LL.B. 1927); Bar. N.S. Wales 1927, and a K.C. 1942; a Justice of High Court of Australia 1950-70; Dep. Chancellor of New England Univ. 1968-70, since when Chancellor: *m.* 1928, Eleanor May, da. of the Rev. William Henry Howard; *cr.* KBE (Civil) 1955, PC 1963. *Jindalee, Biddulph Rd., Armidale, NSW 2350; Australian (Sydney) Club.*

KOTELAWALA, *Col. the Rt. Hon. Sir* John Lionel, *C.H., K.B.E.,* son of the late John Kotelawala; *b.* 1897; ed. at Roy. Coll., Colombo, and at Christ's Coll., Camb.; LL.D. Ceylon 1955; is a Proprietary Planter and Mine Owner, Col. Ceylon L.I., and a J.P. for Ceylon; a Member of Ceylon State Council 1931; appointed Min. for Agriculture and Lands 1933, Min. for Communications and Works 1936, and Min. of Transport and Works 1947; Prime Min. of Ceylon (now Sri Lanka) 1953-56; Grand Cross of Legion of Honour, and of Orders of Merit of Germany, of Merit of Italy, of Rising Sun of Japan, of White Elephant of Thailand, and of the Lion of the Netherlands; an Ass. KStJ; *cr.* KBE (Civil) 1948, PC 1954, CH 1956. *Kandawala, Kotelawalapura, Sri Lanka; Brogues Wood, Biddenden, Kent.*

LANE, *Rt. Hon. Lord Justice (Sir* Geoffrey Dawson), *AFC,* son of the late Percy Albert Lane, of Lincoln; *b.* 1918; ed. at Shrewsbury and Trin. Coll., Camb.; Bar. Gray's Inn 1946, QC 1962, Bencher 1966; Dep. Chm. Rutland Quarter Sessions 1958-62, Chm. 1962-66, Dep. Chm. Beds. Quarter Sessions 1960-66, and a Judge of High Court of Justice (Queen's Bench Div.) 1966-74, since when a Lord Justice of Appeal; Recorder of Bedford 1963-66; Member of Parole Board 1970-72 and Vice Chm. 1972; 1939-45 War as Sqdn.-Ldr. RAF (AFC): *m.* 1944, Jessie (Jan), da. of Donald Macdonald, of Tulloch, Inverness-shire; *cr.* Knt. 1966, PC 1975. *White House, Newlands Lane, Hitchin, Herts.; 2, Crown Office Row, Temple, EC4.*

LANSDOWNE, *Most Hon. the Marquess of; cr.* 1964.

LASCELLES, *Rt. Hon. Sir* Alan Frederick, *G.C.B., G.C.V.O., C.M.G., M.C.; cr.* 1943 [see E. Harewood, colls.].

LAWTON, *Rt. Hon. Lord Justice (Sir* Frederick Horace), son of William John Lawton; *b.* 1911; ed. at Battersea Gram. Sch., and Corpus Christi Coll., Camb.; Bar. Inner Temple 1935, QC 1957, and Bencher 1961; Recorder of Cambridge 1957-61; a Judge of High Court of Justice (Queen's Bench Div.) 1961-72, and Presiding Judge, Western Circuit 1970-72, since when a Lord Justice of Appeal; a Member of Criminal Law Revision Cttee. since 1959; 1939-45 War with London. Irish Rifles (invalided): *m.* 1937, Doreen, da. of Richard Maker Wilton, of Bodmin; *cr.* Knt. 1961. *2, Harcourt Buildings, Temple, EC4; Mordryg, Stoptide, Rock, Wadebridge Cornwall; Garrick Club.*

LEE OF ASHERIDGE, *Rt. Hon. Baroness; cr.* 1966.

LEE OF NEWTON, *Rt. Hon. Baron; cr.* 1964.

LEVER, *Rt. Hon.* (Norman) Harold, *MP,* son of the late Bernard Lever; *b.* 1914; ed. at Manchester Gram. Sch., and Manchester Univ. (LLB); Bar. Middle Temple 1935; Joint Parl. Under-Sec. of State, Dept. of Economic Affairs 1967, Financial Sec HM Treasury 1967-69, and Paymaster Gen. 1969-70; Chancellor of Duchy of Lancaster since 1974; Chm. of Public Accounts Cttee. since 1970, and of Jewish Affairs Research Board since 1971; MP for Exchange Div. of Manchester (*Lab.*) 1945-50, and for Cheetham Div. of Manchester 1950-74, since when for Manchester (Central); 1939-45 War as F/O RAF: *m.* 1962, Diane, da. of Saleh Bashi; 1969. *House of Commons, SW1A OAA.*

LISTOWEL, *Rt. Hon. the Earl of, G.C.M.G.; cr.* 1946.

LLEWELYN-DAVIES OF HASTOE, *Rt. Hon. Baroness; cr.* 1975.

LLOYD, *Rt. Hon.* (John) Selwyn (Brooke), *C.H., C.B.E., T.D., Q.C., M.P.*, son of the late John Wesley Lloyd, T.D., M.R.C.S., L.R.C.P. ; *b.* 1904 ; ed. at Fettes Coll., and at Magdalene Coll., Camb. (Hon. Fellow 1951); Bar. Gray's Inn 1930, a K.C. 1947 and a Bencher 1951; Hon. LL.D. Sheffield 1955, and Liverpool 1957; Hon. D.C.L. Oxford 1960; late Hon. Col. 441st Light Anti-Aircraft Searchlight Regt. R.A. (T.A.); a D.L. of Cheshire; appointed Recorder of Wigan 1948, Min. of State for Foreign Office 1951, Min. of Supply 1954, Min. of Defence 1955, Sec. of State for Foreign Affairs Dec. 1955, and Chancellor of the Exchequer July 1960-62; appointed to enquire into Conservative Party organization 1962; Lord Privy Seal and Leader of House of Commons 1963-64; Speaker of House of Commons since 1971; NW Europe 1944-45 as Brig., Gen. Staff, 2nd Army (despatches, OBE, CBE, Com. of Amer. Legion of Merit); has sat as MP for Wirral Div. of Cheshire (C) since July 1945: *m.* 1951, Elizabeth (from whom he obtained a divorce 1957), da. of Roland Marshall, of W. Kirby, Cheshire; *cr.* O B.E. (Mil.) 1943, C.B.E. (Mil.) 1945, P.C. 1951, CH 1962. *Speaker's House, SW1; Hilbre House, Macdona Drive, W. Kirby, Merseyside; Carlton and Pratt's Clubs.*

LONDON, *Rt. Rev. and Rt. Hon. The Lord Bishop of, DD, cr. 1973.*

§LONG, *Capt. the Rt. Hon.* William Joseph, son of James William Long, of Gt. Ayton, Yorks.; *b.* 1922; ed. at Friend's Sch., Gt. Ayton, and Edinburgh Univ.; Capt. R. Inniskilling Fus. 1940-48; JP of co. Down; Parl. Sec. Ministry of Agric. N. Ireland 1964-Jan. 1966, Senior Parl. Sec. Ministry of Development, Jan. to Oct. 1966; Min. of Education 1966-68, Min. of Home Affairs 1968-69, Min. of Development March to May 1969 and Min. of Education 1969-72; a Member of House of Commons, N. Ireland (U) 1962-73 (Parliament suspended March 1972): *m.* 1942, Elizabeth Doreen, LRCP, LRCSE, LRFPS Glas., da. of John Watson Mercer, of Belfast; *cr.* 1966. *Lisvarna, Donaghadee, co. Down.*

LONGFORD, *Rt. Hon. the Earl of, KG, cr.* 1948.

LOWRY, *Rt. Hon. Sir* Robert Lynd Erskine, son of the late Rt. Hon. Mr. Justice (William) Lowry; *b.* 1919; ed. at Roy. Belfast Academical Inst., and Jesus Coll., Camb. (MA); Bar. N. Ireland 1947, Bencher 1955, QC 1956; Hon. Master of Bench, Middle Temple 1973; a Judge of High Court, N. Ireland 1964-71, since when Lord Ch. Justice of N. Ireland; Hon. Col. 5th Bn. R. Irish Fus. 1967-71, since when of 5th (Vol.) Bn. R. Irish T & AVR; 1939-45 War as Maj. R. Irish Fus. in Tunisia: *m.* 1945, Mary Audrey, da. of John Martin; PC (NI) 1971, and PC (UK) 1974, Knt. 1971. *White Hill, Crossgar, Co. Down; Ulster (Belfast) Club.*

MACANDREW, *Rt. Hon. Baron, T.D.; cr.* 1952.

McBRIDE, *Rt. Hon. Sir* Philip Albert Martin, *KCMG*, son of the late Albert J. McBride, of Adelaide, S. Australia; *b.* 1892; ed. at Burra Public Sch., and Prince Albert Coll.; MHR Commonwealth of Australia 1931-37, Senator 1937-44, and again MHR 1946-58; Assist. Min. for Commerce and Member of War Cabinet 1939-40, Min. for Army Aug. to Oct. 1940, Min. for Supply and Development, and for Munitions 1940-41, Min. for the Interior 1949-50, Min. for Defence 1950-58 (also Min. for Navy and for Air May to July 1951); Leader of Australian Govt. Delegation to Defence Conference, London 1951; Federal Pres. Liberal Party of Australia since 1960: *m.* 1914, Rita I., da. of the late E. W. Crewes, of Kooringa; *cr.* KCMG 1953, PC 1959. 30, *Briar Av., Medindie, S. Aust. 5081; Adelaide, and Australian (Melbourne) Clubs.*

McCARTHY, *Rt. Hon. Sir* Thaddeus Pearcey, *KBE*, son of the late Walter McCarthy, of Napier, New Zealand; *b.* 1907; ed. at St. Bede's Coll., Christchurch, and at Victoria Univ. Coll., Wellington (LLM); Bar. and Solicitor, New Zealand 1930; Judge of Supreme Court of New Zealand 1957-63, since when Judge of Court of Appeal (Pres. 1973); Chm. of Roy. Commns. on State Sers. of NZ 1961-62, on Wage Fixing Procedures in State Sers. 1968 on Racing, and Social Security 1969 and State Services Wages and Salaries 1971; Chm. Winston Churchill

Memorial Trust (NZ); 1939-45 War in Italy: *m.* 1938, Joan Margaret, da. of Francis Joseph Miller, of Wellington; *cr.* Knt. 1964, PC 1968, KBE (Civil) 1974. 100, *Donald St., Wellington 5, New Zealand; Wellington Club.*

§McCONNELL, *Rt. Hon.* Robert William Brian; *cr.* 1964 [see McConnell, Bt. colls.].

MACDERMOTT, *Rt. Hon. Baron, MC; cr.* (N. Ireland) 1940, (UK) 1947.

MACDONALD, *Rt. Hon.* Malcolm John, *OM*, son of the late Rt. Hon. James Ramsay MacDonald, M.P.; *b.* 1901; ed. at Bedales, and at Queen's Coll., Oxford (B.A. 1923, Hon. Fellow 1939, M.A. 1940) ; Hon. LL.D. Hong Kong 1951 ; Hon. D.Litt. Malaya 1951 ; sometime Chm. of National Labour Parliamentary Party : was Parliamentary Under-Sec. of State for Dominion Affairs Oct. 1931 to June 1935, Sec. of State for Colonies June to Nov. 1935, Sec. of State for Dominion Affairs Nov. 1935 to May 1938, again Sec. of State for Colonies May 1938 to May 1940 (also again Sec. of State for Dominion Affairs Oct. 1938 to Jan. 1939), Min. of Health May 1940 to Feb. 1941, High Commr. in Canada for Govt. of United Kingdom, April 1941 to April 1946, Gov.-Gen. of Malayan Union, Singapore and British Borneo April 1946 to May 1948, Commr.-Gen. for United Kingdom in S.-E. Asia May 1948 to Sept. 1955, and High Commr. for United Kingdom in India Sept. 1955 to Oct. 1960 ; Gov. and C.-in-C., Kenya Jan. to Dec. 1963 and Gov.-Gen. and C.-in-C. 1963-64, High Commr. 1964-65, Special Representative in East and Central Africa 1965-67, and Special Representative in Africa 1967-69; elected a Rhodes Trustee 1948; Chancellor of Univ. of Malaya 1949-61, and Visitor of Univ. Coll. Nairobi 1963-64; Chancellor of Durham Univ. since 1970, and Snr. Research Fellow Sussex Univ 1971-73; MP for Bassetlaw Div. of Notts. (Lab.) 1929-35, and for Ross and Cromarty Div. of Invernessshire, Ross-shire, and Cromarty (Nat. Lab.) 1936-45; Grand Cordon of Order of the Trinity of Ethiopia: *m.* 1946, Audrey, da. of Kenyon Fellowes, and widow of Lt.-Col. John Rowley, of Ottawa, Canada; *cr.* 1935, OM 1969. *Raspit Hill, Ivy Hatch, Sevenoaks, Kent.*

McEWEN, *Rt. Hon. Sir* John, *GCMG, CH*, son of David James McEwen; *b.* 1900; MHR Aust. 1937-71; Leader of Aust. Country Party 1958-71; Min. for the Interior 1937-39, Min. of External Affairs 1940, Min. for Air and Civil Aviation 1940-41, a Member of War Cabinet 1940-41, and of War Advisory Council 1941-45, and Min. for Commerce and Agriculture 1949-56, and Min. for Trade (Trade and Industry since 1963) 1956-71; Dep. Prime Min. 1958-67, Prime Minister Dec. 19th, 1967 to Jan. 10th, 1968, and again Dep. Prime Min. 1968-71; 1st Class Order of Rising Sun of Japan, 1971: *m.* 1st, 1921, Dame Ann Mills, DBE, who *d.* 1967, da. of John McLeod of Tongala, Victoria; 2ndly, 1968, Mary Eileen, da. of P. A. Byrne, of Adelaide; *cr.* PC 1953, CH 1969, GCMG 1971. *Stanhope, Victoria, Aust.; 679, Orrong Rd., Toorak, Victoria, Aust. 3142; Melbourne (Aust.) Club.*

McIVOR, *Rt. Hon.* William Basil, son of the late Rev. Frederick McIvor; *b.* 1928; ed. at Methodist Coll., Belfast, and Queen's Univ., Belfast (LLB); Bar. N.I. 1950; Min. of Community Relations, N.I. Govt. 1971-72; Min. of Education, N.I. Exec. 1974; MP for Larkfield (U.) N.I. Parl. 1969-73; a Member of N.I. Assembly for S. Belfast 1973-74: *m.* 1953, Frances Jill, da. of the late Cecil Reginald Johnston Anderson; *cr.* 1971. *Larkfield, River Rd., Lambeg, Lisburn, N.I.*

McKELL, *Rt. Hon. Sir* William John *G.C.M.G., Q.C.*, son of the late R. P. McKell of Pambula, N.S. Wales; *b.* 1891 ; ed. at Public Sch., Surry Hills, N.S. Wales ; Hon. LL.D. Sydney 1952 ; Bar. N.S. Wales 1925, and K.C. 1943; was a M.L.A., N.S. Wales 1917-47, Assist. Min. of Justice N.S. Wales 1920-22, Min. of Justice and Assist. Treasurer 1925-27, Min. for Local Govt. 1930-31, Min. for Justice 1931-32, Leader of the Opposition 1939-41, Premier and Treasurer 1941-47, and Gov.-Gen. and Com.-in-Ch. of Commonwealth of Australia 1947-53 ; a Member of Malayan Constitutional Commn. 1957 : *m.* 1920, Minnie, da of James Pye ; *cr.* P.C. 1948, G.C.M.G. 1951 42/14, *Leura Rd., Double Bay, NSW 2028*

MACLEAN, *Rt. Hon. Baron, KT, GCVO, KBE, cr.* 1971.

McMAHON, *Rt. Hon.* William, *CH*, son of the late William Daniel McMahon, of Sydney; *b.* 1908; ed. at Sydney Gram. Sch., and Sydney Univ. (LlB, BEc); Solicitor, Australia 1933 (practised until 1939); a Member of House of Representatives NSW since 1949; Min. for Navy, and for Air 1951-54 (visited Korea and Japan 1952), for Social Sers. 1954-56, for Primary Industry 1956-58, and for Labour and Nat. Ser. 1958-66, Treas., Commonwealth of Aust. 1966-69, Min. for Foreign Affairs 1969-71, and Prime Min. 1971-72; Acting Min. for Trade May-Aug. and Oct.-Nov. 1956, and i/c CSIRO Oct.-Dec. 1956, Acting Min. for Labour & Nat. Ser. May-Aug. 1957, and for Nat. Development Oct. 1959, for Territories Oct.-Nov. 1961, and for Labour & Nat. Ser. Nov.-Dec. 1966, Sept. 1968, and June-July and Sept.-Oct. 1969, Acting Attorney-Gen. Sept. Oct. 1960 and April-May 1961, and Vice-Pres., Exec. Council 1964-66; Leader Australian Delegation to Commonwealth Parl. Conference, New Delhi 1957-58, and Visiting Min. to ILO Conference, Geneva 1960 and 1964, and Pres. ILO Asian Regional Conference, Melbourne 1962; Dep. Leader of Lib. Party 1966-71, and Leader 1971-72; 1939-45 War as Maj. 1st Inf. Bn., AIF; *m.* 1965, Sonia Rachel, da. of W. E. Hopkins; *cr.* PC 1966, CH 1972. *Parliament House, Canberra, Aust.: Union, Royal Sydney, Elanora and Tattersall's (Sydney), Melbourne, and Commonwealth (Canberra) Clubs.*

MACMILLAN, *Rt. Hon.* (Maurice) Harold, 3rd son of the late Maurice Crawford Macmillan of Birch Grove House, Chelwood Gate, Haywards Heath, Sussex; *b.* 1894; ed. at Eton, and at Balliol Coll., Oxford (Hon. Fellow); Hon. D.C.L. Oxford 1958; D.C.L. Oxford (by diploma) 1960; LL.D. Cambridge 1961; F.R.S. 1962; Hon. LL.D. Sussex Univ. 1963; 1914-19 War as Capt. Grenadier Guards (thrice wounded); was Parliamentary Sec., Min. of Supply 1940-42, Under-Sec. of State for Colonies Feb. to Dec. 1942, Min. Resident in N.-W. Africa Dec. 1942 to May 1945 (also Head of Allied Mission in Italy Nov. 1944 to May 1945), Sec. of State for Air May to July 1945, Min. of Housing and Local Govt. 1951 to 1954, Min. of Defence 1954 to 1955, and Sec. of State for Foreign Affairs April to Dec. 1955, Chancellor of the Exchequer 1955 to 1957, and Prime Min. and First Lord of the Treasury 1957-63; a Joint Pres. of United and Cecil Club since 1957, and Chancellor of Oxford Univ. since 1960; received Freedom of Bromley 1957, and of Toronto 1962; Hon. Freedom of City of London 1961; sat as M.P. for Stockton-on-Tees (C) Oct. 1924 to May 1929, and Nov. 1931 to June 1945, and for Bromley Nov. 1945 to Oct. 1964: *m.* 1920, Lady Dorothy Evelyn Cavendish, GBE, who *d.* 1966, da. of 9th Duke of Devonshire; *cr.* 1942. *Birch Grove House, Chelwood Gate, Haywards Heath, Sussex; Athenæum, Pratt's, Buck's, Carlton, Turf, and Beefsteak Clubs.*

MACMILLAN, *Rt. Hon.* Maurice Victor, *MP* only son of the Rt. Hon. (Maurice) Harold Macmillan; *b.* 1921; ed. at Eton and Balliol Coll. Oxford; late Capt. Sussex Yeo. and Maj. GHQ Liaison Regt. (Phantom); Economic Sec. to Treasury 1963-64; Ch. Sec. to Treasury 1970-72, Sec. of State for Employment, 1972-73, and Paymaster-Gen. 1973-74; MP for Halifax (C) 1955-64, and for Farnham, Surrey since 1966: *m.* 1942, the Hon. Katharine Margaret Alice Ormsby-Gore, da. of 4th Baron Harlech; *cr.* 1972. 12, *Catherine Pl., SW1; Highgrove, Doughton, Tetbury, Glos.; Carlton, Turf, Garrick, Beefsteak and Pratt's Clubs.*

McTIERNAN, *Rt. Hon. Sir* Edward Aloysius, *K.B.E.*, son of the late Patrick McTiernan; *b.* 1892; ed. at Sydney Univ. (B.A. 1911, LL.B. 1914); Bar. N.S. Wales 1916; formerly Privy Chamberlain to Pope Pius XII; a M.L.A. for N.S. Wales 1920-27, Attorney-Gen. 1920-22 and again 1925-27, Lecturer, Faculty of Law, Sydney Univ. 1927, and a Member of House of Representatives, Commonwealth of Australia 1928-30, since when a Judge of High Court of Australia: *m.* 1949, Kathleen, da. of John T. S. Lloyd; *cr.* K.B.E. (Civil) 1951, P.C. 1963. *Breffni, Chilton Parade, Warrawee, N.S. Wales; Australian (Sydney), and Athenæum (Melbourne) Clubs.*

§McVEIGH, *Rt. Hon. Sir* Herbert Andrew, son of the late John McVeigh, of 4, Belmont Park Londonderry; *b.* 1908; ed. at Foyle Coll., Londonderry, and at Queen's Univ., Belfast (BA); Bar. N. Ireland 1931, QC, N. Ireland 1948; Pres. Students Representative Council 1929-30, and Dep. Chm. Boundaries Commn. 1957-65; a Judge of High Court of Justice, N. Ireland 1956-64, and a Lord Justice of Appeal, Supreme Court of Judicature, N. Ireland 1964-73, Judge of Restrictive Practices Court, and Senior Crown Counsel, cos. Fermanagh, Tyrone and Antrim, Chm. of Education Cttee. of Benchers, and of Library and Finance Cttee. of Benchers, Pres. of Queens Univ. Assocn.; a Gov., Victoria Coll., Belfast, Chm., N. Ireland Assocn. for Mental Health, and a Member of Distinction Awards Cttee. (NI) relating to Hosp. Authority Consultants: *m.* 1940, Mary Elizabeth Mabel, da. of the late Adam Reade, of Portstewart, co. Londonderry; *cr.* Knt. 1964, PC 1965. 25, *Cambourne Park, Belfast BT9 6RL; Northern Counties (Londonderry) Club.*

MARA, *Rt. Hon. Ratu Sir* Kamisese Kapaiwai Tuimacilai, *KBE*, son of the late Ratu Tevita Uluilakeba, of Lakeba, Lau, Fiji; *b.* 1920; ed. at Sacred Heart Coll., Fiji, Otago Univ., NZ, Wadham Coll., Oxford (MA, Hon. Fellow), and LSE; Hereditary High Ch. of Lau Is. (Tui Nayau and Tui Lau); MLC 1953, and Elected MLC 1963, MEC 1959; Min. for Natural Resources 1964-66, Leader of Govt. Business 1966-67, Ch. Min. and Member of Council of Mins. 1967-70, since when Prime Min., Min. of Foreign Affairs and Min. of Rural Development (on Independence of Fiji): *m.* 1951, Adi (Lady) Litia Cakobau Lalabalavu, da. of the late Ratu George Cokananuto Tuisawau, OBE (Roko Tui Dreketi); *cr.* OBE (Civil) 1960, KBE (Civil) 1969, PC 1973. 11, *Battery Rd., Suva, Fiji; Tubou, Lakeba, Lau, Fiji; United Oxford and Cambridge University, and Achilles Clubs.*

MARPLES, *Rt. Hon. Baron, FRS; cr.* 1957.

MARSH, *Rt. Hon.* Richard William, son of William Marsh; *b.* 1928; ed. at Jennings Sch., Swindon, Woolwich Polytechnic and Ruskin Coll., Oxford; a Member, Select Cttee. on Estimates 1961, Chm., Interdepartmental Cttee. to Co-ordinate Govt. Policy on Industrial Training 1964, Parl. Sec., Min. of Labour 1964-65, Parl. Sec., Min. of Technology 1965-66, Min. of Power 1966-68, and Min. of Transport 1968-69; Chm. of British Rail Board and of Govs. British Transport Staff Coll., and a Member NEDC since 1971; a Gov. Land Business Sch., since 1974; a Member of Council Foundation Management Education, and of Exec. Political & Economic Planning; MP for Greenwich (Lab.) 1959-71: *m.* 1st, 1950 (m. diss. 1973) Evelyn Mary, da. of Frederick Andrews; 2ndly, 1973, Caroline Dutton, who *d.* 1975; *cr.* 1966. *British Rail Board, 222, Marylebone Rd., NW1.*

MARSHALL, *Rt. Hon. Sir* John Ross, *GBE, CH*, son of the late Allan Marshall, of Wellington, NZ; *b.* 1912; ed. at Victoria Univ. Coll., (BA, LLM); Bar. and Solicitor NZ 1936; Hon. Bencher Gray's Inn; Lecturer in Law, Victoria Univ. 1948-51 (Visiting Fellow); Min. in charge of State Advances Corpn., Public Trust Office, Census and Statistics Dept., and Min. Assist. to Prime Min. 1949-54, of Health 1951-54, and of Information and Publicity 1951-57, Attorney-Gen. and Min. of Justice 1954-57, Min. of Customs 1960-61, and of Industries & Commerce 1960-69; MP (Nat.) NZ since 1946; Dep. Prime Min. of NZ 1957 and 1960-72, and Prime Min. Feb. to Dec. 1972; Dep. Leader, Nat. Party 1957-72, and Min. of Overseas Trade 1960-72, and Min. of Labour & Immigration, and Attorney-Gen. 1969-71; Chm. Nat. Development Council 1969-72; a Dir. Phillips Electrical Industries (NZ) Ltd., Norwich Union Insurance Soc., and other cos.; publication "Law of Watercourses"; 1939-45 War as Maj. 2nd NZEF, Pacific and Italy: *m.* 1944, Margaret, da. of W. E. G. Livingstone, of Perth W. Aust.; *cr.* PC 1966, CH 1973, GBE (Civil), 1974, *Parliament Buildings, Wellington, NZ; United Services (Wellington) and Wellington Clubs.*

MARTONMERE, *Rt. Hon. Baron, GBE, KCMG, cr.* 1962.

MASON, *Rt. Hon.* Roy, *MP.*, son of the late Joseph Mason, of Carlton, nr. Barnsley; *b.* 1924; ed. at Carlton and Royston Elementary Schs., and London Sch. of Econs.; Min. of State, Board of Trade 1964-67, Min. of Defence for Equipment 1967-68, Postmaster Gen. April to June 1968, Min. of Power 1968-69, and Pres. of Board of Trade 1969-70; Sec. of State for Defence since 1974; MP for Barnsley (*Lab.*) since 1953: *m.* 1945, Marjorie, da. of Ernest Sowden, of Royston, W. Riding, Yorks.; *cr.* 1968. 12, *Victoria Av., Barnsley, Yorks.*

MAUDLING, *Rt. Hon.* Reginald, *M.P.*, son of Reginald George Maudling, of Worthing; *b.* 1917; ed. at Merchant Taylors Sch. and at Merton Coll., Oxford; Bar. Middle Temple 1939; Parliamentary Sec. Min. of Civil Aviation 1952, Economic Sec. to Treasury 1952-5, Min. of Supply 1955-7, Paymaster-Gen. 1957-9, Pres. of Board of Trade 1959-61, Sec. of State for the Colonies 1961-62, and Chancellor of Exchequer 1962-64; Dep. Leader of the Opposition 1965-70; Home Sec. 1970-72; Pres. of Nat. Union of Conservative Assocns. 1967-68; MP for Barnet Div. of Herts (*C*) 1950-74, and Barnet (Chipping Barnet) since 1974: *m.* 1939, Beryl, da. of E. Laverick, of Blackheath, SE; *cr.* 1955. *Bedwell Lodge, Essendon, Herts.*

MAYBRAY-KING, *Rt. Hon. Baron; cr.* 1965.

MEGAW, *Rt. Hon. Lord Justice* (*Sir* John), *CBE, TD,* son of the late Hon. Mr. Justice R. D. Megaw, of Belfast; *b.* 1909; ed. at Roy. Academical Instn. Belfast, St. John's Coll., Camb. (Hon. Fellow), and Harvard Law Sch.; Hon. LLD Belfast; Bar. Gray's Inn 1934, a QC 1953, a QC N. Ireland 1954, and a Bencher 1958; a Judge of High Court of Justice (Queen's Bench Div.) 1961-69, since when a Lord Justice of Appeal; Pres. of Restrictive Practices Court 1962-68; 1939-45 War with RA: *m.* 1938, Eleanor Grace, da. of the late W. G. Chapman; *cr.* CBE (Civil) 1956. Knt. 1961, PC 1969. 14, *Upper Cheyne Row, SW3.*

MELLISH, *Rt. Hon.* Robert Joseph, *MP*, son of John Mellish, of Deptford, SE8; *b.* 1913; ed. at St. Joseph's RC Sch., Deptford; PPS Admiralty 1948-49, to Min. of Supply 1949-51, and to Min. of Pensions 1951-64, Parl. Sec., Min. of Housing and Local Govt. 1964-67, and again May to June 1970, Min of Public Buildings and Works 1967-69, Govt. Ch. Whip 1969-70, and Ch. Labour Whip 1970-74, since when Govt. Ch. Whip, MP for Rotherhithe Div. of Bermondsey 1946-50, for Bermondsey 1950-74, since when for Southwark (Bermondsey); 1939-45 as Capt. RE in SE Asia: *m.* 1938, Anne Elizabeth, da. of George Warner, of Bermondsey, SE16; *cr.* 1967. 12, *Downing St., SW1; 4, Crantock Rd., Catford, SE6.*

MENZIES, *Rt. Hon. Sir* Robert Gordon, *K.T., C.H., Q.C.,* son of the late James Menzies, formerly M.L.A. of Victoria; *b.* 1894; ed. at Grenville Coll., Ballarat, at Wesley Coll., Melbourne, and at Melbourne Univ. (LL.M. 1st class Honours 1917, Hon. LLD 1942); Hon. LLD Bristol, Queen's Univ., Belfast, Melbourne, British Columbia, Sydney, McGill, Malta, Laval (Quebec), Tasmania, Camb., Harvard, Leeds, Adelaide, Brisbane, Edinburgh, Birmingham, Australian National Univ. (Canberra), Sussex, Drury Coll. Missouri, Univ. of Cal., and Kent; Hon. DSc. NSW; Hon. DCL Oxford; Hon. DLittW. Australia; Hon. Fellow of Roy. Australasian Coll. of Physicians, of Roy. Australasia Institute of Architects, of Institute of Meat, of Australian Acad. of Science, of FRCP and FRCOG; Roy. Australasian Coll. of Surgs., Zological Soc. of London, Inst. of Builders, London, Australian Coll. of Gen. Practitioners, and FRCS; Bar, Victoria and High Court, Australia, 1918, and a KC 1929; Hon. Bencher, Gray's Inn 1935; a Member of House of Representatives, Commonwealth of Australia 1934-66; a MLC and Hon. Min., Victoria 1928-29, a MLA 1929-34, and Attorney-Gen., Min. for Railways, and Dep. Premier, Victoria 1932-34; Attorney-Gen. and Min. for Industry, Commonwealth of Australia 1934-39, Dep. Leader of United Australia Party 1936-39 and Leader 1939-41; Prime Min. 1939-41 (also Treasurer 1939-40, Min. for Co-ordination of Defence 1939-41, Min. for Trade and Customs Feb. to March 1940, Min. for Information March to Dec. 1940, and Min. for Munitions June to Nov. 1940), a Member of Advisory War Council

1941-44, and Leader of the Opposition 1943-49; Founder and Leader of Aust. Liberal Party 1943-66, and again Prime Min. 1949-66 (also Min. for External Affairs 1960-61); Constable of Dover Castle, and Lord Warden of the Cinque Ports since 1965; Chancellor of Univ. of Melbourne 1967-72; a Freeman of Cities of London, Edinburgh, Swansea, Oxford, Athens, Melbourne, Hastings and Sandwich, an Hon. Freeman of Clothworkers' and Goldsmiths' Cos.; Pres. of Melbourne Scots; a FRS and FRSA; a Ch. Com. of American Legion of Merit; formerly a Member of Council of Melbourne Univ.; Leader of Mission to President Nasser in Cairo to discuss Suez Canal Affairs 1956; has Coronation medals (1937 and 1953): *m.* 1920, Dame Pattie Maie, *GBE,* el. da. of the late J. W. Leckie; *cr.* PC 1937, CH 1951, KT 1963. 2, *Haverbrack Av., Malvern, Melbourne, Australia; Walmer Castle, Deal, Kent; Commonwealth (Canberra), Melbourne Cricket, Melbourne; Scots, and Athenæum (Melbourne); Athenæum, Pratt's, Australian, Savage, and Lord's Taverners Clubs, and MCC.*

MERTHYR, *Rt. Hon. Baron, KBE, TD; cr.* 1964.

MILLAN, *Rt. Hon.* Bruce, *MP,* son of the late David Millan; *b.* 1927; ed. at Harris Acad., Dundee; Chartered Accountant; Parly. Under-Sec. of State for Defence (RAF) 1964-66, and for Scotland 1966-70; Min. of State for Scotland since 1974; MP for Craigton Div. of Glasgow (*Lab.*) since 1959: *m.* 1953, Gwendoline May, da. of the late Reginald John Fairey; *cr.* 1975. 46, *Hardy Rd., SE3.*

§MINFORD, *Rt. Hon.* Nathaniel Owens, son of the late Hugh Minford, of Templepatrick, co. Antrim; *b.* 1912; ed. at Belfast Roy. Acad.; Member of House of Commons NI (*U*) 1951-72 (Leader 1971-72; Parl. Sec. Min. of Development N. Ireland 1967-68 and Sen. Parl. Sec. 1968-69; Min. of State, Min. of Development 1969-72, Parliament suspended March 1972; Member of NI Assemby 1973-74: *m.* 1951, Maureen Helena, da. of Thomas Ferguson Minford, MB, of Randalstown, co. Antrim; *cr.* 1969. 2, *Birch Hill Av., The Steeple, co. Antrim.*

MOLSON, *Rt. Hon. Baron; cr.* 1956.

§MORGAN, *Rt. Hon.* William James; *b.* 1914; Parliamentary Sec. to Min. of Commerce and Assist. Parliamentary Sec. to Min. of Finance, N. Ireland 1959-61, and Min. of Health and Local Govt. 1961-64, since when Min. of Labour and National Insurance; a JP of Belfast; MP for Oldpark Div. of Belfast (*U*) 1949-58, and Clifton Div. of Belfast 1959-73 (Parliament suspended March 1972); Member of NI Assembly 1973-74: *m.* 1942, Dorothy Eileen, da. of Thomas Brennan; *cr.* PC 1961. *Rhanbuoy, Carrickfergus, co. Antrim.*

MORRIS OF BORTH-Y-GEST, *Rt. Hon. Baron, C.B.E., M.C.; cr.* 1951.

MORRIS, *Rt. Hon.* John, *MP,* son of the late David William Morris; *b.* 1931; ed. at Ardwyn, Aberystwyth, Univ. Coll. of Wales, Aberystwyth, and Caius Coll., Camb.; Bar. Gray's Inn 1954; Lt. RWF; Parl. Sec. Min. of Power 1964-66, and Min. of Transport 1966-68; Min. of Defence for Equipment 1968-70; Sec. of State for Wales since 1974; MP for Aberavon (*Lab.*) since 1959: *m.* 1959, Margaret Meinir, da. of the late Edward Lewis, OBE, JP; *cr.* 1970. *House of Commons, SW1A 0AA.*

MOUNTBATTEN OF BURMA, *Adm. of the Fleet the Rt. Hon. Earl, KG, GCB, OM, GCSI, GCIE, GCVO, DSO, FRS; cr.* 1947.

§MOYOLA, *Rt. Hon. Baron; cr.* 1967.

MUIRSHIEL, *Rt. Hon. Viscount, KT, CH, CMG; cr.* 1952.

MULLEY, *Rt. Hon.* Frederick William, *MP,* son of the late William Mulley, of Leamington Spa; *b.* 1918; ed. at Warwick Sch., at Ch. Ch., Oxford (MA); Fellow of St. Catharine's Coll., Camb. 1948-50; BSc Econ London; Bar. Inner Temple 1954; P.P.S. to Min. of Works 1951; a Member of National Exec. Cttee. of Labour Party 1957-58, 1960-64, and since 1965; Dep. Sec. of State for Defence; Min. of Defence for the Army 1964-65, Min. of Aviation 1965-67, Joint Min. of State, Foreign Office 1967-69, and Min. of Transport 1969-70; Min. of Transport, Dept. of Environment 1974-75, since when Sec. of State for Education and Science; 1939-45 War as Lance-Sgt., Worcestershire Regt. (prisoner); MP for

Park Div. of Sheffield (*Lab.*) since 1950: *m.* 1948, Joan, da. of Alexander M. Phillips; *cr.* 1964. *192, Sutherland Av., W9.*

MUNSTER, *Rt. Hon. the Earl of, K.B.E.; cr.* 1954.

MURRAY, *Rt. Hon.* Ronald King, *MP,* son of the late James King Murray, MIEE; *b.* 1922; ed. at George Watson's Coll., Edinburgh, Univ. of Edinburgh, and Jesus Coll., Oxford; 1939-45 War with REME; Bar. Scotland 1953, Advocate-Depute 1964, QC 1967; Lord Advocate since 1974; MP for Leith Div. of Edinburgh (*Lab.*) since 1970: *m.* 1950, Sheila Winifred, da. of Sidney Thomas Gamlin, of Bristol; *cr.* 1974. *38, Primrose Bank Rd., Edinburgh EH5 3JF; 30, Great King St., Edinburgh EH3 6QH; Royal Forth Yacht, and Forth Corinthian Yacht Clubs.*

§NEILL, *Maj. the Rt. Hon. Sir* Ivan; *b.* 1906; ed. at Queen's Univ., Belfast (BScEcon); Snr. Dir. Ivan Neill & Co., Building & Eng. Contractors since 1928; MP N. Ireland 1949-73 (Parliament suspended March 1972); Min. of Labour and Nat. Insurance, N. Ireland 1950-62, Min. of Education 1962-64, and Min. of Finance 1964-65; Min. of Development 1968-69, and Speaker of House of Commons, N. Ireland (*U*) 1969-72; a DL for Belfast; 1939-45 War as Maj RE. Far East: *m.* 1928, Margaret Helena Allen *cr.* 1950, Knt. 1973. *Greenlaw, Ballywilliam, Donaghadee, co. Down.*

NEWE, *Rt. Hon.* Gerard Benedict, *OBE,* son of Patrick Newe; *b.* 1907; ed. at St. Malachy's Coll., Belfast, Queen's Univ., Belfast (MA), and New Univ. of Ulster (D.Litt.); Sec. of N.I. Council of Social Ser. 1948-72; a Min of State, Dept. of PM, (N.I.) 1971-72; Vice-Chm. of Irish Commn. for Justice and Peace 1970-72; Chm. of Assisi Fellowship since 1965, and of Personal Social Sers. Cttee. Northern Health and Social Servs. Board since 1973; *cr.* OBE (Civil) 1962, PC 1971. *Prospect House, Cushendall, Ballymena, co. Antrim, BT44 0RY.*

NOBLE, *Com. the Rt. Hon. Sir* Allan (Herbert Percy), *K.C.M.G., D.S.O., D.S.C.,* son of the late Adm. Sir Percy Lockhart Harnam Noble, *G.B.E., K.C.B., C.V.O.; b.* 1908; ed. at Radley; Com. (ret.) RN (served 1927-45); a DL for Suffolk; ADC to Viceroy of India 1936-8; Govt. Observer, Bikini Atomic Bomb Tests 1946; PPS to the Rt. Hon. Sir (Robert) Anthony Eden, K.G., P.C., M.C., M.P. 1947-51, and Parliamentary and Financial Sec., Admiralty 1951-5, Parliamentary Under-Sec. of State for Commonwealth Relations 1955-6, and Min. of State for Foreign Affairs 1956-9 ; Special Ambassador to Ivory Coast 1961; a Member of Advisory Cttee. on ser. Parliamentary candidates 1963-74; 1939-45 War (despatches, DSC, DSO); MP for Chelsea Oct. 1945 to Sept. 1959: *m.* 1938, Barbara Janet Margaret, only da. of the late Brig. Kenneth Gabbett: *cr.* P.C. 1956, K.C.M.G. 1959. *3, Culford Gdns., SW3; Troston Cottage, Bury St. Edmunds, Suffolk; White's Club.*

NOEL-BAKER [see Baker].

NORTH, *Rt. Hon. Sir* Alfred Kingsley, *KBE,* son of the late Rev. J. J. North, DD; *b.* 1900; ed. at Canterbury Coll., Christchurch, NZ (LL.M. 1925); Bar. 1924, and a KC 1947; appointed a Judge of Supreme Court, NZ 1951, a Judge of Court of Appeal 1957, and Pres. of Court of Appeal 1963-72: *m.* 1924, Thelma Grace, da. of the late William Dawson; *cr.* Knt. 1959, KBE (Civil) 1964, PC 1966. *28, Mahoe Av., Remuera, Auckland, NZ; Wellington (Wellington), and Northern (Auckland) Clubs.*

NORTHUMBERLAND, *His Grace the Duke of, KG, TD; cr.* 1973.

NUGENT OF GUILDFORD, *Rt. Hon. Baron; cr.* 1962.

NUTTING, *Rt. Hon. Sir* (Harold) **Anthony,** Bt.; *cr.* 1954.

O'BRIEN OF LOTHBURY, *Rt. Hon. Baron, GBE; cr.* 1970.

OGMORE, *Rt. Hon. Baron, T.D. ; cr.* **1951.**

O'MALLEY, *Rt. Hon.* (Brian) Kevin, *MP,* son of Frank O'Malley, of Mexborough, Yorks.; *b.* 1930; ed. at Mexborough Gram. Sch., and Manchester Univ. (BA); Assist. Govt. Whip 1964-66, Dep. Ch. Govt. Whip and a Lord Commr. of Treasury 1967-69, Parl. Under-Sec. of State, Dept. of Health and Social Security 1969-70; Min. of State

Dept. of Health and Social Security since 1974; MP for Rotherham (*Lab.*) since 1963: *m.* 1959, Kathleen Sylvia, da. of Herman Curtiss, of Billingborough, Lincs.; *cr.* 1975. *29, Hall Av., Mexborough, Yorks.*

§O'NEILL OF THE MAINE, *Rt. Hon. Baron; cr.* 1956.

§O'NEILL, *Rt. Hon.* Phelim Robert Hugh; *cr.* 1969 [see B. Rathcavan].

ORME, *Rt. Hon.* Stanley, *MP,* son of Sherwood Orme, of Sale, Cheshire; *b.* 1923; 1939-45 War as Warrant Officer, Air-Bomber Navigator, RAF Bomber Command; a Borough Councillor of Sale 1958-65; a Member of AEU (shop steward); Min. of State for N. Ireland since 1974; MP for Salford West (*Lab.*) since 1964: *m.* 1951, Irene Mary, da. of Vernon Fletcher Harris, of Worsley, Lancs.; *cr.* 1974. *47, Hope Rd., Sale, Cheshire.*

ORMROD, *Rt. Hon. Lord Justice* (*Sir* Roger Fray Greenwood), son of Oliver Fray Ormrod, of Whitehaven, Cumberland; *b.* 1911; ed. at Shrewsbury, and at Queen's Coll., Oxford (BA, BM, BCh, Hon. Fellow); Bar. Inner Temple 1936; QC 1958; House Physician, Radcliffe Infirmary, Oxford 1941-42, and Lecturer in Forensic Medicine, Oxford Med. Sch. 1950-57; a Judge of High Court of Justice (Probate Divorce and Admiralty Div. (now Family Div.)) 1961-74, since when a Lord Justice of Appeal; 1939-45 War as Maj. RAMC: *m.* 1938, Doris Anne, da. of Charles Lush, of Ealing; *cr.* Knt. 1961 PC 1974. *4, Aubrey Rd., W8; Garrick Club.*

ORR, *Rt. Hon. Lord Justice* (*Sir* Alan Stewart), *OBE,* son of the late William Orr, of Gt. Wakering, Essex; *b.* 1911; ed. at Fettes, Edinburgh Univ., and Balliol Coll., Oxford (MA); Bar. Middle Temple 1936 and Inner Temple 1961; QC 1963; Barstow Law Scholar; a Member of Gen. Council of the Bar 1953-57, Junior Counsel (Common Law) to Commrs. of Inland Revenue 1957-63, and Recorder of Windsor 1958-64, and Oxford 1964-65; Dep. Chm. Oxford Quarter Sessions 1964-71, a Judge of High Court of Justice (Probate, Divorce and Admiralty Div.) 1965-71, and Presiding Judge for Superior Courts NE Circuit 1970-71, since when a Lord Justice of Appeal; 1939-45 War as Wing Cdr. RAF (despatches, OBE): *m.* 1933, Mariana Frances Lilian, da. of Capt. J. C. Lang, KOSB; *cr.* OBE (Mil) 1944, Knt. 1965, PC 1971. *Highfield, Harmer Green, Welwyn, Herts.; United Oxford and Cambridge University Club*

PAGE, *Rt. Hon.* Rodney Graham, *MBE, MP,* son of the late Lt.-Col. Frank Page, DSO (Mayor of Hertford); *b.* 1911; ed. at Magdalen Coll. Sch., Oxford, and London Univ. (LLB); Solicitor 1934; Min. for Local Govt. and Development, Dept. of the Environment 1970-74; MP for Crosby (*C*) since 1953; 1939-45 War with RAF: *m.* 1934, Hilda Agatha, da. of Edgar John Dixon; *cr.* MBE (Mil.) 1946, PC 1972. *92, Highgate Hill, N6; Myrtle Bank, Crosby Rd. N., Liverpool 22.*

PANNELL, *Rt. Hon. Baron; cr.* 1964.

PEARCE, *Rt. Hon. Baron; cr.* **1957.**

PEARSON, *Rt. Hon. Baron, CBE; cr.* 1961.

PEART, *Rt. Hon.* (Thomas) **Frederick,** *MP,* son of Emerson Featherstone Peart, of Durham; *b.* 1914; ed. at Wolsingham Gram. Sch., and at Durham Univ. (BSc); PPS to Min. of Agric. 1945-51; Min. of Agric., Fisheries and Food 1964-68, and since 1974, and Lord Privy Seal April to Nov. 1968; Lord Pres. of Council and Leader of House of Commons 1968-70; Leader of Labour Delegation to Council of Europe and Western European Assembly 1973-74; Vice-Pres. Council of Europe 1973-74; 1939-45 War as Capt. RA in N. Africa and Italy; MP for Workington Div. of Cumberland (*Lab.*) since 1945: *m.* 1945, Sarah Elizabeth, da. of Thomas Lewis, of Aberystwyth; *cr.* 1964. *House of Commons, SW1A 0AA.*

PENNYCUICK, *Rt. Hon. Sir* John, son of the late Col. John Pennycuick, CSI, of Camberley, Surrey; *b.* 1899; ed. at Winchester, and at New Coll., Oxford (BA); Bar. Inner Temple 1925, a Bencher 1954, and a KC 1947; a Judge of High Court of Justice (Chancery Div.) 1960-70, and Vice-Chancellor 1970-74; JP for Bucks: *m.* 1930, Lucy, who *d.* 1972, da. of Stanley Johnstone, of Birmingham; *cr.* Knt. 1960, PC, 1974. *Old Manor House, Maids Moreton, Bucks.*

PERTH, *Rt. Hon. the Earl of ; cr.* **1957.**

PEYTON, Rt. Hon. John Wynne William, *MP*, son of the late Ivor Eliot Peyton; *b.* 1919; ed. at Eton, and Trin. Coll., Oxford (MA); Bar. 1945; Parl. Sec. Min. of Power 1962-64, Min. of Transport June to Oct. 1970, and for Transport Industries, 1970-74; 1939-45 War as Capt. 15th/19th Hussars (prisoner); MP for Yeovil (C) since 1951: *m.* 1st, 1947 (m. diss. 1966), Diana, da. of the late Douglas Clinch, of Durban; 2ndly, 1966, Mary Constance, da. of the late the Hon (Everard) Humphrey Wyndham, MC [see B. Egremont, colls.]; *cr.* 1970. 32, *Chester Terr., NW1; Lytes Cary, Somerton, Somerset; Boodle's.*

POOLE, Rt. Hon. Baron, CBE, TD.; *cr.* 1963.

§**PORTER, Rt. Hon.** Sir Robert Wilson, *QC*, son of the late Joseph Wilson Porter; *b.* 1923; ed. at Model Sch. and Foyle Coll., Londonderry and Queen's Univ', Belfast (LLB 1949); Bar. N. Ireland 1950, QC 1965; Jun. Crown Counsel, co. Londonderry 1960-63 and co. Down 1964-65, Counsel to Attorney Gen. for N. Ireland 1963-64, and 1965; Parl. Sec. Min. of Home Affairs, and Min. of Health and Social Sers. 1969, and Min. of Home Affairs, N. Ireland 1969-70; a Member of House of Commons, N. Ireland (U) 1966-72 (Parliament suspended March 1972); late RAFVR and RA (TA): *m.* 1953, Margaret Adelaide, da. of the late F. W. Lynas; *cr.* PC 1969, Knt. 1971. *Ardkeen, Marlborough Park North, Belfast 9; RAF and Ulster Clubs.*

POWELL, Rt. Hon. (John) Enoch, *MBE*, son of Albert Enoch Powell; *b.* 1912; ed. at King Edward's Sch., Birmingham, and at Trin. Coll., Camb. (B.A. 1933, M.A. 1937) ; was Professor of Greek, Sydney Univ. 1937-9, Parliamentary Sec., Min. of Housing and Local Govt. 1955-7, and Financial Sec. to H.M. Treasury 1957-8 ; Min. of Health 1960-63; 1939-45 War as Brig., Roy. Warwickshire Regt. (M.B.E.), unsuccessfully contested Normanton Div. of W. Riding of Yorkshire (C) Feb. 1947; MP for S-W Div. of Wolverhampton 1950-74, since when for South Down (UUUC): *m.* 1952, Margaret Pamela, da. of Lt.-Col. L. E. Wilson; *cr.* MBE (Mil.) 1943, PC 1960. 33, *South Eaton Place, SW1.*

PRENTICE, Rt. Hon. Reginald Ernest, *MP*, son of Ernest George Edward Prentice, of 6, Hunter Rd., Thornton Heath, Surrey; *b.* 1923; ed. at Whitgift Sch., and London Sch. of Economics (B.Sc.Econ.); a JP of Croydon; Member of Staff, Transport and General Workers' Union 1950-57; Min. of State for Education and Science 1964-66, Min. of Public Building and Works 1966-67, and Min. of Overseas Development 1967-69; Sec. of State for Education and Science 1974-75, since when Min. for Overseas Development; MP for East Ham (North) (Lab.) 1957-74, since when of Newham (NE); 1939-45 War as Lt. RA in Italy: *m.* 1948, Joan Godwin of S. Norwood, SE25; *cr.* 1966. 5, *Hollingsworth Rd., Croydon, CRO 5RP.*

PRIOR, Rt. Hon. James Michael Leathes, *MP*, son of the late Charles Bolingbroke Leathes Prior; *b.* 1927; ed. at Charterhouse, and Pembroke Coll., Camb. (BA); late Lt. R. Norfolk Regt.; Farmer and Land Agent in Norfolk and Suffolk since 1951; PPS to Pres. of Board of Trade 1963, to Min. of Power 1963-64, and to Rt. Hon. Edward Heath, MBE, MP, Leader of Opposition 1965-70; Min. of Agriculture, Fisheries & Food 1970-72, and Lord President of the Council, and Leader of the House of Commons 1972-74; Opposition Spokesman on Home Affairs, 1974, since when on Employment; MP for Lowestoft (C) since 1959; *m.* 1954, Jane Primrose Gifford, da. of the late Air Vice-Marshal Oswyn George William Gifford Lywood, CB, CBE; *cr.* 1970. *Old Hall, Brampton, Beccles, Suffolk;* 36, *Morpeth Mansions, SW1; MCC.*

PYM, Rt. Hon. Francis Leslie, MC, *MP*, son of the late Leslie Ruthven Pym, MP; *b.* 1922; ed. at Eton, and Magdalene Coll., Camb.; DL for Cambridgeshire; Assist. Govt. Whip 1962-64, Opposition Dep. Ch. Whip 1967-70, Parl. Sec. to Treasury and Govt. Ch. Whip, 1970-73, and Sec. of State for N.I. 1973-74; MP for Cambridgeshire (C) since 1961; 1939-45 War as Capt. 9th Queen's

R. Lancers in Africa and Italy (despatches twice, MC): *m.* 1949, Valerie Fortune, da. of Francis John Heaton Daglish; *cr.* 1970. *Everton Park, Sandy, Beds.; Carlton, and Cavalry Clubs.*

RADCLIFFE, Rt. Hon. Viscount, *G.B.E.*; *cr.* 1949.

RAMGOOLAM, Rt. Hon. Sir Seewoosagur, son of Chaudhury Ramgoolam; *b.* 1900; ed. at Roy. Coll. Curepipe, and Univ. Coll., London (Hon. Fellow 1971); Hon. LLD Delhi; LRCP London and MRCS England; Mayor of Port Louis 1958; MLA Mauritius 1940 and MEC 1948; Min. of Finance 1960-68, Ch. Min. 1961-64, and Premier 1965-68, since when Prime Min.; Grand Cross Nat. Order of Malagasy Republic, Medal of National Assembly of France, Grand Cross of Republic of Senegal, Grand Cross of Order of Merit of Central African Republic, Grand Cross National de Benin of Togo, Grand Officer of the Legion of Honour of France; UN prize for Outstanding Achievements in field of Human Rights: *m.* 1941, Sahoduth, da. of the late Taccordial Ramjoorwon; *cr.* Knt, 1965, PC 1971. 85 *Desforges St., Port-Louis, Mauritius.*

RAMSDEN, Rt. Hon. James Edward, son of Capt. Edward Ramsden, MC, of Breckamore Hall, nr. Ripon; *b.* 1923; ed. at Eton, and Trin. Coll., Oxford (M.A.); Parl. Under-Sec. of State for War and Financial Sec., War Office 1960-63, and Sec. of State for War 1963-64; a Dir. of Prudential Insurance Co.; 1939-45 War as Lt. KRRC attached Rifle Bd. in NW Europe; MP for Harrogate Div. of W. Riding of Yorks. (C) 1954-74: *m.* 1949, Juliet Barbara Anna, yst. da. of Sir Charles Edward Ponsonby, TD, 1st Bt.; *cr.* 1963. *Old Sleningford Hall, Ripon, Yorks.;* 10, *Cleaver Sq., SE11; Brooks's Club.*

RAMSEY OF CANTERBURY, Rt. Rev. and Rt. Hon. Baron, *DD; cr.* 1956.

RATHCAVAN, Rt. Hon. Baron; *cr.* (Ireland) 1921 (N. Ireland) 1922, and (UK) 1937.

RAWLINSON, Rt. Hon. Sir Peter Anthony Grayson, *QC*, *MP*, son of Lt.-Col. Arthur Richard Rawlinson, OBE, of Ferring, Sussex [see Grayson, Bt.]; *b.* 1919; ed. at Downside, and at Christ's Coll., Camb.; Bar. Inner Temple 1946, and QC 1959; Recorder of Salisbury 1961-62, and Solicitor-Gen. 1962-64; Attorney Gen. 1970-74; Vice-Chm. of Senate of the Four Inns of Court 1974; 1939-45 War as Maj. Irish Guards in N. Africa (despatches); MP for Epsom Div. of Surrey (C) 1955-74, since when of Epsom and Ewell: *m.* 1st, 1940, Haidee Kavanagh, from whom he obtained a divorce 1954 (m. annulled by Sacred Rota Rome); 2ndly, 1954, Elaine, da. of the late Vincent Dominguez, of Rhode Island, USA; *cr.* Knt. 1962, PC 1964. 4, *Paper Buildings, Temple, EC4; White's Club.*

REA, Rt. Hon. Baron, *O.B.E.*; *cr.* 1962.

REDMAYNE, Rt. Hon. Baron, DSO, TD; *cr.* 1959.

REES, Rt. Hon. Merlyn, *MP*, son of the late Levi Daniel Rees, of Cilfynydd, S. Wales; *b.* 1920; ed. at Harrow Weald Gram. Sch., Goldsmiths' Coll., London Univ., and L.S.E.; 1939-45 War as Sqdn.-Ldr. RAF; Teacher in Economics and History, Harrow Weald Gram. Sch. 1949-60, Organised Festival of Labour 1960-62, Lecturer in Economics, Luton coll. of Tech. 1962-63; PPS to Chancellor of Exchequer 1964, Parl. Under-Sec. of State MOD (Army) 1965-66, Parl. Under-Sec. of State, MOD (RAF) 1966-68, and Parl. Under-Sec. of State, Home Office 1968-70; Sec. of State for N. Ireland since 1974: MP for S. Leeds (Lab.) since 1973: *m.* 1949, Colleen Faith, da. of Henry Faith Cleveley, of Kenton, Middx.; *cr.* 1974. 50, *Cedar Drive, Hatch End, Pinner, Middx.*

REIGATE, Rt. Hon. Baron; *cr.* 1961.

RENTON, Rt. Hon. Sir David Lockhart-Mure, *KBE, TD, QC, MP*, son of the late Maurice Waugh Renton, M.D., C.M., D.P.H.; *b.* 1908; ed. at Oundle, and at Univ. Coll., Oxford (BCL, MA); Bar. Lincoln's Inn 1933, Member of Bar Council 1939, QC 1954, and a Bencher 1962; a Member of Senate of Inns of Court 1967-71; a DL of Huntingdon and Peterborough; Parl. Sec., Min. of Fuel and Power 1955-57, and of Min. of Power 1957-58, Joint Parl. Under-Sec. of State, Home Office 1958-61, Min. of State, Home Office 1961-62; Recorder of Rochester 1963-68, and of Guildford 1968-71; Pres. Conservation Soc. 1970-71; a Member, Commn. on the Constitution 1971-73; Chm. of Cttee. on the Preparation of Legislation 1973-75; 1939-45 War as Maj. RA; MP for Hunts (C) since 1945: *m.* 1947, Claire Cicely, yst. da. of the late Walter Atholl Duncan; *cr.* PC 1962, KBE (Civil) 1964. *Moat House, Abbots Ripton, Huntingdon;* 1, *Westminster Gdns., Marsham St., SW1; Carlton, and Pratt's Clubs.*

RHODES, *Rt. Hon. Baron, KG, DFC; cr.* 1969.

RHYL, *Rt. Hon. Baron, OBE; cr.* 1955.

RICHMOND, *Rt. Hon. Mr. Justice* (*Sir* Clifford Parris), son of Howard Parris Richmond, QC; *b.* 1914; ed. at Wanganui Collegiate Sch., Victoria Univ., Wellington, NZ, and Auckland Univ. (LLM); Bar. and Solicitor NZ 1936; a Partner in legal firm of Buddle, Richmond & Co., Auckland 1946-60, and a Judge of Supreme Court of NZ 1960-72, since when Judge of Court of Appeal, NZ; 1939-45 War as Maj. 2NZEF in N. Africa and Italy: *m.* 1938, Valerie Jean, da. of Nicholson Hamilton; *cr.* Knt. 1972, PC 1973. 19, *Lower Watt St., Wadestown, Wellington, NZ; Wellington (NZ) Club.*

RIPPON, *Rt. Hon.* (Aubrey) Geoffrey (Federick), QC, MP, son of the late Arthur Ernest Sydney Rippon, of Surbiton; *b.* 1924; ed. at King's Coll., Taunton, and at Brasenose Coll., Oxford (Hon. Fellow 1972); Bar. Middle Temple 1948, and QC 1904; Councillor of Surbiton 1945-54 (Mayor 1951-52), a Member of London Co. Council 1952-61, Leader of Conservative Party Group 1957 59, PPS to Min. of Housing and Local Govt. 1956-57, and to Min. of Defence 1957-59, Parliamentary Sec. to Min. of Aviation 1959-61, Joint Parliamentary Sec., Min. of Housing and Local Govt. 1961-62, and Min. of Public Building and Works 1962-64; Min. of Tech. June to July 1970, Chancellor of the Duchy of Lancaster 1970-72, and Sec. of State for the Environment 1972-74; MP for Norwich South (C) 1955-64 (Cabinet 1963-64 and 1970-74), and for Hexham since 1966: *m.* 1946, Ann Leyland, da. of Donald Yorke, MC, of Prenton, Ches.; *cr.* 1962. *Ellwood House, Barrasford, Hexham, Northumberland; Carlton; White's and Pratt's Clubs, and MCC.*

ROBENS OF WOLDINGHAM, *Rt. Hon. Baron; cr.* 1951.

ROBINSON, *Rt. Hon.* Kenneth, son of the late Clarence Robinson, of Latchford House, Warrington, Lancs.; *b.* 1911; ed. at Oundle; a Co. Sec. 1946-49, Assist. Govt. Whip 1950-51, and Opposition Whip 1951-54; a Member of Exec. Cttee. of National Trust 1951-64, Vice-Pres. of National Assocn. for Mental Health 1958-64, Min. of Health 1964-68, and Min. for Planning and Land, Min. of Housing and Local Govt. 1968-69; Dir. Social Policy BSC 1970-72, Man. Dir. Personnel, BSC 1972-74; Chm. English Nat. Opera since 1972, and of London Transport Exec. since 1975; 1939-45 War as Lt.-Cdr. RNVR, in Mediterranean, Far East, and Pacific; MP for N. Div. of St. Pancras (Lab.) 1949-70: *m.* 1941, Helen Elizabeth, da. of Frederick Hartnoll Edwards; *cr.* 1964. 12, *Grove Terr., NW5.*

RODGERS, *Rt. Hon.* William Thomas, *MP,* son of William Arthur Rodgers; *b.* Oct. 28th, 1928; ed. at Magdalen Coll., Oxford; Borough Councillor, St. Marylebone 1958-62; MP for Stockton-on-Tees (Lab.) 1962-74, since when of Teesside, Stockton; Parly Under-Sec. of State Dept. of Econ. Affairs 1964-67, Leader of UK delegation to Council of Europe and Assembly of WEU 1967-68, Minister of State Board of Trade 1968-69, Treasury 1969-70, Chm. of Expenditure Cttee. on Trade and Industry 1971-74; Minister of State, Min. of Defence since 1974: *m.* 1955, Silvia, da. of Hirsch Szulman; author of "Hugh Gaitskell 1906-63" 1964; *cr.* 1975. 48, *Patshull Rd., NW5.*

ROSKILL, *Rt. Hon. Lord Justice* (*Sir* Eustace Wentworth), son of the late John Roskill, KC; *b.* 1911; ed. at Winchester, and Exeter Coll., Oxford (MA, Hon. Fellow); Bar. Middle Temple 1933, QC 1953, and Bencher 1961; Dep. Chm. of Hants Quarter Sessions 1951-60, and Chm. 1960-71; a Judge of High Court of Justice (Queen's Bench Div.) 1962-71, since when a Lord Justice of Appeal; Vice-Chm. Parole Board

1967-69; Chm. 3rd London Airport Commn. 1968-70; Pres. Senate of Four Inns of Court 1972-74; DL, of Hants.: *m.* 1947, Elisabeth Wallace, da. of the late Thomas Frame Jackson; *cr.* Knt. 1962, PC 1971. *Heatherfield, Newtown, Newbury, Berks.; New Court, Temple, EC4; Reform Club.*

ROSS, *Rt. Hon.* William, *MBE, MP,* son of William Henry Ross, of Ayr: *b.* 1911; ed. at Ayr Acad., and at Glasgow Univ. (MA); Sec. of State for Scotland 1964-70, and again since 1974; 1939-45 War as Maj. Signals (MBE); MP for Kilmarnock Div. of Ayrshire and Bute (Lab.) since (Dec.) 1946: *m.* 1948, Elizabeth Jane Elma, da. of J. Aitkenhead, of Ayr; *cr.* 1964. 10, *Chapelpark Rd., Ayr.*

ROWLING, *Rt. Hon.* Wallace Edward, son of Arthur Rowling; *b.* 1927; ed. at Nelson Coll., NZ (MA); MP for Buller (Lab.) 1962; Min. of Finance NZ 1972-74, since when Prime Min. and Min. of Foreign Affairs: *m.* 1951, Glen Elna, da. of Capt. John Merlin Reeves; *cr.* 1974. *The Residence,* 10, *Lohia St., Khandallah, Wellington, NZ.*

RUSSELL OF KILLOWEN, *Rt. Hon. Baron; cr.* 1975.

SACHS, *Rt. Hon. Sir* Eric, *MBE, TD,* son of Edwin O. Sachs, FRSE, of 5, Ulster Terr., Regents Park, NW1; *b.* 1898, ed. at Charterhouse, and Ch. Ch. Oxford (MA, Hon. Student 1971); Bar, Middle and Inner Temples 1921, KC 1938, Bencher Middle Temple 1947, and Treas. 1967; Recorder of Dudley 1938-43, and of City of Stoke-on-Trent 1943-54, Gresham Prof. of Law 1946-50, a Member of Bar Council and Treasurer 1946-53, a Member of Legal Aid Scheme Making Cttee. 1948-53, and Leader of Oxford Circuit 1952-54; a Judge of High Court of Justice (Probate Div. 1954-60, and Queen's Bench Div. 1960-66), and a Lord Justice of Appeal 1966-72; 1914-18 War as Lt. RA (wounded), 1939-45 War as Brig.: *m.* 1934, the late Janet Margaret, da. of the late Baron Goddard; *cr.* MBE (Mil.) 1942, Knt. 1954, PC 1966. *Walland Oast, Wadhurst, Sussex; Athenæum, and Hurlingham Clubs.*

ST. ALDWYN, *Rt. Hon. Earl, KBE, TD; cr.* 1959.

SALMON, *Rt. Hon. Baron; cr.* 1964.

SANDYS [see Duncan-Sandys].

SCARMAN, *Rt. Hon. Lord Justice* (*Sir* Leslie George), *OBE,* son of the late George Charles Scarman; *b.* 1911; ed. at Radley, and Brasenose Coll., Oxford (MA); Hon. LLD, Exeter, Glasgow, London, Warwick, and Freiburg; Bar. Middle Temple 1936; QC 1957; a Judge of High Court of Justice (Probate, Divorce and Admiralty Div.) 1961-72, since when a Lord Justice of Appeal; Chm., Law Commn. 1965-72; 1939-45 War as Wing Cdr. RAFVR (OBE): *m.* 1947, Ruth Clement, da. of the late Clement Wright; *cr.* OBE (Mil) 1945, Knt. 1961, PC 1972. 77, *Cadogan Sq., SW1.*

SELKIRK, *Rt. Hon. the Earl of, GCMG, GBE, AFC, QC; cr.* 1955.

SELLERS, *Rt. Hon. Sir* Frederic Aked, *MC,* son of the late John Shuttleworth Sellers, of Liverpool; *b.* 1893; ed. at Silcoates Sch., and at Liverpool Univ. (BA 1913, LLB 1920, Hon. LLD 1956); Bar. Gray's Inn 1919, a KC 1935, a Bencher 1938, and Treasurer 1952; Recorder of Bolton 1938-46, and a Judge of High Court of Justice (Queen's Bench Div.) 1946-57, and a Lord Justice of Appeal 1957-68; Chm. of Court of Govs. of Mill Hill Sch. 1951-68; Chm. of Criminal Law Revision Cttee. 1959-69; 1914-18 War as Capt. King's Regt. (MC and two bars): *m.* 1917, Grace, da. of the late William Malin, JP of Derby; *cr.* Knt. 1946, PC 1957. *Highwood Lodge, Mill Hill, NW7; Reform Club.*

SHACKLETON, *Rt. Hon. Baron, KG, OBE; cr.* 1966.

SHAKESPEARE, *Rt. Hon. Sir* Geoffrey Hithersay, *Bt.; cr.* 1945.

SHAW, *Rt. Hon. Lord Justice* (*Sir* Sebag), son of Henry Shaw; *b.* 1906; ed. at Univ. Coll., London (LLB); Bar. Gray's Inn 1931, QC 1962, Bencher 1967; Recorder of Ipswich 1958-68, and a Judge of High Court of Justice (Queen's Bench Div.) 1968-75, since when a Lord Justice of Appeal: *m.* 1928, Sally, da. of Oscar Baumgart; *cr.* Knt. 1968, PC 1975. 69, *Wynnstay Gdns., W8.*

SHAWCROSS, *Rt. Hon. Baron, GBE, QC; cr.* 1959.

SHEARER, *Rt. Hon.* Hugh Lawson, son of James Shearer; *b.* 1923; ed. at St. Simon's Coll., Jamaica; Hon. LLD, Howard Univ., Wash., DC; a Member Kingston and St. Andrew Corpn., Jamaica 1947-51; MHR Jamaica 1955-59; Dep. Chm. Jamaica Mission to UN 1962-66; Min. without Portfolio and Leader of Govt. Business in Senate 1962-67, and Prime Min., Min. of External Affairs, and Min. of Defence, Jamaica 1967-72, since when Leader of Opposition; 1st Dep. Leader and a Member Central Exec. Jamaica Labour Party, and Island Supervisor and Vice-Pres. Bustamante Industrial Trade Union; *cr.* 1969. 7, *Retirement Rd., Kingston 5, Jamaica.*

SHEPHERD, *Rt. Hon.* Baron; *cr.* 1965.

SHINWELL, *Rt. Hon.* Baron, CH; *cr.* 1945.

SHORE, *Rt. Hon.* Peter David, son of Capt. R N Shore; *b,* 1924; ed. at Quarry Bank High Sch., Liverpool, and King's Coll., Camb.; PPS to Prime Min. 1965-66, Joint Parl. Sec., Min. of Technology 1966-67, Sec. of State for Economic Affairs 1967-69, and Min. without Portfolio 1969-70; Sec. of State for Trade since 1974; a Member of Fabian Soc.; MP (*Lab.*) for Stepney 1964-74, since when for Tower Hamlets (Stepney and Poplar): *m.* 1948, Elizabeth Catherine Wrong; *cr.* 1967. 23, *Dryburgh Rd., SW15.*

SHORT, *Rt. Hon.* Edward Watson, MP, son of Charles Short, of Warcop, Westmorland; *b.* 1912; ed. at Bede Coll., Durham Univ. (LLB); Opposition Assist. Whip 1955-61, Dep. Ch. Opposition Whip 1962-64, Parl. Sec. to Treasury and Govt. Ch. Whip 1964-66, Postmaster Gen. 1966-68, and Sec. of State for Education and Science 1968-70; Dep. Leader of Labour Party since 1972; Lord Pres. of The Council and Leader of House of Commons since 1974; 1939-45 War as Capt. DLI; MP for Central Newcastle upon Tyne (*Lab.*) since 1951: *m.* 1941, Jennie, da. of Thomas Sewell, of Newcastle upon Tyne; *cr.* 1964. 4, *Patterdale Gdns., Newcaxtle upon Tyne, 7; Howgarth, Westmorland.*

SILKIN, *Rt. Hon.* John Ernest, MP, [see B. Silkin]; *cr.* 1966.

SILKIN, *Rt. Hon.* Samuel Charles, QC, MP, [see B. Silkin]; *cr.* 1974.

SIMON OF GLAISDALE, *Rt. Hon. Baron,; cr.* 1961.

§SIMPSON, *Rt. Hon.* Robert, MB, BCh, son of Samuel Simpson; *b.* 1923; ed. at Ballymena Acad., and Queen's Univ., Belfast (MB, BCh, BAO); Min. for Community Relations, N. Ireland 1969-71; Member of House of Commons NI (*U*) 1953-73 (Parliament suspended March 1972): *m.* 1954, Dorothy Isobel, da. of Robert Strawbridge, MA, DD; *cr.* 1969. *Random Cottage, Craigbilly, Ballymena, co. Antrim; Royal Over Seas League.*

SKRIMSHIRE [see Anderson.]

SLESSER, *Rt. Hon.* Sir Henry (Herman), younger son of the late Ernest Slesser, of Gerrard's Cross, Bucks; *b.* 1883; ed. at Oundle, St. Paul's Sch., and London Univ.; Hon. LLD, Exeter; Bar. Inner Temple 1906, and a KC and a Bencher 1924; a JP for Devon; Solicitor-Gen. Feb. to Nov. 1924, and a Lord Justice of Appeal 1929-40; unsuccessfully contested Leeds, Central Div. (*Lab.*) Nov. 1922 and June and Dec. 1923; sat as M.P. for S.E. Div. thereof Oct. 1924 to June 1929: *m.* 1910, Margaret, *J.P.,* da. of the late Corrie Grant, K.C., formerly M.P. for Rugby Div. of Warwickshire; *cr.* Knt. 1924, PC 1929. *Holcombe House, Moretonhampstead, Newton Abbot, Devon, TQ13 8PW.*

SMITH, *Col. the Rt. Hon. Sir* Reginald Hugh DORMAN-, *G.B.E.,* son of Major Edward Patrick Dorman-Smith, of Bellamont Forest, Cootehill, co. Cavan; *b.* 1899; ed. at Harrow; Lieut.-Col. Gen. Staff and Hon. Col. 5th Batn. Queen's Roy. Regt. (TA); an Alderman of Surrey co. Council 1931-5, and Pres. of National Farmers' Union 1936-37; High Sheriff of Hampshire 1952; Afghan War 1919 with 15th Sikhs; was Min of Agriculture and Fisheries 1939-40, and Gov. of Burma 1941-6; is a KStJ; Burma 1941-2 (despatches); sat as MP for Petersfield Div. of Hampshire (*C*) Nov. 1935 to Feb. 1941: *m.* 1921, Doreen Agnes Edith, da. of Sir John Watson, 2nd Bt. [see Inglefield-Watson, Bt.]; *cr.* Knt. 1937, PC 1939, GBE (Civil) 1941. *Hunters Croft, Grayswood, Haslemere, Surrey.*

SMITH, *Rt. Hon. Sir* Derek Colclough WALKER-, *Bt., T.D., Q.C.; cr.* 1957.

SMITH, [see Hornsby-Smith].

SMYTH, *Brig. the Rt. Hon. Sir* John George, *Bt., VC, MC; cr.* 1962.

SNEDDEN, *Rt. Hon.* Billy Mackie, QC, MP, son of A. Snedden, of Alva, Scotland; *b.* 1926; ed. at Perth State Sch., and W. Aust. Univ. (LLB); Bar. W. Aust. 1951, and Vic. 1955, and QC 1963; Attorney-Gen., Aust. 1963-66, Min. for Immigration 1966-69, and for Labour and Nat. Ser. 1969-71, Treas., Commonwealth of Aust., and Dep. Leader of Liberal Party 1971-72 since when Leader of Opposition and Leader of Liberal Party; MHR Aust. since 1955 (Leader of House 1966-71): *m.* 1950, Joy, da. of J. Forsyth; *cr.* 1972. 22, *Pine Cres., Ringwood, Victoria, Australia* 3134; *Naval and Military, and Melbourne Scots (Councillor) (Melbourne) Clubs.*

SOAMES, *Rt. Hon. Sir* (Arthur) Christopher (John), *GCMG, GCVO, CBE,* son of the late Capt. Arthur Granville Soames, OBE, of Hays Lodge, Chesterfield Hill, W1; *b.* 1920; ed. at Eton, and RMC; Assist. Mil. Attaché, British Embassy, Paris 1946-47, and PPS to Prime Min. (Rt. Hon. Sir Winston Churchill) 1952-55, Parl. Under-Sec. of State, Air Min. 1955-57, Parliamentary and Financial Sec., Admiralty 1957-58, Sec. of State for War 1958-60, and Min. of Agriculture, Fisheries and Food 1960-64; Ambassador to France 1968-72, since when a Member of European Commn. of EEC, and a Vice-Pres. (external relations), of enlarged EEC since 1973; Pres. of Roy. Agric. Soc. of England 1973; 1939-45 War as Capt. Coldm. Gds., in Middle East, Italy and France (French Croix de Guerre); Grand Officer Legion of Honour; MP for Bedford (*C*) 1950-66: *m.* 1947, the Hon. Mary, *MBE,* da. of the late Rt. Hon. Sir Winston Leonard Spencer-Churchill, KG OM, TD [see D. Marlborough, colls]; *cr.* CBE (Civil) 1955, PC 1958, GCMG 1972, GCVO 1972. *Castle Mill House, North Warnborough, Basingstoke, Hants; White's, Carlton, and Portland Clubs.*

STABLE, *Rt. Hon. Sir* Wintringham Norton, *MC,* son of Daniel Wintringham Stable, of Plas Llwyn Owen, Montgomeryshire; *b.* 1888; ed. at Winchester, and at Ch. Ch., Oxford (MA; Hon. Student 1960); Bar. Middle Temple 1913, KC 1935, and a Bencher 1938; 1914-18 War with Montgomeryshire Yeo., and R. Welch Fusiliers (TF); a Judge of High Court of Justice (King's Bench Div.) 1938-68; Chm. of Quarter Sessions, Merioneth, 1944-67, and Shropshire, 1947-67: *m.* 1916, Lucie Haden, da. of Francis Ford Freeman, of Tavistock, Devon, and widow of R. B. Murphy; *cr.* Knt. 1938, PC 1965. *Plas Llwyn Owen, Llanbrynmair, Montgomeryshire SY19 7BE.*

STAMP, *Rt. Hon. Lord Justice* (Sir (Edward) Blanshard, son of the late Alfred Edward Stamp, CB; *b.* 1905; ed. at Gresham's Sch., Holt, and at Trin. Coll., Camb. (MA); Bar. Inner Temple 1929, Bencher Lincoln's Inn 1956; Junior Counsel to Commrs. of Inland Revenue (Chancery Div.) 1954-64, and to HM Treasury (Chancery Div.), Board of Trade, etc. 1960-64, and a Judge of High Court of Justice (Chancery Div.) 1964-71, since when a Lord Justice of Appeal; *m.* 1st, 1934, Mildred Evelyn, who *d.* 1971, da. of John Marcus Poer O'Shee, of Gardenmorris, co. Waterford; 2ndly, 1973, Mrs. Pamela Joan Peters; *cr.* Knt. 1964, PC 1971. 30, *Hanover House, St. John's Wood, NW8; United Oxford and Cambridge University, and Garrick Clubs.*

STEPHENSON, *Rt. Hon. Lord Justice* (Sir John Frederick Eustace), son of the late Sir Guy Stephenson, CB. [E. Shrewsbury, colls.]; *b.* 1910; ed. at Winchester, and New Coll., Oxford (MA); Bar. Inner Temple 1934 and QC 1960; Recorder of Bridgwater 1954-59, and of Winchester 1959-62, Diocesan Chancellor of Peterborough 1956-62, and of Winchester 1958-62 and Dep. Chm. of Dorset Quarter Sessions 1962-72; a Judge of High Court of Justice (Queen's Bench Div.) 1962-71, since when a Lord Justice of Appeal; 1939-45 War with RE and as Lt.-Col. Intelligence Corps: *m.* 1951, Hon. (Frances) Rose Asquith, yr. da. of Baron Asquith of Bishopstone (ext.); *cr.* Knt. 1962, PC 1971. 30, *Drayton Gardens, SW10; Hurlingham Club, and MCC.*

STEVENSON, *Rt. Hon. Mr. Justice* (Sir (Aubrey) Melford Steed), son of the late Rev. J. G. Stevenson; *b.* 1902; ed. at Dulwich Coll., and London Univ. (LLB); Bar. Inner Temple 1925, KC 1943, Bencher 1950, and

Treas. since 1972; Dep. Judge Advocate, Office of Judge Advocate Gen. 1940-45, and Recorder of Rye 1944-51 and of City of Cambridge 1952-57; a Judge of High Court of Justice (Queen's Bench Div.) since 1957, and Presiding Judge of SE Circuit since 1970: *m.* 1947, Rosalind Monica, da. of the late Orlando Henry Wagner; *cr.* Knt. 1957, PC 1973. *94, Old Church St., SW3; Truncheons, Winchelsea, Sussex; Garrick Club.*

STEWART, *Rt. Hon.* (Robert) Michael (Maitland) *CH, MP,* son of the late Robert Wallace Stewart; *b.* 1906; ed. at Christ's Hospital, and at St. John's Coll., Oxford (Hon. Fellow); Hon. LLD Leeds; a Freeman of Hammersmith; a Lord Commr. of HM Treasury 1945-46; Comptroller and Vice-Chamberlain of HM Household 1946-47, Under-Sec. of State for War 1947-51, and Parl. Sec., Min. of Supply, May to Oct. 1951; Sec. of State for Education and Science 1964-65, Sec. of State for Foreign Affairs 1965-66, Sec. of State for Economic Affairs 1966-67, and First Sec. of State 1967-68, Sec. of State for Foreign Affairs 1968, and Secretary of State for Foreign and Commonwealth Affairs 1968-70; 1939-45 War with Intelligence Corps, and as Capt. Army Educational Corps; MP for E. Fulham *(Lab.)* 1945-55, for Fulham 1955-74, since when Hammersmith (Fulham): *m.* 1941, Mary Elizabeth, *Baroness Stewart of Alvechurch* (Life Baroness), da. of Herbert Birkinshaw, of Barnt Green, Worcs.; *cr.* PC, 1964, CH 1969. *11, Felden St., SW6.*

STODART, *Rt. Hon.* (James) Anthony, *MP,* yr. son of the late Col. Thomas Stodart, CIE, IMS; *b.* 1916; ed. at Wellington; a farmer; Jt. Parl. Under-Sec. of State, Scottish Office 1963-64; Parl. Sec. Min. of Agric., Fisheries and Food 1970-72; Min. of State Min. of Agric., Fisheries and Food 1972-74; MP for Edinburgh West *(C)* since 1959: *m.* 1940, Hazel Jean, da. of Ronald James Usher, DSC, RN [see Usher Bt., colls.]; *cr.* 1974. *Lorimers, N. Berwick, E. Lothian; Caledonian, and New (Edinburgh) Clubs.*

STONEHOUSE, *Rt. Hon.* John Thomson, *MP,* son of William Mitchell Stonehouse, of Southampton; *b.* 1925; ed. at Taunton's Sch., Southampton, and London Sch. of Economics, London Univ.; Parl. Sec. Ministry of Aviation 1964-66, Parl. Under-Sec. of State for Colonies 1966-67, Min. of Aviation 1967, Min. of State, Min. of Tech. 1967-68, Postmaster Gen. 1968-70, and Min. of Posts & Telecommunications 1969-70; MP for Wednesbury *(Lab.)* 1957-74, since when Walsall (North): *m.* 1948, Barbara, da. of Robert Smith; *cr.* 1968. *House of Commons, SW1A 0AA; RAC.*

STOPFORD, *Rt. Rev. and Rt. Hon.* Robert Wright, *KCVO, CBE, DD,* son of John W. Stopford, of Garston, Liverpool: *b.* 1901; ed. at Liverpool Coll., and at Hertford Coll. Oxford (MA, Hon. Fellow 1956); Hon. DCL Durham 1951; DD Lambeth 1957; Hon. DD London 1965; Fellow King's Coll. London 1965; Hon. Fellow Coll. of Preceptors 1965; Prin. of Trin. Coll. Kandy, Ceylon 1934-40 and of Achimota Coll. Gold Coast 1940-45, and R. of Chipping Barnet 1946-48; Moderator of Church Training Colls. 1947-55 and Gen. Sec. Nat. Soc. and Schs. Council 1952-55; appointed a Chap. to HM 1952, Select Preacher Oxford 1959 and 1973, and Camb. 1963, and Prelate of Order of the British Empire and Dean of the Chapel's Royal 1961-73; an Hon. Canon of Canterbury 1951-56; Bishop of Fulham (Suffragan Bishop for Diocese of London) 1955-1956, 33rd Bishop of Peterborough 1951-61, 114th Bishop of London 1961-73 and Vicar-Gen. of Jerusalem 1974-75, Bishop Designate of Bermuda 1976: *m.* 1st, 1935, Winifred Sophia, who *d.* 1942, da. of W. Morgan, of Belfast; 2ndly Kathleen Mary, who *d.* 1973, da. of H. Holt, of Lytham, Lancs.; *cr.* CBE (Civil) 1949, PC, 1961, KCVO, 1973. *Upper House, Up Sombour.e, Stockbridge, Hants, SO20 6RD.*

STOTT, *Rt. Hon.* George Gordon, *QC (Lord Stott); cr.* 1964. [See " LORDS OF SESSION.]

STOW HILL, *Rt. Hon. Baron, QC; cr.* 1948.

STRATHCLYDE, *Rt. Hon. Baron; cr.* 1953.

STRAUSS, *Rt. Hon.* George Russell, *M.P.,* son of the late Arthur Strauss, M.P.; *b.* 1901; ed. at Rugby; was Parliamentary Private Sec. to Min. of Transport 1929-31, Parliamentary Sec., Min. of Transport 1945-47, and Min. of Supply 1947-51; MP

for Vauxhall Div. of Lambeth *(Lab.)* 1929-31, and 1934-1950, and since 1950: *m.* 1932, Patricia, da. of F. O'Flynn; *cr.* 1947. *1, Palace Green, W.8; Naylands, Slaugham, Sussex.*

§STRONGE, *Rt. Hon. Sir* Charles Norman Lockhart, Bt., *M.C.; cr.* 1946.

SUMMERSKILL, *Rt. Hon. Baroness, CH; cr.* 1949.

§TAYLOR, *Rt. Hon.* John David, son of George D. Taylor; *b.* 1937; ed. at Roy. Sch., Armagh and Queen's Univ., Belfast (BSc); AMICEI, AMInstHE; Member of House of Commons, NI *(U)* 1965-73 (Parliament suspended March 1972); Parl. Sec. to Min. of Home Affairs, N. Ireland 1969-70, and Min. of State for Home Affairs 1970-72; Member of NI Assembly *(UUUC)* 1973-74, NI Convention since 1975: *m.* 1970, Mary Frances Todd; *cr.* 1970. *4, Mullinure Park, Portadown Rd., Armagh.*

THATCHER, *Rt. Hon.* Margaret Hilda, *MP,* da. of Alfred Roberts; *b.* 1925; ed. at Kesteven and Grantham Girls' Sch., and Somerville Coll., Oxford (MA, BSc); Bar. Lincoln's Inn 1953; Sec. of State for Education & Science 1970-74; Leader of the Opposition since 1975; MP for Finchley *(C)* 1959-74. since then for Barnet (Finchley): *m.* 1951, Denis Thatcher; *cr.* 1970. *House of Commons, SW1A 0AA; Carlton Club.*

THOMAS, *Rt. Hon.* Peter John Mitchell, *QC, MP,* only son of the late David Thomas, solicitor; of Llanrwst, Denbighshire; *b.* 1920; ed. at Epworth Coll., Rhyl, and at Jesus Coll., Oxford (MA); Bar. Middle Temple 1947, and QC 1965; PPS to Solicitor-Gen. 1955-59, Parl. Sec., Min. of Labour 1959-61, Parl. Under-Sec. of State for Foreign Affairs 1961-63, and Min. of State for Foreign Affairs 1963-64; Chm. of Conservative Party Orgn. 1970-72, and Sec. of State for Wales 1970-74; a JP of Cheshire and Denbighshire, and Dep. Chm. of Cheshire Quarter Sessions and Denbighshire Quarter Sessions 1965-70; 1939-45 War with RAF (prisoner); MP for Conway *(C)* 1951-66, Hendon South 1970-74, since when for Barnet (Hendon South): *m.* 1947, Frances Elizabeth Tessa, only da. of Basil Dean, CBE [E. Warwick); *cr.* 1964. *145, Kennington Rd., SE11; Bath, Llanbedr-y-Cennin, Conway, Caernarvonshire; Carlton Club.*

THOMAS, *Rt. Hon.* (Thomas) George, *MP,* son of the late Zachariah Thomas; *b.* 1909; ed. at Tonypandy Gram. Sch. and Univ. Coll., Southampton; Vice-Pres. Methodist Conference 1959-60, Parl. Under-Sec. of State, Home Office 1964-66, Min. of State, Welsh Office 1966-67, and Commonwealth Office 1967-68, and Sec. of State, Welsh Office 1968-70; Dep. Speaker and Chm. of Ways and Means, since 1974; Freeman of Borough of Rhondda 1970; MP for Central Cardiff *(Lab.)* 1945-50, since when for Cardiff West; *cr.* 1968. *173, King George Drive, Cardiff.*

THOMSON, *Rt. Hon.* George Morgan, son of the late James Thomson, of Monifieth, Angus; *b.* 1921; ed. at Grove Acad., Dundee; Hon. LLD Dundee; Hon. D.Litt. Heriot Watt; MP for E. Div. of Dundee *(Lab.)* 1952-72; Min. of State, Foreign Office 1964-66; Chancellor of Duchy of Lancaster 1966-67, Jt. Min. of State, Foreign Office 1967, Sec. of State for Commonwealth Affairs 1967-68, Min. without Portfolio 1968-69, and Chancellor of Duchy of Lancaster 1969-70; Chm. David Davies Inst. of Internat. Affairs since 1970; a Member of Comm. of European Communities, with special responsibility for Regional Policy since 1973; and of enlarged EEC (Regional Policy) since 1973: *m.* 1948, Grace, da. of Cunningham Jenkins, of Glasgow; *cr.* PC 1966. *Commission of European Communities, 200, Rue de la Loi, Brussels; Europe House Club.*

THORNEYCROFT, *Rt. Hon. Baron; cr.* 1951.

THORPE, *Rt. Hon.* (John) Jeremy, *MP,* son of the late John Henry Thorpe, OBE, KC, JP [see Norton-Griffiths. Bt.], *b.* 1929; ed. at Eton, and Trin. Coll., Oxford; Pres. of Oxford Union 1951; Bar. Inner Temple 1954; Leader of Parl. Liberal Party since 1967; MP for N. Devon *(L)* since 1959: *m* 1968 1st, Caroline, who *d.* 1970, da. of Warwick Allpass, of 3, Beeches Wood, Kingswood, Surrey; 2ndly, 1973, Maria Donata Nanetta Paulina Gustava Erwina Wilhelmina (Marion), da. of the late Erwin

Stein, and formerly wife of 7th Earl of Harewood; *cr.* 1967. *c/o House of Commons, SW1; Reform and National Liberal Clubs.*

§TOPPING, *Rt. Hon.* Walter William Buchanan, *Q.C.*, son of Walter Topping of Belfast ; *b.* 1908 ; ed. at Rossall, and at Queen's Univ., Belfast ; Bar. N. Ireland 1930, and a K.C. 1946 ; was a Member of House of Commons, N. Ireland 1945-60, Ch. Whip 1946-56, and Min. of Home Affairs 1956-60, since when Recorder of Belfast : *m.* 1933, Maureen Osborne, da. of Osborne Gallaher ; *cr.* 1956. *Windyridge, Dunmurry, co. Antrim.*

TRANMIRE, *Rt. Hon.* Baron, *KBE, MC; cr.* 1955.

TREDGOLD, *Rt. Hon. Sir* Robert Clarkson, *K.C.M.G.*, son of the late Hon. Sir Clarkson Henry Tredgold ; *b.* 1899 ; ed. at Prince Edward Sch., Salisbury, S. Rhodesia, at Rondebosch High Sch., and at Hertford Coll., Oxford (Hon. Fellow 1961) ; Hon. LL.D. Witwatersrand 1953 ; Bar. Inner Temple 1923, and a K.C. S. Rhodesia 1936 ; elected a M.L.A., S. Rhodesia 1933 ; appointed Min. of Justice and Defence 1936, Min. of Native Affairs 1941, a Judge of High Court 1943, Ch. Justice 1940, and Ch. Justice, Federation of Rhodesia and Nyasaland 1955 ; resigned 1960 ; European War 1918: *m.* 1925, Lorna Davis, who *d.* 1972 da. of the late Rev. J. D. Keilor; *cr.* CMG 1943, Knt. 1951, KCMG 1955, PC 1957, *Kalanyoni, PO Box* 3545, *Salisbury, Rhodesia.*

TREND, *Rt. Hon.* Baron, *GCB, CVO; cr.* 1972.

TRYON, *Rt. Hon.* Baron, *GCVO, KCB, DSO: cr.* 1971.

TURNER, *Rt. Hon. Sir* Alexander Kingcome, *KBE*, son of the late Joseph Hurst Turner, of Auckland, New Zealand; *b.* 1901; ed. at Auckland Gram. Sch., and at New Zealand Univ. (MA, LLB); Hon. LLD Auckland; Bar. and Solicitor, New Zealand 1922, and a QC 1952; Judge of Supreme Court, New Zealand 1953-62, and a Judge of Court of Appeal 1962-71, and Pres. 1972-73; a Member of Council of Auckland Univ. 1935-59 (Vice-Pres. 1949-50), and Chm. of Research, Massey Agricultural Coll. 1946-53; Co-author of Spencer Bower & Turner on " Law of Estoppel by Representation", " The Doctrine of Res. Judicata", and "The Law of Actionable Misrepresentation": *m.* 1934, Dorothea Frances, da. of Alan Mulgan, of Wellington, New Zealand; *cr.* Knt. 1963, PC 1968, KBE (Civil) 1973. 14, *St. Michael's Cres., Kilburn, Wellington* 5, *New Zealand; Wellington, and Auckland Clubs.*

TWEEDSMUIR OF BELHELVIE, *Rt. Hon. Baroness; cr.* 1974.

VARLEY, *Rt. Hon.* Eric Graham, *MP*, son of Frank Varley, of Poolsbrook, Derbys.; *b.* 1932; ed. at Ruskin Coll., Oxford; Engineer's Turner 1952-55, Mining Industry (Coal) Craftsman 1955-64; Assist. Govt. Whip 1967-68; PPS to PM 1968-69, Min. of State Min. of T. ch. 1969-70, Sec. of State for Energy 1974-75, since when Sec. of State for Industry; MP for Chesterfield (*Lab.*) since 1964: *m.* 1955, Marjorie, da. of Alfred Turner, of Duckmanton, Derbys.; *cr.* 1974. 189, *Middlecroft Rd., Staveley, Chesterfield, Derbys.*

WALKER, *Rt. Hon.* Peter Edward, *MBE, MP*, son of Sydney Walker; *b.* 1932; ed. at Latymer Upper Sch.; Chm. Rose Thomson Young & Co. Ltd., Brokers 1963-70, and Dep. Chm. Slater Walker Securities Ltd. 1964-70; Min. of Housing and Local Govt. June to Oct. 1970, Sec. of State for Environment 1970-72, and Sec. of State for Trade and Industry, 1972-74; MP for Worcester (*C*) since 1961: *m.* 1969, Tessa, da. of Geoffrey Ivan Pout; *cr.* MBE (Civil) 1950, PC 1970. 12, *Cowley St., SW1; Martin Court, Martin Hussingtree, Worcs.; Buck's, Turf, Carlton, and St. Stephen's Clubs.*

WALKER [see Gordon-Walker].

WALKER-SMITH [see Walker-Smith, Bt.].

WAND, *Rt. Rev. and Rt. Hon.* John William Charles, *KCVO, DD*, son of Arthur James Henry Wand; *b.* Jan. 25th, 1885; ed. at King's Sch., Grantham, and St. Edmund Hall, Oxford (B.A. 1st class Theology 1907, M.A. 1911, Hon. D.D. 1934, Hon. Fellow 1938) ; Hon. Fellow Oriel Coll., Oxford 1941, D.Litt. Ripon, U.S.A. 1949 ; S.T.D. Toronto 1947 ; S.T.P. Columbia 1947 ; Hon. D.D. London 1955, and W.

Ontario 1957 ; Fellow of King's Coll., London 1955 ; was Curate of Benwell 1908-11, and of Lancaster 1911-14, V. Choral of Sarum 1914-19, V. of St. Mark's, Sarum 1919-25, Fellow, Dean, and Tutor of Oriel Coll., Oxford 1925-34, Select Preacher at Oxford 1930-32, and Univ. Lecturer in Church History 1931-34 : Senior Chap. (Anglican) 1st Mil. Dist., Australian Mil. Forces 1935-43 ; Sub-Prelate of Order of St. John of Jerusalem 1936 ; a temporary Chap. to Forces 1915-19 ; Hon. Chap. to Forces 1919-22, and since 1925, and of R.N.V.R. since 1947 ; Dean of the Chapels Royal 1945-55 ; appointed Prelate of Order of the British Empire 1946, and Prelate Emeritus thereof 1957 ; consecrated Archbishop of Brisbane and Metropolitan of Queensland 1934 ; translated 72nd Bishop of Bath and Wells 1943, and 112th Bishop of London 1945; ret. 1955; Canon and Treasurer of St. Paul's 1956-69: *m.* 1911, Amy Agnes, who *d.* 1966, da. of William Wiggins, JP; *cr.* PC 1945, KCVO 1955. *Maplehurst Cottage, Maplehurst, Horsham, Sussex.*

WARD OF WITLEY, *Rt. Hon. Viscount ; cr.* 1957.

WATKINSON *Rt. Hon. Viscount, CH; cr.* 1955.

WATT, *Rt. Hon.* Hugh, son of William Watt; *b.* 1912; ed. at Seddon Tech. Coll., NZ; MP Onehunga, NZ, since 1953; Minister of Works, and of Electricity, NZ 1957-60, of Labour and Development 1972-75, since when High Commr. for NZ in UK; Dep. Leader of Labour Party 1963-74, and Dep. P.M. of NZ 1972-74: *m.* 1967, Irene Frances, da. of Percy Hoskins; *cr.* 1974. *c/o New Zealand High Commission, New Zealand House, Haymarket, SW1.*

WATT, *Rt. Hon.* (James) David GIBSON, *MC, MP*, son of the late Maj. James Miller Gibson-Watt, JP, DL, of Doldowlod, Llandrindod Wells; *b.* 1918; ed. at Eton, and Trin. Coll., Camb. (BA); 1939-45 War, as Maj. Welsh Gds., in N. Africa, and Italy (MC, and bar (twice)); a JP and a DL for Radnorshire; PPS to Parl. Under-Sec. of State, War Office 1957, and to Chancellor of the Exchequer 1962-64, Assist. Govt. Whip 1957-59, a Lord Commr. of the Treasury 1959-61, Chm. of Livestock Export Council 1962-74, and Min. of State, Welsh Office 1970-74; MP for Hereford (*C*) since 1956: *m.* 1942, Diana, da. of the late Sir Charles Hambro, KBE, MC; *cr.* 1974. *Doldowlod, Llandrindod Wells, Radnorshire; Boodle's Club.*

WELENSKY, *Rt. Hon. Sir* Roy (Roland), *K.C.M.G.*, son of the late Michael Welensky ; *b.* 1907 ; formerly an Engine Driver ; was a M.L.C., N. Rhodesia 1938-53, and a MEC 1940-53 ; Director of Manpower 1941-45; sometime Leader of N. Rhodesia Labour Party; appointed Chm. of Unofficial Members' Asso. 1946, Min. of Transport and Development, Federation of Rhodesia and Nyasaland 1953, Min. of Transport, Communications and Posts 1954, Dep. Prime Min. and Leader of the Federal Assembly 1955; Prime Min., and Min. of External Affairs 1956-63 (also Min. of Defence 1956-59); Pres. of Federal Party 1956-57, and United Federal Party 1957-63; a Dir. Netherlands Bank of Rhodesia: *m.* 1st, 1928, Elizabeth, who *d.* 1969, da. of W. J. Henderson; 2ndly, 1972, Miriam Valerie, da. of Henry Scott, of Lealholm, Yorks.; *cr.* CMG 1946, Knt. 1953, KCMG 1959, PC 1960. 82, *Queen Elizabeth Rd., Greendale, PO Box* 804, *Salisbury, Rhodesia.*

§WEST, *Rt. Hon.* Henry William, son of the late W. H. West, J.P. ; *b.* 1917 ; ed. at Enniskillen Model Sch. and at Portora Roy. Sch.; a Farmer; N. Ireland Representative on British Wool Marketing Board 1949-58, High Sheriff, co. Fermanagh 1954, and Pres. of Ulster Farmers' Union 1955-56; Min. of Agric., N. Ireland 1960-67, and again 1971-72; Member of House of Commons NI (*U*) 1954-74 (Parliament Suspended March 1972; Member of NI Assembly (*NUUC*) 1973-74 and of NI Convention since 1975: *m.* 1956, Maureen Elizabeth, da. of George Hall, of Enniskillen; *cr.* 1960. *Rossahilly House, Enniskillen, co. Fermanagh.*

WHEATLEY, *Rt. Hon.* Baron; *cr.* 1947.

WHITELAW *Rt. Hon.* William Stephen Ian, *CH, MC, MP*, son of the late William Alexander Whitelaw; *b.* 1918; ed. at Winchester, and Trin. Coll., Camb. (MA); Maj. (ret.) Scots Guards; a Farmer and Landowner in Cum-

THE PRIVY COUNCIL. 1267

berland and Scotland, and a DL of Cumberland; Lord Commr. of the Treasury 1961-62,
and Parl. Sec., Min. of Labour 1962-64;
Opposition Ch. Whip 1964-70, Lord Pres. of
the Council and Leader of House of Commons 1970-72, and Sec. of State for NI
1972-73, and Sec. of State for Employment
1973-74; Dep. Leader of the Opposition
since 1975; 1939-45 War with Scots Gds.
Tank Bn. in Normandy, Germany and
Palestine (MC, despatches); MP for Penrith
and the Border (C) since 1955: m. 1943,
Celia Doriel, yr. da. of the late Maj. Mark
Sprot of Riddell [see Hay Bt., cr. 1635];
cr. PC 1967, CH 1974. Gartshore, Kirkin-
tiloch, Glasgow; Ennim, Penrith, Cumberland; 32, Clabon Mews, Cadogan Sq., SW1;
Guards', Carlton and Pratt's Clubs.

WIDGERY, Rt. Hon. Baron, OBE, TD; cr. 1968.
WIGG, Rt. Hon. Baron; cr. 1964.
WILBERFORCE, Rt. Hon. Baron, CMG, OBE;
cr. 1964.
WILD, Rt. Hon. Sir (Herbert) Richard Churton,
KCMG, ED, son of Dr. L. J. Wild, of Otaki,
NZ; b. 1912; ed. at Feilding High Sch., and
Victoria Univ. of Wellington (LLM); Hon.
LLD, QC, NZ 1957; Solicitor-Gen., NZ,
1957-66, since when Ch. Justice of NZ; Maj.
2nd NZEF in Middle East and Italy: m.
1940, Janet, da. of F. W. Grainger; cr.
KMCG 1966, PC 1966. Supreme Court,
Wellington, NZ; Wellington Club.
WILLEY, Rt. Hon. Frederick Thomas, MP,
son of the late Frederick Willey, FRIBA,
of Durham; b. 1910; ed. at Johnston
Gram. Sch., Durham, and at St. John's Coll.,
Camb.; Bar. Middle Temple 1936; P.P.S.
to Sec. of State for Home Dept. 1946-51,
and Parl. Sec. to Min. of Food 1950-51;
Min. of Land and National Resources'
1964-67; Chm. of Select Cttee. on Members'
Interests, Race Relations and Immigration
and Abortion since 1974; MP for Sunderland
(Lab.) 1945-50, and for N. Div. of Sunderland
since 1950: m. 1939, Eleanor, da. of the late
William H. Snowdon, of Spennymoor; cr.
1964. 11 North Sq., NW11.
WILLIAMS, Rt. Hon. Eric, CH, DPhil, son of
T. H. Williams; b. 1911; ed. at Tranquility
Boys' Sch., Trinidad, and at Queen's Roy.
Coll., Trinidad, and at St. Catherine's Soc.,
Oxford (BA, DPhil), and at Howard Univ.
Washington, USA; Prime Min. since 1962
(also Min. of External Affairs 1961, 1964 and
1967, and Min. of Finance, Planning and
Development since 1967): m. 19—; cr. PC
1964, CH 1969. Prime Minister's Residence,
La Fantaise Rd., St. Anns, Trinidad; Office
of Prime Minister, Whitehall, St. Clair,
Trinidad.
WILLIAMS, Rt. Hon. Shirley Vivien Teresa
Brittain, MP, da. of Sir George Edward
Gordon Catlin; b. 1930; ed. at Summit
Sch., Minnesota, USA, St. Paul's Girls' Sch.,
Somerville Coll., Oxford (Hon. Fellow), and
Columbia Univ., New York; Gen. Sec. of
Fabian Soc. 1960-64; Visiting Fellow,
Nuffield Coll., Oxford since 1967; PPS to
Min. of Health 1964-66, Parl. Sec. Min. of
Labour 1966-67, Min. of State for Education
and Science 1967-69, Min. of State Home
Office 1969-70, and Sec. of State for Prices
and Consumer Protection since 1974; MP
for Hitchin (Lab.) 1964-74, since when for
Herts (Hertford and Stevenage Div.): m.
1955 (m. diss. 1974), Prof. Bernard Arthur
Owen Williams, FBA; cr. 1974. C/o
House of Commons, SW1.
WILLIS, Rt. Hon. Eustace George, son of
the late Walter Willis; b. 1903; ed. at City
of Norwich Sch.; Engine Room Artificer,
RN 1919-30; Min. of State for Scotland
1964-67; 1939-45 War as Sgt. RA; MP for
N. Div. of Edinburgh (Lab.) 1945-50, and
for E. Div. of Edinburgh 1954-70: m.
1929, Mary Swan, da. of Robert Ramsay
Nisbet; cr. 1967. 31, Great King St.,
Edinburgh EH3 6QR.
WILLMER, Rt. Hon. Sir Henry Gordon, OBE,
TD, son of the late Arthur Washington Will-
mer, JP, of Willaston, Wirral, Ches.; b. 1899;
ed. at Birkenhead Sch., and at Corpus Christi
Coll., Oxford (Hon. Fellow 1949); Hon. LLD
Liverpool; Bar. Inner Temple 1924, KC

1939, and Treas. 1969; appointed a Judge of
High Court of Justice (Probate, Divorce, and
Admiralty Div.) 1945, and a Lord Justice
of Appeal 1958; ret. 1969; Pres. of Shipping
Claims Tribunal 1946, a Member of Supreme
Court Committee on Practice and Procedure
1947, and of Gen. Claims Tribunal 1950;
Chm. of Incorporated Inns of Court Mission
1950-63; Chm. Statutory Cttee. of Pharma-
ceutical Soc. of GB 1970, and of Assocn. of
Average Adjusters 1971-72; Chm. of NI
Detention Appeal Tribunal since 1973; a
Trustee of Thalidomide Childrens' Trust
since 1973; 1939-45 War with Coast
Artillery and as Col. with Allied Mil. Govt.
in Italy (OBE): m. 1928, Mary Barbara,
da. of the late Sir Archibald Hurd;
cr. OBE (Mil) and Knt. 1945, PC 1958.
Flat 1, 34, Arkwright Rd., NW3.
WILSON OF LANGSIDE, Rt. Hon. Baron, QC;
cr. 1967.
WILSON, Rt. Hon. (James) Harold, OBE, FRS,
MP, son of the late James Herbert Wilson, of
Huddersfield, Yorks; b. 1916; ed. at
Wirral Gram. Sch., Cheshire, and Jesus
Coll., Oxford (Gladstone Memorial Prize,
1st class Hons. Philosophy, Politics and
Economics); Hon. LLD Lancaster, New
Brunswick, Liverpool, Nottingham and
Sussex; Hon. DCL Oxford; Hon. D. Univ.
Essex; Hon. DTech Bradford; Lect. in
Economics at New Coll., Oxford 1937, Fellow
of Univ. Coll., at Oxford 1938, Economic Assist.
War Cabinet Secretariat 1940-41, Dir. of
Economics and Statistics, Min. of Fuel
and Power 1943-44, and Praelector in Econo-
mics and Domestic Bursar, Univ. Coll.,
Oxford 1945; Chancellor of Bradford
Univ. since 1966; Pres. of Roy. Statistical
Soc. 1972-73; Parl. Sec., Min. of Works
Aug. 1945 to March 1947, Sec. for
Overseas Trade March to Oct. 1947, Pres. of
Board of Trade Oct. 1947 to April 1951;
Leader of Labour Party since 1963 and of
HM Opposition 1963-64, and 1970-74, and
Prime Min. and First Lord of the Treasury
1964-70, and since 1974; MP for Ormskirk,
Lancs. (Lab.) 1945-50, since when for Huy-
ton, Lancs.; an Hon. Elder Brother of Trinity
House: m. 1940, Gladys Mary, da. of the
Rev. D. Baldwin, of The Manse, Duxford,
Cambridge; cr. OBE (Civil) 1945, PC 1947.
10, Downing St., SW1; Grange Farm, Kings-
hill, nr. Gt. Missenden, Bucks.
WINDEYER, Rt. Hon. Sir (William John)
Victor, KBE, CB, DSO, ED, son of the late
W. A. Windeyer, of Hunter's Hill, NSW;
b. 1900; ed. at Sydney Gram. Sch., and
Sydney Univ. (MA, LLB); Bar. NSW 1925,
and KC 1940; Maj.-Gen. (ret.) AMF;
Lecturer in Legal History, Sydney Univ.
1929-36 and in Equity 1937-40, and a
Member of Senate of Sydney Univ. 1949-59
(Dep. Chancellor 1955-58); a Trustee Sydney
Gram. Sch. 1943-70; and a Member of
Council of Austn. Nat. Univ. 1951-55; GOC,
2nd Australian Div. 1950-52, Citizen Force
Member Australian Mil. Board 1950-53,
and Hon. Col. Sydney Univ. Regt. 1957-66;
a Justice of High Court of Australia 1958-72;
Pres. NSW Branch of Austn. Boy Scouts
Assocn. since 1970; 1939-45 War, Middle
East (DSO and Bar), SW Pacific (despatches
thrice, CBE): m. 1934, Margaret Moor,
da. of Robert Vicars, of Cheltenham,
NSW; cr. DSO 1942 (Bar 1943), CBE
(Mil.) 1945, CB (Mil.) 1953, KBE (Civil) 1958,
PC 1963. Peroomba, Turramurra, NSW
2074; Australian and Australasian Pioneers
(Sydney) Clubs.
WINDLESHAM, Rt. Hon. Baron; cr. 1973.
WOOD, Rt. Hon. Richard Frederick, MP;
cr. 1959 [see E. Halifax].
WOODBURN, Rt. Hon. Arthur, son of Matthew
Woodburn; b. Oct. 25th, 1890; ed. at
Bruntsfield and Boroughmuir Public Schs.
and Heriot-Watt Coll., Edinburgh (DLitt);
Scottish Sec. to Labour Party 1932-39,
Parliamentary Private Sec. to Sec.
of State for Scotland 1941-45, Parlia-
mentary Sec. to Min. of Aircraft Production
and Min. of Supply 1945-47, and Sec. of State
for Scotland 1947-50; a Member of Historic
Buildings Council for Scotland and of

Scottish National Trust, and a Trustee Scottish Nat. Library; MP (*Lab.*) for Clackmannan and E. Stirlingshire 1939-70; *m.* 1919, Barbara, da. of Frank Halliday; *cr.* 1947. 83, *Orchard Rd., Edinburgh.*

WOODCOCK, *Rt. Hon.* George, *CBE*, son of Peter Woodcock, of Clayton Green, Lancs.; *b.* 1904; ed. at Brownedge Elementary Sch., and at Ruskin and New (Hon. Fellow 1963) Colls., Oxford; Hon. LLD Sussex, and Manchester; Hon. DCL, Oxford, and Kent; Hon. DSc Aston; Hon. LLD Lancaster and London; Hon. Fellow of LSE 1965, a Member of Roy. Commn. on Taxation of Income and Profits 1951-54, of British Guiana Constitutional Commn. 1954, of Cttee. on working of Monetary System 1957-59, and of Roy. Commn. on Trade Union and Employers Assocns. 1965; Gen. Sec. TUC 1960-69, and Chm. of Commn. on Industrial Relations 1969-71; a Member NEDC 1962-69; Vice-Chm. of National Savings Cttee. since 1952: *m.* 1933, Laura Mary, da. of Frank McKernan; *cr.* CBE (Civil) 1953, PC 1967. 24, *Lower Hill Rd., Epsom, Surrey.*

WOODHOUSE, *Rt. Hon. Mr. Justice (Sir* Arthur Owen), *DSC*, son of Arthug James Woodhouse; *b.* 1916; ed. at Napier BHS, and Auckland Univ. (LLB); 1939-45 War as Lt.-Cdr. RNZNVR, in MTB'S and as liaison officer with Yugo lav Partisans, and Assist. to Naval Attache, British Embassy, Belgrace; Crown Solicitor, Napier 1954-61, a Judge of Supreme Court, Auckland 1961-74, since when a Judge of Court of Appeal, NZ; Counsel to Fluoridation Commn. in NZ 1956-57, and Chm. of Roy. Commn. into Personal Injuries in NZ 1966-67, and in Aust. 1973-74: *m.* 1940, Margaret Leah, da. of Frederick Thorp; *cr.* Knt. 1974, PC 1974. 45, *Portland Rd., Remuera, Auckland 5, New Zealand; Hawkes Bay, Northern, Wellington and Wellesley Clubs.*

WYLIE, *Rt. Hon. Lord; cr.* 1970. [see SCOTTISH LORDS OF SESSION.]

YORK, *Most Rev. and Rt. Hon, the Lord Archbishop of DD; cr.* 1974.

YOUNGER, *Rt. Hon. Sir* Kenneth Gilmour, *KBE; cr.* 1951 [see V. Younger of Leckie].

SCOTTISH LORDS OF SESSION

(AND THE CHAIRMAN OF SCOTTISH LAND COURT) *i.e.* SENATORS OF THE COLLEGE OF JUSTICE IN SCOTLAND,
IN OFFICE OR RETIRED, AND THEIR WIDOWS.

By Royal Warrant Feb. 3rd, 1905, Scottish Lords of Session who have retired are permitted to retain the title of " Hon. Lord," while their wives are also granted the title of " Lady," to be retained after the decease of the husband, but during widowhood only. By Royal Warrant, April 17th, 1912, the above also applies to the Chairman of the Scottish Land Court.]

RT. HON. LORD AVONSIDE.

Rt. Hon. IAN HAMILTON SHEARER, son of Andrew Shearer, O.B.E., J.P.; *b.* Nov. 6th, 1914; ed. at Dunfermline High Sch., at Glasgow Univ. (M.A.) and at Edinburgh Univ. (LLB); Advocate of Scotland 1938, and QC 1952; Sheriff of Renfrew and Argyll 1960-62, Chm. of National Health Ser. Tribunal, Scotland 1954-62, a Member of Scottish Cttee. of Council of Tribunals 1958-62, and Lord Advocate 1962-64; 1939-45 War as Capt. RA; PC 1962; appointed a Lord of Session with title of *Lord Avonside* 1964: *m.* 1st, 1942; 2ndly, 1954, Janet Sutherland, OBE, da. of the late William Murray, MB, ChB, of Paisley.

Residence,—The Mill House, Samuelston, E. Lothian.

LADY BIRNAM.

EDITH LILIAN ARCHER: *m.* 1946, Sir (Thomas) David King Murray, a Lord of Session (with title of *Lord Birnam*), who *d.* 1955.

Residence,— 1, Traquair Park East, Edinburgh, 12.

HON. LORD BIRSAY.

HARALD ROBERT LESLIE, *KT, CBE, TD,* son of the late Robert Leslie, Master Mariner, of Stromness, Orkney; *b.* May 8th, 1905; ed. at Earlston Public Sch., Berwickshire High Sch., Glasgow High Sch., and Glasgow Univ. (MA, LLB); Hon. LLD Strathclyde and Glasgow; FEIS; a DL of Orkney; Advocate 1937, and KC 1949; Advocate Depute 1947-51, Sheriff-Prin. of Roxburgh, Berwick and Selkirk 1956-61, and of Caithness, Sutherland, Orkney and Zetland 1951-65; Chm. of Scottish Advisory Council on Treatment of Offenders 1959, of National Joint Council on Teachers Salaries in Scotland 1960-65, of Scottish Council of Boys' Clubs and Youth Clubs 1962, of Scottish Panel of British Council 1963-69, and of National Savings Cttee. in Scotland 1965-72 (Pres. 1972), and Hon. Pres. of Scottish Council of National Parks 1962-65; Chm. Board of Govs. of Loaningdale Approved Sch., Biggar 1963-68; Pres., Scottish Nat. Dictionary Assocn. 1968; Pres., Scottish Shipwrecked Mariners' Assocn., and United Soc. for Christian Literature (Scotland), Hon. Pres. of Leith Bn. Boys Bde., of Edinburgh, Orkney and Zetland Assocn., and of Glasgow, Orkney and Shetland Assocn., and Chm. of Birsay Cttee. concerning Gen. Med. Sers. in Highlands and Islands; Chm. of Executive Cttee. of Edinburgh Council of Social Ser. 1957-59; Chm., Scottish Advisory Cttee. on Travelling People 1971; Chm. Edinburgh Advisory Board for the Salvation Army 1967 and of Queen's Nursing Inst. Scotland 1973; Hon. Air Commodore, No. 2 (City of Edinburgh) Maritime HQ Unit, R. Aux. A.F.; 1939-45 War as Lt.-Col. R. Scots, served 8th Bn., and at HQ, 15th (Scottish) Div., 8th Corps and 21st Army Group (despatches); Chm. of Scottish Land Court since 1965, with title of *Lord Birsay*; Lord High Commr. to Gen. Assembly of Church of Scotland 1965 and 1966; *cr.* MBE (Mil) 1945, CBE (Civil) 1963, KT 1973: *m.* 1945, Robina Margaret, MB, ChB, only da. of Ex-Provost James George Marwick, FSA (Scot.), of Stromness, Orkney.

Residences,—27, Queensferry Rd., Edinburgh, EH4 3HB ; Queenafjold, Twatt, Birsay, Orkney. *Clubs,*—Caledonian (Edinburgh), Scottish Arts (Edinburgh), Royal Scots.

HON. LORD BRAND.

DAVID WILLIAM ROBERT BRAND, son of the late James Gordon Brand, of Huntingdon, Dumfries; *b.* 1923; ed. at Stonyhurst, and Edinburgh Univ. (MA, LLB); Advocate Scotland 1948, QC 1959; Standing Jnr. Counsel to Dept. of Education for Scotland 1951-53, Advocate Depute for Sheriff Court 1953-55, Extra Advocate-Depute for Glasgow Circuit 1955-57, Advocate-Depute 1957-59; Senior Advocate Depute 1964, Sheriff-Prin. of Dumfries and Galloway 1968-70, Sheriff-Prin. of Roxburgh, Berwick and Selkirk, May to June 1970, and Solicitor-Gen. for Scotland 1970-72; 1939-45 War as Capt. A & SH; appointed a Lord of Session, with title of *Lord Brand* 1972: *m.* 1st, 1948, Rose Josephine Devlin, who *d.* 1968; 2ndly, 1969, Bridget Veronica, da. of

Garrett Russell, and widow of Thomas Patrick Lynch, of Beechmount Mallow, co. Cork.

Residence,—Gospatric House, Dalmeny, W. Lothian, EH30 9TT. *Club,*—New (Edinburgh).

HON. LORD CAMERON.

Sir JOHN CAMERON, *DSC,* son of John Cameron, of Edinburgh, *b.* Feb. 8th, 1900; ed. at Edinburgh Acad. and Univ., Hon. LLD Aberdeen, and Edinburgh LittD. Heriot Watt; Advocate Scotland 1924, and a KC 1936; is a DL for Edinburgh, a FRSE and Hon. Member of Roy. Scottish Acad.; Dean of Faculty of Advocates 1948-55; was Sheriff of Inverness, Elgin and Nairn 1945, and of Inverness, Moray, Nairn, Ross and Cromarty 1946-48; 1914-18 War with RNVR, 1939-45 War with RNVR (despatches, DSC); Knt. 1954; appointed a Lord of Session with title of *Lord Cameron* 1955: *m.* 1st, 1927, Eileen Dorothea, who *d.* 1943, da. of the late Harry Milburn Burrell; 2ndly, 1944, Iris, da. of the late Eric Alfred Henry, and widow of Lambert C. Shepherd.

Residence,—28, Moray Place, Edinburgh, 3.

LADY CARMONT.

BARBARA WILSON CAMPBELL, da. of the late D. Russell Malloy; Dame of British Assocn., Sovereign Mil. Order of Malta: *m.* 1929, John Francis Carmont, a Lord of Session (with title of *Lord Carmont*), and Privy Chamberlain to the Pope, who *d.* 1965.

Residence,—The Avenue, Greenhill Gardens, Edinburgh; *Club,*—University Women's (London).

HON. LORD DUNPARK.

ALASTAIR McPHERSON JOHNSTON, son of the late Rev. A. M. Johnston, BD, of Stirling; *b.* Dec. 15th, 1915; ed. at Merchiston Castle Sch., Jesus Coll., Camb. (BA), and Edinburgh Univ. (LLB, Hon. Fellow); 1939-45 War as Maj. RA (TA) (despatches); Advocate (Scotland) 1946; QC 1958; Sheriff of Dumfries and Galloway 1966-68; Member of Scottish Law Commn. 1968-71; appointed a Lord of Session with title of *Lord Dunpark* 1971: *m.* 1939, Katherine Margaret, da. of Charles Mitchell, of Chislehurst, Kent.

Residences,—8, Heriot Row, Edinburgh, EH3 6HU; Parkend, Stichill, Roxburghshire. *Club,*—New (Edinburgh).

EMSLIE [see Lord Justice-General].

RT. HON. BARON FRASER OF TULLYBELTON.

See Peerage section, FRASER OF TULLYBELTON, BARON.

LADY GRANT.

MARGARET KATHARINE, da. of J. W. Milne: *m.* 1936, William Grant, TD, Lord Justice-Clerk of Scotland (with the title of *Lord Grant*), who *d.* 1972.

Residence,—30, Moray Place, Edinburgh.

HON. LORD GRIEVE.

WILLIAM ROBERTSON GRIEVE, *VRD,* son of the late William Robertson Grieve; *b.* 1917; ed. at Glasgow Acad., Sedbergh, and Glasgow Univ. (MA, LLB); late Lt.-Cdr. RNVR; Advocate Scotland 1947, QC 1957; Jnr. Counsel in Scotland to Board of Inland Revenue 1952-57, Advocate-Depute (Home) 1962-64, and Sheriff-Prin. of Renfrew and Argyll 1964-72; Procurator of Ch. of Scotland 1969-72; 1939-45 War with RN; appointed a Lord of Session with title of *Lord Grieve* 1972: *m.* 1947, Lorna St. John, da. of the late Engineer Rear Adm. Edward Piercy St. John Benn, CB.

Residence,—20, Belgrave Cres., Edinburgh, EH4 3AJ. *Club,*—New (Edinburgh).

LADY GUTHRIE.

JEANNIE HENDRY, da. of T. H. Rutherford, of Auldearn: *m.* 1934, Henry Wallace Guthrie, a Lord of Session (with the title of *Lord Guthrie*), who *d.* 1970.

Residence,—Medwynbrae, West Linton, Peeblesshire.

HON. LORD HUNTER.

JOHN OSWALD MAIR HUNTER; *b.* 1913; B.A. 1934, LL.B. 1936; *m.* 19—; Bar. Inner Temple 1937, Advocate Scotland 1937, and a K.C. Scotland 1951; Sheriff of Ayr and Bute 1957-61; appointed a Lord of Session with title of *Lord Hunter* 1961; Chm. of Scottish Law Commn. 1971.

Address,—Little Ruchlaw, Stenton, Dunbar, East Lothian.

HON. LORD JOHNSTON.

DOUGLAS HAROLD JOHNSTON, *T.D.*, son of the late Joseph Johnston, advocate of Aberdeen ; *b.* 1907 ; ed. at Aberdeen Gram. Sch., at St. John's Coll., Oxford (BA 1929, MA 1937), and at Edinburgh Univ.; Hon. FRIAS; Bar. Inner Temple 1931; Advocate Scotland 1932, and a KC 1947; Chm. of Roy. Fine Art Commn. for Scotland; formerly a Member of Cttee. on Admin. Tribunals; Solicitor-Gen., Scotland 1947-51; 1939-45 War as Lt.-Col. RA; sat as MP for Paisley (*Lab.*) Feb. 1948 to Jan. 1961; appointed a Lord of Session with title of *Lord Johnston* 1961: *m.* 1936, Doris, da. of the late James Kidd.

Residence,—Dunosdale, Cammo Crescent, Barnton, Edinburgh.

RT. HON. THE LORD JUSTICE-CLERK.★

See Peerage Section, WHEATLEY, BARON.

RT. HON. THE LORD JUSTICE-GENERAL.★

Rt. Hon. GEORGE CARLYLE EMSLIE, *MBE,* son of Alexander Emslie; *b.* Dec. 6th, 1919; ed. The High Sch. of Glasgow, and Glasgow Univ. (MA, LLB; Hon. LLD); 1939-45 War in N. Africa, Italy, Greece and Austria (despatches); Bde. Maj. 1944-46; Advocate Scotland 1948; QC 1957; Advocate Depute to Sheriff Courts 1955-57; Junior Assessor to City of Edinburgh 1955-57; Ind. Chm. Discipline Cttees. of Potato and Egg Marketing Boards 1958-65; a Member of Scottish Cttee. of Council on Tribunals 1962-70; Chm. of Scottish Agricultural Wages Board 1968; Sheriff of Perth and Angus 1963-66; Dean of Faculty of Advocates 1965-70, and Senior Assessor to City of Edinburgh 1965-70; Lord Justice-Gen. of Scotland, and Lord Pres. of the Court of Session in Scotland since 1972; MBE (Mil) 1946; appointed a Lord of Session with title of *Lord Emslie* 1970; PC 1972: *m.* 1942, Lilias Ann Mailer, da. of Robert Hannington, of Glasgow.

Residence,—47, Heriot Row, Edinburgh. *Club,*—New (Edinburgh).

HON. LORD KEITH.

HENRY SHANKS KEITH, son of the late Baron Keith of Avonholm [Life Baron]; *b.* Feb. 7th, 1922; ed. at Edinburgh Acad., Magdalen Coll., Oxford (MA), and Edinburgh Univ. (LLB); Bar. Gray's Inn 1951; Advocate Scotland 1950; QC 1962; Standing Jr. Council to Dep. of Health for Scotland 1957-62; a Member of Scottish Valuation Advisory Council 1959-70 (Chm. since 1972), of Law Reform Cttee. for Scotland 1964-70, of Panel of Arbiters under European Fisheries Convention 1964-71, and under Convention on Settlement of Investment Disputes between States and Nationals of other States 1968-71, and of Cttee. on Law of Defamation since 1971; Sheriff-Prin. of Roxburgh, Berwick and Selkirk 1970-71; 1939-45 War in Scots Gds. (despatches); appointed a Lord of Session with title of *Lord Keith* 1971: *m.* 1955, Alison Hope Alan, yr. da. of Alan Brown.

Residence,—33, Heriot Row, Edinburgh.

RT. HON. LORD KILBRANDON.

See Peerage Section, KILBRANDON, BARON.

HON. LORD KINCRAIG.

ROBERT SMITH JOHNSTON, son of W. T. Johnston, iron merchant, of Glasgow; *b.* Oct. 10th, 1918; ed. at Strathallan Sch., St. John's Coll., Camb. (BA), and Glasgow Univ. (LLB); Advocate Scotland 1942; Advocate Depute, Crown Office 1953-55, QC 1955, Home Advocate Depute 1959-62; Sheriff of Roxburgh, Berwick and Selkirk 1964-70; Dean of Faculty of Advocates 1970; a Gov. of Strathallan Sch.; appointed a Lord of Session with title of *Lord Kincraig* 1972: *m.* 1943, Joan, da. of the late Col. A. G. Graham, of Glasgow.

Residence,—Westwood, Longniddry, E. Lothian. *Club,*—Caledonian.

HON. LORD KISSEN.

MANUEL KISSEN, son of the late Lewis Kissen, of Glasgow; *b.* May 2nd, 1912; ed. at Hutcheson's Boys' Gram. Sch., Glasgow, and at Glasgow Univ. (MA, LLB); Hon. LLD Glasgow; Solicitor Scotland 1934, Advocate Scotland 1946, and a QC 1955; Chm. of Law Reform Cttee. for Scotland since 1964, and a Member of Restrictive Practices Court since 1966; 1939-45 War with RAF (despatches); appointed a Lord of Session with title of *Lord Kissen* 1963: *m.* 1964, Victoria, widow of Prof. Edward Solomons, of New York.

Residence,—22, Braid Av., Edinburgh, 10. *Clubs,*—National Liberal (London), and Scottish Liberal (Edinburgh).

★ The Lord Justice-Clerk and the Lord Justice-General are addressed by their judicial titles and not by those with which they take seats on the Bench. (In the case of the present Lord Justice-Clerk who is also a Peer, correspondence on judicial matters is addressed to Lord Justice-Clerk, and socially to Lord Wheatley.)

1272

HON. LORD LEECHMAN.

JAMES GRAHAM LEECHMAN, son of the late Walter Graham Leechman, Solicitor, of Glasgow; *b.* Oct. 6th, 1906; ed. at Glasgow High Sch., and at Glasgow Univ. (MA, BSc, LLB); Advocate Scotland 1932, KC 1949; Advocate Depute 1947-49, Clerk of Justiciary 1949-64, and Solicitor-Gen. for Scotland 1964-65; 1939-45 War with RAF; appointed a Lord of Session with title of *Lord Leechman* 1965: *m.* 1935, Margaret Helen, da. of the late Thomas Wilson Edgar, of Glasgow.

Residence,—626, Queensferry Rd., Barnton, Edinburgh, EH4 6AT.

HON. LORD McDONALD

ROBERT HOWAT MCDONALD, *MC,* son of Robert Glassford McDonald, of Paisley, Renfrewshire; *b.* May 15th, 1916; ed. at John Neilson Instn., Paisley, and Glasgow Univ. (MA, LLB); 1939-45 War with KOSB (despatches); Advocate Scotland 1946, and a QC 1957; Sheriff Prin. of Ayr and Bute 1966-71, a Member of Criminal Injuries Compensation Board 1964-71; Pres. of Industrial Tribunals for Scotland 1972-73; appointed a Lord of Session with title of *Lord McDonald* 1973: *m.* 1949, Barbara, da. of John Mackenzie, of Badcaul, Ross-shire.

Residence,—5 Doune Terr., Edinburgh, EH3 6EA.

HON. LORD MACKENZIE STUART.

ALEXANDER JOHN MACKENZIE STUART, son of the late Prof. A. Mackenzie Stuart, KC; *b.* 1924, ed. at Fettes., Sidney Sussex Coll., Camb. (BA), and Edinburgh Univ. (LLB); Advocate Scotland 1951, QC 1963; Standing Jnr. Counsel to Scottish Home Dept. 1956-57, and Inland Revenue in Scotland 1957-63; Sheriff-Prin. of Aberdeen, Kincardine and Banff 1971-72; a Judge at the Court of the European Communities, Luxembourg since 1973; Hon. Pres. Scottish Lawyers European Gp.; 1939-45 War as Capt. RE; appointed a Lord of Session with title of *Lord Mackenzie Stuart* 1972: *m.* 1952, Anne Burtholme, da. of the late J. S. L. Millar, WS, of Edinburgh.

Address,—Cour de Justice des Communautés Européennes, Kirchberg, Luxembourg, Grand Duchy of Luxembourg.

HON. LORD MACKINTOSH.

CHARLES MACKINTOSH, *M.C.,* son of Hugh Mackintosh, of Nairn ; *b.* May 28th, 1888 ; ed. at Edinburgh Acad. and Univ. (Hon. LL.D. 1949), and at Wadham Coll., Oxford (BA 1911, Hon. Fellow 1959); Advocate Scotland 1914, and a KC 1935; 1914-18 War (MC); Sheriff of Argyll 1937-42, and of Inverness, Elgin, and Nairn 1942-44; a Lord of Session with title of *Lord Mackintosh* 1944-64: *m.* 1921, Mary Lawrie, da. of Sir John Prosser, CVO, WS.

Residence,—55, Northumberland Street, Edinburgh. *Club,*—New (Edinburgh).

HON. LORD MAXWELL.

PETER MAXWELL, son of Cdr. Herries Maxwell, RN, of Munches, Dalbeattie, Kirkcudbrightshire; *b.* May 21st, 1919; ed. at Wellington, Balliol Coll., Oxon. (BA), and Edinburgh Univ. (LLB); Advocate Scotland 1951, QC 1961; Sheriff-Prin. of Dumfries and Galloway since 1970; 1939-45 War as Capt. A & SH and RA in Normandy; appointed a Lord of Session with title of *Lord Maxwell* 1973: *m.* 1941, Alison Susan, da. of James Forest Alexander Readman.

Residence,—46, Heriot Row, Edinburgh, 3.

HON. LORD MIGDALE.

JAMES FREDERICK GORDON THOMSON, son of the late William Thomson, Advocate, of Edinburgh; *b.* June 22nd, 1897; Advocate Scotland 1924, and a QC 1945; Sheriff of Ayr and Bute 1949-52; is a Life Trustee of Carnegie UK Trust; Lord Lt. for Sutherland 1962-72; a Lord of Session with title of *Lord Migdale* 1953-73: *m.* 1938, Louise Carnegie Miller, who *d.* 1947.

Residence,—Ospisdale, Dornoch, Sutherland.

LADY MILLIGAN.

MURIEL JEAN, da. of the late James MacLehose, LLD: *m.* 1925, the Rt. Hon. William Rankine Milligan, a Lord of Session (with title of *Lord Milligan*), who *d.* 1975.

Residence,—38 India St., Edinburgh.

HON. LORD ROBERTSON.

IAN MACDONALD ROBERTSON, *TD,* son of the late James Robertson, of Dundee, Calcutta and Edinburgh; *b.* Oct. 30th, 1912; ed. at Merchiston Castle, Edinburgh, Balliol Coll., Oxford (BA), and Edinburgh Univ. (LLB); Advocate Scotland 1939, and a QC 1954; Sheriff of Ayr and Bute 1961-66, and of Perth and Angus 1966; 1939-45 War as Capt. R. Scots (The Royal Regt.) in Normandy and N-W Europe (despatches); appointed a Lord of Session with title of *Lord Robertson* 1966: *m.* 1938, Anna Love, da. of the late Judge James Fulton Glen, of Tampa, Florida, USA.

Residence,—13, Moray Place, Edinburgh. *Club,*—New (Edinburgh).

LADY RUSSELL.

FLORENCE, da. of Thomas Galloway, of Auchendrane, Ayrshire: *m.* 1913, Albert Russell, a Lord of Session in Scotland (with title of Lord Russell), who *d.* 1975.

Residence,—3 Glenorchy Rd., N. Berwick, E. Lothian.

HON. LORD SORN.

JAMES GORDON MCINTYRE, *M.C.,* son of the late T. W. McIntyre, of Sorn; *b.* July 21st, 1896; ed. at Winchester, at Balliol Coll., Oxford (BA, 1920), and at Glasgow Univ. (Hon. LLD 1957); Advocate Scotland 1922 (Dean of Faculty 1939-44), and a KC 1936; is a JP for Ayrshire; 1914-19 War as Capt. Ayrshire Yeo. (MC and Bar, French Croix de Guerre); a Lord of Session with title of *Lord Sorn* 1944-63: *m.* 1923, Madeline, who *d.* 1954, da. of the late Robert Scott-Moncrieff, of Downhill.

Residence,—Sorn Castle, Mauchline, Ayrshire.

LADY STEVENSON.

SOPHRONIA REYNOLDS, dau. of Michael Gleeson, of Toronto, Canada: *m.* 1919, James Stevenson, a Lord of Session in Scotland (with title of *Lord Stevenson*), who *d.* 1963.

Residence,—Scrabster House, Thurso, Caithness.

HON. LORD STEWART.

EWAN GEORGE FRANCIS STEWART, *MC,* son of the late George Duncan Stewart, CA Edinburgh; *b.* May 9th, 1923; ed. at George Watson's Coll., Edinburgh, and Edinburgh Univ.; 1939-45 War as Capt. 7th/9th (Highlanders) Bn., R. Scots; Advocate Scotland 1949, QC 1960; Advocate Depute 1964-67; Solicitor-Gen. for Scotland 1967-70, and Scottish Law Commr. 1971-75; appointed a Lord of Session with title of *Lord Stewart* 1975: *m.* 1953, Sheila Margaret, da. of the late Maj. Kenneth Gordon Richman.

Residence,—5 Munro Drive, Edinburgh, EH13 0EG., Canty Bay, E. Lothian.

RT. HON. LORD STOTT.

Rt. Hon. GEORGE GORDON STOTT, son of the Rev. G. Gordon Stott; *b.* Dec. 22nd 1909; ed. at Cramond Sch., Edinburgh Acad., and Edinburgh Univ.; Scottish Advocate 1936, Advocate-Depute 1947-51, and a KC 1950; Sheriff of Roxburgh, Berwick and Selkirk 1961-64, and Lord Advocate 1964-67; PC 1964; appointed a Lord of Session with title of *Lord Stott* 1967: *m.* 1947, Nancy, da. of A. D. Braggins.

Residence,—12, Midmar Gdns., Edinburgh.

HON. LORD STRACHAN.

JAMES FREDERICK STRACHAN, son of James K. Strachan, of Glasgow; *b.* Oct. 11th, 1894; ed. at Glasgow Acad. and at Glasgow Univ. (MA 1915, LLB 1921); Hon. LLD Glasgow 1961; Advocate Scotland 1921, and a KC 1938; was Procurator for Church of Scotland 1938-48, Vice-Dean of Faculty of Advocates 1941-8, and Sheriff of Argyll 1942-45, and of Perth and Angus 1945-48; a Lord of Session with title of *Lord Strachan* 1948-67: *m.* 1926, Irene Louise, da. of Timothy Warren, LLD, of Glasgow.

Residence,—Woodville, Canaan Lane, Edinburgh. *Club,*—New (Edinburgh).

MACKENZIE STUART [see Mackenzie.]

HON. LORD THOMSON.

ALEXANDER THOMSON, son of James Stuart Thomson, of Dunfermline; *b.* Nov. 9th, 1914; ed. at Dunfermline High Sch., and at Edinburgh Univ. (MA, LLB); Scottish Advocate 1946, a Member of Faculty of Advocates, Edinburgh since 1946; QC (Scotland) 1955, Sheriff of Renfrew and Argyll 1962-64, Dean of Faculty of Advocates 1964-65; a Judge of Nat. Industrial Relations Court since 1971; 1939-45 War as Capt. RA; appointed a Lord of Session with title of *Lord Thomson* 1965: *m.* 1957, Marie Wilson, da. of the late David G. Cowan, of Milngavie, Glasgow.

Residence,—11, Moray Place, Edinburgh, 3.

LADY WARK.

MARY, dau. of Thomas Wright, of Glasgow: *m.* 1907, John Lean Wark, M.B.E., LL.D., a Lord of Session (with title of *Lord Wark*), who *d.* 1943.

Address,—c/o The Misses Sutherland, 5, Whinnybrae, Broughty Ferry, Dundee.

HILL-WATSON [see Hill].

RIGHT HON. LORD WHEATLEY.

See Peerage Section, WHEATLEY, BARON.

RT. HON. LORD WYLIE.

NORMAN RUSSELL WYLIE, *VRD*, son of the late William Galloway Wylie, of Elderslie, Renfrewshire; *b.* Oct. 25th, 1923; ed. at Paisley Gram. Sch., St. Edmund Hall, Oxford (BA), and Glasgow (LLB) and Edinburgh Univs.; 1939-45 War in Fleet Air Arm; Lt.-Cdr. RNR 1954; Bar. Scotland 1952, Advocate Depute 1959, QC (Scotland) 1964; Solicitor-Gen. for Scotland April to Oct. 1964, and Lord Advocate 1970-74; appointed a Lord of Session with title of *Lord Wylie* 1974; MP for Pentlands Div. of Edinburgh (C) 1964-74; PC 1970: *m.* 1963, Gillian Mary, da. of the late Richard Edward Verney.

Residence,—30 Launder Rd., Edinburgh, EH9 2JF. *Clubs,*—Constitutional and New (Edinburgh), Royal Forth Yacht, and Royal Highland Yacht.

THE BARONETAGE.

The ALPHABETICAL ARRANGEMENT includes (*i.*) the names of Baronets, and (*ii.*) the names of extinct baronetcies that are represented in the female line.

Compound surnames are arranged under the last and principal surname, *e.g.*, Havelock-Allan will be found under the letter A.

The scope of EACH ARTICLE IN THE BARONETAGE is designed to include information concerning every *living* male descended in the male line from the first Baronet, and of all *living* females being issue of males so descended. For remainders to Baronetcies see article on Baronets in Preliminary Section.

DECEASED FEMALE COLLATERALS and their issue are not as a rule referred to in this work.

ISSUE of the members of two families mentioned in the work, who happen to have intermarried, are always referred to under the father's name.

The Christian names of the heir **apparent or** presumptive are given in capital letters.

CREATIONS :—
E. = England (May 22nd, 1611 to April 30th, 1707).
N.S. = Nova Scotia or Scotland (May 28th, 1625 to April 30th, 1707).
I. = Ireland (Sept. 30th, 1619 to Dec. 31st, 1800).
G.B. = Great Britain (May 1st, 1707 to Dec. 31st, 1800).
U.K. = United Kingdom (Jan. 1st, 1801 to present time).

Since 1929, Baronets of England, Ireland, Great Britain, and the United Kingdom have **been** permitted to depict their respective Badges suspended by the ribbon below the shield of arms, as **was** already the case in respect of Baronets of Nova Scotia.

ABDY, Creation (U.K.) 1850, of Albyns, Essex.

Sir ROBERT HENRY EDWARD ABDY, 5th *Baronet*; *b.* Sept. 11th, 1896; *s.* his father, *Sir* HENRY BEADON, 1921; ed. at Charterhouse, and at R.M.C.; is Lieut. 15th/19th King's Hussars (Reserve of Officers); European War 1915-18 in France and Belgium (1914-15 star, two medals): *m.* 1st, 1923, Mrs. Iya Jongeyans (*née* De Gay), who obtained a divorce 1928; 2ndly, 1930 (marriage dissolved 1962), Lady (Helen) Diana Bridgeman, who *d.* 1967, da. of 5th Earl of Bradford; 3rdly, 1962 (m. diss. 1973), Jane Noble, and has issue living by 2nd m.
    Arms—Or, two chevronels between three trefoils slipped sable. Crest—An eagle's head couped proper, beaked azure.
    Residence—Newton Ferrers, Callington, Cornwall.

Firm and faithful.

Son living—By 2nd marriage—VALENTINE ROBERT DUFF (Newton Ferrers, Callington, Cornwall, and Paris), *b.* Sept. 11th, 1937; ed. at Eton.
Sister living—Gladys Erica (6, Landward Court, Harrowby St., W1), *b.* 1892: *m.* 1919, Col. Patrick Campbell Anderson, DSO, MC, Seaforth Highlanders, who *d.* 1965.
Daughter living of 3rd Baronet—Grace Lilian (*Countess of Lanesborough*), *b.* 1887: *m.* 1917, as his second wife, the 8th, Earl of Lanesborough, who *d.* 1950. *Residence*, Swithland Hall, Loughborough, Leicestershire.

ABERCROMBY, Creation (N.S.) 1636, of Birkenbog, Banffshire.
He aims at high things.

Sir IAN GEORGE ABERCROMBY, 10th *Baronet*, only son of Robert Ogilvie Abercromby, el. son of David James Abercromby, 4th son of 5th Bt.; *b.* June 30th, 1925; *s.* his kinsman *Maj. Sir* ROBERT ALEXANDER, *MC*, 1972; ed. at Lancing, and Bloxham Sch., Banbury: *m.* 1st, 1950 (m. diss. 1957), Joyce Beryl, da. of Leonard Griffiths, of Spencer's Wood, Berks.; 2ndly, 1959, Fanny Mary Udale (Mollie), only da. of Dr. Graham Udale-Smith, of Sitio Litre, Puerto de la Cruz, Tenerife, and has issue by 2nd m.

Hrms—Quarterly: 1st and 4th argent, a chevron gules between three boars' head, erased azure, langued of the second; 2nd and 3rd grand quarters: 1st and 4th argent, a lion passant-guardant gules, crowned with an imperial crown: 2nd and 3rd argent, three popinjays vert, beaked and membered gules. Crest—A falcon rising belled proper. Supporters—Two grey-hounds argent, collared gules. Third Motto—Vive ut vivas (*Live, that thou mayst live*).
Residence—Sitio Litre, Puerto de la Cruz, Tenerife, Canarias.

Daughter living—By 2nd m.—Maria Amelia, *b.* 1960.
Widow living of 8th Baronet—ELEANOR (*Eleanor Lady Abercromby*) (202, Cranmer Court, Sloane Av., SW3; East Wing, Leith Hall, Kennethmont, Aberdeenshire), only da. of the late Sir Arthur Anderson, CIE, CBE, of Roffey Pl., Horsham, *m.* 1935, Col. Sir George William Abercromby, DSO, 8th Bt., who *d.* 1964.

Collateral Branch living

Granddaughter of Douglas Charles Abercromby, 4th son of 6th baronet:—
Issue of the late Keith Douglas Abercromby, *b.* 1887, *d.* 1968: *m.* 1st, 1913, Eva Winifred, who *d.* 1930, only da. of the late Harry Millward Wright; 2ndly, 1939, Mrs. Hilda Brocket Lemon (12, Aynho Court, Banbury), da. of Alan Sandys, Bar.-at-Law.
(By 1st m.) Joan Eileen (36, Marlborough Pl., NW8), *b.* 1919: *m.* 1st, 1939 (m. diss. 1948), Alan James Butler Aldridge; 2ndly, 1948, Richard Lloyd Joseph Wills, CBE, MC, who *d.* 1969; 3rdly, 1972, Maj.-Gen. James Alexander Rowland Robertson, CB, CBE, DSO, and has issue living, (by 1st m.) Gail Susan Eva, *b.* 1946: *m.* 1974, Raymond Henry Cornish, of Stoneycroft, Sampford Spiney, Yelverton, Devon.

Sir Alexander Abercromby, of Birkenbog, MP for Banffshire, 7th in descent from George Abercrombie, whose lands were erected into Barony of Pitmedden 1513, was created a Bt. of Nova Scotia 1636 with remainder of his heirs male. The 2nd baronet sat as MP for co. Banff in Scottish Parliament 1694, and the 5th baronet sat as MP for the same co. 1812-8. Sir George William Abercromby, DSO, 8th Bt., was convener of Banff Co. Council 1929-61, and Lord-Lieut. of Banffshire 1946-64.

ACKROYD, Creation U.K.) 1956, of Dewsbury, West Riding of Yorkshire.

PER·FIDEM·ROBUR

Sir JOHN ROBERT WHYTE ACKROYD, 2nd *Baronet*; *b.* March 2nd, 1932; *s.* his father, *Sir* CUTHBERT LOWELL, 1973; ed. at Bradfield, and Worcester Coll., Oxford (MA); an Underwriting Member of Lloyd's, a Member of Central Council, Victoria League for Commonwealth Friendship, and a Churchwarden of St. Mary le Bow, Cheapside, Hon. Sec. Pilgrims of Great Britain 1966: *m.* 1956, Jennifer Eileen McLeod, da. of Henry George Stokes Bishop, of Stow-on-the-Wold, and has issue.

Arms—Azure on a pale between two oak leaves or a sword erect gules. Crest—A goat's head erased azure armed or charged on the neck with a rose argent barbed and seeded proper.

Residence—43, Lansdowne Cres., Holland Park, W11.
Club—Carlton (Cttee-1972).

Sons living—TIMOTHY ROBERT WHYTE, *b.* Oct. 7th, 1958.——Andrew John, *b.* 1961.
Daughters living—Jane Victoria McLeod, *b.* 1957.——Kate Georgina, *b.* 1963.
Brother living—Christopher Lowell, *b.* 1934; ed. at Bradfield, and at Magdalene Coll., Camb. (BA 1957, MA 1961): *m.* 1961, Caroline Rachael, only da. of Eric Lewis of Upper Bridlemere, Woodhall Spa, Lincs., and has issue living, Marcus Lowell, *b.* 1964,—Vivyan Katy, *b.* 1962. *Residence*, Nutfield, Wickhurst Rd., Weald, Kent.
Widow living of 1st Baronet—JOYCE WALLACE (*Joyce, Lady Ackroyd*) (Finches, Bromley, Kent), da. of Robert Whyte, JP, of Chislehurst, Kent: *m.* 1927, Sir Cuthbert Lowell Ackroyd, 1st Bt., who *d.* 1973.
Sir Cuthbert Lowell Ackroyd, 1st Bt., son of Benjamin Batley Ackroyd, of Dewsbury, Yorks, was Lord Mayor of London 1955-56.

ACLAND, Creation (E.) 1678, with precedency from 1644, of Columb-John, Devon.

Unshaken.

Seat—Killerton, Broadclyst, Devon.

Sir RICHARD THOMAS DYKE ACLAND, 15th *Baronet ; b.* Nov. 26th, 1906; *s.* his father, the *Rt. Hon. Sir* FRANCIS DYKE, *M.P.*, 1939; ed. at Rugby, and at Balliol Coll., Oxford (B.A. 1927) ; Bar. Inner Temple 1930; sometime Lance-Bombardier R.A. ; formerly Lieut. R.A. (T.A.); was Assist. Liberal Whip 1935-7, and Leader of Common Wealth Parliamentary Party 1944-5, and Second Church Estates Commr. 1950-51; Senior Lecturer, St. Luke's Training Coll., Exeter; MP for Barnstaple Div. of Devon (*L* and subsequently *Common Wealth*) 1935-45, and for Gravesend Div. of Kent (*Lab.*) 1947-55: *m.* 1936, Anne Stella, ARIBA, da. of R. G. Alford, of 21, Cheyne Walk, Chelsea, S.W., and has issue.

Arms—Checky argent and sable, a fesse gules. **Crest**—A man's hand apaumée couped at the wrist in a glove lying fessewise to the sinister, thereon a falcon perched all proper, jessed and belled or.

Sons living—JOHN DYKE, *b.* May 13th, 1939; ed. at Clifton, and at Magdalene Coll., Camb. (BA, MSc): *m.* 1961, Virginia, ygr. da. of Roland Forge, of The Grange, Banold-le-Beck, Grimsby, and has issue living, Dominic Dyke, *b.* 1962,—Piers Dyke, *b.* 1964,—Holly Dyke, *b.* 1972.— Robert Dyke (Sprydon, Broadclyst, Devon), *b.* 1941; ed. at Bryanston, and at London Univ. (MB, BS); FRCS England, LRCP London: *m.* 1963, Sarah da. of Cdr. James Wood, of Liss, Hants, and has issue living, Daniel James Dyke, *b.* 1969,—Beatrice Maud Dyke, *b.* 1966.— Henry Duke *b.* 1943; ed. at Clifton and at Magdalene Coll., Camb. (BA; DPhil. Oxon): *m.* 1967, Norma, da. of P. N. Gatley, of 28, Cherry Tree Av., Runcorn, Ches.
Brother living—Cuthbert Henry Dyke, *OBE*, (Stagshaw, Ambleside, Westmorland), *b.* 1910; ed. at Trin. Coll., Camb. (BA 1932); Maj. (ret.) RE; High Sheriff of Westmorland 1968; National Trust Regional Agent for NW; OBE (Civil) 1971.

Collateral Branches living.

Issue of the late Arthur Geoffrey Dyke Acland, 2nd son of 14th Bt., *b.* 1908, *d.* 1964: *m.* 1932 (Winifred) Julian Dorothy (Melmore, Burneside, nr. Kendal, Westmorland), da. of Lt.-Col. Sydney Roden Fothergill, J.P., D.L., of Lowbridge House, Kendal:— Oliver Geoffrey Dyke (Millside, Burneside, nr. Kendal), *b.* 1934; 2nd Lt. Border Regt.: *m.* 1959, Judith Veronica, 2nd da. of the late Peter Willans, of 18, Canonbury Park North, N1, and has issue living, Peter Geoffrey Dyke, *b.* 1961,—Francis Oliver Dyke, *b.* 1963,—Christopher John Dyke, *b.* 1966——Robin Julian Dyke, *b.* 1937.——Edward Francis Dyke, *b.* 1942.

Grandchildren of the late Col. Charles Arthur Williams TROYTE, el. son of the late Arthur Henry Dyke TROYTE, 2nd son of 10th baronet:— Issue of the late Major Herbert Walter ACLAND-TROYTE, M.C., *b.* 1882, *d.* 1943 : *m.* 1910, Marjorie Florence, from whom he obtained a divorce 1922, da. of the late Charles Guy Pym (formerly M.P. for Bedford), of Cæsar's Camp, Sandy, Beds :— John (Huntsham House, Tiverton, Devon), *b.* 1914.——Anne WIGNALL, *b.* 1912; assumed by deed poll 1969 the surname of Wignall: *m.* 1st, 1933, the 5th Baron Ebury, who *d.* 1957, and from whom she had obtained a divorce 1941; 2ndly, 1941, as his second wife, Henry Peregrine Rennie Hoare, who obtained a divorce 1946 [M. Bristol]; 3rdly, 1947, as his second wife, Lt.-Col. Frederick Edwin Barton Wignall, Life Gds. (ret.), who *d.* 1956 [Tate, Bt. colls.], 4thly, 1961, Anthony Freire Marreco, and has issue living (by 1st m.) [see B. Ebury],—(by 3rd m.) Caroline Louisa, *b.* 1948: *m.* 1969, Victor Stewart Heron Walker, of Ablington Manor, Bibury, Glos., only son of Sir James Heron Walker, 5th Bt. (cr. 1868). *Residence,*—Huntsham House, Tiverton, Devon.

Grandchildren of the late Capt. John Edward ACLAND (infra):— Issue of the late Capt. Henry Vivian Acland, *b.* 1883, *d.* 1968: *m.* 1st, 1910, Jeanne, who *d.* 1950, only da. of M. Vander Nest, formerly Min. for Belgium in USA; 2ndly, 1951, Mrs. Inez Sweetwood (c/o Toronto-Dominion Bank, Queen and Kent St., Charlottetown, Prince Edward Island), da. of Robert Everett Mutch, of Charlottetown, Prince Edward Island:— (By 1st m.) John Vivian, *b.* 1911; Capt. R. Westminster Rept., Canadian Army: *m.* 1st, 1935, Edith Eleanor, who *d.* 1953, da. of the late John Waterman, of Vancouver, BC; 2ndly, 1954, Joan Wilmot, and has issue living (by 2nd m.) Peter Vivian, *b.* 1955,—Antony Robert, *b.* 1957 ——Peter Theodore, *b.* 1914: Maj. 2nd Canadian Guards, and Maj. (ret.) Indian Army.— Patricia Evelyn, *b.* 1920: *m.* 1945, Robert Browne-Clayton, late Lt., Princess Patricia's Canadian LI, of 4534, Paret Rd., Kelowna, BC, Canada, and has issue living, Patrick Robert, *b.* 1947; ed. at Nôtre Dame Univ., Nelson, BC (BSc),—Peter Shane, *b.* 1949; ed. BC Univ. (BSc): *m.* 1972, Mary Elizabeth, da. of W. C. Law, of Vancouver, BC,—Jeanne Madeline, *b.* 1953.

Grandchildren of the late Col. Charles Arthur Williams Troyte (ante):— Issue of the late Capt. John Edward Acland, 4th King's Own Regt., *b.* 1848, *d.* 1932 (having discontinued the use of the surname Troyte) : *m.* 1882, Norah Letitia Nugent, who *d.* 1938, da. of the late Henry Hyde Nugent Bankes, of Studland Manor, Dorset :— **Arthur Nugent FLOYER-ACLAND**, *CB, DSO, MC* (The Paddock, West Stafford, Dorchester; Army and Navy Club), *b.* 1885; Lt.-Gen. late Duke of Cornwall's L.I.; 1914-18 War in France and Italy (despatches seven times, MC, DSO, Croix de Guerre with two palms), Waziristan 1937-38 (despatches), 1939-45 War; appointed AAG, War Office 1934, and to command 3rd (Jhelum) Inf. Brig. India 1936, and 43rd (Wessex) Div. (TA) 1938; Mil. sec. to Sec. of State for War 1940-42; High Sheriff of Dorset, 1953; a DL for Dorset; assumed by Royal licence 1928 the additional surname of Floyer; DSO 1918, CB (Mil.) 1940: *m.* 1913, Evelyn Stafford, who *d.* 1973, da. of the late Stafford Still, of Lincoln's Inn, and has issue living, Stafford Nugent, *CBE* (The Manor House, West Stafford, Dorchester; United Service Club), *b.* 1916; ed. at Marlborough; Brig. (ret.) late DCLI; OC, 1st Bn. KOYLI 1959-61, GSO 1 (Directing Staff) Australian Staff Coll. 1961-62, Comdg. 130 Inf. Bde. 1963-65; Brig. i/c Admin., and Dep. Cdr. Land Forces, Borneo 1965-66; Brig. A/Q, N. Command 1967/68; Dep. Col. L.I. since 1972; High Sheriff of Dorset 1974-75; 1939-45 War in India, Iraq, W. Desert (prisoner); CBE (Mil.) 1967: *m.* 1950, Patricia Egidia Hastings, da. of the late Lt.-Col. Richard St. Barbe Emmott, Indian Army (ret.) [By Donington (ext.)], and has issue living, Richard Stafford *b.* 1952; ed. at Marlborough; Lt. LI, Andrew Arthur *b.* 1955, Victoria Egidia *b.* 1962.——Charles Edward Bankes (Flat 3, Richmond House, 63, Richmond Rd., Southampton, SO1 3RW), *b.* 1906; ed. at Blundell's Sch.; late Lt.-Col. DCLI; 1939-45 War in France, India and Burma.——Sibell Norah Garteret (2416, Abbott St., Kelowna, BC, Canada), *b.* 1892: *m.* 1919, Lt.-Col. Osborne Victor Maude-Roxby, MBE, MC, who *d.* 1949, and has issue living, Guy Nigel (5527, King George Highway, Surrey, BC, Canada), *b.* 1921: *m.* 1958, Claire Eileen Pollard, and has issue living, Dean Victor *b.* 1961, Craig Leycester *b.* 1965,—Sylvia Norah Grace, *b.* 1926: *m.* 1951, Frederick Molyneux Hackney, Customs Supt., of 21, Tagish Rd., Whitehorse, Yukon, Canada, and has issue living, David Samuel *b.* 1955, Joel Bruce *b.* 1957, Sibell Jeanne *b.* 1952, Gail Patr'cia *b.* 1953.—— Victoria Letitia Troyte, *b.* 1897: *m.* 1928, Maj.-Gen. Nigel William Duncan, CB, CBE, DSO, DL, late RTR, and has issue living, Elizabeth Letitia, *b.* 1929: *m.* 1954, Maj. John Christopher Byron Deverell, RHA (ret.), of Pitlands House, Ramsdell, Basingstoke, and has issue living, John Duncan *b.* 1955; Virginia Letitia *b.* 1957,—Janet Lyndsay Norah, *b.* 1932: *m.* 1956, Maj. Malcolm Vincent Chichester Firth, RA (ret.), of Eastcott Manor, Easterton, Devizes, and has issue living, Richard Lyndsay Martin *b.* 1957, Andrew William Mallaby *b.* 1960, Patrick Nigel Vincent *b.* 1961, David Malcolm Angus *b.* 1964,—Christina Lalage, *b.* 1935: *m.* 1959, Lt.-Col. Roger Halliburton Young, RA, of Creek End, Keyhaven, Lymington, Hants, and has issue living, James Lindsay *b.* 1967, Anthony Halliburton *b.* 1968. *Residence*, The Old Parsonage, Kimmeridge, Wareham, Dorset.

Granddaughter of the late Capt. John Edward ACLAND (ante):—
Issue of the late Capt. John Bevill Acland, *b.* 1890, *d.* 1966: *m.* 1914, Marjorie (Bcx 70, Ganges, Salt Spring Is., BC, Canada), da. of H. Guernsey:—
Ione Vivienne (Box 70, Ganges, Salt Spring Is., BC), *b.* 1915; Headmistress of Strathcona Lodge Sch., Shawnigan Lake, BC 1959-69: *m.* 1936, Charles Clement Guthrie, who *d.* 1966, and has issue living, Barnaby Fairbairn, *b.* 1937; ed. at Univ. of Victoria (BA),—Nicholas Bruce, *b.* 1938; ed. at Univ. of BC (BSc, BEd): *m.* 1966, Anna Scott, and has issue living, Sean Russell *b.* 1967, Ross Cameron *b.* 1968, Ian Benjamen *b.* 1970, Jennifer Sarah *b.* 1974.

Descendants of the late Sir Henry Wentworth Dyke Acland, K.C.B. (4th son of 10th baronet), who was *cr.* a *Baronet* 1890 :—
See Acland, Bt., *cr.* 1890.

Grandchildren of the late Com. Benjamin Dyke Acland, 2nd son of the Rev. Peter Leopold Dyke Acland, 5th son of 10th baronet:—
Issue of the late Lieut.-Col. Baldwyn John Dyke Acland, *b.* 1883, *d.* 1941 : *m.* 1914, Helen Claire, who *d.* 1940, da. of John Breakey, of Chaudière House, Breakeyville, Quebec:—
John Ben Dyke, *b.* 1916; ed. at Rugby: *m.* 1st, 1941 (m. diss. 1950), Beatrice Margaret, who *d.* 1957, da. of William Willes, of Newbold Comyd, Leamington Spa; 2ndly 1950, Lorna Graham, and has issue living (by 1st m), John William Brian Dyke, *b.* 1942: *m.* 1968, Georgina Scarborough, and has issue living, Samantha *b.* 1969, Carina *b.* 1972 (by 2nd m.) Thomas Jeremy Dyke, *b.* 1952,—Diana Jane Dyke, *b.* 1954. *Residence*,—7, St. Andrew St., Tiverton, Devon.
Issue of the late Capt. Hubert Edward Peter Dyke Acland, *b.* 1884, *d.* 1953 : *m.* 1912, Dorothy Marion, who *d.* 1958, da. of Sir John Henry Thorold, 12th Bt. :—
Roger Dyke, *b.* 1920: *m.* 1st, 1945 (m. diss. 1951), Sylvia, only child of the late Nicholas Galperin; 2ndly, 1951, Molly, da. of David McLurg, of Washington, USA, and has issue living, (by 2nd m.) Simon Nicholas Dyke, *b.* 1953.——Anne Dyke, *b.* 1915; formerly Subaltern ATS: *m.* 1948, Ian Graham Gordon. *Residence*, The Old Laundry, Syston, nr. Grantham, Lincolnshire.

Issue of the late Capt. Lauchlan Henry Dyke Acland, MC, *b.* 1889, *d.* 1969: *m.* 1923, Doris Dar (11, Somali Rd., NW2), da. of Hugh Davidson, of 12, Queensbury Pl., SW:—
Julian Dyke (11, Dunton Close, Four Oaks, Sutton Coldfield, Warwicks.), *b.* 1924; ed. at St. Paul's Sch., Magdalen Coll., Oxford (MA, BSc), and Sheffield Univ. (PhD), BM, BCh: *m.* 1964, Alison, da. of Arthur William Chapman, CBE, of 53, Ranmor Cres., Sheffield, and has issue living, Ann Sarah, *b.* 1965.

Granddaughter of the late Rev. Peter Leopold Dyke Acland (ante):—
Issue of the late Rev. Henry Dyke Acland, *b.* 1850, *d.* 1903: *m.* 1878, Adelaide Clementina Hart, who *d.* 1941, da. of the late Richard Vaughan Davis:—
Theodora Julia (Cloud Cottage, Stogumber, Taunton), *b.* 1891.

Granddaughter of the late Rev. Henry Dyke Acland (ante):—
Issue of the late Eng.-Rear-Adm. Edward Leopold Dyke Acland, CB MVO, *b.* 1878, *d.* 1968: *m.* 1910, Phyllis, who *d.* 1973, da. of the late Connell Whipple:—
Adria Margaret, *b.* 1914: *m.* 1st, 1935, Arthur Francis Procter, who *d.* 1970, son of the late Sir Henry Edward Edleston Procter, CBE; 2ndly, 1971, Lt.-Col. James Hawke Dennis, DT, Chevalier of Legion of Honour, of The Dower House, Chippinghurst, Oxon, OX9 9JS, and has issue living (by 1st m.) Susan Caroline, *b.* 1939: *m.* 1969, Timothy Gordon Keown, of Cockslease Farm House, Fawley, Henley-on-Thames, and has issue living, David Nigel *b.* 1971, Alice Belinda *b.* 1972.

Grandchildren of the late Hon. John Barton Arundel Acland, 6th son of 10th baronet:—
Issue of the late John Dyke Acland, *b.* 1863, *d.* 1944 : *m.* 1902, Mary Eveline, who *d.* 1961, el. da. of the late Rev. Canon Harry Woodford St. Hill :—
Thomas St. Hill, *b.* 1910; 1939-45 War with NZEF: *m.* 1963, Margaret Ellen, da. of the late John Musgrove, and widow of Cdr. John Swift Sharp, OBE, RD, RNR.——Emily Mary Dyke, *b.* 1905; is a JP for Somerset; 1939-45 War in ATS. *Residence*, Middle Croft, Porlock, Som.

Issue of the late Henry Dyke Acland, *b.* 1867, *d.* 1942 : *m.* 1906, Elizabeth Grace, who *d.* 1942, da. of the Hon. James Watson, M.L.C., of Sydney, N.S. Wales :—
Phillipa Mabel, *b.* 1914. *Residence*, 8, Dublin Street, Christchurch, New Zealand.

Issue of the late Col. Sir Hugh Thomas Dyke Acland, C.M.G., C.B.E., F.R.C.S., *b.* 1874, *d.* 1956: *m.* 1903, Evelyn Mary, who *d.* 1964, da. of the late J. L. Ovans:—
Sir Hugh John Dyke *KBE* (of Mount Peel Canterbury NZ) *b.* 1904; ed. at Christs Coll. Christchurch; a JP of S. Canterbury; Chm. of New Zealand Wool Board and Vice-Chm. of International Wool Secretariat; a Member of House of Representatives, New Zealand 1942-47; KBE (Civil) 1968: *m.* 1935 Katherine Wilder da. of J. D. Ormond, of Hawkes Bay NZ and has issue living, John Barton Ormond (of Mount Peel, Canterbury, NZ), *b.* 1936: *m.* 1961, Dorothy Rosemary, da. of A. Hobson, of Feilding, NZ, and has issue living, John Barton *b.* 1964, Paul Hobson *b.* 1965, Jessica Emily *b.* 1963, Georgina Katharine *b.* 1969, Alexandra Evelyn *b.* 1970,—Mark Arundel, *b.* 1939,—Rev. Simon Henry Harper (36, Clanricarde Gdns., W2), *b.* 1941,—Audrey Ann, *b.* 1937: *m.* 1960, Hamish McHardy, of Raumati, Waipukarau, Hawkes Bay, NZ, and has issue living Jonathan *b.* 1963, Kate *b.* 1961,—Evelyn Wilder, *b.* 1947,— Sarah Burgoyne *b.* 1951.——Colin Dyke (Woodbourne, Main Rd North, Paraparaumu, NZ), *b.* 1906; 1939-45 War with S. Africa Forces: *m.* 1936, Sybil Marjorie, da. of T. A. Warner, of Durban, Natal, and has issue living, Hugh Thomas Dyke (17, Onehuka Rd., Melling, Lower Hutt, Wellington, NZ), *b.* 1940: *m.* 1965, Fredericka Scott, da. of G. A. Hutton, of Bangor, Dar-

field, N. Canterbury, NZ, and has issue living, Thomas Dyke *b.* 1972, Susannah Scott *b.* 1967, Annabel Emily *b.* 1970,—Mary Ann Warner, *b.* 1936: *m.* 1st, 1964 (m. diss. 1968), Josef Maria Baukes; 2ndly, 1970, Christopher John Hindmarsh, of Nigel St., Havelock North, Hawkes Bay, NZ, and has issue living, John Marcos Acland *b.* 1973, Brigid Acland *b.* 1971, Nicola Acland *b.* 1974.——Michael Dyke, *b.* 1911; 1939-45 War as Lt. NZ Artillery: *m.* 1946, Elizabeth Vibaert da.of H. de C.McArthur, of Dunedin, NZ, and has issue living, Peter McArthur, *b.* 1947,—Alastair Michael, *b.* 1950,—Richard, *b.* 19—. *Residence*,— Christchurch, NZ.——Elizabeth Evelyn Dyke, *b.* 1913; sometime Lt. S. African Women's Auxiliary Army Ser.: *m.* 1944, John Pavey, who *d.* 1952, and has issue living, Timothy John *b.* 1945,—Phillida Ann, *b.* 1946,— Nicola Hornby, *b.* 1948,—Miranda Jane, *b.* 1950. *Residence*, Litton Farm, Otipua, S. Canterbury NZ.

The 1st baronet, Sir John Acland, in the service of Charles I., impaired his fortune by raising and supporting a troop to garrison his house at Columb-John. He was created a baronet, but in the confusion of the civil war the letters patent were destroyed, and on the fall of the royal party he was fined £1,800. After the Restoration, new letters patent were granted, but not till the year 1677, on account of a long minority in the family, in consideration of which the patent specially granted precedency from **1644**. The 10th baronet sat as M.P. for Devon 1812-37, and for N. Devon (*C*) 1837-52, and the Rt. Hon. Sir Thomas Dyke Acland, P.C., 11th baronet, sat as M.P. for W. Somerset 1837-47, for N. Devon (*L*) 1865-85, and for Somersetshire, W., or Wellington, Div. 1885-6. John, grandson of 6th baronet, was also cr. a baronet, 1818 (ext. 1871) and assumed the additional surname of Palmer. The 12th baronet, Sir (Charles) Thomas Dyke, was Dep. Warden of the Stannaries, and sat as M.P. for E. Cornwall (*L*) 1882-5, and for E., or Launceston,Div. of Cornwall 1885-92. The 13th baronet, the Rt. Hon. Sir Arthur Herbert Dyke, P.C., was Vice-Pres. of Committee of Council on Education (with a seat in the Cabinet) Aug. 1892 to June 1895, a Member of Privy Council Committee on Industrial Research, and M.P. for Rotherham Div. of S. Part of W. Riding of York (*L*) 1885-98. The 14th baronet, the Rt. Hon. Sir Francis Dyke, P.C., sat as M.P. for Yorkshire, N. Riding, Richmond Div. (*L*.) 1906-10, for Cornwall, Camborne Div. 1910-22, for Devonshire, Tiverton Div. 1923-4, and for Cornwall, N. Div. 1932-9, and was Financial Sec. to War Depart. 1908-10 and 1911, Under-Sec. of State for Foreign Affairs 1911-15, Financial Sec. to Treasury 1915, and Parliamentary Sec. to Board of Agriculture and Fisheries 1915-16.

ACLAND, Creation (U.K.) 1890, of St. Mary Magdalen, Oxford.

Unshaken.

Sir Hubert Guy Dyke Acland, *DSO,* 4th *Baronet,* *b.* June 8th, 1890; *s.* his brother, *Col. Sir* William Henry Dyke, MC, AFC, TD, 1970; Capt. RN (ret); 1914-19 War and in Baltic with Destroyer Flotilla 1919 (despatches, DSO); in Intelligence Div., Admiralty 1925-27, and Fleet Gunnery Officer, China Station 1928-30; commanded 1st Mine Sweeping Flotilla 1934-35, Fishery Protection Flotilla 1935-36; HMAS *Australia* 1937-38, and HMAS and HMS *Albatross* 1938; Senior Officer, Reserve Fleet (Devonport Div.) 1939; in charge of Chatham Gunnery Sch. 1939-41, and HMS *Vindictive* 1941-42; Maintenance Capt. to Com.-in-Ch., Rosyth 1943, and to Flag Officer-in-Charge, N. Ireland 1943-45; 1939-45 War (Atlantic and N. Africa stars); Silver Jubilee medal (1935) and Coronation medal (1937); DSO 1920: *m.* 1915, Lalage Mary Kathleen, who *d.* 1961, el. da. of the late Capt. John Edward Acland [Acland, Bt., *cr.* 1678, colls.], and has issue.

Arms—Checky argent and sable, a fesse gules, **Crest**—A man's hand apaumée couped at the wrist in glove lying fessewise to the sinister, thereon a falcon perched all proper, jessed and belled or.

Residence,—Abbeyfield, Wyke Oliver Rd., Preston. Weymouth. *Club*,—United Service; Royal Yacht Squadron.

————

Sons living—Antony Guy (Sunny Bank, Totland Bay, I. of W.), *b.* Aug. 17th, 1916; ed. at Winchester and RMA; Maj. (ret.) RA; 1939-45 War in France: *m.* 1st, 1939, Avriel Ann, who *d.* 1943, only child of the late Capt. Mervyn Edward John Wingfield-Stratford, WS [V. Powerscourt, colls.]; 2ndly, 1944, Margaret, el. da. of the late Maj. Nelson Rooke, and has issue living, (by 1st m.) Gail Alison Jane, *b.* 1942: *m.* 1968, Anthony James Rayment, of 30, Lyall Av., Toronto 265, Ont., Canada,—(by 2nd m.) Christopher Guy Dyke, *b.* 1946; ed. at Allhallows' Sch. and RMA; Capt. RA: *m.* 1971, Christine Mary Carden, SRN, yst. da. of John William Brodie Waring, MB, BS, of Waterdip, Totland, I. of Wight, and has issue living, Alexander John Dyke *b.* 1973,—Caroline Barbara Margaret, *b.* 1947; SRN, SCM: *m.* 1972, Peter Desmond George Sleigh, of Waimate, NZ, and has issue living, David Ralph *b.* 1972, John Antony *b.* 1973.—— James Alison, DSO (Keepers Cottage, W. Stafford, Dorchester, Dorset), *b.* 1919; Maj.(ret.) RTR; 1939-45 War in France, N. Africa and Italy (DSO): *m.* 1942, Diana Marcia, only da. of the late James Edward Briggs, of The Elms, Troy, Monmouth, and has issue living, David James Dyke, *b.* 1947; ed. at Nautical Coll., Pangbourne, RNC Dartmouth; Lt. RN,—Ion Andrew Dyke, *b.* 1949; ed. at Nautical Coll., Pangbourne; with P & O Lines Ltd.,—Angela Marcia Dyke, *b.* 1946.

Daughters living of 3rd Baronet—Elizabeth Margaret, *b.* 1919: *m.* 1943 (m. diss. 1968), Maj. Edward Cecil O'Brien, OBE, Parachute Regt. [*see* B. Inchiquin, colls.].——Juliet Mary, *b.* 1922; a JP and a Co. Councillor of Herts.: *m.* 1939, Peter Robert Tabor, RAFVR [D. Somerset, colls.], and has issue living, Robert Simon Dyke (52, Cordrey Gdns., Coulsdon Woods, Surrey), *b.* 1945: *m.* 1970, Brenda Frazer,—James Patrick *b.* 1950,—Rosemary Jill, *b.* 1941; a JP for Avon: *m.* 1962, Richard Hawksworth Horton-Fawkes, of First House, Combe Hay, nr. Bath, and has issue living, David Hawksworth *b.* 1964, Katharine Elizabeth *b.* 1965, Jessica Mary *b.* 1967,—Theresa Mary, *b.* 1943: *m.* 1964, Laurence Atherton Rawstorne, of 70, Bannockburn Rd., Pymble, Sydney, NSW, and has issue living, Patrick Richard Guy *b.* 1968, Joanna *b.* 1966, Amanda Juliet *b.* 1970. *Residence,* Farthings Farm, Glastonbury, Somerset.——(Emily) Patricia, *b.* 1931: *m.* 1953, Kenneth John Coles, and has issue living, Elizabeth Anne, *b.* 1954. *Residence,*—The Old Rectory, Newtimber, Hassocks, Sussex.

Collateral Branches living.

Issue of the late Sir Reginald Brodie Dyke Acland, K.C., 5th son of 1st baronet> *b.* 1856, *d.* 1924: *m.* 1885, Helen Emma, who *d.* **1943,** da. of the late Rev. Thomas Fox, R. of Temple Combe, Wincanton, Somerset :—

Edward Fox Dyke, *b.* 1891 ; ed. at Winchester ; European War 1914-19, with Indian Expeditionary Force as Lieut. Interpreter, and subsequently as a Railway Transport Officer and Lieut. R.A.F., European War 1939-45 as Squadron-Leader R.A.F. Vol. Reserve with Fighter, Bomber, and Maintenance Commands; has Air Efficiency award: *m.* 1924, Beatrice, who *d.* 1972, da. of the late Dr. J. W. Laver, of Grimston, Norfolk, and has issue living, Barbara Elizabeth, *b.* 1929: *m.* 1949, Richard George Adams, of 26, St. Paul's Place, Islington, N1, and has issue living, Juliet Vera Lucy *b.* 1958, Rosamond Beatrice Elizabeth *b.* 1960,—Phyllis Penelope Jane, *b.* 1932: *m.* 1958, Glynn Meirion Owen, of 17, St. Isan Road, Heath, Cardiff, and has issue living, William Edward *b.* 1959, Eleri Jane *b.* 1961, Alys Mair *b.* 1964,—Judith Sarah, *b.* 1942. *Residence,* White Cottage, Eastcourt, Burbage, Wilts.——Ruth Helen, *b.* 1899. *Residence,* Foxlea, Cold Ash, Newbury, Berks.

Granddaughters of the late Sir Reginald Brodie Dyke Acland, K.C. (ante) :—
Issue of the late Wing-Com. Wilfrid Reginald Dyke Acland, D.F.C., A.F.C., *b.* 1894, *d.* 1937: *m.* 1921, Mary Strange (40, Rushfield Rd., Liss, Hants., who *m.* 2ndly, 1939 Air Commodore Thomas Edward Barham Howe, CBE, AFC, who *d.* 1970), da. of the late Thomas Marshall, of Lee-on-Solent:—

Joan Mary Louise, *b.* 1923; European War 1941-5 as 3rd Officer W.R.N.S.: *m.* 1946, Lieut., Com. Peter Allen Ridd Gould, RN, of Hambledon, Stoke Rd., Cobham, Surrey, and has issue living, Timothy Acland Ridd, *b.* 1948,—Angela Mary, *b.* 1950: *m.* 1970, Nicholas David Gooda, and has issue living, Edward Anthony *b.* 1971, Anita Helen *b.* 1973.——Cynthia Helen, *b.* 1928: *m.* 1953, Robert Coston Taylor, of The Farm House, Enton Green, Godalming, Surrey, and has issue living, Frederick Robert Acland, *b.* 1961,—Pamela Harriet, *b.* 1957.

Granddaughters of the late Capt. Francis Edward Dyke Acland, 6th son of 1st baronet:—
Issue of the late Herbert Arthur Dyke Acland, *b.* 1886, *d.* 1968: *m.* 1914, Maud Kathleen (17, Kingsmill, St. John's Wood, NW8), da. of the late Col. G. E. Branson, of Broomgrove, Sheffield:—

Gwyneth Sybil (*Lady Carden*) (North Sydmonton House, Newbury), *b.* 1918: *m.* 1st, 1942, Fl.-Lt. Roderick Stanley Emerson, RAFVR, who *d.* (killed on active ser.) 1944; 2ndly, 1962, Lt.-Col. Sir Henry Christopher Carden, 4th Bt., OBE, and has issue living, (by 1st m.) George Anthony Dyke (Estancia La Ema General Villegas, Buenos Aires, Argentina), *b.* 1943: *m.* 1972, Jilian Graham, da. of F. Graham Roberts, East Farm House, Piddlehinton, Dorset, and has issue living George Mark *b.* 1974.——Stephanie Jane, *b.* 1924: *m.* 1947, Reginald Chase, LDSRCS Eng., of Blue Hills, Finchampstead Ridges, Berks., and has issue living, Phillip Reginald, *b.* 1949,— Douglas Martyn, *b.* 1955.

Issue of the late Capt. Kenneth Francis Dyke Acland, RN, *b.* 1890, *d.* 1975: *m.* 1st, 1915 (m. diss. 1946), Katherine Farquharson, only da. of the late Robert Granbery Baillie; 2ndly, 1946, Jean Elspeth Clare (Bougearel, Quartier St. Michel, 06140 Vence, France), da. of the late Rear-Adm. Colin Mackenzie, CIE, DSO:—
(By 1st m.) Elizabeth Katherine Baillie (12, Eton Terr., Edinburgh 4), *b.* 1920.

Issue of the late Col. Alfred Dyke Acland, C.B.E., 7th son of 1st baronet, *b.* **1858,** *d.* 1937: *m.* 1885, the Hon. Beatrice Danvers Smith, who *d.* 1942, da. of the late Rt. Hon. William Henry Smith, M.P. [V. Hambleden] :—

Arthur William, OBE, MC, TD, *b.* 1897; ed. at Eton; Lt.-Col. late Gren. Gds. and Lt.-Col. late 96th (R Devon Yeo.) Field Regt., RA (TA); 1916-18 War (twice wounded, MC), N-W Europe 1944-45, OBE (Mil.) 1946: *m.* 1926, Violet Gwendolen, da. of the late Rev. Canon the Hon. Robert Grimston [*see* E. Verulam, colls.], and has issue living, David Alfred (The Manor, Notegrove, Cheltenham. *Club,* Royal Yacht Squadron), *b.* 1929: *m.* 1960, Serena Elizabeth, da. of Sir Cyril Hugh Kleinwort [*see* Kleinwort, Bt.], and has issue living, Harry Alexander *b.* 1963, Lucy Henrietta *b.* 1962,—Martin Edward (Standon Green, Ware, Herts.; Roy. Yacht Sqdn.), *b.* 1932; ed. at Eton; a JP of Herts.: *m.* 1956, Anne Maureen, da. of S. Ryder Runton, of Wheatley Chase, Ben Rhydding, Yorks., and has issue living, Michael Christopher Dyke *b.* 1958, Richard Arthur Dyke *b.* 1962, Peter Edward Dyke *b.* 1964,—Charles Robert *b.* 1937; is Capt. Grenadier Gds. *Residence,* Yeoman's, 4, Queens Rd., Cowes, I. of Wight, PO31 8BQ. *Club,* Guards', and Royal Yacht Squadron.——Peter Bevil Edward, OBE, MC, TD (Feniton Court, Honiton, Devon, EX14 0BE), *b.* 1902; ed. at Eton, and at Ch. Ch., Oxford; Hon. Brig.; Hon. Col. R. Devon Yeo. 1953-67; a JP for Devon (High Sheriff 1961), Vice-Lt. 1962, and late Political Ser., Sudan; 1939-45 War in Abyssinia, N. Africa, and Ægean Islands (wounded, despatches, MC, OBE); has 4th class Order of the Nile; OBE (Mil.) 1946: *m.* 1927, Bridget Susan, da. of the late Rev. Herbert Barnett (Hon. Canon of Ch. Ch., Oxford), of Farley Moor, Binfield, Bracknell, Berks [Lethbridge, Bt., colls.], and has issue living, John Hugh Bevil (of Feniton Court, Honiton, Devon. *Club,* Guards'), *b.* 1928; ed. at Eton; Col. Scots Gds.; an Equerry to HRH the late Duke of Gloucester 1956-74; Malaya 1950-51, Cyprus 1951-52; Egypt 1952-53; Zanzibar 1962-63: *m.* 1953, Myrtle Christian Euing, da. of Brig. Alaistair Wardrop Euing Crawford, of La Fougeraie, Gorey, Jersey, and has issue living, Peter John *b.* 1954, Victoria Susan *b.* 1958,—Antony Arthur (17, Fife Rd., E. Sheen, SW14) *b.* 1930; entered Foreign Ser. 1953; Prin. Private Sec. to Sec. of State for Foreign Affairs 1972: *m.* 1956, Clare Anne, el. da of the late Francis Reynolds Verdon, of Littlefields, Sidbury, Devon, and has issue living, Simon Hugh Verdon *b.* 1958, Nicholas Anthony Bevil *b.* 1960, Katharine Mary *b.* 1965.——Sarah Beatrice (*Lady Stafford-King-Harman*), *b.* 1896: *m.* 1917, Lt.-Col. Sir Cecil William Francis Stafford-King-Harman, 2nd Bt., late King's Roy. Rifle Corps. *Residence,*—St. Catherine's Park, Leixlip, co. Kildare.

The 1st baronet, Sir Henry Wentworth Acland, K.C.B., M.D., LL.D., D.C.L., F.R.S. (4th son 10th baronet of creation 1678, *see* ante), a well-known scientist, was Regius Professor of Medicine at Oxford, Hon. Physican to H.M. King Edward VII. when Prince of Wales, and Member and Pres. of Medical Council of United Kingdom. Adm. Sir William Alison Dyke Acland, C.V.O., 2nd Bt., was Naval A.D.C. to Queen Victoria 1896-9, second in command of Channel Squadron 1901-2, and Adm. Sup. of Gibraltar Dockyard 1902-4.

Acland (Fuller-Acland-Hood), see Hood.

ADAIR, Creation (U.K.) 1838, of Flixton Hall, Suffolk.

Loyal to the dead.

Sir ALLAN HENRY SHAFTO ADAIR, *GVCO, CB, DSO, MC,* 6th *Baronet*; *b.* Nov. 3rd, 1897 ; *s.* his father, *Sir* (ROBERT) SHAFTO ADAIR, 1949 ; ed. at Harrow ; Maj.-Gen. (ret.) late Gren. Gds.; Col. Gren. Gds. 1960-74; is a JP for Suffolk, a DL for co. Antrim, and a Patron of seven livings; 1918 War in France and Belgium (wounded, MC and Bar, Croix de Guerre, two medals), 1939-45 War in France (wounded, despatches, DSO, CB, Legion of Honour, Order of Leopold of Belgium); Exon HM's Bodyguard of Yeomen of the Guard 1947-50, Ensign 1950-51, and Lt. 1951-67; DSO 1940, CB (Mil) 1945, CVO 1957, KCVO 1967, GCVO 1974: *m.* 1919, Enid Violet Ida, da. of the late William Humble Dudley Ward [*see* E. Dudley, colls.], and has issue.

Arms—Per bend or and argent, three dexter hands couped at the wrist and erect gules. **Crest**—A man's head affrontée, couped at the neck proper.

Seat—Ballymena, co. Antrim. *Residences*—Holy Hill, Strabane, co. Tyrone; 55, Green St., W. I. *Clubs*—Guards', Turf.

Daughters living—Bridget Mary (*Lady Darell*), *b.* 1928: *m.* 1953, Brig. Sir Jeffrey Lionel Darell, MC, 8th Bt., Coldm. Gds. *Residence*, 55, Green St., WI.——Juliet Enid, *b.* 1930: *m.* 1949, Edward Fitzgerald, MC, late Capt. Irish Gds., and has issue living, Desmond Maurice Allan, *b.* 1953,—Patrick Shafto, *b.* 1954. *Residence*, 25, Burnsall St., SW3.——Annabel Violet, *b.* 1937.

Sister living—Camilla Mary Shafto, *b.* 1895 ; is a J.P. for Suffolk : *m.* 1918, Edmund Henry Apsley Treherne, J.P., who *d.* 1958, and has issue living, David Allan Apsley, *b.* 1919 ; Capt. Green Howards attached Glider Pilot Regt. : *m.* 1st, 1942, Daphne Fairlie, da. of Brigadier Dudley Vere Morley Balders, O.B.E., M.C., of Cleveragh, Waverley Drive, Camberley ; 2ndly, 1946, Mrs. Milly Alice Dorndorf, and has issue living, (by 1st marriage) Allan Apsley *b.* 1943, Julian Dalrymple *b.* 1945,—Robert Philip Dalrymple (Heron's Folly, Mayfield, Sussex), *b.* 1925; formerly Lt. Grenadier Guards: *m.* 1951, Nina Isobel Amy, da. of the late Peter Haig Haig-Thomas [E. Normanton], and has issue living, Thomas Edmund *b.* 1953, Patrick John *b.* 1955, Henry St. George *b.* 1956, Stephen Philip *b.* 1958, Jerome Robert *b.* 1962, Frederick John Owen *b.* 1967, Robert Dunstan John *b.* 1972, Mary Sophie *b.* 1952, Catherine Cornelia *b.* 1960, Margaret Edith Theresa (twin) *b.* 1967,—Geoffrey Avenel (22, Montpelier Sq., SW7), *b.* 1930: *m.* 1968, Bridget Mary Rhona, only child of the late Lt.-Col. Edward Percy Aymer des Graz, Rifle Bde. [see B. Mostyn, colls.], and has issue living, Charles Edward Geoffrey *b.* 1968, Georgina Mary Bridget *b.* 1970. *Residence*,—Heron's Folly, Mayfield, Sussex.

The 2nd baronet, Sir Robert Alexander Shafto, was Lieut. of co. Antrim, he sat as M.P. for Cambridge (L) 1847-52, and 1854-7, and in 1873 was created *Baron Waveney* (peerage of United Kingdom); he died 1886, when the Barony became ext., and the Baronetcy devolved upon his brother.

ADAM, Creation (U.K.) 1917, of Hankelow Court, co. Chester.

The cross gives me welcome rest.

Sir RONALD FORBES ADAM, *G.C.B., D.S.O., O.B.E.*, 2nd *Baronet*; *b.* Oct. 30th, 1885; *s.* his father, *Sir* FRANK FORBES, *C.B., C.I.E.*, 1926 ; ed. at Eton ; Hon. LL.D. Aberdeen 19—; Hon. Fellow Worcester Coll., Oxford 19—; Gen. late R.A. ; European War 1914-18 in France and Italy (despatches thrice, D.S.O., O.B.E., 1914 star, two medals), European War 1939-45 in France and Belgium Comdg. 3rd Corps (despatches, K.C.B., G.C.B.) ; appointed Comdt. Staff Coll., Camberley, Sept. 1937, Dep. Ch. of Imperial Gen. Staff Dec. 1937, and Gen. Officer Comdg.-in-Ch., N. Command June 1940; was A.-G. to the Forces June 1941 to May 1946 ; became Col. Comdt. R.A. and Army Educational Corps 1940 ; Chm. of British Council 1946-54, Pres. of Library Asso. 1949, and Chm. of Executive Board of United Nations Education, Scientific and Cultural Organisation 1952-4 ; Pres. of Marylebone Cricket Club 1946-47; Pres. of National Institute of Adult Education 1948-64, and Principal of Working Men's Coll., N.-W. 1956-60; Chm. of Council of Inst. of Education, London Univ. 1948-67; a Trustee of National Central Library 1953-69; DSO 1918, OBE (Mil) 1919, CB (Mil.) 1939, KCB (Mil) 1941, GCB (Mil.) 1946: *m.* 1915, Anna Dorothy, who *d.* 1972, 2nd da. of Frederick Islay Pitman, of Scarlets, Berks, and has issue.

Arms—Argent, a mullet pierced between three cross-crosslets fitchée gules, a chief of the last thereon a pale or, charged with a rose of the second, barbed and seeded proper. **Crest**—A cubit arm argent holding in the hand a cross-crosslet fitchée in bend sinister, and charged on the wrist with a rose, both as in the arms.

Residence—Carylls Lea, Faygate, Sussex. *Clubs*—United Service, Athenæum.

Daughters living—Barbara Forbes (*Lady Proctor*). *b.* 1917 : *m.* 1953, as his second wife, Sir (Philip) Dennis Proctor, K.C.B. *Residence,* 43, Canonbury Square, N.1.——Bridget Islay Forbes, *MBE, b.* 1927; Lt.-Col. WRAC; MBE (Mil.) 1960.——Isabel Forbes (twin), *b.* 1927.

Brother living—Colin Gurdon Forbes, *C.S.I., b.* 1889; ed. at Eton, and at King's Coll., Camb. (B.A. 1911); entered I.C.S. 1913, and retired 1927; sometime Private Sec. to Gov. of Bombay; JP of E. Riding of Yorks; 1916-18 War in Mesopotamia and Palestine; CSI 1924: *m.* 1920, the Hon. Irene Constance Lawley, da. of 3rd Baron Wenlock, and has issue living, *Rev.* Stephen Timothy Beilby Forbes, *b.* 1923; ed. at Eton, and at Balliol Coll., Oxford: *m.* 1954, Penelope, da. of G. C. Munday, MC, of Leverington Hall, Wisbech, Cambridgeshire, and has issue living, Anna Victoria *b.* 1955, Catherine Mary *b.* 1956, Lucy *b.* 1960,—Sonia Clare *b.* 1966,—Nigel Colin (Skipwith Hall, Selby, Yorks.), *b.* 1930; ed. at Eton, and at King's Coll., Camb.: *m.* 1954, Teresa Hermione Idena, only da. of Cdr. David Robertson, RN, and has issue living, Charles David *b.* 1957, Titus Desmond *b.* 1960, Julian Nigel Peregrine *b.* 1961, Harry Crispin *b.* 1962,— Virginia Mary Forbes (The Grange, Elvington, York), *b.* 1922: *m.* 1948, Capt. Hugo Francis Guy Charteris, MC, Scots Gds., who *d.* 1970, [*see* E. Wemyss and March]. *Residence,*—The Grange, Elvington, York. YO4 5AD.

Sister living—Hetty Clifford Reay, *M.B.E., b.* 1896 ; Co. Sec., Women's Land Army, W. Sussex. *Residence,* Carylls Lea, Faygate, Horsham, Sussex.

Collateral Branches living.

Issue of the late Eric Graham Forbes Adam, C.M.G., 2nd son of 1st baronet
    b. 1888, *d.* 1925 : *m.* 1918, Agatha Perrin, da. of Reginald Walter Macan,
    Master of Univ. Coll., Oxford, and widow of Sidney Spooner :—
CHRISTOPHER ERIC FORBES, *b.* Feb. 12th, 1920 : *m.* 1957, Patricia Anne Wreford, younger
   da. of the late John Neville Wreford Brown. *Residence,* 46, Rawlings Street, S.W.3.

    Grandchildren of Colin Gurdon Forbes Adam, C.S.I. (ante) :—
Issue of the late Desmond Francis Forbes Adam, *b.* 1926, *d.* 1958: *m.* 1949, the Hon.
    Vivien Elisabeth (of 11, Mulberry Walk, SW3), da. of Sir Oswald Ernald Mosley, 6th
    Bt. [see B. Ravensdale.]:—
Rupert Colin, *b.* 1957.——Cynthia Rebecca, *b.* 1950.——Arabella Irene, *b.* 1952.

The 1st baronet, Sir Frank Forbes Adam, C.B., C.I.E., was Pres. of Bombay Chamber of Commerce 1884-9, and Manchester Chamber of Commerce 1893, 1894, and 1903-5.

AGNEW, Creation (N.S.) 1629, of Lochnaw, Wigtownshire.

By counsel not by rashness

Sir FULQUE MELVILLE GERALD NOEL AGNEW OF LOCHNAW, 10th *Baronet,* son of the late Major Charles Hamlyn Agnew, 3rd son of 8th baronet; *b.* 1900; *s.* his uncle, Sir ANDREW NOEL, 1928; ed. at Harrow; sometime Lt. 4th Batn. R. Sussex Regt: *m.* 1937, Swanzie, da. of Capt. Esme Nourse Erskine, CMG, MC, and has issue [The 10th Baronet *d.* Aug. 28th, 1975].

Arms—Argent, a chevron between two cinque-foils in chief gules, and a saltire couped in base azure. **Crest**—An eagle issuant and reguardant proper. **Supporters**—Two heraldic tigers proper collared and chained or.
Address—University of Malawi, Box 280, Zomba, Malawi.

Son living—CRISPIN HAMLYN (2, Lonsdale Terr., Edinburgh, EH3 9HN; Alpine, and Army and Navy Clubs), *b.* May 13th, 1944; ed at Uppingham and RMA; Capt. RHF, a Member of East Greenland Expedition 1966, Leader of Army East Greenland Expedition 1968, a Member of Jt. Sers. Expedition to Elephant Island 1970-71, Leader of Jt. Sers. Expedition to Chilean Patagonia 1972-73, a Member of Army Nuptse Expedition, 1975.

Collateral Branches living.

    Grandsons of the late Col. Quentin Graham Kinnard Agnew, DSO, MVO, 4th
    son of 8th Baronet (ante):—
Issue of the late Col. David Quentin Hope Agnew, *b.* 1900, *d.* 1975: *m.* 1928, Janet May
    Dilkes (Anwoth Cottage, Gatehouse of Fleet, Castle Douglas, Kirkcudbrightshire), da.
    of the late Rev. Charles Herbert Malden, R. of Little Gransden, Beds.:—
Andrew David Quentin (5-6, Clarach Rd., Borth, Dyfed), *b.* 1929; ed. at Trin. Coll., Glenalmond and
   Edinburgh Univ. (BSc); Ph.D. Bangor: *m*' 1957, Shirley, da. of the late James Arnold Smithson,
   of Woodstock, Simonstone, Lancs, and has issue living, David James, *b.* 1960,—Peter Jonathan,
   b. 1963,—Robin Andrew *b.* 1966.——Jonathan Herbert (Barchuill, Gatehouse of Fleet, Castle
   Douglas, Kirkcudbrightshire, and 210, Main Rd., Broomfield, Essex, ard has issue living, George
   Archibald Quentin, *b.* 1962,—Michael Stannus, *b.* 1965,—Susan Louise, *b.* 1963.

    Issue of the late Col. Quentin Graham Kinnaird Agnew, D.S.O., M.V.O., 4th son
    of 8th baronet, *b.* 1861, *d.* 1937 : *m.* 1st, 1899, Evelyn Mary, who *d.* 1913, da. of
    the late Capt. J. H. I. Alexander, C.B., R.N.; 2ndly, 1916, Cicely Anne
    Churchill, who *d.* 1964, youngest da. of the late James Inskip, of Clifton Park
    House, Clifton:—
John Andrew, RN, *b.* 1903; became Com. 1943: *m.* 1934, Ysabel Augusta Aurelia, da. of Don
   Ernesto Larios, of Algeciras, Spain, and has issue living, Fulke Quentin Ernesto, *b.* 1938; Maj.
   RHF: *m.* 1970, Susan Georgina, el. da. of Group Capt. F. H. Tyson, RAF (ret.), of Diss, Norfolk,
   and has issue living, Tomas Quentin *b.* 1972,—Luisa Beatrice, *b.* 1973. *Residence,*—Monte de la
   Torre, Los Barrios, Provincia de Cadiz, Spain. *Club,*—Naval and Military.——Suzanna Mary,
   b. 1907: *m.* 1942, Henry Nicolai Sclater and has issue living, Patrick Henry (23A, High Street
   West, Dorchester, Dorset), *b.* 1944; ed. at Charterhouse, and R. Agric. Coll., Cirencester: *m.*
   1968, Rosalyn Heather, da. of Urban Stephenson, of Stalbridge, Dorset, and has issue living,
   William Patrick *b.* 1969, Alastair James *b.* 1971,—Andrew Agnew (Wallace Court, Westwell,
   nr. Ashford, Kent), *b.* 1949; ed. at Winchester, and Wye Coll.: *m.* 1969, Joëlle, da. of Lucien
   Patient, of Paris, and has issue living, Julien Renand *b.* 1970, Chloë Elise *b.* 1974. *Residences,*—
   The Cottage, Broughton, Stockbridge, Hants., SO20 8AX; Blackloch, Lochhaw, Stranraer,
   Wigtownshire.

Grandchildren of the late Col. Quentin Graham Kinnaird Agnew, D.S.O., M.V.O.
(ante):—
Issue of the late Capt. Patrick Alexander Agnew, Seaforth Highlanders, *b.* 1908, *d.* (killed
in action during European War) 1943: *m.* 1936, Baroness Johanna Elizabeth (who *m.*
2ndly, 1944, Lt.-Col. William Stanley Baird), da. of Baron Barthold Mackay [*see*
L. Reay, colls.]:—
Robin Andrew Patrick Mackay, *b.* 1940: *m.* 1965, Diana Clyde, da. of Humphrey Dinsdale Phillips
and formerly wife of David Allan Bennett, and has issue living, Jordon Alexander Mackay
b. 1967——Rosemary Joanna Evelyn, *b.* 1938: *m.* 1960, Arthur Struan Hannay Robertson, and
has issue living, Duncan Straun Alexander, *b.* 1961,—Jonathan Dougal, *b.* 1962. *Residence,*—

Granddaughters of the late Rev. David Carnegie Andrew Agnew, 3rd son of 7th
baronet:—
Issue of the late Andrew David Carnegie Agnew, *b.* 1856, *d.* 1927: *m.* 1882, Minnie Dale,
who *d.* 1928, da. of David Dale Buchanan:—
Pearl Eleanor Isabella Jane, *b.* 1883.——Amethyst Muriel Dale, *b.* 1892: *m.* 1944, W. Hulley,
who *d.* 1947.——Ivy Diamond Dale (4, St. Johns Av., Glenwood, Durban, Natal), *b.* 1895.

Grandchildren of the late Sir Stair Andrew Agnew, KCB 5th son of 7th baronet:
Issue of the late Stair Carnegie Agnew, *b.* 1872, *d.* 1940: *m.* 1918, Sylvia Bellville, who
d. 1974, da. of the late Alexander Martin Bunster Bremner, Bar.-at-Law, of 1, St.
Petersburg Place, W., and 3, Paper Buildings, Temple, EC:—
Lesley Stair, *b.* 1919 ; Sister Mary Magdalene ; has been Canoness Regular of Order of St.
Augustine since 1945.
Issue of the late Col. Herbert Charles Agnew, O.B.E., late R.E., *b.* 1880, *d.* 1949: *m.* 1919,
Enys (now of Bonjedward House, Jedburgh), da. of the late James Wason, of Merton
Hall, Wigtownshire :—
John Nevin, *b.* 1922; ed. at Rugby, and at Ch. Ch., Oxford (MA): Lt.-Col. (ret.) Coldstream
Guards: *m.* 1951, Margaret Scott, da. of the late Moffat Thomson, of Lambden,
Berwickshire, and has issue living, Andrew Robert *b.* 1956,—James Douglas, *b.* 1959,—Jean
Catherine, *b.* 1953. *Residence,* Bonjedward House, Jedburgh, Scotland.——Patrick William,
b. 1927; ed. at Rugby, and at Trin. Coll., Camb. (B.A. 1947, M.A. 1963): *m.* 1958, Anne Meryl
Turner, and has issue living, David Martin, *b.* 1959,—Stephen William, *b.* 1963,—Hazel Patricia,
b. 1961. *Residence,* North Lodge, Tak-ma-Doon Rd., Kilsyth, Stirlingshire.

Grandson of the late Thomas Frederick Andrew Agnew, 6th son of 7th Bt.:—
Issue of the late Capt. Douglas Agnew, R.N., *b.* 1869, *d.* 1953 : *m.* 1904, Helen Louise
Ann, who *d.* 1962, da. of the late Robert Thorne, of Greenock:—
Frederick Douglas,*TD, b.* 1909; ed. at Repton; Maj. (ret.) The King's Regt. (Liverpool); 1939-45
War at Singapore as DAAG 18th Div. (prisoner): *m.* 1st, 1938, Barbara (from whom he obtained
a divorce 1950), da. of R. T. B. Glasspool, of Calday Grange School, West Kirby; 2ndly, 1951,
Vivien Elizabeth Willoughby, da. of Harold Willoughby Bartlett, of Vine Leigh House, Well
End, Bourne End, Bucks, and has issue living, (by 1st m.) Jocelyn, *b.* 1940: *m.* 1965, Raymond
Graham Jenner, of 1C, Park Hill Close, Carshalton Beeches, Surrey, and has issue living, Angus
Donald Agnew *b.* 1966, Bruce Roderick *b.* 1969. *Residence,* Ellenbank, Kirkcudbright.

Granddaughters of the late Thomas Frederick Andrew Agnew, 6th son of 7th
baronet:—
Issue of the late Percy Reginald Agnew, *b.* 1878, *d.* 1952 : *m.* 1909, Ethel Adelaide Susan
Wakefield, who *d.* 1962:—
Kathleen Julia: *m.* 1940, William Robert Logie of Hillhead, Piper's Lane, Heswall, Cheshire, and
has issue living, William Robert Agnew, *b.* 1942: *m.* 1971, Alison Grant, yr. da. of George Alexander Grant Peterkin, MBE, MB, ChB, of 24, Belgrave Cres., Edinburgh, 4.—Johanna Susan,
b. 1941: *m.* 1966, William John Andrew Mortimer-Harvey, and has issue living, Kate Johanna
b. 1966, Victoria Heather *b.* 1967,—Margaret Kathleen, *b.* 1944: *m.* 1969, Andrew Boyd, and
has issue living, Sarah Kirstie *b.* 1972,—Heather Alexander, *b.* 1945.——Maud Susan Rosemary:
m. 1941, Jarvis H. Campbell, and has issue living, John Agnew, *b.* 1949: *m.* 1974, Kathleen Mary,
yr. da. of Alexander Shaw Ferguson W.lson, of The Orchard, Kilbride, Doagh, co. Antrim,—
Adelaide Elizabeth, *b.* 1943,—Eily Jane, *b.* 1945,—Dinah Mary, *b.* 1953. *Residence,* The Moat
Inn, Donegore, Dunadry, co. Antrim.——Poppy Eily, *b.* 1915.——Denis Francis, *b.* 1917.——
Nancy Marion, *b.* 1919: *m.* 1939, Philip Humphrey Vellacott, and has issue living, Giles Wake-
field, *b.* 1949.—Julia Clare, *b.* 1943,—Teresa, *b.* 1944. *Residence,* Tan y Bryn, Franksbridge,
Llandrindod Wells.

The first three baronets successively represented Wigtownshire in Parliament,—the latter was also
a member of the Grand Convention of Estates 1689. The 5th baronet, a Lieut.-Gen. in the army,
received £4,000 as compensation for the abolition of the office of Sheriff of Wigtownshire, which had
been hereditary in this family for more than 300 years. The 7th baronet was M.P. for Wigtownshire
(L) 1830-38, and the 8th, 1856-68. The 9th baronet was M.P. for Edinburgh, S. Div. (*L.U.*) 1900-
1906.

AGNEW, Creation (U.K.) 1895, of Great Stanhope Street, St. George, Hanover Square, co. London.

Sir (JOHN) ANTHONY STUART AGNEW, 4th *Baronet;*
b. July 25th, 1914 ; *s.* his father *Major Sir* JOHN STUART,
1957.

Arms—Per saltire argent and gules, in pale two cinquefoils and in fesse
as many saltires couped, all counterchanged. Crest—An eagle reguardant,
wings expanded proper, each wing charged with a pale or, holding in its
mouth a sword pointed upwards also proper, and resting the dexter claw on
a saltire couped gules.

Seat—Rougham Hall, Bury St. Edmunds.

Consilio et impetu.
By wisdom and vigour.

Brothers living—GEORGE KEITH, *T.D., b.* Nov. 25th, 1918 ; ed.
at Rugby, and at Trin. Coll., Camb.; is Major Suffolk Yeo. (Reserve),
and a J.P.; European War 1939-45 : *m.* 1948, Baroness Anne Merete
Louise, da. of Baron Schaffalitzky de Muckadell, of Rodkilde, Fyn,
Denmark, and has issue living, John Keith, *b.* 1950,—George Anthony, *b.* 1953. *Residence,*
Blackthorpe Farm, Rougham, Bury St. Edmunds.——Stephen William, *b.* 1921 ; ed. at Rugby,
and at Trin. Coll., Camb.; late Lt. 7th Hussars; 1939-45 War (wounded): *m.* 1st 1947 (*m.* diss.
1966) Elizabeth, da. of the late James Brooks Close; 2ndly, 1967, Mrs. Adene Leona Cookson,
yr. da. of Vincent John Brady, of Sydney, and has issue living (by 1st *m.*) John Stuart (Narford

Farm, Narborough, Kings Lynn), *b.* 1949,—Bolton (24, Baring St., N1), *b.* 1950,—James Brooks Close, *b.* 1953,—Stephen Hardcastle, *b.* 1954,—Theodore Thomas More, *b.* 1961,—St. John Kenneth, *b.* 1964,—Margaret Elizabeth Diana, *b.* 1952. *Residence,* Oulton Hall, Norwich.

Uncle living (son of 2nd baronet)—George Colin, *b.* 1882 ; ed. at Rugby, and at King's Coll., Camb. ; European War 1914-16 as Lieut. (despatches, invalided).   *Residence,* 35, Cheyne Court, S.W.3.

Aunts living (daughters of 2nd baronet)—Mary Emily, *b.* 1880: *m.* 1904, William Burn Anderson who *d.* 1948. *Residence,* 32, Pont St., SW1.——Cicely (twin), *b.* 1891: *m.* 1920, Norman Froggatt Kingzett, MBE, who *d.* 1947, and has issue living, Richard Norman (of 18, Sloane Av., Chelsea, SW3), *b.* 1921: *m.* 1952, Julia Mary, da. of Sir Geoffrey Ernest Tritton, MBE, 3rd Bt., and has issue living, Jan Antony *b.* 1955, Christopher Richard Colin *b.* 1958,—Pamela Sybil, *b.* 1925: *m.* 1949, Dowrish Evelyn Louis Joll, of 7, Pelham Place, SW7, and has issue living, William Evelyn Hinton *b.* 1953, Caroline Laura *b.* 1950: *m.* 1974, Nigel Duck, of Yew Tree Cottage Castleton Gwent, Charlotte Elizabeth *b.* 1955, Harriet Sophia *b.* 1959. *Residence,* 50, Cranmer Court, Chelsea, SW3.

Collateral Branches living.

Grandchildren of the late Charles Morland Agnew, O.B.E. (infra) :—
Issue of the late Charles Gerald Agnew, *b.* 1882, *d.* 1954 : *m.* 1906, Olive Mary, who *d.* 1946, da. of the late Ven. William Danks, Canon of Canterbury :—
Sir Geoffrey William Gerald (11, Alexander Sq., SW3; Brooks's and Garrick Clubs), *b.* 1908; ed. at Eton, and at Trin. Coll., Camb. (MA); Chm. of Thos. Agnew & Sons, Ltd. since 1965, of Soc. of London Art Dealers 1970-74, of Friends of Courtauld Inst. since 1970, of Evelyn (Agnew) Nursing Home, Cambidge since 1955, and of St. Geroge's Art Trust, King's Lynn 1966-73, a Vice-Pres. of Artists Gen. Benevolent Inst. since 1968 (Permanent Steward since 1955); Knt. 1973: *m.* 1934, the Hon. Doreen Maud Jessel, da. of 1st Baron Jessel, and has issue living, Jonathan Geoffrey William (6, Brompton Sq., SW3), *b.* 1941; ed. at Eton, and at Trin. Coll., Camb. (BA): *m.* 1966, Hon. Agneta Joanna Middleton Campbell, yr. da. of Baron Campbell of Eskan (Life Baron), and has issue living, Caspar Jonathan William *b.* 1967, Lara Joanna *b.* 1969, Katherine Agneta *b.* 1971,—Morland Herbert Julian (Magnolia House, 64, Strand-on-the-Green, W4), *b.* 1943; ed. at Eton, and at Trin. Coll., Camb. (BA): *m.* 1973, Elizabeth Margaret, yst. da. of William B. Mitchell, of Gateside, Blanefield, Stirlingshire,—Jennifer Maud, *b.* 1937: *m.* 1962, Paul Lazell, of 55, St. James's Gdns., W11, and The Manor House, Wighton, Norfolk, and has issue living, Sebastian Henry *b.* 1963, Dominic Geoffrey Paul *b.* 1972, Natasha Jennifer *b.* 1967.——Denys Martin (Flat 1, 15, West Halkin St., SW1), *b.* 1919; ed. at Eton, and at Trin. Coll., Camb. (BA); Maj. RA (Emergency Reserve); 1939-45 War; MTAI; former Vice-Pres. American Express Internat. UK and Ireland; Dir. of Sales, Europe, Hotel Representative Inc.: *m.* 1st, 1943, Monica, da. of the Rev. S. Foskett, MD, of Killinghall, Harrogate; 2ndly, 1949, Josephine Ann,da. of Alan Ross, of Natal, S. Africa; 3rdly, 1974, Rosetta Mary, da. of Mrs. Ethel Benjamin, of Johannesburg, S. Africa, and has issue living (by 1st m.) Jeremy Andrew Derrick (3912, Linden Place, Colorado Springs, Colorado, USA), *b.* 1943; ed. at Eton, and Colorado Coll., USA (BA), and Univ. of Colorado (BS): *m.* 1968, Mary Sylvia Perkins, and has issue living, Tracy Marie *b.* 1974,—(by 2nd m.) William George Morland, *b.* 1955,—Emma Christianne Annabel, *b.* 1951.

Issue of the late Lieut.-Col. Kenneth Morland Agnew, D.S.O., O.B.E., M.C., R.A. (re-tired), *b.* 1886, *d.* 1951 : *m.* 1st, 1910, Edith, who *d.* 1950, da. of the late Dr. A. H. Laver, of Sheffield ; 2ndly, 1921, Louise, da. of David Harris, of Leeds ; 3rdly, 1942, Lilian, who *d.* 1951, da. of George Matmerson, of Johannesburg, S. Africa :—
(By 1st marriage) Joyce, *b.* 1913: *m.* 1940, Maj. Edwin Peter Holness, R.A. (ret.). *Residence,* 3, Roehampton Gate, SW15 5JR.

Issue of the late Major Alan Graeme Agnew, *b.* 1887, *d.* 1962: *m.* 1913, Dorothy Cecil who *d.* 1959, da. of the late William Winstanley Strode, of Pole House, King's Langley:—
Peter Graeme, *M.B.E.; b.* 1914; Wing Com. R.A.F. Vol. Reserve; M.B.E. (Mil.) 1946: *m.* 1937, Mary Diana, only da. of the late James Philip Hervey, of Knutsford, Cheshire, and has issue living, Ian Hervey (Oaklands Park House, Newdigate, Dorking, Surrey), *b.* 1941: *m.* 1964, Amanda Barbara, da. of the late Maj. A. Wyndham-Read, and has issue living, Mark Wyndham *b.* 1966, Jonathan Graeme *b.* 1968,—James Philip (Nancarras Mill, The Level, Constantine, nr. Falmouth, Cornwall, TR11 5PU), *b.* 1947: *m.* 1972, Carol Ann only da. of the late Edward Garfield Williams, of Constantine, Cornwall, and has issue living, Emma Victoria *b.* 1972,—Penelope Mary, *b.* 1939: *m.* 1961, Lt.-Col. Norman Thomas Davies, MBE RA, c/o Lloyds Bank, Princes Risborough, Bucks., and has issue living, Edward Peter *b.* 1962, Clare Mary *b.* 1964,—Diana Nicola *b.* 1945: *m.* 1966, Anthony David Mayhew, of Broomham Farm, Chiddingly, Sussex, and has issue living, Anthony James *b.* 1969, Gavin Mark *b.* 1971. *Residence,*—Roscaddon, Manaccan, nr. Helston, Cornwall.——Jacquelin, *b.* 1916: *m.* 1937, Joseph Stanley Desmond Whitaker, of Patervan, Tweedsmuir, by Biggar, Lanarkshire, and has issue living, Graeme Stanley (Askew Rigg, Troutbeck, Penrith), *b.* 1938: *m.* 1959, Penelope Ann, da. of the late Group Capt. E. H. Walker, and has issue living, Charles Allan, *b.* 1962, Anthony John, *b.* 1964, Bridget Ann, *b.* 1960,—Nigel Glynne (Kinton Lodge, Kinton, Nesscliffe, Shrewsbury, Salop), *b.* 1940: *m.* 1964, Patricia Caroline, da. of Ian F. Stewart, of Mollstone Wood, Red Lane, Limpsfield, Surrey and has issue living, Jeremy Stewart *b.* 1964, Patricia Frances *b.* 1967,—David Alan (56, Croft Av., Penrith), *b.* 1941: *m.* 1963, Madeline, da. of the late M. Paux, of Koniz, Switzerland, and has issue living, Jean-Francois *b.* 1965, Patrique *b.* 1969, Marie-Claude *b.* 1964,—Jonathan Milnes, *b.* 1947: *m.* 1974, Christine, da. of William Turner, of Menzion, Tweedsmuir.

Issue of the late Charles Morland Agnew, O.B.E., 2nd son of 1st baronet, *b.* 1855, *d.* 1931: *m.* 1881, Evelyn Mary, who *d.* 1932, da. of William Naylor:—
Hugh Ladas, *b.* 1894; Com. R.N. (ret.): *m.* 1st, 1920, Mary Violet Maud, who *d.* 1932, da. of the late Hugh Davies, of Trinidad; 2ndly, 1934, Gwendolen Ford, who *d.* 1975, da. of the late Ernest Albert Smith, and has issue living (by 1st m.), Susan Elizabeth, *b.* 1930: *m.* 1954, Robert Edward Michael Momber, of Durgan, Weybridge, Surrey, and has issue living, Robert Hugh *b.* 1956, Adrian Michael *b.* 1958. *Residence,* 59, Cranmer Court, S.W.3.

Grandchildren of the late Walter Agnew (infra):—
Issue of the late Victor Charles Walter Agnew, *b.* 1887, *d.* 1929 : *m.* 1913, Phyllis May Claude [(Siloam, Morfa Bychan, Portmadoc, N. Wales) : she *m.* 2ndly, 1932, Air Commodore Andrew George Board, CMG, DSO, DL, RAF, who *d.* 1973], da. of the late Claude Baggallay, KC, of 32, Draycott Place, SW:—
Charles David, *b.* 1916; ed. at Harrow; Lt.-Col. (ret.) 15th/19th Hussars: *m.* 1949, Mary Lorna, da. of the late Rt. Rev. Henry St. John Stirling Woollcombe, Bishop of Selby, Yorkshire, and has issue living, David Richard Charles, *b.* 1953,—Susan Lorna, *b.* 1950,—Vanda Jane, *b.* 1959. *Address,*—c/o Lloyds Bank, 6, Pall Mall, SW1. *Club,* Cavalry.——Elizabeth Moran, *b.* 1914: *m.* 1938, Brig. Brian Kingzett, CBE, MC, of The Close, Bourton, Gillingham, Dorset, and has issue living, Charles David Brian, *b.* 1942,—Sarah Elizabeth, *b.* 1945.

Issue of the late Walter Agnew, 3rd son of 1st baronet, *b.* 1861, *d.* 1915 : *m.* 1886, Mabel, who *d.* 1956, da. of Charles Wilkin, of Gordon Square, W.C. :—

Richard Leslie, *b.* 1900; ed. at Rugby; Major 15th/19th King's Roy. Hussars, and 1st Northants Yeo. and Lieut.-Col. E. Riding Yeo. and 146th (Duke of Wellington's Regt.) Roy. Armoured Corps ; High Sheriff of Northamptonshire 1957 ; unsuccessfully contested Northampton (*U*) Feb. 1950 : *m.* 1st, 1927 (marriage dissolved 1946), Leila May, da. of Brig.-Gen. Anthony Courage, D.S.O., M.C. ; 2ndly, 1953, Hilda Dorothy, da. of the late Thomas Henry Spinks, and has issue living, (by 1st marriage) (Richard) Mark Walter, *b.* 1930; Lieut. (ret.) R.N.: *m.* 1955 (m. diss. 1963), Edwina Ottilie Jane, el. da. of the late Maj.-Gen. Sir Robert Edward Laycock, K.C.M.G., C.B., D.S.O. [*see* E. Dudley, colls.], and has issue living, Leonie *b.* 1956,— Leila Rosemary, *b.* 1928: *m.* 1st, 1948 (marriage dissolved 1959), Kenneth Malcolm Ritchie; 2ndly, 1962, Robert John Lyle, of Old Winders House, Peasmarsh, Rye, Sussex, and has issue living, (by 1st m.) Linda Rosemary Anne *b.* 1951: *m.* 1973, Fl. Lt. Nigel Corbishley, Venetia Claire *b.* 1953: *m.* 1972, Robert Christopher Springett Sanders, of 17, Cricket Lea, Lindford, Bordon, Hants., (and has issue living, Katherine Joan *b.* 1974), (by 2nd m.), Richard Charles Cecil *b.* 1965, Lucinda *b.* 1963,—Lavinia Mary *b.* 1933: *m.* 1st, 1952, Geoffrey Arnold Ellert; 2ndly, 1956, Jonathan Rashleigh, of Dumbledore, Warren Row, nr. Wargrave, Berks, and has, issue living, (by 1st m.) Sallyann Barbara RASHLEIGH, *b.* 1953: assumed by deed poll 1970 the surname of Rashleigh, Serena RASHLEIGH *b.* 1954: assumed by deed poll 1970 the surname of Rashleigh (by 2nd m.) Julian Philip *b.* 1957, Elizabeth Jane *b.* 1961. *Residence,*—Peartree Cott., Turweston, Brackley, Northants.

The 1st baronet, Sir William (many years senior partner in the firm of Thos. Agnew and Sons, of Manchester, Liverpool, and London, and Chm. of Bradbury, Agnew, and Co. (Limited), proprietors and publishers of *Punch*), sat as M.P. for S.E. Lancashire (*L*) 1880-85, and for Lancashire (S.E.), Stretford Div. 1885-6, and the 2nd baronet sat as M.P. for Salford, W. Div. (*L*) 1906-18.

AGNEW, Creation (U.K.) 1957, of Clendry, co. Wigtown.

Sir PETER GARNETT AGNEW, 1st *Baronet,* son of the late Charles Leonard Agnew, of Peover Cottage, Knutsford, Cheshire ; *b.* July 9th, 1900 ; ed. at Repton ; Com. R.N. (retired) ; was A.D.C. to Gov. of Jamaica 1927-8 ; Parliamentary Private Sec. to Pres. of Board of Trade (Rt. Hon. Walter Runciman) 1935-7, and to First Commr. of Works (Rt. Hon. Sir Philip Sassoon) 1937-9, an Assist. Govt. Whip May to July 1945, and a Conservative Whip 1945-50; a Church Commr. for England 1948-68; Chm. of Iran Soc. 1966-73; a Trustee of Historic Churches Preservation Trust since 1968, and Pres. of European Centre of Documentation and Information since 1974; Knt. Cdr. of Order of Homayoon of Iran; 1939-44 War with RN (despatches); MP for Camborne Div. of Cornwall (*C*) 1931-50, and for S. Div. of Worcs. 1955-66: *m.* 1928, Enid Frances, da. of the late Henry Boan, of Perth, W. Australia, and has issue.

Arms—Parted per saltire argent and gules, two cinquefoils in pale, and as many saltires couped in fesse all counterchanged, a bordure azure. Crest—An eagle rising reguardant proper, holding in the dexter claw a sword, hilted and pommelled or.

Residence—2, Smith Sq., SW1. *Club*—Carlton.

Son living—QUENTIN CHARLES SOMERVILLE AGNEW-SOMERVILLE, *b.* March 8th, 1929 ; assumed by Roy. licence 1950 the additional surname of Somerville after that of Agnew and the arms of Somerville quarterly with those of Agnew: *m.* 1963, the Hon. Margaret Irene April Drummond, yst. da. of 15th Baron Strange, and has issue living, James Lockett, *b.* 1970,— Amelia Rachel, *b.* 1965,—Geraldine Margaret, *b.* 1967. *Residence*,—Somerville, Navan, co. Meath.

AINSWORTH, Creation (U.K.) 1916, of Ardanaiseig, co. Argyll.

Sir JOHN FRANCIS AINSWORTH, 3rd *Baronet; b.* Jan. 4th, 1912; *s.* his father *Sir* THOMAS, 1971; ed. at Trin. Coll., Camb. (MA); FRHistS); Inspector, Irish Manuscripts Commn. since 1943; Visiting Lecturer in Mediæval History, Univ. Coll., Cork, 1966-69; Vice-Chm. of Dublin SPCA 1964-65, and since 1968 (Chm. 1965-66): *m.* 1st, 1938 (m. diss. 1946), Josephine, el. da. of Cdr. Walter Randolph Bernard, RN [*see* B. Graves, colls.]; 2ndly, 1946, Anita Margaret Ann, el. da. of the late Harold Arthur Lett, of Kilgibbon and Ballynadara, Enniscorthy, co. Wexford.

Residence,—Carraphuca, Shankill, co. Dublin.

Half-Brother living—(THOMAS) DAVID (Crotanstown, The Curragh, co. Kildare), *b.* Aug. 22nd.
1926; ed. at Eton; late Lt. 11th Hussars: *m.* 1957, Sarah Mary, da. of the late Lt.-Col. Hugh
Carr Walford, 17th/21st Lancers, and has issue living, Anthony Thomas Hugh, *b.* 1962,—
Charles David, *b.* 1966,—Serena Mary, *b.* 1958,—Tessa Jane, *b.* 1959.
Sister living—Iris Helen Hersey, *b.* 1916: *m.* 1939, Nicholas St. Vigor Fox, of Lough Park House,
Castlepollard, co. Westmeath [Sutton, Bt., colls.], and has issue living, John St. Vigor, *b.* 1948,—
Charlotte Sylvia, *b.* 1943.

The 1st baronet, Sir John Stirling Ainsworth ; was a mine-owner, and sat as M.P. for Argyllshire (L) Aug. 1903 to Nov. 1918.

AIRD, Creation (U.K.) 1901, of Hyde Park Terrace, Paddington, co. London.

Vigilantia.

By vigilance,

Sir (GEORGE) JOHN AIRD, 4th *Baronet*; *b.* Jan. 30th,
1940; *s.* his father, *Col. Sir* JOHN RENTON, *MVO, MC,*
1973; ed. at Eton, Ch. Ch., Oxford, and Harvard Univ.;
a Page of Honour to HM 1955-57: *m.* 1968, Margaret
Elizabeth, yr. da. of Sir John Harling Muir, TD, 3rd Bt.,
and has issue.

Arms—Gules, on a chevron between in chief two wolvesheads
erased, and in base a mullet of six points within an increscent all argent,
two falcons' heads erased sable. Crest—On a bull-headed rail fesswise,
a lion rampant holding erect between the paws a spike point downwards
all proper.
Residence,—Grange Farm, Evenlode, Moreton-in-Marsh, Glos.

Daughters living—Rebecca, *b.* 1970.——Belinda Elizabeth, *b.* 1972.
Sisters living—Susan Priscilla, *b.* 1942.——Petra Daphne (*Hon. Mrs
L. David Verney*), *b.* 1944: *m.* 1965, the Hon. Leopold David Verney,
only son of 20th Baron Willoughby de Broke.——Amanda Alecia,
b. 1946.
Aunt living (daughter of 2nd baronet)—Nellie Phyllis, *b.* 1887: *m.* 1910,
William Noel Cunliffe, who *d.* 1933 [*see* Cunliffe, Bt., colls.]. *Residence,*
—3, West Halkin Street, SW1.

Widow living of 3rd Baronet—*Lady* PRISCILLA Heathcote-Drummond-Willoughby (*Lady Priscilla
Aird*) (Forest-Lodge, The Great Park, Windsor; 43 Clabon mews, SW1), da of 2nd Earl of
Ancaster: *m* 1939, Col. Sir John Renton Aird, MVO, MC, 3rd Bt., who *d.* 1973.

Collateral Branches living.

Grandsons of the late Malcolm Rucker Aird (infra):—
Issue of the late Malcolm Henry Aird, OBE, *b.* 1899, *d.* 1965: *m.* 1922, Joan Meredith,
(Neville House, Kintbury, Berks.), da. of Henry Sturgis:—
MALCOLM ROBIN MEREDITH, *b.* Dec. 16th, 1923; ed. at Canford; 1939-45 War as Lt. Irish Guards
(wounded): *m.* 1955, Barbara, da. of J. Addison Wilson, and has issue living, Julian Malcolm,
b. 1955,—Zandra Theresa Jane, *b.* 1960.——Alistair Sturgis, *MVO* (31, St. James's Palace, SW1),
b. 1931; ed. at Eton, and RMC; late Capt. 9th Lancers; Equerry to HM Queen Elizabeth the
Queen Mother 1960-64, and Asst. Private Sec. and Extra Equerry 1964-73, since when Comptroller
of the Household to HM Queen Elizabeth the Queen Mother; MVO (4th class) 1969: *m.* 1963,
Fiona Violet, da. of Lt. Col. Ririd Myddleton, MVO, Coldstream Gds. [see M. Lansdowne], and
has issue living, Caroline Margaret Violet, *b.* 1964,—Henrietta Idina, *b.* 1966,——Jeremy John
(Quarry Wood Cottage, Burghclere, Newbury, Berks.), *b.* 1936; ed. at Eton: *m.* 1967, Mary
Elizabeth, da. of the late Lt.-Col. Sir William Richard De Bacquencourt Des Voeux, 9th Bt., and
has issue living, David William, *b.* 1968,—Catherine Rosemary, *b.* 1972.

Issue of the late Malcolm Rucker Aird, 2nd son of 1st baronet, *b.* 1872, *d.* 1934:
m. 1898, Nellie Margaret, who *d.* 1954, da. of Jeremiah Dummett, formerly
of 54, Porchester Terrace, W. :—
Ronald, *MC, TD* (of Champlain's Well, Great Mongeham, Deal, Kent), *b.* 1902; ed. at Eton,
and at Clare Coll., Camb.; is Capt. and temporary Maj. 4th co. London Yeo. (TA); 1939-45
War in Middle East (wounded, MC); and Assist. Sec. Marylebone Cricket Club 1926-52, and
Sec. 1952-62: *m.* 1925, Viola Mary, who *d.* 1965, da. of Sir Godfrey Baring, KBE, 1st Bt., and has
issue living, Gillian Viola, *b.* 1930: *m.* 1st, 1951 (m. diss. 1961), Robert Ian MacDonald;
2ndly, 1962, Christopher Michael Maude, of Feildings, Hoe Lane, Flansham, Bognor Regis,
and has issue living, (by 1st m.) Ian *b.* 1955, Zara *b.* 1953, (by 2nd m.) Victoria Viola *b.* 1968.——
Ruth Sarah, *b.* 1909: *m.* 1940, Robert Ross Buchanan Brown, CBE, and has issue living, Ian
Robert, *b.* 1946,—Sarah Elizabeth, *b.* 1944,—Margaret Jane, *b.* 1947. *Residence,* Wargrave
Court, Wargrave, Berks.——Elizabeth Mary, *b.* 1912. *Residence,* 12, Gorselands, Wash Common, Newbury, Berks.

The 1st baronet, Sir John, was a partner in the firm of John Aird and Co., contractors (who
carried out the Assuan Dam and Assiut Barrage in Egypt), and sat as M.P. for Paddington, N. Div.
(C) 1887-1906.

AITCHISON, Creation (U.K.) 1938, of Lemmington, co. Northumberland.

Sir CHARLES WALTER DE LANCEY AITCHISON, 4th *Baronet*; *b.*
May 27th, 1951; *s.* his father, *Major Sir* STEPHEN CHARLES DE LANCEY, 1958;
late Lt. 15th/19th KRH.

Residence—Howden Dene, Corbridge, Northumberland.

Brother living—STEPHEN EDWARD, *b.* March 27th, 1954.

Uncle living (son of 2nd baronet).—David Lachlan, *b.* 1928; Chm. and Managing Dir. of Walter
Willson, Ltd., and de Lancey Lands, Ltd.; *m.* 1955, Dorothy Hazel, da. of the late S. K. Walton,
of Wanwood Hill, Alston, Cumberland, and has issue living, Jeremy David, *b.* 1959,—Dawn
Elizabeth, *b.* 1956. *Residence,* The Red House, Apperley Rd., Stocksfield, Northumberland.

Aunt living (daughter of 2nd baronet)—Shena Diana, *b.* 1927. *Residence,* Spindle Lodge, Spindle-
stone, Belford, Northumberland.

Great-Uncle living (son of 1st baronet)—Stephen Villiers, *b.* 1902; ed. at Harrow, and at Christ's
Coll., Camb.: *m.* 1st, 1925, Alice Stamper; 2ndly, 1955, Jessie Ethel, da. of the late Vernon
Lovell, of Shiplake-on-Thames. *Address,* P.O. Box 171, Barberton, Transvaal.

Great-Aunt living (daughter of 1st baronet)—Aline Mary: *m.* 1918, Brig. Harrison.

Widow living of 3rd Baronet—ELIZABETH ANNE MILBURN, *MB, BS,* el. da. of the late Lt.-Col.
Edward Reed. of Ghyllheugh, Longhorsley, Northumberland: *m.* 1st, 1950, Maj. Sir Stephen
Charles de Lancey Aitchison, 3rd baronet, who *d.* 1958; 2ndly, 1974, Roland Antory Cookson,
CBE, DCL, of Howden Dene, Corbridge, Northumberland.

The 1st baronet, Sir Stephen Harry Aitchison (son of John Gordon Aitchison), was a J.P. for City and Co. of Newcastle-upon-Tyne and for Northumberland. The 2nd baronet, Sir Walter de Lancey Aitchison, F.S.A., was Managing Director of Walter Willson, Ltd., and of de Lancey Lands Ltd. The 3rd baronet, Major Sir Stephen Charles de Lancey Aitchison, late 13th/18th Roy. Hussars, was Managing Director of Walter Willson Ltd., and of de Lancey Lands Ltd.

AITKEN, Creation (U.K.), 1916, of New Brunswick, Dominion of Canada.

Sir (JOHN WILLIAM) MAXWELL AITKEN, *D.S.O., D.F.C.*, 2nd *Baronet*, who *s.* as 2nd Baron Beaverbrook, June 9th, 1964, until he disclaimed his peerage, 1964 [see Beaverbrook, Barony of.]

ALBU, Creation (U.K.) 1912, of Grosvenor Place, City of Westminster, and Johannesburg, Province of Transvaal, Union of South Africa.

Sir GEORGE ALBU, 3rd *Baronet*; *b.* June 5th, 1944; *s.* his father, *Sir* GEORGE WERNER, 1963: *m.* 1969, Joan Valerie, da. of the late Malcolm Millar, and has issue.

Arms—Per chevron raguly or and vert, in the dexter chief an acorn, in the sinister a flower of a sugar bush, both slipped and leaved, and in base a bear sejant proper. **Crest**—The battlements of a tower or, issuant therefrom a demi-bear proper, holding in the dexter paw a flower of the sugar plant as in the arms.

Residence—Glen Hamish Farm, Richmond, Natal.

All turns out well.

Daughter living—Camilla Jane, *b.* 1972.

Sisters living—Georgina, *b.* 1930: *m.* 1951, Allan Goodman, and has issue living, James Martin, *b.* 1952,—Charles Anthony, *b.* 1953,—John, *b.* 1963,—Philippa Mary, *b.* 1955,—Victoria, *b.* 1960,—Mary Anne (twin), *b.* 1960.——Susan Nomakepu (*Hon. Mrs. David P. D. Stapleton-Cotton*), *b.* 1932: *m.* 1955, the Hon. David Peter Dudley Stapleton-Cotton, of Papenboom, 42, Newlands Av., Newlands, Cape Town, S. Africa, [*see* V. Combermere].——Julia Mary (*Hon. Mrs. Michael J. H. Grimston*) *b.* 1937: *m.* 1957, the Hon. Michael John Harbottle Grimston [*see* B. Grimston of Westbury]. *Residence*, Penny Hill, Bryanston, S. Africa.——Caroline, *b.* 1943: *m.* 1969, P. G. L. Lorentz, of 16, 4th Av., Melville, Johannesburg, Transvaal, and has issue living, William George, *b.* 1971.

Aunts living (daughters of 1st baronet)—Katherine Victoria, *b.* 1891: *m.* 1913, Erroll Gordon Hay, and has issue living, Ian Bruce David, *b.* 1916,—Kathleen Helen Elizabeth, *b.* 1914.——Alice Ernestine, *b.* 1893: *m.* 1924, Nigel James Bengough, DL, and has issue living, Piers Henry George, *OBE* (Great House, Canon Pyon, Herefords.), *b.* 1929; Lt.-Col. (ret.) R. Hussars (PWO); OBE (Mil.) 1973: *m.* 1952, Bridget Adams, and has issue living, Andrew, Nigel Crosbie *b.* 1954, Jonathan Fiennes *b.* 1955,—Jane, *b.* 1926: *m.* 1952, Richard Bridges St. John Quarry, OBE, of Gaddeshill House, Eversley, Hants., and has issue living, Adam Philip St. John *b.* 1955, Charlotte Louise *b.* 1953. *Residence*, Monkland, Leominster, Herefordshire.

Widow living of 2nd Baronet—ELSIE VIOLET TAYLLR (*Elsie*, *Lady Albu*): *m.* 1959, as his second wife, Sir George Werner Albu, 2nd Bt., who *d.* 1963.

The 1st baronet, Sir George Albu (son of the late Simon Albu, of Berlin), was naturalized as a British subject in Transvaal 1887 and in England 1911, and was Chm. and Managing Director of General Mining and Finance Corporation, Ltd. The 2nd baronet, Sir George Werner Albu, was Chm. of General Mining and Finance Corporation, Ltd.

ALEXANDER, Creation (U.K.) 1921, of Edgehill, Stamford, Connecticut, U.S.A.

Sir DOUGLAS HAMILTON ALEXANDER, 2nd *Baronet*; *b.* June 6th, 1900; *s.* his father, *Sir* DOUGLAS ALEXANDER, 1949; ed. at Princeton Univ. (B.A. 1921).

Arms—Azure, on a chevron between three lymphads, sails furled, oars in action or, as many grenades fired proper. **Crest**—In front of a talbot's head erased sable, gorged with a collar gemelle gules, two crescents or.

Residence—118, Palmers Hill Rd., Stamford, Conn. 06902, USA.

Brother living—ARCHIBALD GILLESPIE (of 44, Woodbine Rd., Stamford, Conn., U.S.A.), *b.* March 29th, 1907: *m.* 1932, Margery Isabel Griffith, of Media, Penn., U.S.A., and has issue living, Douglas, *b.* 1936: *m.* 1958, Marylon Scatterday, of Worthington, Ohio, USA,—Archibald Bonsall, *b.* 1940: *m.* 1967, Catherine Clair Biggins, of Montclair, New Jersey, USA,—Margery Griffith, *b.* 1945: *m.* 1st, 1969 (m. diss. 1971) Richard Danch Cleland; 2ndly, 1972, Frederic James Ramsey, III, of 6, Banksville Av., Greenwich, Conn. 06830, USA.

Sister living—Helen Douglas (118, Palmers Hill Rd., Stamford, Conn. 06902, USA), *b.* 1897.

Vita perit labor non moritur.
Life perishes, labour never dies.

The 1st baronet, Sir Douglas Alexander (son of the late Andrew Alexander, of Errol, Perthshire, and Hamilton, Canada), was for many years Pres. of The Singer Manufacturing Co., of New York.

ALEXANDER, Creation (U.K.) 1945, of Sundridge Park, co. Kent.

Always watchful.

Sir CHARLES GUNDRY ALEXANDER, 2nd *Baronet, b.* May 5th, 1923 ; *s.* his father *Sir* FRANK SAMUEL, 1959 ; ed. at Bishops Stortford Coll., and at St. John's Coll., Camb. (B.A. 1943, M.A. 1947) ; is Chm. of Alexander Shipping Co. Ltd., and a Director of Houlder Bros. & Co. Ltd., Houlder Line Ltd., and other cos. ; Lieut. R.N. (retired) : *m.* 1944, Mary Neale, only child of the late S. R. Richardson, of Maple Lawn, Lyndhurst, Hants, and has issue.

Arms—Barry wavy on ten azure and argent a lion rampant gules holding a trident erect or, on a chief of the second three lymphads sable with pennons flying gules. Crest,—On a bundle of sticks fessewise banded or, a cock proper collared gold.

Residence—Norsted Manor, Orpington, Kent. *Town Address*,—53, Leadenhall St., EC3. *Club*,—RAC.

Son living—RICHARD (Qawra, 1, Norsted Manor, Orpington, Kent), *b.* Sept. 1st, 1947: *m.* 1971, Lesley Jane, da. of Frederick William Jordan, of Bishops Stortford.

Daughter living—Jennifer, *b.* 1949.

Brother living—John Edward, *b.* 1924 ; late Lieut. R.N.V.R. : *m.* 1953, Maureen Dickson, and has issue living, Jonathan Charles, *b.* 1957.—Catherine, *b.* 1954. *Residence*, Dene Court, Oldfield Drive, Heswall, Wirral, Cheshire.

Sisters living—Elizabeth Jane, *b.* 1927 : *m.* 1949, Lieut.-Col. Peter Walter Swinton Boult, T.D., and has issue living, Nigel Peter Alexander, *b.* 1952,—Geoffrey Pattisson, *b.* 1957,— Rosanne Margaret, *b.* 1950,—Alison Judith, *b.* 1955. *Residence*, Lincoln Lodge, Pines Road, Bickley, Kent.——Margaret Mary, *b.* 1929 : *m.* 1951, Neville Manwaring Wells and has issue living, Michael Edward Alexander, *b.* 1956,—Martin Charles Stanley, *b.* 1959,—Frances Mary, *b.* 1954. *Residence*, Wood End, Kent Hatch, Edenbridge, Kent.

The 1st baronet, Sir Frank Samuel Alexander (son of the late Edward Alexander, of Highgate, N.) was a shipowner and shipbroker, and was Lord Mayor of London 1944-5.

CABLE-ALEXANDER, Creation (U.K.) 1809, of the City of Dublin.

Per mare, per terras.
By sea and land.

Sir DESMOND WILLIAM LIONEL CABLE-ALEXANDER, 7th *Baronet* ; *b.* Oct. 4th, 1910 ; *s.* his father, *Major Sir* LIONEL CECIL WILLIAM *ALEXANDER, D.S.O.* 1956 ; ed. at Harrow ; assumed by deed poll 1931, the additional surname of Cable before that of Alexander : *m.* 1st, 1935, Mary Jane (who obtained a divorce 1941), da. of James O'Brien, J.P., of Enniskillen, co. Fermanagh ; 2ndly, 1941, Margaret Wood, da. of the late John Burnett, of Dublin, and has issue by 1st and 2nd marriages.

Arms—Per pale argent and sable a chevron, and in base a crescent counterchanged ; on a canton azure a harp or, in the sinister chief point a mullet of the last. Crest—An armed arm embowed holding a sword proper, charged on the wrist with a mullet or.

Address,—c/o Barclays Bank, Cocks Biddulph Branch, 16, Whitehall, SW1.

Son living—By 1st marriage—PATRICK DESMOND WILLIAM, (c/o Barclays Bank, 63, Terminus Rd., Eastbourne), *b.* April 19th, 1936; ed. at Downside; Maj. R. Scots Dragoon Gds. (Carabiniers and Greys): *m.* 1961, Diana Frances, el. da. of Col. P. H. Rogers, of Bushey, Herts, and has issue living, Melanie Jane, *b.* 1963,—Louise Fenella, *b.* 1967.

Daughters living—By 2nd marriage—Jacqueline, *b.* 1941: *m.* 1962, Dillon Godfrey Welchman, of Pringle House, Priors Hardwick, Rugby, Warwicks., and has issue living, James Dillon, *b.* 1969,— Sara Dawn, *b.* 1964.——Susan, *b.* 1948: *m.* 1970, Richard H. Hardwicke.

Half-Brother living—Nigel William (West Wey House, Charles Hill, Tilford, Surrey), *b.* 1925; ed. at Haileybury; Maj. (ret.) Grenadier Guards; 1939-45 War: *m.* 1964, Anne, da. of Bernard Ambrose Wheatley, of Stolford, Somerset, and has issue living, Hugh William, *b.* 1967,—Charlotte Anne, *b.* 1971.

Aunt living (daughter of 5th baronet)—Eileen Edith Caledon, *b.* 1888 : *m.* 1908, Lieut.-Col. Donald Cuthbertson Dennistoun Sword, D.S.O., who *d.* 1954, having obtained a divorce 1918 ; 2ndly, 1919, Lieut.-Col. Clifford Cyril Scott, M.C., and has issue living (by 1st marriage), Roderick William Denistoun, M.C., *b.* 1909 ; is Capt. Middlesex Regt. ; European War 1939-40 (M.C.) : *m.* 1st, 1938, Pamela Rachel Palles, only da. of Capt. H. E. Rydon, of Arusha, Tanganyika ; 2ndly, 1943, Iris Angela Ernst, da. of Henry Cambronne Dennistoun Sword, of Westcombe House, near Evercreech, Somerset, and has issue living, (by 2nd marriage) Henry Ernest *b.* 1946, (by 1st m.) Sonia Rosalie Dennistoun *b.* 1939. *Residence*,

Widow living of 6th Baronet—HOPEFUL MERRISON ROSE (*Hopeful Lady Alexander*) (2, Honey Hanger, Hindhead, Surrey), da. of the late Capt. George William Hutrell, of Aberdeen: *m.* 1924, as his second wife, Maj. Sir Lionel Cecil William Alexander, DSO, 6th Bt., who *d.* 1956.

Collateral Branches living.

Grandchildren of the late Richard Alexander-Shaw, son of the late William John Alexander-Shaw (who had assumed the additional surname of Shaw 1846), 2nd son of 1st baronet :—

Issue of the late Godfrey William ALEXANDER, *b.* 1861, *a.* 1903, having discontinued the surname of Shaw : *m.* 1800, Alice Maude, da. of James Priestley, of Bankfield, Taylor Hill, Huddersfield :—

Kathleen, *b.* 1892. *Residence,*

Issue of the late Charles Henry Alexander, *b.* 1866, *d.* 1898: *m.* 1890, Susie Macauly, da. of Robert Alexander, of Harwich, Kent, Canada:—
Robert Godfrey, *b.* 1894. *Residence,*

Of this family the Earls of Caledon are a branch. John Alexander (el. son of Capt. Andrew Alexander, of Ballyclose, who was attainted in 1689) had three sons (1) John, ancestor of the Alexanders of Milford, co. Carlow, (2) Nathaniel, ancestor of the Earls of Caledon, (3) William, ancestor of William Alexander, 1st baronet, who was Lord Mayor of Dublin. The 2nd baronet was a Director of the Bank of Ireland, and the 3rd baronet was Attorney-General to H.M. King Edward VII., when Prince of Wales, and a Member of the Council of H.R.H.

HAGART-ALEXANDER, Creation (U.K.) 1886, of Ballochmyle, co. Ayr.

Perseverance conquers.   Without fear.

Sir CLAUD HAGART-ALEXANDER, 3rd *Baronet,* son of the late Wilfred Archibald Alexander, 2nd son of 2nd Baronet ; *b.* Jan. 6th, 1927 ; *s.* his grandfather *Sir* CLAUD, 1945 ; ed. at Sherborne, and at Corpus Christi Coll., Camb. (BA); additional surname of Hagart recognized by decree of Lord Lyon 1948 ; a DL for Ayr: *m.* 1959, Hilda Etain, yr. da. of Miles Malcolm Acheson, late Chinese Maritime Customs Ser. [D. St. Albans, colls.], and has issue.

Arms—Quarterly : 1st and 4th, per pale argent and sable, a chevron between a fleur-de-lys in chief and a crescent in base all counterchanged, within a bordure parted per pale gules and or, *Alexander* ; 2nd, per bend azure and argent, in chief a star of sixteen points or, and in base another star of as many points of the first, on a bend sable a lion passant of the second between two crosses moline of the third, *Hagart* ; 3rd, gules, two straight swords in saltire, points downwards, proper, hilted and pommelled or, between two fleur-de-lys in chief and base of the second and two mullets in the flanks argent, *McCaul.* Crest—1st, an elephant passant proper, *Alexander ;* 2nd, a lion rampant, proper, *Hagart.*

Seat—Kingencleuch House, Mauchline, Ayrshire. *Club*—New (Edinburgh).

Sons living—CLAUD, *b.* Nov. 5th, 1963.——Boyd John, *b.* 1966.
Daughters living—Helenora Etain, *b.* 1960.——Anna Joanna Elizabeth, *b.* 1961.
Sisters living—Mary Primrose, *b.* 1921: *m.* 1947, Lt.-Col. John Edward Margesson, MBE (ret.), S. Wales Borderers, and has issue living, Richard William, *b.* 1948,—John Bertram, *b.* 1950, —Hugh David, *b.* 1954. *Residence,* Maes-y-Gwenith, Llanvair Discoed, Chepstow, Monmouthshire.——Penelope Marion Acheson (*Lady Head*) *b.* 1924: *m.* 1967, as his second wife, Sir Francis David Somerville Head, 5th Bt., of 10, Fairway, Merrow, Surrey.

Uncles living (sons of 2nd baronet)—Claud ALEXANDER, *b.* 1897; ed. at Eton: *m.* 1st, 1928, Maude, who *d.* 1936, da. of Lt.-Col. J. Oswald-Clazey, of Lamorva, Falmouth, 2ndly, 1949, Mrs. Peggy Silley, da. of E. R. Le Mare, of Birchington, Kent, and has issue living (by 1st m.) John Oswald Claude (Rangi Cottage, Hawley Rd., Blackwater, Camberley, Surrey), *b.* 1936; Lt. Col. R. Signals: *m.* 1962, Mary, el. da. of Col. Derek Grant Birkett, OBE, RA, and has issue living, Liza Jane *b.* 1964, Sharon Louise *b.* 1968. *Residence,* Hazels, Downe, Kent.—— Boyd ALEXANDER, *b.* 1902. *Residence,* 7, Hertford Rd., Worthing, Sussex.

Aunt living (daughter of 2nd baronet)—Wilhelmina ALEXANDER, *b.* 1907. *Residence,* Fay Cottage, Faygate, Sussex.

The 1st baronet, Maj.-Gen. Sir Claud Alexander (son of the late Boyd Alexander, of Ballochmyle and Southbar, co. Ayr), served in Crimea 1854-5 and was M.P. for S. Ayrshire (C) 1874-85.

ALISON, Creation (U.K.) 1852. [Extinct 1970].

Sir FREDERICK BLACK ALISON, 5th and last *Baronet*.

Daughter living of 5th Baronet—Phoebe Ann, *b.* 1926: *m.* 1947, Leslie Thomas Allen, of Down Cottage, Lamberhurst Down, Lamberhurst, Kent, and has issue living, Richard Thomas, *b.* 1948,—Bruce Harry, *b.* 1950,—David Frederick, *b.* 1953,—Peter Robert, *b.* 1961.

Widows living of 4th and 5th Baronets—ISA MARGERY (*Margery, Lady Alison*) (c/o Coutts & Co., 440, Strand, WC2), da. of the late Sir Charles Tyrrell Giles, KC, DL, JP, of Copse Hill House, Wimbledon, SW; has Order of Mèrcy: *m.* 1919, Cdr. Sir Archibald Alison, OBE, 4th Bt., who *d.* 1967.——Lilian Phoebe (*Lady Alison*) (Down Cottage, Lamberhurst Down, Lamberhurst, Tunbridge Wells, Kent), da. of the late Louis Charles Phillips, of Sebakwe, Kenilworth, S. Africa: *m.* 1919, Sir Frederick Black Alison, 5th Bt., who *d.* 1970, when the title became ext.

HAVELOCK-ALLAN, Creation (U.K.) 1858, of Lucknow.

Faithfully.

He Bears the cross bravely.

Sir HENRY RALPH MORETON HAVELOCK-ALLAN, 3rd *Baronet*, son of the late Allan Havelock-Allan, 2nd son of 1st baronet; *b.* Aug. 31st, 1899; *s.* his uncle, *Sir* HENRY SPENCER MORETON, 1953; ed. at Charterhouse; formerly Lieut. Scots Gds. [The 3rd Baronet *d.* Nov. 4th, 1975].

Arms—Quarterly, 1st and 4th sable, a cross potent quarter pierced or, charged with four guttes de sang; in chief two lions heads erased of the second, all within a bordure engrailed erminois; a canton ermine, *Allan;* 2nd and 3rd, vert, a castle double-turreted argent between two fleurs-de-lys in chief, and a cross-crosslet fitchée in base or, *Havelock.* **Crests**—1st, a demi-lion rampant argent, ducally crowned gules, charged on the shoulder with a cross-crosslet fitchée sable, holding in the dexter paw a cross potent or, supporting in the sinister a rudder of the second; 2nd, a lion rampant gules, semée of ermine spots, charged on the shoulder with a castle argent, sustaining a Danish battleaxe proper.

Address,—c/o Nat. Westminster Bank, 320, Euston Rd., NW1.

Brother living—ANTHONY JAMES ALLAN (c/o Gorrie Whitson & Sons, 9, Cavendish Sq., W1; RAC), *b.* Feb. 28th, 1904; a Film Producer: *m.* 1939 (m. diss. 1952), Valerie Louise (Film Actress), da. of the late Com. Robert Gordon Hobson, RN, and has issue living, Simon Anthony Henry, *b.* 1944,—Anthony Mark David, *b.* 1951.

Half-Brother living—Gervaise George Michael, *b.* 1921 : *m.* 1946, Rhoda, da. of Thomas Beard, of Swansea, and has issue living, Thomas Allan Spencer, *b.* 1949,—Louise Charlotte, *b.* 1954. *Residence,*

Sister living—Hope Aline, *b.* 1898 : *m.* 1st, 1925, Capt. Graeme Stewart Lockhart Whitelaw, Seaforth Highlanders, from whom she obtained a divorce 1933 ; 2ndly, 1935, as his second wife, the 3rd Baron Allerton, who obtained a divorce 1947. *Residence,* Mabolton Farm, Chiasiellis di Mortegliano, Udine, Italy.

Half-Sisters living—Diana Constance : *m.* 1939, Evelyn Francis Scott.——Nancy Stella : *m.* 1947, Maj. Patrick Thorvald Auchmuty Musters, RA (HQ 1 Wing, AAC, BFPO 41), and has issue living, Patrick Havelock Auchmuty, *b.* 1952,—Fiona Havelock Auchmuty, *b.* 1948,—Gillian Havelock Auchmuty (twin), *b.* 1952,—Nicola Havelock Auchmuty, *b.* 1954.

Widow living of 2nd Baronet—DORIS PAMELA (*Lady Havelock-Allan*), da. of Sir Maurice Levy, JP, DL, 1st Bt. ; a SSStJ; Co. Pres., Durham Co. (Women's Section) and National Vice-Pres., British Legion; Organizer of Women's Vol. Ser., Darlington 1938-44: *m.* 1937, as his third wife, Sir Henry Spencer Moreton Havelock-Allan, 2nd baronet, who *d.* 1953. *Residence,* Whorlton House, Barnard Castle, Co. Durham.

Collateral Branches living.

Granddaughter of George Eric Havelock, yr. son of Capt. Joshua HAVELOCK, next brother of 1st Bt. (who was on special remainder to the Baronetcy):—
Issue of the late Eric Henry Edwardes Havelock, CB, CBE, *b.* 1891, *d.* 1974: *m.* 1st, 1919, Christina Ramsay Scott, who *d.* 1958, da. of the late Alexander Moodie of Edinburgh; 2ndly, 1962, Eileen, who *d.* 1972, da. of the late Col. John W. H. Potts, RHA, and widow of Maj.-Gen. Walter Reginald Paul, CBE:—
(By 1st m.) Elizabeth Kerr, *b.* 1920: *m.* 1946, Konstanty Kosciuszko, of Apart, 2C, 1196 Eastern Parkway, Brooklyn 11213, New York, USA, and has issue living, Stefan Henry, *b.* 1959.

Granddaughters of the late George Broadfoot HAVELOCK, yst. brother of 1st baronet:—
Issue of the late Major Beresford Arthur Jardine Havelock (only son), 2nd Batn. attached 7th Ser. Batn.) Prince of Wales's (N. Staffordshire Regt.), *b.* 1889, *d.* (killed in action at Baku) Sept. 1918 (despatches) : *m.* (March) 1916, Kathleen Margaret (who *m.* 2ndly, 1921, Major Daniel Frederick Bartlett, M.B.E., Indian Army), da. of Sydney Smith, formerly Dep. Inspector-Gen. of Police, Punjab :—
Patricia Margaret Helen, *b.* (Dec.) 1916.——Beres Aileen, *b.* (*posthumous*), Feb. 1919.

Maj.-Gen. Sir Henry Havelock, K.C.B., father of the 1st baronet, distinguished himself by his unparalleled march from Allahabad to Cawnpore and Lucknow, which latter place he held with astonishing bravery against the rebels for two months. A patent of baronetcy in his favour was granted Nov. 26th, 1857, but as he died two days prior to the date thereof, the honour was extended to his son, Henry Marshman, with special remainder, in default of his issue male, to his father's issue. Lieut.-Gen. Sir Henry Marshman Havelock, G.C.B., V.C., 1st baronet, Col.-in-Ch. Roy. Irish Regt., who also served with distinction during the Indian Mutiny, assumed by Roy. licence 1880 the additional surname of Allan, and sat as M.P. for Sunderland (L) 1874-81, and for Durham, S.-E. Div. (*LU*) 1885-92 and 1895-97, when he was murdered by Afridis in the Khyber Pass. Sir Henry Spencer Moreton Havelock-Allan, 2nd baronet, was Parliamentary Private Sec. to Under-Sec. of State for India (Hon. E. S. Montagu, M.P.) 1910-14, and sat as M.P. for Durham Co., Bishop Auckland Div. (L) 1910-18. He served during European War 1916-18 as Major 17th Lancashire Fusiliers (wounded).

MAGNUS-ALLCROFT, Creation (U.K.) 1917, of Tangley Hill, Wonersh, co. Surrey.

By faith and work.

Sir PHILIP (MONTEFIORE) MAGNUS-ALLCROFT, *CBE*, 2nd *Baronet*, son of the late Laurie Magnus, el. son of 1st baronet; *b.* Feb. 8th, 1906; *s.* his grandfather, *Sir* PHILIP *MAGNUS*, 1933; ed. at Westminster, and at Wadham Coll., Oxford (MA); in Civil Ser. 1928-33, and 1945-50; CC for Salop 1952, CA 1968 (Chm. of Planning Cttee.), JP for Salop 1952-72; FRSL, FRHistS, a biographer, and historian; a Gov. of Attingham Coll., and Ludlow Gram. Sch.; a Trustee of Nat. Portrait Gallery since 1970, and a Member of W. Midlands Regional Cttee. of Nat. Trust since 1973; 1939-45 War as Maj. RA and Intelligence Corps in Iceland and Italy; assumed by deed poll 1951 the additional surname of Allcroft; CBE (Civil) 1971: *m.* 1943, Jewell, only da. of the late Herbert John Allcroft [Russell, Bt., *cr.* 1832, ext.].

Arms—Bendy of six gules and vert, on a fesse or an open book proper between two martlets sable. Crest—A magnolia tree flowered proper.

Residence—Stokesay Court, Onibury, Salop, SY7 9BD. *Clubs*—Brooks's, Beefsteak, Pratt's.

Brother living—HILARY BARROW *MAGNUS*, *T.D.*, *Q.C.*, *b.* March 3rd, 1909; ed. at Westminster, and at Ch. Ch., Oxford (MA); Bar. Lincoln's Inn 1933, a QC 1957 and Bencher 1963; a JP for Kent 1948-71; National Insurance Commr. 1964; 1939-45 War as Lt.-Col. Rifle Brig. (TA): *m.* 1950, Rosemary Vera Anne, da. of the late George Henry Masefield, and widow of Quentin Hurst, and has issue living, Laurence Henry Philip, *b.* 1955, Caroline Anne, *b.* 1951. *Residence*, The Gate House, Leigh, nr. Tonbridge, Kent. *Clubs*,—Garrick, Beefsteak.

Sisters living—Jessie Dora: *m.* 1935, David Hugh Sandell, M.D., F.R.C.S., of 44, Burton Court, Chelsea, SW3, and has issue living, Robert Laurie (Calehill House, Little Chart, nr. Ashford, Kent) *b.* 1938; ed. at Eton, and at Ch. Ch., Oxford: *m.* 1969, Stephanie Getz, and has issue living, Adam Jonathon *b.* 1972,—Jenifer Celia Emily, *b.* 1936; Bar. Lincoln's Inn 1958; LSE: *m.* 1962, Nicholas Bridges-Adams, of Hermitage, Waterfall, Bantry, co. Cork.——Ruth Emily: *m.* 1946, as his second wife, Denzil Sebag-Montefiore, of South House, Broadham Green, nr. Oxted, Surrey and has issue living, Charles Adam Laurie *b.* 1949: ed. at Eton and St. Andrew's Univ.,—Mary Pamela, *b.* 1951; Bar. Middle Temple 1974: *m.* 1973, David Murray Davidson.

The 1st baronet, Sir Philip Magnus, a pioneer of technical education, sat as MP for London Univ. (U) 1906-22.

ALLEN, Creation (U.K.) 1933, of Marlow, co. Buckingham. [Extinct 1939.]

Sir FRANCIS RAYMOND ALLEN, 2nd and last *Baronet*.

Daughter living of 1st Baronet—Violet Parkinson, *b.* 1903: *m.* 1st, 1924, Alfred Francis Hope Baldry; 2ndly, 1942, William Fisher-Luttrelle, and has issue living, (by 1st marriage) Felicia, *b.* 1927,—Ann, *b.* 1931. *Residence*, 6, Medallion Place, Thames Reach, Maidenhead, Berks.

Widow living of 2nd Baronet—ALTHEA JOAN (BLACK), da. of Owen Leonard Hanks, of Wallasey Bay, Essex: *m.* 2ndly, 1935, Sir Francis Raymond Allen, 2nd baronet, who *d.* 1939, when the title became ext.; 3rdly, 1941, Capt. Dennis L. Bennett, Staffordshire Yeo., who *d.* (killed in action during European War) 1942; 4thly, 1945, Lieut.-Col. Oliver Charles Berger, Roy. Scots Greys.

ALLEYNE, Creation (G.B.) 1769, of Four Hills, Barbados.

[Name pronounced "Alleen."]

Sir JOHN MEYNELL ALLEYNE, *D.S.O.*, *D.S.C.*, *R.N.*, 4th *Baronet*, son of the late Reynold Henry Newton Alleyne, el. son of 3rd Baronet ; *b.* Aug. 11th, 1889; *s.* his grandfather, *Sir* JOHN GAY NEWTON, 1912; became Lieut. 1910, Lieut.-Com. 1918, and Com. 1924; retired as Capt. 1936; European War 1914-18 (wounded, despatches, D.S.C., D.S.O.), European War 1939-45; D.S.O. 1918: *m.* 1920, Alice Violet, da. of the late James Campbell, of 12, Cornwall Gardens, S.W., and has issue.

Arms—Per chevron gules and ermine, in chief two lions heads erased or. Crest—Out of a ducal coronet a horse's head argent.

Residence—South Lynch, Hursley, near Winchester.

Let not your own interests move you but rather the wishes of the public.

Son living—*Rev.* JOHN OLPHERTS CAMPBELL, (The Rectory, Speke, Liverpool, 24), *b.* Jan. 18th, 1928; ed. at Eton, and at Jesus Coll., Camb.: *m.* 1968, Honor, da. of the late William Albert Irwin, of Belfast, and has issue living, Richard Meynell, *b.* 1972,—Clare Emma Gila, *b.* 1969.

Daughters living—Eileen Violet, *b.* 1923.——Rosemary *b.* 1925 : *m.* (Dec. 6th) 1954, John Perry, who *d.* (Dec. 10th) 1954. *Residence*, 48, Eaton Terr., SW1.

Brother living—Reynold Meynell, *b.* 1892; Com. (retired) R.N. ; European War 1914-18, European War 1939-45. *Residence*, 6, Hazelwood Rd., Duffield, Derby, DE6 4DP.

Sister living—Kathleen. *Residence*, 6, Hazelwood Rd., Duffield, Derby, DE6 4DP.

Sir John Gay, the 1st baronet, represented St. Andrew's in the Barbados House of Assembly 1757-67, and was Speaker of the House 1767-97 ; he had two sisters, one married the 1st Earl of Radnor, and the other, Sir Charles Knowles, 1st baronet.

ANSON, Creation (U.K.) 1831, of Birch Hall, Lancashire.

Never despair.

Sir PETER ANSON, *CB*, 7th *Baronet, b.* July 31st, 1924; *s.* his father, *Sir* EDWARD REYNELL, 1951; Rear-Adm. (ret.); Comdg. Officer, HMS *Alert* 1957-58, on Staff of RN Tactical Sch. 1959-61, Comdg. Officer, HMS *Broadsword* 1961-62, Dep. Dir., Weapons Radio (Naval), Min. of Defence 1963-65, and Dir. 1965-66, Comdg. HMS *Naiad* and Capt. (D) Londonderry Sqdn. 1966-68, and Comdg. HMS *Mercury*, and Capt. HM Signal Sch. 1968-70, Cdr. Naval Forces Gulf 1970-72 and Assist Ch. Defence Staff (Sigs.) 1972-74; SW Pacific 1941-45 (prisoner) CB (Mil) 1974: *m.* 1955, Elizabeth Audrey, da. of the late Rear-Adm. Sir (Charles) Philip Clarke, KBE, CB, DSO, and has issue.

Arms—Argent, three bendlets engrailed gules, a crescent for difference. **Crest**—Out of a ducal coronet or, a spear's head proper. *Residence*—Rosefield, Rowledge, Farnham, Surrey, GV10 4AT.

Sons living—PHILIP ROLAND, *b.* Oct. 4th, 1957.——Hugo William, *b.* 1962.
Daughters living—Louisa Frances, *b.* 1956.——Sarah Elizabeth, *b.* 1966.
Brother living—John, *b.* 1930 ; ed. at Winchester, and at Magdalene Coll., Camb. (MA); Under Sec. H.M. Treasury: *m.* 1957, Myrica, da. of the late Dr. H. Fergie-Woods, and has issue living, Christopher Edward, *b.* 1958,—Timothy John, *b.* 1967,—Rachel Mary, *b.* 1961,—Elizabeth Margaret, *b.* 1968. *Residence*, 18, Church Rd., Barnes, SW13 9HN.

Sisters living of 4th Baronet—Agnes Margaret, *b.* 1883 : *m.* 1st, 1912, Horace Edward Wilkie Young, who *d.* 1914, Vice-Consul at Philippopolis ; 2ndly, 1923, Charles Evelyn David Gladstone, who *d.* 1942 ; 3rdly, 1954, Capt. Henry Whyham, R.A. (retired), who *d.* 1961. *Residence*, 3, Rossetti Gardens Mansions, Chelsea, S.W.3.——Anne Evelyn, *b.* 1886 : *m.* 1912, Capt. Thomas Edmund Sotheron Estcourt, JP, late Roy. Scots Greys (MP for Pontefract Div. of W. Riding of Yorkshire 1931-35), who *d.* 1958, and has issue living, Thomas Desmond George, *b.* 1918 ; European War 1940-42, in Coldstream Guards (invalided),—Eleanor Josephine, *b.* 1915 : *m.* 1937, Major Philip Sheehy-Morris-Keating R. Horse Gds. of Newnton Priory, Long Newnton, Tetbury, Gloucestershire, and has issue living, Sarah Diana Josephine *b.* 1957. *Residence*,—

Widow living of 6th Baronet—FRANCES ALISON (*Dowager Lady Anson*), da. of the late Hugh Pollock [*see* Montagu-Pollock, Bt. colls.] : *m.* 1923, Sir Edward Reynell Anson, 6th baronet, who *d.* 1951. *Residence*, 85, Boundstowe Rd., Rowledge, Farnham, Surrey, GV10 4AT.

The 1st baronet, a younger brother of the 1st Viscount Anson, and uncle of the 1st Earl of Lichfield, greatly distinguished himself during the Peninsular War. The 2nd baronet was killed by a railway accident at Wigan, August 2nd, and 1873. The 3rd baronet, Rt. Hon. Sir William Reynell, P.C., was Warden of All Souls' Coll., Oxford 1881-1914, Vice-Chancellor, Oxford Univ. 1898-9, Parliamentary Sec. to Board of Education 1902-5, M.P. for Oxford Univ. (*LU*) 1899-1914, and a Trustee of National Portrait Gallery and of British Museum. The 4th baronet, Sir Denis George William, was drowned in the Thames July 1914, shortly after his succession to the Baronetcy. The 5th baronet, Sir John Henry Algernon, Lieut. R.N. ; *d.* (on active service during European War) 1918. The 6th baronet, Sir Edward Reynell served in R.N. during European War 1915-19, and as Lieut.-Col. R.A. during European War 1939-45.

ANSTRUTHER, Creation (N.S.) 1694, of Balcaskie, Fife.

PERIISSEM·NI· PERIISET

Sir RALPH HUGO ANSTRUTHER, *CVO, MC,* 7th *Baronet,* son of the late Capt. Robert Edward Anstruther, M.C., only son of 6th Baronet ; *b.* June 13th, 1921 ; *s.* his grandfather, *Col. Sir* RALPH WILLIAM, 1934 ; ed. at Eton, and at Magdalene Coll., Camb. (B.A. 1940) ; is a Member of the Queen's Body Guard for Scotland (Roy. Co. of Archers), a D.L., and Major Coldstream Guards (Regular Army Reserve); Equerry to H.M. Queen Elizabeth the Queen Mother since 1959 and Treasurer since 1961; Assist. Private Sec. 1959-64; 1939-45 War (wounded, MC), Malaya 1948-50 (despatches); CVO 1967.

Arms—Argent, three piles sable, a bordure gules ; in a dexter canton argent a saltire azure surmounted of an inescutcheon or charged with a lion rampant within a double tressureflory counterflory gules (being the addition of Nova Scotia as a Baronet). **Crest**—On a chapeau gules furred ermine, two demi-arms holding a pole-axe with both hands proper, the spike of the said axe being projected sable.

Seats—Balcaskie, Pittenweem, Fife; Watten, Caithness.

———

Mother living—Marguerite Blanche Lily, da. of the late Hugo de Burgh, of Ballinapierce, co. Wexford : *m.* 1919, Capt. Robert Edward Anstruther, M.C. (ante), who *d.* 1921. *Residence,* Balcaskie, Pittenweem, Fife.

Collateral Branches living.

Grandchildren of the late Henry Torrens Anstruther, 2nd son of 5th baronet :—
Issue of the late Douglas Tollemache Anstruther, *b.* 1893, *d.* 1956 : *m.* 1st, 1914, Enid
(who *d.* 1964, having obtained a divorce 1924), da. of the late Lord George Granville
Campbell [D. Argyll, colls.]; 2ndly, 1925, Evelyn Mabel (11, Paradise Walk,
SW3), da. of the late Sir John Wormald, KBE:—
(By 1st m.) IAN FIFE CAMPBELL (Estate Office, Barlavington, Petworth, Sussex; Brooks's
Club), *b.* May 11th, 1922; ed. at Eton and at New Coll., Oxford; an Author; Capt. late R.
Corps of Signals; a Member of Queen's Body Guard for Scotland (R. Co. of Archers); 1939-45
War with Argyll and Sutherland Highlanders, Signals and Intelligence Corps: *m.* 1st, 1951 (m.
diss. 1963), Honor, el. da. of the late Capt Gerald Blake; 2ndly, 1963, Susan Margaret Walker,
da. of H. St. J. B. Paten, and has issue living, (by 1st wife) Emily Kate Campbell, *b.* 1953,—
(by 2nd wife) Sebastian Paten Campbell, *b.* 1962,—Tobias Alexander Campbell, *b.* 1968,—Rachel
Whittome Campbell, *b.* 1965,—Harriet Joan Campbell, *b.* 1967,—Eleanor Thurloe Campbell, *b.*
1971.——Janet Finetta Campbell, *b.* 1920: *m.* 1st, 1945 (m. diss. 1959), the Rev.
William Pritchard Cole, Chap. to Forces; 2ndly, 1968, Clive Ernest Baker, of Wallins Cottage,
Westrop Green, Newbury, and has issue living, (by 1st m.) Michael Henry Campbell, *b.* 1945,—
Janet Barbara Campbell, *b.* 1947.

Grandchildren of the late Adm. Robert Hamilton Anstruther, C.M.G., 3rd son
of 5th baronet :—
Issue of the late Col. Philip Noel Anstruther, D.S.O., M.C., *b.* 1891, *d.* 1960 : *m.* 1st,
1920, Mary Hope (who *d.* 1963, having obtained a divorce 1931), da. of Harold Chaloner
Lewin, of Birchdale, Bromley, Kent; 2ndly, 1937, Mary Were, of New Zealand;
3rdly, 1952, Mrs. Marion Secretan, da. of the late Capt. I. Gregor MacGregor, R.N.R.:—
(By 1st marriage) Robert Lewin, *b.* 1924 ; ed. at Eastbourne Coll. ; is a F.R.I.C.S. : *m.* 1950,
Rosemary Nathalie, only da. of Com. (E.) Guy Ernest Williamson, M.B.E., R.N., and has issue
living, Peter Robert, *b.* 1955,—Catherine Jane, *b* 1951,—Sally Elizabeth, *b.* 1958. *Residence*,
Boundary Cottage, Ightham, Kent.——Jean Mary (The Little House, 2E, Southlands Grove,
Bickley, Kent), *b.* 1921: *m.* 1951, Fl.-Lt. Robert (Robin) Owen Blackall, RAF, who *d.* 1952.
Issue of the late Arthur Wellesley Anstruther, C.B., 4th son of 5th baronet, *b.* 1864,
d. 1938 : *m.* 1st, 1893, the Hon. Mary Elma Hovell-Thurlow-Cumming-Bruce,
who *d.* 1894, el. da. of 5th Baron Thurlow; 2ndly, 1901, (Louise Adèle) Rose,
who *d.* 1962, da. of the late W. H. Trapmann, of Charleston, South Carolina,
U.S.A., and 29, Roland Gdns., S.W.:—
(By 2nd m.) Peter Ralph (One South Balch St., Hanover, NH 03755, USA) *b.* 1907; ed. at Malvern
and at Princeton Univ., USA: *m.* 1st, 1949 (m. diss. 1954), 2ndly, 1962, Mary Virginia, da. of
the late Morgan Berkeley More, of New York City.——Margaret Elizabeth, *b.* 1906; 1940-45
War as Section Officer WAAF. *Residence*, The Chestnuts, Watlington, Oxon.

Grandchildren of the late Lieut.-Col. Robert Hamilton Lloyd-Anstruther, son
of the late Col. James Hamilton Lloyd-Anstruther, son of the late Brig.-
Gen. Robert Anstruther, el. son of 3rd baronet :—
Issue of the late Sir Fitzroy Hamilton ANSTRUTHER-GOUGH-CALTHORPE, Bt., *b.* 1872,
d. 1957, who was cr. a *Baronet* 1929 [*see* that title].

Grandchildren of the late Col. John Anstruther-Thomson, el. son of John An-
struther-THOMSON, el. son of Col. John Anstruther, 3rd son of 2nd baronet:—
Issue of the late Lieut.-Col. William ANSTRUTHER-GRAY, *b.* 1859, *d.* 1938; having assumed
by deed poll 1904, the surname of Gray in lieu of that of Thomson : *m.* 1891, Jessie
Clayre, *C.B.E.*, who *d.* 1958, da. of the late Andrew Tennant, of Essenside, Glenelg,
S. Australia :—
William John St. Clair, *MC*, *PC*, *b.* 1905; cr. a *Baronet* 1956, and *Baron Kilmany* (Life Peer) 1966,
[see that title].

The 1st baronet, Sir Robert Anstruther (third son of the late Sir Philip Anstruther) purchased
Balcaskie in 1698. The 5th Baronet was Lord-Lieut. of co. Fife, and sat as M.P. for co. Fife (*L*) 1864-80,
and for St. Andrews District of Burghs 1885-6. The 6th Baronet was also Lord-Lieut. of co. Fife.

Anstruther-Gough-Calthorpe, see Calthorpe.

CARMICHAEL-ANSTRUTHER, Creations (N.S.) 1700 and 1798 (G.B.), of Anstruther
co. Fife.

I should have   Sir WINDHAM ERIC FRANCIS CAR-
perished had   MICHAEL-ANSTRUTHER, 11th *Baronet* of Nova
I not gone *Always*   Scotia and 8th *Baronet* of Great Britain, son of the
through it. *ready.*   late Gerald Yorke Anstruther and great-grandson
of the 7th Bt. of Nova Scotia and 4th Bt. of Great
Britain ; *b.* May 29th, 1900 ; *s.* his cousin, *Sir*
WINDHAM FREDERICK, 1928 ; ed. at Marlborough ;
is Heritable Carver to and one of the Masters of
Roy. Household in Scotland, and a D.L. for co.
Lanark : *m.* 1st, 1932, Fay Sybil Marie, da. of
Ernest Rechnitzer, of 45, Charles Street, Berkeley
Square, W., and Warninglid Manor, Haywards
Heath ; 2ndly, 1948, Joanne, da. of the late
William Coates, of Brighton.
Arms—Quarterly : 1st and 4th, argent, three piles issuing
from the chief sable ; 2nd and 3rd, argent, a fesse wreathed azure and gules. Crests—1st, two arms
in armour holding a battleaxe with both hands gauntleted proper ; 2nd, a dexter arm in armour
embowed holding in the hand a broken spear proper. Supporters—Two falcons, wings expanded
proper, beaked and membered gules, belled and jessed or.
Seat—Carmichael House, Thankerton, Lanarkshire. *Residence*, 161, Rose St., Edinburgh.

Widow living of 10th Baronet—KATHERINE MARY, da. of the late D. A. Neilson, of Wentbridge House, Pontefract : *m.* 1st, 1925, Sir Windham Frederick Carmichael-Anstruther, 10th
baronet of Nova Scotia and 7th baronet of Great Britain, who *d.* 1928 ; 2ndly, 1930 (divorce
1940), John Robert Follett, who *d.* 1953 [E. Dunmore]. *Residence*,

Collateral Branch living.
Issue of the late Capt. Hugh John Elphinstone Anstruther, uncle of 11th
baronet, *b.* 1875, *d.* 1960 : *m.* 1906, Ada Marie, who *d.* 1958, da. of Thomas
Clark, of Heathdene, Burston Road, Putney, S.W. :—
Averil Nina, *b.* 1907: *m.* 1947, Hugh Thompson Dickinson, of 3, Broadstone Place, W.1.

Sir James Anstruther, 12th in descent from William de Candela, Lord of the lands and barony of Anstruther, co. Fife, was appointed Hereditary Grand Carver by James VI. of Scotland 1585, and one of the Masters to the Household 1592. This family have ranked as Barons of Scotland for upwards of 700 years. John Anstruther (younger) of Anstruther, son of Sir William Anstruther of Anstruther, a Lord of Session in Scotland, with the title of Lord Anstruther, was created a Baronet of Nova Scotia 1700. His grandson, Sir Philip, 3rd Bt., assumed for himself the name of Paterson about 1782, while Sir Philip's brother Sir John, 4th Bt., Chief Justice of Bengal, was created a baronet of Great Britain 1798. The 5th (cr. 1700) and 2nd (cr. 1798) baronet assumed the additional surname of Carmichael, on succeeding to the estates of that family in 1817, and the 8th and 5th baronet sat as M.P. for Lanarkshire S. (C) 1874-80.

ANTROBUS, Creation (U.K.) 1815, of Antrobus, Cheshire.

Mindful of God, grateful to friends.

Sir PHILIP COUTTS ANTROBUS, 7th *Baronet*, son of the late Geoffrey Edward Antrobus, grandson of Gibbs Crawfurd Antrobus, brother of 2nd Bt.; *b.* April 10th, 1908; *s.* 1968; 1939-45 War (prisoner): *m.* 1st, 1937, Dorothy Margaret Mary, who *d.* 1973, da. of the late Rev. W. G. Davis; 2ndly, 1975, Doris Primrose, da. of the late Harry George Watts, and widow of Thomas Ralph Dawkins, and has issue by 1st m.

Arms—Lozengy or and azure, on a pale gules three estoiles of the first. **Crest**—Issuing out of rays proper an unicorn's head couped argent, horned and maned or, gorged with a leaf of laurel proper. **Supporters**—Two horses proper.

Residence—Amesbury Abbey, Amesbury, Wilts.

Sons living—By 1st m.—EDWARD PHILIP (Madingley, 5, Basil St., Ferndale Est. 3, Randburg, S. Africa), *b.* Sept. 28th, 1938; ed. at Witwatersrand Univ. (BSc (Min. Eng.)) and Magdalene Coll., Camb. (MA): *m.* 1966, Janet Sarah Elizabeth, da. of Philip Walter Sceales, of Johannesburg, and has issue living, Francis Edward Sceales, *b.* 1972,—Barbara Joanna, *b.* 1968,—Sarah Diana, *b.* 1970.——Michael Ronald (Longacre, Baroda, CP, S. Africa), *b.* 1939; Dip. of Agric. (S. Africa); *m.* 1968, Sandra, da. of J. H. Moolman, of Middleton, Cape Prov., and has issue living, Philip Michael, *b.* 1973,—Cherie Joann, *b.* 1969,—Elizabeth Ruth, *b.* 1971.

Daughter living—By 1st m.—Patricia Jennifer, *b.* 1948: *m.* 1971, Capt. Michael George Rodgers Montgomery, RE (c/o Lloyds Bank, Gentlemans Walk, Norwich).

Brother living—Crawfurd Ralph (Glen Stuart, Box 151, Cradock, Cape Prov., S. Africa), *b* 1915; 1939-45 War (wounded): *m.* 1943, Sheila, da. of the late Ven. Archdeacon A. E. McKenzie, and has issue living, Geoffrey Gordon, *b.* 1944,—Margaret Jean, *b.* 1947.

Sisters living—Ida Dorothy, *b.* 1909; 1939-45 War in S. African Mil. Nursing Ser.: *m.* 1st, 1937, Frank Thomas Hayes, of Cathcart, Cape Province, S. Africa; 2ndly, 1944, Cyril Embleton Hilton Barber, and has issue living (by 1st m.), Heather Ann, *b.* 1938,—(by 2nd m.) Valerie May Hilton, *b.* 1948: *m.* 1974, William Gerald Sieberhagen, of 307, Mountbow Court, Bower Rd., Wynberg, Cape Prov., S. Africa. *Residence*,—20, Cornwall Rd., Kenton-on-Sea, Cape Prov., S. Africa.——Mary Shakerley, *b.* 1913: *m.* 1937, Edward Mounsey Gilfillan, JP, and has issue living, Edward Crawfurd, *b.* 1940: *m.* 1968, Ruth-Mary MacJannet,—Philip Mounsey, *b.* 1950, Camilla Mary, *b.* 1938: *m.* 1968, Henry Guerney Gush and has issue living, Giles Joseph Guerney *b.* 1968,—Jocelyn May, *b.* 1948. *Residence*, Conway Farm, PO Conway Station, Cape Province, S. Africa.

Uncle living—Ronald Henry, MC, *b.* 1891; Lt.-Col. (ret.) RA, and a DL; High Sheriff of Cheshire 1960; 1914-18 War (despatches, MC), 1939-45 War: *m.* 1921, Muriel Kathleen, da. of the late Richard Henry Gosling, of Hawthorn Hill, Bracknell, Berks. [Dyer, Bt.], and widow of Capt. Henry Miles Chetwynd-Stapylton [*see* V. Chetwynd, colls.], and has issue living, John Ronald Lindsay (The School House, 18, School Lane, Eaton, Congleton, Ches.) *b.* 1926; ed. at Eton, at Magdalene Coll., Camb. (MA), and at Trin. Coll., Oxford; late Lt. Duke of Wellington's Regt., and 8th R. Irish Hussars; Palestine 1947-48 as Lt. 17-21st Lancers: *m.* 1st, 1952 (m. diss. 1960), Ann, el. da. of the late Lt.-Cdr. Denys Royds Brocklebank, RN [*see* E. Crawford and Balcarres, colls.]; 2ndly 1961 (m. diss. 1966), Margaret Jane, only child of the late Dr. J. H. Penman, of Eskbank, Midlothian; 3rdly, 1966, Rochelle Christine, yr. da. of the late Theodore William Candee, of Pasadena, Cal., USA, and has issue living (by 1st m.), Nigel John Lindsay (Hackthorne, Whitcombe Rd., Beaminster, Dorset), *b.* 1953; ed. at Michael Hall Sch., Forest Row, James Hugh Lindsay (Hackthorne, Whitcombe Rd., Beaminster, Dorset), *b.* 1954; ed. at Michael Hall Sch., Forest Row (by 3rd m.) Richard Henry Lindsay *b.* 1967, Charles Edward Lindsay *b.* 1968, Rosemary Caroline Lindsay *b.* 1969, Jane Elizabeth Lindsay *b.* 1972, Catherine Mary Lindsay *b.* 1975. *Residence*,—Eaton Hall, Congleton, Cheshire.

Widow living of 6th Baronet—OLIVE GERALDINE (*Olive, Lady Antrobus*) (West Amesbury House, Amesbury, Salisbury), da. of the late Louis Theobald Dillon FitzGibbon, and widow of Jordan Dumaresq [*see* V. Dillon, colls.]: *m.* 1919, Sir Philip Humphrey Antrobus, MC, 6th baronet, who *d.* 1968.

Collateral Branches living.

Grandsons of John Coutts Antrobus (nephew of 2nd baronet):—
Issue of the late Ralph Edmund Antrobus (uncle of 7th baronet), *b.* 1871, *d.* 1927: *m.* 1901, Millicent, who *d.* 1937, da. of the late Edward Lindsey De Morgan:—
Geoffrey John (2a, 5th Av., Parktown North, Johannesburg, Transvaal, S. Africa), *b.* 1904; ed. at Emmanuel Coll., Camb. (BA 1962): *m.* 1st (Jan.) 1938, Mary Dorothea Van der Byl, who *d.* 1950; 2ndly, 1953, Antonia Marie (BLEW), da. of the late William H. Carlin, of Johannesburg,

S. Africa, and has issue living (by 1st m.) Prunella Mary, *b.* (Oct.) 1938: *m.* 1961, David Burt, of Silton Hoe, Peaslake, Surrey, and has issue living, Lyndon Oliver Antrobus *b.* 1965, Nicola Katherine *b.* 1962,—Chloe Louise, *b.* 1943: *m.* 1969, Alan Douglas Saunders, of Gordon Heights, Constantia, Cape Town, and has issue living, Thandi Antonia *b.* 1973.——Edmund Shakerley Alexander, *b.* 1919; ed. at Magdalene Coll., Camb. (BA 1946), and at McGill Univ., Montreal (MSc 1949, PhD 1955); 1939-45 War as Capt. RA: *m.* 1947, Shelagh Elizabeth Rich, and has issue living, Edmund Bayard, *b.* 1949,—Bryan Ralph, *b.* 1951,—Christopher Adrian, *b.* 1952,—Robin Clive, *b.* 1954. *Address*, c/o Anglo-American Corp. of S. Africa Ltd., 44, Main St., Johannesburg, S. Africa.

Issue of the late Rev. Jocelyn James Antrobus (uncle of 7th baronet), *b.* 1876, *d.* 1953: *m.* 1915, Justine Mary Louisa, who *d.* 1964, da. of the late Maj. William Affleck King [Duckworth-King, Bt., colls.]:—
Charles Hugh, *b.* 1916; ed. at Eton, and at Magdalene Coll., Camb.; is Lieut.-Col. R.A. (retired); European War 1939-45 (despatches): *m.* 1945, Pamela Violet, da. of the Lieut.-Col. Huntly Gordon Spencer, T.D., of South Hill House, Cranmore, Shepton Mallet. *Residence*, Wootton House, Wootton Rivers, near Marlborough, Wilts.——Mary Elizabeth (16, Prospect Place, Camden Rd., Bath), *b.* 1918.

Grandson of Walter Guy Antrobus (infra):—
Issue of the late Robert Michael Antrobus, *b.* 1910, *d.* 1961: *m.* 1st, 1938 (marriage dissolved 1948), Janet Lyle Holmes, da. of the late Neil Mackay, of Seapoint, Cape Town, S. Africa; 2ndly, 1959, Peggy, da. of Douglas Graham, and widow of Donald Halley:—
(By 1st m.) Norman Hugh (17, Plover St., Horizon, Extension, 1, Rooseport, Transvaal), *b.* 1940: *m.* 1963, Barbara Gwen, da. of E. J. M. Gravitt, of Pietermaritzburg, and has issue living, Stephen Craig, *b* 1965,—Liane Mary, *b.* 1966.

Grandchildren of the late John Coutts Antrobus (ante):—
Issue of the late Walter Guy Antrobus (uncle of 7th baronet), *b.* 1879, *d.* 1963: *m.* 1907, Kathleen Frances (of 24, Barry Rd., Pietermaritzburg, Natal, S. Africa, da. of the late Brig.-Gen. Arthur Broadwood, CVO [E. Clanwilliam, colls.]:—
Henry Lindsay (c/o Chief Civil Engineer, Rhodesia Railways, Box 604, Bulawayo, Rhodesia), *b.* 1916; ed. at Witwatersrand Univ.; an AMICE: *m.* 1943, Mary Lammie, da. of Thomas Howie, of Wankie, S. Rhodesia and has issue living, Ronald James, *b.* 1950,—Rosemary Lindsay, *b.* 1947,—Helen Kathleen, *b.* 1951.——Dennis Ronald, *b.* 1920; ed. at Witwatersrand Univ. (BSc 1949): *m.* 1950, Audrey Eleanor, da. of William James McGill, of Rustenberg, and has issue living, Dennis Mark, *b.* 1956, Sally Elizabeth, *b.* 1952.——Frances Joan, *b.* 1912.——Penelope Maud, *b.* 1914.

This Baronetcy was conferred upon Edmund Antrobus, of Antrobus Hall, Cheshire, with special remainder to his nephews Edmund (who *s.* as 2nd Bt.) and Gibbs Crawfurd (ancestor of 7th Bt.).

ARBUTHNOT, Creation (U.K.) 1823, of Edinburgh.

INNOCENT AND TRUE

Sir HUGH FITZGERALD ARBUTHNOT, 7th *Baronet; b.* Jan. 2nd, 1922; *s.* his brother, *Major Sir* ROBERT DALRYMPLE, 1944; ed. at Eton; formerly Capt. Welsh Guards: *m.* 1949, Elizabeth Kathleen, who *d.* 1972, da. of the late Sqdn.-Ldr. G. G. A. Williams, and has issue.

Arms—Azure, a crescent between three mullets, two and one, argent; the whole within a bordure or, charged with three boars' heads, couped gules. **Crest**—A peacock's head proper. **Supporters**—*Dexter*, a wyvern vert vomiting flames proper; *sinister*, a greyhound argent, collared and line reflexed over the back gules.

Residence—Mount Ulston, Jedburgh, Roxburghshire.

Sons living—KEITH ROBERT CHARLES *b.* Sept. 23rd, 1951; ed. at Wellington.—David William Patrick, *b.* 1953; ed. at Wellington.
Daughter living—Christian Aline, *b.* 1950: *m.* 1973, Geoffrey Morley, and has issue living, Aline Elizabeth, *b.* 1974.
Daughter living of 4th Baronet—Rosalind Désirée, *b.* 1906: *m.* 1926, Anthony John Anson [*see* E. Lichfield, colls.]. *Residence*, Highdown, Horam, Sussex.

Collateral Branches living.

Grandchildren of the late Rev. Robert Keith Arbuthnot, 3rd son of 2nd baronet:—
Issue of the late Robert Edward Vaughan Arbuthnot, C.S.I., *b.* 1871, *d.* 1922: *m.* 1899, Ethel Mary, who *d.* 1965, da. of the late Maj. Charles Wyndham, formerly of Bengal Cav.:—
Elnyth Mary Arbuthnot, *b.* 1900: *m.* 1924, Count Ferrante Capponi, Vice-Adm. Italian Navy, who *d.* 1965, and has issue living, *Count* Neri Piero Roberto, *b.* 1925: *m.* 1958, Flavia, younger da. of Romano Lodi-Fè, Min. Plen., Italian Foreign Office (ret.), and has issue living, Niccolo Piero *b.* 1961, Piero Zanobi *b.* 1965, Sebastiano *b.* 1971, Tessa *b.* 1959,—Diamante Tessa Luisa, *b.* 1927: *m.* 1949, Marchese Agostino Cornaggia Medici della Castellanza, and has issue living, Beatrice *b.* 1950: *m.* 1972, Marchese Rolando Rovereto Ilaria *b.* 1954: *m.* 1973, Angiolo Logi. *Residence*, 28, Via de Bardi, 50125, Florence, Italy.

Issue of the late Henry FitzGerald Arbuthnot, b. 1873, d. 1917: m. 1900, Ivy, who d.
     1959, da. of the late John Minchin, of Ootcamund, Madras :—
Hugh FitzGerald, b. 1903: ed. at St. Edward's Sch., Oxford: m. 1928, Kathleen Phyllis (Peggy)
     da. of the late R. W. Sheppard, of Looe, and has issue living, Patrick Stephen FitzGerald (The
     Litten, Grimsdells Lane, Amersham, Bucks.), b. 1936; ed. at Haileybury: m. 1967, Jennifer
     Anne, da. of the late S. G. Roe, and has issue living, Simon Charles FitzGerald b. 1969,—Rose-
     mary Elizabeth FitzGerald, b. 1930; ed. at Headington Sch., Oxford and Bristol Univ. (BA):
     m. 1957, Wiliam Allen Humpherson, FRCO, BDS, of Thornbury Cottage, Winterbourne Stoke,
     nr. Salisbury, and has issue living, Robert William b. 1958, Michael Hugh b. 1962, Edward
     Allen b. 1970, Susan Linley b. 1960. Residence, Greywethers, Uffington, Oxon.——Madeline
     Ivy, b. 1908: m. 1928, Geoffrey Wilmot Teed, and has issue living, Christopher Litherland (5,
     Thackeray St., W8), b. 1933,—Hugh Arbuthnot (65, Fisherton St., Salisbury) b. 1936: m. 1966,
     Marjorie Gillian, BA, da. of the late Charles Theodore Law-Green, Notary Public, of Bradford,
     and has issue living, Jane Arbuthnot b. 1970, Caroline Green b. 1972,—Ruth Sinclair, b. 1930:
     m. 1954, Derek Hale, of Gløde House, 28a London Rd., Great Glen, Leics., and has issue living,
     Jonathan Wilmot b. 1964, Christine Morley b. 1956, Deborah Sinclair b. 1959,—Aurea Wilmot
     b. 1943: m. 1968, Christopher James Collier Hart, of Home Cottage, Marshfield, Chippenham,
     and has issue living, Alexandra Prinz b. 1972. Residence,—Station Cottage, Fairford, Glos.——
     Katherine Rose, b. 1913: m. 1943, Robert Theodore Gladstone, who d. 1962. Residence,—
     Little Colt, Hammerwood Rd., E. Grinstead, Sussex.

                    Grandchildren of the late Col. George Arbuthnot (infra) :—
     Issue of the late Major John Bernard Arbuthnot, M.V.O., b. 1875, d. 1950: m. 1903,
          Olive, who d. 1953, only da. of the late Sir Henry Arthur Blake, G.C.M.G.:—
David George, b. 1905; ed. at Eton, and at Corpus Christi Coll., Camb. (MA); FZS; a CStJ: m.
     1st, 1933 (m. diss. 1946), the Hon. Elizabeth Dorothy Kemeys-Tynte, later Baroness Wharton.
     who d. 1974; 2ndly, 1946, Barbara Margherita, who d. 1974, da. of Francis Chiappini, JP, of
     Wynberg, Cape Province, S. Africa, and widow of Percy Seymour Douglas-Hamilton [see D.
     Hamilton, colls.], and has issue living, (by 1st m.) Hon. Myrtle Olive Felix, b. 1934: co-heiress
     presumptive to Barony of Wharton: m. 1958, Henry MacLeod Robertson (Harry Robinson,
     Musical Dir.), of 9, Gipsy Lane, SW15, and has issue living [see By. Wharton],—Hon. Caroline
     Elizabeth, b. 1935; co-heiress presumptive to Barony of Wharton: m. 1970, Lt.-Cdr. Jonathon Cecil
     Appleyard-List, RN, and has issue living [see By. Wharton]. Residence,—St. Andrews, 8,
     Largo Rd., Newlands, Cape Province, S. Africa.——Terence John (6, Sheridan Court, Barkston
     Gdns.' SW5 oET), b. 1906; ed. at Eton; Group-Capt. RAF (ret.), and an OStJ; Mohmand
     Operations 1935 (despatches), 1939-45 War in France (despatches, Order of Leopold of Belgium,
     Croix de Guerre): m. 1937, Karin, da. of Carl Sundgren, of Hudiksvall, Sweden, and has issue
     living, John Sten Robert, b. 1941: m. 1971, Elizabeth M., da. of Sir (Charles) Henry Plumb, of
     Southfields, Coleshill, Warwicks.,—Susan Christine, b. 1939: m. 1970, B. John Minchin,—Diana
     Karin, b. 1942: m. 1963, Geert Holger Sonderhoff, of 316, Stevens Drive, W. Vancouver, BC,
     Canada, and has issue living, Terence Sven b. 1965, Stefan Andrew b. 1967.——Bernard Kieran
     Charles, DSC, b. 1909; d. 1975, Cdr. (ret.) RN; 1939-45 War (DSC): m. 1939, Rosemary Harold,
     da. of the late Lt.-Col. Harold Thompson, DSO, and has issue living, Shirley, b. 1949: m.
     1970, Nigel Murray, of 20, Gerald Rd., SW1W 9EQ, and has issue living, Simon Peregrine
     Gauvain, b. 1972, Iona Louise Arbuthnot, b. 1974,—Penelope Anne, b. 1953. Residence,—
     Myrtle Grove, Youghal, co. Cork.——Irene Jean Grace, b. 1904.——Patricia Evangeline Anne,
     b. 1914: m. 1st, 1933, Arthur Cecil Byron; 2ndly, 1940, Claud Cockburn, and has issue living,
     (by 2nd m.) Alexander Claud, b. 1941: m. 1968 (m. diss. 1973), The Hon. Emma Christina
     Tennant, da. of 2nd Baron Glenconner, and formerly wife of (i) Sebastian Yorke [see E. Hard-
     wicke, colls.], and (ii) Christopher John Penrice Booker, and has issue living, Daisy Alice b. 1969,
     —Andrew Myles, b. 1947,—Patrick Oliver, b. 1950. Residence,—Brook Lodge, Youghal, co.
     Cork.

               Granddaughter of the late John Alves Arbuthnot, 2nd son of 1st baronet:—
     Issue of the late Col. George Arbuthnot, b. 1836, d. 1912: m. 1870, Caroline Emma Nepean,
          who d. 1927, da. of the late Capt. Andrew Nepean Aitchison, H.E.I.C.S.:—
Mary Christobel, b. 1879: m. 1st, 1907, George Archibald Wallace Young; 2ndly, 1914, Capt.
     Alexander Gifford Ludford-Astley, who d. (killed in action in Mesopotamia) 1917 [Dixie, Bt.];
     3rdly, 1923, Col. Edgar James Bridges, MC, who d. 1960. Residence,—Brockham House,
     Brockham Green, Betchworth, Surrey.

                 Grandson of the late Adm. Sir Geoffrey Schomberg Arbuthnot, KCB, DSO
                      (infra):—
     Issue of the late Michael Geoffrey Henderson, b. 1919, d. 1967: m. 1948, Patricia, (5,
          Egerton Place, SW3), da. of the late Lt.-Col. R. I. H. Collins, of Thurston House,
          Bury St. Edmunds:—
Peter Geoffrey (5, Egerton Place, SW3) b. 1950.

                 Granddaughter of the late Adm. Charles Ramsay Arbuthnot, son of the late
                      George Clerk Arbuthnot, 3rd son of 1st baronet :—
     Issue of the late Adm. Sir Geoffrey Schomberg Arbuthnot, K.C.B., D.S.O., b. 1885,
          d. 1957: m. 1913, Jessie Marguerite, who d. 1947, da. of the late William Henderson,
          of Berkley House, Frome :—
Mary Marguerite, b. 1914: m. 1934, Lt.-Col. Walter Stuart Augustus Clough-Taylor, late RWF, of
     Marvins, Kingston Deverill, Warminster, Wilts. [E. Castle Stewart], and has issue living, Juliet
     Mary, b. 1935: m. 1961, Timothy Charles Austin Horn, and has issue living, Francis William
     Austin b. 1962, Charlotte Mary b. 1965.

                 Granddaughter of the late Maj.-Gen. William Arbuthnot, CB, el. son of the
                      late Archibald Francis Arbuthnot, 4th son of 1st baronet:—
     Issue of the late Gerald Archibald Arbuthnot, Lt. Grenadier Guards, b. 1872, d. (killed
          in action) 1916: m. 1894, (Mary Johanna) Dulce, who d. 1945, da. of the late Charles
          Oppenheim:—
Cynthia Isabelle Theresa (24, Pelham Cres., SW7) b. 1898: m. 1925, Stephen Ian Fairbairn, from
     whom she obtained a divorce 1941, and has issue living, Jennifer Selena (Hon. Mrs. John R. C.
     Manners), b. 1927: m. 1949, the Hon. John Robert Cecil Manners, el. son of 4th Baron Manners.

                 Granddaughter of the late Lt.-Col. Archibald Hugh Arbuthnot (infra):—
     Issue of the late Lt.-Cdr. Archibald Hugh Gough Arbuthnot, R.N., b. 1900; d. 1959:
          m. 1st, 1935 (marriage dissolved 1954), Molly Irene Frances Weeks; 2ndly, 1955,
          Emma Mary (4, Jesmond Rd.), Hove), da. of the late Rev. Gilbert Ambrose Bell, MA:—
By 2nd marriage) Viola Jane, b. 1957.

                 Grandchildren of the late Maj. Archibald Ernest Arbuthnot, 3rd son of Archibald
                      Francis Arbuthnot (ante):—
     Issue of the late Lieut.-Col. Archibald Hugh Arbuthnot, b. 1874, d. 1957 : m. 1st, 1900,
          Gertrude, who d. 1918, da. of the late Rev. Frederick Charles Green, V. of Denmead,
          Hants; 2ndly, 1920, Marjory, who d. 1975, da. of the late Rev. Howard Beech, formerly
          R. of Barlavington and Burton-with-Coates, Sussex:—
(By 1st m.). Patrick Charles (Quay Head, Sampford Peverel, Tiverton, Devon), b. 1902; ed. at
     Haileybury; ret. Tea Planter; 1939-45 War in Middle East as Maj. Indian Army: m. 1952,
     Evelyn Margaret, da. of the late G. R. Crawford, of Leamington, and formerly of Thropton,
     Northumberland, and has issue living, Patrick Hugh Alexander, b. 1954; ed. at Blundell's and
     Sidney Sussex Coll., Camb.,—Colin Hugh David, b. 1957; ed. at Blundell's.——Ernest Douglas
     (Downham Grove, 3 Norwich Common, Wymondham, Norfolk), b. 1905; late Sudan Political Ser.:

m. 1939, Mary Morgan, and has issue living. Anthony, *b.* 1948: *m.* 1974, Frances, da. of Sqdn. Ldr. F. W. Williamson, of Garvestone, Norfolk,—Robin Douglas, *b.* 1951, Ann Faith, *b.* 1941.—— Sheila Gertrude Talmash, *b.* 1917; 1939-45 War as Subaltern, ATS: *m.* 1942, Maj. Robert Dunlop, MBE, Derbyshire Yeo., and has issue living, Robert Andrew, *b.* 1948,—Caroline Jane, *b.* 1944,— Elspeth Marilyn, *b.* 1951. *Residence,* Meadow Cottage, Aldingbourne, Chichester.——(by 2nd m.) Deborah Faith, *b.* 1921; 1939-45 War as Subaltern, ATS: *m.* 1948, Edmund O'Donnel Colley Grattan, FRCS, of Rook's Orchard, Little Wittenham, Abingdon, late Colonial Med. Ser., Kenya, and has issue living, Howard Colley Arnout Hugh, *b.* 1949,—Clive Edmund Hume, *b.* 1953,— Sarah Faith Madalyn, *b.* 1950,—Clare Winifred Melissa, *b.* 1956.

Issue of the late Capt. Ernest Kennaway Arbuthnot, DSO, RN (retired), *b.* 1876 *d.* 1945: *m.* 1st, 1910, Edith Elizabeth (the actress Miss "Evie Greene"), who *d.* 1917, da. of Richard Bentley Greene, formerly of Parnholt, Laburnum Grove, Portsmouth ; 2ndly, 1920, Gladys who *d.* 1946, da. of the late W. B. Mann, of Downe, Broadhampton, S. Devon :—
(By 2nd m.) John Keith, OBE, RN (Baynards, San Pawl Tat Tarea, Naxxar, Malta; United Service Club), *b.* 1927; Lt.-Cdr. RN (ret.); 1939-45 War; Korea 1951 nad 1954; OBE (Mil) 1967: *m.* 1949, Susan Phillipa, only da. of Kenneth Petrie Letts, of Tickerage Mill, Blackboys, Sussex, and has issue living, Richard Keith, *b.* 1950,—Charles Petrie, *b.* 1959,—Sally Anne, *b.* 1954,— Phillipa Jane, *b.* 1961.——Peter Kennaway (Oak Hammer, Plummers Plain, Horsham, Sussex), *b.* 1930; Lt. RN (ret.); Korea 1952: *m.* 1957, Mia. el da. of the late Maj. Percy Montagu Nevile, of Skelbrooke, Yorks., and has issue living, Matthew Kennaway, *b.* 1959.

Issue of the late Col. William Patrick Arbuthnot, R.M. (retired), *b.* 1878, *d.* 1949 : *m.* 1904, Olive, who *d.* 1957, only da. of the late Hon. William Gregory Walker, sometime a Puisne Judge of Supreme Court, N.S. Wales :—
Olive Joan, *b.* 1905 : *m.* 1926, Col. Charles Walter Adair, R.M., and has issue living, Arbuthnot James, *b.* 1931; Maj. RA: *m.* 1959, Gillian Marjorie Mettam, of Farnborough, Hants, and has issue living, William Henry *b.* 1961, Catherine Elizabeth *b.* 1960,—Patrick Charles Hugh, *b.* 1942: *m.* 1968, Gloria Rosalind Ogston, of Solihull, Warwicks., and has issue living, Andrew Patrick *b.* 1970,—Anthea Arbuthnot, *b.* 1928: *m.* 1958, the Rev. John Echlin D'Aeth, of Corner Well House, Butleigh, Glastonbury, Som., and has issue living, Jack Theodore *b.* 1959, Sybil Mary *b.* 1961. *Residence,* Maen House, Burton Bradstock, Dorset.——Patricia Gwyn, *b.* 1906: *m.* 1931, Henry Bartle Jary Frere, only son of Sir Bartle Henry Temple Frere, and has issue living, Henrietta Julia Arbuthnot, *b.* 1942. *Residence,* Halfway House, Scoulton, Hingham, Norfolk.

Grandchildren of the late Robert George Arbuthnot (infra):—
Issue of the late Capt. Robert Wemyss Muir Arbuthnot, MC, *b.* 1889, *d.* 1962: *m.* 1915, Mary (The Golden Wing, Gaddesden Row, Hemel Hempstead), el. da. of Norman Coghill, of Almington Hall, Market Drayton:—
Andrew Robert Coghill, *b.* 1926; European War 1944-45 as Capt. Scots Guards (wounded): *m.* 1952, Mrs. Audrey Dutton-Barker, da. of Denys Johnson, M.C., of Midhurst, Sussex, and has issue living, Charles Robert Denys, *b.* 1956,—Caroline Rose, *b.* 1954. *Residence,* Monksfield House, Tilford, nr. Farnham, Surrey.——Mary Juliet Gough, *b.* 1917: *m.* 1939, Guy Marsden Halsey, TD [*see* Halsey, Bt., colls.]. *Residence,* The Golden Parsonage, Gaddesden Row, nr. Hemel Hempstead, HP2 6HG.——Elizabeth Christian, *b.* 1918: *m.* 1943, Frank Ernest Cameron Cox, and has issue living, Oliver Robert Frank, *b.* 1944,—Christopher Peter, *b.* 1946: *m.* 1969, Sylvie, da. of Jean Escaude, of Brive-la-Gaillarde, France, and has issue living, Gregory Pierre *b.* 1970, Ludovic *b.* 1972,—Virginia Frances Elizabeth, *b.* 1949. *Residence,*—The Jolly Sailors Orchard, Brancaster Staithe, Norfolk.

Granddaughter of the late Archibald Francis Arbuthnot, 4th son of 1st baronet:—
Issue of the late Robert George Arbuthnot, *b.* 1843, *d.* 1890 : *m.* 1885, Helen Mary, who *d.* 1926, da. of the late Sir William Muir, K.C.S.I., of Dean Park House, Edinburgh :—
Elizabeth Gertrude Gough (twin), *b.* 1889. *Residence*—141, Cranmer Court, Sloane Av., SW3.

This family is a branch of the Lairds of Arbuthnot, who have held lands in Kincardineshire from about 1160. The 1st baronet, Sir William, Lord Provost of Edinburgh in 1822, entertained George IV. to a public banquet in that city, and was created a baronet by the King in person, the patent, however bearing date 1823. The 4th baronet, Rear-Adm. Sir Robert Keith Arbuthnot, K.C.B., M.V.O., died (killed in action at the battle of Jutland during European War) June 1916 (despatches, posthumous K.C.B.). The 5th baronet, Brig.-Gen. Sir Dalrymple Arbuthnot, C.M.G., D.S.O., served in S. Africa 1900-1901, and in European War 1914-18 (C.M.G., D.S.O.). The 6th baronet, Major Sir Robert Dalrymple, 24th Lancers, *d.* (killed in action in Normandy) 1944.

ARBUTHNOT, Creation (U.K.) 1964, of Kittybrewster, Aberdeen.

Sir JOHN SINCLAIR-WEMYSS ARBUTHNOT, *M.B.E., TD,* 1st *Baronet,* el. son of the late Maj. Kenneth Wyndham Arbuthnot, Seaforth Highlanders; *b.* Feb. 11th, 1912; ed. at Eton, and at Trin. Coll., Camb. (MA); an Underwriting Member of Lloyd's, a Dir. of Ecclesiastical Insurance Office Ltd., and of other public cos.; Chm. of Halcyon Investments, Ltd., and Folkestone and Dist. Water Co., and a National Vice-Pres. of Trustee Savings Banks Assocn.; Joint Hon. Sec. of Assocn. of British Chambers of Commerce 1953-59, PPS to Min. of Pensions 1952-55, and to Min. of Health 1956-57; a Member of Public Accounts Cttee. 1955-64, Chm. of Cttees., and Temp. Chm. of House of Commons 1958-64, Second Church Estates Commr. 1962-64; Chm. of Archbishop of Canterbury's Commn. on reorganisation of Diocesan Boundaries in SE England 1965-67, a Member of House of Laity in Church Assembly 1955-70; a Trustee of Lambeth Palace Library since 1964, and a Member of Gen. Synod of Church of England since 1970 (a Member of panel of Chm); a Church Commr. for England since 1965, Vice-Chm. Assets Cttee. since 1968, 1939-45 War as Maj. RA (TA Reserve 1948-62); MP for Dover Div. of Kent (C) 1950-64; *cr.* MBE (Mil) 1944: *m.* 1943, Margaret Jean, yr. da. of Alexander G. Duff, and has issue.

Arms—Azure, a crescent between three mullets argent, a bordure gules charged with two escallops in chief and a buck's head cabossed or in base, and in centre chief (overlapping bordure) an inescutcheon argent. Crest—A peacock's head and neck proper, accompanied on either side by a spray of strawberry leaves vert, each flowered of a cinquefoil Argent.

Residences—Poulton Manor, Ash, Canterbury, Kent, CT3 2HW; 7, Fairholt St., SW7 1EG.
Clubs—Carlton, City of London, Royal Commonwealth Society.

Sons living—WILLIAM REIERSON, *b.* Sept. 2nd, 1950; ed. at Eton.——James Norwich, *b.* 1952; ed. at Eton, and Trin. Coll., Camb.

Daughters living—Elizabeth Mary, *b.* 1947; ed. at St. Mary's Sch., Calne, and Kent Univ. (BA).—— Louise Victoria, *b.* 1954; ed. at St. Mary's Sch., Calne, and Exeter Univ.——Alison Jane, *b.* 1957; ed. at Benenden.

Sir John Sinclair-Wemyss Arbuthnot, MBE, TD, 1st Bt., is grandson of William Reierson Arbuthnot, 5th son of George Arbuthnot of Elderslie, brother of Sir William Arbuthnot 1st. Bt. cr. 1823).

ARCHDALE, Creation (U.K.) 1928, of Riversdale, co. Fermanagh.

Follow the destiny allotted.

Sir EDWARD FOLMER ARCHDALE, *D.S.C., R.N.,* 3rd *Baronet : b.* Sept. 8th, 1921 ; *s.* his father, *Vice-Adm. Sir* (Nicholas) Edward, *CBE,* 1955; Capt. RN (ret.); 1939-45 War (despatches, DSC): *m.* 1954, Elizabeth Ann Stewart, da. of Maj.-Gen. William Boyd Fellowes Lukis, CBE, and has issue.

Arms—Quarterly 1st and 4th, azure, a chevron ermins between three talbots passant or, *Archdale;* 2nd, or, a chevron sable, *Mervyn;* 3rd quarterly, 1st and 4th azure, three fleurs-de-lis or ; 2nd and 3rd gules, three gem ring. gold, all within a bordure or, charged with a tressure flory, gules, in the centre point an inescutcheon argent charged with a tilting spear and sword saltireways, points upwards proper, *Montgomery.* Crest—Out of a ducal crest coronet or, an heraldic tiger's head argent, maned, tufted and armed sable.

Residence—Battom Cottage, Owslebury, Winchester, Hants.

Son living—Nicholas Edward, *b.* Dec. 2nd, 1965.
Daughters living—Annabel Frances, *b.* 1956.——Lucinda Grace, *b.* 1958.
Sister living—Alice Gerda (Tadmoor, Avenue Rd., Cranleigh, Surrey), *b.* 1923: *m.* 1949 (m. diss. 1964), Maj Peter Courage, late King's Dragoon Guards, and has issue living, John Mervyn, *b.* 1950,—Gerda Veronica, *b.* 1952,—Susan Rose, *b.* 1956,—Belinda Jane, *b.* 1958.

Uncle living—(son of 1st baronet)—Audley Quintin, *b.* 1886; ed. at Winchester; Lieut.-Col. (ret.) RHA; 1914-18 War; 1939-45 War: *m.* 1922, Mary Edith Haigh, da. of Oliver Bury, of 7, The Vale, Chelsea, SW, and has issue living, Rosemary, *b.* 1923: *m.* 1949, William Anthony Twiston-Davies, of The Mynde, Much Dewchurch, Hereford, and has issue living, Audley William *b.* 1950, Nigel Anthony *b.* 1957, Alexandra Rosemary *b.* 1954, Penelope Auriol *b.* 1959,—Judith Penelope, *b.* 1924,—Anne Alicia, *MBE, b.* 1928; MBE (Civil) 1973. *Residence*, Tre-Evan, Llangarron, Ross on Wye.

Collateral Branches living.

Issue of the late William Porter Palgrave Archdale, C.B.E., 2nd son of 1st baronet, *b.* 1883, *d.* 1956: *m.* 1918, Alice Edith Palgrave, who *d.* 1963, da. of the late Capt. Charles Alexander Price Chetwynd-Talbot [E. Shrewsbury, colls.]:—

Mervyn Talbot, *b.* 1924: *m.* 1951, Aureole Helen, da. of the late Rev. Canon Robert Hamilton Whelan, and has issue living, Peter Mervyn, *b.* 1953,—Geraldine Angel, *b.* 1952. *Residence*, The Cottage Farm, Knockmoyle, Omagh, co. Tyrone.——Angel, *b.* 1919: *m.* 1946, Paul von Benckendorff, and has issue living, Simon Anthony, *b.* 19—,—Carolyn, *b.* 1947,—Phillipa (twin), *b.* 1947.——Kathleen, *b.* 1922: *m.* 1958, Anthony Robert Whelan, BSc, and has issue living, Nicholas Robert, *b.* 1960,—Sarah Deborah, *b.* 1963. *Residence*, Rose Cottage, Hornby, Gt. Smeaton, Northallerton, Yorks.

Issue of the late Capt. Humphrys Archdale, DSC, RN, yst. son of 1st baronet ; *b.* 1896; *d.* 1972: *m.* 1944, Mary Katherine, who *d.* 1975 (2nd Officer (ret.) WRNS), da. of the late Robert Leslie Gilbert:—
Gilbert Humphrys, *b.* 1947; ed. at Tonbridge.
    The 1st baronet, the Rt. Hon. Sir Edward Mervyn Archdale (el. son of the late Nicholas Montgomery Archdale, of Crock na Crieve, co. Fermanagh), was M.P. for N. Div. of Fermanagh (*U*) 1898-1903 and 1916-22, and a Member of House of Commons of N. Ireland 1921-37. He was first Min. of Agriculture, N. Ireland 1921-33, and of Commerce 1921-5. The 2nd baronet, Vice-Adm. Sir Nicholas Edward Archdale, C.B.E. served during European War 1914-18 Comdg. Submarine Flotillas, and was Senior Naval Officer, Copenhagen 1920.

ARMSTRONG, Creation (U.K.) 1841, of Gallen Priory, King's County.

Sir ANDREW ST. CLARE ARMSTRONG, 5th *Baronet ; b.* Dec. 20th, 1912 ; *s.* his father, *Sir* NESBITT WILLIAM, 1953 ; ed. at Wellesley Coll., Wellington, New Zealand ; European War 1939-45 with Australian Imperial Force.

Arms—Quarterly: 1st and 4th, argent, issuing from the sinister side a dexter arm habited gules, the hand grasping the trunk of an oak-tree eradicated and broken at the top proper ; 2nd and 3rd, argent, three pallets azure.   **Crest**— An arm embowed in armour proper, the hand grasping the broken trunk of an oak-tree, as in the arms.

Residence,—20, Cobbleset Lane, Pinetown, Natal.

Sister living—Edith Fisher, *b.* 1910 : *m.* 1933, Clarence Cliff, and has issue living, Frances, *b.* 1938. *Residence*, 33, Freyburg Street, Lyall Bay, Wellington, New Zealand.

I am still unconquered.

INVICTUS·MANEO

Collateral Branches living.

Grandchildren of the late Andrew Charles Armstrong (infra):—
Issue of the late Edmund Clarence Richard Armstrong, Bluemantle Pursuivant of Arms, *b.* 1879, *d.* 1923: *m.* 1906, Mary Frances, who *d.* 1953, da. of the late Sir Francis Richard Cruise, MD, DL, of 93, Merrion Square, West, Dublin:—

ANDREW CLARENCE FRANCIS, *C.M.G., b.* May 1st, 1907 ; ed. at St. Edmund's Ware, and at Christ's Coll., Camb. (B.A. 1928) ; formerly Permanent Sec., Min. of Mines and Power, Federation of Nigeria ; retired 1961 ; C.M.G. 1959 : *m.* 1st, (Jan) 1930, Phyllis Marguerite, who *d.* (Jan.) 1930, da. of the late Lieut.-Col. Roland Henry Waithman, D.S.O.; 2ndly, 1932, Laurel May, el. da. of the late Alfred Wellington Stuart, and has issue living, (by 2nd m.) Christopher John Edmund Stuart, *b.* 1940; ed. at Ampleforth, and RMA; Maj. RCT: *m.* 1972, Georgina Elizabeth Carey, 2nd. da. of Lt.-Col. W. G. Lewis, of Hayling Island, and has issue living, Charles Andrew *b.* 1973, James Hugo *b.* 1974.   *Residence*, Fernacre, Little Marlow, Bucks.——Edmund Charles Mark, *b.* 1914; ed. at St. Edmund's, Ware, and at St. John's Coll., Camb. (BA 1935); 1939-45 War as Lt. (S) RNR; assumed by deed poll 1945, the Christian names of Edmund Charles Mark in lieu of Edmund Clarence Charles: *m.* 1st, 1939, Patricia Phyllis Vassall Adams; 2ndly, 1951, Dorice, da. of the late William Harold Austin, and has issue living, (by 2nd m.) Mark Simon, *b.* 1954,—Sean Andrew (triplet), *b.* 1954,—Patrick Austin (triplet), *b.* 1954.   *Residence*, Litheys Hill, Hambledon, Hants.——Katherine Mary, *b.* 1909: *m.* 1937, Jerrold Vassall Adams, and has issue living, Paul Rory (St. Johns Point, Westbury-on-Severn, Glos.) *b.* 1941; MB, BS; Surg. Lt., RN: *m.* 1967, Nicola, el. da. of Dr. R. Lissau, of Wynstones, Brookthorpe, Glos., and has issue living, Guy Luke *b.* 1969, Daniel Francis *b.* 1971,—Augusta Frances, *b.* 1938: *m.* 1st, 1958 (m. diss. 1972), Alastair Ian Hamish Valentine; 2ndly, 1972, Christopher K. Keele, of 3, Roundacre, Inner Park Rd., Wimbledon SW19, and has issue living (by 1st m.) Hamish Guy *b.* 1958, Alastair Rory *b.* 1961, Ranald Andrew *b.* 1962, Katherine Ann *b.* 1959, (by 2nd m.) Stephanie Jane *b.* 1974,—Sarah Catherine, *b.* 1945: *m.* 1971, Richard Thomas Holland, of 40, Rainsford Rd., Toronto 5, Canada, and has issue living, Camilla Juliet *b.* 1973.   *Residence,*—Knoll Cottage, Medmenham, Gt. Marlow, Bucks.

Issue of the late Andrew Charles Armstrong, 3rd son of 1st baronet, *b.* 1845, *d.* 1895 : *m.* 1st, 1874, Alice Maria, who *d.* 1881, da. of the late Sir Thomas William Clinton Murdoch, K.C.M.G. ; 2ndly, 1888, Annie Beatrice, da. of John Lorrimer, formerly of Aylestone, Leicester :—
(By 2nd marriage) John Andrew, *b.* 1892 ; formerly Capt. Lancashire Fusiliers ; sometime Dist. Commr. Lawra, Gold Coast : *m.* 1935, Pauline, da. of the late Major C. O. N. Williams, of Pulborough, Sussex, and has issue living, Jill Sara, *b.* 1937 : *m.* 1958, Capt. Alexander Bayly Maxwell-Hyslop, 17th/21st Lancers (ret.), of Woodbridge Mill, Bedchester, Shaftesbury, Dorset, and has issue living, Lucinda Francis *b.* 1959, Zara Belinda *b.* 1962. *Address,* c/o Barclays Bank, 53, Sloane St., SW1.——Nadine Alice, *b.* 1889: *m.* 1919, Maj. Vernon Robert Guise, OBE, MC, late RA, who *d.* 1939 [see Guise, Bt., colls.]. *Residence,*—Orford House, Woodcote Park, Coulsdon, Surrey, CR3 2XN.

Grandchildren of the late Montagu Fullerton Armstrong, 5th son of 1st baronet:—
Issue of the late Lieut.-Col. Nevill Alexander Drummond Armstrong, O.B.E., *b.* 1874, *d.* 1954 : *m.* 1902, Mary Anne Katherine (who *d.* 1953, and from whom he had obtained a divorce 1920), da. of the late Andrew Charles Armstrong (ante) :—
Eileen Molly Nevill (Shenley, 42, Howick Park Av., Penwortham, Preston), *b.* 1903.

Issue of the late Jack Proby Armstrong, *b.* 1878, *d.* 1953 : *m.* 1912, Maria Dominga Alvarenga (now of Guatemala City, Guatemala), da. of John Molina :—
Montagu John Proby, *DSC* (Chalet Santa Fe, 2a, Avenida-12-27, Zona 10, Guatemala), *b.* 1913; ed. at Harrow, and at Merton Coll., Oxford; is Lt.-Com. RNVR; 1939-45 War (despatches, DSC). ——Martha Florence, *b.* 1921: *m.* 1st, 1944, Elmer Page Madsen, from whom she obtained a divorce 1956; 2ndly, 1958, James W. Thornton, of 7841, Woodsdale Lane, Jacksonville, Fla. 32216, USA, son of the late Sir Henry Worth Thornton, KBE.

Issue of the late Frederick Edmund John Armstrong, *b.* 1889, *d.* (on active ser. N.-W. Frontier of India) 1919: *m.* 1915, Stella, who *d.* 1966, el. da. of J. R. Morgan, late of Portmore, Weymouth:—
Beatrice, *b.* 1916: *m.* 1937, Com. Edric Guy Philip Bromefield Knapton, DSC, RN, of Old Craven Arms, Inkpen, Newbury, Berks., and has issue living, Guy Augustus Bromfield (c/o Barclays Bank, Godalming, Surrey), *b.* 1940: *m.* 1966, Catherine Margaret Ffoulkes, da. of Francis Herbert Walker,—Julian Richard Anthony, *b.* 1954,—Vanessa Josephine Stella, *b.* 1944,—Marie Victoria Gwendolyn, *b.* 1947,—Louise Elizabeth Teresa, *b.* 1956.——Madeline, *b.* 1917: *m.* 1942 (m. diss. 1967), Bernard Michael Edmund O'Mahoney, and has issue living, Kevin Edmund, *b.* 1943,—Hugh Frederick Michael, *b.* 1948,—Stephen Lawrence Thomas, *b.* 1956,—Philippa Katherine, *b.* 1944,—Deirdre Lillian Mary, *b.* 1958.

Granddaughter of the late Charles Nesbitt Frederic Armstrong, 6th son of 1st baronet:—

Issue of the late George Nesbitt Armstrong, b. 1883, d. 1971: m. 1st, 1906, Phoebe Georgina Frances Ruby (who d. 1939, having obtained a divorce 1908), only da. of Col. Jocelyn Otway; 2ndly, 1913, Evelyn Mary (Coombe Cottage, Coldstream, Vic., Aust.), da. of the late Michael Doyle, of Brisbane:—
(By 2nd m.) Helen Pamela Fullerton (Melba) (*Pamela, Baroness Vestey*), (Coombe Cottage, Coldstream, Vic., Aust.), b. 1918; raised to the rank of a Baron's widow 1955: m. 1939, Capt. the Hon. William Howarth Vestey, Scots Gds., who d. (killed in action in Italy) 1944, only son of 2nd Baron Vestey.

This family was anciently settled on the Scottish Border, and John Armstrong, laird of Gilnockie Hall, Eskdale, the most famous leader of the warlike clans that made frequent inroads into the northern counties of England, was, with many of his retainers, executed about 1530. Andrew Armstrong, his descendant, and ancestor of the present family, migrated to Ireland early in the 17th century, and settled in co. Fermanagh; he greatly distinguished himself in the army of Charles I. Capt. Sir Andrew H. Armstrong, 3rd Bt., was High Sheriff of King's co. 1914.

ARMSTRONG, Creation (U.K.) 1892, of London. [Extinct 1944.]

Sir FRANCIS PHILIP ARMSTRONG, *O.B.E.*, 3rd and last *Baronet.*

Daughter living of 2nd Baronet—Mary, b. 1903; former Member of North Cotswold Rural Dist. Council. *Residence,* The Butts, Guiting Power, Cheltenham, Glos. GL54 5US.

Widow living of 2nd Baronet—MILLICENT (*Lady Armstrong*), da. of the late Adolph Leopold Ortlepp, of Graaff Reinert, Cape Province, S. Africa: m. 1925, as his second wife, Sir George Elliot Armstrong, C.M.G., 2nd baronet, who d. 1940.

ARMYTAGE, Creation (G.B.) 1738, of Kirklees, Yorkshire.

Always ready.

Sir JOHN LIONEL ARMYTAGE, 8th *Baronet;* b. Nov. 23rd, 1901 ; *s.* his father, *Brig.-Gen. Sir* GEORGE AYSCOUGH, *C.M.G., D.S.O.,* 1953 ; ed. at Eton, and at R.M.C.; Capt. King's Roy. Rifle Corps : *m.* 1st, 1927, Evelyn Mary Jessamine (from whom he obtained a divorce 1946), da. of Edward Herbert Fox, of Adbury Park, Hants [*see* Arbuthnot, Bt., cr. 1823 colls.]; 2ndly, 1949, Maria Margarete, da. of Paul Tenhaeff, of Bruenen Nierderhein, and has issue by 1st and 2nd marriages.

Arms—Gules, a lion's head erased between three cross-crosslets argent. Crest—A dexter arm embowed couped at the shoulder, habited or, the cuff argent, holding in the hand proper a staff gules, headed and pointed or.

Seat—Kirklees Park, Brighouse, Yorks. Clubs—Naval and Military, Oriental.

Son living—By 1st marriage—JOHN MARTIN, b. Feb. 26th, 1933.
Daughters living—By 1st marriage—Ann, b. 1928: m. 1948 (marriage dissolved 1960), Francis Richard Anson [see E. Lichfield, colls.].——By 2nd marriage—Christina Mary, b. 1952.
Brother living—Reginald William, GC, CBE (of Wick Cottage, Downton, Wilts.), b. 1903; became Rear-Adm. 1959; was Ch. Inspector of Naval Ordnance 1956-9, Vice-Pres. of Ordnance Board 1959-60, and Pres. 1961; European War 1939-45; AM (now GC) 1928; CBE (Mil.) 1959: m. 1928, Sylvia Beatrice, da. of Lt.-Col. Charles Russell Staveley-Staveley, of Pamflete, Holbeton, Plymouth, and has issue living, David George (Meadow Wood, Penshurst, Kent; United Service and Royal Aero Club), b. 1929; Capt. RN; Comdg. HMS *Minerva* 1968-70, Defence Policy Staff 1970-72, and Naval Assist. to First Sea Lord 1972-74: m. 1954, Countess Antonia Cosima, el. da. of Count Cosmo Diodono de Bosdari [see Walker-Okeover, Bt.], and has issue living, Hugh Antony b. 1955, Charles David b. 1962, Davina Jane b. 1956.—Maurice John Reginald (of Maplehurst, Staplehurst, Tonbridge, Kent), b. 1932: m. 1956, Brioni Katharine, da. of Gerald Wellington Williams, [see D. Northumberland, colls.], and has issue living, Lucinda Jane Brioni b. 1959, Nicola Susan Katharine (twin) b. 1959, Jane Annette b. 1962.—Roderick Charles (Nelson House, East Ilsely, Berks.), b. 1934: m. 1961, Susan, da. of Maj. Reginald T. Whitehead, of Abergavenny, and has issue living, Marcus David b. 1964, Gaye b. 1965.
Sister living—Barbara Ellen, b. 1906: m. 1930 (marriage dissolved 1949), Col. Henry David Makgill-Crichton-Maitland, OBE, REME, who d. 1970 [see E. Lauderdale, colls.]. Residence,—Simon's Seat Farm Cottage, Skyreholme, Skipton, Yorkshire.

Collateral Branches living.

Issue of the late John Hawksworth Armytage, 2nd son of 6th baronet, b. 1873, d. 1944: m. 1912, Everilda Frances (who assumed by deed poll 1938 the additional surname of Creyke), (of 39, Coleherne Court, S.W.5), da. of the late Ralph Creyke [Bacon, Bt.]:—
Walter John, b. 1913 ; formerly Lieut. King's Roy. Rifle Corps ; European War 1939-45 (despatches, prisoner) : m. 1st, 1947, Daphne Frances Mary Lucas (from whom he obtained a divorce 1958), only da. of the late T. G. Fletcher, of Ardmulchan, Navan, co. Meath ; 2ndly, 1959, Marion Elizabeth, only da. of Major David Anderson, D.L., LL.D., of Creevy Rocks, Saintfield, co. Down, and widow of Edward d'Arcy, and has issue living, (by 1st marriage) Julian Ralph Fitzroy, b. 1948: m. 1973, Laura, da. of the late Capt. Ian Galloway,—Clare Frances Elizabeth, b. 1950, (by 2nd m.) Diana Marion, b. 1960. Residences, Halston House, Moyvore, co. Westmeath; Inishlackan Island, Roundstone, co. Galway.——Ellen Elizabeth, b. 1915: m. 1st, 1940, John Antony de Berniere Hallows, who obtained a divorce 1945; 2ndly, 1945, (Henry) Duncan Crow. Residence, Little Bendrose, Finch Lane, Amersham Common, Bucks.

This family is descended (according to a pedigree attested by Sir Henry St. George, Norroy King of Arms) from John Armytage, of Wrigbowls, Lincolnshire, temp. King Stephen. **Two branches of the family at different times have been created baronets.** Brig.-Gen. Sir George Ayscough Armytage, C.M.G., D.S.O., 7th baronet, served in European War 1914-18 as Brig.-Gen. Comdg. an Inf. Brig., D.S.O., C.M.G.

ARNOTT, Creation (U.K.) 1896, of Woodlands, St. Anne, Shandon, co. Cork.

Sir JOHN ROBERT ALEXANDER ARNOTT, 5th *Baronet*; *b.* April 9th, 1927; *s.* his father, *Sir* ROBERT JOHN, 1966; ed. at Harrow; late Lt., R. Irish Fusiliers: *m.* 1974, Ann Margaret, da. of the late T. A. Farrelly, of Kilcar, co. Cavan.

Arms—Per chevron argent and azure, in chief two mullets and in base a crescent, all counterchanged, on a chief of the second three mullets of the first. Crest—On a rock a tower proper, therefrom a pennant of one point flying to the sinister azure.
Residence,—Ashtown House, Castleknock, co. Dublin. *Club*,— Kildare St.

Speratum et completum.
Hoped for and realized.

Brother living—ERIC JOHN (10, Lansdowne Cres., W11; 82, Harley St., W1; Kildare St. Club), *b.* June 12th, 1929; ed. at Harrow, and at Trin. Coll., Dublin (MB and BCch, FRCS): *m.* 1960, Veronica Mary, only da. of Capt. Arvid Langué, of West Green Cottage, Hartley Wintney, Hants., and has issue living, Stephen John, *b.* 1962,—Robert Lauriston John, *b.* 1971,—Tatiana Amelia, *b.* 1963.
Uncle living (son of 2nd baronet)—Thomas John, *b.* 1899; Maj. (ret.) 15th Hussars; 1939-45 War (despatches); Silver Star USA: *m.* 1927, Lettice Mary, da. of the late Lieut.-Col. Charles Montagu Crompton-Roberts, of Drybridge, Monmouth [Greenwell, Bt.], and has issue living, Peter John (Flat 38, Braemar, Kersfield Rd., Putney, SW15; *Club*—Army and Navy) *b.* 1929; late Lt. 15th/19th Hussars,—Guy, *b.* 1932; late Lt. 15th/19th Hussars: *m.* 1963, Diana, da. of D. Staines, of Wahroonga, Queensland,— Mariegold Winifred, *b.* 1931: *m.* 1955, Maj. David Miller [*see* M. Waterford],—Caroline, *b.* 1934. *Residence*, Poole Keynes House, Cirencester. *Club*, Cavalry.

Great-Aunt living (daughter of 1st baronet)—Mary Louisa Mabel (*Lady Brooke*), *b.* 1886: *m.* 1915, Capt. Sir Francis Hugh Brooke, 2nd Bt. (*cr.* 1903), who *d.* 1954. *Residence*,—Pickering Forest, Celbridge, co. Kildare.

Collateral Branch living.

Grandchildren of the late David Taylor Arnott, 2nd son of 1st baronet:—
  Issue the late John Frederic Arnott, MC, *b.* 1892, *d.* 1967: *m.* 1919, Phyllis, who *d.* 1967, da. of James Cundell:—
John) Anthony (Devon Cottage, Bourton, Dorset), *b.* 1921; FRICS; 1939-45 War as Lt.-Cdr. RNVR despatches): *m.* 1944, Jean Barbara, da. of the late Charles Lovett Gill, of Odiham, Hants., and has issue living, John David (87, Ash Grove, Liverpool 15) *b.* 1947; ed. at Cheltenham Coll., Birmingham Univ., and Liverpool Univ. (BA): *m.* 1971, Jennifer Mary Dooley,—(Ann Margaret) Amabel ARNOTT (39, Lilley Rd., Liverpool, L7 0LP), *b.* 1945; assumed by deed poll 19—the names of Amabel Arnott: *m.* 1969, Robert Hughes.——Patricia Ruth (3, Uigshadder, by Portree, I. of Skye), *b.* 1920: *m.* 1961, Evrard Burke (formerly Bourque), who *d.* 1964.

The 1st baronet, Sir John Arnott (son of the late John Arnott, of Auchmuchty, Fiteshire), was a noted philanthropist and largely connected with many Irish industries, and sat as M.P. for Kinsale (L) 1859-63.

ARTHUR, Creation (U.K.) 1841, of Upper Canada.

Sir BASIL MALCOLM ARTHUR, 5th *Baronet*; *b.* Sept. 18th, 1928; *s.* his father, *Sir* GEORGE MALCOLM, 1949; MP for Timaru (*Lab.*); Min. of Transport, and Min. in Charge of State Insurance Office NZ since 1973: *m.* (Jan.) 1950, Elizabeth Rita, da. of Alan Mervyn Wells, of Wakefield, Nelson, New Zealand, and has issue.

Arms—Or, on a chevron azure between two clarions in chief gules and a kangaroo sejant in base proper, two swords the points upwards also proper, points and hilts of the first; on a chief of the third a horse courant argent. Crest—In front of two swords in saltire proper, pommels and hilts or, a pelican in her piety sable. the nest or.
Residence—Seadown, No. 3 Rd., Timaru, New Zealand.

Stet fortuna domûs.
May the fortune of the house stand.

Son living—STEVEN JOHN, *b.* July 1st, 1953.
Daughters living—Marylin Jane, *b.* 1950.——Cheryl Dawn, *b.* 1951.
Sisters living—Helen Fay, *b.* 1931.——Maureen Beatrice, *b.* 1933.
——Elizabeth Adele, *b.* 1948.

Widow living of 4th Baronet—DORIS FAY (*Dowager Lady Arthur*), da. of Joseph Wooding, J.P., of Woodland Grange, Woodbury, and Geraldine, S. Canterbury, New Zealand : *m.* 1928, Sir George Malcolm Arthur, 4th Bt., who *d.* 1949. *Residence*, Wakatu, Nelson, New Zealand.

Collateral Branches living.

Grandsons of the late George Arthur, son of the late Col. Edward Penfold Arthur, Born.S.C., 4th son of 1st baronet :—
  Issue of the late George Frederick Neale Arthur ; *b.* 1878, *d.* 1939 : *m.* 1905, Edith Lavender, da. of the late J. H. Taylor :—
George Leonard, *b.* 1908; Maj. (ret.) S. African Staff Corps; W. Desert 1941-42, Dep. Assist. Adjt.-Gen. British Forces in Palestine 1943-44, Inniskilling Fus. in Italy 1944, and a Member of British Mil. Mission to Greece 1945; DAAG Natal 1949-57; a Member of Provincial Council, Natal (United Party), and Cabinet Min. Natal Exec. Cttee. 1966-70: *m.* 1936, Gladys Raina, da. of George Percy Farr, JP, of Bedford, Cape Province, S. Africa, and has issue living, Gavyn Farr, *b.* 1951; ed. at Harrow, and Ch. Ch., Oxford. *Residence*, Adcote, 105, Hollander Cres., Morningside, Durban, S. Africa.——Archibald John, *b.* 1909. *Residence*,

Grandchildren of the late Sigismund Rayner Arthur (infra):—
  Issue of the late Rev. John Sigismund Arthur, MC, *b.* 1894, *d.* 1974: *m.* 1925, Constance Amy Farquhar (Pucklechurch House, Pucklechurch, Bristol), da. of Joseph Sladen, late ICS:—
Leonard John Henry (Royal Oak Cottage, Church Broughton, Derby), *b.* 1926; ed. at Aldenham and Magdalene Coll., Camb. (MB, BChir.); MRCP; Capt. RAMC (TA): *m.* 1954, the Hon. Janet Stella Brain, da. of 1st Baron Brain, and has issue living, Robert Leonard Sigismund, *b.* 1955,— Linet Stella, *b.* 1956,—Tansy Amy Anne, *b.* 1959,—Elaine Fay, *b.* 1961, Hazel Jane, *b.* 1964,—

Ruth Gilly, b. 1966.——Flora Jessamine Mary, b. 1928: m. 1954, Charles Edward Elliott, BM, BCh., of Cook St., Northgate, Brisbane, Qld., and has issue living, Charles John Peter, b. 1955,—John Michael, b. 1956,—Thomas George, b. 1956,—Jessamine Mary, b. 1960,—Lucy Jane, b. 1972.——Rose Eleanor, b. 1931: m. 1961, the Rev. Edward Longman, of Yardley Vicarage, Birmingham, B33 8PH, and has issue living, Harold John, b. 1962,—Peter George, b. 1965,—George Roland, b. 1969,—Anna Frances, b. 1963,—Alexandra Maxine, b. 1973.——Cecil Lucy Sylvia, b. 1939.

Issue of the late Sir (Oswald) Raynor Arthur, KCMG, CVO, b. 1905, d. 1973: m. 1935, Mary Elizabeth, MBE (36, Argyll Rd., W8), da. of the late Rt. Hon. Sir Cecil Arthur Spring Rice, GCMG, GCVO [see B. Monteagle of Brandon, colls.]:—
Thomas Sigismund Raynor (Ashby Pastures, Melton Mowbray, Leics.), b. 1940; ed. at Eton, and Oriel Coll., Oxford (MA): m. 1966, Angela Susan Clare, da. of the late Lt.-Col. Roland T. W. MacLeod, of Weston, Dunsyre, Lanark, and has issue living, George Raynor Macleod, b. 1969,—Juliet Caroline, b. 1966,—Valentine Bridget, b. 1968.——Caroline Ann Florence, b. 1937: m. 1972, Courtney Kenny.

Grandchildren of the late John Raynor Arthur, 6th son of 1st baronet:—

Issue of the late Sigismund Raynor Arthur, b. 1867, d. 1920: m. 1891, Constance Eleanor, who d. 1947. da. of Sir Charles Parry Hobhouse, 3rd Bt.:—
Lucy Eleanor, MB, BS, b. 1904: m. 1st, 1929 (divorce 1953), Charles Edward Murray Elliott; 2ndly, 1953, Denys Otho Hamson, OBE, MC, who d. 1963, and has issue living, (by 1st m.) Anthony Charles Raynor (c/o Coutts & Co., 440, Strand, WC2), b. 1937, ed. at Trin. Coll., Camb. (BA); Solicitor 1963: m. 1960, Christina, da. of Capt. W. T. Hindson, RN (ret.), and has issue living, Nicholas Charles Raynor b. 1964, Paul William Anthony b. 1967,—Timothy John (Lark Hill, Haynes West End, Beds.), b. 1940; ed. at Trin. Coll., Camb. (MA): m. 1964, Julia Margaret Clare, da. of Donal O'Donovan, and has issue living, Hugh Stephen Murray b. 1965, Lucy Eleanor Catherine b. 1964, Alice Margaret Sophie b. 1970,—Rosalind Ann, MB, BS, b. 1930; DObstRCOG 1955: m. 1956, the Rev. John Dorsett Owen Hinton (Lt.-Cdr. RN ret.), of The Vicarage, Pucklechurch, Bristol, and has issue living, Jeremy Charles Dorsett b. 1961, John Murray Raynor b. 1964, Sarah Margaret, b. 1958. Residence,—3, Courtfield Mews, SW5 0NH.

Issue of the late Major Edmond John Arthur, b. 1873, d. 1953: m. 1921, Kathleen Emily Isabel Ada, da. of George Penn Simkins:—
George Henry Edmond (RD2, Clevedon, Auckland, NZ), b. 1927: m. 1950, Kathleen, da. of Frederick Joseph Bow, of Sea Mills, Bristol, and has issue living, Robert George, b. 1950: m. 1969, Janice Margaret, da. of Gerald Poolman, of 266, Tavy House, Plymouth.——Leonora Kathleen, b. 1923: m. 1945, John Francis Bingham, Fl. Sgt., RAF (ret.), of 7, Norman Rd., Carlton, Nottingham, NG3 6IN.

This family migrated from Cornwall to Plymouth early in the 18th century. The 1st baronet, Lieut.-Gen. the Right Hon. Sir George Arthur, K.C.H., D.C.L., Col. of the 50th Foot, was knighted in 1837. He was successively Governor of Honduras, Van Diemen's Land, Upper Canada, and Bombay and Provisional Gov.-Gen. of India 1846. The 3rd baronet, Capt. Sir George Compton Archibald Arthur, M.V.O., was Private Sec. to F.-M. Earl Kitchener, when Sec. of State for War.

ASHBURNHAM, Creation (E.) 1661, of Broomham, Sussex.

Sir DENNY REGINALD ASHBURNHAM, 12th Baronet : b. March 24th, 1916 ; s. his father, _Sir_ FLEET-WOOD, 1953 ; is Capt. S. Staffordshire Regt, and a co-heir to Barony of Grandison : m. 1946, Mary Frances, da. of Major Robert Pascoe Mair, of Wick, Udimore, Sussex, and has issue.

Arms—Gules, a fesse between six mullets argent. Crest—Out of a ducal coronet or an ash-tree proper.

Residence—Little Broomham, Church Lane, Guestling, Hastings.

Son living—JOHN ANCHITEL FLEETWOOD, b. June 25th, 1951: m. 1975, Corinne A., da. of D. W. J. O'Brien, of Chelwood Farm, Nutley, Sussex.

Will God, and I shall.

Daughters living—Frances, b. 1947.——Honor Rosemary, b. 1949.

Sister living—Honor Elfrida, b. 1920: m. 1951, Ernest James Boorman, of 25, Whitehill Lane, Wootton Bassett, Wilts.

Collateral Branches living.

Issue of the late Lawrence Ashburnham, 4th son of 8th baronet, b. 1870, d. 1944: m. 1904, Rosalie Winifred, da. of the late Talbot Barnard, of The Hoo, Kempston, Bedford :—
Doreen Winifred, b. 1905: m. 1945, Sydney Jackson Ruffner, and has issue living, Virginia Rosalie, b. 194-. Resides in W. Virginia, U.S.A.

Granddaughters of the late John Woodgate Ashburnham, son of the late George Ashburnham, 4th son of 5th baronet :—
Issue of the late John Anchitel Ashburnham, b. 1865, d. 1939 : m. 1894, Jean, who d. 1937, da. of the late Rev. R. Price :—
Phyllis Elizabeth, b. 1895 : m. 1st, 1918, Lieut.-Col. John William James Clark-Kennedy, who d. 1939, S. African Police (ret.) [V. Lifford]; 2ndly, 1961, Colin Charlwood Frye, O.B.E., and has issue living, (by 1st marriage) Margaret Lettice Frances Ashburnham, b. 1921: m. 1947, Major John Ellis Spencer, R.H.A. Address, c/o Country Club, Auckland Park, Johannesburg, S. Africa.——Jean Margaret Julia (c/o Country Club, Auckland Park, Johannesburg, S. Africa), b. 1899: m. 1922, John Pratt-Johnson, MC, MB, BS, who d. 1960, and has issue living, John Ashburnham (750, West Broadway, Vancouver 9, BC, Canada), b. 1929; MB and BCh Witwatersrand 1950; DO England 1955; FRCSE 1955; FRCS, Canada 1962: m. 1957, Elizabeth Jean Stimson, and has issue living, Brian Warren b. 1960, Douglas John (twin) b. 1960,—Jean Ellen Ashburnham, b. 1923,—Elizabeth Grace Ashburnham (twin), b. 1923: m. 1950, William Quinn Nicol, of 39, Fourth Av., Parktown North, Johannesburg, S. Africa, and has issue living, Martin b. 1954, Julia Charlotte b. 1956.

This family, which takes its name from Ashburnham (originally written Esseburnham), in Sussex, is of great antiquity. This line derives from Richard of Broomham, 2nd son of Thomas Ashburnham, temp. Henry VI. The el. son John was ancestor of the Earls of Ashburnham (ext. 1924). Sir Denny Ashburnham, 1st baronet, was M.P. for Hastings, and Victualler of the Navy. The 2nd baronet was Chamberlain of the Exchequer and M.P. for Hastings; the 4th baronet was Bishop of Chichester: and the 7th baronet was Chancellor and Prebendary of Chichester. Sir Anchitel Piers, 9th baronet, assumed by Roy. licence 1899 the additional surname of Clement.

ASKE, Creation (U.K.) 1922, of Aughton, East Riding of Yorkshire.

Rev. Sir CONAN ASKE, 2nd *Baronet; b.*
April 22nd, 1912 ; *s.* his father *Sir* ROBERT
WILLIAM, LL.D., Q.C., 1954 ; ed. at Rugby,
and at Balliol Coll., Oxford (MA): *m.* 1st, 1948,
Vera, who *d.* 1960, yr. da. of the late George
Rowbotham, of Iffley, Oxford, and formerly
wife of Roland Faulkner; 2ndly, 1965,
Rebecca, yr. da. of Hugh Grant, of Wick,
Caithness.

Arms—Argent, a martlet sable between two bars
azure, each charged with as many cross-crosslets of the
first.   Crest—In front of a Saracen's head proper wreathed
around the temples argent and azure, two roses argent.
Residence,—167, Malvern Rd., Worcester, WR2
4NN.

Brother living—ROBERT EDWARD (45, Holland Rd.,
W14), *b.* March 21st, 1915: *m.* 1940, Joan Bingham, only
da. of Capt. Bingham Ackerley, of White Lodge, Cobham, and has issue living, Robert John Bingham,
b. 1941. *Address*—.

Sisters living—Margaret, *b.* 1910: *m.* 1936, Richard du
Vivier, CBE, of 45, Chatsworth Rd., Ealing, W5.——
Audrey Vivienne, *b.* 1917. *Residence,* Willows, Old Av.,
Weybridge, Surrey.

The 1st baronet, Sir Robert William Aske, LL.D., Q.C., (son of the late Edward Aske, of
Hull), was Dep. Sheriff of Hull 1906-8, and sat as M.P. for Newcastle-upon-Tyne E. Div. (*L*)
1923-24, and 1929-45.

Assheton-Smith (Duff-Assheton-Smith), see Duff.

ASTLEY, Creation (U.K.) 1821, of Everleigh, Wiltshire.

Trust, but see whom you trust.

Sir FRANCIS JACOB DUGDALE ASTLEY, 6th
Baronet, son of the late Rev. Anthony Aylmer
Astley, 6th son of 2nd Baronet; *b.* Oct. 26th,
1908; *s.* his kinsman, *Capt. Sir* FRANCIS HENRY
RIVERS ASTLEY-CORBETT, 1943; ed. at Marl-
borough, and at Trin. Coll., Oxford; formerly
Capt. Intelligence Corps; Senior Lecturer, Univ.
Coll., Ghana, 1948-62, and Head of Classics Dept.,
Atlantic Coll., St. Donat's Castle 1962-69: *m.*
1934, Brita Margareta Josefina Nystrom, of
Stockholm, and has issue.

Arms—Azure, a cinquefoil pierced ermine.   Crest—Issuant
from a ducal coronet or, a plume of seven ostrich feathers gules.

Address,—21A, Lindfield Gdns., NW3 6PX.

Daughter living—Bridget Mary, *b.* 1939: *m.* 1960, Capt. John
Pollock Maxwell, R. Tank Regt., c/o Lloyds Bank, Salisbury,
Wilts., and has issue living, Robert Astley Kennedy, *b.* 1962,
—Simon Harrison, *b.* 1965.

Sister living—Dorothea Elisabeth (c/o Bank of NSW, Bowral, NSW 2576), *b.* 1903: *m.* 1929, Cdr.
George Francis Hole, RN (ret.), who *d.* 1964, and has issue living, John, *b.* 1930: *m.* 1st, 1952,
Stephanie, da. of Berisford Burge, of Bellevue Hill, Sydney, NSW; 2ndly, 1973, Margaret Britton,
da. of R. F. Smith, of Cooma, NSW, and has issue living (by 1st m.), Anthony Bruce *b.* 1953,
Martin John Astley *b.* 1956, Camilla Susan *b.* 1957.—Richard Anthony (6, Vista Av., Bayview,
Sydney, NSW 2104), *b.* 1936: *m.* 1959, Beth, da. of W. Robinson, of Moree, NSW, and has issue
living, Michael *b.* 1962, Andrew Richard *b.* 1966, Amanda Louise Angela *b.* 1959,—Christopher
James, *b.* 1943: *m.* 1971, Ann, da. of James Beharell, of Batemans Bay, NSW, and has issue living,
James Astley *b.* 1973, Tegan Francis *b.* 1974.

Sister living of 5th Baronet—Pamela Irene ASTLEY-CORBETT, *b.* 1919 : *m.* 1951, Archibald
Thomas Dunn, and has issue living, Thomas Astley, *b.* 1952,—Archibald John Hugh, *b.* 1955,—
Marcia Mary, *b.* 1953,—Susannah Madeline Sara, *b.* 1956,—Katherine Elizabeth Corisande,
b. 1962. *Residence,* Overbury Hall, Layham, Hadleigh, Suffolk.

Collateral Branch living.

Issue of the late Major Hugh Francis Lethbridge Astley, 2nd son of 2nd baronet
b. 1831, *d.* 1910: *m.* 1st, 1853, Augusta Ellen, who *d.* 1874, da. of the late
James Peel Cockburn; 2ndly, 1898, Jessie (who *d.* 19—, having *m.* 2ndly,
1913, Edwin Raymond Plumbe), da. of Alfred Aves:—
(By 2nd marriage) Joan, *b.* 1899: *m.* 1924, John Cameron Morris, M.B., and has issue living, three
sons.——Dorothy, *b.* 1903: *m.* 1937, Paymaster-Lieut. John Gordon Goodard, RN. *Residence,* 171, Sussex Gdns., W2.

The family of Astley is of great antiquity in Warwickshire. Thomas de Astley, a baron *temp.*
Henry III., was slain at the battle of Evesham, A.D. 1265. He was ancestor of William, Lord Astley,
and of the present baronet, by his 1st wife, and of the Barons Astley, of Reading (extinct 1688), and
of Sir Jacob Astley, Bt., of Melton Constable (title now merged in Barony of Hastings), by his 2nd
wife. The baronetcy conferred on Sir Richard Astley, of Patshull, became extinct in 1771, and a new
patent was granted, 1821, to Sir John Dugdale Astley, of Everleigh, who sat as M.P. for Wilts
1820-32, and for N. Wilts 1832-5, a descendant of Thomas Astley, younger brother of Sir Richard
Astley, Bt., of Patshull. Sir John, 3rd baronet, sat as M.P. for N. Lincolnshire (*C*) 1874-80. Sir
Francis, 4th baronet, assumed by Roy. licence 1890 the additional surname and arms of Corbett.
Sir Francis Henry Rivers, 5th baronet, Capt. Scots Guards, *d.* (killed in action during European
War) 1943.

Aubrey-Fletcher, see Fletcher.

AUSTIN, Creation (U.K.) 1894, of Red Hill, Castleford, West Riding of York.

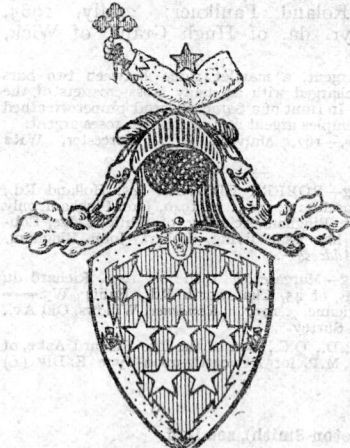

Sir JOHN BYRON FRASER AUSTIN, 3rd *Baronet; b.* July 14th, 1897; *s.* his father, *Sir* WILLIAM MICHAEL BYRON, 1940; ed. at Downside; late Lieut. 7th Hussars, and Major Indian Army, and a Dir. of Austin Properties, Ltd., of Baronetcy Properties, Ltd., and of St. Anthony's Properties, Ltd., served with Somaliland Camel Corps and King's African Rifles, Tanganyika; 1914-18 War as Fl.-Com. RFC and RAF, Burma, and E. Frontier of India 1939-44 Comdg. a Batn. Indian Army (despatches): *m.* 1st, 1953 (marriage dissolved 1958), Sheila Jean (BOYCE), da. of Duncan MacNaught, of Kilmaurs, Ayrshire; 2ndly, 1960, Rhoda Noreen, da. of Herbert Lloyd Pinches, of Eastbourne, and widow of Col. C. Rose.

Trust in God and He will give strength.

Arms—Gules, eight mullets three, three and two argent, within a border dovetailed or, charged with four thistles slipped and leaved proper. **Crest**—A dexter arm embowed in fesse, couped at the shoulder, vested or, cuff indented ermine, the hand proper grasping a cross botony fitchée gules, resting on the arm a mullet of the last.

Residence—Hurstpierpoint, Sussex. *Club*—RAF.

Brother living—WILLIAM RONALD, *b.* July 20th, 1900 ; *m.* 1st, 1926, Dorothy Mary, who *d.* 1957, da. of the late L. A. Bidwell, F.R.C.S. ; 2ndly 1958, Mary Helen Farrell, and has issue living (by 1st marriage), Michael Trescawen (Idestone, Barton, Dunchideock, Devon), *b.* 1927; ed. at Downside; 1939-45 War with RNVR: *m.* (Jan.) 1951, Bridget Dorothea Patricia, da. of the late Francis Farrell, of Miltown, Clonmellon, co. Meath, and has issue living, Mary *b.* (Nov.) 1951, Jane *b.* 1954, Susan *b.* 1956, —Anthony Leonard (Court Barton, Crediton, Devon), *b.* 1930; ed. at Downside: *m.* 1st, 1956 (m. diss. 1966) Mary Annette, da. of Richard Kelly, of Greenogue, Kilsallaghan, co. Dublin; 2ndly, 1967, Aileen Morrisson Hall-Stewart, and has issue living (by 1st m.), Peter John *b.* 1958, Nicholas Michael James *b.* 1960, Caroline Dorothy *b.* 1957 (by 2nd m.), Rebecca Dorothy Mary *b.* 1968. *Residence,*—Holeland House, Dunsford, Devon.

Sisters living—Marjorie Irene Gwendoline (Dairyland, Chalvington, Sussex), *b.* 1901: *m.* 1924, Major Leslie Lawson de Ste Croix, MBE, late RASC, who *d.* 1975, and has issue living, David Austin (c/o National Westminster Bank, Royal Sq., Jersey), *b.* 1927; FSCA: *m.* 1950, Margaret Castle, and has issue living, Peter Henry *b.* 1956, Anne Mary *b.* 1953: *m.* 1973, David Charles Norman, ACA.——Violet Cecily (9, Carlton Hill, Exmouth) *b.* 1906: *m.* 1932, Brig. Douglas Hugh Moffatt Carbery, MC, DFC, late RA, who *d.* 1959, and has issue living, Anne Irene, *b.* 1935: *m.* 1956, Lt.-Cdr. Alexander Leonard Dominic Brown, RN, of 1, Midmar Av., Morningside, Edinburgh, 10, and has issue living, Hamish Alexander Douglas *b.* 1961, Sally-Anne *b.* 1958.——Muriel (c/o Lloyds Bank, Bovey Tracey, Devon). *b.* 1908: *m.* 1930 (m. diss. 1947), Col. Maurice Charles Frye, late Indian Army, and has issue living, John Maurice, *b.* 1935; ed. at Lancing, a Co. Manager: *m.* 1964.

Collateral Branches living.

Issue of the late John Standish Thomas Joseph Austin, 2nd son of 1st baronet, *b.* 1875, *d.* 1941 : *m.* 1908, Gwendolyne Aubrey Beverley, who *d.* 1959, da. of the late Capt. Beverley Robinson, of Hyde Lodge, Winchester :—

John Standish Beverley, *b.* 1909 ; ed. at Ampleforth, and at Downside. *Residence,* 33, Muncaster Gate, Malton Rd., York.——Janetta Agnes Gwendolyne, *b.* 1912.

Issue of the late Joseph Edward Austin, 4th son of 1st baronet ; *b.* 1881, *d.* 1938 : *m.* 1914, Katherine Matilda, who *d.* 1968, da. of the late John Ryan, MD, FRCSI, of Castleconnell, co. Limerick:—

Richard Joseph Byron, *b.* 1926 ; ed. at Ampleforth. *Residence,* 65, Chatsworth Court, Pembroke Rd., W8.——Joan Agnes Mary, *b.* 1917: *m.* 1949, Michael Laurence Bexon, MC, of 19, York Av., SW14, and has issue living, Julian Michael Adrian, *b.* 1950,—Dominic Edmund Christian, *b.* 1954.

The 1st baronet, Sir John Austin, sat as M.P for Osgoldcross Div. of E. Part of W. Riding of Yorkshire (L) 1886-1906.

AVERY, Creation (U.K.) 1905, of Oakley Court, Bray Berks. [Extinct 1918.]

Sir (WILLIAM) ERIC THOMAS AVERY, *M.C.*, 2nd and last *Baronet*, who *d.* (on active ser. during European War) 1918.

Daughters living of 1st Baronet—Sybil Genevieve, *b.* 1906 : *m.* 1928, Jacques Fabry, and has issue living, Gerard, *b.* 1939,—Jean Louis, *b.* 1938,—Florence, *b.* 1934: *m.* 1959, Baron William Desazars de Montgaithard, of 8, Rue Rembrandt, Paris VIII, and has issue living, Roland *b.* 1962, Louis *b.* 1964, Serge *b.* 1970. *Residence,* 7, Quai Voltaire, Paris VII.——Monica Maud, *b.* 1907: *m.* 1st, 1927 (divorce 1930), Gaston, Comte de Béarn, only son of Prince de Béarn et de Chalais; 2ndly, 1930 (divorce 1950), Comte Bertrand de la Salle, and has issue living, (by 2nd m.) Marie Claude, *b.* 1935: *m.* 1963, Comte Jean Dadvisard, and has issue living, Christine *b.* 1963, Véronique *b.* 1964.

AYKROYD, Creation (U.K.) 1920, of Lightcliffe, West Riding of co. of York.

Sir WILLIAM MILES AYKROYD, *MC,* 3rd *Baronet*; *b.* Aug. 24th, 1923; *s.* his father, *Sir* ALFRED HAMMOND, 1965.

Arms—Azure, on a chevron ermine between three stags' heads erased or, as many crosses couped sable. **Crest**—In front of a stag's head erased and gorged with a wreath of oak proper, two crosses as in the arms.

Residence—Buckland Newton Place, Dorchester, Dorset.

Victory in truth.

Sister living — Ann Prudence, *b.* 1920: *m.* 1944, Douglas Ferris Hewat Jaboor, M.B., Ch.B., and has issue living, Philip, *b.* 1953,—Sarah, *b.* 1947: *m.* 1968, Simon James Curzon Willson, of Apt. 61, Garrucha, Almeria, Spain, [see V. Scarsdale],—Victoria Anne, *b.* 1948: *m.* 1967, Paul Barry Paterson, of More Hall, Brockton, Much Wenlock, Salop. *Residence,*—La Maison De la Fontaine, Mont Perrine, St. Lawrence, Jersey.
Aunt living (daughter of 1st baronet)—Mary Hammond, *OBE, b.* 1902; sometime Regional Administrator, Leeds Women's Vol. Sers.; OBE (Civil) 1945. *Residence,* Smithwood House, Cranleigh, Surrey.
Widow living of 2nd baronet—SYLVIA (*Lady Aykroyd*) (Priests House, Stockeld Park, Wetherby, Yorks.), da. of the late Francis Walker, of Huddersfield, and widow of Lt.-Col. Foster Newton Thorne: *m.* 1919, Sir Alfred Hammond Aykroyd, 2nd baronet, who *d.* 1965.

Collateral Branches living.

Issue of the late Harold Hammond Aykroyd, OBE, MC, TD, 2nd son of 1st baronet; *b.* 1896, *d.* 1974: *m.* 1st, 1926, Nina Marguerite (from whom he obtained a divorce 1938), da. of the late Edward J. Hulse, of Oakdene, Duffield Rd., Derby; 2ndly, 1941, Kathleen Ellen (Whixley Hall, Whixley, York), e. da. of the late Harry Tyrrell-Gray, FRCS:—
(By 1st m.) Susan, *b.* 1931: *m.* 1st, 1951 (m. diss. 1958), John Kenneth Benney, RE; 2ndly, 1968, Christopher John Day, of Sandhill House, Gunnislake, Cornwall, and has issue living, (by 1st m.) Cecilia Anne, *b.* 1952.——Sally Mary, *b.* 1934: *m.* 1960, Christopher Boyd Stoddart, and has issue living, Mark Harold Boyd, *b.* 1966,—Margaret Jane, *b.* 1962.——(by 2nd m.) Harriet Louisa, *b.* 1951.

Issue of the late Col. George Hammond Aykroyd, TD, yst. son of 1st baronet, *b.* 1900, *d.* 1972: *m.* 1924, Margaret Roberts (The Priory, Nun Monkton, York), da. of Sir Frederic Alfred Aykroyd, 1st Bt., cr. 1929:—
MICHAEL DAVID (Broxholme, Ripley, Harrogate, Yorks.), *b.* June 14th, 1928: *m.* 1952, Oenone Gillian Diana, da. of Donald George Cowling, MBE, of Leeds, and has issue living, Henry Robert George, *b.* 1954,—Annabel Mary Diana, *b.* 1956,—Sarah Jane, *b.* 1960,—Susannah Margaret, *b.* 1964.——(John) Richard (Ivy Farm, Roecliffe, Boroughbridge, York, YO5 9LY), *b.* 1934: *m.* 1st, 1963 (m. diss. 1974), Catherine Marthe, cl. da. of George Vettier, of La Hulottière, Yvré, L'Evêque (Sarthe), France; 2ndly, 1974, Lavinia Mary, da. of Patrick Thomas Beasley, and formerly wife of Confrey A. Phillips [see E. Wilton], and has issue living (by 1st m.), Bertina Dominique, *b.* (Nov.) 1963.——David Peter (Carlton Farm, Nun Monkton, York), *b.* 1937: *m.* 1958, Lydia Huldine, yr. da. of Richard Beamish, of Castleyons, co. Cork, and has issue living, Nicholas William, *b.* 1962,—Amanda Huldine, *b.* 1960,—Emily Sorrell, *b.* 1970.——Patricia Jean, *b.* 1925.

The 1st baronet, Sir William Henry Aykroyd (son of the late Alfred Aykroyd, of Oakwood, Manningham, Yorkshire), was a Director of T. F. Firth & Sons, Ltd., of Brighouse, and High Sheriff for W. Riding of Yorkshire 1926.

AYKROYD, Creation (U.K.) 1929, of Birstwith Hall, Hampsthwaite, co. York.

Sir CECIL WILLIAM AYKROYD, 2nd *Baronet*; *b.* April 23rd, 1905; *s.* his father, *Sir* FREDERIC ALFRED, 1949; ed. at Charterhouse, and at Jesus Coll., Camb. (B.A. 1926); is Patron of the living of Hampsthwaite.

Arms—Azure, on a chevron ermine between three stags' heads erased or, as many crosses patonce sable. **Crest**—In front of a stag's head erased and gorged with a chaplet of oak proper, two crosses as in the arms.

Seat—Birstwith Hall, near Harrogate.

Victory in truth.

Brothers living—FREDERIC HOWARD, *b.* Oct. 10th, 1907; ed. at Rugby, and at Jesus Coll., Camb. (B.A. 1928): *m.* 1932, Ruth Joan, da. of Carlton Oldfield, of Moor Hill, Harewood, Yorkshire, and has issue living, Mary Elisabeth Wendy Carlton, *b.* 1934: *m.* 1955, Nigel David Sykes Porter,—Joanna Jane, *b.* 1937: *m.* 1960, Christopher Jonathan Pumphrey, of Bolam West Houses, Middleton, Morpeth, Northumberland, and has issue living, Edward Jonathan Lawrence *b.* 1963, Andrew Charles *b.* 1965, Sara Rose *b.* 1962,—Victoria Margaret, *b.* 1939: *m.* 1962, Robin Fleming, of Barton Abbey, Steeple Aston, Oxon, and has issue living, Philip *b.* 1965, Rory David *b.* 1968, Joanna Kate *b.* 1963. *Residence,* The Lodge, Kirkby Overblow, nr. Harrogate.——Bertram, *b.* 1915; ed. at Charterhouse, and at Trin. Coll., Camb.; 1939-45 War as Capt. King's Own Yorkshire LI (despatches): *m.* 1st, 1938, Margot (from whom he obtained a divorce 1947), da. of the late L. Graham Brown, FRCS, of 82, Portland Place, W1; 2ndly, 1949, Catalina, da. of the late Henry Marchington, of Hope Green, Adlington, Cheshire, and has issue living (by 1st m.), James Alexander Frederic (33, Sudeley St., N1), b. 1943; ed. at Eton: m. 1973, Jennifer, da. of Frederick William Marshall, MRCS, LRCP, of 3, Penylan Av., Porthcawl, Glam., —Jean Margaret Elizabeth (2, Willow Court, Moulsford, Wallingford, Oxon.), b. 1940: m. 1962 (m. diss. 1972), Michael Frederick David Morley, and has issue living, Henry Michael Charles b. 1965, Edward James Cecil b. 1967,—(by 2nd m.) Jeremy Charles, b. 1950; ed. at Eton and Trin. Coll., Camb. (BA),—Toby Nigel Bertram, b. 1955; ed. at Eton, and St. Catharine's Coll., Camb.,—Rachel, b. 1952. *Residence*, Treyford Manor, Midhurst, Sussex.

Sister living—Margaret Roberts, b. 1903; is a C.St.J.: *m.* 1924, Col. George Hammond Aykroyd, TD, RA, who d. 1972 [*see* Aykroyd, Bt., *cr.* 1920 colls.]. *Residence*, The Priory, Nun Monkton, York.

The 1st baronet, Sir Frederic Alfred Aykroyd (son of the late William Edward Aykroyd, of Ashdown, Apperley Bridge, Yorks., uncle of Sir William Henry Aykroyd 1st baronet ,(cr. 1920), was a Merchant and High Sheriff of Yorkshire 1941-42.

AYLMER, Creation (I.) 1622, of Donadea, co. Kildare.

Sir FENTON GERALD AYLMER, 15th *Baronet*; b. March 12th, 1901; s. his father, *Sir* GERALD ARTHUR EVANS-FREKE, 1939: *m.* 1928, Rosalind Boultbee, da. of J. Percival Bell, of Hamilton, Ontario, and has issue.

Arms—Argent, a cross sable between four Cornish choughs proper. **Crest**—A Cornish chough proper rising out of a ducal coronet or.
Residence—29, Church Hill, Westmount, Montreal, Canada.

Son living—RICHARD JOHN (28, Madison Av., Watertown, Mass., USA), b. April 23rd, 1937: *m.* 1962, Lise, da. of Paul Demers, of Montreal, and has issue living, Fenton Paul, b. 1965,—Genevieve, b. 1963.
Daughter living—Rosalind Alice, b. 1941: *m.* 1965, Michael Neal Denis White, of Victoria, BC, Canada.
Sister living—Margaret Lydia, b. 1899: *m.* 1924, Donald Henry Macfarlane, M.B.E., M.C., 23, Hackett St., Stanstead, Prov. Quebec, Canada, and has issue living, Margaret Ann Aylmer, b. 1926; is a Sister of Anglican Sisterhood of St. John the Divine, Willowdale, Ontario.—Mona Aylmer, b. 1929,—Rose Aylmer, b. 1935: *m.* 1959, Edmund Hugh McIntyre, of 919, Athol St., Whitby, Ont., Canada, and has issue living, Andrew Bruce b. 1962, Cynthia Margaret b. 1960.

Aunt living—Elfrida Fenton : *m.* 1917, James Henry Nicholson, who d. 1943, and has issue living, Joan Elfrida Aylmer, b. 1918 ; formerly Flight Officer W.A.A.F. : *m.* 1944, J. Carlaw Martin, late Wing Com. R.A.F., and has issue living, Timothy Carlaw b. 1947, Gordon Peter John b. 1949. *Resides* in Bournemouth.

Widow living of 14th Baronet—MABEL HOWARD (*Dowager Lady Aylmer*), da. of the Hon. J. K. Ward, M.L.C., of Quebec : *m.* 1898, Sir Gerald Arthur Evans-Freke Aylmer, 14th baronet, who d. 1939. *Residence*, Pierrefonds Manor, 18465, Gouin Blvd. W, Pierrefonds, Quebec, Canada.

Collateral Branches living.

Grandson of the late Capt. John Evans-Freke Aylmer, 2nd son of 11th baronet :—
Issue of the late Rear-Adm. Henry Evans-Freke Aylmer, C.B.E., b. 1878, d. 1933 : *m.* 1910, Edith Winifred, who d. 1952, da. of the late Vet.-Col. Sir Francis Duck, K.C.B., F.R.C.V.S.:—
John Francis, b. 1910; late RAF. *Residence*,

Granddaughters of the late Rev. William Josiah Aylmer, 3rd son of 7th baronet :—
Issue of the late William Henry Aylmer, b. 1833, d. 1882 : *m.* 1st, 1861, Henrietta, who d. 18—, da. of Dr. Martin ; 2ndly, 1874, Elizabeth, who d. 1936, da. of the late Dr. Gordon, of Sydney, N.S. Wales :—
(By 2nd marriage) Blanche Emily.——Ida Mildred.——Madge Irene.——Muriel Lilian.

Granddaughters of the late William Henry Aylmer (ante):—
Issue of the late Percy Gordon Aylmer, b. 1865, d. 1923 : *m.* 1888, Eliza Anne, who d. 1951, da. of the late William Haddon :—
Inez Amy (c/o Holy Spirit Convent, Brisbane, Qld., Aust.), b. 1895: *m.* 1921, Cyril Frederick Mullins, who d. 1965.——Muriel Eileen (of 75, Wyralla Av., Epping, NSW), b. 1907.

Grandchildren of the late Percy Gordon Aylmer (ante):—
Issue of the late Arthur William Aylmer, b. 1899, d. 1964: *m.* 1924, Daisy (47, Sharon Dr., Poughkeepsie, NY), da. of William Goodall of Firthcliffe, NY :—
Constance Elizabeth, b. 1931: *m.* 1953, Charles T. Brown, and has issue living.
Issue of the late Justin Kenneth Aylmer, b. 1893, d. 1951: *m.* 1918, Winifred Clare Mullins:—
Francis Gordon, b. 1919: *m.* 19—, Dura Marion Onus, of Inverell, N.S. Wales, and has issue living, Michael, b. 19—,—Peter, b. 19—,—Anthony, b. 19—,—Marion Dura, b. 19—.——Ernest Austin (of Clement Terr., Christie's Beach, St. Lawrence, Australia), b. 1921: *m.* 1943, Jean Elsie, da. of the late James Alfred Walker, of Earlwood, N.S. Wales, and has issue living, David Ernest, b. 1945,—Philip Kenneth Raymond, b. 1952,—James Raymond, b. 1953,—Margaret Jean, b. 1944,—Irene Clare, b. 1950.——Kenneth Richard, b. 1922: *m.* 1952, Trudy, da. of W. Everingham.——Bruce William, b. 1927: *m.* 19—, Elizabeth Law, and has issue living, Robert, b. 19—,—Barbara, b. 19—.——Marjorie Irene, b. 1924: *m.* 1946, John Michael McGann, and has issue living, Beverley Gay, b. 1948,—Lynette Joy, b. 1951,—Jeanette Ellen, b. 1953.
Issue of the late Frederick Gordon Aylmer, b. 1900, d. 1954: *m.* 1940, Alma Elton, (48, Maxim St., West Ryde, Sydney, NSW 2114):—
Carolyn Ann, b. 1946; BSc: *m.* 1970, Ronald Bucholtz.——Margaret Susan, b. 1948: *m.* 1969, Alan Underwood.

The Aylmers are found in the cos. of Dublin and Kildare in the 13th century, and John Aylmer got the Manor of Lyons, co. Kildare, about 1400 by marriage with Helen Tyrrell. The present representative of the Lyons, or Elder Branch, is Gerald Valentine Aylmer. Sir Gerald Aylmer, Knt., *cr.* a Baronet 1621-2 (founder of the Donadea branch of the family), was third son of Richard Aylmer, of Lyons, co. Kildare (temp. 1509-1559). The 13th baronet, Sir Fenton John Aylmer, V.C., K.C.B., was a Lieut.-Gen. in the Army.

AYLWEN, Creation (U.K.) 1949, of St. Bartholomew's in the City of London. Extinct 1967.

Sir GEORGE AYLWEN, 1st and last *Baronet*.

Daughter living of 1st Baronet—By 1st marriage—Marjorie Edith Georgina, *b.* 1906: *m.* 1936, Kenneth George Lampson, and has issue living, Michael George, *b.* 1936,—David John *b.* 1939. *Residence,* Park Farm House, Maresfield, Sussex.

Widow living of 1st Baronet—ELENA INGRAA (*Lady Aylwen*), (39, Green St., W1), da. of the late Prof. Alexander Bulgarides (son of the late Diplomat Constantine Bulgarides): *m.* 1951, as his 2nd wife, Sir George Aylwen, 1st baronet, who *d.* 1967, when the title became ext.

BACKHOUSE, Creation (U.K.) 1901, of Uplands, Darlington, co. Durham, and The Rookery, Middleton Tyas, North Riding of Yorkshire.

Confido in Deo.
I trust in God.

Sir JONATHAN ROGER BACKHOUSE, 4th *Baronet, b.* Dec. 30th, 1939; *s.* his father, *Major Sir* JOHN EDMUND, *MC,* 1944; ed. at Ampleforth and Brasenose Coll. Oxford ; a Dir. of W. H. Freeman and Co., Ltd., publishers.

Arms—Per saltire or and azure, a saltire engrailed ermine between two roses in pale gules barbed and seeded proper, and as many passion crosses in fesse of the first. Crest—In front of a rock proper thereon an eagle displayed vert holding in each claw a passion cross or, a serpent on its back, the tail nowed, also proper.

Address—c/o Lloyds Bank, 39, Piccadilly, W.1.

Brother living—OLIVER RICHARD (34, Briarwood Drive, Northwood Hill, Middx. HA6 1PL), *b.* July 18th, 1941; ed. at Ampleforth: *m.* 1970, Gillian Irene, only da. of L. W. Lincoln, of Northwood, Middx.

Sisters living—Jenifer Ann, *b.* 1938: *m.* 1959, Arthur Wreford Reed, of 27, Newhurst Rd., W14, and has issue living, Dominic Wreford, *b.* 1962,—Rupert Wreford, *b.* 1964,—Catherine Anna, *b.* 1960,—Suzanne Belinda, *b.* 1961.——Judith Mary BACKHOUSE (posthumous), *b.* 1945; resumed by deed poll 1968, the surname of Backhouse: *m.* 1st, 1967 (m. diss. 1971), Garth Bentley Gibson; 2ndly, 1973, Filippo Lo Giudice, of Via Cortina d'Ampezzo 221, Rome, Italy.

Aunts living—Florence (*Lady Biggs*), *b.* 1908: *m.* 1934, Vice-Adm. Sir Hilary Worthington Biggs, KBE, CB, DSO, of Hill House, Meonstoke, Southampton, and has issue living, Geoffrey William Roger (Pound House, Meonstoke, Southampton), *b.* 1938; Lt.-Cdr. RN: *m.* 1967, Marcia, el. da. of Lt.-Gen. Sir Henry Lowther Ewart Clark Leask, KCB, DSO, OBE, and has issue living, William Patrick Lowther, *b.* 1968, Anthony Michael Lowther, *b.* 1970, Phillip Henry Lowther *b.* 1972,—Michael Richard, *b.* 1942—Elizabeth, *b.* 1936: *m.* 1958, Maj James Walmsley, RM, of 36, St. Catherines Rd., Hayling Island, Hants., and has issue living, James Patrick *b.* 1960, David Christopher *b.* 1962,—Rachel Mary, *b.* 1944: *m.* 1969, Catp. Michael Curtis, R. Hamps. Regt. and has issue living, Lucinda *b.* 1970, Alexandra *b.* 1973.——Ruth Dora. ARRC (c/o Barclays Bank, Sloane Sq., SW1), *b.* 1913; is an Associate Member of Inst. of Med. Social Workers; 1939-45 War with VAD (ARRC).——Joan Margaret, *b.* 1920: *m.* 1944, Lt. Archibald Norman Macpherson, RN (ret.), and has issue living, Allan Alisdair, *b.* 1951,—Angus John, *b.* 1953,—Susan Margaret *b.* 1947: *m.* 1973, Maj. Harry Alexander Desmond Buchanan, MC, late Gren. Gds., of 168, Walton St., SW3, and Keepers, Totford, nr. Alresford, Hants. *Residence,*—Commonwood, Bearsted, Kent.

Widow living of 3rd Baronet—JEAN MARIE FRANCES, only child of the late Lt.-Col. Gavin Robert Vernon Hume-Gore, MC: *m.* 1st, 1937, Major Sir John Edmund Backhouse, MC, RA, 3rd baronet, who *d.* (of wounds received in action in France) 1944; 2ndly, 1953 (m. diss 1966) (William) Nicol Gray, CMG, DSO; 3rdly, 1970, Norman Renshaw Sharpe, of Twin Pines Orchard, Waimate North, Ohacawai RD1, Bay of Islands, NZ.

Collateral Branches living.

Issue of the late Richard Miles Backhouse, brother of 3rd baronet *b.* 1911, *d.* 1969: *m.* 1st, 1948, Angela May (who obtained a divorce 1951), da. of the late Peter Haig Haig-Thomas [E. Normanton] and widow of Capt. Richard Dudley Melchior Gurowski, Scots Guards); 2ndly, 1951, Edeltraud Margaretha (16, Apsley House, Finchley Rd., NW8), da. of Hans Perz of Vienna:—
(By 2nd m.) Louise Maria Theodora, *b.* 1955.——Julia Maria Florence, *b.* 1956.

Issue of the late Lt.-Col. Miles Roland Charles Backhouse, D.S.O., T.D., yst. son of 1st baronet, *b.* 1878, *d.* 1962: *m.* 1904, Olive, who *d.* 1954, da. of the late Geoffrey Fowell Buxton, C.B. [Buxton, Bt., colls.]:—
Roger Trelawny (Exelby House, Exelby, Bedale, N. Yorks. DL8 2HB), *b.* 1905; ed. at Harrow; Maj. RRC; former local Director of Barclays Bank, Darlington; High Sheriff of Co. Durham, 1962-63: *m.* 1938, Beatrice Ada Janet, da. of the late Capt. Hedleigh St. George Bond, R. Canadian Engs., of Toronto, Canada, and has issue living, Jane Trelawny, *b.* 1939: *m.* 1962, Michael Lake Coghlan, of 109, Manchester Rd., Wilmslow, Ches., and has issue living, Henry Trelawny Lake *b.* 1964, Benjamin Patrick Lake *b.* 1970, Jane Louise Lake *b.* 1962, Serena Mary Lake *b.* 1969,—Avery St. George BACKHOUSE (19, Bradbourne St., SW6) *b.* 1941; resumed the surname of Backhouse 1972: *m.* 1963, Colin Frohawk Burrell, from whom she obtained a divorce 1973 and has issue living Oliver Roy St. George *b.* 1966, Katharine Victoria *b.* 1964,—Elizabeth Ester

b. 1943: *m.* 1969, Angus Hugh Fraser, of The Old Rectory, Clipston, nr. Market Harborough, Leics., and has issue living, Sophie Lavinia *b.* 1971, Camilla Elizabeth *b.* 1973.——Jonathan (Breewood Hall, Gt. Horkesley, Colchester), *b.* 1907; a Merchant Banker: *m.* 1934, Alice Joan, da. of Brig. Gen. Charles Richard Woodroffe, CMG, CVO, CBE, and has issue living, David Miles (15, Ranelagh House, Elystan Pl., SW3), *b.* 1939: *m.* 1969, Sophia Ann, da. of the late Col. C. H. S. Townsend, and has issue living, Benjamin Jonathan *b.* 1974, Cilla Gael *b.* 1972,—— William (Layer Marney Wick, Colchester, Essex, CO5 9UT), *b.* 1942: *m.* 1971, Deborah Jane, da. of Lt.-Col. the Hon. David Edward Hely-Hutchinson [see E. Donoughmore], and has issue living, Harriet Diana *b.* 1975,—Joanna, *b.* 1936: *m.* 1956, Jeremy J. N. Wyatt, of Alresford Hall, Colchester Essex, and has issue living, Thomas *b.* 1967, Sarah *b.* 1957, Nell *b.* 1959, Carina *b.* 1963.——Wilfred Jaspar, *MBE* (Horsey Island, Kirby le Soken, Essex), *b.* 1913; ed. at Rugby; is Maj. Roy, Corps of Signals (TS); 1939-45 War in Middle East (despatches, MBE); MBE (Mil) 1941: *m.* 1946, Nancy Catherine, da. of Lindsay Edward Bury, CBE, and widow of David Haig-Thomas, and has issue living, Joseph, *b.* 1953,—Mary *b.* 1947,—Hanna, *b.* 1948.——Una Patricia (of Hawthorn Farm, Great Missenden, Bucks.), *b.* 1911: *m.* 1938 (m. diss. 1961), Douglas Collins, and has issue living, Christopher Douglas, *b.* 1940,—Benjamin Jasper, *b.* 1952,—Susanna Mary, *b.* 1942: *m.* 1965, Timothy Bertram Abel Smith, of 30, Dawson Place, W2, and has issue living, Lucy *b.* 1969, Julia *b.* 1971,—Belinda, *b.* 1946,—Annabella, *b.* 1947.

The 1st baronet, Sir Jonathan Edmund Backhouse (el. son of the late Edmund Backhouse, J.P., of Trebah, Falmouth), was a D.L. and J.P. for N. Riding of Yorkshire and co. Durham. The 2nd baronet, Sir Edmund Trelawny, was Professor, Peking Univ. 1902-13, and subsequently Professor of Chinese, King's Coll., London. The 3rd baronet, Maj. Sir John Edmund Backhouse, MC, RA, *d.* (of wounds received in action in France) 1944.

BACON, First Creation (E.) 1611, of Redgrave, Suffolk; Second Creation (E.) 1627, of Mildenhall, Suffolk.

Moderation is stable.

Sir EDMUND CASTELL BACON, *KG, KBE, TD* (*Premier Baronet of England*), 13th Baronet of Redgrave, and 14th Baronet of Mildenhall; *b.* March 18th, 1903; *s.* his father, Sir NICHOLAS HENRY, 1947; ed. at Eton, and at Trin. Coll., Camb.; Hon DCL, Univ. of E. Anglia; Lt.-Col. late Comdg. 55th (Suffolk Yeo.) Anti-Tank Regt. RA (TA); Hon. Col. RA (TA) 1947-67; Lord-Lt. and a JP for Norfolk, a KStJ, a Dir. of Lloyds Bank, Ltd. 1949-73, and Pro-Chancellor of Univ. of E. Anglia 1964-73; High Steward of Norwich Cathedral since 1956, and of Gt. Yarmouth since 1968; a Church Commr. 1955-63, and Chm. of British Sugar Corpn. 1957-68; Chm. of Economic Development Cttee. for Agric. 1966-71; N-W Europe 1944 (despatches, OBE); OBE (Mil) 1945, KBE (Civil) 1965, KG 1970: *m.* 1936, Priscilla Dora, da. of Col. Sir Charles Edward Ponsonby, TD, 1st Bt., and has issue.

Arms—Gules, on a chief argent, two mullets pierced sable. **Crest**—A boar passant ermine. **Supporters** (personal to 13th Baronet as a KG),—*Dexter*, A representation of a standard bearer of XIVth Legion of the Army of Ancient Rome, habited, and holding in the dexter hand a spear proper, bearing the vexillum of the Legion (azure an heraldic sea-goat contourny), fringed on the lower edge or; *sinister*, a representation of a standard bearer of the XXth Legion of Ancient Rome, habited, and holding in the sinister hand a spear proper, bearing the vexillum of the Legion (azure a boar courant), fringed on the lower edge or.

Residence—Raveningham Hall, Norwich. *Clubs*—Carlton, Pratt's.

Son living—NICHOLAS HICKMAN PONSONBY *b.* May 17th, 1953; ed. at Eton, and Dundee Univ.; a Page of Honour to HM 1966-69.

Daughters living—Joanna Constance (*Hon. Mrs. Edward R. Palmer*), *b.* 1937; a JP for Inner London: *m.* 1957, the Hon. Edward Roundell Palmer, who *d.* 1974, son of 3rd Earl of Selborne. *Residence*, 3, Holland Park, W11.——Lavinia Winifred, *b.* 1939: *m.* 1972, Stephen Cokayne Gibbs, son of the Hon. Sir Geoffrey Cokayne Gibbs, KCMG [see B. Aldenham and Hunsdon of Hunsdon].——Elizabeth Albinia, *b.* 1944: *m.* 1971, Ronald James Bremner Hoare, of Mainland Trinity, Jersey.——Sarah, *b.* 1947: *m.* 1970, Paul Douglas Nicholson, of Quarry Hill, Brancepeth, co. Durham [*see* Lawson Tancred, Bt.].

Sisters living—Margery Frances (*Margery, Lady Rowley*), *b.* 1894: *m.* 1920, Sir Charles Samuel Rowley, 6th Bt., who *d.* 1962. *Residence*, Holbecks, Hadleigh, Suffolk.——Albinia Joane (244, Cranmer Court, SW3), *b.* 1897: *m.* 1924, Brig. Wilson Theodore Oliver Crewdson, CBE, late RA, who *d.* 1961, and has issue living, Wilson Peregrine Nicholas, *b.* 1926,—Christopher John, *b.* 1930,—Sarah Albinia, *b.* 1929.——Bridget Louisa, *b.* 1897: *m.* 1934, Lt.-Col. William Noel Arnold, MC, TD, who *d.* 1973. *Residence*, Quorn House, Hingham, Norfolk.——Katharine Mary, *b.* 1906: *m.* 1930, John Fowell Buxton, who *d.* 1970 [*see* Buxton, Bt., colls.]. *Residences*, Morley Hall: Ware, Herts.; Easneye, Ware, Herts.

Collateral Branches living.

Issue of the late Thomas Walter Bacon, 4th son of 10th baronet of Redgrave and 11th baronet of Mildenhall, *b.* 1863, *d.* 1950 : *m.* 1901, Edith Mary, who *d.* 1950, da. of the late Alexander Samuel Leslie Melville [E. Leven and Melville, colls.] :—
Anthony Walter, *b.* 1902; ed. at Eton, and at Trin. Coll., Camb. (B.A. 1923); formerly Flight-Lieut. Auxiliary Air Force : *m.* 1941, Lola Mary, da. of the late Charles Stanley Martin, of Dowlais, Glamorgan, and has issue living, Christopher Nicholas (Villa Farm, Otley, Suffolk), *b.* 1945. *Residence*, Crag Pit House Aldeburgh, Suffolk.——Francis Thomas, *OBE, FRS*, *b.* 1904; ed. at Eton, and Trin. Coll., Camb. (MA); OBE (Civil) 1967: *m.* 1934, Barbara Winifred, da. of the late Godfrey Papillon, of Barrasford, Northumberland, and has issue living, Edward Thomas Godfrey (Gateside Farm, Darvel, Ayrshire), *b.* 1939; ed. at Eton, and at Fitzwilliam House, Camb. (MA).—Elizabeth Daphne, *b.* 1935: *m.* 1958, Giles Arthur Vivian-Neal, of Welbeck House, Brooke, Norfolk, and has issue living, Henry Arthur, *b.* 1963, James Francis, *b.* 1968, Gina Rosemary, *b.* 1960, Marianne Clare, *b.* 1961. *Residence*, Westfield, Little Shelford, Cambridge, CB2 5ES. *Club*, Athenaeum.

Grandchildren of the late Thomas Walter Bacon (ante) :—
Issue of the late Christopher Henry Bacon, *b.* 1906, *d.* 1956 : *m.* 1940, Diana Sybil Richmond (of Warren Bank, Broughton, near Chester), da. of the late Frederick Richmond Brown [*see* Brown, Bt.] :—
Richard Anthony (Meerschaum Vale, Lismore, NSW) *b.* 1943: *m.* 1973, Doreen Nan, da. of John Keillar, and has issue living, Georgina Louise, *b.* 1974.——Timothy Roger (626, Kings Rd., SW6) *b.* 1947.——Elizabeth Anne, *b.* 1942: *m.* 1971, Pierre Bartlett, of Yew Tree Cottage, Tilston, Malpas, Ches., SY14 7EZ, and has issue living, Nicholas Michael, *b.* 1972,—Suzannah Louise, *b.* 1973.

Grandsons of the late Rev. Reginald Cazalet Bacon, son of the late Rev. Francis Bacon, son of the late Nicholas Bacon, 2nd son of 8th baronet of Redgrave and 9th baronet of Mildenhall, *b.* 1861 :—
Issue of the late Capt. Francis Rimington Bacon, *b.* 1891, *d.* 1947: *m.* 1919, Winifred Marie, who *d.* 1973, da. of the late Col. George Henry Brook Coats, CB, of 5, Powis Sq., Brighton:—
Roger David Coats (Hadham House, Haig Av., Canford Cliffs, Poole, Dorset), *b.* 1922; ed. at Downside, and at Trin. Coll., Camb.; late Capt. Irish Guards: *m.* 1947, Phyllis Eleanor Claire, da. of the late Roland Oliver, of Hong Kong, and has issue living, Sarah, *b.* 1948,—Fiona Jane, *b.* 1950,—Veronica Claire, *b.* 1953,—Diana Mary, *b.* 1958,—Jennifer, *b.* 19—.——Anthony Peter Coats (of Bramhope, Weaponness Park, Scarborough, Yorks.), *b.* 1924; ed. at Downside, and at Trin. Coll., Camb. (MB, MRCP 1950; MD 1961): *m.* 1947, Helen, da. of Harold Jaques, of Legram's Lane, Bradford, and has issue living, Hugh Francis, *b.* 1952,—Peter Jaques, *b.* 1953,—Annette Susan, *b.* 1959,—Patricia Margaret, *b.* 1962.

This family is descended from Sir Nicholas Bacon (Lord Keeper of the Great Seal to Queen Elizabeth I), who was father of that great luminary of science Sir Francis Bacon, born 1561. Sir Nicholas' el. son Sir Nicholas was the first person to receive a Baronetcy. Sir Hickman Beckett, 12th Bt., was a J.P. and D.L. for Lincolnshire (High Sheriff 1887), and a County Alderman for Lindsey Div. of Lincolnshire (Chm. 1914-24).

BADDELEY, Creation (U.K.) 1922, of Lakefield, Parish of St. Mary Stoke Newington, co. London.

In thee, O Lord, I trust.

Sir JOHN BERESFORD BADDELEY, 3rd *Baronet; b.* Nov. 23rd, 1899; *s.* his father, *Sir* (JOHN) WILLIAM 1951; ed. at Lancing: *m.* 1929, Nancy Winifred, da. of the late Thomas Wolsey, of Smallburgh Hall, Norfolk, and has issue.

Arms—Argent, a sword erect between two crosses couped gules, on a chief of the last a hind trippant between two garbs or. Crest—An arm couped and erect, vested azure, cuff argent, the hand holding an open book buckled and clasped proper between two crosses as in the arms. *Residence*—Street Cottage, Bury, Sussex.

Son living—JOHN WOLSEY BERESFORD (41, School Hill, Storrington, Sussex), *b.* Jan. 27th, 1938: *m.* 1962, Sara Rosalind, da. of Colin Crofts, of Scarborough, and has issue living, Sara Alexandra, *b.* 1964,—Anna Victoria, *b.* 1965,—Emma Elisabeth, *b.* 1972.
Daughters living—Susan Catherine, *b.* 1932 : *m.* 1956, Anthony Philip Harris, and has issue living, Ian Robert Beresford, *b.* 1958,—Michael Anthony, *b.* 1959, —David John Tindall, *b.* 1961,—Peter Wolsey, *b.* 1964,—Andrew Charles, *b.* 1966,—Lucinda Jane, *b.* 1963. *Residence*, Santon House, Reigate Heath, Betchworth, Surrey.——Shirley Anne, *b.* 1934: *m.* 1956, Alan Richard Anthony Grout-Smith, and has issue living, John Alan Beresford, *b.* 1962,—Nicola Susan, *b.* 1958,—Sally Caroline, *b.* 1960. *Residence*,—Hadmans, Childingfold, Surrey.

Sister living—Betty Mary, *b.* 1909; a J.P. of Wilts.: *m.* 1938, Donald George Matthews Blanchard, and has issue living, Peter Donald, *b.* 1945; BSc,—Diana Mary, *b.* 1939: *m.* 1964, Simon John Vaisey Faux of Culleys Farm. Clench Common, Marlborough, Wilts., and has issue living, James Edward Vaisey *b.* 1969, Jenny Anne *b.* 1966, Susan Jane *b.* 1967,—Anne Catherine, *b.* 1942: *m.* 1973, Timothy David Holgate, of 5, Reed's Ground, Marlborough,—Mary Patricia, *b.* 1950. *Residence*, The Manor, Burbage, Marlborough, Wilts.

Collateral Branches living.
Issue of the late Mark Baddeley, 2nd son of 1st baronet, *b.* 1871, *d.* 1930 : *m.* 1918, Mabel Annie, da. of John Frederick Trigg :—
Mark David (Woodberry, King George's Av., Margate), *b.* 1921; ed. at Cliftonville Coll.——Mabel Joyce.

Issue of the late Bernard Beresford Baddeley, 3rd son of 1st baronet, *b.* 1876, *d.* 1956 : *m.* 1900, Ethel Emily, who *d.* 1955, da. of Sir David Burnett, 1st Bt. :—
Paul Bernard (9, Porchester Terr., W2), *b.* 1903; ed. at Charterhouse: *m.* 1954, Mrs. Barbara Joan Hobson, who *d.* 1968, da. of the late Harry Tilling.——Allan Beresford, *b.* 1909; ed. at Christ's Coll., Camb. (BA 1931, MA 1936); formerly Capt. RE: *m.* 1945, Dorothy Ronwen, da. of the late H. J. Head, of Highlands, Wych Cross, Sussex, and has issue living, Paul Allan, *b.* 1948,—John Burnett, *b.* 1951,—Rozanne Mary, *b.* 1946. *Residence*, Hawkins, Tytherington, Wotton-under-Edge, Glos.——Marjorie Gertrude: *m.* 1935, William John Hunt Montgomery Beattie, MD, FRCS, of Ivy Cottage, Reigate Heath, Surrey.

The 1st baronet, Sir John James, head of the firm of Baddeley Bros., wholesale stationers, etc., of 19 and 20, Moor Lane, E.C.2, was Sheriff of City of London 1908-09 and Lord Mayor 1921-22. The 2nd baronet, Sir (John) William Baddeley, was Managing Director of the firm of Baddeley Bros., Ltd., an Alderman (Cripplegate Ward) for City of London, and Master of Stationers' and Newspapermakers' Co. 1937.

BAGGE, Creation (U.K.) 1867, of Stradsett Hall, Norfolk.

Sir JOHN ALFRED PICTON BAGGE, *ED, 6th Baronet;*
b. Oct. 27th, 1914; *s.* his father, *Sir* JOHN PICTON,
CMG, 1967; ed. at Eton; Maj. late Inns of Court
Regt., and a CStJ; 1939-45 War with Cheshire Yeo.;
Military Missions in Ethiopia, Kenya and Bulgaria;
Chm. of Council of Order of St. John of Jerusalem in
Norfolk 1969: *m.* 1939, Elizabeth Helena (Lena), da.
of the late Daniel James Davies, CBE, Commr. for
Newfoundland in London, and has issue.

Arms—Lozengy paly bendy, argent and gules, two flaunches or,
on a chief of the last an annulet between two cinquefoils of the
second. **Crest**—A pair of wings addorsed or, semée of annulets gules.

Residences, Stradsett Hall, King's Lynn, Norfolk; 8, Maunsel
St., SW1. *Club,*—Boodle's.

Sons living—JOHN JEREMY PICTON, *b.* June 21st, 1945; ed. at
Eton; ACA.——Alfred James Stephen, *b.* 1952; ed. at Eton;
2nd Lt. Blues and Royals.——Thomas Philip, *b.* 1955; ed. at
Eton.
Daughters living—Christabel Rosamund, *b.* 1940: *m.* 1963, James
Hinton Scott [V. Downe], of 81, Elgin Cres., W11, and has issue
living, Anthony Crauford, *b.* 1964,—Lucinda Ruth, *b.* 1966,—
Sara Rosamund, *b.* 1968.——Rosaleen Pleasance, *b.* 1947: *m.*
1972, Capt. Jonathan James Buxton [see Buxton Bt., colls.].——
Elizabeth Mary Frances, *b.* 1949.
Brother living—Thomas Peter (Reed Bank, Ashford Rd., Bearsted,
Kent; Boodle's Club), *b.* 1917: ed. at Eton; Maj. late Inns of
Court Regt. (Reserve): *m.* 1st (divorce 1951), Mary Armine,
da. of Brig. Leonard William Henry Mathias, DSO, and widow of
Maj. D. B. Radley, DCLI; 2ndly, 1954, Sorel Venetia, da. of Col.
Clarence Preston Gunter, CIE, OBE.

My hope is in God.

Collateral Branch living.
Issue of the late Major Henry Percy Bagge, M.C., youngest son of 3rd baronet, *b.*
1879, *d.* 1942 : *m.* 1928, Marjorie Aubrey, who *d.* 1951, da. of the late Com.
Alexander Young Crawshay Mainwaring Spearman [Spearman, Bt., colls.] :—
Mary Pleasance (7, Stack House, Cundy St., SW1), *b.* 1929; ed. at Newnham Coll., Camb. (BA):
m. 1952 (m. diss. 1973), Amir Feridur Garakani.
The 1st baronet, Sir William Bagge (son of the late Thomas Philip Bagge, J.P., D.L., of
Stradsett, and Islington, Norfolk), sat as MP for West Norfolk (C) 1837-57 and 1865-80.

**BAILEY, Creation (U.K.) 1919, of Cradock, Province of Cape of Good Hope, Union of
South Africa.**

Sir DERRICK THOMAS LOUIS BAILEY,
D.F.C., 3rd Baronet; b. Aug. 15th, 1918 ; *s.* his
half-brother, *Sir* JOHN MILNER, 1946 ; ed. at Win-
chester, and at Ch. Ch., Oxford ; Capt. S. African
Air Force ; formerly 2nd Lieut. S. African Irish ;
European War 1939-45 (D.F.C.): *m.* 1946, Katherine
Nancy, da. of Robert Stormonth Darling, of Rose-
bank, Kelso, Scotland, and has issue.

Arms—Argent, on a fesse between three martlets gules a
bezant between two sprigs of mimosa proper. **Crest**—A demi-
female figure with arms extended proper, habited azure, round
the neck a ruff, and trimmed at the collar, cuffs and shoulders
argent, holding in the dexter hand a castle or, and in the
sinister a sprig of mimosa also proper.
Seat—Brinsop Court, Hereford. *Residence*—De Poort,
Colesberg, S. Africa.

Sons living—JOHN RICHARD, *b.* June 11th, 1947; ed. at
Winchester.——Thomas Noel, *b.* 1948; ed. at Win-
chester,——William Abe, *b.* 1950; ed. at Winchester.——
Patrick James, *b.* 1959.
Daughter living—Patricia Rosemary, *b.* 1951.
Brother living—James Richard Abe, *D.F.C., b.* 1919 ed.
at Winchester, and at Ch. Ch., Oxford ; formerly Squadr on
Leader R.A.F. Vol. Reserve; European War 1939-45
(D.F.C.): *m.* 1st, 1958 (marriage dissolved 1963), Gillian
Mary, da. of John Kilgour Parker, of Cape Town, S.
Africa; 2ndly, 1964, Barbara (TAYLOR), and has issue living,
(by 1st marriage) Jonathan Alcuin Abe, *b.* 1959,—(by 2nd m.)
Alaric James Abe, *b.* 1965,—Prospero James Thomas,
b. 1969. *Address,*—PO 226, Bryanston, Transvaal.

Virtue is my fortress.

Sisters living—Ann Hester Zia (twin), *b.* 1918 : *m.* 1939,
Capt. Pierce Synnott, C.B., who obtained a divorce 1948, and has issue living, David James
Pierce, *b.* 1941.——Noreen Helen Rosemary, *b.* 1921: *m.* 1st, 1941, Wing-Com. Peter Anker
Simmons, DFC, RAF, who *d.* 1947; 2ndly, 1947, Count Peter Christian Raben, who *d.* 1969, and
from whom she obtained a divorce 1951, and has issue living, (by 1st m.) Richard James Anker,
b. 1944,—Noreen Starr Anker (*Lady Naylor-Leyland*), *b.* 1941: *m.* 1967, Sir Vivyan Edward
Naylor-Leyland, 3rd Bt., of 6, Harbour Mews, Nassau, Bahamas,—(by 2nd m.) Paul Michael,
b. 1949,—Alexandra Louise, *b.* 1948. *Residences,* 6 bis Rue Lavoisier, Paris 8c, France; 94,
Pretoria Av., Athol, Johannesburg.
Widow living of 2nd Baronet—STELLA MARY (*Stella, Lady Bailey*), da. of the late Charles
Chiappini, of 2, Stephen Street, Cape Town, S. Africa : *m.* 1945, as his third wife, Sir John
Milner Bailey, 2nd Bt., who *d.* 1946. *Residence,* 123, Kloof Nek Road, Cape Town, S. Africa.

The 1st baronet, Sir Abe Bailey, K.C.M.G. (son of the Hon. Thomas Bailey, of Queenstown, S. Africa), was engaged in Farming in Cape Colony, and a Company Director ; implicated
in Jameson Raid (sentenced to two years' imprisonment and fined £2,000); S. African War 1899-

1902 as an Intelligence Officer, and Major Gorringe's Flying Column ; S.-W. Africa 1914-15 as Major and D.A.Q.M.G. Union Forces ; in 1908 raised and equipped at own expense 200 Inf. and 100 Mounted Inf. to quell Zululand Rebellion in Natal ; had Corps of Sharpshooters in Flanders during European War 1914-18 ; a Member of House of Assembly, Union of S. Africa 1910-24 ; a M.L.A. of Cape Colony and of Transvaal (Whip in both Parliaments).

BAILLIE, Creation (U.K.) 1823, of Polkemmet, Linlithgowshire.

It shines in the dark.

Sir GAWAINE GEORGE HOPE BAILLIE, 7th *Baronet* ; *b.* March 8th, 1934 ; *s.* his father, *Sir* ADRIAN WILLIAM MAXWELL, 1947 ; ed. at Eton : *m.* 1966, Mrs. Margot Gardner, da. of Senator Louis P. Beaubien, and has issue.

Arms—Azure, nine mullets, three, three, two, and one or within a bordure counter-nebulée argent and sable. **Crest**—Issuant out of clouds proper an estoile or. **Supporters**—Two lions guardant argent.

Residence—33, Wilton Cres., SW1.

Son living—ADRIAN LOUIS, *b.* March 26th, 1973.
Daughter living—Liza Katharine, *b.* 1969.

Collateral Branch living.

Granddaughter of the late Thomas Baillie, 4th son of 1st baronet:—
Issue of the late William Baillie, *b.* 1861, *d.* 1928 : *m.* 1892, Mary, who *d.* 1946, el. da. of the late Rev. Walter Fellows, Incumbent of St. John's, Toorak, Melbourne:—
Julia Mary (Alexandra) (183, Valley Rd., Streatham, SW16), *b.* 1905 : *m.* 1943, Leonhard Adam, LLD, Dr. Phil., who *d.* 1960, and has issue living, Mary Clare, *b.* 1945 : *m.* 1964 (m. diss. 1969), Gabriel A. Michaelides.

The father of the 1st baronet was a Lord of Session (Lord Polkemmet). **Sir William, 2nd** baronet, sat as M.P. for Linlithgowshire (*C*) 1845-7. The 5th baronet, Sir Gawaine George Stuart Baillie, Lieut. 2nd Dragoons, was killed in action during European War 1914. The 6th baronet, Sir Adrian William Maxwell Baillie, sat as M.P. for Linlithgowshire (*C*) 1931-5, and for Tonbridge Div. of Kent 1937-45.

BAIRD, Creation (N.S.) 1695, of Saughton Hall, Edinburghshire.

By strength and valour.

Sir JAMES RICHARD GARDINER BAIRD, MC, 10th *Baronet* ; son of the late Capt. William Frank Gardiner Baird, 2nd son of 8th baronet ; *b.* July 12th, 1913 ; *s.* his uncle, *Maj. Sir* JAMES HOZIER GARDINER, MC, 1966 ; ed. at Eton, and University Coll., Oxford ; formerly Capt. Kent Yeo. ; 1939-45 War (MC) : *m.* 1941, Mabel Ann Tempest, da. of Algernon Gill, of Toronto, and has issue.

Arms—Gules, a sanglier passant or ; on a canton ermine a sword pale-wise proper. **Crest**—A boar's head erased or.

Residence—Wareside, Ware, Herts. *Club*—Bath.

Sons living—JAMES ANDREW GARDINER, *b.* May 2nd, 1946 ; ed. at Eton.——William Julian Gardiner, *b.* 1947 ; ed. at Milton Abbey.

Daughter living—Lavinia Mary Arabella, *b.* 1951.

Brother living—William Henry Gardiner (Manor Barn, Aston Tirrold, Berks.), *b.* 1914 ; ed. at Eton : *m.* 1st, 1946 (m. diss. 19—), Helen, da. of the late Rev. Canon Edward Charles Rich ; 2ndly, 1966, C. Gwendolyn, da. of the late James Smart, OBE, of Ottawa, and has issue living, (by 1st m.) Mervyn Edward Hozier, *b.* 1947,—Roderick Frank, *b.* 1955,—Judith Mary, *b.* 1951.

Collateral Branch living.

Descendants of the late William Baird (el. son of the late William Baird, 2nd surviving son of 1st baronet), whose 2nd son David was *cr.* a *Baronet* 1809 with special remainder to his el. brother Robert.
See Baird, Bt., *cr.* 1809.

King Charles I issued a warrant creating James Baird, of Byth, co. Haddington, Baron Devern, but he died before the patent passed the great seal. His el. son, Sir John Baird, was a Lord of Session under the style of Lord Newbyth, and his son Sir William of Newbyth was *cr.* a baronet (NS 1680, ext. 1745). The 2nd son of James Baird of Byth, Robert of Saughton Hall, Midlothian, an Edinburgh merchant, was *cr.* a baronet with remainder to heirs male of the body. Sir William Baird, 5th baronet, *m.* 1750, Frances, da. of the celebrated Col. James Gardiner, of Bankton, who was killed at the battle of Prestonpans 1745.

BAIRD, Creation (U.K.) 1809, of Newbyth, Haddingtonshire.

Sir DAVID CHARLES BAIRD, 5th *Baronet*, son of the late William Arthur Baird, 2nd son of 3rd baronet ; *b.* July 6th, 1912 ; *s.* his uncle, *Sir* DAVID, *M.V.O.*, 1941 ; ed. at Eton.

Arms—Gules, in chief within an increscent an estoile of eight points argent ; in base a boar passant or ; on a canton ermine a sword erect proper, pommel and hilt gold. **Crests**—1st, a Mameluke mounted on a horse, and holding in his dexter hand a scimitar all proper ; 2nd, a boar's head erased or.
Residence,—Summer Hill, Haugh of Urr, Kirkcudbrightshire.

By strength and valour.

Brother living—ROBERT WALTER STUART, *b.* March 5th, 1914 ; European War 1939-41 with Lothians and Border Yeo. (prisoner) : *m.* 1st, 1938 (marriage dissolved 1960), Maxine Christine, only child of Rupert Darrell, of New York, U.S.A. ; 2ndly, 1960, Maria Florine Viscart, and has issue living, (by 1st marriage) Charles Stuart, *b.* 1939 : *m.* 1965, Jane Joanna, da. of the late Brig. A. Darley Bridge,—(by 2nd m.) Frances, *b.* 1960. *Residence,* Blantyre, Chantago, St. Jean de Luz, B-P, France.

Sisters living—Margaret Stuart, *b.* 1910 : *m.* 1933, Marcus Humphrey Ure Spurway, and has issue living, Humphrey John (Linhouse, Livingston, W. Lothian), *b.* 1942 : *m.* 1968, Rosaline Avril Orr Walker,—George Henry, *b.* 1945,—Kalitza Mary Stuart, *b.* 1939 : *m.* 1961, Patrick Alexander Campbell Fraser, of Borthwickshiels, Hawick, Roxburghshire,—Theresa Frances, *b.* 1941 : *m.* 1966, Richard Dawnay Innes, of Playford Hall, Ipswich [see V. Downe, colls.]. *Residence,* Newpark House, Livingston, W. Lothian.——Hersey Ellen, *b.* 1916 : *m.* 1939, Maj. Lachlan Gordon-Duff, Gordon Highlanders, from whom she obtained a divorce 1959, and has issue living, Simon Lachlan (Bridge House, Hurstbourne Tarrant, Hants.), *b.* 1942 ; Capt. Scots Gds.,—Robert Andrew (18, Ormidale Terr., Edinburgh), *b.* 1945 : *m.* 1973, Caroline Gascoigne, and has issue living, Hersey Diana *b.* 1973. *Residence,*—Blackford, Haugh of Urr, Kircudbrightshire.

Collateral Branches living.

Granddaughter of the late Maj. Robert George Baird (infra):—
Issue of the late Maj. Robert Douglas Baird, MC, *b.* 1893, *d.* 1969: *m.* 1926, Alice Patience (2, Culford Gdns., SW3), da. of the late Cecil Gordon Crawley, CBE, of 19, Cranley Pl., SW7.
Dawn, *b.* 1927: *m.* 1968, Geoffrey Haig Loyd, of Remenham House, Ocle Pychard, Herefords. [see Oakeley, Bt.].

Grandchildren of the late Robert Henry Baird, son of the late Capt. Wynne Baird, R.N., brother of 2nd baronet:—
Issue of the late Robert George Baird, *b.* 1864 *d.* 1938 : *m.* 1893, Mabel Charlotte, who *d.* 1957, da. of the late Rev. William Mondeford Bramston [Chetwode, Bt.] :—
George Henry William, *b.* 1903; ed. at Eton; Maj. (ret.) Seaforth Highlanders; 1939-40 War: *m.* (Jan.) 1931, Catherine Augusta, da. of the late Capt. Francis William Forester [Milbank, Bt.], and has issue living, Angus George David (Hartsfield House, Westland Green, Little Hadham, Herts.), *b.* 1934: *m.* 1961, Fiona Elizabeth Hildred, da. of John Sholto Fitzpatrick Cooke, and has issue living, Andrew James *b.* 1970, Nicola Laura *b.* 1964, Eliza Caroline *b.* 1967,—Diana Catherine, *b.* (Dec.) 1931: *m.* 1953, Julian Charles Lewis Jenkinson, of Folly Faunts House, Goldhanger, Maldon, Essex [see Jenkinson, Bt., colls.]. *Residence,*—Moat House, Monewden, Woodbridge, Suffolk.

The 1st baronet, the Rt. Hon. Sir David Baird, G.C.B., P.C. [2nd son of the late William Baird, el. son of the late William Baird, 2nd surviving son of Sir Robert Baird, 1st Bt. (cr. 1695)], was a distinguished military commander, and was cr. a baronet with special remainder to the heirs male of his brother, Robert. At the capture of Seringapatam he headed the storming party, and as Commander-in-Chief he captured the Cape of Good Hope. In the battle of Corunna he lost an arm. On his death without issue in 1847, he was succeeded under the special remainder by his nephew, David. This family is a junior branch of Baird, baronet of Saughton Hall, to whose title the present Baronet of Newbyth is in remainder. The 3rd baronet, Sir David, served in the Crimea, and in the Indian Mutiny.

BAKER, Creation (U.K.) 1802, of Wembley. [Extinct 1959.]

Sir RANDOLF LITTLEHALES BAKER, *D.S.O.*, 4th and last *Baronet.*

Daughter living of 4th Baronet—Selina Littlehales, *b.* 1925: *m.* 1955, Major William Harry Gibson Fleming, RA (ret.), JP, DL, of Ranston, Blandford, Dorset, and has issue living, James Randolf, *b.* 1958,—Anthea Margaret, *b.* 1956.
Widow living of 4th Baronet—MARY CAROLINE (*Lady Baker*), widow of Lieut.-Col. Frank Preedy : *m.* 1955, as his second wife, Sir Randolf Littlehales Baker, D.S.O., 4th baronet, who *d.* 1959, when the title became ext. *Residence* Green Lines, Childe Okeford, near Blandford, Dorset.

SHERSTON-BAKER, Creation (G.B.) 1796, of Dunstable House, Richmond, Surrey.

Sir HUMPHREY DODINGTON BENEDICT SHERSTON SHERSTON-BAKER, 6th *Baronet* ; *b.* Oct. 13th, 1907 ; *s.* his father, *Lieut.-Col. Sir* DODINGTON GEORGE RICHARD SHERSTON, 1944 ; ed. at Downside, and at Ch. Coll., Camb. (B.A. 1929) : *m.* 1938 (marriage dissolved 1952), Margaret Alice, only da. of H. W. Binns, of 9, Campden Street, W.8, and has issue.

Arms—Argent, a saltire sable charged with five escallops erminois, on a chief azure a lion passant of the third, armed and langued gules. **Crest**—A demi-lion rampant per fesse indented, erminois and pean, holding in the paws an escallop argent charged with an ermine spot.
Club—Carlton.

Fidei coticula crux.
The cross is the test of faith.

Son living—ROBERT GEORGE HUMPHREY, *b.* April 3rd, 1951.
Daughters living—Margaret Elizabeth, *b.* 1939: *m.* 1969, Peter Leggatt.——Sarah Loraine, *b.* 1940: *m.* 1963, Christopher Charles Jervis Johnson-Ferguson, [see Johnson-Ferguson, Bt.].——Jane Magdalen, *b.* 1948.

Collateral Branches living.

Issue of the late John Dunstan Sherston BAKER, 2nd son of 4th baronet, b. 1882, d. 1940 : m. 1915, Anna Josephine, who d. 1952, da. of the late Alexander Wood, F.S.A.:—
Peter, MC (3D, Sheen Gate Gdns., SW14), b. 1918: ed. at Downside; Maj. (ret.) RA; a Queen's Messenger since 1964; 1939-45 War (despatches, MC): m. 1947, Elizabeth, da. of the late Mrs. W. H. Barham, of 1, Camden Park, Tunbridge Wells, and has issue living, Veronica, b. 1948: m. 1969, Christopher Carlton Fulton (52, Shaftesbury Way, Strawberry Hill, Twickenham, Middx.), and has issue living, Guy Charles Jeffreys b. 1970, Robyn Frances Jeffreys b. 1973,—Josephine b. 1950,—Gabrielle, b. 1954.——Loraine Josephine: m. 1938, Count Alexandre Gaston Pierre du Bouzet, and has issue living, Jean Pierre, b. 1938,—Patrick Peter, b. 1939: m. 1968, Susan Böhn, of Stockholm,—Christian Xavier, b. 1942,—Jean Francois, b. 1950,—Marguerite Loraine, b. 1940: m. 1964, Ivan Bruce, c/o National & Grindlays Bank, 13, St. James's Sq., SW1,—Anne France, b. 1943: m. 1966, Peter Meakin, c/o National & Grindlays Bank, 13, St. James's Sq., SW1,—Chantal, b. 1946: m. 1967, J. F. David, of Paris, France,—Beatrice Marie Madeleine, b. 1958. Residence,—21, Avenue du Parc St. James, Neuilly-sur-Seine, Paris, France.

Issue of the late Lieut.-Col. John Chicheley Sherston BAKER, brother of 4th baronet, b. 1850: d. 1913: m. 1884, Louisa Constance, who d. 1936, da. of Sir Thomas Going Bernard Dancer, 6th Bt. :—
Henry Chicheley Dancer Sherston, b. 1893 ; ed. at Queen Elizabeth's Gram. Sch., Wimborne, Dorset; formerly Lieut. Roy. W. Surrey Regt.: m. 19—, Deidri Veronica Dorreen, only da. of the late Lieut.-Col. Edwin Bailey Stuart-Rattray, R.E., of Rickmansworth, Herts. Residence, The Coach House, Dover Road, Branksome Park, Bournemouth West.——Winifred Violet Sherston. Residence, 15, Landseer Rd., Bournemouth, W.

This family was settled in the west of England several centuries before the creation of the baronetcy. The 1st baronet received a baronetcy for raising and maintaining for King George III. a troop of 500 horse styled "The Richmond Rangers," and the 4th Bt. was many years Recorder of Barnstaple and Bideford and a County Court Judge. The 5th Baronet, Sir Dodington George Richard Sherston, Lieut.-Col. (retired) I.M.S., assumed by deed poll 1923 (recorded at Heralds' College) the additional surname of Sherston.

Baker-Wilbraham, see Wilbraham.

BALFOUR, Creation (U.K.) 1911, of Albury Lodge, Albury, Hertfordshire.
[Extinct 1929.]

Sir ROBERT BALFOUR, 1st and last *Baronet.*

Granddaughters living of 1st Baronet—(Issue of the late Alexander Balfour, el. son of 1st baronet, b. 1882, d. 1923 : m. 1910, Ruth Frances, who d. 1940, da. of the late John D. Macfarland, banker, of Lincoln, Nebraska, USA)—Nancy (36E, Eaton Sq., SW1), b. 1911; OBE (Civil) 1965.——Margaret, b. 1917: m. 1948, John B. Ashbrook, and has issue living, Susan Margaret, b. 1950: m. 1973, F. V. Casselman, of Mass., USA,—Katherine Jessie, b. 1955. Residence, Wrango Hall, Denham Village, Bucks.

BALL, Creation (U.K.) 1911, of Merrion Square, City of Dublin, and Killybegs, co. Donegal.

Sir NIGEL GRESLEY BALL, *Sc.D.*, 3rd *Baronet*; b. Aug. 27th, 1892 ; s. his brother, *Sir* (CHARLES) ARTHUR KINAHAN, *M.D.*, 1945 ; ed. at Trin. Coll., Dublin ; was Professor of Botany, Univ. Coll., Colombo 1924-43, Lecturer in Botany, King's Coll., London 1944-55, Reader 1955-7, and Special Lecturer 1957-9 : m. 1922, Florine Isabel, da. of the late Col. Herbert Edwardes Irwin (formerly Roy. Warwickshire Regt.) and has issue.

Arms—Argent, on a chevron gules between three fireballs proper a galley with one mast, sail furled, pennant flottant in stern of the first. Crest—An arm vambraced embowed argent, charged with two ogresses, the hand proper grasping a fireball as in the arms.
Residence,—19, Bernard Rd., W. Worthing, Sussex.

Sons living—CHARLES IRWIN (of Downlands, Seale, nr. Farnham, Surrey), b. Jan 12th, 1924; is a Chartered Accountant and a Dir. of Kleinwort Benson, Ltd.: m. 1950, Alison Mary, da. of Lt.-Col. Percy Holman Bentley, MBE, MC, of Farnham, Surrey, and has issue living, Richard Bentley, b. 1953,—Diana Margaret, b. 1955.——Ronald Herbert (Fifehead Manor, Middle Wallop, Stockbridge, Hants.), b. 1925; is an ARIBA: m. 1st, 1950, Pamela Mary, who d. 1969, da. of the late John Morton, of Hunningham Grange, Warwicks.: 2ndly, 1970, Mrs. Diana Joy Maitland, da. of Lt.-Col. James Pridham, of 55, Elm Park House, Fulham Rd., SW10, and has issue living (by 1st m.), Christopher Nigel Morton (10, South St., Wilton, Salisbury, Wilts.), b. 1951: m. 1974, Melanie, da. of Col. David James Fenner, of Carters Cottage, Stapleford, Salisbury, Wilts.,—Jonathan Gresley, b. 1956,—Rupert Valentine, b. 1958,— Susan Mary, b. 1953.

Daughter living—Valerie Margaret : m. 1953, Christopher Elliott Winn, and has issue living, David Elliott, b. 1958,—Joanna Margaret, b. 1955,—Fiona Anne, b. 1957. Residence, 81, Ennerdale Road, Richmond, Surrey.

Sister living—Annie Muriel Kift. Residence, Freeland House, Freeland, Oxon.

Collateral Branch living.

Issue of the late Ivan Hellicar Ball, 4th son of 1st baronet, b. 1894, d. 1963: m. 1929, Dorothy (of 28, Fairacres Rd., Bebington, Cheshire), da. of the late Charles E. Gill:—
Ursula Pamela Joyce, b. 1930: m. 1959, Herbert John Lewis, of Strath Isla, Wothorpe Drift, Stamford, Lincs., and has issue living, Peter John, b. 1961,—Joanna Mary, b. 1964,—Sarah Catherine, b. 1966.——Dorothy Lucia Annie, b. 1933.

The 1st baronet, Sir Charles Bent Ball, M.D., F.R.C.S.I., was Hon. Surg. to King Edward VII., in Ireland 1904-10 and to King George V. 1910-16. The 2nd baronet, Sir (Charles) Arthur Kinahan Ball, M.D., was appointed Regius Professor of Surgery, Dublin Univ. 1933.

HARMOOD-BANNER, Creation (U.K.) 1924, of Liverpool, co. Lancaster.

Nil sine numine

Nothing without the Deity.

Sir GEORGE KNOWLES HARMOOD-BANNER, 3rd *Baronet*; *b.* Nov. 9th, 1918; *s.* his father, *Sir* HARMOOD, 1950; ed. at Eton, and at Camb. Univ. : *m.* 1947, Rosemary Jane, da. of Col. Maurice Lawrence Treston, C.B.E., and has issue.

Arms—Quarterly, 1st and 4th per pale ermine and or, a fleur-de-lis counterchanged, in chief a lion passant gules, *Banner;* 2nd and 3rd, chequy or and azure, on a bend engrailed ermine an eagle displayed between two roses gules, barbed and seeded proper, *Harmood.* Crests—1st, in front of a sinister arm embowed in armour proper, garnished or, the hand grasping a spear in bend sinister, flowing therefrom a banner gules, fringed argent and gules, and charged with a fleur-de-lis argent, two fleur-de-lis also argent, *Banner;* 2nd, issuant from an antique crown or a demi-stag between two oak branches proper, *Harmood.* *Address*—c/o Bank of Nova Scotia, 11, Waterloo Place, SW1.

Daughters living—Susan, *b.* 1951.——Gillian, *b.* 1953.

Sisters living—Elizabeth, *b.* 1908 : *m.* 1931, Ronald Percy Crawshaw, and has issue living, James, *b.* 1947,—Joanna, *b.* 1934,—Cordelia Anne, *b.* 1937. *Residence,* Chestnut Cottage, Beckley, nr. Rye, E. Sussex.——Frances Cordelia (3, Castle Sq., Tenby, Pembs.) *b.* 1913: *m.* 1941 (m. diss. 1948), Capt. James Jardine-Hunter-Paterson, King's Own Scottish Borderers.

The 1st baronet, Sir John Sutherland Harmood-Banner, was a partner in the firm of Harmood Banner and Sons, chartered accountants, of Liverpool, and sat as M.P. for Everton Div. of Liverpool (C) Feb. 1905 to Oct. 1924. The 2nd baronet, Sir Harmood, was High Sheriff of Montgomeryshire 1920, and Mayor of Montgomery 1928-32.

BANNERMAN, Creation (N.S.) 1682, of Elsick, Kincardineshire.

PRO PATRIA

For my country.

Sir DONALD ARTHUR GORDON BANNERMAN, 13th *Baronet*; *b.* July 2nd, 1899; *s.* his father, *Lieut.-Col. Sir* ARTHUR D'ARCY GORDON, *K.C.V.O., C.I.E.,* 1955; ed. at Harrow and RMC; Lt.-Col. (ret.); Cameron Highlanders; with Control Commn., Germany 1945-8; was an Assist. Master at Fettes Coll. 1952-60; N. Russia 1919, Middle East 1940-43, N.-W. Europe 1945: *m.* 1932, Barbara Charlotte, da. of the late Lieut.-Col. A. Cameron, O.B.E., Indian Medical Ser., of Southwold, Suffolk, and has issue.

Arms—Gules, a banner displayed argent, thereon a canton azure charged with St. Andrew's cross of the second, as the badge of Scotland. Crest—A demi-man in armour holding in his right hand a sword proper. Supporters—Two armed men proper.

Residence—11, Learmonth Place, Edinburgh, 4.

Sons living—ALEXANDER PATRICK (11, Learmonth Pl., Edinburgh, 4), *b.* May 5th, 1933; ed. at Gordonstoun, and Roy. Agric. Coll., Cirencester; formerly with Queen's Own Cameron Highlanders, and at Queen Elizabeth's Training Coll. for The Disabled.——David Gordon (16, Coval Gdns., E. Sheen, SW14), *b.* 1935; ed. at Gordonstoun, and at New Coll., Oxford: *m.* 1960, Mary Prudence, da. of the Rev. Philip Frank Ardagh-Walter, V. of Woolton Hill, Hants., and has issue living, Clare Naomi, *b.* 1961,—Margot Charlotte, *b.* 1962,—Arabella, *b.* 1965,—Clodagh Isobel Rose, *b.* 1975.

Daughters living—Ruth Mary Charlotte, *b.* 1937: *m.* 1958, Dr. Michael Joseph Orgill Massey, of 1. Vernon Av., Handsworth Wood, Birmingham, 20, and has issue living, Jonathan David, *b.* 1962,—William Michael, *b.* 1964,—James Richard, *b.* 1966,—Alexandra Mary, *b.* 1959,—Charlotte Elizabeth, *b.* 1960.——Janet Elizabeth Naomi (twin), *b.* 1937; ARCM 1959: *m.* 1966, Warren Jackson, MA, of 7, Gildridge Rd., Manchester, 16, and has issue living, Catherine Elizabeth, *b.* 1967,—Ruth Helen Isobel, *b.* 1969.

Sister living—Charlotte Elizabeth, *b.* 1902: *m.* 1937, Gerald Derek Lockett, MBE, of Clonterbrook House, Swettenham, Congleton, Ches., and has issue living, Jeffery Bannerman (of Clonter Farm, Swettenham, Congleton, Cheshire), *b.* 1939: *m.* 1961, Anita de Chair, and has issue living, Amanda Elizabeth *b.* 1964, Sarah Patricia *b.* 1966, Isabella Caroline *b.* 1968.—Richard Bannerman (37, Britannia Sq., Worcester), *b.* 1942: *m.* 1968, Gillian Adams-Cairns, and has issue living, William Jeffery *b.* 1970, Katharine Fenella *b.* 1971, Sophia Hannah Elizabeth *b.* 1974.

Daughter living of 11th Baronet—Eve Mary, *b.* 1921: *m.* 1951, Thomas Cecil Leyburn Symmes, of 57A, Pitt St., Wadestown, Wellington, NZ, and has issue living, Howard Alexander, *b.* 1954,—George Weymouth, *b.* 1956.

Widow living of 11th Baronet—JOAN MARY (*Joan, Lady Bannerman*), da. of the late Frederic Dundas Harford, C.V.O., J.P., D.L. (formerly in Diplo. Ser.), of 49, Egerton Gardens, S.W.3 [B. Mowbray, colls.]: *m.* 1920, Lt.-Col. Sir Alexander Bannerman, 11th baronet, who *d.* 1934. *Residence,* 28, Melton Court, South Kensington, SW7.

Collateral Branches living.

Grandchildren of the late Edward Mordaunt Bannerman (infra) :—
Issue of the late D'Arcy Bannerman, *b.* 1875, *d.* 1952 : *m.* 1896, Mary, da. **of the Rev.**
Richard Dennett, D.C.L., formerly R. of Ashton, Chudleigh, Devon :—
Halcro D'Arcy (86, Crouch Hill, N8), *b.* 1898; late Indian Army, E. African Forces, and E. African
Civil Ser.——Thora D'Arcy (383, Avenida Grau, Dept. 1901, Lima, 1, Peru), *b.* 1903: *m.* 1931,
Raymond Frederick Budden, late of Meteorological Office, Air Min., who *d.* 1972.
Issue of the late Com. Bertrand Bannerman, D.S.O., *b.* 1883, *d.* 1954 : *m.* (April) 1909,
Vera (of Sandy Cove, Rock, Cornwall), da. of Edward Stuart :—
Sheila Christina (*Lady Walsham*), *b.* (Dec.) 1909: *m.* 1936, Rear-Adm. Sir John Scarlett Warren
Walsham, 4th Bt., CB, OBE. *Residence*, Ash Beacon, Churchill, nr. Axminster, Devon.

Grandsons of the late Patrick Wilson Bannerman, son of the late Charles Banner-
man, 2nd brother of 6th baronet :—
Issue of the late Edward Mordaunt Bannerman, *b.* 1850, *d.* 1923: *m.* 1st, 1873, Annie
Christina, who *d.* 1902, da. of the late James Hay Mackenzie, W.S. ; 2ndly, 1907, Jean,
who *d.* 1951, el. da. of William Clarke Dale :—
(By 1st m.) Nigel Johnston (c/o Nat. Westminster Bank, 1, St. James's Sq., SW1), *b.* 1892; 1914-18
War, as Lieut. RFA.——(By 2nd m.) Mordaunt Francis (c/o Nat. Westminster Bank, 70, Glou-
cester Gdns., W2), *b.* 1907; 1939-45 War as Sqdn. Ldr. RAFVR: *m.* 1st, 1937, Aileen Salisbury,
yst. da. of Elford Virtue, of Godalming, Surrey; 2ndly, 1950, Edna Gladys, yst. da. of David
Hamilton Thompson, of Cardiff.

Granddaughter of Mordaunt Francis Bannerman (ante):—
Issue of the late Nigel Mordaunt Bannerman, *b.* 1943, *d.* 1975: *m.* 1971, Jane Alison (18,
Pilgrims Close, Farnham, Surrey), el. da. of Paul Taylor, of Milford, Godalming,
Surrey:—
Henrietta Jane, *b.* 1973.

The ancestors of this family were hereditary banner-bearers to the kings of Scotland. The
baronetcy was conferred by Charles II upon Sir Alexander Bannerman for "his constant loyalty
during the Rebellion, and of the heavy calamities he had suffered on that account." The 3rd baronet
raised a regiment, and was with it at the battle of Culloden. His son, the 4th baronet, sold the
Elsick estate for a nominal price, having been threatened with forfeiture on account of his father's
and his own alleged participation in the rebellion of 1745. A portion of the Elsick estate was repurchased by 9th baronet, and passed on his death to his da., the wife of the 10th Earl of Southesk.
Sir Arthur D'Arcy Gordon Bannerman, K.C.V.O., C.I.E., 12th baronet, was Resident, Kashmir
1917-21, and Gentleman-Usher to H.M. 1928-36.

BARBER, Creation (U.K.) 1960, of Greasley, co. Nottingham.

Sir WILLIAM (FRANCIS) BARBER, *T.D.*,
2nd *Baronet*, *b.* Nov. 20th, 1905 ; *s.* his
father, *Col. Sir* (THOMAS) PHILIP, *D.S.O.*,
TD, 1961; Hon. Col. 1961-66; a JP for Notts.,
and High Sheriff 1964-65; 1939-45 War as
Maj. S. Notts Hussars Yeo. RHA in Palestine, Egypt, N. Africa and NW Europe:
m. 1936, Diana Constance, da. of the late
Lt.-Col. Thomas Owen Lloyd, CMG, and has
issue.

Arms—Ermine, two chevronels, between three fleurs-
de-lys gules a bordure embattled also gules. **Crest**—In
front of two swords in saltire points upward proper hilts
and pomels or, a bull's head erased also proper.
Residence,—Lamb Close, Eastwood, Notts., NG16
3QX.

Son living—THOMAS DAVID (17, Sloane Av., SW3),
b. Nov. 18th, 1937; ed. at Eton and Trin. Coll.,
Camb. MA): *m.* 1972, Amanda Mary, da. of Frank
Rabone, of Beacon Bank Farm, Coton, Milwich,
Staffs., and widow of Maj. Michael Healing, Gren.
Gds., and has issue living, Thomas Edward, *b.* 1973.
Daughter living—Diana Mary, *b.* 1939: *m.* 1965, Nicholas
Bache Barlow Davie-Thornhill, of Holt House, Two
Dales, Matlock [*see* Barlow, Bt. cr. 1907.]
Sisters living—Joan (The Old Stables, Lamb Close,
Eastwood, Notts.), *b.* 1907: *m.* 1934, the Rev. Canon
Sydney John Galloway, who *d.* 1969.——Beatrice
Naomi (of The Manse, Moor Green, Newthorpe, Notts.),
b. 1911: *m.* 1939, Flight Lieut. Charles Robert David
Stewart, RAF, who *d.* (killed in action 1940).——Honor (St. George Castel. Guernsey), *b.* 1914:
m. 1947, Cdr. Noel Hunt, RNVR (ret.), who *d.* 1974.

Collateral Branch living.
Issue of the late Thomas Cecil Barber, el. son of 1st baronet, *b.* 1903, *d.* 1930:
m. 1928, Joyce Mary (of 53, Eaton Place, S.W.1) [who *m.* 2ndly, 1933 (marriage
dissolved 1948), Col. John Sydney North FitzGerald, C.V.O., M.B.E., M.C.
[see By. North, colls.]; 3rdly, 1948, Lieut.-Col. Arthur Frederick Reginald
Wiggins, who *d.* 1961], da. of the late Dr. Edward Williams Hedley, of The
Cottage, Thursley, Surrey:—
Susan (156, Barnhorn Rd., Little Common, Bexhill-on-Sea), *b.* 1930: *m.* 1st, 1951 (m. diss. 1965),
Ian Hope Johnstone; 2ndly, 1968, David Day, who *d.* 1970, and has issue living, (by 1st m.)
Robin, *b.* 1956,—Rosanna, *b.* 1958.

The 1st baronet, Col. Sir (Thomas) Philip Barber, D.S.O., T.D. (son of the late Thomas Barber,
of Lamb Close, Greasley, Notts.), was Hon. Col. S. Notts. Hussars Yeo., High Sheriff of Notts.
1907, a Councillor of Notts. Co. Council 1898-1925, and Alderman 1925-61 (Chm. 1931-45), and
Pro-Chancellor of Nottingham Univ. 1955-61.

BARBOUR, Creation (U.K.) 1943, of Hilden, co. Antrim. [Extinct 1951.]

Right Hon. Sir JOHN MILNE BARBOUR, 1st and last *Baronet.*

Daughters living of 1st Baronet—Rebecca Edwards (c/o National Westminster Bank, 36, St.
James's St., SW1), *b.* 1902.—— Mary Davey, *b.* 1908: *m.* 1929, Rowland Morrow Byers. *Resi-
dence,*—Birchwood, Woodlands Rd. West, Virginia Water, Surrey.——Elizabeth Law Milne,
b. 1910: *m.* 1st, 1941, Hugh Chapman MacLean, who *d.* 1945; 2ndly, 1954, Robin Young Paton,
MB, FRCS. *Residences,* Gorse Hill Manor, Gorse Hill Road, Virginia Water Surrey; 9 Astell,
Street, SW3.

BARCLAY, Creation (N.S.) 1668, of Pierston, Ayrshire.

The cross of Christ is our crown.

Sir COLVILLE HERBERT SANFORD
BARCLAY, 14th *Baronet*, el. son of the late Rt.
Hon. Sir Colville Adrian de Rune Barclay,
K.C.M.G., 3rd son of 11th baronet ; *b.* May 7th,
1913; *s.* his uncle, *Sir* ROBERT CECIL DE
BELZIM, 1930 ; ed. at Eton, and at Trin. Coll.,
Oxford (B.A. 1935, M.A. 1946); was a 3rd Sec.
in Diplo. Ser. 1938-41 ; European War 1939-45
as Lieut.-Com. R.N.V.R. : *m.* 1949, Rosamond
Grant Renton, da. of the late Dr. W. Arm-
strong Elliott, of 55, Bournemouth Rd.,
Chandler's Ford, Hants, and has issue.

Arms—Azure, a chevron between three crosses patée
or. Crest—A sword erect proper, hilted and pommelled or.
Residence—Pitshill, Petworth, Sussex.

Sons living—ROBERT COLRAINE, *b.* Feb. 12th, 1950.
——Alistair James Elliot, *b.* 1952.——Colville Edwin
Ward, *b.* 1956.

Brothers living—Cecil Edward Sanford (Oakley House,
Oakley, nr. Diss., Norfolk) *b.* 1914: ed. at Eton and
Magdalen Coll., Oxford (BA): *m.* 1st, 1939 (marriage
dissolved 1957), Yvonne Eleanor Mutch, da. of Sir
William Edward Leonard Shenton; 2ndly 1958,
Marcia Isobel Mary, da. of the late John Horatio
Macoun, and has issue living, (by 2nd m.) Melanie
Sarita, *b.* 1958.——Robert Charles Sanford, *b.* 1918;
ed. at Eton, and at Magdalen Coll., Oxford; formerly
Maj. Intelligence Corps.; a JP, and a Chevalier of
Legion of Honour; Croix de Guerre: *m.* 1st, 1941
(m. diss. 1964), Camilla, da. of Sir George Menteth Boughey, CBE, 9th Bt.; 2ndly, 1964, Alice
Molly, da. of the late Sidney Blackman, and has issue living (by 1st m.) Peter John (134, Somerset Rd., SW19), *b.* 1941: *m.* 1964, Angela Mary, da. of Harold Francis Blackborow, and has
issue living, Alasdair James *b.* 1968, Piers David *b.* 1972,——Michael George (Frostland Farm
Newchurch, Romney Marsh, Kent) *b.* 1945: *m.* 1973, Susan, da. of James Thompson, and has
issue living, Philippa *b.* 1973,——Jonathan Robert (Larks Hill, Stoke Holy Cross, Norwich, NOR
55W), *b.* 1947: *m.* 1969, Clare Amabel, da. of the late Capt. Philip Cecil Langdon Yorke, OBEl RN
[*see* E. Hardwicke, colls.],——Christopher Richard, *b.* 1949. *Residence*, Grundisburgh House
Grundisburgh, Woodbridge, Suffolk.

Mother living—Sarita Enriqueta (*Baroness Vansittart*), da. of the late Herbert Ward, of 105,
Avenue Malakoff, Paris : *m.* 1st, 1912, the Rt. Hon. Sir Colville Adrian de Rune Barclay,
K.C.M.G. (ante), who *d.* 1929 ; 2ndly, 1931, the 1st Baron Vansittart, who *d.* 1957, when the
title became ext. *Residence*, 8, Hyde Park Gdns., W2.

Collateral Branches living.

Grandchildren of the late William Malo de Rune Barclay, 3rd son of 10th
baronet :—
Issue of the late William Malo de Rune Barclay, *b.* 1871, *d.* 1917 : *m.* 1898, Nellie Grace
Inall Hamilton :—
Leslie William Hamilton de Rune, *M.B.E.*, *b.* 1899; ed. at Camden Gram. Sch., Sydney, N.S.
Wales; formerly Engineer Officer Roy. Australian Air Force; is Inspector in charge, Aeronautical
Inspection Directorate, Sydney; European War 1918 with Roy. Australian Engineers; cr.
M.B.E. (Civil) 1963: *m.* 1927, Mabel Dobson Freene, and has issue living, Beverley Lesley
Lorraine, *b.* 1936; ed. at Sydney Church of England Gram. Sch. for Girls. *Residence*, 89,
Oliver Rd., Harbord, via Manly, Sydney, N.S. Wales.

Issue of the late Frederick Arthur d'Epinay Barclay, *b.* 1875, *d.* 1955 : *m.* 1904, Laura,
who *d.* 1939, da. of Cradock Beauchamp, of New Zealand :—
William Cradock de Rune, *b.* 1906 ; European War 1939-43 with New Zealand Forces in Middle
East (invalided) : *m.* 1943, Frances Bernice Aplin, and has issue living, Elizabeth Beauchamp,
b. 1945. *Residence*, 2, Rangiora Av., Kaiwharawhara, Wellington, NZ.

Issue of the late Aubrey Henri de Rune Barclay, *b.* 1880, *d.* 1950: *m.* 1903, Alice Anne,
who *d.* 1969, el. da. of Sir Edward Osborne Gibbes, 3rd Bt.:—
Betty Theodosia: *m.* 1936, Russell Gellatly, of 3, Harbour St., Wollongong 2500, NSW, and has
issue living, Peter Russell, *b.* 1947: *m.* 1967, Marilyn Fay, el. da. of Peter Fletcher, of Dural,
NSW,——Susan Alice (50, Grace Av., French's Forest, NSW), *b.* 1939: *m.* 1961, Roy Lancaster
Lucena, who *d.* 1975, and has issue living, Peter Blair Lancaster *b.* 1964, Karen Jane *b.* 1962,
Belinda Maree *b.* 1969.

Grandchildren of Frederick Arthur d'Epinay Barclay (ante):—
Issue of the late Capt. Beauchamp d'Epinay Barclay, R.A.M.C., *b.* 1911 ; *d.* (killed in action
at Hong Kong) 1941 : *m.* 1935, Margaret Katherine (who *m.* 2ndly, 1945, Ian
Rutherford, of 32, Michie Street, Roslyn, Dunedin, New Zealand), da. of the late James
Begg, of Dunedin, New Zealand :—
James Fergus (Cruachan, RD1, Miller's Flat, Central Otago, NZ), *b.* 1940: *m.* 1964, Sally Elizabeth,
da. of Hugh Stuart Fleming, MB, ChB, of Hove, Sussex, and has issue living, Andrew James,
b. 1967,——Hamish Beauchamp, *b.* 1969.——Margaret Elizabeth, *b.* 1936: *m.* 1958, John Michael
Gibbs, MB, ChB, of 4, Delta St., Dunedin, NZ, and has issue living, David Douglas, *b.* 1966,——
Margaret Jennifer, *b.* 1959,——Hilary Eva, *b.* 1961,——Helen Dorothy, *b.* 1970.——Frances Beauchamp, *b.* 1938: *m.* 1966, Robert Campbell, MICE, MIStructE, of 14, Grove Park, Knutsford,
Ches., and has issue living, James Robert, *b.* 1968,——Alastair John, *b.* 1969,——Margaret Elizabeth,
b. 1966.

Issue of the late Capt. Leslie George de Rune Barclay, son of the late Henry Torrens de
Rune Barclay, 4th son of 10th baronet, *b.* 1879, *d.* 1965: *m.* 1926, Dorothea, who *d.*
1971, el. da. of the Rev. Charles Herbert Griffith:—
Ninian de Rune (81, South Undercliff, Rye, Sussex), *b.* 1927: *m.* 1971,——.——Michael George
(27611 Santa Clarita Rd., Saugus, Cal. 91350, USA), *b.* 1932, late RAF: *m.* 1953, Agnes Joy, yr.
da. of A. Batehup, of Northiam, Sussex, and has issue living, Wendy Margaret, *b.* 1954,——Beverley
Ann, *b.* 1959.

The ancestors of this family were of distinction in Ayrshire in the 12th century. The 8th baronet,
who had been officially employed on the Continent, fell into the hands of the French, 1798. He was
closely confined in the Temple, and twice tried by a Military Commission on account of a mission he
was supposed to have filled at the Hague 1796-8. He was each time acquitted, and in November 1799
was released and sent by cartel to England by the special order of Bonaparte.

BARING, Creation (U.K.) 1911, of Nubia House, Northwood, Isle of Wight.

Sir CHARLES CHRISTIAN BARING, 2nd *Baronet, b.* Dec. 16th, 1898; *s.* his father *Sir* GODFREY, KBE, 1957; ed. at Eton; late Maj. Coldstream Guards; a JP for Isle of Wight (Chm. of Bench 1962-70), a D.L. of Hants, a Member of Cttee. of Management of Board of Visitors, HM Prison, Parkhurst 1956-70, and of RNLI since 1961; 1914-18 War (wounded); 1940-45 War: *m.* 1948, Jeanette, da. of Henry Charles Daykin.

Arms—Azure, a fesse or, in chief a bear's head couped proper, muzzled and ringed of the second. **Crest**—A mullet erminois, two of the points resting on the pinions of a pair of wings conjoined and elevated argent.
Residence—4, Sandlands, Seaview, Isle of Wight.

Sister living—Helen Azalea, *b.* 1901: *m.* 1928, William Piers Thursby, of Piers House, Sandwich, Kent.

Collateral Branch living
Issue of the late Capt. Raymond Alexander Baring, 2nd son of 1st baronet, *b.* 1912, *d.* 1967: *m.* 1938, Margaret Fleetwood (Well House, Malshanger, Basingstoke), yst. da. of the late Col. Robert William Pigott Clarke Campbell-Preston:—

By uprightness and labour.

CHARLES PETER (39, Loxley Rd., SW16), *b.* May 24th, 1939; ed. at Eton; late Lt. R. Horse Gds.: *m.* 1964 (m. diss. 1974), Sarah, da. of the late Col. William Gill Withycombe, of Sutton, Thirsk, Yorks., and has issue living, Arabella, *b.* 1965,—Henrietta, *b.* 1966.——John Francis (34, Bettridge Rd., SW6 3QB), *b.* 1947: *m.* 1971, Elizabeth, yr. da. of Robert D. H. Pillitz, of Juramento 3437, Buenos Aires, Argentina, and has issue living, Julian Alexander David, *b.* 1975.——Andrew Michael Godfrey, *b.* 1949.——Ann Hermione, *b.* 1941: *m.* 1963, Alistair John Buchanan, of Hill Barn, Gt. Bedwyn, Marlborough, Wilts., and has issue living, Catherine Anne Louise, *b.* 1965,—Teresa Margaret, *b.* 1967,—Helen Hermione, *b.* 1973.

Sir Godfrey Baring, K.B.E., 1st Bt., son of the late Lieut.-Gen. Charles Baring [*see* Northbrook, colls.], was Chm. of co. Council for Isle of Wight, an Alderman of London co. Council 1920-22, Parliamentary Private Sec. (unpaid) to Under-Sec. of State for the Colonies 1908, and to Pres. of Board of Education 1911, and sat as M.P. for Isle of Wight (L) 1906-1910, and for N.·W. or Barnstaple Div. of Devonshire 1911-18.

BARLOW, Creation (U.K.) 1803, of Fort William, Bengal.

Love peace.

Sir CHRISTOPHER HILARO BARLOW, 7th *Baronet; b.* Dec. 1st, 1929; *s.* his father, *Wing-Com.* Sir RICHARD HUGH, *A.F.C.*, R.A.F., 1946; ed. at Eton, and at McGill Univ., Montreal: *m.* 1952, Jacqueline Claire de Marigny, el. da. of John Edmund Audley, of Chester, and has issue.

Arms—Argent, on a chevron engrailed gules between three cross-crosslets fitchée azure, two lions passant counter-passant supporting an eastern crown or, in chief between the two cross-crosslets a branch of olive and another of palm in saltire proper. **Crest**—Out of an eastern crown or a demi-lion argent, the paws supporting a cross-crosslet as in the arms, issuing from the crown on the dexter side of the lion a branch of olive and on the sinister another of palm both proper. **Supporters**—On either side an angel proper, vested argent, zoned and on the head an eastern crown or; the dexter holding in the exterior hand a balance or, and in the other a book proper, the sinister bearing in the exterior hand an olive branch, and in the other an escroll proper.
Residence—18, Winter Av., St. John's, Newfoundland.

First of all things be thou pious.

Son living—CRISPIAN JOHN EDMUND AUDLEY, *b.* April 20th, 1958.
Daughters living—Persephone Claire, *b.* 1953.——Caroline Claire, *b.* 1960.
Brothers living—David Peter, *b.* 1931; ed. at Eton, and at Peterhouse, Camb. : *m.* 1958, Mary June Emmerton, of Victoria, British Columbia, and has issue living, Peter Stephen, *b.* 1961,—Richard Owen, *b.* 1963,—Rosemary Sylvia Mary, *b.* 1968. *Residence*, 1335, Franklin Terr., Victoria, BC, V8S IC8.——Anthony Donald (c/o Business Internat. SA 12-14, Chemin Rieu, 1211, Geneva), *b.* 1935; ed. at Stowe: *m.* 1961, Ginette Burki, of Courrendlin, Switzerland.
Sister living—Lucinda Mary, *b.* 1941: *m.* 1962, Edward James Chubb, of Blackbird Cottage, Woodside Lane, King's Stanley, Stonehouse, Glos., and has issue living, Richard John. *b.* 1963,—William Maurice, *b.* 1969.
Uncle living (son of 5th baronet)—Christopher Mark, *b.* 1908; ed. at Stowe, and at King's Coll., Camb. (MA, MusB); 1939-45 War as Sqdn. Ldr. RAFVR. *Residence*, Norman Corner, Kingsgate Rd., Winchester, Hants.
Aunt living (daughter of 5th baronet)—Mildred Hilare, *b.* 1895: *m.* 1923, Richard John Routh, and has issue living, Francis John (Arlington Park House, W4 4HD), *b.* 1927: *m.* 1956, Virginia Raphael, and has issue living, Simon Christopher *b.* 1958, Alexander Francis *b.* 1972, Christina Phoebe *b.* 1961, Belinda Rosalind *b.* 1970,—Richard Michael (Greenhall House, 241, Bolton Rd., Atherton, Lancs.), *b.* 1934: *m.* 1964, Brenda, da. of the late William Parkinson, of Bolton and has issue living, Daniel William *b.* 1965, Christopher Benjamin *b.* 1968, Adam Michael Joseph *b.* 1970,—Hilary Katherine, *b.* 1924: *m.* 1949, Stephen Malet Tunnicliffe, of 4, The Square, Clun, Salop, and has issue living, Timothy Hugh (12, Farrar St., Barnsley, Yorks.) *b.* 1950: *m.* 1952, Christine, da. of Tom Gardner, of Sale, Cheshire, Stephen Jacob Routh *b.* 1952, Richard John *b.* 1958. *Residence*, Egton Cottage, Kid Lane. Clun, Craven Arms, Salop.
Widow living of 6th Baronet—Rosamund Sylvia. da. of the late Francis Swithin Brait h waite Anderton: *m.* 1st, 1928, Wing-Com. Sir Richard Hugh Barlow, A.F.C., R.A.F., 6th

baronet, who *d.* 1946; 2ndly, 1950, the Rev. Leonard Haslett Morrison, MA, Bar.-at-law. *Residence,* Sutton Cottage, Charterhouse Rd., Godalming, Surrey.

Sir George Hilaro Barlow, G.C.B., the 1st baronet, was a Member of the Council of Bengal, Provisional Governor-General of India 1805-7, and Governor of Madras 1807-13. The 2nd baronet was a Judge of the Supreme Court of Calcutta. Sir Morison, the 3rd baronet, who was in the 7th Hussars and 9th Lancers, served during the Indian Mutiny (medal with clasp for Lucknow). The 4th baronet, Sir Richard, was a Member of the Legislative Council of Madras and Chm. of Madras Harbour Trust. The 5th baronet, Col. Sir Hilaro William Wellesley, C.B., C.M.G., was 11 years Sup. of Roy. Laboratory, Woolwich, S.E., and was subsequently in Min. of Munitions. The 6th baronet, Wing-Com. Sir Richard Hugh, A.F.C., served in European War 1939-45 (A.F.C.).

ARLOW, Creation (U.K.) 1902, of Wimpole Street, St. Marylebone, co. London.

Sir THOMAS ERASMUS BARLOW, *DSC, RN,* 3rd *Baronet; b.* Jan. 23rd, 1914; *s.* his father, *Sir* (JAMES) ALAN (NOEL), *GCB, KBE,* 1968; ed. at Winchester; Capt. RN (ret.); 1939-45 War (DSC): *m.* 1955, Isabel, da. of the late Thomas Munn Body, MRCS, LRCP, of Middlesbrough, and has issue.

Arms—Argent, on a pile sable between two torches erect in base fired proper, an eagle displayed with two heads of the field. **Crest**—In front of a staff erect entwined by a serpent proper, an eagle's neck erased with two heads argent, thereon a rose gules.

Residence,—Boswells, Wendover, Bucks.

SICUT·AQUILA·JUVENESCAM

I will renew my youth like the eagle.

Sons living—JAMES ALAN, *b.* July 10th, 1956.——Philip Thomas, *b.* 1960.

Daughters living—Monica Ann *b.* 1958.——Teresa Mary, *b.* 1963.

Brothers living—Erasmus Darwin (4, Downshire Hill, Hampstead, NW3 1BG), *b.* 1915; ed. at Marlborough, and Trin. Coll., Camb. (MB, BChir., MA); MRCS England, LRCP London; DPM; MRC Psych; late Sen. Lecturer and Consultant in Psychiatry, St. Thomas's Hosp.; a Dir. of Group Investors, Ltd.; Chm. of Scientific and Medical Instruments, Ltd., Cambridge Scientific Instruments, Ltd., and Cambridge Medical Instruments, Ltd.: *m.* 1938, Brigit Ursula Hope, da. of the late Ladbroke Black, and has issue living, Thomas Jeremy Erasmus (28, Princes Av., Muswell Hill, N10), *b.* 1939; MA, ARCM: *m.* 1962, Jane (BA), da. of Bernard Hollowood,—Camilla Ruth (9, Grove Terr., NW5), *b.* 1942: *m.* 1st, 1965 (m. diss. 1973), Martin Christopher Mitcheson, MB, BChir, DPM; 2ndly, 1974, Stuart Anthony Whitworth-Jones, and has issue living, (by 1st m.) Luke Thomas *b.* 1966, Amy Brigit *b.* 1967,—Gillian Phyllida, *b.* 1944: *m.* 1966, Fabian Peake, of 57, Camden Park Rd., NW1.——Andrew Dalmahoy, *b.* 1916; ed. at Eastbourne Coll., and at Trin. Coll., Camb. (MA, MB and BChir); MRCP, London: *m.* 1951, Yvonne Tanner, and has issue living, Martin Thomas, *b.* 1953,—Claire, *b.* 1954. *Residence,* 10, Norland Sq., Kensington, W11.——Horace Basil, FRS (Trin. Coll., Camb.), *b.* 1921; ed. at Winchester, at Trin. Coll., Camb. (MB and BChir.) and at Harvard Univ., USA (MD); Fellow of Trin. Coll., Camb., 1950-54, of King's Coll., Camb. 1954-64, and Prof. of Physiology, Berkeley Univ., Calif., USA 1964-73, since when Prof, of Physiology, Camb. Univ.: *m.* 1954, Ruth Chattie, da. of Dr. Myer Salaman, and has issue living, Rebecca Nora, *b.* 1956,—Natasha Helen, *b.* 1958,—Naomi Jane, *b.* 1962, Emily Anne, *b.* 1967.

Sister living—Hilda Horatia, *b.* 1919: *m.* 1944, John Hunter Padel, BA, MB, BS, DPM, and has issue living, Oliver James, *b.* 1948,—Felix John, *b.* 1955,—Adam Frederick, *b.* 1958,—Ruth Sophia, *b.* 1946,—Nicola Mary, *b.* 1951. *Residence,* 12, Broadlands Rd., Highgate, N6.

Widow living of 2nd Baronet—(EMMA) NORA (*Nora, Lady Barlow*) (Sellenger, Sylvester Rd., Cambridge), da. of the late Sir Horace Darwin, KBE, FRS [B. Farrer]: *m.* 1911, Sir (James) Alan (Noel) Barlow, GCB, KBE, 2nd Bt., who *d.* 1968.

Collateral Branch living.

Issue of the late Sir Thomas Dalmahoy Barlow, GBE, 2nd son of 1st baronet, *b.* 1883, *d.* 1964: *m.* 1911, Esther Sophia, JP, who *d.* 1956, da. of Henry Gaselee:—

Basil Stephen (Stancombe Park, Dursley, Glos.), *b.* 1918: ed. at Marlborough, and at Trin. Coll., Camb.: *m.* 1st, 1940, Harriette Alice (from whom he obtained a divorce 1950), da. of His Honour Judge (Robert) Peel, OBE, KC [Worsley-Taylor, Bt.]; 2ndly, 1950, Gerda Theresa Zaar Ferrari da Grado, da. of the late Prof. Dr. Zaar, of Graz, Austria, and has issue living, (by 2nd marriage) Nicholas Dalmahoy, *b.* 1951,—Maria Theresa, *b.* 1953,—Esther Alexandra, *b.* 1956.——Theodora Gertrude (49 Strand on the Green, W4), *b.* 1912: *m.* 1936, Carl Winter, who *d.* 1966, and from whom she obtained a divorce 1953, and has issue living, Robert Stephen, *b.* 1939,—John Barlow, *b.* 1944,—Caroline Helen, *b.* 1942.——Sophia Penelope, *b.* 1914: *m.* 1943, Raymond William Baldwin, of Penn, Macclesfield Rd., Alderley Edge, Cheshire, and has issue living, Thomas Raymond, *b.* 1947: *m.* 1973, Anna, da. of Prof. Barber, of Oxford,—Alice Margaret, *b.* 1944: *m.* 1968, the Rev. Andrew Talbot-Ponsonby [see E. Shrewsbury, colls.],—Rosalind Penelope, *b.* 1949; MB: *m.* 1973, Cameron Kennedy, MB.

The 1st baronet, Sir Thomas Barlow, KCVO, MD, FRCP, FRS (son of the late James Barlow, JP, of Greenthorne, Edgworth), Physician Extraor. to Victoria 1899-1901, Edward VII and George V, Physician to the Households of Queen Victoria 1897-1901 and King Edward VII, 1901-10 and George V 1910-36. The 2nd Bt. Sir (James) Alan Noel Barlow, GCB, KBE, was 2nd Sec. to Treasury 1942, and Chm. of Nat. Gallery 1948-55. He donated his collections of Persian pottery to the Ashmolean 1953, and Chinese porcelain to Univ. of Sussex 1967.

BARLOW, Creation (U.K.) 1907, of Bradwall Hall, Sandbach, co. Chester

Sir JOHN DENMAN BARLOW, 2nd *Baronet*; *b.* June 15th, 1898; *s.* his father *Sir* JOHN EMMOTT 1932; is a Partner in the firm of Thomas Barlow, and Brother, of Manchester and London, Chm. of several Rubber and Tea Producing Cos. and other Cos.; MP for Eddisbury Div. of Cheshire (*Nat.*) 1945-50, and for Middleton and Prestwich, Div. of Lancs (*C*) 1951-56: *m.* 1928, the Hon. Diana Helen Kemp, da. of 1st Baron Rochdale, and has issue.

Arms—Per pale ermine and gules, three chevrons counterchanged, over all two lions combatant or. *Crest*,—A lion sejant affrontée or holding erect in the forepaws a cross-crosslet fitchée gules.

Seat—Bradwall Manor, Sandbach, Cheshire.

Sons living—JOHN KEMP (45, Halsey St., SW3; Bulkeley Grange, Malpas, Cheshire), *b.* April 22nd, 1934; ed. at Winchester, and at Trin. Coll., Camb. (BA 1956): *m.* 1962, Susan, elder da. of Col. Sir Andrew Marshal Horsbrugh Horsbrugh Porter, 3rd Bt., DSO, and has issue living, John William Marshall, *b.* 1964,—Thomas David Bradwall, *b.* (Jan.) 1966,—Andrew Michael Kemp, *b.* (Dec.) 1966,—Charles James Bulkeley, *b.* 1970.——George Bradwall (Robin's Cob, Henbury, Macclesfield, Cheshire), *b.* 1938; ed. at Radley: *m.* 1967, Daphne Anne, da. of H. R. Birtwistle, of Gt. Dudland, Sawley, Clitheroe, Lancs., and has issue living, Jeremy, *b.* 1968,—Edward Bradwall, *b.* 1972,—Deborah Jane Kemp, *b.* 1970.——Mark Henry Denman (Waldridge Manor, Ford, Aylesbury) (twin) *b.* 1938; ed. at Radley: *m.* 1968, Rosemary Alexandra, da. of J. A. Bell, of Anglesey, and has issue living, Andrew Mark Egerton, 1972,—Camilla Frances, *b.* 1970.

Daughter living—Jennifer Beatrice, *b.* 1932.

Brother living—Thomas Bradwell, *b.* 1900; Partner in firm of Thomas Barlow & Bro.; Chm. of Highlands & Lowlands Para Rubber Co. Ltd.: *m.* 1943, Elizabeth Margaret, da. of the late Hon. Bertrand George Sackville-West [see B. Sackville], and has issue living, Henry Sackville, *b.* 1944; ed. at Eton, and at Trin. Coll., Camb,—Anna Elizabeth, *b.* 1949. *Residence*, Thornby House, Thornby, Northampton.

Sister living—Anna Elizabeth, *b.* 1905: *m.* 1930, Humphrey B. C. Davie, J.P., who assumed by Roy. Licence 1959 the surname of Thornhill after his patronymic, and has issue living, Nicholas Bache Barlow (Holt House, Two Dales, Matlock), *b.* 1936: *m.* 1965, Diana Mary, only da. of Col. Sir William (Francis) Barber, 2nd Bt., and has issue living, John Philip Bache *b.* 1966, Adrian George Barber *b.* 1968,—Michael William John, *b.* 1943,—Bettine Eva Frances, *b.* 1933: *m.* 1955, David Francis Ferrand, of Aythorpe Roding House, Dunmow, Essex, and has issue living, Richard Davie *b.* 1956, Thomas David *b.* 1966, Flora Elizabeth Frances *b.* 1959. *Residence*, Stanton-in-Peak, Matlock, Derbyshire.

The first baronet, Sir John Emmott, was senior partner in the firms of Thomas Barlow and Brother of London and Manchester, and Barlow and Co. of Calcutta, Shanghai, Singapore, and Kuala Lumpur (Federated Malay States), and sat as M.P. for Frome Div. of Somerset (*L*) 1892-5, and 1896 to 1918.

MONTAGUE-BARLOW, Creation (U.K.) 1924, of Westminster, co. London.
[Extinct 1951.]

Rt. Hon. Sir (CLEMENT) ANDERSON MONTAGUE-BARLOW, *K.B.E.*, 1st and last *Baronet.*

Widow living of 1st Baronet—DORIS LOUISE (*Lady Montague-Barlow*), da. of H. Edward Reed, of Sandwich, Kent : *m.* 1934, the Rt. Hon. Sir (Clement) Anderson Montague-Barlow, KBE, 1st Baronet, who *d.* 1951, when the title became ext. *Residence*, 20, Charles St., W1.

BARNEWALL, Creation (I.) 1623, of Crickstown Castle, Meath.

Sir REGINALD ROBERT BARNEWALL, 13th *Baronet*; *b.* Oct. 1st, 1924 ; *s.* his father, *Sir* REGINALD JOHN, 1961 ; ed. at Xavier Coll., Melbourne; 1939-45 War with A.I.F. in S.-W. Pacific: *m.* 1st, 1946, Elsie Muriel, who *d.* 1962, da. of Thomas Matthews Frederick, of Brisbane, Queensland; 2ndly, 1962, Maureen Ellen, da. of William Daly, of S. Caulfield, Victoria, and has issue living, by 1st and 2nd marriages.

Arms—Ermine, a bordure engrailed gules. *Crest*—From a plume of five ostrich feathers, or, gules, azure, vert, and argent, a falcon rising of the last.

Residence—Kilbrew, 184, The Esplanade, Point Vernon, Qld., Aust.

Son living—By 2nd marriage—PETER JOSEPH, *b.* Oct. 26th, 1963.

Daughters living—By 1st marriage—Mary Catherine, *b.* 1947.——Frances Patricia, *b.* 1948.——Margaret Anne, *b.* 1952.

I had rather die than be disgraced.

Collateral Branches living.
Issue of the late Arthur Walter Aylmer Barnewall, 2nd son of 11th baronet:
b. 1890, d. 1961: m. 1921, Hilda, da. of the late Thomas Triffit.
Alfred Reginald, b. 1921.——John Robert, b. 1922.——Henry Marcus Joseph, b. 1924.——Kevin
Arthur, b. 1925.——Patrick Thomas, b. 1928.
Issue of the late Alfred George Barnewall, half-brother of 11th baronet, b. 1880,
d. 1952: m. 1915, Sarah, da. of J. Footter, of Violet Town, Victoria,
Australia :—
Patrick Joseph, b. 1915 ; is a J.P. ; Middle East and New Guinea 1940-45 with 2/9th
Australian Field Regt. : m. 1949, Daphne Mavis, da. of Charles Turner Lockhart, and has
issue living, Robert Charles, b. 1957,—Naomi Patricia, b. 1955. Address, c/o Postmaster,
Tootool, N.S. Wales.——John Robert, b. 1917 : m. 1946, Marietza Elizabeth, da. of Henry
James O'Rourke, of Tullamore, N.S. Wales, and has issue living, John Jeffrey, b. 1951,—Marietza
Anne, b. 1947,—Linda Mary, b. 1955,—Dorothea Laree, b. 1959. Residence, Eloora, White-
mark, Flinders Island, Tasmania.——Francis Richard, b. 1922 : m. 1951, Margaret Mary,
da. of L. Lyons, of Euchuca, Victoria, Australia, and has issue living, Brian Francis,
b. 1956,—Kerry Teresa, b. 1952,—Dianne Margaret, b. 1953. Residence, Whitemark, Flinders
Island, Tasmania.——George Raymond, b. 1923.——Terence James, b. 1935.——Kathleen
Joyce, b. 1919. Residence, Tootool, N.S. Wales.

Descendants of Robert Barnewall, who settled in America 1840, and Benjamin,
who went to Australia (uncles of 11th baronet), and Samuel Barnewall and
William Barnewall (great-uncles of 11th baronet), who both emigrated to
America.

This family, the name of which was originally de Barneval, is of great antiquity. Sir Michael
de Barneval, who landed on the coast of Cork in 1172, was the first of the family who settled in Ireland.
The 2nd baronet suffered severely during the Cromwellian usurpation ; and of the extensive possessions then wrested from him, he obtained, after the re-establishment of the monarchy, only his
castle and 2,000 acres of land. The 3rd baronet was M.P. for Meath 1689-90. Sir George, 4th Bt.
(a descendant of the 2nd son of the 1st Bt.), established his right to this title in 1744 ; his cousin,
Thomas, however, did not assume it, and it remained dormant from 1790 until 1821, when the succession of Sir Robert, 8th Bt., was registered at the Ulster Office, Dublin.

**BARON Creation (U.K.) 1930, of Park Street, Parish of St. George, Hanover Square,
co. London. [Extinct 1934.]**

Sir Louis Bernhard Baron, 1st and last Baronet.

Widow living of 1st Baronet—Elsie, da. of Bruno Richter, of New York: m. 1st, 1913, Sir
Louis Bernhard Baron, 1st baronet, who d. 1934, when the title became ext.; 2ndly, 1935, Arthur
Robert Tritton, who d. 1957. Residence, Godmersham Park, Canterbury.

**BARRAN, Creation (U.K.) 1895, of Chapel Allerton Hall, Chapel Allerton, West Riding
of co. York, and of Queen's Gate, St. Mary Abbots, Kensington, co. London.**

The love of country.

Sir John Napoleon Ruthven Barran, 4th
Baronet: b. Feb. 14th, 1934; s. his father, Sir
John Leighton, 1974; ed. at Winchester; late
Lt. 5th R. Inniskilling Dragoon Gds.: m. 1965,
Jane Margaret, da. of Sir Stanley George Hooker,
CBE, of Orchard Hill, Milbury Heath, Wotton-
under-Edge [see B. Bradbury], and has issue.

Arms—Per saltire gules and sable, a bear passant or,
muzzled of the second, between two mascles palewise of the
third. Crest—In front of a tower gules charged with three
mascles intertwined palewise, a lion's jamb fessewise erased or.

Residences,—26, Pond Place, SW3; Lacon Hall, Sawley,
Yorks.

Son living—John Ruthven, b. Nov. 10th, 1971.
Uncles living (sons of 2nd baronet)—Edward Nicholson, b.
1910; ed. at Winchester, and at Trin. Coll., Camb. (BA 1931,
MA 1935); formerly Capt. 5th R. Inniskilling Dragoon Gds.:
m. 1st, 1940, Daphne Margaret, da. of Herbert William Bird,
of Norther, Cranleigh, Surrey; 2ndly, 1955, Patricia Helen,
el. da. of A. G. Blake, and has issue living, (by 1st m.) Nicholas
Dudley Edward (70, St. Peter's St., Islington, N1). b. 1942:
m. 1964, Feliksa, da. of Feliks Pabilionis, of Omaha, Nebraska,
and late of Kaunas, Lithuania, and has issue living, Antony Nicholas b. 1967, Daniel Nicholas
b. 1968,—Stephen William Edward, b. 1944,—(by 2nd m.) Charles Patrick Edward, b. 1955,—
(by 1st m.) Alice Daphne Margarita, b. 1946,—(by 2nd m.) Frances Margarita, b. 1958.——Sir
David Haven, b. 1912; ed. at Winchester, and Trin Coll., Camb. (BA); Pres. Asiatic Petroleum
Corpn. (NY) 1958-61; Chm. of Shell Transport and Trading Co. Ltd. 1967-72, and of Shell Oil
Co. (USA) 1970-72; cr. Knt. 1971: m. 1944, Jane Lechmere. da. of the late Nicholas Lechmere
Cunningham Macaskie, QC, and has issue living, Tristram Cosmo, b. 1945: m. 1973, Miranda Clare
Mitchell, yst. da. of Maj. Sir Robert Crichton Mitchell Cotts, 3rd Bt., and has issue living, Ferdi-
nand b. 1974,—Julian Mark Lechmere (4, Burnley Rd., SW9), b. 1947: m. 1970, Mary, da. of Sir
Edward Wilder Playfair, KCB, and has issue living, Leo David b. 1973, Tabitha Jane b. 1972,—
Marius Peregrine Lechmere, b. 1949: m. 1972, Veronica Teresa, da. of Prof. A. L. d'Abreu, of Ford
House, Coughton, Alcester, Warwicks., and has issue living, Perdita Elizabeth b. 1972, Lorna
Marina b. 1974,—Adrian Stuart Lechmere, b. 1959,—Jane Francesca, b. 1950,—Lalage Margarita,
b. 1957,—Calista Maria, b. 1960. Residences, 36, Kensington Sq., W8; Brent Eleigh Hall,
Suffolk. Clubs, Garrick, River (New York).

Widow living of 2nd Baronet—Esther Frances (Dowager Lady Barran), da. of the late Hon.
F. M. B. Fisher, of Rotorua, New Zealand : m. 1946, as his second wife, Sir John Nicholson
Barran, 2nd Bt who d. 1952. Residence, 2, Phillimore Place, W8.

Collateral Branches living.

Issue of the late Philip Austyn Barran, younger brother of 2nd baronet, *b.* 1876, *d.* 1953 : *m.* 1908, Dorothy Currer, who *d.* 1956, only da. of the late Arthur Currer Briggs, of Leeds :—

Arthur Haworth, *b.* 1911; ed. at Repton, and at St. John's Coll., Camb.: *m.* 1945, Rosa, da. of the late J. R. Greenwood, of The Oval, Tranmere Park, Guiseley, Yorkshire, and has issue living, Jonathan Haworth, *b.* 1946,—Elizabeth Claire, *b.* 1954. *Residence,* Lavender Cottage, Aston Tirrold, Berks.——Donald Austyn Nicholson, *MB, BChir, MRCS, LRCP, FRSM, b.* 1922; ed. at Repton, and at Trin. Coll., Camb. (MB and BChir, MA); FFARCS and FRSM. *Residence,* 3, Gt. Western Terr., Glasgow, W2.——Dorothy Stella Margaret, *b.* 1919: *m.* 1943, Joseph William Sloan Allison, CA, and has issue living, Joseph Philip Sloan, *b.* 1944,—Judith Stella Elaine, *b.* 1948: *m.* 1968, Sub-Lt. Simon Hugh Stone, RN, of Sythian Portwinkle, Torpoint, Cornwall,—Dorothy Lucy Louise, *b.* 1951. *Residence,* Longbarn, Cardross, Dunbartonshire.

Issue of the late Alfred Barran, 4th son of 1st baronet, *b.* 1851, *d.* 1927: *m.* 1st, 1883, Lilly Maria, who *d.* 1885, da. of the late Thomas Scattergood, M.R.C.S., of Leeds; 2ndly, 1904, Anne Mabel, who *d.* 1950, only da. of the late Capt. T. C. Wharton, 97th Regt.:—

(By 2nd marriage) George Fletcher, *MD, BCh, b.* 1908 ; ed. at Wellington Coll., and at Trin. Coll., Camb. (B.A. 1929) ; M.R.C.S. and L.R.C.P. 1933 ; M.B., B.Ch. 1934 ; M.D. 1947 : *m.* 1936, Clare Mary Elizabeth, da. of Albert Dudley, of London, and has issue living, George Wharton, *b.* 1939,—Richard Martin, *b.* 1941,—Hugh Paull, *b.* 1943,—Rosemary Clare, *b.* 1947. *Residence,* Bower Bank, Gawthrop, Sedbergh, Cumbria, LA10 5QQ.

Granddaughters of the late Alfred Barran (ante):—
Issue of the late Claude Roulston Barran, *b.* 1885, *d.* 1942: *m.* 1911, Edith, who *d.* 1973, da. of the late Arthur Gaunt, of Stanningley Hall, Leeds:—
Lilian Joan (Littlecroft, Burton Leonard, Harrogate, HG3 3RW) *b.* 1912.——Katharine Muriel, *b.* 1913; M.B. and Ch.B. Leeds 1940. *Residence,* Prospect House, Scotton, Knaresborough.

Issue of the late Richard Wharton Barran, *b.* 1905, *d.* 1961 : *m.* 1936, Marie Eileen (of Poplar Cottage, Amberstone, Hailsham, Sussex), da. of the late George Crabbe, of Ceylon:—
Valerie Anne Heather, *b.* 1941.

Granddaughters of the late Henry Barran (infra):—
Issue of the late Henry Vernon Flower Barran, *b.* 1894, *d.* 1943: *m.* 1921, Cicely (now of Madehurst Lodge, Arundel, Sussex), da. of the late Vice-Adm. Francis Wade Caulfeild, C.B.E. [*see* V. Charlemont, colls.] :—
Mary Rosalie, *b.* 1922: *m.* 1963, Antony Giles Heron, of Bank House, Glaisdale, Whitby, Yorks.,——Alethea Katharine, *b.* 1925: *m.* 1950, the Rev. John Manifold Courtenay, MA, of The Vicarage, Long Buckby, Northampton, NN6 7QF.——Bridget Flower, *b.* 1927: *m.* 1949, Denis Martin Browne, ARIBA, of 6, Park Rd., Richmond, Surrey, and has issue living, Thomas Martin, *b.* 1951, —Henry Francis, *b.* 1962,—Roland, *b.* 1965,—Helen Mary, *b.* 1952.——Elfrida Cicely, *b.* 1929: *m.* 1957, Martin Bennett Cordeaux, of 15, Lee Rd., Lincoln, and has issue living, Charles Nicholas, *b.* 1958,—Elizabeth Katharine, *b.* 1961,—Cicely Jane, *b.* 1964.——Selina Elizabeth, *b.* 1934: *m.* 1960, Michael Stanley Makower, of Gogar House, Blairlogie, by Stirling [*see* V. Chetwynd, colls.].——Christabel Lucy, *b.* 1939.

Issue of the late Henry Barran, 5th son of 1st baronet, *b.* 1856, *d.* 1942: *m.* 1891, Rosalie Mary, who *d.* 1914, da. of the late Edgar Flower, J.P., of Middle Hill, Broadway, Worcestershire:—
Elaine Isabel Flower, *b.* 189-. *Residence,* Shadwell Grange, Moortown, Leeds, LS17 8AW.

Grandchildren of the late Sir Rowland (Hirst) Barran, 6th son of 1st baronet:—
Issue of the late Capt. Hugh Bradley Barran, MC, *b.* 1889, *d.* 1975: *m.* 1917, Estelle, (Finghall, Leyburn, Yorks.), da. of the late Frank Lockhart Cox, of 85, Cadogan Gdns., SW3:—
Hugh Rowland Murray (Hildenley, Malton, Yorks.), *b.* 1929: *m.* 1957, Diana Buttercup, da. of the late Eric Geoffrey Dawnay [*see* V. Downe, colls.], and has issue living, Patrick Robin, *b.* 1959,—Nicholas Eric Hugh, *b.* 1964,—Annabelle Clare, *b.* 1961,—Verena April, *b.* 1968.——Jean Lockhart, *b.* 1919.——Elspeth Estelle, *b.* 1921.——Ann Lockhart, *b.* 1930: *m.* 1950, Maj. John Francis Leetham Robinson, MC, 12th R. Lancers, of The Normans, Bilbrough, York, and has issue living, Hugh Andrew Leetham, *b.* 1955,—Marion Lockhart, *b.* 1951,—Caroline Mary *b.* 1957,—Joanna Susan, *b.* 1961.

Issue of the late Sir Rowland (Hirst) Barran, 6th son of 1st baronet, *b.* 1858, *d.* 1949 : *m.* 1st, 1887, Rose Cardew (who *d.* 1952, and from whom he had obtained a divorce 1899), da. of the Rev. Gilbert Bradley ; 2ndly, 1909, Louise Buchanan, who *d.* 1947, da. of the late J. Stevenson Brown, of Montreal :—
Gwendoline Cardew, *b.* 1896: *m.* 1919, John Ughtred Thornton Shuttleworth, Indian Army Reserve of Officers, who *d.* 1961. *Residence,* 35, Bark Place, W.2.

The 1st baronet, Sir John Barran, who was founder of the firm of John Barran and Sons merchants, of Leeds, sat as M.P. for Leeds (*L*) 1876-85, and for Yorkshire, W. Riding, E. Part Otley Div. 1886-95. The 2nd baronet, Sir John Nicholson Barran, was Parliamentary Private Sec. to Rt. Hon. H. H. Asquith M.P., and sat as M.P. for Hawick Dist.(*L*) 1909-18.

Barrett-Lennard, see Lennard.

BARRINGTON, Creation (U.K.) 1831, of Limerick.

The ame while I live.

Sir CHARLES BACON BARRINGTON, 6th *Baronet; b.* June 6th, 1902; *s.* his father, *Sir* CHARLES BURTON, *M.B.E.*, 1943; ed. at Eton: *m.* 1930, Constance Doris, da. of E. J. Elkington, and has issue.

Arms—Argent, three chevronels gules and a label of three points vert, on a canton of the second, a trefoil slipped or. Crest—Out of a crown vallery or a hermit's bust with a cowl vested paly argent and gules.

Residence—Barrihurst, Cranleigh, Surrey, GU6 8LQ.

Daughters living—Victoria Elizabeth Josephine, *b.* 1940.——Diana Mary Rose, *b.* 1946: *m.* 1968, Thomas Manuel.

Brother living—ALEXANDER FITZWILLIAM CROKER, *b.* Nov. 19th, 1909. *Residences*, 11, Tedworth Square, SW3; Linhay Farm, Bramshaw, Hants.

Collateral Branches living.

Issue of the late John Beatty Barrington, 4th son of 4th baronet, *b.* 1859, *d.* 1926: *m.* 1887, Catherine Charlotte, who *d.* 1937, el. da. of John Bayly, DL, of Debsborough, co. Tipperary:—

Mary Charlotte Gladys: *m.* 1911, Colin Algernon Campbell, who *d.* 1957, and has issue living, Sir Jock (John Middleton), *b.* 1912; cr. *Baron Campbell of Eskan* (Life Peer) 1966,—Denis Middleton (of Underriver House, nr. Sevenoaks, Kent), *b.* 1915; ed. at Chillon Coll.: *m.* 1st, 1940 (m. diss. 1961), Helen Christian, da. of the late Brig.-Gen. Alexander Duncan Macpherson, CB, CMG, DSO, DL; 2ndly, 1961, Mrs. Barbara Sharpe, da. of Muriel Bowden, and has issue living, (by 1st marriage) Alexander Barrington *b.* 1941, Michael Denis *b.* 1942, Mark Colin *b.* 1947, Bridget Kathleen *b.* 1944, Mary Helen *b.* 1951,—Alexander Middleton, *b.* 1917; ed. at Eton; is Wing-Cdr. RAF: *m.* 1942, Pamela Hazel, da. of Desmond Kinahan, and has issue living, James David *b.* 1945, Alexander Roderick *b.* 1948, Vivien Hazel *b.* 1947, Rose Mary Lorna *b.* 1952, Emma *b.* 1958,—Colin Middleton, *b.* 1926; ed. at Eton,—Lorna Middleton, *b.* 1921: *m.* 1944, John Bayly, of Ballinaclough House, Nenagh, co. Tipperary, and has issue living, John *b.* 1946, Desmond Peter *b.* 1947, Charlotte Mary *b.* 1950, Anne Lorna *b.* 1959. *Residence*, Debsborough, Nenagh, co. Tipperary.——Marjory: *m.* 1915, Capt. Michael King-French, formerly RFA, who *d.* 1950. *Residence*, 77, Merrion Rd., Dublin, 4.

Grandsons of the late Col. Joseph Thomas Barrington, el. son of Daniel Barrington (infra):—
Issue of the late John Frederick Barrington, D.S.O., *b.* 1881, *d.* 1961: *m.* 1916, Christine Mary Stella, who *d.* 1962, da. of the late C. Kuhling, of North Ferriby, E. Yorkshire:—
John William (2216-7th Street, SW Calgary, Alberta), *b.* 1917; ed. at Stowe; Maj. (ret.) Roy. Irish Fusiliers; Palestine 1939 (medal, with two clasps), European War 1939-45 in Italy (1939-45 star, Italy star, two medals), Palestine 1948: *m.* 1949, Annie Wetten, of Coire, Switzerland, and has issue living, Benjamin, *b.* 1950,—Reto, *b.* 1953,—Annette, *b.* 1952.——Peter Malet, *M.C.*, *T.D.*, *b.* 1920; ed. at Wellington Coll.; admitted a Solicitor 1947; European War 1939-45 as Major R.A. and R.H.A. (despatches thrice, M.C. and Bar, 1939-45 star, Africa star, N.-W. Europe star, two medals): *m.* 1945, Joan Warren, da. of Col. Guy Warren Meade, D.S.O., MC, and has issue living, Charles Peter (The Lodge, Gt. Bealings, nr Woodbridge, Suffolk), *b.* 1946: *m.* 1969, Ann Elizabeth, da. of H. B. Foster, and has issue living, Elizabeth Ann *b.* 1973,—Michael, *b.* 1951. *Residence*, Little Prestwick, Chiddingfold, Surrey.

Granddaughter of the late Daniel Barrington, 2nd son of 1st baronet:—
Issue of the late Capt. Richard Williams Barrington, H.E.I.C.S., *b.* 1838, *d.* 1900: *m.* 1873, Henrietta Maria Jane, who *d.* 1933, el. da. of the late John Johnstone, of Halleaths, Lockerbie, and Castelnau House, Mortlake:—
Helen Lucy Johnstone: *m.* 1905, John Molesworth Staples, who *d.* 1948 [*see* Staples, Bt.]. *Residence*, 14, Clyde Rd., Dublin.

Grandson of the late Capt. Richard Williams Barrington, H.E.I.C.S. (ante):—
Issue of the late Richard Irving Williams Barrington, *b.* 1892, *d.* Nov. 1928: *m.* 1922, Constance Elizabeth Mary (who *m.* 2ndly, 1930, Major Alan Murdoch), only child of the late Harry Manders:—
Laurence Hew Williams, *b.* June, 1928; ed. at Eton; Maj. Roy. Wiltshire Yeo.; formerly Capt. Coldstream Guards, Malaya, 1950 (despatches): *m.* 1st, 1950 (m. diss. 1968), Patricia Anne Isabella, da. of Ralph Whitson; 2ndly, 1968, Merle Aurelia, da. of Sir Leonard Ropner, MC, TD, 1st Bt. (cr. 1952), and formerly wife of Christopher John Spence, and has issue living (by 1st m.), Rupert Hew Williams, *b.* 1963,—Serena Henrietta Williams, *b.* 1956,—(by 2nd m.), Shaun Richard Williams, *b.* 1969. *Residence*, Nether Lypiatt Manor, Stroud, Glos.

This family claims to be descended from Odo du Barentin, who came to England with the Conqueror. Fifteenth in descent from Odo, who received grants of land in Essex, and became custodian of Hatfield forest, was Sir Francis Barrington, of Barrington Hall, Essex, created a baronet, 1611. This title became extinct, upon the death of the 10th baronet, in 1833; but prior thereto (1831) a baronetcy had been conferred upon a younger branch, Sir Joseph Barrington, of Limerick, who, with his sons, founded the Limerick Hospital and Infirmary, an institution incorporated by Act of Parliament.

BARROW, Creation (U.K.) 1835, of Ulverstone, Lancashire.

Little suffices.

Sir RICHARD JOHN UNIACKE BARROW, 6th *Baronet*; *b.* Aug. 2nd, 1933; *s.* his father, *Major Sir* WILFRID JOHN WILSON CROKER, 1960; ed. at Beaumont; Capt. (retired) Irish Gds.; joined Internat. Computers and Tabulators, Ltd. 1960: *m.* 1961, Alison Kate, yr. da. of the late Capt. Russell Grenfell, RN (ret.), and has issue.

Arms—Sable, two swords in saltire points upwards argent, pommels and hilts or between three fleurs-de-lis, one in chief and two in flanche, an anchor erect in base of the last. Crest—On a mount vert a squirrel sejant cracking a nut all proper, charged on the shoulder with an anchor.

Residence—36, South Vale, SE19.

Son living—ANTHONY JOHN GREN-FELL, *b.* May 24th, 1962.
Daughters living—Nony Mary Louise, *b.* 1963.——Frances Teresa Catherine, *b.* 1971.
Sisters living—Rosamond Mary Geraldine, *b.* 1927 : *m.* 1956, George Myles Sterling, and has issue living, Myles Patrick, *b.* 1958,—Andrew David, *b.* 1963,—Natalie Rosamond *b.* 1960. *Residence*, Castletown, Coolbawn, Nenagh, co. Tipperary.——Ann Patricia, *b.* 1928: *m.* 1951, Maj. Anthony Richard Carr, from whom she obtained a divorce 1960, and has issue living, Julian Anthony Robie, *b.* 1955. *Residence*, Fellover, St. Breward, nr. Bodmin, Cornwall. ——Angela Mary Philippa, *b.* 1940: *m.* 1968, Geoffrey Swaine, of, 9, Oaktree Close, Ealing, W.5, and has issue living, Jonathon David, *b.* 1971,—Mary Angela, *b.* 1972.
Uncles living (sons of 4th baronet)—Alfred Francis Lendon, *b.* 1904: *m.* 1933, Ruth, da. of William Sydney Milsum, formerly of Frensham, Surrey, and has issue living, John Lendon (31, Lingfield Av., Torkington Park, Hazel Grove, Ches.), *b.* 1934: *m.* 1961, Maureen Ann, da. of Alfred Stanley Gover, and has issue living, Nicola Mary *b.* 1963, Paul Lendon *b.* 1966,—Anthony Francis (Street Farm, Tilford, Surrey), *b.* 1937: *m.* 1962, Alexa, da. of Raleigh Ashlin Skelton, and has issue living, Kevin Mark *b.* 1963, Katharine Laura *b.* 1965,—Simon William, *b.* 1942, —Susanne Mary *b.* 1946: *m.* 1972, Patrick Hugh Walker-Taylor, of 40, Walker Rd., Maidenhead, Berks., and has issue living, Timothy Patrick *b.* 1974,—Catherine Ruth, *b.* 1950. *Residence*, Ulverstone, 7, Mavins Rd., Farnham, Surrey.——Edward Joseph Merriman, *b.* 1912; formerly Paymaster Lt.-Cdr. RNR: *m.* 1938, Mary Allen, of Shrewsbury, Salop, and has issue living, Timothy John *b.* 1946: BVSC; MRCVS: *m.* 1969, Fiona, da. of Eric Lord, of Croydon,—Diana Margaret, *b.* 1938: *m.* 1963, Peter McConnell, of Shrewsbury, and has issue living, Simon John *b.* 1969, Julie Mary *b.* 1966, Sarah Francis *b.* 1971,—Marylin Elizabeth, *b.* 1944: *m.* 1970, John Butler, of Shrewsbury, 12, West Hermitage, Belle Vue, Shrewsbury.
Aunt living (daughter of 4th baronet)—Mildred Mary Winifred, *b.* 1901 : *m.* 1st, 1922, Edward Stanhope Benbow Rowe, who *d.* 1941 ; 2ndly, 1949, Gerard Dun, and has issue living, (by 1st marriage) Edward, *b.* 1929,—John, *b.* 1930,—Anthony, *b.* 1934,—Ursula, *b.* 1923,—Joscelyn, *b.* 1925. *Resides in* Trinidad.
Widow living of 5th Baronet—PATRICIA (*Patricia, Lady Barrow*), da. of the late Richard Gordon FitzGerald Uniacke, FSA: *m.* 1926, Major Sir Wilfrid John Wilson Croker Barrow, 5th baronet, who *d.* 1960. *Residence*, 14, Dowe House, The Glebe, Blackheath, SE3.

The 1st baronet, Sir John Barrow, for many years Secretary to the Admiralty, and Founder of the Royal Geographical Society, was highly distinguished as an author, a traveller, and a meritorious public servant, to whose memory a monumental tower, 100 feet high, was erected by public subscription on the Hoad Hill, Ulverston, his birthplace. The 2nd baronet was Chief Clerk at the Colonial Office and Secretary and Registrar of the Order of St. Michael and St. George, of which he was a Companion The 3rd baronet, Sir John Croker Barrow, was a Bar.-at-law of Lincoln's Inn, and a J.P. for Kent.

BARRY, Creation (U.K.) 1899, of St. Leonard's Hill, Clewer, Berks, and Keiss Castle, Wick, Caithness-shire.

Sir RUPERT RODNEY FRANCIS TRESS BARRY, MBE, 4th *Baronet;* *b.* Dec. 6th, 1910; *s.* his father, *Sir* CLAUDE FRANCIS 1970; Maj. (ret.) Oxfordshire and Bucks LI; Lord of the Manors of Ockwells and Lillibrooke, Berks., and Baron de Barry of Portugal; 1939-45 War; MBE (Mil) 1945: *m.* 1st, 1936, Diana Madeleine, who *d.* 1948, only da. of Rowland O'Brien Thompson, of 8, Harley Gdns., SW10; 2ndly, 1951, Sheila Georgina Veronica, only da. of Maj. George Joseph Francis White, MBE, of Ashford, Kent, and has issue by 1st and 2nd m.

Arms—Azure, two lions passant guardant or.

Residence,—Brisley Rise, Willesborough Lees, Ashford, Kent.

Sons living—By 1st m.—LAWRENCE EDWARD ANTHONY TRESS, *b.* Nov. 1st, 1939; ed. at Haileybury; Capt. Gren. Gds.——(By 2nd m.) Timothy Rupert Francis Tress, *b.* 1952.——Nicholas Mark Francis Tress, *b.* 1957.——Jonathan Rodney Francis Tress, *b.* 1960.
Daughters living—By 1st m.—Armorel Madeleine Frances Tress, *b.* 1936: *m.* 1959, Maj. Peter Miles Lambert, Gren. Gds. [see D. Wellington, colls.].——(By 2nd m.) Tara Caroline Frances Tress, *b.* 1954.——Xandra Georgina Frances Tress, *b.* 1962.

Sisters living—Kathleen Manners Tress, *b.* 1909: *m.* 1934, Edgar Freshman, FRCS, of The Clock House, Challock, Ashford, Kent, and has issue living, Roger David Barry, *b.* 1938: *m.* 1966, Anne Gillivary Cocker—Judy Rosemary, *b.* 1935: *m.* 1957, Robert William Miles Hunt (Post Bag Howick, Natal, S. Africa),—Angela Carolyn Tress, *b.* 1942: *m.* 1967, Maj. Robert Anthony Barntlett, The Queens Regt., of Grove Cottage, Bishopsbourne, Canterbury.——Sheila Yvonne Elizabeth Doris, *b.* 1915: *m.* 1941, Col. John Loftus Carter, RM, [M. Ely, colls.), and has issue living, Brian Loftus, *b.* 1945; Lt. RM: *m.* 1969, Caroline Jane Halsey,—Sally Elizabeth, *b.* 1943: *m.* 1970, David William Mearns Gow. *Residence*, Rose Cottage, Mersham, nr. Ashford, Kent.

Aunts living—(daughters of 2nd baronet)—Cicely Eleanor, *b.* 1892: *m.* 1918, Philip Poore, who *d.* 1937 [*see* Poore, Bt., colls.]. *Residence*, Pakaraka, Bay of Islands, NZ.——Margaret Colquhoun, *b.* 1894; 1914-18 War in VAD Jan. 1917 to Dec. 1918 (two medals): *m.* 1919, Capt. James Clifton Colquhoun, MBE, formerly Highland LI, and has issue living, James Barry, *b.* 1931,—William Baliol, *b.* 1934,—Elizabeth, *b.* 1924.—Margaret, *b.* 1927,——Rosamonde (*Lady Muspratt*), (22, East St., Alresford, Hants.). *b.* 1901: *m.* 1925, Gen. Sir Sydney Frederick Muspratt, KCB, CSI, CIE, DSO, Indian Army, who *d.* 1972, and has issue living, John Scott (47, Dominion Circuit, Forrest, Canberra, ACT), *b.* (Oct.) 1925: *m.* 1957, Elizabeth Barrett, da. of John Davis Canning, of Waipukurau, NZ, and has issue living, David Barry, *b.* 1928: *m.* 1963, Rosemary Anne, el. da. of Col. E. D. Rash, and has issue.

Collateral Branches living.

Issue of the late Douglas Herron Barry, 3rd son of 1st baronet, *b.* 1861, *d.* 1945 : *m.* 1884, Rose Grace, who *d.* **1939,**da. of Peter Gowland:—
Audrey Rose, *b.* 1895: *m.* 1922, Maj. Leslie Fitzroy Richard, formerly RA, from whom she obtained a divorce 1946. *Residence*, Sandy Croft, Heathfield, Sussex.

Issue of the late William James Barry, 4th son of 1st baronet, *b.* 1864, *d.* 1952, *m.* 1896, Lady Grace Murray, *M.B.E.*, who *d.* 1960, da. of 7th Earl of Dunmore :—
Gerald, *M.C., b.* 1896 ; ed. at Eton ; is Lieut.-Col. ; European War 1914-19 with Cold-stream Guards (1914-15 star, M.C.) ; European War 1939-45 with Black Watch : *m.* 1923, Lady Margaret Pleydell-Bouverie, da. of 6th Earl of Radnor, and has issue living, Richard John (The Warren, Gt. Witchingham, Norwich, NOR 65X), *b.* 1938: *m.* 1965, Jillian Frances, da. of Lt.-Col. A. L. Novis, MC, of Fryern House, Storrington, Sussex, and has issue living, James Tress *b.* 1967, Anthony Gerald *b.* 1969,——Anne (*Lady Alastair N. J. Gordon*), *b.* 1924: *m.* 1950, Lord Alastair Ninian John Gordon [*see* M. Aberdeen and Temair],—Diana, *b.* 1927: *m.* 1st, 1951, Kenneth Robert Motion, from whom she obtained a divorce 1959: 2ndly, 1959, Nathaniel Edward Sherwood, of Easthope Green, Marks Tey, Essex, and has issue living, (by 1st m) Richard Peter *b.* 1954, Sarah *b.* 1955, (by 2nd m.) David Gerald *b.* 1960,—Patricia Helen, *b.* 1932: *m.* 1958, Peregrine Michael Hungerford Pollen [*see* Pollen, Bt., colls.],—Rosemary (twin), *b.* 1938: *m.* 1966, Colin Vyvyan Peterson, of 7, Fitzroy Rd., NW1 8TU, son of the late Sir Maurice Drummond Peterson, GCMG, and has issue living, Andrew Drummond, *b.* 1967, Thomas Richard *b.* 1970, Helen Margaret *b.* 1969, Alice Diana *b.* 1974. *Residence*, Lake House, Gt. Witchingham, Norwich.——Hubert Wyndham, *b.* 1898; Cdr. (ret.) RN; 1914-18 War, 1939-45 War: *m.* 1936, Violet Agatha, da. of Sir Edward Archibald Ruggles-Brise, MC, TD, MP, 1st Bt., and has issue living, William Edward (12, Kensington Park Mews, W11), *b.* 1938: *m.* 1965, Juliet Alexandra Sarah, da. of James H. L. Musker [*see* E. Lauderdale, colls.], and has issue living, Catherine Jane *b.* 1968,—James Hubert, *b.* 1947,—Rosemary, *b.* 1939: *m.* 1963, Alastair Pinckard Leslie, late Capt. RHF, of Grays House, Bramley, Basingstoke [*see* E. Rothes],—Susan (*Hon. Mrs. Simon M. Arthur*), *b.* 1945: *m.* 1969, Maj. the Hon. Simon Mark Arthur, of Burnham House, Upavon, Pewsey, Wilts., el. son. of 3rd Baron Glenarthur. *Residence*, Hill House, Broughton, Stockbridge, Hants.——Esther Joyce, *b.* 1906——Nancy Elizabeth, *b.* 1910: *m.* 1935, George Nigel Capel Cure, TD, DL, JP, and has issue living, George Ronald (1, Cambridge Pl., W8), *b.* 1936: *m.* 1968, Caroline, only da. of Giles Yarnton Mills, of Puys sur Dieppe, France, and has issue living, a son *b.* 1971,—Michael, *b.* 1947,—Sarah Virginia (*Hon. Mrs. Thomas R. Lindsay*), *b.* 1938: *m.* 1961, the Hon. Thomas Richard Lindsay, of 3, Netherton Grove, Chelsea, SW10 [*see* E. Crawford]. *Residence*, Blake Hall, Ongar, Essex.

Issue of the late Col. Stanley Leonard Barry, C.M.G., C.B.E., D.S.O., M.V.O, late 10th Hussars, 5th son of 1st baronet, *b.* 1873, *d.* 1943 : *m.* 1906, Hannah Mary, who *d.* 1924, el. da. of James Hainsworth, of 34, Phillimore Gardens, W.8, and formerly wife of Col. W. MacGeorge, 6th Dragoon Guards, from whom she obtained a divorce 1902; 2ndly, 1927, Laline Annette, who *d.* 1969, da. of the late William Harvey Astell, JP, DL (sometime Lt. Grenadier Guards), of Wood-bury Hall, Sandy, Beds, and widow of Lt.-Col. Arthur Preston Hohler, DSO (V. Gort):—
(By 1st m.) Jeanne Irene (*Hon. Mrs. James A. G. McDonnell*), *b.* 1915: *m.* 1939, the Hon. James Angus Grey McDonnell [*see* E. Antrim]. *Residence*, 36, Farley Court, Melbury Rd., W14.

The 1st baronet, Sir Francis Tress Barry, was descended trom Richard Barry, of Eynsham, Oxon, temp. 1476, and the family arms were recorded by Lawrence Barry, of Hampton Gay Manor, Oxon, at the Visitations of Oxfordshire in 1566 and 1574, identical with those recorded for Sir Robert Barry, of Stanton Barry, Bucks., temp. Edward I; Sir Francis was *cr.* Baron de Barry in Portugal 1876, sat as M.P. for Windsor (C) 1890-1906, and was Consul-Gen. in Great Britain for Ecuador. The 2nd baronet, Sir Edward Arthur Barry, was High Sheriff of Berks in **1907,** and Lieut.·Col. Berks Yeo.

BARTLETT, Creation (U.K.) 1913, of Hardington-Mandeville, Somerset.

With fortitude and fidelity.

Sir BASIL HARDINGTON BARTLETT, 2nd *Baronet*, son of the late Hardington Arthur Bartlett, second but el. surviving son of 1st Baronet ; *b.* Sept. 15th, 1905 ; *s.* his grandfather, *Sir* HERBERT HENRY, 1921 ; ed. at Repton, and at Corpus Christi Coll., Camb ; is Lieut.-Col. Intelligence Corps; 1939-45 War (wounded, despatches): *m.* 1937 (m. diss. 1960), Mary, only da. of the late Sir Ian Zachary Malcolm of Poltalloch, KCMG, and has issue.

Arms—Argent, two barrulets dancettée between in chief two cinquefoils and in base a crescent issuant therefrom a cross formée fitchée, all azure. **Crest**—A demi eagle displayed azure, winged or, supporting with the beak a pennon of the first, charged with the arms.

Residence—733C, Holland Park, W11. *Club*—Beefsteak.

Daughters living—Julia Jane, *b.* 1937.——Lucy Mary le Breton, *b.* 1941: *m.* 1969, Adrian Alexander Bridgewater [see B. Vivian].——Annabel Kate, *b.* 1945.

Brother living—HENRY DAVID HARDINGTON, MBE (Harpers, Bledlow Ridge, High Wycombe), *b.* March 18th, 1912; ed. at Stowe, and Corpus Christi Coll., Camb.; Lt.-Col. RA (TA); MBE (Mil) 1944: *m.* 1st, 1936 (m. diss. 19—) Kathlene Rosemond, da. of Lt.-Col. W. H. Stanbury, of 90, West Hill, Putney, SW15; 2ndly, 19—, and has issue living (by 1st m.) John Hardington (c/o Barclays Bank, Church St., Leatherhead, Surrey), *b.* 1938: *m.* 19—, Elizabeth Joyce, da. of George Rayne, of Norbiton Rd., Kingston upon Thames, and has issue living, Andrew Alan *b.* 1973, Stephen *b.* 1975,—Simon Hardington (Whitkirk Cottage, Sheriff Hutton, nr. York), *b.* 1940: *m.* 19—,—Christopher Mandeville (1, Redland Bank Cottages, South Holmwood, Surrey), *b.* 1942: *m.* 19—, and has issue living.

Sister living—Irene Theodora, *b.* 1908.

Collateral Branches living.

Issue of the late Eric Oscar Bartlett, 4th son of 1st baronet, *b.* 1882, *d.* 1968: *m.* 1907, Irene, who *d.* 19—, da. of the late Lawrence Alport, of 100, Lexham Gdns., W.:—

Betty Frances, *b.* 1908: *m.* 1933, Gordon Bushell Hedley, late Bengal Pilot Ser., and has issue living, Richard, *b.* 1940,—Anne Wilhelmina Betty, *b.* 1934.——Mary Augusta, *b.* 1911: *m.* 1st, 1934, Fl.-Lt. Roy James Oliphant Bartlett, RAF, who *d.* 1936; 2ndly, 1941, Group Capt. James Douglas Ferrier Bruce, RAF, and has issue living, (by 1st m.) Peter Howard Oliphant (posthumous), *b.* 1937,—Jill Rose Alyne Charlotte, *b.* (Dec.) 1934: *m.* 1955, Stuart Bollam, and has issue living, Miles Stuart *b.* 1957, Kim Paulin, *b.* 1956, (by 2nd m.) Mhairi Christina Deborah *b.* 1945.

Issue of the late Maj. Norman Edwin Bartlett, yst. son of 1st baronet; *b.* 1888 *d.* 1972: *m.* 1st, 1917 (m. diss. 1928), Mary Adelaide Leslie, da. of Norman R. Foster, of 47, Murray Rd., Wimbledon SW; 2ndly, 1928, Sheila Barton (Flat 1, Spring Grove, Chartris Rd., Sunningdale, Berks., S25 99B), da. of Mrs. Hill, of 11, Bentinck Terr., SW8:—

(By 1st m.) Norman Alaric, RN (c/o Ministry of Defence (Navy), SW1), *b.* 1920; Lt.-Cdr. and Pilot, Flying Branch, RN; 1939-45 War (despatches): *m.* 1945, Mary Paterson Waugh, and has issue living, Michael Alaric, *b.* 1946,—Carol Ann, *b.* 1948.——Hazel Leslie, *b.* 1922: *m.* 1st, 1947, George Edward Short, who *d.* 1962; 2ndly, 1966, Philip John Elwood, of Rylands, Altarnun, Launceston, Cornwall.——(by 2nd m.) Derek (Fiveways, Warfield, Bracknell, Berks.), *b.* 1930; late Maj. LG: *m.* 1956, Joan Patricia, da. of R. J. Breyfogle, and has issue living, Peter Mandeville, *b.* 1960,—Robert Hardington, *b.* 1965,—Jonica Mary, *b.* 1958.——Edwina, *b.* 1933: *m.* 1956, Esmond Dunn Boldero, late Capt. LG, of Gyles Croft, Bellingdon, Chesham, Bucks., and has issue living, Jonathan Dunn, *b.* 1958,—Alexandra, *b.* 1964,—Louisa, *b.* 1966.

Sir Herbert Henry Bartlett, 1st Bt., was many years Chm. of Perry and Co. (Bow), Limited, contractors.

BARTTELOT, Creation (U.K.) 1875, of Stopham, Sussex.

[Name pronounced "Bartlot."]

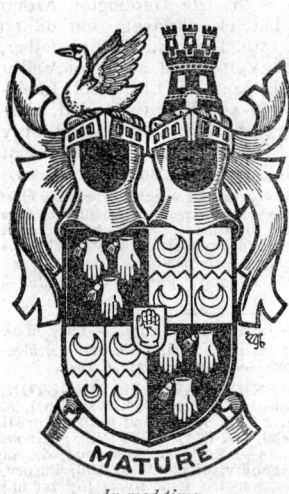

In good time.

MATURE

Sir BRIAN WALTER DE STOPHAM BARTTELOT, 5th *Baronet; b.* July 17th, 1941; *s.* his father, *Brigadier Sir* WALTER DE STOPHAM, *DSO* 1944; ed. at Eton; Maj. Coldstream Gds.; is patron of two livings; Equerry to HM 1970-72: *m.* 1969, the Hon. (Mary Angela) Fiona Weld Forester, yst. da. of the 7th Baron Forester, and has issue.

Arms—Quarterly, 1st and 4th sable, three sinister gloves pendent argent, tasselled or, *Barttelot;* 2nd and 3rd quarterly, per fesse argent and gules, four crescents countercharged, *Stopham.* Crests—1st, a swan couchant wings endorsed argent, *Barttelot;* 2nd, a castle with three turrets sable, *Stopham.*

Seat—Stopham House, Pulborough, Sussex. *Residence*—Keepers, Stopham, Pulborough, Sussex.

Daughters living—Isabel Emily, *b.* 1971,—Sophie Rosalind, *b.* 1973.
Brother living—ROBIN RAVENSCROFT, *b.* Dec. 15th, 1943; ed. at Seaford Coll., and Perth Univ., W. Aust.
Uncle living (son of 3rd baronet)—William Frederick Geoffrey Nelson, *b.* 1905; ed. at Wellington Coll.; formerly Lieut.-Col. R.E.: *m.* 1930, Jane Elizabeth, da. of D. Stirling, of Santiago, Chile, and has issue living, Richard James Walter Stuart, *b.* 1932,—Elizabeth Georgiana Margaret, *b.* 1933: *m.* 1st, 1955 (m. diss. 1973), James Drury Edward Kelly, Essex Regt.; 2ndly, 1973, Nigel John Petrie Mermagen, of 2, Furham Feild, Hatch End, Pinner, Middx., and has issue living (by 1st m.), Thomas James Barttelot *b.* 1956, Rose Jane Elizabeth *b.* 1958.
Residence,—Brooklawn, Lyminster, nr. Arundel, Aussex.

Widows living of 3rd and 4th Baronets—GLADYS ST. AUBYN, da. of the late William Collier Angove, of 83, Onslow Gdns., SW: *m.* 1st, 1903, Lt.-Col. Sir Walter Balfour Barttelot, DSO, 3rd baronet, who *d.* (killed during 1914-18 War while Mil. Attaché at Teheran) 1918; 2ndly, 1920, Capt. Neston William Diggle, C.M.G., R.N., who *d.* 1963. *Residence,* Tellisford House, nr. Bath.——SARA PATRICIA, da. of the late Lt.-Col. Herbert Valentine Ravenscroft, of The Abbey, Storrington, Sussex: *m.* 1st, 1938, Brigadier Sir Walter de Stopham Barttelot, DSO, 4th baronet, who *d.* (killed in action) 1944; 2ndly, 1965, Cdr. James Nigel Walter Barttelot, RN (ret.) (infra).

Collateral Branch living.

Issue of the late Lieut.-Com. Nigel Kenneth Walter Barttelot, R.N., 2nd son of 2nd baronet, *b.* 1883, *d.* (killed in action) 1914: *m.* 1906, Dorothy Maud (*Lady Rose*) (who *d.* 1961, having *m.* 2ndly, 1923, as his second wife, Vice-Adm. Sir Frank Forrester Rose, K.C.B., D.S.O., who *d.* 1955), el. da. of the late Frederick Aldcroft Kay :—
James Nigel Walter, *b.* 1911; Cdr. RN (ret.): *m.* 1st, 1936, Rachel Mildred, who *d.* 1964, da. of Raymond Courage, of Edgcote, Banbury; 2ndly, 1965, Sara Patricia, da. of the late Lt.-Col. Herbert Valentine Ravenscroft, and widow of Brig. Sir Walter de Stopham Barttelot, DSO, 4th baronet (ante) and has issue living, (by 1st m.) Nigel Michael Anthony (The Old Vicarage, Westow, York), *b.* 1941: *m.* 1971, Serena, da. of F. W. Brett, of Sussex Cottage, Burwood Park, Walton-on-Thames, and has issue living, Sasha Rachel *b.* 1972, Olivia Henrietta *b.* 1974,—David James Raymond (47, Belgravia Court, Ebury St., SWI), *b.* 1946: *m.* 1973, Lucinda Jane, da. of Cdr. G. R. Callingham, RN, ret.),—Carol Rachel Mildred, *b.* 1938: *m.* 1961, Torquil Robin Armour Macmillan, of Altyre House, Gt. Horkesley, Colchester, and has issue living, James Armour *b.* 1965, Andrew Giles *b.* 1968, Timothy Iain *b.* 1969, Lucinda Jane Carol *b.* 1963. *Residence,* Old Farm, Wisborough Green, Sussex.
John Barttelot, who *d.* 1428, acquired Stopham in the right of his wife Joan, dau. and co-heir of William de Stopham. The Rt. Hon. Sir Walter Barttelot, C.B., P.C., 1st baronet, sat as M.P. for W. Sussex (C) 1860-85, and for Sussex, N.W., or Horsham, Div. 1885-93. Capt. Sir Walter Barttelot, 2nd baronet, was killed in action in S. Africa 1900, while Comdg. 2nd Vol. Batn. Roy. Sussex Regt. The 3rd baronet, Sir Walter Balfour Barttelot, D.S.O., Major and Brevet Lieut.-Col. Coldstream Guards, was killed during European War while Mil. Attaché at Teheran (Croix de Guerre). The 4th baronet, Brigadier Sir Walter de Stopham Barttelot, D.S.O., late Coldstream Guards, was killed in action in France 1944.

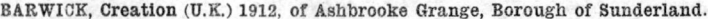

BARWICK, Creation (U.K.) 1912, of Ashbrooke Grange, Borough of Sunderland.

In ouris servata fides.

Sir RICHARD LLEWELLYN BARWICK, 3rd *Baronet; b.* Nov. 4th, 1916; *s.* his father, *Sir* JOHN STOREY, 1953; ed. at Harrow: *m.* 1st 1948 (m. diss. 1968), Valerie Maud (WARD), da. of R. J. Skelton, of Nairobi, Kenya; 2ndly, 1968, Denise, da. of the late Alexander Reginald Pole, of Walton-on-Thames and widow of Hugh Christian Radcliffe, Bar.-at-Law, and has issue by 1st m.

Arms—Azure, a galley or, in chief two bears' heads couped argent, muzzled gules. Crest.—A demi bear rampant argent muzzled gules, holding between the paws an ancient ship's lantern or.

Seat—Thimbleby Hall, Northallerton, Yorkshire.

Daughters living—By 1st m.—Rozanne Valerie, *b.* 1950: *m.* 1970, Alan Bulmer, of Coombe Cross House, East Meon, Petersfield, Hants.——Sandra Anne, *b.* 1952: *m.* 1971, Timothy G. W. Hancock, of the Manor House, Pytchley, Northants.——Victoria Maud Lorraine, *b.* 1961.

Collateral Branch living.

Issue of the late George Short Barwick, 2nd son of 1st baronet, *b.* 1879, *d.* 1937: *m.* 1913, Marianne, who *d.* 1975, da. of the late William Marshall, of Davenham, Ches.:—

Angela Ruth, *b.* 1916 : *m.* 1947, her cousin, John Gilbert Gilbey, and has issue living, Christopher John Barwick, *b.* 1949,—Arabella Clare, *b.* 1953. *Residence,* Inholmes, Woodland St. Mary, nr. Newbury, Berks.——Diana Marianne, *b.* 1917: *m.* 1st, 1945 (marriage dissolved 1955), Lieut. John Bowles, R.N.; 2ndly, 1959, Gerald Leopold Wiener, O.B.E., of 45, Edwardes Sq., W.8, and has issue living (by 1st marriage) George Anthony John, *b.* 1946,—Sarah Margaret Diana *b.* 1949.

The 1st baronet, Sir John Storey Barwick, was a coalowner, and Chm. of several collieries. The 2nd baronet, Sir John Storey, was High Sheriff of Durham 1922.

BATES, Creation U.K.) 1880, of Bellefield, co. Lancaster.

Sir GEOFFREY VOLTELIN BATES, *M.C.*, 5th *Baronet,* son of the late Major Cecil Robert Bates, D.S.O., M.C., 3rd son of 2nd baronet; *b.* Oct. 2nd, 1921 ; *s.* his uncle *Sir* PERCY ELLY, *G.B.E.*, 1946; ed. at Radley; Capt. (ret.) 8th Hussars, and Maj. (ret.) Cheshire Yeo.; High Sheriff of Flintshire 1969; 1939-45 War (MC): *m.* 1st, 1945, Kitty, who *d.* 1956, da. of Ernest Kendall-Lane, of Saskatchewan, Canada; 2ndly, 1957, the Hon. Olivia Gwyneth Zoë Fitz Roy, who *d.* 1969, da. of 2nd Viscount Daventry; 3rdly, 1971, Juliet Eleanor Hugolyn White-ɪocke-Winter, widow of Edward Colin Winter, and has ɪssue by 1st and 2nd m.

Labore et virtute. By labour and virtue.

ᴬᵣᵐˢ—Argent, on a fesse azure a quatrefoil between two fleurs-de-lys argent, between in chief two quatrefoils azure, and in base a fleur-de-lys of the same. ᴄʳᵉˢᵗ—A stag's head erased azure, attired or, transfixed by two arrows crosswise of the second, and charged on the neck with two quatrefoils in pale or.

Residence—Gyrn Castle, Llanasa, Holywell, Clwyd.

Sons living—By 1st m.—EDWARD ROBERT, *b.* July 4th, 1946; ed. at Gordonstoun.——Richard Geoffrey, *b.* 1948.

Daughters living—By 2nd marriage—Celina Zoë, *b.* 1958.——Sarah Rose, *b.* 1960.

Sister living—Audrey Cecil, *b.* 1919 : *m.* 1942, Major the Hon. Thomas Heron Hazlerigg, Leicester-shire Yeo. from whom she obtained a divorce 1956 [*see* B. Hazlerigg]. *Residence,* The Court House, Cold Overton, Oakham, Rutland.

Collateral Branches living.

Issue of the late Col Denis Haughton Bates, MC, TD, 5th son of 2nd baronet, *b.* 1886, *d.* 1959: *m.* 1922, Aline Mary, who *d.* 1974, da. of Edward T. Crook, of Woodlands Hall, Bridgnorth:—

Philip Edward, VRD (Friars Wood, Boldre, Lymington, Hants.) *b.* 1925; ed. at Shrewsbury; Maj. (ret.) RM Force VR; 1943-45 War: *m.* 1952, Mary Patricia Carol, da. of Lt.-Col. Clive Vincent Moberly-Bell, OBE, and has issue living, Hugh Percy, *b.* 1953,—Denis Moberly, *b.* 1954,—Patricia Mary, *b.* 1956,—Carol Elisabeth, *b.* 1957.——Denise Elisabeth, *b.* 1928: *m.* 1958, the Rev. Thomas Michael Rylands, R. of Malpas, Cheshire, and has issue living, Thomas Gordon, *b.* 1959,—Mark James, *b.* 1961,—Alison Joane, *b.* 1963. *Residence,* The Rectory, Malpas, Ches.

Issue of the late Lieut.-Col. Austin Graves Bates, D.S.O., M.C., 6th son of 2nd baronet, *b.* 1891, *d.* 1961 : *m.* 1920, Jean Christian Marguerite (of Anton's Hill, Coldstream, Berwickshire), da. of Col. James Hunter, of Anton's Hill, Coldstream, Berwickshire:—

Jeremy Dickson, *b.* 1932; ed. at London Univ. (BSc 19—).——Martin Graves (Hill Farm, Elmsett, Ipswich), *b.* 1935; ed. at St. Edmund Hall, Oxford (BA); late Queen's Own Cameron High-landers: *m.* 1965, Susan Myfanwy Prudence, da. of Capt. Robert Edward Dudley Ryder, VC, RN [*see* E. Harrowby, colls.], and has issue living, Oliver Robert Hunter, *b.* 1969,—Susannah Hilaré, *b.* 1970.

Issue of the late Maurice Halifax Bates, Lt. RA, 7th son of 2nd baronet, *b.* 1898, *d.* 1925: *m.* 1922, May Frances (who *d.* 1969, having *m.* 2ndly, 1927, Brig. Ralph Emerson Pickering, CBE, late Queen's Roy. Regt., who *d.* 1962), da. of the late Sir Edward Arthur Henry Blunt, KCIE, OBE [Blunt, Bt. colls.]:—

Ann Maurice, *b.* (posthumous) 1925. *Residence,* Brackenside, Hinckley Rd., Wolvey, Leics.

Granddaughter of the late Sydney Eggers Bates (infra) :—

Issue of the late Col. Arthur Sydney Bates, D.S.O., T.D., *b.* 1879, *d.* 1958 : *m.* 1905, Mary da Costa, who *d.* 1962, da. of the late Lieut.-Col. Charles Robert Crosse, C.M.G., M.V.O., formerly Roy. W. Kent Regt.:—

Anne Mary, *b.* 1915 : *m.* 1939, Lieut.-Col. John Oliver-Bellasis, D.S.O., D.L., J.P., Roy. Fusiliers, and has issue living, Charles Arthur John (Montague House, Eastbury, Newbury, Berks.), *b.* 1940; ed. at Winchester, and Roy. Agric. Coll., Cirencester; MRAC; FRICS: *m.* 1972, Julia Elizabeth, da. of Lt. John Errol Manners, DSC, RN (ret.), of Laurel House, Great Cheverell, Devizes, Wilts., and has issue living, Clare Elizabeth *b.* 1974,—Hugh Richard, *b.* 1945; ed. at Winchester, and RMA; Maj. WG: *m.* 1971, Daphne Phoebe, yr. da. of Maj. Arthur Christopher Parsons. [see E. Rosse, colls.]. *Residence,* Wootton House, Wootton St. Lawrence, Basingstoke, Hants.

Issue of the late Sydney Eggers Bates, 3rd son of 1st baronet, *b.* 1851, *d.* 1924 : *m.* 1878, Elizabeth Jessie, who *d.* 1940, da. of the late Lieut.-Col. George Grenville Malet [Malet, Bt., colls.]:—

Edith Mary : *m.* 1923, William Lamb, who *d.* 1936. *Residence,* 32 Bryanston Square, W.1.—— Dorothy Eileen : *m.* (May) 1948, Thomas More, M.B.E., who *d.* (Sept.) 1948. *Residence,* The Gray House, Chadlington, Oxford.

The 1st baronet, Sir Edward, was M.P. for Plymouth (C) 1871-80 and 1885-92. The 4th **baronet** Sir Percy Elly, G.B.E., was Chm. of Cunard Steamship Co., Ltd., and of Cunard-White Star Ltd.

BATES, Creation (U.K.) 1937, of Magherabuoy, co. Londonderry.

Sir (JOHN) DAWSON BATES, *M.C.*, 2nd *Baronet* ; *b.* Sept. 21st
1921 ; *s.* his father, *the Rt. Hon. Sir* (Richard) Dawson, O.B.E., 1949 ;
formerly Major Rifle Brig. ; Middle East 1939-45 (M.C.) : *m.* 1953, Mary
Murray, da. of the late Lieut.-Col. J. M. Hoult, R.A., of Norton Place,
Lincoln, and has issue.
  Residence—Eaton Hastings Grange, Faringdon, Berks.

Sons living—RICHARD DAWSON HOULT, *b.* May 12th, 1956.——Charles Joseph Dill, *b.* 1959.
Daughter living—Drusilla Mary Cynthia, *b.* 1954.

  The 1st baronet, Rt. Hon. Sir (Richard) Dawson Bates, O.B.E. (son of the late Richard
Dawon Bates, Solicitor, of Belfast), was Min. for Home Affairs, N. Ireland 1921-43.

BATHO, Creation (U.K.) 1928, of Frinton, Essex.

Sir MAURICE BENJAMIN BATHO, 2nd
Baronet ; *b.* Jan. 14th, 1910 ; *s.* his father, *Sir*
CHARLES ALBERT, 1938 ; ed. at Uppingham, and
abroad ; formerly Managing Dir. of Reed Paper
and Board Sales Ltd., Sub-Dir. of Syrian Wheat
Collection Scheme of Spears Mission 1943,
Regional Adviser on Cereals Collection to Min.
of Finance, Iran 1944, and Dep. Dir. of Rice
Procurement, Bengal 1945 ; 1939-45 War as
Lt.-Col. KRRC : *m.* 1934, Antoinette Marie,
da. of Baron d'Udekem d'Acoz, of Ghent,
Belgium, and has issue.

Arms—Gules, on a fess argent two castles of the first, over
all a sword in pale point upwards proper. **Crest**—A dragon
sejant or gorged with a mural crown gules, and holding in the
dexter claw a sword as in the arms.

  Residence—Carlton Hall, Saxmundham, Suffolk. *Clubs*—
Constitutional, Naval and Military.

Neither do I hesitate at trifles.

Son living—PETER GHISLAIN (Park Farm, Saxmundham), *b.* Dec. 9th, 1939 ; ed. at Ample-
forth : *m.* 1966, Lucille Mary, da. of Wilfrid F. Williamson, of The White House, Saxmundham,
and has issue living, Rupert Sebastian Ghislain, *b.* 1967,—Alexander Francis Ghislain *b.* 1970,—
Hugh Charles Ghislain, *b.* 1973.——Richard Ghislain (16, Orchard Close, Moreton-on-Lugg,
Hereford, HR4 8DG), *b.* 1941 ; ed. at Ampleforth, and at Wye Coll. (BSc London) : *m.* 1970,
Georgina Catherine Ann Gwynne, da. of the late W. R. G. Chadwick, and has issue living, Charles
William Ghislain, *b.* 1971,—Sarah Catherine Ghislain, *b.* 1974.
Daughters living—Anne Madeline Bessie Ghislaine, *b.* 1938 : *m.* 1964, Stephen Robert Morgan
Oliver, Broadgate, Whepstead, Bury-St. Edmunds, and has issue living, Felix Benjamin Morgan,
b. 1966,—Alban Geoffrey Morgan, *b.* 1968,—Damian Paul Morgan, *b.* 1970.——Jacqueline
Ghislaine, *b.* 1947

  The 1st baronet, Sir Charles Albert Batho (son of the late William Smith Batho, of Highgate, N.),
was an Alderman of City of London (Aldgate Ward) 1921-38, Sheriff 1925-6, and Lord Mayor 1927-8.

HERVEY-BATHURST, (Creation (U.K.) 1818, of Lainston, Hants.
[Name pronounced "**Harvy-Bathurst.**"]

Sir FREDERICK PETER METHUEN HERVEY-
BATHURST, 6th *Baronet* ; *b.* Jan. 26th, 1903 ; *s.*
his father, *Major Sir* FREDERICK EDWARD WILLIAM,
D.S.O., 1956 ; ed. at Eton ; Capt. late Grenadier
Guards : *m.* 1st, 1933 (marriage dissolved 1956),
Maureen Gladys Diana, el. da. of Charles Gordon,
of Boveridge Park, Salisbury ; 2ndly, 1958,
Cornelia, da. of the late Frederic White Shepard, of
New York, U.S.A., and widow of Dr. John Lawrence
Riker, of Rumson, New Jersey, U.S.A., and has
issue by 1st marriage.

Arms—Quarterly, 1st and 4th, sable, two bars ermine, and in
chief three crosses-patée or, a crescent for difference, *Bathurst* ;
2nd and 3rd, gules, on a bend argent three trefoils vert, a martlet for
difference, *Hervey*. **Crest**—1st, a dexter arm embowed in armour
proper, grasping a spiked club or, *Bathurst* ; 2nd, an ounce passant
sable, bezantee ducally gorged and chained or, in the paw a trefoil
slipped vert, *Hervey*.
  Seat—Somborne Park, King's Somborne, Hants. *Residence*—
Bellevue Av., Rumson, New Jersey, USA.

Hold thy faith.

Son living—By 1st marriage—FREDERICK JOHN CHARLES
GORDON, *b.* April 23rd, 1934 ; ed. at Eton, and at Trin. Coll.,

Camb. (B.A. 1957); **is** Lieut. Grenadier Guards (Reserve): *m.* 1957, Caroline Myrtle, da. of Sir William Randle Starkey, 2nd Bt., and has issue living, Frederick William John, *b.* 1965,—Louisa Caroline, *b.* 1959,—Sophia Selina Irene, *b.* 1961. *Residences*, Somborne Park, King's Somborne, Hants.; 450 Kings Rd., SW10.
Daughter living—By 1st m.—Selina Anthea Maureen, *b.* 1936: *m.* 1959, Lt.-Col. Peter Gerald Sandeman Tower, Coldstream Guards [Butler Bt., cr. 1628], and has issue living, William John, *b.* 1963,—Nicola Jane, *b.* 1961. *Residence*, Mouse Lodge, Winkfield, Windsor Forest, Berks.
Half-Brother living—Benjamin Alexander Frederick, *b.* 1920; ed. at Eton, and at Trin. Coll. Camb. (BA); Maj. late Grenadier Guards and Special Forces; a DL of Herefordshire; 1939-45 War (wounded, despatches twice): *m.* 1947, the Hon. (Violet) Elizabeth Virginia Cocks, only child of 6th Baron Somers, and has issue living, James Felton Somers, *b.* 1949,—George Arthur Somers, *b.* 1952. *Seat*, Eastnor Castle, Ledbury, Herefordshire.

Collateral Branch living.

Grandson of the late Lieut.-Col. Lionel PASTON-COOPER, 2nd son of 3rd baronet:—
Issue of the late Capt. Sidney Lionel PASTON-COOPER, *b.* 1887; *d.* 1934: *m.***1927**, Ermyntrude Mary, who *d.* 1936, da. of Henry Caley,of Hovingham, Yorkshire:—
Astley Cecil Hervey, *b.* 1929: *m.* 1950, Jean Louise, da. of Lawrence Dickinson, of **8, Dorset Avenue**, Welling, Kent, and has issue living, Lionel Lawrence Hervey, *b.* 1951,—Sally Ann, *b.* 1953. *Residence*,

The 1st baronet, Sir Felton Elwell Hervey, was a grandson of the late Hon. Felton Hervey, 7th son of 1st Earl of Bristol [*see* M. Bristol], and was A.D.C. to the Duke of Wellington at Waterloo. He assumed in 1801 the additional surname and arms of Bathurst, and on his death without issue in 1819, he was succeeded, under special remainder, by his next brother, Sir Frederick Anne Hervey-Bathurst, 2nd Bt. Lieut.-Col. Sir Frederick, 4th baronet, sat as M.P. for S. Wilts (C) 1861-5. Major Sir Frederick Edward William, 5th Bt., D.S.O., Grenadier Guards, served in Egyptian Campaign 1898, S. Africa 1900, and European War 1914-18 (D.S.O.).

BAYNES, Creation (U.K.) 1801, of Harefield Place, Middlesex.

Rage supplies arms.

Sir RORY MALCOLM STUART BAYNES, 6th *Baronet*; *b.* May 16th, 1886; el. son of the late Rev. Malcolm Charles Baynes, 4th son of 3rd Bt.; *s.* his cousin, *Sir* WILLIAM EDWARD COLSTON, *MC*, 1971; ed. at Harrow; late Lt.-Col. Cameronians (Scottish Rifles); Co. Councillor for Som. 1946-58, and Co. Alderman 1958-68; 1914-18 War (wounded); Palestine 1936; 1939-45 War: *m.* 1925, Audrey, who *d.* 1947, da. of the late Edward Giles, CIE, and has issue.

Arms—Sable, a shin-bone in fesse surmounted of another in pale argent; on a canton of the last, a vulture proper. **Crest**—A cubit arm vested, azure, cuffed erminois, the hand holding a jaw-bone argent. **Supporters**—Two savages wreathed with holly about the head and waist, carrying clubs over their exterior shoulders all proper.
Residence,—The Cottage, Lake Vyrnwy Hotel, via Oswestry, Salop, SY10 0LY.

Son living—JOHN CHRISTOPHER MALCOLM (The Cottage, Lake Vyrnwy Hotel, via Oswestry, Salop., SY10 0LY), *b.* April 24th, 1928; late Lt.-Col. Queen's Own Highlanders; Malaya 1950-53 (despatches): *m.* 1955, Shirley Maxwell, only da. of the late Robert Dodds, of Foxbury, Lesbury, Alnwick, and has issue living, Christopher Rory, *b.* 1956,—Timothy Peter, *b.* 1957,—Simon Robert Maurice, *b.* 1960,—William John Walter, *b.* 1966.
Brother living—Keith Stuart (c/o Lloyds Bank, Rye, Sussex), *b.* 1887; ed. at Harrow, and Trin. Coll., Camb.; Artist.
Sister living—Morah Susan Stuart (Southill House, W. Cranmore, Shepton Mallet, Somerset), *b.* 1893: *m.* 1914, Maj. Ralph Beecroft Horsfield, formerly Essex Regt., who *d.* 1966.

Collateral Branch living.

Grandson of the late Edward Neil Baynes, youngest son of 3rd baronet:—
Issue of the late Edward Stuart Augustus Baynes, OBE, *b.* 1889, *d.* 1972: *m.* 1918, Helen Mary (32, Avondale Cres., Killiney, co. Dublin), da. of G. Meredith, of Epsom, and widow of J. S. White:—
Anthony Edward George (School Hill, Little Minster, Minister Lovell, Oxon.), *b.* 1921; Artist; 1939-45 War as Sub-Lt. RNVR.

The 1st baronet, Sir Christopher, was the son of William Baynes (a Gentleman of the Privy Chamber to George II. and George III.), of Harefield Place, Middlesex, and Kilburn Hall, Yorkshire, descended from the old Yorkshire family of Bayne, originally de Bayeux; Sir Christopher served in Royal Horse Guards 1781-8, and in 1796 was Major-Commandant of the "Uxbridge Gentlemen and Yeomanry Cavalry," which corps he helped to raise; he was also a D.L. for Middlesex.

BAZLEY, Creation (U.K.) 1869, of Hatherop, co. Gloucester.

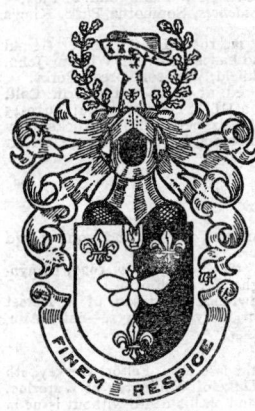

Consider the end.

FINEM RESPICE

Sir THOMAS STAFFORD BAZLEY, 3rd *Baronet*, son of the late Gardner Sebastian Bazley, only son of 2nd baronet; *b.* Oct. 5th, 1907; *s.* his grandfather, *Sir* THOMAS SEBASTIAN, 1919; ed. at Harrow, and at Magdalen Coll., Oxford: *m.* 1945, Carmen, only da. of J. Tulla, of 11, Stanley Gardens, W.11, and has issue.

Arms—Per pale azure and sable, a bee volant or between three fleurs-de-lis argent. Crest—A cubit arm erect proper charged with a bee volant or, the hand holding a chapeau gules, turned up gold; the whole between two branches of oak vert.

Residence—Eastleach Folly, nr. Hatherop, Cirencester, Gloucestershire.

Sons living—THOMAS JOHN SEBASTIAN, *b.* Aug. 31st, 1948.——Anthony Martin Christopher, *b.* 1958.——John Francis Alexander, *b.* 1961.

Daughters living—Catherine, *b.* 1950.——Virginia, *b.* 1953.

Sisters living—Elisabeth Rachel, *b.* 1904: *m.* 1930, Christopher Evelyn Blunt, O.B.E., and has issue living, Simon Wilfrid (Old Angle, Dartmouth Row, Greenwich, SE10), *b.* 1933: *m.* 1964, Julia Miranda Lampson, and has issue living, Christopher Mark *b.* 1967, Amanda Claire *b.* 1966,—Anne Caroline, *b.* 1931: *m.* 1964, Prof. Karl Frederick Morrison, Chicago Univ., USA, and has issue living, Andrew David *b.* 1965, Sarah Christina *b.* 1966,—Judith Elisabeth, *b.* 1937: *m.* 1962, Julian Edwin Hamby Mustoe, of 58, Grafton Terr., NW5, and has issue living, James William *b.* 1963, Sophia Louise *b.* 1967. *Residence*,—Ramsbury, Wilts.——Frances Catharine Ruth, *b.* 1905: *m.* (Jan.) 1932, Richard Arthur Warren Hughes, OBE [*see* Hughes, Bt., *cr.* 1773, colls.]. *Residence*, Mor Edrin, Talsarnau, Merioneth, N. Wales.——Rachel Constance, *b.* 1909: *m.* 1939, Edward John Ronald Bennett, and has issue living, John Sebastian, *b.* 1942: *m.* 1971, Sara Hermione, da. of Maj. Inglis Jones,—Henry Christopher, *b.* 1946,—Edward Alexander, *b.* 1948,—Charles Michael (twin), *b.* 1948,—Victoria, *b.* 1940: *m.* 1964, Henry Alexander Fowell Buxton [*see* Buxton, Bt., colls.]. *Residence*, Hartwell Farm, Poulton, Glos.

Collateral Branch living.

Granddaughter of the late Gardner Sebastian Bazley, only son of 2nd baronet (ante):—

Issue of the late Anthony Gardner Bazley, *b.* 1911, *d.* 1937: *m.* 1934, Anne [(*Baroness Howard of Penrith*), who *m.* 2ndly, 1944, the 2nd Baron Howard of Penrith], da. of the late John Beaumont Hotham [*see* B. Hotham, colls.]:—

Susan Antonia, *b.* 1937: *m.* 1st, 1958 (m. diss. 1970), Peter Humphrey Van Oss; 2ndly, 1970, William John Vicary, of Court Leys, Toot Baldon, Oxford, and has issue living (by 1st m.), Mark Peter Anthony, *b.* 1959,—Anthony Tom Francis, *b.* 1961,—Juliet Anne Favell (twin), *b.* 1961,—Katharine Susanna, *b.* 1964,—(by 2nd m.) William Sebastian, *b.* 1973.

The 1st baronet sat as M.P. for Manchester (*L*) 1858-80, and the 2nd baronet was High Sheriff of Gloucestershire 1874.

BEAUCHAMP, Creation (U.K.) 1911, of Grosvenor Place, City of Westminster.

[Pronounced "**Beecham.**"]

Sir BROGRAVE CAMPBELL BEAUCHAMP, 2nd *Baronet*; *b.* May 5th, 1897; *s.* his father, *Sir* EDWARD, 1925; ed. at Eton; sometime Lieut. Household Cav.; unsuccessfully contested Lowestoft Div. of E. Suffolk(*NL*) Nov. 1922; sat as M.P. for E. Div. of Walthamstow (*C*) Oct. 1931 to June 1945: *m.* 1923, Lady Evelyn Leonora Almina Herbert, da. of 5th Earl of Carnarvon, and has issue.

Arms—Argent, a chevron between three martlets sable. Crest—On a mount vert, a greyhound sejant argent, spotted brown, collared or.

Residence—19, Kingston House, Princes Gate, S.W.7.

Daughter living—Patricia Evelyn, *b.* 1925: *m.* 1949, Major Michael William Thomas Leatham, and has issue living, Simon Anthony Michael. *b.* 1951,—Edward Arthur Martyn, *b.* 1953. *Residence*, Church Hill, Worplesdon, Surrey.

The 1st baronet, Sir Edward Beauchamp, son of the late Rev. William Henry Beauchamp, of Chedgrave, Norfolk [*see* Proctor-Beauchamp, Bt., colls.] was a Member of Lloyds (Chm. 1905 and 1913, and Vice-Chm. 1915 and 1916), and sat as M.P. for N., or Lowestoft, Div. of Suffolk (*L*) Jan. 1906 to Jan. 1910, and Dec. 1910 to Nov. 1918, and for E. Suffolk Lowestoft Div., Dec. 1918 to Oct. 1922.

Always faithful.

TOUJOURS FIDELE

BEAUCHAMP, Creation (U.K.) 1918, of Woodborough, co. Somerset.
[Pronounced **"Beecham."**]

Whatsoever God wishes.

Sir PETER (DOUGLAS CLIFFORD) BEAU-
CHAMP, 2nd *Baronet*; *b.* March 11th, 1903; *s.*
his father, Sir FRANK, *C.B.E.*, 1950; ed. at
Eton: *m.* 1st, 1926, Nancy Esther (who obtained
a divorce 1933), da. of Laurence E. Moss, of
Sydney, N.S. Wales; 2ndly, 1933, Pamela
Dorothy May Chandor, who *d.* 1971; 3rdly,
1972, Mary Elizabeth, el. da. of the late Guy
Harrop Haslewood, of Bridgnorth, and widow
of J. H. Tilbury.

Arms—Azure three grenades fired and a bordure engrailed
or. **Crest**—A tiger statant azure, charged on the shoulder
with a grenade as in the arms.

Residence,—The Pebbles, Fore St., Budleigh Salterton,
Devon.

Sister living—Dorothy Joan, *b.* 1901 : *m.* 1st, 1931, Major
Claude de Lisle Bush, who *d.* 1941 : 2ndly, 1946, Brigadier
Keith Frederick William Dunn, C.B.E., and has issue
living, (by 1st marriage) Michael, *b.* 1938. *Residence,*
Bencombe House, Uley, Gloucestershire.

The 1st baronet, Sir Frank Beauchamp, C.B.E. (son of the late William Beauchamp, of Norton
Hall, near Bath), was Col. in Army, a D.L. for Somerset, and High Sheriff of Somerset 1926.

PROCTOR-BEAUCHAMP, Creation (G.B.) 1745, of Langley Park, Norfolk.
[Pronounced **"Proctor-Beecham."**]

Always faithful.

Sir CHRISTOPHER RADSTOCK PROCTOR-BEAU-
CHAMP, 9th *Baronet*; *b.* Jan. 30th, 1935; *s.* his
father, the *Rev.* Sir IVOR CUTHBERT, *MB, BCh,*
1971; ed. at Rugby, and Trin. Coll., Camb.
(MA): *m.* 1965, Rosalind Emily Margot, da. of
Gerald Percival Wainwright, of 135, Marina,
St. Leonard's-on-Sea, and has issue.

Arms—Argent, a chevron between three martlets sable.
Crest—On a mount vert, a greyhound sejant argent, spotted
brown, collared or.

Residence,—The White House, Harpford, nr. Sidmouth, Devon.

Sons living—CHARLES BARCLAY, *b.* July 7th, 1969.——
Robert Ivor, *b.* 1971.
Daughter living—Rosalind Caroline, *b.* 1967.
Brother living—Anthony Hazlerigg, *b.* 1940; ed. at
Monkton Combe Sch. and at Trin. Coll., Camb. (MA);
AMICE: *m.* 1965, Anne Elise, da. of the late Rev.
Thomas Hewitt, V. of St. George's, Worthing, and has
issue living, Guy James, *b.* 1967,—Julian Thomas, *b.*
1968,—Claire Alexandra, *b.* 1970.
Sister living—Rosemary Jean, *b.* 1936: *m.* 1964, Thomas
Henry Geake, MA, AMIMech.E., and has issue living,
William Beauchamp, *b.* 1968,—Elisabeth Marjorie, *b.*
1965,—Helen Mary, *b.* 1967.

Uncle living (son of 7th Baronet)—Basil Ralph, *b.* 1906; ed. at Marlborough, and at Toronto Univ.
(Diploma in Agriculture 1932): *m.* 1st, 1932 (m. diss. 1957) Joan, da. of Tom Storey; 2ndly,
1957, Diana, da. of Lt.-Col. Bernard H. Elliott, RA (ret.), of Goring House, North Woodchester,
nr. Stroud, Gloucestershire and has issue living, (by 1st m.) Nicholas (162, High St., Teddington,,
Middx.), *b.* 1935); 2ndly, FPWI: *m.* 1964, Pauline, da. of Jacob de Mos, of Rotterdam, and
has issue living, Alison de Mos *b.* 1965, Sarah Jane *b.* 1966, Victoria Isobel *b.* 1967,—Carol
Margot, *b.* 1933: *m.* 1958, Fl.-Lt. Claude de Pina D. Swain of 1, Dumas Close, Bicester, Oxon.,
and has issue living, Charles de Pina Beauchamp *b.* 1959, Claudia Fenella *b.* 1961,—Elisabeth
Waldegrave, *b.* 1934.—(by 2nd m.) Sophie Joy, *b.* 1958. *Residences,* Eastgate House, Narberth,
Dyfed; Ty Castell, Grosvenor Hill, Cardigan.

Widow living of 8th Baronet—CAROLINE MURIEL (*Caroline Lady Proctor-Beauchamp*), da. of the
late Frank Densham [B. Hazlerigg; colls.]: *m.* 1933, the Rev. Sir Ivor Cuthbert Proctor-
Beauchamp, MB, BCh, 8th Bt., who *d.* 1971. *Residence,* 16, Strand Court, Topsham, Exeter.

Collateral Branches living.

Issue of the late Sir Edward Beauchamp [2nd son of the late Rev. William **Henry**
Beauchamp (infra)], who was *cr.* a *Baronet* 1911.
See Beauchamp, Bt., *cr.* 1911.

Granddaughter of the late Rev. William Henry Beauchamp, 2nd son of 3rd
baronet :—
Issue of the late Rev. Canon Henry Woodrooffe Beauchamp, *b.* 1852, *d.* 1915 *m.* 1876,
Katherine Mary who *d.* 1950, da. of the late Rev. Charles Snell [Dashwood, Bt., of
Kirtlington, colls.] :—
Sybil Katherine, *b.* 1889: *m.* 1920, as his second wife, Brigadier Frederick Cromie De Butts, CB,
DSO, MC. *Residence,* The Old Vicarage, Gt. Gaddesden, Hemel Hempstead, Herts.

Grandchildren of Reginald Percy Beauchamp (infra):—
Issue of the late Percy Tremayne Beauchamp, *b.* 1908, *d.* 1959: *m.* 1935, Eileen Alice,
who *d.* 1964, da. of Arthur Edward Croft:—
Anthony Tremayne, *b.* 1937: *m.* 1961, Nancy Ann Jones, of Muddy Creek, Tas., and has issue living,
Christopher Tremayne, *b.* 1964,—Wendy Ann, *b.* 1965.——Suzanne Elizabeth, *b.* 1946.

Grandchildren of the late Robert Beauchamp, 3rd son of 3rd baronet;—
Issue of the late Reginald Percy Beauchamp, *b.* 1873, *d.* 1944: *m.* 1904, Malvina Blanche
Natalie, who *d.* 1967, da. of Jonathan Purdy Plummer:—
Geoffrey Frank (El-Retiro, Rosevears, W. Tamar, Tasmania), *b.* 1914: *m.* 1950, Dorothy Vernon,
who *d.* 1970, da. of Vernon Thomas Lewis, of 9, Hilda Cres., Hawthorne, Vic., and has issue
living, Pamela Nerida, *b.* 1952.——Vonda Laura (5, Queens Av., Vaucluse, Sydney, Aust.): *m.*
1933, Ronsley Miles Ponsonby, who *d.* 1964.——Nerida Nadine (El-Retiro, Rosevears, W.
Tamar, Tasmania) *b.* 1916: *m.* 1935 (divorce 1943), Ronald Breadabane Postle.

Grandchildren of the late Edward Hayes Beauchamp (infra):—
Issue of the late Edward Guy Beauchamp, *b.* 1885, *d.* 1966: *m.* 1918, Louise France
Caroline, da. of the late A. T. Haultain, of Napier, NZ:—
Trevor Haultain (54, Cook St., Howick, Auckland, NZ), *b.* 1919; Capt. 2nd NZEF; 1939-45
War in S.-W. Pacific and Italy: *m.* 1952, Beryl Irene, da. of Herbert Maxwell, of Otorahanga,
King Country, NZ, and has issue living, Robin Max, *b.* 1953,—Christine, *b.* 1960.

Issue of the late Herbert Rolf Haultain Beauchamp, DCM, *b.* 1890, *d.* 1968: *m.* 1st, 1918
Ida, who *d.* 1952, da. of the late John Stevenson, of Naumai, Wanganui, NZ; 2ndly
1955, Mary Joyce, da. of the late Capt. James Stevenson Hempton, of Dunedin, NZ.
(By 1st m.) John Proctor (91, Deep Creek Rd., Torbay, Auckland, 10, NZ), *b.* 1923: 1939-45 War
with New Zealand Forces: *m.* 1947, Barbara, da. of Oliver Coupland, of 18, Grey St., Wanganui,
NZ, and has issue living, Warwick Rolf, *b.* 1952: *m.* 1974, Jan, da. of Lester Wintere, of Parr Terr.,
Milford, NZ —Michael Douglas, *b.* 1957,—Bruce Proctor, *b.* 1963,—Margaret Anne, *b.* 1947: *m.*
1974, Stewart Rankin,—Jane Allison, *b.* 1950: *m.* 1974, Alan Stewart Davis,—Elizabeth Claire,
b. 1955: *m.* 1974, Peter David Anderson.——Jill, *b.* 1926: *m.* 1949, Ronald Parkin, of 26, Huatok
St., New Plymouth, NZ, and has issue living, Jan, *b.* 1952,—Carolyn, *b.* 1950,—Andrea, *b.* 1954.

Granddaughter of the late Capt. Edward Halhed Beauchamp, RN, 3rd son of
George Edward Beauchamp, 2nd son of 2nd baronet:—
Issue of the late Edward Hayes Beauchamp, *b,* 1852, *d.* 1897: *m.* 1881, Elinor L., who *d.*
1926, da. of the late Col. T. M. Haultain, of Auckland, New Zealand:—
Esme Constance: *m.* 1912, George Herbert Ussher, MD, FRCS, and has issue living, Alison Beau-
champ, *b.* 1913,—Geoffrey Arland, *b.* 1915,—Kenneth Edgeworth, *b.* 1925,—Colin George Beau-
champ, *b.* 1929,—Esme Stuart, *b.* 1917,—Shirley Haultain, *b.* 1920.   *Residence,* Faillie, Sefton St.,
Timaru, New Zealand.

Grandchildren of the late Herbert Lloyd Beauchamp, son of Capt. Edward
Halhed Beauchamp, RN (ante):—
Issue of the late Hugh Edward Beauchamp, *b.* 1886, *d.* 1962: *m.* 1st, 1907, Grace Ethel,
da. of F. Quistorf, of Santa Cruz, California, USA; 2ndly, 19—, Tekla, who *d.* 19—, da.
of Carl Viborg, of Stockholm, Sweden:—
(By 1st m.) Dorothy Margaret, *b.* 1909: *m.* 1931, Harry Eugene Lennon.

Issue of the late Herbert Cecil Beauchamp, *b.* 1888, *d.* 1969: *m.* 1913, Dora, who *d.* 1968,
da. of H. Dohrmann, of Reinbeck, Iowa:—
David Dohrmann (830, Overhill Drive, Redding, Cal., USA 96001), *b.* 1916; F/O Air Transport
Command, US Army Air Corps: *m.* 1941, Jean Anita, da. of Wade Greening Moores, of Redding,
Cal., USA, and has issue living, Mark David Beauchamp, *b.* 1952,—Sarah Caroline, *b.* 1954.

Granddaughter of the late Henry Champion Beauchamp, yst. son of the late
George Edward Beauchamp (ante):—
Issue of the late James Lloyd Hobart Beauchamp, *b.* 1862, *d.* 1927: *m.* 1891, Maria
Radford Knight, da. of the late Augustus George Stead:—
Maria Georgiana, *b.* 1892: *m.* 1928, Robert Desmond Carruthers, and has issue living, Marie Lucy
Beauchamp, *b.* 1930.   *Residence,*

Grandchildren of the late Capt. Willoughby George Beauchamp, son of Robert
Willoughby James Beauchamp, 4th son of Henry William Johnson Beau-
champ, el. son of William Henry Beauchamp, 3rd son of 1st baronet:—
Issue of the late Capt. Willoughby Greaves Beauchamp, CBE, VRD, Ceylon, RNVR,
b. 1890, *d.* 1960: *m.* 1912, Kathleen Alice (Little Hollow, 25, Church St., Wiveliscombe,
Taunton), da. of the late Dr. W. B. Benison, of King's Heath, Worcestershire:—
Kathleen Patricia, *b.* 1913; formerly Junior Com. A.T.S.: *m.* 1947, Alfred Thomas Morant, of
West Braynes, 25, Church St., Wiveliscombe, Taunton, Somerset, and has issue living, Wil-
loughby Vivian Paul, *b.* 1950,—Julian Philip, *b.* 1953.—Auriol Ann Melicent, *b.* 1948.——
Elaine Joyce, *b.* 1916: *m.* 1st, 1936, Edward Gordon Windus, from whom she obtained a divorce
1954; 2ndly, 1955, Anthony Edward Davy Windus, of Town House, Holcombe Rogus, Welling-
ton, Som., and has issue living, (by 1st m.) Michael Edward Beauchamp, *b.* 1937: *m.* 1965,
Evelyn Vera Pugh, and has issue living, Dirk Edward Beauchamp *b.* 1966, Fiona Elaine Beau-
champ *b.* 1968,—Stefanie Gail Elaine, *b.* 1940: *m.* 1959, Robin Outram, of Savani Estate, P.O.
Handi Hills, Kenya, and has issue living, Stephen Jeremy *b.* 1960, Christopher James *b.* 1961,
Suzanne Nicola *b.* 1963.——Barbara Meredith, *b.* 1923: *m.* 1943, Ronald Arthur Lushington, late
Maj. Indian Army, and has issue living, Christopher Saxton, *b.* 1947,—Madeleine Dawn, *b.* 1945:
m. 1972, Raynes Lloyd Sherwell, of Meadowend, Bryanston, S. Africa.   *Residence,*—Old Inn,
Langford Budville, Wellington, Som.

Issue of the late Com. Harold Charles Beauchamp, Roy. Indian Navy, *b.* 1891, *d.* 1942: *m.*
1918, Olive (16, Evelyn Close, Cheltenham), da. of the late Maurice Smelt Duke, MRCS,
of 272, Kennington Park Rd., SE:—
Peter Clare, *b.* 1928; ed. at Cheltenham.——Betty (Elisabeth), *b.* 1922: *m.* 1946, James Paten
Cooper, late Maj. King's African Rifles, and has issue living, Charles James Beauchamp Douglas,
b. 1954,—Caroline Elisabeth Beauchamp Paten, *b.* 1949,—Rosemary Deborah Beauchamp, *b.*
1951.   *Residence,* 18, Clarence Hill, Dartmouth, Devon.

Issue of the late Cdr. Lawrence King Beauchamp, RN, *b.* 1900, *d.* 1966: *m.* 1924, Helen
Mary Victoria (8, Evelyn Close, Sandy Lane, Charlton Kings, Cheltenham), da. of the
late Robert Edward Stuart, solicitor, of Gannicox, Stroud, Glos.:—
Julian Lawrence Stuart (Pear Tree Cottage, Bratton, Wilts.) *b.* 1928; MInst. AM, AMBIM, Cdr.
RN; ed. at Kelly Coll.: *m.* 1st, 1951 (m. diss. 1966), Jennifer, da. of the late Harry George
Parkes, of Wolverhampton; 2ndly, 1968, Isobel Mary, da. of the late Thomas Layfield, of
Beckenham, and widow of Cdr. Peter Angus Fickling, RN, and has issue living (by 1st m.),
Timothy Christopher Julian, *b.* 1952; ed. at Kelly Coll., and Birmingham Univ.,—Caroline
Susan, *b.* 1954,—(by 2nd m.) Fenella Jane Isobel, *b.* 1970.——Sheila Frances, *b.* 1925: *m.* 1st,
1946, Jack Eric Jones, who *d.* 1955; 2ndly, 1963, Douglas George Horace Frank, QC, of Little
Northover, Akeley, Buckingham, and has issue living, (by 1st m.) Roger Beauchamp Spencer,
b. 1947: *m.* 1973, Marilyn McGowan, of San Francisco, USA,—Andrew Julian Stuart, *b.* 1950:
m. 1974, Margaret Atkinson, of Edinburgh,—(by 2nd m.) Joanna Helen Louise, *b.* 1965,—Amelia
Phoebe, *b.* 1967.——Daphne Helen Stuart, *b.* 1932.

Grandchildren of the late Willoughby James Beauchamp (ante):—
Issue (by 1st marriage) of the late Capt. Willoughby George Beauchamp, *b.* 1864, *d.* 1922;
  m. 1st, 1888, Emily, who *d.* 1910, da. of the Rev. Joshua Greaves, formerly V. of Great
  Missenden; 2ndly, 1911, Emily Elizabeth, who *d.* 1929, el. da. of the late William Henry
  Herbert, of Havenfield Lodge, Great Missenden:—
Evelyn Frances Joyce, *b.* 1903: *m.* 1928, Richard Feltrim Fagan, MB, BS, DPH, and has issue
  living, Richard Beauchamp Feltrim (of Sauls Farm, Seven Hills Rd., Iver Heath, Bucks),
  b. 1932; ed. at Wellington: *m.* 1957, Gillian, only da. of F. W. Barnes, of South Park House,
  Gerrards Cross, Bucks, and has issue living, Patrick Richard Feltrim *b.* 1959, Timothy Feltrim
  b. 1963, Sheena Feltrim *b.* 1961,—John Willoughby Feltrim, *b.* 1936; ed. at Wellington. *Residence,* Watersplash Farm, Fulmer, Bucks.

Issue of the late Henry King Beauchamp, C.I.E., *b.* 1866, *d.* 1907: *m.* 1897, Mabel, who
  d. 1948, da. of the late H. Hammond-Spencer, of Glendaragh, Teignmouth, S. Devon:—
Henry Rex (Hillside, Bower's Hill, Redlynch, Salisbury, Wilts.), *b.* 1906; ed. at Uppingham, and
  RMA; Brig. RAPC; formerly Capt. R. Leicestershire Regt.; 1939-45 War: *m.* 1st, 1937 (divorce
  1947), Moira Helen, da. of the late G. H. Normand, of Edinburgh; 2ndly, 1954, Mrs. Elizabeth
  Margaret Dobson, da. of A. H. Ford-Moore, of Salisbury, and has issue living (by 1st m.), David
  Fitzgerald, *b.* 1940: *m.* 1971, Victoria Mary, da. of James Clark, of Connecticut, USA, and has
  issue living, Gillian Alexandra *b.* 1973, Catriona Clare *b.* 1974.

**Issue of the late Vernon Francis Beauchamp, *b.* 1869; *d.* 1949: *m.* 1897, Amy, who *d.*
  1948, da. of the late William Henry Herbert, of Great Missenden, Bucks :—**
Francis William Herbert (1020, Union St., San Francisco, Cal. 94133; University (San Francisco)
  Club), *b.* 1898: *m.* 1st, 1927, Anna, who *d.* 1970, da. of the late William H. Lamprecht, of
  Cleveland, Ohio, USA; 2ndly, 1971, Mrs. Catharine Newhall, da. of the late Edward Fitz-
  Randolph Vail, of Santa Barbara, Cal.——Alan Charles Douglas (Route 2, Orono, Toronto,
  Ont., Canada), *b.* 1901: *m.* 1944, Olga, da. of the late W. K. Rhodes, and has issue living, Hugh
  Alan Vernon, *b.* 1945.——Lucien Willoughby, *b.* 1903: *m.* 1937, Nancy Knight, da. of
  Bradford Richards, and has issue living, Peter Willoughby (15, Essex St., Brockton, Mass.,
  USA), *b.* 1943: *m.* 1970, Stacy Ann, da. of Joseph Maurice Scanlon, of Middleboro', Mass.,—
  Sandra, *b.* 1945. *Residence,* 9, Sunset Drive, South Easton, Mass., USA.

Sir William Beauchamp-Proctor, 1st Bt., was MP for Middlesex 1747-68 which latter name he
added by Act of Parliament in compliance with the terms of the will of his maternal uncle, George
Proctor of Langley Park, Norfolk. The 4th Bt. assumed by Roy. licence 1852 the surname of
Proctor-Beauchamp in lieu of Beauchamp-Proctor. The 6th Bt., Col. Sir Horace George, CB,
Norfolk Regt. was killed in action during 1915 War. The Rev. Sir Montagu Harry Proctor-
Beauchamp, 7th Bt., was a Missionary in China 1885-1936.

BEAUMONT, Creation (E.) 1661, of Stoughton Grange, Leicestershire.

Exalted, not elated.

Sir GEORGE HOWLAND FRANCIS BEAU-
MONT, 12th *Baronet*; *b.* Sept. 24th, 1924; *s.* his
father, *Sir* GEORGE ARTHUR HAMILTON, 1933;
ed. at Stowe; formerly Warrant Officer
Australian Army; is patron of one living;
N.-W. Europe 1944-45 with Coldstream
Guards, and as Lieut. 60th Rifles: *m.* 1st, 1949
(marriage annulled 1951), Barbara, da. of
William Singleton; 2ndly, 1963, Henrietta
Anne, da. of the late Dr. Arthur Waymouth,
and has issue by 2nd m.

    Arms—Azure, semée of fleurs-de-lis, a lion rampant
or.   **Crest**—On a chapeau azure, semée of fleurs-de-lis and
turned up ermine, a lion passant or.
    Address—Duntrune Nurseries, Deddington Mill,
Deddington, Oxon.

Daughters living—by 2nd marriage—Georgina Brienne
Arabella, *b.* 1967.——Francesca Renée Henrietta, (twin)
b. 1967.
Sister living—Eleanor Brienne, *b.* 1927: *m.* 1954, Major
Hugh Abdy Collins, The Buffs. *Residence,* Karen,
Kenya.
Widow living of 11th Baronet—RENÉE MURIEL, da.
of Maj.-Gen. Sir Edward Northey, G.C.M.G., C.B.:
m. 1st, 1923, Sir George Arthur Hamilton Beaumont,
11th baronet, who *d.* 1933; 2ndly, 1934, Capt. Oswald
M. D. Bell, who *d.* 1949. *Residence,* The Old Mill, Woolstone, Faringdon, Berks.

Collateral Branch living.

Granddaughter of the late Francis Henry Beaumont, son of the late William
Francis Bertie Beaumont, brother of 8th baronet:—
Issue of the late Major Francis Montagu Beaumont, *b.* 1857, *d.* 1936: *m.* 1904, Sybil Anne,
  who *d.* 1949, da. of Higford Higford, formerly of Hartsfield, Betchworth:—
Crystal Katherine, *b.* 1908: *m.* 1930, Leslie James Earl, of Henspark,Dulverton, Somerset, and
  has issue living, Diana, *b.* 1931: *m.* 1st, 1952 (marriage dissolved 1959); 2ndly, 1959, David
  Bassett, of West Woodburn, East Anstey, Tiverton, Devon, and has issue living, (by 1st marriage) Janice *b.* 1953, (by 2nd m.) Earl Jonathan *b.* 1960, Gwenda Margaret *b.* 1962,—Rosemary
  Margaret, *b.* 1934: *m.* 1953, Vernon Hammett, of West Anstey, S. Molton, Devon, and has
  issue living, Peter *b.* 1962, Joanna *b.* 1960,—Lesley Anne, *b.* 1950.

This family is descended in a direct paternal line from John de Brienne, King of Jerusalem
and Emperor of Constantinople, and his 2nd son, Louis, married Agnes, heiress of Beaumont, in France, whose sons took the name of Beaumont. Henry, the 4th son of Louis and
Agnes seated himself in England, and became Earl of Buchan, in Scotland. His son John,
2nd Lord Beaumont, married Eleanor, 5th daughter of Henry Plantagenet, Earl of Lancaster,
grandson to King Henry III. On the death of William, 2nd Viscount Beaumont, the eldest branch
became extinct in the male line [see B. Beaumont]. A younger branch (descended from Thomas

Beaumont, second son of 4th Baron Beaumont) settled at Cole Orton, *temp.* Edward IV., of which was Nicholas Beaumont, who died 1585, leaving, besides other issue, two sons : (1) Sir Henry, whose son, Sir Thomas, was created a baronet in 1619, and Viscount Beaumont, of Swords, Dublin, in 1622, which titles became extinct on the death of the 3rd viscount, in 1702 ; (2) Sir Thomas, of Stoughton, grandfather of Sir Thomas, the 1st baronet, from whom is descended the present baronet. Sir Thomas, 1st Bt., was M.P. for Leicestershire, and Sir Henry, 2nd Bt., was also M.P. for Leicestershire 1679-87. Sir George, 4th Bt., represented Leicester in Parliament 1702-37, and the 7th Bt., Sir George Howland, sat for Beeralston 1790-96.

WRIXON-BECHER, Creation (U.K.) 1831, of Ballygiblin, Cork.

Sir WILLIAM FANE WRIXON-BECHER, *M.C.*, 5th *Baronet ; b.* Sept. 7th, 1915 ; *s.* his father, *Sir* EUSTACE WILLIAM WINDHAM, 1934; ed. at Harrow, and at Magdalene Coll., Camb. ; is Lieut. and temporary Major Rifle Brig. (Supplementary Reserve) ; European War 1939-45 in Middle East and Italy (twice wounded, M.C.) : *m.* 1st, 1946 (marriage dissolved 1960), the Hon. Ursula Vanda Maud (BRIDGEWATER), 2nd da. of 4th Baron Vivian ; 2ndly, 1960, Yvonne Margaret (MOSTYN), da. of A. Stuart Johnson, of Henshall Hall, Congleton, Cheshire, and has issue by 1st marriage.

Arms—Vair, argent and gules, on a canton or a **stag's** head coupéd sable. **Crest**—Out of a ducal coronet or, a demi-lion ermine gorged with a plain collar vair.
Residence—16, Wilton Place, S.W.1. *Clubs*—White's, M.C.C.

Son living—By 1st marriage—JOHN WILLIAM MICHAEL, *b.* Sept. 29th, 1950; ed. at Harrow.

He lives twice who lives well.

Daughter living—Susannah Elizabeth (Edmonston Lodge, Biggar, Lanarks) *b.* 1948: *m.* 1970, Gordon M. A. P. Whitson, who *d.* 1974, and has issue living, James Alexander, *b.* 1973.

Sisters living—Aileen, *b.* 1910.——Sheila, *b.* 1913.——Rosemary, *b.* 1914: *m.* 1938, Cyril Jeremy Taylor Watson who *d.* 1974, having obtained a divorce 1948. *Residence*, Rose Cottage, Barlavington, Petworth, Sussex.

The 1st baronet, Sir William Wrixon, MP for Mallow, assumed by Roy. licence in 1831, his mother's maiden name of Becher. She was Mary, da. of John Townsend Becher of Annisgrove, co. Cork, and sister and heir of Henry Becher of Creagh. Their ancestor, Fane Becher, was granted lands in co. Cork 1588.

BECKETT, Creation (U.K.) 1921, of Kirkdale Manor, Nawton, N. Riding of Yorkshire.

Sir MARTYN GERVASE BECKETT, *M.C.*, 2nd *Baronet ; b.* Nov. 6th, 1918 ; *s.* his father, *the Hon. Sir* (WILLIAM) GERVASE, 1937; ed. at Eton, and at Trin. Coll., Camb. (BA); RIBA; Capt. Welsh Guards; 1939-45 War (MC): *m.* 1941, the Hon. Priscilla Léonie Helen Brett, da. of 3rd Viscount Esher, and has issue.

Arms—Gules, a fesse between three boars' heads coupéd erminois, a crescent for difference. **Crest**—A boar's **head** coupéd or, pierced by a cross patée fitchée erect gules.
Residences—3, St. Alban's Grove, W.8; Kirkdale Farm, Nawton, Yorks.

Sons living—RICHARD GERVASE, *b.* March 27th, 1944.——Jeremy Rupert, *b.* 1952.

Daughter living—Lucy Caroline, *b.* 1942: *m.* 1st, 1962 (m. diss. 1969), Adrian Whitfield; 2ndly, 1970, John Warrack, of Beck House, Rievaulx, nr. Helmsley, York., and has issue living (by 1st m.) Teresa, *b.* 1963,—Emily, *b.* 1965,—(by 2nd m.), Benedict John, *b.* 1971,—Christopher Martyn, *b.* 1974.

Half-Sister living—Ann Prunella (Flat 21, 27, Onslow Sq., SW7), *b.* 1907: *m.* 1936, Harry Bathurst Norman, GM, MD, who *d.* 1966, and has issue living, Paul Bathurst (Brundon Hall, Sudbury, Suffolk), *b.* 1937: *m.* 1960, Susan Mary, yr. da. of Charles Orbell, of The Hermitage, Clare, Suffolk, and has issue living, Hal Charles *b.* 1969, Arabella Harriet Bathurst, *b.* 1961, Teresa Prunella *b.* 1963, Deborah Mary *b.* 1966,—Harriet Rose, *b.* 1939, —Deirdre Nell, *b.* 1946: *m.* 1st, 1964 (m. diss. 1970), Luciano Billi, of Florence; 2ndly, 1971, Nicholas Paul Beresford-Jones, of The Sett, Leavenheath, Colchester, Essex, and has issue living (by 1st m.) Selina Elizabeth *b.* 1964 (by 2nd m.), Alexandra Juliet *b.* 1973.

To benefit the State.

The 1st baronet, the Hon. Sir (William) Gervase Beckett (second son of the late William Beckett-Denison, and brother of 2nd Baron Grimthorpe), was Principal Proprietor and Editor-in-Ch. of *Saturday Review*, and M.P. for Whitby Div. of N. Riding of Yorkshire (C) 1906-18, for Scarborough and Whitby Div. thereof 1918-22, and for N. Div. of Leeds 1923-9.

PASTON-BEDINGFELD, Creation (E.) 1660, of Oxburgh, Norfolk.

Despising earthly things I look only towards the sun.

Sir EDMUND GEORGE FELIX PASTON-BED-
INGFELD, 9th *Baronet ; b.* June 2nd, 1915 ; *s.* his father,
Sir HENRY EDWARD, 1941 ; ed. at Oratory Sch., and
at New Coll., Oxford ; is a co-heir to Barony of
Grandison, and Major Welsh Guards ; European War
1939-45 (wounded) : *m.* 1st, 1942 (marriage dis-
solved 1953), Joan Lynette, who *d.* 1965, da. of
Edgar G. Rees, of Llwyneithin, Llanelly; 2ndly,
1957, Agnes Danos, who *d.* 1974, da. of the late
Miklos Gluck, of Budapest, Hungary; 3rdly, 1975,
Mrs. Peggy Hannaford-Hill, of Fort Victoria,
Rhodesia and has issue by 1st m.

𝕬rms—Quarterly, 1st and 4th ermine, an eagle, display gules
Bedingfeld ; 2nd and 3rd argent, six fleur-de-lis, **three,** two, and one
azure, a chief indented or, *Paston.* 𝕮rest—1st, an **eagle displayed**
or, *Bedingfeld*; 2nd, a griffin sejant wings elevated or gorged
with a collar gules, therefrom a line held in the beak and terminating in a ring of the last, *Paston.* 𝕭abge—A fetter lock.
        Seat—Oxburgh Hall, King's Lynn, Norfolk. *Residence*—
15, Highgate Close, N6.

Son living—By 1st m. HENRY EDGAR (Paston House, Litcham,
King's Lynn, Norfolk; Bath Club), *b.* Dec. 7th, 1943; ed. at
Ampleforth; Chartered Surveyor: *m.* 1968, Mary, da. of the
late Brig. Robert Denis Ambrose, CIE, OBE, MC, and has
issue living, Richard Edmund Ambrose, *b.* Feb. 8th, 1975,—
Katherine Mary, *b.* 1969,—Charlotte Alexandra, *b.* 1971.
Daughter living—By 1st marriage—Alexandra Winifred Mary, *b.* 1947: *m.* 1970, J. Michael
Yearsley, of Moss Side Cottage, Over Tabley, Knutsford, Cheshire, and has issue living, Nicola,
b. 1971.
Sisters living—Margaret Mary Anastasia *b.* 1905.——Frances Mary Teresa, *b.* 1919: *m.* 1st, 1949,
Frank Douglas Playford, who *d.* 1956; 2ndly, 1957, Maitland Maitland Nimmo, and has issue
living. *Residences,* Oxburgh Hall, King's Lynn, Norfolk; White River, Transvaal, S. Africa.
Widow living of 8th Baronet—SYBIL (*Dowager Lady Paston-Bedingfeld*), el. da. of the late Henry
Alexander Lyne Stephens, of Grove House, Roehampton: *m.* 1904, Sir Henry Edward Paston-
Bedingfeld, 8th baronet, who *d.* 1941. *Residence*, Oxburgh Hall, King's Lynn, Norfolk.

Collateral Branch living.
        Issue of the late Francis Augustus Bedingfeld, 6th son of 7th baronet, *b.* 1874,
        d. 1950: *m.* 1926, Dorothy Mary Hooker, who *d.* 1932:—
Rev. Richard Francis, *b.* 1930.——Elizabeth Mary Teresa, *b.* 1928; is a nun of Convent of Loretto,
Pretoria, S. Africa.
        This family took its name from Bedingfield, Suffolk. Sir Edmund Bedingfeld (*d.* 1446) acquired
the lordship of Oxburgh on marriage with Margaret, sister and co-heir of Robert de Tuddenham.
During the civil wars Sir Henry Bedingfeld, Knt., besides being imprisoned in the Tower, lost
£47,000 in the King's cause. His son claimed this amount of Charles II., but that monarch, being
unable to pay the money, created him a baronet. The 6th baronet assumed, in 1830, by Roy.
licence, the additional surname of Paston, having married Margaret Anne, da. and heir of Edward
Paston of Appleton, Norfolk.

BEECHAM, Creation (U.K.) 1914, of Ewanville, Huyton, co. Palatine of Lancaster.

Nothing without labour.

Sir ADRIAN BEECHAM, 3rd *Baronet ;*
b. Sept. 3rd, 1904 ; *s.* his father, *Sir* THOMAS,
C.H. 1961 ; Mus.B. Durham 1926 : *m.* 1939,
Barbara Joyce, da. of the late Edward Cairn,
and has issue.

𝕬rms—Per fesse gules and sable, a fesse nebuly **plain**
cotised, in chief an escallop between two martlets and the **like**
in base all or. 𝕮rest—A swan's head erased argent, beaked
gules, holding an escallop and between two escallops or.

        Residence,—Compton Scorpion Manor, Shipston-on-
Stour.

Sons living—JOHN STRATFORD ROLAND, *b.* April
21st, 1940.——Robert Adrian, *b.* 1942: *m.* 1969, Daphne
Mattinson, and has issue living, Michael John, *b.* 1972,—
Judith Mary, *b.* 1970.

Daughter living—Jane (Longdon Manor, Shipston-on-Stour),
b. 1945: *m.* 1969, Frederick Charles Brabyn, and has issue
living, Adrian Alexander Benjamin, *b.* 1972.

Brother living—Thomas Welles, *b.* 1909 ; formerly Capt.
R.E. ; is an Asso. Member of Institution of Structural
Engineers : *m.* 1937, Mozelle, da. of the late Edward Cairn,
and has issue living, Thomas Richard, *b.* 1944,—Henry
John, *b.* 1947,—Ann Margaret, *b.* 1949,—Elizabeth
Marion (twin), *b.* 1949: *m.* 1969, Andrew George Richard
Birtwell, of The Corner House, Stourton, Shipston-on-
Stour, and has issue living, Emily Jane *b.* 1970. *Residence,*
Tidmington House, Shipston-on-Stour.
Aunts living (daughters of 1st baronet)—Edith (Avon Lodge, Little Common, Bexhill, Sussex),
b. 1884: *m.* 1910, Frederick Duke Duke-Woolley, MRCS, who *d.* 1937, late Lt.-Col. RAMC
(Special Reserve), and has issue living, Hilary Beecham, *DFC, RAFVR* (Nadur, Gozo, Malta,
GC); *b.* 1912; BA; ARIVA: *m.* 1st, 1938 (m. diss. 1946), the Hon. Elizabeth Alice Cecilia (JOLY
DE LOTBINIÈRE), da. of 4th Baron Hylton; 2ndly, 1947 (m. diss. 1970), Bridget Mary, da.
of the late Philip Melland Armitage; 3rdly, 1970, Mrs. Paula Mary Longmate, da. of the late
Frederick Edwin George Speke, and has issue living, (by 2nd m.) Amanda Clare *b.* 1949,—
Raymond Myles Beecham, *DSO, DFC, b.* 1916; Gp. Capt. RAF (ret.); 1939-45 War (DFC and
Bar, DSO, American DFC); DSO 1943: *m.* 1939, Jocelyn Elizabeth Alice de Satge, who *d.* 1966,
da. of the late Lt.-Col. Cecil Garnett, and has issue living, a son *b.* 1952, Christine Diana Nina *b.*
1940, Rosemary Edith Cecil *b.* 1943, Joanna Sylvia *b.* 1948.——Jessie, *b.* 1886: *m.* 1909, Maj.
Leonce Delphin, DSO, MC, who *d.* 1932.——Elsie Olive, *b.* 1889: *m.* 1915, William Senior Ellis.
——Army Christine, *b.* 1894: *m.* 1st, 1917, Reginald John Wrathall, OTC, who. *d.* (on ser.) 1918;
2ndly, 19—, Rex Walker, who *d.* 19—. Residence,

Mother living—Utica, da. of Dr. Stuart Welles, of New York, U.S.A. : *m.* 1903, Sir Thomas Beecham, C.H., 2nd baronet, who *d.* 1961, having obtained a divorce in Idaho, U.S.A., 1943. *Residence,* Clopton House, Stratford-on-Avon.

Collateral Branch living.

Issue of the late Henry Beecham, 2nd son of 1st baronet, *b.* 1888, *d.* 1947 : *m.* 1914, Ethel Anne, who *d.* 1951, da. of Herbert Baxter, of Keyham Hall, Leicestershire :—

Joseph Michael, *M.B.E., b.* 1917 ; European War **1939-45**, as Major R.A. (M.B.E.) ; M.B.E. (Mil.) 1944: *m.* 1939, Sylvia, only child of the late Frank B. Nathan, of 14, Charleville Mansions, W14, and has issue living, Valerie Anne, *b.* 1941. *Residence,* Trove House, Long Crendon, Aylesbury.——Henry Robert Derrick, *b.* 1921: *m.* 1st, 1943, Annie Ellen (who obtained a divorce 1949), da. of the late Thomas John King; 2ndly, 1951, Shiela, da. of Bertram John Martin, of Bushey Heath, Herts., and has issue living, (by 1st marriage) Jasmine Heather, *b.* 1944,—Priscilla Rosamunde, *b.* 1947,—Susan Jane WHITHEAR, *b.* 1949; adopted 1950, by W. A. Whithear, of 84, Larchwood Drive, Englefield Green, Egham, Surrey, whose surname she assumed.——Paul (Hollybush Farmhouse, Ilmington, Shipston-on-Stour, Warks.) *b.* 1923: *m.* 1952, Mary, da. of William Arthur, of Pill Lawn, Barnstaple, Devon, and has issue living, William Henry Mark, *b.* 1954,—Hugh Joseph, *b.* 1957,—Matthew Arthur, *b.* 1965,—Sarah Caroline, *b.* 1953,—Hannah Charlotte, *b.* 1956,—Emma Ruth, *b.* 1960.——Helen Audrey, *b.* 1915; MA Oxon. 1949. *Residence,* 26, Park Town, Oxford.

Grandchildren of the late Henry Beecham (ante):—
Issue of the late Christopher Beecham, *b.* 1925, *d.* 1970: *m.* 1951, Kathleen Elizabeth (Manor Cottage, Eynesbury, St. Neots, Hunts.) da. of Maj. Bertie Orme Collis, of Pinner, Middx.:—
Philip Henry Orme, *b.* 1962.——Diana Mary, *b.* 1953.——Honor June, *b.* 1955.——Jennifer Kate, *b.* 1957.——Penelope Carol, *b.* 1950.——Sally Helen, *b.* 1965.
The 1st baronet, Sir Joseph Beecham, was the well-known pill manufacturer, of St. Helens, a Director of A. and F. Pears (Limited), and Mayor of St. Helens 1899-1900, and 1910-11-12. The 2nd baronet, *Sir* Thomas Beecham, C.H., the well-known Musical Conductor, was knighted in 1916.

BEEVOR, Creation (G.B.) 1784, of Hethel, Norfolk.

Sir THOMAS AGNEW BEEVOR, 7th *Baronet; b.* Jan. 6th, 1929 ; *s.* his father, *Com. Sir* THOMAS LUBBOCK, R.N., 1943 ; ed. at Eton, and at Magdalene Coll., Camb.: *m.* 1st 1957, (m. diss. 1965), Barbara Clare, yst. da. of Capt. Robert Lionel Brooke Cunliffe, CBE, RN (ret.) [see Cunliffe Bt., colls.]; 2ndly, 1966, Carola, da. of His Honour Judge Jesse Basil Herbert, MC, QC, [see B. Rea], and has issue by 1st marriage.

ᴀʳᵐꜱ—Per pale or and argent, on a chief indented sable, three lions rampant of the first. ᴄʳᵉꜱᵗ—A beaver passant proper.

Residence—Hargham Hall, Norwich.

Son living—by 1st marriage—THOMAS HUGH CUNLIFFE, *b.* Oct. 1st, 1962.

Daughers living—by 1st marriage—Bridget Anastasia, *b.* 1958.——Juliana Clare, *b.* 1960.

Gentle in manner, but vigorous in deed.

Sisters living—Ina Margaret Anastasia, *b.* 1920: *m.* 1942, Capt. John Lewis, R.A., and has issue living, Peter John Elliott, *b.* 1943,—William Beevor, *b.* 1948,—Judith Margaret Anne, *b.* 1946.——Jocelyn Mary (*Lady Warner*), *b.* 1927: *m.* 1949, Sir (Edward Courtenay) Henry Warner, 3rd Bt. *Residence,* The Grove, Great Baddow, Essex.——Christian Chevallier, *b.* 1934: *m.* 1959, George Habib Homsi, of 3401, Slade Run Drive, Falls Church, Virginia 22042, USA.

Widow living of 6th Baronet—EDITH MARGARET, only da. of Frank Agnew, formerly of Eccles Hall, Attleborough: *m.* 1st, 1919, Com. Sir Thomas Lubbock Beevor, R.N., 6th baronet, who d. (killed on active ser. during European War) 1943 ; 2ndly, 1944, Rear-Adm. Robert Alexander Currie, C.B., D.S.C. *Residence,* Thorpe Morieux Hall, Bury St. Edmunds, Suffolk.

Collateral Branches living.

Grandchildren of the late Ralph Jermy Beevor (infra):—
Issue of the late Ralph Branthwayt Beevor, *b.* 1895, *d.* 1970: *m.* 1921, Phyllis Margaret Ashburner, who *d.* 1972, da. of Henry Oliver Minty:—
Ralph Vernon Ashburner, *b.* 1924.——Michael Branthwayt, *b.* 1935; ed. at Gresham's Sch., Holt, and Trin. Coll., Camb. (BA).——Ruth Margaret, *b.* 1929: *m.* 1956, Dennis Frederick Outwin, of Curacao, Ray Park Rd., Maidenhead, and has issue living, Christopher Dennis, *b.* 1960,—Daphne Margaret, *b.* 1958,—Wendy Ruth, *b.* 1964.
Issue of the late Ralph Jermy Beevor, 3rd son of 4th baronet, *b.* 1859, *d.* 1937: *m.* 1894, Sophia Mary, who *d.* 1948, da. of the late Rev. Joseph Preston, of 20, Calvert Street, Norwich:—
Esmond Ayton, *b.* 1902: *m.* 1953, Olive May, da. of the late Henry Joseph Beazley, and widow of William Henderson Gray. *Residence,* The Manor House, Coltishall, Norfolk.——Irene Bedingfeld, *b.* 1898. *Residence,* Driftway, Stoke Holy Cross, Norwich.——Nancy Clover (34, Portadown Av., Pakuranga, Auckland, NZ), *b.* 1899: *m.* 1928, Robert Lawson Bennett, who *d.* 1967, and has issue living, Robert Graham Temple (60, Kirkwood Av., Christchurch, NZ), *b.* 1930; ed. at Canterbury Coll., NZ (MSc, PhD): *m.* 1958, Helen Gertrude Dawber, and has issue living, Robert Hugh *b.* 1960, Bruce Stephen *b.* 1962, Alison Hilda *b.* 1967,—Anne Moyna, *b.* 1928: *m.* 1958, Gavin Albert Loftus Crew, of 74, Bleakhouse Rd., Howick, Auckland, NZ, and has issue living, Miles Gavin *b.* 1964, Paul Thomas *b.* 1965, Fiona Anne *b.* 1967.——Averil Preston, *b.* 1901. *Residence,* Graffham, Petworth, Sussex.
Issue of the late Rowland Beevor, 6th son of 4th baronet, *b.* 1866, *d.* 1942: *m.* 1893, Margaret Frances, who *d.* 1954, da. of George Evans :—
Cecil Thomas Ashworth, *O.B.E., T.D., b.* 1898 ; admitted a Solicitor 1921 ; is Lieut.-Col. R.A. (T.A.), a D.L. for Norfolk and Vice-Pres. of Asso. of Drainage Authorities ; European War 1914-18 (wounded), European War 1939-45 ; O.B.E. (Civil) 1957 : *m.* 1925, Violet Babington, da. of Edward Babington Lenton, of Ivy House, Fritton, Great Yarmouth, and has issue living, Elizabeth Bridget Babington, *b.* 1928 : *m.* 1952, John Clifford Painter, of Myrobella, Upton, Norfolk, and has issue living, Stephen Langman *b.* 1956, Hilary Joanna *b.* 1953, Philippa Jane *b.* 1961. *Residence,* Ivy House, Fritton, Great Yarmouth.——Miles, *b.* 1900; ed. at Winchester. and at New Coll., Oxford (BA 1921); admitted a Solicitor 1925; is a JP for Herts. 1939-45 War as Flight-Lt. RAF Vol. Reserve: *m.* 1st, 1924, Margaret Florence, who *d.* 1934

da. of the late Algernon John Frederick Platt, of Barnby Manor, Newark-on-Trent; 2ndly, 1935, Sybil, only da. of Lt.-Col. John Babington Gilliat, DSO, of The Manor House, Welwyn, Herts., and has issue living, (by 1st m.) John Rowland (6, Campden House, Terr., W8), b. 1930; ed. at Winchester, and at Ch. Ch., Oxford (BA; FCA): m. 1955, Fenella Sybil, da. of Brig. John Gordon Bedford-Roberts, CBE, and has issue living, Timothy James b. 1957, Justin Miles b. 1961, Catrina Margaret b. 1958,—(by 2nd m.) Antony Romer (84, Cambridge St., SW1V 4PS), b. 1940, ed. at Winchester, and at New Coll., Oxford (BA); solicitor 1966: m. 1970, Cecilia, da. of the late John G. Hopton, and has issue living, Mark Andrew Antony b. 1975, Karen Louise b. 1974,—Ronald Hugh b. 1947; ed. at Winchester and Worcester Coll., Oxford (BA): m. 1972, Sabina Margaret Anne, da. of Harman Joseph Gerard Grisewood, CBE,—Helen b. 1943: m. 1966, Norman Jonathon Dudley Foster, of Plowden House, Hatton, Shifnal, Salop, and has issue living, Peter b. 1972, Charlotte Anne b. 1967, Caroline Jane b. 1968, Elizabeth Amy b. 1970. Residences, Parkside, Welwyn, Herts.——Judith Chevallier, b. 1896: m. 1921, James Alister Pope, CIE, who d. 1954, and has issue living, John Rose (12, Chapel Lane, Leicester, LE2 3WE), b. 1924: m. 1956, Patricia Anne Squires, and has issue living, Nicholas James Arend b. 1957, Elisabeth Jane b. 1960,—Margaret Elizabeth, b. 1922: m. 1961, Lt.-Cdr. John Gordon Phillips, RN (ret.), of The Homestead, Hall Rd., Wallington, Surrey, and has issue living, Richard Martin b. 1961, Simon John b. 1963, Catherine Bridget (twin) b. 1961. Residence, Willow Cottage, Blacksmiths Lane, Presbury, Glos.

Sir Thomas Beevor, 1st Baronet (son of Thomas Beevor, of Norwich), was a great Agriculturalist. The 6th Baronet, Com. Sir Thomas Lubbock, R.N., d. (killed on active ser. during European War) 1943.

BEIT, Creation (U.K.) 1924, of Tewin Water, Tewin, co. Hertford.

Sir ALFRED LANE BEIT, 2nd *Baronet;* b. Jan. 19th, 1903; s. his father, *Sir* OTTO (JOHN), *K.C.M.G.*, 1930; ed. at Eton, and at Ch. Ch., Oxford (M.A. 1933); is a Trustee of Beit Trust, a Director of Nyasaland Hotels & Brewery, Ltd., and a member of Advisory Committee of Tanganyika Concessions, Ltd., and Squadron-Leader (retired) R.A.F. Vol. Reserve; was Parliamentary Private Sec. (unpaid) to Financial Sec. to War Office 1935-8, and to Sec. of State for Colonies 1944-45; unsuccessfully contested S.-E. Div. of St. Pancras (C) May 1929; sat as M.P. therefor Oct. 1931 to June 1945 (defeated there July 1945): *m.* 1939, Clementine Mabell Kitty, da. of the late Major the Hon. Clement Bertram Oglivy Mitford, D.S.O. [*see* B. Redesdale, colls.].

Arms—Azure, on a bend argent three tents of the field garnished or. Crest—Out of a circlet or a demi-salamander issuant from flames proper.

FAIT BIEN FAIT TÔT

Residences—Russborough, Blessington, co. Wicklow, Eire; Beach Rd., Gordon's Bay, S. Africa; 2 The Little Boltons, SW10.

Sisters living—Alice Angela, b. 1899: m. 1927, Arthur Clifford Howie Bull, M.B.E., J.P., and has issue living, Nicholas Theodore, b. 1935.—Rosemary Claire, b. 1928.—Diana Jean, b. 1930. Residence, Brynderwen Court, Usk, Monmouthshire.——Lilian Muriel (*Lady Munro*) (Wepham Lodge, Arundel, Sussex), b. 1904: m. 1934, as his second wife, Sir (Richard) Gordon Munro, KCMG, MC, who d. 1967, and has issue living, Alan Gordon, b. 1935,—Neil Gordon, b. 1938.

Sir Otto (John) Beit, K.C.M.G., 1st Bt. (son of the late Siegfried Beit, of Hamburg), was a Director of British S. Africa Co., and of Rhodesia Railways, Ltd., a Trustee of Rhodes Trust, and of Beit Railways Trust (Rhodesia), and Founder of Beit Memorial Fellowships for Med. Research.

BELL, Creation (U.K.) 1885, of Rounton Grange, co. York, and of Washington Hall, co. Durham.

Sir JOHN LOWTHIAN BELL, 5th *Baronet;* b. June 14th, 1960; s. his father, *Sir* HUGH FRANCIS, 1970.

Arms—Argent on a fesse azure, between three hawks' lures of the second, as many hawks' bells of the first. Crest—A hawk's head, holding in its beak a hawk's lure azure, and resting its dexter claw on a sun in splendour or.

Seat—Arncliffe Hall, Ingleby Cross, Northallerton, Yorks.

PERSEVERANTIA
Perseverance.

Brothers living—DAVID HUGH, b. Oct. 8th, 1961.——Andrew Mark, b. 1963.——Thomas Hugh, b. 1964.

Grandmother living—Frances Helena, da. of the late John William Morkill, JP, DL, of Newfield Hall, Bell Busk, Yorks.: m. 1921, The Rev. Hugh Lowthian Bell (ante), who d. 1926.

Widow living of 4th Baronet—MARY, MB, ChB, (*Lady Bell*), (Arncliffe Hall, Ingleby Cross, Northallerton, Yorks.); D. Obst. RCOG; a JP for Yorks., da. of the late George Howson, of The Hyde, Hambledon, Bucks.: m. 1959, as his 2nd wife, Sir Hugh Francis Bell, 4th Bt., who d. 1970.

The 1st baronet, Sir Lowthian Bell, an Ironmaster and Coal-owner, sat as M.P. for Hartlepool (L) 1875-80. The 2nd baronet, Sir (Thomas) Hugh, was Lord-Lieut. for N. Riding of York 1906-31, and Pres. Iron and Steel Institute 1907-10. The 3rd baronet, Sir Maurice Hugh Lowthian Bell, C.M.G., T.D., was Col. Yorkshire Regt., and served in S. Africa 1900-1901, and in European War 1914-19 (C.M.G.).

BELL, Creation (U.K.) 1909, of Mynthurst, Leigh, co. Surrey. [Extinct 1955.]

Sir EASTMAN BELL, M.C., 2nd and last Baronet.

Daughter living of 1st Baronet—Lucy Putnam, b. 1888 : m. 1916, Maurice FitzGerald, and has issue living, Nesta Elizabeth, b. 1918: m. 1940, Arthur Wakefield Selwyn, of 15, Belbroughton Rd., Oxford, and has issue living, Jane b. 1941, Elizabeth b. 1943, Mary b. 1946, Olivia b. 1952. Residence, 15, Belbroughton Rd., Oxford.

MORRISON-BELL, Creation (U.K.) 1905, of Otterburn Hall, Elsdon, Northumberland.

Perseverance.

Sir WILLIAM HOLLIN DAYRELL MORRISON-BELL, 4th *Baronet; b.* June 21st, 1956; *s.* his father, *Capt. Sir* CHARLES REGINALD FRANCIS 1967.

Arms—Quarterly, 1st and 4th, sable, on a fesse ermine between three bells argent, a falcon close between two crescents of the field; 2nd and 3rd, argent, on a fesse azure between three Moors' heads couped at the neck proper, the turbans vert turned up argent, three roses or.   **Crests**—1st, a falcon close proper, belled and jessed or, holding in the beak a bell argent; 2nd, in front of a Moor's head couped at the shoulders as in the arms three roses gules.

Seat—Highgreen, Tarset, Northumberland.

Brother living—JULIAN FRANCIS TARRET, b. Feb. 14th, 1959.
Aunts living (daughters of 2nd baronet)—Kathleen Frances, TD, b. 1906; a JP and an Hon. Alderman for Northumberland (formerly Alderman); formerly Senior Com. ATS. Residence, Charlton Tarset, Northumberland.——Daphne Frances, b. 1908: m. 1950, as his second wife, Brig. Brian Mortimer Archibald, CBE, DSO, RE (ret.), of Wadge Head, Tarset, Hexham, and has issue living, Elizabeth Frances, b. 1951.——Veronica Frances, b. 1911: m. 1942, John Jerome Stonborough, formerly Maj. Canadian Army, and has issue living, Jerome Claude, b. 1943,—John Tarret Christian, b. 1948,—Margaret Isabella, b. 1944. Residences, Toscana Park, Gmunden, Austria; Glendon, Corfe Mullen, Wimborne, BH21 3HB, Dorset.
Widow living of 3rd baronet—PRUDENCE CAROLINE, only da. of the late Lt.-Col. Wyndham Dayrell Davies, 60th Rifles (ret.): m. 1st, 1955, Sir Charles Reginald Francis Morrison-Bell, 3rd Bt., who d. 1967; 2ndly, 1969, Peter Gillbanks, of South Scarletts, Kiln Green, Twyford, Berks.

Collateral Branches living.

Issue of the late (Arthur) Clive Morrison-Bell (2nd son of 1st baronet), who was cr. a Baronet 1923 :—
See Morrison-Bell, Bt., cr. 1923 (ext.).

Issue of the late Ernest Fitzroy Morrison-Bell, O.B.E., 3rd son of 1st baronet, b. 1871, d. 1960 : m. 1902, Maud Evelyn, who d. 1960, da. of the late Lieut.-Col. Frank Henry T.P., formerly 9th Lancers, of Elmestree, Tetbury, Gloucestershire :—
Louise Monica (Hall Barn, Blewbury, Didcot, Oxon., OX11 9QB), b. 1903: m. 1929, Col. Cecil Everard Montague Grenville-Grey, CBE, late KRRC, who d. 1973, and has issue living, Wilfred Ernest, b. 1930: m. 1963, Edith Dlamini, and has issue living, Wilfrid Jonathan, b. 1964, Peter Thulani b. 1967, Susan Thandi (twin), b. 1964,—Susan Monica (Countess of March and Kinrara), b. 1932: m. 1951, the Earl of March and Kinrara, el. son of 9th Duke of Richmond.——Ruth Evelyn, b. 1904.——Claire Wilhelmina Maud, b. 1907: m. 1928, Maj. Robert Moubray, formerly 16th Lancers, who d. 1961, and has issue living, John Robert Fitzroy, b. 1945: m. 1972, Patricia Maeve MacLeod, and has issue living, Belinda Mary Claire b. 1973,—Evelyn Mary, b. 1929,—Anne Catherine Wilhelmina, b. 1931,—Gillian Claire, b. 1933. Residence, Broomlands, Kelso, Roxburghshire.——Mary Ernestine, b. 1910; formerly Sen. Com. ATS: m. 1946, Brig. Geoffrey William Goschen, DSO, MC, late RHA, and has issue living, John Henry, b. 1949,— Mary, b. 1948. Residence, Hill House Farm, Cradley, nr. Malvern, Worcs.

Issue of the late Lieut.-Col. Eustace Widdrington Morrison-Bell, 4th son of 1st baronet, b. 1874, d. 1947: m. 1914, the Hon. Harriet Margaret Hepburn-Stuart-Forbes-Trefusis, who d. 1975, da. of 20th Baron Clinton:—
Anthony Eustace, DFC (Fourways, Bembridge, I. of Wight), b. 1916; ed. at Wton; acting Wing-Com. RAF Vol Res.: 1939-45 War (DFC).——Pamela Elizabeth, b. 1918.——Sylvia Morwenna, b. 1922: m. 1941, Maj. Arthur Thomas Chamberlayne, R. Fusiliers, and has issue living, Michael Thomas (Lower Hearn, Headley, Hants.), b. 1943; ed. at Wellington; ACA. Residence, Clouds Garden House, East Knoyle, Salisbury, Wilts.

The 1st baronet, Sir Charles William Bell, assumed by Roy. licence 1905 the additional surname and arms of Morrison. The 2nd baronet, Sir Claude William Hedley Morrison-Bell, sometime Capt. Argyll and Sutherland Highlanders, served on N.-W. Frontier of India 1897-8 and during European War 1914-18.

MORRISON-BELL, Creation (U.K.) 1923, of Harpford, co. Devon. [Extinct 1956.]

Sir (ARTHUR) CLIVE MORRISON-BELL, 1st and last *Baronet.*

Daughters living of 1st Baronet—Shelagh Jocelyn (*Lady Campbell*), *b.* 1913: *m.* 1st, 1943 (m. diss. 1951), William Cooper Moore; 2ndly, 1968, as his 2nd wife, Sir Ralph Abercromby Campbell, of Lomans Hill, Hartley Wintney, Hants., and has issue living, (by 1st m.), David Anson Clive, *b.* 1944.——Patricia Louisa *b.* 1919: *m.* 1st, 1941 (m. diss. 1956), Maj. John Nevile Wake Gwynne, RA [Wake, Bt.]; 2ndly, 1968, Henry Michael Barclay, of Hanworth Hall, Norfolk, and has issue living (by 1st m.), Nevile Martin (5, Lansdowne Walk, W11), *b.* 1941; ed. at Eton, and at Trin. Coll., Oxford: *m.* 1972, Charlotte, da. of Sir Cyril Hugh Kleinwort [see Kleinwort Bt.] and formerly wife of Richard Lawrence, Baillieu, and has issue living, Chloe Patricia, *b.* 1973,—Jessica Violet, *b.* 1944: *m.* 1966, Charles Cospatrick Douglas-Home [see B. Home of the Hirsel].

Widow living of 1st Baronet—*Hon.* LILAH KATHERINE JULIA WINGFIELD (*Hon. Lady Morrison-Bell*), da. of 7th Viscount Powerscourt : *m.* 1912, Sir (Arthur) Clive Morrison-Bell, 1st baronet, who *d.* 1956, when the title became ext. *Residence,* 11, Cumberland Mansions, George St., W.1.

GRATTAN-BELLEW, Creation (U.K.) 1838, of Mount Bellew, co. Galway.

Sir HENRY CHARLES GRATTAN-BELLEW, 5th *Baronet ; b.* May 12th, 1933 ; *s.* his father, *Lieut.-Col. Sir* CHARLES CHRISTOPHER, *M.C.,* 1948 ; ed. at Ampleforth ; was Assist. Dist. Commr., Kenya Police Reserve 1953-4, and Dist. Officer, Kenya Administration 1954-55: *m.* 1st 1956 (m. diss. 19—) Naomi Ellis, yr. da. of the late Dr. Charles Cyril Morgan, of Chester; 2ndly, 19—, Gillian, da. of   , and has issue by 2nd m.

Arms—Quarterly, 1st and 4th sable, fretty or, a crescent argent or difference, *Bellew* ; 2nd and 3rd, per saltire sable and ermine, over all a lion rampant or, *Grattan.* **Crests**—1st, an arm embowed in armour proper, charged with a crescent for difference, grasping in the hand a sword proper, pommel and hilt or, *Bellew* ; 2nd, a dove proper, holding in its dexter claw a sceptre and standing on a barrel or, *Grattan.*

Residence,—

Tout d'en haut.
All from above.

Daughter living—(By 2nd m.)—Deirdre Sophia, *b.* 19—.

Sister living—Deirdre Maureen, *b.* 1924 : *m.* 1946, Gerald Kiernan, and has issue living Charles Dominck, *b.* 1947,—Henry Gerard, *b.* 1952,—Valerie Maureen, *b.* 1946,—Maureen Gabriel, *b.* 1949,—Dawn Vivien, *b.* 1956. *Residence,* 35, Priory Grove, Stillorgan, Dublin.

Uncle living (son of 3rd baronet)—*Sir* Arthur John, *CMG, QC, b.* 1903; ed. at Downside and at Christ Coll., Camb. (BA 1924); Bar. Lincoln's Inn 1925, and a QC Tanganyika 1952; was Attorney-Gen. Sarawak 1948-52, Member for Legal Affairs and Attorney-Gen., Tanganyika 1952-56, and Ch. Sec. Tanganyika 1956-9; Malaya 1941-45 (prisoner); CMG 1956, Knt. 1959: *m.* 1931, Winifred Mary, da. of the late Edmond R. Mahony, of Kilinan, Kilchreest, co. Galway, and has issue living, (Arthur Henry) Bertram (Hole Farm, Gt. Waldingfield, nr. Sudbury, Suffolk), *b.* 1937; ed. at Downside; 2nd Lt., late 8th Hussars; is a member of Lloyd's: *m.* 1961, Georgina Madeleine Mary, da. of Sir George Edward Mordaunt Milner, 9th Bt., and has issue living, Charles Henry Mordaunt *b.* 1964, Sophie Rose *b.* 1962,—Gillian Barbara, *b.* 1934: *m.* 1967, Peter Haggard Lyster, of Little Chishill Manor, Cambs., and has issue living, Thomas Henry *b.* 1971, Grania Mary *b.* 1968, Anna Gillian *b.* 1969. *Residence,*—Plegdon Green, nr. Henham, Essex. *Club,* United Hunts.

Aunt living (daughter of 3rd baronet)—Helena Barbara (Our Lady of Consolation Nursing Home, Tullamore, co. Offaly), *b.* 1889.

Widow living of 4th Baronet—MAUREEN PEYTON (*Dowager Lady Grattan-Bellew*), niece and adopted da. of the late Capt. Sir Thomas George Segrave, C.B.E.: *m.* 1923, Lieut.-Col. Sir Charles Christopher Grattan-Bellew, M.C., 4th baronet, who *d.* 1948. *Residence,* 35, Priory Grove, Stillorgan, co. Dublin.

Collateral Branches living.

Issue of the late Thomas Henry Grattan-Bellew, 4th son of 3rd baronet, *b.* 1901, *d.* 1967: *m.* 1933, Bettina Idrone Dorothy (Mount Loftus, Goresbridge, co. Kilkenny), el. da. of the late Maj. John Edward Blake Loftus, of Mount Loftus, co. Kilkenny:—

PATRICK EDWARD (Mount Loftus, Goresbridge, co. Kilkenny), *b.* Sept. 26th, 1934; ed. at Univ. Coll., Dublin (BSc), and McGill Univ., Canada (MSc); PhD Camb.; a mineralogist.——Idrone Pauline Mary, *b.* 1936: *m.* 1964, Roger William Brittain, of Wards Garth, Layer-de-la-Haye, Colchester, and has issue living, William Henry Grattan, *b.* 1965,—Charles Francis, *b.* 1966,—James Nickolas, *b.* 1971,—Georgina Mary Idrone, *b.* 1968.

Issue of the late Moira Jane Grattan-Bellew, da. of 3rd baronet, *b.* 1891, *d.* 1971: *m.* 1920, James D'Arcy, DL, JP, of Ardcarne, Ballinasloe, co. Galway:—

William Isidore (Fort William, Ballinasloe co. Galway), *b.* 1920; ed. at Stonyhurst; 1939-45 War as Capt. RA: *m.* 1st, 1955, Shelia Jane, only da. of T. H. MacDonald, of Barguillean, Taynult, Argyllshire, formerly wife of Robert Tyer; 2ndly, 1967, Angela Anne, da. of Thomas Wallace, of Greystones, co. Wicklow, and has issue living, (by 1st m.) Jane Mary, *b.* 1956.——Teresa, *b.* 1922: *m.* 1943, M. B. MacQuaid, of 64, Medway Parade, Weston Av., Perivale, Middx., and has issue living, Philip, *b.* 1945,—Philippa, *b.* 1944,—Judy, *b.* 1946,—Doreen, *b.* 1952.——Doreen Mary (St. O'Hara's Hill, Tullamore, co. Offaly), *b.* 1927.

The 1st baronet was fourth in descent from Michael Bellew of Mount Bellew. a descendant of Christopher Bellew, brother of Sir Patrick Bellew, 1st baronet (cr. 1688) [*see* B. Bellew]. The father of the 3rd baronet assumed by Roy. licence the additional surname and arms of Grattan, The 4th baronet, Sir Charles Christopher, M.C., was Lieut.-Col. King's Roy. Rifle Corps (Reserve).

BELLINGHAM, Creation (G.B.) 1796, of Castle Bellingham, co. Louth.

[Name pronounced "Bellinjum."]

So it is.

A friend to a friend.

Sir NOEL PETER ROGER BELLINGHAM, 7th *Baronet* (of 2nd creation), *b.* Sept. 4th, 1943; *s.* his father, *Sir* ROGER CARROLL PATRICK STEPHEN, *MB*, *ChB*, *DA*, 1973; ed. at Lindisfarne Coll.

ᴀʀᴍꜱ—Argent, three bugle horns sable, stringed gules and garnished or. Cʀᴇꜱᴛ—A buck's head couped or.

Seat—Castle Bellingham, co. Louth. *Residence*— 1, Adswood Lane West. Stockport, Cheshire.

Brother living—ANTHONY EDWARD NORMAN, *b.* March 24th, 1947, ed. at Rossall.

Aunt living—Constance Catherine Mary Pia, *b.* 1912: *m.* 1st, 1935, Brendan Russell, who *d.* 1956; 2ndly, 1963, Oswald Shaw-Hamilton, and has issue living, (by 1st m.) Heber, *b.* 1936: *m.* 1961, Cora Ann Walsh, and has issue living, Nigel Brendon Charles *b.* 1962, Hilary Elizabeth Ann *b.* 1965,—Patrick, *b.* 1942: *m.* 1966, Carol Ann Banbrook, and has issue living, Brendon Daniel *b.* 1967, Nicholas Damian *b.* 1968,—Una, *b.* 1939: *m.* 1965, Patrick Rory White, and has issue living, Sharon Ann *b.* 1966,—Anne (twin), *b.* 1939: *m.* 1967, Charles Fyson, and has issue living, Erik Christopher *b.* 1969. *Residence*, Dromeena House, Castle Bellingham, co. Louth.

Daughter living of 5th Baronet—Gertrude Mary, *b.* 1906: *m.* 1927, Ronald Derwent Hawker [Buxton, Bt.], and has issue living, Martin *b.* 1929; ed. at Stowe, and at Trin. Coll., Camb. (MA). *Residence*, Claydon Hall, Ipswich.

Widow living of 6th Baronet—MARY (*Lady Bellingham*) (1, Adswood Lane West, Cale Green, Stockport, Cheshire; Castle Bellingham, co. Louth), da. of the late William Norman: *m.* 1941, Sir Roger Carroll Patrick Stephen Bellingham, MB, ChB, DA, 6th Bt., who *d.* 1973.

Collateral Branches living.

Grandchildren of the late Maj. Sydney Edwin Bellingham, el. son of the late Lt.-Col. William Johnston Bellingham, 5th son of 2nd baronet:—

Issue of the late Major Alan Mure Bellingham, M.C., *b.*, *b.* 1881; *d.* 1946: *m.* 1st, 1914 Beatrix Laura (who *d.* 1962, having obtained a divorce 1930), da. of the late John Henry Harrison, I.C.S.; 2ndly, 1930, Mabel Theodora Lucy Tirard (138B, Greenwich High Rd., SE10), da. of Theodore Seton Dury, Ch. Master, Supreme Court:—

(By 1st m.) Beatrix Pamela BELLINGHAM-KIGGELL, *b.* 1918; assumed the surname of Bellingham-Kiggell by deed poll 1970: *m.* 1st 1938 (divorce 1945), Ronald Arthur Cleave; 2ndly, 1947 (divorce 1962) John Chatterton Coysgarne Sim, and has issue living, (by 1st m.) Zenia Sophia SIM, *b.* 1938; assumed by deed poll 1948 the name of Sim in lieu of her patronymic,—(by 2nd m.) Carol Ann, *b.* 1950.——(By 2nd m.) Patrick Alan Sydney, *b.* 1936: BA, Oxon: *m.* 1958, Elizabeth Mary, da. of the late Harold Hall Bagnall, of Westerham, Kent, and has issue living Alan Hall, *b.* 1960,—Dorcas Elizabeth, *b.* 1962,—Isobel Marie (twin), *b.* 1962. *Residence*, Tingewick Mill, Buckingham.——Brigid Alaine, *b.* 1933: *m.* 1st, 1954, from whom she obtained a divorce 1969, Brian Deakin; 2ndly, 1970, Richard Barham, and has issue living (by 1st m.) Charles Rupert, *b.* 1956,—Timothy Graham, *b.* 1959,—Helena Judith, *b.* 1958. *Residence*,—

Grandchildren of the late Thomas Eudo Bellingham (infra) :—

Issue of the late William Eudo Bellingham, *b.* (Dec.) 1882, *d.* 1954: *m.* 1906, Louisa Bertha, who *d.* 1935, da. of William Arthur Krick, of Chicago, U.S.A.:—

William Arthur Eudo (2810, Merrimac Blvd., Toledo, Ohio, 43606, USA), *b.* 1909: *m.* 1932, Myrna Arlene, da. of Edwin T. Nester, and has issue living, Kay Arlene, *b.* 1934: *m.* 19—, Thomas Taylor, of 22, Duncan Rd., Ho-Ho-Kus, New Jersey, 07423, USA,—William Eudo (4506, Shadow Glenn Drive, Colorado Springs, Colo. 80909, USA), *b.* 1938,—Jean Carolyne, *b.* 1941: *m.* 19—, Pat Johnson, of 3534, Edgevale, Toledo, Ohio, USA,—Linda Anne, *b.* 1944: *m.* 1970, Richard Allardyce, of 11606, Helmont Drive, Oakton, Va. 22124, USA,—Gwen Francis, *b.* 1946: *m.* 19—, Richard Osenbaugh, of 2810, Merrimac Blvd., Toledo, Ohio, USA.——Frederick Richard (260, 14th St., Vero Beach, Florida, 32960, USA), *b.* 1923: W. 1st, 1944 (divorce 1947), Mary Winifred, da. of Cary C. Winans; 2ndly, 1951, Elizabeth Hayes; 3rdly, 1958, Geraldine Helen Hermanson, and has issue living, (by 1st m.) Patricia, *b.* 1945,—Kathleen, *b.* 1947,—(by 2nd m.) Michelle, *b.* 1952,—(by 3rd m.) Timothy Shane, *b.* 1959.——Vesper Grace, *b.* 1910: *m.* 1941, Roy Arthur Gustofson, and has issue living, Lucy Christine, *b.* 1942: *m.* 1st, 1959 (m. diss. 1966), Ray Victor Soukkola; 2ndly, 1968, Robert Boggiano, of 5131, Sisson Drive, Huntington Beach, Calif, 92649, USA, and has issue living (by 1st m.), Ray Victor *b.* 1960, Laurie Grace *b.* 1961; (by 2nd m.) Jamie Lynn *b.* 1969, Jayne Marie *b.* 1968, Monique Ann *b.* 1971. *Residence*,—311, 89th Avenue West, Duluth, Minnesota 55808, USA.——Louisa Hazel, *b.* 1913: *m.* 1932, Conrad Edward Nelson, and has issue living, Constance Paulette, *b.* 1944: *m.* (March) 1963, Thomas Neil Nelson, of 940, Franklin Terr., Minneapolis, Minnesota, USA, and has issue living, Rodney Kirk *b.* (Nov.) 1963. *Residence*, 1023, South 72nd Avenue West, Duluth, Minnesota, USA.——Laurel Joyce, *b.* 1925: *m.* 1945, Thomas Edward Telando, and has issue living, Thomas Michale, *b.* 1946,—Charlotte Louisa, *b.* 1947. *Residence*,—

Issue of the late John Stuart Bellingham, *b.* 1889, *d.* 1965: *m.* 1937, Doreen, who *d.* 1974, da. of the late Edward O'Brien, of Ambleside, Westmorland:—

Roger Graham (24 Fircroft Close, Hill View Rd., Woking, Surrey) *b.* 1939: *m.* 1965, Pauline, da. of David Rankine, and has issue living, Alan Graham, *b.* 1966,—John Terrance, *b.* 1969.

Grandchildren of the late William Stewart Bellingham, son of the late John Bellingham, brother of 2nd baronet:—

Issue of the late Thomas Eudo Bellingham, *b.* 1849, *d.* 1923: *m.* (March) 1882, Grace, who *d.* 1905, da. of the late Rev. W. Harkness, M.A., of Athea, co. Limerick :—

Thomas Francis Gordon, *b.* 1885 : *m.* 1918, Iva Abigail, da. of A. E. Bridge, and has issue living, Stewart (Bawlf, Alberta, Canada), *b.* 1921: *m.* 19—, and has issue living, Roger *b.* 19—, a da. *b.* 19—,—William Milton, *b.* 1922,—Stephen Ramsay (Calgary, Alberta, Canada), *b.* 1924: *m.* 19—, and has issue living. *Residence*, Bawlf, Alberta, Canada.——Hazel, *b.* 1887: *m.* 1915, Charles Wundabaldt Christen, who *d.* 1961, and has issue living, Charles Patrick Harkness, *b.* 1918: *m.* 1946, Virginia Beane, and has issue living, Charles Patrick *b.* 1947, Julia Hazel *b.* 1949, Christina Helen *b.* 1953,—John Wundabaldt (968, 88th Avenue W. Duluth Minnesota, USA), *b.* 1923: *m.* 1943, Theresa Lucille Lovich, and has issue living, John Charles *b.* 1946, Steven William *b.* 1948: Daniel Thomas *b.* 1952, David Paul *b.* 1953, Patricia Terese *b.* 1944,—Hazel Mary *b.* 1924: *m.* 1st, 1943, Albert Jackson; 2ndly, 1946, Lawrence Robert Hanstein, of Staunton, Illinois, USA, and has issue living, (by 1st marriage) Anthony Lee *b.* 1945, (by 2nd marriage) Laurence Robert *b.* 1948, David *b.* 1953, Mary Lynn *b.* 1951.

Grandson of the late Arthur D'Arcy Bellingham, 5th son of William Stewart
Bellingham (ante):—
Issue of the late Lt.-Col. Arthur Stuart Bellingham, *b.* 1893, *d.* 1969: *m.* 1923, Jean (Glencara, Rathconrath, Mullingar, co. Westmeath; Salar Lodge, Leenane, co. Galway; The Cliffs, Howth, co. Dublin), da. of Andrew Arthur, of Rosemount, Ayrshire:—
John Stuart (5, rue Paul-Louis-Courier, Paris VII), *b.* 1929; ed. at Eton, and Magdalene Coll., Camb. (BA).

Grandchildren of Arthur Stuart Bellingham (ante) :—
Issue of the late (Arthur) Henry Bellingham, Lieut., Leicestershire Yeo., *b.* 1926, *d.* 1959 :
m. 1953, June Marion Cloudesley (who *m.* 2ndly, 1962, Col. Ian Bruce Baillie, Life Gds., of Congham Lodge, Hillington, King's Lynn [see B. Burton, colls.], da. of Arthur Cloudesley Smith, FRCS:—
Henry Campbell, *b.* 1955.——Elizabeth Alison, *b.* 1956.

This ancient family derives its name from Bellingham-in-Tyndale, Northumberland. William de Bellingham was Sheriff of Tyndale 1279. Robert of Bellingham, temp. Henry V, *m.* Elizabeth, da. of Sir Richard Tunstall, KG. His el. son, Sir Henry was cr. Knt. Banneret at Battle of Wakefield 1460, whose son, Sir Robert, was similarly honoured at Battle of Stoke 1487. The present family descend from Alan of Levens, Westmorland, 8th son of Robert (ante). Alan's gt.-grandson, Robert, settled in Ireland and was father of (i) Sir Daniel of Dubber, co. Dublin, Lord Mayor of Dublin, who was cr. a Bt. of Ireland 1687 (title ext. 1699), and (ii) Henry of Gernonstown (later called Castle Bellingham) co. Louth. Henry served as Cornet in a Regt. of Cavalry raised in the north for suppressing the Irish rebellion. By his wife, Lucy Sibthorpe, he was father of Col. Thomas who raised a Regt. of Cavalry and served with William III, where he acted as his guide during the march from Dundalk to the Boyne. After that battle he accompanied the King to Duleek. In consequence, James II's army destroyed Castle Bellingham by fire. His grandson, Alan of Castle Bellingham, *m.* 1738, Alice, da. and co-heir of the Rev. Hans Montgomery of Grey Abbey, co. Down. Alan's 4th son, Sir William, was in 1796 cr. a Bt. of GB with remainder to the heirs male of the body of his father, and was MP for Reigate and Private Sec. to Pitt. He was *s.* by his nephew, Sir Alan (el. son of Alan, el. brother of 1st Bt.) 1826. Sir (Alan) Henry, 4th Bt. was MP for co. Louth and Private Chamberlain to Popes Pius IX, Leo XIII and Pius X. Brig.-Gen. Sir Edward Henry Charles Patrick, CMG, DSO, late R. Scots, was a Senator of Irish Free State 1925-56.

BENN, Creation (U.K.) 1914, of The Old Knoll, Metropolitan Borough of Lewisham

Sir JOHN ANDREWS BENN, 3rd *Baronet ;*
b. Jan. 28th, 1904 ; *s.* his father, *Sir* ERNEST JOHN PICKSTONE, *C.B.E.,* 1954 ; ed. at Harrow, at Princeton Univ., and at Gonville and Caius Coll., Camb.; Chm. of English-Speaking Union of the Commonwealth 1969-72; Chm. of Cincinnati Milacron Ltd.; a Consultant, Benn Bros., Ltd., and Ernest Benn, Ltd.; Maj. KOYLI: *m.* 1929, the Hon. Ursula Helen Alers Hankey, da. of 1st Baron Hankey and has issue.

Arms—Argent, two barrulets indented gules, between in chief as many dragons' heads erased and in base a pencil and a pen in saltire proper, tied with a lace azure, pendent therefrom a torteau, charged with a figure "1914" or. Crest—On a rock a spear erect proper, flowing therefrom a pennon azure, charged with the word "Onward," letters or.
Residence—High Field, Limpsfield, Surrey.

By God's favour.

Sons living—JAMES JONATHAN, *b.* July 27th, 1933 ; ed. at Harrow, and at Clare Coll., Camb. (B.A. 1957, M.A. 1961) : *m.* 1960, Jennifer Mary, el. da. of Dr. Wilfred Vivian Howells, O.B.E., of 73, Walter Rd., Swansea, and has issue living, Robert Ernest, *b.* 1963,—Juliet Clare, *b.* 1966. Residence, Fielden Lodge, Ightham, Kent.—Timothy John (Hickens Cottage, Chiddingstone, nr. Edenbridge, Kent), *b.* 1936; ed. at Harrow, at Princeton Univ., and at Clare Coll., Camb. (MA): Lt. Scots Guards and Man. Dir. of Benn Brothers Ltd.: *m.* 1st, 1959 (m. diss. 1973), Valerie Hamlyn, ygr. da. of the late Capt. P. H. W. Davie; 2ndly, 1973, Susan Elizabeth Hardingham, only da. of George Hodges, of Delray Beach, Florida, USA, and has issue living (by 1st m.), Peter Quentin, *b.* 1961,—William Justin, *b.* 1964,—Thomas Hamlyn, *b.* 1967.

Daughters living—Susan Paschal, *b.* 1930: *m.* 1952, Michael Graeme Compton, and has issue living, Josephine, *b.* 1953,—Ann, *b.* 1956. Residence, 5, Moorhouse Rd., W2.——Christina Frances, *b.* 1948.——Marigold Margaret, *b.* 1950.

Brother living—Edward Glanvill, *b.* 1905; ed. at Harrow, and at Clare Coll., Camb.; Chm. of Benn Bros., Ltd., a Dir. of Ernest Benn, Ltd., and Major E. Surrey Regt.: *m.* 1931, Beatrice Catherine, MBE, da. of the late Claude Newbald, of Lyndhurst, Wallington, Surrey, and has issue living, James Glanvill (121, Church Rd., SW19 5AH), *b.* 1944: *m.* 1st, 1967, Judith, da. of W. H. McMinn, of 15, Ingram House, Hampton Wick, Surrey; 2ndly, 1973, Susan May, da. of Vivian G. Beardsell, of Yellow Flat, Borde Hill, Haywards Heath, W. Sussex, and has issue living (by 2nd m.) Peter Glanvill *b.* 1974, Alistair James *b.* 1975,—Elizabeth, *b.* 1936: *m.* 1961, Kenneth Charles Stewart Young, of Old Rectory, Buckland, nr. Aylesbury, Bucks., and has issue living, Catherine Ann *b.* 1962, Miranda *b.* 1964. Residence, 27, Lennox Gdns., SW1X 0DE.

Sisters living—Elizabeth, *b.* 1907: *m.* 1935, Paul Alfred Shinkman, of New York, and has issue living, Paul Glanvill, (617, Shady Lawn Rd., Chapel Hill, NC 27514, USA), *b.* 1936; ed. at Landon Sch., Harvard Coll. (BA), Univ. of Michigan (MA, PhD): *m.* 1969, Judith Kay, da. of F. E. Barnett, of Charlotte, NC, USA,—Christopher Joseph (101, Eastern Heights Drive, Ithaca, NY 14850, USA) *b.* 1940; ed. at St. Albans Sch., Thiel Coll. (BA), Westminster Coll. (MA), Univ. of Pittsburgh (PhD): *m.* 1965, Marsha Ann, el. da. of Marshall Axel Friberg, of Jamestown, NY, and has issue living, Matthew Christopher *b.* 1972,—Bernard Francis (61, Dawes Rd., SW6 7DT), *b.* 1943; ed. at St. Mark's Sch., Dartmouth Coll. (BA): *m.* 1974, Gillian Clare, yr. da. of Daniel Crawley, of London, SE. *Residence,* 3040, Dent Pl., NW, Georgetown, Wash., DC 20007, USA.——Julia Wedgwood, *b.* 1916: *m.* 1945, Albert Edward Louis Mash, OBE, Public Relations Consultant, and has issue living, John Martin, *b.* 1948: *m.* 1973, Ann Patricia Sweeney,—Jennifer Dorothy *b.* 1946: *m.* 1973, Geoffrey Wade, and has issue living, George William *b.* 1974. *Residence,* The Rookery, N. Bersted, Bognor Regis.

Collateral Branches living.
Issue of the **late** Capt. Frederick Christopher Benn, **3rd** son of 2nd baronet, *b.* 1912, *d.* (killed in action during European War) 1941: *m.* **1937,** Phyllis, da. of the late E. M. Preston, of Slaugham Park, Sussex:—
Oliver Preston (Hackhurst Stud, Lower Dicker, Hailsham), *b.* 1938; ed. at Eton, and Clare Coll., Camb.; 2nd Lieut. Intelligence Corps; Bar. Middle Temple 1970: *m.* 1970. Clarissa Dorothy Jeannette, da. of Guillermo Sergio Santa Cruz y Zerrano, of Weybridge, Surrey, and has issue living, Belinda Alice Irene, *b.* 1970.
Issue living of the late Rt. Hon. (William) Wedgwood Benn, D.S.O., D.F.C., P.C, (2nd son of 1st baronet), who was cr. *Viscount Stansgate* 1942 [*see* that title]

The 1st baronet, Sir John Williams Benn, Chm. of Benn Brothers (Limited), publishers, **was a** Member of London County Council 1889-1922 (Chm. 1904-5), and sat as M.P. for St. George's Div. of **Tower** Hamlets (*L*) 1892-95, and for Devonport 1904-10. The 2nd baronet, Sir Ernest John Pickstone Benn, C.B.E., was a Director (sometime Chm.) of Benn Bros., Ltd., of Ernest Benn. Ltd., and of United Kingdom Provident Institution, Pres. of So. ofIndividualists, and High Sheriff of co. London 1932.

BENN, Creation (U.K.) 1920, of Rollesby, co. Norfolk.

Sir PATRICK ION HAMILTON BENN, 2nd *Baronet,* son of the late Col. Ion Bridges Hamilton Benn, son of 1st baronet ; *b.* Feb. 26th, 1922 ; *s.* his grandfather, *Capt. Sir* (ION) HAMILTON, *C.B., D.S.O., T.D., R.N.V.R.* 1961 ; ed. at Rugby ; is Capt. Reserve of Officers, late Duke of Cornwall's L.I., and Major Norfolk Army Cadet Force; a Trustee and a Gov. of E. Anglian Trustee Savings Bank; Commr. of Great Yarmouth Port and Haven; European War 1941-5 in N. Africa, Italy, and Greece (despatches), Korea 1951-2: *m.* 1959, Edel Jørgine, da. of the late Col. W. S. Løback, formerly Roy. Norwegian Army.

Arms—Argent, on a chevron indented gules between three lions rampant sable, a trefoil slipped or. Crest— A tiger passant argent gorged with a collar dancettee gules charged with a trefoil as in the arms.

COURAGE SANS PEUR
Courage without fear

Seat—Rollesby Hall, nr. Great Yarmouth, Norfolk. *Club*—Norfolk (Norwich).

Sister living—Dorothy Hamilton, *b.* 1917. *Residence,* Flat 14, 50, Cornwall Gdns., SW7.
Mother living—Theresa Dorothy, da. of the late Major F. H. Blacker, formerly 4th Hussars: *m.* 1916, Col. Ion Bridges Hamilton Benn, Duke of Cornwall's L.I. and Norfolk Regt. (ante), who *d.* 1956. *Residence,* Broad Farm, Rollesby, Gt. Yarmouth, Norfolk.

Capt. Sir (Ion) Hamilton Benn, C.B., D.S.O., T.D., 1st baronet (son of the late Rev. John Watkins Benn, R. of Carrigaline and Douglas, co. Cork), was Mayor of Greenwich 1901-2, a Co. Councillor for London 1907-10, M.P. for Greenwich (C) 1910-22, Capt. R.N.V.R., Founder Member of Port of London Authority, and Pres. of Tower Hill Improvement Trust.

BENNETT, Creation (U.K.) 1929, of Kirklington, co. Nottingham.

Sir RONALD WILFRID MURDOCH BENNETT, 3rd *Baronet, b.* March 25th, 1930; *s.* his father, *Sir* (CHARLES) WILFRID, *T.D.,* 1952 ; ed. at Wellington, and at Trin. Coll., Oxford: *m.* 1st, 1953, Audrey Rose-Marie Patricia, only da. of Maj. A. L. J. H. Aubépin, of co. Mayo; 2ndly, 1968, Anne, da. of the late Leslie George Tooker, and has issue by 1st m.

Arms—Gules, a cross moline between three demi-lions rampant or. Crest—In front of a lion rampant gules charged on the shoulder with a cross moline argent, a scaling ladder fessewise or.

Residence—5 Portland Rd., Holland Park, W11.

Daughters living—By 1st m.—Anne-Marie Julia, *b.* 1954: *m.* 1973, Stephen Hickman.——Georgina Marion, *b.* 1956.
Uncle living (son of 1st baronet)—PETER (46, Highpoint, Weybridge, Surrey), *b.* 1938; ed. at Charterhouse, and Pembroke Coll., Camb.: *m.* 1966, Monique Christine, el. da. of Amade Monsempès, of St. Maur, Des Fossès, Seine, France.
Sister living—Anne, *b.* 1928: *m.* 1st, 1961, Gerald Norman Fox-Edwards; 2ndly, 1974, Conrad Lyddon Voss-Bark, of Lyd Cottage, Leat Rd., Lipton, Devon, and has issue living (by 1st m.), Adam, *b.* 1962,—Jane, *b.* 1964.
Aunt living (daughter of 1st baronet)—Audrey, *b.* 1904: *m.* 1928, Douglas Haultain Phillips, son of the Hon. Sir William Watkin Phillips, and has issue living, Susan, *b.* 1929: *m.* 1954, Timothy Ernle Gilpin [By. Ernle],

SERVIR · LE · ROY
To serve the King.

and has issue living, Joanna Clare b. 1955, Henrietta Haultain b. 1957,—Caroline Louise, b. 1931.

Widows living of 1st and 2nd Baronets—LEOPOLDINE (*Dowager Lady Bennett*) (c/o 46, High Point, Weybridge, Surrey), da. of Leopold Armata, of Vienna: *m.* 1938, as his second wife, Sir Albert James Bennett 1st baronet who d. 1945.——(AGNES) MARION DAWES (*Marion, Lady Bennett*) OBE, da. of the late James Somervell, of Sorn Castle, Ayrshire; OBE (Civil) 1953: *m.* 1927, Sir (Charles) Wilfrid Bennett, TD, 2nd baronet, who d. 1952. *Residence*, 63, Cheyne Court, Flood St., Chelsea, SW3.

Collateral Branch living.

Issue of the late Frank Carlton Bennet, 2nd son of 1st baronet, b. 1900, d. 1973: *m.* 1923, Mariella, who d. 1973, da. of the late Algernon Douglas-Pennant [B. Penrhyn, colls.]:—

MICHAEL (Flat 70, Albert Hall Mansions, SW7), b. Feb. 15th, 1924: *m.* 1952, Janet Hazel Margaret, da. of Brig. Edward Joseph Todhunter, TD, and has issue living, Mark Edward Frances, b. 1960,—Caroline Mariella Carleton, b. 1954,—Victoria Serena, b. 1957.——David (The Gate House, Wing, Leighton Buzzard; Guards Club), b. 1927: *m.* 1959, Hilary Sheridan, da. of Bernard F. Clarke, and has issue living, Algernon James, b. 1962,—Sarah Elisabeth, b. 1967.

Sir Albert James Bennett, 1st baronet (son of the late Edward Bennett), sat as M.P. for Mansfield Div. of Notts (*L*) 1922-3, and for Central Div. of Nottingham (*U*) 1924-30. Sir (Charles) Wilfrid Bennett, T.D., 2nd baronet, was Lieut.-Col. Notts Yeo. (Sherwood Rangers), and a Metropolitan Magistrate 1946-52.

Beresford-Peirse, see Peirse.

BERNARD, Creation (U.K.) 1954, of Snakemoor, co. Southampton.

Sir DALLAS GERALD MERCER BERNARD, 1st Baronet, son of the late Edmund Bowen Bernard, J.P., of Snakemoor, Botley, Hants; b. March 22nd, 1888; is a Lieut. for City of London; Managing Dir. of Jardine Matheson & Co., Ltd., 1922-28, a Dir. of Matheson & Co., Ltd., 1928-42, and of Bank of England 1936-49, and Dep. Gov. 1949-54, and Chm. of Courtauld's, Ltd. 1962-64: *m.* 1922, Elizabeth, el. da. of the late Sir Charles (Stewart) Addis, KCMG, and has issue. [The 1st Baronet d. Nov. 26th, 1975.]

Arms—Sable, two greyhounds rampant and addorsed argent in chief as many stags' heads caboshed or. **Crest**—Issuant from a circlet of bezants, a demi bear sable, muzzled or.

Residence,—9, Nun's Walk, Virginia Water, Surrey.

Son living—DALLAS EDMUND, b. Dec. 14th, 1926; ed. at Eton, and at Corpus Christi Coll., Oxford (B.A. 1948, M.A. 1955): *m.* 1959, Sheila Mary, el. da. of Arthur Gordon Robey, of 14, Waggon Rd., Hadley Wood, Herts., and has issue living, Juliet Mary, b. 1961,—Alicia Elizabeth, b. 1964,—Sarah Jane, b. 1968. *Residence*, 36, Marryat Rd., Wimbledon, SW19.

Daughters living—Elizabeth Piercy, b. 1924; ed. at Southover Manor, Lewes, and at London Univ.: *m.* 1949, Gordon William Strang, FCA. *Residence*, Dock House, Beaulieu, Hants.——Margaret Anne (Little Orchard, Lymington Rd., Milton on Sea, Hants.), b. 1929; ed. at Southover Manor, Lewes: *m.* 1952 (m. diss. 1974), William Geoffrey Cleverly, MB, BS.

BERNEY, Creation (E.) 1620, of Parkehall in Redham, Norfolk.

Sir JULIAN REEDHAM STUART BERNEY, 11th Baronet, only son of the late John Reedham Erskine Berney, Lieut R. Norfolk Regt., only son of 10th baronet; b. (posthumous) Sept. 26th, 1952; s. his grandfather, *Sir* THOMAS REEDHAM, *MC*, 1975.

Arms—Quarterly gules and azure, a cross engrailed ermine. **Crest**—A garb argent.

Residence—Finchingfield, Braintree, Essex.

Aunts living—Estelle Elaine, b. 1922: *m.* 1st, 1940, Maj. Kenneth William Bols, Indian Army, who d. (of wounds received in action in Italy) 1944 [Strickland-Constable, Bt., colls.]; 2ndly, 1946, Lieut.-Col. Mark Frederic Strutt, MC, RA (TA) [see B. Rayleigh, colls.], and has issue living, (by 1st m.) Andrew Nevile David, b. 1943,—Erica Sarah b. 1941: *m.* 1966, Nigel Frederick Burch,— (by 2nd m.) [see B. Rayleigh colls.]. *Residence*, Crix, Hatfield Peverel, Essex.——Elizabeth Ann (36, Redcliffe Gdns., SW10), b. 1927: *m.* 1952 (m. annulled 1960), Allan E. Shepherd.—— Claire, b. 1933: *m.* 1956, Lt. Jeremy Michael Lynch, RN, and has issue living, Lewis Reedham, b. 1967,—Nicole, b. 1958,— Tania, b. 1962. *Residence*, Msasa Lane, Old Enterprise Rd., Box HG 160, Highlands, Salisbury, Rhodesia.

Nothing rashly nor with fear

Mother living—Hon. Jean Davina Stuart (*Hon, Mrs. Jesson*) (Finchingfield, Braintree, Essex), da. of 1st Viscount Stuart of Findhorn: *m.* 1st, 1951, John Reedham Erskine Berney, Lieut. R. Norfolk Regt., who d. (killed in action in Korea) 1952; 2ndly, 1954, Percy William Jesson.

Grandmother living—Marjorie Agnew Erskine, da. of William Erskine Gill, of Salisbury, Rhodesia: *m.* 1927, as his 2nd wife (m. diss. 1947), Sir Thomas Reedham Berney, MC, 10th Bt., who d. 1975.

Collateral Branches living.

Issue of the late John Hanson Berney, 2nd son of 9th baronet, *b.* 1868, *d.* 1959: *m.* 1900, Margaret, who *d.* 1948, da. of Sinclair George, of New Zealand :—
HUGH BARTON, *MB, ChB, b.* Jan. 11th, 1902; ed. at New Zealand Univ. (MB and ChB 1925): *m.* (March) 1931, Lilian Irene, da. of Robert William Grigor, of Blenheim, New Zealand, and has issue living, Helen, *b.* (Nov.) 1931; BA: *m.* 1955, the Rev. Edward Maurice Dashfield (St. Matthew's Collegiate Sch. for Girls, Pownall St., Masterton, NZ), and has issue living, Philip Berney *b.* 1958, James Gilbert *b.* 1961, Prudence Ann *b.* 1956,—Ann (twin), *b.* 1931: *m.* 1st, 1955, Dr. Peter Dennis, of Wellington, NZ, from whom she obtained a divorce 1964; 2ndly, 1964, William Edward Willmott, PhD, of 3780 Point Grey Rd., Vancouver 8, BC, Canada, and has issue living, (by 1st m.) Simon Hugh Miller *b.* 1959, Charlotte Jane *b.* 1956, Helen Clare (twin) *b.* 1956, Catherine Ann *b.* 1960, (by 2nd m.) Andrew Mark *b.* 1966,—Janet Douglas, *b.* 1935, BA 1955: *m.* 1960, Terence David O'Leary, of Glenconner, Old Av., Weybridge, Surrey, and has issue living, John Terence *b.* 1960, Daniel Hugh (twin) *b.* 1960, Helen Fiona *b.* 1964. *Residence*, Masterton, NZ.——John Reedham, *b.* 1911: *m.* 1937, Joyce, da. of Donald Bennett, and has issue living, John Reedham Donald, *b.* 1944,—Richard Warwick, *b.* 1946,—Jocelyn Margaret, *b.* 1938, —Juliet Alice, *b.* 1953.——Margaret Lorraine, *b.* 1914: *m.* 1937, Harold Arthur Roland Dunderdale, of Edinburgh, and has issue living, Francis John Berney, *b.* 1939,—David Bruce, *b.* 1942,— Antonia Margaret, *b.* 1944.——Barbara Dorothy (twin), *b.* 1916: *m.* 1942, Melvin Cooper Armstrong, of 15, College Av., Christchurch 5, S. Island, NZ, and has issue living, David Warwick, *b.* 1946,—Richard Thomas, *b.* 1948,—Philippa Jane, *b.* 1943.

Granddaughters of John Hanson Berney (ante):—
Issue of the late Sinclair Henry Hanson Berney *b.* 1906, *d.* 1967: *m.* 1936, Barbara May (17, Lansdowne Cres., Lansdowne, Masterton, NZ), da. of the late Andrew Roby Bloxam, of Christchurch, NZ:—
Jenifer May, *b.* 1938: *m.* 1965, David Kennedy Logan, of 75, Essex St., Masterton, NZ, and has issue living, John Berney Kennedy, *b.* 1968,—Hélen Margaret, *b.* 1966,—Robyn Elizabeth, *b.* 1971.——Diana Margaret (twin), *b.* 1938: *m.* 1962, John Allan D. Burnett, of 21, Lincoln Av., Tawa, Wellington, NZ, and has issue living, Andrew John Hanson, *b.* 1971,—Margaret Jane, *b.* 1967.

Issue of the late Alexander David Berney, 7th son of 9th baronet, *b.* 1877, *d.* 1942: *m.* 1924, Alice, who *d.* 1939, da. of A. J. Moore, of Lowestoft :—
Olive Maud, *b.* 1925: *m.* 19—, Paul Rafoth. *Resides in* U.S.A.

The Berneys, claiming to be of Norse origin, were seated at Berney, near Walsingham, Norfolk, at the time of the Norman Conquest. It is further claimed for the Berneys that they are one of the three families who settled in England before the Conquest and have never wanted a male heir. The 1st baronet, Sir Richard Berney, was Sheriff of Norfolk 1622, and the 4th baronet was Sheriff of Norwich 1762.

BETHUNE, Creation (N.S.) 1683, of Scotscraig, co. Fife.

Kind or gracious.   A crown for a mitre.

DEBONNAIRE   PRO MITRA CORONAM

Sir ALEXANDER MAITLAND SHARP BETHUNE, 10th *Baronet*; *b.* March 28th, 1909; *s.* his father, *Sir* ALEXANDER SHARP, 1917; ed. at Eton, and at Magdalene Coll., Camb.; formerly Capt. Intelligence Corps; is a Co. Director : *m.* 1955, (Ruth) Mary, da. of J. Hurst Hayes, of Marden House, East Harting, Sussex, and has issue.

Arms—Quarterly, 1st, azure, a fesse chequy or and gules between three lozenges of the second, *Bethune*; 2nd, azure, on a St. Andrew's Cross argent, a bleeding heart transpierced with two swords disposed in saltire, points downwards proper, hilted and pommelled or, the heart having over it a mitre of gold placed on the field and tasselled gules surrounded with a bordure or, charged with the Royal Tressure, flowered and counter-flowered of the fourth (the coat of augmentation granted by H.M. Charles II.) ; 3rd, argent, a fesse azure between two cross crosslets fitchée in chief, and in base a mullet sable, *Sharp* ; 4th, argent, on a chevron sable an otter's head erased of the first, *Balfour*. **Crests**— 1st, a demi-otter sable ; 2nd, a celestial crown or.

Residence—21, Victoria Grove, W.8.

Daughter living—Lucy Elizabeth, *b.* 1959.

Sisters living—Marguerite Victoria (c/o Westminster Bank, Cheltenham), *b.* 1890: *m.* 1913, Ernest Costley-White, O.B.E., who *d.* 1941, formerly Ch. Sec. Zanzibar Gov., and has issue living, Colin Robert (of Bafford Croft, Charlton iKng's, Cheltenham), *b.* 1914; formerly Capt. Roy. Warwickshire Regt.: *m.* 1942, Joan Eleanor, da. of the late B. Wade, of Frinton, and has issue living, Timothy Nigel *b.* 1946, Michael Alexander *b.* 1949.——Evelyn Carnegie, *b.* 1892: *m.* 1915, Col. Lionel George Pilkington M.C., formerly Roy. Warwickshire Regt., who *d.* 1955, and has issue living, David Charles Bethune, *OBE* (Appledown, Frilsham-by-Hermitage, nr. Newbury, Berks.), *b.* 1916; formerly Lieut. RA; OBE (Civil) 1954: *m'* 1943, Nancy Gillian, da. of the late Hon. Arnold Nottage Palmer [*see* B. Palmer, colls.], and has issue living, Julian Alexander Bethune *b.* 1946, Susan Elizabeth *b.* 1948: *m.* 1969, John Dallas Scott, of 166, Bellaw St., Melbourne, Aust.,—*Sir* Alastair (Lionel Alexander Bethune), *FRS* (The Crossways, View Rd., Rainhill, Liverpool), *b.* 1920; *cr.* Knt. 1970 [*see* KNIGHTAGE]: *m.* 1945, Patricia Nicholl, da. of Rear-Adm. Frank Elliott, OBE, and has issue living, Rosalind Gay *b.* 1946: *m.* 1969. *Residence*, Frilsham-by-Hermitage, nr. Newbury.——Elizabeth Madeline, *b.* 1897.

Collateral Branch living.

Granddaughter of the late Major Robert Bethune, son of the late Lieut.-Gen. Alexander Sharp (afterwards Bethune), JP DL, de jure, 7th baronet:—
Issue of the late Lieut.-Col. Henry Alexander Bethune, *b.* 1866, *d.* 1946; *m.* 1902, Elinor Mary, who *d.* 1955, da. of John Brown Watt, of Sydney, N.S. Wales :—
Mary Sharp, *b.* 1903: *m.* 1929, Lieut.-Col. Harry Francis Keir Wedderburn, Black Watch (Roy. Highland Regt.), who *d.* (on active ser. during European War) 1943 [*see* Ogilvy-Wedderburn, Bt., colls.]. *Residence*, Featherhouse, Mountquhanie, Cupar, Fife.

Sir William Sharp, Knt., of Scotscraig, co. Fife, was created a baronet 1683. On the death in 1780 of the 6th baronet, Sir William Sharp, who m. Margaret, da. of John Bethune, of Blebo, co. Fife, and sister and eventual heir of Henry Bethune, of Blebo, the Baronetcy became dormant and so remained until 1916. Alexander Bethune (formerly of Blebo), who assumed the additional name of Sharp, having established his right to the title as 9th Baronet before the Baronetage Committee of the Privy Council, as son of the late Capt. Alexander Bethune, J.P., D.L., of Blebo, co. Fife, de jure 8th baronet, grandson of the late Lt.-Gen. Alexander Sharp de jure 7th baronet (who on succession to Blebo in 1815 assumed by Roy. licence the surname of Bethune in lieu of his patronymic), only son of 6th baronet.

EVANS-BEVAN, Creation (U.K.) 1958, of Cadoxton-juxta, Neath, co. Glamorgan.

Sir MARTYN EVAN EVANS-BEVAN, 2nd *Baronet*; *b.* April 1st, 1932; *s.* his father, Sir DAVID MARTYN, 1973; ed. at Uppingham; High Sheriff of Breconshire 1967-68: *m.* 1957, Jennifer Jane Marion, da. of Robert Hugh Stevens, of Eardisley, Herefordshire, and has issue.

Arms—Argent, three boars' heads couped sable on a chief gules a demi lion rampant erased or between two castles of the field. Crest—Issuing from the battlements of a tower argent a demi lion rampant or gorged with a collar gules holding between the paws a boar's head as in the Arms.

Residence—Felin-Newydd, Llande Falle, Brecon, Powys. *Club*—Carlton.

Sons living—DAVID GAWAIN, *b.* Sept. 16th, 1961.——Richard Martyn, *b.* 1963.——Thomas Rhydian, *b.* 1966——Hugh Evan, *b.* 1971.
Sister living—Marigold Evans (*Countess of Rothes*), *b.* 1934: *m.* 1955, the 21st Earl of Rothes. *Residence*, Tanglewood, West Tytherley, Salisbury.
Widow living of 1st Baronet—EIRA WINIFRED (*Eira, Lady Evans-Bevan*), (Val au Bec, Les-Routeurs, St. Peters, Jersey), el. da. of the late Sidney Archibald Lloyd Glanley, of Calcutta, India: *m.* 1929, Sir David Martyn Evans-Bevan, 1st Bt., who *d.* 1973.

BIBBY, Creation (U.K.) 1959, of Tarporley, co. Palatine of Chester.

Sir (ARTHUR) HAROLD BIBBY, *D.S.O.*, 1st *Baronet*, son of the late Arthur Wilson Bibby, of Woolton, Liverpool ; *b.* Feb. 18th, 1889 ; ed. at Rugby ; Hon. LL.D. Liverpool 1959 ; Major late RA (TA) (ret.); Snr. Partner in the firm of Bibby Bros. & Co. 1935-73; Chm. of Bibby Line, Ltd. 1935-69; a DL for Cheshire (High Sheriff 1934-35), and Hon. Freeman of Liverpool; a Gov. of Rugby Sch. 1932-67; 1914-18 War in France and Flanders (despatches twice, DSO); DSO 1918, Knt. 1956: *m.* 1920, Marjorie Guthrie, da. of the late Charles James Williamson, JP, and has issue.

Arms—Azure a saltire parted and fretty argent surmounted in fesse pointby a lion rampant pean between two escallops in pale and as many mullets of six points in fesse of the second. Crest—Upon a plate a cubit arm erect holding a sword in bend sinister proper pomel and hilt or.

Residence—Tilstone Lodge, Tarporley, Cheshire. *Club*—Bath.

Son living—DEREK JAMES, *MC*, *b.* 1922; ed. at Rugby, and at Trin. Coll., Oxford (MA); Snr. Partner in the firm of Bibby Bros. & Co., Chm. Bibby Line, Ltd., Pres. Indefatigable and National Sea Training Sch. for Boys; 1939-45 War as Capt. RA (wounded, MC): *m.* 1961, Christine Maud, da. of the late Rt. Rev. Frank Jackson Okell, Bishop of Stockport, and has issue living, Michael James, *b.* 1963,—Geoffrey Frank Harold, *b.* 1965,—Peter John, *b.* 1969,—David Richard, *b.* 1970,—Jennifer Margaret, *b.* 1962. *Residence*,—Willaston Grange, Hadlow Rd., Willaston, Wirral, Ches.
Daughters living—Patricia Mary, *b.* 1921: *m.* 1st, 1944 (marriage dissolved 1956), Ronald Stuart Kinsey; 2ndly, 1962, Iain Hall Brookes Macdonald, and has issue living, (by 1st marriage) Anne Quenelda Stuart, *b.* 1947,—Hilary Jane Stuart, *b.* 1951. *Residence*, 100, Old Church St., S.W.3.——Joan Elizabeth, *b.* 1926: *m.* 1951, Major Reginald Francis Foster, Indian Army (ret.), of The Puncheon, Charlton Adam, Somerton, Somerset, TA11 7AS, and has issue living, Rachel Frances, *b.* 1955.——Anne Marjorie, *b.* 1928: *m.* 1951, Lt.-Col. John Hamilton Parlairet, who *d.* 1969, and has issue living, Sarah Lillias, *b.* 1953,—Joanna Vivian, *b.* 1955,—Ailsa Jane, *b.* 1957. *Residence*, 35, Redcliffe Rd., SW10 9NJ.

BIDDULPH, Creation (E.) 1664, of Westcombe, Kent.

Sir FRANCIS HENRY BIDDULPH, 9th *Baronet*, 3rd son of the late Walter John Biddulph, el. son of the late Com. Edward Biddulph, R.N., 3rd son of the late Simon Biddulph, 3rd son of the late Walter Biddulph, uncle of 4th baronet ; *b.* June 8th, 1882 ; *s.* his kinsman, *Sir* THEOPHILUS GEORGE, 1948 ; is a Grazier : *m.* 1907, Janet, who *d.* 1956, da. of the late Walter Bain Hannah, of Brisbane, Queensland, and has issue.

Arms—Vert, an eagle displayed argent. Crest— A wolf rampant argent, wounded on the shoulder proper.

Residence—Mount Playfair, Tambo, Queensland.

Sons living—STUART ROYDEN, *b.* June 24th, 1908 : *m.* 1939, Muriel Margaret, 3rd da. of Angus Harkness, of Hamley Bridge, S. Aust., and has issue living, Ian D'Olier (Roma Downs, Roma, Qld.), *b.* 1940: *m.* 1967, Margaret Eleanor, only da. of the late John Gablonski, of Oxley, Brisbane, and has issue living, Paul William *b.* 1967, Julie Denise *b.* 1969, Roslyn Mary *b.* 1971,—Wendy Margaret, *b.* 1946: *m.* 1966, Huan Donald John Fraser, of Claverton Park, Wyandra, Qld., and Sherwood, Condamine, Qld., and has issue living, Gina Margaret *b.* 1969,—Mary Estelle, *b.* 1947: *m.* 1968, Ian Sutherland, of Rosevale, Wyandra, Qld., and has issue living, Timothy Andrew *b.* 1969, Lee-Anne *b.* 1970. *Residence*, Mount Playfair, Tambo, Qld.——Malcolm Francis, *b.* 1910: *m.* 1936, Inez Margaret, da. of James Donnelly, of Longreach, Qld., and has issue living, Peter Michael (Blackhall St., Dingo, Qld.), *b.* 1939: *m.* 1963, Beverley Marie, only da. of the late Wilson Story, of St. George's Heights, Sydney, NSW, and has issue living, Michael Andrew *b.* 1964, Sean Gregory *b.* 1970, Craig *b.* 1973, Anne Marie *b.* 1971,—David Francis, *b.* 1942,—Janice Clare, *b.* 1937: *m.* 1958, Lionel Garth Moody, of Alpha and Macs Creer Stations, Wyandra, Qld., and has issue living, Alison Marie *b.* 1959, Tanya Claire *b.* 1962, Fona Margaret *b.* 1963. *Residence*, Mount Playfair, Tambo, Qld.

Collateral Branches living.

Issue of the late Alice Caroline Biddulph, sister of 9th baronet, *b.* 1873, *d.* 1971: *m.* 1904, Edward Dunbar Wells, who *d.* 1954:—
Doreen Catherine, *b.* 1910: *m.* 1931, Francis Joseph Priddle, of Wood St., Springsure, Qld., and has issue.——Phyllis May, (20, Brae Ross St., Rockhampton, Qld., Aust. 4700), *b.* 1911.

Descendants, if any, of the late Francis Henry Biddulph (who was *b.* 1839, and left issue a son), uncle of 9th baronet.

Descendants, if any, of the late Charles Biddulph (who left issue, one son), 2nd son of the late John Burnet Biddulph (*b.* 1796), 5th son of the late Simon Biddulph (ante), and great-uncle of 9th baronet.

Grandchildren of the late William Burnett Biddulph (infra):—
Issue of the late Ernest William Biddulph, *b.* 1889, *d.* 1963: *m.* 1939, Anna Brando:—
William Burnett (Moria, 158, Heeken St., Vkyheid 3100, Natal), *b.* 1930: *m.* 1955, Helena Hendrina Naude, and has issue living, Erlo William Burnett, *b.* 1965,—Zelda, *b.* 1956,—Janène, *b.* 1962,—Beknadine, *b.* 1974,——Magdalena Suzanna *b.* 1944: *m.* 1964, Raymond Fraser Morris, of 109, South St., Vryheid, Naral, and has issue living, Wayne William, *b.* 1966,—Delainie Anne, *b.* 1970.

Grandchildren of the late Ernest Walstrand Biddulph, 3rd son of the late John Burnet Biddulph (*b.* 1796), 5th son of the late Simon Biddulph, great-grandfather of the 9th baronet:—
Issue of the late William Burnett Biddulph, *b.* 1859, *d.* 1946: *m.* 18—, Florentia Magda-lena, who *d.* 1947, da. of the late James Brookes, of Farm, Welgelegen, Van Reenen, Orange Free State:—
Joseph Gilbert (P.O. Box 22, Sandspruit, Transvaal), *b.* 1891: *m.* 1921, Anna Struwig, and has issue living, William Burnett (of Mount Ngwibi, P.O. Mount Ngwibi, Natal), *b.* 1925: *m.* 1951, Hester Botha, and has issue living, Joseph Gilbert *b.* 1955, Wilma *b.* 1953, Annalise *b.* 1955, Brenda *b.* 1956,—Catherina, *b.* 1922: *m.* 1943, Hans Jurie Vosloo, Box 36, Sandspruit, Trans-vaal, and has issue living, George Sebastiaan *b.* 1944, Joseph Gilbert *b.* 1950, Anna Margaretta *b.* 1955,—Florentina, *b.* 1923: *m.* 1944, Willem Pieter Van Breda, of Sandspruit, Transvaal, and has issue living, Frederic Charles *b.* 1946, Joseph Gilbert *b.* 1948, Willem Pieter *b.* 1952, Burnett *b.* 1956,—Anna, *b.* 1930: *m.* 1950, Desmond Stokes, and has issue living, William *b.* 1951, Joseph *b.* 1954, Ann *b.* 1952, Nellie *b.* 1958, Margaret *b.* 1959, Desiree *b.* 1962,—Josephine, *b.* 1936: *m* 1955, Hilbert Austin Glad, of 14, Marais St., Heidelberg, Transvaal, and has issue living, Hilbert Pierre *b.* 1958, Joseph Alfred *b.* 1959.——Alphonso Charles (of 102, Main Rd., Randfontein, Transvaal), *b.* 1896.——Henry William (P.O. Box 160, Volksrust, Transvaal), *b.* 1898: *m.* 1925, Johanna Elizabeth Francisca Struwig, and has issue living, William Burnett (P.O. 160, Volksrust, Transvaal), *b.* 1927: *m.* 1955, Maria Susanna Johanna Swanepoel, of Estcourt, Natal, and has issue living, Henry William, *b.* 1956, Eleanor Burnett *b.* 1959.——Jacobus Cornelius (of Weltevrede, P.O. Sandspruit, Transvaal) *b.* 1899: *m.* 1930, Miemie Van Reenen, and has issue living, William Burnett, *b.* 1939: *m.* 1960, Gesina Van Aswegen, and has issue living, Reenen Jacobus *b.* 1961,—Elizabeth Susanna, *b.* 1932: *m.* 1954, Hendrick Van Zyl, of 30a, Dan Piernaar Rd., Volksrust, Tranvaal, and has issue living, Susan Mari *b.* 1959.——Simon Thomas (of 102, Main Rd., Randfontein, Transvaal), *b.* 1911: *m.* 1947, Mrs. Jacoba Wilhelmina Dannhauser, da. of Matheus Willemse.——Catherine Maude (P.O. Box 93, Nelspruit, Transvaal), *b.* 1903.——Maria Elizabeth, *b.* 1909: *m.* 1929, Tiberius Neser, P.O. Wakkestroom, Transvaal, and has issue living, Florentina Magdalena, *b.* 1930: *m.* 1953, Roy Goldhill, of 18, St. David's Road, East London, Cape Prov., S. Africa, and has issue living, David Roy *b.* 1958.——Violet Maud, *b.* 1915: *m.* 1939, Hendrik Sebastiaan Kriek, P.O. Box 88, Villiers, Orange Free State, and has issue living, Sebastiaan William, *b.* 1949.

Issue of the late Alphonso Biddulph, *b.* 1860, *d.* 19— : *m.* 1887, Catharina Magdalena Hendrica, da. of the late Joseph Brookes (ante):—
Ernest Walstrand, *b.* 1888.——Joseph Cornelis, *b.* 1889 : *m.* 1924, Anna Maria Grobler, and has issue living, Anna Maria, *b.* 1921.——Henry Stephen, *b.* 1892.——Bertie William, *b.* 1893.——Edward Charles, *b.* 1897.——Alphonso Gilbert, *b.* 1904.——Violet Catherine, *b.* 1895.——Florence Emma Roselin, *b.* 1907. *Residence*,

Granddaughters of the late John Burnet Biddulph (ante) :—
Issue of the late Edward John Biddulph, *b.* 1829, *d.* 1909: *m.* 18—, Fanny, da. of Edward Tunbridge, of Sundays River, Cape Province, S. Africa :—

Ina, *b.* 1879.——Freda, *b.* 1886: *m.* 1912, and has issue living. *Residence,*

Descendants, if any, of the late Thomas Burnet Biddulph, 5th son of the late John Burnet Biddulph (*b.* 1796) (ante).

SELBY-BIGGE, Creation (U.K.) 1919, of King's Sutton, co. Northampton.
[Extinct 1973.]

Sir JOHN AMHERST SELBY-BIGGE, *OBE,* 2nd and last *Baronet.*

Daughters living of 2nd Baronet—Lydia Jane (Limeuce, Dordogne, France), *b.* 1920: *m.* 1941 (m. diss. 1946), Gabriel Morand.——Cornelia Diana, *b.* 1922: *m.* 1947, Hugh Max Bowden, of Port Douglas, N Queensland, and has issue living, Anna Melissa Radclyffe, *b.* 1954,—Joanna Katherine Radclyffe, *b.* 1963.——Mary Elizabeth, *b.* 1924 (23, Cornwall Gdns., SW7): *m.* 1st, 1951, John Sheals Pratt, MD, who *d.* 1956; 2ndly. 1967, Group Gapt. Richard Irwin Knight Edwards, DFC, AFC, RAF (ret.), who *d.* 1967.
Daughter living of 1st Baronet—Evelyn Mary, *b.* 1887: *m.* 1908, Capt. Henry Cecil Pember, Household Batn., who *d.* (killed in action) 1917, and has issue living, Susan Mary, *b.* 1909: *m.* 1936, Henry Frederick Erskine Tufnell [E. Mar and Kellie], of Greenvale Farm, Cross-in-hand, Sussex, and has issue living, David Henry Amherst (8, St. Anne's Cres., Lewes, Sussex), *b.* 1938: *m.* 1968, Frances Elizabeth Watkins (and has issue living, Robert James Henry *b.* 1971, Emma Elisabeth Mary *b.* 1969), Edward Nicholas Pember *b.* 1945, Christina Matilda Beatrice (33, Merthyr Terr., SW13), *b.* 1940: *m.* 1962 (m. diss. 1971), Ian Lindsay Murdoch (and has issue living, Alexander Rupert Lindsay *b.* 1965, Arabella Natasha *b.* 1967). *Residence,* Rodmell Hill Cottage, nr. Lewes, Sussex.

BINGHAM, Creation (U.K.) 1903, of Sheffield. [Extinct 1945.]

Sir ALBERT EDWARD BINGHAM, *O.B.E.,* 2nd and last *Baronet.*

Daughter living of 2nd Baronet—Esmé Lyle, *b.* 1896: *m.* 1918, Major Pierre Elliot Inchbald. M.C., formerly R.H.A., who *d.* 1959, and has issue living, Peter Bingham (of Holdfast Manor, Upton-on-Severn, Worcs.), *b.* 1919: *m.* 1947, Rosemary Alice Anne, da. of Col. Sir Joseph Nall, D.S.O., T.D., 1st Bt., and has issue living, Peter Joseph Nicholas *b.* 1951, Guy William Benjamin *b.* 1952,—Euan (The Old Manse, Rosskeen, by Invergordon, Ross-shire), *b.* 1929; late Capt. Lancashire Fusiliers: *m.* 1st, 1956 (m. diss. 1970), Sally Ann, only da. of W. A. Foster, of Bosham, Sussex; 2ndly, 1971, Patricia Ann, only da. of A. H. Gibb, of St. Georges Sq., SW1, and has issue living (by 1st m.) Michael Christopher *b.* 1957, David Pierre William *b.* 1960, Fiona Esme *b.* 1962 (by 2nd m.) Tara *b.* 1971,—Judy Featherstone, *b.* 1923: *m.* 1947, Lt.-Col. James Thomas Amcotts Wilson, KOYLI [see Wilson, Bt., cr. 1874, colls.], Gillian Elizabeth (*Lady Hammick*), *b.* 1931: *m.* 1953, Sir Stephen George Hammick, 5th Bt. *Residence,* Wraxall Manor, Dorchester, Dorset.

BIRCHENOUGH, Creation (U.K.) 1920, of Macclesfield, co. Chester. [Extinct 1937.]

Sir (JOHN) HENRY BIRCHENOUGH, *G.C.M.G.,* 1st and last *Baronet.*

Daughter living of 1st Baronet—Sylvia Milicent, *b.* 1890: *m.* 1915, Alfred Farr Morcom, MB, BC, MRCS, who *d.* 1952, and has issue living, Anthony John, *b.* 1916,—Henry Richard, *b.* 1922. *Residence,* Flat 8, 14, West Halkin Street, SW1.

BIRD, Creation (U.K.) 1922, of Solihull, co. Warwick.

Sir RICHARD GEOFFREY CHAPMAN BIRD, 4th *Baronet; b.* Nov. 3rd, 1935; *s.* his father *Sir* DONALD GEOFFREY, 1963; ed. at Beaumont: *m.* 1st, 1957, Gillian Frances, who *d.* 1966, da. of Bernard Haggett, of Solihull; 2ndly, 1968, Helen Patricia, only da. of Frank Beaumont, of Pontefract, and has issue by 1st m.

Arms—Vert, on a pale or two popinjays of the field, on a chief ermine three garbs of the second. **Crest**—A garb as in the arms between two roses per pale gules and argent, leaved and slipped proper. *Residence—*

Success is the reward of endeavour.

Sons living—By 1st m.—JOHN ANDREW, *b.* Jan. 19th, 1964.——Mark Richard, *b.* 1965.
Daughters living—By 1st m.—Cecilia Mary, *b.* 1957.—— Frances Bernadette, *b.* 1959.——Brigitte Ann, *b.* 1960. ——Rowena Clare, *b.* 1962.
Brother living—Peter Donald Chapman (3, Hillfoot, Groomsport, co. Down), *b.* 1938; ed. at Beaumont: *m.* 1962, Vera Mary, da. of Albert Seymour, of Northfield, and has issue living, Anthony Donald, *b.* 1964,— Christopher Robert, *b.* 1967.
Sister living—Elizabeth Anne, *b.* 1931: *m.* 1955, John Brigg, and has issue living, David Lockwood John *b.* 1956,—Michael James, *b.* 1957,—Peter Donald (twin), *b.* 1957. *Residence,* The Soundings, Bosham Hoe, Chichester.

Aunts living—Eileen Hilda: *m.* 1st, 1930, John Walter Jones, who *d.* 1934; 2ndly, 1935, Group Capt. Frank Grenville Argyle Robinson, DFC, RAF (ret.), and has issue living, (by 2nd marriage) Ronald Geoffrey Argyle, *b.* 1936,—Josephine Elsie, *b.* 1949. *Residence,* Greys Mallory, near Warwick.——Eleanore Marshall: *m.* 1932, Vernon Harms-Cooke,

and has issue living, Sylvia, b. 1934: m. 1959, Peter John Smith, and has issue living, Nigel Peter b. 1961, Charles Francis b. 1963, Christabel b. 1964,—Annalova, b. 1936: m. 1953, David Stanley Faber, and has issue living, Geoffrey David b. 1961, Rosanne b. 1955, Colleen b. 1957, Anita b. 1959,—Geoffrena, b. 1938: m. 1959, Capt. James William Beachus, RA, and has issue living, Timothy James b. 1962, Lucinda b. 1961,—Eleanore, b. 1940,—Carol, b. 1941: m. 1962, John Edmund Davies, of The Retreat, Sedgeberrow, Evesham, Worcs., WR11 6UA, and has issue living, Anthony William Gordon b. 1968, Tracey Anne b. 1971. Residence, The Wold Furlong, Chipping Camden, Glos.
Daughter living of 2nd Baronet—Pamela Stephanie Helen EVANS, b. 1909; assumed by deed poll 1974 the surname of Evans: m. 1st, 1934 (m. diss. 1946), Reginald William Bell; 2ndly, 1952 (m. diss. 1973), Vicomte Alain de Mauduit de Kervern, and has issue living, (by 1st m.) Robert Reginald, b. 1935,—Thomas Randal, b. 1937,—William Andrew, b. 1940,—(by 2nd m.) Francoise Héléne, b. 1952. Residence, Mille Fiori, Oletta, 20, France.

Sir Alfred Frederic Bird, 1st Bt. (cr. a Knt. 1920, nominated a Baronet Jan. 1st, 1922, d. Feb. 1922), was Chm. of Alfred Bird and Sons (Limited), Manufacturing Chemists, and sat as M.P. for W. Div. of Wolverhampton (Co.U) Jan. 1910 to Feb. 1922. Sir Robert Bland Bird, K.B.E., 2nd baronet, was Chm. of Alfred Bird & Sons, and sat as M.P. for W. Div. of Wolver-hampton (C) 1922-29, and 1931-45.

BIRKIN, Creation (U.K.) 1905, of Ruddington Grange, Ruddington, Notts.

Sir CHARLES LLOYD BIRKIN, 5th *Baronet*, son of the late Col. Charles Wilfrid Birkin, C.M.G., 4th son of 1st baronet; b. Sept. 24th, 1907; s. his uncle, *Sir* ALEXANDER RUSSELL, 1942; ed. at Eton; formerly temporary Capt. Roy. Armoured Corps: m. 1940, Janet, da. of Peter Johnson, and has issue.

Arms—Argent, a cross raguly couped vert between in the 1st and 4th quarters, a bee volant, and in the 2nd and 3rd a birch tree eradicated proper. Crest—A scorpion erect proper.

Club—Carlton.

Son living—JOHN CHRISTIAN WILLIAM, b. July 1st, 1953; ed. at Eton.

Daughters living—Jennifer Claire Eleanor, b. 1941: m. 1971, Charles de Clermont.——Amanda Jane Averill, b. 1943.

Sister living—Winifred May, b. 1894: m. 1st, 1913, the Rt. Hon. William Dudley Ward, who d. 1946, and from whom she had obtained a divorce 1931 [see E. Dudley, colls.]; 2ndly, 1937, Wing-Com. the Marquis de Casa Maury (Spain), who d. 1968, and from whom she obtained a divorce 1954.

Prepared for peace and war.

Daughters living of 3rd Baronet—Pamela Mary, b. 1922: m. 1st, 1941, Major Samuel Luckyn Buxton, M.C., 17th/21st Lancers, who d. (killed in action during European War) 1944 [see Buxton, Bt., colls.]; 2ndly, 1946, Major Aubrey Leland Oakes Buxton, M.C. [see Buxton, Bt., cr. 1840, colls.]. Residence, Norman House, Stansted, Essex.——Sara Margaret, b. 1926: m. 1st, 1950 (m. diss. 1961), Maj. James Robert Hanbury, late Roy. Scots Greys, who d. 1971; 2ndly, 1962, Col. George Anthony Murray Smith, and has issue living (by 1st m.) Evan Robert, b. 1951: m. 1974, Rosalind Jeannette, da. of Derrick Allix Pease [see Pease Bt., cr. 1920],—Timothy James, b. 1952. Residence, Gumley, Market Harborough, Leics.

Collateral Branches living.

Issue of the late Major Philip Austen Birkin, O.B.E., 5th son of 1st baronet, b. 1869, d. 1951 : m. 1900, Frances Emily who d. 1953, 2nd da. of Joseph Littlewood, J.P., of the Park, Nottingham :—
Geoffrey Ivor, TD, b. 1911; Maj. (ret.) RHA, 1939-45 War (despatches). Residence, Rose Cottage, Darmsden, Needham Market, Suffolk.——Frances Marjorie, b. 1905: m. 1st, 1928, Duncan William Grant, who d. 1933; 2ndly, 1938, Douglas Charles Lockwood. Residence, La Adela, Vivorata, Argentina.

Issue of the late Major Harry Laurence Birkin, TC, 6th son of 1st baronet, b. 1872, d. 1951 : m. 1909, Olive Isobel, who d. 1960, da. of the late Rev. Henry Charles Russell, R. of Wollaton, Notts [D. Bedford, colls.] :—
James Michael, CB, DSO, OBE, DFC, AFC (Little Burneston, Ashlake, Fishbourne, I. of Wight; Notts. Club, MCC, Royal Yacht Sqdn.), b. 1912; ed. at Harrow, and at Trin. Coll., Camb.; Group Capt. (ret.) and Hon. Air Commodore RAuxAF; Inspector RAuxAF 1952-62, and an ADC to HM 1957-63; 1939-45 War (AFC, DFC, DSO); DSO 1944, OBE (Mil) 1951, CB (Mil) 1956: m. 1956, Antonia, da. of the late Lt.-Col. A. F. Stanley-Clarke, and has issue living, James Francis Richard, b. 1957,—Abigail Victoria Ann, b. 1959.——David Leslie, DSC, b. 1914; ed. at Harrow, and at Trin. Coll., Camb.; is Lt.-Cdr. RNVR; 1939-45 War (DSC): m. 1943, Judy Mary (Judy Campbell, the actress), da. of the late John Arthur Gamble, OBE (J. A. Campbell), and has issue living, Andrew Timothy, b. 1945,—Jane Mallory, b. 1946,—Linda Mary Deborah, b. 1950. Residence, 65, Deodar Rd., Putney, SW15. Clubs, MCC, Chelsea Arts.

The 1st baronet, Sir Thomas Isaac Birkin (son of the late Richard Birkin, J.P., of Aspley Hall, Nottingham), was a Director of Great Northern Railway Co., and of Mercantile Steamship Co., and High Sheriff of Notts 1892. The 2nd baronet, Sir Thomas Stanley Birkin, was High Sheriff for Notts 1915. The 3rd baronet, Sir Henry Ralph Stanley Birkin, was a well-known Racing Motorist, and holder of several records.

BIRKMYRE, Creation (U.K.) 1921, of Dalmunzie, co. Perth.

Advance.

Sir HENRY BIRKMYRE, 2nd *Baronet; b.* March 24th, 1898; *s.* his father, *Sir* ARCHIBALD, CBE, 1935; ed. at Wellington Coll.; 1914-18 War in France with RFA: *m.* 1922, Doris Gertrude, da. of the late Col. Herbert Austen Smith, CIE, formerly Inspector-Gen. of Civil Hospitals, Bihar and Orissa, and has issue.

Arms—Per chevron argent and sable, in chief two eagles heads erased and in base a thistle leaved and slipped all proper. Crest—In front of a rising sun proper an eagle displayed sable.
Residence—Springbank, Cooden, Bexhill-on-Sea, Sussex.

Son living—ARCHIBALD, *b.* Feb. 12th, 1923; ed. at Radley; Burma 1941-45 as Capt. RA; *m.* 1953, Gillian Mary, only da. of the late Eric M. Downes, O.B.E., and has issue living, James, *b.* 1956,—Alison Mary, *b.* 1954,—Serena Jane, *b.* 1960. *Residence,* Fernhill Cottage, Windsor Forest, Berks.
Daughter living—Jane Henrietta, *b.* 1929 : *m.* 1952, Major Robert Evelyn Russell Smallwood, of Finches, Pembury, Tunbridge Wells, and has issue living, Rosemary Jane, *b.* 1954,—Susan Caroline, *b.* 1957.

Brother living—Archy, *b.* 1904 : *m.* 1940, Doreen, only child of the late Robert Barclay, of Kilbirnie, Ayrshire, and has issue living, David, *b.* 1941,—Adelaide, *b.* 1945: *m.* 1974, John Hugh Borthwick of Borthwick, yr., of The Neuk, nr. Gilston, by Heriot, Midlothian [see L. Borthwick, colls., dormant]. *Residence,* Overdale, Ancaster Rd., Crieff, Perthshire. *Club*—Royal Scottish Automobile.

The 1st baronet, Sir Archibald Birkmyre, C.B.E. (son of the late Henry Birkmyre, of Port Glasgow), was knighted 1917, and was senior partner in the firm of Birkmyre Bros., merchants, of Calcutta.

BLACK, Creation (U.K.) 1922, of Midgham, co. Berks.

Not the cross, but the light.

Sir ROBERT ANDREW STRANSHAM BLACK, *E.D.,* 2nd *Baronet; b.* Jan, 17th, 1902; *s.* his father, *Sir* ROBERT JAMES, 1925 ; ed. at Eton, and at Camb. Univ. ; Major 99th (Bucks and Berks Yeo.) Field Brig. R.A. (T.A.) ; High Sheriff of Berks 1934 : *m.* 1927, Ivy, da. of Brig.-Gen. Sir Samuel Herbert Wilson, K.C.B., K.C.M.G., K.B.E., and has issue.

Arms—Argent, a saltire sable between two crescents in pale and as many mullets in fesse gules, on a chief of the second three trefoils slipped of the field. Crest—Issuant out of a cloud a demi-lion rampant proper, charged on the shoulder with a trefoil vert and holding in the paws a fylfot sable.

Residence—Elvendon Priory, Goring, Reading, Berks.

Son living—ROBERT DAVID (Cavalry Club), *b.* March 29th, 1929; ed. at Eton; Maj. (ret.) R. Horse Guards; Maj. Berks and Westminster Dragoons Yeo., and Joint MFH Garth and S. Berks Hunt: *m.* 1953 (m. diss. 1972), Rosemary Diana, da. of Sir Rupert John Hardy, 4th Bt., and has issue living, Diana Sarah, *b.* 1955,—Fiona Caroline, *b.* 1957,—Joanna Rosemary, *b.* 1966.

Sisters living—Marjorie Rhona Cecilia (East Lodge, Midgham Green, Reading): *m.* 1928, Reginald Michael Currie, who *d.* 1962, and has issue living, James Michael Blyth, *b.* 1931,—John Robert Blyth, *b.* 1933,—Peter Thomas Blyth, *b.* 1937.——Gladys May (of Headlams Well, Ipsden, Oxon.): *m.* 1940, Brig. Leonard Geoffrey Holmes, CBE, and has issue living, Andrew Peter Geoffrey, *b.* 1944; ed. at Radley, and Magdalene Coll., Cambridge.

The 1st baronet, Sir Robert James Black, was Chm. of Mercantile Bank of India, and a Director of Shell Transport Co. (Limited).

BLACKETT, Creation (E.) 1673, of Newcastle, Northumberland.

We will labour in hope.

Sir GEORGE WILLIAM BLACKETT, 10th *Baronet; b.* April 26th, 1906; *s.* his brother, *Sir* CHARLES DOUGLAS, 1968; 1939-45 War: *m.* 1st, 1933, Euphemia Cicely, who *d.* 1960, da. of the late Maj. Nicholas Robinson, of Frankton Grange, Salop; 2ndly, 1964, Daphne Laing, da. of the late Maj. Guy Laing Bradley, of Bridge End House, Hexham.

Arms—Argent, on a chevron between three mullets pierced sable three escallops of the field.
Residence,—Colwyn, Corbridge-on-Tyne, Northumberland.

Brothers living—FRANCIS HUGH, *b.* Oct. 16th, 1907; ed. at Eton; Maj. (ret.) The Royals; 1939-45 War: *m.* 1950, Elizabeth Eily (BARRIE), da. of the late Howard Dennison, of Valparaiso, Chile, and has issue living, Hugh Francis, *b.* 1955,—Marcus Henry, *b.* 1961,—Angela Frances, *b.* 1951,—Charlotte Elizabeth, *b.* 1952. *Residence*, Halton Castle, Corbridge, Northumberland. *Club*,—Cavalry.——Rupert Henry, *b.* 1911; ed. at Eton and Lincoln Coll., Oxford (BA); Maj. (ret.) DLI; 1939-45 War: *m.* 1941, Felicity Mary Audley (CLAPTON), da. of the late Lt.-Col. William Alfred Scudamore Smith, and has issue living, Piers Rupert, *b.* 1941,—Miranda, *b.* 1944. *Residence*, Thorne Close, Constantia, Cape Province, S. Africa.

Daughters living of 9th Baronet—Caroline Ann, *b.* 1936: *m.* 1957, Capt. Geoffrey Thomas Warren Fenwicke-Clennell, late 11th Hussars, of The Weft House, Widdington, Essex, and has issue living, Nicholas, *b.* 1959,—Luke Thomas, *b.* 1961,—Katharine Mary, *b.* 1963.——Lucinda Mary, *b.* 1940: *m.* 1st, 1964 (m. diss. 1971), Ewan Iain Macleod Hilleary; 2ndly, 1971, Michael Henry Basil Peto, of Cliddesden Down House, Basingstoke [see Peto, Bt., cr. 1927], and has issue living (by 1st m.), Iain Douglas, *b.* 1965,—(by 2nd m.) see Peto, Bt., cr. 1927.

Widow living of 9th Baronet—URSULA MARY (*Ursula, Lady Blackett*) (The Estate House, Matfen, Newcastle upon Tyne), da. of the late Maj. Maurice Fearing Cely-Trevilian, of Midelney Manor, Drayton, Som.: *m.* 1935, Sir Charles Douglas Blackett, 9th Bt., who *d.* 1968.

Collateral Branches living.

Grandson of the late Harold Blackett, el. son of the late John Charles Blackett, R.N., 4th son of 5th baronet:—
Issue of the late Henry Beaumont Blackett, *b.* 1886, *d.* 1964: *m.* 1916, Evelyn Nora Mary, who *d.* 1966, da. of J. Booth Lazenby, of Newcastle-on-Tyne:—
John Harold Booth (of West House, Whalton, Morpeth, Northumberland. *Club*, Cavalry), *b.* 1923; ed. at Radley; 1939-45 War as Lieut. 15th/19th King's Roy. Hussars: *m.* 1953, Veronica Heath Stuart, da. of Henry Tegner, of Whalton, Northumberland, and has issue living, John Simon, *b.* 1954,—Rupert Beaumont, *b.* 1957,—Caroline Rose, *b.* 1960,—Juliet Evelyn, *b.* 1965.

Granddaughter of John Charles Blackett, RN (ante):—
Issue of the late Adm. Henry Blackett, C.B.E., *b.* 1867, *d.* 1952 : *m.* 1906, the Hon. Pamela Mary Fisher, who *d.* 1949, youngest da. of 1st Baron Fisher :—
Pamela, *b.* 1911 : *m.* 1957, Clifford Henry Bray. *Residence*, 32, Tongdean Road, Hove, Sussex. *Club*, Curzon.

The 1st baronet, Sir William Blackett (son of William Blackett, of Hoppyland, co. Durham), was M.P. for Newcastle-upon-Tyne 1673-80. The 2nd baronet, Sir Edward, was M.P. of Newcastle-upon-Tyne, and an Alderman and sometime Mayor of that borough. Sir Hugh Douglas Blackett, 8th baronet, was High Sheriff of Northumberland 1914.

BLACKWOOD, Creation (U.K.) 1814.

By right paths.

Sir FRANCIS ELLIOT TEMPLE BLACKWOOD, 6th *Baronet* ; *b.* March 11th, 1901 ; *s.* his brother, *Sir* HENRY PALMER TEMPLE, 1948 ; is *h.p.* to Barony of Dufferin and Clandeboye and to Baronetcy of Blackwood of Ballyleidy (*cr.*1763) [see M. Dufferin and Ava]: *m.* 1921, Lilian Margaret, da. of the late Fulton J. MacGougan, of Vancouver.

Arms—Azure, a fesse or, in chief a crescent argent, and in base a mascle of the third. **Crest**—On a cap of maintenance gules, turned up ermine, a crescent argent.

Residence—114, Casa Mobile Circle, W. Sacramento, California, USA, 95691.

Widow living of 5th Baronet—ETHEL EDITH MARY (*Dowager Lady Blackwood*), da. of the late Humphrey Grenfell Ratcliffe, of Penhellis, Deal, Kent: *m.* 1926, Sir Henry Palmer Temple Blackwood, 5th baronet, who *d.* 1948. *Address*, c/o Lloyds Bank, Epsom, Surrey.

Collateral Branches living.
Issue of the late Capt. Maurice Baldwin Raymond Blackwood, D.S.O., R.N., 3rd son of 4th baronet, *b.* 1882, *d.* (on active ser. during European War) 1941: *m.* 1915, Dorothea, who *d.* 1967, da. of the late Hon. G. Bertrand Edwards, of Huon Park, Sydney, N.S. Wales :—
FRANCIS GEORGE (Uambi, 408, Bobbin Head Rd., N. Turranurra, NSW, 2074), *b.* May 20th, 1916; MIEAust; ARACI: *m.* 1941, Margaret, da. of Hector Kirkpatrick, of Lindfield, NSW, and has issue living, John Francis, *b.* 1944; ed. at Univ. of NSW (BArch): *m.* 1971, Kay Greenhill, of Seaforth, Sydney, NSW,—Peter Maurice, *b.* 1950,—Angela Margaret, *b.* 1942; ed. at Sydney Univ. (BSc): *m.* 1965, Clifton Elliott Barker, BSc, of 141, Campbell Drive, Wahroonga, NSW 2076, and has issue living, Stephen Michael Barker *b.* 1969, Zoë Frances *b.* 1971.——George *OBE*, *DCS* (Myriong, Funtington, Chichester), *b.* 1920; Cdr. RN; OBE (Mil.) 1970: *m.* 1950, Diana, da. of the late Lt.-Col. A. L. A. Flint, and has issue living, Robert George Temple, *b.* 1953,—Michael Francis (37, The Crescent, Vaucluse, 2030, NSW), *b.* 1959,—Clare Mary, *b.* 1956. *Residence*, Myriong, Funtington, W. Sussex.——Henry, *b.* 1922, late Lt. RAustNR; Capt. Merchant Marine: *m.* 1948, Katherine, da. of D. T. Rankin, of Westwood, West Wyalong, NSW, and has issue living, Maurice Henry, *b.* 1954.——Mary, *b.* 1917: *m.* 1st, 1940, John Frankcomb, who *d.* (killed on active ser. as PO RAAF) 1942: 2ndly, 1945, Edward Lister Ifould, DSO, DFC, and has issue living, (by 1st m.) Dorothy Pamela, *b.* 1942,—(by 2nd m.) William Edward *b.* 1947,—Marian, *b.* 1946,—Frances Gay Lister, *b.* 1953. *Residence*, 1762, Pittwater Rd., Bayview, NSW.

Issue of the late Neville Foster Blackwood, 4th son of 4th baronet, b. 1884; d. 1964: m. 1919, Kathleen Nelly, who d. 1959, da. of the late H. S. Mosenthal:—
Robin Henry (1, Gurney Close, Caversham, Reading, Berks.), b. 1926.

The 1st baronet, a Vice-Admiral of the Blue, was the youngest son of Sir John Blackwood, 2nd baronet, of Ballyleidy, whose wife, Dorcas, was, after her husband's decease, created Baroness Dufferin and Clandeboye in her own right [see M. Dufferin, colls.]. He was the bearer of the despatches announcing the victory of Trafalgar. The 4th baronet, Sir Francis, was Capt. R.N., and served in the Crimea.

BLAIR, Creation (U.K.) 1945, of Harrow Weald, co. Middlesex. [Extinct 1962.]

Sir REGINALD BLAIR, 1st and last Baronet.

Granddaughter living of 1st Baronet—[Issue of the late Capt. Malcolm Reginald Blair, Roy. Fusiliers, el. son of 1st baronet, b. 1906, d. (killed in action in France) 1940: m. 1936, Sheila Pasmore], Jenny Mabel, b. 1937: m. 1st 1957 (m. diss. 19—), Robert Alan Cumming Greenleas; 2ndly, 19—, Peter B. Trier, of Alderwood House, Greenham Common, Newbury, Berks.

Daughter living of 1st Baronet—Mary Lile Wieland, b. 1910: m. 1937, Lieut.-Com. G. Vernon W. Harrison, R.N., who d. (killed in action during European War) 1941, and has issue living, Peter Reginald Wallace, b. 1939.

HUNTER BLAIR, Creation (G.B.) 1786, of Dunskey.

Vigilance, trength, pleasure.

Sir JAMES HUNTER BLAIR, 7th *Baronet ; b.* May 7th, 1889 ; *s.* his father, *Capt. Sir* EDWARD, 1945 ; ed. at Wellington Coll., and at Balliol Coll., Oxford (B.A. 1911) ; late Lieut. Seaforth Highlanders ; European War 1914-18 (wounded) : *m.* 1st, 1917, Jean, who *d.* 1953, da. of T. W. McIntyre, of Sorn, Ayrshire ; 2ndly, 1954, Mrs. Norah Collins, who *d.* 1966, el. da. of the late Herbert Edward Byers, and has issue, by 1st marriage.

Arms—Quarterly : 1st, argent, a chevron gules between three bugles vert, vested and stringed of the second, *Hunter* ; 2nd, argent, on a chevron gules between three cross-crosslets fitchée sable a fleur-de-lis or, within a double tressure flory counterflory of the second, *Kennedy of Culzean* ; 3rd, argent, on a saltire sable eight mascles of the field, in chief a star gules, *Blair* ; 4th, argent, a shake-fork sable, and in chief a rose gules, surmounted of a mullet of the field, *Cuninghame of Brownhill.* Crest—A stag's head cabossed proper. Supporters—Dexter, a dog of chase salient argent ; sinister, an antelope [springing proper, gorged with an open crown and a chain hanging thereat or.

Residence—Milton, Maybole, Ayrshire.

Sons living—By 1st marriage—EDWARD THOMAS, b. Dec. 15th, 1920 ; ed. at Eton, and at Balliol Coll., Oxford; 1939-45 War with KOYLI; Member of Kirkcudbright Co. Council since 1970: m. 1956, Norma, who d. 1972, el. da. of W. S. Harris. Residence, Parton House, Castle Douglas, Kirkcudbrightshire.——James (Blairquhan Castle, Maybole, Ayrshire) b. 1926; ed. at Eton, and at Balliol Coll., Oxford, formerly Lt. Scots Gds.; a DL for Ayrshire.

Collateral Branches living.

Issue of the late Com. Gaspard Patrick Hunter Blair, R.N., 2nd son of 6th baronet, b. 1895, d. (killed in action during European War) 1941 (despatches) ; m. 1929, Sophie, who d. 1968, having m. 2ndly, 1945, as his second wife, Rear-Adm. Robert Cathcart Kemble Lambert, DSO, who d. 1950), el. da. of the late Prince Alexis Koudacheff:—
Francis, b. 1930 ; formerly Sub-Lieut. R.N.V.R. : m. 1957, Joyce, da. of Com. James Graham, O.B.E., R.N., and has issue living, Patrick David, b. 1958,—Michael Francis, b. 1959,—Peter James, b. 1961,—Caroline Mary, b. 1963. Residence, Marbrack, Carsphairn, Castle Douglas, Kirkcudbrightshire.——Katherine Isabel, b. 1933; ed. at Oxford Univ. (MA); BA London 1958: m. 1960, Michael R. Stidworthy, of The Old Rectory, Caldecote, Cambridge, and has issue living, John Damian, b. 1967,—Alexander Luke, b. 1969,—Xenia Mary Gabriel, b. 1961,—Imogen Theresa, b. 1963.

Grandchildren of the late Major Reginald Stanley Hunter Blair, M.B.E. (infra):—
Issue of the late Lieut.-Col. David Walter Hunter Blair, b. 1894, d. 1961 : m. 1st, 1919 (m. diss. 1941), Barbara, who d. 1965, da. of the late George Cameron Norman; 2ndly, 1941, Hughe Thelma, who d. 1972, da. of the late Capt. H. E. Reid, R. Scots, and widow of Maj. J. W. Williams, 2nd Punjab Regt.; she m. 3rdly, 1965, Adm. Sir Walter Thomas Couchman, KCB, CVO, DSO, OBE, of Tandymead, Bromeswell, nr. Woodbridge, Suffolk:—

(By 1st marriage) John David, b. 1925 ; ed. at Eton : m. 1952, Jennifer Mary, only da. of Leslie Hamilton Gault, and has issue living, Thomas, b. 1957,—Jane, b. 1956,—Sophie, b. 1960. *Residence*, Muircambus House, Kilconquhar, Fife.——(By 2nd marriage) Neil Malcolm, b. 1944; late Gordon Highlanders.——(By 1st m.) Aline Rosemary, b. 1921: m. 1st, 1944 (m. diss. 1949) Lt.-Col. David Theodor Dobie, DSO, formerly Parachute Regt.; 2ndly, 1949 (m. diss. 1965), as his 2nd wife, Maj. Hugh Cam Hobhouse, N. Somerset Yeo. [*see* Hobhouse, Bt.]; 3rdly, 1965, John Alastair Livingston Timpson, MC, late Scots Gds., of 11, Paultons Sq., SW3.

Issue of the late Cdr. Ronald Hunter Blair, DSC, RN, b. 1898, d. 1968: m. 1929, Nancye (Fiddlers Hall, Charlestown, Fife), da. of the late W. B. Colbeck, of Auckland, NZ:—
Alister (Gilder Lodge, Althorne, Chelmsford, Essex), b. 1930; ed. at Wellington; Lt.-Cdr. RN, (ret.); Korea 1952-53: m. 1958, Jennifer Shirley, el. da. of the Rev. Basil William Greenup, of Rock, Cornwall, and has issue living, Nicholas Patrick Alister, b. 1959.——Reginald Stuart (2, Cobden Rd., Edinburgh), b. 1942; late Lt. Gordon Highlanders: m. 1968, Jennifer Marjorie, el. da. of Jack Paley Yorke, and has issue living, Camilla Louise, b. 1970,—Antonia Claire, b. 1972.——Ronald Patrick (15, Douglas Cres., Edinburgh), b. 1944: m. 1972, Mary Fitzhugh, da. of William T. Stewart, Jr., of Far Hills, New Jersey, USA, and has issue living, James Stewart, b. 1974.——Julia, b. 1932: m. 1st, 1958, Charles Maitland Zane; 2ndly, 1966, Arnold J. Bauer, and has issue living, (by 1st m.) Lucy Sarah Mackenzie, b. 1960, (by 2nd m.) Rebecca, b. 1968. ——Elizabeth Mary (twin), b. 1944.

Issue of the late Major Reginald Stanley Hunter Blair, M.B.E., 7th son of 4th baronet, b. 1861, d. 1948: m. 1893, Emily Gertrude, who d. 1967, da. of the late Robert Heaton Rhodes, of Christchurch, NZ:—
Elisabeth Anne, b. 1909: m. 1933, Eyre Chatterton, MICE, and has issue living, Peter James, b. 1941,—Antony Richard, b. 1946: m. 1974, Mary Angela, da. of John Coyle, of Beechpark West, Athlone, co. Westmeath,—Lorna Laderina, b. 1935. *Residence*, Portaneena, Ballykeeran, Athlone, co. Westmeath.

Sir James Hunter Blair, 1st baronet was MP and Lord Provost of Edinburgh, and a partner in the banking house of Sir William Forbes and Co. He was 2nd son of John Hunter of Mainholm and Brownhill, Ayrshire, yr. son of James Hunter of Abbotshill, Ayrshire, an estate granted to his ancestor James Hunter by charter 1569. The 1st Bt. added the name of Blair about 1774, having m. 1770 Jane, sister and heir of David Blair, and only da. of John Blair of Dunskey, Wigtownshire by Anne Kennedy, sister and co-heir of 10th Earl of Cassillis. The 5th baronet, the Rt. Rev. Sir David Oswald, was Abbot of Dunfermline and Private Chamberlain to Pope Leo XIII.

BLAKE, Creation (I.) 1622, of Menlough, Galway.

Sir THOMAS RICHARD VALENTINE BLAKE, 17th *Baronet; b.* Jan. 7th, 1942; *s.* his father, *Sir* ULICK TEMPLE, 1963; ed. at Bradfield.

Arms—Argent, a fret gules.   **Crest**—A tiger-cat passant guardant proper.

Residence,—

Virtus sola nobilitas.
Virtue alone ennobles.

Mother living—Elizabeth, da. of Arthur Gordon, of Blundellsands, Lancs.: m. 1st, 1940 (marriage dissolved 1950), Sir Ulick Temple Blake, 16th Baronet, who d. 1963; 2ndly, 1965, Vice-Adm. Eric William Longley Longley-Cook, CB, CBE, DSO, of Gathorne Cottage, West Lavant, Chichester.

Collateral Branches living.

Grandchildren of the late Major Cecil Bruce Blake (infra):—
Issue of the late Major Charles Anthony Howell Bruce Blake, Roy. Ulster Rifles, b. 1911, d. (killed in action in Korea) 1951: m. 1948, Elspeth (who m. 2ndly, 1961, Patrick Michael Gardner, MBE, of 44, Hillmorton Rd., Rugby), da. of the late Lt.-Col. A. M. Arnott:—
ANTHONY TEILO BRUCE (posthumous), b. May 5th, 1951; ed. at Wellington——Caroline Bruce, b. 1949.

Grandchildren of the late Surg.-Maj. Walter Blake, 2nd son of the late Walter Blake, grandson of 10th baronet:—
Issue of the late Maj. Cecil Bruce Blake, b. 1880, d. 1937: m. 1909, Effie, who d. 1969, da. of S. Earnshaw Howell, JP:—
Valentine John Bruce, b. 1914 ; European War 1939-45 as Lieut. Indian Army (prisoner); m. 1950, Carla Maria Aïda Wrinch-Schulz, of Gardens, Cape Town, S. Africa, and has issue living Jonathan Luttrell, b. 1953,—Kerry Valentine, b. 1963,—Rosalie Julianne, b. 1951,—Noelle Claire Louise, b. 1959. *Residence*, Careysville, Fermoy, co. Cork.——Elinor Joyce, b. 1910: m. 1933, Cyril Hall Green, and has issue living, Jeremy Dominic Blake (Tim's House, Castlelyons, co. Cork) b. 1934: m. 1965, Gabriel Meredith Benson, and has issue,—Celia Elinor Vadyn, b. 1936: m. 1958, Edward John Mansel Hugh Frampton Child-Villiers [*see* E. Jersey]. *Residence*, Ballyvolane House, Castlelyons, co. Cork.——Patricia Honora, b. 1919: m. 1st, 1942, Samuel Francis Hewitt Haughton, MB, BCh, from whom she obtained a divorce 1957; 2ndly, 1957, Joseph Gerald Caulfield Kirby-Turner, who d. 1961 [B. Kilmaine, colls.], and has issue living, (by 2nd m.) Belinda Shiralee Anne, b. 1959,—Sharon Briar Rose, b. 1960. *Residence*, Stookeen Cottage, Colamaine East, Bantry, co. Cork.

Descendants of the late John Blake, 4th son of 3rd baronet :—

Grandchildren of the late Valentine Joseph Blake (infra):—
Issue of the late Lt.-Col. Arthur Maurice Joseph Blake, MC, LRCP, LRCS, b. 1884, d. 1974: m. 1938, Barbara (Sally Park, Templeogue, Dublin 14), only da. of Raymond Stephenson, of Cranford, Stillorgan Rd., Dublin:—

Martin Joseph, *b.* 1952.——Anne Meriel Josephine, *b.* 1939: *m.* 1964, Patrick Leonard, of Edmonds-
town Park, Rathfarnham, Dublin 14, and has issue living, John Arthur (Sean), *b.* 1967,—Jeremy,
b. 1973,—Natasha Veronica, *b.* 1965.——Erica Mary Josephine, *b.* 1940: *m.* 1966, Bernard
H. C. Corbally, of Glen Trool, Sinclair Lane, Helensburgh, Dunbartonshire, and has issue living,
Simon Herbert Arthur, *b.* 1967,—Colin George Eric, *b.* 1968,—Ruth Ida Mary, *b.* 1974.

> Grandson of the late Valentine O'Connor Blake, son of the late Maurice Blake,
> grandson of the late Maurice Blake (*d.* 1789), grandson of the late John Blake
> (ante):—
> Issue of the late Valentine Joseph Blake, *b.* 1843, *d.* 1912: *m.* 1880, the Hon. Mary French,
> who *d.* 1919, da. of 3rd Baron de Freyne :—

Gerald, *b.* 1896: *m.* 1943, Ann Deegan, and has issue living, Valentine, *b.* 1945: *m.* 1971, Madelene,
ony da. of J. Andrews, of Perivale, Middx.,—Gerald (6, Cambell Court, Campbell Rd., Hanwell,
W7), *b.* 1947: *m.* 1968, Elaine Thomas, of Baglan, Glam., and has issue living, Gervase *b.* 1969,
Emma Josephine *b.* 1972,—Arthur, *b.* 1950. *Residence*, 16, Egerton Gdns., Ealing, W13.

The founder of this family is said to have accompanied King John to Ireland in 1185. The 1st
baronet, Sir Valentine Blake, was Mayor of Galway borough 1611 and 1630. The 6th baronet, Sir
Walter, was the first Catholic gentleman of any distinction who joined William III ; he maintained
and clothed a regiment at his own expense.

BLAKE, Creation (G.B.) 1772, of Langham, Suffolk. [Extinct 1975.]

Cdr Sir CUTHBERT PATRICK BLAKE, *D.S.O., RN.* 6th and last *Baronet.*

Daughter living of 6th Baronet—Veronica Anstace, *b.* 1919; late 2nd Officer WRNS: *m.* 1942,
Maj. Hugh Gilson-Taylor, Suffolk Regt. (ret.), and has issue living, Christopher Gilson (41,
Rowan Rd., W6), *b.* 1943: *m.* 1969, Patricia Anne, da. of Ismay Emanuel, of London, W6, and
has issue living, Andrew Blake *b.* 1972, David Patrick *b.* 1955.—Anstace Felicity, *b.* 1949: *m.*
1971, Gilbert William Peter Wright, and has issue living, Jonathan William Blake *b.* 1972, James
Robert *b.* 1974. *Residence*, Barnfield, Stanstead, Sudbury, Suffolk.

Collateral Branch living.

> Granddaughter of the late Col. George Pilkington Blake, only son of James
> Bunbury Blake, 4th son of 3rd baronet:—
> Issue of the late Eustace James Pilkington Blake, *b.* 1865, *d.* 1940: *m.* 1889, Ethel Minna,
> who *d.* 1943, da. of the late Col. P. B. Schreiber, Roy. Scots:—

Violet Hilda (twin), *b.* 1890: *m.* 1915, Sydney Johnston, and has issue living, Denis Norman
(5, Rivey Lodge, Old Woking Rd., West Byfleet, Surrey), *b.* 1918; 1939-45 War with RAF in
Burma: *m.* 1947, Nona Margaret, da. of Francis Spencer Green, and has issue living, Martin
Blake *b.* 1948, Colin *b.* 1951,—Alexander Frank (Wreacot, Moss Side, Lytham, Lancs.), *b.* 1921;
1939-45 War with E. Surrey Regt., and Glider Pilot Regt.: *m.* 1945, Kathleen, da. of Thomas
Rawsthorn, and widow of Michael Mathew, Queen's Regt., and RAF, and has issue living, Kevin
b. 1950, Patrick Robert *b.* 1959,—Beryl Lander, *b.* 1916: *m.* 1941, Ronald Dermott Shallcross
Jack, of Bramerton, West Byfleet, son of Sir Robert Ernest Jack, and has issue living, Duncan
Robert Lander *b.* 1947, Julia Colleen Shallcross *b.* 1942. *Residence*,—Stroma, Hanger Hill,
Weybridge, Surrey.

BLAKE, Creation (U.K.) 1907, of Tillmouth Park, Cornhill, co. Northumberland.

I shall rise again.

RESURGAM

Sir FRANCIS MICHAEL BLAKE, 3rd
Baronet ; *b.* July 11th, 1943 ; *s.* his father, *Sir*
(FRANCIS) EDWARD COLQUHOUN, 1950; ed. at
Rugby: *m.* 1968, Joan Ashbridge, da. of F. C. A.
Miller, of Ramsay Lodge, Kelso, and has
issue.

Arms—Per chevron argent and sable, a chevron per
chevron between in chief two garbs and in base a frette all
counterchanged. **Crest**—A morion proper, thereon a martlet
argent, holding in the beak a sprig of barley sable.
Residence—The Dower House, Tillmouth Park,
Cornhill-on-Tweed, Northumberland.

Sons living—FRANCIS JULIAN, *b.* Feb. 17th, 1971.——
Nicholas Winston, *b.* 1974.
Sister living—Pamela, *b.* 1925; formerly in WRNS: *m.*
1st, 1944 (m. diss. 1947), Lt. Richard Hosking, RNR;
2ndly, 1947 (m. diss. 1970), Capt. David Clayhills
Henderson, formerly KOSB, and has issue living (by
2nd m.) Edward James, *b.* 1952,—Christopher David,
b. 1963,—Deborah, *b.* 1948,—Joanna, *b.* 1949,—Olive,
b. 1954,—Dinah, *b.* 1960. *Residence*, 629, Kings Rd.,
Fulham, SW6.
Half-Sister living—Caroline Anne Honey, *b.* 1948: *m.* 1975,
Adam Henville Simonds.
Aunt living—(daughter of 1st baronet)—Marjory
Frances, *b.* 1890: *m.* 1st, 1917, Capt. R. N. F. Mills,
R.F.C., who *d.* (killed in action during European War,
1917; 2ndly, 1921, Major Alfred Davis Welch
RMLI, who *d.* 1960. *Address*, Kingarth Hotel, Crieff,
Perthshire.

Widow living of 2nd Baronet—DOREEN MAUD, da. of the late J. B. Sample, of Stoneleigh,
Hexham-on-Tyne, Northumberland : *m.* 1st, 1947, as his second wife, Sir (Francis) Edward
Colquhoun Blake, 2nd Bt., who *d.* 1950; 2ndly, 1961, Wing Com. John Francis Grey, D.S.O.,
DFC, RAF, who *d.* 1964. *Residence*, Oxendean Burn, Cornhill-on-Tweed, Northumberland.

Collateral Branch living.

Issue of the late Patrick Delaval Blake, younger son of 1st baronet, *b.* 1904, *d.* 1961 : *m.* 1st, 1927 (divorce 1944), Phyllis, da. of W. Lee Ellison, of Chester; 2ndly, 1944, Mrs. Ruby Holdsworth, who *m.* 1973, W. E. Sweet, of 18, Spencer Close, Warsash, Southampton, Hants.

By 1st m.) Ian Francis (Slab Cottage, Shepherd's Hurst, Outwood, Surrey), *b.* 1929; Lt.-Cdr. RN: *m.* 1954, Frances Jillian, da. of W. T. Barton, of Shepherd's Hurst, Outwood, Surrey, and has issue living, Philip Ian, *b.* 1955,—Carol Patricia, *b.* 1957.——Mary Douglas, *b.* 1931: *m.* 1965, Dr. Peter Branson, Oaklands Cottage, Wray Common, Reigate, Surrey.

The 1st baronet, Sir Francis Douglas Blake, C.B. (son of the late Francis Blake, of Tillmouth Park, Northumberland) sat as M.P. for Berwick-on-Tweed Div. of Northumberland(*Co.L.*) 1916-22. The 2nd Baronet, Sir Francis Edward Colquhoun Blake, was Capt. R.A. (T.A. Reserve), and served in European War 1914-18 and European War 1939-45.

BLAKER, Creation (U.K.) 1919, of Brighton, Sussex.

Sir JOHN BLAKER, 3rd *Baronet*; *b.* March 22nd, 1935; *s.* his father, Maj. Sir REGINALD *TD*, 1975: *m.* 1st, 1960 (m. diss. 1965), Catherine Ann, da. of the late Francis John Anselon Thorold [see Thorold, Bt., colls.]; 2ndly, 1968, Elizabeth Katherines, da. of Col. John Russell, DSO.

Arms—Ermine three chevronelles, in chief two towers sable. **Crest**—A horse's head sable, charged with three chevronelles argent.

Residence—Knowles Cottage, Ardingly, Sussex.

Sister living—Anne, *b.* 1932: *m.* 1953, Edmund Crosby Cockburn, and has issue living, Crosby Bay, *b.* 1956,—Crosby Kim, *b.* 1958,—Georgina Gay, *b.* 1954. *Residence*, Glebe Farm, Shuckburgh, Daventry, Northants.

Aunt living (daughter of 1st Baronet)—Jessie, *b.* 1891: *m.* 1921, Arthur Newington of St. Georges Retreat, Burgess Hill, Sussex.

Widow living of 2nd Baronet—SHEILA KELLAS (*Sheila, Lady Blaker*) (Knowles, Ardingly, Sussex), da. of Alexander Cran, MB of Little Court, Merrow, nr. Guildford: *m.* 1930, Maj. Sir Reginald Blaker, TD, 2nd Bt., who *d.* 1975.

The 1st baronet, Sir John George Blaker, O.B.E., was Mayor of Brighton 1895-9.

BLAKISTON, Creation (G.B.) 1763, of the City of London.

[Name usually pronounced "**Blackiston.**"]

Sir (ARTHUR) NORMAN HUNTER BLAKISTON, 8th *Baronet*, son of Reginald Norman Blakiston, son of Charles Robert Blakiston (see colls., infra); *b.* April 26th, 1899; *s.* his kinsman, Sir ARTHUR FREDERICK, MC, 1974; Solicitor: *m.* 1962, Mary Ferguson, da. of the late Alfred Ernest Gillingham, of Cave, S. Canterbury, NZ, and has issue.

Arms—Argent, two bars gules, in chief three cocks of the last. **Crest**—A cock gules.

Residence—28, McKenzie St., Geraldine, S. Canterbury, NZ.

DOE WELL & DOUBT NOT

Sons living—FERGUSON ARTHUR JAMES, *b.* Feb. 19th, 1963.——Norman John Balfour, *b.* 1964.
Sisters living—Hilda Mary (18, Melrose, Terr., Nelson, NZ), *b.* 1896.——Annie Constance Olive, *b.* 1905: *m.* 1935, Robert Norman Graham McNab, of 18, Melrose Terr., Nelson, NZ, and has issue living, Graham Norman Anthony, *b.* 1938: *m.* 1961, Jacqueline Tutbury, and has issue living, Jody, *b.* 1961, Jack, *b.* 1969, Mandy, *b.* 1963,—Janice Constance Agnes, *b.* 1942: *m.* 1965, Brian Dennison Maurice, of 13, Vanbrugh Hill, Blackheath, SE3, and has issue living, David Ceri, *b.* 1970.
Widow living of 7th Baronet—ANN HOPE PERCIVAL (*Ann, Lady Blakiston*), (Corton, Warminster, Wilts.), da. of the late Purcell Cooke Jeans, of Cortington Grange, Warminster, Wilts.: *m.* 1954, as his 2nd wife, Sir Arthur Frederick Blakiston, MC, 7th Bt., who *d.* 1974.

Collateral Branches living.

Grandchildren of the late Charles Robert Blakiston, 5th son of 3rd baronet, *b.* 1825, *d.* 1898: *m.* 1858, Mary Anna, who *d.* 1924, da. of the late Most Rev. Henry John Chitty Harper, D.D., sometime Bishop of Christchurch, and Primate of New Zealand:—
Issue of the late Charles Douglas Blakiston, *b.* 1868. *d.* 1950: *m.* 1908, Ethel Anne, who *d.* 1967, da. of the late John Henley Whishaw, of Featherston ,NZ:—

Rev. Peter Henley Douglas, *b.* 1911, is V. of Mount Maunganui, New Zealand: *m.* 1940, Eileen, da. of Dr. John C. Bradshaw, of Christchurch, New Zealand.——Charles Michael Hardy, *b.* 1919: *m.* 1945, Nancy, da. of Charles E. Holmes, of Wellington, New Zealand, and has issue living, David Holmes, *b.* 1946,—Roger Charles *b.* 1948—Simon Michael, *b.* 1952.   *Residence* 1, Cobden Lane, Napier, NZ.——(Phyllis) Anne Whishaw: *m.* 1948, Frederick Harrison Beckett, ANZIA, ARIBA, MRSA, of 26, Orakei Rd., Remuera, Auckland, NZ, and has issue living, Anne Priscilla, *b.* 1949: *m.* 1968, Graham Lester Pitts, BArch, of 37, Cowan St., Auckland, NZ, and has issue living, Jonathan Graham *b.* 1971,—Diana Pauline, *b.* 1950: *m.* 1970, Jeffrey Jamieson, of 26, Orakei Rd., Remuera, Auckland, NZ, and has issue living, Tessa Diana *b.* 1971.—— Patricia Elizabeth Harper: *m.* 1938, John Abercrombie Bolton, of Woodville, and has issue living, Peter David Cheney (PO Box 2050, Stortford Lodge, Hawke's Bay, NZ), *b.* 1939: *m.* 1964, Gael McRae, and has issue living ~ n Abercrombie Collyns *b.* 1965, Michael McRae Cheney *b.* 1966, Ian Sampel Lockett *v.* 1969,—Timothy John, *b.* 1946,—Belinda Anne, *b.* 1941: *m.* 1961, Hugo Ryland Johnston, of Remuera, Auckland, and has issue living, Christopher Hugh *b.* 1963, David *b.* 1966, Sarah Elizabeth *b.* 1964,—Elizabeth Patsy, *b.* 1944: *m.* 1968, Anthony Charles Everard White, of Masterton, NZ, and has issue living, Charles Henry Everard *b.* 1969,—Juliet Barbara, *b.* 1949: *m.* 1969, Michael Gordon Neale, of 78, Kawhai St., Nelson, NZ, and has issue living, Simon *b.* 1972.——Barbara Helen Joan: *m.* 1st, 1940, Henry Frank Seymour, who *d.* (killed in action) 1941; 2ndly, 1945, Allan Frederick Palairet, and has issue living, (by 1st m.) Nicholas Charles (Wensleydale Station, Private Bag, Gisborne, NZ), *b.* 1941: *m.* 1966, Patricia Anne Ingram, of Auckland, and has issue living, Howard Frank *b.* 1970, Andrea June *b.* 1972,— (by 2nd m.) Anthea Gay, *b.* 1949: *m.* 1973, Noel Morris Kershaw, of 17, Christian St., Christchurch, NZ,—Penelope Sue, *b.* 1955.   *Residence*, 5, Kelvin Rd., Remuera, Auckland, NZ.

Granddaughters of the late Maj. John Blakiston, 27th Regt., 2nd son of 2nd baronet:—

Issue of the late John Rochfort Blakiston, *b.* 1840, *d.* 1921 : *m.* 1876, Georgina Helen, who *d.* 1928, da. of the late Rev. Francis William Cubitt [B. Hastings, colls.] :—
Mary Helen (3, Highsett, Hills Rd., Cambridge), *b.* 1889: *m.* 1921, Charles Sumner Durst, OBE, who *d.* 1961, and has issue living, David William (c/o Lloyds Bank, 67, Kingsway, WC2) *b.* 1922; ed. at Marlborough, and at Pembroke Coll., Camb. (MA); AMIEE; 1939-45 War as Capt. REME: *m.* 1953, Margaret Joyce, da. of E. Child, of Southwold, and has issue living, Jennifer Penelope *b.* 1957,—Rosanne Mary Georgina, *b.* 1932: *m.* 1969, John Horace Blight, of 2, Brook St., Windsor, Berks., and has issue living, Francis Charles *b.* 1971.

Grandchildren of the late John Rochfort Blakiston (ante):—

Issue of the late John Francis Blakiston, CIE, *b.* 1882, *d.* 1965: *m.* 1st, 1918, Paula, from whom he obtained a divorce 1930), da. of the late E. Allen Howard, Bar.-at-law; 2ndly, 1937, Margaret Dora (Anelog, Aberdaron, Pwllheli, Caernarvonshire), el. da. of the Rev. G. A. Ward-Jackson, R. of Rousham with Lower Heyford, Oxford:—
(By 2nd marriage) John Alan Cubitt, *b.* 1938.——Susan Anne Margaret, *b.* 1940.——Jane Mary Dora Helen, *b.* 1944: *m.* 1968, Richard Parker, of 2, Culmstock Rd., SW11 62X, and has issue living, Nycolas Sebastian Robert Blakiston *b.* 1970,—Venetia Clare Rosalind, *b.* 1969.

Grandchildren of the late Capt. John Blakiston-Houston (infra) :—

Issue of the late Capt. Richard Blakiston-Houston, *b.* 1864, *d.* 1933 : *m.* 1897, Lilian Agnes, who *d.* 1952, da.of the late George Jardine Kidston, of Finlaystone, Renfrewshire :—
John Matthew, *b.* 1898; ed. at Eton; FLAS (Overseas); Lt.-Col. (ret.) 11th Hussars, Capt. and Brevet Maj. RAC (Reserve); Hon. Col. 5th Bn., Roy. Inniskilling Fusiliers (TA) to 1963; a DL for co. Down (High Sheriff 1944); High Sheriff of co. Tyrone 1954; European War 1916-18; European War 1939-42 in Egypt, Libya, and E. Africa as Lieut.-Col. Comdg. S. Rhodesia Armoured Cars: *m.* 1931, Lettice Arden, da. of Henry Gervas Stobart, of Thornton Hall, Thornton-le-Dale, Yorkshire, and has issue living, Richard Patrick, *b.* 1948,—Mary Bridget, *b.* 1932: *m.* 1956, Gavin Rowan Hamilton, of Stenton House, Stenton, Dunbar, E. Lothian, and has issue living, James (Hamish) John *b.* 1961, Patrick Gawaine *b.* 1964, Catherine Nicola Blanche *b.* 1957,—Anne *b.* 1934: *m.* 1962, Capt. David John Hallifax, RN [Hughes, Bt., cr. 1773], of Scrag End, Vernon Hill, Bishop's Waltham, Hants., and has issue living, Thomas Ronald *b.* 1965, Matthew William Hughes *b.* 1967, Louisa Kate *b.* 1964,—Prudence, *b.* 1936: *m.* 1964, John Archibald Douglas-Menzies, of Mounteagle, Fearn, Ross-shire, and has issue living, John William *b.* 1966, Andrew Edward *b.* 1968, James *b.* 1970,—Elizabeth, *b.* 1939: *m.* 1973, Michael Haines,—Patience Victoria, *b.* 1944.   *Residences*, Beltrim Castle, Gortin, co. Tyrone; Roddens, Ballywater, co. Down.——Marian (*Lady MacMillan of MacMillan of Knap*), OBE, *b.* 1905; is a CStJ; OBE (Civil) 1952: *m.* 1929, Gen. Sir Gordon Holmes Alexander MacMillan of MacMillan of Knap, KCB, KCVO, CBE, DSO, MC, late Argyll and Sutherland Highlanders, and has issue living, George Gordon (of Finlaystone, Langbank, Renfrewshire), *b.* 1930; MA; *m.* 1961, Cecilia Jane, MA, da. of the late Capt. Arthur Spurgin, and has issue living, Arthur Gordon *b.* 1962, Richard Anthony *b.* 1963, Malcolm James *b.* 1967,—John Richard Alexander, OBE, *b.* 1932; MA; Col. late Argyll and Sutherland Highlanders, and Gordon Highlanders; OBE (Mil.) 1973: *m.* 1964, Belinda, da. of Lt.-Col. R. H. Lumley-Webb, MC, of Tunstall House, Sittingbourne, Kent, and has issue living, Gordon John *b.* 1967, Elizabeth Mary *b.* 1966, Diana Belinda *b.* 1971,—David (The White House, Finlaystone, Langbank, Renfrewshire), *b.* 1939: *m.* 1962, Liv Senstad, da. of Rolf Andersen, of Oslo, Norway, and has issue living, Alastair Thomas *b.* 1964. Lilian Victoria *b.* 1968,—Andrew Allardice (FAO, Rome), *b.* 1942; MA, PhD: *m.* 1972, Roberta, da. of the late H. Becher, and has issue living, Harry Julius *b.* 1973,—Elizabeth Judy *b.* 1935: *m.* 1963, Lt.-Cdr. John Robin Hutton, MBE, RN of 83, Burntwood Grange Rd., SW18, and has issue living, James Rupert *b.* 1966, Alice *b.* 1964.   *Residence*, Finlaystone, Langbank, Renfrewshire.

Issue of the late Lieut.-Col. James Edward Blakiston-Houston, O.B.E., *b.* 1877, *d.* 1958 : *m.* 1913, Dorothy Irene, who *d.* 1962, da. of Col. Frederic William Rea, Indian Army:— Sheelah, *b.* 1915 ; formerly Junior Com. A.T.S. : *m.* 1942, Major Robert Dempster Wilson, who *d.* 1956, late R.A.S.C., and has issue living, James Dempster, *b.* 1944.   *Residence*, The Glebe, Killinchy, co. Down.

Granddaughter of the late Richard Bayly Blakiston-Houston, 5th son of 2nd baronet :—

Issue of the late Capt. John Blakiston-Houston, *b.* 1829, *d.* 1920: *m.* 1859, Marian, who *d.* 1890, da. of the late Richard S. Streatfeild, of The Rocks, Sussex :—
Ethel Fanny : *m.* 1st, 1902, James Robert Macalpine-Downie, who *d.* (killed in action during European War) 1918; 2ndly, 1929, Arthur McClintock, who *d.* 1930.   *Residence*, Strathappin House, Appin, Argyll.

Grandchildren of the late John Richard Blakiston, son of the late Rev. Peyton Blakiston, M.D., F.R.S., 6th son of 2nd baronet:—

Issue of the late Ralph Blakiston, *b.* 1861; *d.* 1936: *m.* 1st, 1889, Ellen Anne Fell, who *d.* 1910, da. of the late Rev. Robert Walker, V. of Wymeswold, Leicestershire ; 2ndly, 1916, Rosemary, who *d.* 1972, da. of Edmund Gore, of Crosby:—
(By 1st m.) *Rev.* Robert Ralph Christian (Hillside, Hurstbourne Tarrant, nr. Andover, Hants), *b.* 1890: *m.* 1929, Winifred Muriel, yr. da. of John Frost, of Ripley, Derbyshire, and has issue living, John Robert (Wood Sorrel Cottage, Nutley, Sussex) *b.* 1931; ed. at Haileybury: *m.* 1960, Carol Helen, yst. da. of John C. Durham, of Anniswood, Warninglid, Sussex, and has issue living Michèle Anne *b.* 1964, Rachel Jane *b.* 1966.——John Horace, BSc, *b.* 1897; Lt. RNR (ret.): *m.*

1928, Winifred Kathleen Maybank, da. of Archie William Webb, of Banstead, and has issue living, David (Tara, 65, Curley Hill Rd., Lightwater, Surrey), b. 1934; ed. at Haileybury, and at Loughborough Coll. (honours Dip. Mech. Eng.; MIMechE, CEng): m. 1962, Joanna Averil, da. of Cecil Green, of Kingsthorpe, Northampton, and has issue living, John b. 1967, Anne b. 1970, Carol Clare b. 1972. *Residence*, Applegarth, Bosham Hoe, Sussex.——Anna Marie, b. 1892: m. 1921, Sqdn.-Ldr. George Halstead Whitaker, RAF, who d. 1959, and has issue living, Ellen Frances, b. 1933: m. 1955, Michel Lawrence Watkins, of Valley House, 20, Essenden Rd., Sanderstead, Surrey, and has issue living, Simon Michael b. 1956, Stephen Benedict b. 1957, Robert Francis b. 1961, Mary Thérèse b. 1963, Tamsin Jane b. 1966. *Residence*, Little Croft, 24, Downsview Rd., Seaford, Sussex.

Issue of the late Aubrey Blakiston, b. 1862, d. 1935: m. 1881, Lelia Emily, who d. 1915, da. of the late Edmund Harris, of Rugby :—

Eleanor Lelia Marie: m. 1903, Anthony James Hasslacher, who d. 1950, and has issue living, Harry, b. 19—.——Dorothy Mary (912, Sequeo Av., Santa Cruz, Cal., USA): m. 19—, Newman Brown who d. 1957.——Clare Joseph Mary (Bungalow Blue, Via Porro 22, Chiesanova, Padua, Italy); ed. at Milan Univ. (PhD).

Grandchildren of the late Matthew Folliott Blakiston, son of the late Rev. Peyton Blakiston, M.D., F.R.S. (ante):—

Issue of the late Rochfort Folliott Blakiston, b. 1860, d. 1949 : m. 1st, 1907, Ellen Kate who d. 1929, only da. of the late George Greenleaf, of Great George Street, Westminster, SW; 2ndly, 1930, Elizabeth Lilian Diana, el. da. of the Rev. David Jones, V. of Goodwick, Pembrokeshire.

(By 2nd m.) Digby Rochfort David (Gale How, Pine Rd., Hook Heath, Woking, Surrey), b. 1931; late Lt. RN: m. 1959, Dorothea Irene Louise Walser, and has issue living, Matthew Simon Rochfort, b. 1964,—Louise b. 1961,—Caroline, b. 1962.——Michael Peyton Folliott (Street Farm House, Sheering, Bishops Stortford Herts.) b. 1933; ed at Trin. Coll., Oxford (BA): m. 1973, Mrs. Fanny Marie Francis, el. da. of Henri Roquette, of Lille, France.

This is a branch of the family of Blakiston, of Blakiston, co. of Durham, in which two baronetcies were conferred in 1615 and 1642, expiring respectively in 1619 and 1713. The 1st baronet of the present creation was Sheriff of London 1753, and Lord Mayor 1760.

BLANE, Creation (U.K.) 1812, of Blanefield, Ayrshire. [Extinct 1916.]

Com. Sir CHARLES RODNEY BLANE, *R.N.,* 4th and last *Baronet.*

Daughter living of 4th Baronet—Helen Mary, b. 1913: m. 1940, William Robert Tomkinson, TD, late Capt. Middx. Regt., and has issue living, Robert Charles (Lower Verney Cottage, Kimblewick, nr. Aylesbury, Bucks.), b. 1941: m. 1968, Joanna Sally Hastings, and has issue living, James Robert b. 1970, Simon William b. 1972,—David Edward b. 1945,—Virginia Susan, b. 1943: m. 1964, Maj. W. Andrew Evans, 5th R. Inniskilling Dragoon Gds., and has issue living, Lucinda Emma Katherine b. 1967, Alexandra Louise Harriette b. 1969,—Diana Helena (twin), b. 1943: m. 1969, David Rainald Lewthwaite, [see Lewthwaite, Bt.]. *Residence*, Hilborough, The Warren, Kingswood, Surrey.

BLENNERHASSETT, Creation (U.K.) 1809, of Blennerville, co. Kerry.

Fortune helps the brave.

Sir (MARMADUKE) ADRIAN FRANCIS WILLIAM BLENNERHASSETT, 7th *Baronet ; b.* May 25th, 1940; *s.* his father, *Lieut. Sir* MARMADUKE CHARLES HENRY JOSEPH CASIMIR, RNVR, 1940; ed. at McGill Univ., Imperial Coll., London (MSc) and Cranfield Business Coll. (MBA): m. 1972, Carolyn Margaret, da. of the late Gilbert Brown, and has issue.

Arms—Gules, a chevron ermine between three dolphin embowed argent. **Crest**—A wolf sejant proper.

Residence—41, Park Rd., Chiswick, W4 3EY.

Son living—CHARLES HENRY MARMADUKE, b. July 18th, 1975.

Daughter living—Celina Mary Charlotte, b. 1973.

Collateral Branches living.

Issue of the late Capt. William Lewis Rowland Paul Sebastian Blennerhassett, D.S.O., O.B.E., youngest son of 4th baronet, b. 1882, d. 1958 : m. 1910, Olivia Frances, who d. 1953, da. of Sir Thomas Fraser Grove, 1st Bt. :—

Casimir Paul Francis Rowland, b. 1911; Maj. late Nigeria Regt.; formerly Assist. Comptroller of Customs, Nigeria: m. 1945, Elizabeth Charlotte Josephine, da. of the late Com. Gregory Stapleton, RN [see D. Norfolk, colls.], and widow of Maj. Francis John Angus Skeet, and has issue living, John Rowland, b. 1952,—Rosanna Frances, b. 1946. *Residence*, 17, Campden Hill Rd., Kensington, W.8.

Granddaughter of the late Rowland Ponsonby Blennerhassett, son of the late Richard Francis Blennerhassett, son of the late Rowland Blennerhassett, 4th son of 1st baronet:—

Issue of the late Richard Francis Ponsonby Blennerhasset, b. 1879, d. 1938: m. 1914, Silvia, who d. 1957, only da. of the late Frederic W. H. Myers, of Leckhampton, Cambridge:—

Diana Mary Ponsonby, b. 1916: m. 1939 Richard John Moreton Goold-Adams CBE, only son of the late Maj. Sir Hamilton Goold-Adams, GCMG, CB. *Residence*, Highfield House, Binley, Andover, Hants.

The ancestors of this family were long seated in Cumberland, and took their name from the township of Blennerhasset in that co. Members of the family represented Carlisle in nearly every Parliament from Richard II to James I, and later frequently represented either Kerry co. or the borough of Tralee. Robert Blennerhassett settled in co. Kerry in the reign of James I. The 4th baronet, the Rt. Hon. Sir Rowland, sat as M.P. for Galway (L) 1865-74, and for co. Kerry 1880-85. The 6th baronet, Lieut. Sir Marmaduke Charles Henry Joseph Casimir, R.N.V.R., d. (killed in action during European War) 1940.

BLOIS, Creation (E.) 1686, of Grundisburgh Hall, Suffolk.

[Name pronounced "**Bloyss.**"]

Sir CHARLES NICHOLAS GERVASE BLOIS, 11th *Baronet:* *b.* Dec. 25th, 1939; *s.* his father, *Capt. Sir* GERVASE RALPH EDMUND, *MC*, 1968; ed. at Harrow and Trin. Coll., Dublin: *m.* 1967, Celia Helen Mary, only da. of Cyril George Francis Pritchett, CBE, of Mayfield, and has issue.

Arms—Gules, a bend vair between two fleurs-de-lis argent. **Crest**—A gauntlet proper holding a fleur-de-lis argent.

Residence,—Red House, Westleton, Saxmundham, Suffolk.

Je me fie en Dieu.
I trust in God.

Son living—ANDREW CHARLES DAVID, *b.* Feb. 7th, 1971.
Daughter living—Helen Janet, *b.* 1974.
Brother living—Rodney John Derek (Cockfield Hall, Yoxford, Suffolk), *b.* 1941; ed. at Harrow: *m.* 1968, Lady (Elizabeth) Caroline (Elinor Evelyn) Giffard, da. of 3rd Earl of Halsbury, and has issue living, Camilla Frances Elizabeth, *b.* 1970,—Susanna Gillian Caroline, *b.* 1972.
Sister living—Gillian Frances Audrey (3, Ennismore Gdns., SW7), *b.* 1943: *m.* 1965 (m. diss. 1970), Hugh Christopher Riddle.
Aunts living—(daughters of 9th baronet)—Christian Frances, *b.* 1902: *m.* 1st, 1928 (m. diss. 1940), Edward Archibald Fraser Harding; 2ndly, 1940, Geoffrey Henry Cecil Bing, QC, of Orchard Cottage, Walpole, Suffolk, and has issue living, (by 2nd m.) Inigo Geoffrey, *b.* 1944,—Richard, *b.* 1946.——Flavia Ria Joan (*Baroness Burntwood*) *b.* 1914: *m.* 1948, Baron Burntwood [Life Peer]. *Residences*, Flat 2, 37, Chester Way, SE11; The Thatched Cottage, Walberswick, Southwold, Suffolk.
Mother living—Audrey Winifred, only da. of the late Col. Harry Johnson, DSO, of Boden Hall, Ches.: *m.* 1938 (m. diss. 1948) Capt. Sir Gervase Ralph Edmund Blois, MC, 10th Bt., who *d.* 1968.
Widow living of 10th Baronet—MARGARET LUCIA (*Margaret Lady Blois*) (The Vicarage, Ballyhooly, co. Cork), da. of the late Maj. the Hon. Charles James White [see B. Annaly, colls.]: *m.* 1948 as his 2nd wife, Capt. Sir Gervase Ralph Edmund Blois, MC, 10th Bt., who *d.* 1968.

Collateral Branches living.

Issue of the late Major Eardley Steuart BROOKE, T.D., 3rd son of 8th baronet, *b.* 1869, *d.* 1955, who assumed by Roy. licence 1931 for himself and issue the surname and arms of Brooke in lieu of his patronymic : *m.* 1916, Violet Mary Magdalene, who *d.* 1945, da. of Thomas Sproat, of Port Mary, Kirkcudbright, and Valparaiso :—
Thomas Eardley, *b.* 1918 ; ed. at Wellington Coll. ; is Capt.R.A. (Reserve), and a Fellow of Land Agents' So. : *m.* 1948, Joy, da. of Maj.-Gen. Robert Stedman Lewis, C.B., O.B.E., and has issue living, Thomas Robin Eardley. *b.* 1951,—Jennifer Mary, *b.* 1949,—Elizabeth Anne, *b.* 1953. *Residence*, Cresborough, Rhos, Haverfordwest.——Michael Steuart BLOIS-BROOKE, *R.D., b.* 1919 ; is Lieut.-Com. R.N.R.; re-assumed by deed poll 1953, the surname of Blois in addition to and before that of Brooke : *m.* 1949, Mary, younger da. of Cecil Harvey Mead, of Oak House, Crawley Down, Sussex, and has issue living, Mark Harvey, *b.* 1954,—Susan Penelope, *b.* 1950: *m.* 1973, Nigel Robert Clifford, Bar. at law,—Diana Mary, *b.* 1959. *Residence*, St. Austin's House, Curtis Lane, Sheringham, Norfolk.——Eileen Mary, *b.* 1917: *m.* 1938, Lt.-Col. Edward Douglas Garnett, RA, who *d.* 1964, and has issue living, Anthony Eardley Douglas, *b.* 1939. *Residence*, Redgate House, Wherstead, Ipswich.

Grandchildren of the late Maj. Eardley Steuart Brooke, TD (ante):—
Issue of the late Robert John Brooke, B.L., *b.* 1923, *d.* 1963: *m.* 1949, Ann Hamerton Gordon (St. Aidan's, Morebattle, Kelso), el. da. of Capt. Francis Gordon Troup, of Dunbennan:—
Alastair John, *b.* 1950.——Ian Steuart, *b.* 1953.——Katharine Margaret, *b.* 1961.

Granddaughters of the late Lieut.-Col. Dudley George Blois, D.S.O., R.F.A. (infra) :—
Issue of the late Wing Com. John Dudley Blois, R.A.F. Regt. (late Major Irish Guards), *b.* 1915, *d.* 1954: *m.* 1948, Elizabeth Catherine (Shawfield, Tekels Av., Camberley, Surrey), da. of Rear-Adm. Sir Wellwood George Courtenay Maxwell, KBE, CMG [B. Chesham]:—
Elizabeth Frances Moyra, *b.* 1949.——Sarah Jane, *b.* 1951.
Issue of the late Lieut.-Col. Dudley George Blois, D.S.O., R.F.A., 5th son of 8th baronet, *b.* 1875, *d.* (killed in action) 1916: *m.* 1914, Georgiana Isabella Frances, who *d.* 1967, da. of the late Adm. Sir Compton Edward Domvile, GCB, GCVO [Peel, Bt., *cr.* 1800, colls.]:—
Jane Elizabeth Georgiana Joan (26, Manchester St., WIM 5PG), *b.* 1916; formerly 3rd Officer WRNS.

Issue of the late Rev. Gervase Vanneck Blois, yst. son of 8th baronet, *b.* 1881, *d.* 1961: *m.* 1914, the Hon. Hester Murray Pakington, who *d.* 1973, da. of 3rd Baron Hampton:—
Anthony Gervase, *D.F.C., b.* 1918; ed. at Wellington Coll.; formerly Flight-Lieut, R.A.F. Vol. Reserve, and 2nd Lieut. Welsh Guards; European War 1939-45 (D.F.C.): *m.* 1957, Ivy Tucker, da. of William Charles Bell. *Residence*, 19, Bilton Road, Rugby.——David Pakington, *b.* 1923; Capt. MN: *m.* 1951, Joan, da. of the late Capt. L. R. Brock, and has issue living, Michael David Stuart, *b.* 1955,—Angnea Claire, *b.* 1958. *Residence*, 34, Strawberry Vale, Twickenham, Middx.——Evelyn Hester (*Baroness MacLeod of Borve*), *b.* 1915; *cr. Baroness MacLeod of Borve* (Life Baroness) 1971 [see that title].——Margaret Elaine, *b.* 1916: *m.* 1941, D. Ian Wilson, and has issue living, David Gervase Frederick, *b.* 1954,—Fiona Margaret, *b.* 1942, Sheila Elizabeth, *b.* 1944,—Ann Rosemary, *b.* 1945. *Residence*, Lickfold House, Lodsworth, Sussex.——Elizabeth Mary, *b.* 1921; formerly Subaltern ATS: *m.* 1953, George Francis Smith, of 8681, Shepherd's Way, N. Surrey, British Columbia, and has issue living, Fiona Elizabeth, *b.* 1956,—Gillian Hester, *b.* 1958,—Jennifer Margaret, *b.* 1962.

Issue of the late Lieut.-Col. William Thornhill Blois, brother of 8th baronet, *b.* 1841, *d.* 1889, *m.* 1874, Fanny Elizabeth, who *d.* 1912, el. da. of the late William Arkwright, of Sutton Scarsdale, Chesterfield :—
Ernest Pierrepont, *b.* 1880: *m.* 1900, Lilian Emily, who *d.* 1918, da. of J. W. Moore, and has issue living, Trevor Galfridus, *b.* 1904,—Esmè Ernestine, *b.* 1901,—Agnes Mary, *b.* 1903,—Fanny Elizabeth, *b.* 1911,—Nancy Avril, *b.* 1918.——Basil Frederic, *b.* 1881 ; ed. at Wellington Coll.; formerly Capt. R.F.A. (T.F.): *m.* 19—, Kathleen, who *d.* 1922, da. of the late Robert Overell.—— Geoffrey Stephen, *b.* 1884. *Residence*.

Galfridus de Blois held lands in Walpole, Suffolk, *temp.* Richard I. The family resided at Norton, Suffolk, till *temp.* King Henry VII, and at Grundisburgh Hall, Suffolk. They removed to Cockfield Hall in 1693, which is still in possession ı clamembe rof th eBloisfamily.

BLOMEFIELD, Creation (U.K.) 1807, of Attleborough, co. Norfolk.

Sir THOMAS EDWARD PEREGRINE BLOMEFIELD, 5th *Baronet*, son of the late Com. Thomas Charles Alfred Blomefield, R.N., el. son of 4th baronet ; *b*. May 31st, 1907 ; *s*. his grandfather, *Sir* THOMAS WILMOT PEREGRINE, *C.B.*, 1928 ; ed. at Wellington Coll., and at Trin. Coll., Oxford (B.A. 1930, M.A. 1936) ; European War 1939-45 as Lt.-Cdr. RNVR: *m*. 1947, Mme. Ginette Harting, da. of Dr. RaphaelMassart, of Paris, and has issue.

Arms—Sable, on a chevron argent a branch of laurel between two bomb-shells fired proper ; and on a canton or, a spear's head imbrued proper.   **Crest**—Issuant from a mural crown argent a demi-heraldic tiger azure, armed and tufted or, collared argent, and holding a sword broken in the middle proper.

Residence—16, Campden House, Sheffield Terr., W.8.   *Club*—Turf.

Son living—THOMAS CHARLES PEREGRINE (21B, Parsons Green, SW6), *b*. July 24th 1948; ed. at Wellington, and Mansfield Coll., Oxon.: *m*. 1975, Georgina G., da. of Cdr. Charles Over, RN, of The Meadows, Brockham Green, Surrey.

Sister living—Angela Margaret, *b*. 1905: *m*. 1958, Cary Best, of Diamond Cottage, Rolvenden Layne, Cranbrook, Kent.

Collateral Branches living.
Issue of the late Lieut.-Col. Wilmot Blomefield, O.B.E., R.E., youngest son of 4th baronet, *b*. 1878, *d*. 1926: *m*. 1907, Jessie Leila (4, Cherry Orchard, Stoke Poges, Bucks), only da. of the late William A. Hodges, J.P., of East Bridgeford, Notts:—
His Honour *Judge* Peregrine Maitland, *b*. 1917; ed. at Repton, and Trin. Coll., Oxford (MA); Bar. 1947; Circuit Judge; late Capt. Roy. Signals; 1939-45 War (wounded): *m*. 1941, Angela Catherine Crofton, and has issue living, Adam Peregrine Horatio, *b*. 1946: *m*. 1970, Esther Margaret, da. of Vaughan Lewis, of Swansea, and has issue living, Anna Claudia *b*. 1972.   *Residence*, Dorndon House, Hurst, Berks.——Leila Winifred, *b*. 1908; *m*. 1934, Stephen Charles Hawtrey, CB, and has issue living, Ralph Stephen Wilmot, (Dept. of Classics, Univ. of Auckland, NZ), *b*. 1941: *m*. 1969, Eleanor Mary, da. of Leo Kreusler Waterford, and has issue living, Nicholas Ralph Leo *b*. 1974, Catherine Mary Anne *b*. 1971,—Charles Francis Peregrine, *b*. 1944: *m*. 1966, Veronica Wiggins, and has issue living, Paul Charles *b*. 1971,—David James *b*. 1973,—Anne Lila, *b*. 1937: *m*. 1964, Patrick Jean Bernard Georges Destenay, Aix-en-Provence, France, and heas issue living, Marc Stéphane Henri *b*. 1968, Anna Catherine Leila *b*. 1972.   *Residence*, 52, New St. Henley-on-Thames, Oxon.——Rowan Lilias Augusta, *b*. 1910.——Rosemary Eardley (*Lady Hayman*), *b*. 1914: *m*. 1942, Sir Peter Telford Hayman, KCMG, CVO, MBE, High Commr. in Canada, of Uxmore House, Checkendon, Oxon., and Earnscliffe, Ottawa, Canada, and has issue living, Christopher Wilmot Arden, *b*. 1947,—Virginia Rosemary, *b*. 1944.

Grandchildren of the late Rev. Samuel Edward Blomefield, 3rd son of 2nd baronet :—
Issue of the late Edward Hugh Blomefield, M.V.O., *b*. 1852, *d*. 1938 : *m*. 1888, Lilian Emily, who *d*. 1946, da. of the late Rev. Henry Augustus Marsh, formerly V. of Tuxford, Newark, Notts:—
Allan Herbert, *b*. 1891 : ed. at Charterhouse, and at King's Coll., London : *m*. 1935, Olive Nesfield Cookson, and has issue living, Roger Stanley (14, St. Asaphs Av., Studley, Warwicks.), *b*. 1937: *m*. 1959, Eve Kathleen Bartlett, and has issue living, Adrian Paul *b*. 1964, Dawn Lesley *b*. 1960.   *Residence*, Littledean, Loose, nr. Maidstone.——Edith Alicia, *b*. 1894: *m*. 1913, Robert John Goldsmid Levien of The Stock Exchange, who *d*. 1937.   *Residence*, Moat Bungalow, Station Rd., Otford, Sevenoaks, Kent.

Granddaughters of the late Lawrence Woodyeare Blomefield (infra):—
Issue of the late John Woodyeare Blomefield, *b*. 1903, *d*. 1967: *m*. 1927, Dorothea Mae (P.O. Box 514, E. London, S. Africa), da. of A. Farr:—
Anne Shirley, *b*. 1927: *m*. 1947, Pieter Barendse Botha van Gend, and has issue living, Nardi Anne, *b*. 1949,—Cornelia Mae, *b*. 1952.——Elizabeth Jill, *b*. 1931: *m*. 1954, John Charsley Meyer, of Silverdale, E. London, S. Africa, and has issue living, Mark William, *b*. 1955,—Bruce Woodyeare, *b*. 1957,—Colin John, *b*. 1959.

Granddaughter of the late Rev. John Blomefield, 4th son of 2nd baronet:—
Issue of the late Lawrence Woodyeare Blomefield, *b*. 1870, *d*. 1956 : *m*. 1899, Celia Nora, who *d*. 1961, da. of the late A. B. Caldwell:—
Frances Celia, *b*. 1901: *m*. 1922, Dr. Arnold Klosser van Niekerk, dental surgeon (S. Africa), and has issue living, Olive Joan, *b*. 1926: *m*. 1947, Kenneth Louis Clur, and has issue living, Robert Louis *b*. 1955, Linda Ann *b*. 1948, Beverley Louise *b*. 1952,—Valerie Ellen, *b*. 1928: *m*. 1948, Garth Cox Latimer, who *d*. 1966 and has issue living, Dean Andrew *b*. 1949, Michael Garth *b*. 1951, Alan John *b*. 1953.   *Residence*, 7, Salisbury Rd., East London, S. Africa.

Granddaughter of the late Rev. Robert Allan Blomefield, 5th son of 2nd baronet :—
Issue (by 2nd marriage) of the late Rev. George Pinchin Allan Blomefield, *b*. 1854, *d*. 1923: *m*. 1st, 1879, Madeleine Amelia, who *d*. 1896, da. of the late Rev. Alfred Bligh Hill, V. of St. Paul's, Tiverton ; 2ndly, 1898, Kathleen Ruth, who *d*. 1926, da. of the late Lewis Stephen Woodthorpe, of Glazenwood, Essex :—
May Dorothy Wilmot, *b*. 1901.   *Residence*, Triashill, Rusape, Rhodesia.

Grandchildren of the late Rev. Charles David Blomefield, 6th son of 2nd baronet:—
Issue of the late Charles Allan Blomefield, *b*. 1871, *d*. 1940: *m*. 1902, Minnie, who *d*. 1964, el. da. of Loftus Otway Burrowes:—
Allan Arthur, *b*. 1903; ed. at Witwatersrand Univ. (B.Sc. 1925); is Principal of English Med. Scn., Lichtenburg, Transvaal: *m*. 1930, Dorothy Jane, da. of A. T. Adams, and has issue living, Justine, *b*. 1931,—Jennifer, *b*. 1934.——Loftus Charles (46, Hutchinson Rd., Pietermaritzburg, Natal), *b*. 1905; ed. at Univ. of S. Africa, Pretoria (BVSc 1928, DVSc 1944); formerly Assist. Chief of Vet. Service, Natal: *m*. 1937, Una Innes, da. of the late J. A. Munro, and has issue living, John Alan (PO Box 32, Ixopo, Natal) *b*. 1942: *m*. 1967, Norma Ann, el. da. of B. A. R. Schefermann, and has issue living, Peter Annand *b*. 1970, Monica Ann *b*. 1968,—Thomas Loftus, *b*. 1944; ed. at Univ. of Natal (BSc Agric.), Margaret Otway, *b*. 1938: *m*. 1962, Allan John Nicol, of Nottingham Rd., Natal, and has issue living, Deborah Margaret *b*. 1968, Jacqueline Jennifer *b*. 1970.

The 1st baronet, Maj.-Gen. Sir Thomas, commanded the Artillery in the expedition to Copenhagen 1807.   The 4th baronet, Sir Thomas Wilmot Peregrine, acted as Private Sec. to successive Pres. of Board of Trade (Baron Stanley of Preston, and Sir Michael Hicks-Beach, Bt.), and was Assist. Sec. to Board of Trade (Finance Depart.) 1901-8.

LYNCH-BLOSSE, Creation (I.) 1622, of Castle Carra, Mayo.

Neither rashly nor timidly.

Sir RICHARD HELY LYNCH-BLOSSE, 17th *Baronet, b.* Aug. 26th, 1953; *s.* his father, *Sir* DAVID EDWARD, 1971.

Arms—Azure, a chevron between three trefoils slipped or. **Crest**—A lynx passant coward argent.

Residence,—38, Elmwood, Welwyn Garden City, Herts.

Sisters living—Caroline Susan, *b.* 1951.——Bridget Ruth, *b.* 1958.

Aunt living—Sylvia Diana, *b.* (posthumous) 1928: *m.* 1958, Maj. Robert Basil Sullivan-Tailyour, Worcestershire & Sherwood Foresters Regt., of The Curate's Egg, Dymocks Lane, Sutton Veny, Warminster, Wilts., and has issue living, James Robert, *b.* 1960,—Sarah Jane, *b.* 1963.

Great Uncle living—George Robert (Selwyn Village, Pt. Chevalier, Auckland, NZ), *b.* 1895; sometime a tea planter in Ceylon: *m.* 1929, Lucy Myra, da. of Bertram Adams, of Auckland, NZ, and has issue living, Robert Edward (68, Matipo Rd., Mairangi Bay, Auckland, NZ), *b.* 1932: *m.* 1954, Alannah Marie, da. of John Donald Graham Drought, and has issue living, Robert Mark *b.* 1955, Brendan Scott *b.* 1960, Jennifer Sue *b.* 1957,— Gerald Bertram (25, Kawaha Point Rd. Rotorua, NZ), *b.* 1936: *m.* 1966, Moira Jean, da. of R. B. Johns, of Auckland, and has issue living, Craig Allan *b.* 1967, Catharine Mary *b.* 1970, Joanne Maree *b.* 1972,—Timothy Richard (4, Britton Av., Mount Roskill, Auckland, NZ), *b.* 1939; Snr. Police Sgt.: *m.* 1962, Joan, da. of Richard Wittington, of Auckland, and has issue living, Stephen John *b.* 1964 David Paul *b.* 1966,—Andrew John (3, Gerrrad St., Mt. Roskill, Auckland, NZ), *b.* 1946: *m.* 1968, Janice Marie, da. of E. Swinburne, and has issue living, Christopher Andrew *b.* 1972.

Great-Aunt living—Constance Diana, *b.* 1889: *m.* 1918, Capt. Ernest Norman Bock, formerly S. Lancs. Regt., and has issue living, Margaret, *b.* 1922,—Pauline Ann, *b.* 1927. *Residence,* Casila 189, Concepcion, Chile.——Theodora Mary, *b.* 1893: *m.* 1923, Glenton Hunt, of 48, Tweed St., Mt. Maunganu, NZ, and has issue living, Moira Evelyn, *b.* 1925: *m.* 1951, Archibald Couper, (Box 63, Hensall, Ont., Canada), and has issue living, Donald Alan *b.* 1955, Andrew Glen *b.* 1963, Janet Mary *b.* 1952, Margaret Jean *b.* 1959,—Gillian Frances, *b.* 1927: *m.* 1953, John Burton Camping, of 147, Valley Rd., Mt. Maunganui, NZ. and has issue living, David Falconer *b.* 1955, Stephen James *b.* 1957, Michael John (twin) *b.* 1957, Bridget Ann *b.* 1959.

Daughters living of 15th Baronet—Elizabeth Cicely, *b.* 1916: *m.* 1951, F. C. Gordon Harris, of 164, Oldfield Rd., Stannington, Sheffield, and has issue living, Alan Gordon, *b.* 1952,—Margaret Jane, *b.* 1954.——Susan Frances, *b.* 1917; 1939-45 War with WAAF: *m.* 1942, Wing-Cdr. Brian Noble, RAF (ret.), of Old Inn Cottage, Inwardleigh, Okehampton, Devon, and has issue living, Nigel Brian, *b.* 1947; Capt. RA,—Elizabeth Hilary, *b.* 1945.

Daughters living of 13th Baronet—By 1st m.—Evelyn Mary (of Brambles, Newlands Rd., New Milton, Hants.), *b.* 1912.——By 2nd m.—Frances Clodagh, *b.* 1936: *m.* 1960, Paul Richard Nevell, of 7, Sea Lane, Goring-by-Sea, Worthing, and has issue living, Christopher Paul *b.* 1965,— James Robert, *b.* 1968.

Daughter living of 12th Baronet—Alice Cecil Emily: *m.* 1934, Lt.-Col. Robert Arthur Milne, RE (ret.), and has issue living, Robert Cecil (1, Rumbold Rd., SW6), *b.* 1935; ed. at Wellington: *m.* 1970, Diana Sutton, and has issue living, a son *b.* 1971,—Mary Elizabeth, *b.* 1936: *m.* 1963, the Rev. Peter John van de Kasteele, of The Rectory, Mursley, Bletchley, Bucks. *Residence,* Pengwern House, Oakley St., Shrewsbury.

Grandmother living—Evangeline Margaret Victoria (North Ham, Dolton, N. Devon), da. of the late Charles William Maitland Hudson: *m.* 1922, Hely Richard Lynch-Blosse, who *d.* 1928.

Widow living of 16th Baronet—ELIZABETH (*Lady Lynch-Blosse*), da. of Thomas Harold Payne, of Welwyn Garden City: *m.* 1950, Sir David Edward Lynch-Blosse, 16th Bt., who *d.* 1971.

Collateral Branches living.

Grandsons of the late Capt. Edward Falconer Lynch-Blosse, uncle of 13th baronet, and son of the late Very Rev. Henry Lynch-Blosse, Dean of Llandaff, 2nd son of 8th baronet:—

Issue of the late Maj. Cecil Eagles Lynch-Blosse; *b.* 1890; *d.* 1966: *m.* 1st, 1915 (m. diss. 1940) Dorothy Delahaize, who *d.* 1962, da. of the late Rev. John Delahaize Ouvry, R. of Haydon, Sherborne; 2ndly, 1943, his cousin, Violet Emily (Flat 34, 4, Grand Av., Hove), da. of the late Francis Traherne Lynch-Blosse [see infra]:—

(By 1st m.) (ERIC) HUGH, OBE (The Paddocks, Newnham, Glos.); *b.* July 30th, 1917; Group Capt. RAF (ret.); OBE (Mil) 1952: *m.* 1946, Jean Evelyn, da. of Cdr. Andrew Robertson Hair, RD, RNR, of Edinburgh, and has issue living, David Ian, *b.* 1950; ed. at Blundells,—Valerie Jean, *b.* 1947: *m.* 1974, Irvine Cormack, of Salisbury Rhodesia.——Anthony Cecil (26, Harrison Av., Rockaway, NJ, USA), *b.* 1919; Assist. Branch Manager of Sherwin-Williams Co.; 1939-45 War as Fl. Lt. RAF: *m.* 1st, 1942, Margaret, from whom he obtained a divorce 1946, da. of Maj.-Gen. David Graeme Ridgeway, CB, DSO; 2ndly, 1948, Marjorie Elizabeth, da. of James Joseph William Morris, of Portland Maine, USA, and has issue living, (by 2nd m.) Michael Anthony, *b.* 1950,—Sean James *b.* 1960,—Sharon Delahaize (twin) *b.* 1960.

Grandson of the late Francis Traherne Lynch-Blosse (infra):—

Issue of the late Francis Courtenay Lynch-Blosse, *b.* 1898, *d.* 1943: *m.* 1932, Dorothy Guthrie, who *d.* 1965, da. of Duncan MacRae, of Ruthven, Kingussie, and widow of Charles I. Lynn-Thomas:—

Richard Courtenay (Hugletts Farm, Hugletts Lane, Old Heathfield, Sussex), *b.* 1937; ed. at Wellington: *m.* (March) 1965, Deirdre Geraldine Mary, who *d.* (June) 1965, da. of the late Comdt. Patrick Butler, of Dublin.

Granddaughters of the late Very Rev. Henry Lynch-Blosse (ante):—

Issue of the late Francis Traherne Lynch-Blosse, *b.* 1859, *d.* 1926: *m.* 1885, Emily Vivian, who *d.* 1936, da. of the late Richard Cory, J.P., of Cardiff:—

Violet Emily LYNCH-BLOSSE: *m.* 1st, 1913, Hew James Brown, who *d.* 1934, and from whom she had obtained a divorce 1925, and resumed her maiden name by deed poll; 2ndly, 1943, as his 2nd wife, her cousin, Maj. Cecil Eagles Lynch-Blosse, who *d.* 1966 (ante).——Constance Mabel Frances (of The Vineyard, Berkeley St., Cheltenham): *m.* 1918, Capt. Leonard Robert Arthur

Bate, King's Roy. Rifle Corps, who *d.* 1959, and has issue living, Rosemary Suzanne, *b.* 1920: *m.* 1948, Maj. Michael Thomas Jerome Bate-Williams, RA, and has issue living, Christopher Michael Leonard *b.* 1949, John Robert Alexander *b.* 1951.

The family of Lynch is of great antiquity in Connaught, being among the earliest settlers who were denominated the "Tribes of Galway". Sir Henry Lynch, 1st Bt., and Sir Robuck (Robert) Lynch, 2nd Bt., successively sat as MP for Galway. The 2nd Baronet was Mayor of Galway 1638. Sir Henry Lynch, 3rd Bt., was a Baron of the Exchequer in Ireland 1686. Sir Robert, 6th Bt., assumed the additional surname of Blosse, having *m.* 1749, Elizabeth, da. and heir of Francis Barker, and heir of Tobias Blosse, of Little Belstead, Suffolk.

BLOUNT, Creation (E.) 1642, of Sodington, Worcestershire.

[Name pronounced "**Blunt.**"]

Sir EDWARD ROBERT BLOUNT, 11th *Baronet; b.* Dec. 2nd, 1884; *s.* his brother, *Lieut.-Col. Sir* WALTER ASTON, 1958; late Lt. RFC and RAF: *m.* 1914, Violet Ellen, who *d.* 1969, da. of A. Grant Fowler, MICE, and has issue.

Arms—Barry nebulée of six or and sable.   **Crest**—An armed foot in the sun.

Residence,—Hallinwood, Selsdon Vale, Selsdon, Surrey.

Son living—WALTER EDWARD ALPIN, *D.S.C., b.* Oct. 31st, 1917; ed. at Beaumont Coll., and at Sidney Sussex Coll., Camb. (B.A. 1939, M.A. 1943); Lieut. R.N.V.R.; European War 1939-45 (D.S.C. and two Bars): *m.* 1954, Eileen Audrey, only da. of the late Hugh B. Carritt, and has issue living, Nichola Jane, *b.* 1955. *Residence,* 19, St. Ann's Terrace, St. John's Wood, N.W.8.

Lux tua via mea.
Thy light, my path.

Daughter living—Diana Apollonia, *b.* 1916. *Residence,* Hallinwood, Selsdon Vale, Selsdon, Surrey.

Collateral Branch living.

Granddaughters of the late Henry Edmund Blount, son of the late Sir Edward Charles Blount, K.C.B., son of Edward Blount, M.P., 2nd son of 7th baronet :—
Issue of the late Edward Charles Aston Marie Blount, O.B.E., *b.* 1874, *d.* 1953 : *m.* 1897, Clara Marianne Ghislaine, *O.B.E.,* who *d.* 1953, da. of the late Napoléon, Duc de Bassano :—
Clare Gertrude Mary Ghislaine, *b.* 1898. *Residence,* Tilkhurst, East Grinstead, Sussex.——Marguerite Pauline Mary, *MBE, b.* 1908; formerly a Co. Alderman of E. Sussex; MBE (Civil), 1946. *Residence,* Tilkhurst, East Grinstead, Sussex.

The 1st baronet suffered for his loyalty during the civil war, and was long imprisoned, first at Oxford, and afterwards in the Tower. Sir Walter Kirkham Blount, 3rd Bt., was Sheriff of Worcestershire 1687-8, and Sir Edward, 8th Bt., was High Sheriff of the same county in 1835. The Barons Mountjoy of Thurston, and the Barons of Ixworth in Suffolk (now extinct), were descended from this family.

BLUNDEN, Creation (I.) 1766, of Castle Blunden, Kilkenny.

Sir WILLIAM BLUNDEN, 6th *Baronet; b.* April 26th, 1919; *s.* his father, *Sir* JOHN, 1923; ed. at Repton; Lieut.-Com. R.N. (retired): *m.* 1945, Pamela Mary (formerly 2nd Officer WRNS), da. of John Purser, of Merton House, Dublin, 6, and has issue.

Arms—Quarterly: 1st and 4th argent, ten billets four, three, two, and one, sable; 2nd and 3rd, or a lion passant-guardant per pale gules and sable.   **Crests**—1st, a demi-lion rampant per fesse sable and argent, armed and langued gules; 2nd, a griffin segreant vert, armed, winged and beaked or.

Seat—Castle Blunden, Kilkenny.

Daughters living—Sarah Vanessa, *b.* 1946: *m.* 1970, John Edward Spencer Perceval Maxwell.——Grizelda Jane, *b.* 1948.——Caroline Susan (twin), *b.* 1948.——Rowena Mary Phillida, *b.* 1952.——Elizabeth Anne, *b.* 1955.——Fiona Christine, *b.* 1958.

Brother living—PHILIP OVERINGTON, *b.* Jan. 27th, 1922; ed. at Repton; European War 1942-5 with R.N.: *m.* 1945, Jeanette Francesca (W.R.N.S.), el. da. of Capt. D. Macdonald, R.N.R., of Portree, Isle of Skye, and has issue living, Hubert Chisholm, *b.* 1948,—John Maurice Patrick, *b.* 1955. *Residence,*

We must yield to love.

Collateral Branch living.

Issue of the late Eric Overington Blunden, yr. son of 4th baronet, *b.* 1892, *d.* 1969: *m.* 1918, Bridget Constable (Willows, Collingham, nr. Newark, Notts.), da. of the late Henry George Constable Curtis :—
Josephine Bridget Annette, *b.* 1926: *m.* 1947, Col. George Vicary Kenyon, CBE, TD, of Highfields Lodge, Ware, Herts., and Pier View, Dunmore East, co. Waterford, and has issue living, Robin George Blunden, *b.* 1950; ed. at Charterhouse,—Crispin Simon Vicary, *b.* 1955,—Rowena Josette Caroline, *b.* 1953.

The 1st baronet was M.P. for Kilkenny and a distinguished member of the Irish Bar. Sir **William** Blunden, M.B., 4th Bt., was High Sheriff of co. Kilkenny 1904, and *d.* Oct. 25th, 1923, only three days prior to his son **and** successor, Sir John, 5th Bt.

BLUNT, Creation (G.B.) 1720, of London.

Sir DAVID RICHARD REGINALD HARVEY
BLUNT, 12th *Baronet; b.* Nov. 8th, 1938;
s. his father, *Sir* RICHARD DAVID HARVEY,
1975: *m.* 1969, Sonia Tudor Rosemary, da.
of the late Albert Edward Day, and has issue.

Arms—Per pale or and sable, barry nebuly of six
counterchanged. **Crest**—Issuing out of clouds a sun in
splendour charged with an eye issuing tears, all proper.

Residence,—74, Kirkstall Rd., SW2 4HF.

Thy light is my life.

Daughter living—Davina Angela Rosemary, *b.* 1971.
Half-Sisters living—Georgina Lavinia, *b.* 1945.——Caroline Margaret (Diana Lodge Stud, Purton, Wilts.)
b. 1947.

Uncle living—CHARLES HARVEY DAVID, *b.* Sept. 18th,
1919.

Aunts living—Cecily Maud Helen, *b.* 1910: *m.* 1934,
Robin Whitworth, of Freelands, Westwell, Burford,
Oxon., and has issue living, Anna Maureen Cecily, *b.*
1945.——Doris Julia Sybil, *b.* 1916: *m.* 1945, Maj.
Frederick William Kennedy, Indian Army, who
d. 1972, and has issue living, Amber Julia, *b.* 1946:
m. 1972, Rodger A. Brooks,—Susan Anne, *b.* 1948.
Residence, Springfort, Patrickswell, co. Limerick.

Widow living of 10th Baronet—MARGARET HUNAM
(*Margaret, Lady Blunt*) (The Old Mill, Mayfield,
Sussex), da. of the late William Redhead, and formerly
wife of 2nd Viscount Rothermere: *m.* 1947, as his
2nd wife, Sir John Lionel Reginald Blunt, 10th Bt.,
who *d.* 1969.
Widow living of 11th Baronet—MARGARET (*Margaret, Lady Blunt*) (Diana Lodge Stud, Purton,
Wilts.), da. of John H. Dean, of Duntisbourne Leer, Cirencester: *m.* 1943, as his 2nd wife, Sir
Richard David Harvey Blunt, 11th Bt., who *d.* 1975.

Collateral Branches living.

Issue of the late Charles William Lockhart Blunt, 3rd son of 8th baronet, *b.* 1882, *d.* 1958:
m. 1913, Lilian, who *d.* 1958, da. of the late C. Calcutt, of Goudhurst, Kent :—
Robin Anthony (The Three Wents, Quarndon, Derby), *b.* 1926; ed. at Wellington Coll., CEng,
MIMechE: *m.* 1st, 1949, Sheila Stuart, from whom he obtained a divorce 1962, da. of C. Stuart
Brindley; 2ndly, 1962, June Elizabeth, da. of Charles Wigginton, of The Park, Duffield, and has
issue living (by 1st m.) Jonathan Stuart, *b.* 1955,—(by 2nd m.) Mark Charles, *b.* 1963.

Issue of the late Henry Wilfrid Blunt, youngest son of 8th baronet, *b.* 1887, *d.* 1957,
m. 1915, Maud Etta, da. of the late J. Hyde :—
Gabrielle Hilda, *b.* 1919 : *m.* 1st, 1941, Capt. Tony Thawnton, 3rd King's Own Hussars, from
whom she obtained a divorce 1950 ; 2ndly, 1955, (*m.* diss. 1972), Julian Bond, and has issue
living, (by 1st m.) Paul John Anthony BOND, *b.* 1946, adopted 1955 by his stepfather, Julian
Bond, whose surname he assumed,—Nicholas Peter BOND, *b.* 1947 ; adopted 1955 by his step-
father, Julian Bond, whose surname be assumed,—(by 2nd m.) Stella Mary, *b.* 1956. *Residence,* 3,
Gingerbread Lane, Hawkhurst, Kent.

Grandchildren of the late Capt. Francis Theophilus Blunt, 2nd son of the Rev.
Edward Powlett Blunt, yr. son of the late James Blunt, son of Walter
Blunt, 5th son of 2nd baronet:—
Issue of the late Sir Edward Arthur Henry Blunt, K.C.I.E., O.B.E., *b.* 1877, *d.* 1941 : *m.*
1901, Ada, who *d.* 1958, third da. of the late Com. Charles H. Stone, R.N. :—
John Edward Chicheley, *b.* 1907; ed. at Marlborough ; is Lieut.-Col. R.A.: *m.* 1936, Margaret, da. of
R. Whiteley, of Heath, Wakefield, and has issue living, John Michael Chicheley, *b.* 1937.——
Violet Constance, *b.* 1904: *m.* 1926, Brig. Sydney Henry Persse, DSO, Indian Cav., who *d.*
1945, and has issue living, Burton Richard Edward, *b.* 1941: *m.* 19—, Veronica Anne Delderfield,
and has issue living, Burton Simon Henry *b.* 1965, Edward James Frederick *b.* 1970, Henrietta
Anne *b.* 1971,—Elizabeth Anne Audrey, *b.* 1934: *m.* 1956, George Marcus Telford, and has issue
living, Peter Marcus *b.* 1957, Andrew Richard Thomas *b.* 1962, Alison Anne *b.* 1959, Penelope
Heather *b.* 1964,—Caroline Margaret Seymour, *b.* 1937: *m.* 1959, Capt. Roderick Norman
Alexander MacLeod, RA, and has issue living, Alastair Roderick Donald, *b.* 1960, William Henry
b. 1968, Katherine Flora *b.* 1963, Elizabeth Charlotte *b.* 1965. *Residence,* Rest Harrow, Little
Cheverell, nr. Devizes, Wilts.
Issue of the late Right Rev. Bishop Alfred Walter Frank Blunt, D.D., formerly Bishop
of Bradford, *b.* 1879, *d.* 1957: *m.* 1909, Margaret Catharine, who *d.* 1963, el. da. of
Lieut.-Col. Joshua Duke, formerly Indian Med. Ser.:—
David Alfred Chicheley, *b.* 1915: *m.* 1940, Dorothy Brailsford Booth, and has issue living, Peter
Robin Chicheley (Home Farm, Newburgh, Coxwold, York.), *b.* 1946: *m.* 1969, Angela Shirley,
da. of the late Arthur Benjamin Drane, MA, of 33, Simbalk Lane, Bishopthorpe, York, and has
issue living, Michael Peter Chicheley *b.* 1975, Jenny Elisabeth *b.* 1972,—Patricia Anne Brailsford,
b. 1941: *m.* 1967, Timothy Steuart Hallam Piper, of St. Anselm's, Bakewell, Derbys., and has
issue living, Richard David Steuart *b.* 1969, Nicholas James Steuart *b.* 1970. *Residence,* 21,
Simbalk Lane, Bishopthorpe, York.——Helen Amy, *b.* 1911: *m.* 1st, 1934 (m. diss. 1941),
Christopher Hodgson; 2ndly, 1942 (m. diss. 1948), Geoffrey Dawson; 3rdly, 1962, Richard
Marshall Bond, of Hunter House, Stanstead, Sudbury, Suffolk, and has issue living, (by 2nd m.)
Jane, *b.* 1943: *m.* 1965, Nigel Hartley Dryden Butterworth [see Dryden, Bt.].——Margaret
Dorothy, *b.* 1913: *m.* 1936, Rudolf Paul Gerard Kirchem, and has issue living, Michael Hans
Edward (15, Hunters Hill, Kingsley, nr. Frodsham, Ches.), *b.* 1937: *m.* 1965, Jean Miriam
McKenna, and has issue living, Michael John Geoffrey *b.* 1966, Catherine Marina *b.* 1967,—
Elisabeth Jane, *b.* 1940: *m.* 1971, David George Cross, of Sestri, Linksway, Bookham, Surrey,—
Anthony Peter Francis, *b.* 1953. *Residence,* Adlington Lodge, Albury Rd., Burwood Park,
Walton on Thames, Surrey.

Grandchildren of the late Maj.-Gen. Grant Blunt, RE, yst. son of the Rev.
Edward Powlett Blunt (ante):—
Issue of the late Col. Conrad Edward Grant Blunt, C.B.E., D.S.O., *b.* 1868, *d.* 1948; *m.*
1st, 1900, Aimée, who *d.* 1918, da. of Col. Abel Straghan, C.B. ; 2ndly, 1920, Beatrice,
who *d.* 1946, widow of Frank Fullagar :—
(By 1st marriage) Hugh Clavell, *b.* 1908: *m.* 1939, Elizabeth Marjorie, only da. of W. S. Campbell,
and has issue living, Susan Famela, *b.* 1940. *Residence,* Windermere, British Columbia.——Marjorie
Nina, *b.* 1903: *m.* 1930, George Douglas Laurie Pile, CBE, who *d.* 1965. *Residences,* 30, Wynn-
stay Gdns., W8; Bulkeley House, Barbados, West Indies.

Issue of the late Arthur Powlett Blunt, C.M.G., *b.* 1883; *d.* 1946: *m.* 1919, Winifred **Grace** (who obtained a divorce 1937), da. of Dr. W. H. Fawcett, of Bournemouth :— Grant Anthony Clavell (30, March Court, Warwick Drive, SW15), *b.* 1920; ed. at Bradfield; ACIS; Capt. RM (ret.); 1939-45 War: *m.* 1942, June Dorothy, da. of J. C. Liddle, and has issue living, Alistair Clavell, *b.* 1946; ed. at Bradfield; BA (Hons),—Gene Carol, *b.* 1943; ed. at Cheltenham Ladies' Coll., and Bedford Coll., London (BSc): *m.* 1967, Bertrand Edouard Doger de Speville, of 55, The Avenue, Richmond, Surrey, and has issue living, Guy Rollo *b.* 1971, Claire Anne Maude *b.* 1974.——Evelyn Powlett Clavell, *RD* (c/o Redic Australia Pty. Ltd., PO Box 160, Bayswater, Vic. 3153, Aust.) *b.* 1924; Lt.-Cdr. RNR, 1939-45 War with RNVR: *m.* 1956, Patricia, da. of Col William Joseph Gaunt Beach, MBE, and has issue living, Jonathan Andrew Clavell, *b.* 1959,— Sarah Virginia Clavell, *b.* 1957,—Philippa Mary Clavell, *b.* 1960.

Descendants of the late Lt.-Col. Edward Walter MACKENZIE (who assumed the additional surname of Mackenzie 1905, but subsequently discontinued the use of the surname of Blunt), el. son of Maj.-Gen. Charles Harris Blunt, CB, 4th son of Edward Walter Blunt, 3rd son of Walter Blunt (ante): *m.* 1899, Sibell Lilian, Countess of Cromartie, who *d.* 1962 [see E. Cromartie].

Grandchildren of the late Col. Arthur Blunt, 6th son of the late Edward Walter Blunt (ante):—
Issue of the late Arthur Wharton Blunt, *b.* 1866, *d.* 1939 : *m.* 1906, Mary, who *d.* 1936, da. of Col. Arthur Edward Ward, formerly Roy. Welch Fusiliers:— Arthur Roper Lascelles, *b.* 1925.——Frances Georgina Shirley, *b.* 1907.——Marjory Grace, *b.* 1908.——Joan Evelyn Mary, *b.* 1914: *m.* 1947, Kazimier Wyskinski, Polish Army.——Joyce Cautley, *b.* 1921: *m.* 1946, Peter J. Presnail, of 210, Coromandel Parade, Coromandel Valley, S. Aust. 5051, and has issue living, Richard, *b.* 1947,—Shirley, *b.* 1951,—Hazel, *b.* 1954.

Issue of the late Hugh Roper Blunt, *b.* 1874, *d.* 1931 : *m.* 1915, Agnes Sara, who *d.* 1948 da. of Charles Gray, of Waiohika, Gisborne, New Zealand :— Michael Hugh (21, Seatoun Heights Rd., Seatoun 3, Wellington, NZ), *b.* 1920; PhD; MRCVS; late Capt RAVC: *m.* 1958, Susanne Mary, da. of Lawson Field, of Gisborne, NZ, and has issue living, Gerald Hugh Lawson, *b.* 1959.——Richard Mark (8, Dinsdale Place, Hamersley, W. Aust. 6022), *b.* 1924; late Lt. RN: *m.* 1st, 1952 (m. diss. 1963), Adrien Seldon Truss; 2ndly, 1965, Patricia Eileen, da. of Walter Stanley Lee, of Perth, W. Aust., and has issue living, (by 1st m.), Teresa June, *b.* 1953,—(by 2nd m.) David Mark, *b.* 1967,—Georgia Alison, *b.* 1969.

Issue of the late Lieut.-Col. Allan St. John Blunt, D.S.O., *b.* 1880, *a.* 1931 : *m.* 1914, Doris Elizabeth who *d.* 1948, da. of the late John G. Stephen, of Douglas, Isle of Man:— Elizabeth Shirley, *b.* 1923: *m.* 1944, Harry Batten Poustie, DSC, RD, and has issue living, John David, *b.* 1948,—Michael Ian, *b.* 1954,—Richard Hugh, *b.* 1965,—Charles Christopher (twin), *b.* 1965,—Vivienne Mary, *b.* 1951,—Louise Caroline, *b.* 1964. *Residence*, Hilary, Ashburton Rd., Bovey Tracey, Devon.

According to the pedigree on record at the College of Arms, Sir John, 1st baronet, was the fourth child of Thomas Blunt, of Rochester, Kent. Thomas, "shoemaker and baptist," was baptized at St. Nicholas, Rochester, July 24th, 1665, and was buried at St. Nicholas, Rochester, March, 28th 1703, his father being John Blunt, of St. Sepulchre's, London, "upholder." In 1732 the Court of Chivalry summoned and fined the 1st Bt. for using without right the arms of Sir Charles Blount, Lord Mountjoy, Earl of Devonshire ; he appealed from the sentence, and a day was appointed for hearing his appeal, but he died before any further proceedings took place, and the officially recorded arms of the family are as described above. The 4th baronet sat as M.P. for Lewes (L) 1832-7, and Capt. Sir John Harvey Blunt, 8th Bt., Roy. Dublin Fusiliers, served throughout the Indian Mutiny.

CRAWLEY-BOEVEY, Creation (G.B.) 1784, of Highgrove, Gloucestershire.
[Name pronounced "Crawley-Boovey."]

Sir THOMAS MICHAEL BLAKE CRAWLEY BOEVEY, 8th *Baronet*; *b.* Sept. 29th, 1928; *s.* his father, *Sir* LAUNCELOT VALENTINE HYDE, 1968; ed. at Wellington Coll., and St. John's Coll., Camb. (MA); late 2nd Lt. Durham LI; Editor of *"Money Which?"* 1968: *m.* 1957, Laura, el. da. of Jan Pouwels Coelingh, of Wassenaar, Holland, and has issue.

Arms—Erminois, on a fesse azure between three cranes proper a saltire couped between two cross-crosslets fitchée or, on a chief ermine a bend gules, charged with three guttes-d'or between two martlets sable. **Crest**—A mount vert thereon a crane proper gorged with a collar or, holding in his dexter claw a saltire couped of the last.

Residence,—41, Thornhill Rd., N1.

To be, rather than seem to be.

Sons living—THOMAS HYDE, *b.* June 26th, 1958.—— William Walstan, *b.* 1960.

Brother living—Anthony Francis d'Auvergne (128, Graham Rd., SW19), *b.* 1932; ed. at RNC Dartmouth: *m.* 1968, Gertrud, da. of the late Dr. Johannes Felix Potrykus, of Soerabaya, Java.

Widow living of 7th Baronet—ELIZABETH GOODETH (*Elizabeth, Lady Crawley-Boevey*), (41, Thornhill Rd., N1), da. of Herbert d'Auvergne Innes, late Indian Police: *m.* 1927, Sir Launcelot Valentine Hyde Crawley-Boevey, 7th Baron, who *d.* 1968.

Collateral Branches living.
Issue of the late Capt. Edward Martin Crawley-Boevey, 2nd son of 5th baronet, *b.* 1873, *d.* (killed in action) 1914: *m.* 1905, Rosalie Winifred, who *d.* 1966, da. of the late Col. George Conrad Sartorius, CB, of Thorwald, Godalming:—

Richard Martin, *b.* 1908 ; ed. at St. John's Coll., Camb.: *m.* 1945, Gladys Frances Farrer Young, who *d.* 1955, and has issue living, Timothy Martin, *b.* 1949. *Residence*, Muden, Natal, S. Africa.

 Issue of the late Rev. Canon Arthur Curtis Crawley-Boevey, 3rd son of 5th baronet, *b.* 1874, *d.* 1965: *m.* 1906, Evelyn Rosalie, who *d.* 1962, da. of the late Robert Carnegie, of Terenure, co. Dublin:—

Rev. Robert Arthur (Seer Green Vicarage, Beaconsfield, Bucks), *b.* 1912; ed. at Hertford Coll., Oxford (MA); V. of Seer Green: *m.* 1947, Josephine, da. of the late Joseph Howard, of Evenlode House, Moreton-in-Marsh, Glos., and has issue living, David Alexander, *b.* 1948,—Peter Robert, *b.* 1957,—Juliet Ann, *b.* 1950: *m.* 1975, Andrew Dean.——Nancy Albinia (The Gatehouse, Merevale, Atherstone, Warwickshire), *b.* 1910.——Marjorie Evelyn, *b.* 1916.——Elizabeth Jocosa, *b.* 1918; ed. at Girton Coll., Camb.

 Grandsons of the late Arthur William Crawley-Boevey, 6th son of 4th baronet :—
 Issue of the late Major Martin Crawley-Boevey, D.S.O., M.C., Duke of Cornwall's L.I., *b.* 1883, *d.* 1954: *m.* 1919, Elizabeth Adela, who *d.* 1972, da. of the late Capt. Roger Hall, DL, of Narrow Water, co. Down, and widow of Lieut.-Col. Neville Reay Daniell, DSO [E. Clanwilliam, colls.]:—

Antony, *MBE, b.* 1921; Maj. (ret.) 17th/21st Lancers; 1939-45 War with 7th Hussars; MBE (Mil.) 1964: *m.* 1st, 1950, Cynthia Louise (who obtained a divorce 1957), da. of the late William Hugh Neville Bagot, of Haut du Mont, La Haule, Jersey; 2ndly, 1960, Josephine Beryl, da. of Lt.-Col. N. H. Kindersley, of Sunny Cottage, Piddletrenthide, Dorset, and has issue living, (by 1st m.) Susan Elizabeth Mary, *b.* 1951,—(by 2nd m.) Martin Henry, *b.* 1963,—Simon Antony, *b.* 1967,—Katherine Lucy, *b.* 1964. *Residence*, Churchfields, Rodborough, Stroud, Glos.—— Arthur Martin (c/o Professional Golfers' Association, National HQ, Kennington Oval, SE11), *b.* 1924; Capt. (ret.) RA; 1939-45 War (despatches).

 Grandchildren ot the late Octavius Charles Crawley-Boevey (**infra**):—
 Issue of the late Santiago Carlos Crawley-Boevey, *b.* 1872, *d.* 1913: *m.* 18—, a da. of Alamos Cuadra, of Valparaiso, Chile :—
Charles, *b.* 1897.——Marie, *b.* 1899.

 Issue of the late Octavius Charles Crawley-Boevey, 7th son of 4th baronet, *b.* 1846, *d.* 1897: *m.* 1871, Maria Francisca, da. of Bernardino Murga, Judge of the Corte Superior, Arequipa, Peru :—
Edward Maximo, *b.* 1875.——Mary Isabel, *b.* 1878 : *m.* 1904, Frederico de la Fuenta, and has issue living, Frederico Francisco, *b.* 1906,—Hilda Carmela, *b.* 1911.——Rose Agnes, *b.* 1880.——Lilian Maude Antonia, *b.* 1882.——Leonor Octavia, *b.* 1884.——Blanche Josephine, *b.* 1889 : *m.* 1910, Gerald Bingham [M. Sligo, colls.], and has issue living, Norah Frances, *b.* 1912,—Dorothy Blanche, *b.* 1913,—Eileen Gertrude, *b.* 1915,—Elizabeth Hilda, *b.* 1918.——Ella Margaret, *b.* 1894. ——Hilda Ines, *b.* 1896.

 Grandchildren of the late Thomas William Crawley, el. son of the late Rev. Thomas William Crawley (**infra**):—
 Issue of the late Thomas Charles Rochfort Crawley, *b.* 1882, *d.* 1963: *m.* 1914, Margaret (71, Duke St., Dryden, Ontario, Canada), da. of Charles McKerrow, MB, of Workington, Cumberland:—

Thomas Bryson, *b.* 1918: *m.* 1947, Christina, only da. of H. Vollweiter, of Toronto, Canada, and has issue living, Thomas Henry, *b.* 1958,—Christopher John, *b.* 1963,—Gilda Carolyn, *b.* 1951,— Carla Susan, *b.* 1953,—Lisa Marlene, *b.* 1956.——James Bryan (139, Kingston Row, Winnipeg 8, Man., Canada), *b.* 1921: *m.* 1964, Edith Janice Doreen, da. of Charles Player Halls, of Regina, Sask., Canada, and has issue living, Devin Charles Bryan, *b.* 1968.——Margery, *b.* 1915.

 Issue of the late Rev. Canon John Lloyd Crawley, *b.* 1884, *d.* 1951: *m.* 1921, Marion, who *d.* 1961, da. of Charles McKerrow, MB:—

Rev. John Lloyd Rochfort (The Vicarage, Lorton Rd., Cockermouth, Cumbria, CA13 9DU), *b.* 1922; V. of St. Anthony's, Newcastle 1953-59, V. of Longhoughton and R. of Howick 1959-69, and Master of St. Thomas the Martyr, Newcastle, and Chap. Newcastle Univ. 1969-74, since when V. of Cockermouth: *m.* 1947, Isabell, da. of the late William Robson, of Reaveley Powburn, Alnwick, and has issue living, Michael (5. Bethel St., E. Moreton, Keighley, Yorks.), *b.* 1949; PhD; DIC: *m.* 1971, Greer Anne, only da. of George Williams, of New London, Conn., USA.— Margaret, *b.* 1924: *m.* 1946, Maj. William Vivian Dickinson, MBE, RA, of Sykes Farm, Burnby, York, and has issue living, John, *b.* 1948: *m.* 1970, Dianne Warby,—Michael, *b.* 1955,— Richard, *b.* 1960,—Susan *b.* 1949: *m.* 1971, Kenneth Hope.

 Grandchildren of the Rev. Thomas William Crawley, son of the late Rev. John Lloyd Crawley, 2nd son of 2nd baronet:—
 Issue of the late Lieut.-Col. George Burridge Crawley, *b.* 1858, *d.* 1932: *m.* 1st, 1882 (divorced 1887), Kate Ouseley, da. of the late Surg.-Maj. Henry Sherlock; 2ndly, 1892, Adelaide, who *d.* 1946, da. of the late Charles Bell Syer:—
(By 1st marriage) George Ouseley, *b.* 1883. *Residence*,

 Issue of the late Charles Purrier Crawley, *b.* 1859, *d.* 1896: *m.* 18—, Emily Kent, da. of the late — Hooper:—
Charles Robert Thomas Edmund, *b.* 1880.——Noel George, *b.* 1888.——Albinia, *b.* 18—.—— Hannah Dorothy, *b.* 1887. *Residence*,

 Grandsons of the late Charles James Crawley, only son of the late Rev. Charles Yonge Crawley, son of the late Rev. Charles Crawley, 3rd son of 2nd baronet:—
 Issue of the late (Charles) Alan Crawley, *b.* 1887, *d.* 1975: *m.* 1915, Jean Nairn (830, Sayward Rd., Vic., BC, Canada), only child of David Horn, of Winnipeg:—

(Charles) David (1757, N. Stanley Av., Los Angeles, Calif. 90046, USA), *b.* 1916; ed. at BC Univ. (BA); 1939-45 War as F/O RCAF: *m.* 1st, 1942 (m. diss. 1960), Lois Kathleen, only da of Francis Ritchie, of Vancouver, BC; 2ndly, 1965, Dorothy Fried, of Los Angeles, Calif., and has issue living (by 1st m.) Charles Peter (PO Box 8276, Mammoth Lakes, Calif. 93546, USA), *b.* 1943: *m.* 1963 (m. diss. 1971), Carole Cavalier, of Los Angeles, Calif., and has issue living, Thresa Lyn *b.* 1963, Brandi Michelle *b.* 1969,—Christopher David (1425, Grant St., Vic., BC, Canada), *b.* 1947: *m.* 1972, Erin McMartin, of Sidney, BC, Canada, and has issue living, Aleta *b.* 1974.——Michael (830, Sayward Rd., Vic., BC, Canada), *b.* 1919; ed. at Ravencourt Sch., Winnipeg; 1939-45 War with RCASC.

 Grandson of the late William Savage Crawley, son of the late Rev. William Crawley, 5th son of 2nd baronet :—
 Issue of the late William Evelyn Maddock Crawley, *b.* 1859, *a.* 1926: *m.* 1st, 1894, Fanny Gertrude, who *d.* 1911, da. of the late Arthur Wellesley Critchley; 2ndly, 1913, Harriet Gladys, da. of the late Robert Chambres Chambres:—
By 2nd marriage) Evelyn Myles Chambres, *b.* 1914. *Residence*,

 The 1st baronet, Sir Charles Barrow, sat as M.P. for Gloucester 1751-89 ; his patent of baronetcy was made with remainder to his kinsman, Thomas Crawley-Boevey, grandson of Thomas Crawley, who, on inheriting Flaxley Abbey 1726, took the additional surname of Boevey ; the 6th baronet, Sir Francis Hyde, was a Verderer of the Forest of Dean.

BOILEAU, Creation (U.K.) 1838, of Tacolneston Hall, Norfolk.

DE·TOUT·MON·CŒUR

With all my heart.

Sir GILBERT GEORGE BENSON BOILEAU, 6th *Baronet; b.* Feb. 13th, 1898; *s.* his father, *Sir* FRANCIS JAMES, 1945; ed. at Xavier Coll., Kew, and at Newman Coll., Melbourne Univ. (M.B. and Ch.B. 1923); is Major Australian Army Med. Corps (Reserve) : *m.* 1st, 1924, Chica Patricia (from whom he obtained a divorce 1933), da. of the late James Louis Edgworth-Somers, L.R.C.S.I., of Mornington, Victoria, Australia ; 2ndly, 1941, Mary Catherine, da. of the late Lawrence Riordan, of Cradock, S. Australia, and has issue by 1st and 2nd marriages.

Arms—Azure, a castle triple towered or, masoned sable, and in base a crescent of the second. **Crest**—A pelican in her piety proper charged on the breast with a saltire couped gules.

Residence—Minto Lodge, Dandenong, Victoria, Australia. *Clubs*—Navy, Army and Air Force, Savage.

Daughters living—By 1st marriage—Prudence Despréaux, *b.* 1925: *m.* 1954, Anthony Harvey, of 138, Napoleon St., Eltham, Victoria, Australia, and has issue living, Georgia, *b.* 1955,—Tracey, *b.* 1958.——Angela Mary, *b.* 1927: *m.* 1949, John Stewart Milne, of Casérnè, Croydon, Victoria, Australia, and has issue living, Anthony Stewart, *b.* 1950,—Virginia, *b.* 1951,—Sarah, *b.* 1952,—Jane, *b.* 1954,—Lisa, *b.* 1956,—Elizabeth, *b.* 1967,—Melanie, *b.* 1967.——**By 2nd m.**—Madelon Mary, *b.* 1945.——Elisabeth Ann, *b.* 1948.——Mary Ann, *b.* 1953.

Brothers living—EDMOND CHARLES, *b.* May 28th, 1903; is Capt. Aust. Forces: *m.* 1933, Marjorie Lyle, da. of Claude Monteath D'Arcy, of Launceston, Tas., and has issue living, Guy Francis, *b.* 1935; Lt.-Col.: *m.* 1962, Judith Frances, da. of Senator George Conrad Hannan, of Glen Iris, and Canberra, and has issue living, Nicolas Edmond George *b.* 1964, Christopher Guy *b.* 1969, Simone Terese *b.* 1963, Caroline Virginia *b.* 1968,—Peter Linden (Seaton St., Glen Iris, Vic., Aust.), *b.* 1937: *m.* 1967, Claudia, da. of Alan Edward Mills, of Wanganui, NZ, and has issue living, Dominic Peter *b.* 1968, James Edward *b.* 1971. *Residence*, 61, Erica Av., Glen Iris, Vic., Aust.——Patrick Etienne, *b.* 1912: *m.* 1940, Jean Frances, da. of the late John Jordan Moore, and has issue living, Michael Donald, *b.* 1949,—Patricia Ann, *b.* 1943.

Collateral Branch living.

Grandchildren of the late Edmund William Pollen Boileau, 3rd son of 1st baronet :—

Issue of the late Edmond Charles Boileau, *b.* 1877, *d.* 1940: *m.* 1902, Jean Ballantyne, who *d.* 19— :—

Maurice, *b.* 1904.——Eric, *b.* 1906.——Catherine, *b.* 1908. *Residence*,

This baronet is descended in an unbroken line from Etienne Boileau, Baron de Castelnau and St. Croix (Province of Languedoc), who, in 1250, on the departure of Louis IX. for the Holy Land, was appointed, during his absence, Governor of Paris, and 1st Grand Provost of France. He drew up the first Municipal Code, which is still used. His descendant, Charles Boileau, Baron de Castelnau and St. Croix, fled to England at the Revocation of the Edict of Nantes. Descendants of the same family own the original French property.

BOLES, Creation (U.K.) 1922, of Bishop's Lydeard, Somerset.

Sir JEREMY JOHN FORTESCUE BOLES, 3rd *Baronet; b.* Jan. 9th, 1932; *s.* his father, *Capt. Sir* GERALD FORTESCUE, 1945; ed. at Stowe: *m.* 1st, 1955 (m. diss. 1970), Dorothy Jane, yr. da. of J. A. Worswick, of Enmore, Som.; 2ndly, 1970, Elisabeth Gildroy, yr. da. of E. P. Shaw, of Englefield Green, Surrey, and widow of Oliver Simon Willis Fleming, and has issue by 1st and 2nd m.

Arms—Azure, on a fesse ermine, between three standing bowls argent, out of each a boar's head or, a portcullis also or. **Crest**—In front of a rising sun or a demi-boar azure, pierced in the left shoulder by an arrow proper.

Residence—Lime, House, Tilford Farnham, Surrey.

As I do to thee so will I do to others.

Sons living (By 1st m.)—RICHARD FORTESCUE, *b.* Dec. 12th, 1958.——David Hastings Fortescue, *b.* 1967.
Daughters living (By 1st m.)—Sarah Jane, *b.* 1956.——(By 2nd m.) Jessica Blanche Mary, *b.* 1971.
Aunts living (daughters of 1st baronet)—Violet Beatrice: *m.* 1932, Michael Allen Bucknall, and has issue living, Nicholas Lysaght Allen, *b.* 1939. *Residence*, Triscombe House, Bishop's Lydeard, nr. Taunton. Somerset.——Doreen Frances: *m.* 1936, Cyril Alfred Anderson, who *d.* 1958, and has issue living, Hermione Beatrice Hewitt, *b.* 1937: *m.* 1969, John Richard Lewes, and has issue living, Claire Beatrice *b.* 1974,—Audrey France Hewitt, *b.* 1939: *m.* 1966, Fl.-Lt. Norman Thomas Boulger, RAF, and has issue living, Susannah Frances *b.* 1968. *Residence*, The Glebe House, Crowcombe, Taunton, Som.——Nesta Mary. *Residence*, Paradise Farm, Crowcombe, Taunton.

The 1st baronet, Lieut.-Col. Sir Dennis Fostescue Boles, C.B.E. (son of the late Rev. James Thomas Boles, of Ryll Court, Exmouth, and Moyge, co. Cork), was M.P. for W., or Wellington, Div. of Somerset (C) **1911-18**, and for Taunton Div. of Somerset **1918-21**. The 2nd baronet, Capt. Sir Gerald Fortescue, 17th/21st Lancers, *d.* (on active ser. during European War) 1945.

BOLTON, Creation (U.K.) 1927, of West Plean, co. Stirling.

By industry and courage.

INDUSTRIA ET VIRTUTE

Sir Ian Frederick Cheney Bolton, K.B.E., 2nd *Baronet ; b.* Jan. 29th, 1889 ; *s.* his father, *Sir* Edwin, *M.B.E.*, 1931 ; ed. at Eton; Hon. LL.D. Glasgow 1955; a Chartered Accountant; formerly a Partner in Arthur Young, McClelland, Moores & Co., of Glasgow and London; Part-time Member of British Transport Commn. 1947-59 (Chm. of Scottish Area Board 1955-59), and Lord-Lieut. of co. Stirling 1949-64; past Pres. of Inst. of Chartered Accountants of Scotland; Pres. of Scottish Boy Scout Assocn. 1943-57; a Freeman of Stirling; 1914-18 War in France as Capt. 3rd Bn. Argyll and Sutherland Highlanders (despatches); OBE (Civil) 1946, KBE (Civil) 1957.

Arms—Argent, a falcon close sable, armed, jessed and belled or, on a chief engrailed of the second three bezants. **Crest**—A falcon as in the arms.
Seat—West Plean, Stirling.

The 1st baronet, Sir Edwin Bolton, MBE (son of the late Joseph Cheney Bolton, of Carbrook and West Plean, Stirlingshire), was Convener of Stirlingshire 1919-27, and Vice-Lt. 1926-31.

BONHAM, Creation (U.K.) 1852.

Sir Antony Lionel Thomas Bonham, 4th *Baronet ; b.* Oct. 21st, 1916 ; *s.* his father, *Major Sir* Eric Henry, *C.V.O.*, 1937 ; ed. at Eton ; Major (retired) Roy. Scots Greys: *m.* 1944, Felicity, only da. of the late Col. Frank Lionel Pardoe, D.S.O., of Bartonbury, Cirencester, and has issue.

Arms—Sable, a chevron nebulée between three crosses, patée fitchée at the foot argent ; on a canton of the last a squirrel sejant gules. **Crest**—A mermaid holding in the dexter hand a wreath of coral and in the sinister a mirror proper.

Residence—Ash House, Ampney Crucis, Cirencester, Glos.

To be, rather than to seem to be.

ESSE QUAM VIDERI

Sons living—GEORGE MARTIN ANTONY, *b.* Feb. 18th, 1945.——Simon Philip, *b.* 1947.——Timothy Eric, *b.* 1952.
Sister living—Elizabeth Mary, *b.* 1914: *m.* 1939, Lieut.-Com. Bryan William Richard Curling, V.R.D., R.N.V.R., and has issue living, David Antony Bryan, *b.* 1943: *m.* 1971, Jennifer, da. of John Schlesinger,—Christopher Desmond, *b.* 1947: *m.* 1974, the Hon. Melissa Llewelyn-Davies, da. of Baron Llewelyn-Davies [Life Baron],—Jonathan James, *b.* 1951,—Belinda Jane Mary, *b.* 1940. *Residence*, Fullerton Manor, nr. Andover, Hants.

The 1st baronet, Sir Samuel George Bonham, K.C.B. (son of Capt. George Bonham, H.E.I.C.S., a descendant of Sir John Bonham, of Stanway Hall, Essex), was Gov. of Straits Settlements 1837-47, and Gov. and Com.-in-Ch. at Hong Kong, and Ch. Superintendent of British Trade in China 1847-53. The 2nd baronet, Sir George Francis, was Envoy Extraor. and Min. Plen. to Serbia 1900-1903, and to Swiss Confederation 1905-9. The 3rd baronet, Sir Eric Henry, C.V.O., was Comptroller of the Household to H.R.H. Prince Arthur of Connaught 1913-26.

BONSOR, Creation (U.K.) 1925, of Kingswood, Epsom, Surrey.

Omne bonum Dei donum

Every good thing is the gift of God.

Sir BRYAN COSMO BONSOR, *M.C.*,
T.D., 3rd *Baronet*; *b.* Aug. 26th, 1916; *s.* his
father, *Major Sir* REGINALD, 1959; ed. at
Eton; is Major RA; a DL for Bucks; 1939-45
War (despatches, MC); a DL for Bucks: *m.*
1942, Elizabeth, da. of Capt. Angus Valdimar
Hambro, of Milton Abbas, Dorset, and has
issue.

Arms—Per fesse azure and argent, a pale counterchanged, three lions' heads erased or, on a chief also or
three roses gules, barbed and seeded proper. *Crest*—A
wolf passant sable, collared and chained gold, resting the
dexter fore-paw on a rose as in the arms.

Seat—Liscombe Park, Leighton Buzzard, Bedfordshire.
Residence—

Sons living—NICHOLAS COSMO (Burcott Hill House,
living, Leighton Buzzard, Beds.), *b.* Dec. 9th, 1942;
ed. at Eton, and Ch. Ch., Oxford (BA); Bar. Inner
Temple 1967: *m.* 1969, the Hon. Nadine Marisa Lampson,
da. of 2nd Baron Killearn, and has issue living, Sacha
Henrietta,——Richard Angus, *b.* 1947; ed. at Eton: *m.*
1971, Susan, da. of F/L David Henry Lewis Wigan,
RAFVR [By. Tweedmouth].
Brother living—David Victor, *M.C.*, *b.* 1918; ed. at
Eton; Major late Grenadier Guards; European War
1939-45 (M.C.): *m.* 1945, Sheila, da. of Maj.-Gen. Sir
Miles William Arthur Peel Graham, K.B.E., C.B., M.C.
[E. Lovelace, colls.], and has issue living, Anthony
Miles, *b.* 1948,—Neil Reginald David, *b.* 1950,—Caroline
Sheila, *b.* 1946. *Residence*, Little Stocks, Aldbury,
near Tring, Herts.

Sister living—Daphne Marion, *b.* 1924: *m.* 1st, 1944, Clyde Euan Miles Graham, Flying Officer
R.A.F., who *d.* (on active ser. during European War) 1944 [E. Peel, colls.]; 2ndly, 1948, Alex-
ander David Stewart, M.B.E., T.D. [*see* E. Galloway, colls.]. *Residence*, North Green, Kelsale,
Saxmundham, Suffolk.

Collateral Branch living.

Issue of the late Robert Cecil Bonsor, M.C., 3rd son of 1st baronet, *b.* 1880, *d.* 1932:
m. 1922, Enid, da. of S. Lawrence:—
Michael Cosmo (of Paradise, Waltham St. Lawrence, Berks.), *b.* 1926: *m.* 1951, Ann Marie, da. of
Marc Wallenberg, and has issue living, Celia Jane, *b.* 1954,—Charlotte, *b.* 1956,—Camilla Ann,
b. 1961,—Robert Angus Cosmo, *b.* 1963,——Ann Elizabeth, *b.* 1923.

The 1st baronet, Sir (Henry) Cosmo Orme Bonsor, sat as M.P. for Surrey, N.E., or Wimbledon,
S.W., Div (C) 1885-1900, and was sometime a Director of the Bank of England. The 2nd baronet,
Sir Reginald, was Major Surrey Yeo., Chm. of John Dickinson & Co., Ltd., of Apsley Mills, Hemel
Hempstead, and High Sheriff of Bucks, 1940-41.

BOORD, Creation (U.K.) of 1896, Wakehurst Place, Ardingly, Sussex.
[Name pronounced "**Board**."]

Virtute et industria

By integrity and industry.

Sir RICHARD WILLIAM BOORD, 3rd
Baronet, son of the late Alexander Edgar Boord, 3rd
son of 1st baronet; *b.* Nov. 9th, 1907; *s.* his uncle,
Sir WILLIAM ARTHUR, 1928; ed. at Marlborough,
and at Lincoln Coll., Oxford; formerly Squadron-
Leader R.A.F. Vol. Reserve: *m.* 1st, 1933, Yvonne
Swingler (from whom he obtained a divorce 1944),
da. of Joseph Arthur Hubert Bird, formerly of 23B,
De Vere Gardens, Kensington, W.8; 2ndly, 1944,
Ethel El Marie, who *d.* 1973, da. of H. Moline, of
Duluth, Minnesota, U.S.A., and has issue by 1st m.

Arms—Per fesse azure and gules, a goat's head erased
within an orle of eight martlets argent. *Crest*—A goat
argent, guttee de poix, resting the dexter leg on an escutcheon
gules, charged with a martlet of the first.
Residence—4, Trumpeters House, Old Palace Yard,
The Green, Richmond, Surrey.

Sons living—By 1st marriage—NICOLAS JOHN
CHARLES (Les Aloadès, Batimenl, 94, Traverse Prat,
13008-Marseille, France), *b.* June 10th, 1936: *m.* 1st, 1960
(m. diss. 1965), Françoise Tempra; 2ndly, 1965, Françoise Renée, da. of Marcel Clovis Mouret, of 69, Traverse
de Carthage, 13, Marseilles 8°.——Antony Andrew (18,
Morden Rd., Blackheath, SE3), *b.* 1938: *m.* 1960, Anna
Christina von Krogh, and has issue living, Andrew
Richard, *b.* 1962,—Tamsin Katrina, *b.* 1961.

Sister living—Sybil Katherine (of 5, Embankment Gdns., SW3), *b.* 1906.

The 1st baronet, Sir (Thomas) William Boord (el. son of Joseph Boord, J.P., of Harefield
Grove, Uxbridge), was a partner in the firm of Boord and Son, distillers, and a Director of London
and Provincial Bank Limited), and sat as M.P. for Greenwich (C) 1873-95.

BOOTH, Creation (U.K.) 1916, of Allerton Beeches, City of Liverpool.

Neither rashly nor timidly.

Sir DOUGLAS ALLEN BOOTH, 3rd *Baronet;*
b. Dec. 2nd, 1949; *s.* his father, *Sir* PHILIP,
1960; ed. at Harvard Univ.

    Arms—Per pale and per chevron argent, ermine, and sable,
in chief two boars' heads erased and erect of the last and in base
a like boar's head of the first. **Crest**—A rose gules, barbed,
seeded and encircled by two olive branches proper, thereon a
lion passant argent.

    Residence.—1255, Daniels Av., Los Angeles, Calif.
90035, USA.

Brother living—DEREK BLAKE, *b.* April 7th, 1953.

Uncle living (son of 1st baronet)—Edmund, *b.* 1908 : *m.*
1933, Henrietta Mary, da. of the late Sir Charles (Stewart)
Addis, KCMG, and has issue living, Anthony Edmund
(Watchbury House, High St., Barford, Warwicks.),
b. 1934; ed. at Gordonstoun, and at King's Coll., Camb.
(MB, BCh); FRCS, FRCSE: *m.* 1st, 1957, Margaret Helen
Elizabeth, da. of the late Maj. A. B. Miller; 2ndly, 1969,
Susan Alison Letitia, da. of the late Lt. R. O'Neill Roe,
RN, and has issue living (by 1st m.), Edmund Stuart
b. 1960, Sam Andrew *b.* 1962, Adam Piper *b.* 1963,—Martin
Butler (60, Elmbridge, Churchgate St., Old Harlow,
Essex), *b.* 1936; ed. at Gordonstoun, and at King's Coll.,
Camb. (MA): *m.* 1968, Margaret Hilary, da. of Clifford
Birch, of York,—Philip Addis, *b.* 1946,—Edmund, *b.*
1948,—Mary Rachel, *b.* 1939: da. of Cranborne Chase Sch.:
m. 1967, James William Bruce Douglas, BM, BCh, of 17,
Quick St., N1. *Residence*, Kinderhook, Lock Lane, Birdham,
Chichester.

Widow living of 2nd Baronet—ETHEL, da. of Joseph Greenfield, of New York, USA; has resumed
surname of Booth: *m.* 1st, 1948, as his second wife, Sir Philip Booth, 2nd baronet, who *d.* 1960;
2ndly, 1962 (m. diss. 1965), Prof. Winston R. Weisman, PhD. *Residence,*—1255, Daniels Av.,
Los Angeles, Calif. 90035, USA.

    The 1st baronet, Sir Alfred Allen (son of the late Alfred Booth, J.P., of Liverpool) was a
director of Alfred Booth & Co., Ltd., and sometime chairman of Cunard Steamship Co., Ltd.

GORE-BOOTH, Creation (I.) 1760, of Artarman, Sligo.

Sir MICHAEL SAVILE GORE-BOOTH, 7th *Baronet;*
b. July 24th, 1908; *s.* his father, *Sir* JOSSLYN AUGUSTUS
RICHARD, 1944; ed. at Rugby, and at Trin. Coll., Camb.

    Arms—Quarterly of six : 1st quarterly, 1st and 4th, argent three boars
heads couped and erect sable ; 2nd and 3rd, gules, a fesse between three
cross-crosslets or ; 2nd, argent, on a fesse sable three bezants ; 3rd, argent a
lion's head erased between three crescents gules ; 4th, gules three cinquefoils argent ; 5th, gules on a bend or, three martlets ; 6th, checky azure and
argent a fesse gules. **Crest**—1st, a lion passant, *Booth* ; 2nd, a wolf rampant,
Gore. **Mottos**—over *First Crest*—"Quod ero spero" (*I hope for what I
shall be*) ; over *Second Crest*—"In hoc signo vinces" (*Under this sign thou
shalt conquer*).
    Seat—Lissadell, Sligo.

Genti æquus utrique.
Just to either line.

Brother living—ANGUS JOSSLYN, *b.* June 25th, 1920 : formerly Capt.
Irish Guards ; N.-W. Europe 1945 : *m.* 1948, the Hon. Rosemary
Myra Vane (who obtained a divorce 1954), da. of 10th Baron Barnard,
and has issue living, Josslyn Henry Robert, *b.* 1950,—Georgina Clara
Rosaleen Eirenice, *b.* 1949: *m.* 1970, Capt. Clive Abercromby Blomfield-
Smith, 9th/12th R. Lancers (c/o Officers' Mess, 9th/12th R. Lancers,
BFPO 41). *Residence*, Lissadell, Sligo.

Sisters living—Bridget Mary, *b.* 1911.——Rosaleen Rache., *b.* 1914.——Aideen Joyce, *b.* 1916.

Collateral Branches living.

    Issue of the late Mordaunt Gore-Booth, younger son of 5th baronet, *b.* 1878,
d. 1958: *m.* 1906, Evelyn Mary, who *d.* 1963, da. of the late Robert Stanley
Scholfield, of Sandhall, Howden, E. Yorkshire:—
Paul Henry, GCMG, KCVO (*Baron Gore-Booth*), *b.* 1909; *cr. Baron Gore-Booth* (Life Peer) June
14th, 1969 [see that title].

    Grandchildren of the late Mordaunt Gore-Booth (ante) :—
    Issue of the late Colum Robert Gore-Booth, *b.* 1913, *d.* 1959 : *m.* 1st, 1939, Joan Yvonne
Ballard, adopted da. of the Rev. C. W. Chastel de Boinville; 2ndly, 1947, Mary (who
m. 2ndly, 1971, Michael William McLean Barker, of the Pant Farm, Cross Ash, Aber-
gavenny, Gwent), da. of the late Edward Paget Schofield, JP, of Sandhall, Howden,
York [D. Northimberland, colls.]:—
(By 2nd marriage), Francis Peter, *b.* 1948.——Nicholas Justin, *b.* 1952.——Susan Caroline, *b.* 1950.

    This family has a common origin with Earl Temple of Stowe and Gore Bt. (cr. 1622), [see latter
title]. Nathaniel Gore, father of Sir Gore Booth, 1st baronet, m. 1711, Lettice, da. and heir of
Humphrey Booth of Dublin. Sir Robert Newcomen Gore, 3rd baronet, assumed by Roy. licence
1804, the additional surname and arms of Booth.

BOOTHBY, Creation (E.) 1660, of Broadlow Ash, Derbyshire.

Sir HUGO ROBERT BROOKE BOOTHBY, 15th *Baronet ; b.* Aug. 10th, 1907 ; *s.* his father, *Sir* SEYMOUR WILLIAM BROOKE, 1951; ed. at Lancing Coll., and at Hertford Coll., Oxford; Capt. RA (TA); a JP for Glamorgan (High Sheriff 1953); Lieut. for S. Glamorgan 1974; a Member of National Broadcasting Council for Wales, 1953-6, and of Glamorgan co. Agric. Exec. Cttee. 1953-62, Chm. of Art Cttee. Nat. Museum of Wales 1966-70; a Fellow of Woodward Corporation and S. Wales Regional Dir. of Lloyds Bank: *m.* 1938, (Evelyn) Ann, da. of Herbert Charles Richards Homfray, of Penllyn Castle, Cowbridge, Glamorgan, and has issue.

Arms—Argent, on a canton sable a lion's jamb erased erect or. Crest—A lion's jamb as in the arms.
    Residence—Fonmon Castle, Barry, Glamorgan. *Club*—Travellers'.

The death of Christ is to me the death of death.

Son living—BROOKE CHARLES, *b.* April 6th, 1949, ed. at Eton, and Trin. Coll., Camb.

Daughters living—Penelope Ann, *b.* 1939: *m.* 1959, Lieut. Timothy Hale, RN, and has issue living, Veronica Ann Leslie, *b.* 1960.——Caroline Serena, *b.* 1941: *m.* 1962, Ifor Lewis, of Manton Weir Farm, Manton, Marlborough, and has issue living, Vivienne Serena, *b.* 1966,—Carina Cecilia, *b.* 1969.

Sister living—Serena Margaret, *b.* 1914 : *m.* 1958, Herbert Charles Richards Homfray, who *d.* 1960. *Residence*, Church House, Penllyn, Cowbridge, Glamorgan.

Collateral Branches living.

Grandsons of the late George Boothby (infra):—
Issue of the late George William Bernard Boothby, *b.* 1917, *d.* 1972: *m.* 1942, Aurill Alice (29, Oakfield Rd., Highlight, Barry, Glamorgan), da. of John Edward Innell:—
George William, *b.* 1948.——Richard Charles Brooke, *b.* 1955.

Granddaughters of the late Com. George William Boothby, son of the late Rev. Brooke Boothby, 2nd son of 7th baronet :—
Issue of the late George Boothby, *b.* 1867, *d.* 1921 : *m.* 1904, Mabel Gertrude (of 241, Gladstone Road, Barry, S Wales), da. of Bernard Flanagan :—
Irene Mabel, *b.* 1905; is an Anglican Nun.——Violet Dora, *b.* 1908: *m.* 1935, Ernest Victor Evans and has issue living, Geoffrey Boothby, *b.* 1937. *Residence*, 11, Birch Grove, Barry, Glamorgan.——Edna Frances, *b.* 1910: *m.* 1940, Ronald George Henry Steele, and has issue living, Elizabeth Penelope *b.* 1944. *Residence*, Rangeworthy, 3, West Town Drive, Brislington, Bristol.

Grandchildren of the late Rev. Evelyn Boothby, 2nd son of Rev. Charles Boothby, 3rd son of 7th baronet:—
Issue of the late Capt. William Osbert Boothby, C.V.O., C.B., R.N., *b.* 1866, *d.* 1913: *m.* 1907, Hilda Lambert, who *d.* 1960, da. of the late Capt. Henry Stephen Swiney, 69th Regt.:—
Christopher Evelyn, *b.* 1912 ; ed. at Lancing Coll.; is Major R.M.: *m.* 1940, Pamela Gertrude, da. of the late Frederick Lewis Heriot-Maitland [*see* E. Lauderdale, colls.], and has issue living, Marilyn Susan, *b.* 1944: *m.* 1967, Stanley LeBlanc, of 3123, Tower Trail, Dallas, Texas, USA, and has issue living James Boothby *b.* 1971 Sarah Maria *b.* 1968 —Diana Mary, *b.* 1948: *m.* 1969, John Michael Spiller, of 3, Clos Brynderi, Rhiwbina, Cardiff, S. Wales. *Residence*,—Corner Cottage, Lower Bourne, Farnham, Surrey.——Margaretta Laura, *b.* 1908.——Alice Rafela, *b.* 1911. *Residence*,—12c, Fitzgerald Park, Fitzgerald Av., Seaford, Sussex.
Issue of the late Basil Tanfield Beridge Boothby, *b.* 1873, *d.* 1948 : *m.* 1909, Katharine Georgina who *d.* 1938, only surviving da. of the late Major F. B. Knox, R.A. :—
(Evelyn) Basil, *CMG* (23, Holland Park Av., W11), *b.* 1910; ed. at Winchester, and at Corpus Christi Coll., Camb. (BA); was Counsellor, Brussels 1954-59; Ambassador to Iceland 1962-65, since when a Permanent Repres. to Council of Europe; CMG 1958: *m.* 1946, Susan Penelope, da. of the late Brig.-Gen. the Hon. Arthur Melland Asquith, DSO [*see* E. Oxford Asquith, colls.], and has issue living, John Joseph, *b.* 1947,—Henry, *b.* 1955,—Emily Albertine *b.* 1948: *m.* 1967 Piers Paul Read, of Stonegrave, York, son of Sir Herbert Edward Read, DSO, MC,—Jane Penelope, *b.* 1914: *m.* 1937, St. John Bernard Vyvyan Harmsworth, and has issue living, Penelope Georgina Mary, *b.* 1938: *m.* 1968, Wyndham Parfitt,—Sarah Elizabeth Anne, *b.* 1941: *m.* 1963 (m. diss 1974), Alexander Randal Mark, Viscount Dunluce, el. son of 8th Earl of Antrim, —Laura Jane, *b.* 1944: *m.* 1967, David Henry George Montagu-Douglas-Scott, of 25, Whitelands House Chelsea SW3 [*see* D. Buccleuch]. *Residence*—Valley Home, Horsted, Keynes, Sussex.——(Katharine) Anne, *b.* 1915: *m.* 1939, Col. Hubert Layard Chesshyre, late RE, of Don Jon House, Canterbury, and has issue living, David Hubert Boothby, *b.* 1940; Rouge Croix Pursuivant of Arms since 1970,—William John, *b.* 1943: Capt. RE,—Matthew Henry, *b.* 1944; MA, MB, BCh,—John Francis, *b.* 1948,—Katharine Mildred, *b.* 1947: *m.* 1969, Thomas Peregrine Stansfeld Bryant, and has issue living, William *b.* 1974, Rosemary (twin) *b.* 1974,—Alice Jane, *b.* 1956.

Grandchildren of the late Col. Basil Charles Boothby, 4th son of the late Rev. Charles Boothby (ante):—
Issue of the late Rev. Walter Ralph Jebb Boothby, *b.* 1865, *d.* 1925: *m.* 1900, Mary, who *d.* 1948, da. of the late Rev. George Frederick Prescott, of 10L, Hyde Park Mansions, N.W., formerly V. of St. Michael and All Angels, Paddington, W.:—
Basil Frederick, *MBE, b.* 1904; ed. at Lancing, and at Selwyn Coll., Camb. (BA); late Special Export Officer, CBI; MBE (Civil) 1957: *m.* 1934, Dorothy, da. of Frank Gould, of Ryde, I. of Wight, and Calcutta, and has issue living, Christopher Brooke (13, Rectory Meadow, Fornham All Saints, Bury St. Edmunds), *b.* 1938; ed. at Lancing; MRCP London, MRCS England: *m.* 1969, Anne Barrow Dalston, of Torcross, Devon, and has issue living, Hugo Thomas Brooke *b.* 1972, William Jebb Dalston (twin) *b.* 1972, Margaret Elizabeth Prescott *b.* 1974. *Residence*, 6, Montpelier Row, Blackheath, SE3.
Issue of the late Capt. Evelyn Leonard Beridge Boothby, D.S.O., R.N., *b.* 1876; *d.* 1937: *m.* 1st, 1905, Esmé Frances Nevill Augusta, who *d.* 1913, da. of Sir Edward Beauchamp, 1st Bt., M.P.; 2ndly, 1924, Lucy Margaret Amy, who *d.* 1948, widow of Capt. F. T. Gardiner, Highland L.I.:—

(By 1st m.) Esmé Janet (Rafella Cottage, Wheeler Lane, Witley, Surrey), *b.* 1906.——(By 2nd m.) Walter Evelyn Brooke (64, Morley Crescent East, Stanmore, Middx.), *b.* 1927: *m.* 1st, 1951 (m. diss. 1974), Yvonne, da. of J. S. Capewell, of Harlesden, NW; 2ndly, 1974, Catharine Jane, da. of A. F. Stobart, of Newton Farm, Tregony, Cornwall, and has issue living (by 1st m.), Martin William, *b.* 1953,—Bruce Michael, *b.* 1959.

A baronetcy was conferred, in 1644, upon Henry Boothby, of Claytor Close; but, though the creation received the sign-manual of Charles I., it did not pass the Great Seal, by reason of the confusion of the civil wars. At the Restoration his only son, William Boothby, of Broadlow Ash, Derbyshire, was cr. a Baronet de novo by Charles II., with the date of 1660. Ashbourne Hall, Derbyshire, the seat of the family for 200 years, was sold in 1846, in accordance with the will of the 9th baronet. The 10th baronet, Sir Brooke, was in Diplo. Ser., and the 11th, Sir Charles Francis, was Lieut. N. Mayo Mil.

BOREEL, Creation (E.) 1645, of Amsterdam, Holland.

[Name pronounced "**Borale**."]

Jonkheer Sir FRANCIS DAVID BOREEL, 13th *Baronet*; *b.* June 14th, 1926; *s.* his father *Jonkheer Sir* ALFRED, 1964; Consul-Gen. of the Netherlands, Sao Paulo, Brasil, since 1975: *m.* 1964: Suzanne, da. of Willy Campagne, of Paris, and has issue.

Arms—Argent, on a chevron between three bugle horns sable, two whips thonged proper, on a chief gules a lion passant guardant or. **Supporters**—On clouds two angels proper, vested argent.

Address—c/o Ministry of Foreign Affairs, Casuariestaat 16, The Hague, Netherlands.

Daughters living—Reiniera Adriana, *b.* 1965.—— Christina Wilhelmina, *b.* 1966.——Titia Florence, *b.* 1973.

Sister living—Florence, *b.* 1922: *m.* 1955, H. W Van Lelyveld. *Residence*, 7, Marthalaan, Enschede, Holland.

Collateral Branches living.

Granddaughters of the late Jonkheer William Walter Astor Boreel, son of the late Jonkheer Francis Robert Boreel, son of Lt.-Gen. William Francis Boreel, 3rd son of 7th baronet:—
  Issue of the late Jonkheer Robert John Ralph Boreel, *b.* 1867, *d.* 1904: *m.* 1891, Edith Margaret, who *d.* 1933 (having *m.* 2ndly, 1905, Jacob Pieter Crommelin), da. of Philo Ives, of Hartford, Connecticut, USA:—
Helen Barbara Isabella (c/o Nat. Westminster Bank, 96-97, Strand, WC2), *b.* 1894: *m.* 1921 (m. diss. 1944), Ralph Clarmont Skrine Stevenson, CMG (cr. KCMG 1946 and GCMG 1949), and has issue living, Mark Boreel, *b.* 1924.——(Edith) Wendela Dorothy, *b.* 1896; an Asso. of Roy. So. of Painter Etchers: *m.* 1924, Leslie George Wylde, late Lt. Canterbury Regt. (NZ Forces), who *d.* 1935, and has issue living, James Paxton de Eglesfield, *b.* 1927. *Residence*, 8, Avenue de Sully, 1814, La Tour de Peilz, Vaud, Switzerland.

    Grandchildren of the late Jonkheer James Lucas Boreel (infra):
      Issue of the late Jonkheer Gerard Lucas Boreel, *b.* 1913, *d.* 1970: *m.* 1943, Virginia Rae who *d.* 1972, da. of Frank Gervin Bright, of New York:—
STEPHAN GERARD, *b.* Feb. 9th, 1945.——Maurits, *b.* 1946: *m.* 1971, Tilde Anna Eisma.—— Joan, *b.* 1949.

    Grandchildren of the late Jonkheer Gerard Salomon Boreel, 2nd son of Jonkheer Jacob Otto Bernard Boreel, yr. son of Jonkheer Lucas Boreel, 4th son of 7th baronet:—
      Issue of the late Jonkheer James Lucas Boreel, *b.* 1883, *d.* 1939: *m.* 1911, Baroness Adriana Sophia, who *d.* 1958, da. of Baron Maurits van Randwijck:—
Maurits (Rembrandtlaan 23, Doorn, Holland), *b.* 1914: *m.* 1942, Antoinette Crommelin, and has issue living, Lucas Jacob, *b.* 1945: *m.* 1966, Henriette van Teunenbroek, and has issue living, Elsa-Bertha *b.* 1967, Esther Nanette *b.* 1970,—Paul Marinus, *b.* 1949,—Willem, *b.* 1952,— Jacoba, Francina, *b.* 1943: *m.* 1968, Arnold Hendrik Tieleman.——Henriette, *b.* 1917: *m.* 1947, Dirk J. G. Buurman, of Rembrantlaan 4 Velp, Gelderland, Holland.
      Issue of the late Jonkheer Hugo Boreel, *b.* 1884, *d.* 1962: *m.* 1930, Baroness Emilie Henriette Adele, who *d.* 1970, da. of Baron Cornelis van Tuyll van Serooskerken:—
Lucas Gerard (Eikenhorstlaan, 19, Wassenaar, Holland), *b.* 1931: *m.* 1960, Marie Louise, da. of Pierre van Son.——Cornelis Jan (Beekhuizen-seweg 67a, Velp, (Gld.), Netherlands) *b.* 1932: *m.* 1959, Claudine Wilhelmina Woltera, da. of Willem Jan Royaards, and has issue living, Robert Jan Willem, *b.* 1960,—Lucas Wolter, *b.* 1966,—Claudine Emilie Amarante, *b.* 1963. ——Geert Frans, *b.* 1934: *m.* 1958, Henriette Nancy Leopoldine, da. of Jonkheer B. W. F. van Riemsdijk, and has issue living, Hugo Geert, *b.* 1959,—Barthold Willem Lucas, *b.* 1960,—Pauline Danielle, *b.* 1964. *Residence*, Bruggenbosch, Blikkenweg 15, Twello, Holland.

    Granddaughters of the late Jonkheer Jacob Otto Bernard Boreel (ante):—
      Issue of the late Jonkheer Marius Willem Boreel, *b.* 1856, *d.* 1905: *m.* 1886, Cornelia, who *d.* 1939, da. of the late Jonkheer Theodor Prins van Westdorpe, of Haarlem, Holland:—
Catharina Margaretha, *b.* 1891: *m.* 1918, Henri Louis van Eeghen. *Residence*, Noordhout, Driebergen, Holland.

      Issue of the late Jonkheer Paulus James Boreel, *b.* 1863, *d.* 1938: *m.* 1892, Marie, who *d.* 1945, da. of Jacob Pieter Suermondt:—
Anna, *b.* 1896.——Wendela, *b.* 1898.

    Grandson of the late Jonkheer Paulus James Boreel (ante):—
      Issue of the late Marie Boreel, *b.* 1893, *d.* 1971: *m.* 1925, James Skinner Mackenzie Eddison, OBE, who *d.* 1965.
John Michael (P.O. Box 1216, Bandar Seri Begawan, Brunei), *b.* 1930; BSc, MICE, MIStructE, MASCE, MEIC: *m.* 1956, Marjorie Joyce Hailey.

Grandchildren of the late Jonkheer Hendrik Etienne Gustave Boreel (infra):—
Issue of the late Jonkheer Jacob Gerard Joseph Boreel, *b.* 1891, *d.* 1945: *m.* 1914, Charlotte Susanna (Hanenburglaan 198, The Hague), da. of Eduard Manuel:—
Henri Etienne Gustave (36, 3e Feldepad, The Hague, Holland), *b.* 1915: *m.* 1949 Hendrika Catharina Allegonda, da. of Ferdinand Karel August Luder, and has issue living, Henri Etienne Gustave, *b.* 1952,—Jacqueline Marguérite Charlotte, *b.* 1950,—Margot Jeanne Françoise, *b.* 1955,—Jacqueline Louise, *b.* 1918: *m.* 1943, Jan Arbouw, of The Hague, Holland.

Issue of the late Jonkheer Willem Boreel, *b.* 1893, *d.* 19—: *m.* 1915, Clasine Justine Cornelie, da. of Willem Anton Van Andel:—
Robert Hugo, *b.* 1919; Maj.-Gen. Dutch Army: *m.* 1939, Marie Louise Colette, da. of Wilhelmus Jacobus Antonius Van der Valk, and has issue living, Paul, *b.* 1947: *m.* 1968, Martha Deirdre de Graaf, and has issue living, Daphne Cherette *b.* 1968, Cynthia Jasmine *b.* 1970,—Ernst Boudewijn, *b.* 1948,—Maud, *b.* 1941: *m.* 1964, Frederik Racke.——Paul René, *b.* 1922: *m.* 1946, Audry, da. of Arthur James Ritchie, and has issue living, Robert Willem, *b.* 1947,—Helen Elisabeth, *b.* 1948: *m.* 1970, Wayne McKell.——Jeanne Marie Josephine, *b.* 1916: *m.* 1939, Hendrik Dirk Buurman, of Brussels, Belgium.

Grandchildren of the late Jonkheer Theodoor Gustaaf Victor Boreel, son of the late Jacob Boreel (*b.* 1777), son of the late Jacob Boreel (*b.* 1746), next brother of 7th baronet:—
Issue of the late Jonkheer Hendrik Etienne Gustave Boreel, *b.* 1866, *d.* 1908: *m.* 1889, Jeanne Josephine, who *d.* 1944, da. of Jacob Gerard Joseph Breyman:—
Alfred, *b.* 1894: *m.* 1st, 1920 (m. diss. 1953), Marie Francoise, da. of Frederik Hendrik de Bruine; 2ndly, 1955, Raden Dalia Mingsih, and has issue living (by 1st wife), Jacob Alfred, *MD* (Overveen, Holland), *b.* 1932: *m.* 1959, Albertine, da. of Jan Willem Cornelis De Vietter, and has issue living, Jacob Jan *b.* 1960, David Tibor *b.* 1962, Michiel *b.* 1963,—Eleonore, *b.* 1920: *m.* 1951, Cornelis Ian Reindert Phaff,—Ilse Anetta Jacoba, *b.* 1924: *m.* 1951, Gustaaf Adolf Cordesius, of Vlierboomstraat 614, The Hague, Holland,—(by 2nd wife), David Dradjat, *b.* 1959,—Yvonne Annette, *b.* 1953.——Jacoba, *b.* 1895: *m.* 1917, Rene Johny Kerdijk, of Djkarta, Indonesia, who *d.* 1968.

Issue of the late Jonkheer Johan Jacob Boreel, *b.* 1869, *d.* 1934: *m.* 1893, Sophia Fredrika, who *d.* 1904, da. of Jean Paul Frederik Gericke:—
Willem, *CBE* (Dennenlaan 101, Ede, Holland), *b.* 1895; Capt. (ret.) R. Netherlands Navy; CBE (Hon. Mil.) 1941: *m.* 1923 Ernestina Augusta Maria da. of Professor Dr. Hajo Brugmans, and has issue living, Maria Augusta, *b.* 1924: *m.* 1953, Cornelis Christiaan van Saarloos, MD, of Voorstraat 43 Franeker, Friesland, Holland,—Sophia Fredrika, *b.* 1927: *m.* 1958, Dr. Mario Mancosu, of Piedimonte 35, Terni, Umbria, Italy.——Sophia Alette Désirée, *b.* 1896: *m.* 1927, Jonkheer Dr. Johan Jacob von Schmid, Emeritus Prof. Univ. of Brussels, of 1, Sonnehofstrasse, Egg (Zurich), Switzerland.——Eleonora Jacoba, *b.* 1902: *m.* 1931, Dr. Pieter van Braam van Vloten. *Residence*, Delistraat 2A, The Hague, Holland.

Issue of the late Jonkheer Victor Eduard Anthon Boreel, *b.* 1871, *d.* 1957: *m.* 1897, Adrienne Jeanne, who *d.* 1959, da. of Eduard Jellinghaus:—
Willem (96, Paulinastraat, The Hague, Holland), *b.* 1898: *m.* 1926, Elizabeth Johanna Maria Peman, da. of Dr. Adriaan Marinus Kakebeeke, and has issue living, Victor Eduard, *b.* 1928: *m.* 1955, Gijsberta, da. of Dirk Nicolaas Verschoor, and has issue living, Willem Hendrik *b.* 1956, Victor Cornelis *b.* 1959, Barbara *b.* 19—.

Grandchildren of the late Jonkheer Victor Eduard Anthon Boreel (ante):—
Issue of the late Jonkheer Eduard Boreel, *b.* 1901, *d.* 1967: *m.* 1st (m. diss. 1946), Karin Elisabeth, da. of Jonkheer Maximiliaan Jacob Theodoor van de Poll; 2ndly, 1950, Maria Luisa Marques (Rua Ribeiro Sanches 21-3, Lisbon, Portugal), da. of Dr. José Santos Gouveia:—
(By 1st m.) Victor Charles (5, Rua do Porto, Estoril, Portugal), *b.* 1932: *m.* 1957, Béatrice Marie Louise Andrée, da. of Jonkheer Paul Marie Camille Frédéric de Kerckhove dit van der Varent and has issue living, Frederik Eduard Paul, *b.* 1958.—Christine Ghislaine Béatrice Karin *b.* 1957.——Maximiliaan Willem Felix (Lage Laarderweg 110, Huizen, Holland), *b.* 1935: *m.* 1962, Meta Dorothea Ludmilla, da. of René André Rost Onnes, and has issue living, Ghislaine Cornélie Carine, *b.* 1963,—Eugénie Renée *b.* 1965.——Karin Ghislaine Johanna (21, Av. Herbert Hoover, Brussels) *b.* 1940.

The 1st baronet, an envoy to England, was knighted by King James I in 1619, and it is related that he received from King Charles II on June 28th, 1653, a Royal Warrant as a Baron of England. The 9th baronet was a Member of the Upper House of Representatives in Holland, and was several times President of the Second Chamber of the States-General, and Gov. of North Holland. The 10th Baronet, was Gentleman of the Privy Chamber to the King of the Netherlands and subsequently Chamberlain to the Queen of the Netherlands.

BORTHWICK, Creation (U.K.) 1908, of Whitburgh, Humbie, Co. Haddington.

Sir JOHN THOMAS BORTHWICK, *MBE*, 3rd *Baronet*; only son of the late Hon. James Alexander Borthwick, 2nd son of 1st Bt.; *b.* Dec. 5th, 1917; ed. at Eton, and Trin. Coll., Oxford; late Maj. Rifle Brig. (TA); MBE (Mil) 1945: *m.* 1st, 1939 (m. diss. 1961), Irene, only child of Joseph Heller, of 2, Buckingham Place, SW1; 2ndly, 1962, Irene, da. of the late Leo Fink, of 26, Rue Franqueville, Paris XVI, and has issue living by 1st and 2nd m.

Arms—Argent, a cinque foil sable, on a chief invected of the last two cinquefoils of the first. Crest—A staff raguly fessewise sable, thereon a blackamoor's head in profile couped proper.
Residences,—Fox Hills, Long Cross, Surrey; 10, Cheyne Gdns., SW3.

Sons living—By 1st m.—ANTONY THOMAS (3, Lansdowne Cres., W11), *b.* Feb. 12th, 1941; ed. at Eton: *m.* 1966, Gillian Deirde Broke, da. of the late Nigel Vere Broke Thurston, RN, and has issue living, Matthew Thomas Thurston, *b.* 1968,—Suzanna Claire Irene, *b.* 1970,—

Camilla Fay Broke, b. 1973.——Peter Richard John, b. 1943: m. 1970, Helen, yr. da. of T. C.
Vogel, of Cudgewa, Vic., Aust.——Patrick James Joseph (19, Phillimore Place, W8) b. 1945:
m. 1969, Amanda Rosemary, yr. da. of R. G. A. Wells, of Lines End, Winchelsea, Sussex, and
has issue living, Alexander, b. 1971.——(by 2nd m.) Mark George Alexander, b. 1962.——John
Kelly Leo, b. 1965.

Mother living—[see Barony of Whitburgh.]

Collateral branches living

Issue of the late Hon. **William** Borthwick, 3rd son of 1st baronet, and brother of 1st
Baron Whitburgh, b. 1879, d. 1956: m. 1909, Ruth Margery, who d. 1971 [Bny. of
Whitburgh], only da. of the late Jason Rigby, MICE, of Wimbledon, SW:—
William Jason Maxwell, DSC (North House, Brancaster Staithe, King's Lynn Norfolk) b. 1910;
ed. at Winchester. and at Trin. Coll. Camb.; Bar. Inner Temple 1933; late Com. RNVR; 1939-
45 War (DSC): m, 1937, Elizabeth Cleveland da. of the late Herbert Elworthy, of Timaru, NZ,
and has issue living, Alister Jason (Deepdale House, Brancaster Staithe, King's Lynn, Norfolk),
b. 1945: m. 1970, Verily Anne, da. of Albert Augur East, and has issue living, Jason Matthew
b. 1971, Fiona Anne b. 1974,—Josephine Cleveland, b. 1939: m. 1960, John James Luddington
(Deepdale House, Brancaster Staithe, King's Lynn, Norfolk), and has issue living, Peter William
b. 1966, Julia Ruth b. 1961, Mary Elizabeth b. 1965,—Rosalind Cleveland, b. 1942: m. 1968,
Robert Andrew Spedding, 1 Miles Cottages, Taylors Lane, Bosham, Chichester, Sussex, and has
issue living, Harry George William b. 1973, Joanne Elizabeth b. 1970,—Celia Cleveland, b. 1947.
Brancaster Staithe, Norfolk. *Clubs,*—United University, Royal Thames Yacht.——Brian
Thomas, b. 1920; ed. at Eton; formerly Lt. RNVR: m. 1946, Jennifer Ruth, JP, da. of Maj.
Evelyn Ronald Moncrieff Fryer, MC, Gren. Gds., of Selborne, Hants. [see E. Peel, colls.], and
has issue living, Simon William Frederick, b. 1950,—Nicholas James, b. 1953,—Charles Thomas,
b. 1955,—Timothy Michael, b. 1958,—Sara Marjorie, b. 1951. *Residence,*—Manor Farm, Brancaster, Norfolk. *Club.*—Bath.——Elinor Valerie. b. 1915: m. 1940, Maj. Robert William
Augustus Fane, MBE, RA [see E. Westmorland, colls.]. *Residences,*—Hoo House, Hoo, Woodbridge, Suffolk.——Margaret Ruth, b. 1926: m. 1949, Henry Neville Hemsley, and has issue
living, John Neville, b. 1956,—Oliver Charles, b. 1960,—Clare Margaret, b. 1953,—Patricia Mary,
1964. *Residence,*—Langham Lodge, Oakham, Rutland.

Grandchildren of the late Hon. **Malcolm** Algernon Borthwick (infra):—
Issue of the late Lt.-Col. Algernon Malcolm Borthwick, MC, TD, b. 1907, d. 1975: m. 1935,
Edith Wylde, who d. 1975, da. of James Stanley Addison, of Wethersfield Place, Essex:
Malcolm (Wethersfield Place, Blaintree, Essex; 64, George St., Mackay, N. Qld., 4740, Aust.),
b. 1938: m. 1966, Dorothy Mary Prudence, 2nd da. of Alan M. Barker, of Salisbury, and has issue
living, Benedict, b. 1971,—Sophie Alexander, b. 1967,—Kate Cecile, b. 1969.——Winifred Letitia,
b. 1936: m. 1962, Stephen Tumim, Bar. at Law, of River House, 24, Upper Mall, W.6, and has
issue living, Matilda Edith, b. 1963,—Emma Renée, b. 1964,—Olivia, b. 1968.——Lucilla
Blanche (*Hon. Mrs. S. James Butler*), b. 1942: m. 1960, the Hon. Samuel James Butler [see B.
Butler of Saffron Walden].

Issue of the late Hon. **Malcolm** Algernon Borthwick, yst. son of 1st baronet, and brother
of 1st Baron Whitburgh, b. 1881, d. 1941: m. 1905, Blanche Buckland, who d. 1965, da.
of Henry Thomson Gorrie, of Auckland, NZ:—
Patrick John, b. 1908; ed. at Harrow: m. 1931, Nancy Hope, da. of Guy C. Williams, of Te Parac,
Masterton, NZ, and has issue living, Thomas Malcolm, b. 1933,—Robin John, b. 1938,—Hamish
Charles, b. 1940,—Patricia Mary. b. 1936. *Residence,*—Te Whanga, Masterton, NZ.——Letitia
Blanche, b. 1913: m. 1st, 1934, Capt. Michael Valentine Paul Fleming, who d. (of wounds whilst
a prisoner during 1939-45 War 1940) [Rose, Bt., cr. 1874, colls.]; 2ndly, 1945, James Currie
Thomson, MBE, TD, JP, late Lt.-Col. Queen's Own Cameron Highlanders, and has issue living,
(by 1st m.) Valentine Patrick (Stonewall Park, Chiddingstone Hoath, Kent), b. 1935: m. 1963,
Elizabeth Helen, only da. of the Hon. Sir Geoffrey Cokayne Gibbs, KCMG [see B. Aldenham],
Christopher Michael b. 1937,—David Algernon (Copse Hill, Lower Slaughter, Glos.), b. 1938
m. 1967, Jocelyn Isobel Ann, da. of Sir John MacLeod, TD, late Queen's Own Highlanders [see
B. Dulverton, colls.], and has issue living, Lara Kate b. (Jan.) 1968, Annabel Theodora b. (Dec.)
1968, Katrina Jane b. 1971,—Gillian, b. 1940: m. 1966, Nigel Colin Newberry, and has issue
living, Alexander Douglas b. 1970, Georgina Blanche b. 1967, Beatrice Laura b. 1968,—(by 2nd
m.) James Borthwick b. 1946: m. 1970, Maureen Angela, yr. da. of W. G. Scott, of Forres, and
has issue living, James Angus Wilfred b. 1972,—Clare Neil (twin) (*Hon. Mrs. Robin C. Denison-
Pender*) b. 1946: m. 1966, the Hon. Robin Charles Denison-Pender, of Jessups, Mark Beech,
Edenbridge, Kent [see B. Pender].——Rachel Sybil, b. 1914: is a JP for Wilts: m. 1937, Peter
Sturgis, and has issue living, Julian Russell, b. 1938,—Toby Russell, b. 1947,—Ann Elizabeth,
b. 1945. *Residence,*—Dauntsey Park, Chippenham, Wilts.

Sir **Thomas** Borthwick, 1st Bt., b. 1835, son of Thomas Borthwick of Edinburgh; was Chm.and
Snr. partner of Thos. Borthwick & Sons (Ltd.), Colonial Merchants; was nominated a peer
June 1912, but d. July 1912, before the patent passed the Great Seal. His widow Letitia Mary,
da. of Thomas Banks, received Roy. licence Feb. 1913 to use the title of *Baroness Whitburgh*; she
d. 1935. Their son Sir Thomas Banks, 2nd Bt. was cr. *Baron Whitburgh* Dec. 1912; he d. 1967,
when the Barony became ext., and the Baronetcy passed to his nephew, Sir John Thomas, 3rd
Bt.

BOSSOM, Creation (U.K.) 1953, of Maidstone, Kent.

Hon. Sir CLIVE BOSSOM, 2nd *Baronet*; b. Feb. 4th,
1918; s. his father ALFRED CHARLES, Baron Bossom
(Life Peer), 1965; ed. at Eton; Maj. (ret.) The Buffs,
a Liveryman of Grocers', Paviors' and Needlemakers'
Cos.; FRSA; KStJ; a Co. Councillor for Kent 1949-52;
Pres. Industrial Fire Protection Assocn., Vice-Pres.
Anglo-Belgian Union, Chm. of Europa Insurance Co.,
Ltd., of Europa Assistance, Ltd, of Ex-Ser. War
Disabled Help Depart., of Iran Soc., of RAC, and of
RAC Motor Sports Council, a Dir. of Vosper Thorny-
croft, Ltd.; PPS to Joint Parl. Secs. to Min. of Pensions
and Nat. Insurance 1960-62, to Sec. of State for Air
1962-64, and to Home Sec. 1970-72; MP for Leominster
(C) 1959-74; Cdr. of Order of Leopold II of Belgium:
m. 1951, Lady Barbara Joan North, el. sister of 9th
Earl of Guildford, and has issue.

Arms—Gules a representation of a steel building column and
three floor girders with wind bracing projecting therefrom to the
sinister or, on a chief of the second an antique lamp inflamed sable

between on the dexter a rose gules barbed and seeded proper, and on the sinister a thistle leaved and slipped also proper. Crest,—Upon a mount vert an oak tree fructed charged with an eye irradiated proper.

Residences,—3, Eaton Mansions, SW1.   Parson's Orchard, Eastnor, nr. Ledbury, Hereford-shire.   *Clubs,*—Carlton, RAC, MCC.

———

Sons living—BRUCE CHARLES, *b.* Aug. 22nd, 1952.——Andrew Clive, *b.* 1954.——James Edward, *b.* 1962.

Daughter living—Arabella Emily, *b.* 1968.

Collateral Branch living.

 Issue of the late Doric Bossom, yr. son of Life Baron and 1st Baronet, *b.* 1922, *d.* 1959: *m.* 1949, June (who *m.* 2ndly, 1967, Maj. Kenneth Arnold Gibbs Crawley, TD, of 20, Alexander Sq., SW3 [Crawley-Boevey, Bt., colls.], el. da. of V. B. Longworth, of Port Elizabeth, S. Africa:—

Doric Alfred Howard, *b.* (posthumous) 1960.

———

Bosville Macdonald, see Macdonald.

———

HOUSTOUN-BOSWALL, Creation (U.K.) 1836.
[Name pronounced " **Hoostun-Boswall.**"]

Sir THOMAS HOUSTOUN-BOSWALL, 7th *Baronet* ; *b.* Feb. 13th, 1919 ; *s.* his father, *Major Sir* GORDON 1961 ; European War 1939-45 as Pilot-Officer RAF Vol. Reserve: *m.* 1st, 1945 (m. diss. 1970), Margaret, da. of George Bullen-Smith; 2ndly, 1971, Anne-Lucie, da. of Pierre Naquet, and has issue by 1st and 2nd m.

 Arms—Not recorded at Lyon Office.
 Residence,—Heath Grange, Blindley Heath, Lingfield, Surrey.

———

Son living—By 1st m—THOMAS ALFORD (26, Montpelier St., SW3), *b.* May 23rd, 1947: *m.* 1971, Eliana Michele, da. of Dr. John Pearse, of New York, and has issue living, Alexander Alford, *b.* 1972.

Daughters living—By 1st m.—Amber Georgina, *b.* 1946: *m.* 1969, Alan Moore, and has issue living, Georgina, *b.* 1972.——**By 2nd m.**—Sophie, *b.* 1973.

Brother living—Alistair, *b.* 1931. *Residence,*

Uncle living—Alistair HOUSTOUN-BOSWALL-PRESTON, CBE; *b.* 1888; Maj. RASC; 1939-45 (despatches); CBE (Civil) 1920.

Daughters living of 5th Baronet—Pamela Nanine, *b.* 1916 : *m.* 1938, William Oliver Calvert, who *d.* 1959, and has issue living, Ian Arbuckle, *b.* 1939,—George William, *b.* 1951,—Susan Arbuckle, *b.* 1942.——Patricia Mary, *b.* 1917: *m.* 1939, Maj. Leslie Le Mottee, late RA, and has issue living, Judith Christina, *b,* 1942,—Pamela Mary, *b.* 1947. *Residence,* 34, Kingsway, Ewell, Surrey.——Elizabeth Flora, *b.* 1923: *m.* 1941, Anthony Hawker, MC, formerly Maj. RA, and has issue living, Nicholas George James, *b.* 1942,—Victoria Jane, *b.* 1956. *Residence,*——

Daughter living of 4th Baronet—Elizabeth Phœbe, *b.* 1915: *m.* 1940, Major John Alastair Livingston Timpson, M.C., Scots Guards, from whom she obtained a divorce 1956, and has issue living, Nicholas George Lawrence, *b.* 1941: *m.* 1972, Lady Selina Catherine Meade, el. da. of 6th Earl of Clanwilliam, and has issue living, Lawrence Rupert John *b.* 1974,—Rupert Alastair Hugh, *b.* 1945,—Gerard Brian Sebastian, *b.* 1946: *m.* 1972, Siobahn Anne Southwell, da. of Maurice Fitzgerald, of Hill Place, Haywards Heath, Sussex,—Veronica Naomi Livingston (*Countess Peel*): *m.* 1973, *b.* 1950 the 3rd Earl Peel. *Residence,* The Old Rectory, Lower Basildon, Reading RG8 9NH.

Collateral Branches living.

 Granddaughters of the late Alfred Houstoun Boswall, 5th son of 2nd baronet:—
 Issue of the late Sir William Evelyn Houstoun-Boswall, K.C.M.G., M.C., *b.* 1892, *d.* 1960: *m.* 1921, Margaret Dorothy, O.B.E., who *d.* 1957, da. of the late George Anson Byron [B. Byron, colls.] :—
Diana Mary, *b.* 1925: *m.* 1962, Group Capt. Charles Blundell Owen, DSO, DFC, AFC, of Yew Tree Cottage, Southover, Lewes, Sussex, and has issue living, William Francis Blundell, *b.* 1963,—Oliver Peter Steevens, *b.* 1964.

 Issue of the late Capt. Charles Houstoun-Boswall, R. Scots Greys, *b.* 1894; *d.* 1946: *m.* 1935, Marguerite Yvonne Savage, da. of Herbert Pritchard, of Toronto, Canada, and Nassau, Bahamas:—
Jane Carolyn, *b.* 1936: *m.* 1957, John Clyfford Trevor, and has issue living, Mark Clyfford, *b.* 1961,—Richard Charles *b.* 1969,—Carolyn Elizabeth, *b.* 1959,—Emma Cecil, *b.* 1963. *Residence,* The Cottage, Pinkneys Green, Maidenhead, Berks.

 This baronet is male heir and representative of the ancient family of the Houstouns of Cotrioch **h**ereditary baillees and justiciaries of the Barony of Busbie, Wigtownshire, and of Calderhall, Mid-lothian. Gen. Sir William Houstoun, G.C.B., 1st Baronet, was a Gen. in the Army. The 2nd baronet, Col. in Grenadier Guards, assumed in 1847 the additional surname of Boswall on his marriage with Euphemia, daughter of Thomas Boswall, of Blackadder. The 3rd baronet was Capt. Grenadier Guards and Convener of Berwickshire. The 4th baronet, Capt. Sir George Reginald, Grenadier Guards, was killed in action during European War 1915. The 5th Baronet, Capt. Sir (Thomas) Randolph Houstoun-Boswall served in Royal Scots, and *d.* 1953. His son and heir, George Cleeton Houstoun-Boswall, Lt. Royal Scots, was killed on active ser. at Hong Kong, 1941. The 6th baronet, Maj. Sir Gordon Houstoun-Boswall, 1st Life Guards (whose father, Col. Thomas Alford Houstoun-Boswall-Preston, assumed by Roy. licence in 1886 the additional surname of Preston) discontinued the surname of Preston 1953.

BOUGHEY, Creation (G.B.) 1798, of Newcastle-under-Lyme, Staffordshire.

[Name pronounced "Boey."]

Neither to seek nor to despise distinction.

Sir RICHARD JAMES BOUGHEY, 10th *Baronet* ; *b.* July 30th, 1925 ; *s.* his father, *Sir* GEORGE MENTETH, CBE, 1959 ; ed. at Eton ; a JP for E. Sussex, a DL for Sussex and an OStJ ; Chm. E. Sussex Agric. Exec. Cttee. 1958-67, and of Apple and Pear Develop. Council 1967-72 ; Sheriff of Sussex 1964, and Liaison Officer to Min. of Agric., Fisheries and Food. 1965-72 ; 1939-45 War in N.-W. Europe as Lt. Coldstream Guards : *m.* 1950, Davina Julia, da. of Fitz Herbert Wright [*see* V. Powerscourt], and has issue.

Arms—Quarterly : 1st and 4th, sable, a cross wavy erminois between four plates, each charged with an arrow in bend sable of the first, *Fletcher ;* 2nd and 3rd, argent, three bucks' heads erased and affrontée ermines, *Boughey.* Crests—1st, a plate charged with a pheon per pale ermine and sable ; 2nd, out of an eastern crown gold the points alternate or and argent, a buck's head ermines, attired and collared of the first.

Residence—Ringmer Park, Lewes, Sussex.
Club—Boodle's.

Sons living—JOHN GEORGE FLETCHER, *b.* Aug. 12th, 1959.——James Richard, *b.* 1960.

Daughters living—Julia Mary, *b.* 1952: *m.* 1973, Peregrine James Chadwyck-Healey [see Chadwyck-Healey, Bt.].——Rosalind Jane, *b.* 1954.——Clare Anne *b.* 1957.

Sisters living—Mary Hermia, *b.* 1914: *m.* 1935, Robert Hugh Priestley, of Oakley Manor, Basingstoke.——Camilla (The Old Rectory, Acrise, Folkestone), *b.* 1916: *m.* 1941, Robert Charles Sanford Barclay (from whom she obtained a divorce 1964) [*see* Barclay, Bt.].——Anne, *b.* 1922: *m.* 1946, James Roddy Huff, Lieut. U.S. Army, and has issue living, James David, *b.* 1947,—Elizabeth Anne, *b.* 1949,—Celia, *b.* 1958. *Residence*, 172, North Crest Rd., Chattanooga, Tennessee, U.S.A.

Daughter living of 5th Baronet—Dorothy (*Hon. Mrs. Gerald S. Clegg-Hill*): *m.* 1907, Capt. the Hon. Gerald Spencer Clegg-Hill, who *d.* 1930 [*see* V. Hill]. *Residence*, 119, Grange Road, Ealing, W.5.

Collateral Branches living.

Granddaughters of the late Maj.-Gen. John Boughey, 2nd son of the late Lt.-Col. George Fenton Fletcher Boughey, 3rd son of 2nd baronet:—
Issue of the late Rev. Canon Percy Fletcher Boughey, *b.* 1882, *d.* 1961 : *m.* 1911, Elsie le Strange, who *d.* 1964, da. of the late Lt.-Col. William Herring, J.P. (formerly 27th Inniskillings), of Narborough House, Narborough, Norfolk:—
Elisabeth Margaret, *b.* 1916: *m.* 1940, Richard Quintin Gurney, formerly Major City of London Yeo., and has issue living, David Quinton (Portland Farm, Elkesley, Retford, Notts.), *b.* 1941: *m.* 1965, Jacqueline McLeod, da. of John Rawle, of Estancia el Fortin, Necochea, Argentina, and has issue living, Robert Edward Quintin *b.* 1969, Elisabeth Anne *b.* 1966, Juliet Carolyn *b.* 1973,—Mary Elisabeth, *b.* 1945: *m.* 1968, Stephen Dickinson, of the Manor House, Barrasford, Northumberland, and has issue living, Michael Edward *b.* 1969, James Stephen *b.* 1971,—Sarah Carolyn, *b.* 1949: *m.* 1970, David Acloque, of the White House, Lenwade, Norfolk, and has issue living, Sarah Jane *b.* 1974,—Nicola Ruth, *b.* 1953. *Residence*,—Bawdeswell Hall, Norfolk.

Issue of the late Rev. Anchitel Harry Fletcher Boughey, *b.* 1849, *d.* 1936 : *m.* 1883, Katharine Annie, who *d.* 1935 da. of the late I. S. Lovell, of Thornby, Rugby :—
Katharine Clare (Beda): *m.* 1st, 1915, Robert Mervyn Powys Druce, who *d.* 1949; 2ndly, 1950, Lionel John Treleaven Polgreen, MC, and has issue living, (by 1st m.) Pamela Matilda, *b.* 1918: *m.* 1943, Richard Stratton, of the Manor House, Kingston Deverill, Wilts, and has issue living, David *b.* 1944, Peter William *b.* 1947, Rosemary *b.* 1949, Hilary *b.* 1951,—Evelyn Patricia (Hawks Hill, Gt. Witchingham, Norfolk), *b.* 1922: *m.* 1st, 1942, Lieut. Richard D. Deuchar, RNVR, from whom she obtained a divorce 1949; 2ndly 1960, Philip Wayre, from whom she obtained a divorce 1974, and has issue living, (by 1st m.) Carol *b.* 1943: *m.* 1967, William Alexander, of Hearn Vale Cottage, Headley, Hants. (and has issue living, Juliet Patricia *b.* 1968, Fiona Catherine *b.* 1969), Rosalind *b.* 1945: *m.* 1972, Michael Banks, of Manor Farm, Waresley, Beds. (and has issue living, Melanie Catharine *b.* 1974), Juliet *b.* 1948: *m.* 1969 Adrian John Hants. (and has issue living, Juliet Patricia *b.* 1968, Fiona Catherine *b.* 1969), Rosalind *b.* 1945: *m.* 1972, Michael Banks, of Manor Farm, Waresley, Beds. (and has issue living, Melanie Catharine *b.* 1974), Juliet *b.* 1948: *m.* 1969 Adrian John Taunton, of 105, Piccotts End, Hemel Hempstead, Herts. *Residence*, 156, Sloane St., SW1.

Grandchildren of the late William Fenton Fletcher Boughey, 4th son of 2nd baronet:—
Issue of the late Com. Edward Harry Fletcher Boughey, R.N. (retired), *b.* 1878, *d.* 1953 : *m.* 1902, Ethel Georgina Emily, who *d.* 1959, da. of the late Capt. George Alexander Harrisson [V. Galway, colls.] :—
Edward Peter Fletcher, *OBE* (Ashdown House, Hare St., nr. Buntingford, Herts.; St. James', Pratt's, and Carlton Clubs), *b.* 1911; ed. at Imperial Ser. Coll.; late Lt.-Col. Gen. List; 1939-45 War (OBE); OBE (Mil.) 1945: *m.* 1st, 1945, Halina Anna (from whom he obtained a divorce 1949), da. of the late Count Stanislaw Ambrozewicz, of Lodz, Poland; 2ndly, 1949, Nina Gladys, who *d.* 1966, da. of the late Brinsley Nixon, of Seafield, Westward Ho! ; 3rdly, 1973, Emmeline Amy, da. of the late Brig.-Gen. Vigant William de Falbe, CMG, DSO, of Whittington House, Lichfield, and widow of Lt.-Col. Francis David Eardly Freemantle, TD [see B. Cottesloe, colls.].——Patience, *b.* 1908: *m.* 1943, Denys Vincent Douglas Burke-Gill, of Millfield School, Street, Som., and has issue living, Bridget Persephone, *b.* 1945,—Susan Penelope, *b.* 1947.

Issue of the late Com. Alfred Fletcher COPLESTONE-BOUGHEY, R.N., *b.* 1883, *d.* (killed in action during battle of Jutland) 1916, having assumed by deed poll 1910 the surname of Coplestone before that of Boughey: *m.* 1910, Mary Cliffe, who *d.* 1955, da. of the late Frederick Coplestone, C.B.E., J.P., of Richmond Hill, Chester :—

John Fenton, *b.* 1912; ed. at Shrewsbury, and at Brasenose Coll., Oxford (B.A. 1934); **Bar. Inner Temple** 1935; Judge of Co. Courts 1969: *m.* 1944, Gilian Beatrice, da. of the late Hugh Alfred Counsell, of Appleby, Westmorland, and has issue living, William Fenton, *b.* 1947; ed. at Winchester, and at Brasenose Coll., Oxford (BA),—Mary, *b.* 1946. *Residence,* 82, Oakley St., SW3. *Club,* Athenæum.

Sir Thomas Fletcher, 1st Bt., was High Sheriff of Staffordshire 1783 and 1789. The 2nd baronet (M.P. for Staffordshire 1820-22) assumed by sign-manual 1805 the surname of Boughey, in lieu of his patronymic. The 3rd baronet, Sir Thomas Fletcher Fenton, was High Sheriff of Staffordshire 1832, and the 4th baronet, Sir Thomas Fletcher, was also High Sheriff of that county 1898. The 5th baronet, Sir George, was R. of Forton 1863-1908, and the 7th, Sir Robert, V. of Betley. Sir George Menteth, C.B.E., 9th baronet, was Under-Sec. to Govt. of Punjab 1912-13, and sometime Principal Clerk, Med. Ser. Div., Min. of Pensions.

ROUSE-BOUGHTON, First Creation (E.) 1641, of Lawford Parva, Warwickshire. Second Creation (G.B.) 1791, of Rouse Lench, Worcestershire. [Extinct 1963.]

Sir EDWARD HOTHAM ROUSE-BOUGHTON, 13th and last *Baronet* of Lawford, and 5th and last of Rouse Lench.

Daughter living of 13th Baronet—By 1st marriage—Mary Frances (of Downton Hall, Ludlow, Salop), *b.* 1917.

Widow living of 13th Baronet—ELIZABETH (*Lady Rouse-Boughton*) (Dickens Cottage, Seagrove Bay, Seaview, Isle of Wight, and 39, Rutland Gate, SW7), da. of E. W. Hathaway Hunter, and widow of Geoffrey Swaffer: *m.* 1948, as his 2nd wife, Maj. Sir Edward Hotham Rouse-Boughton, 13th baronet, who *d.* 1963, when the title became ext.

Collateral Branch living

Granddaughter of the late Andrew Johnes ROUSE-BOUGHTON-KNIGHT, 2nd son of 10th baronet:—

Issue of the late Andrew Greville ROUSE-BOUGHTON-KNIGHT, *b.* 1869, *d.* 1928: *m.* 1891, Isabel Harriet, who *d.* 1955, da. of the late Algernon Charles Heber-Percy [D. Northumberland, colls.] :—
Dorothea Emily, *b.* 1892.

BOULTON, Creation (U.K.) 1905, of Copped Hall, Totteridge, Herts.

I WILL · NEVER · QUIT

Sir HAROLD (HUGH CHRISTIAN) BOULTON, 4th *Baronet*; *b.* Oct. 29th, 1918; *s.* his father, *Sir* (DENIS DUNCAN) HAROLD (OWEN), 1968; ed. at Ampleforth Coll.; late Capt. Irish Guards (Sup. Reserve); 1939-45 War: *m.* 1944, Patricia Mary OBE (who re-assumed by deed poll 1951 her maiden name of Maxwell-Scott), da. of the late Maj.-Gen. Sir Walter Joseph Constable-Maxwell Scott, CB, DSO, 1st Bt.

Arms—Argent, on a bend gules two leopards' faces of the field a chief arched of the second thereon two falcons close proper. **Crest**—Upon a hollybush a falcon rising, holding in the dexter claw a bird-bolt in pale, head downwards, and in the beak a sprig of holly all proper. **Supporters**—*Dexter,* a Knight of St. John in armour, robed proper; *sinister,* a female figure representing Charity vested proper, with mantle gules, round the head a fillet argent inscribed "Caritas," and holding in the exterior hand a heart or, inflamed proper.

Residence,—c/o Bank of Montreal, City View Branch, 1481, Merivale Rd., Ottawa, 5, Canada.

Sister living—Marie Louise, *b.* 1921: *m.* 1948, James Russell Smith, and has issue living, Carlton Michael *b.* 1949,—Duncan Rumsey (twin) *b.* 1949,—Marie Louise, *b.* 1952. *Residence,*
Widow of 3rd Baronet—LOUISE (*Louise, Lady Boulton*), (c/o Nat. Westminster Bank, Stanhope Gate, W1), da. of the late Hugh J. McGowan, of USA: *m.* 1918, Sir (Denis Duncan) Harold (Owen) Boulton, 3rd baronet, who *d.* 1968.

Sir Samuel Bagster Boulton, J.P., D.L., A.I.C.E. (Telford Medallist), was Chm. of Burt, Boulton and Haywood (Limited), of London and Paris, Chm. London Labour Conciliation Board, and a pioneer in many industrial and philanthropic movements. The 2nd baronet, Sir Harold Edwin, C.V.O., C.B.E., was Vice-Pres. The Queen's Institute of Dist. Nursing, Founder and Hon. Manager of the House of Shelter, Chm. of Mendicity So., and Founder and Joint Chm. People's Palace Horticultural So.

BOULTON, Creation (U.K.) 1944, of Braxted Park, co. Essex.

Sir EDWARD JOHN BOULTON, 2nd *Baronet*; *b.* April 11th, 1907; *s.* his father, *Sir* WILLIAM WHYTEHEAD, 1949; *ed.* at Eton, and at Trin. Coll., Camb. (BA); late Maj. Staffordshire Yeo.; Lord of the Manors of Alresford, Great Braxted, and Kelvedon Hall; 1939-45 War in Middle East, Italy, and NW Europe (despatches); unsuccessfully contested S. Div. of Ilford (C) July 1945.

Arms—Argent on a bend engrailed couped gules three leopards' faces or. Crest—Upon a holly bush fructed a falcon rising proper, belled or.
Residence,—Quaisné Lodge, Portelet, Jersey. *Club*—Cavalry.

Brothers living—*Sir* WILLIAM WHYTEHEAD, *CBE, TD, b.* June 21st, 1912; *ed.* at Eton, and at Trin. Coll., Camb. (BA honours 1934); Bar. Inner Temple 1936; Hon. Lt.-Col. RHA Essex Yeo. (TA); Sec. to the Senate of the Inns of Court and the Bar; served with Allied Command in Germany 1945-50; 1939-45 War in Middle East; CBE (Civil) 1958, Knt. 1975: *m.* 1944, Elizabeth, only da. of the late Brig. Henry Noel Alexander Hunter, DSO, and has issue living, John Gibson, *b.* 1946,—Julia Rosalind, *b.* 1945: *m.* 1965, Anthony John Nevill Russell, of Elm House, Elmdon, Saffron Walden, and has issue living, William Jonathan *b.* 1968, Jennifer Rosalind *b.* 1969,—Susan Elizabeth, *b.* 1949.
Residences, The Quarters House, Alresford, Colchester, Essex; 37, Rutland Gate, SW7.—Christopher Carmichael, *b.* 1919; *ed.* at Eton, and at Trin. Coll., Camb.; 1939-45 War in France, Middle East, Italy, and Austria as Capt. Intelligence Corps and with Allied Commn. in Austria. *Residence,* Ouaisné Lodge, Portelet, Jersey.

Sir William Whytehead Boulton, 1st Bt. (son of the late William Whytehead Boulton, J.P., of Beverley, Yorkshire), was a Govt. Whip, and a Junior Lord of the Treasury 1940-42, and Vice-Chamberlain of H.M.'s Household 1942-4, and sat as M.P. for Central Div. of Sheffield (C) **1931-45.**

BOWATER, Creation (U.K.) 1914, of Hill Crest, Borough of Croydon.

Omnia Vincit Labor.
Labour conquers all things.

Sir JOHN VANSITTART BOWATER, 4th *Baronet*; *b.* April 6th, 1918, son of the late Capt. Victor Spencer Bowater, 3rd son of 1st baronet; *s.* his uncle, *Sir* (THOMAS) DUDLEY (BLENNERHASSETT), 1972: *m.* 1943, Joan Kathleen, da. of the late Wilfrid Ernest Henry Scullard, of Boscombe, and has issue.

Arms—Argent, on an inescutcheon sable between eight martlets in orle gules a crescent of the field.
Residence—88, Greswolde Rd., Solihull, Warwicks.

Son living—MICHAEL PATRICK, (46, Cole Valley Rd., Hall Green, Birmingham, 28) *b.* July 18th, 1949: *m.* 1968, Alison, da. of Edward Wall, of Knowle, and has issue living, Suzanne, *b.* 1969.

Daughter living—Penelope Ann; *b.* 1954.

Aunts living (daughters of 1st baronet)—Elsie Mary (6, Hillcrest Rd., Hythe, Kent), *b.* 1892.——Doris Margaret (6, Hillcrest Rd., Hythe, Kent), *b.* 1896: *m.* 1916, Capt. Norman Gerald Kerr Salmon, MC, RAPC.

Daughters living of 2nd Baronet—Daphne Audrey, *b.* 1919.——Rowena Maud, *b.* 1926.

Daughter living of 3rd Baronet—Kathleen Stella Mary, *b.* 1921: *m.* 1945, Leslie Colling-Mudge, of Brook Street House, Woodchurch, Ashford, Kent.

Widows living of 2nd and 3rd Baronets—ETHEL MAUD (*Dowager Lady Bowater*), da. of the late John Keeler-Grix, of Keith Lodge, Woodside, SE: *m.* 1914, Sir Rainald Vansittart Bowater, 2nd baronet, who *d.* 1945. *Residence,* 33, St. Margarets, Rottingdean, Sussex.——JESSIE FAITHFULL, (*Jessie Lady Bowater*) (15, Encombe, Sandgate, Folkestone), da. of W. J. Frampton, of Stone, Kent, and widow of Norman Vansittart Bowater (brother of 1st baronet): *m.* 1948, as his 2nd wife, Sir (Thomas) Dudley (Blennerhassett) Bowater, who *d.* 1972.

Sir (Thomas) Vansittart Bowater, 1st Bt. (son of the late William Vansittart Bowater, of Bury Hall, Lower Edmonton, N.), was an Alderman of City of London 1907-38, Lord Mayor 1913-14, and MP 1924-38.

BOWATER, Creation (U.K.) 1939, of Friston, Suffolk.

Difficulties do not daunt.

Sir NOËL VANSITTART BOWATER, *G.B.E.*, *M.C.*, 2nd *Baronet*; *b.* Dec. 25th, 1892 ; *s.* his father, *Major Sir* FRANK HENRY, *T.D.*, 1947 ; ed. at Rugby; past Vice-Chm., Bowater Paper Corporation, Ltd.; (Alderman, City of London 1944-70, and Sheriff 1948-49, Lord Mayor 1953-54); KStJ, and a Knight Com. of Order of Menelik II of Ethiopia, and of the North Star of Sweden; formerly Capt. 91st (4th London) Field Brig., R.A. ; Master of Vintners' Co. 1954-55 ; European War 1914-19 in France and Belgium (M.C. three medals) ; Defence Medal ; G.B.E. (Civil) 1954 : *m.* 1921, Constance Heiton, da. of David Gordon Bett, of Woodbridge, Suffolk, and has issue.

Arms—Argent, an orle of eight martlets gules on an inescutcheon sable a crescent of the field. **Crest**—A rainbow issuant from water proper. **Supporters**—(*personal as a G.B.E.*), *Dexter*, An Exmoor Stag proper ; *sinister*, a Devon bull also proper armed inguled and tufted or, both gorged with a riband azure pendent therefrom a representation of the Jewel of Office of the Lord Mayor of the City of London.

Residences—Conifers, Old Avenue, St. George's Hill, Weybridge ; Riscombe, Exford, Somerset. *Clubs*—St. James', City Livery, Guildhall.

Son living—EUAN DAVID VANSITTART (Coombe Farmhouse, Chagford, Devon), *b.* Sept. 9th, 1935; ed. at Eton, and at Trin. Coll., Camb.; *m.* 1964, Susan Mary Humphrey, da. of A. R. O. Slater, FCA, and has issue living, Moray Vansittart, *b.* 1967,—Lucien Ross Thomas, *b.* 1973,— Jacqueline, *b.* 1965,—Alexis, *b.* 1969.

Daughters living—Anne Patricia, *b.* 1925 : *m.* 1954, Group Capt. Randolph Stuart Mills, D.F.C., R.A.F., and has issue living, Philip Stuart, *b.* 1956,—William Stuart, *b.* 1957. *Residence*, Little Meadow, W. Chiltington, Sussex.——Jane Gillian *b.* 1930: *m.* 1953, Christopher William Restarick Beeson, and has issue living, Mark, *b.* 1954,—Peter, *b.* 1956,—David, *b.* 1957,—Oona, *b.* 1960. *Residence*, Ford Farm, Manaton, Devon.

Brother living—*Sir* Ian Frank, GBE, DSO, TD, *b.* 1904; ed. at Eton, and Magdalen Coll., Oxford; Lt.-Col. (ret.) RA (TA); Lt. and Alderman of City of London (Sheriff 1965-66, Lord Mayor 1969-70); Assist. of Court of Haberdashers' Co. (Warden 1954-55, Master 1967-68), Chm. of Bowater Hotels, Ltd., an OStJ; Grand Decoration of Honour in Silver for sers. to Austrian Republic; Order of El Kawkab of Kingdom of Jordan; Italy 1943-45 (DSO), Knt. 1967: *m.* 1927, the Hon. Ursula Margaret Dawson, da. of 1st Viscount Dawson of Penn, and has issue living, Michael Ian Vansittart (9, Hampstead Hill Gdns., NW3), *b.* 1934; ed. at Eton; Maj. (ret.) Scots Guards; Head of Communications Bowater Corpn.: *m.* 1960, Camilla Caroline, el. da. of Air Commodore Whitney Willard Straight, CBE, MC, DFC [*see* E. Winchilsea], and has issue living, Arabella Charlotte *b.* 1961, Katherine Elisabeth *b.* 1963, Caroline Mary *b.* 1964, Sophie Melissa *b.* 1970,—Susan Vansittart, *b.* 1929 : *m.* 1956, George Crofton Addison Doughty, of 17, Flood St., SW3 5ST, son of the late Sir Charles Doughty, QC, and has issue living, Caroline Susan *b.* 1958,—Charlotte Mary, *b.* 1937: *m.* 1st, 1961, (Denis) Anthony Russell, who *d.* 1966 [*see* Russell, Bt., colls. (*cr.* 1916)]; 2ndly, 1970, J. Watcyn Lewis, of 66, Clifton Hill, NW8, and has issue living (by 1st m.) [see Russell Bt., (cr. 1916), colls.]; (by 2nd m.), Damien Watcyn *b.* 1971, Gareth Hugh *b.* 1973. *Residence*, Hasker House, Woolley Firs., Maidenhead Thicket, Berks. *Clubs*, White's, City Livery.

Sisters living—Ethel May (Knightsbridge House, Hellingly, Hailsham, Sussex), *b.* 1896: *m.* 1916, Capt. Olaus Charles William Johnsen, DFC, who *d.* 1960, and has issue living, William Hugo Gilroy, *MC* (of Gravelye House, Gravelye Lane, Lindfield, Sussex), *b.* 1917; ed. at Eton: *m.* 1947, Maisie, da. of Thomas S. Frazier, and has issue living, William Martin Frazier *b.* 1947; ed. at Eton, Graham Claridge *b.* 1950; ed. at Eton, Marye Rose *b.* 1953,—Peter Bowater (of The Mirrie, Denham, Bucks), *b.* 1923; ed. at Eton: *m.* 1954, Birthe Nina, da. of Baron Raben-Levetzau of Aalholm Castle, Denmark, and has issue living, Hugo Anthony *b.* 1956, James William *b.* 1960, Josephine Nina *b.* 1958,—Richard (of Shalden Manor, nr. Alton, Hants), *b.* 1927; ed. at Eton: *m.* 1960, Patricia Nadejda, da. of Capt. Frank Moxon, MC, and has issue living, William Frank *b.* 1961, Julian Richard *b.* 1963, Arabella Charlotte *b.* 1966,—Michael Robin (Box 40, Via Schaffer 34, Merano, Italy) *b.* 1941: *m.* 1966, Virginia, da. of Count Giovanni Battista Nani-Mocenigo, of Merano, Italy,—Pamela May, *b.* 1918: *m.* 1944, Richard Braddyll Tulk-Hart, MRCS, LRCP, DCH, of The Cottage, Fairwarp, Uckfield, Sussex, and has issue living, Jeremy John Bowater *b.* 1947: *m.* 1974, Sally Virginia Lydall-Alesbury, Nicola *b.* 1948, Tessa Claridge *b.* 1953,— Sheilagh Claridge, *b.* 1920: *m.* 1940, Peter Laurence Candler, FRCOG (PO Box 4, 7964, Nairobi, Kenya), and has issue living, Rowena Ruth *b.* 1940; *m.* 1963, Maj. Cedric Nigel Barry-Taylor (and has issue living, Henry Sebastian *b.* 1965, Polly Anna *b.* 1971).——Beryl Stuart, *b.* 1902: *m.* 1931, Col. Arthur Howard Eckford Howell, DSO, TD, late RHA (*Club*, Army and Navy), and has issue living, David Arthur Russell, *MP* (115, Fentiman Rd., SW8; Carlton Club), *b.* 1936; ed. at Eton, and at King's Coll., Camb.; Min. of State NI 1972-74; MP for Guildford (C) since 1966: *m.* 1967, (Cary) Davina, da. of the late David Wallace, and has issue living, Frances Victoria *b.* 1969, Kate Davina *b.* 1970,—Jane Duncombe, *b.* 1932: *m.* 1957, Lt.-Col. Peter Evan Wyldbore Gibbs, Coldm. Gds. of the Old Rectory, Cholderton, Salisbury, Wilts. and has issue living, Nicholas Roland Antony *b.* 1957, Simon Evan Alexander *b.* 1962, Camilla Jane Evadne *b.* 1959. *Residence*, 5, Headford Place, SW1.

The 1st baronet, Major Sir Frank Henry Bowater, T.D. [son of the late William Vansittart Bowater, of Bury Hall, Lower Edmonton, N., and brother of Sir (Thomas) Vansittart Bowater, 1st Bt. (*cr.* 1914)], sometime Major R.F.A., was a Paper Maker and a Lieut. and Alderman of City of London (Sheriff 1929-30, Lord Mayor 1938-9).

BOWDEN, Creation (U.K.) 1915, of City of Nottingham.

FIDE ET SPE

With faith and hope.

Sir FRANK HOUSTON BOWDEN, 3rd *Baronet;* b. Aug. 10th, 1909 ; *s.* his father, *Sir* HAROLD, G.B.E., 1960 ; ed. at Rugby, and at Merton Coll., Oxford (B.A. 1931, M.A. 1953) ; assumed the additional forename of Houston 1960 ; formerly Lieut. (S) RNVR; 1939-45 War: *m.* 1st, 1934 (m. diss. 1936), Marie José Stiénon de Messey, only da. of Charles Stiénon, of Paris; 2ndly, 1937, Lydia Eveline, da. of Jean Manolovici, of Bucharest, Roumania, and has issue by 1st and 2nd m.

Arms—Quarterly, sable and or, over all a bow in bend of the second, between two cycle wheels charged in the centre with a winged foot, couped at the ankle, all proper. **Crest**—A heron's head erased at the neck proper, gorged with a mural crown gold.
Residence—Thame Park, Thame, Oxon. *Clubs*—White's, Royal Thames Yacht, Bath.

Sons living—By 1st marriage—NICHOLAS RICHARD (Hensting Farm, Fishers Pond, Eastleigh, Hants), b. Aug. 13th, 1935; ed. at Millfield.——**By 2nd marriage** —Adrian Harold Houston (33, Grosvenor Sq., W1; Carlton, White's and Royal Thames Yacht Clubs), b. 1938; ed. at Radley, and at Merton Coll., Oxford (MA); assumed the additional forename of Houston 1960: *m.* 1968, Marjorie Walter, da. of John Dozier Gordan, of New York City, USA, and has issue living, Alexander Gordan, b. 1972,—Stephanie Florence, b. 1975.——Aubrey Francis Houston (Orchard House, Swallowfield, Berks.; Brooks's Club), b. 1940; ed. at Eton, and at Merton Coll., Oxford (MA); assumed the additional forename of Houston 1960: *m.* 1969, Mary Julia, da. of David Richard Colville [see V. Colville of Culross, colls.], and has issue living, James Edward Houston, b. 1975,—Victoria Houston, b. 1973.——Gregory Andrew Houston (Carlton Club), b. 1948; ed. at Eton, and Mansfield Coll., Oxford (BA); assumed the additional forename of Houston 1960.

Sister living—Ruth, b. 1911 : *m.* 1st, 1932, Christopher Bourchier Wrey, from whom she obtained a divorce 1947 [*see* Wrey, Bt.] ; 2ndly, 1947, Ernest Wittmann. *Residence,* 7, Inner Park Road, Wimbledon, S.W.19.

Aunt living (daughter of 1st baronet)—Sylvia: *m.* 1916, Major Leonard Whitaker Owen Taylor, MB, ChB, formerly RAMC. *Residence,* Le Clos du Chemin, St. Peter's, Jersey.

Widow living of 2nd Baronet—VALERIE (*Valerie, Lady Bowden*), da. of the late Richard Raymont Came, and widow of Bertie Renfrew Porter: *m.* 1957, as his fourth wife, Sir Harold Bowden, GBE, 2nd Bt., who d. 1960. *Residences,* 8, Hay's Mews, W1; The Manor, Marsh Court, Stockbridge, Hants.

Sir Frank Bowden, 1st Bt., was Founder, Chm., Managing Director, and Principal Owner of Sturmey-Archer Gears (Limited), and of Raleigh Cycle Co. (Limited). Sir Harold Bowden, G.B.E., 2nd Bt. was Pres. of Raleigh Industries Ltd., and High Sheriff of Notts. 1933.

BOWEN, Creation (U.K.) 1921, of Colworth, co. Bedford.

Audaces fortuna juvat

Fortune favours the brave.

Sir THOMAS FREDERIC CHARLES BOWEN, 4th *Baronet;* b. Oct. 11th, 1921; *s.* his brother, *Sir* JOHN EDWARD MORTIMER, 1939; ed. at Eton: *m.* 1947, Jill Claude, da. of Cyril Lloyd Evans, of Prestea, Ghana, West Africa, and has issue.

Arms—Azure, a lion rampant within an orle, all within four roses or and as many bezants alternately. **Crest**—A lion sejant proper holding in the dexter paw a Bowen knot argent.
Residence—Beechcroft, St. Georges Av., Weybridge, Surrey.

Son living—MARK EDWARD MORTIMER, b. Oct. 17th, 1958.

Daughters living—Julia Rosemary, b. 1950: *m.* 1970, Lt. Robert Andrew Fewings, RN, of 62, Carisbrooke, Southill, Weymouth, Dorset, and has issue living, Paul Stuart, b. 1973.——Margot Claire, b. 1952: *m.* 1974, Malcolm Ivanson Kirkpatrick, of 15, Curzon Rd., Weybridge, Surrey.

Sister living—Angela Betty Isobel, b. 1912: *m.* 1933, Capt. Ivan Francis Low, King's Own Yorkshire L.I., from whom she obtained a divorce 1944, and has issue living, Michael Henry Francis (Howick, Natal), b. 1935: *m.* 1958, Mary Porter, of Cambridge, and has issue living, Paul Francis b. 1960, Martin Henry b. 1965, Geraldine Claire b. 1962. *Residence,* Martin, Howick, Natal.

Collateral Branch living.
Issue of the late Harold Cedric Bowen, younger son of 1st baronet, b. 1896, d. 1959: *m.* 1921, Vera Donnet, who d. 1967:—
Nicholas Edward, b. 1923; is Wing-Cdr. R.A.F.: *m.* 1944, Eve, da. of the late Edward Batty, and has issue living, Michael Edward (Brook House, Ampleforth, York), b. 1944: *m.* 1968, Gillian Margaret, da. of Col. B. R. D. Garside, MC, and has issue living, Nicola Emma b. 1969, Victoria Margaret b. 1972, Anabel Elizabeth b. 1974,—Christopher Anthony Richard, b. 1946.—— Clarissa, b. 1929: *m.* 1954, Mervyn Heald, QC, of Headfoldswood, Loxwood, Sussex, son of the Rt. Hon. Sir Lionel Frederick Heald, QC, MP, and has issue living, Robert Lionel, b. 1974,— Henrietta Sara, b. 1955,—Annabel Clare, b. 1957,—Julia Elizabeth, b. 1959.

Sir Albert Edward Bowen, 1st Bt. (son of Edward Bowen, of Hanley), was Pres. of Buenos Aires Great Southern Railway Co., and of many Cos. in City of London. Major Sir Edward Crowther Bowen, 2nd Bt., 6th Inniskilling Dragoons, served during European War 1914-18 (M.C.).

BOWLBY, Creation (U.K.) 1923, of Manchester Square, Borough of St. Marylebone.

Sir ANTHONY HUGH MOSTYN BOWLBY, 2nd *Baronet*; *b.* Jan. 13th, 1906; *s.* his father, Sir ANTHONY ALFRED, *K.C.B.*, *K.C.M.G.*, *K.C.V.O.*, *F.R.C.S.*, 1929; ed. at Wellington Coll., and at New Coll., Oxford : *m.* 1930, Dora Evelyn, da. of the late John Charles Allen, of York, and has issue.

Arms—Per fesse sable and argent, a pale with three hinds' heads erased two and one, and as many annulets one and two all counterchanged. Crest—Three annulets interlaced one and two or, between two thorn branches proper. *Residence*—The Old Rectory, Ozleworth, Wotton-under-Edge, Glos.

Ne·cede·malis

Yield not to adversity.

Daughters living—Anthea, *b.* 1930 : *m.* 1956, Jolyon Dromgoole, and has issue living, Emma, *b.* 1957,—Julia, *b.* 1961,—Rose, *b.* 1964,—Susanna (triplet), *b.* 1964,—Belinda (triplet), *b.* 1964. *Residence*, 42, Upper Montagu St., W1.——Sophia, *b.* 1945.

Brothers living—(EDWARD) JOHN MOSTYN, CBE, MD, *b.* Feb. 26th, 1907; ed. at Trin. Coll., Camb (MA, BCh, MD); FRCP, FRCPsych; Hon. D. Litt. Leicester; late Lt.-Col. RAMC; CBE (Civil) 1972: *m.* 1938, Ursula, da. of Dr. T. G. Longstaff, and has issue living, Richard Peregrine Longstaff (Boundary House, Wyldes Close, NW11), *b.* 1941: *m.* 1963, Xenia Garrett, and has issue living Benjamin *b.* 1966, Sophia *b.* 1969,—Robert John Mostyn, *b.* 1948,—Mary Hamilton, Rectory Farm House, Evesbatch, Bishop's Frome, Worcs., *b.* 1939: *m.* 1964, Capt. Timothy Richard Holbrook Dawson, RE, and has issue living, Guy Philip Richard *b.* 1965, Patrick Timothy John *b.* 1969,—Pia Rose Whitworth, *b.* 1945: *m.* 1968, Carlos Duran, and has issue living, Xohan *b.* 1968, Xavier *b.* 1973. *Residence*, Wyldes Close Corner, Hampstead Way, NW11.—— Charles James Mostyn *b.* 1908; ed. at St. Catherine's Coll., Camb. *Residence*, Sisters living—Frances Winifred Mostyn, *b.* 1899.——Dorothy Evelyn Mostyn, *b.* 1910: *m.* 1932, Ernest Henry Phelps Brown, MBE, Professor of Economics, London Univ., and sometime Fellow of New Coll., Oxford, and has issue living, Nicholas Anthony Phelps, *b.* 1936,—Thomas Henry Phelps, *b.* 1948,—Juliet Virginia Phelps, *b.* 1934. *Residence*, 16, Bradmore Rd., Oxford.

The 1st baronet, Sir Anthony Alfred Bowlby, K.C.B., K.C.M.G., K.C.V.O., F.R.C.S. (Pres. Coll. of Surgs. 1920-23), was Surg. to Royal Household 1904-10, and an Hon. Surg. to H.M. 1910-29, and served in S. African War 1899-1900 in charge of Portland Hospital (despatches, medal, C.M.G.), and during European War 1914-19 as Maj.-Gen. Army Med. Ser., and as Advisory Consulting Surg. to British Forces in France (American D.S.M.).

BOWMAN, Creation (U.K.) 1884, of Holmbury St. Mary, co. Surrey.
[Name pronounced " Boman."]

Sir JOHN PAGET BOWMAN, 4th *Baronet*; *b.* Feb. 12th, 1904; *s.* his father, the *Rev.* Sir PAGET MERVYN, 1955 ; ed. at Eton ; formerly 2nd Lieut. 98th (Surrey and Sussex Yeo., Queen Mary's) Army Field Brig., R.A. (T.A.) : *m.* 1st, 1931, Countess Cajetana Hoyos, who *d.* 1948, da. of Count Edgar Hoyos, of Schloss Soos, Lower Austria ; 2ndly, 1948, Frances Edith Marian, da. of the late Sir (James) Beethom Whitehead, K.C.M.G. [E. Midleton], and has issue by 1st marriage.

Arms—Or, on a chevron between three bows stringed palewise gules, two lions combatant of the first between as many escallops argent. Crest—Upon a mount vert the stump of a tree proper, around the upper part a belt sable, and pendent therefrom, on the dexter side, a quiver gules filled with arrows argent. *Residence*—Bishops Green House, Greenham Common, near Newbury, Berks.

We conquered formerly with these arms.

Son living—By 1st marriage—DAVID ANTHONY PAGET (Sherwood, Boar's Hill, Oxford), *b.* Oct. 16th, 1935: *m.* 1968, Valerie Winifred, da. of Reginald Cyril Tatham, FRCS, of Spinney Croft, N. Ferriby, E. Yorks.

Daughter living—By 1st marriage—Rachel Elinor, *b.* 1938; SRN: *m.* 1967, Gerald William Wensley Clarkson [see Lane Bt.].

Collateral Branches living.
Issue of the late Guy Eddowes Paget Bowman, 2nd son of 2nd baronet, *b.* 1878, *d.* 1933: *m.* 1907, Ethel Mary, who *d.* 1943, only da. of the late George Cyril Bowman, of Clews, Haslemere :—
Nancy Freda, *b.* 1913: *m.* 1st, 1927, Vernon D. R. Pakenham Gilbert, who *d.* 1965; 2ndly, 1966, James Henry Guy Burney, of Coombe Brook, Peaslake, nr. Guildford, and has issue living (by 1st m.) Anthony Guy Pakenham (48, Cherry Garden Av., Folkestone), *b.* 1939; ed. at Tonbridge, and at Durham Univ. (BA): *m.* 1966, Brenda Hazebroek, and has issue living, Christopher Guy *b.* 1968, John Peter *b.* 1970, Amanda Nancy *b.* 1971,—Richard John Michael (Lyndene, St. Pauls Rd. East, Dorking, Surrey) *b.* 1942; ed. at Lancing; ARICS: *m.* 1st, 1966 (m. diss. 1973), Patricia Butt; 2ndly, 1973, Judith Mary Downton Croft, and has issue living, (by 2nd m.) Joanna Mary Pakenham *b.* 1974.

Grandchildren of the late John Frederick Bowman, 2nd son of 1st baronet:—
Issue of the late Maj. Humphrey Ernest Bowman, CMG, CBE, *b.* 1879, *d.* 1965: *m.* 1st, 1916, Frances Guinevere, who *d.* 1923, da. of the late Lt.-Col. Arthur Henry Armytage

[Armytage, Bt.]; 2ndly, 1925, Elinor Marion, who d. 1957, widow of Arthur William Bowman (infra), and has issue living:—
(By 1st m.) Paul Humphrey Armytage (41, Egerton Cres., SW3 2EB), b. 1921; ed. at Eton; sometime Maj. Coldstream Guards: m. 1st, 1943, Felicitie Anne Araminta (who obtained a divorce 1947), da. of Sir Harold Alfred MacMichael, GCMG, DSO [E. Leven and Melville, colls.]; 2ndly, 1947 (m. diss. 1974), Gabrielle May, formerly wife of Lt.-Col. Walter Currie, US Army; 3rdly, 1974, Elizabeth Deirdre, yr. da. of the late Bruce R. Campbell, of Goorianawa, NSW, and formerly wife of Maj.-Gen. Thomas Bell Lindsay Churchill, CB, CBE, MC, and has issue living, (by 2nd m.) Amanda Caroline, b. 1947,——Cynthia Pamela Mary (33, Malvern Court, Onslow Sq., SW7) b. 1918: m. 1943 (m. diss. 1969), Rear Adm. Josef Bartosik, CB, DSC, RN, and has issue living, Jan Josef, b. 1946,—Conrad, b. 1948,—Matthew, b. 1954,—Christina Cynthia, b. 1945.

Issue of the late Clive Frederick Bowman, MC, b. 1884, d. 1972: m. 1920, Erica Violet, who d. 1972, da. of the late Col. Robert George Wardlaw-Ramsay, DL [B. Magheramorne, colls.]:—
Martin Ramsay (Camusdarach, Morar, Inverness-shire), b. 1928; ed. at Ampleforth, and Ch. Ch., Oxford (MA); Bar. Inner Temple 1953; formerly 2nd Lt. The King's Regt.; CC Inverness-shire 1973-75.——Erica Rosemary, b. 1921: m. 1948, Douglas Burch Law, formerly Maj. Seaforth Highlanders, of Lythe House, Selborne, Alton, Hants., and has issue living, Nicholas Simon, b. 1954,—James Christopher, b. 1956.——Heather Mary, b. 1922: m. 1956, Trevor Cairns, and has issue living, Conrad Thomas, b. 1957,—Edmund Frederick, b. 1960.——Dorothea Vivien, b. 1924; is a Nun.

Granddaughter of the late Rev. Arthur Gerald Bowman, 3rd son of 1st baronet:—
Issue of the late Arthur William Bowman, London Regt., b. 1887, d. (while prisoner, of wounds in action during European War) 1918: m. 1911, Elinor Marion [who d. 1957, having m. 2ndly, 1925, the late Humphrey Ernest Bowman, CMG, CBE (ante)], da. of the late Rev. Charles Conybeare, R. of Tichborne, Hants:—
Barbara Paget, b. 1912 : m. 1932, Wing-Com. Douglas Sender, R.A.F. (retired), and has issue living, Michael Conybeare (Surreyholme, Dartnell Park Rd., W. Byfleet, Surrey), b. 1933; ed. at Wellington Coll.: m. 1962, Judith Olivia Hedley, and has issue living, Richard Paget b. 1964,—Katherine Elizabeth b. 1966,—Penelope Markland, b. 1936: m. 1959, Lt.-Col. Anthony Wells, RA (ret.), now with RAA, of Mount Pleasant Cottage, Mount Pleasant, Guildford, Surrey, and Le Chapeau, Cobbitty, NSW, and has issue living, Pandora Markland b. 1965,—Joanna Paget, b. 1953. Residence, L'Espine, Millbrook, Jersey.

The 1st baronet was an eminent ophthalmic surgeon. Sir W. Paget Bowman, 2nd Bt., was many years Registrar of the Corporation of the Sons of the Clergy. The Rev. Sir Paget Mervyn Bowman, 3rd Bt. was R. of Shere, Rural Dean of Cranleigh and Surrogate 1919-50.

BOWMAN, Creation (U.K.) 1961, of Killingworth, co Northumberland.

Sir James Bowman, K.B.E., 1st Baronet, son of Robert Bowman; b. March 8th, 1898 ; is a J.P. for Northumberland ; was Gen. Sec. Mineworkers' Asso. 1935-49, Vice-Pres. National Union of Mineworkers 1938-49, a Member of Gen. Council of Trades Union Congress 1945-49, Chm. of N. Div. National Coal Board 1950-55, Dep. Chm. of National Coal Board 1955-6, and Chm. 1956-61 ; European War 1914-18 with R.M. ; C.B.E. (Civil) 1952, K.B.E. (Civil) 1957 : m. 1922, Jean, da. of Henry Brooks, of Ashington, Northumberland, and has issue.
Residence—Woodlands, Killingworth Station, Forest Hall, Newcastle-upon-Tyne.

Son living—GEORGE (of Parkside, Killingworth Drive, Killingworth Station, Newcastle-upon-Tyne, 12), b. July 2nd, 1923: m. 1960, Olive Case, of S. Shields, and has issue living, Julie Victoria, b. 1961,—Louise Janet, b. 1963,—Claire Elizabeth, b. 1965.

Daughter living—Mary, b. 1925: m. 1950, John Robert Rayne, of Parkside, Killingworth Drive, Killingworth Station, Newcastle-upon-Tyne, 12, and has issue living, Susan, b. 1952.

Bowyer (Bowyer-Smyth), see Smyth.

BOYCE, Creation (U.K.) 1952, of Badgeworth, co. Gloucester.

DO IT WITH THY MIGHT

Sir Robert (Charles) Leslie Boyce, 3rd Baronet, b. May 2nd, 1962; s. his father, Sir Richard (Leslie), 1968.
Arms—Or on a chevron gules an open book proper edges and clasps of the first on a chief of the second a portcullis chained also of the first between two swords erect also proper pomels and hilts gold. Crest—A demi lion gules grasping in the dexter paw a pen or.
Residence,—Saddlestones, Quenington, Glos., GL7 5BT.

Sister living—Sarah Jane Leslie, b. 1960.

Uncles living (sons of 1st baronet)—JOHN LESLIE (182, Huntingdale Rd., Mt. Waverley, Victoria 3149, Aust.) b. Nov. 16th, 1934 m. 1957, Finola Mary, da. of the late James Patrick Maxwell, of Bansha, co. Tipperary, and has issue, Richard Alan, b. 1968,—Elizabeth Jane Leslie, b. 1958,—Evelyn Mary, b. 1961,—Suzanne Caroline, b. 1963.——Charles Francis Leslie (Greyrocks, Box, Minchinhampton, Glos.), b. 1936: m. 1963, Elizabeth, only da. of William Todd, of 130, Meadoway, Bishop's Cleeve, Cheltenham, and has issue living, Edward Neal Leslie, b. 1965,—Philip William James, b. 1971,—Kathryn Maybery, b. 1966,—Victoria Claire Alexandra, b. 1973.

Widows living of 1st and 2nd Baronets—MAYBERY BROWSE (Maybery, Lady Boyce), only da. of the late Edward Philip Bevan, of Melbourne, Australia; is a DStJ: m. 1926, Sir (Harold) Leslie Boyce, KBE, 1st baronet, who d. 1955. Residence, 16, Queens Court, Queens Rd., Cheltenham, Glos.——JACQUELINE ANNE, only da. of Roland A. Hill, of Brimscombe, Glos.: m. 1st, 1958, Sir Richard (Leslie) Boyce, 2nd baronet, who d. 1968; 2ndly, 1974, Christopher Boyce-Dennis, of Saddlestones, Quenington, Glos., GL7 5BT.

The 1st baronet, Sir (Harold) Leslie Boyce, K.B.E. (son of the late Charles Macleay Boyce, of Sydney, N.S. Wales), was Sheriff of Gloucester 1941-2, and Lord Mayor of London 1951-2, and sat as M.P. for Gloucester (C) 1929-45.

BOYD, Creation (U.K.) 1916, of Howth House, Howth, co. Dublin.

I trust.

Sir ALEXANDER WALTER BOYD, 3rd *Baronet*, son of the late Major Cecil Anderson Boyd, M.C., M.D., late R.A.M.C., 2nd son of 1st baronet ; *b.* June 16th, 1934 ; *s.* his uncle, *Sir* WALTER HERBERT, 1948 : *m.* 1958, Molly Madeline, da. of the late Ernest Arthur Rendell, of R.R.3, Vernon, British Columbia, and has issue.

Arms—Azure, a fesse chequy argent and gules between three estoiles or. Crest—Out of a crest coronet or charged, with three ermine spots, a dexter hand erect having the two last fingers turned in and the rest pointing upwards proper.

Residence—R.R.3, Vernon, British Columbia, Canada.

Sons living—IAN WALTER RENDELL, *b.* March 14th, 1964.——Robert Alexander Rendell, *b.* 1966.
Daughters living—Heather Lynn, *b.* 1959.——Susan Christine, *b.* 1961,—Sandra Molly, *b.* 1967.
Half-Sisters living—Deirdre Anna, *b.* 1925 : *m.* 1944, Walter V. Dunham, and has issue living, David, *b.* 1964,—Ruth Aideen, *b.* 1946,—Patricia Ann, *b.* 1948,—Beverley Jean, *b.* 1951,—Mary Elizabeth, *b.* 1953.——Aideen Gwendolyn, *b.* 1926: *m.* 1947, Robert Laird Russell, and has issue living, Heather Joanne, *b.* 1959.——Ruth Mary, *b.* 1927: *m.* 1951, Anthony Weisgarber, and has issue living, Kathleen Mary *b.* 1957,—Tracy Ann *b.* 1962. *Residence*, 1154, Tolmie Av., Victoria, BC.

Mother living—Marjorie Catharine (ALLAN), el. da. of the late Francis Kinloch [*see* Kinloch, Bt., *cr.* 1686, colls.] : *m.* 1933, as his second wife, Major Cecil Anderson Boyd, M.C., M.D., late R.A.M.C. (ante), who *d.* 1942. *Residence*, Rural Route, 3, Vernon, British Columbia.

Collateral Branches living.

Grandsons of the late Lieut.-Col. Henry Alexander Boyd (infra):—
Issue of the late Major Ronald Walter Boyd M.C., Roy. Ulster Rifles, *b.* 1914, *d.* (killed in action in Italy) 1944; *m.* 1939, Virginia (who *m.* 2ndly 1949, Humphrey Allen Walter, ERD, of Courthay, Little Gatton, Reigate, Surrey, RH2 oHJ), da. of the late John Freeman, of Bexleyheath, Kent:—
Noel Alexander (The Studio, 37, Cranley Gdns., SW7) *b.* 1940; ed. at Canford: *m.* 1968, Sarah Caroline, el. da. of Michael Francis Sherwin, OBE, of Langridge, W. Hoathly, Sussex.——Nigel Cecil John, *b.* 1943; ed. at Seaford.

Issue of the late Lieut.-Col. Henry Alexander Boyd, C.M.G., D.S.O., 3rd son of 1st baronet, *b.* 1877, *d.* 1943 : *m.* 1908, Moya, who *d.* 1959, da. of the late John Shaw Exham, J.P., of Worlington, Suffolk :—
Heather, *b.* 1910. *Residence*, 82, Foster Av., Mount Merrion, co. Dublin.

Issue of the late Robert Reginald Boyd, youngest son of 1st baronet, *b.* 1880, *d.* 1959 : *m.* 1922, Agnes Maria Dorothea, who *d.* 1964, da. of the late Lt.-Col. Charles Harrison, of Ross, Herefordshire:—
Walter Michael Stewart (7, The Parade, Marion, S. Australia) *b.* 1924: *m.* 1951, Janet Brown, and has issue living, Nicholas Michael, *b.* 1954,—Jonathan Peter, *b.* 1956,—Emma Jane, *b.* 1960.——Robert Stanley (28, Canonbury Grove, N1) *b.* 1927: *m.* 1965, Ann, da. of the late Daniel Hopkin, MC, MP.

The 1st baronet, the Rt. Hon. Sir Walter Boyd, P.C., LL.D., was successively Receiver Judge for Ireland, a Judge of the Court of Bankruptcy in Ireland, and one of the Justices of the High Court of Justice in Ireland. The 2nd baronet, Sir Walter Herbert Boyd, K.C., was Ch. Registrar of Bankruptcy (Ireland) 1912-37.

BOYNTON, Creation (E.) 1618, of Barmston, Yorkshire. [Extinct 1966.]

Sir GRIFFITH WILFRID NORMAN BOYNTON 13th and last *Baronet.*

Daughter living of 12th Baronet—Constance Mary, *b.* 1892: *m.* 1922, Douglas Arthur Blundell Hill, late Capt. RAF. *Residence*, 13, Warwick Gdns., W14.
Widow living of 13th Baronet—NAOMI CORALIE (*Lady Boynton*), da. of the late Harry Ethelston Nightingale, [*see* Nightingale, Bt., colls.], *m.* 1914, Cdr. Sir Griffith Wilfrid Norman Boynton, RN, 13th Bt., who *d.* 1966, when the title became ext.

Collateral Branches living.

Granddaughter of the late Charles Boynton, 3rd son of 9th baronet:—
Issue of the late Col. Francis Boynton, *b.* 1859, *d.* 1938 : *m.* 1887, Elsie, who *d.* 1952, only child of the late Maj.-Gen. Thomas Phillips, Col. 18th (Queen Mary's Own) Hussars :—
Elsie Evelyn, (Hillside House, Ashbourne, Derbys.) *b.* 1890: *m.* 1915, Lieut.-Com. Jean Louis Miéville, DSO, late RNVR, who *d.* 1967, [Aird, Bt], and has issue living, Louis Philip (Stone House, Sutton Valance, Kent.) *b.* 1916; 1939-45 War as Capt. Irish Guards: *m.* 1st, 1949, (m. diss. 1968) Janetta Marian Kerr; 2ndly, 1968, Patricia Helen, da. of the late Adm. Sir (Eric James) Patrick Brind, GBE, KCB, and has issue living, (by 1st m.), Marian Susan Julia *b.* 1951, Sara Jane *b.* 1955.

Granddaughter of the late Capt. George Hebblethwaite Luton Boynton, 4th son of 9th baronet :—

Issue of the late George Henry Keeling Boynton, *b.* 1851, *d.* 19—: *m.* 1st, 1873, Charlotte Isabella, who *d.* 1885, da. of the late A. C. Barrett, of Kingston-on-Thames; 2ndly, 1886, Frances, da. of G. W. Smyth, of Dover Street, W.:—

(By 2nd marriage) Lilian Constance Mary, *b.* 1888 : *m.* 1912, Capt. Harry Edward Lionel Pilbrow, formerly RAF, and has issue living, Harry Edward Boynton, MBE (Karmi Village, Kyrenia, Cyprus), *b.* 1915; MBE (Mil) 1945: *m.* 1st, 1947 (m. diss. 1959), Margaret Ingham, Porritt; 2ndly, 1961, Mrs. Florence Mary McGregor, da. of Robert Ambrose Gates,—Constance Mary, *b.* 1913; *m.* 1936, Reginald Petrie, of Grayshott House, Grayshott, Hindhead, Surrey, and has issue living, Susan Patricia Mary *b.* 1937: *m.* 1959, John Hargreaves Horsman, of Carr Wood, Pinecote Drive, Sunningdale, Berks (and has issue living, Caroline Louise *b.* 1962, Samantha Lois *b.* 1966), Janet Elizabeth *b.* 1939: *m.* 1962, Peter David Lumb, of Broadwood House, Avon Rd., West Moors, Dorset (and has issue living, Christopher David Petrie *b.* 1962, Patrick Neil *b.* 1966), Angela Caroline Frances *b.* 1944: *m.* 1968, Donald Neil Rowley Morrison, of Woodbine Cottage, Engleton Lane, Brewood, Staffs. (and has issue living, Stuart John Petrie *b.* 1969, Jamie William Petrie *b.* 1971). *Address,*—Springkell Hotel, Hindhead, Surrey.

BRADFORD, Creation (U.K.) 1902, of South Audley Street, City of Westminster, co. London.

Sir EDWARD ALEXANDER SLADE BRADFORD, 5th *Baronet :* *b.* (posthumous) June 18th, 1952 ; *s.* his half-brother, *Sir* JOHN RIDLEY EVELYN, 1954.

Arms—Argent, on a fesse embattled counter-embattled between three mural crowns sable, as many stags' heads erased or. *Crest*—A stag's head erased or, charged on the neck with a mural crown, and suspended from the mouth a bugle horn stringed sable.
Residence—Faith Cottage, Pett, Sussex.

Half-Sister living—Alison Rose, *b.* 1939: *m.* 1957, James Ronald Creighton Adams, and has issue living, John Evelyn Creighton, *b.* 1959, —Bradford Michael, *b.* 1965. *Residence*, Riverside House, N. Manchester, Indiana, U.S.A.

Uncle living (son of 2nd baronet)—DONALD CLIFTON, *b.* May 22nd, 1914 ; formerly Capt. Seaforth Highlanders : *m.* 1949, Constance Mary, da. of the late C. J. Morgan, of Glyncorrwg, S. Wales, and has issue living, Susan Jane, *b.* 1950,—Katharine Anne, *b.* 1952,—Joanna Mary, *b.* 1957. *Residence*, Woodside, Seal, Sevenoaks, Kent.

Humani nihil alienum.
Nothing concerning man
is indifferent to me.

Mother living of 4th Baronet—Alison, da. of John Lawson of Borrobol, Sutherland : *m.* 1st, 1937, Major Sir Edward Montagu Andrew Bradford, 3rd baronet, who *d.* 1952, and from whom she had obtained a divorce 1947; 2ndly, 1951, John Owen Fisher Davies, CBE, MD, MRCP, of Marylands Farm, Chislehampton, Oxford.

Widow living of 3rd Baronet—MARJORIE (CHAPMAN) (*Lady Bradford*), da. of Samuel Bere of Addiscombe, Surrey : *m.* 1950, as his second wife, Major Sir Edward Montagu Andrew Bradford, 3rd baronet, who *d.* 1952. *Residence*, Faith Cottage, Pett, Sussex.

Collateral Branch living.

Issue of the late Lieut.-Col. Edward Austen Bradford, D.S.O., youngest son of 1st baronet, *b.* 1879, *d.* 1958: *m.* 1908, Margaret Louisa, who *d.* 1972, da. of the late Herbert Carey Hardy, of Danehurst, Sussex:—

Berenger Colborne, D.S.O., M.B.E., M.C., *b.* 1912 ; ed. at Eton ; is Brigadier, late Black Watch (commanded 5th and 2nd Batns.), and a Member of Queen's Body Guard for Scotland (Roy. Co. of Archers) ; European War, 1939-45 (wounded, despatches, M.B.E., M.C., D.S.O. and Bar) ; M.B.E. (Mil.) 1942, D.S.O. 1944 (Bar 1945) : *m.* 1951, Susan, da. of the late Col. Arthur Hanning Vaughan-Lee of Dillington Park, Ilminster, Somerset, and has issue living, Robert Berenger Pickering, *b.* 1952,—Andrew Edward Hanning, *b.* 1955,—Ronald James Knight, *b.* 1958,— Margaret Jane, *b.* 1953. *Residence*, Kincardine, Kincardine O'Neil, Aberdeenshire.——Adela Evelyn, *b.* 1909: *m.* 1933, Lieut.-Col. Fergus Gleeson, Indian Army, who *d.* 1962, and from whom she obtained a divorce 1945, and has issue living, Cassandra Margaret, *b.* 1936,—Bridget Elizabeth, *b.* 1940. *Residence*, 46, Porchester Terr., W2.——Cassandra Felicity, MBE (Taylor's Cottage, Chichester Rd., Midhurst, Sussex), *b.* 1915; formerly Capt. Air Transport Auxiliary; MBE (Civil) 1946: *m.* 1941, Group Capt. Peter Hugh Bragg, RAF, who *d.* 1966, and has issue living, Ronald Wake field, *b.* 1948.——Diana Elizabeth, *b.* 1919: *m.* 1941, Rupert P. Shervington, late Capt. RE, and has issue living, Evelyn Arthur, *b.* 1942, BA, Trin. Coll., Dublin,—Diana Clare, *b.* 1943,—Caroline Faith, *b.* 1954. *Residence*, Cantlesbury, Hinxworth, Herts.

The 1st baronet, Col. Sir Edward Ridley Colborne, was Commr. of Police of the Metropolis 1890-1903. The 2nd baronet, Col. Sir Evelyn Ridley Bradford, Comdg. 2nd Batn. Seaforth Highlanders (Ross-shire Buffs, Duke of Albany's), was killed in action during European War 1914. The 3rd baronet, Sir Edward Montagu Andrew, was Major Cameronians.

BRADY, Creation (U.K.) 1869, of Hazelbrook, co. Dublin, Ireland. [Extinct 1927.]
Sir WILLIAM LONGFIELD BRADY, 4th and last *Baronet.*

Daughter living of 4th Baronet—Ethne Florence, *b.* 1902. *Residence,*
Daughter living of 3rd Baronet—Jessie Elizabeth Maziere *b.* 1901. *Residence,*

BRAITHWAITE, Creation (U.K.) 1954, of Burnham, co. Somerset. [Extinct 1958.]
Sir JOSEPH GURNEY BRAITHWAITE, 1st and last *Baronet.*

Widow living of 1st Baronet—EMILY VICTORIA (*Lady Braithwaite*) (Aran House, 38, Woodville Rd., Ealing, W5), da. of the late Arthur Moreton Lomax: *m.* 1932, as his second wife, Sir Joseph Gurney Braithwaite, 1st Bt., who *d.* 1958, when the title became ext.

BRICKWOOD, Creation (U.K.) 1927, of Portsmouth.

Sir BASIL GREAME BRICKWOOD, 3rd *Baronet*; *b.* May 21st, 1923; *s.* his half-brother, *Sir* RUPERT REDVERS, 1974: *m.* 1st, 1947, Betty Cooper; 2ndly, 1956, Shirley Anne, da. of Richard Wallace Brown, and has issue by 2nd m.

Arms—Argent a pale checky azure and or between two oak trees couped vert on a chief gules three ears of barley slipped and leaved of the third and a sprig of hop slipped and leaved proper in saltire between two billets gold. *Crest*— A demi savage wreathed about the temples with a chaplet of oak holding in the dexter hand a sprig of hop slipped and leaved proper and resting the sinister hand upon a billet or. *Club*, RAF.

NIL·ARDUUM

Nothing arduous.

Daughters living—(by 2nd m.) Tessa Anne, *b.* 1959.——Gail Anne, *b.* 1963.
Daughters living of 2nd Baronet—Sally (Neale), *b.* 1933: *m.* 1956, Nigel William Seville Yonge, of Homefields, Bulls La.. Cowfold, Sussex, and has issue living, William Jonathan Michael, *b.* 1961,—Andrew James Neale, *b.* 1964,—Susannah Mary, *b.* 1957,—Annabel Mary, *b.* 1959.—— Ann Neale, *b.* 1934: *m.* 1959, John Colin Caldecott Bauer, of Little Parks, Woodlands Lane, Stoke D'Abernon, Cobham, Surrey, and has issue living, John William, *b.* 1960,— Nicola Anne, *b.* 1962.

The 1st baronet, Sir John Brickwood, was Chm. and Managing Director of Brickwood & Co., Ltd., brewers, of Portsmouth, and sometime Chm. of Portsmouth Chamber of Commerce.

BRINCKMAN, Creation (U.K.) 1831, of Burton, Yorkshire.

By persevering.

Sir RODERICK (NAPOLEON) BRINCK- MAN, *D.S.O., M.C.*, 5th *Baronet* ; *b.* Dec. 27th, 1902 ; *s.* his brother, *Major Sir* THEODORE ERNEST WARREN, 1954 ; Col. (retired) Grenadier Guards : has been an A.D.C. to Gov.-Gen. and Com.-in-Ch., Canada, and to Gov. of Victoria ; was Ch. of Staff, Mil. Mission to Moscow 1944-5, and Head of Liaison Mission to Netherlands 1945 ; European War 1939-45 (wounded, despatches, D.S.O., M.C., prisoner, escaped) ; D.S.O. 1941 ; *m.* 1st, 1931, Margaret Wilson, da. of Wilson Southam, of Rockcliffe, Ottawa, Canada ; 2ndly, 1943, Rosemary Marguerite (GILBEY), da. of the late Lieut.- Col. James Charles Hope-Vere [*see* M. Linlithgow, colls.], and has issue by 1st and 2nd marriages.

Arms—Argent, three hills azure. *Crest*—A pair of wings quarterly argent and azure.
Residences—Mornington House, Wimbledon Common, SW19; Cross Keys, Sandwich, Kent. *Clubs*—Buck's, Guards', Turf, White's.

Sons living—By 1st m.—THEODORE GEORGE RODERICK (1, Dale Av., Toronto, Canada; St. Helena, St. James, Barbados) *b.* March 20th, 1932; ed. at Millfield, at Trin. Coll. Sch., Port Hope, Ontario, at Ch. Ch., Oxford, and at Trin. Coll., Toronto Univ.: *m.* 1958, Helen Mary Anne, da. of the late Arnold Elliot Cook, of Toronto, Canada, and has issue living, Theodore Jonathan, *b.* 1960,—Roderick Nicholas, *b.* 1964,—Sophia Theresa, *b.* 1963.——John Francis (of 131, Clandeboye Av., Montreal, Canada), *b.* 1933: *m.* 1963, Susan Jennefer, da. of Peter Woodburn Blaylock, of Toad's Tooting, Ile Bizard, Quebec, Canada, and has issue living, Adam Blaylock, *b.* 1965,—Theadora Southam, *b.* 1966.
Daughter living—By 2nd marriage—Theadora Elizabeth, *b.* 1944: *m.* 1964. Gerard Francis Campbell, of 491, Fulham Rd., SW6 [*see* B. Harlech].

Collateral Branches living.

Grandchildren of the late William Edward Brinckman, R.N., 3rd son of 1st baronet :— Issue of the late William Henry Brinckman, *b.* 1860, *d.* 1920: *m.* 1894, Winifred Blanche Victoria, who *d.* 1969, da. of the late C. Cox:—
William Brian (12, Heath Lane, Chester), *b.* 1904: *m.* 1937, Marjorie, da. of the late John Ashbrook Hughes, and has issue living, Hilary Anne, *b.* 1937.——Rosemary, *b.* 1900: *m.* 1941, Col. Harold A. Bazley, FRICS, RE (ret.) of High Beeches, Chaddesley Rd., Kidderminster, Worcs.

Issue of the late Major Rowland Brinckman, O.B.E., *b.* 1861, *d.* 1948 ; *m.* 1st, 1891, Anna Alexander, who *d.* 1910, da. of the late Professor J. E. Cairnes ; 2ndly, 1911, Marian, who *d.* 1941, da. of the late Richard Baxter :—
(By 1st marriage) Christine Phyllida (*Lady Marshall*), *b.* 1907 : *m.* 1931, Sir Hugo Frank Marshall, KBE, CMG, and has issue living, Robert Rowland (22, Edwin Rd., Twickenham, Middx.) *b.* 1942: *m.* 1966, Joan Monica Theresa, da. of Rev. Canon H. Leach, of Johannesburg,—David William, *b.* 1945: *m.* 1969, Lorraine June, da. of C. W. Robbins, of Miami Beach, Florida, and has issue living, William Denvs *b.* 1970, Reuben Grey *b.* 1972,—Janet Mary, *b.* 1937: *m.* 1960, David B. Cunliffe-Jones, of 9, Elson Rd., Formby, Lancs., and has issue living, Andrew Robert *b.* 1962, Peter David *b.* 1964, Judith Elizabeth *b.* 1961, Rosemary Janet Helen *b.* 1968. *Residence*, Murrell House, Limpley Stoke, nr. Bath.

The 1st baronet whose patronymic was Broadhead, in 1842 resumed for himself and issue by Roy. licence, the family name of Brinckman. He sat as M.P. for Yarmouth 1820-26. Sir Theodore, 2nd Baronet. sat as M.P. for Canterbury (*L*) 1868-74. Sir Theodore Francis, C.B., 3rd Baronet, was Hon. Col. The Buffs and sometime Lieut.-Col. London Regt. Sir Theodore Ernest Warren, 4th baronet, was Major 1st Life Guards.

BRISCO, Creation (G.B.) 1782, of Crofton Place, Cumberland.

Take with a grateful hand.

(*Sir*) DONALD GILFRID BRISCO, 8th *Baronet*; *b.* Sept. 15th, 1920; *s.* his father, *Sir* HYLTON MUSGRAVE CAMPBELL, 1968; a Sheep Farmer; a JP; 1939-45 War, as a Pilot with RNZAF and RAF in Europe and Mediterranean (prisoner): *m.* 1945, Irene, only da. of Henry John Gage, of Ermine Park, Brockworth, Glos., and has issue.

Arms—Argent, three greyhounds courant in pale sable. Crest—A greyhound courant sable seizing a hare proper.
Address—Longworth, PO Box 165, Havelock North, NZ.

Daughters living—Barbara Ann, *b.* 1946,——Penny Christine, *b.* 1949.——Jill Kathleen, *b.* 1952.

Sisters living—Joan Elsie, *b.* 1923 : *m.* 1953, F. J. A. McTague, of 33, Kennedy Rd., Napier, Hawke's Bay, New Zealand.——Oriel Patricia, *b.* 1926: *m.* 1950, James C. Waldren. *Residence*, 1111 Allenby St., Hastings, Hawke's Bay, New Zealand.

Uncle living—ORIEL ARTHUR (136, Fraser St., Tauranga, NZ), *b.* June 26th, 1892; 1914-18 War in Egypt, Gallipoli and France: *m.* 1st, 1921, Lilian Fridrica, da. of Francis Dominic Saunderson, of Linwood, Christchurch, NZ; 2ndly, 1960, Sarah Louisa, RRC, who *d.* 1971, da. of Rice Owen Clark, of Hobsonville, Auckland, NZ.——Gilfrid Rimington (53, Durham St., Winton, Southland, NZ), *b.* 1895; is a Sheep Farmer: 1914-18 War with NZF: *m.* 1941, Constance Freda, da. of Charles J. Polson, of Masterton, NZ, and has issue living, Campbell Howard (Kawariri, Hokonui, No. 2 RD, Winton, Southland, NZ) *b.* 1944: *m.* 1969, Kay Janette, da. of Ewan W. McFadzien, of Gt. North Rd., Winton, Southland, NZ, and has issue living, Kent Rimington *b.* 1972,—Rosemary Robyn, *b.* 1943: *m.* 1966, Peter Collin Neale, of 9, Courtenay Rd., Rose Bay, Sydney, Aust. 2029, and has issue living, Adam Hylton *b.* 1968.

Sister living of 6th Baronet—Gwendolen Constance : *m.* 1906, William Clay Baker, who *d.* 19—, and has issue living, Gwendolen Aubrey, *b.* 1912. *Residence*,

Widows living of 6th and 7th Baronets—RUBY PEARL (*Ruby, Lady Brisco*), da. of John Jacob Runck: *m.* 1938, as his second wife, Sir Aubrey Hylton Brisco, 6th Bt., who *d.* 1957. *Address*, Box 22 Bayside, Refugio County, Texas, USA.——KATHLEEN (*Kathleen, Lady Brisco*) (208, Windsor Av., Hastings, Hawke's Bay, NZ), da. of W. Fenwick McAllaum, of NZ: *m.* 1914, Sir Hylton Musgrave Campbell Brisco, 7th Bt., who *d.* 1968.

Sir John Brisco, 1st Bt. of Crofton, was grandson of John Brisco of Crofton, descended from Isold Brisco of Brisco, who acquired the Manors of Crofton, Whinnow, and Dundraw, in right of his wife, Margaret, da. of Sir John Crofton, Knt., of Crofton, and was great-grandson of Robert Brisco, of Brisco, Cumberland. The 5th baronet, Sir Hylton Ralph Brisco, was drowned at sea on a voyage to Bombay 1922; he *m.* 1st, 1904, Lilian Mabel (who obtained a divorce 1915), da. of the late James King; 2ndly, 1916, Grace (from whom he obtained a divorce 1921), da. of the late Henry Vaughan.

BRISCOE, Creation (U.K.) 1910, of Bourn Hall, Bourn, co. Cambridge.

I perform and persevere.

Sir JOHN LEIGH CHARLTON BRISCOE, *D.F.C.*, 4th *Baronet* ; *b.* Dec. 3rd, 1911 ; *s.* his father, *Sir* (JOHN) CHARLTON, *M.D., F.R.C.P.*, 1960 ; ed. at Harrow, and at Magdalen Coll., Oxford (B.A. 1933, M.A. 1950) ; A.C.A. 1937 ; European War 1942-5 as Flight-Lieut. R.A.F. Vol. Reserve (D.F.C.) : *m.* 1948, Teresa Mary Violet, da. of Brig.-Gen. Sir Archibald Fraser Home, K.C.V.O., C.B., C.M.G., D.S.O., and has issue.

Arms—Argent, two greyhounds courant sable, on a chief arched of the last two roses of the first, barbed and seeded proper. Crest—Upon a mount of heather proper a greyhound courant paly of twelve argent and sable.

Residence—Little Acres, Grays Park Road, Stoke Poges, Bucks. *Club*, RAF.

Sons living—JOHN JAMES, *b.* July 15th, 1951.—— Edward Home, *b.* 1955.

Daughter living—Diana Clare, *b.* 1949.

Brother living—Richard Kynaston, *b.* 1914; ed. at Charterhouse, and at Balliol Coll., Oxford (B.A. 1936, M.A. 1947) ; A.C.A. 1940 ; F.C.A. 1960 ; European War 1940-45 as Capt. R.A. : *m.* 1951, Margaret Hamilton, da. of Sir Hugh Mallinson Rigby, 1st Bt., K.C.V.O., F.R.C.S. *Residence*, Maple House, Higher Combe Road, Haslemere, Surrey.

Collateral Branch living.
Issue of the late Hugh Kynaston Briscoe, C.S.I., C.I.E., youngest son of 1st baronet, *b.* 1879, *d.* 1956: *m.* 1919, Noel, who *d.* 1971, da. of the late John E. Worrall, of Langstones, 39, Bidston Rd., Oxton, Birkenhead:—
John Arthur (Frith Haye, Gravel Path, Berkhamsted), *b.* 1925: *m.* 1955, Hilairy Mary, da. of the late S. K. Shaw, of Lynbank, Mill Gap Rd., Eastbourne, and has issue livng, Neil David, *b.*

1956,—Andrew Mark, b. 1960,—Lindsay Ann, b. 1958.——Ellen Kathleen, b. 1920: m. 1945, Maj. Anthony Stanley Purcell Jeans, TD, Wilts. Regt., and has issue living, Michael Anthony Purcell, b. 1947,—Jennifer Rosemary Ellen, b. 1950. *Residence,*—The Manor Farm, Newton Stacey, nr. Stockbridge, Hants.——Nancy Charlton, b. 1921.——Mary Clare, b. 1928: m. 1954, James Anthony Farrer-Halls, and has issue living, Alan Anthony, b. 1961,—Barbara Mary, b. 1955,—Gillian Clare, b. 1958. *Residence,*—The Old Cottage, Broadcommon Rd., Hurst, Berks.

Sir John James Briscoe, 1st baronet, was High Sheriff of Cambridgeshire 1888. Sir (John) Charlton Briscoe, M.D., F.R.C.P., 3rd baronet, was a Consulting Physician to King's Coll. Hospital and to Evelina Hospital for Sick Children.

RUGGLES-BRISE, Creation (U.K.) 1935, of Spains Hall, Finchingfield, Essex.

Sir JOHN ARCHIBALD RUGGLES-BRISE, *C.B., O.B.E., T.D.,* 2nd *Baronet* ; b. June 13th, 1908 ; his father, *Col. Sir* EDWARD ARCHIBALD, *M.C., T.D., M.P.,* 1942; ed. at Eton; is a J.P. for Essex, a Freeman of Chelmsford, Gov. of Felsted and Chigwell Schs., a KStJ, an Under-writing Member of Lloyd's; appointed Lord-Lt. of Essex 1958, and Pro Chancellor of Essex Univ. 1963; Pres. Country Landowners Assocn. 1958-59, Chm. of Standing Council of the Baronet-age 1958-63 and a Church Commr. 1959-65; formerly Hon. Col. 459th (Essex) Heavy Anti-Aircraft Regt. RA (TA); 1939-45 War (OBE); OBE (Mil) 1945, CB (Civil) 1958.

Arms—Quarterly, 1st and 4th, gules, a cross between four mascles argent, all within a bordure sable, charged with eight quatrefoils of the second, *Brise*; 2nd and 3rd argent on a chevron gules, between three roses of the second, barbed, seeded, leaved and slipped proper, as many estoiles or, *Ruggles.* **Crests**—1st, a demi-crocodile sable, *Brise*; 2nd, in front of twelve arrows in saltire proper, heads outwards, a tower or, inflamed proper, *Ruggles.* *Seat*—Spains Hall, Finchingfield, Braintree, Essex.

Brother living—GUY EDWARD, TD, b. June 15th, 1914; late Capt. Essex Yeo.; a DL of Essex; High Sheriff 1967-68; a Member of London Stock Exchange; 1939-45 War in N. Africa (prisoner (Italy), escaped): m. 1940, Elizabeth, only da. of the late James Knox, of Smithstone House, Kilwinning, Ayrshire, and has issue living, Timothy Edward, b. 1945; ed. at Eton: m. 1975, Rosemary E., yr. da. of J. S. Craig, of 12, Browning Close, W2,—James Rupert b. 1947; ed. at Eton,—Samuel Guy, b. 1956. *Residences,* Housham Tye, Harlow, Essex; Ledgowan Lodge, Achnasheen, Wester Ross. *Clubs,* Cavalry, City of London.

Sisters living—Violet Agatha, b. 1907: m. 1936, Com. Hubert Wyndham Barry, R.N. (retired) [*see* Barry, Bt., colls.]. *Residence,* Hill House, Broughton, Stockbridge, Hants.——Cecilia Margaret, b. 1919 ; formerly Section Officer W.A.A.F. : m. 1943, John Julian Riddick, formerly Capt. R.A., and has issue living, Robert John Gurney, b. 1951,—Graham Edward Galloway, b. 1955,—Elspeth Marjorie, b. 1952. *Residence,* Coldstream House, Shipton-under-Wychwood, Oxon.

Widow living of 1st Baronet—LUCY BARBARA (*Lady Ruggles-Brise*), M.B.E., da. of the Rt. Rev. W. R. Pym, Bishop of Bombay ; M.B.E. (Civil) 1957 : m. 1939, as his second wife, Sir Edward Archibald Ruggles-Brise, MC, TD, MP, 1st baronet, who d. 1942. *Residence,* Flat 2, 16 Rupert St., W1.

The 1st baronet, Col. Sir Edward Archibald Ruggles-Brise, M.C., T.D. (son of the late Archibald Weyland Ruggles-Brise, J.P., D.L., of Spains Hall, Finchingfield, Essex), was Lieut.-Col. and Brevet Col. late 104th (Essex Yeo.) Brig., R.A. (T.A.), Vice-Lieut. for Essex, and M.P. for Maldon Div. of Essex (C) 1922-3 and 1924-42.

BROADBENT, Creation (U.K.) 1893, of Brook Street, co. London, and Longwood, Yorkshire.

áλεν áρіετεύειν. *To excel always.*

Sir WILLIAM FRANCIS BROADBENT, 3rd *Baronet* ; b. Nov. 29th, 1904 ; s. his father, *Sir* JOHN FRANCIS HARPIN, *M.D., F.R.C.P., M.R.C.S.,* 1946 ; ed. at Winchester, and at Trin. Coll., Oxford : m. 1935, Veronica Pearl, who d. 1951, da. of the late Benjamin F. Eustace, of Hillside Farm, Glasenvin, Dublin.

Arms—Per pale ermine and azure, a fesse nebulée counter-changed, in the dexter chief quarter a caduceus erect proper. **Crest**—In front of a pheon the staff rompée, a serpent nowed, all proper. *Residence*—21, Porchester Terrace, W.2.

Sisters living—Phyllis Margaret, b. 1896: m. 1923, Capt. Arthur, Henry Parsons, RN, and has issue living, Alan John Maurice (13 Farrin St., Attadale, W. Australia), b. 1928: m. 1960, Jillian Sidney Fergus Prain, and has issue living, Giles Henry William b. 1961, Penelope Barbara b. 1963,—Cynthia Margaret, b. 1926: m. 1955, Paul Bertram Baker, of Red Maples, Salcombe Hill Rd., Sidmouth, and has issue living, John Paul Philip b. 1957, Janet Cynthia b. 1959. *Residence,* Wemyss Cottage, Gorseway, Sidmouth.—— Sylvia Mary (Selwood, Cottage, Minchinhampton, Glos.), b. 1898: m. 1931, William George Dawson, who d. 1972, and has issue living, Richard William (Green End Farm House, Pegsdon Hitchin, Herts.), b. 1932: m. 1957, Mary Heath, and has issue living, Paul Richard b. 1958, Timothy Charles b. 1963,—Rosemary Katherine b. 1935: m. 1958, James Martin Stewart Caldwell, c/o PO Box 2, Naro Moro, Kenya, and has issue living, Marcus Stewart b. 1958, Hazel Katherine, b. 1962.——Katherine Mabel, b. 1899: m. 1953, Philip Lander Birley. *Residence,* Braddens Yard, Long Crendon, Bucks.

Collateral Branches living.

Grandsons of the late Maj. Walter Broadbent, MD, FRCP (*infra*):—
Issue of the late John Graham Monroe Broadbent, b. 1901, d. 1967: m. 1933, Elizabeth Mary Beatrice (2, Ramsay Rd., Windlesham, Surrey), only da. of Robert Arthur Dendy, of 15, Third Av., Hove:—

GEORGE WALTER (c/o Lloyds Bank, Fairford, Glos.), *b.* April 23rd, 1935; Fl.-Lt. RAF: *m.* 1962, Valerie Ann, only da. of Cecil Frank Ward, of Boston Rd., Horncastle, and has issue living, Andrew George, *b.* 1963,—Ione Charlotte Elizabeth, *b.* 1967.——Robert John Dendy, *b.* 1938.

Issue of the late Major Walter Broadbent, M.D., F.R.C.P., 3rd son of 1st baronet, *b.* 1868, *d.* 1951 : *m.* 1896, Edith, O.B.E., who *d.* 1952, da. of the late Rt. Hon. John Monroe, LL.D., Judge of Landed Estates Court, Ireland :—
Hubert William Lonsdale, *MB* (15, Montague Sq., W1), *b.* 1908; ed. at Charterhouse, and at Trin. Coll., Camb.: *m.* 1934, Marjorie, da. of the late Sir Arthur Kirwan Agar, Ch. Justice of British Honduras, and has issue living, Graham Agar (90, Wildwood Rd., Hampstead Garden Suburb, NW11), *b.* 1938: *m.* 1964, Valerie Suzanne Mytton, and has issue living, Charles Richard *b.* 1968, Philip David *b.* 1972,—Judith Anne, *b.* 1935: *m.* 1960, Robin Scoones, of Wychwood, Bryanston, Blandford Forum, Dorset, and has issue living, Ian Christopher *b.* 1962, Simon Richard *b.* 1964, Timothy Graham *b.* 1967.——Moira Edith, *b.* 1905: *m.* 1927, Maj. Colin Davenport, OBE, FRCVS, formerly RAVC, and has issue living, Doreen, *b.* 1928: *m.* 1958, Capt. John Eric Sheldon Ellis, RTR, and has issue living, Christopher Shaun Sheldon *b.* 1958, Colin Peter Sheldon *b.* 1961,—Cicely, *b.* 1934. *Residence*, Brackendene, Burley, Hants.

Sir William H. Broadbent, K.C.V.O., M.D., F.R.C.P., LL.D., F.R.S., 1st Bt., son of John Broadbent, was an eminent consulting Physician and Physician-in-Ord. to King Edward VII. and the Prince of Wales. Sir John Francis Harpin Broadbent, M.D., F.R.C.P., M.R.C.S., 2nd Bt., was Consulting Physician to St. Mary's Hospital, London Fever Hospital, and King Edward VII. Sanatorium, Midhurst.

BROCKLEBANK, Creation (U.K.) 1885, of Greenlands, co. Cumberland and Springwood, co. Lancaster.

Sir AUBREY (THOMAS) BROCKLEBANK, 6TH *Baronet*; *b.* Jan. 29th, 1952; *s.* his father, *Maj.* Sir JOHN MONTAGUE, *TD* 1974; ed. at Eton, and Univ., Coll., Durham.

Arms—Argent, three brocks proper, each on a mount vert; on a chief azure as many escallops of the first. *Crest*—On an anchor fessewise sable, a cock argent, combed and wattled gules, and charged on the shoulder with an escallop of the first.

Residence,—14, Tenter Terr., Durham.

God send grace.

Aunt living (daughter of 3rd baronet)—Angela Grace, *b.* 1908: *m.* 1931, John Vincent Wrigley, MBE, and has issue living, John Patrick, *b.* 1946; ed. at Eton,—Leila Virginia Grace, *b.* 1934: *m.* 1st, 1954, Ross Kearsley Pigot, who obtained a divorce 1973; 2ndly, 1973, Julian Harrison, of Oulton Park House, Tarporley, Cheshire, and has issue living, (by 1st m.) David Kearsley *b.* 1956, Carolyn Jane *b.* 1955, Fenella Clare *b.* 1958; (by 2nd m.) Nicholas Justin *b.* 1974,—Rosamond Catherine, *b.* 1945: *m.* 1966, Christopher Robert Dunbar Woodward, of Stepple Hall, Cleobury Mortimer, Worcs., and has issue living, Nicholas Robert *b.* 1969, Charlotte Jane *b.* 1967. *Residence*,—Delbury Hall, Craven Arms, Shropshire.

Widow living of 5th Baronet—PAMELA SUE (*Lady Brocklebank*) (Il Palazz, Zejtun, Malta, GC), da. of the late William Harold Pierce, OBE, of Oxton, Cheshire, and formerly wife of Maj. Leslie Forshaw-Wilson: *m.* 1950, Maj. Sir John Montague Brocklebank, TD, 5th Bt., who *d.* 1974.

Collateral Branches living.

Grandson of the late Major John Jasper Brocklebank, D.S.O. (infra) :—
Issue of the late Lieut.-Com. John Maurice Brocklebank, R.N.V.R., *b.* 1917, *d.* (on active ser. during European War) 1945: *m.* 1944, Evelyn Margaret (170, Campden Hill Rd., W8), da. of Gordon Pyper, and widow of T. L. Stephenson, 2nd Lieut.:—
JOHN DANIEL (posthumous) (c/o LBI Trust Co., Lloyds & Bolsa International Bank, Ltd., 100, Pall Mall, SW1 45HP), *b.* Sept. 29th, 1945, ed. at Eton and Keble Coll., Oxford: *m.* 1971, Donna J, da. of Maj. Clixby Fitzwilliams, of Hazeldene, Healing, nr. Grimsby, and has issue living, Daniel, *b.* 1975.

Issue of the late Maj. John Jasper Brocklebank, DSO, 2nd son of 2nd baronet, *b.* 1875, *d.* 1942: *m.* 1914, Constance Mary, who *d.* 1965, da. of the late Sir Robert Leonard Powell, JP, of Flowers Hill, Pangbourne:—
Thomas Gordon (80A, Broadlands Rd., Emerald Hill, Salisbury, Rhodesia), *b.* 1921; ed. at Eton; formerly Lt. RNVR (Fleet Air Arm): *m.* 1st, 1952, Gillian Chester, who *d.* 1966, da. of the late William Francis Cardew; 2ndly, 1970, Edith Josephine, da. of the late William Geoffry Ward, and widow of Neville Wells Abbott, and has issue living, (by 1st m.) Robin John, *b.* 1954,—Geoffrey Cardew, *b.* 1959,—Christopher Philip, *b.* 1963,—Anne Frances, *b.* 1962.

Issue of the late Robert Allport Brocklebank, 3rd son of 2nd baronet, *b.* 1878, *d.* 1946: *m.* 1903, Frances, yst. da. of the late John H. Walker, JP for cos. Fife and Forfar:—
Oliver, *RN*, *b.* 1908; became Lt.-Com. 1939: *m.* 1st, 1931, Diana, da. of the late Col. Wilford Boteler, DSO, RA; 2ndly, 1947, Marjorie Joan Snowling, and has issue living, (by 2nd m.) Alison Philippa, *b.* 1948,—Elizabeth Joanna, *b.* 1950,—Edwina Jane, *b.* 1952. *Residence*, Redbourne, Lowestoft Rd., Gorleston-on-Sea, Norfolk.

Issue of the late Harold Brocklebank, 3rd son of 1st baronet, *b.* 1853, *d.* 1936: *m.* 1878, Mary Ellen, who *d.* 1929, da. of the late John Brogden:—
Eleanor Hilda: *m.* 1923, Brig. Edward Rigby Kewley, DSO, MC, who *d.* 1972. *Residence*, Little Dean House, Stockbridge, Hants.

Grandchildren of the late Rev. Charles Henry Brocklebank, 4th son of 1st baronet:—
Issue of the late Charles Gerald Brocklebank, MC, *b.* 1893, *d.* 1940: *m.* 1925, Beatrice Gresley, (The Mill House, Higham, Colchester), da. of the late Falconer Madan:—
Charles William (of Giffords Hall, Stoke-by-Nayland, Suffolk), *b.* 1930; ed. at Eton and Ch. Ch. Oxford: *m.* 1965, Marcia Andrea, MA, da. of Arthur Early, of Hickory Corners, Michigan, USA, and has issue living, James Gerald, *b.* 1970,—Diana Lasswell, *b.* 1968.——Mary, *b.* 1926: *m.* 1948, Michael Guy Molesworth Bevan, and has issue living, Roger Anthony Briscoe, *b.* 1951,—William George Briscoe, *b.* 1958,—James Edward Briscoe, *b.* 1960,—Penelope Anne, *b.* 1955. *Residence*, Longstowe Hall, Cambridge, CB3 7UH.——Ann, *b.* 1928.

The 1st baronet, Sir Thomas, was son of the late Wilson Fisher, of Keekle, Whitehaven; assumed in 1845, by Roy. licence, the surname of Brocklebank, on succeeding to the estate of his maternal uncle Thomas Brocklebank, of Greenlands, Cumberland, and was High Sheriff of Cumberland 1864. The 2nd baronet was High Sheriff of Lancashire 1908, and the 3rd baronet, Sir Aubrey (Chm. of Thomas and John Brocklebank (Limited), and a Director of Suez Canal Co., Cunard Steamship Co. (Limited), and other cos.), was High Sheriff of Cumberland 1921.

BROCKLEHURST, Creation (U.K.) 1903, of Swythamley Park, co. Stafford.

Sir JOHN OGILVY BROCKLEHURST, 3rd *Baronet,* son of the late Lt.-Col. Henry Courtney Brocklehurst, 2nd son of 1st baronet; *b.* April 6th, 1926; *s.* his uncle, *Lt.-Col. Sir* PHILIP LEE, 1975; Lord of the Manor of Heaton Swythamley.

Arms—Paly per pale argent and sable, three chevronels engrailed between as many brocks counterchanges. **Crest**—A brock sable holding in the mouth a slip of oak fructed proper in front of a mount vert, thereon two oak trees proper.
Residence, Breezes, Brighton.

Daughters living of 2nd Baronet—By 1st marriage—Anne Nina, *b.* 1915: *m.* 1940, Major Algernon John Harington Stranack, RA (ret.), of Dendro Moli, Nissaki, Corfu, Greece.——Pamela Margaret, *b.* 1917: *m.* 1st, 1940, James Leslie Milne, who *d.* 1956; 2ndly, 1963, Lt.-Cdr. Francis Henry Inskip Austen, RN (ret.), of Gt. Markly, Heathfield, Sussex.

Truth directs me.   **Aunt living (daughter living of 1st baronet)**—Mabel Annie, *b.* 1886: *m.* 1st, 1905, Jonkheer Frans I. Van Haeften, who *d.* 1964, and from whom she obtained a divorce 1926; 2ndly, 1927, Sir Henry Gordon Ley, 2nd Bt., who *d.* 1944, and from whom she had obtained a divorce 1939, and has issue living, (by 1st m.), Wilhelmina Josephine Philippa, *b.* 1907: *m.* 1939, Lt.-Col. the Hon. (Arthur) Patrick William Seely, TD (later 3rd Baron Mottistone), who *d.* 1966, having obtained a divorce 1949.
Residence, Pitt Manor, Winchester.

This family settled from Derbyshire at Gap House, Taxal, Staffs., early in the 17th century. Maj.-Gen. John Fielding Brocklehurst, late RHG, nephew of 1st baronet, was Lord in Waiting to George V and in 1914 was *cr.* Baron Ranksborough, which peerage became ext. on his death 1921. Sir Philip Lancaster Brocklehurst, 1st baronet of Swythamley Park, Staffs., was 4th son of John Brocklehurst (MP 1832-69), of Hurdsfield House, Cheshire. Sir Philip Lee Brocklehurst, 2nd baronet, accompanied British Antarctic Expedition 1907-09.

BRODIE, Creation (U.K.) 1834, of Boxford, Suffolk.

Sir BENJAMIN DAVID ROSS BRODIE, 5th *Baronet*; *b.* May 29th, 1925 ; *s.* his father, *Sir* BENJAMIN COLLINS, *M.C.,* 1971; *ed.* at Eton; late R. Signals.

Arms—Azure, on a chevron between three mullets argent, three civic wreaths vert. **Crest**—A dexter cubit arm erect, holding a civic wreath as in the arms with three arrows, one in fesse and two in saltire points towards the dexter argent.

Residence—

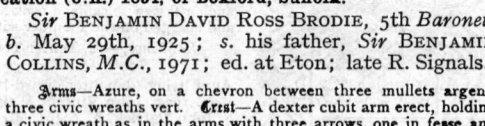

Brother living—COLIN ALEXANDER, *b.* April 19th, 1929; *ed.* at Eton and Magdalen Coll., Oxford; Bar. Middle Temple 1953; late 8th (King's Irish) Hussars: *m.* 1955, Julia Anne Irene, da. of the late Norman E. Wates, of Elmore, Chipstead, Surrey, and has issue living, Christian Norman, *b.* 1957,—Alexander Colin, *b.* 1959. *Address,* 24, Old Buildings, Lincolns Inn, WC2.

Sister living—Angela Mary, *b.* 1933; *ed.* at St. Andrews Univ. (MA, Hons. Econ.). *Residence,* Betchworth Lodge, Betchworth, Surrey.

Aunts living (daughters of 3rd baronet)—Phoebe Mary, *b.* 1889.——Olive Marjory, *b.* 1892. *Residence,* Oakwood House, Box Hill, Tadworth.

Collateral Branch living
Grandson of the late Capt. Edgar Waldegrave Brodie, 3rd son of the late Rev. William Brodie, 2nd son of 1st baronet:—
Issue of the late Capt. Malcolm William O'Callaghan Brodie, *b.* 1887, *d.* 1966: *m.* 1st, 1922, Phyllis Gwavas, who *d.* 1940, da. of Henry Tredenham Fitzherbert Carlyon; 2ndly, 1948, Sybil Barbara (54, Avondale Rd., Taradale, Hawke's Bay, NZ), da. of the late Henry Shearburn Clark, of Fenhill, Hawke's Bay, NZ:—
(By 1st m.) Mark Donald Carlyon William (Ballinahinch, RD2, Napier, NZ), *b.* 1928: *m.* 1955, Patricia, da. of Judge A. A. Whitehead, of NZ, and has issue living, Malcolm Robert, *b.* 1956,—Douglas William, *b.* 1958,—Christopher Mark, *b.* 1961,—Philip John Edgar, *b.* 1964.

The 1st baronet, Sir Benjamin Collins Brodie, D.C.L., F.R.S., a distinguished surgeon, was Pres. of Roy. So., Serjeant-Surgeon to King William IV., and to Queen Victoria, and first Surgeon-in-Ordinary to the late Prince Consort : the 2nd baronet was Waynflete Professor of Chemistry, Oxford Univ., and the 3rd baronet was High Sheriff for Surrey 1912.

BROMHEAD, Creation (U.K.) 1806, of Thurlby, Lincolnshire.

[Name pronounced "**Brumhead.**"]

Sir BENJAMIN DENIS GONVILLE BROM-HEAD, *O.B.E.,* 5th *Baronet,* son of the late Major Edward Gonville Bromhead, el. son of 4th baronet; *b.* May 7th, 1900; *s.* his grandfather, *Sir* BENJAMIN PARNELL, *C.B.,* 1935; *ed.* at Wellington Coll. ; Lieut.-Col. (retired) Frontier Force Regt. (Indian Army) ; was Political Agent N. Waziristan and N.-W. Frontier Province 1945-7 ; Iraq 1920 (medal with clasp), Waziristan 1922-4 (wounded, medal with clasp), N.-W, Frontier of India 1930 (despatches, medal with clasp). Waziristan 1937 (despatches); O.B.E. (Civil) 1943: *m.* 1938, Nancy Mary, only da. of the late T. S. Lough, of Buenos Aires, Argentina, and has issue.

Arms—Azure, on a bend argent, between two leopards' faces or, a mural crown gules, between two fleurs-de-lis sable. **Crest**—Out of a mural crown gules, an unicorn's head argent, armed or, in the mouth a rose gules, slipped and leaved proper.
By concord property is increased.   *Seat*—Thurlby Hall, Lincoln.

Son living—JOHN DESMOND GONVILLE, b. Dec. 21st, 1943; ed. at Wellington.

Daughters living—Diana Jane Gonville, b. 1940: m. 1966, Dr. Paul Sherwood, of 86, Portland Pl., W1, and has issue living, Robin Paul Austen, b. 1969,—Julian George, b. 1974.——Anne Kathleen Gonville, b. 1942: m. 1965, Robin James German, of Lullington House, Lullington, Burton-on-Trent, and has issue living, Patrick Benjamin James, b. 1967,—Robin Piers Gonville, b. 1969,—Alexander Henry Bromhead, b. 1971.

Brother living—Edmund de Gonville Hosking, b. 1903; ed. at Wellington Coll.; Lieut.-Col. (retired) Indian Army; N.-W. Frontier of India 1930 (medal), Burma 1943-5 (1939-45 star, Burma star, Defence medal, British War medal): m. 1938, Joan, da. of the late Brig. Sir Henry Lawrence Scott, CB, DSO, MC, and has issue living, John Edmund Gonville (Duiker House, Fencott, Islip, Oxford,) b. 1939; ed. at RAF Coll., Cranwell; Pilot BOAC,—David Gonville (The Old Bell House Coulston Wilts.), b. 1944; ed. at St. Andrews, S. Africa, and RMA; Capt. R. Regt. of Wales; Gen. Ser. Medal (Clasps), S. Arabia and N. Ireland: m. 1970, Susan, da. of Cdr. R. H. Fyson, DSC, JP, RN, and has issue living, James Henry de Gonville b. 1974, Annabel Suzanne de Gonville b. 1973,—Jaqueline Anne Gonville, b. 1942: m. 1971, James Boonzaier, of 33, Victory Gdns., Heyton Rd., Victory Park, Johannesburg. Address,—c/o Standard Bank, 28, Northumberland Av. WC2.

Sisters living—Dorothea, b. 1898 : m. 1919, Major Roland William Wrigley Grimshaw, formerly Indian Army, who d. 1933, and has issue living, Kathleen Vera Anne, b. 1924 : European War 1939-45 in W.R.N.S. Residence, The White House, Coates, Cirencester, Gloucestershire. ——Anne Marie Gonville, b. 1905 : m. 1928, Brigadier Keith Cyril Darlington Dawson, O.B.E., Indian Army (ret.), of Balaka, 176, Barkly St., Beleura Hill, Mornington 3931, Victoria, Australia.

Collateral Branch living.

Issue of the late Major Benjamin Gonville Bromhead, 2nd son of 4th baronet, b. 1876, d. 1939: m. 1912, Edith Maud, who d. 1975, da. of the late Lt.-Col. R. C. Andrews, Indian Army:—

Robert Benjamin Gonville, CBE (The Wing, Thurlby Hall, Aubourn, Lincoln), b. 1913; ed. at Dover Coll.; Col. (ret.) late Roy. Berkshire (Duke of Edinburgh's R. Regt.); Burma 1943 (MBE), Cyprus 1958 (despatches, OBE); Ser. Adviser to British High Commr. in Nigeria 1960-63; Col. the Duke of Edinburgh's R. Regt. (Berks. and Wilts.) 1965-70; MBE (Mil.) 1943, OBE (Mil.) 1958, CBE (Mil.) 1966: m. 1947, Mary Traill, da. of the late Harold McMeekin, of Bearsden, Dunbartonshire.——Kathleen Constance, b. 1915: m. 1941, Lt.-Col. Cyril Frederick Hembrough Walter, Indian Army, of Hanover House, Curry Rivel, Langport, Som., and has issue living, Jonathan, b. 1944.

Anthony Bromhead of Wheatley, Notts, supported Charles I and was killed at Newark. His el. son Benjamin purchased Thurlby and Bassingham manors, Lincs. and d. 1702. Bordman Bromhead of Thurlby m. 1756, Frances, da. and heir of William Gonville, last male heir of family whose ancestor, Edmund de Gonville founded Gonville Hall (now Gonville and Caius Coll.), Camb., 1348. Their son, Lt.-Gen. Sir Gonville Bromhead, was the 1st baronet.

BROMLEY, Creation (G.B.) 1757, of East Stoke, Nottinghamshire.

Sir RUPERT CHARLES BROMLEY, 10th Baronet; b. April 2nd, 1936; s. his father, Maj. Sir RUPERT HOWE, M.C. 1966; ed. at Michaelhouse, Natal, Rhodes Univ. and Ch. Ch., Oxford; Bar. Inner Temple 1959: m. 1962, Priscilla Hazel, da. of the late Maj. Howard Bourne, HAC, and has issue.

Arms—Quarterly, per fesse indented gules and or. Crest—a pheasant sitting proper.
Residence, Brendon, Selwyn Rd., Kenilworth, Cape Town, S. Africa.

Think firmly.

Sons living—CHARLES HOWARD, b. July 31st, 1963.—— Philip Anthony, b. 1964.——Henry Walford, b. 1970.

Brother living—Maurice David (19, Brent Rd., Baguio City, Philippines), b. 1941: m. 1965, Heather Mary Estcourt-Cutter, and has issue living, Caroline Margaret, b. 1966,—Jennifer Mary, b. 1968.

Daughters living of 8th Baronet—Marion Victoria, b. 1908.——Anne, b. 1915: m. 1939, Capt. Thomas Henry Perceval Lloyd, KOYLI, of 724, Martini Gdns., Gardens, Cape Town, S. Africa, and has issue living, David Anthony Henry, b. 1945,—Mary-Anne, b. 1941, —Arabella Patricia, b. 1954.——Elizabeth Mary, b. 1919: m. 1st, 1940, the 6th Baron Sudeley who d. (on active ser.) 1941: 2ndly, 1965, Maj. Arthur James Robert Collins, CVO, of 38, Clarence Terr., Regent's Park, NW1 4RD; and Kirkman Bank, Knaresborough, Yorks.——Patricia Sophia, b. 1922: m. 1956, John Richard Franco. Residence, Coldstream, Boot Rd., RD3, West Chester, Pennysylvania, USA.

Daughters living of 6th Baronet—Ruperta Sibyl, b. 1901: m. 1924 (marriage dissolved 1933), John Lister Shand, who d. (on active ser. during European War) 1941, son of the late Sir Charles Lister Shand. Residence, Clouds Lodge, East Knoyle, Salisbury.——Esther Lilian, b. 1905: m. 1st, 1927, Major Sir John Donald Alexander Arthur Makgill, 12th Bt., Coldstream Guards, from whom she obtained a divorce 1943; 2ndly, 1946, James J. A. Murray, LL.B., Capt. 1/10th Ghurkha Rifles, who d. 1964. Residence,

Mother living—Dorothy Vera (c/o Standard Bank, Jan Smuts Av., Rosebank, Johannesburg), da. of the late Sir Walford Harmood Montague Selby, KCMG, CB, CVO: m. 1935 (m. diss. 1960), Maj. Sir Rupert Howe Bromley, MC, 9th baronet, who d. 1966.

Collateral Branch living.

Granddaughters of the late Thomas Bromley, 5th son of 3rd baronet :—
Issue of the late Rupert Fitzroy Bromley, b. 1862, d. 1933: m. 1902, Emilye, who d. 1936, da. of the late Capt. Rennie, C.B.:—
Rosemary Sylvia, b. 1906: m. 1939, Alfred John Owston, who d. 1961, and has issue living, Anthony John Wyndham, b. 1940; ed. at Eton; Bar. Inner Temple 1965: m. 1967, Vivien Patricia Bellamy, and has issue living, Vanessa Rosemary b. 1968, Gavin Anthony b. 1970,—Nicholas Adrian Fenton, b. 1947; ed. at Stowe. Residence, 4, Coniger Rd., SW6.

The 1st baronet, Sir George Smith, married Mary Howe, great granddaughter of Prince Rupert Lord Carrington is descended from a younger brother of the first baronet. Sir George Bromley, 2nd baronet, assumed, by sign-manual in 1778, the name of Bromley in lieu of his patronymic. Sir Robert Bromley, 6th baronet, was Administrator of St. Kitts and Nevis. Sir Maurice Bromley-Wilson, 7th Bt. was High Sheriff of Westmorland 1901, and assumed by Roy. licence 1897 the additional surname and arms of Wilson. Rear-Adm. Sir Arthur Bromley, K.C.M.G., K.C.V.O., 8th baronet, was a Gentleman Usher to H.M. 1927-61, and Ceremonial and Reception Sec., Dominion and Colonial Office 1931-53.

BROOKE, Creation (E.) 1662, of Norton Priory, Cheshire.

FASTE WITHOUT FRAUDE

Sir RICHARD CHRISTOPHER BROOKE, 9th *Baronet ; b.* Aug. 8th, 1888 ; *s.* his father, *Sir* RICHARD MARCUS, 1920 ; ed. at Eton, and Ch. Ch., Oxford (B.A., and M.A. 1923) ; late Lieut. Scots Guards and Special Reserve of Officers ; a J.P. and a D.L. ; formerly a County Councillor for Worcestershire (High Sheriff 1931) ; Vice-Chm. of Worcestershire War Emergency Committee 1939-45 ; was Chm. of Bewdley Div. Unionist Assocn. 1945-46: *m.* 1st, 1912, Marian Dorothea, who *d.* 1965, da. of the late Arthur Charles Innes-Cross [D. Roxburghe, colls.]; 2ndly, 1967, Kathleen Enda, da. of the late Francis Gildea, of Dun Laoghaire, Dublin, and has issue by 1st m.

Arms—Or, a cross engrailed per pale gules and sable.   **Crest**— A brock, or badger, passant proper.

Residence—Oaklands, St. Saviour, Jersey.   **Clubs**—Guards', Kildare Street (Dublin).

Son living—RICHARD NEVILLE, *b.* May 1st, 1915; ed. at Eton; a Chartered Accountant; formerly Lt. Scots Guards; a partner in firm of Price, Waterhouse & Co. (European Firms); 1939-45 War (prisoner, escaped): *m.* 1st, 1937 (m. diss. 1959), Lady Mabel Kathleen Jocelyn, da. of 8th Earl of Roden; 2ndly, 1960, Jean Evison (CHEETHAM), da. of the late Lt.-Col. Arthur Cecil Corfe, DSO, and has issue living, (by 1st m.) Richard David Christopher (Cedar House, Shurlock Row, Twyford, Berks), *b.* 1938: *m.* 1963, Carola Marion, el. da. of Sir Robert Eskine Hill, 2nd Bt., and has issue living, Richard Christopher *b.* 1966, Edward Marcus *b.* 1970,—Piers Leighton (37, Yeoman's Row, SW3), *b.* 1940: *m.* 1967, Susan, da. of John Davenport, of New York City, and has issue living, Sebastian Piers *b.* 1974, Arabella Elinor *b.* 1973. *Residences,* Parc Residentiel de L'Esterel, par les Adrets (Var), France; 14, Rue Cognacq-Jay, Paris VII, France. *Clubs,* Boodle's, Travellers' (Paris).

Daughter living—Audley Marian, *b.* 1912: *m.* 1937, Kurt Adolf Seebohm (Guenthergasse 3, Vienna, Austria), and has issue living, Kurt Florian, *b.* 1939,—Andrea Gabrielle, *b.* 1941.

Collateral Branch living.

Issue of the late Victor Alexander Brooke, 4th son of 7th baronet, *b.* 1857, *d.* 1937 : *m.* 1893, Nora, who *d.* 1957, da. of James Linton, of Palmerston North, New Zealand :—

Victor James, *b.* 1899; a JP; an Alderman of Tamworth City Council, NSW 1931-59; 1914-18 War: *m.* 1927, Doris Isabella, who *d.* 1971, da. of John Bull Ware, and has issue living, Bladen James (Panorama Rd., Calala, via Tamworth, NSW), *b.* 1928; a JP: *m.* 1958, Adeline Ruth, da. of Kenneth Field Clemson, JP, of Wyndella, Collarenebri, NSW, and has issue living, Daron James Clemson *b.* 1964, Kim Anabel *b.* 1959, Anthea Kay *b.* 1960. *Residence,* 46, Panorama Rd., Calala, Tamworth 2340, NSW.——Reginald Marcus, *b.* 1905: *m.* 1927, Beth Allender, who *d.* 1957, da. of Andrew John Telfer, and has issue living, Peter Brabazon (22, Welham St., Beecroft, NSW), *b.* 1929; is a JP: *m.* 1954, Beverley Elizabeth, only da. of Francis William George Vincent, of 14, Virginia St., North Wollongong, NSW, and has issue living, Victor Garry *b.* 1956, —Donald John, *b.* 1932,—Lynton Marcus (of 25, Glen St., Eastwood, NSW), *b.* 1933: *m.* 1956, Wendy Vida, only da. of the late David Arthur Kenneth Miller, of 84, Midson Rd., Epping,— Richard Michael, *b.* 1937,—Pamela Elizabeth, *b.* 1935: *m.* 1953, Anthony John Glasgow, of 34, Russell St., Eastwood, NSW, and has issue living, Peter John *b.* 1954, Denise Beth *b.* 1957. *Residence,* 11, Hill St., Port Macquarie, NSW.

The 1st baronet, Sir Henry Brooke, was four times appointed Sheriff of Cheshire by the Parliamentarians. The 2nd baronet, Sir Richard, was Sheriff of the same co. 1667. The 3rd baronet, Sir Thomas, was Gov. of Chester Castle during the greater part of Queen Anne's reign.

BROOKE, Creation (U.K.) 1903, of Summerton, Castleknock, co. Dublin.

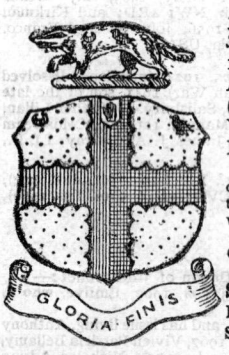

GLORIA FINIS

Glory, the end.

Sir GEORGE CECIL FRANCIS BROOKE, *M.B.E.,* 3rd *Baronet ; b.* March 30th, 1916 ; *s.* his father, *Sir* FRANCIS HUGH, 1954 ; ed. at Stowe ; is Major 17th/21st Lancers ; European War 1939-45 in N. Africa and Italy (wounded, despatches) ; M.B.E. (Mil.) 1949 : *m.* 1959, Lady Melissa Eva Caroline Wyndham-Quin, el. da. of 6th Earl of Dunraven and Mount-Earl, and has issue.

Arms—Or, a cross engrailed per pale gules and sable, in dexter canton a crescent of the second, and in sinister canton a martlet of the third, for difference.   **Crest**—A badger passant proper, charged with a crescent and a martlet gules.

Residence—Glenbevan, Croom, co. Limerick.   **Clubs**— Cavalry, White's, Kildare Street.

Son living—FRANCIS GEORGE WINDHAM, *b.* Oct. 15th 1963.
Daughter living—Emma Nancy, *b.* 1965.
Sister living—Emily Alma (Newnham Park Farm, Crowborough), *b.* 1918.

Uncle living (son of 1st baronet)—Geoffrey Thomas (Knocktoran, Elton, Knocklong, co. Limerick), *b.* 1896; ed. at Winchester; late Lt. 16th/5th Lancers; 1914-18 War (1914 star, Croix de Guerre); *m.* 1942, Millicent Bettine Stewart, who *d.* 1967, da. of Maj. H. H. D. Seaton, of Mount Coote, co. Limerick.

Aunt living (daughter of 1st baronet)—Rose Dorothy. *Residence,* Straffan House Stables, Straffan co. Kildare.

Widow living of 2nd Baronet—MARY LOUISA MABEL (*Mary. Lady Brooke*), da. of Sir John Arnott, 1st Bt. : *m.* 1915, Sir Francis Hugh Brooke, 2nd Bt., who *d.* 1954. *Residence,* Pickering Forest, Celbridge, co. Kildare

Collateral Branches living.

Issue of the late George Brooke, Lt. Ir h Gds., el. son of 1st baronet, *b.* 1877, *d.* (killed in action) 1914: *m.* 1907, Nina, who *d.* 1970, da. of the late Rt. Hon. Lord Arthur William Hill, PC [M. Downshire, colls.)]:—

Nancy Myra, *b.* 1911: *m.* 1st, 1931, John Hollingworth Roberts, from whom she obtained a divorce 1934; 2ndly, 1941, Capt. Michael Stratton, and has issue living, (by 2nd marriage) Patrick Michael, *b.* 1945,—Juliet Nina, *b.* 1942. *Residence,* Hall Farm, Evenley, Brackley, Northants.

Issue of the late Capt. John Brooke, DSC, RN (ret.), 6th son of 1st baronet, *b.* 1887, *d.* 1974: *m.* 1918, Margaret Winifred, MBE (Harts Gorse, Beddingham, Lewes), only da. of the late Col. Francis Tothill, RA, of Roseneath, Fareham:—

Geoffrey Arthur George, *DSC,* (Beech House, Balcombe, Sussex; Army and Navy Club), *b.* 1920; Lt.-Cdr. RN (ret.); 1939-45 War in Europe and Far East (DSC, Atlantic Star, Mediterranean star, Pacific star): *m.* 1956, Venetia Mabel, only da. of the late Capt. the Hon. Oswald Wykeham Cornwallis, OBE, RN (ret.) [see B. Cornwallis, colls.], and has issue living, Caroline Jane, *b.* 1957, —Venetia Anne Margaret, *b.* 1959,—Georgina Emily Rose, *b.* 1963.

Issue of the late Basil Gerald Brooke, 7th son of 1st baronet, *b.* 1894, *d.* 1969: *m.* 1919, Essex Vere, (23 Halsey St., SW3), da. of Sir Charles Vere Gunning, CB, CMG, 7th Bt.:—

Henry Arthur Gunning, MC, *b.* 1923; ed. at Winchester; Col. Queens R. Lancers since 1972; Lt.-Col. Comdg. 16th/5th Queens R. Lancers 1966-69; 1939-45 War in Tunisia and Italy (MC). ——Mary Essex Gunning, *b.* 1928: *m.* 1960, Col. Graham Chatfeild-Roberts, TD, of Jankes Farmhouse, Wakes Colne, Colchester and has issue living, John Henry *b.* 1962,—Essex Jane, *b.* 1963.

This family is a branch of the family of Viscount Brookeborough (of Colebrooke, co. Fermanagh). The 1st baronet, Sir George Frederick was a Director (sometime Gov.) of the Bank of Ireland, over 50 years head of the late firm of George F. Brooke and Son, wine merchants, of Dublin, and High Sheriff for co. Wexford 1882, and for co. Dublin 1898.

BROOKE, Creation (U.K.) 1919, of Almondbury, West Riding of Yorkshire.

Sir JOHN WESTON BROOKE, 3rd *Baronet ; b.* Sept. 26th, 1911 ; *s.* his father, *Major Sir* ROBERT WESTON, *D.S.O., M.C.,* 1942; ed. at Repton, and at Trin. Coll., Camb.; Maj. (ret.) Lovat Scouts; a JP and a DL for Ross-shire: *m.* 1st, 1945 (m. diss. 1963), Rosemary, da. of the late Percy Llewelyn Nevill [see M. Abergavenny, colls.]; 2ndly, 1966, Phoebe Napier Harvey, MB, ChB, widow of Capt. Sir Peter Drummond Macdonald, KBE, and has issue, by 1st marriage.

Arms—Argent, a cross nebulée per pale gules and sable, in the first and fourth quarters a boar's head erased of the last. **Crests**—In front of a sword erect, the blade entwined by two serpents respecting each other proper, a boar's head erased sable.

Seat—Fearn Lodge, Ardgay. Ross-shire. *Clubs*—Royal Ocean Racing, Scottish Conservative (Edinburgh).

Sons living—By 1st marriage—ALISTAIR WESTON, *b.* Sept. 12th, 1947; ed. at Repton.——Charles Weston, *b.* 1951; ed. at Repton.

Sisters living—Elizabeth Jean, *b.* 1910: *m.* 1939, Lieut.-Com. Malcolm Buist, RN, who *d.* 1965, and has issue living, Elizabeth Mary, *b.* 1944,—Jane Christine, *b.* 1947.——Hazel Mary, *b.* 1918: *m.* 1942, Major John Alexander Lochore, Seaforth Highlanders, who *d.* (killed in action) 1944, son of Sir James Lochore, and has issue living, Hamish John (Burgie House, Forres, Morayshire), *b.* 1943; Capt. R. Scots Greys: *m.* 1970, Pollyann Elise, da. of Lt.-Col. the Hon. David Edward Hely-Hutchinson [see E. Donoughmore), and has issue living, Alexander David *b.* 1971. Hugh Mark *b.* 1974,—Fiona Margery, *b.* 1945: *m.* 1971, Lt.-Cdr. Ian Patrick Meiklejohn, RN, of Deer Close, Horse House, nr. Leyburn, Yorks., and has issue living, Clodagh Kirsteen *b.* 1974. *Residence,* Burgie Mains, Forres, Morayshire.

Nor is it by craft.

Sir John Arthur Brooke, 1st baronet, was a Director of John Brooke and Sons (Limited), of Armitage Bridge, Huddersfield, a J.P., and Chm. York House of Laymen.

DE CAPELL BROOKE, Creation (U.K.) 1803, of Oakley, Northamptonshire.
[Extinct 1968.]

Sir EDWARD GEOFFREY DE CAPELL BROOKE, *CBE,* 6th and last *Baronet.*

Collateral Branch living.

Granddaughter of the late Janet Booth (who *m.* 1861, Capt. Joseph Thomas Wetherall, of Loddington House, Kettering), da. of the late Augusta de Capell-Brooke (who *m.* 1835, John Booth, of Glendon Hall, Northants.) yst. da. of 1st Bt.:—

Issue of the late Harold de Capell Wetherall, *b.* 1868, *d.* 1943: *m.* 1905, Laura Burfoot, who *d.* 1955, da. of George Lucas, of Sydney, NSW:—

Noela Eunice (250, Jersey Rd., Woollahra, NSW 2025), *b.* 1907.

BROOKSBANK, Creation (U.K.) 1919, of Healaugh Manor, Healaugh, West Riding of Yorkshire.

Sir EDWARD WILLIAM BROOKSBANK, 2nd *Baronet*, el. son of the late Lieut.-Col. Edward York Brooksbank, 2nd son of 1st baronet ; *b.* June 15th, 1915 ; *s.* his grandfather, *Sir* EDWARD CLITHEROW, 1943 ; ed. at Eton ; Lt.-Col. Queen's Own Yorkshire Yeo. (Hon. Col. 1963-71), and Lord of the Manor of Healaugh: *m.* 1943, Ann, da. of Lt.-Col. Thomas Claud Clitherow, D.S.O., of Hotham Hall, Brough, Yorkshire, and has issue.

Arms—Azure, two bars wavy argent within a bordure or. **Crest**—A white hart's head couped proper, attired or, accolled with two bars wavy azure.

Seats—Healaugh, Tadcaster   Menethorpe Hall, Malton.

Son living—EDWARD NICHOLAS, *b.* Oct. 4th, 1944; ed. at Eton; Capt. The Blues and Royals: *m.* 1970, Emma Myrtle Mary Anne. da. of the Rt. Hon. Richard Frederick Wood, MP [see E. Halifax].

Brothers living—Benjamin John (Tilsmere, Frys Lane, Yateley, Camberley, Surrey), *b.* Sept. 27th, 1918.—Stamp Godfrey (Rock Hill House, Hambledon, Godalming, Surrey), *b.* 1922; ed. at Eton; 1939-45 War with Coldstream Guards: *m.* 1942, Celia Dorothy, da. of the late Maj. the Hon. Sir John Spencer Coke, KCVO [see E. Leicester, colls.], and has issue living, David William, *b.* 1946:   *m.* 1972, Vanessa, el. da. of the late Kenneth A. Whittome,—George Edward Hugh, *b.* 1949.

Sisters living—Diana Hazel (Caixa Postal 34, Rio de Janeiro), *b.* 1914:   *m.* 1936, Robert Froud Norton, who *d.* 1967.——Crystal Elizabeth, *b.* 1924:   *m.* 1st (m. diss. 1960), Henry Desmond Verner Pakenham, CBE [see E. Longford, colls.]; 2ndly, 1960, Ivor George Salmond, OBE, and has issue living, (by 1st m.) [see E. Longford, colls.], (by 2nd m.) Felicity Diana, *b.* 1962.

The 1st baronet, Sir Edward Clitherow Brooksbank (son of the late Edward Brooksbank of Healaugh Manor, Tadcaster, and Newton House, Whitby), was Chm. of Barkston Ash Conservative Asso. for over 40 years.

BROUGHTON, Creation (E.) 1660, of Broughton, Staffordshire.
[Name pronounced "Brawton."]

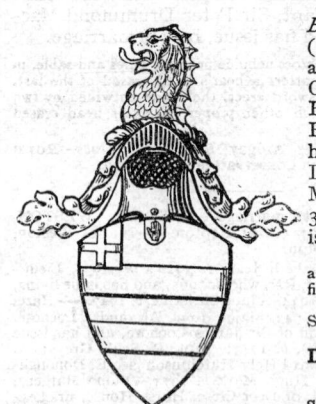

Sir EVELYN DELVES BROUGHTON, 12th *Baronet ; b.* Oct. 2nd, 1915 ; *s.* his father, *Sir* (HENRY JOHN) DELVES, 1942 ; ed. at Eton, and at Trin. Coll., Camb.; formerly 2nd Lieut. Irish Guards (Supplementary Reserve), and Major R.A.S.C. : *m.* 1st, 1947, the Hon. Elizabeth Florence Marion Cholmondeley (from whom he obtained a divorce 1953), da. of 4th Baron Delamere; 2ndly, 1955 (m. diss. 1974), Helen Mary, da. of J. Shore, of Wilmslow, Cheshire; 3rdly, 1974, Mrs. Rona Crammond, and has issue living by 2nd m.

Arms—Argent, two bars gules, on a canton of the second a cross of the field. **Crest**—A sea-dog's head couped gules, finned argent.

Seat—Doddington Park, Nantwich, Cheshire. *Club*—St. James'.

Daughters living—By 2nd marriage—Isabella Delves, *b.* 1958,—Julia Helen Delves, *b.* 1961,—Lavinia Mary, *b.* 1965.

Sister living—Rosamond (*Lady Lovat*), *b.* 1917:   *m.* 1938, the 15th Lord Lovat. *Residences*, Beaufort Castle, Beauly, Inverness-shire; Balblair House, Beauly, Inverness-shire.

Aunt living (daughter of 10th baronet)—Violet Evelyn Delves, *b.* 1894: *m.* 1918, A. Pike, formerly Lieut. Indian Army Reserve, and has issue living, Audley Gareth, *b.* 1931,—Delves Evelyn Mary, *b.* 1919.—Pamela Amice, *b.* 1925. *Residence,* Moonya, Bicheno, Tasmania.

Widow living of 11th Baronet—Diana (*Baroness Delamere*), da. of the late Seymour Caldwell, of Hove, Sussex : *m.* 1st, 19—, Vernon Motion ; 2ndly, 1941, as his second wife, Sir (Henry John) Delves Broughton, 11th Bt., who *d.* 1942; 3rdly, 1943, Gilbert de Preville Colville, who *d.* 1966, having obtained a divorce 1955; 4thly, 1955, as his third wife, the 4th Baron Delamere. *Residences,* 11, Chesterfield Hill, W1; Soysambu, Elmenteita, Kenya.

Collateral Branches living.

Grandchildren of the late Lt.-Col. Geoffrey Delves Broughton, O.B.E. (infra):—
Issue of the late Lt.-Cdr. Peter John Delves Broughton, R.N., *b.* 1915, *d.* 1963:   *m.* 1st, 1940, Nancy Rosemary, yr. da. of the late J. E. Paterson, of Instow; 2ndly, 1948, Evelyn Gunn, da. of the late J. G. Sutherland:—
(By 1st m.) DAVID DELVES, *b.* May 7th, 1942.——(By 2nd m.) Geoffrey Delves, *b.* 1963.——Susan Delves, *b.* 1950.——Patricia Delves, *b.* 1953.——Shelagh Delves, *b.* 1959.

Granddaughters of the late Lt.-Col. Delves Broughton, son of the late Rev. Delves Broughton, 2nd son of 8th baronet :—
Issue of the late Lieut.-Col. Geoffrey Delves Broughton, O.B.E., Welch Regt., *b.* 1880, *d.* 1957 : *m.* 1913, Violet Carnegie, who *d.* 1938, da. of H. Anstey and widow of Talbot Dean-Pitt :—
Elizabeth Jane Delves, *b.* 1918: *m.* 1st, 1940, Lieut. Bernard Willoughby, R.N., who *d.* (on active ser. during European War) 1942 [B. Middleton, colls.]; 2ndly, 194-, Anthony Pim; 3rdly, 1948, Kenneth Phillips, who *d.* 1950; 4thly, 19—, Bruce Clark, and has issue living (by 2nd marriage), Rosemary *b.* 19—.——Ann Joan Delves, *b.* 1922: *m.* 1942 (marriage dissolved 19—), F. P. Lansdell, Lieut R.A. *Residence,*

Descendants (if any) of Vernon Warburton Broughton (*b.* 1864, *d.* 1937), only son of Vernon Delves Broughton, el. son of the Rev. Thomas Delves Broughton, el. son of Thomas Delves Broughton, 3rd son of 6th baronet.

Grandchildren of the late Cdr. Cecil Delves Broughton, RN, 3rd son of the Rev. Thomas Delves Broughton (ante):—
Issue of the late Brigadier Theodore Delves Broughton, *b.* 1872, *d.* 1944 : *m.* 1st, 1897, Marion Julia, who *d.* 1905, da. of the late Charles Augustus Theodore Bouwens ; 2ndly, 1908, Eva Joanna, who *d.* 1959, el. da. of the late Col. John Warre Sill [Sutton, Bt. colls.] :—
(By 1st m.) Brian Charles (Brambles, Grove Lane, Iden, Rye, Sussex), *b.* 1903; ed. at Marlborough: *m.* 1931, Margaret Gwenda, da. of the late Edmund Law, and has issue living, *Rev.* Simon Brian Hugo (Christ Church Parsonage, PO Box 602, Chittagong, E. Pakistan), *b.* 1933; ed. at Marlborough, and at Exeter Coll., Oxford (MA),—Ann Marion (5, Thorncliffe Rd., Mapperley Park, Nottingham), *b.* 1939; a SRN.——Diana Sill, *b.* 1920.

Granddaughter of the late Gen. William Edward Delves Broughton, 2nd son of Thomas Delves Broughton (ante) :—
Issue of the late Maj.-Gen. William Edward Delves Broughton, *b.* 1837, *d.* 1895: *m.* 1870, Laura Margaret Buchan, who *d.* 1906, el. da. of Stephen Lawson, 7th Hussars :—
Ethel Georgina : *m.* 1908, Robert Stoughton, who *d.* 1925, and has issue living, Robert Knyvett Clarke (of Wintour, Crossway Green, Chepstow, Monmouthshire), *b.* 1909 ; is an A.M.I.E.E. and Assist. Ch. Mechanical Engineer, R.N. Propellant Factory, Caerwent, near Chepstow, Monmouthshire : *m.* 1941, Christine Quested Culmer, da. of the late A. G. Hunt, and has issue living, Robert Knyvett Quested *b.* 1942, Sarah Christine Quested *b.* 1943,—Ethel Margaret Mary, *b.* 1912. *Residence,* 8, Cornwall Road, Bedford.

Grandchildren of the late Maj.-Gen. William Edward Delves Broughton (*b.* 1837) (ante):—
Issue of the late Lieut.-Col. Legh Harley Delves Broughton, D.S.O., *b.* 1873. *d.* 1942 : *m.* 1903, Constance, who *d.* 1965, da. of George Randall Johnson, of Feniton Court, Honiton, Devon:—
Legh Randall Delves (18, Trafalgar Sq., Seapoint, Cape Town, S. Africa) *b.* 1904; ed. at Eton, and at Univ. Coll., Oxford (BA); late Nigerian Civil Ser.: *m.* 1st, 1944, Esse Maria, who *d.* 1971, da. of the late C. J. Petersen, of Durban, S. Africa; 2ndly, 1972, Norah Leila Mountjoy, da. of the late H. M. Bartlett, of Cape Town.——John Rowlls, *b.* 1910; ed. at Marlborough: *m.* 1942, Ellen du Toit.——Agnes Laura Margret Delves, *b.* 1906: *m.* 1934, Cdr. Christopher Mildmay Hall, RN [Mordaunt, Bt.], and has issue living, Jocelyn Daphne Margret (*Lady Critchett*), *b.* 1935: *m.* 1964, Sir Ian George Lorraine Critchett, 3rd Bt.,—Judith Anne, *b.* 1936: *m.* 1964, Jonathan A. Coode, of Trebyan House, Bodmin, Cornwall, and has issue living, Victoria Arundel *b.* 1967, Claire Margaret, *b.* 1968, Laura Cicely *b.* 1972,—Catherine Elizabeth, *b.* 1941: *m.* 1967, Wing Cdr. Philip G. Pinney, MVO, of Pond House, Pyrton, Watlington, Oxon., and has issue living, Charlotte Russell *b.* 1969, Ann Margret *b.* 1970. *Residence,* Higher Boswarva, Newbridge, Penzance, Cornwall.

Granddaughters of the late Col. John Delves Broughton, son of the late Gen. William Edward Delves Broughton (ante) :—
Issue of the late Brian Delves Broughton, *b.* 1879, *d.* 1926 : *m.* 1912, Elizabeth Annie, da. of H. K. Osborn, of Ladysmith, Natal :—
Cecilia Dorothy, *b.* 1913 : *m.* 1938, Major Guise Montgomery Foxton Beaumont, E.D., and has issue living, Michael Foxton (9, Leicester St., Grahamstown, Cape, S. Africa), *b.* 1939: *m.* 1966, Marion Egerton, da. of B. E. B. White, of Glen Cliff, Bedford, Cape, S. Africa, and has issue living, Warrick Foxton *b.* 1967, Bruce Egerton *b.* 1969,—Keith Alan (Box 93, Grahamstown 6140, Cape, S. Africa), *b.* 1945: *m.* 1969, Lynda Jean, yst. da. of C. W. Giles, of Pietermaritzburg, Natal, and has issue living, Gavin Guise *b.* 1970, Stephen John *b.* 1972. *Address,* Brushwood, Box 93, Grahamstown, Cape. S. Africa.——Lucy Margaret. *b.* 1914: *m.* 1940, Francis Alfred Heritage, of 170, E. Wilston Rd., Newmarket 4051, Brisbane, Qld., Aust., and has issue.——Joan Christine, *b.* 1916: *m.* 1942, Leonard Newnham Malyon, of Bryanson, PO, Winters Klooff, Natal, S. Africa, and has issue living, Rodney Charles, *b.* 1956,—Sandra Ellen, *b.* 1944: *m.* 1969, Sinclair Stanley Blunden, of Rookwood Tylden, Queenstown, Cape, and has issue living, Merle Iris *b.* 1970.

Grandchildren of the late Edward Walthall Delves WALTHALL, son of the late Edward Delves Broughton, son of the late Edward Delves Broughton, 5th son of 6th baronet :—
Issue of the late Capt. Henry Douglas Delves WALTHALL, O.B.E., *b.* 1880, *d.* 1931: *m* 1911, Hilda Maud (now of The Orchard, St. John's Road, Watford, Herts), da. of the late Frederick Leigh Hancock (J.P. for Flintshire and High Sheriff 1910), of The Warren, Broughton, near Chester :—
Leigh Edward Delves, *C.B.E., D.S.C., R.N.*, *b.* 1914 ; became Capt. 1952 ; was Director of Air Equipment Admiralty 1959-61 ; European War 1939-45 as Fleet Air Arm Pilot (D.S.C.); *m.* 1951, Dorothy Margaret, el. da. of the late Hugh Robert Leonard, of Ladywalk, Heronsgate, Hertfordshire, and has issue living, Fiona Ann, *b.* 1953,—Louisa Delves, *b.* 1956,—Theodora Serena Delves, *b.* 1959. *Residence,* Hillhouse Farm, Sapperton, Cirencester. *Club,* Army and Navy.——Daphne, *b.* 1912.

The annals of this old Staffordshire family extend to *temp.* Henry VI. Sir Brian Broughton 3rd Bt., was M P. for Newcastle 1715-24. He *m.* 1710, Elizabeth, only da. and sole heir of Sir Thomas Delves, 3rd Bt., of Doddington, co. Chester. The 4th baronet, their son, who *s.* also to the Doddington Estates in Cheshire, assumed the additional name of Delves, in compliance with the terms of his grandfather's will. The 6th Bt. was High Sheriff of Staffordshire in 1740, and the 9th in 1859.

BROUN, Creation (N.S.) 1686, of Colstoun, Haddingtonshire.

Let majesty flourish.

Sir LIONEL JOHN LAW BROUN, 12th
Baronet; b. April 25th, 1927; *s.* his father,
Sir (JAMES) LIONEL, 1962.

Arms—Gules, a chevron between three fleurs-de-lis or.
Crest—A lion rampant, holding in the dexter forepaw a
fleur-de-lis or.

Residence,—Coonimba, Coonamble, NSW, Australia
2820.

Widow living of the 11th Baronet—GEORGIE (*Lady Broun*)
(Colstoun, Gunnedah, Pottinger, NSW, Aust.),
yst. da. of the late Henry Law, of Kearon, Burgoyne
St., Gordon, N.S. Wales: *m.* 1925, Sir (James) Lionel
Broun, 11th Bt., who *d.* 1962.

Collateral Branches living.

Issue of the late William Arthur Broun,
2nd son of 10th baronet, *b.* 1876, *d.*
1925: *m.* 1916, Marie Victoria, who
d. 1964, da. of W. McIntyre, of
N. Sydney:—

WILLIAM WINDSOR, *b.* 1917; ACA (Australia); 1939-45 War as Lieut. AIF: *m.* 1952,
D'Hrie, da. of Frank R. King, of Bingara, NSW, and has issue living D'Hrie Sheree, *b.* 1956,—
Rani Beverley, *b.* 1959. *Residence,* 23, Clanalpine St., Mosman, NSW.——Hulance Haddington
(462, Pittwater Rd., N. Manly 2100, NSW), *b.* 1919; 1939-45 War as Sergeant Pilot RAAF,
Middle East 1940-42: *m.* 1947, Joy Maud, da. of A. L. Stack, of Mosmann, NSW, and has issue
living, Robyn Joy, *b.* 1948,—Wayne Hercules, *b.* 1952,—Julie Christine, *b.* 1955.——Lionel
McIntyre, *b.* 1921; 1939-45 War with RAAF: *m.* 1955, Shirley, da. of A. L. Stack (ante) and
has issue living, Walter Leslie, *b.* 1961,—Steven McIntyre, *b.* 1963,—Lucinda Maree, *b.* 1957——
John Hercules August (13, Kilroy St., Gunnedah, NSW), *b.* 1923: *m.* 1st, 1953, Patricia Johnson ;
2ndly, 1962, Margaret, da. of Reginald Chapman, of Dubbo, NSW, and has issue living, (by 1st m.)
Richard, *b.* 1954,—(by 2nd m.) Tracy Lee, *b.* 1963,—Phoebe Margaret, *b.* 1968.

Issue of the late Reginald Augustus Broun, 3rd son of 10th baronet, *b.* 1878, *d.* 1948:
m. 1910, Alice Maude (now of Gunnedah, N.S. Wales), da. of W. B. Wilkinson, of
Mosman, Sydney, New South Wales:—

Reginald William Wilkinson, *b.* 1912. *Residence,* Dalblair, Gunnedah, NSW.——Noel Marian,
b. 1918: *m.* 1944, Charles Edward Robinson, and has issue living, Bernard James, *b.* 1946:
m. 1968, Annie, da. of James Kernihan, and has issue living, Nicole Marie *b.* 1974. *Residence,*
Southern Wood, 15, Cambridge Rd., Mooroolbark, Vic.. Aust. 3138.

Issue of the late Alice Marion Broun, da. of 10th baronet, *b.* 1881, *d.* 1969:
m. 1904, Leslie Sprague, who *d.* 1942:—

Mervyn Broun (60, Douglas St. East, St. Ives, NSW), *b.* 1913: *m.* 1940, Gwendoline Marjorie
Stone, and has issue living, Denzil Mervyn (Killurin, Birregurra, Vic.), *b.* 1941: *m.* 1964, Susan
Margaret Calvert, and has issue living, Steven Denzil Broun *b.* 1966, Andrew Noel Mervyn *b.*
1967,—Leslie Philip (71, Evansdale Rd., Hawthorn, Vic., Aust.), *b.* 1943: *m.* 1970, Kathryn
Ann Herbert.——Ian Broun, *b.* 1920.——Audrey Marion, *b.* 1904: *m.* 1935, Capt. Felix Lionel
Edge, of Binda Vale, Toolamba, Vic., and has issue living, Derek Felix, *b.* 1942,—Wendy Marion,
b. 1939: *m.* 1964, John Seymour Wilson, of 51, Cascade St., N. Balwyn 3104, Melbourne, Vic.,
and has issue living, Bruce John *b.* 1965, Darren Geoffrey *b.* 1967, Philip Felix *b.* 1970.——Dirleen
Muriel, *b.* 1909: *m.* 1936, Richard Molesworth, of 19, Linacre Rd., Hampton, Melbourne, Vic.,
and has issue living, Michael John Leslie, *b.* 1941,—Simon Richard, *b.* 1954,—Corinne Dirleen,
b. 1949.——Zelma Elizabeth, *b.* 1912: *m.* 1939, Reginald John Essington King, of 15, Moralla
Rd., Kooyong, Melbourne, Vic., and has issue living, Jonathan Leslie Essington (Headley Rd.,
Leatherhead, Surrey), *b.* 1942: *m.* 1975, Jane Lewis, and has issue living, Lowanna Katherine
Ruth *b.* 1975,—David James Essington (16, Docker St., Richmond, Vic.), *b.* 1945: *m.* 1971, Susan
Spencer George, and has issue living, Samuel Antonie Essington *b.* 19—.—Julie Essington,
b. 1940: *m.* 1964, Vere David Urquhart Hunt, of 32, Montaito Av., Toorak, Vic., and has issue
living, Peter Anthony Urquhart *b.* 1966, Timothy John McKay *b.* 1970, Sari Amanda *b.* 1968,—
Belinda Essington, *b.* 1949: *m.* 1973, Richard John Barber, of 84, Rae St., N. Fitzroy, Vic.

Grandchildren of the late David Limond Broun (infra):—
Issue of the late William James Broun, *b.* 1882, *d.* 1963: *m.* 1st, 1914, Miriam Rheta,
da. of Sidney T. Peryman, of Mosman, Sydney, NSW; 2ndly, 1947, Dorothea Esther,
who *d.* 1968, da. of David A. Strahley, of Sandy Knowe, Inverell, N.S.W.:—

(By 1st m.) William James Peryman (24a, Gladstone Parade, Lindfield, NSW), *b.* 1922; ed. at
Sydney Univ. (B.E.); formerly Lt. RAN: *m.* 1956, Penelope Jane, da. of the late W. T. H.
Horn, of Canberra, and has issue living, William James Harvey *b.* 1958,—Anthony Fraser
Cameron, *b.* 1960.——Malcolm David (61, Greenwich Rd., Greenwich, NSW 2065), *b.* 1935; ed. at
Sydney Univ. (BA, LLB); Bar. NSW 1959: *m.* 1st, 1962 (m. diss. 1971), Janet Patricia, da. of
the late Allan Douglas Edwards; 2ndly, 1972, Wendy Sue, da. of W. J. Hannelly, and has issue
living (by 1st m.) Alexander Alan Hercules, *b.* 1965,—Charlotte Doriam, *b.* 1963,—Sophie Amelia,
b. 1969,—(by 2nd m.) Nicholas Malcolm, *b.* 1975.——Wilga Joan, *b.* 1917: *m.* 1937, Ian Cecil de
Courcey Dutton, of 59, Barraba Rd., Manilla, NSW, and has issue living, Ian Herbert, *b.* 1940,—
Peter James, *b.* 1952,—Christopher Philip, *b.* 1955,—Anne Wilga *b.* 1938,—Melissa Judith,
b. 1945,—Pauline, *b.* 1946,—Miriam, *b.* 1953.——Mario Rheta, *b.* 1918: *m.* 1st 1943 (m. diss.
1970) Maxwell Charles Halliday, MDS; 2ndly, 1970, the Hon. Mr. Justice (Martin Francis)
Hardie of Linton, 27, Stanton Rd., Mosman, NSW 2088, and has issue living, (by 1st m.) Miriam
Victoria, *b.* 1948.——Catherine Eleanor Broun, *b.* 1952.——Dorothy Lenglen, *b.* 1919: *m.* 1947,
Walter Woods, of The Woods, Boundary Rd., West Pennant Hills, NSW, and has issue living,
Michael William Frank, *b.* 1954,—Adam Lindsay Broun, *b.* 1956,—Justin Thomas, *b.* 1957,—
Margarita Henry, *b.* 1959,—Sara Dorothy Broun, *b.* 1962.——June Joy, *b.* 1921: *m.* 1949, Ross
Abbott Hayes, MB, BS, of 15A, Kulgoa Rd., Bellevue Hill, NSW, and has issue living, Clive
Broun Abbott, *b.* 1950,—James Abbott Broun, *b.* 1953,—David Broun Abbott, *b.* 1954,—Matthew
George Broun, *b.* 1964.

Issue of the late David Limond Broun, son of 9th baronet, *b.* 1855, *d.* 1934: *m.* 1877,
Margaret, who *d.* 1928, da. of the late Martin Kelly, of Stony Creek, Bundarra,
New England, N.S. Wales :—

Eleanor Gale, *b.* 1884: *m.* 1915, Hercules Christian McIntyre. *Residence,* Holmsdale, 32, Cremorne
Rd., Cremorne, NSW, 2090.

Grandchildren, if any, of the late Peter Nicholas Broun, Colonial Sec., of **Swan River**, son of the late William Broun, 2nd son of 6th baronet, *b.* 17—, *d.* 1846, and *m.* 1824, Caroline, da. of James Simpson, by whom he had issue, M'Bride, James, Charles, and five daughters.

Granddaughter of the late Richard M'Bryde Broun, son of the late William Broun (ante):—
Issue of the late Capt. William Luke Broun (P. and O. Co.'s Ser.), *b.* 1850, *d.* 1935: *m.* 1st, 1886, Harriet Louisa, who *d.* 1906, da. of the late William Boodle, solicitor, of Cheltenham; 2ndly, 1909, Alice Glen, who *d.* 1959, widow of Charles Wilson, of Melbourne, Australia :—
(By 2nd m.) Edith Elizabeth McBryde, *b.* 1911: *m.* 1940, Douglas Matthew Duder Raper, of Aldehurst, Aldeburgh, Suffolk, and has issue living, Rosemary Elizabeth Broun *b.* 1949: *m.* 1972, George Antony Alexander Johnson, of 15, Petersham Mews, SW7,—Sarah Christian Broun, *b.* 1952.

This family claims descent from George Broun of Colstoun, who married, 1543, Marion Hay, da. of 2nd Lord Hay of Yester, ancestor of the Marquess of Tweeddale. The dowry of the lady consisted of the famous " Coulston Pear," which her remote ancestor, Hugo de Gifford, of Yester, a famous necromancer, who *d.* 1267, was supposed to have invested with the extraordinary virtue of securing unfailing prosperity for the family who might possess it. This pear is still preserved at Colstoun, and even when shorn of its superstitious surroundings is, nevertheless, a wonderful **vegetable curiosity**. Sir George Broun, 2nd baronet, *m.* 1692, Lady Elizabeth Mackenzie, da. of the 1st Earl of Cromartie, and it is reported that during the first night after her marriage when she slept at Colstoun, she dreamed she had eaten the pear. Her brother-in-law looked upon this as a bad omen, and expressed great fears that she would be an instrument to destroy the house of Colstoun. Be this as it may, Sir George sold the estates, and in 1718 was drowned with his family in the Tyne. On the death of the 5th baronet without male issue, his cousin the Rev. Richard Broun (the next heir) **never** assumed the title as 6th baronet, but his el. son James was served heir-male-general to his cousin, the 5th baronet, in 1826, and assumed the Baronetcy as 7th baronet.

BROWN, Creation (U.K.) 1863, of Richmond Hill.

There is unity among brothers

Sir CHARLES FREDERICK RICHMOND BROWN, 4th *Baronet*, son of the late Frederick Richmond Brown, 2nd son of 2nd baronet ; *b.* Dec. 6th, 1902; *s.* his uncle, *Sir* MELVILLE RICHMOND, 1944 ; ed. at Eton ; is Capt. (retired) Welsh Guards, and Lieut.-Col. Comdg. 7th Batn. Green Howards (T.A.) and a D.L. of N. Riding of Yorks.: *m.* 1st, 1933, Audrey (from whom he obtained a divorce 1948), da. of the late Brig.-Gen. the Hon. Everard Baring, C.V.O., C.B.E. [*see* B. Revelstoke, colls.] ; 2ndly 1951 (m. diss. 1968), the Hon. Gwendolin Carlis Meysey-Thompson, youngest da. of 1st Baron Knaresborough; 3rdly, 1969, Pauline Emily Gwyneth Mansel, da. of the late Arden Henry William Llewelyn Morgan, and widow of Edward John Westgarth Hildyard, FSA, FRES, of Middleton Hall, Pickering, Yorks., and has issue by 1st m.

Arms—Quarterly ; 1st and 4th, gules, a chevron or between two bears' paws erased in chief argent, and four hands conjoined in saltire of the second in base ; on a chief engrailed gold, an eagle displayed sable, *Brown* ; 2nd and 3rd, argent a chevron nebuly sable between two moorhens close in chief proper and a fleur-de-lys in base azure, *Luxmoore*. **Crest**—A bear's paw erased argent, issuant out of a wreath of oak vert, holding a sinister hand proper.
Residence—Stonely Woods, Fadmoor, York. *Club*—Guards'.

Son living—By 1st marriage—GEORGE FRANCIS RICHMOND, *b.* Feb. 3rd, 1938 ; is Lieut. Welsh Guards; Extra Equerry to HRH the Duke of Edinburgh 1961-63, and ADC to Gov. of Queensland 1963-65.

Daughters living—By 1st marriage—Jennifer Richmond, *b.* 1934.——Elizabeth Maud Richmond *b.* 1943: *m.* 1970, Guy M. A. Crawford, of St. Blanes, Dunblane, Perthshire.

Sister living—Diana Sybil Richmond, *b.* 1913 : *m.* 1940, Christopher Henry Bacon, who *d.* 1956 [*see* Bacon, Bt., colls.]. *Residence*, Warren Bank, Broughton, near Chester.

Collateral Branches living.

Grandchildren of the late Col. James Clifton Brown (infra):—
Issue of the late Brig.-Gen. Howard Clifton Brown, *b.* 1868 ; *d.* 1946 : *m.* 1903, Mary Eirene, who *d.* 1951, da. of the late Hon. Sir Henry Edward Agincourt Hodges, a Puisne Judge of Supreme Court, Melbourne :—
Elizabeth Clifton, *b.* 1914 ; formerly Co. Assist. A.T.S.: *m.* 1944, Major Edmund Archibald Calvert, late Roy. Dragoons [Cholmeley, Bt.], and has issue living, Henry Clifton, *b.* 1948,—Jennifer Clifton, *b.* 1947: *m.* 1970, Josceline Crove, of 27, Cloncurry St., SW6, and has issue living, Miranda Clifton *b.* 1974. *Residences*, Kilnwood, Faygate, Sussex; Fasnakyle, Cannich, Inverness-shire.——Katherine Clifton, *b.* 1917: *m.* 1946, Ion H. T. Garnett-Orme.——Margaret Eirene Clifton (*Baroness Amherst of Hackney*), *b.* 1921: *m.* 1939, the 3rd Baron Amherst of Hackney. *Residences*, Shroner Wood, Martyr Worthy, Winchester; 29, Eaton Mews South, SW1.

Issue of the late Edward Clifton CLIFTON-BROWN, *b.* 1870, *d.* 1944 (having assumed by deed poll 1923 (enrolled at College of Arms) the additional surname of Clifton): *m.* 1897, **Dora Winifred**, who *d.* 1962, youngest da. of the late George Hanbury, of Blythewood, Maidenhead:—

Geoffrey Benedict, *b.* 1899; ed. at Eton; Lieut.-Col. (retired) 12th Roy. Lancers; European War 1939-41 (despatches); sat as M.P. for Bury St. Edmunds Div. of W. Suffolk (C) July 1945 to Feb. 1950: *m.* 1927, Robina Margaret Hill, da. of the late Rowland Sutton (*see* Sutton, Bt., colls.], and has issue living, Edward Geoffrey (14, St. James Gdns., W11), *b.* 1928: *m.* 1st, 1953, Jillian Mary (from whom he obtained a divorce 1958), da. of David Walkinshaw, of Bishopton, Hall Moon Hill, Haslemere; 2ndly, 1960, Sarah Simonetta, younger da. of Roger Herbert Frances, OBE, of 7, Clarendon Close, W2, and has issue living, (by 1st marriage) James Benedict *b.* 1956, Margaret Joanna *b.* 1957, (by 2nd marriage) Louisa *b.* 1961, Sarah *b.* 1964,—Robert Lawrence (Little Bradley House, nr. Haverhill, Suffolk), *b.* 1929: *m.* 1952, Florence Elizabeth Lindsay, el. da. of Ronald Arthur Vestey [*see* Vestey, Bt.], and has issue living, Geoffrey Robert *b.* 1953, Ronald Colin *b.* 1963, Jane Elizabeth *b.* 1954, Angela Florence *b.* 1956. *Residence,* The Old Rectory, Cockfield, Bury St. Edmunds.——Anthony George, *TD, b.* 1903; ed. at Eton, and at Trin. Coll., Camb. (BA 1942); an Alderman of City of London 1950-60, Sheriff 1957-58 and a Lt. 1950-60, and an O.St.J.; formerly Maj. RA (TA); 1939-45 War (wounded); a Member of Court of Assists. of Merchant Taylors' Co. (Master 1945-46, Upper Renter Warden 1953-54): *m.* 1st, 1930, Delia Charlotte G., who *d.* 1947, da. of the late George Edward Wade; 2ndly, 1949, Phyllis Adrienne, da. of the late Francis Harvey, of Dublin, and has issue living, (by 1st m.) Georgiana Elmira *b.* 1934: *m.* 1962, Anthony Charles Bailey, LLB, Bar.-at-Law, of 23, Ossulton Way, Hampstead Garden Suburb, N2, and has issue living, Edward Hugh Clifton *b.* 1966, Jane Delia *b.* 1964,—Felicity Caroline *b.* 1970,—Meliora Delia, *b.* 1936: *m.* 1957, John Norman Abell of 451, Russell Hill Rd., Toronto 7, Ont., Canada, yr. son of Sir George Edmond Brackenbury Abell, KCIE, OBE, and has issue living, Martin George *b.* 1962, Antony Philip Norman *b.* 1964, Sarah Elizabeth *b.* 1959,—Julia Mary, *b.* 1942. *Residence,* 7, Via del Moro 10, Rome 00153, Italy.——Rhona (*Lady Cracroft-Amcotts*), *b.* 1901: *m.* 1927, Lt.-Col. Sir Weston Cracroft-Amcotts, MC, late RE, who *d.* 1975, and has issue living, Rosemary Grace (Exton Cottage, Exton, Southampton), *b.* 1928: *m.* 1952, Lt.-Cdr. Gervis Hugh Frere Frere-Cook, RN (ret.), who *d.* 1974, and has issue living, Simon Aubrey Cracroft *b.* 1955, David Bartle Cracroft *b.* 1957, Jane Elizabeth Cracroft *b.* 1954,—Marian Cicely, *b.* 1931: *m.* 1957, Thomas Charles Weguelin Micklem, of Foxbridge Farm, Kirdford, Sussex, and has issue living, Jeremy Charles Cracroft *b.* 1961, Philippa Rhona *b.* 1958, Sylvia Diana *b.* 1964,—Bridget Katharine, *b.* 1933: *m.* 1959, Robert Peel Charles Eley, of Chartfield House, South Carlten, Lincoln, and has issue living, Charles William Amcotts *b.* 1963, Annabel Louise Cracroft *b.* 1961,—Penelope Sylvia, *b.* 1938. *Residence,* Hackthorn Hall, Lincoln.

Issue of the late Douglas Clifton Brown, *b.* 1879, *d.* 1958   *cr. Viscount Ruffside 1951* [see that title] :—

Grandchildren of the late Col. James Clifton Brown, second son of the late Alexander Brown, el. son of 1st baronet:—
Issue of the late Capt. Cedric Clifton Brown, *b.* 1887, *d.* 1968: *m.* 1938, Mary Aymee Lilian, OBE (Lower Farm, South Wootton, King's Lynn, Norfolk), da. of the late Rev. John A. Labouchere:—
Peter Cedric Clifton (Longacres, Finchampstead, Berks.), *b.* 1939: *m.* 1968, Petronelle, yr. da. of S. L. Grubb, of Beechmount, Fethard, co. Tipperary, and has issue living, John Cedric Clifton, *b.* 1970,—Louis Peter, *b.* 1971, Henry Samuel Clifton, *b.* 1974.——Anthony John Clifton (Perces, Greenstead Green, Halstead, Essex, and Congham Manor, Kings Lynn, Norfolk), *b.* 1942: *m.* 1967, Françoise, da. of M. Mooser, of Neuchâtel, Switzerland, and has issue living, Douglas Alexandre Clifton *b.* 1968,—Philippe Anthony, *b.* 1975.——Ursula Mary Clifton, *b.* 1941.

Descendants of the late Alexander Hargreaves Brown (3rd son of the late Alexander Brown, el. son of 1st baronet), who was *cr. a Baronet* 1903:—
See Pigott-Brown, Bt.

Sir William Brown, 1st baronet, an eminent merchant in Liverpool and New York, sat as M.P. for South Lancashire 1846-59, and was High Sheriff of Lancashire 1863. He established the mercantile firm of Brown, Shipley, and Co., Liverpool, and founded, in 1860, the Public Library and Museum in William Brown Street, Liverpool, at a cost of £42,000, and for that and other services to Liverpool he was created a baronet. The 2nd baronet was High Sheriff of Northamptonshire 1873.

PIGOTT-BROWN, Creation (U.K.) 1903, of Broome Hall, Capel, Surrey.

Sir WILLIAM BRIAN PIGOTT-BROWN, 3rd *Baronet, b.* Jan. 20th, 1941; *s.* his father, *Sir* JOHN HARGREAVES, 1942; ed. at Eton.

Arms—Quarterly, 1st and 4th gules, a chevron or between two bears' paws erased in chief argent, and four hands conjoined in saltire of the second in base; a chief engrailed of the last thereon an eagle displayed sable (for distinction), in the honour point a cross-crosslet of the third, *Brown*; 2nd and 3rd ermine, three fusils conjoined in fesse sable, *Pigott*. **Crest**—Issuant out of a wreath of oak vert a bear's paw erect argent, holding a sinister hand couped at the wrist proper.
Residences—Orchard House, Aston Tirrold, Berks.; 25, Chapel St., SW1.

There is unity among brothers.

Aunts living—Joan Terrell Hargreaves (*Lady Prideaux*), *b.* 1911: *m.* 1934, Col. Sir John Francis Prideaux, OBE, and has issue living, Christopher John (Doddershall, Aylesbury; Brook's and City of London Clubs), *b.* 1936; ed. at Eton: *m.* 1959, Celia, da. of P. A. Daniell, of Glebe House, Buckland, Surrey, and has issue living, David John *b.* 1962, Charles *b.* 1966, Lavinia *b.* 1961,—Michael Charles Terrell, *b.* 1950; ed. at Eton, and Trin Coll., Camb.: *m.* 1975, Mrs. Susan H. Monsarrat,—Editha Anne, *b.* 1940: *m.* 1968, Alaster Templeton of The Old Rectory, Whatfield, nr. Ipswich, Suffolk, and has issue living, Katherine Elizabeth, *b.* 1968, Jane Celia *b.* 1970. *Residence,* Elderslie, Ockley, Surrey.——Patience Hargreaves (The Cottage, Ockley, Surrey), *b.* 1915: *m.* 1939, Charles Augustus Lee Steere, AuxAF, who *d.* (killed in action over Dunkirk) 1940, and has issue living, Gordon Ernest (Jayes Park, Ockley, Surrey), *b.* 1939: *m.* 1966, Mary Katherine, da. of Innes Stuart, of Ethie Mains, Arbroath, Angus, and has issue living, Henrietta Clare *b.* 1969, Lucinda Mary *b.* 1971, Marina Jane *b.* 1973.

Widow living of 2nd Baronet—HELEN VIOLA EGERTON, only da. of the late Maj. Gilbert Francis Egerton-Cotton [*see* V. Combermere, colls.]: *m.* 1st, 1940, Capt. Sir John Hargreaves Pigott-Brown, Coldstream Guards, 2nd Baronet, who *d.* (killed in action during European War) 1942; 2ndly, 1948, Capt. Charles Raymond Radclyffe, late Roy. Scots Greys. *Residence,* Lew, Oxfordshire.

Collateral Branch living.

Issue of the late Walter Hargreaves BROWN, 2nd son of 1st baronet, *b.* 1881, *d.* 1936: *m.* 1913, Alberta Laura (who *m.* 2ndly, 1937, Major Alexander Innes, MC [Innes, Bt., *cr.* 1628, colls.]), da. of the late Capt. Guy Mainwaring, RN:—

Susan Henrietta Hargreaves, *b.* 1914 : *m.* 1935, Curtis Delmar-Morgan, D.S.C., R.N.V.R., and has issue living, Michael Walter (Swaynes, Rudgwick, Sussex), *b.* 1936: *m.* 1962, Marjorie, da. of John Kennedy Logan, and has issue living, Benjamin John *b.* 1966, Katharine Susan *b.* 1968, Alexandra Jane *b.* 1971,—Jeremy Hugh, *b.* 1941: *m.* 1966, Nicolie Jane, da. of Howard Eden Smith, and has issue living, a da. *b.* 1970. *Residence,* Fairlight, Sarisbury Green, Hants.—— Margaret Hargreaves, *b.* 1917: *m.* 1st, 1938, Robert Graham Fletcher, who *d.* 1960; 2ndly, 1961, Alexander Ronan Nelson, and has issue living, (by 1st m.) Alastair Robert Leslie, *b.* 1941: *m.* 1965, Maria Lucia Simoes, and has issue living, Robin Simoes *b.* 1972, Monica Simoes *b.* 1966, Katia Simoes *b.* 1967,—Charles Hugh, *b.* 1946: *m.* 1970, Rose Noreen Nugent Sherlock, and has issue living, Andrew Charles *b.* 1972.—Ronald James, *b.* 1948,—Fiona Margaret, *b.* 1939,—Katharine Hargreaves, *b.* 1953. *Residences,* Muckairn, Taynuilt, Argyll; Ardlussa, Isle of Jura, Argyll.

The 1st baronet, Sir Alexander Hargreaves Brown [*see* Brown, Bt., *cr.* 1863, colls.], sat as M.P. for Wenlock (8) 1868-85, and for Mid. or Wellington, Div. of Shropshire (LU) 1885-1906. His el. son Capt. Gordon Hargreaves Brown was killed in action 1914. He *m.* 1910, Edith Ivy, el. da. and co-heir of Adm. William Harvey Pigott of Doddershall Park, Bucks. who in 1925 assumed the additional surname and arms of Pigott for herself and her issue. Their son, Capt. Sir John Hargreaves Pigott-Brown, 2nd Bt. Coldstream Guards, was killed in action 1942.

Browne (Cave-Browne-Cave), see Cave.

BROWNRIGG, Creation (U.K.) 1816.

Virescat vulnere virtus.

Valour strengthens from a wound.

Sir NICHOLAS GAWEN BROWNRIGG, 5th *Baronet,* son of the late Gawen Egremont Brownrigg, 2nd and only surviving son of 4th Baronet; *b.* Dec. 22nd, 1932; *s.* his grandfather, *Rear-Adm. Sir* DOUGLAS EGREMONT ROBERT, *CB,* 1939: *m.* 1st, 1959 (m. diss. 1965), Linda Louise, da. of Jonathan B. Lovelace, of Beverly Hills, California, USA; 2ndly, 1971, Valerie Ann, da. of Julian A. Arden, of Livonia, Michigan, USA, and has issue by 1st m.

Arms—Argent, between three crescents gules, a lion rampant-guardant sable holding in the dexter fore-paw a sword proper, hilt or, thereon a serpent entwined vert ; and for augmentation, on a chief embattled of the last, a representation of the sceptre of the King of Kandy or, and of the banner of the said King, being gules within a bordure with a ray of the sun issuing from each angle a lion passant holding a sword in saltire, the whole ensigned with a representation of the crown of Kandy. Crests—1st, augmentation, a demi-Kandian proper holding in the dexter hand a sword and in the sinister the crown of Kandy ; 2nd, out of a mural crown or, a sword erect in pale proper, hilt or, thereon a serpent entwined vert.

Address—PO Box 361, Ukiah, Calif. 95482, USA.

Son living—By 1st m.—MICHAEL GAWEN, *b.* Oct., 1961.

Daughter living—By 1st m.—Sylvia Alderyn, *b.* 1964.

Mother living—Baroness Lucia, da. of Baron Victor von Borosini, of 1270, Mesa Road, San Marino 9, California, U.S.A.: *m.* 1st, 1931 (divorce in U.S.A. 1936), Gawen Egremont Brownrigg (ante), who *d.* 1938; 2ndly, 1936 (divorce in USA 1941), John Burnham; 3rdly, 1941 (m. diss. 1957), Com. Edmund Lyford Engel, US Naval Reserve; 4thly, Harry Albert Batten, who *d.* 1966. *Residence,* 207, Griegos Rd., NE, Albuquerque, New Mexico 87107, USA.

The 1st baronet, Sir Robert Brownrigg, G.C.B. (son of the late Henry Brownrigg, of Rockingham, co. Wicklow), was a Gen. in the Army, and Col. 9th Foot. The 4th baronet, Sir Douglas Egremont Robert, C.B., was a Rear-Adm. R.N.

BRUCE, Creation (N.S.) 1628, of Stenhouse, Stirlingshire.

We have been.

Sir (Francis) Michael Ian Bruce, 12th *Baronet;* b. April 3rd, 1926; s. his father, *Sir* Michael William Selby, 1957; discontinued use of his Christian name of Francis; US Marine Corps, Amphibious Forces, and Fleet Marines Force 1943-46 (Solomons, Bismarck Archipeligo, and Philippines Campaigns); Member of Sqdn. A, 7th Regt. NY 1948 (ret.); Master's Ticket 1968: *m.* 1st, 1947 (m. diss. 1957), Barbara Stevens, da. of Francis J. Lynch; 2ndly, 1961 (m. diss. 1963), Frances Keegan; 3rdly, 1966, Marilyn Anne,, da. of Carter Mullaly, and has issue by 1st m.

Arms—Or, a saltire and chief gules, in the dexter canton an escutcheon argent charged with a chief sable. Crest—On a cap of dignity an arm from the shoulder couped fessewise holding a sceptre ensigned on the point with an open crown as that worn by Robert I. of Scotland. Supporters—*Dexter*, a knight in armour the vizor open and a plume of feathers in his helmet holding a sceptre in his right hand all proper ; sinister, a lion rampant azure armed and langued gules, crowned with the crown of Robert I., and gored with that of David II., chained with an antique chain or.
Address—c/o Newport National Bank, Westcliff & Dover, Newport, Cal., USA.

Sons living—By 1st marriage—MICHAEL IAN RICHARD b. Dec. 10th, 1950.— Robert Dudley, b. 1952.

Half-Brother living—Michael David Lennon, b. 1948.
Half-Sister living—Corinna Mary Constance, b. 1940.
Widow living of 11th Baronet—MARGARET HELEN (*Margaret, Lady Bruce*), da. of Sir Arthur Lennon Binns, C.B.E., M.C.; late Section Officer, W.A.A.F.: *m.* 1946, as his fourth wife, Sir Michael William Selby Bruce, 11th Bt., who d. 1957. *Residence,*

Collateral Branches living.
Issue of the late William Nigel Ernle Bruce, younger son of 10th baronet, b. 1895, d. 1953: *m.* 1921, Violet Pauline who d. 1970, da. of the late Col. Willington Shelton, of Bruree, co. Limerick:—
Pauline Margaret, b. 1922 : *m.* 1946, Wing-Com. Geoffrey Page, D.S.O., D.F.C., R.A.F. (retired), and has issue living, Nigel Geoffrey, b. 1953,—Jamie Douglas, b. 1958,—Pauline Shelley, b. 1948.
——Jennifer Beryl (Apart. 2, Scala A, Parco del Mimose, Seconda Traversa, Viale Circe, Terracina, Italy), b. 1924: *m.* 1st, 1944, Lt. Jay Gould, USAF, from whom she obtained a divorce 1946; 2ndly, 1947, Arthur Sebastian Gilbey, who d. 1964 [*see* Gilbey, Bt., colls.], and has issue living, (by 1st m.) Jay Bruce, b. 1946,—(by 2nd m.) [*see* Gilbey, Bt. colls.].

Grandchildren of the late Capt. Arthur Neil Bruce, son of the late William Cuningham Bruce, 2nd son of 7th baronet :—
Issue of the late William Cuningham Bruce, b. 1866, d. 1924 : *m.* 1897, Ellen, da. of John Scott:—
Robert Neil, b. 1904.——William Cuningham, b. 1907.——Colin Cadell, b. 1914.——Corinna Joan, b. 1916.——Lornas Dorothy, b. 1919.

Granddaughter of the late Robert Cathcart Bruce, MD, 3rd son of the late Maj.-Gen. Alexander James Bruce, el. son of the late Alexander Fairlie Bruce (b. 1799), 3rd son of 7th baronet:—
Issue of the late Robert Cathcart Bruce, b. 1898, d. 1966: *m.* 1927, Christian Adeline (The Cottage, Bicknoller, Taunton), da. of the late William Henderson, of Berkley House, Frome:—
Fairlie Cathcart, b. 1928: *m.* 1951, Charles William Hutton, BArch, FRIBA, of 56, Brook Green, W6, and has issue living, Fairlie Elizabeth, b. 1952.—Julia Frances, b. 1954,—Anina Mary, b. 1955.

Grandchildren of the late Alexander Fairlie Bruce, b. 1857, son of George Cadell Bruce, 2nd son of Alexander Fairlie Bruce, b. 1799 (ante)
Issue of the late Lieut.-Com. Alan Cathcart Fairlie Bruce, R.N., b. 1894, d. 1927 : *m.* 1919, Barbara (of 56, Arlington Lodge, Monument Hill, Weybridge, Surrey), da. of E. Clarributt Skinner:—
Colin Michael Fairlie (c/o National & Grindlays Bank, 13, St. James's Sq., SW17 4LF), b. 1925; ed. at Christ's Hospital, and at Oxford (MA) and Edinburgh Univs.; Economic Adviser, Agric. and Rural Development Depart. of International Bank for Reconstruction and Development, Washington, since 1965; Far East, 1943-45 as Sub-Lt. RNVR: *m.* 1st, 1946, Patricia Mary Platt; 2ndly, 1963, Georgina Morrison Baker, and has issue living, (by 1st m.) Timothy Michael Fairlie, b. 1948,—Alan Simon Fairlie, b. 1950,—Jonathan Neil Fairlie, b. 1958,—Lindsay Madeleine Fairlie, b. 1953,—Jenny Catriona Fairlie, b. 1960,—(by 2nd m.) Fiona Elspeth, b. 1965.——John Alan Fairlie, b. 1926; ed. at Christ's Hospital, and at Oxford Univ.; Manager, Personnel and Admin. Shell Chemicals UK Ltd.; Far East 1945 as Lieut., RA: *m.* 1950, Joyce Edna Soffe, and has issue living, Iain Alasdair Fairlie, b. 1954,—Andrew Stuart Cathcart (twin), b. 1954,—Alison Jean, b. 1951.——Barbara Jean, b. 1921: *m.* 1941, Col. Robert John Augustine Hornby, OBE (ret.), Queen's R. Surrey Regt., of Airth House, Fairacres, Cobham, Surrey, and The Corner House, Church St., Deddington, Oxford, and has issue living, Vivien Sheena (*Hon. Mrs. Edward F. Northcote*), b. 1942: *m.* 1963, the Hon. Edward Frederic Northcote, of 91, Cottenham Park Rd., Wimbledon, SW20 0DS [see E. Iddesleigh],—Louise Panette, b. 1947: *m.* 1967 Kenneth Dudley Johns Bootes-Johns, of Flat 7, 86, Worple Rd., Wimbledon, SW19.

Grandchildren of the late Col. Elliott Armstrong Bruce, 7th son of the late Alexander Fairlie Bruce, b. 1799 (ante):—
Issue of the late Lieut.-Col. Malcolm Edward Lloyd Bruce, Indian Army, b. 1872, d. 1952: *m.* 1903, Clementina Blyth, who d. 1958, youngest da. of the late W. F. B. Dalzel, M.D., Surg.-Major Bengal Army:—

Robert Graham Dalzel, b. 1910 ; Major (retired) E. Surrey Regt. ; European War 1939-40 (prisoner): m. 1956, Joan Mary Price. *Residence*, Stenhouse, Boundary Rd., Grayshott, Hindhead, Surrey.——Elizabeth Mary Dalzel (twin), b. 1910: m. 1933, Neville Eugene Govett, who d. 1972, and has issue living, Bryan, b. 1934; ed. at St. Paul's Sch.,—Richard, b. 1937; ed. at St. Paul's Sch.,—Robert John, b. 1944. *Residence*, 13, Clydesdale Gdns., Richmond, Surrey.

Grandchildren of the late Michael McCubbin Bruce, 8th son of Alexander Fairlie Bruce, b. 1799 (ante):—
Issue of the late Robert Cathcart Bruce, b. 1878, d. 1968: m. 1916, Emma Dolores (Hamilton House, Brookway Rd., Charlton King's, Cheltenham), da. of the late John Croce:—
Vivian Richard, MB, (Hamilton House, Brookway Rd., Charlton Kings, Cheltenham), b. 1919: m. 1st, 1942, Norah Maeve Yates, who d. 1960; 2ndly, 1962, Bernadette Yates, and has issue living (by 1st m.) Robert James, b. 1946; Lt. RM: m. 1969, Elizabeth Jane Moira, da: of the late David Clement Burgess, and has issue living, Elizabeth Maeve b. 1970, Laura Christian b. 1971,—Michael Alexander, b. 1949,—Richard Hubert, b. 1956,—(by 2nd m.) Paul Cathcart, b. 1963,—Angus Peter, b. 1964,—Joseph Douglas, b. 1970.

Issue of the late Charles Kerr Bruce, b. 1880, d. 1955: m. 1928, Lilian Leonnard, who d. 1959:—
Ian Robert (Shibblers, Boughton Monchelsea, Maidstone), b. 1931: m. 1956, Dorothy Evelyn Knight, and has issue living, Anne, b. 1960,—Caroline Jane, b. 1963——Margaret, b. 1930: m. 1956, Norman Terence Whight, of The Cherries, 15, Fairfield Way, Hildenborough, Kent, and has issue living, Charles Bruce, b. 1963,—Fiona Margaret, b. 1960.——Audrey Mary, b. 1935; m. 1958, George David James Morgan, and has issue living, Christopher David, b. 1962,—Felicity Claire, b. 1960.

Grandchildren of the late Robert Perry Bruce (infra):—
Issue of the late Michael Macaulay Bruce, b. 1904, d. 1964: m. 1937, Louise Françoise (27, Marlborough Rd., Doncaster), da. of Prof. Van der Pot, of the Netherlands:—
Robert William (9, Longfield Drive, Bessacarr, Doncaster), b. 1940: m. 1964, Jennifer Patricia Guilfoyle Brown, and has issue living, Michael Gregory Macaulay, b. 1968,—Rosalind Ellen Macaulay, b. 1966,—Miranda Jane Macaulay, b. 1970.——Michael Zachary, b. 1951.——Mary Louise, b. 1938: m. 1961, Colin Hugh Prince, of 33, Homersham Rd., Kingston upon Thames, and has issue living, Hamish Robin John, b. 1966,—Anna Louise, b. 1966.——Vanessa Bertha Jane, b. 1942: m. 1968, Christopher Ryle, of West Lodge, Umberslade, Solihull, and has issue living, Deborah b. 1968,—Xanthe, b. 1969.——Barbara Lucy, b. 1945: m. 1969, Paul Lewis Henderson, of School House, Philips Lane, Darrington, Yorks., and has issue living, James b. 1974, Juliet b. 1972.

Grandchildren of the late Alexander Fairlie Bruce, b. 1799 (ante):—
Issue (by 2nd marriage) of the late Robert Perry Bruce, b. 1861, d. 1914: m. 1st, 1886, Ethel Blanche, who d. 1911 (from whom he obtained a divorce 1899), da. of the late John Russell, of Merthyr Tydfil ; 2ndly, 1903, Olive Maud, who d. 1968, 2nd da. of the late Joseph Babington Macaulay, formerly of Rosebush, Pembrokeshire, and Paignton, S. Devon:—
Nigel Macaulay (twin), b. 1906; India and Burma 1941-45 as Maj. RA with 14th Army, Burma: m. 1940, Helen Woodhall. *Residence*, Little Grange, Hollesley, nr. Woodbridge, Suffolk. *Club*, Army and Navy.——Edward Macaulay, b. 1908; 1939-45 War in Italy as Maj. Middlesex Regt. (despatches): m. 1939, Nancy Elinor, ygst. da. of Lt.-Col. F. G. C. Humfrey, late Indian Army, and has issue living, David Nigel Macaulay, b. 1947; ed. at Gresham's Sch. and St. Andrew's Univ. (MA),—Elizabeth Mary, b. 1942: m. 1966, Dirk Detert, PhD, of 623, Frankfurt 80, Drosselweg 5, Germany, and has issue living, Niels Bruce b. 1970, Ian Bruce b. 1974. *Residence*, Bartonbury Close, Cirencester.——Olive, b. 1911: m. 1934, Gabriel Grisewood, and has issue living, Daniel, b. 1934: m. 1960, Margaret Pickett, and has issue living, Rachel b. 1961, Sara b. 1962,—Allan Christopher, b. 1936,—Benjamin, b. 1929.——Mary Anne, b. 1937: m. 1962, Calum MacFarlane-Barrow, of Clay Bokie, Mar Lodge Estate, Braemar, Aberdeenshire, and has issue living, Ruth b. 1963,—Lucy, b. 1941. *Residence,*—

Grandchildren of the late Col. Elliott Armstrong Bruce (ante):—
Issue of the late Major John Elliott Lidderdale Bruce, R.A., b. 1870, d. (killed in action) 1915: m. 1900, Charlotte Mabel (who d. 1956 having m. 2ndly, 1920, Ernest Neele, who d. 1937), da. of the late T. J. G. Johnstone, of Ceylon Civil Ser. :—
John Charles Douglas (20, Caroline Court, Scottburgh, Natal), b. 1902; Brig. (ret.) Indian Army: m. 1934, Dorothy Barbara, el. da. of the late Robert Thomas Dundas, CIE, Indian Police (ret.).

Issue of the late Elliott Henry Rochfort Bruce, b. 1874, d. 1933 : m. 1905, Frances Maude, who d. 1949, da. of A. McDonald :—
Elliott McDonald, b. 1906 : m. 1932, Kathleen, da. of G. Clarke, and has issue living, Michael, b. 1939,—Josephine, b. 1945,—Heather, b. 1949. *Residence*, Launceston, Tasmania.——Malcolm Alexander, b. 1913 : m. 1942 (marriage dissolved 19—), Doris Gwynnith, and has issue living, Donald Malcolm, b. 1944,—Geoffrey, b. 1946,—Richard (twin), b. 1946.——Beryl Brenda b. 1919: m. 1947, Herbert Winston Eaton, and has issue living, Geoffrey Winston. b. 1949,—Linda Christine, b. 1952.

Grandchildren of the late Eric Henry Stuart Bruce, only son of the late Gen. Michael Bruce, grandson of the late Patrick Cranfurd Bruce, 5th son of 6th baronet:—
Issue of the late Brigadier Ian Robert Craufurd George Mary Bruce, D.S.O., M.B.E., b. 1890, d. 1956: m. 1926, Joan Mary (of Hampton Court Palace, East Molesey, Surrey), da. of the late Lieut.-Col. Rowland Charles Feilding, D.S.O. [see E. Denbigh, colls.] :—
Anne Mary, b. 1927 : m. 1953, Nicholas Patrick Reyntiens, and has issue living, Dominick Percival Ian, b. 1957,—John Patrick Martin, b. 1964,—Edith Mary Isabel, b. 1954,—Lucy Mary Anne, b. 1959. *Residence*, Burleighfield House, Loudwater, Bucks.——Janet Mary, b. 1928: m. 1950, Peter Michaeljohn Ward, and has issue living, Jonathan Francis Bruce, b. 1954,—Robert Richard Craufurd, b. 1959,—Edmund Giles William, b. 1962,—Damian Peter Michael, b. 1966,—Clare Dorothy, b. 1951,—Catharine Joan, b. 1952,—Magdalen Mary, b. 1955,—Hester Janet Teresa b. 1964. *Residence*, Waterdell House, Croxley Green, Herts.——Helen Mary, b. 1929: m. 1956, Stephen Edward Francis Bally, of MS 201, Calico Creek, Gympre 4570, Qld., Aust., and has issue living, Ian Stephen Edward, b. 1959,—Alexander St. John, b. 1963,—David Anthony, b. 1968,—Louise Frances Joan, b. 1957.——Eynor Mary (Ambassador Suite, Imperial Hotel, Tokyo, Japan), b. 1933: m. 1957, Alfred Edwin Bell, and has issue living, Christopher Michael Ian, b. 1958,—Julian Sebastian, b. 1962,—Theodore Richard John, b. 1972.——Philena Mary Edith, b. 1949.

Issue of the late Alastair La Vallette Eric Mary Bruce, b. 1898, d. 1950 : m. 1923, Winifred Moultrie (of Resthaven, 16, Tilford Road, Farnham, Surrey), da. of the late J. A. E. Wren, of Southsea :—
Anthony Crawford John, b. 1925. *Residence*, Resthaven, 16, Tilford Road, Farnham, Surrey.

This family is a cadet branch of the Bruces of Clackmannan, from whom the Earls of Elgin also derive their descent. Sir William Bruce, who was created a baronet with remainder to his heirs male whatsoever, was a yr. son of William son and heir of Sir Alexander Bruce of Airth 6th in descent from Sir Edward Bruce of Airth, yr. son of the second Sir Robert Bruce of Clackmannan, who d. before 1406.

BRUCE, Creation (U.K.) 1804, of Downhill, Londonderry.

We have been.

Sir HERVEY JAMES HUGH BRUCE, 7th *Baronet*; *b.* Sept. 4th, 1952; *s.* his father, *Sir* HERVEY JOHN WILLIAM, 1971; ed. at Eton; 2nd Lt., Gren. Gds.

Arms— Or, on a saltire gules a harp of the field, stringed argent, on a chief of the second a canton argent, charged with a lion rampant azure.   **Crest**—A lion passant azure holding in his dexter paw a trefoil slipped proper.
Residence,—Petersham House, Falmouth Gdns., Newmarket, Suffolk.

Sister living—Lauretta Chinty, *b.* 1950: *m.* 1971, David Ralph Foster Harbord, Capt. 15th/19th King's R. Hussars, who *d.* 1974 [B. Suffield, colls.].

Uncle living (son of 5th baronet)—RONALD CECIL JUCKES (24 Fairfax Rd., Teddington, Middx.), *b.* Aug. 22nd, 1921: *m.* 1960, Jean, da. of Lewis James William Murfitt, and has issue living, Alan James, *b.* 1964.

Aunt living (daughter of 5th baronet)—Beryl Margaret Gwladys (749, Chelsea Cloisters, SW3), *b.* 1917.

Widow living of 6th Baronet—CHRISTA IRENE VALENTINE (*Lady Bruce*) (Petersham House, Falmouth Gdns. Newmarket, Suffolk), da. of the late Lt.-Col. Chandos de Paravacini, OBE, of Birkholme Manor, Corby, Lincs., and formerly wife of the late Maj. David Charles Innes-Ker [*see* D. Roxburghe, colls.]: *m.* 1949, Sir Hervey John William Bruce, 6th Bt., who *d.* 1971.

Collateral Branches living.

Issue of the late Lt.-Col. Percy Robert CLIFTON, CMG, DSO, TD, JP, DL, 2nd son of 4th baronet, *b.* (twin), 1872, *d.* 1944 (having assumed by Roy. licence 1919 the surname and arms of Clifton only in lieu of his patronymic) : *m.* 1st, 1898, Aletheia Georgina, who *d.* 1904, da. of the Rt. Hon. Sir Richard Horner Paget, 1st Bt. (*cr.* 1886) ; 2ndly, 1909, Evelyn Mary Amelia, **da. of** the late Major Thomas Leith [E. Carnwath] :—
By 2nd m.) Peter Thomas, *DSO*, *b.* 1911; Lt.-Col. (ret.) Gren. Gds.; Clerk of the Cheque and Adjt., Hon. Corps of Gentlemen-at-Arms since 1973; Italy 1943-45 (DSO); a JP for Hants. and a DL for Notts; DSO 1945: *m.* 1934 (m. annulled on her petition 1936) Ursula Sybil, da. of Sir Edward Hussey Packe, KBE [B. Colebrooke, ext.]; 2ndly, 1948, Patricia Mary Adela, da. of the late Maj. J. M. Gibson-Watt, of Doldowlod, co. Radnor, and widow of Maj. Robert Nevill Cobbold, Welsh Gds. [M. Abergavenny, colls.], and has issue living, (by 2nd m.) Georgina Anne (*Hon. Mrs. Richard F. G. Wrottesley*), *b.* 1949: *m.* 1967, the Hon. Richard Francis Gerard Wrottesley, who *d.* 1970, 2nd son of 5th Baron Wrottesley,—Rose Amelia (*Hon. Mrs. Mark W. Vestey*), *b.* 1952: *m.* 1975, the Hon. Mark William Vestey [see B. Vestey]. *Residence,* Dummer House, Basingstoke, Hants.

Issue of the late Henry James Bruce, C.M.G., M.V.O., 4th son of 4th baronet, *b.* 1880, *d.* 1951 : *m.* 1915, Tamara Karsavina, da. of M. Karsavin, of Petrograd, Russia :—
Nikita, *b.* 1916 : *m.* 1st 1940 (marriage dissolved 1946), Kay, da. of Capt. Robert G. Bannerman ; 2ndly, 1957, Dorothy Mary Norah Mostyn, da. of William Mostyn Bell, and has issue living (by 2nd marriage), Nicholas Henry William, *b.* 1960,—Caroline Mary Tamara, *b.* 1958. *Residence,* 38, Longfield Drive, Amersham, Bucks.

Grandchildren of the late Rev. Canon Lloyd Stewart Bruce, 4th son of 2nd baronet:—
Issue of the late Rev. Robert Douglas Bruce, *b.* 1867, *d.* 1944 : *m.* 1894, Alice Margaret who *d.* 1955, da. of the late Henry William Lord, Bar.-at-Law :—
Rev. Henry Douglas, (Society of St. John the Evangelist, Marston St., Oxford) *b.* 1900; ed. at Keble Coll., Oxford (BA 3rd class Honours in Theology 1922); sometime Priest-in-Charge of All Saints' and St. Margaret's, Andros, Bahamas; is a member of So. of St. John the Evangelist, Oxford.——Nigel Patrick, *BM, BCh, b.* 1905; ed. at Keble Coll., Oxford (BA); Hosp. of the Epiphany, Kamdara, Bihar, India 1934-40; 1939-45 War as Capt. RAMC: *m.* 1934, Audrey Patricia Villiers, only child of the late Rev. Owen Samuel Edward Clarendon, V. of Iffley, Oxford, and has issue living, Clare, *b.* 1935: *m.* 1956, Peter Colpoys Paley Johnson, only son of Lt.-Col. Sir John Paley Johnson, 6th Bt. (cr. 1755). *Residence,* Pear Tree Cottage, East End, Fairford, Glos.

Grandchildren of the Rev. Robert Douglas Bruce (ante):—
Issue of the late Rev. Michael Bruce, *b.* 1908, *d.* 1968: *m.* 1935, Jean Stuart (12, Strathearn Place, Edinburgh, EH9 2AL), da. of the late Ian Campbell, LRCP, LRCS, of 11, Herford Rd., Harrogate:—
Robert John (12, Strathearn Place, Edinburgh, EH9 2AL), *b.* 1936.——Elspeth Mary, *b.* 1942: *m.* 1965, Stuart Semple, MB, ChB, of Mounthooly, Winchburgh, W. Lothian, EH52 6PY, and has issue living, Jean, *b.* 1968,—Shelia, *b.* 1970,—Mairi, *b.* 1971.

Grandchildren of the late Rev. Canon Lloyd Stewart Bruce (ante):—
Issue of the late Rev. Francis Rosslyn Courtenay Bruce, DD, *b.* 1871, *d.* 1956: *m.* 1908, Rachel, who *d.* 1971, el. da. of the late Richard Hanbury Joseph Gurney, JP, DL [Buxton, Bt.]:—
Merlin, *OBE, b.* 1909; Cdr. RN (ret.); 1939-45 War; Korea 1950-52 (despatches); Councillor Hemel Hempstead RDC 1961-70; OBE (Mil) 1959: *m.* 1933, Marjorie Joan, only da. of the late William Hitchcock, of Kettlewells Farm, St. Albans, and has issue living, Euslin (37, Clinton Cres., St. Leonards on Sea, Sussex, TN38 0RN), *b.* 1933; late Sub-Lt. RN: *m.* 1957, Enid Pedley, and has issue living, Quinton Bruce *b.* 1959, Roderick Hulme *b.* 1962, Damian Trispen *b.* 1970, Jeremy Larick *b.* 1974, Nicola Jane *b.* 1958, Caroline Fiona *b.* 1964,—Rollo (96, West End Drive, Horsforth, Leeds), *b.* 1939; ed. at St. Catharine's Coll., Camb. (BA): *m.* 1965, Katharine Margaret, BA, da. of Ronald Hill, of Princethorpe, Warwicks., and has issue living, Rory James *b.* 1968, Lucy Helen *b.* 1966. *Residence,* The Orchard, Almsford End, Harrogate.——Erroll, *b.* 1913; Cdr. RN (ret.): *m.* 1939, Silvia Daphne, only da. of the late Col. C. R. Sylvester Bradley, and has issue living, Peregrine (Hazeldell, Broadmead, Lymington, Hants.), *b.* 1940; late Capt. R. Signals: *m.* 1974, Fiona Anne, da. of Gp. Capt. Reginald Bryson Wardman, OBE, AFC,—Peter, *b.* 1941, Lt.-Cdr. RN,—Rosamund, *b.* 1943: *m.* 1962, Terence Patrick Griffin, of 4, Westover Rd., SW18, and has issue living, Benedict James *b.* 1963, Tabitha Rose *b.* 1964, Polly Bridge *b.* 1966, Matilda Victoria *b.* 1968, Flora Rhalou *b.* 1972,—Errollyn, *b.* 1950,—Chloe Siola, *b.* 1965. *Residence,*—Lofts, Lower Pennington, Lymington, Hants. *Club,*—Royal Yacht Sqdn.——Rhalou, *b.* 1911: *m.* 1935, George Hugh Kirkby Peace, MRCVS, of Brighthill Farm, Rollright Stones, Chipping Norton, Oxon, and has issue living, Colin Kirby (The Gables, Newmarket), *b.* 1936; ed. at Pembroke Coll., Camb. (MA, MB (Vet.), MRCVS): *m.* 1967, Anne, el. da. of John Rawle, of Necochea, Argentina, and has issue living, Rosslyn Lucas Kirkby *b.* 1968, Geraldine *b.* 1970,—Hubert Kirkby (Henley Farm, Miserden, Glos.), *b.* 1937: *m.* 1st, 1964

Penelope Claire, da. of Maj. Patrick Joseph Brady; 2ndly, 1974, Priscilla Elizabeth, el. da. of Brig. Charles Phipps, of The Isle of Wight, and has issue living (by 1st m.) Henry Kirkby b. 1964, Anne-Marie Claire b. 1966, Georgina Lucy Rose b. 1971,—Peter Kirkby (c/o Devon and Exeter Hospitals, Devon), b. 1941; BSc. London; MB, BS; LRCP, MRCS: m. 1968, Jane Knight, and has issue living, Catharine b. 1971, Sophie Rhalou b. 1972,—Thomas Kirkby (Moonacre, Highwood Bottom, Speen, Bucks.), b. 1943: m. 1967, Judeth Jane, da. of the late A. Champion, and has issue living, Emily Mary b. 1968, Sarah Lucinda b. 1974,—Benjamin Kirkby (twin), (c/o Sheeplands Farm, Ripe, Lewes), b. 1943: m. 1967, Kathleen Rosemary Denise, da. of Brig. Donald Maxwell Cornah, MBE, DSO, of Seaford, Sussex, and has issue living, Simon Kirkby b. 1967, Robert Antony Kirkby b. 1969,—James Kirkby (Holly Cottage, Whichford, Warwicks.), b. 1947: m. 1973, Margaret Christine, 2nd. da. of Sir Stanley Lewis Prescott, of Perth, Aust.— Verily, b. 1915: m. 1st, 1940, Capt. Donald Clive Anderson, late Indian Army, who d. 1957; 2ndly, 1971, Paul Edward Paget, CVO, FSA, FRIBA, of Templewood, Northrepps, Cromer, Norfolk [see Paget, Bt., colls., cr. 1871], and has issue living, (by 1st m.) Edward, b. 1948: m. 1973, Mrs. Christina Bolt, yr. da. of F. G. Raymond, of East Lodge, Holkham, Norfolk, and has issue living, Evelyn b. 1973,—Marian, b. 1941: m. 1964, James Haldane O'Hare, of 19, Claremont Court, Glasnevin, Dublin XI, and has issue living, Justin b. 1966, Christina b. 1965, Eloise b. 1970,— Rachel, b. 1943: m. 1965, David Henry Bradby, MA, PhD, of 18, King St., Canterbury, and has issue living, Lawrence b. 1968, Donald b. 1973, Hannah b. 1966,—Janie, b. 1952: m. 1971, Charles Hampton, of Samuel Cottage, Oreton, Salop, and has issue living, Daisy Maya b. 1973,—Alexandra, b. 1953: m. 1972, Michael Holgreaves Allerhand, of Sunshine Towers, Vaccarials, Riols, France 34.——Lorema, b. 1920: m. 1942, Alan Wilfrid Gough Goolden, MB, BS, and has issue living, Adrian French, b. 1945,—Robin Massy, b. 1948. Residence,—Orchard House, Summerhouse Lane, Aldenham, Herts.

Issue of the late Capt. Wilfred Montagu Bruce, C.B.E., R.D., R.N.R., b. 1874, d. 1953: m. 1913, the Hon. Dorothy Florence Boot (of Les Pommiers, St. Lawrence, Jersey), da. of 1st Baron Trent:—
Nancy Jessica, b. 1915 : m. 1940, Adriano Guarnieri, and has issue living, Giovanni Bruce, b. 1947,—Antonio Wilfrid, b. 1949,—Andrea, b. 1953,—Francesca Flora, b. 1941. Residences, via Jacopo, da Riva, 19, Lido, Venice, Italy; Palazzo Guarnieri, Feltre, Belluno, Italy— Rosemary June, b. 1919: m. 1939, Alan Burrough, CBE, of Manor Garden, Henley-on-Thames, Oxon.

Grandchildren of the late Henry Barnard Dalrymple Bruce, el. son of the late Lt.-Col. Henry Stewart Beresford Bruce (infra):—
Issue of the late Arthur Bonnycastle Dalrymple Bruce, b. 1890, d. 1934: m. 1916, Marguerite Heloise (now of 85, Clifton Road, Toronto, Canada), da. of Frederick Edward Neale, of Chatham, New Brunswick :—
Arthur Blair Dalrymple (258, S. Taylor Mills Drive, Richmond Hill, Ont., Canada), b. 1924; has assumed the name of Arthur in lieu of his first Christian name of Frederick: m. 1951, Patricia, da. of the late Richard Raymond Jarvis, of Ottawa, and has issue living, Richard Neale Dalrymple, b. 1954,—Susan Elizabeth, b. 1955.——Heloise Patricia, b. 1918: m. 1945, Capt. Robert John McLaughlin, Toronto Scottish Regt., who d. 1949, and has issue living, Robert Bruce (posthumous) b. 1949. Residence, 85, Clifton Rd., Toronto, Canada.

Grandchildren of the late Lt.-Col. Henry Stewart Beresford Bruce, el. son of Adm. Sir Henry William Bruce, 3rd son of 1st baronet:—
Issue of the late Arthur Hill Nunn Bruce, b. 1856, d. 1918 : m. 1900, Rose, who d. 1947, da. of John Steen, of Galetta, Canada:—
Arthur James Henry, b. 1901: m. 1931, Gladys, da. of Edward Bearinger, of Waterloo, Ontario, Canada, and has issue living, Arthur Michael Edward (90, Woodrich Cres., Apart. 206, Ottawa, Canada), b. 1938: m. 1962, Holly, da. of Carl Cunningham, of Toronto, and has issue living, Wendy Raina b. 1968, Susan Ann b. 1969,—Patricia Mary Jane, b. 1934: m. 1956, Robert Arthur Davey, 1842, Village Green, Burlington, Ont., Canada, and has issue living, Robert Bruce b. 1958, Steven Michael b. 1967, Susan Patricia b. 1960, Karen Elizabeth, b. 1962. Residence, 84, Beaver Ridge, Ottawa 5, Ont., Canada.——Reginald Alexander Steen (3440, Richmond Rd., Ottawa, Canada), b. 1904: m. 1933, Marie, da. of George Albert Blouin, of Ottawa, Canada, and has issue living, Robert Arthur Stewart, b. 1936: m. 1963, Karen, da. of James Dunn, of Old Chelsea, Quebec, and has issue living, Reginald Arthur Spencer b. 1964, Alexander James Robert b. 1967, D'Arcy Stewart Anthony b. 1968, Justin Martin Maynard b. 1971,—Marie Elizabeth Clare, b. 1934: m. 1956, Frederick Reginald Anfossie, of 3232, Carling Av., Ottawa 14, Ont., K2H 587, and has issue living, Frederick Bruce b. 1957, Christine Elodie b. 1959, Janet Marie b. 1961, Heather Claire b. 1963, Margo Elizabeth b. 1968,—Sandra Margo Ann, b. 1938: m. 1960, Grant Pereigo McDonald (RR2, Tadoussac Drive, Aylmer East, PQ, Canada), and has issue living, Reginald Albert Stroud b. 1962, Robert Bruce Reid b. 1963, Adam Alfred Grant b. 1964, John Arthur Steen b. 1968.——Stewart Frederick Dundonald, b. 1905; is Lt.: m. 1940, Kathleen Edna, da. of Charles Cook, of Ottawa, Canada, and has issue living, Nona Frances Evelyn, b. 1944: m. 1970, John Douglas Argue, of Labrador City, Labrador, Newfoundland,—Joan Kathleen Susan, b. 1946: m. 1972, Walter William Nibogie, of 113, Bayswater Av., Ottawa, Canada,—Nancy Elizabeth Ann, 1949. Residence, 513, Westminster Av., McKellar Park, Ottawa, Canada.—— Eileen Frances Mariette, (85, Kirby Rd., Ottawa, 14, Canada) b. 1900: m. 1924, David Pattee Kirby, who d. 1953, and has issue living, Bruce Robert William (173, Highland Av., Rowayton, Conn., USA), b. 1929: m. 1956, Margo Alma Dancey, and has issue living, Janice Margo b. 1958, Kelly June b. 1960,—Beverley Eileen Rosemary, b. 1935: m. 1961, David Bruce Brown, of 55 Barnes Cres., Ottawa 6, Canada, and has issue living, David Alexander b. 1966, Pattee Allison b. 1963, Karen Elizabeth b. 1969.

Grandchildren of the late Arthur Hill Nunn Bruce (ante.):—
Issue of the late Allan Ernest Hill Bruce, b. 1907, d. 1973: m. 1930, Maria Ann (Britannia Bay, Ont. Canada), da. of Elidore Sauvé, of Ottawa, Canada:—
Allan Alexander Dundonald, b. 1931: m. 1956, Patricia Ann Leeks.——Hervey William Beresford, b. 1932.——Marie Lorraine Caroline, b. 1934: m. 1957, Patrick Francis Timlin.

Granddaughter of the late Lt.-Col. Henry Stewart Beresford Bruce (ante):—
Issue of the late Col. Stewart Armit Macdonald Bruce, b. 1858, d. 1937: m. 1891, Helen, da. of the late John McGregor, of Balmenach, Cromdale, Morayshire:—
Jean Mariette Isabel Otway, b. 1892: m. 1916, Cyril Gordon Taylor, from whom she obtained a divorce 1932. Residence,

Granddaughter of the late Reginald Archibald Kenneth Bruce, 7th son of the late Lt.-Col. Henry Stewart Beresford Bruce (ante):—
Issue of the late Capt. William Reginald Richard Stewart Bruce, Irish Guards, b. 1910, d. (killed in action in Belgium) 1944 : m. 1934, Mirabel Melville Gray (who m. 2ndly 1946, J. M. Hawkes, of Midwood, Clochan, by Buckie, Banffshire), da. of J. D. Walker, of Balgownie Lodge, Aberdeenshire:—
Mirabel Hermione (2, Walker Place, Torry, Aberdeen), b. 1941: m. 1964 (m. diss. 1972), Alan Hamill, MN.

Granddaughter of the late Rear-Adm. James Minchin Bruce, son of the late Adm. Sir Henry William Bruce, KCB, 3rd son of 1st baronet:—
Issue of the late James Minchin Bruce, b. 1859, d. 19—: m. 1888, Ethelwynne, da. of the Rev. James Powell:—
Minnie, b. 1889. Residence,

Granddaughter of the late Major Stewart Hervey Bruce, son of the late Lieut.-Col. Stewart Craufurd Bruce, 4th son of 1st baronet :—
Issue of the late Rev. Stewart Alexander Bruce, *b.* 1870, *d.* 1956 : *m.* 1911, Ada Frances, who *d.* 1945, da. of the late Dr. R. E. MacDowell :—
Maire Frances Patricia, *b.* 1913: *m.* 1939, Sqdn.-Ldr. Reginald Maurice Cracknell, MBE, late RAFVR, who *d.* 1970, and has issue living, Andrew Alexander Leon, *b.* 1943,—Peter Bruce, *b.* 1947. *Residence,* 4, Ashcroft, Cedar Drive, Hatch End, Middx.

The Bruces of Down Hill, Londonderry, descend from Patrick Bruce of Newton, yr. brother of Sir William Bruce of Stenhouse, 1st baronet (cr. 1628). Sir Henry Harvey Bruce, 1st baronet, was 5th in descent from him. The only brother of the 1st baronet of this creation, Sir Stewart Bruce, also received a patent of baronetcy in 1812 (extinct 1841). The Rt. Hon. Sir Henry Hervey Bruce, P.C., 3rd Bt., was Lieut. and Custos Rotulorum for Londonderry (High Sheriff 1846), and sat as M.P. for Coleraine (C) 1862-74 and 1880-85. The 4th baronet was High Sheriff of co. Londonderry 1903.

Bruce-Gardner, see Gardner.

BRUNNER, Creation (U.K.) 1895, of Druids Cross, Little Woolton, Lancashire; Winnington Old Hall, Winnington, Cheshire; and Ennismore Gardens, Westminster, co. London.

Sir FELIX JOHN MORGAN BRUNNER, 3rd *Baronet*; *b.* Oct. 13th, 1897; *s.* his father, *Sir* JOHN FOWLER, 1929; ed. at Cheltenham Coll., and at Trin. Coll., Oxford (B.A. Honours in History 1921, M.A. 1925); formerly Flying Officer R.A.F. Vol. Reserve; is Chm. of Brunner Investment Trust, Ltd., and other Cos.; was Chm. of Henley Rural Dist. Council 1954-7; Pres. of Liberal Party Organisation 1962-3; 1916-18 War as Lt. RFA: *m.* 1926, Dorothea Elizabeth, OBE, JP, da. of the late Henry Brodribb Irving, and has issue.

Arms—Gules, a fountain playing proper, charged on the basin with a rose gules, in chief two mullets of six points or. **Crest**—In front of a wing erect gules, a fountain as in the arms.

Residence—Greys Court, Henley-on-Thames, Oxon. *Clubs*—Bath, Reform.

If thou art wise, drink.

Sons living—JOHN HENRY KILIAN, *b.* June 1st, 1927; ed. at Eton, and at Trin. Coll., Oxford (B.A. 1950); formerly Lieut. R.A.: *m.* 1955, Jasmine Cicely, da. of the late John Wardrop-Moore [Erskine, Bt., cr. 1821, colls.], and has issue living, Nicholas Felix Minturn, *b.* 1960,—Mark Jonathan Irving, *b.* 1962,—Claire Eliza, *b.* 1958. *Residence*, 13, Glyndon Av., Brighton, Vic., Australia 3186.——Timothy Barnabas Hans, *b.* 1932, ed. at Eton, and at Trin. Coll., Oxford (MA); formerly Lt. Irish Guards: *m.* 1960, Helen Ursula: da. of Norris Marshall, of 17, Oxford Rd., Teddington, Middlesex, and has issue living, Jacob Sebastian, *b.* 1961,—Conrad Orlando, *b.* 1966,—Francesca Laura *b.* 1963,—Imogen Charlotte. *b.* 1965. *Residence*, 24, Bedford Gdns., W8.——Daniel Felix Brodribb, *b.* 1933; ed. at St, Edward's Sch., Oxford: *m.* 1959, Helen Elizabeth, only da. of J. Alan Price, FRCP, of Heaton, Bradford, and has issue living, Rupert James Brodribb, *b.* 1961,—Piers Daniel Carlyle, *b.* 1967,—Rachel Elizabeth, *b.* 1962,—Lucy Charlotte, *b.* 1964. *Residence*, Grey's Green House, Henley-on-Thames, Oxon.——Hugo Laurence Joseph (13, Barnsbury Sq., N1), *b.* 1935; ed. at Eton, and at Trin. Coll., Oxford (MA): *m.* 1967, Mary Rose Catherine, da. of the late Arthur Joseph Lawrence Pollen [see Pollen, Bt., colls.], and has issue living, Joseph Gabriel *b.* 1967,—Samuel Felix, *b.* 1972, Magnus Gregory Nathaniel, *b.* 1974,—Isabel Mary, *b.* 1969.
Sister living—Joyce Morgan (*Joyce, Lady Worsley*) *b.* 1895: *m.* 1924, Col. Sir William Arthington Worsley, 4th Bt., who *d.* 1973. *Residence*, Hovingham Hall, York.

Collateral Branches living.

Grandchildren of the late Harold Roscoe Brunner (infra):—
Issue of the late Anthony Brunner, *b.* 1901; assumed by deed poll 1919 the christian name of Anthony in lieu of his baptismal names of Egbert Sidney Houston; *d.* 1970: *m*: 1934, Amy Phyllis Ivy (Felicity) Whitaker (Highlands, Woodcote, nr. Reading):—
John Kilian Houston (The Square House, Palmer St., South Petherton, Som. TA13 5DB) *b.* 1934; ed. at Cheltenham; author and poet: *m.* 1958, Marjorie Rosamond, only da. of the late Edwin Charles Sauer.——Verena Hilda May, *b.* 1937; MA, and Dip. Ed. Edinburgh: *m.* 1967, Arthur Edward William Thornton, of 6, Mulberry Drive, Dunfermline, Fife.——Jennifer Margaret Felicity, *b.* 1939: *m.* 19—, John Marchant, and has issue living.

Issue of the late Wing-Cdr. Oswald Patrick O'Brien Brunner, RAF, *b.* 1908, *d.* 1966: *m.* 1933, Elaine (Wotton House, Wotton Underwood, nr. Aylesbury, Bucks.), da. of the late Richard Howlett, of Ambassadors' Court, St. James's Palace, SW1:—
Mary Elizabeth April, *b.* 1936: *m.* 1961, David A. S. Gladstone, of 2, Mountfort Terr., Barnsbury, N1, and has issue living, Patrick, *b.* 1969,—Perdita *b.* 1965.

Issue of the late Harold Roscoe Brunner, 3rd son of 1st baronet, *b.* 1871, *d.* 1926 : *m.* 1898, Ethel, who *d.* 1926, el. da. of the late Arthur Houston LL.D., K.C. (Ireland), Bar.-at-law :—
Shelagh Salome Houston, *b.* 1900; granted title of Countess Rietberg in Principality of Liechtenstein 1952: *m.* 1st, 1925 (divorce 1934), HSH Prince Ferdinand Andreas Joseph Maria von und zu Liechtenstein; 2ndly, 1934 (divorce 1952), George Otto Suppancic, and has issue living, (by 1st m.) *Count* Christopher Richard Francis von Rietberg, *b.* 1926; formerly in 15th/19th Hussars: *m.* 1955, Kathleen Hamilton, da. of Alfred Thayer Mahan, of Old Greenbush Rd., Orangeburg, New York State, USA, and has issue living, *Count* Mark Andreas *b.* 1959, *Countess* Gabrielle Catherine, *b.* 1957,—*Countess* (Ethel) Elisabeth Olga Mary von Rietberg, *b.* 1928: *m.* 1st, 1953 (m. diss. 1961) Klaus Bruno von Brehm, of Alt-Aussee, Austria; 2ndly, 1968, Richard Douglas Loftus Onslow (PO Box 41, Knysna 6570, S. Africa) [see E. Onslow, colls.]. *Residence*, 50, Storeys Way, Cambridge.

The 1st baronet, the Rt. Hon. Sir John Tomlinson Brunner, P.C., was second son of the late Rev John Brunner, a native of Zurich, and proprietor of Mere Bank Sch., Everton, Liverpool; he founded Brunner Mond and Co. (Limited), alkali manufacturers, of Northwich, Cheshire, and gave new building and land for the Witton Gram. Sch., Northwich; subscribed liberally to Liverpool Univ. (besides endowing Chairs of Economic Science, Physical Chemistry and Egyptology); also donated to the Nantwich, Winsford, and Middlewich Public Libraries, and in July, 1885, presented to the town of Northwich a Public Library (rebuilt it 1909); gave Village Halls to several villages, and "Guildhalls" to Runcorn and Winsford; sat as M.P. for Cheshire, Northwich Div. (L) 1885-6, when he was defeated; re-elected 1887, and sat until 1910. The 2nd baronet, Sir John Fowler Brunner (who discontinued by deed poll a third christian name of Leece), was a Director of Brunner, Mond and Co. (Limited), and of Madeley Collieries (Limited), and sat as M.P. for Lancashire (S.-W.), Leigh Div. (L) Jan. 1906 to Jan. 1910, for Cheshire, Northwich Div. Jan. 1910 to Nov. 1918, and for Southport Dec. 1923 to Oct. 1924.

BRUNTON. Creation (U.K.) 1908, of Stratford Place, St. Marylebone.

The incitement of glory is the torch of the mind.

God is our refuge and strength.

Sir (EDWARD FRANCIS) LAUDER BRUNTON, 3rd *Baronet; b.* Nov. 10th, 1916; *s.* his father, *Sir* (JAMES) STOPFORD (LAUDER), 1943; ed. at Trin. Coll. Sch., Port Hope, at Bryanston Sch., and at McGill Univ. (B.Sc. MD and CM); Hon. Attending Physician, R. Victoria Hosp. Montreal, a Fellow of International Soc. of Hematology, and of American Coll. of Physicians, and a Member of American Soc. of Hematology; 1940-45 War as Capt. R. Canadian Army Med. Corps: *m.* 1946, Marjorie Grant, only da. of David Sclater Lewis, MSc, MD, FRCP (Canada), and has issue.

Arms—Or, a caduceus sable on a chief azure three pallets argent. Crest—On a mount vert, a beacon fired between two sprigs of laurel proper.

Address—PO Box 140, Guysborough, Nova Scotia, Canada.

Son living—JAMES LAUDER (Apt. 104, 1000, McGregor St., Montreal 112, Canada), *b.* Sept. 24th, 1947: *m.* 1967, Susan, da. of Charles Hons, and has issue living.
Daughter living—Nancy Elizabeth, *b.* 1949.
Sister living—Ethel Alice Bonsall (1765, Vernon St. Halifax, Nova Scotia, Canada), *b.* 1918: *m.* 1942, Ralph Hoskins.

Widow living of 2nd Baronet—ELIZABETH, da. of J. Bonsall Porter, Ph.D., D.Sc., Professor of Engineering, McGill Univ., Montreal, Canada : *m.* 1st, 1915, Sir (James) Stopford (Lauder) Brunton, 2nd Bt., who *d.* 1943; 2ndly, 1948, Francis Hankin, of Guysborough, Nova Scotia.

The 1st baronet, Sir (Thomas) Lauder Brunton, M.D., D.Sc., F.R.S., F.R.C.P., LL.D., was an eminent Consulting Physician. The 2nd baronet, Sir (James) Stopford (Lauder) Brunton, was a Mining Geologist.

Buchan-Hepburn, see Hepburn.

BUCHANAN, Creation (U.K.) 1878, of Dunburgh, Stirlingshire.

Never conquered.

Sir CHARLES JAMES BUCHANAN, 4th *Baronet; b.* April 16th, 1899; *s.* his father, *Sir* ERIC ALEXANDER, 1928; ed. at Harrow; Major (retired) Highland L.I., a Member of Queen's Body Guard for Scotland (Roy. Co. of Archers), a J.P. and D.L. for Notts.; co. Commr. for Notts. of Boy Scouts' Assocn. 1949-62; High Sheriff of Notts. 1962; with N. Russian Relief Force 1919; European War 1939-45 in France and Italy; was A.D.C. to Gov. of Madras 1928-32: *m.* (Feb.) 1932, Barbara Helen, da. of the late Lieut.-Col. the Rt. Hon. Sir George Frederick Stanley, G.C.S.I., G.C.I.E., C.M.G. [*see* E. Derby, colls.], and has issue.

Arms—Or, a lion rampant sable between two otters' heads erased in chief proper and a cinque-foil in base of the second, all within a double tressure flory counter flory of the last. Crest—An armed dexter hand holding a cap of dignity purpure, the facings ermine. Supporters—*Dexter,* a falcon wings elevated and addorsed proper, belled and beaked or ; *sinister,* a gryphon sable; each charged on the breast with two branches of laurel conjoined or.
Residence—St. Anne's Manor, Sutton Bonington, Loughborough. *Club*—Lansdowne.

Sons living—ANDREW GEORGE (Hodsock Priory, Blyth, Worksop), *b.* July 21st, 1937; *ed.* at Eton, at Trin. Coll., Camb., and at Wye Coll., London Univ.; late 2nd Lt. Coldstream Guards a Chartered Surveyor and a Chartered Land Agent: *m.* 1966, Belinda Jane Virginia, da. of Donald C. Maclean, of Thurloe Sq., SW7, and widow of Gresham N. Vaughan, and has issue living, George Charles Mellish, *b.* Jan. 27th, 1975,—Laura, *b.* 1967.——Hugh Charles Stanley, (Lower Farm House, Drayton Beauchamp, Aylesbury, Bucks.), *b.* 1942; *ed.* at Eton, and at McGill Univ., Canada: *m.* 1969, Nony Caroline Vatcher, da. of Lt.-Col. John Johnston Dingwall, DSO, of Lyford Grange, Lyford, Berks, [see V. Galway, colls.], and has issue living, James Ian Stanley, *b.* 1974,—Clarissa Victoria Rosamund, *b.* 1972.
Daughters living—Georgina Mary Gabrielle, *b.* (Dec.) 1932: *m.* 1966, Michael Denzil Grierson Clayton, of 6, Cobden Cres., Edinburgh, and has issue living, Roger Lancelot, *b.* 1969,—Harriet Beatrix Evelyn, *b.* 1971.——Constance Carolyn, *b.* 1934: *m.* 1961, Hugh John Alexander Lindsay, of 91, Lansdowne Rd., W11 [see E. Crawford].
Sister living—Mary Constance Victoria (Holland House Misson, Bawtry, Doncaster) *b.* 1901: *m.* 1921, Maj. Thomas Garrett Mayhew, DL, JP, late E. Yorkshire Regt., who *d.* 1965, and has issue living, Patricia Constance Phyllis, *b.* 1923: *m.* 1st Patrick William Mackenzie Dean; 2ndly, 1952, Derek Sydney Chandos Fisher, who *d.* 1972; 3rdly, 1973, Sqdn. Ldr. John Matthias Oxenham Dyer, DFC, AFC, RAF (ret.) of Kagia Farm, P.O. Box 111, Limuru, Kenya.

This family descends from Archibald Buchanan of Auchintorlie, Dunbartonshire (a cadet of Buchanan of Leny), whose yst. son Andrew was grandfather of the 1st baronet, the Rt. Hon. Sir Andrew Buchanan, successively Ambassador at Berlin, St. Petersburg and Vienna.

Buchanan-Jardine, see Jardine.

LEITH-BUCHANAN, Creation (G.B.) 1775, of Burgh St. Peter, Norfolk.

Sir CHARLES ALEXANDER JAMES LEITH-BUCHANAN, only son of the late John Wellesley Macdonald Leith-Buchanan, el. son of James Macdonald Buchanan Leith-Buchanan, 3rd son of 4th baronet, 7th *Baronet*; *b.* Sept. 1st. 1939; *s.* his kinsman, *Sir* GEORGE HECTOR MACDONALD, 1973: *m.* 1962, Marianne, da. of Col. Earle Wellington Kelly, and has issue.

Arms—Quarterly: 1st and 4th or, a cross-crosslet fitchée sable, between three crescents in chief and as many fusils in base gules; 2nd, or, a lion rampant sable, in the dexter forepaw a heart gules within a double tressure flory counterflory of the second, all within a bordure compony argent and azure. 3rd, counterquartered, 1st argent, a lion rampant gules, 2nd or, a hand couped at the wrist holding a cross crosslet fitchée gules, 3rd, per fesse or and vert in chief a lymphad sable and in base a salmon naiant argent; 4th, argent an oak tree eradicated proper charged with an eagle displayed or, all within a bordure invected gules. **Crest**—1st, a cross-crosslet as in the arms, 2nd, a dexter hand erect proper couped below the wrist, holding a dagger of the last, hilt and pommel or.

Residence—9814, Barlow Rd., Fairfax, Va. 22030, USA.

Daughter living—Mary Elizabeth, *b.* 1964.
Aunt living—Jean Isobel Barbara (645, Chelsea Cloisters, SW3), *b.* 1911.
Stepmother living—Isabel Sim (The Grange, Narre Warren North, Vic., Aust.), da. of the late A. W. Fraser, of Birchwood, Inverness; *m.* 1948, as his 2nd wife, John Wellesley Macdonald Leith-Buchanan (ante), who *d.* 1956.
Widow living of 6th Baronet—BARBARA (*Barbara, Lady Leith-Buchanan*), (Drummakill, Alexandria, Dunbartonshire), da. of Willard Phelps Lesbure, of Springfield, Mass., USA: *m.* 1933, Sir George Hector Macdonald Leith-Buchanan, 6th Bt., who *d.* 1973.

 Granddaughter of the late Charles John Leith-Buchanan (infra):—
Issue of the late Thomas Wellesley Macdonald Leith-Buchanan, *b.* 1907, *d.* 1967: *m.* 1932, Mary C. (100, Sulphur Springs Rd., Ancaster, Ont., Canada) da. of the late Allan J. Cameron, Bar.-at-law, of Halifax, Nova Scotia:—
Eleanor Clare, *b.* 1935: *m.* 1955, William Hugh Shaw, of 99, Carrington Court, Ancaster, Ont., Canada, and has issue living.

  Issue of the late Charles John Leith-Buchanan, 4th son of 4th baronet, *b.* 1875, *d.* 1948: *m.* 1905, Mary Eleanor, who *d.* 1946, da. of William Farmer, of Ancaster, Ontario, Canada:—
Mary Elizabeth Warburton, *b.* 1911. *Residence*,

 Grandchildren of the late Alexander Henry LEITH, son of George Gordon Browne Leith, 2nd son of 2nd baronet:—
Issue of the late Marjorie LEITH, *b.* 1883, *d.* 1960: *m.* 1911, A. Montye Macrae:—
Morson Leith, *b.* 1913; is Lieut. Roy. Canadian Naval Vol. Reserve; European War 1939-44: *m.* 1942, Helen Josephine Slater, of Oakville, Ontario, and has issue living, James Morson, *b.* 1943,—Gordon Stuart, *b.* 1944,—Gordon Eric Alexander, *b.* 1951,—John Ewart Bryant (twin), *b.* 1951,—Lorna Leith, *b.* 1948. *Residence*, 41, Navy Street, Oakville, Ontario, Canada.——John Montye (Lakefield College School, Lakefield, Ontario), *b.* 1916; Lt. RCNVR; 1939-44 War: *m.* 1944, Helen Irene Gilroy, of Oakville, Ontario, and has issue living, Montye Bruce, *b.* 1946,—Alexander Ian, *b.* 1948,—Alison Jane, *b.* 1953.——Donald Gordon, *b.* 1920; is Lieut. RCNVR; 1939-45 War: *m.* 1953, Joan Irwin, of Toronto, Canada, and has issue living, Andrew Leith, *b.* 1955,—Christopher Donald Irwin, *b.* 1958,—Heather Jean, *b.* 1956. *Residence*, 215, Stone St., Gananoque, Ontario, Canada.——Eleanor Ferrier, *b.* 1920: *m.* 1944, Lt.-Cdr. Ralph Patrick Abbott, Roy. Canadian Naval Vol. Reserve, of Toronto, Canada.

This family, of considerable antiquity in Scotland, is in direct descent from William Leith, Provost of Aberdeen 1350. The 1st baronet, Sir Alexander Leith, was Lieut.-Col. 88th Foot ; his father was killed while commanding artillery at siege of Havannah, 1763. The 3rd baronet, Sir Alexander Wellesley William Leith, m. Jemima, da. of Hector Macdonald Buchanan, and their son, Sir George Hector, 4th baronet assumed the additional surname of Buchanan 1877.

Buckworth-Herne-Soame, see Soame.

WILLIAMS-BULKELEY, Creation (E.) 1661, of Penrhyn, Carnarvonshire.

Sir RICHARD HARRY DAVID WILLIAMS BULKELEY, 13th *Baronet*, son of the late Majo͡r Richard Gerard Wellesley Williams-Bulkeley, M.C.ʳ only son of 12th baronet; *b.* Oct. 5th, 1911; *s.* hi grandfather, *Sir* RICHARD HENRY, *K.C.B.*, 1942; ed. at Eton; is Lieut.-Col. Comdt. of Caernarvonshire and Anglesey Army Cadet Force, a J.P. for Anglesey, and a CStJ; Lord-Lt. of Anglesey 1947-74, since when of Gwynedd; S-E Asia 1944-5 as Maj. R. Welch Fusiliers: *m.* 1938, Renée Arundell, da. of Sir Thomas Lewis Hughes Neave, 5th Bt., and has issue.

Arms—Quarterly: 1st and 4th, sable a chevron between three bulls' heads cabossed argent; a canton ermine, *Bulkeley;* 2nd and 3rd, gules, a chevron ermine between three men's, heads couped in profile proper, *Williams.* **Crest**—1st, out of a ducal coronet a bull's head argent, horned or, charged with a chevron sable; 2nd, a stag's head cabossed argent.
Seat—Baron Hill, Beaumaris, Anglesey. **Residence**—Plas Meigan, Beaumaris, Anglesey.

Sons living—RICHARD THOMAS (Glan Aber, Pentraeth, Anglesey, Gwynedd), *b.* May 25th, 1939; ed. at Eton; Capt. Welsh Guards: *m.* 1964, Sarah Susan, el. da. of the late Rt. Hon. Lord Justice (Sir Henry Josceline) Phillimore, OBE, and has issue living, Richard Hugh, *b.* 1968,—Harry David (twin), *b.* 1968,—Victoria Mary, *b.* 1973.——Michael (Pigeon Hill, Lilley, Luton), *b.* 1943; ed. at Eton; Lt. Welsh Gds.: *m.* 1968, Ellen Marie, el. da. of the late L. Falkum-Hansen, of Drammensveien, 50B, Oslo, and has issue living, James, *b.* 1970,—David Haakon, *b.* 1973.

Sister living—Victoria Sylvia Jane (The Reddings, Scaynes Hill, Sussex), *b.* 1910: *m.* 1938, Hubert Alfred Cleary, who *d.* 1965.

Collateral Branch living.

Granddaughter of the late Maj. Arthur Wellesley Williams, 3rd son of 9th baronet:—
Issue of the late Rupert Owain Glendwr Williams, *b.* 1866, *d.* 1939: *m.* 1899, Marion Winkworth, who *d.* 1937, only child of the late Henry Hammond, of Duncton, Sussex:—
Sylvia Mary (69, St. Pauls Rd., Chichester) *b.* 1905.

This family descends in the male line, as did the House of Tudor, from Edynfed Vychan, Chief Minister to Llywellyn the Great. William ap Griffith of Cochwillan, Caernarvonshire, 10th in descent, assisted Henry VII at Bosworth. His son William Williams was the first to adopt that surname. His great-great-grandson, Sir Griffith Williams of Penrhyn (nephew of John Williams, Archbishop of York), was cr. a baronet by Cromwell 1658 and by Charles II 1661. Sir Richard Bulkeley Williams, 10th baronet, assumed the additional surname of Bulkeley in 1826 on succeeding to the estates of Viscount Bulkeley.

BULL, Creation (U.K.) 1922, of Hammersmith, co. London.

Sir GEORGE BULL, 3rd *Baronet;* *b.* June 19th, 1906; *s.* his brother, Sir STEPHEN JOHN, 1942; sometime Cadet R.N.; admitted a Solicitor 1929; Senior partner in the legal firm of Bull & Bull, of 11, Stone Buildings, Lincoln's Inn, WC, Hon. Solicitor to Roy. So. of St. George and Roy. Life Saving So., Gov. of Godolphin and Latymer Sch., of Upper Latymer and of Latymer Foundation, Trustee of Hammersmith United Charities, and Chm. of London Rent Assessment Cttees.; 1939-45 War as Cdr. RNVR: *m.* 1933, Gabrielle, da. of the late Bramwell Jackson, MC, and has issue.

Arms—Sable, three astronomical signs of Taurus or. **Crest**—A bull's head cabossed sable, charged on the forehead with the sign of the Taurus as in the arms.

Residence—3, Hammersmith Terrace, W.6. *Clubs*—1900, MCC, London Corinthian Sailing (Pres.).

Son living—SIMEON GEORGE, b. Aug. 1st, 1934 ; ed. at Eton, Innsbruck, and Paris ; admitted a Solicitor 1959 ; is a partner in the legal firm of Bull & Bull : m. 1961, Annick Elizabeth Renée Geneviève, younger da. of the late Louis Bresson, of Château des Masselins, Chandai, Orne, France, and has issue living, Stephen, b. 1966,—Jacqueline-Hester, b. 1964,—Sophia Ann, b. 1971. *Residence*, 77, Palewell Park, SW14. *Club*, Royal Thames Yacht.

Daughter living—Charlotte Sophia, b. 1938 ; ed. at Roedean, and at Emma Willard'Sch., New York: m. 1964, Christopher A. W. Gibbons, of 4, Hammersmith Terr., W6, and has issue living, Sybil Jemima, b. 1965,—Georgina Loveday, b. 1967.

Brothers living—Anthony, *CBE*, b. 1908; ed. at Gresham Sch., Holt, and at Magdalene Coll., Camb. (MA); Col. late RE; Transport Consultant; Vice-Chm. of London Transport Exec. 1965-71 (Pres. of Inst. of Transport 1960-70), and a CStJ; Transport Div. Control Commr. for Germany (British Element), Berlin 1945-46; 1939-45 War (OBE, American Bronze Star); OBE (Mil) 1944, CBE (Civil) 1968: m. 1946, Barbara, who d. 1947, da. of Peter Donovan, of Great Banks, Rye, Sussex, and has issue living, Caroline (*Lady Chichester-Clark*), b. 1947: m. 1974, as his 2nd wife, Sir Robert Chichester-Clark, MP [see M. Donegall, colls.]. *Residences*, 27, Pelham Place, SW7; Trowland Cottage, Burnham Norton, Norfolk. *Club*, United Oxford and Cambridge University.——Peter Cecil, *DSC*, b. 1912; ed. at Winchester; 1939-45 War as Lt.-Cdr. RNVR (DSC).

The 1st baronet, the Rt. Hon. Sir William (James) Bull, F.S.A., was senior partner in the firm of Bull & Bull, solicitors, of 3, Stone Buildings, Lincoln's Inn, W.C., and King Street, Hammersmith, W., a Director of Equity and Law Life Assurance Co., and of Siemens, Ltd., Pres. of Council of Roy. Albert Hall, Hon. Solicitor to League of Mercy, and to Roy. So. of St. George, first Hon. Freeman of Hammersmith, and Maltravers Herald of Arms Extraor. ; sat as M.P. for Hammersmith (C) 1900-1918, and for S. Div. thereof 1918-29, and was Parliamentary Private Sec. to Rt. Hon. W. H. Long, M.P. (afterwards Viscount Long of Wraxall) 1902-21. The 2nd baronet, Flight-Lieut. Sir Stephen John, R.A.F. Vol. Reserve ; partner in the firm of Bull & Bull ; d. (on active ser. in Java) 1942.

BULLOCK, Creation (U.K.) 1954, of Crosby, co. Palatine of Lancaster. [Extinct 1966.]

Sir (HAROLD) MALCOLM BULLOCK, *MBE*, 1st and last Baronet.

Daughter living of 1st baronet—Priscilla Victoria, b. 1920: m. 1947, Peter Robin Hood Hastings Bass, who d. 1964 [see E. Huntingdon, colls.]. *Residence*,—Well's Head House, Kingsclere, nr. Newbury, Berks.

BULLOUGH, Creation (U.K.) 1916, of Isle of Rhum, co. Inverness, and The Down House, Redmarley, co. Worcester. [Extinct 1939.]

Sir GEORGE BULLOUGH, 1st and last *Baronet*.

Daughter living of 1st Baronet—Hermione (*Countess of Durham*), b. 1906: m. 1931, as his second wife, the 5th Earl of Durham, who d. 1970. *Residence*, West Marden Hall, Chichester.

BUNBURY, Creation (E.) 1681, of Stanney Hall, Cheshire.

To be rather than to seem.

Sir (JOHN) WILLIAM NAPIER BUNBURY, 12th *Baronet; b.* July 3rd, 1915; *s.* his father, *Sir* CHARLES HENRY NAPIER, 1963; ed. at Eton, and at Jesus Coll., Camb.; High Sheriff of Suffolk 1972-73; 1939-45 War as Capt. KRRC: *m.* 1940, Margaret Pamela, da. of the late Thomas Alexander Sutton [see Sutton, Bt., colls.], and has issue.

Arms—Argent, on a bend sable three chess-rooks of the field. **Crest**—Two swords saltire-wise through the mouth of a leopard's face or, the blades proper, hilted and pommelled gold. *Seat*—Naunton Hall, Rendlesham, Suffolk.

Sons living—MICHAEL WILLIAM (14, Kelso Place W8), b. Dec. 29th, 1946; ed. at Eton, and Trin. Coll., Camb. (MA) ——Charles Thomas (Hall Farm, Thurning, Dereham, Norfolk), b. 1950; ed. at Radley, and Roy. Agric. Coll., Cirencester: m. 1971, Sarah Elizabeth, el. da. of W. D. Hancock, of Sherborne Hall, King's Lynn, Norfolk, and has issue living, Emma Sarah b. 1973,—Rebecca Louise, b. 1974.——Christopher Henry (twin), b. 1950; ed. at Radley.

Sister living—Margaret Elinor, b. 1918: m. 1945, Major James Michael Heigham Royce Tomkin, M.C., 5th Roy. Inniskilling Dragoon Gds., of Red House, Wissett, Halesworth, Suffolk, and has issue living, Alastair Peter Royce, b. 1949,—a son, b. 1951,—Caroline Susan, b. 1947.

Collateral Branches living.

Grandsons of the late Lt.-Col. William St. Pierre Bunbury, 3rd son of Col. Henry William St. Pierre Bunbury, CB, son of 7th baronet:—

Issue of the late Lieut.-Col. Gerald Bruce St. Pierre Bunbury, Indian Army, b. 1883, d. 1954 : m. 1909, Frances Mary Olivia, who d. 1952, only da. of the late Francis Peter Dixon, J.P., of Wood View, Carlisle :—

Francis Ramsay St. Pierre, *C.B.E.*, *D.S.O.*, b. 1910; ed. at Rugby; Brigadier (ret.) Duke of Wellington's Regt. ; N.-W. Frontier of India 1935, European War 1939-45 in Persia, Middle

East, and Italy (despatches, D.S.O.), Korea 1953 (Bar to D.S.O.), Cyprus 1958 (despatches C.B.E.) ; D.S.O. 1945 (Bar 1953), C.B.E. (Mil.) 1958 : *m.* 1933, Elizabeth Pamela Somers, who *d.* 1969, da. of the late Francis Reginald Liscombe, of Lansoar House, Lansoar, Monmouth-shire, and has issue living, Charles Napier St. Pierre, *MBE, b.* 1941; ed. at Rugby; Maj. Duke of Wellington's Regt., N. Ireland 1974; MBE (Mil.) 1974,—Ann Geraldine St. Pierre, *b.* 1934. *Residence,* 16, Lancaster Rd., Wimbledon, SW19.

Issue of the late Brig. Noel Louis St. Pierre Bunbury, DSO, *b.* 1890, *d.* 1971: *m.* 1923, Iris Graham, who *d.* 1965, da. of James Baird Whitelaw, of N. Berwick:—
David St. Pierre (1, Hazelwood Rd., Hale, Cheshire), *b.* 1926; ed. at Imperial Coll. of Science and Tech., London (PhD, BSc).

This family traces its origin to a younger branch of the Norman house of St. Pierre. From Hugh Lupus, second Norman Earl of Chester, the family obtained the manor of Bunbury in Cheshire. David de Bunbury, 7th in descent from St. Pierre, acquired by marriage, *temp.* Edward III, the lordship of Stanney, which the family possessed until 1859. 11th in descent from David de Bunbury was Sir Thomas, the 1st baronet. The 6th baronet, Sir Thomas Charles, was forty-three years M.P. for Suffolk. The 7th baronet, Lieut.-Gen. Sir Henry Edward, K.C.B., sat as M.P. for Suffolk, and was Under-Sec. of State for War 1809-16. Sir Edward Herbert Bunbury, 9th baronet, was M.P. for Bury St. Edmunds (*L*) 1847-52.

RICHARDSON-BUNBURY, Creation (I.) 1787, of Augher, co. Tyrone.

Sir (RICHARD DAVID) MICHAEL RICHARD-SON-BUNBURY, *R.N.,* 5th *Baronet,* el. son of the late Richard Richardson-Bunbury, 2nd son of the late Moutray Frederic Richardson-Bunbury, 2nd son of the late William Richardson-Bunbury, 2nd son of 2nd Baronet ; *b.* Oct. 27th, 1927 ; *s.* his kinsman, *Sir* MERVYN WILLIAM, 1953: *m.* 1961, Jane Louise da. of the late Col. A. W. Pulverman, and has issue.

Arms—Quarterly: 1st and 4th, ermine, a chess-rook be-tween two leopards' faces in bend between two bendlets sable, *Bunbury* ; 2nd and 3rd, azure, on a fesse argent between an ancient ship the sails furled in chief, and in base a bull's head couped or, a saltire gules, *Richardson.* **Crests**—1st, in front of a tree proper on a mount vert a leopard's face, paly of six argent and sable, transfixed by two arrows in saltire also proper ; **2nd,** a lion rampant ermine, in the mouth a trefoil slipped vert, be-tween the fore-paws a torteaux charged with a cross-crosslet or. *Residence*—Woodlands, Mays Hill, Worplesdon, Guildford, Surrey.

Virtue appears like an oak.

Sons living—ROGER MICHAEL, *b.* Nov. 2nd, 1962,—Thomas William, *b.* 1965.

Brother living—Roger Hugh Moutray (Fonthill Cottage, Lewannick, Launceston, Cornwall), *b.* 1934; Cdr. RN: *m.* 1965, Carol Irene, da. of F. J. H. Arnold of Rodings, Pilgrims Way, Guildford, and has issue living, Robert Moutray, *b.* 1968,—David, *b.* 1972,—Judith Mervyn, *b.* 1967,—Elizabeth (twin), *b.* 1972.

Sisters living—Margaret Delves, *b.* 1931; SRN: *m.* 1966, James Harvey Woolliams, of Norwich House, Kingham Hill, Kingham, Oxford, and has issue living, Richard Frank, *b.* 1968.—Angela Mervyn, *b.* 1946; BA.

Mother living—Florence Margaret Gordon, da. of Col. Roger Gordon Thomson, C.M.G., D.S.O. [Broughton, Bt., colls.] : *m.* 1925, Richard Richardson-Bunbury (ante), who *d.* 1951. *Residence,* Quarrymead, Hillcrest Road, Hythe, Kent.

Collateral Branches living.

Grandsons of the late Moutray Frederic Richardson-Bunbury (infra):—
Issue of the late James Richardson-Bunbury, *b.* 1901, *d.* 1970: *m.* 1938, Betty Winifred (Flat 2, Moorview, Ashwell Lane, Glastonbury, Som.), da. of Col. Roger Gordon Thomson, CMG, DSO [Broughton, Bt., colls.]:—
Patrick James, *b.* 1939; ed. at Millfield.——William Hedley (77, Talbot Av., S. Como., W. Aust. 6152), *b.* 1940; ed. at King's Sch., Bruton, and Durham Univ. (BA); MACE; Dip. Ed.: *m.* 1964, Jennifer Anne, da. of L. D. Syer, of Folkestone, and has issue living, Alison Claire, *b.* 1969,—Katherine Anne, *b.* 1971.——Andrew, *b.* 1943; ed. at Millfield, and Keble Coll., Oxford (MA).

Grandchildren of the late William Richardson-Bunbury, 2nd son of 2nd baronet:—
Issue of the late Moutray Frederic Richardson-Bunbury, *b.* 1865, *d.* 1917: *m.* 1896, Mary Capel Vines, who *d.* 1949 :—
Kathleen, *b.* 1903: *m.* 1926, Guy Waterman Elkington, MB, MRCP, who *d.* 1967, and has issue living, Edward James, *b.* 1927,—Arthur Guy, *b.* 1929,—Christopher Richard, *b.* 1933,—John Henry, *b.* 1939,—Mary Violet, *b.* 1930. *Residence,* 15, Kershaw St., Sublaco, Perth, W. Aust.
Issue of the late Archibald Edward Richardson-Bunbury, *b.* 1868, *d.* 1937: *m.* 1909, Vida Muriel, who *d.* 1967, da. of the late Arthur Heppingstone:—
Archibald Vernon, *b.* 1916: *m.* 1939, Iris Jensen, and has issue living, Edward Vernon, *b.* 1941,—Richard Archibald, *b.* 1943.—Dorothy Margaret, *b.* 1940,—Wendy Muriel, *b.* 1944,—Patricia Iris, *b.* 1946,—Doreen Jennifer, *b.* 1948. *Residence,* Marybrook House, Busselton, W. Australia.——Caroline Mervyn, *b.* 1910 : *m.* 1935, John Oliver Coote, and has issue living, John Edward, *b.* 1937,—Diana Bunbury, *b.* 1935. *Residence,* 29A, New St., Peppermint Grove, W. Australia.——Dorothy Emelie, *b.* 1911 : *m.* 1st, 1932, Robert Edward Drake Brockman ; 2ndly, 1940, Wilfrid Gordon Johnston, and has issue living, (by 1st marriage) Mervyn Molloy, *b.* 1935,—(by 2nd marriage) Elizabeth Margaret, *b.* 1941,—Judith Bunbury, *b.* 1942,—Margaret Bunbury, *b.* 1944,—Vida Bunbury, *b.* 1948. *Residence,* Box 83, Post Office, Angusta, W. Australia.——Marjorie Vida, *b.* 1918: *m.* 1940, Norman William Malcolm, who *d.* 1972, and has issue living, Miles William Eric Bunbury, *b.* 1944,—Anthony Bunbury, *b.* 1955,—Sabina Bunbury, *b.* 1947. *Residence,* 102, Tyrell St., Nedlands, W. Australia.

This family was originally Scottish ; they became possessed of the Castle of Augher, in Tyrone by the marriage of Archibald Richardson with the da. of Sir James Erskine. Sir James, the 2nd baronet in 1822, assumed his aunt's name of Bunbury.

BURBIDGE, Creation (U.K.) 1916, of Littleton Park, co. Middlesex.

Sir HERBERT DUDLEY BURBIDGE, 5th *Baronet,*
only son of Herbert Edward Burbidge, 2nd son
of 1st baronet; *b.* Nov. 13th, 1904; *s.* his kinsman,
Sir JOHN RICHARD WOODMAN, 1974: *m.* 1933,
Ruby, da. of Charles Ethelbert Taylor, of The
Willows, Comox, Vancouver 1, BC, and has
issue.

Arms—Argent, a chevron sable between in chief two gads
proper and in base an unicorn of the second. **Crest**—A stag's
scalp, between the attires a boar's head erased and erect, all
proper.

Residence,—12549, 27 Avenue, Surrey, BC, Canada.

Labour conquers all things.

Son living—PETER DUDLEY (4724, Tree Top Heights,
Victoria, BC, Canada.), *b.* June 20th, 1942: *m.* 1967,
Peggy Marilyn, da. of Kenneth Anderson, of Ladner,
BC, and has issue living, Kathleen Jean, *b.* 1973.
Daughter living of 3rd baronet—Susan Woodman, *b.* 1927:
m. 1949, Michael Deric Lloyd Pearson, and has issue living,
Robert Lloyd, *b.* 1954,—Teresa Ann, *b.* 1951,—Kate
Alexandra, *b.* 1959. *Residence,* Broughton, 104, Coombe
Lane West, Kingston upon Thames, Surrey.
Daughters living of 2nd baronet—Enid Catherine Wood-
man, *b.* 1902: *m.* 1926, Capt. A. J. Vernon Venables,
who *d.* 1958, and has issue living, John Anthony Woodman
(Sandford House, 39, West St., Farnham, Surrey), *b.* 1928;
late Capt. RASC: *m.* 1956, Hazel Margaret, only da. of
Dr. R. L. Harward, of Odiham, Hants, and has issue living,
Anthony Mark Vernon *b.* 1960, Peter John Vernon *b.* 1964,
Margaret Anne Woodman *b.* 1962,—Jane Carol Woodman, *b.* 1930,—Catherine Dawn Woodman,
b. 1933: *m.* 1963, H. James Petherick, of Court Farm, Heale, Parracombe, N. Devon, and has
issue living, Carol Dawn *b.* 1964, Jill Catherine Julia *b.* 1967. *Residence,* 20, Egerton Gdns.,
SW3.——Sylvia Emily Woodman (*Lady Turnbull*), *b.* 1906: *m.* 1st, 1934, Eric Macleod Mitchell;
2ndly, 1948, Sir Roland Evelyn Turnbull, KCMG, Gov. and Com.-in-Ch. of N. Borneo, who *d.*
1960. *Residence,* 46, Ennismore Gdns., SW7.——Alva Grace Woodman, *b.* 1913: *m.* 1935,
Gerald Rudall Holman, who *d.* 1969, and has issue living, Rodney Woodman, *b.* 1942: *m.* 1973,
Jill Elizabeth Andrew,—Carol Woodman, *b.* 1938: *m.* 1961, John Humphrey Beattie, of Willow
House, Blundel Lane, Stoke D'Abernon, Surrey, and has issue living, Fiona Ann *b.* 1962,—
Nicola Jane *b.* 1966. *Residence,* Stillwater, Oak End Way, Woodham, Weybridge.
Widow living of 3rd baronet—JOAN ELIZABETH (HAMILTON) (*Joan, Lady Burbidge*) (Barons Keep,
Tidmarsh Lane, Tidmarsh nr. Reading) da. of Ernest Reginald Moxey, of London: *m.* 1946,
as his 2nd wife, Sir Richard Grant Woodman Burbidge, 3rd baronet, who *d.* 1966.
Widow living of 4th baronet—BENITA ROXANE (*Benita, Lady Burbidge*), (Albury Farmhouse,
Draycot, Tiddington, Oxon.), da. of the late Adrian Willem Mosselmans, of Ascot, Berks.:
m. 1956, Sir John Richard Woodman Burbidge, 4th baronet, who *d.* 1974.

The 1st baronet, Sir Richard Burbidge, was Managing Director of Harrods (Limited), of
Knightsbridge, S.W., Joint Managing Director of Harrods (Buenos Aires) Limited, Chm. of Dickins
and Jones (Limited), a Director of Hudson's Bay Co., and a Member of Advisory Board of Ministry
of Munitions.

BURDETT, Creation (E.) 1665, of Burthwaite, Yorkshire.

Sir SAVILE AYLMER BURDETT, 11th *Baronet* ;
b. Sept. 24th, 1931 ; *s.* his father, *Sir* HENRY AYLMER,
M.C., 1943 ; ed. at Wellington Coll., and at Imperial
Coll., London; late temporary Sub-Lieut. R.N.V.R.: *m.*
1962, June Elizabeth Campbell, da. of the late Dr. J. M.
Rutherford, of Westside, Knowl Hill, Woking, Surrey, and
has issue.

Arms—Paly of six argent and sable, on a bend gules three martlets or.
Crest—On a tower argent a martlet with wings displayed or.
Residence,—The Shieling, Sibley's Green, Thaxted, Essex, CM6 2NU.

Son living—CRISPIN PETER, *b.* Feb. 8th, 1967.
Daughter living—Felicity Jane, *b.* 1963.
Sisters living—Anne Margaret, *b.* 1929.——Jennifer Joyce, *b.* 1934 : *m.*
1st, 1952, Marian Stachowiak; 2ndly, 1970, Gordon Skinner, and has
issue living (by 1st m.), Nicholas John, *b.* 1959,—Martin Allen, *b.* 1961,
Sarah Margaret, *b.* 1957. *Residence,* 18, Cherry Garden Rd., East-
bourne.
Daughter living of 8th Baronet—Constance Hay BURDETT (c/o National Bank of New Zealand
8, Moorgate, E.C.2), *b.* 1908; resumed her maiden name of Burdett for herself and issue 1953:
m. 1938 (marriage dissolved 1952), Albert Charles Blau, Swiss Diplo. Ser., and has issue living,
Charles Albert BURDETT, *b.* 1942—John Coventry BURDETT, *b.* 1945.
Widow living of 10th Baronet—AUDREY GRACE CHICHESTER (*Audrey, Lady Burdett*), da. of George
Cutcliffe, formerly of 28, Glazbury Rd., W14: *m.* 1928, Sir Henry Aylmer Burdett, MC, 10th
baronet, who *d.* 1943. *Residence,* The Rising, East Knoyle, Wilts.

Collateral Branch living.

Issue of the late Lt.-Col. Ernest Wyndham Burdett, D.S.O., M.C., yst. son of the late
Rev. William Jerome Burdett, yr. son of 6th Bt., *b.* 1887, *d.* 1962: *m.* 1919, Hebe
Etheldreda Ellen Curwen, who *d.* 1967, da. of the late Lt.-Col. Gilbert R. H. Collis, of
24, Ovington Sq. SW:—
Arlington Jerome D'Arcy (Great Trippetts Farm, Milland, Liphook, Hants), *b.* 1922; Lt.-Cdr.,
RN (ret.): *m.* 1948, Elizabeth Alix, el. da. of the late Sir Charles Holditch Bristow, CIE, and
has issue living, Jeremy Francis D'Arcy, *b.* 1951,—Richard Wyndham *b.* 1962,—Susan Priscilla,
b. 1949: *m.* 1973, John Patrick Manley,—Marion Elizabeth, *b.* 1953.——Elizabeth Sylvia, *b.*
1921.

Sir Francis, 1st baronet, was son of Francis Burdett, of Burthwaite co. York.

BURKE, Creation (I.) 1797, of Marble Hill, Galway.

Sir THOMAS STANLEY BURKE, 8th
Baronet : b. July 20th, 1916; *s.* his father,
Sir GERALD HOWE, 1954 ; ed. at Harrow, and
at Trin. Coll., Camb. : *m.* 1955, Susanne
Margareta, el. da. of Otto Salvisberg, of Thun,
Switzerland, and has issue.

Arms—Erminois, a cross gules ; in the first quarter
a lion rampant sable. **Crest**—A cat-a-mountain sejant-
guardant proper, collared and chained or.

Residence—18, Elmcroft Av., NW11 0RR.

Son living—JAMES STANLEY GILBERT, *b.* July
1st, 1956.

Daughter living—Caroline Elizabeth, *b.* 1959.

Half-Sisters living—Bridget Alison, *b.* 1921 : *m.* 1944,
Lieut.-Col. Eugene Dechelette, O.B.E., French Artillery
(Reserve), of 217, Faubourg S-Honoré, Paris VIII, and
has issue living, Edward Henry Charles, *b.* 1950,—
Elizabeth Alison, *b.* 1947,—Anne Marie, *b.* 1949.—
Elizabeth Anne, *b.* 1924.

Collateral Branches living.

One king, one faith, one law.

Grandson of the late Henry Ulick
Burke (infra):—
Issue of the late Lt.-Col. Ulick Richard Samuel
Burke, *b.* 1907, *d.* 1963: *m.* 1930, Cynthia
(132, Marine Court, St. Leonards, Sussex), da.
of H. Darling:—
Jeremy Ulick (Woodleigh, 15, Daltrey Rd., Stevenage, Herts.), *b.* 1931; ed. at Univ. Coll., NW;
C.Eng., FICE, FIArb: *m.* 1st, 1954 (m. diss 1962), Anne, el. da. of J. E. Chinneck, of Berkhamsted, Herts.; 2ndly, 1963, Prudence Mary, el. da. of H. P. Stride, of Milbury Heath, Glos., and
has issue living (by 1st m.), Ulick Simon, *b.* 1957,—(by 2nd m.) Ulick Jacquelyn, *b.* 1964,—
Ulick Karen, *b.* 1966.

Granddaughter of the late Ulick Ralph Burke, son of the late Charles Granby
Burke, 2nd son of 2nd baronet:—
Issue of the late Henry Ulick Burke, *b.* 1874, *d.* 1960: *m.* 1st, 1902, Rose Uvedale, who
d. 1931, da. of the late Lieut.-Col. Parry Okeden, of Turnworth, Dorset; 2ndly, 1934,
Eva Mary (STRIDE), who *d.* 1964, da. of the late Thomas Foster:—
(By 1st marriage) Katrina Marian, *b.* 1904: *m.* 1st, 1927 (marriage dissolved 1949), Guy Louis
Beachim Beauchamp, of Norton Hall, Stratton-on-the-Fosse, nr. Bath; 2ndly, 1950, Surg.-
Com. Francis William Armytage Fosbery, R.N. (ret.), and has issue living, (by 1st marriage),
John Louis, *b.* 1930. *Residence*, Easthill, Upper Westwood, nr. Bradford-on-Avon, Wilts.

Grandson of the late Capt. James Henry Thomas Burke, C.B., R.N., son of Maj.
Gen. James Henry Burke, 3rd son of 2nd baronet :—
Issue of the late James Howe Campbell Ulick Burke, *b.* 1880, *d.* 1946 : *m.* 1st, 1912, Lilian
Maud (who obtained a divorce 1928), da. of William John Whenmouth ; 2ndly, 1930,
Annie Amelia Granville, of 6, Churchfield Road, Ealing, W.13 :—
(By 2nd marriage) James Ulick Hubert, *b.* 1932. *Residence*, 6, Churchfield Road, Ealing, W.13.

Sir Thomas, 1st baronet, raised a Regt. of Foot at his own expense during the Napoleonic
Wars. The 2nd baronet was Vice-Lieut. for co. Galway (High Sheriff 1838), and sat as M.P. therefor
1830-32. The 3rd baronet was also M.P. for co. Galway 1847-65.

BURNETT, Creation (N.S.) 1626, of Leys, Kincardineshire. [Dormant 1959.]

Sir ALEXANDER EDWIN BURNETT OF LEYS, *O.B.E.*, 14th *Baronet*,
d. May 9th, 1959.

Daughter living of 13th Baronet—Elizabeth Rohays Mary (*Lady Boyd-Rochfort*), *b.* 1916: *m.* 1st,
1938, the Hon. Henry Kerr Auchmuty Cecil, Lt. Gordon Highlanders and Army Air Corps.,
who *d.* (killed in action during European War) 1942 [*see* B. Amherst of Hackney]; 2ndly, 1944,
Capt. Sir Cecil Charles Boyd-Rochfort, KCVO, and has issue living, (by 1st m.) [*see* B. Amherst of
Hackney],— (by 2nd m.) Arthur Roger (Tally Ho Stud, Mullingar, co. Westmeath) *b.* 1945; ed.
at Eton: *m.* 1974, Mrs. Lena Margherita Maria Towell, da. of Aldo Berni, of 1, Mariners Drive,
Bristol 9. *Residence*, Kilnahard Castle, Ballyheelan, co. Cavan.

Collateral Branch living.

Descendants of the late Alexander Burnett (2nd son of 6th baronet), who assumed
the surname and arms of Ramsay by Roy. licence, and was *cr.* a *Baronet* 1806.
Of whom *Sir* ALEXANDER WILLIAM BURNETT RAMSAY, 7th *Baronet*, *b.* Aug. 4th, 1938,
is the presumed heir to this Baronetcy.

The lands of Leys are held under a charter from Robert Bruce, dated 1324. The 1st baronet,
Sir Thomas Burnett, though a Covenanter, was much trusted by Charles I., and was a friend of the
great Marquess of Montrose. He was uncle of the famous Dr. Gilbert Burnet, Bishop of Salisbury.
The son of 6th baronet, who assumed the name of Ramsay, was created a baronet 1806. The 12th
baronet, Col. Sir Thomas Burnett, R.A., was Lord-Lieut. and Convener for co. of Kincardine.
The 13th baronet, Maj.-Gen. Sir James Lauderdale Gilbert Burnett, C.B., C.M.G., D.S.O., was
Brigadier of Queen's Body Guard for Scotland (Roy. Co. of Archers), Vice-Lieut. of Kincardineshire, and Col. of the Gordon Highlanders, and commanded the 14th, 153rd and 8th Inf. Brigs.,
and 51st (Highland) Div. (T.A.).

BURNETT, Creation (U.K.) 1913, of Selborne House, County Borough of Croydon.

Firmness in dangers.

Sir DAVID HUMPHERY BURNETT, M.B.E., T.D., 3rd *Baronet ; b.* Jan. 27th, 1918 ; *s.* his father, *Col. Sir* LESLIE TREW, C.B.E., T.D., 1955 ; ed. at Harrow, and at St. John's Coll., Camb. (MA); FRICS, FBIM; a Lt. of City of London, Chm. and Managing Dir., of The Proprietors of Hay's Wharf Ltd., a Dir. of Guardian Roy. Exchange Assurance Ltd., a Member of Port of London Authority since 1962, and Chm. of S. London Botanical Inst. since 1964; Chm. of The London Wharfingers Assocn. 1964-71; Master of Co. of Watermen and Lightermen 1964; late Maj. RA (TA) 1939-45 War in France, Africa, and Italy (despatches, MBE); MBE (Mil) 1945: *m.* 1948 Geraldine Elizabeth Mortimer, da. of the late Sir Godfrey Arthur Fisher, KCMG, and has issue.

Arms—Per chevron or and sable, two holly leaves in chief vert, in base a hunting horn of the first, stringed **argent.** **Crest.**—Issuing from flames a branch of holly erect proper.
Residences—Tandridge Hall, nr. Oxted, Surrey; Tillmouth Park, Cornhill-on-Tweed, Northumberland. *Club*—Turf.

Sons living—ROBERT LESLIE FISHER, *b.* May 24th, 1949.——Charles David, *b.* 1951; ed. at Harrow, and Lincoln Coll., Oxford.——John Godfrey, *b.* 1954; ed. at Harrow.

Brother living—Richard Leslie, *b.* 1932; ed. at Eton, and at King's Coll., Camb.; LRAM 1952, ARCM 1952; formerly 2nd Lt. R. Leicester Regt.: *m.* 1969, Katrina Eveline, only da. of W. Graeme Hendrey, of Snatts Hill, Bletchingley, Surrey. *Residences*, 3, Macaulay Rd., SW4; Finchcocks, Goudhurst, Kent.

Sisters living—Mary, *b.* 1919 : *m.* 1948, Capt. Richard Gilbert Dawson, M.B.E., and has issue living, Richard, *b.* 1951,—John, *b.* 1953,—Teresa Joan *b.* 1950,—Sarah, *b.* 1959. *Residence,* South Fawley Manor, near Wantage, Berks.——Joan Dorothy, *b.* 1920: *m.* 1953, John Clement Herbert Taylor, and has issue living, Geoffrey, *b.* 1958,—Thomas, *b.* 1960,—Marian Joan, *b.* 1956. *Residence,* Braydells, Haywards Heath, Sussex.——Nancy, *b.* 1926: *m.* 1st, 1948 (m. diss. 1960), Ian Alastair Sinclair; 2ndly, 1972, Prof. A. H. Gerrard, of Leyswood, Groombridge, Sussex, and has issue living, (by 1st m.), Guy, *b.* 1951,—Josephine Anne, *b.* 1949,—Karen Lesley, *b.* 1954.

Widow living of 2nd Baronet—JOAN (*Joan, Lady Burnett*), dau. of the late Lieut.-Col. Sir John Humphery : *m.* 1917, Col. Sir Leslie Trew Burnett, C.B.E., T.D., 2nd baronet, who *d.* 1955. *Residence,* Stratton, Godstone, Surrey.

Sir David, 1st baronet, was Lord Mayor of London 1912-13. Sir Leslie Trew, C.B.E., T.D., 2nd baronet, was Hon. Col. 460th Heavy Anti-Aircraft Regt. R.A. (T.A.), and Master of Coopers Co. 1947.

BURNEY, Creation (U.K.) 1921, of Preston House, Preston Candover, co. Southampton

What is done honourably is right.

Sir CECIL DENNISTON BURNEY, 3rd *Baronet; b.* Jan. 8th, 1923; *s.* his father, *Cdr. Sir* (CHARLES) DENNISTOUN, *CMG*; ed. at Eton, and Trin. Coll., Camb.; a Dir. of Hampton Trust, Ltd.; a MLC, N. Rhodesia 1959-64, and an MP for Zambia 1964-68; 1939-45 War with RNVR: *m.* 1957, Mrs. Hazel Marguerite de Hamel, yr. da. of the late Thurman Coleman, of Weymouth, and has issue.

Arms—Azure, a pale argent two bars counterembattled counterchanged between in chief and in base a fountain proper. **Crest**—Out of a naval crown gold a bull's head azure, armed or. **Supporters** (not hereditary)—On either side a sea-bull azure, armed or.

Addresses,—P.O. Box 672, Ndola, Zambia, 5, Lyall St., SW1. *Clubs*,—Carlton, Buck's, Turf, Leander, Bulawayo, Ndola, Salisbury (Rhodesia).

Sons living,—NIGEL DENNISTOUN, *b.* Sept. 6th, 1959.——Philip Julian Gerard, *b.* 1961.
Widow living of 2nd Baronet,—GLADYS, (*Gladys, Lady, Burney*) (Huntley Towers, Paget, Bermuda), da. of George Henry High, of Lake Shore Drive, Chicago, USA: *m.* 1921, Cdr. Sir (Charles) Dennistoun Burney, CMG, 2nd Bt., who *d.* 1968.

The 1st baronet, Adm. of the Fleet Sir Cecil Burney, GCB, GCMG, was 2nd in Command of Grand Fleet at battle of Jutland 1916, and 2nd Sea Lord 1916-1917. Cdr. Sir (Charles) Dennistoun Burney, CMG, RN was inventor of Explosive Paravane and Protector Paravane.

BURRARD, Creation (G.B.) 1769, of Walhampton, Hampshire. [Extinct 1965.]

Daughter living of 8th Baronet—Elizabeth Geraldine (Eagle Cottage, Seend, Melksham, Wilts.), *b.* 1927.

BURRELL, Creation (G.B.) 1774, of Valentine House, Essex.

Sir WALTER RAYMOND BURRELL, *C.B.E., T.D.,* 8th *Baronet ; b.* Dec. 11th, 1903 ; *s.* his father, *Lieut.-Col. Sir* MERRIK RAYMOND, *C.B.E.* 1957 ; ed. at Eton ; late Lt.-Col. R.A. (T.A.); a D.L. for Sussex, and a Trustee of Roy. Agricultural So. of England (Pres. 1964); Pres. of Co. Landowners' Asso. 1952-3, and Vice-Chm. of W. Sussex Co. Council 1953 ; France 1939-40, U.S.A. 1943-4, N.-W. Europe 1944-45 (M.B.E.) ; M.B.E. (Mil.) 1945, C.B.E. (Civil) 1956 : *m.* 1931, the Hon. Anne Judith Denman, *O.B.E.,* da. of 3rd Baron Denman, and has issue.

Per fluctus ad oram.
Through the waves to the shore.

⁂rms—Vert, three! plain shields argent, each having a bordure engrailed or.

Seat—Knepp Castle, Horsham. *Club*—Boodle's.

Sons living—JOHN RAYMOND (Floodgates, West Grinstead, Horsham, Sussex), *b.* Feb. 20th, 1934; ed. at Eton: *m.* 1st, 1959, Rowena Frances, da. of the late Michael H. Pearce, from whom he obtained a divorce 1971; 2ndly. 1971, Margot Lucy, da. of F. E. Thatcher, of Sydney, NSW, and has issue living (by 1st m.), Charles Raymond, *b.* Aug. 27th, 1962,—Joanna Susan, *b.* 1960; (by 2nd m.), Andrew John, *b.* 1974.——Mark William (43a, Reeves Mews, W1), *b.* 1937; ed. at Eton, and Pembroke Coll., Camb. (BA): *m.* 1966, Mrs. Margot Munro, da. ot Westray Pearce, of Killara, NSW, and has issue living, William Westray, *b.* 1967,—Anthony Merrik, *b.* 1969,—Sophia Judith, *b.* 1974.
Daughters living—Penelope Anne, *b.* 1932: *m.* 1953, John Richard Greenwood, of Stone Hall, Balcombe, Sussex, and has issue living, John Simon, *b.* 1955,—James Anthony, *b.* 1959,—Anne Lucinda, *b.* 1957,—Fiona Mary, *b.* 1962.——Julia Mary Rona (twin), *b.* 1934: *m.* 1953, Jeremy Fox Eric Smith, of Balcombe House, Balcombe, Sussex, and has issue living, Julian Raymond Eric, *b.* 1956,—Hugo Jeremy Eric, *b.* 1957,—Dione Angela, *b.* 1954,—Sarah Helen, *b.* 1962.
Brother living—Peter Eustace, *CBE* (Huntland Downs, Ligonier, Pa., USA; Boodle's Club), *b.* 1905; ed. at Eton; formerly Sqdn. Ldr., RAF; Dir. of National Stud 1937-71; 1940-44 War as Sqdn. Ldr. RAF; CBE (Civil) 1957: *m.* 1st, 1929, Margaret Edith Pamela (who obtained a divorce 1940), da. of the late Lt.-Col. Stephen Hungerford Pollen, CMG [*see* Pollen, Bt., colls.]; 2ndly, 1971, Mrs. Constance P. Mellon, of Ligonier, Pa., USA, and has issue living (by 1st m.) Merrik Kay (15, Arlington Court, Arlington Rd., Twickenham, Middx.), *b.* 1937; ed. at Harrow: *m.* 1960 (m. diss. 1968), Julian Sarah, el. da. of David Hugo Burr, and has issue living, Peter, *b.* 1963.
Sister living—Joan Louise, *b.* 1902 : *m.* 1st, 1927, Major Lord North, who *d.* 1940, el. son of 8th Earl of Guilford; 2ndly, 1947, Charles Harman Hunt. *Residence*, Ockenden Garden House, Cuckfield, Sussex.
Half-Sister living—Ethelreda Josephine (*Baroness Tryon*), *b.* 1909 : *m.* 1939, the 2nd Baron Tryon. *Residence*, Church Farm, Great Durnford, Salisbury.

Collateral Branch living.
Issue of the late Peter Timothy Burrell, late Lieut. RN, el. son of Peter Eustace Burrell, CBE (ante), *b.* 1930, *d.* 1975: *m.* 1955, Patricia Clarice Marion, da. of Capt. Arthur Thomas Thompson, of Morcott, Rutland, and formerly wife of Ralph John Hamilton Pollock [see Pollock Bt., colls.]:—
Nicola Pamela Jane, *b.* 1957.

The first baronet was Sir Charles Raymond, who was created with remainder to his son-in-law, William Burrell, who succeeded as 2nd baronet. The 3rd baronet sat as M.P. for Shoreham (*C*) 1806-62, and at the time of his death was "father" of the House of Commons. The 4th baronet was also M.P. for Shoreham (*C*) 1862-76, and the 5th baronet sat as M.P. for New Shoreham (*C*) 1876-85, Lieut.-Col. Sir Merrik Raymond Burrell, C.B.E., 7th Bt., was High Sheriff of Sussex 1918, and Pres. of Roy. Agricultural So. of England 1936, and served in S. Africa 1900-01, and during European War 1914-19 as Lieut.-Col. (C.B.E.).

Sir ERNEST PENNINGTON BURROWS, 3rd and last *Baronet.*
Daughter living of 2nd Baronet—Fanny Beatrice, *b.* 1887: *m.* 1935, Alfred B. Yeates. *Residence,*

Sir HERBERT WALTER BUTCHER, MP, 1st and last *Baronet.*

Daughters living of 1st Baronet—Joy Daphne, *b.* 1936: *m.* 1956, Jonathan Payn Fellows-Smith, of 73, Pymers Mead, Croxted Rd., SE21, and has issue living, Richard Jonathan, *b.* 1957,—Charles Herbert (twin) *b.* 1957,—James William, *b.* 1958.——Pauline Mary, *b.* 1938: *m.* 1960, John Embleton Cardwell, of 12, Woodcote Park Av., Purley, Surrey, and has issue living, David Anthony, *b.* 1963,—William John, *b.* 1968,—Caroline Mary, *b.* 1961,—Jane Elizabeth, *b.* 1967.——Elisabeth Clare, *b.* 1944: *m.* 1966, John Alun Kelvin-Davies, (133, Fishpool St., St. Albans, Herts., AL3 4RY), and has issue living, Clare Elisabeth, *b.* 1967,—Holly Ann *b.* 1969.

Widow living of 1st Baronet—MARY (*Lady Butcher*) (122, Foxley Lane, Purley, CR2 3NB, Surrey) da. of James Odom, of Peterborough: *m.* 1935, Sir Herbert Walter Butcher, MP, 1st baronet, who *d.* 1966, when the title became ext.

BUTLER, Creation (I.) 1628, of Cloughgrenan, co. Carlow, Ireland.

Sir THOMAS PIERCE BUTLER, *CVO, DSO, O.B.E.*, 12th *Baronet* ; *b.* Sept. 18th, 1910 ; *s.* his father, *Lieut.-Col. Sir* RICHARD PIERCE, *O.B.E.*, 1955 ; ed. at Harrow, and at Trin. Coll., Camb. (BA); Col. Lt.-Col. Comdg. Grenadier Guards 1955-59, and Mil. Adviser to High Commr. for UK in NZ 1959-61; Maj. and Resident Gov. of HM Tower of London 1961-71, and Keeper of Jewel House, Tower of London 1968-71, a JP for Co. of London, FRGS, CStJ; Pres. of London (Prince of Wales's) Dist. St. John Ambulance Bde. 1967-70; 1939-45 War (despatches, DSO); DSO 1944, OBE (Mil) 1954, CVO 1970: *m.* 1937 (m. diss. 1972), Rosemary Liège Woodgate, whom he re-married 1973, da. of the late Maj. James Hamilton Davidson-Houston, of Pembury Hall, Kent, and 6, Thurloe Sq., SW7, and has issue.

Arms—Or, a chief indented azure, a bordure indented ermine. **Crest**—Out of a ducal coronet or, a plume of five ostrich feathers, therefrom a falcon rising argent.

As I find.   *Seat*—Ballin Temple, Ardattin, co. Carlow. *Residence*— 6, Thurloe Sq., Kensington, SW7. *Club*—Guards'.

Son living—RICHARD PIERCE (51, Thurloe Sq., SW7), *b.* July 22nd, 1940; ed. at Eton: *m.* 1965, Diana, da. of Col. S. J. Borg, of The Palms, St. Julians, Malta, and has issue living, Thomas Pierce, *b.* 1966,—Stephen Patrick, *b.* 1968,—Rupert Dudley, *b.* 1971, Anne Virginia, *b.* 1973.
Daughters living—Caroline Rosemary, *b.* 1939: *m.* 1958, Lt.-Col. Richard Charles Keightley, 5th Roy. Inniskilling Dragoon Guards, of White Kennels, Tarrant Gunville, Dorset, el. son of the late Gen. Sir Charles Frederic Keightley, GCB, GBE, DSO, and has issue living, Charlotte Joan, *b.* 1961,—Arabella Caroline, *b.* 1962,—Victoria Rosemary, *b.* 1965.——Virginia Pamela Liège, *b.* 1949: *m.* 1970, Capt. Michael Cunningham, The Queen's Own Hussars, of The Old †Rectory Harrington, Northants, and has issue living, Sophia Louisa Caroline, *b.* 1973.
Sisters living—Joan, *b.* 1908: *m.* 1943, Robert Nigel Bright Brunt, CBE, and has issue living Nicholas John Pierce, *b.* 1946; ed. at Marlborough; Capt. R. Fus.,—Nigel Richard Pierce, *b.* 1948; ed. at Harrow,—Rosemary Helen, *b.* 1944; ed. at Lady Eleanor Holles Sch., and at King's Coll., London Univ. (BA): *m.* 1971, the Rev. Anthony Broughton Hawley, MA. *Residence*, Oak Cottage, Knowle Lane, Cranleigh, Surrey.——Doreen Frances, *b.* 1913: *m.* 1934, Maj. Denis William Powlett Milbank, RA (TA) [*see* Milbank, Bt.]. *Address*, PO Ulu, Kenya.

Collateral Branches living.

Grandchildren of the late Richard Pierce Butler, 2nd son of 9th baronet:—
Issue of the late Hans Pierce Butler, *b.* 1880, *d.* 1940 : *m.* 1st, 1908, Agnes Lenore, who *d.* 1931, da. of the late William Edward Spurstow Moulson, of Solsgirth, Manitoba ; 2ndly, 1932, Maude Addison (1032, Cameron Av., Mount Royal, Calgary, Alberta, Canada):—
(By 1st m.) Richard Pierce (Box 87, Swan River, Manitoba, Canada), *b.* 1911: *m.* 1st, 1933, Vida McDonald, who *d.* 1968; 2ndly, 1970, Elsa Butler, of Pinawa, Manitoba, and has issue living (by 1st m.), Arthur Hans Pierce (Erickson, Manitoba, Canada), *b.* 1934; BSA, MSc: *m.* 1955, Elsie Elaine Laycock, and has issue living, Walter Richard Pierce *b.* 1964, Kerrie Lee *b.* 1966,—Kathleen Enid Selena, *b.* 1935: *m.* 1956, John Francis Lockhead, of Basswood, Manitoba, Canada, and has issue living, Richard Francis *b.* 1959, Phyllis Marie *b.* 1961,—Sheila Margaret Era, *b.* 1939: *m.* 1958, John Richard Fawcett (Box 515, Swan River, Manitoba, Canada), and has issue living, Cherylyn Sheila *b.* 1961, Kimberly Dawn *b.* 1963, Lorilee Faye *b.* 1967.——John Edward (Youngstown, Manitoba), *b.* 1916.——Arthur Cecil (Box 26D, RR2 Winnipeg, Manitoba, R3C 2E6), *b.* 1919.——William Hans (Foxwarren, Manitoba), *b.* 1922: *m.* 1943, Betty Atwell, and has issue living, Alan David, *b.* 1944,—Garth Charles, *b.* 1946,—William Grant, *b.* 1957.——Charles Edwin (Solsgirth, Manitoba), *b.* 1926: *m.* 19—, Marian McKay, and has issue living, Morley, *b.* 1951,—Barry, *b.* 1953.——Sidney Clarence (Dugald, Manitoba), *b.* 1928: *m.* 1952, Joan Yardings.——(By 2nd m.) Hans Pierce, *b.* 1939.——(By 1st m.) Agnes Gertrude, *b.* 1913: *m.* 1932, Walter Taylor, of 4604, Victoria Drive, Vancouver, BC, and has issue living, William, *b.* 1942,—Constance Lena, *b.* 1934: *m.* 1952, Mike Rooney.——Eva Constance, *b.* 1915: *m.* 1936, Walter McTavish, of Rossburn, Manitoba, and has issue living, Walter Lloyd, *b.* 1936,—Corinne Gertrude, *b.* 1938: *m.* 1957, Edward James Perrin,—Selina Elsie, *b.* 1944,—Wynona May, *b.* 1952.——(By 2nd m.) Mariana, *b.* 1935.——Maude Brenwin, *b.* 1937.

Issue of the late Lieut.-Col. Walter Selby Butler, 4th son of 9th baronet, *b.* 1845, *d.* 1939 : *m.* 1885, Alice Lucy, who *d.* 1939, da. of the late Edmund Fowler, of Abberley, Edgbaston :—
Vivien Tilla (La Poulido, Avenue Vara Villa, Roquebrune, St. Roman, France) *b.* 1891: *m.* 1913, Kenneth Cookson, OBE, who *d.* 1963, and has issue living, John Butler, *b.* 1924; ed. at Harrow: *m.* 1951, Adene, da. of Vincent Brady, and has issue living, Christopher Alexander Kenneth *b.* 1954, Elizabeth Julia *b.* 1953,—Mary, *b.* 1916: *m* 1st, 1941 (m diss. 1952), Maj. John George Spencer Churchill [*see* D. Marlborough, colls.]; 2ndly, 1954, Jacob Herman Huizinga, of 8, Lennox Gardens Mews, SW1.

Grandchildren of the late Capt. Henry William Paget Butler, 4th son of 8th baronet :—
Issue of the late Francis Frederick Baron Butler, *b.* 1861, *d.* 1926 : *m.* 1891, Bertha Florence, who *d.* 1928, da. of the late P. J. Dunne, of Rockhampton, Queensland :—
Reginald Percy BUTLER-FITZGERALD (71, Regatta Parade, Southport, Qld. 4215, Aust.), *b.* 1896; assumed by authority of Ch. Herald of Ireland 1946, the additional surname and arms of Fitz-Gerald, and discontinued by deed poll 1946 the christian name of FitzGerald: *m.* 1930, Muriel, who *d.* 1971, yst. da. of the late F. J. B. Martin, of New Farm, Brisbane, Qld., and has issue living, Frederick FitzGerald, *b.* 1933,—Geraldine, *b.* 1946: *m.* 1972, John Conoplia, of Brisbane, and has issue living, Rebecca Frances *b.* 1973.——Mabel Florence, *b.* 1905. *Residence*, Adelaide, S. Australia.
Issue of the late Thomas Percy Butler, *b.* 1862, *d.* 1933 : *m.* 1st, 1905, Harriette Gwendoline, who *d.* 1931, da. of the late Col. John Henry Graham Smyth, C.M.G. [E. Mount Cashell, ext.] ; 2ndly, 1932, Rosabel May, who *d.* 1954, only da. of Capt. Charles Walker, 21st Fusiliers, and widow of Sir George Beresford Butler, of Island View, Clifden, co. Galway :—
(By 1st marriage) Tyssen Desmond, *b.* 1906 ; Major (retired) Roy. Welch Fusiliers : *m.* 1940, Dorothy, da. of George Saltonstall West, of Chestnut Hill, Massachusetts, USA, and has issue

living, George Tyssen, *b.* 1943,—Richard Percy, *b.* 1944. *Address,* c/o National and Grindlays Bank, 54, Parliament St., S.W.1.

Granddaughter of the late James Butler, 4th son of 7th baronet :—
Issue of the late Beauchamp Charles Butler, *b.* 1865, *d.* 1919 : *m.* 1896, Elizabeth (who *m.* 2ndly, 19—, — Hamilton), da. of the late T. Findlay Muirhead, of Durban, Natal :—
Eileen Doris, *b.* 1901 : *m.* 19—, — Jones, and has issue living, a son, *b.* 19—. *Residence,* Repson Road, Durban, Natal.

Grandchildren of the late Capt. John Bayford Butler, RN el. son of Capt. Charles George Butler, RN, 5th son of 7th baronet:—
Issue of the late Francis Algernon Butler, *b.* 1878, *d.* 1935 : *m.* 1909, Dorothy Jean, da. of the late Douglas James Chester, of Bedford :—
Doreen, *b.* 19— : *m.* 19— Frank Clear. *Residence,* Esquimault, Canada.——Eileen, *b.* 19—.—— Vivienne, *b.* 19—.

Issue of the late Humphrey Charles Butler, *b.* 1880, *d.* 1969: *m.* 1st 1904, Emily Laura, who *d.* 1916, da. of the late Alexander J. Baxter; 2ndly, 1918, Helen Howard, who *d.* 1919; 3rdly, 1920, Sheila Gertrude Edith (6, Bridge Avenue Mansions, Hammersmith, W6), da. of the late William Bernard Blackwell:—
(By 1st m.) Humphrey de Bohun Bayford (140, Urbano Drive, San Francisco, USA), *b.* 1904; ed. at Haileybury, and at Stanford Univ. (AB 1928): *m.* 1930, Mildred, da. of the late William Erskine Duncan, of Oroville, Cal., USA, and has issue living, Bayford Duncan, (c/o Butler Productions, 442, Post St., San Francisco, Cal., USA), *b.* 1938, ed. at Stanford Univ. (AB): *m.* 1964, Nancy, da. of James F. Grandin, and has issue living, Bayford Duncan *b.* 1965, James Devereux *b.* 1969.——(by 3rd m.) Anthony Bernard (c/o Lloyds Bank, 4/5, King St., Richmond, Surrey), *b.* 1929; Maj. RTR (ret.): *m.* 1st, 1969, (m. diss. 1972), Amanda McBlain, da. of Lt.-Col. W. McBlain Stephen; 2ndly, 1973, Mrs. Harriet Eileen Harland.

Grandson of the late William Charles Butler, 2nd son of Capt. Charles George Butler, RN (ante):—
Issue of the late Lieut.-Col. Charles Walter Butler, O.B.E., Indian Army, *b.* 1880, *d.* 1941: *m.* 1905, Vivien Eleanor, who *d.* 1943, da. of the Rev. Canon Thomas James Bowen:—
Richard Shirley, *b.* 1907 ; ed. at Charterhouse ; is Major (retired) Gloucestershire Regt. ; Burma 1944-5 ; Korea 1950 : *m.* 1940, Auriol Lilian Evelyn, da. of the late Rev. A. R. Biddle, of Temple Hill, East Budleigh, Devon, and has issue living, Patrick James Richard, *b.* 1944; ed. at Wellington, and Auckland Univ., N.Z.—Penelope Eve (c/o Coutts & Co., 440, Stand, WC2) *b.* 1942: *m.* 1968, Maj. Thomas Christopher Peter Brooke, IG, and has issue living, James Richard Henry Ormonde *b.* 1972. *Residence,* Long Ham House, Cornwood, S. Devon.

Grandson of the late Lt.-Col. Charles Walter Butler, OBE (ante):—
Issue of the late Brig. Walter George Ormonde Butler, DSO, MC, *b.* 1917, *d.* 1967: *m.* 1945, Pamela Winsome Muriel (who m. 2ndly, 1970, Brig. Cuthbert Grafton Moore, OBE, of Patches, On the Green, Amport, Andover) da. of Dr. Sidney Owen, of Isleworth, Middlesex:—
David Simon Ormonde (3, Drayson Mews, W8 4LY), *b.* 1947: *m.* 1971, Vivienne Claire, el. da. of Cdr. R. P. FitzGerland, RN, of Petworth, Sussex, and has issue living, Toby George Ormonde, *b.* 1974.

Grandchildren of the late James Thomas Butler, grandson of William Paul Butler, 4th son of 5th baronet. :—
Issue of the late Charles Richard Butler, *b.* 1860, *d.* 1932: *m.* 1895, Ethel Elizabeth Jane, who *d.* 1943, el. da. of the late Philip Charles Newton, J.P.:—
James Humphrey, *b.* 1897; Group-Capt. RAF; 1914-19 War, Indian Frontier 1920 (clasps): *m.* 1st, 1925, Marguerite Kathleen Louise, who *d.* 1938, da. of John Hale, of Donaghcloney House Donaghcloney, co. Down; 2ndly, 1939, Freda, da. of F. E. Peto, of Pietermaritzburg, S. Africa, and has issue living, (by 1st m.) Charles Humphrey John (767, Tamarack Drive, San Rafael, Cal. 94903, USA), *b.* 1927; ed. at Wellington, and at Univ. of Virginia (AB); Lt.-Col. US Army Reserve: *m.* 1957, Elizabeth Ann, da. of Harry F. Mett, of Schenectady, NY, and has issue living, Bradford Frederick, *b.* 1962,—(by 2nd m.) Barbara Anne Sommerset *b.* 1941; 2nd Officer WRNS,—Isobel Louise, *b.* 1945. *Residence,* 34, Easthorpe, Southwell, Notts.——Edward Walter Charles, *b.* 1900; 1918-19 War with 4th Dragoon Guards: *m.* 1939, Iris Courtenay, da. of the late Rev. G. Moriarty, R. of Ergener, co. Tyrone, and has issue living, Walter Richard Courtenay, *b.* 1944; 3rd Officer, Blue Funnel Line,—Maeve Geraldine Audley, *b.* 1940: *m.* 1964, the Rev. Brian Desmond Anthony Hannon, of Christchurch Rectory, 80, Northland Rd., Londonderry, and has issue living, Desmond Pierce O'Brien *b.* 1965, Brendan Gerald *b.* 1968, Edward Neil Anthony *b.* 1970. *Residence,* Springhill, Moneymore, co. Derry.——Blanche Adelaide. *Residence,* 6, Longford Place, Monkstown, Dublin.

Issue of the late Somerset Edward Molyneux Butler, L.R.C.S.I., L.R.C.P.I., *b.* 1867, *d.* 1914 : *m.* 1902, Elise Jessie, who *d.* 1942, only child of Reginald Bearcroft :—
Margaret Elise, *b.* 1902: *m.* 1928, Maj. Philip Anderson, A & SH, who *d.* 1968, and has issue living, Oliver George Bearcroft (Orchard Farm, Kirkmichael, Ayrshire), *b.* 1943; Reserve A & SH: *m.* 1969, Phillipa Kate, da. of the late Maj. C. L. Stephenson, and has issue living, Philip George, *b.* 1970, Emily Mary *b.* 1971. *Residence,* Woodlands Cottage, Kirkmichael, Ayrshire.

Issue of the late George Fitzwalter Butler, *b.* 1868, *d.* 1947 : *m.* 1899, Laura Jean, who *d.* 1945, da. of the late Daniel Teer, land agent :—
Florence Adelaide (101, Albany House, 303, 21st Av. SW, Calgary, Alberta, Canada).

Grandsons of the late Charles Richard Butler (ante):—
Issue of the late Lieut.-Col. Beauchamp Henry Butler, D.S.O., Roy. Inniskilling Fusiliers, *b.* 1902, *d.* (killed in action during European War) 1943 : *m.* 1938, Vera May (who *m.* 2ndly, 1946, Major Charles Patrick Fitzgerald, of Turlough Park, Castlebar, co. Mayo), da. of the late Maj. W. Stewart, MC, JP, of Daisy Hill, Clogher, co. Tyrone:—
Michael Henry (46, Edith Rd., W14), *b.* 1939; formerly in Roy. Signals.——Patrick Beauchamp Rupert (Turlough Park, Castlebar, co. Mayo), *b.* 1943.

The 1st baronet, Sir Thomas Butler, High Sheriff and M.P. for co. Carlow, was the natural son of the Hon. Sir Edmund Butler, 2nd son of 9th Earl of Ormonde. Lieut.-Col. Sir Richard Pierce Butler, O.B.E., 11th baronet, was High Sheriff of co. Carlow 1905, and served in S. African War 1901-2, and in European War 1914-19 (despatches twice, O.B.E.).

BUTLER, Creation (U.K.) 1922, of Old Park, Devizes, Wilts.

Sir (REGINALD) MICHAEL THOMAS BUTLER, *QC*, 3rd *Baronet*; *b.* April 22nd, 1928; *s.* his father, *Sir* (REGINALD) THOMAS, 1959 ; Bar. and Solicitor Ontario 1954 and B.C. 1967; QC 1967: *m.* 1st, 1952 (m. diss. 1967), Marja Margaret Elizabeth, only da. of Ewen H. McLean, of Toronto; 2ndly, 1968, Barbara Anne, da. of Kevin Cahill, of Dublin, and has issue by 1st m.

Arms—Azure, three covered cups in pale between two flaunches or, each charged with a cross-crosslet sable. **Crest**—A demi-horse sable, charged on the shoulder with a covered cup and resting the sinister hoof upon a cross-crosslet or.

Address—Box 381, Brentwood Bay, BC, Canada.

Sons living—By 1st m.—(REGINALD) RICHARD MICHAEL, *b.* Oct. 3rd, 1953.——Geoffrey MacLean, *b.* 1956.——Thomas David, *b.* 1960.
Brother living—Peter Woods, *b.* 1933 : *m.* 1959, Lucia Harris, and has issue living. *Residence*, Vancouver, British Columbia.
Sister living—Patricia Carroll, *b.* 1935: *m.* 1957, William Milburn, of London, England, and has issue living, Peter William Hewlins, *b.* 1958,—Christopher, *b.* 1961.
Aunt living (daughter of 1st baronet)—Gladys Marjorie, *b.* 1897: *m.* 1922, Richard Wayland-Smith, MB, FRCS, who *d.* 1967, and has issue living, Anne Elizabeth, *b.* 1923. *Residence*, Little Close, 3, South Parade, Budleigh Salterton, S. Devon.
Mother living—Marjorie, el. da. of the late Sidney Brown Woods, K.C., of Stirlingswood, Edmonton, Alberta, Canada : *m.* 1st, 1927, Sir (Reginald) Thomas Butler, 2nd baronet, who *d.* 1959, having obtained a divorce 1949 ; 2ndly, 1950, L. M. Crookston. *Residence*, 4146, Torquay Drive, Victoria, British Columbia.
Widow living of 2nd Baronet—DIANE (BERRY) (*Diane, Lady Butler*), da. of William Aubrey Southerton : *m.* 1950, as his second wife, Sir (Reginald) Thomas Butler, 2nd baronet, who *d.* 1959. *Residence*, 45, Eaton Square. S.W.1.

BUTLER, Creation (U.K.) 1926, of Edgbaston, co. Warwick. [Extinct 1939.]

Sir WILLIAM WATERS BUTLER, 1st and last *Baronet.*

Daughter living of 1st Baronet—Edna Mary Ewing, *b.* 1902: *m.* 1924, Edward Victor Horton, MC, JP, who *d.* 1946, and has issue living, Christopher David, *b.* 1928,—Antony Brian (The Old Rectory, Taplow, Bucks.), *b.* 1933: *m.* 1957, Sheila Wendy Morgan, and has issue living, Henrietta Sophie Louise *b.* 1957, Serena Jane Rosabel *b.* 1960, Clemency Mary-Rose *b.* 1963,—Graham Butler, *b.* 1936,—Ann Maureen, *b.* 1926. *Residence*, The Old Bakehouse, Stanton, nr. Broadway, Worcestershire.
Collateral Branch living.

Issue of the late William Owen Butler, only son of 1st baronet, *b.* 1898, *d.* 1935: *m.* 1922, Beatrice Eileen, [who *d.* 1970, having *m.* 2ndly, 1939 (m. diss. 1950), Lt.-Com. Clive Gordon Trencham, RN (ret.)], da. of Thomas Charles Byrne:—
Patricia Ann, *b.* 1924: *m.* 1947, Peter Henry Murray Yeo (c/o Lloyds Bank, 16, St. James's St., SW1), and has issue living, Christopher David, *b.* 1948,—Sally Ann, *b.* 1950,—Murray Clare, *b.* 1953.——Teresa Jill (27261, Sunset Blvd., Lathzup Village, Michigan 48076, USA), *b.* 1928: *m.* 1951 (m. diss. 1747), Robert Arthur Young (43, Quarrendon St., SW6), and has issue living, Robert Mark, *b.* 1951,—Sarah Caroline, *b.* 1954.——Genevieve Owen (posthumous), *b.* 1935.

BUTLIN, Creation (U.K.) 1911, of Harley Street, St. Marylebone. [Extinct 1916.]

Capt. Sir HENRY GUY TRENTHAM BUTLIN, 2nd and last *Baronet*, Cambridgeshire Regt.; *d.* (killed in action during European War) 1916, when the title became ext.

Sister living—Violet Muriel Trentham, *b.* 1881: *m.* 1902, Norman Morice, who *d.* 1943, and has issue living, Geoffrey Norman, *TD*, *b.* 1904; ed. at Malvern and at Corpus Christi Coll., Camb. (MA); Solicitor 1929,—Gerald Charles Trentham *b.* 1907; ed. at Malvern, and at Corpus Christi Coll., Camb.,—Muriel Joan, *b.* 1910: *m.* 1943, John Norwood,—Barbara Frances (twin), *b.* 1910. *Residence*, Edith Lodge, Graham Road, Great Malvern, Worcestershire.

BUTT, Creation (U.K.) 1929, of Westminster, co. London.

Sir (ALFRED) KENNETH DUDLEY BUTT, 2nd *Baronet*; *b.* July 7th, 1908; *s.* his father, *Sir* ALFRED, 1962; ed. at Rugby, and at Brasenose Coll., Oxford; 1939-45 War as Major R.A.; is an Underwriting Member of Lloyd's, and Managing Dir. of Brook Stud Co.: *m.* 1st, 1938, Kathleen Breen, da. of the late E. Farmer, of Shanklin, Isle of Wight; 2ndly, 1948, Marie Josephine, da. of the late John Bain, of Wadhurst, and widow of Lt.-Col. Ivor Watkins Birts.

Arms—Argent, on a chevron engrailed gules between in chief two torteaux and in base a trefoil slipped vert, a portcullis chained or. **Crest**—A lion sejant proper gorged with a collar gemelle or, and supporting with the dexter fore paw a spear, the head fracted and dependent also proper.

Residences—Wheat Hill, Sandon, Buntingford, Herts.: Flat 29, 1, Hyde Park Sq., W.1. *Club*—Junior Carlton.

SVM QVOD SVM

I am what I am.

Widow living of 1st Baronet—WILHELMINE (*Wilhelmine, Lady Butt*) (5, Rue Maurepas, St. Peter Port, Guernsey), da. of Heinrich Wahl, of Gelsenkirchen-Buer: *m.* 1960, as his second wife, Sir Alfred Butt, 1st baronet, who *d.* 1962.

Sir Alfred Butt, 1st .Bt ,son of F. Butt, of Hampshire, was Director of Rationing, Min. of Food 1917-18, Chm. and Managing Dir., Theatre Royal, Drury Lane 1925-31, and M.P. for Wandsworth (Balham and Tooting Div.) (*U*) 1922-36.

BUXTON, Creation (U.K.) 1840, of Belfield, Dorsetshire.

Sir THOMAS FOWELL VICTOR BUX-TON, 6th *Baronet*; *b.* Aug. 18th, 1925 ; *s.* his father, *Sir* THOMAS FOWELL, 1945 ; ed. at Eton, and at Trin. Coll., Camb.; Scots Guards 1943-1948 : *m.* 1955, Mrs. Doris Mary Chisenhale-Marsh, who *d.* 1965, da. of Peter Randall Johnson.

Arms—Argent, a lion rampant tail elevated and turned over the head sable, between two mullets of the second. Crest—A buck's head couped gules, attired or, gorged with a collar of the last, therefrom pendent an escutcheon argent, charged with an African's head sable. Supporters—*Dexter*, an African sable, wreathed about the head and loins vert; *sinister*, a buck gules, attired or.

Residence—Woodredon, Waltham Abbey, Essex.

Sister living—Montagu Lucy, *b.* 1927: *m.* 1965, John Harold Rose, of Evelegh's, Long Wittenham, Abingdon, Oxon.

Aunt living (daughter of 4th baronet)—Lucy Victoria (*Lady Bentinck*), *b.* 1893 : *m.* 1922, the Rev. (Count) Sir Charles Henry Bentinck, K.C.M.G., who *d.* 1955 [D. Portland, colls.]. *Residence*, Ash Tree Cottage, Upshire, Waltham Abbey, Essex.

Great-Uncle living (son of 3rd baronet)—Rt. Rev. Bishop Harold Jocelyn, *b.* 1880; ed. at Harrow, and at Trin. Coll., Camb. (BA 1901, MA 1905); has been Chap. to Bishop of Rangoon, R. of Horley, Assist. Priest of Ch. Ch., Westminster, Chap. St. George's Cathedral, Jerusalem, and Sec. to Lord Mayor's Fund for Armenian Relief; was Archdeacon of Cyprus 1928-33, and Bishop of Gibraltar 1933-47; is a Knight Com. of Order of George 1, of Greece, and Sub-Prelate of Order of St. John of Jerusalem; has Order of St. Sava of Yugoslavia. *Residence*,

Widow living of 5th Baronet—EVA KATHARINE (*Eva, Lady Buxton*), da. of the late Edward Balfour, of Balbirnie, Fife: *m.* 1931, as his second wife, Sir Thomas Fowell Buxton, 5th baronet, who *d.* 1945. *Residence*,

Collateral Branches living.

Branch from 2nd son of 4th Baronet:—
Issue of the late Capt. Roden Henry Victor Buxton, CBE, RN, 2nd son of 4th baronet, *b.* 1890, *d.* 1970: *m.* 1st, 1917, Dorothy Alina, who *d.* 1956, da. of the late Col. Charles William Robert St. John, RE; 2ndly, 1957, Hilda, MBE (Rodwell House, Loddon, Norwich), da. of the late Charles Alfred Meadows, of Rainham, Kent:—
(By 1st m.) JOCELYN CHARLES RODEN, *VRD* (Eastlands, West Wellow, Romsey, Hants.); United Service Club), *b.* Aug. 8th, 1924; Lt.-Cdr. RNVR; 1939-45 War (despatches), Korea 1953: *m.* 1960, Ann Frances, da. of Frank Smitherman, MBE, HM Foreign Ser., and has issue living, Frances Dorothy, *b.* 1960,—Harriet Lucy, *b.* 1962,—Caroline Sarah, *b.* 1964.——Gerard St. John Roden (Pitteadie House, Kirkcaldy, Fife, United Service Club), *b.* 1927; Lt. Cdr. RN; 1944-45 War: *m.* 1954, Judith Averil, da. of the late Hon. Angus Dudley Campbell, CBE [*see* B. Colgrain] and has issue living, Crispin Charles Gerard, *b.* 1958,—Charlotte Anne Gerard, *b.* 1955,—Laura Joan Gerard, *b.* 1961.——Anne Frances Roden, *b.* 1920: *m.* 1945, Henry Winterstein Gillespie, MD, of 41, Thurloe Sq., SW7, and La Lucertola, Tronzano, Lago Maggiore, Italy, and has issue living, Nicola Henrietta St. John, *b.* 1946: *m.* 1st, 1965 (m. diss. 1969), Charles Rupert Raw; 2ndly, 1975, John Latimer Smith, of 104, Earls Court Rd., W8,—Richenda Antoinette de Winterstein *b.* 1949.——Elisabeth Lucy Roden, *b.* 1922: *m.* 1951, Maj. Thomas Arnett Hughes-Ross, MBE, RCT, and has issue living, Timothy Arnett Ross, *b.* 1954,—Joanna Elisabeth Ross, *b.* 1952,—Penelope Jane Ross, *b.* 1956.——Phyllida Dorothy Roden, *b.* 1932: *m.* 1959, Ronald Carlile Buxton (infra).

Branch from 3rd son of 4th Baronet:—
Issue of the late Maj. Clarence Edward Victor Buxton, MC, 3rd son of 4th baronet, *b.* 1892, *d.* 1967: *m.* 1st, 1917 (m. diss. 19—) Mary Aline, MBE, who *d.* 1954, da. of Lt.-Col. Frederic Ewart Bradshaw, DSO; 2ndly, 1945, Mrs. Mavis Jean Fox (Ithanji, Limuru, Kenya, and Kinuni, Vipingo, Kenya Coast), da. of Walter Bromhead:—
(By 1st m.) Maurice (Bear Ash, Twyford, Berks.), *b.* 1919; late Capt. Coldstream Guards; 1939-45 War: *m.* 1941, Alison Mary, da. of L. L. Savill, of Comenden Manor, Cranbrook.——Rupert (PO Box 3122, Umtali, Rhodesia), *b.* 1923; 1939-45 War as Lt. RNVR: *m.* 1st, 1949 (m. diss. 1968), Ann, da. of Prof. Frank Debenham, OBE, of Cambridge; 2ndly, 1972, Betty Webb, of S. Africa, and has issue living, (by 1st m.), Jonathan, *b.* 1950,—Paul Stephen, *b.* 1954,—Colin, *b.* 1957.——Gwendolen, (c/o Barclays Bank, High St., Salisbury, Wilts.), *b.* 1921: *m.* 1960, Terence Leland Bowles, and has issue living, Katherine, *b.* 1963.——Rosemary, *b.* 1927: *m.* 1955, Francis Henry Alastair Julian Lochrane, of The Corner House, Mapleton, nr. Ashbourne, Derbyshire.——(by 2nd m.) Rowena Clarence, *b.* 1945.——Carissa Clarence, *b.* 1946.

Branches from younger sons of 3rd Baronet—
Issue of the late Rt. Hon. Noel Edward NOEL-BUXTON (2nd son of 3rd baronet), who was cr. *Baron Noel-Buxton* 1930 [*see* that title].
Issue of the late Charles Roden Buxton, 3rd son of 3rd baronet, *b.* 1875, *d.* 1942: *m.* 1904, Dorothy Frances, who *d.* 1963, da. of the late Arthur Trevor Jebb, of Ellesmere, Salop:—
David Roden (Old Ellwoods, Bridleway, Grantchester, Cambs.), *b.* 1910; ed. at Trin. Coll., Camb. (MA): *m.* 1st, 1939 (m. diss. 1948), Annelore, da. of H. Albers; 2ndly, 1950, Mary Violet, da. of the late Denis Alfred Jex Buxton (infra), and has issue living, (by 1st m.) Roden Arnold (18, Ellington St. N7). *b.* 1942; ed. at St. Christopher Sch., and Trin. Coll., Camb. (BA); DArch; RIBA: *m.* 1971, Linda Jane, da. of Richard Miller, MRO, of Bromley, Kent, and has issue living, Samuel Roden *b.* 1972,—(by 2nd m.) Charles Benedict, *b.* 1958.—James Andrew, *b.* 1964,—Elizabeth Eglantyne *b.* 1951,—Richenda Mary, *b.* 1953,—Francesca, *b.* 1956.——Eglantyne Roden, *b.* 1906 (Flat 2, 13, Redcliffe Sq., SW10), ed. at Somerville Coll., Oxford (MA).
Issue of the late Leland William Wilberforce Buxton, yst. son of 3rd baronet, *b.* 1884, *d.* 1967: *m.* 1912, Ada Mary, el. da. of the Rev. Thomas Henry Royal Oakes, BD, formerly R. of Thurgarton, Norwich:—

Julian Wilberforce, *TD* (*Club*, Oxford and Cambridge), *b.* 1913; ed. at Ampleforth, and at Trin. Coll., Camb. (BA); Maj. RA (TA); 1939-45 War in Middle East; Canadian Manager for British Leather Corporation 1950-52: *m.* 1939 (m. diss. 1948), Marie Iseult Dunsterville, only child of Walter Frederick Dunsterville, of Lushill, Stock, Essex.——Aubrey Leland Oakes, *MC* (Norman House, Stansted, Essex. *Club*, White's), *b.* 1918; ed. at Ampleforth, and at Trin. Coll., Camb.; Maj. RAC (Supplementary Reserve); 1939-45 War (despatches, MC): *m.* 1946, Pamela Mary, el. da. of Sir Henry Ralph Stanley Birkin, 3rd Bt., and widow of Maj. Samuel Luckyn Buxton, MC, 17th/21st Lancers (infra), and has issue living, Timothy Leland (Norman House Cottage, Stansted, Essex), *b.* 1948: *m.* 1972, Julie Mary, da. of Lt-Cdr. (John) Michael Avison Parker, CVO, and has issue living, Alexandra Louise *b.* 1973,—Aubrey James Francis, *b.* 1956,—Nicola Mary Caroline, *b.* 1947: *m.* 1970, Adrian William Guy Sykes,—Lucinda Catherine, *b.* 1950,— Veronica Frances, *b.* 1953,—Victoria Jane *b.* 1960.——Diana Elizabeth, *b.* 1915: *m.* 1939, Lt. Adrian James Dent, RN, of Dockhead, Beaulieu, Hants., son of Sir Francis Henry Dent, CVO, and has issue living, Simon Adrian, *b.* 1949: *m.* 1972, Brigitte Engelhard,—Jeremy Francis, *b.* 1952: *m.* 1971, Penelope Linton,—Gladys Henrietta, *b.* 1940: *m.* 1963, Simon Aidan Reynolds,— Janet Sylvia, *b.* 1947.——Mary Judith, *b.* 1922; formerly in ATS: *m.* 1st, 1942, Philip Arthur Leo Gompertz, Lt. RE, who *d.* (killed in action) 1942; 2ndly, 1945, Capt. Clement Wynter Lister, RA, Walnut Tree House, Burnham-on-Crouch, Essex, and has issue living, (by 2nd m.) Patrick Thomas Buxton, *b.* 1948,—Philippa Judith, *b.* 1946: *m.* 1971, David John Lloyd Watkins.

Branch from 2nd son of 2nd Baronet—

Grandchildren of the late Samuel Gurney Buxton, 2nd son of 2nd baronet:—
Issue of the late Edward Gurney Buxton, *b.* 1865, *d.* 1929 : *m.* 1895, Laura, *M.B.E.*, who *d.* 1957, da. of the late John Gurney :—
Desmond Gurney, *b.* 1898; ed. at Eton; Lieut.-Col. late 6th Batn. Roy. Norfolk Regt. (T.A.), Major (ret.) King's Roy. Rifle Corps. and a D.L. for Norfolk; 1914-18 War, N.-W. Europe 1945: *m.* 1930, Rachel Mary, da. of the late Lieut.-Col. A. F. Morse, of Coltishall Mead, Norwich, and has issue living, Andrew Edward, (36, Burnsall St., SW3) *b.* 1935; ed. at Eton, and at Magdalene Coll., Camb. (MA): *m.* 1967, Barbara Anne, da. of the late Capt. Cyril Gascoigne Lloyd [see Preston, Bt.], and has issue living, Harry Desmond Gascoigne *b.* 1972, Laura Catherine *b.* 1968, Nicola Rachel Anne *b.* 1971,—James Desmond, *b.* 1947; ed. at Eton and Magdalene Coll., Camb. (BA): *m.* 1975, Anna, yst. da. of the late Douglas Collins, of Gt. Missenden, Bucks.—Annabel Audrey, *b.* 1938,—Rosalinde Rachel, *b.* 1939: *m.* 1965, John Raoul Wilmot Stansfeld [see Eardley-Wilmot, Bt., colls.],—Elizabeth Laura, *b.* 1941: *m.* 1962, William Lister Archibald Pryor, of Summerfields, Oxford, and has issue living, Alexander Timothy William *b.* 1968, Hugh William Arthur *b.* 1974, Victoria Elizabeth *b.* 1965. *Residence*, Hoveton Hall, Wroxham, Norfolk.—— Eric (Old Rectory, Yaxley, Eye, Suffolk), *b.* 1899.——Daphne, *MBE*, *b.* 1905; MBE (Civil) 1974: *m.* 1929, Capt. Russell Thomas Harmer, formerly RE, who *d.* 1940, son of the late Sir Sidney Frederic Harmer, KBE, FRS, and has issue living, Thomas Edward (of The Grange, Rackheath, Norwich), *b.* 1932: *m.* 1960, Ruth MacMillan, da. of David L. Walker, of Old Bank House, Aylsham, Norfolk, and has issue living, Charles Russell *b.* 1962, Edward David *b.* 1967, Nicholas John *b.* 1974, Mary Elizabeth *b.* 1963, Ann Catherine *b.* 1965,—Daniel Sidney (1657, Walnut St., Halifax, Nova Scotia), *b.* 1936: *m.* 1962, Jacqueline Erwin, da. of R. J. Moore, of Halifax, Nova Scotia, and has issue living, Stephen Russell *b.* 1963, Colin John *b.* 1966,—Jean Laura, *b.* 1930: *m.* 1953, David Ian Hird, of Little Orchard, Box Lane, Boxmoor, Herts., and has issue living, Alison Daphne *b.* 1954, Claire Laura *b.* 1955, Isobel Rosalie *b.* 1957, Vivien Anne *b.* 1959, Penelope *b.* 1961. *Residence*, West Grange, Rackheath, Norwich.——Phyllis *b.* 1907: *m.* 1931, Col. Cecil Townley Mitford-Slade, late KRRC; Lord Lt. for Som. [Slade, Bt., colls.], and has issue living, Anthony Cecil Wyndham (Motcombe Meadows, Motcombe, Shaftes-bury, Dorset), *b.* 1932; ed. at Eton; Maj. LI: *m.* 1959, Mary Dawn Rogers, and has issue living, Christopher Neave *b.* 1962, Richard Cecil *b.* 1965, Rosemary Anne *b.* 1960,—Patrick Buxton (Damales House, West Green, Hartley Wintney, Hants.), *b.* 1936; ed. at Eton; late Capt., R. Green Jackets: *m.* 1964, Anne Catharine, el. da. of A. H. Stanton, of Brakeys, Hatfield Peverel, Essex, and has issue living, James Patrick *b.* 1973, Nicola Claire *b.* 1967, Fiona Dawn *b.* 1970,— Carolyn Noel *b.* 1949. *Residence*, Montys Court, Norton Fitzwarren, Taunton.——Enid Laura, *b.* 1914: *m.* 1937, Capt. Laurence Frederick York, Yorks. Hussars, who *d.* 1967, and has issue living, Sonia Elizabeth, *b.* 1940: *m.* 1960, Giles Coode-Adams, of Cuckoos Farm, Little Baddow, Chelmsford, Essex, and has issue living, Benjamin Richard *b.* 1965, Henrietta Mary *b.* 1962,—Bridget Laura, *b.* 1944: *m.* 1969, Arthur William Stevenson, of 2, Flanchford Rd., W12, and has issue living, Henry *b.* 1973, Rebecca *b.* 1971,—Katherine Diana, *b.* 1947: *m.* 1969, Nicholas Fox, of 67, Kyrle Rd., SW11, and has issue living, Harriet *b.* 1973. *Residence*, Meadow Cottage, Stoke-by-Nayland, Colchester.——Monica, *b.* 1916: *m.* 1937, Maj. Robert Henry Calvert, Middx. Yeo, of Picts House, Horsham, Sussex [Cholmeley, Bt.], and has issue living, Monica Julia, *b.* 1939: *m.* 1st, 1964, Maj. John Dominic Morrogh Bernard, Irish Gds., who *d.* 1968; 2ndly 1969, Maj. Shane Gabriel Basil Blewitt, IG, of South Corner, Duncton, Petworth, Sussex, and has issue living (by 1st m.) Alexander Dominic Calvert, *b.* 1966, Katherine Mary, *b.* 1965, (by 2nd m.) Piers Shane Basil Calvert *b.* 1972, Davina Henrietta *b.* 1970,—Diana *b.* 1941,—Patricia Rohays, *b.* 1943: *m.* 1968, Michael Charles Richardson, of 11, Northumberland Place, W2, and has issue living, Mark Jonathan *b.* 1969, Lucinda Patricia *b.* 1971, Anna Monica *b.* 1973,—Georgina Sophia, *b.* 1949: *m.* 1973, John Richard Hull Moore, of 11, Hazlebury Rd., SW6.——Louise Jacinth, *b.* 1918: *m.* 1946, Benjamin Whittaker, and has issue living, Edward Benjamin Buxton, *b.* 1948,—Nigel Buxton, *b.* 1950,—Clive Buxton, *b.* 1953. *Residence*, 3, West Rd., Bury St. Edmunds, Suffolk.

Issue of the late Capt. Harry Gurney Buxton, *b.* 1871, *d.* 1936 : *m.* 1910, Evelyn, who *d.* 1955, da. of the late Richard Musgrave Harvey,—
Grizell Evelyn, *b.* 1919: *m.* 1946, the Ven. Edwin James Greenfield Ward, MVO, Chap. to HM and Archdeacon of Sherborne, and has issue living, Simon Andrew Buxton, *b.* 1952,—Joanna, *b.* 1947: *m.* 1975, Christopher James Evan Spicer, of Home Farm, Pakenham, Suffolk,—Aliso n *b.* 1950. *Residence*, W. Stafford Rectory, Dorchester, Dorset.

Grandchildren of the late Edward Gurney Buxton (ante):—
Issue of the late Hubert Edward Buxton, *b.* 1901, *d.* 1973: *m.* 1932 (m. diss. 1948) Anne Hawise Colleton, da. of the late Col. Arthur Hautayne Bowring, RFA [see Colleton, Bt., ext.]:—
Robert Hugh (44, Pottery Lane, W11), *b.* 1933; ed. at Eton: *m.* 1st, 1963 (m. diss. 1972), Helen Loveday, el. da. of D. M. R. Piesse, of St. Helena; 2ndly, 1973, Mrs. Judith Serena Lourenco, da. of John Richard Rumsey, and has issue living (by 1st m.), David Colleton, *b.* 1964,—Henry Gurney, *b.* 1966.——Sara Carolyn Colleton *b.* 1937: *m.* 1964, Peter James Foot (c/o PO Box 223, Denmark, W. Aust.), and has issue living Lorna Alice, *b.* 1965,—Elizabeth Angela, *b.* 1967.

Issue of the late Mervyn Buxton, Lieut. R.A.P.C., *b.* 1903, *d.* (on active ser. during European War) 1944: *m.* 1932, Carmela Mary Beatrice (now of 27, Kenway Road, S.W.5) da. of George Herbert Lyon:—
Simon Lyon (15/66, Wrights Rd., Drummoyne, NSW), *b.* 1935; ed. at Wellington Coll., and at Magdalene Coll., Camb. (BA): *m.* 1971, Janet Susan, da. of Haille Paine, of Bowral, NSW, and has issue living, Thomas Lyon, *b.* 1973.——Ian Lyon (12, Grand Parade, Tynemouth, Tyne & Wear, NE30 4JS), *b.* 1937; ed. at Wellington Coll., and at Glasgow Univ. (BA, PhD); C.Eng.; Reader in Marine Transport Newcastle Univ.: *m.* 1966, Jean Mary, da. of the late William Coch-rane, of E. Lothian, and has issue living, Keith Mervyn Lyon, *b.* 1974,—Fiona Anne, *b.* 1969.

Issue of Mark Buxton, *b.* 1909, *d.* 1972: *m.* 1949, Penelope Ann Cecil (8, Walker Av., W. Perth, W. Aust.), da. of Edmund C. Clifton, of Perth, W. Aust., and widow of P/O O. K. Fisher, RAF.:—
Jeremy Clifton Gurney, *b.* 1952; ed. at Ch. Ch. Gram. Sch., Perth, and Univ. of W. Aust. (BA).

Granddaughters of the late Samuel Gurney Buxton (infra):—
Issue of the late Capt. Richard Gurney Buxton, *b.* 1887, *d.* 1972: *m.* 1914, Mary Primrose, who *d.* 1972, da. of the late Maj. Anthony Stephen Ralli, 12th Lancers:—
Pamela Chloe, *b.* 1915: *m.* 1948, Michael Desmond MacCarthy, of 25, Wellington Sq., SW3, and Wiveton Hall, Holt, Norfolk, and has issue living, Desmond James, *b.* 1956,—Mary Lisa, *b.* 1950. ——Marian Camilla, *b.* 1919: *m.* 1947, Maj. Richard Peyton, late RHA, of Old Rectory, Little Birch, Hereford, and has issue living, Robin Derek, *b.* 1950,—Nigel Richard, *b.* 1951.

Issue of the late Samuel Gurney Buxton, 2nd son of 2nd baronet, *b.* 1838, *d.* 1909 : *m.* 1st, 1861, Louisa Caroline, who *d.* 1879, da. of the late John Gurney Hoare, of Hampstead ; 2ndly, 1886, Mary Ann, who *d.* 1938, da. of the late Henry Birkbeck, of Stoke Holy Cross, Norwich:—
(By 2nd m.) Minna Alice: *m.* 1914, Major Arthur Thomas McMorrough Kavanagh, MC, late 7th Hussars, who *d.* 1953, and has issue living, Joane, *b.* 1915: *m.* 1st, 1936, Major the Marquess of Kildare (from whom she obtained a divorce 1946), el. son of 7th Duke of Leinster; 2ndly, 1947, as his second wife, Lt.-Col. Archibald James Macalpine-Downie, MBE, Roy. Tank Regt., who *d.* 1958 [Blakiston, Bt., colls.], and has issue living, (by 1st m.) [*see* D. Leinster], (by 2nd m.) Andrew McMorrough *b.* 1948,—Rolline, *b.* 1920: *m.* 1945, Major Phillip Pardoe, King's Roy. Rifle Corps,—Mary Clare McMorrough (*Lady Carr-Ellison*), *b.* 1923: *m.* 1951, Capt. Sir Ralph Harry Carr-Ellison, of Hedgeley Hall, Powburn, Northumberland, and has issue living, John McMorrough *b.* 1952, Ralph Simon *b.* 1954, Andrew Thomas *b.* 1962, Rose Alice *b.* 1958,— Eva Helen McMorrough, *b.* 1926: *m.* 1949, Hugh David Hamilton Wills, CBE, TD, [*see* B. Dulverton, colls.]. *Residence*, Borris House, co. Carlow.

Branch from 3rd son of 2nd Baronet

Grandchildren of the late Gerald Buxton, el. son of Edward North Buxton, 3rd son of 2nd baronet:—
Issue of the late Lieut.-Col. Edward North Buxton, M.C., *b.* 1894, *d.* 1957 : *m.* 1st, 1924, the Hon. Sibyl O'Neill, *M.B.E.*, who *d.* 1946, sister of 3rd Baron O'Neill ; 2ndly, 1951, Daphne Rosemary (of St. Clements, Rushall, Diss, Norfolk), da. of the late Lieut. H. N. Munro, R.N.V.R., of Rushall, Diss:—
(By 1st m.) Mark Gerald Edward North (Coffyns, Spreyton, Crediton, Devon), *b.* 1929; ed. at Harrow and at Trin. Coll., Camb. (BA 1952): *m.* 1962, Leucha Daphne Mary, yr. da. of the late Col. Sir Edward Courtenay Thomas Warner, DSO, MC, 2nd baronet, and has issue living, Edward North, *b.* 1963,—Terence Mark *b.* 1965.——Morna Annabel, *b.* 1926: *m.* 1951, Clive Ernest Arkle, MB, ChB, and has issue living, Alexander Edward Buxton, *b.* 1953,—Alwyn Gerald Buxton, *b.* 1957,—Bridget Ayliffe Buxton, *b.* 1955,—Ann Daphne Buxton, *b.* 1959. *Residence*, Benarth Hall, Conway, Caernarvonshire.

Grandchildren of the late Edward North Buxton (ante):—
Issue of the late Gerald Buxton, *b.* 1862, *d.* 1928 : *m.* 1890, Lucy Ethel, O.B.E., who *d.* 1940, da. of Sir Joseph Whitwell Pease, M.P., 1st Bt. (cr. 1882) :—
Rebekah Mary (*Lady Clarke*), *b.* 1900: *m.* 1921, Col. Sir Ralph Stephenson Clarke, KBE, TD, DL, who *d.* 1970, and has issue living, Robert Nunn Stephenson (Borde Hill, Haywards Heath, Sussex, RH16 1XP), *b.* 1925; late RNVR: *m.* 1st, 1949 (m. diss. 1967), Juana Nidia Gereth, only child of the late Lt.-Col. John Bickersteth-Wheeler, MC; 2ndly, 1967 (m. diss. 1972), Eileen Ann Hay; 3rdly, 1972, Maria Josefa Strelow Williams, da. of the late Maj.-Gen. Stanislav Marian Bulak-Balachowicz, and has issue living, (by 1st m.) Ralph Roland Bickersteth Stephenson *b.* 1953, Andrewjohn Patrick Stephenson *b.* 1955, Marylynn *b.* 1950,—Simon Edward Stephenson (Cridmore Farm, Chillerton, I. of Wight, and The Manor House, High St., Lindfield, Sussex), *b.* 1926: *m.* 1952, Jill Maureen, el. da. of Harry Vos, of Kenwards Farm, Lindfield, Sussex, and has issue living, Christopher Stephenson *b.* 1954, Rupert Stephenson *b.* 1959, Caroline Stephenson *b.* 1956, Alison Stephenson *b.* 1957. *Residence*, Brook Bouse, Ardingly, Sussex.

Issue of the late Maj. Anthony Buxton, DSO, *b.* 1881, *d.* 1970: *m.* 1926, Mary Philomena, who *d.* 1953, da. of the late Hon. Bernard Constable-Maxwell [D. Norfolk, colls.]:—
John Joseph (Horsey Hall, Gt. Yarmouth), *b.* 1927; ed. at Ampleforth, and at Trin. Coll., Camb. (BA): *m.* 1958, Bridget de Bunsen, and has issue living, Robin Anthony, *b.* 1963,—Jane Mary, *b.* 1959,—Clare Margaret, *b.* 1960,—Caroline Mary, *b.* 1965.——Elizabeth Mary, *b.* 1926: *m.* 1951, Michael Walter Bonn, of Oaklands, St. Peters, Jersey, and has issue living, Simon Michael Joseph, *b.* 1953,—Sara Mary Philomena, *b.* 1952,—Mary Elizabeth, *b.* 1956,—Theresa Mary, *b.* 1959.——Jean Mary, *b.* 1930: *m.* 1956, Christopher Richard Miles, of Court Lodge Farm, Bletchingley, Surrey [see Greenwell, Bt.].——Judith Mary (Sister Mary Pia, IBVM, of St. Mary's Convent, S. Ascot, Berks), *b.* 1932; is a Nun.

Branches from 5th, 6th and 7th sons of 2nd Baronet:—

Issue of the late Charles Louis Buxton, 6th son of 2nd baronet, *b.* 1846, *d.* 1906 : *m.* 1873, Maria, who *d.* 1930, da. of the late Rev. Henry James Lee Warner, of Thorpland Hall, Norfolk :—
Melicent Louis, *b.* 1883 : *m.* 1909, Gerard Anstruther Wathen, C.I.E., who *d.* 1958, and has issue living, Mark William Gerard, *TD* (Bolwick Hall, Marsham, Norwich; Talisker House, Isle of Skye. *Clubs*, Brooks's, MCC), *b.* 1912; ed. at Gresham's Sch.; Maj. HAC; a local Dir. of Barclays Bank, Ltd., of Norwich, and a JP of Norfolk; High Sheriff 1968; Master of Mercers' Co. 1962; a Church Commr.: *m.* 1940, Rosemary, da. of Charles Eric Addington Hartridge [Flannery, Bt.], and has issue living, Roderick Mark Hulbert (c/o British Council, Sana'a, Yemen), *b.* 1940; educational adviser to Yemeni Govt.: *m.* 1966, Jacqueline Greville, da. of Air Vice-Marshal Anthony Greville Dudgeon, CBE, DFC (and has issue living, Philip Gerard *b.* 1969, Melanie Rosemary *b.* 1972), Jonathan Mark Gerard *b.* 1951, Primula Rosemary *b.* 1946: *m.* 1970, Hugh Maitland Houston (and has issue living Alastair Hugh *b.* 1972, Katriona Margaret *b.* 1971), Erica Melicent *b.* 1949,—Julian Philip Gerard (14, Brooksby St., Barnsbury, N1 1HA; Woodcock Farm House, Owlpen, Glos., GL11 5TD; Travellers Club), *b.* 1923; ed. at Harrow; formerly Capt. KRRC; Snr. Gen. Mgr., Barclays Bank International: *m.* 1948, Priscilla Florence, da. of Maj.-Gen. Bevil Thomson Wilson, CB, DSO [*see* Starkey, Bt.], and has issue living, Simon Walter Julian *b.* 1950, Penelope Lucy Priscilla *b.* 1952, Henrietta Katharine Priscilla *b.* 1954,— Diana Melicent, *b.* 1914: *m.* 1st, 1938 (m. diss. 1946), Maj. David William Alexander Mure, KRRC [E. Eglinton]; 2ndly, 1947, Dr. W. Hargrave-Wilson, of Pilot's House, Tinderbox, Tasmania, and has issue living, (by 1st m.) George Roger (Tinderbox, Tasmania), *b.* 1939. *Residence*, Bolwick Hall, Marsham, Norwich.

Grandson of the late Francis William Buxton, 7th son of 2nd baronet:—
Issue of the late Hugh Forster Buxton, Lieut. Rifle Brig., *b.* 1882, *d.* (killed in action during European War) 1916 : *m.* 1904, Blanche, who *d.* 1907, 3rd da. of the late Major St. Aubyn, 24th Regt.:—
Philip Olaf, *b.* 1906; a JP of Witney, and Chm. of Witney RDC 1965-68: *m.* 1934, Ruth Christian, JP, da. of the late Aubrey Trevor Lawrence, MBE, KC [*see* Lawrence, Bt., cr. 1867, colls.], and has issue living, Hugh Lawrence (The Clock House, Widford, Burford, Oxon., OX8 4DU), *b.* 1936; ed. at Eton, and at Ch. Ch., Oxford: *m.* 1965, Elizabeth Caroline Tilden Whitelocke, da.

of the late D. A. Abernethy, of Bampton, Oxon, and has issue living, Guy Lawrence *b.* 1969, Belinda Ruth *b.* 1967, Anne Caroline *b.* 1975.   *Residence*, Widford Manor, Burford, Oxford.

Branch from el. son of 2nd son of 1st Baronet:—

Grandchildren of the late Henry Fowell Buxton (infra):—
Issue of the late John Fowell Buxton, *b.* 1902, *d.* 1970: *m.* 1930, Katharine Mary (Morley Hall, Ware, Herts.; Easneye, Ware, Herts.), da. of Sir Nicholas Henry Bacon, 13th Bt.:—
Henry Alexander Fowell (Mardocks Mill, Wareside, Ware, Herts.), *b.* 1937; ed. at Eton: *m.* 1964, Victoria, only da. of (Edward John) Ronald Bennett, of Hartwell Farm, Cirencester [see Bazley, Bt.], and has issue living, Nicholas Fowell, *b.* 1966,—Anthony John, *b.* 1968,—Katharine Louise, *b.* 1971.——Bridget Jane (*Hon. Mrs. Reuben Pleydell-Bouverie*) *b.* 1931: *m.* 1956, the Hon. Reuben Pleydell-Bouverie [see E. Radnor].——Anna Katharine, *b.* 1934: *m.* 1966, George Watkin Myrddin-Evans.——Penelope Mary Albinia, *b.* 1939: *m.* 1956, Richard Christopher Naylor (see Holt, Bt., *cr.* 1935, ext.].——Elizabeth Priscilla, *b.* 1947.——Teresa Constance (twin), *b.* 1947.

Grandson of the late John Henry Buxton, el. son of Thomas Fowell Buxton, 2nd son of 1st baronet:—
Issue of the late Henry Fowell Buxton, *b.* 1876, *d.* 1949: *m.* 1st, 1900, Katharine Tayspel, who *d.* 1945, da. of the late Rt. Hon. James Round of Birch Hall, Essex ; 2ndly, 1945, Mairi, who *d.* 1962, da. of James Milne, and widow of N. Clark Neill, of Home Close, Hursley:—
(By 1st m.) Michael Auriol, *b.* 1914; ed. at Harrow; formerly Lt.-Cdr. RNVR; High Sheriff of Rutland 1953: *m.* 1938, Elizabeth, da. of Robert Hamond Arthur Elwes, of Congham House, King's Lynn, and has issue living, Gervase Michael (Swangles Farm, Cold Christmas, Ware, Herts.), *b.* 1939; ed. at Harrow, and Trin. Coll., Camb., late 2nd Lt. R. Scots Greys: *m.* 1965, Susan Margaret, da. of Malcolm McKenzie, of 13, Lennox Gdns., SW1, and has issue living, Matthew Thomas Gervase *b.* 1967, Jocelyn David *b.* 1972, Lucy Jane, *b.* 1966, Cara Susan *b.* 1969,—Christopher Robert (The Thatches, Kingston, Cambridge), *b.* 1940; ed. at Harrow, FRICS: *m.* 1965 (m. diss. 1970), Judy Francis, el. da. of Gordon Hollingsworth Dixon, of Somerton House, Winkfield Row, Berks.; 2ndly, 1973, Priscilla, da. of Maj. John Gardner, of Naughton Manor, Ipswich, and has issue living (by 1st m.), Timothy James *b.* 1967, Richard Anthony (twin) *b.* 1967; (by 2nd m.) Alexandra *b.* 1975,—Jonathan James (14, Lydon Rd., SW4), *b.* 1943; ed. at Harrow; Maj. late 17th/21st Lancers: *m.* 1972, Rosaleen Pleasance, da. of Sir John Alfred Picton Bagge, 6th Bt., and has issue living, Georgina Elizabeth *b.* 1973, Victoria Rose *b.* 1975 —Charles Joseph *b.* 1951; ed. at Harrow; Lt. 17th/21st Lancers. *Residence —* Mill House Westacre, King's Lynn, Norfolk.

Grandchildren of the late Henry Fowell Buxton (ante) :—
Issue of the late Maj. Robert James Buxton, MB, BChir, MRCS, LRCP, DOMS, *b.* 1908, *d.* 1968: *m.* 1935, Lilla Mary Alyson (Galhampton Manor, N. Cadbury, Yeovil, da. of C. E. Pumphrey, of W. Bitchfield, Belsay, Northumberland:—
James Anthony Fowell (18B, Albert Bridge Rd., SW11), *b.* 1948; ed. at Harrow, and Trin. Coll., Camb. (BA); Bar. Inner Temple 1971.——Richard Moberly, *b.* 1953; ed. at Harrow, and Trin. Coll., Camb. (BA).——Victoria Mary Rose, *b.* 1937: *m.* 1958, David James Faulkner, Maj. Irish Guards [see D. Buccleuch, colls.].——Lavinia Hermione, *b.* 1938: *m.* 1966, Mathew Alexander Thorpe, of Seend Green House, Seend, Wilts., and has issue living, Gervase James Doncaster, *b.* 1967,—Alexander Lambert, *b.* 1969,—Marcus Somerled, *b.* 1971.——Lettice Katharine, *b.* 1941. ——Rosamond Mary Alyson (twin), *b.* 1948.

Issue of the late Capt. Joseph Gurney Fowell Buxton, Grenadier Guards, *b.* 1913, *d.* (killed in action in Tunisia) 1943: *m.* 1938, Elizabeth Langley (who *m.* 2ndly, 1946, Alexander Ludovic Grant, of Marbury Hall, Whitchurch, Salop.), da. of the late Major Robert Barbour, of Bolesworth Castle, Tattenhall, Chester.
Andrew Robert Fowell (Bentley Park, Ipswich, Suffolk), *b.* 1939; ed. at Winchester, and at Pembroke Coll., Oxford (BA); late 2nd Lt. Grenadier Guards: *m.* 1965, Jane Margery, only da. of Lt.-Col. John Peter Grant of Rothiemurchus, MBE [see Cs. of Dysart], and has issue living, Tessa Rose, *b.* 1966, Veronica Mary, *b.* 1970.——Joseph William Henry, *b.* 1943; ed. at Harrow; Capt. Gren. Gds.: *m.* 1972, Sarah Louise, who *d.* 1974, el. da. of Lt.-Col. Richard Patrick Pilkington Smyly, MC, of Eaton Garden House, Eccleston, Chester.——Meriel Rose, *b.* 1940: *m.* 1964, Robert Ivan Kenyon-Slaney, of Hatton Grange, Shifnal, Salop [see B. Kenyon, colls.].

Grandchildren of the late John Henry Buxton (ante):—
Issue of the late Rev. Arthur Buxton, *b.* 1882, *d.* 1958: *m.* 1908, Esmé Caroline, who *d.* 1971, da. of the late Col. Francis William Pixley, VD, DL, JP, FSA, of Wooburn House, Wooburn, Bucks:—
Nigel Arthur, *M.B.*, *B.Chir.*, *M.R.C.S.*, *L.R.C.P.* (of 14, Virgilwood Drive, Willowdale, Ontario, Canada), *b.* 1909; ed. at Harrow, and at Trin. Coll., Camb. (BA), Licentiate of Med. Council of Canada; 1939-45 War as Capt. RAMC: *m.* 1948, Elmira, *MD*, da. of the late William Richli, MD, of Mariposa, Cal., USA, and has issue living, David Edson, *b.* 1949: *m.* 1974, Terri, da. of Gerald Snyder, of Oregon, USA,—John Arthur, *b.* 1950,—Louise Elizabeth, *b.* 1952.——Richenda Dorothy, *b.* 1911: *m.* 1938, George Blaker Blaker, CMG, of Lake House, Ockley, Dorking, Surrey, and has issue living, Richenda Jennifer, *b.* 1955.——Mary, *b.* 1913, Priscilla Peronne, *LRAM*, *b.* 1916; Detachment Officer, British Red Cross Soc.

Grandchildren of the late John Henry Buxton, el. son of the late Thomas Fowell Buxton, 2nd son of 1st baronet:—
Issue of the late Rev. Leonard Buxton, *b.* 1877, *d.* 1946 ; *m.* 1903, Kathleen, who *d.* 1958, da. of the late Capt. John Digby Wingfield-Digby, of Coleshill Park, Warwickshire, and Sherborne Castle, Dorset:—
Rev. Edmund Digby (Farm Cottage, Winchester Rd., Alresford, Hants., SO24 9EZ), *b.* 1908; ed. at Charterhouse, and at Trinity Coll., Camb. (MA): *m.* 1940, Katharine Monsarrat, el. da. of the late John Arthur Hargreaves, of Neston, Cheshire, and has issue living, *Rev.* Edmund Francis (Farm Cottage, Winchester Rd., Alresford, Hants., SO24 9EZ), *b.* 1942; ed. at Sherborne, Trin. Coll., Camb. (MA), and Birmingham Univ. (DPS): *m.* 1969, Jane Mary, only da. of the Rev. Arthur Leslie Jones, of Upwey Rectory, Weymouth, and has issue living, Nicholas Andrew *b.* 1972, Thomas Mark *b.* 1974,—Antony Leonard, *b.* 1950; ed. at Sherborne, and Trin. Coll., Camb.,— Mary Ethel, *b.* 1944: *m.* 1972, David James Grundy, MB, BS, FRCS (Wusasa Hospital, Zaria, Northern Nigeria), and has issue living, Katharine Mary *b.* 1973,—Lucy Jane, *b.* 1947.—— Kenneth Leonard, *FRCS*, *LRCP* (31, Blacketts Wood Drive, Chorleywood, Rickmansworth, Herts.), *b.* 1909; ed. at Charterhouse, and at Trin. Coll., Camb. (Exhibitioner, BA 1930, MA 1935): *m.* 1935, Agnes Josephine, da. of the late Rev. Dr. Tom Bragg, V. of Christ Church, Lowestoft, and has issue living, Paul Kenneth (4896, Lochside Drive, Victoria, BC, Canada), *b.* 1936; ed. at Trin. Coll., Camb. (MA, MB, BChir, MRCP): *m.* 1962, Heather Clive, da. of Lt.-Col. J. C. Edlmann, of Tattenhall, Chester, and has issue living, Jonathan *b.* 1965, Joanna Rachel, *b.* 1967,—Andrew Wakefield, *b.* 1939,—Angela Josephine, *b.* 1944: *m.* 1974, Simon Kendall (PO Box 74748, Nairobi, Kenya),—Susanna Rachel, *b.* 1945: *m.* 1969, Terrence Hookway, of 4, Valley Close, Goring-on-Thames, and has issue living, John *b.* 1973.——Daniel Richard (Ohauiti Rd., RD3, Tauranga, NZ), *b.* 1913; ed. at Bryanston, and at Trin. Coll., Camb.: *m.* 1940, Josephine Burdekin, and has issue living, Timothy Richard Blake (Harbutt Rd., RD1, Cambridge, NZ), *b.* 1942: *m.* 1964, Juliette Gaye, da. of C. W. L. Jex-Blake, of RD2, Whitianga, NZ, and has issue living, Darren Richard Blake *b.* 1966, Shane Laurence Blake *b.* 1968,—David Adrian Leonard

(47, Wallace Terr., Te Awamutu, NZ), *b.* 1945; ed. at Massey Univ., NZ (BSc Ag): *m.* 1970, Lynley Anne, da. of J. O'Conner, of 10, Mere Mere St., Timaru, NZ, and has issue living, Adrian David *b.* 1973.——*Rev.* Digby Hugh (Valcartier Village, Quebec, Canada GOA 450), *b.* 1916; ed. at Stowe Sch., and at Trin. Coll., Camb. (MA); Priest in charge of Valcartier Mission, Quebec.—— Kathleen Hannah, *b.* 1905.——Ruth Lydia, *b.* 1906: *m.* 1941, John Willoughby Harris, and has issue living, Patrick John, *b.* 1946; ed. at Wanganui Collegiate Sch., and at Canterbury Univ. (BE): *m.* 1972,—Elizabeth Hannah, *b.* 1943: *m.* 1963, Alfred Rudolf Bernd Ehrhardt of Arapaepae Rd., Ihakara RD, Levin, NZ, and has issue living, Richard Brent *b.* 1972. *Residence,* Roslyn Rd., Levin, NZ.

Branch from 3rd son of 2nd son of 1st Baronet

Grandchildren of the late Major Geoffrey Charles Buxton, T.D., el. son of the late Geoffrey Fowell Buxton, CB, 3rd son of Thomas Fowell Buxton (ante):—
Issue of the late Major Peter Stapleton Buxton, Leicestershire Yeo., *b.* 1904, *d.* (killed in action during European War) 1944 : *m.* 1934, Julia Victoria (of Mansion House, Gainford, Darlington, co. Durham), da. of the late Claud Edward Pease :—
James Geoffrey Pease (Stone Lodge, Seaton, Uppingham, Leics.), *b.* 1939; ed. at Eton, and at Trin. Coll., Camb.: *m.* 1970, Meriel Jessica Cowen, da. of Maj. Denis Cowen, of E. Farndon Hall, Market Harborough, and has issue living, Rose Emma, *b.* 1973.——Anne Victoria, *b.* 1936: *m.* 1959, Robin Slingsby Pease, of Hill House, Gainford, co. Durham, and has issue living, Peter Charles Gordon, *b.* 1965,—Victoria Julia Diana, *b.* 1962,—Annabel Primrose Robin, *b.* 1971.

Granddaughters of Geoffrey Fowell Buxton (infra):—
Issue of the late Maj. Ivor Buxton, DSO, TD, *b.* 1884, *d.* 1969: *m.* 1918, Phyllis Dorothy (Shelley Hall, Ipswich, Suffolk), da. of the late Col. Hugh Gurney Barclay, CVO, of Colney Hall, Norwich, and widow of Henry Cecil Johnson, DSO:—
Nancy, *b.* 1919; *m.* 1st, 1940, Lt.-Col. John Noel Ronald Loveday, 16th/5th Lancers, who *d.* (killed in action) 1944; 2ndly, 1947, Maj. John Hallifax Weller Poley, MC, of Boxted Hall, Bury St. Edmunds, and has issue living, (by 1st m.) Tessa, *b.* 1942,—(by 2nd m.) Richard Hallifax, *b.* 1949,—Nicholas Toby, *b.* 1951.——Felicity Mary (*Lady Blacker*), *b.* 1921: *m.* 1st, 1942, Maj. John Rew, who *d.* (killed in action) 1943; 2ndly, 1947, Gen. Sir Cecil Hugh Blacker, KCB, OBE, MC, of Whitchurch House, Whitchurch, Aylesbury, and has issue living (by 2nd m.), Terence, *b.* 1948: *m.* 1975, the Hon. Caroline Susan Dean Soper, da. of Baron Soper [Life Baron], —Philip, *b.* 1949.

Granddaughters of the late Thomas Fowell Buxton, 2nd son of 1st baronet:—
Issue of the late Geoffrey Fowell Buxton, C.B., *b.* 1852, *d.* 1929 : *m.* 1878, Mary, who *d.* 1940, da. of the late Rev. the Hon. John Harbord [B. Suffield]:—
Avery (*Hon. Mrs. Guy G. Wilson*), *b.* 1889; *m.* 1911, as his second wife, Lt.-Col. the Hon. Guy Greville Wilson, CMG, DSO, who *d.* 1943 [*see* B. Nunburnholme, colls.]. *Residence,* 29, Campden Hill Gate, W8.——Rose (Box 49666, Nairobi, Kenya), *b.* 1898: *m.* 1923, Algernon Richard Cartwright, who *d.* 1947, and has issue living, Giles Aubrey (Upper Pryors, Cowden, Edenbridge, Kent) *b.* 1924; ed. at Eton; a co. Dir.: *m.* 1954, Helen Celia, da. of the late Maj. John Arthur Pryor,—Prudence Tobina, *b.* 1928: *m.* 1949, Capt. Arthur Gerald Cole, late Irish Guards, of Kekopey, Gil-Gil, Kenya [*see* E. Enniskillen, colls.].
Issue of the late Rev. Barclay Fowell Buxton, *b.* 1860, *d.* 1946 : *m.* 1886, Margaret Maria Amelia, who *d.* 1947, da. of the late William Railton, of 65, Onslow Square, S.W. :—
Barclay Godfrey, M.C., *b.* 1895; ed. at Repton, and at Trin. Coll., Camb. (M.A.); formerly Capt. Duke of Wellington's (W. Riding) Regt. (T.A.); 1914-18 War (wounded, M.C. with Bar): *m.* 1922, Dorothea Reader, who *d.* 1967, yr. da. of the late Reader Harris, K.C., of Clapham, SW, and has issue living, Christopher Godfrey Reader (Kirtlington Park, Oxon.; The Penthouse, 6, The Little Boltons, SW10), *b.* 1929; ed. at Charterhouse, and at Trin. Coll., Camb. (MA); Chm. of Period and Country Houses, Ltd., London; appointed Master of Business Administration, Dartmouth Coll., USA, 1955; sometime 2nd Lt. RA: *m.* 1964 (m. diss. 1969), Margaret Isabel, yr. da. of Lt.-Col. H. B. Watkins, of Knighton, Radnorshire,—Joanna Margaret Reader (21A, Porchester Terr., W2; Hurlingham Club), *b.* 1927; ed. at Sherborne Sch. for Girls, and at Edinburgh Univ.; a Market Research Consultant. *Residence,* Woodend, Crawley Ridge, Camberley, Surrey.—— Rachel Jane, *b.* 1905. *Residence,* Wayside, Stanway, Colchester, Essex.

Grandson of the late Geoffrey Fowell Buxton, CB (ante):—
Issue of the late Com. Bernard Buxton, D.S.O., *b.* 1882, *d.* 1923 : *m.* 1904, Lady Hermione Grimston, who *d.* 1924, da. of 3rd Earl of Verulam :—
Geoffrey Mungo, O.B.E., *b.* 1906; ed. at Harrow, and at Peterhouse, Camb. (George Carter Scholar); Group-Capt. (retired) R.A.F., and a F.R.Ae.S. ; O.B.E. (Mil.) 1946 : *m.* 1929, Horatia Mary, da. of the late Adm. Sir William Wordsworth Fisher, G.C.B., G.C.V O., and has issue living, Carolyn Viola, *b.* 1934,—Juliet Horatia, *b.* 1937,—Rose Vivian, *b.* 1951. *Residence,* Wiveton Green, Holt, Norfolk.

Granddaughter of the late Com. Bernard Buxton, D.S.O. (ante):—
Issue of the late Major Samuel Luckyn Buxton, M.C., 17th/21st Lancers, *b.* 1914, *d.* (killed in action in Italy) 1944: *m.* 1941, Pamela Mary [who *m.* 2ndly, 1946, Major Aubrey Leland Oakes Buxton, M.C., R.A. (ante)], da. of Sir Henry Ralph Stanley Birkin, 3rd Bt.:—
Christina Hermione, *b.* 1944: *m.* 1967, John Millard Barnes, of 28, Bramham Gdns., SW5, and has issue living, Amanda Jane, *b.* 1968,—Sarah Hermione, *b.* 1970.

Branch from 4th son of 2nd son of 1st Baronet

Grandchildren of the late Patrick Alfred Buxton, CMG, FRS, MRCS, LRCP, el. son of Alfred Fowell Buxton, 4th son of Thomas Fowell Buxton (ante):—
Issue of the late Martin Patrick Buxton, *b.* 1920, *d.* 1966: *m.* 1949, Jacqueline Marcelle, who *d.* 1968, da. of Percival James Stokes:—
James Patrick, *b.* 1957.——Eleanor Ruth *b.* 1950: *m.* 1970, Paul Hudson Stanford, of The Old Rectory, South Somercotes, Louth, Lincs.——Rachel Phillida, *b.* 1952: *m.* 1973, Leslie Huson, of Rookery Cottage, Vicarage Lane, Cadney, Brigg.——Alice Richenda, *b.* 1954.

Issue of the late Fl.-Lt. Andrew Patrick Buxton, DFC, late RAF, *b.* 1923, *d.* 1952: *m.* 1949, Kathleen Audrey (who *m.* 2ndly, 1955, Martin Francis Wood, of 27, Northmoor Rd., Oxford), da. of the late Rev. J. H. Stanfield, of Seaton, Devon:—
Robin David, *b.* 1950.——Sarah Margaret, *b.* 1951.

Grandchildren of the late Alfred Fowell Buxton (ante):—
Issue of the late Patrick Alfred Buxton, C.M.G., F.R.S., M.R.C.S., L.R.C.P., *b.* 1892, *d.* 1955 : *m.* 1917, Muryell Gladys (of Saunders' Close, Bledlow, Aylesbury Bucks), da. of the late Rev. the Hon. William Talbot Rice [*see* B. Dynevor, colls.]:—
Helen Muryell, *b.* 1925; ed. at Camb. Univ. (BA 1948); formerly in First Aid Nursing Yeo.: *m.* 1948, Arthur Robert Donald Wright, and has issue living, Simon Nicholas, *b.* 1949,—Patrick Stephen, *b.* 1951,—Hannah Elizabeth, *b.* 1953,—Charlotte Helen, *b.* 1956,—Lesley Rachel, *b.* 1961. *Residence,* The Schools, Shrewsbury.——Marian Elizabeth, *b.* 1927: *m.* 1950, Michael Nicholson, and has issue living, Catherine Muryell, *b.* 1952,—Elizabeth Frances, *b.* 1953,—Rosamond Lillian, *b.* 1956,—Teresa Marian *b.* 1958. *Residence,* Manor Farm, Bucknell, Bicester, Oxon.——Rachel Katharine, *b.* 1930; ed. at Camb. Univ. (BA 1951): *m.* 1952, Christopher Herzig, and has issue living, Stephen Christopher, *b.* 1954,—Francis Patrick, *b.* 1955,—Edmund Martin, *b.* 1958,—Hugh John *b.* 1961,—Harriet Elizabeth, *b.* 1963. *Residence,* Blatchford House, King's Rd., Horsham, Sussex.——Lucy Bertha, *b.* 1932; ed. at

Camb. Univ. (B.A. 1954): *m.* 1955, Geoffrey Chandler, and has issue living, Hilary Jane, *b.* 1957, —Sarah Elizabeth, *b.* 1959,—Clare Marjorie, *b.* 1961,—Susan Ann, *b.* 1964. *Residence,* 57, Blackheath Park, Blackheath, S.E.3.

Issue of the late Denis Alfred Jex Buxton, *b.* 1895, *d.* 1964: *m.* 1923, Emily Mary, who *d.* 1970, da. of the late William Hollins [B. Sherwood]:—

Paul William Jex (of Castle House, Chipping Ongar, Essex; *Club,* Brooks's), *b.* 1925; ed. at Rugby, and at Balliol Coll., Oxford (BA); formerly Capt. Coldm. Gds.; Diplo. Ser. 1950-71; banking 1972-74; Assist. Sec. NI Office since 1974; NW Europe 1945 (wounded): *m.* 1st, 1950 (m. diss. 1971), Katharine, da. of Sir Hubert Hull, CBE; 2ndly, 1971, the Hon. Margaret Evelyn Bridges, da. of 1st Baron Bridges, and formerly wife of Trevor Henry Aston, and has issue living (by 1st m.), Charles Hubert Jex *b.* 1951,—Tobias Richard Valentine, *b.* 1953,—Mary Katharine, *b.* 1956,— (by 2nd m.) Sophia Frances, *b.* 1972,—Hero Elizabeth, *b.* 1974.——Mary Violet, *b.* 1924: *m.* 1950, as his second wife, David Roden Buxton (ante).——Cecilia Rachel (3, Linton Rd., Oxford) *b.* 1927; ed. at Lady Margaret Hall, Oxford (BA); a Fellow of Wolfson Coll., Oxford, and a Univ. Lect.: *m.* 1951 (m. diss. 1968), Marcus Dick, who *d.* 1971, and has issue living, Jasper Henry, *b.* 1956,—Catherine Sophia, *b.* 1953,—Cressida Rose, *b.* 1960.——Elizabeth Rosalind (34, Bracondale, Norwich), *b.* 1929: *m.* 1953 (m. diss. 1964), Tristram Yelin, and has issue living, Francis North Hunter Buxton, *b.* 1957,—Cecilia Mary *b.* 1954,—Natasha Vera *b.* 1959.

Branch from youngest son of 2nd son of 1st Baronet

Grandchildren of the Rev. Barclay Fowell Buxton, 5th son of Thomas Fowell Buxton (ante):—

Issue of the late Capt. Murray Barclay Buxton, M.C., *b.* 1889, *d.* (result of enemy action during European War) 1940: *m.* 1920, Janet Mary Muriel, who *d.* 1942, da. of Sir (Edward) Hildred Carlile, C.B.E., 1st Bt.:—

Ronald Carlile, *b.* 1923; ed. at Eton, and at Trin. Coll., Camb (MA); formerly Capt. REME, is a Co. Dir.; MP for Leyton (C) 1965-66: *m.* 1959, Phyllida Dorothy Roden, yr. da. of Capt. Roden Henry Victor Buxton, CBE, RN (ret.) (ante), and has issue living, Peter Hildred, *b.* 1960,—Robert Victor, *b.* 1964,—Camilla Janet St. John (twin), *b.* 1960,—Vanessa Anne Carlile, *b.* 1962. *Residences,* 67, Ashley Gdns., SW1; Kimberley Hall, Wymondham, Norfolk.

Issue of the late Alfred Barclay Buxton, *b.* 1891, *d.* (result of enemy action during European War) 1940 : *m.* 1916, Edith Mary Crossley (of 70, Pelham Court, S.W.3), da. of C. T. Studd, formerly of 17, Highland Road, Upper Norwood, S.E. :—

Susan Studd, *b.* 1918 : *m.* 1943, Michael Wood, M.B., B.S., F.R.C.S., and has issue living, Mark Lionel, *b.* 1945,—Hugo Charles, *b.* 1948,—Janet Mary, *b.* 1946,—Katrina Susan, *b.* 1951. *Address,* Box 49502, Nairobi.

The family of Buxton were seated for nearly three centuries at Coggeshall, Essex. The 1st baronet, Sir Thomas Fowell Buxton, M.P. for Weymouth (L) 1820-36, was distinguished for his exertions for the abolition of slavery and reform of the penal code. The 3rd baronet, Sir Thomas Fowell, G.C.M.G., sometime a partner in the firm of Truman, Hanbury and Co., sat as M.P. for Lynn Regis (L) 1865-8, and was Gov. of S. Australia 1895-8. The 4th baronet was High Sheriff of Essex 1905. The 5th baronet was High Sheriff of Essex 1928.

BUZZARD, Creation (U.K.) 1929, of Munstead Grange, Godalming, co. Surrey.

Be what you seem to be.

Sir ANTHONY FARQUHAR BUZZARD, 3rd *Baronet*; *b.* June 28th, 1935; *s.* his father *Rear-Adm. Sir* ANTHONY WASS, *CB, DSO, OBE,* 1972; ed. at Charterhouse, Ch. Ch., Oxford (MA), and Ambassador Coll., Pasadena, Cal. (BA); ARCM; freelance educational Consultant and Tutor: *m.* 1970, Barbara Jean, da. of Gordon Earl Arnold, of Mendon, Michigan, USA, and has issue.

Arms—Per chevron azure and argent, in chief two covered cups of the second and in base a rod of Æsculapius proper. Crest—Rising from clouds an eagle proper, gorged with an Eastern crown or.

Residence—Ruhamah, 48, Gallows Hill Lane, Abbots Langley, Herts.

Daughters living—Sarah Jane *b.* 1971 —Claire Judith. *b.* 1974. Brother living—TIMOTHY MACDONNELL (Great Walstead Lindfield Haywards Heath Sussex RH16 2QL) *b.* Jan. 28th 1939; a LRAM and a Graduate of Roy. Schs. of Music: *m.* 1970, Jennifer Mary, da. of the late Peter Patching, and has issue living, Rachel Mary, *b.* 1974. Sister living—Gillian Margaret, *b.* 1944; BSc.

Uncle living (son of 1st baronet)—Edward Miller, *FRCP, b.* 1909; ed. at Charterhouse, and Magdalen Coll., Oxford; MRCP 1937, FRCP 1949; formerly Surg.-Lt.-Cdr. RNVR: *m.* 1937, Sylvia Bevan, da. of the late Dr. John William Fordham, of Hughenden, Loughborough Rd., Leicester, and has issue living, David, *b.* 1950,—Sarah, *b.* 1941,—Judith, *b.* 1944,—Anne, *b.* 1947. *Residence,* The Barn, Oakley Park, Frilford Heath, nr. Abingdon, Oxon.

Aunts living (daughters of 1st baronet)—Margaret Helen, *b.* 1900: *m.* 1925, Harold Gardiner Hill, MBE, MD, FRCP, and has issue living, Peter Farquhar, *b.* 1926,—Michael Anthony, *b.* 1928,— Richard Temple, *b.* 1932. *Residence,* 30 Stanhope Gdns., SW7.——Sylvia Marion, *b.* 1904.—— Isabel May, *b.* 1910: *m.* 1933, Cdr. Herbert William Acworth, RN, and has issue living, William Farquhar (Gt. Hidden Farm, Hungerford, Berks.), *b.* 1934: *m.* 1964, Susan Henrietta, yr. da. of Capt. Roddie Casement, OBE, RN, of Terwick Old Rectory, Rogate, Petersfield, Hants. [see Greenwell, Bt.], and has issue living, William Bernard *b.* 1965, James Michael *b.* 1966, Anna Claire *b.* 1970,—Adam Buzzard, *b.* 1943,—Susan Esmé, *b.* 1936, Jane Marion, *b.* 1941. *Residence,* Old Farm Cottage, Oakley Park, Frilford Heath, nr. Abingdon, Berks.

Widow living of 2nd Baronet—MARGARET ELFREDA (*Margaret Lady Buzzard*) (Todd House, West Clandon, Surrey), da. of the late Sir Arthur Rowland Knapp, KCIE, CSI, CBE: *m.* 1932, Rear-Adm. Sir Anthony Wass Buzzard, CB, DSO, OBE, 2nd Bt., who *d.* 1972.

The 1st baronet, Sir (Edward) Farquhar Buzzard (son of the late Thomas Buzzard, M.D., F.R.C.P., of 74, Grosvenor Street, W.1), was Physician Extraor. to H.M. 1924-32, Physician-in-Ord. 1932-6. and an Extra Physician 1937-45.

BYASS, Creation (U.K.) 1926, of Port Talbot, co. Glamorgan.

Sir GEOFFREY ROBERT SIDNEY BYASS, *T.D.*, 2nd *Baronet ; b.* Sept. 30th, 1895 ; *s.* his father, *Sir* SIDNEY HUTCHINSON, 1929 ; ed. at Winchester ; is a D.L. for Glamorgan and Lieut.-Col. and Brevet Col. T.A. Reserve, late Comdg. 81st (Welsh) Field Brig. R.A. (T.A.) ; European War 1916-18 in Egypt, France, and Belgium (wounded, two medals); Mayor of Port Talbot 1937-38: *m.* 1st 1919, Marian, who *d.* 1968, da. of the late Col. Sir Gerald Trevor Bruce, KCB, CMG, DSO, TD; 2ndly, 1972, Mrs. Winifred Kate Gillespie-Hill, da. of the late William Paton, of Glamorgan, and has issue by 1st m.

Arms—Argent, three wings in bend azure. *Crest*—A wing argent, thereon an escutcheon azure, charged with a fleur-de-lis also argent.

Residence—Camden Place, Chislehurst, Kent.

Daughters living By 1st m.—Gillian Mary, *b.* 1921: *m.* 1948, Kenneth Mackenzie Knight, of Mozartlaan 303, The Hague, and has issue living, Nigel Geoffrey Roy, *b.* 1950,—Simon Gerald, *b.* 1953.——Daphne Caroline, *b.* 1925: *m.* 1st, 1949, Major Ian Guy Mathews, Somerset and Cornwall L.I.; 2ndly, 1962, Lt.-Col. William Roland Lawson, of The Pump Room, Winkfield, Berks., and has issue living, (by 1st m.) Caroline, *b.* 1951: *m.* 1972, Malcolm Turner, of Drumby, Dunino St. Andrews, Fife, and has issue living, Samuel *b.* 1972,—Belinda, *b.* 1952.——Pamela Julia, *b.* 1926: *m.* 1953, Arthur David Veall, of Upper Gade, Little Gaddesden, Herts., and has issue living, Robert John, *b.* 1955,—Christopher Toby, *b.* 1956,—Ivan, *b.* 1964,—Julia Diana, *b.* 1958.——Rosemary Valentine, *b.* 1933: *m.* 1959, Kenneth Michael Bond Wright, of 13, Karoo Av., East Lindfield, NSW, and has issue living, Sarah Caroline, *b.* 1960,—Charlotte Mary, *b.* 1962.——Ursula Marian, *b.* 1940: *m.* 1693, John Dornton, of Manor Lodge, North Rd., Chesham Bois, Bucks., and has issue living, Charles Geoffrey, *b.* 1964,—Elizabeth Henrietta, *b.* 1967,—Susannah Marian, *b.* 1971.

Sister living—Mary Eveline (Woodmans, Bosbury Old Country, Ledbury) *b.* 1899: *m.* 1925, Capt. Thomas Nathaniel Hone, OBE, late KRRC, who *d.* 1946.

The 1st baronet, Sir Sidney Hutchinson Byass, was Chm. of Robert B. Byass, Ltd., of Port Talbot, Pres. of Mid-Glamorgan Conservative Asso., thrice Mayor of Aberavon, and first Mayor of Port Talbot.

Cable-Alexander, see Alexander.

CAHN, Creation (U.K.) 1934, of Stanford-upon-Soar, co. Nottingham.

Sir ALBERT JONAS CAHN, 2nd *Baronet; b.* June 27th, 1924; *s.* his father, *Sir* JULIEN, 1944; ed. at Harrow: *m.* 1948, Malka, da. of the late Reuben Bluestone, and has issue.

Arms—Gules, a cross raguly ermine between in the second and third quarters a fleur-de-lis or. *Crest*,—In front of a fox's head erased two branches of willow in saltire proper.

Seat—Stanford Hall, Loughborough. *Residence*—10, Edgecoombe Close, Warren Rd., Kingston upon Thames, Surrey.

Sons living—JULIEN MICHAEL, *b.* Jan. 15th, 1951; ed. at Harrow.——Edward John, *b.* 1959.

Daughters living—Madeleine Jane, *b.* 1949.——Valerie Janet, *b.* 1954.

Brother living—Richard Ian (Crispa, Bashurst Copse Itchingfield, Horsham, Sussex), *b.* 1927: *m.* 1964, Marietta, da. of Joseph Seidler.

Sister living—Patience, (108, Costa Brava Beach Rd., Sea Point, Capetown, S. Africa), *b.* 1922: *m.* 1st, 1945 (m. diss. 1957), Fl. Lt. Jules V. Silverston, RAF; 2ndly, 1957, Edward Wynne-Jones, MB, ChB, who *d.* 1958; 3rdly, 1972, Henricus Gerardus Godefridus Retrot, and has issue living.

Widow living of 1st Baronet—PHYLLIS MURIEL (*Dowager Lady Cahn*), da. of A. Wolfe, of Bournemouth: *m.* 1916, Sir Julien Cahn, 1st Bt., who *d.* 1944. *Residence*, Sesame, Angmering-on-Sea, Sussex.

The 1st baronet, Sir Julien Cahn (son of Albert Cahn), was Master of Burton Hunt 1926-35, of Woodland Pytchley Foxhounds 1935-7, and of Fernie's Foxhounds 1937-9, and sponsored and captained many cricket teams on tours abroad.

CAIN, Creation (U.K.) 1920, of Wargrave Manor, co. Berkshire. [Extinct 1969.]

Sir ERNEST CAIN, 2nd and last *Baronet.*

Daughters living of 2nd Baronet—Ann, *b.* 1925.——Joan (twin), *b.* 1925: *m.* 1952, Ian Merrick Cuthbertson Hill, and has issue living, Christopher Michael Ian, *b.* 1957,—Susan Elizabeth, *b.* 1955. *Residence,* 66, Elmfield Rd., Gosforth, Newcastle upon Tyne 3.——Vivien Elizabeth, *b.* 1932: *m.* 1st, 1954, Charles William Munro Wilson, from whom she obtained a divorce 1959; 2ndly, 1961, Baron Pierre Cervello, from whom she obtained a divorce 1966, and has issue living, (by 1st m.) Amanda Louise, *b.* 1956.

Daughter living of 1st Baronet—Dorothy Mary, *b.* 1892.

Widow living of 2nd Baronet—ENID BERTHA WILLOUGHBY) (*Lady Cain*) (White House, Ferry Lane, Wargrave, Berks.), da. of George Glasgow, of Liverpool *m.* 1923, Col. Sir Ernest Cain, 2nd Bt. who *d.* 1969, when the title became ext.

CAIRD, Creation (U.K.) 1928, of Glenfarquhar, co. Kincardine. [Extinct 1954.]

Sir JAMES CAIRD, 1st and last *Baronet.*

Daughter living of 1st Baronet—Henrietta Margaret, *b.* 1896: *m.* 1921, Hugh Scudamore, and has issue living, James, *b.* 1922,—Edward, *b.* 1923,—Hugh, *b.* 1926,—Sylvia, *b.* 1930. *Residence,* Waveney, Marryat Road, Wimbledon Common, S.W.19.

ANSTRUTHER-GOUGH-CALTHORPE, Creation (U.K.) 1929, of Elvetham Hall, Elvetham, co. Southampton.

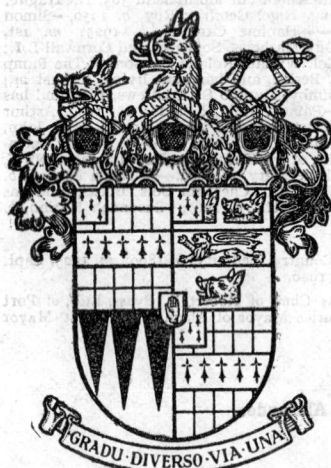

The same way, but by different steps.

Sir RICHARD HAMILTON AN-STRUTHER-GOUGH-CALTHORPE, *C.B.E.,* 2nd *Baronet, b.* March 28th, 1908 ; *s.* his father *Sir* FITZROY HAMILTON 1957 ; ed. at Harrow, and at Magdalene Coll., Camb. (MA); Hon. LLD Birmingham 1950; a DL, a JP and Co. Alderman for Hants (Chm. 1967); Brig. (ret.) R. Scots Greys; a Dir. of Lloyds Bank, Artagen Properties, and Rowton Hotels; 1939-45 War in Norway and Middle East (OBE, CBE, Croix de Guerre); OBE (Mil.) 1940, CBE (Mil.) 1946: *m.* 1939, Nancy Moireach, only da. of the late Vernon Austen Malcolmson, JP [B. Belper], and has issue.

Arms—Quarterly : 1st and 4th checky or and azure, a fesse ermine, and (for distinction) a canton ermine, *Calthorpe*; 2nd, gules, on a fesse argent, between three boars' heads couped or, a lion passant azure, and (for distinction) a canton ermine, *Gough*; 3rd, argent, three piles issuing from the chief sable, *Anstruther.* Crest—1st, a boar's head couped erect argent, charged (for distinction) with an ermine spot azure, *Calthorpe*; 2nd, a boar's head couped argent, pierced through the cheek with a broken spear gules, and charged (for distinction) with an ermine spot azure, *Gough*; 3rd, two arms in armour, pholding in the gauntlet a battle-axe all proer, *Anstruther.*

Seat—Elvetham Farm House, Hartley Wintney, Hants. Clubs—Royal Yacht Squadron.

Grandchildren living,—(Issue of the late Niall Hamilton Anstruther-Gough-Calthorpe, *b.* 1940, *d.* 1970: *m.* 1964, Martha Rodman, who m. 2ndly, 1975, Charles C. Nicholson, da. of Stuart Warren Don, of 1, Hyde Park St., W2) [see Nicholson Bt. (cr. 1912)]:—EUAN HMAILTON, *b.* June 22nd, 1966.——Lara Nancy Don, *b.* 1968.

Sons living—Michael Richard, *b.* 1943; ed. at Harrow, and Coll. of Estate Management; ARICS. ——John Austen, *b.* 1947; ed. at Harrow.

Sisters living—Frances Jean, *b.* 1910: *m.* 1942, His Honour Judge (Frank Alleyne) Stockdale, el. son of the late Sir Frank Arthur Stockdale, GCMG, CBE, and has issue living, James Arthur FitzRoy, *b.* 1948; ed. at Eton, and Southampton Univ. (LLB); Bar. Gray's Inn 1972: *m.* 1974, Jane Mary Gabriel, el. da. of William Hazzard,—Sarah Victoria, *b.* 1943: *m.* 1965, Christopher N. A. Castleman, and has issue living, Jonathan William *b.* 1971, Amanda Lucy *b.* 1967,—Frances Jane, *b.* 1946: *m.* 1967, Charles J. Deacon, and has issue living, Julian Mark *b.* 1972, Rebecca *b.* 1970. *Residence,* 4, Verulam Buildings, Grays Inn, WC1.——Barbara (*Baroness Luke*), *b.* 1911: *m.* 1932, the 2nd Baron Luke. *Residence,* Odell Castle, Bedfordshire, MK43 7BB.

Sir FitzRoy Hamilton Anstruther-Gough-Calthorpe, 1st baronet (el. son of the late Lieut.-Col. Robert Hamilton Lloyd-Anstruther [Anstruther, Bt., colls.]), assumed by Roy. licence 1910, the surname and arms of Anstruther only ; also later by Roy. licence 1910, for himself and issue the surnames of Gough-Calthorpe in addition to, and after that of Anstruther, and the Arms of Gough and Calthorpe quartered with those of Anstruther, having *m.* 1898, the Hon. Rachel Gough-Calthorpe, who *d.* 1951, el. da. and co-heir of 6th Baron Calthorpe.

CAMERON, Creation (U.K.) 1893, of Balclutha, Greenock. [Extinct 1968.]

Sir JOHN CAMERON, 2nd and last *Baronet.*

Daughter living of 1st Baronet—Margaret Lilian (Half Acre House, Northcroft Rd., Englefield Green, Surrey), *b.* 1901.

CAMPBELL, Creation (N.S.) 1628, of Auchinbreck.

Sir ROBIN AUCHINBRECK CAMPBELL, 15th
Baronet, b. June 7th, 1922; *s.* his father, *Sir*
LOUIS HAMILTON, 1970; ed. at Eton; late
Lt. (A) RNVR: *m.* 1948, Rosemary (Sally),
da. of Ashley Dean, of Christchurch, NZ, and
has issue.

Arms—Gyronny of eight or and sable, a bordure checky
ermine and purpure.   **Crest**—A dexter hand proper holding
a spur or.

Residence—Glen Dhu, Motunau, N. Canterbury, NZ.
Clubs—Christchurch (NZ) and Bembridge Sailing.

———

Son living—LOUIS AUCHINBRECK, *b.* Jan. 17th, 1953.
Daughters living—Fiona Rosemary, *b.* 1955.——Sophia
Louise, *b.* 1960.

Daughter living of 12th Baronet—Mary Sara (*Lady Fitz-
patrick*), *TD, b.* 1917: *m.* 1944, Gen. Sir (Geoffrey Richard
Desmond Fitzpatrick, GCB, DSO, MBE, MC, late R.)
Dragoons (ret.), and has issue living Brian Richard Charles,
b. 1950,—Sara Georgina, *b.* 1948.   *Address*—c/o Australia
& NZ Banking Group Ltd., 20, Grafton St., W1.

Daughters living of 10th Baronet—Moira Constance (2, Mopoon Terr., Campbeltown, Argyll)
b. 1887.——Ida Cerise, *b.* 1888: *m.* 1918, G. W. Kells, and has issue living, Robin Burton Campbell, *b.* 1919,—Moira Louise, *b.* 1921,—Judith Carandini, *b.* 1923. *Residence*, Gisborne, NZ.

Widows living of 12th and 14th Baronets—NANCY SARAH (*Nancy Lady Campbell*), only da. of the
late Edward Chapman, of Canterbury, NZ: *m.* 1915, Capt. Sir Charles Ralph Campbell, 12th
baronet, who *d.* 1948. *Residence*, Davaar, Bembridge, I. of Wight.——MARGARET ELIZABETH
PATRICIA (*Margaret, Lady Campbell*), (15, Jacksons Rd., Fendalton, Christchurch, NZ), da. of the
late Patrick Campbell: *m.* 1920, Sir Louis Hamilton Campbell, 14th baronet, who *d.* 1970.

Collateral Branch living.

Descendants of the late Patrick Campbell, of Stuck, co. Bute, brother
of the late Rev. Duncan Campbell, V. of Kilfinnan, great-great-
great-grandfather of 8th baronet :—

Grandsons of the late Archibald Samuels Campbell, great-great-great-grandson
and heir male of the late Rev. Patrick Campbell, of Torblaren, and grandson
and heir male of the late Patrick Campbell, of Stuck, co. Bute (ante) :—
Issue of the late Sir Archibald Young Gipps Campbell, K.C.I.E., C.S.I., C.B.E., V.D. ;
b. 1872, *d.* 1957: *m.* 1910, Frances Irene (*Lady Campbell*), who *d.* 1967, da. of the late
Rev. Henry Savill Young, of Mallard's Court, Stokenchurch, Oxfordshire [Young, Bt.,
cr. 1769, colls.]:—
Archibald Hugh (Ballomill, Abernethy, Perthshire), *b.* 1914; Lieut.-Col. (ret.) Roy. Signals: *m.* 1940,
Mary Alison Nugent, da. of the late Lieut.-Col. Herbert Nugent Young, DSO, Roy. Inniskilling
Fusiliers, and has issue living, Archibald James, *b.* 1943,—Alison Margaret *b.* 1941: *m.* 1966,
Robert Michael. of Ballomill House, Abernethy, Perthshire, and has issue living, Anthony
Richard *b.* 1967, Isobel Margaret *b.* 1969,—Christian Jean Mary, *b.* 1948.——Colin Alan George
(West Stowell House, Oare, Marlborough, Wilts. ; The Old Manse, Lochgair,by Lochgilphead,
Argyll), *b.* 1917; Capt. (ret.) Black Watch, and in Foreign Ser.: *m.* 1st, 1945 (m. diss. 1961)
Mary Cosser, da. of the late Ramsay Young; 2ndly, 1966, Joanna Frances, da. of the late George
Falconer Ball, MC, and has issue living (by 1st m.), Mary Irene Young, *b.* 1946,—Claire Elizabeth,
b. 1949,—Fiona Penelope, *b.* 1955.——Niall Patrick, *b.* 1925; Lt. (ret.) RE: *m.* 1st, 1953 (m. diss.
1965), Gillian Margaret Elizabeth, da. of Arthur John Morris; 2ndly, 1967, Peta Caroline, da. of
William Kelso Paul, and has issue living (by 1st m.), Sarah Caroline, *b.* 1954,—Julia Anne, *b.*
1956,—(by 2nd m.) James William Patrick, *b.* 1968,—Rebecca Louise, *b.* 1971. *Residence*,
Lingmoor, 15, Rutland Rd., Harrogate.

This baronetcy was conferred upon Sir Dugald Campbell. Knight. with remainder to his heirs
male whatsoever. Upon the death of the 6th baronet in 1812, Dugald Campbell, of Kildalloig,
Day-Keeper of the Great Seal in Ireland, is said to have become *de jure* 7th baronet, but not to
have assumed the title, and the baronetcy remained dormant until 1841. when it was claimed by
Dugald Campbell's heir, John Eyton Campbell, of Killdalloig, who proved himself heir to the title,
and was subsequently recognized as 8th baronet *de facto*.

CAMPBELL, Creation (N.S.) 1668 (about), of Aberuchill, Perthshire.

Victory follows the brave.

Sir COLIN MOFFAT CAMPBELL,
M.C., 8th *Baronet* ; *b.* Aug. 4th, 1925 ;
s. his father, *Capt. Sir* JOHN ALEX-
ANDER COLDSTREAM, 1960 ; ed. at
Stowe ; is with James Finlay & Co.,
Ltd. ; European War 1944-5 with
Scots Guards (wounded, M.C.) : *m.*
1952, Mary Anne Chichester, da. of
Brigadier George Alexander Bain,
O.B.E. [*see* M. Donegall, colls.], and
has issue.

Arms—Quarterly : 1st and 4th, gyronny of
eight or and sable ; 2nd, argent, a lymphad with
her oars in action sable ; 3rd, or, a fesse checky
argent and azure ; all within a bordure ermine.
Crest—A lion guardant gules crowned with laurel
and holding in his dexter paw a sword proper,
hilted and pommeled or, and in the sinister a dag,
or Highland pistol. **Supporters**—Two bloodhounds
guardant, proper, collared and leashed or.

Residence—Kilbryde Castle, Dunblane, Perthshire. *Clubs*,—Guards', Turf (Calcutta), Nairobi and Muthaiga (Kenya), Western (Glasgow).

Sons living—JAMES ALEXANDER MOFFAT BAIN, *b.* Sept. 23rd, 1956.——John Alistair Chichester, *b.* 1960.
Daughter living—Janet Mary Bain, *b.* 1953: *m.* 1975, Nicholas John Muir [see Muir Bt.].
Brother living—Alistair Bromley, *b.* 1927 ; *ed.* at Tonbridge : *m.* 1952, Rosemary, da. of the late J. Lindsay Pullar, of Glenfarg House, by Perth, and has issue living, Christopher John *b.* 1954,—Caroline Margaret, *b.* 1956,—Colina Mary, *b.* 1964. *Residence*, Grainston, Kilbryde Dunblane, Perthshire, FK15 9NF.

Collateral Branches living.

Grandchildren of the late Alexander le Grand Campbell, 2nd son of 4th baronet :—
Issue of the late Alexander Bulwer Campbell, *b.* 1855, *d.* 1938: *m.* 1894, Maude, da. of J. Knight:—
Alexander Colin Le Grand, *b.* 1898: *m.* 1922, Mavis Macdonald, who *d.* 1937, and has issue living, Janet Glen, *b.* 1927: *m.* 19—, Neil Lester, of 57, School Rd., Titarangi, NZ.——Clyde Coldstream, *b.* 1905; Solicitor: *m.* 1st, 1936, Mary Fisher, who *d.* 19—; 2ndly, 19—, Eleanor Curnow, of Auckland, and has issue living (by 2nd m.) Margaret, *b.* 1945,—Lindsay, *b.* 1949.——Eleanor Margaret, *b.* 1897: *m.* 1925, Charles Dalrymple Watt, of Kowhai Rd., Waikanee, Gold Coast, NZ, and has issue living, Rosemary Jean, *b.* 1925.——Hester Joan, *b.* 1910: *m.* 1933, Bernard George Matheson Canning, 87, Taukina Rd., Miramar, Wellington, NZ, and has issue living.

Grandsons of the late Col. George Frederick Colin Campbell, C.M.G., V.D., 2nd son of the late Alexander le Grand Campbell (ante):—
Issue of the late Capt. Alan le Grand Campbell, *b.* 1896, *d.* 19—: *m.* 1928, Barbara Alison (Taunton Place, Stoke, Nelson, NZ), da. of the late James Marchbanks of Wellington, NZ:—
John Graham Colin (Avenue Rd., Greenmeadows, Napier, NZ), *b.* 1929: *m.* 1957, Anna Margaret, da. of the late Bertram Kay, of Fulham, London, and has issue, Alexander James le Grand, *b.* 1958,—Robert Neil, *b.* 1960.——Donald James (Campbell St., Karori, Wellington, NZ), *b.* 1930; ANZIA: *m.* 1963, Barbara Mary, da. of Frank Grear, of Nelson, NZ.

Grandchildren of the late William Hunter Campbell, yr. son of the late Robert Stuart Campbell (*b.* 1815), yst. son of William Campbell, WS., 4th son of 3rd baronet:—
Issue of the late Robert Stuart Campbell, *b.* 1873, *d.* 1958: *m.* 19—, Annie, who *d.* 1960, da. of John Holloway:—
Robin Edmund Hunter (Josephine St., Wingham, Ont., Canada), *b.* 1904; matriculated arms as Campbell of Bellsyde, Ont., with Lyon Court 1964: *m.* 1st, 19—, Minerva, who *d.* 1955, da. of W. J. Finlay; 2ndly, 1964, Marjorie, da. of Frank Preston, and has issue living, (by 1st m.) Charles Robert (Seaforth, Ont., Canada), *b.* 1943: *m.* 19—, Margaret Jane, da. of Robert O'Hara, and has issue living, James Robert *b.* 1965, Barry Charles *b.* 1966, Christine *b.* 1969,—Grace Anne Pauline, *b.* 19—: *m.* 19—, Frederick McGee, of Wingham, Ont., Canada, and has issue living,——Stuart William Ivor (Wingham, Ont., Canada), *b.* 1910.——Hubert John Shelley (twin), *b.* 1910.——Annie Elizabeth, *b.* 1906: *m.* 1925, Andrew B. Straughan, of 126, Park St., Goderich, Ont., Canada, and has issue living.
Issue of the late William John Campbell, *b.* 1875, *d.* 1963: *m.* 19—, Mary Hutton, who *d.* 1936:—
James (Wingham, Ont., Canada), *b.* 1904: *m.* 19—, Vivien Castelon.——John, *b.* 1916: *m.* 19—, Muriel Mackay, and has issue living.
Issue of the late George Alexander Campbell, *b.* 1882, *d.* 19—: *m.* 1st, 19—, Jennie Hutton; 2ndly, 19— Flossie Saunders:—
(By 1st m.) John Hunter *b.* 1914: *m.* 1st 19— Margaret Gillies; 2ndly, 19—, Frances Rosetta Gillies, and has issue living (by 1st m.) Harold John Linklater, *b.* 1935: *m.* 19—, Rose-Marie Whitfield, and has issue living John Lewis *b.* 1957, Scott Harold *b.* 1970, Sherri Lou *b.* 1959,—Ronald Keith, *b.* 1939: *m.* 19—, Elizabeth Mary Oliver, and has issue living, Ronald Thomas *b.* 1970,—Gail, *b.* 1941: *m.* 19—, Kenneth Nekon Paterson, and has issue living, (by 2nd m.)——Danny, *b.* 1948,—Mary Barbara, *b.* 1946: *m.* 19—, Douglas Ross Howson, and has issue living.——Mary Haugh, *b.* 1909: *m.* 19—, Edgar McMichael, and has issue living.——Ethel Isabel Sutherland, *b.* 1910: *m.* 1st, 19—, John Johnston; 2ndly, 19—, Alfred Roberts, and has issue living by 1st m.—(by 2nd m.), Harold Alexander, *b.* 1919: *m.* 19—, Adeline Isabel Cardiff, and has issue living, William John, *b.* 1939: *m.* 19—, Diana Teresa Wozniak, and has issue living, Curtis William *b.* 1961, Randall Steven Harold *b.* 1962, Lollie Diana Catherine *b.* 1959, Suzanne Adeline *b.* 1969,—Dwight Alexander, *b.* 1941: *m.* 19—, Lyla Joan Marie Johnston, and has issue living, Grant Dwight *b.* 1961, Charlene Marie *b.* 1960, Sharon Rebecca Jane *b.* 1967,—Nancy Lee, *b.* 1942: *m.* 19—, John Michael Pawitch,—Frances Elizabeth, *b.* 1962.

The 1st baronet, a Lord of Justiciary in Scotland, under the title of Lord Aberuchill, was a Privy Councillor, and sat as M.P. for Perthshire 1690-1702. He lost £17,201 (Scots), from the Highland army under Lord Dundee, and though an Act of Parliament granting him compensation was passed, he did not receive the money. The original patent of baronetcy is lost, and the actual date when it was conferred is not known.

CAMPBELL, Creation (U.K.) 1808, of Succoth, Dunbartonshire.

Labour overcomes everything

Sir ILAY MARK CAMPBELL, 7th *Baronet; b.* May 29th, 1927; *s.* his father, *Capt. Sir* GEORGE ILAY, 1967; *ed.* at Eton, and Ch. Ch., Oxford (BA); Joint Scottish Agent for Christie, Manson & Woods since 1973 (Scottish Agent 1968-73); Pres. of Assocn. for Protection of Rural Scotland: *m.* 1961, Margaret Minette Rohais, only da. of James Alasdair Anderson [*see* E. Halsbury], and has issue.

Arms—Quarterly: 1st and 4th, gyronny of eight engrailed or and sable ; 2nd and 3rd azure, a lion rampant argent, within a bordure counter-compony argent and azure. *Wallace of Elderslie.* **Crest**—A camel's head couped proper; **Supporters**—*Dexter*, a lion rampant guardant proper; *sinister*, a savage wreathed about the temples and loins with oak leaves, all proper.
Residences—Crarae Lodge, by Inveraray, Argyll; Lennel, Coldstream, Berwickshire. *Club*—Turf.

Daughters living—Cecilia Margaret Lucy, *b.* 1963.——Candida Harriett Rohais, *b.* 1964.

Aunt living (daughter of 5th Baronet)—Lucy Katherine Grace, *b.* 1896: *m.* 1925, Charles William Herdman, who *d.* 1956, and has issue living, John Campbell, *b.* 1931,—Susan Elizabeth, *b.* 1926,— Caroline Grace, *b.* 1928. *Residence,* Cutham Hill, Bagendon, Cirencester.

Mother living—Clematis Elizabeth Denys (Belmont, Coldstream, Berwickshire), da. of the late Maj. Walter Waring [M. Tweeddale]: *m.* 1st, 1926 (m. diss. 1935), Capt. Sir George Ilay Campbell, 6th Bt., who *d.* 1967; 2ndly, 1944 (m. diss. 1950) Lt. William Reresby Sitwell, RN.

Sir Ilay Campbell, 1st baronet, was Lord President of Court of Session, with the title of Lord Succoth; and the 2nd baronet Sir Archibald was a Lord of Session 1809-24, with the same designation. The 1st baronet's mother, Helen, who *d.* 1767, was the only da. and heir of John Wallace of Elderslie.

CAMPBELL, Creation (U.K.) 1815.

Sir Guy Theophilus Halswell Camp-bell, *O.B.E., M.C.,* 5th *Baronet*; *b.* Jan. 18th. 1910; *s.* his father, *Major Sir* Guy Colin, 1960; ed. at Eton, and at St. Andrews Univ.; is Col., late 60th Rifles, Camel Corps, Sudan Defence Force, and commanded Kenya Regt. 1952-6; was Head of British Mil. Mission to Libya, 1956-60; European War 1939-45 (wounded, M.C.), Kenya 1954 (O.B.E.), Palestine 1948; O.B.E. (Mil.) 1954: *m.* 1956, Lizbeth Webb, da. of the late Frederick Holton, and has issue.

Arms—Quarterly: 1st and 4th, gyronny of eight or and sable; 2nd, argent, a lymphad, sails furled and oars in action sable, with a flag and pennants flying gules; 3rd, or, a fesse checky azure and argent, all within a bordure embattled ermine. Crest—A boar's head arrachée or.

Clubs—Royal Commonwealth Society, MCC, I Zingari, Royal and Ancient, Puffin's.

Sons living—LACHLAN PHILIP KEMEYS, *b.* Oct. 9th, 1958.——Rory Charles Fitzgerald, *b.* 1961.

Brother living—(Edward Fitzgerald) David, *MC, ERD,* (twin), *b.* 1910; ed. at Eton, and at St. Andrews Univ.; is Major Black Watch (Reserve of Officers), and El Bimbashi, Camel Corps, Sudan Defence Force; European War 1939-45 (wounded, M.C.), Korea 1952-3, Kenya 1954-7. *Residence,* 45, Bramham Gdns., SW5. *Clubs,* New, Caledonian, MCC, I Zingari, Royal and Ancient.

Uncle living (son of 3rd baronet)—Rt. Hon. Sir Ronald Ian, *GCMG, CB, b.* 1890; ed. at Eton, and at Magdalen Coll., Oxford (BA (Honours) History 1912); was Envoy Extraor. and Min. Plen. at Paris 1938-39, at Belgrade 1939-41, and at Washington 1941-5; appointed an Under-Sec. of State Foreign Office 1945, and Ambassador Extraor. and Plen. to Egypt 1946; retired 1950; CMG 1932, CB (Civil) 1937, KCMG 1941, GCMG 1947, PC 1950. *Residence,* Summerfield House, Sidegate, Haddington, East Lothian.

Widow living of 4th Baronet—ALIDA VIRGINIA (ALLAN) (*Alida, Lady Campbell*), only child of Augustus Peeters van Nieuwenrode, Belgium : *m.* 1955, as his second wife, Major Sir Guy Colin Campbell, 4th baronet, who *d.* 1960. *Residences,* 49, Hill Street, W.1 ; Pilmour Place, St. Andrews, Fife. *Clubs,* Guards', St. Rules (St. Andrews).

Collateral Branches living.

Issue of the late Col. John Archibald Campbell, yst. son of 3rd baronet, *b.* 1898, *d.* 1974: *m.* 1st, 1925 (m. diss. 1940), Dorothy, da. of the late John Field, of Perthi, Ruthin; 2ndly, 1944 (m. diss. 1963), Elizabeth, da. of Renard Pearth, of Pittsburgh, USA:—

(By 1st m.) Colin Guy Napier (2, Kildare Terr., W2; White's and Puffins Clubs), *b.* 1930; Capt. late KRRC: *m.* 1965, Lucy Barnett Smith, da. of James A. Barnett, of Bel Air, Cal., USA, and has issue living, Georgina Dorothy, *b.* 1969,—Tessa Sylvia, *b.* 1971.——(by 2nd m.) Henrietta Nina Sylvia, *b.* 1945: *m.* 1971, Andrew Guy Louis de Chappuis Konig, of 6, Molyneux St., W1.

Grandchildren of the late Charles James Napier Campbell, 3rd son of 2nd baronet :—

Issue of the late Major Edward Fitzgerald Campbell, *b.* 1890, *d.* 1950 : *m.* 1915, Agnes Catherine (of Bishopsway, Twyford, Winchester, Hants.), da. of the late Henry Templer Prior, Master of Supreme Court :—

Charles Colin, *b.* 1923 (Woolpit Farm, Ewhurst, Cranleigh, Surrey); ed. at Loretto, and at Pembroke Coll., Camb. (Foundation Scholar) (MA); 1939-45 War as Lt. RE: *m.* 1970, Julia Margaret Rachel, da. of Anthony Smithson Russell, and has issue living, James Charles Anthony, *b.* 1971.——Geraldine Mary, *b.* 1917: *m.* 1941, Maj. Neville Glyn Williams, MC, Indian Army, who *d.* (killed in action during European War) 1945.——Frances Margaret, *b.* 1919 : *m.* 1954 Denys. Newell Pitts Squarey. *Residence,* Bemerton, Salisbury, Wilts.

Granddaughter of the late Percy Fitzgerald Campbell (infra):—

Issue of the late Capt. Ian Percy FitzGerald Campbell, O.B.E., *b.* 1890, *d.* 1963: *m.* 1923, Gwladys Mary, MBE (Huerto de Marquez 24, Marbella, Malaga, Spain), da. of the late Lewis Pugh, KC:—

Graeme Diana, *b.* 1929: *m.* 1954, Louis Paul ffrench-Constant, BM, BCh, of Minack, Sable Rd., P.O. Hillside, Bulawayo, Rhodesia, and has issue living, Edward, *b.* 1958,—Rosamunde Sally, *b.* 1956,—Tanya Mary Louise, *b.* 1963,—Juliet Patricia, *b.* 1967.

Issue of the late Percy Fitzgerald Campbell, 7th son of 2nd baronet, *b.* 1865, *d.* 1907: *m.* 1889, Isabel Annie (who *m.* 2ndly, 1907, Gerald Cecil Dudgeon, C.B.E., who *d.* 1930), da. of the late R. Ballard, of Palumpur, Kangra Valley :—

Joan, *b.* 1904: *m.* 1928 (marriage annulled 1929), Evelyn Bingham Baring, who *d.* 1966 [B. Northbrook, colls.]. *Residence,* Marbella, Spain.

Grandson of the late Ion Douglas FitzGerald Campbell (infra):—

Issue of the late Major Ion Edward FitzGerald Campbell, Duke of Cornwall's L.I., *b.* 1897, *d.* (April) 1936 : *m.* 1933, Evelyn Julia (*Countess of Southesk*) (who *m.* 2ndly, 1952, as his second wife, the 11th Earl of Southesk), da. of Lieut.-Col. Arthur Peere Williams-Freeman, D.S.O., O.B.E. :—

Ion Edward FitzGerald (posthumous) (Dower House, Stagenhoe Park, St. Paul's Walden, Hitchin, Herts.), *b.* (May) 1936: *m.* 1963, Muriel Elisabeth, da. of the late Brig. Leslie Frederick Ethelbert

Wieler, CB, CBE, and has issue living, John Edward FitzGerald, b. 1964,—Leslie James Fitz-Gerald, b. 1965,—Robert Christopher FitzGerald, b. 1967,—Peter Michael FitzGerald, b. 1972.

Issue of the late Ion Douglas FitzGerald Campbell, 8th son of 2nd baronet, b. 1868, d. 1915: m. 1891, Mabel Unsworth, who d. 1931, da. of the late Capt. Unsworth Quin, of Dublin :—
Pamela Georgina Theophila (of The Cottage, Castlebellingham, co. Louth), b. 1899: m. 1919, Rudolph Agnew, and has issue living, Peter Douglas, b. 1922: m. 1946, Margaret Tawse,—Patrick John Alexander, b. 1930: m. 1950, Lucia Murdock,—Rudolph Ion Joseph (29, Queensdale Rd., W11, Cavalry Club), b. 1934: m. 1st, 1957 (m. diss. 1964) Tessa, da. of Sqdn.-Leader John Molony Longley; 2ndly, 1965, Hon. Clare Rosalind Dixon, da. of 2nd Baron Glentoran, and has issue living, (by 1st m.) Charles Edward Molony b. 1961, (by 2nd m.) James Ion Daniel b. 1968, Charlotte Diana Pamela Geraldine b. 1970,—Mary Geraldine, b. 1920: m. 1943, Francis James Nichol,—Pamela Joan, b. 1923: m. 1941, Lt.-Cdr. Peter Piggford, and has issue living, Andrew Donovan b. 1956, Sybil Jane b. 1941.

Issue of the late George Theophilus Campbell, 9th son of 2nd baronet, b. 1872, d. 1924: m. 1917, Winifred Edna Boyd, da. of the late James FitzGibbon Black, of Montreal :—
Elspeth Griselda Theophila, b. 1919: m. 1946, Robin John Patrick Flynn, M.C., D.F.C., and has issue living, Michael George Alexander Robin Fitzgerald Campbell, b. 1949,—Reidy Georgina Campbell, b. 1948. *Residence*

Granddaughters of the late Capt. Frederic Augustus Campbell, 4th son of 1st baronet :—
Issue of the late John St. Clair CAMPBELL-BRABAZON, O.B.E., b. 1865, d. 1942, having assumed by Roy. licence 1923 the additional surname of Brabazon : m. 1900, Caroline Leavett, of Mayford Lodge, Mayford, Woking :—
Pamela Francis, b. 1903 : m. 1st, 1921 (marriage dissolved 1930), Francis Baer ; 2ndly, 1931, Flight-Lieut. Herbert Geoffrey Brookman, R.A.F. (retired), who d. 1936 ; 3rdly, 1937 (marriage dissolved 1956), Robert Walter Guy Grindlay. *Residence*, Shore House, The Quay, Burnham-on-Crouch, Essex.—Geraldine, b. 1904 : m. 1928, Brigadier Edward Hamilton Grant, late Argyll and Sutherland Highlanders, and has issue living, Rosemary Ann, b. 1930. *Residence*, Warner's Hall, Burnham-on-Crouch, Essex.

The 1st baronet, Sir Guy Campbell, C.B. (el. son of the late Lieut.-Gen. Colin Campbell, Lieut.-Gov. of Gibraltar 1809-14), was a Maj.-Gen. in the Army, and Col. of the 3rd West India Regiment; served with distinction throughout the Peninsular war and at Waterloo. The 2nd baronet, Sir Edward FitzGerald, Col. 60th Rifles, served with distinction in the Punjab campaign 1848 and through the Indian Mutiny campaign 1857-8. The 3rd baronet, Sir Guy Theophilus, was Lieut.-Col. 60th Rifles and served in Afghan War 1878-80. The 4th baronet, Sir Guy Colin, was Major 60th Rifles, and served in European Wars 1914-19 and 1941-45.

CAMPBELL, Creation (U.K.) 1831, of Barcaldine and Glenure, Argyllshire.

I am prepared.

Sir IAN VINCENT HAMILTON CAMP-BELL, C.B., 7th *Baronet*, el. surv. son of the late Richard Hamilton Campbell, C.I.E., yst. brother of 4th and 5th Bts., b. May 7th, 1895; s. his cousin, *Capt. Sir* (FRANCIS) ERIC DENNISTOUN, 1963; ed. at Cheltenham, and at Corpus Christi Coll., Oxford; Hereditary Keeper of Barcaldine Castle; 1914-18 War as Lieut. The King's (Liverpool Regt.) (severely wounded); entered Home Civil Ser. 1919 as Assist. Principal, Air Min.; Private Sec. to Ch. of Air Staff 1926-27 and to Permanent Sec. of Air Min. 1927-30, and Assist. Private Sec. to successive Secs. of State for Air 1930-34, Principal, Air Min. 1939, Assist. Sec. Air Min. 1939-45, and Assist. Under-Sec. of State 1945-55; C.B. (Civil) 1951: m. 1st, 1920, Madeline Lowe Reid, who d. 1929, da. of the late H. Anglin Whitelocke, F.R.C.S., of Oxford ; 2ndly, 1932 (marriage annulled on her petition 1942), Iris Constance, da. of the late Lieut.-Col. Ronald Charles Gibb, C.B.E.; 3rdly, 1942, Agnes Louise Watson, da. of the late William Henry Gerhardi, and widow of Victor Vsevolod Watson, M.B.E., and has issue by 1st marriage.

Arms—Quarterly: 1st, gyronny of eight or and sable, *Campbell;* on a canton argent a bend sable, between a unicorn's head in chief and a cross-crosslet fitchée in base gules, *Dennistoun;* 2nd, or, a fesse checky azure and argent, *Stewart of Lorn;* 3rd, argent, a lymphad, sails furled and oars in action sable, *Lorne;* 4th, gyronny of eight or and sable, *Campbell;* on a cantongules two bars or, *Cameron of Lochiel;* the whole within a bordure quarterly or and sable. **Crest**—A Highlander fully armed and equipped, having a claymore in the dexter hand and on the sinister arm a target or. **Supporters**—*Dexter,* a leopard; *sinister,* a stag—all proper.

Seat—Barcaldine Castle, Ledaig, Argyllshire. *Residence*—White Rose, Hawkhurst, Kent.

Son living—By 1st marriage—NIALL ALEXANDER HAMILTON (of 9, West Temple Sheen, SW14); b. Jan. 7th, 1925; ed. at Cheltenham, and at Corpus Christi Coll., Oxford; Bar. Inner Temple 1951; 1939-45 War as Lt. RM; Assist. Sec., St. Mary's Hosp., Paddington 1955-60, Sec., W. Middx. Hosp., Isleworth 1960, and Dep. House Gov., London Clinic 1960-68, since when Sec. to Board of Management, Royal Home and Hosp. for Incurables, Putney: m. 1st, 1949, Patricia Mary (from whom he obtained a divorce 1956), da. of R. Turner; 2ndly, 1957, Norma Joyce, da. of W. N. Wiggin, and has issue living, (by 2nd m.) Roderick Duncan Hamilton, b. 1961,—Angus Charles Dundas b. 1967,—Fiona Madeline Hamilton, b. 1958,—Lucy Catriona Margaret (twin), b. 1967.

Brother living—Richard Henry Dennistoun, b. 1901; ed. at Winchester, and at Corpus Christi Coll., Oxford; formerly Chm. and Managing Director of Shaw Wallace & Co. Ltd., of India; late partner in the firm of R. G. Shaw & Co., 19, Leadenhall St., EC3: m. 1936, Kathleen Adair yst. da. of the late Richard Fallowes Dunn, of Wolverhampton and Sutton, and has issue living, Lorne Mary Dennistoun, b. 1939,—Elizabeth Gay Adair, b. 1942.

Sister living of 6th Baronet—May Lilian, b. 1890: m. 1916, Capt. Henry Harman Wadeson formerly Indian Army, and has issue living, Richard Alexander, b. 1923. *Residence*, 13, Mordon Rd., Seven Kings, Essex.

Daughter living of 5th Baronet—Jean Linda Dennistoun, b. 1893. *Residence*, Hill Crest, Rowlands, Wimborne, Dorset.

Collateral Branches living.

Granddaughter of the late Charlotte Alexandra Norton (infra) :—
Issue of the late Sylvia Marion Norton, b. 1898, d. 1934 : m. 1917, Group Capt. Reginald Stuart Maxwell, M.C., D.F.C., A.F.C., R.A.F. (retired), who d. 1960 :—
Pamela Ann, b. 1920 : m. 1940, Peter Frederick Carter-Ruck, Solicitor and late Capt. R.A., and has issue living, Julie Ann, b. 1941: m. 1967, Doily Scott-Bayfield, and has issue living, Penelope Samantha Juliette b. 1972, Alexandra Miranda Caroline b. 1974. *Residence*, Latchmore Cottage, Gt. Hallingbury, Bishop's Stortford, Herts.

Granddaughters of the late Emily Frances Margaret Begbie, sister of 4th baronet :—
Issue of the late Charlotte Alexandra Begbie, b. 1874, d. 1943: m. 1897, Maj.-Gen. Cecil Burrington Norton, C.M.G., D.S.O., who d. 1953:—
Barbara Frances Millicent (Larkrise, Emmett's Nest, Binfield, Berks.), b. 1900: m. 1st, 1921 (m. diss. 19—), Capt. Roger Harry Allen, Sherwood Rangers; 2ndly, 1929, Wing-Cdr. Ernest Cecil Barlow, RAF, who d. (killed in action) 1940, and has issue living, (by 1st m.) Timothy Eardley (of Spinneys, Tacolneston, Norfolk, NOR 87W), b. 1924: m. 1952, Joy, twin da. of Alfred Jones, of Manor Farm, Reepham, Norfolk, and has issue living, Nicholas Harry Eardley b. 1959, Hilary Meriwether Dennistoun b. 1955,—(by 2nd m.) Fiona Cecile, b. 1930: m. 1960, Guido Targiani, son of the Marquis Felice Targiani, of Rome, Italy, and has issue living, Leopoldo Felix Hermann b. 1963, Francesca Alica b. 1965.——Phyllis Maud Eleanor (twin), b. 1900: m. 1933, Hilary Carol Howard Bull, who d. 1958. *Residence*, 4, Wardour Lodge, Sunningdale, Berks.

Grandchildren of the late Maj.-Gen. John Peter William Campbell, 3rd son of 1st baronet :—
Issue of the late Gerald Edward Lyon Campbell, b. 1863, d. 1902 : m. 1886, Sybil (who d. 1958, having m. 2ndly, 1911, Com. Wentworth Vernon Cole, formerly R.N.), da. of Maj.-Gen. Thomas Ross Church, C.I.E. :—
Mary Hamilton, b. 1888 : m. 1915, Alfred Thomas Duncan Anderson, who d. 1949, and has issue living, Ian Duncan Hamilton, b. 1916,—Alec Vernon b. 1921. *Address,*

This family is descended from Patrick Campbell, of Innerzeldies, legitimated son of Sir Duncan Campbell, 1st baronet of Glenorchy, ancestor of the Earls of Breadalbane (a branch of the Ducal House of Argyll). Sir Duncan Campbell of Barcaldine, 1st Bt. was Capt. Scots Fusilier Guards, and served at Copenhagen, Walcheren, and the Peninsula. He m. 1815, Elizabeth Dreghorn, da. of John Dennistoun of Dennistoun, Dunbartonshire. Sir Alexander, 2nd Bt., was Sergeant-at-Arms in Queen Victoria's Household. The 3rd Bt., Sir Duncan Alexander Dundas, CVO, was Gentleman Usher of the Green Rod 1884-95, and Sec. to Order of the Thistle 1895-1926. The 4th baronet, Sir Alexander William Dennistoun Campbell, was Col. Indian Army. The 5th baronet, Sir Duncan John Alfred Campbell, was sometime a Dist. Judge in Central India, and Acting Commr. in Burma and Central Provinces, India. The 6th baronet, Sir (Francis) Eric Dennistoun Campbell was Capt. S. Lancs. Regt. and served in 1914-18 War and Afghan War 1919.

CAMPBELL, Creation (U.K.) 1913, with precedence of 1804, of Ardnamurchan, Argyllshire.

Sir BRUCE COLIN PATRICK CAMPBELL, 3rd *Baronet* (cr. 1913) (but his name does not, at the time of going to press, appear on the Official Roll of Baronets) ; b. July 2nd, 1904 ; s. his father, *Lieut.-Col. Sir* JOHN BRUCE STUART, *D.S.O.*, 1943; ed. at Edinburgh Acad.; no information concerning this baronet has been received since 1943.

Arms—Not recorded in Lyon Register.

Sisters living—Ena Agnese Lyona, b. 1907 : m. 1928, Matthew Campbell Bain, M.B., Ch.B., J.P., and has issue living, Michael Ian Campbell (c/o Lyall & Evatt, Stock Exchange, Singapore), b. 1929, ed. at Fettes Coll.; a stockbroker: m. 1958, Elaine Scammell, and has issue living, Fiona Campbell, b. 1960, Tiffany Campbell b. 1963, Leonie Campbell b. 1964,—Shirley Lorna Campbell (Foreign Office, SW1), b. 1931; ed. at Lillesden. *Residence*, 6Q, Gallop Rd., Singapore 10.——Noelle Eva Mabel, b. 1909: m. 1929 (m. diss. 1946), Noel Rees; 2ndly, 1946, Maxwell C. Elliot, of La Collina, Boulevard Mistral, Mandelieu, nr. Cannes, France AM, and has issue living, (by 1st m.) John David Campbell (c/o Box 1244, Nairobi, Kenya), b. 1932; ed. at Clifton Coll.; a Tea Broker: m. 1963, Christine Phyllis Wadsworth, and has issue living, Oliver David Campbell b. 1965,—Jeremy Stephen Campbell, b. 1933; ed. at Clifton Coll.; is an Officer in British S. Africa Police, Salisbury, Rhodesia: m. 1956, Laura Kathleen Riddle, and has issue living, Lincoln Noel Campbell b. 1958, Simon Colin Campbell b. 1960, David Jason Campbell b. 1969,—(by 2nd m.) Colin Maxwell Campbell b. 1947: m. 1968, Robina Dogger, of Briars Court, Limpsfield Chart, Oxted, Surrey,—(by 1st m.), Jennifer Ann Campbell, b. 1936: m. 1958, John Bowie, and has issue living, Robin Maxwell John b. 1961, Clare b. 1959.——Marjory Ethelle (10, Marloes Rd., W8), b. 1911: m. 1938, Malcolm Melville, who d. 1942, and has issue living, Pamela Elaine Marguerite, b. 1940: m. 1959, Richard Crockett Knox, and has issue living, Andrew Melville b. 1961, Fiona Heather b. 1964,—Heather Jacqueline Malcolm, b. 1942: m. 1971, Richard Norton Orlando Kingsbury.

Donald Campbell was created a Baronet of Nova Scotia 1628, and resigned his dignity into the King's hands on Aug. 28th, 1643, for a new enfeoffment of it and the lands annexed, in favour of his nephew and heirs male. Upon the decease of Donald, his nephew (George) did not, however, claim the title, neither did the three next succeeding heirs, but about 1790 John Campbell, great-great-grandson of George Campbell (ante) resumed the title as 6th baronet, being followed in turn by his son, John, Lieut.-Gov. of St. Vincent's 1845-53, and his grandson, Maj.-Gen. John William Campbell, C.B. (who served in Crimean Campaign 1855, in China Campaign 1860, and in Afghan War 1879-80), whose claim, however, to be placed on the Roll of Baronets in right of the 1628 creation was not recognized, but upon whom a new Baronetcy of the United Kingdom was conferred in Nov. 1913, with special precedence as above-mentioned. The 2nd baronet d. (whilst a prisoner in Palembang Camp, Sumatra) 1943.

CAMPBELL, Creation (U.K.) 1939, of Airds Bay, co. Argyll, and Bromley, co.Kent.
[Extinct 1954.]

Sir CHARLES DUNCAN MACNAIR CAMPBELL, 2nd and last *Baronet.*

Daughters living of 1st Baronet—Frances Henriette, *b.* 1904 ; is a F.S.A. (Scotland) : *m.* 1930, Rear-Adm. Keith McNeil Campbell-Walter, C.B., who assumed by deed poll and Letters Patent recorded at College of Arms 1952, the additional surname of Campbell before that of his patronymic, and has issue living, Richard Keith (12, Skinner Place, SW1W 8HH), *b.* 1941; ed. at Milton Abbey: *m.* 1st, 1963 (m. diss. 1973), Marion Clare, only da. of F. G. Minter, MBE, of Knock Manor, Wilts.; 2ndly, 1973, Dorothy Ann, yst. da. of the late T. W. Oliver, of Old Bewick Farm, Alnwick, and has issue living (by 1st wife), Lavinia Jane *b.* 1964, Petrina Jean *b.* 1967, (by 2nd wife) Jamie Oliver *b.* 1972,—Michael McNeil CAMPBELL OF AIRDS BAY (twin) (Maison de Bas, Rue d'Egypt, Trinity, Jersey; Guard's, Puffins, and HDYC Clubs), *b.* 1941; ed. at Wellington; Maj. Scots Gds. (ret.); recognized by Lord Lyon as representative of family of Campbell of Airds Bay and discontinued the use of the surname of Walter 1954: *m.* 1963, Anne Catriona, da. of the late Capt. Ian Andrew Tait, Queen's Own Cameron Highlanders, and has issue living, Gillean Lorne Frederick McNeil *b.* 1967, Theresa Anne Henrietta *b.* 1964, Henrietta Constance *b.* 1969,—Fiona Frances Elaine (La Muraz, 1141, Yens, Switzerland), *b.* 1932: *m.* 1956 (m. diss. 1965) Baron Hans-Henrich Thyssen-Bornemisza de Kaszon, and has issue living, Lorne Johannes *b.* 1963, Francesca Anna Dolores *b.* 1958,—Sheila Elspeth, *b.* 1934: *m.* 1957, John William Henry Pretty, MB, BS, late Flt.-Lt. RAF Med. Ser., of 31, Priestfields, Rochester, Kent, and has issue living, Michael John *b.* 1962, Nicola Sheila *b.* 1958, Susan Frances *b.* 1961, Jane Rebecca *b.* 1967. *Residences*, 19A, Princes Gate Mews, SW7 2PS; 10, Ellenabeich, Isle of Seil by Oban, Argyll PA34 4RQ.——Rosemary Jean, BEM, *b.* 1911: *m.* 1943, John Henry Hansard. *Residence*, Hogs Hill Farm, Fernhurst, Haslemere, Surrey.——Elspeth Ada *b.* 1919: *m.*, 1940, Laurence William Orchard, of The Maltings, Cookham, Berks., and has issue living, William Henslow, *b.* 1947,—Lawrence Augustine, *b.* 1950,—Anthony Edward, *b.* 1962,—Gillian Mary, *b.* 1941,—Sarah Elspeth, *b.* 1942: *m.* 1967, Norman Hampel, of Two Oaks, Slade Oak Lane, Denham, Bucks., and has issue living, Simon Mark, *b.* 1968, John Laurence *b.* 1969, Angus James *b.* 1973, Nicola Jane *b.* 1971,—Wendy Frances, *b.* 1944.

COCKBURN-CAMPBELL, Creation (U.K.) 1821, of Gartsford, Ross-shire.
[Pronounced **"Coburn-Campbell."**]

Watchful.

Sir THOMAS COCKBURN-CAMPBELL, 6th *Baronet ;*
b. Dec. 8th, 1918 ; *s.* his father, *Sir* ALEXANDER, 1935 ; ed. at Church of England Gram. Sch., Melbourne, Australia : *m.* 1944, Josephine Zoi, el. da. of Harold Douglas Forward, of Cunjardine, W. Australia, and has issue.

Arms—Quarterly 1st and 4th: quarterly, i. and iv., gyronny of eight or and sable, *Campbell*; ii., argent, a galley or lymphad sails furled, oars in action sable : iii., or, a fesse checky azure and argent, over all a chief argent charged with a rock proper superscribed "Gibraltar," between two medals for Seringapatam and Talavera ; 2nd and 3rd, quarterly, i. and iv., argent, an ostrich feather ensigned with an Imperial crown proper, between three cocks, two and one, gules ; ii. and iii., six mascles three two and one or, *Cockburn*. **Crest**—1st, a dexter hand holding a scimitar all proper, *Campbell.*

Residence—Lot 194, Welshpool Rd., Wattle Grove, 6107, W. Australia.
Son living—ALEXANDER THOMAS (Lot 7, Lewis Rd., Forrestfield 6058, W. Aust.), *b.* March 16th, 1945: *m.* 1969, Kerry Anne, el. da. of Sgt. K. Johnson, of Mt. Hawthorne, W. Aust., and has issue living, Thomas Justin, *b.* Feb. 10th, 1974.

Brothers living—Urban Alfred, *b.* 1921; is Corporal Australian Imperial Force: *m.* 1954, Betty McGuinness.——Alexander Bruce (of 90, Evans St., Shenton Park, W. Australia), *b.* 1923; Leading Aircraftman, Roy. Australian Air Force; S.-W. Pacific 1944-45: *m.* 1951, Beryl, da. of William Elder, of Shenton Park, W. Australia, and has issue living, Susan Peta, *b.* 1954,—Nola Gay, *b.* 1957,—Judith Ann, *b.* 1961,—Alison Lee, *b.* 1964.

Lieut.-Gen. Sir Alexander Campbell, 1st baronet, Col. of 80th Regiment, greatly distinguished himself at Seringapatam, also in the Peninsula, also in 1809-11, where he commanded a division of the British Army. He was created a baronet 1815, and in 1821 obtained a new patent, which extended the limitation to the male issue of his daughter Olympia (Mrs. Cockburn), and afterwards to the male issue of his daughter Isabella Charlotte (Lady Malcolm), which is now extinct. The 2nd baronet assumed in 1824 the additional surname of Campbell. Sir Thomas, 4th baronet, was Pres. of Legislative Council of W. Australia.

HOME-PURVES-HUME-CAMPBELL, Creation (N.S.) 1665, of Purves Hall, Berwickshire.
[Dormant or Extinct 1960.]
[Name pronounced "Hume-Purves-Hume-Campbell."]

Sir JOHN HOME-PURVES-HUME-CAMPBELL, 8th and last *Baronet.*

Daughters living of 8th Baronet—Mabel Jane (L'Olivier, Route de Mons, Tourrettes-Fayence, France 83), *b.* 1905.——Elsie Barbara *b.* 1907: *m.* 1st, 1928, Donovan Storr Allom, who obtained a divorce 1940; 2ndly, 1954, George Moxon Cook, and has issue living, (by 1st m.) Michael Donovan, *b.* 1930; ed. at Wellington Coll., and at Trin. Coll., Camb.,—Bridget Barbara, *b.* 1935,—Sheila Ann, *b.* 1938.

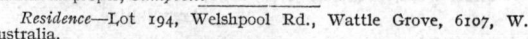

Campbell-Orde, see Orde.

CARDEN, Creation (I.) 1787, of Templemore, Tipperary.

With faith and love.

Sir JOHN CRAVEN CARDEN, 7th *Baronet; b.* March 11th, 1926; *s.* his father, *Sir* JOHN VALENTINE, *M.B.E.*, 1935 ; ed. at Eton : *m.* 1947, Isabel Georgette, youngest da. of the late Robert de Hart, and has issue.

Arms—Argent, a mascle gules between three pheons sable. *Crest*—A pheon sable.

Address—PO Box 4903, Apt. 205, Sulgrave Manor, Cable Beach, Nassau, Bahamas. *Club*—White's.

Daughter living—Isabel Mary, *b.* 1952.

Great-Aunt living (daughter of 4th baronet)—Norah Ierne, *b.* 1873 : *m.* 1903, Capt. Henry Sargeaunt, formerly Cheshire Regt. and Staff-Paymaster Army Pay Depart., and has issue living, Henry Anthony, *C.B.*, *O.B.E.*, *b.* 1907 [*see* "COMPANIONAGE"]: *m.* 1939, Winifred Doris, da. of John Parkinson, and has issue living. *Residence,*

Widow living of 6th Baronet—DOROTHY MARY (*Dowager Lady Carden*), da. of Charles Luckraft McKinnon: *m.* 1925, as his second wife, Sir John Valentine Carden, M.B.E., 6th baronet, who *d.* 1935. *Residence,*

Collateral Branches living.

Grandsons of the late Major Henry Charles Carden, D.S.O., 2nd son of 4th baronet:—
Issue of the late Rev. Canon Henry Craven Carden, *b.* 1882, *d.* 1964: *m.* 1913, Olive, who *d.* 1966, da. of the late Rev. Canon C. V. Gorton:—
DERRICK CHARLES, *CMG* (c/o Lloyds Bank, Winchester), *b.* Oct. 31st, 1921; ed. at Marlborough and at Ch. Ch., Oxford, in Sudan Political Ser. 1942-54; entered HM's Dip Ser 1954; HM Political Agent, Qatar, Persian Gulf 1955-58, Oriental Sec., British Embassy, Tripoli, Libya 1958-62, at Foreign Office, 1962-64 Head of Chancery, Cairo 1964-65, Consul-Gen., Muscat 1965-69, and Dir. Middle East Centre of Arab Studies 1969-73, since when Ambassador to Yemen Arab Republic; *CMG* 1974: *m.* 1952, Elizabeth Anne, da. of the late Capt. Alfred Spalding Russell, DSO, RN, and has issue living, John Craven, *b.* 1953,—Peter James Charles, *b.* 1958,—Elisabeth Louise, *b.* 1956,—Clare Margaret, *b.* 1961.

Issue of the late John Humphrey Carden, *b.* 1886, *d.* 1957 : *m.* 1923, Eileen Winifred Bourke (of 2, Alexandra Road, Brecon), da. of the late Lieut.-Col. Thomas Patrick Shannon, R.A.S.C. :—
Patrick Henry, *b.* 1928; in Trin. House Pilotage Ser.: *m.* 1951, Rosalie Alice, da. of the late Rev. Canon S. W. Groom, formerly V. of Holy Trinity, Lamorbey, Sidcup, and has issue living, Derek Edward Trevor, *b.* 1952,—Nigel John Patrick, *b.* 1954,—Roger Michael Colin, *b.* 1956,—Alison Rosalie, *b.* 1965. *Residence,* The Old Rectory, 91, Windmill St., Gravesend, Kent.——Michael Humphrey *b.* 1929; late Capt. Worcestershire Regt. *Residence,* 2, Alexandra Rd., Brecon.

Issue of the late Frederick Richard Carden, 3rd son of 4th baronet, *b.* 1856, *d.* 1935 : *m.* 1885, Miriam, da. of — Beale :—
Richard Craven, *b.* 1893.——Selwyn, *b.* 18—.——Rodney, *b.* 18—.——Geoffrey, *b.* 18—.——Helen Mary : *m.* 1912, Herbert Roger.——Pattie : *m.* 1915, D A. Morrell. *Residence,*

Issue of the late Capt. Coldstream James Carden, 4th son of 4th baronet, *b.* 1857, *d.* 1925 : *m.* 1891, Rose Margaret Ponton, youngest da. of the late David Johnstone, of Croy Shandon, Dunbartonshire :—
Eileen Margaret, *b.* 1893. *Residence,*

Granddaughters of the late Col. Henry Daniel Carden, 2nd son of 3rd baronet :—
Issue of the late Col. Henry Parry Carden, *b.* 1854, *d.* 1910 : *m.* 1897, Araby, who *d.* 1942, da. of the late Howard Burton, of Cookstown, and widow of Edward Nugent Greer :—
Catherine Constance, *b.* 1898.——Sybil Parry, *b.* 1900 : *m.* 1936, Maj.-Gen. Francis David Rome, CB, CMG, CBE, DSO, late Roy. Fusiliers. *Residence,* Ferne Down, Ham, Marlborough, Wilts, SN8 3QR.

Grandson of the late Lieut.-Col. Henry Westenra Carden (infra):—
Issue of the late Bernard Westenra Carden, *b.* 1887, *d.* 1951 : *m.* 1923, Gwendoline (Ivy Cottage, Boughton Lees, Ashford, Kent), da. of Joseph Price, of Leamington:—
Patrick Westenra, *b.* 1928 ; ed. at Univ. of Wales (B.Sc. 1951) : *m.* 1955, Janet Hilda, da. of William Stickland, of Cambridge, and has issue living, David Westenra, *b.* 1957,—Trevor Courtenay, *b.* 1959,—Angela, *b.* 1961,—Carol Mary, *b.* 1967. *Residence,* The Acre, Mulberry Hill, Chilham, Kent.

Grandchildren of the late Rev. Arthur Carden, 3rd son of 3rd baronet:—
Issue of the late Lieut.-Col. Henry Westenra Carden, *b.* 1857, *d.* 1928: *m.* 1st, 1886, Emily Elphinstone, who *d.* 1918, da. of the late Rev. William Courtenay Clack, R. of Moreton Hampstead, Devon ; 2ndly, 1919, Beatrice, who *d.* 1944, da. of Peter Sharp, formerly of Cannock, Stafford :—
Cecil Courtenay (2185, Wilson Av., Montreal, Canada), *b.* 1892.——Beryl, *MBE* (3, Hyldon Court, Wolsey Gdns., Felixstowe, Suffolk), *b.* 1892; Nursing Matron-in-Ch. (ret.) HM Prison Ser., England and Wales; MBE (Civil) 1946: *m.* 1955, S. Jaggard, who *d.* 1972.——Hazel, *b.* 189-: *m.* 1925, Langshaw Rowland, OBE, son of Sir Leonard Bromfield Rowland. *Residence,* Hoseley House, Gresford, Wrexham.——Sybil Rose Courtenay, *b.* 189-. *Residence,* 78, Royal Hospital Road, SW3.——Muriel Elphinstone, *b.* 1899-: *m.* 1924, Charles Pelham Thursby, and has issue living, Hugh James, *b.* 1931. *Residence* The Bungalow, Clive, Salop.——Christina Annette, *b.* 1900: *m.* 1924, John Elliot Weir, and has issue living, Charles Henry (14003-75th Av., Edmonton, Alberta, Canada), *b.* 1925; MSc, DLS, PEng: *m.* 1949, Kathleen McLellan, and has issue living, Douglas Charles *b.* 1953, Wendy Kathleen *b.* 1954, Sandra Christina *b.* 1957,—Sandra Fraser (63, Atlanta Cres., Calgary, Alberta, Canada), *b.* 1927: *m.* 1950, Freda McCoy, and has issue living, Carlene *b.* 1951, Marion *b.* 1954, Patti *b.* 1961. *Residence,* 814, 21st St. South, Lethbridge, Alberta, Canada.

This family, originally of Lincolnshire, settled at Templemore, co. Tipperary, about 1650.

CARDEN, Creation (U.K.) 1887, of Wimpole Street, Middlesex, and of Mole Lodge, Surrey.

With faith and love.

Sir HENRY CHRISTOPHER CARDEN, *OBE*, 4th *Baronet, b.* Oct. 16th, 1908; *s.* his father, *Maj. Sir* FREDERICK HENRY WALTER, 1966: ed. at Eton; Lt.-Col. (ret.) 17th/21st Lancers; Mil. Attaché, Stockholm 1951-55; N-W Europe 1944-45; OBE (Mil.) 1945: *m.* 1st, 1943, Jane St. Clare (from whom he obtained a divorce 1961); da. of the late Thomas Edward St. Clare Daniell, OBE, MC; 2ndly, 1962, Gwyneth Sybil, FCA, da. of the late Herbert Arthur Dyke Acland, and widow of Fl.-Lt. Roderick Stanley Emerson [see Acland, Bt. (cr. 1890), colls.], and has issue by 1st marriage.

Arms—Per pale sable and gules, a staff sling in bend between four pheons saltirewise, all argent.   Crest—On a fasces fessewise or, a wolf's head erased sable, pierced in the neck with an arrow bendwise or, point downwards gold, embrued proper.

Residence, North Sydmonton House, Newbury.

Son living—By 1st m.—CHRISTOPHER ROBERT (c/o Poste Restaute, GPO, Suva, Fiji), *b.* Nov. 24th, 1946; ed. at Eton: *m.* 1972, Sainimere Rokotuibau, of Suva, Fiji.
Daughter living—By 1st marriage—Melinda Jane, *b.* 1950: *m.* 1975, Andrew James Wilson.

Sister living—Enid Evelyn, *b.* 1902: *m.* 1928, Alfred Henry Michell, who *d.* 1965, and has issue living, John Frederick Carden, *b.* 1933,—Charles Henry Wroughton (10, Wandon Rd., SW6), *b.* 1938: *m.* 1973, Sara Elizabeth, da. of Lt.-Col. Arthur Richard Hanmer, MBE, TD [see Hanmer Bt., colls.],—Clare Winifred Mary (The Old Rectory, Dallington, Heathfield, Sussex), *b.* 1935: *m.* 1st, 1957, (m. diss. 1967), Geoffrey St. George, Schomberg; 2ndly, 1967, Harry Dexter Lyon, and has issue living, (by 1st husband) Laura Caroline *b.* 1960, Julia Rachel *b.* 1961, (by 2nd husband) Giles Roderick *b.* 1965, Selina Rose *b.* 1969.   *Residence,* Linden House, Eye, Suffolk, IP23 7AG.

Collateral Branches living.

Grandchildren of the late Alexander James Carden, 3rd son of 1st baronet:—
Issue of the late Henry Carden, *b.* 1872, *d.* 1948 :   *m.* 1st, 1894, Martha Vinnineda, who *d.* 1918, da. of Ernst Tronson. of Romsdalen, Norway ; 2ndly, 1919, Mildred Kedge, who *d.* 1946:—
(By 1st marriage) Florence Lillian, *b.* 1895: *m.* 1924, Brigadier Francisco Rabia Munōz, Mexican Army.   *Residence,* Antonio Maura, 181, Col Moderna, Mexico, D.F.

Issue of the late Robert Walter Carden, *b.* 1875, *d.* 1943 :   *m.* 1901, Ethel May, who *d.* 1955, el. da. of the late Lemuel Johns, of Christchurch, New Zealand :—
Derick Walter (15, Kingston Park, Fox Pond Lane, Lymington, Hants.), *b.* 1902: *m.* 1929, Lois Leila Frances, da. of the late Daniel Weeks, of Bridport.——Ronald Tracey *b.* 1903: *m.* 1934, Aloysia Frances, who *d.* 1949, da. of the late Frank Machalak, of Plainfield, New Jersey, U.S.A, *Residence,* 19, Windmill Road, W.4.

The 1st baronet, Sir Robert Walter Carden (sometime M.P. for Barnstaple) was Lord Mayor London 1857, and an Alderman 1849-88.   The 2nd Baronet was High Sheriff of Hants 1891. The 3rd Baronet was High Sheriff of Hants, 1922.

CAREW, Creation (E.) 1661, of Haccombe, Devonshire.

Nil conscire sibi.
Conscious of no guilt.

Sir THOMAS PALK CAREW, 10th *Baronet* ; *b.* March 1st, 1890 ; *s.* his father, *Sir* HENRY PALK, 1934 ; ed. at Wellington Coll., and at Pembroke Coll., Oxford ; is Patron of three livings ; European War 1914-19 with Indian Army : *m.* 1st, 1913, his cousin, Ivy Madeleine Laura (from whom he obtained a divorce 1921), da. of the late Col. Arthur John Breakey, O.B.E. ; 2ndly, 1927, Phyllis Evelyn, da. of the late Neville Mayman, of Sydney, N.S. Wales, and has issue by 1st and 2nd marriages.

Arms—Or, three lions passant in pale sable.   Crest—A main-mast, the round top set off with palisadoes or, a demi-lion issuant thereout sable.

Residence—Killyon Manor, Hill of Down, co. Meath.

Son living—By 2nd marriage -RIVERS VERAIN, *b.* Oct. 17th, 1935; ed. at St. Columba's Coll., co. Dublin, and Dublin Univ. (B. Agriculture (Horticulture), MA); Author of " Figures out of Mist ": *m.* 1968, Susan Babington, da. of the late H. B. Hill, and has issue living, Gerald de Redvers, *b.* May 24th, 1975,—Marcella Tamsin, *b.* 1970,—Marina Lys, *b.* 1972,—Miranda Rose (twin), *b.* 1973.   *Residence,* Killyon Manor, Hill of Down, co. Meath.   *Club*—University (Dublin).

Daughters living—By 1st m.—Zia (23, Hill Lands, Wargrave, Berks.), *b.* 1914; 1939-45 War with WAAF: *m.* 1939, Maj. Hugh Richard Stirling, RA, who *d.* (on active ser.) 1944, and has issue living, Anthony Carew (2, Spring Walk, Wargrave, Berks.), *b.* 1942; ed. at Pangbourne Nautical Coll.: *m.* 1968, Geraldine Erica, yst. da. of Fl.-Lt. Walter Frank Barber, of Wargrave,—Valerie Frances, *b.* 1943: *m.* 1969, Jeremy Hamilton Lightly, of 7, Kilfield Rd., Rudgwick, Sussex, and has issue living, Yvonne Susan *b.* 1970.——(By 2nd m.)—Œnone Venetia, *b.* 1929.

Sister living—Dora Gertrude, *b.* 1894 : *m.* 1942, Frederick John Twomey.   *Residence,* Undercliffe Cottage, Dartmouth, S. Devon.

Collateral Branches living.

Grandson of the late Rev. Henry William Carew, son of the late Thomas
Carew, 3rd son of 7th baronet :—
Issue of the late Col. Peter Fitzwilliam Carew, late Suffolk Regt., *b.* 1887, *d.* 1954 : *m.*
1919, Joyce Margaret, who *d.* 1974, da. of the late Capt. the Hon. Arthur Grenville
Fortescue [E. Fortescue colls.]:—
John Mohun, *MC, b.* 1921; formerly Capt. Devonshire Regt.; Burma 1943-44, and Java 1945-46,
with 3rd Gurkha Rifles (wounded, MC): *m.* 1950, Barbara J. S., da. of Maj. Arthur Neil Stewart
Roberts, OBE, and widow of Maj. R. H. B. Shakespear, Roy. Scots Fusiliers, and has issue
living, Nicolas John Stewart, *b.* 1952.   *Residence,* Forge Cottage, Binfield, Bracknell, Berks.

Grandchildren of the late Cdr. Alfred Curtis Carew, RN (infra):—
Issue of the late Thomas Alfred Curtis Carew, *b.* 1895, *d.* 1970: *m.* 1921, Christina, da. of
John Hanna:—
Patrick Henry Curtis, *CD,* (c/o 1380, Cherry Cres., W. Kelowna, BC, Canada), *b.* 1931; ed. at
Trafalgar Sch., Nelson, and Kelowna Senior High Sch.; Lt.-Col. Comdg. R. Canadian Dragoons;
Korea 1952-53 (two medals); NW Europe 1959-63; Cyprus 1966; NW Europe since 1970:
m. 1954, Norma Diane, da. of Claude Rupert Methune Willcox, of Vancouver, BC, Janice Lynn,
b. 1956,—Dene Elizabeth, *b.* 1958,—Suzanne Marie, *b.* 1961.——Verona Lorraine, *b.* 1922: *m.*
1945, Allan Cameron Barton, of 2420, 37th St. SW, Calgary, Alberta, Canada, and has issue
living, Thomas Allan, *b.* 1946,—Gerald Patrick, *b.* 1948,—Allan Bruce, *b.* 1956.——Dorothy
Joan, *b.* 1925: *m.* 1948, Charles Henry de Pfyffer (RR3, KLO Rd., Kelowna, BC, Canada), and
has issue living, Charles Russell, *b.* 1950,—Richard Louis, *b.* 1956,—Christine Marie, *b.* 1951,—
Alice Jerryl, *b.* 1955.

Grandchildren of the late Thomas Carew, 3rd son of 7th baronet :—
Issue of the late Com. Alfred Curtis Carew, R.N., *b.* 1847, *a.* 1927 : *m.* 1893, Susannah,
who *d.* 1939, da. of the late Edmund Grantham:—
Nicholas John, *b.* 1904; ed. at Vernon Senior High Sch.; formerly in British Columbia
Dragoons, Roy. Canadian Armoured Corps: *m.* 1930, Miken Viola, da. of the late George Borg,
and has issue living, Nicolas Darrell, *b.* 1932; ed. at Vernon Senior High Sch., and at British
Columbia Univ.,—Shirley Elizabeth Diane, *b.* 1931: *m.* 1953.——Dorothy Susannah, *b.* 1894:
m. 1932, Hugh Fraser Cunningham.

Granddaughter of the late Charles Robert Sydenham Carew (infra):—
Issue of the late Capt. Peter Gawen Carew, *b.* 1894, *d.* 1966: *m.* 1927, Ruth (Warnicombe House, Tiverton, Devon, and 73, Purser's Cross Rd., SW6), da. of Arthur Chamberlain, JP, of Rackenford Manor, Tiverton:—
Nicola CAREW (Gogwell, Tiverton, Devon); resumed in 1968 the surname of Carew: *m.* 1950 (m.
diss. 1968), Charles Louis Breithmeyer, solicitor, and has issue living, Hugo Charles, *b.* 1951,—
Peter Alan CAREW, *b.* 1953; assumed 1970 the surname of Carew,—Henry John CAREW, *b.* 1957;
assumed 1970 the surname of Carew,—Geoffrey Nicholas CAREW, *b.* 1962; assumed 1970 the
surname of Carew.

Granddaughters of the late Rev. Robert Baker Carew, son of the late Rev.
Thomas Carew, 3rd son of 6th baronet:—
Issue of the late Charles Robert Sydenham Carew, *b.* 1853; *d.* 1939: *m.* 1891, Muriel Mary
Heathcoat, who *d.* 1939 da. of Sir John Heathcoat Heathcoat-Amory, 1st Bt.:—
Nesta Muriel, *b.* 1892: *m.* 1927, Edmund George Coryton [Parker, Bt., cr. 1844, colls.], and has
issue living, Nancy Loveday, *b.* 1930: *m.* 1965, Simon Charles Spencer, of Burtons House,
Burtons Lane, Chalfont St. Giles, Bucks, and has issue living, Charles James *b.* 1966, Andrew
George *b.* 1968,—Jane, *b.* 1933: *m.* 1957, Capt. Philip Peter Davies Cooke, 1st R. Dragoons, of
Gwysaney Hall, Mold, Flintshire [*see* Cooke, Bt., colls.].   *Residence,* Linkincorn House, Yelver-
ton, S. Devon.——Elizabeth Dora, *b.* 1897: *m.* 1959, Col. Colin F. Tod, RA, who *d.* 1973. *Resi-
dence,* The Old Mill House, Wescott, Dorking.——Nancy, *b.* 1899.   *Residence,* Onslow Court
Hotel, Queen's Gate, SW7.

Issue of the late Rev. Walter Gawen Carew, *b.* 1870, *d.* 1923: *m.* 1899, Blanche Gwendolen
who *d.* 1969, da. of the late W. J. Llewellyn, of Southwood, Tiverton:—
Lorna Gwendolen, *b.* 1902.   *Residence,* 52, Lower Sloane St., SW1.

The family of Carew is of great antiquity in Devon and Cornwall, and claims a common descent
with the Dukes of Leinster and Earls of Plymouth from Walter Fitz-Other, who was Castellan of
Windsor 1078.   For several generations the heads of the family are described as Barons of Carew
and Idrone, but none of them sat in Parliament with the exception of Nicholas de Carew, who
subscribed to the celebrated Barons' letter to the Pope in 1300, and from his second son the
present family is descended in a direct line.

Carew Pole, see Pole.

CARGILL, Creation (U.K.) 1920, of Glasgow. [Extinct 1954.]

Sir JOHN TRAILL CARGILL, 1st and last *Baronet.*

Daughter living of 1st Baronet—Allison Hope, *b.* 1896 : *m.* 1922, James Robertson Campbell
Greenlees, D.S.O., M.B., who *d.* 1951, and has issue living, Ronald Cargill Campbell, *b.* 1922,—
Allison Mary Campbell, *b.* 1925.   *Residence,* Eaglescairnie Mains, Haddington, E. Lothian.

CARLILE, Creation (U.K.) 1917, of Ponsbourne, co. Hertford. [Extinct 1942.]

Sir (EDWARD) HILDRED CARLILE, *C.B.E., T.D.*, 1st and last *Baronet.*

Daughter living of 1st Baronet—Eleanor Cicely : *m.* 1927, the Rev. Thomas Vyner Southey,
who *d.* 1928, V. of Ponsbourne.   *Residence,*

CARLILE, Creation (U.K.) 1928, of Gayhurst, co. Buckingham. [Extinct 1950.]

Sir (WILLIAM) WALTER CARLILE, *O.B.E.*, 1st and last *Baronet.*

Widow living of 1st Baronet—KATHARINE ELIZABETH MARY (The Old Cottage, Gayhurst, Newport
Pagnell, Bucks, MK16 8LG), only da. of the late Rev. G. H. Field, of Gayhurst, Newport Pagnell,
Bucks.; is a JP: *m.* 1st, 1940, as his second wife, Sir (William) Walter Carlile, OBE, 1st baronet,
who *d.* 1950, when the title became ext.; 2ndly, 1973, as his second wife, Geoffry Dover.

GIBSON-CRAIG-CARMICHAEL, Creation (N.S.) 1702, of Keirhill, co. Edinburgh, and (U.K.) 1831, of Riccarton, Midlothian.

Live to God, and you shall live.

VIVE · DEO · ET · VIVES

Sir DAVID PETER WILLIAM GIBSON-CRAIG-CARMICHAEL, 15th *Baronet* of Keirhill, and 7th *Baronet* of Riccarton; *b.* July 21st, 1946; *s.* his father *Sir* (ARCHIBALD HENRY) WILLIAM, 1969; ed. at Queen's Univ., Kingston, Canada (BSc): *m.* 1973, Patricia, da. of Marcos, Skarnic, of Santiago, Chile.

Arms—Quarterly: 1st and 4th, ermine, on a fesse sable three crescents argent, *Craig;* 2nd and 3rd, gules, three keys fesseways in pale, wards downwards or, *Gibson.* Crest—A knight on horseback in full armour, his right hand grasping a broken tilting spear shivered all proper. Supporters—Dexter, a man in armour holding in exterior hand a spear all proper; sinister, a war-horse argent, saddled and bridled proper.
        Residence—Quintas, Nova Lima, Brazil. *Address,*—Casilla 2461, Santiago, Chile.
Brothers living—ALASDAIR JOHN, *b.* Feb. 28th, 1948: *m.* 1973, Irene, da. of Bruno Haverbeck, of San tiago, Chile.——Andrew Charles, *b.* 1952.
Sister living—Susan Ann, *b.* 1949: *m.* 1970, Richard John Darling, and has issue living, Christopher John, *b.* 1971,—Nicholas Patrick, *b.* 1973.

Aunts living (Daughters of 13th Baronet)—Emily Edith, *b.* 1915.——Kathleen Joan, *b.* 1919: *m.* 1940, Charles Taylor Darling, of Universidad Nacional de Tucuman, Argentina, and has issue living, Anthony Robin, *b.* 1941,—Richard John, *b.* 1944,—Judith Ann, *b.* 1946.
Great Aunt living—Marjory Violet GIBSON-CRAIG (of 24C, Av. d'Ouchy, Lausanne, Switzerland)
Widows living of 13th and 14th Baronets of Keirhill—EMILY ELLEN (*Emily, Lady Gibson-Craig-Carmichael,* da. of Henry Rummell, of Falkland Islands: *m.* 1914, Sir Eardley Charles William Gibson-Craig-Carmichael, 13th baronet, who *d.* 1939. *Residence,* Casilla 2461, Santiago, Chile. ROSEMARY ANITA (*Rosemary, Lady Gibson-Craig-Carmichael*) (Casilla 2461, Santiago, Chile), da. of George Duncan Crew, of Santiago, Chile: *m.* 1941, Sir (Archibald Henry) William Gibson-Craig-Carmichael, 14th baronet, who *d.* 1969.

Collateral Branches living. (*In remainder to the Nova Scotia (cr. 1702) Baronetcy only.*)
        Issue (by 1st marriage) of the late John Murray Gibson-Carmichael, 3rd son of 10th baronet (cr. 1702), *b.* 1851, *d.* 1923: *m.* 1st, 1892, Amy Katherine, who *d.* 1899, da. of Frederick Archdale; 2ndly, 1921, Beatrice Mary, who *d.* 1964, da. of James Donoghue, of co. Westmeath:—
Violet Penelope, *b.* 1899: *m.* 1929, Dennis Wheeler-Carmichael (who assumed by deed poll 1929 the additional and final surname of Carmichael), of Skirling House, Biggar, Lanarkshire, and has issue living, Thomas Montague (Skirling House, Biggar, Lanarkshire): *b.* 1932: *m.* 1957, Jane, da. of the late Noel Cross, and has issue living, George Alexander *b.* 1959, Charles Edward *b.* 1961,—Margaret Mary (Trewern, 15, Broughton Rd., Biggar, Lanarkshire), *b.* 1930: *m.* 1949, Archibald Colville, who *d.* 1970, and has issue living, Thomas David *b.* 1952, William Henry Archibald *b.* 1955, Rosemary Elizabeth *b.* 1950: *m.* 1974, Neil Robert Colquhoun [see Greenwell, Bt.].

        Grandson of the late James Whitaker Gibson, son of the late William Charles Gibson, C.M.G., a descendant of Alexander Gibson of Durie, brother of 1st baronet :—
        Issue of the late William James Carmichael Gibson, *b.* 1883, *d.* 1955: *m.* 1918, Maude, da. of Roger Buston:—
John Carmichael, *b.* 1919. *Residence,* 10, Clanricarde Gardens, W.2.

        Sir James, 1st Baronet (*cr.* 1831), was second son of the late William Gibson [B. Carmichael, colls.], and assumed the additional surname of Craig 1818. The 2nd baronet, the Rt. Hon. Sir William, P.C., sat as M.P. for Edinburghshire (*L*) 1837-41, and for Edinburgh city 1841-52, and was Lord Clerk Register and Keeper of the Signet of Scotland 1862-78. Sir James, 3rd baronet, was Brigadier Roy. Co. of Archers (King's Body Guard for Scotland). The 4th baronet, Sir Archibald Charles Gibson-Craig, Lieut. Highland L.I., was killed in action during European War 1914 (despatches). The Nova Scotia Baronetcy (cr. 1702) was conferred upon Thomas Gibson, son of Sir John Gibson of Pentland and Addistone, with remainder to his heirs male whatsover, and the 6th baronet (John) of this creation assumed the additional surname of Carmichael on succeeding under the entail of Skirling, Peebles-shire, while Sir Thomas David 11th Bt., was cr. Baron Carmichael 1912. In 1914, Capt. Henry Thomas Gibson-Craig *s.* his brother as 5th Bt. of Riccarton, and in Jan. 1926, his kinsman, the 1st Baron Carmichael, in the N.S. Baronetcy (cr. 1702) of Keirhill; he died in Sept. 1926, having assumed the additional surname of Carmichael.

Carmichael-Anstruther, see Anstruther.

RIVETT-CARNAC, Creation (U.K.) 1836, of Derby.

Thus they go to Heaven.

Rev. Sir THOMAS NICHOLAS RIVETT-CARNAC, 8th *Baronet*, son of the late Vice-Adm. James William Rivett-Carnac, CB, CBE, DSC, 2nd son of 6th baronet; *b.* June 3rd, 1927; *s.* his uncle, *Sir* HENRY GEORGE CRABBE, 1972; ed. at Marlborough; late Capt. Scots. Gds.; Malaya 1950 (despatches); V. of St. Marks, Kennington Oval, SE11 since 1972.

𝔄rms—Quarterly, 1st and 4th quarterly argent and azure, two swords in saltire proper between three mullets, one in chief and two in fesse, and a crescent in base counterchanged, *Carnac*; 2nd and 3rd per pale argent and sable, on a chevron between three lozenges as many martlets counterchanged, *Rivett.* 𝖈rests—1st, a sword erect pommel and hilt or, issuing from a crescent ermine, the internal part gules, *Carnac*; 2nd, an arm erect, couped at the elbow per pale, argent and sable, in the hand proper, a broken sword of the first, hilt and pommel gold, *Rivett. Second Motto*—Holde faste.
Address,—St. Marks Vicarage, Kennington Oval, SE11.

Brother living—MILES JAMES (The Manor House Martyr Worthy, Winchester), *b.* Feb. 7th, 1933; Cdr. RN; Far East Fleet Patrols and Borneo Territories 1964-65 (despatches): *m.* 1958, April Sally, da. of Maj. Arthur Andrew Sidney Villar, of 48, Lowndes Sq., SW1, and has issue living, Jonathan James, *b.* 1962,—Simon Miles, *b.* 1966,—Lucinda Jane, *b.* 1960.

Sister living—Isla Carolyn (*Baroness Abinger*), *b.* 1925; formerly WRNS: *m.* 1957, the 8th Baron Abinger.

Uncle living (son of 6th baronet)—John Temple, *b.* 1906; ed. at Lancing Coll.; late Maj. Duke of Wellington's Regt.: *m.* 1941, Sarah Winifred, only da. of Wilfred Herbert Eglin, of Trimmingham, Halifax, Yorks., and has issue living, Clive, *b.* 1944,—Rosemary Jane, *b.* 1943. *Residence,*

Aunt living (daughter of 6th baronet)—Aileen Mary (108, Beaufort St., SW3), *b.* 1908: *m.* 1945, Edward F. Wakeford, who *d.* 1973.

Daughter living of 5th Baronet—Elinor Maud, *b.* 1887; *m.* 1912, Claud Robert Nightingale, MC, who *d.* 1954 [*see* Nightingale, Bt., colls.]. *Residence,* 8, Berkeley Place, Wimbledon, SW 19.

Collateral Branches living.
Issue of the late Col. Percy Temple Rivett-Carnac, brother of 6th baronet, *b.* 1852, *d.* 1932: *m.* 1898, Alice, who *d.* 19—, da. of Major Sidney Herbert, formerly of Maritzburg, S. Africa :—
Perceval Sydney, *b.* 1904.——Alice Mary, *b.* 1899: *m.* 1924, Capt. — Scott. *Residence,*

Granddaughters of the late William John Rivett-Carnac, 2nd son of 1st baronet :—
Issue of the late Louis Wilfred Guise Rivett-Carnac, *b.* 1854, *d.* 1904: *m.* 1883, Mabel, who *d.* 1951, da. of Lieut.-Col. William Southey :—
Marguerite Mabel, (Thatch Cottage, Eversley, Hants.) *b.* 1885.——Sybil Mary, *b.* 1886: *m.* 1912, Lieut.-Col. Guy Neville Buckland, DSO, RA (ret.) [E. Crawford colls.] who *d.* 1957, and has issue living, John Carnac Lindsay (Beechcrest, Fernhill Rd., Blackwater, Camberley, Surrey), *b.* 1922; ed. at Eton, and New Coll., Oxford (MA honours); 1939-45 War as Fl.-Lt. RAFVR, Burma and Europe: *m.* 1965, Joyce Elizabeth Bursford, and has issue living, William Lindsay Carnac *b.* 1966, James Lindsay Carnac *b.* 1968, Edward Carnac Lindsay *b.* 1973,—Auriol Mary Lindsay, *b.* 1915: *m.* 1948, Lt.-Col. Geoffrey C. Graham, MC, RA, of The Birds House, Weare Gifford, Bideford, Devon, and has issue living, Vanessa Auriol Lindsay *b.* 1949; ed. at St. Hilda's, Oxford (BA), Lindsay Diana *b.* 1951, Diana (twin)—*b.* 1922: *m.* 1947, Donald Tandy, of 8, Normanton Court, Croham Rd., Croydon, Surrey, and has issue living, Timothy John *b.* 1952. *Residence,* Cherrycroft, Grange Rd., Camberley, Surrey.——Ianthe *b.* 1889: *m.* 1912, Norman Kershaw, who *d.* 1966, and has issue living, Sheila Yvonne (18, North Side, Clapham Common, SW4), *b.* 1913: *m.* 1941, Roylance Lynton Parkinson, LRCP, who *d.* (killed in action in Malaya) 1942),—Pamela Ianthe, *b.* 1916: *m.* 1st, 1941, Jack Norfolk; 2ndly, 1957, Reginald Reynolds. *Residence,* 18, North Side, Clapham Common, SW4.

Grandchildren of the late Charles Forbes Rivett-Carnac, 3rd son of 1st baronet :—
Issue of the late Charles James Rivett-Carnac, *b.* 1853, *d.* 1935: *m.* 1st, 1877, Laura Margaret Marion, who *d.* 1905, da. of the late Col. J. S. Ogilvie. B.S.C.; 2ndly, 1906, Frances Clytie, who *d.* 1962, da. of the late Rev. Canon Greenstock:—
(By 2nd *m.*) Douglas Charles Mahisra, *OBE* (Pitt Cottage, Dallington, Heathfield, Sussex), *b.* 1907; ed. at Exeter Coll., Oxford (BA honours); HM Diplo. Ser. (ret.); OBE (Civil) 1956: *m.* 1946, Barbara Joyce, da. of A. R. Pratt, and has issue living, Christopher Charles, *b.* 1947,—John Benedict, *b.* 1949,—Michael Francis, *b.* 1950.——Louis Charles Wykeham (1, The Fradgan, Newlyn, Penzance, Cornwall), *b.* 1912; 1939-45 War; Capt. Sherwood Foresters: *m.* 1939, Alice, da. of the late J. Docherty and has issue living, Clive Anthony Charles (11, Cherrytree Rd., Chinnor, Oxon), *b.* 1940: *m.* 1971, Marilyn, da. of H. C. Wilkes,—Louis Charles James (2, Coastguard House, Gurnards Head, Zennor, St. Ives, Cornwall), *b.* 1942: *m.* 1968, Ann Elsey, and has issue living, Paul Antony *b.* 1968, Andrew Justin *b.* 1970,—Timothy Charles, *b.* 1949; BSc. Hons.,—Nichola Frances *b.* 1947: *m.* 1967, Robin Wentworth Mason, of 77, Hayway, Rushden, Northants, and has issue living, Toby Wentworth *b.* 1970, Christopher Wentworth *b.* 1971.

Granddaughter of the late Charles James Rivett-Carnac (ante):—
Issue of the late Lt.-Col. Charles Francis Rivett-Carnac, Indian Army, *b.* 1909, *d.* 1958: *m.* 1936, Lorna (7, Ormonde Gate, SW3), da. of the late B. Darling:—
Jacqueline Anne (c Chartered Bank, 38, Bishopsgate, EC2), *b.* 1937: *m.* 1957, David Lindsay Millar, and has issue living, Guy McIntyre, *b.* 1959,—Mark Charles Forbes, *b.* 1961,—Nicholas Lindsay *b.* 1962.

Grandchildren of the late John Thurlow Rivett-Carnac (infra):—
Issue of the late Lt.-Col. John Claude Thurlow Rivett-Carnac, MC, KPM, *b.* 1888, *d.* 1975: *m.* 1st, 1923, Ola Jane, who *d.* 1953, da. of S. Wilson, of Maine, USA; 2ndly, 1953, the Hon. Evelyn Hope Balfour, who *d.* 1967, da. of 1st Baron Riverdale, and widow of Gp. Capt. Eustace Jack Linton Hope, AFC, RAF :—
(By 1st *m.*) Sheila Veronica Mary, *b.* 1927: *m.* 1st, 1954 (m. diss. 1969), John Coleman Averill; 2ndly, 1969, A   E   Valentine, of 29, Almorah Rd., Epsom, Auckland, NZ, and has issue living, (by 1st *m.*), John Miles Rochford, *b.* 1958,—Andrew Clive Rochford, *b.* 1960,—Catherine Veronica, *b.* 1955,—Elizabeth Jane Rochford, *b.* 1957.——(by 2nd *m.*) John Charles Malcolm (35, Donnington Court, Donnington Rd., NW10 3TH), *b.* 1955; BBC since 1974.

Grandchildren of the late Charles Forbes Rivett-Carnac (ante):—
Issue of the late John Thurlow Rivett-Carnac, *b.* 1856, *d.* 1948 : *m.* 1887, Edith Emily, who *d.* 1950, da. of the late H. H. Brownlow :—
Edward Charles (Apart. 206, 1035, Belmont Av., Victoria, BC, Canada), *b.* 1901; ed. at East-bourne Coll.; Commr. Roy. Canadian Mounted Police, Ottawa (ret.); attached Field Ambulance Unit with French Army during 1914-18 War: *m.* 1932, Mary Dillon, who *d.* 1970, da. of Col. Francis Bethel Ware, DSO, VD, of London, Ont., and has issue living, Beverley Ann, *b.* 1933: *m.* 1954, A. F. Griffin, of Victoria, BC, Canada, and has issue living, Brenda Gayle *b.* 1956,—Mary Frances *b.* 1940: *m.* 1965, Gerald Edward Marshall Beeney, TD, MA, LLB, of Cherry Tree, Wickhurst Lane, Broadbridge Heath, Horsham.——Edith Maude, *b.* 1895: *m.* 1917, Brig. Edward Temple, RA, who *d.* 1960, and has issue living, Edward Peter (c/o Nat. Westminster Bank, 41, Lothbury, EC2), *b.* 1918; Col. (ret.) RA: *m.* 1st, 1951, Lesley Barnes; 2ndly, 1971, Esther Mary Dick,—John Hugh (Fairfield, Cooling Rd., High Halstow, Rochester), *b.* 1921: *m.* 1952, Joan Eaton, and has issue living, Michael Martyn *b.* 1953, Andrew William *b.* 1957, Jane *b.* 1955,—James David (Witheridge, Tiverton, Devon), *b.* 1936; ed. at Queens' Coll., Camb. (BA), MB); MRCVS: *m.* 1959, Nancy Lewis, and has issue living, Richard David *b.* 1972, Sarah *b.* 1962, Catherine *b.* 1963, Rachel *b.* 1967. *Residence*, Flat 4, Lewes House, Lewes Rd., East-bourne.

Grandsons of the late John Thurlow Rivett-Carnac (ante):—
Issue of the late Lt.-Col. Herbert Gordon Rivett-Carnac, Indian Army, *b.* 1892, *d.* 1962: *m.* 1925, Cushla Margarette, who *d.* 1974, da. of Lt.-Col. Robert Southey Pottinger:—
Eric Gordon, *b.* 1926.——John Southey, *b.* 1929.

Grandchildren of the late Charles Forbes Rivett-Carnac, 3rd son of 1st baronet):—
Issue of the late Harry Moreland Rivett-Carnac, *b.* 1857; *d.* 1948 : *m.* 18—, Eleanor, who *d.* 1965 da. of ———— :—
Flora, *b.* 18—: *m.* 18—, F. Cumming of Bellerive, Tasmania.——Muriel, *b.* 18—: *m.* 18—, M. Haywood, of 126, Cimitiere St., George Town, Tasmania.——Holly, *b.* 18—: *m.* 18—, Herbert L. Bynon. *Residence*, 126 Cimitiere St., George Town, Tasmania.

Issue of the late Col. Seymour Gordon Rivett-Carnac, late R.E., *b.* 1868, *d.* 1931: *m.* 1st, 1893, Martha Ella Maude, who *d.* 1920, da. of John Latch : 2ndly, 1925, Maria, Frances (10, Barlow Rd., Cheltenham), da. of H. W. Rowland, formerly of The Bryn, Wyesham, Monmouth:—
(By 2nd m.) Ann, *b.* 1928; ed. at Newnham Coll., Camb. (BA honours 1950, MA honours 1954): *m.* 1956, Alan Mitchell Burgess, CEng, MIEE, MInstMC, and has issue living, Martin Frank, *b.* 1960,—Janet Rachel, *b.* 1958,—Sarah Kathleen, *b.* 1962. *Residence*, 55, Digswell Park Rd., Welwyn Garden City, Herts.

The 1st baronet was Chairman of the East India Co. two years in succession, many years M.P. for Sandwich, and Governor of Bombay 1838-41. His father, who was son of J. Rivett, in H.E.I.C.S., and M.P. for Derby, assumed by sign-manual the additional surname of Carnac. The 2nd baronet sat as M.P. for Lymington (C) 1852-60. The 4th baronet, Sir Claud James, having been missing for many years, an order was issued in the Chancery Div. in March 11th, 1924, pre-suming his death as Dec. 31st, 1909. Sir William Perceval, 5th Bt., died March 21st, 1924. The 6th baronet, the Rev. Sir George Clennell (sometime R. of Woldingham), was son of William John Rivett-Carnac, 2nd son of 1st Bt.

CARY, Creation (U.K.) 1955, of Withington, co. Lancaster.

Sir ROBERT ARCHIBALD CARY, 1st *Baronet*, son of Robert Cary; *b.* May 25th, 1898 ; ed. at Ardingly, and at R.M.C. ; is Chm. of Lancashire United Transport, Ltd., and of J. Compton, Sons & Webb, Ltd. ; was Parliamentary Private Sec. to Civil Lord of the Admiralty 1939-42, and to Sec. of State for India and Burma 1942-5, an Assist. Govt. Whip 1944-5, and a Junior Lord of the Treasury May to July 1945 ; appointed Parliamentary Private Sec. to Lord Privy Seal and Leader of House of Commons 1951 ; European War 1916-18 with 4th Dragoon Guards, European War 1939-45 with 4th/7th Roy. Dragoon Guards ; M.P. for Eccles (C) 1935-45, and for With-ington Div. of Manchester 1951-74; Knt. 1945: *m.* 1924, the Hon. Rosamond Mary Curzon, da. of the late Col. the Hon. Alfred Nathaniel Curzon [*see* B. Scarsdale]. and has issue.

Arms—Argent, on a bend cotised sable three roses of the field barbed and seeded proper in sinister chief a cinquefoil gules. **Crest**—A swan, wings elevated and addorsed proper between two cinquefoils gules.

Residence—Wrotham Water, Wrotham, Kent. *Clubs*—Turf, and Pratt's.

Son living—ROGER HUGH, *b.* Jan. 8th, 1926 ; ed. at Eton, and at New Coll., Oxford (B.A. Modern History 1949); Lt. Grenadier Guards (Reserve), and an Asso. of Roy. Historical Soc.; was Producer, BBC 1950-56 and Talks Assist., European Ser., 1956-58, Dep. Editor *The Listener* 1958-61, Management Training Organiser, BBC 1961-66, Snr. Assistant Secretariat BBC 1966-74, since when Special Assist. Public Affairs BBC; Sec., Central Music Advisory Cttee. BBC since 1966: *m.* 1st, 1948 (m. diss 1951), Marilda, da. of Maj. Philip Pearson-Gregory, MC; 2ndly, 1953, Ann Helen Katharine, el. da. of Hugh Blair Brenan, OBE, former Assist. Sec. Roy. Chelsea Hosp., SW1, and has issue living, (by 1st m.) Marcia Susan, *b.* 1949: *m.* 1971, Robin Gibson-Watt, of Gelli-Garn, Llanyre, Llandrindod Wells, Radnorshire,—(by 2nd m.) Nicolas Robert Hugh, *b.* 1955,—Roger Nathaniel Blair, *b.* 1957,—Charlotte Rhoda Rosamond, *b.* 1960. *Residence*, 23, Bath Rd., Chiswick, W4. *Club*, Pratt's.

CASSEL, Creation (U.K.) 1920, of Lincoln's Inn, City of London.

Sir HAROLD FELIX CASSEL, *QC, 3rd Baronet;*
b. Nov. 8th, 1916; *s.* his brother, *Sir* FRANCIS
EDWARD, 1969; Bar. Lincoln's Inn 1946; QC
1970; Recorder of Gt. Yarmouth 1968-72,
since when Hon. Recorder; Recorder of Crown
Court since 1972; 1939-45 War, as Capt. RA:
m. 1st, 1940 (m. diss. 1963) Ione Jean, da. of the
late Capt. Evelyn Hugh Barclay [see B.
Somerleyton]; 2ndly, 1963, Mrs. Eileen
Elfrida Smedley, da. of James Rider Faulkner,
and has issue by 1st m.

Arms—Per fesse embattled azure and gules, in chief
a pair of scales or between two swords points upwards,
pommels and hilts of the third and in base a portcullis
also of the third. **Crest**—A lion rampant, gules resting
the dexter paw on a mill-rind gold.
Residence—49, Lennox Gdns., SW1.

Let justice be done.

Sons living—By 1st m.—TIMOTHY FELIX HAROLD
(The Manor House, Aldingbourne, Sussex), *b.* April 30th,
1942; ed. at Eton; Bar. Lincoln's Inn 1965: *m.* 1971,
Mrs. Jenifer Samuel, da. of Kenneth Bridge Puckle,
and has issue living, Alexander James Felix, *b.* May 25th,
1974,—Natalia Hermione, *b.* 1972.——Jeremy James,
b. 1950.——Evelyn Martin, *b.* 1952.
Daughter living—By 1st m.—Miranda Phyllis, *b.* 1946.
Sisters living—Hermione Anna (32, Argyll Rd., W8) *b.* 1910.
——Josephine Helen (twin), *b.* 1916: *m.* 1939, Griffith
Cresswell Evans Pugh, BM, BCh., and has issue living,
David Sheridan Griffith, *b.* 1940.—Simon Francis, *b.*
1945,—Oliver Lewis Evans, *b.* 1955,—Harriet Veronica,
b. 1946. *Residence*, Hatching Green House, Hatching
Green, Harpenden, Herts.

The Rt. Hon. Sir Felix Cassel, QC, 1st Bt. (son of M. S. Cassel, of 2, Orme Sq., W.), was Pres. of
Management Cttee. of Cassel Hosp. for Functional Nervous Disorders, a Member of Council
of King Edward VII Sanatorium, Midhurst, and Chm. of Trustees of Cassel Educational Trust,
Judge Advocate-Gen. 1916-34, and MP for St. Pancras, W. (*C*) 1910-16.

**CAVE, Creation (U.K.) 1896, of Cleve Hill, Mangotsfield, co. Gloucester; Sidbury
Manor, Sidbury, co. Devon; and Stoneleigh House, Clifton, Bristol.**

Sir CHARLES EDWARD COLERIDGE CAVE, 4th
Baronet; b. Feb. 28th, 1927 ; *s.* his father, *Sir* EDWARD
CHARLES, 1946 ; ed. at Eton ; formerly Lieut. Devonshire
Regt.; High Sheriff of Devon 1969: *m.* 1957, Mary
Elizabeth, da. of John Francis Gore, CVO [see E. Arran,
colls.], and has issue.

Arms—Azure, fretty argent, on a fesse or a greyhound courant sable,
collared of the second, a bordure of the third pellettée. **Crest**—A daisy-flower
slipped proper, a greyhound's head issuant therefrom per pale argent and
sable, guttée counterchanged.

Seat—Sidbury Manor, Sidmouth, Devon.

Cave.
Beware.

Sons living—JOHN CHARLES *b.* Sept. 8th, 1958.——Nicholas
Stephen, *b.* 1961.——Thomas Henry, *b.* 1964.——Richard Hugh, *b.*
1967.

Sisters living—Rosemary Betty (Elmside, Newton Poppleford, Sidmouth, Devon), *b.* 1924.——Daphne Frances, *b.* 1930. *Residence*,
Greenhead, Sidbury, Devon.

Mother living—Betty Christabel Gertrude, da. of the late Rennell
Coleridge, of Salston, Ottery St. Mary, Devon : *m.* 1922, Sir Edward Charles Cave, 3rd Bt.,
who *d.* 1946, and from whom she had obtained a divorce 1942. *Residence*, Daisymount House,
Ottery St. Mary, Devon.

Collateral Branches living.

Issue of the late Walter Frederick Cave, 3rd son of 1st baronet, *b.* 1863, *d.* 1939: *m.*
1892, Jessie Maria, who *d.* 1934, da. of the late Hugh Cochrane, of Montreal :—
Richard Walter Dundonald, *b.* 1901 ; ed. at Eton: *m.* 1934, Joan Elizabeth, da. of the late Charles
Lyon Liddell [see B. Ravensworth, colls.]. *Residence*, Overwey, Tilford, Farnham, Surrey.

Granddaughters of the late Maj. Arthur Stephen Cave, 4th son of 1st baronet:—
Issue of the late Ronald Arthur Cave, *b.* 1910, *d.* 1964: *m.* 1936, Audrey Œnone
(Ramblers, Holford, Somerset), da. of Dr. Francis Child, formerly of Penlee, Weybridge:—
Diana Ann, *b.* 1938: *m.* 1957.——Sylvia Margaret, *b.* 1944.

This family is probably a branch of the Caves of Yorkshire and Leicestershire, but their recorded
pedigree commences with John Cave of Leigh Sinton, co. Worcester, *temp.* 15th century, who was
ancestor of Sir Richard Cave, Kt., a distinguished General killed at the battle of Naseby, and also of
John Cave (great-grandfather of 1st baronet), founder of the Cave bank at Bristol. The arms, which
have been confirmed three times by the Heralds' College, were originally granted in the reign of
Henry VII. The 1st baronet, Sir Charles Daniel, was a Director of Union of London and Smith's
Bank (Limited), and the 2nd baronet, Sir Charles Henry, was High Sheriff of Devon 1926.

CAVE-BROWNE-CAVE. Creation (E.) 1641, of Stanford, Northamptonshire.

Sir ROBERT CAVE-BROWNE-CAVE, 16th
Baronet; *b.* June 8th, 1929; *s.* his father, *Sir* CLEMENT
CHARLES, 1945; ed. at St. Georges's Sch., Vancouver,
at Univ. Sch., Victoria, and at British Columbia
Univ.: is Pres. of Cave & Co., Ltd.: *m.* 1954,
Lois Shirley, da. of John Chalmers Huggard, of
Winnipeg, Canada, and has issue.

Arms—Quarterly: 1st and 4th, azure, fretty argent, *Cave;* 2nd
and 3rd, azure, a chevron between three escallops or, a bordure
engrailed gules, *Browne.* *Crest*—1st, a greyhound courant sable,
collared argent; 2nd, a stork, proper, winged and gorged with
a ducal crown or, beaked and membered gules.

Residence—6087, Wiltshire Street, Vancouver, British
Columbia.

Son living—JOHN ROBERT CHARLES, *b.* June 22nd, 1957.

Daughter living—Lisé Irene, *b.* 1955.

Beware.

Great-Uncle living—Anthony Stanhope, *b.* 1879.

Daughter living of 14th Baronet—Phœbe Hyacinthe,
M.B.E., b. 1901; is a Missionary in Uganda; M.B.E. (Civil) 1956. *Residence,*

Widow living of 15th Baronet—DOROTHEA PLEWMAN (*Dorothea, Lady Cave-Browne-Cave*), da.
of Robert Greene Dwen, of Chicago, U.S.A.: *m.* 1923, Sir Clement Charles Cave-Browne-Cave,
15th Bt., who *d.* 1945. *Residence,*

Collateral Branches living.

Grandchildren of the late Rev. Fitzherbert Astley Cave-Browne-Cave, son of the
late Rev. William Astley Cave-Browne-Cave, 2nd son of 9th baronet:—
Issue of the late Cecil Beckwith Cave-Browne-Cave, *b.* 1871, *d.* 1953: *m.* 1st, 1896,
Sara Eleanor, who *d.* 1928, da. of the late John W. Nicholson, of St. John, New
Brunswick; 2ndly, 1929, Edith Beatrice, who *d.* 1948, da. of Alfred Evans, J.P.,
formerly of Chesham Bois, Bucks :—
(By 2nd marriage) Penelope Margaret Cecil, *b.* 1931: *m.* 1965, Timothy Fitzgerald ffrench-Mullen,
of 12, Inkerman Terr., Allen St., W8, and has issue living, Candetta Lydia Cecil, *b.* 1966,—
Tara Eve Siobhan, *b.* 1970.——Catherine Priscilla Astley, *b.* 1937: *m.* 1958, David Bates, and has
issue living, Joanna Catherine, *b.* 1959. *Residence,* Villa Jilguero, la Candia Alta, La Orotava,
Tenerife, Canary Islands.

Issue of the late Courtney Priestley Edwards Cave-Browne-Cave, *b.* 1890, *d.* 1961: *m.*
1915, Helen Freda, who *d.* 1955, only da. of A. J. Cable, of Epping, Essex :—
Paul Astley (11, Westbourne Cres., Highfield, Southampton), *b.* 1917; Printer and Publisher;
formerly Capt. Gen. List; a JP for Southampton: *m.* 1940, Joan Myfanwy, da. of the late Thomas
Norman Jones, JP, of Rhyl, N. Wales, and has issue living, Paul, *b.* 1954,—Jane, *b.* 1943; BSc,—
Adrienne, *b.* 1947; BA, Cambs.,—Sarah, *b.* 1959.——Lyndon Fraser, *b.* 1923; ed. at Liverpool
Univ.; is an ARIBA: *m.* 1952, Betty, only da. of Walter Rush, of Dinnington, Yorks., and has
issue living, Anthony John, *b.* 1952; LLB, London,—Bernard James William *b.* 1954. *Resi-
dence,* 24, Portland St., Leamington Spa.——Anthony, *DSO* (Fossedene Manor, Combrook,
Warwicks.), *b.* 1925; ed. at Birmingham Sch. of Architecture; an ARIBA; Burma 1945 as
Capt. S. Wales Borderers (DSO), Sumatra 1945-46 as Intelligence Officer, 26th Indian Div.;
DSO 1945: *m.* 1957, Dinah Ann, da. of J. W. Mitchell, of Longville, Much Wenlock, Salop, and
has issue living, Genille Anthony, *b.* 1959,—Courtney Peter, *b.* 1961,—Jonathan Lyndon, *b.* 1962,
—William Astley, *b.* 1967.——Bernard Adrian *b.* 1926; 1939-45 War as Lt. Middx. Regt.,
Palestine 1946-47: *m.* 1961, Ann, da. of Richard George William Pritchard, JP, of Roddis
House, Wellesbourne, Warwick, and has issue living, Richard Ambrose, *b.* 1962,—Rowland
Fraser, *b.* 1966,—Helen Ann, *b.* 1963. *Address,* Box 5369, Station A, Toronto 1, Canada.

Grandsons of the late Edward Johnson Cave-Browne-Cave (infra):—
Issue of the late Edward Jordayne Cave-Browne-Cave, *b.* 1885, *d.* 1970: *m.* 1910, Jane
Ella, who *d.* 1968, da. of the late Joseph Hilton Cant, of Appleby:—
Genille Hilton Jordayne (The Crillon, 3500, Mountain St., Montreal 25, Canada), *b.* 1912; ed. at
BC Univ. (MA), and Massachusetts Inst. of Tech. (PhD); Prof. of Chemistry, McGill Univ.,
Montreal: *m.* 1944, Mary Margaret Elizabeth, da. of Lt.-Col. Robert Henry Palmer, DSO [see
Palmer, Bt., cr. 1660, colls.].——Wilmot Wyamarus (902, Parkland Drive, Victoria, BC, Canada),
b. 1915: *m.* 1969, Janet Kyle, da. of the late Thomas Peddie, MA.

Granddaughter of the late Rev. John Walker Cave-Browne-Cave, el. son of the
late Thomas Cave-Browne-Cave 3rd son of 9th baronet:—
Issue of the late Edward Johnson Cave-Browne-Cave, *b.* 1851, *d.* 1930: *m.* 1880, Phoebe,
who *d.* 1923, da. of the late J. Andrews:—
Florence Beatrice, *b.* 1883. *Residence,* 12892, Sandford Av., Ocean Park, British Columbia.

Grandsons of the late William Cave-Browne-Cave, 2nd son of the late Thomas
Cave-Browne-Cave (ante) :—
Issue of the late Stretton Cave-Browne-Cave, *b.* 1878, *d.* 1961: *m.* 1907, Ethel Milbro,
who *d.* 1943, da. of the late W. H. B. Higgin-Birket, of Birket Houses, Lancashire :—
Glen Myles LEVERING, *b.* 1910; ed. at Winchester; is an Aeronautical Engineer; assumed the
name of Glen Myles Levering in lieu of Myles Verney Cave-Browne-Cave 1944: *m.* 1936
(marriage dissolved 1943), Christina Elizabeth, da. of the late Wilfred Bentley, of Inglewood,
Huddersfield, and Westward Ho!, Windermere.——Stretton Patrick, *b.* 1911; ed. at Sedbergh,
formerly in Warwickshire Yeo.: *m.* 1954, Pamela, da. of Col. H. S. Cole, of Stonebank, Ilkley,
Yorkshire. *Residence,* Topham's Farm, Conistone-with-Kilnsey, nr. Skipton, Yorks.——Bryan
William, *OBE, b.* 1915; ed. at Shrewsbury, and at St. Edmund Hall, Oxford (MA); Dir. of
British Forces Broadcasting Ser., Min. of Defence 1963-71; formerly Lt.-Col. Roy. Northumber-
land Fusiliers and on Gen. Staff; OBE (Mil.) 1946: *m.* 1947, Margaret Royston, *MBE,* da. of
A. Cooke, of Linton-on-Wharfe, Wetherby, Yorkshire, and has issue living, Myles Alfred,
b. 1949; ed. at Rugby, and St. Edmund Hall, Oxford (BA),—Claire Birket, *b.* 1948: *m.* 1970,
Stuart William Brown,—Elise Margaret, *b.* 1952: *m.* 1972, Franz Friedrich Nadenau, and has
issue living, Stephan *b.* 1974. *Residence,* Birket Houses, Winster, Windermere.

Grandchildren of the late Sir Thomas Cave-Browne-Cave, CB, 3rd son of the
late Thomas Cave-Browne-Cave (ante):—
Issue of the late Wing-Cdr. Thomas Reginald Cave-Browne-Cave, CBE, RAF, *b.* 1885,
d. 1969: *m.* 1st, 1918, Marjorie Gwynne, who *d.* 1969, da. of the late Albert Wright;
2ndly, 1969, Elsie May (205, Bassett Av., Southampton), da. of the late James Ricks:—
Thomas Milton (Wrens Farm, Castle Lane, N. Baddesley, Southampton), *b.* 1926: *m.* 1964, Anne,
da. of Ralph P. Symons, of Truro, and has issue living, Thomas Edward, *b.* 1968,—Janet Mary
b. 1965.——Gillian Mary, *b.* 1923.

Grandchildren of the late Frank Wyamarus Cave-Browne-Cave (*b.* 1844),
6th son of the late Thomas Cave-Browne-Cave (ante) :—
Issue of the late Frank Wyamarus Cave-Browne-Cave, *b.* 1886, *d.* 1942 : *m.* 1926,
Kathleen, da. of the late John Douglas de Fenzi :—
Norman John, *b.* 1927 : *m.* 1st, 1952 (marriage dissolved 1957), Eveline Fay, da. of the late John
Stanley Hill ; 2ndly, 1957, Margaret Dobbs, da. of John Stanley Maw, and has issue living,
(by 1st marriage) Peter, *b.* 1955. *Residence,* Trefeddian Hotel, Aberdovey, Merioneth.——
Anne Molly, *b.* 1929: *m.* 1952, Selwyn W. Hill, and has issue living, Anthony Wootton, *b.* 1966,—
Frances Anne, *b.* 1954,—Judith Wootton, *b.* 1955,—Stacey Wootton (da.), *b.* 1961. *Residence,*
150, Lordswood Rd., Harborne, Birmingham.

Granddaughters of the late Rev. John Cave-Browne, el. son of Lt.-Col. Edward
Cave-Browne, 4th brother of 9th baronet:—
Issue of the late Edward Cave-Browne, *b.* 1856, *d.* 1895 : *m.* 1886, Norah, who *d.* 1955, da.
of Lieut.-Col. Gorman, formerly Ceylon Rifles :—
Dorothy Sela, *b.* 1887 : *m.* 1922, Robert Flemyng Prideaux, who *d.* 1952, and has issue living,
Roger Cave (of Pen-Banc, Tegryn, Llanfyrnach, Pembrokeshire), *b.* 1926: *m.* 1955, Bridget
Ellison Adams, and has issue living, Jennifer Dorothy *b.* 1959, Trudy Ann *b.* 1962,—Sela Mary,
b. 1923. *Residence,* 17, Claremont Hill, Shrewsbury.
Issue of the late William Charles Cave-Browne. *b.* 1867, *d.* 1916: *m.* 1895, Maude Alice,
who *d.* 1949, da. of the late Maj.-Gen. W. J. Jones, M.S.C.:—
Selina Verney Cleveland (10312, 107 Av., Grande Prairie, Alberta, Canada), *b.* 1899: *m.* 1923,
Alan Kingsford Watts. who *d.* 1957, and has issue living, Patricia Sela, *b.* 1927: *m.* 1947, Harold
Keith Gerow (Box 903, Salmon Arm, BC, Canada), and has issue living, Rodney Dale *b.* 1948,
Donald Keith *b.* 1952, Terry Francis *b.* 1954, Randall Kingsford *b.* 1958, Cameron Lee *b.* 1962,—
Joan Genille, *b.* 1931: *m.* 1949, Iain Blair MacAlister, of Box 184, Wembley, Alberta, Canada,
and has issue living, Laurence Blair *b.* 1950, Robert Kingsford *b.* 1951, Vickie Joan *b.* 1952.——
Joyce Marian Asteley (Box 22, Athabasca, Alberta, Canada), *b.* 1907: *m.* 1934, the Rev. Canon
Florian Morgan Sanger-Davies, who *d.* 1963.

Grandchildren of Edward Raban Cave-Browne, CSI, yst. son of Lt.-Col. Edward
Cave-Browne:—
Issue of the late Maj.-Gen. William Cave-Browne, CBE, DSO, MC, *b.* 1884, *d.* 1967:
m. 1916, Muriel, who *d.* 1971, da. of J. W. Wainwright, AMICE:—
John Raban, *MC* (United Service Club), *b.* 1917; ed. at King's Bruton, and Pembroke Coll.,
Camb. (BA); Brig. late RE (ret.): *m.* 1940, Ulrica Ellen, da. of the late Maj. Frank Paget-
Hoblyn, and has issue living, Susan Margaret, *b.* 1942: *m.* 1969, Richard Laybourne Perry, of
Warren House, Merrion, Pembroke, and has issue living, Nicholas Charles Laybourne *b.* 1972,
Roger Cave (of Pen-Banc, Tegryn, Llanfyrnach, Pembrokeshire), *b.* 1926: *m.* 1955, Bridget
Camilla Margaret *b.* 1970,—Ultrica Sarah, *b.* 1946: *m.* 1969, Patrick Lawrence Cargrave Covern-
ton, and has issue living, Natasha Louise *b.* 1973.——Caroline Jane, *b.* 1926: *m.* 1948, Derek
Marten Brightman, DSC, of Munstead Park House, Godalming, Surrey, and has issue living,
Christopher Marten, *b.* 1949; 2nd Lt. 16/5L,., Jeremy Richard, *b.* 1951,—Elizabeth Jane, *b.* 1953,
—Nicola Anne, *b.* 1959.
Issue of the late Major Horace Cave-Browne, Indian Army, *b.* 1886, *d.* 1960 : *m.* 1920,
Alice Rose, who *d.* 1972, da. of the late Col. P. A. Weir, Indian Med. Ser.:—
Patrick Norman Rose (150, Greenbank Rd., Edinburgh, EH10 5RN), *b.* 1926; ed. at Charterhouse;
Maj. late N. Rhodesia Regt. and late Seaforth Highlanders; Orientation and Mobility Instructor,
Roy. Blind Sch., Edinburgh: *m.* 1956, Mary Davy, da. of the late Lt.-Col. M. F. D. Cobbold,
Indian Army, and has issue living, Margaret Alison, *b.* 1959,—Ann Mary, *b.* 1961.——
Alison Barbara Rose, *b.* 1932: *m.* 1954, Maj. Robin John Ronald Campbell, Queen's Own
Highlanders (Seaforth and Camerons) [*see* E. Cawdor, colls.]. *Address,* c/o Lloyds Bank, High
St., Uckfield, Sussex.

According to a pedigree collected and certified by the Garter King of Arms, 1632, this family
is derived from Jordan de Cave, who inherited the Lordships of North and South Cave, co. York,
1068. Sir Thomas Cave, 1st baronet, was, during the civil war, a strenuous supporter of his
sovereign. The 2nd baronet was M.P. for Coventry, and the 3rd and 7th baronets each sat as
M.P. for Leicestershire. The 3rd baronet, Sir Thomas Cave, of Stanford Hall, *m.* the Hon. Margaret Verney, a descendant of the 1st Baron Braye. Sarah Otway-Cave, of Stanford Hall, only
da. of Sir Thomas, 6th baronet, became Baroness Braye on the termination of the abeyance in
1839, and was grandmother of the present peer. John, father of the 9th baronet, assumed the name
of Browne by Act of Parliament 1752, his mother having been an heiress of that name, and
Sir William 9th baronet assumed the additional surname of Cave by Roy. licence 1839. The
12th baronet, the Rev. Sir Genille, sometime engaged in ranching, and served in Boxer Expedition,
in Spanish-American War 1898-99 and during 1914-18 War; afterwards a Min. in Wesleyan
Methodist Church in America; took Holy Orders in Church of England 1920, and became R. of
Londesborough, Yorkshire. The 13th baronet, Sir Reginald Ambrose, was Capt. RN, and served
at Bombardment of Alexandria 1882.

CAYLEY, Creation (E.) 1661, of Brompton, Yorkshire.

Sir DIGBY WILLIAM DAVID CAYLEY, 11th *Baronet*;
son of Lt.-Cdr. William Arthur Seton Cayley, 2nd son
of Digby Leonard Arthur Cayley (infra); *b.* June 3rd,
1944; *s.* his kinsman, *Maj. Sir* KENELM HENRY ERNEST,
1967; ed. at Malvern, and Downing Coll., Camb. (MA): *m.*
1969, Christine Mary, da. of the late Derek Francis
Gaunt, of Ilkley, Yorks., and has issue.

Arms—Quarterly argent and sable, a bend gules charged with three
mullets of the first. **Crest**—A demi-lion rampant or charged with a bend
gules, thereon three mullets argent, in the paws a battleaxe argent, helved
gules.
Residence—Homestead, Eastham St., Clitheroe, Lancs.
Daughter living—Emma Jane, *b.* 1974.

Callide sed honeste.

*With skill but with
honour.*

Sister living—Josephine Beatrice Seton (twin), *b.* 1944: *m.* 1968,
Giacomo Bertolini, of Via Bergognone 27, Milan, Italy.
Uncle living—CUTHBERT JOHN (Leenane, Maam Cross, co. Galway),
b. June 9th, 1907; ed. at Eton, and Pembroke Coll., Camb.; FRGS;
1939-45 War as F/O RAFVR: *m.* 1938, Cecil Lilla Iris, who *d.* 1972,
da. of the late Adm. George Cuthbert Cayley, CB [Cayley, Bt., colls.].

Daughters living of 10th Baronet—Angela Elizabeth (Brompton, Scarborough, Yorks.), *b.* 1930,
m. 1950, (m. diss. 1959) Sir Robert John Frank, 3rd Bt.——Susan Dorothy Marie Gabrielle,
b. 1934: *m.* 1955, Maldwin Andrew Cyril Drummond [*see* E. Perth, colls.]. *Residence,* Cadland,
Fawley, Southampton.——Virginia Anne (*Hon. Mrs. Richard Storey*), *b.* 1936: *m.* 1961, the
Hon. Richard Storey, of Greystone House, Settrington Malton. Yorks., and 7, Douro Place, W8
[*see* B. Buckton].——Belinda Jane, *b.* 1940: *m.* 1962, Mark Singleton Evans of 6, Argyll Rd.,

W8, and has issue living, Arthur Nicolas Singleton, *b.* 1963,—Alexander Kenelm Singleton, *b.* 1970,—Amanda Elizabeth Singleton, *b.* 1966.——April Mary, *b.* 1945: *m.* 1969, Thomas Vernon Patridge, of 40, Princedale Rd., W11, and has issue living, William Kenelm Thomas, *b.* 1972,—Annabel Elizabeth Diana *b.* 1974.——Alison Rose (twin), *b.* 1945: *m.* 1972, Patrick Dermot Maloney, of 30, Albert Mansions, Albert Bridge Rd., SW11 and has issue living, Elizabeth Mary, *b.* 1974.——Joanna Storm, *b.* 1947: *m.* 1974, Richard Henry Cornwall-Legh, of High Legh House, Knutsford, Cheshire.

Mother living—Natalie Maud (Blackburn House, Hopton, Diss, Norfolk), yr. da. of the late Ernest Grey, of North Beacons, Conway: *m.* 1937, Lt.-Cdr. William Arthur Seton Cayley (ante), who *d.* 1964.

Collateral Branches living.

Granddaughter of Digby Leonard Arthur Cayley (grandfather of 11th baronet), el. son of Digby Cayley, 2nd son of 7th baronet:—
Issue of the late Maj. Digby Coddington Cayley, *b.* 1895, *d.* 1965: *m.* 1924, Beatrice Elizabeth Eleanora (Coolmore House, Thomastown, co. Kilkenny), da. of Robert Charles Campbell-Renton, of Lamberton, and Mordington, Berwick-on-Tweed:—
Pauline Grace, *b.* 1924.——Katherine Sonia (*Baroness ffrench*), *b.* 1926: *m.* 1954, the 7th Baron ffrench.——Amanda Beatrice, *b.* 1938.

Grandchildren of the late Adm. George Cuthbert Cayley, CB, 2nd son of Digby Cayley (ante):—
Issue of the late Capt. Charles Paul Cuthbert Cayley, RE, *b.* 1906, *d.* (on active service during European War) 1945: *m.* 1939, Cassandra Rosamond Elaine (Lullingstone, Bardwell, nr. Bury St. Edmunds, Suffolk, who *m.* 2ndly, 1946, John Sarginson, who *d.* 1972), da. of Sir Digby Algernon Hall Legard, 13th Bt.:—
George Paul (6, Highfield Eye, Suffolk, IP23 7BP), *b.* 1940; ed. at Felsted: *m.* 1967, Shirley Southwell, da. of Frank Woodward Petford, of Kirby Cane, Norfolk, and has issue living, Paul Alistair, *b.* 1971,—Kevin George, *b.* 1974.——Sarah Philadelphia, *b.* 1943.

Granddaughter of the late Digby Cayley (ante):—
Issue of the late Capt. Harry Francis Cayley, D.S.O., R.N., *b.* 1873, *d.* 1954 : *m.* 1900, Margery, who *d.* 1901, da. of Sir Thomas George Freake, 2nd Bt. :—
Alexandra Margery Eileen, *b.* 1901: *m.* 1928, Lt.-Cdr. Arthur Frank Armitage, RN (ret.), of Oldlands Hall, Uckfield, Sussex, and has issue living, Mark Cecil Christopher, *b.* 1937,—Diana Eileen, *b.* 1932: *m.* 1956, John Trevor Lewis, of Gosport House, Laugharne, Carmarthenshire.

Grandchildren of the late Rev. Reginald Arthur Cayley, 3rd son of 7th baronet:—
Issue of the late Capt. Edmund Henry George Cayley, *b.* 1870, *d.* 1945: *m.* 1st, 1898, Marie Olga, who *d.* 1910, da. of Otto Martin, of Valparaiso, Chile; 2ndly, 1914, Laura Eugénie Beatrice, who *d.* 1949, da. of the late George Fox:—
Digby Edgar Martin (c/o Lloyds Bank, Ltd., Golders Green, N.W.11), *b.* 1904; Master Mariner, late Colombo Pilot Ser., and Lt.-Cdr. RNVR: *m.* 1931, Dorothy, who *d.* 1972, da. of the late Thomas Allen Harper, of Edgbaston, Birmingham, and Sandgate, Queensland.——Evelyn Olga Vivienne, *b.* 1899: *m.* 1923, Wilhelm Wilkendorf, of Quilpue, and has issue living, Heinz Ferdinand Otto (of Quilpue, Chile), *b.* 1927: *m.* 1958, Ursula Wilckens, of Valparaiso, Chile, and has issue living, Richard *b.* 1959, Astrid *b.* 1960,—Harold Christian (Casilla 3070, Santiago, Chile), *b.* 1934: *m.* 1966, Senta Schwarzenberg, of Santiago, and has issue living, Robert Christian *b.* 1970, Stephan Alfred (twin) *b.* 1970, Helga Veronica *b.* 1968.

Granddaughters of the late Capt. Edmund Henry George Cayley (ante):—
Issue of the late Squadron Leader Damyon Edmund Martin Cayley, *b.* 1909, *d.* 1957 : *m.* 1944, Mary Ann, who *d.* 1973, da. of Stephen Taylor, of Sheffield:—
Barbara Ann, *b.* 1945: *m.* 1962, Victor Mason, and has issue living, Michael Shaun, *b.* 1965,—Deborah Anne, *b.* 1963.——Patricia Janis, *b.* 1948: *m.* 19—.

Grandsons of the late Rev. Edward Cartwright Cayley (infra):—
Issue of the late Arthur Bowen Cayley, *b.* 1898, *d.* 1973: *m.* 1921, Katherine Vanderwerken, who *d.* 1973, da. of Peleg Howland, of Toronto:—
Edward Cartwright (Holderness School, Plymouth, New Hampshire, USA), *b.* 1922; ed. at Trin. Coll. Sch., Port Hope, and Toronto Univ. (BA); MA Columbia Univ.; Lt-Cdr. RCNVR; Assist. Headmaster of Holderness Sch.; 1939-45 War: *m.* 1st, 1944 (m. diss. 1956) Margaret Noble, of Mansfield, Notts.; 2ndly, 1956, Catherine Norma, dal of the late Alexander Stuart, of Eganville, Ont., and has issue living (by 1st m.) David Cartwright, *b.* 1946,—Susan Margaret, *b.* 1948,—Catherine Jane, *b.* 1952.——Peleg Howland (Glen Lea, High Pitfold, Hindhead, Surrey), *b.* 1924; ed. at The Grove, Lakefield, Ont.; Capt. RCN (ret.): *m.* 1st, 1945 (m. diss. 1953), Freda Rosemary, da. of Alfred Cotter, of 8, Cherryhill, Beechlands, Belfast; 2ndly, 1955, Patricia Challinor, da. of Dr. John C. Poole, of Craig Allen, Lettermore, Argyll, and has issue living, (by 1st m.) Jennifer Margaret, *b.* 1947,—(by 2nd m.) John Howland, *b.* 1956,—Richard Arthur, *b.* 1960,—Christopher Peter, *b.* 1966.

Issue of the late Hugh Cartwright Cayley, *b.* 1901, *d.* 1967: *m.* 1st, 1928, Ethel Ann Farquharson, who *d.* 1934, da. of Wilmot L. Matthews; 2ndly, 1940, Gladys (10, Lamport Av., Apt. 105, Toronto, 5), da. of J. T. Large:—
(By 1st m.), Hugh Cartwright (78A, Chesnut Park Rd., Toronto, 5) *b.* 1932.

Granddaughters of the late Rev. John D'Arcy Cayley, el. son of William Cayley, M.P., 2nd son of John Cayley, *b.* 1761, el. son of John Cayley, *b.* 1730, 2nd son of Cornelius Cayley, *b.* 1692, 5th son of Cornelius Cayley, 4th son of 1st baronet :—
Issue of the late Rev. Edward Cartwright Cayley, D.D., *b.* 1864, *d.* 1921 : *m.* 1895, Alice, who *d.* 1951, da. of the late Rev. A. J. Broughall, formerly R. of St. Stephen's, Toronto :—
Alice Margaret, *b.* 1896: *m.* 1925, Arthur Arundel Harcourt-Vernon, who *d.* 1971 [*see* B. Vernon, colls.]. *Residence*, 137, Heddington Ave., Toronto, Canada.——Sylvia, *b.* 1909: *m.* 1937, the Ven. Terence Patrick Crosthwait, Archdeacon of York. *Residence*, 182, Brook St., Toronto 12, Canada.——Ray D'Arcy, *b.* 1912: *m.* 1947, William Ramsay Osler. *Residence*, R. R. No. 1, Saanichtown, Vancouver Island, BC.

Grandchildren of the late William Cayley, M.P. (ante) :—
Issue of the late Francis Cayley, *b.* 1845, *d.* 1909 : *m.* 1874, Jane Isabel, who *d.* 1920, da. of the late Henry Easton, Collector of Customs, of Cobourg, Ontario :—
William Henry, *b.* 1881.——Emma Robinson, *b.* 1876.——Adelaide Mary, *b.* 1877 : *m.* 19—, R.H. Strickland.——Muriel Isabel, *b.* 1879 : *m.* 19—, Jay Scholefield. *Residence,*

Grandchildren of the late Claud Thornton Cayley, son of the late John Cayley, *b.* 1816 (infra) :—
Issue of the late Claud D'Arcy Cayley, *b.* 1882, *d.* 1948: *m.* 1917, Lilian Gertrude, who *d.* 1943, da. of R. Hall, of Retford, Notts :—
Robert Edward Digby, *b.* 1918: *m.* 1942, Mary Robson. *Residence,*

Issue of the late Capt. Edward St. Quinton Cayley, *b.* 1887, *d.* 1941: *m.* 1916, Sybil Frances, who *d.* 1975, da. of the late Rev. Joseph Alfred Halloran, of The Old Parsonage, Ospringe, Faversham:—

Patricia St. Quintin, *b.* 1922 : *m.* 1948, Anthony Bruce Askew, and has issue living, Rory Anthony Rank, *b.* 1949,—Cleone St. Quintin, *b.* 1952. *Residence*, Tophill Farm, Withyam, near Hartfield, Sussex.

Issue of the late Charles Knightley Cayley, *b.* 1888, *d.* 1916 : *m.* 1915, Alice Leach, of S. Africa :—

Alice Knightley, *b.* 1916 : *m.* 1940, Christian Rosslee, and has issue living, Jean, *b.* 1944,—Gail, *b.* 1946. *Residence*, 50, Hannaben Street, Linksfield Ridge, Johannesburg, S. Africa.

Granddaughter of the late John Cayley, *b.* 1816, 4th son of the late John Cayley, *b.* 1761 (ante) :—

Issue of the late Francis Osmund Cayley, *b.* 1856, *d.* 1921 : *m.* 1882, Marion Louisa, who *d.* 1943, da. of Sir James Lukin Robinson, 2nd Bt. :—

Marjorie Gordon, *b.* 1897: *m.* 1925, John William Gamble Boyd, and has issue living, John William Gamble *b.* 1929; RCAF —Philip Cayley, *b.* 1932; RCAF,—Peter Beverley, *b.* 1935. *Residence*, Toronto, Canada.

Grandson of the late Sir Richard Cayley (infra) :—

Issue of the late Hugh Charles Cayley, *b.* 1869, *d.* 1945 : *m.* 1899, Annie Beatrice, who *d.* 1951, da. of Alfred Wilkins, of 43, Earl's Court Square, S.W.:—

Richard Wilkins, *b.* 1902 ; ed. at Aldenham, and at Imperial Coll. of Science and Technology (B.Sc. Engineering 1924) ; formerly Capt. R.E.M.E.: *m.* 1935, Joan Harvey, da. of the late Dr. E. Harvey Sutcliff, of Torrington, N. Devon, and has issue living, William Richard (33, Geraint's Way, Cowbridge, S. Glam.), *b.* 1944: *m.* 1972, Mary Elizabeth, da. of George Arthur Baillie, of The Riggs, Midlem, Selkirk, and has issue living, Alexander Richard *b.* 1973, Arthur Edward (twin) *b.* 1973,—Mary Catherine, *b.* 1938: *m.* 1963, Richard John Wood, of Blücher, Wellington Coll., Crowthorne, Berks, and has issue living, James Julian *b.* 1965, Jonathan Mark *b.* 1968,—Janet Rose, *b.* 1940: *m.* 1965, Barry Keith Palmer, of The Villa, Kingstone, Hereford, and has issue living, Daniel Barry *b.* 1970, Louise Janet *b.* 1967, Eleanor Mary *b.* 1969. *Residence*, 40, The Woodlands, Esher, Surrey.

Grandchildren of the late Dep.-Surg.-Gen. Henry Cayley, C.M.G., F.R.C.S. 4th son of the late Edward Cayley *b.* 1782, only son of Edward Cayley, *b.* 1733, 3rd son of Cornelius Cayley, *b.* 1692 (ante):—

Issue of the late Cyril Henry Cayley, M.D., *b.* 1865, *d.* 1905 : *m.* 1893, Maria Charlotte, who *d.* 1960, da. of the late William Black, of Christchurch, New Zealand :—

Henry Douglas, *OBE* (Virginia Lodge, Boronia St., Bowral, NSW), *b.* 1904; formerly Ch. Gen. Manager, Nat. & Grindlay's Bank, Ltd., London; OBE (Civil) 1946: *m.* 1940, Nora Innes, da. of the late Maj. Nigel Paton, of Covehithe, Wrentham, Suffolk, and has issue living, Neil Henry (7, Cooleena Rd., Elanora Heights, Sydney, NSW), *b.* 1943: *m.* 1970, Julie, da. of A. I. Bowen, of Melbourne, Aust., and has issue living, Henry James *b.* 1972, Victoria Anne *b.* 1971,—Innes Margaret, *b.* 1941: *m.* 1971, Terence John Benson, and has issue living, Andrew Douglas *b.* 1973, Mark David *b.* 1975,—Lindsay Mary, *b.* 1948: *m.* 1970, Ian Leslie James.——Cyril, *MC, b.* 1905; Maj. (ret.) Indian Army; 1939-45 War in Middle East and Italy (wounded, MC). ——Dorothy St. Quintin, *b.* 1895. *Residence*, Cherrahurst, 50, Connaught Rd., Fleet, Hants.

Granddaughter of Maj.-Gen. Douglas Edward Cayley, C.B., C.M.G., 3rd son of the late Dep.-Surg.-Gen. Henry Cayley, C.M.G., F.R.C.S., (ante):—

Issue of the late Com. Richard Douglas Cayley, D.S.O., R.N., *b.* 1907, *d.* (on active service, 1943: *m.* 1933, Nancy (who *m.* 2ndly, 1943, Herbert Samuel Gild, FRCS, of Little Vinesgate, Brasted, Chart, Kent), yr. da. of Edward Coutts, of Swefling, Fleet, Hants:—

Jennifer Jane, *b.* 1934: *m.* 1956, Sqdn.-Ldr. Arthur Christopher Doggett, RAF [B. Horder], and has issue living, Antonia Clare, *b.* 1958,—Jessia, *b.* 1963.

Grandson of the late Bernard Cayley (infra):—

Issue of the late William Bernard Cayley, *b.* 1907, *d.* 1963: *m.* 1935, Bronwen, da. of R. C. Young, of Yanco, N.S. Wales:—

John William Douglas (Fulford Waters, PO Box 17, Yanco, NSW), *b.* 1938; ed. at Geelong Gram. Sch., Victoria, and at Melbourne Univ. (BSc agriculture): *m.* 1964, Glenys Robertson Wilson, and has issue living, Ross Andrew, *b.* 1965,—Fiona Bronwen, *b.* 1968.

Grandchildren of the late Dep.-Surg.-Gen. Henry Cayley, C.M.G., F.R.C.S. (ante):—

Issue of the late Bernard Cayley, *b.* 1871, *d.* 1914 : *m.* 1904, Gertrude Mary, who *d.* 1942, da. of J. C. Large :—

Hugh Edward (19, Hill Court, Wimbledon, SW19), *b.* 1910; ed. at Clifton Coll., and at Wye Agricultural Coll.; Middle East 1940-43, Burma 1943-45 as Capt. RE; with AVIS.——Agnes Mary (53, Cobham Rd., Fetcham, Leatherhead, Surrey), *b.* 1906: *m.* 1926, Maj. Charles Fraser Raper, late Indian Army, who *d.* 1965, and has issue living, John James, *b.* 1927,—Charles Richard, *b.* 1929.

Issue of the late Rear-Adm. Henry Priaulx Cayley, R Australian Navy, *b.* 1877, *d.* 1942: *m.* 1906, Ethel Mary, who *d.* 1940, da. of Thomas Hewitt, of Sandcroft, Baynards, near Horsham:—

Henry Francis (44A, Shirley Rd., Wollstoncraft, Sydney, NSW), *b.* 1910; ed. at Church of England Gram. Sch., Geelong, Australia: *m.* 1940, Marea, da. of Colin Borthwick, of Sydney, Australia, and has issue living, Charles Francis, *b.* 1943,—Susan Aneva Mary, *b.* 1947,—Mary Lorraine, *b.* 1950.

Grandchildren of the late Arthur Cayley, 6th son of the late Edward Cayley, *b.* 1782 (ante) :—

Issue of the late Osbert Arthur Cayley, *b.* 1869, *d.* 1947 : *m.* 1910, Dorothy, who *d.* 1942, da. of the late Rev. George Herbert Lewis (Indian Ecclesiastical Establishment, retired) ,of Allandale, Burnham, Somerset :—

Forde Everard de Wend, *MBE, MD, FRCP, b.* 1915; formerly Capt. RAMC; 1939-45 War in Far East (prisoner, MBE); MBE (Mil) 1946: *m.* 1941, Eileen Lilian, da. of the late Arthur C. Dalton, and has issue living, Arthur Charles Digby (33, Kenilworth Rd., Ealing, W5), *b.* 1946; ed. at Brighton Coll., and Middx. Hosp.; MB, BS, MRCP: *m.* 1969, Jeanette Ann, MB, BS, da. of the late G. Avery, of Plymouth, and has issue living, George Cornelius Forde *b.* 1971,—Michael Forde *b.* 1950; ed. at Brighton Coll., and St. John's Coll., Oxon (BA). *Residence*, 67, Wish Rd., Hove 3, Sussex——Frances Dorothy, *b.* 1912: *m.* 1941, S. A. Yates. *Residence*, 33, Kenilworth Rd., Ealing, W5.

The Sire de Cailly (or Cayley), from Cailly in Normandy, was one of the followers of William the Conqueror, and is celebrated in the *Roman de Rou*. His descendants were settled in Norfolk for three centuries, when the chief representative of the family removed to Yorkshire, where his descendants have since remained. The 1st baronet, Sir William Cayley, was knighted by Charles I., and created a baronet by Charles II., for his services in the Civil War. He married Dorothy, daughter of Sir William St. Quintin, of Harpham, a lineal descendant of Joan, daughter of Edward I. The 6th baronet, Sir George, was a pioneer of aviation. In 1804 he made a successful model glider, and in 1809 a full sized glider which he flew with ballast in lieu of a pilot. In 1852 he launched the first man-carrying glider. The 9th baronet, Sir George Everard Arthur, Capt. Roy. Defence Corps, *d.* (on active ser. during European War) 1917.

CAYZER, Creation (U.K.) 1904, of Gartmore, co. Perth.

Cautiously but fearlessly.

Sir JAMES ARTHUR CAYZER, 5th *Baronet*; *b.* Nov. 15th, 1931 ; *s.* his brother, *Sir* NIGEL JOHN, 1943 ; *ed.* at Eton.

Arms—Party per chevron azure and argent, in chief two fleurs de lis or, and in base an ancient ship with three masts, sails furled sable, colours flying gules ; a chief invected of the third thereon three estoiles of the first. Crest—A sea-lion erect proper, holding in the dexter paw a fleur-de-lis, and supporting with the sinister an estoile, both or.

Seat—Kinpurnie Castle, Newtyle, Angus.   *Club*—Carlton.

Sisters living—Deva, *b.* 1923: *m.* 1946, Lieut.-Com. John Studholme Brownrigg, DSC, RN, who *d.* 1971, only son of the late Adm. Sir (Henry John) Studholme Brownrigg, KBE, CB, DSO, and has issue living, Henry John Studholme, *b.* 1961. *Residence*, Badgers Wood, Lymore Lane, Milford on Sea, Lymington, Hants.——Angela, *b.* 1926: *m.* 1950, Anthony Malcolm Galliers-Pratt, and has issue living, Rupert Anthony, *b.* 1951: *m.* 1973, Alexandra Mary, da. of Maj. Hugh Rose, of Burton House, Buriton, nr. Petersfield,—Nigel Kenneth, *b.* 1954,—Anthony Charles, *b.* 1958. *Residences*, Mawey Hall, Cleobury Mortimer, Worcs.; 40, Belgrave Sq., SW1.

Aunts living (daughters of 2nd baronet)—Winifred Mary (The Bungalow, Garlenick Manor, Grampound, Cornwall), *b.* 1899: *m.* 1917, Rear-Adm. Niel O'Neill, RN, who *d.* 1953, and has issue living, Bryan Geoffrey, *OBE, DSC, RN* (Spinneys, 26, Park Av., Camberley, Surrey), *b.* 1918; is Cdr.; OBE (Mil) 1964: *m.* 1944, Alison M. MacKenzie, and has issue living Niel *b.* 1953, Susan Clodagh *b.* 1945: *m.* 1967, Lt. Michael Anthony Lynch, RAN, of Sydney (and has issue living, Adam Michael *b.* 1969, Dominic Paul *b.* 1972), Sheelagh Mary *b.* 1950,—Yvonne Mary, *b.* 1919: *m.* 1943, James Macdonald McGlashan, of St. Ives, Cambuskenneth, Stirlingshire, and has issue living, Alan John *b.* 1944, Fiona Mary *b.* 1948,—Dawn, *b.* 1932: *m.* 1960, Ernest A. Ostro, Pugs Corner, Abinger Common, Dorking, Surrey, and has issue living, Ernest Neil Armstrong Simon *b.* 1970, Anne Katherine Winifred *b.* 1961, Linde Elizabeth Tamsin *b.* 1963,—Maureen, *b.* 1934: *m.* 1956, Lt.-Cdr. Jeremy D. Tetley, RN, of Garlenick Manor, Grampound, Cornwall, and has issue living, Robin Neil *b.* 1959, Mark Geoffrey *b.* 1962, Rachel Elizabeth, *b.* 1957.——Estelle Agnes, *b.* 1901: *m.* 1923, Capt. Philip G. Marr, RFC and RAF, who *d.* 1966, and has issue living, Celia, *b.* 1927: *m.* 1958, Noel J. Knights, of Brynhill, The Twitten, Crowborough, Sussex, and has issue living, Julia Carol *b.* 1961, Isabel Elizabeth *b.* 1964,—Janice Estelle, *b.* 1936: *m.* 1961, Brian W. Ford, of Kinpurnie, Quirindi, NSW, and has issue living, Justin Harry *b.* 1966, Simon Philip *b.* 1968, Deborah Estelle *b.* 1969, Jodi Ann *b.* 1963. *Residence*, 14, Victoria Court, Grand Av., Hove, Sussex.——Iris Cecilie (14, Victoria Court, Grand Av., Hove), *b.* 1905: *m.* 1938 (m. diss. 1968), Duncan Alistair McKellar, and has issue living, Heather Joy, *b.* 1943: *m.* 1965, Kenneth Leonard Hyman, of Flat 1, Little Silver, Marsham Way, Gerrard's Cross, Bucks., and has issue living, Jeanne Cecile *b.* 1966, Tara Penelope *b.* 1968.——Bernice Amice *b.* 1906.

Widow living of 3rd Baronet—BEATRICE EILEEN, *O.B.E.* (*Lady Cayzer*), el. da. of the late James Meakin, of Westwood Manor, Staffordshire [E. Sondes]; O.B.E. (Civil) 1963: *m.* 1919, Sir Charles William Cayzer, M.P., 3rd baronet, who *d.* 1940. *Residence*, Kinpurnie Castle, Newtyle, Angus.

Collateral Branches living.

Issue living of the late August Bernard Tellefsen Cayzer, 3rd son of 1st baronet, who was *cr.* a *Baronet* 1921:—
Of whom *Sir* (WILLIAM) NICHOLAS, 2nd *Bt.*, *b.* Jan. 21st, 1910 ; is *h.p.* to this baronetcy.

Issue of the late Arthur Edward Bryant Cayzer, 4th son of 1st baronet, *b.* 1878, *d.* 1909: *m.* 1905, Louise Margaret, who *d.* 1966, da. of John Birkett, of Kendal:—
Nancy Avis Louise, *b.* 1909: *m.* 1936, Alister Curtis Leeson, and has issue living, Ian Arthur (Talana, Esher Close, Esher, Surrey), *b.* 1937: *m.* 1965, Eileen Margaret Tennent, and has issue living, Sally Louise *b.* 1968, Patricia Anne *b.* 1971. *Residence*, Heathfield, Chilworth, Hants.

Issue of the late Sir Herbert Robin Cayzer, 5th son of 1st baronet, who was *cr.* Baron Rotherwick 1939 [see that title].

Issue of the late Major Harold Stanley Cayzer, 6th son of 1st baronet, *b.* 1882 *d.* 1948: *m.* 1908, Mary Kate, who *d.* 1946, el. da. of Joseph Hume Dudgeon, of Merville, Booterstown, co. Dublin:—
Harold Stanley, *b.* 1910; ed. at Eton; Major 11th Hussars (Reserve); 1939-45 War (wounded): *m.* 1st, 1943 (m. diss. 1956), Doussa, da. of Fahmy Bey Wissa, of Ramleh, Egypt; 2nd, 1959 (m. diss. 1967), Pamela, da. of Geoffrey Myers, of Lagos, Nigeria; 3rdly, 1971, Beatrice Fairbanks Murray. *Residences*, 41, Ovington Sq., SW3; 95, Eaton Sq., SW1.

The 1st baronet, Sir Charles Cayzer, was head of the firm of Cayzer, Irvine and Co. (Limited), steamship owners, of London, Liverpool, Manchester, and Glasgow, and sat as M.P. for Barrow-in-Furness (C) 1892 to 1906.   The 3rd baronet, Sir Charles William Cayzer, was M.P. for Cheshire, City of Chester Div. (C) 1922-40, and a Member of Roy. Co. of Archers (King's Body Guard for Scotland.   The 4th baronet, Sir Nigel John Cayzer, Lieut. Scots Guards, *d.* (killed in action in Italy) 1943.

CAYZER, Creation (U.K.) 1921, of Roffey Park, Horsham, co. Sussex.

Sir (WILLIAM) NICHOLAS CAYZER, 2nd *Baronet* ; *b.* Jan. 21st, 1910 ; *s.* his father, *Lieut.-Com. Sir* AUGUST BERNARD TELLEFSEN, 1943 ; ed. at Eton, and at Corpus Christi Coll., Camb. ; is *h.-p.* to his kinsman's Baronetcy (*cr.* 1904), Chm. of Cayzer, Irvine & Co., Ltd., of Clan Line Steamers, Ltd., of British and Commonwealth Shipping Co., Ltd., and of Union Castle Mail Steamship Co., Ltd.; Chm. of Liverpool Steam Shipowners' Asso. 1945, of Gen. Council of British Shipping 1959, and of Chamber of Shipping's British Liner Cttee. 1960-63, Pres. Chamber of Shipping of UK 1959, and of Inst. of Marine Engineers 1963-4, a Member of Min. of Transport's Shipping Advisory Panel 1962-64, and Prime Warden of Shipwrights' Co. 1969-70; *m.* 1935, Betty, el. da. of the late Owain Williams, and has issue.

Caute sed impavide.
Cautiously, but fearlessly.

Arms—Per chevron azure and argent, two estoiles or and an ancient ship with three masts, sails furled sable, colours flying gules, on a chief of the third three fleur-de-lis of the first. **Crest**—A sea-lion erect proper, gorged with a naval crown, holding in his dexter paw a fleur-de-lis gold.

Residences—95, Eaton Sq., S.W.1; The Grove, Walsham-le-Willows, Suffolk.

Daughters living—Nichola, *b.* 1937 : *m.* 1956, Michael Keith Beale Colvin, late Lieut. Grenadier Guards, and has issue living, James Michael Beale, *b.* 1965,—Amanda, *b.* 1957,—Arabella Nichola, *b.* 1960. *Residence*, Tangley House, nr. Andover, Hants.——Elizabeth, *b.* 1946.

Brother living—BERNARD GILBERT STANCOMB, *b.* March 14th, 1914 ; ed. at Eton, and at Magdalene Coll., Camb.; late Major Queen's Westminsters, King's Roy. Rifle Corps (T.A.) ; is a Dep.-Chm. of British & Commonwealth Shipping Co. Ltd., and of Union-Castle Mail Steamship Co. Ltd., and a Director of Cayzer, Irvine & Co., Ltd., and of Clan Line Steamers, Ltd. *Residences*, 52, Eaton Terrace, S.W.1 ; Parish's House, Timsbury, Somerset.

Sister living—Ina Heather, *b.* 1907 : *m.* 1st, 1934, Frederick Herbert Marsden Kaye, who *d* 1952, from whom she had obtained a divorce 1939; 2ndly, 1940, Maj. Richard Buckley, who *d.* 1971, and has issue living (by 1st m.) Pamela Heather, *b.* 1936: *m.* 1956, Lt.-Col. Thomas Nigel Bromage, OBE, Gren. Gds., of Barland House, Presteign, Powys, and has issue living, Charles Nigel *b.* 1960, Nichola *b.* 1963,—(by 2nd m.) Peter Neville (6, Albert Place, Victoria Rd., W8), *b.* 1942: *m.* 1967, Mary Barabel Stewart, and has issue living, Arabella Mary *b.* 1970, Roseanna Neville *b.* 1972,—Hermione Mary, *b.* 1944: *m.* 1975, Paul George Homer Crosfield. *Residences*, Rapkyns, Horsham, Sussex; Westerhall, Langholm, Dumfries-shire.

The 1st baronet, Lieut.-Com. Sir August Bernard Tellefsen Cayzer, R.N. [3rd son of Sir Charles William Cayzer, 1st Bt. (*cr.* 1904)], was Chm. of Cayzer, Irvine & Co., Ltd., and other cos., and a Director of Suez Canal Co.

CHADWICK, Creation (U.K.) 1935, of Bidston, co. Palatine of Chester.

Sir ROBERT (PETER) BURTON CHADWICK, 2nd *Baronet ; b.* June 22nd, 1911 ; *s.* his father, *Sir* ROBERT BURTON *BURTON-CHADWICK*, 1951 ; ed. at St. George's, Harpenden, Herts.; European War 1942-45 with New Zealand Mil. Force in N. Africa and Italy : *m.* 1st, 1937 (marriage dissolved 1949), Rosalind Mary, da. of Harry John Stott ; 2ndly, 1950, Beryl Joan, da. of Stanley Frederick J. Brailsford, and has issue by 1st and 2nd marriages.

Honour in purity.

Arms—Azure, on water in base barry wavy argent and vert an ancient ship or, sail set and banner flying at the stern of the second, each charged with a martlet of the first, at the masthead a pennon gules fimbriated argent, in chief a lion passant between two mullets of the last. **Crest**—Or and azure a demi-sea horse proper gorged with a naval crown and holding between the fins a portcullis chained or.

Residence—29, Myrtle Street, Lower Hutt, New Zealand.

Son living—By 2nd marriage—JOSHUA KENNETH, *b.* Feb. 1st, 1954.

Daughters living—By 1st marriage—Diana, *b.* 1938.——Sally Virginia, *b.* 1940.—**By 2nd marriage** —Wendy Lorraine, *b.* 1951.

Sister living—Gwynfa Burton, *b.* 1906 : *m.* 1935 (marriage dissolved 1955), George D'Arcy Edmondson, C.M.G., C.V.O., O.B.E. *Residence*, 40, Ovington Street, S.W.3.

The 1st baronet, Sir Robert Burton Burton-Chadwick (el. son of the late Joseph Chadwick, of Liverpool), assumed by deed poll 1936, the additional surname of Burton ; was head of the firm of Chadwick & Askew, shipowners, of Liverpool and London and Parliamentary Sec. to the Board of Trade 1924-28. He sat as M.P. for Barrow-in-Furness (C) 1918-22, and for Wallasey 1922-31.

Chadwyck-Healey, see Healey.

CHAMBERLAIN, Creation (U.K.) 1828, of London.

Sir HENRY WILMOT CHAMBERLAIN, 5th *Baronet;*
b. May 17th, 1899; *s.* his father, *Sir* HENRY HAMILTON
ERROL, 1936.

Arms—Gules, within an orle argent charged with eight mullets azure as
armillary sphere or. *Crest*—An eagle displayed proper, the dexter claw
resting on an armillary sphere or.

Address—c/o Church, Adams, Tatham & Co., 23/25, Bell St., Reigate,
Surrey.

Collateral Branches living.

Issue of the late Neville Colin Bowie Chamberlain, 2nd son of
3rd baronet, *b.* 1863, *d.* 1948: *m.* 1893, Jessie Maud, who
d. 1950, only child of the late Frederick Kearsley Hargreaves,
of Bolton:—

Margaret Ursula May, *b.* 1901. *Residence,* Blue Tiles, Beehive Lane,
Ferring, Sussex.

Spes et fides.
Hope and faith.

Granddaughter of the late Neville Colin Bowie
Chamberlain (ante):—
Issue of the late Neville Henry Hargreaves Chamberlain, *b.*
1894, *d.* 1962: *m.* 1922, May (of 7, Swathmore Drive, Great
Crosby, Liverpool, 23), da. of the late Philip Byrne, of Great
Crosby, Liverpool, 23:—

Patricia Ursula, *b.* 1929: *m.* 1951, George Hartley, and has issue living, David Colin, *b.* 1961,—
Jennifer Mary, *b.* 1956. *Residence,* 53, Rosedale Av., Crosby, Liverpool, 23.

Granddaughter of the late Lt.-Cdr. Henry Chamberlain, RN, 2nd son of the
late Rear-Adm. William Charles Chamberlain, 3rd son of 1st baronet:—
Issue of the late Capt. Neville Grahame Chamberlain, *b.* 1896, *d.* 1945: *m.* 1927, Edna Claire,
who *d.* 1951, da. of John Spence-Nicol, of Wellington, New Zealand:—
Pamela Barbara, *b.* 1928 : *m.* 1950, Peter James Pound, and has issue living, William Grahame, *b.*
1951,—Toby James, *b.* 1954,—Hugo Giles Barclay *b.* 1957. *Residence,* 4, Northcote Mansions,
Heath St., Hampstead, NW3.

Sir Henry Chamberlain, 1st baronet, was Consul-General and Chargé d'Affaires in Brazil.

Champion de Crespigny, see de Crespigny.

DALRYMPLE-CHAMPNEYS, Creation (U.K.) 1910, of Littlemead, Nutley, Sussex.

Not afraid to die for my country.

Sir WELDON DALRYMPLE-CHAMPNEYS,
C.B., D.M., 2nd *Baronet ; b.* May 7th, 1892 ;
s. his father, *Sir* FRANCIS HENRY, *D.M.,*
F.R.C.P., 1930 ; ed. at Oriel Coll., Oxford
(MA, BCh, DM, DPH, Hon. Fellow since
1968) ; MRCP London 1925, and
FRCP 1935; was Dep. Ch. Med.
Officer, Min. of Health 1940-56; Past Pres. of
Sections of Epidemiology and State Med.,
of Comparative Medicine, and of History of
Medicine, Roy. Soc. of Medicine, and Pres. of
Haemophilia So., Past Chm. and Fellow of
Roy. Vet. Coll., a Trustee and Member of
Council of Animal Health Trust, Vice-Pres.
Roy. So. of Health (Chm. of Council 1948),
and Pres. Oxon. branch, Mental Health
Assocn.; Member of Council of Roy. Coll. of
Physicians 1948-50, and Milroy Lecturer
1950; Hon. Physician to HM 1941-44; author
of several works on preventive medicine;
Lord of the Manor of Stanwick, Northants;
late Capt. Gren. Gds.; 1914-18 War in
France and Belgium (wounded, 1914-15 star, two medals); assumed by deed
poll 1924 the additional surname of Dalrymple; CB (Civil) 1957: *m.* 1st, 1924,
Anne Alwyn, *OBE,* who *d.* 1968, da. of the late Col. Arthur Spencer Pratt,
CB, CMG, of Orford Hall, Surrey; 2ndly, 1974, Norma Hull, da. of the late
Col. Richard Hull Lewis, of co. Cork, and widow of A. S. Russell, DSc, of
Ch. Ch., Oxford.

Arms—Quarterly, 1st and 4th, per pale ermine and sable a lion rampant or, a bordure engrailed
counter-changed charged with three grenades of the third, *Champneys ;* 2nd and 3rd or, on a saltire
couped azure between two cinquefoils ermine in pale and as many water bougets sable in fesse nine
lozenges of the first, *Dalrymple.* *Crests*—1st, a demi-blackamoor proper wreathed about the temples
or and holding in the dexter hand a ring of the last, garnished with a sapphire, *Champneys;* 2nd,
n front of a rock proper a cinquefoil ermine, *Dalrymple.*

Residence,—6A, Moreton Rd., Oxford. *Clubs*—Athenæum, Guards'.

Sister living—Margaret de l'Etang, *b.* 1887: *m.* 1915, the Rev. Eric George Southam, Canon
Emeritus, and former Provost of Guildford, who *d.* 1952. *Residence,* St. George's Nursing Home,
Ringwood Rd., Ferndown, Dorset.

The 1st baronet, Sir Francis Henry Champneys, D.M., F.R.C.P. (son of the late Very Rev.
William Weldon Champneys, Dean of Lichfield), was Past Pres. of Roy. So. of Med., Vice-Pres,
of British Coll. of Obstetricians and Gynæcologists, and first Chm. of Central Midwives Board :
m. 1876, Virginia Julian, who *d.* 1922, da. of Sir John Warrender Dalrymple, 7th Bt., of Leuchie,
North Berwick.

CHANCE, Creation (U.K.) 1900, of Grand Avenue, Hove, co. Sussex.

Sir ROGER JAMES FERGUSON CHANCE, *M.C.*, 3rd *Baronet*, el. son of the late George Ferguson Chance, 2nd son of 1st baronet ; *b.* Jan. 26th, 1893 ; *s.* his uncle, *Sir* WILLIAM, 1935 ; ed. at Eton, and at Trin. Coll., Camb. (B.A. 1918, M.A. 1921) ; Ph.D., London Univ. 1927 ; is Capt. (retired) Rifle Brig. ; Squadron-Leader R.A.F. Vol. Reserve 1940-41; acting Press Attaché at Berlin 1938; formerly Capt. 4th Dragoon Guards and Rifle Bde.; 1914-18 War (twice wounded, despatches twice, MC): *m.* 1921, Mary Georgina, da. of the late Col. William Rowney, and has issue.

Deo non fortuna.

Through God, not by chance.

Arms—Gules, a saltire vair between two fleurs-de-lis in pale and as many towers in fesse argent. **Crest**—A demi-lion rampant gules, semée of annulets or, holding between the paws a sword erect entwined by a wreath of oak all proper.

Residence—9, Eaton Square, S.W.1. *Club*—Athenæum.

Son living—GEORGE JEREMY FFOLLIOTT (6, Wootton Court, Lillington Av., Leamington Spa., Warwicks.; Rhosgyll Fawr, Chwilog, Pwllheli, Caerns), *b.* Feb. 24th, 1926; late Lt. RNVR; a Dir. of Massey-Ferguson, Ltd., Coventry: *m.* 1950, his cousin, Cecila Mary Elizabeth, da. of Sir (William) Hugh (Stobart) Chance (infra), and has issue living, John Sebastian, *b.* 1954,—Roger William Tobias, *b.* 1960,—Victoria Katharine Elizabeth, *b.* 1952,—Helena Mary ffolliott, *b.* 1957.

Daughters living—Serena Mary Benedicta, *b.* 1928: *m.* 1953, Robert Temple Armstrong, CB, son of Sir Thomas Henry Wait Armstrong, and has issue living, Jane Orlanda, *b.* 1954,—Teresa Brigid, *b.* 1957. *Residence*, 6, Woronzow Road, N.W.8.—Teresa Margaret, *b.* 1930 : *m.* 1955, George Gilbert Kennedy, DFC, of Cashelnagor, Gortahork, co. Donegal, and has issue living, Seamus Michael ffolliott, *b.* 1963,—Miles Thomas Pitt, *b.* 1965.

Brother living—*Sir* (William) Hugh (Stobart), C.B.E., *b.* 1896 ; ed. at Eton, and at Trin. Coll., Camb. (B.A. 1920, M.A. 1924) ; was a Member of Smethwick County Borough Council 1940-45 (Chm. of Education Committee), and a Member of Roy. Commn. on Scottish Affairs 1952 ; has been a County Councillor for Worcestershire since 1946 (Chm. Education Cttee. 1957-64); a D.L.; European War 1914-18 as Lieut. Worcestershire Regt., and R.F.C.; High Sheriff of Worcestershire 1942; Knt. 1945, C.B.E. (Civil) 1958: *m.* 1st, 1926, Cynthia May, da. of the late Major A. F. B. Cresswell, of Cresswell and Harehope, Northumberland; 2ndly, 1961, Rachel (CARR), da. of the late Cyril Cameron R.H.A., of Tasmania, and has issue living, (by 1st marriage) William John Ferguson (of Shepley, Gingindhlovu, Zululand, Natal), *b.* 1929: *m.* 1951, Elizabeth Kathleen, da. V. J. S. Crookes, of Chartwell, Umzinto, Natal, and has issue living, Christopher John Hugh *b.* 1952, James William Frederick *b.* 1953, Richard George Ferguson *b.* 1956, Sarah Elizabeth *b.* 1960.—Hugh Nicolas (Harcourt Farm, Chorley, Bridgnorth, Salop), *b.* 1940: *m.* 1965, Caroline Susan, da. of P. E. M. Holmes, of Stourton House, Stourbridge, Worcs., and has issue living, Timothy William Holmes *b.* 1966, Henry Charles Hugh *b.* 1969, Lucy Emma *b.* 1971,—Kathleen Idonea Cresswell *b.* 1927: *m.* 1st, 1948 (m. diss. 1956), William Henry Dunamace Heaton-Armstrong, son of Sir John Dunamace Heaton-Armstrong, MVO; 2ndly, 1956 (m. diss. 1965), Lt.-Cdr. John Timothy Fetherston-Dilke, RN (ret.); 3rdly 1965, Colin Frederick Rogers, LDSRCS of The Coach House, Birlingham, Pershore, Worcs., and has issue living (by 1st m.), Anthony Eustace John *b.* 1950, Mary Suzanne Bertha *b.* 1949, Bridget Cynthia *b.* 1952, Rachael Catherine *b.* 1954, (by 2nd m.) Timothy Hugh *b.* 1958, Miranda Catherine *b.* 1956,—Cecilia Mary Elizabeth, *b.* 1928: *m.* 1950, her cousin, George Jeremy ffolliott Chance (ante),—Bridget Nicola, *b.* 1931: *m.* 1963, the Rt. Rev. John Richard Gordon Eastaugh, Lord Bishop of Hereford, of Bishops. House, The Palace, Hereford, and has issue living, James Gordon Mark *b.* 1964, Edward John Hugh *b.* 1970, Katharine Elizabeth Sophia *b.* 1967. *Residence*, The Clock House, Birlingham, Pershore, Worcs. *Club*, Leander.

Sister living—Katharine Dorothea, *b.* 1894. *Residence*, Cedar House, Burton, Christchurch, Dorset.

The 1st baronet was for many years head of the firm of Chance Bros. and Co. (manufacturers of dioptric illuminating apparatus for lighthouses, etc.), of Smethwick and Oldbury, near Birmingham.

CHAPMAN, Creation (U.K.) 1958, of Cleadon, co. Durham.

Mildly but firmly.

Sir ROBIN (ROBERT MACGOWAN) CHAPMAN, *C.B.E., T.D.*, 2nd *Baronet*; *b.* Feb. 12th, 1911; *s.* his father *Col. Sir* ROBERT, *C.B., C.M.G., C.B.E., D.S.O., T.D.* 1963; ed. at Marlborough (Senior Scholar) and at Corpus Christi Coll., Camb. (Exhibitioner, MA); a FCA and a Partner in the firm of Chapman, Hilton, Hutchinson and Dunford, of S. Shields, Chm. of James Hogg & Sons (N. Shields) Ltd., and of John W. Pratt Ltd., Chm. and Manager of NE Investment Trust Ltd., Joint Sec. and a Dir. of Shields Commercial Building Soc., a Dir. of Commercial Union Assurance Co., Ltd. (Local Board); a JP for co. Durham (High Sheriff 1960-61); Vice Lord-Lieut. for co. Tyne and Wear; late Lt.-Col. RA (TA); Hon. Col. 463rd Regt. (TA) 1963-67, and of Co. of Durham Regt. (RA) T & AVR 1967-72, and Dep. Hon. Col. Northumbrian Vols. TAVR 1972-4; a Trustee of Ingham

Infirmary, S. Shields 1946-49, of Netherton Approved Sch. 1948-57, a Member of Taxation and Research Cttee. of Institute of Chartered Accountants 1951-53, Chm. of No. Cos. Provincial Area, Conservative and Unionist Party 1954-57, a Member of Standing Joint Cttee. and of Police Authority 1955-59 and 1961-65, Chm. of Jarrow Div. Conservative and Unionist Assoc. 1957-60 (Pres. since 1962), and Pres. of N. Soc. of Chartered Accountants 1958-59, a Gov. of United Newcastle Hosps. 1957-64, Hon. Treasurer of Durham Co. Boy Scouts' Assocn. 1947-67, Manager of Finchdale Abbey Training Centre for the Disabled 1948-68, Chm. of Durham Diocesan Board of Finance 1965-70, and a Member of Durham Co. TA Assocn. 1948-68, and of N. of England TA Assocn. 1968-74; Chm. Durham Co. Scout Council 1972; Vice-Pres. of Northumberland and Durham Assocn. of Building Socs. since 1973; a Member of Cttee. of Northumberland and Durham Assocn. of Building Societies, of Durham Diocesan Synod, Pres. of S. Shields Boy Scouts Assocn., and of South Shields YMCA; 1939-45 War; CBE (Civil) 1961 : *m.* 1941, Barbara May, da. of Hubert Tonks, of Ceylon, and has issue.

Arms—Per chevron argent and gules a crescent counterchanged in dexter chief a portcullis chained sable over all in pale a sword point downwards proper pommel and hilt or. **Crest**—Issuant from a wreath of oak proper a dexter arm embowed vested gules cuffed argent grasping in the hand a harpoon also proper.

Residence—Cherry Tree House, Cleadon, nr. Sunderland, co. Tyne and Wear. *Clubs*—Junior Carlton, Hawks, County (Durham).

Sons living—DAVID ROBERT MACGOWAN (Rosemont, 2, West Meadows Rd., Cleadon, Sunderland, co. Tyne and Wear; Northern Constitutional Club), *b.* Dec. 16th, 1941; ed. at Marlborough, and at McGill Univ., Montreal (BCom); a Dir., North Eastern Investment Trust Ltd., of John W. Pratt, Ltd., and of other cos., and a partner, Wise, Speke & Co., Stock and Share Brokers, Newcastle-upon-Tyne: *m.* 1965, Maria Elizabeth, JP, da. of Dr. N. de Gosztonyi, of Pecs, Hungary, and has issue living, Michael Nicholas, *b.* 1969,—Christina Elisabeth *b.* 1970.——Peter Stuart (8, Chepstow Cres., W11 3EB) *b.* 1944; ed. at Marlborough, at Trin. Coll., Camb. (BA), and LSE (MSc): *m.* 1972, Joan, da. of R. S. V. Hewitt, of Washington, co. Tyne and Wear, and has issue living, Christopher, *b.* 1974.

Daughter living—Elizabeth Mary, *b.* 1946; ed. at Benenden, St. Aidan's Coll., Durham, and Columbia Univ., New York: *m.* 1967, Dr. Mark Ivan Levy, of 126, Corte Madera Av., Mill Valley, Cal. 94941, USA, and has issue living, Noah, *b.* 1970,—Gabriel, *b.* 1972.

Brother living—Henry James Nicholas (of Jerards, Sandford Orcas, Sherborne, Dorset; Travellers Club), *b.* 1914; ed. at Marlborough, and at Corpus Christi Coll., Camb. (Scholar, MA); an Underwriting Member of Lloyd's; in Colonial Admin. Ser. 1937-57; Member of Dorset Co. Council 1962-74 (Alderman 1970): *m.* 1950, Anne Barbara, da. of Sir William Dawson Croft, KCB, KBE, CIE, CVO, and has issue living, Caroline Anne, *b.* 1955.

Sir Robert Chapman, C.B., C.M.G., C.B.E., D.S.O., T.D., son of Henry Chapman, J.P. of Westoe S. Shields, was a Chartered Accountant, M.P. for Houghton-le-Spring Div. of co. Durham (*C*) 1931-35, and High Sheriff of co. Durham 1940-41.

CHARLES, Creation (U.K.) 1928, of The Abbey Grange,   altham Abbey, co. Essex and of Manchester Square, Parish of St. Marylebone, co. London. [Extinct 1975.]

Sir NOEL HUGHES HAVELOCK CHARLES, *KCMG, MC,* 3rd and last *Baronet.*

Widow living of 3rd Baronet—GIPSY JOAN (*Lady Charles*), (St. Christophe, Châteauneuf-de-Grasse, France, AM): *m.* 1957, as his 2nd wife, Sir Noel Hughes Havelock Charles, KCMG, MC, who *d.* 1975, when the title became ext.

CHAYTOR, Creation (U.K.) 1831, of Croft, Yorkshire, and Witton Castle, Durham.

Fortune wills it.

Sir WILLIAM HENRY CLERVAUX CHAYTOR, 7th *Baronet*; *b.* May 4th, 1914; *s.* his father, *Sir* EDMUND HUGH, 1935; is patron (alternately) of Witton-le-Wear V. : *m.* 1947, Mrs. Patricia Alderman, da. of Loftus Joseph McCaffry, and has issue.

Arms—Per bend dancettée argent and azure, four quatrefoils two and two bendwise counter-changed. Crest—A buck's head couped lozengy argent and sable, attired or, in the mouth a trefoil slipped vert.

Residence, Flat 3, Bridlemere, Newmarket.

Daughter living—Carol Miranda, *b.* 1948.

Sister living—Anne, *b.* 1919: *m.* 1946, Peter Dickinson, and has issue living, Simon Clervaux, *b.* 1948,—Mark Chaytor, *b.* 1951, —John Joicey, *b.* 1953. *Residence*, Beech Close Farm, Newton, Stocksfield, Northumberland.

Collateral Branches living.

Grandchildren of the late Reginald Clervaux Chaytor (infra):—
Issue of the late William Richard Carter Chaytor, *b.* 1881, *d.* 1973: *m.* 1st, 1909, Anna Laura, who *d.* 1947, da. of the late George Fawcett, 2ndly, 1949, Clare Ethel, who *d.* 1966, da. of John E. Parker:—
(By 1st m.) GEORGE REGINALD, *b.* ———, 1913.——Florence Berneice, *b.* 1915: *m.* 1942, Thorbjorn Johansen, of 1970-19th Av., Campbell River, BC, Canada, and has issue living, George Edward, *b.* 1943,—Larry Elof, *b.* 1944,—Ronald Douglas, *b.* 1948.——Florinc May, *b.* 1920: *m.* 1951, Edwin John Dauncey, of 7596, Lougheed Highway, N. Burnaby, BC, Canada, and has issue living, Darwin Ross, *b.* 1953,—Dale Allan, *b.* 1956,—Douglas Edwin, *b.* 1960.—— Doreen Isabelle (twin) *b.* 1920: *m.* 1941, Herbert William Scott, of 2857, Noel Drive, N. Burnaby, BC, Canada, and has issue living, Edward William, *b.* 1946,—Beverley Ann, *b.* 1949.

Issue of the late Reginald Clervaux Chaytor, youngest son of 2nd baronet, *b.* 1857, *d.* 1952: *m.* 1878, Margaret Ann, who *d.* 1953, da. of Archibald McCurdie, of Dalhousie, New Brunswick, Canada :—
Herbert Archibald (Hillview Rd., RR No. 1, Lantzville, BC, Canada) *b.* 1884: *m.* 1911, Effie Bell, da. of William Smith, and has issue living, Herbert Gordon (of Honeymoon Bay, BC), *b.* 1922: *m.* 1947, Mary Alice, da. of Thomas Craven, and has issue living, Bruce Gordon (3242, Lodmell Rd., Vic., BC, Canada, V9C 2V7), *b.* 1949: *m.* 1969, Rosemary Lea, da. of Reid Stephen, of Lake Cowichan (and has issue living, John Gordon *b.* 1973, Sharon Kathleen *b.* 1969), Kenneth Reginald *b.* 1952, Robert David *b.* 1958,—Dorothy May, *b.* 1912: *m.* 1936, George Walter Blewett, of Hillview Rd., RR1, Wellington, BC.

Granddaughters of the late Reginald Clervaux Chaytor (ante) :—
Issue of the late Perley Edgar Chaytor, *b.* 1886, *d.* 1939 : *m.* 19—, Dora May Lodge :—
Jean Pearl, *b.* 1908.——Rita Alberta, *b.* 1909.——Irene, *b.* 1912.——Audrey, *b.* 1913. *Residence,*

Grandchildren of the late John Clervaux Chaytor, *b.* 1836 (infra):—
Issue of the late Maj.-Gen. Sir Edward Walter Clervaux Chaytor, K.C.M.G., K.C.V.O., C.B., *b.* 1868, *d.* 1939 : *m.* 1898, Louisa Jane, who *d.* 1948, da. of C. S. Collins :—
Edward John Clervaux, *b.* 1903; Brig. late RA, 1939-45 War in Middle East and N.-W. Europe (despatches twice): *m.* 1st, 1938, Margaret Frances Morgan, who *d.* 1969, only da. of Charles Archibald Vlieland, Malayan Civil Ser.; 2ndly, 1970, Mrs. Carina Mary Marcelle Anderson. *Residence*, 20, Shrewsbury House, Cheyne Walk, SW3. *Clubs*, Cavalry, Somerset County.—— Dorothy Clervaux, *b.* 1902: *m.* 1933, Ian Douglas McNeill, who *d.* 1950, and has issue living, Nigel Edward Ian, *b.* 1938: *m.* 1971, Anna Margaret, el. da. of Maj. J. R. Fogg-Elliott, RSFus (ret.). *Residence*, 38, Wolsey Rd., East Molesey, Surrey.

Issue of the late Alfred Henry Chaytor, K.C., *b.* 1869, *d.* 1931: *m.* 1899, Dorothy Elizabeth, who *d.* 1960, el. da. of Harry Percy Burrell :—
(Alfred) Drewett *b.* 1901; ed. at Eton and at Trin. Coll. Camb. (BA 1922); Bar. Inner Temple 1925: *m.* 1929 Rachel Elizabeth da. of the Rev. William Hartley Carnegie R. of St. Margaret, Westminster, SW, Canon and Sub-Dean of Westminster Abbey, and Chap. to Speaker of House of Commons, and has issue living, William Drewett (The Hall, Croft, Darlington), *b.* 1937: *m.* 1964, Susan Philippa, el. da. of James Lawrence Bunting Ansell, MRSS, LRCP, and has issue living, Clervaux James *b.* 1967, a da. *b.* 1970,—Elizabeth (Scrafton Lodge, Leyburn, Yorks.), *b.* 1934: *m.* 1959, Lt. David Henry Ashwin, and has issue living, Philip David *b.* 1960, Henry William *b.* 1962, Rachel Elizabeth *b.* 1964,—Jane, *b.* 1935: *m.* 1956, John Richard Evelyn Atkinson, of Temple Sowerby House, Penrith, Cumberland, and has issue living, Richard Matthew Clervaux *b.* 1968,—Susannah Albina (*Hon. Mrs. Edward L. Jackson*) *b.* 1939: *m.* 1971, the Hon. Edward Lawies Jackson, of Dunesslin, by Dunscore, Dumfriesshire son of 3rd Baron Allerton. *Residence*, Spennithorne Hall, Leyburn, Yorks.——Edward Drewett, *MC* (Tufton, Culver Lane, Rattery, S. Brent, Devon), *b.* 1913; ed. at Eton; Lt.-Col. (ret.) West Yorks. Regt.: Burma 1944-45 (MC): *m.* 1938, Mary Monica, only da. of the Rev Canon Thomas John Woodall, of The Close, Salisbury, and has issue living, Richard Clervaux, *b.* 1939,—Michael Clervaux, *b.* 1944.——Catharine Beatrice, *b.* 1907. *Residence*, Bridge House, Croft, Darlington.—— Dorothy Anne, *b.* 1912: *m.* 1937, George Egerton Lambert Manley, and has issue living, Robert John Lambert, *b.* 1938,—Christopher Michael, *b.* 1948,—Peter George, *b.* 1949,—Jessica Helen, *b.* 1940: *m.* 1968, Charles James Mansfield, of 5, Borland St., Roma, Qld., son of the Hon. Sir Alan James Mansfield, KCMG, KCVO. *Residence*, 126, Ebury St., SW1, and has issue living, Anthony Roderick *b.* 1969, David William *b.* 1970.——Margaret Clare, *b.* 1918: *m.* 1939, Anthony William Kellie-Smith, Lt. RA, who *d.* 1942, and has issue living, David Anthony, *b.* 1940: *m.* 1963, Griselda, da. of George Williams, of Toronto, and has issue living, Samuel Anthony *b.* 1966, Owen William *b.* 1968. *Residence*, Bridge House, Croft, Darlington.

Issue of the late Elinor Mary Chaytor, *b.* 1874, *d.* 1917 : *m.* 1906, Percy Watt Stuart, of Spring Creek, New Zealand, who *d.* 1948 :—
Elinor Mary, *b.* 1908: *m.* 1st, 1929 (m. diss. 1961), Ronald William Reid, MS, FRCS, who *d.* 1968; 2ndly, 1974, Ronald William Boyd Morris, BL, FSA, of Quarter, Kilmacolm, Renfrewshire, and has issue living, (by 1st m.), David Hugh Lorimer (27, Sloane Av., SW3), *b.* 1946: *m.* 1971, Christine Mary, da. of Benjamin Reeves, of Colchester, and has issue living, James Benjamin Ronald *b.* 1972,—Alison Mary Deirdre (*Countess of Rosebery*), *b.* 1931: *m.* 1955, the 7th Earl of Rosebery,—Griselda Helen, *b.* 1935: *m.* 1956, Peter William Franks, and has issue living, Philip William *b.* 1957, Stephen Hugh *b.* 1959, William Robert David *b.* 1967, Elizabeth Helen *b.* 1963,—Margaret Anne Stuart, *b.* 1940: *m.* 1966, Christopher Charles Burn (39, Palewell Park, SW14), and has issue living, Alexander Paul Stanford *b.* 1968, John Christopher

Maxwell *b.* 1970,—Frances Elizabeth Stuart (twin), *b.* 1940: *m.* 1962, Michael Anthony Eagar (Ingrams House, The Schools, Shrewsbury, Salop), and has issue living, Charlotte Elisabeth Stuart *b.* 1965, Sophie Helen *b.* 1967.——Beatrice Emma, *b.* 1909: *m.* 1941, Maj. Hugh Sykes, RA.——Margaret Clervaux (5, Orpen Close, W. Bergholt, Colchester, CO6 3BG, Essex), *b.* 1913: *m.* 1937, Peter Alfred Friel Lugg, who *d.* 1963, and has issue living, Anthony Alfred Clervaux Friel, *b.* 1941,—Susan Mary Beatrix Clervaux, *b.* 1946: *m.* 1969, Jahes Falconer Stevenson, of The Old Swan Inn, Norfolk St., Cambridge.

Granddaughter of the late John Clervaux Chaytor, *b.* 1806 (infra):—
Issue of the late John Clervaux Chaytor, *b.* 1836, *d.* 1920: *m.* 1867, Emma, who *d.* 1913, da. of the late Edward Fearon, of Nelson, New Zealand:—
Isabel Clervaux. *Residence,* Croft, Picton, Marlborough, New Zealand.

Grandchildren of the late John Clervaux Chaytor (*b.* 1836) (ante) :—
Issue of the late Col. Lawrence Clervaux Chaytor, M.C., V.D., New Zealand Mounted Rifles, *b.* 1892, *d.* 1954 : *m.* 1920, Dorothy Mary Bullen (of Marshlands, Marlborough, New Zealand), da. of the late John Robert Bullen Tripe :—
John Lawrence Clervaux, *b.* 1926 : *m.* 1954, Susan Ruth, da. of G. M. Turrell, of Banks Peninsula, Canterbury, New Zealand, and has issue living, Sarah Frances Clervaux, *b.* 1956,—Miranda Jane **Clervaux,** *b.* 1958.—Frances Alexandra Clervaux, *b.* 1961. *Residence,* Marshlands, Marlborough, New Zealand.——Anthony David Clervaux, *b.* 1934.——Jocelyn Dorothy Clervaux, *b.* 1921: *m.* 1947, Michael Fearon Hall, and has issue living, Michael Timothy Chaytor, *b.* 1949,— Annabel Rose, *b.* 1954,—Georgina Miranda Mary, *b.* 1959. *Residence,* Pendeen Hororata, Canterbury, New Zealand.——Frances Anne Clervaux, *b.* 1922: *m.* 1956, Michael Kenneth Macdonald, of Gallovie, Hastings, NZ, and has issue living, Fiona Anne, *b.* 1958,—Caroline, *b.* 1959.

Issue of the late Col. John Clervaux Chaytor, R.A., *b.* 1896, *d.* 1957 : *m.* 1930, Olive Mary, who *d.* 1957, da. of Col. Reginald Brittan, D.S.O., O.B.E., of Failand Hill, Failand, Somerset :—
Pamela June, *b.* 1934 : *m.* 1959, Capt. Henry Raymond Harvey Fooks, son of Sir Raymond Hatherell Fooks, CBE, of Reves Hall Farm, Eyke, Suffolk, and has issue living, Caroline Mary, *b.* 1961,—Serena Alice, *b.* 1963,—Sarah Clervaux, *b.* 1965.——Jennifer Margaret *b.* 1936: *m.* 1959, Thomas Barrington Cubitt, of Forbury House, Kintbury, Berks., and has issue living, Anabelle Jane, *b.* 1964,—Alicia Mary, *b.* 1965,—Miranda Louise, *b.* 1967,—Sophia Henrietta, *b.* 1968.

Grandchildren of the late Arthur Chaytor, 2nd son of John Clervaux Chaytor, *b.* 1806 (ante):—
Issue of the late Arthur Cuthbert Chaytor, *b.* 1873, *d.* 1948: *m.* 1908, Linda (18, Evelyn Rd., Howick, Auckland, New Zealand), da. of Charles Martin, of Stoke, Nelson, New Zealand:—
Jack Martin (of Arkles Bay, Auckland, New Zealand), *b.* 1913: *m.* 1937, Ida Kathleen, da. of E. A. Russell.——Jose Meiva, *b.* 1909.

Issue of the late Capt. Frank Clervaux Chaytor, *b.* 1884, *d.* 1962: *m.* 1922, Alice, da. of John Hill, of Winslow:—
Joan Clervaux, *b.* 1925: *m.* 1952, Ian McKelvie Bull, and has issue living, Mary Clare, *b.* 1953,— Susan Alice, *b.* 1958.

The 1st baronet of the cr. 1831 was descended from Henry Chaytor, brother of Sir William Chaytor (cr. 1671). He and the 2nd baronet sat in Parliament for Sunderland and Durham respectively. Christopher Chaytor, Surveyor-Gen. to Queen Elizabeth I, obtained a grant of arms in 1571. He married Elizabeth, sole heiress of the Clervaux family, which had owned estates at Croft since 1246. William Chaytor, grandson of Christopher Chaytor, was cr. a Baronet 1671 (title ext. 1721). The 4th baronet was High Sheriff of co. Durham 1902.

CHETWYND, Creation (G.B.) 1795, of Brockton Hall, Staffordshire.

What God wills, let it be done.

Sir ARTHUR RALPH TALBOT CHETWYND, 8th *Baronet,* son of the late William Ralph Talbot Chetwynd, MC, brother of 7th baronet; *s.* his uncle, *Sir* (ARTHUR HENRY) TALBOT, OBE, MC, 1972; *b.* Oct. 28th, 1913; ed. at Vernon Prep. Sch., Vernon, BC, and Univ. of BC; Dir. Remedial Gymnastics BC Workman's Compensation Board 1942; Ch-Instructor Med. Reconditioning RCAF 1943, 45; Associate in Physical and Health Ed., Univ. of Toronto, and Publicity Officer. Univ. of Toronto Athletic Assocn. 1946-52; Pres. and Gen. Man. Chetwynd Films Ltd., Toronto, Canada since 1952: *m.* 1940, Marjory May MacDonald, el. da. of the late Robert Bruce Lang, of Vancouver, BC, and has issue.

Arms—Quarterly, 1st and 4th, azure a chevron between three mullets or; 2nd and 3rd argent, two gules.

Residence,—95, Thorncliffe Park Drive, Leaside Towers, Apt. 402, Toronto, Ont., Canada. *Clubs,* Naval and Military, Empire (Canada), Royal Canadian Yacht.

Sons living—ROBIN JOHN TALBOT (20, Cockburn Drive, Scarborough, Ont., M1C 2T2, Canada), *b.* Aug. 21st, 1941: *m.* 1967, Heather Louise, el. da. of George Lothian, of Baie D'Urfe, Quebec, and has issue living, James Talbot, *b.* 1973,—Kimberly Anne, *b.* 1971.——William Richard Talbot (1090, Sycamore Cres., Oshawa, Ont., L19 657, Canada), *b.* 1946: *m.* 1971, Patricia Anne, da. of the late Geoffrey Senior, of Manchester, and has issue living, Geoffrey Talbot, *b.* 1973.

Mother living—Frances Mary (Suite 1, 627, Superior St., Victoria, BC, Canada), da. of the late James Jupe: *m.* 1912, William Ralph Talbot Chetwynd, MC, who *d.* 1957.

Widow living of 7th Baronet—(FRANCES) AUDREY, (*Audrey Lady Chetwynd*), (Firs Cottage, 63, Balmore Lane, Lymington, Hants.), da. of the late Dr. Thomas Smith, of Boldre, Hants., and formerly wife of the late John Taylour Boumphrey: *m.* 1956, as his 3rd wife, Sir (Arthur Henry) Talbot Chetwynd, OBE, MC, 7th Bt., who *d.* 1972.

Collateral Branches living.

Issue of the late Capt. Walter Hill Chetwynd, 3rd son of 3rd baronet, *b.* 1856, *d.* 1916: *m.* 1890, the Hon. Edome Eliza Theodosia, who *d.* 1950, da. of 8th Baron Monson :—

Phyllis Marion, *b.* 1893. *Residences*, Fetternear, Kemnay, Aberdeenshire ; 57, Carlisle Mansions, S.W.1.

Grandchildren of the late Maj. William Fawkener Chetwynd, M.P., 2nd son of 1st baronet:—

Issue of the late Charles Chetwynd, *b.* 1851, *d.* 1895: *m.* 1888, Mary, who *d.* 1948, el. da. of George Meakin, J.P., of Creswell Hall, Staffs.:—

Charles William George (c/o Barclays Bank, Usk, Monmouthshire), *b.* 1894; ed. at Haileybury; 1914-18 War: *m.* 1st, 1914, Olive Mary (who obtained a divorce 1932), da. of J. Hall, of Huntingdon; 2ndly, 19—; 3rdly, 19—, Mary Elizabeth, da. of Arthur Griffiths, J.P. of Worcester, and has issue living, (by 1st marriage) Basil Charles Fawkener (of Greenacres, Creech St. Michael, Taunton), *b.* 1915: *m.* 1944, Margaret Joan, da. of the late George Ernest Welch, and has issue living, Paul Ernest Fawkener *b.* 1945: *m.* 1972, Shirley Evelyn, el. da. of Raymond Godfrey Manuel, of Creech, Heathfield, Raymond Charles Fawkener *b.* 1950: *m.* 1974, Susan Jane, el. da. of John Kershaw, of Taunton, Som.,—Ronald John Trevor, *b.* 1918: *m.* 19—, Rhona Mary, *b.* 1916: *m.* 1940, Philip Graham Stacey Brinson, of 35, Park Cres., Frenchay, Bristol, and has issue living, John *b.* 1948,—(by 3rd marriage) Valerie Elizabeth, *b,* 1940: *m.* 1961, Pael Carrington.——Beatrice Ada (of 192, The Rye, E. Dulwich, SE15), *b.* 1888.——Mildred Flornce, Mary, *b.* 1890.

A younger branch of the family of Viscount Chetwynd, of great antiquity in Shropshire. The first of this branch to settle in Staffordshire was Sir John de Chetwynd, *temp.* Henry III. The 1st baronet, many years Clerk to the Privy Council, received knighthood in 1787, and the 2nd sat as M.P. for Stafford. Sir George Chetwynd 4th Bt., was High Sheriff of Warwickshire 1875.

CHEYNE, Creation (U.K.) 1908, of Leagarth, Fetlar, and North Yell, co. Zetland.

[Name pronounced "**Chain**."]

He conquers by patience.

PATIENTIA·VINCIT

Sir JOSEPH LISTER WATSON CHEYNE, 3rd *Baronet* ; *b.* Oct. 10th, 1914 ; *s.* his father, *Col. Sir* JOSEPH LISTER, *M.C.*, 1957 ; ed. at Stowe, and at Corpus Christi Coll., Camb. ; European War 1939-45 as Major Queen's Westminsters, King's Roy. Rifle Corps : *m.* 1st, 1938 (marriage dissolved 1955), Mary Mort, who *d.* 1959, da. of Vice-Adm. John Derwent Allen, C.B. ; 2ndly, 1955, Cicely, da. of T. Metcalfe, of Padiham, Lancashire, and has issue by 1st and 2nd marriages.

Arms—Azure, on a bend between six crosses patée fitchée argent an oak tree eradicated proper, fructed or. *Crest*—A cross patée fitchée argent.

Residences—Leagarth, Fetlar Shetland ; 36, Via Roma Grottaferrata, Rome, Italy.

Sons living—By 1st marriage—PATRICK JOHN LISTER (Craneswater House, Craneswater Park, Southsea), *b.* July 2nd, 1941; ed. at Lancing: *m.* 1968, Helen Louise Trevor, da. of Louis Smith, of 18, Helena Rd., Southsea, and has issue living Louis Richard Patrick Lister, *b.* March 25th, 1971,—Elizabeth Henrietta Louise, *b,* 1960,—Mary Catherine Fleur, *b.* 1974.—— By 2nd m.—John Joseph Peter, *b.* 1956.——James Andrew Watson, *b.* 1957.

Daughters living—By 1st marriage—Ann Caroline Lister, *b.* 1939 : *m.* 1961, Major Ronald Eric Croll Adam, Queen's Own Highlanders. *Residence*, Duncryne, Forres, Morayshire.—— **By 2nd marriage**—Helen Margaret Watson, *b.* 1959.

Brother living—Andrew Watson, *b.* 1921; ed. at Stowe, and at Loughborough Coll., Leicester; late Capt. RE, and a FICE; Burma 1942-45, NW Europe 1945 (despatches): *m.* 1946, Joyce, da. of Conway Stanton, of Kensington, SW10. *Residence*, 11, Ropers Orchard, Danvers St., SW3.

Widow living of 2nd Baronet—NELITA MANFIELD (*Nelita, Lady Cheyne*), da. of Andrew Pringle, formerly of Borgue, Kirkcudbright, and Basing House, Banstead : *m.* 1912, Col. Sir Joseph Lister Cheyne, M.C., 2nd baronet, who *d.* 1957. *Residence*, 15, Abingdon Court, W.8.

Collateral Branches living

Issue of the late Brig. William Watson Cheyne, DSO, OBE, 2nd son of 2nd baronet, *b.* 1920, *d.* 1970: *m.* 1946, Laurel Audrey (12, Crondace Rd., SW6), da. of the late Lt.-Gen. Sir Balfour Oliphant Hutchison, KBE, CB [*see* Jervis-White-Jervis, Bt. (ext.), colls.]:—

Julian Lister Hutchison, *b.* 1947.——David Watson, *b.* 1948.——William Gerald, *b.* 1950.—— Bridget Nelita, *b.* 1955.

Issue of the late William Hunter Watson Cheyne, M.B., M.R.C.S., L.R.C.P., 2nd son of 1st baronet, *b.* 1889, *d.* 1957: *m.* 1923, Grizel (20, Chester St., Edinburgh, 3), da. of I. F. Bayley, formerly of Halls, East Lothian:—

George Watson, *b,* 1929; MA., LL.B. Camb.; Bar. Gray's Inn 1955: *m.* 1964, Alison Diane Muir (Bar.-at-law), da. of C. Muir Jones, of Hawarden, Chester, and has issue living, Piers William Watson, *b.* 1965,—Phyllida Alison, *b.* 1968,—Catriona Helen, *b.* 1971. *Address*, 1, Paper Bldgs., Temple, EC4.——Janet Mary Watson (*Hon. R. H. Vere Cochrane*), *b.* 1931: *m.* 1956, the Hon. (Ralph Henry) Vere Cochrane [*see* B. Cochrane of Cults]. *Residence*, Cults, Cupar, Fife.

The 1st baronet, Sir (William) Watson Cheyne, K.C.M.G., C.B., F.R.C.S., F.R.S., an eminent surgeon, and Pres. of Roy. Coll. of Surgs., was Lord-Lieut. of Orkney and Shetland 1919-30, and sat as M.P. for Edinburgh and St. Andrews Univ. (C) 1917-18 and for Edinburgh, St. Andrews, Glasgow, and Aberdeen Univs. (*Co.U*) 1918-22. The 2nd baronet, Sir Joseph Lister Cheyne, M.C., was Col. Comdg. 16/5th Lancers.

CHICHESTER, Creation (E.) 1641, of Raleigh, Devonshire.

Sir (EDWARD) JOHN CHICHESTER, 11th *Baronet ; b.* April 14th, 1916 ; *s.* his father, *Com. Sir* EDWARD GEORGE, *R.N.* (retired), 1940 ; ed. at Radley ; late Capt. Roy. Scots Fusiliers ; is patron of one living ; was King's Foreign Service Messenger 1947-50, and with Imperial Chemical Industries Ltd. 1950-60 ; European War 1939-45 with Roy. Scots Fusiliers, and as Lieut. R.N.V.R. : *m.* 1950, the Hon. Anne Rachel Pearl Douglas-Scott-Montagu, da. of 2nd Baron Montagu of Beaulieu and widow of Major Howel Joseph Moore-Gwyn, Welsh Guards, and has issue.

Arms—Checky or and gules, a chief vair. **Crest**—A heron **rising** with an eel in its beak proper.
Address— Battramsley Lodge, Boldre, nr. Lymington, Hants.

Ferme en foy.
Firm in faith.

Sons living—JAMES HENRY EDWARD, *b.* Oct. 15th, 1951.——Julian John Raleigh, *b.* 1963.
Daughters living—Coral Anne, *b.* 1954.——Georgina Caroline, *b.* 1955.——Mary Rose, *b.* 1957.
Sister living—Mary, *b.* 1917: *m.* 1941, Cdr. John Blakeley Russell, DSC, RN (ret.), of Old Mills, Parkham, Bideford, N. Devon, and has issue living, Christopher John, *b.* 1954,—Hermione Anne, *b.* 1942: *m.* 1962, Robin Labron Johnson, and has issue living, Nicolas Patrick Amyas Labron *b.* 1963, Tristan Alexander Labron *b.* 1965,—Cherry Rose, *b.* 1952.

Uncle living (son of 9th baronet)—Marcus Beresford, *b.* 1896; European War 1914-19 as Capt. Roy. N. Devon Hussars Yeo.: *m.* 1925, Myra Brownrigg, youngest da. of the late Maj. Harvey, Brownrigg Jay, and has issue living, Imogen Ann, *b.* 1926: *m.* 1948, Maj. Arthur John Digby Hamilton, Scots Guards of Stephenstown, Dundalk, co. Louth [Fairlie Cunninghame, Bt.], and has issue living, Philip Arthur Marcus *b.* 1949, Edward Digby Hamilton *b.* 1953, James John *b.* 1959, Thomas Patrick (twin) *b.* 1959, Kate Antonia *b.* 1955,—Jane Catherine, *b.* 1929: *m.* 1957, Roger Longrigg, of Orchard House, Crookham, Hants, and has issue living, Laura Jane *b.* 1958, Frances Angelica *b.* 1961, Clare Selina *b.* 1963. *Residence,* Horseshoe Lodge, Compton Chamberlayne, nr. Salisbury, Wilts.

Aunts living (daughters of 9th baronet)—Edith Mary, *b.* 1891: *m.* 1911, Sir Stephen Charles Bine Renshaw, 2nd Bt., from whom she obtained a divorce 1939.——Fanny, *b.* 1892: *m.* 1930, Capt. Patrick Maitland Campbell, MC, who *d.* 1961, and from whom she obtained a divorce 1943, and has issue living, Fiona Patricia, *b.* 1932: *m.* 1955, Derek Gilbert, of Nutbourne Place Farm, Nutbourne, Pulborough, Sussex, and has issue living, Patrick *b.* 1966, Joanna *b.* 1957, Daphne *b.* 1959, Erica *b.* 1962. *Residence,* Greenford, Mare Hill, Pulborough, Sussex.——Joanna (Instow House, Instow, N. Devon), *b.* 1893.

Mother living—Phyllis Dorothy, da. of the late Henry Francis Compton [Musgrave, Bt., *cr.* 1611], *m.* 1st, 1915, Com. Sir Edward George Chichester, R.N. (retired), 10th Bt., who *d.* 1940, and from whom she obtained a divorce 1924; 2ndly, 1930 (marriage dissolved 19—), Humphrey Seymour Ramsay Critchley-Salmonson, late The Cameronians, who *d.* 1956. *Residence,* 11, Kellett Rd., Shirley, Southampton.

Widow living of 10th Baronet—GLADYS ETHEL, da. of the late J. Fordham, and formerly wife of Major F. H. Cairnes, M.C., 5th Inniskilling Dragoon Guards : *m.* 1st, 1935, as his third wife, Com. Sir Edward George Chichester, R.N. (retired), 10th Bt., who *d.* 1940 ; 2ndly, 1961, Com. Robert S. Heffner, late U.S. Navy. *Residence,* The Flat, Instow, N. Devon.

Collateral Branches living.

Issue of the late Lieut.-Col. Gerard Chichester, 5th son of 8th baronet, *b.* 1859 *d.* 1906: *m.* 1891, Alice Jane Harriette Maude, who *d.* 1932, da. of the late G. Pinckney, of Feniton Court, Devon :—
Alice Mary, *b.* 1892 : *m.* 1923, Capt. Andrew Stuart Hibberd, M.B.E. *Residence,* 2 West Field, Budleigh Salterton, Devon.——Geraldine Maud, *b.* 1895. *Residence,* Hillcroft, Lympstone, Devon.

Issue of the late George Chichester, 6th son of 8th baronet, *b.* 1865, *d.* 1933: *m.* 1st, 1900, Frances Caroline, who *d.* 1904, da. of the late Col. Hugh Robert Hibbert, Roy. Fusiliers, formerly of Birtles Hull, Cheshire, and Broadgate, Barnstaple ; 2ndly, 1908, Essex Mary, da. of the late Col. Hugh Robert Hibbert :—
(By 1st m.) Patrick George, *OBE, b.* 1901; ed. at Sherborne; Group Capt. RAF; 1939-45 War (Greek AFC); OBE (Mil.) 1963: *m.* 1931, Gladys Evelyn Vesta Clemency, da. of William Carnegie Barnes, and has issue living, Jeremy Patrick (Hawthorn Cottage, Congresbury, Som.), *b.* 1932: *m.* 1956, Kay Lloyd, and has issue living, Mark Arlington Raleigh *b.* 1957, Matthew Patrick Lloyd *b.* 1966, Miranda Frances Louise *b.* 1962,—Patricia Gladys Clemency, *b.* 1939: *m.* 1963, Anthony Quinton, MD (c/o Nat. Provincial Bank, High St., Barnstaple, N. Devon), and has issue living, Lucinda Clemency *b.* 1965,—Caroline Sandra Pietre Katrina, *b.* 1944: *m.* 1970, Michael George Temple Harris, Cdr. RN, of The White House, Severn Stars Lane, Tamerton Foliot, Plymouth [*see* B. Harris, colls.],—Clarissa Evelyn Georgette, *b.* 1948: *m.* 1972, Keith James Keating, of Cloncurry, W. Qld., Aust, and has issue living, Melissa Evelyn *b.* 1973, Georgina Naomi *b.* 1974. *Residence,* Hayne Manor, Lewdown, Devon.——Adrian Francis, *b.* 1903. *Residence,* Chelfham, Barnstaple, N. Devon.

Grandson of the late Rev. Charles Chichester (infra):—
Issue of the late Sir Francis Charles Chichester, KBE, *b.* 1901, *d.* 1972: *m.* 1st, 1923, Muriel Eileen, who *d.* 1929, da. of the late M. F. Blakiston; 2ndly, 1937, Sheila Mary (9, St. James's Place, SW1), da. of the late Gerald Craven, of Belle Eau Park, Notts.:—
(By 2nd m.) Giles Bryan, *b.* 1946; ed. at Ch. Ch., Oxford.

Issue of the late Rev. Charles Chichester, 7th son of 8th baronet, *b.* 1868, *d.* 1938: *m.* 1896, Emily Annie, who *d.* 1962, da. of the late Samuel Page, of Chitt's Hill, Wood Green, N.:—
This family took its name from Chichester, Sussex. On the marriage of Thomasine Raleigh with John Chichester in 1384 this family settled at Raleigh, Devon. Sir Roger Chichester was knighted by the king at the siege of Calais, and afterwards served at Poitiers. The 9th baronet, Rear-Adm. Sir Edward Chichester, was a Naval A.D.C. to H.M. Queen Victoria and H.M. King Edward VII 1899-1902.

CHILD, Creation (U.K.) 1868, of Newfield, and of Stallington Hall, Staffordshire and of Glen [Losset, co. Argyll.

[Extinct 1958.]

Sir (SMITH) HILL CHILD, *G.C.V.O., C.B., C.M.G., D.S.O.,* 2nd and last *Baronet.*

Daughters living of 2nd Baronet—Teresa (34A, Campden Hill Gdns., W8), *b.* 1927.——Mary Cornelia, *b.* 1933: *m.* 1959, Henry Charles Whitbread, and has issue living, Caroline Mary, *b.* 1960,—Flora Joscelyne, *b.* 1962,—Angela Helen, *b.* 1965. *Residence,* Greenaway House, Wheathampstead, Herts.

Sisters living of 2nd Baronet—Cicely Helen, *b.* 1884 : *m.* 1906, Col. Wilfrid Wykeham Jelf, C.M.G., D.S.O., R.A., who *d.* 1933, and has issue living, Lilah Margaret, *b.* 1911. *Residence,* 2, Milford Cottage, Milford, Surrey.

CHILD, Creation (U.K.) 1919, of Bromley Palace, Bromley, Kent

Sir (COLES JOHN) JEREMY CHILD, 3rd *Baronet; b.* Sept. 20th, 1944: *s.* his father, *Sir* (COLES) JOHN, 1971; *ed.* at Eton; actor: *m.* 1971, Deborah Jane, da. of Henry Percival Snelling, and has issue.

Arms—Per chevron azure and gules, on a chevron engrailed ermine between three eagles close argent a fylfot sable. **Crest**—An eagle, wings expanded argent charged on the breast with a fylfot sable, holding in the beak by its neck a serpent entwined round the body vert.
Residence—23, Seymour Rd., Hampton Wick, Kingston upon Thames, Surrey.

Daughter living—Honor Melissa, *b.* 1973.
Sisters living—Deirdre Kathleen, *b.* 1934: *m.* 1959, Antony Edward Woodall, of The Old Rectory, Wyddial, Buntingford, Herts [Crawley-Boevey, Bt., colls.], and has issue living, James Henry, *b.* 1960,—Andrew Hugh, *b.* 1963,—Edward Antony John, *b.* 1967.——Honor Diana, *b.* 1936: *m.* 1959, Capt. Noel Hardwick Matterson, late R. Dragoons, of Green Place, Wonersh, Surrey, and has issue living, Charles John Hardwick, *b.* 1960,—Justin George Hardwick, *b.* 1962,—Nicholas Noel Hardwick, *b.* 1963,—Dominic Graham Hardwick, *b.* 1965.
Aunts living (daughters of 1st baronet)—Audrey Eleanor Mary, *b.* 1887.——Norah Phyllis Amy, *b.* 1889: *m.* 1917, the Rev. Charles Hallam Edwards (formerly Maj. RWF, who *d.* 19—), and has issue living, Anne Penelope Hallam, *b.* 1918: *m.* 1944, Capt. Henry Nicholas Straker, MC, RA, and has issue living, Henry *b.* 1948, Caroline *b.* 1945,—Susan Isham, *b.* 1921: *m.* 1949, Maj. William Wheaton Michael Chard, Roy. Fusiliers.

To imitate rather than to envy.

Sir Coles Child, 1st baronet, was son of the late Coles William John Child, J.P., D.L., of Bromley, Kent. The latter's great great grandfather John Child, of Yaxley, Hunts (*d.* 1743): *m.* Isabella, da. of William Coles, of London.

CHITTY, Creation (U.K.) 1924, of The Temple.

Sir THOMAS WILLES CHITTY, 3rd *Baronet* ; *b.* March 2nd, 1926 ; *s.* his father, *Sir* (THOMAS) HENRY WILLES, 1955 ; *ed.* at Winchester, and at Univ. Coll., Oxford : *m.* 1951, Susan Elspeth Russel, da. of R. Glossop, and has issue.
Residence,—Bow Cottage, West Hoathly, Sussex.

Son living—ANDREW EDWARD WILLES, *b.* Nov. 20th, 1953.
Daughters living—Cordelia Anne, *b.* 1955.—Miranda Jane, *b.* 1967.——Jessica Susan, *b.* 1971.
Brothers living—Michael Willes, *b.* 1929 : *m.* 1954, Janet Leonora, da. of W. A. Messenger, of Forest Down, Pyrford, Woking, and has issue living, Sebastian William, *b.* 1958,—Anne-Marie, *b.* 1966. *Residence,* Mayhurst Lodge, Easthill, Woking, Surrey.——John Henry Willes (31, Church Way, Sanderstead, Surrey), *b.* 1932; late Lt. RA: *m.* 1968, Diana Mary, da. of G. D. B. Dear, of Coulsdon, Surrey and has issue living, Antonia Mary Willes, *b.* 1970,—Louise Elizabeth Willes, *b.* 1973.
Aunts living (daughters of 1st baronet)—Diana Willes, *b.* 1890: *m.* 1915, John Erskine Read, Q.C., LLD, DCL, Judge of Internat. Court of Justice who *d.* 1974, and has issue living, Thomas Herbert Willes, *b.* 1920; a Counsellor, Dept. of External Affairs, Canada: *m.* 1947, Penelope, da. of Archer Fortesque Duguid, DSO, OBE [E. Fortescue, colls.], and has issue living, John James Duguid *b.* 1948, Timothy Michael *b.* 1955, Jennifer Duguid *b.* 1953,—Gordon Henry Hale (of 152, Welland Avenue, Toronto, 7, Ontario, Canada), *b.* 1928 ; B.A. 1950, LL.B. 1952 ; a Bar. and Solicitor of Supreme Courts of Ontario and Nova Scotia : *m.* 1952, Catherine Easton, da. of Charles MacKinnon, of Edinburgh, and has issue living, Ian Walter *b.* 1957, Diana Catherine *b.* 1952, Elspeth Anne *b.* 1955. *Residence,* 81, Dunmurray Blvd., Scarborough 755, Ont., Canada.——Elizabeth Willes, *b.* 1892: *m.* 1918, Henry Matthew Philipson-Stow, who *d.* 1953 [*see* Philipson-Stow, Bt., colls.]. *Residence,* Old Vicarage, Farnham, Surrey.

Collateral Branch living.

Issue of the late Robert Michael Willes Chitty, 2nd son of 1st baronet, *b.* 1893, *d.* 1970: *m.* 1922, Norah A. (11, Colin Av., Toronto 7, Canada), da. of W, Cooke, of Toronto:—
Thomas Michael Willes (6550, Spruce Drive, Birmingham, Mich., USA), *b.* 1930: *m.* 1952, Edith Jeremy Weir, of Toronto, and has issue living, Robert Arthur, *b.* 1953,—Diana, *b.* 1956,—Susan Elizabeth *b.* 1957.——Norah Elizabeth, *b.* 1926: *m.* 1958, Ross Alexander Wilson and has issue living, Lesley, *b.* 1959.

The 1st baronet, Sir Thomas Willes Chitty, K.C. (son of Thomas Edward Chitty), was a Master of Supreme Court 1901-20, and Senior Master of Supreme Court and King's Remembrancer 1920-26. The 2nd baronet, Sir (Thomas) Henry Willes Chitty, was a Bar.-at-law of Inner Temple.

CHOLMELEY, Creation (U.K.) 1806, of Easton, Lincolnshire.
[Pronounced 'Chumly.']

Sir MONTAGUE JOHN CHOLMELEY, 6th *Baronet*; *b.* March 27th, 1935; *s.* his father, *Lt.-Col. Sir* HUGH JOHN FRANCIS SIBTHORP, *C.B., D.S.O.,* 1964; ed. at Eton; Capt. Grenadier Guards: *m.* 1960, Juliet Auriol Sally, yst. da. of Maj.-Gen. Sir Eustace John Blois Nelson, KCVO, CB, DSO, MC [*see* D. Grafton], and has issue.

Arms—Gules, two helmets in chief proper, and a garb in base or; a mullet for difference. Crest—A garb or.

Seat—Easton Hall, Grantham. *Residence*—Church Farm, Burton le Coggles, Grantham, Lincs. *Clubs,*—Guards', White's.

Son living—HUGH JOHN FREDERICK SEBASTIAN, *b.* Jan. 3rd, 1968.

Daughters living—Camilla, *b.* 1962,—Davina, *b.* 1964.

Aunt living (daughter of 4th baronet)—Rosamond Mary Edith (*Hon. Mrs. Charles G. Cubitt*), *b.* 1904: *m.* 1927, Col. the Hon. Charles Guy Cubitt, CBE, DSO, TD, DL, RA (TA) [*see* B. Ashcombe]. *Residence*, High Barn, Effingham, Leatherhead, Surrey.

Widow living of 5th Baronet—CECILIA (*Cecilia, Lady Cholmeley*) (of The Dower House, Easton, Grantham), da. of W. H. Ellice, of Ewhurst Manor, Shermanbury, Horsham: *m.* 1931, Lt.-Col. Sir Hugh John Francis Sibthorp Cholmeley, C.B., D.S.O., 5th baronet, who *d.* 1964.

This family is a younger branch of the noble house of Cholmondeley. Henry Cholmeley, **of** Burton Coggles, settled in Lincolnshire in the 16th century, and from him the present baronet is descended in a direct line. The 1st baronet was MP for Grantham 1820-26, and the 2nd baronet sat for many years successively as MP for Grantham and Lincolnshire North (*L*). The 4th baronet, Capt. Sir Montague Aubrey Rowley Cholmeley, Grenadier Guards, was killed in action during European War Dec. 1914.

CHRISTISON, Creation (U.K.) 1871, of Moray Place, Edinburgh.

May it guide my life.

Sir (ALEXANDER FRANK) PHILIP CHRISTISON, *G.B.E., C.B., D.S.O., M.C.,* 4th *Baronet;* *b.* Nov. 17th, 1893; *s.* his half-brother, *Sir* ROBERT ALEXANDER, 1945; ed. at Edinburgh Acad., and Oxford Univ. (BA); Hon. Fellow Univ. Coll. 1973; Gen. (ret.) late Queen's Own Cameron Highlanders and Duke of Wellington's Regt., a DL for Roxburghshire, and a FSA (Scotland); Col. Duke of Wellington's Regt. and 10th Gurkha Rifles, and Hon. Col. 414th (Forth) Coast Regt., RA (TA); commanded 15th Scottish Div. 1941-2, 33rd Indian Corps 1942-43, 15ht Indian Corps, Burma 1943-5, and 14th Army 1945, C-in-C, Allied Land Forces SE Asia 1945, and Allied Com., Netherlands E. Indies 1945-46; GOC-in-C N. Command 1946, and of Scottish Command, and Gov. of Edinburgh Castle 1947-49; ADC Gen. to HM 1947-49; Pres. Clarsach Soc., Chm. of Scottish Salmon Angling, and of Officers' Soc., Chm. of Scottish Salmon Angling Fedn., and of Officers' Assocn. Scotland, Vice-Pres. Officers' Assocn., Pres. Army Cadet Force, Scotland, and Burma Star Assocn., Scotland; 1914-18 War (despatches, MC with Bar), Burma 1943-45 (despatches), Indonesia 1945-46; has Grand Cordon of Order of Cloud and Banner of China; CB (Mil) 1943, KBE (Mil) 1944, DSO 1945, GBE (Mil) 1948: *m.* 1916, Betty, who *d.* 1974, da. of the late Rt. Rev Anthony Mitchell, DD, Bishop of Aberdeen and Orkney; 2ndly, 1974, Jessie Vida Wallace-Smith, and has issue (by 1st m.).

Arms—Or, a chevron sable between three laurel leaves proper. Crest—A passion cross gules on three grieces proper.

Residence—The Croft, Melrose, Roxburghshire. *Clubs*—United Service, New (Edinburgh).

Daughters living—By 1st m.—Alison Ann, *b.* 1924; formerly Junior Com. WAC (India): *m.* 1945, Capt. Denis Clode James, Roy. Indian Army Ser. Corps, of 83, Branksome Gdns., City Beach, Perth, W. Aust., and has issue living, Michael Christison, *b.* 1947,—Philip Christison, *b.* 1949,— Jane Alison, *b.* 1946,—Kandy Ann, *b.* 1953.——Fiona, *b.* 1932: *m.* 1954, Peter Thomson McLintock, of Springfield, Penicuik, Midlothian [*see* McLintock, Bt.].

Sisters living—Dorothea Mary, *b.* 1896: *m.* 1922, Douglas Keith Fenton, and has issue living, Rosamond Mary Elworthy, *b.* 1923: *m.* 1943, Paul Raymond Herman, of The Look-out, Hammersley Lane, Penn, Bucks., and has issue living, John Douglas *b.* 1946, Richard Frederick Alexander *b.* 1959, Christine Elisabeth *b.* 1944, Angela Mary *b.* 1949,—Deirdre Christison, *b.* 1925: *m.* 1st, 1952, Gerald Roy Edwards; 2ndly, 1974, William Stanley Knight, of Middle Farm, Oakley, nr. Bedford, and has issue living (by 1st m.), Paul Christison *b.* 1955, Nicholas Keith *b.* 1957. *Residence*, 8, Darby Crescent, Sunbury-on-Thames, Middlesex.——Irene Victoria Elworthy, *MB, ChB, b.* 1897; ed. at Edinburgh Univ. (MB and ChB 1922).——Alison Florence Alexandra, *b.* 1901: *m.* 1925, Paymaster-Capt. Philip Skelton Graham, RN, who *d.* 1965, and has issue living, Philip Colin Christison, (16, Dumpton Gap Rd., Broadstairs, Kent), *b.* 1926: *m.* 1955, Dorothy, da. of Frederic W. Ireland, and has issue living, Michael *b.* 1957, Eleanor *b.* 1959,— Alison Monica, *b.* 1928: *m.* 1952, (Charles) Patrick Fleeming Jenkin, MP, of 9, Hurst Av., N6

5TX, and has issue living, Charles *b.* 1954, Bernard *b.* 1959, Nicola *b.* 1956, Flora *b.* 1962,—Marion Dorothea, *b.* 1930: *m.* 1960, Michael Richards, of 11, Orchard Cres., Edinburgh, 4, and has issue living, Hugh *b.* 1961, Daniel *b.* 1967, Alison *b.* 1962, Clare *b.* 1964,—Penelope Jean, *b.* 1934. *Residence,* 81, Craigleith Hill Av., Edinburgh, 4.

The 1st baronet, a celebrated physician, was twice President of the Royal College of Physicians, Edinburgh, President of the Royal Society of Edinburgh 1868-73, a Physician in Ordinary to H.M. Queen Victoria in Scotland, and a Member of the General Medical Council of the United Kingdom 1857-73. The 2nd baronet, Sir Alexander, was Surg.-Gen. Bengal Army. The 3rd baronet, Sir Robert Alexander Christison, was British Vice-Consul at Lima 1916-19.

CHURCH, Creation (U.K.) 1901, of Harley Street, co. London, and Woodside, Hatfield, Herts.

Mea spes est in Deo.
My hope is in God.

Sir GEOFFREY SELBY CHURCH, *C.B.E., M.C., T.D.,* 2nd *Baronet; b.* Jan. 11th, 1887; *s.* his father, *Sir* WILLIAM SELBY, *K.C.B, M.D.,* 1928; ed. at Winchester, and at Univ. Co.., Oxford; Col. and Hon. Brig. (ret.) RA (TA), Hon. Col. 86th (Herts Yeo.) Field Regt., R.A. (T.A.), and a J.P. and D.L. for Herts (High Sheriff 1936); European War 1914-19 (M.C.), European War 1939-40 (C.B.E); appointed to command R.A., 54th (E. Anglian) Div. (T.A.) 1939, and an additional A.D.C. to H.M. 1941; C.B.E. (Mil.) 1940: *m.* 1st, 1913, Doris Louise Cleghorn, who *d.* 1917, da. of the late Sir William Somerville, K.B.E., LL.D., D.Sc., Emeritus Professor of Rural Economy, and an Hon. Fellow of St. John's Coll., Oxford; 2ndly, 1920, Helene Elizabeth, who *d.* 1962, da. of the late John L. Traynor, of Michigan, U.S.A.

Arms—Or, on a fesse engrailed between three greyhounds' heads sable, erased gules, collared azure, three bezants. **Crest**—A greyhound's head sable, erased gules, collared azure, and charged on the neck with two bezants.

Residence—St. Michael's, Hatfield, Herts. *Club*—United University.

Collateral Branches living.

Grandchildren of the late John William Church (infra):—
Issue of the late Barbara Brenda Church, *b.* 1910, *d.* 1954: *m.* 1937, Donald Henry Merry (of Charterisville, 77, Burke Rd. North, E. Ivanhoe, 3079, Victoria, Aust.):—
Hugh Geoffrey, *b.* 1940.——Paul Martin, *b.* 1948.——Cynthia Margaret, *b.* 1944.

Issue of the late John William Church, Lt. Hertfordshire Regt., el. son of 1st baronet, *b.* 1878, d. (killed in action during 1914-18 War) 1918: *m.* 1908, Brenda, who *d.* 1951, da. of the late Hugh Lee Pattison, of 85, Linden Gardens, Bayswater, W :—
Lesbia Mary, *b.* 1916: *m.* 1941, Sergei G. Kadleigh, ARIBA, of Flat 5, 6, Coningham Gdns., SW5.

The 1st baronet, Sir William Selby Church. K.C.B., **M.D.,** was Pres. of Roy. Coll. of Physicians 1899-1905, and an Hon. Treasurer of Roy. So. of Medicine 1910-11 and 1912-13 (Pres. 1908-10).

CHURCHMAN, Creation (U.K.) 1938, of Melton, co. Suffolk. [Extinct 1947.]

Sir WILLIAM ALFRED CHURCHMAN, 1st and last *Baronet.*

Daughters living of 1st Baronet—Ida Nancy (Melton Lodge, Woodbridge, Suffolk) *b.* 1900.——Violet, *b.* 1902.

CLARK, Creation (U.K.) 1883, of Cavendish Square, co. Middlesex.

Free for a blast.

Sir ANDREW EDMUND JAMES CLARK, *M.B.E., M.C., Q.C.,* 3rd *Baronet ; b.* July 18th, 1898 ; *s.* his father, *Col. Sir* JAMES RICHARDSON ANDREW, *C.B., C.M.G.,* 1948; ed. at Eton; Bar. Inner Temple 1928, and Lincoln's Inn 1934, a K.C. 1943, and a Bencher (Inner Temple) 1951 ; Col. and Hon. Brigadier late R.A. (Reserve) ; is an O.St.J. ; European War 1914-18 (despatches, M.C.) ; M.B.E. (Mil.) 1941 : *m.* 1st, 1921, Angelica, who *d.* 1922, da. of the late Arthur James Taylor, of Strensham, Worcestershire ; 2ndly, 1924, Adeline Frances, el. da. of Lieut.-Col. Arthur Daniel Derviche Jones, D.S.O., M.C., and has issue by 2nd marriage.

Arms—Or, a fesse vair, in chief a boar's head couped between two crescents, and in base a like boar's head all sable. **Crest**—A demi huntsman winding a horn, holding in his sinister hand a whip all proper between stag's attires, the scalp in front, argent.

Residence—45, Victoria Rd., W8. *Club*—Boodle's.

Daughters living—By 2nd marriage—Jennifer Jane, *b.* 1934 ; Bar. Inner Temple 1955 : *m* 1956, John Bertrand Worsley, of 49, Campden Hill Rd., W.8 [see B. Napier of Magdala, colls.]——Susan Mary, *b.* 1936; Bar. Inner Temple 1958: *m.* 1958, Ian Malcolm Constable-Maxwell-

Scott [see Constable-Maxwell-Scott, Bt., cr. 1642]. *Residence* Grants Hill House, Uckfield, Sussex.

The 1st baronet, Sir Andrew M.D., was an eminent physician. The 2nd baronet, Sir James Richardson Andrew, C.B., C.M.G., was Hon. Col. in the Army and served in S. African War 1899-1900, and in European War 1915-19 with R.A.M.C. (C.M.G.).

CLARK, Creation (U.K.) 1886, of Melville Crescent, Edinburgh.

In God I trust.

Sir THOMAS CLARK, 3rd *Baronet; b.* March 30th, 1886 ; *s.* his father, *Sir* JOHN MAURICE, 1924 ; ed. at Edinburgh Acad., and at Univ. Coll., Oxford ; a DL for City of Edinburgh, and a FRSE ; Chm. of City of Edinburgh T. and AF Assocn. 1947-50; sometime senior partner, T. & T. Clark, publishers; Maj. (ret.) TA (formerly 7th Roy. Scots) ; 1914-18 War ; was Hon. Col. Forth Heavy (later 414th Coast) Regt. RA (TA) 1938-49: *m.* 1914, Ellen Mercy (Elenita), da. of the late Francis Drake, and has issue.

Arms—Azure, a fesse or between a castle triple towered argent masoned sable in chief, and a crescent of the second in base. Crest—A demi-lion rampant azure, holding in his dexter paw a battleaxe proper.

Residence—23, Wester Coates Av., Edinburgh, 12. *Club*—Caledonian United Service and Northern (Edinburgh).

Sons living—JOHN DOUGLAS (23, Wester Coates Av., Edinburgh, 12), *b.* Jan. 9th, 1923; ed. at Gordonstoun: *m.* 1969, Anne, da. of the late Angus Gordon, of Beauly, Inverness-shire.——Francis Drake (of 11, Addison Av., W11), *b.* 1924; ed. at Edinburgh Acad.; 1939-45 War with RN: *m.* 1958, Mary, da. of the late John Alban Andrews, MC, FRCS, and has issue living, Edward Drake, *b.* 1966.

Daughters living—Laura Moubray, *b.* 1916: *m.* 1940, Maj. Hugh M. Renwick. RAC (ret.), of Greenacres, 49, Gogarbank, Edinburgh, 12, and has issue living, William Norman Hugh, *b.* 1950.— Diana Elizabeth, *b.* 1942: *m.* 1967, Allan Miller Duthie, of Carlsgill Lodge, Westerkirk, Langholm, Dumfriesshire,—Cynthia Caroline, *b.* 1947.——Cynthia Adeline (twin), *b.* 1924; 1939-45 War with WRNS.

Brothers living—Henry James Douglas, *M.C., b.* 1888 ; Brigadier (retired) late Argyll and Sutherland Highlanders, and a D.L. for Stirlingshire ; European War 1914-18 (severely wounded, despatches, MC), 1939-45 War as Inf. Brig. Comd., and Col. on Staff: *m.* 1915, Isobel, who *d.* 1969, da. of the late Lt.-Col. Wentworth Forbes, of Glebe House, Brackley, and has issue living, Wentworth Douglas (2, Trevor St., SW7), *b.* 1916; Lt.-Col. Argyll and Sutherland Highlanders (ret.); 1939-45 War (wounded): *m.* 1948, Florence Mary (LESLIE), da. of the late Duncan Richard Ricketts, and has issue living, Wentworth Mary Carolyn *b.* 1949. *Residence*, Kerachbank, Doune, Perthshire. *Club*, United Service.——John Maurice, *MBE, b.* 1903; Hon. Maj. (ret.) RE (Movement Control); MBE (Mil) 1944: *m.* 1933, Winnie Stratton, da. of the late Dr. Campbell Highet, and has issue living, Hugh Lothian (c/o Bank of Scotland, 69, George St., Edinburgh), *b.* 1939; Maj. Argyll and Sutherland Highlanders: *m.* 1967, Deborah Mary Ann, da. of Col. William Innes Moberly, CBE (and has issue living, Hugo Ian Moberly *b.* 1970, Harry James Lothian *b.* 1972), Hamish Douglas, *b.* 1945; Capt. Argyll and Sutherland Highlanders; despatches Aden 1967: *m.* 1969, Wendy Ann Macdonald, only da. of Ian M. Harper, of Redlairdston, Buchlyvie, Stirlingshire (and has issue living, Ian Nicholas Harper *b.* 1971, Mark James Macdonald *b.* 1974). *Residence*,—Shorestones, Seaview, I. of Wight.

Sister living—Isabella Douglas, *A.R.R.C., b.* 1891 ; is an Hon. Life Member, British Red Cross So. : *m.* 1920, Arthur Cedric Mears Coxon, *T.D., M.B., B.Ch., M.R.C.S., L.R.C.P., L.D.S.* (late Capt. 5th Batn. Norfolk Regt.), who *d.* 1968, and has issue living, Arthur John Douglas (2, Elm Grove Lane, Dinas Powis, Glam.), *b.* 1927; Lt.-Cdr. RN: *m.* 1st, 1951 (m. diss. 1971), Pamela Ann, da. of the late Frank A. Longman; 2ndly, 1971, Mrs. Magnolia Sissons, da. of the late Philip Le Couteur Richards, and has issue living (by 1st m.), Mark Peter *b.* 1954.—Helen Florence Howard, *b.* 1923: *m.* 1948, Kenneth Roderick McKilliam, BA, Colonial Ser. (ret.) and Capt. Gordon Highlanders (ret.) of Green Hedges, Boughton Aluph, Ashford, Kent, and has issue living, Robert Douglas *b.* 1950; BSc (Chem. Eng.); ACGI: *m.* 1971, Catherine Anne, el. da. of John Paton Milne, of Montrose, Angus, Isobel Jean *b.* 1952. *Residence*, 8 Queens Court, Canterbury Rd., Ashford, Kent.

Collateral Branches living.

Issue of the late Lt. Ian Campbell Clark, RM, son of Maj. John Maurice Clark, MBE (ante), *b.* 1937, *d.* (killed in action Sarawak, despatches) 1966: *m.* 1962, Melita (who m. 2ndly, 1971, Anthony Hurst of, 27, Gordon Rd., Sevenoaks, Kent), only da. of I. G. Powell, of Woking, Surrey:—
Timothy Ian Hugh, *b.* (*posthumous*) 1966.

Issue of the late Lieut.-Col. Thomas George Clark, **T.D., 2nd son of 1st baronet,** *b.* **1868, *d.* 1948** : *m.* 1st, 1894, Eliza, who *d.* 1943, da. of the late James Reburn; 2ndly, 1944, Evelyn Agnes Nelson-Smith, who *d.* 1054 :—
(By 1st m.) Thomas George, *b.* 1895; a Dir. T. & T. Clark, publishers; Capt. 7th Bn. R. Scots (ret.); 1914-18 War: *m.* 1921, Mary Hall, da. of the late Thomas Aldcorn, of Johannesburg, S. Africa, and has issue living, Thomas George Ramsay Davidson (Tyneford House, Ford, Midlothian), *b.* 1922; is a Chartered Accountant, a Dir. T. & T. Clark, publishers; 1939-45 War with RAF: *m.* 1956, Sheila Campbell, da. of Herbert Campbell Brown, of Littleacre, Strathkinnes Rd., St. Andrews, Fife, and has issue living, Thomas George Nigel *b.* 1965, Sheena Campbell *b.* 1959, Karen Ramsay (twin *b.* 1959, Gillian Davidson *b.* 1962,—Wendy Margaret, *b.* 1935: *m.* 1968, George Gordon Brown, Maj. (ret.) 9/12th R. Lancers; Barrister, of Kingshot, Edward Rd., St. Cross, Winchester, and has issue living, Richard Gordon *b.* 1973, Melanie Ann *b.* 1969. *Residence*, 19, Whitehouse Loan, Edinburgh.——Eliza Lilian, *b.* 1890. *Residence*, Invergowrie, Parsonage Rd., Horsham, Sussex.——Kathleen Muriel, *b.* 1904: *m.* 1936, Hugh MacIntyre, and has issue living, Alison Dora, *b.* (Feb.) 1942, Jessica Margaret, *b.* (Dec.) 1942: *m.* 1966, William Sinclair Hays, MA, of Estancia, Ifoa, Minas de Corrales, Uruguay, and has issue living, Hugh Sinclair *b.* 1970, Catriona Eleanor *b.* 1971. *Residence*, Alticry, Port William, Wigtownshire.

Sir Thomas Clark, 1st baronet (many years senior partner in the publishing firm of T. and T. Clark, of Edinburgh), **was Lord Provost of Edinburgh 1885-8.** Sir John Maurice Clark, 2nd baronet. **M.B.E., V.D., D.L. (sometime senior partner in the publishing firm of T. and T. Clark), was Chm,** Scottish Life Assurance Co. (Limited), and Col. (sometime Comdg.) 7th Batn. Roy. Scots.

CLARK, Creation (U.K.) 1917, of Dunlambert, City of Belfast.

FREE·FOR·A·BLAST

Sir GEORGE ANTHONY CLARK, 3rd *Baronet;*
b. Jan. 24th, 1914 ; *s.* his father, *Sir* GEORGE
ERNEST, 1950 ; ed. at Canford ; is Capt. Black
Watch (Reserve), and a DL for Belfast; a Senator,
N. Ireland 1951-69; Grand Master of Grand
Orange Lodge of Ireland 1957-68, and Imperial
Grand Master of Imperial Grand Orange Council
of the World 1961-63; MP for Dock Div. of
Belfast (*U*) in Parliament of N. Ireland 1938-45;
High Sheriff of co. Antrim, 1954: *m.* 1949, Nancy
Catherine, da. of George W. N. Clark, of Upper-
lands, co. Derry, and has issue.

Arms—Barry wavy of four argent and azure, a galley with
sail set and flags flying all or, on a chief of the second a thistle
slipped with two leaves, between two roses of the third. Crest—
A demi huntsman proper, vested azure, blowing a horn or.

Residence—Tullygirvan House, Ballygowan, co. Down.

Daughter living—Elizabeth Frances Catherine, *b.* 1960.

Brothers living—COLIN DOUGLAS, *M.C., b.* July 20th, 1918; ed. at Eton, and at Camb. Univ.
(B.A. 1939 M.A. 1944) ; European War 1939-45 as Major R.E. (despatches, M.C.) : *m.* 1946,
Margaret Coleman, da. of Maj.-Gen. Sir Charlton Watson Spinks, KBE, DSO, and widow of
Maj. G. W. Threlfall, MC, and has issue living, Jonathan George (Somerset House, Threapwood,
Malpas, Cheshire), *b.* 1947; Capt. R. Green Jackets: *m.* 1971, Susan Joy, da. of Brig. T. I.
Gray, OBE, and has issue living, Polly Caroline *b.* 1973,—Sarah Louise, *b.* 1949,—Gillian Mar-
garet Anne, *b.* 1957. *Residence,* Kinelarty, Creevytenant Ballynahinch, co. Down.——Peter
Aubrey, *b.* 1927; ed. at Campbell Coll., Belfast: *m.* 1951, Rosemary Frazer, da. of T. Frazer
Mackie, of Guincho, Helen's Bay, co. Down, and has issue living, Richard Henry Frazer, *b.*
1952,—Michael Peter George, *b.* 1955. *Residence,* Castle Farm House, Ballygowan, co. Down.

Sister living—Beatrice Norah, *b.* 1911 : *m.* 1st, 1931, Major Theodore Bertram Doxford, R.A.S.C.,
from whom she obtained a divorce 1946 ; 2ndly, 1953, Col. William Buckley Nicholl Roderick,
O.B.E., who *d.* 1957 ; 3rdly, 1961, John Wrench, and has issue living, (by 1st marriage) Angela
Beatrice, *b.* 1935: *m.* 1st, 1958, (m. diss. 1968), Martin W. R. Heinzl; 2ndly, 1968, Ernest
Edward Giles Beeson, of Hoddern Farm, Piddinghoe, Newhaven, Sussex, and has issue living,
(by 1st m.) Philip Carlos Martin *b.* 1960, Robert Peter Douglas *b.* 1962, Martina Georgina
Angela *b.* 1959 (by 2nd m.) Julia Mary *b.* 1969, Sarah Elizabeth *b.* 1970. *Residence,* Casa de Las
Flores, Apartado 103, San Pedro de Alcantara, Malaga, Spain.

The 1st baronet, Sir George Smith Clark (son of James Clark, of Paisley), was M.P. for N. Div.
of Belfast (*C*) 1907-10, and a Member of Senate of N. Ireland 1925-34. The 2nd baronet, Sir
George Ernest Clark, was High Sheriff of co. Antrim 1940, and of co. Down 1941.

STEWART-CLARK, Creation (U.K.) 1918, of Dundas, West Lothian.

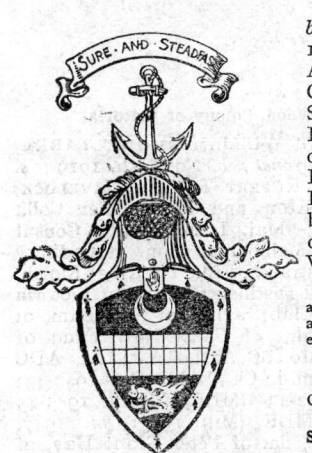

SURE·AND·STEADFAST

Sir JOHN STEWART-CLARK, 3rd *Baronet*;
b. Sept. 17th, 1929; *s.* his father, *Sir* STEWART,
1971; ed. at Eton, and Balliol Coll., Oxford;
AMP Harvard Business Sch.; late Lt. Coldm.
Gds.; Member of Queen's Body Guard for
Scotland (Roy. Co. of Archers); Man.
Dir. of J. & P. Coats, Pakistan, Ltd. 1961-67,
of J. A. Carp's Garenfabrieken, Helmond,
Holland, 1967-70, and Philips Electrical, Ltd.,
London 1971-75, since when of Pye of Cam-
bridge, Ltd.: *m.* 1958, Lydia Frederika,
da. of Jonkheer James William Loudon, of
Valkenswaard, Netherlands, and has issue.

Arms—Sable, a fesse chequy argent and azure between
a crescent or in chief, a boar's head couped of the last, armed
and langued of the third in base, a bordure ermine for difference. Crest—An anchor cabled gules.

Seat—Dundas Castle, South Queensferry, W. Lothian.
Residence—Holmsley House, Holtye Common, nr.
Cowden, Kent. *Club*—White's.

Son living—ALEXANDER DUDLEY, *b.* Nov. 21st, 1960.

Daughters living—Daphne Beatrix Felicia, *b.* 1959.——
Nadia Marie Anne, *b.* 1963.——Zarina Gabrielle, *b.* 1965.——Natalie Frederika Louise, *b.* 1969.

Sister living—Sara Norena Marie, *b.* 1932: *m.* 1961, Patrick Thomas Salvin Bowlby, of Culver-
thorpe Hall, Grantham, and has issue living, Anthony Adrian Francis Salvin, *b.* 1962,—Michael
Stewart Salvin, *b.* 1964,—Karina Jane Maria Minette Salvin, *b.* 1968.

Uncles living (sons of 1st baronet)—John Conran, *b.* 1906.——Alan (twin), *b.* 1914.

Aunts living (daughters of 1st baronet)—Elizabeth Morna (twin), *b.* 1914.——Marie Rona, *b.* 1915.

Widow living of 2nd baronet—JANE PAMELA (*Jane, Lady Stewart-Clark*), (Dundas Castle, South
Queensferry, W. Lothian), da. of the late Maj. Arundell Clarke, of Fremington House, N. Devon:
m. 1927, Sir Stewart Stewart-Clark, 2nd Bt., who *d.* 1971.

The 1st baronet, Sir John, was a Director of Clark and Co. (Limited), and assumed the
additional surname of Stewart 1909.

CLARKE, Creation (U.K.) 1831, of Dunham Lodge, Norfolk.

Sir (CHARLES MANSFIELD) TOBIAS CLARKE, 6th *Baronet*; *b.* Sept. 8th, 1939; *s.* his father, *Sir* HUMPHREY ORME, 1973; adopted the additional christian name of Tobias 1962; ed. at Eton, Ch. Ch. Oxford (MA), Sorbonne, and NY Univ., Graduate Business Sch.; Assist. Vice-Pres. London Branch of Bankers Trust Co., New York: *m.* 1971, Charlotte el. da. of Roderick Walter, of 12, Stanford Court, Cornwall Gdns., SW7.

Arms—Ermine, on a bend cotised gules, three swans argent between three annulets sable. **Crest**—A mount vert, thereon a lark wings elevated or, in the beak an ear of wheat proper, the dexter claw resting on an annulet as in the arms.

Residences—80, Campden Hill Rd., W8 7AA; The Church House, Bibury, Glos. *Clubs*, Boodle's, Pratt's, Jockey (Paris), The Brook (New York), Racquet and Tennis (New York).

Sapientia Melior Fortitudine.

Half brother living—ORME ROOSEVELT (28, Marville Rd., SW6), *b.* Nov. 30th, 1947; ed. at Eton: *m.* 1971, Joanna Valentine, da. of John Barkley Schuster, TD [see B. Wyfold].
Uncle living (son of 4th baronet)—Charles Frederick Orme (twin), *b.* 1909; ed. at Eton: *m.* 1942, Sylvia Vera, da. of the late Leo Kaelin, of Einsiedeln, Switzerland, and has issue living, William Oliver, *b.* 1943,—Katharine Sybil, *b.* 1950. *Residence*, The Little Manor, Tackley, Oxon.

Collateral Branches living.

Grandsons of the late William Peter Dunham Clarke, OBE, el. son of the late William Alexander Clarke (infra):—
Issue of the late Peter Ethelston Clarke, *b.* 1916, *d.* 1975: *m.* 1940, Isabel Helen (1, Kelso Place, W8), da. of Philip Elton Longmore, CBE:—
Peter Alexander, *b.* 1941; ed. at Eton, and Trin. Coll., Camb.: *m.* 1967, Lilah Victoria Mary, da. of John Forrester, of Ardnacross, Isle of Mull, and has issue living, Paul Sebastian, *b.* 1971.——
John Elton, *b.* 1948; ed. at Eton, and Kent Univ.

Grandchildren of the late William Alexander Clarke (3rd son of 2nd baronet) :—
Issue of the late Paul Humphrey Clarke, M.C., *b.* 1891, *d.* 1946 : *m.* 1927, Joyce Chicheley, who *d.* 1934, da. of the late Richard Chicheley Plowden :—
Humphrey, *b.* 1929.——Paul Ivor (Gongwe Farm, Box 77, Kitale, Kenya), *b.* 1931: *m.* 1963, Angela Mary, da. of Thomas George Cleaver, and has issue living, Fiona Mary, *b.* 1964,—Rosemary Ann, *b.* 1965.——Barbara, *b.* 1928: *m.* 1951, Anthony Lucien Noon Arlaud, Satima, Prior's Pocket Rd., Moggill 4068, Queensland, and has issue living, Anthony Stephen, *b.* 1953,—David Paul, *b.* 1955,—Christopher John *b.* 1961.

The 1st baronet, Sir Charles Mansfield Clarke, was Physician to Queen Adelaide. The 3rd baronet, Gen. Sir Charles Mansfield Clarke, G.C.B., G.C.V.O., served on Taptee River with 57th Regt. 1858, in New Zealand Wars 1861 and 1863-6, in Zulu Campaign 1879 (despatches, medal with clasp, C.B.), and in Basutoland 1880-81 (medal with two clasps), and was Gov. of Malta and in command of troops there 1903-7.

CLARKE, Creation (U.K.) 1882, of Rupertswood, Colony of Victoria.

Sir RUPERT WILLIAM JOHN CLARKE, M.B.E., 3rd *Baronet* ; *b.* Nov. 5th, 1919 ; *s.* his father, *Sir* RUPERT TURNER HAVELOCK, 1926 ; ed. at Eton, and at Magdalen Coll., Oxford (M.A.); Maj. Irish Guards, Consul for Monaco in Melbourne, Chm. of Cadbury Schweppes Australia, Ltd., of King Ranch, Aust., of United Distillers Co., and of Victoria Amateur Turf Club; a Dir. of Nat. Bank of Australasia, Ltd., of Capel Nat. Fund of Conzinc Riotinto of Australia, Ltd.; ADC (later PA) to Com.-in-Ch., Middle East 1942-43; N. Africa 1942-43 (MBE), Italy 1943-45 (despatches); MBE (Mil) 1943: *m.* 1947, Kathleen Grant, da. of Peter Grant Hay, of Toorak, Victoria, Aust., and has issue.

Arms—Or, two bars azure between four escallops, three in chief and one in base gules ; two flaunches of the second. **Crest**—In front of a dexter arm embowed in armour, the hand in a gauntlet proper holding an arrow in bend sinister or, flighted argent, three escallops also or.

Residences—Richmond House, Avoca St., S. Yarra, Australia; Bolinda Vale, Clarkefield, Victoria, Australia. *Clubs*—Guards', Lansdowne, Australian, Athenæum Melbourne (Victoria), Union (Sydney), Queensland (Brisbane).

Signum-quærens-in-vellere.

Seeking the sign in the wool.

Sons living—RUPERT GRANT ALEXANDER, *b.* Dec. 12th, 1947.——Peter Robert Justin John, *b.* 1955.

Daughter living—Vanessa Margaret, *b.* 1952.

Sister living—Elizabeth Elsie Faith, *b.* 1924 : *m.* 1952, Willoughby Alfred Lake [*see* Lake, Bt.]. *Residence,* Manor Cottage, Much Hadham, Herts.

Half-Sisters living—Mary Phyllis, *b.* 1887: *m.* 1909, Reginald Clive Power, who *d.* 1951, and has issue living, Faith Mary, *b.* 1918: *m.* 1938, Geoffrey Samuel Whitehead, and has issue living, Margaret Anne *b.* 1943: *m.* 1971, Ernest Buffett, Prudence Mary *b.* 1944: *m.* 1968 Peter Julian Isles Smith, and has issue living, Penelope *b.* 1970. *Residence,* 13, Tintern Av., Toorak, Melbourne, Aust.——Aimée Gwendolyn, *b,* 1894: *m.* 1st, 1915, Col. Charles Robert Tolver Michael Gerard, DSO, OBE, who *d.* 1971, and from whom she obtained a divorce 1930 [*see* B. Gerard, colls.]; 2ndly, 1940, Com. Humphrey Ranulph Brand, RN (ret.), who *d.* 1953 [V. Hampden, colls.]. *Residence,* Glynde Place, Glynde, Sussex.

Collateral Branches living.

Issue of the late Hon. William Lionel Russell Clarke, 3rd son of 1st baronet, *b.* 1876, *d.* 1954 : *m.* 1908, Florence Douglas, who *d.* 1961, da. of the late Col. Henry Douglas Mackenzie [Mackenzie, Bt., *cr.* 1673, colls.] :—

Hon.) Michael Alastair, *b.* 1915; ed. at Harrow, and at New Coll., Oxford (BCL, MA); 1939-45 War as Lieut. Australian Imperial Force; a M.L.C., Victoria: *m.* 1948, Helen Rosalind, da. of Essington Lewis, C.H., and has issue living, Andrea Rosalind, *b.* 1950.—Louise Merilyn, *b.* 1953.—Rosemary Janet, *b.* 1956. *Residence,* Burnewang North, Rochester, Victoria, Australia. ——Janet Marjorie Nina, *b.* 1911: *m.* 1941, Capt. Henry Armstrong Hammond, 5th Light Horse, AIF, of Swift St., Murrumburrah, NSW, and has issue living, Russell Rupert, *b.* 1945: *m.* 1973, Cheryl Gay, da. of W. R. Harvey.

Issue of the late Hon. Sir Francis Grenville Clarke, KBE, 5th son of 1st baronet, *b.* 1879, *d.* 1955: *m.* 1901, Nina Ellis, who *d.* 1948, da. of Thomas Cotton, banker, of Melbourne:—

Margaret Mary, *b.* 1904: *m.* 1st, 1933 (m. diss. 1952), John Egerton Oldham, LLB; 2ndly, 1952, William Haldane, of C'an Pacienci, Pollensa, Mallorca, Spain, and has issue living, (by 1st m.) John Christopher Clarke, *b.* 1934.—Patricia Anne, *b.* 1940: *m.* 1967, Albert Calvert.——Patricia Kathleen (Jaarloo, Camperdown, 3260, Vic., Aust.), *b.* 1906: *m.* 1939, Sqdn. Ldr. Raymond Vincent O'Byrne, who *d.* 1973.——Valerie Janet, *b.* 1920: *m.* 1946, Capt. Robert John Southey, CMG late Coldm. Gds., of Denistoun Av., Mount Eliza, Vic., Aust. 3930, and has issue living, Robert Clarke Allen, *b.* 1948,—Guy Francis, *b.* 1950,—Jonathan Edward, *b.* 1951,—William Blaise, *b.* 1957,—Patrick Richard Christian, *b.* 1963.

Grandchildren of the late Lt.-Col. Reginald Hastings Clarke (infra):—
Issue of the late Reginald Clive Nevil Clarke *b.* 1910, *d.* 1964: *m.* 1935, Elizabeth Macpherson, who *d.* 1965:—

Robin (2, Julie Court, Ashwood, Victoria 3147, Australia), *b.* 1935: *m.* 1958, Prunella, da. of Wilfred Weigall, of Cobden, Vic., Australia, and has issue living, Anthony Clive, *b.* 1963,—Sara Elizabeth, *b.* 1965.——Ernestine, *b.* 1937.

Issue of the late Lieut.-Col. Reginald Hastings Clarke, 6th son of 1st baronet, *b.* 1880, *d.* 1914: *m.* 1904, Ernestine Maud, who *d.* 1926, da. of Edmund Govett, of Melbourne :—

Joan Rosemary, *b.* 1908: *m.* 1st, 1931, John Francis St. Barbe Barclay, who *d.* (killed in action during European War) 1940; 2ndly, 1941, Frederick Norman Hill, and has issue living, (by 2nd marriage) Elizabeth Jane, *b.* 1942: *m.* 1963, Gordon MacQuarie Douglass, of 109, Adelaide Parade, Woollahra, Sydney, SNW, and has issue living, Sybella Jane *b.* 1966.—Susan Diana, *b.* 1944: *m.* 1967, Simon Creswick. *Residence,* 33, Manning Rd., Double Bay, Sydney, NSW. ——Ernestine Elizabeth Hastings, *b.* 1914: *m.* 1937, Timothy Collins, of Fairfield Park, Greta South, Glenrowan, Victoria, Australia, and has issue living, David Timothy Henry, *b.* 1939,— Penelope Anna, *b.* 1943.

This family was settled at Weston Zoyland, Somerset since the beginning of the 18th century. The Hon. William John Turner Clarke, father of 1st baronet, settled in Australia in 1840. The 1st baronet, Hon. Sir William John Clarke, was many years engaged in pastoral pursuits in Victoria and was a M.L.C. there.

Clarke-Jervoise, see Jervoise.

CLAY, Creation (U.K.) 1841, of Fulwell Lodge, Middlesex.

Sir HENRY FELIX CLAY, 6th *Baronet;* *b.* Feb 8th, 1909; *s.* his father, *Sir* (GEORGE) FELIX NEVILLE, 1941 ed. at Gresham's Sch., and at Trin. Coll., Camb. (MA) Sen. Partner in the firm of McLellan and Partners, and a Partner in the firm of Merz and McLellan, of 1, Warwick Row, SW1, and a FIEE: *m.* 1933, Phyllis Mary, yr. da. of the late R. H. Paramore, MD, FRCS, of Rose Cottage, Elstead, Surrey, and has issue.

Arms—Argent, a chevron engrailed paly of eight sable and or between three trefoils of the second. **Crest**—Two wings argent each charged with a chevron engrailed between three trefoils slipped sable.
Residence,—Wheelwrights, Cocking, Midhurst, Sussex.

Per orbem.
Throughout the world.

Son living—RICHARD HENRY (18, De Freville Av., Cambridge, CB4 1HS), *b.* June 2nd, 1940: *m.* 1963, Alison Mary, da. of Dr. James Gordon Fife, and has issue living, Charles Richard, *b.* 1965,—Thomas Henry *b.* 1967,—James Felix *b.* 1969,—Virginia Rachel *b.* 1964,— Catherine, *b.* 1971.

Daughters living—Jenny Elizabeth, *b.* 1936: *m.* 1959, Oswyn Murray, of 88, Southfield Rd., Oxford, and has issue living, James Augustus Henry, *b.* 1961,—Octavia, *b.* 1965.——Sarah Richenda, *b.* 1938.

Brother living—Anthony George Hobhouse, MB, BCh (Darwin House, 2, Darwin St., Shrewsbury), *b.* 1914; ed. at Camb. Univ. (MA, MB, BCh); late Maj. RAMC; 1939-45 War: *m.* 1st, 1938

(m. diss. 1959), Elizabeth Alice, da. of Sir Gilbert Charles Upcott, KCB; 2ndly, 1960, Patricia Barbara, who *d.* 1967, da. of the late Archibald Foulcher, of West Wickham, Kent; 3rdly, 1971, Pamela Joan, da. of Edward Farley Oaten, of Walton-on-Thames, and has issue living, (by 1st m.) Christopher George Anthony (12, Carnarvon Rd., Bristol, 6), *b.* 1940: *m.* 1973, Diana, da. of Edward Hippolyte Joseph Burbridge, and has issue living, Felix Temple *b.* 1974,—(by 2nd m.) Timothy Paul, *b.* 1961.

Sisters living—Margaret Imogen, *b.* 1904: *m.* 1938, Joseph Cleverly Lister, son of the late Col. Sir William Tindall Lister, K.C.M.G., K.C.V.O., M.D., F.R.C.S., and has issue living, Simon Felix (27, Connaught Gdns., N10 3LD) *b.* 1939, *m.* 1968, Penelope Jane Bidwell, and has issue living, Stephen Joseph Shelford *b.* 1971.—Imogen Mary, *b.* 1941: *m.* 1965, Paul Digby Moynagh, MD, FRCS (c/o Coutts & Co., 440, Strand, WC2), and has issue living, Mark Digby *b.* 1967, Rachel Imogen Moynagh *b.* 1970,—Bridget Ann (twin), *b.* 1941: *m.* 1965, Mieczyslaw Zygmunt Wasilewski, of 26, Peter Av., Oxted, Surrey, and has issue living, Thomas Adam *b.* 1969, Margaret Theresa *b.* 1966. *Residence*, Whitebays, Lee Rd., Aldeburgh, Suffolk.——Janet, *b.* 1907: *m.* 1948, Humphrey Seymour Outterson Wood. who *d.* 1971. *Residence*, 4, Hay's Mews, Berkeley Sq., W1.——Theresa Rachel, *b.* 1911; DSc 1955: *m.* 1974, Rodney Q. Searight, of 129, Oakwood Court, W14.

Widow living of 5th Baronet—RACHEL (*Rachel, Lady Clay*), el. da. of the late Rt. Hon. Henry Hobhouse, of Hadspen House, Castle Cary, Somerset : *m.* 1904, Sir (George) Felix Neville Clay, 5th baronet, who *d.* 1941. *Residences*, 18, Kensington Park Gardens, W.11 ; 9, Market Cross Place, Aldeburgh, Suffolk.

This family descends from the Clays **of** Crich, co. Derby. George Clay, of Cambridge, who married Elizabeth, daughter of Felix Calvert, of Ferneaux Pelham, in 1670, was great-grandfather of George Clay, born 1757, who for upwards of half a century was extensively engaged in London as **a** merchant and shipowner, and his son, William, created a baronet, was M.P. for the Tower Hamlets 1832-57, Secretary of the Board of Control 1839-41, and author of numerous works on Joint Stock Banking, Banks of Issue, the Currency, etc.

CLAYTON, Creation (G.B.) 1732, of Marden Park, Surrey.

QUID LEONE FORTIUS

What is braver than the lion.

Sir ARTHUR HAROLD CLAYTON, *D.S.C.*, 11th *Baronet* ; *b.* Oct. 14th, 1903 ; *s.* his father *Sir* HAROLD PHILIP DUDLEY, 1951 ; ed. at Haileybury; is Lieut.-Com. R.N.R.; European War 1939-45 (despatches, D.S.C.) : *m.* 1st, 1927, Muriel Edith, who *d.* 1929, da. of the late Arthur John Clayton (infra) ; 2ndly, 1931 (marriage dissolved 1954), Alexandra, only child of the late Sergei Andreevsky; 3rdly, 1954, Mrs. Dorothy (Jill) Hamer, who *d.* 1964, da. of the late Arthur John Greenhalgh, of Llanrhos, Llandudno; 4thly, 1965, Mrs. Diana Bircham, da. of the late Capt. Charles A. Grazebrook, 60th Rifles, and has issue by 2nd m.

Arms—Argent, a cross sable between four pellets. **Crest**—A leopard's paw erased and erect argent, grasping a pellet. *Second Motto*—Virtus in actione consistit (*Virtue consists in action*).
Residence—Colonsay, Kingswear, Devon.

Son living—By 2nd marriage—DAVID ROBERT (Rock House, Kingswear, Devon), *b.* Dec. 12th, 1936; Capt. MN: *m.* 1971. Julia Louise, da. of the late Charles Henry Redfearn, and has issue living, Robert Philip, *b.* July 8th, 1975.

Daughter living—By 2nd marriage—Ann, *b.* 1933 : *m.* 1951, Alfred Plews. *Residence*, Bardwell, Hookhills Rd., Paignton, Devon.

Brother living—FitzRoy Richard Henry (20, Rozel, Middle Lincombe Rd., Torquay), *b.* 1907; is Lieut. RASC; 1939-45 War in Central Med. Forces and BAOR: *m.* 1st, 1930, Morwen, who *d.* 1941, da. of the late Judge Fedor Andrew Satow [V. Chilston]; 2ndly, 1944, Moira Consuelo, who *d.* 1971, da. of the late Philip Fidelis Ryan, of Ceylon; 3rdly, 1973, Phyllis Margaret, da. of the late Reginald James Tindal, of Wirral, Cheshire, and widow of Sydney James Pullan, of Lillington Manor, Leamington Spa, and has issue living, (by 1st m.) Barry Drew Satow, *b.* 1935,—(by 2nd m.) Roderick John (c/o National Westminster Bank, Drapers Gdns., EC2), *b.* 1945: *m.* 1968, Diana Melissa, yr. da. of Sir Horace Alan Walker, of Eaton Place, SW1, and Alcester, and has issue living, Patrick Justin FitzRoy *b.* 1970, Louisa Jane *b.* 1972,—(by 1st m.) Ailsa *b.* 1932: *m.* 1952, William Findlay Key, of 39, Forest Drive, Pinelands, Cape Town, S. Africa, and has issue living, Richard William *b.* 1960, Philippa Margaret *b.* 1954, Gail Morwen *b.* 1956.

Daughters living of 8th baronet—Cynthia Anne CLAYTON-EAST, *b.* 1914; 1939-45 War as Section Officer WAAF: *m.* 1949, as his second wife, Walter Gerald Cloete Graham, CBE, and has issue living, a son, *b.* 1956,—a da., *b.* 1954. *Residence*, Milland, Hertmonceux, Sussex.——Erica Marcia, *b.* 1915: *m.* 1938 (m. diss. 1958), Col. John Kenneth Maitland Gordon, CBE, late Welch Regt., who *d.* 1967 [V. Torrington, colls.], and has issue living, Alan Julyan Maitland (9, Fawcett St., SW10), *b.* 1941; ed. at Eton, and Trin. Coll. Dublin: *m.* 1968, Diana Margaret Elonwy James, of Salisbury, Rhodesia, and has issue living, Charles Edward Maitland *b.* 1975, Emma Caroline Alexandra *b.* 1971,—Cosmo Gerald Maitland (5, Farm Place, Kensington, W8), *b.* 1945; ed. at Eton; Bar. Middle Temple 1966: *m.* Vanessa Maria Juliet Reilly-Morrison. *Residence*, 19, Victoria Grove, W8.

Widow living of 10th Baronet—LEILA CECILIA (*Dowager Lady Clayton* (The Corners Nursing Home, 3, Greenway Rd., Churston, Brixham, Devon), da. of the late Francis Edmund Clayton (infra): *m.* 1903, Sir Harold Philip Dudley Clayton, 10th baronet, who *d.* 1951. *Residence*, 20, Rozel, Middle Lincombe Rd., Torquay.

Collateral Branches living.

Granddaughters of the late John Lloyd Clayton, R.N., 3rd son of 4th baronet
(cr. 1732):—
Issue of the late Capt. John William Clayton, F.R.G.S., b. 1833, d. 1913: m. 1st, 1862,
Mary Henrietta Charlotte, who d. 1880, da. of Col. Henry Charles Capel Somerset [D.
Beaufort, colls.]; 2ndly, 1892, Kathleen Mary, who d. 1943, da. of the late James Gibson,
M.L.C., of Tasmania:—
(By 2nd m.) Violet, b. 1893: m. 1st, 1914, Maj. Edgar Henry Stocker, formerly 13th
Hussars, who d. 1924, and from whom she had obtained a divorce 1921; 2ndly, 1923 (marriage
annulled on her petition 1926), Major Richard William Rice Jeudwine, formerly Roy. Irish
Fusiliers; 3rdly, 1932, Lt.-Col. Frederick Charles Goddard, Indian Army, who d. 1962. Residence,
The Manor House, Felpham, Sussex.——Winifred Ianthe, b. 1895: m. 1st, 1919, Capt. Martin G.
Byard Copeman, formerly Leicestershire Regt. from whom she obtained a divorce 1936 ; 2ndly,
1943, Col. Philip Herbert Catt, F.R.G.S., late Scots Guards (retired), and has issue living, (by
1st marriage) Michael George Auchel (of Lavender Cottage, Felpham Rd., Bognor Regis, Sussex,
and Northcliffe School, Grove Place, Nursling, Southampton), b. 1920. Residences, The Manor
House, Felpham, Sussex; Lavender Cottage, Felpham, Sussex.

Granddaughter of the late George Augustus Clayton, 2nd son of Rice Richard
Clayton, 4th son of 4th baronet (cr. 1732):—
Issue of the late Emily Maude Clayton, b. 1892, d. 1971: m. 1913, Douglas Cameron
Westall, who d. 1957:—
Sheila Yvonne, b. 1919: m. 1950, Harold Jefferson, of 13, Essex Villas, W8.

Granddaughter of the late Rice Richard Clayton, MP (ante):—
Issue of the late Francis Edmund Clayton, b. 1844, d. 1905: m. 1881, Eliza, who d. 1882, da.
of the late Henry Liggins, of 3, Ladbroke Square. W., and Antigua:—
Leila Cecilia (Dowager Lady Clayton): m. 1903, Sir Harold Philip Dudley Clayton, 10th Bt., who
d. 1951 (ante).

Issue of the late Arthur John Clayton, b. 1846, d. 1922: m. 1893, Alice Rose, who d. 1922,
da. of the late William Jones, of Hereford :—
Marjorie (Ballintua, 4A, Downsview Rd., Hassocks, Sussex), b. 1894: m. 1915, Capt. R. G. Thompson, who d. 1963, Roy. West Surrey Regt.——Mildred Hester Marian, b. 1898 (Ballintua, 4A,
Downsview Rd., Hassocks, Sussex): m. 1st, 1928, Maj. Constantine Hotham Crichton, who
d. 1946; 2ndly, 1954, Lennard Reed Barton, who d. 1967.

Grandson of the late Lieut.-Col. Sir Fitzroy Augustus Talbot Clayton, KCVO,
son of the late Rev. Augustus Philip Clayton, 5th son of 4th baronet:—
Issue of the late Capt. Cecil Fraser Talbot Clayton, b. 1880, d. 1940: m. 1st, 1909, Kathleen
Agnes (who obtained a divorce 1918), da. of the late Lieut.-Col. William E. Bradish-
Ellames, of Manor House, Little Marlow ; 2ndly, 1918, Alice, who d. 1957, da. of the
late John T. Hatton, J.P. :—
(By 2nd marriage) Gilbert Talbot Hatton, b. 1920 ; European War 1943-5 in R.A.F. Vol. Reserve.
Residence, Cobbles, Broadstone, Dorset.

Grandsons of Col. Emilius Clayton (b. 1841) (infra):—
Issue of the late Lt.-Col. Emilius Clayton, OBE, b. 1884, d. 1967: m. 1915, Irene Dorothy
Constance, who d. 1971, da. of the late Col. T. E. Strong, Indian Army:—
Michael Thomas Emilius, OBE (10, Overstrand Mansions, Prince of Wales Drive, SW11), b. 1917;
attached Min. of Defence since 1939; OBE (Civil) 1958: m. 1942, Mary Margery, el. da. of
the late Dr. J. Roberts-Pate, of Oxford, and has issue living, Amanda Rosemary, b. 1949.——
Anthony Hugh Le Quesne, TD (April Cottage, 43, Ford Lane, Farnham, Surrey), b. 1928; MA
and PhD, St. Andrews Univ.; FSA, Scot; Maj. Queen's R. Regt. (TA) and Intelligence Corps (TA);
Kenya Civil Ser. 1952-65, since when Sen. Lect., RMA, Sandhurst: m. 1973, Judith Mary, da. of
P. H. Blackstone, of Rhu, Dunbarton, and has issue living, Robert, b. 1975.

Granddaughter of Capt. Emilius Clayton (b. 1803), son of Lt.-Col. George
Clayton, son of the late William Clayton, 2nd son of 1st baronet (cr. 1732): —
Issue of Col. Emilius Clayton, b. 1841, d. 1921: m. 1883, Ellen, who d. 1947, da. of the late
Richard Laurence Pemberton, of Hawthorn Tower, Seaham, co. Durham:—
Bridget Eleanor, b. 1988: m. 1914, Capt. Winstanley Robert Coverdale Moorsom, OBE, RN, who d.
1966. Residence, Scarth, Winsley, nr. Bradford-on-Avon, Wilts.

Grandchildren of the late Major Sir Edward Gilbert Clayton, C.B., el. son of
the late Maj.-Gen. Henry Clayton, 2nd son of Lt.-Col. George Clayton (ante):—
Issue of the late Lieut.-Col. Henry Edward Gilbert Clayton, b. 1867, d. 1947: m. 1900,
Huberta, da. of Capt. Hubert Grenfell, R.N., formerly of Alverstoke, Hants :—
Henry Hubert, b. 1906 ; M.A. 19—— ; is Head of Theoretical Physics Branch, National Research
Laboratories, Chalk River, Ontario ; European War 1939-45, as Major Roy. Canadian Artillery :
m. 1944, Isobel May, da. of W. G. Winters, of Pembroke, Ontario, and has issue living, William
Edward, b. 1945,—Florence Nancy Thackeray, b. 1947. Residence, Deep River, Ontario,
Canada.——George Edward (Box 413, Ganges, Salt Spring, BC, Canada), b. 1907; BASc,
MCIME, MAIME: m. 1939, Olive, da. of the late H. M. Selfe, of Vancouver, BC.——Petronilla,
b. 1903: m. 1939, Richard Baden Whaley, ARICS, of Valley End, 27, Layton Lane, Shaftesbury,
Dorset, and has issue living, Richard Grenfell, b. 1940.——Grace Cynthia Maude, b. 1909: m.
1934, Philip Hennell Amsden, formerly RN, and has issue living, Michael Phillip, b. 1935,—
Harry Linton, b. 1938 (Box 272, Courtenay, BC, Canada),—Robin Petite, b. 1941,—Stephen
Oliver, b. 1944.

Issue of the late Blanche Georgine Clayton, b. 1865, d. 1951 : m. 1893, the Rev. William
Francis Sorsbie, who d. 1944, formerly R. of Swainswick :—
Sir Malin, CBE, b. 1906; FRGS; CStJ; Gen. Manager of E. African Airways 1947-56: m. 1st, 1928,
Vivian (from whom he obtained a divorce 1945), da. of Nevile Benskin; 2ndly, 1946, Elizabeth
Melmoth, who d. (May) 1955, da. of James McNeice; 3rdly (Oct.) 1955, Constantine, da. of the
late Albert Wheeler Johnston, of Greenwich, Connecticut, USA. Residence, Karura Av.,
Muthaiga, Nairobi, Kenya. Address, PO Box 45337, Nairobi, Kenya. Clubs, Bath, RAF,
Nairobi and Muthaiga Country (Nairobi),——Jean, b. 1904: m. 1928, Walter Norman Hughes,
formerly Housemaster of Whitelaw House, Rugby, and has issue living, Peter, b. 1941,—Joanna
Mary, b. 1931,—Katharine, b. 1934,—Dilys Ann, b. 1940. Residence, Downfield, Brockweir,
Chepstow.

Sir William Clayton, M.P., the 1st baronet (cr. 1732), was a nephew of Sir Robert Clayton,
Knight, Lord Mayor of London 1679. The 2nd, 3rd and 4th baronets were also Members of Parlia-
ment, and the 5th baronet, Gen. Sir William Robert, K.C.B., a distinguished Waterloo officer, sat as
M.P. for Great Marlow (L) 1831-42. The 6th Baronet was High Sheriff for co. Bucks 1876, and at his
death the title devolved upon his kinsman Sir Gilbert Augustus Clayton-East, 3rd Baronet of Hall
Place, whose immediate ancestor was William East, of Hall Place, Berks, created a baronet in 1766,
which title became extinct 1828. His nephew, the 1st baronet of the 2nd creation (1828), of Hall
Place, Sir East George Clayton-East, was 2nd son of Sir William Clayton, 4th baronet (cr. 1838),
and nephew of Sir Gilbert East, the last baronet of the 1st creation. The 2nd baronet took the

surnames of Gilbert-East and the arms of East for his life only by Roy. licence 1839. The 7th baronet, Sir Gilbert Augustus Clayton-East, s. his father 1866 in the Baronetcy cr. 1838 as 3rd Bt., and his kinsman, Sir William Robert Clayton 1914 in the Baronetcy cr. 1732 as 7th Bt., having resumed in 1870 the name and arms of Clayton-East in lieu of Gilbert-East. Sir Robert Alan Clayton-East-Clayton, 9th Bt. of Marden and 5th Bt. of Hall Place, assumed by deed poll 1932 the surnames of Clayton-East-Clayton in lieu of Clayton-East, and d. Sept. 1932, when the Baronetcy of Hall Place became ext., and the baronetcy of Marden Park devolved on his kinsman, Sir Harold Philip Dudley Clayton, 10th Bt.

CLERK, Creation (N.S.) 1679, of Penicuik, Edinburgh.
[Name pronounced "Clark."]

Victory loves care.

Sir JOHN DUTTON CLERK, CBE, VRD, 10th *Baronet : b.* Jan. 30th, 1917 ; s. his father, Sir GEORGE JAMES ROBERT, 1943; ed. at Stowe; Commodore RNR (ret.); a JP for Midlothian since 1955, Vice-Lieut. 1965-72, since when Lord-Lieut.; CBE (Mil.) 1966: m. 1944, Evelyn Elizabeth, da. of the late W. Robertson, and has issue.

Arms—Or, a fesse checky azure and argent between two crescents in chief gules, and a boar's head couped in base sable. **Crest**—A demi-huntsman winding a horn proper. **Supporters**—*Dexter,* a naked man wreathed about the middle with oak, in the dexter hand a bow, over his shoulder a quiver of arrows, and the skin of a wild beast hanging behind his back all proper ; *sinister,* a Druid priest with flowing beard proper, vested and hooded argent, holding in the sinister hand an oak-branch acorned vert.

Seat—Penicuik House, Penicuik, Midlothian.

Sons living—ROBERT MAXWELL, (Lachlanwells, Forres, Morayshire, IV36 0RA), b. April 3rd, 1945; ed. at Winchester and London Univ. (BSc Agric); ARICS: m. 1970, Felicity Faye, yr. da. of Feorge Collins, of Grayshott House, Bampton, Oxford, and has issue living, Goerge Napier, b. 1975,—Julia Elizabeth, b. 1973.— Piers Edward John, b. 1955.

Daughters living—Aymée Lavinia, b. 1947: m. 1969, George Robin Paget Ferguson, of 5, Windsor Terr., Clifton, Bristol, and has issue living, John Spencer Guy b. 1974,—Alice Rose, b. 1971.— Honor Elizabeth, b. 1957.

Sisters living—Susan Rosemary Dacre, b. 1905: m. 1928, Col. Hugh Francis d'Assisi Stuart Law DSO, OBE, MC, TD, DL, late Irish Guards and Border Regt. (TA), and has issue living, Hugh Francis Stephen John, b. 1931; Capt. late 9th Lancers,—Francis Robin Luke Alexander, b. 1946,—Rosemary Bridget Honor Stuart, b. 1930. *Residence*, Barony House, Lasswade, Midlothian.——Aymée Lavender, b. 1907; formerly Junior Com. and temporary Senior Com. ATS: m. 1928, Col. Alan Vincent Gandar Dower, TD, DL, late 2nd Dragoon Guards, and has issue living, Natalie Gay Stuart, b. 1931. *Residences*, Newington House, Warborough, Oxford; 35, Lowndes St., Belgrave Sq., SW1; Swinbrook Cottage, Swinbrook, Oxon.

Collateral Branches living.

Grandsons of the late George Edward Clerk, b. 1850, el. son of the late George Edward Clerk (b. 1815) (infra):—
Issue of the late George Edward Clerk, M.D., C.M., b. 1877, d. 1938: m. 1903, Annie, da. of Eugene Manny :—
Sydney Percy, b. 1912: m. 1938, Thérèse, da. of Louis St. Laurent, and has issue living, Michelle Marie Madeleine, b. 1940,—Héléne, b. 1943.——Joseph Harry, b. 1914: m. 1950, Alberta Therese, da. of Armand Drouin, and has issue living, Irene Gail, b. 1952. *Residence*,

Issue of the late Abel Clerk, b. 1897, d. 1964: m. 1927, Cecile, da. of R. Poisson:—
André Arthur (10430, Meunier St., Ahuntsic, Montreal, Canada), b. 1929: m. 1955, Claire, da. of Armand Charbonneau, and has issue living, Georges, b. 1958,—Benoit, b. 1962,—Bruno, b. 1964, —Micheline, b. 1956.

Granddaughter of the late George Edward Clerk (b. 1815), 2nd son of 6th baronet:—
Issue of the late Dr. Charles François Clerk, b. 1851, d. 1927: m. 1st, 1873, Noemi Bertrand, who d. 1883; 2ndly, 1884, Delphine Barsalo who d. 1951:—
(By 1st m.) Marie b. 1882: m. 1903, Ovide Gelinas, who d. 1958, and has issue living, Ernest Aimé, b. 1917,—Germaine Delphine (23, Presidental Terr., Acushnet, Mass., USA), b. 1908: m. 1931, Frank Peppin, who d. 1967, and has issue living, Jeanne Solange b. 1935: m. 1956, Pierre Senecal, of 3, Westmouth Sq., Montreal, Quebec, Canada (and has issue living, Paul b. 1957, Philippe b. 1963), Susan b. 1940: m. 1972, Paul Charbonneau, of 209, Herson St., New Bedford, Mass., USA.

Grandchildren of the Edmund Antoine Clerk (infra):—
Issue of the late Walter Charles Clerk, *b.* 1891, *d.* 1937 : *m.* 1st, 1915, Jeanne Beauchamp,
who *d.* 1920; 2ndly, 1922, Gabrielle Beauchamp:—
(By 1st marriage) Françoise, *b.* 1917: *m.* 1943, Pierre R. Gendron, D.S.C., Sub-Lieut. Roy.
Canadian Naval Vol. Reserve.——Marguerite, *b.* 1919: *m.* 1943, Jacques de Tonnancour.——(By
2nd marriage) George *b.* 1925: *m.* 1950, Lucette C. Barbeau, and has issue living, Patrice, *b.*
1964,—Philippe, *b.* 1959,—Josée, *b.* 1952,—Michelle, *b.* 1953,—Danie, *b.* 1957. *Residence*,
455, Ardwell, Mount Royal, Montreal, Canada.——Robert, *b.* 1926.——Suzanne, *b.* 1924.

Grandchildren of the ate George Edward Clerk (ante):—
Issue of the late Edmund Antoine Clerk, *b.* 1858, *d.* 1921: *m.* 1886, Malvina Tourville,
who *d.* 1900:—
Guy, *b.* 1893; late Customs Officer: *m.* 1916, Jeanne Mongeau.——Henry, *b.* 1896: *m.* 1918,
Liliane Payette, and has issue living, Gérard (265, Beverley Av., Mount Royal, 304, Quebec,
Canada) *b.* 1919; Capt. Canadian Army: *m.* 1949, Lucille McCaughan, and has issue living,
Joanne, *b.* 1955,—Jacques, *b.* 1922; P/O RCAF: *m.* 19—, Gabrielle Brunet, PhD, and has issue
living, David *b.* 1952, Nathalie *b.* 1950,—Stephen (Chemin Osias Leduc, St. Hilaire, Quebec,
Canada), *b.* 1926; BA and BCL, 1951: *m.* 1954, Thérèse Saint-Jacques, and has issue living,
Eric Fraser *b.* 1955, Nicolas *b.* 1957, Jean (twin) *b.* 1957,—Pierre (of Florence, Italy), *b.* 1928; is
a painter: *m.* 1953, Adriana Bertolini, and has issue living, Jessica *b.* 1954. *Residence*, St.
Hilaire sur Richelieu, co. Rouville, Quebec, Canada.——Paul, *b.* 1890: *m.* 1927, Alice Gascon,
who *d.* 1947, and has issue living, Paul, *b.* 1930,—Andrée, *b.* 1933,—Françoise, *b.* 1928: *m.* 1952,
Léon D. Des Lauriers.——Bernard, *b.* 1902.——Marie, *b.* 1894.——Pauline, *b.* 1896.——Yvette,
b. 1912: *m.* 1937, Jacques Trépanier, LLD, Journalist, and has issue living, François *b.* 1938,—
Maurice, *b.* 1942,—Hélène, *b.* 1943,—Josette, *b.* 1946, Micheline, *b.* 1947. *Residence*, 211,
Walnut Av., St. Lambert, Quebec, Canada.

Issue of the late Alexander Marie Joseph Clerk, *b.* 1861, *d.* 1932: *m.* 1888, Blanche Gelinas,
who *d.* 1942:—
Edouard, *b.* 1889 ; is an Architect and Inventor : *m.* 1917, Fernaude, da. of the Hon. Dr. Ernest
Choquette, MLC, of Quebec, and has issue living, Michel, *b.* 1920; M.Com. 1943: *m.* 1952,
Monique Martineau, and has issue living, Philippe *b.* 1953, Cyril *b.* 1954, Emmanuel *b.* 1960,
Catherine *b.* 1957, Sophie *b.* 1964,—Marc, *b.* 1923: *m.* 1949, Gabrielle Brunet, PhD, and has issue
living, David *b.* 1952, Nathalie *b.* 1950,—Stephen (Chemin Osias Leduc, St. Hilaire, Quebec,
Canada), *b.* 1926; BA and BCL 1951: *m.* 1954, Thérèse Saint-Jacques, and has issue living,
Eric Fraser *b.* 1955, Nicolas *b.* 1957, Jean (twin) *b.* 1957,—Pierre (of Florence, Italy), *b.* 1928; is
a painter: *m.* 1953, Adriana Bertolini, and has issue living, Jessica *b.* 1954. *Residence*, St.
Hilaire sur Richelieu, co. Rouville, Quebec, Canada.——Paul, *b.* 1890: *m.* 1927, Alice Gascon,
who *d.* 1947, and has issue living, Paul, *b.* 1930,—Andrée, *b.* 1933,—Françoise, *b.* 1928: *m.* 1952,
Léon D. Des Lauriers.——Bernard, *b.* 1902.——Marie, *b.* 1894.——Pauline, *b.* 1896.——Yvette,
b. 1912: *m.* 1937, Jacques Trépanier, LLD, Journalist, and has issue living, François *b.* 1938,—
Maurice, *b.* 1942,—Hélène, *b.* 1943,—Josette, *b.* 1946, Micheline, *b.* 1947. *Residence*, 211,
Walnut Av., St. Lambert, Quebec, Canada.

Issue of the late Jean Pio Robert Clerk, *b.* 1870, *d.* 1932: *m.* 1898, Marie Alma, da. of
the late Hon. Senator L. O. David:—
Jacques Donald, *b.* 1904 : *m.* 19—, Elizabeth Labrecque, and has issue living, Robert, *b.* 1929,—
Gilles, *b.* 1931,—Jacques, *b.* 1930,—Lise, *b.* 1929,—Janine, *b.* 1933.——Louis Phillippe Duncan,
b. 1907 : *m.* 1936, Gabrielle, da. of the Hon. G. C. Simond, and has issue living, Henri, *b.* 1941,—
Michelle, *b.* 1937.——Jean Elton, *b.* 1919.——Jeanne Isabella, *b.* 1899 : *m.* 19—, Theodore
Fauteux, and has issue living, Pierre, *b.* 1928,—Louise, *b.* 1927.——Camille Gertrude, *b.* 1902.

Granddaughter of the late Alexander Marie Joseph Clerk (ante):—
Issue of the late Maurice Clerk, *b.* 1893, *d.* 1926 : *m.* 1926, Marguerite Lajoie:—
Louise, *b.* 1926: *m.* 1948, Léopold Brégent. *Residence*,

Granddaughters of the late John Clerk, QC, 3rd son of 6th baronet:—
Issue of the late John Frederick Clerk, *b.* 1848, *d.* 1931 : *m.* 1884, Eleanor, who *d.* 1937, da.
of the late Gustavus Smith, of Goldicote [*see* D. Atholl, colls.]:—
Violet (The Old Vicarage, Chippenham, Wilts.), *b.* 1886: *m.* 1909, Francis Maurice Du Plat Taylor,
JP, MICE, who *d.* 1954, and has issue living, St. John Maurice (twin) (The Old Vicar-
age, Chippenham, Wilts.), *b.* 1917; Capt. R. W. Kent Regt.: *m.* 1945, Katherine Jean, da.
of Col. L. E. Machin, King's Own Scottish Borderers, and has issue living, Thalia Frances *b.*
1946: *m.* 19—, Robert Race, and has issue living (Amos *b.* 1965, Esther (twin) *b.* 1965), Caroline
Mary *b.* 1950: *m.* 1971, Peter Attridge, Joanna Bridget (twin) *b.* 1950, Rosemary Anne *b.* 1953,
Barbara Jean *b.* 1954,—Virginia Mercy, *b.* 1910.——Nancy Eleanor, *b.* 1901: *m.* 1934, Philip
Giles Tennant. *Residence*,
Issue of the late Duncan Edward Clerk, *b.* 1863, *d.* 1941: *m.*1890, Madge, who *d.* 1942,
da. of the Rev. David Bruce, D.D.:—
Mabel Thorold Bruce, *b.* 1895. *Residence*,

Grandchildren of the late Major Edward Clerk, 7th son of 6th baronet :—
Issue of the late William Henry Clerk, *b.* 1867, *d.* 1915 : *m.* 1906, Sarah Cecilia Reeves,
who *d.* 1954 :—
Edward, *b.* 1907 : *m.* 1940, Dora Appleby, and has issue living, Edward Peter, *b.* 1941. *Residence*,
Musk Vale, Foster North, Victoria, Australia.——William Robert (twin), *b.* 1907. *Residence*,
29, St. Georges Road, Armadale, Victoria, Australia.
Issue of the late Herbert Edward Clerk, *b.* 1871, *d.* 1931: *m.* 1908, Helen, who *d.* 1946,
da. of the late Jules A. Heuer :—
Margery Alice, *CBE*, *b.* 1913; ed. at St. Paul's Girls' Sch., and St. Hugh's Coll., Oxford (MA); JP
of City of London; Member of Chelsea Borough Council 1945-56, Co. Councillor for London 1946-
58 (Dep. Chm. 1957-58), and Gov. of Hammersmith Hosp. 1959-65; 1939-45 War as Ensign
Women's Transport Ser. (FANY); CBE (Civil) 1959: *m.* 1937, Maj. Richard Thornton, Roy.
Tank Regt. (ret.), and has issue living, Richard George Clerk, *b.* 1944,—Anthony Christopher
Lawrence, *b.* 1947,—Anna Sara Constance, *b.* 1951. *Residence*, 30, Cheyne Row, SW3.——Mary
Helen, *b.* 1915: *m.* 1939, Michael George Russell Adams, and has issue living, Nicholas Henry
Harvey (c/o The Rifle Depot, Winchester), *b.* 1943, Capt. Light Div. (R. Green Jackets): *m.* 1964,
Leila, da. of Maj. G. M. King, and has issue living, Mark Henry Leo *b.* 1966, Claire Laura Catherine
b. 1971,—George Miles Bramston, *b.* 1956,—Daffodil Jane Florence, *b.* 1946: *m.* 1971, Charles
Brian Marriage, of Lawn View, North Lane, Buriton, Petersfield, Hants. *Residence*, Hazelhurst
Dymock, Glos.

Grandchildren of the late Col. Alexander Clerk, 8th son of 6th baronet:—
Issue of the late Arthur Stanley Clerk, *b.* 1864, *d.* 1948 : *m.* 1897, Edith Maud, who *d.*
1955, da. of the late C. E. Sheffield, of Nova Scotia :—
Charles Beverley, *b.* 1904: *m.* 1925, Angela Herbin, who *d.* 1969, and has issue living, Alexander
Simson (23, Pleasant St., Kentville, Nova Scotia), *b.* 1930: *m.* 1953, Shirley Evangeline, da. of
Robert S. Cook, of Kentville, Nova Scotia, and has issue living, Charles Alexander *b.* 1954,
Thomas Richard *b.* 1956, Katharine Lois *b.* 1958, Susan Berhice *b.* 1961, Faye Marie *b.* 1965,—
Mary Beverley, *b.* 1929: *m.* 1954, William Stevens, of 1245, Agincourt Rd., Ottawa, 3, Canada,
and has issue living, William Charles *b.* 1954, Marylynne Margaret *b.* 1958. *Residence*, Nichols
Rd., Kentville, Nova Scotia, Canada.——Dorothy Evangeline, *b.* 1902: *m.* 1926, Arthur Merlin,
of 82, Broadway Av., Apt. 1, Toronto, 12, Ont., and has issue living, Marilyn, *b.* 1928: *m.* 1st,
(m. diss. 1967) Kenneth Arthur Wynne; 2ndly, 1967, Richard Arthur Kirby, of 32, Willowbank
Blvd., Toronto, Canada, and has issue living (by 1st m.) Kenneth Arthur *b.* 1955, Derrick Andrew
b. 1957.
The family is descended from John Clerk, distinguished for his loyalty and attachment to th
party of Mary Stuart. His great-grandson, John, was created a baronet by Charles II. The 2nd
baronet was a Baron of the Exchequer of Scotland 1707-55. The 6th baronet, a Privy Councillor,
was M.P. for Edinburghshire (C) 1818-32 and 1835-7, for Stamford 1838-47, and for Dover 1847-52,
and during his political career, held office in several administrations. Sir George Douglas 8th Bt.,
was Lieut.-Col. in the Army, and a Commr. of Supply for cos. Midlothian and Peebles.

CLERKE, Creation (E.) 1660, of Hitcham, Buckinghamshire.

[Name pronounced "**Clark**."]

Sir JOHN EDWARD LONGUEVILLE CLERKE, 12th *Baronet*, son of the late Francis William Talbot Clerke, Lieut. Coldstream Guards, el. son of 11th baronet; *b.* Oct. 29th, 1913; *s.* his grandfather, *Sir* WILLIAM FRANCIS, 1930; ed. at Eton, and at Magdalene Coll., Camb. (B.A. 1934); is Capt. Roy. Wilts. Yeo. (T.A.): *m.* 1948, Mary, da. of the late Lieut.-Col. I. R. Beviss-Bond, of Prosperity, Natal, S. Africa, and has issue.

Arms—Argent, on a bend gules between three pellets as many swans of the field; on a sinister canton azure a demi-ram salient of the first, and in chief two fleurs-de-lis or, over all a baton trunked. **Crest**—A ram's head couped proper.

Residence—Westbrook House, Bromham, Chippenham, Wilts.

Son living—FRANCIS LUDLOW LONGUEVILLE, *b.* Jan. 25th, 1953.

Daughters living—Albinia Jennifer, *b.* 1949.——Teresa Mary, *b.* 1951.

Brother living—Rupert Francis Henry, *DFC* (White Ladies, Thornton Av., Warsash, Hants.), *b.* 1916; ed. at Eton, and at Magdalene Coll., Camb.; Group Capt. RAF (ret.) 1939-45 War (DFC): *m.* 1st, 1945 (m. diss. 1972), Ann Jocelyn, da. of the late M. J. Tosswill, of The Top House, Paignton, Devon; 2ndly, 1975, Pamela Emily, da. of the late F. H. Bayliss, of Leamington Spa, Warwicks., and has issue living, (by 1st m.) Robert William, *b.* 1952,—Nicola Frances, *b.* 1950.

Aunt living (daughter of 11th baronet)—Beatrice Janet Elsie, *b.* 1891: *m.* 1916, Robert Evelyn Henderson, who *d.* 1925, sometime Lieut. Household Cav. and A.D.C., and has issue living, Robert Alistair (Ayotbury, Welwyn, Herts), *b.* 1917: *m.* 1947, Bridget Elizabeth, da. of Col. John George Lowther, CBE, DSO, MC, TD [*see* Lowther, Bt., *cr.* 1824], and has issue living, Robert David Charles *b.* 1948, James *b.* 1955, Emma Mary *b.* 1950: *m.* 1971, Hugh Leopold Seymour [*see* M. Hertford, colls.]. *Residence*, 55, Cranmer Court, Sloane Av., SW3.

The first person named in the pedigree of this family (some members of which were benefactors to Magdalen College, Oxford), is Richard Clerke, of Willoughby, *temp.* Henry VI. From him descended in the 4th generation, Sir John Clerke, who, at the battle of "Spurs," 1513, took the Duke of Longueville prisoner, and for that signal service received from Henry VIII. a grant of the canton of honourable augmentation, still borne in the family arms. The 9th baronet served in the 52nd Regt. at Waterloo.

CLIFFORD, Creation (UK.) 1887, of Flaxbourne, Marlborough, New Zealand.

Sir ROGER CHARLES JOSEPH GERRARD CLIFFORD, 6th *Baronet, b.* May 28th, 1910; *s.* his brother, the *Rev. Sir* LEWIS ARTHUR JOSEPH, 1970: *m.* 1934, Elizabeth, da. of Charles R. Kiver, of Christchurch, NZ, and has issue.

Arms—Checky or and azure, a fesse gules. **Crest**—Out of a ducal coronet or, a wyvern rising gules.

Residence—9, Winara Av., Waikanae, nr. Wellington, NZ.

Semper paratus.
Always ready.

Sons living—ROGER JOSEPH (135, Totara St., Christchurch, NZ) *b.* June 5th, 1936: *m.* 1968, Joanna Theresa, da. of Cyril James Ward, [*see* Ward, Bt., *cr.* 1911], and has issue living, Angela Mary Jane,, *b.* 1971.——Charles Joseph (twin), *b.* 1936.

Daughter living—Elizabeth Mary Jane, *b.* 1938.

Sisters living—Agnes Mary Annette (*Hon. Mrs. Francis J. Southwell*), *b.* 1899: *m.* 1924, the Hon. Francis Joseph Southwell, who *d.* 1953 [*see* V. Southwell]. *Residence*, Beechtree House, Market Drayton, Salop.——Rosamond Mary Clare, *b.* 1904; European War 1939-45 as Junior Com. A.T.S.

Daughters living of 2nd Baronet—Beatrice Mary, *b.* 1892: *m.* 1922, George Ranald Macdonald. *Residence*, Cust, New Zealand.——Helen Mary Jane, *b.* 1897: *m.* 1926, Baron Joseph A. Sapio de Belmonte, D.Sc., Marquis de Santa Oliva, and has issue living, Gioia Helen Patricia, *b.* 1927,—Christian Georgette Maria, *b.* 1939. *Residence*,

Collateral Branch living.

Granddaughter of the late Charles William Clifford, 3rd son of 1st baronet:—
Issue of the late Capt. George Gilbert Joseph Clifford, *b.* 1893. *d.* (of wounds received in action during European War) 1940: *m.* 1925, Alcie Mary (*Lady Clifford*) (Garnet House, PO Box 3750, Salisbury, Rhodesia); granted 1958, the same style, title, place, and precedence as if her late husband had survived and succeeded to the title), da. of J. J. Calder, of Ardargie, Perthshire:—

Anne Caroline, *b.* 1926. *Residence*, Benter Coach House, Stratton-on-the-Fosse, near Bath.

The 1st Baronet, Sir Charles (el. son of George Lambert Clifford [5th son of the Hon. Thomas Clifford, 2nd son of 3rd Baron Clifford of Chudleigh]), was Speaker of the House of Representatives, NZ 1853-60.

COATES, Creation (U.K.) 1921, of Haypark, City of Belfast.

Sir FREDERICK GREGORY LINDSAY COATES, 2nd *Baronet; b.* May 19th, 1916; *s.* his father, *Sir* WILLIAM FREDERICK, 1932; ed. at Eton, and RMA; Brig. (ret.) late RTR; was with Min. of Supply 1947-53, Assist. Mil. Attaché, British Embassy, Stockholm 1953-6, and attached to British Joint Sers. Mission, Washington 1956-58, Comdt., Roy. Armoured Corps Sch. of Tank Technology 1958-61, and Col., Gen. Staff, War Office, and Min. of Defence 1961-66 and Dir. Munitions, Defence Research and Development Staff, Asst. Mil. Attaché, Washington, USA 1966-69, and Mil. Adviser Defence Sales, Min. of Defence (Army) 1969-71; 1939-45 War in Libya, and NW Europe (twice wounded): *m.* 1940, Joan Nugent, da. of the late Maj.-Gen. Sir Charlton Watson-Spinks, KBE, DSO, and has issue.

*Arms—*Gules, a chevron cotised argent, on a chief ermine two bells or; on an escutcheon of pretence, quarterly, 1st and 4th argent, a fir tree growing out of a mount in base vert surmounted by a sword in bend supporting a crown in the dexter canton proper, and in chief and base, a lion's head erased armed and langued gules; 2nd and 3rd gules, three bears' heads couped argent, muzzled sable. *Crest—*A cock statant, wings closed, gules.

*Residence,—*Launchfield House, Bryantspuddle, Dorset. *Clubs—*Naval and Military, Royal Motor Yacht, Parkstone Yacht; Royal Yacht Squadron.

Son living—DAVID CHARLTON FREDERICK (17, Dryden Close. St. Ives, Hunts.), *b.* Feb. 16th, 1948; ed. at Millfield; a Dir. of Castle Motors, Thetford, Norfolk: *m.* 1973, Christine Helen, da. of Lewis F. Marshall, of Ely, Cambs.

Daughters living—Elizabeth Sara Ann, *b.* 1941: *m.* 1964, Maj. Carol James Hay Gurney, 2nd Green Jackets (ret.), of Higham Lodge, Higham, Stratford St. Mary, Suffolk, and has issue living, Christopher Hay *b.* 1968,—Sara Catherine, *b.* 1965.——Moira Louise, *b.* 1945: *m.* 1967, Anthony Hunt, of 74, Lynn St., Swaffham, Norfolk, and has issue living, Nigel David Anthony Howard, *b.* 1968,—Michael William Richard, *b.* 1971.

Sister living—Jean Ann Dorothy, *b.* 1919: *m.* 1938, Thomas Roland Lecky Sinclair of Rathlure, Old Towne, Montserrat, W. Indies, son of the late Capt. Sir Kenneth Duncan Lecky Sinclair, DL, RNR, and has issue living, Francis David Nicholas, *b.* 1940: *m.* 1963 (m. diss. 1966), Peggy Elizabeth Biller,—Kenneth Richard Coates (2132, Haycock Rd., Falls Church, Va., USA) *b.* 1946: *m.* 1972, Marion Evans Jefferds, of W. Va., USA,—Eleanor Margaret, *b.* 1943: *m.* 1962, Walter Roger Shope, Maj. US Army and has issue living, Thomas Roger *b.* 1968, Jean Marie *b.* 1964.

The 1st baronet, Sir William Frederick Coates, J.P., D.L. (son of the late David Lindsay Coates, J.P., of Clonallon, Belfast), was senior partner in William F. Coates & Co., stockbrokers, of Belfast, High Sheriff of Belfast 1906, Lord Mayor of Belfast 1920, 1921, 1922, 1929, and 1930, High Sheriff of co. Antrim 1931, a Freeman of City of Belfast, and first Member of the Senate of N. Ireland.

MILNES COATES, Creation (U.K.) 1911, of Helperby Hall, Helperby, North Riding of Yorkshire.

Sir ROBERT EDWARD JAMES CLIVE MILNES COATES, *DSO,* 3rd *Baronet; b.* Sept. 27th, 1907; *s.* his father, *Capt. Sir* (EDWARD) CLIVE, OBE 1971; ed. at Harrow, Queens' Coll., Camb., and RMC; Lt.-Col. (ret.) Coldm. Gds.; a JP for N. Riding of Yorks.; patron of two livings; served with Trans-Jordan Frontier Force 1937-40 (despatches), Italy 1944-45 (despatches); DSO 1945: *m.* 1945, Lady (Ethel) Patricia Hare, da. of 4th Earl of Listowel, and widow of Lt.-Col. Charles Thomas Milnes Gaskell, Coldm. Gds. [E. Ranfurly], and has issue.

*Arms—*Per fesse or and argent, three pallets sable, two flaunches gules, the dexter charged with a rose of the second, barbed and seeded proper, and the sinister with a lion passant also of the second. *Crest—*Upon a rock proper, a cock or, charged on the breast with a quatrefoil gules, and resting the dexter leg on an escarbuncle argent.

*Residence—*Moor House Farm, Helperby, York.

While I breathe I will struggle.

Son living—ANTHONY ROBERT, *b.* Dec. 8th, 1948; ed. at Eton, and St. Thomas' Hosp.; MRCS; LRCP.

Daughter living—Mary Freda, *b.* 1947; ed. at St. Mary's, Wantage, and Univ. Hall, Buckland.

Sisters living—Bridget Sibyl, *b.* 1910; Lady-in-Waiting to HRH The Princess Royal 1953-63: *m.* 1st, 1931, Harold David Cuthbert, Scots Gds., who *d.* 1959, and from whom she obtained a divorce 1944; 2ndly, 1962, Seton Hedley Dearden, MBE, of Butley Priory, nr. Woodbridge, and has issue living, (bv 1st m.) John Aidan (Beaufront Castle, Hexham), *b.* 1934,—Belinda Jane Elizabeth (*Hon. Mrs. Matthew H. Beaumont*), *b.* 1932: *m.* 1973, as his 2nd wife, the Hon. Matthew Henry Beaumont, of Flat 9, 50, Cornwall Gdns., SW7, and Glebe House, Woodlands Rd., Ashurst, Hants. [see V. Allendale],—Caroline Alice Celia (Flat 5, 29, Ennismore Gdns., SW7), *b.* 1940.——— Elizabeth Hermione, *b.* 1914: *m.* 1937, William Barclay Harris, QC, of Moatlands, E. Grinstead, Sussex, and 29, Barkston Gdns., SW5, and has issue living, Jonathan William (9, Addison Gdns., W14), *b.* 1940: *m.* 1966, Nabila, da. of Fares Sarofim Bey, OBE, of Minia and Cairo,— Jessica Elizabeth, *b.* 1938: *m.* 1973, Peter Tcherepnine,—Hermione Mary, *b.* 1943.

Widow living of 2nd baronet—*Lady* CELIA HERMIONE CREWE-MILNES, *JP* (*Lady Celia Milnes-Coates*) (Helperby Hall, Helperby, Yorks.), da. of 1st Marquess of Crewe (ext.): *m.* 1906, Capt. Sir (Edward) Clive Milnes-Coates, OBE, 2nd Bt., who *d.* 1971.

The 1st baronet, Sir Edward Feetham Coates (a member of the firm of Coates, Son and Co., stockbrokers, of Gresham St., EC), MP for Lewisham (C) 1903-18, and W. Lewisham 1918-21. Sir Edward Clive Coates, 2nd Bt., who *m.* 1906, Lady Celia Hermione-Crewe-Milnes, da. of 1st and ast Marquess of Crewe, assumed by deed poll 1946 the surname of Milnes-Coates.

COATS, Creation (U.K.) 1905, of Auchendrane, Maybole, co. Ayr.

Sir ALASTAIR FRANCIS STUART COATS, 4th *Baronet*; *b.* Nov. 18th, 1921; *s.* his father, Lt.-Col. Sir JAMES STUART, *MC,* 1966; ed. at Eton; Capt. late Coldstream Guards: *m.* 1947, Lukyn, da. of Capt. Charles Gordon, and has issue.

Arms—Or, three mascles sable, a chief engrailed azure, semée-de-lis of the field.   Crest—A stag's head erased proper, charged on the neck with an escarbuncle or.

Residence—Birchwood House, Durford Wood, Petersfield, Hants.

Son living—ALEXANDER JAMES, *b.* July 6th, 1951; ed. at Eton.
Daughter living—(Sarah Mary (*Viscountess Ednam*), *b.* 1948: *m.* 1972, William Humble David Jeremy, Viscount Ednam, el. son of 4th Earl of Dudley.
Brothers living—Ivor Paul, *b.* 1923; late Lieut. 12th Lancers: *m.* 1959, Gay, da. of Dr. Charles Pinckney, of 76, Albert Hall Mansions, SW, and has issue living, Dominic Peter, *b.* 1962,—James Charles, *b.* 1964,—Emma Lucinda, *b.* 1960,—Sophie Louise, *b.* 1966.   *Residence,* 55, Onslow Sq., SW7.——James Raymond, *b.* 1928. *Residence,* 24, Lennox Gdns., SW1.
Aunt living (daughter of 2nd Baronet)—Margaret Mary Josephine (*Margaret Viscountess Knollys*), *b.* 1902: *m.* 1928, the 2nd Viscount Knollys, who *d.* 1966.   *Residences*—20, Laxford House, Cundy St., SW1; Old White's Farm, Forest Row, Sussex.

With a faithful heart.

Collateral Branch living.

Issue of the late Alfred Mainwaring Coats, 2nd son of 1st baronet, *b.* 1869, *d.* 1942: *m.* 1895, Elizabeth, who *d.* 1940, da. of the late Morris Barnewall, of Flushing, Long Island, U.S.A. :—
Elizabeth Barnewall, *b.* 1902: *m.* 19— (m. diss. 1938), Kenneth McCall, and has issue living. *Residence,*

The first baronet, Sir James Coats (a Director of J. and P. Coats (Limited), sewing cotton manufacturers of Ferguslie Thread Works, Paisley), was el. son of the late Sir Peter Coats, of Auchendrane, Ayrshire, who was el. surviving son of the late James Coats, of Paisley, and el. brother of the late Thomas Coats, of Ferguslie and Maxwellton [*see* B. Glentanar and Glen-Coats, Bt.]. The second baronet, Sir Stuart Auchincloss Coats, was Private Chamberlain of Sword and Cape to Popes Pius X, Benedict XV, Pius XI and Pius XII, and sat as M.P. for Wimbledon (C) 1916-18, and for E. Div. of Surrey 1918-22.

GLEN-COATS, Creation (U.K.) 1894, of Ferguslie Park, Paisley, co. Renfrew.
[Extinct 1954.]
Sir THOMAS COATS GLEN GLEN-COATS, 2nd and last *Baronet.*
Collateral Branch living.
Issue of the late Alexander Harold Glen-Coats, 2nd son of 1st baronet, *b.* 1883, *d.* 1933: *m.* 1924, Elizabeth Millar, who *d.* 1969, da. of the late Thomas Greenlees, of Newark, Paisley:—
(Margaret) Elizabeth (Clouds Park, E. Knoyle, Salisbury), *b.* 1928.——(Winifred) Lettice (Clouds Park, E. Knoyle, Salisbury), *b.* 1929; a JP of Wilts.

COCHRANE, Creation (U.K.) 1903, of Woodbrook, Old Connaught, Bray, co. Wicklow, Lisgar Castle, Bailieborough, co. Cavan, and Kildare Street, City of Dublin.

Sir DESMOND ORIEL ALASTAIR GEORGE WESTON COCHRANE, 3rd *Baronet, b.* Oct. 22nd, 1918 ; *s.* his father, *Sir* ERNEST CECIL, 1952; ed. at Eton; is Hon. Consul-Gen. of Ireland in Republics of Syria and the Lebanon; 1939-45 War as Major Lancashire Fusiliers in Middle East: *m* 1946, Yvonne, only child of the late Alfred Bey Sursock, of Beirut, Lebanon, and has issue.

Arms—Azure, on chevron engrailed argent, between in chief two boars' heads erased or, and in base a sun in splendour of the last, a thistle proper between two trefoils slipped vert. Crest—In front of two tilting-spears in saltire a bay horse passant all proper.

Residence—Maison Sursock, Beirut, Lebanon. *Club*—Carlton.

By virtue and labour.

Sons living—HENRY MARC SURSOCK (Woodbrook, Bray, co. Wicklow), *b.* Oct. 23rd, 1946; ed. at Eton, and Trin. Coll., Dublin (MA): *m.* 1969, Hala, da. of Fuad Es Said, and has issue living, Alexander Desmond, *b.* 1973,—Faiza Maria Rosebud, *b.* 1971.—— Alfred Marie Stanislas Sursock, *b.* 1948; ed. at Eton, and Univ. of Rome (Dr. Arch.).——Roderick Inigo Marie Sursock, *b.* 1952; ed. at Le Rosay, and American Univ. of Beirut.

Daughter living—Isabelle Maria Elsa Sursock, *b.* 1962.

Sisters living—Elizabeth Margaret, *b.* 1915: *m.* 1939, Robert Elsworth Steen, M.D., F.R.C.P.I., and has issue living, David Michael Cochrane Elsworth, *b.* 1945: *m.* 1971, Rosemary Florence, el. da. of Maj. William Bellingham Denis Dobbs, R. Ulster Rifles (ret.), [see B. Vestey, colls.],— Sarah Fiola Elsworth, *b.* 1942. *Residence,* Mountsandel, Carrickmines, co. Dublin.

Half-Sisters living—Beatrice Dorothea, *b.* 1900: *m.* 1924, Capt. Richard Esmond Curwen Escombe, R.F.A., of Upton House, Upton, Andover.——Jan Asa Helen Grahame, *b.* 1939.

The 1st baronet, Sir Henry Cochrane, was Governing Director of Cantrell and Cochrane (Limited) mineral water manufacturers, of Dublin, and an Alderman of that City for over 25 years. Sir Ernest Cecil, 2nd Bt., was an Hon. Gentleman-in-Waiting to the Lord-Lieut. of Ireland 1908-09, and a dramatist (author of "A Matter of Fact" and "Monica").

COCKBURN, Creation (N.S.) 1671, of That Ilk.

[Pronounced "Coburn."]

He arises with a song.

Watchful and bold.

Sir JOHN ELLIOT COCKBURN, 12th *Baronet ; b.* Dec. 7th, 1925 ; *s.* his father, *Lieut.-Col. Sir* JOHN BRYDGES, *D.S.O.,* 1949: *m.* 1949. Glory Patricia, el. da. of the late Nigel Mullings, of Snitterfield, Stratford-on-Avon, and has issue.

Arms—Quarterly: 1st and 4th argent, three cocks gules, *Cockburn ;* 2nd and 3rd, gules, six mascles or, three, two and one, *Weapont ;* all within a bordure vert. Crest—A cock crowing proper.

Residence—

Sons living—CHARLES CHRISTOPHER, *b.* Nov. 19th, 1950.——James Chandos, *b.* 1952.——Jonathan Mc-Queen, *b.* 1956.

Daughters living—Julia Georgina, *b.* 1954.——Catherine Isabel (twin), *b.* 1956.

Sister living—Frances Isabel, *b.* 1921.

Widow living of 11th Baronet—ISABEL HUNTER *(Dowager Lady Cockburn),* da. of the late James McQueen, of Crofts, Stewartry of Kirkcudbright : *m.* 1919, Lieut.-Col. Sir John Brydges Cockburn, D.S.O., 11th Baronet, who *d.* 1949. *Residence,* 76, Learmonth Court, Edinburgh, 4.

Collateral Branches living.

Granddaughters of the late Col. George William Cockburn, 4th son of 7th baronet :—
Issue of the late Charles Edward Stuart Cockburn, *b.* 1867, *d.* 1917 : *m.* 1894, Lilian, who *d.* 1943, da. of Sir Morton Edward Manningham-Buller, 2nd Bt.:—
Rosalind, *MBE*; MBE (Civil) 1962: *m.* 1921, Cdr. Guy Darracott Millar, RN (ret.), who *d.* 1940. *Residence,* Flat 5, 24, Palace Court, W2.

Issue of the late Donald Graham Cockburn (twin), *b.* 1872, *d.* 1938 : *m.* 1st, 1915, Dorothy Agnes, who *d.* 1916, da. of Lewis Evans ; 2ndly, 1922, Nora, who *d.* 1947, el. da. of G. Walton, and widow of H. D. Douglas :—
(By 1st m.) Edith Penelope, *b.* 1916. *Residence,*

Alexander de Cockburn, ancestor of this family, was Heritable Usher of the White Rod 1373 and later Keeper of the Great Seal of Scotland. Sir James Cockburn of that Ilk 1st Bt. purchased from his cousin Sir Archibald Cockburn, 4th Bt. (whose title became dormant 1880) the lands of Langton, Berwickshire, and office of Usher.

Cockburn-Campbell, see Campbell.

CODRINGTON, Creation (G.B.) 1721, of Dodington, Gloucestershire.

Face to the enemy.

VULTUS·IN·HOSTEM

Sir WILLIAM ALEXANDER CODRING-
TON, 8th *Baronet* ; *b.* July 5th, 1934 ;
s. his father, *Lieut.-Com. Sir* WILLIAM
RICHARD 1961.

Arms—Argent, a fesse embattled counter-embattled
sable fretty gules between three lions passant of the
third. **Crest**—Not recorded at College of Arms.

Residence—99, St. James' Drive, SW17.

Brothers living—GILES PETER, *b.* Oct. 28th,
1943.——Andrew Richard, *b.* 1947.
Sister living—Sally Ann, *b.* 1939: *m.* 1962, Philip
John Francis Collingwood, of 105, St. James' Drive,
SW17, and has issue living, Richard Francis, *b.*
1964,—Sophia Catherine Mary, *b.* 1963,—Charlotte
Mary, *b.* 1966.
Uncle living (son of 6th baronet)—Frank Christopher,
b. 1908 ; ed. at Victoria Coll., Jersey (King Charles
1st Scholarship) and at Pembroke Coll., Oxford :
m. 1933, Bawn, el. da. of Col. Sir James Philip
Reynolds, 1st Bt., D.S.O., M.P., and has issue living,
Christopher Michael (Le Manoir, 1523, Surpierre, Switzerland) *b.* 1937: *m.* 1972, Christine
Beatrice, el. da. of Lt.-Col. Max Emil Bürki, of Château Surpierre, Switzerland. *Address*—c/o
Barclays Bank, 153, Sloane St., SW1.

Mother living—Joan Kathleen Birelli, el. da. of Percy E. Nicholas : *m.* 1933 (marriage dissolved
1952), Lieut.-Com. Sir William Richard Codrington 7th baronet, who *d.* 1961.

Collateral Branches living.

Issue of the late Gerald William Henry Codrington [son of the late Christoper William
Codrington, M.P., grandson of the late Edward Codrington (infra)], who was *cr.* a
Baronet 1876 :—
See Codrington, Bt., *cr.* 1876.

Grandchildren of the late Lt.-Gen. Sir Alfred Edward Codrington, GCVO,
KCB (infra):—
Issue of the late Col. Sir Geoffrey Ronald Codrington, KCVO, CB, CMG, DSO, OBE, TD,
b. 1888, *d.* 1973: *m.* 1923, Cecilia Mary Roche Court, Winterslow, Salisbury), da. of the
late Ernest James Wythes, CBE [Thorold, Bt.]:—
Michael Christopher Alfred (Dene House, Seend, Melksham, Wilts., SN12 6NJ), *b.* 1926; late Maj.
16th/5th Lancers: *m.* 1953, Irene Margaret, da. of the late Col. Mark Edward Makgill-Crichton-
Maitland, CVO, DSO [see E. Lauderdale, colls.], and has issue living, Camilla Anne, *b.* 1957,—
Bridget Margaret, *b.* 1958.—Katherine Alice, *b.* 1965.——James Geoffrey (Poplar Hall, Appledore, Kent), *b.* 1935: *m.* 1961, Lorraine, el. da. of R. G. A. Wells, of Lines End, Winchelsea, Sussex,
and has issue living, Richard Melville, *b.* 1962,—Charles Sebastian, *b.* 1964,—Annabelle Cecilia,
b. 1967.——Mary Alice (*Hon. Mrs. Robert T. Boscawen*), *b.* 1924; a JP of co. London: *m.* 1949,
the Hon. Robert Thomas Boscawen, MC, JP [see V. Falmouth].——(Emma) Cecilia (Roche
Court, Winterslow, Salisbury), *b.* 1930.

Issue of the late Capt. William Melville Codrington, CMG, MC, *b.* 1892, *d.* 1963: *m.* 1935,
Katharine Theodosia (Hambledon Manor, Oakham, Rutland) (who *m.* 2ndly, 1968,
Edward Kirkpatrick, who *d.* 1972), da. of John Houston Sinclair, CMG, CBE [Cock-
burn, Bt., colls.]:—
Jane Evelyn, *b.* 1937: *m.* 1961, Capt. Richard Miles Micklethwait, Grenadier Guards, of Preston
Hall, Uppingham [*see* D. Norfolk, colls.].——Teresa Anne, *b.* 1944.

Grandson of the late Gen. Sir William John Codrington, GCB, MP, son of
the late Adm. Sir Edward Codrington, G.C.B., 3rd son of the late Edward
Codrington, 4th son of 1st baronet :—
Issue of the late Lieut.-Gen. Sir Alfred Edward Codrington, G.C.V.O., K.C.B., *b.* 1854 ; *d.*
1945 : *m.* 1885, Adela Harriet, *C.B.E.*, who *d.* 1935, el. da. of the late Melville Portal, of
Laverstoke House, Whitchurch, Hants [E. Minto]:—
John Alfred *b.* 1898 ; ed. at Harrow, at Ch. Ch., Oxford (BA and MA 1930), and at Strasbourg
Univ.; Lt.-Col. (ret.) Coldstream Guards; 1914-18 War; attached to Mil. Mission, Smyrna
1920, and British Liaison Officer, French Forces in Syria, 1926-29; was ADC to Com.-in-Ch. in
India 1933-36, attached, Foreign Office 1939-42, Assist. Ch. of Staff, Gibraltar 1942-43, and
Special Liaison Officer, Algiers 1943-44; has Greek Mil. Cross; is an OStJ, and a Com. of Order of
Phoenix of Greece: *m.* 1936, Primrose (who obtained a divorce 1942), younger da. of the late
Dr. Vaughan Harley, of Harley St., W1. *Residences*, 1, Ranelagh Cottages, Pimlico, SW1;
Stone Cottage, Hambleton, Oakham, Rutland.

The 2nd baronet, who died 1792, disinherited his son, Sir William, the 3rd baronet, and **bequeathed**
his estates to his nephew, Christopher Bethell-Codrington, whose grandson was *cr.* a baronet **1876.**

CODRINGTON, Creation (U.K.) 1876, of Dodington, Gloucestershire.

True virtue is imperishable.

Sir CHRISTOPHER WILLIAM GERALD HENRY CODRINGTON, 2nd *Baronet;* b. Oct. 6th, 1894; s. his father, *Sir* GERALD WILLIAM HENRY, 1929; ed. at Uppingham; formerly Capt. 19th Hussars; European War (wounded); High Sheriff for Gloucestershire 1938: m. 1st, 1921, Joan Mary, who d. 1961, da. of the late Thomas Reginald Hague Cook, of 46, Portman Square, W. [Elliot, Bt., *cr.* 1874 (ext.)]; 2ndly, 1963, Henrietta Desirée Moutray, da. of the late Maj. Beresford Moutray Read, of Castle Grove, Bampton, Tiverton, Devon, and has issue by 1st marriage.

Arms—Argent, a fesse embattled counter-embattled sable fretty gules between three lions passant of the third. Crest—Issuant from a coronet composed of four roses set upon a rim or a dragon's head gules between two dragon's wings per fesse or and azure.
Seat—Dodington Park, Chipping Sodbury, Gloucestershire. *Residence*—Castle Grove, Bampton, Tiverton, Devon, *Club*—Cavalry.

Son living—By 1st marriage—SIMON FRANCIS BETHELL, b. Aug. 14th, 1923; ed. at Eton; formerly Major Coldstream Guards; European War 1942-5 in Italy: m. 1st, 1947 (marriage dissolved 1959), Joanne, da. of John William Molineaux, of Rock Castle, Kilmacsimon, co. Cork, and widow of William Humphrey Austin Thompson; 2ndly, 1959, Pamela Joy Halliday, da. of Major George Walter Bentley Wise, M.B.E., and has issue living, (by 2nd marriage) Christopher George Wayne, b. 1960,—Bethell, b. 1961,— Hugo John, b. 1964. *Residence*, Dodington, Chipping Sodbury, Gloucestershire. *Club*, Guards'.

This family is a younger branch of the Codringtons, baronets, of Dodington, creation 1721. The Codringtons have been established in Gloucestershire since *temp.* Henry IV. The 1st Bt. was Sir Gerald William Henry Codrington, son of the late Christopher William Henry Codrington, M.P. *see* Codrington Bt., *cr.* 1721, colls.].

COGHILL, Creation (G.B.) 1778, of Coghill Yorkshire.

He does not sleep who keeps guard.

Sir (MARMADUKE NEVILL) PATRICK SOMERVILLE COGHILL, *T.D.*, 6th *Baronet*; b. March 18th, 1896; s. his father, *Sir* EGERTON BUSHE, 1921; ed. at Haileybury; is Lieut.-Col. (retired), late Herts Yeo., R.A. (T.A.), a D.L. for Herts, and an O.St.J., served in the Arab Legion as Col. 1952-6; has 2nd class Order of El Istiqlal of Jordan; European War 1916-18 in France and Belgium (two medals); European War 1939-45 in Middle East (despatches twice); Special Ser. Officer, Turkey and Iraq 1919-25.

Arms—Quarterly: 1st and 4th, ermine a chevron between three cocks gules, *Coghill*: 2nd and 3rd, gules, on a chevron argent three pellets, a chief indented of the second. Crest—On a mount vert a cock gules charged on the breast with a bezant.
Residence—Savran House, Aylburton, Lydney, Gloucestershire.

Brothers living—NEVILL HENRY KENDAL AYLMER, b. April 19th, 1899; ed. at Haileybury, and at Exeter Coll., Oxford (Scholar 1917, B.A. 1922, Fellow 1924-57, M.A. 1925); F.R.S.L., 1950; Merton Professor of English Literature 1957-66; 1914-18 War as 2nd Lt. RFA: m. 1927, Elspeth Nora (who obtained a divorce 1933), da. of the late Dr. Richard James Harley, of Mill Hill House, Inchture, Perthshire, and has issue living, Rosemary Caroline, b. 1928. *Residence*, Savran House, Aylburton, Lydney, Glos.— Joscelyn Ambrose Cramer (Pennsylvania Farm, Newton St. Loe, Bath), b. 1902; ed. at Haileybury; formerly Lt. S. Wales Borderers; 1939-45 War as Lt.-Cdr. RNVR: m. 1st, 1926, Elizabeth Gwendoline (who obtained a divorce 1949), da. of the late John B. Atkins, of 30, Burton Court, SW3; 2ndly, 1949 (m. diss. 1971), Louise, da. of Comdt. Berdonneau, of Paris, and has issue living, (by 1st m.) Egerton James Nevill Tobias (of Aberlour House, Aberlour, Banffshire), b. 1930; ed. at Gordonstoun, and at Pembroke Coll., Camb.; Headmaster of Aberlour House: m. 1958, Gabriel Nancy, da. of Maj. Dudley Claud Douglas Ryder [*see* E. Harrowby, colls.], and has issue living, Patrick Kendal Farley b. 1960, Elizabeth Louise Gay b. 1962,—Faith Patricia Elizabeth, b. 1928: m. 1955, James Leslie Garson, of Hill Farm, Elsfield, Oxford, and has issue living, Jeremy James b. 1961, Elizabeth Lucy b. 1956, Rachel Margaret b. 1958, Isobel Laura b. 1968,—(by 2nd m.) Bridget Olivia Françoise, b. 1949.—Jocelyn Edith Louise, b. 1952: m. 1972, Stephen George Thomas, of 15, Royal Park, Clifton, Bristol 8,—Deborah Katharine Hildegarde, b. 1954.

Sister living—Katharine Adelaide Hildegarde (Savran House, Aylburton, Lydney, Glos.), b. 1906: m. 1944, Major Terence Greer Johnston, who d. 1972.

Collateral Branches living.

Grandchildren of the late Claude Plunket Coghill (infra) :—
Issue of the late Joscelyn Kendal Bushe Coghill, b. 1893, d. 1959 : m. 1925, Maud Evelyn, da. of the late Leslie Phillips Filder, of Crawley, Sussex :—
John Kendal Plunket, b. 1929; ed. at Sherborne; Lt.-Col. RAOC: m. 1951, Diana Mary, da. of the late Frederick Charles Callen, of Tanganyika, and has issue living, Michèle Mary, b. 1957,—

Amanda Patricia, *b.* 1960,—Samantha Jane, *b.* 1967. *Address,* c/o Barclays Bank, 92, Church Road, Hove.——Sheila Mary, *b.* 1926: *m.* 1952, David Polwhele Cooper, and has issue living, Shaun David Coghill, *b.* 1956,—Sally Muara Coghill, *b.* 1954,—Julie Rosalyn Coghill, *b.* 1965,—Lucinda Jane Coghill, *b.* 1966. *Residence,* Arda, M'sonneddi, Rhodesia.

Issue of the late Claude Plunket Coghill, 4th son of 4th baronet, *b.* 1859, *d.* 1922: *m.* 1885, Mary Maude, who *d.* 1948, da. of the late Ferdinand McVeagh, of Drewstown, co. Meath:—

Hester Elfrida Brooke, *L.R.C.S., L.R.C.P.* ; *L.R.C.P.* and *L.R.C.S.* Edinburgh 1916, *L.R.F.P.S* Glasgow; sometime Assist. Sch. Med. Officer, Cornwall. *Residence,* 1, Arlington Road, Eastbourne

The 1st baronet, Sir John Cramer, LLD, of Coghill Hall, Knaresborough (grandson of Oliver Cramer, of Ballyfoile, co. Kilkenny, and his wife Hester, sister of the Rt. Hon. Marmaduke Coghill, Chancellor of the Exchequer, Ireland), succeeded to the family estates of his cousin Hester, da. and heiress of James Coghill, LLD, and widow of the 1st Earl of Charleville, and assumed by Roy. licence the additional surname of Coghill 1774/5. His successor Sir John Thomas Coghill, 2nd Bt., and his brother and successor, Sir Josiah Coghill Coghill, 3rd Bt., assumed by Roy. licence, the surname of Coghill only in 1807 and 1817 respectively. The 4th baronet was High Sheriff of Dublin co. in 1859, and was *s.* by his second son as 5th Bt., the el., Nevill Josiah Aylmer Coghill, VC, Lieut. 24th Regt., having been killed while saving the Colours of his regt. at the battle of Isandhlwana Jan. 22nd, 1879.

WALEY-COHEN, Creation (U.K.) 1961, of Honeymead, co. Somerset.

Sir BERNARD NATHANIEL WALEY-COHEN, 1st *Baronet,* son of the late Sir Robert Waley Cohen, KBE; *b.* May 29th, 1914; ed. at HMS Britannia (RNC Dartmouth), Clifton Coll., and Magdalene Coll., Camb. (MA); Hon. LLD London 1961; assumed by deed poll 1950 his final forename as an additional surname; an Underwriting Member of Lloyd's since 1939; Chm. of Simo Securities Trust Ltd. 1955-70; Dep. Chm. Burston Group Ltd.; a Dir. of Matthews Wrightson Pulbrook, Ltd., Burston and Texas Commerce Bank, Ltd., Central London Region, Lloyds Bank Ltd., Tudor Accessories Ltd., Kleeman Industrial Holdings Ltd., and other cos.; a Liveryman of Clothworkers' Co. (Court 1966, Chm. Finance Cttee. 1971), and Alderman of City of London 1949, Sheriff of City of London 1955-56, and Lord Mayor of London 1960-61; Gov. Hon. Irish Soc. 1973; Chm. Public Works Loan Board since 1972 (Dep. Chm. 1971-72); Member of Council and Board of Govs. Clifton Coll. since 1952, Member of Coll. Cttee. Univ. Coll., London since 1953 (Treasurer 1962-70, Vice-Chm. 1970, Chm. 1971), Member of Senate London Univ. since 1962 and Court since 1966; Chm. Wellesley House Prep. Sch. since 1965; Chm. Devon & Som. Staghounds since 1953, a Member of Finance and Gen. Purposes Cttee. British Field Sports Soc. since 1957 (Treasurer since 1966), Pres. Bath & West Southern Cos. Show 1963, and Pres. Devon Cattle Breeders Soc. 1963; Member of Marshal Aid Commemoration Commn. 1957-60; Treasurer, Jewish Welfare Board 1948-53, Vice-Pres. United Synagogue 1952-61, and of Anglo-Jewish Assocn. since 1962, Pres. Jewish Museum since 1964, and a Member of Central Council of Probation and After Care Cttee. 1965-69, and of Nat. Corpn. for Care of Old People since 1965; a Prin., Min. of Fuel and Power 1940-47; Asso. KStJ; Knt. 1957: *m.* 1943, the Hon. Joyce Constance Ina Nathan, *MA, JP,* only da. of 1st Baron Nathan, and has issue.

Arms—Quarterly, 1st and 4th. argent, on a chevron gules cottised azure, between in chief two roses of the second barbed and seeded proper, and in base a buck's head couped also proper, three annulets or, *Cohen* ; 2nd and 3rd, argent a chevron azure cottised sable between in chief two eagles displayed of the last and in base on a mount vert a hind trippant proper, *Waley.* **Crests**—1st, a buck's head couped argent, attired or, holding in the mouth a rose slipped gules, the neck encircled by a wreath of oak proper between four barrulets gules, *Cohen* ; 2nd, out of a bush of fern a hind's head proper in the mouth a rose argent stalked and leaved also proper, *Waley.*

Residences—Honeymead, Simonsbath, Minehead, Somerset : 11, Little St. James's Street, SW1. *Clubs*—Athenæum, Boodle's, Pratt's, City Livery, University Pitt (Cambridge), Jockey Club Rooms (Newmarket), Harlequin, RFC, and MCC.

Sons living—STEPHEN HARRY (13, Godfrey St., SW3), *b.* June 22nd, 1946; ed. at Eton, and Magdalene Coll., Camb. (MA); Financial journalist *Daily Mail* 1968-73, since when Editor *Money Mail Handbook*; a Dir. Euromoney Publications Ltd., and a Gov. of Wellesley House Sch.: *m.* 1972 Pamela Elizabeth, yr. da. of J. E. Doniger, and has issue living, Lionel Robert, *b.* Aug. 7th, 1974.——Robert Bernard, *b.* 1948; ed. at Eton; New York Representative of Christie, Manson & Wood 1970.

Daughters living—Rosalind Alice, *b.* 1945; ed. at Cranborne Chase Sch.: *m.* 1966, Philip Ralph Burdon, of 157, Pendalton Rd., Christchurch, NZ, and has issue living, Miranda Ruth *b.* 1970,—Rebecca Joyce, *b.* 1972.——Eleanor Joanna, *b.* 1952; ed. at Cranborne Chase Sch., and Girton Coll., Camb.

COLFOX, Creation (U.K.) 1939, of Symondsbury, co. Dorset

Sir (WILLIAM) JOHN COLFOX, 2nd *Baronet*; *b.*
April 25th, 1924; *s.* his father, *Sir* (WILLIAM)
PHILIP, MC, 1966; ed. at Eton; a JP for Dorset;
High Sheriff 1969; 1939-45 War as Lt. RNVR: *m.*
1962, Frederica Loveday, da. of Adm. Sir Victor
Alexander Charles Crutchley, VC, KCB, DSC, and
has issue.

Arms—Sable, three spinning-cogs erect and in fesse or, on
chief argent, as many fox-heads couped at the neck gules.
Crest—A fox proper, charged on the body with two fleurs-de-
lys in fesse sable, and resting the sinister paw on a fleur-de-lys
gules.

Residence, Symondsbury Manor, Bridport, Dorset.

Light, Law, Liberty.

Sons living—PHILIP JOHN, *b.* Dec. 27th, 1962.——Edward Timothy, *b.* 1969.
Daughters living—Victoria Mary, *b.* 1964.——Charlotte Ismay Joan, *b.* 1966.——Constance Ruth, *b.* 1971.
Sisters living—Susan Helen Frances, *b.* 1929: *m.* 1950, William Henry Batten, and has issue living David Henry Cary, *b.* 1952,—Michael John, *b.* 1960,—Tessa Mary, *b.* 1954,—Bridget Caroline, *b.* 1955. *Residence*, Church Farm, Ryme Intrinsica, Dorset.——Bridget Alice, *b.* 1931: *m.* 1st, 1958, Lt.-Col. Peter Amyand Brenton Wickham, late RA, who *d.* 1967; 2ndly, 1968, Alexander David Evelyn Mure, JP, of Pevington Farm, Pluckley, Kent, and has issue living (by 1st m.), Anthony John Macarthur, *b.* 1960,—Mark Andrew, *b.* 1962,—Tania Catherine, *b.* 1959.

COLLETON, Creation (E.) 1661, of London.   [Extinct 1938.]

Sir ROBERT AUGUSTUS WILLIAM COLLETON, *C.B.*, 9th and last *Baronet*.
Daughters living of 9th Baronet—Lorna Colleton (44, Rivermead Court, SW6), *b.* 1887: *m.* 1st, 1913, Lt.-Col. Arthur Hautayne Bowring, RFA, who *d.* (result of active ser.) 1919; 2ndly, 1924, as his second wife, Col. Henry Charles Swinburne Ward, CIE, OBE, who *d.* 1966, and has issue living, (by 1st m.) Anne Hawise Colleton, *b.* 1914: *m.* 1st, 1932 (m. diss. 1948), Lt.-Col. Hubert Edward Buxton, who *d.* 1973, [*see* Buxton, Bt., colls.]; 2ndly, 1949, Lt.-Col. Neville Pierce Wadley, MC.——Gwynnydd Colleton (*Hon. Mrs. Hugh E. Thellusson*), *b.* 1894: *m.* 1914, Lt.-Col. the Hon. Hugh Edmund Thellusson, DSO, who *d.* 1926 [*see* B. Rendlesham].   *Club*, Hamilton.

COLLETT, Creation (U.K.) 1934, of Bridge Ward in the City of London.

Sir IAN SEYMOUR COLLETT, 3rd *Baronet*; *b.*
Oct. 5th, 1953: *s.* his grandfather, *Sir* HENRY
SEYMOUR, 1971; ed. at Lancing Coll.

Arms—Azure, on a chevron couped or between three hinds
trippant proper, collared of the second, an arch sable, between
two open books also proper.   **Crest**—A demi-hind proper,
collared or, resting the sinister foot on an escutcheon gold,
charged with a maul sable.

Residence—11, Collingham Gdns, S.W.5.

Sister living—Joanna Ruth, *b.* 1956.

Uncle living (son of 2nd baronet)—CHRISTOPHER, *b.* June
10th, 1931; ed. at Harrow, and at Emmanuel Coll.,
Camb. (MA); Capt. RA (TA); a FCA, a Freeman of City
of London, and a Liveryman of Glovers' Co; Common
Councilman since 1974: *m.* 1959, Christine Anne, da. of the
late Oswald Hardy Griffiths, of Nunthorpe, Yorks., and has
issue living, Alastair John Calvert, *b.* 1961,—Angus
Christopher Calvert, *b.* 1964,—Alexandra Louise Calvert,
b. 1972. *Residence*, 121, Home Park Rd., Wimbledon,
SW19. *Club*, City Livery.

Aunt living (daughter of 2nd baronet)—Margaret Ruth, *b.* 1922; JP: *m.* 1950, Col. George Victor Nudd Chadd, OBE, TD, JP, DL, and has issue living, Richard Jonathan, *b.* 1953,—Timothy Charles, *b.* 1955,—Nicholas Martyn Philip, *b.* 1958. *Residence*, Woodlands, Elm Tree Rd., Oulton Broad, Suffolk.

Great Uncles living (sons of 1st baronet)—Richard Ionn, *b.* 1901: *m.* 1926, Helen Alice, da. of the late Harry Hayns, and has issue living, Norman Ionn (78, Warren Rd., Donaghadee, co. Down), *b.* 1927: *m.* 1954 Ethne Maureen, da. of Samuel Chadwick, and has issue living, Kevin Samuel Richard *b.* 1955, Norman Michael *b.* 1959, Helen Margaret *b.* 1962,—James Masterman (Owl's Hoot, 23, Bramley Av., Coulsdon, Surrey, CR3 2DS), *b.* 1930: *m.* 1962, Rosalind Mary, da. of John Humphrey Lane, of Meldreth, Woodcote Av., Wallington, Surrey, and has issue living, Lucinda Mary *b.* 1963,—Richard Patrick (Thatches, Hall Lane, Witnesham, Ipswich), *b.* 1932; Capt. RE (TA): *m.* 1958, Gillian Anne, da. of Alfred James Remes, and has issue living, Jane Louise *b.* 1960, Johanna Mary *b.* 1962,—Henry Alexander (Capstone, Mouldsworth, Chester), *b.* 1944, ACA; a Freeman of City of London; a Liveryman of Distillers' Co.: *m.* 1969, Joy Eileen, da. of the Rev. Ross McPherson Heard, of Hatch Beauchamp Rectory, Taunton, and has issue living, Christian Tom *b.* 1972, Ross Tobias *b.* 1973. *Residence*, Mill Farm House, Blythburgh, Suffolk.——*Sir* Thomas Kingsley, *CBE* (of Fairfax Cottage, Wilderness Rd., Chislehurst, Kent; East India, Sports and Public Schools, and City Livery Clubs) *b.* 1906; ed. at Bishop's Stortford Coll.; a Master Printer, a Freeman of City of London, a Liveryman of Distillers' Co. (Master 1960-61) and a Member of City of London TA Assocn., and one of HM Lieuts. for City of London;

a Common Councilman of City of London 1945, Chm. of City Lands Cttee., Ch. Commoner 1955 and Chm. of Special Cttee., Corporation of London 1956-66, Chm. of Policy and Parl. Cttee, 1966-71, and Chm. Board of Govs., Bishop's Stortford Coll. since 1964; Chevalier of Order of Christ of Portugal; CBE (Civil) 1950, Knt. 1968: *m.* 1930, Beatrice Oline, da. of the late Thomas H. Brown, of Englefield, Bickley.——David Brooke, *b.* 1907; a Freeman of City of London, a Fellow of Inst. of Rubber Industry, a Dir. of Dunlop Co. Ltd. 1952-67; Past Pres. of Rubber & Plastics Research Assocn. of Great Britain; a Member of London Electricity Board, and Senior Pro-Chancellor of Loughborough Univ. of Technology: *m.* 1933, Mary Cecily Beatrice, da. of the late Hugh C. Aston, and has issue living, Anthony Hugh (3, The Dorkings, Great Broughton. Cleveland), *b.* 1936; MA Camb.; CEng; MICE; a Freeman of City of London: *m.* 1962, Christine Ann Little, and has issue living, Gail Christine *b.* 1964, Clare Elizabeth *b.* 1967, June Alison *b.* 1969,—Eliza[beth Anne, *b.* 1934; Freeman of City of London: *m.* 1957, David Luard Boult, of Ravelstone, Manley, Ches., and has issue living, David Mark *b.* 1960, Edward William *b.* 1963, Nicola Anne Louise, *b.* 1958,—Bridget Mary, *b.* 1945. *Residence,* West Winds, 149, The Drive, Rickmansworth, Herts.

Mother living—Sheila Joan (11, Collingham Gdns., SW5), only da. of the late Harold Scott, of Inverleith Gdns., Edinburgh; a Freeman of City of London: *m.* 1951, David Seymour Collett, who *d.* 1962, el. son of 2nd baronet.

Widows living of 1st and 2nd Baronets—GRACE AUDREY (*Grace, Lady Collett*), el. da. of the late Thomas Livingstone Ashford, of Gillingham, Beccles, Suffolk: *m.* 1936, as his second wife, Sir Charles Henry Collett, 1st baronet, who *d.* 1938. *Residence,*—Gillingham, Beccles, Suffolk.—— RUTH MILDRED (*Lady Collett*), Flat 1, Orchard Green, Homefield Rd., Bromley, Kent), el. da. of the late William Thomas Hatch, MICE, MIEE: *m.* 1920, Sir Henry Seymour Collett, 2nd Bt., who *d.* 1971.

Collateral Branches living

Issue of the late John Collison Collett, 5th son of 1st baronet, *b.* 1903, *d.* 1956 : *m.* 1928, Ethel Ruth (of Stable End, Windhill, Bishop's Stortford, Herts), da. of the late Benjamin A. Glanvill :— John Brian Glanvill, *b.* 1929 : *m.* 1959, Phyllis Ivy Sybil Kiddy, and has issue living, Robert Glanvill, *b.* 1961,—John Charles, *b.* 1969,—Helen Mary, *b.* 1960. *Residence,* Countess Wells Farm, Framlingham, Suffolk.——Peter Glanvill, *b.* 1933: *m.* 1959, Cecilia Judith, who *d.* 1966, da. of Gerald Eliot Meysey Bromley-Martin, and has issue living, Gerald Henry Glanvill, *b.* 1961, —Thomas John Eliot, *b.* 1962,—Alexander Peter Glanvill, *b.* 1965,—Nicola Mary, *b.* 1959. *Residence,* The Granary, Windhill, Bishop's Stortford.——Sheila Mary *b.* 1931: *m.* 1955, John Donald Sewell, and has issue living, David John Elliott, *b.* 1956,—Andrew William, *b.* 1961,—Michael James, *b.* 1967,—Jean Mary, *b.* 1958. *Residence,* Brettenham Park, nr. Ipswich, Suffolk. ——Diana, *b.* 1940: *m.* 1959, Thomas Joseph Henighan, and has issue living, Stephen Patrick Glanvill, *b.* 1960,—Phoebe Clare, *b.* 1964. *Residence,*

Issue of the late Roger Collett, yst. son of 1st baronet, *b.* 1909, *d.* 1972: *m.* 1934 (m. diss. 19—), Doreen Frances Alvie, da. of the late Sydney Platt:— Roger James (116, Coleraine Rd., Blackheath, SE3 7NU), *b.* 1942; ed. at Ellesmere Coll.: *m.* 1966, Valerie Doreen, da. of the late Prof. Cyril George Beasley, and has issue living, Christopher James, *b.* 1973,—Nicola Valerie, *b.* 1971.——Susan Marjory, *b.* 1939: *m.* 1960, James Stafford Coombe, of Glenmore, Church Lane, Chipstead, Surrey, and has issue living, Andrew James Grant, *b.* 1964,—Caroline Jane, *b.* 1961,—Edwina Gay, *b.* 1963,—Georgina Susan, *b.* 1974.

The 1st baronet, Sir Charles Henry Collett (son of the late Henry John Richard Collett, J.P. of The Hall, Peasenhall, Suffolk), was a Common Councilman of City of London 1912-27, an Alderman 1927-38, Sheriff 1932-3, and Lord Mayor 1933-4.

COLMAN, Creation (U.K.) 1907, of Gatton Park, Gatton, Surrey.

Quick enough if well enough.

Sir MICHAEL JEREMIAH COLMAN, 3rd *Baronet*; *b.* July 7th, 1928; *s.* his father, *Sir* JEREMIAH 1961; ed. at Eton; Capt. Queen's Own Yorks. Yeo. (RARO); Dir. of Reckitt & Colman Ltd.: *m.* 1955, Judith Jean Wallop, da. of Vice-Adm. Sir Peveril Barton Reibey Wallop William-Powlett, KCB, KCMG, CBE, DSO [*see* E. Portsmouth, colls.], and has issue.

  Arms—Ermine, on a pale rayonnée or, between two crosses flory sable, a lion rampant gules. **Crest**—In front of two wings argent, each charged with an estoile azure, a rock proper, thereon a caltrap or. **Badge**—Issuant through an antique crown or, a greyhound's head proper.
  Residence—Malshanger, Basingstoke, Hants.

Sons living—JEREMIAH MICHAEL POWLETT, *b.* Jan. 23rd, 1958.——John Powlett, *b.* 1962.
Daughters living—Olivia Helena Judith, *b.* 1956.——Victoria Rose, *b.* 1960.——Alice Mary *b.* 1965.
Brother living—Oliver James, *b.* 1933: *m.* 1967, the Hon. Cynthia Makins, twin da. of 1st Baron Sherfield, and has issue living, Thomas James, *b.* 1969. *Residence,* 35, Greville Rd., NW6.
Sister living—Gillian Veronica, *b.* 1926.
Widow living of 2nd Baronet—EDITH GWENDOLEN (*Gwen, Lady Colman*), da. of Sir Alfred Ernest Tritton, 2nd Bt. : *m.* 1924, Sir Jeremiah Colman, 2nd Bt., who *d.* 1961. *Residence,* Bartletts Farm, Mattingley, Basingstoke, Hants.

The 1st baronet, Sir Jeremiah Colman (son of the late Jeremiah Colman, of Carshalton Park, Surrey), was Chm. of J. & J. Colman, Ltd., manufacturers of Norwich and London, and a Lieut. for City of London.

COLMAN, Creation (U.K.) 1952, of Reigate, co. Surrey. [Extinct 1966.]

Sir NIGEL CLAUDIAN DALZIEL COLMAN, 1st and last *Baronet.*
Widow living of 1st Baronet—NONA ANN (*Lady Colman*), (Middleton Manor, Winterslow, Salisbury, Wilts.), da. of the late Edward H. M. Willian: *m.* 1952, Sir Nigel Claudian Dalziel Colman, 1st baronet, who *d.* 1966, when the title became ext.

COLQUHOUN, Creation (G.B.) 1786, of Luss, Dumbarton.
[Pronounced "Cohoon."]

If I can.

Sir IVAR IAIN COLQUHOUN OF Luss, 8th *Baronet; b.* Jan. 4th, 1916; *s.* his father, *Lt.-Col. Sir* IAIN, *K.T., D.S.O., LL.D.* 1948 ; ed. at Eton ; is Ch. of the Clan Colquhoun, and Capt. Gren. Gds., DL and JP of Dunbartonshire and Hon. Sheriff Substitute: *m.* 1943, Kathleen, da. of the late Walter Atholl Duncan, and has issue.

Arms—Argent, a saltire engrailed sable. Crest—A hart's head couped gules, attired argent. Supporters—Two ratchhounds argent, collared sable.

Seat—Ross-dhu, Luss, Dunbartonshire. *Clubs*—White's, Puffin's, Royal Ocean Racing.

Son living—MALCOLM RORY, *b.* December 20th, 1947; ed. at Eton.
Daughter living—Iona Mary (*Duchess of Argyll*), *b.* 1945: *m.* 1964, the 12th Duke of Argyll. *Residence*, Inveraray Castle, Argyll.
Brother living—Donald, *b.* 1920 ; European War 1939-45, as Capt. Scots Guards: *m.* 1946, Josephine Griselda, da. of Wilfrid Janson, of 16, Wilton Crescent, S.W.1, and has issue living, James, *b.* 1947,—Iain, *b.* 1949,—Catherine, *b.* 1958. *Residence,* Stuckgowan, Tarbet, Loch Lomond.
Sisters living—Fiona Bryde (*Countess of Arran*), *b.* 1918 : *m.* 1937, the 8th Earl of Arran. *Residence*, Pimlico House, Hemel Hempstead, Herts.——Robina, *b.* 1923 ; sometime in W.R.N.S. : *m.* 1950, Capt. Alan Lewis Wigan, King's Roy. Rifle Corps (Reserve) [*see* Wigan, Bt.].——Frances Mary, *b.* 1925.

The earliest surname under which the family of Colquhoun is traced is that of Kilpatrick Sir John Colquhoun, of Luss, 14th in descent from Umphridus de Kilpatrick (*temp.* Alexander II, was created a baronet of Nova Scotia by Charles I. Sir Humphrey Colquhoun, 3rd baronet, in 1704 resigned his Baronetcy to the Crown, and obtained a new patent with the old precedency, but with the remainder to his son-in-law James Grant (who on succeeding to the Baronetcy assumed the surname of Colquhoun, but resumed that of Grant in 1719) and the heirs male of his marriage with Sir Humphrey's da. [*see* E. Seafield]. In 1786 James, 4th son of the above mentioned James Grant was cr. a Baronet of Great Britain. The 3rd baronet (*cr.* 1786), sat as M.P. for Dunbartonshire in 1802 ; and Sir James, the 4th baronet (who *m.* 1843, Jane, 2nd da. of Sir Robert Abercromby, 5th By., of Birkenbog, co. Banff), was Lord-Lieut. of Dunbartonshire, and M.P. (*L*) therefor 1837-41. Sir James, 5th baronet, was also Lord-Lieut. of Dunbartonshire 1887-1907. Lieut.-Col. Sir Iain Colquhoun, K.T., D.S.O., LL.D., Scots Guards, was Lord-Lieut. of Dunbartonshire, Lord High Commr. for Church of Scotland 1932, 1940, and 1941, and Lord Rector of Glasgow Univ. 1934.

COLT, Creation (E.) 1694, of St. James's-in-the-Fields Liberty of Westminster, Middlesex.

He conquers who endures.

Sir EDWARD WILLIAM DUTTON COLT, 10th *Baronet,* son of the late Major John Rochfort Colt, North Staffordshire Regt., halfbrother of 9th baronet ; *b.* Sept. 22nd, 1936 ; *s.* his uncle *Sir* HENRY ARCHER, *DSO, MC,* 1951; ed. at Douai; MB and BS, London: MRCP; FACP; Ch. of Endocrinology St. Barnabas Hosp., Bronx NY, 10457, and Assist. Attending Physician St. Luke's Hosp., New York, NY 10025: *m.* 1966 (m. diss. 1972), Jane Caroline, da. of James Histed Lewis, of 12, Pont Céard, Versoix, Geneva, and Washington, DC.

Arms—Argent, a fesse between three colts courant sable. Crest—A colt passant or.

Residence—11, Stafford Road, Seaford, Sussex.

Sister living—Joan Margaret Roper, *b.* 1932.

Daughters living of 8th Baronet—Flora Margaret Frances Sophia Dutton Vaughan (Higher Greenhill, Lympstone, Devon), *b.* 1890: *m.* 1921, Maj. John Maunder Webb Gill, formerly Devonshire Regt., who *d.* 1935, and has issue living.——Stella Theodora Dutton Vaughan, *b.* 1893: *m.* 1932, the Rev. Claude Alfred Wiglesworth Russell, Preb. of Exeter Cathedral, who *d.* 1955. *Residence*, Bonython, 18, Forde Park, Newton Abbot, S. Devon.
Mother living—Angela Miriam Kyan : *m.* 1st, 1928, Major John Rochfort Colt, N. Staffordshire Regt. (ante), who *d.* (on active ser. during European War) 1944 ; 2ndly, 1946, Capt. Robert Leslie Cock, N. Staffordshire Regt. *Residence*, 11, Stafford Road, Seaford, Sussex.

The pedigree of this family commences with Thomas Colt, of Carlisle ; his son, Thomas Colt, of Essex and Suffolk (Keeper of the Rolls of Chancery in Ireland, and a Privy Councillor to King Edward IV.), was father of John Colt, whose da. Joan (or Jane) was 1st wife of Sir Thomas More, Lord Chancellor of England. From him descended George Colt (son of Sir Henry Colt, Knt., who was son of George Colt, High Sheriff of Suffolk 1587, and great-grandson of Sir George Colt, Knt.); he was father of the 1st baronet, Sir Henry Dutton Colt, Adj. to Prince Rupert, Ensign of the Yeoman of the Guard, and M.P. for Westminster *temp.* William III. and Anne. His brother, John **Dutton** Colt, was M.P. for Leominster, and his brother, Sir William Dutton Colt, Knt., was Master of the Horse to Prince Rupert, and Envoy at the Courts of Hanover and Dresden.

COLTHURST, Creation (I.) 1744, of Ardrum, Cork.

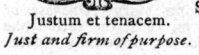

Sir RICHARD LA TOUCHE COLTHURST, 9th *Baronet :* b. Aug. 14th, 1928 ; s. his father, *Sir* RICHARD ST. JOHN JEFFERYES, 1955 ; ed. at Harrow, and at Peterhouse, Camb. (MA); is an Underwriting Member of Lloyd's, and a Liveryman of Grocers' Co.: *m.* 1953, Janet Georgina, da. of L. A. Wilson-Wright, of Coolcarrigan, co. Kildare, and has issue.

Arms—Argent, on a fesse azure between three colts courant sable, **as** many trefoils slipped or. **Crest**—A colt statant sable.

Seats—Ardrum, Inniscarra, co. Cork ; Blarney Castle, co. Cork, *Residences*—Turret Farm, Blarney, co. Cork; Wheatlands, Crockham Hill, Edenbridge, Kent. *Clubs,*—Bath, City University, Cork and County, Kildare St., MCC.

Justum et tenacem.
Just and firm of purpose.

Sons living—CHARLES ST. JOHN (MCC and Pitt (Camb.) Clubs), *b.* May 21st, 1955; ed. at Eton, and Magdalene Coll., Camb.——James Richard (MCC and Lansdowne Clubs) *b.* 1957; ed. at Eton and St. Thomas Med. Sch., London Univ.——Henry Nicholas Almroth, *b.* 1959; ed. at Eton.

Daughter living—Georgina Margaret, *b.* 1961.

Brother living—George Silver Oliver Annesley, *b.* 1931 ; ed. at Harrow and at Trin. Coll., Camb.; late 2nd Lt. Life Gds.; Member of London Stock Exchange: *m.* 1st, 1959 (m. diss. 1966), the Hon. Elizabeth Sophia Sydney, el. da. of 1st Viscount De L'Isle; 2ndly, 1968, Caroline Romaine, da. of Cdr. Anthony Boyce Combe [see Farquhar, Bt., colls.] and has issue living, (by 1st m.) Shaunagh Anne Henrietta *b.* 1961,—(by 2nd m.) Romaine Louisa, *b.* 1969,—Rowena Barbara, *b.* 1971. *Residences*, Pitchford Hall, Salop; 6, Crescent Grove, SW4. *Clubs,* Turf, City University, Kildare St., Cork and County.

Half-Sister living—By 1st m.—Shournagh Dorothy, *b.* 1914: *m.* 1937, Robert Tristram Combe, Lt. Coldm. Gds., who *d.* (of wounds received in action at Dunkirk) 1940, and has issue living, Richard Tristram, *b.* 1938; ed. at Eton; Capt. Coldm. Gds.,—Henry Cecil, *b.* 1940. *Residence*, Eernshill, Hambridge, nr. Langport, Som.

The 1st baronet, Sir John Colthurst (el. son of John Colthurst, of Ardrum and Ballyandy). was M.P. for Doneraile 1751-60, for Youghal 1761-8, and for Castle Martyr 1769-75. Sir John Conway Colthurst, 2nd Bt. *d.* of wounds received in a duel 1787. Sir Nicholas Colthurst, 3rd Bt., was MP for Johnstown, Longford 1783-90, and for Castle Martyr 1791-5, and High Sheriff, co. Cork 1788. Sir Nicholas Conway Colthurst, 4th Bt., was MP for City of Cork 1812-29. Sir George Conway Colthurst, 5th Bt., was MP for Kinsale (L) 1863-74 and High Sheriff, co. Cork 1850. Sir George St. John Colthurst, 6th Bt., was High Sheriff, co. Cork 1884. Sir George Oliver Colthurst, 7th Bt., served in 1914-19 War as Capt. Special Cav. (Croix de Guerre). Sir Richard St. John Jefferyes Colthurst, 8th Bt., was High Sheriff of co. Dublin 1920-21.

Colyer-Fergusson, see Fergusson.

CONANT, Creation (U.K.) 1954, of Lyndon, co. Rutland.

Sir JOHN ERNEST MICHAEL CONANT, 2nd *Baronet;* b. April 24th, 1923; s. his father *Sir* ROGER JOHN EDWARD, *CVO*, 1973; ed. at Eton, and Corpus Christi Coll. Camb. (BA); High Sheriff of Rutland 1960: *m.* 1950, Periwinkle Elizabeth, el. da. of the late Dudley Thorp, of Brothers House, Kimbolton, Hunts., and has issue.

Arms—Per saltire gules and azure billetée or. **Crest**—A stag proper the dexter foreleg resting on a shield gules billetée or.

Residence—Lyndon Hall, Oakham, Rutland.

It shall be given to him who tries
CONANTI·DABITUR

Sons living—SIMON EDWARD CHRISTOPHER, *b.* Oct. 13th, 1958. ——William John Nathaniel, *b.* 1970.

Daughters living—Fiona Elizabeth, *b.* 1955.——Melanie, *b.* 1961.

Brothers living—Guy Timothy Geoffrey, *b.* 1924; ed. at Stowe; formerly Fl. Lt. RAF; a JP, and a DL for Northants, High Sheriff of Northants, 1969: *m.* 1953, Elizabeth; da. of the late A. T. Handley, I. of Wight, and has issue living, Rupert Edward Geoffrey, *b.* 1964,—Sheena Lorraine, *b.* 1954,—Elizabeth Jane, *b.* 1955,—Diana Juliet, *b.* 1960. *Residence,* Bulwick Park, nr. Corby, Northants.——Charles Richard, *b.* 1929; ed. at Eton: *m.* 1958, Katherine Anne Ross, da. of Hubert George Anthony Ross-Wilson, of Gaddesby, Leics., and has issue living, Caroline-Rose, *b.* 1959,—Francesca Louise, *b.* 1962. *Residence,* Rose Cottage, Gaddesby, Leics.

Mother living—Daphne Lorraine, (Catmore Lodge, Oakham, Rutland) da. of the late Alfred Ernest Learoyd, of 36, Princes' Gate, SW1: *m.* 1920, (m. diss. 1972), Sir Roger John Edward Conant, CVO, 1st Bt., who *d.* 1973.

Widow living of 1st Baronet—Mrs MARY BUCHANAN (*Mary Lady Conant*), (14 Lowndes Lodge, Cadogan Place SW1), da. of A. H. Worth, of Hovenden, Lincs.: *m.* 1972, as his 2nd wife, Sir Roger John Edward Conant, CVO, 1st Bt., who *d.* 1973.

CONGREVE, Creation (U.K.) 1927, of Congreve, co. Stafford. [Extinct 1941.]

Com. Sir GEOFFREY CECIL CONGREVE, *D.S.O., R.N.,* 1st and last *Baronet ; d.* (killed in action during European War) 1941.

Daughters living of 1st Baronet—Anne Henrietta, *b.* 1923 : *m.* 1944, Richard M. T. Tyler, formerly Capt. R.E., and has issue living, John Christian Congreve, *b.* 1945,—Richard Henry Felix, *b.* 1954,—Camilla Madeleine Mary, *b.* 1946,—Amelia Henrietta Rose, *b.* 1950. *Residence,* Meesden Hall, nr. Buntingford, Herts.——Marygold Elizabeth, *b.* 1926: *m.* 1953, Maj. Ian Stafford Alexander, Roy. Irish Fusiliers (ret.), and has issue living, Maria Congreve, *b.* 1959. *Residence,* Castle Bank, Stowe by Chartley, Stafford.——Carola, *b.* 1929: *m.* 1948, John Horatio Gordon Shephard, formerly Capt. Gren. Gds., from whom she obtained a divorce 1959, and has issue living, Thomas Horatio Congreve, *b.* 1949,—Henry John, *b.* 1955. *Residence,* 10, First St., SW3.

Widow living of 1st Baronet—HELENA MADELEINE MARY, da. of the late Augustus Henry Eden Allhusen, of Stoke Court, Stoke Poges [*see* B. Stanley of Alderley, colls.] ; formerly Senior Comdt. A.T.S. ; assumed the surname of Stewart-Mackenzie of Seaforth 1944 : *m.* 1st, 1922, Com. Sir Geoffrey Cecil Congreve, D.S.O., R.N., 1st Bt., who *d.* (on active ser. during European War) 1941, when the title became ext. ; 2ndly, 1942, Reginald James Tyler, who *d.* 1956, having assumed the additional surname of Stewart-Mackenzie 1944. *Residence,* Westburton Place, nr. Pulborough, Sussex.

STRICKLAND-CONSTABLE, Creation (E.) 1641, of Boynton, Yorkshire.

To the will of God.

Sir ROBERT FREDERICK STRICKLAND-CONSTABLE, 11th *Baronet; b.* Oct. 22nd, 1903; *s.* his brother, *Sir* HENRY MARMADUKE, 1975; ed. at Magdalen Coll., Oxford (MA, DPhil.); Lt.-Cdr. RNVR: *m.* 1st, 1929 (m. annulled 1931), Rosalind Mary, da. of Arthur Webster; 2ndly, 1936, Lettice, yst. da. of the late Maj. Frederick Strickland (infra), and has issue by 2nd m.

Arms—Quarterly : 1st and 4th, gules and vair a bend or, *Constable* ; 2nd and 3rd, gules a chevron or, between three crosses-pattée argent on a canton ermine a buck's head erased and attired sable, *Strickland.* **Crests**—1st, a ship, sails furled, all or. *Constable* ; 2nd, a turkey cock in his pride proper, *Strickland.*

Residence—Combe Wood, Brasted, Westerham, Kent.

Sons living—(By 2nd m.)—FREDERIC, *b.* Oct. 21st, 1943; ed. at Westminster, and Corpus Christi Coll., Camb. (BA).—— John Robert Francis (128, Ramsden Rd., SW12), *b.* 1949; ed. at. Bryanston, and London Univ. ¡Higher Dip. in Fine Art): *m.* 1971, Christine, da. of D. W. Roberts, of St. Paul's Cray, Kent.

Daughters living—(By 2nd m.)—Miranda, *b.* 1938; ed. at London Univ, (BA).——Elizabeth Diana, *b.* 1940; ed. at Roy. Coll. of Music (ARCM), and Staatliche Höchschule für Musik, Cologne: *m.* 1972, John Maxwell Fairley, BSc., of 7737 Bad Dürrheim, Ludwigstrasse 7, W. Germany, and has issue living, Lucy Fiona, *b.* 1974.

Widow living of 10th Baronet—Countess (ERNESTINE) EDINA (*Edina, Lady Strickland-Constable*), (Wassand Hall, nr. Hull), da. of the late Count Rex, formerly Saxon Min. in Vienna: *m.* 1929, Sir Henry Marmaduke Strickland-Constable, 10th Bt., who *d.* 1975.

Collateral Branches living.

Issue of the late Major Frederick Strickland, 2nd son of 8th baronet, *b.* 1867 *d.* 1934: *m.* 1903, Mary Beatrix, who *d.* 1965, da. of the late Sir John Isaac Thornycroft, LLD, FRS:—

Diana Blanche, *b.* 1911: *m.* 1933, the Rev. Edward Denzil Chetwood Wright, of Brattleby House, Brattleby, Lincoln, and has issue living, Jonathan Michael (Lion House, Brattleby, Lincoln) *b.* 1938: *m.* 1965, Anne Morgan, and has issue living, David Strickland *b.* 1966, Sarah Penelope *b.* 1969,—Peter Philip, *b.* 1941,—Samuel Strickland, *b.* 1948,—Elizabeth Susannah, *b.* 1934: *m.* 1965, Alexander Arbuthnott Dunbar, of Pitgaveny House, Elgin, [*see* Dunbar, Bt., *cr.* 1700]. ——Lettice (*Lady Strickland-Constable*), *b.* 1913: *m.* 1936, as his second wife, Sir Robert Frederick Strickland-Constable, 11th Bt. (ante).

Issue of the late Capt. Henry Strickland, O.B.E., R.N., 4th son of 8th baronet, *b.* 1873, *d.* 1934: *m.* 1910, the Hon. Ida Mary Hazel Willoughby, who *d.* 1965, da. of 10th Baron Middleton:—

Monica Lucy Ann, *B.Sc., b.* 1916 ; B.Sc. London Univ. 1938. *Residence,* Barton Hill House, Whitwell, York., YO6 7JL.

Grandsons of the late Walter Richard Strickland (who assumed by deed poll 1886 the surname of Cholmley, but continued to use the surname of Strickland), son of the Rev. Nathaniel Constantine Strickland, 6th son of 6th baronet:—

Issue of the late Gerald Constantine Strickland, M.M., *b.* 1888, *d.* 1962: *m.* 1st, 1910, (marriage dissolved 1921), da. of John Hampton, of Pretoria; 2ndly, 1922, Magdalene (of 16, Buckingham Court Beach, East London, Cape Prov., S. Africa), da. of Peter Hünten, of Pretoria, S. Africa:—

(By 1st m.) Gerald John (64, Forest Rd., Bramley, Johannesburg, S. Africa), *b.* 1911; ed. at Rand Univ.: *m.* 1940, Patricia, da. of Archibald Edward Benson, of Pretoria, and has issue living, John, *b.* 1950,—Margaret Julia Patricia (Division of Microbiology, Southwest Foundation, PO Box 28147, San Antonio, Texas 78284, USA), *b.* 1942.

Issue of the late Arthur William Strickland, *b.* 1890, *d.* 1970: *m.* 1918, Violet May, who *d.* 1956, da. of Edward S. Margerum, of Merrylands, W. Aust.:—

Stanley Arthur (28, Cavendish Rd., New Malden, Surrey), *b.* 1920: *m.* 1952, Eileen Mary, da. of the late Patrick Henry Keeley, of Surbiton and has issue living, Janet Frances, *b.* 1960.——John Edward (56, Chertsey Drive, N. Cheam, Surrey) *b.* 1923: *m.* 1953, Rose Ena, da. of the late George Thomas William Greenfield, of N. Cheam, Surrey, and has issue living, Christopher Graham, *b.* 1962,—Susan Carol, *b.* 1960,—Alison Ruth, *b.* 1966.

Granddaughters of the late Hugh Strickland; 2nd son of the late Rev. Nathaniel Constantine Strickland, 6th son of 6th baronet:—

Issue of the late Nathaniel Lewis Hugh Strickland, *b.* 1899, *d.* 1955 : *m.* 1923, Unity
Margaret, who *d.* 1975, da. of the late Arthur Birch:—
Mavis Rae, *b.* 1929: *m.* 1952, Eric Richard Earl, of 7, Lombardy Drive, Berkhamsted.——Mary
Joy, *b.* (twin) 1929: *m.* 1952, George Arthur Jones, of 6, Cherry Rise, Chalfont St. Giles, Bucks.
——Margaret Anne, *b.* 1932: *m.* 1953, Lionel Wood. *Residence*, 10, Broomfield Rise, Abbots
Langley, Herts.

Granddaughters of the late Robert Strickland (infra):—
Issue of the late Claude Francis Strickland, C.I.E., *b.* 1881, *d.*1962: *m.* 1915, Dorothy
Lisa, who *d.* 1972, da. of the late G. A. Branson, MD, of Dandaraga, Riddell, Victoria,
Australia:—
Patricia Elizabeth Mary, *b.* 1916: *m.* 1941, Col. Arthur Vyvyan Denton, Loyal Regt., of The
Dial House, Lower Bourne, Farnham, Surrey, and has issue living, Amanda Elizabeth Ann
Vyvyan, *b.* 1943: *m.* 1968, David Frederick James Leathers [see V. Leathers.],—Joanna Mary
Vyvyan, *b.* 1946: *m.* 1974, Martyn Laurence.——Frances Pamela Ann, *b.* 1919: *m.* 1st, 1942,
Anthony William Vivian, RAF Vol. Reserve, who *d.* (killed in action in Mediterranean) 1942;
2ndly, 1946, Capt. Anthony James Parr, of 35, Moore St., SW3, and has issue living, (by 2nd m.)
Francis Nicholas, *b.* 1949: *m.* 1974, Sakiko Fukuda,—Laetitia Mary, *b.* 1948: *m.* 1970, William
Logan Jack, of Huntingdon Court, Kington, Herefords.

Grandson of the late Walter Strickland, el. son of the late George Strickland, 2nd son of 5th baronet:—
Issue of the late Robert Strickland, *b.* 1848, *d.* 1925: *m.* 1876, Mary Katharine, who *d.*
1938, da. of the Rev. Lancelot Arthur Sharpe, R. of Tackley, Oxfordshire :—
Cecil Eustace, *BSc*, *b.* 1889: *m.* 1st, 1923 (m. diss. 1942), Dorothy Enid, 2nd da. of E. Stocker, of
Blackheath, SE; 2ndly, 1949, Galatea, da. of Costas Patzatzis, of Cairo, and has issue living, (by
1st m.) Martin Robert Cecil (PO Box 1975, Salisbury, Rhodesia), *b.* 1927; BSc; MIEE: *m.*
1953, Judith Melvia, da. of Cecil Kerr, and has issue living, Walter Robert Cecil *b.* 1954, Hugh
Edward *b.* 1955, Kenneth William *b.* 1959, Alexander David *b.* 1965,—Walter Nicholas, *PhD*
(c/o Dept. of Biochemistry, Univ. of Cape Town, Private Bag Rondebosch, Cape, S. Africa),
b. 1930: *m.* 1st 1956 (m. diss. 1964), Margaret Brown, of Dunoon, Argyll; 2ndly, 1968, Marie, da.
of Lynn Shields, of Salt Lake City, and has issue living (by 1st m.), Gina Elizabeth *b.* 1963,—(by
2nd m.) Robert Nicholas *b.* 1971, Jessica Helen, *b.* 1951. *Residence*, PO, Borrowdale, Rhodesia.

Grandsons of the late Robert Strickland (ante):—
Issue of the late Clement Cyprian Strickland, *b.* 1892, *d.* 1943 : *m.* 1920, Violet Isobel,
(now of The Nunnery, Hillborough, Thetford, Norfolk), da. of the late Meyrick Edward
Selby-Lowndes, J.P., of Mursley Grange, Winslow. Bucks. :—
Rev. Paul Clement Lowndes (Lakenheath Vicarage, Brandon, Suffolk), *b.* 1921: *m.* 1950, Emily
Hartley, of Pontefract, and has issue living, Janet Elizabeth, *b.* 1951,—Mary Isobel, *b.* 1961.——
Robert Lowndes, *b.* 1924. *Residence*, The Nunnery, Hillborough, Thetford, Norfolk.

Granddaughters of the late Walter Kennedy Strickland, son of the late Charles Strickland, son of the late George Strickland (ante):—
Issue of the late Com. Charles Walter Campbell Strickland, R.N., *b.* 1873, *d.* 1918 : *m.* 1909,
Constance Margaret Lorn Campbell (who *d.* 1959, having *m.* 2ndly, 1928, Benjamin
Charles Apps), da. of the late Major F. W. Campbell, RHA:—
Constance Alice Lorn Campbell, *b.* 1912: *m.* 1940, Alfred Aubone Baden Fuller, of 5, Devas Rd.,
SW20, and has issue living, Charles Walter Frank, *b.* 1948,—Kate Margaret Lorn, *b.* 1942,—
Eleanor Francis Campbell, *b.* 1944: *m.* 1967, Marcus Willmott Smith, and has issue living, Colin
Frederick *b.* 1972, Laura Meg *b.* 1970.——Katarin Jarrard Campbell, *b.* 1914: *m.* 1938, John
Evan Privett, of Priory Cottage, Naish, East Coker, Yeovil, Som., and has issue living, John
Hugh Charles, *b.* 1939: *m.* 1971, Jane Dilys Roland Macqueen, and has issue living, Jonathan
Edward Macqueen *b.* 1972, Philada Jane *b.* 1974,—Robin Jarrard Campbell, *b.* 1940: *m.* 1964,
Penelope Lisbeth Bate, and has issue living, James Jarrard Campbell *b.* 1966, Edward Tobias
b. 1970, Kathryn Louise *b.* 1968,—Alan Frederick, *b.* 1943: *m.* 1975, Carolin Graham Fawcett,—
Christina Katarin *b.* 1946.

Granddaughters of the late Algernon Henry Peter Strickland, son of the late Algernon Augustine de Lille Strickland (infra) :—
Issue of the late Algernon Walter Strickland, *b.* 1891, *d.* 1938 : *m.* 1915, Lady Mary
Charteris (now of Apperley Court, Gloucester ; she *m.* 2ndly, 1943, Major John George
Lyon, R.A.), da. of 11th Earl of Wemyss :—
Pamela Sabina, *b.* 1921: *m.* 1947, Maj. Henry Benjamin Van der Gucht, MC, late R. Northumber-
land Fusiliers, and has issue living, Guy Tristam, *b.* 1951,—Hugo Charles, *b.* 1956,—Juliet
Clare, *b.* 1948. *Residences*, 14, Cromwell Cres., SW5; Apperley Court, Gloucester.——Sara Ann
Mary, *b.* 1926: *m.* 1950, Prof. Albert Raymond Maillard Carr, Warden of St. Anthony's Coll.,
Oxford, and has issue living, Adam Henry Maillard, *b.* 1951,—Matthew Xavier Maillard,
b. 1953,—Alexander Rallion Charles, *b.* 1958,—Laura Selina Madeline, *b.* 1954. *Residences*,
29, Charlbury Rd., Oxford; Woolhanger Manor, Parracombe, N. Devon.

Grandson of the late Algernon Augustine de Lille Strickland, son of the late Augustine Edmund Christopher Strickland (infra) :—
Issue of the late Claud Hugh Strickland, *b.* 1871, *d.* 1938 : *m.* 1st, 1895, Maud Mary
(from whom he obtained a divorce 1903), da. of the late P. R. Gordon Canning, of
Hartbury House, near Gloucester ; 2ndly, 1908, Una Clara Margaret, who *d.* 1959,
da. of the late John Charles Bell, of Langbraugh Hall, Cleveland :—
(By 1st marriage) Walter Claud, *b.* 1896: *m.* 1st, 1932, Charmain Louise (from whom he obtained a
divorce 1946), only child of Lieut.-Col. Harold Cazenove Hessey, of Bethersden, Kent ; 2ndly,
1954, Mary Julanne, el. da. of the late Wilfred Henry Kellam-Harris, of Putney, S.W., and has
issue living, (by 2nd marriage) Walter Hugh Jeremy, *b.* 1960. *Residence*, Lower Telham, Battle,
Sussex.

Grandchildren of the late Claud Hugh Strickland (ante):—
Issue of the late Hugh Baring Strickland, *b.* 1899, *d.* 1972: *m.* 1954, Pauline (Ventonvaise,
Callestick, Truro), da. of P. Wood, of Shaldon, Devon:—
Christopher Claud Hugh, *b.* 1955.——Sarah Janet, *b.* 1962.

Grandchildren of the late Walter Cecil Strickland, son of the late Augustine Edmund Christopher Strickland, 4th son of the late George Strickland, 2nd son of 5th baronet:—
Issue of the late Dudley Herbert Cecil Strickland, *b.* 1860, *d.* 1953: *m.* 1901, Margaret,
who *d.* 19—, da. of Edwin J. Gilbert, of San Bernadino, California, USA:—
Arthur Cecil, *b.* 1902.——Violet St. Leger: *m.* 19—,—Frederick Segrist.

Issue of the late Cecil St. Leger Strickland, *b.* 1876, *d.* 1929: *m.* 1903, Lucy Estes, who
d. 1968, da. of the late Henry Edward Smithes, of Mount Pleasant, Kansas, USA:—
Cecile Daphine, *b.* 1904: *m.* 1939, Cdr. Stuart Erskine Crewe-Read, RN (ret.), and has
issue living, Susan Shira, *b.* 1941,—Anna, *b.* 1947. *Residence*, Fig Tree Cottage, Preston,
Weymouth, Dorset.——Joan, *b.* 1908: *m.* 1933, Maj. George Vilett Rolleston, Worcestershire
Regt. (Supplementary Reserve), and has issue living, George Lancelot St. Leger, *MBE*, *b.* 1939;
Capt. Coldsteam Guards; MBE (Mil.) 1969. *Residence*, Holetown House, Sampford Spiney,
Yelverton, S. Devon.

The 1st baronet, Sir William Strickland, was summoned to Cromwell's House of Peers as Lord Strickland. The 3rd baronet was a distinguished M.P. during the reigns of William, Anne, and George I., and the 4th baronet was a Lord of the Treasury and Secretary for War *temp.* George II. The 7th baronet assumed, in 1865, by royal permission, the surname of Cholmley for himself and those of his heirs male who may succeed to the Cholmley estates. He *m.* 1818, Mary, da. and heir of the Rev. Charles Constable of Wassand, Yorks. Sir Walter William Strickland, 9th Bt., became a Czecho-Slovakian citizen and did not use the title.

Constable-Maxwell-Scott, see Scott.

COOK, Creation (U.K.) 1886, of Richmond, Surrey.

Sir FRANCIS FERDINAND MAURICE COOK, 4th *Baronet*; *b.* Dec. 21st, 1907; *s.* his father, *Sir* HERBERT FREDERICK, 1939; ed. at Bradfield Coll.; FRSA, a Fellow of St. Ives So. of Artists of Cornwall, of Jersey So. of Artists, of Chelsea Arts So., and of Roy. Cornish Soc. (Truro); authority on methods and mediums used by old masters; musician, composer and organist; bears courtesy title of *Visconde de Monserrate* in Portugal: *m.* 1st, 1928, Molly Violet (from whom he obtained a divorce 1930), da. of the late Thomas Wilson Mappin [*see* Mappin, Bt.]; 2ndly, 1933, Dorothea Alice (from whom he obtained a divorce 1935), da. of Col. William Bennett, DSO, OBE, MB, of Belbins, Romsey, Hants; 3rdly, 1937, Joan Loraine (from whom he obtained a divorce 1942), da. of John Aloysius Ashton-Case; 4thly, 1942,

Esse **quam** videri.

To be rather than to seem.

Barbara Frances Lang; 5thly, 1947, Juliet Berry (who obtained a divorce 1951), da. of Christopher Perkins, of The Stone, Sudbury, Suffolk; 6thly, 1951, Jane Audrey Nott (who obtained a divorce 1956), da. of the late Cdr. G. L. Turnbull; 7thly, 1956, Mrs. Bridget Brenda Polland, da. of the late Thomas David Lynch, and has issue by 3rd and 6th m.

Arms—Gules, a rose argent barbed and seeded proper between three crescents of the second; a chief vaire. **Crest**—Issuant from a chaplet of roses gules a dexter arm embowed proper, holding in the hand a mullet of six points or between two branches of oak vert.

Residence,—Le Coin, La Haule, St. Aubin, Jersey. *Address*—The Studio, The Sir Francis Cook Galleries of Fine Art, Augrés, Trinity, Jersey. *Clubs*—Arts, Royal Automobile, Victoria (Jersey).

Son living—By 3rd marriage—CHRISTOPHER WYMONDHAM RAVNER HERBERT (c/o Coutts & Co., 1, Old Park Lane, W1), *b.* March 24th, 1938; late RAF: *m.* 1st, 1958, Mrs. Malina Gunasekera, of Ceylon, from whom he obtained a divorce 1975; 2ndly, 1975, Mrs. Margaret Miller, da. of the late John Murray, and has issue living (by 1st m.), Richard Herbert Aster Maurice, *b.* June 30th, 1959,—Priscilla Melina, *b.* 1968.

Daughter living—By 6th m.—Cleone Willa Johanne Vera Rosemary, *b.* 1952: *m.* 1970, Peter Wilson, and has issue living, Stuart Francis James, *b.* 1971,—Catherine Jane Brenda Rachael, *b.* 1972.

Sisters living—Vera Mary, *b.* 1899: *m.* 1st, 1921, George Mervyn Anstey Hamilton-Fletcher, J.P., who obtained a divorce 1938; 2ndly, **1938** as his second wife, Major Dudley Claud Douglas Ryder, Dorset Regt. [*see* E. Harrowby, colls.], and has issue living, (by 1st marriage) Gareth Mervyn, *b.* 1922,—Timothy Herbert, *b.* **1925**,—Nicholas Francis, *b.* **1929**,—Simon Alexander, *b.* 1931,—(by 2nd marriage) [*see* E. Harrowby, colls.]. *Residence,* Rempstone, Corfe Castle, Dorset. —Rachel Margaret, *b.* 1903: *m.* 1st, 1922, Sir John Serocold Paget Mellor, M.P., 2nd Bt., from whom she obtained a divorce 1937; 2ndly, **1939**, Capt. William Eric Lloyd, Roy. Berks Regt., who *d.* (killed in action during 1939-45 War) 1943. *Residence,* Shrewsbury House, Cheyne Walk, SW3.

Collateral Branch living.

Issue of the late Wyndham Francis Cook, 2nd son of 1st baronet, *b.* 1860, *d.* 1905: *m.* 1887, Frederica Evelyn Stilwell, who *d.* 1925, da. of the late F. J. Freeland, of Chichester :—

Humphrey Wyndham (Kingston House North, Ennismore Gdns., SW7), *b.* 1893; ed. at Harrow, and Ch. Ch., Oxford: *m.* 1st, 1926 (divorce 1934), Gillian, da. of the late Frederick William Hedderley, of Oxford; 2ndly, 1941, Anne Beattie Blakeley, da. of the late John Moffett, of Ballynahinch, N. Ireland, and has issue living, (by 1st m.) William Wyndham Humphrey, *b.* 1928.—— Cecil Emily Freda Wyndham (*Lady O'Connor*) (44, Wynnstay Gdns., Allen St., W8), *b.* 1896: *m.* 1920, Sir Terence James O'Connor, KC, MP, who *d.* 1940, and has issue living, Rachel Ursula, *b.* 1921: *m.* 1942, Cledwyn Lewis,—Rosemary, *b.* 1923.——Ursula Maud Wyndham, *b.* 1900: *m.* 1st, 1921, Highat Cecil Harcourt Smith (from whom she obtained a divorce 1924), son of Sir Cecil Harcourt Smith, CVO; 2ndly, 1924, Cecil Walter Lazenby. *Residence,*

The 1st baronet, Sir Francis Cook (son of the late William Cook, of Roydon Hall, Kent), was cr. *Visconde de Monserrate*, of Cintra, Portugal, and was founder and donor of Queen Alexandra's House (an institution for lady art students), Kensington Gore, and a well-known collector of works of art. Sir Frederick Lucas, 2nd Bt., was head of the firm of Cook, Son and Co., warehousemen and shippers, of St. Paul's Churchyard, E.C., and sat as M.P. for Lambeth, Kennington Div. (**C**) 1895 to 1906. Sir Herbert Frederick, 3rd Bt., Bar.-at-law, was a Trustee of National Gallery 1923-30, and National Portrait Gallery 1916-30, and author of Giorgione, and Reviews & Appreciations and other publications.

COOKE, Creation (E.) 1661, of Wheatley Hall, Yorkshire.

Sir CHARLES ARTHUR JOHN COOKE, 11th *Baronet* (but his name does not, at time of going to press, appear on the Official Roll of Baronets), *b.* Nov. 12th, 1905; *s.* his father, *Sir* WILLIAM HENRY CHARLES WEMYSS, 1964; ed. at Wellington; Maj. 4/7th Roy. Dragoon Guards 1939-45 War in France (prisoner): *m.* 1932, Diana, only da. of Maj.-Gen. Sir Edward Maxwell Perceval, KCB, DSO, JP, and has issue.

Arms—Or, a chevron gules between two lions passant-guardant sable. **Crest**—Out of a mural crown argent, a demi-lion guardant issuant as in the arms gorged with a ducal coronet or.

Residence—15, The Esplanade, Fowey, Cornwall.

Son living—DAVID WILLIAM PERCEVAL (West Wold, Evenlode, Moreton-in-Marsh), *b.* April 28th, 1935; ed. at Wellington; Maj. RCT: *m.* 1959, Margaret Frances, da. of Herbert Skinner, of Knutsford, Ches., and has issue living, Sara Elisabeth Mary, *b.* 1960,—Louise Diana Margaret, *b.* 1962,—Catherine Faith Maria, *b.* 1968.

Daughter living—Amanda Norah Mildred (Porcorum, Sandy Down, Boldre, Lymington, Hants.), *b.* 1939: *m.* 1964, David Old, and has issue living, Amanda Mary Perceval, *b.* 1966.

Half Sister living—Elizabeth Hera, *b.* 1928: *m.* 1968, Group Capt. C. E. A. Garton, RAF (ret.), of Quinta da Boa Vista, Funchal, Madeira, and has issue living, Patrick William, *b.* 1969,—Dorothy Margaret, *b.* 1970.

Collateral Branches living.

Issue of the late William Francis Henry Cooke, el. son of 10th baronet, *b.* 1903, *d.* 1950: *m.* 1946, Irene Mary, widow of Capt. O. Belingham Smith:—
Patricia Irene Mildred, *b.* 1949.

Issue of the late Arthur Gordon Wyatt Cooke, yr. son of 9th baronet, *b.* 1876, *d.* 1969: *m.* 1905, Blanche Elia Catherine, who *d.* 1949, da. of the late Charles Eldon Clarke, of Newton House, co. Tipperary:—
William Bryan (730, Wharncliffe Rd., Duncan, Vancouver Island, BC), *b.* 1909; Capt. late Indian Army: *m.* 1959, Marion June, yr. da. of the late Mervyn Corsellis, and has issue living, Marion Nathalie, *b.* 1960.——Blanche Elia Ruby (Box 14, Mill Bay, Vancouver Island, BC, Canada), *b.* 1908: *m.* 1933, the Rev. John Bernard Valentine White, Chap. to Forces, and has issue living, Anthony John (479, Balliol St., Toronto, Ont., Canada, M4S 1E1), *b.* 1938: *m.* 1972, Sally Rosalind, el. da. of the late I. D. Champion, of Wolverhampton, and has issue living, Bryan Llewellyn *b.* 1974,—Jeremy Nicholas (3214 E 47th Av., Vancouver, BC, Canada), *b.* 1940: *m.* 1964, Beverly Ann, da. of the late G. R. Atchison, of Vancouver, BC, and has issue living, Gordon John *b.* 1965, Nicola Leigh *b.* 1971.

Grandchildren of the late George Bryan Cooke-Yarborough, son of George Cooke-Yarborough (*b.* 1794), son of John Cooke-Yarborough (*b.* 1765), grandson of George Cooke, 2nd son of 3rd baronet:—
Issue of the late George Eustace Cooke-Yarborough, *b.* 1876, *d.* 1938 : *m.* 1914, Daphne Isabel (who *m.* 2ndly, 1950, Capt. Tadeuz Mincer, who *d.* 1969), yr. da. of Henry Cordy Wrinch of Ipswich:—
Edmund Harry, *b.* 1918; ed. at Ch. Ch., Oxford (B.A. 1944, M.A. 1944); is Dep. Ch. Scientist U.K. Atomic Energy Authority : *m.* 1952, Anthea Katharine, da. of John Alexander Dixon, of King Charles Cottage, Colden Common, near Winchester, and has issue living, Anthony Edmund, *b.* 1956,—Jane Anthea, *b.* 1958. *Residence*, Lincoln Lodge, Longworth, near Abingdon, Berks.

Issue of the late Capt. Orfeur Frederick Cooke-Yarborough, *b.* 1878, *d.* 1965: *m.* 1960, Anne (Nancy) Henrietta Lucy, who *d.* 1965, el. da. of the late Rev. William Wyatt, R. of Broughton Brigg, Lincs.:—
Bryan Orfeur Eustace (PO Box 147, Selukwe, Rhodesia), *b.* 1907: *m.* 1938, Ellen Martha (Nellie), who *d.* 1974, da. of the late John Myers, of Mount Silinda, Rhodesia, and has issue living, Edmund Orfeur (28, Banbury Drive, Southwold, Bulawayo, Rhodesia), *b.* 1940: *m.* 1966, Jennifer Anne, da. of Lt.-Col. John Winterton Scott, and has issue living, David John Orfeur *b.* 1970, Nichola Joan *b.* 1966,—Rosemary Anne, *b.* 1945: *m.* 1966, Rodney Franklin Buckley, of 51, Highlands Rd., Pinetown, Natal, and has issue living, Craige Franklin *b.* 1970, Samantha Anne *b.* 1974,—Susan Mary, *b.* 1951: *m.* 1973, Jacobus Petrus van Lelyued (P/Bag 33Z, Zaka, Rhodesia), and has issue living, Darren Richard *b.* 1974.——Thomas Nicholas, *b.* 1910; late RAF: *m.* 1940, Elizabeth Thomson, da. of the late William Gilmore, of Edinburgh, and has issue living, Nicholas Michael, *b.* 1941.——Nancy Penelope Mary, *b.* 1912: *m.* 1939, Lt.-Col. George Michael Donaldson Wingate, RA, of The Riding, Knook, Warminster, and has issue living, Elizabeth Anne, *b.* 1940,—Sarah Penelope, *b.* 1944: *m.* 1964, Lt. Michael R. R. Peever, RN, of Tuck's Rd., Main Ridge, Vic., Aust., and has issue living, Richard Charles *b.* 1971.——Henrietta Rosemary Orfeur, *b.* 1918; formerly in ATS: *m.* 1944, Maj. William Victor Smith, Lancs. Yeo., of March Wall, King's Drive North, Caldy, Wirral, Ches., and has issue living, Richard Orfeur Bateson, *b.* 1949,—Rosemary Julia, *b.* 1945.

Issue of the late Humfrey Charles Cooke-Yarborough, *b.* 1880, *d.* 1955: *m.* 1911, Honor, Lake (Greyroof, Wyfold Lane, Kingswood Common, Henley-on-Thames), da. of the late Col. Henry Lake Wells, CIE, RE:—
Michael Humfrey, *b.* 1915; is an Architect: *m.* 1942, Pamela, da. of the late Sir John Baldwin, KCMG, CB, and has issue living, Ann, *b.* 1944: *m.* 1967, Alain Paul René Nérot, of 46, rue Ernest Renau, 95320, 95, St. Leu la Forêt, France, and has issue living, Lucie *b.* 1974,—Penelope, *b.* 1946: *m.* 1974, George Roger Frank Wallbridge. *Residence*, 7, St. Anne's Close, Highgate West Hill, N6 6AR.——Steven Sandford (5, Flint Av., Larchmont, NY 10538, USA), *b.* 1919; an Engineer; formerly Capt. RE: *m.* 1941, Evelyn, da. of the late Charles Buccleuch Scott, of Trinidad, and has issue living, Christopher, *b.* 1949,—Nicholas, *b.* 1952.——Eustace, *b.* 1921; an Industrial Designer. *Residence*, 49a, Maresfield Gdns., NW3.

Grandchildren of George Cooke-Yarborough (*b.* 1794)ante):—
Issue of the late Alfred Cooke-Yarborough, *b.* 1847, *d.* 1925 : *m.* 1874, Mary, who *d.* 1919, da. of James Ferguson, of Opara, Hokianga, New Zealand :—
Randall Francis, *b.* 1883: *m.* 1917, Norma, da. of George Downes, of Kohu Kohu, Hokianga, New Zealand, and has issue living, Pauline, *b.* 1923: *m.* 1947, Raymond Leslie Gerrard Rogers, of Nilgris S. India, and has issue living, Sandra Francis *b.* 1946, Diana Leslie *b.* 1958.——Mabel Christina Margaret, *b.* 1885: *m.* 1912, George Andrewes, who *d.* 1948, and has issue living, Lancelot George (of Kohu Kohu, Northland, New Zealand), *b.* 1914; European War 1939-45 as Fl.-Lt. Roy. New Zealand Air Force: *m.* 1950, Audrey Winnifred Kemp, and has issue living,

Wayne George Kemp *b.* 1952,—Desmond Yarborough (of 4, Ngapawa St., Sandringham, Auckland, New Zealand), *b.* 1920; 1939-45 War as Navigator, Bomber Command, RAF: *m.* 1945, Joyce Mildred Winter, and has issue living, Russell Peter *b.* 1945, Blake Yarborough *b.* 1952, Lee *b.* 1955, Gillian Mary *b.* 1948, Sherrill Joy *b.* 1950,—Marie Durelle, *b.* 1917 : *m.* 1939, John Wilson Allen, of Main Street, Te Karaka, near Gisborne, New Zealand, and has issue living, Anthony George *b.* 1940, John Desmond *b.* 1944, Brett Yarborough *b.* 1952, Maureen Robin *b.* 1942, Pamela Raewyn *b.* 1946, Bronwyn Margaret (twin) *b.* 1952,—Nancy Ethelwynne, *b.* 1924 : *m.* 1946, Charles Stanley Mathers, of Orewa, Auckland, New Zealand, and has issue living, David *b.* 1947, Max *b.* 1950, Mark (twin) *b.* 1950. *Residence,* Kohu Kohu, Hokianga, New Zealand.——Mildred May *b.* 1889 : *m.* 1917 Roland Octavius Phillips, who *d.* 1944, and has issue living, Diana Wynne, *b.* 1920 : *m.* 1942, George Douglas Brown, of 53, Maskell Street, St. Heliers, Auckland, New Zealand, and has issue living, Grant Victor Roland *b.* 1945, Diana Phillipa *b.* 1952,—Mary Rosalind, *b.* 1924 : *m.* 1948, Raymond George Wagstaff, of Onewhero, Tuakau Auckland, New Zealand,—Constance May, *b.* 1925,—Lindley Mercia, *b.* 1928 : *m.* 1952, Owen Frederick Hood, of 48, Bellevue Av., Northcote, Auckland, N4, New Zealand. *Residence,* Hermiston, 56, Shakespeare Rd., Takapuna, New Zealand.——Ethel Winifred, *b.* 1894: *m.* 1923, James Joseph Molloy, and has issue living, Brian Francis, *b.* 1927 : *m.* 1951, Doris Nancy, el. da. of George Watts, of Avondale, Auckland, New Zealand, and has issue living, Gregory Ian *b.* 1952, David George *b.* 1956, Linda Frances *b.* 1954,—Barry James, *b.* 1930 : *m.* 1952, Margaret Elizabeth, younger da. of S. G. Thompson, of Manurewa, New Zealand, and has issue living Terence Michael *b.* 1956, Colleen Ngaire *b.* 1954,—Marny Mildred, *b.* 1923 : *m.* 1951, John Andrew Smith and has issue living, John Peter *b.* 1952. *Residence,* 42, Gloucester Road, Manurewa, New Zealand.

Issue of the late Arthur Cooke-Yarborough, *b.* 1852, *d.* 1933: *m.* **1877,** Ethel Constance, who *d.* 1935, da. of the late Rev. William Rawlins Capel, of Cairnryan, Bournemouth:—
Edith Muriel. *Residence,* Roughstones, Cottage Rd., Leeds, 6.

Grandchildren of the late Richard Cooke-Yarborough (*b.* 1851), son of Richard Cooke-Yarborough (*b.* 1805), son of John Cooke-Yarborough (ante):—
Issue of the late Francis Michael Cooke-Yarborough, *b.* 1904, *d.* 1970: *m.* 1933, Mary, who *d.* 1965, da. of the late Everett L. Hudson, of Newcastle-upon-Tyne:—
Richard Everett (Ramsay Av., W. Pymble, NSW), *b.* 1935: BSc (Honours) 1961: *m.* 1960, Sheila Margaret, da. of John Hugill, of Strathnaver, Walton, Brampton, Cumberland, and has issue living, Helena Margaret, *b.* 1960,—Claire Mary, *b.* 1963,—Ruth Meryl *b.* 1967.——Jean Christine, *b.* 1937: *m.* 1960, Alan Keith Martin, BSc, PhD, of Dalmore, Greenhead, Mauchline, Ayrshire, and has issue living, Colin Seath, *b.* 1962,—Patricia Anne, *b.* 1964,—Christine Fiona, *b.* 1966,— Mary Kay, *b.* 1967.——Mary Elizabeth *b.* 1942: *m.* 1965, Robert Alexander Porteous, of 65, Lyncroft Gdns., Hounslow, Middx., and has issue living, Alexander Michael, *b.* 1967,—Robert James, *b.* 1968.

Grandchildren of Richard Cooke-Yarborough (*b.* 1805) (ante):—
Issue of the late Rev. Canon John James Cooke-Yarborough, *b.* 1855, *d.* 1941: *m.* 1890, Emily, who *d.* 1947, da. of the late Richard Foster, of Homewood, Chislehurst:—
Margaret Hope, *b.* 1891: *m.* 1915, Herbert Prior Ingram, of Trinidad, who *d.* 1943, and has issue living, Margaret Jane, *b.* 1916: *m.* 1945, Peter Hallett Fraser, and has issue living, Richard Thomas Yarborough *b.* 1951, Robert Peter *b.* 1954, Judy Rosemary *b.* 1947,—Rosamond Marion, *b.* 1918: *m.* 1944, Alan Robson, and has issue living, Anthony Prior *b.* 1946, Alicia Ann *b.* 1950——Mary Honor, *b.* 1893: *m.* 1st, 1920, Lawrence Hodgson Archer-Hind, who *d.* 1923; 2ndly, 1928, Charles Ernest Augustine Jeffery, OBE, who *d.* 1964.——Dorothea Alice (20, Thomas Eyot, Twickenham, Middx.) *b.* 1897: *m.* 1934, Richard Keith van Sickle, who *d.* 1960, and has issue living, James Richard Theodore *b.* 1938.——Jean Lily (*Jean, Countess of Balfour*), *b.* 1900: *m.* 1925, the 3rd Earl of Balfour, who *d.* 1968. *Residence,* West Roundel, Broxmouth Park, Dunbar.——Elizabeth Serena (1, Tufton Court, Tufton St., Westminster, SW1), *b.* 1904: *m.* 1927, Sqd.-Ldr. Philip Jackson-Taylor, RAF, who *d.* (killed on active ser. during European War) 1945, and from whom she had obtained a divorce 1941.

Grandson of the late Charles Edward Cooke (infra):—
Issue of the late Capt. Arthur Charles Darwin Cooke, *b.* 1876, *d.* 1963: *m.* 1913, Muriel, who *d.* 1958, el. da. of the late Leonard Brownlow Horrocks:—
David Charles Darwin (175, Victoria Av., Remuera, Auckland, New Zealand), *b.* 1917; Lt., New Zealand Forces; 1939-45 War: *m.* 1944, Phyllis Edith, da. of the late Capt. Arthur Henry Prosser, OBE, and has issue living, Richard Charles Darwin, *b.* 1947: *m.* 1972, Dorothy Jane, da. of the late Eric George Woollams,—Elizabeth Angela Darwin, *b.* 1948: *m.* 1970, Martin John Beattie, LLB, of 4, Napier Av., Takapuna, Auckland, NZ, and has issue living, Rosemary Ann *b.* 1971, Amanda Jane *b.* 1973.

Issue of the late Philip Bryan Cooke, *b.* 1886, *d.* 1968: *m.* 1st, 1909, Florence Alma, who *d.* 1950, da. of James Leamy, of Vancouver, BC; 2ndly, 1951, Katharine, who *d.* 1963, da. of David Walter Price, of Westerley, Rhode Island, USA:—
(By 1st m.) Bryan Edward (Alford, Boronia Rd., Glenorie, NSW, 2157), *b.* 1910; Maj. AIF (Reserve); 1939-45 War /prisoner): *m.* 1st, 1933 (m. diss. 1945), Margaret Ida, who *d.* 1965, da. of the late Walter Hiskens, of Melbourne; 2ndly, 1946, June Mary, da. of the late Arthur Tregea, of Sydney, and has issue living (by 1st m.) Robin May, *b.* 1936: *m.* 1st, 1956 (m. diss. 1960), Michael Threlfall; 2ndly, 1961, Bruce Arthur Rickard, of 10, Kokoda Av., Wahroonga, NSW 2076, and has issue living (by 1st m.) Philip *b.* 1957, (by 2nd m.) Samuel Bruce *b.* 1962, James Arthur *b.* 1963, Nicholas Lancelot *b.* 1965,—(by 2nd m.), Elizabeth Alice, *b.* 1948: *m.* 1966, John Curley, 18, George Mobbs Drive, Castle Hill, NSW 2154, and has issue living, Louise Alice *b.* 1967, Amanda June *b.* 1970, Penelope Anne *b.* 1971.

Granddaughters of the late Capt. Bryan William Darwin Cooke, 2nd son of the late Bryan William Darwin Cooke (*b.* 1764), only son of the late Bryan Cooke, 2nd son of the late John Cooke, 7th son of 3rd baronet:—
Issue of the late Charles Edward Cooke, *b.* 1846, *d.* 1929 : *m.* 1874, Marion Elizabeth, who *d.* 1936, da. of the late Rev. Arthur Guyon Purchas, of Challinor House, Auckland, New Zealand :—
Ethelwynne Beatrice Victoria, *b.* 1883: *m.* 1911, William Martin Simcox, who *d.* 1956, and has issue living, John William Bertram, *b.* 1917,—Martin Guyon, *b.* 1919,—Henry Truran Heathcote, *b.* 1921,—Ethelwynne Marian, *b.* 1912,—Frances Evelyn, *b.* 1915. *Residence,* 79, Kirk St., Otaki, NZ.——Elsie Mary Emily, *RRC*, *b.* 1885: 1914-18 War as Sister Aust. and NZ Forces (RRC, 2nd class): *m.* 1920, Maj. Lewis Clayton Timperley, late Aust. Forces, who *d.* 1946, and has issue living, Richard Henry (6, Cooper St., Fannie Bay, Darwin, N. Territory 5790), *b.* 1922; Capt. Aust. Army (Reserve); 1941-45 War: *m.* 1952, Hazel Mary, da. of the late Thomas Houlden, MBE, MM, JP, and has issue living, David Clayton, *b.* 1953, Georgina Mary *b.* 1955. *Residence,* Hilltop Lodge, Bentley, W. Aust.——Vera Durelle (Cohi Resthome, Ventnor St., Auckland, NZ), *b.* 1898: *m.* 1926, Capt. John Stuart Robertson, BEM, late Indian Army, and has issue living, Ian Stuart, *b.* 1929,—Mary Stuart, *b.* 1927: *m.* 1948, Victor Norman Cato, of 3, Wharua Rd., Remuera, Auckland, NZ, and has issue living, Alan Stuart *b.* 1952, Geraldine Mary *b.* 1949: *m.* 1969, Owen Erle Hoskin, MA, of 47, Brown St., Dunedin, NZ (and has issue living, Bronwyn Mary *b.* 1971). Cynthia Durelle *b.* 1951.

Grandchildren of the late Rev. Charles Herbert Cooke (infra):—
Issue of the late Lancelot Darwin Cooke, b. 1891, d. 1975: m. 1922, Edith Euphemia
Catherine (The Cottage, Kenfield Hall, Petham, Canterbury), da. of the late Maj.
Allan Ewen Grant. IMS:—
Charles Bryan (Ramanathan Hall, Peradeniya, Sri Lanka), b. 1925: m. 1952, Vajira Wijesinghe
Kannangra, and has issue living, Arjuna Bryan, b. 1953.——Sheila Beatrice (14, Marine Sq.,
Brighton, BNZ 1DL), b. 1923: m. 1943, Capt. John A. Nelson, Med. Corps, US Army, who d.
1963, and has issue living, James Darwin, b. 1946,—Lance Edward, b. 1947,—Richard Crosby
(1932, Brookview Rd., Castleton, New York 12033, USA), b. 1949: m. 1973, Nancy Mack.

Granddaughters of the late Rev. Charles Cooke, 4th son of the late Bryan Darwin
Cooke (b. 1764) (ante):—
Issue of the late Rev. Charles Herbert Cooke, b. 1862, d. 1946: m. 1890, Ida Beatrice, who
d. 1941, da. of the late Rev. G. F. A. Armstrong, R. of Lorum, co. Carlow:—
Grace Dorothy: m. 1931, Samuel Nevill Neild, who d. 1941. Residence, 33, Mile Oak Rd., Old
Portslade, Sussex.——Marjorie Sheila (PO Box 86, Triangle, Rhodesia): m. 19—, Thomas
Murray MacDougal, OBE, MC.——Barbara Helen (4, Fordington Hill House, High St., Dor-
chester, Dorset, DT1 1LZ); ed. at Oxford Univ. (MA).——Betty Mary (The Lodge, Bonmahon,
co. Waterford): m. 1929, Louis Dennis Martin, and has issue living, Patrick Graeme, b. 1930.——
Elinor Beatrice (Boundary House, Udimore, Rye, Sussex).

Grandchildren of the late Maj. Philip Tatton Davies-Cooke, OBE, el. son of the
late Maj. Philip Bryan Davies-Cooke, el. son of the late Philip Davies Cooke,
great grandson of the late Henry Cooke 2nd son of 2nd baronet:—
Issue of the late Col. Philip Ralph Davies-Cooke, CB, TD, b. 1896, d. 1974: m. 1924,
Kathleen Mabel, OBE (Owston Hall, Askern, Doncaster, Yorks.), da. of the late William
Hugh Davies-Cooke (infra):—
Philip Peter (Gwysaney Hall, Mold, Flintshire), b. 1925; late Capt. 1st R. Dragoons: m. 1957,
Jane, da. of Edmund George Coryton [see Carew, Btt., colls.], and has issue living, Richard Piers,
b. 1960, Paul Bryan, b. 1962,—Michael Anthony, b. 1965.——David Ralph (Aspland House,
Wicken, Cambs., and 25, Barkston Gdns., SW5), b. 1930; late Capt. R. Welch Fusiliers: m. 1955,
Henrietta Sarah Angénis, da. of Edward Jan Hoos [see B. Brownlow], and has issue living, Philip
Rupert Hugh, b. 1960,—Nicola Sarah Angénis, b. 1958.——Philippa Marjorie, b. 1938: m. 1961,
William George Antony Warde-Norbury, late Coldm. Gds., of Well House, Shearsby, Lutter-
worth, Leics., and has issue living, Mark William Antony, b. 1962, Alistair George, b. 1966.
Issue of the late Capt. Richard Anthony Davies-Cooke, b. 1909, d. 1962: m. 1934, Berys
who d. 1966, da. of the late T. Fanning-Evans, of Plas Cadnant, Menai Bridge,
Anglesey:—
Doris Caroline (Tal-y-Bont, Dwyran, Anglesey), b. 1935: m. 1971, Arthur Henry Grant, and has
issue living, Arthur Paul, b. 1972.

Grandchildren of the late Bryan Davies POOLE (infra):—
Issue of the late Capt. Bryan Cudworth Halsted Poole, b. 1892, d. 1971: m. 1925, Eleanor
Margaret Lawson, who d. 1948, da. of the Rt. Hon. Sir Adrian Knox, KCMG, KC, LLB.
Adrian Bryan, b. 1927.——Bronwen Margaret Knox, b. 1932: m. 1955, Maj. Basil Hugh Philipse
Heaton, MBE, RA, of Rhûal, Mold, and has issue living, Sara Margaret, b. 1956,—Julia Mary
b. 1959,—Victoria Bronwen b. 1971.

Grandchildren of the late Col. Bryan George Davies-Cooke, son of the late
Philip Bryan Davies-Cooke (ante):—
Issue of the late Bryan Davies Poole, b. 1861, d. 1931: m. 1890, Georgiana Mary, who d.
1944, da. of the late Charles Fenwick :—
Richard Domville, b. 1900; ed. at Charterhouse, and RMC; Lt.-Col. Rifle Bde. Club, Boodle's.——
Judith Mimi (Lady Hay) b. 1891: m. 1st, 1914, Capt. Alfred Spencer Mason Summers, Hussars,
who d. (killed in action) 1916; 2ndly, 1918, Capt. Sir Bache McEvers Athole Hay, 11th baronet
(cr. 1635), who d. 1966. Residence, Crookson, Peebles.
Issue of the late William Hugh Davies-Cooke, b. 1862, d. 1941 : m. 1900, Mabel Louisa,
who d. 1956, da. of the late Capt. E. W. Philips, of Rhûal, Mold :—
Sybil Gwynydd (Langcroft, Leeds Close, PO Highlands, Salisbury, Rhodesia), b. 1901——Kathleen
Mabel, OBE, b. 1903; Chm. of Executive Committee of Girl Guides' Assoc. of Great Britain
1948-51; OBE (Civil) 1964: m. 1924, Col. Philip Ralph Davies-Cooke, CB, TD, who d. 1974
(ante.)——Doris Sara, b. 1907: m. 1940, Lt.-Col. Anthony Lawrence Allpress, JP, who d. 1971,
and has issue living, William Anthony Toulmin (Chemin de Burquenet 27, 1095 Lutry, Switzerland), b. 1942; CA (R): m. 1970, Tamsin Fay Muirhead, and has issue living, Sharon Anne b.
1973,—Alyn Diana, b. 1941: m. 1967, Roger William Newmarch, of M'Sanje Ranch, PO Box
CH 113, Chisipite, Salisbury, Rhodesia, and has issue living, Steven William b. 1968, Christopher
George b. 1969. Residence, Longcroft, Leeds Close, Highlands, Salisbury, Rhodesia. Clubs,
Travellers' (London) and Salisbury (Rhodesia).

This family was settled in the vicinity of Doncaster. Laurence Cooke, Prior of Doncaster
1536-38, was executed at Tyburn 1540 for denying the King's Supremacy. Sir George Cooke of
Wheatley, Yorks., 1st Bt., was great-grandson of the prior's brother William. He received his
baronetcy for his father's and his services for the Royal cause in the Civil War, with remainder
to his next brother, Henry, who s. as 2nd Bt. 1683, and rebuilt Wheatley Hall.

COOPER, Creation (U.K.) 1821, of Gadebridge, Hertfordshire.

Sir PATRICK GRAHAM ASTLEY COOPER, 6th
Baronet, el. son of the late Col. Clifton Graham Astley
Cooper, D.S.O., R.A., 3rd son of the late Major
Loftus Lewis Astley Cooper, 8th son of 2nd baronet ;
b. Aug. 4th, 1918 ; s. his kinsman, Sir HENRY LOVICK,
1959 ; ed. at Marlborough ; formerly Senior Assist.
Land Commr., Min. of Agriculture and Fisheries :
m. 1942, Audrey Anne, younger da. of the late Major
Jervoise Collas, Mil. Knight of Windsor, and has
issue.

Arms—Vert, a fesse embattled or between two pheons in chief,
and as many thigh-bones saltirewise in base argent. Crest—Out of a
mural crown argent, a demi-spear erect proper, fringed or, pointed
argent, and surmounted by two palm-branches in saltire vert.

Residence—Monkton Cottage, Monks Risborough, Bucks.

NIL

MAGNUM · NISI · BONUM

Nothing is great that is not good.

Son living—ALEXANDER PASTON ASTLEY (47, Denholme,
Upholland, nr. Skelmersdale, Lancs.), b. Feb. 1st, 1943: m. 1974,
Minnie Margaret, da. of Charles Harrison.

Daughters living—Patricia Ann, b. 1950.——Helena Rosalind
Collette, b. 1958.

Collateral Branches living.

Granddaughter of the late Rev. Samuel Lovick Astley Cooper, 3rd son of 2nd baronet :—
Issue of the late Francis William Astley Cooper, *b.* 1859, *d.* 1945 : *m.* 1897, Lyonesse Matilda Dora Ida Agnes Ernestine Curson Paulet Wilbraham Joyce Eugenie Bentley Saxonia Dysart Plantagenet, who *d.* 1944, da. of the late Rev. Ralph William Lionel Tollemache-Tollemache [*see* Cs. Dysart, colls.] :—
Theodora Mary Astley, *b.* 1899. *Residence,* Bentley, Albecq, Castel, Guernsey.

Grandchildren of the late Capt. Albert Beauchamp Astley Cooper, O.B.E., 9th son of 2nd baronet :—
Issue of the late Lieut.-Col. Geoffrey Beauchamp Astley Cooper, O.B.E., *b.* 1884, *d.* 1948 : *m.* 1st, 1911, Gladys Mary, who *d.* 1912, da. of Lieut.-Col. Orbell Henry Oakes of Nowton Court, Bury St. Edmunds; 2ndly, 1914, Louisa Maude, who *d.* 1972, da. of the late I. W. H. White, of West Lea, Meanwood, Leeds:—
(By 2nd m.) Gerald Nigel Astley, *b.* 1916; ed. at Wellington Coll.; Maj. (ret.) 1st R. Green Jackets : *m.* 1st, 1941, Mary Constance (who obtained a divorce 1945), da. of the late Capt. Basil Hamilton Piercy, RN (ret.) [B. Forteviot]; 2ndly, 1951, Joan Ryland, da. of Dr. Bernard Wall, of Coleshill, Warwickshire, and has issue living, (by 1st m.) Juliet Jane, *b.* 1942: *m.* 1964, Peter R. Bellfield, of Dial Post Farm House, Rusper, Horsham, and has issue living, Robert James Astley *b.* 1965, Charles Peter *b.* 1969, Edward Jonathan *b.* 1972—(by 2nd m.) Desmond Beauchamp, *b.* 1955; ed. at Wellington Coll. (Scholar), and St. Peters Coll., Oxford,—Felicity Ann, *b.* 1954; ed. at Roy. Sch., Bath, and Durham Univ. *Residence,* Five Bells Cottage, Hessett, nr. Bury St. Edmunds.——Rosemary Anne, *b.* 1920: *m.* 1946, Lt.-Col. Peter Jarrett Lewis, The Buffs, and has issue living, Virginia Rosemary, *b.* 1949: *m.* 1974, Maj. Roderick Alexander Cordy-Simpson, 13th/18th R. Hussars (Queen Mary's Own). *Residence,* Thedwastre, Thurston, nr. Bury St. Edmunds.

Granddaughters of the late Clement Astley Paston Cooper, 10th son of 2nd baronet :—
Issue of the late Stephen Clement Paston Cooper, *b.* 1885, *d.* 1935 : *m.* 1915, Florence Gertrude Taylor, who *d.* 1966:—
Elizabeth Margaret ASTLEY COOPER (Flat 4, 92/94 St. Giles St., Norwich), *b.* 1916; assumed by deed poll 1968 the surname of Astley Cooper: *m.* 1st, 1935 (m. diss. 1949), Maj. Roderick Walter Sholto Douglas, RAC (TA) [*see* E. Morton, colls.); 2ndly, 1949, as his 2nd wife, Sir Basil Antony Trevor Mostyn, 13th Bt., who *d.* 1956; 3rdly, 1939 (m. diss. 1966), David George Longman.——Monica Mary (Flat 4, 2, Harrington Rd., Preston Park, Brighton), *b.* 1917.——Diana Susan, *b.* 1919: *m.* 1st, 1939 (m. diss. 1967), Com. Cecil John Grenfell, RN (ret.) [E. Cavan, colls.]; 2ndly, 1969, Clive Walter Edwin Windsor-Richards, of Golf Lodge, Steepways, Hindhead, Surrey, GU26 6PQ, and has issue living (by 1st m.), John Stephen *b.* 1940; Lt. RN: *m.* 1967, Stephanie Ann (Sophie), da. of Capt. James Marigold, RN, and has issue living, James Christopher *b.* 1969, Nicholas Ian (twin) *b.* 1969,—Richard Francis, *b.* 1944,—Michael Gerrard *b.* 1947,—Sally Angela (twin) *b.* 1947.——Pamela Jane, *b.* 1921: *m.* 1966, Lt.-Cdr. John Woolven Anderton, VRD, RNVR, (ret.) of Tudor Farm, Dodleston, Chester.

The 1st baronet, Sir Astley Paston Cooper (5th son of the late Rev. Samuel Cooper, D.D., R. of Great Yarmouth, Yelverton, and Morley), was an eminent Surg. He was created a Baronet with special remainder, in default of male issue, to his nephew, Astley Paston Cooper (3rd son of his el. brother, the Rev. Samuel Lovick Cooper, R. of Ingoldsthorpe and Barton, Norfolk), by whom he was *s.*

COOPER, Creation (U.K.) 1863, of Woollahra, New South Wales.

Sir CHARLES ERIC DANIEL COOPER, 5th *Baronet* ; *b.* Oct. 5th, 1906 ; *s.* his father, *Sir* (WILLIAM GEORGE) DANIEL, 1954 ; ed. at Harrow ; Major (retired) The Royals : *m.* 1st, 1931, Estelle, who *d.* 1952, da. of the late William Manifold, of Victoria, Australia ; 2ndly, 1953, Mary Elisabeth d'Abo, da. of Capt. J. Graham-Clarke, of Frocester Manor, Gloucestershire, and has issue by 2nd marriage.

Arms—Azure, a chevron engrailed between two lions passant in chief and a star of eight points in base or. Crest—A lion sejant or, collared azure, supporting with the dexter paw a lance erect proper, and suspended therefrom by a chain or an escutcheon also azure charged with a star as in the arms.

Residence—Heywood Manor, Boldre, Lymington, Hants.

Perseverantia omnia vincit.
Perseverance conquers all things.

Sons living—By 2nd marriage—WILLIAM DANIEL CHARLES, *b.* March 5th, 1955.——George John, *b.* 1956.
Brother living—Sydney Michael (Old Merchants Hall, Steeple Ashton, nr. Trowbridge, Wilts., BA14 6EU), *b.* 1909; ed. at Harrow.
Sister living—Joyce Mabel (twin), *b.* 1909 : *m.* 1st, 1932, Brigadier Henry Balfour Scott, 1st Roy. Dragoons, who *d.* 1955 ; 2ndly, 1955, George Beeby, and has issue living, (by 1st marriage) Michael Balfour, *b.* 1933. *Residence,* Clive Cottage, Compton, Berks.

Daughter living of 2nd Baronet—Hilda Susan Ellen, *b.* 1891 : *m.* 1st, 1912, Thomas Uchter Caulfeild, Viscount Northland, Coldstream Guards, who *d.* (killed in action) 1915, only son of 5th Earl Ranfurly ; 2ndly, 1917, as his second wife, Com. the Hon. Geoffrey Edward Mills, RNVR, who *d.* (on active ser.) 1917 [*see* B. Hillingdon]; 3rdly, 1918, Capt. Michael Wardell, 10th H., who *d.* 1969, and from whom she obtained a divorce 1929; 4thly, 1929, Julien Joseph Lezard, Bar.-at-law, and has issue living (by 1st m.) [*see* E. Ranfurly],—(by 3rd m.) Simon John, *b.* 1919,—(by 4th m.) a son, *b.* 1929. *Residence,* The Mill House, Gt. Missenden, Bucks.

Collateral Branch living.

Issue of the late Arthur Hamilton Cooper, 2nd son of 3rd baronet, *b.* 1881, *d.* 1973: *m.* 1910, Mabel Alice, who *d.* 1973, da. of Sir William Henry Smith-Marriott, 5th Bt.:—
Arthur William Douglas, *b.* 1911; ed. at Repton, and Trin. Coll., Camb.; formerly in RAF; Croix de Guerre with Palm.——Geoffrey Mervyn, *b.* 1916; ed. at Eton; 1939-45 War as Capt. R. Sussex Rept.: *m.* 1st, 1941 (m. diss. 1956), Elise Marie, da. of the late George McGregor Rich-

mond, of Balnacraig, Perthshire; 2ndly, 1957, Jean Margaret, da. of William Ross-Brown, of Durban, Natal, and has issue living (by 1st m.), Marie Frances Richmond, b. 1942.——Robert Henry (The Down House, Blandford St. Mary, Dorset; Carlton Club), b. 1922; ed. RN Coll., Dartmouth; a JP of Dorset; 1939-45 War as Lt. RN (wounded): m. 1946, HH Princess Teri, of Albania (niece of HM The late King Zog), and has issue living, William Jeremy Daniel, b. 1951,—Westrow Gerald Alan, b. 1956.

The 1st baronet, Sir Daniel, G.C.M.G., was the first Speaker of Legislative Assembly of N.S. Wales 1856-60.

COOPER, Creation (U.K.) 1905, of Hursley Park, Hursley, co. Southampton.
[Extinct 1961.]

Sir GEORGE JAMES ROBERTSON COOPER, 2nd and last *Baronet*.

Daughter living of 1st Baronet—May Phebe, b. 1893: m. 1915, Lieut.-Col. Archibald Hanning Wilkie, formerly King's Roy. Rifle Corps, and has issue living, David Alexander Hanning WILKIE-COOPER (of Merdon Manor, Hursley, Winchester), b. 1926; late Capt. 6oth Rifles; assumed by Roy. licence 19—, the additional surname of Cooper,—Hazel Penelope, b. 1916: m. 1935, John Gurney Hanning, of Almond Hill, Tokai, Cape Town, S. Africa, and has issue living, Judith Fiona b. 1940, Jane Rohays b. 1944. *Residence*, Cantray House, Croy, Gollanfield, Inverness-shire.

COOPER, Creation (U.K.) 1905, of Shenstone Court, Shenstone, co. Stafford.

Sir FRANCIS ASHMOLE COOPER, 4th *Baronet;* b. Aug. 9th, 1905; s. his brother, *Sir* WILLIAM HERBERT, 1970; MA Camb.; PhD London; MIChemE; Chm. Ashmole Investment Trust Ltd. since 1969: m. 1933, Dorothy Frances Hendrika, da. of the late Emile Deen, and has issue.

Arms—Ermine, on a pile argent three martlets sable, and on a chief gules two boars' heads couped or. Crest—Between two sprigs of holly erect a lion's jamb grasping in the paw a like sprig in bend sinister, all proper.

Residence—Bastide de la Maraouro, 06149 Tourrette S/Loup, France.

Son living—RICHARD POWELL, (Rowler, Brackley, North-ants.), b. April 13th, 1934; ed. at Marlborough: m. 1957, Angela Marjorie, el. da. of Eric Wilson, of Norton-on-Tees, Durham, and has issue living, Richard Adrian, b. 1960,—Jane Alice, b. 1958,—Belinda Gay, b. 1963.

Daughters living—Elizabeth Sally Ann, b. 1936: m. 1962, Peter James Glendinning, of Priory Farm, Thornborough, Buckingham, and has issue living, John Whittingham, b. 1970,—Daphne Dorothy, b. 1974.——Jacqueline Margaret, b. 1939: m. 1962, Peter Desmond Flaherty, of Glen Cottage, Butlers Dene Rd., Woldingham, Surrey, and has issue living, Andrew Niall b. 1970,—Sally Clodagh, b. 1963,—Sheena Mary, b. 1964,—Julia Siobhan, b. 1966.——Dione Frances, b. 1944: m. 1970, Christopher Bruce Jones, of Bexley, RD Manurewa, Auckland, NZ.

Complete things attempted.

Widow living of 3rd Baronet—EILEEN DOLORES PATRICIA (*Patricia, Lady Cooper*), (Shenstone, Berkhamsted, Herts.), da. of the late G. P. Hayes, of Dunloe Castle, co. Kerry, and formerly wife of the late W. P. George, of Gadsden, Alabama, USA: m. 1948, Sir William Herbert Cooper, 3rd Bt., who d. 1970.

The 1st baronet, Sir Richard Powell, was Vice-Pres. of Council of Roy. Agricultural So., and High Sheriff of Staffordshire 1901, and the 2nd baronet was a J.P. for Herts, and sat as M.P. for Walsall (C.) 1910-22.

COOTE, Creation (I.) 1621, of Castle Cuffe, Queen's County, Ireland.

Cost what it may.

Truth conquers.

Sir JOHN RALPH COOTE, *C.B.*, *C.B.E.*, *D.S.C.*, 14th *Baronet ;* b. Jan. 10th, 1905 ; s. his father *Sir* RALPH ALGERNON, 1941 ; Rear-Adm. (retired) ; was Dep. Director of Naval Ordnance (Material) and Ch. Ordnance Engineer Officer 1955-8 ; European War 1939-45 (D.S.C., C.B.E.) ; C.B.E. (Mil.) 1946, C.B. (Mil.) 1957 : *m.* 1927, Noreen Una, da. of the late Wilfred Tighe, of Rossanagh, co. Wicklow, and has issue.

〔rms—Argent, a chevron sable between three coots close proper. ℭrꜩt—A coot proper.
Residence—Monkton House, Melksham, Wilts.

Sons living—CHRISTOPHER JOHN, *b.* Sept. 22nd, 1928 ; ed. at Winchester, and at Ch. Ch., Oxford (B.A. 19—, M.A. 1957) ; sometime Lieut. 17th/21st Lancers : *m.* 1952, Anne Georgiana, da. of Lieut.-Col. Donald James Handford, RA [Bs. D'Arcy de Knayth, colls.], and has issue living, Nicholas Patrick, *b.* 1953,—Vanessa Jean, *b.* 1955. *Residence*, Russets, Blackpond Lane, Farnham Royal, Bucks.——Terence Eyre (Flat 4, 130A, Haverstock Hill, NW3), *b.* 1933; ed. at Winchester.

Brother living—Thomas Charles, *M.B.E.*, *b.* 1907 ; ed. at Tonbridge, and at Univ. Coll., London (BSc Eng, FRTPI): late Prin. Planner Dept. of the Environment; MBE (Civil) 1946: *m.* 1932, Zuilmah Paton, da. of the late W. P. Sherriff, of Delgany, co. Wicklow. *Residence*, 237, Sussex Gdns, W2.

Uncle living (son of 12th baronet)—Maxwell Henry, *b.* 1895: Wing-Cdr. (ret.) RAF; 1914-18 War in Gallipoli and France; 1939-45 War in Middle East, N. Africa, Malta, and Italy (despatches): *m.* 1935, Muriel Evelyn, who *d.* 1970, da. of the late Evelyn Arthur Rich, MRCS [Rich, Bt., colls.], and widow of Walter Jagger, MB. *Residence*, Westacre, Sleepers Hill, Winchester, Hants.

Collateral Branches living.

Issue of the late John Methuen Coote, OBE, 2nd son of 12th baronet, *b.* 1878, *d.* 1967: *m.* 1912, Leonora Wray who *d.* 1969, da. of the late John Townsend Trench, of Kenmare [B. Ashtown, colls.]:—
Joanna Frances (Gins, Beaulieu, Hants.) *b.* 1913; 1939-45 War 1st Officer WRNS; HM Diplo. Ser. 1948-73.——Diana Jean, *MBE*, *b.* 1914; N-W Europe 1944-45 as Senior Cdr. ATS; MBE (Mil.) 1946: *m.* 1946, Edmund Luxmoore, of Crackenthorpe Hall, Appleby, Westmorland, and Staindrop Hall, Staindrop, co. Durham, and has issue living, Michael John, *b.* 1948: *m.* 1973, Margaret, da. of Surg.-Cdr. J. More-Nisbett, of The Drum, Gilmerton, Edinburgh,—Richard Aylmer, *b.* 1955,—Elizabeth Jean, *b.* 1950.

Issue of the late Com. Bernard Trotter Coote, O.B.E., 3rd son of 12th baronet, *b.* 1880, *d.* 1955 : *m.* 1907, Grace Harriet, who *d.* 1958, el. da. of the late Very Rev. John Joseph Robinson, D.D. [B. Avebury] :—
Rev. Denis Ivor, *CBE* (12. Belle Vue Rd., Parkstone, Dorset, BH14 8TW; RAF Club), *b.* 1908; ed. at Woking Gram. Sch.; Group Capt. (ret.) RAF; 1939-45 War (despatches), CBE (Mil.) 1951: *m.* 1933, Olive Sheelagh (late Fl. Officer WAAF), only da. of the late Hugh Crompton Bischoff, of Woodhayes, Woodlands, Southampton, and has issue living, Caragh Mary, *b.* 1949: *m.* 1973, Patrick O'Fáoláin, of 40, Pembroke Rd., Ballsbridge, Dublin 4, and has issue living, Tamsin *b.* 1973.——Michael Henry (Glenaraneen, Brittas, co. Dublin), *b.* 1913; ed. at Woking Gram. Sch.: *m.* 1939, Barbara Netterville, da. of the late Richard Netterville Eaton, of Roslyn Churchtown, Dundrum, co. Dublin, and has issue living, David Brian (Slieve Thoul, Brittas, co. Dublin), *b.* 1942: *m.* 1968, Elizabeth Joy, da. of A. P. Brooks, of 16, Woodside Drive, Castle Park, Rathfarnham, co. Dublin, and has issue living, Susan Barbara *b.* 1972,—Deirdre Joan, *b.* 1940: *m.* 1973, Sean Rowsome, of Grangemoor, Killcullin, co. Kildare,—Sheila Anne (Annaghbeg, Bally Maice, nr. Tallaght, co. Dublin), *b.* 1946: *m.* 1968, Maj. Patrick Brian Hemming Robeson, 6th Queen Elizabeth's Own Gurkha Rifles, and has issue living, Simon Michael *b.* 1970, Nicholas Andrew Hemming *b.* 1973, Philippa Charlotte Hemming *b.* 1969,—Jennifer Hazel, *b.* 1949: *m.* 1969, Peter Stuart Todd, and has issue living, Sarah Stuart *b.* 1972, Jane Stuart *b.* 1974.——*Rt. Rev.* Roderic Norman, *DD* (*Bishop of Colchester*) (The Bishop's House, 32, Inglis Rd., Colchester), *b.* 1915; ed. at Woking Gram. Sch., and at Trin. Coll., Dublin (MA, DD); Bishop of Gambia and the Rio Pongas 1951-57, Bishop of Fulham 1957-66, since when Bishop of Colchester; Archdeacon of Colchester 1969-72: *m.* 1964, Erica Lynette, da. of the late Rev. Eric G. Shrubbs, MBE, R. of Lawshall, Suffolk, and has issue living, Patrick Shrubbs, *b.* 1972,—Antoniette Alexandra, *b.* 1965.—Bernadette Sophie, *b.* 1966.——Brian Philip, *MC* (The Principal's House, Woodlands Rd., Leatherhead, Surrey; RAF Club), *b.* 1919; ed. at Woking Gram. Sch., and at Coll. of St. Columba, Dublin; Wing-Cdr. (ret.) RAF Regt.; Prin. of Queen Elizabeth's Training Coll., Leatherhead; 1939-45 War as Capt. Recce. Corps (MC): *m.* 1949, Elizabeth Helen, da. of the late W. J. Rutt, of Trimley St. Mary, Suffolk, and has issue living, Grace Elizabeth, *b.* 1956.

Granddaughters of the late Com. Bernard Trotter Coote, O.B.E., R.N. (ante) :—
Issue of the late Wing-Com. Patric Bernard Coote, R.A.F., *b.* 1910, *d.* (presumed killed in action) 1941: *m.* 1935, Muriel (Culver Haye, Motcombe, Shaftesbury, Dorset), da. of the late Maj.-Gen. Alexander Montagu Spears Elsmie, CB, CMG:—
Ann Patricia, *b.* 1937.——Susan Brigid, *b.* 1939: *m.* 1970, Geoffrey Maurice Young, of 169, Stoke Lane, Westbury-on-Trym, Bristol, BS9 3RR, and has issue living, Michael Patrick, *b.* 1971,—Catherine Ann, *b.* 1974.

Issue of the late Charles Chenevix Coote, O.B.E., 4th son of 12th baronet, *b.* 1884, *d.* 1944: *m.* 1908, Alice Maud, who *d.* 1968, only da. of the late Most Rev. John Baptist Crozier, D.D., Archbishop of Armagh, and Primate of All Ireland:—
Mervyn Charles, *b.* 1913 ; ed. at Durham Univ. (B.Sc. 1937) ; formerly Major R.E.: *m.* 1949, Inger Dahl, da. of Dahl Sorensen, of Copenhagen, Denmark, and has issue living, Peter Dahl, *b.* 1950. *Residence*, 18, Albany Mews, Montagu Av., Newcastle upon Tyne, NE3 4IW.——Dermot Chenevix, *OBE*, *RN*, *b.* 1915; Cdr. (ret.) 1939-45 War, Operations in Madagascar (despatches); OBE (Mil.) 1967: *m.* 1945, Dorothy Oliver, 2nd Officer, WRNS, and has issue living, Christopher Chenevix, (6, Wildern Close, Locks Heath, Southampton, SO3 6EZ), *b.* 1946; Lt. RN: *m.* 1971, Cheryl, da. of William Bridge, and has issue living, James *b.* 1971, Timothy Charles *b.* 1973,—Anthony Richard *b.* 1950. *Residence*, Willow Brook, Yarley Hill, Wells, Somerset.——Cecilia Maud, *b.* 1911: *m.* 1st, 1935 (m. diss. 1945), Benjamin Thomas Bowman; 2ndly, 1950 (m. annulled 1952), Mortimer Wilmot Bennitt, Under-Sec. of Min. of Works; 3rdly, 1962, John Ainsworth

Gordon, of 28, John's Av., NW4, and has issue living, (by 1st m.) Charles Christopher Benjamin (Mariners, Anglesea Rd., Wivenhoe, Colchester, CO7 9JR), *b.* 1939: *m.* 1961, June Vivian Murray, and has issue living, Timothy Charles *b.* 1968, Sarah Louise *b.* 1962, Emma Lucy, *b.* 1966,— James Thomas, *b.* 1941.——Patricia Aileen, *b.* 1919; formerly Section Officer WAAF, and attached RAF Delegation, Washington, USA: *m.* 1943, Air Commodore Nelles Woods Timmerman, DSO, DFC, RCAF, and has issue living, Mark, *b.* 1945,—Peter, *b.* 1950,—Nicola Mary, *b.* 1952. *Address*, House 407, 55, Waterford Drive, Weston, Ont., Canada.

Issue of the late Arthur Philip Coote, J.P., 5th son of 12th baronet, *b.* 1887, *d.* 1954: *m.* 1918, Margaretta (Wylye Head, Kilmington, Warminster, Wilts), da. of the late Albert Leslie Wright [*see* B. Fitzwalter, colls.]:—
Stephen Arthur (Home Farm, Ashford Carbonell, Ludlow, Salop), *b.* 1925; ed. at Repton, Selwyn Coll. Camb., and Roy. Agric. Coll. Cirencester; formerly Lt. Rifle Bde.: *m.* 1951, Sheila Mary Healey, and has issue living, Michael Philip John, *b.* 1952,—Timothy Stephen, *b.* 1954,—Nicholas Anthony, *b.* 1955,—Peter Richard, *b.* 1965,—Bryony Mary, *b.* 1958. ——Margaretta Anne, Broad Leys, Widdington, Saffron Walden, Essex), *b.* 1919; SRN; late PMRAFNS: *m.* 1946, Geoffrey Cecil Morris, who *d.* 1969, and has issue living, William Philip, *b.* 1947,—Sally Margaretta, *b.* 1948.——Bridget, *b.* 1924: *m.* 1959, Capt. Reginald Fife Whinney, DSC, RN, of Wylye Head, Kilmington, Warminster, Wilts., and has issue living, Alison Bridget, *b.* 1963.

Grandchildren of the late Com. John Pemberton Plumptre Coote (infra) :—
Issue of the late Lieut.-Col. Mervyn Chidley Coote, *b.* 1885 ; *d.* 1950 : *m.* 1915 Cecil Maud Vera (of 3, Stafford Av., Nelson, New Zealand), da. of the late Maj.-Gen. Cecil William Park, C.B.:—
Chidley (Emano St., Nelson, New Zealand), *b.* 1918: *m.* 1954, Mavis Ellen Thompson.——Eleanor Patricia, *b.* 1916: *m.* 1940, James Chilton Francis Hayter, of Rocklands, Golden Bay, Nelson, NZ, and has issue living, Stephen James, *b.* 1945.——Maureen Joyce, *b.* 1923: *m.* 1963, Samuel Nicholson, of 93, Coronation Rd., Morrinsville, Waikato, NZ, and has issue living, Ian Andrew, *b.* 1964.——Rosemary Cecilia, *b.* 1929: *m.* 1951, Joseph Trevor Clark, and has issue living, Anthony Joseph, *b.* 1952,—Peter Andrew, *b.* 1954,—Geoffrey Robert, *b.* 1956,—Jeremy John, *b.* 1961.

Issue of the late Com. John Pemberton Plumptre Coote, 3rd son of 11th baronet, *b.* 1850, *d.* 1938: *m.* 1880, Eleanor Agnes, who *d.* 1925, da. of the late John Osmaston, of Hawkhurst Court, Sussex :—
Joyce Margaretta (of 9, London Rd., Harrow-on-the-Hill, Middlesex), *b.* 1891: *m.* 1924, Frederick Arthur Leaf, who *d.* 1959, and has issue living, John Frederick (Druries, Harrow-on-the-Hill, Middlesex), *b.* 1925: *m.* 1955, Jean Marjorie, da. of Richard S. Witchell, and has issue living, Juliet Susanna Jane *b.* 1966.——Eleanor Marian, *b.* 1928: *m.* 1950, Cdr. John Shapland Fricker, RN, of Pinecombe, Hill Brow, Liss, Hants., and has issue living, Peter Frederick Shapland, *b.* 1951 Andrew John Shapland, *b.* 1956, Jeremy David Shapland *b.* 1958, Elizabeth Marian *b.* 1952, Miranda Joyce *b.* 1966,—Mary Joyce, *b.* 1931.

Grandchildren of the late Cecil Henry Coote (infra):—
Issue of the late John Cecil Coote, M.M., *b.* 1889, *d.* 1937 : *m.* 1915, Edith Blechynden (now of Nelson, New Zealand) :—
John Robin, *b.* 1916 ; European War 1939-45 as Major 20th New Zealand Armoured Regt. : *m.* 1947, Anna May McDonald, and has issue living, John McDonald, *b.* 1949,—Isobel Anne, *b.* 1950. —Alison May, *b.* 1954,—Ann Cecile, *b.* 1956. *Residence*, Hira R.D., Nelson, New Zealand.—— Peter Chidley, *b.* 1921 ; formerly Flying Officer Roy. New Zealand Air Force : *m.* 1942, Nancy Bower Playter, and has issue living, Robin Maxwell, *b.* 1943: *m.* 1968, Jacqueline Phillippa Elliott. *Residence*, Waingaro, Takaka, NZ.——Richard Eyre, *b.* 1929; Korea 1950-52 as Lt. New Zealand Forces: *m.* 1953, Janet Patricia Armatage Holmes, and has issue living, Stephen Richard, *b.* 1955,—David Eyre, *b.* 1959,—Jonathan Robert, *b.* 1966,—Sarah Patricia, *b.* 1965. *Residence*, Ballyfin, Enner Glynn Rd., Nelson, NZ.——Edith Jane, *b.* 1919: *m.* 1953, Ralph Armatage Holmes, and has issue living, Marion Jane, *b.* 1954. *Residence*, Armatage, Wakapuaka Rd., RD1, Nelson, NZ.

Issue of the late Frederick Stanley Coote, OBE, *b.* 1896; *d.* 1967: *m.* 1920, Edith Farquharson Crowe:—
John Oldham (47, Caversham St., SW3), *b.* 1921; Capt. RN (ret.); 1939-45 War: *m.* 1944, Sylvia, el. da. of the late Rear-Adm. J. L. Syson, and has issue living, Judith Sylvia, *b.* 1945: *m.* 19——,— Angela Mary, *b.* 1947,—Belinda Jane, *b.* 1953.

Issue of the late Eric Royds Methuen Coote, *b.* 1902, *d.* 1974: *m.* 1932, Patricia Vercoe (Iwaimea Rd., Nelson, NZ):—
Philip Arthur Cecil (26, Mount St., Nelson, NZ), *b.* 1935: *m.* 1957, Gabrielle Alice Goodman, and has issue living, John Anthony Royds, *b.* 1959,—Richard Philip, *b.* 1964,—Timothy Philip (twin), *b.* 1964,—Thomas Stanley Eyre, *b.* 1967,—Catherine Alice, *b.* 1958,—Bridget Ann, *b.* 1961.——Robert Malcolm (203, Cornelia Rd., Toongabbie 2146, Sydney, NSW), *b.* 1947: *m.* 1971, Rhondda Beverly Kenny, of Sydney, NSW, and has issue living, Deborah Michelle, *b.* 1974.——Jennifer Margaret, *b.* 1933: *m.* 1959, Arthur Edward Maskill, and has issue living, Patricia Ann, *b.* 1960,—Margaret Kaye, *b.* 1961,—Virginia Robyn, *b.* 1964,—Diana Mary, *b.* 1965.

Issue of the late Cecil Henry Coote, 5th son of 11th baronet, *b.* 1856, *d.* 1926 : *m.* 1888, Blanch Mabel, who *d.* 1947, da. of John Oldham, of Werneth, Nelson, New Zealand :—
Ivy Mabel, BEM, (8, Eginton St., Motueka, Nelson, NZ), *b.* 1892: *m.* 1916, Charles William Thorp, who *d.* 1971 [B. Middleton, colls.], and has issue living, John Willoughby, *b.* 1920,— Trevor Cecil, *b.* 1922,—Robert Charles, *b.* 1928.——Myrtle Cecilia, *b.* 1898.

Granddaughter of the late Adm. Robert Coote, C.B., 4th son of 9th baronet :—
Issue of the late Stanley Victor Coote, *b.* 1862, *d.* 1925 : *m.* 1889, Louisa, who *d.* 1939, el. da. of the late Ven. Frederick Bathurst, Archdeacon of Bedford :—
Honor Dorothea, *b.* 1896: *m.* 1920, Lt.-Col. Anthony Charles Barnes, DSO, OBE, who *d.* 1974 [Buxton, Bt., colls.], and has issue living, George Stanley Coote (Mill House, 60, Roman Bank, Long Sutton, Spalding), *b.* 1925: *m.* 1961, Priscilla Ann, da. of the late Walter Post, of Spofford, NH, USA,—Margaret Honor, *b.* 1921,—Catherine Lucy, *b.* 1923: *m.* 1957, Hugh David Phillimore, of 15, Mansel Rd., Wimbledon, SW19, and has issue living, Clare Penelope *b.* 1964. *Residence*, Foxholm, Cobham, Surrey.

Grandchildren of the late Charles Purdon Coote, son of the late Charles Purdon Coote, son of the late Capt. Robert Carr Coote, brother of 9th baronet:—
Issue of the late Major Charles Robert Purdon Coote, *b.* 1875, *d.* 1954 : *m.* 1933, Noel Margaret Jephson, (Fairdown, Vernham Dean, nr. Andover, Hants.), da. of the late Lt.-Col. Ernest Henry Denne Stracey [*see* Stracey, Bt. colls.]:—
Nicola Harriette (*Baroness Clinton*), *b.* 1937: *m.* 1959, the 22nd Baron Clinton.——Margaret Lydia Faith, *b.* 1939: *m.* 1966, Colin Patrick Annesley Martin Hill, of 13, Ladbroke Grove, W11 [*see* E. Annesley, colls.].——Caroline Anne, *b.* 1940: *m.* 1963, Baron Lambert Frederick Casijn van Till, of Fortlaan 1, Bussum, Holland, and has issue living, Rupert Maurice Casijn, *b.* 1967,— Edward Nicholaas Frederick, *b.* 1972,—Lydia Julie, *b.* 1964.——Rosamond Aileen, *b.* 1943: *m.* 1965, Timothy Hetherington Earle Bulwer-Long, 15th/19th King's R. Hussars (ret.), of Heydon, Norfolk, and has issue living, Lucy Wiggett, *b.* 1966,—Charlotte Louise, *b.* 1968.—— Mary Patricia, *b.* 1945.

Sir Charles Coote, 1st baronet, Provost-Marshal and Vice-President of the Province of Connaught, greatly distinguished himself at the relief of Birr, 1642.   The 2nd baronet was created, in 1661, Earl of Mountrath, in the peerage of Ireland, when the baronetcy merged in the peerage.   The 7th earl and 8th baronet, having no heir, obtained in 1800 a new creation, that of Baron Castle Coote, with special remainder, which title became extinct in 1827, when the baronetcy reverted to the great-great-grandson of the 2nd son of 1st baronet.

COPE, Creation (E.) 1611, of Hanwell, Oxfordshire. [Dormant or Extinct 1972.]

Sir MORDAUNT LECKONBY COPE, *MC*, 16th and last *Baronet*.

Daughter living of 14th Baronet—Joan Penelope (*Lady Cope-Strachan*), b. 1926; assumed by deed poll 1969 the surname of Cope-Strachan: m. 1949, Sir Duncan Alexander Grant, 13th Bt. (*cr.* 1688) who d. 1961.   *Residences*, 34, Morehampton Rd., Donnybrook, Dublin; Manzanares 22, Madrid 5, Spain.

Widows living of 14th, 15th and 16th Baronets—EDNA FRANCES (*Lady Peto*) (Onslow Court Hotel Queens Gate, SW7 5LR), da. of the late Edward B. Hilton, of Paris and New York: m. 1st, 1922 Capt. Sir Denzil Cope, 14th Bt., who d. 1940; 2ndly, 1951, as his second wife, Sir Geoffrey Kelsal Peto, KBE, who d. 1956 [*see* Peto, Bt., *cr.* 1855, colls.],——ANGELA ROSE ELIZABETH, da. of James A. S. Wright, AFC, FDS, RCS, of Brighton: m. 1st, 1956, Sir Anthony Mohun Leckonby Cope, 15th Bt., who d. 1966; 2ndly, 1967, Swinton Thomas, Bar.-at-Law, of 36, Sheffield Terr., W8.——EVELINE (*Lady Cope*), (c/o Lloyds Bank, 79, Brompton Rd., Knightsbridge, SW3), da. of the late Alfred Bishop, of Tuffley, Gloucester: m. 1936, as his 2nd wife, Sir Mordaunt Leckonby Cope, MC, 16th Bt., who d. 1972, when the title became ext.

CORBET, Creation (U.K.) 1808, of Moreton Corbet, Shropshire.

*Deeds are
the praise
of valour.*

*While
I breathe,
I hope.*

VIRTVTIS LAVS ACTIO   DUM·SPIRO·SPERO

DEVS·PASCIT·CORVOS

God feeds the raven.

Sir JOHN VINCENT CORBET, *M.B.E.*, 7th *Baronet*, son of the late Archer Henry Corbet, grandson of the late Richard Corbet, 2nd son of 1st baronet ; b. Feb. 27th, 1911 ; s. his kinsman, *Sir* GERALD VINCENT, 1955; ed. at Shrewsbury Sch., RMA, Woolwich, and at Magdalene Coll., Camb. (MA); Lt.-Col. (ret.) RE, a JP, a DL, and a Co. Councillor for Salop (High Sheriff 1966); an OStJ.; a member of Ch. Assembly and Gen, Synod since 1960; NW Frontier of India 1935; India, Burma and Malaya 1939-45 (despatches, MBE); MBE (Mil.) 1946: m. 1st, 1937, Elfrida Isobel Francis; 2ndly, 1948, Doreen Elizabeth Stewart (GRAY), who d. 1964, da. of the late Arthur William Gibbon Ritchie, of Enniskillen; 3rdly, 1965, Annie Elizabeth, MBE, da. of the late James Lorimer, of Christchurch, NZ.

Arms— Or, a raven sable.   *Crests*—1st, An elephant statant argent, tusked or, the trappings sable, fimbriated gold, on his back a castle triple-towered of the last; 2nd, a squirrel sejant cracking a nut or.

Residence—Acton Reynald, Shrewsbury.   *Clubs*—United Service and Royal Aero, Royal Thames Yacht.

Sister living—Helen Anne Evelyn, b. 1913 : m. 1946, John Dennis Russell, who d. 1973, and has issue living, Christopher Corbet, b. 1949,——Georgina Anne, b. 1947.   *Residences*, East Grove, Lymington, Hants; 68, Cheyne Court, Chelsea, SW3.

Daughter living of 4th Baronet—Lesbia (*Lady Lambe*), b. 1905: m. 1st, 1927, Lieut. Victor Ivor Henry Mylius, formerly R.N.; 2ndly, 1940, Adm. of the Fleet Sir Charles Edward Lambe, GCB, CVO, who d. 1960, and has issue living, (by 1st marriage) Andrew (85, Camberwell Grove, SE5; Northwood Cottage, St. Fort, Newport-on-Tay, Fife), b. 1935: m. 1959, Frances Jill, only da. of Charles Sweetman, of 124, Siddeley Av., Coventry, and has issue living, Caspar b. 1960, Jules Andrew Horatio b. 1963,—(by 2nd m.) James Louis (c/o Central Planning Office, Government Buildings, Suva, Fiji), b. 1943: m. 1969, Mrs. Felicia Laflin, da. of Donald Orr Sproule,—Louisa Caroline, b. 1946.   *Residences*, Knockhill House, Newport-on-Tay, Fife; 21, Stafford Pl., SW1.

Collateral Branches living.

Granddaughters of the late Henry Reginald Corbet, son of the late Richard Corbet (*infra*):—
    Issue of the late Reginald Corbet, b. 1857, d. 1945: m. 1891, the Hon. Katharine Russell, M.B.E., who d. 1950, da. of 23rd Baron de Clifford :—
Sybil, b. 1892 : m. 1922, Lieut.-Col. Edmond Waller Browne, formerly R.F.A., who d. 1960.   *Residence*, Devon House, Market Drayton, Salop.

Granddaughter of the late Richard Corbet, 2nd son of 1st baronet:—
    Issue of the late Rev. Athelstan Corbet, b. 1837, d. 1926: m. 1st, 1866, Julia Helen, who d. 1885, da. of Sir Archer Denman Croft, 8th Bt. ; 2ndly, 1887, Octavia Geraldine, who d. 1942, da. of the late Octavius Browne, of Courtlands, Devon.
(By 2nd marriage) Mary Geraldine.   *Residence*, 21A, Beauchamp Avenue, Leamington Spa.

This family is descended in an unbroken male line from Hugh Corbeau (or Corbet), a noble Norman, who with two sons came over with William the Conqueror.   One of these sons, Roger Fitz-Corbet, was father of William de Corbet, who settled at Wattlesborough, Shropshire, and was the common ancestor of the present baronet, and of Peter Corbet, of Caus Castle, who was summoned to Parliament as a baron *temp.* Edward I., which title became ext. 1347.   Moreton Corbet Castle, the ancient family seat, was destroyed by fire during the Civil Wars, and is a beautiful ruin. The present baronet descends from Richard Corbet, younger brother of Sir Vincent Corbet, M.P., who was created a baronet 1642 (title ext. 1688), and whose widow was created Viscountess Corbet, of Linslade, for life.   The 5th baronet, Sir Roland James, Lieut. Coldstream Guards, was killed in action during European War 1915 together with three other possible heirs of his generation

CORNWALL, Creation (U.K.) 1918, of Holcombe Burnell, co. Devon. [Extinct 1962.]

Sir REGINALD EDWIN CORNWALL, 2nd and last *Baronet.*

Daughters living of 1st Baronet—Elizabeth Jane : *m.* 1910, William Thelwell Read.——Laura Ellen.

CORRY, Creation (U.K.) 1885, of Dunraven, co. Antrim.

Sir JAMES PEROWNE IVO MYLES CORRY, 3rd
Baronet; *b.* June 10th, 1892; *s.* his father, *Sir* WILLIAM,
1926; ed. at Eton, and at Trin. Coll., Camb. (B.A. 1914, M.A.
1918) ; sometime Sub-Lieut. R.N.V.R. : *m.* 1st, 1921
(marriage dissolved 1937), Molly Irene, da. of the late
Major O. J. Bell ; 2ndly, 1946, Cynthia, da. of the late
Capt. F. H. Mahony, and widow of Capt. David Polson,
and has issue by 1st and 2nd marriages.

Arms—Gules, a saltire engrailed argent, between in chief, a rose of the
last, in fesse two thistles slipped proper, and in base a trefoil slipped or.
Crest,—A cock combed and wattled proper, and charged on the breast
with a trefoil slipped vert.
Residence—Dunraven, Fauvic, Jersey.

Vigilans et audax.
Watchful and bold. **Son living—By 1st marriage**—WILLIAM JAMES, *R.N., b.* Aug. 1st,
1924 ; is Lieut.-Com. : *m.* 1945, Diana, da. of the late Lieut.-Col. J. B.
Lapsley, MC, and has issue living, James Michael (42, Albert St., Aylesbury, Bucks., HP20
1LX), *b.* 1946: *m.* 1973, Sheridan Lorraine, da. of Arthur Peter Ashbourne,—Timothy William
(28, Johannisburger Allee, W. Berlin), *b.* 1948: *m.* 1971, Bridget Isabella Litherland, and has
issue living, Georgina Katharine *b.* 1974,—Nicholas John, *b.* 1958,—Simon Myles, *b.* 1961,—
Jane Susanna, *b.* 1949,—Patricia Diana, *b.* 1956. *Residence,* The Mount, Portchester, Hants.
Daughters living—by first marriage—Anne (19, Cressages Close, Felstead, Essex), *b.* 1922; 1939-45
War, 3rd Officer WRNS: *m.* 1945 (m. diss. 1970), Norman Wilkins Trembath, Lt. R. Warwickshire
Regt., and has issue living, Anthony David, *b.* 1946: *m.* 1973, Marie Joelle Annick-Galvez,—
Timothy Mark, *b.* 1948: *m.* 1975, Elizabeth Anne Allen,—Sandra Rosalind, *b.* 1949: *m.* 1972,
Adrian Christopher Ransom Brown.——Susan, *b.* 1926.——**By 2nd m.**—Amanda Jane, *b.* 1947:
m. 1972, Hamlyn Gordon Jones, PhD, of 26, Scotsdown Rd., Trumpington, Cambridge, and has
issue living, Katherine Myleta, *b.* 1974.

This family emigrated from Dumfriesshire to co. Down early in the 17th century. The 1st
baronet sat as M.P. for Belfast (C) 1874-85, and for Armagh co., Mid Armagh Div. 1886-91. The
2nd baronet, Sir William, was a Director of Cunard Steamship Co., Ltd.

CORY, Creation (U.K.) 1919, of Coryton, Whitchurch, co. Glamorgan.

Sir CLINTON JAMES DONALD CORY, 4th
Baronet; b. March 1st, 1909; *s.* his brother, *Sir*
VYVYAN DONALD, 1941 ; ed. at Brighton Coll.;
Squadron Leader R.A.F. Vol. Reserve: *m.* 1935,
Mary, da. of Arthur Douglas Hunt, M.D.,
Ch.B., of Park Grange, Duffield Road, Derby,
and has issue.

Arms—Argent, a saltire between two quatrefoils in pale
sable, on a chief azure a griffin's head erased between two
quatrefoils or. Crest—In front of a griffin's head erased or
between two wings per pale of the last and gules three
quatrefoils sable.
Residence—Baytree Cottage, Hinxworth, near Baldock,
Herts.

Cor unum via una.

One heart, one way.

Son living—CLINTON CHARLES DONALD, *b.* Sept
13th, 1937; ed. at Brighton Coll.

Brother living—Philip Cecil Donald, *b.* 1913. *Residence,*
Dawneys Corner, Pirbright, Woking, Surrey, GU24 oJB.

Sisters living—Valerie (*Lady Gane*), *b.* 1905 : *m.* 1st, 1928
(marriage dissolved 1948), Walter W. P. Woolland, who
d. 1949 ; 2ndly, 1954, as his second wife Sir Irving
Blanchard Gane, KCVO, who *d.* 1972, and has issue living,
(by 1st marriage), David Anthony Walter (of Baydon
Manor Cottage, Ramsbury, Wilts.), *b.* 1929,—Peter Donald Cory (of Manor Farm, North Oakley,
Hants.), *b.* 1931. *Residence,* Newmans, Pirbright, Surrey.——Diana Ethel Muriel, *b.* 1918: *m.*

1943, Major Andrew Lyell, DFC, RA, and has issue living, Vivien Diana, b. 1944,—Clementina Lindsay, b. 1949. *Residence*, Whitelands House, Chiddingfold, Surrey.

Aunts living (daughters of 1st baronet)—Edith Winifred, b. 1881: m. 1901, H. T. Thornley, of Broughton, Flat 2, Esher Park, Esher, Surrey.——Jessie Rosalie, b. 1911: m. 1933, Lt.-Col. William Handley Ferguson, late RHA, and has issue living, Shane Steuart Cory, b. 1934; ed. at Eton: m. 1961, Jill, da. of George Huber, of Durban, and has issue living, Kim Cory b. 1963, Dana Cory b. 1965,—Fiona Dawn Cory, b. 1947: m. 1969, Greville Edward Mervyn Vernon, of Newington House, Kingscote, Glos. [see B. Lyveden, colls.]. *Residence*, Ozleworth Park, Wotton-under-Edge, Glos.——Carmen (*Carmen, Baroness McGowan*), b. 1914: m. 1937, the 2nd Baron McGowan, who d. 1966. *Residences*, Bragborough Hall, Rugby; 7, Princes Gate, SW7.

Widow living of 2nd Baronet—GERTRUDE (*Gertrude, Lady Cory*), da. of Henry Thomas Box: m. 1904, Sir Herbert George Donald Cory, 2nd baronet, who d. 1935. *Residence*, Dawneys Corner, Pirbright, Woking, Surrey, GU24 0JB.

The 1st baronet, Sir (James) Herbert Cory (a Director of John Cory & Sons, Ltd., shipowners), was High Sheriff for Glamorgan 1913, and M.P. for Cardiff Dist. (C) Nov. 1915 to Nov. 1918, and S. Div. thereof Dec. 1918 to Nov. 1923.

Cory-Wright, see Wright.

COTTER, Creation (I.) 1763, of Rockforest, Cork.

While I breathe I hope.

Sir DELAVAL JAMES ALFRED COTTER; *D.S.O.*, 6th *Baronet;* b. April 29th, 1911; s. his father, *Sir* JAMES LAURENCE, 1924; ed. at Malvern , Lieut.-Col. (retired) 13th/18th Roy. Hussars ; N.-W. Europe 1944-45 (D.S.O.) ; D.S.O. 1944 : m. 1st, 1943, Roma (who obtained a divorce 1949), da. of Adrian Rome, of Dalswinton Lodge, Salisbury, S. Rhodesia, and widow of Squadron-Leader K. A. K. MacEwen, R.A.F. ; 2ndly, 1952, Eveline Mary, da. of the late Evelyn John Mardon, of Halsway Manor, Crowcombe, Somerset, and widow of Lieut.-Col. John Frederick Paterson, O.B.E., R.H.A., and has issue by 1st marriage.

Arms—Quarterly: 1st and 4th, argent a chevron gules between three serpents proper, *Cotter;* 2nd and 3rd, azure, a fesse between a fleur-de-lis in chief and a mullet in base or, *Rogerson.* **Crest**—A dexter arm embowed, armed and grasping a dart, all proper.
Residence—Castle Widenham, Castletownroche, co. Cork. *Clubs*—Cavalry, Kildare Street (Dublin).

Daughters living—By 1st marriage—Sarah Gay Lisette, b. 1944.——Charnisay Ann, b. 1946: m. 1971, Capt. Charles A. H. Gwyn, Scots Gds., of Easter Lennieston, Thornhill, by Stirling, Perthshire.

Sister living—Violet Rosa Sonia, b. 1909 : m. 1st, 1930, Arthur Alec Banes-Walker, from whom she obtained a divorce 1938; 2ndly, 1941 (marriage dissolved 1955), Basil Kennedy. *Residence*, 168, Cromwell Rd., SW5.

Collateral Branches living.

Issue of the late Laurence Stopford Llewelyn Cotter, 2nd son of 5th baronet, b. 1912, d. (killed in action during European War) 1943: m. 1935, Grace Mary (who m . 2ndly, 1945, Lt.-Col. Geoffrey Rittson-Thomas, late Manchester Regt., of Haytor, nr. Newton Abbot, S. Devon), da. of the late Ivor Downing, of Beverley, Llanishen, Cardiff:—
PATRICK LAURENCE DELAVAL (West Aish, Morchard Bishop, Crediton, Devon), b. Nov. 21st, 1941; ed. at Blundell's and Roy. Agric. Coll., Cirencester: m. 1967, Janet, da. of the late George Potter, of Goldthorne, Barnstaple, and has issue living, Julius Laurence George, b. 1968.— Jermima Grace Mary, b. 1970,—Jessica Lucy, b. 1972.——Peta Natalie b. 1935: m. 1963, George Derek Wilson, of Beggar's Roost, Strete, Dartmouth, and has issue living, Paul Sean, b. 1964,— William Robin, b. 1966,—Adam Edward, b. 1969,—Charlotte Emma, b. 1971.——Primrose Anne (8, Southdean Gdns., SW19), b. 1939: m. 1st, 1960 (m. diss. 1967), Richard Hugh Nicholas Creswell, 2ndly; 1968 (m. diss. 1969), Henry George Herbert, Viscount Throwley, son of 4th Earl Sondes (now 5th Earl Sondes), and has issue living (by 1st m.), Belinda Jane, b. 1960,—Robin Amanda, b. 1962.

Issue of the late Thomas Lombard Cotter, brother of 5th baronet, b. 1888, d. 1923 m. 1912, Victoria Jean Robertson, who d. 1923:—
Ian Peter, b. 1916. *Residence*, Rockgrove, Darlington, Victoria, Australia.——Bettine, b. 1920: m. 1st, 1943, J. Harrison Owen, Roy. Australian Air Force, who d. (killed on active ser. during European War) 1943 ; 2ndly 1946, Wing-Com. Richard C. Cresswell, D.F.C., Roy. Australian Air Force, from whom she obtained a divorce 1956 ; 3rdly 1956, Group-Capt. Alan Graham Douglas, C.B.E., M.C., R.A.F. Regt. *R esidence,*

Grandchildren of the late Col. George Sackville Cotter, C.B., son of the late Rev. James Laurence Cotter, LL.D. (infra):—
Issue of the late James Laurence Cotter, b. 1839, d. 1889: m. 1868, Frances, da. of Capt. Ironside:—
George Sackville, b. 1870.——Wemyss M'Kenzie Osborne. b. 1872.——Henry Martin Stuart, b. 1873.——Oliver Wendell Holmes, b. 1879.——Agnes Mary.——Evadne Kilgour.——Ada Margaret.——Katherine.——Anne Winifred.

Grandchildren of the late James Laurence Cotter (ante) :—
Issue of the late Arthur Douglas Cotter, b. 1878, d. 1918 : m. 1904, Marion Church Solmes :—
James Guthrie Sackville, b. 1906 : m. 19—, and has issue living.——George Clinton Solmes, b. 1905 : m. 19—, and has issue living.——Frances Marion Louise, b. 1908 : m. 1926, Alexander Nicholson Salisbury, who d. 19—, and has issue living, Virginia Puella, b. 1927 : m. 19— Lloyd Fieley, and has issue living, a son, b. 19—, a da., b. 19—, a da. b. 19—. *Residence,*

Granddaughter of the Rev. William Henry Cotter, LL.D. (infra):—
Issue of the late Capt. George Edmund Sackville Cotter, *b.* 1882, *d.* (on active service
during European War) 1917: *m.* 1914, Beatrice Mary Grove (who *m.* 2ndly, 1921,
Brig. John Keily Gordon, DSO, RHA, of Firholt, Crowthorne, Berks.), da. of Com. Hans
Thomas Fell White, JP, late RN, of Springfort Hall, Mallow, co. Cork:—
Benita May, *b.* 1915: *m.* 1st, 1936, Major Arthur William Granville Dobbie, R.E., who *d.* (killed in
action during 1939-45 War) 1944, el. son of Lt.-Gen. Sir William George Shedden Dobbie
G.C.M.G., K.C.B., D.S.O.; 2ndly, 1950, Major Derek Wrey Savile, R.A., and has issue living,
(by 1st marriage), William Ian Cotter, *b.* 1939; Maj. RE,—(by 2nd marriage) George Keith
Wrey, *b.* 1951. *Residence,* Cross Ways, Middle Gordon Rd., Camberley, Surrey.

Granddaughter of the late Rev. James Laurence Cotter, LL.D, el. son of the
late Rev. George Sackville Cotter, 4th son of 1st baronet:—
Issue of the late Rev. William Henry Cotter, LL. D., *b.* 1844, *d.* 1931: *m.* 1st, 1878, Catherine
Letitia, who *d.* 1894, da. of the late George Stawell, of Crobeg, co. Cork; 2ndly, 1896,
Eva, who *d.* 1903, da. of J. T. Sikes, of Elmvale, co. Cork, and Kincora, Ceylon:—
(By 2nd marriage) Eva Maude, *b.* 1901: *m.* 1921, Lt.-Col. Alexander Patrick Cathcart Hannay,
OBE, MC, Queen's Own Cameron Highlander (also Squadron-Leader RAF), of Kenbank House,
Dalry, Castle Douglas, Kirkcudbrightshire, and has issue living, Patrick Victor Cathcart (c/o
Education Dept., Kota Kinabalu, Sabah, Malaysia), *b.* 1923; MA: *m.* 1st, 1948, Elvira Teodora
Fachetti, who *d.* 1964; 2ndly, 1965, Mrs. Iride Antonietta Giuseppina Ercolini, of La Spezia,
Italy,—Timothy John (Sharow Grange, Sharow, Ripon) *b.* 1929, Fl.-Lt. RAF: *m.* 1st, 1956
(m. diss. 1974), Judith Butler; 2ndly, 1974, Linda Jess Elizabeth Callan, of Edinburgh, and has
issue living (by 1st m), Patrick George *b.* 1958, William Victor Bladsworth *b.* 1963.

Grandchildren of the late George Sackville Cotter (*b.* 1829) (infra):—
Issue of the late George Sackville Cotter, *b.* 1858, *d.* 1904: *m.* 1889, Margaret, da. of John
McAvella:—
Marguerite Stewart, *b.* 1892: *m.* 1920 .Major Frank Warren Burnham, M.C., Canadian Machine
Gun Corps (Reserve of Officers). *Residence,*
Issue of the late James Laurence Sackville Cotter *b.* 1864, *d.* 19—: *m.* 1897, Mary Morrison
da. of Henry Ontario Dee:—
James Laurence (of Meadow Creek, Claresholm, Alberta, Canada), *b.* 1900: *m.* 1924, Anna, da.
of R. Harris, of Ohio, U.S.A., and has issue living, James Laurence, *b.* 1925,—Joyce Marie,
b. 1929.

Grandchildren of the late Col. George Sackville Cotter *b.* 1783), 2nd son of the
late Rev. George Sackville Cotter (ante):—
Issue of the late George Sackville Cotter, *b.* 1829, *d.* 1907: *m.* 1858, Frances, who *d.* 1901,
da. of J. Stewart, of Dunville, Ontario:—
Henry Crofts, *b.* 1875: *m.* 1907, Alice, da. of Richard Chambers.——Kate Alfreda: *m.* 1895,
Edward Rand Niblett, banker, and has issue living, Edward Russell, *b.* 1897; is Lieut. Roy.
Hamilton Regt., Canadian Forces; European War 1914-19 in France and Belgium (wounded,
two medals): *m.* 1923, Noreen, da. of the late Dr. J. A. Porter, of Toronto.——Mary Susannah.

Grandsons of the late William Crofts Cotter, 2nd son of the late Col. George
Sackville Cotter (*b.* 1783) (ante):—
Issue of the late James Laurence Cotter, *b.* 18—, *d.* 1943 : *m.* 1916, Jane, who *d.* 19—
da. of William Blyth, of Edinburgh :—
Laurence Meldrum, *b.* 1917. *Residence,* Meadow Creek, Alberta, Canada.——James Lawrence
b. 1919 ; European War 1942-5 with Roy. Canadian Army Ser. Corps : *m.* 1948, Phyllis, da.
of Frank Peters, of Claresholm, Alberta, Canada, and has issue living, Garry Laurence, *b.* 1953,
—Marlane Phyllis, *b.* 1957,—Karen Jean, *b.* 1959. *Address,* Box 473, Claresholm, Alberta,
Canada.——Blyth Sackville, *b.* 1921. *Residence,*

Grandchildren of the late Rev. Richard Henry Cotter, 5th son of the late Rev.
Joseph Rogerson Cotter (*b.* 1790) (ante):—
Issue of the late Joseph Henry Cotter, *b.* 1867, *d.* 1937 : *m.* 1896, Ethel Mary, who *d.*
1960, dau. of the late Surg.-Maj. Samuel Kyle Cotter, M.D. (infra):—
Charles Henry (Apt. 101, 1371, Fir St., White Rock, BC, Canada), *b.* 1898; formerly Lt. RA; is a
Chartered Accountant: *m.* 1924, Louise, da. of John Wesley Ray, of Miami, Manitoba, Canada,
and has issue living, Charles Roy Henry (584, Victoria Av., Belleville, Ont.), *b.* 1927: *m.* 1953,
Gertrude Elizabeth, da. of Hugh V. McCann, of Ottawa, Canada, and has issue living, Joseph
Henry *b.* 1957, Patricia Ann *b.* 1954, Mary Elizabeth *b.* 1960, Barbara Jane *b.* 1963, Catherine
Louise *b.* 1965,—John Raymond (of 338, Hartviksen St., Port Arthur, Ontario, Canada), *b.* 1929:
m. 1957, Vivienne Margaret, da. of Henry A. Patton, of, 4, Cotesbach Rd., Clapton, E5, and
has issue living, Stephen Henry *b.* 1960, Karen Louise *b.* 1959, Susan Margaret *b.* 1961,—Marjorie
Ethel, *b.* 1930: *m.* 1954, John Durward Johnson, of RR No. 5, Truro, Nova Scotia, Canada,
and has issue living, David Robert *b.* 1955, Eric Charles *b.* 1957, Bruce Allan *b.* 1958, John
Andrew *b.* 1965, Susan Elizabeth *b.* 1961.——Laurence Cecil (706, 1710 Portage Av., Winnipeg,
Manitoba R3J 0E2), *b.* 1906.——Adelaide Beatrice Ethel, *b.* 1903: *m.* 1931, Wilfred Joseph
Gagnon, and has issue living, Wilfred Joseph (of 2009, Centre St., Calgary, Alberta, Canada),
b. 1934: *m.* 1954, Glenda Mae Johnston, and has issue living, Garry John *b.* 1962, Robert Allan
b. 1966,—Paul Martin, *b.* 1937 (BE Geology): *m.* 1961, Maureen Walsh, and has issue living, Paul
James *b.* 1964, Deanna Louise *b.* 1962, Yvonne Michele *b.* 1963, Jennifer *b.* 1966,—Winnifred
Alice, *b.* 1932: *m.* 1953, Stephen Berkes, of Box 38, Whitewood, Saskatchewan, Canada, and has
issue living, Stephen Michael *b.* 1958, Linda Ann *b.* 1954, Nancy Lynn *b.* 1956.——Lilian Muriel
Edith (1003-1710, Portage Av., Winnipeg, Manitoba, R3J 0E3), *b.* 1910.

Grandsons of the late Joseph Henry Cotter (ante):—
Issue of the late Walter Richard Cotter, *b.* 1902, *d.* 1971: *m.* 1923, Lois (Route 1, Box
803, Camas, Washington, 98607, USA), da. of George Benton King, of Camas, Washing-
ton, USA:—
Eugene Richard (210E 8th South, Springfield, Utah, USA), *b.* 1924: *m.* 1947, Mary Agnes, da. of
Robert Ramsey, of Temple, Arizona, USA, and has issue living, Charles Eugene, *b.* 1952,—
Neil Edward, *b.* 1957,—Jennifer Marie, *b.* 1954.——George Henry (1015 A-4th St., Woodland,
Cal. 95695, USA), *b.* 1926: *m.* 1st, 1949, (m. diss. 19—), Barbara Gene, da. of Glenn Maxwell, of
Richmond, Cal., USA; 2ndly, 1971, Judith Kay, da. of Rex Clark, of Indianapolis, Indiana
USA, and has issue living, (by 1st m.), Walter Richard, *b.* 1953,—Kevin George, *b.* 1966.

Grandchildren of the late Rev. Richard Henry Cotter (ante):—
Issue of the late Alexander M'Caul Cotter, *b.* 1871, *d.* 1929: *m.* 1896, Mildred Bertha
Eveline, who *d.* 1925, da. of George Edwards:—
Charles Rogerson, *b.* 1897 (109-2300 E. Valley Parkway, Escondido, Calif. 92027, USA): *m.* 1st,
1934, Isabella Millie, who *d.* 1963, da. of Nelson Young: 2ndly, 1970, Iris May Webb, widow of
Lloyd George Cotter (infra).——Felix Alexander, *b.* 1900: *m.* 1929, Ella Elenor Christopherson, of
Brock, Sask., and has issue living, William Leroy, *b.* 1935,—Bernice Eveline, *b.* 1930. *Residence,*
5994, Dumfries St., Van., BC.——Louis Stephen (RR2, Mannville, Alberta, Canada), *b.* 1913;
1939-45 War with Canadian Army: *m.* 1941, Elizabeth Ellen, da. of Harry Thomas, of Mannville,
Alberta, Canada, and has issue living, Gavin Bryson, *b.* 1947: *m.* 1972, Rita Maureen, da. of
Allan McDonell, of St. Albert, Alberta, Canada,—Arlene Berna, *b.* 1942: *m.* 1968, Dr. Richard
Ellis Danziger, Lt. USN, of 19323, Keymar Way, Gaithersburg, Maryland 20760, USA, and has
issue living, Derek Scott *b.* 1972, Kathryn Erin *b.* 1975.——Lillian Kate (Suite 14; 6707-92nd

Av., Edmonton, Alberta), *b.* 1903: *m.* 1927 (m. diss. 1954), Harry Bowers, and has issue living, Alton McCaul (881, Heritage Blvd., N. Vancouver, BC, Canada), *b.* 1930; ed. at Manitoba Univ. (B. Architecture): *m.* 1951, Doreen Enid Willett, and has issue living, Jeremy Alton *b.* 1967, Daniel Edward *b.* 1969,—Henry Keith (41, Murphy Cres., Saskatoon, Saskatchewan); *b.* 1932; ed. at Alberta Univ. (BSc): *m.* 1957, Mary Lynne Houston, and has issue living, Jeffrey Keith *b.* 1963, Susan Diane *b.* 1959,—Michael James (Apt. 1201-9925, Jasper Av., Edmonton, Alberta), *b.* 1938: *m.* 1st, 1958 (m. diss. 1972), Gail Evelyn Green; 2ndly, 1972, Mavis Berguist, and has issue living (by 1st m.), David Michael *b.* 1960, Laurie Eveline *b.* 1959, Colleen Lynn *b.* 1969,— Mildred Clara, *b.* 1934: *m.* 1955, Gerald Douglas Grover, of 6504-87th Av., Edmonton, Alberta, Canada, and has issue living, Rodger Douglas *b.* 1959, James Terrance *b.* 1961, Barbara Diane *b.* 1957.——Florence Mildred, *b.* 1906: *m.* 1929, William James Shury, of 1751, 97th St., N. Battleford, Sask., Canada, and has issue living, David William (1371-100th St., N. Battleford, Sask., Canada), *b.* 1930; ed. at Sask. Univ. (LLB): *m.* 1956, Jane Miller, and has issue living, William Brent Cotter *b.* 1963, Debra Elizabeth *b.* 1956,—Harold Lloyd (3611 118th St., Edmonton, Alberta, Canada), *b.* 1942: *m.* 1961, Alice Hartman, and has issue living, Dale Lloyd *b.* 1962, Kyle Damon *b.* 1971,—Terrance James (3619-50th Av., Lloydminster, Sask.), *b.* 1944: *m.* 1965, Mary, da. of Doyle Edwards, of Saskatoon, and has issue living, Gregory Doyle *b.* 1970, Sandra Lynn *b.* 1966, Laurie Ann *b.* 1971,—Garry Clair (200, Georgian Way, Sherwood Park, Alberta, Canada), *b.* 1938: *m.* 1960, Claudia Fradette, and has issue living, Brian Keith *b.* 1963, Todd Kevin *b.* 1964,—Donaline Elizabeth *b.* 1932: *m.* 1955, Harold Jones, of 10117, Borden Cres., N. Battleford, Sask.), and has issue living, Glenn Harold *b.* 1960,—Evelyn Mildred, *b.* 1933, is a Sch. Teacher: *m.* 1955, Donald MacKenzie, of 959, Herbert Rd., Richmond, BC, Canada, and has issue living, Janice *b.* 1957, Valerie *b.* 1958, Wendy *b.* 1963.

Grandchildren of the late Alexander McCaul Cotter (ante):—
Issue of the late Lloyd George Cotter (twin), *b.* 1916, *d.* 1968: *m.* 1945, Iris May Webb, who *m.* 2ndly, 1970, Charles Rogerson Cotter (ante):—
Burney Thomas (4855, Canada Way, Burnaby, BC, V5G 1L6, Canada), *b.* 1946: *m.* 1969, Rosemarie, da. of Michael Koroluk, Geraldton, Ont., Canada, and has issue living, Christine Michelle, *b.* 1975.——Bonnie Mildred (twin), *b.* 1946: *m.* 1972, Paul Halagaza, and has issue living, Mark Leonard, *b.* 1974.

Grandchildren of the late Rev. Richard Henry Cotter (ante):—
Issue of the late Gerald de Purcell Cotter, *b.* 1881, *d.* 1941: *m.* 1917, Rosalind, who *d.* 1961, da. of James Billington Coughtrie, formerly of Hong Kong:—
Hilary James Coughtrie (38, Jill's Court, Barrie L4M 4L7, Ontario, Canada), *b.* 1918; ed at Westminster, and at Pembroke Coll., Oxford (MA): Lt. (ret.) RN; late ADC to Gov.-Gen. of British Somaliland: *m.* 1957, Patricia Kathleen Angela Mary Esther, only da. of the late James Doyne, of Castlerickard, co. Meath, and has issue living, Godwin Arthur, *b.* (Jan.) 1959,—Hilary Patrick, *b.* (Dec.) 1959,—Marcian Gerald, *b.* 1962,—Rosalind Catherine, *b.* 1958,—Rebecca Claire, *b.* 1961, —Mary Jane Frances, *b.* 1963,—Rowena Josephine, *b.* 1964,—Rachel Anne Monica, *b.* 1967.—— Arthur Gerald Purcell, *MB* (Castle House, Newtownstewart, co. Tyrone), *b.* 1924; ed. at Westminster, at Oxford Univ., and at Trin. Coll., Dublin; late Capt. RE: *m.* 1959, Isabel Adams, of Gortin, co. Tyrone, and has issue living, Colin Arthur, *b.* 1961,—Lynda Marie, *b.* 1962.——Angela Mary Purcell, *b.* 1921: *m.* 1951, Ulick O'Connor Milborne-Swinnerton-Pilkington, of Gortbrack, Castletownsend, Skibereen, co Cork [see Milborne-Swinnington-Pilkington, Bt.].

Issue of the late Joseph Rogerson Cotter, *b.* 1869, *d.* 1957 : *m.* 1913, Ellen Harriet, who *d.* 1948, da. of the late Surg.-Maj. Samuel Kyle Cotter, M.D. :—
Joan Jamieson, *b.* 1916; ed at Trin. Coll., Dublin (BA); late Subaltern ATS: *m.* 1944, Henry Haskins Ferrell, Junior, MD, late Capt. US Army Med. Corps, and has issue living, Henry Haskins, 3rd *b.* 1951,—Leslie Cotter (a da.), *b.* 1949: *m.* 1974, José Manuel Kauffmann,—Joan Pinson, *b.* 1954. *Residence*, 511, Cathedral Drive, Alexandria, Virginia, 22314, USA.

Grandchildren of the late Duncan Donald Darrock Cotter, 6th Regt., 8th son of the late Rev. Joseph Rogerson Cotter (*b.* 1790) (ante):—
Issue of the late Major Arundel John Plunkett Cotter, U.S. Army, *b.* 1883, *d.* 1952 : *m.* 1911, Emma Stothard, da. of William Robert Carter :—
Arundel, *b.* 1912 ; Lieut.-Col. U.S. Army ; European War 1939-45 : *m.* 1st, 1942 (marriage dissolved 1952), Madelyn, da. of Forest Mitchell ; 2ndly, 19—, Gabrielle Pauline, da. of Harry Tarter, of Washington, D.C., and has issue living, (by 1st marriage), Arundel, *b.* 1944,—(by 2nd marriage), Harry Bruce, *b.* 1955,—Robert Darrock, *b.* 1956.——Joyce, *b.* 1914 ; ed. at Connecticut Coll. for Women (B.S. 19—) : *m.* 1948, Lieut.-Col. George Kern, U.S. Army. *Residence*,

Issue of the late Harry Norman Cotter, D.D.S., *b.* 1885, *d.* 1960 : *m.* 1912, Rose Isabel (of 514, Gramatan Avenue, Mount Vernon, New York, U.S.A), da. of Henri Malabre, of Kingston, Jamaica :—
Harry Norman Rogerson (533, Driftwood Rd., North Palm Beach, Florida, 33403, USA), *b.* 1922; ed. at Cornell Univ. (ME 1948): Lt., US Marine Corps (Reserve); 1939-45 War: *m.* 1950, Beverly Jane, da. of Alfred Edmund Hayes, and has issue living, Thomas Joseph, *b.* 1952,—Anthony John, *b.* 1962,—Patrick Hayes, *b.* 1963,—Lark Ellen, *b.* 1951,—Noreen Ann, *b.* 1954,—Andrea Jane, *b.* 1955.——Richard Duncan Rogerson (twin) (of 5333, Ravensworth Rd., N. Springfield, Virginia, U.S.A.), *b.* 1922; ed. at Yale Univ. (B.A. 1947); is Lieut. U.S. Marine Corps (Reserve); European War 1939-45: *m.* 1949, Mary Theresa, da. of James J. Kelleher, and has issue living, Richard Duncan, *b.* 1950,—Michael Patrick, *b.* 1952,—Peter James, *b.* 1953,—David Henry, *b.* 1955,—Matthew, *b.* 1956,—Eileen Mary, *b.* 1956,—Elizabeth Ann, *b.* 1960.——Margaret Charlotte, *b.* 1917: *m.* 1942, Cæsar Leopold Pitassy, LL.B., of 11, Hidden Green Lane, Larchmont, New York, U.S.A., and has issue living, Richard Norman *b.* 1943.

Grandchildren of the late Surg.-Major Samuel Kyle Cotter, M.D., yst. son of the late Rev. Joseph Rogerson Cotter (*b.* 1790) (ante):—
Issue of the late Major Raymond Kyle Cotter, M.C., Indian Army (retired); *b.* 1889, *d.* 1948: *m.* 1914, Beryl Jessie Macdonald, who *d.* 1972, da. of the late Charles Macdonald Wintle, Sup. Frontier Police, India:—
Derek Raymond Kyle (HQ, BSSO (G), BFPO Branch 40, Germany), *b.* 1916: *m.* 1st, 1938, Daphne Cushion who *d.* 19—; 2ndly, 19—, and has issue living (by 1st m.), Anthony Derek, *b.* 1941,—Merril Victoria, *b.* 1942,—Carolyn, *b.* 1948,—(by 2nd m.), Nicholas Paul, *b.* 19—.——Kathleen Beryl Kyle (Susan), (87, Dartford Rd., Sevenoaks, Kent), *b.* 1915: *m.* 1st, 1933, Reginald Barnes Edwin, ICS, who *d.* 1961, and from whom she obtained a divorce 1942, and re-married 1946; 2ndly, 1942, Major Denis Erskine Ward, Roy. Tank Regt. [V. Bangor, colls.] who *d.* (killed in action) 1945, and has issue living, (by 3rd m.) David Michael Harrison, *b.* 1948,—Peter John Ashton, *b.* 1950.—(by 1st m.) Verity Anne, *b.* 1934: *m.* 1959, Terry Nicholas Blows, of 58, Channel View Rd., Campbells Bay, Auckland 10, NZ, and has issue.

This family was seated in co. Cork prior to the fifteenth century. Sir James Cotter of Anngrove, co. Cork, was C.-in-C. of James II's forces in Co's Cork, Limerick and Kerry. His son, James Cotter, executed in 1720, was father of Sir James Cotter of Rockforest, Co. Cork, 1st Bt. who was M.P. for Askeyton in the Irish Parliament. In 1874, Ludlow Cotter, son and heir of 4th Bt. was the last to receive a knighthood as a privilege of the Order under the second Letters Patent. He *dvp* 1882.

COTTERELL, Creation (U.K.) 1805, of Garnons, Herefordshire.

Sir RICHARD CHARLES GEERS COTTERELL, *CBE, TD,* 5th *Baronet; b.* June 1st, 1907; *s.* his father, *Sir* JOHN RICHARD GEERS, 1937; ed. at Eton; Lt.-Col. (ret.) RA (TA), a JP for Herefordshire, a K.St.J., and patron of two livings; late Lt. Roy. Horse Guards; a Forestry Commr. 1945-64, and Lord-Lieut. of Herefordshire 1945-57; Middle East and Italy 1943-45 (despatches); CBE (Civil) 1965: *m.* 1930 (marriage dissolved 1958), Lady Lettice Lygon, who *d.* 1973, da. of 7th Earl Beauchamp; 2ndly, 1958, the Hon. Molly Patricia, da. of 1st Viscount Camrose, formerly wife of 1st Baron Sherwood, and widow of Capt. Roger Charles George Chetwode [see B. Chetwode], and has issue by 1st m.

Arms—Quarterly or and argent, a cross engrailed per pale sable and gules, in the second quarter two escallops, and in the third one, all of the third; over all a bend also sable. **Crest**—An arm in armour embowed proper, garnished or, the hand gauntleted also proper, resting on an escutcheon argent, charged with a talbot's head erased sable, collared and lined or.

I did not seize it, I recovered it.   *Residence*—Garnons, Hereford.   *Club*—White's.

Sons living—By 1st marriage—JOHN HENRY GEERS, *b.* May 8th, 1935 ; ed. at Eton ; is Lieut. Roy. Horse Guards : *m.* 1959. Vanda Alexandra Clare, da. of Major Philip Alexander Clement Bridgewater [*see* B. Vivian], and has issue living, Henry Richard Geers, *b.* 1961,—James Alexander Geers, *b.* 1964,—David George Geers, *b.* 1969,—Camilla Jane, *b.* 1963.——Thomas Richard Geers, *b.* 1939; ed. at Eton.

Daughters living—By 1st marriage—Rose Evelyn, *b.* 1932 : *m.* 1954, Charles Eric Alexander Hambro, son of Col. Sir Charles Jocelyn Hambro, K.B.E., M.C., and has issue living, Charles Edward, *b.* 1959,—Alexander Robert, *b.* 1962,—Clare Evelyn, *b.* 1957. *Residences*, 69, Victoria Rd., W8; Dixton Manor, Gotherington, Cheltenham.——Anne Lettice (*Lady Sinclair*), *b.* 1933: *m.* 1968, the 17th Lord Sinclair. *Residence*, Knocknalling, Dalry, Kirkcudbrightshire.

Sister living—Mildred Katharine (*Lady Falkiner*), *b.* 1902: *m.* 1925, Lt.-Col. Sir Terence Edmond Patrick Falkiner, 8th Bt., late Coldstream Gds. *Residence*, Kingsthorne House, Hereford.

Col. Sir John Geers, 1st baronet, sat as M.P. for Herefordshire 1804-31 ; his grandfather, John Brooks, of Broadway, assumed the surname and arms of Cotterell, by Roy. licence. The 3rd baronet was M.P. for Herefordshire 1857-9, and the 4th baronet was Lord-Lieut. of Herefordshire 1904-33 (High Sheriff 1897).

COTTS, Creation (U.K.) 1921, of Coldharbour Wood, Rogate, Sussex.

Sir ROBERT CRICHTON MITCHELL COTTS, 3rd *Baronet; b.* Oct. 22nd, 1903; *s.* his brother, *Sir* (WILLIAM) CAMPBELL MITCHELL-COTTS, 1964; ed. at Harrow, and at Balliol Coll., Oxford; Maj. (ret.) Irish Guards: *m.* 1942, Barbara Mary Winefride, da. of the late Capt. Herbert John Throckmorton, R.N. [see Throckmorton, Bt., colls.], and has issue.

Arms—Azure, on a chevron between in chief two lions rampant and in base a representation of the Southern Cross, three lymphads sable. **Crest**—A quadriga or.

Residence,—Valley Farm, Clopton, Woodbridge, Suffolk.

Forward trusting in God.

Sons living—RICHARD CRICHTON MITCHELL, *b.* July 26th, 1946; ed. at Oratory Sch.——Hamish William Anthony Mitchell, *b.* 1951; ed. at Ampleforth.

Daughters living—Lucinda Mary Agnes Mitchell, *b.* 1944.——Susan Marie-Joseph Mitchell, *b.* 1945.——Miranda Clare Mitchell, *b.* 1948: *m.* 1973, Tristram Cosmo Barran, son of Sir David Haven Barran [see Barran, Bt.].

Sister living—Agnes Nivison (twin), *b.* 1902: *m.* 1st, 1926, Brigadier Claude Frederick Forestier-Walker, O.B.E., M.C., 3rd Hussars [*see* Forestier-Walker, Bt., cr. 1835, colls.], from whom she obtained a divorce 1930 ; 2ndly, 1941, Squadron Leader Claude Alastair Blyth Rome [B. Blyth], from whom she obtained a divorce, 1951. *Address*, c/o Lloyds Bank Ltd., 132, Regent Street, W.1.

This family was originally spelt Coutts. The 1st baronet, Sir William Dingwall Mitchell Cotts, K.B.E. (son of the late William Cotts, of Sanquhar, Dumfries-shire), was head of the firm of Mitchell Cotts and Co., of London, and of allied firms in S. Africa and elsewhere (merchants, colliery proprietors, and steamship owners), and sat as M.P. for Western Isles (*NL*) 1922-23. Sir (William) Campbell Mitchell-Cotts, 2nd baronet, assumed by deed poll 1932 the additional surname of Mitchell.

COUPER, Creation (U.K.) 1841.

[Name pronounced "Cooper."]

Sir ROBERT NICHOLAS OLIVER COUPER, 6th *Baronet*; *b.* Oct. 9th, 1945; *s.* his father *Maj. Sir* GEORGE ROBERT CECIL 1975; ed. at Eton; Capt. Blues and Royals: *m.* 1972, Curzon Henrietta, da. of Maj. George Macbean, of Loughanmore, Dunadry, co. Antrim.

Arms—Or, a chevron gules charged with another ermine, between three laurel-leaves slipped vert. **Crest**—Out of a mural coronet argent, a hand holding a garland proper.

Residence—Annery, Barton, Monkleigh, Bideford, N. Devon.

By valour.

Sister living—Jennifer Susan Amanda (twin), *b.* 1945.

Uncle living—Jem Ramsay (Los Amigos, Santa Eleadora, FCNGSM, Argentina), *b.* 1904; ed. at Marlborough Coll.; late temp. Capt. 27th Lancers: *m.* 1940, Aileen Jessie, da. of the late Thomas Robert Lamb Abbott, and has issue living, Francis Jem, *b.* 1946, —Caroline, *b.* 1941: *m.* 1968, Enrique Avendano, of Estancia San Miguel, Treinta de Agosto, FCDFS, Argentina, and has issue living, Diego *b,* 1970, Cecilia Maria *b.* 1969.

Aunt living—Doris Helen, *b.* 1907: *m.* 1941, Capt. Thomas Charles Jefferies, 27th Lancers, of Kilcarbery House, Enniscorthy, co. Wexford.

Daughter living of 3rd Baronet—Sybil (350, Station St. Box Hill, Melbourne, Aust.), *b.* 1885.

Widow living of 5th Baronet—MARGARET GRACE (*Margaret, Lady Couper*) (Annery Barton, Monkleigh, Bideford, N. Devon), da. of the late Robert George Dashwood Thomas, of Southwick, Kirkcudbrightshire: *m.* 1941, Sir George Robert Cecil Couper, 5th baronet, who *d.* 1975.

Grandson of the late James Robert Couper (ante):—
Issue of the late Maj. John Every Couper, MBE, *b.* 1900, *d.* 1966: *m.* 1928, Katherine Audrey Mary (18, Montague Rd., Ealing, W13), da. of the late William Ross Alexander, of Cupar, Fife:—. .
JONATHAN EVERY, *b.* Feb. 26th, 1931; ed. at Douai.

Granddaughter of the late Gen. James Kempt Couper, 2nd son of 1st baronet:—
Issue of the late William Lemprière Couper, *b.* 1874, *d.* 1926: *m.* 1919, Isabel Hodgson, who *d.* 1968, having *m.* 2ndly, 1952, Arthur Alfred Hitch, who *d.* 1965:—
Cara Jocelyn Mary, *b.* 1921: *m.* 1952, Verne Barrett Dickey, of 45540, Spruce Drive, Sardis, British Columbia, and has issue living, William Miles, *b.* 1955,—Roy Couper, *b.* 1957,—Alan Verne, *b.* 1960,—Mary Isabel, *b.* 1953.

Col. Sir George, C.B., K.H. 1st baronet, Capt. 92nd Regt. at Copenhagen; served throughout Peninsular War (medal with five clasps); was Mil. Sec. to Sir James Kempt in Canada, and subsequently to Lord Durham; afterwards Comptroller of Household and Equerry to H.R.H. the late Duchess of Kent. The 2nd baronet, Sir George Ebenezer Wilson Couper, K.C.S.I., C.B., C.I.E., of the H.E.I.C.S., was present at the siege of Lucknow as A.D.C. to Sir Henry Lawrence and Sir John Inglis, subsequently becoming Gov. of N.-W. Provinces, India. Sir Guy Couper, 4th Bt., *d.* 1975, when the baronetcy passed to Maj. Sir George Robert Cecil Couper, 5th Bt., el. son of James Robert Couper, 4th son of 2nd Bt.

COWAN, Creation (U.K.) 1921, of the Baltic, and Bilton, co. Warwick.

[Extinct 1956.]

Adm. Sir WALTER HENRY COWAN, *K.C.B., D.S.O., M.V.O.,* 1st and last *Baronet.*

Daughter living of 1st Baronet—Martha Gillian Rosemary, *b.* 1905. *Residence,* Merle Cottage, Scampston, Malton, Yorks.

COXEN, Creation (U.K.) 1941, of Seal, co. Kent. [Extinct 1946.]

Major Sir WILLIAM GEORGE COXEN, 1st and last *Baronet.*

Widow living of 1st Baronet—KATHLEEN ALICE (*Lady Coxen*), da. of the late Edward Doncaster, of Snettisham, Norfolk: *m.* 1912, Maj. Sir William George Coxen, 1st baronet (Lord Mayor of London 1939-40), who *d.* 1946, when the title became ext. *Residence,* Wellswood Park, Torquay.

Cowell-Stepney, see Stepney.

Cradock-Hartopp, see Hartopp.

CRAIG, Creation (U.K.) 1927, of Alsager, co. Chester. [Extinct 1933.]

Sir ERNEST CRAIG, 1st and last *Baronet.*

Daughter living of 1st Baronet—Anna Ernestine, *b.* 1888 : *m.* 1912, Franklin Wheaton-Smith, who *d.* 1946, and has issue living, Craig (Nichols Hill, Dorset, Vermont 05251, USA), *b.* 1917; is Maj. US Army: *m.* 1st, 1943, (m. diss. 1963), Princess Tatiana, da. of Prince Wiasemsky; 2ndly, 1965, Elizabeth Cynthia, da. of the late Robert W. W. Cryan, and has issue living, (by 1st m.), Simon William Gordon (c/o Royal Institution of Great Britain, 21, Albemarle St., W1), *b.* 1945: *m.* 1972, Hilary Christine, da. of Kenneth A. Bird, Tatiana Cleone Anne (*Hon. Mrs. Richard T. G. Parker*), *b.* 1944: *m.* 1967, the Hon. Richard Timothy George Parker [see E. Macclesfield],—Barbara Anne, *b.* 1915. *Residence,* Sherman, New Mexico, USA.

Craig (Gibson-Craig-Carmichael), see Carmichael.

CRAIK, Creation (U.K.) 1926, of Kennoway, co. Fife. [Extinct 1955.]

Sir HENRY DUFFIELD CRAIK, *G.C.I.E., K.C.S.I.*, 3rd and last *Baronet.*

Daughter living of 3rd Baronet—Rose Elizabeth (*Lady Targett*), b. 1905: m. 1st, 1929, Capt·
Kenneth Mackessack, 2nd Seaforth Highlanders; 2ndly, 1947, as his 2nd wife, Sir Robert William
Targett, CIE, who d., 1965 and has issue living, (by 1st m.) David (of 41, Vernon St., Croydon,
Victoria, Australia), b. 1931: m. 1st, 1955, Lola Bloomfield, who d. 1968; 2ndly, 1974, Frances
Evelyn Christie,—Elizabeth Jane, b. 1933: m. 1957, John Dennis Culme-Seymour [see Culme-
Seymour, Bt., colls.].   *Residence*, La Cible, Jersey.

Widow living of 2nd Baronet—MARY FRANCES (*Lady Craik*), da. of the late Rt. Hon. Alfred
Lyttelton, K.C., M.P. [see V. Cobham, colls.] : m. 1928, Sir George Lillie Craik, M.C., 2nd
baronet, who d. 1929.   *Residence*, 5A, Dean's Yard. Westminster, S.W.1.

CRAUFURD, Creation (G.B.) 1781, of Kilbirney, North Britain.

Distinction without a stain.

Sir ROBERT JAMES CRAUFURD, 9th *Baronet*;
b. March 18th, 1937; s. his father *Sir* JAMES
GREGAN, 1970; ed. at Harrow, and Univ.
Coll., Oxford: m. 1964, Catherine Penelope,
da. of the late Capt. Horatio Westmacott.
RN, and has issue.

Arms—Argent, two tilting spears in saltire proper
between four ermine spots sable, a bordure chequy gules and
of the field.   **Crest**—An ermine proper.
Residence—Brightwood, Aldbury, Tring, Herts.

Daughters living—Caroline Anne, b. 1965.——Penelope Jane,
b. 1967.——Veronica Mary, b. 1969.

Sisters living—Jane Elizabeth, b. 1932: m. 1960, Maj.
Michael Cumby Spurrier, late DLI, of 25, Thames Court,
E. Molesey, Surrey.——Margaret Ruth, b. 1934: m. 1962,
John Peter Hudson, of 96, Northchurch Rd., N1, and has
issue living, Alexander Matthew, b. 1965,—Emma Caroline,
b. 1963,—Erica, b. 1968.

Daughters living of 7th Baronet—Isolda Vereker, b. 1912: m. 1945, Maj. James Clement, of Glencairn, Dunlop, Ayrshire, and has issue living, James Robert Alexander, b. 1949,—Helen Alexa
Caroline, b. 1950.——Cynthia, b. 1917: m. 1st 1944, Jacques Pinkasfeld, who d. 1963; 2ndly,
1972, Lt.-Col. Albert Francis Lamb. of 22, Bridport Rd., Drimpton, Beaminster, Dorset, and has
issue living, Peter Charles, b. 1950,—Rosemary; b. 1952.

Widow living of 8th Baronet—RUTH MARJORIE (*Ruth, Lady Craufurd*), (Brightwood, Aldbury,
Tring, Herts.), da. of Frederic Corder, of Ipswich: m. 1931, Sir James Gregan Craufurd, 8th
baronet, who d. 1970.

Collateral Branch living.

Granddaughters of the late Capt. Henry Robert Craufurd (ante):—
Issue of the late Col. Robert Quentin Craufurd, D.S.O., b. 1880, d. 1943 : m. 1st, 1909,
Mildred Mary, who d. 1929, da. of the late Rt. Hon. William Kenny, a Judge of High
Court in Ireland, of Marlfield, Cabinteely, co. Dublin; 2ndly, 1931, Muriel Frances,
who d. 1969, da. of the late George Edward Darroch, of 40, Stanhope Gdns., SW, and
Braidley, Canford Cliffs, Dorset:—
(By 1st m.) Dorothy Mary, b. 1910; a Member of Soc. of the Holy Child Jesus.——Alice Gwendoline,
b. 1913: m. 1959, Maj. William Henry Murray, Irish Guards.   *Residence*, 41B, Onslow Sq.,
SW7.——Mildred Heather Mary (61, Finborough Rd., SW10), b. 1916.

This family descends from John who possessed the Northern part of the Barony of Crawford
1153.   His son, Sir Reginald de Craufurd, m. Margaret, da. and heir of James de Loudoun, and
his descendants inherited the lands of Loudoun which passed to Susan da. and heir of Sir Reginald
Craufurd executed by the English at Carlisle 1307.   She m. Sir Duncan Campbell of Reidcastle,
from whom descend the Earls of Loudoun.   Sir Alexander Craufurd, 1st Bt., was 11th in descent
from Archibald Craufurd of Previck and Thirdpart, living 1401, 2nd son of Thomas of Auchenames, great-grandson of Hugh, yr. brother of Sir Reginald.

CRAVEN, Creation (U.K.) 1942, of Crowhurst, co. Surrey. [Extinct 1946.]

Sir DEREK WORTHINGTON CLUNES CRAVEN, 2nd and last *Baronet.*

Daughter living of 2nd Baronet—Jennifer Anne, b. (posthumous), 1946.

Widow living of 2nd Baronet—MARJORIE KATHLEEN WALLIS (*Lady Craven*), da. of the late
Alfred Henry Hopkins : m. Dec. 1945, as his second wife, Sir Derek Worthington Clunes Craven,
2nd baronet, who d. 1946, when the title became ext.   *Residence*, St. Andrews Cottage, Donhead
St. Andrew near Shaftesbury, Dorset.

Crawley-Boevey, see Boevey.

Crespigny, see de Crespigny.

CRISP, Creation (U.K.) 1913, of Bungay, Suffolk.

Sir (JOHN) PETER CRISP, 4th *Baronet;*
b. May 19th, 1925 ; *s.* his father, *Sir* JOHN
WILSON, 1950 : *m.* 1954, Judith Mary, da. of
the late H. E. Gillett, F.R.I.C.S., and has issue.

Arms—Paly of four ermine and gules, on a chevron or five
horseshoes sable. Crest—A camelopard sejant or, gorged with
a collar with chain reflexed over the back gules, supporting
with the dexter foreleg an oar of the Royal State Barge proper.
Residence—Hollyhocks, Cranleigh, Surrey.

Sons living—JOHN CHARLES, *b.* Dec. 10th, 1955.——
Michael Peter, *b.* 1957.——Charles Frank, *b.* 1960.

Daughter living—Catherine Mary, *b.* 1962.

Widow living of 3rd Baronet—MARJORIE (*Marjorie, Lady
Crisp*), da. of F. R. Shriver : *m.* 1920, Sir John Wilson
Crisp, 3rd baronet, who *d.* 1950. *Residence*, Hollyhocks,
Cranleigh, Surrey,

Collateral Branch living.

Issue of the late Bernard Woodward Crisp, 3rd son
of 1st baronet; *b.* 1875; *d.* 1963; *m.* 1901, Elsa
Florence, who *d.* 1938, da. of Robert Schwarz:—
Joan Veronica, *b.* 1904; *m.* 1st, 1927 (marriage dissolved
1951), Trevor Gayer Fetherstonaugh, M.C., M.B., Ch.M.;
2ndly, 1953, Capt. John Egerton Broome, D.S.C., R.N.
(ret.), of 4, Sprimont Place, S.W.3.——Daphne, *b.* 1909:
m. 1931, Gerald H. Pinckney, of Wards Hill, Chapel Lane,
Bagshot, and has issue living, Jeremy Gerald (45, Black Lion Lane, Hammersmith, W.6), *b.*
1935: *m.* 1960, (Helen) Belinda, da. of Maj. Harcourt Michael Scudamore Gold, M.C., T.D.,
and has issue living, Charles William *b.* 1962, Simon Philip *b.* 1964, Emily Belinda *b.* 1967,—
Julie Ann, *b.* 1933: *m.* 1955, Capt. David Kentish Barnes, of Bolney House, Finchampstead,
Berks., and has issue living, Timothy James, *b.* 1961, Nicola Jane Kentish *b.* 1963.

The 1st baronet, Sir Frank Crisp (son of the late John Shalders Crisp, of Bramfield, Suffolk),
was senior partner in the legal firm of Ashurst, Morris, Crisp & Co., of 17, Throgmorton Avenue,
E.C.

CRITCHETT, Creation (U.K.) 1908, of Harley Street, Borough of St. Marylebone.

Sir IAN GEORGE LORRAINE CRITCHETT, 3rd
Baronet ; b. Dec. 9th, 1920 ; *s.* his father, *Sir* (GEORGE)
MONTAGUE, *M.V.O.*, 1941; ed. at Harrow, and at Clare
Coll., Camb. (B.A. 1942) ; formerly Flight-Lieut.
R.A.F. Vol. Reserve ; entered Foreign Office 1948 ;
was 3rd Sec. (Commercial) in Vienna 1950-51, 2nd
Sec. (Commercial) in Bucharest 1951-53, and 2nd
Sec. in Cairo 1956: *m.* 1st, 1948, Paulette Mary
Lorraine, who *d.* 1962, da. of the late Col. Henry
Brabazon Humfrey, formerly Indian Army; 2ndly,
1964, Jocelyn Daphne Margret, el. da. of Cdr.
Christopher Mildmay Hall, Wellow, Bath, [*see*
Broughton, Bt.], and has issue by 2nd m.

Arms—Azure, a fire chest argent, flames proper, between three
crickets or. Crest—A starling in front of an iris flowered proper.
Residence—Uplands Lodge, Pains Hill, Limpsfield, Surrey.

Son living (By 2nd m.)—CHARLES GEORGE MONTAGUE, *b.* April
2nd, 1965.

Daughter living (By 2nd m.)—Xanthe Clare Lorraine, *b.* 1968.

Aunts living (daughters of 1st baronet)—Dora Sibyl Mary (of
32, Eresby House, Rutland Gate, S.W.7): *m.* 1913, William
Moon Upjohn, Lieut. Welsh Guards, who *d.* (killed in action
during European War) 1918, and has issue living, Clive Henry
Critchett (of 10, Sturges Field, Ashfield Lane, Chislehurst,
Kent), *b.* 1914; ed. at Eton, and at Trin. Coll., Camb. (M.B.
and B.Chir., M.D. and M.A.), M.R.C.S. England and L.R.C.P.
London, D.C.H.; F.R.C.P. London; formerly Surg.-Lieut. R.N.V.R.: *m.* 1962, Anna, M.B.,
B.S., yr. da. of John Leask Warrander, C.B.E., of Edinburgh, and has issue living, Melissa,
Mary *b.* 1964, Charlotte Maryrose *b.* 1970.——Violet Nita: *m.* 1915, Andrew Sinclair Buchanan
MVO, who *d.* 1957 [Buchanan, Bt., colls.]. *Residence*, 34, Eresby House, Rutland Gate, SW7.

Widow living of 2nd Baronet—INNES (*Dowager Lady Critchett*), da. of the late Col. Francis
George Archibald Wiehe, formerly Durham L.I.: *m.* 1914, Sir (George) Montague Critchett,
M.V.O., 2nd baronet, who *d.* 1941. *Residence*, Fernhill Cottage, Fernhill, Horley, Surrey.

The 1st baronet, Sir (George) Anderson Critchett, K.C.V.O., was a K.G.St.J., Pres. of
Ophthalmological So. 1899-1900, and Surg.-Oculist to King Edward VII. 1901-10, and to King
George V. 1910-18, and Surg.-Oculist- in-Ord. to King George V. 1918-25, and the 2nd baronet, Sir
(George) Montague Critchett, M.V.O., was in Lord Chamberlain's Office, St. James's Palace 1912-41.

CROFT, Creation (E.) 1671, of Croft Castle, Herefordshire.

To be rather than to seem.

Sir BERNARD HUGH DENMAN CROFT, 13th *Baronet, b.* Aug. 24th, 1903 ; *s.* his father, *Sir* HUGH MATTHEW FIENNES, 1954 : *m.* 1931, Helen Margaret, da. of H. Weaver, and has issue.

Arms—Quarterly per fesse indented azure and argent ; in the 1st quarter a lion passant guardant or. Crests—1st, a lion passant guardant argent ; 2nd, a wyvern sable vulned in the side gules.
Residence—Salisbury Court, Uralla, NSW, Aust.

Sons living—OWEN GLENDOWER, *b.* April 26th, 1932 : *m.* 1959, Sally, da. of Dr. T. M. Mansfield, of Brisbane, Queensland, and has issue living, Thomas Jasper, *b.* 1962,—Patricia Alice, *b.* 1960. *Residence*, Salisbury Court, Uralla, NSW.— Hugh Denman, *b.* 1942: *m.* 1974, June Johnson, and has issue living, Edwina, *b.* 1974.——Bernard John, *b.* 1943.
Daughters living—Margaret, *b.* 1935: *m.* 1960, David Arundel Wright, and has issue living, Phillip Arundel, *b.* 1963,—Charlotte May, *b.* 1961. *Residence*, Wollomombi, Armidale, N.S. Wales.— Camilla, *b.* 1947.
Brothers living—Herbert Frederick, *b.* 1906: *m.* 1932, Marjorie Valmai, da. of R. Evans, and has issue living, Peter Herbert (Wongalee, Uralla, NSW), *b.* 1933: *m.* 1965, Ann, da. of the late L. G. Carpenter, of Toll-Bar, Cooma, NSW, and has issue living, Guy Herbert *b.* 1966,—Andrew Peter *b.* 1968,—Robert Ryland (Tangley, Guyra 2365, NSW), *b.* 1937: *m.* 1966, Helen, da. of D. J. Fraser, of Tangley, Guyra, NSW, and has issue living, Quentin Stewart, *b.* 1967, Carlisle Robert *b.* 1974.—James Philip (Weebaree, Uralla 2358, NSW), *b.* 1950: *m.* 1972, Elaine, da. of Kenneth Wall, of Darling St., Cowra, and has issue living, Rowena Jane *b.* 1974,—Shirley Anne *b.* 1934: *m.* 1954, David Gill, of Langford, Walcha, NSW, and has issue living, Michael David *b.* 1957, Philippa Shirley *b.* 1955, Katrina Anne *b.* 1958. *Residence*, Bareena, Uralla, NSW.——Frederick James (Lugwardine, Barraba 2347, NSW) *b.* 1009; formerly Flying Officer, RAAF: *m.* 1943, Barbara, da. of Howard Carter, of Barraba, NSW, and has issue living, Edward Hugh Wynfold, *b.* 1944: *m.* 1969, Jennifer Mary, da. of Thomas James Stirton, of Armoobilla, Cheepie, Qld, and has issue living, Edward James Wynford *b.* 1971.—— Richard Marsh, *b.* 1910: *m.* 1941, Mary, da. of F. Ewing, of Walcha, NSW. *Residence*, Dunvegan, Uralla NSW.

Sister living—Phyllis Lucy, *b.* 1901 : *m.* 1923, George Stuart Robertson Park, and has issue living, Walter Stuart (of Browning Vale, Manilla, N.S. Wales), *b.* 1925 : *m.* 1950, June Coates, and has issue living, Elizabeth *b.* 1951: *m.* 1973, Robert John Nicoll, of Sydney, Wendy *b.* 1954, Deborah *b.* 1957,—Ian Croft (Andamooka, Spring Ridge, NSW), *b.* 1936: *m.* 1960, Kay, only da. of A. Shaw, of Lammermoor, Wee Woa, NSW, and has issue living, Kenneth Ian *b.* 1963, Geoffrey Steven *b.* 1964, Nicholas David *b.* 1970, Janine Maree *b.* 1968,—Phyllis Joan, *b.* 1924: *m.* 1949, Roger L'Estrange Rankine, of 100, Upper St., Tamworth, NSW, and has issue living, Timothy Roger *b.* 1951: *m.* 1975, Leticia Forte, of Woolongong, Andrew Stuart *b.* 1954, Steven John *b.* 1960,—Mary Isabel, *b.* 1928: *m.* 1949, John Mervyn Wilshire, of 41, Hyman St., Lamworth 2340, NSW, and has issue living, Malcolm John *b.* 1958, Marilyn Mary *b.* 1950: *m.* 1973, Timothy John O'Keefe, of Lamworth, NSW, (and has issue living, George Alexander *b.* 1974), Christine Linda *b.* 1953: *m.* 1972, Lowell Reardon, of Singleton, NSW, (and has issue living, Melissa Louise *b.* 1973). *Residence*, 250, Johnson St., Lamworth 2340, NSW.

Daughter living of 10th Baronet—Einor (Ynswyth House, Blewett Av., Seaview, Isle of Wight), *b.* 1904: *m.* 1928, Henry Charlton Parr, formerly Lt. Bedfordshire and Herts. Regt. from whom she obtained a divorce 1934 [E. Roden.], and has issue living, June Valerie, *b.* 1931: *m.* 1950, Lt.-Col. Samuel Brian Smith, MC, of Luggershill, Broadway, Worcs., and has issue living, Samuel James *b.* 1953, Richard Peter *b.* 1958, Miranda Jane *b.* 1951, Lucinda Patsy *b.* 1957.

Collateral Branches living.

Issue of the late Archer John Croft, yst. son of 12th baronet, *b.* 1913, *d.* 1971: *m.* 1939, Marcie Isell Heathfield (9, St. Andrews Av., Armidale 2350, NSW), da. of the late Clifton Hazlewood Eliott [see Eliott, Bt., colls.].
Antony John (7, Tarella Drive, Mt. Waverley, Vic. 3149, Aust.), *b.* 1940: *m.* 1966, Kathleen Francis, yr. da. of R. F. Kelsall, of Port Macquarie, NSW, and has issue living, Michael John, *b.* 1967,— Tania Jane, *b.* 1968.——David Archer (12, Proctor St., Armidale 2350, NSW), *b.* 1946: *m.* 1971, Violeta, only child of V. Deikus, of 6, Albert St., Cabramatta, NSW, and has issue living, Justin Damian, *b.* 1973.——Stephen Hugh, *b.* 1953.

Grandson of the late Brig.-Gen. William Denman Croft, CB, CMG, DSO(infra):—
Issue of the late Capt. William Owen Glendower Croft, Indian Army, *b.* 1913, *d.* 1946 : *m.* 1944, Margaret, da. of the late Major — Tobin, Indian Army :—
Richard Owen Glendower (The Oast House, Bakers Mead, Pluckley, nr Ashford, Kent, TN27 0RE), *b.* 1944; ed. at Kent Univ.; Lt. 1st Bn. Cameronians (Scottish Rifles): *m.* 1967, Elizabeth Jillian Allen, and has issue living, James Owen, *b.* 1972,—Emma Kate *b.* 1974.

Issue of the late Brig.-Gen. William Denman Croft, CB, CMG, DSO, 4th son of 9th baronet, *b.* 1879, *d.* 1968: *m.* 1912, Esmé (The Anchorage, Mawnan, Falmouth), da. of Sir Arthur Edwin Sutton, 7th Bt.:—
Rev. John Armentieres, *MC* (The Anchorage, Mawnan, Falmouth; Army and Navy Club), *b.* 1915; ed. at Stowe; Maj. (ret.) RA; late Indian Army; V. of Gwinear 1960-70; N-W Frontier 1935 (despatches), Burma 1944 (wounded, MC): *m.* 1948, Sheila Kathleen, da. of the late Maj. J. A. Ford, of Pengreep, Cornwall, and has issue living, Edmund Hugh Glendower, *b.* 1954,—Patricia Lucy, *b.* 1951.——Violet Lorna, *b.* 1917: *m.* 1942, Lt.-Cdr. Thomas Charteris Black, RNVR, and has issue living, Peter Michael, *b.* 1952,—Jane Margaret, *b.* 1943,—Susan Mary, *b.* 1945.—— Angela Desiree (Stonecrop, Avebury, Wilts.), *b.* 1923: *m.* 1955, Roland Grievson, who *d.* 1974.

Issue of the late Jasper Brodie Croft, 6th son of 9th baronet ; *b.* 1884 ; *d.* 1950 : *m.* 1907, Catherine, who *d.* 1975, da. of F. G. Taylor, of Terrible Vale, NSW:—
Jasper Thomas (c/o Commercial Banking Co. of Sydney, 343, George St., Sydney. NSW) *b.* 1924; Fl. Lt. RAAF, and a JP: *m.* 1948, Editha Deirdre, da. of the late George Westgarth, of Scone, NSW, and has issue living, Jasper David, *b.* 1949,—Bettina Kay, *b.* 1951: *m.* 1973, Peter Leslie, of Beverley, Nevertire, NSW,—Kerrie Leigh (da.), *b.* 1954.——Kitty MacLeod (Unit 21, 48, Harris St., Harris Park, 2150, NSW), *b.* 1908: *m.* 1938, Peter Assheton, who *d.* 1970, and has issue living, Pedir Raif Orme, *b.* 1941: *m.* 1972, Nancy Shaw, and has issue living, Olwen Annaliese *b.* 1975,—Rowena Tydwr, *b.* 1939: *m.* 1966, Zbyszek Lisak, and has issue living, Tamara *b.* 1967, Nadya *b.* 1968.——Ana Lucy McLeod, *b.* 1909; QAIMNS (Reserve): *m.* 1942, Claude

Wallace Grievson, Staff Cdr. Orient Line, who *d.* 1969, and has issue living, Jasper Wallace, *b.* 1944: *m.* 19—, , and has issue living, Jasper Claude *b.* 1975,—Barbara Jasmine, *b.* 1949: *m.* 19—, Graeme Carson.——Isabel McLeod, *b.* 1911: *m.* 1945, Bassett Care, of 39, Brisbane Av., Camp Hill, Brisbane 2, Qld., and has issue living, Frederick, *b.* 1946: *m.* 1969, Jennifer Dianne, da. of the late Arthur Silas Faulk, and has issue living, Amanda *b.* 1970, Sally *b.* 1972.—— Marjorie McLeod, *b.* 1912: *m.* 1943, Cecil Gordon Lowe, RAAF, of 32, North Rd., Woodridge, Qld., and has issue living, Benjamin John, *b.* 1944: *m.* 1962 (m. diss. 1975) Gloria Daphne, da. of W. Williams, of W. Aust., and has issue living, Dallas *b.* 1969,—William James, *b.* 1951: *m.* 1974, Caroline, da. of Kenneth Watson, and has issue living, Daniel William *b.* 1975,—Catherine Jane, *b.* 1947: *m.* 1969, Brian Finnigan, of 65, Ashton St., Kingston, Qld., and has issue living, Jo-Anne *b.* 1972,—Susanne Barbara, *b.* 1950: *m.* 1971, Kenneth Murray,—Elizabeth, *b.* 1953: *m.* 1975, Peter Ware,—Mary Anne, *b.* 1955.——Enid Barbara McLeod, *b.* 1915: *m.* 1959, Maj George Ronald Hyde, of AIF, of Belmore Terr., Sunshine Beach, Qld.——Nancy Perena McLeod *b.* 1921: *m.* 1950, Eric W. Adams, of Pokataroo, NSW.

Grandchildren of the late Richard Benyon Croft, son of the late Rev. Richard Croft 3rd son of 6th baronet:—

Issue of the late Lieut.-Col. Richard Page Croft, *b.* 1872, *d.* 1961 : *m.* 1908, Eva Pansy Millicent Philippa Stanhope, who *d.* 1940, da. of William Sharp Waithman, J.P., D.L. [E. Harrington] :—

Richard Arthur FitzRoy Page, *b.* 1910; late Major RASC; 1939-45 War (despatches): *m.* 1st, 1939 (marriage dissolved 1956), Felice Amy (Peggy) McClymont; 2ndly, 1956, Daphne Frye, and has issue living, (by 1st m.) Richard Nicholas Page (El Patio, El Pinilho, 70, Torremolinos, Spain), *b.* 1941: *m.* 1st, 1967, Teresa Mary, who *d.* 1971, da. of the late Donald Jewell, of Burry Port, Carmarthenshire, and formerly wife of Sverré Wilberg, of Frederikstadt, Norway; 2ndly, 1973, Bruna Campesato,—Hugo Douglas Page, *b.* 1944: *m.* 1969, Dawn Pryde, and has issue living, Richard Page *b.* 1973, Arabella *b.* 1971,—Miriam Anne Page, *b.* 1948: *m.* 1974, Piers Rogers. *Residence*, The Round House, Ware, Herts.

Issue of the late Rt. Hon. Sir Henry Page Croft, C.M.G., T.D., 1st Bt., who was *cr.* Baron Croft 1940 [*see* that title].

Croft Castle, from which the family name is derived, was sold about 1765, having descended from father to son for more than 700 years (but was bought back by the Trustees for the 11th Bt. in **1924, and is now the property of the National Trust**). and members of the family represented Herefordshire in sixteen Parliaments between 1297 and 1874. Sir John Croft of Croft Castle *m.* Janet, da. of Owen Glendower. The father of the first baronet was Bishop of Hereford. The 10th baronet, Sir Herbert Archer Croft, Capt. Herefordshire Regt. *d.* (killed in action during European War) 1915. The 11th baronet, Sir James Herbert Croft, Capt. No. 1 Commando Special Ser. Batn., *d.* (killed on active ser. during European War) 1941.

CROFT, Creation (U.K.) 1818, Cowling Hall, Yorkshire.

To be rather than to seem.

Sir JOHN WILLIAM GRAHAM CROFT, 4th *Baronet*, son of the late William Graham Croft, 4th son of 2nd baronet ; *b.* May 30th, 1910 ; *s.* his uncle, *Sir* FREDERICK LEIGH, 1930 ; ed. at Stowe ; Lieut. R.A.(retired).

Arms—Quarterly per fesse indented or and gules, in the first quarter a lion passant-guardant of the second. **Crest**—A lion passant guardant per pale, indented gules and erminois, the dexter fore paw resting on a shield argent charged with a star of the order of the Tower and Sword. **Supporters**—Dexter, a lion guardant or, gorged with a wreath of laurel vert, therefrom pendent an escutcheon gules, charged with a tower or; sinister, a bull sable, horned crined hoofed and gorged with a wreath of laurel or, therefrom pendent an escutcheon argent, charged with the star of the order of the Tower and Sword.

Residence—57, Chester Row, S.W.1.

Mother living—Marjorie, da. of the late Rev. Thomas Sarsfield Hall, R. of Dodington and Wychling, Sittingbourne: *m.* 1909, William Graham Croft, who *d.* 1928. *Residence*, 57, Chester Row, S.W.1.

Collateral Branches living.

Issue of the late Francis Edgar Croft, 3rd son of 2nd baronet, *b.* 1861, *d.* 1910 : *m.* 1891, Miss Zoë Bromley, who *d.* 1948 :—

Cynthia: *m.* 1916, Wilfrid Holland, who *d.* 1945, and has issue living, Frances, *b.* 1918: *m.* 1940, John Willis Price,—Nancy Cynthia, *b.* 1920: *m.* 1951, Patrick Brian Bradley. *Residence*,

Issue of the late Tom Radcliffe Croft, 6th son of 2nd baronet, *b.* 1878, *d.* 1964: *m.* 1909, Louise, who *d.* 1964, da. of the late Francis Sales, of Charlton, Kent:—

John Archibald Radcliffe (Cornerways, Stodmarsh, Canterbury), *b.* 1910; Maj. W. Yorkshire Regt. (ret.): *m.* 1953, Lucy Elizabeth, da. of the late Maj. William Dallas Loney Jupp, OBE, of Stafford, and has issue living, Thomas Stephen Hutton, *b.* 1959,——Cyril Bernard (Rayham Farm, Whitstable, Kent), *b.* 1918; late Lieut. Buffs: *m.* 1957, Sheila Maisie, da. of Henry Clark Cox, of Whitstable, and has issue living, Diana Louise, *b.* 1959,—Wendy Jane, *b.* 1961.—— Rosalind Editha Louise, *b.* 1914.

This family is of common origin with the Crofts of Herefordshire, and the Crofts of Stillington Hall, Yorkshire. The 1st baronet, a Portuguese Commissioner, Knight of the Portuguese Order of the Tower and Sword, and Baron da Serra da Estrella in Portugal, did considerable service in the Peninsular war by risking his life to obtain information for the Duke of Wellington, and in distributing the British Parliamentary grant of £100,000 for relieving the Portuguese, and was Hon. Chargé d'Affaires at Lisbon 1815.

CROFTON, Creation (U.K.) 1801, of Mohill, Leitrim.

God gives the increase.

Sir (HUGH) PATRICK SIMON CROFTON, 7th *Baronet*, son of the late Major Morgan George Crofton, el. son of 6th baronet; *b.* Dec. 2nd, 1936; *s.* his grandfather, *Lieut.-Col. Sir* MORGAN GEORGE, *D.S.O.*, 1958; ed. at Eton ; late 2nd Lieut. Welsh Guards: *m.* 1967, Mrs. Lene Eddowes, da. of Kai Augustinus, of Copenhagen, and has issue.

Arms—Per pale indented or and azure, a lion passant-guardant counterchanged, a crescent for difference. Crest—Seven ears of wheat, on one stalk proper.

Seat—Mohill Castle, co. Leitrim. *Residence*—Carbrook, Curridge, Newbury, Berks. *Club*—Guards'.

Daughter living—Atalanta Chloe Majken, *b.* 1969.

Uncles living (sons of 6th baronet)—HUGH DENIS, *b.* April 10th, 1937; ed. at Eton, Worcester Coll., Oxford (BA), and Bristol Univ. (BA).——Edward Morgan, *b.* 1945; ed. at Eton and RMA; Capt. Coldm. Gds.

Mother living—Rosalie, da. of the late John Lever Tillotson, of Bidston Court, Cheshire: *m.* 1st, 1934, Major Morgan George Crofton (ante), who *d.* 1947, and from whom she had obtained a divorce 1941; 2ndly, 1947, Lt.-Col. George St. Vigor J. Vigor, O.B.E., late Welsh Guards. *Residence*, Carbrook, Curridge, Newbury, Berks.

Widow living of 6th Baronet—MARGARET AMELIA (*Lady Crofton*), da. of the late Judge Morris Dallett, of Philadelphia, U.S.A.: *m.* 1933, as his third wife, Lieut.-Col. Sir Morgan George Crofton, D.S.O., 6th baronet, who *d.* 1958. *Residence*, Woodbridge, Brockenhurst, Hants.

Collateral Branches living.

Granddaughter of the late Rev. Henry William Crofton, 3rd son of 2nd baronet:—
Issue of the late Major James Cazalet Crofton, *b.* 1847, *d.* 1894 : *m.* 1868, Henrietta Anne, who *d.* 1870, da. of John Edwards, J.P., of Knockrobin, Wicklow; 2ndly, 1876, Charlotte, who *d.* 1894, widow of Capt. — Carpendale, Indian Marines :—
(By 2nd marriage) Norah Gertrude Charlotte : *m.* 1906, Bertram Farmer, and has issue living, Crofton James Langford, *b.* 1908 ; is a farmer : *m.* 1945, Mary Katharine, da. of the Rev. Richard Wells, and has issue living, Michael Richard Crofton *b.* 1946, Katharine Sarah *b.* 1949,—Alan Wentworth, *b.* 1910,—Betty Patricia Marianne (twin), *b.* 1908. *Residence*, 2, Wellington Square, Cheltenham.

Granddaughters of the late Lieut.-Gen. James Crofton (infra) :—
Issue of the late Major Robert Benjamin Crofton, *b.* 1873, *d.* 1904: *m.* 1904, Helena Chute, who *d.* 1974, el. da. of the late Richard Grubb Ridgway, of River View House, Waterford):—
Kathleen *b.* 1908. *Residence*, 20, King George Road, Minehead, Somerset.——Helen Norah, *b.* 1912.

Issue of the late Charles D'Arcy Crofton, *b.* 1879, *d.* 1955 : *m.* 1910, Mary Helen Elizabeth, who *d.* 1960, da. of H. G. Gearing, formerly of Tea Hill, Coonoor, Nilgris, S. India :—
Patience D'Arcy, *b.* 1911 : *m.* 1936, Lieut.-Col. Joseph Richard Waters, O.B.E., R.A., and has issue living, Prudence D'Arcy, *b.* 1937: *m.* 1969, Harry Waugh, of 14, Camden Sq., NW1, and has issue living, Jamie Horsburgh *b.* 1974, Harriet D'Arcy (twin) *b.* 1974,—Ann Gilian, *b.* 1938: *m.* 1961, Peter Llewellyn Sheldon (RFD Casco, Maine, USA), and has issue living, Valentine D'Arcy *b.* 1969, Clare Helen *b.* 1966. *Residence*, Down Cottage, Frant, Tunbridge Wells.——Beatrice Barratt, *b.* 1915: *m.* 1938, Brig. Anthony John le Grand Jacob, MBE, late RE, of The Rose Cottage, St. James's Green, Southwold, Suffolk, and has issue living, John, *b.* 1940,—Rupert, *o.* 1948,—Rosemary, *b.* 1944,—Alice, *b.* 1950.

Issue of the late John Hutchinson Crofton, M.B., M.R.C.S., *b.* 1883, *d.* 1953 : *m.* 1914, Alice, who *d.* 1943, da. of the late Arthur Charles Humphreys-Owen, M.P., of Glansevern, Mongomeryshire :—
Anne Dorothy, *b.* 1915. *Address*, c/o Westminster Bank Ltd., Maidenhead, Berks.——Ruth Margaret, *b.* 1919 : *m.* 1949, Norman Renshaw Sharpe. *Residence*, 24, Gunterstone Road, W.14

Granddaughter of the late Capt. Morgan Crofton, RN, el. son of the late Morgan Crofton, 3rd son of 1st baronet :—
Issue (by 2nd marriage) of the late Lieut.-Gen. James Crofton, *b.* 1826, *d.* 1908 : *m.* 1st, 1858, Mary Susan, who *d.* 1860, da. of Sir Robert Montgomery, G.C.S.I. : 2ndly, 1867, Clara Elizabeth, who *d.* 1890, da. of the late Capt. Edward Lake, R.N. [Lake, Bt.] :—
Lillian, *b.* 1880: *m.* 1st, 1903, Charles Stanhope Foster Crofton, who *d.* 1909; 2ndly, 1911, Maj William Lister Newcombe, formerly Worcestershire Regt., who *d.* 1949, and has issue living (by 2nd m.) William Lister, *b.* 1913; Maj. (ret.) Worcestershire Regt.: *m.* 1944, Heather Margaret, da. of the late Lt.-Col. G. Sanderson, and has issue living, Guy Lister *b.* 1948, Jennifer Jean Olivia *b.* 1945, Sarah Margaret *b.* 1956,—Lillian Clare Isabel, *b.* 1912: *m.* 1933, Morris Milner Woodford, and has issue living, Mary Josephine *b.* 1939: *m.* 1965, John Penrose Rogers, (Bedales School, Steep, Petersfield, Hants) (and has issue living, Lucinda Clare *b.* 1966, Hannah Mary Winifred *b.* 1969)—Jeanette, *b.* 1917. *Residence*, Summer Farm, Crossways, Moreton, nr. Dorchester, Dorset.

Grandchildren of the late Rev. Henry Woodward Crofton, el. son of Capt. Morgan Crofton, RN (ante):—
Issue of the late Rev. Henry Francis Crofton, *b.* 1859, *d.* 1943: *m.* 1886, Catherine Louise, da. of the late H. N. Chipman, MD:—
Janette Melesina, *b.* 1887.——Isabel Ona, *b.* 1892.——Francesca Cecilia, *b.* 1893. *Residence*,
Issue of the late Maj. Geoffrey Hugh Schenley Crofton, late Suffolk Regt., *b.* 1881, *d.* 1955: *m.* 1908, Monica, da. of the late A. W. Hall, of Barton Abbey, Steeple Aston:—
Henry Horatio, *b.* 1910; Capt. W. Yorks. Regt.——Monica Melesina Nem, *b.* 1915.——Angela Catherine, *b.* 1917. *Residence*,
Issue of the late Maj. Charles Woodward Crofton, N. Staffs. Regt., *b.* 1866, *d.* (killed in action) 1915: *m.* 1901, Catherine Mary, who *d.* 1944, da. of the late C. F. W. Stowell:—
Hugh Charles Henry *b.* 1915; ed. at Wellington Coll.; Maj. (ret.) RA: *m.* 1949, Margery, da. of the late T. Summerson, of Sunderland, and has issue living, John Hugh, *b.* 1954.——Kathleen Louisa *b.* 190-.

Grandchildren of the late Francis Blake Crofton, 5th son of the Rev. William
Crofton, 2nd son of Morgan Crofton (ante):—
Issue of the late Algernon Francis Blake, *b.* 1873, *d.* 19— : *m.* 1893, Edith, da. of James
Hall, of Peterborough, Ontario :—
Katharine CEBRIAN; resumed her former surname of Cebrian 19—: *m.* 1st, 1919, Louis de Laveaga
Cebrian, who *d.* 1937; 2ndly, 1938, Douglas Lindsay Pringle, who *d.* 1960, and has issue living
(by 1st marriage) Luis Enrique, *b.* 1933,—José Maria de Laveaga, *b.* 1934: *m.* 1958, Celia King
McNeare, and has issue living, José Algernon Crofton *b.* 1959, Luis Miguel Crofton *b.* 1962.

Issue of the late Arthur Molesworth Crofton, *b.* 1874, *d.* 1945: *m.* 1897, Gwendolin Forrest,
who *d.* 1950, of Quebec, Canada:—
Brian Forrest, *b.* 1905.——Henry Desmond, *b.* 1907: *m.* 1st, 1937, Frances Veron Borgeest, who *d.*
1942; 2ndly, 1951, Marie Jeanne, da. of Joseph Muloin, and widow of Sqn.-Ldr. Oliver J.
Gaboury, RCAF.——Charles Patrick (PO Box 343, Sudbury, Ont., Canada), *b.* 1913: *m.* 1943,
Catherine Kennedy, and has issue living, David Ian, *b.* 1944,—Arthur Blake, *b.* 1946,—Alan,
b. 1953,—Terence (twin), *b.* 1953,—Catherine Patricia, *b.* 1948,—Joan, *b.* 1949.——Francis
Terence, *b.* 1915; is an Organist.

Sir Morgan Crofton, 1st Bt. of Mohill, co. Leitrim, was 5th in descent from Henry Crofton of
Mohill, yst. son of Henry Crofton of Ballymurry (*d.* 1643), el. son of Edward Crofton of Ballymurry
(*d.* 1627). The father of the 4th baronet (Col. Hugh Denis Crofton (who commanded 20th Regt.
at Alma and was wounded at Inkerman) was accidentally shot by a soldier of the 32nd Foot, at
Preston, September 15th, 1861, while commanding the Depôt Battalion; and it is a singular circumstance that the same bullet killed the Adjutant of the Battalion (Capt. J. Hanham), who was
also heir to a baronetcy. Lieut.-Col. Sir Morgan George Crofton, D.S.O., Life Guards, 6th baronet,
served in S. Africa 1899-1902 (severely wounded at relief of Ladysmith), 1914-18 War (D.S.O.),
and in 1939-45 War.

CROFTON, Creation (U.K.) 1838, of Longford House, Sligo.

God gives the increase.

Sir MALBY STURGES CROFTON, 5th
Baronet (but his name does not, at time of going
to press, appear on the Official Roll of Baronets);
b. Jan. 11th, 1923; *s.* his father, *Major
Sir* (MALBY RICHARD) HENRY, *D.S.O.*, 1962; ed.
at Eton; European War 1941-5 as Capt. Life
Guards in Middle East and Italy: *m.* 1961
(m. diss. 1966), Elizabeth Madeline Nina, el. da.
of the late Maj. Rhys Clavel Mansel [see Mansel,
Bt., colls.].

Arms—Per pale indented or and azure, a lion passant-
guardant counterchanged. Crest—Seven ears of wheat on
one stalk proper.

Seat—Longford House, co. Sligo. *Residence*—75,
Victoria Rd., W8.

Sister living—Beatrix Katharine, *b.* 1921; formerly Junior
Com. ATS. *Residence*, 2, Caithness Rd., W14.

Aunt living—(daughter of 3rd baronet)—Dorothy. *Address*,
Arva, Upper Glenageary Rd., Glenageary, co. Dublin.

Collateral Branches living.

Grandchildren of the late Col. Malby Edward Crofton, 3rd son of 2nd baronet:—
Issue of the late Col. Malby Crofton, D.S.O., *b.* 1881; *d.* 1948: *m.* 1911, Sarah Dorothy
Beatrice, *J.P.* (now of 33, Trevor Place, S.W.7), da. of the late Col. William Frederick
Noel Noel, formerly R.E. [*see* E. Gainsborough, colls.]:—
(Ursula) Doryne (Elizabeth), *b.* 1927; European War 1939-45 in Middle East (Africa Star); Section
Officer W.A.A.F.: *m.* 1951, William Robert Castle Cleary, A.R.I.B.A., son of Sir William Castle
Cleary, K.B.E., C.B. *Residence*, 33, Trevor Place, Knightsbridge, S.W.7.

Issue of the late Brig. Roger Crofton, CIE, MC, *b.* 1888, *d.* 1972: *m.* 1st, 1914, Stella
Clifton, who *d.* 1916, da. of the late Judge Thomas Gilbert Carver, KC; 2ndly, 1921,
Dorothy Frances, who *d.* 1953, da. of Col. Henry Melville Hatchell, DSO, formerly R.
Irish Regt.; 3rdly, 1954, Agnes Marjorie (30, Whitehall Court, Rondebosch, Cape Town,
S. Africa), da. of Samuel Osborn, and widow of (1) Capt. Cyril Oswald Denman-Jubb,
Duke of Wellington's Regt., and (2) John Johnston May:—
(By 2nd m.) (HENRY EDWARD) MELVILLE (Haldon, St. Giles Hill, Winchester), *b.* Aug. 16th,
1931; ed. at Hilton Coll., Natal, and Trin. Coll., Camb. (BA Eng); formerly Prin. Admin. Officer,
HM Overseas Civil Ser.: *m.* 1955, Mary Brigid, twin da. of Gerald K. Riddle, of Buttercombe,
Newton Abbot, and has issue living, Julian Malby, *b.* 1958,—Nigel Melville, *b.* 1964,—Nicola
Dorothy, *b.* 1961.

In 1661 a baronetcy was conferred upon Sir Edward Crofton of the Mote, co. Roscommon
(*d.* 1675), grandson of Edward Crofton of Ballymurry, co. Roscommon (*d.* 1627); it became extinct
on the death of the 5th baronet in 1780, and a new baronetcy was granted in 1838 to Sir James
Crofton of Longford House, co. Sligo, descended from Thomas Crofton, uncle of 1st Bt., and subsequent to 1780 the senior male line of Croftons in Ireland.

CROSBIE, Creation (N.S.) 1630, of Maryborough, Queen's County. [Extinct 1936.]
Sir WILLIAM EDWARD DOUGLAS CROSBIE, 8th and last *Baronet*.

Daughter living of 8th Baronet—By 1st marriage—Marjorie Kathleen Crosbie, *b.* 1895 : *m.*
1920, Godfrey Sutcliffe Marsh, formerly Indian P.W.D., and has issue living, Elizabeth Ann
Crosbie, *b.* 1934: *m.* 1960, Seafield Christopher Cousins, of 37, Scarsdale Villas, W8, and has
issue living, Sally Georgina *b.* 1962, Juliet Emma *b.* 1964. *Residence*, 37, Scarsdale Villas, W8.

CROSS, Creation (U.K.) 1912, of Marchbankwood, Kilpatrick-Juxta, co. Dumfries. and City of Glasgow. [Extinct 1962.]

Sir ALEXANDER CROSS, 3rd and last *Baronet.*

Widow living of 2nd Baronet—SHEILA (*Lady Cross*), da. of the late Gilbert Moffit, of Gwalia, W. Australia: *m.* 1939, Sir William Coats Cross, 2nd baronet, who *d.* 1947. *Residence,* 16A, Richardson Av., Claremont, Perth, W. Australia.

CROSS, Creation (U.K.) 1941, of Bolton-le-Moors, co. Lancaster. [Extinct 1968.]

Rt. Hon. Sir RONALD HIBBERT CROSS, KCMG, KCVO, 1st and last *Baronet.*

Daughters living of 1st Baronet—Angela Louise Vereker (*Hon. Mrs. Neil D. Campbell*), *b.* 1925: *m.* 1951 the Hon. Neil Donald Campbell, DSC, son of 2nd Baron Colgrain. *Residence,* Yorks Hill Farm, Ide Hill, Sevenoaks, Kent.——Diana Marion Hibbert, *b.* 1927: *m.* 1955, James Richard Emery Taylor, of Shatwell Farm, Yarlington, Wincanton, Som.——Susanna Carolyn, *b.* 1938: *m.* 1966, Francis Trajan Sacheverell Sitwell, of 20, Ladbroke Grove, W11, [*see* Sitwell, Bt.].—— Karina Mary, *b.* 1942: *m.* 1965, Maj. Sean Michael Barton, 22nd Cheshire Regt., of Hill Farm House, Babcary, Somerton, Som.

CROSSLEY, Creation (U.K.) 1909, of Glenfield, Dunham Massey, co. Chester.

I believe and love.

Sir CHRISTOPHER JOHN CROSSLEY, *R.N.,* 3rd *Baronet,* son of the late Lieut.-Com. Nigel John Crossley, R.N., son of the late Eric Crossley, O.B.E., 2nd son of 1st baronet ; *b.* Sept. 25th, 1931 ; *s.* his great-uncle, Sir KENNETH IRWIN, 1957; ed. at Canford; Lt.-Cdr. RN (ret.): *m.* 1959 (m. diss. 1969), Carolyne Louise, da. of the late L. Grey Sykes and has issue.

Arms—Azure, a chevron between in chief two Tau crosses and in base a hind statant. Crest—A hind's head couped or, holding in the mouth a Tau cross azure.

Residence—6B, Laverton Mews, SW5.

Sons living—NICHOLAS JOHN, *b.* Dec. 10th, 1962.—— Julian Charles, *b.* 1964.

Granddaughters living of 2nd Baronet—(Issue of the late Anthony Crommelin Crossley, M.P., only son of 2nd baronet, *b.* 1903, *d.* 1939: *m.* 1927, Clare (12A Selwood Place, SW7; Brankelow Folly, Whitchurch, Salop.), da. of the late Brig. Alan Fortescue Thomson, DSO:—Penelope Georgina (*Viscountess Garnock*) *b.* 1928: *m.* 1st, 1951 (m. diss. 1969), Maj. Henry Ronald Burn Callander, MC; 2ndly, 1969, David Bethune Lindesay-Bethune, Viscount Garnock, el. son of 14th Earl of Lindsay, and has issue living (by 1st m.), Sarah Alexandra Mary, *b.* 1952,—Victoria, *b.* 1954,—Emma Georgina, *b.* 1959.——(Virginia Charlotte) Theresa, *b.* 1936: *m.* 1956, Alain R. E. Camu, and has issue living, Adrien Bonaventure, *b.* 1957,—François Henri, *b.* 1958,—Nicolas Pascal, *b.* 1961,—Virginie Charlotte, *b.* 1959. *Residences,* 55, Drève des Gendarmes, Brussels, 18, Belgium; Château de Ronsevaal, Alost, Belgium.

Daughters living of 2nd Baronet—Fidelia Josephine, *b.* 1905 : *m.* 1949, as his second wife, Geza Schubert.——Ruth Irwin (Domanda, Hayes, Navan, co. Meath), *b.* 1909: *m.* 1st, 1931, as his second wife, Capt. Michael Wardell, late 10th Hussars; 2ndly, 1944, Capt. Konstanty C. Scheunert, MBE, who *d.* 1970, and has issue living (by 1st m.) Timothy William (Williamstown House, Clonsilla, co. Dublin. *Clubs,* Kildare St., White's, Roy. Yacht Sqdn.), *b.* 1932; Sub.Lieut. (ret.) RN: *m.* 1953, Lady Antonia Pamela Mary Crichton, da. of 5th Earl Erne, and has issue living, Michael John William *b.* 1956, Antony Henry Constantine *b.* 1959, David Stewart Timothy *b.* 1963, Sabrina Mary Louise *b.* 1954: *m.* 1974, Michael L. F. Smith, Henrietta Pamela Mary *b.* 1967.——Catherine Pamela Field, *b.* 1913: *m.* 1st, 1944, Wing-Cdr. Donald Geoffrey Simmons, RAF, who *d.* (killed on active ser. Middle East) 1945; 2ndly, 1950, the Rev. Canon Frank Hay Gillingham, who *d.* 1953. *Residence,* 4, Blvd. des Moulins, Monte Carlo, Monaco.

Uncles living—John Richard Irwin, *b.* 1908 ; ed. at Eton ; European War 1939-45 as Lieut.-Com. (E.) R.N.V.R. *Address,* Pull Scar, Box 121, White River, E. Transvaal, S. Africa.——Michael Nicholson, D.S.O., O.B.E., D.F.C., *b.* 1912 ; ed. at Eton ; is Wing-Com. (retired) R.A.F.; European War 1939-45 in France (despatches, D.S.O., D.F.C., O.B.E.) ; D.S.O. 1940, O.B.E. (Mil.) 1946 : *m.* 1st, 1940 (marriage dissolved 1945), Doreen Maud, only da. of George Tibbitt, of 59, Albert Court, S.W.7 ; 2ndly, 1957, Sylvia, only da. of the late Com. P. A. Heyder, R.N., and has issue living, (by 2nd m.) Sloan Nicholas, *b.* 1958,—Claudia Bettine, *b.* 1959,—Alison Michele, *b.* 1964. *Address,* Loughrigg, Box 379, White River, E. Transvaal, SA.

Aunt living—Barbara Katharine, *b.* 1905 : *m.* 1938, Lieut.-Col. Humphrey Graham Lambert, D.S.O., formerly R.H.A., who *d.* 1959. *Residence,* Milbourne House, Malmesbury, Wilts.

Stepmother living—Marjorie (WINTERBOTTOM), da. of the late John Gilley : *m.* 2ndly, 1932, as his second wife, Lieut.-Com. Nigel John Crossley, R.N., who *d.* (of wounds received in action during European War) 1939 ; 3rdly, 1957, as his second wife, Capt. Richard William Ravenhill, CBE, DSC, RN. *Residence,* Little Paddock, The Ridings, Angmering-on-Sea, Sussex.

Widow living of 2nd Baronet—ELIZABETH JOYCE (*Elizabeth, Lady Crossley*), da. of the late E. Shenton, of Boxmoor, Herts : *m.* 1954, as his second wife, Sir Kenneth Irwin Crossley, 2nd baronet, who *d.* 1957. *Residence,* Little Cheverell House, Devizes, Wilts.

The 1st baronet, Sir William John Crossley (son of Major Francis Crossley, of Glenburn, co. Antrim, descended from the Crossleys of Scaitcliffe, Todmorden), a Director of Manchester Ship Canal, and Chm. of Crossley Bros. (Limited), of Manchester, sat as M.P. for Altrincham Div. of Cheshire (L) 1906-10. The 2nd baronet, Sir Kenneth Irwin Crossley, J.P., was High Sheriff of Cheshire 1919.

Culme-Seymour, see Seymour

GORDON-CUMMING, Creation (U.K.) 1804, of Altyre, Forres.

Sir WILLIAM GORDON GORDON-CUMMING, 6th *Baronet; b.* June 19th, 1928; *s.* his father, *Major Sir* ALEXANDER PENROSE, *M.C.*, 1939 ; ed. at Eton ; late Lieut. Roy. Scots Greys : *m.* 1953, (m. diss. 1972), Elisabeth, da. of Maj.-Gen. Sir William Robert Norris Hinde, KBE, CB, DSO, and has issue.

Arms—Quarterly, 1st and 4th azure three garbs or ; 2nd and 3rd argent three bendlets sable, each charged with as many roses of the field ; on an escutcheon of pretence argent, the following achievement—Arms—Quarterly, 1st and 4th grand quarters counterquartered, 1st, azure three boars' heads couped or, armed and langued gules, *Gordon* ; 2nd, three lions' heads erased gules, *Badenoch* ; 3rd, on three crescents between the Royal tressure gules, *Seton* ; 4th, azure, three fraziers argent, *Frazer* ; 2nd and 3rd grand quarters, gules, three stars or, *Sutherland,* all within a bordure of the last. Crest—A cat salient proper armed azure. Mottoes (*for Cumming*)—" Courage " ; (*for Gordon*),—"Sans crainte" (*Without fear*). Supporters—Dexter, a greyhound proper, gorged with a collar gules charged with two buckles or ; sinister, a savage proper wreathed about the head and middle with laurel vert, brandishing a club proper ; the whole within a bordure or, *Cumming.* Crest—A lion rampant or, in the dexter paw a dagger proper, *Cumming.* Supporters—Two horses argent.

Seat—Altyre, nr. Forres, Morayshire.

Son living—ALEXANDER PENROSE, *b.* April 15th, 1954.

Daughters living—Sarah, *b.* 1955.——Charlotte, *b.* 1958.——Henrietta, *b.* 1959.

Sisters living—Cecily Josephine (Strone House, Bridge of Cally, Blairgowrie, Perthshire; 31, Tite St., SW3), *b.* 1925: *m.* 1st, 1957, as his 2nd wife, 2nd Earl of Woolton, who *d.* 1969; 2ndly, 1969, (m. diss. 1974), the 3rd Baron Forres.——Philippa, *b.* 1933: *m.* 1955, David Archibald Innes [*see* V. Downe, colls.]. *Residence,* Hensill House, Hawkhurst, Kent.

Uncle living (son of 4th baronet)—Michael Willoughby, *b.* 1901: formerly a Midshipman R.N.: *m.* 1st, 1923, Rachel Jean (who *d.* 1968, having obtained a divorce 1943), da. of the late Col. John Anstruther Thomson [Anstruther, Bt., colls.]; 2ndly, 1943, Shirley Barbara, da. of the late Torben Laub, of Rush Court, Wallingford, Berks., and has issue living, (by 2nd m.) Priscilla Jane *b.* 1950,—Catherine Rose, *b.* 1953: *m.* 1972, Desmond Fforde, of Ardress House, Annaghmore, Portadown, co. Armagh. *Residence,* 41, Marryat Rd., Wimbledon, SW19.

Widow living of 5th Baronet—ELIZABETH (*Elizabeth, Countess Cawdor*), da. of J. Topham Richardson, JP, of Harps Oak, Merstham: *m.* 1st, 1924, Maj. Sir Alexander Penrose Gordon-Cumming, MC, 5th baronet, who *d.* 1939: 2ndly, 1961, the 5th Earl Cawdor, who *d.* 1970. *Residence,* Constabulary Garden, Nairn.

Collateral Branches living.

Issue of the late Lt.Com. Roualeyn Geoffrey Gordon-Cumming, RN, and son of 4th baronet, *b.* 1895, *d.* 1928: *m.* 1923, Mary Violet Katharine [(81, Arlington House, SW1); she *m.* 2ndly, 1929 (m. annulled on her petition 1939), John S. Newall; 3rdly, 1941, Geoffrey Hugh Wilkinson (from whom she obtaind a divorce 1948)], da. of the late Capt. W. M. Marter:—

Alexander Roualeyn, *CVO* (2, Wallgrave Rd., SW5), *b.* 1924; Group Capt. RAF; *cr.* CVO 1970: *m.* 1st, 1965, Beryl Joyce MacNaughton, who *d.* 1973, da. of the late Naughton Dunn; 2ndly, 1974, Elizabeth Patricia, da. of Travers, Robert Blackley, CMG, CBE, of Gurrane, Fermoy, co. Cork, and has issue living, (by 1st m.) Ann Penrose, *b.* 1968.

Grandson of the late Henry William Grant Gordon-Cumming (infra):—
Issue of the late Cdr. Henry Ronald Gordon-Cumming, OBE, RN, *b.* 1893, *d.* 1971: *m.* 1927, Lorna Isabelle, who *d.* 1974, da. of Ernest W. Morey, of Johannesburg:—
Rev. Henry Ian (Christchurch Vicarage, Virginia Water, Surrey), *b.* 1928: *m.* 1955, Janet Elizabeth Latimer Cleave, and has issue living, Jane Evelyn, *b.* 1957,—Joanna Mary, *b.* 1959,—Lucille Clare, *b.* 1962,—Deborah Diana, *b.* 1965.

Granddaughters of the late Henry Gordon-Cumming, 3rd son of 2nd baronet:—
Issue of the late Henry William Grant Gordon-Cumming, *b.* 1859, *d.* 1939: *m.* 1892, Evely Agnes, who *d.* 1948, da. of the late Hugh Barlow Lindsay, Bom. C. S. [E. Crawford colls.]:—
Lettice Elizabeth, *b.* 1897: *m.* 1st, 1920 (divorce 1939), Harold Claude Thwaits, S. Rhodesia; Civil Ser.; 2ndly, 1941, Philip Anthony Curtis, R. Indian NR and has issue living (by 1st m.),

Humphrey Lennox, *b.* 1924,—Joy Evelyn, *b.* 1921,—Emmeline Rose, *b.* 1929,—Sylvia Lettice, *b.* 1930. *Address.*

Issue of the late Lieut.-Col. Ludovic Seymour Gordon-Cumming, *b.* 1861, *d.* 1924: *m.* 1895, Constance Mary, who *d.* 1906, only da. of the late Count de Morel, of 20, Beaufort Gardens, S.W. :—
Katherine Marjorie, *b.* 1896. *Residence,* 62, Rutland Gate, SW7.

Granddaughters of the late Maj. Francis Hastings Toone Gordon-Cumming, 6th son of 2nd baronet:—
Issue of the late William Ian Gordon-Cumming, *b.* 1864, *d.* 1949 : *m.* 1891, Rose, who *d.* 1934, da. of A. White, of New Zealand :—
Constance Alexa, *b.* 1892 : *m.* 1925, Guy D'Eresby Goyder. *Residence,* Yana Road, Warrandyte, Victoria, Australia.——Mary Adela Rose, *b.* 1895: *m.* 1915, George Berners Kynvett, and has issue living, Henry Berners, *b.* 1915,—Mark Alastair, *b.* 1918: *m.* 1941, Ola B., da. of G. F. Peters, of Dannevirke, NZ.——Ethel Fredereka, *b.* 1899: *m.* 1926, Harold Sedcole Malcolm. *Residence,*

Issue of the late Charles Lennox Gordon-Cumming, *b.* 1865, *d.* 1948 : *m.* 1901, Mary Elizabeth, da. of W. E. Thomas, of Dallas, Texas, USA:—
Constance Alexa : *m.* 1st, 1922, Clarence Ray Herrington, who *d.* 1946 ; 2ndly, 1949, Q. B. Workman, and has issue living, (by 1st marriage) Phyllis Rae, *b.* 1930 : *m.* 1954, John Snead Billups, and has issue living, Patti Jon *b.* 1956, Molli Elizabeth *b.* 1958. *Residence,* 1st and Floyd Streets, Tulia, Texas, U.S.A.——Marjorie Mary : *m.* 1927, Randle James Culwell, and has issue living, Gordon James *b.* 1929 : *m.* 1948, Grace Elaine da. of Dr. Bascom MacIntosh Puckett, and has issue living, Michael James *b.* 1950, Grace Victoria *b.* 1951. *Residence,* 1121, Broadmoor, Amarillo, Texas, U.S.A.——Kathleen Elizabeth, *b.* 1909 : *m.* 1932, Jerome Maurice Baker. *Residence,* 1306, West 6th Street, Plainview, Texas, U.S.A.

The Cumyn or Cumming family settled in Scotland in the reign of David I. Richard Comyn, of Northallerton received grants of lands in Roxburghshire. John Comyn, of Badenoch, chief of this family, married Eleanor, sister of King John Baliol, by which marriage Sir John of Badenoch " Red Cumyn " was a competitor for the kingdom of Scotland. Robert Cumming, 13th of Altyre, Forres, chief of the family, who bore undifferenced arms, married Lucy, da. of Sir Ludovic Gordon of Gordonstoun, and his great-grandson Sir Alexander Cumming, 1st Bt., took the name of Gordon-Cumming on *s.* to the estates of Gordon of Gordonstoun.

CUNARD, Creation (U.K.) 1859, of Bush Hill, Middlesex

Sir GUY ALICK CUNARD, 7th *Baronet; b.* Sept. 2nd, 1911; *s.* his brother, *Sir* HENRY PALMES, 1973; ed. at Eton; Maj. (ret.) 4th/7th R. Dragoon Gds.

Arms—Azure, on a fesse wavy argent between two barrulets also wavy or, three anchors sable. Crest—On a rock proper, a falcon, wings expanded argent, the dexter claw resting on a cinquefoil azure.

Residences—Naburn Hall, Yorks.; The Garden House, Wintringham, Malton, Yorks.

By perseverance.

Aunt living—Margorie Laura, *b.* 1884: *m.* 1911, Robert Harcourt, who *d.* 1962 [*see* B. Vernon, colls.]. *Residences,* Malwood, Lyndhurst, Hants.; 9, Headfort Place, S.W.1.

Collateral Branch living.

Granddaughters of the late William Cunard, 2nd son of 1st baronet:—
Issue of the late Cyril Grant Cunard, *b.* 1867, *d.* 1914: *m.* 1896, Beatrice Rhoda, who *d.* 1945 (having *m.* 2ndly, 1918, Capt. Walter H. Curran, Canadian Mil. Forces, who *d.* 1931), da. of the late George Louis Monck Gibbs [Elton, Bt.]:—
Laura Kathleen, *b.* 1898. *Residence,* Flat 4, 51, Cadogan Place, S.W.1.——Veronica May, *b.* 1902: *m.* 1927 (marriage dissolved 1948), Major Claud Edward Frederick Hanbury-Tracy, R.A. (T.A.) [*see* B. Sudeley, colls.]. *Residence,* Trinity Cottage, Midhurst, Sussex.——Barbara Haliburton, *b.* 1906; is a Serving Sister of Order of St. John of Jerusalem: *m.* 1932, John Arthur Pepys Charrington, and has issue living, *Rev.* Nicholas John (Christ Church Vicarage, Wellington, Telford, Salop.), *b.* 1936: *m.* 1962, Celia Mary, da. of Leslie Harrison Jaques, and has issue living, James Nicholas *b.* 1965, Edward Mark *b.* 1974, Mary Beatrice *b.* 1963, Lucy Eleanor *b.* 1967,—Thomas Cunard, *b.* 1938,—Giles Antony, *b.* 1944,—Veldes Julia, *b.* 1933: *m.* 1956, Timothy Raison, of 2, Mill Hill Rd., SW13, and has issue living, Paul Timothy Mark *b.* 1963, Naomi Celia *b.* 1957, Laura Veldes *b.* 1959, Katharine Barbara Gabriel *b.* 1962,—Mary Clare, *b.* 1939. *Residence,* Brick Cottage, Lower Wood End, Marlow, Bucks.——Penelope Elton, *b.* 1909: *m.* 1st, 1934, Brig. Nigel Dugdale, CBE, 17th/21st Lancers, who *d.* 1955; 2ndly, 1967, George Arthur Loveday, TD, and has issue living, (by 1st m.) Sam William, *b.* 1948,—Antonia Rosetta, *b.* 1939: *m.* 1969, Nicholas Young, of 7, Hamilton Terr., NW8, [*see* Young, Bt., cr. 1813, colls.],—Teresa Beatrice, *b.* 1946. *Residences,* Bushton Manor, Wootton Bassett, Wilts.; 5, Bywater St., SW3.——Virginia Beatrice, *OBE* (13, The Terrace Barnes, SW13), *b.* 1912; is a CStJ; MBE (Civil) 1946, OBE (Civil) 1956: *m.* 1963, Judge John Harcourt Barrington, who *d.* 1973.

The 1st baronet, Sir Samuel, established the Cunard Line of mail steamers between the United States of America and England.

CUNINGHAME, Creation (N.S.) 1672, of Corsehill, Ayrshire.

Sir JOHN CHRISTOPHER FOGGO
MONTGOMERY CUNINGHAME, 12th *Baronet*;
b. July 24th, 1935; *s.* his brother, *Sir*
WILLIAM ANDREW MALCOLM MARTIN
OLIPHANT, 1959; ed. at Fettes Coll., and at
Worcester Coll., Oxford; late Lieut. Rifle
Brig.: *m.* 1964, Laura Violet, da. of Sir
Godfrey Nicholson, 1st Bt. (*cr.* 1958), and
has issue.
    Arms—Argent, a shake-fork sable, a crescent for differ-
ence. *Crest*—A unicorn's head erased, proper.
    Residence—28, Kelso Place, W8. *Club*—St. James'.

Daughters living—Christian Elizabeth, *b.* 1967.——Georgiana Rose, *b.* 1969.——Elizabeth Clara, *b.* 1971.
Half-Sister living—Pamela Richenda Cubitt, *b.* 1910:
m. 1st, 1932, Capt. Thomas Abdy Combe, Grenadier
Guards (Reserve); 2ndly, 1942, Desmond FitzGerald
Underwood, who *d.* 1968, and has issue living, (by 2nd
m. John Weston (50, Norfolk Av., Sanderstead,
Surrey), *b.* 1943; BSc, MB, BS, FRCS: *m.* 1965, Rosemary McCaw, MB, BS, and has issue living, Charles
Edward *b.* 1973,—(by 1st *m.*) Susan Marian Richenda,
b. 1936: *m.* 1st, 1956 (m. diss. 1965), Christie Pember-
ton; 2ndly, 1965, Nicholas Hallam Stuart Kindersley,
of Newcastle, Ballymahon, co. Longford, and has issue
living, (by 1st *m.*) Anthony Thomas Christie *b.* 1957,
Julian Marina Richenda *b.* 1959, (by 2nd *m.*) Gerald
Sebastian Molesworth *b.* 1966, Pamela Selena Jane
b. 1968,—Elizabeth Jane, *b.* 1939: *m.* 1965, William
Halliday Keatley, TD, of The Old Vicarage, Langley,
Saffron Walden, and has issue living, Annabel Catherine
Richenda *b.* 1966, Juliet Alice des Voeux *b.* 1967.
Residence, Ramparts Cottage, Bakers Lane, Colchester,
CO4 5BD.

Widow living of son of 10th Baronet—Barbara, MBE (*Barbara, Lady Montgomery Cuninghame*),
da. of the late Lt.-Col. Hugh Annesley Gray-Cheape, DSO, of Carse Grey, Forfar, co. Angus;
raised to rank of a baronet's widow 1948; MBE (Civil) 1964: *m.* 1934, Lt.-Col. Alexander
William James Henry Montgomery Cuninghame, DSO, Roy. Scots Fusiliers, who *d.* (killed in
action in Normandy) 1944. *Residence*, Bankhead House, Forfar.

Widows living of 10th and 11th Baronets—NANCY MACAULAY, da. of the late W. Stewart Foggo,
of Aberdeen and Coldstream, British Columbia: *m.* 1st, 1925, as his second wife, Col. Sir Thomas
Andrew Alexander Montgomery Cuninghame, D.S.O., 10th baronet, who *d.* 1945; 2ndly, 1946,
Jan Frederik Christian Killander, formerly of Swedish Foreign Office. *Residence*, Es Figuerelet,
Mancor del Valle, Mallorca, Spain.——SARA CAROLYN, da. of the late Brig.-Gen. Lord Esmé
Charles Gordon Lennox, KCVO, CMG, DSO [*see* D. Richmond and Gordon, colls.]: *m.* 1st,
1956, Sir William Andrew Malcolm Oliphant Montgomery Cuninghame, 11th baronet,
who *d.* 1959; 2ndly, 1959, Ewen Alastair John Fergusson, son of Sir Ewen Macgregor Field
Fergusson. *Residence*, D3, Albany, W1

Collateral Branch living.
    Issue of the late Lieut.-Col. Edward William Montgomery Cuninghame, D.S.O.,
R.H.A., 2nd son of 9th baronet, *b.* 1878, *d.* 1935: *m.* 1909, Mary, who *d.* 1947,
da. of the late James Stewart, of Blackhouse, Skelmorlie, Ayrshire:—
Olive Bridget, *b.* 1910: *m.* 1st, 1934, Lt.-Col. Alexander James Houison-Craufurd, MC, Roy. Scots
Fusiliers, who obtained a divorce 1939 [Dalrymple-Hay, Bt., colls.]; 2ndly, 19—, John Sweeney.
Residence,
    This family descends from Andrew Cuninghame, 1st of Corsehill, 2nd son of 4th Earl of Glencairn
(dormant 1796), to whom the baronet is probably next in line.

FAIRLIE-CUNINGHAME, Creation (N.S.) 1630, of Robertland, Ayrshire.

By   *I am*
fortitude.   *prepared.*

Sir WILLIAM ALAN FAIRLIE-CUNING-
HAME, *M.C.*, 15th *Baronet*; *b.* Jan. 31st, 1893; *s.*
his brother, *Sir* HUSSEY BURGH, 1939; Bachelor
of Engineering, Sydney Univ.; formerly Master in
charge of Preparatory Section, St. John's Sch., Vau-
cluse, Sydney, N.S. Wales, and Lieut. Australian
Forces (Reserve); was Research Officer
Commonwealth Scientific and Industrial Re-
search Organization, Metrology Div. 1943-58;
European War 1915-19 (M.C.): *m.* 1929, Irene
Alice, who *d.* 1970, da. of the late Henry
Margrave Terry, and has issue.

Arms—Quarterly, 1st and 4th argent, a shake-fork between a bugle-horn in chief and two castles in base sable,
Cuninghame; 2nd and 3rd, or, a lion rampant and in chief
three stars gules, *Fairlie*. *Crests*—1st, a unicorn's head proper, armed or, *Cuninghame*; 2nd, a
lion's head or, *Fairlie*. *Supporters*—Two knights in complete armour, holding in their exterior hands
batons or.
    Residence—45, Wyvern Avenue, Chatswood, Sydney, N.S.W.

Son living—WILLIAM HENRY, *b.* Oct. 1st, 1930: *m.* 1972, Janet Menzies, da. of the late Roy
Menzies Saddington, and has issue living, William Robert, *b.* July 19th, 1974.
Brother living—John Hastings, *b.* 1899; Bachelor of Architecture, Sydney Univ.; Lt. (ret.)
Austn. Forces: *m.* 1934, Margaret, da. of Charles Woodhill, of NSW, and has issue living, David
Hastings (1, Myall Av., Wahroonga, Sydney, NSW), *b.* 1937: *m.* 1963, Susan Gai,
da. of Henry White, of Coolah, NSW, and has issue living, Charles Hastings *b.* 1966, Annabel
b. 1967,—Peter, *b.* 1939,—Elisabeth, *b.* 1941: *m.* 1962, William Leslie Murray Robson, of 112,
Paddington St., Paddington, NSW 2021, and has issue living, Andrew Fairlie Murray *b.* 1963,
Hamish Hastings Murray *b.* 1965,—Georgina Jane, *b.* 1947. *Residence*, Glenairn, Goonoo
Goonoo Rd., Tamworth, NSW.

Sisters living—Agnes Henrietta, b. 1896: m. 1920, Herbert Arnold St. John Kent, late 2nd Lt. Aust. Artillery, who d. 1968, and has issue living, William Arnold (Taranaway, Isisford Queensland), b. 1927: m. 1956, Margaret Naomi Cameron Waugh, and has issue living, William St. John b. 1957, Lachlan Cameron b. 1962, Robin Margaret Cameron b. 1960,—Winifred Fairlie, b. 1923: m. 1953, Dietrich Max Schmelzer, of Obergurgl, Jimbour, Qld. 4405, and has issue living, Roland Dietrich Arnold b. 1957, Andreas Jock b. 1968, Barbara Sabine b. 1954, Elisabeth Fairlie b. 1956, Ingrid Bettina b. 1960,—Elizabeth Audrey, b. 1925,—Virginia, b. 1932: m. 1961, John Patrick McConnel Trier, of Dandarbong, Cedar Vale Rd., Cedargrove, Qld., and has issue living, Alister John Kent b. 1963, Susan Audrey b. 1966,—Hastings Loraine, b. 1935: m. 1956, John Danvers Nott, of Newhaven, Rannes, Qld., and has issue living, Christopher John b. 1959, Gregory Kent Nigel b. 1963. Address—Box 48, Beaudesert, Qld.——Amabel Marguerite, b. 1901: m. 1933, Alick Scott Osborne, who d. 1957, and has issue living, William Fairlie Cuninghame, b. 1934: m. 1964, Janet Stewart Stevenson, and has issue living, Alick Stevenson, b. 1968, Stewart William b. 1970, Susan Margaret b. 1967,—Andrew Hastings, b. 1937: m. 1st, 1966, Barbara Constance Heron, who d. 1973; 2ndly, 1974, Judith Nancy Pope, and has issue living, (by 1st m.) Phillip Scott b. 1967, Eleanor Marguerite b. 1969,—Mary Macartney, b. 1933: m. 1959, John William Laurie, of 40, Kenthurst Rd., St. Ives, NSW, and has issue living, William Alick Osborne b. 1963, Margaret Kathleen b. 1961, Sarah Elisabeth (twin) b. 1963, Georgina Mary b. 1969. Residence, 11, Ingalara Av., Wahroonga, NSW.

Daughters living of 14th Baronet—Margaret Alice: m. 1946, Stanley C. Wood, and has issue living, Harold Anthony, b. 1948,—Norma Margaret, b. 1947,—Janice Alice, b. 1952.——Ann: m. 1955, Arlie William Vout, of 26, Cranbrook Av., Cremorne, Sydney, NSW.——Patricia: m. 19—, Peter Goddard Sheldon, of 31, Stanton Rd., Mosman, Sydney, NSW, and has issue living, Robert Stewart, b. 19—,—Antony Stewart, b. 19—,—Jane Stewart, b. 19—.

Widow living of 14th Baronet—ALICE MONA (Dowager Lady Fairlie-Cuninghame), da. of the late Dr. Robert Stewart, of Adelaide, S. Australia : m. 1917, Sir Hussey Burgh Fairlie-Cuninghame, 14th baronet who d. 1939. Residence, 105, Darling Point Road, Darling Point, N.S. Wales.

Collateral Branches living.

Issue of the late Fairlie Percy Cuningham, brother of 13th baronet, b. 18—, d. 1936: m. 1898, Gertrude Constance, da. of the late Richard Randolph Machattie, of N.S. Wales:—
Herbert Alexander, b. 18—.——Kathleen May. Residence,

Granddaughters of the late Charles Rawdon Cuningham (infra) :—
Issue of the late Eric de Burgh Cuningham, b. 1900, d. 1946: m. 1934, Betty Maurice (Closeburn, 197, Walker St., N. Sydney, NSW 2060) (she m. 2ndly, 1952, Henry William Hardess Waller, who d. 1961; 3rdly, 1969, Michael Alexander Addison Kirkpatrick) da. of the late Mrs. M. Barton, of Leura, NSW:—
Anthea, b. 1936: m. 1959, Michael Havelock Marchbank, and has issue living, Jonathan Havelock, b. 1964.—Joanna Cuningham, b. 1960,—Katharine Jane, b. 1962. Residence, 19, North Av., Newcastle-upon-Tyne.——Rhonwen, b. 1943: m. 1971, Jack Aylward Mooney, of Gap Rd., Parkes, NSW, and has issue living, Sean Aylward, b. 1972.

Issue of the late Archibald Loudon Cuningham, Australian Imperial Force, b. 1905, d. (killed in Malayan Campaign) 1942: m. 1936, Nancy Maurice [who m. 2ndly, 1946, Robin Ellison Cuningham (infra)], da. of the late Mrs. M. Barton, of Leura, N.S. Wales:—
Nancy Robin, b. 1939: m. 1964, Peter Edwin Bell (Steamships Trading Co. Ltd., PO Box 496, Port Moresby, Papua/NG), and has issue living, Alastair Christian Loudoun, b. 1967,—Belinda Jane, b. 1965,—Fairlie Louise, b. 1972.

Issue of the late Charles Rawdon Cuningham, brother of 13th baronet, b. 18—, d. 1909 : m. 1894, Harriet Maria, who d. 1953, da. of the late Edward Hardman Macartney (Macartney, Bt., colls.] :—
Alister Gordon (634, Yambla Av., Albury, NSW) b. 1902: m. 1948, Catherine Ida, da. of the late Hugh Rule, of Rockhampton, and has issue living, Robert Gordon, b. 1953.——Robin Ellison (twin), b. 1905: m. 1946, Nancy Maurice, da. of the late Mrs. M. Barton, of Leura, NSW, and widow of Archibald Loudon Cuningham (ante), and has issue living, Georgine Ellison, b. 1951: m. 1975, Robert Ranald Mackay, of Tinagood, Scone, NSW. Residence, 29, Suffolk Av., Collaroy, NSW.

Issue of the late Geraldine Mary, da. of 11th baronet, d. 1940: m. 1905, Capt. Corry Langrishe Connellan, who d. 1923, formerly Buffs (E. Kent Regt.):—
Phyllida Georgina (Skeaghvasteen, Milltown, co. Kilkenny), b. 1906: m. 1937 (m. diss. 1945), Adm. Sir Walter Thomas Couchman, KCB, CVO, DSO, OBE, and has issue living, John Michael David (Johnstown House, Carlow), b. 1943; ed. at Repton: m. 1971, Mary Burrel Mackenzie, of Glenlogan, Sorn, Ayrshire, and has issue living, Sophia Phyllida b. 1973, Alexandra Mary Ruth b. 1975,—Caroline Jansis, b. 1938: m. 1967, Roderick Drevar Murphy, of Sheestown Lodge, Kilkenny,—Fiona Rosamund, b. 1941: m. 1st, 1965 (m. diss. 1970), Capt. Simon Mark Curtis Wrigley, 13th/18th Hussars; 2ndly, 1969, Noel Marshall Bolingbroke-Kent, of 32, Gt. Percy St., WC1, and has issue living (by 2nd m.), Zara b. 1973.

Grandson of the late John Fairlie Cuningham (infra):—
Issue of the late John Henry Cuningham, b. 1898, d. 1969: m. 1924, Kathleen, MB, MS, da. of the late Prof. T. E. Clouston, DD:—
James Fairlie Boyd, b. 1932.

Grandchildren of the late Surg.-Gen. James Macnabb Cuningham, C.S.I., M.D., son of the late Major William Cuningham (infra):—
Issue of the late Arthur Mactier Cuningham, b. 18—, d. 1940: m. 1888, Agnes Murray, of Newby, Williams Road, Toorak, Victoria, Australia :—
Mary Mactier.——Nora: m. 1920, Leslie Albert Austin, Lieut. Australian Forces (Reserve of Officers), and has issue living, Derek Leslie b. 1921. Residence,

Issue of the late John Fairlie Cuningham, b. 1862, d. 1935: m. 1894 Margaret Campbell :—
Donald Macrae, b. 1905: m. 1929, Rose Eleanor, da. of the late Samuel Wilde Wills, and has issue living, John Fairlie, b. 1943,—Florence Ann, b. 1933: m. 1957, David Jones, BVSc, Sydney Univ.——Mary Stewart. Residence,

Grandson of the late Lieut.-Col. Francis George Glencairn Cuninghame (infra):—
Issue of the late William Glencairn Cuninghame, b. 1913; d. 1959: m. 1935, Doris Bishop, of Wiltshire House, Uffcot. Broad Hinton, Swindon, Wilts:—
Anthony Glencairn (of Dunsford House, Uffcott, Broad Hinton, Swindon), b. 1935: m. 1961, Pamela Horton, and has issue living, Andrew Glencairn, b. 1965,—Sally Helen, b. 1962,—Olair Elizabeth, b. 1964.

Granddaughter of the late Francis Goode Cuningham (infra):—
Issue of the late Lieut.-Col. Francis George Glencairn Cuninghame (who adopted the spelling of Cuninghame 19—), b. 1880, d. 1956: m. 1912, Violet Jessie, who d. 1957, da. of Capt. Phipps Hornby, Rifle Brig. (Prince Consort's Own):—
Carol Jean, b. 1915: m. 1950, John Douglas Philip Watney, of Ballarhenny, Orrisdace, Kirk Michael, Isle of Man, and has issue living, Guy Charles Glencairn, b. 1954.

Grandson of the late Major William Cuningham, son of the late Alexander Cuningham, 2nd son of 5th baronet :—

Issue of the late Francis Goode Cuningham, *b.* 1836, *d.* 1911 : *m.* 1st, 1864, Anne Colquhoun, who *d.* 1877, da. of Boyd Alexander Cuninghame ; 2ndly, 1879, Jean Elizabeth, who *d.* 1939, da. of Col. William Forbes Hutton, H.E.I.C.S. :—
(By 2nd marriage) John Loudoun, *b.* 1887. *Residence,*

This family is descended from the Hon. William Cuningham (1st of Craigends), 2nd son of the 1st Earl of Glencairn, by the Hon. William's 2nd marriage in 1499 with Dame Marion Auchinleck. The 1st baronet, Master of the Works to James VI. of Scotland, was created a baronet, with remainder to heirs male whatsoever. At the death of his nephew, Sir David Cuninghame, 4th baronet, the title remained dormant until assumed by William Cuninghame, on being served heir in 1778, to his great-great-grandfather, Sir David Cuninghame, of Robertland, who was grandfather of the 1st baronet. The 5th baronet *m.* Margaret, da. of William Fairlie of Fairlie, co. Ayr, to whose estate he succeeded. The 6th baronet assumed the additional surname of Fairlie, and the 8th received a grant of supporters to himself and his heirs male succeeding him in the baronetcy. The 13th baronet, Sir William Edward, assumed by deed poll 1912, the surname of Fairlie-Cuninghame in lieu of his patronymic Cuningham.

CUNLIFFE, Creation (G.B.) 1759, of Liverpool, Lancashire.

Faithfully.

Sir DAVID ELLIS CUNLIFFE, 9th *Baronet,* *b.* Oct. 29th, 1957; *s.* his father, *Sir* CYRIL HENRY, 1969.

Arms—Sable, three conies courant argent, two and one. **Crest**—A greyhound sejant argent, collared sable.

Residence—17 Gurney Court Road, St. Albans.

Brother living—ANDREW MARK *b.* April 17th, 1959.
Sister living—Susan Nicolette (twin), *b.* 1959.
Widow living of 8th Baronet—EILEEN M. (17, Gurney Court Rd., St. Albans), da. of Frederick William Parkins, and widow of Charles Clifford, of Walton-on-Thames: *m.* 2ndly, 1956, Sir Cyril Henley Cunliffe, 8th Bt., who *d.* 1969; 3rdly, 1970, Frederick Henry Moore.

Collateral Branches living.

Grandchildren of the late David Cunliffe BCS, 3rd son of 4th baronet:—
Issue of the late Col. Ernest William Cunliffe, *b.* 1857, *d.* 1912: *m.* 1st, 1885, Mary Adeline, who *d.* 1899, da. of the late Maj.-Gen. David Limond, CB; 2ndly, 1900, Isabella Fergusson, who *d.* 1940, da. of John Bradford:—
(By 2nd m.) William Lockhart, *b.* 1902; ed. at Wellington Coll.; formerly Chm. of International Standards Brands Incorporated, of New York, USA; 1918 War with Grenadier Guards: *m.* 1923, Maude Ethel, da. of Henry Suthers, of New York, and has issue living, Bruce Fergusson, *b.* 1925; ed. at Dartmouth Coll., USA; Lt.-Col. (ret.) US Marine Corps Korea 1950 (American Bronze Star, and Presidential citation); Vietnam 1965-66 (2nd Bronze Star): *m.* 1947, Joanne, da. of Richard Holbrook, of Keene, NH, USA, and has issue living, Taylor Fergusson *b.* 1950, Orinda *b.* 1949: *m.* 1970, Edward Andrew Jerue, Lt. US Marine Corps, Kailua, Hawaii, USA, Catherine Suthers *b.* 1956,—Stuart Owen (17, Squassick Rd., West Springfield, Mass., USA), *b.* 1931; ed. at Kimball Union Acad., Meriden, New Hampshire; sometime in U.S. Marine Corps: *m.* 1957, Mary, da. of David Berglund, of Albany, New York, USA, and has issue living, Fred Owen *b.* 1958, David William *b.* 1960,—Lorna Margaret, *b.* 1929: *m.* 1949, Amos Webster Gile, of 39 Atlantic Av., Cohasset, Mass., USA, and has issue living, John Lockhart *b.* 1952, Joanne Lorna *b.* 1951: *m.* 1972, Svein Michaelsen, of Bergen, Norway, Pamela Jean *b.* 1954. *Residence,* 49, Border St., North Scitnate, Mass., USA.——Colin Fergusson (Torlundy, 71, Windermere Rd., SW16) *b.* 1909; 1939-45 War, with Grenadier Guards and as Maj., N. Staffordshire Regt.: *m.* 1st, 1934, Muriel Constance Gore, who *d.* 1953; 2ndly, 1954, Sally Marion Mackay.——Audrey Roma, *b.* 1903: *m.* 1932, John Howard Tunley, of Downside Cottage, Polgooth, St. Austell, Cornwall.——Sonia, *b.* 1911: *m.* 1st, 1935, Frank Shaw, from whom she obtained a divorce 1948; 2ndly, 1948, Eric Skead, of 60, Victoria St., Orillia, Ontario, Canada, and has issue living, (by 1st m.) Sandra, *b.* 1936,—(by 2nd m.) Howard, *b.* 1949.

Granddaughter of the late Capt. Ellis Brooke Cunliffe, el. son of Ellis Watkin Cunliffe, 3rd son of 3rd baronet:—
Issue of the late William Noel Cunliffe, *b.* 1877, *d.* 1933: *m.* 1910, Nellie Phyllis (now of 3, West Halkin Street, S.W.1), da. of Sir John Aird, 2nd Bt. :—
Gundred, *b.* 1913: *m.* 1937, Mervyn Cunliffe-Fraser, Kings Farm, Horsham, Sussex, and 14, Shafto Mews, SW1, and has issue living, Valerie, *b.* 1942: *m.* 1972, Mark Trenor Thomasin Foster, of Sandylay House, Great Leighs, Essex.

Grandson of the late Brooke Cunliffe (*b.* 1815), son of the late Brooke Cunliffe (*b.* 1790) (infra):—
Issue of the late Brooke Stewart Cunliffe, *b.* 1848, *d.* 1936: *m.* 1883, Grace Amey, who *d.* 1914, da. of the late Thomas Gordon, of 11, Grosvenor Crescent, Edinburgh:—
Brooke Foster Gordon, *b.* 1889; European War 1914-18 as Capt. Scottish Horse Yeo., attached R.A.F.: *m.* 1921, Catherine Hay, who *d.* 1962, da. of Col. H. R. Peake, and has issue living, Brooke Malcolm, *b.* 1928; Supt., Rhodesian Police (ret.),—Diana Hay, *b.* 1923. *Residence,* 50, Corstorphine Hill Gdns., Edinburgh, 12.

Granddaughter of the late Maj.-Gen. George Gordon Cunliffe, son of the late Brooke Cunliffe (*b.* 1790) (infra) :—
Issue of the late Brig.-Gen. Frederick Hugh Gordon Cunliffe, C.B., C.M.G., late Seaforth Highlanders, *b.* 1861, *d.* 1955 ; *m.* 1895, Ella Sophie, who *d.* 1950, el. da. of David Gaussen, of Marton Hall, Baschurch, Salop :—
Cecile Gertrude, *M.B.E.*, *b.* 1898; is Hon. Sec., Book Depart., Victoria League; M.B.E. (Civil) 1959. *Residence,* 250, Old Brompton Road, S.W.5.

Grandchildren of the late Brooke Cunliffe (*b.* 1790), 4th son of 3rd baronet :—
Issue of the late Col. Foster Lionel Cunliffe, *b.* 1854, *d.* 1927 : *m.* 1st, 1894, Alice Mary, who *d.* 1907, el. da. of Edward Lyon, of Windlesham Hall, Bagshot ; 2ndly, 1912, Rose Nannette, who *d.* 1950, da. of G. J. Fenwick, and widow of J. Dowling :—

(By 1st marriage) Robert Lionel Brooke, *C.B.E.*, *b.* 1895; Capt. R.N. (ret.); S.-E. Pacific 1944 (despatches, C.B.E., Grand Officer of Order of Leopold II. of Belgium); was Admiralty Representative and Naval Assist. to High Commr. for UK in Canada 1946-48; CBE (Mil.) 1944: *m.* 1st, 1926, Barbara Eleanor, who *d.* 1970, da. of Col. Harry Cooper, of Pakenham Lodge, Pakenham, Suffolk; 2ndly, 1971, Christina, da. of the Rev. Canon Sydney Cooper, and has issue living, (by 1st m.) Bridget Eleanor, *b.* 1927: *m.* 1957, Hugh Rosslyn Inigo Sackville-West, MC, of Knole, Sevenoaks, Kent [*see* B. Sackville],—Nicolette Anne, *b.* 1929: *m.* 1954, Robert Charles Cotton [*see* V. Combermere, colls.],—Barbara Clare, *b.* 1936: *m.* 1957 (m. diss. 1965), Sir Thomas Agnew Beevor, 7th Bt. *Residence*, The Garden House, Pakenham, Bury St. Edmunds, Suffolk ——Alice Frances Clare, *b.* 1900. *Residence*, 63A, Netherall Gdns., NW3.

Sir Ellis Cunliffe 1st Bt., M.P. for Liverpool (*d.* 1767), descended from a younger branch of the Cunliffes of Hollins, Lancs. Sir Robert Henry Cunliffe, 4th baronet, a General in the Bengal Army received the honour of knighthood. The 6th baronet, Major Sir Foster Hugh Egerton Cunliffe, Rifle Brig. (Prince Consort's Own), was killed in action during European War July 1916.

Cunliffe-Owen, see Owen.

CUNNINGHAM, Creation (U.K.) 1963, of Crookedstone, Killead, co. Antrim.

Sir (SAMUEL) KNOX CUNNINGHAM, *QC*, 1st *Baronet*, son of the late *Rt. Hon.* Samuel Cunningham, of Fernhill, Belfast; *b.* April 3rd, 1909; ed. at Roy. Belfast. Academical Inst., Fettes, and Clare Coll., Camb. (MA); Bar. Middle Temple 1939, and QC 1959; Chm. of National Council of YMCAs 1949-67, PPS to Rt. Hon. Harold Macmillan, Prime Min. 1959-63; Pres. of Old Fettesian Assocn. 1967-70; Provincial Grand Master Masonic Province of Glos., a Member of Court of Assistants of Drapers' Co., (Master 1973-74); Dep. Grand Master of Ireland of The Loyal Orange Institution, and an Apprentice Boy of Londonderry; 1939-45 War with Scots Gds.; MP for S. Antrim (*UU*) 1955-70: *m.* 1935, Dorothy Enid, JP, da. of the late Edwin Riley, of Bilston, Staffs.

Arms.—Azure, a shake-fork between three mullets or. Crest.—A unicorn's head couped or.

Residence—Derhams House, Minchinhampton, Stroud, Glos. *Clubs*—Carlton, Ulster (Belfast), New (Cheltenham), Hawks (Cambridge), MCC.

DICK-CUNYNGHAM, 1st Creation (N.S.) 1669, Cunyngham of Lambrughtoun, co. Ayr 2nd Creation (N.S.) 1707, Dick, of Prestonfield, Edinburgh. [Extinct 1941.]

Major Sir (COLIN) KEITH DICK-CUNYNGHAM, 9th of 1st and 11th of 2nd creation and last *Baronet* ; *d.* (killed in action during European War) 1941.

Collateral Branch living.

Issue of the late Maj.-Gen. James Keith Dick-Cunyngham, C.B., C.M.G., D.S.O., 3rd son of 7th and 9th baronet, *b.* 1877, *d.* 1935: *m.* 1905, Alice Daisy, who *d.* 1963, da. of the late Lieut.-Col. Sir Harold Arthur Deane, K.C.S.I.:—

Betty, *b.* 1907 : *m.* 1926 (divorce 19—), Capt. Thomas William Robert Hill, R.A., and has issue living, Thomas Colin Neil RANSOM (Horwell Farm, Hardwick, Bicester), *b.* 1932; ed. at Bradfield; formerly Cornet Roy. Horse Guards; adopted by Christopher Ransom, of Monks Wall, Otterton, Budleigh Salterton, S. Devon, whose surname he assumed by deed poll 19— in lieu of his patronymic: *m.* 1959, Rosanna Conning Kilburn, and has issue living, Christopher James *b.* 1961,—Patricia Betty, *b.* 1927: *m.* 1954, Kenneth Diamond Hardie Cattanach, of Bridge House, Hermitage, nr. Newbury, Berks,—Dorothy Joan (Joanna), *b.* 1930; adopted by Christopher Ransom, of Monks Wall, Otterton, Budleigh Salterton, S. Devon, whose surname she assumed by deed poll 19— in lieu of her patronymic: *m.* 1953, Peter Jeremy Pelly [*see* Pelly, Bt., colls.],—Janet Mary DICK-CUNYNGHAM, *b.* 1917, resumed her maiden surname 1963: *m.* 1940, Capt. Roderick Francis Oliver, Roy. Horse Guards, from whom she obtained a divorce 1960 [Grant-Suttie, Bt., colls.], and has issue living, Caroline Stephanie *b.* 1944: *m.* 1965, Nicholas Kilmaine de Courcy-Ireland, of 12, Abingdon Villas, W8, Georgina Mary *b.* 1946. *Residence*, Huerta las Palomas, Coín, Provincia de Malaga, Spain.

CUNYNGHAME, Creation (N.S.) 1702, of Milncraig, Ayrshire.

Sir (HENRY) DAVID ST. LEGER
BROOKE SELWYN CUNYNGHAME, 11th
Baronet ; b. Feb. 7th, 1905 ; *s.* his father,
Lieut.-Col. Sir PERCY FRANCIS, *O.B.E.*,
1941 ; ed. at Eton ; Squadron-Leader R.A.F.
Vol. Reserve ; European War 1939-44 : *m.*
1941, the Hon. Pamela Margaret Stanley,
da. of 5th Baron Stanley of Alderley and
has issue.

    Arms—Argent, a shake-fork sable between three
fleurs-de-lis azure. **Crest**—A unicorn argent, unguled
maned and armed or, lying on a mount vert. **Supporters**—*Dexter*, a knight in armour holding in his
exterior hand a spear ; *sinister*, a countryman habited
azure. in his exterior hand a hay-fork.
    Residence—15, Madeline Rd., SE20. *Club,*—
Athenæum.

Sons living—ANDREW DAVID FRANCIS (69,
    Hillgate Place, W8 ; Brooks's Club), *b.* Dec. 25th,
    1942 ; ed. at Eton ; FCA : *m.* 1972, Harriet Ann,
    da. of Charles Thomas Dupont, of Montreal,
    Canada.——John Philip Henry Michael Selwyn,
    b. 1944 ; ed. at Eton.——Arthur James Angustus,
    b. 1951 ; ed. at Westminster.

    Brother living—Ian Francis Rowland Selwyn, *b.*
1910 ; ed. at Eton ; Ch. Assist., Min. of Production
and attached to British Raw Materials Mission, Washington, U.S.A. 1943-6 : *m.* 1st, 1938, Cicely
Mary, who *d.* 1945, el. da. of the late Francis Chaytor Starkey ; 2ndly. 1947, Eugénie Beatrice
Gwendolen, who *d.* 1962, da. of the late James Howard Allport, and widow of Rear-Adm. J. U.
Penrose-FitzGerald, and has issue living, (by 1st m.) Michael Ian Francis Starkey (39, Hilda
Vale Rd., Farnborough, Kent), *b.* 1945 : *m.* 1970, Penelope Mary, yr. da. of Allan Mortimer, of
Ballinger, Bucks.,—Sarah Albinia Starkey, *b.* 1940 : *m.* 1964, Feico Jan Leemhuis (RR3 Hem-
mingford, Quebec Province, Canada), and has issue living, Adrian Samuel *b.* 1969,—Caroline
Mary Albinia Starkey, *b.* 1943 : *m.* 1968, Barry Lloyd, of 32, Guildford Park Av., Guildford,
Surrey, and has issue living, Hannah Cicely *b.* 1973,—(by 2nd m.) Moira Janet Albinia Allport,
b. 1947 : *m.* 1969, Konstantin Andreevich Stramentov, of Apt. 79, Obrucheva St. 4, Moscow,
V421, USSR, and has issue living, Alexandra Jane Cunynghame *b.* 1973. *Residences,* 67, Marlborough Place, NW8 ; The Cottage, Swanbourne, Bletchley, Bucks. *Club,* Bath.

Collateral Branches living.

    Issue of the late Stuart Cunynghame, yr. son of 9th baronet ; *b.* 1874, *d.* 1962 : *m.* 1915,
    Helen Dorothy, who *d.* 1944, da. of the late Rev. A. Holland Taylor, D.D. :—
Colin Kenneth, *b.* 1918 ; Maj. late Indian Army.——David Francis (BOAC, PO Box 4756,
Durban, S. Africa), *b.* 1920 ; Capt. late Indian Army ; Airline Sales Representative, BOAC :
m. 1st, 1947, (m. diss. 1957) Ruth Armitage, da. of the late Walter Patrick Murray ; 2ndly, 1964,
Renate Maria Dietrich, and has issue living, (by 1st m.) David Stuart, *b.* 1948,—Diana Patricia,
b. 1950,—(by 2nd m.) Christopher Daniel, *b.* 1966,—Deborah Avril, *b.* 1968.

    Grandson of the late James Robertson Thurlow Cunynghame, 4th son of 8th
    baronet :—
    Issue of the late Francis Thurlow Hardinge Cunynghame. *b.* 1880, *d.* 1940 : *m.* 1909,
    Frances Anne, who *d.* 1954, da. of Nicholas Murnane, of Brisbane :—
Frank Vincent, *b.* 1910 : *m.* 1949, Mary Hennessy, and has issue living, Helen Anne, *b.* 1949,—
Diane Frances, *b.* 1952,—Jennifer Anne, *b.* 1955, Frances Mary, *b.* 1957. *Residence,* 18,
Serpentine Parade, Vaucluse, Sydney, N.S. Wales.

    Grandson of the late Gen. Sir Arthur Augustus Thurlow Cunynghame, GCB,
    5th son of 5th baronet :—
    Issue of the late Arthur Hardinge David Cunynghame, *b.* 1853 ; *d.* 1917 : *m.* 1892, Alexandra
    Isabel, who *d.* 1938, da. of the late Alexander Scott :—
David Hardinge, *b.* 1897 ; ed. at Cheltenham Coll. ; Maj. (ret.) Roy. Corps of Signals ; 1914-18 War
in France, Belgium, and the Balkans (wounded) : *m.* 1934, Ruth Ilon Ismay Mary, da. of the
Rev. A. E. Phillips, and has issue living, Francis Arthur David Anthony, *b.* 1935. *Residence,*
Minster Lovell, nr. Oxford.

    This family is a younger branch of the Earls of Glencairn (dormant since 1796), claiming
descent from 2nd son of 1st Earl (*d.* 1488). The 1st baronet, Sir David Cunynghame of Milncraig,
co. Ayr, a distinguished lawyer, and an eloquent member of the Scottish Parliament, was cr. a
Baronet with remainder to his "heirs male in perpetuum." The 10th baronet, Sir Percy Francis,
O.B.E., in Sarawak Civil Ser. 1886-1909, was Lieut.-Col. Middlesex Regt., and served in European
War 1914-18 (despatches).

CURRIE, Creation (U.K.) 1847.

Sir WALTER MORDAUNT CYRIL CURRIE, 5th
Baronet ; b. June 3rd, 1894 ; *s.* his father, *Sir* WALTER LOUIS
RACKHAM, 1941 ; ed. at Sherborne ; is a Member of
Performing Rights So. ; European War 1914-19 with
R.A.O.C.

    Arms—Gules, a saltire couped argent, in the centre chief point a rose
of the last barbed and seeded proper. **Crest**—A cock proper, resting its
foot upon a rose argent, barbed and seeded proper.

    Residence—Chasefield Cottage, Wickham Bishops, Witham, Essex.

Largs.

Collateral Branches living.

Issue of the late Percy George Colin Currie, 3rd son of 2nd baronet, *b.* 1857, *d.* **1932**: *m.* 1885, Agnes Grace Johnstone, da. of the late Charles Paterson, **of** Dumfries:—

Muriel Helen, *b.* 1887: *m.* 1911, Edgar Green, formerly Indian Telegraph Depart., and has issue living, Richard Colin, *b.* 1914,—Agnes Muriel Rachel, *b.* 1915,—Margaret Suzanne, *b.* **1919.**—— Ethel Lilian Adelaide, *b.* 1893. *Residence,*

Grandsons of the late William Close Currie, 3rd son of 1st baronet:—
Issue of the late William John Frederick Currie, *b.* 1852, *d.* **1923**: *m.* 1887, Minnie Euphemia Henrietta McMillan, who *d.* 1953, 2nd da. of G. H. Catania :—

WILLIAM GEORGE CUBITT, *b.* Feb. 29th. 1888 : *m.* **1952**, Mrs. Ellen May Thornton. *Residence,* Sekenke P.O., Singida, Tanzania.——Edward John Charles, *b.* 1892 ; served **with** Malayan Defence Force at Singapore 1942 : *m.* 1935, Mrs. Doris Melrose. *Residence,* Walnut Cottage, Benenden, Kent.

Grandchildren of the late Lucy Marian Alexander Currie (infra):—
Issue of the late Arthur Reynault Gordon, *b.* 1895, *d.* **1965**: *m.* 1921, Jean Rosamond (St. Andrew's Cottage, Haye Lane, Lyme Regis, Dorset), da. of Edward Archdall Ffooks, of Kingscote, Dorchester:—

Peter David (42, Lincoln Drive, Pyrford, Woking, Surrey), *b.* 1923: *m.* 1958, Susan Mary Gladys da. of Donald A. Daniel, of Hawksdown, Lyme Regis, and has issue living, Philip Byrom, *b.* 1960,—Sarah Jane, *b.* 1963.——Joanne, *b.* 1922: *m.* 1945, George Gordon Bennett, and has issue, living, Gordon (16, Ursula St. Battersea, SW11 3DW), *b.* 1947: *m.* 1968, Carol Anne, da. of H. T. Finnigan, 48, Blackwell Lane, Darlington, and has issue living, Simon Peter *b.* 1971,—Nicholas James *b.* 1972,—Bruce (19, Holystone Close, Newsham Farm Estate, Blyth, Northumberland), *b.* 1950: *m.* 1973, Catherine, da. of R. Taylor, of Holywood, 16, Church Rd., Gosforth, Newcastle on Tyne, and has issue living, Timothy *b.* 1973,—Peter, *b.* 1953.——Betty (16, Ursula St., SW11), *b.* 1927.——Nancy Jean (Biel Mill, Dunbar, E. Lothian), *b.* 1936.

Granddaughter of the late Charles Currie, BCS, 4th son of 1st baronet:—
Issue of the late Lucy Marian Alexander Currie, *b.* 1863, *d.* 1962: *m.* 1892, Arthur Byrom Gordon, who *d.* 1914:—

Eileen Catharine (Coggans Farm, Lower Holditch, Axminster), *b.* 1898: *m.* 1923, Edward Cambridge Ffooks (from whom she obtained a divorce 1935), and has issue living, Roger Cambridge (Tittlesfold Farm, Billingshurst, Sussex), *b.* 1924: *m.* 1951, Gillian Melville, da. of Lt.-Col. Basil Ronald Turner, DSO, of Timewell House, Morebath, Devon, and has issue living, Anthony Cambridge *b.* 1952, Jonathan Adrian *b.* 1955, Stephanie Vivien *b.* 1963,—Oliver Owen Fraser, *FRCS* (Lammas House, Scarcroft, Leeds), *b.* 1927: MRCS England and LRCP London 1949; FRCS England 1958: *m.* 1954, Patricia, da. of the late Charles William Scorer, and has issue living, Nigel Quentin *b.* 1956, Matthew Jocelyn *b.* 1963, John William *b.* 1971, Sarah Catherine *b.* 1958,—Edward Arthur (39, Courtfield Rd., SW7), *b.* 1928; MA 19—; a Fellow of Chartered Insurance Institute,—Catherine Mary (twin), *b.* 1928,—Susan Marjorie, *b.* 1934: *m.* 1st, 1953, Peter Sheridan-Patterson (from whom she obtained a divorce 1959); 2ndly, 1963, John Melville Smith, of Sandlin House, Leigh Sinton, Malvern, Worcs., and has issue living (by 1st m.) Alexandra Clare *b.* 1957.

Grandchildren of the late Robert George Currie, B.C.S., 5th son of 1st baronet:—
Issue of the late George Hugh Currie (twin), *b.* 1873, *d.* 1951 : *m.* 1st, 1897, Grace E., da. of A. F. Miller, of Farmington, New Mexico, U.S.A. ; 2ndly, 1925, Adelaide Caroline, da. of the late Gore Ouseley, C.S.I., H.E.I.C.S.:—

(By 1st m.) Alick Bradley (Tenacre Ranch, Bayfield, Colorado, 81122, USA), *b.* 1904; late USA Dept. of Commerce (ret.).——George Donald (Pauma Valley, Cal. 92061, USA), *b.* 1907; is a Stockman: *m.* 1928, Janet, da. of the late James Scott, of Bayfield, Colorado, USA, and has issue living, Donald Scott, *b.* 1930: *m.* 1st 1948 (m. diss. 1951), Charlotte, da. of Charles Johnstone, of Mesa, Arizona, USA; 2ndly, 1952, Barbara Lee, da. of A. P. Garnier, of Cal., USA, and has issue living (by 1st m.) Donald Mark *b.* 1949: *m.* 1st 1969 (m. diss. 1969) Gloria Price; 2ndly, 1969, (m. diss. 1971), Inga Mae Rouse (and has issue living (by 2nd m.), Mark Donald *b.* 1970), Julia Ann *b.* 1950: *m.* 1969, Eugene Gangaware (and has issue living, Elizabeth Ann *b.* 1970), Janet Sue (twin) *b.* 1950: *m.* 1970, Jack D. Hawkins,—(by 2nd m.) Gary Dwayne *b.* 1953: *m.* 1970, Wilma Kathleen Wyatt, of Colorado, USA (and has issue living, Bandy Sue *b.* 1971), Tina Marie *b.* 1955, Kathren Evelyn *b.* 1959,—James Davidson (15603, Espola Rd., Poway, Cal. 92604, USA), *b.* 1932: *m.* 1956, Olga Mary, da. of Miguel Otero, of Tampa, Florida, and has issue living, Lila Jan *b.* 1967,—George Robert, *b.* 1943: *m.* 1962, (m. diss. 1972), Lucy Lavonne, da. of S. M. Gilliam, of Charlotte, N. Carolina 28200, and has issue living, Michael Todd *b.* 1963, Richard Eric *b.* 1967.——Annie Flora, *b.* 1897: *m.* 1920, Clinton B. Fiske Harsh, of Box 1122, Silver City, New Mexico, USA, and has issue living, George Clinton (Gila, New Mexico, USA), *b.* 1920: *m.* 1948, Julia Retmiller, and has issue living, Rhett *b.* 1954, Dian Elizabeth *b.* 1949: *m.* 1968 (m. diss. 1971), Charles D. Mannino (and has issue living, Meridee Francis *b.* 1968),— Robert Currie (1916, Yucca Drive, Silver City, New Mexico, USA), *b.* 1922: *m.* 1948, Majorie Shean, and has issue living, Matthias Brayton *b.* 1955, Alice Anne Thadia *b.* 1949, June Margil *b.* 1950, Alexis Mary *b.* 1958, Cecily Louise *b.* 1960.—Glenn Ray (507, North Park St., Tuscola, Illinois, USA), *b.* 1925: *m.* 1949, Jeanne Prator, and has issue living, Glenn Ray *b.* 1958, Sandra *b.* 1951, Christine *b.* 1954, Nancy *b.* 1956.

Granddaughters of the late Maj.-Gen. Fendall Currie, 6th son of 1st baronet:—
Issue of the late Fendall James Pears Currie, *b.* 1867, *d.* 1946 : *m.* 1890, Christina, da. of David Anderson :—

Veda Mary Fendall, *b.* 1891: *m.* 1922, Thomas Scott MacMillan of 83, Creyke Rd., Ilaen, Christchurch 4, NZ, and has issue living, Mary Christina, *b.* 1924,—Elizabeth Scott, *b.* 1925.

Issue of the late Lieut.-Col. Ivor Bertram Fendall Currie, D.S.O., *b.* 1872, *d.* 1924: *m.* **1906**, May Constance, who *d.* **1937**, da. of the late F.-M. Sir George Stuart White, V.C., G.C.B., O.M., G.C.S.I., G.C.M.G., G.C.I.E., G.C.V.O., LL.D.:—

Sylvia Constance, *b.* 1910 : *m.* 1937, Nigel George Kingsford Burgess, and has issue living, Anthony Malcolm Kingsford, *b.* 1941,—Simon George Fendall, *b.* 1945. *Residence,* 7 Robert Close, Randolph Av., W.9.——Eleanor Frances, *b.* 1918.

Grandson of the late Maj. Disney Rivers Currie, 8th son of 1st baronet:—
Issue of the late Maj. Disney Rivers Currie, MC, *b.* 1894, *d.* 1964: *m.* 1919, Ethel Jeannette Bryce (Hobbs Cottage, Phillips Rd., Marnhull, Dorset), da. of Arnold Bryce Smith:—

Frederick Disney Rivers (Whitehayes, 93 Church St., Willingdon, Eastbourne), *b.* 1921; Burma, 1943 as Capt. Roy. Scots (wounded): *m.* 1949, Jean Alison, da. of Lionel Westropp Jardine, CIE, [see Jardine, Bt., *cr.* 1916], and has issue living, Peter Frederick Rivers, *b.* 1950: *m.* 1973, Mary Rose Veronica, da. of E. J. Goodman,—Jennifer Jean, *b.* 1953: *m.* 1972, Alan Sayers, and has issue living, Jonathan Alan *b.* 1974,—Fiona Alexandra, *b.* 1955.

This family came from Dunse, Berwickshire. William Currie, who *d.* 1781, became a London banker. His grandson, Sir Frederick Currie, 1st baronet, was successively Foreign Secretary to the Indian Government, a Member of the Supreme Council in India, a member of the Court of Directors of the H.E.I.C.S, and one of the Home Council in London.

CURTIS, Creation (U.K.) 1802, of Cullands Grove, Middlesex.

Sir PETER CURTIS, 6th *Baronet,* son of the late Edward Beaumont Cotton Curtis, great-grandson of 2nd baronet ; *b.* April 9th, 1907 ; *s.* his kinsman, *Sir* FRANCIS EDGAR EGERTON, 1943; ed. at Winchester; Lieut. late 16/5th Lancers : *m.* 1934, Joan Margaret, da. of the late Reginald Nicholson [E. Waldegrave], and has issue.

Arms—Paly of six or and azure, a fesse checky argent and sable, on a canton gules a dragon's wing erect of the third, in base a sword proper, pommel and hilt of the first, surmounting a key in saltire of the second. **Crest**—A ram's head couped argent, surmounted by two branches of oak in saltire proper.
Residence—Little Manor, near Bishop's Waltham, Hants. *Club*—Cavalry.

We conquer step by step.

Son living—WILLIAM PETER, *b.* April 9th, 1935.
Daughters living—Rosemary Antonia Joan, *b.* 1943: *m.* 1966, John Clarkson Spink, of Poplars Farm, Rotherwick, Basingstoke, and has issue living, Annabel Louise, *b.* 1970.——Fiona Mary, *b.* 1946: *m.* 1968, Anthony David Findon Littlejohn, of Uplands Cottage, Limpsfield, Oxted, Surrey, and has issue living, Ruth Hermione, *b.* 1971,—Georgina Clare, *b.* 1973.
Brother living—Gerald Edward, *b.* 1909; ed. at Winchester and at Trin. Coll., Oxford (B.A. 1930, M.A. 1935) : *m.* 1939, Philippa da. of the late Capt. Philip Clayton Alcock, D.L., J.P., of Overton Lodge, Ludlow, and has issue living, Edward Philip, *b.* 1940; ed. at Bradfield, and RMA; Maj. 16/5th Lancers,—Sonia Mary, *b.* 1944: *m.* 1971, Charles Hamilton Ewart, of 54, Montagu Sq., W.1, and has issue living, Gabrielle Alice Anne *b.* 1972. *Residence,* Cym Bach Lodge, Glasbury-on-Wye, via Hereford.

Daughter living of 5th Baronet.—Winifred Lotus, *b.* 1904: *m.* 1927, Capt. Alan Walter Dolby, who *d.* 1943, sometime R. Berks. Regt., and has issue living, John Horace Curtis (c/o Coutts & Co., 1 Cadogan Place, SW1), *b.* 1928; ed. at St. Paul's Sch.: *m.* 1959, Anthea Louise Whitamore, and has issue living, Timothy William Curtis *b.* 1964, Caroline Lurleen Curtis, *b.* 1960,—Robert Francis (17, Crowsport, Hamble, Hants.), *b.* 1933; ed. at Christ's Hospital Sch.; is Master Mariner Merchant Navy: *m.* 1960, (m. diss. 1967), Jean Patricia, da. of Sidney Clark, and has issue living, Simon Francis Curtis *b.* 1962, Louise Wynett *b.* 1964. *Residence,* 17, Crowsport, Hamble, Hants.

Collateral Branches living.

Grandchildren of the late William Cotton Curtis, el. son of the late George Lear Curtis, 2nd son of 2nd baronet:—
Issue of the late Lieut.-Col. Hubert Montagu Cotton Curtis, D.S.O., *b.* 1876, *d.* 1948 *m.* 1st, 1915, Lilian, who *d.* 1931 (having obtained a divorce 1929), da. of the late Louis Watson, of Brighton, and widow of Alfred Broadwood; 2ndly, 1929, Marcella Olive Penrose Robinson, who *d.* 1969:—
(By 2nd marriage) William Richard (Abington Lodge, Abington, Cambridge), *b.* 1933; ed. at Eton: *m.* 1961, Janice Clare, da. of William Yates Duckworth, of Garstang, Lancs., and has issue living, William Giles, *b.* 1962,—Timothy David, *b.* 1968,—Anna Clare, *b.* 1963.——Hilda Lucy Penrose (7, Lyston Lane, Long Melford, Suffolk), *b.* 1930: *m.* 1955 (m. diss. 1968) Charles Henry Anderson, Capt. R. Inniskilling Fus., and has issue living, Lucie Rose, *b.* 1956,—Arabella Joan Louisa, *b.* 1960,—Caroline Rebecca, *b.* 1961.

Grandchildren of the late Rear-Adm. Arthur Cecil Curtis, 2nd son of the late George Lear Curtis (ante):—
Issue of the late Brigadier Arthur Drury Curtis, *b.* 1888, *d.* 1950 : *m.* 1st, 1915, Margery May, who *d.* 1943, el. da. of Robert Barlow, of Bombay ; 2ndly, 1946, Evelyn Muriel, who *d.* 1951, da. of Murray Simmons, of Whitton, Middlesex :—
(By 1st marriage) Arthur Derek Edward, M.C., *b.* 1917 ; ed. at St. Catharine's Coll., Camb. (B.A. 1939, M.A. 1960); Lt.-Col. R.E. (ret.); European War 1939-45 in France (M.C.): *m.* 1943, Katherine Mary, da. of the late T. Hadfield, of Sheffield, and has issue living, Arthur Richard Edward, *b.* 1947; Capt. RA; ed. at Haileybury and RMA,—Katherine Margaret, *b.* 1944: *m.* 1969, Capt. M. A. Langdon, RM, and has issue living, Julian Charles Anthony *b.* 1972, Mathilda Mary *b.* 1974. *Residence,* Oak Covert, Kingsley Av., Camberley, Surrey. *Club,* Royal Commonwealth Society.——Robert Cecil, *b.* 1922; ed. at Wellington Coll.; Lt.-Col. RA; 1939-45 War in N. Africa and Italy: *m.* 1952, Pamela Margaret, da. of late Oliver S. Sedgwick, of Chislehurst, Kent, and has issue living, Carol Frances Margaret, *b.* 1956. *Address,* c/o Lloyds Bank, 6, Pall Mall, SW1.——Joan Mary Lavie, *b.* 1916: *m.* 1940, Col. Edward Raymond Lewis, CBE, and has issue living, Robert Edward Curtis, *b.* 1941,—Penelope Alison, *b.* 1947. *Residence,* 8, Queens Park, Chester.

Issue of the late Capt. Cecil Montagu Drury Curtis, OBE, *b.* 1889, *d.* 1966: *m.* 1933, Rosa Marion (73, Dale Av., Hassocks, Sussex), da. of the late R. H. Woodley:—
Christopher Francis, *b.* 1939; BA, Oxford; PhD, Edinburgh: *m.* 1970, Jill Pickup, PhD.——Hazel Rosemary, *b.* 1934: *m.* 1960, Sidney Edward Smith, of 8, Blunts Wood Rd., Haywards Heath, Sussex, and has issue living, David Edward, *b.* 1965,—Rosalind Margaret, *b.* 1961,—Alison Claire, *b.* 1963,—Stephanie Jane, 1968.

Issue of the late Francis Augustus Drury Curtis, *b.* 1891, *d.* 1927: *m.* 1916, Gwendolen Angelo Taylour, who *d.* 1961, da. of the late Edwin Taylour English, of Toronto, Canada:—
Ada Harriette Drury, *b.* 1918 : *m.* 1958, John Bernard Scowcroft, Ch. Engineer, Merchant Navy and has issue living, Sarah Jane, *b.* 1960. *Residence,* Roseland, Cubert, Newquay, Cornwall.

Grandson of the late Capt. Ernest Henry Curtis, 3rd son of the late George Lear Curtis, (ante):—
Issue of the late Edgar Ralph Curtis, *b.* 1883, *d.* 1950: *m.* 1921, Ellen Annie, who *d.* 1963, da. of Thomas Underdown, of Tonbridge:—
Montague Ralph *b.* 1922; ed. at Malvern Coll., and at Trin. Coll., Oxford (M.A.); Capt. late E. Yorkshire Regt.: *m.* 1964, Margaret Winifred Welsby, da. of the late Thomas Welsby Holland, of Chester. *Residence,* La Fougere, Rozel Hill, St. Martin, Jersey.

Descendants, if any of the late Angustus John Curtis, 4th son of 2nd baronet (whose son Maj. Augustus Frederick Curtis *b.* 1840, left issue three sons):—

Granddaughter of the late Lieut.-Gen. William Frederick Curtis, el. son of the
late Timothy Abraham Curtis, 3rd son of 1st baronet:—
   Issue of the late Col. William Frederick de Hubbenet Curtis, *b*. 1842, *d*. 1906 : *m*. 1880,
   Mary Owen. who *d*. 1934, da. of the late John Ward Nicholls, Sec. of Greenwich Hospital :—
Joceline Sophia Lilian: *m*. 1925, Paul Stutfield. *Residence,*

   Grandchildren of the late Capt. George Arthur Hamilton Curtis, RAN, el. son
   of the late Col. James Charles Curtis (infra):—
      Issue of the late Cecil Arthur Hamilton Curtis, *b*. 1895, *d*. 1970: *m*. 1929, Constance May,
      who *d*. 1968, da. of Aubrey E. Webb, of Mel., Aust.:—
Geoffrey Cecil Hamilton (Tigh-na-Ceard, Mt. Cotton Rd., Capalaba, Qld.), *b*. 1932: *m*. 1960,
Barbara Ellen, da. of Peter Angus, of Newmarket, Brisbane, Qld., and has issue living, Fiona
Madeline Hamilton, *b*. 1962,—Helen Mary Hamilton, *b*. 1964.——Anne Eleanor Hamilton, *b*.
1935.

   Grandchildren of the late Col. James Charles Curtis, son of the late Timothy
   Abraham Curtis (ante):—
      Issue of the late Alfred William Hamilton Curtis, *b*. 1864, *d*. 1918: *m*. 1901, Euphemia
      Hilda, McClung, da. of William A. C. Reynolds, and widow of Henry Cooperthwaite:—
James Alfred Percy Hamilton (2057, Topping St., Trail, BC, Canada), *b*. 1907; Lt. 2nd Bn. Rocky
Mountain Rangers (ret.): *m*. 1939, Barbara Milsom, da. of Frank Weldon Russell, of Dartmouth,
Nova Scotia, and has issue living, James Russell Hamilton, *b*. 1941: *m*. 1966, Marion Eileen, da.
of George B. Moore, of Vancouver, BC, and has issue living, James David Hamilton *b*. 1974,—
Alfred William Hamilton, *b*. 1945; *m*. 1971, Barbara Joan, da. of Benjamin Earl Tompkins, of
Terrace, BC, and has issue living, James William Hamilton *b*. 1973.——Grace Anna Delicia
Florence Hamilton, *b*. 1903: *m*. 1923, Laurie E. Wiren (PO Box 248, Gibson's Landing, BC,
Canada), and has issue living, John, *b*. 1930,—James, *b*. 1934,—Margaret, *b*. 1926,—Leonore,
b. 1928.——Margaret Euphemia Cecilia Hamilton, *b*. 1909: *m*. 1940, Lloyd E. Kindleysides
(PO Box 29, Escondido, Cal., 92025, USA).

   Grandchildren of the late Col. Charles Herbert Curtis, el. son of Charles William
   Curtis, el. son of Charles Berwick Curtis, 4th son of 1st baronet:—
      Issue of the late Maj. Timothy Herbert William Curtis, *b*. 1882, *d*. 1966: *m*. (Jan.) 1913,
      Edith Marjorie, who *d*. 1968, da. of the late F. Aldcroft Kay:—
Pamela Kay, *b*. (Oct.) 1913; sometime Junior Com. ATS: *m*. 1943, Maj. John Howard Nickson,
RA, of The Elms, High Easter, Essex, and has issue living, Simon John Curtis, *b*. 1945,—Jeremy
David, *b*. 1947 —Cecelia Anne, *b*. 1953.——Mary Kay. *b*. 1917: *m*. 1939, Col. Alexander George
Jeffrey Readman, DSO, R. Scots Greys, of The Old Rectory, Fairsted, Hatfield Peverell, Essex,
and has issue living, Timothy Christopher George, *b*. 1944,—Teresa Mary, *b*. 1947.

      Issue of the late Maj. Philip Pinckney Curtis, MC, *b*. 1884, *d*. 1974: *m*. 1st, 1925 (m. diss.
      1933), Heléne Ellinor Clare, da. of the late Capt. Glen Kidston, 3rd Bn. Black Watch;
      2ndly, 1941, Marion (Annesley Cottage, Bank, Lyndhurst), only child of George Berkeley
      Wilson, of Long Barn, Ringwood:—
(By 1st m.) Cherry April Ellinor, *b*. 1926: *m*. 1949, Maj. Terence Leslie Gossage, late KOYLI, of
Flexford House, Sway, Lymington, and has issue living, Philip Leslie, *b*. 1951,—Andrew Alex-
ander, *b*. 1963, Julia April Ellinor, *b*. 1954.——Alison Audrey Primrose, *b*. 1928: *m*. 1956,
William Ashe Dymoke Windham, of Crowley Lodge, Crowley, Northwich, Cheshire [see Bowyer-
Smyth, Bt., colls.].——Glenda Kidston, *b*. 1931: *m*. 1st, 1953 (m. diss. 1968), Maj. Herrick
Colin Butchard, late 2nd Gurkha Rifles; 2ndly, 1969, Rodney Frederick Hedderley Ward, late
Coldm. Gds., of the Old Manor, Ickleford, Herts., and has issue living (by 1st m.) William James
Langrishe, *b*. 1956,—Victoria Annabelle Ellinor, *b*. 1954,—Henrietta Matilda, *b*. 1957.——(by
2nd m.) Timothy Malise (The Old Curate's House, Bramdean, Alresford, Hants.), *b*. 1942; ed. at
Eton, Trin. Coll., Camb. (BA), and Harvard Business Sch., USA (MBA): *m*. 1968, Sally Elizabeth,
da. of Ambrose Stevens Higgins, of Bangor, Maine, USA, and has issue living, Timothy George,
b. 1972,—Edward Ambrose (twin), *b*. 1972,—Katherine Pinckney, *b*. 1970.——Giles Philip,
b. 1945; ed. at Eton, and St. Andrews Univ. (BSc): *m*. 1971, Sarah Anne, el. da. of the late Lt.-Col.
Walter George Finney [see E. Perth, colls.], and has issue living, Rowena Mary, *b*. 1972.

   Granddaughters of the late Thomas Reginald Curtis, 3rd son of Charles William
   Curtis (ante):—
      Issue of the late Col. William Patrick Stewart Curtis, OBE, *b*. 1899, *d*. 1965: *m*. 1929,
      Margaret Pamela Adderley (Longbarn, Twyford, Hants.), da. of Lt.-Col. H. Adderley
      Cradock:—
Jill Elizabeth, *b*. 1930: *m*. 1952, Frederick Michael Pelly [*see* Pelly, Bt.].——Dorcas Sara, *b*. 1932:
m. 1965, Robin Ross, RM, of 15, York and Albany Close, Walmer, Deal.——Jocelyn Patricia, *b*.
1936: *m*. 1960, Mark Tress (c/o Barclays Bank DCO, 29, Gracechurch St., EC3), and has issue
living, Oliver James Mark, *b*. 1967,—Amanda, *b*. 1961,—Camilla, *b*. 1963.——Victoria Anne
Dorothea Adderley *b*. 1939: *m*. 1965, Denis Gamberoni, of Ballards Place, Cowlinge, Suffolk, and
has issue living, Tobias Felix *b*. 1970, Justine Louise *b*. 1967.——Tessa Cecilia Evelyn, *b*. 1943.

   Grandchildren of the late Charles William Curtis (ante):—
      Issue of the late Eustace Henry Curtis, *b*. 1863, *d*. 1948: *m*. 1904, Laura, da. of Alfred
      Ibbotson, of 45, Hill Street, Berkeley Square, W.1:—
John Eustace, *b*. 1910.——Corina Laurel Mary, *b*. 1908.

   Granddaughter of Charles Berwick Curtis (ante):—
      Issue of the late James Falconer Curtis, *b*. 1827, *d*. 1879: *m*. 1st, 1861, Josephine Adelaide,
      who *d*. 1868, da. of the late Col. Mangin ; 2ndly, 1872 Mary Helen, who *d*. 1919, da. of
      the late Rev. J. Brown of Langford, Notts :—
Gertrude Madeline (Redhill Nursing Home, Annandale, 28, Warwick Rd., Redhill, Surrey) *b*. 1875:
m. 1913, Imre Knopp, who *d*. 1946.

   Grandchildren of the late Maj.-Gen. Sir Reginald Salmond Curtis, KCMG,
   CB, DSO (infra):—
      Issue of the late Diane Curtis, *b*. 1895, *d*. 1968: *m*. 1914, Brig. Robert Albany Boger
      (E. Guilford, colls.), who *d*. 1957:—
John Reginald Frederick (15, Carnarvon Rd., Roseville, NSW), *b*. 1925; ed. at Marlborough and
London Univ.; FACMA, MRCS England, LRCP London, DCH, DPH; late Lt. 17th/21st
Lancers: *m*. 1965, Benita Annette, da. of Bennison Osborne, of Sydney, NSW, and widow of
John Maclean Folbigg, and has issue living, Christina Diane, *b*. 1967.——Elizabeth (31, Macleay
Gdns., 8, Macleay St., Potts Point, NSW), *b*. 1921; formerly Sen. Cdr. ATS.——Ann (c/o Bank
of NSW, George St., Sydney, NSW), *b*. 1922; SRN.

   Grandchildren of the late Maj.-Gen. Reginald Curtis, 3rd son of Charles Berwick
   Curtis (ante):—
      Issue of the late Maj.-Gen. Sir Reginald Salmond Curtis, K.C.M.G., C.B., D.S.O., *b*. 1863,
      d. 1922: *m*. 1894, the Hon. Hilda Margaret, who *d*. 1929, da. of 9th Viscount Barrington :—
Ivy Agnes (twin) (Little Colesbourne, Cheltenham), *b*. 1908: *m*. 1933, John Malebisse Beckwith,
who *d*. 1969, [D. Richmond], and has issue living, William John Malebisse (64, Airedale Av., W4),
b. 1934; Capt. 4th R. Green Jackets (TAVR); a Member of British Computer Soc.: *m*. 1968,
Flavia Rosamond Hulbert, and has issue living, Edward John Malebisse *b*. 1970, Robert Ralph
William *b*. 1971.

Issue of the late Col. Edward George Curtis, C.M.G., *b.* 1868, *d.* 1923 : *m.* 1903, Ethel (Nynehead Court, nr. Wellington, Somerset): she *m.* 2ndly, 1926, Capt. Norman Hornsby, late Indian Army, who *d.* 1957], da. of the late Walter Coote, FRGS:—
David Sacheverell (3, Lombardy Place, Orme Court, W2) *b.* 1913; a member of Inst. of Petroleum; 1939-45 War as Lt.-Col. R. Fus. with Central Mediterranean Force (despatches four times): *m.* 1st, 1935 (divorce 1945), Annora Beatrice, da. of the late Major Frederick Rowland Williams-Wynn, C.B. [*see* Williams-Wynn, Bt., colls] ; 2ndly, 1948, (divorce 1957), Pamela Ruth, da. of the late Reginald Walter Preston ; 3rdly, 1957, Monica Sarah, da. of the late Mrs. Nina Payne, of Athens, Greece, and has issue living, (by 1st marriage) Edward Peregrine Sacheverell (13, Old Palace Lane, Richmond, Surrey; White's Club) *b.* 1937; ed. at Stowe: late Lt. 8th Hussars: *m.* 1970, Marie-Adèle, da. of the late Francis Le Baron Smoot, of Georgetown, Washington, DC, and has issue living, Charles Edward *b.* 1971, William Francis Peregrine *b.* 1974,—Hugh Frederick (4, Pickwick Place, Harrow-on-the-Hill, Middx.; RTYC) *b.* 1941; ed. at Stowe: *m.* 1970, Maija Kaarina, da. of Aulis Samuli Pyy, of Helsinki, and has issue living, Victoria Ann *b.* 1971, Natasha Kaarina Helena—(by 3rd m.) Isabella Alexandra Nina, *b.* 1959.

Granddaughter of the late Spencer Henry Curtis, 5th son of Charles Berwick Curtis (ante):—
Issue of the late Major Spencer Carey Curtis, T.D., *b.* 1865; *d.* 1945: *m.* 1902, Edith Mabel, who *d.* 1931, da. of the late T. J. Eaton, of Malmesbury, Cape Colony :—
Sylvia Rosamond D'Urban Carey, *b.* 1908: *m.* 1932, Thomas Musgrave Pyke, O.B.E., T.D., HM's Inspector of Schs., (ret.), of Little Orchard, Buckham Thorns, Westerham, Kent, and has issue living, Susan Musgrave, *b.* 1935: *m.* 1966, John Leo Monaghan (54, King Edward's Grove, Teddington, Middx.), and has issue living, David John *b.* 1968, Benjamin Musgrave *b.* 1970,—Anne Curtis, *b.* 1939: *m.* 1962, Dr. John Ferens Turner, of Inveresk, Church Rd., Combe Down, Bath, and has issue living, Edward Thomas *b.* 1966, Sophia Jane *b.* 1964, Jessica Charlotte *b.* 1968.

Granddaughters of the late Wilfred Henry Curtis, 2nd son of the late Spencer Henry Curtis (ante):—
Issue of the late Anthony Edmund Spencer Curtis, *b.* 1906, *d.* 1962: *m.* 1931, M. Nancy (Le Vallon, Longdown Lane South, Epsom, Surrey), [who *m.* 2ndly, 1969, John Ormsby Chapple] only child of the late R. Nesbit Taylor, of Meadow Bank, Epsom:—
Jean Anna, *b.* 1933: *m.* 1960, John Richard Aley, of Brookfield, Bradfield St. George, Bury St. Edmunds.——Brenda Carey, *b.* 1936: *m.* 1960, William John Stickland Budd, of 61, Rue de Stockel, B. 1950, Kraainem, Belgium.

Granddaughter of the late Henry Downing Curtis, yst. son of Charles Berwick Curtis (ante):—
Issue of the late Vice-Adm. Berwick Curtis, CB, CMG, DSO, *b.* 1876, *d.* 1965: *m.* 1st, 1907, his cousin Mildred Henrietta Constable, who *d.* 1927, da. of Frank John Constable Curtis; 2ndly, 1929, Violet Penelope Munro, who *d.* 1973, da. of the late Robert J. B. Thomson, and widow of Lt.-Cdr. George Francis Cholmley, of Thorpe Bassett, Malton, Yorks:—
(By 1st m.) Janet Henrietta (Marrett Cottage, Hoarwithy, Hereford.), *b.* 1908: *m.* 1st, 1927 (m. diss. 1936), Com. William Kenneth Ramsden Cross, RN, who *d.* (killed in action) 1941; 2ndly, 1940 (m. diss.), Major John Congreve; 3rdly, 1951, A. Russell Cowell, who *d.* 1964, and has issue living, (by 1st m.) Giles Berwick (The Garden House, 42, Kidbrooke Grove, SE3), *b.* 1928; Lt.-Cdr. RN (ret.): *m.* 1st, 1953 (m. diss. 19—), Sonia, da. of E. Welsby Williams; 2ndly, 19—, Lavinia, da. of Gp. Capt. P. C. Thomson, and has issue living (by 1st m.), Piers William *b.* 1955, Belinda Jane *b.* 1954,—Henrietta Caroline, *b.* 1931: *m.* 1957, Christopher Jermyn Pratt, of The Clergy House, Marlston, Newbury, [M. Bath, colls.], and has issue living, Roderick Jermyn *b.* 1959, James Berwick, *b.* 1963.

The 1st baronet was Lord Mayor of London 1794-5, and sat as M.P. for the City of London 1790-1820. He was offered a peerage, but declined the honour.

Cusack-Smith, see Smith.

DALRYMPLE, Creation (U.K.) 1887, of Newhailes, Midlothian. [Extinct 1971.]
Sir (CHARLES) MARK DALRYMPLE, 3rd and last *Baronet.*

Widow living of 3rd Baronet—*Lady* ANTONIA MARIAN AMY ISABEL STEWART (*Lady Antonia Dalrymple*) (Newhailes, Musselburgh, Midlothian), only da. of 12th Earl of Galloway: *m.* 1946, Sir (Charles) Mark Dalrymple, 3rd Bt., who *d.* 1971, when the title became ext.

Dalrymple-Champneys, see Champneys.

Dalrymple-Hay, see Hay.

Dalrymple-White see White.

ELPHINSTONE-DALRYMPLE, Creation (U.K.) 1828, of Horn, and Logie. Elphinstone, Aberdeenshire. [Dormant or Extinct 1956.]
Sir FRANCIS NAPIER ELPHINSTONE-DALRYMPLE, *C.B.E., D.S.O.,* 7th *Baronet; d.* Dec. 18th, 1956, and concerning the next heir, his kinsman, HEW DRUMMOND ELPHINSTONE-DALRYMPLE, no information is available. At the time of going to press no name appears on the Official Roll of Baronets in respect of this title.

Daughters living of 7th Baronet—Penelope Eleanore, *b.* 1911: *m.* 1st, 1939, James Peter Henry Balston, Flying Officer, Auxiliary Air Force, who *d.* (killed on active ser. during European War) 1940; 2ndly, 1954, Russell Alexander Lovell, of 9, Jonathan Lane, Sandwich, Cape Cod, Mass. 02563, USA.——Daphne Jean, *b.* 1916: *m.* 1938, Brig. David Meynell, CBE, late Roy. Irish Fusiliers, and has issue living, Timothy, *b.* 1940,—Peter David, *b.* 1945. *Residence*, Willowlands, Willow Lane, Wargrave, Berks.

This family is descended from the Hon. Sir Hew Dalrymple, 3rd son of James, 1st Viscount Stair, sometime Lord President of the Court of Session, and also M.P. for North Berwick, who was created a baronet 1698 [*see* E. Stair, colls.]. Francis Austruther Elphinstone Dalrymple, 5th son of 1st baronet, left issue, Hew Drummond *b.* 1857, and Francis Herbert, *b.* 1862. If they left male issue, the senior in line would be heir to this Baronetcy.

HAMILTON-DALRYMPLE, Creation (N.S.) 1698, of North Berwick, Haddingtonshire.

Sir HEW FLEETWOOD HAMILTON-DALRYMPLE, *CVO*, 10th *Baronet*; *b.* April 9th, 1926; *s.* his father, *Sir* HEW CLIFFORD, 1959; ed. at Ampleforth; Maj. (ret.) Gren. Guards; Ensign and Adjt. of Queen's Body Guard for Scotland (Roy. Co. of Archers); a DL of E. Lothian 1964, Vice-Lieut 1973; Man. Dir. of Scottish & Newcastle Breweries, and a Dir. Scottish American Investment Co., and other cos., CVO 1974: *m.* 1954, Lady Anne-Louise Mary Keppel, da. of 9th Earl of Albemarle, and has issue.

Arms—Quarterly : 1st and 4th grand quarters or, on a saltire azure between two water-bougets in flank sable, nine lozenges of the first, *Dalrymple* ; 2nd and 3rd grand quarters, quarterly 1st and 4th gules, three cinquefoils, ermine ; 2nd and 3rd, argent, a lymphad with sails furled sable, all within a bordure componée argent and azure, the first charged with hearts gules and the second with mullets argent, *Hamilton*. **Crest**—A rock proper. **Supporters**,—*Dexter*, a lion guardant gules ; *sinister*, a falcon proper.

Residence,—Leuchie, North Berwick, East Lothian.   *Club*,—Guards'.

Sons living—HEW RICHARD, *b.* Sept. 3rd, 1955; ed. at Ampleforth, and Corpus Christi Coll., Oxford.——John James, *b.* 1957.——Robert George, *b.* 1959.——William Benedict, *b.* 1965.

Brother living—*Rev.* John David, *b.* 1928 ; is a Roman Catholic Priest.

Sister living—Elsie Margaret Mary, *b.* 1922 : *m.* 1947, Major Martin Antony Gibbs, Coldstream Gds., and has issue living, Antony William Hew, *b.* 1947: *m.* 1974, Virginia, da. of the Hon. (William) Keith Rous [see E. Stradbroke],—Mary Blanche, *b.* 1949: *m.* 1971, Rupert Ridge, Lt. I.T,—Anstice Bridget, *b.* 1951,—Cecily Ann Albinia, *b.* 1952.—Katharine Rose, *b.* 1955,—Julian Margaret, *b.* 1957. *Residence*, Sheldon Manor, Chippenham, Wilts.

Widow living of 9th Baronet—ANN DOROTHEA (*Dowager Lady Hamilton-Dalrymple*), da. of the late Augustus Thorne, J.P., D.L. ; is a J.P. : *m.* 1919, Sir Hew Clifford Hamilton-Dalrymple, 9th baronet, who *d.* 1959. *Residence*, Blackdykes, North Berwick, East Lothian.

Collateral Branch living.

Descendants (if any) of Robert Dalrymple-Horn-Elphinstone (2nd son of Robert Dalrymple-Horn-Elphinstone, 3rd son of Hew Elphinstone, 2nd son of 1st baronet), who was *cr.* a *Baronet* 1828.
See Elphinstone-Dalrymple, Bt.

The 1st baronet, the Hon. Sir Hew Dalrymple, 3rd son of 1st Viscount Stair, sat as M.P. for North Berwick in the Scotch Parliament, and was subsequently Lord President of Session, and one of the Commissioners appointed to arrange the Articles of Union. Sir Hew, the 2nd baronet, was M.P. for co. Haddington, and King's Remembrancer in the Exchequer for Scotland. The 3rd baronet, Sir Hew, M.P. for Midlothian, assumed the additional surname of Hamilton, and the 4th baronet assumed the surname of Hamilton after Dalrymple [*see* E. Stair, colls.], while the 8th baronet assumed it before that of Dalrymple.

DALYELL, Creation (N.S.) 1685, of the Binns.   [Dormant 1935.]

Sir JAMES BRUCE WILKIE-DALYELL, 9th *Baronet, d.* Dec. 12th, 1935.

Grandson of 9th Baronet—Thomas (Tam) Dalyell, *MP* (The Binns, Linlithgow) *b.* Aug. 9th, 1932; probable heir to the baronetcy as heir of tailzie, son of the late Lt.-Col. Gordon Loch, CIE, DL, JP, and his wife Eleanor Isabel (da. of Sir James Bruce Wilkie-Dalyell, 9th Bt.), who in 1938, both assumed the surname and arms of Dalyell of the Binns (officially recognized by Lord Lyon King of Arms); ed. at Eton, and King's Coll., Camb.; Dep. Dir. of Studies, Ship-School, Dunrea 1961-62, Sec. of Labour Standing Conference on the Sciences 1962-64, PPS to Min. of Housing and Local Govt. 1964-66; PPS to Leader of House of Commons 1967-68, and to Sec. of State for Social Security 1968-70; a Member of Public Accounts Cttee., House of Commons 1962-65, and of House of Commons Select Cttee. on Science and Technology 1966-68; Chm. of Parl. Labour Party Foreign Affairs Group 1973, Vice-Chm. of Parl. Labour Party 1974; a Member of Select Cttee. on Weath Tax, and of Select Cttee. of Scrutiny on European Legislation; Political Columnist of *New Scientist* since 1968; MP for W. Lothian (*Lab.*) since 1962: *m.* 1963, the Hon. Kathleen Mary Agnes Wheatley, only da. of Baron Wheatley (Life Baron), and has issue living, Gordon Wheatley, *b.* 1965,—Moira Eleanor, *b.* 1968.

Collateral Branches living.
(*Males and Females in remainder*)

Descendants of George Falconar of Carlowrie, W. Lothian, el. son of Jane Stewart (who *m.* David Falconar of Carlowrie and *d.* 1837), da. and heir of Magdalen (who *m.* Robert Stewart of Binny, W. Lothian), da. of 3rd Bt.:—

Granddaughter of the late George Mercer Falconar, 2nd son of George Falconar of Carlowrie (ante) [see L. Falconer of Halkerton].

Grandchildren of the late Helen Jane (who m. John Monsey Collyer of Gimingham, Norfolk, and d. 1919), yr. da. of George Falconer of Carlowrie (ante):—
Issue of the late Brig.-Gen. John Johnston Collyer, CB, CMG, DSO, b. 1870, d. 1941: m. 1903, Hilda Rochford, da. of Michael Henry Quinn:—
Nellie Rochford, b. 1904.——Freda Falconar, b. 1906.

Issue of the late Roger Messenger Monsey Collyer, b. 1874, d. 19—: m. 1909, Maud Winifred, da. of the late Byron Noel:—
Helen Nova, b. 1911,—Elizabeth Maud, b. 1913,—Ruth Amy, b. 1914,—Winifred Noel, b. 1918,—Judith, b. 1921.

This Baronetcy was created with a special remainder " to heirs male and of tailzie." The right of the 9th baronet, Sir James Bruce Wilkie-Dalyell of the Binns, to be placed on the Official Roll of the Baronetage was admitted by the Baronetage Committee of the Privy Council on July 1st, 1914.

DARELL, Creation (G.B.) 1795, of Richmond Hill, Surrey.

Sir JEFFREY LIONEL DARELL, *M.C.*, 8th *Baronet*, only son of the late Col. Guy Marsland Darell, M.C., 3rd son of 5th Baronet ; *b.* Oct. 2nd, 1919 ; *s.* his cousin, *Sir* WILLIAM OSWALD, 1959; ed. at Eton; Brig. (ret.) Coldstream Guards, and patron of one living; commanded 1st Batn. Coldstream Guards 1957-9, AAG, War Office 1959-61, Coll. Comd., RMA Sandhurst 1961-64, Regimental Lt.-Col. Comdg. Coldstream Guards 1964, and Comdg. 56th (London) Inf. Bde. (TA) 1965-67; Vice-Pres. of Regular Commns Board 1968-70, Comdt. Mons Officer Cadet Sch. 1970-72; ADC to HM 1973-74; 1939-45 War (MC): *m.* 1953, Bridget Mary, da. of Maj. Gen. Sir Allen Henry Shafto Adair, KCVO, CB, DSO, MC, 6th Bt., and has issue.

Arms—Azure, a lion rampant or ducally crowned argent. **Crest**—Out of a ducal coronet or a Saracen's head couped at the shoulders proper, bearded sable, wreathed about the temples or and azure, on his head a cap of the last fretty argent tasselled or, turned up ermine.

Residence—55, Green St., W1. *Club*—Guards'.

Son living—GUY JEFFREY ADAIR, *b.* June 8th, 1961.

Daughters living—Katherine Mary, *b.* 1954.——Camilla Viola, *b.* 1956.

Sister living—Cynthia Mary, *b.* 1916: *m.* 1940, Michael Webster Harrap, and has issue living, Simon Richard, *b.* 1941,—John Michael Darell, *b.* 1943,—Giles Thresher, *b.* 1948. *Residence*, Marsh House, Bentley, nr. Farnham, Surrey.

Daughters living of 6th Baronet—Margaret Eleanor Phyllis: *m.* 1930, Helmut William Bruno Schröder, who *d.* 1969, and has issue living, Bruno Lionel, *b.* 1933,—Charmaine Brenda, *b.* 1935.——Nancy Brenda (*Lady Gordon Lennox*): *m.* 1931, Lt.-Gen. Sir George Charles Gordon Lennox, KBE, CB, CVO, DSO [*see* D. Richmond, colls.]. *Residence*, Gordon Castle, Fochabers, Morayshire.

Sister living of 7th Baronet—Elizabeth Joy, *b.* 1913 : *m.* 1934 (marriage dissolved 1945), Peter Julian Clive [Muir-Mackenzie, By.], and has issue living, Colin George, *b.* 1936; ed. at Eton. *Residence*, 58, Queen's Gate, SW7.

The 1st baronet, Sir Lionel Darell, sat as M.P. for Lyme Regis 1780-84, and for Heydon 1784-1802. The 2nd baronet, Sir Harry Verelst Darell, was extensively engaged in commerce in Bengal. Sir Lionel Darell, 5th Baronet, was High Sheriff of Gloucestershire 1887. The 6th baronet, Col. Sir Lionel Edward Darell, D.S.O., 1st Life Guards, was a Co. Councillor, Co. Alderman, and High Sheriff of Gloucestershire 1924, and Hon. Col. 5th Batn. Gloucestershire Regt. 1936.

DASHWOOD, Creation (E.) 1684, of Kirtlington Park, Oxfordshire.

Sir RICHARD JAMES DASHWOOD, 9th, *Baronet*; *b.* Feb. 14th, 1950; *s.* his father, *Sir* HENRY GEORGE MASSY, 1972; ed. at Eton; Lt. 14th/20th Kings Hussars.

Arms—Argent, on a fesse double cotised gules three gryphons' heads erased or. **Crest**—A griffin's head erminois, erased gules. **Supporters**—On either side a male gryphon argent, gorged with a collar flory counter-flory gules.

Residence—Ledwell House, Sandford St. Martin, Oxon.

Nothing is inaccessible to virtue.

Sister living—Emma Victoria Mildred, *b.* 1955.

Uncle living (son of 7th baronet)—JOHN ARTHUR, *b.* July 17th, 1910: *m.* 1952, Patricia Maud, only da. of Frederick Burrows. *Residence*, Mombasa, Kenya.

Great-Aunt living (daughter of 6th baronet)—Muriel Helen, *b.* 1892. *Residence*, The Old Vicarage, Moulsford, Wallingford, Berks.

Widow living of 8th Baronet—SUSAN MARY (*Lady Dashwood*), (Ledwell House, Sandford St. Martin, Oxon.), el. da. of the late Maj. Victor Montgomerie-Charrington, of Grey Court, King's Sutton, Northants.: *m.* 1948, Sir Henry George Massy Dashwood, 8th Bt., who *d.* 1972.

Collateral Branches living.

Issue of the late Arthur Paul Dashwood, OBE, 3rd son of 6th baronet, b. 1882, d. 1964: m. 1919, Edmée Elizabeth Monica (" E. M. Delafield ", novelist), who d. 1943, da. of the late Count Henry Philip Ducarel de la Pasture:—
Rosamund Margaret, b. 1923: m. 1948, Leslie Harold Truelove, MRCP, late RNZAF, 4825, Drummond Drive, Vancouver 8, B.C., and has issue living, Paul Alexander, b. 1948,—Leslie Simon, b. 1950,—Patrick, b. 1955,—Michael Andrew, b. 1961.

Grandson of the late Thomas Alexander Dashwood, el. son of Thomas Alexander Dashwood, el. son of Thomas John Dashwood, BCS, and of the late Thomas Dashwood, 2nd son of 2nd baronet:—
Issue of the late Thomas Henry Knyvett Dashwood, b. 1876, d. 1929   m. 1910, Florence Kathleen, who d. 1939 (having m. 2ndly, 1937, Capt. John Maurice Figgis, of Farnborough Grange, near Banbury), el. da. of the late Thomas Frederick Hugh Smith, F.R.C.S., of Braeside, Farningham, near Dartford, Kent:—
Thomas John Russell, OBE, b. 1911; ed. at Wellington Coll., and Brasenose Coll., Oxford (MA); late Civil Ser. Commr., Nigeria; OBE (Civil) 1952; Sec. Public Schs. Club 1955-68, and of Roy. Motor Yacht Club 1968-69: m. 1936, Edith Mary, da. of the late William Thomas, of Newport, Monmouthshire. Residence, Summersbury Hall, Shalford, Surrey. Club, East India, Sports and Public Schools.

Grandson of the late Alexander John Dashwood, el. son of Alexander Wilton Dashwood, yr. son of Thomas Dashwood (ante):—
Issue of the late Alexander Thomas Dashwood, b. 1855, d. 1911 : m. 1904, Annie (who d. 1941, having m. 2ndly, 1915, Albert Banister), youngest da. of Henry Morris:—
Alexander John, b. 1905 ; is Capt. R.A. ; European War 1939-45 in Middle East : m. 1947, Mary Whitburn, da. of the late Reginald Frank Thorne, of Southborough, near Tunbridge Wells, and has issue living, Alexander Thomas Whitburn, b. 1950,—Jeremy Charles Whitburn, b. 1957,—Sophia Ann Whitburn, b. 1954.   Residence,

Grandchildren of the late George Lionel Dashwood, yst. son of Alexander Wilton Dashwood (ante):—
Issue of the late Sir Henry Thomas Alexander Dashwood, b. 1878, d. 1959 : m. 1909, Norah Creina Bruce, who d. 1948, da. of Henry Arthur Whately, of Midford Castle, Bath :—
Robert Henry Nevile, b. 1921 ; ed. at Harrow, and at Magdalene Coll., Camb. (B.A. 1942, M.A. 1946) ; formerly Capt. R.A. ; is a J.P. for Northants : m. 1959, Ruth Mary, da. of Dr. W. B. R. Monteith, of Purston Manor, Brackley, Northants, and has issue living, David Henry William, b. 1960,—Ian Bruce Robert, b. 1962.   Residence, Farthinghoe Lodge Farm, Farthinghoe, Brackley, Northants.——Norah Creina Frances, b. 1910: m. 1958, William Nell.   Residence, Mare de la Font, Blanes, Gerona, Spain.

Grandchildren of the late Rev. Robert Lewes Dashwood, yst. son of the Rev. Samuel Francis Dashwood (infra):—
Issue of the late Maj. Claude Burrard Lewes Dashwood, b. 1872, d. (of wounds in action during 1914-18 War) 1916: m. 1907, Letitia, who d. 1963 (she m. 2ndly 1929, Capt. Thomas Harry Lockley Turner, late The Buffs, who d. 1948), el. da. of Henry Le Sueur, ISO, JP, of La Plaisance, Wynberg, Cape Colony:—
Robert Armand Lewes (48, Foxwood Av., Mudeford, Christchurch, Hants.), b. 1916; ed. at Canford; 1939-45 War as Capt. Army Catering Corps: m. 1938, Peggy Violet, who d. 1963, only da. of Herbert Reeves, of Bournemouth, and has issue living, Ian Burrard Lewes (Stanford Lodge, Empire Av., Hout Bay, Cape, S. Africa), b. 1947: m. 1968, Marlene Dolores, el. da. of Pieter Kruger, of Sea Point, Cape, and has issue living, Paul Burrard Lewes b. 1972, Annemarie b. 1969,—Anne, b. 1956.——Joyce Viola (Flat 2, 184, West Hill, Putney, SW15), b. 1908: m. 1935, Harry Vernon de Burgh, who d. 1960.——Sheila Ianthe, b. 1909.   Residence, 1A, The Beacon, Exmouth, Devon.——Diana Mary, b. 1913: m. 1936, Ronald Hugh Foster, and has issue living, William Ronald (10, Croft Rd., Christchurch, Hants.) b. 1940: m. 1971, Susan Mary, da. of Garfield Wilkins, of 5, Orchard Av., Cambridge. Residence, Little Haven, Mudeford Quay, Christchurch, Hants.

Issue of the late Capt. Sidney Lewes Dashwood, MBE, b. 1882, d. 1966: m. 1922, Joan, who d. 1963, da. of Sir Sidney Gerald Burrard, KCSI, 7th Bt.:—
Mary Edith Burrard, b. 1923: m. 1946, John Harry Walrond Simmons, MBE, of Selva, Lincombe Lane, Boar's Hill, Oxford, and has issue living, Geoffrey Philip, b. 1952,—Roland Paul, b. 1957,—Rosemary Jane, b. 1949,—Pamela Anne, b. 1959.

Granddaughters of the late Rev. Samuel Vere Dashwood, only son of Samuel Francis Dashwood, great grandson of Richard Dashwood, yst. son of 1st baronet:—
Issue of the late Edward Vere Dashwood, b. 1846, d. 1919: m. 1888, Laura Frederica Penelope who d. 1931, da. of the late Major Edmund Crofts (Roy. Welch Fusiliers), of Merrieleas Eastleigh :—
Diana Penelope, b. 1891: m. 1923, Maj. Alexander James Fraser, MC, Roy. Berks Regt., who d. 1962, and has issue living, Alexander Hugh (Rose Brae, Upper Colwall, Malvern, Worcs.), b. 1924; Maj. (ret.) Duke of Edinburgh's R. Regt.: m. 1949, Dorothy Mabel, da. of Reginald, Edward Mitchell, of Seend, Wilts, and has issue living, Penelope Angela b. 1950: m. 1974, James Howard, Fiona b. 1953,—James Gerald (Joanda, Gt. Bedwyn, Marlborough), b. 1929: m. 1968, Anne, da. of the late Capt. R. A. Morton. Residence, Seymour Lodge, Seend, Melksham, Wilts.——Iris Laura, MBE (7, Inverleith Terr., Edinburgh 3), b. 1893; MBE (Civil) 1948: m. 1921, James Christopher Bull, who d. 1972, and has issue living, Nicholas Vere (12, Lomond Rd., Edinburgh, EH5 3JR), b. 1928: m. 1962, Cynthia Mary Sefton, da. of the late James Sefton Bickers, of Hovingham, Yorks., and has issue living, Christopher Martin Sefton b. 1967, Diana Mary Sefton b. 1964.

Descendants of the late Henry Dashwood, MP, grandson of Lt.-Col. George Dashwood (who assumed the surname and arms of Peyton, and was cr. a Baronet 1776), brother of 1st baronet (The male line, now ext., was in special remainder to the Baronetcy.)
See Peyton, Bt., (ext).

Alderman George Dashwood, of London, undertook, with others, to farm the whole revenue of the kingdom of Ireland temp. Charles II.   He afterwards, with others, farmed the whole revenues of excise and hearth money in England, and was a Commissioner of Revenue till his death in 1682.   A patent of baronetcy was granted to him, but as he did not take it out, his widow was given the precedence of a baronet's widow, while a new patent of baronetcy was granted to his son with special remainder, in default of male issue, to the male descendants of his father.   The 1st baronet of this creation was M.P. for Banbury, the 2nd was M.P. for Oxfordshire, and the 3rd M.P. for Woodstock.   Alderman Francis Dashwood, of London, elder brother of Alderman George Dashwood (ante), was father of Sir Francis Dashwood, 1st baronet, of West Wycombe.

DASHWOOD, Creation (G.B.) 1707, of West Wycombe, Buckinghamshire.

Sir FRANCIS JOHN VERNON HEREWARD DASHWOOD, 11th *Baronet*, and Premier Baronet of Great Britain; *b.* Aug. 7th, 1925; *s.* his father, *Sir* JOHN LINDSAY, *CVO*, 1966; ed. at Eton, at Ch. Ch., Oxford (MA) and Harvard Business Sch.; a Member of Lloyd's; a Co. Councillor of Bucks. 1951-52: *m.* 1957, Victoria Ann Elizabeth Gwynne, only da. of the late Maj. John Frederick Foley, Baron de Rutzen, Welsh Guards [see Foley-Philipps, Bt.], and has issue.

Arms—Argent, on a fesse double cotised gules, three griffins' heads erased or. *Crest*—A griffin's head erased per fesse, erminois and gules.

Residence—West Wycombe Park, Bucks. *Club*—Brooks's.

For the Great Charter.

Son living—EDWARD JOHN FRANCIS, *b.* Sept. 25th, 1964.

Daughters living—Emily Jane, *b.* 1958.——Georgina Helen, *b.* 1960.——Caroline Sarah, *b.* 1962.

Brother living—John (27, Matham Rd., East Molesey, Surrey), *b.* 1929; ed. at Eton and at Ch. Ch., Oxford: *m.* 1st, 1959 (m. diss. 1964), Susan Boyter Duncombe, el. da. of Maj. Ernest Duncombe Shafto, of Little Beamishe, Aldeburgh, Suffolk; 2ndly, 1965, Harriet Louise, el. da. of J. P. Spencer, of Norbury Park, Mickleham, Surrey, and has issue living (by 2nd m.), Thomas, *b.* 1973,—Rebecca Louise, *b.* 1971.

Sister living—Maud Helen Sarah (*Baroness Aberdare*), *b.* 1924: *m.* 1946, the 4th Baron Aberdare, of 1, St. Peter's Sq., W6 9AE.

Daugher living of 9th Baronet—Ida Helen Lindsay (Clayford, Dulverton, Som.), *b.* 1903.

Widow living of 10th Baronet—HELEN MOIRA (*Dowager Lady Dashwood*) (10, Cumberland House, Kensington High St., W8), da. of the late Lt.-Col. Vernon Eaton, R. Canadian Horse Artillery: *m.* 1922, Sir John Lindsay Dashwood, CVO, 10th baronet, who *d.* 1966.

The 1st baronet was knighted 1702, and sat as M.P. for Winchilsea. The 2nd baronet became 8th Baron LeDespencer in right of his mother, and was successively head of the War Office, Chancellor of the Exchequer, and Postmaster-General. He died without male issue, and the barony fell in abeyance. The 3rd baronet—who was half-brother to the 2nd baronet—assumed the additional surname of King. The 6th baronet sat as M.P. for Bucks (*L*) 1832-5, and for Wycombe 1837-62.

DAVID, Creation (U.K.) 1911, of Bombay. [Extinct 1964.]
Sir PERCIVAL VICTOR DAVID EZEKIEL DAVID, 2nd and last *Baronet*.

Daughter living of 2nd Baronet—Katherine Viola Monica, *b.* 1914: *m.* 1952, William Frederick Taylor. *Residence*, 35, Monkridge, Haslemere Rd., Crouch End Hill, N.8.

Sister living of 2nd Baronet—Louise Leah, *b.* 1882: *m.* 1900, David Sassoon Shellim. *Residence*,

Widow living of 2nd Baronet—SHEILA JANE YORKE (*Lady David*) (53, Gordon Sq., W.C.1.), da. of the late Arthur Yorke Hardy: *m.* 1953, as his 2nd wife, Sir Percival Victor David Ezekiel David, 2nd baronet, who *d.* 1964, when the title became ext.

FERGUSON DAVIE, Creation (U.K.) 1847, of Creedy, Devonshire.

Rev. Sir (ARTHUR) PATRICK FERGUSON DAVIE, *TD*, 5th *Baronet*, son of the late Lt.-Col. Arthur Francis Ferguson Davie, CIE, DSO, 3rd son of 3rd Baronet; *b.* March 17th, 1909; *s.* his uncle, *Sir* WILLIAM JOHN, 1947; ed. at Wellington Coll., and at Lincoln Coll., Oxford (MA); an Hon. Chap. to Bishop of Exeter 1949-73: *m.* 1949, Iris Dawn CABLE-BULLER, da. of Capt. Michael Francis Buller [B. Cable (ext.)], and has issue.

Arms—Quarterly; 1st and 4th, argent, a chevron sable between three mullets pierced gules; 2nd and 3rd, azure, three cinquefoils or, upon a chief of the last a lion passant, gules, *Crests*—1st, a pascal lamb reguardant argent; 2nd, a kingfisher wings elevated proper, in the beak a branch of olive vert. fructed or.

Residences—Creedy Park, Crediton, Devon; Skalatos Klepini, Kyrenia, Cyprus.

Under the auspices of Christ.

Son living—ANTONY FRANCIS (c/o Grindlays Bank, 13, St. James's Sq., SW1), *b.* March 23rd, 1952.

Collateral Branches living.

Issue of the late Sir Henry Augustus Ferguson Davie, CB, 2nd son of 3rd baronet, *b.* 1865, *d.* 1946: *m.* 1897, Adeline, who *d.* 1951, da. of the late Thomas Holdsworth Newman [Newman, Bt., *cr.* 1836, colls.] :—

Evelyn Sybil, *b.* 1901. *Residence*, Upton House, Huntsham, Tiverton, Devon.

Issue of the late Edward Cruger Ferguson Davie, 4th son of 3rd baronet, *b.* 1868, *d.* 1948: *m.* 1905, Blanche Evelyn, who *d.* 1959, da. of the late William Wyndham Hasler, of Aldingbourne House, Sussex:—

John, *b.* 1906 ; ed. at Winchester : *m.* 1942, Joan Zoë, da. of the late Raymond Hoole, of Vancouver, BC, and has issue living, Michael (51, Swaffield Rd., SW18), *b.* 1944: *m.* 1968, Jean, da. of Douglas John Macbeth, of Bowdon, Ches., and has issue living, James Michael *b.* 1970,—Julian Anthony (Flat 10, Melton Drive, Edgbaston, Birmingham 15), *b.* 1950. *Residence,* El Paraiso, Calle San Antonio, Puerto de la Cruz, Tenerife.

Grandchildren of the late Henry Herrick Ferguson-Davie (*b.* 1869) (infra) :—
Issue of the late Henry Herrick Ferguson-Davie, *b.* 1894, *d.* 1952 : *m.* 1919, Julia Victoria, da. of John Stokes, of London:—

Henry Herrick, *b.* 1920: *m.* 1st, 1941 (marriage dissolved 1943), Joyce Sanders, of Brooklyn, Baltimore, U.S.A.; 2ndly, 1951, Anna Marie, da. of Bender Clarke, of Gambrillo, Maryland, U.S.A., and has issue living, (by 1st marriage) Henry Herrick *b.* 194-,—(by 2nd marriage) Anna Louise, *b.* 1952. *Residence,*

Issue of the late Charles Francis Ferguson-Davie, *b.* 1898, *d.* 1967: *m.* 1924, Alice Clarke, who *d.* 1968, da. of Henry Newman, of Potterne, Wilts.:—

Muriel Frances, *b.* 1926: *m.* 1st, 1948 (m. diss. 1952), Basil Anthony King; 2ndly, 1952, Bernard, William Pearce, of 75, Nicoll Rd., Brighton Beach, Durban, S. Africa, and has issue living (by 2nd m.), Michael Stephen, *b.* 1953: *m.* 1975, Judith Melany McClelland,—Geoffrey, *b.* 1956,—Robert Andrew, *b.* 1959.

Grandchildren of the late Capt. William Carey Ferguson-Davie (infra):—
Issue of the late William George Michael Ferguson-Davie, *b.* 1923, *d.* 1974: *m.* 1953, Margaret Mary (635, Granville Cres., Richmond, BC, Canada), da. of the late Capt. William J. Fowler:—

Christopher Mark, *b.* 1956.——Deirdre Ann, *b.* 1955.——Jean Elizabeth, *b.* 1961.

Granddaughter of the late Henry Herrick Ferguson-Davie, 2nd son of the late Rev. Charles Robert Ferguson-Davie, 4th son of 1st baronet:—
Issue of the late Capt. William Carey Ferguson-Davie, *b.* 1900, *d.* 1975: *m.* 1922, Katherine (4, Dundela Av., Sandycove, co. Dublin), da. of the late William Robertson Kay, of Sutton, co. Dublin:—

Jean Anne, *b.* 1932: *m.* 1956, George Hellyer-Crawford, of Anglesea, Killiney Hill Rd., Killiney, co. Dublin, and has issue living, Anne Katherine, *b.* 1959,—Alison Jane, *b.* 1963.

Frances Juliana Davie (only surviving sister of Sir John Davie, 9th baronet (cr. 1641), and niece and heiress of Sir Humphrey Phineas Davie, 10th and last baronet, who *d.* 1846): *m.* 1823, Gen. Henry Robert Ferguson. In the following year the baronetcy was revived in Gen. Ferguson's favour, who had assumed by Roy. licence 1846 the additional surname and arms of Davie after his patronymic.

d'Avigdor-Goldsmid, see Goldsmid.

DAVIS, Creation (U.K.) 1946, of Barrington Hall, co. Cambridge.

Sir JOHN GILBERT DAVIS, 3rd *Baronet*; *b.* Aug. 17th, 1936; *s.* his father, *Sir* GILBERT, 1973; ed. at Oundle Sch., and RNC Dartmouth: *m.* 1960, Elizabeth Margaret, el. da. of Robert Smith Turnbull, of Falkirk, and has issue.

Arms,—Quarterly; 1st and 4th, per saltire sable and argent, two pierced mullets or in pale and a dexter and sinister dragon's wing in fesse gules, *Davis*; 2nd and 3rd, per fesse embattled gules and argent in chief three castles or, *Terrett.* Crest,—In front of a spear erect the shaft couped argent, and in front of a vol of dragon's wings three pierced mullets as in the arms.

Residence—3097, The Boulevard, Montreal H3Y 1R8, Canada.

Son living—RICHARD CHARLES, *b.* April 11th, 1970.

Daughters living—Wendy Elizabeth, *b.* 1962,—Linda Mary, *b.* 1964.

Sister living—Ann, *b.* 1931: *m.* 1956, John Robert Whatley, and has issue living, Mark Gilbert Edward *b.* 1958,—Alison Jane, *b.* 1959. *Residence,* Rest Harrow, Ballfield Rd., Godalming, Surrey.

Uncle living (son of 1st baronet)—Bernard, *b.* 1908: *m.* 1944, Bridget Nora, da. of Frederick John Chapman Downing. *Residence,* 54, Cadogan Sq., SW1 X0JW.

Aunt living (daughter of 1st baronet)—Margaret, *b.* 1904: *m.* 1935, Col. Ernest O. A. Singer, RAMC, who *d.* 1957. *Residence,* 119, Barkston Gardens, SW5.

Mother living—Kathleen Ellinor (Rest Harrow, Ballfield Rd., Frith Hill, Godalming, Surrey, GV7 2HE), da. of Sidney Deacon Ford: *m.* 1st, 1927, (m. diss. 1974), Gilbert Davis (who succeeded as 2nd baronet 1950, and *d.* 1973); 2ndly, 1949, Frederick Cyril George White, who *d.* 1960.

The 1st baronet, Sir (Arthur) Charles Davis (son of George John Davis), formerly of Stone Castle, Greenhithe, Kent, was an Underwriting Member of Lloyd's, High Sheriff of Kent 1934-5, and Lord Mayor of London 1945-46.

Davis-Goff, see Goff.

Davson, see Glyn (cr. 1927).

DAWSON, Creation (U.K.) 1920, of Edgwarebury, co. Middlesex.

Sir HUGH TREVOR DAWSON, *C.B.E.*,
R.N., 2nd *Baronet* ; *b.* Jan. 17th, 1893 ; *s.* his
father, *Sir* (ARTHUR) TREVOR 1931 ; is Com.;
C.B.E. (Civil) 1950 : *m.* 1918, Vera Anne
Loch, da. of the late Major Sir Frederick
Loch Halliday, C.I.E., M.V.O., and has issue.

Arms—Azure, on a chevron ermine between **three**
bird bolts argent a rose gules, slipped and leaved between
two daws respectant proper.   Crest—Out of a naval crown
or a daw proper.

Residence—Casina Lodge, 8, Park Village West,
NW1.   *Club*—United Service.

Son living—HUGH HALLIDAY TREVOR. *b.* June
6th, 1931; ed. at Harrow, and RMA, late Maj. Scots
Guards: *m.* 1955, Caroline Jane, only da. of William
Antony Acton [*see* V. Cowdray, colls.], and has issue
living, Hugh Michael Trevor, *b.* 1956,—Nicholas
Antony Trevor, *b.* 1957. *Residence*, 3, Mulberry Walk,
SW3. *Clubs*, White's, Pratt's, Bath, Turf, Guards',
Royal Aero, Buck's, City of London, MCC.

Daughters living—Ursula Anne Trevor, *b.* 1919.—
Avice Louise Trevor *b.* 1923: *m.* 1942, Maj. Edwyn
Inigo Lloyd Mostyn, MC, Scots Guards, from whom she
obtained a divorce 1964 [*see* B. Mostyn, colls.].—

Deeds not words.

Patricia Elinor Trevor (twin), *b.* 1923: *m.* 1st, 1943,
Maj. Raymond Alexander Carnegie, late Scots Guards,
from whom she obtained a divorce 1953 [*see* E. Southesk]; 2ndly, 1953, John Maxwell Menzies
and has issue living, (by 1st m.) [*see* E. Southesk],—(by 2nd m.) Miranda Jane, *b.* 1954,—
Sarah Jane, *b.* 1955,—Katherine Patricia, *b.* 1960. *Residence*, Kames, Duns, Berwickshire.

Sister living—Eva May, *b.* 1899: *m.* 1917, Brigadier Ralph Micklem, CMG, CBE, late RE, and has
issue living, Hugh Ralph (Tellisford, Slade Oak Lane, Gerrards Cross, Bucks.), *b.* 1918; ed. at
Winchester; formerly Capt. York and Lancaster Regt.: *m.* 1954, Joan Elizabeth, da. of the late
Albert J. Brown, of Trebane, Stanmore, Middx., and has issue living, Peter Guy Ralph *b.* 1955,
Catherine Eve Jane *b.* 1957. *Residence*, Heriots, Stanmore, Middx.

The 1st baronet, Com. Sir (Arthur) Trevor Dawson, R.N. (son of the late Hugh Dawson, Bar.-at-
law), was a Director and Sup. of Ordnance of Vickers, Ltd., Chm. of their Armament and Shipbuilding
Management Board, and Vice-Principal of Council of Imperial So. of Knights Bachelor.

DAWSON, Creation (U.K.) 1929, of Appleton Roebuck, co. York. [Extinct 1974.]

(*Sir*) LAWRENCE SAVILLE DAWSON, 2nd and last *Baronet.*

Daughter living of 2nd Baronet—Barbara Jane, *b.* 1940.

Daughter living of 1st Baronet—Joan Scriven, *b.* 1914. *Residence*, Nun-Appleton, York.

Widow living of 2nd Baronet—RUTH (Oldholme, Gorey, Jersey), da. of the late John Smith Baxter,
Harrogate: *m.* 1971, as his 2nd wife, Sir Lawrence Saville Dawson, 2nd baronet (but did
not use title), who *d.* 1974, when the title became ext.

DE BATHE, Creation (U.K.) 1801, of Kingstown Cashel, co. Meath.   [Extinct 1941.]

Sir CHRISTOPHER ALBERT DE BATHE, *R.A.F. Vol. Reserve*, 6th
and last *Baronet ; d.* (killed on active ser. during European War) 1941.

Daughter living of 6th Baronet—Charlotte Louise, *b.* 1934: *m.* 1967, Arthur Cyril Bryan, of 26,
South End Row, W8.

Half-Sister living of 6th Baronet—Bridget. *b.* 1922: *m.* 1942, Capt. Timothy John Gurney,
Coldstream Guards, and has issue living, Christopher, *b.* 1950,—Jeannine Mary, *b.* 1943: *m.*
1964, John Richard Boyle [*see* E. Cork, colls.], Lucinda Marjorie *b.* 1946: *m.* 1965 (m. diss. 1972),
Capt. Graham Morison Vere Nicoll, Welsh Guards [*see* Madden, Bt.]. *Residence*, The White
House, Hare St., Buntingford, Herts.

Widows living of 5th and 6th Baronets—DEBORAH (*Lady de Bathe*), da. of Samuel
Warschowsky, and formerly wife of Dr. Poul Henius: *m.* 1931, as his second wife, Sir Hugo
Gerald de Bathe, 5th baronet, who *d.* 1940.——EDNA (*Lady de Bathe*), da. of the late Arthur
Terrell, of Melbourne, Australia: *m.* 1932, Sir Christopher Albert de Bathe, 6th baronet, Pilot
Officer R.A.F. Vol. Reserve, who *d.* (killed on active ser. during European War) 1941, when the
title became ext.

DEBENHAM, Creation (U.K.) 1931, of Bladen, co Dorset.

Sir GILBERT RIDLEY DEBENHAM, 3rd *Baronet;* b. June 28th, 1906; s. his brother, *Sir* PIERS KENRICK, 1964; ed. at Eton, and at Trin. Coll., Camb. (BChir): *m.* 1935, Violet Mary (Mollie), el. da. of the late His Honour Judge (George Herbert) Higgins, and has issue.

Arms—Sable, a bend cottised between two crescents or. Crest—In front of a garb or, a sickle erect proper, the blade pointing to the sinister.

Residence—Tonerspuddle Farm, Dorchester, Dorset.

Sons living—GEORGE ANDREW, b. April 10th, 1938; ed. at Bryanston, and Trin. Coll., Camb. (BA): *m.* 1969, Penelopè Jane, da. of John David Armishaw Carter, and has issue living, Thomas Adam, b. 1971,—Anna Rose, b. 1972.——William Michael, b. 1940; ed. at Bryanston, and Trin. Coll., Camb. (BA); MSC: *m.* 1974, Gunnel Birgitta, da. of Holger Elis Valfrid Holmgreen.——Paul Edward, b. 1942; ed. at Bryanston, and Trin. Coll., Camb. (BA, MB, BChir); MRCP: *m.* 1968, Jennifer Mary, MB, ChB, da. of the late G. W. Rees, and has issue living, Edward James, b. 1970,—Michael John, b. 1973.

Daughter living—Virginia Mary, b. 1936: *m.* 1960, Graham Leslie Nicol, of 53, Upper Park Rd., NW3, and has issue living, Stephen Leslie, b. 1961,—Alan Leslie b. 1966,—Lucy Jean, b. 1963.

Daughters living of 2nd Baronet—Caroline Susan, b. 1930: *m.* 1954, Francis Patrick Neill, son of the late Sir Thomas Neill, and has issue living, Timothy Piers Patrick, b. 1955,—Robin Charles Richard, b. 1956,—Jonathan Francis Kenrick, b. 1960,—Matthew Piers Thomas, b. 1965,—Harriet Susan Anne, b. 1962,—Emma Charlotte Angela, b. 1967. *Residence*, 8, Milborne Grove, SW10.——Anne Charlotte, b. 1932: *m.* 1962, Peter Muir Horsfield, of 24, Liverpool Rd., King-ston Hill, Surrey, and has issue living, Andrew Piers, b. 1963,—Charles Peter, b. 1964,—Thomas Martin, b. 1966.

Brother living—Martin Ridley, b. 1909; ed. at Eton, and at Trin. Coll., Camb.: *m.* 1937, Beatrice Sydney, da. of the late Ven. Harry Sydney Radcliffe, and has issue living, James Martin Robert, b. 1951,—Susanna Elizabeth, b. 1943: *m.* 1964, Alexander Surtees Chancellor [see Paget Bt., cr. 1886]. *Residence*, East Farm, Affpuddle, Dorset.

Sisters living—Marjorie Cecily, b. (Dec.) 1893.——Hester Mary (of Hollingden, Church Rd. Woldingham, Surrey), b. 1895: *m.* 1937, Wolmer Narlow, who d. 1963.——Cecil Audrey (43, High St., Amersham, Bucks.), b. 1906: *m.* 1953, Charles Robert Bielby, who d. 1967.

The 1st baronet, Sir Ernest Ridley Debenham (son of the late Frank Debenham, of Fitzjohns Avenue, Hampstead, N.W.3), was Chm. of Debenhams, Ltd.

DE BUNSEN, Creation (U.K.) 1919, of Abbey Lodge, Hanover Gate, Metropolitan Borough of St. Marylebone. [Extinct 1932.]

Rt. Hon. Sir MAURICE WILLIAM ERNEST DE BUNSEN, *G.C.M.G., G.C.V.O., C.B.*, 1st and last *Baronet.*

Daughters living of 1st Baronet—Hilda Violet Helena (*Lady Salisbury-Jones*), b. 1900: *m.* 1st, 1921, Major Richard Guy Cecil Yerburgh, O.B.E., Irish Guards, who d. 1926 ; 2ndly, 1931, Maj.-Gen. Sir (Arthur) Guy Salisbury-Jones, G.C.V.O., C.M.G., C.B.E., M.C., late Coldstream Guards, and has issue living, (by 1st m.) John Maurice Armstrong (Barwhillanty, Parton, Castle Douglas), b. 1923; late Capt. I.G.: *m.* 1973, Ann Jean Mary, da. of Peter Maclaren, of Brooklands, Crocketford, Kircudbrightshire,—Oscar Guy de Bunsen (41, Porchester Terr., W2 3TS), b. 1925 (m. diss. 1970), Alicia, da. of the late Horace Marshall, of Grimston Lodge, Tadcaster,—(by 2nd m.) Raymond Arthur, b. 1933; late 2nd Lt. Coldm. Gds.,—Mariette Helena (*Baroness Saye and Sele*), b. 1936: *m.* 1958, the 21st Baron Saye and Sele. *Residence*, Mill Down, Hambledon, Portsmouth, Hants.——Cicely Elizabeth, b. 1902, a JP for Dunbarton-shire: *m.* 1927, Lt.-Col. Archibald Vivian Campbell Douglas of Mains, JP, late Scots Gds. [B. Swansea], and has issue living, Jean Violet (*Hon. Mrs. David H. Erskine*), b. 1928: *m.* 1953, the Hon. David Hervey Erskine, of Felsham House, Felsham, Bury St. Edmunds, [see E. Mar and Kellie], Catherine Hilda, b. 1929: *m.* 1955, Peter Assheton Joynson, of The Glassert, Aberfoyle, By Stirling. *Residence*, Laraich, Aberfoyle, nr. Stirling.——Mary Berta, b. 1910; is author of "Mount up with Wings." *Residence*, Waddington House, Charmouth, Bridport, Dorset.

de Capel Brooke, see Brooke.

CHAMPION DE CRESPIGNY, Creation (U.K.) 1805, of Champion Lodge, Surrey.
[Extinct 1952].
[Name pronounced " **Champion de Crepiny.**"]

Sir VIVIAN TYRELL CHAMPION DE CRESPIGNY, *O.B.E.*, 8th and last *Baronet.*

Daughter living of 8th Baronet—Fleur (3, Walton Park, Bexhill-on-Sea, Sussex), *b.* 1937: *m.* 1967 (m. diss. 1975), John William Gordon-Harris, and has issue living, William, *b.* 1970,—Victoria Fleur, *b.* 1972.

Sisters living of 8th Baronet—Rosalie Kathleen, *b.* 1900: *m.* 1926, Maurice John Hardy, MBE, of Wychling Court, Wychling, nr. Sittingbourne, Kent, [*see* Hardy, Bt., *cr.* 1876, colls.].——Eileen Ethel CHAMPION DE CRESPIGNY, *b.* 1903; resumed the surname of Champion de Crespigny in lieu of William's 1955: *m.* 1st, 1924, John Cecil Denne Allen, formerly Lt. 4th/7th Dragoon Guards, who obtained a divorce 1934; 2ndly, 1935, Lt.-Col. Leoline Williams, DSO, OBE, 4th/7th Dragoon Guards, and has issue living, (by 1st marriage) Jeremy John, *b.* 1930. *Residence,* Flat A5, Sloane Avenue Mansions, Chelsea, SW3.

Daughter living of 4th Baronet—Valerie (*Dowager Lady Smiley*), *b.* 1883: *m.* 1903, Maj. Sir John Smiley, 2nd Bt., 6th Dragoon Guards, who *d.* 1930. *Residence,* Smiley Knowe, Wentworth, Virginia Water, Surrey.

MALLABY-DEELEY, Creation (U.K.) 1922, of Mitcham Court, co. Surrey.
[Extinct 1962.]

Sir ANTHONY MEYRICK MALLABY-DEELEY, 3rd and last *Baronet.*

Daughter living of 2nd Baronet—Valerie Constance, *b.* 1928: *m.* 1947, Michael Peter Heaslett. and has issue living, Ingrid Ursula, *b.* 1952,—Ilsa Kirsten, *b.* 1954,—Helga Karen, *b.* 1955, —Sigrid Anna, *b.* 1959. *Residence,*

DE HOGHTON, Creation (E.) 1611, of Hoghton Tower, Lancashire.
[Name pronounced " **de Hor-ton.**"]

In spite of wrong.

MALGRÉ-LA-TORT.

Sir (HENRY PHILIP) ANTHONY MARY DE HOGHTON, 13th *Baronet* (but his name does not, at time of going to press, appear on the Official Roll of Baronets); *b.* April 19th, 1919; *s.* his father, *Sir* CUTHBERT, 1958; ed. at Beaumont, and at Magdalen Coll., Oxford.

Arms—Sable, three bars argent. Crest—A bull passant argent, ears, tips of the horns, mane, hoofs, and points of tail, sable. Supporters—Two bulls argent.
Residence—Hoghton Tower, Hoghton, Lancashire.

Half-Brother living—RICHARD BERNARD CUTHBERT (Hoghton Tower, Hoghton, Lancs.), *b.* Jan. 26th, 1945; ed. at Ampleforth, McGill Univ. and Birmingham Univ. (MA).

Aunts living (daughters of 11th baronet)— Joan, *b.* 1891: *m.* 1921, Maj. Charles Robert Thropp Thorp, MC, formerly KOYLI, who *d.* 1934, and has issue living, Angela Barbara Mary, *b.* 1925: *m.* 19—. *Residence,* Windows, Bembridge, I. of Wight.——Barbara, *b.* 1894: *m.* 1st, 1914, Robert Myles Heywood, Lt. The Buffs (E. Kent Regt.), who *d.* (killed in action during 1914-18 War) 1915; 2ndly, 1926, Richard Leveson Vernon, and has issue living, (by 2nd m.) Peter James Leveson, *b.* 1927,— Christopher Miles, *b.* 1936,—Barbara Flavia Rose, *b.* 1931. *Residence,* Keevil Manor, Trowbridge, Wilts.

Widow living of 12th Baronet—PHILOMENA, da. of the late Herbert Simmons, of Walton-le-Dale, Lancashire: *m.* 1st, 1944, as his second wife, Sir Cuthbert de Hoghton, 12th baronet, who *d.* 1958; 2ndly, 1960, Richard Grahame Adams, J.P., formerly of H.M. Colonial Admin. Ser., N. Nigeria. *Residence,* Hoghton Tower, Hoghton, Lancashire.

Collateral Branches living.

Issue of the late Charles James Gilbert de Hoghton, 2nd son of 12th Bt., *b.* 1930, *d.* 1971: *m.* 1957, Winifred Valerie Maud (32A, Blanfield Rd., W9), yr. da. of William Richard Glyn Thomas, of Cefn Coed, Merthyr Tydfil:—
Katharine Anne, *b.* 1959.

Issue of the late Major Vere de Hoghton, 2nd son of 11th baronet, *b.* 1882, *d.* killed in action during European War) 1915: *m.* 1911, Alice Dorothy Patience (who *d.* 1968, having *m.* 2ndly, 1921, Joseph Eccles, who *d.* 1944), da. of Sir Frank Hollins, 1st Bt.:—
Diana, *b.* 1913: *m.* 1937, Major Brian Pierson Doughty-Wylie, M.C., Roy. Welch Fusiliers [*see* V. Chelmsford, colls.]. *Residence,* Pen-y-Craig, Tremeirchion, St. Asaph, Denbighshire.

Issue of the late Major Daniel de Hoghton, M.B.E., brother of 11th baronet, *b.* 1853, *d.* 1929: *m.* 1888, Mary, who *d.* 1933, da. of Henry Jones:—
Sybil. *Residence,* Willow Cottage, Orrisdale, Kirk Michael, I. of Man.

This baronetcy is 5th in precedence of the Roll of the Baronets, but as the 2nd, 3rd, and 4th creations are borne by Earls, it ranks immediately after the Premier baronetcy of Bacon. The property of Hoghton has been in the family since *temp.* King Stephen. The 1st baronet, Sir Richard Hoghton, MP for Lancs., entertained King James I for several days at Hoghton Tower.

The 2nd baronet, Sir Gilbert, MP for Lancs. was Gentleman of the Bedchamber to King Charles I, and a Royalist leader. The 3rd and 4th baronets represented Lancs. in Parliament, and the 5th, 6th and 7th baronets each sat as MP for Preston. The 8th baronet assumed the additional surname of Bold, and the 9th baronet resumed in 1862 by Roy. licence the ancient surname of de Hoghton.

DE LA BERE, Creation (U.K.) 1953, of Crowborough, co. Sussex.

Sir RUPERT DE LA BÈRE, *K.C.V.O.*, 1st *Baronet*, son of Reginald De la Bère ; *b.* June 16th, 1893 ; ed. at Tonbridge ; appointed Sheriff of City of London 1941, and an Alderman City of London 1943 (Lord Mayor 1952-53); Pres. of Proprietors of Hay's Wharf, Ltd., a J.P. for City of London, a K.St.J., and a Knight Com. of Orders of North Star of Sweden, and of Dannebrog of Denmark ; European War 1914-18 as Capt. 6th Batn. E. Surrey Regt., seconded to R.F.C. and R.A.F. ; received Hon. Freedom of Evesham 1953 : sat as M.P. for Evesham (*C*) Nov. 1935 to Feb. 1950, and for S. Div. of Worcestershire Feb. 1950 to May 1955 ; Knt. 1952, K.C.V.O. 1953 : *m.* 1919, Marguerite, who *d.* 1969, da. of the late Lt.-Col. Sir John Humphery, and has issue.

Arms—Argent on a fesse between three crescents sable a lizard of the field. **Crest**—Issuant from an ancient crown or, a plume of five ostrich feathers argent charged with a ladybird proper.

Residence—Crowborough Place, Crowborough, Sussex. *Club*—Carlton.

Sons living—CAMERON (1, Avenue Theodore, Flournay, Geneva, Switzerland), *b.* Feb. 12th, 1933 : *m.* 1964, Clairemonde, only da. of Casimir Kaufmann, of 26, Avenue William Favre, Geneva, Switzerland, and has issue living, Réjane, *b.* 1965.——Adrian, *b.* 1939.
Daughters living—Pamela.——Valerie.——Camilla : *m.* 1953 (marriage dissolved 1959), Louis Georges Bourcier, and has issue living, Andrew Charles, *b.* 1954,—Yolande (twin), *b.* 1954. *Residence*, Quarry Hill, Sevenoaks, Kent.

DE LA RUE, Creation (U.K.) 1898, of Cadogan Square, Chelsea, co. London.
[Name pronounced "Dellarue."]

Seek the truth.

Sir ERIC VINCENT DE LA RUE, 3rd *Baronet ; b.* Aug. 5th, 1906 ; *s.* his father, *Sir* EVELYN ANDROS, 1950 ; ed. at Oundle ; late Capt. Notts Yeo. : *m.* 1st, 1945, Cecilia, who *d.* 1963, da. of the late Maj. Walter Waring [M. Tweeddale] ; 2ndly, 1964, Christine Schellin, of Greenwich, Conn., U.S.A., and has issue by 1st and 2nd marriages.

Arms—Or, three bars gules each charged with as many estoiles of the first, in chief an increscent and a decrescent of the second. **Crest**—Between two olive branches vert a cauldron gules, fired and issuant therefrom a snake nowed proper.

Residence—Caldra, Duns, Berwickshire.

Sons living (by 1st marriage)—ANDREW GEORGE ILAY, *b.* Feb. 21st, 1946.——John Vincent Francis, *b.* 1953,——(by 2nd marriage) Vincent St. George, *b.* 1965.

Brother living—Ian Hector (Ruware Ranch, PO Zaka, Fort Victoria, Rhodesia), *b.* 1910; ed. at Eton: *m.* 1936, Violet Bertha, da. of the late T. Despard Bridges, and has issue living, Anthony St. Vincent (5, Normanton Close, Marlborough, Salisbury, Rhodesia), *b.* 1947: *m.* 1971, Ann, da. of Frederic Roberts Blair, of Lloyds Neck, Long Island, New York, and has issue living, Thomas Edward *b.* 1973, Michael Alexander *b.* 1975.

Sister living—Diana Beryl *b.* 1914. *Residence*, Longfield, Rusper, Horsham, Sussex.

Collateral Branch living.

Issue of the late Stuart Andros de la Rue, 3rd son of 1st baronet, *b.* 1883, *d.* 1927 : *m.* 1912, Margaret Griselda (*Lady Sutton*) (of Little Park House, Brimpton, Reading, who *m.* 2ndly, 1928, Air-Marshal Sir Bertine Entwisle Sutton, KBE, CB, DSO, MC, who *d.* 1946), da. of the late Alexander Dundas Ogilvy Wedderburn, KC (*see* Ogilvy-Wedderburn, Bt., colls.]:—
Wedderburn Anthony, *b.* 1914: *m.* 1st, 1937, Jean Roberts; 2ndly, 1948, Marjorie Holland (MARSH), da. of William Holland Harris. *Residence*, Old School House, Buttermere, Marlborough, Wilts.
——Ann Griselda, *b.* 1918: *m.* 1938, Group Capt. John Norwood, RAF, and has issue living, Janet, *b.* 1939,—Jill, *b.* 1941. *Residence*, Old Coach House, Cannon St., Lymington, Hants.

Sir Thomas, 1st Bt., was many years Chm. of Thomas de la Rue and Co., Limited.

de MONTMORENCY, Creation (I.) 1631, of Knockagh, co. Tipperary.

Sir REGINALD D'ALTON LODGE DE MONT-
MORENCY, 18th *Baronet*, yst. son of John Kiddell
de Montmorency, 2nd son of James Lodge de
Montmorency, grandfather of 16th and 17th Bts.,
b. March 13th, 1899; *s.* his cousin, *Sir* MILES
FLETCHER, 1963; formerly with P & O, Bell Russ
& Co., India and A. Besse, Arabia; on staff of
The Times 1936-67; 1914-18 War with HAC and
RHA: *m.* 1928, Dorothy Victoria, da. of Gilbert
Walter Robinson.

Arms,—Or, a cross gules, between four eaglets displayed
azure. *Crest,*—A peacock in his pride, proper.

Residence—Bristol Cottage, Telegraph Rd., Putney Heath,
S.W.15.

Sister living—Kathleen Letitia (25, Rowley Rd., St. Mary-
church, Torquay), *b.* 1894: *m.* 1924, Paul George Shore
Phillipps-Treby, who *d.* 1938.

Widow living of 16th Baronet—ELEANOR KATHARINE
(*Eleanor, Lady de Montmorency*), da. of the late Rev. Edward
Richard Jefferys Nicolls, R. of Saxelby, Leics.: *m.* 1918,
Sir (Hervey) Angus de Montmorency, OBE, 16th Bt., who *d.*
1959. *Residence*, 8, St. Leonard's Court, St. Leonard's Rd.,
E. Sheen, SW14.

Collateral Branches living.

Granddaughter of the late Major Reymond Hervey de Montmorency, el. son of
the late Major Reymond Henry de Montmorency, son of Lieut.-Col. Reymond
Hervey de Montmorency, M.P. (who had resumed this ancient name by Roy.
licence in lieu of Morres 1815), son of the late Rev. Reymond Morres, nephew
of 1st Viscount Mountmorres, and great-great-grandson of 2nd baronet:—

Issue of the late Reymond Hervey de Montmorency, *b.* 1871, *d.* 1938 : *m.* 1905, Gwynedd
Maud, who *d.* 1936, da. of Lieut.-Col. G. T. Thomas, M.R.C.S., L.R.C.P., D.P.H.,
I.M.S. :—

Ann Marion, *b.* 1911: *m.* 1st, 1935, George Henry Carbutt, who *d.* 1956; 2ndly, 1958, Ernest
William Swanton and has issue living, (by 1st marriage) Francis (of The White House, Langham,
Colchester), *b.* 1936: *m.* 1958, Sally Fenella, da. of James Cole Harris, and has issue living,
George Henry de Montmorency *b.* 1963, Emma Louise *b.* 1961,—Edward Reymond (Mount Hall,
Gt. Horkesley, Colchester) *b.* 1940: *m.* 1966, Susan Elizabeth, twin da. of Robert Peter Healing,
[*see* B. Petre]. *Residence*, Delf House, Sandwich, Kent.

Granddaughter of the late William Reymond de Montmorency, son of the late
Lieut. Edward D'Alton de Montmorency, R.N. (ante):—
Issue of the late Edward D'Alton de Montmorency, *b.* 1870, *d.* 1942 : *m.* 1894, Jane, who
d. 1895, da. of Alexander Cumming:—
Florence Eleanor, *b.* 1895. *Residence*, 10, Priestfield Road, Forest Hill, S.E.23.

Grandchildren of the late James Lodge de Montmorency, son of the late Lieut.
Edward D'Alton de Montmorency, R.N. (ante) :—
Issue of the late James Edward Geoffrey de Montmorency, LL.B, MA, *b.* 1866, *d.* 1934:
m. 1899, Caroline Maud Saumarez, who *d.* 1973, da. of the late Maj.-Gen. James de
Havilland, RA:—
ARNOLD GEOFFROY (2, Garden Court, Temple, EC4; Francis Taylor Building, Temple, EC4),
b. July 27th, 1908; ed. at Westminster Sch., and Peterhouse, Camb. (LL.B, MA); Bar. Middle
Temple 1932; 1939-45 War as Maj. RASC: *m.* 1949 (m. annulled 1953) and re-married 1972,
Nettie Hay, da. of the late William Anderson.——Geraldine Susan Maud (*Lady Lewis*), *b.* 1900;
FLA: *m.* 1957, as his 2nd wife, Sir (William) Hawthorne Lewis, KCSI, KCIE, who *d.* 1970.
Residence, The Bridge House, Wilton, Salisbury.

This baronetcy was granted to John Morres, of Knockagh, in 1631, and on the death of Sir
Nicholas, 8th Bt., in 1796, the title devolved upon the 2nd Viscount Mountmorres. In 1815 the
3rd Viscount, and Lt.-Col. Reymond Hervey Morres, ancestor of the present baronet, resumed by
Roy. licence the surname of de Montmorency. In 1951, on the death of the 7th Viscount Mountmorres (also 7th Baron), the Viscountcy and the Barony became ext. and the Baronetcy passed
to his kinsman, Sir (Hervey) Angus de Montmorency, O.B.E., who *s.* as 16th baronet.

DENNY, Creation (I.) 1782, of Castle Moyle, Kerry.

The harvest also shall be mine.

Sir ANTHONY CONINGHAM DE
WALTHAM DENNY, 8th *Baronet*; *b.* April
22nd, 1925; *s.* his father, the *Rev. Sir*
HENRY LYTTELTON LYSTER, 1953; ed. at
Clayesmore; FRSA; a Designer, partner in
firm of Verity and Beverley, Architects and
Design Consultants; an Hereditary Freeman
of Cork; 1943-45 War with RAF in Middle
East: *m.* 1949, Anne Catherine, da. of
Samuel Beverley, FRIBA, of Wilmead,
Linsdale, Bucks, and has issue.

Arms—Gules, a saltire argent between twelve
cross-crosslets or. *Crest*—A cubit arm vested azure,
turned up argent, holding in the hand proper five
wheat-ears or.

Residences—4, Heath Villas, Vale of Health,
Hampstead, NW3; Daneway House, Sapperton,
Glos.

Sons living—PIERS ANTHONY DE WALTHAM, *b.*
March 14th, 1954.——Thomas Francis Coningham,
b. 1956.

Brothers living—Barry Francis Lyttelton, (22, Hassendean Rd., Blackheath, SE3), *b.* 1928; ed. at Clayesmore and RMA; Maj. RA (ret.); formerly in Queen's

R. Regt., and Cadet Indian Army; a 1st Sec. FO: *m.* 1st, 1951 (m. diss. 1968), Mrs. Gertrude Tamara Crofton, da. of the late Harry Carnet Jex, of Hong Kong; 2ndly, 1969, Anne Rosemary Jordon, da. of Col. James Frederick White, MC, late R. Warwicks. Fus., of Auchenstroan, Moniaive, by Dumfries, and has issue living (by 1st m.) James Barry Lyster, *b.* 1958,—Shelagh Joan Lyttleton, *b.* 1959,—(by 2nd m.) Emma Harriet Lyttelton, *b.* 1970.——Edward Maurice FitzGerald, *b.* 1930; ed. at Clayesmore: formerly in RNAS: *m.* 1953, Anna Rose Frances, da. of G. Teesdale.——Richard William Geoffrey (Cainhoe Manor, Clophill, Beds.), *b.* 1940: *m.* 1961, Andrée Suzanne Louise, el. da. of Marcel Louis Parrot, of 210, Rue de Rivoli, Paris, and has issue living, Lyster Richard Henry, *b.* 1961,—Walter Victor Marcel, *b.* 1963,—Giles Anthony William, *b.* 1964,—Julius André Geoffrey, *b.* 1966.

Widow living of 7th Baronet—JOAN LUCY DOROTHY, el. da. and co-heir of the late Major William Alfred Charles Denny, O.B.E. (infra) : *m.* 1924, her cousin, the Rev. Sir Henry Lyttelton Lyster Denny, 7th Bt., who *d.* 1953; 2ndly, 1957, Victor S. Levy, who *d.* 1969. *Residence,* April Cottage, Ghyll Rd., Heathfield, Sussex.

Collateral Branches living.

Granddaughters of the late Lt.-Col. Richard Denny (infra):—
Issue of the late Maj. Richard Brougham Denny, *b.* 1889, *d.* 1967: *m.* 1st, 1928 (m. diss. 19—), Sybil Nina, da. of the late Francis N. Evans-Freke; 2ndly, 1967, Edith Winifred (2, Ashdown Rd., Bexhill, Sussex), da. of the late G. F. Winstone, of Worcester:—
Diana Brougham, *b.* 1930: *m.* 1960, Ronald Herbert Macintosh, CEng, AMIME, MRINA, of 77, Oriel Av., Tawa, Wellington, NZ.——Juliet Oldfield, *b.* 1932: *m.* 1952, Peter Walter Taylor, PhD, of 1, Henderson Av., Malvern, Mel. 3144, Aust., and has issue living, Christopher Richard de Courcy, *b.* 1957,—Caroline Mary Louise, *b.* 1954,—Catherine Jane, *b.* 1961.

Grandchildren of the late Rev. Henry Denny, 3rd son of 3rd baronet :—
Issue of the late Lieut.-Col. Richard Denny, *b.* 1848, *d.* 1915: *m.* 1881, Mary who *d.* 1939, da. of the late Thomas Stokes Guppy, M.D., of Falmouth:—
Geraldine: *m.* 1918, Col. George Thomas Johnson, late Indian Army who *d.* 1972, and has issue living, Michael Denny, *b.* 1921; formerly Capt. R. Fusiliers; 1939-45 War (despatches, prisoner): *m.* 1959, Lorna Sylvia, da. of the late Rear-Adm. R. Lawson,—Brian Denny, *b.* 1923; formerly Flying Officer RAF; 1939-45 War: *m.* 1958, Truda, da. of the late G. H. Neal, of Bebington, Ches,—Jacqueline Naomi, *b.* 1927: *m.* 1952, Lt.-Cdr. Richard Arthur Fogwill, RN, of Rosneath, Yelverton, Devon. *Residence,* Flat 9, Rock Hotel, Yelverton, Devon.

Issue of the late Edmund Barry Denny, *b.* 1860, *d.* 1945: *m.* 1884, Emily Barclay, da. of Henry Allen, of Dublin :—
Henry Allen Maynard, *b.* 1887 ; late Veterans' Guard of Canada ; formerly Capt. Lincolnshire Regt.; European War 1914-18 (wounded) : *m.* 1st, 1926, Kathleen Mary, da. of the late W. W. Goddard, of Stroud, Gloucestershire ; 2ndly, 1950, Elsi Margaret, da. of the late R. O. Williams, and widow of J. Ryall, and has issue living, (by 1st marriage) Norah Peta, *b.* 1928 : *m.* 1949, Robert Addison King, and has issue living, Keith Allan (Banff, Alta), *b.* 1951: *m.* 1974, Heather Ann, da. of the late William Farquharson, Kathy Diane *b.* 1953, Rachel Ann *b.* 1955,—Kathleen Wendy Elizabeth, *b.* 1930: *m.* 1st, 1952 (m. diss. 1963), James Palmer Lee; 2ndly, 1964, William Ernest Smith, of 2015, Frederick Norris Rd., Victoria, BC, Canada, and has issue living (by 1st m.), Randall *b.* 1953, Teresa *b.* 1955: *m.* 1975, Michael Farup, of Salt Spring Island, BC. *Residence,* Tralee, Duncan, Vancouver Island, British Columbia.——Norah Creina, *ARRC*; 1914-18 War (despatches, ARRC) ; Freeman of City of Duncan; Silver Jubilee medal (1935). *Residence,* Innisfree, Brownsey Av., Duncan, Vancouver Is., BC.——Iris; is Section Officer WAAF; 1914-18 War as Driver RAF. *Residence,* 5807, Banks Rd., Duncan, Vancouver Island, BC.

Grandchildren of the late Edmund Barry Denny (ante):—
Issue of the late Capt. Thomas Hamilton Denny, M.B.E., Indian Army, *b.* 1893, *d.* 1959 : *m.* 1920, Muriel Mary, who *d.* 1974, da. of the late Edward Doncaster, of Silk Willoughby, Sleaford:—
Pamela Diana, *b.* 1924: *m.* 1952 (m. diss. 1969), Anthony Miles Denny, and has issue living, Patrick Jonathan Hamilton, *b.* 1956,—Caroline Peta, *b.* 1955. *Residence,* Barkwith, Lakeside Av., Thorpeness, Leiston, Suffolk.

Issue of the late Arthur de Courcy MacGillycuddy Denny, *b.* 1899, *d.* 1971: *m.* 1st, 1926 (m. diss. 1934) Marie Cecilia, da. of H. Brooke; 2ndly, 1937, Mary Evelyn, who *d.* 1967, only da. of the late Brig.-Gen. Noel Ernest Money, CMG, DSO:—
(By 1st m.) Maynard de Courcy Barry (Barkwith House, E. Barkwith, Lincoln), *b.* 1927; ed. at Trin. Coll., Dublin (BA); served RA 1945-48: *m.* 1966, Christine Mary, da. of Walters S. Browne, of Ipswich, and has issue living, Anthony de Courcy Edmund, *b.* 1973.

Grandchildren of the late Ven. Anthony Denny, 4th son of 3rd baronet:—
Issue of the late George Herbert Denny, *b.* 1851, *d.* 1937: *m.* 1876, Ellen, who *d.* 1937, da. of N. Jarvis :—
Edward Jarvis, *b.* 1879: *m.* 1903, Clara Elizabeth, da. of August Will, and has issue living, Ellen Elizabeth, *b.* 19—,—Catharine Antoinette, *b.* 19—.——Anthony George, *b.* 1882 : *m.* 1910, Mathilda Henrietta, da. of C. Dargeloh.——Catharine Magill : *m.* 1900, Curtis L. Sleeper. *Residence,*

Granddaughters of the late Edward Coningsby Denny (infra):—
Issue of the late William Coningsby Denny, *b.* 1867, *d.* 1935: *m.* 1892, Rose Elizabeth, who *d.* 1947, da of the late Joseph Ingram, of Wellington Square, Hastings:—
Marjorie Ethel, *b.* 1896. *Residence,* Tralee, 54, Privett Road, Alverstoke, Gosport, Hants.
Issue of the late Charles Edward Denny, *b.* 1875, *d.* 1946: *m.* 1902, Alice, who *d.* 1965, da. of Samuel Grantham Baker, of Brighton:—
Letitia Ivy Coningsby, *b.* 1904: *m.* 1940, Woolmore Stewart Duncan. *Residence,* Bowersbury, Bowers Heath, Harpenden, Herts.——Ethel Mildred Coningsby, *b.* 1907: *m.* 1933, Sydney Walter Stubbs, and has issue living, Brian Maurice Denny, *b.* 1936,—Colin Anthony, *b.* 1939,—Richard Ivan, *b.* 1949. *Residence,* Bralo Lodge, Headstone Lane, Harrow, Middlesex.—— Kathleen Mary Coningsby, *b.* 1910 : *m.* 1936, Joseph Harry Smith, and has issue living, Peter Nigel Coningsby, *b.* 1948,—Kathleen Hazel Coningsby, *b.* 1940,—Yvonne Coningsby, *b.* 1944. *Residence,* Inchkeith, 54, Swakeleys Drive, Ickenham, Middlesex.——Geraldine Coningsby, *b.* 1917 : *m.* 1939, Stanley Robson Clarke, and has issue living, Barry Ian Charles, *b.* 1946,— Diana Susan, *b.* 1948. *Residence,* 44, Swakeleys Drive, Ickenham, Middlesex.

Grandsons of the late William Denny, 5th son of 3rd baronet :—
Issue of the late Edward Coningsby Denny, *b.* 1839, *d.* 1888: *m.* 1863, Louisa Mary, who *d.* 1916, da. of the late Augustus Callaway, of Rogate, Sussex :—
Horace, *b.* 1877 : *m.* 1904, Mabel, da. of Adm. Arthur de Bellin, late Roy. Italian Navy, and has issue living, John, *b.* 19—,—a da., *b.* 19—,—a da., *b.* 19—. *Residence,*

Issue of the late Henry Arthur Denny, Lieut. R.F.A., *b.* 1841, *d.* 1888 : *m.* 1870, Emma Florence, who *d.* 1886, da. of the late A. Denny, J.P., of Rockfield, Tramore :—
Frederick Wootton, *b.* 1881 ; formerly Lieut. Duke of Edinburgh's (Wiltshire Regt.): *m.* 1913, Rose, da. of Charles T. G. Bright, of Toronto, and widow of — Cramp, and has issue living, Shirley Geraldine, *b.* 1915. *Residence,*

Granddaughters of the late Lieut. Alfred Edward Denny, R.N., son of the late William Denny (ante) :—

Issue of the late Major William Alfred Charles Denny, O.B.E., *b.* 1871, *d.* **1934**: *m.* **1st,** 1896, Lucy Florence, who *d.* 1931, only da. of the late Maj.-Gen. Herbert Coningham, of 32, Vernon Terrace, Brighton; 2ndly, **1933,** Beatrice Mary Louisa, who *d.* 1942, only child of the late Alfred Boydell Golborne, of Chester, and widow of his cousin, Edmund Henry Denny:—
(By 1st marriage) Joan Lucy Dorothy, *b.* 1899 : *m.* 1st, 1924, her cousin, the Rev. Sir Henry Lyttelton Lyster Denny, 7th Bt., who *d.* 1953 (ante); 2ndly, Victor S. Levy, who *d.* 1969.——
Eileen Mary Diana, *b.* 1903: *m.* 1933, William Samuel Sandes Boxwell, who *d.* 1961. *Residence,* Treliggan, Fowey, Cornwall.

Sir Robert Denny, Knt., was M.P. for Cambridgeshire 1391-3, and Lieut. of the Duke of Bedford, Constable of England, at the time of the siege of Rouen. His descendant, Sir Edmond Denny (son of William Denny, of Cheshunt—High Sheriff of Herts 1480), King's Remembrancer to Henry VII., and a Baron of the Exchequer, was father of the Rt. Hon. Sir Anthony Denny, P.C., M.P., Chief Gentleman of the Privy Chamber and Groom of the Stole to Henry VIII., the only gentleman who dared to inform the King of his approaching end, and received from him a pair of gloves (which still exist) worked with pearls ; he was constituted an Executor of Henry VIII., and one of the Guardians of Edward VI. His grandson, Sir Edward Denny, was created Lord Denny de Waltham 1604, and Earl of Norwich 1626. The present family is descended from Sir Edward Denny, Knight Banneret, M.P. (a younger son of the Rt. Hon. Sir Anthony Denny), who, being Governor of Kerry and Desmond, Gentleman of the Privy Chamber to Queen Elizabeth, and Com. under Adm. Howard, etc., received a grant of the Seignory of Dennyvale and Castlemore, co. Kerry, with the Desmonds' chief castle of Tralee, in 1587, as a reward for his naval and military services. For successive generations the family provided representatives for Tralee and co. Kerry in Parliament. Sir Barry, 2nd Bt., was about to be raised to the peerage when he was killed in a duel 1794. Sir Cecil Edward Denny, 6th Bt. (sometime Archivist and Keeper of Records of Govt. of Alberta, and historian of that Province), founded Calgary (Alberta). There is no such place as "Castle Mo .e,"which is an error in the patent of Baronetcy for Castle More, i.e "the great castle" of Tralee. The Rev. Sir Henry Lyttelton Lyster Denny, 7th Bt., was V. of Winslow-cum-Shipton 1916-18, R. of Horsted Keynes 1918-20, V. of St. Mark's, Myddelton Square, E.C., and Fellow of Sion Coll. 1920-25, R. of Wickham 1925-30, R. of Abinger, Surrey 1930-36, and R. and V. of Burwash 1938-52.

DENNY, Creation (U.K.) 1913, of Dumbarton, co. Dunbarton.

Brave and kind.

Sir ALISTAIR MAURICE ARCHIBALD DENNY, 3rd *Baronet* ; *b.* Sept. 11th, 1922 ; *s.* his father, *Sir* MAURICE EDWARD, *K.B.E.,* 1955 ; ed. at Marlborough ; European War 1939-45 with Fleet Air Arm : *m.* 1949, Elizabeth Hunt, da. of Major Sir Ernest Guy Richard Lloyd, D.S.O., M.P., 1st Bt. (*cr.* 1960), and has issue.

Arms—Azure, three suns in their splendour in chief or, and in the honour point a martlet of the last for difference. **Crest**—A dexter hand erect, pointing with two fingers at a sun in his splendour, all proper.

Residence—Damside of Strathairly, Upper Largo, Fife.

Sons living—CHARLES ALISTAIR MAURICE, *b.* Oct. 7th, 1950, ——Nigel Peter, *b.* 1952.——Mark Richard Leslie, *b.* 1955.

Brother living—Graham Royse, *b.* 1927 ; ed. at Marlborough, and at King's Coll., Camb. *Residence,* Gateside House, Drymen, Stirlingshire.

Sisters living—Rosamund Margaret, *b.* 1917 : *m.* 1941, Lieut. Col. John Malcolm Thorpe Churchill, D.S.O., M.C., Seaforth Highlanders, and has issue living, Malcolm John Leslie, *b.* 1942,—Rodney Alistair Gladstone, *b.* 1947. *Residence,* Sunhill House, Mayford, near Woking, Surrey.——Patricia Leslie, *b.* 1931 : *m.* 1952, Thomas Dunlop Bruce Jones, MC, of House on the Hill, Dunblane, Perthshire [Dunlop Bt.], and has issue living, Veronica Margaret, *b.* 1953,—Victoria Leslie, *b.* 1956,—Claire Patricia, *b.* 1958,—Juliet Mary, *b.* 1966.

Uncle living (son of 1st baronet)—James Murray Tulloch, *b.* 1896 ; sometime Capt. R.E. : *m.* 1934, Ivy Rose, da. of the late Henry Pottle, of Bournemouth. *Residence,* Vancouver, British Columbia.

Aunt living (daughter of 1st baronet)—Eileen Margaret, *b.* 1891 : *m.* 1917, Alexander Muir McGrigor, OBE, late Capt., Glos., Yeo., who *d.* 1963 [Muir, Bt.], and has issue living, Peter Muir, *b.* 1927. *Residence,* Anchorfield, Dunblane, Perthshire.

Widow living of 2nd Baronet—MARJORIE (*Marjorie, Lady Denny*), da. of the late William Royse Lysaght, C.B.E., of Castleford, Chepstow : *m.* 1916, Sir Maurice Edward Denny, K.B.E., 2nd Bt., who *d.* 1955. *Residence,* Gateside House, Drymen, Stirlingshire.

The 1st baronet, Sir Archibald Denny, LL.D. (son of Peter Denny, of Helenslee, Dumbarton), was a Naval Architect and a Director of William Denny & Bros., Ltd., shipbuilders and engineers, of Dumbarton. The 2nd baronet, Sir Maurice Edward Denny, K.B.E., was Pres. of William Denny & Bros., Ltd., Chm. of Air Registration Board, and Pres. of Institute of Marine Engineers 1935-6 and of Junior Institution of Engineers 1943-4.

DERING, Creation (E.) 1627, of Surrenden Dering, Kent. [Extinct 1975.]

Sir RUPERT ANTHONY YEA DERING, 12th and last *Baronet.*

Daughter living of 12th Baronet—Susan Helen, *b.* 1941: *m.* 1967, Henry John Fredman, of Cheriton House, South Cheriton, Somerset, and has issue living, Jenny Annabelle, *b.* 1968.

Daughters living of 10th Baronet—Myrtle, *b.* 1898: *m.* 1st, 1917, Capt. Douglas Charles Leyland Speed, OBE, King's R. Rifle Corps (Res.), who obtained a divorce 1925; 2ndly, 1927, Octavius Hugh Mansfield Sturges, and has issue living, (by 2nd m.) Peter Mansfield (c/o Drummonds Branch, Royal Bank of Scotland, 49, Charing Cross, SW1), *b.* 1929; Maj. Queen's R. Irish Hussars,—Elizabeth Jane, *b.* 1932.——Clare, *b.* 1900: *m.* 1929, Henry Bruce Langworthy, Commr. of Federation of Malaya Police (ret.). *Residence,* Church Farm House, East Brabourne, Ashford, Kent.

Widow living of 12th Baronet,—BETTY BRIDGETT, (*Lady Dering*), (Bellings, Midhurst, Sussex), only da. of the late Lt.-Col. Vere Powys Bruce, of Rose Cottage, Charminster, Dorset: *m.* 1940, Lt.-Col. Sir Rupert Anthony Yea Dering, 12th Bt., who *d.* 1975, 2hen the title became ext.

Collateral Branches living.

Granddaughters of the late Lieut.-Col. Edgar William Wallace Dering, son of the late Cholmeley Charles William Dering, 2nd son of 7th baronet:—
Issue of the late Com. Claud Lacy Yea Dering, D.S.O.,· R.N., *b.* 1885, *d.* 1943 : *m.* 1915, Winifred, who *d.* 1941, da. of Edmund Gellibrand, of V.O.19, Cadet Line, Petrograd :—
Enid Deborah Claud (11, Welbeck Court, Addison Bridge Place, W14), *b.* 1922: *m.* 1942 (m. diss. 1965), Robin Craig Guthrie, Portrait painter, and has issue living, Linnet Marion, *b.* 1946.

Issue of the late Anthony Lionel Yea Dering, *b.* 1890, *d.* 1953 : *m.* 1916, Gertrude Frances Cordelia, who *d.* 1969, only da. of Archibald Henry Boyd, Bar.-at-Law, of Bellevue, Westward Ho! [Denny, Bt.]:—
Joan Rosalind Cordelia, *b.* 1917. *Residence*, 2, Thellusson Lodge, Aldeburgh, Suffolk.——Pamela Mary, *b.* 1919: *m.* 1946, Thomas Ian Arthur, of 44, Canynge Rd., Clifton, Bristol, BS8 3LQ, and has issue living, David Anthony Dering, *b.* 1954,—Rosemary, *b.* 1947,—Sarah Gillian, *b.* 1950.

John Dering, who *d.* 1425, acquired the manor of Surrenden (later Surrenden Dering), Kent, on marriage to Christian, da. and heir of John Hawte by Joan, da. and heir of John Surrenden. The 1st baronet was Lieut. of Dover Castle, and his five immediate successors represented Kent in Parliament, while the 8th baronet sat as M.P. for Wexford 1830, Romney 1831-2, and E. Kent 1852-7 and 1863-8. The 9th baronet was Min. to Mexico 1894-1900, and to Brazil 1900-1906. The 10th baronet, Sir Henry Edward Dering, sold Surrenden Dering in 1928.

DES VŒUX, Creation (I.) 1787, of Indiaville, Queen's County. [Extinct 1944.]

Lieut.-Col. Sir WILLIAM RICHARD DE BACQUENCOURT DES VŒUX, 9th and last *Baronet* ; *d.* (killed in action in Holland) 1944.

Daughters living of 9th Baronet—Mary Elizabeth, *b.* 1940: *m.* 1967, Jeremy John Aird, of Quarry Wood Cottage, Burghclere, Newbury, Berks. [*see* Aird, Bt., colls.].——Patricia Jane, *b.* 1941: *m.* 1965, Penrhyn Charles Benjamin Pockney, of 5, Somerset Sq., Addison Rd., W14, and has issue living, Richard Penrhyn, *b.* 1969,—James Charles, *b.* 1970.——Dorothy Susan, *b.* 1944: *m.* 1973, Lt.-Cdr. John David Caldecott, RN, of Holton House, Wincanton, Som, and has issue living, Jane Cynthia, *b.* 1974.

DE TRAFFORD, Creation (U.K.) 1841, of Trafford Park, Lancashire.

Sir RUDOLPH EDGAR FRANCIS DE TRAFFORD, OBE, 5th *Baronet; b.* Aug. 31st, 1894; *s.* his brother, *Sir* HUMPHREY EDMUND, MC, 1971; ed. at Downside and Trin. Coll., Camb. (BA); past Chm. Atlas Assurance and Philip Hill Higginson and Elliott-Automation; 1914-18 War as Capt. Int. Corps and Gen. Staff (despatches twice); OBE (Mil.) 1919: *m.* 1st, 1924, June Isabel, MBE (who obtained a divorce 1938), da. of Lt.-Col. Reginald Chaplin; 2ndly, 1939, Katherine, el. da. of W. W. Balke, of Cincinnati, USA, and formerly wife of Sebastiano Lo Savio, and has issue by 1st m.

Arms—Argent, a griffin segreant gules. **Crest**—A thrasher proper, his hat and coat per pale argent and gules, sleeves counterchanged, breeches and stockings of the 2nd and 3rd, his flail of the 1st.

Residence, 70, Eaton Sq., SW1.   *Club*—White's.

Son living—By 1st m.—DERMOT HUMPHREY, *VRD* (14, Alexander's Sq., SW3), *b.* Jan. 9th, 1925: *m.* 1st, 1948 (m. diss. 1973), Patricia Mary. da. of Francis Mycroft Beeley; 2ndly, 1974, Xandra Carandini, only da. of Lt.-Col. Geoffrey Trollope Lee, and formerly wife of Roderick Walter and has issue living (by 1st m.), John Humphrey, *b.* 1950; ed. at Ampleforth, and Bristol Univ., BSc,—Edmund Francis, *b.* 1952; ed. at Worth,—Gerard Thomas Joseph, *b.* 1968—Mary Annette, *b.* 1949,— Elizabeth Eugenie, *b.* 1951,—Patricia Clare, *b.* 1955,—Victoria Mary, *b.* 1958,—Cynthia Joan Bernadettc, *b.* 1958,—Antonia Lucy Octavia, *b.* 1966.

Daughters living of 4th Baronet—Ann, *CBE, b.* 1918; Ch. Commr. Girl Guides Assocn.; CBE (Civil) 1972: *m.* 1939, Derek Henry Parker Bowles, of White Oak House, Highclere, Newbury. [*see* E. Macclesfield, colls.].——Mary (*Lady Bowes-Lyon*), *b.* 1920: *m.* 1941, Maj.-Gen. Sir Francis James Cecil Bowes-Lyon, KCVO, CB, OBE, MC, of Highfield House, Slindon, Arundel, Sussex [*see* E. Strathmore, colls.].——Violet (*Lady Aitken*), *b.* 1926: *m.* 1951, as his third wife, the 2nd Group Capt. Sir (John William) Maxwell Aitken, DSO, DFC, 2nd Bt. (who s. as 2nd Baron Beaverbrook 1964, but disclaimed this peerage that year) [*see* By. Beaverbrook]. *Residence*, The Garden House, Cherkley, Leatherhead, Surrey.——Catherine, *b.* 1928: *m.* 1952, Fulke Thomas Tyndall Walwyn, and has issue living, Jane, *b.* 1957. *Residence*, Saxon House Stables, Lambourn, Berks.

Collateral Branches living.

Grandchildren of the late Charles Edmund de Trafford (infra):—
Issue of the late Capt. Hubert Edmund Francis de Trafford, b. 1893, d. 1974: m. 1927, the Hon. Cecilia (Xlendi, Gozo, Malta, GC), da. of 1st Baron Strickland (ext.), and 6th Count Della Catena (Maltese Nobility):—
Gerald Edmund Hubert (Villa Bologna, Attard, Malta, GC), b. 1929; ed. at McGill Univ. (BA), and Oxford Univ.; a Knt. of Sovereign Mil. Order of Malta: m. 1971, (Helena Catherina) Charlotte, only da. of Herman Sybrand Hallo, former Ambassador of the Netherlands, of 27, Verdala St. George's Dragonara, Malta, and has issue living, Jasper, b. 1975,—Aloisia Cecilia Mary, b. 1973.
——Anthony Charles Everard (5, Alley, 1, Our Lady of Angels St., Zebbug, Malta, GC), b. 1935, m. 1966, Gabrielle Frances, da. of Maj. Ronald Edward Boone, of Rockcliffe House, Upper Slaughter, Glos.——Hubert George Joseph (The Garden House. Villa Bologna, Attard, Malte, GC), b. 1937: m. 1st, 1966 (m. diss. 19—), Christine Elizabeth, only da. of Lt.-Cdr. Maurice Sydney Adams, RN (ret.); 2ndly 1975, Mary Kate Willis, da. of the late Lt.-Col. Edward C. A Willis Fleming, of The Old Farm, Bracknell, and has issue living (by 1st m.), Rachel Samantha, b. 1967,—Martha Christine Joanna, b. 1969.——Margaret Annette, b. 1928: m. 1952, Cdr. William John Macnamara Faulkner, RN, of Falconswood, Petersfield, Hants. and has issue living, Hugh Edmund Brooke, b. 1953,—Mark William Bingham, b. 1955,—Rosalinda Mary b. 1958,—Catharine Frances, b. 1961.——Elizabeth Clare Hilda Melita (Lady Turner), b. 1932: m. 1963, Adm. Sir Arthur Francis Turner, KCB, DSC, of 15, West Way, Rickmansworth, Herts. and has issue living. Francis Christopher Neale, b. 1966,—Michael Paul Charles, b. 1969.—— Mary Roma Pia Goditha, b. 1934: m. 1964, Philip James Gooding, of 98, Moor Lane, Rickmansworth, Herts., and has issue living, Edward James Trafford, b. 1974,—Louise Alexandra Mary, b. 1967,—Elizabeth Victoria Pia, b. 1969.

Issue of the late Charles Edmund de Trafford, 2nd son of 2nd baronet, b. 1864, d. 1951 : m. 1892, Lady Agnes Mary Pia Feilding, who d. 1921, da. of 8th Earl of Denbigh :—
(Clare, Lady Wolseley), b. 1895: m. 1916, Sir Edric Charles Joseph Wolseley, 10th Bt., who d. 1954. Residence, Rosethorpe, Finmere, Buckingham.

Granddaughters of the late John Randolphus de Trafford, 3rd son of 1st baronet:—
Issue of the late Galfrid Aloysius Cathcart de Trafford, b. 1856, d. 1924 : m. 1887, Cecile Elizabeth Margaret, who d. 1945. da. of the late Comte Hubert de Stacpoole :—
Daphne Ruth Elizabeth Adelaide Mary, b. 1903. Residence, 16, Lion Gate Gdns., Richmond, Surrey.

Issue of the late Lieut.-Col. Charles Alan Cathcart de Trafford, b. 1871, d. 1950 : m. 1900, Lady Victoria Frederica Wilhelmina Georgina Seymour, who d. 1960, da. of 6th Marquess of Hertford :—
Joan Agnes Mary Seymour, b. 1901 ; formerly Subaltern A.T.S. Residence, Guy's Cottage, Avon Dassett, Warwickshire.

Issue of the late Augustus Henry de Trafford, 5th son of 1st baronet, b. 1823, d. 1895 : m. 1876, Gertrude Mary, who d. 1922, da. of the late Herman Walmesley, of Gidlow, Wigan :—
Gertrude Mary : m. 1909, Lieut.-Col. William Erdeswick Ignatius Butler-Bowdon, D.S.O., who d. 1956, and has issue living, Maurice Erdeswick, OBE (Dapsland, Mayfield, Sussex), b. 1910, Capt. RN (ret.); 1940-45 War (despatches): OBE (Mil.) 1946: m. 1939, Anne, da. of the late Lt.-Col. Arthur James Darlington, DSO [V. Brookeborough, colls.], and has issue living, Humphrey Anthony Erdeswick b. 1951, Rachel Anne b. 1941, Sarah Elisabeth b. 1945: m. 1968, Francis Houghton Leslie Ravenscroft, of Blackdon Hill Cottage, Eridge, Sussex (and has issue living, Sacha Benedict, b. 1969, Benjamin Robert b. 1971, George Maurice Houghton b. 1973,— Anthony William (55, Hawkers Rd., Medindie, S. Australia), b. 1913; ed at Oratory Sch.; late Capt. RE: m. 1955, Marion, da. of John Pollock, of Newlands, S.Africa, and has issue living, Richard Anthony b. 1957, Piers Dominic b. 1959, Edward Rupert b. 1960, Charles William b. 1962, Thomas Mark b. 1967, Teresa Mary b. 1965, Caroline Rose b. 1969. Residence, Dawn, Chideock, Bridport, Dorset.——Agnes Mary (6, Marland House, 28, Sloane St., SW1).

The knightly family of Trafford of Trafford, Lancs. can be traced in the male line to the 12th century. Sir Thomas Joseph Trafford, 1st Bt. in 1842 received a Roy. licence to resume the original name of de Trafford. Sir Humphrey, 4th Bt. owner and breeder of racehorses, and was a snr. steward of the Jockey Club 1936 and 1942-53.

DEVITT, Creation (U.K.) 1916, of Chelsea, co. London

Sir THOMAS GORDON DEVITT, 2nd *Baronet*, son of the late Arthur Devitt, el. son of 1st Baronet ; b. Dec. 27th, 1902 ; s. his grandfather, Sir THOMAS LANE, 1923; ed. at Sherborne, and at Corpus Christi Coll., Camb. (MA), Senior Partner in the firm of Devitt and Moore, Chm. of National Service for Seafarers, and a Gov. of Sherborne Sch.; 1940-45 War as Lt.-Col. Seaforth Highlanders and Officer Comdg. Raiding Support Regt.; has Roy. Order of Phoenix of Greece with swords: m. 1st, 1930, Joan Mary (who obtained a divorce 1936), da. of the late Charles Reginald Freemantle, of Hayes Barton, Pyrford, Surrey; 2ndly, 1937 (marriage dissolved 1953), Lydia Mary, da. of the late Edward Milligen Beloe, of King's Lynn, Norfolk; 3rdly, 1953, Janet Lilian, only da. of the late Col. Hugh Sidney Ellis, CBE, MC, and has issue by 2nd and 3rd marriages.

Arms—Per pale gules and azure a bascule argent, chained or, in chief a fountain. Crest—A merman azure, pointing with the index finger of the dexter hand and holding in the sinister hand a rudder gold.
Residences—Cooks Mill, Fordham Heath, nr. Colchester, Essex, CO3 5TF; 5, Rembrandt Close, SW1.

Son living—By 3rd marriage—JAMES HUGH THOMAS, b. Sept. 18th, 1956.

Daughters living—By 2nd marriage—Georgina Jane (*Hon. Mrs. Nigel G. Parker*), *b.* 1937: *m.* 1965, the Hon. Nigel Geoffrey Parker, of Combe Lane Farm, Wormley, Godalming, Surrey [*see* E. Morley].——Stephanie Gordon, *b.* 1942: *m.* 1966, Lt.-Col. J. N. Dudley Lucas, The R. Scots (The R. Regt.), of Becketts, Chilmark, Salisbury, Wilts., and has issue living, Timothy James Stephen, *b.* 1968,—Chloe Henrietta, *b.* 1967.——**By 3rd m.**—Angela Susan, *b.* 1954.

Sister living—Mary Gordon, *b.* 1898 : *m.* 1924, Dennis John Alsen Fletcher, R.A.F. Vol. Reserve, who *d.* (killed on active ser. during European War) 1942, and has issue living, Ann Priscilla, *b.* 1927: *m.* 1949, Alastair Miller Millar, MRCVS, of Friars Farm, Wimbish, Saffron Walden, Essex, and has issue living, Sandra Penelope *b.* 1949: *m.* 1974, Lt. John William Robert Harris, RN, of 10, Purbeck Drive, Fareham, Hants. PO14 1SA. *Residence*, Little Cozens, Widford, Ware, Herts.

Collateral Branches living.

Issue of the late Howson Foulger Devitt, 2nd son of 1st baronet, *b.* 1869, *d.* 1949 : *m.* 1908, Winifred Lina, who *d.* 1972, el. da. of the late Richard Woollcombe, of Starmead, Wokingham, Berks:—

Howson Charles, *OBE* (Gat-e-Whing, Andreas, I. of Man), *b.* 1909; ed. at Sherborne, and at Trin. Hall, Camb.; an Underwriting Member of Lloyds; 1939-45 War as Wing Com. RAF (OBE); OBE (Mil.) 1941: *m.* 1939, Elizabeth Carola, da. of Edward Fairholme, of Burke's Corner, Beaconsfield, and has issue living, Richard Howson, *b.* 1940,—Carola Waveney, *b.* 1942: *m.* 1962, Peter John Laidlaw Jenkins, of Pages, Shalford, Braintree, Essex, and has issue living, Mark Alan Laidlaw *b.* 1964, Carola Rosemary *b.* 1965, Tamsin Elisabeth *b.* 1970.——Peter Kenneth (c/o Williams & Glyn's Bank, 20, Birchin Lane, EC3), *b.* 1911; ed. at Sherborne; Wing-Cdr. Roy. AuxAF, and a DL for Surrey; 1939-45 War (despatches): *m.* 1st, 1935, Eunice Stephanie, yst. da. of the late Sir Charles Sheriton Swan; 2ndly, 1950, Joan Elizabeth, da. of the late T. Forbes Robertson, of Santa Barbara, Cal., USA; 3rdly, 1953, remarried his 1st wife, Eunice Stephanie (ante), and has issue living, (by 1st m.) Jeremy Peter (Tresco, Forrest Rd., Liss Forest, Liss, Hants), *b.* 1937; Cdr. RN (ret.): *m.* 1961, Elspeth, el. da. of Brig. William Edward Guest, MBE, of The Cottage, Lizard, Cornwall, and has issue living, Mark Edward Peter *b.* 1962, Simon Charles Guest *b.* 1964, Nicholas Jeremy James *b.* 1968, Timothy William Guy (twin) *b.* 1968,—Lorna Stephanie, *b.* 1942: *m.* 1963, Geoffrey Glynn-Jones, and has issue living, Timothy Patrick, *b.* 1965, Lavinia Mary, *b.* 1969,—Jaquette Ann, *b.* 1944,—Vivien Gay, *b.* 1948.—— Ursula Helen, *b.* 1912: *m.* 1935, Maj. Michael Alastair Spencer-Nairn, Fife and Forfar Yeo (TA) [*see* Spencer-Nairn, Bt.].——Sheila Winifred (twin), *b.* 1912: *m.* 1936, Edward Michael Harrison, of Otterton Barton, Budleigh Salterton, Devon, and has issue living, Hugh Michael James (Meadowside, Woodbury, Exeter, Devon), *b.* 1942: *m.* 1st, 1968 (m. diss. 1974), Joanna Mary, da. of Col. W. R. Healing, of Budleigh Salterton; 2ndly, 1974, Stephanie Christine, el. da. of the Rev. Peter Haslewood Shaw, V. of Alderney, CI, and has issue living, (by 1st m.) James Edward *b.* 1969, (by 2nd m.) Camilla Rose *b.* 1975,—Juliet Mary, *b.* 1937: *m.* 1964, Tuckerman Moss, PhD, of 67, Alta Vista, Orinda, Cal., USA, and has issue living, Michael Duval *b.* 1965 Jeremy Gilbert *b.* 1968, Rebecca Alice (twin) *b.* 1968,—Lucy Clare, *b.* 1950: *m.* 1971, Paul Robert Hulme, of Tarr Steps Hotel, Hawkridge, Dulverton, Som., and has issue living, Emma Catherine *b.* 1971.

Grandchildren of the late Herbert Pye-Smith Devitt, MRCS, LRCP (infra):— Issue of the late (Herbert) Lionel Devitt, *b.* 1910; *d.* 1964: *m.* 1st, 1939 (m. diss. 1948), (Myfanwy Rina) Doreen, da. of the late Alwyn H. Holman; 2ndly, 1947 (m. diss. 1954), Sheila Mary da. of Edmond Ironside Bremner; 3rdly, 1954, Fleur Traherne Thomas (11B, Bina Gdns., SW6):— (By 1st m.) Michael Wyn (Farmhill Manor, Braddan, I. of Man), *b.* 1943: *m.* 1967, Susan Gundreda de Warrenne, only child of Walter Kingsley Brett, and has issue living, Roland, *b.* 1972, Madeleine, *b.* 1969.——Judith Anne Mary, *b.* 1940: *m.* 1963, Edward David Beresford Tebbs, of Coombe End Cottage, Golf Club Drive, Coombe, Kingston upon Thames, and has issue living, Andrew, *b.* 1971,—Lucy, *b.* 1965,—Amanda, *b.* 1967.

Issue of the late Herbert Pye-Smith Devitt, M.R.C.S., L.R.C.P., 3rd son of 1st baronet, *b.* 1873, *d.* 1958 : *m.* 1st, 1903, Roberta Mary Cornelia, who *d.* 1934, el. da. of the late Major James George Anderson, Roy. Irish Fusiliers ; 2ndly, 1935, Muriel, who *d.* 1951, da. of the late Reginald M. Snow, of Bideford, Devon, and widow of Flight-Lieut. G. E. Blake, RAF; 3rdly, 1952, Carola Evelyn (50, Mildenhall, West Cliff Rd., Bournemouth), da. of the late E. Howard May, and widow of W. W. Brownlee:— (By 1st m.) Philip Eyre (Whydown Lodge, Little Common, Bexhill-on-Sea, Sussex), *b.* 1907; ed. at Sherborne, and at Gonville and Caius Coll., Camb. (BA 1929); 1919-45 War as Maj. Dorset Regt., and a GSO, Scottish Command: *m.* 1947, Patricia Melicent, el. da. of the late Walter Edward Leslie, of Tarbert, co. Kerry, and has issue living, Desmond Philip, *b.* 1950,—Ann Patricia, *b.* 1954.——Dorrothea (Buckhold, Chestnut Av., Guildford) *b.* 1904: *m.* 1930, Henry Martin Ward Clarke, who *d.* 1963, and has issue living, Rosemary *b.* 1932: *m.* 1958, Michael Herzig, of 1, Vicarage Hill, Farnham, Surrey, and has issue living, Andrew Michael *b.* 1960, Peter John *b.* 1962, Martin Robert *b.* 1966, Catherine Jane *b.* 1969,—Jenifer Jane, *b.* 1935.——Margaret, *b.* 1915: *m.* 1944, Cedric Bramley, and has issue living, Roberta, *b.* 1949. *Residence*, Windrush, 30, Wealden Way, Little Common, Bexhill-on-Sea.

Grandsons of the late Herbert Pye-Smith Devitt, MRCS, LRCP, (ante):— Issue of the late John Desmond Devitt, MRCS, LRCP, *b.* 1917, *d.* 1973: *m.* 1957, Pamela Ruth (Kincranigie, Copp Hill Lane, Budleigh Salterton, S. Devon), da. of the late L. B. Foot, of Egbury, Hants.:— Timothy John Herbert, *b.* 1958.——Jonathan Stephen, *b.* 1960.——(Andrew) James, *b.* 1962.

Issue of the late Philip Henry Devitt [youngest son of 1st baronet (cr. 1916)], who was *cr.* a *Baronet* 1931.
See Devitt, Bt., cr. 1931 (ext.).

Sir Thomas Lane Devitt, 1st Bt. (sometime senior partner in the firm of Devitt and Moore, and Pres. of Chamber of Shipping of the United Kingdom 1890, and of Institute of Marine Engineers 1913-14), was one of the Managers of the Orient Line from its foundation, Pres. of the Shipping Federation 1890 to 1923 (also Chm. 1890-1914), Chm. of Lloyd's Register of Shipping 1911-22, and Founder of the Nautical Coll., Pangbourne.

DEVITT, Creation (U.K.) 1931, of Pangbourne, Berks. [Extinct 1947.]

Sir PHILIP HENRY DEVITT, 1st and last *Baronet*.

Daughters living of 1st Baronet—Theodora Joan, *b.* 1919.——Elizabeth Anne (*Lady Koelle*). *b.* 1921 : *m.* 1948, as his second wife, Vice-Adm. Sir Harry Philpot Koelle, K.C.B., and has issue living, Victoria Anne, *b.* 1949,—Phillipa June, *b.* 1951. *Residence*, Mill House, Thornford, Sherborne.——Jennifer Margaret, *b.* 1923.——Dorothy Susan, *b.* 1931.——Bridget Helen (twin), *b.* 1931: *m.* 1952, Oliver Michael Robin Greenwood, late Capt. Coldstream Guards, and has issue living, Simon Nelson, *b.* 1954,—Christopher Philip, *b.* 1957, James William Dickon, *b.* 1964,— Nicola Jane, *b.* 1954. *Residence*, Hosty Lodge, Cudham, Sevenoaks, Kent.

DEWEY, Creation (U.K.) 1917, of South Hill Wood, Bromley, Kent.

VIR SAPIENS FORTIS EST

The wise man is strong.

Sir ANTHONY HUGH DEWEY, 3rd *Baronet*, el. son of the late Major Hugh Grahame Dewey, M.C., el. son of 2nd Baronet ; *b.* July 31st, 1921 ; *s.* his grandfather, *the Rev. Sir* STANLEY DAWS, 1948 ; ed. at Wellington Coll.; is a J.P. for Somerset ; European War 1940-45 as Capt. R.A. and Major N. Somerset Yeo.: *m.* 1949, Sylvia Jacqueline Rosamund, da. of the late John Ross MacMahon, M.B., C.M., of Branksome Manor, Bournemouth, and has issue.

Arms—1st and 4th per fesse sable and or, three cinquefoils between two barrulets between three dragons' heads erased counterchanged, in each of their mouths a sword in bend proper, pommels and hilts of the second, *Dewey;* 2nd and 3rd sable, a griffin segreant ermine, armed or, the wings erminois, a bordure compony argent and gules, *Ballard.* *Crest*—A dragon's head erased sable, holding in the mouth a sword in bend proper, pommel and hilt or, between two dragons' wings of the last, on each a bend of the first, charged with a cinquefoil of the third.
Residence—Silton Lodge, Gillingham, Dorset. *Club*—Army and Navy.

Sons living—RUPERT GRAHAME, *b.* March 29th, 1953.——Charles Ross, *b.* 1960.

Daughters living—Delia Mary, *b.* 1951.——Carola Jane, *b.* 1955.——Angela Rosamund, *b.* 1957.

Sister living—Hilary Mary, *b.* 1923; B.Sc. London 1944, M.Sc. 1947: *m.* 1953, Paul Faulconer Morgan, and has issue living, Hugh Faulconer, *b.* 1960,——Clare Anne, *b.* 1954,——Stella Margaret, *b.* 1956,——Patricia Hilary, *b.* 1957. *Residence*, Sundial House, Styal, Wilmslow, Cheshire.

Uncles living (sons of 2nd baronet)—Norman Strafford, *M.C.*, *b.* 1896 ; ed. at Winchester, and at Pembroke Coll., Camb. (M.A.); 1914-18 War as Lieut. R.F.A. (M.C.): *m.* 1925, Ursula Marguerite, da. of the late H. D. D. Barman, of Helensburgh, and has issue living, Thomas Norman (4, Beadon Rd., Bromley, Kent) *b.* 1926: ed. at Radley, Pembroke Coll., Camb. (MA), and Brunel Univ. (M.Tech.); CEng.; MIEE, MIMechE: *m.* 1964, Janet Mary, da. of the late B. C. Baxter, of Enfield, Middlesex, and has issue living, Stephen Thomas *b.* 1965, Claire Margaret *b.* 1966,——David Lewis (17, Kewferry Rd., Northwood, Middlesex), *b.* 1927; ed. at Radley, and at Pembroke Coll., Camb. (MA); PhD London 1953: *m.* 1960, Jacqueline Anne, da. of L. F. Curtis, of Dartford, Kent, and has issue living, Nigel Lewis *b.* 1967, Fiona Jane *b.* 1961, Helen Gay *b.* 1964,——Martin Ross (Cherry Cottage, 139, Clinton Lane, Kenilworth, Warwicks.), *b.* 1933; ed. at Radley: *m.* 1964, Barbara, da. of the late David Sharp, of Wokingham, and has issue living, Ross Meredith *b.* 1966,——Olive Rosemary, *b.* 1931; BSc London 1955: *m.* 1962, Peter Gordon Hiam Wilson, of The Willows, Lockfold, Bury St. Edmunds. *Residence*, 5, Kings Court, Kelsey Park Av., Beckenham, Kent.——Theodore Stanley, *b.* 1902; ed. at Rugby, and at Pembroke Coll., Camb. (Scholar, BA Honours, MB): *m.* 1929, Monica, da. of Vincent Daniel, of Copping, Leigh, Kent, and has issue living, Terence Charles (20 Harbour Av., Marblehead, Mass., USA), *b.* 1933; ed. at Ampleforth, and at Pembroke Coll., Camb. (BA honours 1957, MA 1961); commissioned RNVR 1954,——Timothy Hugh (The Cottage, Kelston, Bath), *b.* 1935; ed. at Ampleforth: *m.* 1962, Margaret Mia, da. of the late Dr. T. R. D. Aubrey, of Bitton, Glos., and has issue living, Adrian Charles *b.* 1963, Annabel Mary *b.* 1965, Laura Rose *b.* 1967, Jessica Mia *b.* 1968,——Amanda Jane, *b.* 1931: *m.* 1st 1956 (m. diss. 1966), John Robin Millner; 2ndly 1966, Peter Michael Lloyd Wenham, of Ivy House, Gaston Green, Bishops Stortford, and has issue living (by 1st husband) Julian John *b.* 1958, Piers Theodore *b.* 1960, Giles William *b.* 1961, (by 2nd husband) Susanna Jane *b.* 1964, Arabella Monica *b.* 1966,——Caroline Mary, *b.* 1938: *m.* 1962, Julian Reginald Brinton Clist, MBE, of Woodbury Old Farm, Shelsley Beauchamp, Worcs., and has issue living, Sophia Anne Brinton *b.* 1963, Samantha Gëbrielle Brinton *b.* 1964, Imogen Cecilia Brinton *b.* 1969,——Corinne Rose (twin), *b.* 1938: *m.* 1960, Stanley Keith Knowles, of 64, Woodsford Sq., W14, and has issue living, Tobias Sebastian *b.* 1961, Hugh Stanley Keith *b.* 1962, Benedict Caradoc *b.* 1968, Miranda Vivian *b.* 1964. *Residence*, Warders, East St., Tonbridge, Kent.——*Rev.* Meredith Ballard, *b.* 1907; ed. at Rugby, and at Pembroke Coll., Camb. (Scholar, BA Honours, Two Triposes, MA 1932); appointed Fellow and Dean of Pembroke Coll., 1936, and Assist. Tutor 1945; 1939-45 War as temp. Chap. RNVR. *Residence*, Pembroke College, Cambridge.

Aunt living (daughter of 2nd baronet)—Rose Myfanwy, *OBE*, *b.* 1898; formerly HM Inspector of Schs., Dept. of Ed. and Science; OBE (Civil) 1957. *Residence*, 17, Beechfield Rd., Alderley Edge, Cheshire. *Club*—English Speaking Union.

Mother living—Marjorie Florence Isobell (*Lady Bell*), da. of Lieut.-Col. Alexander Hugh Dobbs, late Indian Army, formerly of Bray, Wicklow: *m.* 1st, 1920, Major Hugh Grahame Dewey, M.C. (ante), who *d.* 1936 : 2ndly, 1940, as his second wife, Sir Robert Duncan Bell, K.C.S.I., C.I.E., who *d.* 1953. *Residence*, Chillaway Lodge, Crondall, Farnham, Surrey.

Collateral Branches living.

Grandchildren of the late Maj. Hugh Grahame Dewey, MC, el. son of 2nd baronet:—
Issue of the late Maj. Michael Grahame Dewey, *b.* 1928, *d.* 1973: *m.* 1954, Anne Cecilia (Warden Grange, Chipping Warden, Banbury, Oxon.) da. of the late Brig. Edward Thomas Arthur George Boylan, CBE, DSO, MC [see O'Brien, Bt.]:—
Christopher Grahame, *b.* 1963.——Philippa Mary, *b.* 1955.——Amanda Julia, *b.* 1957.

Issue of the late Thomas Lewis Dewey, 3rd son of 2nd baronet, *b.* 1900, *d.* 1951: *m.* 1936, Josephine May Sadler (who *m.* 2ndly, 1957, Andrew Mackenzie Ross, MD, DLO, of Cherry Tree Cottage, Nether Compton, Sherborne, Dorset), da. of Joseph Sadler Stockton, of Whitely Woods, Sheffield):—
Peter Lewis, *b.* 1938; ed. at Lancing.——Jennifer Ann, *b.* 1937: *m.* 1966, Maj. David Younger Queen's Own Hussars, of Ravenswood, Melrose, Roxburghshire, and has issue living, William Grahame Ralph, *b.* 1970,——James David, *b.* 1972,——Catherine Belinda, *b.* 1967.

Grandson of the late Marshall Dewey (infra):—
Issue of the late Sidney Maurice Dewey, *b.* 1902, *d.* 1968: *m.* 1931, Dorothy Catherine Holt, who *d.* 1968:—
Anthony Guy (White Cottage, Poulner Hill, Ringwood, Hants.), *b.* 1932; ed. at Repton: *m.* 1968, Mrs. Caroline Rose Hardie, da. of the late L. M. Hanbury-Bateman, and has issue living, Martin Guy, *b.* 1969,——Nicholas George, *b.* 1971.

Issue of the late Marshall Dewey, younger son of 1st baronet, *b.* 1874, *d.* 1919: *m.* 1897, Ethel Julia, who *d.* 1925 da. of the late Charles Harvey:—

Phyllis Muriel, *b.* 1904: *m.* 1936, Leonard Gilbert, and has issue living, Tessa Julia, *b.* 1938: *m.* 1966, Robert Tucker, of Woolmers Farm, Bickington, Barnstaple, Devon, and has issue living, Paul Robert *b.* 1971, Carolyn Kay *b.* 1967,—Sarah, *b.* 1941: *m.* 1963, Rodney George Short, of Uplands, Prince Cres., Staunton, Glos., and has issue living, Melanie Jane *b.* 1964, Rebecca Alison *b.* 1968,—Caryl Jane, *b.* 1947: *m.* 1972, Andrew Ian Seat, MB, BS, of 20A, Post St., Godmanchester, Hunts. *Residence*, 2, Combrew Cottages, Bickington, Barnstaple, N. Devon.

Sir Thomas Charles Dewey, 1st Bt., was Pres. of Prudential Assurance Co. The Rev. Sir Stanley Daws Dewey, 2nd Bt., was Preb. of Exeter Cathedral 1935-43, and High Sheriff of Devon **1945.**

TENNYSON-d'EYNCOURT, Creation (U.K.) 1930, of Carter's Corner Farm, Parish of Herstmonceux, co. Sussex.

Nothing rashly

Forward.

Sir (JOHN) JEREMY (EUSTACE) TENNYSON-D'EYNCOURT, 3rd *Baronet*; *b.* July 8th, 1927; *s.* his father, *Sir* (EUSTACE) GERVAIS, 1971; ed. at Eton, and Glasgow Univ.; served RN 1945-47; a Member of Inst. of Management Consultants: *m.* 1st, 1964, (m. diss. 1972), Sally June, el. da. of Robin Stratford, QC, and formerly wife of Colin Fyfe-Jamieson; 2ndly, 1972, Brenda Mary, 2nd da. of Austin Stafford, LRCSI, LM, of 17, Haling Park Rd., Croydon, and formerly wife of Peter Deitsch.

Arms—Quarterly: 1st and 4th, azure, a fesse dancettée between ten billets, four and six or, *d'Eyncourt* ; 2nd and 3rd, gules, three leopards' faces or, jessant-de-lis azure, over all a bend of the last, *Tennyson.* Crests—1st, a lion passant guardant argent, on the head a crown of fleur-de-lis or, the dexter fore-paw supporting a shield charged with the arms of *d'Eyncourt* ; 2nd, a dexter arm in armour, the hand in a gauntlet or, grasping a broken tilting spear, enfiled with a garland of laurel proper, *Tennyson.*

Residences—39, 7th St. Parkhurst, Johannesburg, S. Africa; 24, Cheyne Court, Flood St., SW3.

Brother living—GILES GERVAIS (1128, Ideal St., Mandaluyong, Rizal, Philippines), *b.* April 16th, 1935; ed. at Eton and Millfield; Capt. Coldm. Gds.: *m.* 1966, Juanita, da. of Fortunato Borromeo, and has issue living, Mark Gervais, *b.* 1967.

Sister living—Philippa Janet (*Lady McAlpine*), *b.* 1928: *m.* 1st, 1953 (m. diss. 1970), Nigel Nicolson, MBE [*see* B. Carnock]; 2ndly, 1970, Sir Robin McAlpine, CBE, of Aylesfield, Alton, Hants. [*see* McAlpine, Bt., colls.].

Widow living of 2nd Baronet—VINNIE LORRAINE ((*Vinnie, Lady Tennyson-d'Eyncout*) (3525, Turtle Creek Blvd., Apt. 16E, Dallas, Texas, 7 52 19, USA), da. of the late Andrew Pearson, of Minneapolis, USA, and widow of Robert J. O'Donnell: *m.* 1964, as his 2nd wife, Sir (Eustace) Gervais Tennyson-d'Eyncourt, 2nd Bt., who *d.* 1971.

The 1st baronet, Sir Eustace Henry William Tennyson-d'Eyncourt, K.C.B., F.R.S., D.Sc., LL.D. (son of the late Louis Charles Tennyson-d'Eyncourt, of Bayons Manor, Market Rasen), was a Naval Architect, Director of Naval Construction, Admiralty, and Principal Technical Adviser 1912-23, and Head of Committee at Admiralty which produced the first tanks.

Dick-Cunyngham, see Cunyngham.

Dick-Lauder, see Lauder.

DILKE, Creation (U.K.) 1862, of Sloane Street, Chelsea.

Leo inimicis amicis columba.

A lion to my enemies and a dove to my friends.

Sir JOHN FISHER WENTWORTH DILKE, 5th *Baronet;* *b.* May 8th, 1906; *s.* his father, *Sir* FISHER WENTWORTH, 1944: ed. at Winchester, and at New Coll., Oxford; in HM's Foreign Ser. 1929-32 ; late staff of *The Times* Foreign Depart. in Govt. Information Sers., and BBC External Ser.: *m.* 1st, 1934 (m. diss., 1949), Sheila, da. of Sir William Seeds, KCMG; 2ndly, 1951, Iris Evelyn, da. of the late Ernest Clark, and has issue by 1st marriage.

Arms—Quarterly of nine : 1st, gules, a lion rampant per pale argent and or ; 2nd, argent, a mullet gules ; 3rd, sable a chevron between three leopards' faces or ; 4th, argent, a cross grady throughout sable ; 5th, paly of six argent and gules a bend counterchanged ; 6th, gules, on a bend argent three escallops azure ; 7th, paly of six argent and sable on a bend gules, three mullets argent ; 8th, quarterly : or and gules on a bend sable, between two fretts or, three escallops of the first ; 9th, ermine two chevrons sable. Crest—A dove proper.

Residence—Ludpits, Etchingham, E. Sussex.

Sons living—By 1st marriage—CHARLES JOHN WENTWORTH, *b.* Feb. 21, 1937; ed. at Winchester, and at King's Coll., Camb. (BA).——Timothy Fisher Wentworth (15, Wemyss Rd., SE3), *b.* 1938; ed. at Winchester and at New Coll., Oxford (MA); BM, BCh; MRCP London: *m.* 1965, Caroline Sophia, da. of Christopher Wentworth Dilke (infra), and has issue living, Felix Wentworth, *b.* 1967,—Rosemary Frances, *b.* 1970.

Brother living—Christopher Wentworth, *b.* 1913 ; is a Novelist ; formerly Lieut.-Col. **R.A.:** *m.* 1939, Alice Mary, da. of the late Hon. James William Best, O.B.E. [*see* B. Wynford, **colls.**] and has issue living, Fisher William Wentworth, *b.* 1948,—Caroline Sophia, *b.* 1940: *m.* 1965' Timothy Fisher Wentworth Dilke (ante),—Annabel Mary, *b.* 1942,—Lucy Catherine, *b.* 1952' *Residences*, 1, Campden Grove, W8; Valehouse Farm, Whitchurch Canonicorum, Bridport' Dorset.

Collateral Branches living.

Issue of the late Michael Clifford Wentworth Dilke, 2nd son of 4th baronet, *b.* 1909, *d.* 1944: *m.* 1940, Rosemary Blanche, who *d.* 1974, da. of Capt. Sir Thomas Herbert Cochrane Troubridge, 4th Bt., and widow of Capt. Roderick Kilgour Mackenzie, younger, of Kincraig:—

Lucilla Rose *b.* 1941: *m.* 1970, Gareth Ulric van den Bogaerde, of 27, Viewfield Rd., SW18, and has issue living, Ulric Michael Amadeus Landrover, *b.* 1970,—Alice Rosemary Patience Lucilla, *b.* 1973.

Issue of the late Clement Wentworth Dilke, younger brother of 4th baronet, *b.* 1878, *d.* 1944: *m.* 1901, Marie Hilda Jessie, who *d.* 1944, only child of William Phelps, M.D.:—

Oswald Ashton Wentworth (Moorfield, Huby, Leeds), *b.* 1915; ed. at Stowe, and at King's Coll., Camb. (MA); DLitt et Phil. Univ. of S. Africa; Lecturer in Classics, Univ. Coll., Hull 1946-50, and Lecturer in Humanity, Glasgow Univ. 1950-67, since when Prof. of Latin, Leeds Univ.; Prof. of Classics, Rhodes Univ., S. Africa 1961-62, and Visiting Prof. in Classics Ohio State Univ. 1969; formerly Capt. Intelligence Corps: *m.* 1949, Margaret Sterndale, *M A*, only da. of George Williamson, of Ashton-under-Lyne, and has issue living, Stephen Wentworth (55, Moorhead Park, Cheltenham), *b.* 1951; ed. at Manchester Gram. Sch, Winchester, and New Coll., Oxford (BA); MSc Sheffield; with FO.——Muriel Mary Wentworth *b.* 1903: *m.* 1930, Herbert Fraser Standen, who assumed by deed poll 1952 the additional surname of McDougal after that of Standen, and has issue living, Rev. John Anthony Phelps (Farnham Rectory, Blandford, Dorset), *b.* 1933: *m.* 1965, Susan Eleanor Kent, and has issue living, Anthony Peter *b.* 1966, Clare Susan *b.* 1970. *Residence*, Hedges, Port Lewaigue, Maughold, I. of Man.——Celia Wentworth, *b.* 1908: *m.* 1933, Otto René Gottlieb Vervuart, and has issue living, Reinhardt James (Buizerdhorst 39, Leyden, Netherlands), *b.* 1934: *m.* 1965, Anita Douwes, and has issue living, Melvin Michael *b.* 1966, Norbert Calmon *b.* 1967,—Gerard Michael (Frederikastraat 6, District Surinam, Surinam, S. America), *b.* 1938: *m.* 1970, Mildred Helna, da. of Stuart Fraser, of Paramaribo, Surinam, and has issue living, Stuart René Gerard *b.* 1971,—Celia Wentworth *b.* 1936: *m.* 1962, Anton F. Smit, of Afobakalaan 88, District Surinam, Surinam, and has issue living, Willem Otto Anton *b.* 1968, Audrey Elizabeth *b.* 1965, Jeanine Annette *b.* 1967. *Residence*, 12, Waterkant, Paramaribo, Surinam.

The 1st baronet took a prominent part in the International Exhibitions of 1851 and 1862, and sat as M.P. for Wallingford (*L*) 1865-8. The 2nd baronet, the Rt. Hon. Sir Charles Wentworth Dilke, was Under-Sec. for Foreign Affairs 1880-82, and Pres. of Local Govt. Board 1882-5, and sat as M.P. for Chelsea (*L*) 1868-86, and for Forest of Dean Div. of Gloucestershire 1892-1911.

DILLON, Creation (U.K.) 1801, of Lismullen, Meath.

Sir ROBERT WILLIAM CHARLIER DILLON, 8th *Baronet*, and a Baron of the Holy Roman Empire, son of the late Robert Arthur Dillon (who *d.* Oct. 1925), great-great-grandson of 1st baronet ; *b.* Jan. 17th, 1914 ; *s.* his kinsman, *Sir* JOHN FOX, Nov. 1925 : *m.* 1947, Synolda, da. of the late Cholmondeley Clarke.

Arms—Argent, a lion rampant between three crescents gules, issuant from each crescent a star with six points of the field, over all a **fesse** azure. **Crest**—On a chapeau gules turned up ermine, a falcon rising argent, beaked, legged and belled or. **Second Motto**—" Auxilium ab alto" (*Help from on high*).

Residence—Knockavon House, Enniscorthy, co. Wexford.

Daughter living of 7th Baronet—Millicent, *b.* 1895. *Residence*, Hendregadred, Pentrefelin, Criccieth, Caernarvonshire.

Whilst I breathe I hope. This family is descended from a common ancestor with the Earls of Roscommon and Barons (ext.) Clonbrock. The 1st baronet, Sir John, M.P., was created a Baron of the Holy Roman Empire, 1782, with reversion to male and female descendants, and was authorized by Roy. licence to bear the title in this country.

Dillwyn-Venables-Llewelyn, see Llewelyn.

DIMSDALE, Creation (U.K.) 1902, of Goldsmiths, Langdon Hills, Essex, and Lancaster Street, Paddington, co. London.

Sir JOHN HOLDSWORTH DIMSDALE, 3rd *Baronet*; *b.* Dec. 31st, 1901 ; *s.* his father, *Sir* JOHN HOLDSWORTH, 1923; ed. at Oundle: *m.* 1949, Gisela Panova, who *d.* 1969.

Arms—Argent on a fesse dancettée azure between three mullets **sable** two bezants. **Crest**—A staff fessewise entwined by a serpent proper, thereon a griffin's head erased argent.

Residence—16, Willis Rd., Swaythling, Southampton, SO2 2NT.

Quod Deus vult fiet.
What God wishes will be done.

The 1st baronet, the Rt. Hon. Sir Joseph Cockfield Dimsdale, KCVO, PC, sometime a Dir. of Prescott, Dimsdale and Co. (Limited), bankers, of Cornhill, was Lord Mayor of London 1901-2, and City Chamberlain 1902-12; he sat as MP for City of London (C) 1900-6.

Dinshaw Manockjee Petit, see Petit.

DIXIE, Creation (E.) 1660, of Market Bosworth, Leicestershire.

Sir (ALEXANDER ARCHIBALD DOUGLAS) WOLSTAN DIXIE, 13th *Baronet; b.* Jan. 8th, 1910; *s.* his father, *Sir* GEORGE DOUGLAS, 1948; ed. at St. Joseph's Coll., Dumfries, and at Prior Park Coll., Bath; is patron of one living (but being a Roman Catholic cannot present), and a Member of Windsor Rural Dist. Council: *m.* 1st, 1940, Phyllis Pinnel (from whom he obtained a divorce 1950), da. of the late Lieut.-Col. Percy John Probyn, D.S.O.; 2ndly, 1950, Dorothy Penelope King-Kirkman, and has issue by 2nd marriage.

Arms—Azure, a lion rampant or, a chief of the last. Crest—An ounce sejant proper, ducally gorged or.

Residence—Bosworth Park, Leics.

Quod dixi, dixi

What I have said, I have said.

Daughters living—By 2nd marriage—Eleanor Barbara Lindsay; *b.* 1952.——Caroline Mary Jane, *b.* 1960.

Sister living—Frances Dorothy Madeleine Barbara de la Motte, *b.* 1912: *m.* 1st, 1944, Ernest Thomas Riley Kirby, who *d.* 1966; 2ndly, 1974, Cdr. John Weddall Pontifex, RN (ret.) of Cloudes Lodge, Bingham Av., Lilliput, Poole, Dorset.

This family was settled at Bosworth *temp.* Queen Elizabeth I. Sir Wolstan Dixie, 1st baronet, received his warrant of baronetcy from Charles I., for his activity and zealousness in the royal cause, however, through the confusion of the times, the patent was not taken out until 1660, in which year Sir Wolstan was Sheriff of Leicestershire.

DIXON, Creation (U.K.) 1919, of Astle, Chelford, co. Palatine of Chester.

Sir JOHN DIXON, 2nd *Baronet; b.* June 13th, 1886; *s.* his father, *Sir* George, 1924; ed. at Eton: *m.* 1910, Gwendolen Anne, who *d.* 1974, da. of Sir Joseph Layton Elmes Spearman, 2nd Bt., and has issue.

Arms—Gules, a fleur-de-lis or, on a chief argent three ermine spots sable. Crest—A demi-lion rampant gules, holding between the paws a fylfot or.

Residence—

Illores componunt hominem.

Manners maketh man.

Sons living—JOHN GEORGE (Chemin de l'Ille de Salagnon, 1815 Clarens, Vand, Switzerland) *b.* Sept. 17th, 1911; ed. at Cranleigh: *m.* 1947, Caroline, da. of the late Charles J. Hiltermann of 31, Melbury Court, W8, and has issue living, Mary Jane, *b.* 1951.——Nigel (Little Woolgarston House, Corfe Castle, Dorset), *b.* 1920; Capt. RN (ret.): *m.* 1948, Margaret Josephine, da. of the late Maurice John Collett, of Aston Lodge, Malvern Wells, Worcs., and has issue living, Jonathan Mark, *b.* 1949.

Daughter living—Beryl (11, Newton Court, Swanage, Dorset), *b.* 1916.

Sir George Dixon, 1st Bt., was High Sheriff for Cheshire 1881.

DODDS, Creation (U.K.) 1964, of West Chiltington, co. Sussex.

Sir RALPH JORDON DODDS, 2nd *Baronet; b.* March 25th, 1928, *s.* his father, *Sir* (EDWARD) CHARLES, *MVO*, 1973; ed. at Winchester, and RMA Sandhurst; late Capt. 13/18th Hussars; an Underwriting Member of Lloyd's since 1964: *m.* 1954, Marion, da. of the late Sir Daniel Thomas Davies, KCVO, and has issue.

Arms—Azure issuant from a chief argent and out of a sunburst a dexter hand proper between two crabs heads downward argent each transfixed by a sword or on the chief a steer's head caboshed sable armed gold between two capons proper. Crest—A demi woman affronty proper vested azure holding an open book proper inscribed with the chemical formula for stilboestrol sable.

Residence—93 Abbotsbury Rd., W14.   *Club*—Cavalry.

Daughters living—Caroline, *b.* 1956.——Arabella, *b.* 1961.

The 1st baronet, Sir (Edward) Charles Dodds, MVO, son of Ralph Edward Dodds, of Darlington, and London, was Pres. Roy. Coll. Physicians 1962-66.

SMITH-DODSWORTH, Creation (G.B.) 1784, of Newland Park, Yorkshire.

Sir JOHN CHRISTOPHER SMITH - DODSWORTH, 8th *Baronet*; *b.* March 4th, 1935; *s.* his father, *Sir* CLAUDE MATTHEW, 1940; ed. at Ampleforth: *m.* 1961, Margaret Anne, da. of Alfred Jones, of Pludds, Gloucestershire, and has issue.

Arms—Quarterly: 1st and 4th, argent, a bend engrailed sable between three annulets gules, *Dodsworth*; 2nd and 3rd, per saltire argent and sable two trefoils slipped in pale gules, *Smith*. Crests—1st, a dexter cubit arm in chain mail or, the hand proper grasping a broken tilting spear or, embrued gules, *Dodsworth*; 2nd, out of a ducal coronet or, a boar's head couped at the neck azure, crined and tusked or, *Smith*.
Residence—Thornton Watlass Hall, Ripon, Yorkshire.

Son living—DAVID JOHN *b.* Oct. 23rd, 1963.

Pro lege senatu qu ege.   **Daughter living**—Cyrilla Denise, *b.* 1962.
Govern in accordance   **Sisters living**—Mary Cyrilla, *b.* 1933.——Julia Agnes, *b.* 1938: *m.* 1963.
with law and parliament.   Brian Maccelari, of Johannesburg, S. Africa, and has issue living, Douglas Charles Dodsworth, *b.* 1965,—Jeremy Christopher Dodsworth (twin), *b.* 1965,—Mary Frances Dodsworth, *b.* 1963,—Angela Josephine Dodsworth, *b.* 1969.

Aunt living (daughter of 6th baronet)—Hilda Monica, *b.* 1903: *m.* 1930, Herbert Brian Taylor, who *d.* 1957, and has issue living, David Jenneson (Box 197, Kericho, Kenya) *b.* 1937: *m.* 1966, Anne Doyle, and has issue living, Nicholas *b.* 1969, Anita *b.* 1966,—Simon Brian, *b.* 1939: *m.* 1970, Amalia Zoe, da. of Patrick Butler-Henderson [*see* B. Faringdon, colls.], and has issue living, Emma Amalia Jane *b.* 1971, Amanda Katherine Zoe *b.* 1973,—Christopher Dodsworth, *b.* 1953, James *b.* 1956, Susan *b.* 1958,—Susan Elizabeth Wendy, *b.* 1932; ARCM, LRAM.

Widow living of 7th Baronet—CYRILLA MARIE-LOUISE VON SOBBE (*Cyrilla, Lady Smith-Dodsworth*), da. of William Ernest Taylor, of Linnet Lane, Liverpool: *m.* 1932, Sir Claude Matthew Smith-Dodsworth, 7th baronet, who *d.* 1940. *Residence*, Thornton Watlass Hall, Ripon, Yorkshire.

Collateral Branch living.

Issue of the late Frederick Cadwallader Smith-Dodsworth, 3rd son of 4th baronet, *b.* 1858, *d.* 1900: *m.* 1888, Hannah Elizabeth, da. of T. Harrison, of Littlerock Farm, Osceola Co., Iowa, U.S.A.:—

Dorothy, *b.* 1891: *m.* 1st, 1913, Geoffrey Hoyer Millar; 2ndly, 1919, Eugene Goossens (cr. a Knt. 1955), who *d.* 1962; 3rdly, 1930, Daniel Joseph Reagan, of U.S. Embassy, Paris, and has issue living, (by 1st marriage) Derrick Norman, *b.* 1914,—(by 2nd marriage) Anne, *b.* 1921: *m.* 1945, Edgar Obermer,—Julia, *b.* 1922: *m.* 1944, Georges Robert Weber, of Maastricht, Holland, and has issue living, Christopher George *b.* 1946, Patrick Robert *b.* 1948,—Jane (twin), *b.* 1922: *m.* 1944, Baron Hans Fritz de Tscharner, and has issue living, Richard Samuel Frederick *b.* 1947, Catherine Jane *b.* 1945.

The 1st baronet, Sir John Silvester Smith (son of John Smith, of Newland Hall, Yorkshire), married the sister and heiress of Frederick Dodsworth, of Thornton Watlass, whose surname their children assumed. Thomas Dodsworth, of Dodworth, W. Riding, co. York, Receiver to Henry, 3rd Lord Fitzhugh, K.G., acquired the Thornton Watlass estate in 1415 by marriage with Agnes, da. and heiress of Hugh Thoresby, Ch. Capt. of Richmondshire, and niece of John Thoresby, Cardinal St. Praxis, Archbishop of York, and Chancellor of England, who built the Choir of York Cathedral. Of this family was Sir Edward Dodsworth, Comy.-Gen. to the Army of the Parliament, and Roger Dodsworth, the famous Yorkshire antiquary. Besides the families of Silvester, Dodsworth and Thoresby the Smiths of Newland represent Howarth of Howarth, co. Lancashire, founded by Osbert Howarth, Master of the Buckhounds to Henry II., and Blayney, Barons Blayney, of Monaghan, which peerage cr. 1621, became extinct in 1874. This family is lineally descended from Lionel, Duke of Clarence, third son of Edward III., through Mortimer, Percy, Clifford, Conyers, D'Arcy, Stapylton and Dodsworth.

DOMVILLE, Creation (U.K.) 1814, of St. Albans, Hertfordshire.

Sir(GERALD)GUY DOMVILLE, 7th *Baronet;* *b.* March 3rd, 1896; *s.* his brother, *Capt. Sir* CECIL LIONEL, 1930; ed. at Wellington Coll.; is Lieut.-Com. R.N.V.R.; European War 1915-18, European War 1939-45: *m.* 1920, Beatrice, Mary (who obtained a divorce 1930), da. of Brig.-Gen. Robert Seymour Vandeleur, C.B., C.M.G. [B. Decies, colls.].

Arms—Quarterly: 1st, azure, a lion rampant argent supporting a sword erect representing the sword of the city of London proper; on a chief of honourable augmentation of the second three oriental crowns the points alternately radiated or, encircled by two branches of olive proper, *Domville*; 2nd, azure, a lion rampant argent gorged with a plain collar gules, *Domville* (*ancient*); 3rd, argent, six lozenges conjoined in bend sable, *Carrington*; 4th, argent, five lozenges conjoined in pale gules, *Lymme*. Crests—1st, out of a mural crown gules a demi-lion issuant argent supporting between the paws an escutcheon azure charged with three crowns as in the arms; 2nd, two lions' jambs erased argent. Second motto—" Qui stat caveat ne cadat" (*Let him that stands take heed lest he fall*).
Residence—60, Knightsbridge, S.W.1.   Clubs—Royal Thames Yacht, Portland.

PAX·ALMA·REDIT
Genial peace returns.

Daughter living of 5th Baronet—Louise, *b.* 1915: *m.* 1st, 1936, Leslie Alexander Mackay, from whom she obtained a divorce 1946; 2ndly, 1946, the Hon. (John) David Coulson Fellowes, 2nd Lieut. Rifle Bde. [see B. De Ramsay], from whom she obtained a divorce 1962, and has issue living, (by 1st marriage) Anthony Raymond Alexander (of Lossenham Farm, Newenden, Hawkhurst, Kent), *b.* 1938: *m.* 1961, Christine Susan. yst. da. of the late Lt.-Col. C. H. P.

Crawfurd, and has issue living, Rupert Alexander Crawfurd *b.* 1964, Damian Charles Alexander *b.* 1967,—(by 2nd m.) [*see* B. De Ramsey]. *Residence*, Rose Cottage, Kirtling, Newmarket, Suffolk.

Daughters living of 6th Baronet—Anne Juliet, *b.* 1923; sometime Section Officer W.A.A.F.; *m.* 1943, Walter Siner, 1st Lieut. U.S.A. Air Force, from whom she obtained a divorce 1959, and has issue living, Guy Domville, *b.* 1947,—Anne Catherine, *b.* 1945. *Residence*, Sandy Knowe Bungalow, Compton, near Guildford, Surrey.——Rosemary Gervaise, *b.* 1924: *m.* 1955, the Rev. Wolfgang Müller, and has issue living, Harald Martin Domville, *b.* 1956,—Mark Bernhard Domville (twin), *b.* 1956,—Steven Rufus Domville, *b.* 1959. *Residence*, St. Matthew's Vicarage, Wigmore, Gillingham, Kent.

Widow living of 6th Baronet—LUCY, da. of Lt.-Col. G. F. Whitehead, of Woodfalls, Rudgwick, Horsham: *m.* 1st, 1920, Capt. Sir Cecil Lionel Domville, MC, 6th baronet, who *d.* 1930; 2ndly, 1932, as his second wife, Lt.-Col. Arthur Patrick Hamilton Cadell, DSO, Indian Army (ret.), who *d.* 1957. *Residence*, 10, Woodrising, Sandbanks, Poole.

This family descends from the Domvilles of Lyme, Cheshire, who were a branch of the Domvilles of Brunstath in that county, who held that manor in the reign of Henry III, and whose line ended in an heiress in the reign of Henry IV. Charles Domville, citizen and clothworker of London, who *d.* 1704, was a grandson of William, 3rd son of William Domville of Lyme. His great-grandson, Sir William, 1st Bt., was Lord Mayor of London 1813-14, and in the latter year presided at the grand banquet given for the Prince Regent, the Emperor of Russia and the King of Prussia.

Don-Wauchope, see Wauchope.

DORMAN, Creation (U.K.) 1923, of Nunthorpe, co. York.

Valour in difficulties.

Virtus-in-arduis

Sir CHARLES GEOFFREY DORMAN, *M.C.*, 3rd *Baronet*; *b.* Sept. 18th, 1920; *s.* his father, *Sir* BEDFORD LOCKWOOD, *C.B.E.*, 1956; ed. at Rugby, and at Brasenose Coll., Oxford (BA 1941, MA 1947); Lt.-Col. (ret.) 13th/18th Hussars; 1939-44 War in Middle East and Italy (MC): *m.* 1954 (m. diss. 1972), Elizabeth Ann (a CStJ), da. of the late George Gilmour Gilmour-White, OBE, JP, of North Cerney, Cirencester, and has issue.

Ⓐrms—Argent, two bars azure, each charged with as many roses of the field, barbed and seeded proper, over all a lozenge sable charged with a lion's head erased or. Ⓒrest—Upon a rock proper, a lion's paw erased sable, grasping a spear in bend sinister proper.

Residence—Hutton Grange, Gt. Rollright, Chipping Norton, Oxon., OX7 5SQ.

Daughter living—Eve Constance, *b.* 1962.

Collateral Branch living.

Issue of the late Arthur John Dorman, youngest son of 1st baronet, *b.* 1881, *d.* 1957: *m.* 1910, Dorothy Helen, who *d.* 1957, da. of the late Col. A. W. P. Inman:—

RICHARD (East Barn, Ditchling, Sussex) *b.* May 25th, 1918: *m.* 1947, Diana, da. of the late Dr. Henry Edward Barrett, of 33, Holland Park, W11, and has issue living, Philip Henry Keppel, *b.* 1954,—Jane Elizabeth Keppel, *b.* 1950.——Patricia Marguerite: *m.* 1933, John Bell Dixon, and has issue living, Robert Clive, *b.* 1936: *m.* 1970, Ginette, da. of Marcel Dubuc,—Peter Richard John, *b.* 1945,—Diana Margaret, *b.* 1942. *Residence*, Nevina, Hollybank Rd., Hook Heath, Woking, Surrey.

The 1st baronet, Sir Arthur John Dorman, K.B.E., was Founder and Chm. of Dorman, Long & Co. Ltd., of Middlesbrough. The 2nd, Sir Bedford Lockwood Dorman, C.B.E., was Dep. Chm. of N. Riding of Yorkshire Quarter Sessions, and Chm. of N. Riding of Yorkshire War Agricultural Executive Committee.

Doughty-Tichborne, see Tichborne.

DOUGLAS, Creation (U.K.) 1831, of Glenbervie, Kincardine.

Sir SHOLTO COURTENAY MACKENZIE DOUGLAS, *M.C.*, 5th *Baronet* (but his name does not, at time of going to press, appear on the Official Roll of Baronets), son of the late Donald Sholto Mackenzie Douglas, son of the late Capt. Donald Douglas, 6th son of 1st Baronet, *b.* June 27th, 1890; *s.* his kinsman, *Sir* KENNETH, 1954; is Capt. Seaforth Highlanders; European War 1914-18 (M.C.), European War 1939-45: *m.* 1929 (marriage dissolved 1959), Lorna Tichborne, da. of Capt. Hugh Nangle, of 22, Onslow Square, S.W., and has issue.

Ⓐrms—Not matriculated at Lyon Office at time of going to press. *Residence*—192, Cooden Drive, Cooden, Sussex.

Daughters living—Jean Mackenzie, *b.* 1930: *m.* 1956 (m. diss. 1968), Capt. Brian Joseph Craig, late R. Signals, and has issue living, Alastair James Mackenzie, *b.* 1960,—Duncan Quinnell Mackenzie *b.* 1963. *Residence*, 18, Portland Av., Hove 3.——Lorna Inga Mackenzie, *b.* 1932: *m.* 1st, 1955, (m. diss. 1972), James Neil Maclay; 2ndly, 1973, Capt. John Edward Homewood, of 22, Coleridge Rd., Ottery-St-Mary, Devon, and has issue living (by 1st m.), Mary Chrstine, *b.* 1955.

Sister living—Edith Mildred Elisabeth Mackenzie, *b.* 1892: *m.* 1921, Hugh Northey, who *d.* 1928. *Residence*, 3, Higher Mill Flats, Lyme Regis, Dorset.

The family of Douglas of Glenbervie had a grant from James V. of Scotland of the right to the first vote in Parliament, to be the King's Lieutenants, and to carry the crown at coronations. The 1st baronet, Lieut.-Gen. Sir Kenneth, was Col. 58th Foot. His patronymic was Mackenzie, but he assumed in 1831, by Roy. licence, the name of Douglas, as representative in the female line of the Douglases of Glenbervie. The 3rd baronet was a member of the House of Representatives, New Zealand. The 4th baronet, Sir Kenneth Douglas, was a Barrister and Solicitor.

DOYLE, Creation (U.K.) 1828.

Sir JOHN FRANCIS REGINALD WILLIAM HASTINGS
DOYLE, 5th *Baronet; b.* Jan. 3rd, 1912; *s.* his father, *Col. Sir*
ARTHUR HAVELOCK JAMES, 1948; ed. at Eton; Major
(retired) Cameronians (Scottish Rifles); formerly Roy.
Irish Fusiliers; Palestine 1938 (medal with clasp), European War 1939-45 in France, Greece, Italy and Austria:
m. 1947, Carmen Diana, da. of Col. Steel, Indian Army,
and has issue.

ᴀrms—Argent, three bucks' heads erased proper within a bordure
counter-compony or and azure. ᴄrest—Out of a ducal coronet or, a buck's
head proper.
Residence—Glebe House, Camolin, co. Wexford. *Club*—Kildare St.

Fortitudine vincit.　**Daughter living**—Sylvia Yolande, *b.* 1948.
He conquers by fortitude. **Sisters living**—Diana Violet Edith Constance, *b.* 1905; unsuccessfully
contested S. Div. of Poplar(C) Nov. 1935, and Central Div. of Hull, July
1945: *m.* 1928 (marriage dissolved 1951), Sir Alexander Cadwallader Mainwaring Spearman,
[*see* Spearman, Bt. colls.].——Margaret Isabella Dorothy Evelyn, *b.* 1907: *m.* 1933, Col.
William Heathcoat-Amory, DSO, late KRRC, [*see* V. Amory]. *Residences*, Calverleigh Court
Tiverton, Devon; Craig Lodge, Glendaruel, Argyll.

A baronetcy granted in 1805 to Gen. Sir John Doyle, G.C.B., became extinct in 1834. His **nephew
Maj.-Gen. Sir Francis**, the 1st baronet of the present creation, was Chairman of the Board of **Excise.
Sir Francis Hastings Charles**, the 2nd baronet, was Professor of Poetry in Oxford Univ. 1867-77.

D'OYLY, Creation (E.) 1663, of Shottisham, Norfolk.

Do no ill, quoth Doyle.

Sir JOHN ROCHFORT D'OYLY, 13th
Baronet; b. April 19th, 1900; *s.* his
brother, *Sir* CHARLES HASTINGS, 1962;
Com. (retired) R.N.; European War
1916-18 with Grand Fleet, European War
1939-45 in Atlantic, E. Indies, and Pacific:
m. 1930 (marriage dissolved 1944), Kathleen, el. da. of the late Robert Brown
Gillespie, of Halgolle, Yatiyantota, Ceylon,
and has issue.

ᴀrms—Gules, three bucks' heads cabossed argent,
ᴄrest—Out of a ducal coronet or, two wings erect sable
bezantée, between which and resting on the strawberry
leaf of the coronet an estoile of six points argent.

Address—c/o Lloyds Bank, 39 Piccadilly, W.1.

Daughters living—Jill Rochfort, *b.* 1931: *m.* 1952,
George Creighton, and has issue living, Glen John,
b. 1953.—Ian Robert, *b.* 1960.—Linden Gay,
b. 1954.——Ann Hastings, *b.* 1936: *m.* 1959,
Thomas Hepburn James, of 2, Culross Av., Haywards Heath, Sussex, RH16 1JF, and has issue
living, Shona Ann, *b.* 1960,—Karen Hepburn,
b. 1964,—Tiffany Carterette, *b.* 1965.

Half-Brother living—NIGEL HADLEY MILLER,
b. July 6th, 1914; ed. at Radley; formerly Maj.
R. Scots: *m.* 1940, Dolores, who *d.* 1971, da. of
R. H. Gregory, of New Lodge, Crowhurst, Sussex
and has issue living, Hadley Gregory, *b.* 1956,—
Carol Dolores, *b.* 1942,—Sherry Angela, *b.* 1946.
Residence,

Sister living—Marjorie Isobel D'OYLY, *b.* 1901;
resumed the surname of D'Oyly by deed poll 1949:
m. 1925 (marriage dissolved 1947), Com. Godfrey F.
Evans, R.N. (retired), and has issue living, David
D'OYLY EVANS (of Old Stones, Cronks Hill, Redhill
Surrey), *b.* 1926: *m.* 1956, Elizabeth Anne Coni, and has issue living, Susan Patricia, *b.* 1957
Carol Jane, *b.* 1959. *Residence*, 28, Park Lodge, Hove.

Half-Sisters living—Maude Ethelind Halliday, *b.* 1912: *m.* 1st, 1934 (marriage dissolved 1947);
Lieut.-Col. John Evelyn Fairlie, Indian Army (retired); 2ndly, 1948, Capt. Tom Gordon Hem
ming.——Beryl Evelyn, *b.* 1916. *Residence*, 3, Sandrock Rd., Tunbridge Wells.

Collateral Branch living:
Issue of the late Edward Halliday D'Oyly, son of 10th baronet, *b.* 1865, *d.* 1957: *m.*
1891, Laura, who *d.* 19—, da. of Herbert George Yatman, formerly of Studley, Wimborne Rd., Bournemouth :—
Mary Edith, *b.* 1892.——Mildred Dorothea, *b.* 1893. *Residence,*

Robert d'Ouilly, who came over with William the Conqueror, and was Baron of Hocknorton, in
Oxfordshire, in 1071-2, built and fortified Oxford Castle, and was made Constable of Oxford. The
3rd Baron of Hocknorton founded the Abbey of Oseney on an island in the Isis. This family
descends from Sir Henry D'Oyly of Pondhall, Sheriff of Suffolk, who *d.* 1564. The 1st baronet,
Sir William D'Oyly, M.P. for Norfolk and Yarmouth, a partisan of the royal cause, was knighted,
and subsequently created a baronet. Sir William D'Oyly, 2nd baronet, a Teller of the Exchequer,
was knighted during the lifetime of his father. Sir John Hadley D'Oyly, 6th baronet, Collector
of Calcutta, sat as M.P. for Ipswich. Sir Charles D'Oyly, 7th Baronet, H.E.I.C.S., was a distinguished amateur artist. Maj.-Gen. Sir Charles Walters D'Oyly, 9th baronet, Bengal Army, served
in Gwalior Campaign and Indian Campaign 1857.

DRUGHORN, Creation (U.K.) 1922, of Ifield Hall, Ifield, Sussex. [Extinct 1943.]

Sir JOHN FREDERICK DRUGHORN, 1st and last *Baronet.*

Daughters living of 1st Baronet—Lucienne Frederique, *b.* 1893 : *m.* 1914, Dacre de Jersey Croudace, AIMM, CE, and has issue living, John Michael Dacre (Dacredale, Borrowdale. Salisbury, Rhodesia) *b.* 1928: *m.* 1952, Heather Margaret Gilmour, and has issue living, Alistair Michael Dacre *b.* 1965, Rosmairi Heather *b.* 1954, Caroline Jean *b.* 1958, Janette Alison *b.* 1962,— William Ian, *b.* 1931: *m.* 1956, Marilyn Patricia Jones, and has issue living, Peter George *b.* 1965, Mark Andrew *b.* 1969, Deborah Lucienne *b.* 1961,—David Brian *b.* 1932: *m.* 1972, Grace Lily Logan,—Elizabeth Lucienne *b.* 1915: *m.* 1945, Robert Cherer Smith, of End of Kingsmead Rd., PO Borrowdale, Salisbury, Rhodesia, and has issue living, Gareth *b.* 1953, Deryn *b.* 1946: *m.* 1966, Michael James Read, Beulah Joy *b.* 1949: *m.* 1971, Graham McGuiness,—Margaret Frederique, *b.* 1916: *m.* 1939, Gerald Alfred O'Reilly, and has issue living, Gerald James *b.* 1940: *m.* 1966, Marie Fitzgibben, Kevin *b.* 1945: *m.* 1966, Wendy Bailey, Patrick *b.* 1948: *m.* 1972, Jennifer Barnard, Anne Bernice *b.* 1942: *m.* 1970, Manuel Tavares,—Eileen Mary, *b.* 1917: *m.* 1940, Keith Alistaire Forbes, and has issue living, Brian Alistaire *b.* 1942: *m.* 1966, Shaughn Watson, Nigel *b.* 1950, Jacqueline *b.* 1953,—Pamela Denise, *b.* 1919: *m.* 1942, Lawrence Stanley Rix, and has issue living, Jeremy *b.* 1952, Graham *b.* 1954, Allan *b.* 1957, Molly *b.* 1947: *m.* 1967, Robin Booth, Patricia *b.* 1950: *m.* 19—, Michael Toronyi. *Residence*, Dacredale, Borrowdale, Salisbury, Rhodesia.——Elizabeth Frederica, *b.* 1894: *m.* 1922, Edward John Bowie, who *d.* 1946, and has issue living, Peggy Drughorn, *b.* 1923: *m.* 1946, Air Commodore John Bagot Curtiss, RAF, and has issue living, Peter Hugh Bagot *b.* 1949, Simon Richard Bagot *b.* 1961, Jonathan Patrick Bagot *b.* 1965, Patricia Jane *b.* 1947: *m.* 1972, Joseph André Maxwell Proctor, and has issue living, Elsbeth Gemma *b.* 1974,—June Drughorn, *b.* 1926: *m.* 1951, John Denham Pinnock, MA, and has issue living, Douglas Denham *b.* 1954, Robert Denham *b.* 1955. *Residence*, Banavie, 37, Buckingham Way, Wallington, Surrey.——Maud Frederica, *b.* 1897: *m.* 1926, Lionel James Berry, BSc, ARIC, of Four Acorns, 38 Orchard Rd., Bromley, Kent, and has issue living, Joyce Ann, *b.* 1928: *m.* 1951, Ronald Lynch, and has issue living, Michael *b.* 1953, James *b.* 1956, Susan *b.* 1958,—Susan Elizabeth Wendy, *b.* 1932; ARCM, LRAM.

Collateral Branch living.

     Issue of the late John Frederic Drughorn, son of 1st baronet, *b.* 1887, *d.* 1919 : *m.* 1914, Marie Elizabeth, who *d.* 1943, da. of George Newport :—
Marie Frederica Elizabeth, *b.* 1915 : *m.* 1945, Charles F. Hudson. *Residence*, Ashley, North Chailey, Sussex.

DRUMMOND, Creation (U.K.) 1922, of Lasswade, co. Midlothian. [Extinct 1924.]

Sir HUGH HENRY JOHN DRUMMOND, *C.M.G.*, 1st and last *Baronet.*

Daughter living of 1st Baronet—Marion Edwina, *b.* 1902 : *m.* 1928, Julius Norton Goodwyn, who *d.* 1968. *Residence*, Burstone Manor, Bow, Crediton, Devon.

WILLIAMS-DRUMMOND, Creation (U.K.) 1828, of Hawthornden, Midlothian.

HOS GLORIA·REDDIT·HONORES

These honours are acquired by glory.

Sir WILLIAM HUGH DUDLEY WIL-LIAMS-DRUMMOND, 6th *Baronet*; *b.* Feb. 13th, 1901; *s.* his cousin, *Sir* JAMES HAMLYN WILLIAMS, 1970; ed. at Eton; a Member of Queen's Body Guard for Scotland (Roy. Co. of Archers).

    Arms—Quarterly: 1st and 4th grand quarters, quarterly, 1st and 4th, or, three bars wavy within a bordure gules, *Drummond*; 2nd and 3rd, azure, three bears' heads couped close argent muzzled gules, *Forbes*; 2nd and 3rd grand quarters argent a lion rampant sable, head, paws, and tuft of tail of the field, *Williams*. **Crest**—A demi-pegasus proper, maned and winged or. **Supporters**—Two naked savages, each wreathed about the head and loins with laurels and over the exterior shoulder of each a club, all proper.

    Residence,—Bryneithen, Llandilo, Carmarthenshire.

    The 1st baronet, Sir John Forbes, Capt. R.N., was cr. a baronet (with special remainder to his son-in-law, Francis Walker and the heirs male of his body) for distinguished Naval Sers., and assumed the additional surname of Drummond on his marriage to Barbara Mary, da. and heir of William Drummond of Hawthornden (cadet of Drummond of Carnock, said to be descended from William, *d.* 1428, yr. brother of Sir John, of Stobhall, ancestor of Earl of Perth). His son-in-law, the 2nd baronet, Sir Francis Walker, also assumed the additional surname of Drummond. The 3rd baronet in Dec. 1858 substituted the name of Williams for that of Walker on his marriage with the heiress of Edwinsford.

DRYDEN, Creation (G.B.) 1733, of Ambrosden, Oxfordshire; and 1795, of Canons-Ashby, Northamptonshire.

Sir JOHN STEPHEN GYLES DRYDEN, 11th *Baronet* of 1st and 8th of 2nd creation; *b.* Sept. 26th, 1943; *s.* his father, *Sir* NOEL PERCY HUGH, 1970; ed. at The Oratory Sch., and Woodcote, Berks.: *m.* 1970, Diana Constance, da. of Cyril Tomlinson, of Highland Park, Wellington, NZ.

Arms—Azure, a lion rampant, and in chief a sphere between two estoiles or. Crest—A demi-lion sustaining in his right paw a sphere as in the arms.

Address—c/o Midland Bank, Redhill, Surrey.

Aunts living—Gladys Ethel Florence, *b.* 1905: *m.* 1934, Maj. Hartley Butterworth, N. Stafford Regt. and has issue living, Nigel Hartley Dryden (July Farmhouse, Gt. Chesterford, Saffron Walden, Essex), *b.* 1936: *m.* 1965, Jane, da. of Geoffrey Dawson [*see* Blunt, Bt., coll.], and has issue living, Julian Richard Nigel *b.* 1970, Fiona Catherine *b.* 1967,—Gillian Alison Joan, *b.* 1939: *m.* 1964, Anthony Nevil Adams, and has issue living, Philip Dawson *b.* 1966, Kate Carol *b.* 1967, Nicola Josephine *b.* 1970. *Residence*, Scotney Lodge, Fleet, Hants. ——Evelyn Kate Mary, *b.* 1909: *m.* 1931, Brig. Gerald Ernest Thubron, DSO, OBE, N. Stafford Regt., and has issue living, Colin Gerald Dryden, *b.* 1939; FRSL. *Residence*, Pheasant's Hatch, Piltdown, Sussex.——Honor Elizabeth Helen, *b.* 1914. *Residence*, Home Farm, St. Leonard's Forest, Horsham, Sussex.

Widow living of 10th Baronet—ROSAMUND MARY (*Rosamund, Lady Dryden*) (c/o Williams & Glyn's Bank, Old Brompton Rd., SW7), da. of the late Stephen Francis Eustace Scrope: *m.* 1941, Sir Noel Percy Hugh Dryden, 10th baronet, who *d.* 1970.

Sir Erasmus Dryden, Sheriff of Northamptonshire, was created a baronet 1619. One of his grandsons was John Dryden, the celebrated poet. The title became extinct at the death of the 7th baronet, when the estates devolved upon his niece, who married John Turner, 2nd son of Sir Edward Turner, 2nd baronet of Ambrosden. Mr. Turner in 1791 assumed by sign-manual the surname and arms of Dryden only, was knighted 1793, and created a baronet 1795. The 4th baronet, of creation 1795, in 1874 succeeded, as 7th baronet, to the Turner baronetcy, creation 1733.

DUCKWORTH, Creation (U.K.) 1909, of Grosvenor Place, City of Westminster.

Perseverance.

Sir RICHARD DYCE DUCKWORTH, 3rd *Baronet*; *b.* Sept. 30th, 1918; *s.* his father, *Sir* EDWARD DYCE, 1945; ed. at Marlborough Coll.; formerly Major R.A. : *m.* 1942, Violet Alison, da. of Lieut.-Col. George Boothby Wauhope, D.S.O., of The Mount House, Highclere, Newbury, and has issue.

Arms—Argent: on a chevron engrailed between two leopards' faces in chief and a garb in base sable, three crosses patée or. Crest—Upon a mount between two palm branches vert, a garb fesseways or charged with two crosses patée in fesse, and surmounted by a duck sable.

Residence,—Dunwood Cottage, Shootash, Romsey, Hants. *Club*—Oriental.

Sons living—EDWARD RICHARD DYCE, *b.* July 13th, 1943; ed. at Marlborough.——Anthony George Dyce, *b.* 1946.

Collateral Branch living.

Issue of the late Capt. Arthur Dyce Duckworth, RN, yst son of 1st Bt., *b.* 1896, *d.* 1973: *m.* 1927, Grace Ella Mary (Alder Shaw House, Southborough, Tunbridge Wells), da. of the late Edmund Lionel Pontifex, of Bishopscourt, Broadwater Down, Tunbridge Wells:—

Geoffrey Loraine Dyce (Alder Shaw House, Southborough, Tunbridge Wells), *b.* 1930; ed. at Stowe; Col. late RTR: *m.* 1961, Philippa Ann, da. of Sir (Edward) Percy Rugg, and has issue living Jeremy Dyce, *b.* 1963,—Juliet Ann, *b.* 1964.——Rosemary Margaret Dyce, *b.* 1931: *m.* 1957, Lt.-Col. Athelwold Colin Devereux Watts, Army Air Corps, and has issue living, Andrew Colin Iremonger, *b.* 1960,—Nigel John Iremonger, *b.* 1962,—Caroline Susan Devereux, *b.* 1958,—Kay Rosemary Devereux, *b.* 1963.

The 1st baronet, Sir Dyce Duckworth, MD, LLD, was an eminent physician, Treasurer, Roy. Coll. of Physicians 1884-1923, Pres. of Clinical So. of London 1891-3, and Hon. Physician to King Edward VII, when Prince of Wales 1890-1901. The 2nd baronet, Sir Edward Dyce, was a Puisne Judge of High Court of Burma 1924-27.

Duckworth-King, see King.

DU CROS, Creation (U.K.) 1916, of Canons, Middlesex.

Sir PHILIP HARVEY DU CROS, 2nd *Baronet; b.* June 19th 1898; *s.* his father, *Sir* ARTHUR PHILIP 1955; *ed.* at Harrow; Capt. 3rd Hussars (Special Reserve); European War 1917-19, European War 1939-45 (despatches): *m.* 1st, 1922, Matilde Dita (who obtained a divorce 1950, and reassumed by deed poll 1951 her maiden name of Mallet), da. of the late Sir Claude Coventry Mallet, C.M.G.; 2ndly, 1950, Rosemary Theresa, *M.B.E.*, da. of Sir John David Rees, 1st Bt., K.C.I.E., C.V.O., M.P., and has issue by 1st m. [The 2nd Bt. *d.* Oct. 11th, 1975.]

Arms—Quarterly; 1st vert, a greyhound courant argent in chief a crescent or; 2nd azure, an eastern crown or; 3rd azure, within the horns of a crescent a heart in chief argent; 4th azure, a saltire or, and on an escutcheon argent, a rose gules, stalked and leaved vert. Crest—Out of an eastern crown or, a demi greyhound sable.

Residence—Little Bocombe, Parkham, N. Devon. *Clubs*—Bath, Carlton.

Son living—By 1st marriage—CLAUDE PHILIP ARTHUR MALLET (Glengarry, St. Peter, Jersey; Carlton and Guards' Club), *b.* Dec. 22nd, 1922; formerly Capt. Welsh Guards: *m.* 1st, 1953 (m. diss. 1974), Christine Nancy (TORDOFF), da. of F. E. Bennett, of Spilsby, Lincs.; 2ndly, 1974, Margaret Roy, da. of the late Roland James Frater, of Gosforth, Northumberland, and formerly wife of Oswald Ernest Harewood Cutler, and has issue living (by 1st m.), Julian Claude Arthur Mallet, *b.* 1955.

Daughters living—By 1st marriage—Edome Dita Mallet, *b.* 1924.——Primrose Millicent Elaine Malet, *b.* 1938. *Residence*, The Manor House, Curry Mallet, Somerset.

Brother living—Arthur Roy Peter, *b.* 1913; ed. at Harrow, and at Magdalen Coll., Oxford; Bar. Inner Temple 1936: Major R.A.S.C.; unsuccessfully contested Caernarvon (C) Nov. 1935: *m.* 1935, Myra (McAREVEY), da. of the late Gerald Mooney, of Killiney, co. Dublin. *Residence*, Le Corteau Fou, Glion, Montreux, Switzerland. *Club*, Carlton.

Sisters living—Renée Maude, *b.* 1897: *m.* 1920, William Edward Hedley-Dent (who assumed the additional surname of Hedley 1927), Hon. Lieut.-Col. 8th Hussars, and has issue living, Ronald Peter (of Shortflatt Tower, Belsay, Northumberland), *b.* 1921; Major Welsh Guards (ret.): *m.* 1964, Nancy, da. of Bryant H. Dixon, of Rockaway Valley, Boonton, New Jersey, USA,—Patrick Graham (Newnham Green Farm, Newnham, Basingstoke; White's and Army and Navy Clubs), *b.* 1923; late Capt. Gren. Gds.: *m.* 1948, Jennifer, da. of Ferdinand Christian Otto Speyer, CBE, and has issue living, Giles Edward *b.* 1949, Christopher Graham *b.* 1952. *Residence*, Newnham Green Farm, Newnham, Basingstoke.——Denise Anne, *b.* 1901: *m.* 1923 (m. diss. 1927), Alan V. Insole, FRGS, FZS, who *d.* 19—.

The 1st baronet, Sir Arthur du Cros (son of the late (William) Harvey du Cros, J.P., formerly M.P. for Hastings), was Founder and sometime Chm. and Pres. of Dunlop Rubber Co., Ltd., and Founder, with his father, of Pneumatic Tyre Industry, a Pioneer of Rubber Growing Industry, and a Founder of Junior Imperial League, and first Chm. of its Committee. He initiated Motor Ambulance Movement during European War 1914-19, and sat as M.P. for Hastings (C) 1908-18, and for Clapham Div. of Wandsworth 1918-22.

Dudley-Williams, see Williams.

DUFF, Creation (U.K.) 1911, of Vaynol Park, Bangor, co. Carnarvon.

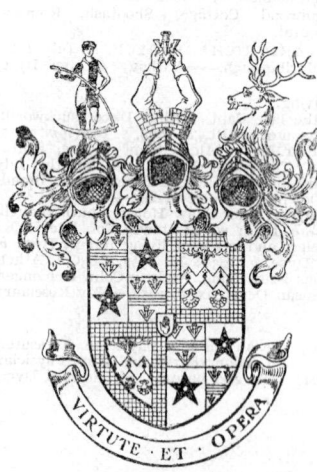

Sir (CHARLES) MICHAEL ROBERT VIVIAN DUFF, 3rd *Baronet; b.* May 3rd, 1907; *s.* his father, *Sir* ROBERT (ROBIN) GEORGE VIVIAN, 1914; High Sheriff of Caernarvonshire 1932, and for Anglesey 1950; is Flying Officer R.A.F. Vol. Reserve, and a K.St.J.; Mayor of Caernarvon 1935-6; Lord-Lt. of Caernarvonshire 1960-74, since when HM Lieut. of Gwynedd; assumed by deed poll 1928, the additional surnames of Assheton-Smith: which he relinquished by deed poll 1945: *m.* 1st, 1935 (m. annulled on her petition 1937), the Hon. (Millicent) Joan Marjoribanks, da. of 3rd Baron Tweedmouth; 2ndly, 1949, Lady (Alexandra Mary) Caroline Cecilia Paget, da. of 6th Marquess of Anglesey.

Arms—Quarterly, 1st and 4th quarterly i and iv azure, two bars between three pheons or, *Smith;* ii and iii argent, a mullet pierced sable, *Assheton;* 2nd and 3rd vert, a fesse dancettée ermine between a stag's head cabossed in chief and two escallops in base or, within a bordure chequy of the last and first, *Duff.* Crests—1st, issuant from a mural crown or, two arms embowed, vested azure, cuffed argent, the hands proper holding a pheon or, *Smith;* 2nd, a mower in the act of mowing, vested per pale argent and sable, sleeves and hose countercharged, cap quarterly argent and sable, scythe handle or, the blade proper, *Assheton :* 3rd, a buck's head erased proper, *Duff.*

By virtue and deeds.

Seats—Vaynol, nr. Bangor, Caernarvonshire: Trefarthen, Anglesey.

This family descends from Patrick Duff of Hatton, Aberdeenshire, yr. brother of William Duff, father of 1st Earl of Fife [*see* D. Fife]. Garden Duff of Hatton, 3rd in descent from Patrick, *m.* Louisa, da. and co-heir of Sir Benjamin Dunbar of Hempriggs, 3rd Bt. The el. son *s.* as *de jure* 5th Bt. [*see* Dunbar, Bt. (cr. 1706).] The 4th son, Robert George Duff: *m.* 1847, Mary, da. of William Bucker Astley by Elizabeth, sister of Thomas Assheton-Smith, of Vaynol Park. His son, the 1st baronet, Sir Charles Garden Duff, assumed by Roy. licence 1905, the surname and arms of Assheton-Smith, in lieu of his patronymic. Sir Robin Duff, 2nd baronet, Lieut. 2nd Life Guards, was killed in action Oct. 1914.

DUFF, Creation (U.K. 1952, of Hatton, co. Aberdeen. [Extinct 1952.]

Lieut.-Col. Sir GARDEN BEAUCHAMP DUFF, *D.S.O.*, 1st and last *Baronet.*

Widow living of 1st Baronet—DORIS (*Lady Duff*), da. of Lindsay Eric Smith : *m.* 1913, Lieut.-Col. Sir Garden Beauchamp Duff, D.S.O., 1st Bt., who *d.* 1952, when the title became ext. *Residence*, Hatton Castle, Turriff, Aberdeenshire.

Duff-Gordon, see Gordon.

DUGDALE, Creation (U.K.) 1936, of Merevale and Blyth, co. Warwick.

Sir WILLIAM STRATFORD DUGDALE, *MC*, 2nd *Baronet; b.* March 29th, 1922; *s.* his father, *Sir* WILLIAM FRANCIS STRATFORD, 1965; ed. at Eton, and at Balliol Coll., Oxford a JP and DL of Warwicks (High Sheriff 1971-72); Solicitor 1949; 1939-45 War as Capt. Grenadier Gds. in N. Africa and Italy (despatches, MC): *m.* 1st 1952, Lady Belinda Pleydell-Bouverie, who *d.* 1961, da. of 7th Earl of Radnor; 2ndly, 1967, Cecilia Mary, da. of Sir William Malcolm Mount, 2nd Bt., and has issue by 1st and 2nd m.

Arms—Quarterly; 1st and 4th, argent a cross moline gules, charged in the centre with a Garter King of Arms, coronet or, and in the 1st quarter a torteau; 2nd and 3rd, barry of ten argent and azure, over all a lion rampant gules. **Crest**—A Griffin's head, wings endorsed or, gorged with a coronet as in the arms.

Seat—Merevale Hall, Atherstone, Warwickshire. *Residence*—Blyth Hall, Coleshill, Birmingham. *Clubs,*—White's, Brooks's, Jockey.

PESTIS · PATRIÆ · PIGRITES

Sloth is the plague of one's country.

Sons living—By 1st m.—WILLIAM MATTHEW STRATFORD, *b.* Feb. 22nd, 1959.——(By 2nd m.) Thomas Joshua Stratford, *b.* 1974.

Daughters living—By 1st m.—Laura, *b.* 1953.——Matilda, *b.* 1955.——Charlotte (twin), *b.* 1955.——(By 2nd m.), Adelaide Margaret Victoria Jane, *b.* 1970.

Brother living—John Robert Stratford (Tickwood Hall, Much Wenlock, Salop; Brooks's, and White's Clubs), *b.* 1923; ed. at Eton, and at Ch. Ch., Oxford; Lord-Lieut. of Salop since 1975: *m.* 1956, Kathryn Edith Helen, CVO, da. of the late Rt. Hon. Oliver Frederick George Stanley, MC, MP [*see* E. Derby, colls.], and has issue living, Edward Stratford, *b.* 1959,—Henry Stratford, *b.* 1963, —Elizabeth Alice, *b.* 1957,—Mary, *b.* 1961.

Sisters living—Susan: *m.* 1950, Timothy Neil Hughes-Onslow, of Benrig, St. Boswells, Roxburghshire, and 32, Godfrey St., SW3 [*see* E. Onslow, colls.].——Judith Margaret: *m.* 1952, Maj. John Evelyn Shirley, KRRC (ret.), of Lough Fea, Carrickmacross, co. Monaghan, and Ettington Park, Stratford-on-Avon, [*see* E. Ferrers, colls.].

The present baronet is descended from Sir William Dugdale, Garter King of Arms 1677-86, and author of *Monasticon Anglicanum* and *Baronage of England*, who *d.* 1686. Richard Geast, maternal nephew of John Dugdale of Blyth, Mowbray Herald Extraordinary, having inherited Blyth Hall, assumed by Royal Licence 1799 the surname and arms of Dugdale. His wife, Penelope Bate, was the el. da. and co-heir of Francis Stratford of Merevale Hall, Warwicks., which was inherited by their son, Dugdale Stratford Dugdale, great-grandfather of 1st baronet.

DUKE, Creation (U.K.) 1849, of London. [Extinct 1935.]

Sir JAMES DUKE, 2nd and last *Baronet.*

Widow living of 2nd Baronet—ELIZABETH MENZIES (*Lady Duke*), da. of the late Neil Macdougall, of Birnam, Dunkeld : *m.* 1932, as his second wife, Sir James Duke, 2nd baronet, who *d.* 1935, when the title became ext. *Residence* 13, Inverleith Place, Edinburgh, 3.

DUNBAR, Creation (N.S.) 1694, of Mochrum, Wigtownshire.

Sir ADRIAN IVOR DUNBAR, 12th *Baronet*, son of the late Clement Adrian Dunbar, 2nd son of the late Lieut.-Col. Thomas Clement Dunbar, brother of 7th baronet ; *b.* 1893 ; *s.* his cousin, *Sir* RICHARD SUTHERLAND, 1953 ; naturalized an American citizen 1939 ; European War 1914-19 in France with Australian Imperial Force : *m.* 1st, 1917, Emma Marie, da. of Jean Wittevrongel ; 2ndly, 1930, Esther Naomi, da. of William Henry Robinson, and has issue by 1st and 2nd marriages.

Arms.—Gules, a lion rampant argent, armed and langued azure, within a bordure of the second charged with eight roses of the first, barbed and seeded vert, in a dexter canton argent a saltire azure, surmounted of an inescutcheon charged with a lion rampant gules within a double tressure flory counterflory gules. Crest— A horse's head argent, bridled and reined gules. Supporters—Two white doves imperially crowned proper.

Seat—Mochrum Park, Kirkcowan, Wigtownshire.

Sons living—By 1st m.—JEAN IVOR, *b.* 1918; late Sgt. Mountain Engineers, USA Army: *m.* 1944, Rose Jeanne, da. of Henry William Hertsch, and has issue living, James Michael, *b.* 1950,—Dennis William, *b.* 1952,—Anne Marie, *b.* 1946.——By 2nd m.—Rowland Adrian, *b.* 1934; late US Med. Corps: *m.* 1957, Janet Lockhart, da. of George Heron, of Newtown Stewart, Wigtownshire, and has issue living, Mary Naomi *b.* 1958, Sylvia Katharine *b.* 1960, Shonna Janet *b.* 1962. *Residence*, 28, Monkhouse Av., Marden Estate, North Shields, Northumberland.——Donald Robert, *b.* 1936; Staff Sgt. US Army AF; formerly in US Med. Corps: *m.* 1st, 1957, Marie F., da. of Douglas Allen, of Newton Stewart, Wigtownshire; 2ndly, 1963, Susan Elizabeth Mary, da. of William Radden Gates, and has issue living, (by 1st m.) Allan William, *b.* 1958,—Roseanne, *b.* 1960,—(by 2nd m.) David Wayne, *b.* 1966,—Linda Anne, *b.* 1969.
Brothers living—William Uthred, *b.* 1902 : *m.* 1924, Theresa Rose Della, da. of Jerome Coe, and has issue living, William Thomas, *b.* 1925 : *m.* 19—.——David Allan, *b.* 1905. *Residence*,
Sisters living—Minnie Emile *b.* 1891 : *m.* 1910, Thomas Harvey, and has issue living, David, *b.* 19—.——Dorothy Joan, *b.* 1894: *m.* 1918, Alan Ashleigh, and has issue living, Alan, *b.* 19—,—David, *b.* 19— *Residence*, 1097 St. Clarens Avenue, Toronto, Canada.——May Hilda, *b.* 1899, *Residence*,
Daughters living of 11th Baronet—Joyce Marguerite, *b.* 1912.——Vida Mary, *b.* 1916. *Residence*, 69, Grandison Road, Battersea, S.W.11.

The present baronet is descended from the Dunbars, the ancient Earls of March and Moray, and is the lineal male representative of the heritable Sheriffs of Elgin and Forres, and chief of that name. The 3rd baronet was Judge-Advocate for Scotland. Sir William, 7th baronet, sat as M.P. for Wigton Burghs (L) 1857-65, was successively a Lord of the Treasury, Keeper of the Privy Seal to H.R.H. Prince of Wales, Keeper of the Great Seal to H.R.H. in Scotland, one of the Council to H.R.H., and Comptroller-Gen. of Exchequer, and Auditor-Gen. of Public Accounts. The 9th baronet, Sir William Cospatrick Dunbar, C.B., was Assist. Under-Sec. for Scotland 1885-1902, and Registrar-Gen. for England and Wales 1902-9. The 10th baronet, Sir James George Hawker Rowland, *d.* Jan. 23rd, 1953, and the 11th baronet, Sir Richard Sutherland, *d.* Jan. 25th, 1953.

DUNBAR, Creation (N.S.) 1698, of Durn, Banffshire.

Hope will give aid.

Sir DRUMMOND COSPATRICK NINIAN DUNBAR, *M.C.*, 9th *Baronet ; b.* May 9th, 1917 ; *s.* his father, *Sir* GEORGE ALEXANDER DRUMMOND, 1949 ; ed. at Radley, and at Worcester Coll., Oxford (B.A. 1938) ; Major (retired) Black Watch ; European War 1939-45 in Middle East, Sicily, and Normandy (twice wounded, M.C.) : *m.* 1957, Sheila Barbara Mary, da. of John Berkeley de Fonblanque, and has issue.

Arms—Quarterly ; 1st and 4th, gules, a lion rampant within a bordure argent, charged with eight roses of the first barbed and seeded vert ; 2nd and 3rd, or, three cushions within the royal tressure gules, all within a bordure nebuly, quartered azure and gules. Crest—Two sprigs of laurel in saltire proper.

Residence—Beaufield House, St. Saviour, Jersey. *Club*—Naval and Military.

Son living—ROBERT DRUMMOND COSPATRICK, *b.* June 17th, 1958.

Collateral Branches living.
Issue of the late Hugh Stephen Dunbar, 3rd son of 7th baronet, *b.* 1881, *d.* 1936: *m.* 1910, Carolie Howard, who *d.* 1948, da. of William James Vere, of Johannesburg, S. Africa:—

Uthred Ninian Vere (Montrose, P.O. Amanzimtoti, S. Coast, Natal), *b.* 1910; 1939-45 War in Middle East, N. Africa, Sicily, and Italy as Sergeant S. African Air Force: *m.* 1942, Susan Kathleen, da. of Arthur George Thompson, and has issue living, Stephen Bruce *b.* 1949,—Eleanor Lynne, *b.* 1947.——William Hancorn Vere (c/o East Driefontein, G. M. Co., P/Bag, Bank, Transvaal, S. Africa) *b.* 1912; 1939-45 War in Middle East and Italy as Warrant Officer (Electrical Technician) S. African Air Force: *m.* 1936, Dorothy Christobel, da. of James Smith Gow, and has issue living, Coral Lisette, *b.* 1939: *m.* 1964, Henry William Walker, and has issue living, Gordon Henry *b.* 1965.——Robert Fyfe, *b.* 1920; Lt. S. African Artillery; 1939-45 War in Middle East and N. Africa: *m.* 1941, Eileen May, da. of Frederick Locke, and has issue living, George Drummond, *b.* 1957,—Beverley Anne, *b.* 1946,—Gail Elizabeth, *b.* 1953,—Dianne Roberta, *b.* 1959. *Residence,* 33, Julia Rd., Overport, Durban, Natal.

Grandson of Hugh Stephen Dunbar (ante):—
Issue of the late Aldred Cospatrick Dunbar, *b.* 1916, *d.* 1971: *m.* 1940, Isidoris Elliott, da. of Maj. William Harrison:—
Raymond Robert, *b.* 1943.
Issue of the late Patrick Martin Borlase Dunbar, 4th son of 7th baronet, *b.* 1884, *d.* 1925: *m.* 1924, Mary (15, Lorite, 25, Chelmsford Rd., Durban, Natal), el. da. of the late Claude F. Shoolbred, of Greenstead Hall, Halstead, Essex:—
Patricia Martin (*posthumous*), *b.* 1926 : *m.* 1951, William Harold Groves, and has issue living, Martin Westley, *b.* 1960,—James Arthur, *b.* 1967. *Residence,* 2, Cumberland Av., Vandia Grove, Randburg, Johannesburg, Transvaal, S. Africa.
Issue of the late Lisette Eleanor, da. of 7th baronet, *b.* 18—, *d.* 1918 : *m.* 1906, Edward FitzGibbon Benson :—
Erin Cuffe (of 7, Altson Rd., Moffatview, Johannesburg, S. Africa), *b.* 1906: *m.* 1948 (marriage dissolved 1961), Frederick Theodore Jensen.——Mia Lisette, *b.* 1908: *m.* 1931, Gordon Kestell-Melvill, and has issue living, Margaret, *b.* 1934: *m.* 1953, Allan Raymond King and has issue living, Gordon Alan *b.* 1955, Diana *b.* 1954.——Eleanor Durris, *b.* 1910: *m.* 1932, William John Knuckey, and has issue living, June Eleanor, *b.* 1933 : *m.* 1955, Donald Alan Rowan, of 8, Minerva Rd., Glendower, S. Africa, and has issue living, Donald Mark *b.* 1956, Robin William *b.* 1957, David Anthony *b.* 1965, Tracey Gillian Lisette *b.* 1968,—Lenore, *b.* 1936: *m.* 1958, Peter John Norman Jefferies, of 13, Hares St., Lyndhurst, Johannesburg, S. Africa, and has issue living, Lindsey-Jane *b.* 1964, Deborah Lisette *b.* 1966, Janine Kendall *b.* 1970. *Residence,* 80, Forest Rd., Bramley, Johannesburg, S. Africa.——Coral Doreen, *b.* 1915: *m.* 1st, 1936 (m. diss. 1941), Coulson Orris Douglas; 2ndly, 1944, Andrew Wallace Cairns (PO Box 1583, Johannesburg, 200, S. Africa), and has issue living (by 1st m.), Barrie Strong (Culemborg, Elizabeth Av., Sandringham, Johannesburg, S. Africa), *b.* 1940: *m.* 1961, Antoinette, da. of Harold Frank Booysen, and has issue living, Graeme *b.* 1969,—(by 2nd m.), Alec McGregor (36, Bob St., Regents Park, Johannesburg, S. Africa), *b.* 1948: *m.* 1970, Teresa Elizabeth, da. of Robert Powrie Sehannie, and has issue living, Leslè Beverley *b.* 1971, Natasha Lee *b.* 1974,—Jennifer, *b.* 1945: *m.* 1971, Robert Arthur Grieve, of 4, Bray St., Barberton, S. Africa, and has issue living, Darryl Robert *b.* 1974, Caroline Tracy *b.* 1972.

This family is lineally descended from James, 4th Earl of Moray, by Isabel Innes, and so from John, 1st Earl of Moray (3rd creation 1371-3), who *m.* Marjorie, da. of Robert II., King of Scots (first of the Stewart Kings), and was brother of George, 10th Earl of Dunbar and uncle of 11th and last of the ancient Earls of Dunbar, whose line was founded by Gospatric, Earl of Northumberland [see following article], grandson of Elgifa, da. of Ethelred II., King of England. The Baronetcy was created with remainder to the heirs male of the body of the grantee and their heirs ma le for ever

DUNBAR, Creation (N.S.) 1700, of Northfield, Moray.

Vigilance strengthens hope.

Sir ARCHIBALD RANULPH DUNBAR, 11th *Baronet; b.* Aug. 8th, 1927; *s.* his father, *Maj. Sir* (ARCHIBALD) EDWARD, MC, 1969; ed. at Wellington, Pembroke Coll., Camb., and Imp. Coll. of Tropical Agric., Trinidad; late Agric. Officer, Uganda Civil Ser., and HMOCS: *m.* 1974, Amelia Millar Sommerville, da of Horace Campbell Davidson, of 10, Forth View Cres., Currie, Midlothian, and has issue.

Arms—Quarterly : 1st and 4th, gules, a lion rampant argent within a bordure of the last charged with eight roses of the field, *Dunbar;* 2nd and 3rd, or, three cushions within the royal tressure gules, *Ranulph;* all within a bordure quartered azure and of the first. **Crest**—A dexter hand apaumée reaching at an astral crown proper.

Residence—The Old Manse, Duffus, Elgin.

Daughters living—Harriet Sophie, *b.* 1974.—Stephanie Clare, *b.* 1975.

Brother living—ALEXANDER ARBUTHNOTT (Pitgaveny House, Elgin)· *b.* March 14th, 1929; ed. at Wellington Coll., and at Pembroke Coll., Camb., Bar. Inner Temple, 1953: *m.* 1965, Elizabeth Susannah, da. of the Rev. Edward Denzil Chetwood Wright, of Brattleby House, Brattleby, Lincs. [*see* Strickland-Constable, Bt., colls.], and has issue living, Crinan James, *b.* 1965,—Clodagh Rebecca Helen, *b.* 1968.

Aunts living—Lilias: *m.* 1921, Lt.-Col. Eustace Clementi Smith, who *d.* 1954, formerly Indian Army. *Residence,* Green Gates, Kintbury, Berks.——Helen: *m* 1911, Lt.-Col. Gerald Ponsonby Sneyd Hunt, CMG, DSO, Princess Charlotte of Wales's (Roy. Berkshire Regt.), who *d.* (killed in action during 1914-18 War) and has issue living, Penelope Helen Carew, *b.* 1914; 1939-45 War with WRNS. *Residence,* Cowleaze, Westbury, Wilts.

Collateral Branch living.

Granddaughters of the late Capt. James Brander DUNBAR-BRANDER, 8th son of 5th baronet, (who in 1869 assumed the name of Brander):—
Issue of the late Capt. James Brander-Dunbar, *b.* 1875, *d.* 1969: *m.* 1922, Noela (37, Lynstone Rd., Bude, Cornwall), da. of Matthew Noel Whiting:—
Juliette, *b.* 1923: *m.* 1957, Herbert Lawrence Miller, of S. Lynstone, Bude, Cornwall, and has issue living, Loveday *b.* 1958.——Una (Little Caton, Ashburton, Newton Abbot, Devon), *b.* 1924.

This family is paternally descended in direct male line (through John Dunbar, Earl of Moray, by his wife, Marjorie, da. of Robert II) from Gospatric, Earl of Northumberland [see preceding article] in right of his mother Ealdgyth, grandda. of Ethelred II., King of England. He had from his cousin, Malcolm III., son of Duncan I, a grant of Dunbar in 1072. Earl Gospatric's father, Maldred, King of Cumbria, was younger brother of Duncan I., who became King of Scots in right of his mother, Bethoc, wife of Crinan the Thane (married *circa* 1000), el. da. and heir of Malcolm II., King of Scots. The 1st baronet died without male issue, and the baronetcy (with remainder to his heirs male whatsoever) devolved upon his brother. The 3rd baronet *d.* in 1763, and his cousin Alexander Dunbar, of Newton, ancestor of the present baronet, was served heir-male, 1776.

DUNBAR, Creation (N.S.) 1706, of Hempriggs, Caithness-shire.

Dame MAUREEN DAISY HELEN DUNBAR OF HEMPRIGGS (*Lady Dunbar of Hempriggs*), *Baroness*, da. of the late Courtenay Edward Moore, el. son of the late Jessie Mona Duff (who *m.* the Rev. Canon Courtenay Moore), da. of *de jure* 5th baronet; *b.* Aug. 19th, 1906; *s.* her kinsman, *Sir* GEORGE COSPATRICK Duff-Sutherland-Dunbar, 1963 (succession recognized by Lyon Court 1965); assumed the name of Dunbar 1963, and recognized in the name of Dunbar of Hempriggs by Lyon Court 1965: *m.* 1940, Leonard James Blake, former Dir. of Music, Malvern Coll., and has issue.

Arms—Quarterly: 1st, gules, a lion rampant within a bordure argent, charged with eight roses of the field, *Dunbar*; 2nd, gules, three mullets or, a crescent of the last for difference, *Sutherland*; 3rd vert, on a fesse dancettée ermine between a buck's head cabossed in chief and two escallops in base or, a mullet of the first for difference, *Duff*; 4th, or, three cushions within a double tressure flory counter-flory gules. *Randolph*; all within a bordure vairy or and gules. **Crest**—A key and sword in saltire proper. **Supporters**—*Dexter*, a lion rampant argent; *sinister*, a savage man holding a baton over his shoulder proper.
Residences—51, Gloucester St., Winchcombe, Cheltenham; Ackergill Tower, Wick, Caithness.

Son living—RICHARD FRANCIS Dunbar of Hempriggs, younger (712, Crossway Rd., Burlingame, Cal. 94010, USA), *b.* Jan. 8th, 1945: *m.* 1969, Elizabeth Margaret Jane, only da. of George Lister, of Gloucester.
Daughter living—Eleanor Margaret BLAKE, *b.* 1949: *m.* 1973, David C. Eldridge, of Brookville, Coberley, nr. Cheltenham.
Widow living of 6th Baronet—DULCIE EDITH, (*Lady Duff-Sutherland-Dunbar*), da. of the late Wescombe Joyce, of Winchester: *m.* 1956, as his 3rd wife, Sir George Duff-Sutherland-Dunbar, 6th Baronet, who *d.* 1962. *Residence*, Windermere, Chandler's Ford, Hants.

Collateral Branches living. (*Males and females in remainder.*)

Grandchildren of Jessie Mona Duff (who *m.* the Rev. Canon Courtenay Moore), da. of *de jure* 5th Bt.:—
Issue of the late Harriet Emma Moore, *b.* 1874, *d.* 1957 : *m.* 1909, Lieut.-Col. Hubert Bernard Tonson Rye, D.S.O., who *d.* 1950, formerly Roy. Munster Fusiliers [Dancer, Bt.] :—
Rudo John (Flaxpool House, Crowcombe, Taunton, Som.), *b.* 1910; formerly Maj. Duke of Cornwall's LI: *m.* 1940, Rosemary Hilda, da. of the late Maj. Guy Hughes, XIIth Bengal Cav., and has issue living, Rohaise Harriet Julia, *b.* 1942: *m.* 1966, Christopher Thomas-Everard, of Boford Farm, Dulverton, Som., and has issue living, Guy Richard *b.* 1969, Lucilla Damaris Mary *b.* 1966,—Caroline Mary Georgina, *b.* 1947,—Amarylde Louise, *b.* 1950: *m.* 1972, Richard Peter Eliot.
Issue of the late Jessie Louisa Rickard (who resumed that surname 1916), *b.* 1876, *d.* 1963: *m.* 1st, 1901, Robert Dudley Innes Ackland, of Boulston, Pembrokeshire; 2ndly, 1908, Lieut.-Col. Victor George Howard Rickard, Roy. Munster Fusiliers, who *d.* (killed in action during European War) 1915; 3rdly, 1916 (marriage dissolved 1935), Lieut.-Col. Tudor Fitzjohn, D.S.O. (formerly Worcestershire Regt.):—
(By 2nd marriage) Justin Victor (of Swiftsden Farm, Hurst Green, Sussex), *b.* 1913: *m.* 1939, Joan, da. of the late Alexander William Haig, of Henley-on-Thames, and has issue living, Alexander, *b.* 1944,—Catherine, *b.* 1949,—Patricia, *b.* 1955.

Grandchildren of Gen. Sir Beauchamp Duff, GCB, GCSI, KCVO, CIE, son of Garden William Duff, next brother of *de jure* 5th Bt.:—
Issue of the late Douglas Garden Duff, OBE, *b.* 1886, *d.* 1968: *m.* 1914, Margaret Crawley, who *d.* 1970, da. of the late J. E. Vincent:—
Robert Beauchamp (of Meldrum House, Old Meldrum, Aberdeenshire), *b.* 1915; ed. at Winchester, and Trin. Coll., Camb.——Margaret Jean, *b.* 1919: *m.* 1st, 1943 (m. diss. 1947), René Dorval, of Montreal, Canada; 2ndly, 1957, Percy Mansfield Scaddan, of Newhouse, Frinton Park, Frinton, Essex, and has issue living, (by 1st m.) Marie Margaret Diane, *b.* 1943: *m.* 1964, Henry Robert Denholm Hallam, of Fir Trees, 9, Dorley Close, Shepperton, Middx., and has issue living, Alison Jeanette *b.* 1966, Paul Ian Douglas *b.* 1969.
Grandson of the late Charles Garden Assheton-Smith, who was *cr.* a Bt. 1911, 2nd son of the late Robert George Duff, brother of *de jure* 5th Bt.:—
See Duff, Bt. (*cr.* 1911).

Descendants of Louisa Alice Duff, da. of Robert George Duff (ante), *b.* 1853, *d.* 1926: *m.* 1876, the 3rd Baron Vivian, who *d.* 1893:—
See B. Vivian.

Granddaughters of the late Col. James Duff of Knockleith, yst. brother of *de jure* 5th Bt.:—
Issue of the late Rev. Canon Garden Llanoe Duff, *b.* 1858, *d.* 1938: *m.* 1885, Elizabeth, who *d.* 1944, da. of Andrew Anderson Dunlop, younger of Keppoch:—
Kathleen Jane (Granary, W. Peckham, Maidstone, Kent), *b.* 1891.——Helen Mary (The Old Vicarage, W. Peckham, Maidstone, Kent), *b.* 1894.

Grandchildren of the late James Duff Duff (infra):—
Issue of the late Maj.-Gen. Alan Colquhoun Duff, CB, OBE, MC, *b.* 1896, *d.* 1973: *m.* 1935, Diana Frances (Rider's Croft, Little Chesterford, Essex), el. da. of the late Col. Richard Parry Crawley, DSO, OBE, MVO:—
James Richard Valentine, *b.* 1941.——Lindsay Margaret, *b.* 1937: *m.* 1st, 1959 (m. diss. 1972), Stephen Francis Robertson; 2ndly, 1972, Colin M. Carden, of Dormers, Grundisburgh, Woodbridge, Suffolk, and has issue living, (by 1st m.) Patrick John, *b.* 1962,—Penelope Ann, *b.* 1964,— (by 2nd m.) Charles Anthony, *b.* 1973.——Christian Frances, *b.* 1942.

Grandchildren of the late Col. James Duff of Knockleith (ante):—
Issue of the late James Duff Duff, *b.* 1860 (twin), *d.* 1940: *m.* 1895, Laura Eleanor, da. of Sir William Fitzwilliam Lenox-Conyngham, K.C.B.:—
Patrick William, *b.* 1901, ed. at Winchester, and at Trin. Coll., Camb. (BA 1922, MA 1926); Regius Prof. of Civil Law, Camb., 1945-68; Warden of Winchester Coll., 1959-62. *Address*, Trinity Coll., Cambridge.——Mary Geraldine (11, Sherlock Close, Cambridge), *b.* 1904.——Hester Laura Elisabeth, *b.* 1912. *Residence*, Low Middleton Hall, Middleton-One-Row, Darlington.
Issue of the late Adm. Victor Alexander Stanley Duff, GCB, GBE, KCVO, *b.* 1862; *d.* 1933: *m.* 1st, 1886, Janet Douglas, who *d.* 1908, da. of the late Garden William Duff; 2ndly, 1924, Marjorie, da. of the late Charles Hill-Whitson, of Parkhill, Perths.:—

(By 1st m.) Helen Douglas, b. 1887: m. 1923, Lieut.-Com. Edgar Dolphin, DSO, RN, and has issue living, Peter Western (32, The Street, Aldermaston, Berks.), b. 1924; Lt.-Com. RN (ret.): m. 1955, Margaret Sally, da. of Cdr. Patrick Rycroft Maurice, OBE, RN (ret.), and has issue living, Mark Patrick b. 1958, Jane Douglas b. 1957, Sarah Katherine b. 1962,—Ann Douglas, b. 1924. Residence, Road Farm Cottage, Churt, Surrey.

Grandsons of the late Dorothy Alexandra Duff (Lady James), OBE, da. of the late Adm. Sir Alexander Ludovic Duff, GCB, GBE, KCVO, (ante):—
Issue of the late Capt. Christopher Alexander James, RN, b. 1916, d. 1969: m. 1938, Cynthia, who d. 1971, da. of the late Douglas Swire [E. Glasgow, colls.]:—
Julian Alexander Ludovic (The Lodge, St. Aubyns, Rottingdean, Brighton, BN2 7GA), b. 1939: m. 1965, Hilary, da. of Thomas Browne, of Misbrooks Cottage, Capel, Surrey, and has issue living, Christopher Mark William, b. 1967,—David Hugh Geoffrey, b. 1969.——David Robin Millais JAMES-DUFF (Cushnie, Auchterless, Turriff, Aberdeenshire), b. 1945; assumed by deed poll, 1963, the additional surname of Duff after his patronymic: m. 1970, Monica, da. of Thomas Browne, of Misbrooks Cottage, Capel, Surrey, and has issue living, Fiona Louise b. 1971,—Tania Robin, b. 1973.——Simon Christopher, b. 1946.

Grandchildren of the late Rev. Charles Edmund Duff, son of the late Col. James Duff, of Knockleith (ante):—
Issue of the late Capt. Ian Archibald James Duff, M.C., b. 1895, d. 1949: m. 1916, Kathleen Frances, who d. 1932, da. of Patrick Vernon Chinnery Haldane:—
Patrick Charles, b. 1920.——Alexander Ian, b. 1922. Residence,

Granddaughter of the late Col. James Duff of Knockleith (ante):—
Issue of the late John Duff, b. 1864, d. 1936; m. 1st, 1897, Constance Evelina Pratt, who d. 1898; 2ndly, 1904, Lily Clough, who d. 1905:—
(By 1st m.) Evelina Frances Helen (1048, Ripple Av., Pacific Grove, Cal. 93950, USA), b. 1898. ——(By 2nd m.) Lily Katharine, b. 1905. Residence, 26, Matham Rd., East Molesey, Surrey.

This Nova Scotia Baronetcy was conferred with remainder to heirs whatsoever, i.e., it can be and has been inherited through or by a female representative of the family. The 1st Bt., the Hon. James Sutherland, advocate, 2nd son of 2nd Lord Duffus m. Elizabeth, da. and ultimate heiress of Sir William Dunbar of Hempriggs, 1st Bt. (cr. 1700) [Dunbar, Bt., of Northfield] whose surname and arms he assumed. After the death in 1875 of Sir George Dunbar, 4th Bt. the male issue of the 1st Bt. became ext., and the Baronetcy devolved on Capt. (Sir) Benjamin Duff, de jure 5th Bt. (son of his sister Louisa, who married, 1805, Garden Duff of Hatton, Aberdeenshire), but he did not prove his right to the title. Sir George Duff-Sutherland-Dunbar, grandson of the de jure 5th Bt., who assumed the additional surnames of Sutherland-Dunbar on succeeding to the Hempriggs and Ackergill estate, established his right as 6th Bt. at Lyon Court 1899. His son Sir George Cospatrick Duff-Sutherland-Dunbar, 7th Bt., d. 1963, and was s. by Dame Maureen Daisy Helen Dunbar, granddaughter of Jessie Mona (who m. 1869 the Rev. Canon Courtenay Moore), da. of de jure 5th Bt. and established her right as Baronetess at Lyon Court 1965.

HOPE-DUNBAR, Creation (N.S.) 1664, of Baldoon.

The more prepared, the more powerful.

Sir DAVID HOPE-DUNBAR, 8th Baronet, b. July 13th, 1941 ; s. his father, Major Sir BASIL DOUGLAS, 1961; ed. at Eton, and Roy. Agric. Coll., Cirencester; ARICS: m. 1971, Kathleen Ruth, yr. da. of the late J. Timothy Kenrick, and has issue.

Arms—Quarterly, 1st, gules, a lion rampant argent, armed and langued azure, a bordure of the second charged with ten roses of the field, barbed and seeded vert, Dunbar; 2nd, azure, on a chevron or between three bezants a bay leaf slipped vert, a mullet of the second in chief for difference, Hope; 3rd, argent, a man's heart imperially crowned proper, on a chief azure three mullets of the field, Douglas; 4th, counter-quartered, 1st and 4th, gules, three cinquefoils ermine, 2nd and 3rd, argent, a lymphad sails furled, sable, flagged gules, Hamilton. Crest—A horse's head couped argent, bridled gules. Supporters—Two lions rampant guardant argent, armed and langued gules, each holding in one of the forepaws a rose slipped proper.

Residence—Banks Farm, Kirkcudbright.

Son living—CHARLES, b. March 5th, 1975.

Daughter living—Philippa, b. 1973.

Widow living of 7th Baronet—EDITH MAUDE MACLAREN (Lady Hope-Dunbar), da. of the late Malcolm Cross: m. 1940, as his second wife, Maj. Sir Basil Douglas Hope-Dunbar, 7th Bt., who d. 1961. Residence, Crofthead Cottage, by Kirkcudbright.

Collateral Branches living. (Males and females in remainder).
Issue of the late Helen Jacqueline Hope, M.B.E., sister of 6th baronet, b. 1875, d. 1923: m. 1901, Alan Burns, of Cumbernauld, co. Dunbarton :—
John Alan, b. 1905; ed. at Harrow, and at Trin. Coll., Camb.; is Lt.-Col. late Scots Gds., and a Member of Queen's Body Guard for Scotland (R. Co. of Archers): m. 1944, Joyce Margaret, da. of G. A. B. August, of Bedford, and has issue living, Felicity Margaret, b. 1945: m. 1974, Francis Michael Morton Peto, of Sorrowlessfield, Earlston, Berwicks. [see Peto, Bt., cr. 1855],—Marion Jacqueline, b. 1948: m. 1968, Maj. Peter Guy Chamberlin, R. Green Jackets, of Sherwood Cottage, Little London, nr. Andover, Hants., and has issue living, Edward Alan b. 1974, Lucinda Geraldine b. 1970. Residence, Godminster Wood House, Bruton, Som.——George, b. 1909; ed. at Eton, and Trin. Coll., Camb.; late Lt.-Cdr. RNVR. Residence, Kilmalieu, Ardgour, Argyll.——Jean Douglas, b. 1903. Residence. Cowdenknowes, Earlston, Berwicks.

Grandchildren of the late Helen Jacqueline Burns, M.B.E. (ante) :—
Issue of the late Charles Hope Burns, b. 1912, d. 1958: m. 1949, Barbara Delscey (of Cowdenknowes, Earlston, Berwickshire), da. of the late Dr. E. Macmillan, of Pretoria, S. Africa:—
Geoffrey Douglas John, b. 1954.——Delscey Hope, b. 1951.

This baronetcy was granted to David Dunbar, of Baldoon, co. Wigtown, in 1664, with remainder "provydit to his heirs male and tailzie." On the death of the grantee the baronetcy became dormant, and so remained until 1916, when Major Charles Dunbar Hope-Dunbar [see M. Linlithgow, colls.], grandson of Lady Isabella Ellen Hope, da. of 5th Earl of Selkirk, and a descendant of Mary (who m. Lord Basil Hamilton) grand-da. of the 1st Bt., in 1916, successfully proved his claim before the Baronetage Committee of the Privy Council, to be placed on the Official Roll of Baronets.

DUNCAN, Creation (U.K.) 1905, of Horsforth Hall, Guiseley, West Riding of Yorkshire. [Extinct 1964].

Sir (CHARLES EDGAR) OLIVER DUNCAN, 3rd and last *Baronet.*

Widow living of 3rd Baronet—ETELKA DE VANGEL (*Lady Duncan*): *m.* 1958, Sir (Charles Edgar Oliver Duncan, 3rd baronet, who *d.* 1964, when the title became ext.

DUNCAN, Creation UK 1957, of Jordanstone, co. Perth. [Extinct 1974.]

Sir JAMES ALEXANDER LAWSON DUNCAN, 1st and last *Baronet.*

Widow living of 1st Baronet—BEATRICE MARY MOORE (*Lady Duncan*) (Jordanston, by Alyth, Perthshire), da. of Thomas Laurence O'Carroll, of Ballinvullen, co. Cork, and widow of Maj. Philip James Kington Blair-Oliphant, of Ardblair Castle, Perthshire: *m.* 1966, as his 2nd wife, Sir James Alexander Lawson Duncan, 1st baronet, who *d.* 1974, when the title became ext.

PAUNCEFORT-DUNCOMBE, Creation (U.K.) 1859, of Great Brickhill, Buckinghamshire

Sir PHILIP DIGBY PAUNCEFORT-DUNCOMBE, 4th *Baronet; b.* May 18th, 1927; *s.* his father, *Maj. Sir* EVERARD PHILIP DIGBY, *DSO,* 1971; ed. at Stowe; Maj. (ret.) late Gren. Gds.; DL of Bucks.: *m.* 1951, Rachel Moyra, da. of Maj. Henry Gerald Aylmer [*see* B. Aylmer, colls.], and has issue.

Arms—Quarterly : 1st and 4th, per chevron engrailed gules and argent, three talbots' heads erased counterchanged, a chief ermine, *Duncombe;* 2nd, gules, three lions rampant argent, *Pauncefort;* 3rd azure. **Crests**—1st, out of a ducal coronet or a horse's leg sable, the shoe argent, charged with a cross-crosslet gold, *Duncombe;* 2nd, a lion rampant argent ducally crowned or, and charged on the shoulder with an escallop sable, *Pauncefort.*

Non fecimus ipsi.
We have not done it ourselves.

Residence—Great Brickhill Manor, Bletchley, Bucks. *Club,* Guards'.

Son living—DAVID PHILIP HENRY, *b.* May 21st, 1956.

Daughters living—Diana, *b.* 1953: *m.* 1974, Jeremy David Trevor West [see B. Graves, colls.]——Charlotte, *b.* 1967.
Sister living—Sophia, *b.* 1925: *m.* 1957, Archibald Evariste Yuill, of Lucas's, Haywards Heath, Sussex, and has issue living, William George Henry, *b.* 1961.
Widow living of 3rd Baronet—EVELYN ELVIRA (*Evelyn, Lady Pauncefort-Duncombe*) (Lane End, Great Brickhill, Bletchley, Bucks.), da. of the late Frederick Anthony Denny [Quilter, Bt.], *m.* 1922, Maj. Sir Everard Philip Digby Pauncefort-Duncombe, DSO, 3rd Bt., who *d.* 1971.

The father of the 1st baronet, Philip Pauncefort, assumed by Roy. licence, in 1804, the additional surname of Duncombe.

DUNDAS, Creation (U.K.) 1821, of Beechwood, Midlothian.

Sir ROBERT WHYTE MELVILLE DUNDAS, 6th *Baronet; b.* Oct. 31st, 1881; *s.* his father, *Sir* GEORGE WHYTE MELVILLE, 1934: *m.* 1926, Dorothea Emilie Victoria, who *d.* 1963, da. of the late A. W. Wiseman, Mus.B., of Monmouth.

Arms—Argent, a lion rampant gules within a bordure engrailed ermine. **Crest**—A lion's head affronté gules surrounded by an oak bush vert, fructed proper. **Supporters** — *Dexter,* a horse rampant ; *sinister,* an elephant ; each charged upon the shoulder with a thistle.

Seat—Comrie House, Comrie, Perthshire.

Try.

This family descends from James, son of Sir James Dundas of Arniston (d. 1679) by his 2nd wife Janet Hephurne, Sir Robert D ndas, 1st baronet was one of the principal Clerks in the Court of Session in Scotland,

DUNDAS, Creation (U.K.) 1898, of Arniston, Borthwick, Midlothian.
[Extinct 1970.]

Sir THOMAS CALDERWOOD DUNDAS, *MBE,* 7th and last *Baronet.*

Daughters living of 7th Baronet—Alice Kirsty, *b.* 1937: *m.* 1960, Antony Pilkington, of Crofton, Lodge, Kingsley, Ches., and has issue living, Jerome Antony Simon, *b.* 1961,—David Christopher: *b.* 1963,—Simon Benedict, *b.* 1972,—Miranda Kirsty *b.* 1966.——Davina Margaret, *b.* 1939. *m.* 1966, Martin Charles Findlay, of Ledburn Manor, Leighton Buzzard, Beds. [*see* E. Dartmouth],

Daughters living of 4th Baronet—Althea Enid Philippa, *b.* 1939: *m.* 1970, Aedrian Bekker, of Arniston, Gorebridge, Midlothian, and has issue living, Kirsty Jean, *b.* 1973.——Myfanwy Elizabeth Jean, *b.* 1946.——Joanne Montgomerie, *b.* 1949: *m.* 1974, Richard Henry James Kerr-Wilson, MB, BChir., of 30, Albany Mansions, Albert Bridge Rd., SW11.

Widows living of 4th and 7th Baronets—JEAN MARIAN, da. of James A. Hood, of Midfield, Lasswade, Midlothian: *m.* 1st, 1936, Sir Philip Dundas, 4th Bt., who *d.* 1952; 2ndly, 1953, Alastair Stewart of La Colline, Chemin Davel 22, 1009 Pully, Vaud, Switzerland.——ISABEL (*Lady Dundas*) (Field Gate, Ditchling, Sussex), da. of the late Charles Goring [*see* Goring, Bt., colls.]: *m.* 1933, Maj. Sir Thomas Calderwood Dundas, MBE, 7th Bt., who *d.* 1970, when the title became ext.

DUNLOP, Creation (U.K.) 1916, of Woodbourne, co. Renfrew.

Deservedly.

Sir THOMAS DUNLOP, **3rd** *Baronet;* *b.* April 11, 1912; *s.* his father, *Sir* THOMAS, 1963; ed. at Shrewsbury, and at St. John's Coll., Camb.; a Chartered Accountant, a partner in the firm of Thomas Dunlop & Sons, ship and insurance brokers, of 50, Wellington St., Glasgow; late Chm. of Savings Bank of Glasgow; an O.St.J.; 1939-45 War as Maj. Roy. Signals: *m.* 1947, Alison, da. of the late T. A. Smith, of Lindsaylands, Biggar, and has issue.

Arms—Argent, a double-headed eagle displayed gules, armed and membered azure; on a chief of the last, a three-masted galley under full sail proper, flagged of the second, at her stern the banner of Scotland, all between two garbs or. **Crest**—A dexter hand couped at the wrist, grasping a dagger all proper.

Residence—The Corrie, Kilmacolm, Renfrewshire.

Son living—THOMAS, *b.* April 22nd, 1951.

Daughters living—Jennifer Margaret, *b.* 1948.——Alison Mary, *b.* 1955.

Sister living—Dorothy Frances, *b.* 1921: *m.* 1948, Ernest Forrester Fortune, MBE, TD, of 11, Douglas Cres., Edinburgh, and has issue living, George Dunlop, *b.* 1953,—Susan Elizabeth, *b.* 1949.

Aunt living (daughter of 1st baronet)—Mary Boyd (2, St. Michael's Drive, Helensburgh, Dunbartonshire).

Collateral Branches living.

Issue of the late Capt. William Beckett Dunlop, RHA yr. son of 2nd baronet, *b.* 1915, *d.* 1970: *m.* 1947, Charmian Katherine Chauncy (19, Marchmont Rd., Ayr), da. of the late Col. Gavin Charteris Towers Speirs, of Hume, Bearsden, Dunbartonshire:—
Anthony Charles Beckett, *b.* 1948; ed. at Rossall.——Michael William Beckett, *b.* 1951; ed. at Rugby.——Simon Speirs Beckett, *b.* 1955; ed. at Millfield.

Issue of the late Peter Mitchell Dunlop, 2nd son of 1st baronet, *b.* 1883, *d.* 1962: *m.* 1915, Florence Leathard (of Dalglennan Lodge, Helensburgh, Dunbartonshire), da. of John Gardner Brewis:—
Mary Mitchell, *b.* 1924: *m.* 1963, Walter A. Bishop, of Larchfield, Old Rd., Buckland, Betchworth, Surrey.

Issue of the late Robert Jack Dunlop, youngest son of 1st baronet, *b.* 1891, *d.* 1952: *m.* 1918, Maude Rowena (now of Findhorn, Helensburgh, Dunbartonshire), da. of the late William C. Teacher, of Bellcairn, Cove, Dunbartonshire:—
George Teacher, *b.* 1923 : *m.* 1950, Margaret Jane Schoelles, and has issue living, Nicholas George Teacher, *b.* 1956,—Rosalie Anne, *b.* 1951,—Carolyn Jane, *b.* 1954,—Philippa Christine, *b.* 1961,— Sally Margaret, *b.* 1963. *Residence,* Torwood, Rhu, Dunbartonshire.——Robert Jack, *b.* 1927: *m.* 1950, Dorothy Shirley Dixon, and has issue living, Robert Alastair, *b.* 1951,— Timothy Dixon, *b.* 1953,—Andrew James, *b.* 1959,—Gillian Elizabeth, *b.* 1956. *Residence,* Lynton, Helensburgh, Dunbartonshire.——Audrey Dorothy, *b.* 1932: *m.* 1952, Antony Leonard Cullen, M.C., T.D., and has issue living, Michael Robert Antony, *b.* 1955,—Roderick Leonard Dunlop, *b.* 1958,—John Hamish Charles, *b.* 1965,—David Alastair Thomas, *b.* 1971,—Rowena Gay, *b.* 1959,—Audrey Hilary, *b.* 1963. *Residence,* New House, Cressing, Essex.

The 1st baronet, Sir Thomas Dunlop, G.B.E. (son of Thomas Dunlop, of Glasgow), was head of the firm of Thomas Dunlop & Sons, shipowners and grain merchants, of Glasgow, and Lord Provost of Glasgow and Lord-Lieut. of co. of City of Glasgow 1914-17.

DUNN, Creation (U.K.) 1921, of Bathurst, Province of New Brunswick, Dominion of Canada.

Watchful and bold.

Sir PHILIP GORDON DUNN, 2nd *Baronet;* b. Oct. 26th, 1905 ; s. his father, Sir JAMES HAMET, Q.C., 1956 : m. 1933, Lady Mary Sybil St. Clair-Erskine (who obtained a divorce 1944, and whom he re-married 1969), da. of 5th Earl of Rosslyn, and has issue.

Arms—Azure, an eagle displayed between three maple leaves or.   Crest—In front of four holly trees proper a lizard gold.
Residence—Stowell Park, Marlborough.

Daughters living—Serena Mary (*Hon. Mrs. N. C. Jacob Roths-child*), b. 1934: m. 1961, the Hon. (Nathaniel Charles) Jacob Rothschild, of 28, Warwick Av., W9, and Doves House,Ham, Wilts., son of 3rd Baron Rothschild.——Nell Mary, b. 1936: m. 1957, Jeremy Christopher Sandford. *Residence,*
Sisters living—Joan Molesworth (*Baroness Sherborne*): m. 1st, 1928, Capt. Hubert John Duggan, MP, Life Guards, who d. (on active ser. during 1939-45 War) 1943, having obtained a divorce 1930; 2ndly, 1930, John Anthony Jenkinson [Jenkinson, Bt., colls.], who d. 1935; 3rdly, 1943, the 7th Baron Sherborne, and has issue living, (by 1st m.) a son, b. 1929. *Residence*, Lodge Park, Aldsworth, Cheltenham, Glos.——Leila Brigid.: m. 1st, 1939, Count Peter Wolff-Metternich, who d. (killed in action in Ukraine) 1941; 2ndly, 1944, Joseph Bromovsky, of Dub, Czechoslovakia, and has issue living, (by 1st m.) *Count* Tassilo Peter Franziskus Paul Maria, b. 1940,—(by 2nd m.) Anthony, b. 1948,—Francis Philip, b. 1958,—Josette, b. 1945. *Residence*, 42, Ovington Street, Chelsea, SW3.

Half-Sister living—Anne, b. 1929 : m. 1st, 1951 (marriage dissolved 1960), Michael Wishart ; 2ndly, 1960, Rodrigo Moynihan, and has issue living (by 1st marriage), Francis Dominic, b. 1951,—(by 2nd marriage) Daniel Henry, b. 19——. *Residence*, 70, Avenue du Leman, Lausanne, Switzerland.

Widow living of 1st Baronet—MARCIA ANASTASIA (*Baroness Beaverbrook*), da. of John Christoforides, of Leyswood, Groombridge, Sussex; Hon LLD Dalhousie; Chancellor of Dal-housie Univ. since 1968: m. 1st, 1942, as his third wife, Sir James Hamet Dunn, QC, 1st baronet, who d. 1956; 2ndly, 1963, as his 2nd wife, the 1st Baron Beaverbrook, who d. 1964. *Residence*, Saint Andrews, New Brunswick, Canada.

The 1st baronet Sir James Hamet Dunn (son of the late Robert Dunn of Bathurst, New Brunswick), was Bar. Nova Scotia and N.W. Territory 1898, and Province of Quebec 1901, and a K.C. 1948.

DUNNING, Creation (U.K.) 1930, of Beedinglee, Lower Beeding, Sussex.

Sir SIMON WILLIAM PATRICK DUNNING, 3rd| *Baronet;* b. Dec. 14th, 1939; s. his father, Sir WILLIAM LEONARD, 1961; ed. at Eton: m. 1975, Frances Deirdre Morton, da. of Patrick Lancaster, of Wapsbourne Manor, Sheffield Park, Sussex, and formerly wife of Capt. Nigel Edward Corbally Stourton [see B. Mowbray, colls.].

Residences—Low Auchengillan, Blanefield, by Glasgow, G63 9AU; 13, Winton Lane, Glasgow, W2.

Widow living of 2nd Baronet—KATHLEEN LAWRIE (*Lady Dunning*), only child of J. Patrick Cuth-bert, MC, of Barclayhills by Perth: m. 1936, Sir William Leonard Dunning, 2nd baronet, who d. 1961. *Residence*, Barclayhills, Guildtown, Perth.

The 1st baronet, Sir Leonard Dunning (son of the late Simon Dunning, of Warwick Square, S.W.), was an Inspector of Constabulary at Home Office 1912-30.

Dunnington-Jefferson, see Jefferson.

DUNTZE, Creation (G.B.) 1774, of Tiverton, co. Devon.

Sir GEORGE EDWIN DOUGLAS DUNTZE, C.M.G., 6th *Baronet;* b. June 1st, 1913 ; s. his father, Sir GEORGE PUXLEY, 1947 ; formerly a Pro-vincial Commr., Uganda; CMG 1960: m. 1st, 1941, (m. diss. 1966), Joan who d. 1972, da. of the late Maj. Frederick Edgar Bradstock, DSO, MC; 2ndly, 1966, Mrs. Nesta Evill, da. of the late T. R. P. Herbert, of Newport, Mon., and has issue by 1st m.

Residence—25, Ennismore Gdns., SW7.

Daughter living—By 1st marriage—Elizabeth Joan, b. 1944: m. 1966, Nicholas Lowther James Grove, of Church Hill Cottage, Church Lane, Aldington, Ashford, Kent, and has issue living, Richard Nicholas Dougal, b. 1970,—Iain Anthony Douglas, b. 1973.

Sisters living—Ivy Harriette (PO, Bothas Hill, Natal), b. 1909: m. 1940, Brian Dougherty, who d. 1962.——Esmée Ida (6, Barons Court, Mitchell Rd., Greendale, Salisbury, Rhodesia), b. 1911: m. 1937, Vyvyan Mackenzie, who d. 1974, and has issue living, Brenda Rosalind, b. 1941,—Lorna Esmée, b. 1943.

Collateral Branches living.

Grandchildren of the late John Alexander Duntze, son of the late Adm. John Alexander Duntze, grandson, of 1st baronet :—

Issue of the late John Alexander Ralph Duntze, *b.* 1878, *d.* 1950 : *m.* 1st, 1905, Carrie Fairchild, who *d.* 1927, da. of Edward J. Godfrey, formerly of St. Paul, Minnesota, U.S.A.; 2ndly, 1929, Louise Marie Berthelon, of Box 36, Mesilla Park, New Mexico, U.S.A.:—

(By 1st marriage) JOHN ALEXANDER, *b.* Nov. 13th, 1909; is a Mechanical Engineer: *m.* 1935, Emily Ellsworth, da. of Elmer E. Harlow, of New Bedford, Massachusetts, U.S.A. *Residence*, St. John's Place, Westport, Connecticut, U.S.A.

Issue of the late George Douglas Duntze, *b.* 1882, *d.* 1946 : *m.* 1920, Mabel Lillian (now of 8049, Gannon Street, St. Louis, Missouri, U.S.A.), da. of Daniel Evans, of St. Louis, U.S.A. :—

Daniel Evans, *b.* 1926 : *m.* 1954, Marietta Welsh, and has issue living, Daniel Evans, *b.* 1960,— Jill Alison, *b.* 1957,—Robin Evans (da.), *b.* 1959.——Dorothy Jane, *b.* 1923 : *m.* 1950, Hal Roach, of 9, Woodhill Rd., Birmingham, Alabama, U.S.A., and has issue living, Michael Todd, *b.* 1952,—Scott Evans, *b.* 1953,—Brooke Normile, *b.* 1955,—Todd Douglas, *b.* 1957.

The 1st baronet, an eminent merchant of Exeter, was sometime M.P. for Tiverton. The 2nd baronet was Receiver-General of the taxes of the co. of Devon.

DUPREE, Creation (U.K.) 1921, of Craneswater, Portsmouth, co. Southampton.

Le·monde·est·mon·pré

The world is my field.

Sir VICTOR DUPREE, 4th *Baronet*; *b.* Dec. 19th, 1887; *s.* his brother *Capt. Sir* VERNON, 1971; Capt. (ret.) late 3rd Dragoon Gds. and Tank Corps.; 1914-18 War (wounded, prisoner): *m.* 1st, 1910, Gladys, who *d.* 1922, da. of Charles Henry Lawson; 2ndly, 1922, Margaret Cross, and has issue by 2nd m.

Arms—Vert, on a bend between two calves passant or three mullets of the field. **Crest**—A lion sejant proper supporting with the dexter forepaw a flagstaff proper, flowing therefrom a banner vert, charged with a mullet or.

Residence—16A, Montpelier Cres., Brighton.

Son living—By 2nd m.—PETER (Great Seabrights, Galley Wood, nr. Chelmsford, Essex), *b.* Feb. 10th, 1924: *m.* 1947, Joan, da. of the late Capt. James Desborough Hunt.

Daughter living—By 2nd m.—Mary, *b.* 1926: *m.* 1948, George Dutton Gibb, of Yenda, Haw Lane, Bledlow Ridge, High Wycombe, Bucks., and has issue living, Elizabeth, *b.* 1951,—Jennifer, *b.* 1954.

Half-Brother living—Thomas William (Riant-Mont, 1816 Chailly s/Clarens, Switzerland; White's and Household Brigade Yacht Clubs), *b.* 1913; ed. at Harrow; late Lt. Gren. Gds.; sometime Private Sec. to HM's Ambassador, Paris; Hon. Attaché at HM's Embassy, Madrid 1936-8, in News Depart., Foreign Office 1938-43, Dept. Assist. to British Resident Min., Allied Force Headquarters, Algiers 1943-44, Press Attaché (local rank of 1st Sec.), HM's Embassy, Paris 1944-46, Foreign Office Observer (Press Relations) at Trials of Major War Criminals, Nuremberg 1946, and again in News Depart. Foreign Office April to Oct. 1946: *m.* 1st, 1938 (m. diss. 1953), Anne, da. of Sir Henry Getty Chilton, GCMG; 2ndly, 1953, Mrs. Jacqueline Harari, da. of Commendatore Leo Goldschmied, and has issue living, (by 1st m.) Delia, *b.* 1939: *m.* 1962, Peter Guy, of 33, Bancroft Av., Highgate, N2, and has issue living, Dominic William *b.* 1963, Susannah *b.* 1965,—Sarah Anne, *b.* 1942.

Sister living—Norah Decima Mary, *b.* 1893: *m.* 1920, John Fulton Houston, and has issue living, Sheila, *b.* 1921: *m.* 1946, Leslie Sachs, of Johannesburg, S. Africa. *Residence*, Birch Tree Cottage, St. Catherine's Rd., Hayling Island, Hants.

Half-Sisters living—Irene Amy Marion : *m.* 1936, John Gerrard Brendan O'Hagan, Squadron-Leader R.A.F., and has issue living, Timothy David Brendan, *b.* 1945.——Margaret Marcella Marion : *m.* 1939, Capt. Donald Harris Browne and has issue living, David William Harris, *b.* 1946,—Susan Marion, *b.* 1940. *Residence*, Courtyards, Crawley Winchester.

Daughter living of 3rd Baronet—Mary Marcella Lucy: *m.* 1941, Terence Patrick Lawrence, of The Glebe House, N. Fawley, Wantage, son of the late Sir Walter Lawrence, JP, of Hyde Hall, Sawbridgeworth, and has issue.

Widow living of 3rd Baronet—LOUISA JENNIE (*Louisa Lady Dupree*) (Little Downings, Prinsted, Chichester, Sussex), da. of George Hillyard, of Southsea: *m.* 1955, as his 2nd wife, Capt. Vernon Dupree, 3rd Bt., who *d.* 1971.

Collateral Branches living.

Issue of the late Eric Dupree, 4th son of 1st baronet, *b.* 1895, *d.* 1932 : *m.* 1928, Gwendoline Violet (43B, York St., Broadstairs, Kent), da. of Henry Harvey:—

Monica Mary (Ride Court Cottage, Woodlands Ride, Ascot, Berks), *b.* 1930: *m.* 1954 (m. diss. 1974), Robin Gordon Hazlitt Morris, and has issue living, Anthony John David, *b.* 1955,—John Richard Hazlitt, *b.* 1958,—Andrew Quentin Dupree, *b.* 1963.——Barbara Jane (Ride Court Cottage, Woodlands Ride, Ascot, Berks.), *b.* 1931: *m.* 1st, 1954, Lt. John Richard Haward, RN, who *d.* 1956; 2ndly, 1957, (m. diss. 1967), Ronald Mitchell, and has issue living, (by 2nd m.), Terence Roger Anstey, *b.* 1957,—Robert Killian, *b.* 1959,—Simon Paul Adam, *b.* 1966.

Issue of the late Lt.-Cdr. James Dupree, RNVR, 5th son of 1st baronet, *b.* 1899, *d.* 1972: *m.* 1928, Mary Ethel Gillott, who *d.* 1949, da. of the late T. W. Reid, and widow of A. Stuart Elsworth:—

Thomas William James) David (Little Fircliff, Whitworth Rd., Darley Dale, nr. Matlock), *b.* 1930.——Jennifer Rosemary Gillott, *b.* 1933: *m.* 1962, Roberto Lorenzo Mercadaz, and has issue living, a son, *b.* 19—,—a son, *b.* 19—,—Maria-Victoria, *b.* 1964,—a da., *b.* 1975.

Issue of the late Capt. John Rupert Dupree, 7th son of 1st baronet, *b.* 1915, *d.* 1965: *m.* 1946, Ann Margaret Frances (BETHELL) (who *m.* 3rdly, 1965, Roger Thornycroft, DSC, of The Home Farm, Bembridge, I. of Wight, son of the late Sir John Edward Thornycroft, KBE), only da. of the late Lt.-Col. Robert George Barlow, Seaforth Highlanders (ret.):—

Michael John, *b.* 1947.

The 1st baronet, Col. Sir William Thomas Dupree, V.D., T.D. (son of the late William Dupree) **was Mayor of Portsmouth 1901-3 and 1909-10 and Hon. Col. R.F.A. The 2nd baronet, Sir William was Chm. and Managing Director of the Portsmouth and Brighton United Breweries, Ltd.**

DURAND, Creation (U.K.) 1892, of Ruckley Grange, Salop.

[Name pronounced "Du-rand."]

Rev. Sir HENRY MORTIMER DICKON MARION ST. GEORGE DURAND, 4th *Baronet*, son of Lt.-Cdr. Mortimer Henry Marion Durand, RN, yst. son of 1st baronet; *b.* June 19th, 1934; *s.* his uncle, *Brig. Sir* ALAN ALGERNON MARION, *MC*, 1971 : *m.* 1971, Stella Evelyn, el. da. of Capt. Christopher L'Estrange, of Dun Laoghaire, co. Dublin, and has issue.

Arms—Azure, five fusils conjoined in fesse within a bordure or; on a chief embattled of the last, a pair of manacles of the first.   **Crest**—Over a rock proper, a crescent argent between two laurel branches or.
Residence—

Esperance en Dieu.
Hope in God.

Son living—EDWARD ALAN CHRISTOPHER PERCY, *b.* Feb. 21st, 1974.
Daughter living—Rachel Elizabeth Marion, *b.* 1972.
Sister living—Elizabeth Pamela Marion, *b.* 1932: *m.* 1957, Maj. George Naismith Bowden, Loyal Regt. (ret.), of Higher Shute Farm, Huish Champflower, Taunton.
Daughter living of 3rd Baronet—Patricia Marion, *b.* 1925: *m.* 1st, 1960, Wing-Cdr. Howard Rex English Rumsey, who *d.* 1964; 2ndly, 1969, Kenneth Alec James Booth, MBE, FILA, of Perreys, Camden Park, Tunbridge Wells, and has issue living (by 1st m.), Alan, *b.* 1962,—Fiona Marion, *b.* 1964.

Aunt living (Daughter of 1st Baronet)—Beryl Marion, *b.* 1887: *m.* 1915, Wilfred Pollen Haviland, MBE, late Capt. 8th Batn., Argyll and Sutherland Highlanders, who *d.* 1947, and has issue living, Gwendolen Mary Beryl, *b.* 1916: *m.* 1946, Peter Herbert Sparks, Maj. (ret.) Indian Army, of The Old Vicarage, Compton Abdale, Cheltenham,—Daphne Marion, *b.* 1923; late 3rd Officer WRNS: *m.* 1950, Com. Edward Adams Nicholson, RN (ret.), of The Lea, Upper Sapey, Worcs. *Residence*, The Old Vicarage, Compton Abdale, Cheltenham.

Mother living—Beatrice Garvan, da. of Judge Sheridan, of Sydney, NSW: *m.* 1931, as his 2nd wife Lt.-Cdr. Mortimer Henry Marion Durand RN, who *d.* 1969.

Widow living of 3rd Baronet—EVELYN SHERBROOKE, CBE (*Evelyn Lady Durand*), (Ellerncroft, Wotton-under-Edge, Glos.);   CBE (Civil) 1955, da. of the late Charles Arnold Crane, and widow of Sir Stanley William Tubbs, 1st Bt. (ext.): *m.* 1944, as his 2nd wife, Brig. Sir Alan Algernon Marion Durand, MC, 3rd Bt., who *d.* 1971.

Sir Edward Law Durand, 1st Bt., Resident in Nepal 1888-91 was el. son of Maj.-Gen. Sir Henry Marion Durand, KCSI, CB, Lt.-Gov. of Punjab 1870, and a descendant of the Ducal House of Northumberland.

DURRANT, Creation (G.B.) 1784, of Scottow, Norfolk.

Sir WILLIAM HENRY ESTRIDGE DURRANT, 7th *Baronet* ; *b.* April 1st, 1901 ; *s.* his father, *Sir* WILLIAM HENRY ESTRIDGE, 1953 ; is a J.P.; S.-W. Pacific 1939-45 (three medals), *m.* 1927, Georgina Beryl Gwendoline, who *d,* 1968, da. of Alexander Purse, of Kircubbin, co. Down, and has issue.

Arms—Or, a cross-crosslet ermines between four ermine spots sable.   **Crest**—A boar passant per fesse wavy argents and gules, bristled and tusked azure, and pierced through the body with a broken lance bendwise sable, point downwards, gold.

Residence—Woodside Gardens, Yardley Av., Waitara NSW, 2077.

Son living—WILLIAM ALEXANDER ESTRIDGE, Nov. 26th, 1929; is Capt. 12th/16th Hunter River Lancers, and a J.P.: *m.* 1953, Dorothy, *B.A.*, da. of Ronal Croker, of Quirindi, N.S. Wales, and has issue living, David Alexander, *b.* 1960,—Susan Elizabeth, *b.* 1962. *Residence*, Spring Park, Gaspard via Quirindi, N.S. Wales.
Daughter living—Beryl Elizabeth Wildbredt, *b.* 1928 : *m.* 1952, Douglas James Weaving (PO Box 142, Rochester Vic. 3561, Aust.), and has issue living, John Laurence *b.* 1956,—Peter Douglas, *b.* 1958,—Elizabeth Anne *b.* 1953.
Brother living—Reginald Walter Estridge, *b.* 1905 : *m.* 1937, Joy Minnie Smith, of Manly, N.S. Wales, and has issue living, Beverley Joy, *b.* 1938,—Kaye Lorraine, *b.* 1944. *Residence*, Burns Rd., Turramurra, NSW.

A dishonouring stain is worse than death.

Sister living—Pearlie May Wildbredt (72, Hopetown Village, Castle Hill, NSW 2154) *b.* 1903: *m.* 1931, Thomas Henry Downs, who *d.* 1971.

This family was established in Rutland and Derbyshire.   William Durrant, from whom the present baronet is in direct descent, migrated to Scottow, Norfolk, and *d.* 1700.   Sir Thomas, 1st baronet, was High Sheriff of Norfolk 1784.

DYER, Creation (E.) 1678, of Tottenham, Middlesex.

Sir (HENRY) PETER FRANCIS SWINNERTON
DYER, *FRS*, 16th *Baronet; b.* Aug. 2nd, 1927; *s.* his
father, *Sir* LEONARD SCHROEDER SWINNERTON,
1975; ed. at Eton, and Trin. Coll., Camb. (Fellow
1955, Dean 1962); FRS; Master of St. Catharine's
Coll., Camb. since 1973.

Arms—Or, a chief indented gules. **Crest**—Out of a ducal
coronet or a goat's head argent, horned gold.

Residence,—St. Catharine's Coll., Cambridge, CB2 1RL.

TERRERE·NOLO TIMERE·NESCIO

*Unwilling to frighten, un-
acquainted with fear.*

Sister living—Anne Winnifred Swinnerton, *b.* 1932.

Daughter living of 12th Baronet—Jacqueline Christine Swinnerton
(*posthumous*), *b.* 1918; late Asst. Section Officer WAAF:
m. 1st, 1943 (m. diss. 1949), Colin E. C. Campbell; 2ndly, 1949,
Col. Vincent Paravicini, TD, and has issue living (by 1st and
2nd m.). *Residences,* 38 Belgravia Court, Ebury St., SW1;
Nutley Manor, Basingstoke, Hants., RG25 2HL.

Widow living of 15th Baronet—BARBARA (*Lady Dyer*) (Westhorpe Cottage, Craven Arms, Salop,
SY7 9JN), da. of Hereward Irenius Brackenbury, CBE, of Seaton Barn House, Northumberland;
JP of Salop; Chm Nat. Fedn. of Women's Insts. 1957-61: *m.* 1925, Sir Leonard Schroeder
Swinnerton Dyer, 15th Bt., who *d.* 1975.

Collateral Branches living.

Grandson of the late Major Frederick Carr Swinnerton Dyer, 3rd son of 9th
baronet :—
Issue of the late Frederick Stewart Hotham DYER-BENNET, *b.* 1862, *d.* 1923 (having
assumed the additional surname of Bennet 1894): *m.* 1885, Adelaide, who *d.* 1942, da.
of George Taylor :—
RICHARD STEWART (98, Mayplace Rd. E., Barnehurst, Kent, DA7 6EH), *b.* Oct. 6th, 1886; Maj.
(ret.) Leics. Regt.; 1914-18 War (twice wounded): *m.* 1912, Miriam Wolcott, who *d.* 1973, da.
of the late Prof. Edward B. Clapp, of California Univ., USA, and has issue living, Richard
(Blue Hill Rd., Monterey, Mass. 01245, USA), *b.* 1913; a musician: *m.* 1st, 1936 (m. diss. 1941),
Elizabeth Hoar Pepper; 2ndly, 1942, Melvene Ipcar, and has issue living, (by 1st m.) Ellen
b. 1937, Eunice *b.* 1939, (by 2nd m.) Brooke *b.* 1946, Bonnie *b.* 1943,—John (907, Winona St.,
Northfield, Minn. 55057, USA), *b.* 1915; Prof. of Mathematics at Carleton Coll., Northfield,
Minn.: *m.* 1951, Mary Abby, da. of the late George B. Randall, and has issue living, David
b. 1954, Barbara *b.* 1965,—Frederick (154, Hillcroft Way, Walnut Creek, Calif. 94596, USA),
b. 1918; Architect: *m.* 1941, Patricia Esther Arndt, and has issue living, Oliver *b.* 1945, John
b. 1947, Cynthia *b.* 1949,—Christopher (7325, Chili Hill Rd., Newcastle, Calif. 95658, USA),
b. 1920,—Miriam, *b.* 1922: *m.* 1963, Kenneth O. May, of 16, Douglas Cres., Toronto, Ont.,
Canada, M4W 2E7.

Grandson of the late Capt. Stewart John Dyer, 4th son of 9th baronet, *b.* 1842,
d. 1925: *m.* 1873, Emily Mary Elizabeth, who *d.* 1912, only child and heir of
the late Henry Edmund Bythesea, of Nettleton, Wilts.
Issue of the late Major Stewart Barton Bythesea Dyer, D.S.O., and Life Guards, *b.* 1875,
d. 1917: *m.* 1906, Mai (she *m.* 2ndly, 1921, Baron A. Pontenani, who *d.* 1937), da. of
the late Capt. S. L. Osborne, RN, of Shanklin, Isle of Wight:—
Thomas Musgrave Swinnerton, *b.* 1907; ed. at Oratory Sch., and at St. Catharine's Coll. Camb.,
formerly Lieut. The Buffs ; European War 1939-44 in Middle East : *m.* 1936, Violet Elizabeth
(from whom he obtained a divorce 1948), da. of Ebenezer Cunningham. *Residence.*

Grandchildren of the late Capt. Edward Dyer, son of the late Edward Dyer, brother
of 8th baronet :—
Issue of the late Thomas Richard Dyer, *b.* 1842, *d.* 1916 : *m.* 1897, Kate Constance Swinnerton, who *d.* 1945, da. of Frederick Swinnerton Dyer, grandson of Edward Dyer
(ante):—
Frederick Thomas Swinnerton, *b.* 1898; ed. at Haileybury, and at Gonville and Caius Coll.,
Camb. (B.A. 1922, M.A. 1946) ; a Member of Roy. So. of Teachers: formerly Major Roy.
Indian Army Ordnance Corps; sometime Lieut. Alleyn's Sch. O.T.C. (late Hampshire Regt.):
m. 1927, Beatrice Henrietta, da. of Charles John Davies, and has issue living, John Frederick
(of 94, Whyke Rd., Chichester), *b.* 1928; late Fl.-Lt. RAF; Sen. Capt. BOAC: *m.* 1950, Linda
Mary, da. of Thomas Rees James and has issue living, Martin John Swinnerton *b.* 1955, Richard
Kenneth Swinnerton *b.* 1960,—Julian Swinnerton (55, Freshfield Bank, Forest Row, Sussex),
b. 1936; late PO RAF; Co. Sec., Vickers Group of Cos.; Assist. Sec. Vickers Ltd. 1973: *m.* 1961,
Patricia Newman, and has issue living, Jeremy Swinnerton *b.* 1964, Ann-Louise *b.* 1966,—Jean
Anne, *b.* 1931: *m.* 1952, A. W. Gransden, of 23, Mavis Close, Ewell, Surrey, and has issue living,
Jonathan Kim *b.* 1953, Joanna *b.* 1957. *Residence,* 19, Mortimer Cres., Worcester Park, Surrey.
——Hugh Swinnerton, ED, *b.* 1902; ed. at Haileybury; is Capt. Roy. Berks, Regt., and RE,
and a JP for Ceylon; sometime in Ceylon Planters' Rifle Corps: *m.* 1933, Barbara Eileen Home-
wood, and has issue living, David Swinnerton (Apt. 417, 371, S. Ellesmere Av., Burnaby, BC),
b. 1934; with Dept. of Attorney-Gen. (Sheriff Office): *m.* 1971, Beverley, da. of Robert W. Steep,
—Patrick Swinnerton (2, Park Farm Cottage, Shaldon Park Farm, Alton, Hants.), *b.* 1937; ed.
at Haileybury: *m.* 1st, 1960 (m. diss. 1970), Elizabeth Rule, da. of the late Air Marshall Sir Thomas
Arthur Warne-Brown, KBE, CB, DSC; 2ndly, 1971, Angela Evelyn Caldicott, and has issue
living, (by 1st m.) Thaila Elisabeth Swinnerton *b.* 1962, Lucinda Jane Swinnerton *b.* 1963,
Sussanah Swinnerton *b.* 1966. *Residence,* Bottor Gate, Hennock, Newton Abbot, S. Devon.——
Gordon Swinnerton, *b.* 1907; 1939-45 War as 2nd Lt. RASC (invalided).

Issue of the late Frederick Campbell Spencer Dyer, *b.* 1845, *d.* 1924 : *m.* 1867, Ellen, who *d.*
1908, da. of the late Charles Weavings, of Salisbury :—
Campbell Charles Frederick, *b.* 1871: Matabele War 1896-7: *m.* 1902, Eleanor Augusta Louise, who
d. 1935, da. of Samuel Bignell, of Andover, and has issue living, Gweneth Mary Bignell, *b.* 1905:
m. 1928, Charles Milo Davine, Bar.-at-law, and has issue living, Milo Charles *b.* 1929, John
Frederick *b.* 1931, Marie Thérèse *b.* 1932.——Benjamin Archibald, *b.* 1882; 1914-18 War with
Hon. Artillery Co. (wounded): *m.* 1908, Mabel Maude, da. of William Moore, and has issue living,
Benjamin Frederick Swinnerton (of Koilamari Tea Estate, North Lakhimpur PO, Upper Assam,
India), *b.* 1910; ed. at Brighton Coll.; late Major Roy. Indian Army Ser. Corps.; served with

Mounted Police in Palestine 1934-38; sometime in Assam Light Horse: *m.* 1945, Betty Taylor, da. of William Thomas Smithies, of Worthing. *Residence,*

Grandchildren of the late Frederick Campbell Spencer Dyer (ante):—
Issue of the late Thomas Harry Dyer, *b.* 1878, *d.* 1937: *m.* 1904, Kate, who *d.* 1953, da. of John Willis :—
John Arnold Swinnerton, *b.* 1905 ; European War 1939-45 as Sergt. Coast Regt. R.A. : *m.* 1st, 1930, Theresa Sylvester, who *d.* 1947, da. of Henry Sylvester Stannard ; 2ndly, 1949, Elizabeth Mahala, da. of Edward Valentine Johnson, of Bedford, and has issue living, (by 1st marriage) Thomas John Swinnerton, *b.* 1931,—(by 2nd marriage) Philip John, *b.* 1952,—Linda Theresa, *b.* 1950.——Nellie Jane Kathleen, *b.* 1906: *m.* 1957, Francis Coyle.——Patricia Swinnerton, *b.* 1912: *m.* 1940, John Eric Mackenzie, Staff Sergeant, Roy. Corps of Signals, and has issue living, Alan Ronald, *b.* 1946,—Valerie Jean, *b.* 1950 *Residence,* 2, Greenville Rd., Stradbrook Rd., Blackrock, co. Dublin.
Issue of the late Frank Stanley Dyer, *b.* 1880, *d.* 1961: *m.* 1910, Ellen Knight, of Suite 9, 1660, Fairfield Rd., Victoria, British Columbia:—
Benjamin Stanley, *b.* 1914: *m.* 1937, Lillian Averina, da. of C. H. Gillan, and has issue living, Althea Dawn, *b.* 1938: *m.* 1956, Allan Francis Millin, of 939, Florimond St., Vancouver-Richmond, British Columbia, and has issue living, Montgomery Allan *b.* 1956, Andrew Brian *b.* 1961, Cynthia Dawn-Marie *b.* 1958. *Residence,* Chisholm Rd., Maple Bay, British Columbia.—— Frederick Douglas, *b.* 1916: *m.* 1941, Myrtle Winifred Foster, and has issue living, Barbara Louise (R11-105, Menzies St., Victoria, BC, Canada) *b.* 1942 : *m.* 1965 (m. diss. 1966) Derry Allan McDonell,—Carol Ann, *b.* 1947: *m.* 1967, Ronald Douglas Robb (157, Robertson, Victoria, BC, Canada)—Nancy Mary, *b.* 1957. *Residence,* 5287, Parker Av., Cordova Bay, Victoria, BC.

Sir **William**, 1st baronet, married Thomazine, only da. and heir of Thomas Swinnerton, of Stanway Hall, Essex. Col. Sir John Swinnerton, 6th baronet, was a Groom of the Bedchamber to the Prince of Wales (afterwards George IV.). Lieut.-Gen. Sir Thomas Richard, 7th baronet, was Aide-de-Camp to Sir Ralph Abercromby in Egypt, and to Sir John Moore at Corunna. Com. Sir Thomas Swinnerton, R.N., 8th baronet, was present at numerous naval actions during the Peninsular war, and his brother, Lieut.-Col. Sir John, K.C.B., was present at Badajoz, Vittoria, St. Sebastian, Pyrenees, Nievelle, Nive, Orthes, and Toulouse. The 10th baronet served in Crimean war, and was present at Sebastopol, both assaults on the Redan, and at the bombardment and surrender of Kimburne. The 12th baronet, Sir John Swinnerton Dyer, M.C., Capt. Scots Guards, was killed in action during European War 1917. The 15th baronet, Sir Leonard Schroeder Swinnerton Dyer, was Chm., Salop Co. Council 1969-72.

Prest à Faire.
Ready to act.

DYKE, Creation (E.) 1677, of Horeham, Sussex.

Sir DEREK WILLIAM HART DYKE, 9th *Baronet*; *b.* Dec. 4th, 1924; *s.* his father, *Sir* OLIVER HAMILTON AUGUSTUS HART, 1969; late RAF: *m.* 1st, 1953 (m. diss. 1963), Dorothy Moses, of Hamilton, Ont., Canada; 2ndly, 1964 (m. diss. 1972), Margaret Dickson Elder, and has issue by 1st m.

Arms—Or, three cinquefoils, sable. Crest—A cubit arm in armour, the hand in a gauntlet sable, garnished or, holding a cinquefoil slipped also sable.

Residence,—Apt. 1105. 23, Spring St., Hamilton, Ont., L8N 2PI, Canada.

Son living—By 1st m.—DAVID WILLIAM, *b.* Jan. 5th, 1955.

Daughter living—By 1st m.—Diana, *b.* 1957.

Brother living—Oliver Guy Hart (Lullingstone Castle, Eynsford, Kent), *b.* 1928: *m.* 1974, Sarah Alexander Hart, da. of the late Rev. Eric Hart Dyke [see colls., infra].

Sister living—Rosemary June, *b.* 1930: *m.* 1st, 1952, (m. diss. 1969) Jack Farr; 2ndly, 1969, Michael Prince, of 23, Cadogan Gdns., SW3, and has issue living (by 1st m.) Amanda Zoe Frances, *b.* 1953,—Katie Victoria Felicity, *b.* 1957.

Widow living of 8th Baronet—MILDRED TURNOVER (*Mildred, Lady Dyke*), (The Homestead, Fordown, Nottingham Rd., Natal, S. Africa), da. of James Blackwood, and widow of Cecil Berens, JP [E. Winterton, colls.]: *m.* 1945, as his 2nd wife, Sir Oliver Hamilton Augustus Hart Dyke, 8th baronet, who *d.* 1969.

Collateral Branches living.

Issue of the late Percyvall Hart Dyke, el. son of 7th baronet. *b.* 1871, *d.* 1922: *m.* 1908, Edythe, who *d.* 1937, da. of the late W. G. Harrison, Q.C.:—
Edythe Frediswide (Marion, Connecticut, USA, 06444), *b.* 1909: *m.* 1st, 1935 (m. diss. 1949), Frederic Andrew Milward, late of Public Works Dept., Burma; 2ndly, 1950 (m. diss. 1956), Herbert Samuel Gallagher; 3rdly, 1956, Austin Edward Marsh, late Maj. RASC, who *d.* 1963.

Issue of the late Reginald Charles Hart Dyke, 4th son of 6th baronet, *b.* 1852, *d.* 1943: *m.* 1st, 1891, Guinevere Eva, who *d.* 1894, da. of the late Gen. Lord Alfred Paget, C.B. [M. Anglesey, colls.]; 2ndly, 1897, Millicent Ada, who *d.* 1946, da. of the late R. C. L. Bevan, of Trent Park, New Barnet:—
(By 2nd m.) Ashley Francis Hart, *b.* 1899; ed. at Eton: *m.* 1940, Marie, da. of Johan Voldengen, of Lier, Norway, and has issue living, Margaretha Millicent Hart, *b.* 1946. *Residence,* Trent Farm, Bathurst, Cape Province, S. Africa.

Grandchildren of the late Thomas Dyke, son of the late Rev. Thomas Hart Dyke, 2nd son of 5th baronet :—
Issue of the late Col. Percyvall Hart Dyke, D.S.O., Indian Army, *b.* 1872, *d.* 1952 : *m.* 1900, Louisa Catherine, who *d.* 1961, da. of Adm. John Halliday Cave, C.B. :—
Trevor Hart, *DSO* (Clough House, Bamford, Derbys.; Army and Navy Club), *b.* 1905; ed. at Marlborough; is Brig. late Queen's R. Regt.; 1939-45 War in France and Burma (DSO); DSO 1944: *m.* 1st, 1933 (marriage dissolved 1965), Eileen Joyce, da. of the late J. H. Niblock-Stuart; 2ndly, 1965, Mary Eliot, widow of Maj. D. E. Lockwood, and has issue living, (by 1st m.) Terence Percyvall Hart (Green Lane House, Ivinghoe, Bucks.; Cavalry Club), *b.* 1934; ed. at Marlborough;

Capt. The Royals: *m.* 1964, Wanda Hermione Krystyna, only da. of the late Lt.-Col. Joseph Mostyn, of Barcliffe, Tamworth, Staffs. [*see* Mostyn, Bt.], and has issue living, Paul Percyvall Hart *b.* 1965, James Terence Hart *b.* 1966,—Jennifer Hart, *b.* 1939: *m.* 1967, Lt. Oliver Nicholas Vaudrey, RN (ret.), of Buckland Court, Buckland, Betchworth, Surrey, and has issue living, David Clough Percyvall *b.* 1969, Annabel *b.* 1972.——Cicely Hart, *b.* 1907: *m.* 1936, Lt.-Col. William Radclyffe Dugmore, KOYLI (ret.), and has issue living, William Radclyffe, *b.* 1940: *m.* 1974, Patricia Elizabeth, 2nd da. of the late F. B. Jarvis, of Hen Ard, Morya Bychan, Gwynedd,—Janet Elvyn Catherine, *b.* 1938: *m.* 1964, John Peter Merrett, of Bank End, Plumgarth, Kendal, and has issue living, Peter William *b.* 1965, Sophie Catherine *b.* 1968, Nicola Mary *b.* 1971. *Residence*, Airieland, Kippford, Dalbeattie, Kirkcudbrightshire.

Grandchildren of the late Col. Percyvall Hart Dyke, DSO (ante):—
Issue of the late Rev. Eric Hart Dyke, *b.* 1906, *d.* 1971: *m.* 1935, Mary (Jane Taylor's Cottage, Shilling St., Lavenham, Suffolk), da. of the late Robert Alexander [see Shaw-Stewart, Bt., colls.]:—
David (Elmswater House, Sussex Rd., Petersfield, Hants.), *b.* 1938; ed. at St. Lawrence Coll., Ramsgate and RNC; Cdr. RN: *m.* 1967, Diana Margaret, da. of Sir William Henry Tucker Luce, GBE, KCMG, and has issue living, Miranda Katharine, *b.* 1972,—Alice, *b.* 1975.——Jane Hart, *b.* 1936: *m.* 1959, David Charles Holland, ERD, of Hill Court Farm, Four Elms, Edenbridge, Kent, and has issue living, Charles Thurstan, *b.* 1962,—Caroline Mary, *b.* 1960,—Clare Lucinda, *b.* 1966.——Sarah Alexander Hart, *b.* 1946: *m.* 1974, Oliver Guy Hart Dyke (ante).

Grandson of the late Rev. Percival Hart Dyke, son of the late Rev. Thomas Hart Dyke (ante) :—
Issue of the late Robert Percyvall Hart Dyke, *b.* 1864, *d.* 1954 : *m.* 1908, Mary Harriette Theodore, who *d.* 1974, da. of the late Rev. John Shephard (sometime V. of Eton), Hon. Canon of Ch. Ch., Oxford, of 33, Craven Hill Gardens, W.:—
Michael Percyvall Hart, *b.* 1909 ; ed. at Marlborough ; Middle East 1940-45 as Major R.A.S.C. ; *m.* 1955, Jean MacGlashan, and has issue living, Timothy Percyvall Hart, *b.* 1959, Jeremy Percyvall Hart, *b.* 1963,—Jennifer Mary Hart, *b.* 1956. *Residence*, 13, Manilla Rd., Clifton, Bristol, 8.

Grandchildren of the late Lieut.-Col. John Dixon Dyke, 3rd son of 5th baronet:—
Issue of the late Col. Edward Hart Dyke, *b.* 1837, *d.* 1930: *m.* 1893, Elizabeth Grace, who *d.* 1936, da. of Col.T.S. MacAdam, of Blackwater, co. Clare :—
Charles Hart, *b.* 1901: *m.* 1958, Kathleen Edith Gregory. *Residence*, Shalom, Dockenfield, Farnham, Surrey, GU10 4HA.——Percyvall Hart, *b.* 1902: *m.* 1931, Helen Leonora, da. of Philip MacAdam, JP, Colonial Med. Ser., of British Guiana, and has issue living, Michael Percyvall Hart, *b.* 1932,—Patrick Alan Hart (34, Weydon Hill Rd., Farnham, Surrey), *b.* 1938: *m.* 1969, Elzbieta Isabela, da. of Eugeniusz Lotocki, of Warsaw, and has issue living, James Paul *b.* 1972. *Residence*, Mahaicony, Shortheath Rd., Farnham, Surrey, GV9 8SL.

Issue of the late Lieut.-Col. Frederick Hotham Dyke, *b.* 1840, *d.* 1934 : *m.* 1871, Emily, who *d.* 1941, da. of the late Rev. Charles Faunce Thorndike, of Villa Freeland, Trieste:—
Winifred Amy, *b.* 1881: *m.* 1911, Cyril Arthur Mileham, solicitor, and has issue living, Barbara Dera, *b.* 1918: *m.* 1936, Eric Adrian Milne, and has issue living, Adrian Edward *b.* 1940, Ian Hugh Milne *b.* 1950, Rosemary Faith *b.* 1942: *m.* 1966, Dr. Christopher John Bretherton Hundleby, of 606, Forest Hills, Mowbray, Cape Town (and has issue living, Alison Mary *b.* 1967). *Residence*, Bure Acre, Aylsham, Norfolk, NOR 07Y.

Issue of the late Col. George Hart Dyke, *b.* 1847, *d.* 1922 : *m.* 1895, Edith Louise, who *d.* 1952, da. of the late Thomas William Kinder, Master of Mints of Hong Kong and Japan :—
Helen Sandra Millicent, *b.* 1897: *m.* 1920, Lieut.-Col. Esdaile Addison Burkitt Orr, M.C., late Roy. Berkshire Regt., and has issue living, Elizabeth, *b.* 1923: *m.* 1947, William Edward Penlygon Moon, who *d.* 1965, and has issue living, Sandra Anne *b.* 1953. *Residence*, 2, St. Peter St., Marlow, Bucks.

Sir Thomas Dyke, of Horeham, Sussex (whose father migrated from Cranbrook, Kent), married 1639, Catherine, da. of Sir John Bramston, Lord Chief Justice of the King's Bench. His son Sir Thomas Dyke, 1st Bt. was Commr. of Public Accounts 1696. The 2nd baronet removed from Horeham to Lullingstone Castle, having married Anne, da. and heir of Percival Hart of that place. Sir Percival Hart Dyke, 5th baronet, unsuccessfully claimed the Barony of Brayes, of which he was a co-heir through the Harts, 1836. The 7th baronet, Rt. Hon. Sir William Hart Dyke, sat as M.P. for W. Kent (C) 1865-8, for Mid. Kent 1868-85, and for Kent, Dartford Div. 1885-1906, and was Sec. to the Treasury 1874-80, Ch. Sec. for Ireland 1885-6, and Vice-Pres. of Council on Education 1887-92.

Eardley-Wilmot, see Wilmot.

EARLE, Creation (U.K.) 1869, of Allerton Tower, Woolton, Lancashire.

Sir HARDMAN ALEXANDER MORT EARLE, 5th *Baronet* ; *b.* Aug. 19th, 1902 ; *s.* his father, *Lieut.-Col. Sir* (THOMAS) ALGERNON, *T.D.*, 1945 ; ed. at Eton; is Capt. RA (T and AVR); 1939-45 War, in N. Africa and Italy (wounded): *m.* 1931, Maie, da. of John Drage, of Chapel Brampton, Northampton, and has issue.

Arms—Argent, three pallets ermines. Crest—A lion's jamb erased sable, holding a harpoon argent.
Residence—14, Kensington Gate, W8. *Clubs*—Cavalry Anglo-Belgian.

Son living—HARDMAN GEORGE ALGERNON (Abington, Murroe, co. Limerick), *b.* Feb. 4th, 1932; ed. at Eton: *m.* 1967, Diana Gillian Bligh, da. of the late Col. Frederick Ferris Bligh St. George, CVO [*see* St. George, Bt., colls.], and has issue living, Robert George Bligh, *b.* 1970,—Katharine Susan, *b.* 1968.
Daughter living—Belinda Mary, *b.* 1937: *m.* 1st, 1959, Patrick John Boteler Drury-Lowe, from whom she obtained a divorce 1968 [see M. Linlithgow, colls.]; 2ndly, 1973, Anthony David Arnold William Forbes, of Wakerley Manor, Oakham, Leics. [see B. Faringdon, colls.].
Sisters living—Rosemary, *b.* 1904.——Myrtle Valentine, *b.* 1911: *m.* 1st, 1933 (marriage dissolved 1947), Robert Owen Symon; 2ndly, 1948, Sydney Vernon, who *d.* 1961; 3rdly, 1962, Brig. Maurice Robert Lonsdale, D.S.O., O.B.E., of Bignor Farm, Kirdford, Billingshurst, Sussex, and has issue living, (by 1st marriage) Máiri Edith, *b.* 1935.

Preserv dium

Collateral Branches living.

Issue of the late Charles Frederic Earle, 6th son of 2nd baronet; *b.* 1867, *d.* 1939; *m.* 1911, Alice Adelaide, who *d.* 1942, da. of Henry Cleveland, and widow of Patrick Cumin Scott, M.B., of Blackheath, S.E. :—

Evelyn Alice, *b.* 1912. *Residence,* 175, King's Hall Road, Beckenham, Kent.——Josephine Noelle, *b.* 1914: *m.* 1941, Douglas Swinscow, M.B., and has issue living. *Residence,* Everley, London Road, Knebworth, Herts.——Rosamond Cleveland, *b.* 1918: *m.* 1939, the Rev. Eric Albert Metcalfe, of 165, Barcombe Av., SW2, and has issue living.

Grandchildren of the late Cecil Arthur Earle, el. son of the late Arthur Earle (infra):—

Issue of the late Capt. Guy Fife Earle, *b.* 1891, *d.* 1966: *m.* 1st 1918 (m. diss. 1922), Isabel Bridget, who *d.* 1971, da. of the late Andrew Greville Rouse-Boughton-Knight [Rouse-Boughton, Bt.]; 2ndly, 1924 (m. diss. 1928), Helen Alice who *d.* 1967, da. of the late Ninian Lowis Elliott [E. Minto, colls.]; 3rdly, 1935, Bridget Joan (Mulberry House, Maperton, Wincanton, Som.), da. of the late Peter Sherston, of Hill House, Templecombe, Som. :—

(By 1st m.) Audrey Bridget (Arnolds, Burnham Market, Kings Lynn), *b.* 1920.——(by 3rd m.) Michael Guy (Mount Gow, Shelford, Vic. 3329, Aust.), *b.* 1942; ed. at Harrow, and Roy. Agric. Coll., Cirencester: *m.* 1969, Morrell Francis Armytage, el. da. of Sqdn. Ldr. John Robert Nassau Molesworth, DFC [*see* V. Molesworth, colls.], and has issue living, Guy Robert, *b.* 1973,—Amanda Morrell, *b.* 1971.——Susan Mary, *b.* 1940.——Virginia Ida, *b.* 1945: *m.* 1971, Frederick Jackson, and has issue living, Conrad Guy Frederick, *b.* 1973.

Issue of the late Brig. Eric Greville Earle, DSO, *b.* 1893, *d.* 1965: *m.* 1st, 1918, Noel (from whom he obtained a divorce 1931), da. of Capt. Edward Downes-Martin, formerly of Killoskehane Castle, co. Tipperary; 2ndly, 1931, Diana Mary, who *d.* 1964, da. of the late Dr. Vaughan Harley, of Walton Hall, Bletchley:—

(By 1st m.) David Eric Martin, OBE, *b.* 1921; ed. at Stowe, and at Ch. Ch., Oxford; Lt.-Col. RA; Burma 1945; OBE (Mil.) 1969: *m.* 1947, Betty Isobel Shield, and has issue living, Charles Henry Diccon, *b.* 1951,—George Eric, *b.* 1953,—Victoria Gay, *b.* 1952,—Charlotte Mary, *b.* 1959.—— Robin Denys Michael, *b.* 1922; ed. at Wellington Coll.; formerly Lt. Fleet Air Arm; SE Asia 1939-45: *m.* 1st, 1946 (m. diss. 1962), Rosemary, da. of Maj. F. A. Latter, of Birkdault, Lindfield; 2ndly, 1963, Anne, da. of the late Capt. Lawford, and has issue living, (by 1st marriage) Toby Dick, *b.* 1951,—Penelope Jane, *b.* 1947,—Jemima Tasmin, *b.* 1949,—Lucy Noel, *b.* 1954. ——Peter Noel Desmond (Chestnuts, Beckley, E. Sussex), *b.* 1923; ed. at Wellington Coll., and at Ch. Ch., Oxford (BA 1949, MA 1954); formerly Lt. RNVR; Atlantic and S.-E. Asia 1939-45: *m.* 1952, Shirley Hope, da. of Wallace MacGregor, of Vancouver, British Columbia, and has issue living, Virginia Melanie, *b.* 1963.

Grandsons of the late Arthur Earle, 4th son of 1st baronet:—

Issue of the late John Greville Earle, *b.* 1869, *d.* 1933: *m.* 1920, Jacobina Reid, who *d.* 1970, da. of the late James Clark, of Kilmarnock:—

John Arthur (15, via Eufrate, Rome 00144, Italy), *b.* 1921; ed. at Winchester, and at Trin. Coll., Camb. (BA 1948); European War 1939-45 in Middle East and Central Mediterranean as Capt. Rifle Brig. (wounded): *m.* 1947, Anna Maria, da. of Magg. Cav. Uff. Lorenzo Tiziani, of Trecenta, Italy, and has issue living, Lawrence Hardman, *b.* 1948,—Arabella Ida, *b.* 1955.—— William Hardman, *b.* 1924; ed. at Winchester, and at Trin. Coll., Camb. (BA 1945, MA 1954); S.-E. Asia 1945 as Capt. RE: *m.* 1958, Vera Charteris, da. of Colin Black, of Fryars, West Chiltington, Sussex, and has issue living, Rupert Langton, *b.* 1960.—Greville Hoare, *b.* 1963,— Alice Jacobina, *b.* 1970. *Residence,* The Walnuts, Beanacre, Melksham, Wilts. *Club,* Oxford and Cambridge.——Richard Greville, *b.* 1925; ed. at Winchester, and at Trinity Coll., Camb. (BA 1949, MA 1959); formerly Sub-Lt. (A) RNVR: *m.* 1956, Joanna Mary, da. of Com. H. K. B. Mitchell, RN (ret.), of Folke Manor, Sherborne, Dorset, and has issue living, Elizabeth Mary, *b.* 1957,—Susan Helen, *b.* 1959. *Residence,* Frankham Farm, Ryme Intrinseca, Sherborne, Dorset.

Issue of the late Lawrence Mathew Earle, *b.* 1881, *d.* 1968: *m.* 1916, Helen Elizabeth Dunkin, who *d.* 1963, da. of the late Capt. Frederic Street, of Dulverton:—

Adrian Mathew, *b.* 1922: ed. at Winchester, and at Worcester Coll., Oxford.——Nigel Lawrence (Sywell Grange Farm, Northampton, NN6 0BE), *b.* 1926; ed. at Radley; 1944-45 War with R. Armoured Corps.: *m.* 1951, Jean, da. of the late Dr. Hugh McClintock, and has issue living, Brian Lawrence, *b.* 1953,—Patrick Nigel, *b.* 1958.

This family was settled at Warrington in the 16th century, and in 1709 died John Earle (son of Gregory Earle), a **principal** inhabitant of the place. His son John settled in Liverpool, and was Mayor thereof 1709. His grandson, Thomas, Mayor of Liverpool, was father of William, also Mayor of Liverpool, as well as of Sir Hardman, 1st baronet. Sir Henry, D.S.O., 3rd baronet, was Lieut.-Col. King's Own Yorkshire L.I. Sir (Thomas) Algernon, T.D., 4th baronet, was Lieut.-Col. sometime Comdg. Lancashire Hussars.

EBRAHIM, Creation (U.K.) 1910, of Bombay.

Sir (MAHOMED) CURRIMBHOY EBRAHIM, 4th *Baronet ;* *b.* June 24th, 1935 ; *s.* his father, *Sir* (HUSEINALI) CURRIMBHOY, 1952 : *m.* 1958, Dur-e-Mariam, da. of Minuchehir Ahmed Nurudin Ahmed Ghulam Ally Nana, of Karachi, Sind, W. Pakistan, and has issue.

Arms—Argent, in base on waves of the sea a Chinese junk sailing to the sinister, in chief also on waves two dhows sailing to the dexter all proper, and a chief per pale gules and or thereon a pale azure between a rose of the first and a lotus flower also proper, and charged with a mullet issuant from a crescent above five mullets in crescent also of the first. Crest—Above an Indian lily on water proper, a mullet radiated or.

Residence—Baitullah, 33, Baitul-Aman Mirza, Kalig Beg Rd., Jameshed Quarters, Karachi, Pakistan.

God leading, nothing hurts.

Sons living—ZULFIQAR ALI, *b.* Aug. 5th, 1960.—— Murtaza Ali, *b.* 1963.——Raza Ali, *b.* 1964.
Daughter living—Durre Najaf, *b.* 1969.
Half-Sisters living—Mumtaz, *b.* 1922 : *m.* 1941, Ahmed Rahim Valimahomed Peermahomed.—— Munira, *b.* 1923 : *m.* 1941, Fazal Rahemtulla Maherali Chinoy. *Residence,*

Great-Uncle living (son of 1st baronet)—Ismailbhoy Currimbhoy, *b.* 1906: *m.* 1925, Zarina, da. of Gulam Husain Sachedina, and has issue living, Aziz, *b.* 1927,—Suraiya Ismail, *b.* 1929: *m.* 1951, Asif Currimbhoy Ebrahim (infra).

Great-Aunts living (daughters of 1st baronet),—Jenabai, *b.* 1880: *m.* 1896, Gulamhusein Ladhabhoy Ebrahim.——Sherbanu, *b.* 1882: *m.* 1899, Gulamhusein Rehemtullah Khairaj.——Labai, *b.* 1883: *m.* 1902, Abdullabhoy Gulamhusein Allana.——Shireenbai, *b.* 1888: *m.* 1911, Rahin Vali Mahomed Pirmahomed.——Khairubai (Khairunisha), *b.* 1894: *m.* 1916, Currimbhoy Nensey Khairaz.——Mariumbai, *b.* 1896 : *m.* 1916, Cassumali Subjeally.——Sharifabai, *b.* 1899: *m.* 1921, Sulieman Rahimtulla Sayani.——Khatijabai, *b.* 1901 : *m.* 1923, Yusufali Moosabhoy Jaffer Pradham. *Residence,* Pabaney Villa, Warden Road, Bombay, India.

Widow living of 3rd Baronet—ALHAJA AMINA KHANUM (*Alhaja, Lady Ebrahim*), da. of Al-Qassamally Jairazbhoy, of Gulshanabad, Peddar Rd., Bombay: *m.* 1926, as his second wife (marriage dissolved 1944), Sir (Huseinali) Currimbhoy Ebrahim, 3rd baronet, who *d.* 1952, and whom she re-married 1949. *Residence,* 33, Baitul-Aman Mirza Kalig Beg Rd., Jamshed Quarters, Karachi, Pakistan.

Collateral Branches living.

Issue of the late Sir Fazulbhoy Currimbhoy Ebrahim, CBE, 4th son of 1st baronet, *b.* 1873. *d.* 1970: *m.* 1889, Sakinabai, who *d.* 1930, da. of the late Datoobhoy Ebrahim, of Cutch Mandvi:—

Ahmedbhoy Fazulbhoy, *b.* 1902: *m.* 1923, Zarina, da. of the late Ahmedbhoy Currimbhoy Ebrahim (infra), and has issue living, Ariff, *b.* 1926,—Niamat, *b.* 1928.——Mohamedali, *b.* 1904.——Gulamali, *b.* 1905: *m.* 1928, Hamida, da. of the late Rehemtullah Currimbhoy Ebrahim (infra).——Hoosein, *b.* 1911.——Amir Ali, *b.* 1913.

Granddaughter of the late Ebrahim CURRIMBHOY (infra):—
Issue of the late Allen CURRIMBHOY, *b.* 1924, *d.* 1960: *m.* 1958, Pritee Misra:—
Alia, *b.* 1961.

Grandchildren of the late Gulamhusein Currimbhoy Ebrahim (infra):—
Issue of the late Ebrahim CURRIMBHOY, *b.* 1897, *d.* 1969: *m.* 1923, Zarina, da. of Ahmed Curmally Janmahomed:—

Zinet, *b.* 1925.——Asif Currimbhoy (20, Nepean-Sea Rd., Bombay 6, India), *b.* 1928: *m.* 1951, Suraiya Ismail, da. of Ismailbhoy Currimbhoy Ebrahim (ante), and has issue living, Tabrik, *b.* 1952,—Tarek, *b.* 1954,—Nahed, *b.* 1959.

Issue of the late Gulamhusein Currimbhoy Ebrahim, 6th son of 1st baronet, *b.* 1879, *d.* 1918 : *m.* 1896, Khanoobai, da. of Datoobhoy Ebrahim, of Cutch Mandvi (ante):—

Ali Mahomed, *b.* 1902.——Aziz, *b.* 1915.——Ammeena, *b.* 1896: *m.* 1916, A. O. Jamal, of Calcutta.

Grandchildren of the late Ahmedbhoy Currimbhoy Ebrahim (infra):—
Issue of the late Hooseinali Ebrahim, *b.* 1908, *d.* 1968: *m.* 1928, Nazli, da. of the late Rehemtullah Currimbhoy Ebrahim (infra):—
Semine, *b.* 1929.——a da., *b.* 1933.

Issue of the late Ahmedbhoy Currimbhoy Ebrahim, 7th son of 1st baronet, *b.* 1885, *d.* 1925: *m.* 1902, Shireen, da. of Dost Mahomed Allana, of Bombay:—

Habibbhoy, *b.* 1910.——Zarina, *b.* 1904: *m.* 1923, Ahmedbhoy Fazulbhoy Ebrahim (ante). *Residence,*

Issue of the late Rehemtullah Currimbhoy Ebrahim, 8th son of 1st baronet, *b.* 1887, *d.* 1928 : *m.* 1908, Sakinabai, da. of Jafferbhoy Ratansey, formerly of Bombay:—

Nazli, *b.* 1909: *m.* 1928, Hooseinali Ebrahim, who *d.* 1968, (ante).——Hamida, *b.* 1912: *m.* 1928, Gulamali Ebrahim (ante).

Issue of the late Habibbhoy Currimbhoy Ebrahim, *b.* 1889, *d.* 1949: *m.* 1913, Khatijabai da. of Nensey Khairaj, of Bombay:—

Nazim, *b.* 1915: *m.* 1941, Zarina, da. of Ahmed S. Moloobhoy, of Bombay, and has issue living, Reisa, *b.* 1944.——Sultan, *b.* 1921: *m.* 1949, Munira, da. of the late Sir Fazal Ibrahim Rahimtoola, CIE, and has issue living, Habib, *b.* 1950.——Husem, *b.* 1924.——Aziz, *b.* 1927.——Munira, *b.* 1926.

Sir Currimbhoy Ebrahim, 1st Bt., was a leading member of the Khoja Community, and an opium, yarn, cotton, silk, tea, sugar, and cloth merchant of Bombay, Hong Kong, Kobe, Shanghai, and Calcutta ; owned the Currimbhoy, the Mahomedbhoy, the Ebrahimbhoy Pabaney, the Fazulbhoy, the Crescent, the Indore Malwa United Mills, the Pearl Mills, and many other factories (ginning and pressing), and the Indian Bleaching, Dyeing, and Printing Works ; established a Girls' Sch., a Madressa at Mandvi, the Currimbhoy Ebrahim Khoja Orphanage in Bombay, and Dharmsalas at Mandvi and Bhuj ; gave large donations to Bombay New Museum Fund, for the new Science Sch. for Bombay, and for Scholarships for Mahomedans. The 2nd baronet, Sir (Mahomedbhoy) Currimbhoy Ebrahim, was a partner in the firm of Currimbhoy Ebrahim and Sons. Each Baronet on succession assumes the name of the 1st Bt.

ECHLIN, Creation (I.) 1721, of Dublin.

[Name pronounced "Ecklin."]

Sir NORMAN DAVID FENTON ECHLIN, 10th *Baronet; b.* Dec. 1st, 1925 ; *s.* his father, *Sir* JOHN FREDERICK, 1932, Capt. (retired) Indian Army : *m.* 1953, Mary Christine, only da. of John Arthur, of Oswestry, Salop.

Non sine prædâ
Not without prey.

Arms—Quarterly, 1st and 4th or, an antique galley, sails furled sable, a forked pennon gules ; 2nd and 3rd gules, a fesse chequey argent and azure, a chief of the last thereon a hound in full chase after a stag, both proper. Crest—A talbot passant proper.
Residence—Nartopa, Marina Av., Appley, Ryde, I. of Wight.

Sister living—Patricia Hazel, *b.* 1928 : *m.* 1951, Fred Tiller, and has issue living, Fred, *b.* 1966,—Hazel Jean, *b.* 1952,—Heather Valerie, *b.* 1956. *Residevce,* Treemeadow, Lavender Rd., Hordle, Lymington, Hants.
Aunt living—Aileen Alexandra : *m.* 1919, John Atkinson, who *d.* 1923. *Residence,*

The Echlin family is of ancient Scottish origin, and formerly possessed princely estates in Scotland, and also large domains in the counties of Kildare, Carlow, Dublin, Galway, and Mayo. Andrew Echlin, of Pittadro, Fifeshire, was Constable and Deputy-Gov. of Edinburgh Castle during the siege of 1572. The Right Rev. Dr. Echlin, Bishop of Down and Connor, who *d.* in 1635, was great-grandfather of Sir Henry Echlin, Knight, a Baron of the Court of Exchequer in Ireland, who was created a baronet in 1721. The 2nd baronet sat as M.P. for Newry. The 3rd baronet dissipated the family estates. The 4th baronet was one of the gentlemen before whom Hamilton Ronan knelt in the Court of King's Bench to beg the King's pardon. The Kildare estates were dissipated by the 4th, 5th, and 6th baronets. Sir Henry Frederick, 8th baronet, was sometime Landlord of The Cider House, Haddenham, Bucks, and Sir John Frederick, 9th baronet, was Sergeant in Roy. Ulster Constabulary.

EDEN, Creations (E.) 1672, of West Auckland, Durham, and (G.B.) 1776, of Maryland, America.

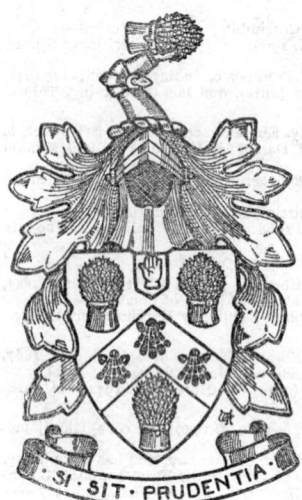

Rt. Hon. Sir JOHN BENEDICT EDEN, *MP,* 9th *Baronet* of 1st and 7th of 2nd creation; *b.* Sept. 15th, 1925; *s.* his father, *Sir* TIMOTHY CALVERT, 1963; ed. at Eton, and at St. Paul's Sch., USA; a Member of House of Commons Estimates Cttee. 1960-64, Delegate to Council of Europe and W. European Union 1960-62, and to NATO Parliamentarians Conference 1962-66; Min. of State for Technology June to Oct. 1970, Min. for Industry, 1970-72, and Min. of Posts and Telecommunications 1972-74; a Member of House of Commons Expenditure Cttee. since 1974; 1939-45 War as Lt. Rifle Bde.; 2nd KEO Gurkha Rifles and the Gilgit Scouts; MP for W. Div. of Bournemouth (C) since 1954; PC 1972: *m.* 1958 (m. diss. 1974), Belinda Jane, only da. of the late Sir (Frederick) John Pascoe, and has issue.

Arms—Gules, on a chevron argent between three garbs or, banded vert, as many escallops sable. **Crest**—A dexter arm embowed in armour, couped at the shoulder proper and grasping a garb fessewise as in the arms, banded vert.

Residences—41, Victoria Rd., W8; Knoyle Place, E. Knoyle, Salisbury. *Clubs*—Boodle's, Pratt's.

If there be but prudence.

Si· SIT· PRUDENTIA

Sons living—ROBERT FREDERICK CALVERT, *b.* April 30th, 1964.——John Edward Morton, *b.* 1966.
Daughters living—Emily Rose, *b.* 1959.——(Arabella) Charlotte, *b.* 1960.
Sisters living—Ann Caroline, *b.* 1923: *m.* 1951, Peter Noel Negretti, and has issue living, Alexandra Mary, *b.* 1953,—Emma Frances, *b.* 1954,—Cristina Gabrielle, *b.* 1956,—Sarah Ann *b.* 1959. *Residence*, Fritham House, Lyndhurst, Hants.——(Meriall) Rose, *b.* 1927: *m.* 1959, James Dalton Murray, CMG, and has issue living, William Andrew Eden, *b.* 1960. *Address*, c/o British Embassy, Port-au-Prince, Haiti.——Amelia Mary, *b.* 1933: *m.* 1958, Giovanni Borrelli, of Fritham Cottage, Lyndhurst, Hants, and has issue living, Timoteo Raffaele, *b.* 1962,—Matteo Francesco Antonio, *b.* 1965,—Chiara Maria Concetta, *b.* 1959.——Elfrida Charlotte *b.* 1940: *m.* 1963, Richard Gordon Fallowfield, of 22, Strickland St., Rose Bay, NSW 2029, and 56, Lansdowne Rd., W11, and has issue living, Timothy Gordon, *b.* 1965,—Nicholas John, *b.* 1967,—Laura Louise, *b.* 1974.
Uncle living (son of 7th baronet)—Rt. Hon. Sir (Robert) Anthony, *K.G., M.C., P.C. (Earl of Avon), b.* 1897; *cr. Earl of Avon* 1961 [see that title].
Widow living of 8th Baronet—PATRICIA (EDITH) (*Patricia, Lady Eden*) (of Fritham Cottage, Lyndhurst, Hants., and 41, Victoria Rd., W8), da. of Arthur Prendergast: *m.* 1923, Sir Timothy Calvert Eden, 8th baronet, who *d.* 1963.

Collateral Branches living.

Grandson of the late Frederick Morton Eden, son of the late Rt. Rev. Robert Eden, D.D., Primus of Scotland, and Bishop of Moray and Ross, 3rd son of 2nd baronet, of Maryland:—
Issue of the late Rowland Frederick Eden, *b.* 1874, *d.* 1948: *m.* 1900, Marie Bernadett Anita, who *d.* 1959, da. of the late Col. Henry George Saunders, ISC [Rugge-Price, Bt., colls.]:—
Frederick Augustus Morton, *b.* 1904; is Lieut.-Com. R.N. (Emergency List): *m.* 1929 Everil Mary, el. da. of the late John Stephen Lang Whiteaway, of Tankerville, Kingston Hill, Surrey, and has issue living, David Frederick Edward, *b.* 1934; ed. at Ampleforth Coll.; is Pilot Officer R.A.F.—John Graham Walter, *b.* 1948,—Mary Alexandra Morton, *b.* 1945. *Club*, Naval and Military.

Descendants of Sir Robert Eden, 1st baronet of Maryland, who was 2nd son of 3rd Baronet of West Auckland :—

Grandson of the late Charles Calvert Eden, son of the late Lieut.-Gen. George Morton Eden, 4th son of 2nd baronet of Maryland :—
Issue of the late Morton Frederic Eden, M.B.E., *b.* 1865, *d.* 1948 : *m.* 1909, Marie Thérèse MacMahon, who *d.* 1962:—
Robert Charles Frederick, *M.B.E., b.* 1916 ; ed. at Zuoz Coll., Switzerland and at Camb. Univ. (B.A. 1940) ; European War 1939-45 as Capt. Intelligence Corps ; M.B.E. (Mil.) 1948 : *m.* 1958.

Barbara, second da. of the late George Reginald Benson, and has issue living, Michael Anthony, *b.* 1960,—Joanna Mary, *b.* 1962. *Residence*, Marchligen, 3112, Allmendingen, Berne, Switzerland. *Club*—Alpine.

Descendants of the late Rt. Hon. William Eden (3rd son of 3rd baronet of West Auckland), who was *cr Baron Auckland* 1789 [*see* that title].

Grandchildren of the late Rev. John Patrick Eden, son of the late Thomas Eden (*b.* 1787), el. son of the late Thomas Eden, 4th son of 3rd baronet:—
Issue of the late Lieut.-Col. John Henry Eden, *b.* 1851, *d.* 1931 : *m.* 1893, Lady Florence Lowry-Corry, who *d.* 1943, da. of 4th Earl of Belmore :—
George Wilfred, *CBE* (Norchard Farm, Stanton St. Gabriel, Morcombelake, Bridport, Dorset), *b.* 1903; ed. at Charterhouse; Brig. (ret.) late The Green Howards (Alexandra, Princess of Wales's Own Yorks. Regt.); Col. The Green Howards 1959-65; Waziristan 1937 (despatches), 1939-45 War (wounded); Col. in Charge of Administration, Land Forces, Hong Kong 1947-49, Brig. A/Q., HQS. Command 1949-52, Dep. Dir. of Movements, War Office 1952-55, and Dir. of Pioneers and Labour and Inspector of R. Pioneer Corps, and an ADC to HM 1955-57; a Cdr. of Order of St. Olav of Norway; CBE (Mil) 1952: *m.* 1946, Katharine Margaret Dorothy, *MBE*, da. of the late Rev. Edward Henry Good, Chap. RN, and has issue living, John Patrick Edward. *b.* 1950,—Philippa Catherine, *b.* 1948.——Christian Florence (c/o Terrace House Hotel, Richmond, Yorks.), *b.* 1894.——Norah Madeline, *b.* 1898. *Residence*, Oaksey Cottage, Galphay, Ripon, Yorks.

Grandchildren of the late Right Rev. George Rodney Eden, DD (infra):—
Issue of the late Sqdn. Ldr. Gerald Balfour Eden, *b.* 1896, *d.* 1970: *m.* 1929, Anne, da. of the late Maj. T. Macey, late Indian Army:—
John Hamilton Rodney (c/o National Westminster Bank, 117/119, Oxford Rd., Reading, Berks.), *b.* 1939; ed. at Nautical Coll., Pangbourne; Sgt. Air QM, RAF: *m.* 1964, Sandra Anne, da. of Dennis Rowland Toms, and has issue living, Anthony Winston Richard, *b.* 1965,—Jeremy Rodney Hugh, *b.* 1967,—Françoise Geraldine, *b.* 1968.——Margaret Anne, *b.* 1929: *m.* 1955, John William Howard Kirkbride, of 318, Wingrove Rd., Fenham, Newcastle upon Tyne, 4, and has issue living, Nicholas George, *b.* 1959,—Amanda, *b.* 1957,—Katherine, *b.* 1961.

Granddaughter of the late Rev. John Patrick Eden (ante):—
Issue of the late Right Rev. George Rodney Eden, D.D. (Lord Bishop of Wakefield 1897-1928), *b.* 1853, *d.* 1940: *m.* 1889, Constance Margaret, who *d.* 1906, da. of the late Rev. Henry John Ellison, Hon. Canon of Canterbury, and Chap.-in-Ord. to H.M. Queen Victoria:—
Dorothy Frances, *b.* 1893; 1914-18 War in TF Nursing Ser. (despatches): *m.* 1920, the Rt. Rev. Clement Mallory Ricketts, sometime Suffragan Bishop of Dunwich, who *d.* 1961 [*see* Ricketts, Bt., colls.). *Residence*, Nyetimber Forge, Bognor Regis, Sussex.

Grandson of the late Charles Hamilton Eden, OBE, 4th son of the late Rev. John Patrick Eden (ante):—
Issue of the late Brig. Henry Charles Hamilton Eden, C.B.E., M.C., *b.* 1889, *d.* 1963: *m.* 1st, 1916, Violet Alice, who *d.* 1956, da. of Capt. Henry Percy Pulleine, of Sandford House, Richmond, Yorks.; 2ndly, 1957, Penelope Glynne (Pine Close, Carroll Av., Ferndown, Dorset), da. of H. W. Sitwell, of Leamington Hastings, and widow of Lt.-Col. R. Temple, R.A.:—
(By 1st m.) Robert John Pulleine (Badlake Farm, West Anstay, S. Molton, Devon), *b.* 1920; Capt. TA: *m.* 1st, 1947 (m. diss. 1969) the Hon. Rosemary Winifred Vivian, da. of 3rd Baron Swansea; 2ndly, 1969, Mrs. Elizabeth Stanley Cleverly, da. of Alan Crowe Rawlinson, and has issue living, (by 1st m.) Sarah, *b.* 1948,—(by 2nd m.), Catherine, *b.* 1969,—Emily Rose, *b.* 1972.

Grandson of the late Brig. Henry Charles Hamilton Eden, C.B.E., M.C. (ante):—
Issue of the late Michael Charles Eden, *b.* 1921, Lieut. R.E.; *d.* (killed in action at Arnhem) 1944: *m.* 1944, Patricia (who *m.* 2ndly, 1946, Robert Everett, of Roeburn Scar, Roeburndale, Lancaster), da. of the late Col.Reginald James Brook, CBE,DSO,ED:—
Peter Michael (posthumous) (Garrachoran, Glen Lean, by Dunoon, Argyll), *b.* 1944: *m.* 1965, Rosemary Frances, da. of Kenneth Charles Bishop, MBE, TD, Evans House, Sedbergh School, Yorks., and has issue living, Rupert Michael, *b.* 1972,—Caroline Rose, *b.* 1967,—Claire Louise, *b.* 1969.

Grandson of the late Gen. John Eden, C.B., son of the late Thomas Eden, 4th son of 3rd baronet :—
Issue of the late Lieut.-Com. George Henry Eden, R.N. (retired), *b.* 1849, *d.* 1921 : *m.* 1901, Miriam Sophia who *d.* 1919, el. da. of the late W. Farnham :—
Hugh Morton (30, Daleham Gdns., Hampstead, NW3), *b.* 1903: *m.* 1938, Monica, da. of the late Lt.-Com. Eustace William Clitherow Stracey-Clitherow [*see* Stracey, Bt., colls.].

Grandchildren of the late Charles Henry Eden, son of the late Robert Eden, son of the late Thomas Eden (ante) :—
Issue of the late Guy Ernest Morton Eden, *b.* 1864, *d.* 1954 : *m.* 1897, Ethel, who d. 1956, da. of the late William Henry Holman, of 30, Gledhow Gardens, S.W. :—
Rodney Guy Morton, *b.* 1899 ; ed. at Eton ; Lieut. Scots Guards (Reserve) ; European War 1917-19 in France (two medals). *Address*, c/o Lloyds Bank, Shipston-on-Stour, Warwickshire.——*Rev.* Adrian Arthur, *b.* 1911 ; ed. at Eton ; is V. of North Elmham with Billingford, Norfolk and Hon. Lieut.-Col. (retired) R.A. : *m.* 1939, Margaret Anne, da. of the late H. Edgar Bushell, of Golborne Manor, Tattenhall, Cheshire, and has issue living, Robin Guy, *b.* 1943,—John Kenneth, *b.* 1949.——Kathleen Ethel, *b.* 1902: *m.* 1924, Charles Ronald Graham, OBE, who *d.* 1933. *Residence*, Inces, Scaynes Hill, Haywards Heath, Sussex.

Grandson of the late Guy Ernest Morton Eden (ante) :—
Issue of the late Charles Egerton Eden, *b.* 1908, *d.* 1957 : *m.* 1936, Eileen Antoinette (of 3, St. James's Court, St. John's Road, Woking, Surrey), da. of the late H. H. Menzies, of Taplow :—
David Guy Egerton, *b.* 1937. *Residence*, 3, St. James's Court, St. John's Road, Woking, Surrey.

Descendants of the late Morton Eden (5th son of 3rd baronet of West Auckland), who was *cr. Baron Henley* 1799 [*see* that title].

Sir Robert Eden, 1st Bt. of W. Auckland, co. Durham, was son of Col. John Eden, who raised a Regt. for Charles I. Sir Robert Eden, Gov. of Maryland 1776, the 2nd son of the 3rd baronet of West Auckland was created a baronet of Maryland, and the 3rd and 5th sons were respectively created Baron Auckland and Baron Henley. The 5th baronet of West Auckland assumed the additional surname of Johnson. On his death without issue in 1844, he was *s.* by Sir William, 4th Bt., of Maryland, the two baronetcies thus becoming merged.

EDGE, Creation (U.K.) 1937 of Ribble Lodge, Lytham St. Annes, co. Lancaster.

Sir KNOWLES EDGE, 2nd *Baronet; b.*
Dec. 31st, 1905; *s.* his father, *Sir* WILLIAM,
1948; ed. at Bolton Sch., and at Trin. Hall,
Camb.; is a Chemical Manufacturer, and a
J.P.; *m.* 1932, Dorothea Eunice, da. of Robert
Walker, of New Haven, Connecticut, U.S.A.,
and has issue.

Arms—Sable, an eagle displayed argent between four
cinquefoils or. Crest—In front of a reindeer's head erased
two rose sprigs in saltire proper flowered gules.

Residence—1, Seafield Road, Lytham, Lancashire.

OFFICIO·EGERE·NOLO

I do not wish to fail in my duty.

Sons living—WILLIAM, *b.* Oct. 5th, 1936 : *m.* 1959, Avril,
Elizabeth Denson, and has issue living, Edward Knowles,
b. 1965,—Martin William *b.* 1968,—Christina Jane, *b.*
1963,—Susannah Clare, *b.* 1971. *Residence*, 8, Ansdell
Road North, Lytham St. Annes, Lancashire.——John
Robert, *b.* 1939.
Sister living—Mary Margaret, *b.* 1917 : *m.* 1940, Gilbert Roy
Fletcher, and has issue living, David Nicholas, *b.* 1942,—
Rosemary Ann, *b.* 1945.—Elizabeth Jane, *b.* 1947,—Gillian
Mary, *b.* 1950. *Residence,* Field House, Meole Brace,
Shrewsbury.
    The 1st baronet, Sir William Edge (son of the late Sir
Knowles Edge, of Great Marld, Smithills, Bolton), sat as
MP for Bolton-le-Moors (*L*) 1916-18 and 1918-23, and for
Leicestershire, Bosworth Div. 1927-45, and was knighted in
1922.

EDMONSTONE, Creation (G.B.) 1774, of Duntreath, Stirlingshire.

Sir ARCHIBALD BRUCE CHARLES
EDMONSTONE, 7th *Baronet: b.* Aug.
3rd, 1934; *s.* his father, *Sir* ARCHI-
BALD CHARLES, 1954 ; ed. at Stowe :
m. 1st, 1957 (m. diss. 1967), Jane, el.
da. of Maj.-Gen. Edward Charles
Colville, CB, DSO [see V. Colville of
Culross]; 2ndly, 1969, Juliet Elizabeth-
da. of Maj.-Gen. Cecil Martin Fother,
gill Deakin, CB, CBE [see Grant, Bt.,
cr. 1705], and hass issue by 1st and 2nd
m.

Arms—Or, an annulet gules, stoned azure
between three crescents of the second within a
double tressure flory-counter-flory of the last.
Crest—Out of a ducal coronet or a swan's head and
neck proper. Supporters—Two lions rampant gules,
Seat—Duntreath Castle, Blanefield, Stirlingshire.

VIRTUS·AUCET·HONOREM

Virtue adds to honour.

Sons living—By 1st m.—ARCHIBALD
EDWARD CHARLES, *b.* Feb. 4th, 1961.——
Nicholas William Mark, *b.* 1964.——By 2nd
m.—Dru Benjamin Marshall, *b.* 1971.
Daughter living—By 1st m.—Philippa Carolyn,
b. 1958.——By 2nd m.—Elyssa Juliet, *b.* 1973.
Sisters living—Mary Bettine (*Lady McGrigor*),
b. 1927: *m.* 1948, Capt. Sir Charles Edward
McGrigor. 5th Bt., late Rifle Brig. *Residences,*
Upper Somachan, by Dalmally, Argyll; Dal-
mally, 18, Cranmer Court, SW3.——Jane Fiona *b.* 1931: *m.* 1950 (m. diss. 1975), Maj. Sir Andrew
Rupert John Buchanan-Jardine, MC, R. Horse Gds., 4th Bt.——Susan Morag, *b.* 1941: *m.* 1964,
Robert Keith Erskine, of Cliftonwood, Newbridge, Midlothian [see E. Buchan, colls.].——Anne
Sibylla, *b.* 1943: *m.* 1970, James Manwaring Robertson, of Struan House, Kilchrenan, Taynuilt,
Argyllshire.

Uncle living (son of 5th baronet)—Edward St John, *b.* 1901 ; Com. R.N. (retired) : *m.* 1936, the
Hon. Alicia Evelyn Browne, da. of 5th Baron Kilmaine, and has issue living, William Henry
Neil, *b.* 1942,—Helen Antonia, *b.* 1937: *m.* 1960, Michael Edmund Hubert Gibbs, of 19, Caroline
Place, W2 [Smith-Marriott, Bt., colls.], and has issue living, Patrick Michael Evan *b.* 1962,
Edward Michael John *b.* 1964, Adrian Michael Philip *b.* 1967, Arabella Marina Clare *b.* 1969.
Residence, Barcombe Old Rectory, nr. Lewes, Sussex.

Widow living of 6th Baronet—GWENDOLYN MARY (*Dowager Lady Edmonstone*), da. of the late
Marshall Field: *m.* 1923, Sir Archibald Charles Edmonstone, 6th baronet, who *d.* 1954.
Residence, Lettre Cottage, Killearn, Glasgow.

    This family is probably descended from an Edmundus of the powerful race of Seton, amid whose
lands Edmonstone, the original family seat, is situated. Mary, daughter of King Robert III of
Scotland, *m.* (as her fourth husband) Sir William Edmonstone of Culloden, and to her and her
husband the lands of Duntreath were granted in 1445. The 1st baronet, Sir Archibald, was eldest
son of Archibald Edmonstone of Duntreath, and Red Hall, co. Antrim, and sat as M.P. for Dunbartonshire and the Ayr and Irvine Burghs 1761-95 ; the 2nd and 4th baronets (Sir Charles and Adm.
Sir William, C.B.) were M.P. for Stirlingshire (*C*) 1812-21 and 1874-80 respectively. Sir Archibald
Edmonstone, C.V.O., 5th baronet, was a Groom-in-Waiting to King Edward VII 1907-10 and *d.*
(April) 1954. Sir Archibald Charles, 6th baronet was sometime an A.D.C. to Gov. of Madras
and *d.* (June) 1954.

EDWARDS, Creation (U.K.) 1866, of Pye Nest, Yorkshire.

Sir CHRISTOPHER JOHN CHURCHILL EDWARDS, 5th *Baronet; b.* Aug. 16th, 1941; *s.* his father, *Sir* HENRY CHARLES SERRELL PRIESTLEY, 1963; ed. at Frensham Heights Sch., and Loughborough Coll: *m.* 1972, Gladys Irene Vogelgesang, and has issue.

Arms—Azure, on a bend nebulée argent, cotised or, a fleur-de-lis between two martlets of the field. **Crest**—Out of a crown vallery or, a talbot's head argent, semée-de-lis azure.
Residence—6133, Laurel Grove Av., N. Hollywood, Calif., 91606, USA.

Omne bonum Dei donum
Every good is the gift of God.

Son living—DAVID CHARLES PRIESTLEY, *b.* Feb. 22nd, 1974.
Brother living—Peter Henry, *b.* 1944.
Widow living of 4th Baronet—DAPHNE MARJORY HILDA (47, Redcliffe Gdns., SW10), el. da. of William George Birt, of Kensington, W: 1st, 1935, as his 2nd wife, Sir Henry Charles Serrell Priestley Edwards, 4th baronet, who *d.* 1963; 2ndly, 1972, Leonard Mallett.
The 1st baronet, Sir Henry Edwards, CB, Provincial Grand Master of Freemasons, W. Riding, sat as MP for Halifax (C) 1847-52, and for Beverley 1857-68. The 3rd baronet, Sir John Henry Priestley Churchill Edwards, *d.* on active ser. 1942, whilst serving with Aust. Forces.

EDWARDS, Creation (U.K.) 1921, of Treforis, co. Glamorgan.

Sir JOHN CLIVE LEIGHTON EDWARDS, 2nd *Baronet; b.* Oct. 11th, 1916; *s.* his father, *Sir* JOHN BRYN, 1922; ed. at Winchester; European War 1940-45 with R.A.S.C., and as Capt. Roy. Pioneer Corps.

Arms—Per chevron sable and argent, in chief two **lions** rampant, and in base a castle counterchanged. **Crest**—A stag's head erased proper, gorged with a coronet composted of eight roses set upon a rim or, between the attires an escarbuncle gold.

Residence—Milntown, Lezayre, Ramsey, Isle of Man.

Nothing without labour.

Edwards-Moss, see Moss.

GREY EGERTON, Creation (E.) 1617, of Egerton and Oulton, Cheshire.
[Name pronounced "Edgerton."]

Sir PHILIP JOHN CALEDON GREY EGERTON, 15th *Baronet, b.* Oct. 19th, 1920; *s.* his father, *Sir* PHILIP REGINALD LE BELWARD, 1962; ed. at Eton; late Capt. Welsh Guards; European War 1939-45, in N. Africa and Italy: *m.* 1952, Margaret Voase, who *d.* 1971, el. da. of the late Rowland Rank, of Aldwick Place, Aldwick, W. Sussex, and widow of Sqdn. Leader Robert Alexander Ullman, RAF.

I trust not in arms, but in valour.

Arms—Quarterly, 1st and 4th, argent, a lion rampant gules between three **pheons** sable. *Egerton*; 2nd and 3rd, barry of six argent and azure, a label of five points gules, *Grey.* **Crest,**— 1st, three arrows, two in saltire argent, and one in pale, pointed downwards or, barbed and feathered able, banded with a ribbon gules; 2nd, on a dexter glove argent, a falcon rising or. **Supporters**—

Dexter, a lion argent ducally crowned or; *sinister*, a wyvern or; each gorged with a plain collar azure, and pendent therefrom an escutcheon gules charged with three pheons argent.

Address,—c/o The Estate Office, Oulton Park, Tarporley, Ches.   *Club*—Pratt's.

Brother living—BRIAN BALGUY LE BELWARD *EGERTON*, *b.* Feb. 5th, 1925; ed. at Repton. *Residence*, Rhue 58, by Ullapool, Ross-shire.

Sister living—Mary Blanche Aveys, *b.* 1916; formerly Section Officer, W.A.A.F.: *m.* 1939, Vincent Akroyd Palliser Costobadie, who *d.* 1959. *Residence*, Singmore Farm, Stover, Newton Abbot, S. Devon.

Daughter living of 12th Baronet—Cecely Alice Grey, *M.B.E.*, *b.* 1893; M.B.E. (Civil) 1920 *m.* 1918, Lieut.-Col. Denys Edward Prideaux-Brune, D.S.O. [B. Brabourne], who *d.* 1952, and has issue living, Philip Egerton Edmund (Myrtle Hill, Andreas Rd., Ramsey, Isle of Man), *b.* 1921; ed. at Harrow; late Warrant Officer RAF: *m.* 1944: Pamela Maud, da. of the late Capt. George Norman Ferrers-Guy, Worcestershire Regt. [B. Avebury, colls.), and has issue living, Richard John Ferrers *b.* 1946, Denys Edmund Charles *b.* 1947, George Brian Philip *b.* 1948, Timothy Rowland Edward *b.* 1953, Philippa Anne Madeleine, *b.* 1961,—Rowland Denys Charles (Dorchester Rd., San Mateo, California, USA), *b.* 1925; ed. at Eton, and at Camb. Univ.; sometime Capt. Rifle Brig.: *m.* 1957, Genevieve McLaren, and has issue living, Cynthia Mary Dean *b.* 1958, Diana Evelyn *b.* 1960,—Cynthia Mary Denise, *b.* 1919; is a JP; *m.* 1942, Brian Alexis Fenwick Stephens of Tollgate House, Wing, Bucks., and has issue living, Nicholas Edward Egerton *b.* 1946, Hugo Offley Prideaux, *b.* 1956, Cecely Isobel Rich *b.* 1958. *Residence*, Plumber Manor, Sturminster Newton, Dorset.

Widow living of 14th Baronet—KATHLEEN (*Kathleen*, *Lady Grey Egerton*), da. of Peter Crook, of Borwick Lodge, Ambleside, and widow of Brian Thorburn Dickson: *m.* 1961, as his 2nd wife, Sir Philip Reginald Le Belward Grey Egerton, 14th Bt., who *d.* 1962. *Residence*, Weston, Lulworth Cove, Dorset.

Collateral Branches living.

Grandchildren of the late F.-M. Sir Charles Comyn Egerton, G.C.B., D.S.O., 3rd son of the late Maj.-Gen. Caledon Richard Egerton (infra) :—
Issue of the late Vice-Adm. Wion de Malpas Egerton, D.S.O., *b.* 1879, *d.* (killed in action during European War) 1943: *m.* 1913, Anita Adolphine, who *d.* 1972, da. of the late A. R. David, of Eastfield, Grimsby:—
David Boswell, *CB, OBE, MC, b.* 1914; Maj.-Gen. (ret.); late RA; FIMechE; Dir-Gen. of Artillery, Min. of Defence, 1964-67, Vice-Pres., and Sen. Army Member of Ordnance Board 1967-69, and Pres. 1969-70; Col. Comdt. RA; 1939-45 War (MC); OBE (Mil) 1956, CB (Mil) 1968: *m.* 1946, Margaret Gillian, da. of the late Rev. Canon Charles Cuthbert Inge, of Streatley, Berks, and has issue living, William de Malpas (8, Grove Av., Twickenham, Middx.), *b.* 1949; ed. at Sherborne; MA Camb: *m.* 1971, Ruth, only da. of the Rev. George Watson, of St. Albans Vicarage, Westcliff-on-Sea,—Charlotte Mary, *b.* 1950; BA, Oxford—Margaret Caroline, *b.* 1955. *Residence*, Pendrys, West Clandon, Surrey; Senior United Service Club.——Penelope, *b.* 1919; formerly 2nd Officer WRNS: *m.* 1955 (m. diss. 1967), Maj. John Michael de Burgh Ibberson, late 16th/5th Lancers, and has issue living, Erika Mary, *b.* 1956. *Residence*, Church Cottage, Martinstown, nr. Dorchester, Dorset.——Alison, *b.* 1922; formerly 3rd Officer WRNS: *m.* 1955, Lt.-Col. Richard Boutcher Gregory, RA (ret.), and has issue living, Andrew Richard, *b.* 1957,—Jane Patricia, *b.* 1960. *Residence*, Lockbank Lodge, Sedbergh, Yorks.

Grandson of the late Sir Reginald Arthur Egerton, C.B. (infra) :—
Issue of the late Reginald Francis le Belward Egerton, *b.* 1880, *d.* 1927: *m.* 1907, Elsie Lillian Rose Harris:—
Rowland le Belward, (1165, Bay St., Apt. 10, San Francisco, Calif. 94123, USA) *b.* 1914: *m.* 1945, Denise, da. of the late Capt. Denis Hayes, M.B.E.

Grandchildren of the late Maj.-Gen. Caledon Richard Egerton, 5th son of 9th baronet :—
Issue of the late Sir Reginald Arthur Egerton, C.B., *b.* 1850, *d.* 1930 : *m.* 1877, Margaret, who *d.* 1919, da. of the late Hon. J. Baker, of Morialta, S. Australia :—
Mary Caledon, *b.* 1878 ; is a nun.——Hilda Dupre, *b.* 1883 ; is a Sister of Mercy.

Issue of the late Adm. Sir George le Clerc Egerton, K.C.B., *b.* 1852, *d.* 1940: *m.* 1st, 1882, Frances Emily, who *d.* 1926, da. of the late Murray Gladstone ; 2ndly, 1932, Margaret Stella (now of Little Hanford, Blandford, Dorset), da. of the late Col. C. A. Maunsell, R.A.M.C., and widow of R. W. Prentice, of Beauworth Manor, Alresford, Hants:—
(By 1st m.) Dorothy (Beechwood, Faygate, Horsham): *m.* 1911, Adm. Philip Wylie Dumas, CB, CVO, RN, who *d.* 1949, and has issue living, Philip Anthony Egerton (Swan Cottage, Goudhurst, Cranbrook, Kent), *b.* 1913; Lt.-Col. (ret.) 8th Gurka Rifles, NW Frontier 1937-40; 1939-45 War: *m.* 1940, Betty, yst. da. of the late C. W. C. Hine, of Moleway, Dorking, and has issue living, Hugh Philip Egerton (c/o Green Jackets Depot, Winchester), *b.* 1942; Maj. R. Green Jackets: *m.* 1966, Christina Ang la, only da. of Lt.-Col. A. T. J. Graham, RA (ret.), of Bowhay Farm, Aish, Totnes (and has issue living, Caroline Mary *b.* 1968, Celia Louise *b.* 1970), Markham Cres-well *b.* 1951: *m.* 1973, Nicola Ada, da. of Herbert Bradley, of Mount Hybla, Castle-Knock, Dublin, Sarah Hine *b.* 1941: *m.* 1st, 1963 (m. diss. 1968), Maj. J. B. B. Pollard (ret.) Coldm. Gds.; 2ndly, 1969, Kenneth St. John Rae, of Exmoor House, Castle Hill, Brenchley, Kent (and has issue living (by 2nd m.) James Henry George *b.* 1964 (by 2nd m.) Angus William Broderick *b.* 1970, Isobel Julie *b.* 1972,—David Brian Gladstone (515, Pine St., Sausalito, Cal. 94965, USA), *b.* 1915; Lt.-Cdr. (ret.) RN: *m.* 1942, Lalage Helen, who *d.* 1974, el. da. of the late Cdr. C. M. I. Scott, RN (ret.), of Lelant, Cornwall, and has issue living, Patrick David Charles *b.* 1944; Capt. US Marine Corps; DFC and bar: *m.* 1972, Mary Anne, el. da. of Cdr. Henry Standt, US Navy (ret.), of 10, Cusick Av., Kings Park, Long Island, New York, USA, Brian Rodney Laurence *b.* 1948,—Patrick George Fairie, *RN, b.* 1917; is Sub-Lt.; 1939-41 War (missing),—Timothy Christopher Charles (of Moat House Farm, Brockham, Surrey), *b.* 1921; formerly Major Roy. Welch Fusiliers: *m.* 1945, Ann, da. of Alec Davidson, of Health Cottage, Dorking, and has issue living, Simon Charles Stuart *b.* 1955, Nicola Dorothy Ann *b.* 1946: *m.* 1970, Neville Blatch, of Swires Farm, Beare Green, Dorking, Surrey (and has issue living, Philip Herbert *b.* 1974, Kath-erine Emily *b.* 1973),—Phillipa Dorothy Dinah, *b.* 1919: *m.* 1942, Maj. David B. Milne, formerly RA, of Mpanda, Highlands, Rhodesia, and has issue living, Murray *b.* 1948: *m.* 1974, Julie Leigh, da. of the late Gilbert Leigh Matthews, of Malta, Phillipa, *b.* 1943: *m.* 1963, Simon Faed, of Cairnsmore, Concession, Rhodesia (and has issue living, Stuart Alastair Ferguson *b.* 1964, Janet Frances Fairrie *b.* 1968).

Grandchildren of the late John MARJORIBANKS-EGERTON, el. son of Philip Henry Egerton (infra):—
Issue of the late Lt.-Col. John Louis Gerard Marjoribanks-Egerton, *b.* 1901, *d.* 1965: *m.* 1936 (Cecilia Mary), Penelope, who *d.* 1974, da. of the late Maj. J. B. Barstow:—
John Caledon Richard, *b.* 1940.——Mary Penelope Jane, *b.* 1938, MA, Oxford, MSc., Alberta: *m.* 1963, John L. Bannister, c/o Lloyds Bank, 6, Pall Mall, SW1, and has issue living, William John, *b.* 1967,—Katherine Penelope, *b.* 1964,—Caroline Nancy, *b.* 1968.——Sarah Cecilia

Geraldine, b. 1942; MA Oxon.: m. 1964, Charles B. Strouts, AMICE, of 32, Cleaver Sq., SE11, and has issue living, Henry Gerard Egerton, b. 1966,—Emma Louise Penelope, b. 1968.—— Frances Mary Caroline, b. 1948.

Issue of the late Lt.-Col. Philip Morys Marjoribanks-Egerton, MBE, b. 1903, d. 1969: m. 1933, Adeline Barbara (Greenogue, 15, Folly Lane, Armagh, co. Armagh), da. of Maj. Osborn Augustin Chambers (late R. Warks. Regt.):—

Philippa Anne Mary, b. 1936: m. 1959, Brian Edgar Ford, of 24, Wesley Av., Peverell, Plymouth, and has issue living, Philip Richard, b. 1963,—Elizabeth Anne, b. 1960,—Sarah Jane, b. 1964,— Susan Lillian, b. 1965.

Grandchildren of the late Philip Henry Egerton, son of the late William Egerton, 3rd son of the late Philip Egerton, father of 8th and 9th baronets :—
Issue of the late Graham Egerton, b. 1861, d. 1922 : m. 1886, Julia Donegan, da. of T. Easley, of Dickson Co., Tennessee, U.S.A. :—

William Graham, b. 1896; with USA Air Force: m. 19—, Rebecca Crenshaw White, of Kentucky, and has issue living, William Graham, b. 19—,—John, b. 19—,—a da., b. 19—,—a da., b. 19—— ——Philip Marjoribanks, b. 1899; in US Dept. of Agriculture; 1914-18 War with US Naval Air Force: m. 19—, Susan Candler, of Corinth, Miss., USA.

Issue of the late William Egerton, b. 1870, d. 1917 : m. 1895, Louisa Marie, who d. 1923, da. of the late Edward Algernon Le Mesurier, banker, of Genoa and Guernsey :—
Mary Elizabeth, b. 1906; MB and BS London; MRCS England and LRCP London; FRCOC London. Residence, 5, Chawton Close, Harestock, Winchester, Hants.

Grandchildren of the late William Egerton (ante):—
Issue of the late William le Belward Egerton, b. 1901, d. 1947: m. 1931, Angela Doreen Loftus, who d. 1972, da. of the late Brig.-Gen. Edward Humphry Bland, CB, CMG, RE (ret.):—

Stephen Loftus (31, Crescent Wood Rd., SE26; Travellers' Club), b. 1932; ed. at Eton and at Trin. Coll., Camb.; formerly 2nd Lt. KRRC; entered HM Foreign Ser. 1956: Private Sec. to Under Sec. of State for Foreign Affairs 1961-62, Oriental Sec. at Baghdad 1963-67, and Counsellor at British Embassy, Tripoli, 1972; Head of Energy Depart. FO since 1973: m. 1958, Caroline da. of Maj. Eustace Thomas Edward Cary-Elwes, TD, late R. Norfolk Regt. of Thurton Hall, Norfolk, and has issue living, William Luke le Belward, b. 1966,—Louisa Charlotte, b. 1963.——Susan Kirsteen, b. 1936; ed. at Reading Univ. (BA 1959); entered HM Foreign Ser. 1960: m. 1962, Jeremy Sandford Cohen, of Oxley House, Abberton, Colchester, CO5 7NR, and has issue living, Thomas William Otway, b. 1965,—Lucy Jane, b. 1968.

Grandchildren of the late Sir Robert Eyles Egerton, KCSI, CIE, yst. son of the late William Egerton (ante):—
Issue of the late Lieut.-Gen. Sir Raleigh Gilbert Egerton, K.C.B., K.C.I.E., b. 1860, d. 1931 : m. 1st, 1894, Bridget Watson, who d. 1894, el. da. of Watson Askew-Robertson [B. Marjoribanks, ext.]; 2ndly, 1903, Maude Helen, who d. 1935, only da. of the late Sir George Rendelsham Prescott, 4th Bt. :—

Joanna Mary, M.R.C.S., L.R.C.P., b. 1905 : m. 1934, Kenneth Hampden Pridie, M.D., F.R.C.S., and has issue living, Jonathan George Egerton, b. 1939,—David Mark Hampden, b. 1942,— Angus Kenneth, b. 1945,—Diccon Charles, b. 1947,—William Raleigh, b. 1949,—Patricia Philippa, b. 1935,—Judith Joanna, b. 1937. Residence, 58, St. John's Road, Clifton, Bristol.

Issue of the late Lieut.-Col. Charles Philip Egerton, b. 1863, d. 1943 : m. 1889, Lilian Isabel, who d. 1950, da. of Lieut.-Gen. Hugh Rose, Indian Army :—
Rowland Philip, b. 1891 : m. 1918, Constance Alice, da. of Edward Courtenay Pratt, of Montreal, and has issue living, Piers Brian Philip, b. 1927 : m. 1948, Lorna, da. of Lorne Green, of Ottawa, Canada, and has issue living, Brian Philip b. 1949.

Grandchildren of the late Lt.-Col. Philip Egerton (ante):—
Issue of the late Robert Charles Egerton, MIEE, b. 1903, d. 1969: m. 1929, Mary Elizabeth Shaw, da. of the Rev. Charles Morris Trownsell, R. of Gidleigh, Devon:—
Julian Robert, (14, Gladsville Rd., Gladsville, Sydney, NSW), b. 1940; MSc, PhD: m. 1966, Kay Lewis, da. of George M. Stewart, of Pennant Hills, Sydney, NSW.——Una Mary, b. 1939; MCSP: m. 1963, Peter John Bayley Wassell, Hong Kong Police (c/o Police HQ, Arsenal St. Hong Kong), and has issue living, Mark Peter, b. 1966,—Amanda Claire, b. 1969,—Victoria Jane, b. 1970.

Grandchildren of the late Piers Egerton-Warburton (infra) :—
Issue of the late Capt. John Egerton-Warburton, Scots Guards, b. 1883, d. (wounds in action) 1915: m. 1908, the Hon. Lettice Legh, (who d. 1968, having m. 2ndly, 1919, Lt.-Col. John Dallas Waters, CB, DSO, who d. 1967), da. of 2nd Baron Newton:—
Elizabeth (Viscountess Ashbrook), b. 1911 : m. 1934, the 10th Viscount Ashbrook. Residence, Arley Hall, Northwich, Cheshire.——Priscilla (Baroness Newton), b. (posthumous) 1915 : m. 1st, 1936, Major Viscount Wolmer, who d. (on active ser. during European War) 1942, el. son of 3rd Earl of Selborne ; 2ndly, 1948, the 4th Baron Newton. Residence, Vernon Hill House, Bishop's Waltham, Hants.

Issue of the late Col. Geoffrey Egerton-Warburton, D.S.O., T.D., b. 1888, d. 1961 : m. 1927, the Hon. Georgiana Mary Dormer, M.B.E., who d. 1955, da. of 14th Baron Dormer :—
Peter (Mulberry House, Bentworth, Hants.), b. 1933; ed. at Eton, and RMA; late Capt. Coldm. Gds.: m. 1st, 1955 (m. diss. 1958), Belinda Vera. da. of the late J. R. A. Young, of Cowdrays, East Hendred, Berks; 2ndly, 1960 (m. diss. 1967) Sarah Jessica Norman, el. da. of Maj. Willoughby Rollo Norman, Gren. Gds. [see Norman, Bt.]; 3rdly, 1969, the Hon. Marya Anne Noble, da. of Baron Glenkinglas, and has issue living, (by 2nd m.) Charles Piers, b. 1961,—James Willoughby b. 1963,—(by 3rd m.), Christopher Geoffrey, b. 1971,—Louisa Jane (twin), b. 1971.——Anne, b. 1928: m. 1954, His Hon. Judge James Eccles Malise Irvine (c/o C. Hoare & Co., 37, Fleet St., EC4), and has issue living, David Peter Gerard, b. 1963,—Susan Caroline Jane, b. 1961.—— Jane (23, Yeoman Row, SW3), b. 1931.

Granddaughter of the late Rowland Eyles Egerton-Warburton, el. son of Rev. Rowland Egerton-Warburton, 7th son of Philip Egerton, father of 8th and 9th baronets:—
Issue of the late Piers Egerton-Warburton, b. 1839, d. 1914 : m. 1880, the Hon. Antoinette Elizabeth Saumarez, who d. 1918, da. of 3rd Baron de Saumarez:—
Lettice, b. 1894. Residence, 8, Avenue Court, Draycott Av., SW3.

Granddaughter of the late Rev. James Francis Egerton-Warburton, 2nd son of the late Rev. Rowland Egerton-Warburton (ante):—
Issue of the late Arthur Egerton-Warburton, b. 1848, d. 1927 : m. 1874, Edna, who d. 1901, da. of James Stowe:—
Ruth: m. 1952, Edgar Hunt, who d. 1959.

Grandchildren of the late Rowland James Egerton-Warburton, 2nd son of Maj. Peter Egerton-Warburton, CMG (infra):—
Issue of the late John Egerton-Warburton, b. 1873, d. 1943: m. 1913, Winifred Vaughan, of 131, Cambridge Terrace, Malvern, S. Australia:—
Richard John, b. 1916; Capt. Australian Imperial Force (Reserve of Officers): m. 1946, Audrey Doreen Roberts, of Melbourne, Victoria, Australia, and has issue living, Jill Rosalind, b. 1948, —Elizabeth Jane, b. 1952,—Bronwyn Grey, b. 1954. Residence, 10, Palmer Avenue, Myrtle

Bank, S. Australia.——Margaret (18, Superba Parade, Mosman, NSW), *b.* 1919: *m.* 1st, 1940, Lt. Robert Paine, who *d.* (killed in action in New Guinea) 1943; 2ndly, 1947, Maxwell Dunn, who *d.* 1966, and has issue living, (by 1st marriage) Frances Margaret, *b.* 1941.
      Issue of the late Peter Augustus Egerton-Warburton, *b.* 1877, *d.* 1944: *m.* 1906, Ellen, da. of W. Fountain, of Saffron Walden:—
Wilbraham, *b.* 1911; late RAAF: *m.* 19—, Olive Foureur.——Elizabeth; is a Nursing Sister Australian Imperial Force: *m.* 19—, Frank Mosey, of Weeroona Ngapala, via Robertstown, S. Australia.
      Issue of the late Rowland Egerton-Warburton, *b.* 1885, *d.* 1963: *m.* 1914, Isabel, da. of W. F. Langdon, of Caulfield, Australia:—
Francis (Bromefield, Glenrowan, Victoria, Australia), *b.* 1917: *m.* 1944, Joan, da. of P. A. Ewing of Bridgetown, W. Australia, and has issue living, Anne, *b.* 1945: *m.* 1966, Herbert Timothy Lee-Steere, of Narrogin, W. Aust., and has issue living, Peter Timothy *b.* 1968.——Annie Isabel, *b.* 1915: *m.* 1939, Harold Vernon Bray, of 27, Clydesdale St., Como, W. Aust., and has issue living, Robert Harold, *b.* 1942: *m.* 1968, Margaret Esme, da. of T. W. Maxwell, of Como, W. Aust.,—Ian Michael, *b.* 1943,—Marjorie Alison, *b.* 1940: *m.* 1963, William Francis Richardson, of Riverlea, Mardella, W. Aust., and has issue living, Michael James *b.* 1966, Felicity Jane *b.* 1970,—Gillian Margaret, *b.* 1948.

      Granddaughter of the late Maj. Peter Egerton-Warburton, CMG, 4th son of the late Rev. Rowland Egerton-Warburton (ante):—
      Issue of the late William Egerton-Warburton, *b.* 1847, *d.* 1906: *m.* 1877, Edith, da. of W. M. Sandford:—
Mary, *b.* 1885: *m.* 1909, Herbert Wilfred Pownall, and has issue living, Robert Alfred, *b.* 1913,—Elizabeth, *b.* 1910,—Frances Mary, *b.* 1917. *Residence,*

      Grandchildren of the late William Egerton-Warburton (ante):—
      Issue of the late Richard Sandford Egerton-Warburton, *b.* 1880, *d.* 1959 : *m.* 1908, Emily Meredith who *d.* 1965, da. of Bayfield Moulden:—
Peter Bayfield (8 Coolidge Av., Lower Mitcham 5062, S. Australia), *b.* 1909; served with 2nd AIF: *m.* 1937, Roma Ballands Hosking, da. of Frank Becker, of Adelaide, S. Australia, and has issue living, Richard Francis (86, Artarmon Rd., Artarmon, NSW 2064, Aust.), *b.* 1940: *m.* 1966, Susan Elizabeth Chandler, of Perth, W. Aust., and has issue living, Bayfield James *b.* 1970, Matthew Robert *b.* 1973,—Elizabeth Louise, *b.* 1938: *m.* 1962, Ian Wesley Giles, of Pomona Rd., Stirling West, S. Aust., and has issue living, Benjamin Peter Wesley *b.* 1969, Anna Louise *b.* 1963, Sally Elizabeth *b.* 1964.——William Arnold (66, Yacca Rd., Seacliff 5049, St. Aust.), *b.* 1918; Capt. AIF (Reserve); 1939-45 War (despatches): *m.* 1940, Letty Dorian Parsons, and has issue living, Michael Philip, *b.* 1948.——Meredith, *b.* 1913: *m.* 1936, Donald Thomas Mitchell, of 15, Cudmore Av., Toorak, 5056, S. Aust., and has issue living, Alan, *b.* 1940,—Jean Meredith, *b.* 1938,—Frances Egerton, *b.* 1943.——Alice Elizabeth Grey, *b.* 1924: *m.* 1947, Robert C. Bell, of 22, Pleasant View Cres., Glen Waverley 3150, Vic., Aust., and has issue living, Hugh, *b.* 1954,—Helen, *b.* 1948,—Barbara, *b.* 1950,—Judy, *b.* 1952.

      Grandchildren of the late Richard Sandford Egerton-Warburton (ante):—
      Issue of the late Edward Howard Egerton-Warburton, *b.* 1910, *d.* 1974: *m.* 1938, Margaret Newland (21, Haig St., Netherby, S. Aust., 5062):—
Peter Ridgeway (Woolibar Station, Kalgoorlie, W. Aust.), *b.* 1941: *m.* 1966, Vanda Sue, da. of J. B. Wood, of Bunbury, W. Aust., and has issue living, David Peter, *b.* 1967,—Deanna Sue, *b.* 1969,—Rosa Margaret, *b.* 1972.——Ann, *b.* 1946: *m.* 1969, James William Clarke, and has issue living, Benjamin James, *b.* 1970.

      Grandchildren of the late William Egerton-Warburton (ante):—
      Issue of the late Philip Egerton-Warburton, *b.* 1882, *d.* 1965: *m.* 1912, Olive Rigarlsford, da. of Alfred Palmer, late of Kapunda, S. Australia:—
Patience Anne, *b.* 1916.——Cecily, *b.* 1918.

      Grandchildren of the late George Grey Egerton-Warburton (infra) :—
      Issue of the late Philip Grey Egerton-Warburton, *b.* 1877, *d.* 1954 : *m.* 1909, Verna Grace, who *d,* 1939, da. of S. J. Rowe, formerly of Perth, W. Australia :—
Geoffrey Grey, *b.* 1911 : *m.* (Jan.) 1940, Marjorie Vere, da. of the late Nelson Hamilton-Taylor, of Mount Barker, W. Australia, and has issue living, Arley Geoffrey, *b.* (Dec.) 1940,—Colin Yorke, *b.* 1947,—Ione Vere, *b.* 1942,—Vivien Gay, *b.* 1944,—Caroline Marjorie, *b.* 1952. *Residence,* Yeriminup, Cranbrook, W. Australia.——Ronald Grey, *b.* 1914: *m.* 1937, Edith Mabel, da. of G. J. A. Swiney, of Albany, and has issue living, Philip Alexander, *b.* 1938: *m.* 1968, Sheila, da. of Donald La Claire, of Vancouver, BC, Canada, and has issue living, Brooke Elizabeth *b.* 19—Michael George (Mirinup, Frankland River, W. Aust.), *b.* 1941: *m.* 1966, Lois Elizabeth, da. of H. O. Grimbly, of Attadale, Perth, W. Aust., and has issue living, Antony Michael Grey *b.* 1967 Grey Edward *b.* 1972,—David Ronald, *b.* 1945: *m.* 19—, Margaret Elizabeth, da. of A. E. Challenor, of Dandallup, W. Aust., and has issue living, Nathan Detroit *b.* 1970, Blanche Elizabeth *b.* 1971,—Jennifer Mary, *b.* 1940: *m.* 1964, John Mattiske, of Norla, Kojonup, W. Aust., and has issue living, Peter Rex *b.* 1972, Marie Louise *b.* 1966, Philippa Jane *b.* 1968,—Diana Margaret, *b.* 1943: *m.* 1972, Ivan Johnson, of Perth, W. Aust. *Residence,* Tambellilup, Frankland River, W. Aust.——Dorothy Antoinette, *b.* 1909: *m.* 1934, George Alexander Swiney, and has issue living, Wayne Haig Egerton, *b.* 1935,—Graham Haig, *b.* 1940. *Residence,* Franklands, Frankland River, W. Aust.

      Grandchildren of the late George Edward Egerton-Warburton, yst. son of the Rev. Rowland Egerton-Warburton (ante) :—
      Issue of the late George Grey Egerton-Warburton, *b.* 1843, *d.* 1913 : *m.* 1872, Amy, da. of Edward Hester:—
Winifred Amy, *b.* 1880: *m.* 1st, 1907, John Hassell, who obtained a divorce 1926; 2ndly, 1932, Thomas Elliot, and has issue living, (by 1st marriage) Theodosia Ellen, *b.* 1911 : *m.* 19—, Percy Augustus Roe, of W. Australia, and has issue living, a da. *b.* 19—,
      Issue of the late Rowland Egerton-Warburton, *b.* 1845, *d.* 1902: *m.* 1881, Mary, who *d.* 1938, da. of John M'Kail:—
Philip Augustus (RMB 222, W. Pingelly, W. Aust.), *b.* 1894; 1914-18 War with AIF: *m.* 1928 Alice Mary Price, and has issue living, Rowland, *b.* 1928: *m.* 1953, Laurel Gloria Ferguson and has issue living, Graeme *b.* 1954, Trevor *b.* 1958, Maxine *b.* 1955,—Ross, *b.* 1931: *m.* 1954 Wilma Joan Smoker, and has issue living, Dean Ross *b.* 1961, Evan Mark *b.* 1966, Alison Joy *b.* 1955, Robya Lois *b.* 1957, Coral Janet *b.* 1960,—Philip (RMB 512, Williams, W. Aust. 6391), *b.* 1934: *m.* 1959, Georgina May, da. of H. F. J. Higginson, of Kanandah, Pingelly, W. Aust., and has issue living, Michael Philip *b.* 1959, Brett Francis *b.* 1970, Debra Susanna *b.* 1961,—Peter (twin), *b.* 1934.

      Grandchildren of the late Horace Egerton-Warburton (infra) :—
      Issue of the late John Le Belward Warburton, *b.* 1882, *d.* 1949: *m.* 1913, Blanche Josephine van Zuilecom, of Yeenyellup, Kojonup, W. Australia :—
John Egerton (Box 20, Kojonup, W. Aust.), *b.* 1916: a Farmer: *m.* 1939, Celia Maltby, da. of Allan Douglas Robinson, of Subiaco, Perth, W. Aust., and has issue living, Quentin (Korellup, RMB 328, Kojonup, 6395, W. Aust.), *b.* 1942: *m.* 1965, Mary Heath, da. of J. W. Rowe, of Claremont, Perth, W. Aust., and has issue living, David Grey *b.* 1970, Robert John Quentin

b. 1972, Megan Alan *b.* 1967,—Alan (Yeenyellup, Box 20, Kojonup, W. Aust.), *b.* 1947: *m.* 1971, Cynthia Margaret, da. of C. D. Lee, of Royston Park, Kojonup, W. Aust., and has issue living, Rachael Margaret *b.* 1972, Emily Jane *b.* 1974,—Celia Ruth, *b.* 1940: *m.* 1960, Anthony Randall Egerton-Warburton, infra).

Issue of the late Horace Grey Egerton-Warburton, *b.* 1891, *d.* 1956 : *m.* 1st, 1915, Ruth, who *d.* 1918, da. of Randle Egerton-Warburton (ante) ; 2ndly, 1920, Vera (of St. Werburgh's, Mount Barker, W. Australia), da. of Charles F. Lake, of Dandenong Road, Malvern, Melbourne, Australia :—
(By 1st marriage) Mary Ruth, *b.* 1916 : *m.* 1st, 1941, Edward Henry Finch, Roy. Australian Air Force, who *d.* (killed in action during European War) 1943 ; 2ndly, 1946, Vernon Wells, Roy. Australian Air Force, and has issue living, (by 1st marriage) Penelope, *b.* 1942,—(by 2nd marriage) Grey Egerton, *b.* 1947,—Peter Randell Scott, *b.* 1950,—Diana Ruth, *b.* 1948. *Residence*, Ceylon Pastures, Kenderup, W. Australia.——Joan, *b.* 1918 : *m.* 1941, Henry Graham Johnson, Australian Imperial Force, and has issue living, Richard Grey, *b.* 1944,—Anthony Peter, *b.* 1946.——(By 2nd marriage) Edward Grey, *b.* 1928.——Yexley Selina, *b.* 1921 : *m.* 1946, Gordon Maitland-Roberts, Australian Imperial Force, and has issue living, Wade Maitland, *b.* 1947,—Bruce Gordon, *b.* 1950,—Helen Ena, *b.* 1948. *Residence*, Chelsea, Moora, W. Australia.—— Patricia Ann, *b.* 1923 : *m.* (Jan.) 1946, William Adolphus Chaffey, M.L.A., and has issue living, David Frank *b.* 1957, Mary Ann *b.* (Nov.) 1946,—Elizabeth Patricia, *b.* 1949. *Residence*, 119, Fitzroy Street, Tamworth, N.S. Wales.——Ann Vera (twin), *b.* 1928 : *m.* 1952, Donald Charles Keir Collins, and has issue living, Bradford Keir, *b.* 1958,—Scott Charles Egerton, *b.* 1962,—Joanne Margaret, *b.* 1953,—Jacqueline Anne, *b.* 1955. *Residence*, 47, Martin Street, Mount Barker, W. Australia.——Helen Maud, *b.* 1931: *m.* 1957, John Halley Arnold, and has issue living, Richard John Halley, *b.* 1960,—Brooke Egerton Halley, *b.* 1962,—Amanda Jane, *b.* 1958,—Michelle Tracey, *b.* 1959. *Residence*, Selsiey Downs, Kojonup, W. Australia.—— Carlene Alice (twin), *b.* 1931: *m.* 1957, John Ronald Penn, and has issue living, Fiona Carlene, *b.* 1958,—Sally Louise, *b.* 1960. *Residence*, Parsons St., Mount Barker, W. Australia.

Grandchildren of the late AugustusEgerton-Warburton, son of the late George, Edward Egerton-Warburton (ante):—
Issue of the late Angus Egerton-Warburton, *b.* 1889, *d.* 1960: *m.* 1925, Dorothy (RMB 406 Euretta, Kojonup, W. Australia), da. of John Weston, of Eastwood, Notts.:—
Brian Wayne, *b.* 1933.——Ian Angus, *b.* 1942: *m.* 1965, Robin, da. of Dr. Robert Elphick, of Shenlon Park, and has issue living, Barney, *b.* 1968,—Simone Elissa, *b.* 1966.——Joan Irma (South Parkfie.d, N. Danalup, W. Australia), *b.* 1926: *m.* 1st, 1950, Ross Bovell, who *d.* 1950; 2ndly, 1955, John Griffin Money, who *d.* 1962.——Evelyn Isabel, *b.* 1928: *m.* 1953, Frank Devine, of Hillside, Frankland River, W. Australia, and has issue living, Peter John, *b.* 1954,—Christopher James, *b.* 1956, Garry Matthew, *b.* 1962,—Leonie Frances, *b.* 1957.——Margaret, *b.* 1931.—— Dorothy June, *b.* 1937: *m.* 1961, John Kitto, of Mayo Flats, 9, Colin St., West Perth, W. Aust., and has issue living, Johnson Grey, *b.* 1966,—Grantham Angus, *b.* 1868.

Issue of the late Reginald Hubert Egerton-Warburton, *b.* 1894, *d.* 1962: *m.* 1925, Lena Mary Lambe (Woolareen, Konjonup, W. Aust.):—
Rex (Woolareen, Kojonup, W. Aust.), *b.* 1928 : *m.* 1946, Muriel Faith Weise, and has issue living, Diane, *b.* 1946 : *m.* 1968, John William Partridge, of Priory Park, Kojonup, W. Aust., and has issue living, Craig John *b.* 1969, Cindy Karen *b.* 1968,—Denise, *b.* 1947 : *m.* 1965, Kevin William Brown, of Denvin Brook, Muradup, W. Aust., and has issue living, Darrin Kevin *b.* 1966, Gavin William *b.* 1967, Byron Rex *b.* 1971,—Maree, *b.* 1953: *m.* 1970, John James Matthews, of Konjonup, W. Aust., and has issue living, Chad James *b.* 1972, Damon John *b.* 1974,—Dawn (Cherryton, Konjonup, W. Aust.), *b.* 1926.

Grandchildren of the late Randle Egerton-Warburton (infra):—
Issue of the late Piers Edward Egerton-Warburton, *b.* 1895, *d.* 1961: *m.* 1920, Winsome, who *d.* 1971, da. of John Ewing, MLC, of W. Australia:—
Diana, *b.* 1924: *m.* 1945, Julian B. Goyder, and has issue living, Piers Bruce, *b.* 1950,—Melody Anne, *b.* 1946,—Elizabeth, *b.* 1947.——Pamela, *b.* 1929: *m.* 1953, Samuel Forster Clarkson, of 16, Cliff Way, Claremont, W. Australia, and has issue living, Simon Nicholas, *b.* 1957,—Eve, *b.*, 1954.——Jenefer, *b.* 1933: *m.* 1956, Ian P. Johnston, of Dardanup, W. Australia, and has issue living, Ian Justin, *b.* 1958,—Julia, *b.* 1956,—Andrea *b.* 1963,—Diana, *b.* 1965.——Angela, *b.* 1941: *m.* 1964, John Charles Roberts, of 51, Saunders St., Mosman Park, W. Aust., and has issue living, Andrew Timothy, *b.* 1966,—Timothy Andrew, *b.* 1970.

Issue of the late George Grey Egerton-Warburton, *b.* 1899, *d.* 1975: *m.* 1929, Ethe Vernon, da. of Edmund Vernon Drake-Brockman, JP:—
Anthony Randall (Brackenhurst, Bridgetown, W. Aust.), *b.* 1935: *m.* 1960, Celia Ruth, da. of John Egerton-Warburton (ante), and has issue living, Randle, *b.* 1963,—Nicholas, *b.* 1966,— Belinda Jane, *b.* 1961.——Vernon Grey, *b.* 1938.——Dorothy Vernon, *b.* 1929: *m.* 1954, John Gordon Boyle, of 40, Tyrell St., Nedlands, 6009, W. Aust., and has issue living, Angela Egerton, *b.* 1955,—Erica Egerton, *b.* 1960.——Fleur, *b.* 1933: *m.* 1956, John Aitken, of Hau-ora, Havelock North, Hawkes Bay, NZ, and has issue living, Timothy Murray, *b.* 1957,—Hamish Egerton, *b.* 1960,—Judith Hill, *b.* 1962.

Granddaughters of the late George Edward Egerton-Warburton (ante):—
Issue of the late Randle Egerton-Warburton, *b.* 1860, *d.* 1938: *m.* 1890, Eva, who *d.* 1931, da. of Edward Hester:—
Cecely Alice (Banyandah Farm, Esperance, W. Aust.), *b.* 1892: *m.* 1919, Maitland John Drake Brockman who *d.* 1969, and has issue living, Egerton Charles (of Laverton Downs, Laverton, W. Aust.), *b.* 1927: *m.* 1948, Daphne Anderson, and has issue living, John *b.* 1949, Philip *b.* 1950, Viki *b.* 1954, Elizabeth *b.* 1961,—Mollie Agatha *b.* 1920: *m.* 1949, Brig. James Roy Anderson, CBE, late R. Sussex Regt. (Barn House, Denton, Harleston, Norfolk; United Service Club), and has issue living, Hamish Warburton Findlater *b.* 1952, Sheena Fiona Egerton, *b.* 1954,—Cecily Jean (Currajugg, Clyde Mountain, Braidwood, NSW), *b.* 1921; reverted to surname of Drake-Brockman: *m.* 1st, 1944 (m. diss. 1955), Richard Smallpiece Whitington; 2ndly, 1962 (m. diss. 1972), Maj.-Gen. Paul Alfred Cullen, CBE, DSO, ED, and has issue living, (by 1st m.) Richard Mark *b.* 1947, James Jerome *b.* 1951,—Frances Margaret, *b.* 1923: *m.* 1951, John Fenwick, of Dempster St., Esperance, W. Aust., and has issue living, Jane Deborrah *b.* 1959.——Margaret Augusta, *b.* 1903: *m.* 1st, 1932, Robert Willgress, BSc, who *d.* 1956; 2ndly, 1956, William Francis Dudley Allison, of Protea Rd., George, Cape Province, S. Africa.

The House of Egerton, one of the most ancient and distinguished in Cheshire, traces its descent to William le Belward, who was Baron of Malpas under the Norman Earl Palatine of that county. David, great-grandson of William le Belward, took the name of Egerton from the Lordship of Egerton, which he had inherited ; and from him, in a direct line, is descended the present baronet. Sir Roland Egerton, 1st Bt., *m.* Bridget, sister and co-heir of 15th Lord Grey of Wilton. The 7th Bt. was created Earl of Wilton, with remainder to his maternal grandson, Hon. Thomas Grosvenor. At his death in 1814 the baronetcy passed to his kinsman John Egerton of Oulton descended from a yr. son of the 1st Bt. By Roy. Warrant dated 30th June, 1825, King George IV granted to the Rev. Sir Philip Egerton, 9th Bt., and all subsequent baronets on succeeding to the title the right to assume for themselves only the additional surname of Grey and the Arms of Grey of Wilton. The 10th baronet sat as M.P. for Chester (C.) 1830, for Cheshire West 1835-68, and for Cheshire West 1868-81. The 13th baronet, the Rev. Sir Brooke de Malpas Grey-Egerton, was R. of Stoke-on-Terne, and Rural Dean of Hodnet 1901-13.

ELEY, Creation (U.K.) 1921, of Sagamore, Shiplake, co. Oxford. [Extinct 1951.]

Sir FREDERICK ELEY, 1st and last *Baronet.*

Daughter living of 1st Baronet—Audrey Mary: *m.* 1925, Alexander Ritchie Lamb, and has issue living. *Residence,* Bradford House, The Common, Frenchay, near Bristol.

ELIOTT, Creation (N.S.) 1666, of Stobs, Roxburghshire.

Be wise.

Sir ARTHUR FRANCIS AUGUSTUS BOSWELL ELIOTT OF STOBS, 11th *Baronet*; *b.* Jan. 2nd, 1915; *s.* his father, *Sir* GILBERT ALEXANDER BOSWELL, 1958; ed. at Harrow, and at King's Coll., Camb. (B.A. 1936, M.A. 1949) ; is Chief of the Clan Elliot, and a Member of Queen's Body Guard for Scotland (Roy. Co. of Archers); 1939-45 War as Maj. KOSB; E. Africa and Burma 1941-45 with King's African Rifles: *m.* 1947, Frances Aileen, el. da. of Sir Francis Kennedy McClean, AFC, and has issue.

Arms—Gules, on a bend or, a baton azure ; in a dexter canton argent, a saltire azure surmounted of an inescutcheon or charged with a lion rampant within a double tressure flory counterflory gules, being the addition of Nova Scotia as a Baronet.

Crest—A hand couped at the wrist in armour holding a cutlass in bend proper. *Supporters*—*Dexter,* a ram : *sinister,* a goat ; both proper and gorged with a laurel branch vert, horned and hooved or.
Residence—Redheugh, Newcastleton, Roxburghshire. *Clubs*—New (Edinburgh), Leander, Puffins.

Daughter living—Margaret Frances Boswell, *b.* 1948: *m.* 1974, Anthony E. B. Vaughan-Arbuckle.

Sisters living—Charlotte Elgitha Veronica Boswell, *b.* 1913: *m.* 1st, 1936 (marriage dissolved 1941), Landon Ketchum Thorne; 2ndly, 1946, Stanley Herbert Maxted, who *d.* 1963; 3rdly, 1964, Thomas Talfourd Mosby, of 3442, Flamingo Drive, Bay Island, Sarasota, Florida, USA.——Jean Cecelia Constance (1/6, Fettes Rise, East Fettes Av., Edinburgh, EH4 1QH), *b.* 1920: m. 1st, 1940, Maj. Alfred Nigel Parker, Queen's Own Cameron Highlanders (SR), who *d.* (killed in action) 1944; 2ndly, 1953, Maj. Alan Edward Seton Jackson, MBE, MC, KOSB, who *d.* 1964, and has issue living, (by 1st m.) Alwyn Colin John (Orchard House, Great Sampford, Essex), *b.* 1940: *m.* 1966, Sarah, da. of H. S. Hays, and has issue living, Nigel Henry *b.* 1968, Lucinda Jane *b.* 1971,—Veronica Gillean (45, West Court, Ravelston House Park, Edinburgh 4), *b.* 1942,—(by 2nd m) Andrew Conway, *b.* 1954; 2nd Lt. KOSB,—Roderick Edward, *b.* 1956.

Widow living of 10th Baronet—DORA FLOURNOY ADAMS (*Dowager, Lady Eliott of Stobs*), only da. of the late Alexander Hopkins, of Atlanta, Georgia, U.S.A. : *m.* 1912, Sir Gilbert Alexander Boswell Eliott of Stobs, 10th baronet, who *d.* 1958. *Residence,* 4/1, Fettes Rise, East Fettes Av., Edinburgh, EH4 1QH.

Collateral Branches living.

Grandchildren of the late Alexander Boswell Vassal Eliott (infra):—
Issue of the late Charles Rawdon Heathfield Eliott, *b.* 1901, *d.* 1972: *m.* 1925, Emma Elizabeth Harris (72, Derby St., Rockhampton, Qld., Aust.):—
CHARLES JOSEPH ALEXANDER (27, Cohoe St., Toowoomba, Qld., Aust., 4350), *b.* Jan. 9th, 1937: *m.* 1959, Wendy, da. of   Bailey, of Ilfracombe, Qld., and has issue living, Rodney Gilbert Charles, *b.* 1966,—Elizabeth, *b.* 1960,—Jenny, *b.* 1961,—Josephine, *b.* 1963.——Keith Robert Vincent (65, Bunya St., Grunslopes, Brisbane, Qld. 4120), *b.* 1942: *m.* 1965, Annette May Nielsen-Kijrgaard, of Roehampton, and has issue living, Brett Robert, *b.* 1966.——Raymond Francis, *b.* 1946.——Irene Gertrude, *b.* 1930: *m.* 1950, Peter Brown (c/o PO Box 4, Yeppon, Qld.).——Myrtle Davies, *b.* 1936.——Bella Loraine, *b.* 1939.

Issue of the late Alexander Boswell Vassal Eliott, half-brother of 9th baronet, *b.* 1867, *d.* 1924: *m.* 1891, Hannah Josephine McKavanagh, who *d.* 1943:—
Gertrude May, *b.* 1893: *m.* 1929, Henry Wilson Mercer.——Annabella Carmichael, *b.* 1897: *m.* 1927, James Bryson. *Residence,* Denham Terr., Rockhampton, Queensland.——Constance Elizabeth, *b.* 1894: *m.* 19—, Clarence Quinn. *Residence,*

Grandsons of Charles Rawdon Heathfield Eliott (ante):—
Issue of the late Clive John Eliott, *b.* 1940, *d.* 1971: *m.* 1961, Estelle Maude Kelland:—
Bradley John, *b.* 1962.——Anthony Charles, *b.* 1966.——Dale Thomas, *b.* 1969.

Granddaughters of the late Gilbert William Eliott, son of the late Gilbert Eliott, C.M.G., 3rd son of 6th baronet:—
Issue of the late Gilbert Francis Eliott, *b.* 1859, *d.* 1943 : *m.* 1887, Emily Kate, who *d.* 1936, da. of W. H. Palmer, of Gippsland, Victoria :—
Joan Mary, *b.* 1897: *m.* 1925, Otto Saddler Hirschfeld, Chancellor of Queensland Univ. who *d.* 1957, and has issue living. *Residence,* 32 Palm Av., Ascot, Qld., Aust.——Emily Innes, *b.* 1901: *m.* 1928, Eric S. Newman, of 39 College Rd., Stanthorpe, Qld. 4380, Aust.

Grandson of the late Gilbert William Henry Eliott, son of the late Francis Willoughby Eliott (infra):—
Issue of the late Gilbert William Eliott, *b.* 1894, *d.* 1961: *m.* 1921, Lilian Mary, who *d.* 1968, da. of William Towle, of Nottingham, and widow of Neville Dalley:—

Gilbert Rowley Roxburgh (53, Epping Rd., Epping, NSW), b. 1923; ed. at Sydney Univ. (BDS); late F/Lt. RAAF: m. 1944, Helen Ross, yr. da. of A. H. Martin, MA, PhD, of Sydney, NSW, and has issue living, Gilbert William Heathfield, b. 1961,—Christine, b. 1945; ed. at Univ. of New England, NSW (BSc), and Sydney Univ. (Dip. Ed.),—Virginia Ruth, b. 1947.

Grandchildren of the late Francis Willoughby Eliott, son of the late Gilbert Eliott, C.M.G. (ante):—
Issue of the late Edward Percy Eliott, b. 1860, d. 1931 : m. 1890, Annie, who d. 1944, el. da. of John Connolly, of Gayndah, Queensland :—
Gilbert, b. 1891 : m. 1929, Barbara, second da. of the late Charles Saddlier, of Gayndah, Queensland.——Marjorie, b. 1892 : m. 1938, Robert Livingston Boyd. Residence.

Grandson of the late Clifton Hazlewood Eliott (infra):—
Issue of the late Francis Heathfield Eliott, b. 1908, d. 1970: m. 1939, Florence Nell (Congi, Woolbrook, NSW.), da. of the late O. B. Briggs:—
Graham Francis Heathfield (26, Kerferd St., Watson, ACT 2602), b. 1941: m. 1970, Karen Joyce, el. da. of Robert John Taylor, of Mt. Druitt, NSW.——Geoffrey Osmer Heathfield (Congi., Woolbrook, NSW), b. 1942: m. 1974, Sally Green, of Moorabinda, Taroom, Qld.

Grandchildren of the late Francis Willoughby Eliott (ante):—
Issue of the late Clifton Hazlewood Eliott, b. 1872, d. 1938 : m. 1905, Mary Isabel, who d. 1960, el. da. of the Rev. R. W. Wilson, of Walcha, New England, N.S. Wales :—
Roger Clifton Heathfield (85, Oak St., S. Tamworth 2345, NSW), b. 1909; late AIF: m. 1st, 1942 (divorce 19—), Winifred Maud, only da. of the Rev. H. E. West, V. of Lenterfield, NS Wales; 2ndly, 1948, Betty Muriel, el. da. of H. Williams, of Landsbrough, Queensland, and has issue living, (by 2nd m.) Roger John, b. 1955,—Robyn Jeannette, b. 1949: m. 1974, Jeffrey Alan Henderson, of 224, East Kurrajong Rd., Kurrajong, NSW,—Wendy Sue, b. 1954: m. 1973, Alan John Hillier, of 3, Jonathon St., S. Tamworth, NSW.——Lyndsay Raine Heathfield, b. 1919; in Australian Imperial Force: m. 1949, Rosemary Margaret, younger da. of Gordon W. Phillips, of 1, Carlos Rd., Artarmon, NS Wales, and has issue living, Andrew Clifton Heathfield, b. 1954,—Gaeling Heathfield, b. 1950,—Ruth Heathfield, b. 1952,—Rosemary Ann Heathfield, b. 1956. Residence, Greenwells, Walcha, New England, NS Wales.——Isabel Heathfield, b. 1906: m. 1st, 1941, Victor French, Australian Imperial Force, who d. 1943; 2ndly, 1950, Donald Finlay, and has issue living, (by 1st m.) Patricia, b. 1932,—Ann, b. 1935. Residence, Vicorarra, Kingsley Terrace, Manly, E2, Queensland.——Madge Heathfield, b. 1907: m. 1943, Alec Euston Gidley King, Australian Imperial Force, and has issue living, Robert Gidley, b. 1946, Sally, b. 1950: m. 1974, Keith Granville (Neutral Bay, Sydney, NSW). Residence, Calala, Box 282, PO Armidale, NS Wales.——Dorothy Mary Heathfield (Nioke Place, Charlestown NSW), b. 1911: m. 1933 (m. diss. 1957), Archibald John Kilpatrick, and has issue living, John Eliott, b. 1936,—Owen Heathfield, b. 1942,—Jillian Mary b. 1934.——Marcie Issell Heathfield (9, St. Andrews Av., Armidale, 2350, NSW), b. 1917: m. 1939, Archer John Croft, who d. 1971 [see Croft, Bt. cr. 1671, colls.].

Grandsons of the late Lt.-Col. Francis Augustus Heathfield Eliott, DSO, (infra):
Issue of the late Heathfield George Henry Eliott, b. 1897, d. 1975: m. 1922, Rhoda Isadora (4, Mayfair Flats, Roslyn Rd., Rondebosch, Cape Town, S. Africa), da. of Frederick William Augustus Daly:—
Ian Cecil Heathfield (PO Box 65006, Benmore 2010, Transvaal), b. 1923: m. 1945, Berenice Louise, da. of George Joseph Washington, and has issue living, Anthony John, b. 1949: m. 1974, Sheila Kirkness,—Christopher Thomas, b. 1953.——Ivor Keith Heathfield (300, Lister Rd., Rembrant Park, Johannesburg, S. Africa), b. 1926: m. 1962, Edythe Gloria, da. of John Marshall Harrison, and has issue living, Graeme, b. 1964,—Kevin John, b. 1973,—Lynette, b. 1963,—Louise, b. 1967.

Grandchildren of the late Major George Augustas Eliott, son of the late Adm. George Augustus Eliott, 5th son of 6th baronet :—
Issue of the late Lieut.-Col. Francis Augustus Heathfield Eliott, D.S.O., b. 1867, d. 1937: m. 1896, Evelyn Georgina Stirling, who d. 1937, da. of Richard William McDermott, of Dublin :—
Hugh Herbert Heathfield, OBE, TD, b. 1903; formerly Lieut.-Col. Roy. Fusiliers: European War 1939-45 in France, N.-W. Europe and Palestine; OBE (Mil.) 1946: m. 1927, Barbara, da. of John Cullen Marsh, of Penge, SE, and has issue living, Ann Georgina Heathfield, b. 1929: m. 1954, William John Bullock, of Upper Leapyatt, Guarlford, Malvern, and has issue living, Anthony John b. 1957, Nigel Timothy b. 1960. Residence, 3, College Mews, Somers Rd., Malvern.—— Evelyn Heather, b. 1898: m. 1923, Horatio Wellesley Burgess, late Lt. Dragoon Gds., and has issue living, John Francis Wellesley (Barnfield House, Ewhurst, Robertsbridge, Sussex), b. 1929: m. 1953, Angela Mildren, and has issue living, Jonathan Nigel b. 1955, Grace Clare b. 1958,—Margaret Jean, b. 1924 : m. 1951, Richard Andrews, of The Lodge, Hampden Road, High Wycombe, Bucks, and has issue living, Christopher John b. 1952, Peter Richard b. 1957,— Jennifer Evelyn, b. 1938. Residence, 7, Wiltshire Gardens, Bransgore, Hants.——Marie Ida, b. 1900 : m. 1923, William Joseph Merrifield, and has issue living, Daphne Joan, b. 1925 : m. 1954, Lt.-Col. John Neil Reeve, RA. Residence, 10, Hambledon Vale, Woodcote Green, Epsom, Surrey.——Dymphna Helen Cynthia, b. 1906 : m. 1930, John Richard Vernon, Nigerian Civil Ser. (retired), and has issue living, Joanne Georgina Dymphna, b. 1933 : m. 1953, Jorgen Lagoni, of Copenhagen, Denmark. Residence, Fossa, Crow Hill, Ringwood, Hants.

The Eliotts or Elliots (then known as Elwalds or Ellots), are reputed to have come from Angus and settled as a clan in Liddesdale under grant of lands from Robert the Bruce, whose purpose was to strengthen the Scottish defences of the Middle March. Their chief built a tower on a bank overlooking Hermitage Water near its junction with the Liddel and was thereafter known as Robert Ellot of Redheugh. His successors for several generations were Captains of Hermitage Castle. The Eliotts of Stobs are descended from Gilbert Eliot of Stobs, son of Robert Eliot, of Redheugh, and his wife, Jean Scott, known as " Gibbie wi' the gowden gartins," who bought Stobs in 1607 from the heirs-portioners of his step-father, Gavin Eliot of Stobs. The Elliots, Earls of Minto, are also descended from this first laird of Stobs. Gen. George Augustus Eliott (Lord Heathfield) the famous defender of Gibraltar, was yst. son of the 3rd baronet. Sir William Francis Eliott, 7th baronet: m. 1826, Theresa, da. of Sir Alexander Boswell, of Auchinleck, 1st Baronet, el. son of James Boswell, biographer of Johnson, and sister and heir of Sir James Boswell, 2nd Baronet, who d. 1857.

ELLERMAN, Creation (UK) 1905, of Connaught Square, Paddington. [Extinct 1973]

Sir JOHN REEVES ELLERMAN, 2nd and last Baronet.

Widow living of 2nd Baronet—Esther (Lady Ellerman), el. da. of the late Clarence de Sola, of Montreal, Canada: m. 1933, Sir John Reeves Ellerman, 2nd Bt., who d. 1973, when the title became ext.

ELLIOTT, Creation (U.K.) 1917, of Limpsfield, Surrey.

Sir HUGH FRANCIS IVO ELLIOTT-
O.B.E., 3rd Baronet ; b. March 10th, 1913 ;
s. his father, Sir IVO D'OYLY, 1961 ; ed. at
Eastbourne Coll., and at Univ. Coll., Oxford
(MA); entered Tanganyika Admin. Ser.
1937; Administrator of Tristan da Cunha
1950-52, and Permanent Sec., Min. of
Natural Resources (later Min. of Agric. and
Co-operative Development), Tanganyika
1958-61; Hon. Sec. British Ornithologists'
Union 1962-67, Vice-Pres. 1970-73, and
Chm. 1972-74; Editor and Special Con-
sultant for International Union for Conserva-
tion of Nature since 1970 (Sec.-Gen. 1964-66;
Liaison Officer in London 1961-70); Chevalier
of the Order of Golden Ark of Netherlands;
OBE (Civil) 1953: m. 1939, Elizabeth
Margaret, da. of the late A. G. Phillipson, of
N. Finchley, N12, and has issue.

Arms—Argent, on a chevron sable between three
bunches of grapes proper as many bezants. Crest—A
garb purpure charged with a fleur-de-lis or.

With others, for others.   *Residence*—173, Woodstock Road, Oxford.

Son living—CLIVE CHRISTOPHER HUGH, b. Aug. 12th, 1945; ed. at Bryanston, and Univ. Coll., Oxford (BA); DPhil; Research Officer, Cape Town Univ. since 1968: m. 1975, Marie Therese, da. of H. Ruttimann of Hohenrain, Switzerland.

Daughters living—Susan Elspeth, b. 1940: m. 1969, Maj. Timothy James Tedder, Gren. Gds. (c/o Westminster Bank, 46, Terminus Rd., Eastbourne), and has issue living, Zara Elizabeth, b. 1971,—Laura, b. 1974.——Judith Margery, b. 1942: m. 1968, Erik Geissler, DPhil, and has issue living, Beatrice Alison, b. 1974.

Brother living—Thomas Anthony Keith, CMG (c/o FCO, Downing St., SW1), b. 1921; ed. at Eton, and at Balliol Coll., Oxford (MA); formerly Capt. KSLI; entered Foreign Ser. 1947; 1st Sec., HM's Embassy, Peking 1957-59, and 1st Sec., Athens 1960; Counsellor Foreign Office, 1964; Polit. Adviser to Hong Kong Govt. 1965-68; Counsellor, Brit. Embassy, Wash. 1968-70, Min. 1970-72, since when Ambassador to Finland; CMG 1968: m. 1951, Alethea Helen, el. da. of the late Maj. Alistair B. H. Richardson, King's Dragoon Gds. [B. Hotham, colls.], and has issue living, Thomas Anthony William, b. 1959, Victoria Carey, b. 1952,—Catherine Frances, b. 1954,—Anne Louisa, b. 1956.

Sisters living—Anne Carey b. 1914; ed. at Lady Margaret Hall, Oxford (BA 1938): m. 1939, John Thomson, late Capt. RASC (The Knoll, Fulbrook, Burford, Oxon.), and has issue living, Robert Hugh Gordon b. 1947,—Andrew John, b. 1949,—Janet Carey, b. 1941: m. 1963, Keith Gilbert Robbins, and has issue living, Paul Gilbert John b. 1965, Daniel Henry Keith b. 1967, Adam Edward Ivo b. 1972, Lucy Helen b. 1970.——Pauline Margery, b. 1917; ARCM (Hon. Fellow 1972).

The 1st baronet, Sir Thomas Henry Elliott, K.C.B. (son of the late Thomas Henry Elliott, of Rue Ruhmkorff, Paris), was Sec. to Board of Agriculture and Fisheries 1892-1913, Dep. Master and Comptroller of the Mint, and *ex-officio* Engraver of H.M.'s Seals 1913-17. The 2nd baronet, Sir Ivo D'Oyly Elliott, was Under-Sec., Depart. of Commerce and Industry, Govt. of India 1916-19, Sec. to Govt. United Provinces, India 1926-31, and Financial Commr. Mauritius 1931.

Ellis-Griffith, see Griffith.

ELPHINSTON, Creation (N.S.) 1701, of Logie, co. Aberdeen.

Not by strength but by valour.

Sir JOHN ELPHINSTON OF GLACK, 11th *Baronet*
son of the late Thomas George ELPHINSTON, 2nd son
of *de jure* 9th baronet; b. Aug. 12th, 1924; s. his
uncle, *Maj. Sir* ALEXANDER LOGIE ELPHINSTONE,
1970 (petition to Court of Lord Lyon pending);
ed. at Repton, and Emmanuel Coll., Camb. (BA);
late Lt. RM; claimant to dormant Baronetcy
of Elphinstone (cr. 1628), and feudal Barony of
New Glasgow, Nova Scotia: m. 1953, Margaret
Doreen, da. of Edric Tasker, of Cheltenham, and
has issue.

Arms—Argent, on a chevron sable between three boars'
heads erased gules, armed and langued azure, an episcopal mitre of the first.
Crest—A dexter hand proper holding a garb or.

Residence—Pilgrims, Churchfields, Sandiway, Northwich
Cheshire.

Sons living—ALEXANDER, b. June 6th, 1955 ; ed. at Repton.——Charles, b. 1958; ed. at Repton, and St. John's Coll., Durham Univ.——Andrew James, b. 1961.——William Robert, b. 1963.

Sister living—Marjorie Mary, b. 1915: m. 1939, Maj.-Gen. Reginald Carteret de Mussenden Leathes, CB, MVO, OBE, RM, of Oaklands, Highbrook, Ardingly, Sussex, and has issue living, Rupert de Mussenden (146, Faversham Southill, Weymouth), b.1941: m.1967, Nicole Foucaud, and has issue living, Thomas de Mussenden b. 1970,—Simon William de Mussenden, b. 1948: m. 1971, Belinda Haire,—David Burlton de Mussenden, b. 1949, —Rosemary Sarah de Mussenden, b. 1944.

Aunt living—(daughter of *de jure*, 9th baronet)—Marjorie Rose: *m.* 1916, Lt.-Col. Charles Hector Congdon, late RM, who *d.* 1958, and has issue living, Timothy Colin Elphinston (c/o Brooke Bond & Co., Box 22, Mufindi, Tanzania), *b.* 1933; late Lt. RM: *m.* 1964, Edwina, da. of Col. W. E. B. Milner, late Indian Army, and has issue living, Simon Charles Elphinstone *b.* 1968, Rosemary Diana *b.* 1966,—Marjorie Jean *b.* 1917: *m.* 1940, Charles Owen Hilary Tripp, who *d.* (at sea at result of enemy action during 1939-45 War); 2ndly, 1947, Lt.-Col. Nigel Stanley Sykes, York and Lancaster Regt. of Rakes Holt, Cove, Tiverton, Devon [Blakiston, Bt., colls.], and has issue living, (by 2nd m.) Peter Samuel *b.* 1948, Colin Roland *b.* 1952, William George *b.* 1954, Daphne Hilda *b.* 1950,—Elizabeth Pamela (of Fairbrook Cottage, Faversham, Kent), *b.* 1919: *m.* 1940 (m. diss. 1950), Capt. John Lewis Jaquet, RM, and has issue living, Jeremy John Louis *b.* 1945, Pepita *b.* 1943, Cherry Virginia *b.* 1948,—Bridget Joy (8, Lansdowne Rd., Bedford), *b.* 1929; ed. at Camb. Univ. (MA: LRAM). *Residence*, 12, Shaftesbury Rd., Canterbury.

Widow living of 10th Baronet—MURIEL EILEEN (*Lady Elphinstone of Glack*) (Kingsway, 5, Bath Rd., Worthing), da. of the late John MacCornish, and widow of James Patterson Sayles: *m.* 1962, as his 2nd wife, Maj. Sir Alexander Logie Elphinstone of Glack, 10th Bt., who *d.* 1970.

Collateral Branches living.

Issue of the late John William Robert Elphinstone, 3rd son of *de jure* 9th baronet, *b.* 1884, *d.* 1949 : *m.* 1st, 1912, Vera Mary (who obtained a divorce 1924), da. of Lloyd W. Griffith, of Westbourne Mansions, Folkestone ; 2ndly, 1924, Bettine Ariana (who *d.* 1969, having obtained a divorce 1931), da. of Sir William Michael Curtis, 4th Bt. (*cr.* 1802); 3rdly, 1938, Edna M. Nethersole:—
(By 3rd m.) John Philip, *b.* 1940: *m.* 1967, Beverley Madge Fisher, and has issue living, Colin Edward, *b.* 1967,—Angela, *b.* 1971.

Issue of the late Lieut.-Col. Alexis ELPHINSTON, Argyll and Sutherland Highlanders (retired), son of *de jure* 8th baronet, *b.* 1873, *d.* 1958 : *m.* 1905, Ethel Margaret, who *d.* 1946, da. of Louis M. Cantloon, Bar.-at-law :—
Colin Anthony John, *b.* 1906: *m.* 1952, Mrs. Margaret Douglas Fisher, who *d.* 1971, da. of the late Frederick Ramsay Palmer.

On Nov. 30th, 1927, Alexander Logie Elphinstone (ante) proved his right (as 10th Bt.) to this Baronetcy (cr. with remainder to heirs-male whatsoever) before the Baronetage Committee of the Privy Council, being a direct descendant of Nicholas Elphinstone of Glack, a grandson of Sir Henry Elphinstone of Pittendreich (who *s.* to the Elphinstone estates in Stirlingshire 1435) [*see* B. Elphinstone], and cousin of Sir John Elphinstone, 4th Bt. of Logie, since whose death in 1743 the title had remained dormant.

ELPHINSTONE, Creation (U.K.) 1816, of Sowerby, Cumberland.

Always ready.

Sir (MAURICE) DOUGLAS WARBURTON ELPHINSTONE, *TD*, 5th *Baronet*, son of the late Rev. Canon Maurice Curteis Elphinstone, 4th son of 3rd Baronet; *b.* April 13th, 1909; *s.* his cousin, *Sir* HOWARD GRAHAM, 1975; ed. at Loretto, and Jesus Coll., Camb. (MA); Fellow Faculty of Actuaries, and FRSE; 1939-45 War as Maj. London Scottish: *m.* 1943, Barbara, da. of the late George Ramsay Main, of Kilmalcolm, and has issue.

Arms—Argent guttée de sang, on a chevron embattled sable between three boars' heads erased gules, two swords proper, pommels and hilts or. **Crest**—Out of a mural crown gules a demi-woman affrontée habited, and in the dexter hand a sword erect proper, pommel and hilt or, in the sinister an olive-branch vert.

Residence—South Park Lodge, South Park, Sevenoaks, TN13 1EL.

Son living—JOHN HOWARD MAIN, *b.* Feb. 25th, 1949; ed. at Loretto.

Daughter living—Janet Christine Helen, *b.* 1953; BA Manchester.

Brothers living—*Rev.* Kenneth John Tristram (3, Enterpen Hall, Hutton Rudby, Yarm, Cleveland. *Club*, Athenæum), *b.* 1911; ed. at Loretto, and at Jesus Coll., Camb. (MA); Bar. Inner Temple 1934, and Lincoln's Inn 1938; Chancellor of Diocese of Chester 1950, Hereford 1953, and York 1971; V. of Southstoke 1966-74, Vicar-Gen. of Province of York since 1972; formerly Capt. Rifle Brig.; 1939-42 War in Middle East (prisoner): *m.* 1938, Felicity, da. of the late Sir Gerald Berkeley Hurst, QC, and has issue living, Margaret Norah, *b.* 1948; BA Dunelm: *m.* 1969, John David Button, BA, M. Phil, of Compass House, Sandwich, Shetland, and has issue living, Rosalind Margaret *b.* 1972, Catherine Joanna *b.* 1974.——Rowland Henry, *MB* (of 48, York Hill, Loughton, Essex), *b.* 1915; ed. at Loretto, and at Jesus Coll., Camb. RNVR: *m.* 1954, Hester Bull, and has issue living, Henry Charles, *b.* 1958,—Mary Georgiana, *b.* 1955,—Constance Hester, *b.* 1957.

Sister living—Norah Christine, *MB, BS, DCH, FRCP(C)*: *m.* 1st, 1968, George Rex Renouf, who *d.* 1971; 2ndly, 19—, William Joseph Browne, PC, QC, of 97, Rennies Mill Rd., St. Johns, Newfoundland, A1B 2PI.

Daughters living of 4th Baronet—Elizabeth Mary, *b.* 1926: *m.* 1952, Cdr. Giles Anthony St. George Poole, RN (ret.), of Murrens, Reading Rd., Crownmarsh Gifford, Wallingford, Berks., and has issue living, Philip Anthony Howard, *b.* 1955,—Timothy Giles Elphinstone, *b.* 1956,—Rosalind Kate Elizabeth, *b.* 1961.——Rosalind Constance, *b.* 1930: *m.* 1950, Robert William Atherstone, and has issue living, Howard Ian Damant, *b.* 1954,—Anne Margaret Herschël, *b.* 1950,—Rosemary Jane Herschël, *b.* 1956,—Katherine Sarah Damant, *b.* 1961,—Audrey Patricia Damant (twin), *b.* 1961. *Address,* Bamburi, PO Box 975, Bindura, Rhosesia.

Sister living of 4th Baronet—Lucy Constance (8, Orchard Mount, Southampton Rd., Ringwood, Hants.), *b.* 1897.

Aunt living—(daughter of 3rd baronet)—Gladys Christine, *b.* 1884: *m.* 1913, the Rev. Harold Frederick Edward Wigram, who *d.* 1946 [*see* Wigram, Bt., colls.]. *Residence,* Helena House, Reading.

Widow living of 4th Baronet—ALICE MARY EMERTON (*Mary, Lady Elphinstone*) (Rectory Farm, Castle Bytham, Grantham, Lincs., NG33 4RJ), da. of Philip John Emerton Brown, of 58, Madeley Rd., Ealing, W5: *m.* 1924, Sir Howard Graham Elphinstone, 4th baronet, who *d.* 1975.

This branch of the Elphinstones descends from Réné de Elphinstone, probably a descendant of Jock Elphinstone, a Member of Scots Guard in France 1494. Réné came to Scotland with Robert Stewart, Earl of Orkney, and *d.* 1587. His yr. son Robert was page to Prince Henry, son of James VI whose gt. gt. grandson, John Elphinstone, was Capt. RN and Adm. Russian Navy. His 6th son, Sir Howard, was the first baronet. He was a distinguished Peninsular veteran, and Col. Comdt. RE, and greatly distinguished himself at the capture of the Cape of Good Hope, in Egypt, and elsewhere. Sir Howard, 2nd baronet, sat as MP for Hastings (L) 1835-7, and for Lewes 1841-7.

Elphinstone-Dalrymple, see Dalrymple.

ELTON, Creation (G.B.) 1717, of Bristol.

Sir CHARLES ABRAHAM GRIERSON ELTON, 11th *Baronet*; *b.* May 23rd, 1953; *s.* his father, *Sir* ARTHUR HALLAM RICE, 1973; ed. at Eton, and Reading Univ. *Residence*—Clevedon Court, Som.

Sisters living—Julia Margaret Hallam, *b.* 1949.——Rebecca Wiggin, *b.* 1951.
Widow living of 10th Baronet—MARGARET ANN (*Lady Elton*) (Clevedon Court, Som.); BA; da. of Olafur Bjornson, MD, FRCS, of Winnipeg, Canada: *m.* 1948, Sir Arthur Hallam Rice Elton, 10th Bt., who *d.* 1973.

Collateral Branches living.

Grandchildren of the late Rev. Henry George Tierney Elton, 5th son of 6th baronet :—
Issue of the late Charles Henry Elton, *b.* 1857, *d.* 1929 : *m.* 1st, 1879, Emily Grace, da. of the late Thomas Christmas, 8th Hussars; 2ndly, 1897 (divorce 1927), Edith May, da. of J. F. Ward, of Hallam House, Walmer, Port Elizabeth, S. Africa:—
(By 2nd m.) CHARLES TIERNEY HALLAM, *b.* 1898: *m.* 1924, Helen, who *d.* 1963, da. of the late Capt. Frederick Patrick Waud, Mercantile Marine, and has issue living, Heather Agnes Campbell, *b.* 1928.——Arthur Hallam (of 25, Sunny Rd., Glenhazel, Johannesburg, S. Africa), *b.* 1901: *m.* 1926, Georgina, who *d.* 1963, da. of the late A. W. Hemming, and has issue living, Anthony Charles Hallam, *b.* 1942,—Rosemary Patricia, *b.* 1930,—June Margaret, *b.* 1933.—— Kathleen Patricia Hallam Elton, *b.* 1908; has resumed the surname of Elton in lieu of that of Baker: *m.* 1940 (divorce 1947), Frank Baker. *Residence*, 58, Hurd St., Newton Park, Port Elizabeth, S. Africa.

Grandson of the late Edmund Hallam Elton (infra):—
Issue of the late Hallam Edmund Arthur Elton, *b.* 1898, *d.* 1963: *m.* 1930, Beryl, who *d.* 1966, da. of the late William Marwood-Elton (infra):—
Timothy Hallam (Thaba'Nchu, Box 1, Cashel, Rhodesia), *b.* 1933: *m.* 1964, Linda Susan, da. of George Richard Paton Pollitt, and has issue living, Simon Marwood Hallam, *b.* 1965,—Anthony Hallam, *b.* 1966,—Sarah Katherine, *b.* 1970,

Granddaughter of the late Rev. Henry George Tierney Elton, (ante):—
Issue of the late Edmund Hallam Elton, *b.* 1860, *d.* 1925: *m.* 1887, Ada Constance, da. of J. H. Webbe, of Crown Lands Depart., Cape Town :—
Lily Avice Hallam, *b.* 1896: *m.* 1st, 1934 (divorce 1946), L. J. Lake; 2ndly, 1968, Henry Adrian Harington, who *d.* 1969. *Address,* Apple, PO Magoebas Kloof, via Pietersburg, Transvaal S. Africa.

Granddaughter of the late Cdr. William Hallam Elton, 2nd son of the Rev. William Tierney Elton 3rd son of Isaac Elton (*b.* 1771), 2nd son of Isaac Elton (*b.* 1739), great-grandson of Jacob Elton, 3rd son of 1st baronet:—
Issue of the late Maurice Arthur Elton, *b.* 1868, *d.* 1943: *m.* 1898, Ellen Mary, da. of William Henry Laxton, of Dudley, Worcestershire:—
Violet Mary Agnes, *b.* 1907: *m.* 1931, Francis Martin Shirey, and has issue living, Richard Francis Elton (108, Howard St., Ashland, Va., USA), *b.* 1933; ed. at Coll. of William and Mary, Virginia (BA 1959); sometime in US Air Force: *m.* 1958, Sandra Andrews Berg, and has issue living, Frederick Elton, *b.* 1962, Mary Melissa *b.* 1960. *Residence,* Gloucester, Virginia, 23061, USA.

Grandchildren of the late Frederick Bayard Elton, son of Isaac Elton (*b.* 1771) (ante):—
Issue of the late Com. Frederick Elton, R.N., *b.* 1854, *d.* 1922: *m.* 1893, Ernestine, who *d.* 1951, da. of the late Ernest White, J.P., of Beaudesert Estates, Logan River, Queensland:—
Frederick Ernest Bayard (32, The Close, Harpenden, Herts., AL5 3NB), *b.* 1895; ed. at Radley; formerly Lieut. 3rd Batn. Welch Regt. (Special, Reserve): *m.* 1st, 1914, Dorothy (who obtained a divorce 1925), da. of Adm. Thomas Young Greet (ret.), of Horsham; 2ndly, 1925, Vera Ida (who obtained a divorce 1932), da. of Hugh Goldie, of Osborne Grange, Bournemouth; 3rdly, 1930, Katherine Mary, da. of Arthur Hamilton Hackett, and has issue living, (by 1st m.) Daphne (El Cipres, La Oratava, Santa Cruz de Teneriffe, Canary Islands), *b.* 1917: *m.* 1936, Derek Maxwell Sanderson [*see* Sanderson, Bt.],—Stephanie *b.* 1920: *m.* 1947, Eden James Hungerford Morgan, of Filham House, Ivybridge, S. Devon,—(by 3rd m.) John Arthur Bayard, *b.* 1940:

m. 1971, Jennifer Elizabeth, el. da. of William George Thomson, of 25, Mill Lane, Shoreham-by-Sea, and has issue living James Edmund Bayard *b.* 1972.——Cedric Edward Bayard (Bucklebury Place, Woolhampton, Berks.) *b.* 1904; Capt. Roy. Fusiliers: *m.* 1930, Barbara Mary Parrott, and has issue living, Nicholas Edward Bayard (22, Darlington Rd., Darlington, Perth, W. Aust. 6070), *b.* 1931: *m.* 1960, Eileen Dorothy, da. of Arthur Preece, of Ross-on-Wye, and has issue living, Patrick Edward Bayard *b.* 1966, Nicola Jane *b.* 1961.——Muriel Agnes (36, Mount Part Rd., Ealing Broadway, W5), *b.* 1897: *m.* 1st, 1921, Major Edward Darling, MC, RA, from whom she obtaind a divorce 1934; 2ndly, 1935, Wing-Com. Charles Lennox Gilbert RAF, who *d.* 1944, and has issue living, (by 1st m.) Fiona Muriel Ruth Elton, *b.* 1928,—(by 2nd m.) Dierdre Anne Elton, *b.* 1935.——Cynthia Ernestine (C1, Hatfield Court, Salisbury Rd., Hove), *b.* 1902: *m.* 1933, Hon. Mr. Justice Cecil Harry Andrew Bennett, CBE, who *d.* 1967, and has issue living, Timothy Dudley Elton, *b.* 1935,—Andrew Paul, *b.* 1939,—Felicia Marjorie, *b.* 1938.

Granddaughter of the late Col. Frederick Coulthurst Elton, CB, grandson of the late Jacob Elton, 3rd son of the late Isaac Elton (*b.* 1739) ante :—
Issue of the late Brig.-Gen. Frederick Algernon George Young Elton, late R.A., *b.* 1867, *d.* 1921 : *m.* 1902, Katherine Elizabeth who *d.* 1955, da. of the late Rev. Nesfield Andrewes, V. of Southwater, Sussex :—
Mary Katherine Gloria, *b.* 1904: *m.* 1920, Maj. Stanley George Reeves Elton Barratt, late 16th/5th Lancers (Reserve) (who assumed by Roy. Licence 1970 the additional surname of Elton before that of Barratt), son of the late Sir Albert Barratt, JP, and has issue living, John Charles Stanley ELTON BARRATT (Millfield Cottage, Bury Green, Little Hadham, Herts. *Club*, Special Forces), *b.* 1930; ed. at Harrow; late 12th R. Lancers; assumed by Roy. Licence 1970 the additional surname of Elton before that of Barratt: *m.* 1957, Olivia Golding Milward, only da. of Lt.-Col. C. W. M. Rogers, TD, of Coopers Farm House, Lawshall, Suffolk, and has issue living, Thomas George Sinclair *b.* 1964, Katherine Joanna Milward *b.* 1961,—Frederick James Young ELTON BARRATT (Home Farm, Swalcliffe, Banbury, Oxon.), *b.* 1934; ed. at Millfield; late Roy. Horse Gds.; assumed by Roy. Licence 1970 the additional surname of Elton before that of Barratt,—Gloria Anne Rosemary (Ballyrankin, Bunclody, co. Wexford), *b.* 1928: *m.* 1960, Cdr. Charles John Skrine, RN, who *d.* 1966, and has issue living, David Charles Sinclair, *b.* 1961, Susan Nesta Rosemary *b.* 1963. *Residence*, Blackwell Hall, Chesham, Bucks.

Grandson of the late William Warry Elton, grandson of Edward Elton, brother of Isaac Elton (*b.* 1739) (ante):—
Issue of the late Lieut.-Col. William MARWOOD-ELTON, *b.* 1865, *d.* 1931 (having assumed by deed poll 1910, the additional surname of Marwood): *m.* 1909, Juliet, who *d.* 1964, only child of Robert Spelman Marriott:—
Nigel William David, *D.F.C.*, *b.* 1911; Group Capt. (retired) R.A.F.; European War 1939-45 (despatches twice, D.F.C., prisoner): *m.* 1952, Daphne (LEE), da. of Gordon Richards, of Chiltern Court, NW3. *Residence*, Higher Penpoll, St. Veep, Lostwithiel, Cornwall. *Club*, Royal Ocean Racing.

The 1st and 2nd baronets were successively Mayors of Bristol, and each sat as M.P. for that City. The 7th baronet sat as M.P. for Bath (*L*) 1857-9, and the 8th was High Sheriff of Somerset 1895.

ERRINGTON, Creation (U.K.) 1963, of Ness, in co. Palatine of Chester.

Sir GEOFFREY FREDERICK ERRINGTON, 2nd *Baronet*; *b.* Feb. 15th, 1926; *s.* his father, *Sir* ERIC, 1973; ed. at Rugby, and New Coll., Oxford; Col. late King's Regt., AMBIM; GSO3 (Int.) HQ 11 Armd. Div. 1950-52, GSO3 (Int.) M13 (b) War Office 1955-57, Bde. Maj. 146 Inf. Bde. 1959-61, Coy. Comd. RMAS 1963-65, Mil. Assist. to Adjt.-Gen. 1965-67, CO 1st Bn. King's Regt. 1967-69, GSO1, 1 (BR) Corps 1969-71, and Col. GS HQ N-W Dist. 1971-74, since when Assist. Adjt.-Gen. M1 (MOD); Chm. Man. Cttee. Kings and Manchester Regt's. Assocn. since 1971: *m.* 1955, Diana Kathleen Forbes, da. of Edward Barry Davenport, of Edgbaston, and has issue.

Arms—Or an open book clasped on a chief azure a spur rowel upwards between two portcullises chained or. Crest—A liver bird supporting with the dexter claw an oak sapling proper.
Residence—Stone Hill Farm, Sellindge, nr. Ashford, Kent.

Sons living—ROBIN DAVENPORT, *b.* July 1st, 1957; ed. at Eton.——John Davenport, *b.* 1959; ed. at Eton.——Andrew Davenport (twin), *b.* 1959; ed. at Eton.

Brother living—Stuart Grant (Earleywood Lodge, Ascot, Berks.), *b.* 1929; ed. at Rugby, and Trin. Coll., Oxford (MA): JP of Cheshire: *m.* 1954, Anne, yr. da. of A. Eric Baedeker, of Edgbaston, and has issue living, David Grant, *b.* 1957; ed. at Rugby,—Charles Stuart, *b.* 1961; ed. at Rugby, —Elizabeth Anne, *b.* 1958.

Sister living—Anne Jacqueline, *b.* 1935; ed. at Wycombe Abbey; Community Relations Officer, RAF Bentwaters since 1964.

Sir Eric Errington, 1st Bt., was MP for Bootle (*C*) 1935-45 and Aldershot 1954-70.

ERSKINE, Creation (U.K.) 1821, of Cambo, Fife.

Watchful and valiant.

Sir (THOMAS) DAVID ERSKINE, 5th *Baronet; b.* July 31st, 1912 ; *s.* his father, *Lieut-Col. Sir* THOMAS WILFRED HARGREAVES JOHN, *D.S.O.*, 1944 ; ed. at Eton, and at Magdalene Coll., Camb. ; Maj. (ret.) Indian Corps of Engineers ; is a JP and DL for Co. Fife; Chm. Fife Co. Council 1970: *m.* 1947, Ann, da. of the late Lieut.-Col. Neil Fraser-Tytler, DSO, TD, and has issue.

Arms—Quarterly, 1st and 4th, gules, an imperial crown within a double tressure flory counter-flory or ; 2nd and 3rd, argent, a pale sable ; the whole within a bordure wavy ermine. **Crest**—On a garb fessewise or, banded azure, a cock wings elevated proper charged with a bendlet wavy sinister of the second.

Seat—Cambo House, Kingsbarns, Fife.

Sons living—THOMAS PETER NEIL, *b.* March 28th, 1950: *m.* 1972, Catherine, da. of Col. G. H. K. Hewlett.
——William, *b.* 1952: *m.* 1973, Sarah Jane McElroy, el. da. of Charles William McElroy Pratt, MD, of Orwell Grange, Orwell, Royston, Herts.
Daughter living—Caroline Sarah, *b.* 1948: *m.* 1974, E. C. H. Sharpe.
Sisters living—Diana Mildred, *b.* 1915: *m.* 1st, 1941, Major N. R. M. Skene, D.S.C., R.M., who *d.* (on active ser. during European War) 1942 ; 2ndly, 1945, David Grant Buxton, late Capt. Middlesex Regt., and has issue living, (by 2nd marriage) Andrew Ralph, *b.* 1947, —Lucinda Dierdre, *b.* 1945: *m.* 1973, Tudor Venn. *Residence*, Rectory Cottage, Shimpling, Diss, Norfolk.
——Victoria Margaret, *b.* 1919; formerly 2nd Officer WRNS. *Residence*, 79, Bolingbroke Grove, SW11.—Penelope Anne, *b.* 1920; formerly 3rd Officer WRNS: *m.* 1941, Lt.-Com. Peter Goldthorpe Sugden, DSC, RN, who *d.* (on active ser.) 1943, and has issue living, Paul Ralph, *b.* 1942; Maj. The Black Watch: *m.* 1966, Janet Mary Rumsey, of Beaminster, Dorset, and has issue living, Thomas Peter *b.* 1969, Caroline Anne *b.* 1968. *Residence*, Cambo House, Kingsbarns, Fife.——Constance Gertrude, *b.* 1921: *m.* 1942, Maj. Oliver Patch, DSO, DSC, RM, and has issue living, Janet Mary, *b.* 1945,—Olivia Cynthia, *b.* 1946: *m.* 1972, Dimitri Tiomkin, of Three Oaks, Courtenay Av., Highgate, N6,—Emily Dorothea, *b.* 1949,—Diana Elizabeth *b.* 1953,—Penelope Margaret Christian, *b.* 1957. *Residence*, Conduit, Barkers Hill, Semley, Shaftesbury, Dorset.——Harriet Katherine Lucinda, *b.* 1924: *m.* 1945, Lt.-Cdr. Hugh Doheny, Roy, Canadian Naval VR, and has issue living, Hugh Erskine, *b.* 1946,—Penelope Ann, *b.* 1949: *m.* 1972, Ronald Carter, of Brunwall, Norwich,—Kathleen Janet, *b.* 1951: *m.* 1972, Brian Hanna, Grandmere, Quebec,—Mary Harriet, *b.* 1952,—Lucinda Margaret Ruth, *b.* 1956,—Victoria Diana, *b.* 1960. *Residence*, Moulton Hill, Lennoxville, Quebec Province, Canada.

Collateral Branches living.

Grandson of the late Capt. David Holland Erskine, 2nd son of 1st baronet:—
Issue of the late Sir James Malcolm Monteith Erskine, *b.* 1863, *d.* 1944: *m.* 1898, Cicely Grace, who *d.* 1969, da. of the late Rev. Charles Penrose Quicke, R. of Ashbrittle, Som.:—
Sir Derek Quicke (PO Box 40132, Nairobi, Kenya), *b.* 1905 ; ed. at Eton, and at RMC; Maj. King's Dragoon Gds.; MLC Kenya 1948-51 and 1961-63; knt. 1964: *m.* 1927, Elisabeth Mary Stretton, da. of the late Maj. R. S. Spurrier, King's Dragoon Gds., and has issue living, Francis David Monteith, *MC* (Gilgil, Kenya), *b.* 1929; Kenya 1954 (MC): *m.* 1958 (m. diss. 1963), Marie-Claude Irene, da. of the late Roland M. A. Manage, of Kenya, and has issue living, Clive Patrick Monteith *b.* 1959, Guy Francis *b.* 1961,—Charles Malcolm, *b.* 1949,—Jane Petal, *b.* 1928: *m.* 1st, 1950 (m. diss. 1963), William Lee Harragin, son of the late Sir Walter Harragin, CMG, QC; 2ndly, 1963 (m. diss. 1972), Robert William Young; 3rdly, 1973, David Wanric Allen (PO Box 174, Nanyuki, Kenya), and has issue living, (by 1st m.) Mark Savile Austin *b.* 1956, Vanessa Jane *b.* 1951, Robin Elisabeth *b.* 1953, Georgia Frances *b.* 1954, Serena Claire *b.* 1959.

Grandchildren of the late Sir James Malcolm Monteith Erskine (ante):—
Issue of the late Denys Malcolm Erskine, *b.* 1903, *d.* 1966: *m.* 1923, Aleda Julia, who *d.* 1971, da. of E. C. Brownfield.:—
Denise Elizabeth Grace, *b.* 1924: *m.* 1st, 1949, Richard Pigott, from whom she obtained a divorce, 1965; 2ndly, 1966, John James Delaney, MC, of Hooklands, Scaynes Hill, Haywards Heath, Sussex.——Margaret Lucile, *b.* 1927: *m.* 1960, Anthony Colin Radclyffe, of 3, Rectory Close, St. Matthew's Rd., St. Leonards-on-Sea.
Issue of the late Keith David Erskine, *b.* 1907, *d.* 1974: *m.* 1st, 1936 (m. diss. 1940), Kathleen Diana, da. of C. W. Kayser, of Eaton Hall, Retford; 2ndly, 1944, Audrey Skinner (Beech Hurst, Waterhouse Lane, Kingswood, Surrey):—
(By 2nd m.) Simon David, *b.* 1953.——Sarah Gay, *b.* 1946: *m.* 1967, Alex Ryan, of Church Cottage, Church Lane, Bletchingley, Surrey, and has issue living, Robert Keith, *b.* 1973,—Audrey Mary, *b.* 1970.——Aleda Grace Elizabeth, *b.* 1948.——Fiona Margaret, *b.* 1949: *m.* 1971, Richard Mottram, of 8, Randolph Rd., Epsom, Surrey.——Deborah Mary, *b.* 1951: *m.* 1974, David Langford Holt, of Pixie, Sandy Lane, Kingswood, Surrey.——Kathrina Jane, *b.* 1956.
Issue of the late James Monteith Erskine (twin), *b.* 1907, *d.* 1965: *m.* 1931, Kathleen Brookes (6, Drake Court, Cranes Park Av., Surbiton, Surrey):—
David Monteith (58, Kingston Rd., E. Ewell, Surrey), *b.* 1933; ed. at Camb. Univ. (MA); Solicitor 1960: *m.* 1960, Tessa Victoria, da. of Dr. James Vernon, of Ascot, Berks, and has issue living, Dominic James Monteith, *b.* 1962,—Malcolm David Vernon, *b.* 1963,—Susan Eileen, *b.* 1970.——Shirley Monteith (twin), *b.* 1933; ed. at Camb. Univ. (BA): *m.* 1954, Barry Michael Clarke, of The Long House, Woodgreen, Hants., and has issue living, Thomas James Woodchurch, *b.* 1958,—Eleanor Margaret, *b.* 1962.

Grandchildren of the late Capt. David Holland Erskine (ante):—
Issue of the late David Wingfield Erskine, *b.* 1868, *d.* 1931: *m.* 1899, Emily Margarette, who *d.* 1904, da. of the late John Burden Blandy:—
Winifred, *b.* 1901: *m.* 1923, Col. Charles Maxwell Orr Sawers, OBE, Indian Cav., who *d.* 1968, and has issue living, David Maxwell, *b.* 1939,—Julia Anne, *b.* 1928: *m.* 1949, Martin Erskine Welford, and has issue living, Christopher Charles *b.* 1951, Stephen Maxwell *b.* 1956, Joanna Valerie *b.* 1953: *m.* 1974, David Charles Lewin. *Residence*, Buckburns, Brancepeth, co. Durham
Issue of the late Mary Silence Erskine, *d.* 1945 : *m.* 1889, John Milberne Leacock, who *d.* 1915:—

David John, *b.* 1890 ; ed. at Wellington Coll., and at Gonville and Caius Coll., Camb. (B.A. 1913): *m.* 1st, 1914, Jessie, who *d.* 1933, da. of John Charles Etchell ; 2ndly, 1934, Florence, da. of W. C. Church, and has issue living, (by 1st marriage) Philip David, *b.* 1917,—Richard, *b.* 1921,— Elizabeth, *b.* 1915,—Ursula, *b.* 1920,—(by 2nd marriage) Martha, *b.* 1939. *Residence*, Cazdar, Gran Canaria, Canary Is.——Edmund Erskine (PO Box 8, Quinto da Casa Brarrea, Funchal, Madeira), *b.* 1891; ed. at Wellington Coll.: *m.* 1st, 1916, Muriel Hobhouse, da. of Ernest Hebble-thwaite; 2ndly, 1939, Eileen Vina, da. of the late John Addie, and has issue living, (by 2nd m.) William Erskine, *b.* 1941; ed. at Harrow,—(by 1st m.) Mary Patricia Erskine (*Lady Rigby*), *b.* 1926: *m.* 1946, Sir (Hugh) John Macbeth Rigby, 2nd Bt., of Ridgehill, Sutton, Macclesfield, Ches.

Sir David Erskine, 1st Bt., was a natural grandson of 9th Earl of Kellie. The 4th baronet, Sir Thomas Wilfred Hargreaves John Erskine, D.S.O., was Lieut.-Col. Queen's Own Cameron Highlanders, and served during European War 1914-16 (D.S.O.).

Erskine-Hill, see Hill.

ESMONDE, Creation (I.) 1629, of Ballynastragh, Wexford.

Sir ANTHONY CHARLES ESMONDE, 15th *Baronet, b.* Jan. 18th, 1899 ; *s.* his brother, *Sir* JOHN LYMBRICK, 1958 ; L.R.C.S. and L.R.C.P. Ireland 1921 ; elected a Member of Dail Eireann 1951, and of Irish National Health Council 1956 ; has been a Member of the Committee of Agriculture, Council of Europe since 1954, and of Committee of Non-Represented Nations, Council of Europe since 1957; Knt. of Sovereign Mil. Order of Malta : *m.* 1927, Eithne Moira Grattan, da. of Sir Thomas Henry Grattan Esmonde, 11th Bt. (infra), and has issue.

Arms—Ermine, on a chief gules three mullets argent. **Crest**—Out of a mural crown a Saracen's head all proper.

Seat—Ballynastragh, Gorey, co. Wexford.

Had rather die than be dishonoured.

Sons living—JOHN HENRY GRATTAN, SC, *b.* June 27th, 1928 ; ed. at National Univ. of Ireland (B.Com. 1950); Bar. King's Inn, Dublin 1950; Senior Councellor 1971: *m.* 1957, Pamela Mary, el. da. of Francis Stephen Bourke, FRCPI, MRIA, and has issue living, Thomas Francis Grattan, *b.* 1960,—Harold William Grattan, *b.* 1964,—Richard Anthony Grattan, *b.* 1969,—Karen Maria Grattan, *b.* 1965,—Lisa Marion Grattan, *b.* 1968. *Residence*, 6, Nutley Av., Donnybrook, Dublin, 4.——Bartholomew Thomas Grattan, *b.* 1937.——Anthony James Grattan, *b.* 1943.

Daughters living—Alice Mary Grattan, *b.* 1929 ; ed. at National Univ. of Ireland (B.Sc. 1951),—— Eithne Marion Grattan, *b.* 1931 ; is a L.R.A.M.——Anne Caroline Grattan, *b.* 1940.

Half-Brothers living—Owen James (Cloneen, Glendalough, co. Wicklow; 5, Ijong St., Braddon, Canberra, ACT), *b.* 1905; ed. at Downside: *m.* 1938, Eira Margaret Antonia, da. of the late George Henry Louis Mackenzie [*see* Mackenzie, Bt., *cr.* 1673, colls.], and has issue living, Eugene Patrick Mackenzie (c/o 5, Ijong St., Braddon, ACT), *b.* 1942; ed. at Blackrock Coll., co. Dublin, and Christian Brothers, ACT; Capt. RAA,—Deborah Anne Barbara, *b.* 1939: *m.* 1968, Peter John Fraser Coutts, BEE, MSc, MA, PLD,—Gillian Mary Antonia, *b.* 1940: *m.* 1963, Colin Leslie Rosewarne, and has issue living, Andrew John *b.* 1964, Allison Mary *b.* 1966, Maria Patricia *b.* 1969,—Vivienne Mary Patricia, *b.* 1945: *m.* 1970, Charles Timothy Cresswell, of Cilwychfach, Bwlch, Brecon, Powys.,—Rosemary Carolyn, *b.* 1946: *m.* 1966, Capt. Robert Keith Peterswald, RAR, and has issue living, Charlotte Antonia *b.* 1968.——*Rev.* Donald, *b.* 1906; ed. at Downside; is a member of St. Joseph's, Foreign Missionary So., Mill Hill.——John Witham, *OBE, DSC, RN*, *b.* 1907; is Capt.; 1939-45 War (DSC, OBE); OBE (Mil.) 1943: *m.* 1940, Aileen, da. of Harold Harold-Barry, of Ballyvonare, co. Cork, and has issue living, Peter Witham, *b.* 1945,—Kevin Harold, *b.* 1948,—Helen Mary Karin, *b.* 1950.——James Bartholomew (twin), *b.* 1909; a MIMM. *Residence*, Cloneen, Glendalough, co. Wicklow.——Patrick MC (46, Alderney St., SW1), *b.* 1914; LRCP and LRCS Ireland; late Maj. RAMC; Colonial Med. Sers. 1945-63; 1939-45 War (MC): *m.* 1943, Norah Marcia, da. of William Cooper, of Malton, Yorks., and has issue living, Margaret Shane, *b.* 1944: *m.* 1966, Peter Alexander Henderson, Cheshire Regt., and has issue living, Dominic Patrick Alexander *b.* 1968, Oliver Thomas Alexander *b.* 1971,—Mary Grania, *b.* 1947: *m.* 1970, Denis Edward Chambers (PO Box 512, Johannesburg, S. Africa), and has issue living, Laragh Victoria *b.* 1971.

Half-Sister living—Mary Carmel. *b.* 1912: *m.* 1935, Dermot St. John Gogarty, Flying Officer R.A.F. Vol. Reserve, of Nairobi, Kenya, and has issue living, Michael Dermot St. John, *b.* 1936.

Daughters living of 11th Baronet—Patricia Alison Louisa Grattan, *b.* 1894 ; is a Lady of Order of the Holy Sepulchre : *m.* 1927, Rear-Adm. John Baptist Heffernan, U.S.A. Navy, and has issue living, *Rev.* Henry Grattan, S.J., *b.* 1930,—Patricia Grattan. *b.* 1929,—Eithne Mary Grattan. *b.* 1933: *m.* 1958, Thomas Michael Hartnett, and has issue living, Thomas Michael *b.* 1960, John Joseph *b.* 1963, Joseph Grattan *b.* 1970, Kathleen Frances *b.* 1959, Elizabeth Ann *b.* 1961, Eithne Grace *b.* 1964, Patricia Grattan *b.* 1967,—Kathleen Barbara Grattan, *b.* 1937: *m.* 1960, Raymond Joseph Wach, and has issue living, Raymond Penafort Edward *b.* 1961, Damian, Aquinas *b.* 1963, Kathleen Therese *b.* 1964, Marie Olukemi *b.* 1967. *Residence*, 3029, Que St., NW, Washington, DC 20007, USA.——Aingelda Barbara Mary Grattan, *b.* 1897. *Residence*, St. Thomas's, Dublin Rd., Arklow, co. Wicklow.——Eithne Moira Grattan (*Lady Esmonde*), *b.* 1902: *m.* 1927, Sir Anthony Charles Esmonde, 13th Bt. (ante).

Widow living of 14th Baronet—ELEANOR (*Eleanor, Lady Esmonde*), da. of the late Laurence Fitzharris, of Dublin : *m.* 1922, Sir John Lynbrick Esmonde, 14th baronet, who *d.* 1958. *Residence*, 37, Court Flats, Wilton Place, Dublin.

The Esmondes are descended from a family which was seated in co. Wexford, and one of whose members was Bishop of Ferns in 1340, and another Bishop of Emly 1356. In the reign of Elizabeth I. Sir Lawrence Esmond, abandoning the creed of his ancestors, espoused the cause of H.M., professed himself a Protestant, and was created Lord Esmonde. He married a Roman Catholic lady, one of the O'Flaherties of Connaught, by whom he had a son. The mother fearing that her child would be reared a Protestant, ran off with the boy, whom she brought up as a strict Catholic. By the statute of Kilkenny, the marriage was voidable in law. The son subsequently gained possession of the Wexford estate, and would probably have gained the peerage, but for the confusion wrought by civil war. He raised a troop of horse for the service of Charles I., and commanded a Regt. in the Duke of Buckingham's expedition to Rochelle, on his return from which he was created a baronet in his father's lifetime. The 9th baronet, the Right Hon. Sir Thomas, sat as M.P. for Wexford (L) 1841-7, and the 10th baronet sat as M.P. for Waterford (L) 1852-76. The 11th baronet Sir Thomas Henry Grattan (sometime a Chamberlain to Vatican Household), sat as M.P., for S. Div. of Dublin co. (N.) 1885-92, for W. Kerry Div. of co. Kerry 1892-1900, and for N. Wexford, Div. of Wexford co. 1900-18, and was a Senator of Irish Free State. The 12th baronet, Sir Osmond Thomas Grattan, was a Member of Parliament of Irish Free State 1923-7 and 1927-36. The 14th baronet, Sir John Lymbrick Esmonde, was a Bencher of King's Inns, Dublin, and Senior Counsel, and sat as M.P. for Tipperary, Co., N. Tipperary Div. (N) 1915-18. He was a Member of Dial Eireann 1937-44, and 1948-51.

ESPLEN, Creation (U.K.) 1921, of Hardres Court, Canterbury, Kent.

Be faithful.

Sir WILLIAM GRAHAM ESPLEN, 2nd *Baronet; b.* Dec. 29th, 1899; *s.* his father, *Sir* JOHN, *K.B.E.*, 1930; ed. at Harrow: *m.* 1928, (marriage dissolved 1951) Aline Octavia, da. of the late Octavius Hedley, and has issue.

Arms—Sable, on a pile between two mascles or, a lymphad of the field. Crest—In front of a demi-eagle displayed sable charged on each wing with a mascle as in the arms, an anchor fessewise or.

Residence—Heron Bridge, Newsham, Richmond, Yorkshire.

———

Son living—JOHN GRAHAM, *b.* Aug. 4th, 1932: *m.* 1956, Valerie Joan, younger da. of Maj.-Gen. Albert Percy Lambooy, C.B., O.B.E., and has issue living, William John Harry, *b.* 1967,—Wendy Anne, *b.* 1959,— Fiona Mary, *b.* 1960,—Mary Caroline, *b.* 1962. *Residence*, Orchards, W. Clandon, Surrey.

Sister living—Laura Ray (*Lady Hoare*): *m.* 1929, Sir Peter William Hoare, 7th Bt. (cr. 1786), who *d.* 1973. *Residence*, Luscombe Castle, Dawlish, Devon.

The 1st baronet, Sir John Esplen, K.B.E. (son of the late William Esplen, of The Willows, Blundellsands), was sometime Senior Director of Esplen, Sons and Swainston (Limited), consulting engineers and naval architects, and Ch. Technical Advisor to Min. of Shipping during European War 1914-18.

EVANS, Creation (U.K.) 1902, of Tubbendens, Farnborough, Kent. [Extinct 1970.]

Daughter living of 1st Baronet—Gwladys Marie de Grasse (c/o Messrs. Child & Co., 1, Fleet St., EC4), *b.* 1877; is a Dame of Grace of Order of St. John of Jerusalem, and has Order of Mercy: *m.* 1st, 1898, the Hon. Arthur Harold Webster, who *d.* 1902, only son of 1st Viscount Alverstone (ext.); 2ndly, 1905, Capt. Iain Ramsay, JP, Argyll and Sutherland Highlanders, who *d.* 1959.

EVANS, Creation (U.K.) 1920, of Wightwick, near Wolverhampton, co. Stafford.

With faith and virtue.

Sir ANTHONY ADNEY EVANS, 2nd *Baronet*, *b.* Aug. 5th, 1922; *s.* his father, *Sir* WALTER HARRY, 1954: *m.* 1948, Rita Beatrice, da. of Alfred David Kettle, of Souldern, Oxon.

Arms—Gyronny of eight gules and or, over all a lion passant, between two fleur-de-lis in pale sable. Crest—In front of a wall embattled and masoned proper, a lion as in the arms.

Address—c/o Nat. Westminster Bank, 103, Colmore Row, Birmingham, 3.

———

Sister living—Diana Gillian Mary (The White House, St. Paul's Alley, Malta, GC), *b.* 1926: *m.* 1st, 1948 (divorce 1954), Capt. John Richard Pugh, RA; 2ndly, 1959, Alan Joseph Webber, and has issue living, (by 1st m.) Vanessa Gillian WEBBER, *b.* 1950; adopted 1959 by her step-father whose surname she assumed,—(by 2nd m.) Daryl Adney, *b.* 1960.

The 1st baronet Sir Walter Harry Evans (son of the late Joseph Evans, JP, of The Lindens, Wolverhampton) was an hydraulic engineer, and a Co. Councillor for Staffordshire.

EVANS, Creation (U.K.) 1963, of Rottingdean, co. Sussex.

Sir (SIDNEY) HAROLD EVANS, *CMG, OBE*, 1st *Baronet*, son of the late Sidney M. Evans, of Mousehole, Cornwall; *b.* April 29th, 1911; ed. at King Edward's Sch., Stourbridge; Ch. Information Officer, Colonial Office 1953-57; Adviser on Public Relations to Prime Min. 1957-64, and Head of Information and Research, ITA 1964-66, since when Adviser on Public Relations to Vickers Board; a Member of Council of Inc. Soc. of British Advertisers since 1972; Chm. of Health Education Council since 1973; OBE (Civil) 1945, CMG 1957; *m.* 1945, Elizabeth, da. of William Jaffray, of Aberdeen, and has issue.

Arms—Gules two chevronels between in chief two suns in splendour, and in base a griffin serjeant or. Crest—A representation of the Rottingdean Windmill proper between two cogwheels sable.
Residence—3, Challoner's Close, Rottingdean, Sussex. *Address*—Vickers House, Millbank Tower, SW1.

___

Daughter living—Annabel Frances, *b.* 1956.

___

GWYNNE-EVANS, Creation (U.K.) 1913, of Oaklands Park, Awre, co. Gloucester.

Heb Elynion Heb Gymmeriad
Without enemies, without character.

Sir IAN WILLIAM GWYNNE-EVANS, 3rd *Baronet*; *b.* Feb. 21st, 1909; *s.* his father, *Sir* EVAN GWYNNE, 1959 : *m.* 1st, 1935, Elspeth, da. of the Rt. Hon. Sir Godfrey Pattison Collins, K.B.E., C.M.G., M.P. ; 2ndly, 1946, Monica Dalrymple, da. of Douglas Clinch, of Durban, and has issue.

Arms—Quarterly 1st and 4th per pale sable and gules, a fesse or, in chief a dagger erect within an annulet, both of the last, between two boars' heads couped argent and the like in base, *Evans*; 2nd and 3rd or, a lion rampant reguardant sable holding between the paws a fleur-de-lis azure, between in the sinister chief and dexter base a bugle horn stringed of the last, *Gwynne*. Crests—1st, on a rock proper a boar's head couped sable between two daggers erect or, *Evans*; and, between two branches of palm proper, a demi-lion sable collared or pierced by a sword in bend sinister point upwards also proper, holding between the paws a fleur-de-lis as in the arms, *Gwynne*.

Seat—Oaklands Park, Newnham, Gloucestershire. *Residence*—57, Eastwood Rd., Dunkeld, Johannesburg, S. Africa.

___

Daughters living—By 1st m.—Sylvia Ada, *b.* 1938: *m.* 1967, Duncan Godfrey Stableford Smith, of 1, Almond Way, Annaty Bank, Tokai, Cape Town, S. Africa.——Gwenllian Mary Hope, *b.* 1939: *m.* 1963, Robert Chumley Bryce Neill (PO Box 885, Johannesburg), and has issue living, Robert Ian Grant, *b.* 1965,—Angela Elspeth, *b.* 1970,—Belinda Gwen, *b.* 1973.

rother living—FRANCIS LORING, *b.* Feb. 22nd, 1914; assumed by deed poll 1943 the name of Francis Loring Gwynne Evans-Tipping in lieu of those of Francis Loring Gwynne-Evans and reverted to his patronymic by deed poll 1958 : *m.* 1st, 1937 (marriage dissolved 1958) Elisabeth Fforde, da. of J. Fforde-Tipping, of Bellurgan Park, Dundalk, Eire ; 2ndly, 1958 Gloria Marie Reynolds, and has issue living, (by 1st m.) David Gwynne, *b.* 1943,—Christopher Evan, *b.* 1946,—Carolyn Eve, *b.* 1947,—(by 2nd m.) Francis Tristan, *b.* 1960,—Teo Leslie, *b.* 1962,—Melody Louise Bernadette, *b.* 1958,—Clelia Marie, *b.* 1965,—Soraya Charlotte, *b.* 1967. *Residences*, Maywood, Wadhurst Park, Wadhurst, Sussex; The Hall Studio, 23B, Grove End Rd., NW8.

Uncle living (son of 1st baronet)—John (c/o Barclays Bank DCO, PO Box 1004, Johannesburg, S. Africa), *b.* 1910.

Aunt living (daughter of 1st baronet)—Bettina May GWYNNE-EVANS, *b.* 1912; resumed the surname of Gwynne-Evans in lieu of Przysiezny 1950: *m.* 1944 (m. diss. 1950), J. H. Przysiezny of Torun, Poland, and has issue living, Richard William, *b.* 1945. *Residence*, Flat 1, 24, Cottesmore Gdns., W8.

Widow living of 2nd Baronet—ADA JANE (*Ada, Lady Gwynne-Evans*), da. of the late Walter Scott Andrews of New York, U.S.A.; an O.St.J.: *m.* 1908, Sir Evan Gwynne Gwynne-Evans, 2nd baronet, who *d.* 1959. *Residence*, Oaklands Park, Newnham, Gloucestershire.

___

The 1st baronet, Sir William Gwynne-Evans (only son of Evan Evans, of Wain, Cardiganshire by Mary Gwynne, widow of Charles Gwynne Pryse, of Gogerddan, Cardiganshire), received Roy licence 1913, to continue to use the additional surname of Gwynne. Sir Evan Gwynne Gwynne, Evans, 2nd baronet, was High Sheriff of Gloucestershire 1943.

WORTHINGTON-EVANS, Creation (U.K.) 1916, of Colchester, Essex. [Extinct 1971.]

Sir (WILLIAM) SHIRLEY WORTHINGTON WORTHINGTON-EVANS, 2nd and last *Baronet.*

Daughters living of 2nd Baronet—Sarah, *b.* 1929: *m.* 1st, 1957 (m. diss. 1971), Wing Cdr. the Hon. Keith Alexander Henry Mason, DFC, (now 3rd Baron Blackford); 2ndly, 1972, Eric Ivor Hopton, of 37, Chesham Place, SW1.——Anne-Louise (Annielou) (*Baroness Jeffreys*) *b.* 1934: *m.* 1967, the 2nd Baron Jeffreys. *Residence*—Marden Grange, Devizes, Wilts.

Widow living of 2nd Baronet—HAZEL WELLS (*Lady Worthington-Evans*) (29, Eaton Sq., SW1), only da. of the late Fearnley Wells Owen: *m.* 1945, as his 2nd wife, Sir (William) Shirley Worthington-Evans, 2nd Bt., who *d.* 1971, when the title became ext.

EVERARD, Creation (U.K.) 1911, of Randlestown, co. Meath.

Virtue consists in action.

Sir NUGENT HENRY EVERARD, 3rd *Baronet*; *b.* Feb. 28th, 1905; *s.* his father, *Major Sir* RICHARD WILLIAM, July 1929; ed. at Harrow; Col. Duke of Wellington's Regt. (W.Riding): *m.* 1933, Frances Audrey, who *d.* 1975, da. of John C. Jesson, and has issue.

Arms—Argent, a fesse wavy between three estoile gules. **Crest**—A pelican in her piety proper.
Residence—

Son living—ROBIN CHARLES (Great House, Layer de la Haye, Colchester), *b.* Oct. 5th, 1939: *m.* 1963, Ariel Ingrid, el. da. of Col. Peter Cleasby-Thompson, MBE, MC, of Red House, West Tofts, Thetford, Norfolk, and has issue living, Henry Peter Charles, *b.* 1970,—Catherine Mary, *b.* 1964,—Victoria Frances, *b.* 1966.
Daughter living—Susan Louise, *b.* 1935: *m.* 1957, Capt. Henry George Dormer, R.A., and has issue living, Sara Louise, *b.* 1958,—Charlotte Rose, *b.* 1962. *Residence,*

Collateral Branch living.

Issue of the late Matthias Richard Everard, 2nd son of 2nd baronet, *b.* 1906, *d.* 1949 : *m* 1938, Maighréad Mary (now of White Mills, Castlebellingham, co. Louth), da. of Michael Joseph Macardle, of Miltown Grange, Castlebellingham:—
Patrick Michael, *b.* 1943: *m.* 1968, Felicity Anne Brigid, da. of Brig. Ralph Nevill Thicknesse, of The Old Farm House, Standon Manor, Hungerford, Berks.

Sir Nugent Talbot Everard, 1st Bt. (appointed High Sheriff of co. Meath 1883, and H.M.'s Lieut. 1906), was a Senator of the Irish Free State 1922-8, and *d.* July 11th, 1929. Major Sir Richard William Everard, 2nd Bt., *d.* July 22nd, 1929.

EVERY, Creation (E.) 1641, of Egginton, Derbyshire.

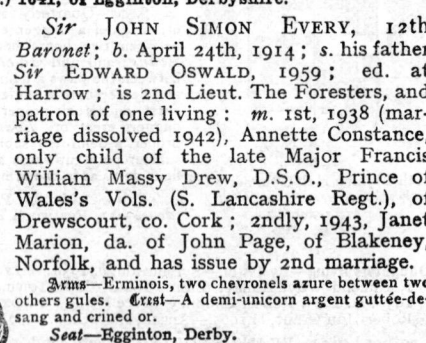

Every man to his own.

Sir JOHN SIMON EVERY, 12th *Baronet*; *b.* April 24th, 1914 ; *s.* his father *Sir* EDWARD OSWALD, 1959 ; ed. at Harrow ; is 2nd Lieut. The Foresters, and patron of one living : *m.* 1st, 1938 (marriage dissolved 1942), Annette Constance, only child of the late Major Francis William Massy Drew, D.S.O., Prince of Wales's Vols. (S. Lancashire Regt.), of Drewscourt, co. Cork ; 2ndly, 1943, Janet Marion, da. of John Page, of Blakeney, Norfolk, and has issue by 2nd marriage.

Arms—Erminois, two chevronels azure between two others gules. **Crest**—A demi-unicorn argent guttée-desang and crined or.
Seat—Egginton, Derby.

Son living—By 2nd marriage—HENRY JOHN MICHAEL, *b.* April 6th, 1947; ed. at Malvern: *m.* 1974, Susan, el. da. of Kenneth Beaton, of Eastshotte, Hartford, Hunts.
Daughters living—By 2nd marriage—Celia Jane, *b.* 1944: *m.* 1965, Nicholas Charles Harcourt Stephens of Harcourt Farm, PO Honeydew, Tvl., S. Africa, and has issue living, Jasper Roland Every, *b.* 1972,—Toby Oliver Every, *b.* 1974,—Candida Imogen Every, *b.* 1969.——Juliet Frances, *b.* 1945: *m.* 1964, John Coltman McCullagh, of The Corner House, Laleham, Middlesex, and has issue living, Andrew John, *b.* 1968,—Diana Mary, *b.* 1965.
Brother living—Charles Henry Sherard, *b.* 1916 ; ed. at Harrow: *m.* 1950 (marriage dissolved 1953), Deirdre Veronica, da. of the late Dr. du Toit, of Johannesburg, S. Africa, and has issue living, a da., *b.* 1950. *Residence,*
Sister living—Leila Penelope, *b.* 1911 : *m.* 1935, Capt. Vivian H. Ward, 5th Batn. Sherwood Foresters (T.A.), and has issue living, Peter Every, *b.* 1938,—Simon Charles Vivian, *b.* 1942. *Residence,* Long Meadow House, Little Cornard, Suffolk.

Great-Uncle living (son of 10th baronet)—Ernest Hollond, *b.* 1870: *m.* 1902, Beatrice May, who *d.* 1949, da. of the late Harvey Young, of Colorado Springs, U.S.A., and has issue living, Ernest Henry (of 14411, S. Biscayne River Drive, Miami, Florida, U.S.A.), *b.* 1906: *m.* 1949, Virginia Kelly,—Patricia, *b.* 1904: *m.* 1st, 1937, Friedrich Schiller, who *d.* 1947; 2ndly, 1952 (marriage dissolved 1956), Valentin Benedict, of West Palm Beach, Florida, U.S.A., and has issue living, (by 1st m.) Friedrich Every Herdern, *b.* 1940: *m.* 1962, Carol Ann Kendrick. *Club*, Boodle's.

Widow living of 11th Baronet—IVY LINTON (*Ivy, Lady Every*), da. of the late Major Alfred Meller, J.P. (formerly 3rd Batn. Norfolk Regt.), of The Limes, Rushmere, Ipswich [B. Sherard, colls.] : *m.* 1909, Sir Edward Oswald Every, 11th baronet, who *d.* 1959. *Residence*, Egginton, Derby.

Collateral Branches living.

Grandsons of the late Capt. Oswald W. Every (infra):—
Issue of the late Edward Every (*b.* 1865), three sons.
   Issue of the late Capt Oswald W. Every, 75th Regt., brother of 10th baronet, *b.* 1835, *d.* 1892: *m.* 1st, 1862, Cecilia Charlotte, who *d.* 1882, da. of the late Henry Charles Burney, LL.D., of Richmond Green, Surrey ; 2ndly, 1885, Florence Amy, da. of the late William Sherwin, of Fawsley, Torquay :—

(By 1st m.) Mabel (Beachlawn Nursing Home, Beachlawn Rd., Liverpool 22).——(by 2nd m.) Francis Flower (48, Millwey Av., Millwey Rise, Axminster, Devon), *b.* 1890: *m.* 1912, Mary Louisa, who *d.* 1965, da. of W. J. Murton, and has issue living, Christy Oswald (8, St. Davids Drive, Millwey Rise, Axminster, Devon), *b.* 1920: *m.* 1948, Winifred Jessie, 2nd. da. of L. Richards, and has issue living, Geoffrey Francis *b.* 1949: *m.* 1971, Rosemarie, da. of G. H. Plec Barnet, Stephen Victor *b.* 1950, Virginia Dawn *b.* 1953: *m.* 1972, Alan Colyton.

Grandchildren of the late Thomas Edward Every-Clayton, son of Lt.-Col. Edward Every-Clayton, 2nd son of 9th baronet:—
Issue of the late Edward Every Every-Clayton, *b.* 1867, *d.* 1936: *m.* 1st, 1892, Mary Fetherstonhaugh, who *d.* 1905, da. of Alexander Heylin, of Newcastle-upon-Tyne ; 2ndly, 1907, Emily May, da. of Arthur Edward Tooze, Bar.-at-law :—

(By 1st m.) Edward Arthur, *b.* 1899: a Purser in Merchant Ser.; European War (torpedoed, two medals, torpedo badge): *m.* 1926, Elsie, who *d.* 1968, da. of A. Ritchie Reid, of Waynflete, New Barnet, Herts. *Residence*, Hardwicks, Egginton, Derby.——Dorothy Mary, *b.* 1895.—— Edith Margaret, *b.* 1897.——Ruth Fetherstonhaugh, *b.* 1905.

Grandchildren of the late Leopold Ernest Valentine Every-Clayton, MD, FRCS (infra):—
Issue of the late Cecil Edward Every, *b.* 1901; relinquished the surname of Clayton 1937; *d.* 1974: *m.* 1927, Viola, who *d.* 1966, da. of the late Edward Ledger, of Hampstead, NW:—

Simon Flower (The White House, Crawley, Winchester), *b.* 1929: *m.* 1956, Diana Mary Jennifer, da. of the late Cdr. L. J. F. Howard-Mercer, RN (ret.), and has issue living, James Edward, *b.* 1961,—Jennifer Ann, *b.* 1958,—Frances Elizabeth, *b.* 1964.——Ann, *b.* 1933.

Grandchildren of the late Thomas Edward Every-Clayton (ante):—
Issue of the late Leopold Ernest Valentine Every-Clayton, M.D., F.R.C.S., *b* 1869, *d.* 1954 : *m.* 1898, Dorothy Anne Elizabeth, who *d.* 1954, da. of Edward Bennett, formerly of Marsden Hall, Lancashire :—

Marion, *b.* 1905. *Residence*,—Springvale, 6, Edward Rd., Clevedon, Som.
   Issue of the late George Frederick William Every-Clayton, *b.* 1871, *d* 1928 : *m.* 1st, 1892, Sarah, who *d.* 1912, da. of William Whittaker; 2ndly 1913, Evelyn May Yeates:—

Herbert Edward, *b.* 1892 : *m.* 1913, Gwendolin Cox, who *d.* 1931, and has issue living, Herbert Newbery, *b.* 1917,—Andrita Valentine, *b.* 1919 : *m.* 1938, William Kenneth Franklin, and has issue living, Daniel William *b.* 1941, Christine Louise *b.* 1939.——John Oswald, *D.S.C.*, *b.* 1898 ; ed. at Univ. Sch., Victoria, British Columbia ; is a Master Mariner ; European War 1914-19 (torpedoed, two medals), European War 1939-45 as Lieut. Canadian Navy Reserve and Capt. Merchant Navy (D.S.C. 1939-45 War Medal, Canadian Vol. Medal, Africa Star, Italy Star, Atlantic Star, 1939-45 Star): *m.* 1925, Marie, da. of William Lloyd, of Liverpool, and has issue living, George William, *b.* 1929 ; ed. at Canadian Public Schs., and at British Columbia Univ. : *m.* 1950, Margot, da. of William Forrest of Victoria, British Columbia.——Thomas Edgar *b.* 1899: *m.* 1943, Ellen May Hill, and has issue living, Wayne *b.* 1944, Frederick Harri, *b.* 1906: *m.* 1937, Ann Brown Morrison, and has issue living, Barbara Ann Gail, *b.* 1939: *m.* 19—, Donald Anderson, of Campbell River, British Columbia, and has issue living, Nancy Janet *b.* 1959, Cindy Donna *b.* 1962. *Residence*, Campbell River, British Columbia.——Arthur Eric Francis, *b.* 1910: *m.* 1948, Edna Beatrice Longley.——Beatrice Mary, *b.* 1895: *m.* 1932, David Erfyl-Evans, and has issue living, David Every, *b.* 1932, ed. at Qualicum Coll.: *m.* 1967, Caryl Margaret Anne, da. of W. F. Scott, of 84, Seventh Av., St. Lucia, Brisbane, Qld., and has issue living, Louise Every *b.* 1967, Georgina Dorothy *b.* 1969, Rosemary Scott *b.* 1971,—Norman Erfyl, *b.* 1932; ed. at Qualicum Coll.: *m.* 1964, Lillian Nora, da. of James Henry Nixon, of Powell River, B.C.—Patricia Mary, *b.* 1935,—Marjorie Erfyl, *b.* 1938: *m.* 1957, John Edward Redding Harris, of Montney, Fort St. John, B.C., and has issue living, John David *b.* 1958, Susan Katherine *b.* 1959, Deb rah Josephine *b.* 1962. *Residence*, Evan's Turkey Farm, R.R.2, Courtenay, Vancouver Island, British Columbia.——Penelope Maud Valentine, *b.* 1903: *m.* 1934, George Anderson Churchill-Emery, who *d.* 1941, and has issue living, Elizabeth Joy, *b.* 1937: *m.* 1955, Arthur Frederick Thompson, of Heriot Bay, British Columbia, and has issue living, Gordon Anthony *b.* 1958, Michael Arthur George *b.* 1959.——Edith Minnie, *b.* 1912: *m.* 1943, Norton Hopkins, who *d.* 1961. *Residence*, Fanny Bay P.O., Vancouver Island, British Columbia.

Granddaughter of the late Reginald Arthur Eric Every-Clayton (infra):—
Issue of the late John Arthur Every-Clayton, *b.* 1903, *d.* 1969: *m.* 1937, Martha Parker (210, West Main St., Danville, Indiana 46122):—

Margaret Lois, *b.* 1940 : *m.* 1959, Terry Lee Williams, attorney for Bank of America, of 29273, Sealion Place, Malibu, Cal., USA.

Grandchildren of the late Thomas Edward Every-Clayton (ante):—
Issue of the late Reginald Arthur Eric Every-Clayton, *b.* 1874, *d.* 1965: *m.* 1902, Fanny, who *d.* 1958, 3rd da. of William Wilding, of Bolton, Lancashire:—

William Wilding (of 51, Church Hill, Honiton, Devon), *b.* 1905: *m.* 1940, Joan Adelaide, da. of the late Ronald John Bennett, of Exeter, and has issue living, Henry John (31, Blackfriars Drive, Droitwich, Worcs.), *b.* 1941: *m.* 1963, Frances Anne Sangster, BA, of London, and has issue living, Catherine *b.* 1967, Tessa *b.* 1969,—Alan William (33, Clyst Valley Rd., Clyst St. Mary, Exeter), *b.* 1945: *m.* 1968, Myra Wynn Arthur, of Axminster, and has issue living, Richard William *b.* 1971,—Robert Edward *b.* 1948; BA,—David Stuart, *b.* 1955,—Pamela Nora Anne (twin), *b.* 1955.——Thomas Edward (of 13, Deanhill Rd., East Sheen, SW14), *b.* 1906: *m.* 1938, Irmgard Adele, da. of Arthur Jackel, of Tallin, Estonia, and has issue living, Glenn Thomas, *b.* 1941; ed. at Kingston Gram. Sch., and Christ's Coll., Camb. (BA); BD; ALBC: *m.* 1972, Winifred, el. da. of Hugh McKee, of Randalstown, co. Antrim,—Clive William (Rue des Ecoles

17, 1490, Court St. Etienne, Belgium), b. 1942; ed. at Kingston Gram. Sch., and London Bible
Coll. (BD, ALBC): m. 1971, Dorothy, da. of Archibald M. O. Dobbie, of Dalry, Ayrshire, and
has issue living, Esther Josette b. 1973.——George Herbert (617 S-W 21st Circle, Boynton Beach,
Florida 33435, USA), b. 1907: m. 1931, Jane Welsh, of New Brunswick, New Jersey, USA, and
has issue living, Donald George, (Zamora 107-6, Col. Condesa, Mexico 11, DF), b. 1935: m. 1957,
Celia Garcia y Garcia, of Mexico City, Mexico, and has issue living, Geoffrey, b. 1961, Lisa
b. 1959, Jennifer b. 1963, Noreen b. 1969,—Jon Arthur (438, Old Trail Rd., Baltimore, Maryland,
21212, USA), b. 1938; Capt. US Army; Viet Nam 1966-71; Bronze Star Medal for Valour (wounded): m. 1968, Janet T. Sabo, of Lakewood, New Jersey, and has issue living, Jon Ernest b. 1970,
Janina Theresa b. 1973,—June M., b. 1940: m. 1969, Daniel H. Young, and has issue living,
Jonathan Herbert b. 1970, Heather Jane b. 1972.

Granddaughters of the late Edward Every-Clayton (ante):—
Issue of the late Major Charles Edward EVERY-HALSTED, b. 1857, d. 1935 (having assumed
by Roy. licence 1886 the name of Every-Halsted in lieu of Every-Clayton): m. 1892, Lucy
Clara (who m. 2ndly, as his second wife, Thomas FitzRoy Phillipps Fenwick, who d.
1938 [Phillipps, Bt., colls.]), da. of the late Lieut.-Col. G. F. Dallas :—
Evelyn Stella, b. 1893: m. 1915, Major Arthur George Pardoe, late RE (TF), who d. 1951.——Mary
Ruth, b. 1898: m. 1st, 1919 (m. dissolved 1942), Capt. Gerald Hargreave Mawson, MC, RE;
2ndly, 1951, the Rev. Henry William John Lancelot Reed Haywood, who d. 1957, and has issue
living (by 1st marriage) John Arthur Hargreave b. 1923,—Charles Edward Hargreave, b. 1926,—
Mary Patricia Hargreave, b. 1920. _Residence,_

Sir Simon Every, 1st Bt., originally of Chardstock, Dorset (who m. Anne, da. and co-heir
Sir Henry Leigh, of Egginton, Derbyshire, and removed to that place), was a loyal supporter
Charles I. Sir John Every, 4th Bt., Capt. R.N., served in cause of William III with distinction.

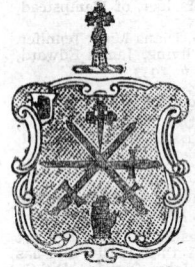

EWART, Creation (U.K.) 1887, of Glenmachan, Strandtown, co. Down, and of Glenbank, Belfast, co. Antrim.

Sir WILLIAM IVAN CECIL EWART, _DSC_, 6th _Baronet_,
son of the late Maj. William Basil Ewart, ygst. son of
the late Frederick William Ewart, 7th son of 1st baronet;
_b._ July 18th, 1919; _s._ his kinsman, _Sir_ TALBOT, 1959; ed.
at Radley; is a JP of co. Antrim, and Chm. of William
Ewart & Son, Ltd., of Belfast; 1939-45 War as Lt.
RNVR (prisoner, DSC): _m._ 1948, Pauline Chevallier,
who _d._ 1964, da. of Wing-Cdr. Raphael Chevallier Preston,
OBE, AFC, of Derry Hill, Ballydugan, Downpatrick,
co. Down, and has issue.

_Hrms—_Or, three swords crossed, two in saltire and one in fesse,
between in chief a cross-crosslet fitchée, and in base a dexter hand couped
at the wrist gules. _Crest—_A hand erect gauntleted proper, holding a
cross-crosslet fitchée gules.

In cruce spero.
In the cross I hope.

_Residence—_Woodlands, Ballynahinch, co. Down. _Clubs—_Ulster (Belfast), Naval.

Son living—WILLIAM MICHAEL, b. June 10th, 1953.

Daughters living—Susan Eveleen, b. 1950: m. 1973, Colin R. Cunningham.——Patricia Rébé,
b. 1951.

Sister living of 3rd Baronet—Mary Gundreda: m. 1927, Col. John Vincent Forrest, CB, CMG,
MB, Army Med. Ser. (ret.), who d. 1953, and has issue living, William Adrian John (14, Rath-
more Rd., Limavady, co. Londonderry) b. 1929; ed. at Wellington Coll., and at Queen's Coll.,
Camb. (BA 1952): m. 1957, Marjorie Ann, el. da. of the late Leslie Rolleston, of Leicester, and
has issue living, Humphrey James b. 1959, Josephine Lucy b. 1961, Isobel Mary b. 1962,—Rachel
Primrose, b. 1928: m. 1949, Capt. Oscar William James Henderson, formerly Irish Guards, of
Glenalmond, Strandtown, Belfast, and has issue living, Mary Gail b. 1950: m. 1971, Reginald
Alan Clarke, of 27, Marlborough Cres., Carryduff, Belfast, Jacqueline Kelso b. 1952, Penelope
Primrose b. 1956. _Residence,_ Glenmachan, Strandtown, Belfast.

Collateral Branches living
Issue of the late George Herbert Ewart, 6th son of 1st baronet. b. 1857, d. 1924:
m. 1886, Alice Flora, who d. 1945, ygst. da. of the late Richard Tipping
Hamilton, of Willowbank, Kingstown, Dublin:—
Frances Madeline, b. 1896: m. 1917, Paymaster Lt.-Com. Philip Smiles, RN (ret.), of 6, St. James
Av., Farnham, Surrey, GU9 9QF, and has issue living, Alan, b. 1924,—Roger Philip, b. 1927,—
Honor Madeleine,—Margaret.——Helen Flora (3, Church Av., Newtownabbey, co. Antrim), b.
1898: m. 1920, Lt.-Col. Louis Sydney Henshall, DSO, who d. 1957, and has issue living, Herbert
Ewart, b. 1923,—James Arthur, b. 1926,—Enid b. 1921.

Grandchildren of the late Frederick William Ewart, 7th son of 1st baronet:—
Issue of the late Maj. Gerald Valentine Ewart, OBE, DL, b. 1884, d. 1936: m. 1911,
Annie Ruth (Pearl) (of Clontagh House, Crossgar, co. Down), da. of the late Rev. T. R.
S. Collins, BD Chap. to the Archbishop of Dublin:—

Eileen Geraldine: m. 1939, Lieut-Com. George Lennox Cotton, DSC, RNVR, and has issue living,
Caroline Mourne Lennox, b. 1942.——Elizabeth Grania Lennox, b. 1944,—Kathleen Anne Lennox,
b. 1945. _Residence,_ Clontagh House, Crossgar, co. Down.

The 1st baronet, Sir William Ewart (son of the late William Ewart, of Glenbank, near Belfast),
was MP for Belfast (C) 1878-85, and for Belfast (N. Div.) 1885-89, and head of the firm of William
Ewart & Son, Ltd., of Belfast. The 2nd Baronet, Sir William Quartus, was head of the firm of
William Ewart & Son, Ltd. of Belfast, and a KStJ. The 3rd baronet, Sir Robert Heard, was a
Director of William Ewart & Son, Ltd., of Belfast.

ORR EWING, Creation (U.K.) 1886, of Ballikinrain, Stirlingshire, and Lennoxbank, co. Dunbarton.

Boldly.

Sir RONALD ARCHIBALD ORR EWING, 5th *Baronet; b.* May 14th, 1912; *s.* his father *Brig.-Gen. Sir* NORMAN ARCHIBALD ORR, *CB, DSO,* 1960; ed. at Eton; Maj. (ret.) Scots Guards; is a Member of Queen's Body Guard for Scotland (Roy. Co. of Archers), and a JP and a DL for Perthshire; 1939-45 War (prisoner): *m.* 1938, Marion Hester, da. of the late Col. Sir Donald Walter Cameron of Lochiel, KT, CMG [*see* D. Montrose], and has issue.

Arms—Argent, a chevron gules, issuant therefrom a banner of the second thereon in the first quarter the arms of St. Andrew—viz., azure a saltire argent; between in chief two mullets gules and in base the sun in its splendour, the whole within a bordure indented gules charged with three martlets argent, two in chief and one in base. Crest—A demi-lion rampant gules holding in its dexter paw a mullet as in the arms.

Seat—Cardross, Port of Menteith Station, near Stirling. *Clubs*—Army and Navy, New (Edinburgh).

Sons living—ARCHIBALD DONALD, (Camilty Mill, Harburn, West Calder, Midlothian; Brooks's Club), *b.* Dec. 20th, 1938; ed. at Gordonstoun, and at Trin-Coll., Dublin; a Member of Queen's Body Guard for Scotland (Roy. Co. of Archers): *m.* 1st, 1965 (m. diss. 1972), Venetia Elizabeth, da. of Maj. Richard Turner; 2ndly, 1972, Nicola Jean-Anne, da. of Reginald Baron Black, of Creagh Castle, Doneraile, co. Cork [*see* D. Roxburghe, colls.].——Ronald James, *b.* 1948; ed. at Gordonstoun, and Dundee Univ.; LLB St. Andrews.

Daughters living—Janet Elizabeth, *b.* 1940: *m.* 1969, John Malcolm Wallace, of The Furnace, Ashburnham, Battle, Sussex, and has issue living, Jasper Simon, *b.* 1973,—Jemma Louise, *b.* 1971.——Fiona Marion, *b.* 1946: *m.* 1968, Adrian Peter Drewe, of Mansfields Cross, Brays Hill, Ashburnham, Battle, Sussex, and has issue living, Jonathan James, *b.* 1971.

Brother living—Alan Lindsay *MC, b.* 1915; ed. at Eton, and at Edinburgh Univ. (BSc Forestry 1939); Master of Forestry, California Univ. 1952; PhD British Columbia Univ. 1956; is Forest Geneticist, British Columbia Forest Ser.; formerly 2nd Lieut. Argyll and Sutherland High-landers; 1939-40 War in France (twice wounded, despatches, MC, prisoner): *m.* 1945, Helen Isabelle, da. of the late William Evans, of Toronto, Canada, and has issue living, Alexander Evans, *b.* 1947: *m.* 1973, Louise Cantin, of Montreal, Canada,—Isobel Laura, *b.* 1954. *Residence,* 3220, Exeter Rd., Vic., BC.

Sister living—Jean Marjorie, *b.* 1918: *m.* 1941, Alexander Robert Webster, of 35, Broadway, New Germany, Natal, and has issue living, Robert Alexander, *b.* 1942,—Yvonne Jean, *b.* 1944.

Collateral Branches living.

Grandchildren of the late Capt. John Orr Ewing, 4th son of 1st baronet:—

Issue of the late Archibald Ian Orr Ewing, *b.* 1884, *d.* 1942: *m.* 1911, Gertrude Bertha, who *d.* 1974, da. of the late Charles Herman Runge, of Chilworthy House, Chard, Somerset:—

(Charles) Ian (*Baron Orr-Ewing*), *OBE, b.* 1912; *cr. a Baronet* 1963 *and Baron Orr-Ewing* 1971.—— Phoebe Gertrude, *b.* 1915.

Grandsons of the late Charles Lindsay Orr Ewing, MP (infra):—

Issue of the late Sir Ian Leslie Orr Ewing, M.P., *b.* 1893, *d.* 1958 : *m.* 1917, Helen Bridget, *M.B.E.* (of Adcombe Edge, Corfe, Taunton, Somerset), da. of the late Hon. Henry Lloyd Gibbs [*see* B. Aldenham, colls.] :—

Anthea Helen, *b.* 1917: *m.* 1938, Major Wilfrid Michael Fox, Coldstream Guards, of Thorn Falcon House, Taunton, Som., and has issue living, Charles St. Vigor (Longhill Farm, Cucklington, Win-canton, Som.), *b.* 1941: *m.* 1964, Charlotte Certhia, da. of Mervyn Jeffery Ingram, MB [see Ingram, Bt.], and has issue living, Laurence St. Vigor *b.* 1965, Nina Jane *b.* 1970,—Helen Mary *b.* 1939: *m.* 1962, Lt.-Col. Blair Aubyn Stewart-Wilson, Scots Gds., of 3, Browning Close, Ran-dolph Av., W9, and has issue living, Alice Helen *b.* 1963, Sophia Mary *b.* 1966, Belinda Anthea *b.* 1970.

Issue of the late Capt. David Orr Ewing, DSO, RN, *b.* 1900, *d.* 1964: *m.* 1930, Helen Mary Stuart (Dunskey, Portpatrick, Wigtownshire), da. of the late Benjamin Noaks, of Bloemfontein, S. Africa:—

Edward Stuart (Dunskey, Portpatrick, Stranraer, Wigtownshire), *b.* 1931; Maj. Black Watch (ret.); a DL of Wigtownshire: *m.* 1958, Fiona, yr. da. of Anthony Farquhar, of Hastingwood House, Harlow, Essex ,and has issue living, Alastair Lindsay, *b.* 1964,—Jane Helen *b.* 1961,—Victoria Susan, *b.* 1962.——Charles David (Torhousemuir, Wigtown, Wigtownshire), *b.* 1936; Lt.Cdr, RN: *m.* 1962, Bridget Juliet, da. of Sir Thomas Astley Woolaston White, 5th Bt. (*cr.* 1802), and has issue living, David Robert, *b.* 1964,—Robert Charles, *b.* 1966.

Issue (by 2nd marriage) of the late Charles Lindsay Orr Ewing, MP, 5th son of 1st baronet, *b.* 1860, *d.* 1903: *m.* 1st, 1888, the Hon. Beatrix Mary Leslie Hore-Ruthven, who *d.* 1930 (from whom he obtained a divorce 1894), da. of 8th Baron Ruthven; 2ndly, 1898, Lady Augusta Helen Elizabeth Boyle (who *d.* 1967, having *m.* 2ndly, 1914, the 1st Viscount Caldecote, who *d.* 1947), da. of 7th Earl of Glasgow:—

(By 2nd marriage) Barbara Dorothea, *b.* 1902: *m.* 1931, Lt.-Cdr. William Edmund Halsey, RN (ret.), of The Knowe, Skelmorlie, Ayrshire [*see* Halsey, Bt.].

Sir Archibald Orr Ewing (7th son of the late William Ewing, of Ardvullen House, Argyllshire, a merchant of Glasgow, and his wife Susan, da. of John Orr, Provost of Paisley), 1st baronet, Dean of Faculties in Glasgow Univ., and an Ensign-Gen. in Roy. Co. of Archers (H.M.'s Body Guard for Scotland) ; M.P. for Dunbartonshire (C) 1868-92. Sir William, 2nd Bt., was a Member of Queen's Body Guard for Scotland (Roy. Co. of Archers). Brig.-Gen. Sir Norman Archibald Orr Ewing, 4th Bt., was a Lieut. Queen's Body Guard for Scotland (Roy. Co. of Archers) and was Hon. Col., 7th Bn. Argyll and Sutherland Highlanders 1932-48.

FAGGE, Creation (E.) 1660, of Wiston, Sussex.

Sir JOHN WILLIAM FREDERICK FAGGE 11th *Baronet*, son of the late William Archibald Theodore Fagge, 4th son of 8th Baronet; *b.* Sept. 25th, 1910; *s.* his uncle, *Sir* JOHN HARRY LEE, 1940; is a Farmer: *m.* 1940, Ivy Gertrude, da. of William Edward Frier, of 15, Church Lane, Newington, Kent, and has issue.

Arms—Gules, two bends vaire. **Crest**—An ostrich with wings expanded argent, beaked, legged and ducally gorged or, holding in the beak a horseshoe proper.

Residence—26, The Mall, Faversham, Kent.

Son living—JOHN CHRISTOPHER, *b.* April 30th, 1942.

Daughter living—Pauline Joy, *b.* 1943.

Sister living—Gwendoline Beatrice May, *b.* 1914.

Daughter living of 10th Baronet—Lucy Harriet Gertrude, *b.* 1913. *Residence*, Boston, U.S.A.

Collateral Branch living.

Safe if upright.

Granddaughter of the late Rev. John Frederick Fagge, 4th son of 6th baronet:—

Issue of the late Sarah Elizabeth Fagge, *d.* 1946 : *m.* 1889, George Goldie, J.P., who *d.* 1904 :—

Ethelreda Marie Teresa, *b.* 1899: *m.* 1936, Lawrence Henry Shattock, FRIBA (Knight of St. Gregory). *Residence*, Little Wiston, Crescent Rd., Wimbledon, SW20.

The 1st baronet, Sir John Fagge (son of the late John Fagge, of Brensett, Kent), sat as M.P. for Rye 1645-53, and for Sussex 1654-9 and 1681-5, and for Steyning 1660-81 and 1685-1701, and was a Col. in Parliamentary Army. He purchased the estate of Wiston, Sussex, from Dr. Thomas Shirley, which passed from Sir Robert Fagge, 4th Bt. to his sister Elizabeth was *m.* 1743, Sir Charles Goring, 5th Bt.

FAIRBAIRN, Creation (U.K. 1869), of Ardwick, Lancashire.

Always the same.

Sir (JAMES) BROOKE FAIRBAIRN, 6th *Baronet*; *b.* Dec. 10th, 1930; *s.* his father, *Sir* WILLIAM ALBERT, 1972; ed. at Stowe: *m.* 1960, Mary Russell, only da. of William Russell Scott, MB, ChB, FFARCS, of 59, Wyke Rd., Weymouth, and has issue.

Arms—Argent, on a chevron between three boars' heads couped gules three bezants. **Crest**—The sun in his meridian splendour or.

Residence—9, High St., Barkway, Royston, Herts.

Sons living—ROBERT WILLIAM, *b.* April 10th, 1965. ——George Edward, *b.* 1969.

Daughter living—Fiona Mary, *b.* 1967.

Brother living—William Andrew (Midway Cottage, Norton, nr. Chichester), *b.* 1934; ed. at Stowe; FCA: *m.* 1961, Elspeth Alison, only da. of the late Robert Hally, of Brookfield, Barnham, Sussex, and has issue living, James Andrew, *b.* 1967,—Nicola Christine, *b.* 1962,—Katharine Alison, *b.* 1964.

Sister living—Angela Christine *b.* 1940: *m.* 1965, Brooke Elliot Mackelcan Johns, FCA, of Lynch Lodge, Lynch Lane, Kensworth, Beds., and has issue living, Jeremy Elliot Mackelcan, *b.* 1967,—Anthony Patrick Mackelcan *b.* 1971.

Aunts living (daughters of 4th baronet)—Violet Edith *b.* 1883.——Mildred Dorothy, *b.* 1903.——Rosalind Gordon, *b.* 1905.——Constance Matilda, *b.* 1908.

Widow living of 5th Baronet—CHRISTINE RENEE COTTON (*Christine, Lady Fairbairn*), (Loom House, Radlett, Herts.) da. of the late Rev. Canon Robert William Croft, V. of Kelvedon, Essex: *m.* 1925, Sir William Albert Fairbairn, 5th baronet who *d.* 1972.

Collateral Branches living.

Issue of the late Reginald Fairbairn, 3rd son of 2nd baronet, *b.* 1856, *d.* 1921: *m.* 1880, May Elizabeth, da. of J. F. Holt:—

Ada, *b.* 1882. *Residence*,

Grandchildren of the late Rev. William Murray Fairbairn, son of the late William Andrew Fairbairn (infra) :—

Issue of the late Vice-Adm. Bernard William Murray Fairbairn, C.B.E., *b.* 1880, *d.* 1960, *m.* 1905, Alice Mary, who *d.* 1970, only da. of the late William Phillipps, of Leigham Villas, Plymouth:—

Alan Bernard Murray (Watchers Lodge, Linchmere Rd., Haslemere, Surrey), *b.* 1906; ed. at Sherborne; Cdr. RN (ret.): 1939-45 War (despatches): *m.* 1943, Adeline Hilda, da. of Lt.-Col. Edward Herbert Sweet, CMG, DSO, and has issue living, John Alan, *b.* 1946; ed. at Wellington, and Trin. Coll., Camb. (MA).——David Patrick, *b.* 1919; ed. at Sherborne; C.Eng., MIMechE, MIMarE; Lt.-Cdr. RN (ret.); with Mirlees Blackstone Ltd., of Stamford: *m.* 1950, Margaret Winifred Ferrers (formerly 2nd Officer WRNS), da. of Ronald Ernest Ferrers Courage, of Redcross Dulverton, and has issue living, William David Murray, *b.* 1953; ed. at Radley, and Magdalene Coll. Camb.; Sub-Lt. RN,—Anne Mary, *b.* 1951. *Residence*, The Firs, Ryhall, Stamford,

Lincolnshire.——Betty Rosemary Alice, b. 1913: m. 1st, 1937, Capt. Colin Gordon Irving Bell, R. Norfolk Regt., from whom she obtained a divorce 1948; 2ndly, 1974, the Rev. Julian Lloyd, of Maycroft, 48, Clarence Hill, Dartmouth, Devon), and has issue living, (by 1st m.) Raymond Gordon (Fincal os Andes, Guatalon, Guatemala), b. 1944; formerly RN,—Angela Rosemary, b. 1940: m. 1964, Colin John Bruce Campbell, RM (c/o Clydesdale Bank, 30, Lombard St., EC3), and has issue living, Shuna Catherine Islay b. 1965, Fiona Jane Alison b. 1967.

Issue of the late Aubrey John Murray Fairbairn, b. 1888, d. 1961: m. 1920, Adela, da. of the late Col. T. A. Rawlins, of Clifton, Bristol, and Berrow, Somerset:—
Ian Aubrey, b. 1927. Residence,

Grandsons of the late William Andrew Fairbairn, 4th son of 1st baronet :—

Issue of the late Edward Percy Fairbairn, b. 1866, d. 1931: m. 1st, 1894, Mary, who d. 1903, da. of the late John Sholto Douglas, of Tilquhillie, Kincardineshire; 2ndly, 1908, Constance, who d. 1952, da. of William Gaven Eden [B. Henley, colls.] :—
(By 2nd marriage) George William, b. 1911; formerly Capt. R.E.; is an A.R.I.B.A.: m. 1940, Katherine Elizabeth, da. of the late Dr. William Deane, of Waddington, Lincoln, and has issue living, Jacqueline Elizabeth, b. 1948. Residence, Swallow House, Canwick, Lincoln.——Patrick Yelverton (Annagh, The Warren, Mayfield, Sussex), b. 1913; ed. at Charterhouse: m. 1940, Dorothy Mary, da. of the late Lewis Henshaw, OBE, of Madras, and has issue living, Edward James, b. 1950: m. 1974, Fiona Catherine, da. of Maj. M. C. Gray, of Steep, Hants.,—Judith Constance, b. 1946: m. 1970, Keith Anthony Delgardo Hornby, barrister, and has issue living, Katya Eugenie b. 1974.

Grandsons of the late Rev. Adam Henderson Fairbairn, 7th son of 1st baronet :—

Issue of the late William Fairbairn, b. 1869, d. 1930: m. 1907, Mary Louisa Henrietta, who d. 1935, da. of the late William F. Swindell, of Melyniog Hall, Salop :—
William Alan Thomas, T.D., b. 1908; ed. at Uppingham, and at Trin. Coll., Camb. ; Major late R. Hampshire Regt.; 1939-45 War (despatches); received Freedom of Alost, Belgium 1945: m. 1944, Marian Ruth, da. of the late Capt. W. T. Wyllie, and has issue living, Stephen Alan ('Alfhólsvegur 87, Kópavogur, Iceland), b. 1947; ed. at Radley: m. 1970, Margrét Jóelsdóttir, and has issue living, Hilda, b. 1973,—Susan Mary, b. 1953; ed. at Stonar: m. 1974, Richard Ivor Sommerin, and has issue living, James Adrian b. 1974. Residence, Beauchamps, Milford-on-Sea, Hants.

Issue of the late Major David Alexander Fairbairn, O.B.E., Duke of Wellington's (W. Riding) Regt., b. 1882, d. 1950: m. 1920, Emmeline Mary, who d. 1964, da. of the late Alfred Coxon, of Surbiton, and widow of Capt. T. A. Abbott, R.F.A.:—

Norman David Nigel, b. 1921; ed. at Wellington Coll., and at Cape Town Univ. (B.A. 1950); is an A.R.I.B.A., and a M.I.A.; European War 1939-45, with R.A. and 17th/21st Lancers: m. 1951, Mary Josephine, da. of Hector Hillaby, Bar.-at-law, and has issue living, Jonathan David, b. 1952,—Mark Benson Hector, b. 1960,—Carol Evangeline Mary, b. 1954,—Alexandra Josephine Margaret, b. 1957.

Sir William Fairbairn, 1st Bt., el. surviving son of Andrew Fairbairn of Smailholm, Roxburghshire, was a celebrated engineer who was associated with Stephenson in erecting the tubular bridge across the Menai Straits 1848. He was a founder of the British Assocn. for the Advancement of Science.

Fairfax (Ramsay-Fairfax-Lucy), see Lucy.

Fairlie-Cuninghame, see Cuninghame.

FALKINER, Creation (I.) 1778, of Annemount, Cork.

[Name pronounced "Fawkner."]

Sir TERENCE EDMOND PATRICK FALKINER, 8th *Baronet ; b.* March 17th, 1903 ; *s.* his father, *Sir* LESLIE EDMUND PERCY RIGGS, 1917; Lieut.-Col. (ret.) Coldstream Guards, a DL for Herefords., and a KStJ; 1939-45 War (wounded): *m.* 1925, Mildred Katharine, da. of Sir John Richard Geers Cotterell, 4th Bt., and has issue.
Arms—Or, three falcons close proper, belled gules. Crest—A falcon's lure proper, between two wings azure.
Residence—Kingsthorne House, Hereford.

Sons living—EDMOND CHARLES, b. June 24th, 1938: m. 1960, Janet Iris, da. of Arthur Edward Bruce Darby, of The Park, Stoke Lacey, Bromyard, Herefordshire, and has issue living, Benjamin Simon, b. 1962,—Matthew Terence, b. 1964. Residence, 37, Salisbury Rd., Barnet, Herts.—— Henry Leslie Basil (Dormer Cottage, Frensham, Surrey), b. 1940: m. 1967, Angela, da. of Peter Wolfe-Taylor, of Chimneys, Ockham, Surrey, and has issue living, Tobias Peter Riggs, b. 1972,—Max Henry Wolfe, b. 1974.
Daughters living—Elizabeth Anne Thérèse, b. 1929 : m. 1956, Michael David Hogg [see Hogg, Bt. colls.]. Residence, 19, Woodlands Road, S.W.13.——Mar; Clare, b. 1934 : m. 1956, Noel John Taylor, and has issue living, Paul John, b. 1957,— Mark Robert, b. 1965,—David James, b. 1969,—Jane Clare, b. 1961,—Sarah Kate, b. 1971. Residence, Citterdine Mordiford, Hereford.——Veronica Cicely, b. 1935: m. 1956, William David Brown, of Pear Tree Cottage, Upper Oddington, Stow-on-the-Wold, and has issue living, Adrian William, b. 1958,—Edward David, b. 1960,—Rupert Duncan, b. 1963,— Dominic George Andrew, b. 1966.
Brother living—Gervase Leslie, b. 1909; formerly Maj. Coldm. Gds.; 1939-45 War (wounded): m. 1934, Rosemary Hastings, da. of Herbert Smith, of Tower, Mold, Flintshire, and has issue living, Richard Gervase (15, Yarrell Mansions, Queens

Club Gdns., W.14), b. 1936: m. 1959, Gabrielle Mary, only da. of Frank Woodgate, of Ledley House, Ebrington, Chipping Campden, Gloucestershire, and has issue living, Sebastian b. 1963, Sophia Mary b. 1962,—Michael George Patrick (Globemon Hall, Ferns, co. Wexford), b. 1940: m. 1970, Joanna Rosamond, el. da. of Walter Peter Baxter [see V. Hawarden], and has issue living, Caroline Helen b. 1972, Emily Rosemary b. 1974.

Sister living—Naomi Elaine Mary, b. 1905 ; is a Nun. *Address*, Convent of the Holy Sepulchre, New Hall, Chelmsford, CM3 3HT, Essex.

Sir Riggs Falkiner, MP, 1st Bt. of Annemount, co. Cork, was great-grandson of Michael Falkiner of Brigart, Leeds, who settled in Ireland about 1651. Sir Charles Leslie Falkiner, 4th Bt., was Capt. R.N., and as Lieut. in 1810 headed the "Shannon" main deck boarders at capture of American ship "Chesapeake" (promoted Com.). His brother, Lt.-Col. Sir Samuel Edmund Falkiner, 5th Bt., served throughout the Peninsular war, was present at Talavera, Busaco, Salamanca, Ciudad Rodrigo, Fuentes d'Onore, and was wounded three times.

FARQUHAR, Creation (G.B.) 1796, of Cadogan House, Middlesex.
[Name pronounced "**Farkwer**."]

By mind and hand.

Sir PETER WALTER FARQUHAR, *D.S.O.*, 6th *Baronet*; b. Oct. 8th, 1904; s. his father, *Capt. Sir* WALTER RANDOLPH FITZROY, 1918; ed. at Eton; is Lieut.-Col. 16th/5th Lancers (commanded 3rd Hussars 1942-4), and a J.P. for Dorset; European War 1939-44 in France, Middle East and Italy (twice wounded, D.S.O. and Bar); D.S.O. 1943 (Bar 1944): m. 1937, Elizabeth Evelyn (Mrs. Andrew Knowles), da. of the late Francis Cecil Albert Hurt, of Alderwasley, near Derby, and has issue.

Arms—Argent, a lion rampant sable between two sinister hands apaumée couped in chief gules, and a crescent in base azure. **Crest**—An eagle rising proper.
Residence—West Kington House, Chippenham, Wilts. *Club*—White's.

Sons living—MICHAEL FITZROY HENRY, b. June 29th, 1938: m. 1963, Veronica Geraldine, el. da. of Patrick Hornidge, of Newton Ferrers, S. Devon, and has issue living, Charles Walter Fitzroy, b. 1964,—Edward Peter Henry, b. 1966. *Residence*, Home Close Farm, Burford, Oxon.——Anthony Charles (Harford Farm House, Naunton, Glos.), b. 1942: m. 1969, Elizabeth Jane, da. of Col. T. M. Braithwaite, of Burghope, Winsley, Bradford-on-Avon, and has issue living, Alexandra Elizabeth, b. 1971,—Annabelle Jean, b. 1973.——Ian Walter, *MVO* (The Kennels, Stratton Audley, Bicester, Oxon.), b. 1945; Capt. Queen's Own Hussars; MVO 1972: m. 1972, Pamela Jane, da. of Charles L. Chafer, of Kirkgate Lodge, Sawdon, Scarborough, Yorks.

Brother living—Charles Richard, *M.C.*, b. 1906; ed. at Eton; is Lieut.-Col. Staffordshire Yeo.; European War 1939-43 (M.C. and Bar): m. 1939, Dorothy Nancy, da. of Major James Gerald Thewlis Johnson, D.S.O. [Alleyne, Bt.], and has issue living, Daphne Violet, b. 1945,—Angela Dorothy, b. 1948. *Residence*, Cubley Lodge, Cubley, Derbyshire.

Sister living—Ruth Violet Mary (*Baroness Dulverton*), b. 1910: m. 1st, 1932 (marriage dissolved 1961), Major Richard Gennys Fanshawe, 16th/5th Lancers, son of Lieut.-Gen. Sir Edward Arthur Fanshawe, KCB; 2ndly, 1962, the 2nd Baron Dulverton, and has issue living, (by 1st m.) David Valentine (c/o Coutts Bank, 440, Strand, WC2), b. 1933; Lt.Col. Gren. Gds.: m. 1963, Sheila Christine, el. da. of Maj.-Gen. John Malcolm McNeill, CB, CBE, and has issue living, Angus Edward b. 1965, Robert Leighton b. 1967, William David b. 1971,—Brian Edward (Ballymore House, Craughwell, co. Galway), b. 1936; Capt. 9th/12th R. Lancers: m. 1960, Elizabeth, da. of Geoffrey Pugh, of Temple Guiting House, Glos., and has issue living, James Robert b. 1961, Anthony Geoffrey b. 1954, Sarah Rose b. 1967. *Residences*, Batsford Park, Moreton-in-Marsh, Glos.; Fassfern, Fort William, Inverness-shire.

Collateral Branches living.

Issue of the late Col. Francis Douglas Farquhar, D.S.O., Coldstream Guards, 2nd son of 4th baronet, b. 1874, d. (killed in action) 1915 : m. 1905, Lady Evelyn Hely-Hutchinson, who d. 1962, having m. 2ndly, 1923, Sir Dougal Orme Malcolm, K.C.M.G., who d. 1955), da. of 5th Earl of Donoughmore:—

Norah Frances Sapphire (The Gate House, Hunsdonbury, Hunsdon, Ware, Herts.), b. 1906; assumed (with her husband) the additional surname of Farquhar 1931: m. 1st, 1925, Mark Oliver, OBE, Lt., 2nd Dragoons (Scots Greys) Res. of Officers; 2ndly, 1948, John Roland Preece, who d. 1974, and has issue living, (by 1st m.) Robert Mark, b. 1925: m. 1968, Penelope Anne Keddie,—Catriona Mary, b. 1928: m. 1952 (m. diss. 1966), Theobald Mathew John Smyth, Lt. Irish Gds. (Reserve),—Norah Elizabeth (*Countess of Lindsey and Abingdon*) (Hunsdonbury, Hunsdon, Ware), b. 1932: m. 1957, 14th Earl of Lindsey, and 9th Earl of Abingdon.——Sybil Barbara, b. 1909: m. 1st, 1930, Lt.-Cdr. Anthony Boyce Combe, late RN; 2ndly, 1946, as his third wife, Charles Robert Archibald Grant, who d. 1972 [E. Rosebery], and has issue living, (by 1st m.) Georginia, b. 1931: m. 1951, Robert Humphrey Gordon Edmunds, CMG, MBE, of Forge House, Burnham Thorpe, King's Lynn. Norfolk, and has issue living, Charles Gervase b. 1952, Simon Dominic Antony b. 1955, Robert David Francis b. 1957, James George Benedict, b. 1960,—Caroline Romaine, b. 1935: m. 1968, George Silver Oliver Annesley Colthurst, of Pitchford Hall, Salop, and 6, Crescent Grove, SW4 [see Colthurst, Bt.]. *Residence*, 17a, Crescent Grove, SW4.

Grandchildren of the late Grenville Frederick Richard Farquhar, 4th son of 3rd baronet:—

Issue of the late Guy William John Farquhar, b. 1899, d. 1962: m. 1928 (marriage dissolved 1947), Daphne Mary Christian, da. of the late Lieut.-Col. Vivian Henry, C.B. [Millbank, Bt.]:—

Edward Vivian (Pitt House Farm, Ashford Hill, Newbury, Berks., RG15 8BN), *b.* 1929; ed. at Eton: late Capt. 11th Hussars; a Dir. of Watney Mann & Truman Brewers Ltd.: *m.* 1956, Polly, da. of the late Adm. of the Fleet, Sir Philip Louis Vian, GCB, KBE, DSO, and has issue living, Peter Christopher Edward, *b.* 1959,—Alastair Vian, *b.* 1966,—Diana Susan, *b.* 1961.——Peter Guy Powlett (March Close, Kings Lane, Flore, Northants), *b.* 1936: *m.* 1961, Rosemary Anne Eaton, only da. of Eaton Hammond, of Hill House, Wroxham, Norfolk, and has issue living, Richard Charles, *b.* 1962,—James Edward, *b.* 1963.——Antonia Daphne Diana, *b.* 1932: *m.* 1956, Antony Noel Gordon Leaf.

> Issue of the late FitzRoy James Wilberforce Farquhar, O.B.E., 5th son of 3rd baronet, *b.* 1858, *d.* 1941: *m.* 1884, Ada Mary, who *d.* 1944, da. of Sir John William Cradock-Hartopp, 4th baronet:—

Arthur Ronald, DSC, *b.* 1888; became Com. 1924, and Capt. (ret.) 1934, War, 1914-18 (wounded), 1939-45 War. *Club,* White's.

> Grandsons of the late Ernest Farquhar, son of the late Harvie Morton Farquhar 2nd son of 2nd baronet :—
> Issue of the late Sir Harold Lister Farquhar, K.C.M.G., M.C., *b.* 1894, *d.* 1953 : *m.* 1917, Constance Audrey, who *d.* 1963, da. of the late Hon. Arthur Algernon Capell [E. Essex, colls.]:—

Ian Rupert, *b.* 1918 ; is Major Grenadier Guards : *m.* 1944, Margaret Eugenie, da. of the late Francis John Gordon Borthwick, W.S. [*see* L. Borthwick, colls.], and has issue living, Francis Rupert, *b.* 1952. *Residences,* Hamlyns, Chudleigh, S. Devon; 48, Paultons Sq., SW3. *Clubs,* White's, Pratt's.——Adrian, *b.* 1924; 1943-44 War, as Capt. 60th Rifles: *m.* 1955, Ann Johnston-Noad, and has issue living, Annabel Cristina, *b.* 1958. *Residence,* Redlynch House, Salisbury. *Clubs,* Boodle's, St. James's.

Sir Robert Farquhar, Knt., of Munie, a younger son of the ancient family of Farquhar of Gilmilnscroft, was Deputy-Receiver of Scotland 1644, and Provost of Aberdeen 1646. His great-great-great nephew, Sir Walter, 1st baronet, was Physician to George IV. when Prince Regent, and had a second son, Robert (first British Gov. and Com.-in-Ch. of the Mauritius), who also was *cr.* a Baronet in 1821 (*ext.* 1924). The 5th baronet, Sir Walter Randolph Fitzroy Farquhar, Capt. R.F.A., *d.* (killed in action during European War) 1918.

FARRAR, Creation (U.K.) 1911, of Bedford, Province of Transvaal, Union of South Africa. [Extinct 1915.]

Sir GEORGE HERBERT FARRAR, *D.S.O.,* 1st and last *Baronet.*

Daughters living of 1st Baronet—Helen Mabel, *b.* 1894 : *m.* 1917, Major Basil Hobson Turner who *d.* 1948, sometime R.F.C., and has issue living, George Hobson, *b.* 1921,—Michael John Farrar, *b.* 1924,—Helen Felicity, *b.* 1918. *Residence,* Bedford, P.O. White River, Eastern Transvaal, S. Africa.——Ella Marguerite (*Ella, Lady Watson*), *b.* 1941: *m.* 1935, Sir Thomas Aubrey Watson, 4th Bt., *cr.* 1866, who *d.* (on active ser. during 1939-45 War) 1941. *Residence,* Court Farm House, Sherbourne, Barford, Warwicks.

FARRINGTON, Creation (U.K.) 1818, of Blackheath, Kent.

Sir HENRY FRANCIS COLDEN FARRINGTON, 7th *Baronet; b.* April 25th, 1914; *s.* his father, *Sir* HENRY ANTHONY, 1944 ; ed. at Haileybury ; Major (retired) late R.A. : *m.* 1947, Anne, el. da. of the late Major William Albert Gillam, D.S.O., Border Regt., and has issue.

Arms—Ermine, on a chevron gules between three leopards' faces sable as many bombs or, fired proper. **Crest**—A dragon wings elevated tail nowed vert bezanty, gorged with a mural crown argent and a chain reflexed over the back or, the body charged with two caltraps fessewise of the last.

Residence—Quarry Cleeve, Wiveliscombe, Taunton, Somerset.

Le bon temps viendra.   **Son living**—HENRY WILLIAM, *b.* March 27th, 1951; ed. at Haileybury.
    Daughter living—Susan Maria, *b.* 1949.
There's a good time coming.   **Sister living**—Margaret, *b.* 1913 : *m.* 1st, 1933, Edward Hugh Lee Rowcliffe, T.D.; 2ndly, 1959, Arthur Wilfrid Nicholson, and has issue living, (by 1st m.) Anthony Hugh Lee, *b.* 1937, ARICS; ALAS,—Pamela Elizabeth (*Baroness Newall*), (Wotton Underwood, Aylesbury, Bucks.), *b.* 1934: *m.* 1956, the 2nd, Baron Newall,—Margaret Matilda, *b.* 1949: *m.* 1972, Capt. John William Matthews, the Blues and Roys. [E. Dartmouth]. (Combermore Barracks, Windsor, Berks.). *Residence,* All Saints House, Axminster, Devon.

Collateral Branches living.

> Issue of the late Alexander Farrington, 2nd son of 5th baronet, *b.* 1872, *d.* 1958 : *m.* 1905, Ellen Katharine, who *d.* 1965, da. of the late William Wilberforce Howard (formerly H.M.'s Senior Inspector of Schools), of Stanmore, Mitcham, N. Devon:—

William Howard, *b.* 1907; Com. (ret.) RN: *m.* 1934, Barbara, who *d.* 1975, da. of Herbert Smale, of 15, Harley St., W1, and has issue living, Andrew James (Cheyneys, Hedgerow, Chalfont St. Peter, Bucks.), *b.* 1942; at Marlborough, and Birmingham Univ. (BSc): *m.* 1965, Susan Kathleen, BSc, da. of Ronald Hugh Wylsher Britton, MRCS, LRCP, of 10, Lane Head Close, Croyde Bay, Braunton, N. Devon, and has issue living, William James *b.* 1967, Eleanor *b.* 19—, Alice Joanna *b.* 1973,—Susan, *b.* 1937,—Jenifer, *b.* 1938: *m.* 1965, Maj. Martin Rothery Sheldon, R. Scots Greys (ret.), of 43, Station Rd., Amersham, Bucks., and has issue living, Bryany Claire *b.* 1966, Camilla Frances *b.* 1968,—Angela, *b.* 1941: *m.* 1966, Andrew Arthur Rose, of Sonachan House, Portsonachan, by Dalmally, Argyll, and has issue living, David Andrew *b.* 1967, Susannah Angela *b.* 1968. *Residence,* Minal Woodlands House, Marlborough, Wilts.

> Issue of the late John Marsden Farrington, yst. son of 5th baronet, *b.* 1874, *d.* 1965: *m.* 1917, Lynda May (26, Congreve Rd., Worthing), da. of George T. Simmonds, of Forest Hill, SE23:—

John Anthony (Chauntsingers, Ryton, Shrewsbury), *b.* 1934; ed. at Eastbourne Coll.: *m.* 1958, Patricia Rose, da. of John William Fowler, of Norwich, and has issue living, Charles Henry, *b.* 1963, Richard John, *b.* 1964.——Mary Joyce, *b.* 1918: *m.* 1st, 1942, Capt. Thomas Southall Porter, Carlton and York Regt., Canadian Forces, who *d.* (killed in action) 1943; 2ndly, 1946, Vincent Allison White, who *d.* 1950; 3rdly, 1955, Philip Challis, of Balaton, Alinora Cres., Goring-by-Sea, Sussex.

Granddaughter of the late Anthony Charles Farrington, M.R.C.S., L.R.C.P.E.,
4th son of 4th baronet:—
Issue of the late Charles Anthony Beevor Farrington, *b.* 1873, *d.* 1939: *m.* 1908, Mabel,
who *d.* 1970, da. of the late George Hastings Rust D'Eye:—
Marjorie Joan Cicely (8, Naish Rd., Barton-on-Sea, New Milton, Hants), *b.* 1910.

Granddaughter of the late Rev. Edward Holmes Farrington, 2nd son of 3rd
baronet:—
Issue of the late George Walker Farrington, *b.* 1850, *d.* 1928: *m.* 1894, Constance May, who
d. 1922, da. of Francis Newton Lowe, formerly of Lincoln:—
Maude Mary, *b.* 1895 : *m.* 1930, Josiah Samuel Gist Billett, who *d.* 1954. *Residence,* Lydcote,
Ventnor, Isle of Wight.

Grandchildren of the late Francis John Farrington, 4th son of the Rev. Edward
Holmes Farrington (ante):—
Issue of the late George Edward Marshall Farrington, *b.* 1882, *d.* 1960: *m.* 1911, Mary
Ellen Johnston, who *d.* 1968, only da. of William B. Fraser, of Griqualand East,
S. Africa:—
Marshall Frances William, *b.* 1912 : *m.* 1939, Crystal Johana, da. of the late William John
MacSeveney, of Nsoko, Swaziland, and has issue living, Alastair Edward, *b.* 1946,—Graham
William, *b.* 1947,—Ian Fraser, *b.* 1948,—Jacqueline Valerie, *b.* 1941.——Lorna Margaret, *b.*
1918: *m.* 1945, Barend Chrisstoffel Pretorius, and has issue living, Chrisstoffel, Marshall, *b.*
1954. *Residence,* 18, Walker St., Pietermaritzburg, Natal.

Sir Anthony Farrington, 1st Bt. of this creation, was a Gen. in the Army, Director-Gen. of R.A.
and Field Train, and an Hon. D.C.L., Oxford, and *m.* 1766, Elizabeth, da. of Alexander Colden,
Lieut.-Gov. of New York. Sir Henry Anthony, 6th Bt., was Ch. Conservator of Forests, Central
Provinces India 1923-7.

Paudel-Phillips, see Phillips.

FAYRER, Creation (U.K.) 1896, of Devonshire Street, St. Marylebone, co. London.
[Name pronounced "**Fairer.**"]

Sir JOSEPH HERBERT SPENS FAYRER, *D.S.C.*, 3rd
Baronet ; b. Oct. 20th, 1899 ; *s.* his father, *Sir* JOSEPH, 1937 ;
ed. at Wellington Coll. ; is Lieut.-Com. R.N.V.R. ; formerly
Lieut. 1st Batn. King's Own Scottish Borderers ; European War
1939-43 with Channel Convoys (D.S.C.) : *m.* 1st, 1926, Mary
Elizabeth Dulsabel (from whom he obtained a divorce 1936),
da. of the late Capt. William Claude Frederick Vaudrey-
Barker-Mill [*see* B. Collins] ; 2ndly, 1939, Helen Diana Scott,
who *d.* 1961, only da. of the late Capt. John Lang,
Edinburgh; 3rdly, 1964, Noreen Christian May, only
da. of the late Rev. John Yuill Walker, of Innerleithen,
and has issue by 2nd marriage.

Ne tentes aut perfice.
*Do not attempt, or else
accomplish.*

Arms—Argent, on a bend invected sable between in chief an Eastern
crown gules and in base an esculapius proper enfiled with an Eastern
crown of the third, three horseshoes or. **Crest**—In front of a sword erect,
point upward proper, pommel and hilt or, a horseshoe or between two
wings erect gules.

Residence,—Over Hailes, Haddington, E. Lothian.

Son living—By 2nd marriage—JOHN LANG MACPHERSON, *b.* Oct. 18th, 1944; ed. at
Edinburgh Acad.

Daughter living—By 2nd marriage—Eleanor Jean Spens (31, Aberdeen Place, NW8), *b.* 1940: *m.*
1967, Michael Ronald Henbrey, and has issue living, Samantha, *b.* 1968.

Sister living—Phyllis Bethia Josephine, *b.* 1898: *m.* 1921, Capt. A. Keith Tod, of Shilfies, Lasswade, Midlothian, and has issue living, Andrew Leonard Fayrer Keith (of Edenkerry,
Lasswade, Midlothian), *b.* 1924: *m.* 1951, Eileen June, da. of the late Rev. Edward Labouchere
Ruthven Thornton, and has issue living, Christopher Edward Keith *b.* 1954, Eileen Bridget
b. 1952, Jennifer Phyllis (twin) *b.* 1954,—Priscilla Ann Josephine, *b.* 1928: *m.* 1952, Lt.-Col. Alan
Patrick Smith, OBE, RE [Boughey, Bt.], of Longhirst Grange, Longhirst, Morpeth, Northumber-
land, and has issue living, Alan Simon Nicholas *b.* 1954, Richard Michael Patrick *b.* 1956, Ann
Elizabeth Phyllis *b.* 1962, Lucy Jane Mary *b.* 1964,—Elizabeth Rosemary Phyllis, *b.* 1930: *m.*
1967, Graham Johnson, of Library House, Kelso, Roxburghshire, and has issue living, James
Graham *b.* 1971, Philippa Marjorie *b.* 1970.

Collateral Branches living.
Issue of the late Lt.-Col. James Outram Spens Fayrer, 4th son of 1st baronet,
b. 1861, *d.* 1918: *m.* 1892, Katherine, who *d.* 1959, da. of F. Steward:—
Evelyn Bethia, *b.* 1894: *m.* 1st, 1926 (m. diss. 1940), Reginald Hamilton Fyers Turner;
2ndly, 1957, Frederick Righton. *Residence,* Apt. 5W, 60E 94th St., New York 10028, NY,
USA.——Wynifred Georgiana Joscelyn (107, Summerhill Av., Toronto 7, Canada), *b.* 1898:
m. 1928, Joseph Pearson Evans, who *d.* 1959, and has issue living, Pamela Joscelyn Bold, *b.*
1928: *m.* 1961, Clifford Joseph Leeb, of 48, Duggan Av., Toronto, 7, Canada, and has issue
living, Gavin Joseph Ignatius *b.* 1962, Kira Hermione *b.* 1964.

Issue of the late Lieut.-Col. Frederick Durand Stirling Fayrer, 6th son of 1st
baronet, *b.* 1869, *d.* 1933: *m.* 1898, Amy Gertrude, who *d.* 1969, da. of the late
Thomas Wilkinson Tetley, of Claughton, Ches.:—

Colin Robert, *b.* 1907: *m.* 1946, Evelyn Elinor May, el. da. of the late Thomas A. Carey, Ceylon
Civil Ser., and has issue living, Anne Patricia, *b.* 1947,—Wendy Elizabeth, *b.* 1949: *m.* 1974,
David L. Allworthy, of 14, Whitstable Rd., Blean, Canterbury, Kent. *Residence,* 7, Lauderdale
Drive, Petersham, Surrey.

The 1st baronet, Sir Joseph, was a F.R.C.S., F.R.C.P., an Hon. Physician to H.M. Queen
Victoria, and an Hon. Physician (Mil.) and Physician Extraordinary to H.M. King Edward VII ;
Gov. of Wellington Coll., and many years Surg.-Gen. and Pres. of Med. Board at India Office.

FEILDEN, Creation (U.K.) 1846, of Feniscowles, Lancashire.

Sir WILLIAM MORTON BULLER FEILDEN,
M.C., 5th *Baronet* ; *b.* May 20th, 1893 ; *s.* his father,
Sir WILLIAM HENRY, 1946 ; was Dist. Remount
Officer, W. Command 1919-37, and Comdt. No. 6
Group, Roy. Observer Corps 1938-45 ; European
War 1914-16 Comdg. Derbyshire Yeo. at Evacu-
ation of Gallipoli (wounded, despatches twice,
M.C., Italian silver medal for valour) : *m.* 1st, 1922,
Margery Hannah, who *d.* 1925, da. of Robert Knowles,
of Ednaston Lodge, near Derby; 2ndly, 1927,
Reva Sarah Mary, who *d.* 1971, da. of the late
Martin Morrison, of Faceby Manor, Yorkshire,
and widow of Maj. Guy Winterbottom.

Arms—Argent, on a fesse cottised azure, between two
martlets in chief and a rose in base gules, barbed and
seeded proper, three lozenges or. **Crest**—A nuthatch perched upon a
hazel-branch fructed, holding in its beak a rose gules, slipped
proper. **Second Crest and Motto**—A palm-tree weighted proper.
"Crescit sub pondere virtus" (*Virtue grows under its imposed
weight*).

Seat—Feniscowles, Lancashire. *Residence*—The Yelt
Farm, Doveridge, Derbyshire. *Club*—Boodle's.

Honor is the reward of virtue. **Sister living**—Cynthia Evelyn: *m.* 1937, Maj. Geoffrey Charles
Barff Charlesworth, Yorkshire Hussars, and has issue living,
William Brian, *b.* 1947; ed. at Eton and Roy. Agric. Coll., Cirencester: *m.* 1971, Annabel Jean,
ARICS, yst. da. of J. Rowse, of Lower Brook Farm, Worminghall, Bucks. *Residence,* The
Chantry, Church Side, Methley, Leeds, LS2 69BJ.

Collateral Branches living.

Issue of the late Major Edward Leyland Cooke Feilden, O.B.E., 2nd son of 3rd
baronet, *b.* 1868, *d.* 1921 : *m.* 1907, the Hon. Marjorie Graham Murray, who
d. 1967, da. of 1st Viscount Dunedin:—

Esmè Mary Graham, *b.* 1913: *m.* 1935, George Richard Shaw, of Crossbank Hill, Hurworth-on-
Tees, Darlington, and has issue living, Graham, *b.* 1948,—Angela Mary Graham, *b.* 1936: *m.*
1955, Group Capt. Anthony Walkinshaw Fraser, RAF (RAF Club), and has issue living, Robert
Walkinshaw *b.* 1963, Amanda Evelyn *b.* 1956, Antonia Esmé *b.* 1958, Alexandra *b.* 1960,—
Fiona Gilroy, *b.* 1944: *m.* 1962, Maj. Fane Travers Gaffney, Welsh Guards (Guards'
Club), and has issue living, Bay Travers *b.* 1963, Richard Desmond *b.* 1964, Adrian Tobias
George Hannaford, *b.* 1972, Miranda *b.* 1966,—Gelda Susan Marjorie Feilden, *b.* 1947: *m.* 1968,
Robert Harding Churton, Capt. 15th/19th King's R. Hussars (c/o Midland Bank, City Branch,
33, Park Row, Leeds, CS1 1CD), and has issue living, Thomas Edward Harding *b.* 1972.

Issue of the late Col. Wemyss Gawne Cunningham Feilden, C.M.G., 3rd son
of 3rd baronet, *b.* 1870, *d.* 1943 : *m.* 1915, Winifred (of All Farthings, Mayfield,
Sussex), da. of the late Rev. William Cosens, D.D. :—

HENRY WEMYSS (Littledene, Heathfield Rd., Burwash, Etchingham, Sussex, TN19 7HN; MCC),
b. Dec. 1st, 1916; ed. at Canford: *m.* 1943, Ethel May, da. of the late John Atkinson, of Newcastle,
and has issue living, Henry Rudyard, *b.* 1951; ed. at Kent Coll., Canterbury,—Jennifer May,
b. 1944: *m.* 1972, Philip Andrew Cooper, of Oak Beams, Holdenhurst Rd., Bournemouth,—Anne
Margaret (c/o Nat. Westminster Bank, 250, Regent St., W1R 6AV) *b.* 1947: *m.* 1970, William
Hugh Stokoe.——Randle Richard, *b.* 1923: ed. at Marlborough, at Corpus Christi Coll., Camb.
(MA) and at Cuddesdon Theological Coll.; Bar. Lincoln's Inn 1949; Curate of St. Andrew's,
Moulsecoomb 1955-57, and of Steyning 1957-58, Tutor-Organiser for Workers' Educational
Assocn. for NE Lancs. 1958-63, and HM Inspector of Schs. 1963-66; Assist. Editor (Political
Affairs), of *Keesing's Contemporary Archives* since 1967, and a Member Gen. Synod of Ch. of
England since 1970: *m.* 1957, Leonora Mary, da. of John Lawrence Marshall, of Leicester.
Residence, 14, Royal Cres., Bath. *Clubs,* Junior Carlton, MCC.

Issue of the late Lt.-Col. Randle Montague Feilden, CBE, 4th son of 3rd baronet,
b. 1871, *d.* 1965: *m.* 1924, Rachel Mary Gordon, who *d.* 1933, da. of the
late Horace Gordon Lowe, of Truro:—

John Randle, *b.* 1931.——Fay Adah Rachel (10, St. Barnabas St., SW1), *b.* 1925; BA, PhD
London, Dip. Psych.; Lecturer Inst. of Psychiatry, London Univ. 1962-65; Personal Research
Award, Mental Health Research Fund 1965-67; Senior Lecturer, Roy. Free Hosp. Medical Sch.,
Univ. of London 1971: *m.* 1st, 1948, Anthony John Fransella, RAF, from whom she obtained a
divorce 1955; 2ndly, 1968, John Royden Cole Hodson.

This family has been settled near Blackburn, Lancashire, for more than four centuries. The 1st
Baronet was M.P. for Blackburn (C) 1832-47.

Ferguson-Davie, see Davie.

JOHNSON-FERGUSON, Creation (U.K.) 1906, of Springkell, co. Dumfries, Kenyon, Newchurch-in-Culcheth, co. Palatine of Lancaster, and Wiston, co. Lanark.

Sir NEIL EDWARD JOHNSON-FERGUSON, *T.D.*, 3rd *Baronet: b.* May 2nd, 1905; *s.* his father, *Col. Sir* EDWARD ALEXANDER JAMES, *T.D.*, 1953; ed. at Winchester, and at Trin. Coll., Camb. (BA); Lt.-Col. Roy. Corps. of Signals, and a JP and Vice-Lieut. for Dumfriesshire; has American Legion of Merit: *m.* 1931, Sheila Marian, da. of the late Col. Herbert Swynfen Jervis, MC, Roy. Munster Fusiliers, of Tilford, Surrey, and has issue.

Arms—Quarterly, 1st and 4th per fesse indented gules and or a pale counterchanged, in chief two boars' heads couped of the second and in base a thistle slipped proper ; 2nd and 3rd azure, on a pile or a lion statant of the first, on a chief azure, between two sprigs of oak slipped, a pale or, thereon a like sprig of oak, all counterchanged. Crest—1st, in front of a thistle erect thereon a bee volant proper, a boar's head couped or ; 2nd, between two oak branches erect proper, a lion statant per pale azure and or, holding in the mouth a sprig of oak also proper.

Know thyself

Residence—Fairyknowe, Eaglesfield, Dumfriesshire.

Sons living—IAN EDWARD, *b.* Feb. 1st, 1932; ed. at Ampleforth, and at Trin. Coll., Camb.: *m.* 1964, Rosemary Teresa, da. of C. J. Whitehead, of The Old House, Crockham Hill, Edenbridge, and has issue living, Mark Edward, *b.* 1965,—Paul Duncan, *b.* 1966,—Simon Joseph, *b.* 1967.——Christopher Charles Jervis, *b.* 1933; ed. at Ampleforth: *m.* 1963, Sarah Loraine, da. of Sir Humphrey Dodington Benedict Sherston Sherston-Baker, 6th Bt., and has issue living, Charles, *b.* 1972,—Victoria Margaret, *b.* 1965,—Lucy Mary, *b.* 1974.——Michael Herbert (Springkell, Eaglesfield, Dumfriesshire), *b.* 1934, Capt. Lowland Yeo; a JP for Dumfriesshire: *m.* 1963, Jennifer, el. da. of Lt.-Col. H. Green, of Manor House, Carlton Husthwaite, Thirsk, Yorks., and has issue living, James Herbert, *b.* 1963,—Robert Charles, *b.* 1969,—Sarah Catherine, *b.* 1965,— Fiona Marion, *b.* 1966,—Laura Rose, *b.* 1967.——Nichois Swynfen (Rue Centrale, Hermancé, Geneva, Switzerland), *b.* 1938: *m.* 1963, Mabel, da. of L. Dawson, of Wendover, Bucks, and has issue living, Alona Francesca, *b.* 1964,—Karina Alicia, *b.* 1966.

Brothers living—Brian Charles, *T.D.*, *b.* 1908 ; ed. at Winchester, and at Ch. Ch., Oxford ; in Major Lanark Yeo., and a J.P. for Dumfriesshire : *m.* 1947, Daphne Louie, da. of Brigadier Walter Andrew Stirling, D.S.O., M.C., R.A., of Polstead, Suffolk and has issue living, Torquil Charles, *b.* 1949,—Denzil Crispin, *b.* 1955,—Merlin Louie, *b.* 1950,—Lorraine Giselle, *b.* 1952. Residence, Solwaybank, Canonbie, Dumfriesshire.——Raymond Patrick, *T.D.*, *b.* 1912 ; ed. at Pembroke Coll., Oxford (B.A. 1934) ; is a D.L. for Cumberland ; late Lieut.-Col. Westmorland and Cumberland Yeo., RA (TA); 1939-45 War (despatches). Residence, Westerkirk Mains, Langholm, Dumfriesshire.

The 1st baronet, Sir (Jabez) Edward (son of Jabez Johnson, J.P., of Kenyon Hall, near Manchester), Chm. of Jabez Johnson, Hodgkinson and Pearson (Limited), assumed by Roy. licence 1881 the additional surname of Ferguson, and sat as M.P. for Mid, or Loughborough, Div. of Leicestershire (L) 1885-6, and 1892-1900. The 2nd baronet, Sir Edward Alexander James Johnson-Ferguson, T.D., was Lieut.-Col. and Brevet Col. late Comdg. Lanarkshire Yeo., and a Director of Tredegar Coal & Iron Co., Ltd.

FERGUSSON, Creation (N.S.) 1703, of Kilkerran, Ayrshire.

Sweeter out of difficulties.

Sir CHARLES FERGUSSON, 9th *Baronet*; *b.* May 10th, 1931; *s.* his father, *Sir* JAMES, LLD, 1973; ed. at Eton: *m.* 1961, the Hon. Amanda Mary Noel-Paton, da. of Baron Ferrier (Life Peer), and has issue.

Arms—Azure, a buckle argent between three boars' heads couped or, in a dexter canton argent a saltire azure, surmounted of an inescutcheon or charged with a lion rampant within a double tressure flory counterflory gules. Crest—A bee on a thistle proper. Supporters—Two gryphons or, armed and beaked gules.

Residence—Gigmagog, Kilkerran, Maybole, Ayrshire.

Sons living—ADAM, *b.* Dec. 29th, 1962.——Joseph Victor, *b.* 1965.

Brother living—Adam Dugdale (9, Addison Cres., W14), *b.* 1932; ed. at Eton, and at Trin. Coll., Camb.: *m.* 1965, (Elizabeth Catherine) Penelope, da. of (Thomas) Peter Hughes, of Furneaux Pelham Hall, Herts., and has issue living, James, *b.* 1966,—Marcus Francis, *b.* 1972,—Petra Christian, *b.* 1968,—Lucy Josephine, *b.* 1970.

That I may profit others.

Sister living—Alice Blanche Helen, b. 1934: m. 1960, Ronald Timothy Renton, MP, of Mount Harry House, Offham, Lewes, and has issue living, Alexander James Torre, b. 1961,—Daniel Charles Antony, b. 1965,—Christian Louise, b. 1963,—Katherine Chelsea (twin), b. 1965,—Penelope Sally Rosita, b. 1970.

Uncles living (sons of 7th baronet)—*Rev.* Simon Charles David (Alton Albany, Barr, Girvan, Ayrshire), b. 1907; ed. at Eton; Lt.-Col. (ret.) Argyll and Sutherland Highlanders; Min. of Barr, Ayrshire 1957-75; Middle East 1939-44, NW Europe 1944-45: m. 1945, Auriole Kathleen, da. of the late Com. Sir Geoffrey Henry Hughes-Onslow, KBE, DSC, RN [see E. Onslow, colls.], and has issue living, Alexander Charles Onslow, b. 1949: m. 1974, Jane Merryn, da. of Group Capt. Bertram Barthold, of Langarth, St. Meryn, Cornwall, and has issue living, a son b. 1975,—John Geoffrey Onslow, b. 1954,—Henrietta Charity Onslow, b. 1952.——Bernard Edward, KT, GCMG, GCVO, DSO, OBE (*Baron Ballantrae*), b. May 6th, 1911; *cr.* Baron Ballantrae (Life Peer) June 1st, 1972 [see that title].

Widow living of 8th Baronet—LOUISE FRANCES BALFOUR STRATFORD (*Louise, Lady Fergusson*) (Kilkerran Maybole, Ayrshire), da. of Edgar Trevelyan Stratford Dugdale [E. Balfour, colls.]: m. 1930, Sir James Fergusson LLD, 8th Bt., who d. 1973.

Collateral Branches living.

Issue of the late Adm. Sir James Andrew Fergusson, K.C.B., K.C.M.G., 2nd son of 6th baronet, b. 1871, d. 1942: m. 1901, Githa Enid, who d. 1964, da. of the late Thomas C. Williams, of Wellington, New Zealand:—
Margaret Edith, b. 1903 : m. 1961, Ralph B. Scholfield. *Residence*, 8, St. Leonards Terrace, SW3.——Augusta Susan (Longwood, Bishop's Waltham, Hants.), b. 1904: m. 1932, Capt. George Francis Locke Marx, OBE, RN, who d. 1965, and has issue living, Andrew John Locke (25, Bolton Gdns., Teddington, Middx. TW11 9AX), b. 1933; Cdr. RN: m. 1963, Rosemary Evangeline, da. of Christopher William Edward Collins, of The Old Rectory, Lackford, Bury St. Edmunds, and has issue living, John William Francis b. 1973, Caroline Elizabeth b. 1964, Annabelle Mary b. 1967,—David George Locke, b. 1936; Managing Dir. of John Rigby & Sons.—— Jean Annie, b. 1908: m. 1930, Edward Lindsay Orr Ewing, MC, Lt. Roy. Highlanders, who d. 1930 [Ewing, Bt., colls.]. *Residence*, Flat C, 7, Tite St., SW3.——Anne Mary, b. 1919. *Residence*, 8, Palace Gardens Terr., W8.

Descendants of the late Rt. Hon. Charles Dalrymple Fergusson (3rd son of 5th baronet), who assumed the surname and Arms of Dalrymple 1849, and was *cr.* a *Baronet* 1887.
See Dalrymple, Bt.

Issue of the late Col. John Adam Fergusson, 4th son of 5th baronet, b. 1845, d. 1900: m. 1871, Sarah, who d. 1936, da. of the late Joseph Gilbert, of Pewsey Vale, S Australia:—
Sarah Faith (Strathmore Rest Home, 27/29, Sandford Mill Rd., Cheltenham, Glos. GL53 7QH), b. 1889.

Granddaughter of the late George Hermand Fergusson, 3rd son of 4th baronet:—
Issue of the late Lieut.-Col. George James FERGUSSON-BUCHANAN of Auchentorlie, b. 1862, d. 1928 : m. 1886, Grace, who d. 1935, da. of Claud Hamilton, of Barns:—
Avril Nora, b. 1892 : m. 1921, Com. Mervyn Boyd Alexander-Sinclair, R.N., son of the late Adm Sir Edwyn Sinclair Alexander-Sinclair, GCB, MVO, and has issue living, David Boyd (c/o Midland Bank, 69 Pall Mall, SW1), b. 1927; ed. at Eton; Brig. late R. Green Jackets: m. 1958, Ann Ruth, da. of the late Lt.-Col. Graeme Daglish, of The Thatched Cottage, E. Haddon, Northants. *Residence*, 58, Campden Hill Gate, NW8 7QJ.

Grandsons of the late Robert Henry Duncan Fergusson (infra) :—
Issue of the late Robert Arthur George Fergusson, b. 1878, d. 1939: m. 1912, Laura Gwendolen, who d. 1962, da. of the late Arthur William English, of Wisbech, Cambridgeshire:—
Irwine Arthur, b. 1913; ed. at Fettes: m. 1939, Pamela Vera, el. da. of Col. P. R. Ayers, M.C., of Newton Abbot, S. Devon, and has issue living, Peter John Charles (High Trees, 53, Whartons Lane, Ashurst, Hants.), b. 1943: m. 1966, Angela Star, da. of Capt. W. H. Behenna, of Bitterne, Southampton, and has issue living, Sean James b. 1973,—Christopher Simon Arthur, b. 1949: m. 1970, Susan Ann, yst. da. of A. Probert, of Knowle, Bristol,—Valerie Ann, b. 1941,—Sheena b. 1958.——Donald Andrew, b. 1920; ed. at Fettes: m. 1958, Patricia Dorothy, da. of D. K. Orton, of Entebbe, Uganda, and has issue living, Colin Ivan Paul, b. 1960,—Martin Arthur, b. 1963,—Heather Dorothy (twin), b. 1963.——Michael Ramsay, b. 1922; ed. at Fettes, and at Rhodes Univ., Grahamstown (BA 1948): m. 1961, Joanna Rosalind, da. of the late H. Stratton, of Warminster, Wilts, and has issue living, Richard Anthony, b. 1963.

Granddaughter of the late Henry Duncan Fergusson, W.S., 6th son of 4th baronet:—
Issue of the late Robert Henry Duncan Fergusson b. 1849, d. 1904: m. 1877, Mabel Frances, who d. 1930, da. of the late Robert Balfour Wardlaw-Ramsay, of Whitehill :—
Irene Hilda : m. 19—, Douglas Langhorne, and has issue living. *Residence*, 313, Petersham Road, Ham Common, Surrey.

Grandson of the late Robert Dundas Octavius Fergusson, 8th son of 4th baronet:—
Issue of the late Robert Dundas Arthur Graham Fergusson, b. 1851, d. 1896: m. 1877, Mary Rachel, who d. 1923, da. of the late Francis Whitworth Russell [Russell, Bt., *cr.* 1812, colls.]:—
A son, b. 1880.

The 1st baronet was an eminent advocate. The 2nd baronet, sometime M.P. for Sutherland, was afterwards a Lord of Session (Lord Kilkerran). The 3rd baronet sat as M.P. for Ayrshire 1774-84 and 1790-96 and for Edinburgh 1784-9. He claimed in 1796 the Earldom of Glencairn (created 1488); the Lords decided that he had proved himself to be heir-general to Alexander, Earl of Glencairn, who died 1670, but had not proved his right to the Earldom. The 6th baronet, the Rt. Hon. Sir James, G.C.S.I., K.C.M.G., C.I.E., P.C., LL.D., Grenadier Guards (killed in Jamaica earthquake 1907), served in Crimean War (wounded at battle of Inkerman), sat as M.P. for Ayrshire 1854-7 and 1859-68, and for N.-E. Div. of Manchester 1885-1906, and was Under-Sec. of State for India 1866-7, Under-Sec. at Home Office 1867-8, Gov. and Com.-in-Ch. of S. Australia 1868-73, Gov. of New Zealand 1873-5, and of Bombay 1880-85, Under-Sec. of State for Foreign Affairs 1886-91, and Postmaster-Gen. 1891-2. Sir Charles, G.C.B., G.C.M.G., D.S.O., M.V.O., LL.D., 7th baronet, was Gen. in the Army, Gov.-Gen. and Com.-in-Ch., New Zealand 1924-30, Chm. W. Indies Closer Union Commn. 1933, and Lord-Lieut. of Ayrshire 1937-50.

COLYER-FERGUSSON, Creation (U.K.) 1866, of Spitalhaugh, Peeblesshire.

By strength and skill.

Sir JAMES HERBERT HAMILTON COL-YER-FERGUSSON, 4th *Baronet,* son of the late Max Christian Hamilton Colyer-Fergusson, Lieut. R.A.S.C., el. son of 3rd baronet ; *b.* Jan. 10th, 1917 ; *s.* his grandfather, *Sir* THOMAS COLYER, 1951 ; ed. at Harrow, and at Balliol Coll., Oxford (B.A. 1939, M.A. 1945); formerly Capt. The Buffs; 1939-45 War (prisoner); Officer BR.

Arms—Argent, a lion rampant azure armed and langued gules, on a chief engrailed of the last a mullet between two cinquefoils of the first. Crest—A dexter hand grasping a broken spear in bend sinister all proper.

Residence—Flat 8, 61, Onslow Square, S.W.7. *Club*—Bath.

Aunts living (daughters of 3rd baronet)—Phillis Katherine St. Leger, *b.* 1900: *m.* 1st, 1922, Capt. John Naylor Hodgson-Wilson, RA, who *d.* 1960, and from whom she had obtained a divorce 1934; 2ndly, 1938 (m. diss. 1949), Theobald Henry Hinkson, and has issue living, (by 1st m.) Rosemary Janet St. Leger Hodgson, *b.* 1923: *m.* 1955, Charles Kenneth Moncreiff Stewart of Coll, JP of Acha House, Island of Coll, by Oban, Argyll, and has issue living, Fiona Katharine Moncreiff *b.* 1956, Fenella Rosemary Lorne *b.* 1959, Nicola Jane Riversdale *b.* 1963,—Marjorie Cecile Mary Hodgson, *b.* 1925: *m.* 1957, Charles Alexander MacDonald (Box 582, Ashcroft, BC, Canada) and has issue living, Charles Alexander Hamilton *b.* 1958.

Collateral Branch living.

Issue of the late Sir Louis Forbes FERGUSSON, K.C.V.O., 3rd son of 2nd baronet, *b.* 1878, *d.* 1962: *m.* 1922, Elizabeth Frances Ethel (*Lady Fergusson*) (18a, Homefield Rd., Wimbledon, SW19), da. of Seth Lewis, of Gt. Bookham, Surrey:—
Christine Forbes, *b.* 1934: *m.* 1966, Charles Raymond Evans, MA, of 16E, Cumberland Rd., Kew Gdns., Surrey.

The 1st baronet, Sir William, LL.D., F.R.S., a distinguished surgeon, was many years Sergeant-Surgeon to H.M. Queen Victoria. Sir James Ranken Fergusson, 2nd Bt., was Vice-Lieut. for Peeblesshire, and a Member of Roy. Co. of Archers (King's Body Guard for Scotland). Sir Thomas Colyer, 3rd Bt., was High Sheriff of Kent 1906, and assumed the additional surname of Colyer 1890.

FFOLKES, Creation (G.B.) 1774, of Hillington, Norfolk.

[Name pronounced "Foaks."]

Sir ROBERT FRANCIS ALEXANDER, FFOLKES, 7th *Baronet; b.* Dec. 2nd, 1943; *s.* his father, *Sir* (EDWARD JOHN) PATRICK BOSCHETTI, 1960.

Arms—Per pale vert and gules, a fleur-de-lis argent. Crest—A dexter arm embowed vested per pale vert and gules, cuff ermine, holding in the hand a spear proper.

Residence—Starlings, Yoxford, Suffolk.

Sister living—Sara Elizabeth, *b.* 1946: *m.* 1968, Maj. Jocelyn James Rhys Wingfield, LI, of Holly Tree Farm, Walpole, Halesworth, Suffolk [see V. Powerscourt, colls.].

Widow living of 6th Baronet—GERALDINE (*Lady ffolkes*), da. of the late William Roffey, of Writtle, Essex : *m.* 1939, Sir (Edward John) Patrick Boschetti ffolkes, 6th baronet, who *d.* 1960. *Residence,* Starlings, Yoxford, Suffolk.

Collateral Branches living.
Granddaughter of the late Martin William Browne ffolkes, el. son of 2nd baronet :—
Issue of the late Martin William Browne ffolkes, *b.* 1849, *d.* 1901: *m.* 1882, Wilhelmine Mary Emily, who *d.* 1943, da. of the late Lieut.-Col. J. D. Brett, 17th Lancers :—
Dame Barbara (*Dame Barbara Strickland*), DBE, *b.* 1884; DBE (Civil) 1923: *m.* 1st, 1911, Capt. Francis Joseph Cresswell, Norfolk Regt., who *d.* (killed in action) 1914; 2ndly, 1918, Gen. Sir Edward Peter Strickland, KCB, KBE, CMG, DSO, who d. 1951, and has issue living, (by 1st m.) Wilhelmine Margaret Eve (*Lady Harrod*) (The Old Rectory, Holt, Norfolk), *b.* 1911: *m.* 1938, Sir (Henry) Roy Forbes Harrod, and has issue living, Henry Mark, *b.* 1939: *m.* 1965, Lady Lucinda Lambton, el. da. of Antony Claud Frederick Lambton, [*see* E. Durham] (and has issue living, Henry Barnaby *b.* 1965, Nathaniel *b.* 1967), Dominick Roy *b.* 1940: *m.* 1974, Mrs. Christina Gavrelle Williams, da. of the late Christopher Hobhouse,—Eve Dorothy Kathleen (of South Raynham Grove, nr. Fakenham, Norfolk), *b.* 1914: *m.* 1st, 1944, John Wiseman; 2ndly, 1948, Gordon le Strange, who *d.* 1960, [M. Huntly, colls.],—(by 2nd m.) Lavender Jane *b.* 1922: *m.* 1st, 1946 (m. diss. 1966), George Seebohm; 2ndly, 1969, Frank Charles Layfield Broadribb, of Knotley Green, Sandon, Buntingford, Herts., and has issue living (by 1st m.), Frederick Hugh

What will happen, will happen.

b. 1949, Henry *b.* 1951, Phillippa Jane *b.* 1948, Patience *b.* 1953. *Residence*, The Old Hall, Snettisham, Norfolk.

Granddaughter of the late Rev. Henry Edward Browne ffolkes, 3rd son of 2nd baronet :—
Issue of the late Robert Walling Everard ffolkes, *b.* 1865, *d.* 1931 ; *m.* 1884, Ada, who *d.* 1906, da. of Col. William Brierly :—
Evelyn Maud (King St., Port Hope, Ont., Canada), *b.* 1889.

This family, in the person of Simon ffolkys, owned lands in Westley Waterless, Cambridgeshire, in 1490. Martin ffolkes, Pres. of Roy. and of Antiquarian Sos., inherited the Hovell estates in Norfolk through his mother, wife of Martin ffolkes, Attorney-Gen. to Queen-Dowager of Charles II. The 5th baronet, the Rev. Sir Francis Arthur Stanley, M.V.O., was an Hon. Chap. to Queen Victoria, a Chap.-in-Ord. to King Edward VII. and King George V., and a Chap. to King Edward VIII. and King George VI.

TWISLETON-WYKEHAM-FIENNES, Creation (U.K.) 1916, of Banbury, co. Oxford.

Look for a brave spirit.

Sir RANULPH TWISLETON-WYKEHAM-FIENNES, 3rd *Baronet* ; *b.* (posthumous) March 7th, 1944 ; *s.* his father, *Lieut.-Col. Sir* RANULPH, *D.S.O.,* 1944; ed. at Eton; late Capt. R. Scots Greys; attached 22nd SAS Regt. since 1966, seconded SAF 1968; White Nile Hovercraft Expedition 1969; British Jostedals Glacier Expedition 1970; Scots Greys Headless Valley Expedition 1971; a Liveryman of Vintners' Co.; author of " Talent for Trouble " 1970, "Icefall in Norway", and "The Headless Valley" 1972, and "Where Soldiers Fear to Tread" 1975: *m.* 1970, Virginia Pepper.

Arms—Quarterly, 1st and 4th azure, three lions rampant or, *Fiennes* ; 2nd and 3rd argent, a chevron between three moles sable, *Twisleton.* Crests—1st, a wolf sejant proper, gorged with a spiked collar, the line therefrom reflexed over the back or, *Fiennes* ; 2nd, an arm embowed, vested sable, cuffed argent, holding in the hand proper a mole spade or, headed and armed of the second.
Address—c/o St. Peters Well, Lodsworth, Petworth, Sussex.

Sisters living—Susan Valerie, *b.* 1933; ed. at Cape Town Univ. (BA 1951): *m.* 1957, John Jervoise Fitzgerald Scott, Maj. the Blues and Roys., of 9, Ladbroke Gds., W11, and has issue living, Arabella Caroline, *b.* 1959,—Venetia Lucy, *b.* 1963.——Celia Florence, *b.* 1936; ed. at Trin. Coll., Dublin (MB and BCh): *m.* 1964, Dr. Robert Savage Brown (c/o Project Hope, Ife, Nigeria), and has issue living, Anthony Newson *b.* 1966,—Deirdre Ann, *b.* 1965,—Nicola Lois, *b.* 1969.——Gillian Audrey *b.* 1938: *m.* 1960, T. George Hoult, of Lower Octon Grange, Foxholes, Driffield, N. Humberside, and has issue living, Andrew George, *b.* 1966,—Rosalind Elfrida, *b.* 1962,—Rachel Celia, *b.* 1963.

Widow living of 2nd Baronet—AUDREY JOAN (*Audrey, Lady Twisleton-Wykeham-Fiennes*), da. of the late Sir Percy Wilson Newson, 1st Bt.: *m.* 1931, Lt.-Col. Sir Ranulph Twisleton-Wykeham-Fiennes, DSO, 2nd baronet, Roy. Scots Greys, who *d.* (of wounds received in action in Italy) 1943. *Residence*, St. Peter's Well, Lodsworth, Sussex.

The 1st baronet, the Hon. Sir Eustace Edward Twisleton-Wykeham-Fiennes, 2nd son of 17th Baron Saye and Sele), was M.P. for Oxfordshire N., or Banbury Div. (*L*) 1906-10 and 1910-18, and Gov. and Com.-in-Ch. of Seychelles 1918-21, and of Leeward Islands 1921-9. The 2nd baronet Sir Ranulph, D.S.O., Lieut.-Col. Roy. Scots Greys, *d.* (of wounds received in action in Italy) Nov. 1943.

FINDLAY, Creation (U.K.) 1925, of Aberlour, co. Banff.

Sir ROLAND LEWIS FINDLAY, 3rd *Baronet; b.* July 14th, 1903; *s.* his brother, *Sir* (JOHN) EDMUND RITCHIE, 1962; ed. at Harrow; Lt.-Col. (ret.) 2nd Dragoons (Roy. Scots Greys): *m.* 1st, 1927 (m. diss. 1964), Barbara Joan, JP, da. of the late S. H. Garrard, of Welton, Northants; 2ndly, 1964, Marjory Mary (CRIPPS), da. of the late Hon. Claud William Biddulph [see B. Biddulph, colls.], and has issue by 1st marriage.

Arms—Or, a chevron purpure between two thistles slipped proper, in chief and in base a rose gules, barbed and seeded vert. Crest—A figure of Mercury holding a caduceus in the sinister hand all proper.
Residence—Chapel Farm, Burley, Oakham, Rutland. *Club*—Cavalry.

Daughter living—by 1st marriage—Barbara Jane (*Countess of Westmorland*), *b.* 1928: *m.* 1950, the 15th Earl of Westmorland). *Residence*, 19, South Eaton Place, SW1.

Daughter living of 2nd Baronet—Moira Juliet, *b.* 1927: *m.* 1951, Meyrick Adam Ovens, of Gains House, Green Hammerton, Yorks., YO5 8BQ.——Gillian, *b.* 1930: *m.* 1953, Maj.-Gen. John Myles Brockbank, CBE, MC, 12th Lancers, Manor House, Steeple Langford, Salisbury.

DEBRETT'S ILLUSTRATED BARONETAGE.

Sister living—Lætitia Florence (*Lady Munro-Lucas-Tooth*), O.B.E., *b.* 1904; O.B.E. (Civil) 1958: *m.* 1925, Lt.-Col. Sir Hugh Vere Huntly Duff Munro-Lucas-Tooth, 1st Bt., Queen's Own Cameron Highlanders. *Residence*, Burgate Court, Fordingbridge, Hants.

Widow living of 2nd Baronet—Laura Hawley Elsom (*Laura, Lady Findlay*), da. of the late Percival Hawley, of Hull: *m.* 1947, as his 2nd wife, Sir (John) Edmund Ritchie Findlay, who *d.* 1962. *Residence,*

Collateral branch living
Issue of the late Peter Findlay, 3rd son of 1st baronet, *b.* 1910, *d.* 1967: *m.* 1933, Helen, who *d.* 1965, da. of W. S. Brewer, of New York:—
Caroline Grace, *b.* 1935: *m.* 1967, Wing-Cdr. Lester Humphries, of Twyford, Hants.

The 1st baronet, Sir John Ritchie Findlay, K.B.E., was proprietor of *The Scotsman*, Chm. of Board of Trustees of National Galleries of Scotland, and of National Housing Co., and Lord-Lieut. of co. Banff. Sir (John) Edmund Ritchie Findlay, 2nd Bt., was M.P. for Banffshire (C) 1935-45.

FINLAY, Creation (U.K.) 1964, of Epping, co. Essex.

Sir Graeme Bell Finlay, *ERD, 1st Baronet*, son of the late James Bell Pettigrew Finlay, of Portskewett House, nr. Chepstow; *b.* Oct. 29th, 1917; ed. at Marlborough, and at Univ. Coll., London; Bar. Gray's Inn 1946 (Sr. Exhibitioner); Assist. Govt. Whip 1957-59, Lord Commr. of Treasury 1959-60, and Vice-Chamberlain of HM Household 1960-64; 1939-45 War, as acting Maj. S. Wales Borderers, attached 5th R. Gurkha Rifles (FF), and as DAAG; Hon. Capt. R. Regt. of Wales; MP for Epping Div. of Essex (C) 1951-64; a Dep. County Court Judge and Dep. Circuit Judge 1967-72, since when Assist. Juge D'Instruction and Judge of Petty Debts Court of Jersey: *m.* 1953, June Evangeline, yr. da. of Col. Francis Collingwood Drake, OBE, MC, DL, 10th R. Hussars, of Mill Hurst, Harlow, Essex, and has issue.

Arms,—Argent on a chevron azure between in chief two roses gules barbed and seeded proper, and in base an estoile of eight points gules within two wings conjoined and erect azure an ancient coronet or. Crest,—In front of an oak tree fructed a whippet sejant proper gorged with an ancient coronet pendent therefrom by the chains a portcullis azure.
Residence,—La Campagne, Rozel, St. Martin, Jersey *Clubs,*—Travellers', United (Jersey).

Son living—DAVID RONALD JAMES BELL, *b.* Nov. 16th, 1963.
Daughters living—Fiona Daphne Margaret Bell, *b.* 1956.——Catrina Mary Bell, *b.* 1959.

FISON, Creation (U.K.) 1905, of Greenholme, Burley-in-Wharfedale, West Riding of Yorkshire.

Trust in God.

Sir Richard Guy Fison, *DSC, 4th Baronet,* *b.* Jan. 9th, 1917; *s.* his father, *Capt. Sir* (William) Guy, *MC* 1964; ed. at Eton, and at New Coll., Oxford; 1939-45 War with RNVR (DSC): *m,* 1952, Elyn, da. of Mogens Hartmann, of Bordeaux. and has issue.

Arms—Per fesse azure and ermine, in chief three battle-axes argent, the staves or, and in base an heraldic tiger passant of the last. Crest—A demi-heraldic tiger or, collared gules, holding between the paws a shield argent, charged with a battle-axe sable.

Residence—The Gate House, Shrubbs Hill, Chobham, Surrey.

Son living—Charles William, *b.* Feb. 6th, 1954.
Daughter living—Isabelle Frances, *b.* 1957.
Brother living—John Michael, *b.* 1920; ed. at Eton; 1939-45 War with RA. *Residence,* 13, Kensington Court, W8.
Sister living—Elizabeth Rees, *b.* 1915: *m.* 1946, Maj.-Gen. William Richard Beddington, CBE, who *d.* 1975, and has issue living, Guy Francis, *b.* 1949. *Residence,* The Old Rectory, Winterborne Stickland, Blandford Forum, Dorset.
The 1st baronet, Sir Frederick William, sat as MP for Doncaster Div., W. Riding, Yorkshire (C) July 1895 to Jan. 1906.

FITZGERALD, Creation (U.K.) 1880, of Valencia, co. Kerry.

Sir GEORGE PETER MAURICE FITZGERALD, MC (*The 23rd Knight of Kerry*), 5th *Baronet*; *b.* Feb. 27th, 1917; *s.* his father, *Capt. Sir* ARTHUR HENRY BRINSLEY, 1967; ed. at Harrow; Maj. (ret.) Irish Guards; Palestine 1939 (despatches), 1939-45 War in Italy (MC): *m.* 1939, Angela Dora, da. of the late Capt. James Rankin Mitchell, of 2, Mansfield St., W1, and has issue.

Arms—Ermine, a saltire gules; in centre point a cross pattée argent. **Crest**—A chevalier in complete armour on horseback at full speed, with his sword drawn and visor raised, proper; saddle gules, saddle-cloth or.

Residence—Cedar Court, Alderton, Woodbridge, Suffolk.

Mattachar-a-buadh.

My presence is victory.

Son living—ADRIAN JAMES ANDREW DENIS (16, Clareville St., SW7, and Lackaneask, Valentia Island, co. Kerry), *b.* June 24th, 1940; ed. at Harrow; a Councillor Roy. Borough of Kensington and Chelsea 1974.

Daughter living—Rosanna, *b.* 1945: *m.* 1964, Count Richard Gurowski, of North End House, Damerham, Fordingbridge, Hants., and has issue living, Iona, *b.* 1967, —Anya, *b.* 1970.

Sister living—Finola Mary, *b.* 1919: *m.* 1st, 1940 (m. diss. 1949), Lt.-Col. Henry Steuart Phillpotts, MC, Irish Gds. of Russelstown Park, co. Carlow; 2ndly, 1949, Maj. Richard Rashleigh Shelley, CVO, R. Scots Greys, who *d.* 1971, and has issue living, (by 2nd m.) Sean David Arthur, *b.* 1953,—(by 1st m.) Rebecca Aimée, *b.* 1943: *m.* 1967, Michael Goodbody,—(by 2nd m.) Emma Finola, *b.* 1951. *Residence*, Yoxford Place, Saxmundham, Suffolk.

Collateral Branches living.

Grandsons of Robert John FitzGerald, 2nd son of 1st baronet:—
Issue of Lt.-Col. Peter Francis FitzGerald, DSO, *b.* 1879, *d.* 1968: *m.* 1909, Baroness Adrienne de Geer, who *d.* 1973, da. of the late Baron Gustave de Geer, of Zeist, Holland:—
Peter Desmond (Querns House, Cirencester, Gloucestershire), *b.* 1910; Capt. late R. Tank Regt.: *m.* 1945, Elizabeth J. C. Norman, and has issue living, Anthony Desmond, *b.* 1953,—Caroline Rosemary, *b.* 1946: *m.* 1970, Maj. Philip Statham, RA,—Olivia Margaret, *b.* 1948,—Louise Elizabeth, *b.* 1951.——Mervyn Robert Gustav (Pen Mill Farm, Penselwood, Wincanton, Som.), *b.* 1911: *m.* 1940, Hilary da. of Percy Houghton Brown, LLD, and has issue living, Alastair Mervyn Malcolm (Rodmead, Maiden Bradley, Warminster, Wilts.), *b.* 1941: *m.* 1964, Penelope Jane, el. da. of Lt.-Col. John Stewart Eyre, and has issue living, Colin John *b.* 1970, Fiona Margaret *b.* 1965, Katherine Lucy *b.* 1967—Peter Robin, *b.* 1943; ed. at Canford, and Trin. Coll., Oxford,—Elizabeth Ann, *b.* 1945: *m.* 1969, Francis Mark Dineley, of Woodlands, Berwick St. John, Shaftesbury, Dorset, and has issue living, Alexander Perin *b.* 1973, Maria Frances *b.* 1971.

Grandson of the late Capt. Peter David FitzGerald (infra):—
Issue of the late Capt. James Brinsley Peter FitzGerald, *b.* 1894, *d.* 1962: *m.* 1924, Lady Moyra Marjorie Dawson-Damer, who *d.* 1962, da. of 5th Earl of Portarlington:—
Michael George Maurice (Gawcombe, Kingham, Oxford, and Parkwood, Three Springs, W. Aust.; Farmers' Club), *b.* 1925: *m.* 1959, F. Ruth, da. of Maj. P. A. F. Spence, of Deddington Manor, Oxon., and has issue living, Peter Desmond Philip *b.* 1961,—Sarah Moyra, *b.* 1962,—Ann Rachael (twin), *b.* 1962.

Issue of the late Peter David FitzGerald, 3rd son of 1st baronet, *b.* 1855, *d.* 1935: *m.* 1st, 1890, Helena Mary Elizabeth, who *d.* 1904, da. of Major William Francis Percy, Norfolk Regt., and widow of Capt. Leslie Martin, 12th Lancers; 2ndly, 1906, Charlotte Honor, who *d.* 1929, da. of the late Lieut.-Col. Thomas S. MacAdam, of Blackwater, co. Clare:—
(By 1st m.) Peter John, *b.* 1900; Com. (ret.) RN; 1914-18 War; 1939-45 War: *m.* 1928, Penelope, da. of Lt.-Col. Leonard Markham Crofts, DSO. *Residence*, Mondellihy, Adare, co. Limerick. *Clubs*, White's, Kildare St., Irish Turf.

The title of Knight of Kerry was conferred upon his son Maurice by John Fitz Thomas FitzGerald, Earl of Decies and Desmond, by virtue of his royal seigniory as a Count Palatine, and his descendants have ever since been so styled in Acts of Parliament, patents under the Great Seal, and other legal documents. The 1st baronet was the 19th Knight of Kerry. The 2nd baronet, Capt. Sir Maurice FitzGerald, C.V.O., served in Ashanti 1873-4 (several times mentioned in despatches, medal with clasp), and was an Extra Equerry to H.R.H. the Duke of Connaught.

FITZGERALD, Creation (U.K.) 1903, of Geraldine Place, St. Finn Barr, co. Cork.

Rev. (*Sir*) EDWARD THOMAS FITZGERALD, 3rd Baronet; *b.* March 7th, 1912; *s.* his father, *Sir* JOHN JOSEPH, 1957, but does not use the title; a Roman Catholic Priest.

Arms.—Ermine, on a saltire gules charged with two arrows saltirewise points downwards or, a chief arched of the second thereon a lymphad between two towers or. **Crest.**—In front of three oak trees a knight mounted in full armour proper bearing on his sinister arm a shield argent charged with a civic crown gules.

Residence—Mayfield, Cork.

muir nA 3-cpann

A sea of trees.

Brother living—*Rev.* DANIEL PATRICK, *b.* June 28th, 1916.
Uncle living—(Son of 1st baronet)—William, *b.* 1892: *m.* 1943, Kathleen O'Mahoney.

Collateral Branch living

Issue of the late Andrew Fitzgerald, 4th son of 1st baronet, *b.* 1885, *d.* 1969: *m.* 1916, Elizabeth Barry-Murphy, who *d.* 1952:—

John Finnbarr (Meadowlands, Wilton Rd., Cork), *b.* 1918:— *m.* 1940, Margaret Hogg, and has issue living, Andrew Peter, *b.* 1950,—Geraldine, *b.* 1953.——Andrew Joseph (60, Glenbrooke Park, Rathfarnham, Dublin, 14), *b.* 1922: *m.* 1953, Patricia Clark, and has issue living, Paul Andrew, *b.* 1966,—Anne, *b.* 1955,—Helen, *b.* 1959.——Margaret Mary, *b.* 1920.——Katherine, *b.* 1925.

The 1st baronet, Sir Edward (son of Daniel FitzGerald, of Gurstmaurane, Treleary, co. Cork) was Lord Mayor of Cork, 1903.

FITZHERBERT, Creation (G.B.) 1784, of Tissington, Derbyshire.

Une (only) will I serve.

Sir JOHN RICHARD FREDERICK FitzHerbert, 8th *Baronet*; el. son of the late Ven. Henry Edward FitzHerbert, yst. son of 5th baronet; *b.* Sept. 15th, 1913; *s.* his uncle, *Sir* WILLIAM, 1963; ed. at Charterhouse; formerly Lt. 8th Bn., Sherwood Foresters; 1939-45 War (prisoner): *m.* 1957, Anne (ASTELL), da. of the late H. J. Rees.

Arms—Gules, three lions rampant or. Crest—A cubit arm in armour erect, the hand appearing clenched within the gauntlet all proper.

Seat—Tissington Hall, Ashbourne, Derbyshire.

Brothers living—*Rev.* DAVID HENRY, *MC* (Dennington Rectory, Woodbridge, Suffolk), *b.* Sept. 9th, 1918; late Maj. 7th (Queen's Own) Hussars; 1939-45 War (MC): *m.* 1962, Charmian Hyacinthe, yr. da. of the late Samuel Ranulph Allsopp [see B. Hindlip, colls.], and has issue living, Richard Ranulph) *b.* 1963,—Selina Helen, *b.* 1965,—Juliet Sarah (twin) *b.* 1965,—Lucy Hyacinthe, *b.* 1967.——Alec Benjamin (of Hall Cottage, Quarndon, Derby), *b.* 1923.

Sisters living.—Mary Ida (of Trusley Manor West, Sutton-on-the-Hill, Derby), *b.* 1908.——Sybil Helen (Corner House, Dennington, Woodbridge, Suffolk), *b.* 1909.——Elinor Ruth (Meadowside, Brook Lane, Sutton-on-the-Hill, Derbys., DE6 5JA), *b.* 1911: *m.* 1st, 1936, Raymond Johnson German, TD, who *d.* (killed in action 1944); 2ndly, 1947, John Puxley White Jamie, MC, TD, DL, who *d.* 1972, and has issue living, (by 2nd m.) John Robert FitzHerbert (The Cottage, Blanch Croft, Melbourne, Derbys.), *b.* 1948: *m.* 1973, Jane, da. of T. D. Weston, of Rothley, Leics.——Ann (2, The Park, Duffield, Derbys.), *b.* 1916.

Collateral Branches living.

Grandchildren of the late Lieut.-Col. Richard Henry FitzHerbert, 2nd son of 3rd baronet :—

Issue of the late Major Walter Hepburn Melitas FitzHerbert, *b.* 1842, *d.* 1930: *m.* 1886, Mary Joanna Sophia, who *d.* 1937, da. of the late Rev. Thomas William Carr, R. of Barming, Maidstone :—

Harriet Marjorie, *b.* 1891. *Residence,* Somersal Herbert, Derby.

Issue of the late Arthur Richard FitzHerbert, Trooper in New Zealand Forces, *b.* 1853, *d.* (wounds in action during European War) 1917 : *m.* 1881, Mary Lucy, who *d.* 1942, da. of Major Marshall (formerly of 65th Regt.), of Tutu Totara, Marton, New Zealand :—

Mildred Mary (48, Hadfield Cres., Wanganui, NZ), *b.* 1891.

Grandchildren of the late Arthur Richard FitzHerbert (ante):—

Issue of the late Arthur Geoffry Marshall FitzHerbert, *b.* 1882, *d.* 1974: *m.* 1908, Hilda Eunice, who *d.* 1966, da. of the late W. Gray, of Marton, NZ:—

Arthur William (Tuatenui Rd., Marton, NZ,, *b.* 1922; 1939-45 War with RNZAF, and as Pilot Officer RAF: *m.* 1952, Noeline Carol, da. of Richard Kerkham, of Suva, Fiji, and has issue living, Arthur Gray, *b.* 1954,—Madeline Grace, *b.* 1953: *m.* 1971, Barry Edward Fairburn, of Wanganui, NZ, and has issue living, Aaron Karl *b.* 1972, Daniel Craig *b.* 1974.——Eileen Mildred, *b.* 1919: *m.* 1956, John Charles Shere, of Green's Rd., NO4 ED, Palmerston Borth, NZ.

Issue of the late Beresford Close FitzHerbert, *b.* 1884, *d.* 1969: *m.* 1918, Gladys Ruby (8, Brookfield St., St. Heliers Bay, Auckland, 5, NZ), da. of John Owens, of Epsom, Auckland, NZ:—

Adeline Beryl (284, Kohimarama Rd., Kohimarama, Auckland, NZ), *b.* 1919: *m.* 1946 (m. diss. 1961), Maxwell Robert Moore, F/O RNZAF, who *d.* 1967, and has issue living, Beverley Robin, *b.* 1955,—Jennifer Beryl, *b.* 1947: *m.* 1973, John Charles Mortland, of Waituna West, Feilding, NZ,—Alison Anne, *b.* 1951.——Dorothy Grace, *b.* 1920: *m.* 1945, Robert William Smith, F/O RNZAF, of Pukenana, Taihape, NZ, and has issue living, Robert Phillip Beresford, *b.* 1951,—Dorothy Christine, *b.* 1946,—Pauline Beresford, *b.* 1947,—Barbara Anne, *b.* 1954.——Ngaire Beresford (23, Rutherford Terr., Remuera, Auckland, NZ), *b.* 1923: *m.* 1950 (m. diss 1972), John McRobert Calder, F/O RNZAF, and has issue living, John Beresford, *b.* 1953,—Peter McRobert, *b.* 1955.

Granddaughters of the late Lt.-Col. Richard Henry FitzHerbert (ante):—

Issue of the late Anthony Francis FitzHerbert, *b.* 1863, *d.* 1925 : *m.* 1893, Catherine Anne, who *d.* 1954, da. of the late Charles Bull, of Aorangi, Fielding, New Zealand :—

Cicely Beresford, *b.* 1900: *m.* 1931, Henry William Petre [*see* B. Petre, colls.]. *Address.* R.D.1, Motueka, S. Island, New Zealand.——Nellie, *b.* 1905 : *m.* 1927, Strachan Agnew Goldingham, late Squadron Leader Roy. New Zealand Air Force. and has issue living, Heather Linda, *b.* 1929: *m.* 1953, 1st (m. diss. 1963), Lt.-Cdr. Michael Clinton Danby, RN; 2ndly, 1964, (Lionel) Peter Winterton Twiss, OBE, DSC, of Nettleworth, Titchfield, Hants, and has issue living, (by 1st marriage) Edward Strachan Clinton, *b.* 1960, Brigette Anne Rosemary *b.* 1956. *Residence,*—7, Wigan Place, Palmerston North, New Zealand.

Grandchildren of the late Herbert Haffenden FitzHerbert, el. son of the late Rev. Alleyne FitzHerbert (infra) :—

Issue of the late Egbert FitzHerbert, *b.* 1863, *d.* 1944: *m.* 1st, 1891, Florence Grace, who *d.* 1905, da. of the late Edward Gregory, of Feilding, New Zealand ; 2ndly, 1912, Margaret, da. of the late Benjamin John Holloway, of Thame, Oxon, and widow of Charles Joseph Little, of Eldon Road, Kensington, W. :—

(By 1st marriage) John Alleyne, *M.C.*, *b.* 1896; European War 1914-19 in France with 1st Australian Tunnelling Co. (despatches, MC).——Herbert Haffenden, *b.* 1905: *m.* 1934, Stella Marguerite, da. of the late W. F. Seymour, of Auckland, NZ.——Margaret Eunice, *b.* 1893: *m.* 1921, Robert Hugh Oakley Caldwell, and has issue living Robert Egbert, *b.* 1924,—Richard Pringle, *b.* 1930,—

Barbara, *b.* 1922,—Nancy, *b.* 1927. *Residence*, 101, Messines Road, Karori, Wellington, New Zealand.

Grandchildren of the late Horace FitzHerbert (infra) :—
Issue of the late Herbert FitzHerbert, *b.* 1887, *d.* 1958 : *m.* (Jan.) 1915, Winifred, who *d.* 1932, da. of William Walpole :—
William Michael, *b.* (Nov.) 1915 : *m.* 1947, Elsie Lillian, da. of Charles Ogle, and has issue living, William Anthony, *b.* 1950,—Annette Margaret, *b.* 1948,—Jennifer Ann, *b.* 1953. *Residence*, The Kestrels, Hunterville, New Zealand.——Mary Winifred, *b.* 1917 : *m.* 1941, Raymond Windelborn.——Eleanor Margaret, *b.* 1919. *Residence*, 5, Clifford Road, Johnsonville New Zealand.

Grandchildren of the late Herbert Haffenden FitzHerbert (ante) :—
Issue of the late Horace FitzHerbert, *b.* 1865, *d.* 1931 : *m.* 18—, Elizabeth, da. of — Drury :—
Norman, *b.* 1889 : *m.* 1919, Evelyn, da. of the late Robert M. Pemberton, C.E., of Waikane, New Zealand, and has issue living, John Anthony, *b.* 1920 : *m.* 1942, Martha Betty, da. of William George Hope, and has issue living, David Anthony *b.* 1945, Timothy John *b.* 1951, Catherine Mary *b.* 1947, Margaret Alison *b.* 1952,—Richard Gurden, *b.* 1922. *Residence,*
Issue of the late Augustus FitzHerbert, *b.* 1872, *d.* 1908 : *m.* 1902, Ellen, da. of the late John Curd:—
James Bruce, *b.* 1908 : *m.* 1940, Eileen Olson, of New Plymouth, New Zealand. *Residence*, Donnett Street, Opunake, New Zealand.——Janet Ruth, *b.* 1904 : *m.* 1939, Robert Steele Martin, Engineer, and has issue living, Luke Steele, *b.* 1942. *Residence*, Opunake, New Zealand.——Maude Mount Cashel, *b.* 1906. *Residence,*

Grandchildren of the late Rev. James FitzHerbert, son of the late Rev. Alleyne FitzHerbert (infra) :—
Issue of the late Humphrey Beresford FitzHerbert, *b.* 1879, *d.* 1951 : *m.* 1st, 1907, Kathleen, who *d.* 1941, da. of Charles Alexander, of Liverpool ; 2ndly, 1941, Winifred Ivy Bing, who *d.* 1962:—
(By 2nd m.) Humphrey Bing Vivian (36, West over Rd., Broadstairs, Kent), *b.* 1942: *m.* 1971, Pamela Joan, da. of James Sidney Pitt, of 7, Streete Court Rd., Westgate on Sea, Kent.—— Susan Eirene Angelina, *b.* 1945: *m.* 1964, Robert Viggo Jensen (6, Balliol Rd., Broadstairs, Kent), and has issue living, Jetta Elva, *b.* 1965.

Issue of the late Capt. Douglas Cecil FitzHerbert, *b.* 1882, *d.* 1933 : *m.* 1924, Daphne (now of South Collingham, Newark-on-Trent), da. of the late Henry Joseph Wigram [*see* Wigram, Bt., colls.] :—
Alleyne John, *b.* 1931 ; ed. at Denstone ; is Capt. Sherwood Rangers Yeo. (T.A.) : *m.* 1959, Judith Mary, da. of the late Ernest T. Walker, and has issue living, Amanda Sara, *b.* 1964. *Residence,* The Old Forge, Barkestone-le-Vale, Nottingham.

Grandson of the late Rev. Alleyne FitzHerbert, 3rd son of 3rd baronet:—
Issue of the late Henry Ralph FitzHerbert, *b.* 1852, *d.* 1917 : *m.* 1881, Martha, who *d.* 1909, da. of W. F. Kennedy, of Wellington, New Zealand :—
Claude Kennedy, *b.* 1884: *m.* 1910, his cousin, Averil Alexandra, who *d.* 1962, da. of the late, Rev. William Alexander Woodward. *Residence*, 7, The Fosseway, Clifton, Bristol, 8.

Grandchildren of the late Anthony FitzHerbert, 4th son of 3rd baronet:—
Issue of the late Gerard Horne FitzHerbert, *b.* 1853, *d.* 1899 : *m.* 1875, Emma, who *d.* 1937, el. da. of Thomas Fantam :—
Leonard, *b.* 1886.
Issue of the late Francis FitzHerbert, *b.* 1854, *d.* 1929 : *m.* 1902, Edith, who *d.* 1935, da. of the late John Knight FitzHerbert (infra):—
Geoffrey Francis, *b.* 1903 ; ed. at Sherborne : *m.* 1929, Violet Wrench (who obtained a divorce 1938), da. of the late James Watts Wyncoll, of Lynholme, Bridgwater.——Elizabeth (c/o Standard Bank, Main Rd., Claremont, Cape, S. Africa), *b.* 1905: *m.* 1937, Tom Bokenham Reddick, and has issue living, Robert Laird, *b.* 1945,—Sara, *b.* 1939.

Grandsons of the late Godfrey White FitzHerbert (infra) :—
Issue of the late Henry FitzHerbert, *b.* 1908, *d.* 1960: *m.* 1940, Betty, (who m. 2ndly, 19—, Robert Fulton, da. of Arthur W. Barnley, of Kiriga Estate, Thika, Kenya:—
Henry Nicholas, *b.* 1952.——Simon John, *b.* 1953.

Granddaughters of the late John Knight FitzHerbert, 5th son of 3rd baronet :—
Issue of the late Godfrey White FitzHerbert, *b.* 1864, *d.* 1939 : *m.* 1900, Anna Rachel, who *d.* 1961, da. of the late Henry Alleyne Pile [Alleyne, Bt., colls.] :—
Joan, *MRCS, LRCP, DPM*, (c/o Bible College of Wales, Derwen Fawr Rd., Swansea), *b.* 1902: *m.* 1923, Lt. John Hugh Lloyd Lloyd-Owen, RN (ret.).——Judith Agnes (c/o Emmanuel Grammar School, Derwen Fawr Rd., Swansea), *b.* 1914.

The 1st baronet was 9th in male descent from Nicholas, 2nd son of John FitzHerbert, of Somersal Herbert, whose ancestors possessed it from the beginning of the 13th century. Nicholas, died 1472, having acquired Tissington by his marriage with Margaret, da. of Robert Fraunceys, of Foremark, and grand-da. and co-heir of Sir Thomas Clinton (2nd son of 3rd Baron Clinton).

FLANNERY, Creation (U.K.) 1904, of Wethersfield Manor, Essex. [Extinct 1959.]

Sir HAROLD FORTESCUE FLANNERY, *M.B.E.*, 2nd and last *Baronet.*

Daughter living of 1st Baronet—Enid Fortescue (Plough Cottage, Church St., Rudgwick, Sussex), *m.* 1916, Capt. David Crawford Moore Lindsay, Black Watch (Roy. Highlanders) (ret.), who *d.* 1939, and has issue living, David Fortescue Moore (of Elmhurst, Little Bookham, Surrey), *b.* 1917: *m.* 1949, Sylvia Mason, and has issue living, David Ian Strickland *b.* 1953, Peter Crawford *b.* 1958, Elizabeth Romer, *b.* 1951,—Elizabeth Eve, *b.* 1919: *m.* 1944, Capt. Lennox William Napier, DSO, DSC, RN (ret.) (Plough Cottage, Church St., Rudgwick, Sussex), and has issue living, Christopher Lennox *b.* 1944, Paul Morillyon *b.* 1949, Lucilla Eve *b.* 1952,—Rosamund Romer, *b.* 1930.

Daughter living of 2nd Baronet—Joan Fortescue, *b.* 1918: *m.* 1940, Geoffrey Montague Fenwick Stow, Assist. Marshal of Diplo. Corps, and has issue living, Timothy Montague Fenwick, *b.* 1943,—Michael Montague Fenwick, *b.* 1948,—David Montague Fenwick, *b.* 1950,—Rebecca Rosamond, *b.* 1945. *Residence*, 84, Park St., W1.

Widow, living of 2nd Baronet—MAUD (*Lady Flannery*), da. of St. George Boswell, of Quebec: *m.* 1917, Sir Harold Fortescue Flannery, M.B.E., 2nd baronet, who *d.* 1959, when the title became ext. *Residence*, 3, Alde House, Aldeburgh, Suffolk.

FLAVELLE, Creation (U.K.) 1917, of Toronto, Dominion of Canada.

Sir (JOSEPH) ELLSWORTH FLAVELLE, 2nd
Baronet; *b.* May 25th, 1892; *s.* his father, *Sir*
JOSEPH WESLEY, 1939; is a Gov. of St.
Andrew's Coll.: *m.* 1917, Muriel, da. of William
N. McEachren, and has issue.

Arms—Per chevron azure and sable in chief two cylindrical
shells and in base issuant a dexter hand erect, the fingers reaching towards an estoile in fesse point all counterchanged.
Crest—A cubit arm erect argent, winged or, the hand holding a
torch sable, fired proper.

Residence—Kingswold RR2, King, Ontario, Canada.
Club—York (Toronto).

Sons living—JOSEPH DAVID ELLSWORTH, *b.* Nov.
9th, 1921: *m.* 1942, Muriel Barbara, da. of Reginald Morton,
and has issue living, Muriel Catherine, *b.* 1944,—Virginia
Ann *b.* 1947, Elizabeth Ann *b.* 1950.——William Ellsworth,
b. 1926.

Daughter living—Clara Elizabeth, *b.* 1918: *m.* 1941, Gage
Hayward Love, and has issue living, Gage Ellsworth, *b.*
1942,—David Hayward, *b.* 1946,—Peter Flavelle, *b.* 1948,—
William Geoffrey, *b.* 1951. *Residence*, West Winds, RR2,
King, Ontario, Canada.

The 1st Baronet, Sir Joseph Wesley Flavelle (son of
John Flavelle), was Chm. of Imperial Munitions Board of
Canada and of Grand Trunk Railway of Canada.

Prepared for peace and war.

AUBREY-FLETCHER, Creation (G.B.) 1782, of Clea Hall, Cumberland.

Sir JOHN HENRY LANCELOT AUBREY-FLETCHER, 7th
Baronet; *b.* Aug. 22nd, 1912; *s.* his father, *Maj. Sir*
HENRY LANCELOT, *CVO, DSO*, 1969; ed. at Eton, and
New Coll., Oxford (BA); Bar. Inner Temple 1937; JP
for Bucks; Dep. Chm. of Quarter Sessions 1959-71; a
Metropolitan Magistrate 1959-71; Recorder of Crown
Court 1972-74; High Sheriff of Bucks. 1961; 1939-45
War as Lt.-Col. Gren. Gds. (SR): *m.* 1939, Diana Fyn-
vola, only child of the late Lt.-Col. Arthur George
Edward Egerton, Coldm. Gds., and has issue.

Arms—Quarterly : 1st and 4th, argent, a cross engrailed sable between
four pellets each charged with a pheon argent, *Fletcher*; 2nd and 3rd
azure, a chevron between three eagles' heads erased or, *Aubrey*.
Crests—1st, a horse's head argent, *Fletcher*; 2nd, an eagle's head erased
or, *Aubrey*.

Martis, non cupidinis.
Of war, not of love.

Residences,—13, Lowndes Sq., SW3; The Gate House, Chilton, Aylesbury.

Son living—HENRY EGERTON, *b.* Nov. 27th, 1945; ed. at Eton.

Daughter living—Susan Mary Fynvola (*Hon. Mrs. Richard O. Stanley*), *b.* 1940: *m.* 1965, the Hon.
Richard Oliver Stanley [see E. Derby].

Brothers living—Nigel Chilton, *b.* 1914 (Chilton Croft, Hinton Waldrist, Faringdon, Oxon., SN7
8SE), ed. at Eton; Fl. Lt. RAFVR; 1939-45 War: *m.* 1942, Areta Mae Lees, and has issue living,
Philip Nigel (Blakeney, Buckland, Faringdon, Berks.), *b.* 1944: *m.* 1969, Susan Anne, only da. of
Wing-Cdr. M. L. Bathe, RAF (ret.), and has issue living, Caroline Susan *b.* 1973,—David Lancelot
(twin), *b.* 1944 (126, Munster Rd., Fulham, SW6): *m.* 1974, Carolyn Cochrane, only da. of Kenneth
F. Neale.——Lancelot Philip, *b.* 1919; ed. at Eton; Capt. (ret.) Grenadier Guards; 1939-45 War
(wounded, prisoner): *m.* 1952, Audrey Muriel, only da. of (Frederick) Ronald Oliver [see B.
Hindlip, colls.], and has issue living, Mark Lancelot, *b.* 1964,—Jane Elizabeth, *b.* 1961. *Residence*, Wychden, Chobham, Surrey.——Edward Henry Lancelot (Gatherum Farm, Ryehurst
Lane, Binfield, Berks.), *b.* 1930; ed. at Eton, and New Coll., Oxford; Lt.-Col. Gren. Guards:
m. 1953, Bridget Mary, el. da. of Brig. Sir Henry Robert Kincaid Floyd, CB, CBE, 5th Bt., and
has issue living, Richard Edward Henry, *b.* 1954,—Patrick John Kincaid, *b.* 1955,—Gillian
Mary, *b.* 1958

Sister living—Mary Elizabeth, *b.* 1923: *m.* 1951, Algernon Putland Devaynes Smyth, and has issue
living, Charles Henry Devaynes, *b.* 1955,—Caroline Dorothy, *b.* 1952. *Residence*, Rye House,
Silchester, Reading.

Widow living of 6th Baronet—NANCY CECIL (*Nancy, Lady Aubrey-Fletcher*), (Barnfield, Delly End,
Hailey, Witney, Oxon), da. of Joseph Cecil Bull, and widow of Maj. Charles Reynolds: *m.* 1965,
as his 2nd wife, Maj. Sir Henry Lancelot Aubrey-Fletcher, CVO, DSO, 6th Bt., who *d.* 1969.

Collateral Branch living.
Issue of the late John Lowther FLETCHER, 6th son of 3rd baronet, *b.* 1851, *d.* 1928:
m. 1893, Emily, who *d.* 1937, da. of the late William Burkwood, and widow of
Cecil H. Weston:—
Grace Vaughan, *b.* 1891.——Jacquetta May, *b.* 1894: *m.* 1919, Ronald G. Seaburne-May, Capt.
Sherwood Forresters, who *d.* 1940, and has issue living, Daphne, *b.* 1923,—Jacquetta Jane,
b. 1929. *Residence,*

Henry Fletcher, of Cockermouth, entertained Mary, Queen of Scots, on her journey from
Workington to Carlisle, 1568, and presented her with robes of velvet, for which she returned him a
letter of thanks. From him descended Sir Richard Fletcher, whose son, Henry, was created a baronet,
1640. He raised a regiment for Charles I., and was slain at Rawton Heath. This baronetcy expired
with Sir Henry, 3rd baronet, who died a monk at Douay 1712. Sir Henry, 1st baronet of the present
creation, was a Cdr. in Navy of HEICS; a distinguished Director of the East India Co., and MP
for Cumberland 1768-1802. The 4th baronet, the Rt. Hon. Sir Henry Aubrey-Fletcher, CB, PC,
sat as MP for Horsham (C) 1880-85, and for Lewes, 1885-1910. He was Parliamentary Groom-in-
Waiting to Queen Victoria 1885-86, and assumed by Roy. licence 1903 the additional surname and
arms of Aubrey. His brother Sir Lancelot, 5th baronet, also assumed by Roy. licence 1910 this
additional surname and arms. Maj. Sir Henry Lancelot Aubrey-Fletcher, 6th baronet, was Lord
Lieut. of Bucks. 1954-61, and HM Lieut. of Body Guard of Hon. Corps. of Gentlemen-at-Arms
1956-57.

FLOYD, Creation (U.K.) 1816.

Sir GILES HENRY CHARLES FLOYD, 7th
Baronet; *b.* Feb. 27th, 1932; *s.* his father, *Lt.-Col.*
Sir JOHN DUCKETT, *TD*, 1975; ed. at Eton; High
Sheriff of Rutland 1968: *m.* 1954, Lady Gillian
Moyra Katherine Cecil, da. of 6th Marquess of
Exeter, and has issue.

Arms—Sable, a lion rampant-reguardant argent, on a
chief embattled or a sword erect proper, pommel and hilt or,
the blade passing through an eastern crown gules, between
two tigers' faces also proper. **Crest**—A lion rampant-
reguardant argent, murally crowned gules, bearing a flag
(representing the standard of Tippoo Sultaun) flowing to the
sinister proper.

Residence—Tinwell Manor, Stamford, Lincs.

Bearing patiently the dust and
the sun.

Sons living—DAVID HENRY CECIL, *b.* April 2nd, 1956; et. at
Eton.——Henry Edward Cecil, *b.* 1958.
Brother living—John Edmund Kincaid (North Ecchingswell
House, Newbury, Berks.), *b.* 1936; late Capt. 15th/19th
Hussars: *m.* 1965, Victoria Jane, el. da. of Richard N.
Cannon, OBE, of Combe Place, Lewes, and has issue living,
Clare Victoria, *b.* 1966,—Nicola Anne, *b.* 1967,—Marina
Jocelin, *b.* 1971.
Daughter living of 5th Baronet—Bridget Mary, *b.* 1930: *m.*
1953, Lt.-Col. Edward Henry Lancelot Aubrey-Fletcher, of
Gatherum Farm, Ryehurst Lane, Binfield, Berks. [*see*
Aubrey-Fletcher, Bt.].
Aunt living—(daughter of 4th Baronet)—Elizabeth Anne
(Gold Acres, High St., East Meon, Petersfield, Hants.),
b. 1897: *m.* 1929, John Humphrey Nicholson, MC, who *d.* 1971 [E. St. Aldwyn, colls.].
Widow living of 5th Baronet—Hon. Kathleen Fanny Gretton (*Hon. Lady Floyd*), (Chearsley Hill
House, Aylesbury, Bucks.), da. of the 1st Baron Gretton: *m.* 1929, Brig. Sir Henry Robert
Kincaid Floyd, CB, CBE, 5th Bt., who *d.* 1968.
Widow living of 6th Baronet—JOCELIN EVADNE, JP (*Jocelin, Lady Floyd*), (Lovington House,
Ovington, nr. Alresford, Hants.), da. of the late Sir Edmund Charles Wyldbore Smith [see
Smith-Marriott, Bt., colls.]: *m.* 1929, Lt.-Col. Sir John Duckett Floyd, TD, 6th Bt., who *d.*
1975.
Collateral Branches living.
Issue of the late Lt.-Col. Charles Murray Floyd, OBE, RE, yst. son of 4th
baronet, *b.* 1905, *d.* 1971: *m.* 1948, Mary Elizabeth (Great Chalfield, Melksham,
Wilts.), only child of Robert Fleetwood Fuller, of Great Chalfield, Melksham,
Wilts., and widow of Lt.-Col. Patrick John Salvin Boyle, RSF [see E. Glasgow
colls.]:—
Robert Charles, *b.* 1949; ed. at Eton, and Keble Coll., Oxford.——Thomas Henry, *b.* 1951; ed. at
Eton.——William Duckett, *b.* 1956; ed. at Eton.

Grandson of the late Rev. Charles Greenwood Floyd, 4th son of 2nd baronet:—
Issue of the late Lt.-Col. Arthur Bowen Floyd, DSO, OBE, *b.* 1888, *d.* 1965: *m.* 1922, Iris Clare who *d.* 1975, da. of D. Turner Belding, of East Dereham, and widow of Capt. A. Stewart Ritchie, MC:—
John Anthony (26, Park Village East, NW1), *b.* 1923: *m.* 1948, Margaret Louise, da. of Maj. H. Rosselli, of Worlington, Suffolk, and has issue living, Elizabeth Joanna, *b.* 1951,—Caroline Philippa, *b.* 1953.

Issue of the late Charles Ashburnham Floyd, 6th son of 2nd baronet, *b.* 1838, *d.* 1920: *m.* 1867, Mary, who *d.* 1907, da. of George Pomeroy, of Exeter:—
Julia Miranda Laura: *m.* 1926, as his second wife, Col. John Spottiswoode Purvis, C.B.E., late R.E., who *d.* 1927.——Gertrude Frederica Mary Ashburnham. *Residence.*

Issue (by 2nd marriage) of the late Walter Combermere Lee Floyd, M.I.C.E., 7th son of 2nd baronet, *b.* 1841, *d.* 1917 : *m.* 1st, 1869, Elizabeth Jane, who *d.* 1870, el. da. of the late Richard Dunning, of Townsend, Winkleigh, Devon ; 2ndly, 1882, Cecilia Mary Louisa, who *d.* 1928, da. of the late James Findlay, of Easterhill, Lanarkshire :—
Cecilia Margaret, *b.* 1891: *m.* 1930, Claude George Coventry Mallet, who *d.* 1966, son of Sir Claude Coventry Mallet, CMG. *Residence,* 1, Andar D., Rua Presidente Wilson, 4, Arieiro, Lisbon, Portugal.

This family, of Welsh origin, was settled in Cheshire and Shrewsbury. Gen. Sir John Floyd, 1st Bt., Col. 8th Light Dragoons, distinguished himself in India as Col. of 19th Light Dragoons, and was 2nd in command at the taking of Seringapatam, 1799. His daughter, Julia, married the statesman Sir Robert Peel. Brig. Sir Henry Robert Kincaid Floyd, CB, CBE, 5th Bt., late 15th/19th Hussars (Col. 1947-57) was Equerry to HRH the Duke of Gloucester 1927-28; BGS 8 Corps 1944, and Ch. of Staff 8th Army 1944-45, Lord Lieut. of Bucks. 1961-68; HM Lieut of Body Guard of Hon. Corps of Gentlemen-at-Arms 1966-68.

Foley-Philipps, see Philipps.

FORBES, Creation (N.S.) 1630, of Craigievar, Aberdeenshire.

Hon. Sir EWAN FORBES OF BRUX, 11th *Baronet*; *b.* Sept. 6th, 1912; *s.* his brother, WILLIAM FRANCIS, AFC, 19th Lord Sempill 1965; ed. at Munich, and Aberdeen Univ.; MB and ChB Aberdeen 1944: *m.* 1953, Isobel, da. of the late Alexander Mitchell, of Glenrinnes.
ᴀrms,—Not yet matriculated in the line of the present baronet.

Residence,—Brux Lodge, Alford, Aberdeenshire.

Collateral Branches living.
Issue of the late Rear-Adm. the Hon. Arthur Lionel Ochoncar Forbes-Sempill, yst. son of 17th Lord Sempill, *b.* 1877, *d.* 1962: *m.* 1st, 1903, Muriel Emily (who *d.* 1954, having obtained a divorce 1914), da. of the Rev. Walter Spencer, formerly of Fownhope Court, Hereford; 2ndly, 1919, Helen Mabel, who *d.* 1921, da. of the late Maj. John Allen, of Brackley House, Brackley, Northants; 3rdly, 1926, Mary Cutting Holland, who *d.* 1940, da. of the late Arthur J. Cumnock, of 521, Park Av., New York:—
(By 3rd marriage) JOHN ALEXANDER CUMNOCK (3, Mallord St., SW3; Naval and Military Club), *b.* Aug. 29th, 1927; late Capt. Seaforth Highlanders; Actor-Manager: *m.* 1st, 1958 (m. diss. 1964), Penelope Margaret Ann, da. of Arthur Gordou Grey-Pennington; 2ndly, 1966, Jane Carolyn, only da. of C. Gordon Evans, of Chelsfield, Kent.——(By 2nd m.) Janet, *b.* 1920; formerly Sergeant ATS: *m.* 1958, Norman Walker, of Stonecote, Presteigne, Radnorshire, who assumed 1958, by deed poll the additional surname of Forbes before his patronymic, and has issue living, Ian, *b.* 1960.

Descendants of the late Hon. James Ochoncar Forbes, brother of 17th Lord Sempill:—
See Ly. Sempill.

Granddaughters of the late Alexander Kinloch Forbes, yst. son of the late John Forbes-Mitchell, of Thainstone, 4th son of the late Duncan Forbes-Mitchell, 2nd son of 4th Bt.:—
Issue of the late Rev. John Fraser Forbes, *b.* 1847, *d.* 1887: *m.* 1878, Edith Palin, who *d* 1914, da. of the late Henry Wenden, of Barnes, Surrey:—
Agnes Dorothy Mary, *b.* 1880.——Emmeline Brita Cahusac, *b.* 1882.——Edith Margaret Lyndhurst, *b.* 1884: *m.* 1919 (m. diss. 19—), Capt. Hugh Percival Cotton, RN (ret.), who *d.* 1956. *Residence,*—

Descendants of Duncan Forbes (who m. the Hon. Sarah Forbes, sister of 17th Lord Sempill), el. son of Alexander Forbes, 5th son of Duncan Forbes-Mitchell (ante):—
See Ly. Sempill.

Granddaughters of the late Capt. Arthur Newton Forbes-Gordon, el. son of the late Arthur Forbes-Gordon (infra):—
Issue of the late Maj. Arthur Dalrymple Forbes-Gordon of Langlee, Cameron Highlanders, *b.* 1872, *d.* 1931: *m.* 1902, Dorothy Ione Helen, who *d.* 1964, da. of the late Frederick Morton Eden [Eden, Bt., colls.]:—
Christian Dorothy ROYLE, *b.* 1910; resumed the surname of Royle 1959: *m.* 1st, 1934, Maj. Frederick George Margaritus Grey, Highland LI, who obtained a divorce 1938; 2ndly, 1939, Maj. John Popplewell Royle, Glider Pilot Regt., who *d.* (killed in action at Arnhem) 1944; 3rdly, 1950, Lt.-Cdr. John Charles Grattan, DSC, RN, and has issue living, (by 2nd marriage) Mark John Forbes, *b.* 1941.——Catherine Helen (Spinal Hostel, Stoke Mandeville Hospital, Aylesbury, Bucks.), *b.* 1915; late VAD: *m.* 1st, 1938 (m. diss. 1939), Robert Sinclair Scott, Lt. Highland LI; 2ndly, 1941 (m. diss. 1954), Charles Albert Andres, of Brussels.

Grandson of the late Arthur Forbes-Gordon, son of the late Lt.-Col. Arthur Forbes, 5th son of 4th Bt.: —
Issue of the late Capt. William Balfour Forbes, AM, RN, *b.* 1845, *d.* 1928: *m.* 1889, Helen, who *d.* 1958, da. of the late Capt. Walter B. Persee, 90th Regt.:—
William, *b.* 1905.

Grandson of the late Capt. William Balfour Forbes, AM, RN (ante):—
Issue of the late Lt. Arthur Walter Forbes, DSO, RN, b. 1892, d. (lost at sea during
1914-18 War) 1918: m. 1917, Elizabeth (Eveline Betty), [who d. 1961, having m. 2ndly,
1919, Cdr. John Gordon Aitchison, OBE, RN [Aitchison, Bt.], who d. 1964], da. of the
late William Tudor Sutherland, of Skibo Castle, Sutherland:—
Arthur Michael Gerald Sutherland (*posthumous*), b. 1918; Maj. (ret.) King's Own Scottish Bor-
derers: m. 1947, Phœbe Mabel, da. of the late Lt.-Col. Cyril Charles Johnson Barrett, CSI,
CIE, and has issue living, Christine Helen, b. 1949,—Lorna Betty-May b. 1952: m. 1974, Martin
John Guy Knights, BA. *Residences*,—1, Walton Place, SW3; 9, Seafield Terr., Seaview, I. of
Wight; The Shirling, Killin, Perthshire. *Club*—Army and Navy.

The Forbes of Craigievar, Aberdeenshire, descend from Patrick Forbes of Corse, 2nd son of
2nd Lord Forbes. Sir William Forbes of Craigievar, el. son of William, 2nd son of William Forbes
of Corse and nephew of Sir Arthur Forbes [see E. Granard] was cr. a *Baronet* of Nova Scotia with
remainder to his heirs male 1630. He commanded a troop of horse in the Civil Wars, sat as MP
for Aberdeen, and received a grant of 16,000 acres in New Brunswick. Sir William Forbes, 5th
Bt., m, 1780, the Hon. Sarah Sempill, el. da. of the 12th Baron Sempill, and Sir William, 8th Bt.
(who s. 1846), s. as 17th Lord Sempill 1884, and assumed in 1885 the additional and principal surname of Sempill. On the death of 19th Lord Sempill 1965, the Lordship descended to his daughter
[see L. Sempill], and the baronetcy to his brother.

FORBES, Creation (U.K.) 1823, of Newe, Aberdeenshire.

*They will attain a higher point, who
strive at things the most exalted.*

Sir JOHN STEWART FORBES,
D.S.O., 6th *Baronet*; *b.* Jan. 8th, 1901;
s. his father, Sir CHARLES STEWART, 1927;
ed. at Wellington Coll.; Col. (retired)
late R.E.; Hon. Col. 51st (Highland)
Div. Engineers 1960-67; JP, and Vice-Lt.
for Aberdeenshire; served in Norway
1940 (despatches, DSO), and Burma
1944-45 (despatches) *m.* 1933, Agnes
Jessie, da. of Lieut.-Col. David Lorraine
Wilson-Farquharson, DSO, of Allargue,
Corgarff, Aberdeenshire, and has issue.

Arms—Quarterly: 1st and 4th, azure, three
bears' heads couped argent, muzzled gules, *Forbes*;
2nd and 3rd, azure, three cinquefoils argent,
Fraser. **Crest**—A falcon rising proper. **Supporters**—Two bears argent, muzzled gules.

Residence—Allargue, Corgarff, Aberdeenshire.
Clubs—St. James', Royal Northern.

Daughters living—Bridget Rosemary Zilla, b.
1935: m. 1962, Maj. Francis Mitchell Kent
Tuck, R.E., c/o Lloyds Bank, 6, Pall Mall,
SW1, and has issue living, Rosemary Jean
Winter, b. 1963,—Caroline Frances Stewart,
b. 1964,—Ellen Alexandra Farquharson, b.
1968.——Elspeth Ann, b. 1937; ed. at Aber-
deen Univ. (MA honours): m. 1960, George
Hardie, DA, of 29, Marchbank Rd., Bieldside,
Aberdeenshire, and has issue living, Jonathan Forbes, b. 1967,—Katherine Ann, b. 1961,—Ruth
Mary, b. 1964.——Veronica Jean b. 1938: m. 1958, Edward Lancaster, DA, ARIBA, FRIAS,
(31, McLeod Rd., Balloch, Inverness-shire), and has issue living, Alan Stewart, b. 1961,—Kevin
Edward, b. 1965,—Fiona Margaret, b. 1958.——Margaret Xanthe Patricia, b. 1940, MB, ChB,
Aberdeen: m. 1964, James Colquhoun Petrie, MB, ChB, MRCP, of 126, Desswood Place, Aberdeen,
and has issue living, John Ross, b. 1965,—Mark Colquhoun, b. 1969,—Rachel Xanthe Anne,
b. 1967,—Paula Jane, b. 1970.——Alison Stewart, b. 1946: m. 1968, T. Angus Ouchterlony, of
West Wing, The Guynd, by Arbroath, Angus, and has issue living, Peter Anthony Heathcote,
b. 1971,—James Angus Heathcote, b. 1973,—Teresa Mary, b. 1969.

Sisters living—Katherine Stewart (Newe, Aberdeenshire), b. 1903.——Mary Veronica, b. 1904: m.
1929, Edward Collins, who d. 1948. *Residence*, Newe, Aberdeenshire.

Collateral Branch living.

Granddaughters of the late Lt.-Col. James Stewart Forbes (infra):—
Issue of the late George Stewart Forbes, MRCVS, b. 1911, d. 1969: m. 1st, 1938 (m. diss.
1949), Mrs. Violet Mabel Doyle, da. of Kenward Stuart Barker; 2ndly, 1949, Joan
(Burley Lodge Shinfield, Berks.), da. of the late Frederick Turvey:—
(By 2nd m.) Fiona Hay Lavens, b. 1950: m. 1970, Nicholas Ashmead Cliff Vigors, and has issue
living, Charles Stewart Cliff, b. 1973,—Sarah Louise, b. 1974.——Alison Feridah, b. 1952: m.
1973, John Albert King,——Teresa Frances Ida, b. 1953.——Joanna Grace, b. 1955.——Sarah
Georgina, b. 1967.——Nicola Jane Stewart, b. 1969.

Grandchildren of the late George Stewart Forbes, 2nd son of 3rd baronet:—
Issue of the late Lieut.-Col. James Stewart Forbes, b. 1872, d. 1957: m. 1st, 1896, Lady
Angela Selina Bianca St. Clair-Erskine (who d. 1950, having obtained a divorce 1906),
da. of 4th Earl of Rosslyn; 2ndly, 1910, Feridah, who d. 1953, da. of Hugh Lewis
Taylor:—
(By 2nd m.) HAMISH STEWART, MBE, MC, b. Feb. 15th, 1916; ed. at Eton; Maj. (ret.) Welsh
Gds.; 1939-45 War (prisoner, MC, MBE); MBE (Mil) 1945: m. 1945, Jacynthe Elizabeth Mary,
da. of the late Eric Gordon Underwood, and has issue living, James Thomas Stewart, b. 1957,—
Caroline Serena, b. 1947,—Jane Henrietta Mary, b. 1950,—Christian Clare, b. 1961. *Residence*,
Hambleden Cottage, Henley-on-Thames. *Club*, Turf.——Ian Dudley Stewart, *DSC* (Quhyte-
woollen House, Lockerbie, Dumfriesshire; *Club*, Turf), b. 1919; Cdr. RN, and a yr. Brother of
Trinity House; 1939-45 War: m. 1st, 1950, Lady Penelope Anne Rous (who obtained a divorce
1960), da. of 4th Earl of Stradbroke; 2ndly, 1961, Gunilla, da. of the late Fritz Ryman, and has
issue living, (by 1st m.) Charles Stewart, b. 1956,—Catriona, b. 1951,—Caroline Ianthe, b. 1952.
——Mevagh (of The Garage, 10A, Edith Grove, SW10), b. 1914: m. 1948, Julius Joseph Alfred
Horton, who d. 1963.——Juanita Ann Stewart, b. 1929: m. 1st, 1949, Capt. Anthony Maitland
Steel, from whom she obtained a divorce 1954; 2ndly, 1961, Richard Currier Stickney, and has
issue living, (by 2nd m.) Francis Robin Christopher, b. 1962. *Residence*, Longmeadow, Chiswick
Mall, W4.

Sir Charles Forbes, 1st Bt., merchant of Bombay, was in 1833 served heir male to 3rd Lord
Forbes of Pitsligo (peerage attainted 1745) when Lord Lyon allowed him the Pitsligo arms and

supporters, being descended from William Forbes of Daach and Newe, **yr.** brother of Sir Alexander Forbes of Pitsligo (d. *c.* 1496, from whom 1st Lord Forbes of Pitsligo was 5th in descent) and gt. grandson of Sir William Forbes of Kynnaldy (*d.* 1446), next brother of 1st Lord Forbes.

STUART-FORBES, Creation (N.S.) 1626, of Pitsligo, and Monymusk, Aberdeenshire.

Neither timidly, nor rashly.

Greater than adversity, a match for prosperity.

Sir CHARLES EDWARD STUART-FORBES, 12th *Baronet* ; *b.* Aug. 6th, 1903 ; *s.* his brother, *Sir* HUGH, 1937; ed. at Ocean Bay Coll.; a Co. Manager (ret.): *m.* 1966, Ijah Leah MacCabe, who *d.* 1974, of Wellington, NZ.

Arms—1st and 4th, grand quarters, azure, on a chevron between three bears' heads couped argent, muzzled **gules**, a heart of the last ; 2nd and 3rd, grand quarters, quarterly, 1st and 4th, azure, three bears' heads couped argent, muzzled gules ; 2nd and 3rd, azure, three cinquefoils argent. **Crest**— Out of a baron's coronet a hand holding a scimitar all proper. **Supporters**—Two bears proper.

Address,—33, Dillon's Point Rd., Blenheim, NZ.

Sisters living—Lilian May: *m.* 19—,——— Everett.—— Ilene Myrtle: *m.* 1926, William Houslow, who *d.* 1957, and has issue living, Kenneth Charles Patrick *b.* 1929. ———Gertrude Ellen: *m.* 1939, Jack Jennings of 90, The Esplanade S2, Wellington, NZ, and has issue living, John David (23, Mountbatten Grove, Upper Hutt, NZ), *b.* 1944: *m.* 1968, Beryl Margaret, yst. da. of Eric Weightman, of Notts., and has issue living, Richard David *b.* 1968, Stuart Craig *b.* 1970. ———Merlin (68, South St., Blenheim, NZ), *m.* 1936, Ernest Edward Williams, who *d.* 1974, and has issue living, Hugh Edward, *b.* 1937,—Lillian June, *b.* 1938,—Barbara Joan (twin), *b.* 1938,— Karen Anne, *b.* 1957.———Gwendoline Rose: *m.* 1952, Leonard Lowe, who *d.* 1965, and has issue living, Peter Morris, *b.* (Jan.) 1956,—Barbara Theresa, *b.* (Nov.) 1956,—Yvonne Maria, *b.* 1959.

Aunt living (daughter of 9th baronet)—Beatrice Fullarton: *m.* 1914, James Royston Callender, and has issue living, William Stuart (of 42, Renfrew Av., Mount Albert, Auckland, New Zealand), *b.* 1915: *m.* 1952, Ella Jean Skuse, and has issue living, David Gordon *b.* 1953, Robert Andrew *b.* 1956, Linda Margaret *b.* 1955,—Hugh Royston, *b.* 1919: *m.* 1949, Mary Lorna Elliot, of Artarmon, Sydney, N.S. Wales, and has issue living, Warwick Elliot *b.* 1951, Vivien Elliot *b.* 1953. *Residence,*

Widow living of 11th Baronet—ANN WALLACE SCOTT (*Ann, Lady Stuart-Forbes*): *m.* 1929, Sir Hugh Stuart-Forbes, 11th baronet, who *d.* 1937.

Collateral Branches living.

Issue of the late William Kenneth Stuart-Forbes, 3rd son of 10th baronet, *b.* 1906, *d.* 1946: *m.* (March) 1932, **Marjory** Gilchrist, of Mahakapawa, Marlborough, New Zealand :—

WILLIAM DANIEL (of Omaka Valley, Marlborough, New Zealand), *b.* Aug. 21st, 1935: *m.* 1956, Jannette MacDonald, and has issue living, Kenneth Charles, *b.* (Dec.) 1956,—Daniel Dawson, *b.* 1962,—Reginald MacDonald, *b.* 1964,—Catherine Florence, *b.* 1958,—Eileen Jane, *b.* 1960.—— Avis Ilene, *b.* (Dec.) 1932: *m.* 1954, William Charles Russell, and has issue living, Stuart William, *b.* 1961,—Janice Katheryn, *b.* 1955,—Dianne Avis, *b.* 1956,—Susan Margaret, *b.* 1958.

Issue of the late Reginald Alexander Stuart-Forbes, yst. son of 10th baronet, *b.* 1909, *d.* 1974: *m.* 1940, Florence Annie Gilchrist (Hammericks Rd.), Blenheim, NZ):—

Dorothy Anne, *b.* 1947.———Marilyn, *b.* 1951: *m.* 1972, Alister James McAlpine.

Issue of the late William Forbes, 3rd son of 9th baronet, *b.* 1876, *d.* 1938: *m.* 1906, Lillian Marian (now of 29, Ballance Street, Shannon, New Zealand), da. of the late James Moore:—

William John, *b.* 1908. *Residence,* Shannon, New Zealand.——Gwendoline.——Moya: *m.* 1942, Owen Alfred Wiley, and has issue living, Andrew Owen, *b.* 1943,—Kerin Francis, *b.* 1944,— Noel William, *b.* 1946,—Paul Royson, *b.* 1948. *Residence,* Awapuni, Palmerston South, New Zealand.

Grandchildren of the late George Edward Forbes, son of George Forbes, 3rd son of 6th baronet:—

Issue of the late Rev. Edward Archibald Forbes, *b.* 1869, *d.* 1929: *m.* 1922, Enid Blackburn, who *d.* 1971, da. of the late Rev. Canon Garden Llanoe Duff Dunbar, Bt. cr. 1706, colls.]:—

Andrew Garden Duff, *b.* 1925; ed. at Trin. Coll., Glenalmond, at Wellington Coll., New Zealand, and at Trin. Coll., Camb. (B.A. 1950, M.A. 1954) : *m.* 1953, Alison, da. of E. St. Clair Wilson, of Wellington, New Zealand, and has issue living, Alexander Duff, *b.* 1955,—Barbara Elizabeth, *b.* 1954,—Christian Margaret, *b.* 1957,—Louisa Mary, *b.* 1961. *Residence,* The Old Vicarage, West Peckham, Maidstone, Kent.——Elizabeth Helen, *b.* 1923; B.Sc. (Engineering) London 1950: *m.* 1951, Cdr. Ralph Crichton Rupert Brooke, VRD, CEng., FIEE, RNR, and has issue living, John Ralph, *b.* 1953,—Peter William, *b.* 1957,—Jane Elizabeth, *b.* 1955. *Residence,* 34, Vineyard Hill Rd., SW19 7JH.

Issue of the late Com. Spencer Dundas Forbes, R.N., *b.* 1874, *d.* (killed in action) Nov. 1st, 1914: *m.* 1913, Ethel, youngest da. of the late Lieut.-Col. J. S. Walker, Black Watch (Roy. Highlanders), of Wilbury, Sunningdale, Berks :—

Spencer Malcolm Edward, *b.* (posthumous), 1914 : *m.* 1st, 1940, Marie Terese (from whom he obtained a divorce 1947), da. of Boleshaw Sulikowski, of Warsaw, Poland ; 2ndly, 1954, Elizabeth Lechmere, da. of the late Sandys Stuart Macaskie, of Lustleigh, S. Devon, and has issue living, (by 2nd marriage) James Fergus Spencer, *b.* 1956,—Camilla Elizabeth, *b.* 1958. *Residence,* Billingham Manor, Newport, I. of Wight ; Royal Yacht Squadron.

Grandsons of the late Capt. James Arthur Forbes, RN, 4th son of George Forbes, (ante):—

Issue of the late Capt. Charles Hay Forbes, C.B.E., *b.* 1873, *d.* 1919 : *m.* 1901, Emily Fawcus, who *d.* 1964, da. of the late James Carrall, H.M. Commr. of Customs, China :—

Reginald Arthur (Ley of Cushnie, Alford, Aberdeenshire; *Club,* Challoner), *b.* 1905; Lt.-Cdr. RN (ret.): *m.* 1st, 1930, Margaret Evelyn (who obtained a divorce 1944), da. of the late Gideon Macpherson Rutherford [see E. Ancaster, colls.]; 2ndly 1944, Joyce Charlotte Newton, of Quebec, Canada, and has issue living, (by 1st m.) James Hay (5708, Longfellow St., Riverdale, Maryland, USA), *b.* 1931: *m.* 1958, Helen Reddy, of Montreal, Canada, and has issue living, Peter Jonathan *b.* 1960, Michael Todd *b.* 1963, Susan Catherine *b.* 1959,—(by 2nd m.) William Henry, *b.* 1944,— (by 1st m.) Margaret Christine, *b.* 1933: *m.* 1959, John Jervis Murray Bankes, solicitor, of Cottage Farm, Lovedean Lane, Horndean, Hants., and has issue living, Henry Francis John *b.* 1966,

Caroline Margaret *b.* 1964.——Cyril Louis (*Dom James*) (St. Benet's Hall, Oxford), *b.* 1913; ed. at Ampleforth, and at Oxford Univ. (MA); is a Benedictine monk, and Chap., Knights of Malta; Master of St. Benet's Hall, Oxford, since 1964.

Grandchildren of the late Capt. Charles Hay Forbes, C.B.E. (ante):—
Issue of the late Lieut.-Com. John Hay Forbes, D.S.O., R.N., *b.* 1906, *d.* (on active ser. during European War) 1940 : *m.* 1930, Edith Sheilah (who *d.* 1951, having *m.* 2ndly, 1943, as his second wife, Lt.-Col. the Hon. Richard Martin Peter Preston, DSO, who *d.* 1965 [V. Gormanston, colls.]), da. of the late Reginald de Crecy Steel, of Walton-on-Thames:—
Charles Hay (Litein Tea Factory Co., Ltd., PO Box 2040, Litein, Kericho Kenya), *b.* 1931; is a Tea Planter: *m.* 1959, Juliet Rosalind Murray, and has issue living, John Hay, *b.* 1960,—George Louis, *b.* 1961,—Drostan Gerard, *b.* 1962,—Sheila Emily, *b.* 1963.——Angus John Reginald (*posthumous*) (1236, East Vine St., W. Covina, Cal., USA), *b.* 1941: *m.* 1963, Victoria Seward, of California, USA, and has issue living, Richard Leland John, *b.* 1965,—Caroline Lilah Jo, *b.* 1963.——Fiona Eileen, *b.* 1937: *m.* 1961, Anthony Haig Morse, of Laughton Manor Farm, Laughton Hills, Lutterworth, Leics., LE17 6QA, and has issue living, Claire Emma, *b.* 1962,—Rachel Elizabeth, *b.* 1965.

Grandson of Capt. Charles Hay Forbes, CBE, RN (ante):—
Issue of the late Air-Commodore James Louis Forbes, OBE, *b.* 1880, *d.* 1965: *m.* 1919, Marjorie, da. of Sir Thomas Putnam, and widow of Capt. Philip Picot:—
James Alexander (Mill Cottage, Fulmer, Bucks.), *b.* 1919; 1939-45 War as Maj. Gordon Highlanders: *m.* 1946, Susan Elizabeth, da. of Maj.-Gen. Alan Hugh Hornby, CB, CBE, MC, and has issue living, Michael James, *b.* 1949,—Caroline Susan, *b.* 1952.

Sir William Forbes, of Monymusk, Aberdeenshire (4th in descent from Duncan Forbes of Corsindae, 2nd son of 2nd Lord Forbes) was cr. a Baronet with remainder to heirs male whatsoever. Sir Charles Hay Hepburn Stuart-Forbes, 10th baronet assumed the additional surname of Stuart. Sir Walter Scott, in his Notes to " Marmion ", speaking of Sir William, the 6th baronet, an Edinburgh banker, says: " He was unequalled, perhaps, in the degree of individual affection entertained for him by his friends, as well as in the general esteem and respect of Scotland at large". Sir William Forbes, 7th baronet, *m.* 1797, Williamina Wishart, only child and heir of Sir John Belshes-Wishart, afterwards Stuart, 4th Bt. of Fettercairn, who was descended in the maternal line from Stuart of Castlemilk. Sir John Stuart Hepburn Forbes, 8th baronet assumed the additional surname and arms of Hepburn. He was heir general of the last Lord Forbes of Pitsligo (his ancestor, the 4th Bt., having *m.* Mary, da. of the 3rd and sister of the 4th Lord). His only child married the 20th Baron Clinton, to whom the whole of the estates descended.

Forbes-Leith of Fyvie, see Leith of Fyvie.

FORD, Creation (U.K.) 1929, of Westerdunes, co. of East Lothian.

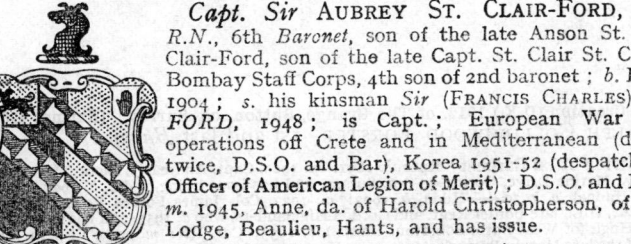

Sir HENRY RUSSELL FORD, 2nd *Baronet;* *b.* April 30th, 1911 ; *s.* his father, *Sir* PATRICK JOHNSTON, 1945; ed. at Winchester, and at New Coll., Oxford : *m.* 1936, Mary Elizabeth, da. of the late Godfrey F. Wright, of Whiddon, Bovey Tracey, and has issue.

Arms—Vert, a chevron between a dexter and a sinister wing in chief and in base a pyramid all or. Crest—A sphinx wings elevated, the head ensigned with a plume and supporting between the fore-paws a papyrus stalk flowered and leaved or.
Residence—Seaforth, Gullane, East Lothian.

Son living—ANDREW RUSSELL (30, Boundary Rd., Chippenham, Wilts.), *b.* June 29th, 1943; ed. at Winchester, and New Coll., Oxford: *m.* 1968, Penelope Anne, only da. of Harry Relph, of Wildwinds, Rotherby, Leics., and has issue living, Toby Russell, *b.* Jan. 11th, 1973,—Julia Mary, *b.* 1970.
Daughters living—Jill Dorothy, *b.* 1937.——Alison Patricia, *b.* 1946: *m.* 1970, Robert M. Cowe, of Beanston Mill, Haddington, E. Lothian.——Belinda Christine, *b.* 1951: *m.* 1974, Graeme P. C. McWilliam, of 60, Winchendon, Rd., SW6.
Brother living—Harold Frank (Broomhill, by Stanley, Perth; 22, India St., Edinburgh), *b.* 1915: *m.* 1948, Lucy Mary, da. of the late J. R. Wardlaw Burnet, K.C., of Edinburgh, and has issue living, Patrick John, *b.* 1952,—Claire Lucy, *b.* 1949,—Harriet Mary, *b.* 1955,—Katharine Anne, *b.* 1958.
Sisters living—Joan Cassels, *b.* 1909: *m.* 1933, John Calthrop, of 8, The Island, Thames Ditton, Surrey.——Marjorie Elaine, *b.* 1913: *m.* 1941, Alan Murray, of 26, Gordon St., Mosman, NSW.

The 1st baronet, Sir Patrick Johnston Ford (son of James Ford, of Edinburgh), sat as M.P. for Edinburgh, N. Div. (*U*) 1920-23 and 1924-35, and was a Junior Lord of the Treasury 1922-3.

ST. CLAIR-FORD, Creation (G.B.) 1793, of Ember Court, Surrey.

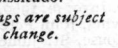

Capt. **Sir** AUBREY ST. CLAIR-FORD, *D.S.O.*, *R.N.*, 6th *Baronet*, son of the late Anson St. Clair St. Clair-Ford, son of the late Capt. St. Clair St. Clair-Ford, Bombay Staff Corps, 4th son of 2nd baronet ; *b.* Feb. 29th, 1904 ; *s.* his kinsman *Sir* (FRANCIS CHARLES) RUPERT FORD, 1948 ; is Capt. ; European War 1939-45, operations off Crete and in Mediterranean (despatches twice, D.S.O. and Bar), Korea 1951-52 (despatches twice, Officer of American Legion of Merit) ; D.S.O. and Bar 1942: *m.* 1945, Anne, da. of Harold Christopherson, of Penerley Lodge, Beaulieu, Hants, and has issue.

Arms—Per pale gules and or, two bends vaire ; on a canton of the second a greyhound courant sable. Crest—A greyhound's head sable erased gules, muzzled or.

Omnium rerum
vicissitudo.

*All things are subject
to change.*

Residence—Corner House, Sandle Copse, Fordingbridge, Hants.

Son living—JAMES ANSON, *b.* March 16th, 1952; ed. at Wellington.

Daughter living—Julia Mary, *b.* 1954.

Brother living—*Sir* Peter, K.B.E., C.B., D.S.O., *b.* 1905 ; Maj.-Gen. (retired) late King's Own Yorkshire L.I. ; GOC 1st Federated Div., Malaya 1954-57, and Dep. Ch. of Staff, HQ, Allied Land Forces Central Europe 1958-60; 1939-45 War in Italy (DSO and Bar), Malaya 1951-52 (CBE); DSO 1944 (Barr 1945), CBE (Mil) 1952, CB (Mil) 1954, KBE (Mil) 1960. *Residence,* Cotswold Lodge, Littlestone-on-Sea, New Romney, Kent.

Sister living—Daphne Jane Anson, *b.* 1914 : *m.* 1934, Capt. Geoffrey William Preston, R.E., and has issue living, Roger St. Clair, *b.* 1935; Capt. K.O.Y.L.I.: *m.* 1964, Polly Mary, da. of the late Robin Marriott,—Judith Mary, *b.* 1946. *Residence,* Beck Cottage, Menethorpe, Malton, Yorks.

Daughters living of 5th Baronet—Beryl Cicely FORD, *b.* 1921 : *m.* 1951, James Arthur Peter Peirce, M.B., Ch.B., and has issue living, Martin Charles Arthur, *b.* 1952,—Sarah Jane Charlotte, *b.* 1955. *Residence,* St. Annes, 4, Hill Rd., Swanage, Dorset.——Janetta Olive FORD, *b.* 1925, *m.* 1964, David Ryland Pullinger, of 16, Hollow Oak Rd., Stoborough, Wareham, Dorset.

Widow living of 5th Baronet—KATHERINE OLIVE (*Lady Ford*), da. of James Charles Yorke, J.P., of Langton, Dwrbach, Pembrokeshire [*see* E. Hardwicke, colls.]: *m.* 1918, Sir (Francis Charles) Rupert Ford, 5th Bt., who *d.* 1948. *Residence,* Treown, Wilfred Road, Boscombe, Bournemouth.

Collateral Branches living.

Issue of the late Lt.-Cdr. Drummond St. Clair-Ford, RN, 2nd brother of 6th baronet, *b.* 1907, *d.* (killed on active ser.) 1943: *m.* 1933, Norah Elizabeth (who *m.* 2ndly, 1945, Rear-Adm. Peter Noel Buckley, CB, DSO (ret.), of Forest Cottage, Sway, Hants.), da. of Capt. Charles James Astley Maberly, late 17th Lancers:—
Colin Anson (Kilmelford, Chiltern Hills Rd., Beaconsfield, Bucks.), *b.* 1939: *m.* 1964, Gillian Mary, da. of Rear-Adm. Peter Skelton, CB, and has issue living, Kate Mary, *b.* 1967,—Fiona Elizabeth, *b.* 1969.——Robin Sam, *b.* 1941.——Elizabeth Jane, *b.* 1937: *m.* 1961, John Nigel Courtenay James, of April Cottage, Fulmer, Bucks., and has issue living, Simon, *b.* 1966,—Annabel Clare, *b.* 1964.

Issue of the late Cdr. Vernon John St. Clair-Ford, MBE, RN, yst. brother of 6th baronet, *b.* 1918, *d.* 1952: *m.* 1947, Patricia Mary (who *m.* 2ndly, 1954, Lt.-Cdr. Michael Ainsworth, RN, of Blendon Lodge, Finchampstead Rd., Wokingham, Berks.), da. of the late F. G. H. Bedford, of Petersfield, Hants.
Timothy Bedford, *b.* 1948.——Gordon Sam, *b.* 1950.

Grandchildren of the late Rev. Charles FORD, 3rd son of 1st baronet :—
Issue (by 2nd marriage) of the late Henry Stuart FORD, *b.* 1843, *d.* 1895 : *m.* 1st, 1873, Sophia Sarah, who *d.* 1881, da. of E. Gregory; 2ndly, 1883, Mary, da. of Thomas Wells :—
Reginald Severne, *b.* 1888 ; formerly Lieut. 1/9th Hampshire Regt.

Issue of the late Rev. Charles Primrose FORD, *b.* 1849, *d.* 1922 : *m.* 1875, Mary Jane, who *d.* 1930, da. of the late Rev. I. B. Turner :—
Alice Constance, *b.* 1885: *m.* 1907, Cuthbert Bailey, and has issue living, David Anson Steele, *b.* 1917; Prior of Blackfriars, Leicester,—John Cuthbert, *b.* 1921: *m.* 1947, Diana Mary Derrington, da. of Cdr. Charles Edward Hudson, OBE, RD, RNR, of Seatown House, Chideock, Dorset, and has issue living, Hugh John Cuthbert Mowbray *b.* 1957, Mark Charles Francis Derrington *b.* 1959, Philippa Mary St. Clair *b.* 1948, Catherine Ann Vernon *b.* 1949, Juliet Elizabeth Anson *b.* 1950, Fiona Francesca Helen *b.* 1952, Alexandra Christian Isobel *b.* 1954,—Barbara Vernon, *b.* 1910; is a Canoness Regular of The Lateran at Our Lady's Priory, Hayward's Heath,—Betty Primrose, *b.* 1912: *m.* 1938, Thomas Charles Edwards, of Ampleforth Coll., Yorks., and has issue living, David Lewis *b.* 1941, Thomas Mowbray *b.* 1943, Mary Imelda *b.* 1949,—Peggy Mary Anson, *b.* 1914: *m.* 1935, Charles Reginald Braybrooke, and has issue living, Perilla Ann *b.* 1942,—Judith St. Clair, *b.* 1918.

Grandchildren of the late Rev. Charles Primrose FORD (ante):—
Issue of the late Rev. Roger Anson FORD, *b.* 1878, *d.* 1932 : *m.* 1916, Kathleen Orme, da. of the late Montague Torridge Morris, Colonial Civil Ser. :—
Montague Patrick (Langass Lodge, Lochmaddy, North Uist, Inverness-shire), *b.* 1918; BSc, MRCVS; late Colonial Ser., N. Nigeria: *m.* 1st, 1951 (m. diss. 1967), Rosalind Elizabeth, da. of Lt.-Col. Thomas Harold Barnes, of Castle Cary; 2ndly, 1969, Ivy Lillian Lowden, da. of William Buckell, and has issue living (by 1st m.), Sara Kathleen, *b.* 1959.——Charles Primrose, *b.* 1922; Fl. Lt. RAF: *m.* 1949, Margaret Watson, and has issue living, Victoria Primrose, *b.* 1953.—— Dorothy Vernon, *b.* 1930.

The 1st baronet was a Member of the Council in Barbados, and in 1790 sat as MP for Newcastle-under-Lyme. Capt. St. Clair Ford, yst. son of 2nd Bt., and grandfather of the 6th Bt., assumed the additional surname of St. Clair 1878.

Forestier-Walker, see Walker.

FORSTER, Creation (U.K.) 1912, of The Grange, Sutton, co. Surrey   [Extinct 1930.]
Sir RALPH COLLINGWOOD FORSTER, 1st and last *Baronet.*

Daughters living of 1st Baronet—Ruth, *b.* 1891: *m.* 1920, Capt. Andreas J. Floor, of Tamarisk House, 44A, Marine Drive, Goring-on-Sea, Sussex, and has issue living, a da., *b.* 1921,—a da., *b.* 1924,—Hannah *b.* 1930.——Hilda, *b.* 1893: *m.* 1927, Col. James Forbes Robertson, V.C., D.S.O., M.C., D.L., late Border Regt. and Gordon Highlanders, who *d.* 1955, and has issue living, Kenneth Hugh (of West Barn, Soberton, Hants.), *b.* 1933; Cdr. RN: *m.* 1959, Elspeth Janet, only da. of the late Marvin Puttock, of Medwyn House, Somerton, Somerset, and has issue living, Fiona Doon *b.* 1960, Kirsten *b.* 1962, Grania Helen *b.* 1966,—Ann, *b.* 1929: *m.* 1951, Lt.-Col. John Douglas Watson, MBE, RE, of Well Cottage, Hatchford End, Cobham, Surrey, KT11 1NA, and has issue living, James Douglas *b.* 1955, Sally v. 1952,—Jean *b.* 1930: *m.* 1960, Lt.-Cdr. Peter Brian Godley, RN, of Nut Ash, Headley, Surrey, and has issue living, John Peter *b.* 1962, Sarah Jean *b.* 1960, Joanna *b.* 1968. *Residence,* Flat 318, Minster House, St. James' Court, Buckingham Gate, SW1.

FORWOOD, Creation (U.K.) 1895, of The Priory, Gateacre, Childwall, co. Palatine of Lancaster.

Sir DUDLEY RICHARD FORWOOD, 3rd *Baronet,*
b. June 6th, 1912; *s.* his father, *Lieut.-Col. Sir* DUDLEY
BAINES, C.M.G., 1961; ed. at Stowe Sch.; formerly
Capt. and temporary Major Scots Guards (Reserve); is
an Underwriting Member of Lloyd's; Master of New
Forest Buckhounds 1957-65; Hon. Attaché British
Legation, Vienna 1934-37, and Equerry to HRH the Duke
of Windsor 1937-39; Official Chm. New Forest Consultative Panel 1970; Chm. of Crufts since 1973, and Verderer
of New Forest since 1974; Hon. Dir. Roy. Agric. Soc. of
England: *m.* 1952, Mary Gwendoline (CULLINGFORD), da.
of Basil S. Foster.

Fide virtute et labore.
By faith, virtue and
labour.

Arms—Per fesse or and azure, in chief a cormorant sable, beaked
and membered gules, between two fleurs-de-lis of the second, in base an
ancient galley or, sail argent. Crest—Between two wings argent the
battlements of a tower, thereon in front of a stag's head two hatchets in
saltire all proper.

Residences—The Old House, Burley, Ringwood, Hants; 43, Addison
Rd., W14.

Collateral Branches living.

Issue of the late Arthur Noel Forwood, 3rd son of 1st baronet *b.* 1881, *d.* 1960,
m. 1st, 1903, Evelyn Agnes Heathcote (who obtained a divorce 1923), only
da. of W. Forrester Addie, J.P.; 2ndly, 1923, Hyacinth, da. of the late
Henry Pollard, of Chester :—

(By 2nd marriage) PETER NOEL, *b.* Oct. 15th, 1925; ed. at Radley; 1939-45 War with Welsh
Guards: *m.* 1950, Roy, da. of James Murphy, MBE, FRCS, LRCP, of Horsham, Sussex,—
Susan Noel, *b.* 1951,—Diana Geraldine, *b.* 1953,—Jane *b.* 1954,—Joanna Baines, *b.* 1956,—
Caragh Vivien, *b.* 1958,—Amanda Elizabeth, *b.* 1963. *Residence,* Newhouse Farm, Shillinglee,
Chiddingfold, Surrey.——Enid, *b.* 19—: *m.* 1950, Herbert J. Water. *Residence,* Stanford Park,
nr. Rugby.——Wendy Baines, *b.* 1931.

Issue of the late Eric Baines Forwood, youngest son of 1st baronet, *b.* 1884, *d.*
1949: *m.* 1911, Mary Katharine, who *d.* 1965, da. of John Herbert, of Spring
Cottage, Kenilworth:—

Judith, *b.* 1912.

The Rt. Hon. Sir Arthur B. Forwood, 1st Bt., sat as M.P. for Lancashire (S.W.), Ormskirk
Div. (C) 1885-98, and was Sec. to the Admiralty 1886-92.

FOSTER, Creation (U.K.) 1831, of Stonehouse, Louth. [Extinct 1947.]

Sir AUGUSTUS VERE FOSTER, 4th and last *Baronet.*

Daughter living of 4th Baronet—Dorothy Elizabeth Charlotte Vere, *b.* 1903: *m.* 1940,
Lieut.-Col. Arthur Charles William May, M.C., Highland L.I. [E. Ellesmere, colls.]. *Residence,*
Glyde Court, Ardee, co. Louth.

Sister living of 4th Baronet—Alice Jane Blanche : *m.* 1912, as his second wife, Maj.-Gen. Fitz-
gerald Wintour, CB, CBE, who *d.* 1949, and has issue living, Charles Vere (Flat 32, Cranfield
House, Southampton Row, WC1), *b.* 1917: *m.* 1940, Eleanor, da. of Professor Ralph J. Baker, of
Cambridge, Mass., USA, and has issue living, James Charles *b.* 1947, Patrick Walter *b.* 1954,
Anna *b.* 1949, Hilary Nora *b.* 1953,—Cordelia Mary (*Baroness James of Rusholme*), (Penhill
Cottage, West Witton, Leyburn, N. Yorks.), *b.* 1912: *m.* 1939, Baron James of Rusholme (Life
Peer).

FOSTER, Creation (U.K.) 1838, of Norwich. [Extinct 1960.]

Sir HENRY WILLIAM BERKELEY FOSTER, *M.C.,* 4th and last
Baronet.

Daughter living of 4th Baronet—Janet Elizabeth (56A, Ladbroke Grove, W.11), *b.* 1930.

Daughters living of 3rd Baronet—Aileen Cavendish, *b.* 1886 : *m.* 1915, Dwight Carlton Harris,
of 3, E. 77th St., New York 10021, NY, USA.——Dorothy Harlie, *b.* 1890: *m.* 1920, Maj. James
Gerard Berkeley Portman Graham, Highland LI, who *d.* 1964, and has issue living, Gerard Colin
Berkeley, *b.* 1922; 1939-45 War as Lt. RA: *m.* 1973, Hannelöre, da. of Carl Heinrich August
Hoefle, of Hamburg. *Residence,* Quinta do Eirado, 472, Rua Santos Dias San Mamede de
Infesta, Portugal.——Georgina Patricia, *b.* 1902. *Residence,* Flat 5, Woodridge House, Wood-
ridge Close, Bracknell, Berks., RG12 3Q7.

Collateral Branches living.

Issue (by 2nd marriage) of the late Charles Foster, 2nd son of 1st baronet, *b.* 1828,
d. 1906: *m.* 1st, 1858, Charlotte, who *d.* 1888, 3rd da. of the late Capt. Thomas
George Wills, R.N.; 2ndly, 1890, Georgina Gertrude, who *d.* 1922, da. of the late
Lieut.-Col. E. G. Cubitt, 7th Hussars :—

Georgina Fanny Julia, *b.* 1891. *Residence,* Park Lane Cottage, Southwold, Suffolk.

Granddaughter of the late Francis Gostling Foster, 3rd son of 1st baronet :—
Issue of the late Charles Blackwell Foster, *b.* 1861, *d.* 1915 : *m.* 1891, Emily Caroline Phyllis
who *d.* 1911, da. of the late James Ray, M.R.C.S. :—

Beryl Ray, *b.* 1896. *Residence,* Wilby House, near Diss, Norfolk.

FOSTER, Creation (U.K.) 1930, of Bloomsbury, co. London.

Sir JOHN (GREGORY) FOSTER, 3rd *Baronet;* b. Feb. 26th, 1927; s. his father, Sir THOMAS SAXBY GREGORY, 1957; ed. at Michaelhouse Coll., Natal, and at Witwatersrand Univ. (M.B. and B.Ch. 1951); M.R.C.P. Edinburgh 1955; Physician; European War 1944-5 with S. African Artillery: *m.* 1956, Jean Millicent, da. of the late Elwin Watts, F.R.C.S.E., of Germiston, S. Africa, and has issue.

Address—122, York St., P.O. Box 325, George, Cape Prov., S. Africa. *Club*—Johannesburg Country.

Son living—SAXBY GREGORY, b. Sept. 3rd, 1957.
Daughters living—Deborah Jean Gregory, b. 1959,——Carolyn Gregory, b. 1962.——Rosemary Gregory, b. 1963.
Sister living—Barbara Maude Gregory, b. 1929.
Widow living of 2nd Baronet—BERYL (*Beryl, Lady Foster*), da. of the late Alfred Ireland, M.D., of Cradock, Cape Province, S. Africa : *m.* 1925, Sir Thomas Saxby Gregory Foster, 2nd baronet, who d. 1957. *Residence*, 13, Donegal Avenue, Park View, Johannesburg, Transvaal.
Collateral Branch living
Issue of the late Lewis Marshall Gregory Foster, yr. son of 1st Baronet, b. 1904, d. 1970: *m.* 1931, Margaret Amy (11, Vernon Close, Leamington Spa), da. of Max Tillard, formerly of Johannesburg:—
Richard Tillard (PO Box 86, Southbroom, Natal, S. Africa), b. 1935: *m.* 1st, 1964 (m. diss. 1973), Carola Margaret, da. of the Rev. George Henry Talbot Roe, R. of Wheathampstead, Herts.; 2ndly, 1975, Mrs. Winifred Moira Cameron, da. of — Walker, and has issue living (by 1st m.), Polly Tillard, b. 1965,—Candy Tillard, b. 1970.——Eve Tillard, b. 1932: *m.* 1954, Donald Miller Croudace, of Little Woodcote, Rouncil Lane, Kenilworth, Warwicks., and has issue living, Brigid Lucy, b. 1959,—Charlotte Polly, b. 1962.

The 1st baronet, Sir (Thomas) Gregory Foster (el. son of the late Thomas Gregory Foster, Bar.-at-law), was Provost of Univ. Coll. 1907-29, and Vice-Chancellor of the Univ. of London 1928-30.

LISTON-FOULIS, Creation (N.S.) 1634, of Colinton, Edinburgh.

[Pronounced "**Liston Fowls.**"]

Ready with heart and hand.

Sir IAN PRIMROSE LISTON-FOULIS, 13th *Baronet,* son of the late Lieut.-Col. James Alastair Liston-Foulis, son of the late Lieut.-Col. Archibald Primrose Liston-Foulis, 4th son of 9th baronet; b. Aug. 9th, 1937; s. his kinsman *Sir* ARCHIBALD CHARLES, 1962.

Arms—Argent, three bay-leaves slipped vert. **Crest**—A dexter hand couped, holding a sword in pale, sustaining a wreath of laurel all proper.

Residence—Menendez Pelayo 13, Piso 7, Izqda, Madrid, Spain.

Sisters living—Simone Primrose, b. 1934: *m.* 1973, Geoffrey Richard Hall, of Flat 4, Warren House, 55, Magdalen Rd., Exeter, Devon.——Susan, (Calle Mayor 3, Berdun, Huesca, Spain), b. 1941: *m.* 1962 (m. diss. 1974), Peter John Lely, and has issue living, Edward James Mountenay, b. 1965,—Josephine Anne, b. 1963.

Sister living of 12th Baronet—Gwynneth Beryl, b. 1912: *m.* 1940, John Carl Pietersen, of Rhodesian Railways. *Address*, P.O. Box 1700, Bulawayo, Rhodesia.

Aunt living—Avril Primrose, b. 1915: *m.* 1946, Major Desmond Allhusen, late King's Royal Rifle Corps. *Residence*, Meerhay Cottage, Beaminster, Dorset.

Mother living—Kathleen, da. of the late Lieut.-Col. John Moran, late Indian Army: *m.* 1934, Lieut.-Col. James Alastair Liston-Foulis, who d. (on active ser. during European War) 1942. *Residence*, 26, Mathon Court, Crosslanes, Guildford.

Collateral Branches living.
Grandchildren of the late James Foulis, M.D., F.R.C.P.E., son of the late John Foulis, M.D. (infra) :—
Issue of the late Wilfrid Venour Foulis, b. 1884, d. 1951 : *m.* 1st, 1909, Clara Millington, who obtained a divorce 1923, da. of Alfred Dow, of King's Lynn; 2ndly, 1924, Ida (18, Osborne Villas, Hove, BN3 2RE), da. of the Rev. Joshua Brookes, Canon of Lahore:—
(By 2nd marriage) Ursula Patricia Carey, b. 1926: *m.* 1947, William Joseph Kiernan.

Granddaughter of the late John Foulis, M.D., 2nd son of 7th baronet :—
Issue of the late William Foulis, b. 1848, d. 1912 : *m.* 1874, Louisa May, who d. 1939, da. of the late John Bell, of Sydney, N.S. Wales.—
Louisa May, b. 1885. *Residence*, 92, Vaughan Street, Lidcombe, N.S. Wales.

Alexander Foulis of Colinton, co. Edinburgh, was created a baronet with remainder to heirs male whatsoever. Sir James, the 2nd baronet, MP for Midlothian and a Privy Councillor, who was knighted during the lifetime of his father, was actively engaged in the wars in Scotland after the death of Charles I. He was, with his companions, the Earls of Leven, Crawford, and other gentlemen of rank, betrayed into the hands of the English, while attending a convention of Committee of Estates, at Alyth, in Angus. After the Restoration he was appointed Lord Justice Clerk, with the title of Lord Colinton. The 3rd baronet sat in the last Scottish Parliament 1706, and afterwards for Midlothian in the British Parliament. He was a Lord of Session and a Privy Councillor. On the death in 1825 of Sir James Foulis of Colinton, 6th Bt., the male line from the grantee and his father became ext., and the baronetcy passed to his 6th cousin and heir male, Sir James Foulis, 7th Bt., who was descended from George Foulis of Ravelston, uncle of the 1st Bt. of Colinton. [George's son, Sir John Foulis of Ravelston, was cr. a Baronet in 1661, with remainder to heirs male of the body. The baronetcy of Ravelston was forfeited by the 2nd Bt. for taking part in the 1745 campaign, for which he was beheaded at Carlisle in 1746. The heir to this baronetcy, but for the attainder, is the Baronet of Colinton.] Sir William Foulis of Colinton, 8th Bt. (cr. 1634), added the additional name of Liston, having *m*. 1843, Henrietta Ramage Liston of Millburn Tower, great-niece and testamentary heir of Rt. Hon. Sir Robert Liston, GCB.

FOWKE, Creation (U.K.) 1814, of Lowesby, Leicestershire.

[Name pronounced "Foke."]

Arms are the guardians of peace.

Sir FREDERICK WOOLLASTON RAWDON FOWKE, 4th *Baronet*; *b.* Dec. 14th, 1910; *s.* his father, *Sir* FREDERICK FERRERS CONANT, 1948; ed. at Uppingham ; sometime Capt. Derbyshire Yeo ; European War 1939-43 (wounded) : *m*. 1948, Barbara Ethel, da. of the late L. P. Townsend, and has issue.

Arms—Vert, a fleur-de-lis argent. Crest—1st, a dexter arm embowed, vested and cuffed argent, the hand proper grasping an arrow in bend sinister or, barbed and flighted silver ; and, an Indian goat's head erased vert, armed and eared argent.
Residence—Woolstone Farm, Bishop's Tawton, Barnstaple, N. Devon.

Daughters living—Sarah Elisabeth, *b.* 1949.——Belinda Barbara, *b.* 1955.

Brother living—Michael Gustavus (c/o Lloyds Bank, Chichester, Sussex), *b.* 1919; Cdr. RN (ret.); 1939-45 War (despatches twice): *m*. 1943, Mrs. Esme M. Howard-Johnston, da. of the late Philip Fitz-Gibbon, of Crohana, Stonyford, co. Kilkenny.

Sister living—Betty Mirabelle, *b.* 1912: *m*. 1934, Major Charles Chichester, Roy. Devon Yeo., and has issue living, Penelope Anne, *b.* 1935: *m*. 1959, Maj. Martin Frederick William Maxse, Coldm. Gds., of Catercross, Fittleworth, Pulborough [see Bs. Berkeley, colls.],—Diana Margaret, *b.* 1939: *m*. 1967, Jerome Mahony,—Helena Elizabeth, *b.* 1940. *Residence*, Hall, Barnstaple, N. Devon.

Aunt living—Isabel Margaret, *b.* 1885: *m*. 1923, the Rev. Percy Lane Hooson, and has issue living, Peter Lane Fowke, *b.* 1925.—Mark William Rolleston, *b.* 1927,—Margaret Eva Conant (twin), *b.* 1927. *Residence*, South Lawn, Stamford.

Collateral Branch living

Issue of the late Lt.-Col. Gerrard George Fowke, 2nd son of 3rd baronet, *b.* 1915, *d.* 1969: *m*. 1946, Daphne (4, Queens Park Rd., Bondi Junction, NSW, 2022), da. of A. Monasteriotis, of Corfu:—

DAVID FREDERICK GUSTAVUS, *b.* Aug. 28th, 1950.——Caroline Daphne, *b.* 1948: *m*. 1970, Bruce Theodore Davies.

Sir Frederick Gustavus Fowke, 1st Bt., was son and heir of Lt.-Gen. Sir Thomas Fowke of Lowesby, Leics., Groom of the Bedchamber to the Duke of Cumberland.

FOWLER, Creation (U.K.) 1890, of Braemore, Ross-shire. [Extinct 1933.]

Rev. Sir MONTAGUE FOWLER, 4th and last *Baronet.*

Daughters living of 4th Baronet—By 2nd marriage—Evelyn Denise (The Grange, Felcourt, East Grinstead, Sussex, and Tigh-na-Mara, Ardendrean, Lochbroom, Ross-shire), *b.* 1915: *m*. 1st, 1936, Douglas Hamilton Watt, who *d.* 1973; 2ndly, 1955, Lt.-Col. Alfred John Newling, CB, CBE, MVO, TD, who *d.* 1957, and has issue living, (by 1st m.) Donald George FOWLER (Brambletye, E. Grinstead, Sussex), *b.* 1937; assumed the additional surname of Fowler 1956: *m*. 1960, Sheila Mary Beynon, and has issue living, Andrew James *b.* 1961, Duncan John *b.* 1963, Susanna Jane *b.* 1969.——Elizabeth Joan Daphne, *b.* 1917: *m*. 1st, 1941, Capt. Thomas Wilson; 2ndly, 1951, Peter Drummond-Hay, and has issue living, (by 1st m.) Elisabeth Anne, *b.* 1942,—(by 2nd m.) Peter Neil, *b.* 1954. *Residence*, St. Kessogs, Glencarse, Perths.

Widow living of 4th Baronet—DENISE MARCELLE CHAILLIEY (*Lady Fowler*): *m*. 1914, as his second wife, the Rev. Sir Montague Fowler, 4th baronet, who *d.* 1933, when the title became ext. *Residence*, The Grange, Felcourt, East Grinstead, Sussex.

Collateral Branch living.

Issue of the late Capt. Alan Arthur Fowler, 2nd son of 2nd baronet, *b.* 1887, *d.* (killed in action) 1915 : *m*. 1912, Alice Mary, who *d.* 1932, da. of the late Sir Charles Stuart Bayley, G.C.I.E., K.C.S.I., I.S.O. :—

Marjorie Mary, *b.* 1913: *m*. 1935, Alan Anthony Maxwell Gardiner, and has issue living, Alan David Fowler, *b.* 1942: *m*. 1968, Annesley Louise Brownrigg,—Timothy John Charles, *b.* 1945: *m*. 1969, Angela Jane Willis,—Susan Mary, *b.* 1936: *m*. 1963, James Collingwood Dickson Brown, of Hollandtide House, Berrick Salome, Oxford. *Residence*, 34, Combe St. Lane, Yeovil, Som.

FOX, Creation (U.K.) 1924, of Liverpool, co. Palatine of Lancaster. [Extinct 1959.]

Sir GIFFORD WHEATON GREY FOX, 2nd and last *Baronet.*

Daughter living of 2nd Baronet—By 1st marriage—Georgina Myra Albinia, *b.* 1930 : *m*. 1951, Patrick Tobias Telfer Smollett of Bonhill, M.C., D.L., Highland L.I. (retired), and has issue living, David Alexander Douglas Tobias, *b.* 1953,—Gabrielle Georgiana, *b.* 1960. *Residences*, Cameron House, Alexandria, Dunbartonshire; Garrett House, 9, Cleveland Row, SW1.

Daughter living of 1st Baronet—Adeline Betty (*Lady Holman*): *m*. 1st, 1929, Capt. Basil Holmsdale Allfrey, late 9th Lancers, from whom she obtained a divorce 1939; 2ndly, 1940, as his second wife, Sir Adrian Holman, KBE, CMG, MC, and has issue living (by 1st m.) Anthony Rodney (6, Culford Gdns.,SW3), *b.* 1930: *m*. 1955, the Hon. Julian Mary, who *d.* 1974, da. of Baron Russell of Killowen (Life Baron), and has issue living, Charles Sebastian Holmesdale *b.* 1959, Arabel

Mary *b.* 1956, Georgiana Rose, *b.* 1957,—Peter (of 67 Park Walk, SW10), *b.* 1932: *m.* 1962, Susanna Gabrielle, da. of the late Capt. George Wareing Drewry Ormerod, RA, and has issue living, Richard James Nugent *b.* 1963, Alexander Peter *b.* 1965, Candida Elizabeth *b.* 1970. *Residence,* Bohunt, Liphook, Hants.

Widow living of 2nd Baronet—*Lady* MARYOTH CHRISTINA HAY (Forbes Lodge, Gifford, E. Lothian), da. of the late Lt.-Col. Lord Edward Douglas John Hay, Gren. Gds. [*see* M. Tweeddale], and formerly wife of Lt.-Col. George Richard Trotter, R. Scots Greys [E. Eglinton]; resumed the surname of Hay 1971: *m.* 2ndly, 1954, as his second wife, Sq.-Ldr. Sir Gifford Wheaton Grey Fox, RAFVR, 2nd baronet, who *d.* 1959, when the title became ext.; 3rdly, 1963 (m. diss. 1971), Sir John Hastings James, KCVO, CB.

FRANK, Creation (U.K.) 1920, of Withyham, co. Sussex.

Sir ROBERT JOHN FRANK, 3rd *Baronet ; b.* March 16th, 1925 ; *s.* his brother, *Sir* HOWARD FREDERICK, 1944; ed. at Harrow; a Chartered Surveyor, Auctioneer and an Estate Agent, and a Co. Dir.; 1944-45 War as Flying Officer R.A.F. Vol. Reserve : *m.* 1st, 1950 (marriage dissolved 1959), Angela Elizabeth, el. da. of Sir Kenelm Henry Ernest Cayley, 10th Bt. ; 2ndly, 1960, Margaret Joyce, only da. of Herbert Victor Truesdale, of Heswall, Cheshire, and has issue by 1st and 2nd marriages.

Residence—Ruscombe End, Waltham St. Lawrence, Reading.

Son living—By 2nd marriage—ROBERT ANDREW, *b.* May 16th, 1964.

Daughters living—By 1st marriage—Maria Elizabeth Jane, *b.* 1952: *m.* 1975, Vivian Murray Bairstow.——Katharine Lucy, *b.* 1954.

Half-Sister living—Mary Doreen: *m.* 1st, 1922 (marriage dissolved 1936), Lieut. Kenneth Norman Mackenzie Macrae, R.N. (retired), who *d.* 1958 ; 2ndly, 19—, D. Green, and has issue living, (by 1st marriage) Charles Alexander Mackenzie, *b.* 1924,—Pamela Helen Sylvia, *b.* 1923. *Residence,* Heatherways, Linkside East, Beacon Hill, Hindhead, Surrey.

Widow living of 1st Baronet—ANNIE MURIEL, *O.B.E.* (*Lady Coningham*), da. of John Brooks, O.B.E. (Civil) 1955 : *m.* 1st, 1922, as his second wife, Sir Howard George Frank, G.B.E., K.C.B., 1st baronet, who *d.* 1932 ; 2ndly, 1932, Air Marshal Sir Arthur Coningham, K.C.B., K.B.E., D.S.O., M.C., D.F.C., A.F.C., R.A.F., who *d.* 1948. *Residence,* 42, Duchess of Bedford House, Campden Hill, W.8. *Club,* Bath.

The 1st baronet, Sir Howard George Frank, G.B.E., K.C.B., was senior partner in the firm of Knight, Frank, and Rutley, of 20, Hanover Square, W., 90, Princes Street, Edinburgh, and Ashford, Kent, a Director of Norwich Union Fire Insurance So., of Livett, Frank, and Son, of London and Southampton, and of Victoria and Albert Docks, and Director-Gen. of Lands to War Office and Air Min. and Min. of Munitions 1917-22. The 2nd baronet, Sir Howard Frederick, Lieut. Grenadier Guards ; *d.* (killed in action during European War) 1944.

Frankland-Payne-Gallwey, see Gallwey.

FRASER, Creation (U.K.) 1806, of Ledeclune and Morar, Inverness-shire.

JE LUIS PREST.
I am ready.

Sir KEITH CHARLES ADOLPHUS FRASER, 6th *Baronet* ; *b.* Sept. 14th, 1911 ; *s.* his father, *Major Sir* KEITH ALEXANDER, 1935 ; ed. at Eton, and at Camb. Univ. (B.A. 19—) ; formerly Leading Aircraftsman Roy. Canadian Air Force : *m.* 1st, 1934, Blanca de Undurraga y Sandiford (from whom he obtained a divorce 1946), da. of Julio de Undurraga, of 132, Rue de Longchamp, Paris ; 2ndly, 1947, Mrs. Sybil Craven, da. of George Savage.

Arms—Quarterly: 1st and 4th, azure, a bend engrailed between three cinquefoils (or frasers) argent ; a canton gyronny of eight or and sable : 2nd and 3rd, argent, three antique crowns gules. **Crest**—A buck's head erased gules. **Supporters**—Two stags proper, attired and unguled or, collared azure and pendent from each collar an escutcheon gyronny of eight or and sable, each supporter resting one foot on an anchor of the last.

Address—c/o Brown, Shipley & Co., Ltd., Founders Court, E.C.2.

Sir Simon Fraser, *temp.* Alexander III., received by charter the lordship of Loveth, and he and his brother (Sir Francis), his cousin (Sir Richard Fraser), and William Fraser, Archbishop of St. Andrew's and Lord Chancellor of Scotland, were appointed auditors in the competition for the Scottish crown between Bruce and Baliol, in 1291. From the 2nd son of Hugh Fraser, created Baron Lovat by James I, of Scotland, the present baronet is descended in a direct male line. Sir James, the 3rd baronet, served with distinction in the Peninsula and was on the staff at Waterloo. The 4th baronet sat as M.P. for Barnstapie 1852-3 and 1857-9, for Ludlow (C) 1863-5, and for Kidderminster 1874-80. The 5th baronet, Major Sir Keith Alexander, served in European War, 1914-18, and was M.P. for Harborough Div. of Leicestershire (U) 1918-23.

FRASER, Creation (U.K.) 1921 of Cromarty, and of Vale Avenue, Metropolitan Borough of Chelsea.

Through hardships to the stars.

Sir BASIL MALCOLM FRASER, 2nd *Baronet*; *b.* Jan. 2nd, 1920; *s.* his father *Sir* (JOHN) MALCOLM, *G.B.E.,* 1949; ed. at Eton, and at Camb. Univ.; Capt. R.E. ; European War 1939-45 with Madras Sappers and Miners (despatches).

Arms—Argent, an anchor with cable entwined proper between three cinquefoils **gules,** **Crest**—In front of a demi-eagle displayed **proper** an escutcheon argent, charged with a **cinquefoil** gules.   **Supporters**—On either side an **eagle** rising or, gorged with a naval crown azure.

Residence—175, Beach St., Deal, Kent.

Sister living—Betty Moyra, *b.* 1908: *m.* 1935, Capt. John Gerald Watson Till, RA, who *d.* 1966, and has issue living, John Alistair (127, Copse Hill, SW20), *b.* 1938; ed. at Eton: *m.* 1961, Valerie Ann Winifred, da. of Thomas James Turner of Oldham,—Charmian, *b.* 1946. *Residence,* Kilcarne Lodge, Navan, co. Meath.

The 1st baronet, Sir (John) Malcolm Fraser, G.B.E. (son of the late William John Fraser, of **London**), was Asst. Editor *The Standard,* Editor *Evening Standard and St. James's Gazette,* Day Editor *Daily Express,* and Editor-in-Ch. *Birmingham Gazette, Despatch,* etc., High Sheriff of Surrey 1937-8, and Lord-Lieut. thereof 1939-49.

FRASER, Creation (U.K.) 1943, of Tain, co. Ross.

Deliverance and help.

Sir JAMES DAVID FRASER, 2nd *Baronet;* *b.* July 19th, 1924; *s.* his father, *Sir* JOHN, *K.C.V.O., M.C.,* 1947; ed. at Edinburgh Acad., at Magdalen Coll., Oxford (B.A.), and at Edinburgh Univ. (M.B. and Ch.B.; F.R.C.S. Edinburgh); Ch.M.; Maj. late R.A.M.C., Prof. of Clinical Science in Surgery, Southampton Univ., and Hon. Consulting Surg., Southampton Group of Hosps.; formerly Sen. Lect. in Clinical Surgery, Edinburgh Univ., Hon. Consulting Surg. Edinburgh Roy. Infirmary, and Surg. Colonial Med. Ser.: *m.* 1950, Maureen, da. of the Rev. John Reay, MC, of Bingham Rectory, Notts, and has issue.

Arms—Azure, three cinque foils argent, on a chief **of** the last three bears' heads couped of the field muzzled **of** the second.   **Crest**—A buck's head erased proper.   *Residence*—Rothiemurchus, St. Cross Hill, Winchester, Hants.

Sons living—IAIN MICHAEL, *b.* June 27th, 1951.— Christopher John *b.* 1954.

Sister living—Jean Margaret, *b.* 1019: *m.* 1944, Denis Johnston Cadzow, of Duncrahill, Pencaitland, E. Lothian, and has issue living, Sally Jean, *b.* 1945,— Joan Margaret, *b.* 1947,—Norah Denise, *b.* 1949.

Widow living of 1st Baronet—NINA (*Dowager Lady Fraser*), da. of the Rev. William David Herald, of The Manse, Duns, Berwickshire : *m.* 1918, Sir John Fraser K.C.V.O., M.C., 1st baronet, who *d.* 1947. *Residence* 2, Lennox Street, Edinburgh.

The 1st baronet, Sir John Fraser, K.C.V.O., M.C. (son of James Fraser, of Tain, Ross-shire), was Hon. Surg. to H.M. in Scotland, Regius Professor of Clinical Surgery, Edinburgh Univ., and Surg., Edinburgh Roy. Infirmary 1925-48, and Principal and Vice-Chancellor of Edinburgh Univ. 1944-48.

FRASER, Creation (U.K.) 1961, of Dineiddwg, co. Stirling.

Sir HUGH FRASER, 2nd *Baronet,* who *s.* as 2nd Baron Fraser of Allander, Nov. 6th 1966, until he disclaimed his peerage, 1966 [see Fraser of Allander, By.].

FREAKE, Creation (U.K.) 1882, of Cromwell House, Kensington, and Fulwell Park, co. Middlesex. [Extinct 1951.]

Sir CHARLES ARLAND MAITLAND FREAKE, 4th and last *Baronet.*

Daughter living of 4th Baronet—Sheila Winifred, *b.* 1933: *m.* 1957, John David O'Brien, son of Sir David Edmond O'Brien, 6th Bt. *Residence,* Courtown House, Kilcock, co. Kildare.

FREDERICK, Creation (G.B.) 1723, of Burwood House, Surrey.

Prudent simplicity blesses.

Sir CHARLES BOSCAWEN FREDERICK, 10th *Baronet ; b.* April 11th, 1919 ; *s.* his father, *Lieut.-Col. Sir* EDWARD BOSCAWEN, *CVO,* 1956; ed. at Eton; Maj. (ret.) Gren. Gds.; a JP of Bucks.; a Member Gen. Commn. of Income Tax since 1966, of Stock Exchange Council since 1973, and Chm. of Provincial Unit of Stock Exchange since 1973; a Member of London Stock Exchange 1954-62; N. Africa and Italy 1943-45 (despatches), Palestine 1946-47 (despatches), Malaya 1948-49, Egypt 1952-53: *m.* 1949, Rosemary, el. da. of the late Lt.-Col. Robert John Halkett Baddeley, MC, of Home Close, Donhead St. Mary, Shaftesbury, and has issue.

Arms—Or, on a chief azure three doves argent. **Crest**—On a chapeau azure turned up ermine a dove as in the arms, holding in its beak an olive-branch proper.
Residences—Symon's Granary, Lerryn, Lostwithiel, Cornwall. *Club*—Royal Fowey Yacht.

Sons living—CHRISTOPHER ST.JOHN, *b.* June 28th, 1950.——James Boscawen, *b.* 1963.
Daughters living—Anne Rosemary, *b.* 1952.—— Jill Elizabeth, *b.* 1956.

Sister living—Kathleen Patricia, *b.* 1914 : *m.* 1935, Capt. George Edward Shiffner, late Oxfordshire and Bucks L.I., who *d.* 1956 [*see* Shiffner, Bt., colls.]. *Residence,* Cutt Mill, near Watlington, Oxon.

Collateral Branches living.

Grandchildren of the late George Septimus Frederick, son of the late Lieut.-Col. Thomas Frederick, son of the late Maj.-Gen. Marescoe Frederick, brother of 4th baronet:—

Issue of the late Henry Penrice Frederick, *b.* 1857, *d.* 1942: *m.* 1st, 1891, Margaret, who *d.* 1904, da. of Sir Thomas Beevor, 4th Bt.; 2ndly, 1908, Diana, who *d.* 1940, da. of Sir William Foster, 2nd Bt.:—

(By 1st marriage) Roger (Bowness, 11, Langstone Av., Havant, Hants., PO9 1RW), *b.* 1900 Com. (ret.) RN: *m.* 1928, Nora Mary, da. of the late Col. Herbert Mansfield Whitehead, OBE, of The Grange, Penkridge, Staffordshire, and has issue living, Roger Mansfield (of 5, Waltacre, Yealmpton, S. Devon), *b.* 1930: *m.* 1959, Valerie Anne Watts, and has issue living, Alan Marescoe *b.* 1960, Jonathan Denley *b.* 1962, Thomas Russell *b.* 1966, Catherine Mary *b.* 1967,—Rowena Mary, *b.* 1935: *m.* 1957, Lt.-Col. Ralph Plant, Roy. Signals, and has issue living, Naomi Elizabeth *b.* 1958, Alison Mary *b.* 1959, Stephanie Ann *b.* 1961, Nicola Ruth *b.* 1964, Vanessa Jane *b.* 1965,—Briony Margaret, *b.* 1941: *m.* 1960, Sqdn.-Ldr. John Hamilton, RAF, and has issue living, Roger, *b.* 1961, David Nicholas *b.* 1963.——Mary *b.* 1894: *m.* 1922, the Rt. Rev. George Ernest Ingle, Bishop of Willesden, who *d.* 1964, and has issue living, George Thomas David (7, The Cedars, Buckhurst Hill, Essex), *b.* 1925: *m.* 1st, 1953 (m. diss. 1961), Janet, da. of the late Dr. Campbell Andrews; 2ndly, 1963, Lydia, da. of the late Judge Pablo S. Riviera, of Philippine Is., and has issue living (by 1st m.), Jane Sarah *b.* 1955, (by 2nd m. John Paul David *b.* 1967, Mark James Lee *b.* 1970, Angela Nina *b.* 1966,—Patrick Maynard, (8, Park Av., SW14) *b.* 1929; MA; MIPA; MInstMSM: *m.* 1954, Jennifer Mary Brook, of Totnes, and has issue living, Andrew Patrick George *b.* 1964, Susan Mary *b.* 1955, Victoria Jane *b.* 1957,—Jean Mary, *b.* 1923: *m.* 1955, Christopher Lawrence Penn, of 3, Waterside Place, Princess Rd., NW1 8JT, and has issue living, Caroline Jane *b.* 1957. *Residence,* Flat 2, 27, Thurlow Rd., NW3.

Grandchildren of the late Ernest Prescott Frederick, 3rd son of the late George Septimus Frederick (ante):—

Issue of the late Capt. John Cromwell Frederick, RN, *b.* 1920, *d.* 1974: *m.* 1st, 1942 (m. diss. 1965), Mary Oliveria, da. of the late Rev. Wynyard Warner, MC; 2ndly, 1966, Margaret Lilian (Belliver, Hoo Meavy, Yelverton, Devon), da. of Richard Henry Dalbiac [B. Sherwood]:—

(By 1st m.) John Peter, *b.* 1945: *m.* 1972, Janie Mary, da. of Scott Gundersen, of NZ.——Sarah Ann, *b.* 1943.

Grandchildren of the late George Septimus Frederick (ante):—

Issue of the late Arthur Marescoe Frederick, *b.* 1869, *d.* 1963: *m.* 1900, Petrona Elena, who *d.* 1965, da. of the late C. J. F. Davie, of Montevideo:—

Arthur Roland (of Casilla Correo, 248, Montevideo, Uruguay), *b.* 1901: *m.* 1930, Maria Esther, da. of the late Francisco Costa, of Montevideo, and has issue living, Richard Frank (of Montevideo, Uruguay), *b.* 1935: *m.* 1960, Gloria, da. of Carlos Garcia Arocena, and has issue living, Ricardo *b.* 1963, Odile Maria *b.* 1962, Madelon Maria *b.* 1965,—Lilian Susan *b.* 1932: *m.* 1959, Hugo Sapelli, of Montevideo, Uruguay.——John Davie Geoffrey, *b.* 1903, *d.* 1975: *m.* 1st, 1929, Maria Mercedes, who *d.* 1950, da. of the late Luis Labadie, of Montevideo; 2ndly, 1952, Elisa, da. of the late Juan Lotero, and has issue living, (by 1st m.) John (of Santa Rosa, Canelones, Uruguay), *b.* 1930: *m.* 1961, Martha Rosa, da. of the late Oscar Gulla, of Santa Rosa, Canelones, Uruguay), and has issue living, Carlos Alberto *b.* 1962, Rafael Daniel *b.* 1964, Oscare Geoffrey *b.* 1966,—Henry (POB 204, Montevideo, Uruguay), *b.* 1933: *m.* 1958, Lia, da. of Julio Arocena Capurro, of Buenos Aires, Argentina, and has issue living, Henry Martin *b.* 1959, Diego Jose *b.* 1962, Jaime Luis *b.* 1966, Mercedes Ines *b.* 1961.——Louisa Carmen (c/o A. R. Frederick, Esq., PO Box 248, Montevideo, Uruguay), *b.* 1905: *m.* 1934, W. J. H. Van Wijngaarden, who *d.* 1964.

Grandchildren of the late Edward Gurdon Frederick, MRCS, LRCP, 8th son of
George Septimus Frederick (ante):—
Issue of the late Edward Vincent Frederick, b. 1902, d. 1969: m. 1946, Joan Olive (Ajanta,
Telscombe Cliffs, Sussex), da. of A. Dunford, of Brighton:—
Christopher Hugh, b. 1948.——Helen Mary, b. 1947.——Auriol Rosalind, b. 1952.

Granddaughter of the late George Septimus Frederick (ante):—
Issue of the late Herbert Frederick, b. 1874, d. 1949: m. 1900, Alice Louisa, who d. 1943, da.
of the late W. H. Priest, of H.M's Civil Ser.:—
Edith Nora, b. 1901. Residence, 40, Rousham Rd., Eastville, Bristol, BS5 6XJ.

Sir John Frederick, Knight, a wealthy merchant, Lord Mayor of London 1662, and M.P. for that
city 1663, was a munificent benefactor of Christ's Hospital, and, after the great fire of 1666, rebuilt the
hall at a cost of £5,000. Sir John, the 1st baronet, was his grandson. The 5th baronet was for
several years M.P. for Surrey. The 8th baronet, Sir Charles Edward St. John Frederick, O.B.E.,
was High Sheriff of Northants 1934. The 9th baronet, Lieut.-Col. Sir Edward Boscawen Frederick,
C.V.O., Roy. Fusiliers (retired), was an Exon of King's Body Guard of Yeoman of the Guard
1925-37, and Ensign 1937-50.

FREEMAN, Creation (U.K.) 1945, of Murtle, co. Aberdeen.

Sir (JOHN) KEITH (NOEL) FREEMAN, 2nd
Baronet; b. July 28th, 1923; *s.* his father, *Air Ch. Marshal Sir* WILFRID RHODES, *G.C.B., D.S.O., M.C.,* 1953;
ed. at Rugby, and at Ch. Ch., Oxford; a Dir. Associated
Leisure, Ltd.; 1939-45 War in Europe and Middle
East as Fl. Lt. RAF: *m.* 1946, Patricia Denison,
da. of the late C. W. Thomas, and has issue.

Arms—Per fess azure and viar ancient, three fusils in chief and
a crescent in base or, a bordure engrailed gules. Crest—A fusil or
between two wings displayed azure.

Residence—12, Monckton Court, Strangeways Terr., W14.

Son living—JAMES ROBIN, b. July 21st, 1955.
Daughter living—Katharine Noël, b. 1950.
Sister living—Bridget Anne Elizabeth, b. 1920: m. 1st, 1942
(marriage dissolved 1946), John Vernon Rob; 2ndly, 1954, Godfrey
Henry Beese, of Kimpton House, nr. Andover, Hants., and has
issue living, (by 1st marriage) Joanna Elizabeth, b. 1943, (by 2nd
marriage) Christopher David, b. 1955,—Thomas Jolyon, b. 1957,—
Deborah Helen, b. 1956,—Philippa Lucy, b. 1960.
Half-Sisters living—Joan Margaret, b. 1936: m. 1955, John Richard Bine Morgan-Grenville
[see Ly. Kinloss]. Residence, Upperton House, Petworth, Sussex.——Susan Hilary Philippa,
b. 1939: m. 1962, Robin Neill Lochnell Malcolm, of Nether Largie, Kilmartin, Argyll, and has
issue living, Ian Rory, b. 1963,—Andrew Neill, b. 1965,—Kirsty Elizabeth, b. 1964,—Josephine
Clare, b. 1969.
Widow living of 1st Baronet—ELIZABETH, M.B.E. (Dowager Lady Freeman), da. of the late
Ernest Tatham Richmond, F.R.I.B.A. [B. Avebury, colls.]; M.B.E. (Mil.) 1945: m. 1935, as his
second wife, Air Ch. Marshal Sir Wilfrid Rhodes Freeman, 1st Bt., G.C.B., D.S.O., M.C., who
d. 1953. Residence, Loch Caol Cottage, by Bunessan, Isle of Mull.

The 1st baronet, Air Ch. Marshal Sir Wilfrid Rhodes Freeman, G.C.B., D.S.O., M.C. (3rd
son of William Robert Freeman), commanded Headquarters, Transjordan and Palestine 1930-34;
was Comdt. Roy. Air Force Staff Coll. 1934-36; appointed Air Member of Research and Development on Air Council 1936 (also for Production 1938-40), and Vice-Ch. of Air Staff 1940; Ch.
Executive, Min. of Aircraft Production 1942-45.

Be faithful.

FRY, Creation (U.K.) 1894, of Woodburn, Blackwell, co. Durham.

Sir JOHN NICHOLAS PEASE FRY, 4th *Baronet*;
b. Oct. 23rd, 1897; *s.* his brother, *Sir* THEO-
DORE PENROSE, 1971; ed. at Clifton Coll. and
Trin. Coll., Camb. (BA): *m.* 1927, Helen
Murray, da. of the late William Gibson Bott,
MRCS, JP, of London, NW11, and has issue.

Arms—Per fesse gules and sable, three horses courant
in pale argent. Crest—A dexter arm embowed in armour
proper, garnished or, charged on the upper arm with a
horseshoe sable, the hand grasping a sword fesswise also
proper, pommel and hilt gold.
Residence—Kenmore, Sandy Down, Boldre, Lymington,
Hants., SO4 8PL.
Daughter living—Margaret Jane (6, Turners Wood Drive,
Chalfont St. Giles, Bucks.), b. 1928: m. 1956, Arthur
Keith Redway, MSc, and has issue living, Jeremy Nicholas
Fry, b. 1958.

Brother living—FRANCIS WILFRID, OBE, b. May 2nd,
1904; ed. at Clifton, and at Trin. Coll., Camb. (BA);
JP, MIMinE, OBE (Civil) 1967: m. 1954, Anne Pease, JP,
el. da. of the late Kenneth Henry Wilson, OBE, JP, of
Park Hall, Kidderminster, Worcs. Residence, Cleveland
Lodge, Gt. Ayton, Middlesbrough, Cleveland, TS9 6BT.

Sisters living—Margaret Isobel, BEM, b. 1900; ed. at Newnham Coll., Camb.; Co. Commr. for Girl
Guides, Cambridgeshire and Isle of Ely 1945-57: m. 1923, Miles Crawford Burkitt, JP, FSA,
who d. 1971, and has issue living, John Francis Crawford, b. 1926,—Miles Theodore Crawford
(The Grape House, Grantchester, Cambridge), b. 1932; ed. at Eton and Trin. Coll., Camb. (BA):
m. 1962, Caroline Marion Kennedy Shaw, and has issue living, Francis William Miles b. 1964,
Charles Edward Crawford b. 1967,—Judith Amy Sophia, b. 1925; ed. at Newnham Coll., Camb.
(MA): m. 1960, the Rev. Timothy Bruce Fyffe, BA, of 279, Oulton Rd., Lowestoft, and has issue
living, Francis John b. 1963, Margaret Sophia b. 1961. Residence, The Grape House, Grant-
chester, Cambs.——Sophia Geraldine, b. 1902; ed. at Newnham Coll., Camb. (MA); formerly
Prin. Lecturer in English, Yorkshire Training Coll. of Housecraft (Leeds). Residence, 1 Symonds
Lane, Grantchester, Cambs.

Aunt living (daughter of 1st baronet)—Gabrielle Iris, b. 1906: m. 1933, Edwin Basil Kleu, and
has issue living, Basil Guy (of 34, Boshoff St., Westering, Port Elizabeth, S. Africa), b. 1937:
m. 1961, Cecily Ann Sutcliffe, of Port Elizabeth, S. Africa, and has issue living, Patrick Sean
b. 1964, Roger Mark b. 1067, Jennifer Lesley b. 1962, Moira Ann b. 1965,—Paul Theodore Robert,
b. 1941: m. 1965, Ethlin M. Langford and has issue living, Christopher Paul b. 1971, Valerie b.
1968,—Michael Daniel, b. 1943: m. 1966, Thea Tromp, of Port Elizabeth, and has issue living,
Gary Tyerk b. 1968, Robert Michael b. 1970, Shirley Nicola b. 1966,—Malcolm Peter, b. 1946,—
Gabriel Mary Judith, b. 1948. Residence, 63, Chudleigh Rd., Plumstead, Cape Town, S. Africa.

Collateral Branch living.

Issue of the late Walter Raymond Fry, 3rd son of 1st baronet, b. 1870, d. 1944: m.
1897, Lilian, who d. 1956, da. of the late M. Vallauri, Ch. Dragoman to Turkish Embassy at St. Petersburg :—
Eleanor Priscilla (Box 338, Patchogue, NY, USA), b. 1898: m. 1923, Frank Edwin Ransome,
who d. 1959, and has issue living, Frank Fellows, (124, Hillside Av., Livingston, NJ, USA), b.
1924: m. 1950, Lois Pape, and has issue living, Steven b. 1951, Patricia b. 1954,—John Fry,
(674, Old North Ocean Av., Patchogue, NY, USA), b. 1927: m. 1950, Marjorie Ann Fisher, and
has issue living, Blair E. b. 1951, Meredith b. 1970, Barbara F. b. 1955, Sara Jane b. 1958.

The 1st baronet. Sir Theodore Fry, F.S.A., J.P., D.L. (younger brother of the late Francis
James Fry, of Cricket St. Thomas Chard, father of Sir Geoffrey Storrs Fry, KCB, CVO, 1st Bt.,
cr. 1929, ext. 1960), was a Dir. of Iron, Coal and Shipping cos., and MP for Darlington (L) 1880-95.

FRY, Creation (U.K.) 1929, of Oare, co. Wilts. [Extinct 1960.]

Sir GEOFFREY STORRS FRY, K.C.B., C.V.O., 1st and last Baronet.

Daughter living of 1st Baronet—Ann Jennifer Evelyn Elizabeth, b. 1916: m. 1st, 1942,
Robert Vernon Heber-Percy, from whom she obtained a divorce 1947 [see D. Northumberland,
colls.]; 2ndly, 1949, Alan Ross. Residence,—Clayton Manor, Sussex.

FULLER, Creation (U.K.) 1910, of Neston Park, Corsham, Wiltshire.

Deo Duce Confido.

Sir (JOHN) GERARD HENRY FLEETWOOD
FULLER, 2nd Baronet; b. July 8th, 1906; s. his
father, Sir JOHN MICHAEL FLEETWOOD,
K.C.M.G., 1915; Major (retired) The Life
Guards, a J.P. for Wilts; elected a Co.
Councillor of Wilts 1947, and a Co. Alderman
1961; was Master of Avon Vale Foxhounds
1947-61; European War 1939-42 in Middle
East (despatches) : m. 1st, 1931, Lady Fiona
Pratt (who obtained a divorce 1944), da. of
4th Marquess Camden ; 2ndly, 1945, Kath-
leen Elizabeth, M.B.E. (D.St.J.), who d.
1964, da. of Sir George Herbert Farrar,
DSO, 1st Bt. (ext.); 3rdly, 1966, Mrs. Mary
Leventon, da. of Dr. D. Leigh Spence, of
Melksham, Wilts., and has issue by 1st
marriage.

Arms—Per pale nebuly azure and ermine two bars
counterchanged, over all six martlets two, two, and two or.
Crest—Issuant from a coronet flory or, a lion's head per
pale nebuly azure and ermine. Supporters—Dexter, a lion
reguardant proper; sinister, a wolf reguardant argent;
each gorged with a collar or, pendant therefrom an escutcheon per pale nebuly azure and or,
charged with six martlets counter-changed.
Residences—Neston Park, Corsham, Wilts ; Balmore, Cannich, by Beauly, Inverness.

Sons living—By 1st m.—JOHN WILLIAM FLEETWOOD (Ganbrook Farm, Broughton Gifford,
Melksham, Wilts.), b. Dec. 18th, 1936; Maj. (ret.) The Life Gds.: m. 1968, Lorna Marion, only
da. of F. R. Kemp-Potter, of Hillside, Findon, Sussex, and has issue living, James Henry Fleet-
wood, b. 1970,—Andrew William Fleetwood, b. 1972.——Anthony Gerard Fleetwood (The Old
House, Hare Hatch, Berks), b. 1940; late Lt. The Life Gds.: m. 1964, Julia Mary, el. da. of Lt.-
Col. Eric Astley Cooper-Key, MBE, MC, of 67, Eaton Sq., SW1, and has issue living, William
Gerard Fleetwood, b. 1968,—Camilla Fleetwood, b. 1966.

Brother living—Christopher Herbert Fleetwood, T.D., b. 1908: ed. at Winchester, and at Oxford
Univ. ; Lieut.-Col. (retired) Roy. Wilts. Yeo ; High Sheriff of Wilts. 1956-7: m. 1939, Susan, da.
of the late Maj.-Gen. Sir Percival Otway Hambro, K.B.E., C.B., C.M.G., and has issue living,
Charles Christopher Fleetwood, b. 1945,—Penelope Susanne Fleetwood, b. 1942: m. 1966,
George Oliver Worsley [see Worsley, Bt.], Victoria Henrietta Fleetwood, b. 1944: m. 1966, John
Philip Starkey, el. son of Sir William Randle Starkey, 2nd Bt.,—Georgina Jacintha Fleetwood,
b. 1951. Residence, Jaggards, Corsham, Wilts. Clubs, Carlton, Pratt's.

The 1st baronet, Sir John Michael Fleetwood, K.C.M.G., was a Junior Lord of the Treasury
(unpaid) 1906-7, Vice-Chamberlain of H.M.'s Household 1907-11, and sat as M.P. for W., or Westbury, Div. of Wilts (L) 1900-1911, and Gov. of Victoria 1911-14.

Fuller-Acland-Hood, see Hood.

FURNESS, Creation (U.K.) 1913, of Tunstall Grange, West Hartlepool.

Sir STEPHEN ROBERTS FURNESS, 3rd *Baronet*; *b.* Oct. 10th, 1933; *s.* his father, *Sir* CHRISTOPHER 1974; Lt. RN (ret.): *m.* 1961, Mary, da. of Jack Fitzroy Cann, of Newland, Cullompton, S. Devon, and has issue.

Arms—Per saltire argent and or, a talbot sejant sable, on a chief wavy gules three plates. Crest—Issuant from a wreath of cinquefoils vert, a bear's paw erect argent, charged with a torteaux, grasping a javelin in bend sinister sable, pendent therefrom by the straps proper two spurs or.

Residence—Milbanke, Bedburn, Bishop Auckland, co. Durham.

Son living—MICHAEL FITZROY ROBERTS, *b.* Oct. 12th, 1962.

Daughter living—Serena Mary, *b.* 1964.

Brothers living—Simon John (Netherbyres, Eyemouth, Berwickshire; Army and Navy Club), *b.* 1936; Maj. The LI.——Colin Gerard (of The Mill Farm, Eyemouth, Berwickshire), *b.* 1939: *m.* 1958, Margaret Grace, only da. of Alfred J. Haddock, and has issue living, Francis Christopher *b.* 1963,—Fiona Elizabeth, *b.* 1959,—Julia Margaret, *b.* 1960,—Nicola Jane, *b.* 1964.

Sister living—Patricia Flower, *b.* 1931: *m.* 1960, Maj. Paul Ian Craven Payne, late R. Scots, of Whitehall, Old Cleeve, Minehead, Som., and has issue living, Brian Wyndham *b.* 1961,—Paul Frederick Craven, *b.* 1964.

Uncle living (son of 2nd baronet)—Frank Wilson, MBE, *b.* 1906; ed. at Pembroke Coll., Camb. (MA); is a JP; MBE (Civil) 1967: *m.* 1949, Georgeana Anne, da. of Col. Victor Alexander Henry Daly, OBE, MC, and widow of Alan Guthrie, Flying Officer RAF, and has issue living, John Wilson, *b.* 1952. *Residence,* Knowle House, Kirby Knowle, Thirsk, Yorks. YO7 2JB. *Club,* Yorkshire (York).

Aunt living (daughter of 2nd baronet)—Eleanor Mary, *b.* 1904. *Residence,* Otterington Hall, Northallerton, Yorkshire.

Widow living of 2nd Baronet—VIOLET FLOWER CHIPCHASE, OBE (*Flower, Lady Furness*), (Netherbyres, Eyemouth, Berwicks); OBE (Civil) 1970; da. of the late Lt.-Col. Gerard Chipchase Roberts, of Hollingside, Durham: *m.* 1930, Sir Christopher Furness, 2nd Bt., who *d.* 1974.

The 1st baronet, Sir Stephen Wilson, was Chm. of Furness, Withy and Co. (Limited), and sat as M.P. for Hartlepool (*L*) 1910-14.

FRANKLAND-PAYNE-GALLWEY, Creation (U.K.) 1812.

Sir PHILIP FRANKLAND-PAYNE-GALLWEY, 6th *Baronet*, only son of Lt.-Col. Lowry Philip Payne-Gallwey, OBE, MC, el. son of the Rev. Francis Henry Payne-Gallwey, 4th son of Capt. Philip Payne-Gallwey, yst. son of 1st Bt.; *b.* March 15th, 1935; *s.* his kinsman *Sir* REGINALD FRANKLAND, 1964; ed. at Eton; late Lt. 11th Hussars; assumed by Roy. Licence 1966 the additional surname of Frankland before that of Payne and Gallwey.

Arms—Quarterly: 1st and 4th, per fesse or and gules, in chief an eagle displayed with two heads of the last, in base a bridge of three arches double towered argent, *Gallwey* ; 2nd, gules, a fesse between two lions passant argent, *Payne*; 3rd, azure, a dolphin naiant or, on a chief of the last two saltires couped gules, *Frankland.* Crests—1st, a cat-a-mountain passant guardant proper, gorged with a collar gemelle and charged on the body with a cross patée or, *Gallwey* ; 2nd, a lion's jamb erased erect argent, holding the lower part of a tilting spear in bend sinister gules, *Payne* ; 3rd, an anchor erect azure, stock or, the shank entwined by a dolphin hauriant argent, *Frankland.*

Residence—The Little House Boxford, Newbury, Berks.

I would rather die than be dishonoured.

Daughter living of 5th Baronet—Joan Flower, *b.* 1914: *m.* 1940, Robert Vincent Steven, and has issue living, Patricia Susan, *b.* 1942: *m.* 1968, Timothy John Charsley, BSc (c/o Geological Survey Dept., Zomba, Malawi),—Margaret Sheila, *b.* 1945: *m.* 1969, Michael John Wigginton, of Flat 4, 35, Eccleston Sq., SW1. *Residence*, 227, Route St., Maurice, 1814 La Tour de Peilz, Vaud, Switzerland.

Daughter living of 3rd Baronet—Dorothy FRANKLAND-PAYNE-GALLWEY, *b.* 18—.

Aunt living—Helen Isabel, *b.* 1898: *m.* 1925 Robert Douglas Leigh-Pemberton MC who *d.* 1964 [D. Atholl. colls.] and has issue living Robert (of Torry Hill, Sittingbourne, Kent) *b.* 1927; ed. at Eton and at Trin. Coll. Oxford (BA 1951 MA 1955); Bar. Inner Temple 1953; late Grenadier Guards: *m.* 1953, Rosemary Davina, da. of the late Lt.-Col. David Walter Arthur William Forbes, M.C., Coldstream Guards [B. Faringdon, colls.], and has issue living, John David *b.* 1955, James Henry *b.* 1956, Edward Douglas *b.* 1959, Thomas Robert Arnold *b.* 1961, William Francis *b.* 1964,—Nigel Douglas, *b.* 1929; ed. at Eton, and Oxford Univ.; late Life Guards: *m.* 1973, Alexandra Valerie Roper,—Jeremy (Vitters Oak, Bethersden, Kent), *b.* 1933; ed. at Eton, and at Oxford Univ.; late Gren. Gds.: *m.* 1968, Mary, da. of John S. Ames, of Boston, Mass., and has issue living, Richard Ames *b.* 1971. *Residence*, Kippen, Frimsted, Sittingbourne, Kent.

Mother living—Janet (of The Little House, Boxford, Newbury, Berks.), da. of the late Albert Philip Payne-Gallwey (infra): *m.* 1933, Lt.-Col. Lowry Philip Payne-Gallwey, OBE, MC (ante), who *d.* 1958.

Collateral Branches living.

Issue of the late Lionel Philip Payne-Gallwey, 3rd son of 2nd baronet, *b.* 1851, *d.* 1891: *m.* 1881, Caroline Lucille (who *d.* 1946, having *m.* 2ndly, 1899, F. E. Taylor, of Jamaica, who *d.* 1943), da. of E. B. Lynch:—

Sybil Norah: *m.* 1911, John Louis Granville Sharpe, who *d.* 1940, and has issue living, John Lionel (Wall Farm, Elmsett, Ipswich), *b.* 1912: *m.* 1st, 1940, M. R. L Auster, who *d.* 1963; 2ndly, 1963, M. M. Collins, and has issue living, (by 1st marriage) Patricia Marjorie *b.* 1943—Kathleen Margaret (of 8, Headon Gdns., Countess Wear, Exeter, Devon), *b.* 1913: *m.* 1940, Capt. P. C. Murphy, MC, who *d.* (killed in action during European War) 1943, and has issue living, John Patrick *b.* 1941, Peter David *b.* 1943,—Evelyn Caroline, *b.* 1917: *m.* 1944, the Rev. Neville Walter Lucas Auster, The Vicarage, Dullingham, Newmarket, Suffolk, and has issue living, Martin Lucas *b.* 1946,—Maureen Francis, *b.* 1925: *m.* 1952, Christopher T. Reichwald, MC, of Whitnage Chart, Uplowman, Tiverton, S. Devon, and has issue living, David C. T. *b.* 1953, Rosemary M. (twin) *b.* 1953. *Residence*, Walden, Eagle Lane, Dullingham, nr. Newmarket, Suffolk.

Granddaughter of the late Albert Philip Payne-Gallwey (infra):—
Issue of the late Lt.-Col. Peter Payne-Gallwey, DSO, *b.* 1906, *d.* 1971: *m.* 1953, Ann Josephine (The Old Manor, Upper Lambourn, Berks.), da. of Roger John Linloch Barber-Starkey [Legard, Bt., colls.]:—
Nicola, *b.* 1955.

Issue of the late Albert Philip Payne-Pallwey, yst son of 1st baronet, *b.* 1871, *d.* 1931: *m.* 1900, Katherine Mary, who *d.* 1962, da. of the late Maj. Vaughan Hanning Vaughan Lee, M.P., of Dillington Park, Som.:—
Janet, *b.* 1903: *m.* 1933, Lt.-Col. Lowry Philip Payne-Gallwey, OBE, MC, 7th Queen's Own Hussars (ante), who *d.* 1958.

The 1st baronet, Gen. Sir William Payne, younger half-brother of Ralph Payne, Lord Lavington (ext. 1807), Gov. of Leeward Islands, assumed by Roy. licence 1814 the additional surname of Gallwey in compliance with will of Tobias Wall Gallwey of St. Kitts, his maternal uncle. The 2nd baronet, Sir William Payne-Gallwey, sat as M.P. for Thirsk (C) 1851-80. The 3rd Bt., Sir Ralph William assumed by Roy. licence 1914 for himself and issue the additional surname of Frankland. The 4th baronet, Sir John Frankland-Payne-Gallwey assumed by Roy. licence 1919 the additional surname of Frankland.

GAMBLE, Creation (U.K.) 1897, of Windlehurst, St. Helens, Co. Palatine of Lancashire.

Vix ea nostra voco.
I scarce call these things ours.

Sir DAVID ARTHUR JOSIAS GAMBLE, 4th Baronet *; b.* Dec. 9th, 1907 *; s.* his father, *Sir* DAVID, 1943; ed. at Shrewsbury, and Wadham Coll., Oxford (MA); Chm. of Cirencester RDC 1958-59: *m.* 1st, 1932, Elinor Mary, who *d.* 1961, da. of Henry E. Cole, formerly of Summers, Long Sutton, Hants.; 2ndly, 1965, Evelyn Gamble, and has issue by 1st marriage.

Arms—Or, on a pile gules between two trefoils slipped in base vert, a fleur-de-lis of the first, a chief ermine. Crest—On a mount between two trefoils slipped vert a stork argent, holding in the beak a rose gules, stalked, leaved, and slipped proper.
Residence—Wood End, Tregony, Truro, Cornwall.

Son living—By 1st marriage—DAVID (St. Josephs, North St., Wincanton, Som.), *b.* June 5th, 1933; ed. at Shrewsbury: *m.* 1956, Dawn Adrienne, da. of the late David Hugh Gittins, Pilot Officer RAF, of The Manor House, W. Hagley, Worcestershire, and has issue living, David Hugh Norman, *b.* 1966,—Caroline, *b.* 1957,—Elinor Josephine, *b.* 1961.
Brothers living—Robert Meredith (Rookwood, 4, Abbot Rd., Caversham, Reading, Berks.), *b.* 1909; formerly Capt. Wilts Regt.: *m.* 1st, 1931 (m. diss. 1940), Phyllis Mary, da. of the late Charles E. Bradbury; 2ndly, 1940, Diana Burnaby, da. of the late Walter F. Drayson, and has issue living, (by 2nd *m.*) Hugh Robert George,

b. 1946.—Catherine Frances Dorothy, *b.* 1940: *m.* 1962, Anthony David Weguelin Bertram, of Whistlers, 6, The Mount, Caversham, Reading, Berks., and has issue living, Helen Diana Elizabeth *b.* 1965, Isobel Catherine Joan *b.* 1966, Laura Margaret Diana *b.* 1970, Victoria Susannah Mary *b.* 1974,—Sylvia Helen Jean, *b.* 1944: *m.* 1967, John Alan Goodale and has issue living: Benjamin *b.* 1968, Thomas *b.* 1971,—Rosemary Diana Margaret, *b.* 1948: *m.* 1967, Nicholas Rooker Roberts, and has issue living, Andrew Arthur *b.* 1970, Eleanor Burnaby *b.* 1972.——John Christopher (Gleneva, Latrobe, Tas.), *b.* 1910: *m.* 1939, Pamela Margaret Grace, da. of Arthur Grayhurst Hewat [Aylmer, Bt.], and has issue living, Antony Aylmer (Evandale, Tas.), *b.* 1941: *m.* 1961, Julie Leslie, and has issue living, David Antony *b.* 1962, Christine *b.* 1964, Kathleen Doris *b.* 1967, Jeanne *b.* 1971,—Ann, *b.* 1943: *m.* 1962, David J. F. Bailey, RAN, of Perth, Tas. ——William, *b.* 1913; ed. at Shrewsbury, and at St. John's Coll., Camb. (BA 1935, MA 1946); formerly Lt. RASC: *m.* 1948 Christine Mary, who *d.* 1967, only child of the late Robert Permain. *Residence*, 17, Wickridge Close, Folly Lane, Uplands, Stroud, Glos.

Collateral Branches living.

Issue of the late John Arthur Gamble, 4th son of 2nd baronet, *b.* 1883, *d.* 1947: *m.* 1910, Lilian Jane Emily, who *d.* 1913, da. of the late Rev. Arthur Raggett Cole, of Hurstbourne Priors, Hants :—

Robin Arthur Norman, *b.* 1912; ed. at Uppingham ; formerly Capt. 61st (S. Lancashire) Searchlight Regt., R.A. (T.A.): *m.* 1st, 1939, Emily Goodall, who *d.* 1944 ; 2ndly, 1947, Muriel Maud. da. of the late John Hale, of Knowsley, Lancashire, and has issue living, (by 1st marriage) Elaine Lilian, *b.* 1941: *m.* 1970, Malcolm Charles Gubbins,—Olga Evelyn, *b.* 1944. *Residence*, Tregorland, St. Just-in-Roseland, Truro.

Grandchildren of David Gamble, 3rd son of 1st baronet (infra):—
Issue of the late Conrad Dorner Gamble, *b.* 1881, *d.* 1931: *m.* 1910, Edith Annie, who *d.* 1938, da. of the late Ven. Percy Harris Bowers, R. of Market Bosworth, Leicestershire, and Archdeacon of Loughborough:—

Rodney Dorner, *b.* 1911: *m.* 1st, 1937 (m. diss. 1946), Hester Vernon, da. of W. Vernon Judd; 2ndly, 1948, Marjorie Maud, da. of Jonathan Smithson, and has issue living, (by 1st m.) Prudence Dorner, *b.* 1941.

Issue of the late Lorentz Harry Gamble, *b.* 1893, *d.* 1968: *m.* 1917, Annie Marian, who *d.* 1972, da. of F. T. Clarke, of Stony Stratford:—
Diana May (46a, de Parys Av., Bedford), *b.* 1920; formerly Jun. Com. ATS.

Issue of the late David Gamble, 3rd son of 1st baronet, *b.* 1856, *d.* 1933 : *m.* 1st, 1880, Josephine Henriette, who *d.* 1899, da. of Conrad von Dorner ; 2ndly, 1901, Marion, who *d.* 1955, da. of Griffith Parsonage, of Australia :—
(By 2nd m.) Graeme Neil (Coombe Cottage, Plainsfield, Over Stowey, Bridgwater, Som.), *b.* 1904; ed. at Radley, and at Selwyn Coll., Camb (BA): *m.* 1936, Mary George, of Chislehurst, and has issue living, Sheila Ann, *b.* 1937: *m.* 1959, James Brindley Douglas Bateman, of Lodmore Farm, E. Harptree, Bristol, and has issue living, James Graeme Richard *b.* 1967, William John Douglas *b.* 1974, Fiona Valerie *b.* 1964, Sylvia Mary *b.* 1966, Rosalind Ann *b.* 1969,—Judith, *b.* 1940: *m.* 1962, Hagen Volken Dietrich Stöckl, and has issue living, Alexander Duncan Dietrich *b.* 1963, Natasha Judith *b.* 1964,—Jane Elizabeth, *b.* 1943,—Tessa, *b.* 1952.——Alan Lionel, *b.* 1905. *Residence*, 14, Lower Common South, Putney, SW15.——Keith Desmond (14, Lower Common South, Putney, SW15), *b.* 1911.——(By 1st m.) Josephine Henriette, *b.* 1886: *m.* 1912, Sutherland Jameson, who *d.* 1926.——Elizabeth, *b.* 1888: *m.* 1918, John Wynne Paynter Reece, who *d.* 1956. *Residence*, Tanycoed, Llanfair Talhaiarn, Abergele, Denbighshire.——(By 2nd m.) Jean Marion (14, Lower Common South, Putney, SW15), *b.* 1908.

Grandchildren of the late George Gamble, 4th son of 1st baronet:—
Issue, if any (by 2nd m.) of the late Charles Lancelot Gamble, *b.* 1885, *d.* 19—: *m.* 1st, 1906, Zoë Armstrong, from whom he obtained a divorce 1908; 2ndly, 1909.

Issue of the late Henry Gamble, 6th son of 1st baronet, *b.* 1868, *d.* 1927 : *m.* 1895, Ethel, who *d.* 1924, da. of the late Thomas Brewis :—
David Harry, *b.* 1911 : *m.* 1949, May, only child of Olivier Swithenbank, J.P., of Leeds. *Resides* in Italy.——Enid Kathleen, *b.* 1896: *m.* 1924, Archibald Todrick, MB, ChB, who *d.* 1945. *Residence*, 51, Popes Avenue, Twickenham, Middlesex.——Winifred Kathleen, *b.* 1899 : *m.* 1927. Fred Russell Roberts, who *d.* 1953. *Residence*, 14, First Cross Road, Twickenham Green, Middlesex.——Agnes Grace, *b.* 1908 : *m.* 1930 (divorce 1945), Ronald Kerr, and has issue living. Merry, *b.* 1934: *m.* 1961, John Woodeson, of 4, Martindale Rd., Hounslow, Middlesex, and has issue living, Ben Charles *b.* 1965. *Residence*, Flat 3A, 235, Sussex Gdns., W2.

The 1st baronet, Sir David, K.C.B., was Mayor of St. Helens 1868-70, 1882-3, and 1886-7, a pioneer of the Volunteer Movement, and first Hon. Col. (VD) 2nd Vol. Batn. Prince of Wales' Vols. (S. Lancashire Regt.). The 2nd baronet, Sir Josias Christopher, was also Mayor of St. Helens, 1888-9. The 3rd baronet, Sir David, was also Mayor of St. Helens 1913-15

GAMMANS, Creation (U.K.) 1956, of Hornsey, co. Middlesex. [Extinct 1957.]

Sir (Leonard) David Gammans, *M.P., 1st and last Baronet.*

Widow living of 1st Baronet—Muriel (*Lady Gammans*), el. da. of the late Frank Paul, of Warblington, Hants; FRSA; MP for Hornsey Div. of Middx. (C) 1957-66; Order of Sacred Treasure (2nd class) of Japan: *m.* 1917, Sir (Leonard) David Gammans, MP, 1st baronet, who *d.* 1957, when the title became ext. *Residence*, 34, Ashley Gdns., Ambrosden Av., SW1.

BRUCE-GARDNER, Creation (U.K.) 1945, of Frilford, co. Berks.

Sir Douglas Bruce Bruce-Gardner, 2nd *Baronet; b.* Jan. 27th, 1917; *s.* his father, *Sir* Charles, 1960; ed. at Uppingham, and Trin. Coll., Camb.; Chm. of GKN Rolled & Bright Steel, Ltd. 1968-72; Dir. of Guest, Keen & Nettlefolds, Ltd., 1960; Dep. Chm. GKN, Ltd. 1974; Chm. of GKN Steel Co., Ltd. 1965-67; Pres. of Iron and Steel Inst. 1966-67; Pres. of British Independent Steel Producers' Assocn. 1972: *m.* 1st, 1940 (m. diss. 1964), Monica Flumerfelt, da. of the late Professor Sir Geoffrey Jefferson, CBE, FRS; 2ndly, 1964, Sheila Jane, da. of Roger Stilliard, of Seer Green, Bucks., and has issue by 1st and 2nd marriages.

Arms—Or, a saltire couped gules, charged with five bezants, on a chief of the second a bee volant proper between two roses argent, barbed and seeded also proper. Crest—In front of a miner's pick and gad in saltire a thistle leaved and slipped all proper.
Residence—Bishopswood Grange, Ross-on-Wye.

Sons living—By 1st m.—Robert Henry, *b.* June 10th, 1943; ed. at Uppingham and Reading Univ.—— (By 2nd m.) James Graham, *b.* 1969.

Daughters living—By 1st m.—Erica Judith, *b.* 1941: *m.* 1962, Paul H. Blackburn, and has issue living, Richard Martin, *b.* 1965,—Robert Paul, *b.* 1967,—Katharine Mary, *b.* 1963,—Emma Louise (twin), *b.* 1965.—— Sarah Tanis, *b.* 1952.——(By 2nd m.) Joanna Margaret, *b.* 1966.

Brother living—Bryan Charles, *b.* 1924: *m.* 1952, Helen Rosemary, da. of Digby B. Sowerby, of Kirmington House, nr. Ulceby, Lincolnshire, and has issue living, Edwin Charles, *b.* 1954,—Robin Digby, *b.* 1955,—Stephen Bryan, *b.* 1957,—Ian Douglas, *b.* 1963. *Residence*, The Laurels, Mount Rd., Tettenhall Wood, Tettenhall, Wolverhampton.

Sister living—Gertrude Doreen, *b.* 1913: *m.* 1941, Paul de Kantzow Dykes, late Maj. R.A., and has issue living, Daphne Jane, *b.* 1942,—Sheila Rosemary, *b.* 1946. *Residence*, Maryland, Grange Rd., Cambridge.

Widow living of 1st Baronet—Gertrude Amy (*Gertrude, Lady Bruce-Gardner*), da. of the late Charles Rivington Shill : *m.* 1911, Sir Charles Bruce-Gardner, 1st Bt., who *d.* 1960. *Residence*, Flat 21A, Grosvenor House, Park Lane, W.1.

Sir Charles Bruce-Gardner, 1st Bt. (son of the late Henry Gardner, of Stanstead Lodge, S.E.23), was Chm. of British Iron & Steel Corporation, Ltd., and John Lysaghts, Ltd., and Pres. of British Iron & Steel Research Assocn.

GARTHWAITE, Creation (U.K.) 1919, of Durham.

Sir William Francis Cuthbert Garthwaite, *D.S.C.*, 2nd *Baronet ; b.* Jan. 3rd, 1906; *s.* his father, *Sir* William, 1956; ed. at Bradfield Coll., and at Hertford Coll., Oxford ; Lt.-Com. (A) RNVR; 1939-45 War with Fleet Air Arm (despatches thrice, DSC and Bar, Air Crew Europe Star, Atlantic star, Africa star, 1939-45 Star, Defence Medal); Coronation Medal (1953): *m.* 1st, 1931, the Hon. Dorothy Duveen (who obtained a divorce 1937), da. of 1st Baron Duveen; 2ndly, 1945 (m. diss. 1952), Patricia Beatrice Eden, da. of the late Cdr. Charles Eden Neate, RN, and widow of Cdr. Barry Leonard, RN; 3rdly, 1957, Patricia Merriel, only da. of Sir Philip d'Ambrumenil, and has issue, by 2nd and 3rd marriages.

Arms—Azure, a cross between in the first and fourth quarters five ears of wheat banded, and in the second and third quarters a greyhound rampant, all or. Crest—In front of capstan sable, garnished gold, and fleur-de-lis also gold.
Cuique suum.
To each his own.
Residence—Matfield House, Matfield, Kent. *Clubs*—Bath, Royal Thames Yacht, Portland, Naval, Royal Aero, Royal Automobile.

Sons living—By 2nd marriage—William Mark Charles, *b.* Nov. 4th, 1946; ed. at Gordonstoun, and Univ. of Pennsylvania.——By 3rd m.—John William Philip, *b.* 1958.—— Andrew William David, *b.* 1962.——Simon William James (twin), *b.* 1962.

Half-Brother living—Michael William Gladwin (c/o Barclays Bank, 160, Piccadilly, W1), *b.* 1937.

Half-Sister living—Josette Garthwaite, *b.* 1913 ; has resumed the surname of Garthwaite in lieu of Mouzillat : *m.* 1940 (divorce 1955), Capt. Robert Mouzillat, and has issue living, Elizabeth Jeanette Marguerite Garthwaite, *b.* 1942: *m.* 1965, Capt. John de la Vallette Browne, late Gren. Gds., of 10, Gayfree St., Westminster, SW1,—Dominique Garthwaite (12, Eaton Mews South, SW1), *b.* 1943. *Residence*,—

Widow living of 1st Baronet—Gladys (GALIE), (*Gladys, Lady Garthwaite*), da. of Daniel Hardy: *m.* 1937, as his third wife, Sir William Garthwaite, 1st Bt. who *d.* 1956. *Residences,* 52, Boulevard d'Italie, Monte Carlo, Monaco. *Club,* Women's British and Commonwealth (Paris).

Collateral Branch living.

Issue of the late Anthony William Garthwaite, 2nd son of 1st baronet, *b.* 1917, *d.* 1972: *m.* 1950, the Hon. Waveney Mancroft Samuel (98, Bickenhall Mansions, W1), da. of the 1st Baron Mancroft:—

Nicholas Anthony William Mancroft, *b.* 1952.

The 1st baronet, Sir William Garthwaite (son of the late William Garthwaite, of Staindrop, Durham), was a shipowner and was engaged in sugar planting. He rendered sers. in developing relations between Canada and France, and inaugurating direct line of shipping between those countries, and Special Ser. to Admiralty in European Wars 1914-18 and 1939-45.

Gervis (Tapps-Gervis-Meyrick), see Meyrick.

GETHIN, Creation (I.) 1665, of Gethinsgrott, Cork.

Sir RICHARD PATRICK ST. LAWRENCE GETHIN, 9th *Baronet; b.* May 15th, 1911 ; *s.* his father, *Col. Sir* RICHARD WALTER ST. LAWRENCE, *C.M.G., D.S.O.,* 1946 ; ed. at Oundle ; is Lieut.-Col. R.E.M.E.; European War 1939-45 in France, N. Africa and Malta: *m.* 1946, Fara (2nd Officer, W.R.N.S.), da. of the late J. H. Bartlett, and has issue.

Arms—Vert, a stag salient argent armed or. Crest—On a cap of dignity proper, a stag's head erased argent armed and ducally gorged or.

Residence—Easter Cottage, Bredon, Tewkesbury.

Son living—RICHARD JOSEPH ST. LAWRENCE, *b.* Sept. 29th, 1949.

Daughters living—Helen Mary Elizabeth, *b.* 1947.—— Fara Mary Nicola, *b.* 1948: *m.* 1969, Michael Smee, of 2, Myrtle Rd., Hampton Hill, Middx., and has issue living, Oliver Leo, *b.* 1971.——Georgina Jennifer Mary, *b.* 1952.——Mary Valentine Harriet, *b.* 1945.

Brother living—William Allan Tristram, *MC* (Sun Cottage, Tumblers Hill, Sutton Valence, Kent), *b.* 1913; ed. at Oundle; Lt.-Col. (ret.) RA; 1939-45 War in Mauritius, France and Germany (despatches, MC): *m.* 1937, Nancy Ruth, only child of the late Lieut.-Col. H. G. MacGeorge, late RE, of Paignton, and has issue living, Anthony Michael (Vale House, Loose, Maidstone), *b.* 1939; ed. at Oundle, and at Magdalene Coll., Camb. (MA): *m.* 1965, Vanse, da. of the late Col. Cecil Disney Barlow, OBE, KSLI, and has issue living, Nicholas Richard Tristram *b.* 1965, William Anthony David St. Lawrence *b.* 1970,—Emma Kirstie *b.* 1968,—Patricia Jane, *b.* 1944.

Sister living—Norah Helen Catharine, *b.* 1907: *m.* 1938, James Andrew Paton Charles (PO Box BW 313, Borrowdale, Rhodesia), and has issue living, Michael James Paton (Lower Lodge, Friday St., E. Sutton, Kent), *b.* 1939: *m.* 1st, 1964 (m. diss. 1969), Barbara Elizabeth, da. of A. M. Turner, of Strathfield, NSW; 2ndly, 1969, Maureen, da. of J. Taylor, of Kiama, NSW, and has issue living (by 2nd m.), Julian Andrew Paton *b.* 1973,—Edward William (Serowe, Botswana), *b.* 1944; BSc Agric. and Trop. Dip. Trinidad: *m.* 1973, Rosemarie, da. of K. Kramer, of Winnipeg, Canada,—Elizabeth Anne (twin), *b.* 1944.

Collateral Branches living.

Grandchildren of the late Lt.-Col. Frederick Durrant Gethin (infra):—

Issue of the late John Amory Forrest Gethin, *b.* 1916, *d.* 1965: *m.* 1941, Barbara Damarel Cicely (Rew, Ashburton, S. Devon), da. of Alan Robert Cecil Westlake, of Rowledge, Farnham, Surrey:—

Christopher John Forrest, *b.* 1945.——Nicholas Geoffrey Forrest, *b.* 1950.——Stephen Amory Forrest (twin), *b.* 1950.——Elizabeth Amoret, *b.* 1942: *m.* 1965, Nicholas John du Cane Wilkinson, Lt.-Cdr. RN (ret.), Strathyre, Nairn, and has issue living, Piers Nicholas, *b.* 1973,—Samantha Karen, *b.* 1967,—Claire Felicity, *b.* 1968.

Issue of the late Lieut.-Col. Frederick Durrant Scott Gethin, 2nd son of 7th baronet, *b.* 1879, *d.* 1959 : *m.* 1915, Margaret Cecilia, who *d.* 1955, da. of L. R. W. Forrest, of Beech Holme, Wimbledon Common, S.W. :—

Margaret Joan, *b.* 1920. *Residence,* Higher Ausewell, Ashburton, S. Devon.

Issue of the late Percy Edward Lovell Gethin, yst. son of 7th baronet, OBE, AFC, *b.* 1884, *d.* 1969: *m.* 1918, Norah, who *d.* 1960, da. of James Norwood Stapledon:—

Robert Hugh (22, Glenmoor Rd., Winton, Bournemouth), *b.* 1918; ed. at Stowe, and Corpus Christi Coll., Camb. (MA); 1939-45 War with Intelligence Corps, and 1st Airborne Div.: *m.* 1946, Marjorie Gertrude, da. of B. E. Elliott, and has issue living, Rupert Mark Lovell, *b.* 1957,—Damaris Alicia Honor, *b.* 1952.——Percy Amorey Beaufort (8, Bowers Croft, Cambridge) *b.* 1925; ed. at King's Sch., Canterbury; BA London; 1939-45 War: *m.* 1948, Sylva, da. of B. Olters, of Gothenburg, Sweden, and has issue living, Terence Bertil Amorey, *b.* 1956.

Grandchildren of the late Percy Addison Hayward Gethin, el. son of the late William St. Lawrence Gethin, 2nd son of the late Capt. Richard Gethin, son of 5th baronet :—

Issue of the late Lieut.-Col. Percy St. Lawrence Gethin, M.B.E., b. 1889, d. 1959 : m. 1913, Margery (of Namanga, Kenya), da. of the late Kames J. Cleverly, of Walfish Bay, Cape Province, S. Africa :—
Patrick St. Lawrence Cleverly, b. 1914 ; ed. at Cheltenham ; Major (retired) Roy. Inniskilling Fusiliers ; European War 1939-42 (wounded) : m. 1940, Dagmar May, only child of the late N. H. Daniell, of Race View, Coonoor, S. India, and has issue living, Rowene Margaret, b. 1944,— Elaine Patricia, b. 1946: m. 1968, Paul Disbury Marsh (PO Box 72682, Nairobi, Kenya), and has issue living, Nicola Clare b. 1970. Residence, Namanga, Kenya.——Sheelagh Grace b. 1923: m. 1947, James Wilson Lindsay, and has issue living, Ian Gethin, b. 1951.

Grandchildren of the late Capt. George Gethin, son of the late Richard Gethin (infra) :—
Issue of the late Major Randolph George Gethin, M.B.E., b. 1871, d. 1945 : m. 1911, Georgina Mary, who d. 1956, da. of the late Rev. George Beresford Power [Power, Bt., colls., cr. 1836] :—
Desmond Richard le Poer (North Wing, Kilruddery, Bray, co. Wicklow), b. 1919; ed. at Stowe; Maj. (ret.) Parachute Regt. and late R. Irish Fusiliers (SR); 1939-45 War (wounded): m. 1950, Susan Frances, da. of Brig. F. Talbot Baines, and has issue living, Martin Anthony, b. 1952,— Deirdre Anne, b. 1951.——Kathleen Beatrix (Rincurran, Ardbrack, Kinsale, co. Cork), b. 1912.

Grandchildren of the late Richard Gethin, grandson of the late John Gethin, 2nd son of 4th baronet :—
Issue of the late Francis Reid Gethin, b. 1848; a. 1940 : m. 1882, Harriette Georgina, who d. 1940, da. of the late Very Rev. Arthur Moore, Dean of Achonry :—
Richard (Ashdown Cottage, Westerham Hill, Kent), b. 1886; Capt. (ret.) E. African Corps, Mil. Police; formerly Comdt. Italian Prisoner of War Camp, Kenya; formerly Lt. King's African Rifles; 1939-45 War in Abyssinia and Kenya: m. 1st, 1927, Mary Hunter, da. of Willoughby J. Bond, of Farragh, co. Longford; 2ndly, 1953, Winifred Louise, da. of Frank James Hall, of Sandon Lodge, Edgbaston, Birmingham, and has issue living (by 1st m.), Richard Reid (of Box 64, Kisii, Kenya), b. 1931,—Alexander Willoughby (c/o Lloyds Bank, 6, Pall Mall, SW1), b. 1935; ed. at Jesus Coll., Camb. (MA): m. 1964, Patricia, da. of Alfred Sweeney, of Gerrards Cross, and has issue living, Alexandra Mary, b. 1965, Frances Sheilagh (twin) b. 1965, Elizabeth Alice, b. 1970.

Richard Gethin of Mallow, co. Cork, b. about 1615, was MP for Clonmell 1639-45, and Newton Limavady 1661-66. He received large grants of land from Charles II, upon the understanding that he should establish an English colony and erect manufactories. He received letters patent by which the lands of Cariglemleary were erected into a manor by the name of Gethinsgrott. The 1st wife of the 2nd baronet, Grace Norton, was remarkable for her talent and piety, and a monument to her memory is erected in Westminster Abbey. The 8th baronet, Col. Sir Richard Walter St. Lawrence Gethin, CMG, DSO, late RA, served in S. Africa 1899-1901, and in 1914-18 War.

OSBORNE-GIBBES, Creation (G.B.) 1774, of Springhead, Barbados. [Extinct 1940.]
Sir PHILIP ARTHUR OSBORNE-GIBBES, 4th and last Baronet.
Collateral Branch living.
Issue of the late Philip Ernest Osborne-Gibbes, 7th son of 2nd baronet, b. 1862, d. 1934 : m. 1904.
Dulcie; m. 1932, W. E. Bendrey, and has issue living, Michael, b. 1938. Residence, Lakemba, Sydney, N.S. Wales.

GIBBONS, Creation (G.B.) 1752, of Stanwell Place, Middlesex.

Sir JOHN EDWARD GIBBONS, 8th Baronet; b. Nov. 14th, 1914 ; s. his father, Major Sir ALEXANDER DORAN, 1956 ; ed. at Charterhouse, and at Peterhouse, Camb. ; European War 1939-45 as Capt. Dorset Regt. : m. 1937, Mersa Wentworth (who obtained a divorce 1951), youngest da. of the late Major Edward Baynton Grove Foster, of Warmwell, Dorset, and has issue.

Arms—Gules, a lion rampant or debruised by a bend argent charged with a torteau between two crosses patée-fitchée sable. Crest—A lion's jamb erased and erect gules, charged with a bezant and holding a cross as in the arms.

Residence—2, Malt Cottages, Preston, Weymouth.

Son living—WILLIAM EDWARD DORAN (Pencraig Cottage Cefndyrys, Builth Wells, Radnorshire), b. Jan. 13th, 1948; ed. at Pangbourne, RNC Dartmouth, and Bristol Univ. (BSc.): m. 1972, Patricia Geraldine Archer, LLB, Barrister at Law, da. of Roland Archer Howse.
Daughters living—Charlotte Anne Wentworth, b. 1939; a JP for Som.: m. 1963, Hylton Henry Bayntun-Coward, of Dunkerton Grange, nr. Bath, Somerset, and has issue living, Edward William George, b. 1966,—Jonathan Henry Alexander, b. 1972,—Emma Louise Wentworth, b. 1964,—Polly Jane Constance, b. 1970.——Jane b. 1942: m. 1966, Neville James Henry Grant, of Swan Yard House, 33, East St., Coggeshall, Essex, and has issue living, Thomas Paul Wentworth, b. 1969,—Alexander Hugh Wentworth, b. 1973.
Sisters living.—Dorothea Charlotte (The Old Rectory, Cleggan, co. Galway), b. 1904: m. 1st, 1925, Ernest G. Byng, who obtained a divorce 1934: 2ndly, 1934, Conrad Ormond, and has issue living, (by 1st marriage) Robert Doran (50, Upper

It is more agreeable coming from a pious king.

Mall, W6), *b.* 1926; ARIBA: *m.* 1951, Daphne Tanner, and has issue living, Mathew *b.* 1957,
Hannah *b.* 1953,—Jane, *b.* 1928: *m.* 1955, Christopher Robert Simpson, of The Clock House,
Roman Rd., Birstall, Leicestershire, and has issue living, David Robert *b.* 1957, Charlotte Jane
b. 1959,—(by 2nd m.) John Francis, *b.* 1934: *m.* 19—, Flavia Grant Duff, and has issue living,
—Timothy Conrad (of Sheppard's Farm, Draycot Foliat, Chisledon, nr. Swindon, Wilts.),
b. 1935: *m.* 1960, Pamela Mary Slade, and has issue living, Emma Charlotte *b.* 1961, Jemima
Mary, *b.* 1963, Nicola Rose *b.* 1965, Rebecca Lucy *b.* 1967, Rachel Frances *b.* 1970,—Richard
Louis (8, Holly Terr., Highgate, N6), *b.* 1939: *m.* 1963, Leonée Jasper, and has issue living,
Augustus Jasper *b.* 1972, Marcus Conrad *b.* 1974,—Emily Jane, *b.* 1944.——Betty Lydia, *b.*
1906: *m.* 1931, Capt. Alexander Hamilton Wheeler, MC, who *d.* 1942. *Residence*, Buttermead,
Manaton, Newton Abbot, Devon.——Vera Gladys, *b.* 1908; is a JP: *m.* 1927, Geoffrey Fenwick
Jocelyn Cumberlege, DSO, MC, and has issue living, Geoffrey Mark (of Little Drove Cottage,
Singleton, Chichester), *b.* 1930: *m.* 1954, Shirley Lancaster, and has issue living, Belinda *b.* 1956,
Elizabeth *b.* 1959, Sarah *b.* 1960, Patricia *b.* 1962,—Patrick Francis (Vuggles Farm, Newick,
Lewes, Sussex), *b.* 1933: *m.* 1961, Julia Camm, and has issue living, Christopher Mark *b.* 1962,
Justin Francis *b.* 1964, Oliver Richard *b.* 1968,—*Rev.* Francis Richard, *b.* 1941,—Elizabeth
Blanche, *b.* 1928: *m.* 1951, Patrick B. Brown, of 12342, New McLelland Rd., RR1, Cloverdale,
BC, and has issue living, Stephen *b.* 1952, Nigel *b.* 1954, Geoffrey *b.* 1959, Caroline *b.* 1955,
Jennifer Catherine *b.* 1965. *Residence*, Idlehurst Cottage, Birch Grove, Horsted Keyes, Sussex.

Collateral Branches living.

Grandchildren of the late Capt. Frederick Gibbons, brother of 5th baronet :—
    Issue of the late Capt. Frederick Kenrick Colquhoun Gibbons, R.N., *b.* 1865, *d.* 1954 : *m.*
        1895, Edith Kapiolani, who *d.* 1959, da. of the late A. T. Atkinson, of Honolulu,
        Hawaii :—
Marjorie Kapiolani, *b.* 1896 : *m.* 1925, Lieut.-Col. Pillans Scarth Whitehead, O.B.E., R.A., and
    has issue living, Belinda Kapiolani, *b.* 1929 : *m.* 1956, Archibald Peter Brown and has issue
    living, Archibald Stephen *b.* 1958, William Lambert *b.* 1964, Isobel Clare *b.* 1960, Judith Margaret
    (twin) *b.* 1964. *Residence*, Little Hayes, Broadwindsor, Dorset.——Nancy Alatau, *b.* 1907: *m.*
    1939, Hugo Wilhelm Runfelt, and has issue living, Anne Marie, *b.* 1941. *Residence*, Bastad,
    Sweden.

Grandchildren of the late Robert Gibbons (infra) :—
    Issue of the late Com. Robert Reginald Gibbons, O.B.E., R.N., *b.* 1894, *d.* 1959 : *m.* 1st,
        1922, Olive (from whom he obtained a divorce 1930), da. of William Blane, C.B.E. ;
        2ndly, 1930 (marriage dissolved 1939), Ellery, da. of the late Maj.-Gen. Sir Amyatt
        Hull, of Beacon Downe, nr. Exeter; 3rdly, 1939, Joan Winifred, da. of F. S. Pater-
        son, of Southborough, Kent:—
(By 3rd m.), Robert John (52, Norroy Rd., Putney, SW15), *b.* 1944: *m.* 1st, 1966 (m. diss. 1971),
    Pauline Elizabeth, da. of Stanley Charles March, of 41, Deerswood Rd., West Green, Crawley,
    Sussex; 2ndly, 1973, Anne Marie, da. of Charles Lundberg, of 19, Jeymer Drive, Greenford,
    Middx.——Susan, *b.* 1941: *m.* 1959, Dennis Gordon Pollard, of 27, School Lane, Ashurstwood,
    E. Grinstead, Sussex, and has issue living, Peter Dennis, *b.* 1964,—Lesley Susan, *b.* 1960,—Janet
    May, *b.* 1969.

Grandchildren of the late Sir William Gibbons, K.C.B., youngest son of
        Robert Kenrick Gibbons, 2nd son of Robert Gibbons, 4th son of 2nd baronet:
    Issue of the late Sir William Kenrick Gibbons, C.B., *b.* 1876, *d.* 1957 : *m.* 1915, Aileen
        Margaret Dale, who *d.* 1969, da. of George J. E. Trotter:—
Diana Maynard (Bernadene, The Green, Letchmore Heath, Watford, Herts.), *b.* 1916.——Priscilla
    Doreen, *b.* 1918.——June Cecilia, *b.* 1926.

    Issue of the late Lieut.-Col. Edward Stephen Gibbons, D.S.O., Duke of Cambridge's Own
        (Middlesex Regt), *b.* 1883, *d.* (killed in action during European War) 1918 : *m.* 1914,
        Annie Macgregor, who *d.* 1968, da. of the late John Lyle, of Finnart House, Wey-
        bridge:—
John William, *R.N.* (10, Compton Rd., Winchester), *b.* 1917; Lieut.-Cdr.: *m.* 1st, 1940 (marriage
    dissolved 1947), Alix, da. of the late Bertram Lenox-Simpson; 2ndly, 1964, Mary Lammin, yst.
    da. of the late G. E. Woof, and has issue living, (by 1st marriage) Alan Clive, *b.* 1941.—
    Elisabeth Margaret, *b.* 1915: *m.* 1936, Lieut.-Cdr. John Edgar Burstall, R.N., and has issue
    living, Mark Stephen, *b.* 1945.—Elisabeth Ann, *b.* 1937,—Gillian Margaret, *b.* 1939.
    Residence, Orcheston House, Orcheston St. Mary, Shrewton, Wilts.

Grandchildren of the late Lt.-Col. William Barton Gibbons, 3rd son of the
        late Robert Gibbons (ante) :—
    Issue of the late John Abel Gibbons, *b.* 1854, *d.* 1894: *m.* 1884, Katharine Alice, who *d.*
        1937, da. of Joseph Seymour Salaman, formerly of 143, Sutherland Avenue, W. :—
Dorothy Margaret Maxwell : *m.* 1914, John Brook (in Imperial Yeo. during S. African War, and
    as a Gunner in Canadian Field Artillery during European War), and has issue living, John
    Burbridge (1394, Mount Pleasant, Toronto, Canada), *b.* 1914; is a Chemical Engineer: *m.*
    1940, Joanne Price, of Cleveland, Ohio, USA, and has issue living, David Jeremy *b.* 1947, Calvin
    Price *b.* 1955, Martha Lyn *b.* 1942,—Philip Roy, *DFC*, *b.* 1918; is Fl. Lt. Roy. Canadian Air
    Force, and an Architect: 1939-45 War (DFC): *m.* 1949, Sonia Dixon, of Bournemouth, and has
    issue living, Michael Brian *b.* 1951, Gregory Laurence *b.* 1953, Matthew Ian *b.* 1959, Deborah
    Jane *b.* 1955, Dinah Louise *b.* 1957,—June Rosemary, *b.* 1920: *m.* 1940, Charles H. Doty, of 49,
    Huntly St., Toronto, Canada, and has issue living, Stephen Charles *b.* 1942, Susan Jane *b.* 1944:
    m. 19—, Jacobsen, of St. Anne de Sorel, Quebec, Barbara Jane *b.* 1949. *Residence*,

Granddaughter of the late Charles Kenrick Gibbons (infra):—
    Issue of the late Charles William Kenrick Gibbons, *b.* 1893, *d.* 1969: *m.* 1922, Winifred
        Maud Ethel, who *d.* 1966, da. of the late George Eccles, of Mayaro, Trinidad:—
Rose Margaret Emily (Eccleston, 4C, Upper Brighton Rd., Surbiton, Surrey), *b.* 1926; late Lt.
    QARANC.

Grandson of the late Lt.-Col. William Barton Gibbons (ante):—
    Issue of the late Charles Kenrick Gibbons, *b.* 1856, *d.* 1918 : *m.* 1890, Emily Hinds, who
        d. 1958, da. of the late Charles F. Corbin, of The Beacon, Surbiton :—
Edward John Kenrick, *b.* 1900; ed. at Dover Coll., and at Jesus Coll., Camb. (MA,
    LLB); Solicitor 1929; formerly Town Clerk of Falmouth: *m.* 1938, Marguerite Leslie, da. of
    the late Nicolas Eyare Toke, of Penfillan House, Folkestone, and has issue living, Carol Leslie
    Kenrick, *b.* 1939. *Residence*, Hillside, Harlequin Lane, Crowborough, Sussex.

Grandchildren of the late John Crookenden de Courcy Gibbons (infra):—
    Issue of the late John Hayton Gibbons, *b.* 1909, *d.* 1963: *m.* 1945, Phyllis (who *m.* 2ndly,
        19—, Donald Sheehan, of 24, Springdale Rd., Killara, NSW), da. of   :—
John William, *b.* 1954.——Victoria Hayton, *b.* 1948.——Elizabeth, *b.* 1951.

Grandchildren of the late Lieut.-Col. Frederick FitzRoy Gibbons, el. son of the
        late Lieut.-Col. William Barton Gibbons (ante) :—

Issue of the late John Crookenden de Courcy Gibbons, *b.* 1874, *d.* 1944 : *m.* 1907, Gladys Russell Jones, of Sydney, N.S. Wales:—
Marjorie Mary, *b.* 1922 : *m.* 1944, Clive Stanley Willey, and has issue living, Lyn Gladys, *b.* 1947,—Rae Marjorie (twin), *b.* 1947,—Sue Phillis, *b.* 1951. *Residence*, 6, Maple Road, Melrose, Mass., USA, 02176.

Issue of the late Charles Coulthurst Gibbons, *b.* 1884, *d.* (April) 1926 : *m.* 1st, 19— (marriage dissolved 1923), Muriel Tidswell, who *d.* 1949 ; 2ndly, 1924, Constance Winifred (Broad Acres, 2, St. Johns Rise, Woking, Surrey), da. of David George Edward Wilkinson:—
(By 2nd marriage) Peta Jane Coulhurst (posthumous), *b.* (Nov.) 1926: *m.* 1957, James William Edward Brown. *Residence*, 73, Addiscombe Road, Croydon, Surrey.

Issue of the late Kathleen Tarifa Gibbons, *b.* 1873, *d.* 1955: *m.* 1st, 1897, Hon. Mr. Justice Lionel Mabbott Woodward (Ch. Judicial Commr., Federated Malay States; knighted 1912), who *d.* 1925, having obtained a divorce 1912; 2ndly, 1912, Edward King, who *d.* 1955:—
(By 2nd m.) Joan Patricia, *b.* 1916: *m.* 1st, 1942, Eustace Melville Dougall, from whom she obtained a divorce 1973; 2ndly, 1973, Sydney Burgis Parish, of 8, Webster Gdns., Ealing, W5 5ND, and has issue living, (by 1st m.) Ennis de Courcy Melville (3, Manor Rd., Ealing, W13), *b.* 1948: *m.* 1973, Sally Ann, da. of Brian Percy Emblem, and has issue living, Daniel de Courcy Melville *b.* 1974.

The 1st baronet was Speaker of the House of Assembly, Barbados, and the 2nd baronet sat as M.P. for Wallingford.

GIBSON, Creation (U.K.) 1926, of Great Warley, co. Essex.

Rev. Fr. Sir DAVID GIBSON; *b.* July 18th, 1922; *s.* his father, *Sir* ACKROYD HERBERT, 1975.

Address—c/o Garnet Jones & Co., 78, St. Thomas St., Weymouth.

Sisters living—Joan Ingerid, *b.* 1919: *m.* 1942, Ronald Coad, of Trewhella, Cury, Helston, Cornwall. ——Patricia Ann, *b.* 1929: *m.* 1955, Ronald Wilsdon, and has issue living, Nicholas John, *b.* 1956.

Daughters living of 2nd Baronet—Diana Lilian, *b.* 1915: *m.* 1943, Maj. Anthony Peter Howorth Greenly, late R. Berks. Regt., of Everington House, Newbury, son of the Lt.-Col. Sir John Henry Maitland Greenly, KCMG, CBE, and has issue living, Richard Anthony Howorth, *b.* 1948, —Sarah Mary, *b.* 1947: *m.* 1968, Capt. Charles Edric Holdsworth Hunt, Coldstream Guards [see B. Forester, colls.],—Dorian Isobel, *b.* 1951.——Pamela Mary *b.* 1922: *m.* 1941, Maj. Robert George Pollok-McCall, DL, JP, late Black Watch, and has issue living, Angus John Kenneth, *b.* 1949,—Camilla, *b.* 1942. *Residence*, Kindeace, Delny, Ross-shire.

The 1st baronet, Sir Herbert Gibson, was a Solicitor, a member of the legal firm of Deacon & Co. of 9, Great St. Helens, E.C., and Pres. of Law So. 1925 (Centenary year).

GIBSON, Creation (U.K.) 1931, of Linconia, and of Faccombe, co. Southampton.

Sir CHRISTOPHER HERBERT GIBSON, 3rd *Baronet;* *b.* Feb. 2nd, 1921; *s.* his father, *Sir* CHRISTOPHER HERBERT, 1962; European War 1940-45 as Capt. Canadian Armoured Corps (five medals): *m.* 1941, Lilian Lake, da. of the late Dr. George Byron Young, of Colchester, Essex, and has issue.

Residence—Candlemass Manor, (La Candelaria), Cassilla de Correo 139, Alta Gracia, Sierras de Cordoba, Argentina.
Son living—CHRISTOPHER HERBERT *b.* July 17th, 1948.
Daughters living—Penelope Lake, *b.* 1946.——Pamela Dorothy Madeleine, *b.* 1950.——Dawn, *b.* 1953.
Brother living—Ian Herbert, *b.* 1927; is a FZS. *Residence*, San Martin 296, Buenos Aires, Argentina.
Uncle living (son of 1st baronet)—Clement Herbert (751, Avenida Julio A Roca, Buenos Aires, Argentina), *b.* 1900; ed. at Eton, and at Clare Coll., Camb.: *m.* 1933, Marjorie Julia, da. of the late Robert Anderson, and has issue living, Geoffrey (San Martin, 448, Buenos Aires), *b.* 1934: *m.* 1964, Anne-Marie, da. of the late Martin de Selincourt, and has issue living, Robert Herbert *b.* 1966, Alexander Herbert *b.* 1973, Clemency Rose *b.* 1968,—Clement Herbert (Higham Farm, Northiam, Sussex), *b.* 1936: *m.* 1966, Mrs. Barbara Peel,—Thomas (18, Crescent Grove, SW4), *b.* 1943: *m.* 1966, Anthea Fiona Catherine, da. of the late Lt.-Col. G. A. Palmer, RE, and has issue living, Miles Cosmo Archdale *b.* 1968, Sebastian Thomas Maximilian *b.* 1972, Benjamin Hugh George *b.* 1973.
Widow living of 2nd baronet—DOROTHY EDITH ORME (*Dowager Lady Gibson*), da. of Maj. W. D. Bruce, of Vancouver, British Columbia: *m.* 1919, Sir Christopher Herbert Gibson, 2nd baronet (who adopted Christian name of Christopher in lieu of Meredith by declaration in Scotland 1934), who *d.* 1962. *Residence*, San Martin 296, Buenos Aires, Argentina.

Collateral Branches living.

Issue of the late Gerald Herbert Gibson, 3rd son of 1st baronet, *b.* 1902, *d.* 1951: *m.* 1924, Ursula Marion Wilson, of San Martin 296, Buenos Aires, Argentina, da. of the late W. Greenwell-Robson:—
Roy Herbert, *b.* 1933: *m.* 1970, Georgina Oddette, da. of Santiago Even, and has issue living, Valerie, *b.* 1971.——Diana Madeleine, *b.* 1926.

Issue of the late Cosmo Livingstone Herbert Gibson, yst. son of 1st baronet, *b.* 1904, *d.* 1964: *m.* 1937, Josephine Austin, da. of James Austin Brown:—
Herbert, *b.* 1938: *m.* 1964, Margaret Jean, da. of John Bruce Donald, and has issue living, James Bruce, *b.* 1965,—Herbert Mark, *b.* 1966,—Josephine Jean, *b.* 1966,—Michel, *b.* 1969,—Madeleine, *b.* 1972.——Cosmo David, *b.* 1944.——Noel Gerald *b.* 1954.——David Hope, *b.* 1956.—— Yvonne, *b.* 1939: *m.* 1962, Baron Gaston Carlos Perkins Peers de Niewburgh, and has issue living, Thomas Gaston, *b.* 1964,—Enrique Gaston, *b.* 1968,—Yvonne Cecilia, *b.* 1967.—— Roxana, *b.* 1943: *m.* 1963, Eduardo Francisco Pampillo, and has issue living, Veronica Roxana, *b.* 1964,—Edwina, *b.* 1966,—Victoria, b. 1968.

Sir Herbert Gibson, K.B.E., 1st baronet (son of the late Thomas Gibson, of Edinburgh), was a Landowner and Merchant in the Argentine Republic.

Gibson-Craig-Carmichael, see Carmichael.

GILBEY, Creation (U.K.) 1893, of Elsenham Hall, Essex.

Sir (WALTER) DEREK GILBEY, 3rd *Baronet*, son of the late Walter Ewart Gilbey, el. son of 2nd baronet; *b.* March 11th, 1913 ; *s.* his grandfather, *Sir* (HENRY) WALTER, 1945, ed. at Eton ; Lieut. Black Watch ; European War 1939-45 (prisoner) : *m.* 1948, Elizabeth Mary, da. of Col. K. G. Campbell, of Standen House, Newport, Isle of Wight, and has issue.

Arms—Gules, a fesse nebulée or, in chief a horse rampant between two estoiles, and the like in base, all of the last, Crest—In front of a tower proper, issuant from the battlements thereof a dragon's head gules, a fleur-de- lis or, all between two ostrich feathers argent.
Residence—Culross, Faygate, nr. Horsham, Sussex. Club—Portland.

Son living—(WALTER) GAVIN, *b.* April 14th, 1949; ed. at Eton.

Daughter living—Camilla Elizabeth, *b.* 1953.

Uncle living—(son of 2nd baronet)—Walter Anthony (Ballacallin Mooar, Marown, Crosby, Isle of Man), *b.* 1935; assumed by deed poll 1958 the name of Walter Anthony in lieu of that of Anthony Walter: *m.* 1964, Jenifer Mary, da. of James Timothy Noel Price, of Langlee, Jedburgh, Roxburghshire [see O'Brien, Bt.], and has issue living, Walter Anthony *b.* 1966,—Caroline Anne, *b.* 1967.

Widow living of 2nd Baronet—MARION (*Dowager Lady Gilbey*), da. of the late James Roberts, of Farnley Tyas, near Huddersfield, and widow of Wilson Broadhead, of Elland, near Huddersfield: *m.* 1934, as his second wife, Sir (Henry) Walter Gilbey, 2nd baronet, who *d.* 1945. *Residence,* Barton Mill House, Cirencester, Gloucestershire.

Collateral Branches living.

Grandchildren of the late Sebastian Walter Gilbey (infra):—
Issue of the late Arthur Sebastian Gilbey, *b.* 1919, *d.* 1964: *m.* 1947, Jennifer Beryl (GOULD) (Apart. 2, Scala A, Parco del Mimose, Seconda Traversa, Viale Circe, Terracina, Italy), da. of the late William Nigel Ernie Bruce [*see* Bruce, Bt., cr. 1628, colls.]:—
Christopher Sebastian Bruce, *b.* 1955.——Patricia, *b.* 1949: *m.* 1973, Andrew Michael Talbot Millar, of Flat 3, 21, de Vere Gdns., W8 [Cockburn, Bt., colls.].——Linda, *b.* 1952: *m.* 1971, Michael Christopher Gilbey, of 89, Archway St., Barnes, SW13 [*see* B. Vaux of Harrowden].

Grandchildren of the late Arthur Nockolds Gilbey (infra):—
Issue of the late Sebastian Walter Gilbey, *b.* 1893, *d.* 1971: *m.* 1916, Jean, who *d.* 1970, da. of the late George Milner, of St. James's Sq., Holland Park, W.:—
Giles Milner, *MC*, (Via Fontebella 17, 06081 Assisi, Italy; White's Club), *b.* 1923; ed. at Harrow, and Brasenose Coll., Oxford; late Capt. 12th Lancers; 1939-45 War (MC): *m.* 1962, Mrs. Diana Mary Ryerson, da. of the late W. E. Melville-Cook, of Parkstone, Dorset, and has issue living, Lisa Maria, *b.* 1965.

Issue of the late Rupert Sydney Gilbey, *b.* 1900, *d.* 1959: *m.* 1927, Anne Penelope, who *d.* 1970, da. of the late E. S. Prince:—
Simon Rupert, *b.* 1929; ed. at Eton; formerly Capt. 8th Hussars: *m.* 1st, 1953 (m. diss. 1966), Chloë Rio, who *d.* 1966, el. da. of Col. Christopher Rawlinson Cadge, of Ballygate House, Beccles, Suffolk; 2ndly, 1966, Mrs. Sara Jane Twiston Davies, da. of Augustus Frederick Coryton, of Goleigh Farm House, Greatham, Hants., and has issue living, (by 1st m.) Rupert John, *b.* 1960,—Juliet Rio, *b.* 1955,—Rachel Anne, *b.* 1957,—(by 2nd m.) Lisa, *b.* 1967. *Residence,* Manor Farm, Sapperton, nr. Cirencester, Glos.——Sarah Anne *b.* 1933: *m.* 1953, Patrick Philip Bagshawe, and has issue living, Anthony William Newton, *b.* 1956,—Jasper Philip Adam, *b.* 1960,—Charlotte Anne, *b.* 1954. *Residence,* Church Farm, Whelford, nr. Fairford, Glos.

Issue of the late Arthur Nockolds Gilbey, 2nd son of 1st baronet, *b.* 1861, *d.* 1939: *m.* 1885, Beatrice, who *d.* 1936, da. of the late Henry Gold, JP, DL, (High Sheriff of Berkshire 1897):—
Diana Beatrice, *b.* 1909. *Residence,* Barrymore, Wargrave, Berks.

The 1st baronet, Sir Walter Gilbey, fifth son of late Henry Gilbey, of Bishop's Stortford, Herts, served in Pay Depart. during Crimean War 1854-6 ; and was sometime Chm. of W. & A. Gilbey, Ltd., wine merchants and distillers, of The Pantheon, Oxford Street, W ; also a well-known Agriculturist and Stock-breeder, and a Past Pres. of Smithfield Club, of Hackney Horse So., of the Shire Horse So., Roy. Agricultural So., and of Hunters' Improvement So. The 2nd baronet, Sir (Henry) Walter, was Chm. of W. & A. Gilbey, Ltd., and a prominent figure in the horse-breeding and sporting worlds.

GILLETT, Creation (U.K.) 1959, of Bassishaw Ward, City of London.

Sir (SYDNEY) HAROLD GILLETT, 1st
Baronet, M.C., son of the late William Henry
Gillett, of Highgate, N. ; b. Nov. 27th, 1890 ;
ed. at Marlborough; a Vice-Pres. of Chartered
Accountant Students Soc. of London, a Con-
sultant, Dixon, Wilson, Tubbs and Gillett,
Vice-Chm. of Baden-Powell House Cttee.,
Hon. Col. 8th Essex (517 Light Anti-Aircraft)
Cadet Regt., a Gov. of Nat. Corporation for
Care of Old People, of Grey Coat Hosp., of
Queen Anne's Sch., and of United West-
minster Schs., a Vice-Pres. of London Chamber
of Commerce (Chm. 1956-57); a Past Prime
Warden of Basketmakers' Co., and a K.St.J.;
a Common Councilman of City of London
1930-48, an Alderman 1948-69, Sheriff 1952-53,
and Lord Mayor 1958-59; has 2nd class
Order of Homayoun of Iran, Gold Medal of
Madrid 1959, and Boy Scouts Award of Silver
Wolf 1961; 1914-18 War in France with
Middlesex Regt. (TA) (despatches, MC); Knt.
1953: m. 1919, Audrey Isabel Penrose, who
d. 1962, da. of the late Capt. Edgar Penrose
Wardlaw, and has issue.

Arms—In front of a ship's helm proper, an early nineteenth century waistcoat azure
semée de lys and purfled or on a chief of the second between two estoiles a balance of the
first.   Crest—A grey horse's head and neck erased proper gorged with a coronet composed of six
fleur de lys affixed to a circlet and chained or.

Residence,—12, Kingston House East, SW7.   Clubs—City of London, City Livery.

Son living—ROBIN DANVERS PENROSE, RD (4, Fairholt St., Knightsbridge, SW7 1EQ), b.
Nov. 9th, 1925; ed. at Nautical Coll., Pangbourne; Hon. Cdr. RNR, Master mariner, Yr.
Brother of Trin. House, Liveryman and Warden of Hon. Co. of Master Mariners, a Founder
Member of Nautical Inst., a Dir. of Wigham Poland Home Ltd., Underwriting Member of
Lloyd's, a Fellow of Inst. of Admin. Management, Pres. City of London Civil Defence Instructors
Assocn., Hon. Treas. City of London Centre St. John Ambulance Assocn., Vice-Pres. City of
London Dist. Red Cross, Order of St. John, a Gov. of Pangbourne Coll.; Common Councilman
City of London 1965-69, Alderman 1969, Sheriff 1973; Chm. Civil Defence Cttee. 1967-68; Officer
Order of Leopard of Zaire, Cdr. Order of Dannebrog of Denmark, Order of Johan Sedia Mahkota
of Malaysia: m. 1950, Elizabeth Marion Grace, el. da. of the late John Findlay, JP, of Busby
House, Busby, Lanarks., and has issue living, Nicholas Danvers Penrose, b. 1955,—Christopher
John, b. 1958.

**GILMOUR, Creation (U.K.) 1897, of Lundin and Montrave, Parishes of Largo and
Scoonie, co. Fife, and South Walton, Mearns, co. Renfrew.**

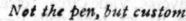

Not the pen, but custom.

Sir JOHN EDWARD GILMOUR, D.S.O., T.D.,
M.P., 3rd Baronet ; b. Oct. 24th, 1912 ; s. his
father, the Rt. Hon. Sir JOHN, G.C.V.O., D.S.O.,
LLD, MP, 1940; ed. at Eton, and at Trin. Hall,
Camb.; Lt.-Col. Fife and Forfar Yeo. 1947-51;
Brevet Col. 1952; Hon. Col. Highland Yeo.
RAC, TAVR 1971-75; a JP and a DL for Fife;
Ensign, Queen's Body Guard for Scotland (R.
Co. of Archers); NW Europe 1944-45 (wounded,
DSO); MP for E. Div. of Fife (U) since 1961;
DSO 1945: m. 1941, Ursula Mabyn, da. of the
late Frank Oliver Wills, and has issue.

Arms—Argent, on a chevron between three trefoils slipped
vert, as many bugle horns of the first.   Crest—A hand fessewise couped at the wrist proper, holding a pen argent.

Seat—Montrave, Leven, Fife.

Sons living—JOHN (Balcormo Mains, Leven, Fife), b. July
15th, 1944: m. 1967, Valerie Jardine, da. of the late G. W.
Russell, and has issue living, John Nicholas, b. 1970,—
Corinna Valerie, b. 1972,—Victoria Juliet, b. 1975.——
Andrew Frank (Bankhead, Leven, Fife), b. 1947: m. 1971,
Mary Spiers, adopted da. of the late Sir Henry Campbell
de la Poer Beresford-Peirse, CB, 5th B., and has issue living,
Andrew Robert Campbell, b. 1972,—David Edward, b. 1974.

Sister living—Dame Anne Margaret, DBE, b. 1909; Chm. of Roy. Free Hosp. 1968-74; Vice-Chm. of
Exec. Cttee. BRCS, a Member Area Health Authority, Camden and Islington, of Council for
Professions Supplementary to Medicine, and of Council of Florence Nightingale Hosp., Vice-Pres.
of Roy. Coll. of Nursing, and a CStJ; Dir. and Commr. for Middle East, British Red Cross and

St. John War Org. 1943-45; CBE (Civil) 1945, DBE (Civil) 1957: *m.* 1932, Lt.-Cdr. John Reginald Bryans, RN (ret.), and has issue living, John Patrick Gilmour (17, Smuggles Way, Rhu, Dunbarton-shire), *b.* 1933; Lt.-Cdr. RN: *m.* 1st, 1959 (m. diss 1970), Rosemary Ann, da. of the late Group Capt. H. G. Wheeler, RAF; 2ndly, 1972, Patricia Mary, da. of the late W. A. MacPherson, and has issue living (by 1st m.), Anthony James Gilmour *b.* 1960, Edward John Gilmour *b.* 1963, Robert Henry Charles *b.* 1965. *Residence*, 7, Harriet Walk, Lowndes St., SW1.

Half-Sister living—Daphne Mary, *b.* 1922: *m.* 1943, Group Capt. Everett Large Baudoux, DSO, DFC, RCAF (ret.), and has issue living, Michael Alfred, *b.* 1951,—Patricia Mary, *b.* 1944: *m.* 1966, Raymond Wayne Docker, of 108, Clarence Av. N., Saskatoon, Saskatchewan, Canada, and has issue living, Thomas Everett *b.* 1970, Philip Ian *b.* 1972,—Sharon Jane, *b.* 1948: *m.* 1974, Lewis MacKay. *Residence*, Big Island, Merigomish, Nova Scotia.

Widow living of 2nd Baronet—VIOLET AGNES (*Violet, Lady Gilmour*), da. of the late Edward Tiley Lambert, J.P., of Telham Court, Battle, Sussex : *m.* 1920, as his second wife, the Rt. Hon. Sir John Gilmour, G.C.V.O., D.S.O., LL.D., M.P., 2nd baronet, who *d.* 1940. *Residence*, Middleton, Fairfield Close, Lymington, Hants.

Collateral Branch living.

Issue of the late Douglas Gilmour, 5th son of 1st baronet, *b.* 1889, *d.* (of wounds in action during European War) 1916: *m.* 1910, Doris Hyacinth (1, Elm Cottage, Sonning, Berks.), da. of the late Charles Paget Hooker, of Cirencester, son of the late Sir Joseph Dalton Hooker, OM, GCSI, CB:—

Doris Pamela Yvonne, *b.* 1914: *m.* 1940, Maj. Philip Donald Howitt Marshall, late Middlesex Regt., of The Malt House, Sonning, Berks., and has issue living, Nicholas Charles Gilmour, *b.* 1950: *m.* 1974, Rosemary Anne, da. of the late Maj. W. J. Kingdom, RA,—Sarah Gilmour, *b.* 1948,—Teresa Gilmour, *b.* 1953.——Myrtle (1, Elm Cottage, Sonning, Berks.), *b.* 1915: *m.* 1st, 1938, John William Hathorn, Flying Officer, RAF (Reserve), who *d.* (killed in a flying accident whilst on active ser.) 1940; 2ndly, 1940 (m. diss. 1949), Capt. Cecil Horace Power Bellwood, Gloucestershire Regt.; 3rdly, 1949 (m. diss. 1952), Col. Patrick Curran Perfect, late KOSB.

Sir John Gilmour, 1st Bt. (el. son of the late Allan Gilmour, of Lundin and Montrave, Fifeshire, and South Walton, Renfrewshire), was a J.P. and D.L. for co. Fife. The 2nd Bt., the Rt. Hon. Sir John, G.C.V.O., D.S.O., P.C., sat as M.P. for Renfrewshire, E. Div. (C) 1910-18, and for Glasgow, Pollok Div. 1918-40, and was a Junior Lord of the Treasury 1921-2, Sec. for Scotland 1924-6, Sec. of State for Scotland 1926-9, Min. of Agriculture and Fisheries 1932-5, Sec. of State for Home Depart. 1932-5, and Min. of Shipping 1939-40.

GILMOUR, Creation (U.K.) 1926, of Liberton and Craigmillar, co. Midlothian.

Not the pen, but custom.

Sir JOHN LITTLE GILMOUR, 2nd *Baronet; b.* June 5th, 1899; *s.* his father, *Brig.-Gen. Sir* ROBERT GORDON, *C.B., C.V.O., D.S.O.,* 1939; ed. at Eton; formerly Lieut. Grenadier Guards; is a Stockbroker: *m.* 1st, 1922, the Hon. Victoria Laura Cadogan, *O.B.E., T.D.* (who obtained a divorce 1929), da. of the late Henry Arthur, Viscount Chelsea [*see* E. Cadogan] ; 2ndly, 1930, Lady Mary Cecilia Rhodesia, da. of 3rd Duke of Abercorn, and has issue by 1st and 2nd marriages.

Arms—Quarterly, 1st and 4th, azure, three writing pens paleways argent, *Gilmour*; 2nd and 3rd, sable, on a saltire argent a crescent gules, *Little*. *Crest*—A dexter hand holding a scroll of paper within a garland of laurel proper.
Seat—Carolside, Earlston, Berwickshire.

Sons living—By 1st marriage—Rt. Hon. IAN HEDWORTH JOHN LITTLE, *MP, b.* July 8th, 1926; ed. at Eton, and at Balliol Coll., Oxford; Bar. Inner Temple 1952; late Lieut. Gren. Gds.; Editor of *The Spectator* 1954-59; an Under-Sec., Min. of Defence 1970-71, Min. of State for Defence Procurement, Min. of Defence 1971-72, Min. of State for Defence 1972-74 and Sec. of State for Defence 1974; Chm. of Conservative Research Dept. since 1974; MP for Central Norfolk (C) 1972-74, since when for Chesham and Amersham; PC 1973: *m.* 1951, Lady Caroline Margaret Montagu-Douglas-Scott, da. of 8th Duke of Buccleuch and Queensberry, and has issue living, David Robert, *b.* 1952: *m.* 1975, Sarah Anne, da. of Michael Hilary George Bradstock, of Donnington Castle House, Newbury [see V. Hawarden, colls.],—Oliver John, *b.* 1953,—Christopher Simon, *b.* 1956,—Andrew James, *b.* 1964,—Jane Victoria *b.* 1959. *Residences*, The Ferry House, Old Isleworth, Middx.; Thwaite House, Aldborough, Norwich. *Clubs*, White's, Norfolk.——**By 2nd m.**—Alexander Clement, *b.* 1931: *m.* 1954, Barbara Marie-Louise, el. da. of the Hon. Denis Gomer Berry, TD [*see* V. Kemsley], and has issue living, Rory Calryn, *b.* 1958,—Christian Alexander, *b.* 1970,—Lucinda Roberte, *b.* 1956. *Residence*, Denchworth Manor, Wantage, Berks. *Club*, White's.

Daughter living—By 1st m.—Diana (*Lady Beith*), *b.* 1923: *m.* 1st, 1943, Col. Alexander Marshall Horace Gregory-Hood, OBE, MC, Grenadier Guards, from whom she obtained a divorce 1949 [*see* V. Hood, colls.]; 2ndly, 1949, Sir John Greville Stanley Beith, KCMG, late HM Foreign Ser., and has issue living, (by 1st m.) [*see* V. Hood, colls.],—(by 2nd m.) Ian Mark, *b.* 1950: *m.* 1975, Mary Jane, da. of Selwyn Few, of Oakington House, Cambridge,—Emma *b.* 1956. *Residence*, Dean Farm House, Sparsholt, Winchester, Hants.

Sister living—Mary (*Lady Knatchbull-Hugessen*), *b.* 1890: *m.* 1912, Sir Hughe Montgomery Knatchbull-Hugessen, KCMG, who *d.* 1971 [*see* B. Brabourne, colls.]. *Residence*, 4, South Close, The Precincts, Canterbury.

The 1st baronet, Sir Robert Gordon Gilmour, C.B., C.V.O., D.S.O. (son of the late Henry Wolrige-Gordon, of Esslemont and Hallhead, Aberdeenshire), assumed the surname of Gilmour

on succession to the estates of his gt. uncle, Walter James Little Gilmour.   He was a Brig.-Gen.
Capt. of King's Body Guard for Scotland (Roy. Co. of Archers), and Gentleman Usher of the Green
Rod (Order of the Thistle).

GLADSTONE, Creation (U.K.) 1846, of Fasque and Balfour, Kincardineshire.

By fidelity and valour.

Sir (Erskine) William Gladstone, 7th
Baronet; *b.* Oct. 29th, 1925; *s.* his father
(*Sir*) Charles Andrew, 1968; ed. at Eton,
and Ch. Ch., Oxford (MA); Assist. Master at
Eton Coll. 1951-61, and Headmaster of
Lancing Coll. 1961-69; Chief Scout of the
UK and Overseas Branches since 1972;
1939-45 War as Sub.-Lt. RNVR: *m.* 1962,
Rosamund Anne, da. of the late Maj. Robert
Alexander Hambro, and has issue.

Arms—Argent, a savage's head affrontée, distilling drops
of blood and wreathed about the temples with holly proper
within an orle fleury gules, all within eight martlets in orle
sable.   **Crest**—Issuant from a wreath of holly proper, a
demi-griffin sable, supporting between the claws a sword,
the blade enfiled by a wreath of oak also proper.

Residences—Hawarden Castle, Deeside, Clwyd;
Fasque, Laurencekirk, Kincardineshire.

Sons living—Charles Angus, *b.* April 11th, 1964.——Robert Nicolas, *b.* 1968.
Daughter living—Victoria Frances, *b.* 1967.
Brothers living—Peter (The Wildfowl Trust, Martin Mere, Burscough, nr. Ormskirk, Lancs.), *b.*
1928; ed. at Eton, and Ch. Ch., Oxford (MA); Curator of Wildfowl Trust: *m.* 1972, Jean Loveday, da. of Allan Roy, of The Hawes, Ainsdale, Southport, and has issue living, Thomas Xeno-
phan, *b.* 1973.——James Francis (68, Stockwell Park Rd., SW9), *b.* 1941; ed. at Eton and Ch. Ch.
Oxford: *m.* 1st, 1963, Janet Barbara, who *d.* 1970, da. of Rudi Schumacher, of Kenya; 2ndly,
1972, the Hon. Josephine Jones, da. of Baron Elwyn Jones (Life Baron), and has issue living
(by 1st m.), Melissa Janet, *b.* 1970,—(by 2nd m.) Andrew Elwyn, *b.* 1974.——Andrew Victor
(3d, The Boltons, SW10), *b.* 1945; ed. at Eton: *m.* 1975, Nicola, da. of Lt.-Col. M. L. D. Skewes-
Cox, of Uphill House, Ponsworthy, Devon.
Sisters living—Penelope Ann, *b.* 1930.——Sara Helen, *b.* 1943: *m.* 1970, Philip John Young, of
East End Farm, Ringstead, Hunstanton, Norfolk, and has issue living, James Edward, *b.* 1971,—
John Anthony, *b.* 1974.
Aunt living—Edith: *m.* 1923, Thomas Henry Gilborn Stamper, CIE, MC, and has issue living,
Henry William Gilborn (Tewes, Little Sampford, nr. Saffron Walden, Essex) *b.* 1926; ed. at
Eton; Lt. RN (ret.): *m.* 1950, Betty Eleanor, da. of Col. Roy Morell, and has issue living,
Catherine Ione Eleanor, *b.* 1951, Elizabeth Julia *b.* 1954, Anna Felicity *b.* 1959,—Elizabeth Noel,
b. 1924: *m.* 1950, Walter Edward Ormerod, of The Old Rectory, Padworth, Berks., and has issue
living, Henry *b.* 1951, William Patrick *b.* 1952, Thomas Caton *b.* 1961, Anne *b*, 1953, Sarah *b.*
1954, Philippa *b.* 1958, Edith Mary *b.* 1959.   *Residence*, Wath Cottage, Damerham, Fordingbridge, Hants.

Daughter living of 4th Baronet—Olive Mary, *b.* 1893 : *m.* 1919, Major Robert Lindsay Loyd,
O.B.E., M.C., Life Guards (retired), and has issue living, Zelda Mary, *b.* 1923: *m.* 1954, Malcolm
Coit Dunlop, of Ravenswood, Gregories Road, Beaconsfield, Bucks, and has issue living, Lindsay
Fergus *b.* 1958, Teressa Mary *b.* 1956, Celina Elizabeth *b.* 1960.   *Residence*, Kings Walden,
Windsor, Berks.

Widow living of 6th Baronet—Isla Margaret (North Park, Hawarden, Deeside, Clwyd), da. of
the late Sir Walter Erskine Crum: *m.* 1925, (Sir) Charles Andrew Gladstone, 6th Bt. (but did not
use the title), who *d.* 1968.

Collateral Branch living.
  Issue of the late Capt. Stephen Deiniol Gladstone, MC, brother of 5th and 6th baronets,
      b. 1891, *d.* 1965: *m.* 1923, Mary St. Clair (Alltdinnie, Aboyne, Aberdeenshire), da. of
      Lt.-Col. Charles Davidson, of Aboyne:—
Stephen Charles (31, Broad St., Alresford, Hants.), *b.* 1924; ed. at Eton; late Lt. Welsh Guards:
m. 1952, Susan Valerie, da. of John Lindsay Guise, of Dolphin Cottage, Portleven, Cornwall,
and has issue living, Stephen James, *b.* 1955,—Clare Elizabeth, *b.* 1953,—Catherine Mary, *b.*
1959,—Juliet Anne, *b.* 1960,—Victoria Jane, *b.* 1963.——John Neville (Beechcroft, Church
Lane, Oxted), *b.* 1932; ed. at Eton: *m.* 1959, Jane Gordon, da. of Maj.-Gen. Robert Alexander
Stephen, CBE, and has issue living, David Gordon William, *b.* 1960,—Peter Robert John, *b.*
1963,—Claire Jane, *b.* 1962.——Mary Felicity, *b.* 1926.——Anne, *b.* 1928: *m.* 1957, Nigel John
Robson, of Pinewood Hill, Wormley, Godalming, Surrey, and has issue living, Andrew Stephen,
b. 1958,—William Nigel, *b.* 1960,—Hugo John, *b.* 1962.

  The 1st baronet assumed, by Roy. licence, the surname of Gladstone in lieu of his patronymic
Gladstones.   Sir Thomas, 2nd baronet, sat as M.P. for Queenborough (C) 1830, for Portarlington
1832-5, for Leicester 1835-7, and for Ipswich 1842, and was Lord-Lieut. of Kincardineshire.   Sir
John Evelyn, 4th baronet, was a J.P. and D.L. for Wilts. (High Sheriff 1897).   Rt. Hon.
William Ewart Gladstone, Prime Min. 1868-74, 1880-85, 1886 and 1892-94, was yst. son of 1st
baronet, and grandfather of 5th and 6th baronets.

Glen-Coats, see Coats.

GLYN, Creation (G.B.) 1759, of Ewell, Surrey, and (G.B.) 1800, of Gaunt's House, Dorsetshire.

Firm to my trust.

Sir RICHARD HAMILTON GLYN, OBE, TD, 9th *Baronet*, of Ewell, and 5th *Baronet*, of Gaunt's House; *b.* Oct. 12th, 1907; *s.* his father, *Sir* RICHARD FITZGERALD, *DSO*, 1960; ed. at Worcester Coll., Oxford (MA 1962): Bar. Lincoln's Inn 1935; late Hon. Col. Queen's Own Dorset and W. Somerset Yeo. Medium Regt. (T.A.), and a D.L. for Dorset; an ADC to HM 1958-63; Commr. of Commonwealth War Graves Commn. 1965; MP for N. Div. of Dorset (C) 1957-70; OBE (Mil) 1955: *m.* 1st, 1939 (m. diss. 1969), Lyndsay Mary, who *d.* 1971, only da. of T. H. Baker, of 20, Morland Av., Stoneygate, Leicester; 2ndly, 1970, Barbara. da. of William Charles Ritchie Jardine, and formerly wife of Gp. Capt. F. Henwood, and has issue by 1st m.

Arms—Argent, an eagle displayed with two heads sable guttée d'or, with a crescent for difference. **Crest**—An eagle's head erased sable, guttée d'or, holding in the beak an escallop argent.

Seat—Gaunt's House, Wimborne, Dorset.

Sons living—By 1st m.—RICHARD LINDSAY (Ashton Farmhouse, Stanbridge, Wimborne, Dorset), *b.* Aug. 3rd, 1943; ed. at Eton; late 2nd Lt. 1st Bn. R. Hampshire Regt.; photographer and designer, Studio Orange, and Gaunts Property Co. and Erbus Antiques 1966-71: *m.* 1970, Carolyn Ann, da. of Roy Frank Williams, of Pasadena, Calif., USA, and has issue living, Richard Rufus Francis, *b.* Jan. 8th, 1971,—Eliza Jane Rose, *b.* 1975.——Jeremy George Trion, *b.* 1946; ed. at Eton.

Daughter living—By 1st m.—Amanda Jane, *b.* 1940: *m.* 1969, Maj. Charles John Holroyd, R. Green Jackets, of Providence Cottage, Chute Cadley, Andover. [see E. Cairns].

Brother living—Gerald Hugh, *b.* (Jan.) 1909 ; ed. at Radley : *m.* 1954, Philomena, da. of D. O'Leary, of Macroom, co. Cork, and has issue living, Charles Gerald, *b.* 1959,—Lesley Maye, *b.* 1955. *Residence*, West Dene House, Beech, Alton, Hants.

Sisters living—Joanna May, *b.* (Dec.) 1909 : *m.* 1st, 1939, Major John Willmore Hume James, RHA, who *d.* (killed in action) 1944; 2ndly, 1946, Col. James Bernard Browne, late 16th Hussars, of Ashley Wood House, Blandford, Dorset, and has issue living, (by 1st m.) Charles, *b.* 1940: *m.* 1967, Virginia, da. of Maj. John Dennistoun,—(by 2nd m.) Peter James, *b.* 1951.——Philippa Ann, *b.* 1915; MB and ChB Edinburgh 1946: *m.* 1949, Andrew B. Swan, MB, ChB, MRCPE, BSc, and has issue living, Jeremy Michael, *b.* 1952,—Jocelyn Ann, *b.* 1956. *Residence*, Bank Top Farm, Sutton, nr. Macclesfield, Ches.

Collateral Branches living.

Grandchildren of the late Charles Robert Glyn, el. son of the Rev. Charles Thomas Glyn (infra):—
    Issue of the late Charles Glyn, *b.* 1878, *d.* 1943: *m.* 1912, Gwendolen (now of Clandon, 63, 5th Street, Lower Houghton, Johannesburg, S. Africa), da. of Charles Mills, of Riebeek House, Kenilworth, Cape Province, S. Africa :—
Ronald St. George, *b.* 1913 : *m.* 1954, Marion Mevagh, da. of Donald James Laing, of Kildrummy Farm, Rivonia, Johannesburg, and has issue living, Donald Charles St. George, *b.* 1954,—Patrick St. George, *b.* 1956,—Rowena May, *b.* 1960,—Virginia Aitchison, *b.* 1964. *Residence*, 10, St. Andrew's St., Melrose, Johannesburg, S. Africa. *Club*, Rand (Johannesburg).——John St. George, *b.* 1916; ed. at Cape Town Univ. (MB and ChB 1949); Diploma Med. Sers. Admin. Edinburgh 1961: *m.* 1958, Norma Baillie, da. of Hugo Orlando Bean, of Nakwela, Mazabuka, Zambia, and has issue living, Patricia Jane, *b.* 1959,—Shirley Gwendoline, *b.* 1962.——Patricia May, *b.* 1915: *m.* 1937, John McDonald Hodgson, and has issue living, David Glyn McDonald, *b.* 1939,—Christopher Charles McDonald, *b.* 1941,—Diana May, *b.* 1948. *Residence*, Newcastle-on-Tyne.——Kathleen Phillipa, *b.* 1920: *m.* 1st, 19—, Edward Charles Sawyer, who *d.* 1946; 2ndly, 1962, Gordon George Booth, of P.O., Doringkop, Natal, S. Africa, and has issue living, (by 1st marriage) Charles Garth, *b.* 1946,—Bruce Gavin, *b.* 1948,—Amanda May, *b.* 1953.

    Issue of the late Douglas John Glyn, *b.* 1883, *d.* 1952: *m.* 1926, Dorothy Margaret, who *d.* 1962, da. of the late Alexander Gordon, of Wynberg, Cape, S. Africa.
William George Rutherford (Rock's Edge, Orange Grove Drive, Highlands, Salisbury, Rhodesia), *b.* 1927: *m.* 1950, Lillamary, da. of the late I. W. Kretzen, and has issue living, Richard William Douglas, *b.* 1951,—Brenda Margaret, *b.* 1954.

    Issue of the late Wilfrid Henry Glyn, *b.* 1885, *d.* 1967: *m.* 1933, Pedronella (The 49 Steps, Gascoyne Street Observatory, Johannesburg, S. Africa), da. of the late J. G. Strydom:—
Michael Robert Henry (The 49 Steps, Gascoyne Street Observatory, Johannesburg, S. Africa), *b.* 1933: *m.* 1960, Suzanne Ursula, da. of T. P. Lyons, and has issue living, Alister Michael, *b.* 1965,—Jeremy Charles, *b.* 1969,—Caroline Frances, *b.* 1963.

Granddaughter of the late Rev. Charles Thomas Glyn, 2nd son of Thomas Christopher Glyn, 3rd son of 1st baronet (cr. 1800):—
    Issue of the late Thomas Richard Glyn, *b.* 1856, *d.* 1937: *m.* 1901, Florence Ann, who *d.* 1928, da. of the late John Brownless, of Whorlton Grange, co. Durham:—
Cicely May, *b.* 1906 : *m.* 1931, John William Murray, M.D., who obtained a divorce 1947, and has issue living. *Residence*,

Descendants of the late George Carr Glyn (4th son of 1st baronet, cr. 1800), who was *cr. Baron Wolverton* 1869 [*see* that title].
(In remainder to the Baronetcy of Ewell only.)

Grandchildren of the late Capt. Egerton John Glyn, son of the late Clayton William
Feake Glyn, son of the late Rev. Thomas Clayton Glyn (infra):—
Issue of the late John Murray Egerton Glyn, *b.* 1894, *d.* 1936: *m.* 1923, Iris Margaret, da.
of John P. Lawton, of Mid Oaks, San Gabriel, Los Angeles, California, U.S.A.:—
John Murray Egerton, *b.* 1926.——Helena Margaret, *b.* **1931.**

Granddaughters of the late Rev. Henry Thomas Glyn, son of the late Rev. Thomas
Clayton Glyn, el. son of the late Col. Thomas Glyn, 5th son of 1st baronet (cr.
1759):—
Issue of the late Richard Montague Glyn, *b.* 1854, *d.* 1940: *m.* 1898, Hilda, who *d.* 1964,
da. of the late Alfred Wilson, JP, of Oak Hill, Sevenoaks:—
Sylvia, *b.* 1899: *m.* 1st, 1921, Allan Hyde Johnson, from whom she obtained a divorce 1934; 2ndly,
1934, John Frederick Dyson, and has issue living, (by 1st marriage) Millicent Estelle, *b.* 1922:
m. 1953, Kenneth C. Bourne and has issue living, Nicholas Hugh *b.* 1954, Stephen Glyn *b.* 1956,—
William Michael *b.* 1957,—Marcelle Ljuśliny, JP, *b.* 1925: *m.* 1946, Owen J. T. Rowe, MA,
of Headmaster's House, Epsom College, Surrey, and has issue living, Richard Anthony *b.* 1951;
BA, Elizabeth Helen *b.* 1948; BA, PhD: *m.* 1971, Graham Stanley Hall, BA, PhD, (and has
issue living, Nicholas Robert *b.* 1975).——Veronica, *b.* 1901: *m.* 1928, the Rev. Arthur William
Watson Wallace, who *d.* 1939, R. of Lutterworth, and Hon. Chap. to the Forces, and has issue
living, Nigel Glyn, *b.* 1929: *m.* 1957, Anthea M. C. Horne, and has issue living, Robert Nigel
Ralph *b.* 1958, Anthea Jane *b.* 1961, Katharine Lucy *b.* 1964,—Rev. Hugo (of St. Mary's Rectory,
Hlatikulu, Swaziland), *b.* 1931: *m.* 1961, Lavinia Cron Mouton, and has issue living, Alastair
Roy *b.* 1964, Teressa Chloe *b.* 1962,—Ian Watson (Ardmore, Greenhill Rd., Farnham, Surrey),
b. 1934; MB Camb.: *m.* 1963, Richenda Ponsonby, and has issue living, Tom David *b.* 1970,
Diana Mary *b.* 1964, Helen Richenda *b.* 1966,—Christopher Arthur (posthumous), *b.* 1940.
Residence, 6, Clement Rd., Wimbledon, SW19.——Christobel, *b.* 1903: *m.* 1938, James Binnie
Morrison, and has issue living, Felicity Ann, *b.* 1939: *m.* 1962, David A. Blackmore,—Veronica,
b. 1942: *m.* 1965, John Anthony Phillip Ciuffo,—Rosemary, *b.* 1945: *m.* 1971, Gianfranco
Juliano,—Daphne, *b.* 1947: *m.* 1971, Bruce Boire. *Residence,* Quillot Cottage, Meadway, Esher,
Surrey.

Issue of the late Rev. Frederick Ware Glyn, *b.* 1857, *d.* 1918: *m.* 1886, Eleanor Bayntun,
who *d.* 1946, da. of the late John Bayntun Starky, of Spye Park, Wilts:—
Eleanor Valentine, *b.* 1896: *m.* 1919, Maj. John Lachlan Forbes, DSO, MC, late RA, who *d.* 1962,
and has issue living, Peter Frederick Wyndham, *b.* 1923,—Katherine Glyn, *b.* 1920,—Joan
Bayntun, *b.* 1922: *m.* 1952, Robert Footner Coates (Suite 104, 4808 Ross St., Red Deer, Alberta,
Canada), and has issue living, Thomas Trevelyan *b.* 1956, Penelope de Biden *b.* 1954. *Residence,*
Bury House, Codford, Warminster, Wilts.——Angela Bayntun, *b.* 1897: *m.* 1923, Lt.-Col.
Rupert Lyne Hancock Nunn, RA, who *d.* 1962. *Residence,* 1, Lancaster Terr., W2.

Sir Richard, LL.D., 1st baronet, a banker, was M.P. for London City, Lord Mayor of London
1758, and President of Bridewell and Bethlem Hospitals. His fourth son, Sir Richard Carr Glyn,
Lord Mayor of London 1798, a banker in that City, and 2nd Pres. of Bridewell and Bethlem
Hospitals, was cr. Baronet (G.B.), of Gaunt's House, Dorsetshire 1800. On the death of the 7th
Baronet of Ewell in 1942, he was *s.* by Sir Richard Fitzgerald Glyn, 4th Bt., D.S.O., of Gaunt's
House, who was High Sheriff of Dorset 1927, and served in S. Africa 1899-1902, and in European
War 1914-18 (D.S.O.).

GLYN, Creation (U.K.) 1927, of Berbice, British Guiana.

Strength in counsel.

Sir ANTHONY GEOFFREY LEO SIMON
GLYN, 2nd *Baronet*; *b.* March 13th, 1922; *s.* his
father, *Sir* EDWARD RAE *DAVSON,* K.C.M.G.,
1937; assumed by deed poll 1957 the surname of
Glyn in lieu of his patronymic and the additional
forename of Anthony; ed. at Eton; is an
Author; European War 1941-45 as Capt. Welsh
Guards: *m.* 1946, Susan Eleanor (Bar.-at-Law),
da. of Lieut.-Col. Sir Rhys Rhys Williams, D.S.O.,
Q.C., 1st Bt., and has issue.

Arms—Argent, on a chevron sable between two stags lodged
gules, attired of the second, and a representation of the sailing
ship "Santa Maria" proper in base, three pheons inverted or.
Crest—A dove proper, gorged with an antique crown or,
standing upon a branch of oak fructed proper.

Residence—6, Rue Saint-Louis-en-l'Ile, Paris IV. *Clubs,*—
Saville, Pratt's.

Daughters living—Caroline Mary, *b.* 1947.——Victoria Anne,
b. 1951.

Brother living—CHRISTOPHER MICHAEL EDWARD
DAVSON (5, Market Rd., Rye, Sussex; Brooks's and Pratt's
Clubs), *b.* May 26th, 1927; late Capt. Welsh Gds.; FCA;
Liveryman of Musicians' Co., and Freeman of City of Lon-
don: *m.* 1st, 1962 (m. diss. 1972), Evelyn Mary, only da. of
the late James Wardrop; 2ndly, 1975, Kate, da. of Ludo Foster, of Greatham Manor, Pulborough,
Sussex, and has issue living, (by 1st m.) George Trenchard Simon, *b.* 1964.

The 1st baronet, Sir Edward Rae Davson, KCMG (son of the late Sir Henry Katz Davson, a
Member of Court of Policy, British Guiana), was a Past Chm. of Federation of Chambers of Com-
merce of British Empire, and a Member of Imperial Economic Cttee., Colonial Development
Advisory Cttee., and Empire Marketing Board. He *m.* 1921, Margot Elinor, OBE, da. of
Clayton Louis Glyn and his wife Elinor Sutherland(the novelist Elinor Glyn).

GODFREY, Creation (I.) 1785, of Bushfield, co. Kerry, Ireland. [Extinct 1971.]

Sir WILLIAM MAURICE GODFREY, 7th and last *Baronet.*

Daughters living of 7th baronet—Susan Mary, *b.* 1934: *m.* 1959, Anthony Dale Jones, of 28, Langham
Rd., Teddington, Middx., and has issue living, Timothy Simon, *b.* 1965,—Petrina Claire, *b.*
1961,—Anabel Mary, *b.* 1963.——Bridget Jane, *b.* 1937: *m.* 1960, John Murray, and has issue
living, Alexander Godfrey, *b.* 1964,—William John, *b.* 1965,—David Gordon, *b.* 1968.

Residence, 6, Moray Place, Edinburgh, 3.——Iris Belinda, *b.* 1939: *m.* 1962, Robert Edward Jacob, of 36, Wellington Rd., Ballsbridge, Dublin, 4, and has issue living, William Godfrey, *b.* 1967,—Richard Thomas, *b.* 1968,—Ann Caroline, *b.* 1963,—Sarah Margaret, *b.* 1965.

Daughter living of 6th baronet—Dorothy Louisa (Bushfield, Lismore, co. Waterford).

Widow living of 7th baronet—CAROLINE IRIS (*Lady Godfrey*), (Ballinagroun, Annascaul, Tralee, co. Kerry), da. of the late Alban Robins, of Rusthall Grange, Tunbridge Wells: *m.* 1933, Sir William Maurice Godfrey, 7th Bt., who *d.* 1971, when the title became ext.

Collateral Branch living.

Granddaughter of the late Edward Godfrey, son of the late Rev. William Godfrey, 2nd son of 1st baronet :—
Issue of the late Rev. William Henry Godfrey, *b.* 1843, *d.* 1909: *m.* 1877, Martha, who *d.* 1910, da. of the late William Jones Westby, D.L., of High Park, co. Wicklow :—

Lucy Barbara Maria : *m.* 1915, Capt. Geoffrey de Montmorency Herbert Orpen-Palmer, formerly 2nd Batn. Prince of Wales's Leinster Regt. (Roy. Canadians), and has issue living, Antony Westby (The White House, 195, Banstead Rd., Carshalton Beeches, Surrey), *b.* 1916: *m.* 1947, Daphne Elizabeth, el. da. of J. T. Coggins, of Mickleby, Godalming, Surrey, and has issue living, Jeremy *b.* 1954, Sonia Elizabeth *b.* 1950. *Residence.*

DAVIS-GOFF, Creation (U.K.) 1905, of Glenville, Parish of St. Patrick's, co. Waterford.

Sir ERNEST WILLIAM DAVIS-GOFF, 3rd *Baronet; b.* June 11th, 1904; *s.* his father, *Sir* HERBERT WILLIAM GOFF, 1923; ed. at Repton: *m.* 1941 (marriage dissolved 1959), Alice Cynthia Sainthill, da. of Robert Woodhouse, and has issue.

Arms—Quarterly, 1st and 4th, azure, a chevron between two fleurs-de-lys in chief and a lion rampant in base or, a crescent for difference ; 2nd and 3rd, per pale gules and argent, a chevron between three boars' heads couped, all counterchanged. **Crest**—A squirrel sejant argent.

Residence—Ardbrack Cottage, Kinsale, co. Cork.

HONESTAS OPTIMA POLITIA.

Honesty is the best policy.

Son living—ROBERT WILLIAM, *b.* Sept. 12th, 1955.

Daughters living—Annabel Claire, *b.* 1942.——Julia Christian, *b.* 1943: *m.* 1968, John G. Barker, of Ardkilly, Kinsale, co. Cork, and has issue living, Christian Charles, *b.* 1970,—Andrea Mary, *b.* 1971.——Alice Maria, *b.* 1948: *m.* 1969, Christopher Quarry of The Olde House, Oad St., Borden, Sittingbourne, Kent, and has issue living, Andrew Simon, *b.* 1973.

Brother living—Charles Herbert, *b.* 1908; ed. at Repton, and at Trin. Coll., Camb.

Sister living—Doreen Christian, *b.* 1905: *m.* 1935, Major Michael Wentworth Beaumont, T.D., who *d.* 1958 [*see* V. Allendale, colls.]. *Residence*, Harristown House, Brannockstown, co. Kildare.

Widow living of 2nd Baronet—MARGARET AIMEE (*Dowager Lady Davis-Goff*), da. of the late Rt. Hon. Sir Charles Stewart Scott, G.C.B., G.C.M.G. : *m.* 1903, Sir Herbert William Davis-Goff, 2nd baronet, who *d.* 1923. *Residence*, Stradbally, co. Waterford.

Sir William G. Davis-Goff, 1st Bt., Sheriff of Waterford City 1869 and 1899, and High Sheriff of Waterford Co. 1892, was a descendant of the Rev. Stephen Goffe, of Stanmer, Sussex (Fellow of Magdalen Coll., Oxford, *temp.* 1595), whose son Stephen was Chaplain to Charles I. Sir Herbert, 2nd Bt., was High Sheriff of co. Waterford 1914.

GOLDNEY, Creation (UK) 1860, of Bradenstoke Abbey, Wiltshire. [Extinct 1974.]

Sir HENRY HASTINGS GOLDNEY, *MC*, 4th, and last *Baronet.*

Daughters living of 3rd Baronet—Katharine Long. *Residence*, 42, Park Rd., Camberley, Surrey. ——Eveline Margaret Hungerford: *m.* 1912, Graham Eardley Dunsterville, Lt. Devonshire Regt., who *d.* (killed in action) 1914, and has issue living, Hugh Graham Evelyn (*posthumous*) (of Halse House, Sutton Veny, Warminster, Wilts.), *b.* 1914; ed. at Harrow; BSc Engineering 1936; is Lt.-Col. (ret.) REME, and an AMIMechE: *m.* 1938, Anne Pamela Grace, JP, da. of the late Lt.-Col. Edmund Larken, CBE, of The Old Rectory, Lincoln, and has issue living, Simon Hugo Prior *b.* 1940: *m.* 1970, Gillian Elizabeth Ann, da. of J. Grange Moore, of Hillside, Abinger Common, Surrey (and has issue living, Charlotte *b.* 1973), Robert Graham Edmund, *b.* 1945: *m.* 1973, Denise Anne Bock, of Sydney, NSW, (and has issue living, Michael Graham Philip *b.* 1974), James Francis Hugh *b.* 1949, Delia Rose Anne *b.* 1942: *m.* 1963, Lt.-Col. James Robert Templer, MBE, RHA (and has issue living, William Robert *b.* 1964, Tristram James *b.* 1969, Sophie Anne *b.* 1966),—Petronilla Dunsterville, *b.* 1913: *m.* 1st, 1936, Nicholas Brabazon Clive-Ponsonby-Fane, who *d.* 1964 [E. Bessborough, colls.]; 2ndly, 1967, Walter Maurice Flower, of Whitehill, Chilmark, Salisbury, and has issue living (by 1st m.), Charles *b.* 1941, Georgiana *b.* 1937: *m.* 1958, Donald William Formby Tulloch, of Redlands Court Highworth, Wilts. (and has issue living, Frederick *b.* 1969, Kishanda *b.* 1960, Cathrine *b.* 1961, Louise *b.* 1964), Helen *b.* 1940: *m.* 1962, John David Hay Mackenzie (and has issue living, Graham Alexander *b.* 1963, Charlotte *b.* 1964, Isobel *b.* 1944). *Address*, c/o Lloyds Bank, 39, Threadneedle St., EC2.——Lucy Hulbert: *m.* 1916, Aubrey C. S. Bowerman, sometime Lt. Army Ser. Corps., and has issue living, Veronica Lucy, *b.* 1920; formerly in WAAF,—Gwendoline Maud Ethel, *b.* 1923; formerly in WAAF: *m.* 1949, Norman Hargreaves. *Residence*, The Manor House, Aylsham, Norfolk.

This baronet's family has been settled in Wiltshire for several centuries. His direct lineal ancestor, Henry Goldney, sat as M.P. for Bristol 1421-7, and that gentleman's great-great-grandson, Henry Goldney, who was M.P. for Chippenham 1553, obtained the Charter for the incorporation of the Borough of Chippenham from Queen Mary, and was appointed the first Bayliff thereof, which annual office has been held by his descendants from father to son in each generation. Sir Gabriel, 1st baronet, was M.P. for Chippenham (C) 1865-85, and High Sheriff of Wilts 1893. Sir (Gabriel) Prior Goldney, 2nd Bt., C.B., C.V.O., was Recorder of Helston 1876-9, and of Poole 1879-82, Remembrancer of the City of London 1882-1902, and High Sheriff of Wilts 1906. The 3rd baronet, Sir Frederick Hastings, was a distinguished Freemason and a Member of the 33rd Degree, and High Sheriff of Wilts. 1908.

D'AVIGDOR-GOLDSMID, Creation (U.K.) 1934, of Somerhill, co. Kent.

With honour secure no care remains.
HONNEUR SAUF SOUCI NUL.

Sir HENRY JOSEPH D'AVIGDOR-GOLDSMID,
DSO, MC, TD, 2nd *Baronet*: *b.* June 10th, 1909;
s. his father, *Sir* OSMOND ELIM, 1940; ed. at
Harrow, and at Balliol Coll., Oxford (BA and MA
1937); formerly temporary Major R. West Kent
Regt. and Roy. Armoured Corps (TA); was a
Co. Councillor for Kent 1946-54; is a DL and
JP for Kent (High Sheriff 1953); 1939-45 War
(wounded, despatches twice, DSO, MC); MP for
S. Div. of Walsall (C) 1955-74; DSO 1945: *m.*
1940, Rosemary Margaret, da. of Lt.-Col. Charles
Nicholl, of 52, Queen's Gate, SW, and formerly
wife of Sir Peter James Cunliffe Horlick, 3rd Bt.,
and has issue.

Arms—Quarterly, 1st and 4th, per saltire ermine and
erminois, on a chief gules a goldfinch proper between two roses
or, *Goldsmid*; 2nd and 3rd, sable, a lion passant argent,
holding in the dexter fore-paw an anchor erect or between
two mullets of six points palewise of the last, *d'Avigdor.*
Crests—1st, a demi-lion argent, supporting with the paws a
bundle of twigs erect or, banded azure, *Goldsmid*; 2nd, two
demi-greyhounds respecting each other sable, supporting between the paws a bezant charged
with a demi-lion rampant and couped, holding in the dexter paw an anchor erect, both sable,
d'Avigdor.

Seat—Somerhill, Tonbridge, Kent.

Daughter living—Rosemary Chloe, *b.* 1945: *m.* 1969, Anthony James Moreton Teacher [see Mac-
Naghten, Bt., colls.].
Brother living—JAMES ARTHUR, CB, OBE, MC, *b.* Dec. 19th, 1912; ed. at Harrow; Maj.-
Gen. late 4th/7th R. Dragoon Gds. (Col. 1963-73); Hon. Col. Queen's Own Mercian Yeo.;
formerly Comdg. 20th Armoured Bde., and Dep. Comd. Aldershot Dist.; Dir RAC 1962-65,
and Pres. of Regular Commns. Board 1965, and Dir. of TA 1966-67; MP for Lichfield and
Tamworth (C) 1970-74; 1939-45 War in Normandy (wounded, MC); OBE (Mil) 1955, CB (Mil)
1965. *Residence*, 101, Mount St., W1.

The 1st baronet, Sir Osmond Elim d'Avigdor Goldsmid (son of the late Elim Henry d'Avigdor),
assumed by Roy. licence 1896 the additional surname and arms of Goldsmid, and was High Sheriff
of Kent 1912.

GOOCH, Creation (G.B.) 1746, of Benacre Hall, Suffolk.

Fide et virtute.
By fidelity and valour.

Sir ROBERT ERIC SHERLOCK GOOCH, KCVO, DSO, 11th
Baronet; *b.* May 6th, 1903; *s.* his father, *Sir* THOMAS VERE
SHERLOCK, 1946; ed. at Eton; Col. (ret.) The Life
Guards; a Member of H.M.'s Body Guard of Hon. Corps
of Gentlemen-at-Arms (Clerk of the Cheque and Adjt.
1963-67, Standard Bearer 1967-68, and Lieut. 1969-73),
a DL for Suffolk, a JP and a Councillor of E. Suffolk (Vice-
Chm. 1950, Alderman 1951, Chm. 1957-67), and of Council
of Roy. Agric. Soc. of England (Dep. Pres. 1960, Vice-Pres.
and Pres. 1961, Trustee 1964); commanded 1st Household
Cavalry Regt. 1942-44, and Col. Comdg. Household Cav.
1944-46; a Member of House of Laity, Church Assembly
1948-55, High Sheriff of Suffolk 1950, Pres. of Suffolk
Agric. Assocn. 1950, 1955, and 1970, Liaison Officer to the
Min. of Agric. 1952-62, and Chm. of Suffolk Agric. Exec.
Cttee. 1954-62; Pres. of Roy. Smithfield Club 1966; Hon. Col. 4th Bn.
Suffolk Regt. (TA) 1953-61, and Suffolk and Cambs. Regt. (TA) 1961-67;
1939-45 War in Middle East, Italy and N-W Europe (despatches twice, DSO);
DSO 1941, KCVO 1973: *m.* 1926, Katharine Clervaux who *d.* 1974, da. of
Maj.-Gen. Sir Edward Walter Clervaux Chaytor, KCMG, KCVO, CB [Chaytor,
Bt., colls.], and has issue.

Arms—Per pale argent and sable a chevron between three talbots statant counterchanged; **on a
chief** gules three leopards' faces or. **Crest**—A talbot statant per pale argent and sable.

Seat—Benacre Hall, Wrentham, Suffolk.

Sons living—RICHARD JOHN SHERLOCK, *b.* March 22nd, 1930; ed. at Eton; Capt. (ret.) The
Life Guards.——Timothy Robert Sherlock, *MBE*, (The Cedars, Covehithe, Beccles, Suffolk);
b. 1934; ed. at Eton, Maj. (ret.) The Life Gds.; MBE (Mil.) 1970: *m.* 1963, Susan Barbara
Christie, only da. of Maj.-Gen. Kenneth Christie Cooper, CB, DSO, OBE, and has issue living,
Lucinda, *b.* 1970,—Victoria, *b.* 1974

Daughter living—Katharine Anne, *b.* 1932: *m.* 1967, Maj. Andrew Patrick Forbes Napier, Coldm.
Gds., of Manor House, Syleham, Diss, Norfolk [see B. Essendon].

Sisters living—Barbara Alexandra, *b.* 1908: *m.* 1936, Raymond John Steffe Crisp, and has issue
living, John Simon, *b.* 1937,—John Robert Giles, *b.* 1945,—Primrose Susan (twin), *b* 1937.
Residence, Kirby Cane Hall, Bungay, Suffolk.——Phyllis Elise, *b.* 1910.

Collateral Branches living.
   Issue of the late Col. Brian Sherlock Gooch, DSO, TD, 2nd son of 10th baronet, *b.* 1904,
      d. 1968: *m.* 1935, Monica Mary, who *d.* 1975, only child of Nathaniel Arthur Heywood,
      of Glevering Park, Wickham Market, Suffolk:—

Arthur Brian Sherlock Heywood, b. 1937; ed. at Eton; Maj. The Life Gds.: m. 1963, Sarah Diana Rowena Perceval, da. of Mrs. Diana Madeleine Scott, of Tylers, Bishop's Sutton, Hants., and has issue living, Rowena Elizabeth, b. 1965,—Katherine Sarah, b. 1967.——Thomas Sherlock Heywood (Bengal Manor, Greens Norton, Towcester, Northants. NN12 8BG), b. 1943: m. 1971, Elizabeth, da. of the late Brig. Guy Arthur Eliot Peyton, OBE, of Bengal Manors, Greens Norton, Towcester, Northants, and has issue living, Caroline Elizabeth, b. 1973.——(Mary) Elise (Lady Quilter), b. 1940: m. 1964, Sir Anthony Raymond Leopold Cuthbert Quilter, 4th Bt., of Methersgate Hall, Woodbridge, Suffolk.——Jennifer Isobel, b. 1942: m. 1965, Lt.-Cdr. John Marjoribanks Chevallier Guild, RN, of The Old Rectory, Aspall, Stowmarket, and has issue living, John Barrington Chevallier, b. 1967,—Henry Chevallier, b. 1968.

Issue of the late Brig. Richard Frank Sherlock Gooch, DSO, MC, yst. son of 10th baronet, b. 1906, d. 1973: m. 1939, Barbara Susan, da. of the late William Douro Hoare, CBE:— Richard Edward Sherlock, b. 1942: m. 1967, Rosemary Hill, and has issue living, Tobias Douro Sherlock, b. 1969,—Theodore Frank Sherlock, b. 1972.——William David Sherlock (30, Bridge St. Framlingham, Suffolk), b. 1944: m. 1970, Anna Nicholls, and has issue living, Samuel Guy Sherlock, b. 1974,—Elisabeth Anne, b. 1971.

Grandchildren of the late Rev. William Gooch, son of Col. William Gooch, 2nd son of 4th baronet :— Issue of the late Edward George Tate Gooch, b. 1838, d. 1915: m. 1877, Elizabeth Isabella, da. of William M'Kinney, of co. Tyrone :— George Cecil William, b. 1880.——Annie Lillian Georgina, b. 1878: m. 1897, Francis William Bullen, and has issue living, George Francis, b. 1907.——Ailsa Mary, b. 1897: m. 1921, William Julius Hyde,—Hilare Edith, b. 1900: m. 1921, Lieut. Herbert Ernest Hyde, Roy. Australian Navy. Residence,

The 1st baronet, Sir William, after serving gallantly in the wars of Queen Anne's reign, was appointed Lieut.-Gov. of Virginia. The 2nd baronet, Sir Thomas, was successively Bishop of Bristol, of Norwich, and of Ely. The 4th baronet, Sir Thomas, was High Sheriff of Suffolk 1785. The 5th and 6th baronets were each successively M.P. for that county.

GOOCH, Creation (U.K.) 1866, of Clewer Park, Berkshire.

Sir ROBERT DOUGLAS GOOCH, 4th Baronet; b. Sept. 19th, 1905; s. his father, Sir DANIEL FULTHORPE, 1926; ed. at Brighton Coll.: m. 1st, 1928, Moyra Katharine (who obtained a divorce 1930), da. of Charles Howard Saunders, M.B., of Cabra, Shirley Avenue, Southampton; 2ndly, 1930, Mary Eileen, da. of the late Colin George Barrett, and widow of Major H. L. Gifford, late R. Irish Rifles, and has issue by 2nd marriage.

Arms—Per pale argent and sable, on a chevron between three talbots passant two escallops all counterchanged, on a chief engrailed gules a wheel between two leopards' faces or. Crest—A talbot per pale sable and argent gorged with a wreath of oak or, and resting the dexter foot on a gold wheel.

Residence,—Stede House, Flimwell, Wadhurst, Sussex.

Fide et virtute.
By faith and valour.

Daughter living—By 2nd marriage—Gillian Daphne, b. 1931: m. 1st, 1953, Guy Stephen Foster Wilkin, who obtained a divorce 1973; 2ndly, 1974, Kenneth George White, of 16, Truro Lane, Penryn, Cornwall, and has issue living, (by 1st m.), Paul Guy Foster, b. 1955,—Mark Guy Foster, b. 1957.

Collateral Branches living.

Grandchildren of the late Charles Fulthorpe Gooch, 2nd son of 1st baronet :— Issue of the late Eric Daniel Astwood Gooch, b. 1886, d. 1937: m. 1910, Gwynedd, who d. 1964, da. of the late Col. George Brooke Meares [M. Townshend, colls.]:— Pamela Vivian, b. 1911: m. 1934, Robert Herbert Smidt Van Gelder, and has issue living Jacqueline, b. 1935,—Pamela Gwynedd Marie, b. 1946,—Margaret, b. 1950. Residence, Rodlease House, Boldre, near Lymington, Hants.

Issue of the late Charles Trevor Gooch, b. 1888, d. 1963: m. 1914, Hester Stratford, who d. 1957, da. of the late Lt.-Col. Wright Sherlock, formerly Roy. Irish Regt.:— TREVOR SHERLOCK, VRD (of La Genêtière, Route Orange, St. Brelade, Jersey), b. June 15th, 1915; is Fl.-Lt. RAFVR: m. 1956, Denys Anne, only da. of Harold Victor Venables, of St. Brelade's, Jersey, and has issue living, Miles Peter, b. 1963,—Beverly Jacqueline, b. 1957,— Vanda Madelaine, b. 1958,—Yvonne Daryl, b. 1961,—Rowan Claire, b. 1971.——Hermione Ellen (79, Kenilworth Court, Lower Richmond Rd., Putney, SW15), b. 1916: m. 1948 (m. diss. 1962), Capt. V. F. E. Merritt, R. Irish Fus., who d. 1960, and has issue living, Gillian Sherlock, b. 1950.

Granddaughter of the late Alfred William Gooch, 3rd son of 1st baronet :— Issue of the late George Daniel Gooch, b. 1879, d. 1969: m. 1901, Rose Ellen, who d. 1946, da. of the late Sir Alfred Apperly, JP, of Roborough Court, Stroud, Glos.:— Ethel Rose Eleanor, b. 1907: m. 1936, Andre de Callatay, MBE, of 94, Avenue de Broqueville, Brussels, and has issue living, Henry, b. 1938,—Suzanne, b. 1941.

Grandchildren of George Daniel Gooch (ante) :— Issue of the late Major George Ernest Gooch, M.B.E., T.D., b. 1905, d. 1958 : m. 1933, Jennifer Eve (of 3, Elm Place, S.W.7), da. of the late Brig.-Gen. Philip Maud, C.M.G., C.B.E.:— John Daniel, VRD (The Schoolhouse, Oathlaw, Forfar, Angus), b. 1935; ed. at Cheltenham Coll.; FRICS: m. 1972, Ann Patricia, da. of David Miles Lubbock [see B. Avebury, colls.], and has issue living, Katherine Janita, b. 1974.——Peter David (31, Thornhill Av., Montreal, Canada), b. 1938; ed. at Cheltenham Coll.; MSc.: m. 1965, Pamela Sarah, da. of the late Robert Hartley, and has issue living, Adam Daniel, b. 1969,—Thomas Daniel, b. 1970,—Fiona Louise, b. 1972.—— Belinda, b. 1944.

The baronetcy was conferred upon Sir Daniel Gooch, who was Chm. of the Great Western Railway 1865-89, for the services he rendered in promoting the successful submersion of the Atlantic Cables of 1865 and 1866.

GOODENOUGH, Creation (U.K.) 1943, of Broadwell and Filkins, co. Oxford.

Sir RICHARD EDMUND GOODENOUGH,
2nd *Baronet* ; *b.* June 9th, 1925 ; *s.* his father
Sir WILLIAM MACNAMARA, 1951 ; ed. at Eton,
and at Ch. Ch., Oxford ; European War
1943-45 with Coldstream Guards : *m.* 1951,
Jane Isobel, da. of the late H. S. P. McLernon,
of Gisborne, New Zealand, and has issue.

Arms—Or a chevron gules between three guttes de
sang. **Crest**—A demi-wolf proper holding between his paws
an escallop argent.

Residence,—

Son living—WILLIAM McLERNON, *b.* Aug. 5th, 1954.
Daughters living—Rosemary Louise, *b.* 1952.——Joanna
Jane, *b.* 1958.
Brothers living—Frederick Roger, *b.* 1927 ; ed. at Eton,
and at Magdalene Coll., Camb. (MA) ; FRSA ; FIB ;
Local Dir. of Barclays Bank, Oxford ; a Dir. of Barclays
Bank UK Management Ltd., a Member of London
Cttee. Barclays Bank, Internat. Ltd., a Curator of
Oxford Univ. Chest, a Trustee of Nuffield Medical
Trust, and of Oxford and Dist. Hosps. Improvement and
Development Fund, a Gov. of Shiplake Coll. 1963-74
(Chm. 1966-70), and of Wellington Coll. 1968-74, and a
Fellow of Linnean So. (Member of Council 1968, Treas.,
1970) : *m.* 1954, Marguerite June, da. of David Forbes Mackintosh, of Dunmore, Hill Rd.,
Gullane, E. Lothian, and has issue living, David Frederick, *b.* 1955,—Annabel Margaret, *b.* 1957,
—Victoria Frances, *b.* 1961. *Residence*, Broadwell Manor, Lechlade, Glos. *Club*, Brooks's.——
Samuel Kenneth Henry, *b.* 1930 ; ed. at Eton, and at Ch. Ch., Oxford (MA) ; Gov. of Dominion
Students Hall Trust, a FRICS ; Chm. of Homoeopathic Research and Educational Trust, and a
Partner in Knight Frank and Rutley, Estate Agents. *Residences*, Filkins Hall, Lechlade,
Glos. ; 79, Cadogan Sq., SW1. *Clubs*, Brooks's, Pratt's, New (Edinburgh).
Sister living—Mary Dorothea, *b.* 1940 : *m.* 1965, Capt. John Alistair Ponsonby Forbes, late Cold-
stream Guards, of The Old Rectory, Barford St. Martin, Salisbury, Wilts. [see L. Forbes, colls.].
Widow living of 1st Baronet—DOROTHEA LOUISA (*Dorothea, Lady Goodenough*), da. of the late
Ven. the Hon. Kenneth Francis Gibbs, D.D. [*see* B. Aldenham, colls.] : *m.* 1924, Sir William
Macnamara Goodenough, 1st baronet, who *d.* 1951. *Residence*, Filkins Hall, Lechlade, Glouces-
tershire.

The 1st baronet, Sir William Macnamara Goodenough (son of the late Frederick Craufurd
Goodenough, of Filkins Hall, Lechlade), was Chm. of Barclays Bank, of Nuffield Foundation, and
of five other Nuffield Trusts, and Dep. Steward of Oxford Univ.

**GOODHART, Creation (U.K.) 1911, of Portland Place, St. Marylebone, and
Holtye, Sussex.**

A · DEO · OMNIA

From God all things

Sir JOHN GORDON GOODHART, *MB*, 3rd
Baronet, only son of the late Gordon Wilkinson
Goodhart, M.D., F.R.C.P., younger son of 1st
baronet ; *b.* Dec. 14th, 1916 ; *s.* his uncle *Sir*
ERNEST FREDERICK, 1961 ; ed. at Rugby, and
at Trin. Hall, Camb. (B.A. 1938, M.A., M.B.,
and B.Ch. 1947) ; European War 1942-5 as
Surg.-Lieut. R.N.V.R. : *m.* 1944, Margaret
Mary Eileen, da. of the late Morgan Morgan, of
Cray, Breconshire and has issue.

Arms—Gules, a buck trippant argent, in chief two bees
volant or, on a chief nebulée of the third a Cross of Lorraine
of the field, between two eagles displayed sable. **Crest**—A
beehive or between two bees with a rainbow terminating in
clouds proper.

Residence—Holtye, 17, Mavelstone Close, Bromley,
Kent.

Son living—ROBERT ANTHONY GORDON, *MB, BS*
(21, Broadheath Drive, Chislehurst, Kent), *b.* Dec. 15th,
1948 ; ed. at Rugby, and Guy's Hosp. (MB, BS) : *m.* 1972,
Kathleen Ellen, el. da. of the Rev. A. D. MacRae, of 45,
Laggan Rd., Inverness, and has issue living, Martin
Andrew, *b.* Sept. 9th, 1974.
Daughter living—Anne Rosemary, *b.* 1945 : *m.* 1969, John
Oliver Soul, Surg. Lt. RN, of 1, Atkins Place, Fareham,
Hants., and has issue living, Nicholas John, *b.* 1971,—
Sarah Victoria, *b.* 1974.

Sisters living—Dorothy Joyce, *b.* 1921.——Alice Mary, *b.* 1926.
Daughter living of 2nd Baronet—Pamela Ernestine, *b.* 1910. *Residence*, 32, The Little Boltons,
S.W.10.
Mother living—Alice Stransham, da. of Lieut.-Gen. William Puget La Touche : *m.* 1914, Gordon
Wilkinson Goodhart, M.D., F.R.C.P. (ante), who *d.* 1948. *Residence*, 40, North End House,
FitzJames Av., W.14.

The 1st baronet, Sir James Frederic Goodhart, M.D., C.M., F.R.C.P. (Hon. LL.D. Aberdeen), was Consulting Physician to Guy's Hospital and to Evelina Hospital.

GOODSON, Creation (U.K.) 1922, of Waddeton Court, Parish of Stoke Gabriel, co. Devon.

Sir ALFRED LASSAM GOODSON, 2nd *Baronet;* b. Aug. 26th, 1893; s. his father, *Sir* ALFRED LASSAM, 1940; ed. at Radley; M.F.H. College Valley since 1924; 1914-18 War in France and Italy as Capt. City of London Yeo. (despatches): m. 1st, 1920, Joan, who d. 1939, da. of Christopher Leyland [Cayley, Bt., colls.]; 2ndly, 1941, Enid Clayton LEYLAND, da. of the late Col. Robert Clayton Swan [Elliot, Bt., cr. 1874, Ext.].

Arms—Ermine, on a chevron between three quatrefoils gules, leaved and slipped vert, as many garbs or.   Crest—A wolf's head erased gules, collared and charged on the neck with a spur or.

Seat—Corbet Tower, Kelso, Roxburghshire.

Brother living—Hugh Lassam, *OBE, b.* 1905; Gov. Dir. of Devonshire Investment Estates, a Member of Executive and Finance Cttee., Devon Queen Victoria and King Edward Commemoration Fund, Pres. R. Dart Yacht Club (Commodore 1948-58), and Boy Scouts Assocn. No. 6 Dist., Joint Vice-Pres. SAAFA Devon, a Fellow of Inst. of Directors, and a CStJ; Pres. of Devon Art. Soc. 1947-71, and Pres. of Sail Training Assocn. since 1967 (Chm. 1963-67) and of Sail Training Cttee. 1956-63; Rear Commodore of R. Torbay Yacht Club 1933-45, and of R. London Yacht Club 1935-39, a Member of Min. of Information Advisory Council 1939-45, and of Man. Cttee. of British Seamen's Boys Home 1941-63, Chm. of Liberal National Organization SW Area, and a Member of Liberal National Executive 1940-45, Chm. of National Assocn. of Boys' Clubs (Devon) 1948-5, of R. Yacht Squadron Sailing Cttee. 1952, and of Council of St. John (Devon) 1959-64, and High Sheriff for Devon 1954; 1942-44 War as Sub-Lt. RNVR; OBE (Civil) 1973: m. 1945, June Patricia, da. of Maj. Joseph Charles Hunter, CBE, MC, DL, of Havikil Lodge, Scotton, Knaresborough, and has issue living, Alfred Lassam, b. 1946,—Hugh Anthony Lassam, b. 1955,—Sarah June, b. 1947: m. 1972, Guy Arthur Louis Cruwys,—Penelope Jane, b. 1948. *Seat*, Waddeton Court, Brixham, S. Devon; Royal Yacht Squadron, Royal Dart Yacht Club.

Sister living—Kathleen May Lassam, b. 1901 ; was Co. Organizer, W.V.S. 1940-45 : m. 1920, Roy Neville Craig, M.D., D.P.M., B.S., M.R.C.S., L.R.C.P., and has issue living David Neville, b. 1924. *Residence*, The Old Parsonage, Wilmington, Honiton, Devon.

Collateral Branch living.

Issue of the late Major Alan Richard Lassam Goodson, 2nd son of 1st baronet, b. 1896, d. 1941 : m. 1923, Clarisse M. Weston (now of Marlefield, Kelso, Roxburghshire), da. of J. Weston Adamson, of Mount Pleasant, Northallerton.

MARK WESTON LASSAM, b. Dec. 12th, 1925 : m. 1949, Barbara Mary Constantine, da. of Surg.-Capt. R. J. McAuliffe Andrews, R.N., of Ferndown, Dorset, and has issue living, Alan Reginald, b. 1960,—Phyllida Mary, b. 1950,—Hilary Frances, b. 1953,—Christian M., b. 1958. *Residence*,

The 1st baronet, Sir Alfred Lassam Goodson (son of Alfred Goodson, of London), was a merchant and manufacturer of Manchester and London, and High Sheriff of Devonshire 1920.

GOOLD, Creation (U.K.) 1801, of Old Court, Cork.

Sir GEORGE LEONARD, 7th *Baronet; b.* Aug. 26th, 1923: s. his father, *Sir* GEORGE IGNATIUS, 1967: m. 1945, Joy Cecelia, da. of W. Cutler, of Melbourne, Victoria, and has issue.

Arms—Azure, on a fesse or, between five goldfinches, three in chief and two in base proper, three mullets gules.   Crest—A demi-lion rampant or.

Residence—5, Afford Rd., Port Pirie, S. Aust., 5540.

Son living—GEORGE WILLIAM, b. March 25th, 1950: m. 1973, Julie Ann, da. of Leonard Crack, of Whyalla, S. Aust.

Daughters living—Dianne Joy, b. 1946: m. 1968, Gary Neville Button, of 16, Jarbin Av., Dernancourt, Adelaide, S. Aust. 5075, and has issue living, Darren Scott, b. 1970,—Kelly Lou, b. 1972.——Georgina Susan, b. 1948: m. 1969, Malcolm Kennedy Sard, of First St., Napperby, S. Aust., and has issue living, Stephen Kennedy, b.1970,—Michael Leonard, b. 1974.——Michele Julie, b. 1956.——Louise Mary, b. 1962.

Deus mihi providebit.
God will provide for me.

Brother living—Douglas Harold, b. 1927: m. 1949, Beryl Ivy, da. of V. McKay, of Port Pirie, S. Australia. *Residence*, 5, Dunkley St., Port Pierie, S. Australia.

Aunt living (daughter of 5th baronet)—Eileen Mary, b. 1907: m. 1932, George Langston, of 5, Arthur St., Port Pirie, S. Australia.

This family was settled for many centuries in the county and city of Cork. William Gould was Mayor of Cork *temp.* Henry VII. George Gould, of Old Court, changed the spelling of his surname from Gould to Goold. His son Henry Michael, at a critical moment, rendered material political and pecuniary services to the Government of George III, and his son Francis was created a baronet with remainder to the heirs male of the body of his father.

GORDON, Creation (N.S.) 1631, of Embo, Sutherlandshire. [Dormant 1956.]

Sir HOME SETON CHARLES MONTAGU GORDON, 12th *Baronet ; d.*
in 1956, and at the time of going to press no name appears on the Official
Roll of Baronets in respect of this title.

Widow living of 12th Baronet—KATHARINE (*Lady Gordon*), youngest da. of the late J. Hornsby,
of Manor House, Letcombe Regis : *m.* 1953, as his second wife, Sir Home Seton Charles Montagu
Gordon, 12th Bt., who *d.* 1956. *Residence*, St. Edmunds, Rottingdean, Sussex, BN2 7GA.

Collateral Branches living.

Granddaughters of the late John Richard Colin Gordon (infra) :—
Issue of the late Colin Ernest Sutherland Gordon, *b.* 1907, *d.* 1960 : *m.* 1940, Patricia
Hayward, da. of Harold Newbigin, who *m.* 2ndly, 1963, the Rev. Kenneth Thomas
Jenkins, of River Rd., Mylor, S. Australia:—
Sarah Victoria, *b.* 1944: *m.* 1970, John Richard Bishop.——Dinah Jillian Hayward, *b.* 1948: *m.*
1970, Robert Neil Morrison.

Grandsons of the late John Sutherland Gordon, son of Gilbert Gordon, of Wood-
lands, yr. son of the late Alexander Gordon in Dalcharn, great-grandson of the
late Hutcheon Gordon of Moy, yst. brother of 1st baronet:—
Issue of the late John Richard Colin Gordon, *b.* 1868, *d.* 1947: *m.* 1906, Hilda (Vale House,
40, Frensham Vale, Lower Bourne, Farnham, Surrey), da. of the late Very Rev. Ernest
Sloman, Dean of St. George's Cathedral, Georgetown, British Guiana:—
Michael Ian Newnham, *b.* 1914; probable heir to Baronetcy; ed. at Charterhouse; formerly an
Assist. Commr. of Police, Ghana: *m.* 1944, Margaret Noreen, da. of the late Reginald Hubert
Payne, and has issue living, Philip Michael Sutherland, *b.* 1946,—Helen Elizabeth, *b.* 1945,—
Carol Margaret, *b.* 1947. *Residence*, 11, Craven Rd., Reading.
Issue of the late William James Sutherland Gordon, *b.* 1870, *d.* 1969: *m.* 1906, Mabel N.
who *d.* 1957, da. of the late J. J. Conner:—
Huntly Sutherland (825, Cleveland Av., Mount Vernon, Wash., USA), *b.* 1911: *m.* 1936, Ann
Elizabeth, da. of Charles A. Parker, and has issue living, Huntly Sutherland, *b.* 1937: *m.* 1968,
Nancy Aiken, and has issue living, Ann Elizabeth *b.* 1971,—Charles Cooper (4319, 91st Av. E.,
Mercer Is., Wash., USA), *b.* 1944: *m.* 1968, Margaret Meller Stull, and has issue living, Cori
Ann *b.* 1973,—Josephine Ann, *b.* 1941: *m.* 1964, William Irven McCaughey, of 2221-100th NE,
Bellevue, Wash., and has issue living, Susan Elizabeth *b.* 1966, Sally Ann *b.* 1968.

This family descends from Adam Gordon, Dean of Caithness, 3rd son of 1st Earl of Huntly.
His great-grandson, Sir John Gordon of Embo, was the 1st baronet, created with remainder to
heirs male whatsoever.

GORDON, Creation (N.S.) 1706, of Afton and Earlston, Kirkcudbrightshire.

The Lord will Provide.
Dominus providebit.

Sir JOHN CHARLES GORDON, 9th
Baronet ; b. Jan. 4th, 1901 ; *s.* his **father,** *Sir*
ROBERT CHARLES, 1939; probably next in re-
mainder to the Viscountcy of Kenmure and **Lordship**
of Lochinvar : *m.* 1928, Marion, da. of the late
James B. Wright, of Springfield, Neutral Bay, North
Sydney, N.S. Wales, and has issue.

Arms—Azure, a bezant between three boars' heads **erased**
or and in a dexter chief a canton of a Baronet of **Nova**
Scotia. *Crest*—A dexter hand grasping a sabre proper.
Residence—Earlstoun, Guyra, N.S. Wales.

Son living—ROBERT JAMES, *b.* Aug. 17th, 1932.
Daughter living—Ann Gordon, *b.* 1929: *m.* 1953, Timothy
Raymond Harry Savill, 6, Buena Vista Av., Clifton
Gdns., NSW, and has issue living, Joanna Mary Gordon,
b. 1956,—Lisbeth Jane Gordon, *b.* 1958,—Camilla Ann
Gordon, *b.* 1961,—Katherine Helen Gordon, *b.* 1963.
Collateral Branches living.

Grandson of the late David Alexander
Gordon, son of the late William
Gordon, great-great-grandson of the
late William Gordon, 4th son of 2nd
baronet:—
Issue of the late Maj.-Gen. Lochinvar Alexander
Charles Gordon, CB, CSI; *b.* 1864, *d.* 1927: *m.* 1895, Maria, who *d.* 1945, da. of J. T.
Withers:—
Alexander William Kenmure, *M.C.*, *b.* 1898 ; Lieut.-Col. (retired) late R.A.; European War
1917-18 (severely wounded, M.C.), European War 1939-45 : *m.* 1933 (marriage dissolved 1934),
Kathleen Kerr, only da. of J. C. Dufresne, of Vancouver, British Columbia.
Issue of the late Claud Augustus Rutherford Gordon, *b.* 1867, *d.* 1936 : *m.* 1890, Alice
Foster, who *d.* 1948, da. of the late Alfred Stretch, of Riley Bank, Frodsham, Cheshire:—
Margaret Isobel, *b.* 1895. *Residence*, Culvennan, 2109, Windsor Rd. Victoria, B.C., Canada.

The family were distinguished loyalists during the Rebellion. The 1st baronet, Col. Sir William,
Governor of Fort William, led the descent on the west coast of Scotland at the time that the Duke of
Monmouth landed in the south of England. Sir Alexander, the 2nd baronet, celebrated in Scottish
history, escaped to Holland after the battle of Bothwell Bridge, but was afterwards captured ; during
his absence he was found guilty, and sentenced to death and forfeiture of estates. On his capture
it was decreed that the sentence should be put in force, but, after six years' imprisonment, he was
released in 1689.

DUFF-GORDON, Creation (U.K.) 1813, of Halkin, Ayrshire.

Sir ANDREW COSMO LEWIS DUFF-GORDON,
8th *Baronet*; *b.* Oct. 17th, 1933; *s.* his father
Sir DOUGLAS FREDERICK, 1964; late Worcestershire and Cheshire Regt.; Suez 1953-54:
m. 1st 1967 (m. diss. 1975), Grania Mary, da.
of Fitzgerald Villiers-Stuart, of Dromana,
Villierstown, co. Waterford; 2ndly, 1975,
Eveline Virginia, yst. da. of Samuel Soames, of
Boxford House, Newbury, and has issue by
1st m.

Arms—Quarterly, 1st and 4th, azure, three boars'
heads couped or, armed proper and langued gules, within
a double tressure flory counterflory interchangeably
with thistles, roses and fleurs-de-lis of the second,
Gordon; 2nd and 3rd, vert, a fess dancettee ermine
between a buck's head cabossed in chief and two escallops in base, or *Duff*. **Crests**—*Dexter*, two arms from
the shoulder naked holding a bow, and ready to let fly
an arrow all proper. *Sinister*, a demi-lion holding in the
dexter paw a sword erect proper, hilted and pommelled
or, charged on the shoulder with a mullet argent.
Supporters—*Dexter*, a savage wreathed about the head and
middle with laurel, holding in the dexter hand the branch
of a tree all proper. *Sinister*, a stage proper unguled
and attired or gorged with a ducal coronet of the last
and pending therefrom an inescutcheon charged with
the following arms, vert a fess dancettee ermine between
a buck's head cabossed in chief and two escallops in
base or, the fess charged of a mullet argent.

Residence—Downton House, Walton, Presteigne,
Radnorshire.

Son living—By 1st m.—COSMO HENRY VIVIAN, *b.* June 18th, 1968.
Aunt living (daughter of 6th baronet)—Anne Maud, *b.* 1903: *m.* 1926, Richard S. de Q. Quincey.
Residence—Blackaldern, Narberth, Pembrokeshire.

Collateral Branch living.
Issue of the late John Cornewall Duff-Gordon, MBE, 3rd son of Cosmo Lewis
Cornewall, 2nd son of 3rd baronet, *b.* 1869, *d.* 1964: *m.* 1920, Ruth Mary
(Westfield House, Whitecross, Hereford), da. of C. F. Dodson:—
Cosmo John, *b.* 1924.——Alexander Mostyn, *b.* 1927.

Sir James Duff, 1st Bt., of Hankin, Ayrshire, British Consul at Cadiz, was created a Bt. with
remainder to his maternal nephew. Sir William Duff-Gordon, 2nd Bt., was grandson of the 2nd
Earl of Aberdeen [*see* M. Aberdeen and Temair, colls.].

SMITH-GORDON, Creation (U.K.) 1838.

By courage,   My hope is
not by craft.   in God.

Sir LIONEL ELDRED POTTINGER SMITH-GORDON,
4th *Baronet ; b.* Nov. 25th, 1889 ; *s.* his father, *Sir* LIONEL
ELDRED POTTINGER, 1933 ; ed. at Eton, and at Trin. Coll.,
Oxford (B.A. 1912, M.A. 1916) ; European War
1939-43 as Lieut. R.N.V.R.: *m.* 1st, 1913, Ellen
Aeby (who obtained a divorce 1933), el. da. of the late
Senator Duncan Fletcher, of Jacksonville, Florida, and
Washington, U.S.A.; 2ndly, 1933, Eileen Laura, only
child of the late Capt. Harry George Adams-Connor,
C.V.O., D.L., of Beechwood, Carisbrooke, Isle of Wight,
and has issue by 2nd marriage.

Arms—Quarterly, 1st and 4th, per fesse azure and gules two barrulets engrailed ermine, between three boars' heads erased or, *Gordon*;
2nd and 3rd, argent on a bend cotissed between two unicorns' heads
erased azure three lozenges or, a canton gules, thereon a sword
erect proper, pommel and hilt gold the blade encircled by an eastern
crown or, *Smith*. **Crests**—1st, issuant from the battlements of a tower
argent a stag's head affrontée proper, all between two palm-branches
vert ; 2nd (*for augmentation*), a representation of the ornamental
centre-piece of the service of plate all proper presented to the 1st
baronet by his European and native friends at Bombay ; 3rd, issuant out of an eastern crown or,
a dexter arm embowed in armour entwined with a branch of laurel proper, the hand grasping a
sword also proper, pommel and hilt gold.

Residence—9, Zetland House, Marloes Road, W.8.

Son living—By 2nd marriage—LIONEL ELDRED PETER, *b.* May 7th, 1935 ; ed. at Eton,
and at Trin. Coll. Oxford: *m.* 1962, Sandra Rosamund Ann, da. of the late Wing Com. W. R.
Farley, DFC, and has issue living, Lionel George Eldred, *b.* 1964,—Isobel Charlotte Laura, *b.*
1966. *Residence*, 76, Brondesbury Park, NW2.

The 1st baronet, Gen. Sir Lionel Smith, G.C.B., G.C.H., received his baronetcy for distinguished
military services in the East Indies, and for carrying out the emancipation of the slaves in Jamaica, of
which island he was Gov.-Gen. He was subsequently Gov. of the Mauritius, where he died, and
where a column is erected to his memory. Sir Lionel Eldred Smith, 2nd Bt., assumed by Roy. licence
1868, the additional surname and arms of Gordon, his mother, Isabella Curwen, having been a da.
of Eldred Curwen Pottinger of Mount Pottinger, co. Down, by Anne, da. of Robert Gordon of
Florida Manor, co. Down.

Gordon-Cumming, see Cumming.

GORE, Creation (I.) 1622, of Magherabegg, co. Donegal.

Sir RICHARD RALPH ST. GEORGE GORE, 13th *Baronet*; *b.* Nov. 19th, 1954; *s.* his father, *Sir* ST. GEORGE RALPH (Nov.) 1973 [son of St. George Richard Gore, son of Frederick Dundas Corbet Gore (*b.* 1853), brother of 9th Bt.].

Arms—Gules, a fesse argent between three cross-crosslets fitchée or. Crest—A wolf rampant argent, collared gules.
Residence—Wycanna, Talwood, Qld., 4322, Aust.

Sola salus servire Deo
To serve God is the only Salvation.

Sisters living—Annabel St. George, *b.* 1951.——Elizabeth St. George, *b.* 1952.——Juliet St. George, *b.* 1957.
Uncle living—NIGEL HUGH ST. GEORGE (Eurone, Goondiwindi, Qld.), *b.* Dec. 23rd, 1922: *m.* 1952, Beth Allison, da. of R. W. Hooper, of Allawah, Tambo, Qld., and has issue living, Seonaid Beth, *b.* 1955.
Aunts living—Phyllis Ruth St. George, *b.* 1912.——Margaretta Leonie St. George, *b.* 1921: *m.* 1958, John Henry Cory, of St. George, Qld., and has issue living, Alan Fitzroy, *b.* 1961,—Janet Ruth, *b.* 1959.
Daughter living of 11th Baronet—Maxine Marjorie St. George, *b.* 1947: *m.* 1968, Capt. Timothy Basil Edward Eugster, Irish Gds., of Deanlands, Vines Cross, Horam, Sussex, and has issue living, Maxmilian Brian Michael, *b.* 1969,—Alexandra Marcia Gabrielle, *b.* 1971,—Juliaf Clare Elizabeth, *b.* 1974.

Widows living of 10th, 11th and 12th Baronets—BEATRICE MILDRED (*Beatrice, Lady Gore*), da. of the late Com. the Hon. Conyngham Albert Denison, RN [see B. Londesborough], and widow of Lt.-Col. Algernon Corbet Turnor, MC, R. Horse Guards: *m.* 1943, as his second wife, Sir Ralph St. George Claude Gore, 10th baronet, who *d.* 1961. *Residence*, Eastgate House, Malmesbury, Wilts.——IRENE LAMONT (Old House, Willards Hill, Etchingham, Sussex), el. da. of Albert James Marshall, of Stranraer, Wigtownshire: *m.* 1st, 1971, as his 3rd wife, Lt.-Col. Sir Ralph St. George Brian Gore, 11th Bt., who *d.* June 1973; 2ndly, 1975, James Biggar.——SHIRLEY (*Lady Gore*), (Wycanna, Talwood, Qld. 4322), da. of C. Tabor, of Wauchope, NSW: *m.* 1950, Sir St. George Ralph Gore, 12th Bt., who *d.* Nov. 1973.

Collateral Branches living.

Grandchildren of the late Frederick Dundas Corbet Gore (*b.* 1853) (infra):—
Issue of the late Frederick Dundas Corbet Gore, *b.* 1885, *d.* 1964: *m.* 1919, Ella Maud, who *d.* 1967, da. of Charles Sydney Jones, of Brisbane:—
Dundas Corbet, *b.* 1921; ed. at Sydney Univ. (BEng); 1939-45 War as Flt.Lt. RAAF.——Hugh Frederick Corbet (7, Romney Rd., St. Ives, NSW) *b.* 1934: *m.* 1963, Jennifer Mary, el. da. of Milton Gordon Copp, of Rose Bay, NSW, and has issue living, Penelope Mary Corbet, *b.* 1965,—Virginia Louise, *b.* 1967.——Rosemary Ella Corbet, *b.* 1920; 1939-45 War with AIF: *m.* 19—, Nicholas Adams, of Hambledon Sugar Mill, Cairns, Queensland.——Barbara Corbet, *b.* 1926.

Issue of the late Frederick Dundas Corbet Gore, brother of 9th baronet, *b.* 1853, *d.* 1921: *m.* 1881, Margaretta Stenhouse, who *d.* 1943, el. da. of Donald Gunn, formerly of Pikedale, Queensland :—
Emily Margaretta St. George, *b.* 1898. *Residence*,

Grandchildren of the late Francis Arthur Gore, el. son of the late Rev. William Francis Gore, yst. son of the late Rev. Thomas Gore, brother of 7th baronet:—
Issue of the late Francis William Baldock Gore, *b.* 1873, *d.* 1937 : *m.* 1920, Mary Isabel Kirsteen (now of Strawberry House, Church Road, Barnes, S.W.13.), da. of the late Francis Corbet-Singleton, formerly of Finchampstead, Berks :—
Francis St. John Corbet, *b.* 1921 ; ed. at Wellington Coll.; Capt. (retired) Roy. Northumberland Fusiliers ; European War 1939-45 : *m.* 1951, Priscilla Margaret, da. of Cecil Harmsworth King, of The Pavilion, Hampton Court, and has issue living, William Ralph St. John, *b.* 1956,—Catharine Harriet Cecilia, *b.* 1954. *Residence*, 21, Pelham Place, S.W.7.——Alan Charles Corbet, *b.* 1926 ; ed. at Wellington Coll. : *m.* 1953, Ann Sabine, da. of W. D. K. Thellusson, of Disley, Gloucestershire, and has issue living, Francis Charles Storar, *b.* 1957, —Thomas Corbet, *b.* 1960. *Residence*, Strawberry House, Church Road, Barnes, S.W.13.

Issue of the late Cyril Gerard Gore, *b.* 1876, *d.* 1954: *m.* 1911, Gladys Marie Howard, who *d.* 1974, da. of Allan A. Spowers, Surveyor-Gen. of Queensland:—
Francis Arthur, *b.* 1921 : *m.* 1947, Leonore, dau. of Leonard Lee, of Queensland, and has issue living, Simon Gerard, *b.* 1955,—Leonie Christine, *b.* 1948,—Amanda Leonore, *b.* 1954.——Nancy Emlyn (c/o Commercial Banking Co. of Sydney, Brisbane, Qld.), *b.* 1912: *m.* 1st 1937, Leslie Brierly Hirst, 10th Ghurka Rifles; 2ndly, 1942, Maj. John Lytton Bellamy, Indian Army; 3rdly, 1948, Alastair Roderick Holmes-Tarn, who *d.* 1967.——Leonie Frances, *b.* 1918: *m.* 1st, 1938, Hugh John Walsh; 2ndly, 1956, Shane Page, and has issue living, (by 1st marriage) Joanna Leonie, *b.* 1939: *m.* 1959, Mervyn Fitzhenry, of Shamrock, Jansenville, Cape Prov., S. Africa, and has issue living, William Hugh Shaun *b.* 1961, Brendan Mervyn *b.* 1964, Shamus Terence *b.* 1968, Bridgit Madeline *b.* 1963,—Emlyn Anna, *b.* 1942: *m.* 1960, John Thompson (c/o National Bank, Kulin 6365, W. Aust.), and has issue living, Simon Patrick *b.* 1963, Leonie Helen *b.* 1961.

Grandson of the late William Wyndham Gore (infra):—
Issue of the late Lt.-Col. Thomas Gerard Gore, DSO, OBE, *b.* 1907, *d.* 1965: *m.* 1933, Mrs. Barbara Young:—
Gerard Anthony St. George, *b.* 1936; ed. at Radley; late Lt. 60th Rifles, and Cyprus Police: *m.* 1957, Wendy, da. of Mrs. C. V. Rippon, of Umkomaas, Natal, and has issue living, Sean Ralph St. George, *b.* 1961,—Nicole Holly St. George, *b.* 1965.

Granddaughter of the late Lt.-Robert William Gore, RN (infra):—
Issue of the late William Wyndham Gore, *b.* 1884, *d.* 1957 : *m.* 1906, Martha (of 21, Tedworth Square, S.W.3), da. of Walter Lord, of Todmorden, Yorkshire :—
Margaret Wyndham, *MBE*, *b.* 1913; formerly Air Com. Transport Auxiliary; MBE (Civil) 1944. *Residence*, 21, Tedworth Sq., SW3.

Grandchildren living of the late Rev. William Francis Gore (ante) :—
Issue of the late Lieut. Robert William Gore, R.N., *b.* 1851, *d.* 1895: *m.* 1883, Ella, who *d.* 1949, da. of George Wyndham, formerly of Dalwood, Hunter River, N.S. Wales :—
St. George Arthur (8/200, Pacific Highway, Greenwich N, Sydney, NSW), *b.* 1886: *m.* 1st 1914, Muriel Mary, who *d.* 1954, da. of John Broughton, Surveyor-Gen. of NSW; 2ndly, 1954, Mildred Prudence, da. of the late Charles James Vyner, MRCVS, of London, and has issue living (by 1st m.), Thomas William St. George (Cardross, Vic., Aust.), *b.* 1915: *m.* 1948, Jane Nichols,

only da. of Samuel Bennett, of W. Aust., and widow of Lt. Donald Stewart Fletcher, RAA, and has issue living, Donald Stewart St. George *b.* 1952,—Patrick St. George (Homeleigh, O'Connell, NSW), *b.* 1921: *m.* 1948, Coralie May, da. of Mark Ruben Venn, of Tasmania, and has issue living, Robert Ralph St. George *b.* 1949, Jonothan Ian St. George *b.* 1953, Peter Simon St. George *b.* 1955.——Maud Gwendolen, *b.* 1888: *m.* 1911, Archibald Turnbull, and has issue living, Elizabeth Ella, *b.* 1912: *m.* 1934, Herbert Clinton Kennan, BVSc, of 29, Allenby Rd., Panmure, Auckland, NZ, and has issue living, Peter Perry (250, Dover Drive, Walnut Creek, Calif. 94598, USA) *b.* 1937; BSc, B.Com.; a Chartered Accountant: *m.* 1966, Genarina Reyes (and has issue living, Peter Timothy *b.* 1967, Charles Clinton *b.* 1973), Jill *b.* 1936,—James Archibald Francis, *DFM, b.* 1913; 1939-45 War with RAAF (DFM): *m.* 1940, Elsie Dorothy, da. of O. Watson, of Singleton, NSW, and has issue living, Bruce James Douglas *b.* 1945, Robyn Dorothy *b.* 1941, Diana Mary (twin) *b.* 1945, Sarha Virginia *b.* 1949,—Joan Winifred, *b.* 1915: *m.* 1948, Roderick Whitaker, of Nunton, Glen Innes, NSW, and has issue living, Elizabeth Wyndham Whitaker *b.* 1953, Caroline Margaret *b.* 1955.—Deirdre Margaret, *b.* 1919; 1939-45 War as Section Officer Women's Aust. AF: *m.* 1947, Clifford Frederick Bunce, and has issue living, Charles Clifford *b.* 1952, Victoria Turnbull *b.* 1950, Julia Elizabeth Brodie *b.* 1953. *Residence,* Meade St., Glen Innes, NSW.

Grandchildren of the late Gerard Ralph Gore, 4th son of the late Rev. William Francis Gore (ante):—
Issue of the late Phyllis Emlyn Gore, *b.* 18—, *d.* 1967: *m.* 1906, John Elworthy Trude, who *d.* 1952:—
John Gerard (125, Sherwood Rd., Toowong, Brisbane, Qld.), *b.* 1910; ed. at Sydney Univ. (B. Arch.); 1939-45 War as Maj. RAA: *m.* 1946, Joan Sidney Steddy, da. of the late William Sidney Page, and has issue living, John William, *b.* 1947,—David Dundas, *b.* 1949: *m.* 1973, Peta Jane, da. of James Alexander Atwill, of Qld.,—Sally, *b.* 1952.——Everil Mary (Oakwal, Bush St., Windsor, Brisbane, Qld.), *b.* 1908: *m.* 1935, George Owen Capper, who *d.* 1973, and has issue living, George Owen John (23, Packham Cres., Glen Waverley, Melbourne, Vic., Aust.), *b.* 1936: *m.* 1970, Margaret Julie, da. of Frederick Keith Warner, of Perth, W. Aust., and has issue living, Michael Owen John *b.* 1972, Georgina Margaret *b.* 1974,—Peter James Gerard (48, Queens Rd., Brisbane, Qld.), *b.* 1939: *m.* 1968, Margaretha Emmy Renate, da. of Alexander Johannes Rotteyeel, of Qld., and has issue living, Elizabeth Mary *b.* 1970, Katrina Bowvine *b.* 1972.

Grandson of the late Nathaniel Gore, son of the late Col. William Gore, M.P., grandson of 3rd Bt.:—
Issue of the late Brig.-Gen. Robert Clements Gore, C.B., C.M.G., *b.* 1867, *d.* (killed in action during 1914-18 War) 1918: *m.* 1899, Rachel Cecilia (who *d.* 1971, having *m.* 2ndly, 1921, Capt. Arthur Marsden, CBE, RN (ret.), who *d.* 1960), da. of Llewellyn Traherne Bassett Saunderson [E. Clonmell]:—
Adrian Clements, *DSO* (Horton Priory, Sellindge, Kent), *b.* 1900; ed. at Eton; Brig. (ret.) late Rifle Bde.; 1939-45 War in N. Africa and Italy (DSO and Bar); DSO 1943 (Bar 1945): *m.* 1972, Enid Aimée, da. of the late John Jameson Cairnes, and has issue living, Toby Clements, *b.* (Dec.) 1927; Maj. Rifle Bde.: *m.* 1959, I. Marian, yr. da. of Edward Macintosh, of Rebeg, Kirkhill, Inverness-shire, and has issue living, Fiona Marian *b.* 1960, Juliet Carolyn *b.* 1962, Tessa Jane *b.* 1968, Stephanie Serena *b.* 1969,—Dinah Priscilla, *b.* 1930: *m.* 1958, Maj. J. Richard S. Besly, Gren. Gds., and has issue living, Adrian Thomas *b.* 1963, Michael John *b.* 1966, Emma Belinda *b.* 1958, Lucinda Mary *b.* 1960, Sara-Jane Beatrice *b.* 1964,—Belinda Beatrice, *b.* 1940: *m.* 1970, Anthony Frederick Millbank, of Blind Knights, Layer de la Haye, Colchester [*see* Millbank, Bt., *cr.* 1882].

Descendants of the late Arthur Gore (2nd son of 1st baronet), who was *cr.* a *Baronet* 1662 [*see* E. Arran].

Sir Paul, or Poule, Gore, 1st Bt. Capt. of Horse (brother of Sir John Gore, Lord Mayor of London 1624, ancestor of Earl Temple of Stowe), was granted lands in co. Donegal in the reign of Elizabeth I which he designated Manor Gore. From his 2nd son Sir Arthur descended the Earls of Arran and from his 4th son Sir Francis, of Lissadill baronets (now Gore-Booth).
The 3rd baronet was a Privy Councillor and Custos Rotulorum of co. Limerick. The 4th baronet, a Privy Councillor, was M.P. for co. Donegal, Chancellor of the Exchequer, and afterwards Speaker of the House of Commons in Ireland. The 5th baronet sat as M.P. for co. Donegal; and the 6th baronet, a distinguished military officer, was, after representing Donegal co. in Parliament, created Baron Gore (1764), Viscount Belleisle (1768), and Earl of Ross (1771), and died without surviving male issue. Sir Ralph Gore, 10th baronet, was elected Commodore of Roy. Yacht Squadron 1947, Pres. of Yachting Assocn. 1945, and of Roy. Yachting Assocn. 1953.

Gore-Booth, see Booth.

GORING, Creation (E.) 1678 (with precedency of 1627), of Highden, Sussex.

Renascentur.
They will rise again.

Sir WILLIAM BURTON NIGEL GORING, 13th *Baronet* ; son of the late Major Frederick Yelverton Goring, 6th son of 11th baronet ; *b.* June 21st, 1933 ; *s.* his uncle, *Sir* FORSTER GURNEY, 1956 ; ed. at Wellington Coll. ; late Lieut. 1st Roy. Sussex Regt. : *m.* 1960, the Hon. Caroline Thellusson, el. da. of 8th Baron Rendlesham.

Arms—Argent, a chevron between three annulets gules. *Crest*—A lion rampant-guardant sable.
Residence—89, Cornwall Gardens, S.W.7.

Brother living—EDWARD YELVERTON COMBE, (Lee Farm Cottage, Free St., Bishops Waltham, Hants), *b.* June 20th, 1936; ed. at Wellington Coll.; Lt.-Cdr. RN: *m.* 1969, Daphne Christine Seller, and has issue living, Elizabeth Christine, *b.* 1970,—Joanna Margaret, *b.* 1972.

Mother living—Freda Margaret, da. of Nigel Ainsworth, of Woolbeding Glebe, Midhurst, Sussex : *m.* 1931, Major Frederick Yelverton Goring (ante), who *d.* 1938. *Residence*, Woolbeding Glebe, Midhurst, Sussex.

Collateral Branches living.

Issue of the late Craven Charles Goring, 3rd son of 11th baronet, *b.* 1881, *d.* 1952: *m.* 1908, Mary Elizabeth, da. of John Conlon, of Roscommon :—
Beryl Elizabeth (2, Clifton Av., Comberford Rd., Tamworth, Staffs), *b.* 19—: *m.* 1930, George Frederick Thawley, who *d.* 1958, and has issue living, Peter Frederick (2, Old Malmesbury Rd., Wootton Bassett, Wilts.), *b.* 1940: *m.* 1966, Christine Mary, da. of Charles Henry Jones Payne, and has issue living, Nicholas *b.* 1971, Lisa *b.* 1969.

Issue of the late Barry Yelverton Goring, brother of 11th baronet, *b.* 1851, *d.* 1929 : *m.* 1893, Marion Haslewood, who *d.* 1898, da. of Charles Pitt Pynsent, of Wellington, New Zealand :—
Barbara Yelverton (Glebe House, Upton Magna, Shrewsbury): *m.* 1922, Com. Francis John Lambert, DSC, RN, who *d.* 1969 [E. Westmorland, colls.], and has issue living, Eloise Marion Grace Georgina, *b.* 1926.

Grandchildren of the late Rev. John Goring, son of the late Charles Goring, M.P., 2nd son of 5th baronet:—
Issue of the late Charles Goring, *b.* 1862, *d.* 1924: *m.* 1906, Beatrice Gabrielle Mary, who *d.* 1970, da. of the late Rev. Arthur Osborne Alleyne, R. of St. Edmund's, Exeter:—
John, *CBE, TD, b.* 1907; ed. at Eton; a DL of Sussex; 2nd Lt. Coldstream Guards 1928-31, Sussex Yeo. (Lt. 1933, Capt. 1939) 1933-46, Maj. 21st Anti Tank Regt. RA, 1940-45, Comdg. Norfolk Yeo. 1945 (despatches twice); Co. Councillor of W. Sussex 1946-52; a Member of W. Sussex Agric. Executive Cttee. 1947 (Chm. 1949-67); a Chevalier of Order of Crown with Palm of Belgium, and Croix de Guerre with Palm of Belgium; CBE (Civil) 1964: *m.* 1947, Lady Hersey Margaret, da. of 8th Earl of Glasgow, and widow of Cdr. the Hon. John Montagu Granville Waldegrave, DSC, RN [*see* By. Radstock, ext.], and has issue living, Richard Harry (Lower Chancton, Wiston, Steyning, Sussex), *b.* 1949: *m.* 1972, Penelope Ann, da. of J. K. Broadbent, of Van Rheede, Wynberg, Cape Town, and has issue living, Eloise Isabella, *b.* 1974, Catherine Clare *b.* 1975,—John James, *b.* 1953,—Corinna Jane, *b.* 1948: *m.* 1969, Nigel Vere Nicoll [*see* Madden, Bt., colls.],—Anne Elizabeth, *b.* 1951. *Residence,* Findon Park House, Findon, Sussex.
——Isabel (*Lady Dundas*) *b.* 1909: *m.* 1933, Maj. Sir Thomas Calderwood Dundas, MBE, 7th Bt. [*cr.* 1898], who *d.* 1970, when the title became ext. *Residence,* Field Gate, Ditching, Sussex.

Issue of the late Major Alan Goring, *b.* 1873, *d.* 1945 : *m.* 1901, Violet Isabel, who *d.* 1945, da. of the late Col. Gerald Charles Penrice Onslow [Onslow, Bt., colls.] :—
Harold, *b.* 1903; ed. at Cheltenham; Lt.-Col. Indian Army (ret.); formerly Lt. Roy. Sussex Regt.; 1939-45 War: *m.* 1929, Mary Frances Eleanor (Kaisar-i-Hind medal), who *d.* 1975, da. of the late Capt. Hamilton Augustus Woodruffe, of Garsington, Oxon, and has issue living, Brian, *b.* 1935: ed. at Cheltenham; Maj. R. Sussex Regt.: *m.* 1958, Prudence Mary, da. of George Baker, of Dickhurst, Lurgashall, Sussex, and has issue living, Alice Lucinda *b.* 1959, Sya Charlotte *b.* 1964, Lydia Mary *b.* 1965,—George, *b.* 1937; ed. at Cheltenham; Maj. Queens' Regt.: *m.* 1969, Nicola Jean, da. of William Ian Gordon, of Skeldon Estate, Berbice, Guyana, and has issue living, Michael, *b.* 1974, Fiona Mary *b.* 1972. *Residence,* Holland House, Warnham, Sussex.——Arthur, *b.* 1907; ed. at Cheltenham; Lt.-Col. Indian Cav. (ret.); Assist. Commr.-in-Ch., St. John Ambulance 1957-72; KStJ; NW Frontier of India 1936-39; 1939-45 War (despatches); has Order of Cloud and Banner of China. *Residence,* 2, Briardale Gdns., Hampstead, NW3. *Club,* Army and Navy.

Henry Goring, of Highden, Sussex, succeeded Feb. 1679-80 as 2nd Bt. (by virtue of the special remainder in the patent of 1678), Sir James Bowyer, 3rd Bt., of Leighthorne, Sussex (younger son of Sir Thomas Bowyer, cr. a baronet July 23rd, 1627), surrendered by fine his patent, and was granted a new patent dated May 18th, 1678, for life with remainder after his death to Henry Goring, of Highden, Sussex (ante), and the heirs male of his body, with precedence of the former patent of July 23rd, 1627. The Goring family is of great antiquity in Sussex, and John Goring was M.P. for Sussex 1467. A member of the family was created Baron Goring 1628, and Earl of Norwich 1644, titles that became extinct on the death of the 2nd Earl (cr. 1644) in March 1672. The 2nd baronet was M.P. for Sussex 1660, for Steyning 1661-79, and again for Sussex 1685-7; the 4th baronet, Col. 31st Foot, was M.P. for Horsham 1707-8, Steyning 1708-15, and again for Horsham 1715, and the 6th baronet was M.P. for Shoreham 1790-6; the 7th baronet was High Sheriff of Sussex, 1827, and the 8th baronet sat as M.P. for Shoreham 1832-41. The 12th baronet, Sir Forster Gurney Goring, was appointed a Capt. of Invalids, Roy. Hospital, Chelsea 1912.

GOSCHEN, Creation (U.K.) 191, of Beacon Lodge, Highcliffe, co. Southampton.

For peace.

Sir EDWARD CHRISTIAN GOSCHEN, *D.S.O.*, 3rd *Baronet ; b.* Sept. 2nd, 1913 ; *s.* his father, *Sir* EDWARD HENRY, 1933 ; ed. at Eton, and at Trin. Coll., Oxford ; European War 1939-45 in Italy as Major Tower Hamlets Rifles, Rifle Brig. (T.A.) (D.S.O.) ; D.S.O. 1944: *m.* 1946, Cynthia, da. of the late Rt. Hon. Sir Alexander George Montagu Cadogan, OM, GCMG, KCB [*see* E. Cadogan, colls.], and has issue.

Arms—Argent, a human heart gules flamant and transfixed by an arrow bendwise point upwards proper. **Crest**—Upon an arrow fessewise the point to the dexter a dove wings endorsed, all proper. *Residence*—Jesmond Hill, Pangbourne, Berks.

Son living—EDWARD ALEXANDER, *b.* March 13th, 1949; ed. at Eton.
Daughter living—Caroline Clare, *b.* 1950.

Sisters living—Dorothy Jean, *b.* 1909 : *m.* 1936, Col. Hugo Meynell, M.C., who *d.* 1960 [*see* V. Halifax, colls.]. *Residence,* Hollybush Park, Newborough, Burton-on-Trent.——Joyce Clara, *b.* 1912 : *m.* 1942, Paymaster-Lieut.-Com. Francis Charles Sackville Tufton, R.N.V.R. [*see* B. Hothfield, colls.]. *Residence,* Crowbury, Watton-at-Stone, Herts.

Collateral Branch living.
Issue of the late George Gerard Goschen, younger son of 1st baronet, *b.* 1887, *d.* 1953: *m.* 1930, Vivienne, who *d.* 1957, da. of the late Bernard de Watteville:—
David Bernard (Ilsington Farmhouse, Puddletown, Dorset), *b.* 1931: *m.* 1954, Angela, only da. of James Macnabb, and has issue living, Sébastien Bernard, *b.* 1959,—Orlando Amadeus, *b.* 1960,—

Chrysoula Angela, *b.* 1955,—Mariora Vivienne, *b.* 1957.——Tana Mary, *b.* 1932: *m.* 1962, John Alais Fletcher, and has issue living, Mark Alais, *b.* 1963,—Miranda Clare, *b.* 1964,—Katherine Alice, *b.* 1966,—Alexandra Sophia, *b.* 1970. *Residence*, Dolphin Cottage, Altwood Rd., Maidenhead.

The 1st baronet, the Rt. Hon. Sir (William) Edward Goschen, G.C.B., G.C.M.G., G.C.V.O., was Envoy Extraor. and Min. Plen. at Belgrade and Copenhagen 1898-1905, Ambassador Extraor. and Min. Plen. at Vienna and Berlin 1905-14, and Gentleman Usher to the Sword of State 1919-24. Sir Edward Henry Goschen, 2nd Bt., was sometime Controller of Secretariat, Egyptian Min. of Finance.

Gough (Anstruther-Gough-Calthorpe), see Calthorpe.

GOULDING, Creation (U.K.) 1904, of Millicent, Clane, co. Kildare, and Roebuck Hill, Dundrum, co. Dublin.
[Name pronounced "**Goolding**."]

VIRTUTE·ET·VALORE

By virtue and valour.

Sir WILLIAM BASIL GOULDING, 3rd *Baronet; b.* Nov. 4th, 1909; *s.* his father, *Sir* (WILLIAM) LINGARD AMPHLETT, 1935; ed. at Winchester, and at Oxford Univ.; Chm. of Fitzwilton Ltd., a Dir. of Bank of Ireland Ltd., of Rio Tinto Zinc Corporation, and of other Cos.; European War 1939-45 as Wing-Com. RAF Vol. Reserve: *m.* 1939, the Hon. Valerie Hamilton Monckton, only da. of 1st Viscount Monckton of Brenchley, and has issue.

Arms—Per bend or and argent, a gryphon segreant within an orle of martlets sable. Crest—A dexter hand apaumée and couped at the wrist, encircled with a chaplet of oak leaves bendwise, and transfixed with an arrow bend sinisterwise, all proper. *Seat*—Ballyrusheen, co. Cork. *Residence*—Dargle Cottage, Enniskerry, co. Wicklow.

Sons living—WILLIAM LINGARD WALTER, *b.* July 11th, 1940; ed. at Winchester, and Trin. Coll., Dublin.—Timothy Adam, *b.* 1945; ed. at Winchester: *m.* 1971, Patricia Mohan, of Dublin.——Hamilton Paddy, *b.* 1947; ed. at Winchester, and Trin. Coll., Dublin; 2nd Officer BEA: *m.* 1970, Yvonne Denise, el. da. of S. V. Holmes Thompson, of Tir-Owen, Viewfort Park, Dunmurry, co. Antrim.

Brother living—Ossian, (of Rafters, E. Chiltington, nr. Lewes, Sussex), *b.* 1913: *m.* 1st 1936 (marriage dissolved 1943), Felice Marteil, of Montreal, Canada; 2ndly, 1943 (marriage dissolved 1962), Yasu Elisabeth Katherine, da. of Lennart Tham, of Husqvarna, Sweden; 3rdly, 1962, Margaret Angela, da. of the late Frank Chadwick, of Eastbourne, Sussex, and has issue living, (by 1st m.) Lynn *b.* 1937: *m.* 1st, 1958, Richard Edgeson Cathcart, Lt. RN; 2ndly, 1966, Ken Irwin—(by 2nd m.) Richard George Michael, *b.* 1951,—Carola Nesta Katherine, *b.* 1946,—Sara Elizabeth Louise, *b.* 1947.

Aunts living (daughters of 1st baronet)—Ada Gladys: *m.* 1915, Capt. Kenneth Blair Harbord, formerly RHA, who *d.* 1959, and has issue living, Tonita Maureen (c/o Glyn, Mills & Co., Whitehall, SW1), *b.* 1916: *m.* 1945, Hugo Cra'ster Wakeford Ironside, Brig. (ret.) late RTR, of Redbridge House, Moreton, Dorset, and has issue living, Nigel Hugo Wakeford *b.* 1947, Jacolyn Tonita *b.* 1949. *Residence*, Cloneen, Curragh, co. Kildare.—— Kathleen: *m.* 1912, Capt. Maurice Falkine Dennis, formerly Seaforth Highlanders, who *d.* 1960. *Residence*, Batlyngmede, Cannon Hill, Maidenhead.

GRAAFF, Creation (U.K.) 1911, of Cape Town, Cape of Good Hope Province of Union of South Africa.

JUSTIS·CREATOR·FAVET

The Creator favours the just.

Sir DE VILLIERS GRAAFF, *M.B.E.*, 2nd *Baronet; b.* Dec. 8th, 1913; *s.* his father, SIR DAVID PIETER DE VILLIERS, 1931; ed. at Cape Town Univ. (B.A. 1932), and at Magdalen Coll., Oxford (B.A. 1935, M.A. 1944); B.C.L. 1936; Bar. Inner Temple 1937; Advocate of Supreme Court of S. Africa 1938; has been a Member of House of Assembly of Union of S. Africa since 1948; elected Leader of United Party 1956; European War 1939-45 with S. African Defence Force (prisoner, M.B.E.); M.B.E. (Mil.) 1946: *m.* 1939, Helena le Roux, da. of Frederick Carel Marthinus Voigt, of Claremont, Cape Province, S. Africa, and has issue.

Arms—Argent, a Paschal Lamb proper, on a chief azure five stars of the first (representing the constellation of the Southern Cross). Crest—In front of three spades erect

in pale, a dexter arm embowed in armour, the hand holding a scimitar, all proper. **Supporters**—*Dexter*, a Boer farmer supporting with the exterior hand a rifle *sinister*, a Cape miner supporting with the exterior hand a pickaxe, both proper.
Seat—De Grendel, Tÿgerberg, near Cape Town, S. Africa.

Sons living—DAVID DE VILLIERS, *b.* May 3rd, 1940; ed. at Diocesan Coll., S. Africa, Stellenbosch Univ. (BSc Agric.), Grenoble Univ., and Magdalen Coll., Oxford (BA).——Johann Frederick de Villiers, *b.* 1946.

Daughter living—Geneé de Villiers, *b.* 1948.

Brother living—Johannes de Villiers, *b.* 1928; ed. at Cape Town Univ., and at St. John's Coll., Camb. (Fellow 1951): *m.* 1951, Lilian Clare, da. of Sir George Paget Thomson, and has issue living, Pieter Johannes, *b.* 1958,—Janet Kathleen, *b.* 1954,—Teresa Clare, *b.* 1955,—Anna Louise (twin), *b.* 1955,—Monica Suzanne, *b.* 1960,—Linda Elaine, *b.* 1966. *Residence*, Morgenrood Rd., Kenilworth, Cape Province, S. Africa.

The 1st baronet, the Hon. Sir David Pieter de Villiers Graaff, was Mayor of Cape Town 1891-2, Min. without portfolio, Cape Colony 1908-10, Min. of Public Works, Posts, and Telegraphs of Union of South Africa 1910-12, again Min. without portfolio 1912-3, and Min. of Finance 1915-6; acted as High Commr. for S. Africa in London 1914.

GRACE, Creation (G.B.) 1795, of Minchenden House, co. Middlesex.

My deeds agree with my name.

Sir RAYMOND EUSTACE GRACE, 6th *Baronet*; *b.* Jan. 6th, 1903; *s.* his father, *Sir* VALENTINE RAYMOND, 1945; ed. at Downside, and at Trin. Coll., Dublin; late Maj. R. Inniskilling Fusiliers: *m.* 1st, 1930 (m. dissolved 1935), Anita Elizabeth Othwell Ash, da. of Percival David William Campbell Gaussen, K.C., of Shanemullagh House, co. Londonderry; 2ndly, 1940, Molly Rosamond Evelyn, who *d.* 1942, da. of the late Maj.-Gen. Robert St. Clair Lecky, CB, CMG, of Ballykealey, co. Carlow; 3rdly, 1946, Evelyn, da. of the late William Schomberg Henchie, of Dublin.

Arms—Gules, a lion rampant per fesse argent and or. **Crest**—A demi-lion rampant as in the arms.
Residence—13, Leeson Park, Dublin.

Sisters living—Aileen Mary Violet, *b.* 1901: *m.* 1st, 1933, William Bruce Hamilton, MB, BCh, Capt. RAMC, who *d.* 1947; 2ndly, 1954, Louis Zeyfert, of 7, Lovell Rd., Cranbourne Village, Windsor Forest, Berks., and has issue living (by 1st m.), Edward Bruce (Kalafat House, Sorrento Rd., Dalkey, co. Dublin), *b.* 1937; BA Dublin: *m.* 1960, Daphne Theodora, BA, da. of Judge Ian Rawdon Green, of Malindi, Rocky Valley, co. Wicklow, and has issue living, Michael Raymond Maurice Bruce *b.* 1960, David Edward Louis *b.* 1964, Christopher Ian Bruce *b.* 1967, Venetia Eileen *b.* 1963,—Patricia Margaret Anna, *b.* 1939: *m.* 1960, Fl.-Lt. Rex Hamilton-Turley, RAF (ret.), of 4, Collemore Rd., Dalkey, co. Dublin, and has issue living, Myles Konrad *b.* 1961, Simon Marcus *b.* 1964, Hereward Christopher Rex *b.* 1967, Lucy Grace *b.* 1963, Ingrid Daphne Mary *b.* 1966.——Kathleen Frances Marguerite (40, Weir View Drive, Dublin), *b.* 1904.——Pansy Rita Henrietta (Cherryhill, Kilmaconogue, Bray, co. Wicklow), *b.* 1907: *m.* 1940, Frederick Robert Hill who *d.* 1955, and has issue living, John Frederick Raymond (Bellerive 217, Zürich 8008, Switzerland), *b.* 1943: *m.* 1968, Ann Marie, da. of Zefferimo Battazzi, and has issue living, Finn *b.* 1970,—Vanessa Kathleen Mary (1, Yard Cottage, The Willows, Maidenhead Rd., Windsor, Berks.), *b.* 1941: *m.* 1969 (m. diss. 1974), Allen Newton Hill, and has issue living, Jane Mechelle *b.* 1971.——Mary Lilian, *b.* 1912: *m.* 1st, 1930 (m. diss. 1969), Maj. Paul McConnell, Ches. Regt. (ret.); 2ndly, 1969, Lt.-Col. Clive O'Neill Wallis (ret.) E. Surreys, of Old Brookside House, Winkfield Rd., N. Ascot, Berks.

Collateral Branch living

Granddaughter of the late Col. Sheffield Hamilton-Grace (nephew of 2nd baronet):—
Issue of the late Major Raymond Sheffield Hamilton-Grace, *b.* 1881, *d.* (killed in action) 1915: *m.* 1912, Gladys, *C.B.E.* [(now of Knowle, Frant, near Tunbridge Wells) ; she *m.* andly, 1919, Col. Joseph Benskin, D.S.O., O.B.E., who *d.* 1953], da. of Michael Paul Grace, of 40, Belgrave Square, S.W.:—
Anne Veronica, *b.* 1914 ; European War 1939-45 as Flight Officer W.A.A.F. (despatches) : *m.* 1948, Com. William Francis Roderick Segrave, DSC, RN (ret.), who *d.* 1974, and has issue living, Nicholas John Paul, *b.* 1953,—Roderick Alan Neil, *b.* 1956,—Elisa Mary, *b.* 1949. *Residence*, Isfield Place, Isfield, near Uckfield, Sussex.

This is one of the oldest Anglo-Norman families that settled in Ireland. Sir Richard Grace, who sat for twenty years as MP for Winchester was cr. a Bt. with remainder to Richard Grace of Boley, Queen's Co. (gt. grandson of Oliver Grace of Gracefield, Queen's Co., his father's el. brother). As Richard Grace, *d.* 1801 before the 1st Bt., his el. son, Sir William, *s.* as 2nd Bt. in 1818. The 5th baronet, Sir Valentine Raymond, was a DL for Queen's Co. (High Sheriff 1907).

GRAHAM, Creation (E.) 1629, of Esk, Cumberland.

Sir MONTROSE STUART GRAHAM, 12th
Baronet; b. Aug. 4th, 1904; *s.* his father, *Sir*
MONTROSE STUART, 1939: *m.* 1932, Elizabeth
Ann, da. of John Gerken, and has issue.

Arms—Quarterly: 1st and 4th, or, on a chief sable three
escallops of the first, *Graham;* 2nd and 3rd, or, a fesse
checky argent and azure in chief a chevron gules, *Stuart.*
Crest—Two wings addorsed or.
Residence—45, Aster Avenue, North Merrick, Long
Island. New York, U.S.A.

Daughters living—Lynne Elizabeth, *b.*1937:*m.*1959,Robert
Jager, of 110, Elward Av., West Islip, Long Island,
New York, and has issue living, Marie Lynne, *b.* 1960,—
Cindy Kay, *b.* 1961.——Dana Stuart, *b.* 1940: *m.* 1961,
Robert Brust, of 2501, Rutler St., Bellmore, Long
Island, New York, and has issue living, Robert George,
b. 1961,—William Edward, *b.* 1965,—Elizabeth Lynne,
b. 1971.

Sister living—Jessie Louise, *b.* 1907: *m.* 1936, Robert
S. Bolton, who *d.* 1944. *Residence,* 185, Marine Avenue,
Brooklyn 9, New York, U.S.A.

Collateral Branches living

Issue of the late Percival Harris
Graham, 2nd son of 10th baronet,
b. 1877, *d.* 1954: *m.* 1901, Louise,
who *d.* 1934, da. of John Wolfe, of
Brooklyn, USA:—
RALPH WOLFE (134, Leisureville Blvd., Boynton
Beach, Fla., 33435, USA), *b.* July 14th, 1908: *m.* 1st,
1939 (m. diss. 1949), Gertrude, da. of Charles Kaminski, of Brooklyn, New York, USA; 2ndly,
1949, Geraldine, da. of Austin Velour, of Brooklyn, New York, USA, and has issue living, (by
2nd m.) Ralph Stuart, *b.* 1950; *m.* 1972, Roxanne, da. of Mrs. Lovette Gurzan, of Elmont, Long
Island, NY,—Robert Bruce Graham, *b.* 1953: *m.* 1974, Denise, da. of T. Jurnarich, of Floral
Park, Long Island, NY.

Issue of the late Robert Vernon Graham, 3rd son of 10th baronet, *b.* 1883, *d.* 1943:
m. 1904, Charlotte Elizabeth, who *d.* 1938, da. of the late Gilbert Baldwin Smith
of Brooklyn, U.S.A.:—
Douglas Duncan, *b.* 1912; formerly in USA Navy: *m.* 1st, 1937 (m. diss. 1948), Harriet, da. of
Thomas Lloyd, of Brooklyn, USA; 2ndly, 1948, Sally, da. of Thomas Gale, of Southampton,
Long Island, USA, and has issue living, (by 1st m.) Harriet Mable, *b.* 1938,—(by 2nd m.) James
Robert, *b.* 1952,—Roland, *b.* 1954,—Brenda Gale, *b.* 1949. *Residence,* 1428, Bellmore Av.,
Bellmore, New York, USA.—Violet Beatrice, *b.* 1905: *m.* 1929, Leonard S. Higgs, of 53,
Willard Circle, Islington, Mass. USA, and has issue living, Ralph Leonard (Wheeling Ill.,
USA), *b.* 1932: *m.* 1953 Megan Williams and has issue living, Jeffrey Wayne *b.* 1957, Janet
b. 1960,—Phyllis Jane, *b.* 1938: *m.* 1957, Edward Thomas, of Belchertown, Mass., USA, and has
issue living, Edward Leonard *b.* 1958, Christopher Michael *b.* 1972, Sharon Lisbeth *b.* 1960, Lisa
Anne *b.* 1961, Lauren Lynne *b.* 1962.——Mildred Jane Elizabeth, *b.* 1916: *m.* 1st, 1942 (m. diss.
1953) William E. Young, RM; 2ndly, 1965, F. W. Rementer, of 829, Spruce St., Collingdale,
Pa. 19023, USA, and has issue living (by 1st m.), William Ernest, *b.* 1944; formerly US Navy.

Granddaughters of the late Robert Vernon Graham (ante):—
Issue of the late James Robert Stuart Graham, *b.* 1907, *d.* 1960: *m.* 1929, Agnes, da. of
the late Dennis Harvey, of Brooklyn, U.S.A.:—
Roberta Naomi, *b.* 1930: *m.* 1957, James Joseph Munson, of 226, Beach 119th St., Rockaway
Park, New York, USA, and has issue living, James, *b.* 1958,—John, *b.* 1959,—Joseph, *b.* 1964,—
Marilyn, *b.* 1963.——Joan Charlotte, *b.* 1933: *m.* 1958, Herbert John Nicol, of Merrick, NY,
USA, and has issue living, Robert, *b.* 1959,—Catherine, *b.* 1962,—Linda, *b.* 1967.

Issue of the late Howard George William Graham, *b.* 1910, *d.* 1957: *m.* 1938, Madelyn.
da. of Joseph Fitzsimmons, of Archbold, Pennsylvania, U.S.A.:—
Charlotte Elizabeth, *b.* 1940: *m.* 1960, Daniel Coladi, of Rockville, Maryland, USA, and has
issue living, Robert, *b.* 1961,—Kenneth, *b.* 1963,—Andrew, *b.* 1965.

Issue of the late George Edward Graham, yst. son of 10th baronet, *b.* 1890,
d. 1969: *m.* 1912, Florence Ethel (Sky View Acres, RD1, Pomona, N.Y. 10970,
USA), da. of the late George Alfred Milne, of Brooklyn, New York:—
George Edward (329, Benton St., Orlando, Fla. 32809, USA), *b.* 1920; Lt.-Col. USAF: *m.* 1945,
Jean Myra MacRury, and has issue living, Stuart George, *b.* 1949,—Leslie Jean, *b.* 1951.——
Dorothy, *b.* 1917: *m.* 1938, Ralph Alfred Hassler, and has issue living, Donald Evan, *b.* 1950,—
Laura Jean, *b.* 1948,—Judith Ann, *b.* 1953.

Issue of the late Edward Charles Graham, 2nd son of 9th baronet, *b.* 1850, *d.* 1913:
m. 1st, 1879, Sarah Frances Swartz, who *d.* 1881; 2ndly, 1894, Ida van
Swearengen, who *d.* 1927 (having *m.* 2ndly, 19—, — Kennedy):—
(By 1st m.) Ada Ellen, *b.* 1880: *m.* 1901, Harry C. Lester, who *d.* 1946.——(By 2nd m.) Donald
Bruce (130, E. 9th St., N. Canton, Ohio 44720, USA), *b.* 1898; 1917-19 War in France as Machine
Gun Sergeant (wounded, Purple Heart, Silver Star, Divisional and Presidential Citation): *m.* 1st,
1919 (m. diss. 1936), Pearl Marie Brownewell; 2ndly, 1941, Gertrude Lysle, da. of Thomas M.
Cowie.

Granddaughters of the late Maj.-Gen. Stuart Frederick Graham (infra):—
Issue of the late Lieut.-Col. Frederick Graham, *b.* 1849, *d.* 1914: *m.* 1877, Charlotte Barbara
Roche, who *d.* 1940, da. of Capt. Edward Joseph Thackwell, 3rd King's Light Dragoons :—
Gladys Eupheme Stuart, *b.* 1884: *m.* 1915, Harold E. Hutteroth, and has issue living,
Charlotte Mary Stuart, *b.* 1923.——Vera Patricia Stuart, *b.* 1888; formerly Junior Com. A.T.S.
Residence, Esk, Princess Street, Burnham-on-Sea, Somerset.

Granddaughter of the late Lieut.-Col. Frederick Graham (ante):—
Issue of the late Stuart Menteith Graham, *b.* 1886, *d.* 1957: *m.* 1919, Leonoré (Mollie),
da. of the late Capt. W. Morrish, Rifle Brig.:—
Marjorie Barbara Stuart, *b.* 1921: *m.* 1963, David Sherwin Walker, of 13315-129 St., Edmonton,
Alberta, Canada.

**Grandchildren of the late Maj.-Gen. Stuart Frederick Graham, 5th son of 8th
baronet :—**
Issue of the late Major William Bannatyne Graham, *b.* 1858, *a.* 1897 : *m.* 1884, Mary Beatrice,
who *d.* 1941, da. of the late Rev. E. H. Hansell, R. of East Ilsley, Berks :—
Edward William Harold, *b.* 1888; formerly in Eastern Extension Telegraph Co., Cocos Keeling
Islands; European War 1916-18 in Italy. *Residence,* Maison du Coin, St. Brelade, Jersey.——

Stuart Douglas, *M.C.*, *b.* 1890; Brigadier (ret.) late R.A.; is a Jurat of Roy. Court, Jersey; European War 1914-18 in Salonika and France (despatches twice, M.C.), European War 1939-45 (wounded): *m.* 1916, Marjorie Helen , el. da. of H. Le Maistre. *Residence,* Maison du Coin, St. Brelade, Jersey.——Mary Dorothy: *m.* 1916, Wilfrid Saunders, formerly India Education Dept. *Residence,* Trinity House, Hazelbury Bryan, Dorset.

Issue of the late Malcolm Macleod Graham, *b.* 1872, *d.* 19— : *m.* 1896, Leopoldine (now of Buenos Aires, Argentine Republic), da. of Mark Gallacher, of Rosario, Argentine Republic:—
Richard Walter Malcolm, *b.* 1903: *m.* 19—.——Oswald Charles, *b.* 1906.——Agnes Beatrice, *b.* 1897: *m.* 19—, Jack Maclaughlin.

Descendants of the late James Graham (2nd son of the late Rev. Robert Graham, D.D., 2nd son of the late Very Rev. William Graham, D.D., 3rd son of 2nd baronet), who was cr. a *Baronet* 1783:—
See Graham, Bt. cr. 1783.

Grandchildren of the late Major Fergus Graham, son of the late Rev. William Paley Graham, son of the late Rev. Fergus Graham, LL.D., 4th son of the late Rev. Robert Graham (ante) :—
Issue of the late Col. Fergus Reginald Winsford Graham, D.S.O., M.C., *b.* 1884, *d.* 1961: *m.* 1915, Egeria Marion Spottiswood, who *d.* 1973, da. of Vice-Adm. Casper Joseph Baker, formerly of Oaklands, Petherton, Somerset:—
Dominick Stuart, *MC, b.* 1920; Maj. (ret.) RA; PhD; Associate Prof. of History, Univ. of New Brunswick; 1939-45 War (wounded twice, despatches, MC): *m.* 1947, Valerie Mary, da. of the late Farleigh H. Greig, of Fleet, Hants, and has issue living, Anita Caroline, *b.* 1949,—Patricia Robin, *b.* 1952. *Residence,* University of New Brunswick, Canada.——Caroline Egeria Malise, *b.* 1929: *m.* 1952, Maj. Thomas Wemyss Muir, Queen's Dragoon Guards, and has issue living, James Fergus Wemyss, *b.* 1963,—Elizabeth Anne, *b.* 1955,—Sarah Jane, *b.* 1957,—Alexandra Caroline, *b.* 1959. *Residence,* Torquhan, Stow, Midlothian.

The 1st baronet, Sir Richard Graham (son of the late Fergus Graham), was Gentleman of the Horse to Charles I., and distinguished himself at the battle of Edgehill. The 3rd baronet, Sir Richard, was cr. *Viscount Preston* (peerage of Scotland) 1680, was British Ambassador to France, and sometime a Sec. of State to James II. ; after the Revolution he was condemned for high treason, but subsequently pardoned. The Baronetcy remained merged in the Viscountcy until the death of the 3rd Viscount in 1739, when it devolved upon his kinsman, the Rev. Sir William, 6th Bt.

GRAHAM, Creation (E.) 1662, of Norton Conyers, Yorkshire.

Sir RICHARD BELLINGHAM GRAHAM, *O.B.E.*, 10th *Baronet; b.* May 17th, 1912 ; *s.* his father, *Major Sir* (REGINALD) GUY, *D.S.O.*, 1940; ed. at Eton, and at Magdalene Coll., Camb.; formerly Wing-Com. R.A.F. Vol. Reserve ; is a J.P. and D.L. for N. Riding of Yorkshire; High Sheriff of Yorkshire 1961; European War 1939-45 (despatches thrice, O.B.E.) ; O.B.E. (Mil.) 1946 : *m.* 1939, Beatrice Mary, only da. of the late Lieut.-Col. Michael Seymour Hamilton-Spencer-Smith, D.S.O., M.C. [*see* Hamilton-Spencer-Smith, Bt., colls.], and has issue.

Arms—Quarterly : 1st and 4th or, on a chief sable three escallops of the field, *Graham* ; 2nd and 3rd, or, a fesse checky argent and azure in chief a chevronel gules, *Stuart* ; in the centre of the quarters a crescent of the last ; all within a border engrailed of the third. *Crest*—Two wings addorsed or.

Seat—Norton Conyers, Melmerby, near Ripon.

Sons living—JAMES BELLINGHAM, *b.* Oct. 8th, 1940.——William Reginald, *b.* 1942.——Jeremy Richard, *b.* 1949: *m.* 1976, Judith E. A. L., da. of G. L. McCann, of West Lodge, Newton-le-Willows, Bedale, Yorks.
Brothers living—Alastair, *M.C., b.* 1915; ed. at Eton; Major (ret.) Roy. Dragoons; European War 1939-45 (M.C.): *m.* 1942, Gundreda Margaret, da. of the late J. L. Graham Jones, M.B., of Bockhampton House, Dorchester, Dorset, and has issue living, Patrick Martin, *b.* 1948: *m.* 1972, Fiona, da. of Maj. K. Leslie F. Forshaw-Wilson,—Caroline Susan, *b.* 1943,—Priscilla Ann (twin), *b.* 1948: *m.* 1968, Peter Norman Bingham Kennedy, of Doonholm, Ayr, and has issue living, Sara Margaret *b.* 1971, Annabel Deborah *b.* 1973.——Jeremy Frank, *b.* 1926: *m.* 1950, Susan Mary, *JP,* da. of Col. Thomas Eustace Smith, of Barton Hall, Darlington, and has issue living, Robin Guy, *b.* 1953,—Nigel Ronald, *b.* 1957,—Elizabeth Jacoba, *b.* 1951: *m.* 1971, Capt. Christopher Russell Oldham, R. Hussars (ret.), of 78, Paxton Rd., W4 2QX, and has issue living, Justin Russell *b.* 1974. *Residence,* Plaster Pitts, Ripon, Yorks.
Residence, The Old House, Middleton Quernhow, Ripon. *Club,* Cavalry.

The 1st baronet of Norton Conyers, received his baronetcy from Charles II, 1662, for services rendered to the Royal cause during the Civil Wars. He was the 2nd son of Sir Richard Graham, 1st Bt. (cr. 1629), of Esk, a distinguished Royalist and Gentleman of the Horse to King James I, and fought at Edgehill and Marston Moor. The 9th Bt., Major Sir (Reginald) Guy, D.S.O., served in S. Africa 1899-1902 and in European War 1914-19 (D.S.O.).

GRAHAM, Creation (G.B.) 1783, of Netherby, Cumberland.

Sir (FREDERICK) FERGUS GRAHAM, *K.B.E., T.D.,* 5th *Baronet; b.* March 10th, 1893 ; *s.* his father, *Sir* RICHARD JAMES, 1932 ; ed. at Eton, and at Ch. Ch., Oxford (MA); formerly Capt. Irish Guards (Special Reserve); Lt.-Col. late 6th Bn. Border Regt (TA), a JP and DL for Cumberland, and patron of two livings; Lord Lieut. of Cumberland 1958-68; Hon. Col. 4th Batn. Border Regt. 1951-56; 1914-18 War (wounded, despatches); appointed P.P.S. to Min. of Pensions March 1933, and to Postmaster-Gen. June 1935; MP for Cumberland, N. Div. (C) 1926-35, and for Darlington 1951-59; KBE (Civil) 1956: *m.* 1918, Mary Spencer Revell, *CBE,* da. of the late Maj.-Gen. Raymond Northland Revell Reade, CB, CMG [V. Churchill, colls.], and has issue.

Arms—Quarterly : 1st and 4th or, on a chief sable three escallops of the field, *Graham*; 2nd and 3rd or, a fesse checky argent and azure in chief a chevronel gules, *Stuart*; in the centre of the quarters a crescent of the last; all within a bordure engrailed azure. *Crest*—Two wings addorsed or.

Seat—Netherby, Longtown Cumberland. *Club*—Farmers'.

Son living—CHARLES SPENCER RICHARD, *b.* July 16th, 1919; ed. at Eton; formerly Maj. Scots Gds.; a DL of Cumberland (High Sheriff 1955-56); Pres. of County Land Owners Assocn. 1971-73; 1939-45 War (despatches), Malaya 1949-50: *m.* 1944, Susan, only da. of Maj. Robert Lambton Surtees, OBE, of Redworth Cottage, Littlestone, Kent, and has issue living, James Fergus Surtees, *b.* 1946: *m.* 1973, Serena Jane, yr. da. of Ronald Frank Kershaw [see E. Lindsey and Abingdon, colls.], Malise Charles Richard, *b.* 1948: *m.* 1974, Pamela Winifred, da. of the Rt. Hon. William (Stephen Ian) Whitelaw, CH, MC, MP, of Ennim, Penrith, Cumberland [see Hay Bt. 1635],—Susanna Anne Mary, *b.* 1951. *Residence,* Crofthead, Longtown, Cumberland.

Brother living—(Richard) Preston GRAHAM-VIVIAN, *MVO, MC,* · 1896; ed. at Eton, and at Trin. Coll., Camb. (BA 1919); 1915-18 War as Lt. KRRC (twice wounded, prisoner, MC); Bluemantle Pursuivant of Arms 1933-47, Windsor Herald 1947-66, and Norroy and Ulster King of Arms 1966-72, Earl Marshal's Sec. 1954-61; assumed by Roy. licence 1929 the additional surname of Vivian, MVO (4th class) 1961: *m.* 1921, Audrey Emily, da. of the late Maj. Henry Wyndham Vivian [see B. Swansea, colls.], and has issue living, Henry Richard (Bosahan, Manaccan, Helston, Cornwall), *b.* 1923; ed. at Eton, and Ch. Ch., Oxford (BA); JP of Cornwall; High Sheriff of Cornwall 1965-66; NW Europe 1944-45 as Lt. Coldm. Gds.: *m.* 1955, Rosemary, only da. of Col. Giffard Tyringham, and has issue living, Richard John *b.* 1957, Lavinia *b.* 1959,—Catherine Maude (Ludgates, Nutbourne, Pulborough), *b.* 1926: *m.* 1947, Lt.-Col. John Peter Thomson-Glover, MC, 9th/12th Roy. Lancers, who *d.* 1968, and has issue living, Michael William (20, Crondace Rd., Fulham, SW6), *b.* 1948; ed. at Wellington, and Trin. Coll., Camb. (BA): *m.* 1974, Katherine, da. of John David Summers, Peter James *b.* 1953, Caroline Veronica *b.* 1950. *Residences,* Wealden House, Warninglid, Sussex; 26, Clabon Mews, Cadogan Sq., SW1. *Club,* Travellers'.

Sister living—Daphne (*Lady Barnes*), *b.* 1903; 1939-45 War as Wing Officer WAAF: *m.* 1925, Sir Kenneth Ralph Barnes, who *d.* 1957. *Address,* PO Box 77, Kyrenia, Cyprus.

Collateral Branches living.

Issue of the late Hugh Graham, 2nd son of 3rd baronet, *b.* 1860, *d.* 1921: *m.* 1888, Jessie, who *d.* 1934, da. of the late Andrew Low, of Savannah, Georgia, USA:—
Alastair Hugh, *b.* 1904; ed. at Wellington Coll., and at Brasenose Coll., Oxford.——Sibyl Hattie Hermione, *b.* 1893: *m.* 1920, Lt.-Col. Lionel Henry Hickson, DSO, and *d.* 1951, and has issue living, Jane Hermione, *b.* 1921: *m.* 1946, Robert Felpts Davidson, and has issue living, Christopher Robert *b.* 1947,—Mary Katherine, *b.* 1928: *m.* 1950, Maj. C. E. Macduff-Duncan, MC, of Redfield, Tore, Ross-shire, and has issue living, Colin Robert *b.* 1951, Alastair Ross *b.* 1954. *Residence,* The Manor House, Bishops Tachbrook, Leamington Spa.

Issue of the late James Reginald Graham, 3rd son of 3rd baronet, *b.* 1864, *d.* 1910: *m.* 1892, Florence Rose (*Lady Graham*), who *d.* 1934, having *m.* 3rdly, 1927, Sir Richard James Graham, 4th Bt. of Netherby (ante)], da. of the late J. Carter Wood, and widow of Capt. Cyprian Knollys:—
Iris Enid Florence (of 10, bis Rue Piccini, Paris, XVI), *b.* 1892: *m.* 1st, 1912, Noel Van Raalte, who obtained a divorce 1920; 2ndly, 1923, Louis Coatalen, who *d.* 1963, and has issue living, (by 1st m.), Iris Charmian, *b.* 1916: *m.* 1940, Maj. Alaric Charles William Russell [see B. Ampthill, colls.],—(by 2nd m.) Iris Marjolie, *b.* 1924: *m.* 1946, Harold Geoffrey Dixon, MB, BS, FRCP, FRCPG, of Mount Edgecombe, Westmoreland, Jamaica, and has issue living, Diana Madeleine *b.* 1951, Louise Marjorie Iris *b.* 1954, Nicola Ann *b.* 1963,

Grandson of the late Rev. Malise Reginald Graham, 2nd son of 2nd baronet:—
Issue of the late Reginald Graham, *b.* 1867, *d.* 1908: *m.* 1897, Helen Dacia, da. of G. S. Herck, of St. Petersburg:—
Ernest Reginald, *b.* 1898.

This family is descended from the Very Rev. William Graham, DD, 4th son of Sir George Graham, 2nd Bt., of Esk (cr. 1629). The 2nd baronet of Netherby, Sir James, GCB, PC, an eminent statesman, sat as MP successively for Hull, East Cumberland, Carlisle, Pembroke, Dorchester, and Ripon, and filled various high offices of State.

GRAHAM, Creation (U.K.) 1906, of Larbert House, Larbert and Househill, Dunipace, co. Stirling.

Forget not.

Sir (John) Reginald Noble Graham, *VC, OBE,* 3rd *Baronet; b.* Sept. 17th, 1892; *s.* his father, *Sir* (John) Frederick Noble, 1936; ed. at Eton and at Trin. Coll., Camb.; 1914-18 War as Maj. Princess Louise's (A & SH) (TF), and in Mesopotamia with Machine Gun Corps (VC), 1939-45 War as temp. Lt.-Col. A & SH attached Staff and AQMG (Movements), Scottish Command; appointed Gentleman Usher of the Green Rod to Order of the Thistle 1959; OBE (Mil) 1946: *m.* 1920, Rachel Septima, da. of Col. Sir Alexander Sprot, CMG, MP, 1st Bt. (ext.), and has issue.

Arms—Or, on a chief invected ermine three escallops of the first. Crest—A falcon proper, beaked and armed or, killing a stork argent armed gules.

Residence—The Mailens, Gullane, E. Lothian.

Son living—JOHN ALEXANDER NOBLE, *CMG* (Caerlaverock House, Bankend, Dumfries; Army and Navy Club), *b.* July 15th, 1926; ed. at Eton, and at Trin. Coll. Camb.; Lt. Gren. Gds., Palestine 1946-47; 3rd Sec. Bahrain 1951-52, and Amman 1953-54, Asst. Private Sec. to Foreign Sec. 1954-57, Second (later First) Sec. Belgrade 1957-60, First Sec. and Consul Benghazi 1960-61, FO 1961-66, Counsellor Kuwait 1966-69, Prin. Private Sec. to Foreign Sec. 1969-72, and Head of Chancery, Washington 1972-74, since when Ambassador to Iraq; CMG 1972: *m.* 1956, Marygold Ellinor Gabrielle, da. of Lt.-Col. Clive Grantham Austin, RHA, JP, DL, [*see* E. Scarbrough], and has issue living, Andrew John Noble, *b.* 1956,—George Reginald Clive, *b.* 1958,—Christian Rachel, *b.* 1961.

Daughter living—Lesley, *b.* 1921: *m.* 1945, Jock Wykeham Strang Steel, son of Sir Samuel Strang Steel, 1st Bt. *Residence*, Logie, Kirriemuir, Angus.

Brothers living—Bevis Royal, *CBE, b.* 1902; ed. at Eton; formerly Senior Representative in the East of Anchor Line, Ltd., Pakistan, Chm. of Pakistan Oxygen and Acetylene Co., Ltd., and Aluminium Pakistan, Ltd., and a Dir. of Associated Electrical Industries (Pakistan), Ltd.; 6 years Chm. of Karachi Chamber of Commerce; 3 years Pres. of Associated Chambers of Commerce, Pakistan; OBE (Civil) 1949, CBE (Civil) 1953: *m.* 1934, Lena, da. of Matthew Alexander Murphy, CBE, of Barbados. *Residence*, Pentire, Bear's Lane, Hingham, NOR 23X. *Clubs*, Oriental, Sind (Karachi).——Frederick Clarence Campbell, *CB, DSO, b.* 1908; ed. at Eton; Maj.-Gen. (ret.) late Argyll and Sutherland Highlanders, and a Member of Queen's Body Guard for Scotland (R. Co. of Archers); Hon. Col. WRAC (T & AVR) Scotland 1962-72; Hon. Col. Argyll and Sutherland Highlanders of Canada since 1972; a DL of Perth; Col. Argyll and Sutherland Highlanders 1958-72, and Col. Comdt. Scottish Div. 1968-69; Assist. Comdr. RMA Sandhurst 1953, Dep. Com. Land Forces, Hong Kong, 1955, Brig. Adviser on Recruiting, Min. of Defence 1955, and Gen. Officer Comdg. Highland Dist., and 51st Highland Div. TA 1959-62; Mohmand Operations 1934, 1939-45 War in Crete, Italy, W. Desert, Syria, and India (despatches thrice, DSO); DSO 1945, CB (Mil.) 1960: *m.* 1936, Phyllis Mary, da. of the late Maj.-Gen. Hugh Francis Edward MacMahon, CB, CSI, CBE, MC, and has issue living, Colin Hugh Campbell, *TD* (Morham Burn, Morham, Haddington, E. Lothian; New (Edinburgh) Club), *b.* 1940; late Capt. 51st Highland Volunteers (TAVR) since 1967; a Dir. of Grahams (Oporto) Ltd. 1963-67; Joint Man. Dir. Cockburn & Co. (Leith), Ltd., Wine Merchants, Edinburgh: *m.* 1963, Joanna, da. of the late David Chancellor, of Pencaitland, E. Lothian, and has issue living, William Frederick Chancellor *b.* 1963, David Campbell *b.* 1969, Suzanna Lucy *b.* 1967,—Ewan Alastair MacMahon (c/o Lloyds Bank, Cox's & King's Branch, 6, Pall Mall, SW1) *b.* 1944; Capt. Argyll and Sutherland Highlanders: *m.* 1967, Sara Diones, da. of Maj.-Gen. A. Reginald Geoffrey Stirling Hobbs, CB, DSO, OBE, and has issue living, Calum James MacMahon *b.* 1970, Fergus Hugh Stirling *b.* 1973,—(Kenneth) James (48, Crabtree Lane, SW6), *b.* 1947; ed. at Eton; late 2nd Lt. Argyll and Sutherland Highlanders; Exec. Honeywell Informations Systems, Ltd.: *m.* 1972, Victoria Margaret Anne, yst. da. of the late Maj. Andrew Stirling Home Drummond Moray, of Easter Ross, Comrie, Perthshire, and has issue living, Magnus James *b.* 1974. *Residence*—Mackeanston House, Doune, Perths. *Clubs*—Caledonian, Army and Navy.

Sister living—Glenda Victoria Maude, *b.* 1897; DBHS; Authoress and Journalist, and Founder, and Chm., Ponies of Britain Club: *m.* 1934, Capt. Hugh Spooner, 19th Lancers, Indian Army (ret.), Sup. Air Operations, Egyptian Airlines, who *d.* 1935. *Residence*, Brookside Farm, Ascot, Berks.

This family is a cadet branch of Graham of Tamrawer, descended from Graham of Auchincloich, nr. Kilsyth, Stirlingshire, who derive from John, 3rd son of Sir David Graham (d. c. 1376,) ancestor of Dukes of Montrose. The 1st baronet, Sir John Hatt Noble Graham (a member of the firm of William Graham and Co., merchants, of 400, Cathedral St., Glasgow, and of Grahams Co. (London), East India merchants) was a cadet of Graham of Tamrawer, descended from Graham of Auchincloich.

GRAHAM, Creation (U.K.) 1964, of Dromore, co. Down.

Sir John Moodie Graham, 2nd *Baronet; b.* April 3rd, 1938; *s.* his father, *Sir* Clarence Johnston, 1966; ed. at Trin. Coll., Glenalmond and Queen's Univ., Belfast (BSc): *m.* 1970, Valerie Rosemary, da. of the late Frank Gill, of 5, Greenview Park, Belfast, 9, and has issue.

Residence—Lisroyan, 154, Malone Rd., Belfast, BT9 5LJ.

Daughters living—Suzanne Margaret, *b.* 1971.——Alyson Rosemary, *b.* 1974.

Sir Clarence Johnston Graham, 1st baronet, was Chm. of Standing Cttee., Ulster Unionist Council 1947-63, and a Dir. of John Graham (Dromore) Ltd., Engineering Contractors.

GRANT, Creation (N.S.) 1688, of Dalvey.

Under thy favour will I flourish.

Sir PATRICK ALEXANDER BENE-DICT GRANT, 14th *Baronet*; *b.* Feb. 5th, 1953; *s.* his father, *Sir* DUNCAN ALEXANDER 1961; ed. at Abbey Sch., Fort Augustus.

Arms—Gules, three antique crowns or within a bordure engrailed of the last with the Baronet's badge of Nova Scotia in the dexter canton. **Crest**—The trunk of an oak-tree sprouting out some leaves with the sun shining thereon all proper. **Supporters**—*Dexter*, a Highlander; *sinister*, a negro proper.

Residence, Daire-nan-Guithas, Duncanston, Conan Bridge, Ross-shire.

Brothers living—DENZIL MOHUN BEDE *b.* April 19th, 1955.——Drostan John, *b.* 1956

Sisters living—Fiona Mary Julia, *b.* 1950: *m.* 1966 Christopher Kanthack St. John Bird, of 27, Crestway, Roehampton, SW15, and has issue living, Christopher Kenelm Anthony, *b.* 1967,——Theodore Denzil Drostan, *b.* 1971,——Penelope Frances Julia, *b.* 1968.——Maria Teresa, *b.* 1951: *m.* 1969, Ramon Anthony Cooke, BE, C.Eng., MIEI, of 2, Upper Mount St., Dublin 2, and has issue living, Jessica Fiona, *b.* 1969.

Aunt living—Diana Mary, *b.* 1931; ed. at St. Leonard's Sch., and at London (B.A. 1954) Univ.: *m.* 1954, Jean-Pierre Dalcher, and has issue living, Claude Francis, *b.* 1957,——Derrick Albert Alexander, *b.* 1959,——Anne, *b.* 1956. *Residence*, Villa Fidelis, Chemin du Blessoney, 1092, Belmont-sur-Lausanne, Vaud, Switzerland.

Great-Aunts living (daughters of 12th baronet)—Esther GRANT (Weston Town, Evercreech, Som.), *b.* 1915; resumed by declaration surname of Grant: *m.* 1st, 1936, Cecil Paul Jones; 2ndly, 1944, Fl.-Lt. Francis Ernest Appleyard Kitto, RAF, who *d.* 1964, and has issue living, (by 1st m.) Luke Kitto, *b.* 1941; assumed, by certificate of adoption 1945, the surname of Kitto: *m.* 1966, Mary Woolacot, and has issue living, Mathew Alexander *b.* 1967, Louise Victoria *b.* 1969,—(by 2nd m.) Alexander, *b.* 1944: *m.* 19—, Susan Appleby, and has issue living, Jonas *b.* 1972, Sasha *b.* 1974,—Crispin, *b.* 1951,—(by 1st m.) Julia, *b.* 1938: *m.* 1960, Nigel Keen, and has issue living, Alexander Hamilton *b.* 1961, Gabriel *b.* 1965, Flora Vivian *b.* 1962,—(by 2nd m.) Belinda, *b.* 1948: *m.* 1973, Mark Clothier, and has issue living, Luke *b.* 1973, Abby Isabel *b.* 1975,—Grace, *b.* 1955.——Guinevere (*Lady Tilney*), *b.* 1916; formerly 2nd Officer WRNS; DL for Lancs.; Member of BBC Gen. Advisory Council since 1967, Pres. Nat. Council of Women of Gt. Britain 1968-70, Chm. Women's National Commn. 1969-71, British Rep. of UN Status of Women Commn. 1970-73; Co-Chm. Women Caring Trust since 1972: *m.* 1st, 1944, Capt. K. Lionel Hunter, R. Canadian Dragoons, who *d.* 1947; 2ndly, 1954, Col. Sir John Dudley Robert Tarleton Tilney, TD, JP, and has issue living (by 1st m.) Tony Lionel HUNTER-TILNEY, *b.* 1947; ed. at Eton, and Magdalen Coll., Oxford (BA); assumed by deed poll 1954 the additional surname of Tilney: *m.* 1970, Juliet Faller, and has issue living, Ludovic John Grant *b.* 1971. *Residence*, 25, Fulwood Park, Liverpool, 17; 3, Victoria Sq., SW1.

Daughter living of 11th Baronet—Rosalind Margaret Innes, *b.* 1893: *m.* 1918, Capt. Edward Coverley Kennedy, R.N., who *d.* (on active ser. during European War) 1939 [*see* M. Ailsa, colls.]. *Residence*, The Sunbury Homes, Thames St., Sunbury-on-Thames, Surrey.

Grandmother living—Mary Angela, da. of the late Rev. Henry Arthur Mackenzie, DD, MusB V. of Shotley Bridge, co. Durham: *m.* 1st, 1926, Alexander Lovett Grant, el. son of 12th baronet who *d.* 1935; 2ndly, 1936 (m. diss. 1955), Capt. Denis Francis Keegan, MBE, who *d.* 1966 *Address*, c/o Royal Bank of Scotland, 60-62, Lombard St., EC3.

Widow living of 13th Baronet—JOAN PENELOPE (*Lady Cope-Strachan*); assumed be deed poll 1969 the surname of Cope-Strachan, da. of Capt. Sir Denzil Cope, 14th Bt. (*cr.* 1611): *m.* 1949, Sir Duncan Alexander Grant, 13th baronet, who *d.* 1961. *Residences*, 34, Morehampton Rd., Donnybrook, Dublin; Manzanares, 22, Madrid 5, Spain.

Collateral Branch living.

Issue of the late Percy Frere Grant, M.B., 4th son of 10th baronet, *b.* 1869, *d.* 1909: *m.* (Feb.) 1905, Theodora, who *d.* 1938, da. of J. H. Goodrich:—
Winifred Anne St. John, *b.* (Nov.) 1905; ed. at Cape Town Univ. (BA): *m.* 1930, Gerard Anthony Thomson, of 55, Kings Way, Warner Beach, S. Coast, Natal 4125.——Susan Ursula (10, Westerford Rd., Newlands, Cape, S. Africa), *b.* 1907: *m.* 1930, Christian Arnold Wahl, who *d.* 1967.

This baronetcy was conferred with remainder to heirs male whatsoever, and on the death of the 1st baronet without issue in 1695 the title remained unassumed until Patrick Grant, of Inverladinen, a distant relative, was served heir male general to the 1st baronet in 1752. The 8th baronet, M.P. for Cambridge, was Chairman of Committees in Parliament 1826-30, a member of the Board of Control 1835, and subsequently a Commissioner for Auditing the Public Accounts. The 10th baronet was Principal and Vice-Chancellor of Edinburgh University 1868-84. The 11th baronet was Regius Professor of Public Law and of the Law of Nature and of Nations in Edinburgh Univ. 1890-1922. The 12th baronet was Foreign Sec. to Gov. of India 1914-19, and Ch. Commr., N.-W. Frontier Province 1919-21.

GRANT, Creation (N.S.) 1705, of Cullen, co. Buchan.

Sir ARCHIBALD GRANT, 13th *Baronet*; *b.*
Sept. 2nd, 1954: *s.* his father, *Capt. Sir*
FRANCIS CULLEN, 1966.

Arms. Gules, three antique crowns or, within a
border ermine. **Crest,**—A Bible expanded proper.
Supporters—Two Angels proper, wings or.

Seat—House of Monymusk, Monymusk, Aberdeenshire.

Brothers living—FRANCIS TOLLEMACHE, *b.* Dec. 18th,
1955.——Duncan John Cullen, *b.* 1957.

Sisters living—Catriona Charmiane, *b.* 1959.——Sarah
Jean, *b.* 1961.

Aunts living (daughters of 10th baronet)—Evelyn Mary
Frances, *b.* 1910: *m.* 1934, Maj.-Gen. Cecil Martin
Fothergill Deakin, CB, CBE, late Grenadier Guards,
and has issue living, Charles Cullen William, *b.* 1939:
m. 1973, Pamela, only da. of Brig. Gerald L. Fitz Gerald,
of River Cottage, Longparish, Hants.;—Juliet Elizabeth
(*Lady Edmonstone*), *b.* 1943: *m.* 1969, as his 2nd wife,
Sir Archibald Bruce Charles Edmonstone, 7th Bt.
Residence, Stocks Farm House, Beenham, Berks.——Elspeth (18b, Barclay Rd., SW6), *b.* 1913:
m. 1933 (m. diss. 1963), Richard Luis Owen Waddington, and has issue living, Frances Elspeth
Luise, *b.* 1934: *m.* 1961, Alastair Manson, of 69, West Hill Rd., SW18 1LE, and has issue living,
William Giles *b.* 1965, Lucy Elspeth *b.* 1962, Alice *b.* 1967.——Catherine Jean (*Lady Legge-
Bourke*) (9, Wilbraham Place, SW1), *b.* 1917: *m.* 1938, Maj. Sir Edward Alexander Henry Legge-
Bourke, KBE, MP, DL, R. Horse Gds., who *d.* 1973 [*see* E. Dartmouth, colls.].——Christian Mona,
b. 1920: *m.* 1st, 1942, Michael Fife William Angas, Gren. Gds., from whom she obtained a divorce
1951; 2ndly, 1953, John Gordon Ogston Miller, of The Old Stables, Newtown, Newbury, Berks.,
and 21, Burton Court, SW3, and has issue living, (by 1st m.) Auburn Carolyn Catherine, *b.* 1945,—
Cherill Melmere, *b.* 1947: *m.* 1966, Charles Heckstall, of Virginia, USA, and has issue living,
Cyprian Carolus *b.* 1967.

Daughters living of 11th Baronet—*see* Baroness Tweedsmuir of Belhelvie.

Widows living of 10th, 11th and 12th Baronets—EVELYN ALICE LINDSAY (*Dowager Lady Grant*),
da. of the late Collingwood Lindsay Wood [B. Hotham, colls.]: *m.* 1909, Col. Sir Arthur Grant
CBE, DSO, 10th baronet, who *d.* 1931.——PRISCILLA JEAN FORTESCUE (*Baroness Tweedsmuir
of Belhelvie*), da. of Brig. Alan Fortescue Thomson, DSO; *cr.* Baroness Tweedsmuir of Belhelvie
(Life Peerage) 1970: *m.* 1st, 1934, Maj. Sir Arthur Lindsay Grant, 11th baronet, who *d.* (killed
in action) 1944; 2ndly, 1948, the 2nd Baron Tweedsmuir. *Residences*, 40, Tufton Court, SW1;
Potterton House, Balmedie, Aberdeenshire. *Club*, Guards'.——JEAN MARGHERITA (*Lady
Grant*), (House of Monymusk, Monymusk, Aberdeenshire), da. of the late Capt. Humphrey
Douglas Tollemache, RN [*see* B. Tollemache, colls.]: *m.* 1953, Capt. Sir Francis Cullen Grant,
12th baronet, who *d.* 1966.

    This family is a branch of the noble house of Grant (Earls of Seafield). Archibald Grant of
Ballentomb, progenitor of this line was 4th son of James Grant, 3rd of Freuchie (now Castle
Grant), who *d.* 1553. The 1st baronet, Sir Francis (Lord Cullen), a Senator of the College of
Justice (4th in descent from Archibald) was created a baronet by Queen Anne. The 2nd baronet,
Sir Archibald, carried out extensive agric. reforms and tree planting. The 10th baronet, Col.
Sir Arthur Grant, CBE, DSO, served in S. Africa 1899-1902, and during 1914-18 War (severely
wounded). The 11th baronet, Maj. Sir Arthur Lindsay Grant, Grenadier Guards, *d.* (killed in
action) 1944. The 12th baronet, Capt. Sir Francis Cullen Grant, RE, served in Normandy
campaign (despatches).

GRANT, Creation (U.K.) 1926, of Househill, co. Nairn. [Extinct 1932.]

Sir JAMES AUGUSTUS GRANT, 1st and last *Baronet.*

Daughters living of 1st Baronet—Margaret (*Lady Guise*), *b.* 1897: *m.* 1924, Sir Anselm William
Edward Guise, 6th Bt., who *d.* 1970. *Residence*, Elmore Court, nr. Gloucester.——Hester, *b.*
1899: *m.* 1st, 1923 (m. diss. 1937), Brig. Arthur Darley Bridge, MC, formerly Coldm. Gds.;
2ndly, 1945, Col. Alexander Frederick Gordon Renton, O.B.E., M.C., T.D. *Residence*, Easton
Town Farm, Sherston, near Malmesbury, Wilts.

MACPHERSON-GRANT, Creation (U.K.) 1838, of Ballindalloch, Elgin.

*With sword
and courage.*

Sir EWAN GEORGE MACPHERSON-
GRANT, 6th *Baronet*, son of the late Capt.
George Bertram Macpherson-Grant,
O.B.E., J.P., D.L., 2nd son of 3rd
baronet; *b.* Sept. 29th, 1907; *s.* his
cousin, *Sir* GEORGE, 1951; ed. at
Winchester, and at Ch. Ch., Oxford;
is a Member of Queen's Body Guard for
Scotland (Roy. Co. of Archers), and
of Scottish Faculty of Advocates, and a
D.L. for Banffshire; formerly Major
R.A.: *m.* 1937, Evelyn Nancy Stopford,
da. of the late Maj. Edward Spencer
Dickin [E. Courtown, colls.], and has
issue.

Arms. 1st and 4th, gules, a target
between three antique crowns or, *Grant of Ballindalloch;* 2nd and 3rd, per fesse or and azure a
lymphad of the first, masts, oars, and tacklings proper,
ensigned gules, between a hand couped fessewise
holding a dagger in pale in the dexter canton, and
in the sinister a cross-crosslet fitchée gules, all

within a bordure of the last, *Macpherson of Invereshie*. Crests—1st, a dexter hand erect, holding a dirk in pale proper ; and, a cat sejant-guardant proper with fore-foot erect.

Seats—Craigo House, Montrose ; Ballindalloch Castle, Ballindalloch. *Club*, New (Edinburgh).

Daughter living—Clare Nancy, *b.* 1944: *m.* 1967, Oliver Henry Russell, of Sudbrook Lodge, Ham Common, Richmond, Surrey, son of Adm. the Hon. Sir Guy Herbrand Edward Russell, GBE, KCB, DSO [see B. Ampthill.].

Sister living—Mary, *b.* 1905 : *m.* 1928. Col. Andrew Hamilton Farquhar Fausset-Farquhar, D.S.O., TD, JP, Cameron and Gordon Highlanders, and has issue living, Angus Hamilton Macpherson, *b.* 1934,—Hamish Bertram Mainwaring, *b.* 1947,—Pamela Mary *b.* 1929,—Daphne Primrose, *b.* 1945. *Residence*, Farr, Kincraig, Kingussie, Inverness-shire.

Collateral Branch living.

Issue of the late Alastair Macpherson-Grant, 3rd son of 3rd baronet, *b.* 1874, *d.* 1949: *m.* 1904, Hester Charlotte, who *d.* 1945, da. of the late Arthur C. Kennard, of 17, Eaton Place, S.W. :—

Nina Marion, *OBE* (*Nina, Baroness Deramore*), *b.* 1905; is a CStJ and Branch Patron British Red Cross So., E. Riding, Yorks.; OBE (Civil) 1956: *m.* 1929, the 5th Baron Deramore, who *d.* 1964. *Residence,* 6, Eaton Place, SW1.——Susan Hester, *b.* 1910. *Club*, Service Women's. ——Anne Frances, *b.* 1914: *m.* 1939, Lt.-Col. William D. Keown-Boyd, OBE, 60th Rifles, and has issue living, Alexander, *b.* 1949,—Jennifer, *b.* 1942. *Residence*, 12, Queensmead, St. Johns Wood Park, NW8.

The Macphersons of Invereshie descend from Gillies, *temp.* Alexander III, younger son of Ewan Ban, 2nd son of Muriach, Chief of Clan Chattan. The name Macpherson signifies " son of the Parson." Sir George Macpherson-Grant, 1st Bt., of Invereshie assumed the additional surname of Grant 1806, being heir to his great-uncle, Col. William Grant of Ballindalloch.

Grant-Suttie, see Suttie.

Grattan-Bellew, see Bellew.

Graves-Sawle, see Sawle.

GRAY, Creation (U.K.) 1917, of Tunstall Manor, Hart, co. Durham.

Sir WILLIAM GRAY, 2nd *Baronet*; *b.* Aug. 18th, 1895 ; *s.* his father, *Sir* WILLIAM CRESSWELL, 1924; ed. at Loretto Sch.; a DL for co. Durham (High Sheriff 1938); 1914-18 War as Capt. Yorkshire Regt. (wounded, despatches, prisoner) : *m.* 1st, 1929, Josephine, who *d.* 1943, da. of W. H. Eveleigh; 2ndly, 1947, Beryl (HENSHAW), da. of Alfred Stott, of Crowborough, Sussex, and has issue by 1st marriage.

Arms—Barry of six argent and azure, a lion rampant gules, on a chief of the second two lymphads or. **Crest**—An anchor or in front of and supported by two lions jambs erased gules.

Residence—Orchard Cottage, Egglestone, Barnard Castle, co. Durham.

Grandchildren living—[Issue of the late William Talbot Gray, el. son of 2nd baronet, *b.* 1931 *d.* 1971: *m.* 1954, Rosemarie Hume (Egglestone Hall, Egglestone, Barnard Castle, co. Durham), da. of Air Commodore Charles Hume Elliott-Smith]:—

WILLIAM HUME, *b.* July 26th, 1955; ed. at Eton.——Victoria, *b.* 1958.——Emma, *b.* 1962.

Son living—By 1st m.—NICHOLAS ANTHONY (Skutterskelfe House, Hutton Rudby, Yarm, Yorks.; 43, Markham Sq., SW3), *b.* 1934: *m.* 1956, Amanda, only da. of H. W. Edwards, of Ashmore Green, Newbury, Berks., and has issue living, Edward Dylan, *b.* 1964,—Matthew Barnaby, *b.* 1969,—Daisy, *b.* 1970.

Sister living—Edith, b. 1894: m. 1919, Capt. Stephen Godlee, formerly RA, who d. 1940, and has issue living, Peter Lister, b. 1924. *Residence*, Crakehall House, Bedale, Yorkshire.

The 1st baronet, Sir William Cresswell Gray, Chm. of the firm of William Gray and Co. Limited), and a Member of *Lloyds Register* Committee, founded the S. Durham Steel and Iron Co. Limited) in 1889.

GRAYSON, Creation (U.K.) 1922, of Ravenspoint, co. Anglesey.

Virtue is the safest tower.

Sir RONALD HENRY RUDYARD GRAY-SON, 3rd *Baronet* ; *b.* Nov. 15th, 1916 ; *s.* his father, *Sir* DENYS HENRY HARRINGTON, 1955 ; ed. at Harrow ; European War 1941-5 with R.A.F. : *m.* 1st, 1936 (divorce 1944), Babette Vivienne, da. of the late Count Vivien Hollender; 2ndly, 1946, Dorothy Vera Hoare, da. of Charles Serrell.

Arms—Sable, on a fesse between a portcullis in chief and a lymphad in base or, two ravens of the first. **Crest**—In front of a rising sun or, a tower proper, issuant therefrom a demi-lion sable resting between the paws a spur gold.

Address—Vaucluse, Sydney, N.S. Wales.

Uncles living (sons of 1st baronet)—RUPERT STANLEY HARRINGTON, b. July 22nd, 1897; ed. at Harrow; Knt. of Order of Holy Sepulchre; 1914-18 War as Lt. Irish Guards; King's Foreign Ser. Messenger 1939-45: m. 1st, 1919, Ruby Victoria, da. of Walter Henry Banks; 2ndly, 1950, Vari Colette, da. of Maj. Henry O'Shea, late Roy. Dublin Fusiliers, of Cork.——Brian Harrington, b. 1900; ed. at Harrow, and at Pembroke Coll., Camb.; a Member of National Assocn. of Prison Visitors; 1939-45 War as Capt. RASC; has Humane Soc.'s silver medal for saving life: m. (1st, 1930, Sofia (from whom he obtained a divorce 1946), da. of the late George Buchanan Commercial Counsellor, Chilian Embassy in London), of 7, Addison Rd., W14; 2ndly, 1949, Ruth, da. of the late O. L. Anders, of Littlethorpe Hall, Ripon, and has issue living, (by 1st marriage) Jeremy Brian Vincent (17, Bramerton St., SW3), b. 1933; ed. at Downside: m. 1958, Sara, da. of C. F. Upton, and has issue living, Simon Jeremy b. 1959, Paul Francis b. 1965, Mark Christopher b. 1968, Caroline Mary b. 1961, Anna Katherine b. 1962, Lucy Kate, b. 1970,—Jane Angela, b. 1931,—(by 2nd m.) Alicia Lorraine, b. 1953: m. 1973, Clive Trevor Thorne Rogers. *Residence*, Summerfield, Ditchling, Sussex.——Tristram Hugh Harrington, OBE, b. 1902; ed. at Harrow, and at Clare Coll., Camb.; Col. late Irish Gds.; was Comdt. Roy. Mil. Police Depot 1947-50; Provost Marshal Far East Land Forces, 1952, and Ch. Constable, UK Atomic Energy Auth. Constab. 1954-67, OBE (Mil) 1951: m. 1928, Barbara, who d. 1974, da. of Morgan Ignatius Finucane, MRCS, JP, Bar.-at-law, of 10, Ashley Pl., SW1, and has issue living, Patrick Tristram Finucane (Clements House, The Terrace, Wokingham, Berks.), b. 1942: ed. at Downside, and RMAS; Maj. late Irish Gds.: m. 1965, Vivienne Mary, da. of Hector Rowcliffe Munro, of Javea, Alicante, Spain, and has issue living, Mark Patrick Munro b. 1974, Louise Mary Munro b. 1968, Nicola Kathryn Munro b. 1970,—Mary Dora Finucane, b. 1931: m. 1958, John Owen Blaksley, of The White House, Gosmore, Hitchin, Herts, and has issue living, John Patrick b. 1959, Richard Edmund b. 1961,—Angela Mary Finucane, b. 1934: m. 1955, Maj. Michael John Drummond-Brady, The Queen's Regt., of Stonechats, Chelwood Gate, Sussex, and has issue living, Simon Michael Grayson b. 1955, Mark Frederick Grayson b. 1957, Emma Angela Grayson b. 1962. *Residence*, Flat 12, 25, Cheyne Pl., SW3.——Ambrose Desmond Harrington (Le Groignet, Kings Mills, Catel, Guernsey), b. 1913; formerly a King's Foreign Ser. Messenger: m. 1966, Lilian, da. of Gerald Westwood Potter, of Park Gates, East-bourne and widow of Dr. Lydiard Wilson.——Godfrey Ramsay Harrington (twin), b. 1913: m. 1939, Ida, da. of the late Sextus Hassing, of Frederica, Denmark, and has issue living, Simon Anthony b. 1952,—Karen Grethe Maria, b. 1940: m. 1960, Colin Ross, and has issue living, Nicholas b. 1962,—Lila Marianna, b. 1945: m. 1966, Colin Michael Creswell, son of Sir Michael Justin Creswell, KCMG,—Lorna Theresa, b. 1848. *Residence,*

Aunts living (daughters of 1st baronet)—Ailsa Margaret Harrington, b. 1895: m. 1916, Lt.-Col. Arthur Richard Rawlinson, OBE, of Quaves, South Drive, Ferring, Sussex, and has issue living, Rt. Hon. Sir Peter Anthony Grayson, QC, MP (4, Paper Buildings, Temple, EC4) [see PRIVY COUNCIL], b. 1919: m. 1st, 1940, Haidée (from whom he obtained a divorce 1954, and annulled by Sacred Rota Rome), da. of the late Gerald Kavanagh, of Dublin; 2ndly, 1954, Elaine, da. of the late Vincent Dominguez, and has issue living, (by 1st m.) Mikaela b. 1941: m. 1964, Jonathan Irwin, of Ivy House, Leixlip, co. Kildare (and has issue living, Charles b. 1965, Luke b. 1967, Job b. 1972), Dariel b. 1943: m. 1965, Harry Garnett (and has issue living, Sophia b. 1968, Natasha b. 1970), Haidée b. 1948: m. 1968, Richard Annesley (and has issue living, Peter b. 1970, Arabella b. 1972), by 2nd m. Michael Vincent b. 1957, Anthony b. 1963, Angela b. 1962.——Auriol Dora Harrington (Maison du Guet, Amherst, Guernsey), b. 1903: m. 1927, Walter Bruce Harvie, from whom she obtained a divorce 1937, and has issue living, John Bruce, b. 1928,—Jill Auriol Mary, b. 1929: m. 1st, 1952, Cyprian Waller-Bridge, who d. 1960; 2ndly, 1973, Geoffrey R. Hamber, of 29, Pembroke Place, W8, and has issue living (by 1st m.), Michael Cyprian b. 1953,—Susan Dora b. 1933.——Meryl Lorraine Harrington, b. 1909.——Angela Decima Harrington, b. 1910: m. 1st, 1934, Vincent Luis Dominguez, from whom she obtained a divorce 1946; 2ndly, 1946, C. Mathew Dick, of Newport, Rhode Island, USA, and has issue living, (by 1st m.) Luis Carlos, b. 1939,—Elaine Angela, b. 1935. *Residence*, Clover Patch, Newport, Rhode Island, USA.

Widow living of 2nd Baronet—JEANETTE (*Jeanette, Lady Grayson*) (c/o Williams & Glyns Bank, 22, St. Mary Axe, EC2), da. of the late John Evan Glen, of Edinburgh: m. 1951, as his third wife, Sir Denys Henry Harrington Grayson, 2nd Bt., who d. 1955.

The 1st baronet, Sir Henry Mulleneux Grayson, K.B.E. (son of the late Henry Holdrege Grayson, J.P., of Liverpool) was Lieut.-Col. R.M., a Director of several Shipping and Shipbuilding Cos., and High Sheriff of Anglesey 1917-18, and sat as M.P. for W. Div. of Birkenhead (Co. U.) 1918-22.

GREEN, Creation (U.K.) 1886, of Wakefield, Yorkshire, and Ken Hill, Norfolk.

Waste not.

Sir EDWARD STEPHEN LYCETT GREEN, *C.B.E.* 4th *Baronet* ; *b.* April 18th, 1910 ; *s.* his father, *Sir* EDWARD, ARTHUR LYCETT, 1941 ; ed. at Eton, and at Magdalene Coll., Camb.; Bar. Lincoln's Inn 1933; a J.P. and D.L. for Norfolk 1959-74; Chm. E. Anglian Regional Hosp. Board; Dep. Chm. Norfolk Quarter Sessions 1948-71; formerly Maj. RA; a County Councillor for Norfolk 1946-9; 1939-45 War; CBE (Civil) 1964: *m.* 1935, Constance Mary (Co. Councillor for Norfolk), da. of the late Ven. Harry Sydney Radcliffe, Archdeacon of Lynn, and has issue.

Arms—Vert, guttee d'eau, three stags trippant or, in fesse two roses argent. Crest—In front of a mount vert thereon a stag trippant or, collared vert, three roses argent.

Residence,—Ken Hill, Snettisham, King's Lynn. *Clubs*—White's, Pratt's, Norfolk (Norwich).

Daughter living—Livia Lycett, *b.* 1937: *m.* 1961, Robert Edmond Buscall, and has issue living, Harry Charles, *b.* 1963,—Patrick Edward, *b.* 1965. *Residence,* Low Farm, Carbrooke, Thetford, Norfolk.

Brother living—SIMON LYCETT, *T.D.*, *b.* July 11th, 1912 ; ed. at Eton, and at Magdalene Coll., Camb. ; is a D.L. for W. Riding of Yorkshire, and a J.P. for Wakefield ; Lieut.-Col. Comdg. Yorkshire Dragoons Yeo. 1947-51; 1939-44 War: *m.* 1935 (m. 1st, diss. 1971), Gladys, da. of the late Arthur Ranicar, JP, of Springfield, Wigan; 2ndly, 1971, Mary, da. of the late George Ramsden, of Dale House, Wakefield, and has issue living (by 1st m.), Diana Rose Francis, *b.* 1935: *m.* 1964, Capt. Ronald Eden Wallace, of Eyford Knoll, Upper Slaughter, nr. Cheltenham [see Lindsay-Hogg, Bt.] *Residence,* Cliff Bank, N. Rigton, Leeds. *Club,* White's.

Collateral Branch living.

Grandchildren of the late Cdr. David Cecil Lycett Green, RN (infra):—
Issue of the late Richard David Rafe Lycett Green, *b.* 1925, *d.* 1969: *m.* 1st, 1948 (Marie) Patricia (from whom he obtained a divorce 1956), da. of Michael Maguire, of Melbourne, Aust., and widow of Capt. the Hon. Peter Rudyard Aitken, R. Fus. [see By. Beaver-brook]; 2ndly, 1958, Margaret Alison, da. of Maj. Geoffrey Denis Lock, MBE, MC, of Rainbow Wood, Bath, and formerly wife of Yan Kai-Nielsen:—
(By 1st m.) Edward Patrick Lycett (Orchard Dene, Church Lane, Welford-on-Avon), *b.* 1950; ed. at Stowe: *m.* 1971, Cordelia Sarah, da. of C. B. Stretton Wilson, of Stratford-on-Avon.— Mary Angela, *b.* 1949.

Issue of the late Cdr. David Cecil Lycett Green, R.N., 2nd son of 2nd baronet, *b.* 1892, *d.* 1960 : *m.* 1st, 1923, Angela (from whom he obtained a divorce 1944), youngest da. of Edward Hubert Courage, of Kirkby-Fleetham Hall, Bedale; 2ndly, 1948, Margery Dora Helen, who *m.* 3rdly, 1970, Alec Pilking-ton, of 43, Cadogan Sq., SW1, da. of Lt.-Col. Henry Ross, CIE, OBE, and formerly wife of Col. Tom C. Williamson, DSO:—
(By 1st m.) Rupert William Lycett (Blackland House, Calne, Wilts), *b.* 1938; late 2nd Lt. Roy. Armoured Corps.: *m.* 1963, Candida Rose, da. of Sir John Betjeman, CBE [see B. Chetwode], and has issue living, David Lycett, *b.* 1975,—Lucy Rose, *b.* 1964,—Imogen Rose, *b.* 1966,— Endellion Rose, *b.* 1969——Catherine Auriol Lycett, *b.* 1935: *m.* 1967, Raja Ranbir Singh, of 4, Tregunter Rd., SW10, and has issue living, Xenia, *b.* 1968,—Tamara, *b.* 1970,—Alexia, *b.* 1972.

Sir Edward Green, 1st Bt. (el. son of the late Edward Green, of Wakefield); Capt. 1st W. Yorkshire Yeo.; sat as M.P. for Wakefield (C) 1874 (but was unseated) and July 1885 to July 1892 (when he resigned). Sir Edward Arthur Lycett Green, T.D., 3rd Bt., was Lieut.-Col. and Brevet Col. Yorkshire Dragoons Yeo.

GREEN, Creation (U.K.) 1901, of Belsize Park Gardens, Hampstead, co. London.
[Extinct 1959.]

Sir GEORGE ARTHUR HAYDN GREEN, 4th and last *Baronet.*

Daughter living of 2nd Baronet—Evelyn Kate, *b.* 1905. *Residence,* 11, Cumberland Mansions, West End Lane, Hampstead, N.W.6.

Green-Price, see Price.

GREENAWAY, Creation (U.K.) 1933, of Coombe, co. Surrey.

Either do not attempt, or complete.

Sir DEREK BURDICK GREENAWAY, *CBE, TD,* 2nd *Baronet, b.* May 27th, 1910 ; *s.* his father, *Sir* PERCY WALTER, 1956 ; ed. at Marlborough ; Maj. RA, a JP and a DL of Kent (High Sheriff 1971-72), and Chm. and Managing Dir. of Daniel Greenaway & Son, Ltd., printers ; Joint Master of Old Surrey and Burstow Fox Hounds 1958-66, and Pres. of Sevenoaks Div. Conservative Assocn. 1963-66 (Chm. 1960-63) ; Assist. Hon. Treasurer of S-E Area Conservative and Unionist Assocn. 1966-69, Treasurer since 1969 ; Master, Stationers' & Newspaper Makers' Co. 1974-75 ; Hon. Col. 44 (HC) Signal Regt., (Cinque Ports) (TA) 1966-67 and Hon. Col. 36th (Eastern) Signal Regt. (V) 1967-74 ; CBE (Civil) 1974 : *m.* 1937, Sheila Beatrice, only da. of the late Richard Cyril Lockett, of 58, Cadogan Pl., SW1, and has issue.

Arms,—Quarterly : 1 and 4, gules, a chevron between in chief two covered cups and in base a closed book clasps downwards or, *Greenaway*; 2 and 3, vert an ancient ship with three masts sails set or, between four seagulls close proper, *Burdick.* *Crest,*—A griffin's head erased or, semée of roses gules, barbed and seeded proper, suspended from the beak an annulet gold.

Residence—Dunmore, Four Elms, Edenbridge, Kent. *Clubs*—Carlton, City of London.

Son living—JOHN MICHAEL BURDICK, *b.* Aug. 9th, 1944; ed. at Harrow; Lt. Life Gds. (ret.); a Dir. of Daniel Greenaway & Sons, Ltd.

Daughter living—Anne Jennifer: *m.* 1969, Capt. David Patrick Lewis Hewson, Blues and Royals, of 103, Abbotsbury Rd., W14, and Attyflin, Patrickswell, co. Limerick [B. Merthyr], and has issue living Annabel Mary, *b.* 1971,—Clare Louise, *b.* 1973.

Brother living—Alan Pearce, *b.* 1913; late Capt. King's Regt.; a JP for Co. London (an Alderman of City of London 1965-72) and Dep. Chm. of Daniel Greenaway & Sons Ltd., printers, and their subsidiary and assoc. Cos.; Sheriff of City of London 1962-63; elected Court of Common Council 1952; Chm. of Central Markets Cttee. 1964: *m.* 1948, Patricia Frances, da. of Sir Frederick Michael Wells, 1st Bt. (*cr.* 1948), and has issue living, Michael Philip *b.* 1949,—Susan Mary, *b.* 1952. *Residence,* The Doone, Byfleet Rd., Cobham, Surrey.

Sisters living—Doreen Lydie, *b.* 1908; a JP: *m.* 1936, Harold Francis Ralph Sturge, Metropolitan Magistrate (ret.), and has issue living, Martin Greenaway, *b.* 1938,—Simon Harold (Linersh Cottage, Linersh Wood, Bramley, Surrey), *b.* 1940: *m.* 1967, Hilary Barbara Highet, and has issue living, Charles Campbell *b.* 1969, Alexander James *b.* 1972. *Residence,* 85, Woodlands Rd., Surbiton.—Jasemine Amy, *b.* 1911: *m.* 1938, Charles Anthony Hinds Howell, DM, FRCP, and has issue living, Penelope, *b.* 1940: *m.* 1965, William B. Fraser, of 1, Alleyn Rd., Dulwich, SE21, and has issue living, Camilla Anne *b.* 1967, Emma Mary *b.* 1968,—Rosamund, *b.* 1942,—Marguerite, *b.* 1946: *m.* 1970, Peter Bainbridge. *Residence,* The Manor, Pootings, Edenbridge, Kent.

The 1st baronet, Sir Percy Walter Greenaway (son of the late Daniel Greenaway, Dep. of City of London), was Chm. of Daniel Greenaway & Sons, Ltd., printers and stationers, and of other Cos., a Member of Court of Common Council of City of London (Alderman 1923, Senior Sheriff 1931-2, and Lord Mayor 1932-3), and Master of Stationers' and Newspaper Makers' Co., 1932 (re-elected 1933), and Treasurer 1951.

GREENWELL, Creation (U.K.) 1906, of Marden Park, Godstone, co. Surrey, and Greenwell, Wolsingham, co. Durham.

I become green.

Sir PETER McCLINTOCK GREENWELL, *T.D.*, 3rd *Baronet* : *b.* May 23rd, 1914 ; *s.* his father, *Sir* BERNARD EYRE, *M.B.E.*, 1939 ; ed. at Winchester, and Trin. Coll., Camb.; late Capt. 98th (Surrey and Sussex Yeo.) Field Brig., RA (TA); High Sheriff of Suffolk 1966, a DL 1973; 1939-45 War (despatches, prisoner): *m.* 1940, Jean Henrietta Rose, da. of Peter Haig Haig-Thomas [E. Normanton], and has issue.

    Arms—Or, two bars azure between three ducal coronets gules. Crest—A stork statant proper, beaked and legged gules, gorged with a wreath of laurel vert.

    Seats—Butley Abbey Farm, Woodbridge, Suffolk ; Greenwell, co. Durham.

Sons living—EDWARD BERNARD, *b.* June 10th, 1948: *m.* 1974, Sarah Louise da. of the late Lt.-Col. Philip M. G. Anley, of Sculthorpe House, Fakenham, Norfolk.——James Peter, *b.* 1950.

Daughter living—Julia Henrietta, *b.* 1946: *m.* 1970, Alexander Richard Trotter, of Charterhall, Duns, Berwickshire, and has issue living, Henry Peter, *b.* 1972,—Edward John, *b.* 1973.

Sisters living—Joyce Marjorie, *b.* 1903: *m.* 1927, Maj. Walter Harold Miles, MBE, Dorsetshire Regt. (ret.), and has issue living, Christopher Richard (of Court Lodge, Bletchingley, Surrey), *b.* 1928: *m.* 1956, Jean Mary, da. of the late Anthony Buxton, D.S.O. [*see* Buxton, Bt. colls.], and has issue living, Richard John *b.* 1957, Hubert Christopher *b.* 1959, Mary Anna Theresa *b.* 1960, Sophia Mary *b.* 1967,—Philip David (Hinton Hall, Lea Cross, Shrewsbury, Salop), *b.* 1931: *m.* 1960, the Hon. Julian Isabella Joan Chetwynd, da. of 9th Viscount Chetwynd, and has issue living, Charles Philip Chetwynd *b.* 1962, Sara Isabella *b.* 1961,—Rosemary Joyce, *b.* 1935: *m.* 1957, Michael Harper Gow, of The Manor House, Woughton-on-the-Green, Bucks., and has issue living, Christopher Michael Harper *b.* 1961, Fergus Benjamin Harper *b.* 1965, Lucinda Rosemary *b.* 1959, Amelia Jean *b.* 1967. *Residence*, North Park Farm, Godstone, Surrey.——Barbara Patience (*Lady William-Powlett*), *b.* 1906: *m.* 1st, 1929, Capt. Newton James Wallop William-Powlett, DSC, RN, who *d.* 1963; 2ndly, 1966, Vice-Adm. Sir Peveril Barton Reibey Wallop William-Powlett, KCB, KCMG, CBE, DSO [*see* E. Portsmouth, colls.] ——Elisabeth Kathleen, *b.* 1908: *m.* 1931, Capt. Roddie Casement, OBE, RN, and has issue living, Michael Bernard (Dene Cottage, West Hartling, Petersfield, Hants.), *b.* 1933; Cdr. RN: *m.* 1956, Christina Rose, da. of Capt. J. C. Maclean, and has issue living, William Rory John *b.* 1961, Rachel Christina *b.* 1957, Flora *b.* 1959,—Patrick John, *b.* 1935: *m.* 1966, Margaret Rose, da. of A. G. Lloyd, and has issue living, Hanna *b.* 1968, Isabella *b.* 1970,—Elisabeth Ann, *b.* 1942: *m.* 1963, Anthony John Howard, of Drove Cottage, Newbridge, Cadnam, Hants., and has issue living, Tom Peter *b.* 1967, Kate Elisabeth *b.* 1965, Emma (twin) *b.* 1967,—Susan Henrietta, *b.* 1944: *m.* 1964, William Farquhar Acworth, of Gt. Hidden Farm, Hungerford, Berks. [*see* Buzzard, Bt.]. *Residence*, Terwick Old Rectory, Rogate, Petersfield, Hants.—— Anna Margaret *b.* 1913: *m.* 1st, 1940, Sir James Henderson-Stewart, MP, 1st Bt., who *d.* 1961; 2ndly, 1965, Geoffrey Walford Wilks, CBE, TD, of Walnut House, Ufford, Stamford and 64, Cadogan Sq., SW1.——Ruth Veronica, *b.* 1916: *m.* 1st, 1936, William Reginald Colquhoun, TD, who *d.* 1971; 2ndly, 1972, Peter Birchall, of Cecily House, Cirencester and has issue living (by 1st m.), William Patrick (2, Thornton Close, Girton, Cambridge), *b.* 1939: *m.* 1971, Frances Elspeth, only da. of Archibald Cameron, of 5, Denman's Close, Lindfield, Sussex, and has issue living, Anna Elizabeth *b.* 1973,—Alastair Peter, *b.* 1941,—John Humphrey, *b.* 1943: *m.* 1969, Susan Elizabeth, el. da. of Michael Ingram, of Driffield Manor, Cirencester, and has issue living, Mark Humphrey *b.* 1973,—Neil Robert, *b.* 1947: *m.* 1974, Rosemary Elizabeth, da. of the late Archibald Colville [see Gibson-Craig-Carmichael, Bt.],—Anna Margaret, *b.* 1946: *m.* 1968, Nigel Guthrie McNair Scott, of Cotswold Farm, Cirencester, Glos., and has issue living, Robert William *b.* 1970, Alastair Guthie *b.* 1972, David Ronald *b.* 1973.

Aunt living—(daughter of 1st baronet)—Margery Eyre, *b.* 1885: *m.* 1915, Capt. Frank Somerville Beauford, formerly Roy. Fusiliers (City of London Regt.), who *d.* 1959. *Residence*, Troston Hall, Bury St. Edmunds.

Collateral Branches living.

Issue of the late Maj. Aynsley Eyre Greenwell, 2nd son of 1st baronet, *b.* 1876, *d.* 1944: *m.* 1906, Beatrice Lilian, who *d.* 1966, da. of the late Rev. Canon Edward Sanderson, Preb. of Chichester (formerly R. of Uckfield):— Whitfield Ava Aynsley, *b.* 1907; Lieut.-Cdr. R.N.V.R.: *m.* 1935, Eve Turner, and has issue living, William Maxwell Walpole, *b.* 1942,—Eve Jennifer, *b.* 1939. *Residence*, Shermanbury Place, Shermanbury, nr. Horsham, Sussex.——Ivor Desmond, *b.* 1911; is Lieut.-Cdr. R.N.V.R.: *m.* 1939, Diana Ward, and has issue living, Jane Elizabeth, *b.* 1954,—Mary Claire (twin), *b.* 1954. *Residence*, Upper House, West Burton, nr. Pulborough, Sussex.——Basil Evelyn, *b.* 1915; is Lieut. R.N.V.R.: *m.* 1st, 1948 (marriage dissolved 1952), Phyllis Joyce, da. of the late K. L. Weatherall Pepper, of Lewes, Sussex; 2ndly, 1955, Sarah, da. of the late Capt. the Hon. Walter Seymour Carson, R.N. [By. Carson, ext.], and has issue living, (by 2nd marriage) Simon Lloyd, *b.* 1956,—Giles Henry, *b.* 1957,—Joanna Beatrice Taswell, *b.* 1962, Virginia Annette *b.* 1965. *Residence*, Tanners, River, Petworth, Sussex.——Walpole Edward (Wiler, Lötschental, Valais, Switzerland), *b.* 1920; 1939-45 War as FO RAFVR: *m.* 1963 (m. diss. 1972), Rosemary Heather

Bunn, da. of John Pares-Wilson, and has issue living, Rupert John Walpole *b.* 1964.——Verona Beatrice, *b.* 1910: *m.* 1935, Maurice Arthur Pryor, who *d.* 1959, and has issue living, Timothy Arthur, *b.* 1941,—Penelope, *b.* 1938,—Sarah Anne, *b.* 1944,—Anna Aynsley, *b.* 1951. *Residence,* Gallops, Ditchling, Sussex.

Issue of the late Geoffrey Eyre Greenwell, youngest son of 1st baronet, *b.* 1894, *d.* 1949: *m.* 1922, Mildred (who *m.* 2ndly, 1956), da. of the late J. Evans, of Norwood, SE:—

John Evelyn (East Field, Henfold Hill, Beare Green, Dorking, Surrey) *b.* 1924; ed. at King's Sch., Canterbury; 1939-45 with RAFVR: *m.* 1956, Frances Valerie Anne, da. of the late Marnix Cremer, of Lovelocks, Horley, and has issue living, Andrew John, *b.* 1959,—Jane Frances, *b.* 1963.

Sir Walpole Lloyd Greenwell, 1st Bt. (2nd son of the late Walpole Eyre Greenwell), was High Sheriff of Surrey 1903.

GRESLEY, Creation (E.) 1611, of Drakelowe, Derbyshire.

Sir WILLIAM FRANCIS GRESLEY, 13th *Baronet*; yst. son of William Stukeley Gresley, 3rd son of the Rev. John Morewood Gresley, yr. brother of 9th baronet, *b.* Oct. 10th, 1897; *s.* his kinsman *Sir* NIGEL, 1974: *m.* 1924, Ada Mary, da. of the late George Miller.

Arms—Vaire, ermine and gules. **Crest**—A lion passant ermine, armed angued, and collared gules.

Residence—59A, Grand Av., Southbourne, Bournemouth.

Collateral Branches living.

Meliore fide quam fortuna.

With better fidelity than good fortune.

Granddaughters of the late Rev. Nigel Gresley, 2nd son of 9th baronet :—

Issue of the late Nigel Bowyer Gresley, *b.* 1870, *d.* 1915 : *m.* 1903, Mabel Constance Talbot, who *d.* 1957, da. of the late Nicholas Jeffrey, of London, Ontario :—

Eleanor Constance, *b.* 1904: *m.* 1925, Capt. Roger Shawe Manley, and has issue living, Michael Roger (Northwood, Northwood Park, Sparsholt, Winchester), *b.* 1938; ed. at Canford Sch.: *m.* 1964, Sally Anne, el. da. of Cdr. Milner, and has issue living, Mark Shawe *b.* 1969, Jane Louise *b.* 1966,—Bridget Eleanor, *b.* 1926: *m.* 1951, Lt.-Cdr. Ian Gilmour Lovesy, RN, of Dane End Cottage, Therfield, Royston, Herts., and has issue living, Mark Gilmour *b.* 1955, Christopher Ian *b.* 1956, Neil Alastair *b.* 1959,—Gillian Gresley, *b.* 1934: *m.* 1956, David Gordon Glennie, of Green Acres, Hewshott Lane, Liphook, Hants, son of Adm. Sir Irvine Gordon Glennie, KCB, and has issue living, Nigel Gordon *b.* 1957, Timothy David, *b.* 1959, Simon Roger *b.* 1964, Caroline Juliet *b.* 1962. *Residence*, The Old Mill House, Bramshott, Liphook, Hants.——Maud Victoria (Yew Tree Cottage, Hammer Vale, Haslemere, Surrey), *b.* 1909: *m.* 1941, Capt. Peter M. Aldridge, Queen's Own Cameron Highlanders, who *d.* (killed in action in France) 1944, and has issue living, Peter Nigel (posthumous), *b.* 1945.

Issue of the late Sir (Herbert) Nigel Gresley, C.B.E., D.Sc., *b.* 1876, *d.* 1941 : *m.* 1901, Ethel Frances, who *d.* 1929, da. of the late W. P. Fullagar, solicitor, of St. Anne's-on-Sea, Lancashire :—

Violet, *b.* 1904: *m.* 1937, Maj. Geoffrey Edward Michael Godfrey, M.B.E., R.E.M.E., son of the late Sir Daniel Eyers Godfrey, and has issue living, Timothy Dan (69, Richmond Rd., Wolverhampton), *b.* 1938: *m.* 1960, Penelope Anne, da. of Lawrence Kelly Silvester, and has issue living, Nicholas Dan *b.* 1961, Selena Anne *b.* 1964,—Benjamin Michael (Belle Vue, The Folley, Layer de la Haye, Colchester, Essex), *b.* 1942: *m.* 1965, Hjørdis Andersen Bøgeskov, and has issue living, James Michael *b.* 1969, Nina Louise *b.* 1971,—Louise Gresley, *b.* 1939: *m.* 1970, Alexander Wellwood Jameson, of Crecy, Isle of Whithorn, Newton Stewart, Wigtownshire. *Residence*, Fyfield House, Fyfield, nr. Ongar, Essex.——Marjorie, *b.* 1909. *Residence*, 13, Lewes Cres., Brighton, Sussex.

Issue of the late Nigel Morewood Gresley, el. brother of 13th baronet, *b.* 1892, *d.* 1966: *m.* 1921, Mary Mansfield (3, Park View Court, Mount Pleasant Rd., Poole), da. of the late R. M. Hobill:—

Mary Penelope, *b.* 1928: *m.* 1959, Brian Stacy Warham Rigby-Hall, of 46, Queen's Park West Drive, Bournemouth, and has issue living, Robert Gresley, *b.* 1965,—Frances Margaret, *b.* 1968.

Granddaughter of the late Maj. Francis Gresley, son of the late Richard Gresley, uncle of 9th baronet:—

Mary Lillian, *b.* 1887: *m.* 1912, Christopher George, who *d.* 1954. *Residence*, Green Meadows, Bepton, Midhurst, Sussex.

Nigel de Stafford, ancestor of this family, held Drakelowe and other Derbyshire manors of the King in 1086. Dugdale considers him to have been a brother of Robert de Stafford. If so, he would have been son of Roger de Tony or Tosni (*d.c.* 1039), grandson of Hugh de Calvacamp, a Norman noble living in mid-10th century. Sir George Gresley, 1st baronet, was a patron of learning, who introduced Sir William Dugdale to the Earl of Arundel (Earl Marshal).

Grey (cr. 1711), see Lambert (cr. 1711).

GREY, Creation (U.K.) 1814, of Fallodon, Northumberland.

To serve the king with good will.

Sir ANTHONY DYSART GREY, 7th *Baronet*; *b.* Oct. 19th, 1949; *s.* his grandfather, *Sir* ROBIN EDWARD DYSART, 1974; Man., Fibre Glass Div. Bel Art Corpn: *m.* 1970, Donna (Museum Curator), da. of Donald Daniels, of 60, Park Lane, W1.

Arms,—Gules, a lion rampant within a bordure engrailed argent, a mullet for difference. **Crest.**—A scaling ladder in bend sinister or, hooked and pointed sable.

Residence—Van Riper Hopper House, 533, Berdan Av., Wayne, NJ 07470, USA.

***

Great Aunt living—Annette Dysart, *b.* 1890: *m.* 1928 Arthur Fraser Sutton, MBE, of 75, Warrimoo Av. St. Ives, NS Wales.

Mother living—Nancy (86, Kingsway Gdns., 38, King's Park Rd., Perth, W. Aust.), da. of the late Francis John Meagher, of Winning Station, W. Aust.: *m.* 1946, Edward Elton Grey, who *d.* 1962, only son of 6th Bt.

Widow living of 5th Baronet—GWLADYS (*Gwladys*) *Lady Grey*), (Arrandale, 111, Westmorland Rd., Bromley, Kent), yst. da. of the late William Maxwell: *m.* 1920, Sir Harry Martin Grey, MRCS, LRCP, 5th baronet, who *d.* 1960.

The 1st baronet, the Hon. Sir George Grey, was third son of the 1st Earl Grey; the 2nd baronet, the Rt. Hon. Sir George, G.C.B., P.C., sat as M.P. for Devonport (*L*) 1832-47, for Northumberland North 1847-52, and for Morpeth 1853-74; was Sec. of State for Home Department 1846-52, 1855-8 and 1861-6, Sec. of State for the Colonies 1854-5, and Chancellor of the Duchy of Lancaster 1841 and 1859-61; the 3rd baronet, Rt. Hon. Sir Edward, K.G., sat as M.P. for Berwick-on-Tweed (*L*) 1885-1916, and was Under-Sec. of State for Foreign Affairs 1892-95, and Sec. of State for Foreign Affairs 1905-16, and Ambassador to U.S.A. (on special mission) 1919; *cr. Viscount Grey of Fallodon*, co. Northumberland 1916 (ext. **1933**).

Grey Egerton, see Egerton.

GRIERSON, Creation (N.S.) 1685, of Lag, Dumfriesshire.

Safer by this

Sir RICHARD DOUGLAS GRIERSON, 11th *Baronet*; *b.* June 25th, 1912; *s.* his father, *Major Sir* ROBERT GILBERT WHITE, 1957; ed. at Imperial Ser. Coll., Windsor.

Arms—Gules, on a fesse or, between three fetterlocks argent a mullet azure. **Crest**—A lock as in the arms.

Residence—4, Modena Rd., Hove.

***

Collateral Branches living

Issue of the late Lieut.-Col. Alexander George William Grierson, R.M. (retired), 2nd son of 9th baronet; *b.* 1884, *d.* 1951: *m.* 1920, Violet Ethel (now of 6, The Beach, Walmer, Kent), da. of Lieut.-Col. Arthur Edward Bewes, C.M.G., of Walmer, Kent:—

MICHAEL JOHN BEWES (71, Wyatt Park Rd., Streatham Hill, SW2), *b.* July 24th, 1921: *m.* 1971, Valerie Anne, da. of Russell Wright, of Gidea Park, Essex.——Pamela Violet, *b.* 1925: *m.* 1955, Richard Wallace Vernon [*see* Vernon, Bt.]. *Residence*, Scotch Corner, Wildernesse Avenue, Sevenoaks, Kent.

Issue of the late Frederick Vedast Grierson, Lieut. King's Own Scottish Borderers, ygst son of 9th baronet, *b.* 1888, *d.* 1922: *m.* 1909, Frederica, who *d.* 1941, da. of Arthur Frederick Skipp, of Cheltenham:—
Lorna Mary Sheila : *m.* 1941, Carl Berger, who obtained a divorce 1951. *Residence,*

This family claim descent from Gilbert, younger son of Malcolm MacGregor of MacGregor (*d.* 1374). Sir Robert Grierson, Knight, of Lag, who sat as MP for Dumfries 1678-86, was created a baronet with remainder to heirs male whatsoever. He was a great persecutor of the Covenantors, and presided at the trial and execution of two women known as the Wigtown Martyrs who refused to take the abjuration oath. He was " Sir Robert Redgauntlet " of Wandering Willie's tale in Sir Walter Scott's *Redgauntlet.* Sir Gilbert Grierson, 4th baronet, joined the Jacobite Rising 1715.

NORTON-GRIFFITHS, Creation (U.K.) 1922, of Wonham, Betchworth, co. Surrey.

For King and Empire.

Sir PETER NORTON-GRIFFITHS, 2nd *Baronet*; *b.* May 3rd, 1905 ; *s.* his father, Sir JOHN, *K.C.B., D.S.O.,* 1930; ed. at Eton, and at Magdalen Coll., Oxford ; Bar. Inner Temple 1931 ; was Assist. Mil. Attaché, Madrid 1941-42, Gen. Manager of Shell Co. of Portugal Ltd. 1951-3, and Managing Director of Belgian Shell Co., S.A. 1953-60 ; is an Officer of Order of Crown of Belgium and of Order of Oak Leaf Crown of Luxembourg ; European War 1940-45 as Major Intelligence Corps : *m.* 1935, Kathryn, da. of the late George F. Schrafft, of Newton, Massachusetts, U.S.A., and has issue.

Arms—1st and 4th, sable, a flaming sword erect between two griffins combatant or, *Griffiths*; 2nd and 3rd argent, on a fesse raguly between two fleur-de-lis azure, a fleur-de-lis between two crescents or, *Norton.* Crests—1st, a demi-lion rampant gules, grasping in the paws a flaming sword erect, *Griffiths*; 2ndly, a dexter gauntlet clasped sable between two ostrich feathers argent, *Norton.* Supporters—Dexter, a Colonial soldier in the uniform of a trooper of the Second Regiment King Edward's Horse, resting the exterior hand upon a terrestrial globe in frame environed with a meridian; *sinister,* a labourer holding in the exterior hand a Jackhammer drill all proper.
Address—Quinta do Torneiro, Paço d'Arcos, Portugal.

Sons living—JOHN (26, Burnt Bridge Av., Bricktown, NJ, 08723, USA), *b.* Oct. 4th, 1938; ed. at Eton; late Sub-Lt. RN; a Chartered Accountant: *m.* 1964, Marilyn Margaret, el. da. of Norman Grimley, of 40, Hillcrest Rd., Gt. Crosby, Liverpool.——Michael (24, Horwood Close, Headington, Oxford), *b.* 1941; ed. at Eton, and at Keble Coll., Oxford (DPhil, Zoology); Ecologist, Serengeti Research Inst 1970-74: *m.* 1965, Ann, only da. of the late Group Capt. Blair Alexander Fraser, RAF, of Dolphin House, Batheaston, Bath [E. Dundonald, colls.].
Daughter living—Anne, *b.* 1936: *m.* 1956, Richard Hathaway Morgan, and has issue living, Kathryn, *b.* 1957,—Christina, *b.* 1958,—Pascale, *b.* 1960. *Residence,* Chateau d'Oursières, 28420, Beaumont-les-Autels, France.
Sisters living—Ursula (Stonewalls, Limpsfield, Surrey), *b.* 1903; is a JP for Surrey (Co. Councillor 1948-61): *m.* 1922, John Henry Thorpe, OBE, KC, JP, Recorder of Blackburn, who *d.* 1944, and has issue living, Rt. Hon. (John) Jeremy, MP [see PRIVY COUNCIL]; *b.* 1929: *m.* 1st, 1968, Caroline Julia, who *d.* 1970, da. of Warwick Allpass, of 3, Beeches Road, Kingswood, Surrey; 2ndly, 1973, Maria Donata Nanetta Paulina Gustava Erwina Wilhelmina (Marion), da. of the late Erwin Stein, and formerly wife of 7th Earl of Harewood, and has issue living (by 1st m.), Rupert Jeremy *b.* 1969,—Lavinia, *b.* 1923: *m.* 19—, Col. Eric Thompson Bradley, OBE, of 82, North Lane, E. Preston, Sussex, and has issue living, Caleb Rupert *b.* 1947, Jason Adrian *b.* 1953, Lydia Jane *b.* 1949.——Phoebe (Pear Tree Cottage, Churt, Surrey), *b.* 1906: *m.* 1947, Edward Bromilow Joynson, MBE, who *d.* 1972.

Collateral Branch living.

Issue of the late Capt. Michael Norton-Griffiths, R.E., 2nd son of 1st baronet, *b.* 1908, *d.* (killed in action) 1940: *m.* 1936, Mrs. Elizabeth Gertrude Colclough, who *m.* 3rdly, 1946, George Paul Minchin Woodward, of New Jersey, USA, and 4thly, 1954, Ralph Arthur Hubbard, of 1, Shorecroft, Aldwick, Bognor Regis [see B. Addington, colls.], yr. da. of the late Stephen Cozens, of Mackney Manor, Wallingford, Berks:—
Johanna, *b.* 1936: *m.* 1969, Keith Martin Butt, MA, MB, MRCVS, of Burhunt Farm, Selborne, Hants., and has issue living, Matthew Martin, *b.* 1972,—Martha, *b.* 1971.

The 1st Baronet, Lieut.-Col. Sir John Norton-Griffiths, K.C.B., D.S.O. (son of the late John Griffiths, of Brecon), assumed by deed poll 1917, the additional surname of Norton, and was Governing Director of Sir John Norton-Griffiths & Co., Ltd., public works contractors and engineers : served in S. African War, first in Colonial Div., and afterwards as Capt. and Adj. Lord Roberts' Body Guard, Head Quarter Staff, and in European War 1914-16 when he raised a Special Cav. Regt., subsequently being on Staff of Engineer-in-Ch. to organize and start Tunnelling Cos, R.E., and went on special mission to Roumania for destruction of oil wells and corn stores (despatches thrice, D.S.O.) : M.P. for Wednesbury (C) Jan. 1910 to Nov. 1918, and for Central Div. of Wandsworth Dec. 1918 to Oct. 1924.

GROTRIAN, Creation (U.K.) 1934, of Leighton Buzzard, co. Bedford.

By courage and faith.

Sir JOHN APPELBE BRENT GROTRIAN, 2nd *Baronet*; *b.* Feb. 16th, 1904; *s.* his father *Sir* HERBERT BRENT, K.C., 1951; ed. at Eton, and at Trin. Coll., Oxford; European War 1939-45 (despatches).

Arms—Gules, a wyvern or, in chief two roses argent, barbed and seeded proper. Crest—A wyvern or, resting the dexter leg upon a rose argent, barbed and seeded proper.

Residences—Raughmere House, Lavant, Chichester, Sussex; 40, Hamilton Terr., St. Johns Wood, NW8.

Sisters living—Lilian Désirée, *b.* 1914.——Mary Joizelle Elizabeth Pearl, *b.* 1918 : *m.* 1947, John Gifford Ormerod, and has issue living, Elizabeth Mary, *b.* 1949,—Caroline Anne, *b.* 1955. *Residence*, 142, Tuffley Avenue, Gloucester.

Collateral Branches living.

Issue of the late Major Charles Herbert Brent Grotrian, T.D., B.C.L., J.P., R.A. (T.A.), el. son of 1st baronet, *b.* 1902, *d.* (killed in action in Burma) 1944 : *m.* 1936, Aileen Georgina (of 17, Hogarth Road, Hove, 3, Sussex), only da. of the late George Ernest Etlinger :—

Charlotte Elizabeth, *b.* 1941.

Issue of the late Squadron Leader Robert Philip Brent Grotrian, 3rd son of 1st baronet, *b.* 1908, *d.* (on active ser. in Far East) 1945 : *m.* 1st, 1931, Elizabeth Mary, only da. of the late Major Herbert Hardy-Wrigley ; 2ndly, 1939, Margaret (CHAUDOIR) (who *m.* 3rdly, 1950, His Honour Judge (Richard Geraint) Rees, of Fellside, 23, Heath Rd., Weybridge, Surrey), da. of the late George Green :—

(By 1st marriage) PHILIP CHRISTIAN BRENT, *b.* March 26th, 1935; ed. at Eton, and at Univ. of Trin. Coll., Toronto: *m.* 1960, Anne Isabel, da. of Robert Sieger Whyte, of Toronto, Canada, and has issue living, Philip Timothy Brent, *b.* 1962. *Residence*, 295, Glen Rd., Toronto 5, Canada.——(By 2nd marriage) Jane Felicity, *b.* 1942: *m.* 1964, Peter Lewis Andrews, of Old Timbers, Shere Rd., W. Horsley, Surrey, and has issue living, Philip Kenneth, *b.* 1964,—Sarah Jane, *b.* 1967.

The 1st baronet, Sir Herbert Brent Grotrian, K.C., D.L., B.C.L. (2nd son of the late Frederick Brent Grotrian, M.P.), was Recorder of Scarborough 1918-46, sat as M.P. for S.-W. Div. of Kingston-upon-Hull (C.) 1924-29, and was High Sheriff of Bedfordshire 1931.

GROVE, Creation (U.K.) 1874, of Ferne, Wiltshire.

Neither above nor below.

Sir CHARLES GERALD GROVE, 5th *Baronet*; *b.* Dec. 10th, 1929; *s.* his brother, *Sir* WALTER FELIPE PHILIP, 1974.

Arms—Ermine, on a chevron engrailed gules ; three scallops, the centre one or, the others argent. Crest—A talbot statant sable, collared argent.

Resides in USA.

Brother living—HAROLD THOMAS, *b.* Dec. 6th, 1930.

Mother living—Elena, da. of the late Felipe Crosthwaite : *m.* 1926, Walter Peel Grove, who *d.* 1944, having obtained a divorce in Mexico 1933. *Resides in USA.*

This family claims descent from John Grove, who settled in Wilts. from Bucks. *temp.* Henry VI. William Grove, M.P., for Shaftesbury, who died 1589, purchased Ferne in 1563 and Sedghill in 1582. Sir Thomas Fraser Grove, 1st Bt., was M.P. for S. Wilts. (L) 1865-74, and for Wilts. S., or Wilton, Div. 1885-92.

GUINNESS, Creation (U.K.) 1867, of Ashford, co. Galway.

My hope is in God.

Sir KENELM ERNEST LEE GUINNESS, 4th *Baronet*, son of the late Kenelm Edward Lee Guinness, M.B.E., R.N.V.R., 2nd son of the late Capt. Benjamin Lee Guinness, 2nd son of 1st baronet; *b.* Dec. 13th, 1928; *s.* his uncle *Sir* ALGERNON ARTHUR ST. LAWRENCE LEE, 1954; ed. at Eton and at Mass. Institute of Technology, U.S.A.; late 2nd Lieut. Roy. Horse Guards: *m.* 1961, Mrs. Jane Nevin Dickson, and has issue.

Arms—Quarterly: 1st and 4th per saltire gules and azure, a lion rampant or, on a chief ermine a dexter hand couped at the wrist of the first, *Guinness*: 2nd and 3rd argent, on a fesse between three crescents sable a trefoil slipped or, *Lee*. Crests—1st, a boar passant, quarterly or and gules; 2nd, on a pillar argent, encircled by a ducal coronet or, an eagle preying on a bird's leg erased proper. **Supporters**—On either side a stag gules, attired and gorged with a collar gemmel or, pendant therefrom by a chain gold an escutcheon, the dexter charged with the arms of Guinness, and the sinister with those of Lee. [The supporters in the arms were granted to Sir Benjamin Lee Guinness, 1st baronet, and his heirs male, upon whom the dignity of a baronet may descend, as a special mark of favour for the public spirit and munificent liberality manifested by him in the restoration of St. Patrick's Cathedral, Dublin.]

Residence—2814, 35th St., NW, Washington, DC, USA.   *Club*—Buck's.

Sons living—KENELM EDWARD LEE, *b.* Jan. 30th, 1962.——Sean St. Lawrence Lee, *b.* 1966.

Sister living—Geraldine St. Lawrence, *b.* 1930: *m.* 1956, Mikael Essayan, and has issue living, Martin Sarkis, *b.* 1959,—Joanna Consuelo, *b.* 1958.   *Residence*, 6, Chelsea Sq., SW3.

Daughter living of 3rd Baronet—Susan (Shoonan) Rosemary Lee, *b.* 1931 : *m.* 1st, 1953, Samuel Charles Gillchrest, from whom she obtained a divorce 1956 ; 2ndly, 1958, Keith Rawlings Hall, of Yarhampton House, Astley, Worcs., and Farm Cottage, Beenham, Berks., and has issue living, (by 2nd m.) Simon Patrick Rawlings, *b.* 1959,—Timothy Mark Lee, *b.* 1967,—Susan Felicity, *b.* 1960,—Jennifer Margaret, *b.* 1963.

Mother living—Josephine, daughter of Sir Thomas Joseph Strangman: *m.* 1928, Lieut. Kenelm Edward Lee Guinness, M.B.E., R.N.V.R., from whom she obtained a divorce 1936.   *Residence*, Casa Ferrer, Cala San Vicente, Pollensa, Majorca.

Widow living of 3rd Baronet—WINIFRED (MOUNTENEY) (*Winifred, Lady Guinness*), da. of the late John George Hall: *m.* 1928, Sir Algernon Arthur St. Lawrence Lee Guinness, 3rd baronet, who *d.* 1954.   *Residence*, Jays Wood, Beenham, Berks.

Sir Benjamin Lee Guinness, M.P., LL.D., 1st Bt., sat as M.P. for Dublin City (*C*) 1865-8, and at his own cost restored the Cathedral of St. Patrick, Dublin.   His el. son, Sir Edward, 2nd Bt., sat as M.P. for Dublin (*C*) 1868-9 and 1874-80, when he was cr. *Baron Ardilaun*, of Ashford, co. Galway (peerage of United Kingdom), which Barony became ext. at his death in 1915.

GUISE, Creation (G.B.) 1783, of Highnam Court, Gloucestershire.

[Name pronounced "**Gyze**."]

Sir JOHN GRANT GUISE, 7th *Baronet*; *b.* Dec. 15th, 1927; *s.* his father, *Sir* ANSELM WILLIAM EDWARD, 1970; ed. at Winchester; Capt. (ret.) Queen's Own Hussars; patron of one living.

Arms—Gules, seven lozenges conjoined vaire, three, three, and one, on a canton or a mullet of six points pierced sable. **Crest**—Out of a ducal coronet or a swan wings elevated argent, gorged with a ducal crown and chain over the back or. **Supporters** (to descend with the baronetcy)—*Dexter*, a swan with wings endorsed argent crusilly and langued gules, beaked and membered sable, collared and chained or ; *sinister*, a bear sable, billetty, collared and chained or, langued and armed gules.

Seat—Elmore Court, nr. Gloucester

QUO · HONESTIOR · EO · TUTIOR

The more honest, the more safe.

Brother living—CHRISTOPHER JAMES (97, Hurlingham Rd., SW6), *b.* July 10th, 1930; ed. at Stowe: *m.* 1969, Mrs. Carole Hoskins Benson, el. da. of Jack Master, of The Dower House Crawley, Winchester, Hants., and has issue living, Anselm Mark, *b.* 1971,—Ruth Victoria Margaret, *b.* 1972.

Sister living—Philippa Margaret, *b.* 1926: *m.* 1950, Maj. Alastair Hugh Joseph Fraser, MC, Lovat Scouts [*see* L. Lovat, colls.].   *Residences*, Coddenham House, Coddenham, Ipswich; Moniack Castle, Kirkhill, Inverness-shire.

Widow living of 6th Baronet—MARGARET (*Lady Guise*), (Elmore Court, nr. Gloucester), da. of Sir Sir James Augustus Grant, 1st Bt.; *cr.* 1926 (Ext.): *m.* 1924, Capt. Sir Anselm William Edward Guise, 6th baronet, who *d.* 1970.

Collateral Branches living.

Issue of the late Col. Christopher Dering Guise, 3rd son of 4th baronet, *b.* 1855, *d.* 1926 : *m.* 1903, Ella Letitia, who *d.* 1928, da. of the late Vice-Adm. Gerard John Napier :—

Valérie Napier, *b.* 1907.   *Residence*,

Grandson of the late Major Henry John Guise, 2nd son of 3rd baronet :—

Issue of the late William Verner Guise, *b.* 1856, *d.* 1935 : *m.* 1879, Emilie Annie, who *d.* 1921, da. of Lee Vyner, of Ceylon :—

Anselm Verner Lee, *C.B.E.*, *b.* 1881 ; formerly Major in the Army; has Portuguese Red Cross medal, and Order of Leopold of Belgium ; C.B.E. (Civil) 1918.   *Residence*,

Grandchildren of the late Rivett Francis Guise, 2nd son of the late Francis Edward Guise, 3rd son of 3rd baronet:—

Issue of the late Lt.-Cdr. Jack Francis Vernon Guise, *b.* 1882, *d.* 1964: *m.* 1917, Catherine Renée, who *d.* 1970, da. of the late Gilbert Ireland-Blackburne, of Bristol:—

John Nicholas (63, Bywood Way, Lynwood, W. Aust.) *b.* 1920: *m.* 1st 19—, (m. diss. 19—) Valerie Parker; 2ndly, 19—, Beverley Parker, and has issue living, (by 1st m.), Anthony, *b.* 1951,—Nikki (da.), *b.* 1952,—Judith Anne, *b.* 1955,—(by 2nd m.) James Nicholas, *b.* 1969.——Christopher Rivett (86, Varden St., Kalgoorlie 6430, W. Aust.), *b.* 1921: *m.* 19—, Marion Strang, and has issue living, Christopher John, *b.* 1949,—Georgina Elizabeth, *b.* 1951,—Penelope Jane, *b.* 1955.——Reginald Ireland (Box 51, Coorow 6515, W. Aust.), *b.* 1923: *m.* 1951, Gladys Constance, only da. of Robert Alexander Baxter, of 44, Bedford St., Cunderin, Aust., and has issue living Larry Steven, *b.* 1958,—Neil Reginald, *b.* 1960,—David Nigel, *b.* 1970,—Wendy Nola, *b.* 1954.——Marguerite Renee, *b.* 1918: *m.* 19—, Ralph James Lang, of 48, Adair Parade, Mount Lawley, 6050, W. Aust., and has issue living.——Diana Mary, *b.* 1925: *m.* 19—, Graham Johnson, of 40,

Welwyn Av., Manning, 6152, W. Aust., and has issue living.——Tacy Avena, *b.* 1927: *m.* 1st, 19— (m. diss. 19—), Thomas Turbett; 2ndly, 19—, Bernard Kelly, of 23, Kooham Way, Balga 6061, W. Aust., and has issue living, (by 1st m.),.........................; (by 2nd m.), ...——Georgina Frances, *b.* 1930: *m.* 19—, Jack Pritchard, and has issue living.

Issue of the late Capt. Francis Edward Boissier Guise, *b.* 1892, *d.* 1970: *m.* 1st, 1914, Ethel Mary, who *d.* 1943, da. of Edward Valentine Holme; 2ndly, 1944, Gertrude Joyce (10, Harrow Rd., Brislington, Bristol 4), da. of E. F. Taylor, of Kingswood, Bristol:—

(By 2nd m.) Christopher Francis (97, Somerset Rd., Knowle, Bristol), *b.* 1945; late RN: *m.* 1973, Gwynneth Harock, of Bristol, and has issue living, Nicola, *b.* 1974,—Rhian (twin) *b.* 1974.—— Penelope Catherine, *b.* 1946: *m.* 1966, Nigel Wilkinson, of 2, Trent Way, Riverdene, Basingstoke, and has issue living, Simon, *b.* 1970,—Nicholas, *b.* 1972.——Elizabeth Anne, *b.* 1950: *m.* 1973, David Richard Fynn, of 50, Littledean, Yate, nr. Bristol.——Rosemary Caroline, *b.* 1954.

Issue of the late Lieut.-Col. John William Guise, *b.* 1894, *d.* 1963: *m.* 1924 (marriage dissolved 1937), Dorothy Alma, da. of Theodore Hewitt English:—
Patricia Frederica, *b.* 1929.

Issue of the late Christopher Probyn Guise, *b.* 1899, *d.* 1965: *m.* 1st, 1931, (m. diss. 1956), Hope, da. of the late F. G. P. Neison, of Lahore; 2ndly, 1959, (m. diss. 1963), Catherine Elizabeth de Villiers:—

(By 1st m.) Anselm Neison (Grays Rd., P.O. Box 54092, Plimmerton, nr. Wellington, NZ), *b.* 1935: *m.* 1959, Eileen Mary, da. of Col. Patrick Henry Cummins, IMS (ret.) [see E. Lauderdale, colls.], and has issue living, Edward William. *b.* 1962,—Christopher Patrick, *b.* 1973,—Laura Joan, *b.* 1960, —Susan Mary, *b.* 1965.——John Francis, *b.* 1947.——Dinah Gabrielle, *b.* 1936: *m.* 1957, Peter Maunder, of 51, Winchendon Rd., Teddington, Middx.

Issue of the late Rivett Arthur Guise, *b.* 1902, *d.* 1965: *m.* 1924, Beatrice Geraldine (Conifers, Ringwood Rd., Ferndown, Dorset), da. of the late Edward Charles Rudge, of Abbey Manor, Evesham:—
Peter Rivett John (Highnam, St. Mary's Rd., Hay-on-Wye, Hereford), *b.* 1928: *m.* 1953, Morfydd Meredydd, da. of the late Lewis Morris, of St. Harman, Rhayader.——Shelia Mae, *b.* 1925: *m.* 1952, Francis Brian Collis, of Collingwood, Crowsley Rd., Shiplake, Oxon., and has issue living, David Brian, *b.* 1954,—Simon Christopher, *b.* 1957.

Granddaughter of the late Francis Edward Guise (ante):—
Issue of the late John Wright Guise, *b.* 1855, *d.* 1916: *m.* 1st, 1884, Helen Edith, who *d.* 1885, da. of His Honour the late Judge Sumner, of Hempsted Court, Gloucester; 2ndly, 1888, Charlotte, who *d.* 1931, da. of the late Edwin Crawshay:—
(By 2nd m.) Lesa Frances, *b.* 1893: *m.* 1920, Capt. Kingsmill Foster Manley Power, MC, Gloucestershire Regt. Reserve, who *d.* 1963, and has issue living, Manley Anselm, *b.* 1920,—Charlotte Lesa, *b.* 1922. *Residence,*

Granddaughters of the late Rev. Vernon Lane Guise, son of the late Rev. Vernon George Guise, 4th son of 3rd baronet :—
Issue of the late Maj. Vernon Robert Guise, OBE, MC, *b.* 1885, *d.* 1939: *m.* 1919, Nadine Alice (Orford House, Woodcote Park, Coulsdon, Surrey), da. of the late Andrew Charles Armstrong [*see* Armstrong, Bt., *cr.* 1941, colls.]:—
Veronica Louise, *b.* 1921 : *m.* 1946, Alan Falconer, F.R.C.S., Surg.-Lieut.-Com. R.N., and has issue living, John Hedley, *b.* 1951,—Alastair, *b.* 1955,—Jennifer Anne, *b.* 1947,—Catherine Scott, *b.* 1949. *Residence*, 71, Alexandra Park Road, Muswell Hill, N.10.——Elizabeth Mary Joanna, *b.* 1923 : *m.* 1954, Francis John Clark Mennell, and has issue living, Andrew Guise, *b.* 1955,— Susan Lilias, *b.* 1956. *Residence*, 7, Friars Rise, Woking, Surrey.

In 1262 Nicholas de Gyse (having *m.* a near relative of Sir John de Burgh, el. son of Hubert Earl of Kent), received in right of his wife the manor and lordship of Elmore in Gloucestershire. Sir Anselm de Gyse, son of Nicholas, received (temp. 1274) a confirmation of this manor by a further grant (still in possession of the family), and assumed the De Burgh arms, differenced by a canton. His descendant, Christopher Guise, el. son of William Guise, of Elmore (Sheriff of Gloucestershire 1647), was *cr.* a Baronet 1661, which Baronetcy became ext. at the death of the 5th baronet in April 1783 ; but eight months after, in Dec. 1783, his cousin and heir male, John Guise (of the younger branch), of Highnam Court, co. Gloucester, great-grandson of Henry Guise, a younger son of William Guise, of Elmore (ante), younger brother of 1st Baronet of 1st creation, was also *cr.* a Baronet. The 2nd baronet (of the 2nd creation) sat as M.P. for Gloucestershire. Gen. Sir John Guise, 3rd Bt., G.C.B., was granted supporters to descend to heirs male of the body on succession to the baronetcy 1863, and the 4th and 5th Baronets were High Sheriffs of Gloucestershire.

GULL, Creation (U.K.) 1872, of Brook Street.

Without God labour is in vain.

Sir MICHAEL SWINNERTON CAMERON GULL, 4th *Baronet;* *b.* Jan. 24th, 1919; *s.* his father *Capt. Sir* RICHARD CAMERON, 1960 ; ed. at Eton ; formerly 2nd Lieut. Scots Guards (Supplementary Reserve) : *m.* 1950, Yvonne (BAWTREE), da. of the late Albert Oliver Macarius Heslop, of Cape Town, S. Africa, and has issue.

Arms—Azure, a serpent nowed or between three sea-gulls proper ; a canton ermine, thereon an ostrich feather argent, quilled or, enfiled by the coronet which encircles the plume of the Prince of Wales, gold. *Crests*—1st, a lion passant guardant or, supporting with his dexter fore paw an escutcheon azure, thereon an ostrich feather argent, quilled or, enfiled with a coronet as in the canton ; 2nd, two arms embowed, vested azure, cuffs argent, the hands proper holding a torch or fired proper.
Residence—2, Harcourt Rd., Claremont, Cape Town, S. Africa.

Son living—RUPERT WILLIAM CAMERON, *b.* July 14th, 1954.
Daughter living—Katherine Dona Mary, *b.* 1951.
Sister living—Pamela Dona Anne, *b.* 1922 : *m.* 1946, Col. Alistair James Strang Martin, CBE, Queen's Own Highlanders (ret.), and has issue living, Christopher Thomas, *b.* 1948,—Michael Richard Alistair, *b.* 1953.
Uncle living (son of 2nd baronet)—John Evelyn, MC, *b.* 1914; 1939-45 War, Capt. Coldstream Guards (despatches, MC): *m.* 1957, Margaret Colquhoun, da. of the late Capel Berger of Hatfield, Herts. and has issue living, Angus William John, *b.* 1963. *Residence*, Trowley Hill Farm, Flamstead, nr. St. Albans, Herts.

Aunts living (daughters of 2nd baronet)—Mary Edith, *b.* 1887: *m.* 1st, 1911, William Herbert Watney, Lieut. Rifle Brig., who *d.* (killed in action during European War) 1915; 2ndly, 1926, William Houldsworth McConnel, who *d.* 1943, and has issue living (by 2nd m.), William Roger (Exstable, Alvescot, Oxon. OX8 2QJ), *b.* 1929: *m.* 1955, Susan Ingersoll, da. of W. T. Lyall, of Montreal, Canada, and has issue living, William Timothy *b.* 1957, Andrew Jamie *b.* 1967, Patricia Heidi *b.* 1960, Robyn Ingersoll *b.* 1962.——Dorothea Susan, *b.* 1897: *m.* 1923, Maj. Vernon Cyprian Knollys, Rifle Brig. (ret.), who *d.* 1973, and has issue living, David Cyprian (Woodlands Codds Hill, Beenham, Reading, RG7 5QG), *b.* 1925: *m.* 1952, Pamela Jane Sharman, and has issue living, Deborah Claire *b.* 1954, Catherine Anne *b.* 1956, Elizabeth Fay *b.* 1959, Veronica Frances *b.* 1963, Caroline Louise *b.* 1964,—Susan Anne, *b.* 1927: *m.* 1949, Maj.-Gen. Peter Hudson, CBE, Rifle Bde. (Little Orchard, Frilsham, Hermitage, Berks.), and has issue living, Jessica Rosemary *b.* 1963. *Residence*, St. Martins, Yattendon, Newbury, Berks.——Rosemary Violet, *b.* 1912: *m.* 1954, Maj. R. S. Schreiber, late Coldm. Gds. *Residence*, Campsea Ashe House, Woodbridge, Suffolk.

This baronetcy was conferred on William Withey Gull, M.D., an eminent Physician (subsequently Physician in Ordinary to H.M. Queen Victoria), in recognition of services rendered to H.R.H. Albert Edward, Prince of Wales, during his severe illness in the winter of 1871; and H.M. Queen Victoria also, in 1872, granted the canton as an augmentation to the arms. The 2nd baronet, Sir (William) Cameron, sat as M.P. for Devonshire N.-W. Div. (*LU*) 1895-1900.

GUNNING, Creation (G.B.) 1778, of Eltham, Kent.

Sir ROBERT CHARLES GUNNING, 8th *Baronet*, son of the late Charles Archibald John Gunning, son of the late Major Charles George Gunning, son of the late Major John Gunning, 6th son of 2nd baronet; *b.* Dec. 2nd, 1901; *s.* his kinsman, *Brig.-Gen. Sir* CHARLES VERE, C.B., C.M.G., 1950; ed. at St. Paul's Sch., and at Leeds Univ.; European War 1939-45 as Lieut. R.A. (T.A.) with Anti-Aircraft Command: *m.* 1934, Helen Nancy, da. of the late Vice-Adm. Sir Theodore John Hallett, K.B.E., C.B., and has issue.

Arms—Gules, on a fesse erminois between three doves argent, as many crosses formée per pale gules and azure. *Crest*—A dove holding in its dexter claw a caduceus proper.

Residence—Peace River, Alberta, Canada. *Club*—Caledonian.

He rules alone with impartial sway

Sons living—CHARLES THEODORE (2940, McCarthy Rd., Ottawa K1V 8K6, Ont., Canada), *b.* June 19th, 1935; BEng., CEng., AMIMechE, AMIMarE; RCN: *m.* 1969, Sarah, da. of Col. Patrick Arthur Easton, of Tonbridge, Kent, and has issue living, Caroline Ann, *b.* 1971.——John Robert, (Box 1793, Peace River, Alberta, Canada), *b.* 1944: *m.* 1969, Alina Tylicki, and has issue living, Derek John Robert, *b.* 1972,—Lori-Ann, *b.* 1969.——Joseph Jeremy (PO Box 2409, Peace River, Alberta, Canada) *b.* 1946: *m.* 1968, June Smith, and has issue living, Diana Elizabeth, *b.* 1968,—Theressa Kathleen, *b.* 1971,—Michelle Wendy, *b.* 1973.——David Laurence, *b.* 1948.——Henry Michael (Poole, Dorset), *b.* 1949: *m.* 1970, Rita Bruneau, and has issue living, Holly Michelle, *b.* 1970,—Melanie Dawn, *b.* 1975.——Bernard Christopher (Charlottown, PEI), *b.* 1951; Land Surveyor.—— George Peter, *b.* 1953: *m.* 1974, Pauline Maud Karpiak.——Anthony Andrew Simon, *b.* 1955. **Daughters living**—Iseult Sara, *b.* 1936: *m.* 1970, Klaus Krey (Box 1241, Peace River, Alberta TOH 2XO, Canada), and has issue living, Andrew Lee, *b.* 1974,—Suzanne Nicole, *b.* 1972.——Elaine Beatrice, *b.* 1939: *m.* 1958, Arnold Nelson Jones (Box 772, High Prairie, Alberta, Canada), and has issue living, Michael Robert, *b.* 1959,—Charles Mark, *b.* 1960,—George Marion, *b.* 1961,— Bruce Gordon, *b.* 1963,—Christopher John Peter, *b.* 1971,—Kathryn Ann, *b.* 1967. **Daughter living of 7th Baronet**—Essex Vere: *m.* 1919, Basil Gerald Brooke, formerly Lieut. 17th Lancers, who *d.* 1969 [*see* Brooke, Bt., colls., *cr.* 1903]. *Residence*, 23, Halsey St., SW3. **Sister living**—Josephine (7, Hawthorn Way, Storrington, Sussex), *b.* 1904.

Collateral Branches living.

Granddaughter of the late Col. George Hamilton Gunning, D.S.O., uncle of 8th baronet :—

Issue of the late Major Jack Hamilton Gunning, Indian Army, *b.* 1907, *d.* 1956 : *m.* 1st, 1938, Judith Clowes, who *d.* 1942, da. of the late Capt. Norton Clowes Castle, Roy. Irish Regt.; 2ndly, 1951, Kathleen Irene (107, Twickenham Rd., Isleworth, Middx.), da. of P. W. A. Wilson, of Shirley, Surrey:—

(By 1st m.) Cherry Hamilton, *b.* 1939: *m.* 1962, John Benjamin Lionel Underwood, Maj. King's Own Roy. Border Regt., of Halfacre, France Hill Drive, Camberley, Surrey, and has issue living, Michael John Benjamin, *b.* 1966,—Catherine Louise, *b.* 1964,—Jennifer Elizabeth, *b.* 1967.

Granddaughters of the late Brig.-Gen. Orlando George Gunning, C.M.G., D.S.O. (infra):—

Issue of the late Sir (Orlando) Peter Gunning, C.M.G., *b.* 1908, *d.* 1964: *m.* 1940, Patricia Mary (*Lady Gunning*) (25C, Upper Cheyne Row, SW3 5JL), da. of the late Capt. Dermot O'Connor, MC:—

Susan Mary, *b.* 1944.——Diana Rosemary *b.* 1947: *m.* 1971, Patrick Durnford, of 74, Shinfield Rd. Reading, and has issue living, Richard Peter Henry, *b.* 1975.

Granddaughters of the late Col. John Campbell Gunning, son of the late Maj. John Gunning, 6th son of 2nd baronet :—

Issue of the late Brig.-Gen. Orlando George Gunning, C.M.G., D.S.O., Indian Army, *b.* 1867, *d.* (on active ser. during European War) 1917 : *m.* 1902, Margaret Cecilia, who *d.* 1951, da. of the late Clinton George Dawkins:—

Elizabeth Margaret Mary, *b.* 1905: *m.* 1934, Rupert Macnaghten Cecil Thursfield, of Castle Mound, Weedon Lois, Towcester, Northants.——Lilian Jessie Isabella, *b.* 1906. *Address*, c/o National and Grindlays Bank, Parliament St., SW1.

Issue of the late Capt. Henry Ross Gunning, *b.* 1879, *d.* 1951 : *m.* 1st, 1904 Charlotte Henrietta, who *d.* 1908, da. of the late Anthony Harley Bacon ; 2ndly, 1914, Violet Gwendoline, who *d.* 1973, da. of the late Robert Cubitt:—

(By 2nd m.) John Robert (Apt. 1204, 155, Navy St., Oakville, Ont.) *b.* 1916; ed. at Queen's Univ., Kingston, Ont. (BSc Eng.); a Professional Engineer: *m.* 1941, Eleanor, da. of the late John William Elley, of Dublin, and Windsor, Ontario.——Richard Ross, *b.* 1928: *m.* 1951, Hilda, da. of John Ronald Staniforth, and has issue living, Christopher John Ross, *b.* 1955,—Timothy Robin, *b.* 1959,—Heather Jean, *b.* 1954. *Residence*, 5665, Oakglen Drive, South Burnaby, British Columbia.——(By 1st m.) Henrietta Marion (1305, West 13th Av., Vancouver 9, BC.), *b.* 1905.——Evelyn Briliana (15, Rylstone Rd., Eastbourne, Sussex), *b.* 1907.

The 1st baronet was successively Minister Plenipotentiary at the Courts of Berlin and St. Petersburg and the 2nd baronet was successively M.P. for Wigan (1800-1802), Hastings (1802-6), and East Grinstead (1812-18). Sir Robert, 3rd baronet, sat as M.P. for Northampton 1830-31, and was High Sheriff of Northamptonshire 1841-2, and Sir Henry, 4th baronet, was successively R. of Knockyn, Incumbent of Horton, and R. of Wigan, and Rural Dean. The 7th Baronet. Brig.-Gen. Sir Charles Vere Gunning, C.B., C.M.G., served in S. Africa 1900-02 and during European War 1914-18 (despatches twice).

GUNSTON, Creation (U.K.) 1938, of Wickwar, co. Gloucester.

Sir DERRICK WELLESLEY GUNSTON, *M.C.*, 1st *Baronet*, son of the late Capt. Bernard H. Gunston [D. Wellington, colls.] ; *b.* Feb. 26th, 1891 ; ed. at Harrow, and at Trin. Coll., Camb. (B.A. honours 1913) ; is Major 7th Batn. Gloucestershire Regt. (T.A.), and Capt. Irish Guards (Reserve) ; European War 1914-19 as temporary Major and 2nd in command of 1st Batn. Irish Guards (M.C.) ; a Member of Parliamentary Mission to Newfoundland 1943 ; appointed Parliamentary Private Sec. (unpaid) to Min. of Health 1926, to Chancellor of the Exchequer Nov. 1931 (resigned Feb. 1936), and to Under-Sec. of State for War 1940 ; sat as M.P. for Gloucestershire, Thornbury Div. (*C*) Oct. 1924 to June 1945 (defeated there July 1945) : *m.* 1917, Evelyn Bligh, *O.B.E.*, da. of the late Howard Bligh St. George [*see* St. George, Bt., colls.], and has issue.

꠆rms—Not exemplified at time of going to press.
Residences—Fram Cottage, Bembridge, I. of Wight; 14, Pelham Cres., SW7. *Clubs*—Carlton, Royal Yacht Squadron.

Son living—RICHARD WELLESLEY (Carlton, Pratt's, and East India and Sports Clubs), *b.* March 15th, 1924; ed. at Harrow and at Clare Coll., Camb.; 1942-45 War in RAF (aircrew); Colonial Ser., Nigeria, Nyasaland, Bechuanaland 1948-60: *m.* 1st, 1947, Elizabeth Mary (from whom he obtained a divorce 1956), da. of Sir Arthur Colegate, MP [Worsley, Bt.]; 2ndly, 1959, Joan Elizabeth Marie, da. of Mrs. Marie Louise Walker, of Somerset West, Cape, and has issue living (by 1st m.) Caroline Jane, *b.* 1950: *m.* 1971, Jonathan Robert F. Peel, and has issue living, Victoria Mary *b.* 1972,—(by 2nd m.) John Wellesley, *b.* 1962.

GUNTER, Creation (U.K.) 1901, of Wetherby Grange, Collingham, West Riding of Yorkshire.

Sir RONALD VERNON GUNTER, 3rd *Baronet*; *b.* March 8th, 1904; *s.* his father, *Lieut.-Col. Sir* ROBERT BENYON NEVILL, 1917; 1939-45 War as Lt.-Cdr. R.N.V.R.: *m.* 1st, 1925, Anne Daisy (who *d.* 1963, having obtained a divorce 1932), da. of C. Lovell Simmonds; 2ndly, 1932, Dorothy Eleanor (JOHNSTON), da. of H. E. Capes; 3rdly, 1950, Vera Irene (WYNN PARRY), who *d.* 1962, having obtained a divorce 1954, da. of Sir Henry Philip Price, 1st Bt. (*cr.* 1953); 4thly, 1955, Phyllis Lesley Wallace, da. of William St. Clair Johnston, and has issue by 1st marriage.

꠆rms—Sable, a chevron invected between in chief two gauntlets and in base a stag's head erased or. ꠆rest—On a gauntlet fessewise or, a stag's head erased proper.
Residence—Mill Hamlet Cottage, Sidlesham, nr. Chichester, Sussex.

Val y Gallo.

Daughter living—**By 1st marriage**—Hazel Ursula Anne, *b.* 1927: *m.* 1948, Kjell Christian Andresen, and has issue living, Peter Christian Gunter, *b.* 1952,—Hazel Anne Christine Gunter, *b.* 1955. *Residence*, Endsleigh, Crossway, Walton-on-Thames, Surrey.——Jane Hilda Clara, *b.* 1929: *m.* 1950, Harry Ian Lee-Duncan, and has issue living, Linda-Jane Gounter, *b.* 1952,— Diana Charlotte Gounter, *b.* 1954,—Alexandra Karen Gounter, *b.* 1959. *Residence*,—Tree Tops, Wessels Rd., PO Rivonia, Sandton, Transvaal, S. Africa.

The 1st baronet, Sir Robert (son of Robert Gunter, of Earl's Court, Middlesex), served as Capt. 4th Dragoon Guards during Crimean War, and sat as M.P. for Knaresborough (*C*) 1884-5, and for Barkston Ash Div. of E. Part of W. Riding of Yorkshire 1885-1905. The 2nd baronet, Lieut.-Col. Sir Robert Benyon Nevill, *d.* (on active ser. during European War) 1917.

GUTHRIE, Creation (U.K.) 1936, of Brent Eleigh Hall, co. Suffolk.

Sir GILES CONNOP MCEACHARN GUTHRIE, *O.B.E., D.S.C.*, 2nd *Baronet*; *b.* March 21st, 1916; *s.* his father, *Capt. Sir* CONNOP THIRLWALL Robert, *KBE*, 1945; ed. at Eton, and Magdalene Coll., Camb.; a JP for W. Sussex 1955-1969; a Merchant Banker (ret.); formerly Man. Dir. Brown Shipley & Co. Ltd.; Dep. Chm. North Central Finance Ltd., a Dir. of Prudential Assurance Co. Ltd., and of other Cos.; Chm. and Ch. Exec. of BOAC 1964-68, a Member of Board of BEA 1959-68; Chm. of Air Transport Insurance Ltd., Bermuda 1969-71; a Gov. and Vice-Chm. of The London Hosp. 1965-69; Lt.-Cdr. RNVR 1943; 1939-45 War with Fleet Air Arm (DSC); winner of Schlesinger trophy with the late C. W. A. Scott in Portsmouth-Johannesburg Air Race 1936; OBE (Mil) 1946: *m.* 1939, Rhona, only da. of the late Frederic Stileman, and has issue.

꠆rms—Per chevron argent and azure, in chief two eagles displayed of the second, and in base a lymphad with oars and sails furled of the first, pennons flying gules. ꠆rest —A cubit arm in armour proper, charged with two crosses patée fitchée in pale azure, holding in the hand proper a grenade sable, fired also proper.

Residence—Rozel, St. Martin, Jersey.   *Clubs*—Royal Yacht Squadron, MCC.

Sons living—MALCOLM CONNOP (Brent Eleigh, Belbroughton, Stourbridge, Worcs.), *b.* Dec. 16th, 1942; ed. at Millfield: *m.* 1967, Victoria, da. of the late Brian Willcock, and has issue living, Giles Malcolm Welcome, *b.* 1972,—Islay Mary Welcome, *b.* 1968.——Alastair Peter (24, Pembroke Rd., W8), *b.* 1944; ed. at Eton, and at Magdalene Coll., Camb.: *m.* 1966, Elizabeth, yr. da. of the late Valentin Schaposchnikoff, and has issue living, Alexander Valentine Connop, *b.* 1966,—Barnaby Giles, *b.* 1969.

Sister living—Diana Mary.

The 1st Baronet, Sir Connop Thirlwall Robert Guthrie, K.B.E., was a financier and a director of public companies. In 1914-18 War he was Capt. Grenadier Guards (wounded), a Special Representative in U.S.A. of Min. of Shipping 1916-19, and a Member of U.S.A. Govt. Shipping Control Cttee. 1918-19.   In 1939-45 he was Head of Security Div. of British Security Co-ordination in W. Hemisphere 1941-5, and an Hon. Air Commodore Auxiliary Air Force.

Gwynne-Evans, see Evans.

Hagart-Alexander, see Alexander.

Haggerston, see Constable-Maxwell-Scott, Bt., cr. 1642.

HALL, Creation (N.S.) 1687, of Dunglass, Haddingtonshire.

Vigilance ensures tranquillity.   Sir NEVILLE REYNOLDS HALL, 13th *Baronet*, son of Capt. Lionel Erskine Hall, 2nd son of Capt. Basil Sidmouth de Ros Hall, RN, el. son of Capt. Basil Hall, RN, 2nd son of 4th baronet; *b.* Feb. 16th, 1900; *s.* his brother, Col. Sir LIONEL REID, MC, 1975; ed. at Oundle, Keble Coll., Oxford (BSc), and R. Coll. of Science, S. Kensington (Assocn.); formerly Demonstrator at RN Eng. Coll., Devonport, and Sen. Lect. at RN Coll., Dartmouth: *m.* 1957, Dorothy Maud, da. of the late William Lawrence Jones.

Arms—Azure, a chevron argent between three cranes' **heads** erased at the necks or.   *Crest*—A crane or, standing upon a mount vert holding in the dexter claw a stone proper.

Residence—Ash Collage, Ash, Dartmouth, S. Devon.

Brother living—Sir DOUGLAS BASIL, *KCMG*, *b.* Feb. 1st, 1909; ed. at Radley, and at Keble Coll., Oxford (MA); a JP of Devon, and a Member of Police Authority for Devon and Cornwall Police; entered Overseas Civil Ser. as a Cadet, N. Rhodesia 1930; Dist. Officer 1932-50, Sen. Dist. Officer 1950-53, Provincial Commr. 1953, Administrative Sec. 1955-56, Sec. for Native Affairs 1956, and Gov. and Com.-in-Ch. of Somaliland Protectorate 1959-60; CMG 1958, KCMG 1959: *m.* 1933, Rachel Marion, da. of the late Maj. Ernest Gartside-Tippinge, RA, and has issue living, John Douglas Hoste (2, Combe Cottages, Staverton, Totnes, S. Devon), *b.* 1945; ed. at Dover Coll., at Gonville and Caius Coll., Camb. (BA), and Southampton Univ. (Cert. Ed.); schoolteacher, King Edward VI Comprehensive Sch.: *m.* 1972, Angela Margaret, da. of George Keys,—Marion, *b.* 1940; ed. at Trin. Coll., Dublin (MA): *m.* 1965, John Francis Fuller-Sessions, MA, of 9, Holbeck Av., Scarborough, Yorks., and has issue living, Nicholas Francis Blair *b.* 1974, Ruth *b.* 1967, Sara *b.* 1969,—Ruth, *b.* 1942: *m.* 1963, Anthony Bernard Cragg, of 83, Milton Rd., Lombardy E., Johannesburg, S. Africa, and has issue living, Stephen Browning *b.* 1966, Christopher Douglas *b.* 1968, Timothy Hugh *b.* 1970, Ann Louise *b.* 1965.   *Residence*, Barnford, Ringmore, nr. Kingsbridge, Devon.   *Club*, Royal Commonwealth Society.

Daughters living of 12th Baronet—Mary Jane Rosamond, *b.* 1922; 1939-45 as 3rd Officer WRNS: *m.* 1946, Mark Peter Whitlock, solicitor, of 112, Ashley Gdns., SW1, and has issue living, John Mark, *b.* 1955,—Paul Mark, *b.* 1957,—Martin Mark, *b.* 1959,—Mary Louise, *b.* 1947,—Jane Frances Mary, *b.* 1949.——Elizabeth Katharine Marion, *b.* 1925; ed. at Edinburgh Univ. (BSc); MRCVS: *m.* 1949, Oliphant Fairburn Jackson, PhD, MRCVS, of Stagenhoe Home Farm, St. Paul's Warden, Hitchin, Herts., and has issue living, James Ellis, *b.* 1959,—Anthony Oliphant, *b.* 1961,—Rosemary Frances, *b.* 1955.——Teresa Madeleine, *b.* 1930: *m.* 1952, Herbert Norman Constantine, of Laskill, Hawnby, York, and has issue living, Robert Francis, *b.* 1953,—Nigel Loudon, *b.* 1954,—Neville Egerton, *b.* 1959,—Serena Mary, *b.* 1963.

Widow living of 12th Baronet—MARY MARJORIBANKS MOORE (*Mary, Lady Hall*) (The Lodge, Scorton, Richmond, Yorks.), da. of the late Maj.-Gen. Sir Gerard Moore Heath), KCMG, CB, DSO, and widow of Capt. James Douglas Gaussen MacNeece, MC, RFA [Grey-Egerton, Bt., Colls.]: *m.* 1921, Col. Sir Lionel Reid Hall, MC, 12th baronet, who *d.* 1975.

Sir James Hall, 4th baronet, MP for St. Michael's, was President of the Royal Society of Edinburgh.   Sir Martin Julian Hall, OBE, 10th baronet, was Director of Food Section, Min. of Munitions during 1914-19 War, and Ch. Reconstruction Officer for Scotland, Min. of Labour.

HALL, Creation (U.K.) 1919, of Burton Park, Sussex.

In Deo Fides

Sir JOHN BERNARD HALL 3rd *Baronet; b.* March 20th, 1932; *s.* his father, *Lieut.-Col. Sir* DOUGLAS MONTGOMERY BERNARD, *D.S.O.,* 1962; ed. at Eton, and at Trin. Coll., Oxford; Lt. R. Fus. (RARO); Lord of Manors of Barlavington, Burton and Crouch; a Dir. of Bank of America Internat.: *m.* 1957, Delia Mary, da. of the late Lt.-Col. James Archibald Innes, DSO [*see* V. Downe, colls.], and has issue.

Arms—Vert, on a fesse or, between in chief a cross-crosslet fitchée between two talbots' heads erased argent collared and ringed gules, and in base a like talbot's head, three escallops sable. Crest—A talbot's head erased sable, ears argent, gorged with a chaplet or, garnished with roses gules, between two cross-crosslets fitchée gold.

Residences—Penrose House, Patmore Heath, Albury, Ware, Herts.; Inver House, Lochinver, Lairg, Sutherland.

Son living—DAVID BERNARD *b.* May 12th, 1961.

Daughters living—Caroline Evelyn, *b.* 1959.——Julia Nancy, *b.* 1965.

Half-Sister living—Pamela Mary, *b.* 1916: *m.* 1st, 1936 (marriage dissolved 1944), Richard Haliburton Bentley; 2ndly, 1944 (marriage dissolved 1948), Ivan Lorn Buchanan; 3rdly, 1949, Norman Percy Hackforth. *Residence*, Honeysuckle Cottage Wittersham, Kent.

Mother living—Nancie Walton, only da. of the late John Edward Mellor, C.B., J.P., D.L.: *m.* 1st, 1925, as his 2nd wife, Lt.-Col. Sir Douglas Montgomery Bernard Hall, D.S.O., 2nd Bt., from whom she obtained a divorce 1950; 2ndly, 1962, Col. Peter James Bradford, D.S.O., M.C., T.D. *Residences*, Long Crumples, Alton, Hants.; Tumore Lodge, Lairg, Sutherland.

The 1st baronet, Sir Douglas Bernard Hall (son of the late Bernard Hall, J.P., of Villa Mariposa, Cannes, France), sat as M.P. for Isle of Wight (*C*) Jan. 1910 to Oct. 1922 and was High Sheriff of Sussex 1907.

HALL, Creation (U.K.) 1923, of Grafham, co. Surrey.

Ready.

Sir (FREDERICK) JOHN (FRANK) HALL 3rd *Baronet; b.* Aug. 14th, 1931; *s.* his father *Sir* FREDERICK HENRY, 1949; ed. at Bryanston: *m.* 1st, 1956 (m. diss. 1960), Felicity Anne, da. of the late Edward Rivers-Fletcher, of Norwich; 2ndly, 1961 (m. diss. 1967) Patricia Ann, da. of Douglas Atkinson, of Greystead, Longlands Rd., Carlisle; 3rdly, 1967, re-married his 1st wife, Felicity Anne (ante), and has issue by 2nd and 3rd m.

Arms—Sable, a cross moline between in the first and fourth quarters a talbot's head erased and in the second and third a chaplet of oak or. Crest—A demi-griffin sable holding between the claws a portcullis or.

Residence—Carradale, 29, Embercourt Rd., Thames Ditton, Surrey, KT7 OLH.

Daughters living—By 2nd m.—Nicola Jane, *b.* 1962.—— Samantha Mary, *b.* 1965.——(by 3rd m.) Antonia Anne, *b.* 1970.——Victoria Joy, *b.* 1973.

Brother living—DAVID CHRISTOPHER (Inverene, 368, Queens Rd., Aberdeen), *b.* Dec. 30th, 1937: *m.* 1962, Irene, da. of William Duncan, of 2, Tollohill Pl., Kincorth, Aberdeen, and has issue living, John Christopher, *b.* May 22nd, 1965,—Olwen Evelyn, *b.* 1967.

Sister living—Mary Olwen Primrose, *b.* 1928.

Aunt living (daughter of 1st baronet)—Annie Elsie (PO Box 106, Kyrenia, Cyprus): *m.* 1926, Maurice Henry Drake.

Mother living—Olwen Irene, da. of the late Alderman Frank Collis, of Stokeville, Stoke-on-Trent, and Mira Mar, Deganwy, near Llandudno : *m.* 1st, 1924, Sir Frederick Henry Hall, 2nd baronet, who *d.* 1949, and from whom she had obtained a divorce 1944 ; 2ndly 1957, Arthur Borland Porteous, MD, DPH. *Residence*, 14, Coalecroft Rd., Putney, SW15.

The 1st baronet, Sir Frederick Hall, K.B.E., D.S.O., Chm. and Managing Director of Mercantile Marine Finance Corporation, Ltd., and a Member of Lloyd's and the Baltic Exchange, sat as M.P. or Dulwich Div. of Camberwell (*C*) 1910-32.

HALSEY, Creation (U.K.) 1920, of Gaddesden, co. Hertford.

Rev. Sir JOHN WALTER BROOKE HALSEY (*the Rev. Brother John Halsey*), 4th *Baronet*; *b.* Dec. 26th, 1933; *s.* his father, *Capt. Sir* THOMAS EDGAR, *DSO, RN,* 1970; ed. at Eton and Magdalene Coll., Camb. (BA).

Arms—Argent, on a pile sable three griffins' heads erased of the field. **Crest**—A dexter cubit arm proper, habited gules, the cuff argent, holding a griffin's claw erased or.

Residence—The Fraternity, 23, Manse Rd., Roslin, Midlothian.

Sister living—Margaret Anne, *b.* 1938: *m.* 1961, John Farnon, of Old Bell House, Market Lavington, Devizes, and has issue living, Jennifer Anne, *b.* 1962,—Nicola Jane, *b.* 1964,—Alison Sarah, *b.* 1966.

Uncle living (son of 2nd baronet)—WILLIAM EDMUND, *b.* Jan. 8th, 1903; Lt.-Cdr. (ret.) RN: *m.* 1931, Barbara Dorothea, da. of the late Charles Lindsay Orr Ewing, MP [*see* Orr Ewing, Bt., colls.], and has issue living, Bridget, *b.* 1934: *m.* 1958, Edward Alfred Heycock, of Kilmory, West Glen Rd., Kilmacolm, Renfrewshire, and has issue living, Susan Mary *b.* 1959, Caroline Bridget *b.* 1961, Jennifer Lucy *b.* 1966. *Residence*, The Knowe, Skelmorlie, Ayrshire.

The spoken word cannot be recalled.

Aunts living (daughters of 2nd baronet)—Marion Blanch: *m.* 1925, Thomas Selwyn Pryor, MC, who *d.* 1929, and has issue living, Elizabeth Jane (Middleway House, Kingston Gorse, Littlehampton, Sussex), *b.* 1926: *m.* 1st, 1949 (m. diss. 1962), Michael Brian Hickling; 2ndly, 1967, George Seddon, and has issue living, (by 1st m.) Carola Margaret Elizabeth *b.* 1950, Susan Lovegrove *b.* 1952, Olivia Marion *b.* 1955, Angela Jane *b.* 1956,—Mary Julia, *b.* 1927: *m.* 1949, Eric Charles Marsden [*see* V. Dillon],—Adeline Margaret, *b.* 1929: *m.* 1960, Maj.-Gen. William Digby Manifold Raeburn, CB, DSO, MBE [*see* Raeburn, Bt., colls.]. *Residence*, Gaddesden Place, Hemel Hempstead, Herts.—Jean: *m.* 1931. Gilbert Graham Balfour, and has issue living, Belinda Mary, *b.* 1937: *m.* 1960, Maj. Lionel David Wood (infra),—Elzabeth Rhoda, *b.* 1938: *m.* 1971, David Shelley. *Residence*, Rough Close, Upper Hardres, Canterbury.—Agatha: *m.* 1942, Alan Edmondson Bainbridge, and has issue living, Thomas Howard, *b.* 1943,—Andrew Halsey, *b.* 1944,—David James Macalpine, *b.* 1950,—Patricia Mary, *b.* 1946, Jean Vivien, *b.* 19—.——Evelyn Cecilia: *m.* 1944, Brig. Frederick Manus De Butts, CMG, OBE, late SCLI, of The Old Vicarage, Gt. Gaddesden, Hemel Hempstead, Herts., and has issue living, David Frederick, *b.* 1950,—Caroline Mary, *b.* 1952: *m.* 1974, Anthony Hugh Bond.

Collateral Branches living.

Issue of the late Adm. Sir Lionel Halsey, G.C.M.G., G.C.V.O., K.C.I.E., C.B., 4th son of 1st baronet, *b.* 1872, *d.* 1949 ; *m.* 1905, Morwenna, who *d.* 1959, da. of Major Bevil Granville, of Wellesbourne Hall, Warwick :—

Joan, *b.* 1910 ; is a J.P. for Herts : *m.* 1933, George Lockhart Wood, who *d.* 1959, and has issue living, John Lockhart (The Hoo, Gt. Gaddesden, Hemel Hempstead), *b.* 1935: *m.* 1963, Rosemary Sonia Despard, da. of Richard Graham Hensley Hopkins, and has issue living, George Edmund Richard *b.* 1966, Kirstin Rebecca *b.* 1968,—Lionel David (c/o HQ, Welsh Gds., Birdcage Walk, SW1), *b.* 1938; Maj. Welsh Gds.; Extra Equerry to HRH the Duke of Edinburgh 1965-67: *m.* 1960, Belinda Mary, da. of Gilbert Graham Balfour (ante), and has issue living, James Lionel Norman *b.* 1963, Sarah Morwenna *b.* 1961, Alexandra Louise *b.* 1965,—Richard George (Markham House, Badminton, Avon), *b.* 1939: *m.* 1963, Penelope Gay, da. of Lt.-Col. John Bertie Harris Daniel, MBE, MC, and has issue living, Andrew John *b.* 1966, Emma Ruth *b.* 1965,—Edmund Michael (The Old Rectory, Holwell, Hitchin, Herts.), *b.* 1943: *m.* 1971, Elizabeth Anne, da. of Sqd.-Ldr. Robert Roland Patrick Fisher, RAF (ret.), and has issue living, Sarah Georgina *b.* 1974,—Ruth Mary, *b.* 1945: *m.* 1973, James Henry Wood Ritchie, of Creagan Farm, Appin, Argyll. *Residence*, The Old Rectory, Whipsnade, Dunstable, Beds.——Ruth, *b.* 1915. *Residence*, Parsonage Piece, Whipsnade, Dunstable, Beds.

Issue of the late Rev. Canon Frederick Halsey, 3rd son of 1st baronet, *b.* 1870, *d.* 1952: *m.* 1901, Audrey Katharine, who *d.* 1969, da. of the late Lt.-Col. William Marsden, of Cedar Court, Farnham :—

Patrick Johnston, *b.* 1905 (The Little House, Torrington Rd., Berkhamsted, Herts.); ed. at Eton, and at Magdalen Coll., Oxford (BA).——Guy Marsden, *TD* (The Golden Parsonage, Gaddesden Row, Hemel Hempstead, HP2 6HG), *b.* 1908; ed. at Eton; is a JP for Herts.; 1939-45 War as Lt.-Col. Herts Regt. (TA) (despatches): *m.* 1939, Mary Juliet Gough, da. of the late Capt. Robert Wemyss Muir Arbuthnot, MC [*see* Arbuthnot, Bt., colls.], and has issue living, Nicholas Gay, *b.* 1948,—Robert Frederick, *b.* 1950.——Katharine Audrey (The Little House, Torrington Rd., Berkhamsted),——Barbara: *m.* 1961, John Parr Curgenven (Church Cottage, Iffley, Oxford), el. son of the late Sir Arthur Joseph Curgenven.

This family is descended from John Halsey of Great Gaddesden, Herts, who was living 1512. The 1st Baronet the Rt. Hon. Sir (Thomas) Frederick Halsey (son of Thomas Plumer Halsey, M.P.), sat as M.P. for Herts. (*C*) 1874-85, and for W. Herts. 1885-1906 and *d.* 1927.

HAMBLING, Creation (U.K.) 1924, of Yoxford, co. Suffolk.

Sir HERBERT HUGH HAMBLING, 3rd *Baronet,*
b. Aug. 3rd, 1919; *s.* his father, *Sir* (HERBERT)
GUY (MUSGRAVE), 1966; ed. at Eton; late
Flt.-Lt. RAF; formerly in BOAC, Montreal;
1939-45 War: *m.* 1950, Anne Page, da. of the
late Judge Hugo Edmund Oswald, of Seattle,
USA, and has issue.

Arms—Argent, a sword erect sable between two flaunches azure, each charged with a hank of cotton of the field.
Crest—A falcon supporting with the dexter claw a distaff
proper, and charged on the body with a bezant.

Seat—Rookery Park, Yoxford, Suffolk. *Addresses*—
c/o British Overseas Airways, Boeing Airplane Co., Box
707, Renton, Washington, USA; Rookery Park, Yoxford, Suffolk.

Discern and decide.

Son living—HERBERT PETER HUGH, *b.* Sept. 6th,
1953.

Sisters living—Margherita, *b.* 1912: *m.* 1937, Fl.-Lt. Maurice Hare, yst. son of Maj.-Gen. Sir
Steuart Welwood Hare, KCMG, CB, and has issue living, David Steuart (Kitt's Farm, Churt,
Farnham, Surrey), *b.* 1942: *m.* 1969, Julie, da. of Walter Pierre Courtauld, and has issue living,
Lucas Welwood Bruno *b.* 1972, Samuel James *b.* 1974,—Robin Gordon (Fordley Hall, Middleton,
Saxmundham, Suffolk), *b.* 1944: *m.* 1973, Caroline Mary, da. of Edward Felix Mason, and for-
merly wife of William Oscar Watson, and has issue living, Reuben Edward Hare *b.* 1975,—
Philippa, *b.* 1938: *m.* 1st, 1959 (m. diss. 1965), Timothy Peckover Burrill; 2ndly, 1967, Simon
Pierre Courtauld, of Chieveley Manor, Newbury, Berks., and has issue living, (by 1st m.) Rebecca
Nina *b.* 1961; (by 2nd m.) Kim Guy Augustine *b.* 1973. *Residence,* Fordley Hall, Middleton,
Saxmundham, Suffolk.——Mollie Gordon, *b.* 1915: *m.* 1958 Robert Geoffrey Smith, of Sutton
Hall, Woodbridge, Suffolk.

The 1st baronet, Sir (Henry) Herbert Hambling, was Dep. Chm. of Barclays Bank (Limited),
of Barclays Bank (France) (Limited), Barclays Bank (Dominion, Colonial and Overseas), and of
Barclays Bank S.A.I., first Govt. Director of Imperial Airways, Ltd. 1924-30 (formed as a result of
report presented by Hambling Committee of which he was Chm.), and a Director of North Britishand
Mercantile Insurance Co., and of Ocean Marine Insurance Co. (Limited); Financial Member of
Min. of Munitions during European War 1914-19 (Knt.).

HAMILTON, Creation (N.S.) 1646, of Silvertonhill, Lanarkshire.

Sir (ROBERT CHARLES) RICHARD CARADOC
HAMILTON, 9th *Baronet*; *b.* Sept. 8th, 1911;
s. his father, *Major Sir* ROBERT CARADOC, 1959;
ed. at Charterhouse, and at St. Peter's Coll.,
Oxford: *m.* 1952, Elizabeth Vidal, da. of Sir
William Pell Barton, K.C.I.E., C.S.I., and has
issue.

Arms—Gules, a gillie flower stemmed and leaved proper
between three cinquefoils ermine, all within a bordure or.
Crest—A horse's head and neck couped argent, maned or.

Residence—Briery Hill, Walton, Warwick.

Son living—ANDREW CARADOC, *b.* Sept. 23rd, 1953.

Daughters living—Susanna Eve, *b.* 1956.——Sophia Louisa,
b. 1964.——Penelope Katherine, *b.* 1966.

Brother living—Oliver Anson, *b.* 1916: *m.* 1957, Barbara
Mary, da. of Frank Willcox, of Perranporth, Cornwall.
Residence, The White House, Lifton, Devon, PL16 0AN.

Sister living—Cynthia, *b.* 1909. *Residence,* Collaven Manor,
Sourton, Okehampton, Devon.

Collateral Branches living.

Issue of the late Frank Hamilton, 2nd son of 7th baronet, *b.* 1878, *d.* 1934: *m.*
1913, Mary Elizabeth, who *d.* 1961, da. of the late John Williams Batterham,
M.B., F.R.C.S., of St. Leonards-on-Sea:—
Ian Frank Howden (Church Cottage, Blean, Canterbury), *b.* 1916: *m.* 1950, Zelma, da. of Laurence
Theodore Snyman, and has issue living, Paul Howden, *b.* 1951,—Mark Howden, *b.* 1955,—
Warwick Howden, *b.* 1959.——Arthur Hugh Claud, *b.* 1925.——Joan Mary Hamilton, *b.* 1915:
m. 1941, Stanley Silson, and has issue living, Ian Frank, *b.* 1943,—Raymond Robert Hamilton,
b. 1946,—Simon Hatchard, *b.* 1957,—Mary Elizabeth Joy, *b.* 1952. *Residence,* Terra Firma, 4,
Sylvania Av., Westville, Durban, S. Africa.

Grandchildren of the late Howden Anson Philip Hamilton, el. son of Capt.
Frederick William Hamilton, 3rd son of 5th baronet:—
Issue of the late Frederic Howden Faulconer Hamilton, *b.* 1877, *d.* 1959: *m.* 1st, 1899,
Jessie Jean, who *d.* 1929, elder da. of the late W. McMinn; 2ndly, 1930, Beatrice
Agnes, who *d.* 1955, only da. of the late Samuel Banfield of Exeter:—
(By 1st m.) Howden McMinn (21, Calderstone Av., Liverpool, 16) *b.* 1900: *m.* 1935, Patricia Camp-
bell, only child of Matthew Currie, of Ayr, and has issue living, Gloria Constance Barbara, *b.* 1937:
m. 1956, Edward Watson, and has issue living, Andrew Charles Hoden *b.* 1958.——Frederic

William Seymour (215, West 6th Av., Oliver, Box 797, BC, Canada) *b.* 1906: *m.* 1930, Florence Maud, da. of George John Saby, of Cambridgeshire, and has issue living, Kathleen Anita, *b.* 1931, —Barbara Joanna, *b.* 1933: *m.* 1955, Oscar Mitchell Taylor.——Constance, *b.* 1912: *m.* 1941, Richard Haugh, of Screel, Fishers Brae, Coldingham, Berwicks., and has issue living, Howden Hamilton, *b.* 1950.—Robert Seymour (twin), *b.* 1950: *m.* 1974, Marion Henderson Cunningham, only da. of Frederick Lenz, of Linlithgow.

Issue of the late Capt. Henry Rudston STUART-HAMILTON, Gordon Highlanders (who assumed by deed poll 1920, the additional surname of Stuart), *b.* 1883, *d.* 1962: *m.* 1920, Mabel Mary, who *d.* 1968, el. da. of the late Rev. Edmund Milnes Ellerbeck:— Donald Maclaren (of Butanben, Preston Bagot, Henley-in-Arden, Warwickshire), *b.* 1926; ed. at Harrow, and King's Coll., Camb.; Capt. The Black Watch (TA); MIMSM: *m.* 1956, Jill, MSAOT, yr. da. of the late Lt.-Col. David Guy Porteous, OBE, JP, of St. Cyrus, Angus, and has issue living, Clova Claire Ducarol, *b.* 1959,—Alison Fenella, *b.* 1967.

Granddaughter of the late Lieut.-Col. Henry Charles Hamilton, son of the late Henry Charles Hamilton, C.S.I., 4th son of 5th baronet:—
Issue of the late Charles Norman Maclean Hamilton, *b.* 1885, *d.* 1957: *m.* 1926, Molly Eileen (24, Oakleigh Court, Oxted, Surrey), da. of the late D. Crowe, MB, of Melfield, Blackrock, co. Dublin:—
Anne Maclean, *b.* 1927.

This is the nearest branch of the Ducal House next to the great family of Abercorn, descending from Alexander Hamilton of Silvertonhill, brother of 1st Lord Hamilton. Sir Robert Hamilton, 1st Bt., a steady loyalist, was a favourite of Charles I; his patent of baronetcy was not, however, recorded in the General Register owing to the then confusion and distraction of the country.

HAMILTON, First Creation (G.B.) 1776, of Marlborough House, Hampshire.
Second Creation (U.K.) 1819, of Trebinshun House, Brecknockshire.

Virtue is the only nobility.
Sola nobilitas virtus.

Sir EDWARD SYDNEY HAMILTON, 7th *Baronet* of 1st, and 5th *Baronet* of 2nd creation; *b.* April 14th, 1925; *s.* his father, *Sir* (THOMAS) SYDNEY PERCEVAL, 1966; ed. at Canford; late RE.

Arms—Quarterly : 1st and 4th, gules, three cinquefoils pierced ermine, 2nd and 3rd, argent, a lymphad with her sails furled sable. Crest—Out of a ducal coronet or, an oak-tree proper fructed of the first and penetrated transversely in the main stem by a frame-saw proper, the frame also of the first, and the blade inscribed with the word "Through."

Residence—The Cottage, East Lavant, Sussex.

Sister living—Favoretta Sydney Annina, *b.* 1923: *m.* 1941, Wing-Cdr. Roy Stuart Kingsford, RAF (ret.), of Old Straddles, Cross Oak Lane, Salfords, Surrey, and has issue living, Colin Roy, *b.* 1942,—Michael Ian, *b.* 1950,—Sandra Diana, *b.* 1946.

Capt. Sir John Hamilton, R.N., 1st Bt. of Trebinshun, grandson of William Hamilton (one of the five " Kentish Petitioners " in 1701), brother of 6th Earl of Abercorn, distinguished himself at the Siege of Quebec 1775. Adm. Sir Edward Joseph Hamilton, younger son of 1st Bt. (*cr.* 1776) was *cr.* a Bt. of Marlborough House, Hants, 1819. Sir Edward Archibald Hamilton, 2nd Bt.[(*cr* 1819), *s.* in 1892 as 4th Bt. (*cr.* 1776).

HAMILTON, Creation (U.K.) 1937, of Ilford, co. Essex.

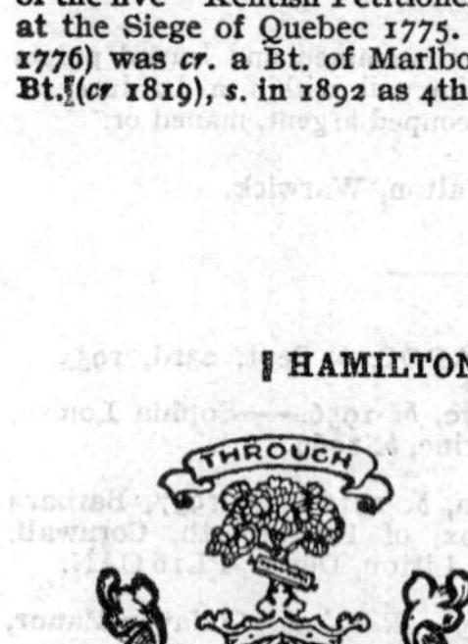

Sir PATRICK GEORGE HAMILTON, 2nd *Baronet; b.* Nov. 17th, 1908; *s.* his father, *Maj. Sir* (COLLINGWOOD) GEORGE CLEMENTS, 1947: ed. at Eton and at Trin. Coll., Oxford (MA): *m.* 1941, Winifred Mary (Pix) (STONE), OBE, MA, only da. of the late Hammond B. Jenkins, of Maddings, Hadstock.

Arms—Quarterly, 1st and 4th gules and argent, three cinquefoils pierced ermine and a canton of the second, charged with a trefoil slipped vert; 2nd and 3rd, a lymphad, sails furled, oars in action sable. Crest—Out of a ducal coronet, or, an oak-tree proper fructed gules, cut with a frame-saw of the first.

Residence—23, Cheyne Walk, S.W.3. *Club*—Carlton.

The 1st baronet, Maj. Sir (Collingwood) George Clements Hamilton (son of the late Ven. George Hans Hamilton, VD, DD, JP, Archdeacon of Northumberland, and Canon of Durham), was MP for Altrincham Div. of Cheshire (C) 1913-23, and for Ilford 1928-37.

Virtue is the only nobility

Hamilton-Dalrymple, see Dalrymple.

STIRLING-HAMILTON, Creation (N.S.) 1673, of Preston, Haddingtonshire.

For my country.

Capt. Sir ROBERT WILLIAM STIRLING-HAMILTON, 12th *Baronet ; b.* April 5th, 1903 ; *s.* his father, *Sir* WILLIAM, 1946 ; Capt. (retired) R.N. ; is a J.P. for W. Sussex ; formerly Commodore, R.N. Barracks, Portsmouth ; European War 1939-45 (despatches) : *m.* 1930, Eileen, da. of the late Rt. Rev. Henry Kemble Southwell, C.M.G., D.D., formerly Bishop Suffragan of Lewes [see V. Southwell, colls.], and has issue.

Arms—Gules, three cinquefoils within a bordure argent. **Crest**—An armed man from the middle brandishing a sword aloft proper.

Residence—Puriton Lodge, Hambrook, Chichester, Sussex.

Son living—BRUCE (c/o Glyn, Mills & Co. (Holts Branch), Kirkland House, Whitehall, SW1), *b.* Aug. 5th, 1940; Capt. late Queen's Own Highlanders: *m.* 1968, Stephanie, el. da. of William Campbell, LRCP, LRCS, of Cozac, 32, Alloway, Ayr, and has issue living, Georgina Claire, *b.* 1970.

Daughters living—Joanna Eileen, *b.* 1930: *m.* 1955, Maj. Ian Kroyer MacKinnon, Queen's Own Highlanders, *Address,* c/o Puriton Lodge, Hambrook, Chichester, Sussex.——Eila Mary, *b.* 1939: *m.* 1st, 1959, Lt. Timothy Martin Woodford, RN, who *d.* 1966 [Crofton, Bt., cr. 1801, colls.]; 2ndly, 1967, George Rudolf Wratislaw Walker, MA, of The Old House, Stoke Fleming, Devon, and has issue living, (by 1st *m.*) Charlotte Amanda, *b.* 1960.——Amanda Caroline, *b.* 1962,—(by 2nd m.) Harriet Nicola *b.* 1970,—Emily Mary, *b.* 1972.

Collateral Branches living.

Grandchildren of the late Hubert Hamilton, 2nd son of 9th baronet:—
Issue of the late William Stirling Hamilton, *b.* 1869, *d.* 1958: *m.* 1898, Kathleen, who *d.* 1961, da. of the late George Robert Elsmie, CSI :—

Robert William (Haskers, Westleton, Suffolk), *b.* 1905: *m.* 1935, Eileen Hetty, el. da. of the late Francis Goldworth Lowick, and has issue living, *Rev.* Andrew Robert, *b.* 1937; ed. at New Coll., Oxford (MA): *m.* 1972, Josephine Mary, da. of Reginald Sargant,—William Alexander Hubert (c/o Coutts Bank, 440, Strand, WC2), *b.* 1941; ed. at Trin. Coll., Camb. (BA): *m.* 1966, Cecilia Louise Somerville, da. of the late Maj. Charles Erling Bernard Catt [Somerville, Bt., colls., ext.], and has issue living, Alexander James Erling *b.* 1967, Anna Cecilia Louise *b.* 1969,—Thomas Hamilton, *b.* 1952,—Penelope Frances, *b.* 1936: *m.* 1960, Maj. Robert Alan Mountcastle Seeger, MC, RM, of Windwhistle, Saltern's Way, Lilliput, Poole, Dorset, BH14 8JR, and has issue living, Frances Clare *b.* 1955, Katharine Anne *b.* 1966,—Katharine Jane Patricia *b.* 1955.——Kathleen Elizabeth (27, Pier Av., Southwold, Suffolk), *b.* 1899: *m.* 1934, Edward Reginald Pierssené, who *d.* 1954, and has issue living, Anne Gillian, *b.* 1936: *m.* 1960, Lancelot Maurice Ieler, of Stoke Wood House, Limpley Stoke, Bath, BA3 6JB.

Grandchildren of the late Lt.-Col. William Gavin Hamilton (infra):—
Issue of the late Capt. John William Stirling Hamilton, MC, *b.* 1919, *d.* 1959: *m.* 1945, Kathleen Dorothea (Tordarroch, Helensburgh, Dunbartonshire), da. of John Alexander Thomson, MBE, of Tordarroch, Helensburgh:—

Alastair Colin Stirling, *b.* 1954.——Alison Lesley, *b.* 1947.——Daphne Helen, *b.* 1950.

Grandchildren of the late Thomas Hamilton, M.D., F.R.C.S. (infra) :—
Issue of the late Lieut.-Col. William Gavin Hamilton, *b.* 1874, *d.* 1937: *m.* 1st, 1908, Louise, who *d.* 1914, da. of the late Alison Cunningham, of Peterborough ; 2ndly, 1916, Helen, who *d.* 1950, da. of the late Dugald Stewart Macphee, of Glasgow :—

(By 2nd *m.*) Alastair Gavin, DSC, *b.* 1922; Lt. Cdr. RN (ret.); 1939-45 War (DSC): *m.* 1956, Gillian Bomford, and has issue living, Jock, *b.* 1962,—Gail, *b.* 1960,—Katherine, *b.* 1964.——Margaret Audrey, *b.* 1918; is 2nd Officer WRNS; 1940-45 War: *m.* 1946, Charles Ian Turcan, of Oxey Barn, Woodside, Lymington, Hants, and has issue living, Gavin Charles, *b.* 1948,—Alan Ronald Hamilton, *b.* 1952,—Lydia Helen, *b.* 1950.

Issue of the late Thomas Hamilton, M.D., F.R.C.S., 3rd son of 9th baronet, *b.* 1843, *d.* 1918 : *m.* 1873, Helen, who *d.* 1932, da. of the late J. W. Nutt :—

Helen Gladys, *b.* 1890: *m.* 1921, John Watson Simpson, M.B., who *d.* (result of European War) 1929 [Watson, Bt., *cr.* 1895], and has issue living, John Anthony, *b.* 1923,—Moyra Anne Margaret, *b.* 1924: *m.* 1951, David John Luther [see E. Gainsborough, colls.],—Rosemary Hamilton, *b.* 1926: *m.* 1954, Sydney Anthony Holden Garnar, of Spicklewood, Seal Chart, nr. Sevenoaks, Kent, and has issue living, Clive Robert Sydney *b.* 1963, Yvonne Alison Lindsay *b.* 1960. *Residence,* The White House, Godden Green, nr. Sevenoaks, Kent.

This family descends from Sir John Hamilton of Fingalton, yr. brother of Sir David Hamilton of Cadzow (d.c. 1392) ancestor of Duke of Hamilton. Sir William Hamilton, 1st Bt. was cr. a Baronet with remainder to his heirs male whatsoever. On the death of Sir Robert, 2nd Bt. 1701, the baronetcy passed to his kinsman Sir Robert of Airdrie, 5th in descent from John who was killed at Flodden 1513, yr. brother of Robert of Preston, ancestor of 1st Bt., but the baronetcy was not re-assumed until 1834 by Sir William *de jure,* 9th Bt., who had been served heir male to the 2nd Br. 1816. He was Prof. of Logic and Metaphysics at Edinburgh Univ. Gen. Sir William, CB, 10th Bt. assumed by deed poll, in 1889, the additional surname of Stirling, his grandmother Elizabeth being a da. of William Stirling of Drumpellier, whose son established in 1818 representation of the family of Stirling of Cadder.

HAMMICK, Creation (U.K.) 1834, of Cavendish Square, London.

To be praised by one already praised.

Sir STEPHEN GEORGE HAMMICK, 5th *Baronet* b. Dec. 27th, 1926; s. his father, Sir GEORGE FREDERICK, 1964; ed. at Stowe: m. 1953, Gillian Elizabeth, yr. da. of the late Maj. Pierre Elliot Inchbald, M.C. [*see* Bingham, Bt. (ext.)], and has issue.

Arms—Paly of four or and vert, a bordure ermine charged with seven hurts, on a chief azure a lion passant argent. **Crest**—A demi-lion per pale or and vert holding an escarbuncle gold.

Residence—Badgers, Wraxall, Dorchester, Dorset.

Sons living—PAUL ST. VINCENT, b. Jan. 1st, 1955,—Jeremy Charles, b. 1956.

Daughter living—Wendy Jane, b. 1960.

Widow living of 4th Baronet—MARY ADELIZA (*Dowager Lady Hammick*) (Spring Hayne, Offwell, Honiton, Devon), da. of the late Lt.-Col. Henry Welch-Thornton, formerly RAOC, of Curtisknowle, Halwell, S. Devon: m. 1925, as his 2nd wife, Sir George Frederick Hammick, 4th Bt., who d. 1964.

Collateral Branches living.

Issue of the late Rear-Adm. Alexander Robert Hammick, brother of 4th baronet, b. 1887, d. 1969: m. 1918, Nancy, who d. 1964, el. da. of D. Ross-Johnson:—
Anne Felicity (The Old House, Lodsworth, Sussex), b. 1919.

Issue of the late Stephen Hammick, 3rd son of 2nd baronet, b. 1846, d. 1934: m. 1885, Constance, who d. 1937, da. of the late Lieut.-Gen. Frederick Schneider, of Wateringbury, Kent:—
St. Vincent Frederick, b. 1886; Major (retired) Indian Army: m. 1919, Annie Caroline Massingberd, da. of Aubone Aldrich Pyke, of The Hermitage, Netley Abbey, and has issue living, Stephen Aubone, DSC (The Old House, Brighstone I. of Wight), b. 1922; Cdr. RN; 1939-45 War (DSC, despatches twice): m. 1943, Mary Elizabeth, da. of John Laurence Westmacott [*see* Hamilton Spencer-Smith, Bt., colls.], and has issue living, Stephen Timothy John b. 1946: m. 1969, Raymonde, da. of Maj. Eugene I. J. Carson, of S. Africa, Susan Patricia b. 1945,—Aubone St. Vincent, RN (444, Unthank Rd., Norwich), b. 1925; is Lt.-Cdr.: m. 1948, Cynthia Florence Katharine, da. of William George Shiell [B. Airedale], and has issue living, Marion b. 1949: m. 1967, Ian Donald Pickett, BA, of 57, Salisbury Av., St. Albans, Herts., (and has issue living, Melissa Juliette b. 1967, Eleanor Theresa (twin) b. 1967), Imogen Katherine b. 1952: m. 1972, John Blandford, Miranda Jane b. 1958,—Mary Désirée Massingberd, b. 1930: m. 1953, Colin Edward Foster, of 6365, Elm St., Vancouver, Canada, and has issue living, Michael Colin b. 1954, Christopher John b. 1956, Caroline Antonia b. 1957,—Adrianne Elaine Patricia, b. 1937: m. 1964, Vincent George Jarvis Ball of Lynchetts, Chandler's Ford, Hants., and has issue living, Anthony St. Vincent b. 1965, Stephen Jarvis b. 1967, David Jonathan b. 1971. *Residence*, Crofters, Warsash, Southampton.

Issue of the late Capt. Stephen Frederick Hammick (Oxfordshire and Bucks L.I.), only son of 3rd baronet, b. 1871, d. (of wounds in action during European War, 1916: m. 1906, Muriel Katharine, who d. 1924, da. of Capt. Andrew Hamilton Russell, formerly 58th Regt., of The Heath House, Petersfield, Hants:—
Penelope Katherine, MB, BS (of 46, Castle Rd., Salisbury), b. 1910.

Grandchildren of the late Sir Murray Hammick, KCSI, CIE (infra):—
Issue of the late Maj. Henry Alexander Hammick, OBE, MC, b. 1890, d. 1968: m. 1919, Mabel Emily (May) (Delvers, Pyrford, Woking), da. of Sir Philip Edward Pilditch, MP, 1st Bt.:—
Henry Edgar Murray (Avonsleigh, Ramley Rd., Pennington, Lymington, Hants.), b. 1919; late Lt. RNVR; 1939-45 War: m. 1949, Eleanor Macleod, da. of Cdr. Patrick Bruce Lawder, RN, and has issue living, Elizabeth Helen Macleod, b. 1951,—Anne Olivia Mary, b. 1953.——Charles Cyril Willmott (Sutton Warblington, Long Sutton, Basingstoke), b. 1927; late Maj. Gren. Guards: m. 1st, 1953 (m. diss. 1959), Mary Rose, only da. of Col. Walter Hugh Crichton, CIE; 2ndly, 1961, Georgina, da. of the late Maj.-Gen. George Douglas Gordon Heyman, CB, CBE, and has issue living, (by 1st m.) Piers St. Vincent Charles, b. 1954,—Charlotte Emily Dorothea, b. 1955,—(by 2nd m.) Thomas Henry Heyman St. Vincent, b. 1963,—Katherine Emily Amanda, b. 1965,—Rose Sophia, b. 1970.——Alexander Philip (The Priory, Woodbury, Exeter), b. 1928: m. 1954, Pamela Mary, da. of C. Prosper-Liston, of Penang, and has issue living, Murray Philip St. Leger, b. 1957,—Melinda Mary, b. 1955,—Victoria Rosanne, b. 1958,—Nicola May, b. 1961.——Anthea Elizabeth Eve, b. 1922: m. 1949, Dennis John Dale Shepherd, and has issue living, Justin Philip William, b. 1952,—Miranda Dorothy Emila, b. 1950,—Zoë Alexandra Denise, b. 1954,—Isobel Anthea, b. 1956,—Melissa May, b. 1966.

Issue of the late Sir Murray Hammick, K.C.S.I., C.I.E., 7th son of 2nd baronet, b. 1854, d. 1936: m. 1883, Ada Constance, who d. 1950, da. of Maj.-Gen. Arthur Thaddeus Searle, I.S.C.:—
Dorothy Constance: m. 1921, Lt.-Col. Alexander Charles Broughton Mackinnon, CBE, Indian Army (ret.), who d. 1942, and has issue living, Mairi Cynthia, b. 1924: m. 1954, James Arnold Adams, FRCS.

Sir Stephen Love Hammick, F.R.C.S., 1st baronet (el. son of Stephen Hammick, Alderman of Plymouth), was an eminent surgeon and physician, and 1st Surg. of R.N. Hospital, Plymouth. The 3rd baronet, Sir St. Vincent Alexander Hammick, served in New Zealand War 1864-5 (medal, and specially mentioned).

Hamond-Græme, see Græme.

HANHAM, Creation (E.) 1667, of Wimborne, Dorsetshire.

Sir MICHAEL WILLIAM HANHAM, *DFC*, 12th *Baronet, b.* Oct. 31st, 1922; only son of Patrick John Hanham, yst. son of Col. Phelips Brooke Hanham, brother of 9th baronet; *s.* his Kinsman, *Sir* HENRY PHELIPS, 1973; ed. at Winchester; 1939-45 War as Fl.-Lt. RAFVR (DFC): *m.* 1954, Margaret Jane, only da. of Wing-Cdr. Harold Thomas, RAF, of Marine Court, St. Leonards-on-Sea, and has issue.

Arms—Quarterly, or and gules, on a bend sable three crosses paté fitchée of the first. *Crest*— A griffin's head erased, beaked sable.

Residences—Deans Court, Wimborne, Dorset; Trillinghurst Farmhouse, Goudhurst, Cranbrook, Kent.

Son living—WILLIAM JOHN EDWARD, *b.* Sept. 4th, 1957; ed. at Winchester.

Daughter living—Victoria Jane, *b.* 1955.

Mother living—Dulcie (Pond Farm, Biddenden, Kent), da. of the late William George Daffarn, of Valewood, Haslemere, and widow of Lynn Hartley: *m.* 1921 (m. diss. 1943), Patrick John Hanham, who *d.* 1965, son of the late Col. Phelips Brooke Hanham, grandson of 7th baronet.

To be, rather than to seem.

Sir John Alexander Hanham, 9th baronet, and his son Sir John Ludlow Hanham, 10th baronet, were Apparitors-Gen. of Province and Diocese of Canterbury.

HANMER, Creation (G.B.) 1774, of Hanmer, Flintshire.

Sir (GRIFFIN WYNDHAM) EDWARD HANMER, 7th *Baronet*; *b.* Aug. 30th, 1893; *s.* his father, *Sir* WYNDHAM CHARLES HENRY, 1922; ed. at Wellington Coll.; is Lieut.-Col., a J.P. for Flintshire (High Sheriff 1932), and patron of four livings; was Senior Steward of Jockey Club 1944-5; European War 1914-18 as Capt. Yeo., and attached RAF: *m.* 1st, 1921, Aileen Mary, who *d.* 1967, da. of the late Capt. John Edwin Rogerson, OBE, MP, of Mount Oswald, Durham; 2ndly, 1968, Angela Mary, widow of Richard Nightingale Bromley, and has issue by 1st m.

Arms—Argent, two lions passant guardant azure. *Crest*—On a chapeau azure turned up ermine a lion sejeant guardant argent.
Seat—Bettisfield Park, Whitchurch, Salop. *Clubs*—Cavalry, Jockey.

Son living—By 1st m.—JOHN WYNDHAM EDWARD, *b.* Sept. 27th, 1928; Capt. (ret) R Dragoons; a JP for Flintshire: *m.* 1954, Audrey Melissa, da. of Maj. A. C. J. Congreve, of Notre Dame, Carces Var, France, and has issue living, Wyndham Richard Guy, *b.* 1955,—Edward Hugh, *b.* 1957. *Residence,* The Mere House, Hanmer, Whitchurch, Salop.
Daughters living—By 1st m.—Joan Essex, *b.* 1922.—Pamela Aileen (*Lady Wilson*), *b.* 1923: *m.* 1947, Capt. Sir Thomas Douglas Wilson, MC, 4th Bt., of Lillingstone Lovell Manor, Buckingham.——Evelyn Mary, *b.* 1926.
Sister living—Heather, *b.* 1897. *Residence,* 27, Manor Av., Kidderminster, Worcs.

Keep fast honour.

Collateral Branches living.

Grandchildren of the late Rev. Henry Hanmer, brother of 3rd and 4th baronets:—
Issue of the late John Hanmer, *b.* 1854, *d.* 1936: *m.* 1890, Constance Catherine, who *d.* 1954, da. of the late Alexander Busby, of Cassilis, N.S. Wales :—
Henry Ivan, *DFC, b.* 1893; Group Capt. RAF; 1914-18 War (DFC with bar, Order of the Nile): *m.* 1st, 1937, Margaret Florence Mary, who *d.* 1947, only da. of the late Rev. Henry Kenneth Warrand, of Westhorpe Hall, Southwell, Notts; 2ndly, 1954, Lady Frances Jane Cole, da. of 5th Earl of Enniskillen, and has issue living, (by 1st m.) John Henry Warrand (Colston House, Colston Bassett, Notts.), *b.* 1938; Capt. 17th/21st Lancers (ret.): *m.* 1964, Penelope Clare, da. of Sir Denis Le Marchant, 5th Bt., and has issue living, Thomas Stephen *b.* 1971, Isabel Jane *b.* 1965, Harriet Mary *b.* 1969,—William Richard, *b.* 1945,—Flora Elizabeth, *b.* 1939: *m.* 1967, Frederick John Sasse, of Hyde Cottage, Willingale, Ongar, Essex, and has issue living, Stephen John *b.* 1968, Matthew Alexander *b.* 1971, Selina Margaret *b.* 1974,—(by 2nd m.) Thomas Edward Trevor, *b.* 1956. *Residence,* Westhorpe Hall, Southwell, Notts.——Charles Gordon, *b.* 1898; sometime Lt. Indian Army; 1914-18 War, Afghan War 1919, and 1939-45 War: *m.* 1940, Winifred Beatrice, da. of Reginald Walter Harvey of Stone, Tenterden, Kent. *Residence,* Inyanga Downs, P. Bag 31, Rusapi, Rhodesia.——William Francis Busby (PO Box 18, Troutbeck, Rhodesia), *b.* 1899; formerly Lt. RA (TA): *m.* 1st, 1927, Margaret, who *d.* 1967, da. of Archibald Cameron Norman, of The Rookery, Bromley Common [Wake, Bt., colls.]; 2ndly, 19—, Bethia Ann, da. of

the late Joseph Condy, of Umtali, and has issue living, (by 1st m.) John Anthony, *b.* 1928: *m.* 1952, Margaret May, da. of I. G. Morrison, of Cape Town, and has issue living, Quentin William *b.* 1952, Andrew Ian *b.* 1958, Deborah Anne *b.* 1954,—Richard Norman Montagu (Shabanie Mine, Shabani, Rhodesia), *b.* 1937, BSc, Cape Town; AMSAIMechE, PEng, MEIC: *m.* 1963, Joyce Catherine, who *d.* 1973, da. of the late Ernest Philpot, of Beckenham, Kent, and has issue living, Anthony David *b.* 1967, Gillian Margaret *b.* 1964,—Phoebe Margaret, *b.* 1931,—Janet Virginia, *b.* 1932: *m.* 1971, Charles George Davis Sutherland, of Auckland, NZ, and Salisbury, Rhodesia, and has issue living, George Francis Hanmer *b.* 1972,—Catherine Yvonne, *b.* 1936: *m.* 1958, Keith Allen, of Cranstead, St. Georges Av., Weybridge, Surrey, and has issue living, John Hanmer *b.* 1958, Charles William *b.* 1960, Stephen Guy *b.* 1963, Caroline Elizabeth *b.* 1965.

Grandson of the late Edward Wingfield Hanmer (infra):—
Issue of the late Edward Henry John Hanmer, MC, MM, *b.* 1888, *d.* 1969: *m.* 1922, Aileen Ethel, who *d.* 1954, da. of John Agnew Finlay, of Belfast, and Rio de Janeiro:—
John Richard, *b.* 1925.

Grandchildren of the late Rev. Henry Hanmer (ante):—
Issue of the late Edward Wingfield Hanmer, *b.* 1856, *d.* 1901: *m.* 1885, Catherine, who *d.* 1939, da. of the late Humphrey Hanmer (infra):—
Florence Catherine Alicia, *b.* 1895: *m.* 1921, Philip Tudor Newling, formerly Lt. RFC, and has issue living, June Hanmer, *b.* 1925: *m.* 1949, Robert Alan Reid, late Lt.-Com. RNVR, of 2371, Riley Av., Ottawa, 5, Ont. and has issue living, David Ian *b.* 1950, Philip James *b.* 1953. *Residence,* 33, Inglis St., Motueka, Nelson Prov., NZ.

Issue of the late Thomas Hanmer, *b.* 1857, *d.* 1923: *m.* 1891, Edith Mary, who *d.* 1905, younger da. of the late George A. Brittain, of The Lilies, near Aylesbury:—
Joan Florence (twin) (Milestones, Playden Lane, Iden, nr. Rye, Sussex), *b.* 1894: *m.* 1st, 1917, Capt. John Theobald Milne, MC, RFC, who *d.* (killed in action) 1917; 2ndly, 1923, Stuart Eddington Gay, who *d.* 1967, and has issue living, (by 2nd m.) Timothy Thomas Stuart (Roserrans, Tregatillian, St. Columb Major, Cornwall), *b.* 1927: *m.* 1958, Heather Margaret Grange, and has issue living, Emma Margaret *b.* 1961, Camilla Joan *b.* 1964,—Ivor Philip Eddington (Franklyns Farm House, Itchen Abbas, Winchester), *b.* 1930: *m.* 1954, Mary Rosalind Merrett Stock, and has issue living, Anthony Christian Eddington *b.* 1956, Sarah Elizabeth *b.* 1959,—Judith Marion, *b.* 1934: *m.* 1955, Capt. K. G. I. Hart, late 7th Hussars, of 10, Taylors Av., Grange Court, Hoddesdon, Herts., and has issue living, Jonathan Eugene *b.* 1963, Julia Gay *b.* 1957.

Grandson of the late Rev. Hugh Hanmer (infra):—
Issue of the late Robert Hugh Hanmer, OBE, MC, *b.* 1895, *d.* 1971: *m.* 1922, Mary Helen, who *d.* 1945, da. of the late Nathaniel Spens, of 1, St. Mary Abbot's Court, Kensington W14:—
Hugh Niel (The Old Granary, Great Eversden, Cambridge), *b.* 1926: *m.* 1953, Diana, da. of Robert Hurst, of Lustleigh, Devon, and has issue living, Robert Davi,d *b.* 1957,—Lucia Caroline, *b.* 1956.

Grandchildren of the late Rev. Henry Hanmer (ante):—
Issue of the late Rev. Hugh Hanmer, *b.* 1862, *d.* 1939: *m.* 1894, Margaret Maude, who *d.* 1943, da. of Robert Peel Ethelston:—
Arthur Richard, *MBE, TD* (The Barn, Berriew, Welshpool, Powys), *b.* 1899; ed. at Pembroke Coll. Camb. (BA); Lt.-Col. RWFus (TA); MBE (Mil) 1944: *m.* 1929, Violet Millicent, who *d.* 1968, da. of the late Maj. William John Corbett-Winder, of Vaynor Park, Berriew, Montgomeryshire, and has issue living, John Richard Lyon, *b.* 1940; ed. at Eton,—Sara Elizabeth, *b.* 1938: *m.* 1973, Charles Henry Wroughton Michell, of 10, Wandon Rd., SW6 [see Carden, Bt., cr. 1887].——Stephen Henry, *TD* (Chains Cottage, Racecourse, Oswestry), *b.* 1906; ed. at Shrewsbury, and at St. John's Coll., Camb. (BA); Hon. Maj. Durham LI (TA Reserve); 1939-45 War (wounded).——John Michael, *DSO, OBE* (of Tarrant Monkton, Blandford, Dorset; United Service Club), *b.* 1907; Brig. (ret.) late Durham LI; NW Europe 1944-45 (despatches, DSO); a Chevalier of Order of Crown of Belgium with Palm; has Croix de Guerre with Palm; DSO 1945, OBE (Mil) 1951: *m.* 1934, Esther, yst. da. of Reginald Black, DL, JP, of Prees Hall, Whitchurch, Shropshire, and has issue living, Michael David Adam (11, Georgian Village, Castleknock, co. Dublin; Hibernian United Service Club), *b.* 1935; ed. at Stowe, and at Clare Coll., Camb. (BA): *m.* 1964, Judy Carol, yr. da. of Cecil Jack Fairchild, of 54, Claremont Rd., Tunbridge Wells, and has issue living, Clare Lucinda *b.* 1965, Julia Caroline *b.* 1968,—*Rev.* Richard John, *b.* 1938; ed. at Winchester, and Peterhouse, Camb. (BA),—Henry, *b.* 1943; ed. at Shrewsbury.——Margaret Evelyn, *CBE* (Glenwood, Queens Park, Oswestry; VAD Club), *b.* 1896; a JP of Salop; CBE (Civil) 1957: *m.* 1936, Maj. Bertie Edward Parker Leighton, who *d.* 1952 [Leighton, Bt., colls.].——Ruth Henrietta, *b.* 1905: *m.* 1934, Fitzherbert Edward Shallcross Jacson, of Tedsmore Hall, Oswestry [B. Hatherton], and has issue living, Edward Shallcross Owen, *b.* 1938,—Susan Margaret, *b.* 1937.

Granddaughter of the late George Hanmer (infra) :—
Issue of the late Humphrey George Hanmer, *b.* 1886, *d.* 1927: *m.* 1st, 1914 (marriage dissolved 1924), Beatrice Winnifred, da. of the late George Sumpter, of Oamaru, New Zealand; 2ndly, 1925, Muriel Emma, da. of George Henry Bostock, of Ranui, Perth, W. Australia :—
(By 2nd marriage) Elizabeth Muriel, *b.* 1929 : *m.* 1951, Arthur Cecil John Coates, and has issue living, David John, *b.* 1953,—Anne Muriel. *b.* 1955. *Residence,* 53, Duncan Street, Wanganui, New Zealand.

Granddaughter of the late Humphrey Hanmer, son of the late Rev. John Hanmer, 3rd son of 2nd baronet :—
Issue of the late George Hanmer, *b.* 1859, *d.* 1934: *m.* 1885. Ruth, who *d.* 1946, da. of C. Percy Cox, of Christchurch, New Zealand :—
Municent Clara, *b.* 1891: *m.* 1917, Lt.-Col. Vincent Lee Dean, VD, Indian Army, who *d.* 1942, Railway Dept. Govt. of India, and Auxiliary Force, India, and has issue living, Jacquelyne Mercy Hanmer, *b.* 1918: *m.* 1st, 1938, Lt.-Col. Charles Brown Bennett, Indian Cav., who *d.* 1946; 2ndly, 1948, Maj. Morris Edward Gervais, Canadian Army (ret.), and has issue living (by 1st m.) Humphrey Charles *b.* 1946: *m.* 1966, Susan Katherine, da. of   , (and has issue living, Charles David Thompson *b.* 1967, Thomas Christopher Edward *b.* 1969), (by 2nd m.) Municent Ella *b.* 1949. *Residence,* 1234, Hillhurst Rd., Oakville, Ont., Canada.

Grandson of the late Thomas Hanmer, son of the late William Hanmer, 6th son of 2nd baronet :—
Issue of the late Thomas William Hanmer, *b.* 1868, *d.* 1950,: *m.* 1911, Ivy Mira Frances, who *d.* 1965, only da. of the late Charles John Dodd, of The Belfry, Uckfield, Sussex:—
Patrick William Talgai (Quillet, Erskine Rd., Gullane, E. Lothian) *b.* 1915; Capt. RN (ret.).——Nicholas Brian, *MBE* (Westholme West, Cumberland St., Woodbridge, Suffolk; Naval and Military Club) *b.* 1921; Maj. (ret.) R. Sussex Regt.; formerly Sen. Dist. Commr., Colonial Ser.; MBE (Civil) 1960: *m.* 1st, 1944, Felicity Mary, who *d.* 1969, only da. of Frank William Sly, of Bruton; 2ndly, 1970, Betty May, da. of Harry Smith, of Sudbury Hill, and has issue living (by 1st m.), David Nicholas Frank (c/o Barclays Bank, 17/21, High St., E. Grinstead), *b.* 1944; Maj. Parachute Regt.: *m.* 1968, Susan, da. of George Inverarity, DFC, of Brighton, and has issue living, Guy David *b.* 1971, Emma Jane *b.* 1969, a da. *b.* 1973,—Oliver William, *b.* 1955,—Jill Elizabeth, *b.* 1951.——Moyra Frances, *b.* 1942; late 3rd Officer WRNS: *m.* 1943, Capt. Markham Evelegh, *MVO, RN,* of Brook House, Netherbury, Bridport, Dorset, and has issue living, Patrick

John Markham *b.* 1944; with P & O Steam Nav. Co.,—Nicola Anne Moyra, *b.* 1950.——Sheelagh
Helen, *b.* 1913; formerly in ATS: *m.* 1st, 1941 (m. diss. 1946), Donald Harry Muuro, 2nd Lt. RA;
2ndly, 1958, Ronald Coleridge.——Denys Beryl (Dancerwood, 4631, Pipe Line Rd., Vic., BC,
Canada), *b.* 1917: *m.* 1st, 1939 (m. annulled 1942), Maj. Charles Harry Campbell, Indian Army,
who *d.* 1944; 2ndly, 1943, Maj. Peter Michael Harry Dalzell McLaughlin, CD, Canadian Army
(ret.) and Maj. Indian Army (ret.), who *d.* 1971, and has issue living, (by 2nd m.) Kevin Michael
Dalzell (1739, Albert Av., Vic., BC, Canada), *b.* 1949: *m.* 1969, Bonnie Shirley Davies, and has
issue living, Dalzell Michael Talgai *b.* 1969, Maya Denys Shirley *b.* 1972,—Shawn Denys Dalzell,
b. 1955,—Maureen Daphne Hamer, *b.* 1944: *m.* 1967, David Walter Carter, of 866, Latoria Rd.,
Vic., BC, Canada, and has issue living, Blair Alexander *b.* 1974,—Meira Petricia Hanmer, *b.*
1951: *m.* 1970, Gary Wayne Tennent, of 2060, Whitebirch Rd., Sidney, BC, Canada, and has issue
living, Leah Michelle *b.* 1975.

> Grandchildren of the late Rear-Adm. John Graham Job Hanmer, **son of the lat e**
> Capt. Job Thomas Syer Hanmer, R.N., son of the late Capt. Job Hanmer,
> R.N., 2nd son of 1st baronet :—
> Issue of the late Lieut.-Col. Lambert Alfred Graham Hanmer, D.S.O., Indian Army, *b.*
> 1868, *d.* (of wounds in action) 1918: *m.* 1901, Ethel Elizabeth, who *d.* 1964, da. of
> the late Col. Thomas Heaton Lovett, of Belmont, Salop:—
> Richard Graham, *b.* 1906 ; ed. at Wellington Coll. ; is Lieut.-Col. Indian Cav. (retired) : *m.* 1939
> Helen, youngest da. of the late Dr. A. W. Campbell, of Sydney, N.S. Wales, and has issue living
> David Graham (40, Edge St., Kensington, W8) *b.* 1940; ed. at Wellington Coll.; late Capt. R.
> Dragoons: *m.* 1968, Susan Evelyn, da. of Brig. I. M. Christie, and has isuse living, Piers Christie
> Graham *b.* 1971. *Residence*, Forbury Farm, Kimbolton, Leominster, Herefordshire. *Club*,
> Cavalry.——Rosemary Elizabeth (Lower Pyke, Kimbolton, Leominster), *b.* 1905.

> Issue of the late Thomas Walden Hanmer, *b.* 1875, *d.* 1949: *m.* 1903, Ida, who *d.* 1961,
> 2nd da. of A. Whitby Simpson, of Armidale, N.S. Wales:—
> John Walden, E.D., *b.* 1915; is a J.P.; 1939-45 War with Australian Imperial Force: *m.* 1949,
> Jean Eileen Davies, el. da. of Arthur Archibald Sterling Nixon, of Claremont, Oaklands, N.S.
> Wales, and has issue living, Ruth Madeleine, *b.* 1950,—Jean Anne, *b.* 1955,—Patricia Margaret,
> *b.* 1957. *Residence*, Claremont, Oaklands, nr. Corowa, N.S. Wales.——Helen Walden (20, Bertha
> Rd., Cremorne, Sydney, NSW), *b.* 1903: *m.* 1958, Ernest Charles Stumm, who *d.* 1974.——
> ——Mildred Walden, *b.* 1905: *m.* 1932, Douglas Melliar Phelps, and has issue living, Michael
> Melliar, *b.* 1941. *Address*, c/o Bank of N.S. Wales, Lane Cove, Sydney, N.S. Wales.——Beatrice
> Walden, *b.* 1910; 1939-45 War as Capt. Australian Army Nursing Ser.

This family is of considerable antiquity in Flintshire. Sir John de Hanmer, of Hanmer, **was**
Constable of Carnarvon Castle *temp.* Edward I. His great-grandson, Sir Jenkin Hanmer, joined
Owen Glendower in his rebellion against Henry IV, and was killed at the battle of Shrewsbury in
1403. The 1st baronet (cr. 1774), Sir Walden, M.P. for Sunbury in two Parliaments, was 15th in
descent from Sir John de Hanmer. The 3rd baronet sat as M.P. for Shrewsbury (L) 1832-37,
for Hull 1841-47, and for Flint 1847-72, when he was created Baron Hanmer; he died *s.p.* in
1881, when the Peerage became extinct, and the Baronetcy reverted to his brother. The 6th
Baronet was High Sheriff of Flintshire 1902. There was an earlier Baronetcy (cr. 1620) **in the**
Hanmer family, which became ext. in 1746.

HANSEN, Creation (U.K.) 1921, of Bideford, co. Devon.
[Extinct 1958.]

Sir SVEN WOHLFORD HANSEN, *M.B.E.*, 1st and last *Baronet.*

Daughter living—By 1st marriage—Kathleen, *b.* 1900: *m.* 1925, Major Thomas Wilson
Stephens, M.B.E., T.D., Monmouthshire, Regt., and has issue living, Robert Humphrey Wilson,
b. 1934. *Residence*, Corner Lodge, Burnham Market, King's Lynn.

HANSON, Creation (U.K.) 1887, of Bryanston Square, co. Middlesex.

Sir ANTHONY LESLIE OSWALD HANSON,
4th *Baronet ; b.* Nov. 27th, 1934 ; *s.* his half-
brother. *Sir* RICHARD LESLIE REGINALD, 1951,
ed. at Gordonstoun; late RNVR: *m.* 1964,
Denise Jane, da. of R. S. Rolph, of Stoke-
sub-Hamdon.

Arms—Or, a chevron counter compony gules and argent,
cotised of the second, between three martlets sable ; in the
centre chief point a crescent also of the second. **Crest**—On
a fasces fessewise or, a martlet rising sable.

Residence—

By the fear of God and assiduity.

Collateral Branch living.
Issue of the late Sir Francis Stanhope
Hanson, 2nd son of 1st baronet, *b.*
1868, *d.* 1910: *m.* 1897, Pearl Norcott,
who *d.* 1960; (she *m.* 2ndly, 1926,
Maj. Henry Noel Winter, late Roy.
Fusiliers, who *d.* 1952), da. of the late
Charles Albert Winter, JP, of 33,
Hyde Park Sq., W:—
Violet Gwendoline Pearl, *b.* 1899: *m.* 1st, 1919 (m. annulled
on her petition 1923), William Bullivant; 2ndly, 1924,
Capt. Donald Selfe Leonard Gregson, formerly Indian
Cav., from whom she obtained a divorce 1944; 3rdly,
1946, John Roland Adams, QC. *Residence*, Gubbions
Hall, Great Leighs, Chelmsford, Essex.

The 1st baronet, Sir Reginald, was Lord Mayor of
London 1886-7, and sat as MP for City of London (C)
1891-1900.

HANSON, Creation (U.K.) 1918, of Fowey, Cornwall.

SEMPER PARARE.

To be ready always.

Sir (CHARLES) JOHN HANSON, 3rd *Baronet*; *b.* Feb. 28th, 1919; *s.* his father, *Sir* CHARLES EDWIN BOURNE, 1958; ed. at Eton, and at Clare Coll., Camb.: late Capt. Duke of Cornwall's LI: *m.* 1st, 1944 (m. diss. 1968), Patricia Helen, only child of the late Adm. Sir (Eric James) Patrick Brind, GBE, KCB; 2ndly, 1968, Violet Helen, da. of the late Charles Ormonde Trew, and formerly wife of the late Capt. Philip Cecil Langdon Yorke, OBE, RN [see E. Hardwicke, colls.], and has issue by 1st m.

Arms—Argent, three lions rampant in chevron between as many mascles azure. Crest—A lion rampant azure, holding in the dexter forepaw an antler or, and resting the sinister paw upon two mascles fesseways and interlaced of the last.

Residence—7, Abingdon Gdns., Abingdon Villas, W8.

Son living—By 1st m.—CHARLES RUPERT PATRICK, *b.* June 25th, 1945.

Daughter living—By 1st m.—Bridget Clare, *b.* 1948: *m.* 1969, Michael Grahame Cloete Graham-Cloete, (Albany Cottage, Bryanston, Johannesburg, S. Africa), and has issue living, James, *b.* 1975.

Sisters living—Violet Alice Rosalind (Farleigh Cottage, Farleigh Hungerford, nr. Bath), *b.* 1909: *m.* 1930 (m. diss. 1970) Capt. Robert Godmond Poole, RN (ret.), and has issue living, Scilla Rosalind, *b.* 1935: *m.* 1964, Anthony Francis Raikes, of The White House, Woodchurch, nr. Ashford, Kent, and has issue living, Simon Anthony *b.* 1965, Vanessa Rosalind *b.* 1972,—Serena Mary, *b.* 1944.——Edwina Marjorie Clare, *b.* 1912: *m.* 1940, Maj.-Gen. Ralph Cyril Cruddas, CB, DSO, DCLI, and has issue living, Sarah Joslyn, *b.* 1942: *m.* 1968, Ronald Murray Brown, of 18, St. George's Terr., Perth, W. Aust. 6005, and has issue living, Katharine Rose, *b.* 1969, Anna Mary *b.* 1971,—Julia Rose, *b.* 1949,—Joanna Clare, *b.* 1951.   Residence, Springfield House, Nunney, nr. Frome, Som.

The 1st baronet, Sir Charles Augustin Hanson (a partner in the firm of Coates, Son & Co., stockbrokers, of 99, Gresham Street, E.C.), was Lord Mayor of London 1917-18, and sat as M.P. for S.-E., or Bodmin, Div. of Cornwall (U) 1916-22.   The 2nd baronet, Sir Charles Edwin Bourne Hanson, was a partner in the firm of Coates, Son & Co., stockbrokers, of 99, Gresham Street, E.C.2 Major Duke of Wellington's Regt., and High Sheriff of Cornwall 1939.

HARDINGE, Creation (U.K.) 1801, of Lurran, Fermanagh.
[Name pronounced "Harding."]

POSTERA·LAUDE·RECENS

Fresh in the praise of posterity.

Sir ROBERT ARNOLD HARDINGE, 7th *Baronet*; *b.* Dec. 19th, 1914; *s.* his father, *Sir* ROBERT, 1973 (but at the time of going to press his name does not appear on the Official Roll of Baronets).

Arms—Gules, on a chevron argent fimbriated or three escallops sable, a chief wavy argent, thereon the representation of a French frigate wholly dismasted, towed towards the dexter by an English frigate in a shattered state, all proper. Crests—1st, a dexter hand couped in naval uniform grasping a sword, surmounting a Dutch and French flag in saltire, on the former inscribed "Atalanta," on the latter "Piedmontaise," the sword passing through a wreath of laurel near the point, and a little below through one of cypress, all proper; 2nd, a mitre gules thereon a chevron argent fimbriated or charged with three escallops sable.

Address,—

Daughter living of 4th Baronet—Muriel Emily, *b.* 1884: *m.* 1911, John Christie MacLeod, of Pythouse, Tisbury, Wilts., and has issue living, John Edmund Hardinge (Elbury Edge, Compton Abbas, nr. Shaftesbury, Dorset), *b.* 1913; is Maj. Cameronians (Scottish Rifles): *m.* 1941, Dorothy Irene, only da. of Aidan Long, of Elbury Edge, Compton Abbas, Dorset,—Donald Norman (73, Worcester Cres., Woodford Green, Essex), *b.* 1915; Capt. RA (ret.).

Mother living—Emma Abbott, (Colturn Hotel, 980, Grant St., Room 405, Denver, Colorado, 80203, USA), da. of Charles Arnold: *m.* 1st, 1911 (m. diss 1938), Robert Hardinge, later 6th baronet, who *d.* 1973; 2ndly, 1944, Leonard O. Anderson, who *d.* 1959.

Collateral Branches living.

Grandchildren of the late Bradford Hardinge, son of the late Maj.-Gen. Richard Hardinge, el. son of the late Rev. Henry Hardinge, brother of 1st baronet (infra):—

Issue of the late George Nicholas Hardinge, *b.* 1865, *d.* 1943: *m.* 1923, Lady Lilian Frances who *d.* 1974, da. of the late Lt.-Col. James Otway Graham-Toler [*see* E. Norbury]:—
NICHOLAS WILLIAM (White House, Fingringhoe, Essex), *b.* Oct. 11th, 1928: *m.* 1973, Mrs. Anne Curtis, da. of Lt.-Col. W. T. Delamain.——Phyllis Lilian (Rose Cottage, Bramdean Common, Alresford, Hants.), *b.* 1925.

Descendants of the late Field-Marshal the Rt. Hon. Henry Hardinge, G.C.B. (brother of 2nd baronet, and 3rd son of the late Rev. Henry Hardinge, el. brother of 1st baronet), who was *cr. Viscount Hardinge* 1846 [*see* that title].

Richard Hardinge (3rd son of the late Nicolas Hardinge, Clerk of the House of Commons and secretary to the Treasury), was *cr.* a Baronet with special remainder to the heirs male of his father. Sir Robert Hardinge, 6th Bt., grandson of Robert James, 3rd son of the 3rd Bt., did not appear on the Official Roll of Baronets.

HARDY, Creation (U.K.) 1876, of Dunstall Hall, co. Stafford.

Armed with faith bold.

Sir RUPERT JOHN HARDY, 4th *Baronet; b.* Oct. 24th, 1902 ; *s.* his father, *Sir* BERTRAM, 1953 ; ed. at Eton, and at Trin. Hall, Camb. (B.A. 1925) ; Lieut.-Col. (retired) The Life Guards: *m.* 1930, the Hon. Diana Joan Allsopp, da. of 3rd Baron Hindlip, and has issue.

Arms—Argent, on a bend invected plain cotised gules, three catherine wheels or ; on a chief of the second as many leopards' faces of the third. **Crest**—A dexter arm embowed in armour proper, garnished or, entwined by a branch of oak vert, charged with two catherine wheels, the one above, the other below the elbow gules, the hand grasping a dragon's head erased proper.
Residence—Spratton House, Spratton, Northampton. *Club*—Turf.

Son living—RICHARD CHARLES CHANDOS, *b.* Feb. 6th, 1945: *m.* 1972, Venetia Wingfield, da. of Simon Wingfield Digby, MP, of Haydon Gate, Sherborne.
Daughter living—Rosemary Diana (The Glebe House, Guilsborough, Northampton), *b.* 1931: *m.* 1953 (m. diss. 1972) Robert David Black, only son of Maj. Sir Robert Andrew Stransham Black, ED, 2nd Bt.
Brother living—Hugh Bertram (Box 148, Limuru, Kenya), *b.* 1907; ed. at Eton, and Trin. Coll., Camb. (BA) ; Lt.-Col. (ret.) 3rd King's Own Hussars; late Staffs. Yeo. (TA): *m.* 1933, Joan Stella Gwendolyn, da. of Charles Hammond Dracott, and formerly wife of James Alexander Guthrie, and has issue living, Audrey Elizabeth Una, *b.* 1936: *m.* 1965, Charles Frederick Backhouse (c/o Bank of Montreal, Calgary, Alberta, Canada), and has issue living, David Hugh *b.* 1971, Isabelle Joan *b.* 1969.

Collateral Branch living.

Issue of the late Rt. Hon. Laurence Hardy, 4th son of 1st baronet, *b.* 1854, *d.* 1933: *m.* 1886, Evelyn Emily, who *d.* 1911, da. of John Gathorne Wood, of Thedden Grange, Alton :—
Arthur Evelyn, *b.* 1893 ; ed. at Eton ; is Major Coldstream Guards (Reserve) ; European War 1914 in France and Belgium (1914 star, two medals) : *m.* 1918, Nancy Marion, da. of Horace George Devas, formerly of Nizels, Hildenborough, Kent [E. Cawdor, colls.], and has issue living, Gerald Alan (of Hillhurst Farm, Hythe, Kent), *b.* 1926 : *m.* 1953, Carolyn, da. of the late Maj.-Gen. Arthur Tarver Evanson, C.B., M.C., and has issue living, Sarah *b.* 1957, Jane *b.* 1958.—Ruth, *b.* 1919 : *m.* 1940, Col. Charles Reginald Tuff, Buffs (retired), of Hogs Green, Sandling, Hythe, Kent, and has issue living, Timothy Charles *b.* 1947, Geoffrey *b.* 1954, Prunella Primrose *b.* 1942. *Residence*, Sandling Park, Hythe, Kent.——Maurice John, *M.B.E.*, *b.* 1902 ; ed. at Eton, and at Ch. Ch., Oxford ; European War 1939-45 as Major R.E. ; M.B.E. (Mil.) 1946 : *m.* 1926, Rosalie Kathleen, da. of the late Brig.-Gen. Tyrell Other William Champion de Crespigny [*see* Champion de Crespigny, Bt.], and has issue living, Jane, *b.* 1931: *m.* 1955, Peter Leonard Eckersley, of Ewhurst Pl., Ewhurst, Robertsbridge Sussex, and has issue living, Peter David Charles *b.* 1957, Clare Arabella *b.* 1960, Suzanne Jane *b.* 1962. *Residence*, Wychling Court, Wychling, Sittingbourne, Kent.

Sir John, 1st baronet, sat as M.P. for Midhurst (C) 1859, for Dartmouth 1860-68, and for S. Warwickshire 1868-74. Sir Bertram, 3rd baronet was High Sheriff of Staffordshire 1925.

HARE, Creation (U.K.) 1818, of Stow Hall, Norfolk.

N on videri sed esse.
Not to seem, but to be.

Sir RALPH LEIGH HARE, 4th *Baronet ; b.* Jan. 19th, 1903 ; *s.* his father, *Sir* (GEORGE) RALPH LEIGH, 1933 ; ed. at Eton ; Major (retired) Coldstream Guards : *m.* 1st, 1928 (marriage dissolved 1944), Doreen Pleasance Anna, da. of Major Sir Richard Ludwig Bagge, D.S.O. ; 2ndly, 1945 (marriage dissolved 1958) Natalie Alexandria Elizabeth Julia, da. of the late Capt. Baron Oscar Gerard de Langué ; 3rdly, 1960, Barbara Mary Theodora, youngest da. of the late Joseph Arthur Walton, and has issue by 1st, 2nd and 3rd marriages.

Arms—Gules two bars or, a chief indented of the last. **Crest**—A demi-ion rampant argent, gorged with a ducal coronet or.
Residence—Stow Bardolph, King's Lynn, Norfolk. *Club*—Guards'.

Son living—By 1st marriage—THOMAS, *b.* July 27th, 1930; ed. at Eton, and at Magdalen Coll., Camb. (MA) ; ARICS; is Lt. Coldm. Gds. (Reserve): *m.* 1961 Lady Rose Amanda Bligh, da. of 9th Earl of Darnley and has issue living, Lucy Rose, *b.* 1962,—Elizabeth Florence, *b.* 1964. *Residence*, Stow Bardolph, King's Lynn, Norfolk.

Daughters living—By 1st m.—Jean Bridget, *b.* 1929: *m.* 1st, 1949 (m. diss. 1957), N. E. Beard; 2ndly, 1957 (m. diss. 1971), R. J. Wallis, and has issue living, (by 1st m.) Jeremy Nigel Thomas, *b.* 1953,—Laraine Susan, *b.* 1950,—(by 2nd m.) Robin John, *b.* 1961. *Residence*, 21, Narrow Lane, Histon, Cambridge.——**By 2nd m.**—Angela Florence Natalie, *b.* 1948.——Lorna Lillianne Katrina, *b.* 1957.——**By 3rd m.**—Mary Ann, *b.* 1961.

Sisters living—Mary Leigh (Wings, Stow Bardolph, Kings Lynn), *b.* 1896.——Joan Muriel Leigh, *b.* 1905. *Residence*, Ilsington, nr. Newton Abbot, S. Devon.

Collateral Branch living.

Issue of the late Edward **Philip Leigh** Hare, youngest son of 2nd baronet, *b.* 1869, *d.* 1954 ; *m.* 1st, 1906 (marriage annulled on his petition 1910), Mabel Newton, el. da. of John Taylor, of Brookdale, Newton Heath, Manchester ; 2ndly, 1914, Iris Trelawny Rutherfurd (who *d.* 1974, having obtained a divorce 1920), da. of William Rutherfurd Lamb, of Ryton Hall, co. Durham; 3rdly, 1920, Lady Kathleen Florence Mary, who *d.* 1971, da. of 9th Earl of Harrington, and widow of Edward John Harry Eden Morant, JP, of Brockenhurst Park, Hants.

(By 3rd m.) Philip Leigh (Darlingscott Farm, Darlingscott, Shipton-on-Stour), *b.* 1922: *m.* 1950, Anne Lisle, da. of Maj. Geoffrey Nicholson, CBE, MC [E. Annesley, colls.], and has issue living, Nicholas Patrick *b.* 1955.—Louisa Kathleen (twin), *b.* 1955.——(By 2nd m.) Elizabeth Mildred Leigh (The Old Tiled House, Red Cross Lane, Cambridge), *b.* 1915

Sir Nicholas Hare, twice Speaker of the House of Commons and sometime Master of the Rolls a Commissioner to execute the Office of Lord Chancellor and Keeper of the Great Seal 1555), purchased Stow Bardolph in 1553. His great-great-great-nephew Ralph Hare (son of Sir John Hare, Knt.) was *cr.* 1st Baronet of Stow Bardolph in 1641. Mary, second da. of his son Sir Thomas Hare, 2nd Bt. (*cr.* 1641), and sister and eventual co-heiress of the 5th Bt. (at whose death in 1764 that Baronetcy became ext.), married Thomas Leigh, of London, son of Edward Leigh, of Iver, Bucks (will proved 1689) and in common descent with the Stoneleigh Abbey family, from the Leighs of Cheshire. Her grandson, Thomas Leigh, who succeeded to Stow Bardolph (son of Thomas Leigh, of Iver, Bucks), served with distinction in the American war, assumed in 1791 by Act of Parliament the surname of Hare in lieu of his patronymic of Leigh, and was *cr.* a Baronet in 1818, becoming Sir Thomas Hare, 1st Bt. The 2nd baronet was Capt. 2nd Life Guards, while the 3rd was Lieut. 2nd Life Guards, and High Sheriff of Norfolk 1906.

HARFORD, Creation (U.K.) 1934, of Falcondale, co. Cardigan.

Inter utrumque tene.

Hold between the two.

Sir (John) Timothy Harford, 3rd *Baronet*; *b.* July 6th, 1932; *s.* his father, Lt.-Col. *Sir* George Arthur, *OBE*, 1967; ed. at Harrow, Worcester Coll., Oxford, and Harvard Business Sch.: *m.* 1962, Carolyn, da. of Brig. Guy John de Wette Mullens, OBE, **of North House**, Weyhill, Andover, and has issue.

Arms—Sable, two bendlets argent between three cross-crosslets fitchée in pale of the last. **Crest**—In front of flames issuant therefrom a phœnix proper, two cross-crosslets fitchée in saltire argent.

Residence—South House, South Littleton, Evesham.

Sons living—MARK JOHN, *b.* Aug. 6th, 1964.——Simon Guy, *b.* 1966.

Daughter living—Clare Elisabeth, *b.* 1963.

Brother living—Piers Scandrett (c/o Stock & Co., Bristol & West Building, Broad Quay, Bristol 1), *b.* 1937, ed. at Eton, and at Worcester Coll., Oxford: *m.* 1st, 1961 (m. diss. 1972), Hyacinthe Cecilia, da. of Lt.-Col. Nigel Walter Hoare, OBE, TD [*see* Portal, Bt., colls.]; 2ndly, 1975, Patricia Jane, da. of Air Commodore Patrick Bennett, and has issue living (by 1st m.), Henry Scandrett, *b.* 1963,—Charlotte Anstice, *b.* 1965.

Sister living—Robina Elspeth, *b.* 1934: *m.* 1956, Jeremy Christopher Glyn [*see* B. Wolverton, colls.]. *Residence*, The Bury, Little Hadham, Herts.

Widow living of 2nd Baronet—ANSTICE MARION (*Anstice*, *Lady Harford*), (Lockeridge Down, Marlborough), da. of Sir Alfred Tritton, 2nd Bt.: *m.* 1931, Lt.-Col. Sir George Arthur Harford OBE, 2nd Bt., who *d.* 1967.

The 1st baronet, Major Sir John Charles Harford (son of the late John Battersby Harford, of Falcondale, co. Cardigan, and of Blaise Castle, Henbury, Bristol) was created a baronet June 1934, and *d.* July 1934.

HARINGTON, Creation (E.) 1611, of Ridlington, Rutland.

NODO·FIRMO·

With a firm knot.

Sir RICHARD DUNDAS HARINGTON,
13th *Baronet; b.* Oct. 16th, 1900 ; *s.* his father,
Sir RICHARD, 1931 ; ed. at Eton, and at Sidney
Sussex Coll., Camb.

Arms—Sable, a fret argent. **Crest**—A lion's head erased
or, langued and collared gules, buckled of the first.
Seat—Whitbourne Court, Worcester.

Brother living—*His Honour* JOHN CHARLES DUNDAS,
QC, *b.* June 27th, 1903 ; Bar. Inner Temple 1928, and a
QC 1957; is Lt.-Com. RNVR; was Recorder of New
Windsor 1955-8; appointed Chm. Herefordshire
Quarter Sessions 1957, and a Judge of Co. Courts
(Hampshire Circuit) 1958-73: *m.* 1941, Lavender
Cecilia, da. of the late Maj. Ernest Wriothesley Denny,
DSO [E. Dartmouth, colls.], and has issue living,
Nicholas John, *b.* 1942,—David Richard, *b.* 1944,—
Susan Alexandra, *b.* 1948. *Residence*, Whitbourne
Court, Worcester.

Collateral Branches living.

Grandchildren of the late Rev. Charles
Harington, 2nd son of 11th baronet:—
Issue of the late Sir Charles Robert Harington,
KBE, *b.* 1897, *d.* 1972: *m.* 1923, Jessie
McCririe, who *d.* 1975, da. of the Rev. James
Craig, of The Manse, Kirkpatrick-Durham,
Kirkcudbright:—

Michael (64, Burlington Av., Kew Gdns., Richmond, Surrey), *b.* 1924; MB, BChir; MRCP: *m.*
1958, Marta Rosenfeld, and has issue living, Robert Michael, *b.* 1963,—Amanda, 1967.—Alison
Mary, *b.* 1927: *m.* 1952, Derek Raymond Bangham, of 4, Crown Close, Highwood Hill, NW7,
and has issue living, Charles Richard Mark, *b.* 1955,—Humphrey Bernard, *b.* 1957,—Celia
Elizabeth, *b.* 1954,—Jessica Francis, *b.* 1961.—Margaret Jane, *b.* 1931.

Issue of the late His Honour Judge Edward Harington, 3rd son of 11th baronet,
b. 1863, *d.* 1937: *m.* 1906, Louisa Muriel, who *d.* 1963, only da. of the late
Herbert C. Erskine Vernon:—
(Edward Henry) Vernon (Woodlands House, Whitbourne, Worcs.; Guard's Club), *b.* 1907; ed.
at Eton; Bar. Inner Temple 1930; was Private Sec. to Lord Chancellor and Dep. Sergeant-at-
Arms in House of Lords 1934-40; appointed Assist. Sec. of Commns. to Lord Chancellor 1945,
a Dep. Judge Advocate 1946, and Assist. Judge Advocate Gen. 1955; Dep. Chm. Herefordshire
Quarter Sessions 1969-72, since when a Recorder of Crown Court; a Gold Staff Officer at Coronation of King George VI; 1939-45 War as Maj. Coldm. Gds.: *m.* 1937, Mary Elizabeth (from whom
he obtained a divorce 1949), da. of the late Louis Edwin William Egerton [M. Hertford, colls.];
2ndly, 1950, Mary Johanna Jean, JP, da. of the late Lt.-Col. R. G. S. Cox, MC, and has issue
living, (by 1st m.) Victoria Jane, *b.* 1941: *m.* 1974, Sidney Morgan Whitteridge, VRD, MRCS,
LRPC, of Inverlael, Ullapool, Ross-shire, and has issue living, Mary Ruth, *b.* 1974,—(by 2nd
m.) Marie Louisa, *b.* 1951,—Susan Anne, *b.* 1953.——Kenneth Douglas Evelyn Herbert, *b.* 1911;
ed. at Stowe Sch.; Bar. Inner Temple 1952; Hon. Attaché, British Legation, Stockholm 1930-32;
a JP and Acting Dep. Chm. of Quarter Sessions in Greater London 1966-67, since when a
Metropolitan Magistrate; 1939-45 War as Maj. Coldm. Gds.: *m.* 1st, 1939, Lady Cecilia Bowes-
Lyon, who *d.* 1947, da. of 15th Earl of Strathmore; 2ndly, 1950, Maureen Helen, da. of the late
Brig.-Gen. Sir Robert (Chaine Alexander) McCalmont, KCVO, CBE, DSO, and has issue living,
(by 2nd m.) Michael Kenneth, *b.* 1951; ed. at Eton,—Jonathan Edward McCalmont, *b.* 1955.
Residences, Sotchers, Bury Gate, Pulborough, Sussex; 21, Milner St., SW3. *Club*, Guards'.

Issue of the late Brig.-Gen. John Harington, C.B., C.M.G., D.S.O., 5th son of 11th
baronet, *b.* 1873, *d.* 1943: *m.* 1908, Lady Frances Aline Temple-Gore-Langton
who *d.* 1952, da. of 4th Earl Temple of Stowe :—
John Temple, *D.S.O., M.B.E., b.* 1909; ed. at Winchester; is Major Rifle Brig.; appointed an
A.D.C. 1939; European War 1939-45 (M.B.E., D.S.O.); M.B.E. (Mil.) and D.S.O. 1945: *m.* 1946,
Catherine Mary, da. of Lieut.-Col. Donald Cameron, of Fordon, The Nile, Tasmania, and has
issue living, Richard Donald John, *b.* 1948,—Serena Catherine Lucy, *b.* 1947: *m.* 1971, Julian G.
Barrow,—Cecilia Aline, *b.* 1953.——Aline Lucy (Hon. Mrs. Walter A. C. Keppel), *b.* 1918:
m. 1941, Lt.-Com. the Hon. Walter Arnold Crispian Keppel, DSC, RN [see E. Albemarle].
Residence, Barton House, Meonstoke, Hants.

Granddaughter of the late Arthur Champernowne, son of Henry Champernowne, el. son of Arthur Champernowne (infra):—
Issue of the late Arthur Melville Champernowne, *b.* 1871, *d.* 1946 : *m.* 1907, Helen Iris,
who *d.* 1950, el. da. of Lieut.-Col. Herbert John Ouchterlony Walker, late R.A., formerly
of Leeford, Budleigh Salterton:—
Katharine Iris (Morley Cottage, Halse, Taunton, Som.), *b.* 1912: *m.* 1949, Wing-Cdr. Adrian Henry
Paull, AFC, who *d.* 1965, and has issue living, Angela Iris Constance, *b.* 1951.

Grandson of the late Rev. Richard Champernowne, son of the late Arthur
CHAMPERNOWNE (who assumed the surname and arms of Champernowne 1774),
son of the late Rev. Richard Harington, 2nd son of 6th baronet :—
Issue of the late Francis Gawayne Champernowne, *b.* 1866, *d.* 1921 : *m.* 1911, Isabel Mary,
who *d.* 1969, da. of the late George Burvill Rashleigh, Bar.-at-law, of Riseley, Horton-
Kirby, Dartford and 5, Stone Buildings, Lincoln's Inn, WC [E. Darnley]:—
David Gawen, *b.* 1912; ed. at Winchester, and at King's Coll., Camb. (Fellow 1937-48); a Fellow of
Trin. Coll., Camb.; Prof. of Statistics, Oxford Univ. 1948-59; Prof. of Economics & Statistics,
Camb. Univ. since 1970: *m.* 1948, Wilhelmina Barbara Maria, da. of the late Petrus Ludovicus
Dullaert, of Zutphen, Holland, and has issue living, Arthur Francis, *b.* 1949,—Richard Peter, *b.*
1953. *Residence*, 230, Hills Rd., Cambridge.

John, son of Robert de Haverington, of Haverington (now Harrington), Cumberland, was one
of the barons summoned to Parliament by Edward II. His lineal descendant, Sir John Harington
of Exton, co. Rutland, brother of the 1st baronet, and tutor to the Princess Elizabeth, daughter of
James I., was created Baron Harington, which title became extinct on the death of the 2nd baron.
Sir James, 3rd baronet, one of the Judges commissioned (but who refused to sit) to try Charles I.,
was, by an Act of 13 Car. II., nevertheless excepted at the Restoration out of the general acts of
indemnity, and with Lord Monson, Sir Henry Fieldings, and others subjected to personal degradation

from his honours and rendered personally incapable of bearing arms or title of dignity (but the penalty did not forfeit the honours or attaint the blood). Sir Richard, 11th Bt., was a Metropolitan Police Magistrate 1871-2, and a Judge of County Courts 1872-1905. Sir Richard, 12th Bt., was a Puisne Judge of High Court, Calcutta 1899-1913.

STAFFORD-KING HARMAN, Creation (U.K.) 1914, of Rockingham co. Roscommon.

The safest hope is in heaven.

Sir CECIL WILLIAM FRANCIS STAFFORD-KING-HARMAN, 2nd *Baronet*; *b.* Jan. 6th, 1895; *s.* his father, *the Rt. Hon. Sir* THOMAS JOSEPH STAFFORD, *C.B.,* 1935; M.A. (Agriculture) Oxford 1922; has been Midshipman R.N.; formerly Major and temporary Lieut. Col. King's Roy. Rifle Corps; was A.A.G. Scottish Command 1942-3; appointed a Member of Irish Council of State 1956; European War 1914-18 (despatches); assumed by Roy. licence 1932 the additional surnames of King-Harman: *m.* 1917, Sarah Beatrice, da. of the late Col. Alfred Dyke Acland, C.B.E. [*see* Acland, Bt., *cr.* 1890, colls.], and has issue.

Arms—Quarterly, 1st and 4th, quarterly, i and iv, sable, a chevron between three rams passant argent, attired or, *Harman;* ii and iii, gules, two lions rampant combatant, supporting a dexter hand couped at the wrist and erect argent, *King;* 2nd and 3rd, per chevron, or and argent, a chevron engrailed and a canton gules, *Stafford.* **Crest**—1st, out of a ducal crest coronet or, a dexter arm, armed and erect in pale proper, cuffed argent, the hand also proper, grasping two slips of roses, one gules, the other argent, stalked, seeded, and leaved proper, *Harman;* 2ndly, out of a ducal crest coronet or, a dexter hand erect, the third and fourth fingers turned down proper, *King;* 3rd, out of a ducal crest coronet azure, a swan rising proper, charged with a torteau, *Stafford.*

Residence—St. Catherine's Park, Leixlip, co. Kildare. *Clubs*—Boodle's, Kildare Street, Irish Turf.

Daughters living—Cicely Joan, *b.* 1918: *m.* 1943, Capt. George Heffernan Dennehy, late Irish Guards, and has issue living, Rosemary Anne *b.* 1944: *m.* 1964, Charles Ralph Nicolas Tindal, of Ballyloughan, Bruckless, co. Donegal, and has issue living, Nicolas Henry Charles *b.* 1965, Richard Mark *b.* 1968, Matthew Thomas *b.* 1973, Katherine Mary *b.* 1966, Emma Caroline *b.* 1970, Victoria Jacqueline Frances *b.* 1971,—Sarah Elizabeth, *b.* 1949: *m.* 1970, Don Leopoldo de Bolivar Torres, of Seville, and has issue living, Isabel *b.* 1970, Alexandra Rose *b.* 1974,—Mary Katharine, *b.* 1951,—Caroline Jean, *b.* 1954. *Residences*, 64, Cadogan Sq., SW1; Lotham's Farm, Odiham, Hants.——Elizabeth Anne, *b.* 1919. *Residence*, St. Catherine's Park, Leixlip, co. Kildare.

Collateral Branch living.

Issue of the late Capt. Edward Charles Stafford-King-Harman, Irish Guards, el. son of 1st baronet, *b.* 1891, *d.* (killed in action) 1914, having assumed by Roy. licence 1900 the additional surname of King-Harman: *m.* 1914, Olive (now of Strokestown Park, co. Roscommon; she *m.* 2ndly, 1921, Wilfred Stuart Atherstone Hales-Pakenham-Mahon), only da. of the late Capt. Henry Pakenham-Mahon [*see* E. Longford, colls.]:—

Lettice Mary (*posthumous*), *b.* 1915: *m.* 1935 (m. diss. 1971), Col. Robert Humphrey Lomer, MBE, Gren. Gds., and has issue living, Caroline Mary, *b.* 1937: *m.* 1st, 1957 (m. diss. 1964), Patrick Haselden Wood; 2ndly, 1964, Maj. Neil Gordon Ramsay, late Scots Guards, of Farleyer, Aberfeldy, Perthshire, and has issue living (by 2nd marriage) Melanie Mary *b.* 1966,—Lavinia Rohays, (184, Latymer Court, W6), *b.* 1939: *m.* 1968 (m. diss. 1973), Cdr. Harry James Startin, RN. *Residence*, 21, Lancaster Close, St. Petersburgh Place, W2.

The 1st baronet, the Rt. Hon. Sir Thomas (Joseph) Stafford, C.B. (son of the late John Stafford, J.P., of Portobello, co. Roscommon, descended from the Staffords of Gillstown, co. Roscommon), was a L.R.C.P.I. and L.R.C.S.I., a D.L. for co. Roscommon, and sometime a Member of Local Govt. Board, Ireland, and of Lord-Lieut. of Ireland's Advisory Council. He *m.* 1890, Frances Agnes, da. and heir of the Rt. Hon. Edward Robert King-Harman, MP [E. Kingston]. Thomas Edward Stafford-King-Harman, Lt. Irish Guards, only son and heir of 2nd Bt., *b.* 1921, was killed in action in Normandy 1944.

Harmood-Banner, see Banner.

HARMSWORTH, Creation (U.K.) 1918, of Moray Lodge, Royal Borough of Kensington.

He who acts diligently acts well.

Sir (ARTHUR) GEOFFREY (ANNESLEY) HARMSWORTH, 3rd *Baronet*; *b.* March 29th, 1904 ; *s.* his brother, *Sir* ALFRED LEICESTER ST. BARBE, 1962; *ed.* at Harrow; Sqdn.-Ldr. RAFVR, Chm. of Harmsworth Press, Ltd., of West Country Publications, Ltd., and of Western Morning News Co., Ltd., and a Dir. of *Daily Mail,* and General Trust Ltd.; FSA; a War Correspondent 1939-40.

Arms—Azure, two rolls of paper in saltire or, banded in the centre gules, between four bees volant of the second. **Crest**—A cubit arm, the hand holding a roll of paper fessewise proper between two ostrich feathers or.

Residence—White Cottage, Tealby, Lincoln. *Club*—Royal Automobile.

Sisters living—Annie Mary Geraldine, *b.* 1900 : *m.* 1921, Terry Colley Durham, of Univ. of Richmond, Virginia, U.S.A., who *d.* 1949, and has issue living, Rosemary Virginia Margaret Harmsworth, *b.* 1923 : *m.* 1950, Peter Cecil Clarke, 7th Hussars, and has issue living, Charles Vivian, *b.* 1955, Virginia Audrey Mary, *b.* 1952, Georgina Rosemary Frances, *b.* 1957,—Anne Katharine, *b.* 1925,—Vivian Muriel Mary, *b.* 1928; MA, MSc, DPhil: *m.* 1960, Denis Gregory Mash, and has issue living, Julian Paul Vivian *b.* 1961, Richard Terry Bernard *b.* 1966, Rosalind Elizabeth *b.* 1963, Helen Jane Emily *b.* 1970,—Veronica Thérese, *b.* 1932; BA: *m.* 1954, Neas Adrian Fuller Stokes, and has issue living, Teresa Mary *b.* 1956, Felicity Madeline Rosemary *b.* 1958, Enid Anastasia Maria *b.* 1961, Mary Anne Vivian *b.* 1963. *Residence,* Hollingdene, 22, Upper Church Rd., St. Leonards-on-Sea, Sussex.——Violet Lilian Rosemary (Wychwood Cottage, West St., Mayfield, Sussex), *b.* 1902: *m.* 1926, Alexander Godfrey Crosbie Collins, who *d.* 1932, son of the late Rt. Hon. Sir Godfrey Pattison Collins, KBE, CMG, MP, formerly Sec. of State for Scotland, and has issue living, Harold Godfrey Leicester, *b.* 1927, *d.* 1975: *m.* 1st, 1949, Joan Pamela (who obtained a divorce 1957), da. of B. W. Hodge, of Exmouth; 2ndly, 1957, S. Peters, of Exeter, and has issue living, (by 1st m.) Richard William Harold *b.* 1951, Elizabeth Rosemary Joan *b.* 1955, (by 2nd m.) Nigel Robin Harold *b.* 1958.——Margaret Rosabelle Northcliffe, *b.* 1911. *Residence,* 7, Campden House Court, Gloucester Walk, W8.

The 1st baronet, Sir Robert Leicester Harmsworth (son of the late Alfred Harmsworth, Bar.-at-law), was a younger brother of the 1st Viscount Northcliffe (ext.), and the 1st Viscount Rothermere, and sat as MP for Caithness (L) 1900-18, and for Caithness and Sutherland 1918-22.

HARMSWORTH, Creation (U.K.) 1922, of Freshwater Grove, Parish of Shipley, co. Sussex.

He who acts diligently acts well.

Sir HILDEBRAND ALFRED BERESFORD HARMSWORTH, 2nd *Baronet ; b.* May 27th, 1901 ; *s.* his father, *Sir* HILDEBRAND AUBREY, 1929; *ed.* at Harrow : *m.* 1925, Elen, da. of Nicolaj Billenstein, of Randers, Denmark, and has issue.

Arms—Azure, two rolls of paper in saltire or, banded in the centre gules, between four bees volant of the second. **Crest**—Issuant out of a coronet composed of three roses set upon a rim or, a cubit arm erect, the hand grasping a roll of paper fessewise proper.

Residence—Deepdene, Shottermill, Haslemere, Surrey.

Son living—HILDEBRAND HAROLD (Ewlyn Villa, 42, Leckhampton Rd., Cheltenham), *b.* June 5th, 1931; *ed.* at Harrow, and Trin. Coll., Dublin: *m.* 1960, Gillian Andrea, only da. of William John Lewis, of Tetbury, and has issue living, Hildebrand Esmund Miles, *b.* 1964,—Claire Elen Mary, *b.* 1961,—Kirsten Elizabeth Ashley, *b.* 1963.

Daughter living—Ingeborg Kathleen Elen, *b.* 1926 : *m.* 1951, Capt. Thomas James Johnson, R.A., who *d.* 1963, and has issue living, Ingeborg Caroline Kathleen Elen, *b.* 1952,—Melissa Eugenie Ingeborg Thomasine, *b.* 1954,—Atalanta Kathleen Ingeborg Elen, *b.* 1962. *Residence,* Chiffley Grange, Staplefield, Sussex.

Collateral Branch living.

Issue of the late (Chamberlain) Michael Hildebrand Harmsworth, 3rd son of 1st baronet, *b.* 1903, *d.* 1955 : *m.* 1st, 1931, Barbara Irene, who *d.* 1941, da. of Henry Savile Dean ; 2ndly, 1945, Lucette Charlotte, only da. of Jean Riché, of Paris :—

(By 2nd marriage) John Hildebrand, *b.* 1949.——Charles Hildebrand, *b.* 1951.——(By 1st marriage) Josephine Angela, *b.* 1932.——Melanie Barbara, *b.* 1934.

Sir Hildebrand Harmsworth, 1st Bt. (son of the late Alfred Harmsworth, Bar.-at-law), was a younger brother of the 1st Viscount Northcliffe (ext.), and the 1st Viscount Rothermere ; edited *New Liberal Review* 1901-4, and was sometime Proprietor of *The Globe.*

HARRIS, Creation (U.K.) 1932, of Bethnal Green, co. London.

Sir JACK (WOLFRED) ASHFORD HARRIS, 2nd *Baronet*, *b.* July 23rd, 1906 ; *s.* his father, the *Rt. Hon. Sir* PERCY ALFRED HARRIS, 1952 ; ed. at Shrewsbury, and at Trin. Hall, Camb. (B.A. 19—) ; is Governing Director of Bing, Harris & Co., Ltd., warehousemen and manufacturers, of Wellington, New Zealand, and Pres. of New Zealand Wholesale Soft Goods Federation ; sometime Pres. of Wellington Chamber of Commerce ; European War 1939-45 with New Zealand Forces : *m.* 1933, Patricia, da. of A. P. Penman, of Wohroonga, near Sydney, N.S. Wales, and has issue.

Residence—Te Rama, Waikanae, near Wellington, New Zealand. *Clubs*—Royal Automobile, Wellington (New Zealand).

Sons living—CHRISTOPHER JOHN ASHFORD, *b.* Aug. 26th, 1934 : *m.* 1957, Anna, da. of F. de Malmanche, of Auckland, New Zealand, and has issue living, Andrew Frederick Ashford, *b.* 1958,—Charlotte Anna, *b.* 1960,—Phoebe Jane Ashford, *b.* 1963. *Residence*, 21, Anne St. Wadestown, Wellington, NZ.——Paul Percy, *b.* 1945.

Daughter living—Margaret, *b.* 19—.

Brother living—Thomas Nicholas Robinson, *b.* 1908 ; ed. at King's Sch., Bruton, and at Trin. Hall, Camb.; is Lieut. R.N.V.R.: *m.* 1942, Lucille, only child of D. H. Jonas, and has issue living, Antony Guy David Bloxham, *b.* 1943.

The 1st baronet, the Rt. Hon. Sir Percy Alfred Harris (son of Wolf Harris, of 197, Queen's Gate, S.W.), was M.P. for S. (or Harborough) Div. of Leicestershire 1916-18, and for S.-W. Div. of Bethnal Green 1922-45, and was Ch. Liberal Whip 1935-45.

HARRIS, Creation (U.K.) 1953, of Chepping Wycombe, Bucks.

Marshal of the R.A.F. Sir ARTHUR TRAVERS HARRIS, *G.C.B.*, *O.B.E.*, *A.F.C.*, 1st *Baronet*, son of George S. T. Harris, of PWD India; *b.* April 13th, 1892 ; Hon. LL.D. Liverpool 1946 ; is Marshal of the RAF; 1914-18 War with 1st Rhodesian Regt., RFC and RAF in S.-W. Africa, France, India, Mesopotamia and Middle East (despatches); 1939-45 War (despatches, CB, KCB, GCB, 1st class Order of Suvorov of Russia, **Grand Cross of Orders of Restitution of Poland, and of Southern Cross of Brazil, Grand** Officier, Legion of Honour, Ch. Com. of American Legion of Merit, American D.S.M., Croix de Guerre with palm) ; was Air Officer Comdg. R.A.F., Palestine and Transjordan 1938-39, and No. 5 Group 1939-40, Dep. Ch. of Air Staff 1940-41, Head of R.A.F. Delegation to U.S.A. 1941, and Air Officer Comdg.-in-Ch., Bomber Command 1942-45 ; received Freedom of Honiton 1945, and of Chepping Wycombe 1946 ; O.B.E. (Mil.) 1927, C.B. (Mil.) 1940, K.C.B. (Mil.) 1942, G.C.B. (Mil.) 1945 : *m.* 1st, 1916, Barbara, da. of Lieut.-Col. E. W. K. Money ; 2ndly, 1938, Thérèse, da. of Major E. P. Hearne, and has issue by 1st and 2nd marriages.

Arms—Azure a chevron ermine between in chief two hedgehogs and in base an eagle displayed or. *Crest*—Issuant from an astral crown or a mount vert thereon a hedgehog gold. *Supporters*—(*personal as a G.C.B.*)—*Dexter*, a lion ; *sinister*, an eagle or, both gorged with an astral crown azure.

Residence—The Ferry House, Goring-on-Thames, Oxon.

Son living—By 1st marriage—ANTHONY KYRLE TRAVERS, *b.* March 18th, 1918 ; ed. at Oundle ; European War 1939-45 with Queen Victoria's Rifles and Wiltshire Regt. *Address*, c/o Barclays Bank, Queen's Gate, S.W.7.

Daughters living—By 1st marriage—Marigold Patricia, *b.* 1920 : *m.* 1946, Robert William Armitage, TD, of Grove House, Marishes, Malton, Yorks.,—and has issue living, Rupert Dudley, *b.* 1947,—Peter James, *b.* 1950.——Rosemary Jeanne, *b.* 1923.——By 2nd marriage—Jacqueline Jill (*Hon. Mrs. Nicholas Assheton*) *b.* 1939: *m.* 1960, the Hon. Nicholas Assheton [*see* B.Clitheroe]. *Residence*, 5, Astell St., SW3.

HARRISON, Creation (U.K.) 1922, of Eaglescliffe, co. Durham.

While I breathe, I hope.

Sir (ROBERT) COLIN HARRISON, 4th *Baronet : b.* May 25th 1938 ; *s.* his brother, Sir (JOHN) WYNDHAM, 1955; ed. at Radley, and at St. John's Coll., Camb.: *m.* 1963, Maureen Marie, da. of E. Leonard Chiverton, of Garth Corner, Vivers Place, Kirkbymoorside, Yorks., and has issue.

Arms—Per chevron azure and or, in chief two demi-lions rampant of the second and in base a lymphad sable. Crest—Upon a fernbrake a falcon rising proper, belled and charged upon the sinister wing with a fleur-de-lis or.
Residence—Keld Close, Hutton-le-Hole, York.

Son living—JOHN WINDHAM FOWLER, *b.* Dec. 14th, 1972. Daughters living—Rachel Deborah, *b.* 1966,—Claire Grace, *b.* 1974.
Sister living—Judith May *b.* 1935: *m.* 1962, Paul Standing, of Hill Farm, Langley, Stratford-upon-Avon, and has issue living, Christopher Hugh, *b.* 1965,—Jane Kathleen, *b.* 1963.
Aunt living (daughter of 1st baronet)—Marjorie, *b.* 1901: *m.* 1926, Cyril E. M. Robinson, and has issue living, Pamela Elizabeth, *b.* 1927: *m.* 1950, Anthony Faber, of Brackenrigg, Osmotherley, Northallerton, Yorks., and has issue living, David Anthony *b.* 1951, Jeremy Edward *b.* 1954,—Anne Rosemary, *b.* 1930. *Residence*, Ganavan, Hutton Rudby, Yarm, Yorks.

Widow living of 2nd Baronet—KATHLEEN (*Kathleen, Lady Harrison*), da. of Robert Livingston, of The Gables, Eaglescliffe, co. Durham: *m.* 1930, Sir (John) Fowler Harrison, 2nd Bt., who *d.* 1947. *Residence*, 135, Guisborough Rd., Nunthorpe, Middlesbrough, Cleveland.

The 1st baronet, Sir John Harrison (son of John Harrison, of Stockton-on-Tees), was Mayor of Stockton 1903, 1906, 1916, 1917, and 1918.

HARRISON, Creation (U.K.) 1961, of Bugbrooke, co. Northampton.

Sir (JAMES) HARWOOD HARRISON, *T.D., M.P.,* 1st *Baronet,* son of the late Rev. Ernest Wivelsfield Harrison, of Bugbrooke, Northampton ; *b.* June 6th, 1907 ; ed. at Northampton, and at Trin. Coll., Oxford (B.A. 1928, M.A. 1946) ; is a Co. Director ; Brevet Col. (retired) 4th Suffolk Regt. (T.A.) ; was Parliamentary Private Sec. to Rt. Hon. Harold Macmillan 1953-4, Assist. Govt. Whip 1954-6, a Lord Commr. of the Treasury 1956-9, and Comptroller of H.M. Household 1959-61; Pres. of E. Area, Conservative Party 1963-66 (Chm. 1956-59); Chm. of Unionist Club since 1966, and of Select Sub. Cttee. on Defence and Overseas Affairs since 1971; MP (*C*) for Eye Div. of Suffolk since 1951: *m.* 1932, Peggy Alberta Mary, da. of the late Lt.Col. V. D. Stenhouse, TD, JP, and has issue.

Residence—Little Manor, Hasketon, Woodbridge, Suffolk. *Clubs*—Carlton, Pratt's.

Son living—MICHAEL JAMES HARWOOD (35, Paulton's Sq., SW3) *b.* March 28th, 1936; ed. at Rugby; a Member of Lloyds, and of Council of Sail Training Assocn., a Liveryman of Mercer, Co., and a Freeman of City of London: *m.* 1967, Rosamund Louise, da. of Edward Clive, of Swanmore Lodge, Swanmore, Southampton, and has issue living, Auriol Davina, *b.* 1968,—Priscilla Caroline, *b.* 1971.
Daughter living—Joanna Kathleen *b.* 1939: *m.* 1966, William Ashton Sanders, of Nine Chimney House, Balsham, Cambridge, and has issue living, James William Ashton, *b.* 1968.

CRADOCK-HARTOPP, Creation (G.B.) 1796, of Freathby, Leicestershire.

Sir JOHN EDMUND CRADOCK-HARTOPP, *T.D.,* 9th *Baronet,* son of the late Francis Gerald Cradock. Hartopp, son of the late Col. Edmund Charles Cradock-Hartopp, 2nd son of 3rd baronet ; *b.* April 8th, 1912 ; *s.* his kinsman, *Sir* GEORGE FRANCIS FLEETWOOD, 1949 ; ed. at Uppingham ; European War 1939-45 as Major R.E. (despatches twice) : *m.* 1953, Prudence, 2nd da. of Sir Frederick William Leith-Ross, G.C.M.G., K.C.B., and has issue.

Arms—Quarterly : 1st and 4th, sable, a chevron argent between three otters passant argent, *Hartopp*; 2nd and 3rd, per saltire gules and argent crusily, three boars' heads two and one, couped counterchanged, *Cradock.* Crest—Out of a ducal coronet or a pelican argent vulning herself proper, *Hartopp.*

Residence—The Cottage, 27, Wood Rd., Wimbledon Common, SW20. *Clubs*—East India and Sports, Bombay, Royal Colombo Yacht.

Daughters living—Melinda Anne, *b.* 1954.——Nicola Jane, *b.* 1957.——Joanna Elizabeth, *b.* 1960.
Sister living—Gwendoline Mary, *b.* 1909: *m.* 1938, Group Capt. John Stanton Fleming Morrison, DFC, RAFVR, who *d.* 19—, and has issue living, Elizabeth Mary, *b.* 1942. *Residence*, The Lea, Dogmersfield, Basingstoke, Hants.
Sister living of 6th Baronet—Susan Cynthia Frances, *b.* 1898 : *m.* 1924, Lindsay Drummond, who *d.* 1951 [see E. Perth, colls.]. *Residence*, Sissinghurst Place, Sissinghurst, Cranbrook, Kent.

Collateral Branch living.

Granchildren of the late Col. Edmund Charles Cradock-Hartopp, younger son
of 3rd baronet :—
Issue of the late Major Louis Montague Cradock-Hartopp, *b.* 1884, *d.* 1957 : *m.* 1916,
Marjorie Somerville, who *d.* 1971, only da. of James Falshaw Watson, MICE, MIME,
formerly of Park House, Codsall Wood, Staffs.:—
KENNETH ALSTON, *MBE, DSC, b.* Feb. 26th, 1918; Lt.-Com. (ret.) RN; an Assoc. Member of
Institute of Management; American Legion of Merit; MBE (Mil) 1946: *m.* 1942, Gwendolyn
Amy Lilian Upton, and has issue living, Christina, *b.* 1948. *Residence,* Meadowcroft, Stock,
Essex.——Virginia Anne, *b.* 1922: *m.* 1952, Michael Henry Tindall Carter, and has issue living,
Christopher Henry James, *b.* 1953,—Geraldine Anne, *b.* 1956,—Paula Margaret, *b.* 1962. *Resi-
dence,* Paget Hall, Tydd St. Giles, Wisbech, Cambridgeshire.

Edward Hartopp, M.P. for Leicestershire, was created a baronet 1619, and the baronetcy
became extinct 1762, on the death, without male issue, of Sir John, 4th baronet, whose granddaughter and heiress, Anne Hurlock, married 1777, Edmund Bunney, of The Newark, Leicester,
who assumed the surnames of Cradock-Hartopp, and was created a baronet 1796. Sir Charles
William Everard Cradock-Hartopp, 6th Bt., was a 1st Sec. in Diplo. Ser.

HARTWELL, Creation (U.K.) 1805, of Dale Hall, Essex.

Sir BRODRICK WILLIAM CHARLES ELWIN
HARTWELL, 5th *Baronet* ; *b.* Aug. 7th, 1909 ; *s.* his father,
Sir BRODRICK CECIL DENHAM ARKWRIGHT, 1948 ; ed.
Bedford Sch. ; sometime Pilot Officer R.A.F., and Capt.
Leicestershire Regt.: *m.* 1st, 1937 (marriage dissolved
1950), Marie Josephine, da. of S. P. Mullins ; 2ndly, 1951,
Mary Maude, *M.B.E.,* da. of J. W. Church, and has issue
by 1st marriage.

Arms—Sable, a buck's head cabossed argent, attired or, between the
attires a cross patée-fitchée of the last ; in chief a lion passant guardant per
pale of the second and third ; on a canton ermine two bars per pale azure
and gules. **Crest**—On a mount vert within seven pales or, the second and
fifth charged with a spear-head argent imbrued proper, a hart lodged
argent, the dexter foot on a well of the last, and in the mouth a sprig of
oak vert.

Sorte suâ contentus.
Contented with his lot.

Residence—50, High St., Lavendon, Olney, Bucks.

Son living—By 1st m.—FRANCIS ANTONY CHARLES PETER (c/o Barclays Bank, 11, High
St., Olney, Bucks.), *b.* June 1st, 1940; ed. at Thames Nautical Training Coll., HMS *Worcester*;
Cadet RNR: *m.* 1968, Barbara Phyllis Rae, da. of H. Rae Green, of Sydney, Aust., and has
issue living, Timothy Peter Michael Charles, *b.* 1970.
Sister living—Kathleen Edyth Doreen Augusta, *b.* 1918 : *m.* 1940, Lieut. Michael William
Bramston Hicks Beach, DSC, RNVR [*see* E. St. Aldwyn, colls.]. *Residence,* 40, Burton Court,
SW3.
Half-Sister living—Leila Ruth Madeleine, *b.* 1903 : *m.* 1st, 1925, Charles St. Clair Parsons;
2ndly, 1928, Gen. André Beaufre, Tirailleurs Morrocaines ; 3rdly, 1950, Jean-Edouard Bonnet,
Police Commr., 4th Div., Algiers. *Residence,* Dar-Uvina, Bouzarea, Algiers.

Collateral Branches living.

Grandchildren of the late Sydney Charles Elphinstone Hartwell, 3rd son of
2nd baronet:—
Issue of the late Capt. Barry Hartwell, *b.* 1880, *d.* (killed in action) 1914 : *m.* 1912, Emily
Maybell, da. of the late Joseph Dobbs, of Castlecomer, co. Kilkenny.
Evelyn Patricia, *b.* 1913. *Residence,* Dunloe Cottage, Herbert Rd., Bray, co. Wicklow.

Issue of the late Maj.-Gen. John Redmond Hartwell, CB, DSO, *b.* 1887, *d.* 1970: *m.* 1st,
1911 (m. diss. 1921), Nina Oliver, da. of the late Gen. George Francis William St. John,
CB; 2ndly, 1929, Hazel Hay Liston, who *d.* 1945, da. of the late Sir John Benton,
KCIE; 3rdly, 1946, Edith Elizabeth (4A, De Walden Court, Eastbourne), da. of the
late F. W. Frosdyke:—
(By 1st m.) Diana Marion, *b.* 1912: *m.* 1st, 1934, Lt.-Col. Sidney Clive Blaber, RA, who *d.* (killed
in action in Belgium) 1944; 2ndly, 1951, Stephen Terrell, OBE, TD, QC, of 37, Greycoat Gdns.,
SW1, and has issue living (by 1st m.) Marcus, *b.* 1942,—Carol Ann, *b.* 1940: *m.* 1973, Charles
Bruce Nairn [see Nairn, Bt.],—(by 2nd m.) Peter, *b.* 1951,—Paul, *b.* 1953.——(by 2nd m.)
Barry Benton (Yew Tree House, N. Waltham, Basingstoke), *b.* 1933; Cdr. RN: *m.* 1st, 1956 (m.
diss. 1968) Lois Maureen, yst. da. of Eric C. Bratt, of Bexhill, Sussex; 2ndly, 1970, Elizabeth
Linley, yst. da. of Linley Underwood, of Linden House, Countesthorpe, Leics., and has issue
living (by 1st m.), Karen Fiona, *b.* 1961,—(by 2nd m.) Charlotte Linley *b.* 1973.

Issue of the late Frederick Edward Hartwell, youngest son of 2nd baronet, *b.* 1857, *d.*
19—: *m.* 1881, Susan Mary Ann, da. of William Green, of Wannamboor, Victoria,
Australia :—
Frederick Sydney, *b.* 1886.——Broderick William, *b.* 1889.——John Malcolm, *b.* 1903.——George
Rollen, *b.* 1905.——Ada Wilhelmina, *b.* 1887.——Frances Mary Ann, *b.* 1895.——Julia Sarah, *b.*
1901.——May Alicia, *b.* 1908. *Residence,*

Capt. Humphrey Hartwell received grants of land in co. Limerick and Kings co. 1666.
The 1st baronet Adm. Sir Francis John Hartwell, was Col. Deptford and Woolwich Volunteers,
and Director of Greenwich Hospital.

HARTY, Creation (U.K.) 1831, of Prospect House, Roebuck, Dublin. [Extinct 1939.]

Sir LIONEL LOCKINGTON HARTY, 4th and last *Baronet.*

Daughter living of 4th Baronet—Eileen Rhoda. *Residence,* Belrobin, Newtown Park Avenue,
Blackrock, Dublin.

HARVEY, Creation (U.K.) 1868, of Langley Park, Bucks. [Extinct 1931.]

Sir ROBERT GRENVILLE HARVEY, 2nd and last *Baronet.*

Daughter living of 2nd Baronet—Diana Blanche, *b.* 1897: *m.* 1921, the 1st Baron Balfour of Inchrye,
from whom she obtained a divorce 1946. *Residence,* 63, Whitelands Hse., Chelsea, SW3.

HARVEY, Creation (U.K.) 1933, of Threadneedle Street, City of London.

Sir RICHARD MUSGRAVE HARVEY, 2nd *Baronet* ; *b.* Dec. 1st, 1898 : *s.* his father, *Sir* ERNEST MUSGRAVE, *K.B.E.*, 1955 ; Lieut.-Com. R.N. (ret.): *m.* 1930, Frances Estelle, el. da. of the late Lindsay Crompton Lawford, and has issue.

Residence—Chisenbury Priory, Pewsey, Wilts.

Son living—CHARLES RICHARD MUSGRAVE (The University, Lusaka, Zambia), *b.* April 7th, 1937; ed. at Marlborough, and at Pembroke Coll., Camb.: *m.* 1967, Celia Vivien, da. of George Henry Hodson, and has issue living, Paul Richard, *b.* 1971.
Daughter living—Joanna Musgrave, *b.* 1934: *m.* 1958, Angus Donald Macintyre, Fellow of Magdalen Coll., Oxford, of 8, Linton Rd., Oxford, and has issue living, Benedict Richard Pierce, *b.* 1963,—Magnus William Lachlan, *b.* 1971,—Katherine Cressida Eve, *b.* 1962.
Sisters living—Ruth Musgrave (Church Farm Cottage, Sixpenny Handley, Salisbury), *b.* 1902: *m.* 1930, George MacGowan Harper, and has issue living, Jane Alison, *b.* 1932: *m.* 1959, Lt.-Col. Justus Michael Molitor Lenschau, US Army, of 41, Holmehurst Av., Cotonsville, Baltimore, USA, and has issue living, James Gabriel Molitor *b.* 1961, Katherine Jane *b.* 1964.——Eleanor, Paget Musgrave, *b.* 1905: *m.* 1930, Edward Kent Haliburton Karslake [Darell, Bt., colls.], and has issue living, Antony Edward Kent (Parsonage House, Watchfield, Oxon.), *b.* 1932; Lt.-Col. R. Green Jackets: *m.* 1956, June Pauline, el. da. of Henry William Harris Eastwood, and has issue living, John Burgess *b.* 1956, William Edward Kent *b.* 1963, Caroline Sarah *b.* 1960, Henrietta Sarah *b.* 1965,—Sophia Susan, *b.* 1935: *m.* 1964, Donald Watkins Brown, of 6, Hilltop Rd., Silver Spring, Maryland, USA, and has issue living, Stephen Scott *b.* 1969, Geoffrey Mark *b.* 1972, Bridget Joan *b.* 1967,—Mary Leonora, *b.* 1944: *m.* 1966, Andrew Nicholas Dakin Goodhart, of 15, The Knoll, W13, and has issue living, Rachel Mary *b.* 1970, Catherine Jervis Ruth *b.* 1973.
Residence, Nymet St. George Hse., George Nympton, South Molton, N. Devon.

The 1st baronet, Sir Ernest Musgrave Harvey, K.B.E. (son of the late Rev. Charles Musgrave Harvey, V. of Hillingdon, Middlesex, and Preb. of St. Paul's) was a Director and Dep. Gov. of Bank of England.

Harvie-Watt, see Watt.

Havelock-Allan, see Allan.

HAWKEY, Creation (U.K.) 1945, of Woodford, co. Essex.

Sir ROGER PRYCE HAWKEY, 2nd *Baronet* ; *b.* June 25th, 1905 ; *s.* his father, *Sir* (ALFRED) JAMES HAWKEY, 1952 : *m.* 1st, 1931 ; 2ndly 1947, Mabel Dorothy McMullan, da. of the late Sir Thomas Edward McConnell, C.B.E., M.P., of Belfast, and has issue by 1st marriage. [The 2nd Bt. *d.* Nov. 11th, 1975, when the title became ext.]

Arms—Azure two bars gemel between in chief as many hawks and in base a leopard's face or. Crest—A hawk resting his dexter claw upon a martlet or.

Residence—Great Coopers, Takeley, Essex. Club—M.C.C.

Daughter living—By 1st marriage—Sarah Elizabeth, *b.* 1935.
Sister living—Dinah Mary, *b.* 1910: *m.* 1931, Edward Clarke Pratt. Residence, Bracken Hill, Bay View Road, Westward Ho!, N. Devon.

The 1st baronet, Sir (Alfred) James Hawkey (son of the late Richard Hawkey, of Sunnycroft, Woodford Green, Essex) was Charter Mayor, Mayor, and first Freeman of Borough of Wanstead and Woodford.

By serving.

HAWKINS, Creation (G.B.) 1778, of Kelston, Somersetshire.

Sir HUMPHRY VILLIERS CÆSAR HAWKINS, *M.B.*, *Ch.B.*, 7th *Baronet* ; *b.* Aug. 10th, 1923 ; *s.* his father, *Sir* VILLIERS GEOFFREY CÆSAR, 1955 ; M.B. and Ch.B. 19— ; European War 1942-5, with 6th S. African Armoured Div.: *m.* 1952, Anita, da. of Charles H. Funkey, and has issue.

Arms—Argent, on a saltire engrailed sable a quatrefoil between four fleurs-de-lis or. Crest—On a mount vert a hind lodged or, the dexter forefoot resting on a gunstone.

Residence, 41, Hume Rd., Dunkeld, Johannesburg, S. Africa. Club—Johannesburg County.

Sons living—HOWARD CÆSAR, *b.* Nov. 17th, 1956.——Richard Cæsar, *b.* 1958.
Daughters living—Carol Lee, *b.* 1953.——Kathryn Anne, *b.* 1954.
Sister living—Joy Blanche, *b.* 1921 : *m.* 1944, John Stobart Longworth, and has issue living, Humphrey John, *b.* 1945,—Veronica Anne, *b.* 1951.

For God and the king.

Widow living of 6th Baronet—(MARJORIE) BLANCHE (*Blanche, Lady Hawkins*), da. of A. E.
Hampden-Smithers, of Springs, Transvaal : *m.* 1920, Sir Villiers Geoffrey Cæsar Hawkins, 6th
Bt., who *d.* 1955. *Residence*, 187, Lynnwood Road, Brooklyn, Pretoria, Transvaal, S. Africa.

Collateral Branches living.

Grandchildren of the late Arthur Cæsar Hawkins, 7th son of 3rd baronet :—
Issue of the late Percy Cæsar Hawkins, *b.* 1863, *d.* 19— : *m.* 18—, Catherine Ripkin, who
d. 1937:—
Rupert Cæsar, *b.* 1901.——Oscar Cæsar, *b.* 1908 : *m.* 19—, Zella Bunn, and has issue living,
John Michael Cæsar, *b.* 19—,—Patrick Cæsar, *b.* 19—.——Percy Cæsar, *b.* 1910.——Julia Louisa,
b. 19—.——Kathleen Laura, *b.* 19—.——Cecelia Margaret, *b.* 19—.——Adeline Daisy, *b.* 19—.
Residence,
Issue of the late Cyril Cæsar Hawkins, *b.* 1878, *d.* 1955 : *m.* 1909, Lulu, who *d.* 1955, da.
of W. H. E. During:—
Marie, *b.* 1910. *Residence*, Johannesburg, S. Africa.

Grandchildren of the late Reginald Hawkins, son of the late Rev. Henry
Annesley Hawkins (infra) :—
Issue of the late Lieut.-Col. Eustace Fellowes Sinclair Hawkins, D.S.O., O.B.E., R.A.S.C.,
b. 1881, *d.* 1954 : *m.* 1908, Patience, da. of Capt. J. Henderson, late 12th Lancers :—
Patrick Reginald Cæsar, *b.* 1918.——Honour Marie Marguerite, *b.* 1913.

Grandchildren of the late Rev. Henry Annesley Hawkins, son of the Rev.
Charles Hawkins, 4th son of 1st baronet :—
Issue of the late Arthur Cockburn Hawkins, *b.* 1852, *d.* 19— : *m.* 1883, Agnes, da. of
H. Carmichael :—
Henry Cecil Carmichael, *b.* 1884 : *m.* 1907, Winnifred, da. of John Robinson, and has issue living,
Cecil Arthur Robinson, *b.* 1908,—Harold Percy, *b.* 1909,—Winnifred Agnes Ruth, *b.* 1910.
——Arthur Charles, *b.* 1885.——Reginald Cæsar, *b.* 1890.——Agnes Isabel, *b.* 1889.——Frances
Kathleen, *b.* 1892. *Residence*,

Granddaughter of the late Com. Cæsar Hugh Hawkins, R.N., son of the late Rev.
Charles James Hawkins, son of the late Rev. Charles Hawkins (ante):—
Issue of the late Cæsar Hugh George Wills Hawkins, *b.* (posthumous) 1889, *d.* 1947 : *m.* 1st,
1914, Margaret Edith (who obtained a divorce 1926), da. of the late James Shaw Robertson,
of The Vache, Chalfont St. Giles; 2ndly, 1930, Diodata, who *d.* 19—, da. of the late
Count Bernhard Caboga, of Dubrovnik, Ragusa:—
(By 1st m.) Margaret Elizabeth Anne (947, Green St., San Francisco, Cal. 94133, USA), *b.* 1917:
m. 1st, 1940, Lt. Hilliard Baxley Wilson, USNR, who *d.* 1961; 2ndly, 1967, James Rowland
Lowe, who *d.* 1969, and has issue living, (by 1st m.) Penelope Jane, *b.* 1944: *m.* 1972, Michael
McClure.

Granddaughter of the late Cæsar Hugh George Wills Hawkins (ante):—
Issue of the late Lieut. Cæsar Charles Hawkins, D.S.C., R.N., *b.* 1915, *d.* (on active service
during European War) 1940 : *m.* 1937, Mary Redwood Vachell (who *m.* 2ndly, 1945,
Desmond John Dudley Torrens, M.B.E., M.B., late Lieut.-Col. R.A.M.C., of Dewlands
Gate, Rotherfield, Sussex), da. of Edmund Hann :—
Alice Penelope, *b.* 1938: *m.* 1961, Robin Audley Clinton Vivian, of 7, Moncorvo Close, Ennismore
Gdns., SW7 [see B. Vivian, colls.].

Grandchildren of the late Annie Caroline Woodhead, da. of the late Rev. Charles
James Hawkins (ante) :—
Issue of the late Cæsar Hawkins Copley Woodhead, *b.* 1873, *d.* 1944 : *m.* 1903, Lydia, who
d. 1943, da. of the late William Scrafield :—
Alfred Hawkins, *b.* 1910 : *m.* 19—, Katherine Broadfoot, of Ottawa, Canada, and has issue living,
Peter, *b.* 1944,—Wendy, *b.* 1941,—Patricia, *b.* 1946,—Debra, *b.* 1954.——Muriel Edna, *b.* 1906:
m. 1937, Randolph Harwood Bridgman, Solicitor, who *d.* 1951, and has issue living, John Har-
wood, *b.* 1940; ed. at Lower Canada Coll.,—Brenda Barbara, *b.* 1943. *Residence*, 776, Lexington
Ave., Westmount, PQ, Canada.

Granddaughter of the late Cæsar Richard Hawkins, son of the late Rev. Edward
Hawkins, D.D., el. son of the late Rev. Edward Hawkins, 5th son of 1st
baronet:—
Issue of the late Edward Cæsar Hawkins, *b.* 1876, *d.* 1960 : *m.* 1899, Blanche Marianne,
who *d.* 1951, da. of the late Rev. Charles Blomfield Smith. R. of Shelton :—
Richard Pennell Cæsar, *b.* 1899; Cdr. R.N. (ret.): *m.* 1929, 1st, Enid Helen (from whom he obtained
a divorce 1952), da. of the Rev. John Warren Corbould-Warren, R. of Caistor with Markshall;
2ndly, 1964, Mary Constance Emily, da. of the Rev. Frank Percy Law, R. of Shelton, Norfolk,
and has issue living, (by 1st m.) Diana Elizabeth, *b.* 1930: *m.* 1953, Anthony Pott (c/o Nat.
Westminster Bank, Abingdon, Berks.). *Residence*, Shelton Hall, Long Stratton, Norfolk.

Granddaughters of the late Rev. Charles Halford Hawkins, 2nd son of the late
Francis Hawkins, 2nd son of the late Rev. Edward Hawkins (ante):—
Issue of the late Henry Vaughan Hawkins, *b.* 1879, *d.* 1940: *m.* 1906, Mary Mackenzie,
who *d.* 1946, da. of the late Alexander Francis Mackenzie Downie, of Holybourne
Cottage, Alton, Hants:—
Susette Henrietta Mary, *b.* 1907: *m.* 1937, Lt.-Col. Theobald Frederick Stephen Church, Roy.
Sussex Regt., and has issue living, Anna Caroline, *b.* 1938: *m.* 1959, Brig. Nigel Thomas Bagnall,
MC 4th/7th R. Dragoon Guards,—Jessica Jane, *b.* 1942. *Residence*, Powderham, Exeter, S.
Devon.——Hester Pamela, *b.* 1915: *m.* 1954, Cecil Lancelot Harman. *Residence*, Hill Grounds,
Evenly, Brackley, Northants.

Grandson of the late Rev. Robert Hawkins, 4th son of the late Rev. Edward
Hawkins (ante) :—
Issue of the late Col. Herbert Pennell Hawkins, C.B.E., *b.* 1859, *d.* 1940: *m.* 1910, Hester
Vera, who *d.* 1972, da. of Fleetwood Rynd, formerly of Mount Armstrong, co. Kildare:—
Gerald Francis Cæsar (Sunflower Cottage, Tedburn St. Mary, Exeter), *b.* 1912; ed. at Eton, and at
Oxford Univ. (BM and BCh), MRCS England and LRCP London; 1939-45 War as Maj. RAMC:
m. 1940, Patricia Enid Lambart, da. of Maj. Alexander George Lambart Sladen, MC, of Crabtree
Furlong, Haddenham, Bucks, and has issue living, Julia Margaret, *b.* 1946: *m.* 1971, Ilgvars
Spruntulis.

The 1st baronet, Sir Cæsar Hawkins (son of the late Cæsar Hawkins), was Serjeant-Surg. to
George II and George III.

HAWLEY, Creation (G.B.) 1795, of Leybourne Grange, Kent.

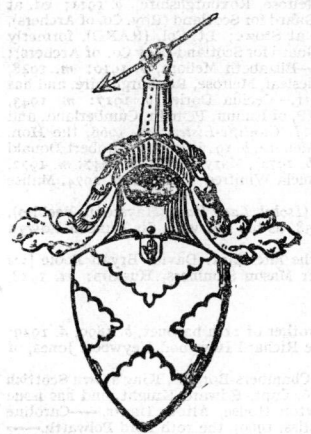

Sir DAVID HENRY HAWLEY, 7th
Baronet, son of the late Capt. Cyril Francis
Hawley, 2nd son of 5th baronet ; *b.* May 13th,
1913 ; *s.* his uncle, Capt. *Sir* HENRY CUSACK
WINGFIELD, 1923 ; ed. at Eton, and at Magdalene
Coll., Camb. (MA); FRICS; Major (ret.)
King's Roy. Rifle Corps, and patron
of one living; is a Member of the firm of James
Martin & Co., land agents, of 8, Bank Street,
Lincoln; a D.L. of Lincs. (High Sheriff
1962-63); 1939-45 War (despatches, prisoner):
Mare Gregson, OBE [E. Lichfield], and has
issue.

Arms—Vert, a saltire engrailed or. *Crest*—A dexter
arm in armour proper, garnished or, holding in the hand
a spear in bend sinister, point downwards, also proper.

Residence—Tumby Lawn, Boston, Lincs., PE22 7TA.

Son living—HENRY NICHOLAS, *b.* Nov. 25th, 1939,
ed. at Stowe.

Daughters living—Margaret Serena, *b.* 1946.——Penelope Marion, *b.* 1948: *m.* 1971, Richard M.
Mansell-Jones.

Aunt living (daughter of 5th baronet)—Olive Victoria : *m.* 1920, the Rev. Henry Cecil Marriott
Spurrier, who *d.* 1954, and has issue living, Henry Francis (of Christ's Hospital, Horsham,
Sussex), *b.* 1924 : *m.* 1957, Bridget Eleanor Fairfax Piper, and has issue living, Peter Henry
b. 1960, Sarah Rosamond *b.* 1961, Philippa Claire *b.* 1966,—Roger Hawley (of The Old Rectory,
Blankney, Lincoln), *b.* 1928: *m.* 1955, Margret Judith Briony Richards, and has issue living,
Timothy John *b.* 1957, Roger Dermot *b.* 1958,—Rosamond Mary Cecile, *b.* 1923: *m.* 1946,
Peter Gwynne Grundy, of 7, Walpole Av., Richmond, Surrey, and has issue living, William
Brandon *b.* 1956. *Residence*, The Old Rectory, Blankney, Lincoln.

HAWORTH, Creation (U.K.) 1911, of Dunham Massey, co. Chester.

Sir (ARTHUR) GEOFFREY HAWORTH, 2nd
Baronet ; *b.* April 5th, 1896 ; *s.* his father, *Sir*
ARTHUR ADLINGTON, 1944 ; ed. at Rugby, and at
New Coll., Oxford (BA 1919, MA 1935); a
JP for Chester 1937-70; 1914-19 War as
Lieut. Queen's Own Roy. W. Kent Regt. and
Machine Gun Corps (despatches) : *m.* 1926,
Emily Dorothea, da. of H. E. Gaddum, of The
Priory, Bowdon, Cheshire, and has issue.

Arms—Azure, on a bend between two stags' heads couped
or, as many garbs gules. *Crest*—Issuant out of grass proper
a stag's head gules arme and collared with a chain or.

Residence—The Red Brook, Lower Peover, Cheshire.

Sons living—PHILIP, *b.* Jan. 17th, 1927 ; ed. at Reading
Univ. (B.Sc. 1948) : *m.* 1951, Joan Helen, da. of the late
Stanley Percival Clark, of Ipswich, and has issue living,
Christopher, *b.* (Nov.) 1951.—Mark, *b.* 1956,—Simon
Nicholas, *b.* 1961,—Adam Ewart, *b.* 1964,—Penelope
Jane, *b.* 1953. *Residence*, Free Green Farm, Over
Peover, Knutsford, Cheshire.——Jeremy Geoffrey, *b.*
1931.

Daughters living—Jennefer, *b.* 1928 : *m.* 1952, Herbert
Hilton Minnis, and has issue living, Sterling Herbert, *b.*
1953,—Russell Harold, *b.* 1954,—Quentin Geoffrey, *b.* 1963,—Jedda Alison, *b.* 1957,—Sonya
Jennefer, *b.* 1960. *Address*, P.O. Box 1720, Nassau, Bahamas.——Alison, *b.* 1934: *m.* 1958,
Richard Crosfield Godlee, of The Grange, Clay Lane, Handforth, Wilmslow, Ches., and has issue
living, Deborah Claire, *b.* 1961,—Sarah Haworth, *b.* 1965.

Sisters living—Lois Adlington, *b.* 1892.——Mary Suzette, *b.* 1899 : *m.* 1930, Harry Goodhart, and
has issue living, Mark Henry, *b.* 1931.—Harry James, *b.* 1933. *Residence*, West Thorpe, Lymington, Hants.

The 1st baronet, Sir Arthur Adlington Haworth (son of the late Abraham Haworth, J.P., of
Bowdon, Cheshire), sat as M.P. for S. Div. of Manchester (*L*) 1906-12, and was a Junior Lord of
the Treasury Feb. to March 1912.

**HAY, Creation (N.S.) 1635, of Smithfield, and Haystoun, Peeblesshire.
[Dormant 1966.]**

Sir BACHE McEVERS ATHOLE HAY, 11th *Baronet*; *d.* in 1966, and at time of
going to press no name appears on the Official Roll of Baronets in respect
of this title.

Daughter living of 9th Baronet—Meliora: *m.* 1909, Maj. Mark Sprot of Riddell, who *d.* 1946, R. Scots Greys, and has issue living, John (Riddell, by Melrose, Roxburghshire), *b.* 1911; ed. at Stowe; late Maj. KOSB and a Member of Queen's Body Guard for Scotland (Roy. Co. of Archers), —Aidan Mark, *MC* (Haystoun, Peebles), *b.* 1919; ed. at Stowe; Lt.-Col. (RARO), formerly Comdg. R. Scots Greys and a Member of Queen's Body Guard for Scotland (Roy Co. of Archers); a JP and a DL for Peeblesshire; 1939-45 War (MC),—Elizabeth Meliora, *b.* 1910: *m.* 1948, Capt. John William Grant, DSO, RN, of Clerklands, Lilliesleaf, Melrose, Roxburghshire, and has issue living, Andrew Seafield *b.* 1952, Penelope *b.* 1951,—Cecilia Doriel, *b.* 1917: *m.* 1943, the Rt. Hon. William Stephen Ian Whitelaw, CH, MC, MP, of Ennim, Penrith, Cumberland, and has issue living, Elizabeth Susan (*Hon. Mrs. Nicholas J. Cunliffe-Lister*): *m.* 1966, the Hon. Nicholas John Cunliffe-Lister [see E. Swinton], Carolyn Meliora, *b.* 1946: *m.* 1973, Robert Donald Macleod Thomas (and has issue living, Miranda Cecilia *b.* 1974), Mary Cecilia, *b.* 1947: *m.* 1972, David Alexander Coltman [see B. Hothfield, colls.], Pamela Winifred, *b.* 1951: *m.* 1974, Malise Charles Richard Graham [see Graham, Bt., cr. 1783].

Widows living of 10th and 11th Baronets—ISOBEL ROSE (*Isobel, Lady Hay*) (Haystoun, Peebles), el. da. of the late Sir Alexander Walker, KBE: *m.* 1958, as his 2nd wife, Sir Duncan Edwyn Hay, 10th baronet, who *d.* 1965.

JUDITH MIMI (*Lady Hay*), (Crookston, Peebles), da. of the late Capt. Davies Bryan Poole [*see* Cooke, Bt., colls.], and widow of Capt. Alfred Spencer Mason Summers, Hussars: *m.* 1918, Sir Bache McEvers Athole Hay, 11th Bt., who *d.* 1966.

Collateral Branches living.

Issue of the late Capt. Robert Athole Hay, el. brother of 11th baronet, *b.* 1890, *d.* 1939: *m.* 1914, Margaret, who *d.* 1928, da. of the late Richard Heywood Heywood Jones, of Badsworth Hall, York:—

Elizabeth, *b.* 1915 : *m.* 1st, 1938, Major David Hammond-Chambers-Borgnis, King's Own Scottish Borderers, who *d.* (on active service) 1943; 2ndly, 1946, Capt. Edward Knight, and has issue living (by 1st and 2nd marriages). *Residence*, Chawton House, Alton, Hants.——Caroline Margaret (3, Manresa Rd., SW3), *b.* 1916: *m.* 1943 (m. diss. 1969), the 10th Lord Polwarth.—— Sarah, *b.* 1924: *m.* 1946, David Rimington Tetley, and has issue living. *Residence*, Brawby Parks, Malton, Yorks.

Issue of the late Robert Butler Hay, 4th son of 8th baronet, *b.* 1864, *d.* 1912 : *m.* 1899, Ella Franklyn, who *d.* 1950, da. of the late F. B. Bulkeley Johnson:—

Grisel Butler, *b.* 1900: *m.* 1924, Lt.-Cdr. Robert Harvey Combe, RN (ret.), of Gledswood House, Chagford, Devon, and has issue living, David Robert (64, Ardross St., Applecross 6153, Perth, W. Aust.), *b.* 1927; ed. at Canford: *m.* 1957, Sarah Helen, da. of Lt.-Col. J. Moulding, of Budleigh Salterton, and has issue living, James Robert *b.* 1958, Nicholas John *b.* 1960, Simon David *b.* 1963,—Christopher John (PO Box 446, Somerset West, Cape Prov., S. Africa), *b.* 1930; ed. at Canford: *m.* 1958, Catherine Patricia, da. of Col. Robert Mair Stevenson, OBE, of Banstead, Surrey, and has issue living, Duncan John *b.* 1960, Caroline *b.* 1962.

Descendants of John, 3rd Lord Hay of Yester, great-great-uncle of 1st baronet, of whom the Marquess of Tweeddale is the presumed heir to the baronetcy.

The 1st baronet was an Esquire of the body of James VI. With his patent of baronetcy he received eighteen square acres of land in Nova Scotia. The 3rd baronet inherited only the title, which on his death, in 1683, became dormant. In 1762 James Hay, M.D., claimed and assumed the baronetcy, was served heir to his great-great-grandfather, John Hay of Kingsmeadows—a younger brother of the grandfather of the 1st baronet—by a jury assembled at Perth 1805, and subsequently, in 1806, matriculated arms as a baronet in the Lyon Office.

HAY, Creation (N.S.) 1663, of Park, Wigtownshire.

Sir ARTHUR THOMAS ERROLL HAY, *ISO*, 10th *Baronet; b.* April 13th, 1909; *s.* his father, *Sir* LEWIS JOHN ERROLL, 1923; ed. at Fettes Coll., Edinburgh; is an ARIBA: *m.* 1st, 1935, Hertha Hedwig Paula Louise (who obtained a divorce 1942), da. of the late Ludwig Stölzle, of Nagelberg, Austria, and widow of Walter Biheller; 2ndly, 1943, Mrs. Rosemary Anne Weymouth, da. of the late Vice-Adm. Aubrey Lambert, and has issue by 1st marriage.

Arms—Argent, three escutcheons gules and in chief an ox-yoke fesseways proper.
Address—c/o Lloyds Bank, Farnham, Surrey.

Son living—By 1st marriage—JOHN ERROLL AUDLEY, *b.* Dec. 3rd, 1935; ed. at Gordonstoun, and at St. Andrew's Univ. (MA honours 1960). *Address*, c/o National Westminster Bank, Fitzroy Square, W.1.

Sisters living—Elspeth Minna Erroll, *b.* 1898 : *m.* 1924, Colin H. P. Campbell Penney, M.C., who *d.* 1947, and has issue living, Michael Erroll, *b.* 1926: *m.* 1957, Eve Pilkington Jackson, and has issue living,—Patrick Joseph (9, Corremmie Gdns., Edinburgh), *b.* 1931: *m.* 1962, Joyce Armstrong, and has issue living, Bridget Mary *b.* 1964, Sarah Frances *b.* 1965,—Sonia Elizabeth Tuchet, *b.* 1929. *Residence*, 92, Murrayfield Gdns., Edinburgh.——Lizabel Ailsa Macdonald (Balendoch, Rogart, Sutherland, and 17, Cadogan St., SW3), *b.* 1903: *m.* 1942, Thomas Pilkington Burns, who *d.* 1951, and has issue living, Jean Hay (35, The Little Boltons, SW10), *b.* 1943: *m.* 1st, 1963 (m. diss. 1969), Anthony Le Quesne Herbert; 2ndly, 1969, Nigel Edmund Kippax Openshaw, and has issue living (by 2nd m.), Elspeth Jane *b.* 1970.——Lilias Erroll Audley Beresford (c/o Barclays Bank, Warminster, Wilts.), *b.* 1906: *m.* 1957, the Rev. Edward Constable Alston.——Margaret Audrey Theresa, *b.* 1907.——Betty Louise Macdonald, *b.* 1913.

Collateral Branch living.

Issue of the late Arthur George Beresford Hay, 3rd son of 8th baronet, *b.* 1878, *d.* 1949 : *m.* 1913, Louise Emily May, who *d.* 1939, da. of the late Lieut.-Col. Henry Robert Carden, D.L., of Fishmoyne, Tipperary :—

Evelyn Alice Carden, *b.* 1914: *m.* 1945, Charles John Barton, late Palestine Police, and has issue living, Mary Hay, *b.* 1948.

The present baronet is senior male representative of Sir Gilbert Hay, of Dronlaw, 2nd son of Sir Thomas Hay, of Erroll, Constable of Scotland. By the marriage of Sir John Hay, 7th Bt. of Park, with Sarah Beresford Cossins (da. of John Cossins by the Hon. Elizabeth Susannah Thicknesse Tuchet, da. of 19th Baron Audley), his descendants are in remainder to the Barony of Audley.

HAY, Creation (N.S.) 1703, of Alderston.

Spare Nought.

Sir FREDERICK BADEN-POWELL HAY, 10th *Baronet*, son of the late Frederick Howard Hay, next brother of 9th baronet ; *b.* June 24th, 1900 ; *s.* his uncle, *Sir* EDWARD HAMILTON, 1936 ; is an Agent; formerly a Grocer; *m.* 1935, Henrietta Margaret, da. of Herbert William Reid.

Arms—Quarterly : 1st and 4th, azure, three fraises, *Fraser*; 2nd and 3rd, gules, three bars ermine, *Gifford of Yester*; over all, upon an escutcheon of pretence **argent** three escutcheons gules, in the centre a key fesseways wards downwards sable, *Hay.* **Crest,**—A goat's head erased, argent, armed or.

Residence—Unit 14, 32, Mentone Parade, Mentone, Victoria 3194, Australia.

Brother living—RONALD NELSON, *b.* July 9th, 1910 : *m.* 1940, Rita, dau. of John Munyard, and has issue living, Ronald Frederick Hamilton, *b.* 1941,—Pamela Rosemary, *b.* 1945. *Residence,* Murrumbeena, Melbourne, Australia.

Sisters living—Lucy, *b.* 1901.—Thelma Violet, *b.* 1914: *m.* 1938, Frank Coulton, and has issue living. *Residence,* 14, Bluegum Cres., French's Forest, NSW.

Mother living—May Elizabeth, da. of George Tomlinson, of Fitzroy, Melbourne, Australia: *m.* 1899, Frederick Howard Hay (*ante*), who *d.* 1934. *Residence,* Poath Road, Hughesdale, Melbourne, Australia.

Collateral Branches living.

Issue of the late Howard Augustus Hay, 4th son of 6th baronet, *b.* 1828, *d.* 1884 : *m.* 1853, Sarah, who *d.* 1902, da. of Henry Harris, of Bitterne, Southampton :—

Douglas Hector, *b.* 1869: *m.* 1896, Amy Margaret, da. of Alexander Jansen, formerly of Ridgway Ontario, Canada, and has issue living, Douglas Howard Jerome, *b.* 1898,—Thelma Arline, *b.* 1903,——Jane Sophia Louisa : *m.* 1902, William Watts, and has issue living, Ernest Hay, *b.* 1904,

Grandchildren of the late James Shaw Hay (infra):—
Issue of the late Conran Ker Hay, *b.* 1882, *d.* 1958: *m.* 1908, Grace, who *d.* 1960, da. of Thomas B. Horsfield, of Manchester:—

Alexander Horsfield (Westtown School, Westtown, Pa., USA 19395), *b.* 1912; MA; a Sch. Teacher: *m.* 1st, 1939, Bernice Louise, who *d.* 1968, da. of Walter C. Woodward, of Richmond, Indiana, USA; 2ndly, 1969, Agnes Marshall, da. of George Ferguson Finnie, of Glasgow, and has issue living (by 1st m.), Conran Alexander, *b.* 1946,—Thomas Carlton, *b.* 1951,—Arminal Elizabeth, *b.* 1943.——Gordon Conran (689, Westmount Hill's Drive, London, Ont., Canada), *b.* 1919, BA; a High Sch. Prin.: *m.* 1943, Elizabeth Jean, da. of Edward Henry Stevenson, of Renfrew, Ont., Canada, and has issue living, Stuart Gordon, *b.* 1946,—Alexander Edward, *b.* 1949,—Elizabeth Grace, *b.* 1951,—Jean Anne, *b.* 1957.——Arminal Grace, *b.* 1916; a nurse of Victorian Order: *m.* 1951, Charles Sweeney, and has issue living, Ross Joseph, *b.* 1957.

Issue of the late Thomas Corlett Hay, VD, *b.* 1883, *d.* 1952: *m.* 1930, Muriel (17, Oakhill Av., NW3), da. of the Rev. Charles Harry Dant, R. of Babcary, Taunton:—

Pamela Jane, *b.* 1931: *m.* 1957, John G. Ewing.——Bettine Muriel, *b.* 1932; a SRN: *m.* 1962, René Bouganon, of Johannesburg.

Granddaughter of the late Alexander Murray Hay, el. son of the late Capt. John Hay, half-brother of 5th baronet :—
Issue of the late James Shaw Hay, *b.* 1850, *d.* 1908 : *m.* 1st, 1880, Charlotte Anne, da. of William Corlett, of Ramsey, Isle of Man ; 2ndly, 1889, Arminal Walmsley, da. of James Scotson, of Liverpool:—

By 2nd marriage) Muriel Scotson, *b.* 1891: *m.* 1921, Georges Louis Bard. *Residence,* 40, Lambolle Rd., NW3.

Grandchildren of the late Loraine Geddes Hay (infra):—
Issue of the late Loraine Macdonald Hay, *b.* 1883, *d.* 1961: *m.* 1917, Mequeline Eugenie Hamel-Smith (of 44, Belmont Circular Rd., Belmont, Trinidad):—

Sydney Bertram Macdonald, *b.* 1918: *m.* 1945, Joan Reis, and has issue living, Phillip Michael Macdonald, *b.* 1946,—Roger Macdonald, *b.* 1948,—Aubrey Andrew Macdonald, *b.* 1949,—Edmund Macdonald, *b.* 1954,—Anthony Macdonald, *b.* 1956,—Ann Maureen, *b.* 1951,—Kathleen, *b.* 1953. *Residence,* 44, Belmont Circular Rd., Belmont, Trinidad.——Denise Rita, *b.* 1920: *m.* 1st, 1940, Rudolph Armine Moze, who *d.* 1942; 2ndly, 1948, Roberto Pelgo Lopez; 3rdly, 1954, Rupert Loraine Hay (infra), and has issue living, (by 1st m.) Patricia Angela, *b.* 1941: *m.* 1970, Senator Conrad O'Brien, and has issue living, Jason Errol *b.* 1973, Sharon Mary *b.* 1971,—Roslyn Ann, *b.* 1944: *m.* 1962, M. Challon Jones, and has issue living, Duglas Challon Lynch *b.* 1962, Suzann Elizabeth Lynch *b.* 1964, Robin Ann Lynch *b.* 1967.——Mequeline Phyllis, *b.* 1922: *m.* 1941, Max Marsan, of 33, Strathmore Av., La Horquette Rd., Glenco, Trinidad, and has issue living, Douglas Martin (c/o Neal & Massy, Ltd., 94-98, Gooding Village, San Fernando, Trinidad), *b.* 1949: *m.* 1974, Alison Mary Ferguson, and has issue living Andrew Douglas, *b.* 1975,—Stanley Sydney (30, Hillisboro Av., Apt. 2306, Toronto, Ont. M5R 1S7), *b.* 1951,—Richard Francis, *b.* 1953: *m.* 1975, Gail Maria Thomas,—Brenda Mary, *b.* 1942: *m.* 1964, Ian Crawford Macintyre,—Judith Ann, *b.* 1943: *m.* 1963, Richard Anthony Frost, and has issue living, Roger Anthony *b.* 1963, Lyndon Maria *b.* 1964, Carolyn Ann *b.* 1968, Lyann *b.* 1972,—Cecile Mildred (30, Hillisboro Av., Apt. 2306, Toronto, Ont. M5R 1S7), *b.* 1947,—Susan Mary, *b.* 1959.——Mary Mildred, *b.* 1942: *m.* 1948, Aldred Mitchell, of 44, Belmont Circular Rd., Port of Spain, Trinidad, and has issue living, Alfred Bernard, *b.* 1950,—William Joseph, *b.* 1958,—Bernadette Mary, *b.* 1949: *m.* 1969, Michael David Diaz, and has issue living, Pamela Bernadette *b.* 1970,—Denise Mequeline, *b.* 1951: *m.* 19—, John A. C. Forster, and has issue living, Andrew Donald *b.* 1969,—Nanette Celine, *b.* 1954,—Susan Marie, *b.* 1955,—Sidney Debra, *b.* 1959.

Issue of the late James Carrington Hay, *b.* 1888, *d.* 1961: *m.* 1921, Maria Cynthia Fifi, who *d.* 1956:—

Rupert Loraine (Alderston, Smart St., St. Augustine ,Trinidad), *b.* 1924: *m.* 1954, Denise Rita (ante), da. of the late Loraine Macdonald Hay.——Ranald Louis (RR3, Caledon East, Ont., Canada), *b.* 1925; ed. at St. Francis Xavier Univ. (BSc), and McGill Univ. (BEng), PEng. Ont.: *m.* 1955 Lorraine Marianné, da. of the late Frederick John Fecteau, of Toronto, and has issue living, Ranald Joseph, *b.* 1956,—Dominic Louis, *b.* 1958,—Cynthia Maria, *b.* 1959,—Genevieve Anne, *b.* 1960,—Marianne Noel, *b.* 1962,—Laurie Elizabeth, *b.* 1965.——Donald Joseph (Smart St., Curepe, Trinidad), *b.* 1927: *m.* 1955, Lola Sue Martin, and has issue living, Donald Roger Paul, *b.* 1956,—Bruce Victor Joseph, *b.* 1959,—Christopher Michael Charles, *b.* 1967,—Paula Emily Rebecca, *b.* 1966.

Granddaughter of the late Lieut.-Col. Thomas Pasley Hay, son of the late Capt. John Hay (ante):—
Issue of the late Loraine Geddes Hay, *b.* 1847, *d.* 1904: *m.* 1879, Emily Alice, who *d.* 1934, da. of the late Donald Macdonald, H.E.I.C.S.:—

Hilda Rose: *m.* 1919, A. R. Davidson Kemp. *Residence,*

Grandchildren of the late Maj.-Gen. Woulfe Hay, son of the late Lieut.-Col. Thomas Pasley Hay (ante) :—

Issue of the late Lieut.-Col. Henry Thomas Horatio Hay, *b.* 1863, *d.* 1934 : *m.* 1896, Mary Margaret, who *d.* 1940, da. of the late Rev. George James Corser, of Burrington, Ludlow :—
Alida Mary (Wood End, Wormley, Godalming, Surrey), *b.* 1899: *m.* 1921, Col. John Kaye Tickell RE (ret.), who *d.* 1969, and has issue living, Douglas John (38, Cromwell Rd., Teddington, Middx.), *b.* 1924; formerly Lt. RE: *m.* 1963, Rozann Parnell, and has issue living, Alexander, John *b.* 1968, Samantha Elizabeth *b.* 1972.

Issue of the late Alexander Hay, *b.* 1872, *d.* 1925 : *m.* 1909, Kathleen, da. of the late Gordon Styles Hare, of Croydon :—
James Woulfe, *b.* 1910: *m.* 1933, Edith Mary, da. of Arthur Henry Myrton, of Johannesburg, S. Africa, and has issue living, Bertha Lillian, *b.* 1934,—Hilda Rose, *b.* 1937.——William Henry Ker, *b.* 1912 : *m.* 1938, Violet Mary da. of the late Harold Mortimer, of Manchester, and has issue living, Lynette Florence, *b.* 1939,—Evadne Felicity, *b.* 1943,—Merilyn Wendy, *b.* 1951. *Residence*, Summer Place, 4, Sunbird St., Elspark, Elsburg, Transvaal, S. Africa.

Descendants of the late Thomas Hay (Lord Huntingdon, a Scottish Lord of Session), grandfather of 5th baronet :—

Grandchildren of the late William Montgomery Hay, son of the late Capt. Henry Hird Hay, 5th Dragoon Guards, great-grandson of the late Thomas Hay (ante):—

Issue of the late Vincent Henry Hay, *b.* 1889, *d.* 1949 : *m.* 1915, Edicel Bassett, who *d.* 1959 :—
Wayne W., *b.* 1918: *m.* 1942, Harriet Johnson, and has issue living, Michael William, *b.* 1943,— Robert Wayne, *b.* 1950,—Ronald Patrick, *b.* 1957,—Barbara Ann, *b.* 1945,—Becky Ann, *b.* 1948, —Jacqueline Marie, *b.* 1953,—Catherine Marie, *b.* 1960.——Helen Francis, *b.* 1922: *m.* 1946, Richard Connell, and has issue living, Thomas Richard, *b.* 1949,—Timothy Peter Joseph, *b.* 1959 —Mary Theresa Louise, *b.* 1947,—Mary Catherine, *b.* 1952,—Mary Anita, *b.* 1954,—Mary Jennifer, *b.* 1956,—Mary Elizabeth, *b.* 1958. *Residence*,

Granddaughter of the late Capt. Henry Hird Hay, 5th Dragoon Guards (ante):—
Issue of the late Vincent Henry Fulford Hay, *b.* 1868, *d.* 1936 : *m.* 1905, Olive Ellen, da. of Thomas John Richards, of Liskeard, Cornwall :—
Majorie Letitia, *b.* 1907: *m.* 1937, Frederick Guy Darvall, banker, and has issue living, Diana Hay, *b.* 1938. *Address*, c/o National Bank of Australasia, Ltd. Jandowaae, Queensland.

This family, anciently seated at Huntingdon, E. Lothian, and at Mordington and Thornydykes Berwickshire, is descended in direct line from the old House of Lockerwort and Yester, whose progenitor was William de Haya (cup bearer to Malcolm IV and William the Lion), who *d.* 1170. Sir John Hay, 1st baronet [el. son of Thomas Hay, of Alderston, E. Lothian (lineally descended from Sir Edmond Hay, of Linplum (*v.* 1429-49), younger brother of Sir David Hay of Yester (*v.* 1475), ancestor of the Marquesses of Tweeddale)], was cr. a Baronet with remainder to heirs male forever. The 8th Baronet, Sir William Henry, a Housepainter by trade, *d.* in Australia in 1927, and was *s.* by his brother, Sir Edward Hamilton, who *d.* 1936, without proving his succession or using the title.

DALRYMPLE-HAY, Creation (G.B.) 1798, of Park Place, Wigtownshire.

Sir JAMES BRIAN DAL-RYMPLE-HAY, 6th *Baronet*, son of the late Lieut.-Col. Brian George Rowland Dalrymple-Hay, son of the late George Houston Dalrymple-Hay, son of the late Col. George James Dalrymple-Hay, 2nd son of 2nd baronet ; *b.* Jan. 19th, 1928 ; *s.* his kinsman, Sir CHARLES JOHN C.V.O., 1952 ; sometime Lieut. R.M.: *m.* 1958, Helen Sylvia, da. of the late Stephen Herbert Card, and has issue.

Arms—Quarterly: 1st and 4th, or, on a saltire azure nine lozenges of the field, all within a bordure gules ; 2nd and 3rd, argent, three escutcheons gules in chief an ox yoke lying fess-ways proper. Crests—1st, a rock per pale azure and or ; 2nd, between two piles or issuant from the torse a falcon proper, charged on the breast with an escutcheon gules. Supporters—Two volunteers belonging to the Corps of Wigton in their uniforms of the year 1800 all proper.
Residence—The Red House, Church St., Warnham, Horsham.

Daughters living—Fiona Louise, *b.* 1963.——Charlotte Ann, *b.* 1966.——Lucie Helen, *b.* 1969.
Brothers living—JOHN HUGH (Wheltones, Long Grove, Seer Green, Bucks.), *b.* Dec. 16th, 1929; ed. at Blundell's Sch.; late Capt. R. Scots Fusiliers: *m.* 1962, Jennifer Phyllis Roberta, da. of the late Brig. Robert Johnston, CBE, and has issue living, Malcolm John Robert, *b.* 1966.—— Ronald George Inglis, *b.* 1933; ed. at Blundell's Sch.
Half-Brother living—Christopher Hamish (Klein Constantia, PO Box 160, Letsitele, 0885, N. Transvaal), *b.* 1941: *m.* 1968, Margaret Linda Smith, and has issue living, Hamish Ian, *b.* 1971,— Amanda Jane *b.* 1975.
Uncle living—Hugh Brereton, D.S.O., *b.* 1900; Lieut.-Col. (retired) Indian Armoured Corps; European War 1939-45 (prisoner, D.S.O.); D.S.O. 1945: *m.* 1939, Gwendyth Margaret, da. of the late Lt.-Col. N. L. Callard, and has issue living, Janet Margaret, *b.* 1941: *m.* 1963, Anthony D. Stericker, of Diamond Cottage, Church End, Gt. Dunmow, Essex, and has issue living, Johanna Margaret *b.* 1966, Sophia Harriett *b.* 1968, Lucinda Jean *b.* 1969. *Residence*, Brownings, Pytches Rd., Woodbridge Suffolk.
Aunt living—Lorna Alice Emily, *b.* 1899: *m.* 1922, Alexander Izat Walker, MC. *Residence,* 134, Welbeck Cres., Troon, Ayrshire.

Collateral Branches living:

Granddaughter of the late Col. George James Dalrymple-Hay, 2nd son of 2nd baronet:—

Issue of the late Sir Harley Hugh Dalrymple-Hay, *b.* 1861, *d.* 1940: *m.* 1891, Agnes Yelland, who *d.* 1956, da. of the late Frederick Waters, of Clarence House, Gosport :— Alison Hathorn Compton, *b.* 1909: *m.* 1938, John Berger, and has issue living, Ann Priscilla Dalrymple, *b.* 1938. *Residence*, Bilbrook House, Bilbrook, Minehead, Som.

Granddaughter of the late Lt.-Col. Stair Francis Barton Dalrymple-Hay, yst. son of the late Col. George James Dalrymple-Hay (ante):—
Issue of the late Com. Christopher Montague Vernon Francis Dalrymple-Hay, D.S.C., R.N., *b.* 1896; *d.* (on active ser. during European War) 1944 : *m.* 1st, 1919, Mary Teresa (who obtained a divorce 1929), younger twin da. of the late Lieut.-Col. Edward Henry Joseph Mostyn [*see* Mostyn, Bt., colls.] ; 2ndly, 1929, Helen Violet, da. of H. K. Grierson, formerly of Castle Douglas :—
(By 1st marriage) Mary Cecily Edith Teresa, *b.* 1920: *m.* 1947, John Walter Ferlex Lloyd-Johnes. *Residence*, Lower Hill Farm, Prestbury, Cheltenham.

Granddaughter of the late Houston Stewart Dalrymple-Hay, 3rd son of 2nd baronet :—
Issue of the late James Stewart Dalrymple-Hay, *b.* 1860, *d.* 1931: *m.* 1886, Emily, da. of William Irving :—
Mary Grace (Glenluce, Woy Woy, N.S. Wales), *b.* 1888.

Grandchildren of the late Richard Tycho Dalrymple Hay (infra):—
Issue of the late Charles Stewart Dalrymple-Hay, MC, *b.* 1891, *d.* 1972: *m.* 1922, Barbara (22, Amaroo Pl., Yass, NSW), da. of the late Warwick Chambers, of Sydney, NSW :—
John Warwick, *b.* 1928; a writer and journalist: *m.* 1953, Barbara Deidre, da. of M. Moir, of Canberra, and has issue living, Heather Nan, *b.* 1954,—Ann Louise, *b.* 1956.——Ann, *b.* 1924; 1939-45 War with WRANS: *m.* 1947, David Thompson, stockbroker, of St. Ives, NSW.

Grandchildren of the late Houston Stewart Dalrymple-Hay (ante):—
Issue of the late Richard Tycho Dalrymple-Hay, *b.* 1861, *d.* 1943: *m.* 1888, Bessie, who *d.* 1941, da. of J. W. Cheesbrough, grazier of New England Dist.:—
Margaret Fordyce (11, Bay View Hill Rd., Rose Bay, NSW), *b.* 1889; is a JP; Coronation Medal (1953).——Kahtleen Alice (c/o Richmond House, 5, Richmond Rd., Rose Bay, NSW), *b.* 1894: *m.* 1st, 1919, William Hay, of Yass, NSW, from whom she obtained a divorce 1933; 2ndly, 1946, Lt.-Cdr. W. de Burgh Thomas, RNR, who *d.* 1962.

Issue of the late Claude Thomas Hugh Vans Dalrymple-Hay, *b.* 1865, *d.* 1953: *m.* 1898, Belle (who *d.* 1967, having obtained a divorce 1921), da. of Frank Wheelhouse:—
Houston Francis Wilfred, *b.* 1907; an Assoc. of Australian Soc. of Accountants: *m.* 1st, 1938, Marie Hawke, from whom he obtained a divorce, 1943; 2ndly, 1967, Olive May, da. of the late John Jacob Worner. *Residence*, 11, Bay View Hill Rd., Rose Bay, NSW.——Isobel Ellen Ruby, *b.* 1904: *m.* 1924, Arthur John Peverly Hall, LLB, of 57, King St., Wollstonecraft, NSW, and has issue living, Isobel Wendy Anne, *b.* 1928.

Issue of the late Houston Stewart Dalrymple-Hay, *b.* 1871, *d.* 1956: *m.* 1906, Daisy Annie, who *d.* 1928, da. of David Davis, of Christchurch, New Zealand :—
Houston Stewart, *b.* 1909 ; formerly Capt. 2nd Australian Imperial Force : *m.* 19—, Peggy Fitzmaurice, da. of Argyle Charles Charleston Loftus, of Brighton, Victoria, and has issue living, Charles Stewart, *b.* 1949,—Helene Fitzmaurice, *b.* 1951. *Residence*, 96, Raglan Street, Mosman, N.S. Wales.——Barbara (of 4, Howell Av., Lane Cove, Sydney, N.S. Wales), *b.* 1913: *m.* 1938, Charles John Newhill Leleu, O.B.E., formerly Roy. Australian Air Force, who *d.* 1961, and has issue living, John Stewart Newhill, *b.* 1939,—Antonia Blanche Newhill, *b.* 1945.——Nancy Stair, *b.* 1915: *m.* 1940, Frank Lawrence Fletcher, and has issue living, James Lawrence, *b.* 1941,—Susan Stair *b.* 1945: *m.* 1970, Peter Brian Barton Pollock, of 5, Lofberg Rd., Pymble, NSW, and has issue living, Peter James *b.* 1972, Simon Stewart *b.* 1974,—Josephine Daisy, *b.* 1948: *m.* 1972, Timothy Martin Harpur, of 22, Suffolk Av., Collaroy, NSW, and has issue living, Sophie Irene *b.* 1974. Elizabeth Nancy (twin) *b.* 1974. *Residence*, 16, Cremorne Rd., Cremorne Point, NSW.——Elizabeth Mary, *b.* 1921: *m.* 1947, Roy Charles Cooper, and has issue living, Peter Charles, *b.* 1951,—Donald Stewart, *b.* 1957,—Sally Victoria, *b.* 1948. *Residence*, 89, Tryon Rd., East Lindfield, NSW.

The 1st baronet, Col. Sir John Dalrymple, of Dunragit, Wigtownshire, married the daughter of Sir Thomas Hay, 3rd Bt., of Park, on inheriting whose estates in 1794 he assumed by Roy. licence the name of Hay. The 3rd baronet, Adm. the Rt. Hon. Sir John Charles, sat as M.P. for Wakefield (C) 1862-65, for Stamford 1866-80, and for Wigton Burghs 1880-85. The 5th baronet, Sir Charles John Dalrymple-Hay, C.V.O., was a Clerk in Foreign Office 1887-95, and in Privy Council Office 1895-1928.

HEAD, Creation (U.K.) 1838, of Rochester, Kent.

Sir FRANCIS DAVID SOMERVILLE HEAD, 5th *Baronet* : *b.* Oct. 17th, 1916 ; *s.* his father, *Sir* ROBERT POLLOCK SOMERVILLE 1924 ; ed. at Eton and at Peterhouse, Camb. (B.A. 1937) ; Major (retired) Queen's Own Cameron Highlanders; 1939-45 War (wounded, prisoner): *m.* 1st, 1950 (m. diss. 1965), Susan Patricia, da. of the late Arthur Douglas Ramsay, OBE [*see* Ramsay, Bt., *cr.* 1806, colls.]; 2ndly, 1967, Penelope Marion Acheson, da. of the late Wilfrid Archibald Alexander, [see Hagart-Alexander, Bt.] and has issue by 1st marriage.

Arms—Argent a chevron ermines between three unicorns, heads couped sable. Crest—A unicorn's head, couped ermine.

Residence—10, Fairway, Merrow, Surrey. *Club*—Naval and Military.

STUDY QUIET

Son living—(by 1st m.)—RICHARD DOUGLAS SOMERVILLE, *b.* Jan. 16th, 1951; ed. at Eton, and Magdalene Coll., Camb.; DipAD.
Daughter living—(by 1st m.)—Diana Mary Frances, *b.* 1954.
Brother living—John Kenelm Somerville, *b.* 1918; ed. at Wellington Coll., and at Oriel Coll., Oxford (MA); BEd. Calgary; 1939-45 War, with Intelligence Corps: *m.* 1942, Lilah Doreen Prittie Wingfield, da. of the late Lt.-Col. Samuel James Chatterton Prittie Perry, FRCS [V. Powerscourt, colls.], and has issue living, Patrick John Somerville (P.O. Box 456, Consort, Alberta, Canada), *b.* 1943: *m.* 1971, Karen Carla, da. of Emanuel Karl Schaufele, of Schuler, Alberta, Canada, and has issue living, Kathleen Patricia *b.* 1974,—David Charles Somerville, *b.* 1949,—

Sarah Grace Edith, *b.* 1947: *m.* 1972, Ronald James Zezulka, of Lethbridge, Alberta, Canada,—Angela Lilah Mary (twin) *b.* 1949: *m.* 1973, Joseph Andrew Panter, of 1813-4 St SW, Calgary, Alberta, Canada, and has issue living, David James *b.* 1974. *Residence*, 123, First St., NW, Medicine Hat, Alberta, Canada.

Sister living—Angela Grace Mary, *b.* 1922: *m.* 1941, Henry Paddison Granlund, D.S.C., late Lt. RNVR, and has issue living, Hew Richard Paddison, *b.* 1943; Lt. RN,—Karen Mary, *b.* 1945,—Margaret Jane, *b.* 1950: *m.* 1973, Anthony Hewitt-Hicks. *Residence*, Cushat Law, Crawley Lane, Balcombe, Sussex.

Aunt living (daughter of 3rd baronet)—Florence Mary, *b.* 1881: *m.* 1922, Percy Meyrick Morris-Davies, V.D., who *d.* 1934, second son of the late Morris-Davies, J.P., D.L., of Ffosyrhydgaled, Llanfarian, Cardiganshire. *Residence*, 6, Hayward Road, Oxford.

Collateral Branches living.

Granddaughters of George Burges Digby Head (infra):—
Issue of the late Com. Robert Digby Head, DSC, RN, *b.* 1917, *d.* 1956: *m.* 1946, Lorraine, ARRC (of 79, Cotes Rd., Barrow-upon-Soar, Leics.), who *m.* 2ndly, 1967 (m. diss. 1973), William Gerard Fallon, da. of Walter Dowding, of Dolphin Sq., SW1:—
Pauline Anne, *b.* 1948.——Linda Mary, *b.* 1951: *m.* 1971, Paul Richard Wilder, of 49, Prince George's Av., Raynes Park, SW20, and has issue living, Robert James, *b.* 1972.

Issue of the late George Burges Digby Head, yr. son of 3rd baronet, *b.* 1888, *d.* 1963: *m.* 1st, 1912, Annie, who *d.* 1940, da. of the late William Stockhill, of York; 2ndly, 1946, Olive Peggy (of 270, Berg St., Muckleneuk, Pretoria, S. Africa), da. of the late George Baker, of Ealing, W.5:—
(By 1st m.) Rosemary Gabriella (c/o Lloyds Bank, 12, High St., Banbury, Oxon.), *b.* 1920.

The 1st baronet, the Right Hon. Sir Francis Bond Head, K.C.H., P.C. (grandson of Moses Mendes, of Old Buckenham, Norfolk, and London, who *m.* Anna Gabriella, elder da. and co-heir of the Rev. Sir Francis Head, 4th Bt., of The Hermitage, Kent (*ext.*), and whose surname her heirs of the body were authorised to assume by Roy. licence 1770), was sometime Lieut.-Gov. of Upper Canada.

CHADWYCK-HEALEY, Creation (U.K.) 1919, of Wyphurst, Cranleigh, co. Surrey, and New Place, Luccombe, Somerset.

Sir EDWARD RANDAL CHADWYCK-HEALEY, *M.C.*, 3rd *Baronet; b.* Jan. 23rd, 1898; *s.* his father, *Sir* GERALD EDWARD, *CBE*, 1955; ed. at Eton, and RMA; Maj. RA; 1914-18 War (MC, Belgian Croix de Guerre), France, N. Africa and Italy 1939-45 (wounded, Bar to MC): *m.* 1924, Rachel (late Ch. Com. ATS), da. of L. C. Whitehead Phillips, of Unsted Park, Godalming.

Arms—1st and 4th gules, four fusils engrailed and conjoined in bend, ermine between two lilies leaved and slipped proper, *Healey*; 2nd and 3rd gules, an anchor cabled within an orle argent, charged with eight martlets of the field (*Chadwyck*). **Crest**—1st, in front of four fusils engrailed and conjoined fessewise ermine a lily as in the arms, *Healey*; 2nd, a talbot's head gules, charged on the neck with an escutcheon argent, thereon a martlet as in the arms, *Chadwyck*.

Residence—The Mill House, Hook, Hants. *Clubs*—Athenæum, Bath.

Believe in me.   **Brother living**—CHARLES ARTHUR, *OBE*, *TD*, *b.* May 27th, 1910; ed. at Eton, and at Trin. Coll., Oxford (B.A. 1932, M.A. 1936); is Lieut.-Col. R.A. (T.A.); European War 1939-45 in N. Africa, Sicily and Italy (despatches twice, O.B.E.); O.B.E. (Mil.) 1945: *m.* 1939, Viola. *J.P.*, da. of the late Cecil Lubbock [*see* B. Avebury, colls.], and has issue living, Charles Edward (Rookwoods, Little Dunmow, Gt. Dunmow, Essex), *b.* 1940; ed. at Eton, and Trin. Coll., Oxford (MA): *m.* 1967, Angela Mary Metson, and has issue living, Edward Alexander *b.* 1972, Catherine *b.* 1970,—Nicholas Gerald, *b.* 1946,—Peregrine James, *b.* 1950: *m.* 1973, Julia Mary, el. da. of Sir Richard James Boughey, 10th Bt.,—Philippa Harriet, *b.* 1943: *m.* 1974, Jeremy Michael Lubbock, of Rowan House, 3, Stockwell Park Rd., SW9 [see B. Avebury, colls.].—Serena Margaret, *b.* 1948: *m.* 1971, Jeremy D. Nickson, of 60, Bromfelde Rd., SW4, and has issue living, Francesca Verena, *b.* 1975. *Residence*, Old Middleton, Westmeston, Hassocks, Sussex. *Club*, Brooks's.

Sister living—Rosa Mary Philippa, *b.* 1907: *m.* 1933, Cyril George Holland-Martin, *J.P.*, and has issue living, Timothy David, *b.* 1936; ed. at Eton; late 2nd Lt. R. Armoured Corps,—Robert George, *b.* 1939; ed. at Eton,—Faith Mary, *b.* 1949: *m.* 1972, Lt. Anthony Hallett, RN. *Residence*, Silver Rill, Overbury, Tewkesbury, Gloucestershire.

Uncle living (son of 1st baronet)—Hilary Philip, *b.* 1888; ed. at Eton; Capt. E. Surrey Regt. late TA Reserve. *Residence*, 49, Hallam St., W1. *Club*—Brooks's.

Collateral Branch living.

Issue of the late Oliver Nowell Chadwyck-Healey, 3rd son of 1st baronet, *b.* 1886, *d.* 1960: *m.* 1916, Gwendoline Mary (of New Place, Porlock, Somerset), da. of Major Hugh Charrington, of Hill Cottage, Taplow, Bucks:—
John Hugh, *b.* 1922; ed. at Eton; formerly Capt. Rifle Brig.; N. Africa and Italy 1943-5 (wounded). *Residence*, New Place, Porlock, Somerset.——Patience Mary, *b.* 1917; late Junior Com. A.T.S.: *m.* 1946, Lieut.-Col. Peter St. George Hereward Maxwell, M.C., Highland L.I., and has issue living, Philip Hugh, *b.* 1947,—Ian Peter, *b.* 1949,—Gillian Mary, *b.* 1954,—Penelope Frances, *b.* 1956. *Residence*, Pettistree Grange, Woodbridge, Suffolk.

The 1st baronet, Sir Charles Edward Heley Chadwyck Chadwyck-Healey, K.C.B., K.C., Hon. Capt. R.N.R., was Chm. Admiralty Vol. Committee 1903-14, commanded a Hospital Ship during European War 1915-18, and was cr. a baronet for valuable service on Admiralty Transport Arbitration Board. The 2nd baronet Sir Gerald Edward Chadwyck-Healey, C.B.E., was Director of Materials and Priority, Admiralty 1918.

HEATH, Creation (U.K.) 1904, of Ashorne Hill, Leamington, Warwickshire.
[Extinct 1942.]

Sir JAMES HEATH, 1st and last *Baronet.*

Widow living of 1st Baronet—DOROTHY MARY (*Lady Heath*), B.Sc., da. of the late C. M. Hodgson, Indian Forest Ser. (retired) : *m.* 1935, as his fourth wife, Sir James Heath, 1st baronet, who *d.* 1942, when the title became ext. *Residence,* 48, Lowndes Square, S.W.1.

HEATHCOTE, Creation (G.B.) 1733, of Hursley, Hampshre
[Name pronounced "Hethcut."]

Et Dieu mon appui.
And God my help.

Sir MICHAEL PERRYMAN HEATHCOTE, 11th *Baronet,* b. Aug. 7th, 1927; *s.* his father, *Sir* LEONARD VYVYAN, 1963; ed. at Winchester, and at Clare Coll., Camb.; late 2nd Lieut. 9th Lancers; in remainder to the Earldom of Macclesfield: *m.* 1956, Victoria, el. da. of Com. J. E. R. Wilford, R.D., R.N.R., of Ackland Cottage, Shirley Holms, Lymington, Hants, and has issue.

    Arms—Ermine, three pomels each charged with a cross or. **Crest**—On a mural crown azure, a pomey charged with a cross or between two wings displayed ermine. **Second Motto**—"Deus prosperat justos " (*God prospers the just*).

    Residence—Warborne Farm, Boldre, Lymington, Hants.

Sons living—TIMOTHY GILBERT, *b.* May 25th, 1957.
——George Benjamin, *b.* 1965.
Daughter living—Harriet Louise, *b.* 1962.
Sister living—Pamela Mary, *b.* 1923: *m.* 1945, John Gilbert Jones (c/o Lloyds Bank, 46, Victoria St., SW1), and has issue living, Richard Edmund, *b.* 1947,—Rosemary Anne, *b.* 1948.

Collateral Branches living.
    (*All male line in special remainder to Earldom of Macclesfield*)

    Granddaughters of the late Rev. Gilbert Vyvyan Heathcote, father of 9th and 10th baronets :—
Issue of the late Rev. Gilbert Arthur Heathcote, *b.* 1854, *d.* 1907 : *m.* 1878, Mary Susan who *d.* 1935, da. of the late Major William James Rind, Bengal Army :—
Mary Gertrude Caroline, *A.R.R.C.,* *b.* 1884 ; has Order of St. Sava of Serbia (5th class). *Residence,* Waverley, High St., Findon, Sussex.

    Issue of the late William Charles Perceval Heathcote, *b.* 1867, *d.* 1937 : *m.* 1921, Ruth, who *d.* 1950, da. of the late Arthur Malcolm Heathcote (infra) :—
Anne, *b.* 1923: *m.* 1945, Baron Diederic W. van Lynden, Ambassador Netherlands Foreign Ser. of Lange Voorhout, 48, The Hague, and has issue living, Jan Willem Alexander, *b.* 1948,—Carel Diederic Aernout, *b.* 1954,—Carola, *b.* 1947: *m.* 1969, Jonkheer A.G. Beelaerts van Blokland.

    Grandchildren of the late Reginald St. Alban Heathcote, DM, FRCP, yst. son of the late Rev. Gilbert Vyvyan Heathcote (ante):—
Issue of the late Anthony Giles Salvin Heathcote, CD, *b.* 1919, *d.* 1970: *m.* 1953, Kathleen Joan (276, McKee Av., Willowdale, Ont., Canada), only da. of H. Dawson, of Burton-on-Trent, Staffs.:—
William Reginald Salvin, *b.* 1955.——Andrew Henry Salvin, *b.* 1962.——Jean Viola, *b.* 1954.——Catherine Dawson, *b.* 1959.——Ann Elisabeth, *b.* 1960.——Ruth Margaret, *b.* 1963.

    Issue of the late Col. Charles George Heathcote, 4th son of 5th baronet, *b.* 1843, *d.* 1924: *m.* 1884, Lucy Lyttelton, *M.B.E.,* who *d.* 1934, da. of the late Richard Tanfield Vachell, of Coptfold Hall, Essex :—
Maud Lyttelton, *ARRC* (Park House, Park Rd., Winchester), *b.* 1885; 1914-18 War (ARRC). ——Frances Gwendolen, *b.* 1890: *m.* 1921, Maj. Albert Parrott, late Green Howards, of Coach House Cottage, Headbourne Worthy, Winchester, Hants.

    Grandson of the late Arthur Malcolm Heathcote (infra):—
Issue of the late James Shirley Heathcote, *b.* 1887, *d.* (of wounds received in action during European War) 1917 : *m.* 1912, Agnes Ethel, da. of James Hatcher, of Brandon, Canada :—
Martin Shirley (Wandinong, Mullaley, NSW), *b.* 1914; ed. at Sherborne; late Lt. RA (Supplementory Reserve); 1939-45 War (prisoner): *m.* 1948, Mary Gertrude, da. of Dr. H. H. Nowland,

of Sydney, NSW, and has issue living, Richard Desmond, *b.* 1950: *m.* 1973, Carmel Montgomery, and has issue living, James Martin *b.* 1974,—Pamela Shirley, *b.* 1949: *m.* 1971, Casper Rey i de Crife,—Ann Margaret, *b.* 1956.

Issue of the late Arthur Malcolm Heathcote, 6th son of 5th baronet, *b.* 1847, *d.* 1934 ; *m.* 1879, Mary Forbes, who *d.* 1903, da. of the late Rev. James Gavin Young, V. of Hursley:—

Marion (Sycamore Cottage, Upton Grey, Basingstoke, Hants.), *b.* 1884: *m.* 1st, 1907, Maj. Robert Maxwell Grenfell Knight RGA; 2ndly, 1921, Com. Ralph Cotesworth, RN (ret.), a King's Foreign Ser. Messenger, who *d.* 1937, and has issue living, (by 1st m.) Barbara Elizabeth, *b.* 1911: *m.* 1933, Cdr. Nigel C. B. Cox, RN, of Sycamore Cottage, Upton Grey, Basingstoke, Hants.

Grandson of the late Adm. Edmund Heathcote, son of the late Rev. Samuel Heathcote, 3rd son of 3rd baronet:—

Issue of the late Capt. Arthur Cleveland Heathcote, R.N., *b.* 1854, *d.* 1933: *m.* 1886, Florence Georgina, who *d.* 1938, da. of Thomas Vance, of Blackrock, co. Dublin:—

Eustace Cleveland, *b.* 1805 ; ed. at Haileybury ; Major (retired) R.M. : *m.* 1926, Marie Macmurrough, da. of the late J. J. Kavanagh, and has issue living, Michael Edmund (Hill Vista, Dockenfield, nr. Farnham, Surrey), *b.* 1931: Capt. RM: *m.* 1959, Jean, el. da. of D. J. V. Hamilton-Miller, of Shrewsbury House, Ditton Hill, Surrey, and has issue living, Kathryn Gay *b.* 1961, Georgina Anne (twin) *b.* 1961, Jenny Louise *b.* 1964,—Valerie, *b.* 1929; 2nd Officer WRNS. *Residence,* 1, Halsdon Close, Exeter Rd., Exmouth, S. Devon.

Grandchildren of the late Charles Heathcote, 5th son of William Lovell Heath-cote, el. son of Adm. Sir Henry Heathcote, 4th son of 3rd baronet:—

Issue of Frederick Lovell Heathcote, *b.* 1875, *d.* 1968: *m.* 1901, Mimie Ethel Ziervogel, who *d.* 1938:—

Geoffrey Charles (Crestwood, P.O. Newton Park, Port Elizabeth, S. Africa), *b.* 1906: *m.* 1939, Megan Edith Pugh-Jones and has issue living, Charles William (Crestwood, P.O. Newton Park, Port Elizabeth, S. Afirca), *b.* 1942: *m.* 1967, Hester de Lange,—Warwick Geoffrey, *b.* 1946,— Gerard Lovell, *b.* 1951,—Eleanor May, *b.* 1948.——Albert Ziervogel (Glenfield, PO Box 7071, Newton Park, Port Elizabeth, S. Africa), *b.* 1909: *m.* 1943, Doreen Oke Thomas, and has issue living, Frederick Malcolm (PO Box 7071, Port Elizabeth, S. Africa), *b.* 1944: *m.* 1972, Elenor Fourie,—Albert Dennisson (PO Box 252, Humansdorp, S. Africa), *b.* 1946: *m.* 1969, Elizabeth Stoutjesdyk, and has issue living, Yvonne Sharon *b.* 1970,—Richard John (PO Box 252, Humans-dorp, S. Africa), *b.* 1948: *m.* 1969, Finette van Gend, and has issue living, Charmaine Sunette *b.* 1969,—Richelle Doreen *b.* 1970,—Hilary Oke, *b.* 1950.——Kathleen Mary (Hayfields, Cradock, Cape Prov., S. Africa), *b.* 1902: *m.* 1922, W. A. Copeman, who *d.* 1938, and has issue living, William Lovell Heathcote, *b.* 1923: *m.* 1948, Maureen Distin, and has issue living, Anthony *b.* 19—, Kathleen, *b.* 19—,Dorothy *b.* 19—, Camilla *b.* 19—, Philip Frederick Heathcote, *b.* 1927: *m.* 1958, DoreenHouston, and has issue living, Roy *b.* 1959, Louis *b.* 1960,—Joyce Belle Heathcote, *b.* 1926: *m.* 1950, Martin Luther Coetzee, and has issue living, Martin St. Leger *b.* 1952, Philip Fitzroy *b.* 1954, Christopher Collett (twin) *b.* 1954,—Hazel Heathcote, *b.* 1930: *m.* 1957, Rodney Spenser, of 14, The Triangle, Pinelands, Cape Town, S. Africa, and has issue living, Christopher *b.* 19—, Rosemary *b.* 19—.——Mimie Lovell. *b.* 1904: *m.* 1929, Andrew Gerald Lovemore, of Hand-field, PO Box2, Sandflats, Paterson, Cape Prov., S. Africa, and has issue living, Frederick Charles Handfield (127, Silverleaf Av., Birchleigh, via Kempton Park, Transvaal), *b.* 1930: *m.* 1961, Jennifer May, da. of William H. Cable (infra), and has issue living, Rowan Handfield *b.* 1965, Dawn Grace *b.* 1962,—David Gerald (Handfield, PO Box 2, Paterson, Cape Prov., S. Africa), *b.* 1931: *m.* 1965, Gayle Ackermann, and has issue living, Russell Loxton *b.* 1967, Theresa Lovell *b.* 1966,—Geoffrey Andrew (Island View, PO Box 2, Sandflats, Paterson, Cape Prov., S. Africa), *b.* 1932: *m.* 1961, Eugénie Merula van Notten, and has issue living, Colin Peter *b.* 1964, Richard Andrew *b.* 1967, Susan Eugénie *b.* 1963,—Brian Lovell (Springfield, Box 31, Grahamstown, S. Africa), *b.* 1937: *m.* 1962, Sonia Mercia Berrington, and has issue living, James Andrew *b.* 1967, Philip George *b.* 1970, Joan Melanie *b.* 1963, Bridgid Charmaine *b.* 1966.——Beryl *b.* 1907: *m.* 1939, Sydney James Gilfillan, of Balmoral, Alexandria, Cape Prov., S. Africa, and has issue living, Heathcote, *b.* 1940: *m.* 1965, Trudie Clair Rose, da. of the late Dr. H. Schoeman, and has issue living, Michael Sydney Lovell *b.* 1968, Jacqueline Beryl *b.* 1967,—Jean, *b.* 1942: *m.* 1966, John Waldy Bartie, of 14, Dreyer St., South Crest, Alberton, Transvaal, and has issue living, Shane Waldy *b.* 1967, Lara Channette *b.* 1968.——Joan, *b.* 1910: *m.* 1938, Maurice E. Wilmot, of The Ghio, PO Alexandria, CP, S. Africa, and has issue living, Chester George, *b.* 1948,—Felicity Mary, *b.* 1940: *m.* 1964, John St. Laurence Beaufort, and has issue living, Sandra *b.* 1966.—— Esmé Helen (Crestwood, Kragga Kamma, Port Elizabeth, CP, S. Africa), *b.* 1913.

Grandchildren of the late Charles William Heathcote (infra):—

Issue of the late Frederick Lennox, Heathcote, *b.* 1903, *d.* 1969: *m.* 1932, Mildred Walkenshaw Shaw, who *d.* 1974:—

Leon Geoffrey, (PO Box 998, Gwelo, Rhodesia), *b.* 1934: *m.* 1957, Gillian Jean Lawson, and has issue living, Frederick Garth, *b.* 1958,—Mark Andrew, *b.* 1962,—Jean Pamela, *b.* 1960.——Roy (PO Box 354, Que Que, Rhodesia), *b.* 1938: *m.* 1965, Gillian Helen Dalling, and has issue living, Paul Roy, *b.* 1972,—Amanda Kim, *b.* 1968.——Frederick Noel, *b.* 1945: *m.* 1967, Catherine Carlyn Barry, and has issue living, Clive Noel, *b.* 1968,—Wayne Douglas, *b.* 1972.——Stella Lenore, *b.* 1933: *m.* 1950, Bruce John Humpage (PO Box 15, Karoi, Rhodesia), and has issue living, Denise Marie, *b.* 1953: *m.* 1971, John Sealy, and has issue living, Gail *b.* 1971, Leigh-Anne *b.* 1974,—Carol Gail, *b.* 1955: *m.* 1974, Neville Thompson.——Colleen, *b.* 1936: *m.* 1954, Errol Dennis Roberts (59, Clyde Rd., Eastlea, Salisbury, Rhodesia), and has issue living, Cheryl Gail, *b.* 1955,—Melody Gaynor, *b.* 1957,—Fiona Gayland, *b.* 1958,—Beverley Colleen, *b.* 1959.—— Cleone, *b.* 1942: *m.* 1963, Rodney E. M. Roberts, of 35, Diamond Drive, Four Winds Est., Bulawyok Rhodesia, and has issue living, Shane Favin, *b.* 1965,—Felicity Ann, *b.* 1967.

Grandchildren of the late Charles Heathcote (ante):—

Issue of the late Charles William Heathcote, *b.*1877, *d.* 1918: *m.* 1st, 19—, Sophie Kichner, who *d.* 1910; 2ndly, 1911, Nellie van Heerden, who *d.* 1918:—

(By 1st m.)—Ellen Cecilia, *b.* 1906: *m.* 1934, William H. Cable, and has issue living, Jennifer May, *b.* 1936: *m.* 1961, Frederick Charles Handfield Lovemore (ante),—Helen Grace (5, Las Vegas, 30, Seventh St., Linden, Johannesburg, S. Africa) *b.* 1939: *m.* 1963 (m. diss. 1969), Michael Dennis Alexander Baerveldt, and has issue living, Alexander Michael *b.* 1964, Hugh William *b.* 1967, Noel Grace *b.* 1965. *Residence,* 14, Greenfield Rd., Greenside, Johannesburg, S. Africa.—— Millicent Pearl, *b.* 1908: *m.* 1937, Harry Dale, and has issue living, Margaret Ann *b.* 1939.——(By 2nd m.) Kathleen Mary, *b.* 1912: *m.* 1933, the Rev. Martin Luther Janse van Rensburg, and has issue living, Luther Calvyn *b.* 1935: *m.* 1959, Anne Elizabeth Nieuwoudt, and has issue living, Johanna Maria *b.* 1960,—Marleen, *b.* 1938: *m.* 1960, Johannes Daniel Nieuwoudt, of Hoopstad, Orange Free State, S. Africa.——Emma Ida May, *b.* 1915: *m.* 1937, Jacobus Wessel Janse van Rensburg, and has issue living, Jacobus Hendrikus, *b.* 1938,—Martin Luther, *b.* 1946,—Jacobus Wessel, *b.* 1949,—Kathleen Mary, *b.* 1943,—Alida Jacoba, *b.* 1949. *Residence,* Hertzogville, Orange Free State, S. Africa.

Issue of the late Fitzroy Hamilton Heathcote, *b.* 1881, *d.* 1938: *m.* 1903, Edith Beamish who *d.* 1947:—

Grace Sybil Beamish, *b.* 1904: *m.* 1930, Norman Sharwood, of 5 Brickmakerskloof, Port Elizabeth, S. Africa, and has issue living, Norma Dorothy, *b.* 1931: *m.* 1954, Tristan McGibbon Maynier, c/o Standard Bank, Queenstown , S. Africa, and has issue living, Derek *b.* 1959, Nicolette *b.* 1956.——Ida Beamish, *b.* 1906: *m.* 1932, William Leslie Lyddon Farrant, c/o Box 375, Pretoria, S. Africa, and has issue living, Leslie Heathcote, *b.* 1935: *m.* 1961, Antoinette du Toit,—David

Heathcote (c/o Box 375, Pretoria, S. Africa), b. 1937.——Olive Ellie Beamish, b. 1909: m. 1st, 1927 (divorce 1936), Henry Southey Scott; 2ndly, 1937, Keith Wynn Hill, P.O. Box 143, Grahamstown, S. Africa, and has issue living, (by 1st marriage) Keith Heathcote (P.O. Box 143, Grahamstown, S. Africa), b. 1929: m. 1953, Valda Beryl, da. of Samuel Thomas Smith, and has issue living, Keith Dennis Heathcote b. 1954, Chiquita Gayle Haethcote b. 1958.—— Winifred Beamish, b. 1917: m. 1st, 1935, John Rennie, who d. (killed in action) 1942; 2ndly, 1944, Patrick Dairmid Dolan, of 9, Avon Place, Cowies Hill, Natal, S. Africa, and has issue living (by 1st m.), Myrle Allison, b. 1938: m. 1963, Paul de Vere Noake, of 7, Delta Rd., Winston Ridge, Johannesburg, and has issue living, John de Vere b. 1964, Susan b. 1966,—(by 2nd m.) Elizabeth Ann, b. 1945: m. 1965, Alan Tucker, of 21, Cheltondale Court, Cheltondale, Johannesburg.—— Edith Ann Beamish, b. 1920: m. 1st, 1943 (divorce 1946), Gordon Sidney Lingfield Shepperson; 2nd, 1946 (m. diss. 1956), Llewelyn Howell, DFC; 3rdly, 19—, Albert Goodrick, and has issue living, (by 3rd m.) Sharon b. 1960.

Issue of the late Cecil Heathcote, b. 1883, d. 1918: m. 1911, Engela Starr, who d. 1941 (having m. 2ndly, 1930, Maurice Meek, formerly of P.O. Willoughby's Siding, S. Rhodesia), el. da. of Ambrose George Campbell Shaw:—
Cecil Starr, b. 1912: m. 1935, Norah Edith, da. of Walter James, and has issue living, Cecil Walter (11, Belgrave Gardens, NW8), b. 1936; Maj.: m. 1st, 1955, Sylvia Ann Boyd Varty, who d. 1959; 2ndly, 1961, Jennifer Gaie Brinsley, and has issue living (by 1st m.), Susan Norah b. 1958 (by 2nd m.), Debbie Gaie b. 1962, Carol Jean b. 1964, Linda Heidi b. 1971,—Janet Mary, b. 1949. Residence, Four Streams Farm, PO Somabula, Rhodesia.——Ambrose Carl Starr, b. 1915: m. 1940, Dorothy, yr. da. of W. B. Richards, of Fort Victoria, Rhodesia, and has issue living, David Starr, b. 1952,—Sylvia Starr, b. 1956. Residence, Fernhill, Essexvale, Rhodesia.——Mary Lesley Starr, b. 1913: m. 1937, Harry Edward Smith. Residence, Stanhope Farm, Somabula, Rhodesia.

Issue of the late Albert Jerrold Heathcote, b. 1887, d. 1964: m. 1st, 1914 (m. diss. 19—, Dorothy Twycross; 2ndly, 1945, Mrs. Muriel Korsten, who d. 1961, and has issue:—
(By 1st m.) William Jerrold, b. 1915: m. 1959, Johanna Hofmeyr.——John Albert (32, Benroy St., Flamewood, Klerksdorp, Transvaal), b. 1916; formerly Sergt., Union Defence Force, S, Africa: m. 1944, Mrs. Rosemary Hilda Beresford Carter, da. of Oswald Beresford Lonsdale. and has issue living, Charles John Beresford, b. 1948,—Phyllis May Beresford, b. 1945,—Rosemary Alice Beresford, b. 1953.——George Twycross (Stutterheim, E. Cape, S. Africa), b. 1918: m. 1943, Elizabeth Mary Allport, and has issue living, Michael John, b. 1954,—Dorothy Ann, b. 1955.

Grandchildren of the late William Lovell Heathcote (ante):—
Issue of the late Henry Heathcote (youngest son), b. 18—, d. 1893: m. 18—, Lætitia Murray [she m. 2ndly, 19—, the Rev. F. Stewart]:—
Henry Gage, b. 1877.——Clifford, b. 18—.——Mary, b. 18—: m. 18—, Clem Will.——Alice Eleanor, b. 1886: m. 1905, Arthur James Ford, Div. Sec. Boy Scouts' Asso., and has issue living, John Lovell Heathcote, b. 1906—Frank Stewart Heathcote, b. 1915,—Arthur Dymond Heathcote, b. 1920,—Muriel, b. 1908,—Evelyn (twin), b. 1908.——Ine, b. 18—. Residence,

Grandchildren of the late Lieut. George Gage Heathcote, R.N., son of the late Adm. Sir Henry Heathcote (ante):—
Issue of the late Gage Charles Heathcote, b. 1842, d. 1895: m. 1879, Hermina Aletta Fourie, da. of A. Van Wych:—
Edward Munro, b. 1882.——Aletta Caterina, b. 1879: m. 1898, Gerhadus Jacobus Van de Nerve ——Emily, b. 1887: m. 1902, Ernest Alfred Hornby.——Hermina Aletta, b. 1889: m. 1905, William George August. Residence,

Granddaughters of Lt. George Gage Heathcote, RN (ante).
Issue of the late William Heathcote, b. 1884, d. 1961: m. 19—, Helena Cathrina Faure (PO Box 37, Keetmanshoop, SW Africa):—
William Charles (Box 439, Keetmanshoop, SW Africa), b. 1929: m. 19—, Connie Danie van Neikerk, and has issue living, William, b. 1958,—Conrad, b. 1960,—Raymond, b. 1963.—— Maria Wilhelmina, b. 1919: m. 19—, Norman Charles Venables, of Lushington Park, PO Kidds Beach, East London, S. Africa, and has issue living, Keith Norman, b. 1942,—Peter Kevin, b. 1956,—Bernadette, b. 1945.——Thora, b. 1922: m. 19—, William Herbert van Schoor (PO Box 2013, Johannesburg, S. Africa), and has issue living, Denise Thora, b. 1944: m. 1965, Alva Felix Walter Oldknow, of 39, The Willows, 4th Av., Florida, Transvaal,—Marlene Diedré, b. 1948: m. 1969, Lukas Matthee Auó.——Maureen Cathrine b. 1937: m. 1961, Petrus Jacobus Alwyn van der Merwe (P.O. Box 315, Mossel Bay, Cape, S. Africa), and has issue living, Petrus b. 1962, Rudolph b. 1965, Marina b. 1966.

Granddaughters of the late Gage Charles Heathcote (ante):—
Issue of the late Thomas Munro Heathcote, b. 1848, d. 1890: m. 1879, Augusta Euphine, dau. of the late E. Philipps:—
Emma Katherine, b. 1882.——Marian, b. 1885. Residence,

Granddaughter of the late Rev. Gilbert Heathcote, son of the late Capt. Gilbert Heathcote, 5th son of 3rd baronet :—
Issue of the late Frederick Arthur Heathcote, b. 1851, d. 1925: m. 1887, Evelyn Constance, who d. 1938, da. of the late Frederick Elin, of Hazlemount, Ryde, Isle of Wight :—
Gertrude Evelyn Atherley, b. 1893: m. 1920, Richard Picton Rosser, M.B., Ch.B., and has issue living, John Gilbert Heathcote, b. 1922,—Charles, b. 1929. Residence,

Granddaughters of the late Thomas Jenkyns Heathcote, el. son of the late Rev. Thomas Heathcote, son of the late Samuel Heathcote, 4th son of the 2nd baronet:—
Issue of the late Rev. Wyndham Selfe Heathcote, b. 1862; d. 19—: m. 1888, Agnes, who d. 1934, da. of the Rev. James Macdonall:—
Catherine Moultrie Maud (of Los Angeles, U.S.A.), b. 1891: m. 19—.
Issue of the late George Wadham Bruce Heathcote, O.B.E., b. 1868, d. 1944: m. 1895, Mary, da. of Mark Bate:—
Grace Mary, b. 1896: m. 1923, Thomas B. Randall.

Granddaughter of the late John Cuthbert Heathcote, son of the late Rev. Samuel John Heathcote, 2nd son of the late Rev. Thomas Heathcote (ante):—
Issue of the late Lt.-Col. John Robert Campbell Heathcote, b. 1879; d. 1947: m. 1st, 1898, Margaret McClellan, from whom he obtained a divorce 1920; 2ndly, 1920, Mary Gertrude, da. of the late Oscar Brandt:—
(By 1st marriage) Evelyn Marie, b. 1899.

The 1st baronet, Sir William, M.P. for Southampton and Buckingham, married Elizabeth, only daughter of the 1st Earl of Macclesfield (Lord Chancellor), to whose peerages Sir William's heir is in remainder. The 3rd baronet was M.P. for Hampshire; the 4th baronet, also M.P. (C) for Hants, assumed the additional surname of Freeman. The 5th baronet, the Rt. Hon. Sir William, P.C., D.C.L., sat as M.P. for Hampshire (C) 1826-32, for N. Hampshire 1837-49, and for Oxford University 1854-68. The 9th baronet, the Rt. Rev. Sir Francis, D.D., was Bishop of New Westminster, British Columbia, 1941-50.

HENNIKER HEATON, Creation (U.K.) 1912, of Mundarrah Towers, Sydney, Australia.

There is light in letters.

Sir Yvo Robert Henniker Heaton, 4th *Baronet; b.* April 24th, 1954; *s.* his father, Wing-Cdr. *Sir* (John Victor) Peregrine, 1971.

Arms—Argent on a bend sable three bulls, heads couped of the first, over all on an escutcheon of pretence, quarterly of six; 1st, vert, three escutcheons argent, each charged with a bordure engrailed or, *Burrell;* 2nd, argent, three battering rams fesseways in pale proper headed and garnished azure, *Bertie;* 3rd, or, fretty azure, *Willoughby;* 4th, vert, three eagles displayed fesseways or, *Owen Gwynedd;* 5th, gyronny of eight or and sable, *Campbell;* 6th, per pale sable and gules, on a cross between four fleurs-de-lys argent, five pheons azure, *Banks.* **Crest**—Out of a crest coronet gules, a bull's head argent.

Residence—14, Woodville Rd., Ealing, W.5.

Sister living—Priscilla Margaret, *b.* 1949.

Half Sisters living—Jacqueline, *b.* 1931: *m.* 1959, Michael Ferris, and has issue living, Rory, *b.* 1959,—Michaela, *b.* 1961.——Anthea Jennifer, *b.* 1934.

Uncles living (sons of 2nd baronet)—Peter Joseph, *b.* May 9th, 1907; ed. at Wellington Coll., and at Corpus Christi Coll., Oxford (MA 1925); Admiralty 1930-38 (Private Sec. to Parl. Sec. 1936); on Editorial Staff of *Punch* 1949-52, and of *The Christian Science Monitor* 1952-63, since when Editorial Consultant to The Christian Science Board of Dirs.: *m.* 1934, Rose Maddock, only da. of the late Amyas Morse, of P. W. D., India. *Residence*, 100, Memorial Drive, Cambridge, Mass., USA.——Clement Algernon Charles, *CBE, b.* 1909; ed. at Wellington Coll.; late Maj. TA (Reserve), FIL; Dir. of Cotton Spinners' Fedn.; UK Employers' Delegate to ILO 1969, and a Companion of Textile Institute 1970 (Pres. 1973); 1939-45 War with 14th/20th Hussars; CBE (Civil) 1965: *m.* 1940, Marjorie, da. of W. E. Speight, of Bournemouth, and has issue living, John Lindsey, *b.* 1946; ed. at Wellington, and Emmanuel Coll., Camb.,—Charles Peter, *b.* 1956,—Hilary Rose, *b.* 1948. *Residence,* Southdene, Goring-on-Thames, Reading, Berks. *Club,* Travellers'.

Widow living of 3rd Baronet—Margaret Patricia (*Lady Henniker Heaton*) (14, Woodville Rd., Ealing, W5), da. of the late Lt. Percy Wright, Canadian Mounted Rifles: *m.* 1948, as his 2nd wife Wing-Cdr. Sir (John Victor) Peregrine Henniker Heaton, 3rd Bt., who *d.* 1971.

Collateral Branches living.

Issue of the late Sir Herbert Henniker Heaton, K.C.M.G., 3rd son of 1st baronet, *b.* 1880, *d.* 1961 : *m.* 1st, 1909, Susan Angèle Phœbe, who *d.* 1922, da. of the late Lindsey Talbot-Crosbie, of Ardfert Abbey, Ardfert, co. Kerry ; 2ndly, 1926, (Helena) Iris, who *d.* 1927, da. of the late Sir Henry Edward McCallum, G.C.M.G. ; 3rdly, 1947, Gladys Meta, who *d.* 1962, da. of the late Col. Claud Francis, and widow of Col. George Going, S. Staffordshire Regt.:—
(By 1st m.) Dermot Wynne, *b.* 1922: *m.* 1956, Joan Townsend, and has issue living, Colin Edward Richard, *b.* 1956,—Keith Patrick, *b.* 1962.——(By 2nd m.) Christopher Robin (Oak Cottage, Watermill Lane, Bexhill on Sea, Sussex), *b.* 1927; late Nigerian Civil Ser.: *m.* 1st, 1952 (m. diss. 1967), Elizabeth, da. of H. Curtis, MD, of Bermuda; 2ndly, 1967, Estelle Patricia, da. of Samuel John Newing, of Cheshunt, Herts., and has issue living, (by 1st m.) Elizabeth, *b.* 1954.——(By 1st m.) Rose Phoebe Anne, *b.* 1914: *m.* 1945, Maj. Norman Keith Czameron, Coldm. Gds., and has issue living, Alastair, *b.* 1951,—Donald, *b.* 1953,—Jane, *b.* 1950,—Susan, *b.* 1956. *Residence,* Port San Carlos, Falkland Islands.——Priscilla Moira, *b.* 1916: *m.* 1940, Walter Theodore Ballantyne, and has issue living, Prisckla Sarah Anne, *b.* 1943. *Residence,*

Issue of the late Capt. Arthur Henniker Heaton, RN, 4th son of 1st baronet, *b.* 1883, *d.* 1965: *m.* 1913, Vera Isabel, who *d.* 1965, da. of the late Hamilton Atherley:—
Michael Hamilton Henniker, *b.* 1914: 1939-45 War as Maj. R. Signals: *m.* 1st, 1937; 2ndly, 1956, Brenda (Miller), da. of Morrison Davies; 3rdly, 1957, Elizabeth Catherine, FLA, da. of Maurice Budgett.——Robin John Henniker, *b.* 1915; formerly Assist. Treasurer, Sarawak; 1939-45 War as Paymaster-Lt.-Cdr. RNVR (despatches): *m.* 1st, 1951, Sylvia Elizabeth, da. of Julian Charles Grumbar, MBE; 2ndly, 1958 Barbara, da. of William Newman Ayers, and has issue living, (by 2nd marriage) Anthony, *b.* (Nov.) 1958,—Sally, *b.* 1961.

The 1st baronet, Sir John Henniker Heaton, introduced a motion in House of Commons (1886) for Universal Ocean Penny Postage, and was instrumental in carrying a large number of postal reforms, and especially in reducing Postal Rates to India and Australia 1890, and Penny Postage to America 1908; carried Imperial Postage Resolution 1898, and sat as MP for Canterbury (C) 1885 to 1910. The 2nd baronet, Sir John, assumed the surname of Henniker Heaton.

Henderson-Stewart, see Stewart.

HENNIKER, Creation (U.K.) 1813, of Newton Hall, Essex.

Sir MARK CHANDOS AUBERON HENNIKER, *C.B.E., D.S.O., M.C.,* 8th *Baronet*, son of the late Frederick Chandos Henniker, great-grandson of 1st baronet ; *b.* Jan. 23rd, 1906 ; *s.* his cousin, Lieut.-Col. *Sir* ROBERT JOHN ALDBOROUGH, *M.C.,* 1958 ; ed. at Marlborough, and at King's Coll., Camb.; Brig. (ret.) late RE; Hon. Col. REME 1964-68; a DL of Gwent; Mohmand Operations 1933 (MC), 1939-45 War in France, N. Africa, Sicily, and Italy (wounded, OBE, DSO), Malaya 1952-54 (despatches, CBE), Suez 1956 (despatches); OBE (Mil.) 1944, DSO 1945, CBE (Mil.) 1953: *m.* 1945, Kathleen Denys, da. of the late John Anderson, of Pilgrim's Way, Farnham, Surrey, and has issue.

Arms—Or, on a chevron gules between two crescents in chief, and in base an escallop azure, three estoiles argent.   **Crest**—An escallop or, charged with an estoile gules.

God is the greatest support.   **Residence**—Pistyll, Began Road, St. Mellons, Monmouthshire. **Club**—United Service and Royal Aero.

MAJOR COLUMNA

DEUS

Son living—ADRIAN CHANDOS (49, Woodvale Av., Cyncoed, Cardiff), *b.* Oct. 18th, 1946; ed. at Marlborough: *m.* 1971, Ann, da. of Stuart Britton, of Malvern House, Fairwater Rd., Llandaff, Cardiff.

Daughter living—Fiona Jane, *b.* 1951.

Sister living—Alison Margaret, *b.* 1909.   *Residence*, 117, Thoroughfare, Woodbridge, Suffolk.

Daughter living of 7th Baronet—Ann Margaret, *b.* 1915 : *m.* 1946, John Holroyd Bairstow. Flying Officer, RAFVR, who *d.* 1968, and has issue living, Janet Margaret, *b.* 1948,—Susan Mary, *b.* 1951.   *Residence*, 18, Savile Park, Halifax, Yorkshire.

Daughters living of 6th Baronet—Beryl Inger HENNIKER-HUGHAN, *b.* 1904. *Residence,* Airds, Parton, Kirkcudbrightshire.——Rhona Mary HENNIKER-HUGHAN, *b.* 1906: *m.* 1936, Wing-Com. Francis Lenox Ingall, Roy. Auxiliary Air Force [Crawley-Boevey, Bt., colls.], and has issue living, Simon Henniker (119, Oakwood Court, W14) *b.* 1939: *m.* 1971, Anne Mary Amelia Gillespie, and has issue living, James Peter Henniker *b.* 1972,—Michael Lenox, *b.* 1941,— Sarah Anne, *b.* 1946: *m.* 1968, Lindsay Claud Neils Bury, of Millichope Hall, Munslow, Craven Arms, Salop, and has issue living, Frank Simon *b.* 1970, Harriet Mary *b.* 1972.   *Residence*, Corsock House, Castle Douglas, Kirkcudbrightshire.——Alison Frances HENNIKER-HUGHAN (4/77, The Drive, Hove, Sussex), *b.* 1910: *m.* 1936, John Gladstone, who obtained a divorce 1947 [E. Shrewsbury, colls.].

Collateral Branch living.

Grandson of the late Rev. Robert Henniker, 3rd son of the late Aldeborough Brydges John Henniker, 3rd son of 1st baronet :—
Issue of the late Col. Alan Major Henniker, C.B.E., R.E., *b.* 1870, *d.* 1949: *m.* 1902, Blanche Marie, who *d.* 1961, da. of the late James Gadsden, of Lannion, Brittany:—
Richard Frederick, *b.* 1906; ed. at Camb. Univ. (MA); a FRIBA; 1939-45 War as Maj. RE: *m.* 1938, Daphne Irene, da. of the late Capt. C. J. Maxwell. *Residence*, Haddon Fields, Membury, Axminster, Devon.

Grandchildren of the late Aldborough Henniker, Q.C., el. son of Aldeborough Brydges John Henniker (ante):—
Issue of the late Mary Constance Henniker, *b.* 18—, *d.* 1952: *m.* 1st, 1888, William George Vallancey Wetherall, who *d.* 1903; 2ndly, 1916, Walter Forder, who *d.* 1927:—
(By 1st marriage) Aldborough Thomas Vallancey (of 10, Branksome Dene Rd., Bournemouth W.), *b.* 1888: *m.* 1918, Ada, el. da. of Alfred David Beynon, and has issue living, Peter de Valence (of Mount Grace Cottage, Mount Grace Drive, Lilliput, Poole, Dorset; United University Club), *b.* 1921; ed. at Canford Sch., and at Corpus Christi Coll., Camb. (LL.B., M.A.); Solicitor 1953; Sqdn.-Ldr. R.A.F. Vol. Reserve; Burma and Malaya 1943-45 (despatches, 1939-45 star, Burma star, Defence medal): *m.* 1951, Christine Margaret, da. of Archibald Sutcliffe Knight, and has issue living, Michael Richard Brydges *b.* 1953, Colin Peter *b.* 1958,—Pamela de Valence (444, Christchurch Rd., Bournemouth), *b.* 1923: *m.* 1943 (m. diss. 1951), Thomas Henry Vernon Haydon,—Rosemary de Valence (Idelwynd, 106, Canford Cliffs Rd., Poole, Dorset), *b.* 1926. ——Kathleen Ada Violet (The Grove, Bridgham, Norwich, NOR 16X), *b.* 1898; has Civil Defence medal; adopted the additional surname of Henniker by deed poll 1964.

Grandson of the late Mary Constance Wetherall (ante):—
Issue of the late Cyril George Trecothic Wetherall, *b.* 1890, *d.* 1957: *m.* 1914, Vera Constance (Heather Dene, The Street, Carlton Colville, Lowestoft), da. of Samuel John Dawson:—
Dennis Selwyn (15, Y Rhos., Cardigan), *b.* 1921: *m.* 1947, Gwendoline, da. of the late William Street, and has issue living, Susan Anne, *b.* 1951.

The Hon. Sir Brydges Trecothick Henniker, 1st baronet, was youngest son of 1st Baron Henniker, he sat as M.P. for Kildare in the last Irish Parliament, the 4th baronet was Private Sec. to Local Govt. Board 1877-80, and Registrar-Gen. of Births, Deaths, and Marriages 1880-1900. The 6th baronet, Adm. Sir Arthur John Henniker-Hughan, C.B., assumed the additional surname of Hughan 1896, and served during European War 1914-16 with Grand Fleet (1914-15 star); was Adm. Sup-Devonport Dockyard 1916-19, and sat as M.P. for Galloway (U) 1924-5. The 7th baronet, Lieut.-Col. Sir Robert John Aldborough Henniker, M.C., served in European War 1914-18 (M.C.), and in European War 1940-45.

HENRY, Creation (U.K.) 1918, of Campden House Court. [Extinct 1931.]
Sir EDWARD RICHARD HENRY, *G.C.V.O., K.C.B., C.S.I.,* 1st and last *Baronet*.
Daughter living of 1st Baronet—Margaret Hermione (of Baily Cottage, Winkfield Rd., Ascot, Berks), *b.* 1902.

HENRY Creation (U.K.) 1923, of Cahore, co. Londonderry.
Sir JAMES HOLMES HENRY, *C.M.G., M.C., T.D.,* 2nd *Baronet; b.* Sept. 22nd, 1911; *s.* his father, the *Rt. Hon. Sir* DENIS STANISLAUS, 1925; ed. at Mount St. Mary's Coll., Chesterfield, at Downside Sch., and at Univ. Coll.,

London (B.A.); Bar. Inner Temple 1934; appointed Crown Counsel, Tanganyika 1946, Legal Draftsman 1949, Solicitor-Gen. 1952, and Attorney-Gen. Cyprus 1956, QC, Tanganyika 1953, and Cyprus 1957; a Member of Foreign Compensation Commn. since 1960; 1939-45 War in Middle East and Italy as Capt. London Irish Rifles (R. Ulster Rifles) (wounded, MC); CMG 1960: *m.* 1st, 1941, Susan Mary (from whom he obtained a divorce 1948), da. of Arthur G. Blackwell; 2ndly, 1949, Christina Hilary, da. of Sir Hugh Oliver Holmes, KBE, CMG, MC, QC, and widow of Lt.-Cdr. Christopher Hayward Wells, RN [*see* Wells, Bt., *cr.* 1944, colls.], and has issue by 2nd m.

Residence, Kandy Lodge, 18, Ormond Av., Hampton-on-Thames, Middlesex. *Clubs,* —Travellers', Royal Commonwealth Society.

Daughters living—By 2nd marriage—Teresa Violet, *b.* (Nov.) 1949.——Christina Mary, *b.* 1951. ——Rosemary Jane, *b.* 1955.

Brother living—DENIS VALENTINE (of 9, White Rd., Blackburn, Lancs.), *b.* June 29th, 1917; ed. at Shrewsbury, and at Clare Coll., Camb. (B.A. honours 1939, M.A. 1944); formerly Lieut. Roy. Ulster Rifles: *m.* 1956, Elizabeth, da. of Rowland Walker, and has issue living, Patrick Denis, *b.* 1957,—Jessica Ellen, *b.* 1960,—Martha Olive, *b.* 1961.

Sisters living—Denise Olive, *MB, BS, MRCS, LRCP* (7, Morley Rd., Farnham, Surrey).——Alice Ellen, *BSc: m.* 1946, Alan Newton, of 15, Sweetwater Close, Shamley Green, Surrey.——Lorna Mary (7, Morley Rd., Farnham, Surrey).

The 1st baronet, the Rt. Hon. Sir Denis Stanislaus Henry, LL.D., sat as M.P. for S. Div. of Londonderry co. (*Co.U*) 1916-21, and was Solicitor-Gen. for Ireland 1918-19, Attorney-Gen. 1919-21, and Lord Ch. Justice of N. Ireland 1921-5.

BUCHAN-HEPBURN, Creation (U.K.) 1815, of Smeaton-Hepburn, Haddingtonshire.

[Pronounced "**Bukkan-Hebburn.**"]

DOMUM · ANTIQUAM · REDINTEGRARE

To restore an ancient house.

Sir NINIAN BUCHAN ARCHIBALD BUCHAN-HEPBURN, 6th *Baronet*; *b.* Oct. 8th, 1922; *s.* his father, *Sir* JOHN KARSLAKE THOMAS 1961; Burma 1943-5 with Queen's Own Cameron Highlanders: *m.* 1958, Bridget, el. da. of the late Sir Louis (Leisler) Greig, K.B.E., C.V.O.

Arms—Quarterly: 1st and 4th, gules, on a chevron argent a rose between two lions rampant of the first, *Hepburn*; 2nd, argent, three lions, heads erased gules, *Buchan*; 3rd, argent an anchor in bend azure, on a chief of the last three cranes or, *Beck.* **Crests**—1st, a horse argent, furnished gules, tied to a yew tree proper, over it the motto "Keep traist"; 2nd, the sun in the dexter chief with a sunflower in full blow open to it proper, over it the motto "Non inferiora secutus" (*Not having followed mean pursuits*). **Supporters**—*Dexter*, a lion, gules; *sinister*, a heron with an eel in its beak proper.

Residence—Logan, Port Logan, Wigtownshire. *Club*—Puffins (Edinburgh).

Sister living—Primrose Eda, *b.* 1917; European War 1939-45 in First Aid Nursing Yeo.: *m.* 1949, Major Ulick Edmund Burke Roche, S. Wales Borderers [*see* B. Fermoy, colls.]. *Residence,* Ynysfor, Penrhyndeudraeth, Merionethshire.

Collateral Branch living

Grandchildren of the late Capt. John Buchan-Hepburn, el. son of John Buchan of Clune, co. Fife, 2nd son of 2nd Bt:—

Issue of the late John Trant Buchan-Hepburn, *b.* 1890, *d.* 1953: *m.* 1927, Edith Margaret (MITCHELL) (now of Chagford, St. Andrews, Fife). da. of William Robb:—

JOHN ALISTAIR TRANT KIDD, *b.* June 27th, 1931; ed. at Charterhouse; Capt. (ret.) late 1st King's Dragoon Guards; was ADC to Gen. Officer Comdg. Malaya 1956-7: *m.* 1957, Georgina Elizabeth, only da. of the late Oswald Morris Turner, and has issue living, John Christopher Alastair, *b.* 1963,—Caroline Georgina, *b.* 1958,—Sarah Elizabeth, *b.* 1960,—Louise Mary, *b.* 1966. *Residence,* Chagford, St. Andrew's, Fife.——Elizabeth Joyce Agnes, *b.* 1933; ed. at St. Leonard's Sch., St. Andrew's, and at St. Andrews Univ. (MB and BCh 1956): *m.* 1957, James Archibald Scott, MVO, of 38, Queen's Cres., Edinburgh, 9, and has issue living, Thomas James Buchan, *b.* 1962,—Robert Alastair Howie, *b.* 1964,—Hector Michael Hepburn, *b.* 1969,—Rachel Elizabeth Frances, *b.* 1960.

This family descends from the Buchans, lairds of Auchmacoy, Aberdeenshire, who claim descent from the Celtic Mormaers and Earls of Buchan. The 13th laird was recognised in 1792 as Chief of the name of Buchan. The lands of Alexander were erected into a barony 1598. His 2nd son, George, was ancestor of John Buchan of Letham, East Lothian, whose 1st wife, Elizabeth (*d.* 1742) was sister and heir of George Hepburn of Smeaton Hepburn, East Lothian. Their son and heir George in 1764 *s.* his maternal uncle as heir of line of Hepburn of Smeaton-Hepburn and to that barony, and was recognized in the name and arms of Buchan-Hepburn. He was Advocate 1763, Judge of Admiralty Court 1790-1 and Baron of the Exchequer, Scotland 1800-14. On retirement he was *cr.* a Baronet in 1815.

The Hepburns of Smeaton-Hepburn descended from Adam 3rd son of Patrick Hepburn of Waughton to whom his father granted these lands in 1538. The Hepburns of Waughton descended from Sir Patrick of Waughton, uncle of Sir Patrick Hepburn of Hailes, who was *cr.* Lord Hailes 1452/3. The 2nd Lord Hailes was in 1482 *cr.* Earl of Bothwell, but both dignities were forfeited 1567 on attainder of James 4th Earl (and 1st Duke of Orkney), 3rd husband of Mary, Queen of Scots. He *d.* without legitimate issue 1578.

Herne (Buckworth-Herne-Soame), see Soame.

Heron (Heron-Maxwell), see Maxwell.

HERSCHEL, Creation U.K.) 1838. [Extinct 1950.]

Rev. Sir JOHN CHARLES WILLIAM HERSCHEL, 3rd and last *Baronet.*

Collateral Branch living.
Issue of the late Arthur Edward Hardcastle Herschel, 2nd son of 2nd baronet, *b.* 1873, *d.* 1924 : *m.* 1904, Ellen Katharine, who *d.* 1926, only da. of the late Lieut.-Col. A. S. Macartney (formerly R.A.), of Torrington :—
Eileen Dorothea, *b.* 1905: *m.* 1934, Christopher William Shorland, Malayan Civil Ser. (ret.) and has issue living, John Herschel HERSCHEL-SHORLAND (5, Vicarage Rd., Lillington, Leamington Spa), *b.* 1935; assumed by deed poll 1966, the additional surname of Herschel: *m.* 1959, Christian Esther Flowerdew Nicholls, and has issue living, William Paul *b.* 1966, Amanda Jane Herschel *b.* 1961, Catherine Anne Herschel *b.* 1962,—Caroline Claire, *b.* 1939: *m.* 1972, Anthony Rushbrooke,—Prudence Mary, *b.* 1942. *Residence,* Meadens, Warfield, nr. Bracknell, Berks.—Caroline Winifred, *b.* 1906. *Residence,* Brooklyn, Warfield, nr. Bracknell, Berks.

Hervey-Bathurst, see Bathurst.

HEWETT, Creation (U.K.) 1813, of Nether Seale, Leicestershire.

Seek nothing beyond your sphere.

Sir JOHN GEORGE HEWETT, *M.C.,* 5th *Baronet; b.* Oct. 23rd, 1895 ; *s.* his father, *Sir* HARALD GEORGE, 1949; ed. at Cheltenham ; British East Africa during European War **1914-18** as Capt. King's African Rifles : *m.* 1926, Yuilleen Maude, da. of the late Samuel Frederick Smithson, of Lauriston, Camberley, Surrey, and has issue.
Arms—Gules, on a chevron embattled argent, between three owls of the second, each crowned with an eastern coronet or, as many bombs fired proper. Crest—Out of a mural crown or, the stump of an oak-tree with branches, thereon a hawk proper gorged with an eastern coronet, belled gold. Supporters—Dexter, a tiger proper gorged with an eastern crown or ; sinister, a buffalo charged on the shoulder with a trefoil slipped, all proper.

Residence—Ol'Morogi, Naivasha, Kenya.

Sons living—PETER JOHN SMITHSON, *M.M.,* *b.* June 27th, 1931; ed. at Bradfield Coll., and at Jesus Coll., Camb. (B.A. 1953); Bar. Gray's Inn 1954: *m.* 1958, Jennifer Ann Cooper, da. of E. T. Jones, of Nairobi, Kenya, and has issue living, Richard Mark John, *b.* 1958,—David Patrick John, *b.* 1968,—Joanna Yuilleen, *b.* 1960. *Address,* P.O. Box 34, Nairobi, Kenya.——Richard Harald, *b.* 1933; ed. at Gordonstoun: *m.* 1959, Bridget Elizabeth Anne, only da. of the late Alistair John Kirkman Finlay, and has issue living, Anthony John Finlay, *b.* 1962,—Julia Caroline, *b.* 1960. *Address,* Box 6591, Nairobi, Kenya.

Sister living—Margaret, *b.* 1894: *m.* 1923, Joshua Rupert Ingham Brooke, M.B.E., who *d.* 1934, and has issue living, John Ingham, *b.* 1924 : *m.* 1954, Pauline Durling,—David William Ingham (Strangers Place, Brightwell, Wallingford, Oxon), *b.* 1932; late Lt. RN: *m.* 1957, Isabel, da. of Nicholas Cheshire, of Clacks Cottage, Ballinger, Great Missenden, Bucks. [see V. Addison], and has issue living, Luke *b.* 1958, Joshua *b.* 1962,—Anne Theodosia Margaret, *b.* 1925: *m.* 1948, Gordon Minard, of Vancouver, British Columbia, and has issue living, a son *b.* 19—, a son *b.* 19—, a da. *b.* 19—. *Residence,* Ashampstead, nr. Reading.

Collateral Branches living.
Issue of the late George Nele Hewett, yst. son of 4th baronet, *b.* 1901, *d.* 1972: *m.* 1931, Margaret Skaife (Vitré, Coldash, Newbury), da. of G. T. Denis de Vitré:—
Denis Nele, *b.* 1932; Lt. RN (ret.).——Jeremy Patrick Nele (2770, Seaview, Victoria, BC), *b.* 1935: *m.* 1963, Norma Shirley Garnett Smith, and has issue living, Geoffrey Alexander, *b.* 1966,—Harald Randall Marsh, *b.* 1969,—Kari Denise, *b.* 1964.

Grandchildren of the late Capt. Charles William Hewett, RN, 2nd son of the late Frank William Hewett (infra):—
Issue of the late Brig. William George Hewett, OBE, MC, *b.* 1894, *d.* 1973: *m.* 1st, 1922 (m. diss. 1931), Louise Susan, da. of the late Francis R. Wolfe; 2ndly, 1932, Beatrice, who *d.* 1961, da. of the late Lt.-Col. James Francis Donegan, CB:—
(By 1st m.) Richard William (The Croft, Almshouse, Common, Haslemere, Surrey), *b.* 1923; Maj. RA (ret.); Malaya 1953 (despatches): *m.* 1954, Rosemary, yr. da. of Basil Cridland, MC, TD, of Fernhurst, Sussex, and has issue living, Vanessa Annabel, *b.* 1957,—Virginia Carolyn Rose, *b.* 1960.——(by 2nd m.) Sarah Margaret Arianwen, *b.* 1942.

Issue of the late Capt. George Stuart Hewett, C.B.E., Roy. Indian Navy, *b.* 1863, *d.* 1937 : *m.* 1899, Maude Mary Brind, who *d.* 1958, da. of Surg.-Gen. Henry Kendall, formerly Army Med. Depart. :—
George Kendall Shuckburgh (29, Anne St., Devonport, Auckland, 9, NZ), *b.* 1904; ed. at Haileybury; Lt.-Col. (ret.) RASC.——Neale Brind Stuart (4, Hazard St., Russell, Bay of Islands, NZ), *b.* 1906; Cdr. (ret.) Roy. Indian Navy Reserve ; a JP of NZ: *m.* 1930, Thecla Edana, yst. da. of A. J. David, and has issue living, Neale John Patrick, BEM (PO Box 208, Manurewa, NZ), *b.* 1931; ed. at Ampleforth; Kenya 1953 (BEM) *m.* 1960, Felicity Ann. da. of the late B. H.

Kerby, and has issue living, Matthew Patrick George b. 1969, Merri Bernard Neale, b. 1961, Felicity Sheena b. 1963, Anita Noreen b. 1967,—George Andrew Kendall (4, Gladys Av., Glenfield 10, Auckland, NZ), b. 1942: m. 1967, Sharon Rose, yst. da. of W. Souster, of Takapuna, Auckland, NZ, and has issue living, Jason Conrad Neale b. 1969, Brind Nicholas Andrew b. 1974, —Jeanne Marie Thecla, b. 1933: m. 1955, Alan Dever, of Glenbrook Station, c/o Putorino PO, Hawkes Bay, NZ, and has issue living, Neale Alan Kendall b. 1958, Alan Guy b. 1961, Wendy Janet Thecla b. 1956, Penelope Jeanne b. 1959, Catherine Adelaide b. 1967.

Gen. the Right Hon Sir George, GCB, the 1st baronet, Col. 61st Regt., and C.-in-C. of the Forces in India, and in Ireland. The 2nd baronet, a Col. in the Army, was a distinguished Officer n Peninsular War.

HEWITT, Creation (U.K.) 1921, of Barnsley, West Riding, co. Yorkshire.

Always the same.

Sir NICHOLAS CHARLES JOSEPH HEWITT, 3rd *Baronet*; *b.* Nov. 12th, 1947; *s.* his father *Maj. Sir* JOSEPH, 1973: *m.* 1969, Pamela Margaret, only da. of Geoffrey J. M. Hunt, TD, of Broadacres, Scalby, Scarborough, and has issue.

Arms—Sable, a chevron in chief three owls or.   **Crest**— Upon the battlements of a tower argent an owl proper.

Residence,—The Forge, Hutton Bushel, Scarborough.

Sons living—CHARLES EDWARD JAMES, b. Nov. 15th, 1970. ——Michael Joseph, b. 1973.
Brother living—Timothy George, b. 1950.
Sister living—Elizabeth Margaret, b. 1945.
Daughter living of 1st Baronet—Kathleen, b. 1896: m. 1921, Hugh Parry Smith, formerly Maj. 1st/5th York and Lancaster Regt., who d. 1956, and has issue living, Kathleen Parry, b. 1922,—Elizabeth Josephine Parry, b. 1925. *Residence,* Gristhorpe Hall, Filey, Yorks.
Widow living of 2nd Baronet—MARGUERITE (*Marguerite, Lady Hewitt*) (Lebberston Hall, nr. Scarborough), da. of Charles Burgess, of Deepdene, Filey: m. 1940, Maj. Sir Joseph Hewitt, 2nd Bt., who d. 1973.

HEYGATE, Creation (U.K.) 1831, of Southend, Essex.
[Name pronounced "Haygate."]

Boulogne et Cadiz.
Boulogne and Cadiz.

Seat—Bellarena, Londonderry.

Sir JOHN EDWARD NOURSE HEYGATE, 4th *Baronet*, son of the late Arthur Conolly Gage Heygate, 3rd son of 2nd baronet; *b.* April 19th, 1903; *s.* his uncle, *Sir* FREDERICK GAGE, 1940; ed. at Eton, and at Balliol Coll., Oxford (BA); a retired Writer; 1939-45 War as Bombardier RA: *m.* 1st, 1930, the Hon. Evelyn Florence Margaret Winifred WAUGH (who obtained a divorce 1936), da. of 1st and last Baron Burghclere; 2ndly, 1936, Gwyneth Eliot (who obtained a divorce 1947), da. of the late John Eliot Howard Lloyd; 3rdly, 1951, Dora Luz, who *d.* 1968, da. of the late John Harvey, of Malin Hall, co. Donegal, and has issue by 2nd m.

Arms—Gules, two bars argent, on a bend or, a torteau between **two** leopards' faces azure.   **Crest**—A wolf's head erased gules.

Sons living—By 2nd marriage—GEORGE LLOYD, b. Oct. 28th, 1936; ed. at Repton (Scholar) and at Trin. Coll., Camb.: m. 1960, Hildegard Mathilde, da. of August Anton Kleinjohann, ——Richard Gage, b. 1940; ed. at Repton, and at Balliol Coll., Oxford: m. 1968, Carol Rosemary, da. of Cdr. Richard Michell, of Leith House, Amberley, Sussex.

Collateral Branches living.

Grandchildren of the late Major William Howley Beaumont Heygate, son of the late William Unwin Heygate, 2nd son of 1st baronet :—
Issue of the late Lieut.-Col. Gerald Heygate, D.S.O., R.F.A., b. 1882, d. 1954 : m. 1916, Cynthia, who d. 1963, da. of C. Darley, of Thorne:—
Katherine Raymonde Anne (c/o National Westminster Bank, 185, Sloane St., SW1), b. 1917: m. 1940, Capt. John Bayley Middleton Horner, Irish Guards, from whom she obtained a divorce 1953, and has issue living, Sarah Elizabeth Raymonde Anne, n. 1942: m. 1962, Virgil Pomfret of 25, Sispara Gdns., SW18, and has issue living, Virgil Alexander b. 1966, Emma Louise b. 1965.

——Felicity Cynthia June, *b.* 1926: *m.* 1950, Lt.-Cdr. Charles Owen, DSC, RN (ret.) (28, Hyde Park Gdns., W2 2NB), and has issue living, Rupert Charles, *b.* 1956,—Caroline Angela, *b.* 1954.

Issue of the late Maj. Lionel Clement Heygate, *b.* 1893, *d.* 1947: *m.* 1st, 1918, Janet Leigh, who *d.* 1923, only da. of the late Richard Jeston Ogle, of Christchurch, NZ; 2ndly, 1935 (m. diss. 1943), Yvonne Sylvia (Eze, Grove Rd., Mandeville, Jamaica), da. of the late W. F. Tyler:—
(By 1st m.) Diana Juliet Beaumont, *b.* 1920: *m.* 1946, Lt.-Col. John Francis Rush, RASC, of The Boundary House, Northiam, Rye, Sussex, and has issue living, Charles Burlison OGLE-RUSH *b.* 1947; ed. at Uppingham; assumed by deed poll 1968 the surname of Ogle-Rush,—Diana Louise, *b.* 1949: *m.* 19——.——(By 2nd m.) Marilyn Jennifer, *b.* 1938: *m.* 1966, John Brigg Charles Fountaine, of Moor Farm, Great Bircham, King's Lynn, and has issue living, Alexandra Juliet Catherine, *b.* 1973.

Grandchildren of the late Major Edward Nicholas Heygate, 3rd son of 1st baronet :—
Issue of the late Capt. Richard Lionel Heygate, *b.* 1859, *d.* 1926 : *m.* 1895, Eleanor Mary Gwenllian, who *d.* 1958, da. of the late Edward James Evans :—
Mary Ursula, *b.* 1896: *m.* 1930, Capt. Eustace King-King, formerly Queen's R. Regt., who *d.* 1975, and has issue living, Edward Michael, *b.* 1931; ed. at Stowe. *Residence*, Deerfold House, Lingen, Bucknell, Salop.——Gladys Henrietta, *b.* 1898: *m.* 1st, 1924, Major Brereton Rigby, who *d.* 1931; 2ndly, 1934, Richard Thomas, and has issue living, (by 1st marriage) Richard Arthur, *b.* 1926: *m.* 1950, Margaret Stocker, and has issue living, Janice Anita *b.* 1951, Yvonne Linda *b.* 1953,—Walter Oswald, *b.* 1931,—(by 2nd marriage) Harold Mostwyn, *b.* 1936: *m.* 1960, Kathleen Ada Hughes, and has issue living, Elizabeth Mary *b.* 1960. *Residence*, Buckland, Leominster.

Issue of the late Walter Beaumont Heygate, *b.* 1861, *d.* 1940 : *m.* 1902, Edith Maud, who *d.* 1947, da. of Stephen Robinson, of Lynhales, Kington, Herefordshire:—
Edward Stephen, M.C., *b.* 1906 ; ed. at Wellington Coll. ; Lieut.-Col. (retired) Roy. W. Kent Regt. ; Palestine 1938 (despatches), European War 1939-45 in N. Africa and Italy (M.C.) : *m.* 1st, 1939, Margaret Moss, of London, who *d.* 1961; 2ndly, 1962, Joyce Marian Gerrard, of Broadstairs, Kent. *Residence*, Tuck Mill, Eaton Bishop, Hereford.

The 1st baronet was Lord Mayor of London 1822, City Chamberlain 1843-4, and M.P. for Sudbury in two Parliaments. Thomas Heygate, of Hayes, was Provost Marshal General under the Earl of Essex at the capture of Cadiz ; his father held the same position in the Army, and was present before St. Quintin ; he was afterwards Provost Marshal in Scotland. Nicholas Heygate, the celebrated collector of curious books and writings, was of this family. Sir Frederick, 2nd baronet, was M.P. for co. Londonderry (C) 1859-74, and the 3rd baronet, Sir Frederick Gage, was Parliamentary Under Sec. to Lord-Lieut. of Ireland 1887-8.

HEYWOOD, Creation (U.K.) 1838, of Claremont, Lancashire.

Sir OLIVER KERR HEYWOOD, 5th *Baronet*, son of the late Maj.-Gen. Cecil Percival Heywood, C.B., C.M.G., D.S.O., 3rd son of 3rd baronet ; *b.* June 30th, 1920 ; *s.* his uncle, *Lieut.-Col. Sir* (GRAHAM) PERCIVAL, *C.B.*, *D.S.O.*, *T.D.*, 1946 ; ed. at Eton, and at Trin. Coll., Camb. (B.A. 1940) ; European War 1940-45 as Capt. Coldstream Guards (despatches): *m.* 1947, Denise (KENWORTHY), yr. da. of the late Jocelyn William Godefroi, MVO, and has issue.

Arms—Argent, three torteaux in bend between two bendlets gules ; on a canton of the last a cross-patée or. **Crest**—On a mount vert the trunk of a tree with two branches sprouting therefrom and entwined with ivy thereon a falcon wings displayed all proper.

Residence—Viner's Wood, Wickstreet, Stroud, Gloucestershire.

Altè volo.
I fly high.

Sons living—PETER (23, Moor Lane, Bunny, Notts.), *b.* Dec. 10th, 1947: *m.* 1970, Jacqueline Anne, da. of Robert Frederick Hunt, CBE, of Greenacre, Charlton Park Gate, Cheltenham.——Michael (twin) (Viner's Wood, Wickstreet, Stroud, Glos.), *b.* 1947: *m.* 1972, Carolyn Awdry Greig.——James Philip, *b.* 1951.
Sister living—Joan Margaret, *b.* 1919: *m.* 1950, John Marsden Preston, and has issue living, Nicolas, *b.* 1952. *Residence*, Wetherby Cottage, Wetherby Place, SW7.
Aunt living (daughter of 3rd baronet)—Isabel Effie. *Residence*, Moor Gate, Brookhouse, Lancaster.

Collateral Branches living.

Issue of the late Lieut.-Col. Gerald Graham Percival Heywood, T.D., youngest son of 2nd baronet, *b.* 1867, *d.* 1954 : *m.* 1898, Mary, who *d.* 1948, da. of the late Ven. the Hon. Berkeley Lionel Scudamore-Stanhope [E. Chesterfield, colls.] :—
Graham Scudamore Percival, *b.* 1903 ; ed. at Winchester, and at New Coll., Oxford (B.A. 1925, B.Sc. 1926, M.A. 1934) ; formerly Director of Roy. Observatory, Hong Kong : *m.* 1937, Valerie, da. of Lieut.-Col. Railton Wyatt, of Locks Heath, Hampshire, and has issue living, Susan Mary, *b.* 1938: *m.* 1961, John Michael Knight, of 1, Waldens Park Rd., Horsell, Woking, and has issue living, Timothy John *b.* 1963, Nicola Susan *b.* 1962, Deborah Ann *b.* 1965, Bridget Julia *b.* 1970,—Veronica Anne, *b.* 1942. *Residence*, Critchells, Lockerley, Hants.

Grandchildren of the late Rev. Henry Robinson Heywood (infra):—
Issue of the late Henry Arthur Heywood, *b.* 1859, *d.* 1943: *m.* 1899, Katharine Louisa, who *d.* 1937, da. of the late Rev. Ernest Alured Waller [Waller, Bt., *cr.* 1814, colls.]:—
Geoffrey Henry, CBE (14, Alexandra Court, 171, Queens Gate, SW7 5HG), *b.* 1903; ed. at Repton; FRICS; Pres. of R. Inst. of Chartered Surveyors 1962-63; Chm. Skelmersdale Development Corpn. 1969-75, and Pres. Manchester Rent Assessment Panel 1965-74; CBE (Civil) 1972: *m.* 1931, Magdeleine Jeanne Georgette Marie, yr. da. of the late Jean Herpin, of Paris, and has issue living, Claude Geoffrey (RRI, Orangeville, Ont., Canada), *b.* 1933; ed. at Repton, and at Gonville and Caius Coll., Camb. (BA); late Lt. RA; HM Overseas Civil Ser., Kenya 1957-62: *m.* 1960, Anne Helen Wilding-Davies, and has issue living, James Claude *b.* 1962, Peter Geoffrey *b.* 1965, Sarah Anne *b.* 1963,—Claire Margaret, *b.* 1938: *m.* 1st, 1961, Mark Hugh Learoyd Piercy (from whom she obtained a divorce 1968); 2ndly 1973, Alexander Campbell Newton

Ferguson, of Bernisdale, Hook Heath, Woking, Surrey, and has issue living (by 1st m.), Giles Hugh Scott b. 1966, Emma Magdeleine b. 1963.——Rev. Charles Richard (5, Stoney Furlong Rd., Baslow, Bakewell, Derbys.), b. 1908; ed. at Repton, and at Gonville and Caius Coll., Camb. (MA): m. 1939, Alice Ruth, da. of Dr. W. Henry Dobie, of Chester, and has issue living, Richard Henry Norman, b. 1946: m. 1971, Melody Dawn, el. da. of Col. J. A. H. Nicholson, of Knoll House, Bamford, Sheffield,—Margaret Anne, b. 1950.

Issue of the late Charles Christopher Heywood, M.B., M.R.C.S., M.R.C.P., b. 1865, d. 1948; m. 1893, Mildred Ella, who d. 1957, el. da. of the late Capt. Percy Reid Lempriere, R.A. :—
Very Rev. Hugh Christopher Lempriere (Ashleigh, 31, Church St., Southwell, Notts.), b. 1896; ed. at Haileybury, and at Trin. Coll., Camb. (MA); formerly Capt. Indian Army; 1914-18 War (wounded, despatches); was Fellow and Dean of Gonville and Caius Coll., Camb. 1928-45; appointed an Examining Chap. to Bishop of Southwark 1932, and to Bishop of Southwell 1942, and Provost of Southwell 1945-69: m. 1920, Margaret Marion, da. of the late Herbert Vizard, of Whitepost House, Redhill, and has issue living, Peter (Ashleigh, Southwell, Notts.) b. 1922; ed. at Haileybury, and at Gonville and Caius Coll., Camb. (MA); formerly Capt. Oxford and Bucks LI; Headmaster of William Sharp Comprehensive Sch., Nottingham since 1968,—Ann Rosemary, b. 1930: m. 1954, Thomas Strachan James, of The Mill House, Linton, Cambridge, and has issue living, Christopher William b. 1955, Timothy Robert b. 1956, Pamela Susan b. 1961.——Basil Lempriere, b. 1903; ed. at Haileybury; late Sgt. RAF Regt.: m. 1930, Phyllis Miriam, da. of the late John Orchard, Bar.-at-Law, an Inspector Min. of Health, of Haigh Moor, Topsham, Exeter, and has issue living, John Basil Sumner, b. 1933; CEng., MIEE,—Christopher Richard (Silverdene, 42, Wood Ride, Haywards Heath, Sussex) b. 1949: m. 1971, Susan Rosa, da. of Thomas William Howarth, of Anworth, The Drive, Lymm, Cheshire, and has issue living, Nicola Jane b. 1974,—Diana Ruth, b. 1937: m. 1963, Michael John Evans, of Rozel, 3, Old Smithy Lane, Lymm, Ches., and has issue living, Andrew Michael b. 1964, Christopher Philip b. 1966, Jennifer Lesley b. 1968. Residence, Clavis, Hillside Drive, Woolton, Liverpool, L25 5NS.—— Ella Marjorie Lempriere, b. 1906; France 1939-40 with Queen Alexandra's Imperial Mil. Nursing Ser.——Mildred Ursula Lempriere, b. 1909; formerly Petty Officer WRNS. Residence, Rozel, 18, Orchard Green, Alderley Edge, Ches.

Grandsons of the late Charles Christopher Heywood, M.B., M.R.C.S., M.R.C.P. (ante) :—
Issue of the late Alan Lempriere Heywood, b. 1899, d. 1960 : m. 1925, Constance (of Franklyn, Old Sticklepath Hill, Barnstaple, N. Devon), da. of Mrs. Frederick Swales, of Simla :—
Denys Guy Lempriere (c/o Williams Glyn's Bank, London Rd., Alderley Edge, Cheshire), b. 1926; ed. at Denstone and Caius Coll., Camb.; Gp. Capt. RAF; commanded No. 94 (F.) Sqdn., and No. 617 Sqdn. (Dambusters): m. 1957, Elizabeth Ann, da. of the late J. Jeffrey Baker, of Windyridge, Altwood Rd., Maidenhead, and has issue living, Robin Guy, b. 1958,—Simon John, b. 1966,—Annabel Jane, b. 1961,—Carol Elisabeth, b. 1962.——Adrian Christopher Lempriere (c/o Mansfield & Co. Ltd., Phoenix Building, 11, Palmer Rd., Singapore, 2), b. 1928; ed. at Denstone, and at Selwyn Coll., Camb. (MA); formerly 2nd Lt. RA: m. 1962, Patricia Mollie Gardner, da. of Guy Goulden, of 16, Grange Rd., Eastbourne, and has issue living, Christopher Lempriere, b. 1962,—Guy Lempriere, b. 1965.

Grandchildren of the late Rev. Henry Robinson Heywood, 5th son of 1st baronet:—
Issue of the late Rt. Rev. Bernard Oliver Francis Heywood, D.D., formerly Lord Bishop of Ely, b. 1871, d. 1960 : m. 1895, Marion Maude, who d. 1957, 2nd da. of the late Capt. Percy Reid Lempriere :—
Michael Henry Lempriere, b. 1900; ed. at Haileybury: m. 1941, Marjorie, da. of C. B. Wood, of High Green, Sheffield, and has issue living, Charles Michael Lempriere (14, North End, Osmotherley, Northallerton DL6 3BB, N. Yorks.), b. 1942: m. 1963, Robina Anne Pattison, and has issue living, Benjamin Michael Lempriere b. 1971,—Peter Bernard Martin, b. 1946,—David Mark, b. 1947,—Margaret Adamson, b. 1944. Residence, The Hollies, Barningham, Richmond, Yorks, —Oliver Martin, b. 1904; ed. at Haileybury, and at Selwyn Coll., Camb.: m. 1946, Eileen Maud Liebert, and has issue living, Timothy David Lempriere, b. 1948; ed. at Haileybury; F/O RAF: m. 1972, Kathleen Ellen, da. of J. L. Waldman, of Caracas, and has issue living, Benjamin Michael b. 1973,—Jonathan Martin (twin) b. 1948; ed. at Haileybury. Residence, Orchard Lea, Bishton Lane, Tutshill, Chepstow.——Charles Bernard Mark, b. 1906; ed. at Haileybury, and at Emmanuel Coll., Camb. (MA); late Capt. Oxford and Bucks LI: m. 1941, Julia Veronica, da. of the late John Denis Cronin. Residence, 16 Argyll Mansions, Hammersmith Rd., W14.—— Francis Melville (The Old Bakery, Catcott, Bridgwater, Som.), b. 1908; ed. at Haileybury, and at Gonville and Caius Coll., Camb. (MA); an Assist. Master at Haileybury 1931-35; Fellow of Trinity Hall, Camb. 1935-39; Master of Marlborough Coll. 1939-52, and Warden of Lord Mayor Treloar Coll., Froyle, Hants 1952-69; m. 1937, Dorothea Kathleen, da. of Sir Basil Edgar Mayhew, KBE, and has issue living, Simon Paget (37, Innston St., Oxford), b. 1945; ed. at Marlborough, New Coll., Oxford (BA, DPhil.), and Harvard Univ. (Kennedy Memorial Scholar 1967): m. 1967 (m. diss. 1972), Sheila Madeleine, only da. of Sir Frank Stannard Gibbs, KBE, CMG,—Susan Frances, b. 1939: m. 1965, Jean Marc Duquesne, of Atp. 1, Residence de Rosendal, Dieppe 76, France, and has issue living, Marc Dominic b. 1966, Benjamin Piers b. 1969, Sebastian Paul b. 1972,—Janion Lempriere b. 1947: BSc London; MB, BS, MRCS, LRCP: m. 1972, Robert John LeQuesne, MB, BS, MRCS, LRCP, of Copse Close, Baughurst, Tadley, Basingstoke, Hants.——Percival Meredith, LRAM, b. 1912; ed. at Haileybury, at King's Coll., and at Trin. Hall, Camb. (MA); Assist. Master Leys Sch. 1937-45; Musical Dir., Rydal Sch., Colwyn Bay.——Maude Lempriere, b. 1897: m. 1923, the Rev. Herbert Bowman, who d. 1930, V. of St. Mark's, Leeds, and Hon. Chap. to Forces, and has issue living, Iris Margaret Lempriere, b. 1924; ed. at Edinburgh Univ. (MB and ChB 1947): m. 1951, Michael Atkinson, MD, FRCP, of 121, Lambley Lane, Burton Joyce, Nottingham, and has issue living, Gillian Lempriere b. 1953, Catherine Veryan b. 1955, Judith Margaret (twin) b. 1955, Alison Clare b. 1962. Residence— 3, Buckingham Drive, Leeds 6.——Ella Marion (Cotchett, Burycroft Rd., Hook Norton, Banbury, Oxon.), b. 1898: m. 1923, the Rev. Canon Thomas Arnold Lee, who d. 1973, and has issue living, John Richard Crispin (64, William St., Richmond, Nelson, NZ), b. 1933; ed. at Durham Sch., and Emmanuel Coll., Camb. (MA); formerly Sub-Lt. RNVR; formerly Supt., Guelph Corrective Center, Ont.; is with Nelson Dept. of Social Sers.: m. 1960, Elizabeth Mary, da. of Arthur Pring Farmer, MB, BS, and has issue living, Benjamin Mark b. 1962, Crispin Oliver b. 1963, Philippa Claire b. 1967,—Ruth Patricia Heywood, b. 1924; BSc London 1946: m. 1949, Michael Bridgman, BSc, ANZIC, of 9, Rutherford Terr., Auckland 5, NZ, and has issue living, David Nicholas b. 1957, Jane Tamsin Lee b. 1953,—Tamsin Margaret Romanis, b. 1926; MB and BCh St. Andrew's 1948, DCH 1951: m. 1959, Lt.-Col. Adrian Goodenough Hayter, MBE, MC, of Takaka, by Nelson, NZ, and has issue living Sarah Ann b. 1960, Rebecca Margaret b. 1963, —Frances Mary Cotchett, b. 1927; BSc London 1948; a Counsellor (Commercial) NZ High Commn., Haymarket, SW1.

The 1st baronet, an eminent banker of Manchester, led the Reform Agitation in Lancashire, and sat as M.P. for that county in the Parliament preceding the passing of the Reform Bill of 1832. His youngest brother, James Heywood, F.R.S., who d. 1897, sat as M.P. for North Lancashire (L) in the Parliaments of 1847 and 1852. The 2nd baronet was High Sheriff of Lancashire 1851. The 3rd baronet was High Sheriff of Derbyshire 1899. The 4th baronet, Lieut.-Col. Sir (Graham) Percival, C.B., D.S.O., T.D., T.A. (retired), served in European War 1914-18 (D.S.O.).

HICKMAN, Creation (U.K.) 1903, of Wightwick, Tettenhall, Staffordshire.

By fire and sword.

IGNE ET FERRO.

Sir(ALFRED) HOWARD WHITBY HICKMAN, 3rd *Baronet*; *b.* Jan. 29th, 1920; *s.* his father, *Major Sir* ALFRED EDWARD, 1947; *ed.* at Eton : *m.* 1948, Margaret D. (THATCHER), only da. of Leonard Kempson, of Potters Bar, Middlesex, and has issue.

Arms—Party per saltire sable and or, two leopards' faces iessent-de-lis in pale and as many fleur-de-lis in fesse, all counterchanged. Crest—A phœnix issuing out of flames, transfixed through the mouth by a tilting-spear palewise proper, each wing charged with two annulets erect and interlaced or.
Residence—Shenley Cottage, Radlett, Herts.

Son living—RICHARD GLENN, *b.* April 12th, 1949.
Brother living—Patrick Nelson (5, The Vale, Chelsea, SW3; Hale Park, Fordingbridge, Hants.; St. James' Club), *b.* 1921; F/L RAFVR (ret.); a Freeman of City of London, and a Liveryman of Fishmongers' Co.: *m.* 1st, 1944 (m. diss. 1950), Mary Lena, da. of Capt. J. A. D. Perrins; 2ndly, 1953, Gail, da. of Col. C. R. St. Aubyn, of Paris, France, and has issue living, (by 1st m.) Patrick Rupert, *b.* 1945,—Rozanna Mariette, *b.* 1946,—(by 2nd m.) Patrick Sloan, *b.* 1955, Vivien Anne, *b.* 1957.
Widow living of 2nd Baronet—NANCY BERYL (*Beryl, Lady Hickman*), da. of Capt. Trevor George Morse-Evans: *m.* 1940, as his second wife, Sir Alfred Edward Hickman, 2nd baronet, who *d.* 1947. *Residence*, Charringworth Court, Winchcombe, Gloucestershire.

Collateral Branches living.

Granddaughters of the late Alfred William Hickman, el. son of 1st baronet :—
Issue of the late Lieut.-Col. Arthur Hickman, *b.* 1891, *d.* 1959 ; *m.* 1914, Dorothy Gwendolen, R.R.C., who *d.* 1957, da. of the late Edward Charles Rudge, J.P., D.L., of Abbey Manor, Evesham :—
Christine Gwen, *T.D.*, *b.* 1920 ; is Major W.R.A.C. (T.A. Reserve).——Pamela Jill, *b.* 1921; formerly Subaltern A.T.S. *Residence*, 308A, Barkham Rd., Wokingham, Berks.

Grandchildren of the late Brig.-Gen. Thomas Edgecombe Hickman, C.B., D.S.O. (infra) :—
Issue of the late Capt. Thomas Alfred Kenneth Hickman, *b.* 1912 ; *d.* (killed in action during European War) 1940 : *m.* 1936, Leila Philippa (who *m.* 2ndly, 1945, Major Eric Inman Scott, MC, of Iron Cross Fram, Byfield, Daventry), el. da. of Lt.-Col. Montagu Martindale Parry-Jones, MC, Roy. Fusiliers [Borrowes, Bt.]:—
Thomas (of Iron Cross, Byfield, nr. Daventry), *b.* 1940; *ed.* at Eton; Capt. The Life Gds.: *m.* 1967, Lieselotte Brawdstetter, of Vienna, and has issue living, Thomas Michael, *b.* 1927—Lucinda Ann, *b.* 1970.——Mary Elizabeth, *b.* 1937: *m.* 1962, Timothy Haworth, of The Dower House, Chastleton, Moreton-in-Marsh, Glos.

Issue of the late Brig.-Gen. Thomas Edgecombe Hickman, C.B., D.S.O., 4th son of 1st baronet, *b.* 1859, *d.* 1930 : *m.* 1907, Elizabeth Maud Mackenzie, who *d.* 1960, da. of the late Surg.-Major James Alexander Smith, D.S.O. :—
Michael, *b.* 1922 ; *ed.* at Eton ; late Lieut. 11th Hussars : *m.* 1st, 1944 (divorce 1947) Vivienne Loraine, da. of Lieut.-Col. M. I. Clutterbuck, of Windmill House, Rowington, Warwickshire ; 2ndly, 1951, Phyllis, da. of W. R. Robinson. *Address*, George Hotel, Hatherleigh, S. Devon.
——Elizabeth Anne, *b.* 1915 : *m.* 1939, Patrick George Grey, and has issue living, Diana Patricia, *b.* 1940. *Residence*, Coole Abbey, Clonmel, co. Tipperary.

Grandchildren of the late Edward Hickman (infra):—
Issue of the late Maj. Charles Edward Hickman, *b.* 1890, *d.* 1963: *m.* 1st, 1915, Edith Barbara, who *d.* 1915, da. of the late Frank Spencer, J.P., of Egerton, Harrow-on-the-Hill; 2ndly, 1921, Dorothy, who *d.* 1966, da. of the late W. Deans Forster, of Pontland, Newcastle-upon-Tyne:—
(By 2nd marriage) David Michael Roy (Ackleton Manor, Ackleton, Wolverhampton), *b.* 1930: *m.* 1959, Eileen Elizabeth, yr. da. of the late Brian Robert Boyd, of Belfast, and has issue living, Charles John, *b.* 1960,—Timothy Robert, *b.* 1964,—Peter Richard (twin), *b.* 1964.——Catherine Elaine, *b.* 1926: *m.* 1st, 1949, Giles Reid Walker, who *d.* 1951 [see Walker-Okeover, Bt., colls.]; 2ndly, 1955, Patrick Campbell Hall, of Champ de Brent, 1861, Auliens, Vaud, Switzerland, and has issue living, (by 1st m.) [see Walker-Okeover, Bt., colls.] (by 2nd m.) Andrew Campbell, *b.* 1957.
Issue of the late Wilfred Haden Hickman, *b.* 1892, *d.* 1973: *m.* 1915, Kathleen Mary Stuart (Queens Holm, Pittville Circus Drive, Westbourne Drive, Cheltenham, Glos.), da. of Edward Noel Mason MD, of Nuneaton:—
Wilfred Ian Edward (Clifton Manor, Clifton upon Dunsmore, Rugby), *b.* 1916; JP for Warwicks.: *m.* 1940, Muriel Claire, da. of the late William Horsnall, of Nuneaton, Warwicks.——Denis Stewart, *MC* (The Royal Victoria Hotel, Nassau, Bahamas), *b.* 1918; late Capt. RASC; 1939-45 War in Italy (MC, 1939-41 Africa and Italy stars, prisoner): *m.* 1st, 1947 (m. diss. 1964) Peggy Barbara (McALPINE), da. of the late John Ernest Saunders, of Gresford; 2ndly, 1965, Jean, da. of A. Urwin, of Tynemouth, and has issue living, (by 2nd m.) Tara Jane, *b.* 1966,—Rona Stuart, *b.* 1967,—Anya Lucy, *b.* 1969.——Christopher Wolf Arden (Home Farm, Guiting Power, Cheltenham), *b.* 1925; 1939-45 War with RASC: *m.* 1949, Daphne Esther, da. of John Alec Clift, and has issue living, Rachel, *b.* 1951,—Rosemary, *b.* 1953,—Gillian, *b.* 1955,—Joanna, *b.* 1964.——Jocelyn Cecilia, *b.* 1919; SRN: *m.* 1946, Brian Newton Shawe-Taylor, of The Old Forge, Brockhampton, nr. Andoversford, Glos., and has issue living, Richard Arland, *b.* 1951,—John Stewart, *b.* 1953,—Desmond Philip, *b.* 1955.——Rona Kathleen, *b.* 1921; 1939-45 War with WRNS: *m.* 1943, Reginald Alfred Reardon Smith, of Green Farm Cottage, Farmborough, nr. Bath, and has issue living, Christopher John Henry, (Cabramatta, Sydney, NSW) *b.* 1946: *m.* 1967 Frances Barnes, and has issue living, Marcia Paula *b.* 1967, Jeremy William, *b.* 1949,—Anthea Kathleen, *b.* 1944,—Janice Caroline, *b.* 1953.

Issue of the late Edward Hickman, 5th son of 1st baronet, *b.* 1860, *d.* 1941: *m.* 1887, Cecilia, who *d.* 1958, el. da. of the late Col. Thompson, J.P., of Milton Hall, Carlisle :—
Lucy, *MBE*, *b.* 1889; is a JP for Staffs.; MBE (Civil) 1939. *Residence*, Leckie Hse., Pattingham, nr. Wolverhampton.——Amy Cecilia, *b.* 1894. *Residence*, Brabourne, Codsall, nr. Wolverhampton.

Grandchildren of the late Victor Emanuel Hickman (infra):—
Issue of the late Cdr. Geoffrey Victor Hickman, DSC, RN, b. 1890, d. 1975: m. 1st, 1914,
Josephine Helen, who d. 1933, da. of Lt.-Col. Walter Reginald Fox, formerly RA; 2ndly,
Gwendoline Dorothy Miell (South View, Leigh, nr. Tonbridge, Kent):—
(By 1st m.) Hugh Geoffrey, b. 1916; 1939-45 War as Lt. S. Staffs. Regt.——Geraldyne Rosemary
Margaret, b. 1917: m. 1946, Richard Wiltshire, of 4, Claverdon Close, Solihull, and has issue
living, Hugh Richard, b. 1947: m. 1970, Barbara Gwenyth Price.

Issue of the late Victor Emanuel Hickman, 6th son of 1st baronet, b. 1863, d.
1935: m. 1889, Ethel Margaret, who d. 1969, da. of the late Edward Brown
Fitton, of Fair Lea, Great Malvern:—
Margaret Hilda May, b. 1894: m. 1917, Lt.-Col. Richard Dalrymple Lauder, formerly Roy. Scots,
who d. 1961, and has issue living, Philip Dalrymple Scott (The Glebe House, Halstock, Yeovil,
Som.), b. 1918; Col. late 11th Hussars: m. 1941, Frances Tertia Elliot, da. of the late Sydney
Paterson, of Bournemouth, and has issue living, Desmond Frank Michael Scott b. 1947, Gillian
Roberta Scott b. 1942: m. 1966, Maj. Charles John Radford, 16th/5th Queen's R. Lancers, (and
has issue living, Toby Rupert John b. 1967, Charlotte b. 1971), Brigid Philippa Scott b. 1944:
m. 1964, Francis Henry Tindal, who d. 1971, (and has issue living, Marcus Francis b. 1969),
Joanna Margaret Scott b. 1954,—Margot Ethel Ramsay (33, Melrose Rd., West Hill, SW18),
b. 1921; sometime Junior Com. ATS: m. 1951, George Holmes, JP, who d. 1973, and has issue
living, James Philip Scott b. 1954, Andrea Margaret b. 1958. Residence, Hill Paddock, Sevenoaks, Kent.

Issue of the late John Owen Hickman, 7th son of 1st baronet, b. 1870, d. 1949:
m. 1903, Nancy Viola, who d. 1963, da. of Harry Barlow:—
Michael Ranulf, b. 1922 ; ed. at Wellington Coll., and at Trin. Hall, Camb. ; Bar. Middle Temple
1949; formerly F/L RAFVR; appointed a Circuit Court Judge 1974: m. 1943, Diana, da. of
Col. D. C. H. Richardson, 10th Hussars, and has issue living, Peter Derek, b. 1951: m. 1974,
Hilary Clare, da. of Don Sadler, of Gwelo, Rhodesia,—Susan Marilyn, b. 1948: m. 1972, Aris
Alexander Pierre Zarpanely, of, 37, Mall Rd., Hammersmith W6. Residence, Acorn Cottage,
Bovingdon, Herts.——Vera Charlotte Nancy, b. 1908.——Audrey Violet Elsie, b. 1912: m. 19—,
Geoffrey May.——Angela Mary, b. 1924: m. 1st, 1943, Charles Gordon Richards, who d. (killed
in action during 1939-45 War) 1943; 2ndly, 1948, William Freshwater, and has issue living, (by
2nd marriage) Michael David Latimer, b. 1950,—Martin Walter James, b. 1958,—Jane Elizabeth
Mary, b. 1948,—Christine Ellen Nancy, b. 1962. Residence, Chaiya, Ball Hill, Newbury, Berks.

Grandchildren of the late John Owen Hickman (ante):—
Issue of the late John Barlow Hickman, b. 1904, d. 1932: m. 1925, Joan (14, Shepherd's
Way, Cirencester, Glos.), da. of the late Kyrle Chatfield Hankinson, of Eden Mount,
Tunbridge Wells:—
John Kyrle (3, Weltje Rd., W6), b. 1927; ed. at Tonbridge, and at Trin. Hall, Camb. (BA), Diplo.
Ser.: m. 1956, Jennifer, da. of Reginald Kendall Love, and has issue living, Matthew
John Kyrle, b. 1964,—Andrew Giles Lovell, b. 1966,—Catherine Lucy, b. 1960.——
Richard Malim (The Malt Shovel, Vigo, Burcot, Bromsgrove, Worcs.), b. 1930; ed. at Ton-
bridge, and at Pembroke Coll., Camb. (BA); m. 1962, Judy Penelope Sylvia, da. of Brig. Charles
Douglas Armstrong, CBE, DSO, MC, and has issue living, Marcus Sebastian Charles, b. 1963,——
Jonathan Edward Barlow, b. 1964.——Dinah, b. 1929: m. 1953, John Frederick Saunders, and
has issue living, Richard Neville, b. 1955,—Joanna Elizabeth, b. 1958. Residence, Aldermoor
Farm, Advent, nr. Camelford, Cornwall.

The 1st baronet, Sir Alfred Hickman, Chm. of Alfred Hickman (Limited), sat as M.P. for
Wolverhampton (C) 1885-6, and 1892-1906.

HILL, Creation (I.) 1779, of Brook Hall, Londonderry.

Sir (George) Cyril Row-
ley Hill, 8th Baronet b. Dec. 18th,
1890 ; s. his father, Sir George
Rowley, 1954 ; ed. at Wellington
Coll.: m. 1919, Edith Muriel, da.
of W. O. Thomas, of Oakhurst,
Liverpool, and Bryn Glas, Mold,
N. Wales.

Arms—Sable, a chevron erminois be
tween three leopards' faces argent. Crest—
A talbot's head couped sable, guttés d'eau,
collared gules, studded and ringed or.

Residence—2, Dawlish Drive, Leigh-
on-Sea.

Net tentes aut perfice.
Attempt not, or accomplish.

Collateral Branches living.
Issue of the late Alfred Rowley
Hill, brother of 7th baronet, b.
1868, d. 1946 : m. 1893, Jean,
who d. 1943, da. of T. Cunningham :—

GEORGE ALFRED ROWLEY, b. Oct.
11th, 1899 ; ed. at Melville Coll., Edinburgh ; formerly Lieut. Bengal Nagpur
Railway Batn. Auxiliary Force (India) ;
N. Russia 1919, European War 1940-44
as Lieut. R.N.V.R.: m. 1st, 1924
(marriage dissolved 1938), Rose Ethel
Kathleen, M.B.E., da. of the late William Spratt ; 2ndly, 1938, ——, and has issue living, (by 1st
marriage) Richard George Rowley, b. 1925 ; ed. at Clayesmore Sch., and at Glasgow Univ. ; is
Capt. KOSB: m. 1954, Angela Mary, who d. 1974, only da. of Lieut.-Col. Stanley Herbert Gallon,
of Berwick-on-Tweed,—(by 2nd marriage) Joh Rowley, b. 1940,—Margaret Ann, b. 1942.
Residence, 5, Cranley Gardens, SW7.

Granddaughters of Rowley John Hill (infra):—
Issue of the late Leslie Thomas Hill, b. 1897, d. 1958: m. 1920, Irene Howlett:—
Joan Maria b. 1925: m. 1945, Leslie Bailey, and has issue living, Kenneth Leslie, b. 1946,—Cheryl
Larraine, b. 1948.——Dorothy Irene, b. 1928: m. 1947, Herbert Alfred Morley, and has issue
living, Christopher John, b .1950,—Carol Anne, b. 1948. Residence,

Grandchildren of Marcus Hill, el. son of Capt. Rowley John Hill, 2nd son of the
Rev. John Beresford Hill, 2nd son of 1st baronet:—
Issue of the late Rowley John Hill, b. 1873, d. 1960: m. 1896, Anne Elizabeth Morrow,
who d. 1912:—
Claude Adam James (3, Robinson St., Sunshine, Vic., Aust.), b. 1901: m. 1928, Ruby Alice Mallett,
and has issue living, Allan Claude (72, Tyquin St., Laverton, Vic., Aust.), b. 1936: m. 1970,
Rachel St. Just,—Joyce Patricia, b. 1933: m. 1951, Geoffrey Paul, of 8, Lancaster Rd., Moorool-
bark, Vic., Aust., and has issue living, Allan Geoffrey b. 1952, Cheryl Therese b. 1955.——Marcus
George (46, Armstrong St., Sunshine, Victoria, Aust.), b. 1904: m. 1929, Lydia May Liddle, and
has issue living, George Frederick, b. 1930: m. 1951, Jean Craggel, and has issue living, Anthony
Rowland b. 1961, Debra b. 1964, Sallyanne b. 1966,—Kevin Leslie (49, Fraser St., Sunshine, Vic.,
Aust.), b. 1935: m. 1959, Wendy Chandler, and has issue living, Mark b. 1961, Paul b. 1963,—
Patricia Miriam, b. 1932: m. 1954, Rolf Ludvisken, of 26, Poole St., Deer Park, Vic., Aust., and
has issue living, John b. 1955, Leanne b. 1960,—Dawn Anne, b. 1939: m. 1963, John Justin, of
7, Bellair Av., Glenroy, Vic., Aust., and has issue living, Kenneth 1964, Darren b. 1966, Glen
b. 1971,—Lorraine Margaret, b. 1941: m. 1963, Frank Kelynack, of 1, Laming Rd., Deer Park,
Vic., Aust., and has issue living, Janine b. 1969.——Cyril Edward (Unit 16/2, Highfield Rd.,
Canterbury 3126, Vic., Aust.), b. 1908: m. 1939, Mary Elizabeth Tinker, and has issue living,
James Rowland Edward (Lot 7, 9, Arnold St., Kilsyth, Mel., Vic., Aust.), b. 1943: m. 1969,
Lynette Jean Berry, and has issue living, Jason James b. 1972, Christophe Eric b. 1974,—Janice
Ann, b. 1940: m. 1962, Ronald Arthur Haynes, of 39, Sandy St., Nunawading, Vic. 3131, Aust.,
and has issue living, Diane Mary b. 1964, Michelle Lucy b. 1966, Joanne Lisa b. 1969, Belinda
Jane b. 1975,—Elizabeth Dianna, b. 1945: m. 1967, Constantine Politis, and has issue living,
Andrew Edward b. 1973, Jeanette Ann b. 1969, Debra Lee b. 1971.——Albert John, b. 1912:
m. 1935, Annie Melba, da. of Edgar William Johnstone.——Vera Maria, b. 1902: m. 1st, 1926,
Tim Burke, who d. 1957; 2ndly, 1957, Francis Hill.

Issue of the late James Henry Sale Hill, b. 1885, d. 1954: m. 1910, Phyllis Ethel Wood-
bury, of Albury, NSW, who d. 1967:—
Roy Ernest (72, Canterbury Rd., Ringwood, Vic., Aust.), b. 19—: m. 19—, Phyllis Allen, of
Paxton St., Ringwood.——James Herbert (Rau St., Albury, NSW), b. 19—: m. 19—, Charlotte
Ethel Bastion.——Olive May, b. 19— : m. 19—, Allan Klinberg (16, Elm St., Wodonga, Vic.,
Aust., NSW).

Issue of the late Philip Ernest Hill, b. 1887, d. 1960: m. 1913, Hilda Maria Ambrosina
Cooper, who d. 1966:—
Clem Ernest, b. 1913.——Stanley George (27, Summerhill Av., E. Malvern, Vict., Aust.), b. 1935:
m. 1964, Patricia Ann McLellan, and has issue living, Philip William Adrian, b. 1966,—Paul
Timothy, b. 1968.——Philis May, b. 1917: m. 1938, George Lewis Robinson, of 49, Hardy Av.,
Wagga Wagga, NSW, and has issue living, Helen, b. 1940: m. 1960,   ,—Shirley, b.
1942: m. 1962   ,—Dawn, b. 1950,—Maree, b. 1956.——Thelma Rose, b. 19—: m.
19—, Ronald Charles Wheeler, and has issue living, Garry, b. 19—,—Robert, b. 19—,—Janet,
b. 19—.

Grandchildren of the late Marcus Henry Sale Hill (infra):—
Issue of the late Wilfred Henry Hill, b. 1906, d. 1972 : m. 1936, Thelma Mattingly (31A
Meridian St., Port Chalmers, Otago, NZ):—
Robert Maxwell, b. 1938.——Lesley Robin Gael, b. 1949: m. 1966, Gavan McEntee, and has issue
living, Gavan Chayne, b. 1966,—Brett Owen, b. 1968,—Stephen Robert, b. 1969.——Dawn
Adeline, b. 1937: m. 1963, Raymond Wilkins, and has issue living Lionel David, b. 1964,—
Deborah Margery, b. 1967,—Dionne Beryl, b. 1970.

Grandchildren of the late George Henry Hill, 3rd son of Capt. Rowley John
Hill (ante):—
Issue of the late Marcus Henry Sale Hill, b. 1870, d. 1946 : m. 1903, Emma Frances,
da. of Henry Kenton, of Lower Harbour, Port Chalmers, New Zealand :—
Henry George (Coreys Bay, Port Chalmers, Otago, NZ), b. 1909: m. 1944, Eileen Webb, of Dunedin,
and has issue living, Harold, b. 19—,—Francis, (twin), b. 19—,—Owen, b. 19—,—Michael,
b. 19—,—Angela, b. 19—,—Sharon, b. 19—,—Eileen, b. 19—.——Edward Albert, b. 1911: m.
1935, Jessie Margaret McWilliam, da. of Robert Wilson, of Whakatane, NZ, and has issue living,
Edward Wilson Sale, b. 1936,—Robert George, b. 1940,—Leonard James, b. 1943,—Marwyr
Albert, b. 1955,—Margaret Elizabeth, b. 1938.——Russell Sale (c/o Diving Company, Opotaki,
NZ), b. 1913: m. 1946, Marie O. Coralyn, and has issue.——Ernie Parker (Deborah Bay, Port
Chalmers, NZ) b. 1916: m. 1946, Jessie May Court, of Waimate, S. Canterbury, NZ, and has issue
living, Malcolm Ross, b. 1947,—Donald Graeme, b. 1962,—Janice Audrey, b. 1950,—Nellie May,
b. 1952,—Barbara Ann, b. 1959.——Eva Frances, b. 19—: m. 1st, 19—, (m. diss. 19—),   ;
2ndly, 19—, John Campbell, of Coreys Bay, Port Chalmers, Otago, NZ, and has issue living, (by
1st m.), Ronald Parkhurst, b. 19—,—(by 2nd m.), Marcus, b. 19—,—Bronwyn, b. 19—.——
Myra Edith, b. 1922: m. 1945, Bruce Bannerman, of 6, Wigan St., Gore, Southland, NZ, and has
issue living, Kevin Bruce, b. 1947,—Andrew Henry, b. 1950,—Neville William, b. 1955,—Nola
Mae, b. 1946: m. 1967, Norman Anderson, and has issue living, Ernest Keith b. 1973, Dianne
b. 1969, Glenis b. 1970,—Marion Frances, b. 1949: m. 1967, Ian Ross Lamberth, and has issue
living, Steven Ross b. 1968, Susan b. 1970,—Loraine Joy, b. 1953: m. 1971, Peter Donaldson,
and has issue living, Joanne Robyn b. 1972,—Denise Myra, b. 1960.——Rita Elizabeth, b. 1917:
m. 1939, Hector Thomas Ralph Gibson, of 109, Taita Drive, Avalon, Lower Hutt, NZ, and has
issue living, Keith Ralph, b. 1944: m. 1972, Marylin Ann Rew,—Jule Ryall, b. 1942: m. 1963,
Ian Norris, and has issue living, Craig Julian b. 1971, Stacy Jule b. 1966, Justine Helen b. 1968.
——Thelma Alice, b. 1920 : m. 19—, Walter McLay, of 56, Kenrock St., Te Aroka,
N. Island, NZ, and has issue living, Ernest, b. 19—: m. 19—, and has issue,—Douglas, b. 19—:
m. 19—, and has issue.——Dorothy Loraine, b. 1924: m. 1955, James Barclay, of 22, Farnham
Av., Palmerston N, NZ, and has issue living, Bruce, b. 19—,—Christopher, b. 19—, Sandra,
b. 19—.——Muriel Margaret, b. 1927: m. 1946, John Stevenson, of 11, Mure St., Mosgiel, Otago,
NZ, and has issue living, Neil, b. 1947: m. 1968, Judith Buckley, of Mosgiel, and has issue living,
Buckley John b. 1971,—Raymond, b. 1948: m. 1969, Karen Miller, of Mosgiel, and has issue
living, David Wayne b. 1969, Kerry b. 1971,—George Ross, b. 1951,—Yvonne, b. 1956.

Grandsons living of the late Marcus Henry Sale Hill (ante) :—
Issue of the late Leonard Graham Hill (twin), b. 1911, d. (killed in action) 1942: m. 1935,
Christina Agnes Allan Wilson, of Section 3, Awakaponga, R.D. Whakatane, New
Zealand :—
Graham Robert Marcus (Corner of Pakeha and Mar Sts., Matata, Bay of Plenty, NZ), b. 1936:
m. 1958, Shirley Fay Whan, of Sydney, Australia, and has issue living, Michael Peter John,
b. (Jan.) 1960,—Leonard Graham, b. (Dec.) 1960,—Warren Stephan, b. 1962,—Stanley Norman,
b. 1963,—Deborah Joy, b. 1964.——Allan Henry (5, Okona Cres., Ngongotaha, Rotorua, NZ),
b. 1938: m. 1959, Raewyn Alice Smith, of Whakatane, New Zealand, and has issue living, Douglas
Allan, b. 1960,—Gordon France, b. 1962,—Rowley Wilson, b. 1964,—Murray Richard, b. 1967.

Grandchildren of the late George Henry Hill (ante):—
Issue of the late George Rowley Sale Hill, b. 1874, d. 19— : m. 19—, Elizabeth Attfield,
who d. 19— :—
Three sons.——Five daughters.

Issue of the late Louis Hill, b. 1878, d. 19— : m. 19—, Elizabeth Walker, who d. 19— :—
Two sons and a daughter.

Issue of the late Percy Graham Hill, b. 1883, d. 1953 : m. 1905, Mary Ellen Wilson :—
George Arthur Graham, b. 1905 : m. 1931, Kathleen Geary, and has issue living, David Graham,
b. 1931,—Donald Percival, b. 1937,—Russell George, b. 1942,—Douglas John, b. 1943,—Valerie

May, b. 1946.——Percival Thomas, b. 1913: m. 1939, Maude Monk.——Helen Caroline, b. 1910, m. 1927, W. R. Lewis, and has issue living, William Leonard (Makerewa Junction, Southland, New Zealand), b. 1932: m. 1956, Jeanette McGregor, and has issue living, Bruce David b. 1958: Donald James b. 1959, Rodney William b. 1961, Susan Gay b. 1960,—Mary Catherine, b. 1928: m. 1952, M. M. Murphy, of 49, Peel St., Westport, New Zealand, and has issue living, Brian William b. 1955, Anthony Maxwell b. 1958, Patrick Thomas b. 1961, Helen Margaret b. 1954: m. 1973, Anthony Robertson, of Westport, NZ, Gloria Mary b. 1957, Kathleen Ann b. 1963, Julie Maureen b. 1964,—Vera Joy, b. 1930: m. 1954, J. J. Walsh, of Menzies Ferry No. 1 R.D., Edendale, Southland, NZ, and has issue living, Angela Mary b. 1956, Gillian Caroline b. 1960, Maree Jane b. 1962, Leanne Ruth b. 1966, Denise Louise b. 1968,—Lorna Ellen, b. 1939: m. 1958, John Desmond Wright, of South Rd., Wyndham, Southland, NZ, and has issue living, Darrell John b. 1959, Graham Norman b. 1960, Paul Robert b. 1961,—Dawn Margaret, b. 1942: m. 1961, Stuart Gray, of 69, Forth St. Mataura Southland, NZ, and has issue living, David Andrew b. 1962, Julie Margaret Irene b. 1964,—Sonia Carol, b. 1947: m. 1965, Alexander George Kelly, of 7, Cunningham St., Invercargill, Southland, NZ, and has issue living, Allen Peter b. 1966, Katrina May b. 1969. *Residence*, South Rd., Wyndham, Southland, NZ.

Granddaughters of the late Capt. Rowley John Hill (ante):—
Issue of the late George Henry Hill, b. 1842, d. 19—: m. 1868, Ellen Sarah, da. of Thomas Daly, of Ealing, W5:—

Charlotte (18, Stonehaven Cres., Palmerton North, NZ), b. 18—: m. 1st, 19—, Edward Crawley, who d. 19—; 2ndly, 19—, William Bennett, who d. 19—.——Margaret Mary (Pearl), b. 18—: m. 19—, George Victor Percy, who d. 1955, and has issue living, William, DSC, b. 1929: m. 1955, Shelley, da. of Robert Cockerton, and has issue living, Mark b. 1956, Dean b. 1960, Leanne b. 1961, Andrea b. 1963,—Andrew, b. 19—,—Colin, b. 19—,—Jean, b. 1921: m. 1947, Graham,. Leslie Scott, of 8, Sherwood Av., Whangarei, NZ, and has issue living, Peter b. 1953, Barbara, b. 1949,—Fay, b. 19—,—Gwen, b. 19—: m. 19—, S. Crozier, of 10, Berkshire Grove, Porirna, NZ,—Joy, b. 19—: m. 19—, F. Hubbersty, of 1, Cordelia Place, Auckland, NZ.

The 1st baronet, Sir Hugh Hill (son of the late Rowley Hill, M.P.), was M.P. for Londonderry. The 2nd baronet, a Privy Councillor, sat as M.P. for city and co. of Derry 1795-1830; he was successively Clerk of the Irish House of Commons, Vice-Treasurer of Ireland, Governor of the Island of St. Vincent, and Governor of Trinidad. The 4th baronet, Major Sir John Hill, served throughout the Indian Mutiny with Bengal Light Cav. The first ancestor of this family, originally of Buckinghamshire, was Treasurer of Ireland under Oliver Cromwell.

HILL, Creation (U.K.) 1916, of Bradford.

Attempt not, or else accomplish.

Sir JAMES HILL, 3rd *Baronet;* b. May 29th, 1905; s. his father, *Sir* ALBERT, 1946; ed. at Wrekin Coll.; is Chm., Sir James Hill & Sons, Ltd., of Bradford: m. 1930, Marjory, J.P., da. of the late Frank Croft, of Brocka, Lindale, Grange-over-Sands, and has issue.

Arms—Or, on a fesse between three leopards' faces sable, as many roses leaved and seeded proper. Crest—Upon a rock charged with two roses as in the arms a merino ram statant proper.

Residence—Brea House, Trebetherick, Wadebridge, Cornwall. *Club*—Bradford.

Son living—JAMES FREDERICK (Brookleigh, Burley Rd., Menston, nr. Ilkley, Yorks.) b. Dec. 5th, 1943: m. 1966, Sandra Elizabeth, da. of J. C. Ingram, of Lenner House, Beamsley, Bolton Abbey, and has issue living, James Laurence Ingram, b. Sept. 22nd, 1973,—Juliet Clare, b. 1969,—Georgina Margaret, b. 1971.

Daughters living—Anita Joan, b. 1931: m. 1953, Michael John Riley, and has issue living, Peter James Wynne, b. 1956,—Christopher John, b. 1960,—Wendy Jeanne, b. 1954. *Residence*, Beech Croft, Bramhope, Leeds.—— Judith Mary, b. 1933: m. 1960, Dixon Donkin, c/o Dunelm Estates, Ltd., P.O. Box 180, Chipata, Zambia, and has issue living, Dixon, b. 1961,—Deborah Marjory, b. 1963,— Nicola Dawn, b. 1969.——Ellen Barbara, b. 1936: m. 1960, Edward Norman Robson, of Windrush, Apperley Bridge, nr. Bradford, and has issue living, Susan Joy, b. 1960,—Jacqueline Ann, b. 1963,—Penelope Jane, b. 1967. ——Florence Margaret (twin), b. 1943: m. 1965, Terence John Coombs, of 1, Oakhampton Rd., Stirling, E. London, S. Africa, and has issue living, Tessa Annette, b. 1965,— Linda Margaret, b. 1967,—Tracey Elizabeth, b. 1973.

Collateral Branch living.

Issue of the late Arthur James Hill, el. son of 1st baronet, b. 1876, d. 1935: m. 1898, Eleanor Beatrice Hindle (now of Denton Park, Ben Rhydding, Yorkshire), da. of the late Thomas Duxbury, FCS, AMICE, of Temple Moyle, Darwen:—
Annie Dulcie (Borwick Lodge, Hawkshead, Ambleside), b. 1900: m. 1st, 1923 (m. diss. 1946), Cdr. Robert Derek Stawell Crosse, OBE, RN; 2ndly, 1946, Paul William Manzi-Fé, and has issue living.——Eleanor Kathleen, b. 1904.——Nelloe Elizabeth Audrey, b. 1907: m. 1st, 1931 (m. diss. 1939), Peter Sime Douty, who d. 1948; 2ndly, 1949, Cecil Denbigh Hannam, MC, and has issue living, (by 1st m.) Juliette Eleanor Sime, b. 1934: m. 1955, John Gordon Londley, late Lt. RN, of Theberton Grange, nr. Leiston, E. Suffolk, and has issue living, Charles Arthur b. 1965, Antonia Eleanor b. 1957, Bridget Alexandra b. 1959. *Residence*, Deerstones, Bolton Abbey, Yorks.——Noeline Etrenne (*Lady Aarvold*), b. 1909: m. 1934, His Honour Judge (Sir Carl Douglas) Aarvold, OBE, TD, DL, JP, Recorder of London, and has issue living, Christopher Olaf, b. 1943,—James Hillary, b. 1946,—John Merriman, b. 1947. *Residence*, Foxbury, West-humble, Dorking.

The 1st baronet, Sir James Hill (son of the late William Hill, of Harden, Bingley, Yorkshire). was head of the firm of Sir James Hill & Sons, wool merchants (which he founded in 1891), and sat as M.P. for Central Div. of Bradford (L) 1916-18.

HILL, Creation (U.K.) 1919, of Green Place, Stockbridge, co. Southampton.
[Extinct 1944.]

Lieut.-Col. Sir NORMAN GRAY HILL, *M.C.*, 2nd and last *Baronet;*
d. (killed on active ser. during European War) 1944.

Daughters living of 1st Baronet—Beatrice Birkbeck ; M.A. Oxford. *Residence*, Quanterness
Portinscale, Keswick, Cumbria.——Rosalind Mary Theodosia ; MA and BLitt Oxford ; Prof.
of History, London Univ.; FRHistS; FSA. *Residence*, 7, Loom Lane, Radlett, Herts.

ERSKINE-HILL, Creation (U.K.) 1945, of Quothquhan, co. Lanark.

Sir ROBERT ERSKINE-HILL,
2nd *Baronet* ; *b.* Feb. 6th, 1917 ; *s.* his
father, *Sir* ALEXANDER GALLOWAY,
K.C., 1947 ; ed. at Eton, and at Trin.
Coll., Camb. (B.A. 1936) ; is a Partner
in the firm of Chiene & Tait, chartered
accountants of Edinburgh, and a Member of Queen's Body Guard for Scotland (Roy. Co. of Archers) ; European
War 1939-42 as Lieut. R.N.V.R. : *m.*
1942, Christine Alison, only da. of the
late Capt. Henry James Johnstone, of
Alva, R.N. [*see* Johnstone, Bt., colls.],
and has issue.

Arms—Quarterly: 1st grand quarter, azure,
a hill argent, charged with two pens, points
downwards in saltire, quills or, feathers sable, in
chief the sun in his splendour, *Hill* ; 2nd grand
quarter, counterquartered, 1st and 4th, argent,
on a pale sable, a cross-crosslet fitches or,
Erskine of Shielfield ; 2nd, azure, a bend between
two cross-crosslets fitchees or, *Mar* ; 3rd, or,
on a bend azure three mascles of the field, and
in the sinister chief a round buckle of the
second, *Haliburton* ; all within a bordure per
pale azure and sable, a canton charged with
a fleur de lys of the second, for difference ; 3rd grand quarter, counterquartered, 1st argent,
on a mount in base a lion rampant vert, on a chief of the second a crescent between two mullets
or, *Halcro* ; 2nd, or a fesse chequy azure and argent, a border gules charged with eight round
buckles of the first, *Stewart of Barscube* ; 3rd, or, on a bend gules, three buckles of the first.
Bonkyll of that ilk ; 4th, argent a heart purpure ensigned with an imperial crown proper, on a chief
gules, three pallets or, *Keith of Galston* ; 4th grand quarter, argent, a lion rampant, azure, armed
and langued gules, on a chief of the second, an elephant's head, cabossed of the first, tusked or,
accompanied by two lymphads of the first under full sail proper, *Galloway*. **Crest**—1st, a stag's head
couped proper, attired sable ; 2nd, a dexter arm from the elbow, couped proper, the hand grasping
a cross-crosslet fitchee or.

Residence—Quothquhan Lodge, Biggar, Lanarkshire.

Sons living—ALEXANDER ROGER, *b.* Aug. 15th, 1949 ; ed. at Eton, and Aberdeen Univ. (LLB).
——Henry James, *b.* 1953.
Daughters living—Carola Marion, *b.* 1943: *m.* 1963, (Richard) David Christopher Brooke, of Cedar
House, Shurlock Row, Berks. [see Brooke, Bt., *cr.* 1662].——Alison, *b.* 1945: *m.* 1966, John
Selby North Lewis, of Walwick Hall, Humshaugh, Hexham, Northumberland, and has issue
living, Selby James, *b.* 1968,—Harriet Alison, *b.* 1970.
Brother living—John Colville, *DSC, VRD, b.* 1921 ; ed. at Eton, and Trin. Coll., Camb.;
European War 1939-45 as Lieut. R.N.V.R. (despatches, D.S.C.) : was an A.D.C. to Gov. of
Bombay 1945-6 : *m.* 1959, Myra Elizabeth, da. of Com. R. Homewood, R.N., and has issue
living, Mark Colville, *b.* 1960,—David John, *b.* 1962. *Residence*, South Lodge, Forest Row,
Sussex.
Sister living—Jean Halcro, *b.* 1928 : *m.* 1st, 1950, Derek John Seth-Smith, who *d.* 1964 ; 2ndly,
1972, George Henry Smith-Wright, and has issue living (by 1st m.), Frederick Alexander, *b.*
1963,—Kay Christian, *b.* 1951,—Rosemary Jean, *b.* 1954,—Mary Jane, *b.* 1957. *Residence*, 34,
Moore St., SW3.

The 1st baronet, Sir Alexander Galloway Erskine-Hill, K.C. (son of Robert Alexander Hill)
was a Director of London & NE Railway and sat as MP for N. Div. of Edinburgh (*U*) 1935-45.

Hill-Wood, see Wood.

HILLS, Creation (U.K.) 1939, of Hills Court, co. Kent. [Extinct 1955.]
Sir ANDREW ASHTON WALLER HILLS, 1st and last *Baronet.*

Mother living of 1st Baronet—Mary Grace (*Lady Hills*), da. of the late Leon Dominic Ashton,
of Cairo, Egypt ; is a Novelist ; granted February 9th 1939, the same style, title, place, and
precedence as if her late husband had survived and been cr. a Baronet ; unsuccessfully contested
N. Div. of Hendon (*L*) Oct. 1959 : *m.* 1931, as his second wife, Major the Rt. Hon. John Waller
Hills, M.P., J.P., D.C.L., who *d.* 1938. *Residence*, 34, Brunswick Gardens, W.8.

Hoare, Creation I. 1784, of Annabella, Cork.

The hour approaches

Sir TIMOTHY EDWARD CHARLES HOARE, 8th *Baronet*; *b.* Nov. 11th, 1934; *s.* his father, *Maj. Sir* EDWARD O'BRYEN, 1969; ed. at Radley, and Worcester Coll., Oxford: *m.* 1969, Felicity Anne, da. of Peter Boddington, JP, of Stratford-upon-Avon, and has issue.

Arms — Sable, a double-headed eagle displayed within a bordure engrailed argent. **Crest**—A deer's head and neck proper, erased argent.

Residence—10, Belitha Villas, Barnsbury, N1.

Son living—CHARLES JAMES, *b.* March 15th, 1971.
Daughters living—Louisa Hope, *b.* 1972.——Kate Annabella (twin), *b.* 1972.
Sister living—Catherine Mary, *b.* 1937: *m.* 1963, David James Clark, and has issue living, David Noah, *b.* 1966,—Ezra David, *b.* 1968,—Abel David, *b.* 1971, —Hester Catherine, *b.* 1973.
Uncle living (son of 6th baronet)—Terence O'Bryen, *b.* 1904: *m.* 1939, Elizabeth, da. of the late William James Cambridge. *Residence*, Cherry Croft, Nepcote Lane, Findon, Sussex.
Widow living of 7th Baronet—NINA MARY (*Nina, Lady Hoare*), 61, Flask Walk, NW3), da. of the late Charles Nugent Hope-Wallace, MBE [see M. Linlithgow, colls.]: *m.* 1932, Maj. Sir Edward O'Bryen Hoare, 7th Bt., who *d.* 1969.

Collateral Branches living.

Grandchildren of the late John Hoare (infra):—
Issue of the late James O'Bryen Hoare, *b.* 1910, *d.* 1967: *m.* (Jan.) 1941, Helen Dorey Hardie (37, Turama Rd., Royal Oak, Auck., NZ):—

RICHARD JAMES O'BRYEN (27, Grange Rd., Mt. Eden, Auckland 4, NZ), *b.* 1947: *m.* 1971, Sally Ann, da. of John Cornwell, of Northcote, Auckland, NZ, and has issue living, David O'Bryen, *b.* 1974.——Stewart John, *b.* 1949.——Janet O'Bryen, *b.* (Nov.) 1941: *m.* 1965, William Frank Richardson, of 45, St. Leonard's Rd., Mt. Eden, Auckland 4, NZ, and has issue living, Michael George, *b.* 1970,—Diana Helen, *b.* 1967.

Grandchildren of the late Rev. James O'Bryen Dott Richard Hoare, el. son of Joseph James Parish Hoare, 3rd son of 3rd baronet:—
Issue of the late John Hoare, *b.* 1874, *d.* 1954: *m.* 1904, Margaret Jane Leversedge, who *d.* 1959:—

John Leslie (7, Pavo St., Camp Hill, Brisbane 4152, Qld., Aust.), *b.* 1919: *m.* 1945, Maxine Heaslip, and has issue living, Susan Elizabeth, *b.* 1946: *m.* 1970, Michael Clifford Quinnell, of 78, School Rd., The Gap, Brisbane, Qld., Aust.,—Jane Victoria, *b.* 1950.——Joan Mary Frances, *b.* 1905: *m.* 1931, Harry Albert Cameron, and has issue living, John Bruce, *b.* 1933,—Margaret Anne, *b.* 1932,—Diana Molly, *b.* 1943. *Residence*, Geera St., Coorparoo, Brisbane, Qld., Aust.——Margaret Alice, *b.* 1912: *m.* 1943, Jack Steane Comport, who *d.* 1961, and has issue living, Stephen (98, Collins Rd., St. Ives, Sydney, NSW), *b.* 1944: *m.* 1st, 1966 (m. diss. 1972), Mary Boyd Thomson; 2ndly, 1973, Gillian Elizabeth Sinton. *Residence*, 28, Latimer St., Greenslopes, Brisbane, Qld.——Molly Gertrude, *b.* 1913: *m.* 1942, Patrick Shine, of 50, Seventh Av., Palm Beach, Qld., Aust., and has issue living, John, *b.* 1946,—Richard, *b.* 1950,—Judith Mary, *b.* 1948.

Issue of the late Denys Hoare, *b.* 1876, *d.* 1958: *m.* 1906, Frances York, who *d.* 1959:—
Norah Frances O'Bryen, *b.* 1907: *m.* 1940, John Edward Buxton, and has issue living, Joanna Elizabeth, *b.* 1941: *m.* 1964, Maj. Christopher Timothy Rawdon Leefe, of West Farm House, Harriotts Lane, Ashtead, Surrey, and has issue living, Mark Rawdon *b.* 1966, Thomas Rawdon *b.* 1968,—Frances Jane *b.* 1944: *m.* 1967, John Edward Holford (Kings Cottage, Elmdon, Saffron Walden), and has issue living, Rebecca Jane *b.* 1968, Melanie Sarah *b.* 1970,—Annabel Mary, *b.* 1948: *m.* 1971, Michael Bonhote Rodney Foster, of 5, King Charles Walk, Prince's Way, SW19, and has issue living, Lucy Annabel Henriette *b.* 1974. *Residence*, Rostellan, Pilgrim's Close, Westhumble, Dorking, Surrey.

Grandsons of the late Joseph George Wallace Hoare, RN, 2nd son of Joseph James Parish Hoare (ante):—
Issue of Helen Susan Kathleen Hoare, *b.* 1867, *d.* 1935: *m.* 1894, John Meek, of Liverpool, formerly of Perth, who *d.* 1907:—
John Wallace (La Floresta, 55, Arundel Rd., Littlehampton, Sussex), *b.* 1902; ed. at Rossall; 1939-45 War: *m.* 1934, Marjorie Evans, only da. of Ernest Edward Cheney, of Bognor Regis, and has issue living, John O'Bryen, *b.* 1935.——Francis Forward O'Bryen, *b.* 1905; ed. at Churchers Coll.: *m.* 1935, Carolina Perez, of Barranquilla, Colombia, and has issue living, Wallace O'Bryen, *b.* 1936,—Carmen Kathleen, *b.* 1938.

Granddaughter of the late Cyril Bertie Edward Hoare (infra):—
Issue of the late Wing-Com. Bertie Rex O'Bryen Hoare, D.S.O., D.F.C., *b.* 1912, *d.* 1947: *m.* 1945, Lucy, who *d.* 1970, da. of Richard Nimmo Watson, of Harrogate:—
Rosemary Verity O'Bryen (posthumous), *b.* 1947.

Granddaughter of the late Edward Senior Hoare, 7th son of the late Joseph James Parish Hoare (ante):—
Issue of the late Cyril Bertie Edward Hoare, *b.* 1882, *d.* 1940: *m.* 1907, Isabel Mary (of D'Avigdor House, Hove, Sussex), da. of Edward Fielder, of Anerley, S.E. :—
Hermione Sophia O'Bryen, *b.* 1910 : *m.* 1952, as his second wife (marriage dissolved 1954), the 2nd Baron Colwyn, who *d.* 1966. *Residence*, D'Avigdor House, Hove, Sussex.

Grandson of the late Edward Hoare, son of the late Rev. Thomas Hoare, 3rd son of 2nd baronet:—
Issue of the late William Wallis Hoare, M.D., F.R.C.S., L.R.C.P., *b.* 1871, *d.* 19—: *m.* 1903, Kathleen Mary Bolton, of Ascot, Brisbane, Queensland :—
Edward Bryan, *b.* 1905.

Granddaughters of the late Edward Wallis Hoare, FRCVS (infra):—
Issue of the late Edward William Wallis Hoare, *b.* 1902, *d.* 1966: *m.* 1936, Elizabeth, da. of the late Angus Baillie, of Glasgow:—
Elizabeth McLean, *b.* 1937.——Margaret Wallis, *b.* 1941: *m.* 1964, Duncan MacPherson Muir, BDS, of 11, Crocus Grove Estate, Irvine, Ayrshire, and has issue living, Caroline Elizabeth, *b.* 1966,—Rebecca, *b.* 1970.——Barbara, *b.* 1948.

Granddaughters of the late Capt. William Jesse Hoare, son of the late Rev. Thomas Hoare (ante):—
Issue of the late Edward Wallis Hoare, F.R.C.V.S., *b.* 1863, *d.* 1920: *m.* 1899, Emily, who *d.* 1961, da. of the late Henry Lindsay Helen, of Dublin:—
Alma Violet Lloyd, *b.* 1900: *m.* 1941, Desmond FitzMaurice, of Avon Lee, Hollymount, Lee Rd. Cork.——Emily Alexandra (Duncan, Hollymount, Lee Rd., Cork), *b.* 1903.——Freesia Helen, *b.* 1909.——Viola Cecilia, *b.* 1913: *m.* 1939, Richard Roberts Gorsuch, and has issue living, Diarmind Roberts, *b.* 1941: *m.* 1970, Jane, el. da. of Arthur Stanley Peacock, of Vancouver,—Terence Richard, *b.* 1947: *m.* 1969, Patricia, da. of Arthur Stanley Peacock, of Vancouver,—Deirdre Cecilia, *b.* 1943: *m.* 1970, Michel le Bell,—Maeve Emily, *b.* 1946: *m.* 1972-Keith Harrison, of Ch. Ch., NZ. *Residence,* 6811, 236th St., RR6, Langley, BC, Canada.—— Myrtle Jesse, *b.* 1918: *m.* 1940, William Henry Hall, who *d.* 1951; 2ndly, 1956, Basil Lionel Baker, of Hanley House, Harmby Rd., Leyburn, Yorks.

The 1st baronet, Sir Joseph, M.P. for Askeaton in the Irish House of Commons, was many years Advising Counsel at Dublin Castle. It has been represented that he lived in *three centuries*—viz., from Dec. 25th, 1699, to Dec. 24th, 1801. Recent researches, however, show that he was born on Dec. 25th, 1707, and died on Dec. 24th, 1801. At the age of 93 he attended in his place in Parliament to vote against the Union. Sir Edward, the 2nd baronet, sat as M.P. for Carlow 1769-76.

HOARE, Creation (G.B.) 1786, of Barn Elms, Surrey.

Sir PETER RICHARD DAVID HOARE, 8th *Baronet, b.* March 22nd, 1932; *s.* his father, *Sir* PETER WILLIAM, 1973; ed. at Eton: *m.* 1961, Jane, from whom he obtained a divorce 1967, only da. of Daniel Orme, of Bulleigh Barton, Ipplepen, S. Devon.

Arms—Sable, an eagle displayed with two heads argent, charged on the breast with an ermine spot, a bordure engrailed of the second. **Crest**—An eagle's head and neck erased argent charged with an ermine spot.
Address—C/o Hoare & Co., 37, Fleet St., EC4.

Brother living—DAVID JOHN (37, Fleet St., EC4), *b.* Oct. 8th, 1935; ed. at Eton: *m.* 1965, Mary Vanessa, yst. da. of Peter Cardew, of Westhanger, Cleeve, Bristol, and has issue living, Simon Merrick, *b.* 1967.

Aunt living—Joyce Norah (The Patch, Ilsington, Newton Abbot, S. Devon), *b.* 1902.

In ardua.

For arduous under-takings.

Widow living of 7th Baronet—LAURA RAY (*Lady Hoare*) (Luscombe Castle, Dawlish, Devon), da. of Sir John Esplen, KBE, 1st Bt.: *m.* 1929, Sir Peter William Hoare, 7th Bt., who *d.* 1973.

Collateral Branches living.

Issue of the late Renée Julia, sister of 6th baronet, *d.* 1953 : *m.* 1889, Charles Cunningham Church, who obtained a divorce 1903 :—
Charles John Douglas, *b.* 1896 ; Capt. (retired) King's Own Scottish Borderers : *m.* 1925, Catherine Cecily, da. of the late Capt. William Francis Annesley Wallace [D. Beaufort, colls.]. *Residence,* 68, Kingston House North, Princes Gate, SW7.

Granddaughters of the late Peter Merrik Hoare (ante) :—
Issue of the late Lennox Merrik Noel Colt Hoare, *b.* 1871, *d.* 1924: *m.* 1895, Evelyn Augusta, who *d.* 1952, da. of the late Thomas Gerard, of Claughton, near Birkenhead, Cheshire :—
Dorothy Augusta Edith, *b.* 1897: *m.* 1920, Capt. F. N. Mitchell, formerly Indian Army, who *d.* 1927 and has issue living, Jane *b.* 1923: *m.* 1954, Capt. John Charles Montague, RE, of Manorside, Cowley, Exeter, and has issue living, Peter John Edward *b.* 1957, William Charles Lennox *b.* 1958, Susan Jane *b.* 1955,—Ruth, *b.* 1926: *m.* 1st, 1949 (m. diss. 1965) Charles Derek Sydney Wintle; 2ndly, 1965, Roger John Mules, MB, BS, of Cliffden, Teignmouth, Devon, and has issue living, (by 1st m.) David Michael Charles *b.* 1961, (by 2nd m.) Anthony John *b.* 1966, Frances Jane *b.* 1968. *Residence,* Halmeston, Dawlish Rd., Teignmouth, Devon.——Alda Evelyn, *b.* 1905: *m.* 1929, Brig. Henry Anthony Lampen Shewell, OBE, late RE, who *d.* 1974, and has issue living, John Michael Henry (c/o C. Hoare & Co., 37, Fleet St., EC4), *b.* 1931; Maj. ACC: *m.* 1959, Alison Averil Jones, and has issue living, Christopher John Henry *b.* 1961, Anthony Martin Edward *b.* 1962,—Alda Mary *b.* 1933: *m.* 1962, John Charles Allday Mousley, of Stanford House, Pirbright, Surrey, and has issue living, Peter John Hunter, *b.* 1963, Claire Alda Louisa *b.* 1964. *Residence,* Rock Close, Ashburton, Devon.

Grandchildren of the late Charles Arthur Richard Hoare, son of the late Peter Richard Hoare (*b.* 1803), son of Peter Richard Hoare, 5th son of 1st baronet:—
Issue of the late Wilfrid Arthur Richard Hoare, *b.* 1876, *d.* 1971: *m.* 1915, Helen Adria da. of the late Col. Harry Hepenstall Rose Heath, CB:—
Richard Michael St. George, *b.* 1918: *m.* 1947, Gladys Margaret Tysack, and has issue living, Richard Charles, *b.* 1947: *m.* 19—, Helen, da. of , and has issue living, Michael John *b.* 19—,—Nigel, *b.* 1949,—John Michael, *b.* 1950.——Jacquetta Adria Margaret (Sorley Farm, Kingsbridge, S. Devon), *b.* 1916: *m.* 1st, 1940 (m. diss. 1946) Terrence Stafford, Lt. RAPC; 2ndly, 1946, Dudley Fisher, who *d.* 19—, and has issue living, (by 1st m.) Rebecca, *b.* 19—: *m.* 19—, , and has issue living, Bridget *b.* 19—,—(by 2nd m.) Noel Hugh, *b.* 1949,—Philipa Jacquetta (twin), *b.* 1949,—Heather Sophia, *b.* 1953.

Issue of the late Reginald Arthur Hoare, *b.* 1878, *d.* (killed in action during European War) 1918 : *m.* 1909, Una Mildred, who *d.* 1951, da. of Thomas C. Williams, of Wellington, New Zealand :—
Reginald Merrick, *b.* 1918: *m.* 1950, Barbara Jean, da. of Francis John Buckland [B. Melchett], and has issue living, Charles Mark, *b.* 1961,—Paul Reginald Richard, *b.* 1963,—Diana Charlotte, *b.* 1956,—Clare Githa, *b.* 1958. *Residence,* 27, Holland Villas Rd., W.14.——Anne Temple, Githa (Old Larkhayes, Dalwood, Axminster, Devon), *b.* 1916: *m.* 1945, Vere Justin Tweedie MC, son of the late Adm. Sir Hugh Justin Tweedie, KCB, and has issue living, Simon Vere, *b.* 1954,—Sarah Patricia, *b.* 1947: *m.* 1968, Edward Charles Townsend,—Amanda Jane, *b.* 1948,

Issue of the late Ralph Francis Hoare, *b.* 1881, *d.* 1956: *m.* 1906, Katherine Hallen, who *d.* 1969, da. of R. J. Sumner Drinkwater, of Northbrook, Orillia, Canada:—
Hugh John Francis, *b.* 1911: *m.* 1947, Margaret Edith, da. of George Thomas Williams of Toronto, Canada. *Residence,* 230, Heath Street West, Toronto, Canada.——Eric Reginald (13, Wellington Cres., Edmonton, Alberta), *b.* 1918: *m.* 1949, Rosemary Brodie Hallowell, da. of Francis Vickerman Lumb, and has issue living, Geoffrey Charles Brodie, *b.* 1953,—Richard Sumner Anthony, *b.* 1955,—Wendy Pamela, *b.* 1961.——Peter Richard (64, Holford Cres., Toronto, Canada), *b.* 1920.——Margaret Katherine Dorothy (11, Jarvis St., Orillia, Ont., Canada), *b.* 1907: *m.* 19—, William Stephan Gill, who *d.* 19—.——Natalie Kathleen Grove (115, Chaplin Cres., Ont., Canada), *b.* 1915.

The 1st baronet's father was Lord Mayor of London 1745. Sir Henry Ainslie Hoare, 5th Bt., was M.P. for Windsor (*L*) 1865-6 and for Chelsea 1868-74.

HOARE, Creation (U.K.) 1962, of Fleet Street, City of London.

For arduous undertakings.

Sir FREDERICK ALFRED HOARE, 1st *Baronet*; son of the late Frederick Henry Hoare, of Woodlands Corner, Ewshott, Surrey; *b.* Feb. 11th, 1913; ed. at Wellington; Managing Partner of C. Hoare & Co., a Member of Court of Assists. of Goldsmiths' Co., a Dir. of Trust Union, Ltd.; elected a Common Councilman of City of London 1948, an Alderman 1950 (Sheriff 1956-57), and Lord Mayor 1961-62; Prime Warden of Goldsmiths' Co. 1966-67; Chm. of Family Welfare Assocn. 1961-68, and of Gen. Practice Finance Corpn. 1966-73; Dep. Chm. National Mutual Life Assurance Soc. 1969-72; Knt. Great Band of Liberian Humane Order of African Redemption, and Grand Officer of Order of Nat. Republic of Ivory Coast; Knt. 1958: *m.* 1st, 1939, Norah Mary, who *d.* 1973, da. of Addison James Wheeler; 2ndly, 1974, Oonah Alice, da. of the late Brig.-Gen. David Ramsay Sladen, CMG, DSO, of Rhydoldog, Rhayader, Powys, and formerly wife of (i) Maj. Keith Hathorn Johnston Stewart, KOSB, and (ii) Lt.-Col. Norman Peter Dew, OBE, and has issue by 1st m.

Arms—Sable, an eagle displayed with two heads argent, charged on the breast with an ermine spot, within a bordure engrailed of the second.
Crest—An eagle's head erased argent, charged with an ermine spot.

Residence,—34, Cadogan Sq., SW1.   *Clubs*—Garrick, Flyfishers', City Livery.

Daughters living—By 1st m.—Mary Rose, *b.* 1944.——Marinella, *b.* 1952.

HOBART, Creation (U.K.) 1914, of Langdown, co. Southampton.
[Name pronounced "Hub'bert."]

The giver makes the gift valuable.

Sir ROBERT HAMPDEN HOBART, 3rd *Baronet ; b.* May 7th, 1915 ; *s.* his father *Lieut.-Col. Sir* (CLAUD) VERE CAVENDISH, *DSO, OBE,* 1949; Lt.-Com. (ret.), RN; 1939-45 War (wounded, two medals, four stars): *m.* 1942, Sylvia, who *d.* 1965, only da. of Henry A. Argo, of Durban, Natal, and has issue.

Arms—Quarterly, 1st, sable, an estoile of six rays or between two flaunches ermine, *Hobart;* 2nd, argent, a saltire between four eagles displayed azure, *Hampden;* 3rd, argent, three battering-rams fessewise in pale proper, armed and garnished azure, *Bertie;* 4th, quarterly, gules and or, in the first quarter a mullet argent, *Vere.* Crest—A bull statant per pale sable and gules bezanté, in his nose a ring or.

Residence—Gatcombe Park, Isle of Wight.   *Clubs*—Travellers', Royal Yacht Squadron, Royal Southern Yacht, Royal London Yacht, Royal Northern Yacht. Royal Southampton Yacht, Bembridge Sailing.

Sons living—JOHN VERE, *b.* April 9th, 1945.——Robert Henry, *b.* 1948.——Anthony Hampden, *b.* 1956.
Daughter living—Penelope Diana, *b.* 1954.

The 1st baronet, Sir Robert Henry Hobart, K.C.V.O., C.B. (el. son of the late Very Rev. the Hon. Henry Lewis Hobart, D.D., Dean of Windsor and Wolverhampton [E. Buckinghamshire, colls.]), was Private Sec. to Sec. of State for War, Postmaster-Gen., Ch. Sec. for Ireland, and Sec. of State for India 1863-74 and 1889-95, and to four Secs. for Scotland 1886-7 and 1892-5, Sec. for Coronation of King Edward VII 1902, Gold Staff Officer at Coronation of King George 1911, M.P. for Hampshire, New Forest Div. (*L*) Jan. 1906 to Jan. 1910, and Official Verderer of the New Forest 1907-27. The 2nd baronet, Sir (Claud) Vere Cavendish Hobart, D.S.O., O.B.E., was Major Grenadier Guards, and Lieut.-Col. Hampshire Regt., and was Gold Staff Officer at Coronations of King Edward VII. and King George V.

HOBHOUSE, Creation (U.K.) 1812, of Broughton-Gifford, Bradford-on-Avon, and of Monkton Farleigh, Wiltshire.

The hope of a better life.

Sir CHARLES CHISHOLM HOBHOUSE, *T.D.*, 6th *Baronet; b.* Dec. 7th, 1906; *s.* his father *Sir* REGINALD ARTHUR, 1947; ed. at Eton; formerly Maj. N. Somerset Yeo. (Hon. Col. 1966-67): *m.* 1st, 1946, Mary (Charlotte), who *d.* 1955, da. of the late John Park, of Benton, Northumberland, and widow of Walter Horrocks, of Salkeld Hall, Penrith; 2ndly, 1959, Elspeth Jean, yr. da. of the late Thomas George Spinney, of Mazagan, Morocco, and has issue by 2nd m.

Arms—Per pale azure and gules, three crescents, two and one, argent, issuing therefrom as many estoiles irradiated or. *Crest*—Out of a mural crown per pale azure and gules, a crescent and estoile as in the arms.
Residence—The Manor, Monkton Farleigh, Bradford-on-Avon, Wilts.

Son living—By 2nd marriage—CHARLES JOHN SPINNEY, *b.* Oct. 27th, 1962.

Brothers living—John Spencer, *A.F.C.*, *b.* 1910; ed. at Eton, and at Oxford Univ.; formerly Squadron Leader R.A.F.: *m.* 1940, Mary, da. of the late Llewelyn Roberts, M.D., of Porthcawl. *Residence*, Farleigh Court, Farleigh Hungerford, nr. Bath.——Hugh Cam, *b.* 1917; ed. at Eton; late Maj. N. Somerset Yeo.: *m.* 1st, 1939 (m. diss. 1947), Diana, da. of Philip George; 2ndly, 1949 (m. diss. 1965), Aline Rosemary (DOBIE), da. of the late Lt.-Col. David Walter Hunter Blair [*see* Hunter Blair, Bt., colls.]; 3rdly, 1965, Judy Margaret, da. of the late J. D. Tisdall, of Butcombe, Som., and has issue living, (by 1st m.) Mark Cam, *b.* 1940.—(by 2nd m.) James Charles, *b.* 1951: *m.* 1974, Sarah, yst. da. of David Sladen,—Martin Hugh John, *b.* 1955,—Julia Mary, *b.* 1956,—(by 3rd m.) Sophie Victoria, *b.* 1967. *Residence*, Ashwick Court, Oakhill, Som.

Sisters living—Mary Elspeth (*Hon. Mrs. Alexander B. Money-Coutts*), *b.* 1908 : *m.* 1930, the Hon. Alexander Burdett Money-Coutts, O.B.E. [*see* B. Latymer]. *Residence*, Askett House, near Aylesbury, Bucks.——Audrey, *b.* 1912 : *m.* 1934, Maj.-Gen. Cecil Llewellyn Firbank, C.B., C.B.E. D.S.O., late Somerset L.I., who obtained a divorce 1952, and has issue living, Simon Christopher, *b.* 1937: *m.* 1962, Caroline Anne, only da. of Major J. T. C. Howard, of Tregatreath, Coverack, Cornwall. *Residence*, Harptree Lodge, Priddy, Wells.

Collateral Branch living

Issue of the late Benjamin Arthur Hobhouse, 3rd son of 5th baronet, *b.* 1914, *d.* 1970: *m.* 1942, Valerie Cuthbertson (Estcott Farm, Wheddon Cross, Minehead, Somerset), da. of the late Dr. John Cuthbertson Walker, of Barnwell, Troon, Ayrshire:—

John Cam (Eastcott Farm, Withiel Florey, Wheddon Cross, Minehead, Som.), *b.* 1947: *m.* 1971, Mary Angela Deakins, da. of Arthur George Newton.——Carol Ann, *b.* 1943: *m.* 1964, George Rogers, of 35, Sunnyhill Rd., Salisbury, Wilts.

Sir Benjamin Hobhouse, 1st Bt., descended from the Hobhouses of Minehead, Somerset, was Ch. Sec., Board of Control, India 1801-03, and 1806-07. Rt. Hon. Sir John Cam Hobhouse, 2nd baronet, created Baron Broughton 1851, was one of the poet Byron's most intimate friends. He was Secretary at War 1832-3. Secretary for Ireland 1833, Chief Commissioner of Woods and Forests 1834, President of the Board of Control 1835-41 and 1846-51, and author of several important works. He died 1869, when the barony became extinct, and the baronetcy passed to his nephew, The 4th baronet, the Rt. Hon. Sir Charles Edward Henry Hobhouse, T.D., sat as M.P. for Wilts, E. or Devizes Div. (L) 1892-5, and for Bristol, E. Div. 1900-1918, and was Church Estate Commr. 1906-7, Under-Sec. of State for India 1907-8, Financial Sec. to Treasury 1908-11, Chancellor of Duchy of Lancaster 1911-14, and Postmaster-Gen. 1914-15.

HODGE, Creation (U.K.) 1921, of Chipstead, co. Kent.

Glory the reward of virtue.

Sir JOHN ROWLAND HODGE, *M.B.E.*, 2nd *Baronet, b.* May 1st, 1913 ; *s.* his father, Sir ROWLAND FREDERIC WILLIAM, 1950 ; ed. at Wrekin Coll. ; formerly Lieut.-Com. R.N.V.R.; formerly Lieut. Oxfordshire and Bucks L.I.; European War 1939-40 (M.B.E.) ; M.B.E. (Mil.) 1940 : *m.* 1st, 1936, Peggy Ann (from whom he obtained a divorce 1939), only da. of Sydney Raymond Kent ; 2ndly, 1939, Joan, only da. of the late Sydney Foster Wilson; 3rdly, 1962, (m. diss. 1967), Jeanne Wood Anderson, da. of the late Cdr W. E. Buchanan, of Edinburgh; 4thly, 1967, Vivienne, da. of Alfred Knightley, of Norwood, and has issue by 2nd and 4th m.

Arms—Sable, an eagle wings addorsed and inverted or between three crescents argent. *Crest*—An eagle as in the arms supporting with the dexter claw an increscent argent and looking at the rays of the sun issuant from clouds proper.
Residence—Casa Toro, St. Andrews Rd., St. Andrews, Malta GC. *Clubs*—Naval, British Racing Drivers, Royal Malta Yacht.

Son living—By 4th marriage—ANDREW, *b.* Dec. 3rd, 1968.
Daughters living—By 2nd m.—Wendy Madeline, *b.* 1941: *m.* 1st, 1962 (m. diss. 1971), Michael Dennis Whiting; 2ndly, 1973, John Edward Aitken Kidd, of Old House, Ewhurst Green, Surrey [see By. Beaverbrook], and has issue living (by 1st m.), Nicholas D'Arcy, *b.* 1962,—Deborah Joanna, *b.* 1964.——Sally Joan, *b.* 1943.——Vicki Alexandra, *b.* 1946: *m.* 1969, George Ian Alexander Heath.——(by 2nd m.) Louise Vivienne, *b.* 1970.

D.—54

1686   DEBRETT'S ILLUSTRATED BARONETAGE.

Brother living—Peter Rowland (Villa Domizia, Ghollieqa Lane, Kappara, Malta), *b.* 1915; late Capt. 2nd Commando Bde.: *m.* 1st, 1940, (m. diss. 1945), Mia, da. of the late Capt. Sir (Albert) Noel Campbell Macklin, of Fairmile, Cobham, Surrey; 2ndly, 1951, Margaret Norma, da. of Harold Plow, of Broadway, Barnton, Ches., and has issue living, (by 2nd m.), Jacqueline Jane, *b.* 1954,—Bridgitte Michele, *b.* 1956.

Sisters living—Margaret Viola (*Lady Isaacson*), *b.* 1908: *m.* 1st, 1927, Jorge Yvan Lage; 2ndly, 1938, Sir Robert Spencer Isaacson, KBE, CMG, who *d.* 1972, and has issue living, (by 1st m.), Elaine Margaret Elizabeth, *b.* 1928: *m.* 1951, Tomas Payne, and has issue living, Vivien Elizabeth Lage *b.* 1953.   *Residence*, The Old Manse, Broughton, Stockbridge, Hants.——Vivien Rosemary, *b.* 1911: *m.* 1st, 1930, St. John Henry Legh Clowes [B. Clanmorris]; 2ndly, 1941, Hugh Gordon Murton-Neale, of Black Barn, Wittersham, Kent, and has issue living, (by 1st m.) Timothy Legh, *b.* 1932,—Susan Carol, *b.* 1935.

Widow living of 1st Baronet—VERA ESTELLE (*Dowager Lady Hodge*), da. of the late John Fraser, widow of Capt. de Grey Warter, 4th Dragoon Guards, and formerly wife of 5th Earl Cathcart : *m.* 1930, as his second wife, Sir Rowland Frederic William Hodge, 1st baronet, who *d.* 1950.   *Residence,*

The 1st baronet, Sir Rowland Frederic William Hodge (son of John Rowland Hodge), was a Shipbuilder and Chm. of Eltringhams, Ltd., of Quay-on-Tyne, Northumberland.

HODSON, Creation (I.) 1787, of Holybrooke House, Wicklow.

Peace and love.

Sir MICHAEL ROBIN ADDERLEY HODSON, 6th *Baronet; b.* March 5th, 1932; *s.* his father, *Maj. Sir* EDMOND ADAIR, *DSO,* 1972; ed. at Eton; Capt. (ret.) Scots Gds.: *m.* 1963, Katrin Alexa, da. of the late Erwin Bernstiel, of St. Andrew's House, St. Andrew's Major, Dinas Powis, Glam., and has issue.

Arms—Sable, a chevron between three martlet, or. **Crest**—A dove close azure, beaked and membered or, holding in her beak an olive-branch proper.

Residence—The Grange, Bucklebury, Berks.

Daughters living—Tania Elizabeth, *b.* 1965.—— Alexa Adderley, *b.* 1966.——Jane Katrina, *b.* 1970.

Brother living—PATRICK RICHARD (Shipton Slade Farm, Woodstock, Oxford) *b.* Nov. 24th, 1934; ed. at Eton; Capt. (ret.) Rifle Bde.; *m.* 1961, June, only da. of H. M. Shepherd-Cross, of The Old Rectory, Brandsby, Yorks., and has issue living, Mark Adair, *b.* 1964,—James Patrick, *b.* 1966,—Rupert Edward, *b.* 1972.

Uncle living—Cecil George (Knockbaun House, Kingstown, Clifden, co. Galway), *b.* 1900: *m.* 1934, Betty Estelle, da. of the late Capt. Arthur Jewel North, MC, of Vale Mascal, Bexley, Kent.

Widow living of 5th Baronet—ANNE ELIZABETH ADDERLEY (*Anne, Lady Hodson*), (The White House, Awbridge, Romsey, Hants.), da. of Lt.-Col. Adderley Craddock, formerly of Hill House, Sherborne St. John, Basingstoke: *m.* 1928, Maj. Sir Edmond Adair Hodson, DSO, 5th Bt., who *d.* 1972.

Collateral Branches living.

Granddaughters of the late Richard Edmond Hodson, 3rd son of 3rd baronet:—
Issue of the late Gilbert Stanley Hodson, *b.* 1895, *d.* 1972: *m.* 1948, Felicity Margaretta (Luska, Puckane, Nenagh, co. Tipperary), yr. da. of the late Lt.-Col. the Hon. Claud Patrick Brabazon, OBE [see E. Meath, colls.]:—
Kathleen Margaret, *b.* 1949.——Marion Felicity, *b.* 1951.

Issue of the late Gilbert Neville Hodson, 4th son of 3rd baronet, *b.* 1859, *d.* 1918: *m.* 1900, Etheldreda Marjory (who *d.* 1961, having *m.* 2ndly, 1929, as his 2nd wife, Capt. Francis Walter Montagu-Douglas-Scott, who *d.* 1942 [D. Buccleuch, colls.]), da. of the Rev. Thomas Lane Coulson Bridges (formerly R. of Barton, Segrave, Kettering), of West Lydford, Taunton :—
Eva Meriel Violet (Curfew House, Sandwich, Kent), *b.* 1901: *m.* 1927, Rev. Charles Sydney Hardy, who *d.* 1965, and has issue living, John, *b.* 1928,—Robert (Villiers House, Eton Coll., Windsor), *b.* 1932; is a House Master, Eton.

Sir Robert Hodson, 1st baronet, was descended in direct line from the Rev. John Hodson, who belonged to a family long settled at Houghton, Staffordshire, and who assisted in the escape of King Charles I. from Oxford in 1646.   After the Restoration, Dr. Hodson was successively Dean of Clogher and Bishop of Elphin; he died 1686.

HOGG, Creation (U.K.) 1846, of Upper Grosvenor Street, co. Middlesex.

Glory gives strength.

Sir KENNETH WEIR HOGG, O.B.E., 6th *Baronet* ; son of the late Guy Weir Hogg, J.P., el. son of the late Charles Swinton Hogg, 2nd son of 1st baronet ; *b.* Sept. 13th, 1894 ; *s.* his kinsman, *Sir* RONALD TRACY *McGAREL-HOGG*, 4th Baron Magheramorne 1957 ; ed. at Haileybury, and at Ch. Ch., Oxford ; Lieut.-Col. Irish Guards ; European War 1914-18 (wounded) ; O.B.E. (Mil.) 1946 : *m.* 1936, the Hon. Aline Emily Partington, da. of 2nd Baron Doverdale.

Arms—Argent, three boars' heads erased azure, langued gules, between two flaunches of the second, each charged with a crescent of the field. **Crest**—Out of an eastern crown argent, an oak-tree fructed proper, and pendent therefrom an escutcheon azure charged with a dexter arm embowed in armour, the hand grasping an arrow in bend sinister, the point downwards also proper.

Residence—2, Curzon Place, Park Lane, W.1.

Collateral Branches living.

Grandchildren of the late Charles Swinton Hogg, 2nd son of 1st baronet :—
Issue of the late Ernest Charles Hogg, *b.* 1863, *d.* 1907 : *m.* 1893, Lucy, who *d.* 1924, da. of the late William Felton Peel, of Alexandria, Egypt :—

ARTHUR RAMSAY, *M.B.E.*, *b.* Oct. 24th, 1896 ; ed. at Sherborne, and at Ch. Ch., Oxford ; European War 1914-18 as Capt. Roy. W. Kent Regt. (twice wounded), European War 1940-45 as Major Gen. List (M.B.E.) ; M.B.E. (Mil.) 1945 : *m.* 1924, Mary Aileen Hester Lee, da. of the late P. H. Lee Evans, and has issue living, Michael David (19, Woodlands Rd., Barnes, S.W.13), *b.* 1925 ; ed. at Sherborne, and at Ch. Ch., Oxford ; European War 1943-45 as Capt. Grenadier Guards : *m.* 1956, Elizabeth Anne Thérèse, el. da. of Sir Terence Edmond Patrick Falkiner, 8th Bt., and has issue living, Piers Michael James *b.* 1957, Adam Charles *b.* 1958, Oliver John *b.* 1961,—Mark Arthur Philip (59, Castle Rd., Salisbury, Wilts.), *b.* 1928 ; ed. at Sherborne, and at Ch. Ch., Oxford (BA honours 1949, BSc 1950, MA 1953) : *m.* 1955, Jennifer Mary, da. of the late Michael F. Spurrell, and has issue living, Stephen Mark *b.* 1960, Philippa Aileen (twin), *b.* 1956, Sally Elizabeth *b.* 1958, Nicola Frances *b.* 1962,—Simon Charles, *b.* 1936,—Anthea Victoria Anthea *b.* 1966. *Residence*, 27, Elgin Rd., Bournemouth.——Irene Constance (The Blenheim Hotel, Brimley Lane, Bovey Tracey, S. Devon, TQ13 9DH), *b.* 1898.

Granddaughter of the late Sir Stuart Saunders Hogg, 4th son of 1st baronet:—
Issue of the late Stuart James Hogg, *b.* 1865, *d.* 1947 : *m.* 1890, Margaret Alice, who *d.* 1943, da. of the late Andrew Muir, of 42, Holland Park, W. :—
Alison Mary, *b.* 1892 : *m.* 1914, Philip Hope Edward Bagenal, O.B.E., D.C.M.. F.R.I.B.A. (sometime Sergeant RAMC). *Residence*, Leaside, Hertingfordbury, Hertford.

Granddaughter of the late Sir Frederick Russell Hogg, K.C.I.E., C.S.I., 5th son of 1st baronet:—
Issue of the late Charles John Haldane Hogg, *b.* 1861, *d.* 1940 : *m.* 1892, Annie Evelyn, who *d.* 1945, da. of the late Rutherford Haldane, M.D., LL.D., of Edinburgh :—
Nancy Evelyn Lowthorpe, *b.* 1893. *Residence*, 16, St. Martin's Church Street, Salisbury, Wilts.

Grandchildren of the late Quintin Hogg, 7th son of 1st baronet:—
Issue of the late Rt. Hon. Sir Douglas McGarel Hogg (*Viscount Hailsham*), *b.* 1872; *cr.* *Viscount Hailsham* 1929 [*see* B. Hailsham of St. Marylebone].
Issue of the late Sir Malcolm Nicholson Hogg, *b.* 1883, *d.* 1948 : *m.* 1910, Lorna, da. of the late Sir Frank Clement Offley Beaman, sometime a Puisne Judge of High Court of Judicature, Bombay :—

Sir John Nicholson, *TD* (of The Red House, Shedfield, Southampton, and 11, Melton Court, SW7; Brooks's Club) *b.* 1912; ed. at Eton, and at Balliol Coll., Oxford; Dep. Chm. of Williams & Glyn's Ltd., of 67, Lombard St., EC3 of Gallaher, Ltd., and of Prudential Assurance Co. Ltd., Chm. of Brown, Harriman & International Banks, Ltd., and a Dir. of National & Commercial Banking Group Ltd., and of Honeywell, Ltd.; Sheriff of co. London 1960, a Fellow of Eton 1951-70, and Chm. of Abu Dhabi Investment Board since 1967; Chm. Export Guarantees Advisory Council 1962-67, and a Member of Commonwealth War Graves Commn. 1958-64; 1939-45 War as Maj. KRRC (TA in Greece, Crete, W. Desert, N. Africa and NW Europe): *m.* 1948, Barbara Elisabeth, da. of Capt. Arden Franklyn, of New Place, Shedfield, Hants., and widow of Brig. Viscount Garmoyle, DSO, late Rifle Bde., el. son of 4th Earl Cairns, and has issue living, Malcolm David Nicholson, *b.* 1949,—Susan Elisabeth, *b.* 1954.——Vivien Yzabel Suzanne Nicholson (58. Ferry Rd., Barnes, SW13), *b.* 1915: *m.* 1st, 1939, Cdr. Henry Morland, R. Indian Navy, who obtained a divorce 1946; 2ndly, 1947 (m. diss. 1954), John R. Caldwell; 3rdly, 195 5, Thomas Melmoth Walters, who *d.* 1974, and has issue living, (by 1st m.) Michael Henry, *b.* 1941,—Miles Quintin, *b.* 1943.

The 1st baronet, Rt. Hon. Sir James Weir Hogg, Registrar of the Supreme Court of Judicature and Vice-Admiralty Court, Calcutta 1815-33, was twice elected Chm. of E. India Co. and sat as M.P. for Beverley (C) 1834-47 and for Honiton 1847-57. The 2nd baronet, Sir James Macnaghten, K.C.B., was Chm. of Metropolitan Board of Works 1870-89, and was M.P. for Bath, (C) 1865-8, for Truro 1871-85, and for Middlesex, Hornsey Div., 1885-7, when he was *cr. Baron Magheramorne*, having in 1877 assumed the additional surname of McGarel. The Barony of Magheramorne became ext. in 1957 on the death of 4th Baron and 5th baronet.

LINDSAY-HOGG, Creation (U.K.) 1905, of Rotherfield Hall, Rotherfield, Sussex.

Sir WILLIAM LINDSAY LINDSAY-HOGG,
3rd *Baronet*; *b.* Aug. 12th, 1930; *s.* his
father, *Sir* ANTHONY HENRY, 1968; ed. at
Stowe; formerly Lt. 17th/21st Lancers;
Dir. of Roebuck Air Charter, Ltd. 1966-72:
m. 1961 (m. diss. 1967), Victoria, twin da. of
John Pares, of Priory House, Kingsclere,
Hants, and has issue.

    Arms—Per pale indented vert and azure, on a bend
or three boars' heads couped sable.   Crest—Issuant out
of a mural crown argent a boar's head erect sable holding
in the mouth a sprig of oak fructed proper.

    Residence—Underwoods, Edgefield, Melton Con-
stable, Norfolk, N24 2AR.

    Daughter living—Sarah Frances, *b.* 1961.

    Uncle living—EDWARD WILLIAM, *b.* May 23rd, 1910; ed.
at Eton: *m.* 1st, 1936 (divorce 1946), Geraldine, da. of
C. M. Fitzgerald; 2ndly, 1957, Mrs. Kathleen Mary
Cadell, da. of James Cooney, of Carrick-on-Suir, co.
Tipperary, and has issue living, (by 1st m.) Michael, *b.*
1940. *Club*, St. Stephen's Green (Dublin).

Great Aunt living (daughter of 1st baronet)—Cecily Lindsay (Milford Lodge, Craven Arms, Salop),
b. 1898: *m.* 1918, Lt.-Col. Eden George Wallace, JP, who *d.* 1968 [B. Auckland, colls.], and has
issue living, Ronald Eden (Eyford Knoll, Upper Slaughter, Glos.), *b.* 1919; ed. at Eton, and
Ch. Ch., Oxford; late Capt. RGH: *m.* 1st, 1941 (m. diss. 1946), Jean Spencer, twin da. of the late
Spencer Ruthven Thornton; 2ndly, 1947 (m. diss. 1950), Valerie Willes, da. of Dr. Oswald
Smith; 3rdly, 1954 (m. diss. 1964), Mrs. Margaret Cecil Mundy, yr. da. of the late Capt. Arthur
Lacy Compton Clarke; 4thly, 1964, Diana Rose Frances, only da. of Simon Lycett Green [see
Green, Bt., cr. 1886], and has issue living (by 4th m.) David Lycett *b.* 1967,—Vivian George
(Milford Lodge, Craven Arms, Salop), *b.* 1921; ed. at Eton; Col. WG.,—Lindsay Alexander
(Earlsdale House, Pontesford, Salop; Cavalry Club); *b.* 1932; FRICS; Maj. Shrops. Yeo.; late
Lt. WG: *m.* 1964 (m. diss. 1970), Pamela Geraldine Downing, da. of Frank Strickland Skailes.

    The 1st baronet, Sir Lindsay Hogg, assumed by Roy. licence 1906, the additional surname of
Lindsay, and sat as M.P. for S., or Eastbourne, Div. of Sussex (C) Oct. 1900 to Jan. 1906.

HOLCROFT, Creation (U.K.) 1921, of Eaton Mascott, Berrington, co. Salop.

Constant and faithful.

Sir REGINALD CULCHETH HOLCROFT,
T.D., 2nd *Baronet ; b.* April 6th, 1899 ; *s.* his
father, *Sir* GEORGE HARRY HOLCROFT, 1951 ;
ed. at Radley, RMC and Exeter Coll., Oxford,
Lt. Indian Cav. (ret.), Maj. Shropshire
Yeo., and a J.P. for Shropshire (High Sheriff
1950-51): *m.* 1st, 1928, Mary Frances, who *d.*
1963, da. of William Swire, CBE, of Longden
Manor, Salop; 2ndly, 1965 (Maybel) Elizabeth,
da. of Raymond Playfair, of Nairobi, and
formerly wife of 5th Earl of Bandon, and has
issue (by 1st marriage).

    Arms—Argent, a cross engrailed between in the 1st and
4th quarters an eagle wings elevated sable, preying upon
an infant proper, swaddled gules, banded or.   Crest—Upon
a log lopped proper, a raven sable holding in the dexter paw
a sword erect, also proper.

    Seat—Wrentnall House, Pulverbatch, Salop.

    Sons living—By 1st marriage—PETER GEORGE CUL-
CHETH, *b.* April 29th, 1931; High Sheriff of Salop
1969-70: *m.* 1956, Rosemary Rachel, da. of the late Capt
George Nevill Deas, 8th Hussars [M. Anglesey, colls.]
and has issue living, Charles Anthony Culcheth, *b* 1959,—
Thomas Marcus Culcheth, *b.* 1967,—Alexander James
Culcheth, *b.* 1969.—Tania Melanie, *b.* 1961. *Residence*,
Eaton Mascott Hall, Cross Houses, Shrewsbury.——
Michael William Culcheth (The White House, Sutton
Montis, Yeovil) *b.* 1935; ed at Radley; Lt.-Cdr. RN
(ret.): *m.* 1968, Amanda Victoria, da. of Wing-Cdr
I. R. C. Macpherson, of Winterbourne Abbas, Dorset.

Daughters living—Ann Cherida, *b.* 1929: *m.* 1952, John Dewé Neville Lake, of The Old Mill, South
Moreton, Didcot, Berks. [see Walsham Bt., colls.].——Mary Virginia, *b.* 1939: *m.* 1960, Maj.
William Kemp Trotter, 11th Hussars, and has issue living, James, *b.* 1964,—Henry Edward
Dale, *b.* 1966,—Philip George Dale, *b.* 1969,—Victoria, *b.* 1962. *Residence*, The Deanery,
Staindrop, co. Durham.
Sister living—Phyllis Evelyn, *b.* 1901. *Residence*, King's Chantry, Binsted, Alton, Hants.
Collateral Branch living.

    Issue of the late John Culcheth Holcroft, Lieut. 3rd Co. London Yeo., 3rd son of
    1st baronet, *b.* 1905, *d.* (killed in action during European War) 1941 : *m.* 1932,
    Beatrice Mathewson (now of Northbrook, Bentley, Hants), da. of the late
    George F. Feathers :—
Timothy Gilbert Culcheth (of Kitcombe House, Newton Valence, Alton, Hants), *b.* 1934; ed. at
Radley; Capt. (ret.) 11th Hussars: *m.* 1958, Joanna Eve, da. of Adm. Sir Stuart Sumner
Bonham-Carter, KCB, CVO, DSO, and has issue living, Alexandra Jane, *b.* 1962,—Caroline
Joanna, *b.* 1966.

    The 1st baronet, Sir George Harry Holcroft (son of the late William Holcroft, J.P., of Prescot
House, Stourbridge), was Chm. of Littleton Collieries (Limited), High Sheriff of Staffordshire
1913-14, and rendered notable sers. to Birmingham Univ.

HOLDEN, Creation (U.K.) 1893, of Oakworth House, Keighley, Yorkshire.

EXTANT·RECTE·FACTIS·PRÆM

Sir EDWARD HOLDEN, 6th *Baronet; b.*
Oct. 8th, 1916 ; *s.* his father, *Sir* ISAAC HOLDEN,
1962 ; M.R.C.S. England and L.R.C.P. London
1942 ; D.A. England 1945, Fellow of Faculty of
Anæsthetists 1958 : *m.* 1942, Frances Joan, el. da.
of John Spark, J.P., of Ludlow, Stockton-on-
Tees.

Arms—Or, a chief azure, over all a bend nebulée between
two roses gules. Crest—Issuant from a chaplet of oak vert,
an eagle's head erased or, gorged with a collar gemel azure.
Residence—Brigante, Stanwick St. John, Richmond,
Yorks.

Brother living—PAUL, *b.* March 3rd, 1923 : *m.* 1950, Vivien
Mary, younger da. of the late Hedley Broxholme Oldham, of
Allesley, Coventry, and has issue living, Michael Peter, *b.*
1956,—Judith Margaret, *b.* 1952: *m.* 1974, Robert
Forrest, of 68 Chesham Rd., Bury, Lancs.—Susan Diana,
b. 1953. *Residence*, Glenside, Rowhills, Heath End,
Farnham, Surrey.

Sisters living—Ruth, *b.* 1915.——Helen, *b.* 1918: *m.* 1947, William Herbert Chapman, MB, ChB,
of 6, Jennifer Way, Rossmoyne, W. Aust. 6155, and has issue living, Andrew, *b.* 1948,—Richard
Holden, *b.* 1953.—Bridget, *b.* 1950: *m.* 1971, Peter Herbert Stone,—Ann, *b.* 1957.——Janet,
b. 1920: *m.* 1946, Capt. George Richmond Aagaard Welsh, RAOC, of 12, Bylands, White Rose
Lane, Woking, Surrey, and has issue living, Geoffrey Peter, *b.* 1948,—Raymond Michael, *b.* 1949,
—Malcolm Nigel, *b.* 1950.

Collateral Branch living
Issue of the late Peter Wood Holden, 2nd son of Edward Holden, 2nd son of 1st baronet,
b. 1872, *d.* 1965: *m.* 1901, Margaret Jane, who *d.* 1946, da. of the late Utrick A. Ritson,
DL, of Calf Hall, Muggleswick:—
Duncan (Te Mara, Miller Rd., Havelock North, NZ), *b.* 1907: *m.* 1930, Helen, da. of Kinross
White, of Hawkes Bay, NZ, and has issue living, Peter Ritson (Forest Gate, Onga Onga, Hawkes
Bay, NZ), *b.* 1933: *m.* 1958, Juliet, da. of Keith de Castro, of Christchurch, NZ, and has issue
living, Duncan Dudley *b.* 1963, Matthew Keith *b.* 1967, Deborah Elizabeth *b.* 1959, Caroline
Jane *b.* 1961,—Diana Margaret, *b.* 1930: *m.* 1955, John Morris Williams, of Kaiaua, Tolaga
Bay, NZ, and has issue living, Michael *b.* 1956, Philip *b.* 1960, Fiona *b.* 1958, Jennifer *b.* 1961.

The 1st baronet, Sir Isaac Holden (son of Isaac Holden, of Gunends, Alston, Cumberland), was
senior partner in the firm of Isaac Holden and Sons, Wool combers, of Alston Works, Bradford, and
sat as M.P. for Knaresborough (*L*) 1865-68, for Yorkshire, W. Riding, N. Div. 1882-85, and for
Yorkshire, W. Riding, N. Part, Keighley Div. 1885-95. The 2nd baronet, Sir Angus Holden sat
as M.P. for Bradford, E. Div. (*L*) 1885-86, and for Yorkshire, E. Riding, Buckrose Div., 1892-1900,
and was cr. *Baron Holden*, of Alston, co. Cumberland (peerage of United Kingdom) 1908. In 1951,
on the death of the 3rd Baron Holden, the peerage became ext., but the baronetcy passed to his
cousin, Sir Isaac Holden Holden (nephew of 1st Baron Holden), who succeeded as 5th baronet

HOLDEN, Creation (U.K.) 1919, of The Firs, Leigh, co. Lancaster.

Deo omnia debeo

I owe all things to God.

Sir GEORGE HOLDEN, 3rd *Baronet; b.*
Dec. 6th, 1914 ; *s.* his father, *Sir* GEORGE, 1937;
ed. at Oundle : *m.* 1937, Betty, da. of the late
William Shaw, of Portland Place, W.1, and has
issue.

Arms—Sable, on a pale ermine between two chevrons or,
a covered cup of the last. Crest—In front of a rising sun in
its splendour or, a moorcock sable, jelloped and wattled
gules.
Residence—Lynnville, Portland Rd., Dorking, Surrey.

Grandson living—[Issue of David George Holden, el. son
3rd baronet, *b.* 1938; *d.* 1971: *m.* 1964, Nancy (Cheescake
Farm, Weldrake, York), da. of H. W. D. Marwood,
Foulrice, Whenby, Brandsby, Yorks.—John David,
b. Dec. 16th, 1968.
Son living—Brian Peter John, *b.* 1944.
Daughters living—Patricia Margaret Anne, *b.* 1942: *m.*
1963, David Coates Mitchell, of Lynden Royd, 60, Scott
Lane West, Riddlesden, Keighley, Yorks.——Deirdre
Rosemary, *b.* 1949: *m.* 1969, David Marsh, of 20, Impstone
Rd., Pamber Heath, Tadley, Basingstoke, and has issue
living, Andrew David, *b.* 1974,—Nicola Katherin *b.* 1972.
Granddaughter living—[Issue of the late Christopher
William Holden, 2nd son of 3rd baronet, *b.* 1940, *d.*
1968: *m.* 1965, June (who *m.* 2ndly, 1970, Barry Har-
greaves Beaumont, of Manor Farm, Wyton, Hull), da. of
Stephen Carrington]:—Sara, *b.* 1968 (posthumous).

Brothers living—John (The Penthouse, Lancaster Lodge, Birkdale, Southport), *b.* 1918: *m.* 1940,
Margaret Lois, da. of Ivan Sharpe, of Southport, and has issue living, Robin John (Burn Brae,
Castleway, Hale Barns, Ches.), *b.* 1942: ACA: *m.* 1964, Margaret Susan, da. of G. I. Rushton, of
Birkdale, and has issue living, Richard Ingham *b.* 1966, Jonathan Robin *b.* 1969,—Anthony Ivan
(7, Old Bricket Wood, Garston, nr. Watford, Herts.), *b.* 1947; ed. at Oundle and Merton Coll.,
Oxford (MA): *m.* 1971, Amanda Juliet, MA, LRAM, ARCM, da. of Sir Harold Brian Seymour
Warren, MRCS, LRCP, of Kingston House South, Ennismore Gdns., SW7.——James Temple
(Greenways, 93, School Rd., Thornton-Cleveleys, Lancs.), *b.* 1922: *m.* 1st, 1948 (m. diss. 1956),
Olive, da. of Henry Thompson Kirby; 2ndly, 1957, Golda Bracey, da. of Clifford Shirley, and
has issue living (by 1st m.), Peter James, *b.* 1954,—Jacqueline Peta, *b.* 1950 (by 2nd m.), Carl
Temple, *b.* 1963.

Sister living—Margaret, *b.* 1916: *m.* 1942, Maj. E. R. Webster, R. Corps of Signals, of Green Banks,
Culcheth, nr. Warrington, Lancs., and has issue living, Pamela Pixie Anne, *b.* 1946: *m.* 1970,

Timothy Joseph Cahill, and has issue living, Joanne Amanda *b.* 1971, Rachael Louise *b.* 1972, —Carol Yvonne Margaret, *b.* 1949: *m.* 1973, Kenneth G. Wilcock, and has issue living, Jennifer Louise *b.* 1975.

Uncles living (sons of 1st baronet)—Arthur, *b.* 1897; 1914-18 War with R.F.C.: *m.* 1st, 1920, Laura, who *d.* 1949, da. of H. Williams; 2ndly, 1949, Dorothy, da. of Nathan Seddon, of Eccles, and has issue living (by 1st m.) Arthur John (Eagley Bank, Andrew Lane, Bolton), *b.* 1921: *m.* 1949, Ethel Hall, of Bolton,—Henry David (Anglezarke, Belmont Rd., Penn., Wolverhampton), *b.* 1922: *m.* 1947, Marjorie, da. of T. A. Brown, of Astley Bridge, Bolton, and has issue living, David Lawrence *b.* 1948, Andrew Charles *b.* 1949, William John *b.* 1953, Madeline Julie *b.* 1967. *Residence,* Agincourt, Woodlands Av., Rustington, Sussex.——John, *b.* 1900: *m.* 1925, Rita, only da. of H. Walton, of Reedley, Burnley, and has issue living, Derek John (5, Alamain Av., Kloof, Natal), *b.* 1927: *m.* 1951, Patricia Kathleen, da. of F. Mansfield, of Heaton Moor, and has issue living, Richard John *b.* 1960, Elizabeth Anne *b.* 1955,—Norman Michael (7, Trafford Av., Westville, Durban, S. Africa), *b.* 1928: *m.* 1957, Enid N., da. of M. Smith, of Adelaide, S. Aust., and has issue living, Christopher Derek *b.* 1959, Peter James *b.* 1960,—Gillian Nancy, *b.* 1935: *m.* 1964, Dennis George Edwin Cox, of Highlands, Berden, Bishop's Stortford, and has issue living, Gordon Michael *b.* 1967, Julia Alison *b.* 1965. *Residence*—Tulloch, Trearddur Bay, Holyhead.

Sir John Henry Holden, 1st Bt. (son of John Holden), was twice Mayor of Leigh, Lancashire. The 2nd baronet, Sir George, was also twice Mayor of Leigh.

HOLDER, Creation (U.K.) 1898, of Pitmaston, Moseley, Worcestershire.

Nisi Dominus frustra.
It is in vain without the Lord.

Sir JOHN ERIC DUNCAN HOLDER, 3rd *Baronet; b.* Aug. 2nd, 1899; *s.* his father, *Sir* HENRY CHARLES, 1945 ed. at Uppingham and at Brasenose Coll., Oxford (MA): *m.* 1927 (m. diss. 1971), Evelyn Josephine, da. of the late William J. F. Blain; 2ndly, 1971, Marjorie Emily, da. of the late Frank R. Markham, and has issue by 1st m.

Arms—Per pale indented or and gules three chevronels ermine, in chief two trefoils slipped and counterchanged. **Crest**—On the battlements of a tower per pale or and argent, charged with a cross gules, a lion sejant per pale indented azure and of the third supporting with the dexter paw an anchor argent.
Residence—6, Church Street, Hampton, Middlesex.

Son living—By 1st m.—JOHN HENRY (Beechcroft, Harold Rd., Abergavenny, Mon.), *b.* March 12th, 1928: *m.* 1960, Catharine Harrison, yr. da. of Leonard Baker, of Stone Lane, Kinver, Staffs., and has issue living, Nigel John Charles, *b.* 1962,—Hugo Richard (twin), *b.* 1962,— Bridget Georgina, *b.* 1964.

Daughters living—By 1st m.—Anthea Josephine, *b.* 1930: *m.* 1961, Peter Wilbraham Swayne, of Aley Farm, Over Stowey, Bridgwater.——Meryl Evelyn, *b.* 1936.

Brother living—Henry Nigel, *b.* 1906 : *m.* 1st, 1929, Anne, da. of the late Lewis Harris Kittredge, of Cleveland, Ohio, U.S., and Mrs. Woodward, of 85, Avenue Kleber, Paris ; 2ndly, 1946, Kathleen Mary, who *d.* 1971, da. of the late A. R. Pratt. *Residence*, Greenways, The Oxdrove, Burghclere, Newbury, Berks.

Sisters living—Kathleen Joyce, *b.* 1902 : *m.* 1945, Frank Osborne Cooke, who *d.* 1959. *Residence*, Applegarth, Tydehams, Newbury, Berks.——Nancy Lilian (of 115, Colherne Court, S.W.5), *b.* 1907.

Collateral Branches living.

Issue of the late Capt. John Alexander Holder, 2nd son of 1st baronet, *b.* 1876, *d.* 1957 : *m.* 1904, Ida Muriel Sybil, who *d.* 1969, da. of the late Very Rev. Robert William Forrest, DD, Dean of Worcester:—
John Terence, *b.* 1905. *Residence* Durford, Sandy Lane, Cobham, Surrey.——Muriel Lettice, *b.* 1912.

Issue of the late Alfred Ernest Holder, 3rd son of 1st baronet, *b.* 1879, *d.* 1963: *m.* 1909, Gwendoline Louisa Ryland (of Hood Manor, Totnes, S. Devon), da. of the late Sir Thomas Chavasse, M.D., of The Linthurst Hill, Barnt Green, Worcs.:—
Charles Frederic Chavasse (Balsam House, Wincanton, Somerset), *b.* 1910; ed. at Cheltenham; Lieut.-Col. R.A. (ret.) : *m.* 1951, Margaret, youngest da. of A. E. Wrigley, of Gaines, Whitbourne, Worcs., and has issue living, Lucy Margaret, *b.* 1953,—Judith Mary, *b.* 1954.—— Gwendoline Mary Chavasse, *b.* 1913: *m.* 1943, Lawry Knight, of Kiddicott, Clyst St. Mary, Exeter, and has issue living, William, *b.* 1945,—Caroline, *b.* 1944.——Phyllis Margaret Chavasse, *b.* 1918: *m.* 1st, 1956 (m. diss. 1967), as his second wife, William Raymond John Evelyn Whatley, now Balfour, [*see* Page-Wood, Bt., colls.]; 2ndly, 1697, Lt.-Col. Matthew Wakefield Drury Evelyn Wood [*see* Page-Wood, Bt., colls.].

HOLDERNESS, Creation (U.K.) 1920, of Tadworth, co. Surrey.

Sir RICHARD WILLIAM HOLDERNESS, 3rd *Baronet; b.* Nov. 30th, 1927; *s.* his father, *Sir* ERNEST WILLIAM ELSMIE, *CBE,* 1968; ed. at Corpus Christi Coll., Oxford (MA): *m.* 1953, Pamela, da. of Eric Chapman, CBE of 34, Upper Mall, W6, and has issue.
Residence—Rosetree House, Boxgrove, Sussex.

Sons living—MARTIN WILLIAM, *b.* May 24th, 1957.——Andrew James, *b.* 1962.

Daughter living—Jane Carleton, *b.* 1955.

Sister living—Margaret Carleton, *b.* 1929; MB, ChB Edinburgh 1954; FFARCS: *m.* 1965, William Frederick Walter Southwood, MD, MCh, FRCS, of Upton House, Bathwick Hill, Bath, and has issue living, Robert William, *b.* 1966,—John Carleton, *b.* 1967.

The 1st baronet, Sir Thomas William Holderness, G.C.B., K.C.S.I. (son of the late John William Holderness, of Liverpool), was sometime Permanent Under-Sec. of State for India.

HOLLAND, Creation (U.K.) 1917, of Westwell Manor, co. Oxford.

To do (one's) duty in good hope.

Sir JIM SOTHERN HOLLAND, *T.D.*, 2nd *Baronet;* b. March 31st, 1911 ; s. his father, Sir (ALFRED REGINALD) SOTHERN 1948 ; ed. at Marlborough, and at Trin. Coll., Oxford (MA); formerly a Manager and alternate Dir. of Charter Consolidated, Ltd., a Dir. of Central Mining & Investment Corpn., Ltd., of Rand Mines Ltd., and of Price & Pierce Ltd.: ADC to Gov. and C-in-C, Malta 1942-44; 1939-45 War (1939-45 star, Africa star, Defence and War Medals): *m.* 1937, Elisabeth Hilda Margaret, only child of Thomas Francis Vaughan Prickard, CVO, CA, FRICS, of Dderw, Rhayader, Radnorshire, and has issue.

Arms.—Azure, a lion rampant guardant within an orle, surrounded by four mullets and as many fleur-de-lis alternately all argent. Crest.—A fox séjant gules, collared argent, supporting with the dexter forepaw an anchor or.

Seat—Westwell Manor, Burford, Oxon. *Club*—Bath.

Daughters living—Jennifer Lisabeth Gwynllyn, *b.* 1940 —Claerwen Belinda, *b.* 1942.

Brother living—GUY HOPE (Sheepbridge Hill Barn, Eastleach, nr. Hatherop, Cirencester, Glos.; Brooks's and Pratt's Clubs), *b.* July 19th, 1918; ed. at Ch. Ch., Oxford; late Capt. Roy. Scots Greys: *m.* 1945, Joan Marianne, only da. of the late Capt. Herbert Edmund Street, 20th Hussars, and has issue living, Davina Huntley, *b.* 1946,—Georgina, *b.* 1951.

The 1st baronet, Sir (Alfred Reginald) Sothern (son of the late Ben Herbert Holland, Registrar of Deeds for Cape Colony), was H.M. Trade Commr., S. Africa 1908-14, Director-Gen. of Inspection of Munitions 1916, Chm., Central Mining and Investment Corporation Ltd. 1924-31, and 1941-5, and Rhodes Trustee 1932-48.

HOLLINS, Creation (U.K.) 1907, of Greyfriars, Broughton, co. Palatine of Lancaster [Extinct 1963.]

Sir FRANK HUBERT HOLLINS, 3rd and last *Baronet.*

Daughter living of 1st Baronet—Rotha Mary (of The Uplands, Shifnal, Salop), *b.* 1884: *m.* 1928, Capt. Christopher Charles Abraham, Northants Regt., who *d.* 19—, [Parker, Bt., *cr.* 1681].

Collateral Branches living.

Issue of the late Philip Leslie Hollins, 3rd son of 1st baronet, *b.* 1878, *d.* 1933: *m.* 1919. Doris Mary, da. of Charles Arthur Abraham [Parker, Bt. *cr.* 1681]:—

Pamela May, *b.* 1920.——Anne, *b.* 1923: *m.* 1st, 1947 (marriage annulled 1951), Major Percy de Courcy Jones, King's Shropshire LI; 2ndly, 1953, Peter Robert Gibson, of The Pines, Links Lane, Rowlands Castle, Hants.

Issue of the late John Chard Humphrey Lancelot Hollins, 4th son of 1st baronet, *b.* 1890, *d.* 1938: *m.* 1914, Ruth (now of Gelston, Whittle-le-Woods, nr. Chorley, Lancashire), da. of the late John Kiel Tullis, of Glasgow:—

Ruth Jean, *b.* 1928.

HOLT, Creation (U.K.) 1916, of Cheetham, co. Palatine of Lancaster. [Extinct 1968.]

Sir EDWARD HOLT, 2nd and last *Baronet.*

Widow living of 2nd Baronet—MARGARET (*Lady Holt*), (Holmacre, Congleton Rd., Alderley Edge, Cheshire), da. of T. S. Lupton, formerly of Runswick, Cheadle Hulme, Cheshire: *m.* 1931, Sir Edward Holt, 2nd Bt., who *d.* 1968, when the title became ext.

HOLT, Creation (U.K.) 1935, of Liverpool, co. Palatine of Lancaster. [Extinct 1941.]

Sir RICHARD DURNING HOLT, *LL.D.*, 1st and last *Baronet.*

Daughters living of 1st Baronet—Anne Durning, *b.* 1899.——Dorothy Isabel Durning (Shellbrook Hill, nr. Ellesmere, Salop), *b.* 1902: *m.* 1935, Thomas Humphrey Naylor, who *d.* 1966, and has issue living, Richard Christopher (Birch Lane House, Flaunden, nr. Hemel Hempstead, Herts.), *b.* 1936; ed. at Eton: *m.* 1966, Penelope Mary Albinia, da. of the late Maj. Fowell Buxton [*see* Buxton, Bt. colls.],—David Murray (West Green Cottage, Hartley Wintney, Hants.), *b.* 1938; ed. at Eton; Capt. Sg: *m.* 1965, Rosemary Gillian, yr. da. of the late Maj. William Whitehead Hicks Beach, TD, DL, of Witcombe Park, Gloucester [see E. St. Aldwyn, colls.], and has issue living, Nicholas John *b.* 1967, Duncan Hugh *b.* 1968, Christopher William *b.* 1972,—Carolyn Georgina, *b.* 1940: *m.* 1963, David Gardiner,—Rosemary Anne, *b.* 1941: *m.* 1971, Oliver Onions, of Borris House, Port Laoise.

HOME, Creation (N.S.) 1671, of Blackadder, co. Berwick.

[Name pronounced "Hume."]

Look to the end.

Sir David George Home, 13th Baronet ; *b.* Jan. 21st, 1904; *s.* his father, Sir John 1938 ; ed. at Harrow, and at Jesus Coll., Camb. (B.A. 1925); Major late Argyll and Sutherland Highlanders ; claims dormant Scottish Earldom of Dunbar (*cr.* 1607) ; is a Member of Queen's Body Guard for Scotland (Roy. Co. of Archers) : *m.* 1933, Sheila, da. of the late Mervyn Campbell Stephen, and has issue.

Arms—Quarterly : 1st, azure on a chevron argent three roses gules, *Blackadder ;* 2nd, vert, a lion rampant argent langued and armed gules, *Home ;* 3rd, argent, three popinjays, vert beaked and limbed gules, *Pepdie ;* 4th, argent, a cross engrailed azure, *Sinclair.* **Crest**—An adder sable in pale, holding in its mouth a rose gules, leaved and stalked vert. **Supporters**—*Dexter,* an otter ; *sinister,* a falcon, both proper.

Residence—Winterfield, North Berwick, East Lothian.   *Clubs*—Brooks's, New (Edinburgh).

Sons living—JOHN (6, Henrietta St., Double Bay, NSW, 2028); New (Edinburgh) and Union (Sydney) Clubs), *b.* June 1st, 1936; ed. at Harrow, and at Jesus Coll., Camb. (BA): *m.* 1966, Nancy Helen, da. of H. G. Elliott, of Perth, W. Aust., and widow of Cdr. Ian Macgregor, RAN, and has issue living, William Dundas, *b.* 1968,—Georgina Helen, *b.* 1969.——Patrick, *b.* 1941; ed. at Harrow.

Daughters living—Hermione, *b.* 1934; ed. at Lady Margaret Hall, Oxford (BA); a JP for Inner London: *m.* 1959, David Peter Michael Malcolm, of 15, Cromwell Cres., SW5, only son of Maj. Sir Michael Albert James Malcolm, 10th Bt.——Anne, *b.* 1942: *m.* 1962, Michael Franks, of 12, Cromwell Cres., SW5, and has issue living, Lucinda Home, *b.* 1964,—Miranda Home, *b.* 1966.

The Homes of Blackadder descend from John, 4th son of Sir David Home of Wedderburn, who fell at Flodden 1513, whose sons present there were known as the "Seven Spears of Wedderburn." John Home of East Blackadder *m.* 1518, Beatrix, el. da. and co-parcener of Robert Blackadder of that Ilk.   On the failure of descendants of her yr. sister who *m.* Robert Home, another of "the Spears," the whole barony passed to this family.   The Homes of Wedderburn descend from Sir David Home (living 1453), yr. son of Sir Thomas Home of that Ilk, ancestor of the Earls of Home.   Sir John Home, 5th in descent from John of Easter Blackadder, was cr. a baronet with remainder to heirs male of his body.   Sir George Home, 7th baronet, was Vice-Adm. of the Blue.   The 10th baronet in 1878 assumed the additional surname of Speirs.

Home-Purves-Hume-Campbell, see Campbell.

HONYWOOD, Creation (E.) 1660, of Evington, Kent.

Sir William Wynne Honywood, *M.C.*, 10th Baronet ; *b.* April 7th, 1891 ; *s.* his brother, Sir Courtenay John, 1944; ed. at Downside; Col. (ret.); Maj. late 17th/21st Lancers, and Lt.-Col. late KSLI, 1914-18 War in France, Belgium, and German E. Africa (despatches thrice, MC), 1939-45 War in France and Cyrenaica; Adj. Ceylon Mounted Rifles and Ceylon Planters' Rifle Corps 1928-31; was Dep. Director of Pioneers and Labour, Cyrenaica Dist. 1945-6, and Comdt. Roy. Pioneer Corps Depot, Middle East, and Officer Comdg. Troops, Qassasin 1946-8: *m.* 1923, Maud Naylor, who *d.* 1953, da. of the late William Hodgson Wilson, of Hexgreave Park, Southwell, Notts, and has issue.

Arms—Argent, a chevron between three hawks' heads erased azure.   **Crest**—A wolf's head couped ermine.

Address—c/o Lloyds Bank, Ltd., 6, Pall Mall, S.W.1.

OMNE·BONUM·DESUPER

Every good thing is from above.

Son living—FILMER COURTENAY WILLIAM (Greenway Forstal Farmhouse, Hollingbourne, Maidstone, Kent), *b.* May 20th, 1930; ed. at Downside, at RMA, Sandhurst, and at Roy. Agric. Coll., Cirencester (Diploma); ARICS; late 3rd Carabiniers (Prince of Wales' Dragoon Gds.); Assist. Surveyor Min. of Agric. Fisheries and Food, Maidstone 1966-73, Surveyor, Cockermouth, Cumbria 1973-74, since when Sr. Lands Officer S.E. Region Central Electricity Generating Board: *m.* 1956, Elizabeth Margaret Mary Cynthia, da. of the late Sir Alastair George Lionel Joseph Miller, 6th Bt. (*cr.* 1788), and has issue living, Rupert Anthony Pagan, *b.* 1957,—Simon Joseph, *b.* 1958,—Mary Caroline, *b.* 1961,—Judith Mary Frances, *b.* 1964.

Daughters living—Rosamund Iseulte Mary, *b.* 1924; 1939-45 War with WRNS: *m.* 1947, Paul Anthony Prior, late Lt. RNVR (11/15, Av. de L'abreuvoir, 78160 Marly-le-Roi, France), and has issue living, Jacqueline Mary, *b.* 1950: *m.* 1972, Timothy Charles Feline,—Helen Catherine, *b.* 1953,—Sarah Jane, *b.* 1956,—Emma Charlotte Claudia, *b.* 1962.——Zaidée Maud Elsie, *b.* 1926; is a State Registered Nurse, SCM, Edinburgh: *m.* 1954, Lieut.-Com. Douglas Inglefield Haywood, RN, and has issue living, Richard Douglas, *b.* 1964,—Elizabeth Zaidée, *b.* 1955,—Katherine Mary, *b.* 1962.—Patricia Anne, *b.* 1967.   *Residence,* Little Romanys, Lawbrook Lane, Peaslake, Surrey.

Brother living—Philip Sydney, *b.* 1893: *m.* 1st, 1916, Helen, da. of the Rev. H. B. Hudson, of New York; 2ndly, 1928, Rachel Gray, da. of Dr. O. M. Jones, formerly of Norfolk, Virginia, U.S.A., and has issue living, (by 2nd marriage) Elodie Constance Joyce, *b.* 1935. *Residence,* Woodcliff Lake, New Jersey, U.S.A.

Collateral Branches living.

Issue of the late Reginald Ernest Honywood, 6th son of 7th baronet, *b.* 1863, *d.* 1917: *m.* 1906, Victoria Henrietta Ezilda Carr, who *d.* 1974:—

Flora Victoria, *b.* 1907: *m.* 1957, Maurice Edward Grubb. *Residence,* 81, Portsea Hall, Portsea Place, W.2.

Issue of the late Guy Honywood, 8th son of 7th baronet, *b.* 1871, *d.* 1912: *m.* 1900, Margaret Bennett Adamson:—

Thomas Guy, *b.* 1903. *Residence,* 64, McMaster Street, Invercargill, New Zealand.

The 1st baronet was Sir Edward Honywood (son of the late Sir John Honywood, High Sheriff of Kent 1607-9). Sir John Honywood, 4th baronet, was M.P. for Steyning 1784-5 and 1788-90, for Canterbury 1790-1802, and for Honiton 1802-6. Sir John William Honywood, 8th baronet, was an Alderman of Kent County Council.

HOOD, Creation (U.K.) 1922, of Wimbledon, co. Surrey.

Sir HAROLD JOSEPH HOOD, *T.D.,* 2nd *Baronet ; b.* Jan. 23rd, 1916 ; *s.* his father, *Sir* JOSEPH, 1931 ; ed. at Downside ; is Lieut. R.A. (T.A.); a Dir. of Catholic Herald, Ltd.; appointed Editor of *The Catholic Who's Who* 1952; a Knt. of St. Gregory the Great, and of Sovereign Mil. Order of Malta: *m.* 1946, the Hon. Ferelith Rosemary Florence Kenworthy, only da. of 10th Baron Strabolgi, and has issue.

Arms—Argent, on a mount vert an oak tree fructed proper, a chief sable, thereon a bow stringed also proper. **Crest**—A demi-stag proper resting the sinister foot on a fret or.

Residence—31, Avenue Road, St. John's Wood, NW8 6BS. *Clubs,*—Challoner, MCC, RAC.

Sons living—JOHN JOSEPH HAROLD, *b.* Aug. 27th, 1952. ——Basil Gervase Francis Gerard, *b.* 1955.

Daughters living—Josepha Ferelith Emma Margaret-Mary, *b.* 1953.——Margaret Marie Elizabeth Felicia, *b.* 1965.

Brother living—Robin Adrian, *b.* 1924 : *m.* 1949, Miriam Teresa (Special Attaché, Venezuelan Embassy, London), da. of the late Don Humberto Blanco-Fombona, and has issue living, Simon Joseph Paul Blanco, *b.* 1951,—Martin Joseph Blanco, *b.* 1953,—Bernadette Marie Blanco (twin), *b.* 1953, —Anne-Marie Elena Kathleen Blanco, *b.* 1957. *Residences,* 29, Campden Hill Road, W.8 ; Rose Tree Cottage, Borley Green, near Sudbury, Suffolk.

Half-Sisters living—Winifred Edith, *b.* 1901: *m.* 1927, Basil Raymond Worthington, who *d.* 1968, and has issue living, Colleen Mary. *Residence,* 164, Cranmer Court, SW3.——Kathleen Muriel (20, Regency Court, London Rd., Brighton, 6), *b.* 1905: *m.* 1st, 1929, Thomas Percival Durant Beighton, who obtained a divorce 1938; 2ndly, 1939, Jessel Anidjar Romain, who *d.* 1961.

The 1st baronet, Sir Joseph Hood, a solicitor, sometime a Dep. Chm. British American Tobacco Co., Ltd., sat as M.P. for Wimbledon (*U*) 1918-24, and was Mayor of Wimbledon 1930-31.

FULLER-ACLAND-HOOD, Creations (U.K.) 1806 of Hartington, co. Derby, and 1809, of St. Audries, co. Somerset.

Sir (ALEXANDER) WILLIAM FULLER-ACLAND-HOOD, 8th Baronet of Hartington and 6th Baronet of St. Audries, son of the late William Fuller-Acland-Hood, 5th son of 3rd Bt. (*cr.* 1809), *b.* March 5th, 1901; *s.* his cousin, the 2nd Baron St. Audries (also 7th and 5th Bt.) 1971; in remainder to Irish Barony of Bridport; *cr.* 1794 [see V. Bridport]; naturalised an American citizen 1926; ed. at Wellington Coll., RMA, and Univ. of Cal. (MA); late Lt. RE: *m.* 1925, Mary V., da. of the late Augustus Edward Jessup, of Philadelphia, USA, and has issue.

Arms,—Quarterly: 1st and 4th, azure, a fret argent on a chief sable three crescents or, *Hood;* 2nd, checky argent and sable, a fesse gules, *Acland;* 3rd, argent, three bars and a canton gules, *Fuller.* **Crests,**—1st, a Cornish chough holding an anchor on the dexter side in bend sinister proper, *Hood;* 2nd, a man's hand couped at the wrist in a glove lying fessewise, thereon a falcon perched all proper, *Acland;* 3rd, out of a ducal coronet gules, a lion's head argent, *Fuller.*

Address,—Box 577, Star Route 2, 29 Palms, Cal., USA 92277.

Daughter living—Elisabeth Anne (11216, Jumper Mesa Rd., SR1, Box 38 D6, Littlerock, Cal, 93543, USA), *b.* 1931:

m. 1952 (m. diss. 1960) Richard C. Pferdner; 2ndly, 1968, Wallace G. Henry who *d.* 1972, and has issue living (by 1st m.) Richard Charles, *b.* 1959,—Kathleen Marie, *b.* 1957,—(by 2nd m.), Eric William, *b.* 1969.
Collateral Branch living.
　　　　　Issue of the late Lt.-Col. Arthur ACLAND-HOOD-REYNARDSON, OBE, 2nd son of 3rd baronet (cr. 1809), *b.* 1859, *d.* 1929 (received Roy. licence to drop the surname of Fuller and assume that of Reynardson after Acland-Hood, and to bear the arms of Reynardson quarterly in lieu of those of Fuller): *m.* 1896, Miriam Anne, *ARRC*, who *d.* 1921, da. of the late Col. C. Birch-Reynardson, of Holywell Hall, Lincolnshire:—
Agatha Isabel (*Hon. Mrs. Mountjoy J. C. W. Fane*), *b.* 1903: *m.* 1926, Maj. the Hon. Mountjoy John Charles Wedderburn Fane, TD, who *d.* 1963 [see E. Westmorland]. *Residence,*—The Old Rectory, Careby, Stamford.

　　This family has common ancestry with Viscount Hood and Viscount Bridport. Sir Samuel Hood, 1st Bt. was cr. 1809 with remainder to his nephew Alexander Hood, who *s.* as 2nd Bt. The Baronetcy of Hartington (cr. 1806) was conferred upon Sir Hugh Bateman with remainder to the male descendants of his daus, Catherine Juliana (who afterwards *m.* Sir Edward Dolman Scott, 2nd Bt. of Great Barr), and Amelia Anne (who afterwards *m.* Sir Alexander Hood, 2nd Bt.). The Baronetcy descended to the former's son, who *s.* at birth, but this title expired in 1905 when the Baronetcy reverted to Sir Alexander Fuller-Acland-Hood, 4th Bt. (who was subsequently cr. Baron St. Audries in 1911, and whose father Sir Alexander Hood added by Roy. licence 1849 the additional names of Fuller-Acland on marriage to Harriet, da. and heir of Sir Peregrine Palmer Fuller-Acland, 2nd and last Bt.). On the death in 1971 of Alexander Peregrine, 2nd Baron St. Audries, the Barony became ext., and the Baronetcies of 1806 and 1809 devolved upon Sir Alexander William, grandson of the 3rd Bt. (cr. 1809).

HOOPER, Creation (U.K.) 1962, of Tenterden, co. Kent.

Sir ANTHONY ROBIN MAURICE HOOPER, 2nd *Baronet*; *b.* Oct. 26th, 1918; *s.* his father, *Sir* FREDERIC COLLINS, 1963; a Dir. of Couper Gallery: *m.* 1970 (m. diss. 1973), Cynthia Theresa Mary, da. of the late Lt.-Col. William James Holdsworth Howard, DSO.

Arms—Azure two swans volant in pale proper on a chief gules an open book proper edged or bound argent between two lyres gold. **Crest**—In front of a swan statant proper five annulets or.

Residence—3, St. Georges' Court, Gloucester Rd., SW7.

Sister living—Bobyl Jane, *b.* 1924: *m.* 1945, Lt.-Cdr. Bernard Vann, M.B.E., D.S.C., R.N., and has issue living, Michael Vann *b.* 1946,—James Vann, *b.* 1949.
Half sister living—Emma Charlotte HOOPER, *b.* 1949; resumed the surname of Hooper: *m.* 1968, (m. diss. 1973), Razek Mamarbachi.
Widow living of 1st Baronet—PRUDENCE AVERY (NEILL) (*Prudence, Lady Hooper*) (40, Pont St., SW1), da. of the late Basil Wenham, of Armscote, Warwicks.: *m.* 1945, as his 2nd wife, Sir Frederic Collins Hooper, 1st baronet, who *d.* 1963.

　　Sir Frederic Collins Hooper, 1st Bt., only son of the late Frederic Stephen Hooper, of Bruton, Somerset, was Managing Dir. of Schweppes Ltd. He was Dir. of Business Training, Min. of Labour and National Ser. 1945-46, and Chm. of Advisory Board, Regular Forces Resettlement Ser. 1957-60.

HOPE, Creation (N.S.) 1628, of Craighall, co. Fife.

But hope is unbroken.

Sir ARCHIBALD PHILIP HOPE, *O.B.E.*, *D.F.C.*, 17th *Baronet*; *b.* March 27th, 1912; *s.* his father, *Sir* JOHN AUGUSTUS, *O.B.E.*, 1924; ed. at Eton, and at Balliol Coll., Oxford (B.A. 1934); formerly Wing-Com. and acting Group-Capt. Auxiliary Air Force; European War 1939-45 (despatches twice, D.F.C., O.B.E.); O.B.E. (Mil.) 1945: *m.* 1938, Ruth, da. of Carl R. Davis, of Fryern, Storrington, Sussex, and has issue.

Arms—Azure, a chevron or between three bezants. **Crest**—A broken terrestrial globe surmounted by a rainbow issuing out of a cloud at each end all proper. **Supporters**—Two female figures representing Hope in vestments vert, on their heads garlands of flowers, each resting her exterior hand on an anchor all proper.

Residence—Upton Grey Lodge, near Basingstoke, Hants.

Sons living—JOHN CARL ALEXANDER (10, Furlong Rd., N7), *b.* June 10th, 1939; ed. at Eton: *m.* 1968, Merle Pringle, da. of Robert Douglas, of Southside, Holbrook, Ipswich, and has issue living, Alexander Archibald Douglas, *b.* 1969,—Natasha Anne, *b.* 1971.——Charles Archibald, *b.* 1945; ed at Eton, and Balliol Coll., Oxford (BA); MA London; a Jr. Research Fellow, Kings Coll., Camb.

Brother living—Hugh Alexander, *O.B.E.*, *M.C.*, *b.* 1914 ; ed. at Eton, and at Worcester Coll., Oxford; Lieut.-Col. (ret.) late King's Royal Rifle Corps; a Mem. of Hon. Corps of Gentlemen at Arms; 1939-45 War (despatches, M.C.), E. Africa 1955-56 (despatches); O.B.E. (Mil.) 1956: *m.* 1949, Cynthia Evelyn, da. of the late Lieut.-Col. Algernon Corbet Turnor, M.C., Roy. Horse Guards [*see* B. Londesborough], and has issue living, Andrew Hugh, *b.* 1951. *Residence*, Fosters, Mattingley, nr. Basingstoke, Hants.

Sister living—Katharine Anne, *b.* 1916: *m.* 1st, 1939, Flight-Lieut. Carl Raymond Davis, D.F.C., Auxiliary Air Force, who *d.* (killed in action during Battle of Britain) 1940 ; 2ndly, 1945, Major Eric George Ewart Rayner, RA, and has issue living, (by 1st m.) Carl Michael (Bagmoor, Hambledon, Henley-on-Thames, Oxon.), *b.* 1940: *m.* 1963, Carolyn Rachel, da. of John White, of Cushat Wood, Potten End, Berkhamsted, and has issue living, Carl Robert *b.* 1971, Helen Rachel *b.* 1966, Julie Theresa, *b.* 1968,—(by 2nd m.) Gillian Mary, *b.* 1948. *Residence*, Horsemoor House, Chieveley, Newbury.

Collateral Branches living.

Granddaughter of the late Capt. Graham Archibald Hope, son of the late Archibald Godfrey Hope, 2nd son of the late Maj.-Gen. Archibald Hugh Hope, son of the late Hugh Hope, 4th son of 9th baronet:—

Issue of the late Sqdn.-Ldr. Nigel Hope, *b.* 1907, *d.* (on active ser. during European War) 1939 : *m.* 1936, Evelyn Di (of Trelaske, Launceston, Cornwall; she *m.* 2ndly, 1950, William Bryant), yr. da. of the late Harry Arnaud Watson, of Emsworth, Hants:—

Alison (*posthumous*), *b.* 1940.

Grandson of the late Major Richard Berwick Hope, son of the late Archibald Godfrey Hope (ante) :—

Issue of the late Alexander Erskine Hope, Lieut. Bedfordshire and Herts Regt., *b.* 1917, *d.* (killed in action during European War) 1944 : *m.* 1941, Lilias Mary Phyllis (who *m.* 2ndly, 19—, C. H. K. Daly), da. of the late Rev. William Herbert Austwick:—

Alexander David Austwick (posthumous), *b.* 1945.

Granddaughter of the late Maj.-Gen. Archibald Hugh Hope (ante) :—

Issue of the late Lewis Anstruther Hope, C.B., *b.* 1855, *d.* 1929 : *m.* 1887, Lucy Elizabeth, who *d.* 1952, da. of the late George Palmer, J.P. (formerly M.P.), of The Acacias, Reading :—

Olive Georgina, *b.* 1891 : *m.* 1915, Col. Norman Valentine Blacker, D.S.O., M.C., who *d.* 1958, and has issue living, *Gen.* Sir Cecil Hugh, *KCB*, *OBE*, *MC* (Whitchurch House, Aylesbury) *b.* 1916, [*see* " Knightage "]: *m.* 1947, Felicity Mary, da. of Maj. Ivor Buxton, DSO, TD [*see* Buxton, Bt. colls.], and widow of Maj. John Rew, and has issue living, Terence *b.* 1948, Philip *b.* 1949,—Joan Olive, *b.* 1919: *m.* 1943, Flight-Lt. C. Booth, RAF, who *d.* (killed in action during 1939-45 War) 1945, and has issue living, Wendy Joan *b.* 19—. *Residence*, Charity Farm, South Walsham, Norwich.

Granddaughter of the late Major Cecil Arthur Hope, 2nd son of the late James Hope, W.S., *b.* 1818, 4th son of late John Hope, M.D., F.R.S., grandson of the late Sir Archibald Hope (Lord Rankeillour of the Court of Session), 2nd son of 2nd baronet:—

Issue of the late Lieut.-Col. Arthur Clement Hope, M.B.E., *b.* 1891, *d.* 1961 : *m.* 1933, Elizabeth Hale, da. of Frederick W. Wallace, of Redjacket, Washington, U.S.A.:—

Jean Elizabeth, *b.* 1937: *m.* 1960, Sergio Pizzicaria. *Residence,*

Grandchildren of the late Edward William Hope, O.B.E., M.D., D.Sc. (infra):—

Issue of the late John Edward Bowring Hope, *b.* 1901, *d.* 1957: *m.* 1927, Catherine (of 26, Roman Road, Shrewsbury, Shropshire), da. of Robert Stephen Hubbersty, M.D., of Avenue House, Sunderland :—

Michael Stephen Edward (Twillingate, 5, Condover Park, Condover, Salop), *b.* 1928; late 2nd Lieut. RHG: *m.* 1st, 1957, Edith Rosemary Byrne, who *d.* 1962, da. of Mrs. Margaret Roberts, of Bexhill-on-Sea; 2ndly, 1964, Catherine Emily, da. of the late Frederick Bradshaw, and widow of William Kenneth Latham, of Newfoundland, and has issue living, (by 1st m.) Nigel John Charles *b.* 1959,—Michelle Catherine Margaret, *b.* 1958,—(by 2nd m.) Catherine Charlotte, *b.* 1964,—Louise Joan, *b.* 1969.——Christopher John (1, Port Hill Drive, Shrewsbury), *b.* 1931; late 2nd Lt. King's Shropshire LI: *m.* 1956, Louise Alicia, da. of Joseph Hall, of St. John's, Newfoundland, and has issue living, Peter John, *b.* 1959,—Susan Louise, *b.* 1960.——Catherine Eve, *b.* 1941: *m.* 1963, Alastair John Padriac Hardie, of 52, Friars Stile Rd., Richmond, Surrey, and has issue living, Jane Catherine Sheelagh, *b.* 1964,—Lucy Anne, *b.* 1967.

Granddaughters of Robert Wallis Hope, el. son of the late Col. Robert Hope, *b.* 1763, son of Capt. Robert Hope, grandson of Sir Archibald Hope (ante):—

Issue of the late Edward William Hope, O.B.E., M.D., D.Sc., *b.* 1856, *d.* 1950 : *m.* 1899, Charlotte Rennie, who *d.* 1962, da. of John Bowring, of Liverpool:—

Marjory Mary, *b.* 1901: *m.* 1940, Francis Stephen Hubbersty, of 34, The Grove, Marton, Middlesbrough.——Elsa Rennie (51, Caldy Rd., W. Kirby, Cheshire), *b.* 1905: *m.* 1925, Lionel Bishop Ridley, who *d.* 1965.

Granddaughter of the late Col. John Urmson Hope, DSO (infra):—

Issue of the late Lt.-Col. John Patrick Molesworth Hope, *b.* 1913, *d.* 1975: *m.* 1938 (m. dis. 1947) (Margaret) Clare Aida, da. of Lionel Julian Walford, of Middleton Stoney, Bicester, Oxon:—

Virginia Anne (77, Troy Court, Kensington High St., W8), *b.* 1942.

Grandchildren of the late Maj.-Gen. John Edward Hope, el. son of Col. John Isaac Hope, yr. son of Col. Robert Hope (*b.* 1763) (ante):—

Issue of the late Col. John Urmson Hope, DSO, *b.* 1881, *d.* 1967: *m.* 1907, Christine Jessie Shelton (181, Lauderdale Mansions, Lauderdale Rd., Maida Vale, W9), da. of Augustus Shelton Hooper, JP, of Hong Kong:—

Christine Mary Shelton (32, Moberly Rd., Salisbury), *b.* 1909: *m.* 1st, 1929, Capt. Frank Wilson Houghton, RA, from whom she obtained a divorce 1934; 2ndly, 1938, Maj.-Gen. Harry Pratt Sparks, CBE, MC, who *d.* 1965, and has issue living, (by 2nd m.) Charles Pratt, *b.* 1941: *m.* 1967, Brigitte Marie-Louise Marcelle Jeanneau, and has issue living, William Xavier Pratt *b.* 1972, Marie-Ann Ruth *b.* 1970,—Jane, *b.* 1939: *m.* 1964, Eric Hugh Legat, of The Cleve, Woodgreen, Fordingbridge, Hants., and has issue living, Patricia Jane *b.* 1965, Vanessa Sarah *b.* 1967, Joanna Mary *b.* 1971.

Issue of the late Rev. George Archibald Hope, *b.* 1882, *d.* 1950 : *m.* 1929, Edith Margaret Aston (now of 35, Kent Rd., Southsea), da. of the late Martin Aston Key, O.B.E., M.D.:—

Robert Frank Molesworth, *b.* 1934 ; ed. at Marlborough, and at New Coll., Oxford (B.A. 1957) : *m.* 1957, Jacqueline Pierrette Regine, da. of Paul Marcel Albert Forer, of 9, Rue de Lille, Marseilles, France, and has issue living, Frank George Aston, *b.* 1959,—Patrick James Mailhe, *b.* 1960.

Residence, 35, Kent Rd., Southsea.——Charles Aston (4, West Av., Exeter), *b.* 1940; *ed.* at Marlborough and Emmanuel Coll., Oxford (BA); Solicitor 1968: *m.* 1967, Kathryn Elizabeth, da. of Capt. Wilfred Williams, Merchant Navy (ret.), and has issue living, Philip Aston, *b.* 1968,—Nicholas Astley, *b.* 1970.——Margaret Mary, *b.* 1932: *m.* 1958, Cdr. Brian Thomas Tippetts, RN, of Priory Cottage, Hinton Charterhouse, Bath, and has issue living, Thomas Edward Hope, *b.* 1965,—Rebecca Mary, *b.* 1959,—Lucinda Ann Margaret, *b.* 1961,—Alice Elizabeth, *b.* 1963.——Elizabeth, *b.* 1937: *m.* 1966, the Rev. (John) Nigel Rowe, of St. Mary's Vicarage, Newchurch-in-Pendle, Fence, Burnley, Lancs.——Clare Urmson (62, Chelsea Gdns., Chelsea Bridge Rd., SW1), *b.* 1943.

Descendants of the late Sir Charles Hope, K.T. (son of the late John Hope, son of the late Sir James Hope, K.B., 6th son of 1st baronet), who was *cr. Earl of Hopetoun*, 1703 [*see* M. Linlithgow].

The 1st baronet, Sir Thomas, Lord Advocate of Scotland, had fourteen children, two of whom were upon the Bench when he pleaded as Lord Advocate ; from this circumstance, it is imagined, arises the privilege which that officer of the Crown enjoys of pleading with his head covered, it having been considered derogatory for a father to uncover before his sons.   In 1643 he was appointed Commissioner to the General Assembly of the Church of Scotland, a dignity which was not again enjoyed by any commoner for nearly three centuries.   The 11th baronet was M.P. for Midlothian (C) 1845-53. Sir John Augustus, O.B.E., 16th baronet, was M.P. for Midlothian (Edinburghshire) (C) Sept. 1912 to Nov. 1918, and for N. Div. of Midlothian and Peeblesshire, Dec. 1918 to Oct. 1922.

HOPE, Creation (U.K.) 1932, of Kinnettles, co. Angus.

AT SPES·NON·FRACTA.

But hope is unbroken.

Sir JAMES HOPE, *M.M.*, 2nd *Baronet ; b.* May 2nd, 1898 ; *s.* his father *Sir* HARRY, 1959 ;   European War 1916-19 with Black Watch (M.M.).

𝔄rms—Azure, a chevron between two bezants in chief and the sun in his splendour in base or. 𝔠rest—A broken terrestrial globe surmounted by a rainbow proper.
  Residence—Eastbarns, Dunbar, East Lothian.

Brother living—ROBERT HOLMS-KERR, *b.* April 12th, 1900 : *m.* 1928, Margaret Eleanor, da. of the Very Rev. Marshall Lang, D.D., of The Manse, Whittingehame, East Lothian. *Residence*, Barneyhill, Dunbar, East Lothian.
Sister living—Margaret Ralston, *b.* 1902 : *m.* 1939, Wing-Cdr. Dudley Lloyd-Evans, MC, DFC, and has issue living, Thomas Harry Hope Lloyd, *b.* 1940; *ed.* at Fettes, and at St. Andrews Univ. (BSc),—Robert Dudley James Lloyd, *b.* 1942, *ed.* at Glenalmond, and at Trin. Coll., Camb. (BA).
  The 1st baronet, Sir Harry Hope (younger son of the late James Hope, of Eastbarns, Dunbar), was M.P. for Buteshire (C) 1910-18, for W. Div. of Stirlingshire and Clackmannanshire 1918-22, and for Forfarshire 1924-31.

Hope-Dunbar, see Dunbar.

HOPKINS, Creation (U.K.) 1929, of St. Pancras, co. London.   [Extinct 1946.]

Sir JOHN WELLS WAINWRIGHT HOPKINS, 1st and last *Baronet.*

Daughter living of 1st Baronet—Elizabeth Joan: *m.* 1925, Com. Leslie Graeme Herbert Farmer, R.N. (retired), and has issue living, James Arthur, *b.* 1930,—Jane Ann, *b.* 1934 : *m.* 1954, Major Arthur Guy Racovita Ellerington, Grenadier Guards (ret.), of 39, Thurloe Sq., SW7,—Elizabeth Geraldine, *b.* 1935: *m.* 1954, John William Bowring Wimble, of Bush Farm, North Chailey, Lewes, Sussex. *Residence*, Tompset's Bank, Forest Row, Sussex.

HORLICK, Creation (U.K.) 1914, of Cowley Manor, co. Gloucester.

Labore et scientia.

By labour and knowledge.

Sir JOHN JAMES MACDONALD HORLICK, 5th *Baronet, b.* April 9th, 1922; *s.* his father, *Lt.-Col. Sir* JAMES NOCKELLS, *OBE, MC,* 1972; *ed.* at Eton; late Capt. Coldm. Gds.; Dep. Chm. of Horlicks Ltd., 1968-72: *m.* 1948, June, da. of Douglas Cory-Wright, CBE [*see* Cory-Wright, Bt.], and has issue.
  𝔄rms—Argent, a lion rampant and on a chief gules between two bulls' heads cabossed a garb of barley or. 𝔠rest—In front of a garb of barley or a lion's head erased gules.
  Residences,—Woodlands House, Henley-on-Thames, Oxon., 43, Montpelier Sq., SW7; Tournaig, Poolewe, Ross-shire.

Son living—JAMES CUNLIFFE WILLIAM, *b.* Nov. 19th, 1956.
Daughters living—Harriet Anne, *b.* 1950; BA London: *m.* 1970, Antony Lansdown Granville, of Tachbrook House, Stourton, nr. Shipston-on-Stour, Warwicks. [*see* Rose, Bt. cr. 1909].——Araminta, *b.* 1953: *m.* 1975, Edward Rory Carson, only son of the Hon. Edward Carson [*see* By. Carson].
Sister living—Ursula Priscilla Marie Gabrielle, *b.* 1916: *m.* 1st, 1936, Capt. Stafford Vaughan Stepney Howard, Coldstream Guards (Reserve), from whom she obtained a divorce 1940 [*see* D. Norfolk, colls.]; 2ndly, 1940, Lt.-Col. John Frederick Herron Weaver, 1st King's Dragoon Gds. (ret.), and has issue living, (by 1st m.) [*see* D. Norfolk, colls.], (by 2nd m.) Christopher Giles Herron, *b.* 1946; *ed.* at Eton. *Residence*, Greywalls, Gullane, E. Lothian.

Daughters living of 3rd Baronet—Natasha, *b.* 1935.——Anna (62, Redcliffe Rd., SW10), *b.* 1938: *m.* 1st, 1960 (m. diss. 1971), Peter Gammon; 2ndly, 19—, and has issue living (by 1st m.), Anthony John, *b.* 1965,—Tama Jane, *b.* 1962.

Daughters living of 2nd Baronet—Roma Ernestine (*Roma, Countess of Dartmouth*) (15B, Bedford Towers, Brighton), *b.* 1903: *m.* 1923, the 8th Earl of Dartmouth, who *d.* 1962.——Elizabeth Ann (Couch, Kate St., Alexandra Headland, Sunshine Coast, Qld.), *b.* 1914: *m.* 1933, John Balfour Symington Coats, and has issue living, Callum (Parsley Place, Montville, Sunshine Coast, Qld.) *b.* 1939: *m.* 1967, Emily Jane Archer, and has issue living, Angus Orlando *b.* 1968, Guy Oliver Balfour *b.* 1972,—Christopher David (47 Hopetoun St., Paddington, Sydney, NSW), *b.* 1943: *m.* 1966, Margaret Helen Van Etten, and has issue living, Mercedes Jane,—Ian Forester Mungo, *b.* 1953,—Mary Manuela, *b.* 1937: *m.* 1959, Francis Skorka, of Essendon Rd., Moggill, Brisbane, Qld., and has issue living, Lester Carl *b.* 1963, Darius Brian Christopher *b.* 1970, Catherine Benita *b.* 1966.

Widows living of 2nd, 3rd and 4th Baronets—SOPHIE SONIA THEOLESCO (*Dowager Lady Horlick*): *m.* 1931, as his second wife, Sir Ernest Burford Horlick, 2nd baronet, who *d.* 1934.——BERYTA (MURRAY) (*Beryta, Lady Horlick*), only da. of Roland Allport, of Sydney, NSW: *m.* 1934 (m. diss. 1948), as his second wife (re-married 1957, as his 4th wife), Sir Peter James Cunliffe Horlick, 3rd Bt., who *d.* 1958.——JOAN ISOBEL (*Joan, Lady Horlick*), (Timbers, Nuffield, Henley-on-Thames, Oxon.), da. of the late James Barrie Macgill: *m.* 1956, as his 2nd wife, Lt.-Col. Sir James Nockells Horlick, 4th Bt., OBE, MC, who *d.* 1972.

Sir James Horlick, 1st Bt., son of James Horlick of Ruardean, Glos. was Lord of Manor of Cowley, Glos., High Sheriff of Glos. 1902, and Chm. and Pres. of Horlicks Ltd.

HORNBY, Creation (U.K.) 1899, of Brookhouse, St. Michael, Blackburn, County Palatine of Lancaster. [Extinct 1971.]

Sir HENRY RUSSELL HORNBY, 2nd and last *Baronet*.

Daughter living of 2nd Baronet—Jean Margaret (Cranford, Worlington, Mildenhall, Suffolk), *b.* 1915: *m.* 1946, Maj.-Gen. Lionel Charles Manners-Smith, CBE, who *d.* 1975, and has issue living, Maurice Charles Hornby, *b.* 1948; Capt. R. Green Jackets: *m.* 1974, Elizabeth, yst. da. of Maj.-Gen. Allan Elton Younger, DSO, OBE, of 408, Collingwood House, Dolphin Sq., SW1.

Daughters living of 1st Baronet—Olivia Letitia, *b.* 1890.——Margaret Grace (Flat 25, Elm Park Gdns., SW10), *b.* 1901.——Annette Mary (Flat 25, Elm Park Gdns., SW10), *b.* 1905.

Widow living of 2nd Baronet—DOROTHY ELMA (*Lady Hornby*), (Barraclough, Clitheroe, Lancs.), da. of the late Maj.-Gen. Sir William Fry, KCVO, CB: *m.* 1913, Sir Henry Russell Hornby, 2nd Bt., who *d.* 1971, when the title became ext.

HORNE, Creation (U.K.) 1929, of Shackleford, Surrey.

Sir ALAN EDGAR HORNE, *M.C.*, 2nd *Baronet*; *b.* Sept. 19th, 1889; *s.* his father, *Sir* (WILLIAM) EDGAR, 1941; ed. at Eton, and at Univ. Coll., Oxford; European War 1914-19 in France and Balkans as Capt. Surrey Yeo. and on Staff (despatches four times, M.C., French Croix de Guerre), European War 1939-45 in Middle East as Lieut.-Col. Roy Pioneer Corps: *m.* 1st, 1915, Henriette, who *d.* 1918, da. of Arthur W. Kelly; 2ndly, 1923 (marriage dissolved 1931), Roslyn, who *d.* 1961, da. of John Brian Robinson, having had issue by 1st and 2nd marriages.

Arms—Gules, a fret vair between two boars passant one in chief and one in base or. Crest—A dexter arm vested gules, cuffed or, holding in the hand proper a hunting horn, and charged on the sleeve with a fret gold.

Residence—4/1, The Paragon, Blackheath, S.E.3. Club —Cavalry.

Fronti Nulla Fides.

Grandson living—[Issue of the late Antony Edgar Alan Horne, only son of 2nd baronet, *b.* 1924, *d.* 1954: *m.* 1945, Valentine Antonia (Château du Basty, Thenon, Dordogne, France), da. of Valentine Dudensing, of Château du Basty, Thenon, Dordogne, France]:—

(ALAN) GRAY (ANTONY), *b.* July 11th, 1948.

Daughter living—By 1st marriage—Edith Margery Jay, *b.* 1916; European War 1939-45 as Junior Com. ATS: *m.* 1944, Maj. Thomas Fiddian Reddaway, who *d.* 1967, and has issue living, Edgar James Fiddian, *b.* 1945.—William Thomas, *b.* 1948.—Henry Sills, *b.* 1950,—Richard Alan, *b.* 1952,—Michael Jay, *b.* 1956,—Susan Mary, *b.* 1949. *Residence*, Garden Hill, Totteridge, N20.

Brother living—William Guy (twin), *b.* 1889; ed. at Eton; late Maj. 10th R. Hussars (Reserve); 1914-19 War in France and Belgium (prisoner, 1914 star, two medals); 1939-45 War: *m.* 1st, 1920 (m. diss. 1949), Louisa Carey, who *d.* 1961, da. of the late Herbert Hardy, of Danehurst, Sussex; 2ndly, 1961, Hortense Amandine, da. of Henri Barbotin, of Hordain, France. *Club*, Cavalry.

The 1st baronet, Sir (William) Edgar Horne (el. son of the late Edgar Horne, of Witley, Surrey), was Chm. of Prudential Assurance Co., and MP for Surrey, Guildford Div (U) 1910-22.

Horsbrough-Porter, see Porter.

HORSFALL, Creation (U.K.) 1909, of Hayfield, Glusburn, West Riding of Yorkshire.

By industry and honour.

Sir JOHN MUSGRAVE HORSFALL, MC, TD, 3rd *Baronet*: *b.* Aug. 26th, 1915; *s.* his father, *Sir* (JOHN) DONALD, 1975; ed. at Uppingham; late Maj. Duke of Wellington's (W. Riding) Regt.; Underwriter at Lloyd's; Joint Man. Dir. of John C. Horsfall & Sons, Ltd., a Dir. of Worsted Spinners Fedn., Ltd. (Pres. 1962-64), and of Skipton Building Soc.; a JP for W. Riding of Yorks.; Burma 1939-45 (MC): *m.* 1940, Cassandra Nora Bernardine, da. of the late George Wright, of Brinkworth Hall, Elvington, York, and has issue.

Arms—Gules, in chief two horses' heads couped argent bridled azure, and in base a rose of the second, barbed and seeded proper. Crest—A horse's head couped ermine, issuing from a chaplet of roses gules.

Residence,—Greenfield House, Embsay, Skipton' Yorks.

Sons living—EDWARD JOHN WRIGHT, (Shoebridge, East-burn, Keighley, Yorks.), *b.* Dec. 17th, 1940; ed. at Uppingham: *m.* 1965, Rosemary, da. of Frank N. King, of East Morton, Keighley, and has issue living, David Edward, *b.* 1966,—Robert Ian, *b.* 1968,—James Christopher, *b.* 1971.——Donald James Linton, (110, Chain Lane, Littleover, Derby), *b.* 1942; ed. at Uppingham, and Jesus Coll., Camb. (MA): *m.* 1965, Angela Mary, da. of Henry Firth, of Ilkley, and has issue living, Peter Linton, *b.* 1970,—Richard Michael, *b.* 1973,—Elizabeth Jane, *b.* 1968.
Daughter living—Henrietta Nora, *b.* 1947.
Brothers living—Donald Fawcett, *TD* (twin), *b.* 1915; ed. at Uppingham, and King's Coll., Camb. (MA); formerly Capt. Duke of Wellington's (W. Riding) Regt.; is an Underwriter at Lloyd's: *m.* 1947, Jeanne Elizabeth, da. of Col. F. Longden Smith, of Woodlands, Skipton, and has issue living, Michael Fawcett, *b.* 1948,—Peter John, *b.* 1953,—Patricia Jane, *b.* 1950: *m.* 1974, Thomas Andrew Hoyle,—Susan Elizabeth, *b.* 1955,—Sara Louise, *b.* 1966. *Residence,* High Royd, Glenlyon Drive, Keighley, Yorks.——Patrick David (Greenhill, Borwick, Carnforth, Lancs.), *b.* 1921; ed. at Uppingham; is an Underwriter at Lloyds; formerly Capt. Duke of Wellington's (W. Riding) Regt.: *m.* 1947, June, da. of Capt. S. H. Clough, of Milton House, Gargrave, Skipton-in-Craven, and has issue living, Christopher David (11, Joe Lane, Catterall, Garstang, nr. Preston, Lancs., PR3 0QD), *b.* 1948: *m.* 1970, Sally, da. of Frank S. Greenwood, of Ingleton, and has issue living, Jonathan David *b.* 1973, Philip Edward *b.* 1975,—Carol Anne, *b.* 1951: *m.* 1975, Anthony Raymond Collinson.
Widow living of 2nd Baronet—GLADYS (*Gladys, Lady Horsfall*). (Field Head, Keighley, W. Yorks.), da. of the late Robert Buck Broster, of Keighley, and widow of Percy Taylor, of Knowle Spring House, Keighley: *m.* 1953, as his 2nd wife, Sir (John) Donald Horsfall, 2nd Bt., who *d.* 1975.

The 1st baronet, Sir John Cousin, Chm. of W. Riding of Yorkshire County Council, was a worsted spinner and banker, and provided Glusburn Technical Institute.

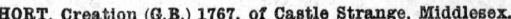

HORT, Creation (G.B.) 1767, of Castle Strange, Middlesex.

WELL-WIN WELL-WEAR

Sir JAMES FENTON HORT, 8th *Baronet;* *b.* Sept. 6th, 1926; *s.* his father, Sir FENTON GEORGE, 1960; ed. at Marlborough, and at Trin. Coll., Camb. (BA, MB, BChir): *m.* 1951, Joan, da. of the late Edward Peat, of Swallownest, Sheffield, and has issue.

Arms—Azure, a cross or between in the first and fourth quarters a rose argent, barbed and seeded proper. Crest—An eagle reguardant, wings expanded, holding in the beak a chaplet of laurel all proper.
Residence—17, Portland Rd., East Grinstead, Sussex.

Sons living—ANDREW EDWIN FENTON, *b.* Nov. 15th, 1954.——Timothy George, *b.* 1960.
Daughters living—Jane Antonia, *b.* 1958.——Diana, *b.* 1962.

Brothers living—Richard Patrick Arthur, *b.* 1931 ; ed. at Harrow, and at Trin. Coll., Camb. (B.A. 19—, M.A. 1959) : *m.* 1956, Agnete Mannheimer, and has issue living, Nicholas Patrick Fenton, *b.* 1962—Rebecca Maria, *b.* 1957,—Cathrina, *b.* 1960. *Address,* Askrikevägen 13, Lidingö, Sweden.——Robert William Lucas (Portora Royal School, Enniskillen, co. Fermanagh), *b.* 1936; ed. at Marlborough, and at Trin. Coll., Camb. (MA).
Sisters living—Elizabeth, *b.* 1925: *m.* 1951, Squadron Leader Eric George Holmes, M.B.E., R.A.F., and has issue living, Helen Margaret, *b.* 1952,—Georgina Slaney *b.* 1954. *Residence,* Clarkhill, Castlewellan, co. Down'——Barbara Anne, *b.* 1929: *m.* 1961, George Bruce Sackville Berkeley, of Lisbuoy, Omagh, co. Tyrone, and has issue living, Martin Sackville Hamilton, *b.* 1964,—Emma Louise Diana, *b.* 1962,—Sara Jane Arabella, *b.* 1966.

Uncle living (son of 6th baronet)—Aylmer Victor Dyson, M.B.E., T.D., *b.* 1897 ; ed. at Harrow and at Brasenose Coll., Oxford ; Major (retired) Roy. Corps of Signals (T.A.) ; European War 1917-19 with R.E. in Egypt and Palestine (wounded, two medals), European War 1939-45 with Roy. Signals; M.B.E. (Civil) 1958: *m.* 1927, Lois Mary, da. of the late Col. Clifford Phillips, V.D., T.D., D.L., of Coolgreany, Malpas, Newport, Monmouth, and has issue living, John

Aylmer Laybourne (239, Bramcote Lane, Wollaton, Nottingham) b. 1931; ed. at Marlborough, and Trin. Coll., Camb. (MA): m. 1958, Leela Senan, and has issue living, Peter Senan Aylmer b. 1958, Michael John Laybourne b. 1960, Patrick Marcus Govind b. 1971,—Daphne Lois, b. 1930; ed. at Lady Margaret Hall, Oxford (MA); Deaconess Community of St. Andrew,—Frances Mary, b. 1937: m. 1963, John Cameron Simpson, MB, FFARCS, of 37, Strathaven Rd., Lee, SE12, and has issue living, James Aylmer b. 1964, David Cameron b. 1966. *Residence*, Compton Chamberlayne, Salisbury.

Aunt living (daughter of 6th baronet)—Iris Elizabeth, b. 1904 ; ed. at Lady Margaret Hall, Oxford. *Residence*, High Craigenfeoch, Johnstone, Renfrewshire.

Widow living of 7th Baronet—GWENDOLENE (*Gwendolene, Lady Hort*), da. of the late Sir Walter Galpin Alcock, M.V.O., Mus.D., of The Close, Salisbury: m. 1922, Sir Fenton George Hort, 7th baronet, who d. 1960. *Residence*, Mountjoy Cottage, Omagh, co. Tyrone.

Collateral Branch living.

Issue of the late Rev. Francis Fitzgerald Hort, brother of 6th baronet, b. 1868, d. 1942: m. 1912, Margaret Charis, who d. 1972, da. of the late Rev. Joseph Henry Gray, Fellow of Queens' Coll., Camb.:—

Margaret Frances, b. 1913 ; ed. at Girton Coll., Camb. (B.A. 1935, M.A. 1950) : m. 1952, John Hunter Terry, and has issue living, Stephen John Anthony, b. 1955,—Rosemary Frances, b. 1953. *Residence*, Brafield, Eastbury Avenue, Northwood, Middlesex.

The 1st baronet was Consul-General at Lisbon, the 2nd baronet sat as M.P. for Kildare 1831-2 ; the 3rd baronet, a Lieut.-Gen. in the Army, served with distinction throughout the Crimean war 1854-5, and the 6th baronet, Sir Arthur Fenton, was 33 years a Master at Harrow School.

HOSKYNS, Creation (E.) 1676, of Harewood, Herefordshire.

VINCULA·DA·LINGUÆ·VEL·TIBI·LINGUA·DABIT

Bind the tongue, or the tongue will bind thee.

Sir BENEDICT LEIGH HOSKYNS, 16th *Baronet*; b. May 27th, 1928 ; s. his brother, Sir JOHN CHEVALLIER, 1956 ; ed. at Haileybury, and at Corpus Christi Coll., Camb. (M.B. and B.Chir. 1952) ; Capt. R.A.M.C. (retired) : m. 1953, Ann, da. of Harry Wilkinson, and has issue.

Arms—Per pale azure and gules, a chevron between three lions rampant or. **Crest**—A lion's head erased or, with flames of fire out of his mouth proper, ducally crowned of the first.

Residence—Harewood, Great Oakley, near Harwich, Essex.

Sons living—EDWYN WREN, b. Feb. 4th, 1956; Senior Chorister, King's Coll., Camb. 1969.——John Chandos, b. 1961.

Daughters living—Janet Mary, b. 1954.——Sarah Leigh, b. 1959.

Brother living—Anthony Hungerford (of 25, Hamilton Gdns., N.W.8), b. 1932; ed. at Marlborough; formerly Lt. Roy. Fusiliers; Korea 1952: m. 1958, the Hon. Katharine Margaret Kaldor, el. da. of Baron Kaldor [Life Baron], and has issue living, Nicholas Clement, b. 1967,—Jane Frances, b. 1962, Teresa Mary, b. 1963.

Sister living—Catherine Mary Trym, b. 1935: m. 1967, Sol Picciotto.

Daughter living of 10th Baronet—Muriel, b. 1889.

Daughter living of 11th Baronet.—Catherine Emma, b. 1888: m. 1915, Ronald Herbert Acland Holbech, OBE, JP [B. Waleran], who d. 1956, and has issue living, Geoffrey Victor Leigh, b. 1918; ed. at Stowe: m. 1st, 1949, Clara Joan (from whom he obtained a divorce 1944), da. of G. Eckard, of Bulawayo, Rhodesia; 2ndly, 1950, Elizabeth Ariana, da. of the late Lionel George Everson Harrisson [Curtis, Bt.], and has issue living, (by 2nd m.) David Ronald Leigh b. 1951, Caroline Olivia b. 1954,—John Ronald Christopher (8, Callcott St., W8) b. 1921; ed. at Stowe: m. 1st, 1946, Jean Suzanne (from whom he obtained a divorce 1950), da. of H. Palethorpe, of Stone Manor, Kidderminster; 2ndly, 1962, Elizabeth Anne, da. of Royston Henry Matthews, of Brasted, Kent, and has issue living (by 2nd m.), Charles Edward b. 1965, William Henry (twin) b. 1965. *Residence*, Farnborough Hall, Banbury.

Widow living of 13th Baronet—MARY TRYM (*Mary, Lady Hoskyns*), da. of the late Edwin Budden, M.A., B.Sc., of Macclesfield; M.A. 1922; late Research Fellow of Newnham Coll., Camb.: m. 1922, the Rev. Sir Edwyn Clement Hoskyns, M.C., 13th baronet, who d. 1937. *Residence*, 25, Hamilton Gdns., NW8.

Collateral Branches living.

Grandson of the late Rear-Adm. Peyton Hoskyns, C.M.G., M.V.O. (infra):

Issue of the late Major Oswald Peyton Latham Hoskyns, b. 1883, d. 1922 : m. 1913, Evelyn Mary, who d. 1965, da. of Joseph Herbert Blacklock, formerly of Overthorpe House, Banbury:—

Rev. John Algernon Peyton (Riverknoll, Hoarwithy, Hereford) b. 1920; ed. at Pembroke Coll., Camb. (MA); formerly Maj. R. Signals; m. 1st, 1944, Ann Veronica, who d. 1968, da. of C. Harrison, of King's Worthy, Winchester; 2ndly, 1970, Andrea Evelyn, da. of the late Adm. Sir Henry Bertram Pelly, KCVO, CB [see Pelly, Bt., colls.], and has issue living (by 1st m.), Oswald Christopher Peyton, b. 1954; Police Constable, Hants Constabulary,—Rachel Susan, *b.* 1946: *m.* 1969, F/O Robert Andrew Lund, RAF, of 12, Gordon Rd., Windsor, Berks, and has issue living, Mark Edward *b.* 1973, Jane Elizabeth Carol, *b.* 1947: *m.* 1972, Rodney Alexander Sinclair, of Hobbit House, 16, Millers Rd., Brookfield, Tauranga, NZ, and has issue living, Charlotte Ann Hoskyns *b.* 1973,—Juliet Ann, *b.* 1951: *m.* 1973, Ian Richard Doswell, MRIPHH.

Issue of the late Rear-Adm. Peyton Hoskyns, C.M.G., M.V.O., 5th son of 9th baronet, *b.* 1852, *d.* 1919: *m.* 1882, Grace MacDuff, who *d.* 1935, da. of D. MacDuff Latham, J.P., D.L. :—

John Walter, *b.* 1892; Cdr. RN (ret.); 1914-19 War, 1939-45 War (wounded, despatches): *m.* 1917, Magdalen Rose Wyndham, da. of the late Peter Hawker, of Longparish House, Hants, and has issue living, Hungerford Robert Leo (Pembroke House, PO Box 31, Gilgil, Kenya), *b.* 1921; ed. at Charterhouse, and Camb. Univ. (MA); late Lt. Rifle Bde.,—Rosemary Eleanor Peyton, *b.* 1919: *m.* 1949, Maj. Geoffrey Nelson Stanton (ret.), KOYLI, of Wynchlows, Greenway Lane, Bath, and has issue living, David John Nelson *b.* 1958, Juliet Rose Brailsford *b.* 1952, Sarah Dorothy Macduff *b.* 1955,—Zara Stephanie Jardine, *b.* 1929; Flying Officer, WRAF (Reserve). *Residence,* Eagle Lodge, Ballylickey, Bantry, co. Cork.——Dorothea, *b.* 1888: *m.* 1916, Com. Walter Macdonald Nash, OBE, RN (ret.), who *d.* 1952, and has issue living, Jeremy, *b.* 1920,—Jillian, *b.* 1923,—Jenifer Dorothea, *b.* 1931. *Residence,* Deptford Cottage, Greywell, Hants.

Grandchildren of the late Ven. Benedict George Hoskyns (infra):—

Issue of the late Lieut.-Col. Chandos Benedict Arden Hoskyns, *b.* 1895, *d.* (of wounds received in action during European War) 1940: *m.* 1920, Joyce (of Cowden House, Cholderton, Wilts.) da. of Austin Taylor, of 30, Eccleston Square, S.W.:—

John Leigh Austin Hungerford (83, West Side, Clapham Common, S.W.4), *b.* 1927; formerly Capt. Rifle Brig.: *m.* 1956, Miranda, only da. of Tom Mott, and has issue living, Barnaby Chandos Tom, *b.* 1959,—Benedict John Hungerford, *b.* 1963,—Benedicta Tamasine Maria, *b.* 1961.——David Chandos Benedict (The Oast House, Wittersham, Kent) *b.* 1929: *m.* 1958, Sheelagh Maion, da. of the Hon. Sir Patrick Redmond Joseph Barry.——Benedicta Lucia, *b.* 1922: *m.* 1955, Richard E. Vernon, of 33, Church Av., SW14, and has issue living, Thomas Richard Adam, *b.* 1958,—Sarah Benedicta, *b.* 1956.

Issue of the late Ven. Benedict George Hoskyns, 6th son of 9th baronet, *b.* 1856, *d.* 1935 : *m.* 1893, Dora Katharine, who *d.* 1950, el. da. of the late H. W. Franklyn, of Shedfield Lodge, Botley, Hants :—

Diana Mary Katharine (*Diana, Lady Thomas*), *b.* 1899: *m.* 1924, the Rt. Hon. Sir Godfrey John Vignoles Thomas, 10th Bt., GCVO, KCB, CSI, who *d.* 1968. *Residence,* Royal Cottage, Kew Green, Richmond, Surrey.

Descendants, if any surviving, of the late Edwin Bennett Hoskyns (el. son of the late John Hoskyns, M.D., 4th son of 6th baronet), who had three sons, John, Chandos, Bennett, and two daus.

Grandson of John Hoskyns (*b.* 1872), 4th son of John Hoskyns, MD, (ante):—
Issue of the late John Hoskyns, *b.* 1872, *d.* 1963: *m.* 1911, Florence May, who *d.* 1966, da. of Alfred Taylor, of Sydney, NSW:—
Chandos John (of 29, Woodcroft Av., St. Georges, Adelaide, S. Australia), *b.* 1915: *m.* 1938, Harriet Anderson, da. of Andrew Anderson Sundquist, of NSW, and has issue living, Max, *b.* 1940,—Craig, *b.* 1944,—Paul, *b.* 1945.

Grandchildren of the late James Hoskyns-Abrahall, 2nd son of the late Rev. John Charles James Hoskyns-Abrahall, el. son of the late Rev. John Hoskyns-Abrahall (*b.* 1773), el. son of the late Rev. John Hoskyns-Abrahall, grandson of the late Rev. John Hoskyns-Abrahall (who assumed the additional surname and arms of Abrahall), yst. son of 2nd baronet:—

Issue of the late Major John Hoskyns Hoskyns-Abrahall, *b.* 1864, *d.* 1924: *m.* 1900, Frances Elizabeth, who *d.* 1941, da. of the late J. H. Vessey, of Halton Manor, Spilsby, Lincolnshire:—

Dorothea Frances, *b.* 1916: *m.* 1st 1942 (m. diss. 1961), Charles Robert Gardiner; 2ndly, 1962, Lt.-Cdr. Alliston Temple Clough Hazledine, RNR, of 24, Blackall Rd., Exeter, and has issue living, (by 1st m.), Christopher Charles (The Welkin, Clavering, Essex), *b.* 1942: *m.* 1967, Janet Marie Lack, and has issue living, Rebehah Jane *b.* 1968,—Peter Patrick Fairfax, *b.* 1945,—Catherine Juliet, *b.* 1944: *m.* 1970, Richard George Stephen Sale, Barrister, of 33, Westwood Rd., Barnes, SW13, and has issue living, George William Alexander *b.* 1972, Mary Margaret *b.* 1971,—Victoria, *b.* 1947: *m.* 1972, Derrick William Swain, of Freedom Av., Kitwee, Zambia.

Issue of the late Major Christopher Henry Hoskyns-Abrahall, *b.* 1871, *d.* (killed in action) 1915: *m.* 1895, Alice Maude Mary, da. of — Allen :—
James, *M.M.*, *b.* 1897 ; European War 1914-19 with Australian Forces (wounded, M.M.).

Grandchildren of the late Theophilus Bennet Hoskyns-Abrahall, 2nd son of the late Rev. John Hoskyns-Abrahall (*b.* 1773) (ante):—
Issue of the late Bennet Hoskyns-Abrahall, C.B.E., *b.* 1858, *d.* 1951 : *m.* 1897, Edith Louise, who *d.* 1954, da. of the Rev. Egerton Tapp :—

Rt. Rev. Anthony Leigh Egerton, *b.* 1903; sometime Lt. RN; was a Chap. RNVR 1939-45, V. of Aldershot 1945-54, and Rural Dean thereof 1949-54; Bishop of Lancaster (Suffragan for Diocese of Blackburn) 1955-75, since when Hon. Assist. Bishop of Lancaster: *m.* 1937, Margaret Ada. da. of the late F. G. Storey, Bar.-at-Law, of Sunderland, and has issue living, John Benedict Leigh (Earby Hall, Newsham, Richmond, Yorks.), *b.* 1939: *m.* 1970, Mary Delamain, da. of the late Lt.-Col. Mansel Jackson, DSO, MC, of Clipsham House, Oakham, and has issue living, Bennet Mansel Leigh *b.* 1971, Harry *b.* 1975,—Anthony David Wren (Milford Rise, Catisfield, Fareham, Hants), *b.* 1943; Lt. RN (ret.): *m.* 1965, Phyllis Penrose, yr. da. of the late Rear-Adm. William Penrose Mark-Wardlaw, DSO, and has issue living, Mark Egerton Wren *b.* 1966, Sarah Katherine Phyllis *b.* 1971,—Janet Elizabeth Rosemary, *b.* 1938: *m.* 1962, Nicholas George Hurry, of 110, Elm Grove Rd., SW13, and has issue living, Fiona Elizabeth *b.* 1963, Victoria Mary *b.* 1967. *Residence,* Pedders Wood, Scorton, nr. Preston, Lancs.——(Andrew) John Chandos, *b.* 1905; ed. at Charterhouse, and at Univ. Coll., Oxford; a Dir. of Unilever Ltd., 1961-68; 1939-45 War as acting Sqdn.-Ldr. RAFVR (despatches): *m.* 1935, Awdry Lorraine, da. of Sir Norman Alexander Leslie, KBE, and has issue living, John Hungerford Leslie (Quakertown, Pa., USA), *b.* 1945: *m.* 1974, Winifred Scherer, of Calif., USA,—Harriet, *b.* 1939: *m.* 1965, Edward Brendan Lynch, WS, of Freeport, Grand Bahama,—Lucinda, *b.* 1940: *m.* 1972, Graham de Putron Tardif, of 76, Larkhill Rise, SW4 6LB, and has issue living, Benjamin Charles de Putron *b.* 1972, Kate Amanda *b.* 1975,—Amanda (twin), *b.* 1940: *m.* 1972, Burton K. Fox, of Quakertown, Pa., USA. *Residence,* The Gate House, Dell Quay, Chichester, Sussex.

Issue of the late Chandos William Hoskyns-Abrahall, M.R.C.S., *b.* 1859, *d.* 1899: *m.* 1892, Gertrude, da. of Robert Kearsley :—

Grandchildren of the late Chandos William Hoskyns-Abrahall, MRCS (ante):—
Issue of the late Sir (Theo) Chandos Hoskyns-Abrahall, CMG, b. 1896, d. 1975: m. 1st,
1925, (m. diss. 1944), da. of Lt.-Col. Richard Frederick Drury, CBE, 2ndly, 1944,
Lois Jennet (6, The Green, Colne Engaine, Colchester), da. of the late the Rev. Canon
Hugh Lambert Ogle, Canon of Ripon:—
(By 1st m.) Robin Chandos (Woodlands House, Cupid Green, Herts.), b. 1928; ed. at Haileybury;
1939-45 War as Lt. Sherwood Foresters: m. 1st, 1950 (m. diss. 1962), Petronella Elisabeth, da. of
John E. Cantlon, of co. Carlow; 2ndly, 1962, Margaret Angela, da. of Frank Keggins, of Knowle,
Warwicks, and has issue living (by 1st m.), Scarlett, b. 1952,—Gail, b. 1955,—(by 2nd m.),
Charles Chandos b. 1964.——Follett Peter (Holt, Anglesea Rd., Wivenhoe, Essex), b. 1934: m.
1960, Carole, da. of Edwin Alexander Marks, of Chigwell, Essex, and has issue living, Edwin
Follett Eden, b. 1965,—Emma Clare Elizabeth, b. 1963.

The 1st baronet, Sir Bennet, M.P. for Herefordshire, was son of Serjeant John Hoskyns M.P.,
whose courageous and patriotic eloquence in the House of Commons, *temp.* James I., against the
encroachments of the Stuart dynasty upon the liberty of Parliament and the people, occasioned
his confinement in the Tower,—hence the motto since borne by his descendants. Sir John, 2nd
baronet, one of the founders of the Royal Society, succeeded his friend Sir Christopher Wren as
President thereof, and received the honour of knighthood. Sir Hungerford, 4th baronet, a distinguished soldier throughout Marlborough's campaigns, was MP for Hereford. The 9th baronet,
the Rev. Sir John Leigh, was R. of Aston Tyrrold and Hon. Canon of Ch. Ch., Oxford. The 12th
baronet, the Rt. Rev. Sir Edwyn Hoskyns, DD, Bishop of Burnley (Suffragan for Diocese of
Manchester) 1901-4, and Lord Bishop of Southwell 1904-25. The 13th baronet, the Rev. Sir
Edwyn Clement, MC, DD, Chap. to Bishop of Derby, Pres., Fellow, Dean and, Librarian of
Corpus Christi Coll., Camb., and Hon. Canon of Derby Cathedral. The 14th baronet, Sir Chandos
Wren, F/O RAF VR, d. (killed on flying operations over Norway) 1945.

HOULDSWORTH, Creation (U.K.) 1887, of Reddish, Manchester, co. Lancaster, an Coodham, Symington, Ayrshire.

[Name pronounced "Hoaldsworth."]

To be bent, not to be broken.

Sir REGINALD DOUGLAS HENRY
HOULDSWORTH, O.B.E., T.D., 4th *Baronet*;
b. July 9th, 1903; s. his father, *Col. Sir*
WILLIAM THOMAS REGINALD, C.B.E., T.D.
1960; ed. at Shrewsbury Sch., and at Camb.
Univ.; is Hon. Col. Ayrshire Yeo. (T.A.)
(Lt.-Col. comdg. 1940); a DL of Ayrshire;
OBE (Mil) 1945: m. 1934, Margaret May,
da. of the late Cecil Emilius Laurie [*see*
Laurie, Bt., colls.], and has issue.

Arms—Ermine, the trunk of a tree in bend raguly
eradicated at the base proper, between three foxes' heads
erased gules. *Crest*—A stag's head erased gules, attired and
collared or, the attires banded with a hank of cotton argent.
Residence—Kirkbride, Maybole, Ayrshire. *Club*—
Cavalry.

Son living—RICHARD THOMAS REGINALD (Park
fairn, Crosshill, Ayrshire), b. Aug. 2nd, 1947: m. 1970
Jane, only da. of Alistair Orr, of Sydehead, Beith, and
has issue living, Simon Richard Henry, b. 1971,—
a son, b. 1975.
Daughters living—Myrtle Janet Mary, b. 1935: m.
1959, Philip Charles Nicholas Howard, and has issue
living, John Henry Nicholas, b. 1961,—Juliette Margaret, b. 1960.——Rosemary Margaret, b. 1939: m.
1962, (William) John Tevenar Usher [*see* Usher, Bt.,
colls.].
Brother living—Walter William Whitmore, T.D., b.
1906; is Major Sherwood Foresters: m. 1945, Hazell
Marcella, da. of the late J. P. Shepherd, of Barbados, and has issue living, Charles William
Shepherd (Braydon Cottage, Leigh, Swindon, Wilts.), b. 1946: m. 1971, Jacqueline, only da. of
Paul Smith, of Biddestone, Wilts., and has issue living, Zoë Anne b. 1974,—Hazell Mary Fiona,
b. 1954. *Residence*, Kineton, Guiting Power, Glos.
The 1st baronet, Sir William Henry Houldsworth, sat as M.P. for Manchester (C) 1883-5, and
for N.-W. Div. of Manchester 1885-1906. The 3rd baronet, Sir William Thomas Reginald,
Houldsworth, C.B.E., T.D., was Hon. Col. Ayrshire Yeo. (Lieut.-Col. Comdg. 1923).

HOULDSWORTH, Creation (U.K.) 1956, of Heckmondwike, West Riding of Yorkshire.

Sir (HAROLD) BASIL HOULDSWORTH, 2nd *Baronet;* b. July 21st
1922; s. his father, *Sir* HUBERT STANLEY, Q.C., (Feb.) 1956; M.R.C.S.
England and L.R.C.P. London 1946; D.A. England 1951; F.F.A., R.C.S.,
England 1954; late Capt. R.A.M.C.; is Consultant Anæsthetist, Barnsley
and Dist. Hospitals: m. 1946, Norah Clifford, da. of Arthur Halmshaw.

Residence—Shadwell House, Lundhill Road, Wombwell, near Barnsley, Yorkshire.

Daughter living—Sarah Belinda Clifford, b. 1949.
Widow living of 1st Baronet—HILDA FRANCES (*Hilda, Lady Houldsworth*), da. of Joseph Clegg:
m. 1919, Sir Hubert Stanley Houldsworth, Q.C., 1st Bt., who d. 1956. *Residence*, 19, Cardigan
Road, Leeds, 6.
The 1st baronet, Sir Hubert Stanley Houldsworth, Q.C., D.Sc., LL.D. (son of the late Albert
Edward Houldsworth), was Regional Controller, Min. of Fuel and Power 1942-43, and Controller-
Gen. 1943-45, Recorder of Doncaster 1946-8, Chm. E. Midlands Div., National Coal Board 1946-51,
and Chm., National Coal Board 1951-6. Pro-Chancellor Leeds Univ. 1949-56; he was cr. a
Baronet Jan. 1956 and d. Feb. 1956.

Houstoun-Boswall, see Boswall.

HOWARD, Creation (U.K.) 1955, of Great Rissington, co. Gloucester.

Sir (HAMILTON) EDWARD DE COUCEY HOWARD, GBE, 2nd *Baronet*; *b.* Oct. 29th, 1915; *s.* his father *Sir* (HAROLD WALTER) SEYMOUR 1967; ed. at Radley, and Worcester Coll., Oxford; Hon. DSc. London; Lord Mayor of London 1971-72; an Alderman of City of London; Senior Partner of the firm of Charles Stanley & Co., Stockbroker; a Member of The Stock Exchange, and a Liveryman of Gardeners' Co. (Master 1961-62); Chm. of LRC Internat.; 1939-45 War as F/O RAF (despatches); GBE (Civil) 1972: *m.* 1943, Elizabeth Howarth, da. of Maj. P. H. Ludlow, and has issue.

Arms—Azure, two wings conjoined in lure and in chief as many cross-crosslets fitchée or, a chief of the last thereon between two leaves of the india rubber tree proper a pale vert charged with a bezant. **Crest**—A toucan holding in the dexter claw and feeding on an apple slipped and leaved all proper.
Residence—Courtlands, Bishops Walk, Shirley Hills, Surrey. *Clubs*—City Livery, City of London.

Sons living—DAVID HOWARTH SEYMOUR (18, Finsbury Circus, EC2), *b.* Dec. 29th, 1945; ed. at Radley, and Worcester Coll., Oxford (MA); Common Councilman City of London, Councillor of London Borough of Sutton, and a Member of Stock Exchange: *m.* 1968, Valerie Picton, only da. of the late Derek W. Crosse, of Chase House, Callis Court Rd., Braodstairs, and has issue living, Robert Picton Seymour, *b.* Jan. 28th, 1971,—Caroline Picton Seymour, *b.* 1970.——John Ludlow Seymour, *b.* 1948; ed. at Grenville Coll., Devon.

Collateral Branch living.
Issue of the late David Seymour de Coucey Howard, yr. son of 1st Bt., *b.* 1919, *d.* 1954:
m. 1942 (m. diss. 1949) Jean McMurdo, da. of the late Thomas McMurdo Heywood:—
Jennifer Anne de Coucey (Bericote, Peachfield Rd., Malvern Wells, Worcs.) *b.* 1945.

HUDSON, Creation (U.K.) 1942, of North Hackney, co. Middlesex.
[Extinct 1956.]

Sir AUSTIN UVEDALE MORGAN HUDSON, *M.P.*, 1st and last *Baronet.*
Widow living of 1st Baronet—MARGARET SYLVIA (*Lady Hudson*), only child of the late Charles Harold Broadbent, JP [Brunner, Bt.]; is a JP for Dumfries-shire: *m.* 1930, Sir Austin Uvedale Morgan Hudson, M.P., 1st baronet, who *d.* 1956, when the title became ext. *Residence*, Kirtleton, Waterbeck, Lockerbie, Dumfriesshire.

Hudson-Kinahan, see Kinahan.

HUGHES, Creation (G.B.) 1773, of East Bergholt, Suffolk.

Sir DAVID COLLINGWOOD HUGHES, 14th *Baronet*; *b.* Dec. 29th, 1936; *s.* his father, *Sir* RICHARD EDGAR 1970; ed. at Oundle and Magdalene Coll., Camb. (MA): *m.* 1964, Rosemary Ann, MA, only da. of the Rev. John Pain, of Framfield Vicarage, Uckfield, Sussex, and has issue.

Arms—Quarterly, 1st azure, a lion rampant or, *Hughes*; 2nd gules, a lion rampant reguardant or, *Elistan Glodrydd*; 3rd, azure, three crowns in pale or, *Beli Mawr*; 4th, per bend sinister ermine and ermines, a lion rampant or, *Tudor Trevor*; 5th, or, a lion rampant reguardant sable, *Gwaeth Voyd*; 6th, per pale azure and sable, three fleur-de-lis or, *Ynyr, King of Gwent*; 7th, sable, a chevron between three goats' heads erased or, *Ithel Velyn*; 8th, azure, a lion cowed passant guardant or, *Llewellyn Aur Dorchog.*
Residence—The Old Fox, Balsham, Cambs., CB1 6E2.

Sons living—THOMAS COLLINGWOOD, *b.* Feb. 16th, 1966.——Timothy John Pell, *b.* 1968.—— Benjamin Richard, *b.* 1969.——Anthony George David, *b.* 1972.
Sister living—Elizabeth Barbara, *b.* 1933: *m.* 1964, Paul Ronald Scott Lever, of Chantry House, Turvey, Beds., and has issue living, Christopher Mark, *b.* 1965, Alison Clare, *b.* 1967,—Catherine Elizabeth, *b.* 1969.
Uncles living—Alfred Marcus, OBE, *b.* 1900; Com. RN; ret. 1936; 1914-18 War NW Europe and SE Asia 1939-45 (OBE); OBE (Mil) 1946: *m.* 1934, Hope Frances, da. of the late Arthur George Pritchard, and has issue living, Pamela Mary, *b.* 1939: *m.* 1965, Maj. Colin Humphrey Cowley Howgill, RM, of Teratak, Whitmore Vale Rd., Grayshott, Hants., and has issue living, Michael Colin *b.* 1968, David Charles *b.* 1970, Susan Rosemary *b.* 1967. *Residence*, Little Hatch, Churt Rd., Hindhead, Surrey.——Charles Collingwood, *b.* 1907; 1939-45 War as Capt. RA: *m.* 1937, Sheila Dorothea, da. of the late Col. Walter Henry Patrick Law, DSO [Brooke, Bt., *cr.* 1919], and has issue living, Peter Collingwood (22, Stewards Close, Epping, Essex), *b.* 1943; ed. at Oundle, and at Pomfret Sch., Conn., USA: *m.* 1965, Susan Elizabeth Ann Cubitt, and has issue living, Natasha Sarah *b.* 1957, Kate *b.* 1970, Victoria *b.* 1972. *Residence*, Hill Farm, Hessett, Bury St. Edmunds.
Aunts living—Pamela Mary, *b.* 1901: *m.* 1927, Arthur Frederick Vavasour McConnell, TD, JP, who *d.* 1961, and has issue living, Robert Frederick (The Priest's House, Puddington, Ches.) *b.* 1937: *m.* 1965, Diana Mary Temple, and has issue living, Frederick Bruce *b.* 1970, Anne Helen *b.* 1968,—Hugh Alexander, *b.* 1943,—Jean Mary *b.* 1929: *m.* 1950, Brian Norris Midwood, of The

Willows Farm, Burrington, nr. Ludlow, Salop, and has issue living, Peter Norris b. 1954, Roger
Norris b. 1962, Joanna Susan b. 1957, Susan Margaret b. 1965, Mary Diana (twin) b. 1965,—
Patricia Helen, b. 1932,—Margaret Pamela, b. 1934: m. 1957, Philip Norris Agnew, of Bainton
Farm, nr. Stamford, and has issue living, Jonathan Philip b. 1960, Christopher Norris b. 1962,
Felicity Margaret b. 1966. *Residence*, Hampton Hall, Worthen, Salop.——Evangeline Gratiana,
(The Stables, Browick, Wymondham, Norfolk), b. 1904: m. 1927, Philip William John Fryer,
MBE, who d. 1974, and has issue living, Richard Philip (Browick Hall, Wymondham, Norfolk)
b. 1936: m. 1969, Sandra Westmacott, and has issue living, Peter Richard b. 1970,—Joan Evange-
line, b. 1930: m. 1958, Hugh Anthony Earle Tilney-Bassett, of Stocks House, Faldingworth,
Market Rasen, Lincs., and has issue living, James Philip Hugh b. 1962, Carolyn Margaret b. 1959,
—Diana Mary, b. 1933: m. 1955, John Martin Thomas Hughes, of Glebe Farm, Gt. Rissington,
Glos., and has issue living, Nicholas John b. 1961, Andrew Gordon b. 1963, Helen Diana b. 1958.
——Rosemary Sybil, b. 1909: m. 1937, Col. George William Browning, OBE, Welsh Gds., and
has issue living, John Montague George, b. 1944: m. 1970, Mary-Grace Feachem, and has issue
living, Christopher George John b. 1972,—Mary Joan, b. 1938: m. 1962, the Rev. Andrew
Alexander Macintosh, of St. John's College, Cambridge, and has issue living, George Alexander
John b. 1967, Thomas Andrew Charles b. 1974, Rachel Alison Mary b. 1964,—Frances Evangeline,
b. 1941: m. 1964, Maj. John Granville Beaumont Rigby, R. Regt. Fus., and has issue living,
Peter Alexander Beaumont b. 1965, Simon William Granville b. 1967. *Residence*, Weatherhill
Farm, Icklingham, Bury St. Edmunds, Suffolk.

Daughters living of 12th Baronet—Elizabeth Mary Theodora (*Lady Best-Shaw*), b. 1896: m.
1921, Com. (E) Sir John James Kenward Best-Shaw, 9th Bt., R.N. (*cr.* 1665). *Residence*, Boxley
Abbey, Maidstone, Kent.——Barbara Frances (The Malt House, E. Cholderton, Andover), b.
1897: m. 1918, Com. Paul Alaric Masters Long, who d. 1936, and has issue living, Jane Mary
b. 1919: m. 1951, Charles Edward Willis House, of Haydown House, East Cholderton, Hants,
and has issue living, Richard James b. 1954, Sarah Jane b. 1952, Charlotte Frances b. 1958.——
Diana Margaret (*Dowager, Lady Mowbray*), b. 1905: m. 1927, Sir George Robert Mowbray, KBE,
5th Bt., who d. 1969. *Residence*, Starvehill House, Mortimer, Berks.

Widow living of 13th Baronet—JESSICA (*Jessica, Lady Hughes*) (233, Kennington Lane, SE11
5DF), da. of the late B. C. Broomhall, FRCS; BA: m. 1967, as his 2nd wife, Sir Richard Edgar
Hughes, 13th baronet, who d. 1970.

Collateral Branches living.

   Issue of the late Ralph Townsend Hughes, 4th son of 9th baronet, b. 1864, d. **1925** :
      m. 1892, Mary, who d. 1949, da. of the late John Addison Birkbeck, of The Priory,
      Grosmont, Yorkshire :—

Sybil Mary (3, Madeira House, Madeira Rd., West Byfleet, Surrey), b. 1893: m. 1921, William
Eden Walker, who d. 1962, and has issue living, Ralph Eden, b. 1923, formerly Capt. R. Corps of
Signals: m. 1954, Joyce Cownie, and has issue living, Charles Eden b. 1955, Richard b. 1959,—
Clive Eden (PO 76 MP, Salisbury, Rhodesia), b. 1927; late Merchant Navy: m. 1st, 1962, Patricia
Lloyd Spencer; 2ndly, 1971, Helen Douglas, and has issue living (by 2nd m.) Alice Megan b.
1973,—Louise, b. 1931: m. 1954, John Hereward Allix (RR1, Parksville, BC, Canada), and has
issue living, Timothy Peter b. 1959, Jane Catherine b. 1955.

      Grandchildren of the Rev. Robert Edgar Hughes, 2nd son of 8th Bt.:—
   Issue of the late Beatrice Mary Hughes, b. 1858, d. 1947: m. 1884, Jerome James Guiry,
      JP:—

Bryan (RR1, Delta, BC, Canada), b. 1894: m. 1922, Eileen, da. of the late Peter O'Donnell, and has
issue living, Bryan Patrick, b. 1923; ed. at Vancouver Coll.,—Peter (Box 1102 Rt. 2, Carmel,
Cal., USA), b. 1926; ed. at Vancouver Coll., and Univ. of BC, Canada.——Mary (Clonmore
House, Piltown, co. Kilkenny), b. 1884: m. 1909, Michael Archdale Morris, MD,
who d. 1934, and has issue living, Richard Archdale (Newrath House, Waterford), b.
1913; ed. at Stonyhurst: m. 1st, 1951, the Hon. Faith Gabriel French, who d. 1962, yst. da,
of 6th Baron de Freyne; 2ndly, 1963, Elizabeth, da. of the late Randal Archange Brereton.
and widow of Christopher Martin, and has issue living, (by 1st m.) Charles Maxwell Archdale,
b. 1951, Michael Lauriston Francis b. 1959, Victoria Mary b. 1954, Alicia Mary b. 1957,—Arthur
(Clonmore Glebe, Piltown, co. Kilkenny), b. 1915; ed. at Stonyhurst: m. 1945, Mary, da. of
Joseph McCan of Ballyowen, co. Tipperary, and has issue living Geoffrey Simon Joseph b. 1954,
Pamela Cecily Mary b. 1947, Clodagh Hilary Ann b. 1948, Joyce Deirdre Gabriel b. 1951,
Jacqueline Krystyne (twin) b. 1956,—George Henry Hubert (Berden Old Vicarage, Bishops
Stortford), b. 1924; ed. at Stonyhurst: m. 1959, Joyce Elizabeth, da. of Justin Robinson
of Toronto, and has issue living, Blaise Hugo Archdale, b. 1961, Jessica Louise b. 1963,—Fred-
erick Reginald, (Beechfield House, Monkstown, Dublin); b. 1929; ed. at Univ. Coll., Dublin
(BL): m. 1955, Valerie Rose, da. of Riocard Farrell, of Summerville, Waterford, and has issue
living, Milessa Jane b. 1957, Melanie Rose Josephine b. 1958,—Anna, b. 1910: m. 1943, Gerald
Fitzgerald, of Clonbeg, Rathgar, Dublin,—Emily Frances Mary, b. 1917,—Dorothy Cecil, b.
1919: m. 1945, Noel Lube Peart, of Dublin, and has issue living, John David Basil b. 1948,
Arthur James Noel b. 1962, Mary Veronica Ruth b. 1946, Gillian Esselde b. 1949, Dorothy
Gabriel b. 1959,—Beatrice Florence, b. 1922,—Gertrude Mary, b. 1927: m. 1952, John Edward
Powell, Solicitor, of 95, North End House, Fitz James Av., W14, and has issue living, Edward
John b. 1967, Marian Katherine Sandra b. 1956, Alison Louise b. 1958.——Margaret Cecil, b.
1891: m. 19—, Richard Anglim, of Ladner, Feltham, co. Tipperary.——Violet Beatrice, b.
1899: m. 1920, Thomas Anthony Frizelle, of 18, Upper George St., Wexford.

         Granddaughters of the late Capt. John William St. John Hughes, 5th son of 8th
            baronet:—
      Issue of the late Major Frederick St. John Hughes, M.V.O., O.B.E., b. 1866, d. 1956:
         m. 1908, Mabel, who d. 1965, da. of the late David Evans, of Ffrwdgrech, Breconshire:—
Alpha Jessie Ruth, b. 1910: m. 1938, Group Capt. James McLaughlin, DSO, DFC, and has issue
living, Deirdre, b. 1940: m. 1967, James C. Hanna, and has issue living, James Owen b. 1970,—
Rona Mary, b. 1945: m. 1967, Lyndhurst Rhys-Davies, and has issue living, Louise b. 1967.——
Beta Mira Grace (twin), b. 1910: m. 1938, Group Capt. Benjamin Heywood-Jones, RAF, who d.
(kille d in action) 1943, and has issue living, Cherry Bronwen, b. 1939,—Gypsy Gail, b. 1943:
m. 1967, Robin Horley, and has issue living, Samantha b. 1969.——April Mary, b. 1913: m.
1939, Sqdn.-Ldr. Hugh Smeddle, DFC, and has issue living, Robert Adam Hughes, b. 1948,—
Susan Ostara Mary, b. 1947. *Residence*, Ford Bridge, Caton, Lancashire.

         Granddaughters of the late William Collingwood Hughes, son of William Hughes,
            Bar.-at-law, 4th son of 3rd baronet:—

      Issue of the late Collingwood James Hughes, b. 1872, d. 1963: m. 1899, Lilian, da. of
         John Crocker, Head Master of the Roy. Naval Engineering Coll., Keyham:—

Helen Lily Collingwood, b. 1903.——Diana Crocker Collingwood, b. 1905.

         Grandchildren of the late Arthur Hughes, b. 1836, son of the late William
            Hughes, Bar.-at-law (ante) :—
      Issue of the late Arthur Hughes, b. 1861, d. 1906 : m. 1897, Louisa Grace, who d. 1930, da.
         of the late Ernest Warren :—

Richard Arthur Warren, *O.B.E.*, *b.* 1900; ed. at Charterhouse, and at Oriel Coll., Oxford; is an Author; formerly Dep. Principal Priority Officer, Admiralty; O.B.E. (Civil) 1946: *m.* (Jan.) 1932, Frances Catharine Ruth, da. of the late Gardner Sebastian Bazley [*see* Bazley, Bt.], and has issue living, *Rev.* Robert Elistan-Glodrydd (32, Kensington Rd., Birmingham 29), *b.* 1932; ed. at Trin. Coll., Oxford (MA); (Lodgings Warden, Birmingham Univ.: *m.* 1960, Sheila Basketts, and has issue living, Claire Frances Rosemary *b.* 1961, Rachel Catherine *b.* 1964,—Owain Gardner Collingwood, *b.* 1943,—Penelope, *b.* 1934; ed. at Oxford Univ. (MA): *m.* 1958, Robin Paul Minney, of Kings Head, Church St., Matlock, Derbys., and has issue living, Thomas *b.* 1960, Hugo Benjamin Paulus *b.* 1962, James *b.* 1963, Richard *b.* 1967,—Lleky Susannah, *b.* 1936,— Catharine Phyllida, *b.* 1940: *m.* 1960, Colin Michael Wells, of 39, Charles St., Ottawa, Canada, and has issue living, Christopher William Llewellyn *b.* 1961, Dominic Richard Alexander *b.* 1963. *Residence*, Mor Edrin, Talsarnau, Merioneth, N. Wales.

Issue of the late Alfred Collingwood Hughes, *b.* 1864, *d.* 1915: *m.* 1897, Ada Mary, who *d.* 1940, da. of Edmond Drage:—
Stanley Collingwood, *b.* 1903.——Jack Collingwood, *b.* (twin) 1903.——Harry Leonard Collingwood, *b.* 1906: *m.* 19—, Pamela Phillips, and has issue living, a son, *b.* 1943. *Residence*,

Issue of the late Robert Hughes, *b.* 1870, *d.* 19—: *m.* 1900, Ella Fanny, da. of Frederick Boldero:—
Robert Bernard (47, Sheen Rd., Richmond, Surrey), *b.* 1906.——Mary Doris Winefride (Calle Obispo Severo 8, 3, Villa Carlos, Minorca, Spain) *b.* 1904.——Margaret Rosemary, *b.* 190-.

This ancient family, according to the College of Arms, is descended from Elistan Glodrydh, Earl of Hereford (*b.* 933). The 1st baronet, Capt. Sir Richard Hughes, R.N., when Commissioner of Portsmouth Dockyard (1773), entertained George III. Sir Richard, the 2nd baronet, Adm. of the Red, was second in command under Lord Howe at the relief of Gibraltar; he also captured the "Solitaire," and gained victory against the French off Barbados 1782. The 10th baronet, Sir (Alfred) Collingwood Hughes, served during European War 1914-18, as Major 4th Vol. Batn. Suffolk Regt. (despatches), and was High Sheriff of Suffolk 1923-4.

HUGHES, Creation (U.K.) 1942, of Denford, co. Berks. [Extinct 1958.]

Sir THOMAS HARRISON HUGHES, 1st and last *Baronet*.

Widow living of 1st Baronet—ANNE (*Lady Hughes*), da. of the late John R. Humphreys, of Llwyn Hall, Carmarthenshire and widow of Gen. D. Van Voorst Evekink (formerly Dutch Mil, Attaché in London): *m.* 1952, as his second wife, Sir Thomas Harrison Hughes, 1st baronet, who *d.* 1958, when the title became ext. *Residences*, 12, Hyde Park Gardens, W.2; The Mill House, Hungerford, Lower Denford, Berks.

Hughes-Hunter, see Hunter.

HULSE, Creation (G.B.) 1739, of Lincoln's Inn Fields

To be rather than to seem.

Sir (HAMILTON) WESTROW HULSE, 9th *Baronet*; *b.* June 20th, 1909; *s.* his father, *Sir* HAMILTON (JOHN), 1931; ed. at Eton, and at Ch. Ch., Oxford; Bar. Inner Temple 1932; formerly Wing-Com. R.A.F. Vol. Reserve; European War 1939-45 (despatches): *m.* 1st, (Jan.) 1932 (marriage dissolved 1937), Philippa Mabel, da. of the late A. J. Taylor, of Strensham Court, Worcestershire; 2ndly, 1938, Ambrosine Nellie Orr, who *d.* 1940, only da. of the late Capt. H. S. Orr Wilson, R.H.A., of Rockfield Park, Monmouthshire; 3rdly, 1945 (marriage dissolved 1954), Dorothy, only da. of the late William Durran, of 80, Church Street, W., and widow of James A. M. Hamilton; 4thly, 1954, Elizabeth Smythet, da. of Col. George Redesdale Brooker Spain, CMG, TD, and has issue by 1st m.

Arms—Per fesse argent and ermine, three piles, one issuing from the chief, between the others reversed, sable. **Crest**—A buck's head couped proper attired or, charged on the neck with a plate surmounted by two bezants; between the attires a sun of the last.

Residence—Breamore, Hants. *Clubs*, Carlton, Bath.

Sons living—By 1st marriage—EDWARD JEREMY WESTROW, *b.* Nov. 22nd, 1932; ed. at Eton; late Capt. Scots Guards: *m.* 1957, Verity Ann, da. of William Pilkington, of Shipton-under-Wychwood, Oxon, and has issue living, Edward Michael Westrow, *b.* 1959,—Camilla Ann, *b.* 1962.

Residence,—Flat 4, 30, Queens Gate Gdns., SW7.——Richard Arthur Samuel (The Nell, Sherfield English, Romsey, Hants.), *b.* 1936; ed. at Eton; late 2nd Lt. Scots Gds.: *m.* 1963, Caroline Susan Joan, da. of Lt.-Col. Sir George David Elliott Tapps-Gervis-Meyrick, 6th Bt., MC, and has issue living, George Richard, *b.* 1967,—Frances Caroline, *b.* 1968.

This family descends from the Hulses of Norbury, Cheshire, and has common orgin with the Holles Earls of Clare, of whom the 4th and last Earl was cr. Duke of Newcastle (cr. 1694, ext. 1711), when his Holles estates were devised to his nephew, Thomas Pelham who was cr. Duke of Newcastle 1715.

The 1st baronet **was** Physician to Queen Anne, and to Kings George I. and George II.

HULTON, Creation (U.K.) 1905, of Hulton Park, Parish of Deane, and co. Palatine of Lancaster.

A mind that knows not how to yield

Sir GEOFFREY ALAN HULTON, 4th *Baronet*; *b.* Jan. 21st, 1920; *s.* his father, Sir ROGER BRADDYLL, 1956; ed. at Marlborough; Capt. RM (ret.), a JP for Lancs., a DL for Greater Manchester, Ch. Scouts Comnr., Pres. of Westhoughton Constituency Conservative Assocn., Vice-Pres. of Country Landowners' Assocn. (Lancs.), and Lancs. Co. Cricket Club; Far East 1941-45 (prisoner); Knt. Cdr. of Order of St. Gregory The Great; Knt. of Order of Holy Sepulchre: *m.* 1945, Mary Patricia, el. da. of P. A. de Vere Reynolds, of Farnborough, Hants.

Arms—Quarterly, 1st and 4th, argent, a lion rampant gules, *Hulton of Hulton*; 2nd and 3rd, argent, a lion rampant gules crowned or, *Hulton of Farnworth*. **Crest**—Out of a ducal coronet or, a hart's head argent between two branches of hawthorn proper.

Residence—The Cottage, Hulton Park, Over Hulton, Bolton, BL5 1BH.

Sister living—Barbara Joan, *b.* 1921; formerly Junior Com. A.T.S.: *m.* 1945, Capt. John Edward Vincent Butterfield, Duke of Wellington's Regt., and has issue living, Hugh Alan John, *b.* 1946,—Neil Roger, *b.* 1949,—Gillian Diana, *b.* 1955. *Residence*, Maltmans End, Maltmans Lane, Gerrards Cross, Bucks.

Collateral Branch living
Issue of the late Arthur Hyde Hulton, 4th son of 1st baronet, *b.* 1873, *d.* 1966: *m.* 1899, Violet Eugenia, who *d.* 1962 da. of the late Capt. Arthur Lister-Kaye [Lister-Kaye, Bt.]:—
Beatrix Eugenia (Chervil Meadow, Speen, Aylesbury), *b.* 1910.

The 1st baronet was Constable of Lancaster Castle 1892-1907.

Hume-Campbell, see Campbell.

Hume-Williams see Williams.

Hunter Blair, see Blair

Huntington-Whiteley, see Whiteley.

HUTCHISON, Creation (U.K.) 1923, of Hardiston, co. Kinross. [Extinct 1972.]
Sir ERIC ALEXANDER OGILVY HUTCHISON, 2nd and last *Baronet*.

Daughters living of 2nd Baronet—By 1st m.—Morna, *b.* 1925: *m.* 1947, Desmond Berry, and has issue living, Bruce Graham, *b.* 1948,—Michael John, *b.* 1950,—Patricia Fayrer, *b.* 1949,—Morna Lilian, *b.* 1952,—Marian Loraine (twin), *b.* 1952.——Sheila, *b.* 1926: *m.* 1956, Eric Alexander Masterton Wood, MB, ChB, MRCP, MRCPE, DPM, of 75, Morningside Park, Edinburgh, 10, and has issue living, Jonathan Paul Masterton, *b.* 1958,—Christopher Malcolm Fayrer, *b.* 1962,—Alastair Graham Spens, *b.* 1964,—Jeremy Douglas, *b.* 1966.——Patricia, *b.* 1928: *m.* 1950, 1st, Julian St. Leger, from whom she obtained a divorce 1954 [*see* B. Bagot, colls.]; 2ndly, 1955, Michael Cain, FRIBA, and has issue living, (by 1st m.) [*see* B. Bagot, colls.],—(by 2nd m.) Sebastian, *b.* 1957,—Marius, *b.* 1958,—Benedict, *b.* 1960. *Residence*, 3, Rosemont Rd. Richmond, Surrey.——By 2nd m.—Jane Moir Ogilvy *b.* 1958.

HUTCHISON, Creation (U.K.) 1939, of Thurle, Streatley, co. Berks.

Sir PETER HUTCHISON, 2nd *Baronet ; b.* Sept. 27th, 1907 ; *s.* his father, *Sir* ROBERT, *M.D., F.R.C.P.,* 1960 ; ed. at Marlborough, and at Lincoln Coll., Oxford (MA); admitted a Solicitor 1933; Dep. Clerk of the Peace and of the County Council, E. Suffolk 1947-71, and Clerk of the Peace and County Solicitor 1971-72: *m.* 1949, Mary-Grace, da. of the late Very Rev. Algernon Giles Seymour [*see* Culme-Seymour, Bt., colls.], and has issue.

Residence—Melton Mead, nr. Woodbridge, Suffolk.

Sons living—ROBERT, *b.* May 25th, 1954.——Mark Seymour, *b.* 1960.
Daughters living—Elspeth, *b.* 1950: *m.* 1975, John Richard Feneran Bryers, of Highwood Cottage, Kilnwick, Driffield, Yorks., YO25 9JF.——Alison Margaret, *b.* 1951.
Brother living—Michael Duncan, *b.* 1912 ; ed. at Eton, and at Magdalen Coll., Oxford : *m.* 1945, Margery Betty Martin, and has issue living, Paul Michael, *b.* 1959,—Sara Laetitia, *b.* 1949, —Margaret Ann, *b.* 1953. *Residence*, 16, Denbigh Gdns., Richmond, Surrey.
Sister living—Ann Felicity, *b.* 1917; JP of Surrey: *m.* 1945, Geoffrey Martin Greenwood, and has issue living, John Gerald, *b.* 1946,—Alan Graham, *b.* 1948,—Charles Duncan, *b.* 1954,—Victoria Jean, *b.* 1950. *Residence*, Saxons, Frensham, Farnham, Surrey.

The 1st baronet, Sir Robert Hutchison, M.D., C.M. (son of Robert Hutchison, of Carlowrie, Kirkliston) was Pres. of Roy. So. of Med. 1934-6, and of Roy. Coll. of Physicians 1938-41.

HUTCHISON, Creation (U.K.) 1956, of Rossie, co. Perth.

Sir JAMES RILEY HOLT HUTCHISON, *D.S.O., T.D.,* 1st *Baronet,* son of the late Thomas Holt Hutchison ; *b.* April 10th, 1893 ; ed. at Harrow; Hon. LLD Glasgow; OStJ; formerly a Dir. of Grampian Holdings, Ltd., 1, Newton Place, Glasgow, C3, and other cos., and a JP for Perthshire; Glasgow Representative to Chamber of Shipping 1933-35, National Pres., Incorporated Sales Managers' Assocn. 1949-51, Pres., Assocn. British Chambers of Commerce 1960-62, Parliamentary Chm., Dock and Harbour Authorities Assocn. 1949-51, and Parliamentary Under-Sec. of State and Financial Sec., War Office 1951-54; Pres. of Assembly of W. European Union 1957-59; Hon. Col. Lanarkshire Yeo. 1948-58; 1914-18 War with Lanarkshire Yeo. and Indian Cav., 1939-45 War in France and N. Africa (DSO, Chevalier of Legion of Honour, Croix de Guerre); sat as MP for Central Div. of Glasgow (*U*) June 1945 to Feb. 1950 (when he was defeated), and for Scotstoun Div. of Glasgow Oct. 1950 to Sept. 1959; DSO 1945: *m.* 1928, Winefryde Eleanor Mary, da. of the late Rev. R. H. Craft, and has issue.

Arms—Argent, an arrow fessways vert, feathered gules and barbed or, between two lymphads vert, sails furled gules, in chief, and a parachute azure, stringed vert and ringed or, in base ; in dexter chief the canton of a Baronet of the United Kingdom. *Crest*—A parachute as in the arms, the ring transversed of an arrow fessways also as in the arms.
Residences—Rossie, Forgandenny, Perthshire; 32, Moore St., SW3. *Clubs*—Cavalry, Western (Glasgow).

Son living—PETER CRAFT (Milton House, Milton, by Dumbarton), *b.*, June 5th, 1935; ed. at Eton, and at Magdalene Coll., Camb.; Lt. late R. Scots Greys, a Dir. of Hutchison & Craft Ltd., insurance brokers, Glasgow: *m.* 1966, Virginia, da. of John M. Colville, of Gribloch, Kippen, Stirlingshire, and has issue living, James Colville, *b.* 1967.

Imbert-Terry, see Terry.

INGILBY, Creation (U.K.) 1866, of Ripley Castle, Yorkshire.

My right.

Sir THOMAS COLVIN WILLIAM INGILBY, 6th *Baronet; b.* July 17th, 1955; *s.* his father *Maj. Sir* JOSLAN WILLIAM VIVIAN, 1974.

Arms—Sable, an estoile argent within a bordure engrailed gobony or and gules. *Crest*—A boar's head couped and erect argent, tusked or, in the mouth an estoile of the last.

Seat—Ripley Castle, Harrogate, Yorkshire.

Sisters living—Caroline Diana Colvin, *b.* 1949.——Katherine Benita Colvin, *b.* 1951: *m.* 1974, Richard Denis Kingsmill Wallace.

Widow living of 5th Baronet—DIANA (*Lady Ingilby*) (Ripley Castle, Harrogate, Yorks.), da. of the late Brig.-Gen. Sir George Lethbridge Colvin, CB, CMG, DSO: *m.* 1948, Maj. Sir Joslan William Vivian Ingilby, 5th Bt., who *d.* 1974.

Collateral Branch living.

Issue of the late Lt.-Col. John Uchtred Macdowall Ingilby, OBE, brother of 4th baronet, d. 1948: m. 1904, Marjorie Cecily, MBE, who d. 1957, el. da. of the late William Robert Phelips, of Montacute House, Stoke-under-Ham:—

Cecily Eleanor, b. 1905. Residence, Lockyers Cottage, Ash Priors, Taunton.——Joan Alicia, b. 1911. Residence, Coleshouse, Askrigg, Leyburn, Yorkshire.

This family, of great antiquity, has been seated at Ripley Castle since temp. Edward III., and has three times received the honour of a baronetcy. Sir William Ingilby of Ripley was created a baronet in 1642, which became ext. in 1772, on the death of his gt-grandson, Sir John Inglby, 4th Bt. In 1781, John Ingilby, natural son of the 4th Bt., who inherited his estates was cr. a baronet in 1781. This title became ext. in 1854 on the death of his son, Sir William Ingleby-Amcotts, 2nd Bt. (who also inherited, by special remainder in 1805, the baronetcy conferred in 1796 upon his maternal grandfather, Sir Wharton Amcotts). Sir Henry John Ingilby of Ripley, 1st Bt. of the third creation in 1866 was el. son of the Rev Henry Ingilby, brother of the 1st Bt. of the second creation (1781) succeeded by devise to the family estates.

Inglefield-Watson, see Watson.

INGLIS, Creation (N.S.) 1703, of Glencorse, Midlothian (formerly Mackenzie of Gairloch, Ross-shire.)
[Name pronounced "Ingles."]

Sir RODERICK JOHN INGLIS OF GLENCORSE, 10th Baronet; b. Jan. 25th, 1936; s. his father, Sir MAXWELL IAN HECTOR, 1974; ed. at Winchester, and Edinburgh Univ. (MB, ChB): m. 1st, 1960 (m. diss. 1975), Rachel Evelyn, da. of Lt.-Col. N. M. Morris, of Dowdstown, Ardee, co. Louth; 2ndly, 1975, Geraldine, yr. da. of R. H. Kirk, of Thaxted, Essex, and has issue by 1st m.

Arms—Azure, a lion rampant argent, armed and langued gules, on a chief of the second three mullets sable. Crest—A demi-lion as in the arms, holding in his dexter fore-paw a mullet argent.

Residence,—Glencorse House, Penicuik, Midlothian. Club,—New Edinburgh.

Son: living—By 1st m.—ALASTAIR MACKENZIE, b. July 28th, 1971.——Ian Richard, b. 1965.——Alexander Colin (twin), b. 1965.
Daughter living—By 1st m.—Amanda Fiona, b. 1963.

Collateral Branches living.

Grandchildren of the late Lt.-Col. Harry Maxwell Mackenzie, RA, grandson of 4th baronet:—

Issue of the late Engineer-Com. Harry Ponsonby MACKENZIE, RN (ret.), b. 1877, d. 1948: m. 1915, Gladys Dalziel who d. 1966, yr. da. of the late William Weatherly of Woolongong, Mortlake, Victoria, Australia:—

Alastair John, b. 1922; formerly Lt. Roy. Australian Naval Vol. Reserve; European War 1939-45 (despatches twice): m. 1955, Isabel Anne, da. of Andrew Kelt, of Pickdick, Brede, Sussex, and has issue living, Roderick Andrew John, b. 1962,—Kythé Jane, b. 1956 —Iona Margaret, b. 1957,—Mairi Anne, b. 1959,—Margaret Isabel Alexandra, b. 1970. Residence, Hillside, Ararat, Victoria, Australia.——Kenneth William, b. 1928: m. 1962, Jennifer Margaret, only da. of the late Col. Patrick Hyde, OBE, and has issue living, Caroline Margaret, b. 1963,—Elizabeth Georgina, b. 1965,—Fiona Jennifer, b. 1970. Residence, Trawalla, Victoria, Australia.

Issue of the late Major Kenneth Gordon MACKENZIE, Canadian Inf., b. 1878, d. (killed in action during European War) 1916 : m. 1911, Minnie Hamilton (of 1041, St. Charles Street, Victoria, British Columbia), el. da. of Charles Henry Strutt, of Kamloops, British Columbia :—

Cicely Kythé Mary Hamilton, b. 1916 ; European War 1943-5 in Women's Roy. Canadian Naval Ser. : m. 1946, Squadron Leader William Anderson Beaumont, OBE, Roy. Aux. A.F., and has issue living, Kythé Victoria, b. 1958. Residence, Athill Lodge, St. Helens Lane, Adel, Leeds, 16, Yorkshire.

Issue of the late Colin Rae MACKENZIE, b. 1887, d. 1973: m. 1913, Nora Constance (Balnain Cottage, Canal Rd., Inverness), da. of the late Herbert Guernsey, of Vic., BC, Canada:—

Margaret Elaine, b. 1914: m. 1st, 1937, (m. diss. 1958), Gerald Ashby Wodehouse Garland, who d. 1965; 2ndly, 1958, C. R. Cuthbert, of Glen Cottage, Ness Castle, Inverness, and has issue living, (by 1st m.) Angela Robin, b. 1938,—Jenifer Sarah, b. 1942: m. 1965, Edward John Roberts, and has issue living, Benjamin Alexander b. 1966, Nicholas Justin b. 1967, William Wayland b. 1970.——Nora Kythé, b. 1917; 1939-45 War as Section Officer WRCAF: m. 1944, Capt. Victor Browne, RCN, of 8193, Alec Rd., Saanichton, Vancouver, BC, Canada, and has issue living, Colin Victor Alleyne, b. 1946,—Susan Kythé, b. 1949.——Christine Ponsonby, b. 1928: m. 1953, Adrian C. Boehme, of 228, Williams Rd., Toorak, Vic. 3142, Aust., and has issue living, Justin Christian, b. 1959,—Nicholas Christian, b. 1962,—Anna Kythé, b. 1958.

Kenneth Mackenzie, created a Baronet of Nova Scotia 1703, was son of Alexander Mackenzie, 7th of Gairloch, and sat as M.P. for Ross-shire 1702. Sir Kenneth John Mackenzie, 7th Bt., was King's and Lord Treasurer's Remembrancer for Scotland 1900-21, and a Scottish Ecclesiastical Commr. 1925-9. On the death in 1958 of the 8th baronet, Sir Hector Mackenzie, MC, Lord-Lt. of Ross-shire, the baronial estate of Gairloch, held from 1476, devolved on his niece, Marjory Charlotte Stirling, Mrs. Stevenson, as Mrs. Mackenzie. 15th of Gairloch, whilst the baronetcy passed to the heir male as Sir Maxwell Ian Hector Inglis of Glencorse, 9th baronet, under this name and designation, pursuant to the entail of the Rt. Hon. John Inglis, Lord Glencorse, Lord Justice-General of Scotland. Sir Maxwell was son of Hector Ian Maxwell Mackenzie-Inglis of Glencorse (who both assumed 1929 the additional surname of Inglis of Glencorse), son of Lt.-Col. Harry Maxwell Mackenzie, RA, son of John Mackenzie, 4th son of 4th Bt. In 1958 Sir Maxwell was recognized by decree of Lyon Court in the surname of Inglis of Glencorse. He was in Political Ser. Gold Coast 1928-37, and Lord Lt. of Midlothian 1964-72.

INGRAM, Creation (U.K.) 1893, of Swineshead Abbey, Lincolnshire.

Sir HERBERT INGRAM, 3rd *Baronet*; *b.* April 18th, 1912; *s.* his father, *Sir* HERBERT, 1958; ed. at Winchester, and at Balliol Coll., Oxford; Major late Grenadier Guards and REME; 1939-45 War (despatches): *m.* 1935, Jane Lindsay, da. of the late James Palmer-Tomkinson, of Totterdown, Inkpen, Newbury and has issue.

Arms—Quarterly, argent and or, gutée de poix, on a **fesse** invected gules four escallops of the second. Crest—On a rock proper, issuant from a wreath of cinquefoils or, a griffin's head erased quarterly gules and argent, charged on the neck with an escallop countercharged.

Residence—Hurst Lodge, near Reading, Berks.

In hoc signo vinces.
Under this sign you shall conquer.

Son living—(HERBERT) ROBIN (South Farm, Water Eaton, Cricklade, Wilts.), *b.* Jan. 13th, 1939; ed. at Eton: *m.* 1st, 1963 (m. diss. 1971), Shiela, only da. of the late Charles Peczenick, of 7, Grosvenor Sq., W1; 2ndly. 1973, Sallie Willoughby, da. of Frank Hilary Minoprio, of Hessle Well House, Heswell, Cheshire, and has issue living, (by 1st m.) James Herbert Charles, *b.* 1966,—Frances Jane, *b.* 1964,—(by 2nd m.) Nicholas David, *b.* 1975.

Daughters living—Marion Judith, *b.* 1937: *m.* 1969, Graham H. Harvey-Evers, of Prestwood Farm, Gt. Missenden, Bucks.——Vivian Helen (twin), *b.* 1937: *m.* 1963, Oliver Turnbull, of High Wells, Natland, Kendal, Cumbria [*see* E. Stamford].——Anne Carolyn, *b.* 1952: *m.* 1974, Alan C. Weston Peck. *Residence*, Hurst Lodge, nr. Reading, Berks.

Brother living—Michael Warren, *b.* 1917; ed. at Winchester, and at Balliol Coll., Oxford (BA 1945); is a JP for Gloucestershire, Maj. late Gren. Gds.: *m.* 1944, Auriol Blanche, el. da. of Lt.-Gen. Sir Arthur Francis Smith, KCB, KBE, DSO, MC [*see* Kintore, colls.], and has issue living, Andrew David Michael (Lypiatt House, Stroud, Glos.), *b.* 1945: *m.* 1969, Carole Letitia, da. of Maj. John David Summers, of 16a, Cadogan Sq., SW1, and has issue living, Matthew William Michael *b.* 1971, Toby David Warren *b.* 1972,—Susan Elizabeth, *b.* 1947: *m.* 1969, John Humphrey Colquhoun, of Brooke House, Frocester, Stonehouse, Glos., and has issue living, Mark Humphrey *b.* 1973, James Arthur *b.* 1975, Nicola Mary, *b.* 1951: *m.* 1970, Paul Archer Tyler, of 29, Cleaver Sq., SE11, and has issue living, Dominick Michael Archer *b.* 1975, Sophie Grzce Auriol *b.* 1972,—Auriol Jacqueline, *b.* 1957. *Residence*, Driffield Manor, Cirencester.

Uncle living (son of 1st baronet)—Collingwood, *b.* 1880; 1914-18 War as Capt. R.A.F.: *m.* 1906, Florence, Maude, only child of Henry Rudolph Laing, of 5, Cadogan Gdns., S.W., and has issue living, Ivor Laing (of Marlowe, Vyner Road South, Birkenhead), *b.* 1907; Flt.-Lt. late R.A.F.; 1939-45 War (despatches): *m.* 1936, Winifred, da. of W. B. Waterhouse, of Wallasey, and has issue living, John Anthony (White Gates, Over Tabley, Knutsford) *b.* 1941: *m.* 1963, Jacqueline Lockley-Cook (and has issue living, Christopher William Ivor Lockley *b.* 1965, Louis Anthony Lockley *b.* 1968, Jennifer *b.* 1938: *m.* 1958, Michael Derek White, of Wayside, Vyner Rd. North, Birkenhead, Jill Susan Rosemary *b.* 1948: *m.* 1969, Clyde Dennis Gordon Coltart, of Browfield, Dale End Rd., Barnston, Wirral (and has issue living, Rupert Gordon *b.* 1971, Amanda Jane *b.* 1973),—Mervyn Jeffery, *MB, BCh, MRCS, LRCP* (of Hill House, Langport, Som.), *b.* 1909; MRCS England and LRCP London 1933; MB, BCh (Camb.); Capt. late RAMC: *m.* 1936, Joan Doreen, da. of the late Engineer-Capt. A. P. L. Dupen, RN, and has issue living, Collingwood William Malcolm *b.* 1939, Priscilla Jane *b.* 1937: *m.* 1963, Dudley Allen Doust, of 6, Diamond Terr., Greenwich, SE10) and has issue living, Hannah Victoria *b.* 1963, Elinor Jane *b.* 1966), Charlotte Certhia *b.* 1944: *m.* 1964, Charles St. Vigor Fox, of Longhill Farm, Cucklington, Wincanton, [*see* Orr-Ewing, Bt., colls., cr. 1886],—Certhia Mary, *b.* 1917: *m.* 1940, Charles Gerald Harden, of Springhill Farm, Iden Green, Benenden, Cranbrook, Kent, and has issue living, Alastair Geoffrey *b.* 1943, Richard Charles *b.* 1946, Veryan Penelope *b.* 1941: *m.* 1964, Ernest Pollard, of Horseshoe Cottage, Woodhurst, Hunts (and has issue living, John Collingwood *b.* 1968, Tessa Mary *b.* 1966) Frances Mary *b.* 1956. *Residence*,The Grange, Benenden, Cranbrook, Kent.

Collateral Branches living.

Issue of the late Sir Bruce Stirling Ingram, OBE, MC, son of 1st Bt., *b.* 1877, *d.* 1963: *m.* 1st, 1904, Amy, who *d.* 1947, da. of John Foy, of 16, Bolton Gdns., SW; 2ndly, 1947, Lily, who *d.* 1962, da. of Sydney Grundy:—
(By 1st marriage) Averil Stirling, *b.* 1905: *m.* 1945, Capt. Jean Prost, of 81, rue de La Pompe, Paris XVI, France.

Grandchildren of Collingwood Ingram (ante):—
Issue of the late Maj. William Alastair Ingram, *b.* 1913, *d.* 1975: *m.* 1947, Daphne (Frame Farm, Beneden, Cranbrook, Kent), el. da. of the late Reginald Bramley Van Wart, OBE, of Llwyngwril, Merionethshire:—

Peter William Irving, *b.* 1950; ed. at Winchester.——Heather Anne, *b.* 1948: *m.* 1969, Michael Paget Bowyer, of Lockerley Water House, Lockerley, Romsey, Hants., and has issue living, Cardine Sarah, *b.* 1972.

The 1st baronet, Sir William James Ingram, sometime Managing Director of the *Illustrated London News*, sat as MP for Boston (L) 1874-80, 1885-6, and 1892-5.

INNES, Creation (N.S.) 1628, of Balvenie, Banffshire.

[Name pronounced "**Innez.**"]

Let it be done without crime.

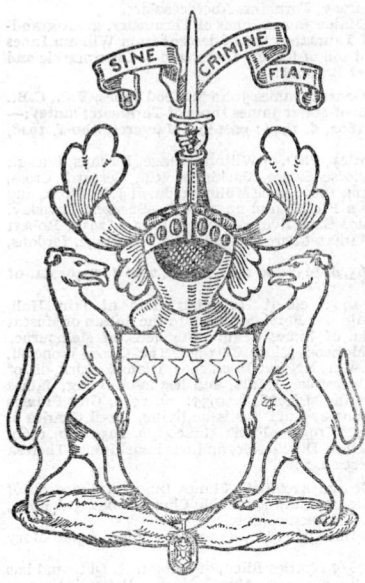

Sir WALTER JAMES INNES OF BALVENIE, 15th *Baronet*, son of the late Hector Innes, 6th son of 11th baronet; *b.* Aug. 8th, 1903; *s.* his cousin, Sir JAMES BOURCHIER, 1950.

Arms—Argent, three mullets in chief azure. **Crest** —A dexter arm, armed and couped at the elbow, holding a broadsword in pale proper. **Supporters**— Two greyhounds argent.

Seats—Balvenie Castle, Banffshire; Edingight Grange, Banffshire. *Residence*—Carlos Pellegrini 485, 4 piso, Dep. B., Buenos Aires, Argentina. *Club*—Union (Mendoza, Argentina).

Sister living—Lily Eileen, *b.* 1901 : *m.* 1925, Hubert Brunel Mallet, of Canning 2638, 5° Piso Depto. E., Buenos Aires, Argentina, and has issue living, Myra, *b.* 1927: *m.* 1952, Oliver Miles Dawe, of 39, Onslow Rd., Walton-on-Thames, and has issue living, Michael Charles *b.* 1954, Angela Katherine *b.* 1956,—Nancy, *b.* 1929: *m.* 1951, Charles Brandon, of Canning 2638, 5° Piso Depto. E., Buenos Aires, Argentina, and has issue living, John *b.* 1956, Diana Lily *b.* 1953.

Collateral Branches living.

Grandchildren of the late Alexander Innes, *b.* 1846, son of the late Alexander Innes, *b.* 1812, el. son of William Innes, son of Alexander Innes of Breda and Cowie, 2nd son of John Innes of Edingight, grandfather of 9th baronet:—

Issue of the late Capt. James William Guy Innes, C.B.E., J.P., D.L., R.N., *b.* 1873, *d.* 1939 : *m.* 1906, Sheila, who *d.* 1949, (having *m.* 2ndly, 1940, the 2nd Marquess of Aberdeen and Temair), da. of the late Lieut.-Col. John Foster Forbes, J.P. D.L., of Rothiemay Castle, Banffshire :—

RONALD GORDON BEROWALD, O.B.E., *b.* July 24th, 1907 ; *ed.* at Harrow ; Lieut.-Col. (retired) Seaforth Highlanders ; European War 1939-45 in Middle East, Sicily, and N.-W. Europe (wounded, O.B.E.) ; O.B.E. (Mil.) 1943: *m.* 1st, 1933, Elizabeth Haughton, who *d.* 1958, el. da. of the late Alfred Fayle, of Merlin, Clonmel, co. Tipperary ; 2ndly, 1961, Elizabeth Christian, el. da. of the late Lieut.-Col. Charles Henry Watson, D.S.O. and has issue living, (by 1st m.) Peter Alexander Berowald (25, Aster Rd., Kempshott Hill, Basingstoke; Naval and Military Club), *b.* 1937; *ed.* at Bristol Univ. (BSc); a MICE: *m.* 1959, Julia Mary, nr. da. of A. S. Levesley, MSc, FRIC, of Burlington Rd., Bristol, and has issue living, Alexander Guy Berowald *b.* 1960, Alastair John Peter *b.* 1965, Fiona Julie *b.* 1963,—George Guy Alfred, *b.* 1941,— Catherine Eytham, *b.* 1940: *m.* 1st, 1962 (m. diss. 1970) Mark Grant Oliver; 2ndly, 1974, Hugh Leslie Sanderson, of Lesmurdie House, Lesmurdie, W. Aust., and has issue living (by 1st m.), Karen Elizabeth *b.* 1965, Alison Mary *b.* 1967. *Residence*, Pinkney Pound, Malmesbury, Wilts. *Club*, Naval and Military.——William Alexander Disney, *b.* 1910; *ed.* at Marlborough; Lt.-Col. (ret.) Gordon Highlanders; Vice-Lt. for Banffshire; 1939-45 War: *m.* 1939, Mary Alison, only da. of the late Francis Burnett-Stuart, of Howe Green, Hertford, and has issue living, Michael Alexander, *b.* 1954,—Jonathan Berowald, *b.* 1955. *Residence*, The Old Manse, of Marnoch, Huntly, Aberdeenshire.——Elizabeth Kathrine Mary, *b.* 1918: *m.* 1st, 1943 (divorce 1948), Maj. James Robertson-McIsaac; 2ndly, 1948, Col. Eric Dighton Mackenzie, CMG, CVO, DSO, who *d.* 1972, and has issue living, (by 2nd m.) [see Mackenzie, Bt., *cr.* 1890]. *Residence*, Calgary House, Tobermory, Isle of Mull.

Issue of the late Sydney Armitage Innes, DSO, *b.* 1879, *d.* 1960: *m.* 1903, Constance Edith, who *d.* 1957, da. of the late Samuel Blain:—

Berowald Alfred, *b.* 1904 ; *ed.* at Rugby ; formerly Lieut.-Col. The Black Watch ; European War 1939-45 (wounded) : *m.* 1931, Betty Ida, da. of the late Alastair C. Sandeman, of Fonab, Pitlochry, Perthshire, and has issue living, Colin Berowald, *b.* 1936 ; *ed.* at Wellington; is Maj. The Black Watch: *m.* 1961, Clovannis Jane, da. of the late Lt.-Col. Charles Frederick Cathcart, DSO [see E. Cathcart, colls.], and has issue living, Andrew Berowald *b.* 1963, Katherine Candida, *b.* 1967, Emily Jane *b.* 1969,—Malcolm Alastair (55, Ovington St., SW3), *b.* 1939; *ed.* at Wellington, and at Trin. Hall, Camb.; late 2nd Lt. Scots Gds.,—James Alexander (twin), (New Belses, Ancrum, Roxburghshire), *b.* 1939: *m.* 1969, Frances, yst. da. of Hugh Leggat, of Pirnie House, Kelso, and has issue living, Melissa Jane *b.* 1972. *Residence*, Tulchan, Glenalmond, Perthshire. *Clubs*, Farmers', Royal and Ancient.——Sylvia, *b.* 1909: *m.* 1944, Maj.-Gen. Frank McLean Richardson, CB, DSO, OBE, RAMC, and has issue living, Hugh Alexander, *b.* 1947,—Alastair Neil, *b.* 1953,—Jennifer Jane, *b.* 1944. *Residence*, The Shaws, West Barnton Av., Edinburgh.

Grandchildren of the late Lt.-Col. Francis Newell Innes of Learney, (infra):— Issue of the late Sir Thomas Innes of Learney, GCVO, LLD, FSA (Scot.), Lord Lyon King of Arms 1945-69, *b.* 1893, *d.* 1971: *m.* 1928, Lady Lucy Buchan (The Laigh Riggs, Torphins, Aberdeenshire, da. of 18th Earl of Caithness:—

Thomas of Learney (Learney, Torphins, Aberdeenshire, AB3 4NB; Roy. Northern Club, Aberdeen); *b.* 1930; *ed.* at Edinburgh Univ. (BSc Agric); late R. Signals; OStJ; Pres. of Deeside Field Club: *m.* 1958, Rosemary Elizabeth, yr. da. of Brig. Cecil Vivian Staveley Jackson, CIE, CBE, of Burnside, Aboyne, Aberdeenshire, and has issue living, Maureen Cecilia, *b.* 1962.——Berowald Fortescue, FSA(Scot) (Inverisla, Rothiemay, Huntly, Aberdeenshire), *b.* 1931; *ed.* at Melville Coll.——Malcolm Rognvald of Edingight, FSA (Scot), *WS* (Edingight, Keith, Banffshire, and 35, Inverleith Row, Edinburgh; New (Edinburgh) and Puffin's Clubs), *b.* 1938; *ed.* at Edinburgh Acad, and Edinburgh Univ. (MA, LLB); OStJ; Falkland Pursuivant Extraor. 1957-58, and Carrick Pursuivant 1958-72, since when Marchmont Herald; Lyon Clerk and Keeper of the Records, Lyon Court since 1966; a member of Queen's Body Guard for Scotland (Roy. Co. of Archers): *m.* 1963, Joan, only da. of Thomas D. Hay, of 31, Ravelston Dykes, Edinburgh, and has issue living, John Berowald, *b.* 1965,—Colin William, *b.* 1967,—Michael Thomas, *b.* 1970.—— Sybil Marjorie, *b.* 1934.

Granddaughter of the late Col. Thomas Innes of Learney, CVO, LLD, 2nd son
of the late William Innes (ante):—
Issue of the late Lt.-Col. Francis Newell Innes of Learney, b. 1845, d. 1907: m. 1892,
Margaret Anne, who d. 1923, da. of the late Archer Irvine-Fortescue, of Kingcausie,
Kincardineshire [E. Fortescue, colls.]:—
Helen Christian, b. 1895.   Residence, Calliebrae, Learney, Torphins, Aberdeenshire.
Descendants of the late Major James Innes of Thrumster, great-grand-
son of James Innes of Thursater, 5th in descent from William Innes
of Thursater, youngest son of Robert Innes, 2nd of Innermarkie and
great-great-uncle of 1st Baronet:—

Grandchildren of the late Lieut.-General James John McLeod Innes, V.C., C.B.,
only son of James Innes, 5th son of Major James Innes of Thrumster (ante):—
Issue of the late Hugh McLeod Innes, b. 1862, d. 1944: m. 1894, Margaret, who d. 1948,
da. of James Bird:—
Christina McLeod, b. 1902: m. 1925, Frank Vigor Morley, PhD, of Wilton Cottage, Jordans, Bucks.;
and has issue living, John Donald Innes (Packhorse House, Packhorse Rd., Gerrards Cross,
Bucks.), b. 1926; ed. at New Coll., Oxford (MA): m. 1962, Alice Millicent, da. of J. T. Flook, and
widow of George Boast,—Hugh Oliver, b. 1928; a FRCO, and an ARCM,—Susanna Loveday,
b. 1932: m. 1956, John Guthrie Smithson, and has issue living, Michael John b. 1957, Robert
Hugh b. 1963, Deborah Mary b. 1959,—Christina Margaret Peregrine (c/o Wilton Cottage, Jordans,
Bucks., b. 1940.
Issue of the late Arthur Donald Innes, b. 1865, d. 1938: m. 1901, Helen, who d. 1948, da. of
Edward Arnold Pittis:—
Neil McLeod (Thursater, Uplyme, Lyme Regis), b. 1903; ed. at Haileybury and at Trin. Hall,
Camb. (MA); Sudan Political Ser. 1926-52, and Min. for Foreign Affairs to the Sultan of Muscat
and Oman 1953-58: m. 1931, Nancy Audrey, da. of James Temple Stephens, of Melbourne,
Aust., and has issue living, Roderick Temple McLeod (Close Cottage, The Close, Wonersh,
Guildford), b. 1938; ed. at Marlborough Coll.; Lt.-Cdr. RN (ret.): m. 1962, Diana Selkirk, da. of
the late Eric S. Drew, of The Gabled House, Alverstoke, Hants, and has issue living, James
McLeod b. 1966, Charles McLeod b. 1969,—Catherine McLeod, b. 1935: m. 1954, Guy Francis
Symondson, of Heathfield House, Windlesham, Surrey, and has issue living, Bevil Charles b.
1955, Robin Francis b. 1957, Alastair James Guy b. 1958,—Fiona McLeod, b. 1939: m. 1960,
Simon Noel Chick, of Manor Farm, Compton Valence, Dorchester, and has issue living, Theresa
Nicola b. 1960, Philippa Helen b. 1963, Sarah Rebecca b. 1967.
Grandchildren of the late Ven. George Archibald Clunes Innes, Archdeacon of
Hamilton, Vic., Aust., son of the late Maj. Archibald Clunes Innes, 3rd Buffs,
6th son of Maj. James Innes of Thrumster (ante):—
Issue of the late George Archibald Clunes Innes, b. 1870, d. 19—: m. 1900, Agnes Mary
Gowthorpe, who d. 1937:—
Charles McLeod, b. 1902: m. 1931, Elspeth Anne, da. of Charles Bilbe, of Dululu, N. Qld. and has
issue living, Lorraine, b. 1932,—Ian, b. 1933,—Colin, b. 1935,—Alan, b. 1947,—Patty, b. 1935,—
Mary, b. 1938,—Jillian, b. 1941.——Enid Emily, b. 1904: m. 19—, Donald James Mackay, and
has issue living, Shirley, b. 1931.
Issue of the late Lilian Emily MacLeay Innes, b. 1872, d. 1942 : m. 1889, Frank Sweet-
nam :—
Reginald Innes, M.B., B.S., b. 1894 ; M.B. and B.S. Melbourne 1923 ; m. 1st, 1923 ; 2ndly, 1940,
Joan Finlay, and has issue living, (by 1st marriage) John, b. 1929.   Residence, 32, Marne Street,
South Yarra, Victoria, Australia.
Descendants of Captain Peter Innes, 79th Foot, 3rd son of William
Innes in Olliclate, and younger brother of Major James Innes of
Thrumster (ante):—

Granddaughters of the late Peter Innes (infra):—
Issue of the late Lt.-Col. Robert Innes, b. 1891, d. 1963: m. 1913, Charlotte Lloyd Heming,
who d. 1972:—
Frances Mary, b. 1918: m. 1946, James Thomas, who d. 1965.——Charlotte Elizabeth, b. 1921:
m. 1939, William Young, of Waterville, King's Co., Nova Scotia, and has issue living, Peter
William, b. 1949,—Sidney Allen, b. 1953,—Patricia Kathleen, b. 1940: m. 1971, John Odak, of
Vancouver, BC,—Charlotte Joy, b. 1941: m. 1961, John Robert Wilkinson, of Toronto, and has
issue living, John William b. 1963, Debra Lee b. 1961,—Sandra Vaughan, b. 1944: m. 1964,
Donald Wade Perry, of Waterville, Kings Co., Nova Scotia, and has issue living, Shannon
Rae b. 1965, Shelley Lynn (twin), b. 1965.——Margaret Joan, b. 1925: m. 1952 Douglas Comrie,
of Main St., Kentville, Nova Scotia, and has issue living, Laurie Douglas, b. 1954,—Michael
Raoul, b. 1962,—Charlotte Ann, b. 1953,—Mary Jane, b. 1963.
Descendants of John Innes of Coxton, grandson of Patrick Innes of the Keam
of Duffus, great-great-great uncle of 1st baronet [see that title].

The limitations of this baronetcy are to heirs male whatsoever, as contained in the " signature,"
or warrant for the patent and heredibus masculis quibuscunque in the latter, on record in Lyon
Court, and on the death of the 8th baronet in 1817, John Innes, of Edingight (having been served
heir male general to his predecessor in the title on Jan. 12th, 1818), assumed the baronetcy as 9th
Bt., and as heir male of John Innes, of Edingight, great-great-uncle of the 1st baronet. The 12th
baronet was Vice-Lieut. for Banffshire.

INNES, Creation (N.S.) 1686, of Coxton, Co. Moray.

Sir CHARLES KENNETH GORDON INNES OF
COXTON, 11th Baronet; b. Jan. 28th, 1910;
s. his father, Maj. (Sir) CHARLES GORDON
DEVERELL, de jure 10th baronet, 1953;
placed on Official Roll of Baronets 1973; ed.
at Haileybury; Capt. late 151st Field Regt.
RA (Ayrshire Yeo.); a Dir. of G. & J. Kitcat,
Ltd.; 1939–45 War: m. 1936, Margaret
Colquhoun Lockhart, el. da. of Frederick
Charles Lockhart Robertson [Colquhoun, Bt.]
and has issue.

Arms—Argent, three mullets within a bordure
embattled azure, in dexter canton argent a saltire
Azure surmounted of an inescutcheon or charged with a
lion rampant within a double tressure flory counterflory
gules (for his Baronetcy of Nova Scotia). Crest, A
dexter arm in armour, the hand naked holding a skean in
pale, both proper, issuing from an embattled tower Argent
masoned sable, port gules.
Residence, October Cottage, Kemnal Park, Haslemere, Surrey.

Son living—DAVID CHARLES KENNETH GORDON (28, Wadham Close, Shepperton, Middlesex), *b.* April 17th, 1940; ed. at Haileybury, and at London Univ (BScEng): *m.* 1969, Marjorie Alison, da. of Ernest W. Parker, and has issue living, Alastair Charles Deverell, *b.* Sept. 17th, 1970,—Dione Elizabeth Colquhoun, *b.* 1974.

Daughter living—Daphne Margaret Colquhoun, *b.* 1948: *m.* 1971, Nigel Geoffrey Wolseley Haig, of 102, Albert Palace Mansions, Lurline Gdns., SW1.

Sister living—Eleanor Joan, *b.* 1913: *m.* 1938, Trevor Walter Mimpriss, MB, MS, FRCS, and has issue living, Timothy John (c/o Westminster Bank, 149, Arthur Rd., SW19), *b.* 1940; MA, MB, BChir, Camb.; FFARCS): *m.* 1964, Wendy Anne, da. of Donald Pryce, and has issue living, Robert Charles *b.* 1971, Rosemary Jill *b.* 1965, Hilary Anne *b.* 1967,—John Graham (Orchard Close, The Downs, Givons Grove, Leatherhead, Surrey), *b.* 1944: *m.* 1966, Lorraine, da. of Donald Lovell, and has issue living, Graham Donald *b.* 1968, James Christopher *b.* 1970,—Jill Alison, *b.* 1942: *m.* 1966, Lt. David Richard Monro Gregory, RN, of The Old School House, Lumphanan, Aberdeenshire, son of Vice-Adm. Sir (George) David (Archibald) Gregory, KBE, CB, DSO, and has issue living, Peter James *b.* 1967, Caroline Joan *b.* 1969, Nicola Helen *b.* 1972. *Residence*, Muskoka, Square Drive, Kingsley Green, Haslemere, Surrey.

Collateral Branches living.

Grandchildren of the late Edward George Innes son of Edward Innes, next brother of *de jure* 9th Baronet:—
Issue of the late Edward David Ballantyne Innes, *b.* 1884, *d.* 1967: *m.* 1st, 1906, Ethel Agnes Isobel, who *d.* 1929, da. of Charles Lucas: 2ndly, 1933, Viney Isobel, da. of Patrick Keogh, of Gawlis, NWC, Tasmania:—
(By 1st m.) John Holdsworth, *b.* 1915: *m.* 1960, ——.——Robert Maxwell, *b.* 1917: *m.* 19—Jean Marshal, and has issue living.——Gwendolen Eleanor (6, Randall St., Sandy Bay, Hobart, Tasmania), *b.* 1906.——Marjory Betty, *b.* 1913: *m.* 1939, James Benjamin Greer.——(by 2nd m.) George Berowald, *b.* 1938.——Jean Elizabeth, *b.* 1934.——Pauline Margaret, *b.* 1939.

Issue of the late Vivian Oswald Innes, *b.* 1888, *d.* 1971: *m.* 1912, Teresa, da. of Matthew Fitzpatrick:—
Gordon Vivian, *b.* 1922.——Cecil Alfred, *b.* 1923.——Leila Anne (Glen Fern, Port Cygnet, Tasmania), *b.* 1913.

Issue of the late Eric Edward Innes, *b.* 1891: *m.* 1st, 1917, Winifred Shelma, who *d.* 1921, da. of Edward Charles O'Brien; 2ndly, 1925, Doris Cecilia, da. of Brian Kilmartin:—
(By 1st m.) Edward George (Linga Longa, Port Cygnet, Tasmania), *b.* 1919: *m.* 1942, Ruth Minnie, da. of Ralph Norris, and has issue living, Nigel David, *b.* 1944;—Christopher Wayne, *b.* 1948.

Issue of the late Atholl Rupert Innes, *b.* 1893, *d.* 1973: *m.* 1922, Kathleen (Kia Ora Mail Box, Lymington Rd., Cygnet, 7H2, Tasmania), da. of Edward Crease:—
William James, *b.* 1924: *m.* 1st, 1950, Avis Lorraine, da. of Victor Eugene Yelland; 2ndly, 1967, Claire Adelaide, da. of R. A. Bathy, of Adelaide, NZ, and has issue living, (by 1st m.), Wendy Beryl Ann, *b.* 1951,—Josephine Lillian, *b.* 1953,—(by 2nd m.) Bronwyn Heather, *b.* 1971.——Sheila Jean, *b.* 1927: *m.* 1957, James Florance Turnover, of 58, Union St., E. Brighton, Vict., Aust., and has issue living, Keppel John, *b.* 1959,—Quentin David, *b.* 1962,—Louise Margaret, *b.* 1958.

Grandchildren of the late Edward Innes (*b.* 1827), next brother of *de jure* 10th baronet:—
Issue of the late Edward George Innes, *b.* 1854, *d.* 1904: *m.* 1st, 1880, Jane, who *d.* 1884, da. of Philip Ballantyne ; 2ndly, 1886, Marjory, who *d.* 1946, da. of Jacob Christie :—
(By 2nd m.) Adrian Arthur (48, Bayfield St., Bellerive, Tasmania), *b.* 1900: *m.* 1927, Daisy, da. of Francis Calvert Smith, and has issue living, Roy Edward (Clifton Beach Rd., Sandford, Tasmania), *b.* (Dec.) 1927: *m.* 1963, Shirley Esther, da. of Victor Richardson Clements, and has issue living, Shane Edward *b.* 1969, Kim Nyree *b.* 1972,—George Calvert (1, Lanena St., Bellerive, Tasmania), *b.* 1932: *m.* 1965, Chou Seng, da. of Thar Yu Mok, and has issue living, Andrew Gary *b.* 1969, Trevor Craig *b.* 1971.——Ismay Anne, *b.* 1898. *Residence.*

Issue of the late William Innes, *b.* 1859, *d.* 1928 : *m.* 1887, Adelina Bianca Alexandrina, who *d.* 1946, da. of William Allsopp :—
Francis Allsopp, *b.* 1888 ; Lieut.-Com. R.N.R.; European War 1914-18 (Croix de Guerre with palms) : *m.* 1926, Marjorie Rolleston, da. of William Tucker Pyke, and has issue living, Berowald Francis, *b.* 1928,—William, *b.* 1935. *Residence*, 61, Seaview Street, Balgowlah, Sydney, N.S. Wales.——William Edward Allsopp, *b.* 1893 : *m.* 1923, Lyla Alta, da. of Frederick Charles Thomson-Brown, of Launceston, Tasmania, and has issue living, Desmond Erick, *b.* 1926,—Patricia Joan, *b.* 1925.——Arthur Berowald, *b.* 1800: *m.* 1926, Irene Eva Eastman, and has issue living, Graeme Alastair, *b.* 1932,—Darren Arthur, *b.* 1936,—Janet Lucille, *b.* 1930,—Sandra Ann, *b.* 1938.——Gordon Tulloh, *b.* 1904: *m.* 1931, Brienetta Grace, da. of Leonard Harold O'Brien.——Clothilde, *b.* 1897. *Residence*, Hobart, Tasmania.

Grandchildren of the late George Innes, yst. brother of *de jure* 9th Bt., and Edward Innes (*b.* 1827) (ante):—
Issue of the late George Peacock Innes, *b.* 1863, *d.* 1936 : *m.* 1893, Susanna Robina, da. of Robert Mills :—
George Donald, *b.* 1905 ; is Municipal Engineer at Miniwa : *m.* 1932, Florence Elizabeth Younger —Myrtle Robina, *b.* 1894.——Elizabeth Stuart, *b.* 1898 ; Emergency Ambulance Corps 1939-44. *Residence*, 56, Shirley Road, Wollstonecroft, Sydney, N.S. Wales.

Grandson of the late Rev. Dr. James Innes, uncle of *de jure* 9th Bt.:—
Issue of the late Edward Henry Innes, Fleet Paymaster, R.N., *b.* 1864, *d.* 1930 : *m.* 1st, 1889, Mary Laughlin, who *d.* 1921, da. of R. D. Fraser, Controller of Customs, Bermuda; 2ndly, 1924, Mary Sheena Butler, who *d.* 1925 :—
(By 1st m.) George William Holt, MBE, (49, Vicarage Rd., East Sheen, SW14; Hurlingham Club) *b.* 1900; Lt.-Col. (ret.) W. Yorks. Regt.; Kurdistan 1923 (medal with clasp), Palestine 1936 (clasp); 1939-45 War (France and Germany star, NW Europe star, Defence medal, 1939-45 War medal); MBE (Civil) 1966: *m.* 1931, Alexandra, da. of Dunbar Marshall, of Natchez, Mississippi, USA, and has issue living, Vivien Holt, *b.* 1932: *m.* 1959, John Kennedy Wagstaff, of 52, Salmons Lane, Whyteleafe, Surrey, and has issue living, Clarissa Christine *b.* 1960, Martine Charis *b.* 1962, Vanessa Jacynth *b.* 1971,—Valerie Evelyn, *b.* 1935: *m.* 1958, Mervyn Russell Chute, of 137, Westhall Rd., Warlingham, Surrey, and has issue living, Nigel Anthony *b.* 1960, Rosalind Alexandra *b.* 1962.

This baronetcy was conferred on Sir Alexander Innes, of Coxton, M.P. for Moray (with remainder to heirs male whatsoever). The Coxton family is a younger branch of Innes of Balvenie, cr. Bt. 1628, descending from Patrick, in the Keam of Duffus, 5th son of Walter Innes of Innermarkie (*d.c.* 1499). Sir Alexander Innes' direct line became ext. with his gt-grandson, Sir David, 6th Bt, who *d.* 1803. The baronetcy descended to Sir Alexander, gt.-grandson of John, 1st of Inaltrie, yr. brother of 1st Bt. On the death in 1886 of Sir George, 8th Bt., succession reverted to (Sir) Charles Innes, FRIBA, *de jure* 9th Bt., son of Edward Innes (*b.* 1792) and 6th in descent from John, 3rd son of John Innes, 2nd of Coxton, and gt-uncle of 1st Bt. Sir Charles Kenneth Gordon, grandson of (Sir) Charles, was placed on the Roll of Baronets in 1973, as 11th Baronet of Coxton.

ISHAM, Creation (E.) 1627, of Lamport, Northamptonshire.

[Name pronounced "Eye-sham."]

I show, I sham not.

OSTENDO NON OSTENTO

Sir GYLES ISHAM, 12th *Baronet;* b. Oct. 31st, 1903 ; s. his father, *Sir* VERE 1941 ; ed. at Rugby, and at Magdalen Coll. Oxford (MA); FSA; a co. Councillor for Northants 1955-64 (High Sheriff 1958); a Trustee of National Portrait Gallery 1964-71; a DL for Northants, and a Knight of Obedience of Sovereign Mil. Order of Malta; Pres. of Assocn. of Independent Hosps.; Middle East 1940- 5 as Lt.-Col. KRRC, latterly on Gen. Staff.

Arms—Gules, a fesse wavy and in chief three piles also wavy, points meeting in fesse argent. **Crest**—A demi-swan, wings displayed argent, beaked sable. **Second Motto**—"On things transitory resteth no glory."

Seat—Lamport Hall, Northampton. *Club*—Beefsteak.

Sister living—Virginia (9, Mill Lane, Kingsthorpe, Northants.), b. 1898.

Collateral Branches living.

Granddaughter of the late Rev. Arthur Isham, son of the late Rev. Henry Charles Isham, 3rd son of 7th baronet :—
Issue of the late Arthur Charles Isham, b. 1847, d. 1897 : m. 1887, Evelyn Rose, who d. 1909 (having m. 2ndly, 1904, the Rev. Clement Eustace Macro Wilson, who d. 1945), da. of the late Richard William Selby-Lowndes, of Elmers, Bletchley :—
Dorothy Evelyn Vere, b. 1888: m. 1917, Lt.-Col. Harry Norton Schofield, VC (formerly RA), HM's Hon. Corps of Gentlemen-at-Arms, who d. 1931, and has issue living, Christopher Corty Isham (of Poynatt's Manor, Skirmett, nr. Henley-on-Thames, Oxfordshire), b. 1921: m. 1949, Angela Marilyn Honor Suzanne, da. of the late Capt. Richard Cecil Kelly, OBE, and has issue living, Harry Richard Vere b. 1950, Vere Michael Christopher b. 1952, Peter Charles Vere b. 1956, Joanna Mary Katherine b. 1957.—Diana Mary Evelyn, b. 1920: m. 1957, Norman Ellison, Waugh, of Mill Leat, Heamoor, Penzance, Cornwall, and has issue living, Richard Christopher b. 1959, Letitia Dorothy Mary b. 1958. *Residence*, 14, Onslow Gdns., SW7.

Grandchildren of the late Arthur Charles Isham (ante):—
Issue of the late Lt.-Col. Vere Arthur Richard Isham, MC, b. 1889, d. 1968: m. 1922, Edith Irene, who d. 1973, da. of Harry Brown:—
IAN VERE GYLES (Vincent House, Pembridge Sq., W2), b. July 17th, 1923; formerly Capt. Co. of London Yeo.; 1939-45 War.——Norman Murray Crawford (5, Copping Close, Park Hill, Croydon, Surrey), b. 1930; B.Arch; RIBA: m. Joan, da. of the late Leonard James Genet, of Umtali, Rhodesia, and has issue living, Richard Leonard Vere b. 1958,—Vere Murray Gyles b. 1960,— Elizabeth Angela, b. 1957.

Issue of the late Elizabeth Mary Victoria Isham, b. 1891, d. 1956: m. 1916, **Neville** Hollings Ogilvie, who d. 1958 :—
Graham Euseby Hollings, b. 1917 ; formerly Lieut. S. African Forces : m. 1940, Evelyn May Horley, and has issue living, Robert Chester Eric, b. 1943.—Carol Madeleine Victoria, b. 1945. *Residence*, 504, Granton Heights, Humewood, Port Elizabeth, S. Africa.——Vere Neville Hollings, b. 1922; formerly Lieut. S. African Forces: m. 1944, Margaret Eleanor, da. of Robert Millar Duff, of Bournemouth, and has issue living, Bruce Neville Duff Hollings, b. 1951,—Marilyn Anne, b. 1949. *Residence*, Durham Farm, Box 308, Gwelo, S. Rhodesia.——Bettine Florence Rose, b. 1920: m. 1st, 1940, Paul Wallis Grice; 2ndly, 1947, Ralph Charles Benjamin Fincham Ryan, and has issue living, (by 1st m.) Michael David Wallis (109, 4th St., Parkmore, Johannesburg), b. 1943; assumed the surname of Ryan: m. 1967, Carol Ann Crangle, and has issue living, Robert Benjamin Victor b. 1971, Elizabeth Jane Victoria b. 1968. *Residence*, 104, Tiber Mansions, Tyrwhitt Close, Rosebank, Johannesburg, S. Africa.

The Isham family, took their name from the village of Isham in Northamptonshire, where they were found holding land under William I. A cadet branch of the family was established at Pytchley in the 13th century, from whom the present family descend. Robert Isham of Pytchley was Escheator of Northamptonshire under Henry VI, and Solicitor to Elizabeth, Queen of Edward IV. Gyles Isham was M.P. for Peterborough twice in the reign of Queen Mary I. His younger brother, John, a prosperous Mercer, established himself at Lamport in 1560, and his grandson Sir John, High Sheriff of Northamptonshire, was created a baronet in 1627, having previously been knighted by James I. His son, Sir Justinian, a staunch Royalist, suffered severely for his loyalty, but became M.P. for Northamptonshire on the Restoration. Sir Justinian, the 4th baronet, M.P. for Northamptonshire, upon the landing of the Prince of Orange, appeared in arms against James II. at Nottingham. The 5th and 6th baronets were also M.P.s for Northamptonshire.

ISHERWOOD, Creation (U.K.) 1921, of Raggleswood, Chislehurst, Kent. [Extinct 1946.]

Sir WILLIAM ISHERWOOD, 2nd and last *Baronet*.

Daughters living of 2nd Baronet—Annette Marie, b. 1934: m. 19—, J. D. Smyth.——Diane Joan, b. 1936: m. 19—, F. B. Green. *Residence*.

Widow living of 2nd Baronet—IRENE JEANNE, da. of C. Pittolo : m. 1932, Sir William Isherwood, 2nd baronet, who d. 1946, when the title became ext. ; 2ndly, 1947, David Stevenson Watt. *Residence*, Harvard House, Pine Rd., Bickley, Kent.

JACKSON, Creation (U.K.) 1815, of Arlsey, Bedfordshire.

Sir JOHN MONTRÉSOR JACKSON, 6th
Baronet; b. Oct. 14th, 1914; *s.* his father, *Sir*
ROBERT MONTRÉSOR, 1940; ed. at Tonbridge,
and at Clare Coll., Camb. (BA); formerly a
Member of the London Stock Exchange: *m.*
1953, Mrs. Enid Beatty, da. of Stanley Hugh
Groome.

Arms—Argent, on a fesse between a goat's head couped
in chief gules and a ship in full sail in base proper, **a**
greyhound courant between two pheons or, within a bordure
of the second charged with eight bezants. **Crest**—A goat's
head couped argent guttée de sang, armed and bearded or,
gorged with a collar gules charged with three bezants, from
the collar a line reflexed of the third, the rings gold.

Residence—Rose Cottage, Charing, Kent.

Sister living—Bernice Evelyn Abrey, *b.* 1917: *m.* 1st, 1940,
Wing-Com. Patrick Edward Geoffrey Gunnell Connolly,
R.A.F.; 2ndly, 1954, Frederick John Ralph, and has
issue living, (by 1st marriage) Richard Edward Geoffrey
Gunnell, *b.* 1942,—Penelope Ann, *b.* 1941. *Residence,*
Hawkswood, Stevens Couch, Battle, Sussex.

Collateral Branches living.

Issue of the late Major Francis Gorham Jackson, late R.E., 2nd son of 4th
baronet, *b.* 1878, *d.* 1942: *m.* 1st, 1908, Ana Maria, da. of the late Pedro
Biscar, of Montevideo, Uruguay; 2ndly, 1919, Dorothy Hattie, da. of Albert
Edward Willis, of Teddington, Middlesex :—
(By 1st marriage) ROBERT, *b.* March 16th, 1910: *m.* 1943, Maria E. Casamayou, of Montevideo,
Uruguay, and has issue living, Victoria M., *b.* 1945,—Bertha Mary, *b.* 1949. *Residence*, Santiago
de Chile, 1241, Montevideo, Uruguay.

Grandchildren of the late Welby Charles Jackson (infra) :—
Issue of the late John Keith Jackson, *b.* 1872, *d.* 1957: *m.* 1914, Anna Maria Bertha,
who *d.* 1953, da. of — Arnold, of Freeling, South Australia :—
Keith Arnold, *b.* 1921: *m.* 19—, Pauline Mona, da. of B. P. Climo, of Wellington, New Zealand,
and has issue living, Neil Keith, *b.* 1952,—Colin Paul, *b.* 1954,—Bruce John, *b.* 1957,—Kenneth
Grant, *b.* 1961,—Claire Alison, *b.* 1954. *Residence*, Coast Rd., Wainuiomata, NZ.——Noela
Grace, *b.* 1915: *m.* 1945, Arthur Lambourn. *Residence,*

Issue of the late William Alfred Jackson, *b.* 1878, *d.* 1965: *m.* 1904, Emily, who *d.* 1952,
da. of John Hale, formerly of Westport, NZ:—
Grace Irene, *b.* 1906: *m.* 1937, Stephen Frederick Louis Cooper, of Gladstone, Wairarapa, NZ,
and has issue living, Stephen Jackson, *b.* 1952.——Elizabeth, *b.* 1911: *m.* 1937, Arthur David
McKay, of Gladstone, Wairarpa, NZ, and has issue living, Arthur Thomas, *b.* 1937,—Rex David,
b. 1953,—Colleen Mary, *b.* 1941,—Marie Elizabeth, *b.* 1943.

Grandchildren of the late John Jackson, 2nd son of 1st baronet :—
Issue of the late Welby Charles Jackson, *b.* 1839, *d.* 1926: *m.* 1866, Elizabeth, who *d.* 1926,
da. of John Grace, of Wellington, New Zealand :—
Sydney Leybourne, *b.* 1886: *m.* 1915, Daphne, who *d.* 1948, da. of William Halse, of Wellington,
New Zealand, and has issue living, Peggy Elinor, *b.* 1917: *m.* 1941, Archibald Douglas Wallace,
of Fitzroy Rd., Havelock North, Hawkes Bay, New Zealand, and has issue living, James
Leybourne *b.* 1946, Simon John Lewis *b.* 1949, Judith Margaret *b.* 1943: *m.* 1964, Lt. Thomas
Arthur Aldridge, RNZ Inf. Regt., P.O. Box 156, Waipukurau, NZ (and has issue living, Louise
Elizabeth *b.* 1965),—Sheila, *b.* 1924: *m.* 1950, Roy James Grant, and has issue living, Neil
James *b.* 1951, David Peter *b.* 1952.——Gordon Francis Welby, *b.* 1888: *m.* 1917, Kathleen
Florence, da. of John Haldane, of Takaka, NZ, and has issue living, John Richard (103, Linwood
Av., Christchurch, NZ), *b.* 1924: *m.* 1947, Leslie Kay, da. of James McKay Heise, of Raetihi,
NZ and has issue living, Peter *b.* 1951, John Terence *b.* 1956, James *b.* 1964, Margaret Gail
b. 1949: *m.* 1968, Teeh Sing, of Melbourne, Vic., Aust. (and has issue living, Geoffrey Peter *b.*
1968), Kathleen *b.* 1954. *Residence*, 59, Glen Rd., Kelburn, Wellington, W1, NZ.

Issue of the late Hugh Whiteman Jackson, *b.* 1842, *d.* 1929: *m.* 1869, Charlotte, who *d.*
1929, da. of A. W. Hayward, of Wellington, New Zealand:—
Sons and daughters living.

Issue of the late Murray James Hamilton Jackson, *b.* 1849, *d.* 1935: *m.* 1877, Selina Spearink,
who *d.* 1942:—
William John (31, Antonio St., Stratford, Taranaki, NZ), *b.* 1895: *m.* 1924, Ella, da. of the late
George Guppy, and has issue living, Alan Hamilton (Kupe, Stratford, NZ), *b.* 1924: *m.* 1949,
Lynn, da. of the late John Lindsay, and has issue living, William Lindsay *b.* 1956, Murry Grant
b. 1959, Anne Agnes *b.* 1953, a teacher,—Robert John, *b.* 1939: *m.* 1962, Ruth Margaret
Lamb, and has issue living, Stephen *b.* 19—, Andrew *b.* 19—, Brendan *b.* 19—, Pauline
b. 19—,—Esme Ruth, *b.* 1927: *m.* 1950, Cecil Edmund Rawhiti Smith,
of 20, Bracken Av., Epsom, Auckland, NZ, and has issue living, Cecil David *b.* 1951, Bruce
Edmund *b.* 1953, Peter Raymond *b.* 1954, Paul Barry *b.* 1959, Rodney John *b.* 1964, Margaret
Ann *b.* 1957, Beverley Joy *b.* 1962,—Evelyn Isabel, *b.* 1931: *m.* 1956, Ashley Gordon Howan,
(Box 401, Ba, Fiji), and has issue living, Lance *b.* 1959, Philip *b.* 19—, Cherry *b.* 1957.——
Murray Spearink (twin), *b.* 1895: *m.* 1921, Mary, da. of William Robinson, and has issue living,
David Murray James, *b.* 1921; is a Salvation Army Officer: *m.* 1950, Olive, da. of Reginald
Frederick Wilde, of Yeovil, Som., and has issue living, Paul Murray *b.* 1951, Verna Elizabeth,
b. 1954,—Edmund Robinson, *b.* 1923; is a Sheep Farmer: *m.* 1945, Thelma, da. of the late Hans
Ries, of Pohokura, Taranaki, NZ, and has issue living, Peter Edmund *b.* 1948, Geoffrey Kendall
b. 1952, Raewyn Ada *b.* 1954, Linda Mary *b.* 1954, Zoe *b.* 1957,—Harold Stuart (Parua Bay,
Whangerei, NZ), *b.* 1926: *m.* 1961, Eleni, da. of Savvas Michalis, of Dhymes, Limassol, Cyprus,
and has issue living, Andros Vassilis *b.* 1962, Nikos Manolis *b.* 1963,—Graham George, *BA, MD,*
—*b.* 1935.——Verna Gladys, *b.* 188-. *Residence*, 65, Cole St., Masterton, NZ.

**Grandchildren of the late Elphinstone Jackson, son of Welby Brown Jackson,
3rd son of 1st baronet:—**

Issue of the late Mountstuart Hungerford Jackson, *b.* 1860, *d.* 1925: *m.* 1886, Ethel Beatrice, who *d.* 1954, da. of David Cowie, a Member of Viceroy of India's Council:—
Cecil Hungerford, *b.* 1887; Col. Indian Army (ret.): *m.* 1916, Marian Blanche, who *d.* 1971, da. of the late, Com. Francis S. Wheeler, R.N., and has issue living, Audrey Madeline Hungerford, *b.* 1920: *m.* 1944, Robert Douglas Howe, M.B.E., I.C.S., and has issue living, Peter Mountstuart *b.* 1948, Veronica Joan *b.* 1946: *m.* 1968, James William Goodford, (and has issue living, Andrew Christopher John *b.* 1970, Richard Michael James *b.* 1972.   *Residence*, Manor House, Martock, Somerset.——
Laurence Hungerford, *b.* 1889; Col. Indian Army (ret.): *m.* 1919, Freda Mary, da. of the late Col. E. H. Dalgety, CB, and has issue living, Peter Hungerford, *b.* 1925; is Maj. RE: *m.* 1953, Joyce Thomasina, da. of Lt.-Col. V. H. Wells-Cole, late KOYLI, and has issue living, Amelia Mary Hungerford *b.* 1955, Catherine Ann Hnngerford *b.* 1957.   *Residence*, Veils Field, Trevone, Padstow, Cornwall.——Dorothy Hungerford, *b.* 1890: *m.* 1922, Col. Spence Daer Reid, late RAMC, who *d.* 1954, and has issue living, Peter Daer, *b.* 1925; is Maj. 1st Roy. Dragoons: *m.* 1958, Catherine Fleetwood, da. of W. A. Carmichael Boodle, of 50, Sloane Street, S.W.1, and has issue living, Duncan Andrew Daer *b.* 1959,—Ian Daer (of 1, Cedar Cres., Woy Woy, N.S. Wales), *b.* 1927; ed. at Edinburgh Univ. (M.B. and Ch.B. 1950): *m.* 1956, Olive Jean Courtenay, da. of W. Courtenay Snook, of St. Veep, Lostwithiel, Cornwall, and has issue living, Hamish Ian Daer *b.* 1957, Angus Courtenay Daer *b.* 1962, Heather Susan Daer *b.* 1959,—Joan Pamela Daer, *b.* 1924: *m.* 1956, Martin Vlaanderen, of Eigen Haard, Piccadilly Rd., Crafters 5152, S. Australia, and has issue living, Martin Richard *b.* 1957, Robert Laurens *b.* 1964, Rosemarie Anne *b.* 1958, Fiona Veronica *b.* 1960.   *Residence*, Dunmar, Tighnabruaich, Kyles of Bute, Argyll.

Grandchildren of the late Maj.-Gen. George D'Aguilar Jackson, 3rd son of 1st baronet:—
Issue of the late Harold Frederick D'Aguilar Jackson, *b.* 1877, *d.* 1942: *m.* 1903, Anna Lillian, widow of Count von Stadie, of Kœnigsberg, Germany:—
William Douglas D'Aguilar, *b.* 1904; ed. at California Institute of Technology, and at S. California Univ.; is Col. U.S. Army, and Ch. of Research and Development Div., Office of Q.M.G., U.S. Army; has Legion of Merit with Oak Leaf Cluster: *m.* 1933, Margaret Williams, and has issue living, Margaret Anne, *b.* 1938,—Susan, *b.* 1940.——Hyacinthe Lillian D'Aguilar, *b.* 1908; ed. at S. California Univ.: *m.* 1933, John Machell Procter, who *d.* 1941.   *Residence*, 6836½, Camrose, Hollywood, California, U.S.A.

The 1st baronet, an East India Co. Director, sat as MP for Dover, and the 3rd baronet was murdered Lucknow (1857) during the Indian Mutiny.

JACKSON, Creation (U.K.) 1902, of Stansted House, Stansted, Essex.

Sir MICHAEL ROLAND JACKSON, 5th *Baronet*; *b.* April 20th, 1919; *s.* his father, *Sir* (WALTER DAVID) RUSSELL, 1956; ed. at Stowe, and at Clare Coll., Camb.; formerly Fl. Lt. RAFVR: *m.* 1st, 1942 (m. diss. 1969), (Hilda) Margaret, da. of Cecil George Herbert Richardson, CBE; 2ndly, 1969, Hazel Mary, da. of Ernest Harold Edwards, and has issue by 1st m.

Arms—Ermine, on a pile azure, between two fountains proper, a sheldrake or. Crest—On a fountain proper a sheldrake or.
Residence—Dragon Cottage, Dragon's Green, Horsham, Sussex.

Son living—By 1st m.—THOMAS ST. FELIX, *b.* Sept. 27th, 1946.
Daughter living—By 1st m.—Sally Ann, *b.* 1944.

Aut mors aut victoria.
Either death or victory

Daughter living of 2nd Baronet—Nancy Amelia, *b.* 1924: *m.* 1948, Michael John Bowman-Vaughan, and has issue living, Michael Thomas, *b.* 1959,—Annabel Leslie, *b.* 1949,—Juliet Euphrosyne, *b.* 1951,—Venetia Mary, *b.* 1954.   *Residence*, 9 Cope Place, W8.

Daughters living of 3rd Baronet—Dawn Nesta (Farthaig Cottage, Gun Hill, Heathfield, Sussex), *b.* 1909.——Joyce Katherine (6, Chesham Rd., Kemp Town, Brighton), *b.* 1910: *m.* 1937 (m. diss. 1954), Lt.-Col. John Ralph Walker, and has issue living, Gay, *b.* 1941.——Meryl Julian (twin) (6, Manor Gate, St. John's Av., Putney, SW15), *b.* 1910: *m.* 1939, Herbert Sharpe Currie, who *d.* 1964, and has issue living, Julian David, *b.* 1944,—Caroline Joyce, *b.* 1941.——Daphne Myddleton (Garden Hill Cottage, Steep, Petersfield, Hants.), *b.* 1914: *m.* 1st, 1939, Sqdn. Ldr. Frederick U. Hollins, AFC, RAFVR, who *d.* (killed on active ser.) 1942; 2ndly, 1948, Maj. Malcolm Comrie Gray, Worcestershire Regt., and has issue living, (by 1st m.) Sarah Daphne, *b.* 1941,—(by 2nd m.) Fiona Catherine, *b.* 1949.

Widow living of 3rd Baronet—NESTA KATHERINE (*Nesta, Lady Jackson*), el. da. of Hedworth Barclay, of Gaddesby Hall, Leicestershire, *m.* 1909, Sir (George) Julius Jackson, 3rd baronet, who *d.* (Feb.) 1956.   *Residence*, Great Posbrooke, Titchfield, Fareham, Hants.

The 1st baronet, Sir Thomas, was Chm. and Director (sometime Ch. Manager) of Hong Kong and Shanghai Bank, Hong Kong. The 2nd baronet, Brig.-Gen. Thomas Dare Jackson, D.S.O., M.V.O., late King's Own Roy. Regt., was Assist. Mil. Sec. to Gov. of Gibraltar 1910-14, and served in S. African War 1901-2 and European War 1914-17.

JACKSON, Creation (U.K.) 1913, of Eagle House, Wimbledon, Surrey.

Sir HUGH NICHOLAS JACKSON, 2nd *Baronet*; *b.* Jan. 21st, 1881; *s.* his father, *Sir* THOMAS GRAHAM, 1924; ed. at Winchester; Lieut. 26th Indian Cav. 1901-8, and Roy. Welch Fusiliers 1908-12; Major (retired) Special Reserve; European War 1914-18: *m.* 1931, Violet Marguerite Loftus, da. of the late Loftus St. George [*see* St. George, Bt., colls.], and has issue.

Arms—Argent, a greyhound courant ermines, between three eagles' heads erased sable. **Crest**—A demi-horse argent, guttée de sang, maned and hoofed sable.
Residence—38, Oakley Street, Chelsea, S.W.3. *Club*—Brooks's.

Son living—NICHOLAS FANE ST. GEORGE (38, Noel Rd., N1. *Club*, Barb), *b.* Sept. 4th, 1934; ed. at Radley, and Wadham Coll., Oxford: Harpsichordist, a Liveryman of Drapers Co., and Dir. of Soho Music Soc., and of St. James's Piccadilly, Music Soc.; Organist at St. Anne's Ch., Soho 1963-71, and of St. James's Piccadilly 1971-74, since when St. Lawrence Jewry-next-Guildhall; Recitals and Broadcasts in Berlin 1967, and Recitals Paris 1972, and 1975, and USA 1975: *m.* 1st, 1961 (m. diss. 1968), Jennifer Ann, da. of F. A. Squire, of 8, Marylebone St., W1; 2ndly, 1972, Nadia Françoise Genevieve, da. of Georges Michard, Director de la Maison de la Culture, St. Etienne, 42, France.

Daughter living—Louise Loftus, *b.* 1946.

Brother living—Basil Hippisley, *M.C.*, *b.* 1887; ed. at Winchester, and at Balliol Coll., Oxford; Maj. (ret.) RHA (TA); 1914-18 War (despatches, MC); 1939-45 War; FRIBA: *m.* 1950, Helen (NICHOLSON), da. of the late Stanley Brotherhood, of Thornhaugh Hall, nr. Peterborough. *Residences*, Warmington Manor, Banbury, and 24, Lowndes Sq., SW1. *Clubs*, Bath, Travellers'.

Sir Thomas Graham Jackson, R.A., 1st Bt., was an architect who designed many churches, private houses, and scholastic and public buildings in Oxford and Cambridge and elsewhere, and was author of many books on architecture.

MATHER-JACKSON, Creation (U.K.) 1869, of The Manor House, Birkenhead.

Sir (GEORGE) CHRISTOPHER MATHER MATHER-JACKSON, 5th *Baronet*, son of the late William Birkenhead Mather Jackson, 2nd son of 2nd baronet; *b.* March 12th, 1896; *s.* his cousin *Sir* EDWARD ARTHUR, 1956; assumed the additional surname of Mather, 1957; ed. at Wellington Coll.; formerly Lieut. Notts and Derbyshire Regt.; is a J.P. for Derbyshire (High Sheriff 1951); European War 1915-18 (wounded, despatches): *m.* 1941, Victoria Emily Ford, da. of Indrick Freyberg, of Mitau, Latvia.

Arms—Azure, a fesse between two goats' heads couped in chief, and a fleur-de-lis in base argent, two flaunches of the last. **Crest**—On a ragged staff fessewise sable, a goat's head couped argent, semée of trefoils vert.
Residence,—West Court, Crondall, Farnham, Surrey. *Club*—White's.

Brother living—ANTHONY HENRY MATHER *JACKSON*, *b.* Nov. 9th, 1899; ed. at Harrow; formerly Lieut. Grenadier Guards (Reserve); is a D.L. and J.P. for Nottingham: *m.* 1923, Evelyn Mary, da. of Lieut.-Col. Sir Henry Kenyon Stephenson, D.S.O., V.D., 1st Bt., and has issue living, Angela Mary Mather, *b.* 1925: *m.* 1947, Francis Ambrose More O'Ferrall, of 36, Curzon Street, W.1, and Hermongers, Rudgwick, Sussex, and has issue living, Susan Angela (*Hon. Mrs. Maxwell W. H. Aitken*), *b.* 1948: *m.* 1974, the Hon. Maxwell William Humphrey Aitken [*see* By, Beaverbrook]; Theresa Mary (*Hon. Mrs. Wentworth P. I. Beaumont*), *b.* 1950: *m.* 1975, the Hon. Wentworth Peter Ismay Beaumont, el. son of 3rd Viscount Allendale, Emma Rose *b.* 1956,—Elizabeth Georgiana Mather (*Viscountess Cowdray*), *b.* 1926: *m.* 1953, as his second wife, the 3rd Viscount Cowdray,—Sarah Gillian Mather (Appletrees, Barton Mills, Bury St. Edmunds), *b.* 1929: *m.* 1955, Henry Lester Louis Morriss, who *d.* 1963, and has issue living, James Nicholas *b.* 1958, Annabel Ruth *b.* 1957, Henrietta Sarah *b.* 1961. *Residence*, Archway House, Kirklington, Newark-on-Trent. *Club*, White's.

Boldly, faithfully, successfully.

Daughter living of 3rd Baronet—Gwladys Ada, *b.* 1888: *m.* 1923, the Ven. Reginald Palmer, DSO, MC, who *d.* 1945. *Residence*, 1, Don Terrace, St. Helier, Jersey, Channel Islands.

Collateral Branches living.
Issue of the late Capt. Henry Mather-Jackson, 9th Lancers, el. son of 3rd baronet, *b.* 1894, *d.* 1928 : *m.* 1920, Florence (now of Monks Orchard, East Hendred, Berks), da. of the late Granville W. Garth, of New York :—
Rosemary, *b.* 1924: *m.* 1949, Stanley Joe Legouix, and has issue living, Geoffrey John Henry, *b.* 1954,—Susan Yvette, *b.* 1950. *Residence*, Greensands, East Hendred, Berks.

Grandchildren of the late William JACKSON, 2nd son of 1st baronet :—
Issue of the late William JACKSON, *b.* 1870, *d.* 1951 : *m.* 1899, Blanche Whitworth, who *d.* 1953, youngest da. of the late George Atkin, J.P., of Egerton Park, Rock Ferry, Cheshire, and Isallt Fawr, Anglesey :—
William, *b.* 1902; ed. at Harrow, and at Balliol Coll., Oxford; formerly Maj. R. Armoured Corps (Border Regt.) (TA): *m.* 1st, 1927, Lady Ankaret Cecilia Caroline Howard who *d.* 1945, da. of 10th Earl of Carlisle; 2ndly, 1966, Ina, da. of the late I. J. Joyce, FRCS, of Reading, and has issue living, (by 1st m.) William Thomas (Routen, Ennerdale, Cleator, Cumberland), *b.* 1927; ed. at Mill Hill, and at Roy. Agricultural Coll., Cirencester: *m.* 1951, Gilian Malise, el. da. of John Stobart, of Farlam Ghyll, Brampton, Cumberland, and has issue living, William Roland Cedric *b.* 1954, Piers Anthony *b.* 1955, Jolyon Thomas *b.* 1957,—Ankaret Tarn, *b.* 1934: *m.* 1955, Capt. Timothy Richard Riley, Rifle Brig., of Burbank House, Blencow, Cumberland, and has issue living, Nicola Ankaret Katherine *b.* 1959, Antonia Elizabeth Tarn *b.* 1962. *Residence*, St. Mary's Vale, Lanercost, Brampton, Cumberland. *Club*, Farmers'.—
Pamela Blanche, *b.* 1900. *Residence*, Parkside, Neston, Cheshire. *Clubs*, VAD, English Speaking Union.

Grandchildren of the late Rt. Hon. Frederick Huth JACKSON (infra):—
Issue of the late Frederick Huth Jackson, *b.* 1896, *d.* 1966: *m.* 1st, 1920 (m. diss. 1929), Helen, da. of the late Prof. Sir Paul Vinogradoff, LLD; 2ndly, 1940, Frederica Frances, da. of Duncan Tucker, of Burnham-on-Sea:—
(By 1st m.) Patrick Huth, *b.* 1922; late Capt. KRRC.—Laura Huth, *b.* 1922: *m.* 1st, 1943 (m. diss. 1948), Eric Dyson; 2ndly, 1954, Capt. William Leys Geddes, 16th/5th Lancers, of The Old Rectory, Rowberrow, Winscombe, Somerset.

Grandchildren of the late Brig.-Gen. Geoffrey Meinertzhagen JACKSON, TD (infra):—
Issue of the late Lt.-Col. Henry Humphrey Jackson, OBE, MC, TD, *b.* 1895, *d.* 1969: *m.* 1924, Georgina, who *d.* 1974, da. of H. Howard Middleditch, JP, of Tamworth House, Duffield:—
Thomas Geoffrey Henry (Freefolk House, Martyr Worthy, Winchester), *b.* 1926; ed. at Harrow; Lt.-Col. R. Green Jackets: *m.* 1957, Judith Margaret, da. of Capt. Henry Mangles Denham, CMG, RN, and has issue living, Catherine Margaret, *b.* 1958,—Victoria Georgina, *b.* 1960,—Louise Sarah, *b.* 1963,—Joanna Henrietta (twin), *b.* 1966.——John Guy Carmichael, *b.* 1931; ed. at Harrow: *m.* 1973, Flora Mary Margaret, da. of Lt.-Col. William Herbert Olivier, TD, and has issue living, Georgina Mary, *b.* 1974.——Ann Georgina Laird, *b.* 1928: *m.* 1952, Maj. Colville Graham Wemyss, Rifle Bde., son of the late Gen. Sir Henry Colville Barclay Wemyss, KCB, KBE, DSO, MC, and has issue living, Henry Graham, *b.* 1956,—Alice Caroline, *b.* 1953.
Issue of the late Capt. Guy Rolf Jackson, MC, *b.* 1896, *d.* 1966: *m.* 1937, Shelagh (St. Andrews, Higham, Derby), da. of the late A. Ignatius Tolhurst, of Gravesend:—
Geoffrey Laird (Glasfryn Hall, Caerwys, Mold, Clwyd), *b.* 1940; ed. at Ampleforth: *m.* 1963, Ruth Clare, da. of D. F. N. Campion, of Okirai, Wanganui, NZ, and has issue living, Jonathan Guy Campion, *b.* 1964,—Charles Desmond Bertram, *b.* 1965,—Rupert James Humphrey *b.* 1968,—William David Geoffrey, *b.* 1970.——Robert Humphrey (Bath Club), *b.* 1943; ed. at Ampleforth, and Brasenose Coll., Oxford: *m.* 1971, Margaret Letitia, da. of James Matthew Barrie, of South Grove House, Highgate, N6.——Jane Mary, *b.* 1938.

Granddaughters of the late Thomas Hughes JACKSON (*b.* 1834), 3rd son of 1st baronet.
Issue of the late Rt. Hon. Frederick Huth JACKSON, *b.* 1863, *d.* 1921 : *m.* 1895, Clara Annabel Caroline, who *d.* 1944, da. of the late Rt. Hon. Sir Mountstuart Elphinstone Grant-Duff, G.C.S.I., C.I.E., F.R.S., of 11, Chelsea Embankment, S.W., and Lexden Park, Colchester :—
Anne Marie Huth (*Hon. Mrs. Christopher E. Fremantle*), *b.* 1909; ed. at Cheltenham Ladies' Coll., and at Lady Margaret Hall, Oxford (MA); *m.* 1930, the Hon. Christopher Evelyn Fremantle [*see* B. Cottesloe]. *Residence*, Privada del Santisimo 19, Mexico DF20.——Clare Annabel Huth, *b.* 1911: *m.* 1935, Louis de Loriol.
Issue of the late Brig.-Gen. Geoffrey Meinertzhagen JACKSON, T.D., *b.* 1869, *d.* 1946 : *m.* 1893, Jessie Cowper Coles, who *d.* 1945, da. of the late Henry H. Laird, of Birkenhead :—
(Hermine) Joan Carmichael, *b.* 1900; is a JP for Derbyshire.——Margaret Beatrice Meinertzhagen, *b.* 1903; was County Commr., Girl Guides, Derbyshire 1947-58; a Councillor, Chesterfield RDC. *Residence*, Handley House, Clay Cross.——(Elizabeth) Bridget Huth (Mount Hall, Llanfair Caereinion, Powys) *b.* 1909; formerly Controller ATS.

Issue of the late Thomas Hughes JACKSON, *b.* 1872, *d.* 1926 : *m.* 1910, Eileen, da. of the late Edward Devery, of Gisborne, New Zealand :—
Hermine Catherine, *b.* 1911: *m.* 1939, Lt.-Cdr. (S.) George Henry Lloyd Davies, RNZNVR, and has issue living, Thomas Hughes Lloyd (20, Foster Cres., Belmont, Lower Hutt, NZ), *b.* 1942: *m.* 1966, Anne Mary, da. of N. J. McHugh, of Lower Hutt, NZ, and has issue living, Guy William Lloyd *b.* 1972, Caroline Jane Lloyd *b.* 1975,—David William Lloyd, *b.* 1947: *m.* 1970, Alison Margaret, da. of Prof. D. A. Kidd, of Christchurch, NZ, and has issue living, Bronwen Sara Lloyd *b.* 1973, Megan Kate Lloyd *b.* 1975,—Susan Hermine Lloyd (11, Timaru Grove, Lower Hutt, NZ), *b.* 1948: *m.* 1974, Wilhelmus Julicher, of Swalmen, Netherlands. *Residence*, 1, St. Andrews Grove, Lower Hutt, NZ.——Barbara Eileen Marian, *b.* 1918: *m.* 1947, Lt. Thomas Joseph Bourke, RNZNVR, and has issue living, Gerard Thomas Hughes, *b.* 1948,—John Patrick, *b.* 1955. *Residence*, Ratanui, Waterloo Rd., Lower Hutt, NZ.

Issue of the late John Peter JACKSON, yst. son of 1st baronet, *b.* 1843, *d.* 1899: *m.* 1869, Florence, who *d.* 1945, da. of the late William Evans:—
Mary Florence, *b.* 1880: *m.* 1907, Capt. Clement Loftus Long, RN, who *d.* 1964 [Wigram, Bt., colls.], and has issue living, Richard Samuel (The Old Vicarage, Sydenham, Oxford), *b.* 1908; ed at Rugby, and at Trin. Coll., Oxford; late Capt. RA (TA); FRICS: *m.* 1939, Mary, da. of Sir John Charrington [B. Sherwood], and has issue living, *Rev.* Simon Richard (Portales, New Mexico), *b.* 1940: *m.* 1969, Suzanne, da. of Col. Lee J. Humphrey, USAAF, (and has issue living, Michael Shawn *b.* 1972, Teresa Linette *b.* 1970), William John (5, Mallord St., SW3), *b.* 1943; a Member of London Stock Exchange: *m.* 1969, Sarah Jane, da. of Phillip Barton Lockwood, of Holywell Hall, Stamford (and has issue living, Samuel Phillip William *b.* 1974, Jane Elizabeth 1972), Charles Timothy *b.* 1951, Christine Elizabeth *b.* 1946,—Elizabeth Anne, *b.* 1910: *m.* 1st, 1933, Christopher John Carruthers, who *d.* 1938 [M. Queensberry, colls.]; 2ndly, 1952, Peter Horace Gordon Clark, of 15, Edwardes Sq., W8, and has issue living, (by 1st m.) Harriet Anne *b.* 1935, Olivia Mary *b.* 1937: *m.* 1961, John Hanby Holmes, of 15, Alleyn Rd., Dulwich, SE21, and has issue living, Andrew Timothy *b.* 1963, Peter Edward *b.* 1965,—Timothy John *b.* 1969. *Residence*, 54, Vicarage Court, W8.

Sir William Jackson, 1st Bt., son of Peter Jackson of Warrington, Surg., by his wife, Sarah, only da. of Henry Mather of Warrington, |was MP (L), Newcastle-under-Lyme 1847-65 and N. Derbys. 1865-68. The 3rd baronet, Lord Lieut. of Mon., assumed in 1886 the additional surname of Mather.

JAFFRAY, Creation (U.K.) 1892, of Skilts, Studley, Warwickshire.

Post nubila Phœbus.
After clouds sunshine.

Sir WILLIAM OTHO JAFFRAY, 5th *Baronet;* b. Nov. 1st, 1951 ; s. his father, *Col. Sir* WILLIAM EDMUND, T.D., 1953 ; is patron of one living.

Arms—Argent, three pallets sable on a fesse cotised gules, four mullets or. Crest—On a mound in front of two palm branches in orle vert, a mullet as in the arms.

Residence—The Manor House, Priors Dean, Petersfield, Hants.

Widow living of 4th Baronet—ANNE (WORSLEY-TAYLOR) (*Lady Jaffray*), only da. of the late Capt. J. Otho Paget, M.C., of Thorpe Satchville Hall, nr. Melton Mowbray, and formerly wife of the late Sir John Godfrey Worsley-Taylor, 3rd Bt., a Member of Petersfield RDC since 1954, and of Hants Co. Council since 1964: *m.* 1950, as his second wife, Col. Sir William Edmund Jaffray, TD, 4th baronet, who *d.* 1953. *Residence*, The Manor House, Priors Dean, Petersfield, Hants.

The 1st baronet, Sir John, founded the Jaffray Chronic Hospital, Birmingham, and was many years connected with the *Birmingham Daily Post*. The 3rd baronet, Sir John Henry Jaffray (Lt. Worcestershire Yeo.), *d.* (killed in action during 1914-18 War) 1916. The 4th baronet, Sir William Edmund Jaffray, TD, was Col. (ret.) late Comdg. Warwickshire Yeo. and a JP and DL for Warwickshire.

JAMES, Creation (U.K.) 1823, of Dublin. [Dormant 1955.]

Sir FULLARTON JAMES, *CBE,* 6th *Baronet, d.* in 1955, and at the time of going to press no name appears on the Official Roll of Baronets in respect of this title.

Arms,—Quarterly, vert and gules, a cross argent charged with a ship in full sail between four anchors erect azure; in the 1st and 4th quarters, a dolphin naiant of the third between three crosscrosslets or; in the 2nd and 3rd, a lion passant-guardant of the last between three fleurs-de-lis argent. Crest,—Issuing from a ducal coronet or, a swan proper, beaked gules, holding therein a dart gold, feathered argent, pointed towards the breast.

Daughter living of 6th Baronet—Isobel Mary Fullarton, *b.* 1900. *Residence*, The Chantry, Fore St., Shaldon, nr. Teignmouth, S. Devon.

Collateral Branches living

Granddaughters of the late Charles Pierce Rowley James (infra):—
Issue of the late Rowley Kingston James, *b.* 1901, *d.* 1938: *m.* 1926, Vera Léontine (Wintergreen, Blackdown Av., Pyrford, Surrey), da. of Arnold Fatio Bideleux:—
Elisabeth Virginia, *b.* 1928: *m.* 1953, William John Hindmoor Youdale, of St. Martin, Mougins, France, 06, and has issue living, James Robert, *b.* 1954,—Peter William, *b.* 1958,—Frederic Michael, *b.* 1969,—Angela Jane, *b.* 1956.——Sheila Margaret, *b.* 1931: *m.* 1955, Nigel Henry Whitfeld, of 50, Parkstone Av., Parkstone, Dorset, and has issue living, Nicholas Rowley, *b.* 1958,—Toby Martin, *b.* 1959,—Lisa Gabrielle, *b.* 1966.—— Patricia May, *b.* 1933.

Grandchildren of the late Charles Henry James, 4th son of 1st baronet:—
Issue of the late Charles Pierce Rowley James, *b.* 1864, *d.* 1929: *m.* 1893, Florence, who *d.* 1946, da. of the late James Edmund Cuppaidge, of Tamnagharrie, co. Down:—
Helen Mary, *b.* 1898: *m.* 1921, Lawrence Gameson, MB, BCh, who *d.* 1972, and has issue living, Felix Rowley, *b.* 1921: *m.* 1971, Gillian, widow of George Robert Lansdowne, and has issue living, Paul Rowley Stuart *b.* 1973,—Arthur Lawrence Hugh (of 32, Oakfields Av., Knebworth, Herts.), *b.* 1925; MA 1950: *m.* 1960, Margaret, da. of Herbert Litherland of Hemel Hempstead, Herts, and has issue living, Clive Philip Hugh *b.* 1961, Amanda Valerie *b.* 1965,—Maureen, *b.* 1923: *m.* 1965, John Vivian Garrett, DM, of Springvale, Wicker Lane, Hale Barns, Cheshire.

Issue of the late Kingston Gerald Henry James, *b.* 1870, *d.* 1920 : *m.* 1898, Pauline Estelle, who *d.* 1957, da. of Armand d'Oursy :—
Gerard Bowes Kingston, *b.* 1899; ed. at Wellington; late RAF.

This family came originally from Somersetshire. Thomas,—whose father, Capt. Thomas James, undertook, by the command of Charles I, a voyage to discover the north-west passage,—sold his estates in Somersetshire, went to Ireland as an officer in Cromwell's army at the time of the Rebellion, and eventually settled in King's County. The 1st baronet, Sir John Kingston, K.B., was Lord Mayor of Dublin 1821-2 and 1840-41, and the 2nd baronet, as eldest son of a baronet, received knighthood 1854. The 6th baronet, Sir Fullarton, C.B.E., was Ch. Constable of Radnorshire and Northumberland.

Jamsetjee Jejeebhoy, see Jejeebhoy.

JARDINE, Creation (N.S.) 1672, of Applegirth, Dumfriesshire.

Beware; I am present!

CAVE·ADSUM

Sir WILLIAM EDWARD JARDINE of APPLEGIRTH, *OBE, TD*, 11th *Baronet*: *b.* April 15th, 1917; *s.* his father, *Sir* ALEXANDER, 1942; Maj. (ret.) KOSB; Bt.-Col., RARO, a Member of Queen's Body Guard for Scotland (Roy. Co. of Archers), and a co. Councillor, a JP, and a DL of Dumfries; 1939-45 War (wounded); OBE (Mil) 1966: *m.* 1944, Ann Graham Maitland, da. of the late Lt.-Col. Claud Archibald Scott Maitland, Gordon Highlanders, of Dundrennan and Cumstoun, Stewartry of Kirkcudbright, and has issue.

Arms—Argent, a saltire and chief gules, the last charged with three mullets of the field pierced of the second. **Crest**—A spur-rowel of six points argent. **Supporters**—*Dexter*, a horse at liberty proper; *sinister*, a man in armour having a scimitar at his side proper.

Residence—Denbie, Lockerbie, Dumfriesshire. *Clubs.*—Army and Navy, Puffin's.

Sons living—ALEXANDER MAULE, *b.* Aug. 24th, 1947; ed. at Gordonstoun,——William, *b.* 1952; ed. at Sedbergh.

Sister living—Christian Maule: *m.* 1940, Lieut.-Col. Charles Patrick Anderson, Argyll and Sutherland Highlanders, and has issue living, Charles Adair, *b.* 1946: *m.* 1972, Patience Howard,——Roderick William, *b.* 1959,——Andrena Christian, *b.* 1943: *m.* 1969, Maj. Alastair Scott-Elliot, A & SH,——Araminta Patricia, *b.* 1950. *Residence*, Ulva Ferry, I. of Mull, Argyllshire.

Collateral Branches living.

Granddaughter of the late Rev. Charles John Jardine (infra):—
Issue of the late Edward William Ratcliff Jardine, *b.* 1872; *d.* 19—: *m.* 1910, May Janet, da. of Capt. J. Huddy, of El Toro, California, U.S.A. :—
Dorothea Twining, *b.* 1911. *Residence,*

Issue of the late Rev. Charles John Jardine, 3rd son of 7th baronet, *b.* 1839, *d.* 1917, *m.* 1870, Martha, who *d.* 1918, el. da. of the late Edward Twining, M.R.C.S., of Walthamstow:—
Eric Hamilton, *b.* 1874: *m.* 1910, Alma Anderson.——Peter St. John, *b.* 1879: *m.* 1919, Monica Maud, da. of the late Capt. Leonard Head, E. Lancashire Regt., and has issue living, Piers Leonard, *b.* 1921.——Margaret Dorcas Mary: *m.* 1901, Frank Fullerton Dyas, and has issue living, Maxwell Wing, *b.* 1902.

Grandchildren of the late Capt. John Jardine, 4th son of 6th baronet :—
Issue of the late Francis Lascelles Jardine, *b.* 1841, *d.* 1919: *m.* 1873, Sana Solia, who *d.* 1923, niece of Moliatoa, King of Samoa:—
Bertie Bootle Arthur Lascelles, *b.* 1884; European War 1915-19 (wounded), European War 1940-45 with Australian Forces and U.S.A. Army Transportation Corps in S.-W. Pacific: *m.* 1919, Elizabeth Duffy, of Brisbane, Queensland, and has issue living, Marie Dempster Lascelles, *b.* 1920,——Elizabeth Margaret Lascelles, *b.* 1927.——Elizabeth Hamilton Sana Lascelles, *b.* 1895: *m.* 1919, Major Charles Richard Sheldon, Australian Staff Corps, who *d.* (killed by Japanese whilst a prisoner of war) 1942, and has issue living, Betty Pamela, *b.* 1920. *Residence,*

Issue of the late John Robert Jardine, *b.* 1846, *d.* 1911: *m.* 1883, Elizabeth Catherine, da· of Thomas Lodge Murray Prior:—
Francis Alexander Lascelles, *b.* 1893; European War (wounded) : *m.* 1924, Madge Dorothy Blackman, of Brisbane, Queensland, and has issue living, Murray Hugh Lascelles, *b.* 1925. *Residence,* Broadwater, Stanthorpe, Queensland.

Grandchildren of the late Francis Lascelles Jardine (ante) :—
Issue of the late Alice Maude Lascelles Jardine, *b.* 1878, *d.* 1961 : *m.* 1900, Herbert Graham Vidgen, who *d.* 1960 :—
Herbert Somerset, *b.* 1901 ; Major Roy. Australian Engineers (Reserve) ; S.-W. Pacific 1939-45: *m.* 19—, Beatrice Werna Reid, of Woombye, Queensland, and has issue living, Grayhame Lascelles, *b.* 1941,——John Newton, *b.* 1944,——Bruce Somerset (twin), *b.* 1944. *Residence,* Chelmer Street West, Chelmer, Brisbane, Queensland.——Cholmondeley Gordon, *b.* 1903 ; late Roy. Australian Naval Reserve : *m.* 1930, Philomena Lynch, of Nundah, Brisbane, Queensland, and has issue living, Frank Anthony, *b.* 1931,——Peter Gordon Grahame, *b.* 1934 : *m.* 1957,——, ——Cholmondeley John, *b.* 1938,——Mary Philomena, *b.* 1932 : *m.* 1953, John Patrick Sexton,—— Margaret Alice, *b.* 1936,——Josephine Lascelles (twin), *b.* 1938. *Residence,* Somerset, Cape York, P.O. Box 39, Thursday Island, N. Queensland.——Frank Graham, *b.* 1909 ; Major late Australian Imperial Force ; S.-W. Pacific 1939-45. *Residence,*

Sir Alexander Jardine was cr. a baronet of Nova Scotia with remainder to his heirs male whatsoever. This line are Chiefs of the Name of Jardine.

JARDINE, Creation (U.K.) 1916, of Godalming, co. Surrey.

Beware, I am here.

Sir IAN LIDDELL JARDINE, *OBE, MC,* 4th
Baronet ; *b.* Oct. 13th, 1923 ; *s.* his father, *Maj.-
Gen. Sir* COLIN ARTHUR, *C.B., D.S.O., M.C.,* 1957 ;
ed. at Charterhouse; Brig. Coldstream Guards;
OC (Col), Coldstream Guards and Regimental Dist.
Coldstream Guards since 1967; 1939-45 War (MC);
OBE (Mil) 1966: *m.* 1948, Priscilla Daphne, da. of
Douglas Middleton Parnham Scott-Phillips, of
Halkshill, Largs, Ayrshire, and has issue.

    Arms—Gules, a saltire argent charged in the centre point
with a lotus flower proper, on a chief of the second six mullets of
the first. Crest—A mullet of six points pierced gules, between
two palm branches proper.

    Residence,—Coombe Place, Meonstoke, Southampton.

Sons living—ANDREW COLIN DOUGLAS, *b.* Nov. 30th,
1955.——Michael Ian Christopher, *b.* 1958.

Daughters living—Harriet Anne, *b.* 1949: *m.* 1972, Anthony
Malcolm Douglas Palmer, R. Green Jackets.——Jean Margaret,
b. 1951.

Sisters living—Elizabeth, *b.* 1921 : *m.* 1946, John Edward
Sharpley, B.M., B.Ch., and has issue living, Mark Alastair,
b. 1947.—Oliver John, *b.* 1949,—Sarah Marily, *b.* 1952. *Residence,* Field House, Fulbrook, near Burford, Oxon.——Gillian
Fiona, *b.* 1930 : *m.* 1954, Ian Grant MacKenzie, M.D., F.R.C.S.,
and has issue living, Alistair Grant, *b.* 1955,—Angus Colin, *b.*
1957,—Andrew Kenneth, *b.* 1958. *Residence,* Upper Kings
Mill, Kingswell, Aberdeenshire.

Uncle living (son of 1st baronet)—Lionel Westropp, *C.I.E., b.* 1895 ; ed. at Charterhouse, and at
Wadham Coll., Oxford (Exhibitioner); entered I.C.S. 1921; appointed to Foreign and Political
Depart. 1924, Revenue and Div. Commr., N.-W. Frontier Province 1937, and Resident for Baroda
and Gujarat States 1943; 1914-19 War with 5th Bn. Queen's Roy. Regt. (wounded, despatches),
Iraq 1920-21 (medal with clasp), N.-W. Frontier of India 1930-31 (medal with clasp); C.I.E. 1939:
m. 1922, Marjorie Mildred, da. of Major Richard John Woods, O.B.E., of Englefield Green, and has
issue living, John Alexander, *b.* 1939: *m.* 1971, Catherine Marie, da. of André Trentesaux, of
Lille, France,—Barbara Ann, *b.* 1925: *m.* 1964, Neville John Cooper, of 17, The Little Boltons,
SW10, and has issue living, Susan Ann *b.* 1964, Henrietta Jane *b.* 1967,—Jean Alison, *b.* 1928:
m. 1949, Frederick Disney Rivers Currie [see Currie, Bt., colls.]. *Residence,* 6, Victoria Rd.,
W8 5RD. *Club,* Naval and Military.

Widow living of 3rd Baronet—JEAN EVELYN LIVESEY (*Jean, Lady Jardine*), da. of the late Maj.-
Gen. Sir William Andrew Liddell, K.C.M.G., C.B. : *m.* 1919, Maj.-Gen. Sir Colin Arthur Jardine,
CB, DSO, MC, 3rd Bt., who *d.* 1957. *Residence,* 46, Abingdon Court, Abingdon Villa, W8.

Collateral Branch living.

    Issue of the late Rev. Canon Kenneth William Seymour Jardine, 4th son of 1st baronet,
b. 1899, *d.* 1960: *m.* 1926, Katharine Frances, who *d.* 1932, da. of W. Cranswick
Noad, formerly of Mount Tabor House, Perth :—

Rev. David Eric Cranswick (St. Saviour's Vicarage, Colemore Rd., Iford, Bournemouth, BH7 6RZ),
b. 1930; ed. at Corpus Christi Coll., Oxford (MA, Dip. Th. 1954); Priest-in-Charge of St. Wilfrid,
Horley 1962-65, and V. of Christ Church, Mitcham 1965-72, since when of St. Saviour's, Iford:
m. 1955, Elsie Vera Susan Shanks, and has issue living, Charles Kenneth Herbert, *b.* 1960,—
Katharine Shelagh Margaret, *b.* 1957,—Rachel Heather Agnes, *b.* 1965.——Julian Francis,
b. 1932. *Residence,* 32 Oppidans Rd., NW3.

    The 1st baronet, Sir John Jardine, K.C.I.E., LL.D., J.P., was a Puisne Judge of Bombay High
Court 1885-97, and sat as M.P. for Roxburghshire (L) 1906-18. The 3rd baronet, Maj.-Gen. Sir
Colin Arthur Jardine, C.B., D.S.O., M.C., D.L., late R.A., was Dep. Gov. of Gibraltar, a Member of
House of Laity, Church Assembly, Mil. Sec. to Com.-in-Ch., British Expeditionary Force 1939-40,
and Director of Army Welfare 1943.

JARDINE, Creation (U.K.) 1919, of Nottingham. [Extinct 1965.]

Sir JOHN JARDINE, *OBE, TD,* 2nd and last *Baronet.*

Daughter living of 1st Baronet—Edna Winifred, *MBE, b.* 1891; MBE (Civil) 1920: *m.* 1st, 1919,
Harold Augustus Fortington, OBE, from whom she obtained a divorce 1943; 2ndly, 1954,
Harold Whitman, and has issue living, (by 1st marriage) Nadia: *m.* 1st, 1938, the Hon. Graham
Charles Kinnaird, Master of Kinnaird (from whom she obtained a divorce 1940), el. son of 12th
Lord Kinnaird; 2ndly, 1957, Col. Ronald Altham Moulton-Barrett, OBE, of House of Glennie,
by Huntly, Aberdeenshire. *Residences,* Bedford Honour, Bedford Village, N.Y. 10506, USA;
But and Ben, Tuckerstown, Bermuda.

BUCHANAN-JARDINE, Creation (U.K.) 1885, of Castle Milk, co. Dumfries.

Beware; I am present!

Sir ANDREW RUPERT JOHN BUCHANAN-JARDINE, MC, 4th *Baronet, b.* Feb. 2nd, 1923; *s.* his father, *Capt. Sir* JOHN WILLIAM, 1969; ed. at Harrow; Maj. RHG: *m.* 1950 (m. diss. 1975), Jane Fiona, da. of Sir Archibald Charles Edmonstone, 6th Bt., and has issue.

Arms—Quarterly 1st and 4th per pale argent and or a saltire gules, on a chief engrailed of the third three mullets of the first, *Jardine*; 2nd, or, a lion rampant gules with a double tressure flory counter-flory sable, *Buchanan*; 3rd, sable, a chevron, between three bears' heads argent, muzzled gules, *Leny*. **Crests** —1st, a spur rowel of six points gules, *Jardine*; 2nd, a sword erect in pale proper, hilted and pommelled or.

Seat—Castle Milk, Lockerbie, Dumfries-shire. *Residence*—Dixons, Lockerbie, Dumfries-shire. *Club,*—MCC.

Son living—JOHN CHRISTOPHER RUPERT, *b.* March 20th, 1952; ed. at Harrow: *m.* 1975, Pandora Lavinia, yr. da. of Peter Murray Lee.

The lion's anger is noble.   **Daughter living**—Diana Gwendolyn Jean, *b.* 1955.

Half Brother living—Charles James (5, Campden Grove, W8; Turf Club), *b.* 1946; ed. at Stowe, and Trin. Coll., Camb.: *m.* 1967, Lady Susan Ankaret Howard, da. of the 11th Earl of Carlisle, and has issue living, Flora Jane, *b.* 1971.

Half Sister living—Caroline Anne, *b.* 1952.

Mother living—Jean Barbara (39, Eaton Sq., SW1), da. of the late Capt. Lord Ernest William Hamilton [see D. Abercorn, colls.]: *m.* 1921 (m. diss. 1944), Capt. Sir John William Buchanan-Jardine, 3rd Bt., who *d.* 1969.

Widow living of 3rd Baronet—PRUDENCE AUDREY (*Prudence, Lady Buchanan-Jardine*), (Castle Milk, Lockerbie, Dumfries-shire, and Moulin de la Mourachonne, Mouans Sartoux, France, AM), da. of William Haggie, of Knayton, Thirsk, Yorks.: *m.* 1944, as his 2nd wife, Capt. Sir John William Buchanan-Jardine, 3rd Bt., who *d.* 1969.

The 1st baronet, Sir Robert Jardine, and the 2nd baronet, Sir Robert William Buchanan Jardine, were successively head of the firm of Jardine, Matheson and Co., merchants in China. The 1st baronet also sat as M.P. for Ashburton (*L*) 1865-8, for Dumfries Burghs 1868-74, and for Dumfriesshire 1880-92. The 3rd baronet assumed the additional surname of Buchanan since his grandmother, Margaret Seton, wife of the 1st baronet, was da. of John Buchanan Hamilton of Leny, Perthshire, and sister and heir of John Hamilton-Buchanan, Ch. of Clan Buchanan.

JARVIS, Creation (U.K.) 1922, of Hascombe Court, co. Surrey. [Extinct 1965.]

Sir (ARNOLD) ADRIAN JARVIS, 2nd and last *Baronet.*

Daughters living of 1st Baronet—Joyce Jeanne (*Baroness Lyle of Westbourne*), *b.* 1902: *m.* 1927, 2nd Baron Lyle of Westbourne, of Bakersgate, Pirbright, Woking, Surrey.——Brenda Beryl (*Lady Williams*), *b.* 1907; a JP for Denbighshire: *m.* 1932, Sir Francis John Watkin Williams, 8th Bt., QC, JP, of Llys, Meirchion, Denbigh.

DUNNINGTON-JEFFERSON, Creation (U.K.) 1958, of Thorganby Hall. East Riding of Yorkshire.

Salvation by the Cross

Lt.-Col. Sir JOHN ALEXANDER DUNNINGTON-JEFFERSON, *DSO*, 1st *Baronet,* son of the late Capt. Mervyn Dunnington-Jefferson, JP; *b.* April 10th, 1884; ed. at Eton; Hon. LLD Leeds; Hon. D. Univ. York; formerly Capt. and Brevet Maj., R. Fus. (ret. as Lt.-Col. in the Army 1919); is a JP and DL for E. Riding of Yorks.; Chm. of E. Riding County Council 1936-68; 1914-18 War (despatches six times, DSO, Belgian Order of the Crown, Italian Order of SS. Maurice and Lazarus, Croix de Guerre, Legion of Honour); DSO 1917, Knt. 1944: *m.* 1938, Isobel, da. of Col. Herbert Anderson Cape, DSO, of Thorganby, York, and has issue.

Arms—Quarterly: 1st and 4th, gules a griphon sejant wings addorsed argent, a bordur engrailed of the last charged with eight pellets, *Jefferson*; 2nd and 3rd, paly of six **argent and azure** on a chief gules a bezant between two annulets or, *Dunnington*. **Crest**—1st a griphon as in the Arms gorged with a collar gemel, azure in the beak a lily slipped proper, *Jefferson*; 2nd, **a** horse current argent gorged with a collar gules charged with a bezant between two annulets or, *Dunnington*.

Residence—Deighton House, Escrick, York. *Club*—Travellers'.

Son living—MERVYN STEWART (26, Chipstead St., SW6), *b.* Aug. 5th, 1943: *m.* 1971, Caroline Anna, only da. of John Bayley, of Hillam Hall, Monk Fryston, Yorks., and has issue living, Annabelle Mary, *b.* 1973.

Daughter living—Rosemary Nicolette, *b.* 1941.

JEHANGIR, Creation (U.K.) 1908, of Bombay.

Sir HIRJI JEHANGIR, 3rd *Baronet, b.* Nov. 1st, 1915; *s.* his father, *Sir* COWASJEE, *G.B.E., KCIE* 1962; ed. at St. Xavier's Sch., Bombay, and at Magdalene Coll., Camb.; Chm. of Jehangir Art Gallery, Bombay: *m.* 1952, Jinoo, da. of K. H. Cama, and has issue.

Arms—Azure, a sun in splendour within an orle of mullets, or, on a canton argent a rose gules slipped proper in bend surmounting a lotus flower in bend sinister also proper. **Crest**—Upon a mount a column, thereon flames of fire all proper. *Residences*—Radaymoney House, Nepeansea Rd., Bombay 400 006; 24, Kensington Court Gdns., W8. *Clubs*—St. James' (London), Willingdon (Bombay).

Sons living—JEHANGIR HIRJI, *b.* Nov. 23rd, 1953.——Ardeshir, *b.* 1956.
Sister living—Sylla, *b.* 1914: *m.* 1946, Richard Holmes, of 24, Kensington Court Gdns., W.8.
Widow living of 2nd Baronet—HILLA HORMARJI (*Hilla, Lady Jehangir*), *MBE*, da. of the late Hormarji Wadia, of Lowji Castle, Bombay; has Kaisar-i-Hind gold medal and bar, MBE (Civil) 1919: *m.* 1911, Sir Cowasjee Jehangir, GBE, KCIE, who *d.* 1962. *Residence*, Readymoney House, Malabar Hill, Bombay.

By special Act of Legislative Council of India 1911 (dissolved 1964), all future holders of the title were to relinquish their own names and assume those of the 1st baronet. The 1st baronet, Sir Cowasjee Jehangir (who assumed the name of Cowasjee Jehangir in lieu of Jehangir Cowasjee), was nephew and adopted son and heir of the late Sir Cowasjee Jehangir, C.S.I., a Leader of the Parsee Community, a great Philanthropist, and Industrialist, and a lineal descendant of Hirji Jehangir Readymoney, who resided in Bombay in 1717, and was the Banker to the East India Company. Sir Cowasjee Jehangir, G.B.E., K.C.I.E., 2nd Bt., was a Member of Bombay Corporation 1902-21, and Chm. 1914-15, a MEC Bombay 1923-28, and a MLA Delhi 1930-47.

JEJEEBHOY, Creation (U.K.) 1857, of Bombay.

Sir JAMSETJEE JEJEEBHOY, 7th *Baronet*, el. son of the late Rustamjee Jamsetjee Jejeebhoy, nephew of 4th Baronet; *b.* April 19th, 1913; *s.* his kinsman, *Sir* Jamsetjee, 1968, when he assumed the name of Jamsetjee Jejeebhoy, in lieu of Maneckjee Rustamjee Jejeebhoy; ed. at Bombay Univ. (BA): *m.* 1943, Shirin Jehengir H. Cama, and has issue.

Arms—Azure, a sun rising above a representation of "the Ghauts" (mountains near Bombay) in base, and in chief two bees volant, all proper. **Crest**—A mount vert, thereon a peacock (close) amidst wheat, and in the beak an ear of wheat all proper. *Residence*—Beaulieu, 95, Worli Seaface, Bombay 18.

Son living—Rustomjee, *b.* Nov. 16th, 1957.
Daughter living—Ava, *b.* 1952.
Daughters living of 6th Baronet—Shireen, *b.* 1952. Deanna, *b.* 1953.——Geeta, *b.* 1955.
Daughters living of 5th Baronet—Ratanbai, *b.* 1911: *m.* 1936, Naval Kaikushroo Dubash, who *d.* 1943, and has issue living, Rustom *b.* 1940,—Jamshed, *b.* 1943. *Residence*, Sett Minar, Pedder Rd., Bombay 26, India.——Aimai, *b.* 1918: *m.* 1942, Nozer Erach D. Pandole. *Residence*, Silverene, Worli Parade, Bombay India.

Widow living of 6th Baronet—SOONOO (*Soonoo, Lady Jejeebhoy*), (Sett Minar, Pedder Rd., Bombay 26; Fountain Hall, 372, Koregaon Park, Poona), da. of the late Hormusji F. Commissariat, of msetjee Jejeebhoy, 6th bt., who *d.* 1968.

Collateral Branch living.

Issue of the late Jamsetjee Cursetjee Jamsetjee Jejeebhoy, brother of 4th baronet, *b.* 1860, *d.* 1916: *m.* 1882, Awabai Shapurjee Dhunjeebhoy, who *d.* 1926 :—
Cursetjee, *b.* 1897 : *m.* 1937, Mary Feroze Jehangir, and has issue living, Pirojbai, *b.* 1938.——
Cursetbai, *b.* 1887 : *m.* 1911, Jeejeebhoy Rustamjee B. Jeejeebhoy, who *d.* 1960, and has issue living, Jamsetjee, *b.* 1912 ; B.A. Bombay 1938 : *m.* 1957, Dinoo Cooverjee Jussawalla, and has issue living, Jeroo *b.* 1962,—Rustomjee, *b.* 1924; B.A. Bombay 1946.   *Residence*, The Cliffiet, Worli Hill, Bombay.

The 1st baronet, Sir Jamsetjee, Knt., a wealthy Parsee merchant; was renowned for his benevolence, charity, munificence, and loyalty, a reputation that was also earned by his son, the 2nd baronet. In 1860 a special Act of the Legislative Council of India was passed, with the sanction of H.M. Queen Victoria, by which all future holders of the title are to relinquish their own names and assume those of the 1st baronet. The 3rd baronet was a M.L.C. of Bombay. The 4th baronet was Sheriff of Bombay 1900. The 5th baronet was Dep. Pres. of Indian Legislative Assembly 1921-31. The 6th baronet was an Industrialist and Banker.

JENKINSON, Creation (E.) 1661, of Walcot, Oxfordshire, and Hawkesbury, Gloucestershire.

Sir ANTHONY BANKS JENKINSON, 13th *Baronet ;* son of the late Capt. John Banks Jenkinson, el. son of 12th Baronet ; *b.* July 3rd, 1912 ; *s.* his grandfather, *Sir* GEORGE BANKS, 1915 ; ed. at Eton, and at Balliol Coll., Oxford : *m.* 1943, Frances, da. of Harry Stremmel, of New York, U.S.A., and has issue.

Arms—Azure, on a fesse wavy argent, a cross-patée gules, in chief two estoiles or. **Crest**—A sea-horse assurgent or, maned azure, supporting a cross-patée as in the arms.

Seat—Hawkesbury, Chippenham, Wilts. *Residence*—Bear's House, Wentworth, Virginia Water, Surrey.

Son living—JOHN BANKS, *b.* Feb. 16th, 1945; ed. at Eton.
Daughters living—Jennifer Ann, *b.* 1947.——Emily Frances Joan, *b.* 1953.
Sister living—(Elizabeth) Deborah, *b.* 1908 : *m.* 1938, Dr. Henry Dreyfus, who *d.* 1944. *Residence*, 19, Montagu Street, W.1.
Aunt living (daughter of 12th baronet)—Georgina Isabel, *b.* 1899.

I obey, I do not serve.

Collateral Branch living.

Grandchildren of the late Lt.-Col. George Seymour Charles Jenkinson, DSO, son of the late John Henry Jenkinson, brother of 11th baronet:—
Issue of the late Capt. Robert Charles Horace Jenkinson, *b.* 1900, *d.* 1970: *m.* 1st, 1925, the Hon. Barbara Vernon Harcourt, OBE, (who *d.* 1961, having obtained a divorce 1936), da. of 1st Viscount Harcourt; 2ndly, 1938, Gwyneth, da. of A. Llewellyn Mathews, of 15, Bryanston Sq., W1:—
(By 1st m.) Julian Charles Lewis (Folly Faunts House, Goldhanger, Maldon, Essex), *b.* 1926; ed. at Eton: *m.* 1953, Diana Catherine, only da. of Maj. George Henry William Baird [*see* Baird, Bt., *cr.* 1809, colls.], and has issue living, Dermot Julian, *b.* 1954,—Karen Barbara, *b.* 1957,—Laura Louise Diana, *b.* 1966.——Lavinia Mary, *b.* 1928.——Clare Barbara, *b.* 1933: *m.* 1955, William McCully, of Leitrim Farm, Loughries, Newtownards, co. Down, and has issue living, Patrick William, *b.* 1965,—Lucinda Barbara, *b.* 1962.——(by 2nd m.) Frances Caroline, *b.* 1942.

The 1st, 2nd, 3rd, 4th, and 5th baronets were successively Members of Parliament for Oxfordshire; the 7th baronet, celebrated statesman, was created Earl of Liverpool, and his son, the 8th baronet and 2nd earl, was for many years Prime Minister of England. The peerage became extinct on the death of the 3rd earl, when the baronetcy devolved upon his cousin, Sir Charles, 10th baronet, M.P. for Dover, who was nephew of the 1st Earl of Liverpool. Sir George, 11th baronet, sat as MP for Wiltshire, N. (C) 1868-80.

JENKS, Creation (U.K.) 1932, ot Cheape, in the City of London.

I seek honour honourably.

Sir RICHARD ATHERLEY JENKS, 2nd *Baronet*; *b.* July 26th, 1906 ; *s.* his father, *Sir* MAURICE, 1946 ; ed. at Charterhouse : *m.* 1932, Marjorie Suzanne, Arlette, da. of Sir Arthur Philip du Cros, 1st Bt., and has issue.

Arms—Per fesse indented sable and argent, on a pile or a boar's head, and in base two boars' heads all couped sable ; on a chief ermine a representation of the sword and mace of the City of London in saltire proper. **Crest**—A sinister arm embowed vested sable, cuffed argent, grasping in the hand a sword in bend proper, pommel and hilt or, enfiled with a ducal coronet gold.
Residence—42, Sussex Sq., W2 2SP.

Sons living—MAURICE ARTHUR BRIAN (Manor Farm House, Binfield Rd., Wokingham, Berks), *b.* Oct. 28th, 1933; ed. at Charterhouse: *m.* 1962, Susan L., da. of Leslie Allen, of Glenside, Star Lane, Hooley, Surrey, and has issue living, Marjorie Emma, *b.* 1964.——Richard John Peter (26, Ilchester Place, W14), *b.* 1936; ed. at Charterhouse: *m.* 1963, Juniper Li-Yung, el. da. of Tan Sri Y. C. Foo, of 18, Golf Club Rd., Ipoh, Malaysia, and has issue living, Richard Albert Benedict, *b.* 1965,—Melissa Kate Rosalind *b.* 1967,—Serena Anne Louise, *b.* 1970.
Brother living—Robert Fergus, *DSC, b.* 1909; Cdr. RN; 1939-45 War (despatches thrice, DSC, Croix de Guerre with Palm): *m.* 1st, 1933, Joyce Wynne (from whom he obtained a divorce 1938), da. of A. E. Booth; 2ndly, Mrs. Molly Estelle Dales, da. of the late Lt. Albert Edward Griffiths, RN (ret.), of Parkstone, Dorset, and has issue living (by 2nd. m.) Robert Philip, *b.* 1948,—Sally Elizabeth, *b* 1945.

Widow living of 1st Baronet—CONSTANCE EDITH (*Constance, Lady Jenks*), da. of W. R. Currie, of Beckenham, Kent : *m.* 1939, as his second wife, Sir Maurice Jenks, 1st baronet, who *d.* 1946. *Address*, c/o 71, Midhurst Hill, Bexleyheath, Kent.

The 1st baronet, Sir Maurice Jenks (son of the late Robert Isaac Jenks, of Clapham, S.W.), was an Alderman of City of London (Sheriff 1930-31, and Lord Mayor 1931-2).

JEPHCOTT, Creation (U.K.) 1962, of East Portlemouth, co. Devon.

Sir HARRY JEPHCOTT, 1st *Baronet*, son of the late John Josiah Jephcott, of Redditch; *b.* Jan. 15th, 1891; ed. at King Edward's Gram. Sch., Birmingham; B.Sc. 1915; Pharmaceutical Chemist 1916, M.Sc. 1918; Hon. D.Sc. Birmingham, and Hon. Fellow Roy. Soc. of Medicine-Bar. Middle Temple 1925; a Member of Phar; maceutical Soc., and Fellow of Roy. Institute of Chemistry; Manufactured Foods Adviser to Min. of Food 1941; Chm. of Council, Sch. of Pharmacy, London Univ. 1948-69, and a Gov. of London Sch. of Economics 1952-58, and of N. London Collegiate Sch. since 1957; Chm. of Glaxo Group, Ltd., 1945-63, of Assocn. of British Chemical Manufacturers 1947-52 (Pres. 1952-55) and of Cttee. on Detergents 1953-55, Pres. of Roy. Institute of Chemistry 1953-55, a Member of Advisory Council, Scientific Policy 1953-56, and Chm. of Council for Scientific and Industrial Research 1956-61; *cr.* Knt. 1946: *m.* 1919, Doris, *FPS*, da. of Henry Gregory, and has issue.

Arms,—Azure two chevronels between in chief a mortar and pestle between two escallops or and in base an open book proper edged and clasped or. **Crest**,—A dove supporting with dexter claw a rod of Esculapius proper the serpent vert.

Residence—Weetwood, 1, Cheney St., Pinner, Middlesex. *Club*—Athenæum.

Sons living—(JOHN) ANTHONY (7, Anne St., Highland Park, Wellington, NZ), *b.* May 21st, 1924: *m.* 1949, Sylvia Mary, da. of Thorsten F. Relling, of Wellington, NZ.——Neil Welbourn (Penvrane, Carnon Downs, Truro, Cornwall), *b.* 1929: *m.* 1951, Mary Denise, da. of Arthur Muddiman, of Abbots Mead, West Clandon, Surrey.

JERVIS-WHITE-JERVIS, Creation (I.) 1797, of Bally-Ellis, Wexford.
[**Extinct 1947.**]

Sir HENRY FELIX JERVIS-WHITE-JERVIS, 5th and last *Baronet*.

Daughter living of 5th Baronet—Aline, *b.* 1890: *m.* 1915, Col. Richard Hynman Andrew, C.B.E., MC, who *d.* 1964, and has issue living, Aline Mary *b.* 1916,—Lucy Catherine, *b.* 1921: *m.* 1945, Elison Pott, of 785, Foxe St., Peterborough, Ont. K9H 6Y6, Canada, and has issue living, Edmund Elison Andrew *b.* 1951: *m.* 1973, Diane, da. of Roland Morency, of Toronto, Ont., Canada, Barry James *b.* 1955, Catherine Aline *b.* 1947: *m.* 1969, Reginald Eadie (and has issue living, Sarah Dawn *b.* 1974), Lucy Diana *b.* 1948: *m.* 1973, Robert Sare, of Thunder Bay, Ont., Canada. *Residence*, Honeysuckle House, Back Lane, Nazeing, Essex.

Collateral Branch living.

Issue of the late Herbert Jervis-White-Jervis, brother of 4th baronet, *b.* 1858, *d.* 1934: *m.* 1893, Beatrice Georgiana, who *d.* 1939, da. of the late Col. Sir Samuel Brise Ruggles-Brise, K.C.B. [Bowyer-Smijth, Bt.]:—

Audrey (*Lady Hutchison*), *b.* 1895: *m.* 1920, Lieut.-Gen. Sir Balfour Oliphant Hutchison, K.B.E.; CB, who *d.* 1967, having had issue, Julian Jervis Oliphant, *b.* 1921: 2nd Lt. 10th Hussars, *d.* (killed in action during 1939-45 War) 1942,—Andrew Balfour, *b.* 1924; Lt. 10th Hussars; *d.* (killed in action in Italy) 1944,—Rowan Balfour, *b.* 1926: *m.* 1956, Alison, da. of Alastair MacLeod, of 5, Parkside Gdns., SW19,—Laurel Audrey (12, Crondace Rd., SW6): *m.* 1946, Brig. William Watson Cheyne, DSO, OBE, who *d.* 1970 [*see* Cheyne, Bt., colls.], Rosanne Beatrice, *b.* 1932: *m.* 1962, William Oates, Yale Univ., of Greensboro, Vermont, USA. *Residence,* Rendham Court, Saxmundham, Suffolk.——Beatrice *b.* 1898; ed. at Newnham Coll., Camb. (BA 1919, MA 1920), and at London Univ. (MB and BS 1925); MRCS England and LRCP London 1924: *m.* 1937, Erst Ellis, who *d.* 1952. *Residence,* Lincoln Cottage, Rosebery Rd., Felixstowe, Suffolk.

CLARKE-JERVOISE, Creation (U.K.) 1813, of Idsworth Park, Hampshire.
[Extinct 1933.]

Sir DUDLEY ALAN LESTOCK CLARKE-JERVOISE, 7th and last *Baronet.*

Daughter living of 7th Baronet—Gladys Agnes, *b.* 1909: *m.* 1936, Kenneth Southam, MRCS, LRCP, and has issue living, Gilian Margaret, *b.* 1938,—Bridget Anne, *b.* 1940: *m.* 1966, Henry Charles Frank Wickham-Smith, of Threeways, Canon's Close, Craigweil-on-Sea, Bognor Regis, Sussex, and has issue living, Simon James Southam *b.* 1968. *Residence,* 78, Bowes Hill, Rowlands Castle, Hants.

JESSEL, Creation (U.K.) 1883, of Ladham House, Goudhurst, co. Kent.

Sir GEORGE JESSEL, *M.C.,* 2nd *Baronet;* *b.* May 28th, 1891; *s.* his father, *Sir* CHARLES JAMES, 1928; ed. at Eton, and at Balliol Coll., Oxford (B.A. and M.A. 1917); Capt. late The Buffs (E. Kent Regt.); Pres. of Imperial Continental Gas Assocn., and a Dir. of other cos.; a JP for Kent; High Sheriff of Kent 1958-59; European War 1914-18 (severely wounded, despatches, M.C.): *m.* 1st, 1923, Muriel Gladys, who *d.* 1948, da. of the late Col. J. W. Chaplin, V.C., C.B., and widow of Major Foster Swetenham, Roy. Scots Greys; 2ndly, 1948, Joan Betty, da. of the late Dr. David Ewart, O.B.E., M.D., F.R.C.S., of Chichester, and formerly wife of the 2nd Baron Russell of Liverpool, and has issue by 1st marriage.

Arms—Azure, a fesse raguly ermine, between three eagles heads erased argent, in the centre chief point a torch erect fired proper. **Crest**—A torch fessewise fired proper, surmounted by an eagle volant argent, holding in the beak a pearl of the last.

Residence—Ladham House, Goudhurst, Kent. *Clubs*—Garrick, Brooks's, Army and Navy, MCC

Son living—By 1st marriage—CHARLES JOHN, *b.* Dec. 29th, 1924; ed. at Eton, and at Balliol Coll., Oxford ; is a J.P. for Kent ; European War 1943-5 as Lieut. 15/19th Hussars (despatches) : *m.* 1956, Shirley Cornelia, da. of John Waters, of Northampton, and has issue living, George Elphinstone, *b.* 1957,—Alastair John, *b.* 1959,—Cornelia Sarah, *b.* 1963. *Residence,* South Hill Farm, Hastingleigh, nr. Ashford, Kent. *Club,* Cavalry.

Brother living—*Sir* Richard Hugh, *b.* 1896 ; ed. at Eton ; sometimes Lieut. 5th Batn. The Buffs (E. Kent Regt.) ; was a Member of Export Credits Guarantee Depart. Advisory Council 1951-60 (Dep. Chm. 1959-60); a Commr., Public Works Loan Board 1949-61, European War 1914-18 with Hampshire Regt.; Knt. 1960: *m.* 1st, 1923, Margaret Ella, who *d.* 1953, 2nd da. of Sir George James Graham Lewis, 2nd Bt.; 2ndly, 1954, Daphne, who *d.* 1971, da. of the late William Buckley Gladstone, and widow of Maj. Thirlwall G. Philipson, MC, Life Gds.; 3rdly 1972, Diana Mary, yr. da. of Maj. William Edward Gatacre, of de Wiersse, Vorden, Holland, widow of Col. George Richard Trotter, R. Scots Greys, and formerly wife of James Edward Michael Clark-Hall, and has issue living, (by 1st m.) David Charles George (of Collyers, Steep, Petersfield, Hants. *Club,* Carlton), *b.* 1924; ed. at Eton; Fellow of Inst. of Bankers, and Chm. of Jessel, Toynbee & Co., Ltd., 1939-45 War as Capt. Coldm. Gds.: *m.* 1950, the Hon. Amelia Grace FitzRoy, da. of 2nd Viscount Daventry, and has issue living, Richard James *b.* 1954, Davina Jane (*Hon. Mrs. Richard T. Kenyon*), *b.* 1952: *m.* 1970, the Hon. Richard Tyrell Kenyon, of The Cumbers, Hanmer, Whitchurch, Salop [see B. Kenyon],—Robin Richard (Beacon Cottage, Staplecross, Sussex; *Club,* Garrick), *b.* 1930; ed. at Eton, and at Balliol Coll., Oxford (BA); Bar. Lincoln's Inn 1953: *m.* 1957, Audrey Gertrude, el. da. of the late Alexander Newman Howard, of The Beacon, Staplecross, Sussex and has issue living, Simon Dana *b.* 1958, Alexander Robin *b.* 1961, Michael Richard *b.* 1965, Virginia Penelope *b.* 1967,—Edith Marie, *b.* 1926: *m.* 1947, William Joseph Straker-Smith, late Capt. Coldm. Gds., of Carham Cornhill-on-Tweed, and has issue living, Peter Dalrymple, *b.* 1951, Richard David *b.* 1959, Tessa Diana *b.* 1949: *m.* 1969, John Robert Robson, of Melbourne Stud, Ayot Green, Welwyn, Herts., (and has issue living, James *b.* 1973, Claire *b.* 1972). *Residence,* The White House, 50, Hay St., Steeple Morden, Royston, Herts., SG8 0PE. *Club,* Brooks's.

Sister living—Nina Dorothy, *b.* 1893. *Residence,* 29/2, Mansfield St., WIM 9FF.

The 1st baronet, Charles James (High Sheriff of Kent 1903), was el. son of the late Rt. Hon. **Sir George Jessel**, P.C., Master of the Rolls and one of the most eminent Judges of his time. The 2nd son, Herbert Merton, was cr. a Baronet 1917 and Baron Jessel 1924.

JOHNSON, Creation (G.B.) 1755, of New York, in North America.

Deo regique debeo.
I owe all to God and the King.

Sir JOHN PALEY JOHNSON, *M.B.E.,* 6th *Baronet,* son of the late Capt. Robert Warren Johnson, R.N., grandson of the late Col. Charles Christopher Johnson, 7th son of 2nd baronet ; *b.* June 12th, 1907 ; *s.* his kinsman, *Sir* (EDWARD) GORDON, 1957; ed. at Wellington Coll.; Lieut.-Col. (retired) R.A.; a Member of London Stock Exchange 1929-33 ; and M.F.H., W. Kent Foxhounds 1958-61; author of " The North American Johnsons "; a Co. Councillor of Kent; MBE (Mil.) 1946: *m.* 1st, 1929, Carol Louise Glorney, da. of the late Edmund Haas, of Essex House, New York City, USA; 2ndly, 1940, Jasmine Lydia, da. of Lt.-Col. the Hon. Noel Gervase Bligh, DSO [*see* E. Darnley]; 3rdly, 1949, Rosemary, da. of the late Arthur Cohen, of 29, Great Cumberland Place, W1, and has issue by 1st and 2nd m. (The 6th Baronet *d.* Dec. 14th, 1975.)

Arms—Argent, two lions counter-rampant supporting a dexter hand gules, in chief three estoiles of the last, and in base a salmon naiant in water proper. **Crest**—An arm gules, encircled with a ducal coronet or, the hand grasping a sword proper, pommel and hilt gold.

Residence—Warrigal Farm, Green Street Green, Dartford, Kent. *Clubs*—Carlton, United Service, RAC, MCC, English-Speaking Union.

Not even difficulties frighten me.

Son living—By 1st marriage—PETER COLPOYS PALEY (Dene End, Buckland Dene, Lymington, Hants.: Royal Ocean Racing, and Royal Southern Yacht Clubs), *b.* March 26th, 1930; ed. at Wellington Coll.; late Capt RA: *m.* 1st, 1956 (m. diss. 1972), Clare, da. of Nigel Patrick Bruce, BM, BCh [*see* Bruce, Bt., *cr.* 1804, colls.]; 2ndly, 1973, Caroline Elisabeth, twin da. of the late Wing-Cdr. Sir (Eric) John Hodsoll, CB, and has issue living, (by 1st m.),—Colpoys Guy, *b.* 1965,—Marina Grace, *b.* 1960,—Alison Fiona, *b.* 1961.

Daughters living—By 1st marriage—Wanda Helene Paley, *b.* 1933 : *m.* 1955, Paul Weychan, of Passage House, Aust, Bristol, and has issue living, Paul Corydon, *b.* 1960,—Charlotte Sophia Carol, *b.* 1956.——**By 2nd marriage—Sarah** Jack Paley (Easton Lodge, Newbury, Berks.), *b.* 1942: *m.* 1st, 1964 (m. diss. 1970) Ezra Mager, of New York City; 2ndly, 1972, Nels Royden Johnson, and has issue living, (by 1st m.) Dickon Porter *b.* 1969, Emma Rachel, *b.* 1964, (by 2nd m.) Daniel Alexander *b.* 1972.

Brother living—Peter Warren, *D.S.O., O.B.E., D.F.C., A.F.C., b.* 1908; late Group-Capt. R.A.F. and Civil Air Attaché, British Embassy, Bonn; 1939-45 War (despatches, D.F.C., A.F.C., D.S.O.); D.S.O. 1945, O.B.E. (Civil) 1954: *m.* 1st, 1934 (marriage dissolved 1961), Joan Agnes, da. of the late Capt. Percy Richard Hare, T.D. [*see* E. Listowel, colls.]; 2ndly, 1961, Margaret Anne, da. of Capt. Guy Wychelo Bower, D.S.C., R.N. (ret.), of Rose Cottage, Fordwich, Kent, and has issue living, (by 1st marriage) Hugo Robert Warren, *b.* 1939,—Virginia, *b.* 1936: *m.* 1961, Marchese Umberto Valdambrini-Accoramboni, of 6, Rutland Rd., Maidenhead, and has issue living, Robert *b.* 1963, Richard Warren *b.* 1965, Julia Louise *b.* 1971. *Residence,* 69, Hambleden, Henley-on-Thames, Oxon. *Clubs*, Bath, RAC.

Sister living—Elizabeth Freda, *b.* 1913.

Collateral Branches living.

Granddaughters of the late Major Frederick Colpoys Ormsby Johnson, 2nd son of the late Vice-Adm. John Ormsby Johnson (infra):—
Issue of the late Brigadier Guy Allen Colpoys Ormsby Johnson, C.B.E., M.C., *b.* 1886, *d.* 1957: *m.* 1911, Mary Isabella (Garry, Victoria Rd., Fleet, Hants), da. of the late Col. Benjamin Geale Humfrey [E. Ranfurly, colls.]:—
Emily Mary Ormsby, *b.* 1912 : *m.* 1st, 1934, Group-Capt. Edward Stephen Dru Drury, R.A.F., who *d.* 1948; 2ndly, 1951, Major Miles Garrick, of Kennel Cottage, Herriard, Basingstoke, Hants. and has issue living, (by 1st m.) Stephen Guy Dru, *b.* 1939,—Michael Humphrey Dru, *b.* 1942.—— Eileen Ormsby, *b.* 1918: *m.* 1945, Finlay George Mackintosh, MB, ChB, of Dunsfold, Moor Rd., Bramhope, Leeds, and has issue living, Alan Finlay, *b.* 1948,—Fiona Mary, *b.* 1945,—Diana Barbara, *b.* 1952.——Grace Ormsby, *b.* 1924: *m.* 1st, 1948, George Acheson Gidney, who *d.* 1969; 2ndly, 1971, Irving Nicholas Wilson, and has issue living (by 1st m.), Mark Henry, *b.* 1949,— David Guy, *b.* 1952,—Alison Jane, *b.* 1953. *Residence,* Shierglas, Victoria Rd., Fleet, Hants.

Grandchildren of the late Vice-Adm. John Ormsby Johnson, son of the late Col. Charles Christopher Johnson, 7th son of 2nd baronet :—
Issue of the late Capt. Alexander Adair Johnson, F.R.C.V.S., *b.* 1873, *d.* 1927: *m.* 1894, Emma Jane, who *d.* 1940, da. of ——:—
Ralph Harold Ormsby, *b.* 1897; late New Zealand Mounted Rifles; 1914-18 War: *m.* 1923, and has issue living, Alexander Ormsby, *b.* 1929. *Residence,* 90, McFadden's Road, St. Albans, Christchurch, New Zealand.——John Ormsby, *b.* 1909: *m.* 1936.—— *Address,* Corner of Guys Rd. and Factory Rd., Janefield, Mosgiel, Dunedin, New Zealand.—— Gertrude, *b.* 1895: *m.* 1928, James Augustus Williamson. *Residence,* 66, Wiggins St., Sumner, Christchurch, New Zealand.——Sybil Renira, *b.* 1909: *m.* 19——, — Derrett.——Phyllis Ormsby, *b.* 1917: *m.* 19——, — Savage. *Residence,*

Grandson of the late Capt. Edward Colpoys Johnson, son of the late Col. Charles Christopher Johnson (ante):—
Issue of the late Hubert Colpoys Johnson, *b.* 1878, *d.* 1925: *m.* 1916, Mary Anne, da. of Thomas Philip Howe, formerly of Newport Pagnell, Bucks:—
Graham Christopher Colpoys, *b.* 1917: *m.* 1951, Joan Winifred Mary, who *d.* 1958, da. of John Bernard Colbeck, of Wakefield, Yorkshire, and has issue living, Anne Winifred Mary, *b.* 1952. *Residence,*

The 1st baronet, Gen. Sir William Johnson, of an ancient family in Ireland named Macshane, went in early life to America, and conducted the expedition to Crown Point, and gained the battles of Crown Point and Niagara, for which services he was created a baronet, and received £5,000 from the Government, and also large grants of land in the Province of New York, then part of the British dominions. He settled on the Mohawk river, and brought the Seneccas—one of the revolted tribes, and inveterate enemies of the English—to a treaty in 1764. He was sole representative of Indian affairs for the northern parts of America for George II., and Col. of the six united nations, their allies and dependants. Sir John, the 2nd baronet, was also Superintendent-Gen. of Indian Affairs in North America. He remained loyal to the Crown at the outbreak of the American Revolution, and raised two battalions of Roy. New York Regt. which he commanded. He was largely responsible for loyalist settlement in Canada.

JOHNSON, Creation (U.K.) 1818, of Bath.

Thou hast conquered, and we live.

Never unready.

Sir VICTOR PHILIPSE HILL JOHNSON, 6th *Baronet*, el. son of Capt. Hugh Walter Beaumont Johnson, 2nd son of Capt. William Victor Johnson, 2nd son of 2nd Bt.; *b.* May 7th, 1905; *s.* his kinsman, Lt.-Col. Sir HENRY ALLEN BEAUMONT, 1965; ed. at Cheltenham; 1939-45 War as Flying Officer RAFVR.

Arms—Per pale sable and azure, on a saltire argent between three towers or, fired proper, one in chief and two in fesse, and two tilting spears saltirewise in base of the second, five cocks of the first. Crest—A tower argent, on the battlements a cock proper. Supporters—*Dexter*, a grenadier habited and accoutred, arms ordered proper; *sinister*, a light infantry man habited and accoutred, arms trailed proper, supporting with his exterior hand a flag-staff also proper, therefrom flowing a banner gules, inscribed " New Ross " in letters of gold.

Residence,—64, Sea Lane, Goring-by-Sea, Sussex.

Daughters living of 5th Baronet—Barbara Patty, *b.* 1918: *m.* 1942, Charles Frederic Roetter, of 5, Balmoral Mansions, Twickenham, Middlesex, and has issue living, Martyn Frederick Alexander Gurney, *b.* 1944; ed. at St. Paul's Sch. (Foundation Scholar), and at Brasenose Coll., Oxford (Scholar); Research Fellow, Univ. Coll., Oxford,—Christine Frances Ada, *b.* 1946: *m.* 1971, Stephen A. Rhodes.——Monica Lena, *b.* 1921: *m.* 1st, 1941 (m. diss. 1952), Marshall Douglas Clare; 2ndly, 1957, Dr. Florencio Enrique Escardo, of Juncal 1335-1°C, Buenos Aires, and has issue living, (by 1st m.) Michael Charles Allen, *b.* 1945: *m.* 1969 (m. diss. 1974), Diane, da. of Bruce Hamilton Wardrope, of 758, Waterford Av., Winnipeg, Manitoba,—Marcia Dorothy, *b.* 1943: *m.* 1965, Michael Bennie, who *d.* 1974, and has issue living, Christopher Michael *b.* 1966, Claire Julia *b.* 1969,—(by 2nd m.) Florencio Julian, *b.* 1958,—Monica Carmen, *b.* 1960,—Pilar, *b.* 1963.

Mother living—Winifred Mena, da. of the late Charles Hill, of Fern Lea, Southampton: *m.* 1st, 1904, Capt. Hugh Walters Beaumont Johnson, who *d.* 1916; 2ndly, 1916, Capt. Allan Fenton Livingstone, who *d.* 1947. *Residence,* Beach House, 64, Sea Lane, Goring-by-Sea, Sussex.

Collateral Branches living.

Granddaughter of the late Maj. Arthur Cyril Beaumont Johnson (infra):—
   Issue of the late Lt.-Col. Charles Robert Johnson, *b.* 1902, *d.* (of wounds received in action) 1941: *m.* 1935, Mrs. Eileen Agnes Johnson, da. of the late G. C. Mothersill, of Bedford:—
Diana Evelyn, *b.* 1935.

Grandson of the late Gen. Sir Charles Cooper Johnson, GCB, 6th son of 2nd baronet:—
   Issue of the late Maj. Arthur Cyril Beaumont Johnson, *b.* 1863, *d.* 1904: *m.* 1901, Roberta Joanna, da. of the late Inspector-Gen. R. Pottinger, RN:—
CYRIL MARTIN HUGH (posthumous) (La Ermita Estanco, Villajoyosa, Alicante, Spain), *b.* Jan. 15th, 1905; 1939-45 War.

Grandson of the late Brig.-Gen. Eliot Philipse Johnson, C.B., 3rd son of the late Gen. Sir Charles Cooper Johnson, G.C.B. (ante):—
   Issue of the late Maj. Percy Eliot Johnson, *b.* 1893, *d.* 1962: *m.* 1925, Molly, da. of the late James Payn, of Harding, Natal:—
Robin Eliot, *b.* 1929; ed. at St. John's Coll., Johannesburg: *m.* 1954, Barbara Alfreda, da. of the late Alfred T. Brown, of Germiston, Transvaal, and has issue living, Patrick Eliot, *b.* 1955,—Judith Marguerite, *b.* 1956,—Heather Mary, *b.* 1959.

Granddaughter of the late Maj.-Gen. Alured Clarke Johnson, C.B., 8th son of 2nd baronet :—
   Issue of the late Lieut.-Col. Gilbert Ward Johnson, *b.* 1866, *d.* 1924 : *m.* 1923, Marion, da. of C. H. Truslove, of Sale :—
Patricia Danino, *b.* (*posthumous*) 1924.

Grandson of the late Col. Archibald Acheson Johnson, 9th son of 2nd baronet:—
   Issue of the late Lt.-Col. Allen Edwin Johnson, DSO, *b.* 1878, *d.* 1972: *m.* 1913, Phoebe Dora Wynn, who *d.* 1961, da. of the late Maj. Alfred Elias:—
Allen Anthony Wynn (Furzedown, Berkhamsted, Herts.), *b.* 1916; ed. at Charterhouse, and St. John's Coll., Oxford; formerly RA: *m.* 1939, Helen Janet Margaret, only da. of W. A. Annett, of Greystoke, Berkhamsted, and has issue living, Mark Allen William Wynn, (30, Irene Rd., SW6), *b.* 1946; ed. at St. John's Coll., Oxford: *m.* 1969, Caroline Jane, only da. of C. R. E. Bowles of London, and has issue living, Alexander Mark Wynn *b.* 1970,—Christopher Wynn, *b.* 1948; ed. at E. Anglia Univ.

The 1st baronet, Gen. Sir Henry, GCB, son of Allen Johnson of Kilternan, co. Dublin, and yr. brother of Sir John Johnson-Walsh, 1st Bt., of Ballykilcavan, (ext. 1953), was Col. of the 5th Regt. and Governor of Ross Castle. The 2nd baronet, Sir Henry Allen, was a distinguished military officer in the Peninsular War. The 3rd baronet, Sir Henry Franks Frederic, was Col. Comdg. Forces in Jamaica, Windward and Leeward Islands. The 4th baronet, Sir Henry Allen William, CB, was Brig.-Gen. late KOYLI.

Johnson-Ferguson, see Ferguson.

Johnson-Walsh, see Walsh.

JOHNSTON, Creation (N.S.) 1626, of Caskieben, Aberdeenshire.

Live that you may live hereafter.

Sir THOMAS ALEXANDER JOHN-
STON, 13th *Baronet*; *b.* Sept. 7th, 1916;
s. his father, *Sir* THOMAS ALEXANDER
1959; an Attorney-at-Law, a partner
in the legal firm of Howell, Johnston,
Langford, Finkbohner and Lawler, of
E. A. Roberts Building, Mobile, Alabama, USA; a Member of Alabama
Constitution Revision Comrs.; Pres.
of Mobile Bar Assocn. 1963, and
of Mobile Branch of English-Speaking
Union 1963-64; sometime a Member of
Senate of State of Alabama: *m.* 1941,
Helen Torrey, da. of Benjamin Franklin Du Bois, and has issue.

Arms—Quarterly: 1st and 4th, argent, a saltire
sable, on a chief gules, three cushions or, *Johnston*;
2nd and 3rd, azure, on a bend or between three
harts' heads erased argent, attired of the second,
as many cross-crosslets fitchée of the second, *Mar*
and *Garioch of Caskieben*, composed together on
one coat. **Crest**—A phœnix in flames proper,
Supporters—Two naked Indians proper, wreathed
about the head and middle with laurel vert.

Residence—350, W. Delwood Drive, Mobile,
Alabama, 36606, USA.

Son living—THOMAS ALEXANDER, *b.* Feb. 1st, 1956.

Daughters living—Helen Du Bois, *b.* 1944: *m.* 1969, Phillip Thomas Sargent, of 9783, Aldbury
Court, Beverly Hills, Cal. 90210, USA, and has issue living, John Harrison, *b.* 1972.——Leslie
Sheldon, *b.* 1951: *m.* 1972, David Charles Krempa, of PO Box 4319, University, Alabama 35486,
USA.

Sisters living—Dianne, *b.* 1926: *m.* 1948, Samuel H. Andrews III, and has issue living, Samuel
Henry, *b.* 1949,—Bruce Sheldon, *b.* 1950,—John Norville, *b.* 1960,—Mark Alexander, *b.* 1961,—
Paula Burke, *b.* 1952,—Lucia Dianne Andrews, *b.* 1958. *Residence*, Citronelle, Alabama, USA.
——Pauline Sheldon, *b.* 1929: *m.* 1947, Leroy C. Baggett, and has issue living, Jennifer Ann,
b. 1950. *Residence*, 2764, Brookwood Drive, Mobile, Alabama, USA.

Uncle living (son of 11th baronet)—Kenneth Douglas (PO Box 323, Point Clear, Alabama, 36564,
USA), *b.* 1903; is Proprietor of South Alabama Realty Co., of 80, St. Michael St., Mobile,
Alabama.

Collateral Branches living.

Issue of the late William Norville Johnston, 2nd son of 11th baronet, *b.* 1894,
d. 1959: *m.* 1921, Catherine, da. of Thomas Murray, of Mobile, Alabama,
USA:—

William Norville (1754, Hunter Av., Mobile, Alabama, USA), *b.* 1922: *m.* 1952, Kathrine Pauline,
da. of Herbert Sigfred Solberg of Mobile, and has issue living, William Norville *b.* 1955,—Stephen
Gregory, *b.* 1958,—Paul Brady, *b.* 1959,—Kathryn Mary *b.* 1953.——Claude Edward (Ridgetown
Circle, Dallas, Texas, USA), *b.* 1930: *m.* 1960, Lucy, da. of Bernard Teague Mahorner, of Mobile,
and has issue living, Edward Ryan *b.* 1961,—Bernard Mathias, *b.* 1965,—Mary Teague, *b.* 1960,—
Laura Jean, *b.* 1964, Courtney Anne, *b.* 1971,—Elizabeth Leigh (twin), *b.* 1971.——Marian,
b. 1924: *m.* 1955, Thomas Ross Johnson, of 7, Dogwood Circle, Spring Hill Station, Mobile,
Alabama, USA, and has issue living, Thomas Ross III, *b.* 1957,—Margaret Murray, *b.* 1956,—
Elizabeth Barry, *b.* 1961.——Helen Jean, *b.* 1926: *m.* 1855, William Earle Bidez, of Birmingham,
Alabama, USA, and has issue living, William Earle, *b.* 1957,—Jeanne Marie, *b.* 1956,—Erin
Anne (twin), *b.* 1957,—Catherine Leary, *b.* 1961.

Issue of the late Frederick Rukard Johnston, 3rd son of 11th baronet, *b.* 1897,
d. 1962: *m.* 1925, Grace (of 203, Glenwood St., Mobile, Alabama, USA), da. of
John A. McRae, of Clio, Alabama, USA:—

Joyce Rukard, *b.* 1926: *m.* 1951, Wallace Abney Burgess, US Navy (ret.), of 1007, Whitestone
Lane, Houston, Texas, USA, and has issue living, Douglas Abney, *b.* 1956,—Patricia Olivia,
b. 1952,—Suzanne McRae, *b.* 1954,—Joyce Johnston, *b.* 1957,—Carolyn Norville, *b.* 1962.
——Mary Norville, *b.* 1928.

Sir George Johnston (son of the late John Johnston, of Caskieben, Aberdeenshire), Sheriff of
Aberdeen, was created a baronet of Nova Scotia 1626 with remainder to his heirs male whatsoever.
Sir Thomas Alexander Johnston 12th baronet was Ch. of Hydro-Power Branch, Dist. Office, Mobile,
Alabama.

JOHNSTONE, Creation (N.S.) 1700, of Westerhall, Dumfriesshire.

Sir FREDERIC ALLAN GEORGE JOHNSTONE, 10th *Baronet*: *b.* Feb.
23rd, 1906; *s.* his father, *Sir* GEORGE FREDERIC THOMAS TANKERVILLE, 1952;
ed. at Imperial Ser. Coll.: *m.* 1st, 1933, Gladys Hands, from whom he obtained
a divorce 1941; 2ndly, 1946, Doris, da. of the late W. L. Shortridge, of Blackheath, S.E., and has issue by 2nd marriage.

Arms,—Not matriculated at Lyon Office at time of going to press.
Residence—Urry's Cottage, Freshwater, Isle of Wight.

Sons living—By 2nd marriage—GEORGE RICHARD DOUGLAS, *b.* Aug. 21st, 1948.——Ian
Allan, *b.* 1954.

Sisters living—Laura Adeline, *b.* 1902. *Residence*, Claymore, The Parade, Cowes, Isle of
Wight.——Violet Florence Ernestine, *b.* 1903: *m.* 1924, Capt. George Thomas Vincent Watson,
formerly Indian Army, of Bellevue, Alberta, Canada, and has issue living, Thomas Frederic
Vincent, *b.* 1925: *m.* 1946, Margaret Elizabeth Payne, and has issue living, Thomas Richard
Vincent *b.* 1958, Judith Anne *b.* 1947, Margaret Aileen *b.* 1950,—Pauline Margaret Dorothy, *b.*
1926: *m.* 1950, Allan Ronald Theodore Tiley, of 69, Galt Av., Toronto, Ontario, Canada, and
has issue living, Diana Joyce Ernestine *b.* 1956,—Anne Philippa Rose, *b.* 1933: *m.* 1954, Reno
Angelo John Bosetti, MEd, and has issue living, Shelly Anne Marie *b.* 1958, Beverly Lynn,

*b.*1959.——Dorothy Katherine Frances (RRI, Maple Bay Rd., Duncan, Vancouver, BC, Canada), *b.* 1904: *m.* 1934, James Hastings, who *d.* 1964, and has issue living, Peter James, *b.* 1938: *m.* 1962, Margaret Judith, el da. of Nëville Hall, of Aldergrove, British Columbia,——Joan Florence (twin), *b.* 1938: *m.* 1st 1955 (m. diss. 1966), Irvyn Percy Ross; 2ndly, 1967, John David Hagar, of Duncan, Vancouver, BC, and has issue living (by 1st m.), Leilani Joan *b.* 1956, (by 2nd m.) John David *b.* 1969, Alisa Joan *b.* 1968.

Collateral Branches living.

Grandchildren of the late Major James Henry L'Estrange Johnstone, M.V.O. (infra):—
Issue of the late Capt. Henry James Johnstone, R.N., *b.* 1895, *d.* 1947 *m.* 1923, Alison (9, Chancellor House, Hyde Park Gate, SW7), da. of the late T. W. McIntyre, of Sorn Castle, Ayrshire:—
John Raymond (The Myretoun, Menstrie, Clackmannanshire), *b.* 1929; ed. at Eton, and at Trin. Coll., Camb.; Managing Dir. of Murray Johnstone & Co., Glasgow.——Christine Alison (*Lady Erskine-Hill*), *b.* 1924: *m.* 1942, Sir Robert Erskine-Hill, 2nd Bt. *Residence*, Quothquhan Lodge, Biggar, Lanarkshire.

Grandson of the late James Johnstone, el. son of the late James Raymond Johnstone, only son of the late John Johnstone, M.P., 5th son of 3rd baronet:—
Issue of the late Major James Henry L'Estrange Johnstone, M.V.O., *b.* 1865, *d.* 1906: *m.* 1891, Amy Octavia (who *d.* 1949, having *m.* 2ndly, 1927, Capt. Alfred Seton Christopher, J.P., late Seaforth Highlanders, who *d.* 1934). da. of the late Andrew Wauchope:—
Andrew Wauchope, *BSc, b.* 1903; ed. at Eton, and King's Coll., London (BSc); MIMechE, MIEE, a Member of Eng. Inst. of Canada, AMICE: *m.* 1932, Eleanor Blanche Helen Margaretta Vere-Laurie, da. of the late Lt.-Col. George Brenton Laurie, RIR, [*see* V. Massereene, colls.], and has issue living, James Andrew Francis, *b.* 1939, *m.* 1963, Helen Christina, el. da. of Ivan F. Wade of 4, Montée St. Jean, Pointe Claire, PQ: Canada, and has issue living, Sheila Christine *b.* 1964, Anne Laurie *b.* 1965, Jennifer Frances *b.* 1968, Kathleen Helen *b.* 1970,—Gillian Margaret, *b.* 1935: *m.* 1957, the Rev. Edmund Selwyn Haviland, of East Peckham Vicarage, Tonbridge, Kent, and has issue living, Andrew Mark James *b.* 1965, Margaret Vivienne *b.* 1958, Angela Helen *b.* 1960, Jane Eleanor *b.* 1963,—Jacquelina, *b.* 1936: *m.* 1966, Thomas Patrick Fitzgerald, of 6, Hampden Rd., Artarmon, NSW 2064, and has issue living, Jon Wauchope *b.* 1967. *Address*, Post Box 39, 86, Hazelwood Av., Hudson, Prov. of Quebec, Canada. *Club*, Junior Charlton.

Grandsons of the late Lieut.-Com. Somerset James SOMERSET-JOHNSTONE, R.N. (infra):—
Issue of the late Major FitzRoy Augustus Beauclerk Johnstone, *b.* 1878, *d.* 1931: *m.* 1915, Alida Helen, who *d.* 1969, da. of the late Andrew Veitch:—
FitzRoy Dawyck Somerset, *b.* 1921.——FitzRoy Montague Veitch (Cornaa Mill, Maughold, Isle of Man), *b.* 1922; ed. at Bradfield Coll., and Wadham Coll., Oxford; 1939-45 War, as Fl. Lt., Bomber Command, RAFVR: *m.* 1956, Dora, da. of the late Alexander Lofthouse, and has issue living, FitzRoy Jonathan, *b.* 1957; ed. at Stowe Sch.,—Judith Helen, *b.* 1959,—Jennifer Alison, *b.* 1962.——James Veitch, (50, Lowther Rd., Barnes, SW13), *b.* 1924: *m.* 1949, Nancy Hayes, da. of Henry Atkinson, and has issue living, Ian James FitzRoy, *b.* 1952.

Grandsons of the late Gen. Montague Cholmeley Johnstone, 3rd son of the late James Raymond Johnstone (ante):—
Issue of the late Lieut.-Com. Somerset James SOMERSET-JOHNSTONE, *b.* 1846, *d.* 1942, having assumed by deed poll 1900 the additional surname of Somerset: *m.* 1st, 1877, Elizabeth Ann, who *d.* 1886, da. of William Jackson Johnson, of Hootton, Cheshire; 2ndly, 1887 (divorce in America 1900), Isabel Ann, who *d.* 1934, da. of Joseph Charles Mappin, formerly of 38, Harrington Gardens, S.W.; 3rdly, 1900, Louisa Hodder, who *d.* 1914 (having obtained a divorce 1910):—
(By 2nd marriage) James Montague Cholmeley, *b.* 1889; ed. at Bedford Sch.; a Master Mariner; late Lieut. R.N.R.; sometime in Australian Navy; European War 1914-17, present at surrender of German New Guinea Sept. 1914, and at destruction of the *Emden* Nov. 1914: *m.* 1917, Alice Maud, da. of Frederick Witham, and has issue living, Fitzroy Somerset, *b.* 1927; European War 1943-5 as Radio Officer in Merchant Navy: *m.* 1952, Francesca Hodson, da. of Edward Wareing, of 20, Craven Gardens, Wimbledon, S.W., and has issue living, Peter James *b.* 1955, Susan Frances *b.* 1953,—Mauriel Sydney, *b.* 1918,—Audrey Philippa, *b.* 1923,—June Octavia, *b.* 1932.—— Malcolm Bruce SOMERSET, *b.* 1893; ed. at Sherborne; European War 1914-18 on Staff 2nd Army Head Quarters for defence of Sussex, Capt. Reserve of Cav. attached Army Remount Ser., and Comdg. 49th Remount Squadron in Salonika (despatches); assumed by deed poll 1932, the surname of Somerset only.

Grandchildren of the late Col. Montague George Johnstone, D.S.O., 2nd son of the late Gen. Montague Cholmeley Johnstone (ante):—
Issue of the late Major Montague Joseph Charles Somerset Johnstone, *b.* 1882, *d.* 1953: *m.* 1st, 1900, Victoria Louise, who *d.* 1916, da. of the late James Stewart, of Glasgow; 2ndly, 1916, Mary Marion Spottiswood (who *d.* 1949, having obtained a divorce 1928), da. of the late George Bayley, of Manuel, Stirlingshire; 3rdly, 1928, Margaret, da. of the late Sir John Foster Fraser :—
(By 2nd m.) Roy Henry Montague, *MBE, b.* 1919; ed. at Eton, and at Magdalene Coll., Camb.; 1939-45 War as Maj. 60th Rifles, on Staff, War Office, and in France and Germany (despatches, MBE); MBE (Mil.) 1945; a Member of London Stock Exchange 1956-74: *m.* 1st, 1939 (m. diss. 1959), Barbara Marjorie, da. of the late Maj. Felix Walter Warre, OBE, MC, of Wytherston, Powerstock, Dorset; 2ndly, 1961, Mme. Francois Terlinden, and has issue living, (by 1st m.,) Roland Richard Montague (17, Airedale Av., Chiswick, W4 2NW), *b.* 1941; ed. at Eton; late Lt. 60th Rifles; Solicitor 1967: *m.* 1968, Sara Outram Boileau, da. of Lt.-Col. John Garway Outram Whitehead, MC, of 10, Blackfriars St., Canterbury, and has issue living, Andrew Henry Montague, *b.* 1969,—William Arthur Montague, *b.* 1973,—Mark Montague, *b.* 1944; ed. at Eton; 2nd Lt. Queen's R. Rifles (TA): *m.* 1971, Rosalind Margaret, da. of Donald Macphee, of Bukuru, Nigeria,—Torquil James Montague, *b.* 1953; ed. at Eton,—Fiona Montague, *b.* 1946, (by 2nd m.) Carol Peter Montague *b.* 1961. *Residence*, Poorton Hill, Powerstock, Bridport, Dorset. *Clubs*, Brooks's, Pratt's.——(By 1st m.) Désirée Barbara Montague, *b.* 1908.—— Eileen Agnes Montague, *b.* 1909: *m.* 1931, Raymond Horwood Hazell, and has issue living, Charles Jonathan, *b.* 1938,—Louise, *b.* 1933,—Anastasia, *b.* 1936. *Residence*, 20, Brendon St., W1.——Rosemary Maud Montague, *b.* 1913: *m.* 1936 Nicholas Desborough Burnell.——(By 2nd m.) Gloria Montague, *b.* 1918.——(By 3rd m.) Alastair Montague, *b.* 1928.

Granddaughters of the late Gen. Montague Cholmeley Johnstone (ante):—
Issue of the late Lieut.-Col. Francis Fawkes Johnstone, *b.* 1849, *d.* 1919: *m.* 1st, 1878, Henrietta Jane [divorced 1886], da. of James Sullivan; 2ndly, 1887, Harriet Lavinia, who *d.* 1910, da. of the late Richard Sargent and widow of Capt. Charles Francis Gregg, of 7th Hussars and 6th Inniskilling Dragoons:—
(By 1st marriage) Mary Louisa Leonora: *m.* 1897, Percy Kitchin.——Frances Geraldine Jane.

Granddaughters of the late Lieut.-Col. Francis Fawkes Johnstone (ante):—
Issue of the late Major Charles Campbell Gosling Johnstone, *b.* 1889, *d.* 1942: *m.* 1st, 1912, Laura Mary (who obtained a divorce 1927), da. of the late Lieut.-Col. Willoughby B. Hemans, R.A.; 2ndly, 1928, Nina, da. of the late Col. Valentine de Sventorgetsky, Russian Imperial Guard:—
(By 1st marriage) Violet Mary St. Clair, *b.* 1914.——Jean Hermione, *b.* 1922. *Residence*,

Granddaughters of the late Gen. Montague Cholmeley Johnstone (ante):—
Issue of the late Caroline Mysie Johnstone, b. 1859, d. 1952: m. 1886, Frederick Gomer,
formerly 7th Dragoon Guards and Indian Rifles, who d. 1926:—
Ethel Winifred (4624, West 7th Av., Vancouver 8, BC, Canada), b. 1895: m. 1926, James Stuart
Crabb, who d. 1968, and has issue living, Margaret Stuart, b. 1928; ed. at British Columbia
Univ. (BA Honours, BLS): m. 1968, W. John Bese, of 10485-155 A St., North Surrey, BC,
and has issue living, Jonathan Mark b. 1971.——Gwendolyn Maud (of 1332, Tatlow, N. Van-
couver, British Columbia), b. 1897: m. 1914, Haydn Newton, who d. 1939, and has issue living,
Phyllis Audrey (of Los Angeles, California, USA), b. 1919: m. 1939 (m. diss. 1963), Dennis A.
Pearman, and has issue living, John b. 1945, Joyce Irene b. 1940, Clara Louise (twin) b. 1945.——
Mabel Edwina Phyllis, b. 1899: m. 1920, Cyril George Deavin, of 1350, Sowden Av., N. Van-
couver, British Columbia, and has issue living, Norma Dorothy, b. 1921: m. 1951, Wilfred Jack
Elder, of 6253, Overstone Drive, W. Vancouver, British Columbia.

Granddaughters of the late John Heywood Johnstone, MP, son of the late Rev.
George Dempster Johnstone, 4th son of the late James Raymond Johnstone
(ante):—
Issue of the late George Horace Johnstone, O.B.E., D.L., b. 1882, d. 1960: m. 1910,
Alison (of Trewithen, Grampound Road, Truro, Cornwall), da. of the Ven. Stamford
Raffles Raffles-Flint (Archdeacon of Cornwall, and Canon of Truro), of Nansawsan,
Ladock, Cornwall:—
Elizabeth Alison, b. 1911.——Rachel Mary, b. 1916: m. 1st, 1934 (marriage dissolved 1944),
Robert Washbourne Money; 2ndly, 1946 (marriage dissolved 1949), James Henderson; 3rdly,
1957, Jack Spenceley-Collins, c/o Trewithen, Grampound Road, Truro, and has issue living, (by
1st m.) Stuart Washbourne, MBE, b. 1935; Maj. SCLI; MBE (Mil) 1964,—Robert Graham
Ernlie Washbourne b. 1936.——Jennifer Ruth, b. 1921: m. 1942, John Edgar Galsworthy, CMG,
HM Foreign Ser., and has issue living, Arthur Michael Johnstone, b. 1944,—Alison Merryn, b.
1947,—Bridget, b. 1952,—Amanda Elizabeth, b. 1959. Address: Trewithen, Grampound Rd.,
Truro, Cornwall.

Descendants of the late Richard Johnstone (el. son of the late Col. John Johnstone,
2nd son of 2nd baronet), who was cr. a Baronet 1797 (with special remainder
to the male issue of his brother, Charles John) [see B. Derwent].

Descendants of the late Charles John Johnstone [2nd son of the late Col. John
Johnstone (ante)], [see B. Derwent].

This family descend from Matthew Johnstone of Pettinain (later called Westraw), Lanarkshire, said to have been a yr. son of Sir Adam Johnstone of that Ilk (d. 1454), ancestor of the
Marquesses of Annandale (dormant 1792). Sir John Johnstone of Westershall, 8th in descent from
Matthew was cr. a Baronet with remainder to his heirs male. He represented Dumfries in the
Scottish Parliament, and voted for the Union. Sir William, the 5th baronet, assumed the surname
of Pulteney on marriage to Frances Pulteney, heir to her cousin the Earl of Bath, and died
without male issue 1805; his only child Henrietta, Laura, was created Countess of Bath, and died
without issue 1808. The 6th baronet, Sir John Lowther, M.P. for Weymouth 1810-11, twice
declined a peerage that was offered to him by Spencer Perceval.

JONES, Creation (U.K.) 1917, of Pentower, Fishguard, co. Pembroke. [Extinct 1952.

Sir TOM BARRY JONES, 2nd and last Baronet.

Daughter living of 1st Baronet—Mary Harris: m. 1st, 1913, Major George Malcombe Nixon
Harman, D.S.O., Rifle Brig., who d. (killed in action during European War) 1914 ; 2ndly, 1917,
Capt. Alfred Hans Waring Caulfeild, M.B., Canadian Army Med. Corps, who d. 1940, and from
whom she had obtained a divorce 1934 [see V. Charlemont, colls.]. Residence, 4, Lyndhurst
Court, Toronto 10, Canada.
Widow living of 2nd Baronet—JEAN (Lady Jones), widow of Herbert Costain, Lieut. R.A.F.: m.
1922, Sir Tom Barry Jones, 2nd baronet, who d. 1952, when the title became ext.

JONES, Creation (U.K.) 1919, of Treeton, West Riding of Yorkshire.

Sir SIMON WARLEY FREDERICK BENTON
JONES, 4th Baronet; b. Sept. 11th, 1941; s.
his father, Sir PETER FAWCETT BENTON, OBE,
1972; ed. at Eton, and Trin. Coll., Camb.
(MA); JP for Lincs.: m. 1966, Margaret
Fiona, da. of David Rutherford Dickson, of
Barrow Lodge, Bury St. Edmunds, and has
issue.

Arms—Per chevron argent and sable, in chief two dragons
heads erased gules, and in base two crosses patée fitchée in
saltire or. Crest—A demi gryphon gules, grasping a miner's
pickaxe, head downwards in pale or.

Seat—Irnham Hall, nr. Grantham, Lincs.

Sons living—JAMES PETER MARTIN, b. Jan. 1st, 1973, —
David William Anthony, b. 1975.

Daughters living—Fiona Charlotte, b. 1967.——Fleur
Alexandra, b. 1970.

Sister living—Jill Benton, b. 1937: m. 1959, William
Hepburn McAlpine, of Fawley Hill, Fawley Green,
Henley-on-Thames, el. son of Sir (Robert) Edwin
McAlpine [see McAlpine, Bt.].

Aunts living (daughters of 2nd baronet)—Pamela Benton (Villa Beauregard, 34 Bl, Garavan, 06500 Menton, France), *b.* 1908: *m.* 1930 (m. diss. 1948). Percival John Parker Stephenson, who *d.* 1973, [*see* Stephenson, Bt., colls.].——Rachel Mary Benton, *b.* 1918: *m.* 1941, George Ronald Murray Kydd, and has issue living, Ian Murray, *b.* 1945,—Donald Hamish, *b.* 1947: *m.* 1970, Christine, da. of —— and has issue living, Loraine Grace *b.* 1971. *Residence*, Cruglas, Swyddffynon, Ystrad Meurig, Cardiganshire.

Great-Aunt living (daughter of 1st baronet)—Katharine Mary: *m.* 1933, Lt.-Col. William Herbert Olivier, TD, JP, DL, LLD, and has issue living, Jasper William Dacres, *b.* 1938: *m.* 1973, Virginia Whitaker,—James Stephen, *b.* 1944; Capt. RHG: *m.* 1968, Sally Anne Simonds: *m.* 1973, John Guy Carmichael Jackson,—Flora Mary Margaret, *b.* 1936,—Julie Katharine, *b.* 1941: *m.* 1966, Patrick Julian Dawnay [see V. Downe, colls.]. *Residence*, Ashford Hall, Bakewell, Derbyshire, DE4 IQA.

Collateral Branch living.

> Issue of the late Capt. Charles Frederick Ward Jones, yr. son of 1st baronet, *b.* 1884, *d.* 1971: *m.* 1921, Dorothy, who *d.* 1962, only da. of the late R. H. Allen, of Hemingfield, Worksop, Notts.:—

David Robert Ward (Orchard House, Firbeck, nr. Worksop, Notts.), *b.* 1925; ed. at Repton; Capt. RHG (Reserve): *m.* 1954, Sally, da. of Col. H. Cantan, of Bridport, Dorset, and has issue living, Emma, *b.* 1956,—Kathryn, *b.* 1960,—Harriet, *b.* 1963.——Anne Ward, *b.* 1922: *m.* 1950, Charles Douglas Pain, of Windy Corner, Kingston Gorse, East Preston, Sussex, and has issue living, Michael Ward Eames, *b.* 1957.——Beth Ward, *b.* 1924: *m.* 1950, Michael William Ollyver Antill, of Woodhouse Hall, Holbeck, Worksop, Notts., and has issue living, Timothy William, *b.* 1954,—Sarah Penelope, *b.* 1952.

Sir Frederick John Jones 1st Bt. was Pres., Mining Assocn. of Gt. Britain, Chm., S. Yorks. Coal Trade Assocn., and Miners' Conciliation Board.

LAWRENCE-JONES, Creation (U.K.) 1831, of Cranmer Hall, Norfolk.

Sir CHRISTOPHER LAWRENCE-JONES, 6th *Baronet, b.* Jan. 19th, 1940; *s.* his uncle, *Sir* LAWRENCE EVELYN, *MC, TD,* 1969; ed. at Sherborne, and Gonville and Caius Coll., Camb. (MA, MB, BChir); DIH England; FRSM; Lord of Manor of Fakenham, Norfolk; assumed by deed poll 1969 the surname of Lawrence-Jones: *m.* 1967, Gail, da. of Cecil Arthur Pittar, FRACS, of Auckland, NZ, and has issue.

Arms—Azure, on a fesse or, three grenades fired proper; in chief a castle, and over it the word "Netherlands" in letters of gold; in base a lion couchant argent, gorged with a ribbon gules fimbriated azure, therefrom suspended a representation of the gold medal presented to the 1st baronet for his services at Badajoz. **Crest**—In front of a castle a lion couchant argent gorged with a wreath of laurel, and pendent therefrom an escutcheon gules charged with a representation of the Badajoz medal as in the arms.

Marte et arte.
By war and art.

Residence—Silwood House, London Rd., Ascot, Berks.

Sons living—MARK CHRISTOPHER, *b.* Dec. 28th, 1968.——John Alexander, *b.* 1971.

Daughters living of 5th Baronet—Nancy Lawrence, *b.* 1913: *m.* 1941, David Vivian Morse, FRCS, of The Old Vicarage, Doddington, Wooler, Northumberland, and has issue living, Jonathan Patrick, *b.* 1942,—Oliver James, *b.* 1949,—Annabel Harriet, *b.* 1944.——Vivien Lawrence, *b.* 1923: *m.* 1942, Simon Anthony Roland Asquith, who *d.* 1973 [*see* E. Oxford and Asquith, colls.]. *Residence*, 15, Castello Av., Putney, SW15.——Lavinia Lawrence, *b.* 1925. *Residence*, 28, Radnor Walk, SW3.

Aunt living (daughter of 4th baronet)—Rachel Margaret Lawrence, *b.* 1891. *Residence*, 13, Richmond Court, 200, Sloane St., SW1.

Mother living—Margaret Louise (Broadcroft, Lymington, Hants), da. of the late Geoffrey Montague Cookson, of Howes Eype, Bridport: *m.* 1938, as his 2nd wife, Cdr. Bertram Edward Jones, RN, who *d.* 1958, 3rd son of 4th baronet.

Collateral Branch living.

> Issue of the late Rt. Rev. Herbert Edward Jones, Suffragan Bishop of Lewes, 2nd son of 3rd baronet, *b.* 1861, *d.* 1920: *m.* 1888, Madeline Long, who *d.* 1928, da. of Edward Long Fox, M.D., F.R.C.P., formerly of Church House, Clifton :—

Violet Madeline, *b.* 1894. *Residence*, Bottle Knapp, Long Bredy, Dorchester.

This family was settled at Sunny Hill, Carmarthenshire for several generations. David Jones moved to Norfolk in the 17th century. Maj.-Gen. Sir Thomas Jones, 1st Bt., was a distinguished officer in RE, serving in the Peninsular War. He *m.* 1816, Catherine, da. of Effingham Lawrence, of Long Island, NY. Sir Lawrence Jones, 2nd Bt. was murdered at Macri, in Turkey, 1845. Sir Lawrence Jones, MC, 5th Bt., was author of "Victorian Boyhood," "Edwardian Youth" and "Georgian Afternoon."

PRICHARD-JONES, Creation (U.K.) 1910, of Bron Menai, Dwyran, Llangeinwen, Anglesey.

Sir JOHN PRICHARD - JONES, 2nd *Baronet*; *b.* Jan. 20th, 1913; *s.* his father, Sir John, 1917; ed. at Eton, and at Ch. Ch., Oxford (B.A. honours 1934); Bar. Gray's Inn 1936; Capt. late The Queen's Bays: *m.* 1st, 1937, Heather Vivian Mary (from whom he obtained a divorce 1950), da. of Sir Walter Richard Nugent, 4th Bt., *cr.* 1831 (of Donore); 2ndly, (Feb.) 1959, Helen Marie Thérèse, da. of J. F. Liddy, Dental Surg., of 20, Lawrence St., Drogheda, and has issue by 1st and 2nd marriages.

Arms—Gules, a lymphad in full sail or, on a chief of the second, two escutcheons of the first. **Crest**—A demi-lion gules, resting the sinister paw on a boar's head erased or. *Residence*—Allenswood House, Lucan, co. Dublin.

Son living—By 1st marriage—DAVID JOHN WALTER, *b.* March 14th, 1943; ed. at Ampleforth, and at Ch. Ch., Oxford (BA Hons).

Daughter living—By 2nd marriage—Susan Marie, *b.* (Nov.) 1959.

Brother living—Richard William, *b.* 1914 ; ed. at Eton, and at Brasenose Coll., Oxford ; is Capt. R.A. : *m.* 1943, Margaret Woodburn (Sally), da. of Squadron-Leader R. H. W. Davidson, and has issue living, Richard Stephen, *b.* 1952,—Marie Ann, *b.* 1948. *Club*, St. James'.

Sir John, J.P., D.L., LL.D., 1st baronet, sometime head of the firm of Dickins and Jones (Limited), of 226-244, Regent Street, W., founded and endowed the Prichard-Jones Institute and Cottage Homes, Newborough, Anglesey, and donated the Prichard-Jones Hall of Univ. Coll. of N. Wales, of which he was Senior Vice-Pres. ; he assumed by deed poll (registered at the College of Arms) 1917 the surname of Prichard-Jones.

PROBYN-JONES, Creation (U.K.) 1926, of Rhyl, co. Flint.   [Extinct 1951.]

Sir ARTHUR PROBYN PROBYN-JONES, 2nd and last *Baronet*.

Widow living of 2nd Baronet—EILEEN (*Lady Probyn-Jones*), da. of the late James Evans, and of Mrs. James Evans, of The Old Hall, Helsby, Cheshire: *m.* 1919, Sir Arthur Probyn Probyn-Jones, 2nd baronet, who *d.* 1951, when the title became ext. *Residence*, Spur Cottage, South Lodge, Ham Common, Surrey.

PRYCE-JONES, Creation (U.K.) 1918, of Dolerw, co. Montgomery. [Extinct 1963.]

Sir PRYCE VICTOR PRYCE-JONES, 2nd and last *Baronet*.

Widow living of 2nd Baronet—SYRA ROANTREE (*Lady Pryce-Jones*) (of The Manor House, Great Ryburgh, Norfolk), only da. of the late Francis O'Shiel, of Omagh, co. Tyrone: *m.* 1938, Capt. Sir Pryce Victor Pryce-Jones, 2nd Bt., who *d.* 1963, when the title became ext.

JOSEPH, Creation (U.K.) 1942, of Stoke-on-Trent, co. Stafford. [Extinct 1951.]

Sir FRANCIS L'ESTRANGE JOSEPH, *K.B.E.*, 1st and last *Baronet*.

Daughters living of 1st Baronet—Rosamond Mary BIRLEY (26, Trevor Place, S.W.7), *b.* 1919, resumed by deed poll 1962 her former surname of Birley: *m.* 1st, 1942 (m. diss. 1956), Maj. Peter Rouse Addison Birley, 17th/21st Lancers; 2ndly, 1957, Christopher Bevis Sanford; 3rdly, 1968, Daniel Vincent O'Donovan, Barrister, and has issue living, (by 1st m.) David Peter Francis *b.* 1943; ed. at Harlow, and at Ch.Ch., Oxford, (by 2nd m.), Francis L'Estrange, *b.* 1957.——Cynthia Violet Maud, *b.* 1921: *m.* 1946, Col. Peter Stanley Walter Dean, R. Anglian Regt. (ret.), of The Rookery, Rougham, Bury St. Edmunds.

JOSEPH, Creation (U.K.) 1943, of Portsoken, City of London.

Rt. Hon. Sir KEITH SINJOHN JOSEPH, *M.P.*, 2nd *Baronet; b.* Jan. 17th, 1918; *s.* his father, *Sir* SAMUEL GEORGE, 1944; ed. at Harrow, and at Magdalen Coll., Oxford; Fellow of All Souls' Coll. 1946-60, and since 1972; Bar. Middle Temple 1946; appointed Parliamentary Private Sec. to Under-Sec. of State for Commonwealth Relations 1957, Parliamentary Sec., Min. of Housing and Local Govt. 1959, Min. of State, Board of Trade 1961-2, and Min. of Housing and Local Govt., and Min. for Welsh Affairs 1962-64; Sec. of State for Social Sers. 1970-74; formerly an Underwriting Member of Lloyd's; a Fellow of Institute of Builders, and Liveryman of Vintners' Co.; an Alderman of City of London 1946-49; a Dir. of Gilbert-Ash Ltd. 1949-59, and Bovis Holdings, Ltd., 1951-59 (Dept. Chm. 1964-70), and Chm. Bovis Ltd., 1958-59; co-founder and first Chm. of Foundation of Management Education 1959; Founder of Mulberry Housing Trust 1965 (First Chm. 1965-69); Chm. of Jewish Affairs Research Board 1966-70; Founder and Chm. of Management Cttee. of Centre for Policy Studies Ltd., 1974; 1939-45 War in Italy as Capt. RA (wounded, despatches); MP for NE Div. of Leeds (*C*) since 1956; *cr* PC 1962: *m.* 1951, Hellen Louise, yr. da. of Sigmar Guggenheimer, of New York, USA, and has issue.

᚛rms—Per chevron gules and barry wavy of ten azure and or a fesse embattled of the last masoned sable in chief a sun in splendour gold. ᚛rest—In front of an annulet azure encircling a tower gules two sprigs of honesty leaved and slipped saltire-wise proper. *Residence*—23, Mulberry Walk, SW3 6DZ. *Club*, Carlton.

———

Son living—JAMES SAMUEL, *b.* Jan. 27th, 1955.
Daughters living—Emma Catherine Sarah, *b.* 1956.——Julia Rachel, *b.* 1959.——Anna Jane Rebecca *b.* 1964.
Widow living of 1st Baronet—EDNA CICELY (*Edna Lady Joseph*), da. of the late P. A. S. Phillips, of Portland Place, W.1 : *m.* 1916, Sir Samuel George Joseph, 1st baronet, who *d.* 1944. *Residence*, Flat 12, Grosvenor House, W1A 3AA.

The 1st baronet, Sir Samuel George Joseph (son of the late A. Joseph), Co-Chm. and Managing Director of Bovis, Ltd., an Underwriter of Lloyd's, and Hon. Col. 56th (1st London) Div. R.E.; was Mayor of St. Marylebone 1928-30, Sheriff of City of London 1933-4, Alderman thereof 1933, and Lord Mayor 1942-43 ; served during European War 1914-19 (wounded, despatches).

———

KABERRY, Creation (U.K.) 1960, of Adel cum Eccup, City of Leeds.

Sir DONALD KABERRY, *T.D., M.P.*, 1st *Baronet*, son of A. Kaberry ; *b.* Aug. 18th 1907; ed. at Leeds; Solicitor 1930; a Crown Repres. of Court and Council of Leeds Univ. 1964-74; a DL for W. Yorks.; a Gov. of Leeds Gram. Sch.; a Member Leeds City Council 1930-39, and 1946-50; Hon. Alderman Leeds; a Member of Council of Law Soc. 1950-55, Assist. Gov. Whip 1952-55, Parl. Sec., Board of Trade April to Oct. 1955, and Vice-Chm. Cons. and Unionist Party 1955-61; Pres., Yorks. Prov. Area Council of Cons. Party since 1966 (Chm. 1951-55, Dep. Pres. 1956-65), Chm. of Assocn. of Conservative Clubs since 1961, and of Board of Govs., of United Leeds Hosps. 1961-74; Chm. of Yorkshire Chemicals, Ltd., W. H. Baxter, Ltd., and Ernest Walker & Co., Ltd.; 1939-45 War in RA (despatches twice); has sat as MP for N-W Div. of Leeds (*C*) since Oct. 1950: *m.* 1940, Lily Margaret, da. of Edmund Scott and has issue.

᚛rms—Per fesse argent and azure and a pile reversed counterchanged three double-warded, keys wards upwards also azure each enfiled by a chaplet of holly fructed proper and of roses argent barbed and seeded also proper. ᚛rest—On a wreath or sable and azure a weeping willow tree proper pendent from the trunk thereof by a ring a fleece or.
Residence,—Adel Willows, Leeds, 16. *Clubs*—Carlton, Constitutional, Leeds.

Sons living—CHRISTOPHER DONALD, *b.* March 14th, 1943: *m.* 1967, Gaenor Elizabeth Vowe, da. of C. V. Peake, of Durkar House, Durkar, Wakefield, and has issue living, James Christopher, *b.* April 1st, 1970,—Angus George, *b.* 1972,—Claire Elizabeth, *b.* 1974.——Andrew Murdoch Scott, *b.* 1946.——Simon Edmund John, *b.* 1948.

KAYE, Creation (U.K.) 1923, of Huddersfield, co. York.

Sir STEPHEN HENRY GORDON KAYE, 3rd *Baronet;* *b.* March 24th, 1917; *s.* his father, *Sir* (HENRY) GORDON, 1956; ed. at Stowe, and at Trin. Coll., Camb.

Arms—Or, a bend cotissed invected between two escutcheons sable each charged with a rose argent, barbed and seeded proper. **Crest**—Upon a staff raguly fessewise or a goldfinch proper, holding in the beak a rose argent, barbed, seeded, leaved and slipped proper.

Residence—Mortimore's, New Buildings, Sandford, Crediton, Devon, EX17 4PP.

Brothers living—DAVID ALEXANDER GORDON, *b.* 1919; ed. at Camb. Univ. (BA); MRCS Eng. and LRCP London 1943: *m.* 1st, 1942 (m. diss. 1950), Elizabeth, only da. of Capt. Malcolm Hurtley, of Baynards Manor, Horsham, Sussex; 2ndly, 1955, Adelle, da. of Denis Thomas, of Brisbane, Qld., and has issue living, (by 2nd m.) Paul Henry Gordon, *b.* 1958,—John Egidio Gordon, *b.* 1967,—Yvonne Marie, *b.* 1956,—Denise Anne, *b.* 1960,—Alaine Freda *b.* 1962,—Marita Margaret, *b.* 1970. *Residence*, Yerinandah, Moggill Rd., The Gap, Brisbane, Qld.
——Brian Joseph Gordon, *b.* 1920: *m.* 1947, Anne, only da. of Frederick Henry Grisewood, OBE, of Hewshotts, Liphook, Hants, and has issue living, Angus Frederick Gordon, *b.* 1962. *Residence*, Chaffcombe Farm, Copplestone, Crediton, Devon.

The 1st baronet, Sir Joseph Henry, was Senior Director of Kaye and Stewart (Limited), of Huddersfield, and a Director of London, Midland and Scottish Railway Co., and of Lloyds Bank (Limited).

Let us be judged by our actions.

LISTER-KAYE, Creation (U.K.) 1812, of Grange, Yorkshire.

Sir JOHN CHRISTOPHER LISTER LISTER-KAYE, 7th *Baronet;* *b.* July 13th, 1913; *s.* his father, *Sir* LISTER, 1962; ed. at Oundle, and at Loughborough Coll.: *m* 1942, Audrey Helen, da. of E. J. Carter, of Westbury-on-Trym, Bristol, and has issue.

Arms—Quarterly, 1st and 4th, argent, two bendlets sable, *Kaye;* 2nd and 3rd, ermine on a fesse sable three mullets or, the whole within a bordure wavy azure, *Lister*. **Crests**—1st, a goldfinch proper, charged on the breast with a rose gules; 2nd, a buck's head proper, erased wavy or, attired sable, and in the mouth a bird-bolt bendwise of the third, flighted argent.

Residence—Woodsome, Bannerdown, Bath. *Club*—Farmers'.

Son living—JOHN PHILLIP LISTER (The Old Kennels, Guisachan, Tomich, Beauly, Inverness-shire. *Clubs*—Highland, Caledonian, Farmers'), *b.* May 8th, 1946; ed. at Allhallows Sch.: *m.* 1972, Sorrel Deirdre, el. da. of Count Henry Noel Bentinck [see D. Portland, colls.], and has issue living, John Warwick Noel, *b.* Dec. 10th, 1974.
Daughter living—Mary Eugenia Helen, *b.* 1944: *m.* 1970, Nigel Carrel, of Fforddlas, Builth Wells, Brecons., and has issue living, Christopher-James, *b.* 1971.
Brother living—Aubrey Robert Lister, *b.* 1917; ed. at Oundle: *m.* 1965, Nora May Gratton.
Sister living—Rosamond Eugenia Mary, *b.* 1912: *m.* 1945, Major Edward Osmond Thornhill Simpson, and has issue living, Mark Thornhill, *b.* 1951,—Sarah Thornhill, *b.* 1946,—Julia Thornhill, *b.* 1947. *Residence*, 7275, Balaclava St., Vancouver 13, BC, Canada.

Keep your own kin kind

Daughter living of 4th Baronet—(Frances) Lois (*Lois, Viscountess de Vesci*) *b.* 1882: *m.* 1st, 1905, the 5th Earl of Rosse, who *d.* 1918; 2ndly, 1920, the 5th Viscount de Vesci, who *d.* 1958. *Residence*, Womersley Park, Doncaster.

Collateral Branches living.

Grandchildren of the late Arthur Lister-Kaye (infra):—
Issue of the late John Arthur Lister-Kaye, b. 1895, d. 1974: m. 1923, Emily Alice, da. of
James Henry Cooper, of Hayling Island:—
Warwick Arthur, b. 1929.——Stella Maud, b. 1924: m. 1943, William John Stewart Boyd, of Vic.,
BC, Canada.

Issue of the late Arthur Lister-Kaye, brother of 6th baronet, b. 1876, d. 1943 : m. 1st
1895, Lottie Emmeline, da. of John Woodward ; 2ndly, 1900, Gertrude, who d. 1945,
da. of J. Hall, formerly of Gore House, New Milton, Hants :—
(By 1st m.) Helen, b. 1896.——(By 2nd m.) Arthur Lister (30, Newcombe Rd., Southampton), b.
1903.

Sir John Kaye, of Woodsome, Almondbury, Yorks, was created a baronet in 1642. This
baronetcy became extinct on the death of the 6th Bt. in 1809, but in 1812 Sir John Lister-Kaye,
natural son and testamentary heir of the 5th Bt. received a Baronetcy. The 3rd Bt., Sir John
Pepys Lister-Kaye, was a Groom-in-Waiting to King Edward VII 1908-10.

KEANE, Creation (U.K.) 1801, of Cappoquin, co. Waterford.

The stroked cat is meek.

Sir RICHARD MICHAEL KEANE, 6th
Baronet ; b. Jan. 29th, 1909 ; s. his father,
Sir JOHN, 1956 ; ed. at Sherborne, and at
Oxford Univ. : m. 1939, Olivia Dorothy,
da. of Oliver Hawkshaw, T.D., of Chisenbury
Priory, Wilts., and has issue.

Arms—Gules, three trouts naiant in pale argent.
Crest—A cat-a-mountain sejant proper, in his dexter paw
a staff displaying the Banner of Great Britain.

Residence—Cappoquin House, co. Waterford. *Club*—
Kildare Street.

Sons living—JOHN CHARLES, b. Sept. 16th, 1941;
ed. at Eton. and Ch. Ch., Oxford.——David Richard,
b. 1950; ed. at Eton, and Bailliol Coll., Oxford: m.
1973, Julia, da. of Henry Bowring, of The Old Orchard,
Bembridge, Isle of Wight.
Daughter living—Vivien Eleanor, b. 1940 : m. 1961,
Simon Pleydell-Bouverie [see E. Radnor, colls.].
Residence, The Castle House, Deddington, Oxon.

Sisters living—Adelaide Mary, b. 1907 : m. 1933,
Cecil Denis Pegge, of Carrigeen, Cappoquin, co. Water-
ford, and has issue living, a son, b. 1937.——Sheila,
b. 1911: m. 1935, Christopher Edward Knight,
and has issue living, Michael John, b. 1939 ; ed. at
Eton, and at New Coll., Oxford: m. 1970, Caroline
Francesca, el. da. of Alexander Kendal Humphrey
Fletcher—Jonathan Christopher, b. 1943; ed. at Eton.—
Martin David, b. 1946, ed. at Eton, and Trin. Coll.,
Dublin: m. 1971, Eleanor Clare, da. of James Malcolm
Harrison,—Susan Jane, b. 1937. *Residence*, Landfall,
Crawley Down, Sussex.——Madeline Lucy; b. 1914:
m. 1938, Donald Godfrey Emerson, CBE, of Meads,
House, Leighterton, Tetbury, Glos., GL8 8UW, and
has issue living, James Seymour (Sunningdale, Skelton,
Saltburn, N. Yorks.), b. 1941; ed. at Marlborough,
and at Trin. Coll., Dublin: m. 1st, 1964 (m. diss. 1971),
Bridget Eileen Mary, da. of Lt.-Col. Wyndham
Marsden Knatchbull [see B. Brabourne, colls.], 2ndly,
1971, Jennifer Ruth Clement, and has issue living
(by 1st m.), Suzanne Mary b. 1964, Gillian Lucy
b. 1966, (by 2nd m.) Richard Donald b. 1971,—Judith Lucy, b. 1943: m. 1967, Michael Maurice
Fletcher Watson,—Carol Georgena, b. 1944: m. 1971, Robert Lorne Hyndham, of Ottawa,
Canada,—Mary Eleanor, b. 1953.

Collateral Branches living.

Issue of the late Capt. George Michael Keane, R.N., 2nd son of 4th baronet, b. 1875,
d. 1957: m. 1909, Violet, who d. 1974, da. of the late Theodore McKenna, of 22, Portland Place, W1:—
Ann Patricia, b. 1910: m. 1934, Christopher Leslie Thompson, Group Capt. RAF (ret.), and has
issue living, Christopher Mark, b. 1935,—Jonathan Michael Adrian, b. 1938: m. 1970, Barbara
Anne, da. of F. Scrowcroft,—Andrew Theodore, b. 1941. *Residence*, Coldenhale, Eastham,
Tenbury Wells, Worcs.

Granddaughters of the late Lieut.-Col. Richard Henry Keane, C.B.E. (infra):—
Issue of the late Robert Lumley Keane, b. 1910, d. 1946: m. 1938, Mary Nesta (now of
Dysert, Ardmore, co. Waterford), da. of the late Walter C. Skrine, of Ballyrankin
House, Ferns, co. Wexford :—
Adele Sara, b. 1940: m. 1972, George Phipps.——Virginia, b. 1945: m. 1969, Kevin Brownlow.

Issue of the late Lieut.-Col. Richard Henry Keane, C.B.E., 3rd son of 4th baronet,
b. 1881, d. 1925: m. 1906, Alice Gabriel, who d. (result of enemy action during
European War) 1944, da. of the late His Honour Judge Sir Lumley Smith,
K.C., of 25, Cadogan Square, S.W. :—
Sibyl Elfrida, b. 1908 : m. 1939, Major Hugh Jocelyn Delmege, and has issue living, Caroline
Stella, b. 1940. *Residence*, The Green Farm, Fethard, co. Tipperary,——Diana Dorothy (St.
Andrew's Hospital, Northampton, NN1 5DG), b. 1915: m. 1940 (m. diss. 1973), Air Commodore Æneas Ranald Donald MacDonell of Glengarry, CB, DFC, RAF, 22nd Ch. of Glengarry,
and has issue living, (Æneas) Ranald Euan (92, Mostyn Rd., SW19), b. 1941; ed. at Bryanston
and St. John's Coll., Camb. (MA): m. 1969 (Dorothy) Ann el. da. of the late Stanley James
Hind, of Guildford, and has issue living, Fiona Jane b. 1971, Victoria Ann b. 1972,—Colin Patrick,
b. 1968: m. 1968, Ursula, da. of Kurt Eichert, of Cologne, and has issue living, Angus Kurt
b. 1970, Sonia Dee b. 1971,—Lindsay Alice, b. 1947: m. 1974, B. C. U. Cuthbertson, late Canadian Army, of Apt. 1210, Somerset Place, 1030, South Park St., Halifax, Nova Scotia, B3H 2W3.

The 1st baronet was successively M.P. for Bangor and Youghal, the 2nd baronet sat as M.P. for Waterford (L) 1832-5, and the 3rd baronet was High Sheriff for co. Waterford in 1856 and the 4th Baronet in 1881.   Sir John Keane, 5th baronet was a Senator of Irish Free State for 26 years a Councillor of State, Republic of Ireland, Gov. of Bank of Ireland, and High Sheriff of co. Waterford in 1911.

KELLETT, Creation (U.K.) 1801, of Lota, Cork.

Feret ad astra virtus.

Virtue will bear you to the skies.

Sir STANLEY EVERARD KELLETT, 6th *Baronet*, el. son of the late Francis Stanley Kellett, 2nd son of 3rd baronet; *b.* 1911; *s.* his kinsman *Sir* HENRY DE CASTRES, 1966: *m.* 1938, Audrey Margaret Phillips, and has issue.

Arms—Quarterly: 1st and 4th, argent, on a mount vert a boar passant sable, armed, bristled, and chained or *Kellett*; 2nd and 3rd, argent, a cross gules, in the first quarter a fleur-de-lis of the second, *Haddock*.   Crest—An armed arm proper, holding a truncheon or.

Residence,—33, Caroma Av., Kyeemagh, NSW

Son living—STANLEY CHARLES (47, May Rd., Dee Why, Sydney, NSW), *b.* March 5th, 1940: *m.* 1st, 1962 (m. diss. 1968), Lorraine May, da. of F. Winspear; 2ndly, 1968, Margaret Ann, da. of J. Bofinger.

Daughter living—Margaret Joy, *b.* 1942: *m.* 1963, Percival William Horton, of 78, Battye Av., Kogarah, NSW, 2217, and has issue living, Phillip William, *b.* 1967,—Colin Stanley, *b.* 1969,—Deborah Jane, *b.* 1964.

Brothers living—Charles Rex (26, Mutch Av., Kyeemagh, 2216, NSW), *b.* 1916: *m.* 1940, Florence Helen Bellamy, and has issue living, Maxwell Rex, (4, Daisy St., Roselands 2195, NSW), *b.* 1947; AASA: *m.* 1968, Jennifer, da. of N. Maher, and has issue living, Jane Maxine *b.* 1974,—Peter Charles, (18, Sirius St., Ruse 2560, NSW), *b.* 1949: *m.* 1973, Jennifer, da. of K. Pike, of W. Aust.,—Marilyn Helen, *b.* 1942: *m.* 1966, Bruce Malcolm Morgan, of 52, Endeavour St., Kentlyn 2560, NSW, and has issue living, Gavin Charles *b.* 1974, Karen Lee *b.* 1969, Joanne Lynne *b.* 1971. ——Ray Weaver (14, Mutch Av., Kyeemagh, 2216, NSW), *b.* 1916: *m.* 1940, Daisy Miriam Payne, and has issue living, Rev. John Raymond (183, Havannah St. Bathurst, 2795, NSW), *b.* 1942; ed. Univ. of NSW (BSc), and Melbourne Coll. of Divinity (BD): *m.* 1965, Sandra, da. of N. Holman, and has issue living, David John *b.* 1973, Michelle Ruth *b.* 1971,—Bruce Lawrence (10, Roy St., Belmore 2192, Sydney, NSW), *b.* 1945: *m.* 1969, Susan, da. of J. Butler, and has issue living, Bronwyn Jane *b.* 1973, Jacqueline Ruth *b.* 1975,—Graham Edward (3/3, Nelson St., Penshurst, NSW, 2222), *b.* 1948; BSc: *m.* 1970, Leonie, da. of R. Adams.

Sisters living—Greta Vessey, *b.* 1907: *m.* 1935, Albert Hector Bartrop, of 4/50, Rawson Av., Bealey, NSW, 2207.——Freda Gertrude (7/55, Banks St., Brighton le Sands, NSW), *b.* 1908.

Daughters living of 3rd Baronet—Myrtle Marcella, *b.* 1892: *m.* 1918, William Abel Gray, who *d.* 1955, and has issue living, John de Castres (of 12, St. Elmo St., Clifton Gdns., Sydney, NSW), *d.* 1924: *m.* 1951, Margaret Grace Connelley, and has issue living, Michael John *b.* 1952, Peter Andrew *b.* 1954, Robert William *b.* 1955, David Francis *b.* 1959, John Anthony *b.* 1963, Marianne *b.* 1957,—Joan de Castres, *b.* 1921: *m.* 1944, Francis Dale Mealey, of 37226, Emery Drive, Mount Clemens, USA, and has issue living, David William *b.* 1955, Jan Elizabeth *b.* 1950.   *Residence*, 3/12, Clifford St., Mosman, Sydney, NSW.——Doris, *b.* 1894.——Reenie Florence (Unit 2, 23 Ross St., Surrey Hills, Vic., Aust.), *b.* 1898: *m.* 1926, Herbert William Jones, who *d.* 1956, and has issue living, Shirley *b.* 1926: *m.* 1951, Terence Shircore, and has issue living, Mark Gregory *b.* 1953, Jan Maree *b.* 1955, Jill Penelope *b.* 1959, Amande Lee *b.* 1962.

Widow living of 5th Baronet—IDA MARY GRACE WEAVER (*Ida Lady Kellett*): *m.* 1952, Sir Henry de Castres Kellett, 5th Bt., who *d.* 1966.

Collateral Branch living.

   Issue of the late William Angustus Kellett, 3rd son of 3rd baronet, *b.* 1889, *d.* 1952: *m.* 1919, Janet Victoria, who *d.* 1936, da. of Andrew Peart:—
William Andrew Henry (5, Railway Parade, Glen Waverley, Victoria, Australia), *b.* 1920: *m.* 1945, Florence, da. of Leslie James Williamson, of Koornang Rd., Carnegie, Victoria, and has issue living, James Andrew, *b.* 1952,—Anne Louise, *b.* 1947,—Christine Elizabeth, *b.* 1950.

   This baronetcy was created with special remainder to the heirs male of Richard Kellett, of Lota, co. Cork, the father of the 1st baronet.   On the death of the 2nd baronet, Sir William, in 1886 the title passed (in accordance with the special remainder) to the descendants of the younger brother (Henry de Castres Kellett, *b.* 1776) of the 1st baronet, whose third son was Henry de Castres Kellett, father of Sir Henry de Castres Kellett, 3rd Bt. (for 40 years a Councillor of Kew, Melbourne.   He did not assume the title until 1906.   Sir Henry de Castres Kellett, 4th baronet, *d.* July 25th 1966.   His only son Sir Henry de Castres Kellett, 5th baronet, *d.* Aug. 6th 1966.

KEMP, Creation (E.) 1642, of Gissing, Norfolk. [Extinct 1936.]

Sir KENNETH HAGAR KEMP, *C.B.E.*, 12th and last *Baronet*.

Collateral Branch living.

   Issue of the late Capt. Robert Hamilton Kemp, only son of 12th baronet, *b.* 1877, *d.* 1933: *m.* 1908, Violet Mary, da. of the late Capt. R. C. Dalrymple Stewart-Muirhead, Roy. Horse Guards:—
Margaret Violet Nancy, *b.* 1910: *m.* 1932, Henry Richard Hurrell, of Kerry, Mappowder, Sturminster Newton, Dorset.——Peggy Isabelle, *b.* 1914: *m.* 1939, Major Richard Harold Arnaud Painter, Essex Regt., of Copse View, Huggler's Hole, Semley, Shaftesbury, Dorset, and has issue living, Richard Hamilton, *b.* 1947,—Gillian Mary, *b.* 1943.

KENNARD, Creation (U.K.) 1891, of Fernhill, co. Southampton.

Sir GEORGE ARNOLD FORD KENNARD, 3rd *Baronet*; *b.* April 27th, 1915; *s.* his brother, *Sir* LAURENCE URY Charles, 1967; ed. at Eton; Lt.-Col. (ret.) late Comdg. 4th Queen's Own Hussars; 1939-45 War (despatches twice, prisoner): *m.* 1st, 1940 (m. diss. 1958), Cecilia Violet Cokayne, only da. of Maj. Cecil John Cokayne Maunsel, JP; [see E. Munster, colls.]; 2ndly, 1958 (m. diss. 1974), Mrs. Molly Jesse Rudd Miskin, yr. da. of the late Hugh Wyllie, of Fishbourne, Sussex, and has issue by 1st m.

Arms— Per chevron gules and azure, a chevron engrailed argent between in chief two keys, wards downwards, or, and in base a sword erect proper, pommel and hilt or. **Crest**—A dexter cubit arm erect in armour proper, charged with a buckle gules, the hand grasping a key in bend or, and a broken sword in bend sinister proper.

At spes non fracta.

But hope is not broken.

Residence—Cogwell, Tiverton, Devon.　　*Club*—Cavalry.

Daughter living.—By 1st m.—Zandra, *b.* 1941: *m.* 1962, Maj. John Middleton Neilson Powell, Queen's R. Irish Hussars (c/o Barclays Bank, Marlborough, Wilts.), and has issue living, Edward Coleridge Cockayne, *b.* 1964,—Louise Cecilia, *b.* 1966.

Queen Victoria signified her intention of bestowing a Baronetcy upon Coleridge John Kennard but he having died before the patent was gazetted, the dignity was conferred on his grandson Coleridge Arthur FitzRoy Kennard, only child of the late Hugh Coleridge Downing Kennard.

KENNAWAY, Creation (G.B.) 1791, of Hyderabad, East Indies.

Sir JOHN LAWRENCE KENNAWAY, 5th *Baronet*; *b.* Sept. 7th, 1933; *s.* his father, *Sir* JOHN, 1956; ed. at Harrow, and at Trin. Coll., Camb.; patron of one living: *m.* 1961, Christina Urszenyi, M.B., Ch.B., and has issue.

Arms—Argent, a fesse azure between two eagles displayed in chief gules, and in base, through an annulet of the third, a slip of olive and another of palm in saltire proper. **Crest**—An eagle rising proper, from the beak an escutcheon pendent azure, charged with the sun in splendour also proper.

Seat—Escot, Ottery St. Mary, Devon.

Son living—JOHN MICHAEL, *b.* Feb. 17th, 1962.

Daughters living—Julia Frances, *b.* 1965,—Irma Annabelle, *b.* 1968.

Brother living—Richard Noel (19, MacMillan Av., Christchurch, NZ) *b.* 1935; ed. at Eton (King's Scholar) and at King's Coll., Camb. (Scholar); Sen. lecturer in Political Science.

Sister living—Mary Joyce, *b.* 1940.

Widow living of 4th Baronet—MARY FÉLICITÉ (*Mary, Lady Kennaway*), da. of the late Rev. Stewart Gordon Ponsonby [Buxton, Bt.]: *m.* 1931, Sir John Kennaway, 4th Bt., who *d.* 1956. *Residence*, Leat Cottage, Plymtree, Cullompton, Devon.

I shall ascend.

Collateral Branches living.

Granddaughter of the late Lieut.-Col. Charles William Kennaway, 2nd son of 2nd baronet :—
Issue of the late Major Charles Noel Kennaway, R.A., *b.* 1877, *d.* 1944: *m.* 1906, Florence Lucie, who *d.* 1966, da. of H. S. Poole, of Halifax, Nova Scotia :—
Monica Evelyn Tindal, *b.* 1910. *Residence*, Greenlaw, The Close, Wonersh, Guildford, Surrey.

Granddaughters of the late Rev. Richard Arthur Kennaway, 4th son of 2nd baronet :—
Issue of the late Mark John Kennaway, *b.* 1880, *d.* 1960 : *m.* 1920, Dorothy, who *d.* 1958, da. of the late Edward Hick, formerly of Chartridge, Chesham :—
Anne, *b.* 1922: *m.* 1946, Gerald Wardlaw Scott, BSc (Eng.), FIMech.E, FInst.Pet., of 15, Warren Av., Richmond, Surrey, and has issue living, Philip Wardlaw, *b.* 1950.—Deborah, *b.* 1948.—
Mary Elizabeth, *b.* 1924: *m.* 1948, Bernard Stratton Davis, OBE, Malayan Civil Ser. (ret.), and has issue living, Mark John Stratton, *b.* 1952,—Sarah Elizabeth, *b.* 1951,—Maroulla Judith, *b.* 1954. *Residence*, Blue House, Churchill Av., Kyrenia, Cyprus.—Philippa Jane, *b.* 1927: *m.* 1962, Alexander Keith Boyle, of 46, Manor View, Finchley, N3, and has issue living, David Kennaway, *b.* 1964,—Michael Kennaway, *b.* 1967,—Kirsteen Susan, *b.* 1965.——Susan Helen, *b.* 1928: *m.* 1966, John Reginald Whitley, of Kingsrod, Kingsley Green, Haslemere, Surrey, and has issue living, Elizabeth Rose, *b.* 1967.

Grandchildren of the late Rev. Charles Edward Kennaway, 2nd son of 1st baronet :—
Issue of the late Rev. Charles Lewis Kennaway, *b.* 1847; *d.* 1940: *m.* 1877, Edith Letitia, who *d.* 1932, da. of the late Charles Joseph Parke, of Henbury House, Wimborne, Dorset :—
Ruth Lettice : *m.* 1915, the Rev. Hugh Speke, Major Lancashire Fusiliers, who *d.* (killed in action) 1915. *Residence*, John's House, Spetisbury, Blandford.——Cicely Joan : *m.* 1st, 1908, Major Gerald Vernon Carter, 1st Dorsetshire Yeo., who *d.* 1937 ; 2ndly, 1956, Leonard Curtis Rawlence who *d.* 1957, and has issue living, (by 1st marriage) Barbara Joan (*Lady Willis*), *b.* 1910, *m.* 1st, 1936 (divorce 1948), Basil John Ringrose; 2ndly, 1959, the Hon. Mr. Justice (Sir John Ramsay) Willis, Q.C., of 1, Verulam Buildings, Grays Inn, WC1, and Waterfields, Snape, Saxmundham, Suffolk, and has issue living, (by 1st m.) Nigel John Carter (3, St. Michael's Gdns., Winchester, Hants.), *b.* 1938: *m.* 1963, Angela Hoyle, (and has issue living, Simon Nigel Olav *b.* 1964, Timothy John *b.* 1966, Amelia Angela Wendy *b.* 1966, Tamsin Alexandra *b.* 1972,)—Lavinia Mary *b.* 1920: *m.* 1945, Howard Lewis Brinsley Sheridan (Spyway Farm, Langton Matravers, Swanage, Dorset), and has issue living, Richard Brinsley *b.* 1945: *m.* 1970, Patricia

Warin, (and has issue livng, Richard Brinsley b. 1972), Rollo Hugh Motley b. 1951, Carol Lavinia Linley b. 1946: m. 1965, William George Lear Hewett, of Portsmouth, (and has issue living, Larissa Jane Linley b. 1967, Georgia Isabelle Davina b. 1968), Davina Jane b. 1953.

Grandson of the late Rev. Charles Lewis Kennaway (ante) :—
Issue of the late Charles Roger Kennaway, b. 1880, d. 1914: m. 1907, Margaret Evelyn, who d. 1917, da. of the Rev. Robert Bagot Chester Everard [B. Bagot, colls.] :—
Roger Charles Lewis, b. 1910; ed. at Harrow; Capt. late Oxfordshire and Bucks L.I. (Supplementary Reserve): m. 1st, 1936 (m. diss. 1947), Alethea Winifrede, da. of the late F. N. Lloyd; 2ndly, 1947, Pamela Lavender, da. of the late Lt.-Cdr. T. C. M. Bellairs, RN, and widow of Group-Capt. Patrick Bruce Bine Ogilvie, DSO, DFC [Renshaw, Bt., colls.], and has issue living, (by 1st m.) Roger Ian (Hafod, Glan Conwy, Colwyn Bay, Clwyd), b. 1938: ARICS: m. 1964, Gabrielle Mary Anna, da. of Lt.-Col. D. I. C. Tennant, of Bosham, Sussex, and has issue living, Charles Lewis b. 1966, Hugh Edward b. 1969, Anthony Francis b. 1973,—(by 2nd m.) Rose Margaret Ruth, b. 1949: m. 1970, Quintin Gerald Wyvern Batt, of Trebell Green Farm, Lanivet, Bodmin, Cornwall, and has issue living, Camilla Louise b. 1973. Residence, Reperry Manor Farm, Lanivet, Bodmin, Cornwall.

The 1st baronet, Sir John, in 1788 was appointed Resident at the Court of the Nizam, with whom, on the breaking out of the war with Tippoo Sultan, he concluded a treaty of alliance, for which service he was created a baronet. In 1792 he concluded treaties of peace between the allied powers and Tippoo, who ceded half his dominions and paid £3,300,000 to the Allies. The 3rd baronet, the Rt. Hon. Sir John Henry, P.C., C.B., sat as M.P. for Devonshire (C) 1870-85, and for Honiton Div. of Devonshire 1885-1910.

KENNEDY, Creation (U.K.) 1836, of Johnstown Kennedy, co. Dublin.

I adhere to virtue.

Sir DERRICK EDWARD DE VERE KENNEDY, 6th Baronet; b. June 5th, 1904; s. his cousin, Sir JAMES EDWARD, 1974; Maj. late R. Ulster Rifles; 1939-45 War: m. 1st, 1926 (m. diss. 1945), Phyllis Victoria, da. of the late Gordon Fowler; 2ndly, 1945, Barbara Mary, who d. 1959, da. of the late William Shepherd, and has issue by 1st m.

Arms—Sable, on a fesse between three esquires' helmets argent, a fox courant proper. Crest—A dexter arm embowed in armour, the hand grasping an oak-branch all proper.
Seat—Johnstown Kennedy, Rathcoole, Co. Dublin.

Sons living—By 1st m.—GEORGE RONALD DERRICK (c/o Lloyds Bank, Newbury); b. Nov. 19th, 1927: m. 1949, Noelle Mona, da. of Charles Henry Green, and has issue living, Michael Edward, b. 1956,—Carolyn Phyllis, b. 1950.——Mark Gordon, b. 1932.
Daughter living—By 1st m.—Julia Maureen Patricia, b. 1934: m. 1961, George Hector Miller, of Middle Chantry, Carter's Lane, Wickham Bishops, Essex, and has issue living, Rupert Leslie Derrick, b. 1965,—Katrina Phyllis Evelyn, b. 1962,—Rachel Susan, b. 1964,—Grania Sarah, b. 1968.
Collateral Branches living.

Granddaughter of the late Capt. Francis Kennedy, 4th son of 1st baronet:—
Issue of the late John Arthur Kennedy, b. 1858, d. 1913: m. 1881, Evelyn Maude, who d. 1921, da. of the late H. G. Bromilow, of Southport:—
Olive Eileen, b. 1889. Residence, 11, Fircroft Av., N. Lancing, Sussex.

Grandchildren of the late Robert Kennedy, 5th son of 1st baronet:—
Issue of the late Edward Robert Kennedy, b. 1860, d. 1925: m. 1905, Doris (now of Newcastle-Lyons, co. Dublin), da. of E. Lumsdaine, of Sydney, N.S. Wales :—
Robert, b. 1911: m. 1935, Catherine Frances, da. of the late Maj. Robert Gregory, of Coole Park, co. Galway, and has issue living, Robert Edward, b. 1940: m. 1969, Sandra Joan, da. of S. A. Giles, of W. Aust., and has issue living, Catherine b. 1972,—Benjamin James, b. 1942,—Susan, b. 1936: m. 1970, Wing Cdr. Ian Traill Sutherland, RAAF,—Margaret Jane b. 1937: m. 1964, Lt.-Col. David, A. R. Murray Brown, Queen's R. Irish Hussars, c/o Midland Bank, Lichfield, and has issue living, Robin David b. 1964, Belinda Jane b. 1966. Residence, Loughananna House, Kilbehenny, co. Limerick.——Percy William, b. 1914: m. 1936, Vivienne Gloria, da. of James O'Shea, and has issue living, William Roger, b. 1940: m. 1966, Vivienne Gloria, da. of James O'Shea, and has issue living, John Edward b. 1967, Darby James b. 1971,—Richard August, b. 1943,—Rosemary Ann Caroline, b. 1937: m. 1957, Allan Ross, of Irishtown, Rathfreigh, Tara, co. Meath,—Evelyn Geraldine Margaret, b. 1942,—Judith Patricia Wilhelmena, b. 1953. Residence, Weston Park, Leixlip, co. Dublin.——Sabia: m. 1929 (m. diss. 1953), the Hon. (Henry) Gerald Valerian Francis Wellesley [see E. Cowley].——Maeve: m. 1932, George John Robinson, who d. 1958, and has issue living, John Edward Bernard, b. 1933,—George William Richard (Stepaside, The Curragh, co. Kildare), b. 1934: m. 1964, Susan, da. of Maj. Cyril Hall, of Gilltown, Kilcullen, co. Kildare, and has issue living, Emma Jane Anna b. 1965, Lara Camilla Patricia b. 1969,—Bryan Patrick Valentine, b. 1940,—Mary Rose, b. 1936: m. 1961, Seamus Hayes,—Doris Teresa, b. 1943. Residence, Phepotstown, Kilcock, co. Meath.——Clodagh Rose (Countess of Roden); an Officer Sister of Order of St. John: m. 1937, the 9th Earl of Roden. Residence, Bryansford, co. Down.——Patricia: m. 1938, Dermot McGillycuddy, late Sqdn.-Ldr. RAFVR, who d. 1974, and has issue living, Dermot Patrick Donough (Nortoft Grange, Guilsborough, Northants), b. 1939; ed. at Eton, and City of Leicester Polytechnic (Diplo. Management Studies); late Lt. Irish Gds.: m. 1964, Wendy O'Connor, da. of the late George Spencer, JP, of Winwick Manor, Northants, and has issue living, Piers Donough Edward George b. 1965, Michael Dermot b. 1968, Jocelyn Patrick Spencer b. 1970, Lavinia O'Connor b. 1966. Residence, Bishopscourt, Staffan, co. Kildare.——Grania Geraldine: m. 1947 (m. diss. 1956), Capt. Edward de Lérisson Cazenove, late Coldm. Gds., and has issue living, Patrick Ralph de Lérisson b. 1947, Nicola Louise, b. 1949. Residence, Springhill, Killenaule, co. Tipperary.

Issue of the late Adm. Francis William Kennedy, C.B., b. 1862, d. 1939: m. 1898, Amy, who d. 1960, da. of Col. Henry Hills Goodeve, late R.A. :—
Francis Henry, b. 1900; Capt. RN (ret.); 1914-18 War: m. 1931, Magdalen Frances, da. of the late George FitzAdam-Ormiston, of Pockeridge Park, Wilts, and has issue living, Robert Francis, b. 1935; Maj. Irish Guards,—John Ormiston (17, Canons Close, Radlett, Herts.), b. 1938: m. 1969, Margaret Lee, of Frome, and has issue living, Christopher Patrick b. 1971, Annabel Margaret b. 1973,—Bridget, b. 1942. Residence, Tout Hill House, Shaftesbury.——Judith Eileen. Residence, 43, Crediton Hill, Hampstead, NW6.——Leila Emilie: m. 1936, Lieut.-Col. Cyril Gough Richards, late RA, who d. 1969, and has issue living, Michael Robert, b. 1946,—Caroline

Kennedy, b. 1937: m. 1960, Norman Peter Herbert of 3026, Montague St., Regina S4S 125, Sask., Canada, and has issue living, Andrew Mark b. 1963, David Neil b. 1965, Simon Paul b. 1972,—Georgina Kennedy, b. 1940: m. 1970, George Colgan, of 23, Brillee St., Waterman 6020, W. Aust., and has issue living, Nicola Elizabeth b. 1974. Residence, 27, Churchill Cres., Sheringham, Norfolk.

Sir John Kennedy, 1st Bt. was great grandson of Darby O'Kennedy of Ballikeiroge Castle, co Waterford.

KIMBER, Creation (U.K.) 1904, of Lansdowne Lodge, Wandsworth, co. London.

You may break, but you shall not bend me.

FRANGAS NON FLECTES

Sir CHARLES DIXON KIMBER, 3rd *Baronet;* b. Jan 7th, 1912; s. his father, *Sir* HENRY DIXON 1950; ed. at Eton, and at Balliol Coll., Oxford (B.A. 193–): m. 1st, 1933, Ursula (who obtained a divorce 1950), da. of the late Ernest Roy Bird, M.P.; 2ndly, 1950, (m. diss. 1965), Margaret only da. of Francis John Bonham, of 13, Dudley Rd., Wimbledon, SW, and has issue by 1st and 2nd marriages.

Arms—Argent, a torteau between three choughs proper, on a chief engrailed gules, three estoiles of the first. Crest— A bull's head cabossed sable horned argent, between the horns an estoile or.

Residence—2, Duxford, Hinton Waldrist, Faringdon, Oxon.

Sons living—By 1st marriage—TIMOTHY ROY HENRY, b. June 3rd, 1936; ed. at Eton: m. 1960 (m. diss. 19—), Antonia Kathleen Brenda, da. of Sir Francis John Watkin Williams, 8th Bt., QC, (cr. 1798), and has issue living, Rupert Edward Watkin, b. 1962,—Hugo Charles, b. 1964.—— Nicholas John, b. 1937; ed. at Eton.——Robert, b. 1941: m. 1964, Carolyn Evelyn Garth, da. of Frederick Griffiths-Jones, of Beacon Wood, Penn, Bucks., and has issue living, Jane Guthrie, b. 1967,—Amanda, b. 1969.

Daughter living—By 2nd marriage—Rhys Catherine, b. 1951.

Sister living—Audrey Patricia (Delamere, Mount Boone, Dartmouth), b. 1913.

Half-Sisters living—Ella Florence Irene, b. 1903.——Helen Margaret, b. 1907: m. 1933, Richard Harrington Franklin, CBE, FRCS, MB, BS, and has issue living, Richard Kimber, b. 1936,— Peter James, b. 1948. Residence, Wolsey House, 4, Montpelier Row, Twickenham, Middlesex.

Collateral Branches living.

Issue of the late Percy Dixon Kimber, 3rd son of 1st baronet, b. 1867, d. 1952: m. 1892, Janet Margaret, who d. 1943, da. of the late William Mackenzie, of Cramond, Natal :—

Guy Mackenzie (7, Clarendon Rd., PO Box 60, Howick, 3290, S. Africa), b. 1899: m. 1926, Ellen Elizabeth Margaret, da. of the late Rev. J. Jardine-Lockhart, of Paignton, Devon, and has issue living, David Percy (of Maritzdaal, Dargle, Natal), b. 1930: m. 1953, Elizabeth Mary Paterson, da. of Tom Paterson Owens, CBE, of Weybridge, Surrey, and has issue living, Richard Guy b. 1956, Christopher David b. 1961, Jeannet Elizabeth b. 1954, Georgina Louise b. 1957,—Michael Jardine (Selsley, Dargle, Natal), b. 1932: m. 1957, Mary Elizabeth, da. of the late J. A. Dales, of Pietermaritzburg, Natal, and has issue living, James Michael b. 1958, Guy Barrington b. 1962, Kathryn Mary b. 1966.

Grandchildren of the late Walter Dixon Kimber (infra) :—

Issue of the late Eric Dixon Kimber, b. 1898, d. 1956: m. 1926, Gwendolen Isa Dow (of Greytown, Natal), da. of the late Lawrence C. French, High Trees, Godalming:—

Anthony Dixon (of Greytown, Natal) b. 1927: m. 1957, Joan Lilian Patterson, and has issue living, Brett, b. 1960,—Erica-Jane, b. 1959.——Roger Dixon, b. 1929: m. 1957, Sandra, da. of Leslie Guy Gold, M.C., of Sussex House, 35, Sussex Place, W.2, and has issue living Richard Orlando Dixon, b. 1957,—Eric Guy Piers, b. 1961,—Catherine Miranda, b. 1959. Residence, Berwyn, 2, Osten Mews, Kensington, S.W.7.——Winifred Margaret, b. 1930: m. 1959, Lawrence Kevin Tonkin, MB, BS, of 10, Nelson St., Woollahra, Sydney, NSW, and has issue living, Lawrence Eric, b. 1963,—Shauna Kerry, b. 1960.

Issue of the late Walter Dixon Kimber, 4th son of 1st baronet, b. 1869, d. 1916: m. 1897, Florence, da. of John Brown, of Natal, and widow of T. J. Holmden:—

Allan Dixon (101, Berea Park Rd., Durban, Natal) b. 1903: m. 1st 1939 (m. diss 1959) Daphne Mary, da. of Richard Guy Chaloner Ogle, of Natal; 2ndly, 1964, Sylvia Margaret, da. of the late Garnet Edwin Driver, solicitor, of Natal, and has issue living, (by 1st m.), Daphne Jane, b. 1940: m. 1st, 1964, (m. diss. 1966), John Campbell, of Natal; 2ndly, 1968, Peter Glen Cox, of Kloof, Natal, and has issue living, (by 1st m.) Paula Catherine b. 1965, (by 2nd m.) Glen Alexander Marc b. 1969, Michael Piers b. 1970, Joshua Richard Alan b. 1971,—Susan Mary, b. 1942: m. 1963, George Desmond Fairfoot, of Iron Latch Cottage, Selsey, Sussex, and has issue living, Samuel Christian b. 1964, Thomas Jason b. 1968, Matthew Adam b. 1969,—Nancy Florence, b. 1946.—— Joyce Dixon (2, Westcliff Drive, Westcliff, Johannesburg), b. 1900: m. 1924, John George William Stevens, who d. 1963, and has issue living, Lovell John (of Mohales Hoek, Lesotho), b. 1929: m. 1953, Olga Mary, da. of Douglas Henry Dare, OBE, of Yarningdale, Marine Parade, Durban, and has issue living, Ann Louise b. 1954, Pamela Jean b. 1956,—June Ruth, b. 1926: m. 1953, Peter August Illing, of 15, Loch Av., Parktown, Johannesburg, S. Africa, and has issue living, Jeremy August b. 1957, Peter Anthony b. 1958, Virginia Ruth b. 1954.——Evelyn Dixon, b. 1911: m. 1936, John Pillinger, of Hilton Rd., Natal, and has issue living, William John, b. 1942: m. 1967, Robyn, da. of Alfred Richardson, of Morden, Surrey, and has issue living, Samantha Ann b. 1969, Justine Eve b. 1971,—Simon Dixon, b. 1945,—Patricia Jill, b. 1937: m. 1963, Peter Bannatyne, of 126, Burnside Rd., PO Hillside, Bulawayo, Rhodesia, and has issue living, Roger Edward b. 1968.

The 1st baronet, Sir Henry, founded the legal firm of Kimber and Ellis, and sat as the first MP for Wandsworth (C) 1885-1913. The 2nd baronet, Sir Henry Dixon, was Ch. Commoner, City of London 1919, and Senior Partner in the legal firm of Kimber, Williams, Sweetland & Stinson.

KING, Creation (U.K.) 1815, of Charlestown, Roscommon.

Sir WAYNE ALEXANDER KING, 8th *Baronet*; *b.* Feb. 2nd, 1962; *s.* his father, *Sir* PETER ALEXANDER, 1973.

Arms—Sable, a lion rampant double queued or. **Crest**—An escallop gules.

Residence—Charlestown, 365, London Rd., Upper Deal, Deal, Kent.

Spes tutissima cœlis.

Our safest hope is in Heaven.

Sister living—Dorothy Jane *b.* 1964.
Great-Aunt living—Grace: *m.* 1915, Maj. Reginald Taylor, RM, and has issue living, Frank Reginald Alexander D., *b.* 1919; Lt.-Col. (ret.) RM: *m.* 1951, Jennifer, da. of Hugh H. Munro, of Chile, and has issue living, Jeremy King *b.* 1959. *Residence*, Burkitt House, Alphington Rd., Exeter.
Daughter living of 4th Baronet—Mary Rowley (Bridport Private Hotel, Stocker Rd., Bognor Regis): *m.* 1932, James King-Currie.
Widow living of 7th Baronet—JEAN MARGARET (*Lady King*), (Charlestown, 365, London Rd., Upper Deal, Kent), da. of Christopher Thomas Cavell, of Deal: *m.* 1957, Sir Peter Alexander King, 7th Bt., who *d.* 1973;

Collateral Branch living.
Issue of the late Douglas James King, brother of 6th baronet, *b.* 1895, *d.* 1962: *m.* 1913, Dorothy Aylett, da. of C. Collins:—
Zena Dorothy, *b.* 1915: *m.* 1932.

KING, Creation (U.K.) 1888, of Campsie, Stirlingshire.

Honour is the reward of industry.

Sir JAMES GRANVILLE LE NEVE KING, T.D., 3rd *Baronet*; *b.* Sept. 17th, 1898; *s.* his father, *Sir* JOHN WESTALL, 1940; ed. at Eton, and at King's Coll., Camb.; formerly Major 99th (Bucks and Berks Yeo.) Field Brig. R.A. (T.A.): *m.* 1928 Penelope Charlotte, da. of the late Capt. Edmund Moore Cooper Cooper-Key, C.B., M.V.O., R.N. [Wigram, Bt.. colls.], and has issue.

Arms—Azure, on a fesse argent between a lion's head erased or in chief, and two billets of the third in base, three roundbuckles of the field. **Crest**—A redbreast proper.

Residence—The Old Vicarage, King's Somborne, Hants. *Clubs*, Brooks's, Travellers'.

Son living—JOHN CHRISTOPHER, *b.* March 31st, 1933. ed. at Eton: *m.* 1958 (m. diss. 1972), Patricia Monica, only da. of the late Lieut.-Col. Kingsley Osbern Nugent Foster DSO, OBE, and has issue living, James Henry Rupert, *b.* 1961,—Melanie Avril, *b.* 1963. *Residence*, Edwins Hall, Woodham Ferrers, Essex.

Daughters living—Susan Penelope, *b.* 1929: *m.* 1957, Christopher Marsden-Smedley, and has issue living, Timothy Charles, *b.* 1959,—Philip John, *b.* 1961,—Catherine Penelope, *b.* 1964. *Residence*, Church Farm, Burrington, Somerset.——Diana Bridget, *b.* 1935: *m.* 1957, Francis Hoare [E. Coventry], and has issue living, James Alexander, *b.* 1959,—Edward Eustace, *b.* 1961,—Richard Francis, *b.* 1967,—Arabella Peggy Marian, *b.* 1968. *Residence*, West Bergholt Hall, Colchester.

Brother living—John Alastair, *b.* 1905; ed. at Eton, and at Trin. Coll., Camb.: *m.* 1st, 1929 (m. diss. 1939), Veronica Mary, da. of the late Col. Bertram Abel Smith, DSO, MC; 2ndly, 1939 (m. diss. 1956), Ruby Enid. da. of the late George C. Atkinson-Clark; 3rdly, 1957, Pierina Holt, and has issue living, (by 1st m.) Rhona Lavinia, *b.* 1932,—(by 2nd m.) Elisabeth Jane, *b.* 1941,—(by 3rd m.) Sarah Rosemary, *b.* 1959. *Residence*, Downs Farmhouse, Baunton, Cirencester, Glos.

Sister living—Margaret Westall, *b.* 1902: *m.* 1930, Capt. Ewen Aymer Robert Ramsay-Fairfax-Lucy, who *d.* 1969, [*see* Ramsay-Fairfax-Lucy, Bt. colls.]. *Residence*, Bryhers, West Broyel Drive, Chichester, Sussex.

Sir James King, 1st baronet (son of John King, of Campsie, co. Stirling, a merchant of Glasgow), was Lord Provost of Glasgow 1886-89. He received Queen Victoria on her visit to Glasgow in 1888.

King (Stafford-King-Harman), see Harman.

DUCKWORTH-KING, Creation (G.B.) 1792, of Bellevue, Kent. [Extinct 1972.]

Sir JOHN RICHARD DUCKWORTH-KING, 7th and last *Baronet*.

Daughters living of 6th Baronet—Anne Eva Katharine *b.* 1915: *m.* 1940 Christopher Willoughby Jardine, CB, and has issue living, Theresa Barbara Lettice (62, Gassiot Way, Sutton, Surrey), *b.* 1942: *m.* 1961 (m. diss. 1973), Anthony Harold Hazell, and has issue living, James Christopher *b.* 1962, Deborah Anne *b.* 1963,—Victoria Agnes, *b.* 1945: *m.* 1968, Peter Nicholas Christian Bordewich, of 116, Hemingford Rd., N1, and has issue living, Luke George Batchelor *b.* 1974,— Cassandra Caroline Mary, *b.* 1954. *Residence*, 8, St. Loo Court, St. Loo Av., Chelsea, SW3.—— Caroline Agnes (16, Culford Mansions, Culford Gdns., SW3), *b.* 1916.

Sister living—Violet Caroline DUCKWORTH-BRADSHAW, *b.* 1894; assumed by deed poll 1950, enrolled at College of Arms, the additional surname of Duckworth before that of Bradshaw : *m.* 1920, Major Cecil Bradshaw, formerly The Queen's Bays (2nd Dragoon Guards), who *d.* 1949, and has issue living, Dudley Cecil, *b.* 1921,—John Duckworth, *b.* 1929,—Valerie Mary, *b.* 1933. *Residence*, Bystock, near Exmouth.

Widows living of 6th and 7th Baronets—BARBARA MADALEN JEAN (*Barbara, Lady Duckworth-King*), da. of the late Hugh James Elibank Scott Makdougall, of Eastcote House, Eastcote, Middlesex [Johnstone, Bt., colls.], *m.* 1915, Maj. Sir George Henry James Duckworth-King, 6th Bt., who *d.* 1952. *Residence*, 16, Culford Mansions, Culford Gardens, SW3.——ALICE PATRICIA (*Lady Duckworth-King*), (47, Avenue de Hassan 11, Tangier, Morocco), da. of Thomas Rutledge, of Fugar House, Ravensworth, co. Durham; *m.* 1943, as his 2nd wife Sir John Richard Duckworth-King, 7th Bt., who *d.* 1972, when the title became ext.

KINLOCH, Creation (N.S.) 1686, of Gilmerton, East Lothian.

I aspire higher.

ALTIUS TENDO

Sir ALEXANDER DAVENPORT KINLOCH, 12th *Baronet ; b.* Sept. 17th, 1902 ; *s.* his father, *Brig.-Gen. Sir* DAVID ALEXANDER, *C.B., M.V.O.,* 1944 ; ed. at Eton ; Major Grenadier Guards ; is a Member of Queen's Body Guard for Scotland (Roy. Co. of Archers) : *m.* 1st, 1929, Alexandra (who obtained a divorce 1945), da. of Frederick Y. Dalziel, of New York, USA ; 2ndly, 1946 (mar. diss. 1965), Hilda Anna, da. of the late Thomas Walker, of Edinburgh ; 3rdly, 1965, Ann, da. of Group-Capt. F. L. White, and has issue by 1st, 2nd and 3rd marriages.

Arms—Azure, a boar's head erased between three mascles or. **Crest**—An eagle rising proper. *Seat*—Gilmerton House, North Berwick, East Lothian. *Clubs*—White's, New (Edinburgh).

Sons living—By 2nd m.—DAVID, *b.* Aug. 5th, 1951 ; ed. at Gordonstoun.——By 3rd m.—James Alexander, *b.* 1967.

Daughters living—By 1st marriage—Emily Lucy (*Hon. Mrs. Hugh W. Astor*), *b.* 1930 : *m.* 1950, the Hon. Hugh Waldorf Astor [*see* B. Astor of Hever]. *Residence*, Folly Farm, Sulhamstead, Berks.——Jean Alexandra, *b.* 1934.—— By 2nd m.—Victoria, *b.* 1947.——Harriet, *b.* 1949 : *m.* 1967, Colin John Weddell, of Snowdon, Gifford, E . Lothian, and has issue living, Jennifer Katherine Graham, *b.* 1968.—— Ann (twin), *b.* 1951.

Collateral Branches living.

Issue of the late Francis Kinloch, 3rd son of 10th baronet, *b.* 1863, *d.* 1916 : *m.* 1896, Marion Eva, da. of the late Charles Nairne Marshall, of Curriehill, New Zealand :— Marjorie Catherine, *b.* 1896 : *m.* 1st, 1919,— Allan ; 2ndly, 1933, as his second wife, Major Cecil Anderson Boyd, M.C., M.D., late R.A.M.C., who *d.* 1942 [*see* Boyd, Bt., cr. 1916]. *Address*, Rural Route 3, Vernon, British Columbia.—— Lucy Margaret, *b.* 1899.

Granddaughter of the late Charles Henry Alexander Frederick Camillo Everard John James Rocheid, great-grandson of Alexander Kinloch (who assumed the surname of Rocheid), 4th son of 3rd baronet:— Issue of the late Colin William Hilmar Otto Rocheid, *b.* 1881, *d.* 1954 : *m.* 1st, 1911, Elizabeth, who *d.* 1935, da. of the late Ernst von Schröder ; 2ndly, 1942, Catherine Jung, who *d.* 1959 :—

(By 1st marriage) Elisabeth Marie Olga Harriet Ernestine, *b.* 1912: *m.* 1936, Capt. Joachim von Sametzki, who *d.* 1946. *Residence*, Hartwicusstrasse 196, Hamburg, 22, Germany.

The 1st baronet, Sir Francis Kinloch (son of Andrew Kinloch, merchant of Rochelle), was Lord Provost of Edinburgh. The 10th Baronet, Capt. Sir Alexander Kinloch, Grenadier Guards, served in Crimea 1854-5. The 11th Baronet, Brig.-Gen. Sir David Alexander Kinloch, CB, MVO, served with Grenadier Guards in S. Africa 1899-1902, and in European War 1914-19.

KINLOCH, Creation (U.K.) 1873, of Kinloch, co. Perth.

Not degenerate.

Sir JOHN KINLOCH, 4th *Baronet;* b. Nov. 1st, 1907; *s.* his father, Sir GEORGE, O.B.E., 1948; ed. at Charterhouse, and at Magdalene Coll., Camb. : *m.* 1934, Doris Ellaline, el. da. of the late Charles Joseph Head, of 24, Imber Close, Esher, Surrey, and has issue.

Arms—Quarterly; 1st, grand quarter azure, a boar's head erased between three mascles or, a crescent of the second in chief for difference, *Kinloch;* 2nd, grand quarter gules, a chevron embattled between three crescents argent, *Oliphant;* 3rd, grand quarter parted per fesse argent and sable, a chevron between three cinquefoils counter-changed, *Balneavis;* 4th, grand quarter counter-quartered; 1st, gules, a broken spear and a standard saltireways argent, the last charged with a cross of the field and fringed or; 2nd, azure, a cat salient argent; 3rd, argent, on a saltire sable nine mascles of the first within a bordure azure; 4th, or, three bars wavy gules, each charged with an escallop of the field, all *Smyth.* **Crest**—A young eagle perched, looking up to the sun in his splendour all proper.

Residence—Northlands, Warnham, Horsham, Sussex.

Son Living—DAVID OLIPHANT (c/o Cathay Securities Ltd., Hong Kong) b. Jan. 15th, 1942; ed. at Charterhouse; CA: *m.* 1968, Susan Minette, yst. da. of Maj.-Gen. Robert Elliott Urquhart, CB, DSO, and has issue living, Katherine Cecilia, b. 1972,—Emily Nicole, b. 1974.

Daughters living—Susan Cecilia, b. 1935: *m.* 1960, Malcolm Henry Rogers, of 17, Mapledene Rd., Scone, New Perth, Perthshire, and has issue living, John Andrew, b. 1965,—Wendy Diana, b. 1962.——Diana Evelyne, b. 1940: *m.* 1960, William Stewart Addis, son of Sir William Addis, KBE, CMG, and has issue living, William Dickson, b. 1962,—Sarah Diana, b. 1963,—Madelaine Rosemary, b. 1968. *Address*, c/o Hongkong & Shanghai Banking Corporation, Hong Kong.

Sister living—Barbara Cecilia, b. 1913: *m.* 1937, Charles Gairdner Dalrymple Tennant, Maj. late RASC, and has issue living, Thomas Peregrine, b. 1939; Lt. RN (ret.): *m.* 1972, Finella Susan, da. of Geoffrey Hooper,—Edward Kinloch, b. 1943,—Tanera Cecilia, b. 1940: *m.* 1962, Michael Charles Averdieck, of Byfield Cottage, Bythorn, Hunts. and has issue living, William John b. 1963, Charles Edward b. 1965, James Ulric (twin) b. 1965,—Victoria Margaret, b. 1950. *Residence*, Cruivie, Rosemount, Blairgowrie, Perthshire.

Collateral Branch living.

Issue of the late James Kinloch, 2nd son of 2nd baronet, b. 1884, d. 1950: *m.* 1909, Julia Madeline, who d. 1962, da. of the late George W. Boase, of Broughty Ferry:—

Colin David (26, Curtis Rd., Ashdell Park, Alton, Hants.), b. 1918; a Chartered Engineer: *m.* 1945, Gertrude L. M., da. of E. R. Bollom, and has issue living, Nigel George, b. 1951,—Bridget Eleanor Mary, b. 1948.——Sheila Maysie, b. 1910: *m.* 1938, Brigadier Arthur Catchmay Tyler, CBE, MC, late Welch Regt., and has issue living, Richard Hugh (c/o Williams & Glyn's, 22, Whitehall, SW1), b. 1939; Capt. R. Regt. of Wales: *m.* 1963, Suzan Gaynor, da. of Lt.-Col. Sam. Griffith, OBE, and has issue living, Christopher Charles Griffith, b. 1965, Nicholas Hugh Griffin b. 1966,—Andrew James, b. 1950,—John Philip, b. 1951,—Mary Joyce, b. 1941: *m.* 1966, Bruce George Draper, of 25, Odenwald Rd., Eaglemont, Vic. 3084, Aust., and has issue living, Jeremy Charles Bruce b. 1971, Catherine Louise b. 1969. *Residence*, 24, Sandy Lane, Cheam, Surrey.——Elspeth, b. 1912: *m.* 1938, Lt.-Cdr. Malcolm David Wanklyn, VC, DSO (two Bars), RN, who d. (killed in action in the Mediterranean) 1942, and has issue living, Ian David Kinloch (c/o National Westminster Bank, Bexhill-on-Sea, Sussex), b. 1939, Lt.-Cdr. RN: *m.* 1971, Penelope, el. da. of Capt. Charles Wickham Malins, DSO, DSC, RN. *Residence*, 31, Wealden Way, Bexhill-on-Sea.——Isla Florence, b. 1915. *Residence*, 31, Wealden Way, Bexhill-on-Sea.

The lands of Kinloch of that Ilk were situated at the head of Rossie Loch, Fifeshire, of which family charters date from 1210, but were sold in the 16th century. David Kinloch, physician and traveller, a descendant of this line, acquired lands in Perthshire which were erected into the Barony of Kinloch temp. James VI. His grandson, Sir David Kinloch of that Ilk was created a baronet 1685, said to have been with remainder to his heirs male whatsoever though no record exists in the Great Seal Register. Sir James Kinloch, 3rd Baronet, took part in the 1745 rising, was tried and condemned to death, and the baronetcy became forfeited, but having escaped to France was subsequently pardoned. His son William, who d.s.p., sold Kinloch to his kinsman, Capt. George Oliphant Kinloch (grandson of James, yr. brother of 1st baronet), whose son George Kinloch of Kinloch fled to France as an outlaw 1819 for advocating reform, but in 1832 was el. M.P. for Dundee. His son, Sir George Kinloch, was the 1st Baronet of the present creation.

KIRKPATRICK, Creation (N.S.) 1685, of Closeburn, Dumfriesshire.

Sir IVONE ELLIOTT KIRKPATRICK, 11th *Baronet;* b. Oct. 1st, 1942; *s.* his father, Sir JAMES ALEXANDER, 1954; ed. at Wellington Coll., and at St. Mark's Coll. Univ. Adelaide.

Arms—Argent, a saltire and chief azure, the last charged with three cushions or. **Crest**—A hand holding a dagger in pale, distilling drops of blood. **Supporters**—Two talbot hounds argent. *Address*—c/o ANZ Banking Group, Ltd., 32, Grenfell St., Adelaide, S. Aust. 5000.

Brother living—ROBIN ALEXANDER, b. March 19th, 1944; ed. at Wellington Coll.

Mother living—Ellen Gertrude, only da. of Capt. R. P. Elliott, late R.N.R.: *m.* 1st, 1941, Sir James Alexander Kirkpatrick, 10th Bt., who d. 1954, and from whom she had obtained a divorce 1953; 2ndly, 1955, John Ogilvie Corbin, MB, BS, FRCS.

Collateral Branches living.

Granddaughters of the late Charles William Sharpe Kirkpatrick, 4th son of 6th baronet:—
Issue of the late Thomas Stripling Kirkpatrick, b. 1867, d. 1937: m. 1903, Amy Louisa, who d. 1962, da. of Walter Norris:—
Grace Amy May, b. 1905: m. 1926, William Henry Williams, and has issue living, Derek Henry (of 44, Ammersham Av., Paddonhurst, Bulawayo, Rhodesia), b. 1929: m. 1953, Kathleen Elizabeth Knipe, and has issue living, Peter Duncan b. 1956, Paul Arnold b. 1957, Margaret Ann b. 1959,—Olive Amy, b. 1932: m. 1954, John Faulding Sissison, of 16, Willow Way, Pinelands, Cape Province, S. Africa, and has issue living, Michael Faulding b. 1959, Noel Faulding b. 1961,— Janet Ann, b. 1943: m. 1960, Roger Stewart Johnson, and has issue living, Susan Barbara b. 1960 Shirley Catherine b. 1961.

Grandchildren of the late Thomas Frederick Kirkpatrick (infra):—
Issue of the late Leslie Maurice Kenneth Kirkpatrick, b. 1925, d. 1962: m. 1948, Rose Lillian May (26, Brunel Rd., Luton, Beds. LU4 ORX), da. of the late Frederick George Walker:—
David Christopher, b. 1950.——Paul Anthony, b. 1953.——Stephen Robert b. 1960.——Maureen Ann b. 1952.

Grandchildren of the late Charles Bartram Kirkpatrick (b. 1873) (infra):—
Issue of the late Thomas Frederick Kirkpatrick, b. 1894, d. (on active ser.) 1940: m. 1920, Mabel who d. 1971, da. of the late John James Childs:—
Beryl (4 Foster Drive, Bodmin, Cornwall), b. 1920: m. 1941, Stanley R. Fairbrass, and has issue living, Alan, b. 1942,—Brian Malcolm, b. 1944,—Melvyn Denis, b. 1948,—Geoffrey, b. 1950,— Keith Anthony, b. 1958.

Issue of the late Charles Bartram Kirkpatrick, b. 1899, d. 1936: m. 1921, Lillian (who m. 2ndly, 1950, George Albert May, of 63, The Fairway, Bickley, Bromley, Kent), da. of Samuel Charles Podd:—
Charles Bartram, b. 1922: m. 1944, Winifred Rosa, da. of George Gaffney, and has issue living, Charles Bartram (49, Norheads Lane, Biggin Hill, Kent) b. 1945: m. 1967, Angela Mary, da. of Sidney Ernest MacClaren Dooley, and has issue living, Paul Charles b. 1972. Residence, 16, Foyle Drive, South Ockendon, Essex.——Donald, b. 1934.——Edna Florence, b. 1924: m. 1946, Henry Crook, of Kelsey, 30, Hillcrest Rd., Cam berley, Surrey, and has issue living, John David, b. 1951,—Hilary June, b. 1955.——Lilian, b. 1926: m. 1945, Sydney Thew, and has issue living, Sydney Charles, b. 1946,—Colin James, b. 1947,—Robert John, b. 1948,—Donald Patrick, b. 1950,—Michael Allan, b. 1952. Residence, Bali H., 8, Natasha St., Wynnum West, Brisbane, Queensland.

Issue of the late James Arthur Kirkpatrick, b. 1902, d. 1935: m. 1929, Ruby, da. of Charles Heat, of Brixton, S.W.:—
Barbara, b. 1931. Residence,

Grandson of Charles William Sharpe Kirkpatrick (ante):—
Issue of the late Charles Bartram Kirkpatrick, b. 1873, d. 1944: m. 1893, Helena Sarah Riches, who d. 1936, da. of William Minns, of Peckham, S.E.:—
Sydney Frank, b. 1912; late Flying Officer R.A.F. Vol. Reserve; 1939-45 War as Flight-Sergeant R.A.F. (Belgian Croix de Guerre with Palm): m. 1943, Margaret Elizabeth Cowell, and has issue living, Valerie, b. 1946; BA,—Sandra Kirkpatrick, b. 1953: m. 1974, Stephen Gent, of 32, Thompson Rd., Brighton, Sussex. Residence, 23, Grange Rd., Orpington, Kent.

Grandson of the late Robert Herries Kirkpatrick, 5th son of 6th baronet:—
Issue of Wallace Herries Kirkpatrick, b. 1886, d. 1967: m. 1920, Lilian Ivy (Closeburn, The Park, Mitcham, Surrey), da. of the late Walter Oughton Hill:—
Wallace Bruce (Duke's Lodge, Alresford Rd., Winchester), b. 1921; late Lt. N. Staffs. Regt.: m. 1946, Irene Sylvia, da. of the late Harold Victor Colls, and has issue living, Scott Herries (Pentons, Chilbolton, Stockbridge, Hants.), b. 1947: m. 1970, Sandra Jean, da. of Leonard Arthur Charles Hall, and has issue living, Gavin James b. 1972, Victoria Jane b. 1974,—Gavin Bruce, b. 1951 (The New Bungalow, Bradley, Alresford, Hants.), b. 1951: m. 1973, Linda, da. of William Prosser, of Llandrindod Wells.

Grandchildren of the late Dep. Surg.-Gen. James Kirkpatrick, MD, son of the late Roger Kirkpatrick (b. 1779), 2nd son of 4th baronet :—
Issue of the late Maj.-Gen. Charles Kirkpatrick, C.B. C.B E.. b. 1879, d. 1955 : m. 1909, Elsie Isobel, who d. 1970, da. of the late Herbert John Hamilton Fasson, ICS:—
Herbert James, CB, CBE, DFC (Rectory Hill Cottage, East Bergholt, Colchester, CO7 6TH), b. 1910; ed. at Cheltenham, and at Trin. Coll., Oxford (MA); Air Vice-Marshal RAF (ret.); 1939-45 War (despatches twice, DFC, CBE); CBE (Mil.) 1945, CB (Mil.) 1957: m. 1937, Pamela Evelyn Darvill, da. of the late Lt.-Col. H. D. Watson, Indian Army (ret.), and has issue living, Roger Hugh (2, Victoria Cottages, Sandycombe Rd., Kew Gdns., Surrey), b. 1939: m. 1965, Julia Margaret, da. of John W. Mortimore, of Broadstone, Dorset and has issue living, Amanda Dorothy b. 1964, Julian Gwinell b. 1966, Dustin John b. 1971,—Christopher Charles, b. 1948,—Elizabeth Elizabeth, da. of Patrick Johnston, of Guildford, Surrey, and has issue living, Jeremy Mark b. 1964, Julian Gwinell b. 1966, Dustin John b. 1971,—Christopher Charles, b. 1948,—Elizabeth Susan, b. 1942: m. 1966, Fl.-Lt. Kenneth A. D. Evans, RAF (c/o Lloyds Bank, 6, Pall Mall, SW1), and has issue living, Nicholas Christopher b. 1966, Rebecca Kate b. 1968,—Grizelda Jean (twin), b. 1948: m. 1st, 1967, Hugh John Allen; 2ndly, 1974, Alan Graham Stuck, of 14, Archery Steps, Albion St., W2, and has issue living (by 1st m.), Jonathan Spencer b. 1968.——Hilda May BUTLER (Ashdean, Whiteparish, Salisbury), b. 1920: m. 1st, 1940, Maj. James Michael Jourdier, E. Surrey Regt.; 2ndly, 1954, David Arthur Yellowlees; 3rdly, Brian Butler, and has issue living, (by 1st m.) Anthony Maxwell Kirkpatrick, b. 1946: m. 1974, Cecilia Maye, da. of Lt.-Col. R. A. Conner, of Maldon, Essex,—Avril Patricia, b. 1947: m. 1969, John Hamish Carysfort Loch, of Monksford Cottage, St. Boswells, Roxburghshire, and has issue living, Rupert John Carysfort b. 1970, Rosalind Cecilia Carysfort b. 1972.

Grandchildren of the late Dep. Surg.-Gen. James Kirkpatrick, M.D. (ante):—
Issue of the late James Ivone Kirkpatrick, C.A., b. 1866, d. 1918 : m. 1905, Elizabeth Margaret, who d. 1959, da. of David Thomson, of Edinburgh :—
Ivone (Knockhill, Fort Grey, East London, S. Africa (PO Box 5031, Greenfields, East London, S. Africa), b. 1907; ed. at Edinburgh Acad., and Edinburgh Univ.; WS 1933; 1939-45 War as Group-Capt. AuxAF: m. 1936, Ruth, da. of the late W. R. Peterson, of East London, S. Africa, and has issue living, Ivone William (58, 10th St., Parkhurst, Johannesburg, S. Africa), b. 1944: a Co. Dir.: m. 1967, Velia Elizabeth Mignon, da. of John Hartdegan, of Parys, Orange Free State, and has issue living, Sean Roger b. 1968, Anne Margaret b. 1971.——Margaret Jean (Easter Sunnyside, Methven, Perth), b. 1912.

The 1st baronet, Sir Thomas Kirkpatrick was created a baronet with remainder to heirs male whatsoever. He built the mansion of Closeburn, which was burnt to the ground through the carelessness of drunken servants on August 29th, 1748, and all the portraits, plate, &c., with most of the family papers, were consumed. Two boxes of papers dating back to the 16th century were de- posited in Register House, Edinburgh in 1952. H.I.M. the Empress Eugenie, widow of H.I.M. Napoleon III, formerly Emperor of the French, was descended from the Kirkpatricks, Barons of Closeburn. Her great-grandfather was William Kirkpatrick, of Conheath, and her lineage traces back through the Conheath and Kirkmichael branches of the family to Alexander Kirkpatrick, of Kirkmichael, who was younger brother of Sir Thomas Kirkpatrick (who d. 1502), ancestor of the 1st baronet. Sir James Alexander Kirkpatrick, 10th Bt. was Flight-Lieut. R.A.F. Vol. Reserve and Assist. Game Warden, Kenya.

KLEINWORT, Creation (U.K.) 1909, of Bolnore, Cuckfield, Sussex.

Sir ALEXANDER SANTIAGO KLEINWORT,
2nd *Baronet ; b.* Oct. 31st, 1892 ; *s.* his father, *Sir*
ALEXANDER DRAKE, 1935 ; ed. at St. John's
Coll., Oxford : *m.* 1938, Yvonne, da. of the late
John Bloch.

Arms—Or, a lion rampant sable, on a chief of the last
three oak trees eradicated proper. Crest—On a mount vert,
three leaves of clover proper.
Residence—1, Third Av., Hove, Sussex.

Nil sine labore.
Nothing without labour.

Brothers living—ERNEST GREVERUS, *b.* Sept. 13th,
1901 ; ed. at Jesus Coll., Camb. (B.A. 1922) ; late Flight-
Lieut. R.A.F. Vol. Reserve : *m.* 1932, Joan Nightingale,
M.B.E., J.P., da. of the late Professor Arthur William
Crossley, C.M.G., C.B.E., F.R.S., D.Sc., LL.D., and has
issue living, Kenneth Drake (of Wallhurst Manor,
Cowfold, Sussex; and 3, Balfour Place, W.1), *b.* 1935:
m. 1st, 1959, Lady Davina Rose Pepys, who *d.* 1973, da. of
7th Earl of Cottenham; 2ndly, 1973, Madeleine Hamilton,
el. da. of Ralph Taylor, of Larrea 1152, Buenos Aires,
and has issue living (by 1st m.), Richard Drake, *b.* 1960,
Marina Rose, *b.* 1962,—(by 2nd m.), Alexander Hamilton *b.* 1975,—Gillian Mawdsley, *b.* 1937: *m.* 1957,
Michael Raymond Warren, JP, of Banks Farm, Barcombe, Lewes, and has issue living, Charles Raymond
b. 1963, Davina Mary *b.* 1958. *Residences*, Heaselands,
Haywards Heath, Sussex; 50, South Audley St., W1.——*Sir* Cyril Hugh, *b.* 1905; late Lt.-Cdr.
RNVR; Chm., Kleinwort, Benson, Lonsdale Ltd. 1971; Chm. Cttee. on Invisible Exports, and a
Member of British Overseas Trade Board; Joint Vice-Chm. Commercial Union Assurance Co.;
Knt. 1971: *m.* 1933, Elisabeth Kathleen, da. of Francis Forde, of Newbury, and has issue living,
Serena Elizabeth, *b.* 1936: *m.* 1960, David Alfred Acland [*see* Acland, Bt., *cr.* 1890, colls.],
Charlotte, *b.* 1938: *m.* 1st, 1965, Richard Lawrence Baillieu, 2ndly, 1972, (Nevile) Martin Gwynne
[*see* Morrison-Bell, Bt. (ext.)], and has issue living (by 1st m.), a da. *b.* 1968 (by 2nd m.) [*see* Morri-
son-Bell, Bt. (ext.)],—Susanna, *b.* 1942: *m.* 1962, David Alphy Edward Raymond Peake, of 15,
Ilchester Place, W14, son of Sir Harald Peake [*see* V. Ingleby]. *Residences*, Sezincote, Moreton-
in-Marsh, Glos., 20, Cheyne Walk, SW3; Royal Yacht Sqdn.

Sister living—Henrietta Hortense (*Lady Evill*), *b.* 1893 : *m.* 1920, Air Ch. Marshal Sir Douglas
Claude Strathern Evill, GBE, KCB, DSC, AFC, DL, RAF (ret.), who *d.* 1971, and has issue
living, Henry Claude Strathern (Cleeves, Weydown Rd., Haslemere, Surrey), *b.* 1931: *m.* 1960,
Irene Joan, da. of J. G. Moncrief, of Crieff, Perthshire, and has issue living, Stephen Boyd
Strathern *b.* 1962, Gillian Annette *b.* 1960, Katrina Louise *b.* 1964,—Annette Strathern,
b. 1921: *m.* 1949, Alan David Donger, TD, JP, Lt.-Col. (ret.) RA (TA), of Taylors Mead, Sparsholt,
nr. Winchester, Hants, and has issue living, William Alan *b.* 1953, Alison Sophie *b.* 1951,—
Sophie Sybella Strathern, *b.* 1929: *m.* 1957, Maj. Reginald Allan Chenevix Trench, RE [*see*
B. Ashtown, colls.]. *Residence*, Cottage No. 20, Headbourne Worthy House, nr. Winchester.

Sir Alexander Drake Kleinwort, 1st baronet (son of the late Alexander Frederic Henry Kleinwort), was a Banker and Partner in the firm of Kleinwort, Sons & Co., of 20, Fenchurch Street, E.C.3.

KNILL, Creation (U.K.) 1893, of The Grove, Blackheath, Kent.

Sir JOHN KENELM STUART KNILL, 4th Baronet (but his
name does not, at the time of going to press, appear on the
Official Roll of Baronets); *b.* April 8th, 1913; *s.* his father,
Sir (JOHN) STUART, 1973; ed. at Downside; Lt. RNVR;
1939-45 War: *m.* 1951, Violette Maud Florence, Martin, da.
of Leonard Martin Barnes, of Durban, S. Africa, and has
issue.

Arms—Gules, semée of crosses botonnée fitchée a lion rampant, all or,
on a chief of the last a fasces fessewise, head to the dexter proper.
Crest—A demi-lion or, holding in the dexter paw a cross botonnée fitchée
azure, and supporting with the sinister a fasces in bend proper.
Residence—Canal Cottage, Bathampton, Somerset.

Nil desperandum.
Never despairing.

Sons living—THOMAS JOHN PUGIN BARTHOLOMEW, *b.* Aug. 23rd, 1952;
a PC City of London Police.——Kenkyn Martin Benedict Stuart,
b. 1954.

Half-Brothers living—Gyles Braose Hamish Stanislas Stuart, *b.* 1945,
——Rognvald Gabriel Nigel Alistair Stuart, *b.* 1946.

Half-Sister living—Gloriana Leonora Dorothea Marie, *b.* 1938: *m.* 1959, CPO William Charles Morehead, RN (ret.), of 33, Brompton Walk, Darlington, co. Durham.

Widow living of 3rd Baronet.—RUTH EVELYN (FOORD) (7, Barton Close, Berrow, Burnham-on-
Sea, Som.), da. of Archibald Barnes: *m.* 1941, as his 2nd wife, Sir (John) Stuart Knill, 3rd Bt.,
who *d.* 1973.

Sir Stuart Knill, 1st baronet, was head of the firm of John Knill and Co., wharfingers, and Lord
Mayor of London 1892-3. Sir John Knill, 2nd baronet, was Lord Mayor of London 1909-10.

KNOTT, Creation (U.K.) 1917, of Close House, Heddon-on-the-Wall, Northumberland.

[Extinct 1949.]

Sir (THOMAS) GARBUTT KNOTT, 2nd and last *Baronet.*

Widow living of 1st Baronet—ELIZABETH, da. of the late Col. V. C. Gauntlett, of St. Helier,
Jersey : *m.* 1st, 1932, as his second wife, Sir James Knott, 1st baronet, who *d.* 1934 ; 2ndly,
1943, Com. Edward Owen Obbard, D.S.C., G.M., R.N., who *d.* 1951. *Residence*, Samares
Manor, Jersey.

KNOWLES, Creation (G.B.) 1765, of Lovell Hill, Berkshire.

Always ready.

Sir CHARLES FRANCIS KNOWLES, 7th *Baronet*; *b.* Dec. 20th, 1951; *s.* his father, *Sir* FRANCIS GERALD WILLIAM, *FRS*, 1974.

Arms—Azure, a naval crown between four crosses crosslet in cross, all within a cross resarcelly disjoined between as many crosses crosslet all or. **Crest**—An elephant statant argent, supporting with the trunk an anchor or.
Residence—Avebury Manor, Wilts.

Sisters living—Averina Constance Frances, *b.* 1950: *m.* 1969, Dr. Martin Dacre Northmore-Ball.——Emma Irene Ann (twin), *b.* 1951.——Christiana Joan Kathleen Ruth, *b.* 1956.
Great-Aunt living (daughter of 4th baronet)—Eileen Beresford (of Pinfold, Chelmondiston, Ipswich), *b.* 1890: *m.* 1914, Capt. George Alfred Cooke, RN, who *d.* 1957, and has issue living, Joan Irwin, *b.* 1920: *m.* 1942, Geoffrey Clive Davies, OBE, of Greenshaw, Holbrook, Ipswich (Chm. of Board of Theo. H. Davies & Co., Ltd., Honolulu), and has issue living, Peter Francis *b.* 1965, Susan Catherine Beresford *b.* 1944: *m.* 1974, Patrick Robert Richard Sinclair, of 1, New Sq., Lincoln's Inn, WC2 [see Sinclair, Bt., colls.], Cynthia Elizabeth *b.* 1947: *m.* 1970, Nigel M. S. Rich, Alison Mary *b.* 1951: *m.* 1974, Lt. Graham M. Day, RN.
Widow living of 6th Bt.—RUTH (*Lady Knowles*), (Avebury Manor, Wilts.), da. of the late Rev. Arthur Brooke-Smith, and widow of P/O Richard Guy Hulse, RAF: *m.* 1948, Sir Francis Gerald William Knowles, FRS, 6th Bt., who *d.* 1974.

Collateral Branch living.
Issue of the late Robert Cosby Knowles, 5th son of 4th baronet, *b.* 1888, *d.* 1972: *m.* 1929, Phyllis Eve (Namarva, Winton, Qld., Aus.), da. of the late Rev. Canon Ward Thomas, of Lorna, Vic., Aust.:—
PETER COSBY (Namarva, Winton, Qld., Aust.), *b.* June 27th, 1930: *m.* 1957, Gloria, da. of H. Oaten, and has ssiue living, Richard Cosby, *b.* 1969,—Sandra, *b.* 1959,—Kerry, *b.* 1964,—Judith Anne, *b.* 1967.——Michael Cosby (Farrer Hall, Monash University, Clayton, Vic., Aust.), *b.* 1936; M. Com. Qld.; PhD Edinburgh; Sr. lecturer, Monash Univ., Aust.: *m.* 1965, Ann, da. of R. Mountain, MA, of Malvern, Vic., Aust.. and has issue living, Stephen Francis, *b.* 1970,—Fiona Mary, *b.* 1972.

The 1st baronet, Sir Charles, Adm. of the White, and Rear-Adm. of Great Britain, a distinguished naval commander, was Governor of Louisburg, Cape Breton, 1745-6, and of Jamaica 1752-6, and in 1770 was appointed, by the Empress Catherine II. of Russia, Chief President of H.I.M.'s Admiralty, with a seat in the Russian Council. Adm. Sir Charles Henry, G.C.B., the 2nd baronet, distinguished himself in his profession, and commanded the "Goliath" in the memorable battle off Cape St. Vincent, Feb. 14th, 1797, when the Spanish fleet was defeated. This family claims to be descended from Charles Knollys, titular 4th Earl of Banbury *temp.* James II. Vice-Adm. Sir Charles G. F. Knowles, 4th Bt.; served in Burma War 1852-3, commanded Niger Expedition 1864, and was thanked by Admiralty for services on Coast of Cuba during insurrection of 1870-71, and for quelling in 1880 insurrection in Danish Island of Santa Cruz, and by Colonial Office for services on Newfoundland Fisheries when in command of the "Lapwing" 1872. The 5th baronet, Sir Francis Howe Seymour Knowles, was Physical Anthropologist to Geographical Survey, Canada, and a prehistorian of note.

LACON, Creation (U.K.) 1818, of Great Yarmouth, Norfolk.

[Name pronounced "**Laykon.**"]

Probity is true honour.

Sir GEORGE VERE FRANCIS LACON, 7th *Baronet*; *b.* Feb. 25th, 1909; *s.* his father, Lieut.-Col. *Sir* GEORGE HAWORTH USSHER, *D.S.O.*, 1950; ed. at Eton: *m.* 1st, 1935 (marriage dissolved 1956), Hilary Blanche, da. of C. J. Scott, of Adgar, Walberswick; 2ndly, 1957, Kathlyn, da. of the late Edward Pillbrow, of 1, Carlisle Square, Chelsea, S.W.3, and has issue by 1st marriage.

Arms—Quarterly, per fesse indented erminois and azure, in the 2nd quarter a wolf's head erased or. **Crest**—On a mount vert a falcon proper, belled or, collared and charged on the breast with a cross flory gules.
Residence—Cliff House, Southwold, Suffolk.

Sons living—By 1st m.—EDMUND VERE (Milbrook, Holton St. Peter, Halesworth, Suffolk), *b.* May 3rd, 1936; ed. at Woodbridge Sch.: *m.* 1963 Gillian, only da. of J. H. Middleditch, of Wrentham, Suffolk, and has issue living, Edmund Richard Vere *b.* 1967,—Anna Kathryn, *b.* 1965.——George Julius (P.O. Box 30390, Nairobi, Kenya), *b.* 1938; ed. at Duncan Hall Sch.: *m.* 1968, Elizabeth Rodger, only da. of Archibald Kelly, of Sheffield, and has issue living, Sarah Elizabeth, *b.* 1970,
—Emma Blanche, *b.* 1973.
Sister living—Cecil Mallise Knyvett (Cliff House, Southwold, Suffolk), *b.* 1914.

Daughter living of 5th Baronet—Dorothy Beecroft (*posthumous*), *b.* 1912: *m.* 1st, 1932, Robert Desmond Ropner (Knt. 1959), from whom she obtained a divorce 1946 [see Ropner, Bt., *cr.* 1904, colls.]; 2ndly, 1946, Capt. D. B. M. Curtis, and has issue living, (by 1st marriage) [see Ropner, Bt., *cr.* 1904, colls.],—(by 2nd marriage) Amanda Murray, *b.* 1948. *Residence*,
Collateral Branches living.

Grandson of the late Thomas Beecroft Ussher Lacon, 2nd son of 3rd baronet :—
Issue of the late Henry Reginald Dunbar Lacon, *b.* 1884, *d.* 1960: *m.* 1912, Hilda Mary, who *d.* 1965, da. of the late William Bruce Slayter, MD, FRCS, of Halifax, Nova Scotia:—

Reginald William Beecroft, *D.S.C.*, *b.* 1913; Cdr. R.N. (ret.); 1939-45 War (despatches four times, D.S.C. and Bar): *m.* 1948, Joan Denyer Briscoe (DUNOLLY), da. of the late Albert J. George. *Residences*, Denman Island, Vancouver, British Columbia; Norris Castle, East Cowes. Isle of Wight.

Granddaughters of the late Capt. Henry Sidney Hammet Lacon, 3rd son of 3rd baronet:—

Issue of the late Gordon Massy Lacon, *b.* 1886, *d.* 1918: *m.* 1909, Phyllis, who *d.* 1962 (having *m.* 2ndly, 1920, John Alan Clutton-Brock, of Oakfield, Weybridge, who *d.* 1925, and 3rdly, 1926, Charles Geoffrey Keith Hulbert, who *d.* 1963), da. of His Honour the late Judge Woodfall, Judge of County Court Circuit No. 44, of Nutfield, Weybridge:—

Barbara Cicely, *b.* 1910: *m.* 1st, 1933, Gilbert Townley Gamble, from whom she obtained a divorce 1948; 2ndly, 1952, Geoffrey Allan Cavendish Frost, RNV(S)R, of Mayfield, Norwich Rd., Acle, Norfolk, and has issue living (by 1st m.), Priscilla Wendy, *b.* 1936: *m.* 1958, Jordi Comerma Tubau, formerly of Barcelona, Spain.——Pamela Abbott *b.* 1912: *m.* 1st, 1936, John Edward Hodgson, from whom she obtained a divorce 1946; 2ndly, 1949, Wing-Cdr. Philip S. Gage, RAF, of Green Cottage, Kington Langley, Chippenham, Wilts. and has issue living (by 1st m.) Robert John (c/o Lloyds Bank, 6, Pall Mall, SW1), *b.* 1937: *m.* 1963 (m. diss. 1971), Caroline Joan Eve Kingdon, and has issue living, Jonathan Charles *b.* 1968, Sarah Jane *b.* 1965,—Penelope Jane, *b.* 1939: *m.* 1964, John Harmon Clary, from whom she obtained a divorce 1967, and has issue living, James Alistair *b.* 1965.

Issue of the late Major Sidney John Boileau Lacon, Roy. Warwickshire Regt., *b.*1889, *d.*(killed in action during European War) 1918: *m.* 1912, Doris, who *d.* 1931, da. of Charles Gibson, of Aberdeen:—

Joan Wendy Moyra, *b.* 1915: *m.* 1st, 1937, Norman Richard Rowley Brooke, from whom she obtained a divorce 1947; 2ndly, 1949, Michael John Rouse.

The present baronet is in direct descent from Edmund Lacon, who settled in Yorkshire early in the seventeenth century, belonging to a younger branch of the very ancient family of Lacon settled in Salop *temp.* Edward III. The 3rd baronet was M.P. for Great Yarmouth (C) 1852-7, and 1859-68, and for Norfolk N. 1868-88. The 5th baronet was Capt. 12th Lancers, and served in S. African War 1899-1901 (Queen's medal with 3 clasps, King's medal with 2 clasps). The 6th baronet, Sir George Haworth Ussher Lacon, D.S.O. served in S. Africa 1901, and during European War 1914-19 as Lieut.-Col. Roy. Warwickshire Regt. (D.S.O.).

LACY, Creation (U.K.) 1921, of Ampton, co. Suffolk.

Honours are enhanced by deserts.

Sir HUGH MAURICE PIERCE LACY, 3rd *Baronet* (but his name does not, at time of going to press, appear on the Official Roll of Baronets); *b.* Sept. 3rd, 1943; *s.* his father, *Sir* MAURICE JOHN PIERCE, 1965; ed. at Aiglon Coll., Switzerland: *m.* 1968, Deanna, da. of Howard Bailey, of Stourbridge.

Arms—Gyronny or and gules, on a bend sable a Lacy knot between two martlets of the first. Crest—An eagle rising or, gorged with a collar gemelle gules and resting the dexter claw on a Lacy knot sable.

Residence—The White House, Instow, N. Devon.

Brother living—PATRICK BRYAN FINUCANE, *b.* April 18th, 1948; ed. at Downside: *m.* 1971, Phyllis Victoria, da. of Edgar P. H. James, of 6, Berkeley Rd., Barnes, SW13.

Sister living—Jeanne Clare, *b.* 1942: *m.* 1965, David Leslie Morgan, and has issue living, Dominic Maurice David, *b.* 1969,—Miranda Jean, *b.* 1967.

Half Sister living—Susan Mary, *b.* 1936: *m.* 1961, Michael John Gemmell, of Great Budds, Shipbourne, Tonbridge, and has issue living, Andrew James, *b.* 1969,—Catriona Sarah, *b.* 1963,—Lucy Charlotte, *b.* 1964.

Aunts living (daughters of 1st Baronet)—Angela Florence, *b.* 1905: *m.* 1931, Col. Godfrey Sturdy Incledon-Webber, TD, DL, MA, late RA, of Buckland Manor, Braunton, N. Devon, and has issue living, Diana Mary, *b.* 1932: *m.* 1961, John Edward Bury, of Carpenter's Field, Puttenham, Guildford, Surrey [see Le Marchant, Bt.],—Elizabeth Angela, *b.* 1934: *m.* 1956, Capt. David John Bigelow Dodge, Gren. Gds., of Woodtown, Alverdiscott, Bideford, N. Devon, and has issue living, John Incledon *b.* 1957, Julian Patrick Bigelow *b.* 1964, Caroline Elizabeth *b.* 1959, Frances Camilla *b.* 1961, Cecilia Charlotte *b.* 1967,—Priscilla Mary, *b.* 1945: *m.* 1969, Maj. Jeremy David Smith-Bingham, Blues and Royals, of St. Brannocks, Braunton, N. Devon, and 1A, Ennismore Gdns., SW7, and has issue living, Richard David Incledon *b.* 1970, Alexander John *b.* 1973.——Eveline Mary Elise, *b.* 1908: *m.* 1939, George Frederick Pinney, CBE, and has issue living, Charles Frederick, *b.* 1947; BA Camb.,—Veronica Beatrice, *b.* 1941,—Julia Margaret, *b.* 1942: *m.* 1970, Ulrich von Bertele y Areilza, and has issue living, Maurice Hans George *b.* 1974, Marceline Veronica *b.* 1971, Isobel Eveline *b.* 1973,—Angela Rose, *b.* 1944: *m.* 1969, David Thomas Alan Boyle [see E. Glasgow, colls.]. *Residence*, Staplefield Court, nr. Hayward's Heath, Sussex.——Vivien Margaret, *b.* 1911; a JP: *m.* 1939, Col. Nathaniel John Wilson, OBE (ret.) late RA, and has issue living, *Rev.* Peter John *b.* 1939; MA; ACA,—Christopher Francis, *b.* 1947,—Mary Angela, *b.* 1941; ARCM: *m.* 1966, Roy McLeod, of 125, Woodford Sq., W14, and has issue living, Fiona Caroline *b.* 1967, Amanda Mary *b.* 1969, Joanna Margaret *b.* 1971, Sarah Jane (twin) *b.* 1971,—Elizabeth Anne, *b.* 1944; SRN: *m.* 1970, Samuel Antoine Frederic Ozanam McNamara, MB, BS, LRCP, MRCS, DObst. RCOG, of Nasty, Ware, Herts., and has issue living, Hugh Daniel *b.* 1970, Ruth Margaret Mary *b.* 1972. *Residence*, Thurston Croft, nr. Bury St. Edmunds, Suffolk.

Widow living of 2nd Baronet—NANSI JEAN (*Nansi, Lady Lacy*), (The White House, Instow, N. Devon), da. of the late Myrddin Evans: *m.* 1940, as his 2nd wife, Sir Maurice John Pierce Lacy, 2nd baronet, who *d.* 1965.

The 1st baronet, Sir Pierce Thomas Lacy (2nd son (by 2nd m.) of John Pierce Lacy, of Oak Mount, Edgbaston, Birmingham) was Chm. of Birmingham Stock Exchange, and Founder of British Trusts Asso. and of British Shareholders' Trust.

LAKE, Creation (G.B.) 1711, of Edmonton, Middlesex.

Sir (Atwell) Graham Lake, 10th *Baronet*; *b*. Oct. 6th, 1923; *s*. his father, *Capt*. Sir Atwell Henry, CB, OBE, RN, 1972; ed. at Eton; Sr. Tech. Adviser MOD; Gilbert and Ellice Is. Mil. Forces 1944-45; Colonial Admin. Ser. 1945-55 (Sec. to Govt. of Tonga 1950-53); British High Commn. New Delhi 1966-68; FCO 1969-72.

Arms—Quarterly: 1st, (coat of augmentation) gules, a dexter arm embowed in armour, issuing from sinister side of the shield, holding in the hand a sword erect, all proper, thereto affixed a banner argent charged with a cross between sixteen escutcheons gules, on the centre of the cross a lion of England; 2nd, sable, a bend, between six crosslets fitchée, argent; 3rd, quarterly, argent and sable, on a bend gules, three mullets argent; 4th, argent, a chevron between three boars' heads couped sable. **Crests**—1st, a cavalier in a fighting posture, his scarf gules, his left arm hanging down as wounded and useless, holding the bridle in his teeth, his face, sword, armour, and horse embrued, all proper; 2nd, a horse's head argent, charged with a fesse, cottised gules.

Un Dieu, un roy, un cœur.
One God, one king, one heart.

Residence,—70, Cadogan Sq., SW1.

Brothers living—Willoughby Alfred, *b*. Aug. 31st, 1925; ed. at Eton: *m*. 1952, Elizabeth Elsie Faith, da. of Sir Rupert Turner Havelock Clarke, 2nd Bt., and has issue living, Susan Kathleen, *b*. 1961,—Catherine Jane, *b*. 1962. *Residence*, Manor Cottage, Much Hadham, Herts.——Edward Geoffrey (11, Mayflower Way, Ongar, Essex), *b*. 1928; ed. at Eton: *m*. 1965, Judith Ann, da. of John Fox, and has issue living, Mark Winter, *b*. 1968,—Sophie Louise, *b*. 1971.

Widow living of 9th Baronet—Kathleen Marion (*Lady Lake*) (Ford Hill, Little Hadham, Ware, Herts.), da. of the late Alfred Morrison Turner, of Broughton, W. Derby, Liverpool: *m*. 1922, Capt. Sir Atwell Henry Lake, CB, CBE, RN, 9th Bt., who *d*. 1972.

Collateral Branch living.

Grandsons of the late Winter Atwell Edward Lake, son of the late Capt. Andrew Winter Lake, 5th son of 4th baronet :—
 Issue of the late Lieut.-Col. Ernest Atwell Winter Lake, C.B.E., Indian Army (retired), *b*. 1886, *d*. 1945: *m*. 1924, Phyllis Marjorie, da. of J. G. Silcock, formerly I.C.S.:—
John Winter Atwell, *b*. 1925 : *m*. 1955, Elsie, da. of R. Milburn, of Long Marton, Westmorland. ——Winter Philip Edward, *b*. 1930: *m*. 1956, Vera, da. of A. G. Liddell, of Durham. *Residence*,

Sir Edward Lake, Chancellor of the Diocese of Lincoln, and Advocate-General in Ireland, was, for his loyalty and services to Charles I., granted by that monarch the coat of augmentation now borne by the family, and the exceptional privilege of nominating a person to be created a baronet. He did not, however, avail himself of this privilege, and, in consequence, a baronetcy was in 1711 conferred on his great-nephew and heir, Bibye Lake, Sub-Governor of the African Co.

LAKIN, Creation (U.K.) 1909, of The Cliff, Borough of Warwick.

Sir Henry Lakin, 3rd *Baronet* ; *b*. Oct. 8th, 1904 ; *s*. his father, *Sir* Richard, 1955 ; ed. at Eton, and at Jesus Coll., Camb. (B.A. 1926) : *m*. 1st, 1927, Bessie, who *d*. 1965, da. of J. Anderson, of Durban, S. Africa; 2ndly, 1965, Grace, da. of John Kyme, of Manchester, and has issue by 1st m.

Arms—Quarterly : indented argent and azure, in the 1st and 4th quarters a pellet charged with a lion's head erased of the first. **Crest**—A dexter cubit arm vested sable cuffed azure, the hand grasping a plasterer's trowel proper.

Address—Torwood, Post Office, Rosetta, Natal, S. Africa.

Son living—By 1st m.—Michael (Torwood, PO Box 40, Rosetta, Natal, S. Africa), *b*. Oct. 28th, 1934; ed. at Stowe: *m*. 1st, 1956 (m. diss. 1963), Margaret, da. of Robert Wallace, of Mount Norris, co. Armagh; 2ndly, 1965, Felicity Ann, da. of A. D. Murphy, of Londiani, Kenya, and has issue living (by 2nd m.), Richard Anthony, *b*. 1968,—Mary Jane, *b*. 1966.

Sister living—Cynthia, *b*. 1907. *Residence*, Sherwood Hill, Tunley, Cirencester.

One God, one king, one heart.

Collateral Branches living.

Issue of the late Henry Gilbert Lakin, 2nd son of 1st baronet, *b*. 1875, *d*. 1964: *m*. 1902, Sybil, who *d*. 1938, da. of the late Sir Patteson Nickalls, of Fallowfield, Chislehurst:—
John, *T.D.* (Hammerwood House, Iping, Midhurst, Sussex), *b*. 1910; a J.P. and a D.L.; Lt.-Col. late Warwickshire Yeo.: *m*. 1939, the Hon. (Helena) Daphne Pearson, da. of 2nd Viscount Cowdray, and has issue living, Michael Simon, *b*. 1955.

Issue of the late Edward Lyon Lakin, 3rd son of 1st baronet, *b*. 1879, *d*. 1922: *m*. 1912, Dorothy Barklie, who *d*. 1969, da. of Col. Barklie Cairns McCalmont, CB [B. Kingsale]:—
Richard Barklie, *DSO, DSC, b*. 1914; is Lt.-Cdr. RN (ret.); 1939-43 War (despatches, DSO, DSC and Bar, USA Legion of Merit); DSO 1943: *m*. 1936, Pamela Mary Helen, da. of the late Philip Jackson-Taylor, and has issue living, Robin Lyon (1709, Pacific Highway, Wahroonga, NSW 2076, Aust.), *b*. 1938; ed. at Eton: *m*. 1964, Gillian Claire, da. of Peter Baily, of South Farm, Gt. Whittington, Northumberland, and has issue living, Jessica Honor *b*. 1966, Nicola Anne Pamela *b*. 1970,—Mark Philip, *b*. 1941; ed. at Eton,—Julian Barklie (20, Standish Rd., W6), *b*. 1948; ed. at Eton: *m*. 1973, Penelope Jane, da. of John Almond of Burghclere, Berks.,—Amanda Joy, *b*. 1947,—Caroline Madeline, *b*. 1953,—Serena Pamela (twin), *b*. 1953. *Residence*, Anick Hall, Hexham, Northumberland. *Clubs*, Army and Navy, Northern Counties.

Issue of the late Major Michael Lawrence Lakin, D.S.O., M.C., 11th Hussars, 4th son of 1st baronet, b. 1881, d. 1960 : m. 1914, Kathleen, who d. 1930, da. of the late Lord Maurice FitzGerald [D. Leinster, colls.] :—

Maurice Victor, M.C., b. 1919 ; ed. at Eton ; late Capt. 17th/21st Lancers ; European War 1940-44, in N. Africa (wounded, MC): m. 1st, 1951 (m. diss. 1956), Huguette Paule Clemence, da. of Robert Cauvin of Paris ; 2ndly, 1959 (m. diss. 1971), Silvanni, da. of Ngot-Vong, of Pnom-penh, Cambodia, and has issue living, (by 2nd marriage) Michael, b. 1960,—Richard, b. 1964. Residence, Cabrol, Flayosc, Var, France.

Sir Michael Henry Lakin, 1st Bt. (son of the late Henry Lakin, of Malvern), was Mayor of Warwick, Vice-Chm. of County Council for Warwickshire, and High Sheriff of that County.

LAMBART, Creation (U.K.) 1911, of Beau Parc, co. Meath.

Prepared on every side.

Sir OLIVER FRANCIS LAMBART, 2nd Baronet; b. April 6th, 1913; s. his father, Lieut.-Col. Sir (GUSTAVUS) FRANCIS WILLIAM, C.V.O., 1926; sometime Lieut. Supplementary Reserve Roy. Ulster Rifles ; European War 1939-44 with R.A.S.C.

Arms—Gules, three gillieflowers pierced argent. Crest—On a mount vert, a centaur drawing a bow or.

Seat—Beau Parc, co. Meath.

Widow living of 1st Baronet—KATHLEEN BARBARA SOPHIA (Lady Lambart), da. of the late Col. John Arthur Henry Moore Brabazon, of Tara Hall, co. Meath: m. 1911, Lieut.-Col. Sir (Gustavus) Francis William Lambart, C.V.O., 1st baronet, who d. 1926. Residence, Beau Parc, co. Meath.

The 1st baronet, Sir (Gustavus) Francis William Lambart, son of the late Gustavus William Lambart, of Beau Parc, co. Meath [see E. Cavan, colls.], was Chamberlain to Viceroy of Ireland 1876-80, Gentleman-in-Waiting 1885-6, Comptroller 1902-3, and again Chamberlain 1903-6; also Sec. to Order of St. Patrick.

LAMBERT, Creation (G.B.) 1711, of London.

By pursuing one attains.

Sir GREVILLE FOLEY LAMBERT, 9th Baronet (but his name does not, at time of going to press, appear on the Official Roll of Baronets), son of the late Lionel Foley Lambert, 4th son of 6th baronet; b. Aug. 17th, 1900; s. his cousin, *Sir* JOHN FOLEY GREY, 1938; ed. at Rugby: m. 1932, Edith Roma, da. of Richard Batson, and has issue.

Arms—Argent, on a mount an oak-tree vert, and a grey-hound courant gules. Crest—Out of a ducal coronet or three ostrich feathers, the dexter feather gules, the centre argent, and the sinister azure.

Residence—1, Linden Court, Hampton Lane, Solihull, Warwicks.

Daughters living—Isabel Pamela, b. 1933.——Roma Ann, b. 1934: m. 1956, Wing Cdr. Colin John Phillips, RAF (c/o Williams & Glyn's Bank, Bennetts Hill, Birmingham), and has issue living, David Jonathan, b. 1958,—Adrian Greville, b. 1959,—Carolyn Ann, b. 1962.—— Carole Joy, b. 1940: m. 1st, 1960, Ray Bennett, from whom she obtained a divorce 1963; 2ndly, 1968, Nicholas Jason Hill, of Silverstone, Bishampton Rd., Flyford Flavell, Worcs., and has issue living (by 2nd m.), Jason Stirling, b. 1970,—Michelle Jane, b. 1973.

Daughter living of 8th Baronet—Eileen GREY, b. 1922: m. 1942, the 11th Earl of Harrington, who obtained a divorce 1946 ; 2ndly, 1947, John Phillip Bissill, MC, and has issue living (by 1st m.) [see E. Harrington],—(by 2nd m.) Alexandra Diana, b. 1950. Residence, Enville Hall, Stourbridge, Worcs.

Daughters living of 7th Baronet—Dorothy Catherine, b. 1884 : m. 1st, 1912, John Edric Lloyd, who obtained a divorce 19—— ; 2ndly, 1926, Ray Patterson, who d. 1945 ; 3rdly, 1947, Earl G. Terry, from whom she obtained a divorce 1955, and has issue living, (by 1st marriage) Jane Catherine Phyllis, b. 1913 : m. 1934, Carl Skelton, of Geyser, Montana, U.S.A., and has issue living, Jerry James b. 1937, Thomas Milton b. 1943, Phyllis Dorothy b. 1936 : m. 1956, William Patrick O'Brien (and has issue living, Patrick James b. 1957, Charles Phillip b. 1959, Catherine Lee b. 1958, Julie Anne b. 1964 Joan Catherine b. 1942).——Phyllis Kathleen Y, b. 1887. Residence, Elm House, Enville, Stourbridge.

Collateral Branches living.

Grandchildren of the late Rev. William Henry Lambert, 6th son of 5th baronet :—

Issue of the late Hugh Biddulph Lambert, *b.* 1867, *d.* 1924: *m.* 1907, Mabel Ellen, **who** *d.* 1965, second da. of Frederick Wells, of Cridmore, Isle of Wight:—

JOHN HUGH, *b.* May 31st, 1910; 1939-45 War with RAF: *m.* 1947, Edith Davies, and has issue living, Peter John Biddulph, *b.* 1952. *Residence*, 123, Admiral Rd., Toronto 5, Canada.—— Robert William (1237, Delmont, Richardson, Texas 75080, USA) *b.* 1911; sometime in Merchant Navy: *m.* 1948, Margaret Daphne Harvey.——Mabel Joyce, *b.* 1908. *Residence*, 503, Fulham Rd., SW6.——Nina Joan *b.* 1916: *m.* 1st, 1941, Guy Duncan Tucker, from whom she obtained a divorce 1948; 2ndly, 1951, Eric Harold Dehn, and has issue living, (by 1st m.) Michael Duncan Hugh, *b.* 1942, (by 2nd m.) Jacqueline Tessa, *b.* 1954.——Nicola Louisa, *b.* 1954. *Residence*, 3, Trewlawney Rd., Bristol, 6.——Julia Margaret, *b.* 1920; 1939-45 War in WAAF. *Residence*, Priory Cottage, Heythrop, Chipping Norton, Oxon.

Grandchildren of the late Alan Lambert, son of the late Francis John Lambert, 3rd son of 4th baronet :—

Issue of the late Mortan Lambert, *b.* 1866, *d.* 1926 : *m.* 1902, Clotilde, who *d.* 1949, da. of Victor Jaccoud, formerly of Rumilly, Haute Savoie, France :—

Montague Victor, *b.* 1904 : ed. at Winchester, and at New Coll., Oxford ; European War 1941-5 as Group Capt. RAFVR: *m.* 1st, 1931, Ena Sylvia Victoria, who *d.* 1944, da. of the late George Grossmith; 2ndly, 1948, Janis Mary, da. of the late Capt. Wilfrid Brittain Squirl-Dawson, of Higham, Suffolk, and has issue living, (by 2nd m.) Charles Geoffrey Mortan, *b.* 1956. *Residence*, 19, Norfolk Rd., Tunbridge Wells, Kent.——Gisele Joan (c/o Westminster Bank, Red Lion St. Norwich), *b.* 1907: *m.* 1st, 1934, Olivier le Mire, 4th Zouaves (French Army), from whom she obtained a divorce 1938; 2ndly, 19—, Hugh Pearson Gee, who *d.* 1965.

Issue of the late Jasper Lambert, *b.* 1872, *d.* 1949: *m.* 1898, Cecil, who *d.* 1964, da. of the late William Forsyth, Q.C., LL.D., of 61, Rutland Gate, S.W.:—

Alan Forsyth (1, Burwood Close, Ringley Park Rd., Reigate, Surrey) *b.* 1901: *m.* 1935, Olive Edith, da. of the late Frederick Long, and has issue living, Philip Jasper, *b.* 1936.——Marjorie Cecil, *b.* 1899. *Residence*, 91, Willifield Way, NW11.——Joyce Marion, *b.* 1908: *m.* 1941, Gerald McPherson, and has issue living, David William Alan, *b.* 1943,—Jasper Alexander Cecil, *b.* 1947. *Residence*, 75, Hatherop Rd., Hampton, Middlesex.

Granddaughter of the late Capt. Robert Lambert, son of the late Gen. Sir John Lambert, GCB, son of the late Capt. Robert Alexander Lambert, RN, son of 2nd baronet:—

Issue of the late Major Robert Lambert, D.S.O., *b.* 1873, *d.* 1955 : *m.* 1898, Henrietta Isabella, *M.B.E., J.P.*, who *d.* 1950, da. of the late George William Lowther [Lowther, Bt., cr. 1824] :—

Alice Winsome, *b.* 1899. *Residence*, Ash Grove, Whitchurch, Salop. *Club*, V.A.D.

Sir John Lambert, the 1st baronet, of the Isle of Rhé, France, settled in England as a merchant, and was one of the Directors of the South Sea Co. In 1710 he supplied the Treasury with money, and for this service was created a baronet. The 7th baronet, Sir Henry Foley, assumed by Roy. licence, 1905, for himself and issue, the surname of Grey in lieu of his patronymic, and the arms of Grey quarterly with those of Lambert, and was High Sheriff of Worcestershire 1901.

LANE, Creation (U.K.) 1913, of Cavendish Square, St. Marylebone.   [Extinct 1972.
Sir WILLIAM ARBUTHNOT LANE, *CBE*, 2nd and last *Baronet*.

Daughter living of 2nd Baronet—Susan Charlotte Arbuthnot, *b.* 1938: *m.* 1964, John Nicolas Bowker, Pinchers Hill, E. Chiltington, nr. Lewes, Sussex, and has issue living, Mark James Arbuthnot Lane, *b.* 1967,—Katy Louise, *b.* 1968.

Daughters living of 1st Baronet—Irene Briscoe Arbuthnot, *b.* 1889, Licentiate of Coll. of Violinists 1938; has Defence and Long Service Medals: *m.* 1911, Harold Chapple, MC, FRCS, FRCOG, who *d.* 1945, and has issue living, Harold Arbuthnot Lane (Lantern Cottage, Queen Camel, Somerset), *b.* 1915; ed. at Stowe, and at Camb. Univ.; sometime Maj. Wilts Regt.: *m.* 1940, Sheila, da. of Dr. Geoffrey Hobbs. of Broughton, Hants, and has issue living, Stephen Andrew Harold *b.* 1947, Sarah Elizabeth *b.* 1942: *m.* 1967, Richard Smith, (and has issue living, Bridget Caroline *b.* 1969, Deborah Jane *b.* 1970),—Peter Arbuthnot Lane (Koryfi, Royal Av., Worcester Park, Surrey), *b.* 1920; ed. at Rugby, and at Camb. and Leeds (MB and ChB, DPM, MRCPsych) Univs.: *m.* 1942, Dorothy, da. of Arthur Sugden, of Roundhay, Leeds, and has issue living, John Harold Lane, *b.* 1946: *m.* 1972, Louise Hamlin Wright, Paul Anthony *b.* 1948, Rosemary *b.* 1951. *Address*, Onslow Court Hotel, SW7.——Eileen Caroline Arbuthnot, *b.* 1893: *m.* 1913, Nathan Mutch, MD, FRCP, and has issue living, Eileen Barbara (2, Fernshaw Close, SW10), *b.* 1915: *m.* 1937 (m. diss. 1953), Patrick Wensley Clarkson, MBE, FRCS, who *d.* 1969, and has issue living, Gerald William Wensley (60, Duggan Av., Toronto 7, Ont., Canada), *b.* 1938: MA: *m.* 1967, Rachel Elinor, da. of Sir John Paget Bowman, 3rd Bt. (cr. 1884) (and has issue living, James Hugo Wensley, *b.* 1970, Alexandra Juliet Cajetana *b.* 1974, Ronald Wensley (6, Sutherland St., SW1) *b.* 1941; MA: *m.* 1972, Amanda, da. of Arnold Hagenbach (and has issue living, Sophie Julia *b.* 1974). *Residence*, Pitt White, Uplyme, Devon.

Widow living of 2nd baronet—FRITZI (*Lady Lane*), (72, Drayton Gdns., SW10 9SB), da. of the late Capt. Fritz Számvald, of Vienna: *m.* 1937, Sir William Arbuthnot Lane, CBE, 2nd Bt., who *d.* 1972, when the title became ext.

LANGHAM, Creation (E.) 1660, of Cottesbrooke, Northamptonshire.

Sir JAMES MICHAEL LANGHAM, 15th *Baronet*; *b.* May 24th, 1932; *s.* his father, *Sir* JOHN CHARLES PATRICK, 1972; ed. at Rossall; Capt. N. Irish Horse: *m.* 1959, Marion Audrey Eleanor, da. of Oswald Barratt, of Tanzania, and has issue.

    Arms—Argent, three bears' heads erased sable, muzzled or. Crest—A bear's head as in the arms.

    Residence,—Claranagh, Tempo, Enniskillen, co. Fermanagh.

Sons living—JOHN STEPHEN, *b.* Dec. 14th, 1960.—— Rupert William, *b.* 1963.
Daughter living—Lucinda Jane, *b.* 1966.
Widow living of 14th Baronet—ROSAMOND CHRISTABEL (*Rosamond, Lady Langham*), (Tempo Manor, Enniskillen, co. Fermanagh), da. of the late Arthur Rashleigh [Emerson-Tennent, Bt. (ext.)]: *m.* 1930, Sir John Charles Patrick Langham, 14th Bt., who *d.* 1972.

    The 1st baronet, Sir John, was knighted by Charles II. at The Hague, being one of a deputation from the city of London to wait on H.M. in Holland. When Sheriff of London in 1642, he, with several other gentlemen, was imprisoned for refusing to publish "An Act for the exheridation of the Royal line, the abolishment of Monarchy in the Kingdom, and the setting up of a Commonwealth. Sir John, the 6th baronet, left £6,000 to the Corporation of London to found a society for the relief of poor soldiers, sailors, and their wives. Sir (Herbert) Charles Arthur, the 13th baronet, was High Sheriff of co. Fermanagh 1930.

Nor suffers them to be savage.

LANGMAN, Creation (U.K.) 1906, of Eaton Square, City of Westminster.

Sir JOHN LYELL LANGMAN, 3rd *Baronet;* *b.* Sept. 9th, 1912; *s.* his father, *Sir* ARCHIBALD LAWRENCE, *C.M.G.*, 1949; ed. at Eton, and at Ch. Ch., Oxford; formerly N. Somerset Yeo.: *m.* 1936, Iris Pamela Gaskell, only da. of Capt. Spencer Kennard, formerly of Purslow Hall, Craven Armss Shropshire, and has issue.

    Arms—Argent, on a pile engrailed sable a water bouget of the first between two flaunches of the second, each charged with a water bouget also of the first. Crest—In front of a mount vert thereon a portcullis with chains sable, three water bougets fessewise of the last.

    Residence—Perrotts Brook House, near Cirencester, Gloucestershire. *Club*, Lansdowne.

Daughters living—Josephine Frances, *b.* 1938.——Judith Ann Camilla, *b.* 1949: *m.* 1972, Ian K. Gibson.

Sisters living—Mary Eleanor, *b.* 1908.——(Nora) Elizabeth Ferrar, *b.* 1919: *m.* 1955, John Archibald Montgomery, and has issue living, Archibald John, *b.* 1957,—James Lyell, *b.* 1961,—Katherine Elizabeth, *b.* 1956. *Residence,* North Cadbury Court, Somerset.

Be just and fear not.

LANGRISHE, Creation (I.) 1777, of Knocktopher Abbey, Kilkenny.

Sir HERCULES RALPH HUME LANGRISHE, 7th *Baronet*; *b.* May 17th, 1927; *s.* his father, *Capt. Sir* TERENCE HUME, 1973; ed. at Eton; late Lt. 9th Lancers: *m.* 1955, the Hon. Grania Sybil Enid Wingfield, only da. of the 9th Viscount Powerscourt, and has issue.

    Arms—Quarterly, or and sable, four covered cups counterchanged. Crest—A lion rampant per fesse or and sable.

    Residences—Knocktopher Abbey, co. Kilkenny; Ringlestown House, Kilmessan, co. Meath. *Clubs*—Cavalry, Kildare Street.

Son living—JAMES HERCULES, *b.* March 3rd, 1957.
Daughters living—Miranda Grania, *b.* 1959.——Georgina Emma, *b.* 1961.——Alalanta Sue, *b.* 1963.
Brothers living—Patrick Nicholas, *TD*, (The Manor House, Sellindge, Ashford, Kent), *b.* 1932; ed. at Eton; Maj. Yeo. TA, RARO (formerly Leicestershire and Derbyshire Yeo. (TA)) and a Member of Lloyds: *m.* 1957, Penelope Jill, only child of the late Lt.-Cdr. Kenneth Horley, RN, and has issue living, Caroline, *b.* 1958,—Marianne Stuart, *b.* 1961.——Robert Gore (9, York Mansions, Prince of Wales Drive, SW11), *b.* 1936; ed. at Eton: *m.* 1966, Eleanor Barbara

Medio tutissimus ibis.
You will walk safest in a middle path.

Muriel, da. of Reginald Arthur Lygon [*see* E. Beauchamp, colls.], and formerly wife of William James Cavendish-Bentinck [D. Portland, colls.], who *d.* 1966, and has issue living, Robin Stuart, *b.* 1967.

Widow living of 6th Baronet—JOAN STUART (*Joan, Lady Langrishe*) (Dormy Cottage, Wentworth, Virginia Water, Surrey), el. da. of the late Maj. Ralph Stuart Grigg [Gore, Bt.]: *m.* 1926, Capt. Sir Terence Hume Langrishe, 6th Bt., who *d.* 1973.

Collateral Branches living.

Grandson of Henry Hoadly Langrishe (infra):—
Issue of the late Lt.-Col. Roger Patrick Hercules Langrishe, *b.* 1905, *d.* 1969: *m.* 1949, Doris May (4, Kearsney Court, Kearsney, Dover), da. of the late Thomas S. Bott, of 16, Beech Rd., Oxford:—
James Hoadly, *b.* 1951; ed. at King's Sch., Canterbury; Sub. Lt. RN.

Grandchildren of the late Richard Langrishe, **5th son of 3rd baronet**
Issue of the late Henry Hoadly Langrishe, *b.* 1872, *d.* 1958 : *m.* 1903, Norah Isabel, who *d.* 1948, da. of the late Rev. Thomas Coney, J.P., Chap. to the Forces, of Braywick Grove, Maidenhead :—
Beatrice Aileen, *b.* 1908; is a Sister in Religion. *Address*, Le Bon Sauveur, Holyhead, Anglesey.

Issue of the late Lieut.-Col. John du Plessis Langrishe, D.S.O., *b.* 1883, *d.* 1947 : *m.* 1914, Helen Dorothy, da. of the late Philip George Collins, of The Park, Beckenham:—
Philip John Duppa (Birches, Pembroke Rd., Woking, Surrey), *b.* 1917: ed. at Pembroke Coll., Camb. (BA 1938). formerly Capt. R.A.: 1939-45 War (prisoner, escaped): *m.* 1st, 1948 (m. dissolved 1963), Phyllis Edwina, da. of C. V. Vanbergen, of Bassett, Hildenborough, Kent; 2ndly, 1963, Isabel Angus, yr. da. of Sir (Alexander) Knox Helm, G.B.E., K.C.M.G., of The Old Rectory, Tewin, Herts, and has issue living, (by 1st marriage) Charles William John, *b.* 1949,— Patrick du Plessis, *b.* 1952.——Hugh Richard, *b.* 1923; ed. at Cheltenham; formerly Lt. R.N.V.R. (Air Arm): *m.* 1955, Pamela Mary, da. of William E. Downes, of Bourton Hall, Much Wenlock, Shropshire, and has issue living, John William, *b.* 1959,—Jane Dorothy, *b.* 1956. *Residence*, Llanfallteg House, Llanfallteg, Whitland, Dyfed.——Dorothy Pratt, (Forest Glen, Lower Densome, Woodgreen, Fordingbridge, Hants.), *b.* 1921: *m.* 1946 (m. diss. 1972), Clifford Anthony Weston, formerly Capt. RA, and has issue living, Richard Anthony, *b.* 1947,—Christopher Nigel, *b.* 1949,—Douglas Neil, *b.* 1951.

Issue of the late Lieut.-Col. Richard Bellingham Langrishe, *b.* 1884, *d.* 1960 : *m.* 1909, Mabel Katherine, who *d.* 1955, da. of Henry F. H. Gibson :—
Richard Courtenay Gibson, *b.* 1912; ed. at Cheltenham Coll.; Lt.-Col. (ret.) late Royal Hampshire Regt. and Parachute Regt.; 1939-45 War in N. Africa, Sicily, Italy, and N.-W. Europe (despatches): *m.* 1940, Jean Gertrude Abercrombie, da. of the late Dr. G. D. Thomson, FRCS, of 10, Belvedere, Bath, and has issue living, Richard Dingwall (c/o Lloyds Bank, Cox's & King's Branch, Pall Mall, SW1Y 5NH), *b.* 1941; ed. at Cheltenham, and London Univ. (BScEng); Maj. RAPC: *m.* 1964, Angela W. Marett, el. da. of D. W. Marett Tims, of Crookham Village, Hants, and has issue living, Belinda Jane Marett *b.* 1967, Rebecca Kate *b.* 1970,—Nicholas du Plessis (14, Dunstable Rd., Richmond, Surrey; Bristol Aero Club), *b.* 1942; ed. at Cheltenham: *m.* 1966, Anna Victoria Airy, only da. of Sq. Ldr. M. E. Townsend, RAF, of Old Castle, Maldon, Essex, and has issue living, Oonagh Richarda du Plessis *b.* 1972. *Residence*, Mount Haviland, Upper Weston, Bath.——Beryl Edith Frances (22, Beacon Heath, Exeter), *b.* 1910: *m.* 1938, Lt.-Col. Gordon Evelyn Porter Cable, 2/7th Rajput Regt. (ret.) and has issue living, Hamish Gordon Langrishe, *b.* 1949,—Andrew Duncan, *b.* 1953,—Barbara Anne, *b.* 1949: *m.* 1963, Michael Ewart Thomas, Solicitor, of Cobbles, Rockbeare, Devon, and has issue living, Nicholas Michael Guy *b.* 1966, James Duncan *b.* 1973, Penelope Anne *b.* 1964, Sarah Jane *b.* 1970.

Issue of the late Richard Langrishe, 5th son of 3rd baronet, *b.* 1834, *d.* 1922: *m.* 1st, 1863, Fannie, who *d.* 1867, da. of Stafford Chaine; 2ndly, 1871, Sarah Ogle, who *d.* 1873, da. of the late Very Rev. Ogle William Moore, Dean of Clogher; 3rdly, 1882, Amitia Sneade, who *d.* 1941, da. of the late Rev. Frederick Brown, of Fern Bank, Beckenham:—
(By 3rd m.) Mary Frances, *b.* 1885. *Residence*, 17, Talbots Inch, Kilkenny.——Marjorie Grace, *b.* 1894. *Residence*, 17 Talbots, Inch, Kilkenny.

This family is descended from Sir Nicholas Langrish, Kt., who was seized of the Manor of Langrish, Hants., A.D. 1273. The Irish branch is descended from Rafe, or Ralph (or Borden), 3rd son of Nicholas Langrishe, of Langrishe. Ralph Langrishe of Borden died between 1542-59; the 3rd in descent from him was Major Hercules Langrishe, Carver in Ordinary to Queen Henrietta Maria, who prevented the arrest of the "Five Members" by Charles I., and the 7th was the 1st baronet, Sir Hercules, who sat for forty years as M.P. for Knocktopher in the Irish Parliament. He was a Privy Councillor, and foremost in his advocacy for repealing the severe laws enacted against Roman Catholics.

LARCOM, Creation (U.K.) 1868.

Sir (CHARLES) CHRISTOPHER ROYDE LARCOM, 5th *Baronet*; *b.* Sept. 11th, 1926; *s.* his father *Sir* PHILIP, 1967; ed. at Radley, and Clare Coll., Camb. (MA); a FCA: *m.* 1956, Barbara Elizabeth, da. of Balfour Bowen, and has issue.

Arms—Argent, on a mount a hawthorn bush proper, and in chief an eagle displayed gules. Crest—On a cap of maintenance azure turned up ermine a martlet sable, with a fleur-de-lis in its beak or. *Residence*—Butlers, Hatfield Peverel, Essex. *Club*, Bath.

Le Roy, la Loy.
The King, the Law.

Daughters living—Mary Elizabeth, *b.* 1957.——Jane Catherine, *b.* 1958.——Julia Dorothy, *b.* 1961.——Anna Balfour, *b.* 1962.
Sister living—Monica Rosemary Georgina, *b.* 1921: *m.* 1942, William Eric Walrond, of 7, Old House Close, Church Rd., Wimbledon, SW19, and has issue living, Patricia Mary, *b.* 1943,—Anne Carol, *b.* 1947,—Christine Diana, *b.* 1953.

Widow living of 4th Baronet—AILEEN MONICA ROYDE (*Aileen Lady Larcom*), (Bridge View Cottage, Blandford St. Mary, Dorset), da. of the late Rev. Arthur George Colbeck, formerly R. of Hasketon, Woodbridge: *m.* 1920, Sir Philip Larcom, 4th Bt., who *d.* 1967.

The 1st baronet, Maj.-Gen. the Rt. Hon. Sir Thomas Aiskew Larcom, K.C.B., P.C. (son of the late Capt. Joseph Larcom), served in R.E., and was subsequently Under-Sec. of State for Ireland. The 2nd baronet, Lieut.-Col. Sir Charles Larcom served in NZ War 1863-4. The 3rd baronet, Major Sir Thomas Perceval Larcom, D.S.O., served with R.A. during European War 1914-18.

LATHAM, Creation (U.K.) 1919, ot Crow Clump, Walton-upon-Thames, co. Surrey.

Sir RICHARD THOMAS PAUL LATHAM, 3rd
Baronet : b. April 15th, 1934 ; *s.* his father,
Sir (HERBERT) PAUL, 1955 ; ed. at Eton, and
at Trin. Coll., Camb. (B.A. 1957, M.A. 1962) ; late
Lieut. Queen's OwnWorcestershire Hussars(T.A.):
m. 1958, Marie-Louise Patricia, da. of Frederick
H. Russell, of Vancouver, British Columbia, and
has issue.

𝔄rms—Gules, an eagle displayed or, between two bezants
in fesse, on a chief of the second a cross moline sable between
two roses of the field. 𝔠rest—An eagle, wings elevated, inverted and addorsed or, resting the dexter claw on a torteaux
and charged on the wing with a cross as in the arms.
Residence—830, Rockbridge Rd., Santa Barbara, Cal.
93108, USA.

By fortune and labour.

Daughters living—Nicola Patricia, *b.* 1959,—Alison Kathleen,
b. 1965.
Aunts living (daughters of 1st baronet)—(Violet) Irene,
b. 1895 : *m.* 1920, Cuthbert Francis Hamilton, who *d.*
1938, and from whom she had obtained a divorce 1926.
Residence, Bournebrook Cottage, Chobham, Surrey.——
Audrey Clara Lilian (*Lady Menzies*), *b.* 1899: *m.* 1st, 1921,
Henry Ralph Stanley Birkin (afterwards 3rd Bt.), who
d. 1933, and from whom she had obtained a divorce 1927; 2ndly, 1928, as his second wife, Lt.-Col.
Lord Edward Douglas John Hay, Gren. Guards [*see* M. Tweeddale], who *d.* (killed on active ser.
during 1939-45 War) 1944; 3rdly, 1948, the Hon. Niall Greville Chaplin, who *d.* 1963, and from
whom she obtained a divorce 1952 [V. Chaplin]; 4thly, 1952, Maj.-Gen. Sir Stewart Graham
Menzies, KCB, KCMG, DSO, MC, who *d.* 1968. *Residence*, The Manor, Davies St., W1.

The 1st baronet, Sir Thomas Paul Latham, was many years Joint Managing Director, and sometime Dep. Chm. of Courtaulds, Ltd., also rendered sers. to Min. of Pensions during European War
1914-19. The 2nd baronet, Sir (Herbert) Paul Latham was a Co. Councillor for London, E.
Lewisham Div. 1928-34, and sat as M.P. for Scarborough and Whitby Div. of N. Riding of Yorkshire (C) 1931-41.

LATTA, Creation (U.K.) 1920, of Portman Square, St. Marylebone, co. London.
[Extinct 1946.]

Sir JOHN LATTA, 1st and last *Baronet.*

Daughter living of 1st Baronet—Mary, *b.* 1899: *m.* 1st, 1924, Maurice Paul Richard Fontaine,
7th Marquis de Cramayel, who *d.* 1943 ; 2ndly, 1947, Count Henri Urbain Chevreau d'Antraigues,
and has issue living, (by 1st marriage) Guy François Philippe, *b.* 1925 ; *s.* his father as 8th
Marquis de Cramayel (*cr.* France 1773) 1943 : *m.* 1951 Edith Broemme, of Lausanne, Switzerland, and has issue living, Dominique Guilaine, *b.* 1952. *Residence*, l'Élysée, Ouchy-Lausanne,
Switzerland.

DICK-LAUDER, Creation (N.S.) 1690, of Fountainhall, Haddingtonshire.

Prudence is the guardian of the tower.

Sir GEORGE ANDREW DICK-LAUDER,
12th *Baronet ; b.* Nov. 17th, 1917 ; *s.* his
father, *Lieut.-Col. Sir* JOHN NORTH DAL
RYMPLE, 1958; ed. at Stowe; Maj. (ret.)
Black Watch; Author of " Let Soldiers
Lust ", " Our Man for Ganymede", and
a " Skull and Two Crystals" 1939-45 War in
Palestine, E. Africa, Middle East and Crete
(prisoner): *m.* 1945, Hester Marguerite, da. of
the late Lt.-Col. George Cecil Minett Sorel-
Cameron, CBE [B. Tollemache], and has issue.

𝔄rms—Gules, a griffin salient within a bordure argent.
𝔠rest—A tower with portcullis down, the head and
shoulders of a sentinel appearing above the battlements
in a watching posture proper. 𝔖upporters—Two lions
rampant argent.
Residence—6A, Succoth Gdns. Edinburgh, EH12
6BS. *Club*—Puffin's.

Dwell as if about to depart.

Sons living—PIERS ROBERT, *b.* Oct. 3rd, 1947.——
Mark Andrew, *b.* 1951.

Daughters living—Georgina Jane, *b.* 1949: *m.* 1973
Nicholas Ernest Kerr-Smiley [*see* Smiley, Bt., colls.]
——Selina Rose, *b.* 1955.

Sister living—Patricia Mary, *b.* 1920: *m.* 1940 (m. diss.,
1970), Maj. Ian Alastair George Davy, TD, and has
issue living, Alastair John George (Low Oxque Farm,
Marrick, Richmond, Yorks.), *b.* 1944; ed. at Charterhouse; Lt. Queen's Own Highlanders: *m.*
1968, Olivia, da. of the late Noel Butler-Madden, and has issue living, Ewan Alastair Baynton

b. 1971, Catriona Noel, *b.* 1969,—Charlotte Jane, *b.* 1942,—Jean Patricia, *b.* 1947,—Lila Christabel, *b.* 1950,—Alice Lorna Mary, *b.* 1961. *Residence*, 51, Prince's Gate Mews, SW7.

Widow living of 11th Baronet—PHYLLIS MARY (*Phyllis, Lady Dick-Lauder*), da. of the late Brig.-Gen. Herbert Augustus Iggulden, CIE: *m.* 1914, Lieut.-Col. Sir John North Dalrymple Dick-Lauder, 11th baronet, who *d.* 1958. *Residence*, Springfield, Tain, Ross shire.

This family is of Norman origin. De Lavedre being mentioned among the barons who accompanied Malcolm Canmore into Scotland. Sir Robert de Lawedre, a companion in arms of Sir William Wallace, was several times Ambassador to England from Robert I. William Lauder was Bishop of Glasgow and Chancellor of Scotland 1423, and his brother was Bishop of Dunkeld. Many of the family attained knightly honours. The 2nd baronet was a Senator of the College of Justice, with the courtesy title of Lord Fountainhall ; and the 5th baronet, who assumed the additional surname of Dick, married his cousin, Isabel, heiress of William Dick, of Grange, who was in direct descent from the Royal House of Plantagenet. Sir John North Dalrymple Dick-Lauder, 11th Bt., was Lt.-Col. Indian Army.

LAURIE, Creation (U.K.) 1834, of Bedford Square, Middlesex.

Virtue is always flourishing.

Sir JOHN EMILIUS LAURIE, *C.B.E.*, *D.S.O.*, 6th *Baronet*; *b.* Aug. 12th, 1892; *s.* his father, *Sir* WILFRID EMILIUS LAURIE, 1936; *ed.* at Eton; Hon. Maj.-Gen. (retired), Col. late Comdg. 2nd Batn. Seaforth Highlanders (Rossshire Buffs, the Duke of Albany's); 1914-18 War (despatches, DSO with Bar, Legion of Honour), 1939-41 War (despatches, CBE, Haakon VII. Liberty Cross of Norway); appointed to command Tientsin Area 1939, 157th (Highland L.I.) Inf. Brig. 1940, and 52nd (Lowland) Div. 1941 ; was Col. Seaforth Highlanders 1947-57; D.S.O. 1916 (Bar 1919), C.B.E. (Mil.) 1940 : *m.* 1922, Evelyn Clare, da. of the late Lieut.-Col. Lionel James Richardson-Gardner, 14th Hussars, and has issue.

Arms—Sable, a cup argent with a chaplet between two laurel branches, all issuing out of the same, vert. **Crest**—Two laurel branches in saltire proper.

Residence,—Woodlands, Westonbirt, Tetbury, Glos. *Clubs*—Army and Navy, Caledonian.

Son living—ROBERT BAYLEY EMILIUS (Heath House, Ardleigh, nr. Colchester, Essex), *b.* March 8th, 1931; ed. at Eton: *m.* 1968, Laurelie Meriol Winifrida, da. of the late Sir Reginald Lawrence William Williams, MBE, ED, 7th Bt. (cr. 1798), and has issue living, Clare Meriol, *b.* 1974.

Daughters living—Rosemary Evelyn Anne, *b.* 1924: *m.* 1949, Com. Robin Henry Ramsay Moodie, R.N. (retired), and has issue living, John Ramsay, *b.* 1955,—Edward Robin, *b.* 1956. *Residence*, Norman Court Farm, Upper Clatford, Andover, Hants.——Marian Clare, *b.* 1927 : *m.* 1950, Hector Laing, and has issue living, Mark Hector, *b.* 1951,—Robert John, *b.* 1953,— Anthony Rupert, *b.* 1955. *Residence*, High Meadows, Gerrards Cross, Bucks.

Sisters living—Evelyn Mary, *b.* 1894: *m.* 1923, Lt.-Col. Noel Edward Baxter, formerly Hampshire Regt., who *d.* 1950, and has issue living, Alan George Laurie (of Gilston, Largoward, Fife), *b.* 1927.——Jean Winifred (c/o National Provincial Bank, S. Audley St., W1), *b.* 1895: *m.* 1948, Ronald Schofield, who *d.* 1964.——Eila Isabel, *b.* 1901: *m.* 1928, as his second wife, Rear-Adm. James Uchtred Farie, CMG, who *d.* 1957. *Residence*, Church Lane House, Lymington, Hants.

Collateral Branches living.

Granddaughter of the late Sir Lyttelton Holyoake BAVLEY, 2nd son of 2nd baronet :—
Issue of the late Vernon Batthyány Fector BAVLEY, *b.* 1860, *d.* 1920: *m.* 1894, Mary Frederica, who *d.* 1949, da. of the late Maj.-Gen. Alexander Clark-Kennedy, I.S.C. :—
Frederica Mary Isabel (94, Chelverton Rd., Putney, SW15), *b.* 1897: *m.* 1920, Henry Theodore Warren Oswell, Malayan Civil Ser., who *d.* 1970 [Warren, Bt., colls.], and has issue living, Hugh Henry Bayley (of Acomb House, Hexham, Northumberland), *b.* 1925; ed. at Stowe; Lieut. Com. RN (ret.): *m.* 1st, 1953 (m. diss. 1974), Helen Jocelyn McMillan, da. of Frank Harvey; 2ndly, 1974, Mary Claire, da. of Frank Bailey, and has issue living (by 1st wife) Rupert Hugh Bayley, *b.* 1966, (by 2nd wife), Rosamond Helen *b.* 1969,—Quintin Miles Bayley (c/o Child & Co., 1, Fleet St., EC4), *b.* 1935; ed. at St. Paul's Sch.; Sqdn. Ldr. RAF: *m.* 1956, Ingerid, da. of Torvald Strømnes, and has issue living, Isabel Susan Ingerid, *b.* 1957,—Rosamund Theodora Mary, *b.* 1920: *m.* 1941 (m. diss. 1952), Graham G. Hough, and has issue living, Julian Graham Theodore, *b.* 1947, Felicity Mary, *b.* 1942,—Anthea Priscilla Frederica, *b.* 1927: *m.* 1955, Ronald Alley, of 61, Deodar Rd., SW15, and has issue living, Fiona Fiammetta Ann *b.* 1955, Antonia Melissa Ann *b.* 1962.

Issue of the late Cecil Emilius Laurie, 3rd son of 3rd baronet, *b.* 1862, *d.* 1919 : *m.* 1900, Helen Janet Douglas, who *d.* 1919, da. of the late Lieut. Robert Douglas Campbell, R.N. [B. Blythswood, colls.] :—
Archibald Montague, *b.* 1904:——Alice Helen, *b.* 1901: *m.* 1935, Norman Edward Feasey, of 124, Queens Gate, S.W.7.——Cassandra Gladys, *b.* 1905.——Margaret May (*Lady Houldsworth*), *b.* 1908: *m.* 1934, Col. Sir Reginald Douglas Henry Houldsworth, 4th Bt., *cr.* 1887, O.B.E., T.D. *Residence*, Kirkbride, Maybole, Ayrshire.——Frances Muriel, *b.* 1909: *m.* 1938, the Rev. James Bruce Harington Evans, R. of St. Marylebone, who *d.* 1958, and has issue living, Anthony James Cecil, *b.* 1940,—Judith Frances, *b.* 1946.——Christina Eve, *b.* 1912: *m.* 1938, Kenneth Murray McCall, and has issue living, David, *b.* 1941,—William, *b.* 1944,—Patricia Helen, *b.* 1942,—Joan, *b.* 1948. *Residence*, Caitloch, Moniaive, Dumfriesshire.——Elizabeth Janet, *b.* 1915: *m.* 1st, 1947 (m. diss. 1960), Francis Marshall; 2ndly, 1960, Francis Dudley Rose, who *d.* 1968, and has issue living, (by 1st m.) Julian Emilius Harold, *b.* 1950,—Janet Philippa Ann, *b.* 1949.

Grandchildren of the late Cecil Emilius Laurie (ante) :—
Issue of the late Ronald Edward Laurie, *b.* 1911, *d.* 1952: *m.* 1941, Rosemary Lillan
Fullerton, of 2, Lostock Av., Poynton, Stockport, Cheshire, SK12 1DR:—
Andrew Ronald Emilius (51, Derwentdale Gdns., Newcastle-upon-Tyne, 7), *b.* 1944: *m.* 1970,
Sarah Anne, el. da. of C. D. Patterson, of Hexham, and has issue living, John Christopher
Emilius, *b.* 1971,—Michael James Edward, *b.* 1973.——Rosemary Helen, *b.* 1942: *m.* 1966,
David McMullan, of 2, Lostock Av., Poynton, Stockport, Cheshire, SK12 1DR, and has issue
living, Andrew David Sean, *b.* 1970.

Grandchildren of the late Kennett BAYLEY, son of the late Rev. Kennett
Champain Bayley, 2nd son of 1st baronet :—
Issue of the late Kennett Champain BAYLEY, *b.* 1873, *d.* 1935: *m.* 1902, Norah Kathleen,
who *d.* 1963, only da. of the late Capt. Henry William Roberts, formerly 98th Regt., of
Hollingside, Durham:—
John Maurice, DSC, *b.* 1905; ed. at Rugby; Cdr. (ret.) RN: *m.* 1935, Mary Boyd. da. of F. M.
Osborn, of Sheffield, and has issue living, *Rev.* Michael John (27, Thornsett Rd., Sheffield,
S7 1NB), *b.* 1936; ed. at Rugby, and at Corpus Christi Coll., Camb. (MA): *m.* 1963, Fleur, da.
of J. Jones, of Calverley, and has issue living, Robin Kennett *b.* 1966, Andrew John *b.* 1968, Jill
Ruth *b.* 1964, Emma Susan *b.* 1970,—Kennett Ian (*Club*, Army and Navy), *b.* 1941; ed. at
Bradfield; Capt. 1st R. Green Jackets: *m.* 1955, Helen Julia, da. of P. D. Benjafield, of Shalford,
Surrey, and has issue living, Benjamin George Robson *b.* 1967, Sarah Mary Helen *b.* 1969,—
Peter Charles, *b.* 1943; ed. at Durham. *Residence*, Scargill Lodge, nr. Barnard Castle. *Club*,
United Service.——Ethel Meverell (*Hon. Mrs. John F. A. Roche*), *b.* 1906: *m.* 1928, the Hon.
John Fenwick Adair Roche [*see* B. Roche], and has issue living, Joanna Mary, *b.* 1932: *m.* 1954,
Dr. John Rideal Scarr, of PO Box 969, Gwelo, Rhodesia, and has issue living, James *b.* 1955,
Thomas *b.* 1957, Alison *b.* 1958, Jennifer Anne *b.* 1961. *Residence*, Hospital End, Moreton-in-
Marsh.

Issue of the late Col. Arthur George BAYLEY, C.B.E., D.S.O., *b.* 1878, *d.* 1949: *m.* 1923,
Katharine Mary Frederica, who *d.* 1952, da. of the late Brig.-Gen. Francis Alexander
Fortescue, C.B., C.M.G. [E. Fortescue, colls.] :—
Elizabeth Frances Mary Louise, *b.* 1924: *m.* 1st, 1947 (m. diss. 1953), John David Nicholas Retallack,
late Maj. Welsh Gds.; 2ndly, 1953, Francis Trelawny Williams, of Tofthill, Gattonside, Melrose,
Roxburghshire [Salusbury-Trelawny, Bt.], and has issue living, (by 2nd m.) Trelawny Michael,
b. 1957.

The 1st baronet, the Right Hon. Sir John Bayley, was for many years a Judge of the Queen's
Bench, and subsequently a Baron of the Exchequer. The Rev. Sir John Robert Laurie Emilius
Bayley, 3rd baronet, assumed by Roy. licence 1887 the surname and arms of Laurie of Maxwelton,
in lieu of his patronymic. The 4th baronet, Col. Sir Claude Villiers Emilius Laurie, C.B., D.S.O.,
served in S. Africa 1900-1902 (despatches, D.S.O.).

LAWES, Creation (U.K.) 1882, of Rothamsted, co. Hertford.

Sir JOHN CLAUDE BENNET LAWES, 4th
Baronet ; b. Sept. 9th, 1898 ; *s.* his father, *Sir* JOHN
BENNET *LAWES-WITTEWRONGE*, 1931 ; Euro-
pean War 1917-19 as 2nd Lieut. R.F.A.; relinquished
the surname of Wittewronge by deed poll in Guernsey 1951 : *m.* 1st, 1928, Kathleen Marjorie Livingstone, who *d.* 1938, da. of the late Gerald Tylston
Hodgson; 2ndly, 1938, Naomi Constance Helen, da.
of the late Lancelot Wykeham Badnall, and has issue
by 1st and 2nd marriages.

Arms—Quarterly : 1st and 4th argent, three bendlets gules
on a chief sable, a barrulet dancettée or ; 2nd and 3rd or, two
flaunches azure, on a chief nebuly of the second three estoiles or.
Crests—1st, a Saracen's head affrontée, and couped below the
shoulders proper, wreathed about the temples, and tied in a bow
or and gules ; 2nd, on a mount vert the trunk of a tree fessewise
eradicated and sprouting to the dexter, surmounted by an ermine passant proper.

Pour la Foi.
For the faith.

Residence—Le Clos du Coudré, St. Pierre du Bois, Guernsey, Channel Islands.

Son living—By 1st marriage—JOHN MICHAEL BENNET, *b.* Oct. 24th, 1932; ed. at Elizabeth
Coll., Guernsey.

Daughter living—By 2nd marriage—Janet Caroline, *b.* 1940: *m.* 1964, John Christopher Berney-
Ficklin.

The 1st baronet, Sir John Bennet Lawes, DSc, FRS, achieved considerable fame as a practical
experimental agricultural chemist. He was grandson of Thomas Lawes, who inherited Rothamsted
from his maternal uncle John Bennet. Rothamsted was inherited by the last named from his
cousin Thomas Wittewronge in 1763, as the maternal grandson of James Wittewronge of Rothamsted, Recorder of St. Albans. The 2nd baronet, Sir Charles Bennet, assumed by Roy. licence 1902,
for himself and issue, the additional surname and arms of Wittewronge.

LAWRENCE, Creation (U.K.) 1858, of Lucknow.

Sir JOHN WALDEMAR LAWRENCE, *OBE*, 6th *Baronet*; *b.* May 27th, 1907; *s.* his brother, *Sir* HENRY EUSTACE WALDEMAR, 1967; *ed.* at Eton, and New Coll., Oxford; Editor of *Frontier;* late Press Attaché at Moscow; Officer of Order of Orange Nassau of the Netherlands; OBE (Civil) 1945: *m.* 1948, Mrs. Jacynth Donaldson-Hudson, da. of the late Rev. Francis George Ellerton.

Arms—Ermine, on a cross raguly gules an eastern crown or; on a chief azure two swords in saltire proper, pommels and hilts gold, between as many leopards' heads argent.   **Crest**—Out of an eastern crown or, a cubit arm entwined by a wreath of laurel and holding a dagger all proper.
Residence—24, St. Leonards Terr. SW3.

Never give in.

Brother living—GEORGE ALEXANDER WALDEMAR, *b.* Sept. 22nd, 1910; *ed.* at Eton and at Trin Coll., Camb.: *m.* 1949, Olga, da. of Peter Schilovsky, and has issue living, Henry Peter, *b.* 1952,—Natalia Honoria, *b.* 1951,—Letitia Catherine, *b.* 1953. *Residence,* Brockham End, Bath.

Daughter living of 2nd Baronet—Norah Margaret, *b.* 1891.

Sir Alexander Hutchinson Lawrence, the 1st baronet, was cr. a Baronet with remainder to his issue male, failing which to his younger brother, and was accidentally killed, Aug. 27th, 1864 by the falling of a bridge on the Tibet road, India.   He was eldest son of the illustrious Sir Henry Montgomery Lawrence, KCB, who fell in defence of Lucknow in 1857.

LAWRENCE, Creation (U.K.) 1867, of Ealing Park, Middlesex.

Sir WILLIAM LAWRENCE, 4*th Baronet;* *b.* July 14th, 1913; *s.* his father, *Sir* WILLIAM MATTHEW TREVOR, 1934 ; *ed.* at Bradfield Coll. ; European War 1939-45 as Major E. Surrey Regt. : *m.* 1st, 1940 (marriage dissolved 1945), Zoe, da. of H. S. Pether, of Grazeley House, Iffley, Oxon; 2ndly, 1945, Pamela Mary, younger da. of J. E. Gordon, of Beechbank, Bromborough, Wirral, Cheshire, nd has issue by 2nd marriage.

Arms—Ermine, a cross raguly gules, in the first and fourth quarters a serpent nowed proper.   **Crest**—A griffin's head couped argent, in front thereof a serpent nowed proper.

Residence—The Knoll, Walcote, near Alcester, Warwick-shire.

By mind and work.

Son living—By 2nd marriage—WILLIAM FETTIPLACE, *b.* Aug. 23rd, 1954; *ed.* at King Edward VI Sch., Stratford on Avon.

Daughters living—By 2nd marriage—Lavinia Margaret, *b.* 1947: *m.* 1971, Julian Conway Seymour [*see* M. Hertford, colls.].——Carolyn Mary (c/o Barclays Bank, 29, High St., Alcester, Warwicks.), *b.* 1949: *m.* 1972, Nicholas Peter Evelyn, and has issue living, Rupert Peter, *b.* 1973.

Sisters living—Mary Barbara, *b.* 1909: *m.* 1933, His Honour Judge Alfred Alexander Gordon Clark, who *d.* 1958, and has issue living, Rev. Charles Philip Gordon (King Charles Vicarage, Frant Rd., Tunbridge Wells, Kent), *b.* 1936, ed. at Eton, and at Worcester Coll., Oxford (MA): *m.* 1965, Thalia Elizabeth, da. of Cdr. Frederick William Fitzjohn Oldham, OBE, RNVR, and has issue living, Alexander David *b.* 1970, Sophia Jane *b.* 1967,—Alexander Mary Gordon, *b.* 1938; ed. at London Univ. (BA): *m.* 1963, Hugo Martin Wedgwood, of Pixham Mill, Pixham Lane, Dorking, el. son of Sir John Hamilton Wedgwood, TD, 2nd Bt.,—Cecilia Mary Gordon, *b.* 1944; ed. at Lady Margaret Hall, Oxford (BA): *m.* 1972, Roderick Saxon Snell, of 75, Florence Rd., Brighton, and has issue living, Maurice Saxon *b.* 1973. *Residence*, Berry's Croft, Westhumble, Dorking, Surrey. ——Elizabeth Anne, *b.* 1910: *m.* 1937, Clement Nelson Swann, F/O RAF, who *d.* 1938, and has issue living, Clemency Anne Rosemary (posthumous), *b.* 1939: *m.* 1962, Michael Selby Gray, of 113, Warwick Av., W9, and has issue living, Ossian *b.* 1966, Hester Amanda Jessica *b.* 1964, Lucy Emily *b.* 1965.——Naomi, *b.* 1915: *m.* 1st, 1939, Richard Peppercorn Duckham; 2ndly, 1957, Flt-Lt. Vivian James, RAF, and has issue living, (by 2nd m.) Siriol Anne, *b.* 1960. *Residence,* Swiss Cottage, Box Hill, Tadworth, Surrey.

Collateral Branch living.

Issue of the late Aubrey Trevor Lawrence, M.B.E., K.C., 2nd son of 2nd baronet, *b.* 1875, *d.* 1930 : *m.* 1901, Constance Emily Fanning, who *d.* 1957, da. of the late Joseph McGaw, of Mickleham Downs, Dorking, and Kooba, N.S. Wales:—
Peter Stafford Hayden (The Great House, Gt. Milton, Oxford; Eton College, Windsor), *b.* 1913; ed. at Eton, and Ch. Ch., Oxford (MA); Assist. Master at Eton since 1936 (House Master 1951-68); 1939-45 War as Lt.-Cdr. RNVR, Radar Officer (despatches): *m.* 1940, Helena Frances, da. of the late Hon. George William Lyttelton [*see* V. Cobham, colls.], and has issue living, Aubrey Lyttelton Simon, *b.* 1942,—Robin Peter Charles, *b.* 1950,—Pamela Jane, *b.* 1945,—Anthea Mary, *b.* 1947,—Jemima Rachel, *b.* 1956,—Susanna Lucy, *b.* 1958.——Ruth Christian, *b.* 1904: is a JP: *m.* 1934, Philip Olaf Buxton, of Widford Manor, Burford, Oxford [*see* Buxton, Bt., colls.].

The 1st baronet, a distinguished surgeon, was a F.R.S., Corresponding Member of Institute of France, a Member of the principal scientific sos. of Europe and America, twice President of the College of Surgeons, and for many years Sergeant-Surgeon to H.M. Queen Victoria.   The 2nd baronet, Sir Trevor, sat as M.P. for Mid Surrey 1875-85 and for S.-E. Div. of Surrey 1885-92, and was 28 years Pres. of Roy. Horticultural So. and 12 years Treasurer of St. Bartholomew's Hospital.

LAWRENCE, Creation (U.K.) 1906, of Sloane Gardens, Chelsea.

GWAITH · GYDA · GOBAITH

Sir DAVID (ROLAND WALTER) LAWRENCE, 3rd *Baronet*; *b.* May 8th, 1929; *s.* his father, *Lieut.-Col. Sir* (PERCY) ROLAND (BRADFORD), *M.C.,* 1950; *ed.* at Radley; sometime Capt. Coldstream Guards: *m.* 1955, Audrey, dau. of Brigadier Desmond Young, M.C., and formerly wife of 11th Duke of Leeds.

Arms—Ermine, an escarbuncle or, surmounted by a lotus flower proper, on a chief arched gules a dragon passant or. *Crest*—A cubit arm, vested gules, cuffed ermine, holding in the hand a plane leaf proper, and charged on the sleeve with a trefoil slipped or. *Supporters* —On either side a heron holding in the beak a sprig of plane fructed proper.

Residence—28, High Town Rd., Maidenhead, Berks.

Brother living—CLIVE WYNDHAM (Whites, Goudhurst, Kent), *b.* Oct. 6th, 1939; *ed.* at Gordonstoun; late Lt. Coldm. Gds.: *m.* 1966, Sophia Annabel Stuart, da. of Ian Hervey Stuart Black, of The Old Manse, Balfron, Stirlingshire, and has issue living, James Wyndham Stuart, *b.* 1970,—Simon Roland Stuart, *b.* 1973.

Sisters living—Jean Jacqueline, *b.* 1926: *m.* 1950, Harold Channing Quitman, and has issue living Jeremy Roland Channing, *b.* 1953,—Annabel Susan Maud, *b.* 1951. *Residence,* 3, Ormonde Gate, SW3.——Susan Louise, *b.* 1944: *m.* 1965, Norman Gardner, of Montreal, and has issue iving, Suzanne Vanessa *b.* 1965,—Amanda Sarah, *b.* 1968.

Widow living of 2nd Baronet—SUSAN (*Susan, Lady Lawrence*), da. of **Sir Charles Stewart Addis,** K.C.M.G.: *m.* 1925. Lieut.-Col. Sir (Percy) Roland (Bradford) Lawrence, M.C., 2nd baronet, who *d.* 1950. *Residence,* 33, Edith Grove, SW10.

Collateral Branch living.

Issue of the late Capt. (Henry Walter) Neville Lawrence, 2nd son of 1st baronet, *b.* 1891, *d.* 1959 : *m.* 1933, Sarah, who *d.* 1947, da. of Nicholas Murray Butler, of New York, U.S.A. :—

Walter Nicholas Murray, *b.* 1935: *m.* 1961, Sally Louise, da. of Lt.-Col. A. B. O'Dwyer, and has issue living, Sarah Louise, *b.* 1962,—Catherine Jane, *b.* 1964. *Residence,* Grey Walls, Hook Heath, Woking.

The 1st baronet, Sir Walter Roper Lawrence, G.C.I.E., G.C.V.O., C.B. (son of the late George Lawrence, J.P., of Trevella, Llangwm, Monmouthshire), was Private Sec. to Viceroy of India 1898-1903, Ch. of Staff for visit of T.R.H. the Prince and Princess of Wales to India 1905-6, and a member of Council of India 1907-9. The 2nd baronet Sir (Percy) Roland (Bradford) Lawrence, M.C., was Lieut.-Col. Coldstream Guards.

Lawrence-Jones, see Jones.

LAWSON, Creation (U.K.) 1841, of Brough Hall, Yorkshire.

LEVE ET RELUIS.

Arise, and re-illumine.

Sir WILLIAM HOWARD LAWSON, 5th *Baronet,* *b.* July 15th, 1907; *s.* his brother, *Sir* RALPH HENRY, 1975; *ed.* at Ampleforth; DL of Cumbria; *Knt.* of Malta 1965: *m.* 1933, Joan Eleanor, da. of the late Maj. Arthur Cowie Stamer, CBE [see Stamer, Bt., Colls.], and has issue.

Arms—Argent, a chevron between three martlets sable. *Crest*—On a cap of maintenance gules turned up ermine, a martlet proper.

Residence—Wood House, Warwick Bridge, Carlisle.

Sons living—JOHN PHILIP HOWARD (Corby Castle, Carlisle), *b.* June 6th, 1934; assumed by Roy. Licence 1962 the surname and arms of Howard: *m.* 1960, Jean Veronica, da. of the late Col. John Evelyn Marsh, DSO, OBE, and has issue living, Philip William, *b.* 1961,— Thomas John, *b.* 1963,—Julia Frances Veronica, *b.* 1964. ——Hugh William *LAWSON* (Croftlands, Heads Nook, Carlisle), *b.* 1936; *ed.* at Ampleforth: *m.* 1961, Margaret Ann, da. of the late Maj. Richard Gubbins Mounsey Heysham, of Castletown, Carlisle, and has issue living, Simon David, *b.* 1962,—Philippa Joan, *b.* 1963,— Pollyanne Lucy, *b.* 1971.——Arthur Mark *LAWSON* (Innes Mill, Urquhart, by Elgin, Moray), *b.* 1940; *ed.* at Ampleforth: *m.* 1968, Rosemary Veronica, da. of Samuel Parkington Vickery, of Ardwell, Newlands, Glasgow, and has issue living, Henry Benedict, *b.* 1970.

Daughter living—Mary Frances, *b.* 1947: *m.* 1969, Julian Rupert Smithers, of Paynes Farm, Radwinter, Saffron Walden, Essex, and has issue living, William Rupert John, *b.* 1973,—Louise Jane, *b.* 1971.

Daughters living of 4th Baronet—Valerie Anne, *b.* 1936: *m.* 1960, Benjamin Worthington [E. Aylesford], of Milbourne Hall, Ponteland, Newcastle upon Tyne, and has issue living, Greville Thomas, *b.* 1963,—Ursula, *b.* 1962,—Lucy-Mary, *b.* 1967.——Alethea Jill Clare, *b.* 1940.

Sisters living—Mary Catherine, *b.* 1900: *m.* 1926, Geoffrey Grosvenor Eccles Bradley, who *d.* 1945. *Residence,* The Clints, Great Corby, Carlisle.——Aurea Clare, *b.* 1901 : *m.* 1926, Alberic Waterkeyn, and has issue living, Denis Gerard HOWARD (Beach House, Fairlie, Ayrshire), *b.*

1929; assumed by Roy. Licence 1962, the surname and arms of Howard: *m.* 1957, Betty Plant, da. of Howard Greenham, Agent-Gen. of S. Australia, and has issue living, Francis *b.* 1960, Catherine Anne *b.* 1959,—Cecilia Mary, *b.* 1926: *m.* 1947, Philip Marland Rambaut, of Beck House, Bosley, Macclesfield, Cheshire, and has issue living, Michael Adrian, *b.* 1948, Anthony Howard *b.* 1950, Benedict Peter *b.* 1954, Andrea Clare Mary *b.* 1957. *Residence*, Corby Castle, Carlisle.

Widow living of 4th Baronet—HELEN BERESFORD, (*Beres, Lady Lawson*) (Wood House, Catterick, York.), da. of Richard Cornelius, and formerly wife of (i) Capt. Kenyon Goode, and (ii) Capt. Edward Joseph Algernon Petre (see B. Petre, colls.): *m.* 1970, as his 2nd wife, Sir Ralph Henry Lawson, 4th Bt., who *d.* 1975.

Sir William, 1st baronet, was son of John Wright, of Kelvedon, by Elizabeth. **da. of Sir** John Lawson, 5th baronet (*cr.* 1665), of Brough Hall, whose surname he assumed. Sir Henry Joseph Lawson, 3rd baronet. In 1899, Ursula Mary, who *d.* 1960, only child and heir of Philip John Canning Howard of Corby Castle, Cumberland, descended from Col. Sir Frances Howard, of Corby Castle, son of Lord William Howard, 3rd son of 4th Duke of Norfolk, and yr. brother of Sir Philip Howard ancestor of the Earls of Carlisle.

LAWSON, Creation (U.K.) 1900, of Weetwood Grange, Headingley-cum-Burley, West Riding of Yorkshire.

Arise, and shine forth.

Sir JOHN CHARLES ARTHUR DIGBY LAWSON, *D.S.O., M.C.*, 3rd *Baronet*; *b.* Oct. 24th, 1912; *s.* his father, *Maj. Sir* DIGBY, *TD*, 1959; ed. at Stowe, and RMC; Chm. of Fairbairn Lawson, Ltd. and subsidiary cos.; a Member of Council Univ. of Leeds; Chm. of Univ. of Leeds Industrial Sers. Ltd.; OC, Inns of Court Regt. 1945-47; Col. 11th Hussars 1965-69, Hon. Col. The R. Hussars 1969-71, since when Col.; US Legion of Merit; 1939-45 War in Middle East, N. Africa and NW Europe (despatches twice, MC, DSO); DSO 1943: *m.* 1st, 1945 (m. diss. 1950), Rose, who *d.* 1972, da. of the late David Cecil Bingham, Lt. Coldm. Gds. [E. Lucan, colls.], and widow of William M. L. Fiske, Pilot Officer RAF, who *d.* (of wounds received in action in Battle of Britain) 1950; 2ndly, 1954, Tresilla Anne Eleanor (DE PRET ROOSE), da. of Maj. Eric Buller Leyborne Popham, MC, of Folly Cottage, Chewton Mendip, Somerset, and has issue by 2nd m.

Arms—Per chevron argent and or, a chevron invected sable, plain cotised vert, between two martlets in chief of the third and a trefoil slipped in base of the fourth. **Crest**—Between two arms embowed, proper the hands holding a sun in splendour a trefoil, as in the arms the whole surmounted by a rainbow also proper.

Residence—Littlethorpe House, Ripon, Yorks.   *Clubs*—Cavalry, MCC.

Son living—By 2nd marriage—CHARLES JOHN PATRICK, *b.* May 19th, 1959.

Brother living—Patrick William, *b.* 1914: *m.* 1939, Jean Mary, da. of the late Col. Sydney Ernest Smith, CBE, of Stuckeridge, Oakford, Devon, and has issue living, Nicholas Patrick David (Morestead, Windlesham Rd., Chobham, Surrey; MCC); *b.* 1940: *m.* 1st, 1962 (m. diss. 1970), Anne Sommerville de Laval Harvie; 2ndly, 1971, Jill, da. of Clifford Wendover Beeson, and formerly wife of Duncan M. Atkinson and has issue living, (by 1st m.) Julian Alexander Nicholas *b.* 1963, Rebecca de Laval *b.* 1965,—(by 2nd m.) Rupert Christopher David *b.* 1972,—Timothy James (Bourn Lodge, Bourn, Cambs.; MCC), *b.* 1942; FRICS: *m.* 1965 Elizabeth White, and has issue living, Mark James *b.* 1968, Simon Alexander *b.* 1970, Peter John *b.* 1974,—Michael Shaun (Garton, Loxwood, Sussex), *b.* 1945: *m.* 1970, Jane Hamilton, and has issue living, James Patrick *b.* 1972, Richard Shaun, *b.* 1973. *Residences*, The Old Rectory, Wrington, Somerset; 10, Eaton Mews, SW1.

Half-Brothers living—Arthur Simon Albert (Staithe Cottage, Steeple Aston, Oxon.), *b.* 1925; is Lt.-Col. N. Somerset Yeo.; formerly Lieut. 11th Hussars: *m.* 1st, 1953 (m. diss. 1961), Virginia Elizabeth Grace, da. of the late Maj. William Steel Huddleston, RHA; 2ndly, 1961, Alison Deirdre, el. da. of Lt.-Col. Ian Balmain, and has issue living (by 1st m.), Piers James, *b.* 1957,—(by 2nd m.), Frances Lisa Victoria, *b.* 1962,—Louise Christian, *b.* 1963,—Clare Alison, *b.* 1968.——Simon Digby, *b.* 1945: *m.* 1972, Georgina Mary, da. of Sqdn. Ldr. J. C. G. Surll.

Sister living—Daphne Olive, *b.* 1910: *m.* 1936, Maj. Richard Edwin Fearing Cely Trevilian, TD, and has issue living, John Maurice Richard, *b.* 1948: *m.* 1971, Penelope, yst. da. of Raymond Hodgson, of Craig, Balmaclellan, Kirkcudbrightshire,—Jane Mary, *b.* 1938: *m.* 1960, Adam Stanislaus Kwiatkowski, and has issue living, Damian Michael Richard *b.* 1965, Sophia Helena *b.* 1963,— Susanna Rose, *b.* 1939: *m.* 1962, Jeremy Gwynne Pilcher, and has issue living, Jonathan Swaine *b.* 1965, Katharine Alexandra *b.* 1963, Charlotte Serena (twin) *b.* 1963,—Teresa Melliscent, *b.* 1946: *m.* 1971, Edward Anthony Dawson. *Residence*, Midelney Manor, Langport, Somerset.

The 1st baronet, Sir Arthur Tredgold Lawson, was Chm. of Fairbairn, Lawson, Combe-Barbour. Ltd., and a Director of Great Eastern Railway and the *Yorkshire Post*. The 2nd baronet, Major Sir Digby Lawson, T.D., was Chm. of Fairbairn, Lawson, Combe-Barbour, Ltd., of Leeds and Belfast, and of Urquhart Lindsay & Robertson Orchar, Ltd., of Dundee.

LAWSON, Creation (U.K.) 1905, of Knavesmire Lodge, City of York. [Extinct 1973.]

Sir PETER GRANT LAWSON, 2nd and last *Baronet*.

Daughter living of 1st baronet—Griselda Grant, *b.* 1905. *Residence*, Cottesbrooke Grange, Northampton.

Widow living of 2nd Baronet—Virginia (*Lady Grant Lawson*), (Venards House, N. Gorley, Fording-bridge, Hants.), yst. da. of the late Sidney Butler Dean, of St. Paul, Minnesota, USA: *m.* 1940, Col. Sir Peter Grant Lawson, 2nd Bt., who *d.* 1973, when the title became ext.

Lawson-Tancred, see Tancred.

LEA, Creation (U.K.) 1892, of The Larches, Kidderminster, Worcestershire, and Sea Grove, Dawlish, Devon.

Sir THOMAS CLAUDE HARRIS LEA, 3rd *Baronet; b.* April 13th, 1901; *s.* his father, *Sir* (THOMAS) SYDNEY, 1946; ed. at Lancing Coll., and at Clare Coll., Camb. (B.A. and LL.B. 1923), is Com. R.N.V(S).R.: *m.* 1st, 1924, Barbara Katharine, *O.B.E., J.P.,* who *d.* 1945, da. of the late Albert J. Pell, J.P., D.L. [Greene, Bt.]; 2ndly, 1950, Diana (BANNAR-MARTIN), only da. of Howard Thompson, of Coton Hall, Bridgnorth, Salop., and has issue by 1st marriage.

Arms—Or, a fesse indented gules, between in chief two lions passant of the second, in base a rock, thereon a beaver proper, spotted ermine, holding in the mouth a sprig of willow slipped vert. *Crest*—In front of a mount vert, thereon a demi-heraldic antelope argent, supporting a bird bolt erect or, three pheons fessewise sable.

Semper fidelis.
Always faithful. *Residence*, Coneybury, Bayton, near Kidderminster, Worcestershire.

Son living—By 1st m.—THOMAS JULIAN (Batchelors Hall, Hundon, W. Suffolk), *b.* Nov. 18th, 1934; Lt. RN (ret.): *m.* 1970, Gerry Valerie, only da. of the late Capt. Gibson Clarence Fahnestock, USAF, and has issue living, Thomas William, *b.* 1973,—Rebecca Barbara, *b.* 1972.

Daughters living—By 1st marriage—Barbara Mary, *b.* 1925 : *m.* 1951, James Blackley Hague Goble, and has issue living, Timothy James Lea, *b.* 1957.—Jonathan Julian, *b.* 1961. *Residence,* Bonningtons, Takeley, Bishop's Stortford, Herts.—Rosemary, *b.* 1927.—Philippa Margaret, *b.* 1929: *m.* 1960, Orlando Michael Philip Kenyon-Slaney [*see* B. Kenyon, colls.]. *Residence,* Oakwood, St. Michael's, Tenterden, Kent.—Lavinia Ann, *b.* 1932: *m.* 1960, Andrew Bethell Marsden-Smedley [*see* B. Westbury, colls.]. *Residence,* Glebe House, Bayton, nr. Kidderminster, Worcs.

Brothers living—Robert Francis Gore, *O.B.E.,* b. 1906; ed. at Lancing Coll., and at Clare Coll., Camb. (B.A. 1927, M.A. 1934): is acting Wing-Com. Auxiliary Air Force (Reserve); O.B.E. (Mil.) 1942 : *m.* 1st, 1939, Valerie Josephine, who *d.* 1948, da. of Lieut. Sir James Henry Domville, R.N., 5th Bt. ; 2ndly, 1956, Susan, da. of John Greenwood, of The Priory of Lady St. Mary, Wareham, Dorset, and has issue living, (by 2nd marriage) Francis Rupert Chad, *b.* 1957.— (by 1st marriage) Annabel Ophelia Clare, *b.* 1945. *Residence,* Temple Mill, Duxford, Cambridgeshire.——John Sydney Birch, *b.* 1911 ; ed. at St. Edward's Sch., Oxford : *m.* 1954, Elisabeth Edith Maunsell, da. of Lieut.-Col. Philip Victor Willingham Gell, of Hopton Hall, Wirksworth, Derbyshire, and has issue living, Richard John Philip, *b.* 1957.—Sarah Caroline Aileen, *b.* 1956. *Residence,* Dunley Hall, Stourport, Worcestershire.

Sister living—Mary Truda, *b.* 1904: *m.* 1954, Cyril Reginald Egerton [*see* D. Sutherland, colls.]. *Residence,* Hall Farm, Newmarket, Suffolk.

Collateral Branch living.

Issue of the late Rev. Percy Harris Lea, son of 1st baronet, *b.* 1872, *d.* 1957: *m.* 1896, Katharine Ellen Margaret, who *d.* 1941, da. of the late Rev. R. A. Gent :—

George Francis Percivale, *b.* 1901 ; ed. at Westminster, and at Trin. Coll., Camb. (B.A. 1923): *m.* 1934, Maria, da. of W. Schulz, of Bratislava, Czechoslovakia, and Vienna, and has issue living, William Francis Peter, *b.* 1944. *Residence,* Rua Traipu, 589, São Paulo, Brazil.

William Butcher: *m.* 1792, Elizabeth, da. of Francis Lea, of Kidderminster. Their son, George Butcher Lea, assumed by Roy. Licence 1834, the surname of Lea. His son, Sir Thomas Lea, of the Larches, Kidderminster, MP for Kidderminster, co. Donegal and S. Londonderry, was cr. a Baronet 1892.

LECHMERE, Creation (U.K.) 1818, of The Rhydd, Worcestershire.

[Name pronounced "Letchmere."]

Sir BERWICK HUNGERFORD LECHMERE, 6th *Baronet; b.* Sept. 21st, 1917; *s.* his father, *Capt. Sir* RONALD BERWICK HUNGERFORD, 1965; ed. at Charterhouse, and at Magdalene Coll., Camb.: *m.* 1st, 1952 (marriage annulled on her petition 1954), Susan Adele Mary, only child of Cdr. G. H. Maunsell-Smyth, RN; 2ndly, 1954, Norah G., el. da. of Col. Christopher Garrett Elkington, DSO, DL, of Mount Pleasant, W. Malvern.

Arms—Gules, a fesse, and in chief two pelicans vulning themselves or. *Crest*—A pelican as in the arms.

Residence,—Severn End, Hanley Castle, Worcester.

CHRISTUS · PELICANO
Christ in the pelican.

Sister living—Joan Penelope Alice, *b.* 1919.

Widow living of 5th Baronet—CONSTANCE MARGUERITE (*Marguerite Lady Lechmere*), (Whittemere, Hanley Castle, Worcs.), da. of the late Lt.-Col. Charles Wigram Long, RA: *m.* 1915, Capt. Sir Ronald Berwick Hungerford Lechmere, 5th Baronet, who *d.* 1965.

Collateral Branch living.

Issue of the late Anthony Hungerford Lechmere, 3rd son of 3rd baronet, *b.* 1868, *d.* 1954: *m.* 1920, Cicely Mary, who *d.* 1964, da. of the late Rev. Charles Bridges, R. of Bredenbury, Herefordshire, and widow of William George Lupton, of The Green, Bromyard, Herefordshire:—

REGINALD ANTHONY HUNGERFORD (of Primeswell, Evendine Lane, Colwall, nr. Malvern, Worcs.), *b.* Dec. 24th, 1920; ed. at Charterhouse, and at Trin. Hall, Camb.; formerly Capt.

5th Roy. Inniskilling Dragoon Guards: *m.* 1956, Anne Jennifer, da. of the late A. C. Dind, of Orbe, Switzerland, and has issue living, Nicholas Anthony Hungerford, *b.* 1960,—Adam Francis, *b.* 1962,—Mark Edmund Dind, *b.* 1966,—Jennifer Sarah, *b.* 1959.

This family obtained lands at Hanley, Worcestershire, in the eleventh century, which have been in the family ever since. Sir Nicholas Lechmere, of Severn End, MP for Bewdley, was a Baron of the Exchequer temp. William III. His grandson, Nicholas, sometime Solicitor and Attorney-General, Chancellor of the Duchy of Lancaster, was created Baron Lechmere of Evesham 1721. The 3rd baronet sat as MP for Tewkesbury (C) 1866-68, for Worcestershire W. 1876-85, for Worcestershire W., or Bewdley Div. 1885-92, and for Worcestershire S. or Evesham Div. 1892-94.

LEEDS, Creation (U.K.) 1812, of Croxton Park, Cambridgeshire.

Sir GEORGE GRAHAM MORTIMER LEEDS, 7th *Baronet; b.* Aug. 21st, 1927; *s.* his father, *Cdr. Sir* REGINALD ARTHUR ST. JOHN, *RN,* 1970; ed. at Eton; late Capt. Gren. Gds.: *m.* 1954 (m. diss. 1965), Nicola, da. of Douglas Robertson McBean, MC, and has issue.

Arms—Argent, a fesse gules between three eagles displayed sable, within a bordure wavy of the second. **Crest**—A staff raguly vert, thereon a cock gules wings expanded, combed, wattled, beaked, and legged or, debruised by a bendlet wavy sinister ermine.

Residence—Roche Bois, Mont'es'Tours, St. Aubin, Jersey. *Clubs*—White's, Guards', Pratt's.

Vigilate !
Watch ye!

Daughters living—Miranda Noel Winnaretta, *b.* 1956.——Anthea Jane, *b.* 1958.——Harriet Annabelle, *b.* 1962.
Sister living—Rhodanthe Winnaretta, *b.* 1929: *m.* 1952, Ronald David Hutton, MC, late Capt. RE, and has issue living, Matthew Charles Arthur, *b.* 1953; ed. at Eton, and Ch. Ch., Oxford,—Deborah Helen, *b.* 1955,—Cecilia Paris (twin), *b.* 1955,—Louisa Winn, *b.* 1957. *Residence,* Langley Grange, Langley, Norwich, Norfolk, NR14 6BL.
Aunt living—Rosamond Edith Lilian (Rosehill, Parabola Rd., Cheltenham, Glos.), *b.* 1900: *m.* 1922, Major Douglas Stewart Davison, DSO, 2nd Lancers (Indian Army), who *d.* 1929, and has issue living, Nigel St. John (c/o Music Dept., Bristol Univ.), *b.* 1929; MA, MusB Camb, DMus Edinburgh, FRCO: *m.* 1965, Kirstine Grahame, da. of Graham William Churchill Meikle, and has issue living, Robert Metcalfe *b.* 1966, Michael Douglas *b.* 1970, Anna Churchill *b.* 1968,—Stella Stewart, *b.* 1923; late 2nd Officer WRNS: *m.* 1946, Maurice Gerald Low, MB, ChB, Surg.-Lt. Cdr. RNVR (ret.), of Lyndhurst, Middlecave Rd., Malton, Yorks., and has issue living, Donald *b.* 1948, Hamish Stewart *b.* 1960, Fiona *b.* 1947, Catriona *b.* 1951,—Alison Daphne (twin), *b.* 1923; formerly in WRNS: *m.* 1959, John Clement Ball, MD, CM, formerly Roy. Canadian Artillery, of 29, Parklane Cres., St. Catherines, Ont., Canada, and has issue living, John Clement *b.* 1960, Rosamond Eleanor *b.* 1962.
Widow living of 6th Baronet—WINNARETTA (*Winnaretta, Lady Leeds*) (Little Oldway, Paignton, S. Devon), da. of the late Paris Eugene Singer: *m.* 1926, Cdr. Sir Reginald Arthur St. John Leeds, RN, 6th Bt., who *d.* 1970.

Collateral Branches living.

Issue of the late Maj. Geoffrey Hugh Anthony Leeds, brother of 6th baronet, *b.* 1911, *d.* 1962: *m.* 1st, 1934, Yolande, who *d.* 1944, da. of James Alexander Mitchell; 2ndly, 1945, Florence (of Croxton, 39, Rabling Rd., Swanage, Dorset), da. of the late Arthur Marshall Longfield:—
(By 1st m.) CHRISTOPHER ANTHONY (Croxton, 39, Rabling Rd., Swanage, Dorset), *b.* Aug. 31st, 1935; ed. at King's Sch, Bruton, London Univ. (BScEcon), and Univ. of S. Cal., USA (MA): *m.* 1974, Elaine Joyce, da. of the late Sq. Ldr. C. H. A. Mullins.

Grandchildren of the late Henry Leeds, 2nd son of 2nd baronet :—
Issue of the late Very Rev. Joseph Edward Henry Leeds, B.D., *b.* 1857, *d.* 1907 : *m.* 1882 (marriage dissolved 1891), Elizabeth Massey, da. of the late Richard Quin, J.P., of Firgrove House, Innishannon, co. Cork :—
Marion Adelaide Lucy, *b.* 1882.——Lilian Anna Marian, *b.* 1884 : *m.* 1907, H. Davison. *Residence,*
Issue of the late Edward Adderley Oglander Leeds, *b.* 1869, *d.* 1923 : *m.* 1895, a da. of R. F. Vevers, of Hereford :—
Vera Mary, *b.* 1898. *Residence,*
Issue of the late Charles George Stretton Leeds, M.D., *b.* 1875, *d.* 1909 : *m.* (March) 1905, Louisa Christian (who *d.* 1960, having *m.* 2ndly, 1921, Archibald Clark, of Ferryden, Montrose, who *d.* 1936, and 3rdly, 1940, John McLinden, of Glasgow, who *d.* 1960), only da. of the late James Barker Duncan, W. S., of 6, Hill Street, Edinburgh :—
Lilian Margaret, *b.* 1908 : Diploma of Art, Edinburgh Coll. of Art 1929. *Residence,* 56, South Trinity Road, Edinburgh, EH5 3NX.

Grandson of the late Capt. William Montagu Leeds, 3rd son of 2nd baronet:—
Issue of the late William Henry Montagu Leeds, *b.* 1858, *d.* 1947 : *m.* 1892, Mary, who *d.* 1956, el. da. of the late James Fyfe-Jamieson, of Monisbrock, Renfrewshire, and 9, Queen's Gate, S.W. :—
Aubrey, *b.* 1903: *m.* 1933, Barbara, only child of J. Travis, of Lightcliffe, Yorks., and has issue living, Antony Hildyard (33, Fairfield Rd., Toronto, Ont., Canada), *b.* 1937: *m.* 1966, (m. diss 1973), Elizabeth Helen Cornell, of Toronto,—Sally Gillian, *b.* 1936: *m.* 1961, John A. Nation, BSc, PhD, of 203, Winston Av., Ithaca, NY14850, USA, and has issue living, Philip David Oliver *b.* 1962, Robert James Anthony *b.* 1964,—Sharman, *b.* 1953. *Residence,* 17, Atwood Av., Kew Gdns., Surrey.

Grandchildren of the late Charles Frederick Augustus Leeds (infra):—
Issue of the late Charles Hildyard Denham Leeds, *b.* 1902, *d.* 1975: *m.* 1940, Merran Elizabeth (Box 927, Claresholm, Alberta, Canada), da. of the late J. H. Drew, of Kitscoty, Alberta, Canada:—
John Charles Hildyard (6307, Dalmarnock Cres., NW, Calgary 49, Alberta Canada), *b.* 1941; BSc, Civil Eng.: *m.* 1965, Eileen Rose, da. of Joseph F. Shalka, of Fort Kent, Alberta, and has issue living, Diane Katherine, *b.* 1967,—Brenda Merran, *b.* 1971.——Charles Eric Montagu (Claresholm, Alberta, Canada), *b.* 1945: *m.* 1971, Patricia Marlene, da. of Irwin E. Brown, of Stavely, Alberta, and has issue living, Charles Montagu, *b.* 1975.——James Douglas Logie (Claresholm, Alberta, Canada), *b.* 1948: *m.* 1972, Irene Mary, da. of J. A. Hughes, of Longview, Alberta.——Helen Merran, *b.* 1951; BSc Pharmacy.

Grandchildren of the late Capt. William Montagu Leeds (ante):—
Issue of the late Charles Frederick Augustus Leeds, *b.* 1868, *d.* 1951 : *m.* 1902, **Mildred** Katharine Mary, who *d.* 1938, da. of the late Denham Robinson, of St. Hilda's, Hampton Wick :—
Eric Edward, *b.* 1907: *m.* 1934, Freda Foster, and has issue living, Jacqueline May, *b.* 1935: *m.* 1955, Robert Raleigh Hugh Tatham, and has issue living, Roderick Hugh *b.* 1958, Catherine Ann *b.* 1956, Carolyn Jill *b.* 1960, Susan Margaret *b.* 1963.——Marjorie Mary Mildred (Box 401, Claresholm, Alberta, Canada), *b.* 1904: *m.* 1935, Henry Sharples, who *d.* 1972, and has issue living, Mildred Joanne, *b.* 1939: *m.* 1962, Anthony Perlich, of Lethbridge, Alberta, Canada, and has issue living, David Anthony *b.* 1969, Jeanne Marie *b.* 1971,—Carol Barbara, *b.* 1940: *m.* 1st, 1960 (m. diss. 1973), Donald Charles Stewart; 2ndly, 1973, Terence Willard Henker, of Claresholm, Alberta, Canada, and has issue living (by 1st m.), Donald Charles Henry *b.* 1964, Barbara Joan *b.* 1962, Patricia Marjorie *b.* 1967,—Kathleen Marjorie, *b.* 1943: *m.* 1966, Kenneth Eugene Tratch, of Lethbridge, Alberta, Canada, and has issue living, Robert Kenneth *b.* 1971, Carole Anne, *b.* 1967, Karen Kathleen *b.* 1968,—Judith Susan, *b.* 1945: *m.* 1966, Helmet Charles Meckelborg, of 2502-23 Av., S. Lethbridge, Alberta, and has issue living, Douglas Charles *b.* 1969, James Joseph *b.* 1970, Susan Kathleen, *b.* 1967.

Granddaughter of the late George Leeds, 3rd son of 1st baronet:—
Issue of the late Rev. William Howard Leeds, *b.* 1853, *d.* 1893: *m.* 1886, **Ethel Beatrice**, who *d.* 1937, el. da. of Charles H. Perkins, of the Admiralty:—
Gabriel Frances (Pythouse, Tisbury, Wilts.), *b.* 1889.

Granddaughters of the late Edward Montagu Leeds, 5th son of 1st baronet:—
Issue of the late Edward Ernest Leeds, *b.* 1859, *d.* 1919: *m.* 1884, **Emma Seddon**, who *d.* 1939, da. of the late S. Seddon Walbank, MD, of Duluth, Minnesota, USA:—
Jessie Louisa, *b.* 1886: *m.* 19—, Fitzgerald Moore.——Kate Frances, *b.* 1887: *m.* 19— Philip Seddon Mellor.
Issue of the late Lieut.-Col. Thomas Louis Leeds, C.M.G., D.S.O., *b.* 1869, *d.* 1926: *m.* 1904, Clara Guion, who *d.* 1940, da. of Lieut.-Col. Henry S. Kilbourne, U.S. Army:—
Sylvia Guion, *b.* 1914: *m.* 1943, Douglas Campbell Ward-Campbell, and has issue living, Iain Gordon Leeds, *b.* 1944; ed. at Marlborough, and at Trin. Coll., Camb.,—Nicholas Carlton Guion, *b.* 1947; ed. at Marlborough. *Residence*, 45A, High St., Wimbledon, SW19.

Sir George William Leeds, 1st Bt. of Croxton Park, Cambs. was Equerry to the Duke of Sussex. The manor of Croxton was purchased by an ancestor of this family about 1568.

LEES, Creation (U.K.) 1804, of Blackrock, Dublin.

I have accomplished.

Sir Thomas Harcourt Ivor Lees, 8th *Baronet*; *b.* Nov. 6th, 1941; *s.* his father, Sir Charles Archibald Edward Ivor, 1963.

Arms—Azure, a fesse checky argent and sable, between six cross-crosslets fitchée, three in the chief and three in the nombril points or, and three billets, two in the honour and one in the base, points of the second. **Crest**—A dexter hand couped above the wrist and erect proper, grasping a crescent or.

Residence—

Daughter living of 5th Baronet—Mary Helen, *b.* 1928: *m.* 1949, David Stuart Hahn, and has issue living, Stuart Arthur, *b.* 1949.—Harold Daniel, *b.* 1953. *Address*, 3, Valsayn Av., Valsayn Park, Curepe, Trinidad.

Aunt living (daughter of 6th baronet)—Constance Lilian Norah, *b.* 1900: *m.* 1923, Henry George Knight, and has issue living, Janet Norah Rosemary, *b.* 1928. *Residence*, 5, Cricket Field Rd., Horsham, Sussex.

Widows living of 4th and 5th Baronets—Louise, da. of—Hayes, of USA: *m.* 1st, 1899, as his third wife Sir Harcourt James Lees, 4th Bt., who *d.* 1917; 2ndly, 1925, George R. Snowden.—Helen Agnes Marion (*Helen, Lady Lees*) (3, Valsayn Av., Valsayn Park, Curepe, Trinidad), da. of the late Charles C. Chittick, of Belle Vue, Nevis, W. Indies, and widow of Thomas Orr Gibb: *m.* 1927, Sir Arthur Henry James Lees, 5th Bt., who *d.* 1949.

Collateral Branches living.

Issue of the late Edwin Leslie Lees, 4th son of 4th baronet, *b.* 1886, *d.* 1937: *m.* 1900, Annie, who *d.* 1961, da. of Jabez Charlton, of Southall, Middlesex:—
Charlotte Anne Dorothy (The Chantry, Gerrans, Portscatho, Truro), *b.* 1908: *m.* 1936, Arthur John Porter, and has issue living, John Richard *b.* 1937,—Mark Edwin, *b.* 1939.——Margaret Monica Laure (The Chantry, Gerrans, Portscatho, Truro), *b.* 1908: *m.* 1936, Arthur John Porter, and has issue living, Geraldine Barbara Elizabeth, *b.* 1910.——Josephine Edwina Agnes, *b.* 1917: *m.* 1940, Edmund Ross Spencer (The Chantry, Gerrans, Portscatho, Truro).

Issue of the late Capt. Cecil Harcourt Folder Lees, 6th son of 4th baronet, *b.* 1873, *d.* 1921 : *m.* 1st, 19—, Nellie Hayes, who *d.* 1903 ; 2ndly, 1905, Frances Louisa Wegg, who *d.* 1913; 3rd, 1917, Jeannie King, who *d.* 1967, da. of George Paterson, of Edinburgh:—
(By 1st marriage) Constance Lilian (of 307, Bulwer St., Pietermaritzburg, S. Africa), *b.* 1900: *m.* 1920, Ernest Wilson, who *d.* 1963, and has issue living, Douglas Ernest, *b.* 1921,—Leslie Erroll, *b.* 1924,—Cynthia Esther, *b.* 1927: *m.* 1st, 1949, Howard Raymond Comins, from whom she obtained a divorce 1054; 2ndly, 1959, Raymond Richard Allison, and has issue living (by 2nd marriage) Lee Constance *b.* 1962, Wendy Edith (twin) *b.* 1962.——(By 2nd marriage) Stella, *b.* 1908: *m.* 1938, John Henry Flack, and has issue living, David Wyndham (12, Churston Rd., Ashwood Park, Pinetown, Natal), *b.* 1943: *m.* 1967, Glenys Ann, da. of Henry Samuel Taylor, and has issue living, Allan Dean *b.* 1969, Wayne Garth *b.* 1972,—Joan Denise, *b.* 1939: *m.* 1960, Noel Barry, Futter, of, 25, Albers Rd., Highland Hills, Pinetown, Natal, and has issue living, Bradley Dale *b.* 1961, Gordon Barry *b.* 1962, Sharon Lynne *b.* 1964, Vanessa Rae *b.* 1967, Lorelle Carol *b.* 1969. *Residence*, 5, Meyerton, 162, Moore Rd., Durban, Natal.——Esmé Frances (Kloof Rest Home, Kloof, Natal), *b.* 1910: *m.* 1938, George Franklin James, from whom she obtained a divorce 1946, and has issue living, Veronica Anne, *b.* 1939: *m.* 1963, James Anthony Gordon, of Brookview Towers, 1340, Danforth Rd., Scarborough M1J 192, Toronto, Ont., Canada, and has issue living, Michael James *b.* 1965, Melissa Anne Helga *b.* 1967, Nicola Barbara Janetta *b.* 1969, Gillian *b.* 1972.

Grandchildren of the late John Cathcart Lees (infra):—
Issue of the late John Rutherfoord d'OLIER-LEES, b. 1887, f. 1972: m. 1923, Margery,
who d. 1975, da. of Thomas H. Scott, of Sunderland:—
JOHN CATHCART (5, Pound Close, Ringwood, Hants.; Naval and Military Club), b. Nov. 12th,
1927; formerly Lt. 2nd Bn. Border Regt. and SAS Regt. (Artists Rifles) TA: m. 1957, Wendy
Garrold, yr. da. of the late Brian Garrold Groom, of Craig Elm, Esbank, nr. Edinburgh, and has
issue living, John Cathcart, b. 1961,—James Scott Lewis, b. 1963.——Edmund Campbell (Lapley
Farm, Coaley, Dursley, Glos.), b. 1929; ACA: m. 1960, Hilary Vernon, da. of John Harbord, of
Englewick, Englefield Green, Surrey, and has issue living, Robert Arthur Campbell, b. 1963,—
Caroline Margery, b. 1961,—Deborah Helen, b. 1962.——Thomas Rutherfoord (40, Worcester
Rd., Chichester, Sussex), b. 1931: m. 1960, Anne Elizabeth, da. of William Simpson Dalgetty, MB,
ChB, of 1, Polwarth Terr., Edinburgh, 11, and has issue lliving, Guy Rutherfoord, b. 1962,—Mark
Angus, b. 1964,—Catherine Anne, b. 1966,—Julia Elizabeth, b. 1968.——Elizabeth, b. 1925: m.
1956, Geoffrey John Martin, and has issue living, Timothy John, b. 1958,—Robin Geoffrey,
b. 1959.——Helen Campbell, b. 1926.

Granddaughters of the late Cathcart Lees, MD, son of 2nd son of 1st baronet:—
Issue of the late Robert Shaw Lees, b. 1844, d. 1904: m. 1883, Anna Magdeléna, da. of the
Ven. Alexander Stuart, Archdeacon of Ross, co. Cork:—
Madeliene Elinor, b. 1885: m. 1918, Henry William Crosthwait, who d. 19—. Residence,

Issue of the late John Cathcart Lees, b. 1854, d. 1922: m. 1886, Helen Campbell, who d.
1948, da. of the late John Rutherfoord d'Olier, of Herbert House, Booterstown :—
Helen Campbell d'Olier, b. 1889: m. 1926, John Richard Matthew, MICE (late Capt. RE), who d.
1953, and has issue living, Helen Mary d'Olier b. 1929; MA London 1955: m. 1971, Basil Graham
Conrade Webb, barrister, of 2, Plowden Bldgs., Middle Temple Lane, EC4. Residence, 46,
Brunswick Gdns., Kensington, W8.

Grandchildren of the late Edward Lees, 2nd son of William Eden Lees, 5th son
of 1st baronet:—
Issue of the late Harcourt Lees, b. 1843, d. 1939: m. 1867, Mary Masey, who d. 1914, da. of
Joseph Burke, formerly of The Lodge, Templemore :—
Harcourt Edward, b. 1884: m. 1961, Eileen, widow of Edward Byron de Lacy. Residence,
Flat 25, Brunswick Manor, Bangor, co. Down.——Ethel Sophia Harriet Western (22, Harcourt
Terr., Adelaide Rd., Dublin 2).

Granddaughters of the late Thomas Orde Hastings Lees, only son of the late
Rev. John Lees, el. son of the late Thomas Orde Lees, 6th son of 1st baronet:—
Issue of the late Lt.-Col. Thomas Orde Hans Lees, O.B.E., A.F.C., b. 1877; d. 1958: m.
1st, 1902, Rhoda Isabel, who d. 1930, da. of the late P. Musgrave, and widow of
R. Lovat Fraser; 2ndly, 1932, Ellaline Hisako:—
(By 1st marriage) Grace Isabel Renée, b. 1909: m. 1st, 1932, Prof. Alfred Jules Ayer, Prof. of
Philosophy of Mind and Logic, Oxford Univ.; 2ndly, 1961, Stuart Newton Hampshire, Prof. of
Philosophy, Dept. of Philosophy, Princeton University, Princeton, New Jersey, U.S.A., and has
issue living (by 1st marriage), David Julian b. 1939, Valerie Jane b. 1936.——(By 2nd marriage),
Zoe Orde Eloise, b. 1936. Residence,

Grandchildren of the late Henry Rowland John Lees, son of the late Maj.
Henry Lees, son of the late Thomas Orde Lees, 6th son of 1st baronet:—
Issue of the late Capt. Henry Orde McAllister Lees (Merchant Ser.), b. 1880, d. 1933: m.
1902, Marion Paul Scott, who d. 1951 :—
Henry Orde Westwater, b. 1903: m. 1944, Dorothea Joan, da. of John Evans, of H.M. Customs
and Excise, Edinburgh.——Dorothy Ann, b. 1904: m. 1943, Capt. Robert William Nicholson
Evans (TA), solicitor, of Edinburgh, and has issue living, Morag Pauline, b. 1945,—Dorothea
Ann Joan, b. 1946. Residences, 40, Garscube Terrace, Murrayfield, Edinburgh; 9, Balfour Street,
North Berwick; Linden Lea, Carlops, Peeblesshire.

Sir John Lees, 1st Bt., son of Adam Lees of Cumnock, Ayrshire, distinguished himself with
the British troops in Germany under the Marquess of Granby. He was afterwards successively
Usher of the Black Rod, Secretary of War, and Secretary to the Post Office in Ireland.

LEES, Creation (U.K.) 1897, of South Lytchett Manor, Lytchett Minster, Dorset.

Sir THOMAS EDWARD LEES, 4th *Baronet*; *b.*
Jan. 31st, 1925; *s.* his father, *Col. Sir* JOHN VICTOR
ELLIOTT, *D.S.O., M.C.,* 1955; ed. at Eton, and at
Magdalene Coll., Camb.; is a J.P. for Dorset (High
Sheriff 1960); European War 1943-5 as Aircraftman
R.A.F. (wounded): *m.* 1949, Faith Justin, only da. of
George Gaston Jessiman, O.B.E., of Swaynes Living,
Great Durnford, Wilts, and has issue.

Arms—Per chevron dovetail argent and gules, in chief two millrinds
sable, and in base an owl of the first. Crest—On a millrind fessewise
sable an owl argent.

Residence—Post Green, Lytchett Minster, Dorset.

Without haste, without rest.

Son living—CHRISTOPHER JAMES, b. Nov. 4th, 1952; ed. at Eton.,
Daughters living—Sarah Margaret, b. 1951.——Bridget Selina, b.
1954.——Elizabeth Jane, b. 1957.

Sisters living—Katharine Margaret, b. 1918: m. 1944, Gerald Henry Rawlinson, of Old Vicarage,
Lytchett Minster, Dorset, and has issue living, Carol Margaret (Sitterton, Bere Regis, Dorset),
b. 1945: m. 1967, (m. diss. 1969), Robert Simmons, and has issue living, Rebecca Margaret b. 1968.
——Rosamond Elizabeth, b. 1921: m. 1943, Professor Dominick John Conway, MD, MRCP,
D.C.H., Flying Officer R.A.F. Vol. Reserve, and has issue living, James Robin, b. 1945,—Oliver
Patrick, b. 1951,—Bryony May, b. 1946,—Dawn Madeline, b. 1948,—Alison Elizabeth, b. 1949,—
Diana Rosemary, b. 1956,—Florentia Anne, b. 1959,—Emily Rosamund, b. 1960. Residence,
720, Lonsdale Rd., Manor Park, Ottawa, Canada.——(Benita) Anne, b. 1923: m. 1949, Lt.-
Col. John Anthony Sandbach Barkworth, 3rd Carabiniers, of Cherry Tree Cottage, Curry
Rivel, Somerset, and has issue living, Anthony Julian Sandbach, b. 1955,—Primrose Madeline,
b. 1951,—Clare Helena, b. 1953.——Jane Madeline (Jarvis, Lytchett Minster, Dorset), b. 1926:
m. 1st, 1946 (m. diss. 1962), Sq. Ldr. Simon Hugh Kevill-Davies, RAF; 2ndly, 1966 (m. diss.
1971), Michael Vaughan Brian, DSc, and has issue living, (by 1st m.) Hugh John b. 1948,—Sheila
Anne, b. 1950,—Benita Jane b. 1954.

Aunts living (daughters of 1st baronet)—Eleanor Juliet Anne (of 13, Oak Hill, Epsom, Surrey), *b.* 1894; *m.* 1919, Capt. Eustace Howard Marsden, Roy. Indian Navy (ret.), who *d.* 1959, and has issue living, Joan Margaret, *b.* 1921: *m.* 1st, 1942, B. Torry; 2ndly, 1967, John Michael Liudzius, HM Diplo. Ser., OBE, of 5, Spencer Rd., Bromley, Kent, and has issue living (by 1st m.), Keith Howard *b.* 1945: *m.* 1972, Peter James *b.* 1948, Janice Elizabeth *b.* 1943: *m.* 1974,— Elizabeth Howard, *b.* 1923: *m.* 1949, Thomas Edmund Pickard (Apartado 160, Algeciras, Spain), and has issue living, Sara Caroline *b.* 1952: *m.* 1974, Deborah Anne *b.* 1954.——Alice Irene Dieudonné (Sunnymead, Bath Rd., Sturminster Newton, Dorset), *b.* 1902: *m.* 1929, Lt.-Col. Gerald Stewart Oxley, MC, King's Roy. Rifle Corps, who *d.* 1960, and has issue living, John Elliott (of Hurworth House, Newmarket, Suffolk), *b.* 1930: *m.* 1959, Annabel Serena, da. of William Arthur Fearnley-Whittingstall, QC, and has issue living, John Arthur Gerald *b.* 1961, Alice Georgina *b.* 1963,—Margaret Geraldine, *b.* 1932: *m.* 1955, Anthony Derek Maxwell Oulton, of 35, St. John's Wood Terr., NW8, and has issue living, Harry Derek Gerald *b.* 1968, Mary Elizabeth *b.* 1956, Caroline Margaret *b.* 1958, Susan Isabella Helen *b.* 1963.

Collateral Branch living.

Issue of the late Capt. Bernard Percy Turnbull Lees, M.C., 3rd son of 1st baronet, *b.* 1891, *d.* 1922: *m.* 1919, Mary (now of Shepherd's Cottage, Whatcombe, Blandford, Dorset), da. of the late Col. Philip John Joseph Radcliffe, C.M.G. [*see* Radcliffe, Bt., colls.] :—

Michael (Lislee House, Courtmacsherry, co. Cork), *b.* 1921; Queen's Own Dorset Yeo. and SOE; 1939-45 War (severely wounded): *m.* 1944, Gwendolen, el. da. of the late E. Stanley Johnson, and has issue living, Christine Mary, *b.* 1946; Bar. Inner Temple 1967: *m.* 1966, Antonio de Padua Jose Maria Bueno, Bar.-at-Law, of 10, Clavering Av., Barnes, SW13, and has issue living, Nicola Anna Christina *b.* 1967, Julia Catherine Mary *b.* 1972,—Michèle Ann, *b.* 1954.——Dolores, *b.* 1920; 1939-45 War with French Red Cross (French Croix de Guerre): *m.* 1953, Cdr. Harry Selby Bennett, RN, of Slepe Green, Organford, Poole, Dorset, and has issue living, James Sebastian Selby, *b.* 1954,—Dominic Bruce Selby, *b.* 1958.——Bernadette Mary, *b.* (*posthumous*) 1923; formerly 3rd Officer WRNS: *m.* 1st, 1943, Fl.-Lt. Richard Osborne Curtis, RAF Vol. Reserve, who *d.* (killed in action during 1939-45 War) 1944; 2ndly, 1956, Lt.-Col. Gordon Robin Kingston Lyon, OBE, 3rd Carabiniers, of, 450 Riverton Drive, Riverton, Perth, W. Aust., 6155, and has issue living, (by 2nd m.) Kim Philip, *b.* 1960.

The 1st baronet, Sir Elliott Lees, D.S.O., sat as M.P. for Oldham (C) 1886-1892, and for Birkenhead 1894-1906, and served during S. African War 1900-1901. The 2nd baronet, Sir Thomas Evans Keith Lees, Lieut. Dorset Yeo., *d.* of wounds in action during European War 1915. **The 3rd baronet, Sir John Victor Elliott Lees, D.S.O., M.C., was Lieut.-Col. (retired) King's Roy. Rifle Corps and subsequently Col. Comdg. 5th Batn. Dorset Regt., and was twice wounded during European War 1914-18.**

LEES, Creation (U.K.) 1937, of Longdendale, co. Chester.

PERGE·SED·CAUT

Go on, but cautiously.

Sir WILLIAM HEREWARD CLARE LEES, 2nd *Baronet*; *b.* March 6th, 1904; *s.* his father, *Sir* (WILLIAM) CLARE, *O.B.E., LL.D.,* 1951; ed. at Leys Sch., Camb.; former Dir. of Bleachers Assocn. Ltd. and Manchester Dist. Board of Martin's Bank: *m.* 1930, Dorothy Gertrude, da. of Francis Alexander Lauder, and has issue.

Arms—Sable, two bars argent, on a chief of the last a garb or, between two roses gules, barbed and seeded proper. Crest—Upon a rock proper, a lion rampant gules, supporting a flagstaff, also proper, flowing therefrom a banner sable, charged with a garb or.
Residence—Ardeevin, Chapel-en-le-Frith, Derbyshire.

Son living—WILLIAM ANTONY CLARE, *b.* June 14th, 1935; ed. at Eton, and at Magdalene Coll., Camb.

Daughter living—Jennifer Dorothy Clare, *b.* 1932: *m.* 1953, John Benn Arnold Wallinger. *Residence,* Beechland Farmhouse, Newick, Sussex.

Sister living—Enid Clare, *b.* 1901. *Residence,* The Cottage, Chinley, Derbyshire.

The 1st baronet, Sir (William) Clare Lees, OBE, LLD (son of the late William Lees, of Birkdale), was Chm. of Bleachers' Asso., Ltd., Dep. Chm. of Martins Bank, and Chm. of Martins Bank, Ltd. (Manchester Board)

LEESE, Creation (U.K.) 1908, of Send Holme, Send, Surrey.

Life is dear, liberty is dearer.

Sir OLIVER WILLIAM HARGREAVES LEESE, *K.C.B., C.B.E., D.S.O.*, 3rd *Baronet; b.* Oct. 27th, 1894 ; *s.* his father, *Sir* WILLIAM HARGREAVES, 1937 ; ed. at Eton ; Lieut.-Gen. (retired) late Coldstream Guards, and a J.P. and D.L. for Shropshire ; appointed High Sheriff of Shropshire 1958; Patron Midland Area, British Legion 1948-62, and Pres., Combined Cadet Force Asso. 1950-72; 1914-18 War (wounded despatches, DSO), 1939-45 War in France, Middle East, Sicily, Italy and Burma (despatches, CBE, CB, KCB, 5th class Order of Virtuti Militari of Poland, Com. of Legion of Honour, French Croix de Guerre, American Order of Merit, Grand Cordon of El Nichan Iftiquar of Tunisia) ; appointed a GSO, Staff Coll., Quetta 1938, to command 30th Corps 1942, 8th Army 1943, and Allied Land Forces S-E Asia 1944; was Gen. Officer Comdg.-in-Ch. E. Command 1945-6; and Hon. Col. Shropshire Yeo. 1947-62; elected Pres. of Old Etonian Asso. 1946 (Chm. 1964-73) ; Lt. of Tower of London 1954-7; National Pres. of British Legion 1962-71, Pres. of Warwickshire Co. Cricket Club 1959-75, of Shropshire Co. Cricket Club 1963-73, and MCC 1965; a Dir. of Securicor; DSO 1916, CBE (Mil) 1940, CB (Mil) 1942, KCB (Mil) 1943: *m.* 1933, Margaret Alice, who *d.* 1964, da. of the late Cuthbert Leicester-Warren [Leighton, Bt.].

Arms—Gules, a fesse embattled counterembattled between in chief two falcons belled or and in base a hand erect couped at the wrist, holding a dagger in pale proper, pommel and hilt gold. **Crest**—A falcon belled or, supporting with the dexter paw a flagstaff proper, beaded and tasselled or, therefrom flowing to the dexter a banner gules charged with a dagger inpale proper, pommel and hilt gold.

Residence—Worfield House, Bridgnorth, Salop.

Brother living—ALEXANDER WILLIAM, *b.* Sept. 27th, 1909 ; ed. at Eton; formerly Capt. Coldstream Guards (Supplementary Reserve). *Residence*, 88, **Cranmer Court, Sloane Avenue, S.W.3.**

Collateral Branches living.

    Issue of the late Vernon Francis Leese, O.B.E., 2nd son of 1st baronet, *b.* 1870, *d.* 1927 : *m.* 1900, Gwendoline Edytha, who *d.* 1929, da. of the late Charles Stevenson :—

John Henry Vernon, *b.* 1901. *Residence*,

    Issue of the late Lieut.-Col. Neville Leese, D.S.O., O.B.E., R.A.S.C., 3rd son of 1st baronet, *b.* 1872, *d.* 1948 : *m.* 1893, Matilda, da. of J. Saunders :—

Cicely Violet : *m.* 1921, Leonard Hay Mottram, and has issue living, Peter Hay, *b.* 1922; European War 1941-5 in R.A.S.C.,—Joe Neville (c/o Barclays Bank, Wimborne, Dorset), *b.* 1927; is Maj. RCT, late RASC and Dorset Regt.: *m.* 1954, June Patricia Mary, only child of Lt.-Col. C. F. Garfit, IMS (ret.), of Alhama Springs, 91, Altea La Vieja, Altea, Alicante, Spain, and has issue living, Richard Neville Garfit *b.* 1957, David Leonard Garfit *b.* 1963,—Pamela Mary, *b.* 1924.——Mary Aurelia Neville: *m.* 1928, John Frederick Fawcett, and has issue living, Joan Mary, *b.* 1928,—Rosemary Ann, *b.* 1938.—— Joyce Alice Noreen: *m.* 1936, William Eric Oldnall, and has issue living, William Neville Russell, *b.* 1943,—Felicity Ann Russell, *b.* 1937,—Tessa Mary Russell, *b.* 1939.

    Issue of the late Major Clive Leese, M.B.E., 6th son of 1st baronet, *b.* 1888, *d.* 1932: *m.* 1916, Dorothy, who *d.* 1949, da. of the late Alfred Dickson, of Chester :—

Cynthia Hilary, *b.* 1919; Lt.-Col. WRAC. *Residence*, 54, Gordon Place, W8.

    The 1st baronet, Sir Joseph Francis (cr. a Knt. 1895), sat as M.P. for Lancashire (N.-E. Accrington Div. (*L*) 1892-1910, and was Recorder of Manchester 1893-1913.

le FLEMING, Creation (E.) 1705, of Rydal, Westmorland.

Pax, copia, sapientia.
Peace, plenty, wisdom.

Sir WILLIAM KELLAND LE FLEMING, 11th *Baronet; b.* April 27th, 1922; *s.* his father, *Sir* FRANK THOMAS, 1971 ; 1939-45 War: *m.* 1948, Noveen Avis, da. of C. C. Sharpe, of Rukuhia, Hamilton, NZ, and has issue.

Arms—Gules, a fret argent. **Crest**—A serpent nowed holding in its mouth a garland of olive and vine all proper.

Residence, 6, Kopane Rd., Palmerston North, NZ.

Sons living—QUENTIN JOHN (147, Stanford St., Ashhurst, Manawatu, NZ), *b.* June 27th, 1949: *m.* 1971, Judith Ann, da. of C. J. Peck, JP, of Ashhurst, Manawatu, NZ, and has issue living, Josephine Kay, *b.* 1973.——Peter Douglas, *b.* 1958.——Murray Kelland, *b.* 1960.

Daughters living—Rosemary Lynette, *b.* 1951.——Elaine Dawn, *b.* 1953.——Marie Louise, *b.* 1955. ——Vicki Karen, *b.* 1964.

Brothers living—Gordon Halsey (of Auroa Rd., Manaia, Taranaki, NZ), *b.* 1925: *m.* 1962 Lorna Marjorie, da. of R. F. Trim, of Trimoana, R. D. Eltham, NZ, and has issue living, Mark Ronald Feltham, *b.* 1965,—Roderick Gordon Hudleston, *b.* 1970,—Ruth Maree, *b.* 1963,—Helen Lorna, *b.* 1964,—Alison Halsey, *b.* 1967.——Lindsay Craig (of Auroa Rd., Manaia, Taranaki, NZ), *b.* 1927: *m.* 1955, Jean Irene, da. of F. G. Campbell, of Patea, Taranaki, NZ, and has issue living, John Fraser, *b.* 1958,—Hugh Vincent, *b.* 1959,—Frances Mary, *b.* 1956,—Annette Isabel, *b.* 1963, —Louise Joy, *b.* 1969.

Uncle living (son of 9th baronet)—Stanley Hudleston (c/o Rydal Hall, Ambleside, Cumbria, LA22 9LX) *b.* 1898; late Chm. of Waimate, W. Div. County Council (NZ): *m.* 1925, Isabel Christina, da. of the late William Mackay, of Riversdale, Otago, NZ and has issue living, Eoin Stanley, *b.* 1926.

Aunts living (daughters of 9th baronet)—Eliza Ann (143, Mangorei Rd., New Plymouth, NZ), *b.* 1892.——Fanny Lindsay (143, Mangorei Rd., New Plymouth, NZ), *b.* 1896.

Widow living of 10th Baronet—ISABELLA ANNIE FRASER (*Isabella, Lady le Fleming*), (Rydal Lovat, Auroa Rd., RD Manaia, Taranaki, NZ), da. of the late James Craig, of Manaia, Taranaki, NZ: *m.* 1921, Sir Frank Thomas le Fleming, 10th Bt., who *d.* 1971.

Collateral Branches living.

Grandchildren of the late Richard Thomas le Fleming (infra) :—
Issue of the late Richard Henry Edward le Fleming, *b.* 1892, *d.* 1960 : *m.* 1918, Mabel Gladys (of 151, Seaview Road, Westown, New Plymouth, New Zealand), da. of Henry Parslow :—

Albert Edward, *b.* 1923 ; European War 1939-45 with Roy. New Zealand Air Force : *m.* 1946, Eileen Ellen, da. of John Moffet, and has issue living, Richard John, *b.* 1953,—Judith Merle, *b.* 1949.   *Residence,* Dudley Road, Inglewood, Taranaki, New Zealand.——Noala Doris, *b.* 1920: *m.* 1942, Raymond Peterson, and has issue living, Janice Margaret, *b.* 1945,—Fay Maralyn, *b.* 1948.   *Residence,* Manutake, Hawera, New Zealand.

Granddaughter of the late William le Fleming, 2nd son of 6th baronet :—
Issue of the late Richard Thomas le Fleming, *b.* 1863, *d.* 1955 : *m.* 1891, Emma Louisa Jones, who *d.* 1935 :—

Elizabeth Louisa (31, Beresford St., New Brighton, Christchurch, NZ), *b.* 1893: *m.* 1st, 1909, Leonard Willis, who *d.* 1918; 2ndly, 1923, Emile Oscar Jean-Baptiste Jayet, who *d.* 1955; 3rdly 1964, Lionel H. Grafton, who *d.* 1966, and has issue living, (by 1st m.) Walter Leonard (31, Grafton St., Linwood, Christchurch, NZ), *b.* 1911: *m.* 1946, Yvonne Eileen (Bonnie) Sanders, and has issue living, William Jean Francis *b.* 1950, Cherryl Diane *b.* 1959,—Louise Elizabeth (41, Bristol St., Levin, NZ), *b.* 1909: *m.* 19—, Yonston,—(by 2nd m.) Leon le Fleming (24, Tomrich St., Aranui, Christchurch, NZ), *b.* 1929: *m.* 1950, Joan Yvonne Remi, and has issue living, André Philip le Fleming *b.* 1952, Mark le Fleming *b.* 1956, Glenn de Denton *b.* 1959, Darron Francoise *b.* 1961,—Yvonne le Fleming, *b.* 1936: *m.* 1955, Eric John Gay, of 9, Reaby St., Winsor, Christchurch, NZ, and has issue living, Wayne Eric *b.* 1957, Darryl Paul *b.* 1964, Sharon *b.* 1960.

This family claims to be descended from Sir Michael le Fleming, of Furness living in 1127. The Visitation of Westmorland 1665 carried the pedigree down to Sir Daniel Fleming of Rydal Hall, Cumberland, father of 1st baronet.   The 1st baronet sat as MP for Westmorland 1696-1707, and the 2nd baronet was Bishop of Carlisle 1734-47.

LEGARD, Creation (E.) 1660, of Ganton, Yorkshire.

By the cross to heaven.

Sir THOMAS DIGBY LEGARD, 14th Baronet ; *b.* Oct. 16th, 1905 ; *s.* his father, *Sir* DIGBY ALGERNON HALL 1961 ; ed. at Lancing Coll., and at Magdalene Coll., Camb. ; is Capt. R.A. : *m.* 1935, Mary Helen, da. of Lieut.-Col. Edmund George Savile L'Estrange-Malone [E. Feversham, colls.], and has issue.

Arms—Argent, on a bend between six mullets pierced or the field gules, a cross-patée or.   **Crest**—A greyhound passant or, collared sable, studded argent.

Residence—Scampston Hall, Malton, Yorks.

Sons living—CHARLES THOMAS (Bishopton Grange, Ripon, Yorks.), *b.* Oct. 26th, 1938; ed. at Eton; MInstM: *m.* 1962, Elizabeth, da. of John M. Guthrie, of Church Meadows, Hutton Buscel, Scarborough, and has issue living, Christopher John Charles, *b.* 1964,— Edward Thomas, *b.* 1966,—Louise Elizabeth, *b.* 1969. ——William Robert (North Grimston House, Malton, Yorks.), *b.* 1943; ed. at Eton, and at Roy. Agric. Coll., Cirencester: *m.* 1967, Sally Ann, da. of the late W. H. Craig.——James Digby (Knaith Hall, Gainsborough, Lincs.), *b.* 1946; ed. at Eton: *m.* 1969, Daphne Jane, el. da. of Denis West, of Belgrave Lodge, Chester, and has issue living, Thomas James St. Quintin, *b.* 1971,— Sophie Jane, *b.* 1973.

Sister living—Cassandra Rosamond Elaine, *b.* 1917: *m.* 1st, 1939, Capt. Charles Paul Cuthbert Cayley, RE, who *d.* 1945 [*see* Cayley, Bt., colls.]; 2ndly, 1946, John Sarginson, who *d.* 1972, and has issue living, (by 1st m.) [*see* Cayley, Bt., colls.],—(by 2nd m.) Jonathan James D'Arcy, *b.* 1947.   *Residence,* Lullingstone, Bardwell, nr. Bury St. Edmunds, Suffolk.

Collateral Branches living.

Issue of the late William Ernest Legard, F/O RAF, yst. son of 13th baronet, *b.* 1911, *d.* (killed in action) 1940: *m.* 1939, Alice (of Appleton House, Appleton Street, Malton, Yorks., who *m.* 2ndly, 1943, Col. Basil Perry Beale, OBE, MC, DL, who *d.* 1967), da. of the Hon. George Ellis Vestey [*see* B. Vestey, colls.]:—

Anne, *b.* 1940: *m.* 1965, Harry O'theil Seymour (PO Box 311, De Funiak Springs, Florida, USA).

Grandchildren of the late Col. Sir James Digby Legard, KCB, el. son of the late Capt. James Anlaby Legard, RN, el. son of the late Rev. William Legard, 4th son, of 5th baronet:—
Issue of the late Col. Alfred Digby Legard, C.B.E., *b.* 1878, *d.* 1939: *m.* 1902, Winifred (who *d.* 1962, having *m.* 2ndly, 1947, as his second wife, Maj.-Gen. George Henry Addison, C.B., C.M.G., D.S.O. who *d.* 1964), only da. of the late Col. Sir William George Morris, K.C.M.G., C.B.:—

Diana, *b.* 1918 : *m.* 1950, John Percival Wheeler, and has issue living, Michael John, *b.* 1952,— Bridget Diana, *b.* 1954.   *Residence,* Bockingfold, near Marden, Kent.

Issue of the late Lieut. George Percy Legard, R.N., *b.* 1879, *d.* 1921: *m.* 1905, Andolie Susannah, who *d.* 1955, da. of the late Percy Luck, of Stockholm :—

Charles Percy Digby, *b.* 1906 ; ed. at Cheltenham Coll. ; Lieut.-Col. (retired) 5th Roy. Inniskilling Dragoon Guards: *m.* 1934, Gertrude Kate, who *d.* 1969, da. of Arthur Thomson, late of Heathside, Wimbledon Common, SW, and Java, and has issue living, Sarah Anthea, *b.* 1939: *m.* 1966, Capt. Malcolm James Sherwin, Queen's Own Hussars, of Manor House, Thornton Steward, Ripon, Yorks., and has issue living, Simon Patrick *b.* 1967, Amanda Kate *b.* 1969,—Dinah Annabel, *b.* 1941: *m.* 1964, James Holt, of Ravenswick, Kirbymoorside, York, and has issue living, Philip James Harrison *b.* 1965, Michael Vernon Charles *b.* 1966, Elizabeth Rebecca *b.* 1969,—Lavinia Anlaby, *b.* 1944. *Residence*, Sheriff Hutton Park, York.——Vendela Susan Esther, *b.* 1911: *m.* 1938 (divorce 1947) Maj. Colin Clement Geoffrey Milward, Northumberland Fusiliers, who *d.* (killed in Korea) 1951, son of Maj.-Gen. Sir Clement Arthur Milward, KCIE, CB, CBE, DSO, and has issue living, Gervase Colin, *b.* 1944,—Susan Mary, *b.* 1939. *Residence*, Netherby, Huttons Ambo, York.

Issue of the late Richard Anlaby Legard, *b.* 1880, *d.* 1973: *m.* 1929, Dorice (Lonsdale Villa, Lonsdale Rd., South Cliff, Scarborough), da. of the late Harold Ostler, of Hull:— Richard Digby (Warren House Farm, Brandsby, Yorks.), *b.* 1930: *m.* 1966, Mrs. Jean H. Dodd, of York, and has issue living, James Richard Anlaby, *b.* 1967.

Grandsons of the late Rev. Francis Digby Legard, son of the late George Legard, el. son of the late Digby Legard (infra) :—
Issue of the late Brig.-Gen. D'Arcy Legard, C.M.G., D.S.O., *b.* 1873, *d.* 1953 : *m.* 1908, Lady Edith Margaret Emily Mary Foljambe, who *d.* 1962, da. of 1st Earl of Liverpool (*cr.* 1905):—
Robert Francis, *TD* (12A, Circus Lodge, Circus Rd., NW8), *b.* 1909; ed. at Shrewsbury; formerly in Child's Bank; late Lt. RA; 1939-45 War (despatches).——Antony Ronald, *MBE*, *b.* 1912; ed. at Winchester, and at Trin. Coll., Oxford; formerly Maj. RE (TA); 1939-45 War (MBE); MBE (Mil) 1940: *m.* 1946, Maud, da. of Clifford Schwabe, of Cuddington Grange, Northwich, Ches., and has issue living, Simon Littledale, *b.* 1947,—David Antony, *b.* 1953,—Diana May, *b.* 1950. *Residence*, Fairway, Delamere, Northwich, Ches.——Peter Herbert, *b.* 1917; ed. at Shrewsbury, and at Edinburgh Univ.; late Lt. Lanarkshire Yeo: *m.* 1959, Brenda Valerie, only da. of the late Lt.-Col. S. Kidd, TD, DL, of Haresgill, Penrith, Cumberland, and has issue living, Jonathan Antony, *b.* 1961,—Edith Veronica Jane *b.* 1964. *Residence*, 11, Glan Aber Park, Chester.

Grandchildren of the late Rev. Digby Charles Legard, 2nd son of the late Digby Legard, 5th son of 5th baronet:—
Issue of the late Digby Charles Legard, *b.* 1851, *d.* 1924: *m.* 1880, Eleanor Clementina, who *d.* 1935, da. of the late Rev. David Bruce, Hon. Canon of Durham:—
Rev. Charles, *M.C.*, *b.* 1887 ; ed. at Cheltenham Coll., and at New Coll., Oxford ; formerly R. of Burghclere, near Newbury ; European War 1914-18 as Capt. Lincolnshire Regt., and A.D.C. Personal Staff; MC 1916: *m.* 1918, Ethel Gertrude, who *d.* 1973, da. of the late Rev. George Strickland Marriott, R. of Sigglesthorne, and has issue living, John Bruce (75, Holland Park, W11), *b.* 1924; ed. at Cheltenham Coll. *Residence*, Brendon Nursing Wing, Park Rd., Winchester.——Muriel Dundas, *b.* 1897. *Residence*, Mynchon, Huttons Ambo, York.

Grandchildren of the Rev. Charles Legard, MC (ante):—
Issue of the late Lt.-Cdr. George Hugo Digby Legard, MBE, RN, *b.* 1920, *d.* 1966: *m.* 1944, Eve Lillian [who *m.* 2ndly, 1973, Guy Alexander Hughes, of Frith House, 24, High St., Amersham, Bucks.], da. of the late Capt. Francis Howard, DSC, RN:— Robin Hugo Charles, *b.* 1945; ed. at Milton Abbey, and Selwyn Coll., Camb. (BA).——Joanna Frances, *b.* 1948.——Hilary Jane, *b.* 1951.

This family is of great antiquity in Yorkshire, and possessed the manor of Anlaby as early as the 13th century, and a portion of the mano. is still in possession of the family. The 1st baronet, Sir John, was M.P. for Scarborough, and an eminent royalist. Sir Charles, 11th baronet, was Chm. of E. Riding of Yorkshire County Council, and M.P. for Scarborough (*C*) 1874-80.

LEICESTER, Creation (I.) 1671, of Timogue, Queen's co. [Extinct 1968.]

Sir CHARLES BYRNE WARREN LEICESTER, 9th and last *Baronet.*

Daughters living of 8th Baronet—By 2nd marriage—Meriel Jeanne, *b.* 1931 : *m.* 1956, Sidney John Winder, and has issue living, Michelle Ann, *b.* 1958,—Nicola Jane, *b.* 1960,—Robyn Marte, *b.* 1968. *Residence*, Montego Bay, Jamaica.——Margaret Mary, *b.* 1937: *m.* 1959, James D. O'Dowd, of Shearwater, Downderry, Cornwall, and has issue living, David Peter, *b.* 1961,— Lynne Avril, *b.* 1960,—Ruth Darrell, *b.* 1964.

Widow living of 8th Baronet—MARTHE (*Lady Leicester*), el. da. of Louis de Miéville de Rossens: *m.* 1930, as his second wife, Sir Peter Fleming Frederic Leicester, 8th Bt., who *d.* 1945. *Residence*, Shearwater, Downderry, Cornwall.

Collateral Branches living.
Issue of the late Lieut.-Col. Byron Leicester, brother of 8th baronet, *b.* 1868, *d.* 1929 : *m.* 1895, Guendolen Margaret, who *d.* 1908, da. of the late John Brooke, of Honley, Yorkshire :—
Meriel Guendolen (c/o National Westminster Bank, 75, Cornhill, EC3), *b.* 1899: *m.* 1922, Col. Eric Adrian Hayes-Newington, DSO, OBE, Indian Army (ret.) and has issue living, Patricia Margaret (c/o National Westminster Bank, 75, Cornhill, EC3), *b.* 1924: *m.* 1946 (m. diss. 1953), John Sheridan, and has issue living, Sarah Jane *b.* 1947, Bridget Ann *b.* 1948,—Erica, *b.* 19—: *m.* 1956, Kenneth Roland Tull, of 85, Abernathy Rd., NW, Atlanta 19, Georgia, USA.——Lesbia Evelyn Margaret, *b.* 1908; assumed by deed poll 1926 the name of Margaret Leicester FLETCHER-TOOMER in lieu of Lesbia Evelyn Margaret Leicester. *Residence*, Yetholm, West Malvern Rd., Malvern.

Granddaughter of the late Major William Frederick Leicester, son of the late Charles
Byrne Leicester (ante):—
    Issue of the late Lieut.-Col. George William Frederic Leicester, *b.* 1895, *d.* 1944: *m.* **1932,**
Katharine Anne (who *m.* 2ndly 1945, Lt.-Col. A. Frankland, of The Gables, Hopton
Cangeford, Ludlow), da. of the late Col. Lawrence Chenevix Trench, CMG, DSO [*see*
B. Ashtown, colls.]:—
Elizabeth Meriel Anne, *b.* 1935.

LEIGH, Creation (U.K.) 1918, of Altrincham, Cheshire.

Sir JOHN LEIGH, 2nd *Baronet, b.* March
24th, 1909; *s.* his father, *Sir* JOHN, 1959; ed. at
Eton, and at Balliol Coll., Oxford (MA): *m.*
1959, Ariane, da. of the late Joseph William
Allen, of Beverly Hills, California, and widow
of Harold Wallace Ross, of New York City.

  Arms—Argent, on a cross engrailed quadrant gules, a
barb or between in chief two roses of the second, barbed and
seeded proper. Crest—A cubit arm bested gules, cuffed
argent, grasping a staff in bend sinister proper, pendant
therefrom a banner of the second, charged with a cross-
couped of the first.
    Residence—23, Quai du Mont Blanc Geneva, Switzer-
land. *Clubs,* St. James', Travellers) (Paris).

Brothers living—ERIC, *b.* April 13th 1913; ed. at Radley;
European War 1939-44 as Lieut.-Com. R.N.V.R.: *m.* 1st,
1934, Joan Fitzgerald Lane (from whom he obtained a
divorce 1939), el. da. of M. C. L. Freer; 2ndly, 1939, Mary
Babette, el. da. of the late J. H. Jaques, and has issue
living, (by 1st m.) Richard Henry, *b.* 1936: *m.* 1962,
Barbro Anna Elizabeth, el. da. of the late Stig Carl
Sèbastian Tham, of Sweden,—(by 2nd m.) Christopher
John (The Spinney, Wendens Ambo, Saffron Walden,
Essex, *b.* 1941; ed. at Radley: *m.* 1963, Gillian Ismay, only
da. of W. K. Lowe, of Fox Farm, Stow-on-the-Wold, Glos.,
and has issue living, Edward John *b.* 1970, Caroline Nicola *b.* 1967,—Victoria Anne, *b.* 1945: *m.*
1967, Capt. Jasper Rodney Archer, 4/7th R. Dragoon Gds., of 15, Lamont Rd., SW10, and has
issue living, a son *b.* 1971. *Residences,* Langley's New House, Hawkedon, Bury St. Edmunds;
14, Donne Place, Chelsea, SW3. *Club,* Royal Thames Yacht.——David, BM, BCh, *b.* 1921; ed.
at Eton and at New Coll., Oxford (MA): *m.* 1945, Rosemary Eleanor, da. of the late W. H.
Wyburn-Mason, of Clytha Park, Newport, Monmouth, and has issue living, Peregrine William
Roger, *b.* 1955,—Eleanor Elizabeth Corinna Wyburn, *b.* 1951. *Residence,* Childrey Manor, nr.
Wantage, Berks.
Sister living—Marjorie Joan, *b.* 1910: *m.* 1939, Capt. William Frederick Bovill, OBE, JP, 5th Roy.
Inniskilling Dragoon Guards, and has issue living, Bristow Charles (Moorlands, Rosalie Plains,
Towowba, Qld.), *b.* 1940; Capt. R. Inniskilling Dragoon Guards: *m.* 1968, Kerry Anne, da. of the
late S. B. Reynolds, of Qld., Aust.,—Miles William, *b.* 1945,—Rex Anthony, *b.* 1948. *Residence,*
Armscote Manor, Stratford-on-Avon, Warwicks.

  The 1st baronet, Sir John Leigh, (son of the late John Leigh, J.P., of Brooklands, Cheshire), was
Proprietor of *The Pall Mall Gazette* (before amalgamation with *Evening Standard*). In European
War 1914-18 he equipped a hospital for wounded officers at Altrincham, and founded, main-
tained, and was Chm. of Canadian Officers' Club. He sat as M.P. for Clapham Div. of Wandsworth
(C) 1922-45

LEIGHTON, Creation (E.) 1693, of Wattlesborough, Shropshire.

Sir MICHAEL JOHN BRYAN LEIGHTON, 11th
Baronet; *b.* March 8th, 1935; *s.* his father, Col. *Sir*
RICHARD TIHEL, *T.D.,* 1957; ed. at Stowe; is patron
of one living; Member of British Ornithologists' Union:
m. 1974, Mrs. Amber Mary Ritchie.

  Arms—Quarterly, per fesse indented or and gules. Crest—A wyvern
with wings expanded sable.
  Seat—Loton Park, Shrewsbury. *Clubs*—Bath, MCC.

Sisters living—Lavinia Ann, *b.* 1932: *m.* 1958, Major Edward Arthur
Trevor Bonnor-Maurice, Coldstream Guards, and has issue living,
Emma Mary, *b.* 1959.—Frances Flavia, *b.* 1962. *Residence,* Bodynfoel
Hall, Llanfechain, Montgomeryshire.——Judy Johanna Kathleen, *b.*
1937.——Elizabeth Linda Mary *b.* 1938.
Widow living of 10th Baronet—KATHLEEN IRENE LINDA (*Lady
Leighton*), da. of Major Albert Ernest Lees, of Rowton Castle, Shrews-
bury: *m.* 1932, Col. Sir Richard Tihel Leighton, T.D., 10th baronet,
who *d.* 1957. *Residence,* Loton Park, Shrewsbury.

Dread shame.

Collateral Branch living.

  Granddaughter of the late Rev. Francis Leighton, son of the late Maj.-Gen.
Thomas Leighton, 3rd son of the late Capt. Baldwin Leighton, 2nd son of 2nd
baronet:—
    Issue of the late Capt. Edward William Forester Leighton, *b.* 1839, *d.* 1932: *m.* 1886
Beatrice Jane, who *d.* 1940, da. of the late John Eyre, of Eyrecourt Castle, Ireland:—
Olga Beatrice: *m.* 1st, 1920, Frank Jay Mackey, of USA, who *d.* 1927; 2ndly, 1927, Antonio Marqui.
de Portago, Grandee of Spain, who *d.* 1942; 3rdly, 1943, Don Isidro Martin Montis. *Residence,*
56, Av. Foch, Paris XVI.

  The Leightons derive their name from Leighton in Shropshire, where they were seated in the 12th
century. They inherited, *temp.* Edward IV., the estates of Wattlesborough and Loton, through the
Mawddwys and the Burghs by the marriage of John Leighton with a coheiress of the last-named

family. The county of Salop was represented in Parliament by Richard de Leighton, A.D. 1312-18, and has since often been represented by members of this family. Sir Edward Leighton, 2nd baronet changed the residence from the ancient castle of Wattlesborough to the house at Loton, which he greatly enlarged in 1712. Sir Baldwyn Leighton, 8th Bt., sat as M.P. for Shropshire S. (C) 1877-85. Col. Sir Richard Tihel Leighton, 10th baronet, Shropshire Yeo., was High Sheriff of Salop 1956.

LEITH, Creation (U.K.) 1919, of the City and County of the City of Newcastle-upon-Tyne. [Extinct 1956.]

Sir ALEXANDER LEITH, *M.C.*, 1st and last *Baronet*

Widow living of 1st Baronet—MARY (HOLROYD) (*Lady Leith*), da. of the late Leonard Asquith, of Brook House, Cleckheaton, Yorkshire : *m.* 1955, as his second wife, Sir Alexander Leith, MC, 1st baronet, who *d.* 1956, when the title became ext. *Residence*, 30, Queen's Close, Harrogate.

FORBES-LEITH OF FYVIE, Creation (U.K.) 1923, of Jessfield, co. Midlothian.

I wait in hope. God assisting.

TRUSTIE TO THE END.
SPE EXPECTO
DEO JUVANTE

Sir ANDREW GEORGE FORBES-LEITH OF FYVIE, 3rd *Baronet*; *b.* Oct. 20th, 1929; *s.* his father , *Sir* (ROBERT) IAN (ALGERNON), *KT, MBE,* 1973; ed. at Eton: *m.* 1962, Jane Kate, who *d.* 1969, only da. of the late David McCall-McCowan, of Dalwhat, Moniaive, Dumfries, and has issue.

Arms—Quarterly, 1st grand quarter or, a cross-crosslet fitchee sable between three crescents in chief and as many fusils in base gules, *Leith;* 2nd grand quarter quarterly, 1st and 4th azure, on a chevron between three bears' heads couped argent, muzzled gules, a man's heart proper, between two skenes of the first, pommelled or, *Forbes of Balfing;* 2nd azure, a fesse chequy argent and of the first between three boars' heads erased or, within a bordure indented of the second, *Gordon of Badensoth;* 3rd argent, a fir-tree growing out of a mount in base vert, surmounted of a sword in bend, supporting on its point an Imperial head erased azure, armed and langued gules, *Gregory;* crown proper, in sinister chief and dexter base a lion's 3rd grand quarter, parted per fesse azure and argent, in chief three bears' heads couped of the second, muzzled gules, and in base as many unicorns' heads erased sable, *Forbes of Ballogie;* 4th grand quarter argent, on a bend gules between two mullets in chief, and in base a hunting horn, sable, stringed of the second, three buckles or, *Burn.* **Crests**—1st, a cross-crosslet fitchee sable *Leith;* 2nd, a bear's head and neck couped argent, muzzled azure, *Forbes;* 3rd a dexter cubit arm in armour bendways, the hand naked proper holding a cross-crosslet fitchée erect in pale gules, *Burn.*

Residences—Fyvie Castle, Fyvie, Aberdeenshire; Dunachton, Kingussie, Inverness-shire. *Clubs*—Royal Northern (Aberdeen), Highland (Inverness).

Sons living—GEORGE IAN DAVID, *b.* May 26th, 1967.——John Charles, *b.* 1969.
Daughters living—Miranda Jane, *b.* 1963.——Louisa Mary, *b.* 1965.
Sisters living—Anne Rosdew, *b.* 1932: *m.* 1959, Angus Maitland Pelham Burn, of Knappach, Banchory, Kincardineshire, and has issue living, Amanda Mary, *b.* 1961,—Lucy Rosdew, *b.* 1963,—Emily Louise, *b.* 1964,—Kate Ruth, *b.* 1966.——Mary Elizabeth, *b.* 1934: *m.* 1961, Maj. James Gresley McGowan, 15th/19th King's Roy. Hussars, of Benridge Hall, Ponteland, Northumberland [*see* Gresley, Bt., colls.].
Aunt living (daughter of 1st baronet)—Zorna Marsalie, *b.* 1893: *m.* 1st, 1916, Capt. Conyers Frederick Woodroffe Lang (formerly Devonshire Regt.), who *d.* 1969, and from whom she obtained a divorce 1933; 2ndly, 1933, Lt.-Col. George Edward Redvers Prior, DSO, MC, who *d.* 1956, and has issue living, (by 1st m.) Charles Douglas, *b.* 1918,—Robin Arthur (Ras-il-Wied, Gudja, Malta), *b.* 1928: *m.* 1964, Pierrette Bertrand, of Bordeaux, and has issue living, Claire *b.* 1965, Dominique *b.* 196—. *Residence*, Thorpe Mandeville Manor, Banbury.

Sir Charles Rosdew Forbes-Leith of Fyvie, OBE, 1st Bt., yst. son of Gen. Robert Burn, Col. Comdt. RA *m.* 1891, the Hon. Ethel Louise Forbes-Leith, OBE, only da. and heir of 1st Baron Leith of Fyvie (*ext.*), and by edict of Lord Court 1925, assumed the surname and arms of Forbes-Leith of Fyvie, for himself, his wife and son, under terms of the will of his father-in-law; MP for Torqu— (U) 1910-23, Col. TA and Lt.-Col. R. Dragoons; served in Hazara Expedition 1888, S. African War 1900 and 1914-18 War. His el. son Arthur Herbert Rosdew was k. in action, nr. Ypres 1914; the yr. son, Sir (Robert) Ian (Algernon) Forbes-Leith of Fyvie, KT, MBE, was Lord Lt. of Aberdeenshire 1959-73.

Alexander Burn bought Kingston, East Lothian 1765, which was sold in 1813 by his son, John Burn, grandfather of 1st Bt. Baron Leith of Fyvie was el. son of Rear-Adm. John James Leith (descended from the Leiths, successively of Barnis, co. Aberdeen, Edingarioc, New Leslie in the Garioch, and Leith Hall) by his wife Margaret, da. of heir of Alexander Forbes of Blackford, Aberdeenshire, descended from Duncan Forbes of Corsindae, 2nd son of 2nd Lord Forbes.

Leith-Buchanan, see Buchanan.

LE MARCHANT, Creation (U.K.) 1841, of Chobham Place, Surrey.

Sir DENIS LE MARCHANT, 5th *Baronet; b.* Feb. 28th, 1906 ; *s.* his father, *Brig.-Gen. Sir* EDWARD THOMAS, *K.C.B., C.B.E.,* 1953 ; ed. at Radley ; Capt. late Cheshire Yeo. (Reserve), and Lieut. Nottingham (Sherwood Rangers) Yeo. ; was High Sheriff of Lincolnshire 1958-9 : *m.* 1933, Elizabeth Rowena, da. of Arthur Hovenden Worth, of Hovenden House, Fleet, Lincolnshire, and has issue.

Arms—Azure, a chevron or between three owls argent. Crest—Out of a ducal coronet an owl's leg erect or.
Residence—Hungerton Hall, Grantham, Lincolnshire.

Me Minerva lucet.
Minerva is my light.

Son living—FRANCIS ARTHUR, *b.* Oct. 6th, 1939 ; ed. at Gordonstoun.
Daughter living—Penelope Clare, *b.* 1944: *m.* 1964, Capt. John Henry Warrand Hanmer [see Hanmer Bt., colls.].
Brother living—Alfred Gaspard (twin), *b.* 1906 ; ed. at Radley : *m.* 1929, Turdis, da. of the late Einar Mortensen, of Holte, Denmark, and has issue living, Spencer, *MP* (Hillside, Whitehough, Chinley, via Stockport, Ches.), *b.* 1931; ed. at Eton; MP for High Peak (C) since 1970; PPS to Ch. Sec. to Treasury 1972-74; Opposition Whip since 1974: *m.* 1955, Lucinda Gaye, da. of Brig. Hugh Nugent Leveson-Gower, late RA [see D. Sutherland, colls.], and has issue living, Perronelle Jane *b.* 1956, Geva Ann *b.* 1958,—Michael (Heale House, Curry Rivel, Som.), *b.* 1937; ed. at Eton: *m.* 1963, Philippa, el. da. of R. B. Denby, and has issue living, Piers Alfred *b.* 1964, Dickon John *b.* 1968, Melissa Winifred *b.* 1965, Antonia Ruth *b.* 1970,—Pamela, *b.* 1933: *m.* 1957, Henry Douglas-Pennant [see B. Penrhyn, colls.]. *Residence*, Wolford Lodge, Dunkeswell, Honiton, Devon.
Sisters living—Ruth Alice (*Lady Fisher*), *b.* 1900: *m.* 1st, 1924, Col. John Bury, OBE, late 17th/21st Lancers, who *d.* 1970, having obtained a divorce 1939; 2ndly, 1939, Brig. Sir Gerald Thomas Fisher, KBE, CSI, CIE, Indian Political Ser., who *d.* 1965, and has issue living, (by 1st m.) John Edward (of Carpenter's Field, Puttenham, nr. Guildford, Surrey), *b.* 1927: *m.* 1961, Diana Mary, el. da. of Col. Godfrey Sturdy Inceldon-Webber, TD, late RA [see Lacy, Bt.], and has issue living, Henry Inceldon *b.* 1962, Mary Helen *b.* 1964, Anne Ruth *b.* 1965, Eleanor Frances *b.* 1967, Jane Angela *b.* 1971, Clare Elizabeth *b.* 1972,—Rosemary, *b.* 1930: *m.* 1960, Maj. John Angus McKay Forbes, RE, of The Lake House, Crookedwood, co. Westmeath, and has issue living, Robert Angus *b.* 1964, Joanna Elizabeth *b.* 1962,—Margaret, *b.* 1931: *m.* 1958, Christopher Eldred Hindson [Lawrence, Bt., *cr.* 1858], of Watlands, Scaynes Hill, Haywards Heath, Sussex, and has issue living, Richard Charles *b.* 1959, Catherine Margaret *b.* 1961. *Residence*, Cross, Little Torrington, N. Devon.——Joan Margaret, *b.* 1901: is a JP: *m.* 1921, Maj. Noel Brand Brooks, MC, TD, Cheshire Yeo [see B. Crawshaw, colls.]. *Residence*, Fairgreen Farm, Churchill, Oxfordshire.

The father of Sir Denis Le Marchant, 1st baronet, Maj.-Gen. John Gaspard Le Marchant (a lineal descendant of Peter Le Marchant, President of the States, and Lieut.-Governor of Guernsey in the 13th century), was killed at the battle of Salamanca, while leading the heavy brigade of cavalry. Brig.-Gen. Sir Edward Thomas Le Marchant, K.C.B., C.B.E., 4th baronet, was High Sheriff of Nottinghamshire 1930, Chm. of Nottinghamshire T.A. Asso. 1931-45, and Dep. Chm. of Quarter Sessions, Nottinghamshire 1933-45.

LENNARD, Creation (U.K.) 1880, of Wickham Court, co. Kent.

Sir STEPHEN ARTHUR HALLAM FARNABY LENNARD, 3rd *Baronet ; b.* July 31st, 1899 ; *s.* his father, *Sir* HENRY ARTHUR HALLAM FARNABY, 1928; ed. at Winchester; Lt.-Col. (ret.) Scots Guards; formerly Pres. of S. H. Lennard & Co. Investment Dealers of 789, W. Pender St., Vancouver; 1914-18 War, 1939-45 War in France, Belgium, Middle East, Persia, Iraq, and India (1939-45 star, African star with 8th Army clasp): *m.* 1st, 1928, Mary Isabel, who *d.* 1970, el. da. of Lawrence Bruce Latimer, of Vancouver; 2ndly, 1970, Margaret Jean, only da. of Daniel Hockin, of Vancouver, and widow of Group Capt. William Neville Cumming, OBE, DFC, RAF.

Arms—Quarterly, 1st and 4th, or, on a fesse gules, three fleurs-de-lis or within a bordure invected sable, *Lennard ;* 2nd and 3rd, ermine, on a pale gules a lion passant or, in base two salmon in pale azure, *Cate...* Crests—1st, out of a ducal coronet or, a griffin's head argent, debruised by a bendlet wavy sinister sable; 2nd, a lion's head rased erminois charged with two bars invected gules.

Residences—Glenhead, Whonnock, BC; 41015-837, West Hastings St., Vancouver, BC.

Sisters living—Mary Grace Hallam, *b.* 1895 : *m.* 1st, 1929, Ronald George Campbell, who *d.* 1940; 2ndly, 1946, Sidney Gilchrist Thompson. *Residence*, The Oast House, Harrietsham, Kent.—— Barbara Julia Hallam, *b.* 1906. *Residence*, Milkhurst Cottage, Broad Oak, Heathfield, Sussex.——Elizabeth Penelope Hallam, *b.* 1908. *Residence*, Ashfield, Harrietsham, Kent.

The mother of the first baronet was only daughter of the late Sir John Farnaby, 4th baronet (extinct 1861), of Kippington, Sevenoaks, who married Mary, granddaughter of the late Sir Samuel Lennard, M.P. for Hythe, 3rd baronet (extinct 1727), of Wickham Court. John Lennard, of Knole and Chevening, who was Custos brevium in the reign of Elizabeth I, purchased the Manor of West Wickham of Sir William Heydon, Knt. The wife of his eldest son became Baroness Dacre in her own right, and his youngest son received the honour of knighthood, and was father of Sir Stephen Lennard, 1st baronet (ext.). Sir John Farnaby Cator, 1st baronet (cr. 1880), had in 1861 assumed by Roy. licence the surname of Lennard in lieu of his patronymic. The 2nd baronet, Sir Henry Arthur Hallam Farnaby Lennard, Hon. Col. Kent R.G.A. (T.A.), served with Hunzar-Naga Expedition 1891-2, (medal with clasp), and during European War 1914-18, Comdg. 11th Batn. Cheshire Regt., and on Staff (Croix de Guerre).

BARRETT-LENNARD, Creation (U.K.) 1801, of Belhus, Essex.

Sir (THOMAS) RICHARD FIENNES BARRETT-LENNARD, OBE, 5th *Baronet*; *b*. Dec. 12th, 1898; *s*. his father, *Sir* RICHARD FIENNES, 1934; ed. at Brighton Coll., and at Clare Coll., Camb. (MA); is a KStJ; OBE (Civil) 1970: *m*. 1922, Kathleen Finora, da. of the late Hon. John Donohoe Fitzgerald, KC [B. Fitzgerald], and has issue.

Arms—Quarterly: 1st and 4th, or, on a fesse gules three fleurs-de-lis or, within a bordure wavy, *Lennard;* 2nd and 3rd, party per pale barry of four counterchanged argent and gules, *Barrett;* all within a bordure wavy sable. **Crest**—Out of a ducal coronet or an Irish wolf dog's head per fesse argent and ermine, charged with an escallop per fesse nebuly, gules and sable. [The 1st baronet also obtained from the Lyon office in Edinburgh a grant of supporters, viz.—two lions rampant or, each charged with a collar quarterly argent and gules; but the grantee's domicile being in England this grant was illegal.]

To wish well.   *Residence*—3, Swallowfield Park, Reading, Berks. RG7 1TG.
                Clubs—Leander, RAC.

Daughter living—Anne, *b*. 1923 : *m*. 1949, the Rev. John Charles Pollock [*see* Pollock, Bt., *cr*. 1866, colls.]. *Residence*, Rose Ash House, South Molton, Devon.

Collateral Branches living.

Granddaughter of the late Rev. Dacre Barrett-Lennard, brother of 2nd baronet:—
Issue of the late Dacre Barrett-Lennard, *b*. 1884, *d*. 1948 : *m*. 1915, Mabel Ella (now of Gable Cottage, Aldham Hadleigh, Suffolk), da. of James Sage, of The Yew Tree Farm, Aldham, Suffolk:—
Viva Dacre, *b*. 1923. *Residence*, Gable Cottage, Aldham Hadleigh, Suffolk.

Grandson of the late Capt. Thomas George Barrett-Lennard (infra):—
Issue of the late Sir Fiennes Cecil Arthur Barrett-Lennard, *b*. 1880, *d*. 1963: *m*. 1916, Winifrede Mignon, who *d*. 1969, da. of Alfred Berlyn:—
Rev. HUGH DACRE (of The Oratory, S.W.7), *b*. June 27th, 1917; ed. at Radley; formerly Capt. Essex Regt.; 1939-45 War (despatches); is Priest of London Oratory.

Issue of the late Trenchard Goodenough Barrett-Lennard, *b*. 1872, *d*. 1945 : *m*. 1903, Rosa, who *d*. 1962, da. of W. I. Hall, of Cheadle Hulme, Cheshire:—
Roy, *b*. 1909 : *m*. 1939, Joyce Christine Elizabeth, da. of Stuart Robert Drinkwater, of Coventry, and has issue living, Richard Fynes, *b*. 1941,—Peter John, *b*. 1942,—Penelope Anne, *b*. 1948.

Granddaughter of the late Trenchard Goodenough Barrett-Lennard (ante):—
Issue of the late Dacre Barrett-Lennard, *b*. 1906 ; *d*. (killed in action during European War) 1944 : *m*. 1938, Una, da. of Leo Burn, of Wallasey, Cheshire :—
Paula, *b*. 1943.

Grandsons of the late Edmund George Lennard Barrett-Lennard, son of the late Edmund Thomas Henry Barrett-Lennard, son of George Barrett-Lennard, 3rd son of 1st baronet:—
Issue of the late Edmund Thomas Dacre Barrett-Lennard, *b*. 1881, *d*. 1945 : *m*. 1907, Kathleen Rosina who *d*. 1939, da. of Thomas D. Pettigrew :—
Geoffrey, *b*. 1908 : *m*. 1933, Lorna Margaret, da. of A. B. Lodge, of York, W. Australia, and has issue living, John, *b*. 1949,—Sarah Margaret, *b*. 1936: *m*. 1963, Archibald Stewart Fraser, of 17, Euston Av., Highgate, S. Aust., and has issue living, John Buchanan *b*. 1966, Geoffrey Lodge *b*. 1968, Catherine Margaret *b*. 1971,—Judith (77, Forrest St., Beverley, 6304, W. Aust.), *b*. 1938: *m*. 1969, Robert Henry Magill, who *d*. 1974, and has issue living, Peter John *b*. 1962,—David James Henry, *b*. 1974,—Catherine Elizabeth, *b*. 1970. *Residence*, Annandale, Beverley, W. Aust.——Anthony Leslie (Box 64, Beverley, W. Aust.), *b*. 1913: *m*. 1943, Ethel Barbara, da. of R. F. Adams, of Sydney, NSW, and has issue living, Antony John William, *b*. 1953,—Carmen Lesley. *b*. 1944,—Jill Kathleen, *b*. 1946: *m*. 1974, Allan Wall, of 63, Hardy Rd., Nedlands, W. Aust.,—Sally Ann, *b*. 1951.

Grandchildren of the late Edmund Thomas Dacre Barrett-Lennard (ante):—
Issue of the late Edmund Thomas Keith Barrett-Lennard, *b*. 1911, *d*. 19—: *m*. 1938, Margaret (Woonderlin, Beverley, W. Aust.), da. of A. V. Clarke, of Beverley, W. Aust.:—
Edmund Timothy Dacre, *b*. 1941.——Douglas John (Woonderlin, Beverley, W. Aust.), *b*. 1944: *m*. 1974, Dorothy Marianne, el. da. of Gordon Derwent Crosthwaite, of Glenroa, Margaret River, W. Aust.——Richard, *b*. 1950.——Helen Mary, *b*. 1939.

Grandchildren of the late Edmund George Lennard Barrett-Lennard (ante):—
Issue of the late Francis Barrett-Lennard, *b*. 1882, *d*. 1960: *m*. 1910, Elsie Selina, who *d*. 1950, da. of Thomas George Walker, of Beverley, W. Australia:—
Thomas Edmund (of Drumclyer, Beverley, W. Australia), *b*. 1916; is a Farmer: *m*. 1948, Lesley Vernon, da. of Vernon Paind Gibson, of Perth, W. Australia, and has issue living, Graham Francis, *b*. 1953,—Felicity Anne, *b*. 1949,—Jennifer Jane, *b*. 1950,—Dinah Louise, *b*. 1955,—Launa, *b*. 1911: *m*. 1940, Horace Arnold Butler, of Beverley, W. Australia, and has issue living, Lennard Wilfred, *b*. 1944, Frances Merrilyn *b*. 1943.

Issue of the late Henry Barrett-Lennard, *b*. 1884, *d*. 1960: *m*. 1912, Muriel Ellen, da. of John Trevelyan:—
Trevor Henry (of Camblebren, Gairdner River, W. Australia), *b*. 1922, is a Farmer; European War 1939-45, with Australian Imperial Force: *m*. 1951, Audrey, younger da. of Albert E. Wilhelm, of Beverley, W. Australia, and has issue living, Cameron, *b*. 1952,—Brent, *b*. 1957,—Leonie Gaye, *b*. 1954,—Belinda Anne, *b*. 1963.

Issue of the late Alexander Forrest Barrett-Lennard, *b*. 1895, *d*. 1941: *m*. 1917, Eva Mary (of Beverley, W. Australia), da. of Edward Berry:—
Alexander Dacre (Belhus, Box 58, Beverley, W. Aust.), *b*. 1921; Sgt. RAAF: *m*. 1949, Dorothea Ann, da. of James Davidson Weaver, of Beverley, W. Aust., and has issue living, Gregory Dacre

b. 1958,—Susan, *b.* 1950: *m.* 1971, Kenneth Charles Baston, of Ella Valla Station, Carnarvon, W. Aust., and has issue living, George Derek *b.* 1974,—Meredith, *b.* 1953: *m.* 1973, Philip Anthony Cockerill, of Geraldton, W. Aust.,—Vicki, *b.* 1955.——Peggy Amy, *b.* 1918: *m.* 1946, Durward Toleman, and has issue living, David Forest, *b.* 1952,—Michael Fiennes, *b.* 1955. *Residence,* 15, Caravan St., Balwyn, E8, Victoria, Australia.

Grandchildren of George Hardey Barrett-Lennard (infra):—
Issue of the late George Graham Barrett-Lennard, *b.* 1887, *d.* 1968: *m.* 1911, Maud
    Gladys Hastings (Unit 9, Freshwater Apts., 42, Victoria Av., Claremont, W. Aust. 6010)
    da. of G. W. Hester, of Dalgarup Park, Bridgetown, W. Australia:—
Fynes (St. Leonards, Kondut, W. Australia), *b.* 1915: *m.* 1949, Florence Ray, da. of W. C. Williams,
    of Nedlands, W. Australia, and has issue living, Kingsley Ian Michael, *b.* 1954,—William Ashley
    Dacre, *b.* 1957,—Wendy Roslyn, *b.* 1950: *m.* 1972, Ralph Dunstan Pomery, of Valetta Rd.,
    Fulham Gdns., S. Aust., and has issue living, Sharon Anne *b.* 1974,—Helen Elizabeth, *b.* 1951:
    m' 1974, Kimberley John Clifton.——Douglas Graham (The Crescent, Gingin, W. Aust.), *b.*
    1916: *m.* 1943, Olive Davidson, and has issue living, David Thomas, *b.* 1945 (Belhus, Upper
    Swan, W. Aust.),—Joan, *b.* 1946: *m.* 1970, Keith McMullan, of Caprice Rd., Geraldton, W. Aust.,
    —Kaye Julie, *b.* 1959.——Lancelot (Averley Downs, Kondut, W. Aust.), *b.* 1918; MB and BS
    Adelaide 19—: *m.* 1945, Patricia Ida, da. of J. Porter, of Northam, W. Aust., and has issue
    living, Michael Scott, *b.* 1949,—Richard John Stirling (Byfields, Kondut, W. Aust.) *b.* 1951: *m.*
    1973, Rosalind, da. of the late Robert Willis, of St. James, Perth, W. Aust.,—Simon Hugh
    b. 1957,—Patricia Ruth, *b.* 1947: *m.* 1972, Richard Stevenson,—Kathleen Ann, *b.* 1954.——
    Godfrey Trevor (475, Parkwood Court, Waterloo, Ont., Canada), *b.* 1926; ed. at Perth Univ.,
    W. Aust. (BSc, BA and at Chicago Univ. (Dr. in Psychology 1959); Prof. in Psychology, Univ.
    of Waterloo, Ont.: *m.* 1948, Helen, da. of William Love, of 40, Harvey St., Mosman Park, W.
    Aust., and has issue living, John Graham, *b.* 1953,—Lance Godfrey, *b.* 1955,—Sirri Anne, *b.*
    1960,—Katherine Gail (twin), *b.* 1960,—Judith Helen, *b.* 1966.——Irwin Prescott (St. Leonards,
    Kondut, W. Australia), *b.* 1929; ed. at W. Australia Univ. (BSc Agriculture, MSc): *m.* 1953,
    Berwine Ruth, da. of Dr. Leigh Cook, of Stirling Highway, Claremont, W. Australia, and has
    issue living, Edward Graham, *b.* 1953,—Hugh Anthony, *b.* 1955,—James Irwin, *b.* 1961,—Ann
    Mary, *b.* 1958.——Hester, *b.* 1913: *m.* (Feb.) 1937, Hubert Leake Shields, of Glenvar, Wongan
    Hills, W. Aust. 6603, and has issue living, Graham Michael, *b.* 1946: *m.* 1969, Lynette, da. of
    John Gale, of Yelbeni, W. Aust., and has issue living, Michael Graham *b.* 1973, Marnie Jane
    b. 1974,—Peter William Hubert, *b.* 1950,—Anthony Hubert, *b.* 1955,—Robin Wendy, *b.* (Dec.)
    1937: *m.* 1961, Dr. Roy Montague Green, MSc (17, Piridari Rd., City Beach, W. Aust.) and has
    issue living, Julie Anne *b.* 1964, Cathy Susan *b.* 1965,—Waverley Hester, *b.* 1939: *m.* 1970,
    Robin Ladyman, of Katanning, W. Aust., and has issue living, Lara *b.* 1972, Tanya *b.* 1974,—
    Christine Mary, *b.* 1944: *m.* 1967, Robert Weise, of Highbury 6313, W. Aust., and has issue living,
    Michael William *b.* 1969, Timothy *b.* 1971, Anthony *b.* 1973,—Elizabeth Ann, *b.* 1953.
Issue of the late Trevor St. Aubyn Barrett-Lennard, *b.* 1889, *d.* 1970: *m.* 1st, 1912,
    Susan Mary, who *d.* 1939, da. of C. W. Ferguson, of Houghton, Swan, W. Aust.; 2ndly,
    1942, Edith Mary, who *d.* 1968, da. of John Edward Wedge:—
(By 1st m.) Ferguson (W. Swan, W. Aust.) *b.* 1913:——Donald (Houghton, Middle Swan, W. Aust.),
    b. 1916: *m.* 1940, his cousin, Dorothy, da. of C. O. Ferguson (infra), and has issue living, Brian,
    b. 1952,—Flora, *b.* 1947.——(by 2nd m.) Barbara, *b.* 1948: *m.* 1968, Stuart William Green, of 4,
    Hudson Rd., Bunbury, W. Aust., and has issue living, Philip Edward Spencer, *b.* 1968,—Julian
    St. Aubyn, *b.* 1973,—Rosemarie Catherine, *b.* 1970.——Elizabeth, *b.* 1949: *m.* 1968, Gregory
    Allan Harris, and has issue living, Trevor Allan, *b.* 1968,—Daniel Raymond, *b.* 1974.
Issue of the late St. Aubyn Edward Barrett-Lennard, *b.* 1899, *d.* 1956: *m.* 1933, Betty
    Corona (of Belhus, Upper Swan, W. Aust. 6056), da. of Edward Sidney Simpson, DSc,
    of Millpoint, South Perth, W. Australia:—
Richard St. Aubyn (Belhus, Upper Swan, W. Aust.), *b.* 1938: *m.* 1965, Sandra, el. da. of Keith
    Irwin Bedford Smith, of Alfred Cove, W. Aust., and has issue living, Nigel Dacre, *b.* 1968,—
    Philip St. Aubyn, *b.* 1972,—Amy Wilson *b.* 1966.——John Dacre, *b.* 1940: *m.* 1970, Lynette
    Marie, el. da. of Robert Atkinson of W. Perth, W. Aust., and has issue living, Mark Robert,
    b. 1970,—Timothy Stewart, *b.* 1972.

Grandchildren of the late St. Aubyn Edward Barrett-Lennard (ante):—
Issue of the late George Simpson Barrett-Lennard, *b.* 1934, *d.* 1972: *m.* 1961, Angela
    Clare (Belhus, Upper Swan, W. Aust.), da. of Alfred Raymond Stevens, of W. Swan,
    W. Aust.:—
David Anthony, *b.* 1966.——Michael John, *b.* 1972.——Susan Fairlie, *b.* 1963.

Grandchildren of the late Edward Graham Barrett-Lennard, el. son of Edward
    Pomeroy Barrett-Lennard, 5th son of 1st Bt.:—
Issue of the late George Hardey Barrett-Lennard, *b.* 1862, *d.* 1917: *m.* 1886, Amy, who *d.*
    1937, da. of the late Hon. Edmund Ralph Brockman, M.L.A., of Henley Park, W.
    Australia:—
Hebe Dorothy: *m.* 1911, C. O. Ferguson, and has issue living, Dorothy, *b.* 1914: *m.* 1940, her
    cousin, Donald Barrett-Lennard (ante). *Residence,* Houghton, Middle Swan, W. Australia.——
Vera: *m.* 1918, C. T. P. Ewing. *Residence,*
Issue of the late Victor Dacre Barrett-Lennard, *b.* 1874, *d.* 1930: *m.* 1906, Blanche Isabel
    (now of Mobedine, York, W. Australia), da. of Robert Allen:—
Dacre, *b.* 1906: *m.* 1943, Maisie, da. of J. Vile, of Aubury, N. S. Wales, and has issue living,
    John Dacre, *b.* 1944.——Victor Dudley, *b.* 1908: *m.* 19— Jane Harper, da. of G. H. Lukin,
    of Guildford, W. Australia.——Ernest Stuart, *b.* 1910: *m.* 19—, Lorraine, da. of Allen Mair,
    of Swanbourne, W. Australia and has issue living, Rupert Allen *b.* 1941,—Sandra, *b.* 1943,—
    Jennifer, *b.* 1947.——Lucille, *b.* 1014: *m.* 19—, John Hill Chellew, and has issue living, John
    Alexander, *b.* 1949,—William Lennard, *b.* 1051,—Margaret Anne, *b.* 1947,—Mary Dianne, *b.*
    1951.——Flora Grace, *b.* 1919 : *m.* 19—, John Richard Fontayne-England, and has issue, John
    Dacre, *b.* 1945,—Jane Anne, *b.* 1950. *Residence,*
Issue of the late Arthur St. Aubyn Barrett-Lennard, *b.* 1876, *d.* 1953: *m.* 1906, Fanny
    Susan, who *d.* 1949, da. of Samuel Henry Viveash:—
Arthur Viveash (Tooldyay Rd., Gidgannup, W. Aust.) *b.* 1910: *m.* 1952, Joan, da. of Frederick
    Short, of Claremont, W. Aust., and has issue living, Jane Margaret, *b.* 1953: *m.* 1973, Bernard
    Drag.——Frank St. Aubyn (Nonutarra Station, Onslow, W. Aust., *b.* 1912: *m.* 1942, Constance
    Rosalie, da. of the Ven. Archdeacon L. D. Parry, of Perth, W. Aust., and has issue living, Ronald
    Susan, *b.* 1945: *m.* 1966, Ian Maxwell Greenham, of 67, Campbell St., Glen Waverley Vic. 3150,
    Aust., and has issue living, Anthony Ian St. Aubyn *b.* 1970, Deborah Susan *b.* 1968,—Marian
    Ruth, *b.* 1947,—Constance Anne, *b.* 1951: *m.* 1972, Neil Bates, RAAF,—Jennifer Robyn, *b.* 1954.
    ——Edward Guy (Mount Stuart Station, Onslow, W. Aust.), *b.* 1919: *m.* 1960, Dymity Ann, da. of
    V. W. Shotter, of Perth, W. Aust., and has issue living, Edward William, *b.* 1967,—Guy St.
    Aubyn, *b.* 1969,—Lindal Dymity, *b.* 1963.
Issue of the late John Evelyn Barrett-Lennard, *b.* 1881, *d.* 1967: *m.* 1911, Frances Amy,
    who *d.* 1954, da. of Edward Kay Courthope, of Perth, W. Australia:—
Frances Josephine, *b.* 1913: *m.* 1940, Geoffrey Howard Gwynne, of 5, Browne Av., Dalkeith, W.
    Aust. 6009, and has issue living, John Howard, *b.* 1946; ed. at W. Aust. Univ. (BSc): *m.* 1969,
    Deborah Judith, da. of A. B. Walton, of Perth, W. Aust., and has issue living, Belinda Judith
    b. 1972, Katherine Anne (twin) *b.* 1972,—Geraldine Frances, *b.* 1941: *m.* 1967, Jens Dalhoff
    Jorgensen, of Aalborg, Denmark, and has issue living, Michael Dalhoff *b.* 1971,
    Frances Dalhoff *b.* 1968,—Angela Madeline, *b.* 1953.——Judith, *b.* 1914: *m.* 1941, Ashburton
    Hall Clark, of 78, Webster St., Nedlands, W. Aust., and has issue living, John Jeremy, *b.* 1941:
    m. 1969, Geraldine Lesley, da. of L. J. Locke, of Perth, W. Aust., and has issue living, Anthony

Phillip *b.* 1974, Catherine Rosanne *b.* 1971,——Frances Louise, *b.* 1946: *m.* 1974, Trevor William Tyson, of 101, Townshend Rd., Subiaco, W. Aust.——Anne, *b.* 1916: *m.* 1946, Edward Alexander Glyn Watkins, of Kerralong, Arthur River, W. Aust., and has issue living, Jonathan George Glyn, *b.* 1948.——Daniel Glyn, *b.* 1955,——Miranda Glyn, *b.* 1952.——Prudence, *b.* 1918: *m.* 1946, Frank Ernest Heymanson, of 13, Vix St., Nedlands, W. Aust., and has issue living, John Simon, *b.* 19——,——Janet Louise, *b.* 19——,——Jennifer Anne, *b.* 19——.——Charlotte Virginia, *b.* 1920: *m.* 1945, Alleyne Bruce Giles, of Undoolya, N. Dandalup, W. Aust., and has issue living, John Nicholas, *b.* 1946: *m.* 1974, Christine, da. of Peter Lynfoot, of Perth, W. Aust.,——Richard Courthope, *b.* 1953: *m.* 1974, Barbara, da. of W. Flower, of Sydney, NSW,——Susanne Virginia, *b.* 1949: *m.* 1971, John Herbert Dowling, of Lower King, via Albany, W. Aust.

Grandchildren of the late William Barrett-Lennard (infra) :—
Issue of the late Walter James Barrett-Lennard, <i>b.</i> 1883, <i>d.</i> 1954: <i>m.</i> 1904, Mary, who
d. 1967, da. of the late James Lawther, of Russell, Manitoba:—

Walter James, *b.* 1914: *m.* 1947, Beatrice Elizabeth, da. of Dr. C. T. Crowdy, of Montreal, Canada, and has issue living, James Thomas, *b.* 1956,——Elizabeth Jane, *b.* 1948,——Deborah Dacre, *b.* 1949,——Naomi Barbara, *b.* 1952. *Residence*, 5190, Maple St., Vancouver 13, British Columbia.——Caroline Mary, *b.* 1908: *m.* 1931, Capt. Richard Walter Underhill, OBE, and has issue living.——Margaret, *b.* 1911: *m.* 1936, Col. Donald Spankie, OBE, Canadian Inf. *Residence*,

Grandchildren of the late Walter James Barrett-Lennard, 8th son of 1st
baronet :—
Issue of the late William Barrett-Lennard, <i>b.</i> 1857, <i>d.</i> 19— : <i>m.</i> 1st, 1880, Margaret, who <i>d.</i>
1890, da. of Capt. Boswell, of Peterborough, Ontario ; 2ndly, 1892, Laura Sophia, who <i>d.</i>
1910, da. of Thomas Garnier Johnson, of The Oaklands, Biuscarth, Manitoba, Canada:—

(By 1st marriage) Hardinge, *b.* 1890; European War 1915-18 : *m.* 1922, Annie, da. of Harry Wyles, of Victoria, British Columbia.——Georgina Boswell : *m.* 1903, D'Arcy E. Boulton, and has issue living, Dacre, *b.* 1906,——Charles Keppel, *b.* 1908,——Angus, *b.* 1911,——Zaidee, *b.* 1907,——Rhoda, *b.* 19——.——Mary Caroline Pearl: *m.* 1911, Vice-Adm. Harry Rowlandson Godfrey, CB, DSO, who *d.* 1947, and has issue living, Derek Charles (15, Redlands Way, Streetly, Sutton Coldfield), *b.* 1922; Lt.-Cdr. RN (ret.): *m.* 1964, Evelyn Mary, da. of the Rev. Dacre Fiennes Barrett-Lennard (infra),——Jocelyn Marion, *b.* 1920: *m.* 1947, Roger N. H. Whitehouse, of The Murrays, Pathhead, Midlothian, EH37 5UL, and has issue living, Godfrey David Hately, *b.* 1948: *m.* 1974, Jill, da. of Dr. R. Emberton,——Christopher Paul Rowlandson, *b.* 1950,——Anthony Adrian Gray, *b.* 1951,——Caroline Anne, *b.* 1954: *m.* 1974, Christopher Bousfield Cox, of 4, Wakefield St., Wanganui, NZ.——Gladys Dacre: *m.* 1909, Frederick Jancowski, formerly of Stewart, British Columbia, and has issue living, Richard William, *b.* 1915,——Frederick Barrett-Lennard, *b.* 1917,——Charles Hardwick, *b.* 1924,——Mildred Dacre, *b.* 1910,——Margaret Kepple, *b.* 1912.—— (By 2nd m.) William Louis, *MC*, *b.* 1893; formerly Lt. Canadian Inf.; European War 1915-18 (wounded, MC): *m.* 1920, Agnes Mildred, da. of the late Nathanial Dowsett, of Lethbridge, Alberta, Canada.——Charles, *b.* 1895; European War 1914-18 with Canadian Inf., and in RAF: *m.* 19——, Florence Sylvia Shafer, of Vancouver, British Columbia.——Mabel Sophia: *m.* 1918, Brigadier Arthur Harry Langham Godfrey, DSO, MC, Australian Mil. Forces, who *d.* (killed in action during European War) 1942, and has issue living, John Elliott, *b.* 1919; is in Australian Mil. Forces: *m.* 19——, Patricia, only da. of Air Commodore Owen (Washington) de Putron, CBE,——Edward Arthur, *b.* 1921,——Charles Lovett, *b.* 1924,——Mildred Isabel, *b.* 1922. *Residence*

Grandchildren of the late Lt.-Col. John Barrett-Lennard, CBE, 3rd son of
Walter James Barrett-Lennard, 8th son of 1st baronet:—
Issue of the late Rev. Dacre Fiennes Barrett-Lennard, <i>b.</i> 1888, <i>d.</i> 1975: <i>m.</i> 1st, 1910,
Charlotte Dorothy Evelyn, who <i>d.</i> 1937, da. of the late Rev. Henry Chichele Hart
Bampton [E. Albemarle, colls.]; 2ndly, 1940, Irene Phyllis (Lytel Mansions, Quendon,
Saffron Walden, Essex), da. of Mark Moss, of Rook Hall, Cressing:—

(By 1st m.) Richard Dacre, *b.* 1921.——Michael Henry, *b.* 1923.——John Fiennes, *b.* 1926.——Evelyn Mary, *b.* 1927: *m.* 1964, Lt. Cdr. Derek Charles Godfrey RN (ret.) (ante).——Rachel Margaret, *b.* 1928.——(By 2nd m.), Philip Francis Dacre, *b.* 1947.

Grandchildren of the late Villiers Barrett-Lennard (infra):—
Issue of the late Richard Barrett-Lennard, <i>b.</i> 1892, <i>d.</i> 1967: <i>m.</i> 1917, Kathleen (85,
Compton Place, Carpenders Park, Herts), da. of Alfred Blake, of Duxmere, Ross-on-Wye:—

Robert Villiers, *b.* 1924.——June Rosemary, *b.* 1922.

Granddaughter of Walter James Barrett-Lennard (ante):—
Issue of the late Villiers Barrett-Lennard, <i>b.</i> 1865, <i>d.</i> 1903 : <i>m.</i> 1885, Laura, who <i>d.</i> 1954,
da. of the late George Clement, of Nottingham:—

Dorothy Mabel, *b.* 1890: *m.* 1914, John Hugh Cecil Murray; 2ndly, 1931, Percival Robert Hopkins, who *d.* 1956, and has issue living, (by 1st marriage) John Keith Lennard, *b.* 1916: *m.* 1939, Evlyn Dawn, da. of the late Col. E. V. Anderson, and has issue living, Evelyn Anne *b* 1944. *Residence*, 19, Kyarra Rd., Glen Iris, Melbourne, Australia.

The 1st baronet, Sir Thomas, of Belhus, Essex, (natural son and testamentary heir of Thomas Barrett-Lennard, 17th Lord Dacre), was MP for S. Essex, and the 2nd, Sir Thomas, was High Sheriff of co. Monaghan 1868.

LEON, Creation (U.K.) 1911, of Bletchley Park, Bletchley, Buckinghamshire.

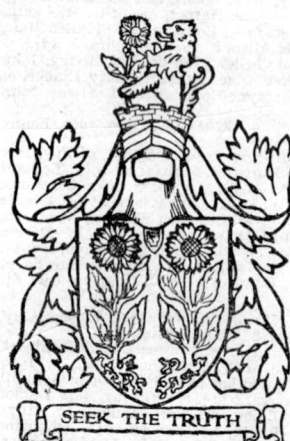

SEEK THE TRUTH

Sir JOHN RONALD LEON, 4th *Baronet*; *b.* Aug. 16th, 1934; *s.* his father, *Sir* RONALD GEORGE, 1964; ed. at Eton; late 2nd Lt. King's Roy. Rifle Corps; an Actor (" John Standing"): *m.* 1961, (m. diss. 1972), Jill, da. of Jack Melford, actor, and has issue.

Arms—Gules: two sunflowers erect, slipped, leaved, and eradicated or, seeded sable. *Crest*—Issuant out of a mural crown or, a demi-lion gules supporting between the paws a sunflower erect, slipped and leaved gold, seeded sable.

Residence—98, Ebury St., SW1.

Son living—ALEXANDER JOHN *b.* May 3rd, 1965.

Brother living—Timothy Michael George (49, Dewhurst Rd., W14), *b.* 1938; ed. at Stowe; late Sub-Lt. RNVR: *m.* 1969, Suzanne, da. of Col. M. Kinnear, late KOYLI.

Half-Sister living—Anne Elizabeth (Villa Elena, Calle Batista 33, Genova, Palma de Mallorca, Spain), *b.* 1925: *m.* 1950 (m. diss. 1964), Michael Gough, and has issue living, Emma Frances, *b.* 1953.

Mother living—Dorothy Katharine (the actress Kay Hammond) (*Lady Clements*) (7, Royal Cres., Brighton, Sussex), da. of the late Cdr. Sir Guy Standing, KBE:

m. 1st, 1932, as his 2nd wife, (m. diss. 1945), Sir Ronald George Leon, 3rd Baronet, who *d.* 1964; 2ndly, 1946, as his 2nd wife, Sir John Selby Clements, CBE.

Widow living of 3rd Baronet—ALICE MARY (*Dowager Lady Leon*) (83, Lexham Gdns., W8), da. of the late Dr. Thomas Holt: *m.* 1947, as his third wife, Sir Ronald George Leon, 3rd Baronet, who *d.* 1964.

Collateral Branch living.

Issue of the late Reginald Herbert Leon, 2nd son of 1st baronet, *b.* 1882, *d.* 1960: *m.* 1st, 1906, Rita Ethel (who *d.* 1966, having obtained a divorce 1916, and *m.* 2ndly 1927, Andrew G. C. Gibson, of Stanley House, King's Stanley, Glos.), da. of the late Abram de Mattos Mocatta; 2ndly, 1920, Mary Millicent, who *d.* 1950, da. of James Blagborough:—

(By 1st marriage) Richard Neville, *b.* 1909: *m.* 1941, Margery Frances, only da. of Sir William Henry Robinson, K.C.M.G., C.B.E., and has issue living, David Richard, *b.* 1946. *Residence,* Slough Place, Cuckfield, Haywards Heath, Sussex.

The 1st baronet, Sir Herbert Samuel Leon (High Sheriff of Bucks 1909), sat as M.P. for Bucks N., or Buckingham, Div. (*L*) 1891-5.

LESLIE, Creation (N.S.) 1625, of Wardis and Findrassie, Morayshire [Dormant 1967].

Sir (HENRY JOHN) LINDORES LESLIE, *9th Baronet*, d. in. 1967, and at the time of going to press no name appears on the Official Roll of Baronets in respect of this title.

Daughter living of 9th Baronet—Elizabeth Jean (*Lady Parker*) *b.* 1952: *m.* 1972, Sir Richard William Hyde Parker, 12th Bt., of Melford Hall, Long Melford, Suffolk.

Daughter living of 8th Baronet—Nancy Jean, *b.* 1923: *m.* 1946, Col. William Henry Gerard Leigh, Life Guards, and has issue living, John Norman Gerard, *b.* 1949.—David William Philip, *b.* 1958.—Carolyn Jane Gerard, *b.* 1947,—Camilla Madelaine Gerard *b.* 1952. *Residences,* 4, Eaton Mansions, Cliveden Place, SW1; Bartlett House, Holyport, Maidenhead, Berks.

Widows living of 8th and 9th Baronets—BETTY ELISE (*Dowager Lady Leslie*), da. of the late John Thomas Beadsworth Sewell, CBE, LLD: *m.* 1919, Wing-Cdr. Sir Norman Roderick Alexander David Leslie, CMG, CBE, 8th baronet, who *d.* 1937. *Residence,* 23, Melville Rd., Barnes, SW. ——COLETTE KATHLEEN (RUSSELL-WALLING), (*Lady Leslie*), (Otten Hall, Belchamp Otten, Sudbury, Suffolk), da. of the late George Theodore Cregan, MC, MD, of 57, Sloane St., SW1: *m.* 1950, Capt. Sir (Henry John) Lindores Leslie, 9th baronet, who *d.* 1967.

Collateral Branches living.

Grandchildren of the late John Leslie, el. son of the late Thomas Leslie, 3rd son of 4th baronet:—

Issue of the late Frank Harvey Leslie, *b.* 1874, *d.* 1965: *m.* 1st, 1915, Amelia Caroline, who *d.* 1918, da. of Alexander Russon; 2ndly, 1918, Agnes Maude, who *d.* 1948, da. of Frank Spooner:—

(By 1st marriage) PERCY THEODORE (38, Borough Rd., Kingston Hill, Surrey), *b.* Nov. 19th, 1915; presumed heir to Baronetcy.

Issue of the late Eliza Myhill Leslie, *b.* 1872, *d.* 1946: *m.* 1897, John Leslie Brown, who *d.* 1928 :—

Alexander Leslie (11, Goddens Close, Northiam, Sussex), *b.* 1903: *m.* 1939, Mary Snadden, da. of George Joseph Rogers.——Margaret Elizabeth Leslie, *b.* 1900: *m.* 1926, John Brougham Harrison, and has issue living, John Brougham, *b.* 1928: *m.* 1950, Ingledubina Louise de la Rosa, of California, USA, and has issue living, James Leslie, *b.* 1958, John Eric, *b.* 1965,—Peter Brougham (of Casilla, 2717, Lima, Peru), *b.* 1933: *m.* 1958, Mary M. Fusilier, of New Orleans, USA, and has issue living, Peter Alexander Brougham Harrison, *b.* 1959, Madelyn Mary Leslie *b.* 1967. *Residence,* Casilla 2045, Lima, Peru.

(*In remainder.*)

Descendants of George Leslie of Crichie, uncle of 1st baronet [see Leslie, Bt., cr. 1876].

On the death of the 2nd baronet the baronetcy reverted to his uncle, William, 2nd son of John Leslie, of Wardis, father of the 1st baronet. but he declined to assume the title as the Wardis estates did not accompany it. His four sons, all died without issue. The baronetcy remained dormant for many years, until it was assumed (without service of heirship) by John Leslie, who was 4th in descent from Norman, next brother of 3rd Bt. The baronetcy was conferred with remainder to heirs male whatsoever, and the Baronets of Glaslough, co. Monaghan *cr.* (UK) 1876, are therefore in remainder.

LESLIE, Creation (U.K.) 1876, of Glaslough, co. Monaghan.

Sir JOHN NORMAN IDE LESLIE, 4th *Baronet*; *b.* Dec. 6th, 1916: *s.* his father, Sir (JOHN RANDOLPH) SHANE, 1971; ed. at Downside, and Magdalene Coll., Camb. (BA); Capt. Irish Gds., K.St.J., Knt. of Honour and Devotion Sovereign Mil. Order of Malta, and Knt. Cdr. Order of St. Gregory the Great; 1939-45 War (prisoner).

Arms—Quarterly, 1st and 4th argent, on a bend azure between two holly leaves vert, three buckles or; 2nd and 3rd or, a lion rampant gules, debruised by a ribbon sable. **Crest**—A griffin's head erased gules.

Residence—19, Piazza in Piscinula, Rome, Italy. *Clubs*—Travellers', Circolo della Caccia (Rome).

GRIP FAST

Brother living—DESMOND ARTHUR PETER (Castle Leslie, Glaslough, co. Monaghan), *b.* June 29th, 1921; ed. at Ampleforth, and Trin. Coll., Dublin; Composer, Author, Film Producer, and Discologist; late Fl. Sgt. Pilot RAF: *m.* 1st, 1945, Agnes, only da. of Rudolph Bernauer, of Budapest, Hungary; 2ndly, 1970, Helen Jennifer, da. of the late Lt.-Col. E. I. E. Strong, of Tor House, Wiveliscombe, Som., and has issue living (by 1st m.), Shaun Rudolph Christopher, *b.* 1947,—Christopher Mark, *b.* 1952,—Antonia Kelvey Leslie, *b.* 1963,—(by 2nd m.) Samantha Helen, *b.* 1966,—Camilla Patricia, *b.* 1968.

Sister living—Anne Theodosia Moyra (Anita) LESLIE, *b.* 1913; is an author; resumed by deed poll 1947 the surname of Leslie in lieu of Rodzianko; served with S. African Army 1940-42 and with 1st French Armoured Div. 1944-45 (French Croix de Guerre, Africa Star, and S. African ser. medal): *m.* 1st, 1937 (m. annulled 1948), Col. Paul Rodz anko, CMG, who *d.* 1965; 2ndly, 1949, Com. William Donald Ælian Leslie-King, DSO, DSC, RN (ret.), who assumed by deed poll 1955 the additional surname of Leslie before that of King, and has issue living, (by 2nd m.) Tarka Richard Bourke, *b.* 1949; Lt. Blues & Royals,—Leonie Rose, *b.* 1951. *Residence*, Oranmore Castle, Oranmore, co. Galway.

Uncle living (son of 2nd baronet)—William Seymour, *b.* 1889; formerly Sec. Queen Charlotte's Maternity Hospital, Hammersmith, W.: *m.* 1929, Gwyneth Rawdon, da. of Rawdon Roden, and has issue living, Jennifer Constance, *b.* 1930. *Residence*, Castle Leslie (West), Glaslough, co. Monaghan. *Club*, Travellers'.——Lionel Allistair David, *b.* 1900; ed. at Eton; late Capt. Cameron Highlanders; 1939-45 War in France and Italy (despatches): *m.* 1942, Barbara Yvonne, da. of Edwin Alexander Enever, and has issue living, Leonie Deirdrie Elise, *b.* 1944. *Residence*, Grasspoint, Isle of Mull.

Widow living of 3rd Baronet—IRIS CAROLA (*Lady Leslie*), (Old Parsonage Farm, Hanley Castle, Worcs.), yst. da. of the late Charles Miskin Laing, Bar.-at-Law, of Bury Knowle, Headington, Oxford, and widow of Capt. Donald Alexander Frazer: *m.* 1958, as his 2nd wife, Sir (John Randolph) Shane Leslie, 3rd Bt., who *d.* 1971.

John Leslie, DD, Bishop of the Isles, Scotland, translated to Raphoe, Ireland 1633, and Clogher 1661, was the first of this family to possess Castle Leslie or Glaslough. He was son of George Leslie of Crichie, 2nd son of Walter Leslie of Wardis and uncle of 1st Bt. (cr. NS 1625), to which baronetcy his line is in remainder.

The 2nd baronet, Sir John, CBE, was Lt. Grenadier Guards and Lt.-Col. Roy. Irish Fusiliers, and served in Egypt 1882, in S. Africa 1900, and in 1914-19 War (CBE). The 3rd baronet was the writer Sir (John Randolph) Shane Leslie.

LETHBRIDGE, Creation (U.K.) 1804, of Westaway House, and Winkley Court, Somerset.

Sir HECTOR WROTH LETHBRIDGE, 6th *Baronet ; b.* Aug. 26th, 1898 ; *s.* his father, *Sir* WROTH PERIAM CHRISTOPHER, 1950; ed. at Radley ; formerly Acting Capt. Rifle Brig. ; European War 1917-18 (prisoner, invalided), European War 1939-45 in W. Africa (invalided) : *m.* 1946, Evelyn Diana, da. of the late Lieut.-Col. Francis Arthur Gerard Noel, O.B.E. [*see* E. Gainsborough, colls.], and widow of Major John Vivian Bailey, Roy. Scots Fusiliers, and has issue.

Arms—Argent, over water proper, a bridge of five arches embattled gules, and over the centre arch a turret, in chief an eagle displayed sable charged on the breast with a bezant. **Crest**—From a bridge embattled of one arch gules a demi-eagle displayed sable, wings erminois charged on the breast with a leopard's face or. **Motto over Crest**—"*Truth.*"

Residence—Long Sutton House, Langport, Somerset. *Clubs*, Junior Carlton, County (Taunton).

My hope is in God.

Son living—THOMAS PERIAM HECTOR NOEL, *b.* July 17th, 1950.

Daughter living—Mary Jacintha, *b.* 1948: *m.* 1974, Maj. Richard I ilywood, Coldm. Gds., of Manor Farm House, Ingoldis Thorpe, King's Lynn, Norfolk.

Collateral Branches living.

Issue of the late Col. Ernest Astley Edmund Lethbridge, C.M.G., D.S.O., 2nd son of 4th baronet, *b.* 1864, *d.* 1943 : *m.* 1919, Ruth Mary, who *d.* 1960, da. of the late Lieut.-Col. the Hon. Edward Alexander Holmes à Court [B. Heytesbury, colls.], and widow of Major Charles Evelyn Forrest, D.S.O. :—

Diana Ruth, *b.* 1922 : *m.* 1950, Alexander Haig Anderson, and has issue living, Charles Ernest Haig, *b.* 1951,—Fiona Diana, *b.* 1953. *Residence*, Rookery Wood, Slinfold, Sussex.

Issue of the late Thomas Buckler Valentine Lethbridge, 3rd son of 4th baronet, *b.* 1866, *d.* 1914 : *m.* 1901, Eva Henrietta Wyndham, who *d.* 1936, da. of Reginald William Templer, of Powderham House, Teignmouth:—

Wroth Thomas Cont, *b.* 1904; formerly Capt., P. and O. Steam Navigation Co.'s Ser.: *m.* 1954, Edith Maria , da. of the late W. H. N. Edwards, and widow of Hugh Wansey Bayly, M.C., M.R.C.S., L.R.C.P. *Residence*, Clevency Cottage, Great Snoring, Norfolk.——Linda Cecely Ger ine (Little Farthings, Wheeler St., Witley, Surrey), *b.* 1906: *m.* 1946, Michael Harold Selby, who *d.* 1965.

Issue of the late Hugh Francis Hesketh Lethbridge, 4th son of 4th baronet, *b.* 1867, *d.* 1935: *m.* 1912, Edith Maude, da. of Thomas Mellor Robinson, of Metford, Natal:—

Hugh Mytton Fitzwarine, *b.* 1913 : *m.* 1945, Elsie Murray, da. of the late Very Rev. Dean Bartlet, of Aberdeen, and has issue living, Hugh George, *b.* 1948,—Jennifer Murray, *b.* 1946.——Wroth Thomas Hesketh Bourchier, *b.* 1914.——Delphine Edith Conyers Bourchier, *b.* 1922.

Grandchildren of the late John Acland Musgrave Lethbridge (infra):—
Issue of the late Duncan John Leghe Lethbridge, *b.* 1898, *d.* 1962; *m.* 1922, Phyllis Muriel (ANDERSON), who *d.* 1971, da. of T. Stanley Chappell, of Chadshunt, Warwicks.:—

Jacqueline Avril, b. 1923: m. 1961, Orpheus F. Quartullo, of 230, Nurmi Drive, Fort Lauderdale, Florida, USA.——June Florence, b. 1926: m. 1944, Mario A. Fog, of Spring Hill Rd., Cold Spring Harbor, Long Island, NY, USA, and has issue living, Duncan Lethbridge, b. 1948,—Stephen Chase, b. 1952.——Ann, b. 1930: m. 1951, Graham Lusk Platt, of 40, Walnut Tree Lane, Cold Spring Harbor, Long Island, New York, USA, and has issue living, Graham Leghe, b. 1959,—Gordon Lethbridge, b. 1960,—Christina May, b. 1956.

Issue of the late Harold Reginald Lethbridge, b. 1901, d. 1972: m. 1942, Shirley Ivy Grace (LIDSTONE), da. of William Mascall, of Cambridgeshire:—
Duncan Stuart, b. 1943.——Reginald Martin Peter, b. 1946.——Richard Christopher Noel, b. 1949.

Issue of the late John Acland Musgrave Lethbridge, 5th son of 4th baronet, b. 1869, d. 1934: m. 1894, Florence Martin, who d. 1931, da. of Sidney Wood Cooper, of New York, U.S.A.:—
Annie Gwendoline, b. 1896: m. 1st, 1916, Capt. Guy Clavering Wetherall, formerly RASC; 2ndly, 1945, Capt. Thorold Murray Smith, MC, of Ridge Cottage, 22, Bellewan Rd., Pietermaritzburg, Natal, S. Africa, and has issue living, (by 1st m.) Robert Guy, b. 1917,—Peter Martin, b. 1919.——Phyllis Henrietta, b. 1897: m. 1933, George Francis Ackroyd, who d. 1938.

Grandchildren of the late Capt. Walter Alexander Charles Lethbridge (infra):—
Issue of the late Walter Miguel Lethbridge, M.C., b. 1886, d. 1964: m. 1st (Jan.) 1907 (marriage dissolved), Anna Agnes, da. of V. Gunter; 2ndly, 1913 (marriage annulled 19—), Catherine Matilda, da. of F. M. Marsh; 3rdly, 1919, Carmela, da. of Miguel I. Aguilera:—
(By 1st m.), Frances Rose, b. (Nov.) 1907.——(by 3rd m.), Walter Miguel (45, Pitman Court, Gloucester Rd., Bath BA1 8BD), b. 1923: m. 1st, 1949 (m. diss. 1956), Nora, da. of Eduardo Barrios; 2ndly, 1957, Jill Margaret, da. of Robert G. Nethery, MRCS, LRCP, of 5, St. Patricks Court, Barh, and has issue living (by 1st m.), Walter Alexander (73, Rue de la Pleine, (75) Paris XX, France), b. 1950: m. 1971, Elsie, da. of Guy Derozieres-Le comte, of Lille, France, and has issue living, Alexis Guillaume b. 1971,—(by 2nd m.), Arabella Margaret, b. 1962.——Rodney Thomas (980 N.W., 45th Av., Miami, Florida, USA), b. 1925: m. 1st, 1942 (m. annulled 1944), Sara, da. of R. Miranda; 2ndly, 1949 (m. diss. 1955), Fedora, da. of Ernesto Moya; 3rdly, 1956, Marcelle Goulet, and has issue living, (by 2nd m.) Doris Elizabeth, b. 1950,—(by 3rd m.) Rodney Thomas, b. 1957,—Michael Walter, b. 1964,—Suzanne Carmen, b. 1962.——Douglas Nelson (155 W 7th St., Apt. 46, Hileah, Florida 33010, USA), b. 1933: m. 1954, Margaret, da. of George Isnor, and has issue living, Michael, b. 1955,—Maureen, b. 1956.——Carmen Rosa, b. 1927: m. 1st, 1950, (m. diss. 19—), Luis F. Pineiro; 2ndly, 19—,   Menendes, of 1230, Milan Av., Coral Gables, Florida, USA, and has issue living (by 1st m.), Luis Felipe, b. 1952,—Rose Marie, b. 1959,—Katherine, b. 1968.

Grandson of the late Walter Buckler Lethbridge, 6th son of 3rd baronet:—
Issue (by 1st marriage) of the late Capt. Walter Alexander Charles Lethbridge, b. 1865, d. 1931: m. 1st, 1885, Rosa Maria (from whom he obtained a divorce in U.S.A.), da. of Miguel del Monte, of Havana ; 2ndly, 1902, Blanche (from whom he obtained a divorce in France 1922), da. of John Bingham, a Judge of the High Court, New York ; 3rdly, 1922, Marie José Léona, youngest da. of the late Josef Léon Mondron, of The Chateau des Hamendes, Charleroi, Belgium :—
John George Jules, b. 1888; formerly in US Navy, and Fl. Lt. RAF; 1914-18 War: m. 1917, Dorothy Josephine, da. of Le Roy M. Taylor, of Washington, USA, and has issue living, John George, b. 1917,—Robert Mortimer, b. 1921.

Grandchildren of the late Ambrose Yarburgh Lethbridge, el. son of the late Charles Lethbridge, el. son of the late Rev. Thomas Prowse Lethbridge (infra):—
Issue of the late Thomas Charles Lethbridge, b. 1901, d. 1971: m. 1st, 1924 (m. diss. 1943), Sylvia Frances, who d. 1973, only child of the Rev. Arthur Gordon Robertson (Canon of Salisbury Cathedral), of Rowdens, Netherhampton, Salisbury; 2ndly, 1944, Mina Elizabeth (Gillcott, Higher Broad Oak Rd., West Hill, Ottery St. Mary, Devon), only da. of the Rev. Matthew Graham Leadbitter, of The Rectory, Moretonhampstead, Devon:—
(By 1st m.) Christopher John (South Farmhouse, Upton Lovell, Warminster, Wilts.), b. 1925; ed. at Wellington Coll., and St. John's Coll., Camb.——Belinda Mary, b. 1930.

Granddaughter of the late Rev. Thomas Prowse Lethbridge, 3rd son of 2nd baronet :—
Issue of the late Capt. Edward Lethbridge, b. 1846, d. 1894: m. 1877, Constance, who d. 1930 (having reverted by Roy. licence, 1922, to her patronymic of BROOKE), da. of the late Francis Capper Brooke, of Ufford Place, near Woodbridge:—
Joan (Lady Maconachie): m. 1921, Sir Richard Roy Maconachie, K.B.E., C.I.E., who d. 1962, and has issue living, Martin Osbert (Claremont Lodge, 49, Claremont Rd., Tunbridge Wells), b. 1925: m. 1950, Evelyn Vera, youngest da. of the late Raymond Kateley, and has issue living, Adrian Simon b. 1955, Amanda Joan b. 1958. Residence—Kingston House, Odiham, Hants.

Granddaughter of the late Capt. Edward Lethbridge (ante) :—
Issue of the late Sibyl Lethbridge, d. 1927 : m. 1909, Major Charles Francis Sewell, late King's Roy. Rifle Corps :—
Diana, b. 1913: m. 1944, James Byng Wright. Residence, The Pytle, Coach Hill, Titchfield, Hants.

Sir John Lethbridge, 1st baronet, was the only son of John Lethbridge, of Westaway House, Pilton, and married Dorothea, el. da. and co-heir of William Buckler, of Boreham, Wilts. The 2nd baronet, Sir Thomas Buckler Lethbridge, sat as M.P. for Somersetshire 1806-12 and 1820-30.

LETT, Creation (U.K.) 1941, of Walmer, co. Kent. [Extinct 1964.]

Sir HUGH LETT, *K.C.V.O., C.B.E., D.C.L., Sc.D., M.B., F.R.C.S.*, 1st and last *Baronet.*

Daughters living of 1st Baronet—Margery Buckston, b. 1907: m. 1933, Stanley Redler, who d. 1947, and has issue living, Joyce Helen, b. 1934: m. 1956, Kenneth Gordon Garrod, of The Old Vicarage, Kneeton, Nottingham, and has issue living, Hugh Charles Gordon b. 1960, Diana Jane b. 1958,—Pamela Lorna, b. 1941: m. 1965, William Flack, of Appledore, Mayfield Park, Wadhurst, Sussex, and has issue living, Pamela Gillian b. 1969. Residence, 2, Walford Hse., Silverdale Rd., Eastbourne.——Sheila Buckston, b. 1910: m. 1946, Maj. Gordon Appleford Lett, DSO, and has issue living, Hugh Brian Gordon, b. 1949; Bar. Inner Temple 1972,—Valerie Buckston, b. 1947; LRAM. Residence, Langton, Warwicks Bench, Guildford, Surrey.——Joan Buckston, b. 1918: m. 1941, Hugh William Cochrane Bailie, MB, FRCS (Edin.), late Capt. RAMC, and has issue living, Hugh Richard Molyneux, b. 1950,—Lyndon Lett, b. 1942; MB, BCh, DO: m. 1974, Richard Austen Bloxham, MB, BS, of 32c, Thames Rd., Chiswick, W4,—Fiona Buckston, b. 1944; MB, BCh, FRCS (Edinburgh). Residence, Rock House, Portstewart, co. Derry, N. Ireland.

LEVER, Creation (U.K.) 1911, of Hans Crescent, Chelsea.

Sir (TRESHAM) CHRISTOPHER ARTHUR LINDSAY LEVER, 3rd *Baronet, b.* Jan. 9th, 1932; *s.* his father, *Sir* TRESHAM JOSEPH PHILIP, *FRSL*, 1975; ed. at Eton, and Trin. Coll., Camb. (MA); late 2nd Lt. 17th/21st Lancers; author: *m.* 1970 (m. diss. 1974), Susan Mary, da. of the late John Armytage Nicholson, of Enniscoe, Crossmolina, co. Mayo, and Milestown, Dunboyne, co. Meath; 2ndly, 1975, Linda Weightman McDowell, da. of the late James Jepson Goulden, of Tennessee, USA.

Arms—Quarterly 1st and 4th, tierce in pairle sable, gus and azure, three bear's heads one and two erased, muzzled or; 2nd and 3rd argent, a chevron invected ermines between two keys erect the wards to the dexter in chief sable, and an Esquire's helmet in base proper. Crests—1st, in front of a rising moon proper, a cormorant sable; 2nd, a dexter arm embowed in armour, the hand proper holding a key in bend sinister, the wards upwards sable, and encircled above the elbow with a chaplet of roses argent, leaved vert.

By courage and faith.

Residence—Rye Mead House, Winkfield, Windsor Forest, Berks. *Club*—Buck's.

Widow living of 2nd Baronet—(CLODAGH) PAMELA (*Pamela, Lady Lever*) (Lessudden, St. Boswells, Roxburghshire), only child of the late Lt.-Col. the Hon. Malcolm Bowes-Lyon, CBE [see E. Strathmore, colls.], and formerly wife of the late Lord Malcolm Avondale Douglas-Hamilton, OBE, DFC [D. Hamilton]: *m.* 1962, as his 2nd wife, Sir Tresham Joseph Philip Lever, FRSL, 2nd Bt., who *d.* 1975.

Sir Arthur, 1st baronet, a J.P. for Essex, was a younger brother of Sir Maurice Levy, 1st Bt. (*cr.* 1913), of Great Glen House, co. Leicester, and son of the late Joseph Levy, of Leicester; he was a member of Roy. Commn. on Coast Erosion, and sat as MP for Harwich (L) 1906-10, and Hackney, Central (NL) 1922-23; assumed by deed poll 1896 and by Roy. licence 1911 the additional surname of Lever; Sir Tresham Joseph Philip, 2nd Bt., was author of various historical works including *The Life and Times of Sir Robert Peel, The House of Pitt*, and *The Herberts of Wilton*.

LEVINGE, Creation (I.) 1704, of High Park, Westmeath.

Sir RICHARD VERE HENRY LEVINGE; *M.B.E.*, 11th *Baronet; b.* April 30th, 1911; *s.* his father, *Sir* RICHARD WILLIAM, 1914; ed. at Eton, and at Balliol Coll., Oxford (B.A. 1933); is Major Lovat Scouts (T.A.); European War 1939-43 (M.B.E.), Far East 1944-5 (despatches), M.B.E. (Mil.) 1941: *m.* 1935, Barbara, da. of George Kidston, of Hazelbury Manor, Box, Wilts, and has issue.

Arms—Vert, a chevron or, three escallops argent in chief. Crest—An escallop argent, within a garland proper.

Residences—Grange Hill, Sandy Ford, co. Dublin; Clohamon House, Ferns, co. Wexford.

Sons living—RICHARD GEORGE ROBIN, *b.* Dec. 18th, 1946: *m.* 1969, Hilary Jane, da. of Dr. Derek Mark, of Wingfied, Bray, co. Wicklow.——Michael James, *b.* 1948.

Daughters living—Elizabeth Anne, *b.* 1937: *m.* 1957, Walter Wright Lee.——Susan Maureen, *b.* 1944: *m.* 1965, Douglas P. W. Wright.——Mary Irene, *b.* 1952.

No footsteps backwards.

Widow living of 10th Baronet—MARGUERITE, el. da. of the late H. C. Pix, of Bradford: *m.* 1st, 1910, Sir Richard William Levinge, Lieut. Household Cav., 10th baronet, who *d.* (killed in action) 1914: 2ndly, 1916, Col. Robt. Vere Buxton, who *d.* 1953 [Buxton, Bt., colls.]. *Residence*, Abbey House, Itchen Abbas, Winchester.

Collateral Branches living.

Issue of the late Major Thomas Vere Levinge, 2nd son of 9th baronet, *b.* 1880, *d.* 1949: *m.* 1928, Dorothy (Wardington House, nr, Banbury, Oxon), da. of J. Ingman, of Northampton:—

William James (41, Bridge Rd., Welwyn Gdn. City, Herts.) *b.* 1929: *m.* 1954, Heather Mary Johnson, of Brackley, Northants, and has issue living, Nicholas Vere, *b.* 1955,—Edward James, *b.* 1957.—Sarah Jennifer Louise, *b.* 1961.——Thomas Gerald, *b.* 1934: *m.* 19—, Stella Field, and has issue living, a son, *b.* 1964.

Issue of the late Bernard George Levinge, 5th son of 9th baronet, *b.* 1887, *d.* 1953: *m.* 1912, Stella Parsons:—

Percy Douglas (31, Brown St., Penrith, NSW), *b.* 1919: *m.* 1953, Mary, da. of Thomas E. G. Munday.——Reginald Noel (9, Dent St., Penrith, NSW), *b.* 1927: *m.* 1950, Pearl Kathleen, da. of late Walter Wright Armstrong, and has issue living, Geoffrey Paul, *b.* 1952,—Maureen Ann, *b.* 1956,—Sharon Maree, *b.* 1963.

Issue of the late Major George Edward Levinge, brother of 9th baronet, *b.* 1862, *d.* 1926: *m.* 1895, Elizabeth Louisa, da. of John Wiley, of Brisbane, Queensland:—

George Onslow, *b.* 1896.——William John, *b.* 1903.

Granddaughter of the late Harry Corbyn Levinge, son of 6th baronet :—
Issue of the late Sir Edward Vere Levinge, K.C.I.E., C.S.I., *b.* 1867, *d.* 1954 : *m.* 1900, Alys Adéle, who *d.* 1952, da. of Maj.-Gen. Charles Frederic Thomas :—
Vera Alys, *b.* 1911: *m.* 1938, Count (Michael) Karl Althann, and has issue living, *Count* (Michael) Robert, *b.* 1939,—*Count* (Michael) Alexander, *b.* 1940,—*Count* (Michael) Victor, *b.* 1944: *m.* 1972, Maria de la Natividad del Valle, of Haverford, Pa., USA,—*Countess* Maria Olga, *b.* 1941,—*Countess* Maria Christina *b.* 1942: *m.* 1966, Don José Manuel de Ruiz Gonsalez, of Ronda, Malaga, Spain, and has issue living, José Carlos *b.* 1967, Alejandro Miguel *b.* 1970,—*Countess* Maria Therese Margarethe, *b.* 1949. *Residence*, A3435, Zwentendorf, a.d. Donau, Lower Austria.

Grandchildren of the late Charles William Levinge (infra) :—
Issue of the late Richard William Chaworth Levinge, *b.* 1843, *d.* 1905 : *m.* 1873, Fanny Ellen, who *d.* 1941, da. of the late George David Donkin (formerly Lieut. 7th Roy. Fusiliers), of Wyfold Court, Oxfordshire :—
Frederick Rufane, *b.* 1890; formerly a Tea Planter in Assam and in Assam Valley Light Horse Vol. Cav. Corp.; 1914-18 War with Indian Defence Corps. Res.: *m.* 1929, Rona Elizabeth, who *d.* 1971, da. of the late Richard M. Hawker, of Bungaree, Clare, S. Aust., and has issue living, Frederick Charle Richard (Messamurray, Box 20, Naracoorte, S. Aust. 5271), *b.* 1939: *m.* 1969, Tessa Mary,only da. of R. W. Barton, of Gisborne, NZ, and has issue living, Charles Richard Wynn. *b.* 1973, Georgina Rona *b.* 1971.——Violet Frances, *b.* 1876: *m.* 1914, Charles Victor George Scott, MICE, Indian Ser. of Engineers, who *d.* 1945, and has issue living, Richard Levinge Colhurst (Dyers Mead, Hugglers Hole, Semley, Shaftesbury, Dorset), *b.* 1915; Maj. (ret.) RASC; 1939-45 War (despatches): *m.* 1946, Peggy Amelia Parfitt, and has issue living, Susan Margaret *b.* 1950: *m.* 1974, John Christopher Monnet Webb, of 5, Southwood Mansions, Southwood Lane, Highgate, N6.

Grandchildren of the late Richard William Chaworth Levinge (ante):—
Issue of the late Capt. Richard Hugh Levinge, *b.* 1879, *d.* 1926 : *m.* 1914, Jennie Moncrieth Howitt (21, Ridgeway Rd., Headington, Oxford), only da. of the late George Bell McCreedy of Belfast, and S. Africa:—
Rev. Evelyn Hugh Jenoyr, *RN* (Wellingore Vicarage, Lincoln) *b.* 1915; ed. at King's Coll., London (Asso. honours); Chap. RN 1952-72; HM Hon. Chap. 1971; R. of Navenby, Lincoln: *m.* 1955, Sheila Joy, da. of S. L. R. Etherton, LLB, BSc, of Detroit, USA, and has issue living, Richard St. John, *b.* 1956. *Address*, c/o Min. of Defence (Navy), SW1.——May Frances Jenoyr (21, Ridgeway Rd., Headington, Oxford) *b.* 1918; SRN; Nursing Officer, Churchill Hosp., Oxford.

Grandchildren of the late Surg.-Maj. Edward Levinge, son of the late Charles William Levinge, son of the late Richard Hugh Levinge, 4th son of 4th baronet :—
Issue of the late Edward Vere Bryce Levinge, *b.* 1889, *d.* 1922 : *m.* 1916, Ethel Violet, who *d.* 1924, da. of the late George Cardwell Porter, M.D., of Castleacre, Norfolk [infra] :—
Bryce Leonard, *b.* 1922 ; is a Farmer.——Avice Ethel Mary : *m.* 1st, 1944, Ward Shepard, who *d.* 1953 ; 2ndly, 1953, George Alfred Robinson, and has issue living, (by 1st marriage) Carol Jean, *b.* 1946,—(by 2nd marriage) Bryce Levinge, *b.* 1954,—Guy Herrick, *b.* 1957. *Address*, P.O. Box 275, Falls Church, Virginia, U.S.A.

Grandchildren of the late Marcus Anthony Levinge, son of the late Mark Anthony Levinge, 5th son of 4th baronet :—
Issue of the late Tenison Francis Levinge, *b.* 1848, *d.* 1920 : *m.* 1882, Naomi, who *d.* 1933, da. of the late Hon. George C. Hawker, of Bungaree, S. Australia :—
Ierne Althea: *m.* 1908, Iver Edmund de Breon MacLaverty, formerly Lt. Hampshire Regt., who *d.* 1956, and has issue living, Deirdre, *b.* 1923.

Issue of the late Robert Degennes Levinge, *b.* 1850, *d.* 1940 : *m.* 1889, Hester M., who *d.* 1907, el. da. of the late — Shine, of Cashel :—
Walter Hodson, *b.* 1894 ; European War 1914-18 with Roy. Canadian Vol. Reserve : *m.* 1945, Marion Blanche, da. of the Rev. Francis Cockle, R. of Aasleagh, Leenane, co. Galway, and has issue living, Hester Sylvia, *b.* 1947.—Daphne Elaine Sybil, *b.* 1950,—Marion Alison Patricia, *b.* 1951. *Residence*, Creaghduff, Athlone, co. Meath.——Vera Hester S., *b.* 1904: *m.* 1948, Charles Sutton Hillis, LRCS, LRCP. *Residence*, 8, Leeson Park, Dublin.

The 1st baronet, the Right Hon. Sir Richard Levinge, was Lord Chief Justice of the Common Pleas in Ireland and the 7th baronet, sat as M.P. for co. Westmeath (L) 1857-65. The 10th baronet, Sir Richard William, Lieut. 1st Life Guards, was killed in action during European War, Oct. 1914.

LEVY, Creation (U.K.) 1913, of Humberstone Hall, co. Leicester.

[Name pronounced "**Levvy**."]

Sir EWART JOSEPH MAURICE LEVY, 2nd *Baronet*; *b.* May 10th, 1897 ; *s.* his father, *Sir* MAURICE, 1933; ed. at Harrow; sometime Assist. Sec. (unpaid) to Adm. Sup. at Devonport; (High Sheriff of Leics. 1937-38); 1940-45 War with 21st Army Group as Lt.-Col. Roy. Pioneer Corps (despatches): *m.* 1932, Hylda, who *d.* 1970, el. da. of the late Sir Albert Levy, of Devonshire House, W1, and has issue.

Arms—Argent, a chevron inverted ermines between two keys erect, the wards to the dexter, in chief sable, and an Esquire's helmet in base proper. **Crest**—A dexter arm embowed in armour, the hand holding a key in bend sinister, the wards upwards sable, and encircled above the elbow with a chaplet of roses argent, leaved vert.
Residence—Welland House, Weston-by-Welland, Market Harborough, Leics. *Club*—Reform.

Daughter living—Caroline Anne Patricia, *b.* 1933: *m.* 1st, 1965, George Robert Paterson Coles, from whom she obtained a divorce 1971; 2ndly, 1971, Terence John McInnes Skinner, of John O'Gaunt House, Melton Mowbray, Leics.

Sister living—Doris Pamela (*Lady Havelock-Allan*) *b.* 1891; a SS.StJ; National Vice-Pres, British Legion (Women's Section); Pres. of co. Durham British Legion (Women's Section); Organiser of Women's Vol. Ser., Darlington 1938-44; *m.* 1937, as his third wife, Maj. Sir Henry Spencer Moreton Havelock-Allan, JP, DL, 2nd Bt. *Residence*, Whorlton House, Barnard Castle, co. Durham.——Alix Cordelia (11, Beech Grove House, Beech Grove, Harrogate, Yorks.), *b.* 1894.——Norah Sybil Carlotta, *q.* 1898: *m.* 1st, 1921, John Richard Duckworth-King (afterwards 7th Bt.), who *d.* 1972, and from whom she obtained a divorce 1933: 2ndly, 1945, Capt. Kenneth Frederick Every Woods, late Roy. Inniskilling Dragoon Guards. *Residence*, The Manor House, Morestead, Winchester.

By courage and faith.

The 1st baronet, Sir Maurice Levy, sat as M.P. for Mid, or Loughborough, Div. of Leicester-shire (*L*) 1900-18, and was a J.P. and D.L. for Leicestershire (High Sheriff 1926), and knighted 1907.

LEWIS, Creation (U.K.) 1902, of Portland Place, Marylebone, co. London, and The Danish Pavilion, Overstrand, Norfolk. [Extinct 1945.]

Lieut.-Com. Sir GEORGE JAMES ERNEST LEWIS, *O.B.E.*, *R.N.V.R.*, 3rd and last *Baronet ; d.* (killed on active ser. during European War) 1945.

Daughter living of 2nd Baronet—Elizabeth Bertha, *b.* 1897 : *m.* 1928, George Wansbrough from whom she obtained a divorce 1938, and has issue living, Joseph, *b.* 1934,—Miriam Beatriz, *b.* 1932. *Residence,* Broughton Poggs, Lechlade, Gloucestershire.

ORR-LEWIS, Creation (U.K.) 1920, of Whitewebbs Park, Enfield, co. Middlesex.

Faithful to fatherland.

Sir (JOHN) DUNCAN ORR-LEWIS, 2nd *Baronet ; b.* Feb. 21st, 1898 ; *s.* his father, *Sir* FREDERICK, 1921 ; ed. at Eton, and at Camb. Univ. ; is Major R.A.S.C. ; European War 1939-45, in Persia, Middle East, and N.-W. Europe : *m.* 1st, 1921, Marjory, who *d.* 1926, da. of the late James Milne, of 3, Buckingham Gate, S.W. ; 2ndly, 1929, Doris Blanche (who *d.* 1960, having obtained a divorce 1936)—formerly Lady (Walter) Gibbons—da. of Charles Lee, J.P., of Cavendish Court, W. ; 3rdly, 1940, Mrs. Phyllis Ann Maitland Allan (from whom he obtained a divorce 1949), da. of the late W. J. Bibby, of Chester ; 4thly, 1950, Anna, da. of the late P. Filipoff, of Rostov, Russia, and has issue by 1st marriage.

Arms—Quarterly, 1st and 4th, per chevron argent and sable, in chief three spear-heads gules and in base a lion rampant of the first, *Lewis* ; 2nd and 3rd, ermine, three piles gules issuant from a chief or, thereon an annulet of the second between two maple leaves vert, *Orr.* **Crests**—1st, a lion sejant supporting with the dexter foreleg a banner sable, charged with a lion rampant argent, *Lewis* ; 2nd, out of the battlements of a tower argent a dexter cubit arm proper, holding in the hand a cross-crosslet or, *Orr.* *Residences*—8, Rue Du Bois, Beaudoir, Cely-en-Biere 77, France ; 1R 22 Ett, Maghtab, Malta, GC. *Clubs,*—White's Travellers' (Paris), Mount Royal (Montreal).

Daughter living—By 1st marriage—Marie Ardyn, *b.* 1922 : *m.* 1942, A. Macpherson, and has issue living, Alastair Duncan, *b.* 1960,—Marjorie Gay, *b.* 1945. *Residence,*

The 1st baronet, Sir Frederick (son of the late William Thomas Lewis, of Swansea, co. Glamorgan, and Montreal, Canada), assumed the additional surname of Orr, and was Pres. of Lewis Brothers (Limited), of Montreal, and Founder and Pres. of Canadian Vickers (Limited).

LEWTHWAITE, Creation (U.K.) 1927, of Broadgate, Parish of Thwaites, co. Cumberland.

Virtue reaching towards heaven.

Sir WILLIAM ANTHONY LEWTHWAITE, 3rd *Baronet ; b.* Feb. 26th, 1912 ; *s.* his father, *Sir* WILLIAM, 1933 ; ed. at Rugby, and at Trin, Coll., Camb. (BA 1933) ; Solicitor 1937 ; formerly a partner in the firm of Southall & Co. ; a Member of Council of Country Landowners' Assocn. 1949-64 ; 1939-45 War in R. Signals, and as Lt. Gren. Gds. : *m.* 1936, Lois Mairi, only child of the late Capt. Struan Robertson Kerr-Clark [E. Drogheda], and has issue.

Arms—Ermine, a cross flory azure, fretty or **Crest**—A garb or, bound by a serpent nowed proper, holding in the mouth a cross-crosslet fitchée gules.

Residence—73, Dovehouse St., SW3 6JZ.

Daughter living—Catherine Jane, *b.* 1954.

Brother living—RAINALD GILFRID, *CVO, OBE, MC,* *b.* July 21st, 1913 ; ed. at Rugby and at Trin. Coll., Camb. (BA) ; Brig. late Scots Gds. ; Mil. Attaché 1964, and Defence Attaché at British Embassy, Paris, 1965-68 ; 1939-45 War in Middle East (MC) ; France, Belgium, Holland, Germany, and Italy ; OBE (Civil) 1974, CVO 1975 : *m.* 1936, Margaret Elizabeth, *MBE,* da. of Harry Edmonds, of New York, USA, and has issue living, David Rainald (49, Ranelagh Grove, W1W 3PB), *b.* 1940 : *m.* 1969, Diana Helena, twin da. of William Robert Tomkinson, TD [see Blane, Bt. (ext.)], and has issue living, Emma Victoria *b.* 1917, Mary-Claire *b.* 1972,—John Valentine (46, Lansdowne Rd., W11 2LR), *b.* 1944 : *m.* 1967, Elizabeth Georginaa, da. of Richard John Bramble Mildmay-White [see By. Mildmay of Flete], and has issue living, Alice Georgiana, *b.* 1969, Martha Grace, *b.* 1970,—Margaret Sylvia, *b.* 1937. *Residences,* 14, Edwardes Sq., W8 6HE ; Broadgate, Millom, LA1B 5JZ, Cumbria.

Sir William Lewthwaite, 1st baronet (Vice-Lieut. of Cumberland 921-2 and 1923-4, and Dep-Chm. of Quarter Sessions) was Chm. Conservative Asso. of Egremont Div. of Cumberland 1904-24 many years Treasurer).

LEY, Creation (U.K.) 1905, of Epperstone Manor, Epperstone, co. Nottingham.

[Name pronounced "Lee."]

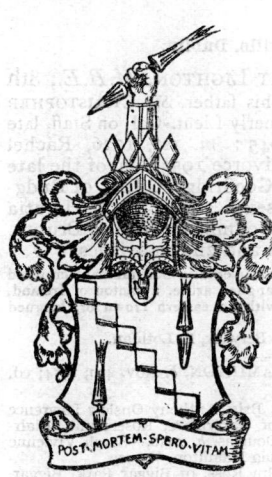

I hope for life after death.

Sir GERALD GORDON LEY, *T.D.*, 3rd *Baronet*, *b.* Nov. 5th, 1902; *s.* his father, *Sir* HENRY GORDON, 1944; ed. at Eton, and at New Coll., Oxford; is Capt. 1st Derbyshire Yeo. Roy. Armoured Corps (T.A.); High Sheriff of Cumberland 1937: *m.* 1st, 1936 (m. diss. 1957), Mrs. Rosemary Catherine Cotter, da. of the late Capt. Duncan Macpherson, RN; 2ndly, 1958 (m. diss. 1968), Grace Foster, and has issue by 1st m.

Arms—Argent, six lozenges conjoined in bend between two broken tilting spears gules. Crest—In front of a cubit arm in armour a hand grasping a broken tilting spear, four lozenges conjoined fesseways gules.
Residence—Lazonby Hall, near Penrith, Cumberland.

Daughters living—By 1st marriage—Elizabeth Bridget Rhoda, *b.* 1937: *m.* 1965, Roger Humphrey Boissier, of Easton House, The Pastures, Repton, Derby DE6 6GG, and has issue living, Rupert John *b.* 1967,—Clare Louise, *b.* 1968.——Annabel Alison, *b.* 1939: *m.* 1960, David Eric Cramer Stapleton, of Rivenhall Place, Witham, Essex, and has issue living, Serena Jane Clare, *b.* 1961,—Charlotte Jessica Louise, *b.* 1963,—Victoria Lucy Annabel, *b.* 1967, —Lara Alexandra Mary-Rose, *b.* 1974.——Caroline Sheila (Barbary House, S. Cheriton, Templecombe, Somerset), *b.* 1943.

Brother living—FRANCIS DOUGLAS, *M.B.E.*, *T.D.*, *b.* April 5th, 1907: ed. at Eton, and at Magdalene Coll. Camb.; is Major Derbyshire Yeo. Roy. Armoured Corps (T.A. Reserve), and a J.P. and D.L.; High Sheriff of Derbyshire 1956; M.B.E. (Civil) 1961: *m.* 1931, Violet Geraldine, da. of the late Maj. James Gerald Thewlis Johnson, D.S.O. [Alleyne, Bt.], and has issue living, Ian Francis (of Fauld Hall, Tutbury, Staffs.), *b.* 1934: *m.* 1957, Caroline Margaret da. of Major George H. Errington, M.C., of Monkton Farm, Fig Tree, Rhodesia, and has issue living, Christopher Ian *b.* 1962, Virginia Mary *b.* 1960,—Susan Alison, *b.* 1937: *m.* 1960, Charles Edward Weatherby, of Mixbury Lodge Farm, nr. Brackley, Northants., and has issue living, Camilla Jane *b.* 1963, Fiona Mary *b.* 1965. *Residence*, Shirley House, Brailsford, Derbyshire.
Sister living—Mary Rhonda (Nesley Down, Westonbirt, Tetbury, Glos.), *b.* 1906: *m.* 1944, Maj. Geoffrey Charles Bishop, 9th Lancers, who *d.* 1970.
Widow living of 2nd Baronet—DOROTHEA GERTRUDE (*Dorothea, Lady Ley*) (Amberley Cottage, Amberley, Sussex), da. of the late Charles Gray, of Anerley, SE, and formerly wife of 2nd Baron Borwick: *m.* 1939, as his 3rd wife, Sir Henry Gordon Ley, 2nd baronet, who *d.* 1944.

Sir Francis Ley, 1st baronet, Gov., Director, and Founder of Ley's Works in Derby, was High Sheriff of Notts 1905.

NAYLOR-LEYLAND, Creation (U.K.) 1895, of Hyde Park House, Albert Gate, co. London.

Faithful and bold.

Sir VIVYAN EDWARD NAYLOR-LEYLAND, 3rd *Baronet*; *b.* March 5th, 1924; *s.* his father, *Sir* ALBERT EDWARD HERBERT, 1952; ed. at Eton, and at Oxford Univ.; formerly Lieut. Gren. Gds.: *m.* 1st, 1952 (m. diss. 1960), the Hon. Elizabeth Anne Marie Gabrielle Fitzalan-Howard, da. of 2nd Viscount Fitz Alan of Derwent; 2ndly, 1967, Noreen Starr Anker, da. of the late Wing.-Cdr. Peter Anker Simmons, DFC, RAF [see Bailey, Bt.], and has issue by 1st and 2nd m.

Arms—Quarterly, 1st and 4th, ermine, on a fesse engrailed sable, between nine ears of barley, three, three, and three vert, banded or in chief, and three like ears in base, a lion passant of the last between two escallops argent and for distinction a canton gules, *Leyland*; 2nd and 3rd, per pale or and argent, a pale sable fretty of the first between two lions rampant of the third, and for distinction a canton gules, *Naylor*. Crests—1st, A mount vert, thereon an escallop argent, surmounted by a demi-eagle erminois, wings endorsed azure, bezantée, in the mouth three ears of barley vert, and charged for distinction with a cross-crosslet gules, *Leyland*; 2nd, a lion passant sable, charged on the body with two saltires or, resting the dexter forepaw upon a shield, charged with the arms of Naylor, and charged further for distinction with a cross-crosslet also or, *Naylor*.
Residence—6, Harbour Mews, Nassau, Bahamas.

Son living—By 1st m.—PHILIP VYVYAN, *b.* Aug. 9th, 1953; ed. at Eton; 2nd Lt. I.G.
Daughter living—By 2nd marriage—Cleonie Mary Veronica, *b.* 1968.
Brothers living—Michael Montagu George, *MC*, *b.* 1926; formerly Capt. The Life Guards: *m.* 1953, Jacqueline Marie Françoise, yst. da. of Maj. Ides Floor, DSO, MBE, of Lullenden, East Grinstead, Sussex, and has issue living, David George Edward, *b.* 1955,—Joanna Rosemary Jane, *b.* 1961. *Residence*, Church Farm, Coates, Cirencester.——Alick David Yorke, *MVO* (135 E. 54th St., New York City, USA). *Clubs*, White's, The Brook (New York), *b.* 1929; formerly Lt. Gren. Gds.; MVO (4th class) 1952: *m.* 1st, 1953 (m. diss. 1962), Diana Elizabeth Lea, da. of Roy Galway, of St. Ronans, Winkfield Row, Ascot, Berks.; 2ndly, 1962 (m. diss. 1969), Dita Douglas (AMORY), da. of Gordon Douglas, Jr., of Price's Neck, Newport, Rhode Island, USA; 3rdly, 1973, Carolyn Neilson, and has issue living, (by 1st m.) Michael Alexander Robert, *b.* 1956, Amanda Jane *b.* 1954, (by 2nd m.) Nicholas Edward *b.* 1962, (by 3rd m.) a son *b.* 1975.
1ster living—Veronica Rosemary, *b.* 1932: *m.* 1955, Peter Cyril Alexander Munster, of Allemogne, Thoiry, Ain 01170, France [see E. Dudley, colls.].

The 1st baronet, Sir Herbert Scarisbrick, was M.P. for Colchester (C) 1892-95, and for Lancashire (S.-W.), Southport Div. (L) 1898-9. The 2nd baronet, Sir Albert Edward Herbert, was Sheriff of Denbighshire 1921, and was sometime an Hon. Attaché, British Legation, Berne, and British Embassy, Paris.

LIGHTON, Creation (I.) 1791, of Merville, Dublin.

Sir CHRISTOPHER ROBERT LIGHTON, *M.B.E.*, 8th *Baronet*; *b.* June 30th, 1897; *s.* his father, *Sir* CHRISTOPHER ROBERT, 1929; ed. at Eton; formerly Lieut.-Col. on Staff, late 60th Rifles; M.B.E. (Mil.) 1945: *m.* 1st, 1926, Rachel Gwendoline (who obtained a divorce 1953), da. of the late Rear-Adm. Walter Somerville Goodridge, C.I.E., of Rudgwick Grange, Rudgwick, Sussex; 2ndly, 1953, Horatia Edith, da. of A. T. Powlett, of Godminster Manor, Bruton, Somerset, and has issue by 1st and 2nd marriages.

Arms—Barry of eight argent and vert, over all a lion rampant crowned with an eastern crown or, armed and langued azure, a canton of Ireland. Crest—A lion's head erased crowned with an eastern crown or, langued azure.

Fortitudine et prudentia.   *Residence*—Elphinstone House, N. Berwick, E. Lothian.
*By fortitude and
prudence.*   Son living—By 2nd m.—THOMAS HAMILTON, *b.* Nov. 4th, 1954; ed. at Eton.

Daughters living—By 1st m.—Bridget Mary, *b.* 1927: *m.* 1949, Brig. Anthony Onslow Lawrence Lithgow, MC, late Black Watch (RHR) [E. Onslow, colls.], of Garrymore, Rosemount, Blairgowrie, Perthshire, and has issue living, Nigel Christopher Douglas, *b.* 1950,—Sarah Vivienne Hamilton, *b.* 1952,—Claire Graina Bridget, *b.* 1953.——Virginia Hamilton, *b.* 1929.
Sisters living—Winifred Helen, *b.* 1891: *m.* 1922, Horatio John Ross, of Biggar Park, Biggar, Lanarks., and has issue living, Marjorie Hamilton (*Hon.* Mrs. *Francis M. Hepburne-Scott*), *b.* 1925: *m.* 1946, Maj. the Hon. Francis Michael Hepburne-Scott, MC, late Lothians and Border Horse [see L. Polwarth].——Florence Hamilton, *b.* 1894: *m.* 1923, Maj. Alexander Caldwells Stewart, MC, 6th Bn. The Cameronians (TA), who *d.* 1927, and has issue living, Robert Christie (of Arndean, Dollar, Scotland), *b.* 1926; formerly Lt. Scots Gds.: *m.* 1953, Ann Grizel, da. of Air Ch. Marshal the Hon. Sir Ralph Alexander Cochrane, GBE, KCB, AFC [see B. Cochrane of Cults].—Grizel Margaret Lighton, *b.* 1925: *m.* 1951, Michael Shaw-Stewart [see Shaw-Stewart, Bt., colls.]. *Residence*, Birkhill, Muckhart, Dollar, Clackmannanshire.

Sir Thomas Lighton, 1st Bt., son of John Lighton of Raspberry Hill, co. Derry, was a Dublin banker, High Sheriff of co. Dublin 1790 and co. Tyrone 1801, and MP for Tuam 1790-97, and Carlingford 1798-1800. At the time of his death his firm was known as Lighton, Needham & Shaw. The last named partner, Robert Shaw, was also created a baronet.

LINDSAY, Creation (U.K.) 1962, of Dowhill, co. Kinross.

Sir MARTIN ALEXANDER LINDSAY OF DOWHILL, *C.B.E.*, *D.S.O.*, 1st *Baronet*, son of the late Lt.-Col. A. B. Lindsay; *b.* Aug. 22nd, 1905; ed. at Wellington Coll.; a Member of Queen's Body Guard for Scotland (Roy. Co. of Archers), 1939-45 War in Norway and as Lt.-Col., N.-W. Europe (despatches twice, D.S.O wounded); M.P. for Solihull Div. of Warwickshire (C) 1945-64; D.S.O. 1945, C.B.E. (Civil) 1952: *m.* 1st, 1932 (m. diss. 1967), Joyce Emily, da. of the late Major the Hon. Robert Hamilton Lindsay [see E. Crawford, colls.]; 2ndly, 1969, the Hon. Loelia Mary, da. of 1st Baron Sysonby, and formerly wife of 2nd Duke of Westminster and has issue (by 1st m.).

Arms—Gules, a fess chequy argent and azure, between a mullet of the second in chief and the base barry undy or and of the third; in a dexter canton argent a sinister hand couped apaume erect of the first. Crest—A castle triple-towered proper, port gules, tower-caps argent. Supporters—Two doves proper, gorged of collars chequy argent and azure.
Residence—The Old Vicarage, Send, Woking.

Sons living—By 1st m.—RONALD ALEXANDER (21, Campden Hill Sq., W8), *b.* Dec. 6th, 1933; a Member of Queen's Body Guard for Scotland (R. Co. of Archers): *m.* 1968, Nicoletta, yr. da. of Capt. Edgar Storich, Italian Navy (ret.), and has issue living, James Martin Evelyn, *b.* 1968. —Hugo Edgar, *b.* 1970,—Robin Ronald Edward *b.* 1972,—Lucia Linda, *b.* 1974.——Oliver John Martin (Brookwood House, Brookwood, Surrey), *b.* 1938; Maj. Gren. Gds.; Member of Queen's Body Guard for Scotland (R. Co. of Archers): *m.* 1964, Lady Clare Rohais Antonia Elizabeth Giffard, yr. da. of the 3rd Earl of Halsbury, and has issue living, Mark Oliver Giffard, *b.* 1968,—Victoria Louise Elizabeth Clare, *b.* 1964,—Fiona Emily Margaret, *b.* 1972.
Daughter living—By 1st m.—Jacynth Rosemary (*Lady Mark Fitzalan Howard*), *b.* 1934: *m.* 1961, Lord Mark Fitzalan Howard [see D. Norfolk]. *Residence*, 13, Campden Hill Sq., W8.

Sir Martin Alexander Lindsay, 1st Bt., of Dowhill, Kinross-shire, is 22nd in descent from Sir William Lindsay, 1st of Dowhill (*b.* 1350), uncle of 1st Earl of Crawford. The estate was sold by James 12th of Dowhill and his son Martin, 13th, in the 18th century. The coat of arms of Adam Lindsay, 5th of Dowhill (*d.* 1544) is set forth in a book by Sir David Lindsay, Lyon King of Arms.

Lindsay-Hogg, see Hogg.

Lister-Kaye, see Kaye.

Liston Foulis, see Foulis.

LITHGOW, Creation (U.K.) 1925, of Ormsary, co. Argyll.

By sea and land.

Sir WILLIAM JAMES LITHGOW, 2nd *Baronet, b.* May 10th, 1934; *s.* his father *Sir* JAMES LITHGOW, *G.B.E., C.B., M.C., T.D.,* 1952; ed. at Winchester; MRINA; FBIM; a DL of Renfrewshire; a Member of Queen's Bodyguard for Scotland (Roy. Co. of Archers), of Nat. Ports Council, of Exec. Cttee. Scottish Council of Development and Industry, of Scottish Regional Council CBI; Chm. of Lithgows (Holdings), Ltd., of Port Glasgow, of Western Ferries, Ltd., of Campbeltown Shipyard, Ltd., and of Scott Lithgow Drydocks, Ltd., Vice-Chm. of Scott Lithgow, Ltd., and a Dir. of Bank of Scotland, of Hunterston Development Co., Ltd., of Gailic Oil Ltd., and other associated Cos.: *m.* 1st, 1964, Valerie Helen, who *d.* 1964, da. of the late Denis Herbert Scott, CBE, of Farley Grange, Westerham, Kent; 2ndly, 1967, Mary Claire, da. of Col. Frank Moutray Hill, CBE, of East Knoyle, Salisbury, Wilts., and has issue by 2nd m.

Arms—Per chevron sable and argent three estoiles in chief of the second, and in base in a seaundy azure and of the second a galley, sails furled of the first, flagged gules. Crest—An otter on a rock proper.

Seat—Ormsary, by Lochgilphead, Argyllshire. *Residence*—Drums, Langbank, Renfrewshire.

Sons living—By 2nd m.—JAMES FRANK, *b.* June 13th, 1970.——John Alexander, *b.* 1974.
Daughter living—By 2nd m.—Katrina Margaret, *b.* 1968.
Sisters living—Margaret Helen, *b.* 1928: *m.* 1951, Geoffrey Robert Rickman, and has issue living, Stephen Lithgow, *b.* 1952,—Robert James, *b.* 1957,—Andrew George, *b.* 1960,—Catherine Margaret, *b.* 1953. *Residence,* Brookham Lodge, Stoke d'Abernon, Cobham, Surrey.——Ann Barlow *b.* 1931: *m.* 1952, William Simon Wilson, and has issue living, Mark Lithgow, *b.* 1960,—Sarah Rosalind, *b.* 1953,—Judith Clare, *b.* 1957.

The 1st baronet, Sir James Lithgow, G.B.E., C.B., M.C., T.D., D.L., J.P., LL.D. (son of the late W. T. Lithgow, of Drums, Renfrewshire), was a Shipbuilder of Port Glasgow, a Member of Board of Admiralty 1940-46, Vice-Lieut. for Renfrewshire, Hon. Col. T.A., and first Freeman of Burgh of Port Glasgow.

LLEWELLYN, Creation (U.K.) 1922, of Bwllfa, Aberdare, co. Glamorgan.

Character is destiny.

Sir RHYS LLEWELLYN, 2nd *Baronet ; b.* March 9th, 1910; *s.* his father, *Sir* DAVID RICHARD, *LL.D.,* 1940; ed. at Oundle, and at Trin. Coll., Camb. (BA 1931, MA 1935); Lt.-Col. Welsh Guards; Sup. Reserve of Officers 1939; 1939-45 War in N-W Europe (despatches); RARO 1945-61; a CStJ; High Sheriff of Glamorgan 1950-51.

Arms—Per chevron or and gules, in chief a lion passant and in base three chevronels all counterchanged. Crest—A demi-dragon holding in the mouth a dexter hand couped proper.

Residence—8c, Bedford Towers, Brighton, BN1 2JG.

Brothers living—HENRY MORTON, *CBE, b.* July 18th, 1911; ed. at Oundle, and at Trin. Coll., Camb. (MA); High Sheriff of Mon. 1966-67; Pres. of Whitbread Wales, Ltd., Davenco (Engineers) Ltd., Chm. of Whitbread International, Ltd., and Sports Council for Wales; Vice-Chm. of Civic Trust for Wales, Member of Wales Tourist Board and a DL of Mon.; a Member of Nat. Hunt Cette since 1946, and Jockey Club since 1969; Pres. of British Show Jumping Assocn. 1975-76; joined Warwicks. Yeo. 1939 and Staff of 21st Army Group 1944; became Lt.-Col. 1944; 1939-45 War in Iraq, Syria, N. Africa, Sicily, Italy, and NW Europe (despatches twice, OBE, American Legion of Merit); has Roy. Humane Soc.'s Medal: show jumping Olympic Gold Medallist, Helsinki 1952; OBE (Mil) 1945, CBE (Civil) 1953: *m.* 1944, the Hon. Christine Saumarez, da. of 5th Baron de Saumarez, and has issue living, David St. Vincent, *b.* 1946,—Roderic Victor, *b.* 1947,—Anna Christina, *b.* 1956. *Residence,* Llanvair Grange, nr. Abergavenny, Monmouthshire. *Clubs,* Cavalry, Cardiff and County.——*Sir* David Treharne, *b.* 1916; ed. at Eton, and at Trin. Coll., Camb. (BA); Capt. late Welsh Guards; a Journalist; author of 'Nye The Beloved Patrician', and 'The Adventures of Arthur Artfully'; a Member of Broadcasting Council for Wales (BBC) 1960-61, and of Welsh Advisory Cttee. for Civil Aviation 1961-62, and Parl. Under Sec. of State for Home Affairs 1951-52; N.-W. Europe

1944-45; MP for N. Div. of Cardiff (C) 1950-59; Knt. 1960: *m.* 1950, Joan Anne, *OBE*, da. of Robert Henry Williams, of Bonvilston House, nr. Cardiff, and has issue living, Robert Crofts Williams, *b.* 1952: *m.* 1975, Susan Constance, el. da. of Hubert Miller-Stirling,—David Rhidian, *b.* 1957,—Emma Victoria, *b.* 1951: *m.* 1974, Bruce H. Dinwiddy, of 1, North Gate, NW8. *Residence,* The Old Rectory, Yattendon, Berks.——William Herbert Rhydian, *MC, b.* 1919; ed. at Eton; Maj. late Welsh Gds.; DL of Cardiganshire, High Sheriff 1967-68; Member Cardiganshire Co. Council 1961-70, Member of Cardiganshire Agric. Exec. Cttee., and Traffic Commr., S. Wales; and a Member of Court of Govs., Nat. Library of Wales 1967-68, and Univ. of Wales 1968-70; 1939-45 War in France, N. Africa, Italy and Greece (despatches, MC): *m.* 1943, Lady Honor Morvyth Malet Vaughan, da. of 7th Earl of Lisburne, and has issue iving, Trefor Wilmot, *b.* 1947: *m.* 1973, Heather Mary, da. of Richard Lucas, of The Lydiate, Heswall,—Cordelia, *b.* 1949: *m.* 1969, Angus Lamont, of The Crown Inn, Chiddingfold, Surrey,—Gaynor Malet, *b.* 1952. *Residence,* Brynreithin, Ffair Rhos, Ystrad Meurig, Cardiganshire. *Clubs,* Cavalry and Guards'; St. David's (Aberystwyth).

Sisters living—Margaret Elaine (*Lady Anderson*), *b.* 1913: *m.* 1935, Sir Donald Forsyth Anderson, who *d.* 1973, son of the late Sir Alan Garrett Anderson, GBE, and has issue living, Gillian Elizabeth, *b.* 1936: *m.* 1966, William Peter Grant Davis, of Johnniefields, Marulan, NSW.—Je nnifer Forsyth, *b.* 1937: *m.* 1965, Anthony David Loehnis, of 8, St. Peters Sq., W6 [see E. Harrowby, colls.],—Lindsay Garrett, *b.* 1942: *m.* 1962, Robert Trench Fox, of Cheriton House, nr. Winchester,—Susan Elaine (*Hon. Mrs. Adam I. S. Bligh*), *b.* 1945: *m.* 1965, the Hon. Adam Ivo Stuart Bligh, of Hambledon House, nr. Portsmouth [*see* E. Darnley]. *Residence,* 9, Hamilton House, Vicarage Gate, W8 4AG.——Elizabeth Aileen Maud, *b.* 1914; formerly Wing Officer WAAF; 1939-45 War: *m.* 1946, Lt.-Col. David Mathew Caradoc Prichard, Roy. Welch Fusiliers, and has issue living, Robert David Caradoc, *b.* 1947,—Colin Hubert Llewellyn, *b.* 1949,—William de Burgh, *b.* 1953. *Residence,* Gobion Manor, nr. Abergavenny, Monmouth.——Magdalene Clare, *b.* 1922: *m.* 1948, Alexander Wyndham Hume Stewart-Moore, of 1, Stavordale Lodge, Melbury Rd., W14, and Seaport Lodge, Portballintrae, co. Antrim, and has issue living, Christopher Wyndham Hume, *b.* 1949,—Michael David, *b.* 1950,—James Anthony, *b.* 1953,—Gillian Clare, *b.* 1956.

The 1st baronet, Sir David Richard Llewellyn (son of the late Rees Llewellyn, J.P., of Bwllfa House, near Aberdare), was Chm. of Welsh Associated Collieries, Ltd. Lysaght Iron & Steel, Ltd., and other Cos., and Pres. of Cardiff Univ. Coll.

LLEWELLYN, Creation (U.K.) 1959, of Baglan, co. Glamorgan.

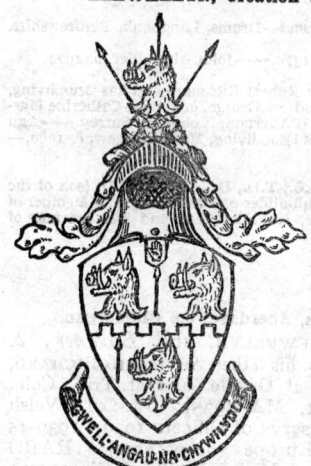

Gwell angau na chywilydd.

Sir (ROBERT) GODFREY LLEWELLYN, *C.B., C.B.E., M.C., T.D.,* 1st *Baronet,* son of the late Robert William Llewellyn, D.L., J.P., of Cwrt Colman, Bridgend, and Baglan Hall, Briton Ferry; *b.* May 13th, 1893; ed. at R.N. Colls., Osborne and Dartmouth; in R.N. 1906-14; served with Montgomeryshire Yeo. Cav. 1915-19; attached 25th Roy. Welch Fusiliers 1917; commanded 6th Mounted Brig. Signal Troop 1917, 4th Cav. Div. Signal Squadron 1918, and 53rd Div. Signals, T.A. 1920-29; Dep. Ch. Signal Officer, W. Command 1929-37; Hon. Col. 53rd Div. Signals 1929-33; became Brevet Lieut.-Col. 1924, Lieut.-Col. 1925, and Brevet Col. 1928; 1914-18 War in Egypt, Palestine, and Syria (despatches twice, M.C., two medals); Col. in charge of Administration, Home Guard, S. Wales 1940-44; Hon. Col. 38th Div. Signals 1941-47; Comdt. Glamorgan Army Cadet Force 1943-49; Hon. Col. 16th (Welch) Parachute Batn. (TA) 1952-55; is a Dir. of Cos., a Gov. of Univ. Coll. of S. Wales and Monmouthshire, a JP and DL for Glamorgan, DL for Monmouthshire, and a K.St.J.; Chm. of Neath Conservative Assocn. 1921-38, and of Welsh Hosp. Board 1959-65; Treasurer of Wales and Monmouth Conservative Assocn. 1947-48, Chm. 1949-56 and Pres. 1958, 1962, 1966, 1967, 1968 and 1969; High Sheriff of Glamorgan 1947, and of Monmouthshire 1963; Vice-Chm. of National Union of Conservative and Unionist Assocns. 1952 and 1953, Chm. 1954 and Pres. 1962; Chm. of Glamorgan TA and Air Force Assocn. 1953-58; Chm. of Organizing Cttee. for VIth British Empire and Commonwealth Games 1958; OBE (Mil) 1927, CBE (Mil) 1942, CB (Mil) 1950, Knt. 1953: *m.* 1920, Frances Doris, who *d.* 1969, da. of Rowland S. A. Kennard, JP, of Little Harrow, Christchurch, Hants, and has issue.

Arms—Per fesse embattled azure and or a javelin erect between two boars' heads erased in chief, and a like boar's head erased between two javelins in base all counter charged. Crest—Upon a rock proper a boar's head erased or in front of three javelins, one in pale and two in saltire, also proper.

Residence,—Tredilion Park, near Abergavenny. *Clubs*—Carlton, Pratt's, United Service, Royal Thames Yacht, Royal Automobile, and Cardiff and County.

Son living—MICHAEL ROWLAND GODFREY, *b.* June 15th, 1921; ed. at Harrow; is Capt. Grenadier Guards (Reserve); Italy 1943-4: *m.* 1st, 1946, Bronwen Mary (who obtained a divorce 1951), da. of Sir (Owen) Watkin Williams-Wynn, 8th Bt.; 2ndly, 1956, Janet Prudence: youngest da. of Lieut.-Col. Charles Thomas Edmondes, D.L., J.P., of Ewenny Priory, Bridgend, Glamorgan, and has issue living, (by 2nd marriage) Sarah Janet, *b.* 1958,—Carolyn Frances, *b.* 1959,—Lucy Mary, *b.* 1963. *Residence,* Glebe House, Penmaen, nr. Swansea, Glamorgan.

Daughter living—Wenllian Kennard, *b.* 1923: *m.* 1949, Maj. Wyndham Jermyn Hacket Pain, late Gren. Gds., of Parkstone House, Ashwood Rd., Woking, Surrey, and has issue living, Nicholas Wyndham Llewellyn, *b.* 1953; ed. at Harrow, and RMA; 2nd Lt. Gren. Gds. (despatches, Ulster 1974),—Simon Michell, *b.* 1956; ed. at Harrow.

DILLWYN-VENABLES-LLEWELYN, Creation (U.K.) 1890, of Penllergaer, Llangyfelach and Ynis-y-gerwn, Cadoxton juxta Neath, Glamorganshire.
[Pronounced "Dilwin-Venables-Hlooellin."]

Sir (CHARLES) MICHAEL DILL-WYN-VENABLES-LLEWELYN, *M.V.O.*, 3rd *Baronet* ; *b.* Feb. 23rd, 1900 ; *s.* his father, *Col. Sir* CHARLES LEYSHON, *C.B.*, 1951 ; ed. at Eton; Brig. Gren. Gds., and a JP for Radnorshire; Lord-Lt. of Radnorshire 1949-74, since when a Lieut. of Powys; MVO (4th Class) 1937 : *m.* 1934, Lady Delia Mary Hicks-Beach, da. of the late Capt. Michael Hugh Hicks-Beach, MP, Viscount Quenington [*see* E. St. Aldwyn], and has issue.

𝕬rms—Quarterly: 1st and 4th, argent, gutée de poix, three chevronels gules, in base a lamb passant proper, *Llewelyn* ; 2nd, azure, two bars each cotised between five mullets, three in chief and two in base all argent, and for difference a cross-crosslet or, *Venables* ; 3rd, gules, on a chevron nebulée argent, five trefoils slipped of the first, *Dillwyn* ; on an escutcheon of pretence the Arms of *Venables* without distinctions. 𝕮rests—1st, on the trunk of a tree fessewise eradicated and sprouting to the dexter, a lamb passant proper, bearing a banner gules charged with three chevronels argent, *Llewelyn* ; 2nd, a wyvern wings expanded gules, each wing charged with a fesse argent, issuant from a weir basket proper, the dexter claw resting on a mullet azure, charged for difference as in the arms, *Venables* ; 3rd, in front of a stag's head couped proper three trefoils slipped vert, *Dillwyn.*

Dread shame.

Residence—Llysdinam, Newbridge-on-Wye, Radnorshire.

Son living—JOHN MICHAEL, *b.* Aug. 12th, 1938; ed. at Eton, and at Magdalene Coll., Camb.: *m.* 1963 (m. diss. 1972), Nina, da. of the late Lt. J. S. Hallam, KRRC, and has issue living, Georgina Katherine, *b.* 1964,—Emma Susan, *b.* 1967.

Daughter living—Mary Julia, *b.* 1936: *m.* 1971, Michael B. Elster, of 26, Lady Margaret Rd., NW5, and has issue living, Jake, *b.* 1972,—Caitlin, *b.* 1974.

Sister living—Agnes Barbara, *CVO*, *b.* 1894; MVO (4th class) 1960; CVO 1967; Lady-in-Waiting to HRH the Duchess of Gloucester 1951-69, since when an Extra Lady-in-Waiting: *m.* 1925, Vice-Adm. Cedric Swinton Holland, CB, who *d.* 1950, and has issue living, John Swinton, *b.* 1929,—Katharine Joan, *b.* 1928. *Residence*, 38, St. Georges Court, Gloucester Rd., SW7.

The 1st baronet, Sir John Talbot Dillwyn-Llewelyn (son of the late John Dillwyn-Llewelyn, F.R.S., of Penllergaer, co. Glamorgan), was Mayor of Swansea 1890, and sat as M.P. therefor (C) July 1895 to Oct. 1900. The 2nd baronet, Col. Sir Charles Leyshon Dillwyn-Venables-Llewelyn, C.B., was High Sheriff of Radnorshire 1924, and Lord-Lieut. 1929-49, and sat as M.P. for Radnorshire (C) Jan. to Nov. 1910.

LLOYD, Creation (U.K.) 1960, of Rhu, co. Dunbarton.

Sir (ERNEST) GUY (RICHARD) LLOYD, *D.S.O.*, 1st *Baronet*, son of the late Major Ernest Thomas Lloyd [Green-Price, Bt.] ; *b.* Aug. 7th, 1890 ; ed. at Rossall, and at Keble Coll., Oxford (B.A. 1913, M.A. 1919) ; is a D.L. for Dunbartonshire ; formerly Major King's Shropshire L.I. ; European War 1914-17 (despatches, D.S.O.), European War 1939-40 with Roy. Warwickshire Regt. in France ; sat as M.P. for Renfrewshire, E. Div. (U) May 1940 to Sept. 1959 ; D.S.O. 1917, Knt. 1953 : *m.* 1918, Helen Kynaston, da. of the late Col. Ernest William Greg, C.B., V.D. and has issue.

𝕬rms—Per bend, sable and gules, a lion rampant regardant argent, goutté of the second, surmounted of a fess or, charged with a barrulet dancette azure, a bordure invected of the fourth. 𝕮rest—A demi-lion argent goutté and langued gules, holding in bend forward two spears sable points upwards or.

Residence—Rhu Cottage, Carrick Castle, Loch-goilhead, Argyll.

Son living—RICHARD ERNEST BUTLER, *b.* Dec 6th, 1928 ; ed. at Wellington Coll., and at Hertford Coll., Oxford ; late Capt. Black Watch : *m.* 1955, Jennifer, da. of Brigadier Ereld Cardiff, of Easton,

Court, near Ludlow Shropshire, and has issue living, Richard Timothy Butler, *b.* 1956,—Simon Wingfield Butler, *b.* 1958,—Henry Butler, *b.* 1965. *Residence*, Sundridge Place, Sundridge, Sevenoaks.

Daughters living—Margaret Kynaston, *b.* 1920 : *m.* 1948, Percy Bruce Southmayd **Fowler**, D.M., F.R.C.P., late Maj. R.A.M.C. *Residence*, Shirley Holms, Gerrards Cross, Bucks.—— Pamela Rathbone, *b.* 1922: *m.* 1954, Robert Petrie Hall, A.M.I.Mech.E. *Residence*, Gable Cottage, Burnham Green, Welwyn, Herts.——Elizabeth Hunt (*Lady Denny*), *b.* 1924: *m.* 1949, Sir Alistair Maurice Archibald Denny, 3rd Bt. (*cr.* 1913). *Residence*, Damside of Strathairly, Upper Largo, Fife.

SINCLAIR-LOCKHART, Creation (N.S.) 1636, of Murkle, co. Caithness, and Stevenson, co. Haddington.

Corda serrata fero.
I bear a locked heart.

Sir MUIR EDWARD SINCLAIR-LOCKHART, 14th *Baronet*; *b.* July 23rd, 1906; *s.* his brother Sir JOHN BERESFORD, 1970: *m.* 1940, Olga Ann, da. of Claude Victor White-Parsons, of Hawkes Bay, NZ, and has issue.

Arms—Quarterly : 1st and 4th, argent, a man's heart proper within a fetter-lock sable, on a chief azure three boars' heads erased argent all within a bordure, ermine, charged with three crosses patee gules ; 2nd and 3rd, argent, on a saltire engrailed gules, four bezants. **Crest**—A boar's head erased argent.

Address—Camnethan, RD10, Feilding, NZ.

Son living—SIMON JOHN EDWARD FRANCIS (14, Selwyn Rd., Havelock North, NZ), *b.* July 22nd, 1941: *m.* 1973, Felicity Edith, only da. of the late I. L, C. Stewart, of Havelock North, NZ, and formerly wife of Cdr. Michael Newcome Waymouth, RNZN, and has issue living, Robert Muir, *b.* Sept. 12th, 1973,—James Lachlan, (twin), *b.* 1973.

Daughter living—Sara Ann May, *b.* 1942: *m.* 1968, Nicholas Welcome Willcock, of Bodenham House, Wolverley, Kidderminster, Worcs.

Sister living—Elizabeth Sinclair (4, Endeavour St., Nelson, NZ), *b.* 1903: *m.* 1929 (Walter) Raleigh Grace, who *d.* 1950, and has issue living, Angela Elizabeth, *b.* 1933: *m.* 1957, Keith Grace McKenzie, MB, ChB, DTM and H, MRCGP, of 105, Lynbrooke Av., Blockhouse Bay, Auckland 7, NZ, and has issue living, Heather Grace *b.* 1958, Jennifer Grace *b.* 1960, Elizabeth Grace *b.* 1965.

Widow living of 13th Baronet—WINIFRED RAY (GRAHAM), (*Winifred, Lady Sinclair-Lockhart*), (The Chantry, Church Lane, Whitwell, I. of Wight), da. of the late Tom Ray Cavaghan, of Aglionby Grange, Carlisle: *m.* 1949, Sir John Beresford Sinclair-Lockhart, 13th Bt., who *d.* 1970.

Collateral Branch living.

Issue of the late Bruce Sinclair-Lockhart, LLM, yst. son of 11th baronet, *b.* 1910, *d.* 1965: *m.* 1940 (m. diss. 1949), Joan Marian Belle Quilliam, of New Plymouth, NZ:—

Sally Elisabeth, *b.* 1942: *m.* 1964, Stuart William Veitch, c/o Private Bag, Waimata, Gisborne, NZ, and has issue living, Guy Bruce, *b.* 1966,—William Ronald *b.* 1968,—Michael Richard, *b.* 1970,—Katie Jane, *b.* 1973.

Sir John Sinclair (son of George Sinclair of Edinburgh) was created a baronet of Nova Scotia with remainder to heirs male whatsoever. Sir Robert, 3rd baronet was a Privy Councillor and a Baron of the Exchequer. Sir John Sinclair, 4th baronet: *m.* 1698, Martha, da. and eventually heir of Sir John Lockhart of Castlehill, a Lord of Session (Lord Castlehill). Sir John Gordon Sinclair, 8th baronet, a distinguished Admiral, served sixty-three years in the Royal Navy. On the death of his son Sir Robert Charles Sinclair, 9th baronet in 1899 the baronetcy passed to a descendant of James Sinclair, yr. son of the 5th baronet, who on inheriting Castlehill 1764 assumed the surname of Lockhart. The 10th baronet Maj.-Gen. Sir Graeme A. Lockhart, CB (who served during Persian and Indian Mutiny Campaigns) assumed the additional surname of Sinclair. Sir Robert Duncan Sinclair, Lockhart, 11th baronet, was son of the late George Duncan Lockhart (whose grandfather assumed the surname of Lockhart in lieu of his patronymic), a descendant of the late James Lockhart Sinclair, 2nd son of 5th baronet.

LOCOCK, Creation (U.K.) 1857, of Speldhurst, Kent. [Extinct 1965.]

Sir CHARLES BIRD LOCOCK, 3rd and last *Baronet*.

Daughters living of 3rd Baronet—Dorothy Christine (Godolphin Bungalow, Wheal Venture Rd., St. Ives, Cornwall, TR26 2PQ), *b.* 1902.——Vera Frances, *b.* 1920: *m.* 1st, 1939, Capt. Philip McDonald Bottome, RASC; 3rdly, 1946, Cyril Stevens: *m.* 3rdly, 1972, Malcolm Paul Holman, of Top Flat, Chy-an-Gweal House, Main Rd., Carbis Bay, St. Ives, Cornwall, and has issue living, (by 2nd marriage) Anthony Charles, *b.* 1948,—(by 1st marriage) Nigel Derek, *b.* 1951,—(by 1st marriage) Patricia Ann, *b.* 1941: *m.* 1960 (m. diss. 1966), Raymond Bey-Leveld, and has issue living, Kevin Wayne, *b.* 1961, Barry Gordon, *b.* 1963,—(by 2nd m.) Anita Janet Christine, *b.* 1956.

Granddaughter living of 3rd Baronet—[Issue of the late Charles Bardolf Locock, *b.* 1905, *d.* 1961, *m.* 1950, Frances Daphne, who *d.* 1974, el. da. of the late Cdr. Ralph Hicks, RN, of Pryrford, Surrey]—Frances Ann, (Two Ways, Maderia Rd., W. Byfleet, Surrey), *b.* 1951.

Collateral Branches living.

Granddaughter of the late Rev. Alfred Henry Locock, 2nd son of 1st baronet :—

Issue of the late Charles Dealtry Locock, *b.* 1862, *d.* 1946: *m.* 1889, Ida Gertrude, who *d.* 1962, da. of the late Col. Herbert Locock, 5th son of 1st baronet:—

Elsa, *b.* 1891. *Residence*, 44, Rusholme Road, Putney, S.W.15.

Granddaughter of the late Col. Herbert Locock, C.B., R.E., 5th son of 1st baronet:—

Issue of the late Sir Guy Harold Locock, C.M.G., *b.* 1883, *d.* 1958 : *m.* 1906, Esther Mary Eleanor, who *d.* 1955, only child of William James Reade :—

Rosemary Esther, *b.* 1907: *m.* 1938, John Wyndham Stanton, of Purlieus Farmhouse, Ewen, Cirencester, Glos., and has issue living, Richard Holbrow, *b.* 1940: *m.* 1974, Janet Vanessa Watson, —Anthony Guy, *b.* 1943: *m.* 1970, Julia Mary Osborn-King,—Susan Mary, *b.* 1947: *m.* 1970, Dr. Martin Fraser, and has issue living, Anthony Charles *b.* 1971, Rosemary Susan *b.* 1974.

LODER, Creation (U.K.) 1887, of Whittlebury, Northamptonshire, and of High Beeches, Slaugham, Sussex.

A sound conscience is a wall of brass.

Sir GILES ROLLS LODER, 3rd *Baronet*, son of the late Capt. Robert Egerton Loder, son of 2nd Baronet; *b.* Nov. 10th, 1914; *s.* his grandfather, *Sir* EDMUND GILES, 1920; ed. at Eton, and at Trin. Coll., Camb. (B.A. 1936, M.A. 19—); formerly Lieut. 98th (Surrey and Sussex Yeo.) Field Brig. R.A. (T.A.); High Sheriff of Sussex 1948; is a J.P. for Sussex, and a FLS: *m.* 1939, Marie Violet Pamela (an OStJ) only da. of the late Bertram Hanmer Bunbury Symons-Jeune, of Runnymede House, Old Windsor, and has issue.

ₐ𝔯𝔪𝔰—Azure, on a fesse between two escallops or, three bucks' heads cabossed proper. 𝔠𝔯𝔢𝔰𝔱—Between two escallops or, a buck's head cabossed and pierced with an arrow bendwise point to the sinister proper.

Residence—Leonardslee, Horsham, Sussex. *Club*—Royal Yacht Squadron.

Sons living—EDMUND JEUNE (Eyrefield Lodge, The Curragh, co. Kildare), *b.* June 26th, 1941; ed. at Eton; FCA: *m.* 1966 (m. diss. 1971), Penelope Jane, da. of Ivo Forde, and has issue living, Gillian Marie, *b.* 1968.—— Robert Reginald (Selehurst, Lower Beeding, Horsham), *b.* 1943; ed. at Eton, and at Trin. Coll., Camb. (BA): *m.* 1967, Quenelda Jane, da. of Sir John Ledward Royden, 4th Bt., and has issue living, Christopher Giles, *b.* 1968,—Peter Thomas, *b.* 1972,—Catherine Marie Violet, *b.* 1970,—Mary Charlotte (twin), *b.* 1972.

Collateral Branches living.

Issue of the late Wilfrid Hans Loder 2nd son of 1st baronet, *b.* 1851, *d.* 1902: *m.* 1878, Sarah Winifred, who *d.* 1943, da. of Charles Rowe:—

Hubert Sydney (Mill Hamlet House, Sidlesham, Chichester), *b.* 1888; ed. at Eton, and at Magdalen Coll., Oxford; sometime Lt. Roy. E. Kent Yeo.: *m.* 1918 (m. diss. 1944), Brenda, da. of Charles McNeill, and has issue living, Simon John (of Resthill Farm, Over Worton, Middle Barton, Oxon.; White's, and Lansdowne Clubs), *b.* 1932; ed. at Eton; late Capt. Grenadier Guards: *m.* 1962, Kathleen Alexandra, el. da. of Richard Evelyn Fleming, MC, TD [*see* B. Wyfold], and has issue living, David Richard, *b.* 1964, Alexander Hugh *b.* 1965, John Alistair *b.* 1968,—Jean Mary, *b.* 1919: *m.* 1939, Stephen Dane Player, of Ednaston Manor, Brailsford, Derby, and has issue living, Peter Dane *b.* 1941, James Stephen (Knowles Farm, Brailsford, Derby) *b.* 1945: *m.* 1969, Phillippa Hedley, da. of Frank Hedley Richardson (and has issue living, Andrew Hedley *b.* 1970), Karen Jean *b.* 1940: *m.* 1963, Dermot Kelly, of Somersal Herbert Grange, Doveridge, Derbys. (and has issue living, Patrick Dermot Stephen *b.* 1968, Doone *b.* 1963, Anna *b.* 1966),—Gillian, *b.* 1925: *m.* 1952, John Johnston Kirkpatrick, of Little Rissington Manor, Glos., and has issue living, Christopher James *b.* 1953, Nicholas Yvone John *b.* 1959, Francis Hugh *b.* 1962, Robin Kenneth Antony *b.* 1969, Rose Cecilia *b.* 1955, Sara Gillian *b.* 1956.

Grandson of the late Alfred Basil Loder, 3rd son of 1st baronet:—

Issue of the late Major Basil Charles Robert Loder, *b.* 1885, *d.* 1934: *m.* 1908, Kate, who *d.* 1957, da. of W. Davies, of Pembroke, S. Wales :—

Robert Eric, *CBE* (The White Cottage, Slaugham, Sussex; Bucks and United Service Clubs), *b.* 1911; ed. at Lancing; Brig. (ret.) late R. Sussex Regt.; ADC to Gov. of NSW 1939, OC 4th/5th (Cinque Ports) Bn., R. Sussex Regt. (TA) 1950-53, Comdt. R. Mil. Sch. of Music, Kneller Hall 1958-61, Head of Commonwealth Mission UN to Korea 1961-62, and Comd. Glos. and Somerset Sub-Dist. 1962-65; Dep. Col. The Queen's Regt. since 1968: a DL for Sussex; Cdr. Order of House of Orange of the Netherlands; 1939-45 War (prisoner); CBE (Mil) 1965.

Issue of the late Gerald Walter Erskine Loder (5th son of 1st baronet), who was cr. *Baron Wakehurst* 1934 [see that title].

Issue of the late Reginald Bernhard Loder, 6th son of the 1st baronet, *b.* 1864, *d.* 1931: *m.* 1895, Lady Margaret Ernestine Augusta Hare, who *d.* 1951, el. da. of 3rd Earl of Listowel :—

Marjorie Kathleen, *b.* 1897: *m.* 1921, Lt.-Col. Cuthbert Henry Dawnay, MC, who *d.* 1964 [*see* V. Downe, colls.]. *Residence*, 16, Hale House, de Vere Gdns., W8.

MORRISON-LOW, Creation (U.K.) 1908, of Kilmaron, co. Fife.

Perils delight me. Prudence excels.

Sir JAMES RICHARD MORRISON-LOW, 3rd *Baronet* : *b.* Aug. 3rd, 1925 ; *s.* his father, *Sir* WALTER JOHN, 1955: *m.* 1953, Anne Rawson, da. of the late Air-Commodore Robert Gordon, C.B., C.B.E., D.S.O., and has issue.

ₐ𝔯𝔪𝔰—Quarterly, 1st and 4th argent, two wolves counterpassant sable, armed and langued gules, on a chief of the last three fleurs-de-lis of the first, *Low ;* 2nd and 3rd per chevron or and ermine three saracens' heads couped at the neck proper, turbaned vert, *Morrison.* 𝔠𝔯𝔢𝔰𝔱𝔰—1st, an eagle's head between two thistles slipped proper, *Low ;* 2nd, a saracen's head proper, turbaned vert, *Morrison.*

Seat—Kilmaron Castle, near Cupar, Fife.

Son living—RICHARD WALTER, *b.* Aug. 4th, 1959.

Daughters living — Alison Dorothy, *b.* 1955.——Jean Elspeth, *b.* 1957.——Susan Elizabeth, *b.* 1963.

Brother living—Colin John (No. 6, Ol Molog, W. Kilimanjaro, Tanzania), *b.* 1928: *m.* 1953, Susan Desiree MacDougall, da. of P. C. M. Watson, of George, S. Africa, and has issue living, Katherine Dorothy, *b.* 1955,—Corinna Helen, *b.* 1959.

Aunt living (daughter of 1st baronet)—Emily Low, b. 1895.

Widow living of 2nd Baronet—(HENRIETTA) WILHELMINA MARY (*Dowager Lady Morrison-Low*), da. of the late Maj. Robert Walter Purvis, of Gilmerton, Fife [Gilmour, Bt., *cr.* 1897]: *m.* 1948, as his second wife, Sir Walter John Morrison-Low, 2nd baronet, who *d.* 1955. *Residence,* Kingsbarns House, Kingsbarns, Fife.

Sir James Low, Knt., 1st Bt., el. son of William Low, of Kirriemuir, by Janet, his wife, da. of Alexander Morrison, of Kirriemuir, was Lord Provost of Dundee 1893-6. Sir Walter John Morrison-Low, 2nd Bt., assumed by deed poll (enrolled at College of Arms) 1924, the additional surname of Morrison.

LOWE, Creation (U.K.) 1918, of Edgbaston, City of Birmingham.

I hope for better things

Sir FRANCIS REGINALD GORDON LOWE, 3rd *Baronet*; *b.* Feb. 8th, 1931; *s.* his father, *Sir* FRANCIS GORDON 1972; ed. at Stowe, and Clare Coll., Camb. (BA, LLB); Bar. Middle Temple 1959; South Eastern Circuit: *m.* 1st, 1961 (m. diss. 1971), Francesca Cornelia, da. of Siegfried Steinkopf, of Berlin; 2ndly, 1971, Helen Suzanne, da. of the late Sandys Stuart Macaskie, solicitor, and has issue by 1st m.

Arms—Erminois, on a bend engrailed cottised plain **azure** between two Stafford knots sable, three wolves' heads erased or. **Crest**—A demi-gryphon erminois, resting the sinister paw on a Stafford knot sable.

Residences—6, Parkfields, Putney, SW15; Rose Cottage, Roud, I. of Wight.

Sons living—By 1st m.—THOMAS WILLIAM GORDON, *b.* Aug. 14th., 1963.—Christopher Francis, *b.* 1964.

Widow living of 2nd Baronet—(DOROTHY) HONOR (*Honor, Lady Lowe*), (8, Seymour Walk, SW10), da. of the late Lt.-Col. Humphry Stephen Woolrych, of Croxley: *m.* 1926, as his 2nd wife, Sir Francis Gordon Lowe, 2nd Bt., who *d.* 1972.

Collateral Branches living

Issue of the late Arthur Holden Lowe, 2nd son of 1st baronet, *b.* 1886, *d.* 1958: *m.* 1924, Evelyn Philpot, who *d.* 1949:—

John Evelyn, *b.* 1928: *m.* 1956, Susan Sanderson, and has issue living, Mark John, *b.* 1957,—Dominic Simon, *b.* 1961,—Judith Anne, *b.* 1962. *Residence,* Duffryn, Liphook, Hants.——Jill Rosemary, *b.* 1937: *m.* 1957, Peter Gibbons, and has issue living, Nicholas Arthur, *b.* 1960,—Caroline Evelyn, *b.* 1958,—Lucinda Mary, *b.* 1961,—Julia Anne, *b.* 1963,—Mary Jane, *b.* 1967. *Residence,* 28, Beverley Rd., Barnes, SW13.

Issue of the late Wing Cdr. John Claude Malcolm Lowe, yst. son of 1st baronet, *b.* 1888, *d.* 1970: *m.* 1912, Winifred Olsson, who *d.* 1968:—

Anthony John (The Oast House, Sandy Lane, Ightham Common, Kent), *b.* 1913: *m.* 1948, Rosemary Richards, and has issue living, Charles *b.* 1949,—Nicholas (twin), *b.* 1949,—Timothy, *b.* 1953,—Joanna, *b.* 1958.——Pauline Muriel *b.* 1917: *m.* 1943, Desmond Kirkness, of Clifton Cottage, Chilham, Kent, and has issue living, Alister, *b.* 1947: *m.* 1973, Marie Ekströmer,—Simon, *b.* 1949,—Christopher, *b.* 1954,—Julian, *b.* 1958,—Jane, *b.* 1944: *m.* 1967, Jeremy Mercer.——Elizabeth Jane, *b.* 1928: *m.* 1957, Edward C. Richardson, of Upper Panshill Farm, Murcott, Islip, Oxford OX5 2RQ, and has issue living, Henry Edward Carleton, *b.* 1961,—Conan Sacheverell Carleton, *b.* 1963,—Emma, *b.* 1958,—Sophie, *b.* 1959.

The 1st baronet, Rt. Hon. Sir Francis William Lowe, D.L., was sometime a partner in the legal firm of Lowe and Jolly, and sat as M.P. for Birmingham, Edgbaston Div. (C) 1898 to 1929.

LOWSON, Creation (U.K.) 1951, of Westlaws, co. Perth.

Sir IAN PATRICK LOWSON, 2nd *Baronet*; *b.* Sept. 4th, 1944; *s.* his father, *Sir* DENYS COLQUHOUN FLOWER-DEW, 1975; ed. at Eton, McGill Univ., Canada, and Duke Univ., USA; an OStJ.

Arms—Quarterly; 1st and 4th per saltire argent and azure, in chief a sealion sejant and in base a fleur-de-lys sable, in each flank a garb or, *Lowson*; 2nd per chevron argent and pean a chevronel invected on the upper side between two sealions segant sable in chief and another in base of the first, *Flowerdew*; 3rd erminois, three catherine-wheels two and one sable within a bordure engrailed azure, over all a chief gules thereon a hill with lines of defence all proper, in dexter chief a mullet argent, *Scott*. **Crest**—1st a garb or; 2nd a demi-man habited azure, garnished gules wreathed about the temples argent and sable holding in the right hand a sprig of two roses, one of the second, the other of the third, stalked and leaved proper.

Residence—Bandirran, Perthshire. *Clubs*—Boodle's, Buck's, MCC.

Sisters living—Gay Ann (*Countess of Kinnoull*), *b.* 1938: *m.* 1961, the 15th Earl of Kinnoull (15, Carlyle Sq., SW3; Pier Hse., Seaview, I. of Wight).——Melanie Fiona Louisa, *b.* 1940: *m.* 1964, Charles Archibald Adam Black, of 1, Astell St., SW3 [D. Roxburghe], and has issue living, Adam Sebastian, *b.* 1965 —Holly Patricia Louisa, *b.* 1968.

Widow living of 1st Baronet—*Hon.* ANN PATRICIA MACPHERSON (*Hon. Lady Lowson*) (Oratory Cottage, 33, Ennismore Gdns. Mews, SW7 1HZ; Carmurie, Elie, Fife), da. of 1st Baron Strathcarron; an OStJ: *m.* 1936, Sir Denys Colquhoun Flowerdew Lowson, 1st Bt., who *d.* 1975.

Sir Denys Colquhoun Flowderdew Lowson, 1st Bt., son of James Gray Flowerdew Lowson JP, PhD, of Balthayock, Perthshire, was Lord Mayor of London 1950-51 (Festival of Britain Year),

LOWTHER, Creation (U.K.) 1824, of Swillington, Yorkshire.

The magistrate shows the man.

Sir WILLIAM GUY LOWTHER, *O.B.E.*, 5th *Baronet* ; *b.* Oct. 9th, 1912 ; *s.* his father *Lieut.-Col. Sir* CHARLES BINGHAM, *C.B. D.S.O.*, 1949 ; *ed.* at Winchester ; Lieut.-Col. late Comdg. 8th Hussars, a Member of Hon Corps. of Gentlemen-at-Arms; CStJ, and a DL of Denbighshire (High Sheriff 1959); Palestine 1936 (despatches), 1939-45 War in W. Desert (prisoner), Korea 1952 (despatches); OBE (Mil) 1952: *m.* 1939, Grania Suzanne, da. of the late Maj. Archibald James Hamilton Douglas Campbell, OBE, of Blythswood House, Renfrew [By. Clarina, ext.], and has issue.

Arms—Or, six annulets sable, a crescent for difference. **Crest**—A dragon passant argent.

Seat—Erbistock Hall, near Wrexham. **Club**—Cavalry.

Son living—CHARLES DOUGLAS (10, Henning St., SW1; Cavalry Club), *b.* Jan. 22nd, 1946; Capt. Queen's R. Irish Hussars: *m.* 1st, 1969 (m. diss. 1975), Melanie Pensee FitzHerbert, da. of the late Roderick Christopher Musgrave; 2ndly, 1975, Florence Rose, yst. da. of Col. Alexander James Henry Cramsie, OBE, of O'Harabrook, Ballymoney, Co. Antrim.

Daughter living—Grizelda Leonora, *b.* 1948: *m.* 1968, Capt. Timothy Michael Bell, Scots Gds., and has issue living, Matthew Guy, *b.* 1974,—Katherine, *b.* 1971.

Sister living—Doreen Margaret, *b.* 1910. *Residence*, The Grange, Overton, near Wrexham.

Uncle living (brother of 4th baronet)—John George, *C.B.E., D.S.O., M.C., T.D.*, *b.* 1885 ; *ed.* at Winchester ; Capt. late 11th Hussars, and Col. late Comdg. Northamptonshire Yeo. and 4th Batn. Northamptonshire Regt. (T.A.) ; is a J.P. and D.L. for Northants, and patron of two livings ; elected a Co. Councillor for Northants 1939, and a Co. Alderman 1949 ; European War 1914-19 (wounded, despatches, M.C., D.S.O.) ; D.S.O. 1919, C.B.E. (Civil) 1953 : *m.* 1911, the Hon Lilah Charlotte Sarah White, da. of 3rd Baron Annaly, and has issue living, George Hugh (of Holdenby House, Northampton. *Club*, Beefsteak, *b.* 1912; Capt. late Life Guards: *m.* 1938, Shiela Rachel Isabel, da. of the late Major Phipps Foster, and has issue living, James *b.* 1947, Shiela Ann *b.* 1943: *m.* 1964, John Carleton Paget,—John Luke (of The Old House, Guilsborough, Northampton), *b.* 1923: Capt. late KRRC: *m.* 1952, Jennifer Jane, el. da. of John Henry Bevan, CB, MC [E. Lucan], and has issue living, Hugh William *b.* 1956, Sarah Charlotte Margaret *b.* 1954, Lavinia Mary *b.* 1958,—Bridget Elizabeth *b.* 1921: *m.* 1947, Robert Alistair Henderson [*see* Clerke, Bt.]. *Seat*, Guilsborough Court, Northampton. *Residence*, 2, Wesley St., W.1. *Club*, Buck's

Widow living of 4th Baronet—RUTH KYNASTON (*Dowager Lady Lowther*), da. of Charles Francis Kynaston Mainwaring [Rankin, Bt., *cr.* 1808] : *m.* 1936, as his second wife, Lieut.-Col. Sir Charles Bingham Lowther, C.B., D.S.O., 4th baronet, who *d.* 1949. *Residence*, Lightwood, Lightwood Green, Overton, Wrexham.

The 1st baronet, many years M.P. for Cumberland, was brother to William, 1st Earl of Lonsdale, and the 2nd baronet was successively M.P. for Cockermouth, Wigton, and York. The **4th baronet**, Lieut.-Col. Sir Charles Bingham, C.B., D.S.O., was Lieut.-Col. Northants Yeo. and High Sheriff of Northants 1926.

LOWTHER, Creation (U.K.) 1914, of Belgrave Square, City of Westminster.

[Extinct 1916.]

Right Hon. Sir GERARD AUGUSTUS LOWTHER, *G.C.M.G., C.B.*, 1st and last *Baronet*.

Daughters living of 1st Baronet—Edith Alice Cecilia, *b.* 1906: *m.* 1st, 1933, Baron Jacques Thenard, who *d.* (killed in action during European War) 1940 ; 2ndly, 1945, Roger Leveque de Vilmorin, and has issue living, (by 1st marriage) Arnould (La Ferté sur Grosne, Sennecey le Grand, France, S. et L.), *b.* 1940: *m.* 1963, Anne de MacMahon, and has issue living, Jacques *b.* 1965, Stanislas *b.* 1966, Henri *b.* 1968,—Anne Henriette Alice, *b.* 1934: *m.* 1958, Jean Lemut, of 15, rue Maître Albert, Paris V, France, and has issue living, Lorraine *b.* 1960, Thomas *b.* 1961, Marthe *b.* 1963,—Irène Marie, *b.* 1936: *m.* 1st, 1956, Nicolas Leveque de Vilmorin, who *d.* 1967; 2ndly, 1973, Count Jean de Luppé, of 11, Av. Raymond Poincaré, 75116 Paris, and has issue living (by 1st m.), Louis *b.* 1957, Mathieu *b.* 1960, Pauline *b.* 1958, Marie *b.* 1962,—(by 2nd m.) Philippe Victor, *b.* 1948,—Eleonore, *b.* 1947: *m.* 1972, Comte Guy de Dampierre. *Residence*, Verrieres le Buisson, Essonne, France.——Gladys Mabel, *b.* 1908: *m.* 1st, 1933, Capt. Charles Nevile Fane, Coldstream Guards, who *d.* (killed in action) 1940 [*see* B. Clinton, colls.]; 2ndly, 1942, Lt.-Col. James Hayton Greenhill Black, late Argyll and Sutherland Highlanders, who *d.* 1966, and has issue living (by 1st m.) [*see* B. Clinton, colls.], (by 2nd m.) Lois Roberta, *b.* 1944: *m.* 1967, Peter Burke, of Holly Hse, Crawley Down, Sussex, and has issue living, Nicholas James *b.* 1969, Matthew Piers *b.* 1970, Laura Melissa *b.* 1974. *Residence*, West Monkton Hse, Taunton.

LUCAS, Creation (U.K.) 1887, of Ashtead Park, Surrey, and of Lowestoft, co. Suffolk.

Sir Joscelyn Morton Lucas, *K.B.E.*, MC, 4th *Baronet*; *b.* Aug. 27th, 1889; *s.* his father, *Sir* Edward Lingard, 1936 ; ed. at Eton; late Capt. (Hon. Maj.) 4th Bn. R. Warwickshire Regt., Chm. of British Sportsman's Club 1958-67; a Vice-Pres. and Member of Council of Roy. Overseas League since 1940, and Chm. of Hospitality Cttee. since 1938, and Founder and Chm. of Allies Welcome Cttee., of Returned Prisoners of War Advice Cttee., and of Empire War Memorial Fund; 1914-19 War (wounded, prisoner, MC); special Welfare Liaison Officer with Dominion Forces in London Command 1940-48; a Member of Council of Roy. Vet. Coll. 1944; Cdr. of Order of Orange Nassau of the Netherlands; 1st Class Czechoslovakian Mil. Medal of Merit; MP for S. Portsmouth (*C*) 1939-66; KBE (Civil) 1959: *m.* 1st, 1933, Edith, who *d.* 1956, da. of the late Very Rev. David Barry Cameron, DD, JP, of Dundee, and widow of Sir Trehawke Herbert Kekewich, 1st Bt. (ext.); 2ndly, 1960, M. Thelma Grace de Chair, who *d.* 1974, da. of Harold Dennison Arbuthnot, of Field Place, Compton, Surrey.

SPES·ET·FIDES.

Hope and faith.

Arms—Per bend argent and gules, a bend dovetailed between six annulets, all counterchanged. **Crest**—Issuant from a wreath of oak or a dragon s head, wings addorsed gules, semée of annulets argent,

Residences—Michelmersh Court, Romsey, Hants; 14, Clabon Mews, Cadogan Sq., SW1. *Clubs*—Carlton, Bath, Kennel, Royal Commonwealth Society.

Collateral Branches living.

Issue of the late Major Ernest Murray Lucas, 3rd son **of** 1st baronet, *b.* 1861, *d.* 1936: *m.* 1900, Ada Catherine, who *d.* 1962, da. of the late J. Fletcher Moore, J.P., D.L., of Manor Kilbride, co. Wicklow:—

Carlton George (Rose Mount, Lustleigh, Newton Abbot, Devon), *b.* 1907: *m.* 1950, Daphne Gertrude, da. of G. W. Bryant, Malayan Civil Ser. (ret.).——Mary Gladys (Hakins, Rose Green, Chappel, Colchester, Essex), *b.* 1902: *m.* 1943, Arthur Cyril Jennings, OBE, MICE, who *d.* 1954; 2ndly, 1955, Wilfred Brinton, JP, who *d.* 1972.——Margery Dorothy Bertha (*Baroness Upjohn*), *b.* 1913: *m.* 1947, Baron Upjohn, CBE (Life Baron), who *d.* 1971. *Residence*, Orpen's Hill House, Birch, Colchester.

Grandsons of the late Major Ernest Murray Lucas (ante) :—
Issue of the late Ralph John Scott Lucas, Lieut. Coldstream Guards, *b.* 1904, *d.* (killed in action) 1941 (despatches): *m.* 1929, Dorothy (now of Icomb Lodge, Icomb, Stow-on-the-Wold), da. of the late Major H. T. Timson, of Tatchbury Mount, Totton, Hants:—

Thomas Edward (c/o Williams & Glyn's Bank, 22, Whitehall, SW1), *b.* Sept. 16th, 1930; ed. at Wellington Coll., and at Trin. Hall, Camb. (MA): *m.* 1958, Charmian Margaret, who *d.* 1970, da. of Col. J. S. Powell, of Drayton Court, SW10, and has issue living, Stephen Ralph James, *b.* 1963.——Patrick Timson, *VRD* (The Hollies, Court Green Heights, Hook Heath, Woking, Surrey; Royal Naval Club), *b.* 1933: ed. at Wellington Coll.; Maj. RM (Reserve): *m.* 1958, Anne da. of J. Westcott, of Yeovil, Som., and has issue living, Simon James Timson, *b.* 1960,—Julian Patrick, *b.* 1962.

Issue of the late Rev. Francis Granville Lewis Lucas, 4th son of 1st baronet, *b.* 1862, *d.* 1939 : *m.* 1892, Mary Frances, who *d.* 1958, da. of the late John E. Bovill, of Sondes Place, Dorking :—

Hubert Francis, CBE, *b.* 1897; ed. at Harrow; Brig. (ret.) late RE; was Brig. in charge of Administration, Malaya 1940-42 (prisoner, CBE 1939-45 and S.-W. Pacific Stars, Defence and Gen. Ser. Medals); European War 1914-18 in Mesopotamia (despatches, two medals), Iraq 1919-20 (medal with two clasps); OBE (Mil.) 1926, CBE, (Mil.) 1946: *m.* 1921, Evelyn Irene Sophie Phipps, da. of the late Brig.-Gen. Edmund John Phipps Hornby, VC, CB, CMG, and has issue living, Diana Joan, *b.* 1931: *m.* 1954, Capt. John Brian St. Vincent Hawkins, Dorset Regt. (ret.), of Orchard House, 7, Clarence Rd., Dorchester, Dorset, and has issue living, Rowena Fay *b.* 1955, Wendy Susan *b.* 1957,—Rosemary Anne, *b.* 1932: *m.* 1962, Lt.-Cdr. William Beauchamp Tower, RN (ret.), of The Home House, Stoke St. Michael, Bath [Johnson, Bt., colls., cr. 1755], and has issue living, Alan Francis Beauchamp *b.* 1964, Christopher John *b.* 1972, Annabel Jane *b.* 1965, Sophie Elizabeth *b.* 1967. *Residence*, Linch Close, Charminster, Dorchester, Dorset.——Arthur John, *b.* 1903: ed. at Harrow; formerly Maj. RE: *m.* 1930, Margaret Ruth, da. of the late Col. Joseph Francis Noel Baxendale, CB, TD [Heathcote, Bt.], and has issue living, James Granville (Laundry Cottage, Froxfield Green, Petersfield, Hants.), *b.* 1932; ed. at Harrow; Lt.-Cdr. RN (ret.): *m.* 1st, 1957, (m. diss. 1973), Suzanne Molly, da. of Edward Fitzroy Talbot-Ponsonby [see E. Shrewsbury, colls.]; 2ndly, 1973, Ann Marie Mason, and has issue living, (by 1st m.), Jonathan Delight *b.* 1964, Charles Granville (twin) *b.* 1964,—Jennifer, *b.* 1936: *m.* 1972, Hugh Cecil Toomer, 5, Eccleston Sq., SW1. *Residence*, Venthams Farm, Froxfield Green, Petersfield, Hants.

Issue of the late Major Evelyn Penn Lucas, M.C., youngest son of 1st baronet, *b.* 1875, *d.* 1950 : *m.* 1902, Mary Georgetta, who *d.* 1948, only da. of the Rev. Richard Stovin Mitchison, late R. of Barby, Rugby :—

Timothy Stovin, MC, TD, *b.* 1916; is Capt.; European War 1939-45 (MC): *m.* 1942, Joanna Repington, only child of C. B. Mathews, of Lob's Wood, Ilkley, Yorkshire, and has issue living, Charles Evelyn Penn (Hill House, Ellington, Hunts.), *b.* 1943: *m.* 1967, Antoinette, only da. of Baron von Westenholz, of Blabesware, Much Hadham, Herts., and has issue living, Piers *b.* 1970, Nina Antoinette *b.* 1971,—Charlotte Theresa Stovin (48, Victoria Rd., W8) *b.* 1945: *m.* 1966 (m. diss. 1971), Christopher Irwin, and has issue living, Alexander Christian Stovin *b.* 1970, Sophia Georgetta Kate *b.* 1968. *Residence*, Sharow Hall, Ripon, Yorks.

Lucas (Munro-Lucas-Tooth), see Tooth.

RAMSAY-FAIRFAX-LUCY, Creation (U.K.) 1836, of The Holmes, Roxburghshire.

Sir EDMUND JOHN WILLIAM HUGH RAMSAY-FAIRFAX-LUCY, 6th *Baronet; b.* May 4th, 1945; *s.* his father, *Maj. Sir* BRIAN FULKE, 1974; ed. at Eton; Dip. RA Schs: *m.* 1974, Sylvia, da. of Graeme Ogden, of The Old Manor, Rudge, Somerset.

Arms—1st and 4th grand-quarters, gules, 1st semée of cross-crosslets, three lucies haurient argent, a canton of the last, *Lucy;* 2nd and 3rd grand quarters, quarterly 1st and 4th argent, three bars gemel sable surmounted by a lion rampant gules, armed and langued azure, *Fairfax;* 2nd, per pale argent and or, an eagle displayed sable, armed, beaked and membered gules, *Ramsay;* 3rd, counter-quartered, 1st and 4th azure, a branch of palm between three fleurs-de-lis or, 2nd and 3rd gules, three annulets or, stoned azure, in the centre of these counter-quarters a crescent or for difference, *Montgomerie.* **Crests**—1st, out of a ducal coronet gules a boar's head argent gutée de poix, between two wings sable: billettée or, charged on the neck, with a cross-crosslet sable, *Lucy;* 2nd, a lion passant guardant proper, *Fairfax.*

MOTTOES—*Dexter*, By truthe and diligence, *Lucy; sinister*, Fare fac, *Fairfax.*

Residences—The Mill, Fossebridge, Glos.; Charlecote Park, Warwick.

Sister living—Mary Caroline Alys Emma, *b.* 1946: *m.* 1967, James Empsom Scott, MA, BM, BCh, FRCS, of Bloxham House, Fossebridge, Cheltenham, and has issue living, Sophie Katherina Rosie, *b.* 1970,—Charlotte Christina Bianca, *b.* 1974.

Aunt living (daughter of 3rd baronet)—Alianore Mary Christina, *b.* 1894; MRCS and LRCP 1943. *Residence*, The Malt House, Charlecote, Warwick.

Widows living of 3rd and 5th Baronets—NORAH (*Lady Ramsay-Fairfax-Lucy*), da. of the late John Hugh Munro Mackenzie, OBE, of Mornish: *m.* 1944, as his 2nd wife, Sir Henry William Cameron-Ramsay-Fairfax-Lucy, CB, 3rd Bt., who *d.* 1944. *Residence*, Fair Rule, Hawick, Roxburghshire.——Hon. ALICE CAROLINE HELEN BUCHAN (*Hon. Lady Ramsay-Fairfax-Lucy*), (The Mill Fossebridge, Glos.; Charlecote Park, Warwick), only da. of 1st Baron Tweedsmuir: *m.* 1933, Maj. Sir Brian Fulke Ramsay-Fairfax-Lucy, 5th Bt., who *i.* 1974.

Collateral Branches living.

Issue of the late Capt. Ewen Aymer Robert Ramsay-Fairfax-Lucy, yst. son of 3rd baronet, *b.* 1899, *d.* 1969: *m.* 1930, Margaret Westall (Bryhers, West Broyle Drive, Chichester), da. of Sir David Westall King, 2nd Bt. (cr. 1888):—

DUNCAN CAMERON (13, Shooters Hill Rd., Blackheath, SE3), *b.* Sept. 18th, 1932; FCA: *m.* 1964, Janet Barclay, da. of P. A. B. Niven, of The Old School House, N. Mundham, Chichester, and has issue living, Spencer Angus, *b.* 1966,—Anna Margaret Barclay, *b.* 1969.——Robin Spencer, *b.* 1937.——Jennifer Frances, *b.* 1935: *m.* 1962, Ronald Ian Talbot Cromartie, c/o FCO, SW1, and has issue living, Alan Duncan Talbot, *b.* 1964,—David Francis Ian, *b.* 1970,—Selina Margaret Lucy, *b.* 1967.——Christina Alison, *b.* 1943: *m.* 1964, John Anthony Chandley Pugh, FCA, of Sprangewell, Poles Lane, Ware, Herts., and has issue living, Jonathan Chandley, *b.* 1966,—Rosanna Lucy, *b.* 1968,—Martha Elizabeth, *b.* 1971.

Issue of the late Com. William George Astell RAMSAY-FAIRFAX, C.M.G., D.S.O., R.N., 3rd son of 2nd baronet, *b.* 1876, *d.* 1946: *m.* 1909, Lilian Kate, who *d.* 1957, da. of the late Henry Rich, of Abbey Lodge, Malmesbury :—

John William (145, Oakwood Court, W14; Challoner Club), *b.* 1909; ed. at Gonville and Caius Coll., Camb. (BA 1931); Lt.-Col. (ret.) Army Catering Corps; Pilgrimage Sec., Aylesford Priory 1958; House Manager to Roy. Commonwealth So. 1959-61; 1939-45 War in Egypt and Palestine; Dep. Chm. Friends of Malta, GC, 1972-73: *m.* 1st, 1947 (m. annulled 1958), Audrey (SCOTT-GIBSON), da. of the Rev. Lewis Richardson; 2ndly, 1964, Mary Dolores, only da. of the late Daniel Carroll, of Dublin.——Victor George Hargrave, *DSC, b.* 1912; Lt.-Cdr. (ret.) RN; 1939-45 War (despatches, DSC): *m.* 1939, Christian Geraldine Mary. who *d.* 1967, only child of the late Lt.-Col. Frederick Arthur Irby [B. Boston, colls.], and has issue living, Victor Ferdinand Desmond, *b.* 1944,—Pepita Christian, *b.* 1942. *Residence*, The Well House, Brettenham, Ipswich, Suffolk, IP7 7PD. *Club*, Army and Navy.

This family claims descent from the same stock as Lord Fairfax of Cameron. Vice-Adm. Sir William George Fairfax, a distinguished naval officer, was made a Knight Banneret for the bravery displayed by him at the battle of Camperdown, and in consideration of his services a baronetcy was conferred upon his only surviving son, Col. Sir Henry Fairfax, who *m.* 1830 (as his 1st wife) Archibald, Montgomerie, da. and eventually heir of Thomas Williamson (afterwards Williamson-Ramsay), by Elizabeth, da. and co-heir of Robert Ramsay of Camno and Arthurstown, Forfar. The 2nd baronet, Col. Sir William George Herbert Taylor, assumed the additional surname and arms of Ramsay 1876, and the 3rd baronet, Sir Henry William, C.B., assumed by Roy. Licence the additional surname of Lucy 1892, and of Cameron 1921, having *m.* 1892, Ada Christina, da. and heir of Henry Spencer Lucy, of Charlecote, Warwickshire.

LUSHINGTON, Creation (G.B.) 1791, of South Hill Park, Berkshire.

Sir HENRY EDMUND CASTLEMAN LUSHING-TON, 7th *Baronet; b.* May 2nd, 1909; *s.* his father, *Sir* HERBERT CASTLEMAN, 1968; ed. at Dauntseys Sch., and Birkbeck Coll., London Univ.; late Supt. Metropolitan Police; 1939-45 War as Fl.-Lt RAFVR: *m.* 1937, Pamela Elizabeth Daphne, el. da. of the late Maj. Archer Richard Hunter, of The White Cottage, Rectory Rd., Wokingham, and has issue.

Arms—Or, on a fesse wavy between three lions' heads erased vert, as many ermine spots or. Crest—A lion's head erased vert, charged on the erasure with three ermine spots or, ducally gorged argent.

Residence—Carfax, Crowthorne, Berks.

Fides nudaque veritas.
Faith and naked truth.

Son living—JOHN RICHARD CASTLEMAN (Standen, Longbottom, Seer Green, Bucks.), *b.* Aug. 28th, 1938; ed. at Oundle: *m.* 1966, Bridget Gillian Margaret, da. of Col. John Foster Longfield, of Knockbeg, Saunton, Braunton, Devon, and has issue living, Richard Douglas Longfield, *b.* 1968,—Greville Edmond Longfield, *b.* 1969.
Daughters living—Caroline Elizabeth, *b.* 1942: *m.* 1964, Patrick Donald Bloss, FCA, of 51, Summersbury Drive, Shalford, Guildford, and has issue living, James Patrick, *b.* 1972,—Diana Elizabeth, *b.* 1967,—Victoria Caroline *b.* 1970.——Penelope Daphne, *b.* 1945: *m.* 1967, Ronald Gulliver, LLB, FCA, of Chase End, Long Grove, Seer Green, Bucks., and has issue living, Christopher Ronald, *b.* 1974.
Brothers living—Algernon Herbert Greville (257, Orrong Rd., Armadale, SE3, Victoria, Australia), *b.* 1910; S.-W. Pacific 1944-45 as Capt. Australian Imperial Force (despatches): *n.* 1st, 1948, Mary Elizabeth Gwenyth, who *d.* 1959, da. of C. J. Dunbar, of Dunbarton, Bairnsdale, Victoria, Australia; 2ndly, 1961, Marjory Lorrainé Breheny, da. of C. W. Le Plastrier, of Woodend, Victoria, Australia.——Stephen Arthur Hay, *b.* 1914: *m.* 1941, Joyce, da. of J. Crump, of Melbourne, Australia. *Address*, Gelliondale, South Gippsland, Victoria, Australia.
Half-Brother living—Patrick Hay Castleman (56, Suzanne Av., Morphett Vale, S. Aust.) *b.* 1931; late RAF: *m.* 1957, Ann Marie, el. da. of Ferdinand Mohr, of 37, Neutorstrasse, Mainz, Germany, and has issue living, Kurt, *b.* 1958,—Werner, *b.* 1960,—Horst, *b.* 1966,—Elke, *b.* 1964.
Half-Sister living—Pamela Anne, *b.* 1929: *m.* 1952, Peter Lindsay Jones, of 19, Aberdare Av., Drayton, Cosham, Portsmouth, PO6 2AT, and has issue living, Alistair, *b.* 1953,—Laurence, *b.* 1959,—Martin Edward, *b.* 1964,—Margaret Amanda, *b.* 1955,—Rosemary Anne, *b.* 1957,—Sarah Louise, *b.* 1966.

Collateral Branches living.

Grandson of the late Sydney George Lushington (infra):—
Issue of the late Lt.-Col. Franklin Lushington Lushington, *b.* 1892, *d.* 1964: *m.* 1st, 1916 (marriage dissolved 1948), Mary Marjorie Bridget, da. of Ernest Howard; 2ndly, 1949, Eleanora, who *d.* 1964, da. of Niels Illeris, of Bagsvaerd, Denmark:—
(By 1st m.) Stephen (Bellboys, Northiam, Sussex), *b.* 1917; ed. at Eton, and at New Coll., Oxford; late RA: *m.* 1st, 1941 (m. diss. 1951), Maureen, da. of Maj. John Pook; 2ndly, 1951 (m. diss. 1972), Sonia, da. of Harry Ratoff; 3rdly, 1972, Beatrice, da. of Irvan O'Connell, of Winchester, Va., USA, and widow of Theodore Roethke, and has issue living, (by 1st m.) Mark, *b.* 1942: *m.* 1966, Cora, da. of Sidney Caplon, of Northampton, Mass., USA, and has issue living, Jacob *b.* 1968,—(by 2nd m.) Catherine Rachel, *b.* 1953: *m.* 1975, Richard Marc Greenblatt.

Granddaughter of the late Edward Harbord Lushington, son of the late Rt. Hon. Stephen Lushington, MP, DCL, 2nd son of 1st baronet:—
Issue of the late Sydney George Lushington, *b.* 1859, *d.* 1909: *m.* 1890, Georgina Caroline Elizabeth Chippindall, who *d.* 1900, da. of Capt. Henry Chippindall Healey, of 25, Lorna Road, Hove, Sussex:—
Mary Frances, *b.* 1897: *m.* 1923, John Dudley Lucie-Smith, M.B.E., who *d.* 1943, Assist. Colonial Sec. Jamaica, and has issue living, John Edward McKenzie, *b.* 1933; ed. at King's Sch., Canterbury, and at Merton Coll., Oxford. *Residence*, 24, Sydney St., Chelsea, S.W.3.
This family was settled in E. Kent from the 14th century. Sir Stephen Lushington, 1st baronet, of South Hill Park, Berks (grandon of Stephen Lushington, of Sittingbourne, who purchased the Manor of Rodmersham) was Chm. of Hon. East India Co. 1790.

LYLE, Creation (U.K.) 1929, of Glendelvine, co. Perth.

Sir GAVIN ARCHIBALD LYLE, 3rd *Baronet,* son of the late Capt. Ian Archibald de Hoghton Lyle, Black Watch, el. son of 2nd baronet; *b.* Oct. 14th, 1941; *s.* his grandfather, *Col. Sir* ARCHIBALD MOIR PARK, *MC,* 1946; ed. at Eton: *m.* 1967, Susan, only da. of John Vaughan Cooper, and has issue.

Arms—Gules, fretty or surmounted of a galley, oars in saltire, sails furled sable, flagged gules, the sails charged with a crescent of the second for difference. Crest—A cock or crested gules.
Residence—Glendelvine, Caputh, Perthshire, PH1 4JN.

Sons living—IAN ABRAM, *b.* Sept. 25th, 1968.——Jake Archibald, *b.* 1969,—Matthew Alexander, *b.* 1974.
Daughter living—Rachel, *b.* 1971.
Sister living—Lorna, *b.* 1939: *m.* 1959, Timothy Cyprian George Thomas Elwes, [see B. Rennell].
Uncle living (son of 2nd baronet)—Archibald Michael, *b.* 1919; ed. at Eton, and at Trin Coll., Oxford; Lt.-Col. (ret.) Scottish Horse, and late Maj. Black Watch; a DL and a JP for Perthshire, and a Member of Queen's Body Guard for Scotland (Roy. Co. of Archers); *m.* 1942, the Hon. Elizabeth Sinclair, yr. da. of 1st Viscount Thurso, and has issue living, Veronica, *b.* 1943: *m.* 1967, Magnus Duncan Linklater, of 31, Gibson Sq., N1, and has issue living, Alexander Ragnar, *b.* 1968, Saul Archibald Robert *b.* 1970,—Janet, *b.* 1944: *m.* 1975, Richard Cooper. *Residence*, Riemore Lodge, Dunkeld, Perths.

Aunt living (daughter of 2nd baronet)—Dorothea, *b.* 1914, *m.* 1937, Rear-Adm. Viscount Kelburn, CB, DSC (subsequently 9th Earl of Glasgow) from whom she obtained a divorce 1962. *Residences*, Marwell House, Owlesbury, nr. Winchester, and Albany, Piccadilly, W1.

Mother living—*Hon.* Lydia Yarde-Buller, da. of 3rd Baron Churston : *m.* 1st, 1938, Capt. Ian Archibald de Hoghton Lyle, Black Watch (ante), who *d.* (killed in action during European War) 1942 ; 2ndly, 1947, the 13th Duke of Bedford, from whom she obtained a divorce 1960. *Residence*, Little Ribsden, Windlesham, Bagshot, Surrey.

Sir Alexander Park Lyle, 1st Bt., was a shipowner, and gt.-grandson of Abram Lyle, of Greenock, who founded the firm of Abram Lyle & Sons in 1796 (previously MacDonald & Lyle). The 1st Lord Lyle of Westbourne was a nephew of the 1st Bt.

Lynch-Blosse, see Blosse.

Lynch-Robinson, see Robinson.

McALPINE, Creation (U.K.) 1918, of Knott Park, co. Surrey.

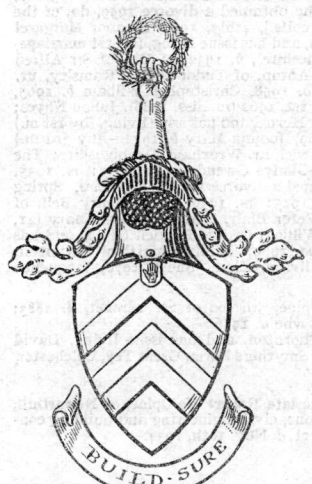

BUILD·SURE

Sir THOMAS GEORGE BISHOP McALPINE, 4th *Baronet*; *b.* Oct. 23rd, 1901; *s.* his cousin, *Sir* (ALFRED) ROBERT, 1968; a Dir. of Sir Robert McAlpine & Sons, Ltd.: *m.* 1st, 1934, Doris Frew, who *d.* 1964, da. of the late D. C. Campbell, of Roseneath, Gosforth, Newcastle-upon-Tyne, and widow of W. E. Woodeson; 2ndly, 1965, Kathleen Mary, da. of the late Frederick Best, and widow of Charles Bantock Blackshaw.

Arms—Per chevron vert and or, two chevronelles one in chief argent the other in base azure. *Crest*—A cubit arm grasping a chaplet of pine fructed all proper.
Residence—The Torrs, Colvend, Dalbeattie, Kirkcudbrightshire.

---

rothers living—*Sir* (ROBERT) EDWIN (Benhams, Fawley Green, nr. Henley-on-Thames), *b.* April 23rd, 1907; a Dir. of Sir Robert McAlpine & Sons, Ltd.; Knt. 1963: *m.* 1930, Ella Mary Gardner, da. of J. G. Garnett, formerly of N. Vancouver, BC, Canada, and has issue living, William Hepburn (Fawley Hill, Fawley Green, Henley-on-Thames), *b.* 1936; a Dir. of Sir Robert McAlpine & Sons Ltd.: *m.* 1959, Jill Benton, only da. of the late Lt.-Col. Sir Peter Fawcett Benton Jones, 3rd Bt., and has issue living, Andrew William *b.* 1960, Lucinda Mary Jane *b.* 1964,—Robert Alistair (West Green House, Hartley Wintney, Hants.), *b.* 1942; a Dir. of Sir Robert McAlpine & Sons Ltd.: *m.* 1964, Sarah Alexandra, da. of the late Paul Hillman Baron, of 72, Bryanston Court, (The Dower House Roydon, E. Peckham, Kent(, *b.* 1946. George St., W1, and has issue living, Mary Jane *b.* 1965, Victoria Alice *b.* 1967,—David Malcolm; a Dir. of Sir Robert McAlpine & Soans Ltd.: *m.* 1971, Jennifer Anne, da. of Eric Hodges, of White Gates, Westfield Farm, Medmenham, Bucks, and has issue living, Katherine Alexandra Donnison *b.* 1972, Elizabeth Louise *b.* 1973,—Patricia Garnett (*Hon. Mrs. Robin S. Borwick*), *b.* 1932: *m.* 1950, the Hon. Robin Sandbach Borwick, Lt. Life Gds. (ret.), of Casa de Rohan, Zebbug, Malta, GC [see B. Borwick].——Malcolm Donnison (The White House, Burton Lazars, Melton Mowbray), *b.* 1909; a Dir. of Sir Robert McAlpine & Sons Ltd.: *m.* 1939, Diana Mary, da. of Sidney Bruce Askew, of Nutfield, Surrey, and has issue living, Ian Malcolm *b.* 1942: *m.* 1967, Caroline Mary, da. of W. H. Ward, of Wisbech, Cambs.,—Bruce Andrew, *b.* 1947,—Susan Mary, *b.* 1945: *m.* 1968, Maxwell Harvey, of Menehay House, Budock, Cornwall.

Sisters living—Agnes Hepburn, *b.* 1903: *m.* 1924, James Henderson Mann, MBE, late Maj. Cameronians (Scottish Rifles), of Terregles, Thicket Corner, Maidenhead, Berks., son of Sir John Mann, KBE, and has issue living, John Michael, *b.* 1930,—Ian Henderson, *b.* 1932,—Margaret Noble, Somerset.——Margaret Elizabeth Henderson (Foxbury, W. Burton Lane, Pulborough, Sussex), *b.* 1905.

Daughters living of 2nd Baronet—Lillias Elizabeth (Naida) (67, Chatsworth Court, Pembroke Rd. W8), *b.* 1900: *m.* 1925, Wing-Cdr. Claude Alward Ridley, DSO, MC, RAF, who *d.* 1942, and has issue living, Robert Louis *b.* 1926: *m.* 1949, Jacqueline, only da. of Charles Bernard, of Paris, and has issue living, Alain Patrick *b.* 1950, Dominique Claudia *b.* 1952,—Elizabeth Lillias, *b.* 1927: *m.* 1952, William John Colin Kitto, of Reef House, Douglas St., Castletown, I. of Man, and has issue living, Nicholas John *b.* 1954, Joanna Elizabeth, *b.* 1957,—Eleanor Jean, *b.* 1933: *m.* 1957, Paul Longmire, of 47, Egerton Cres., SW3, and has issue living, Rupert *b.* 1964, Edward *b.* 1967.——Zelie Agnes Elise Conde, *b.* 1910: *m.* 1934, Surg.-Cdr. Wilfred Treize Rougier Chapman, VD, RNVR, MRCS, LRCP, of Lower Stonehurst Farm, East Grinstead, Sussex, and has issue living, Zeralda Lillias, *b.* 1939: *m.* 1962 (m. diss. 1970), Trevor Adrian Soutry, and has issue living, Giles Robert Adrian, *b.* 1964, Lucinda Caroline *b.* 1969,—Nonie Elizabeth, *b.* 1942,—Penelope Margaret, *b.* 1944: *m.* 1966, David Ronald Adam, of Lower Sandhill House, Halland, nr. Uckfield, Sussex, and has issue living, Angus Ronald *b.* 1969, Annabelle Jane *b.* 1968, Katherine Lucy *b.* 1972.

Uncle living (son of 1st baronet)—Archibald Douglas, MD, FRCP, *b.* 1890; ed. at Cheltenham Coll., and at Glasgow Univ. (MB and ChB 1913, MD 1923); MRCP London 1921; FRCP 1932; Col. and temporary Brig. late RAMC; 1914-18 War as Lt. RAMC and Surg.-Lt. RN (despatches), 1939-45 War (despatches): *m.* 1st, 1917, Elizabeth Meg Sidebottom, who *d.* 1941; 2ndly, 1945, Diana, da. of the late Bertram Plummer, and has issue living, (by 1st m.) Robert Douglas Christopher, CMG (81, Dovehouse St., SW3), *b.* 1919; ed. at Winchester, and New Coll., Oxford (MA); Foreign Office 1946-47, Assist. Private Sec. to Sec. of State 1947-49, Control Commn. for Germany as 2nd, and later 1st Sec. 1949-52; Foreign Office 1952-54, British Embassy, Lima 1954-56, and Moscow 1956-59, Foreign Office 1959-62, Dep. Consul-Gen., New York 1962-64, and

Counsellor, British Embassy, Mexico City 1965-68; a Dir. of Baring Bros. & Co., Ltd.; 1939-45 War as Lt.-Cdr. RNVR (Fleet Air Arm) (CMG 1967): *m.* 1943, Helen, da. of the late Capt. Astley Cannan, and has issue living David Douglas Christopher *b.* 1949, Robert John *b.* 1953, Sarah Margaret *b.* 1946,—(by 2nd m.) Alastair Bertram,   1945: *m.* 1968 (m. diss. 1973), Ann, da. of Maj. Bernard Winchester,—(by 1st m.) Florence Mary, *b.* 1922; formerly 3rd Officer WRNS: *m.* 1952, Peter Alexander MacDonell, of Rose Court, Fortrose, Ross-shire, and has issue living, Charlotte Anne *b.* 1954, Maria Christian *b.* 1958. *Residence*, Lovells Mill, Marnhull, Dorset.

Collateral Branches living.

Issue of the late Sir (Thomas) Malcolm McAlpine, KBE, 3rd son of 1st baronet, *b.* 1877, *d.* 1967: *m.* 1903, Maud, who *d.* 1969, da. of James Gibson Dees:—
Sir Robin, CBE, (Aylesfield, Alton, Hants.), *b.* 1906; assumed by deed poll 1939, the christian name of Robin in lieu of Robert; Chm. of Sir Robert McAlpine & Sons, Ltd. and Newarthill, Ltd.; Pres. Fedn. of Civil Engineering Contractors 1966-71; CBE (Civil) 1957, Knt. 1969: *m.* 1st, 1939, Nora Constance, who *d.* 1966, da. of F. H. Perse; 2ndly, 1970, Mrs. Philippa Janet Nicolson, da. of Sir (Eustace) Gervais Tennyson d'Eyncourt, 2nd Bt.——Malcolm Hugh Dees (Highfields, Withyham, Hartfield, Sussex), *b.* 1917; late Lt.-Col. RE; a Dir. of Sir Robert McAlpine & Sons Ltd.: *m.* 1944, Sheila Margaret, el. da. of the late Maj. F. Raeburn Price, of Fordyce, N. Foreland, Thanet, and has issue living, Adrian Neil Raeburn, *b.* 1944,—Cullum (Malcolm Robert), *b.* 1947: *m.* 1973, Amanda Lamdin—Hamish, *b.* 1954.——Kenneth (The Priory, Lamberhurst, Kent), *b.* 1920; late F/O RAFVR; High Sheriff of Kent 1973-74; a Dir. of Sir Robert McAlpine & Sons Ltd.: *m.* 1955, Patricia Mary, da. of the late Capt. Francis William Hugh Jeans, CVO, RN, and has issue living, Richard Hugh, *b.* 1958,—James Thomas Hemery, *b.* 1960.

Issue of the late Sir Alfred (David) McAlpine, 4th son of 1st baronet, *b.* 1881, *d.* 1944: *m.* 1907, Ethel May, who *d.* 1962, da. of the late James Williams, of Aboyne, Aberdeenshire:—
Alfred James, *b.* 1908 ; is Chm. of Sir Alfred McAlpine & Son Ltd. : *m.* 1st, 1931, Peggy Barbara (who obtained a divorce 1940), da. of the late John Ernest Sanders, of Gresford, Denbighshire ; 2ndly, 1940, Mary Kinder (who obtained a divorce 1951), da. of Frank Musgrave Read ; 3rdly, 1951 (marriage dissolved 1959), Rosemary (LAVERY), who obtained a divorce 1959, da. of the late Major Charles Hugh Gregory-Hood [*see* V. Hood, colls.], 4thly, 1959, Eleanor Margaret Rangel, da. of the late John Nicholson Wallace, of Lisbon, and has issue living, (by 1st marriage) Robert James (Lower Carden Hall, Tilston, Malpas, Cheshire), *b.* 1932; a Dir. of Sir Alfred McAlpine & Son Ltd.: *m.* 1956, Jane, el. da. of James Anton, of Tudor House, Rumsley, nr. Bridgnorth, Salop, and has issue living, Euan James *b.* 1958, Christopher William *b.* 1965, Sara Jane *b.* 1961,—(by 2nd m.) Valerie Ann, *b.* 1942: *m.* 1st, 1962 (m. diss. 1966), Julian Noyes; 2ndly, 1967, Peter Shaw, of Barley End, Aldbury, Tring, Herts., and has issue living, (by 1st m.) William *b.* 1963, (by 2nd m.) Samantha Margaret *b.* 1969, Joanna Mary *b.* 1972.—(by 3rd m.) Sally Dorothy, *b.* 1952. *Residences*, Gerwyn Hall, Marchwiel, nr. Wrexham, Denbighshire; The Towers, Llanarmon, Dyffryn Ceiriog, Denbighshire.——Gladys Gwendolen, *b.* 1911: *m.* 1935, Charles Phipps Brutton, CBE, who *d.* 1964, having obtained a divorce 1943. *Residence*, Spring Hill, Compton, Abdale, Gloucester.——Ethel Mary, *b.* 1915: *m.* 1939, Peter Henry Bell, of Marchwiel Hall, Wrexham, and has issue living, John Peter Blair, *b.* 1950,—Susan Mary (41, Ovington Sq., SW3), *b.* 1940: *m.* 1960 (m. diss. 1968), William George Rendell Gibbs, and has issue living, Camilla Josephine *b.* 1962,—Jane, *b.* 1943: *m.* 1969, William Matthew Patterson, of Oakfield Park, Raphoe, co. Donegal, and has issue living, Kiera Jane *b.* 1970, Jacqueline Christina Mary *b.* 1971.

Issue of the late Granville Ramage McAlpine, 5th son of 1st baronet, *b.* 1883; *d.* 1928: *m.* 1922, Beatrice Mary Donald, who *d.* 1936:—
Maureen Agnes, *b.* 1925 : *m.* 1949, Frederick Stanley Thornton, and has issue living, David Malcolm, *b.* 1950,—Andrew William, *b.* 1953. *Residence*, Smythers Farm, Great Tey, Colchester, Essex.

The 1st baronet, Sir Robert McAlpine, J.P. (son of the late Robert McAlpine, of Newarthill, Lanarks.), founded the firm of Sir Robert McAlpine & Sons, civil engineering and building contractors, and *d.* Nov. 3rd, 1934. The 2nd baronet, Sir Robert, *d.* Nov. 16th, 1934.

MACARA, Creation (U.K.) 1911, of Ardmore, St. Anne-on-the-Sea, co. Lancaster.

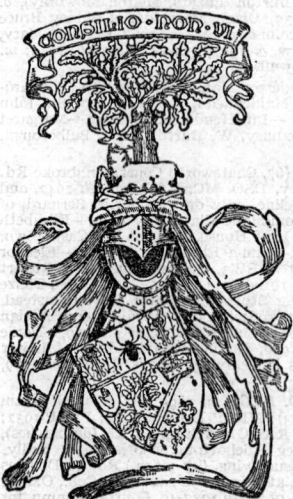

By wisdom not by might.

Sir (CHARLES) DOUGLAS MACARA, 3rd Baronet ; *b.* April 19th, 1904 ; *s.* his father, *Sir* WILLIAM COWPAR, 1931 ; ed. at Fettes : *m.* 1926, Quenilda Mary (who obtained a divorce 1945), da. of the late Herbert Whitworth, of St. Anne's-on-Sea, and has issue.

Arms—Ermine, an oak tree eradicated in bend dexter, surmounted by a sword proper, hilted and pommelled or, in bend sinister, supporting on its point an Imperial Crown of the second, on a chief of the third, a spider sable between two thistles also proper. Crest—A stag reguardant lodged in front of an oak tree proper.

Residence—9, Queen's Parade, Cheltenham.

Daughters living—Pamela Alison, *b.* 1927 : *m.* 1954, John Gordon Raymond Romer, and has issue living, Charles John, *b.* 1958.—Gordon Clive, *b.* 1960,—Gillian Avril, *b.* 1955.—Susan Claire, *b.* 1970. *Residence*, 22, Cranston Grove, Gatley, Ches.——Quenilda Jennifer, *b.* 1929: *m.* 1954, Peter Graham Dobson, and has issue living, Trevor William, *b.* 1957,—John Keith, *b.* 1963,—Susan Jane, *b.* 1954,—Valerie, *b.* 1956,—Kay Elizabeth, *b.* 1960. *Residence*, 35, Banbury Park, Torquay.

Brothers living—JOHN KEITH, *b.* Oct. 29th, 1905 : *m.* 1948, Joan Florence Mary (BENNETT), who *d.* 1956, da. of the late Oswald Francis Gerald Stonor, C.M.G. [*see* B. Camoys, colls.]. *Residence*, Flat 10, Cliff Castle, Seaton, Devon.——William Donald, *b.* 1909: *m.* 1939, Rosalind Verena, who *d.* 1973, da. of the late Frederick Harrild, of Clare Bank, Sevenoaks, Kent. *Residence*, Mallards, Prideaux Rd., Eastbourne.——Hugh Kenneth, *b.* 1913.

Sisters living—Aileen Lillah, *b.* 1908.——Margaret Alison, *b.* 1912 : *m.* 1933, Rogers Edwards who *d.* 1955, and has issue living, Roger Macara, *b.* 1934,—Beverly Alison, *b.* 1935,—Lillah Cherry, *b.* 1942. *Residence*, Flat 9, Cliff Castle, Seaton, Devon.

The 1st baronet, Sir Charles Wright Macara (son of the Rev. William Macara, Min. of Free Church, Strathmiglo, Fife), was Chm. of Henry Bannerman & Sons, Ltd.

MACARTNEY, Creation (I.) 1799, of Lish, Armagh.

It stimulates, but it adorns.

Sir JOHN BARRINGTON MACARTNEY, 6th *Baronet*, el. son of the late John Barrington Macartney, 3rd son of 3rd baronet ; *b.* 1917 ; *s.* his uncle, *Sir* ALEXANDER MILLER, 1960 ; is a Dairy Farmer : *m.* 1944, Amy Isobel Reinke, and has issue.

Arms—Or, a stag trippant, within a bordure gules. **Crest**—A hand holding a slip of a rose tree with three roses thereon all proper.

Residence—37, Meadow St., N. Mackay, Queensland.

Son living—JOHN RALPH (189, St. Anne St., Nowra 2540, NSW), *b.* 1945; RAN : *m.* 1966, Suzanne Marie Fowler, of Nowra, NSW, and has issue living, Donna Maree, *b.* 1968.
Sisters living—Evelyn Catherine, *b.* 1910: *m.* 1931, Albert Edward Ellwood, of 23, Milne Lane, W. Mackay, Qld. 4740, and has issue living, Alan John (4740, Gargett via Mackay, Qld.), *b.* 1935: *m.* 1963, Hester. da. of H. Lewis, of Mackay, Qld., and has issue living, Derek John *b.* 1968, Charmaine Mary *b.* 1964, Dianne Lucy *b.* 1966,—Edward Graham (11, Neumeyer St., Page, Canberra, ACT 2611), *b.* 1945: *m.* 19—, Helen Mary, da. of Thomas Chadwick of Dalby, Qld.,— Audrey Philome, *b.* 1932: *m.* 1952, Noel Nathaniel Perry, of Matcham, Gracemere, via Rockhampton, Qld. 4702, and has issue living, Gregory John *b.* 1957, Christine Anne *b.* 1953, Janette Patricia *b.* 1955, Judith Marie *b.* 1956, Kathleen Ellen *b.* 1959,— Marie Claire, *b.* 1934: *m.* 1956, Franciscao Antonius Brieffres, of 4740, Kuhabul, via Mackay, Qld., and has issue living, Frank John *b.* 1957, Peter Eugene *b.* 1961, Anthony John *b.* 1964, Lynette *b.* 1958, Trudy Bernadette *b.* 1959, Melita Maree *b.* 1963, Yvonne *b.* 1966.——Constance, *b.* 1911: *m.* 1939, Stanley Dan Desbois, 352, Mail Service, Mackay, Qld., and has issue living, Kevin, *b.* 1941: *m.* 1966, Janet Elizabeth Gordon, of Mackay, Qld., and has issue living, Michelle Maree *b.* 1968, Andrea Jane *b.* 1969,—Clive John, *b.* 1948.

Collateral Branches living.

Issue of the late Herbert Charles Macartney, 4th son of 3rd baronet, *b.* 1876, *d.* 1953 : *m.* 1913, Frances, da. of Mountiford Tooker, of Yeppoon, Queensland :—
Patricia Catherine, *b.* 1917: *m.* 1941, Leslie John Campbell, of Inverness, Calliope, Gladstone, Qld., and has issue living, Alan Leslie John Macartney, *b.* 1952,—Diana Ruby, *b.* 1942,—Rosemary Frances, *b.* 1945,—Ailsa Catherine, *b.* 1947.——Frances Evelyn, *b.* 1924: *m.* 1953, John Smith. *Residence*, Brisbane, Qld.
Issue of the late David Edwin Macartney, 6th son of 3rd baronet, *b.* 1880, *d.* 1957 : *m.* 1st, 1912, Flora Gordon, who *d.* 1914, da. of R. K. Ogg, of Rockhampton, Queensland; 2ndly, 1920, Ella Margaret (Palm Lodge, 424, Bowen Terr., New Farm, Brisbane, Qld. 4005), da. of Daniel Craig, of Longreach, Qld. :—
(By 2nd m.) Alexander Macdonald, *b.* 1921; formerly Flight-Lt. RAAF: *m.* 1959, Penelope, da. of C. B. Freeman, of Brisbane, Qld., and has issue living, John Alexander, *b.* 1961,—Deborah Anne, *b.* 1963.——David Edwin *b.* 1924; formerly in R. Austn. Navy: *m.* 1948, Elizabeth Lillias, da. of L. Ewert, of Rotorua, NZ, and has issue living, David, *b.* 1951,—Anthony Craig, *b.* 1956,—Diane, *b.* 1952.——John Craig (Benson Rd., Mount Nebo, Qld 4529) *b.* 1927; formerly in AIF: *m.* 1951, Betty, da. of Dr. Leckie, of Ingham, Qld., and has issue living, Paul Alexander *b.* 1955,—Belinda Lee, *b.* 1952.——Wallace Herbert, (49, Nevin St., Aspley, Brisbane, Qld. 4034), *b.* 1929: *m.* 1973, Judith Anne, da. of K. W. Addison, of Brisbane.——Margaret Miller, *b.* 1923: *m.* 1949, Capt. David Horton, Austn. Nat. Airways, of 19, Millins St., Edge Hill, Cairns, N. Qld., and has issue living, John Macartney, *b.* 1951,—Peter Coulter, *b.* 1955.——Jason Craig, *b.* 1926.——Catherine Ella, *b.* 1962: *m.* 1962, Donald Grayling, RN, of 13, Cliff Av., Winston Hills, Sydney, NSW 1253, and has issue living, Donald David, *b.* 1968,—Fiona Ella, *b.* 1964.
Issue of the late Victor Alan Macartney, yst. son of 3rd baronet, *b.* 1887, *d.* 1969: *m.* 1915, Elsie Maria, da. of the late Robert McKie, of Brisbane:—
Harold Kenneth (Marama, Ourimbah, NSW), *b.* 1919; Singapore 1941 with AIF (prisoner): *m.* 1951, Beatrice, da. of Henry Apsley Carlyle Lowe, of Burling, Terrigall, NSW, and has issue living, William John, *b.* 1959,—Diana Eileen, *b.* 1955.——Elinor Macartney, *b.* 1917: late Sister Austn. Army Nursing Ser.; Middle East 1940-41: *m.* 1942, Maj. Francis Stephen Small, AIF, of Royston Park, Ourimbah, NSW, and has issue living, Roderick Cameron Macartney, *b.* 1943,—Robert Francis, *b.* 1949,—Rosemary Elinor, *b.* 1945,—Margaret Anne (twin), *b.* 1949.

Issue of the late William George Macartney, 2nd son of 2nd baronet, *b.* 1835, *d.* 188– : *m.* 1872, Bessie, da. of the late Robert Bayley Tyser, of Wellington, New Zealand :—
Ernest George, *b.* 1880.——**Eileen Agnes.** *Residence*,

Granddaughter of the late Very Rev. Hussey Burgh Macartney, yr. son of 1st baronet:—
Issue of the late Edward Hardman Macartney, *b.* 1835, *d.* 1903 : *m.* 1862, Georgiana Henrietta, who *d.* 1923, da. of the late James Moore, of Kew, Melbourne :—
Charlotte Mary, *b.* 1889.

Grandchildren of the late Edward Hardman Macartney (ante):—
Issue of the late Edward Hussey Burgh Macartney, *b.* 1867, *d.* 1930: *m.* 1st, 1904, Jane Alexandra, who *d.* 1909, da. of Alexander Richardson McNab; 2ndly, 1910, Constance May, who *d.* 1960, da. of Edward Griffith, :—

(By 2nd m.) James Edward, b. 1911.——John Hussey Burgh (7, Tutus St., Balgowlah, NSW 2093), b. 1915; Lt.-Cdr. RAN (ret.): m. 1945, Geraldine, da. of Eli Leach, of Darwen, England, and has issue living, Francesca May, b. 1948; BA, LLB, Sydney.——(By 1st m.) Jean Marion Isobel, b. 1908: m. 1954, William Balston, who d. 1960.——(By 2nd m.) Catherine Frances, b. 1913: m. 1933, A. N. Magnus.——Constance Eleanor, b. 1922: m. 1950, David Rowley.

Issue of the late Charles Perry Macartney, b. 1880, d. 1947: m. 1912, Daphne Violet, da. of Henry King:—

Violet Moore, b. 1914. *Residence*, 33, Proctors Road, Dynnyrne, Hobart, Tasmania.——Nancy Gower, b. 1920: m. 1958, Leonard J. Basterfield, of 503, Balcombe Rd., Beaumaris, Melbourne, Vic., Aust., and has issue living, Josephine Nancy, b. 1960.——Elizabeth Catherine, b. 1923: m. 1945, Frederick J. Byrne, and has issue living, Frederick Michael, b. 1946,—Damien Charles, b. 1947,—Anthony Gerard, b. 1962,—Paul Leonard Dominic, b. 1966,—Catherine Anne, b. 1949: m. 1972, Geoffrey Francis Taylor, and has issue living, Gabriel Francis b. 1973, Simone Elizabeth b. 1974,—Margaret Louise, b. 1957. *Residence*, 48, York St., Bellerive, Hobart, Tasmania.

The 1st baronet, Sir John, MP (yr. son of William Macartney of Lish, co. Armagh, MP for Belfast), prior to his being created a baronet, received knighthood for his services in promoting inland navigation in Ireland.

McCONNELL, Creation (U.K.) 1900, of The Moat, Strandtown, Belfast.

A conqueror amidst difficulties.

VICTOR IN ARDUIS

Sir ROBERT MELVILLE TERENCE McCONNELL, *V.R.D.*, 3rd *Baronet; b.* Feb. 7th, 1902 ; *s.* his father, *Sir* JOSEPH, *D.L.*, *M.P.*, 1942 ; ed. at Glenalmond, and St. John's Coll., Camb.; Cdr. RNVR (ret.): *m.* 1st, 1928 (m. diss. 1954), Rosamond Mary Elizabeth, da. of the late James Stewart Reade, JP, of Clonmore, Lisburn, co. Antrim; 2ndly, 1967, Mrs. Alice A. M. Hillis, and has issue by 1st marriage.

Arms—Per pale azure and gules, to the dexter a ship in full sail proper, to the sinister an arm embowed and couped at the shoulder argent, the hand grasping a trefoil slipped vert, on a chief of the fourth, three stags' heads cabossed sable. *Crest*—A stag's head erased azure attired and charged on the neck with a bee volant or.

Residence—Quoilequay, Downpatrick, co. Down.

Sons living—By 1st marriage—ROBERT SHEAN, *b.* Nov. 23rd, 1930; ed. at Stowe, at Queens' Coll., Camb., and at British Columbia Univ.——James Angus, *b.* 1933; ed. at Stowe: *m.* 1957, Elizabeth Jillian, da. of the late Derek Harris, of Sydenham, Belfast, and has issue living, Terence Reade, *b.* 1959,—Edmund Fraser, *b.* 1961,—Joanne Christina, *b.* 1958,—Victoria Wylie, *b.* 1965,—Emma-Jane Wylie, (twin), *b.* 1965,—Alison Clare, *b.* 1967. *Residence*, Rory's Glen, Knocknagoney, Holywood, co. Down.——William Donn (The Stables, The Moat, Old Holywood Rd., Strandtown, Belfast), *b.* 1938; ed. at Stowe: *m.* 1963, Daphne Elisabeth, da. of Robert Simms, of Bangor, co. Down, and has issue living, Robert Randal, *b.* 1966,—Stewart Neale, *b.* 1972.

Daughter living—By 1st m.—Elisabeth Moyne, *b.* 1935: *m.* 1958, Robert Henry Cooke Jurn Ramsay (Ardreagh, Marino, Holywood, co. Down), and has issue living, Richard Patrick James, *b.* 1960,—Magnus Robert Neale, *b.* 1967,—Roslyn Moyne Elisabeth, *b.* 1962.

Brother living—(Jackson) Desmond, *b.* 1912 ; late Lieut. R.N.V.R. : *m.* 1948, Honor Muriel, da. of Robert Henry Cooke Ramsay, of The Moat, Old Holywood Road, Belfast, and widow of Squadron Leader Richard Ashton Shuttleworth, R.A.F., and has issue living, Rory Desmond Ramsay, *b.* 1957,—Kathryn Fiona, *b.* 1948: *m.* 1970, Maj. Anthony Randall, and has issue living, Sophia *b.* 19—. *Residence*, Galleon's Lap, Craigavad, co. Down.

Sister living—Josephine Patricia, *b.* 1908 : *m.* 1930, John Dermot Campbell, D.L., M.P., who *d.* (presumed killed in missing aircraft on mission to Italy) 1945, and has issue living, Godfrey Garrett, *b.* 1934,—Colin Walter Joseph, *b.* 1939,—Lisa Alice Frieda, *b.* 1931: *m.* 1956, Wing-Cdr. Peter H. T. Lewis, MBE. *Residence*, 22, Castlehill Rd., Belfast.

Collateral Branch living
Issue of the late Alfred Edward McConnell, 2nd son of 1st baronet, *b.* 1880, *d.* 1963: *m.* 1919, Emma (Yvonne) Dougal, who *d.* 1957:—

Rt. Hon. Robert William Brian (Aughnahough, Lisburn, co. Antrim), *b.* 1922; ed. at Sedbergh, and at Queen's Univ., Belfast (B.A., LL.B.); Bar. N. Ireland 1948; Dep. Chm. of Ways and Means, N. Ireland Parliament 1962-63, Parl. Sec. Min. of Health and Local Government 1963-64, and Min. of Home Affairs 1964-66, and Min. of State, Min. of Development 1966-67, and Leader of House of Commons NI 1967-68; MP for S. Antrim, NI Parliament (*U*) 1951-68; Pres. of Industrial Court NI since 1968; PC N. Ireland 1964: *m.* 1951, Sylvia Elisabeth Joyce, da. of the late Samuel Agnew, of Belfast, and has issue living, Richard Alfred, *b.* 1955,—Samuel James, *b.* 1958,—Helen Elizabeth, *b.* 1964.

The first baronet, Sir Robert John McConnell (son of Joseph McConnell, of Clougher, co. Antrim), was Lord Mayor of Belfast 1900, and the 2nd baronet, Sir Joseph, was M.P. for Antrim Co. (*U*) May 1929 to Aug. 1942.

McCOWAN, Creation (U.K.) 1934, of Dalwhat, co. Dumfries.

We press forward to heaven.

Sir HEW CARGILL McCOWAN, 3rd *Baronet;* b. July 26th, 1930; s. his father, *Sir* DAVID JAMES CARGILL, 1965.

Arms—Argent, a saltire between four anchors sable roped or. **Crest**—An eagle rising proper.

Residence—Auchenheglish, Alexandria, Dunbartonshire.

Brother living—DAVID WILLIAM CARGILL, *b.* Feb. 28th, 1934.

Aunt living (daughter of 1st Baronet)—Margaret Elisabeth, *b.* 1894: *m.* 1931, Alexander Osborne Bonnar. *Residence,* 1, Walker St., Edinburgh, 3.

Widow living of 2nd Baronet—MURIEL EMMA ANNIE (*Lady McCowan*) (Auchenheglish, Alexandria, Dunbartonshire), da. of William Charles Willmott, of Deal: *m.* 1928, Sir David James Cargill McCowan, 2nd baronet, who *d.* 1965.

The 1st Baronet, Sir David McCowan (son of Hew McCowan, of Ayr), was a Senior Partner in the firm of William Euing & Co., marine insurance brokers, of 8, Royal Exchange Buildings, Glasgow, and Hon. Pres. of Scottish Unionist Assocn.

McCULLAGH, Creation (U.K.) 1955, of Lismara, Parish of Carnmoney, co. Antrim.
[Extinct 1974]

Sir JOSEPH CRAWFORD McCULLAGH, 2nd and last *Baronet.*

Widow living of 2nd Baronet—ELIZABETH (*Lady McCullagh*), (Lismara, Shore Rd., Newtownabbey, co. Antrim), da. of James Copeland: *m.* 1937, Sir Joseph Crawford McCullagh, 2nd Bt., who *d.* 1974, when the title became ext.

BOSVILLE MACDONALD, Creation (N.S.) 1625, of Sleat, Isle of Skye.

By sea and land. Virtue for its own sake.

Sir IAN GODFREY BOSVILLE MACDONALD OF SLEAT, 17th *Baronet* and 25th *Chief of Sleat*; *b.* July 18th, 1947; *s.* his father, *Sir* (ALEXANDER) SOMERLED ANGUS, *MC,* 1958: *m.* 1970, Juliet Fleury, only da. of Maj.-Gen. John Ward-Harrison, of Hazel Bush House, Malton Rd., York, and has issue.

Arms (as recorded at Lyon Office)—Quarterly, 1st and 4th grand quarters counterquartered, 1st argent, a lion rampant gules, armed and langued azure, 2nd or, a hand in armour fessewise proper, holding a cross-crosslet fitchée gules, 3rd argent a lymphad, sails furled and oars in action sable, flagged gules, and 4th vert a salmon naiant in fesse proper, *Macdonald;* 2nd and 3rd grand quarters, argent, five lozenges conjoined in fesse gules and in chief three bears' heads erased at the neck sable, muzzled or, a canton, ermine, *Bosville.* **Crests**—1st, a hand in armour fessewise, holding a cross-crosslet fitchée gules, *Macdonald;* 2nd, a bull passant argent, armed or, issuing from a hurst of oaks, charged on the shoulder with a rose proper, *Bosville.* **Supporters**—Two leopards proper, collared or.

Seat—Thorpe Hall, Rudston, Driffield, Yorks.

Daughter living—DEBORAH FLEURY, *b.* 1973.
Brother living—JAMES ALEXANDER, *b.* April 11th, 1949; ed. at Ardingly.
Sisters living—Janet Elizabeth, *b.* 1950.——Annabel Celia Dorothy, *b.* 1953.

Uncle living (son of 15th baronet)—Nigel Donald Peter CHAMBERLAYNE-MACDONALD, M.V.O., b. 1927; Maj. (ret.) late Scots Guards; a Member of the Queen's Body Guard for Scotland (Roy. Co. of Archers); Equerry to H.R.H. the Duke of Gloucester 1954-55, and again 1958-60, and Assist. Private Sec. to H.R.H. the Duke of Gloucester 1958-60; Extra Equerry to H.R.H. the Duke of Gloucester since 1964; High Sheriff of Hants. 1974; OStJ; assumed by deed poll 1958 the surname of Chamberlayne before his patronymic; Chm. of Hants and I. of Wight Assocn. of Boys' Clubs, and a Vice-Chm. of Nat. Assocn. of Boys' Clubs; MVO (4th class) 1960: m. 1958, Penelope Mary Alexandra, only child of the late Tankerville Chamberlayne, of Cranbury Park, Hants, and has issue living, Alexander Nigel Bosville, b. 1959,—Thomas Somerled, b. 1969,— Diana Mary, b. 1961,—Frances Penelope, b. 1965. Residences, Cranbury Park, Winchester; 17, William Mews, Lowndes Sq., SW1.

Aunts living (daughters of 15th baronet)—Jean Alice, b. 1919 : m. 1952, Lieut.-Col. Basil John Ringrose, DSO, TD, of Morton House, Swinderby, Lincoln.——Angela Daphne Rachel, b. 1923: m. 1957, James Michael Gardner Fell, and has issue living, Peter James, b. 1960,—Rachel Mary, b. 1959. Address, University of Pennsylvania, Philadelphia, USA.

Widows living of 15th and 16th Baronets—Hon. RACHEL AUDREY CAMPBELL (Hon. Lady Bosville Macdonald of Sleat), da. of 1st Baron Colgrain : m. 1917, Sir Godfrey Middleton Bosville Macdonald of Sleat, MBE, 15th baronet, who d. 1951. Residence, Eden Croft, Stick Hill, Edenbridge, Kent.——MARY ELIZABETH, (Lady Bosville Macdonald of Sleat), da. of the late Lt.-Col. Ralph Crawley-Boevey Gibbs: m. 1946, Sir (Alexander) Somerled Angus Bosville Macdonald of Sleat, MC, 16th baronet, who d. 1958. Residence, Thorpe Hall, Rudston, Driffield, Yorkshire.

Collateral Branches living.

Descendants of Godfrey William Wentworth Macdonald, 4th Baron Macdonald, 3rd (but el. born after the English marriage of his parents) son of the late Godfrey Macdonald, 3rd Baron Macdonald and 11th baronet [see B. Macdonald].

Descendants of the late Donald Macdonald 1st of Castleton, 2nd son of of 1st baronet :—

Grandson of the late James Alexander Macdonald, 9th of Castleton, el. son of the late James Macdonald, 8th of Castleton, 6th in descent from Donald Macdonald (ante) :—

Issue of the late Rev. James Alexander Donald John Macdonald, 10th of Castleton, b. 1855, d. 1947: m. 1887, Harriet Emma Corderoy, who d. 1932 :—
Donald John, 12th of Castleton, b. 1897: m. 1932, Cecilie Frances Jess, da. of Ernest George Evan-Williams, of Johannesburg, and adopted da. of Maj. James Alexander Macdonald, DSO, MC and has issue living, Ranald Alasdair (5, Halford Rd., Richmond, Surrey), b. 1937; late Cameron Highlanders: m. 1964, Eleanor Russell, of London, and has issue living, Shona b. 1965, —Cecilie Ruth Faith, b. 1933,—Catherine Stella, b. 1941: m. 1962, Graham R. Harvey, of Ferndale, Forres, Morayshire, and has issue living, David Ranald Macdonald b. 1965, Dawn Caroline b. 1968, Louise Robertson b. 1969,—Frances Ruth, b. 1944: m. 1968, Austin Bankhead, of The Square, Duncraig Castle, Plockton, Ross-shire, and has issue living, Jamie Macdonald b. 1969, Patrick Augustine b. 1971. Residence, 2, Boswall Rd., Edinburgh, 5.

Grandson of the late Edward William Johnstone Macdonald (infra):—
Issue of the late Roderick Norman Douglas Macdonald, b. 1886, d. 1971: m. 1912, Eleanor Davison, of Toronto, who d. 1969:—
Alexander Douglas (RR1 Box 166, Charlotte Lake, Ontario), b. 1923: m. 1941, Gertrude Noreen Davis, of Toronto, and has issue living, Geoffrey Alex, b. 1952,—Pamela, b. 1948.

Granddaughter of the late James Alexander Macdonald, 9th of Castleton (ante):—
Issue of the late Edward William Johnstone Macdonald, b. 1858, d. 1931 : m. 1884, Emily Hurst, who d. 1958 :—
Marjorie Johnstone, b. 1895: m. 1932, Augustus Frederick Weiss, and has issue living, Marjorie Eileen, b. 1933: m. 1957, John Ross Crumplin, of 25, Plough Lane, Purley, Surrey, and has issue living, Timothy John Ross b. 1958, Nicholas Macdonald b. 1961, Russell Iain b. 1966,—Pamela Jean, b. 1935: m. 1960, Dr. John Cyril Oakley, of Greyfriars, 95, Old Road East, Gravesend, Kent, and has issue living, Julian Richard b. 1964, Karen Pamela b. 1961,—Alison Macdonald, b. 1939. Residence, 30, The Pines, St. James' Rd., Purley, Sussex.

Grandsons of the late Inspector-Gen. Sir John Denis Macdonald, KCB, MD, FRS, 3rd son of the late James Macdonald, 8th of Castleton (ante):—
Issue of the late Capt. John Denis Macdonald, Roy. Canadian Veterinary Corps, b. 1873, d. 1940 : m. 1908, Minnie Gunter :—
Geoffrey John Gunter, b. 1910 : m. 1939, Muriel Eleanor Tingle, and has issue living, Michael Douglas, b. 1940,—Heather Margaret, b. 1942,—Janet Elizabeth, b. 1947.——James Edward Somerled, b. 1912.——Ewen Reginald, b. 1915 ; European War 1939-45 with Gordon Highlanders: m. 19—, Elsie Glanville, and has issue living, Angus John, b. 1943,—Alison Celia, b. 1947. Residence,
Issue of the late William Richard Macdonald, b. 1876, d. 1950 : m. 1st, Olive —— ; 2ndly, 19—, Erina Archer :—
(By 2nd marriage) Richard John, b. 1940. Residence,

This Baronetcy was created with remainder to heirs male whatsoever and a special clause of precedency, placing it (at the time of its creation) second of that order in Scotland—now it is the premier existing Nova Scotia Baronetcy. In 1776, Sir Alexander Macdonald, 9th Bt., was created Baron Macdonald, of Slate, co. Antrim (peerage of Ireland). Godfrey Macdonald (afterwards 3rd Baron and 11th Baronet) assumed by Roy. licence 1814, on inheriting the estates of Bosville of Thorpe and Gunthwaite, the surname of Bosville in lieu of his patronymic. On succession to the titles in 1824 he resumed the surname of Macdonald after that of Bosville. He died in 1832, having m. (in an English Church) Dec. 15th, 1803, Louisa Maria La Coast, da. of H.R.H. Prince William Frederick, 2nd Duke of Gloucester by Lady Almeria Carpenter, and ward of Farley Edsir, the validity of a Scottish marriage said to have taken place with the same lady in 1799 having been disputed ; he was s. in the Irish peerage by his son Godfrey William Wentworth, born after the date of the English marriage, but according to a decree of the Court of Session in June 1910, the father being domiciled in Scotland, that marriage legitimated according to the law of Scotland, Alexander William Robert Macdonald, b. Sept. 12th, 1800, prior to the date of the English marriage, who had s. to the Thorpe and Gunthwaite estates, and to whom therefore the Nova Scotia baronetcy of 1625 passed de jure. On entering into possession of the Bosville estates in 1832 he assumed by Roy. licence the surname of Bosville in lieu of Macdonald. His grandson, Alexander Wentworth Macdonald Bosville, thus became 14th Baronet in 1910, and resumed the family surname of Macdonald after that of Bosville (recognised by Court of Lord Lyon 1910). The present baronet is heir-male and representative of Sir Donald Macdonald, 1st Bt. (descended from Hugh Macdonald, first of Sleat, a son of Alexander, Lord of the Isles, Earl of Ross, by a da. of Gillepatrick Roy), and representative of the family of Macdonald of Sleat, in the Island of Skye.

McEWEN, Creation (U.K.) 1953, of Marchmont, co. Berwick, and Bardrochat, co. Ayr.

REVIRESCO

Dieu Premier Servi.

Sir ROBERT LINDLEY MCEWEN, 3rd *Baronet*; b. June 23rd, 1926; s. his brother, Sir JAMES NAPIER FINNIE, 1971; ed. at Eton (KS), and Trin. Coll., Camb.; Bar. Inner Temple 1951; late Gren. Gds.; Sublector of Trin. Coll., Camb. 1953-55, an Hon. Sheriff of Roxburghe, Berwick and Selkirk 1971: m. 1954, Brigid Cecilia, da. of James Laver, CBE, and has issue.

Arms—Quarterly: 1st and 4th, or, a lion rampant azure, gorged with a ducal crown proper, on a chief of the second three garbs of the field, *McEwen*; 2nd and 3rd, gules, three headless cranes argent, *Finnie*. *Crest*—The trunk of an oak tree sprouting proper.

Residence—Marchmont, Greenlaw, Berwickshire. *Club*, Brooks's.

Sons living—JAMES FRANCIS LINDLEY, b. Aug. 24th, 1960.—— John Roderick Hugh, b. 1965.
Daughters living—Mary Christian, b. 1956.——Catherine Veronica b. 1958.——Helena Mary Elizabeth, b. 1961.——Isabella Gabriel Anne, b. 1968.
Daughters living of 2nd Baronet—Margaret, b. 1959,—Mary, b. 1963,—Christina, b. 1964.

Brothers living—Roderick (Bardrochat, Colmorrell, Ayrshire), b.1932; ed. at Eton, and at Trin. Coll., Camb.; late Queen's Own Cameron Highlanders: m. 1958, Romana, da. of Raimund von Hofmannsthal, and has issue living, Adam Hugo, b. 1965,—Flora Mary, b. 1959,—Samantha Mary, b. 1960,—Christabel Mary b. 1962.——Alexander Dundas (New Club), b. 1935; ed. at Eton; late Queen's Own Cameron Highlanders: m. 1960 (Princess) Cecilia, da. of HSH Franz, 2nd Prince Weikersheim, of 50, Seymour Walk, SW10, and has issue living, Alexander Francis, b. 1962,—Hugo Gabriel, b. 1965,—Sophia, b. 1961. *Residence*, Whiteside, Greenlaw, Berwickshire.——David Fraser (Turf Club), b. 1938; ed. at Eton, and at Trin. Coll., Camb.; late Queen's Own Cameron Highlanders.——John Sebastian, b. 1942; ed. at Eton, and at Trin. Coll., Camb.
Sister living—Christian Mary (*Baroness Hesketh*), b. 1929: m. 1949, the 2nd Baron Hesketh, who d. 1955. *Residences*, Easton Neston, Towcester, Northants; 20a, Tregunter Rd., SW10.

Widow living of 2nd Baronet—CLARE ROSEMARY, only child of Col. John William Eric Graves Sandars, OBE, TD, of Gate Burton Hall, Gainsborough, Lincs. [B. Graves]: m. 1st, 1958, Sir James Napier Finnie McEwen, 2nd Bt., who d. 1971; 2ndly, 1973, Kenneth Wagg, of Ridge House, Sunningdale, Berks.

Sir John (Helias Finnie) McEwen, 1st Bt., was M.P. for Berwick and Haddington (C) 1931-45, Parliamentary Under-Sec. of State for Scotland 1939-40, and a Lord Commr. of the Treasury 1942-44.

McFARLAND, Creation (U.K.) 1914, of Aberfoyle, co. Londonderry.

This I'll defend

Sir BASIL ALEXANDER TALBOT McFAR-LAND, C.B.E., E.R.D., 2nd *Baronet*; b. Feb. 18th, 1898; s. his father, Sir JOHN, 1926; ed. at Neuwied-on-Rhine, Germany, at Brussels, and at Bedford Sch.; Hon. Col. 9th Londonderry HAA Regt. RA (SR); Chm. of Londonderry and Lough Swilly Railway Co., of Lanes (Derry), Ltd., of Alexander Thompson & Co., Ltd., of J. W. Corbett & Sons, Ltd., of Londonderry Gaslight Co. Ltd., of Sir Alfred McAlpine & Sons (N. Ireland) Ltd., and of Lanes (Fuel Oils) Ltd., a Dir. of Robert) C. Malseed & Co., Ltd., of Lanes Business Equipment), Ltd., of Lanes (Patent Fuels), Ltd., of J. & R. Waterson, Ltd., and of Holmes Coal, Ltd.; Local Dir. of Commercial Union Assurance Co., Ltd.; a Member of Londonderry Port and Harbour Commrs. (Chm. 1952-67) and of the Commandery of Ards, a Commr. of Irish Lights, and a CStJ; Chm. TA & AFA, co. Londonderry 1947-69, and Pres. of N. Ireland TA & VR Assocn. 1968-69; High Sheriff of co. of City of Londonderry 1930-38, and High Sheriff of co. Londonderry 1952; HM Lt. for City of Londonderry since 1939; a Senator of N. Ireland 1939 and 1945-50; Mayor of Londonderry 1939, and 1945-50 (Hon. Freeman); a Member of N. Ireland Air Advisory Council 1946-65, and a Trustee of Magee Univ. Coll. 1962-65; Middle East 1939, and Italy 1939-45 with Londonderry HAA Regt. RA (despatches); CBE (Civil) 1954: m. 1st, 1924, Annie Kathleen, who d. 1952, da. of the late Andrew Henderson, JP, of Parkville, Whiteabbey, Belfast; 2ndly, 1955, Mary Eleanor, who d. 1973, da. of the late William Dougan, of Londonderry, and has issue by 1st m.

Arms—Argent, a saltire engrailed gules, between two roses in pale and a thistle and shamrock in fesse all proper. *Crest*—A demi-savage holding in the dexter hand an antique crown all proper.
Seat—Aberfoyle, Londonderry. *Clubs*—Bath, Kildare Street (Dublin), Ulster (Belfast).

Son living—By 1st marriage—JOHN TALBOT, TD, b. Oct. 3rd, 1927; ed. at Marlborough, and at Trin. Coll., Oxford; a DL of City of Co. of Londonderry; Councillor, Londonderry Corp. 1955-69, High Sheriff of co. Londonderry 1958, and of City of Co. of Londonderry 1965 and

1966; a Member of Londonderry Port and Harbour Commrs. 1966; Chm. ,Board of Govs., Londonderry High Sch. since 1971: *m.* 1957, Mary Scott, el. da. of the late Dr. W. Scott Watson, of Dunmore House, Carrigans, co. Donegal, and has issue living, Anthony Basil Scott, *b.* 1959,— Stephen Andrew John, *b.* 1968,—Shauna Jane, *b.* 1957,—Fiona Kathleen, *b.* 1963. *Residence,* Dunmore House, Carrigans, co. Donegal.

The 1st baronet, Sir John, was a partner in the firm of McCrea and McFarland, engineering contractors, of Belfast and Londonderry, Chm. of Mulhollands (Limited), drapers and of Brewsters (Limited), bakers, of Londonderry, Proprietor of Lough Swilly Steamship Co., and Chm. of Lough Swilly Railway Co.

MACGREGOR, Creation (U.K.) 1828, of Savile Row, Middlesex.

Sir EDWIN ROBERT MACGREGOR, 7th *Baronet*; *b.* 1931; *s.* his father, *Sir* ROBERT JAMES McCONNELL, M.M., 1963; ed. at Univ. of British Columbia (B.A. Sc. 1955, M.A. Sc. 1957): *m.* 1952, Margaret Alice Jean, da. of A. Peake, of Haney, British Columbia, and has issue.

Arms—Argent, from a mount base an oak-tree surmounted by a sword in bend proper, and in chief two eastern crowns gules, all within a bordure engrailed of the last. Crest—A human hand couped at the wrist and holding a dagger erect proper, pommel and hilt gold.

Address—3152, Marine View Place, Victoria, BC, V9C 1Y6, Canada.

Sons living—ROBERT LIONEL FREDERICK, *b.* May 10th 1953.——Ian Grant, *b.* 1959.

Daughters living—Valerie Jean, *b.* 1956.——Marlene Elizabeth, *b.* 1963.

Brother living—Arthur Joseph, *b.* 1933; ed. at Univ. of British Columbia (M.D. 1958): *m.* 1957, Carole Isabel, da. of W. L. Valens, M.D., of Victoria, British Columbia. *Residence,* 3550, Redwood Av., Victoria, British Columbia.

Sisters living—Margaret Gertrude, *b.* 1937: *m.* 1963, Cyril George White, of 1617, Henry St., Halifax, Nova Scotia.——Patricia Elizabeth, *b.* 1939: *m.* 1966, John Peramaki, of 981, Gloria Pl., Victoria, BC, Canada.——Nancy Lane, *b.* 1942: *m.* 1972, Hubert Foulds, of 24205, Alouette Rd., Maple Ridge, BC, Canada.

Widow living of 6th Baronet—ANNIE MARY, da. of the late Joseph Lane, of Nanaimo, BC: *m.* 1st, 1930, Sir Robert James McConnell Macgregor, MM, 6th baronet, who *d.* 1963; 2ndly, 1973, John Kampe, of 290, Homer St., Vic., BC, Canada.

Collateral Branch living.

Issue of the late Brig.-Gen. Charles Reginald Macgregor, C.B., D.S.O., 2nd son of 3rd baronet, *b.* 1847, *d.* 1902 : *m.* 1893, Maud (who *m.* 2ndly, 1903, Addison Yalden Thomson), da. of A. dés Monstiers Campbell, formerly of Oakley House, Abingdon, Berks :—

Helen Maud, *b.* 1894. *Address,* c/o Westminster Bank, Terminus Road, Eastbourne, Sussex.

Sir Patrick Macgregor, 1st Bt., son of James Macgregor of Bellimore, Inverness-shire, was Serjeant-Surgeon to King George IV.

MAC GREGOR of MAC GREGOR, Creation (G.B.) 1795, of Lanrick, co. Perth.

Srioghal mo dhream.
Royal is my race.

E'en do and spair not.

Sir GREGOR MAC GREGOR OF MAC GREGOR, 6th *Baronet*; *b.* Dec. 22nd, 1925 ; *s.* his father, *Capt. Sir* MALCOLM, C.B., CMG, RN, 1958; ed. at Eton; Col. Comdg. Scots Gds., a Member of Queen's Body Guard for Scotland (Roy. Co. of Archers), and 23rd Chief of Clan Gregor: *m.* 1958, Fanny, only da. of Charles Hubert Archibald Butler, of Le Pavillon, Newport, Essex, and has issue.

Arms—Argent, an oak-tree eradicated and fructed in a bend sinister proper, surmounted of a sword in a bend azure, carrying on its point in the dexter canton an antique crown gules. Crest—A lion's head proper crowned with an antique crown or. Supporters—Dexter, a unicorn argent, crowned and horned or ; sinister, a stag proper, tyned azure. Clan Slogan—"Ard Choille."

Seat—Edinchip, Lochearnhead, Perthshire. *Clubs* —Guards', Pratt's, and Puffin's.

Sons living—MALCOLM GREGOR CHARLES, *b.* March 23rd, 1959.——Ninian Hubert Alexander *b.* 1961.

Sister living—Anna Gylla, *b.* 1929 : *m.* 1950, James Christopher Ellis, AADip, ARIBA, and has issue living, Giles Christopher, *b.* 1951,—Conrad James, *b.* 1965,—Anna Gabrielle, *b.* 1953,—Katherine Gylla *b.* 1957. *Residence,* 100, Cheyne Walk, Chelsea, SW10.

Widow living of 5th Baronet—*Hon.* GYLLA CONSTANCE SUSAN (*Hon. Lady Mac Gregor of Mac Gregor*) O.B.E., da. of the late Hon. Eric Norman Rollo [*see* L. Rollo] ; has 1st class Order of Vasa of Sweden ; O.B.E. (Civil) 1948 : *m.* 1925, Capt. Sir Malcolm Mac Gregor of Mac Gregor, C.B., C.M.G., R.N. (retired), 5th baronet, who *d.* 1958. *Residence,* Craggan House, Lochearnhead, Perthshire.

Collateral Branches living

Issue of the late Alexander Ronald Mac Gregor, yr. son of 4th baronet, *b.* 1878, *d.* 1960 : *m.* 1907, Gertrude Blanche, who *d.* 1959, da. of the late Charles Archibald Murray [E. Mansfield, colls.] :—

Malcolm Findanus, *b.* 1908; European War 1939-45 as Lt.-Cdr. R.N.V.R.: *m.* 1st, 1930, Rachel Katharine (who obtained a divorce 1940), da. of the Hon. Eustace Scott Hamilton-Russell, O.B.E. [*see* V. Boyne]; 2ndly, 1941, Mariquita Gwen Alison, da. of A. J. Webbe, and has issue living. (by 2nd m.) Alpin Findanus (79, Stockwell Park Rd., SW9), *b.* 1941: *m.* 1965, Maria Christina, Elisabeth, da. of D. C. Brunow, of Kotka, Finland, and has issue living, Euan Alexander *b.* 1972. *Residence,* Cardney, Dunkeld, Perthshire.

Grandchildren of the late Alexander Ronald Mac Gregor (ante):—

Issue of the late Maj. Dunnchadh Tearlach Mac Gregor, ERD, R. Scots Greys, *b.* 1914, *d.* 1974: *m.* 1st, 1944, Nighean (from whom he obtained a divorce 1949), da. of Col. Alastair Norman Fraser, DSO, MB; 2ndly, 1954, Roxana Mary Jocelyn (Ballacooiley, Ballaugh, I. of Man), da. of Jocelyn Walker, of Oaklands, Isfield, Sussex:—
(By 1st m.), Randal Alasdair (Ballacooiley, Ballaugh, I. of Man), *b.* 1945, Capt. R. Scots Dragoon Gds.: *m.* 1973, Lynn Vanessa, da. of Maj. Tommy Vale, MBE, of Farthings, Kingston Broadway, Shoreham by Sea, Sussex.——(By 2nd m.) Isoabel Maryel, *b.* 1956.——Catriona Gabrielle, *b.* 1968.

Issue of the late Alexander Ronald Mac Gregor (ante):—

Dorviegelda Malvina, *b.* 1910: *m.* 1st, 1939, Sqdn.-Ldr. the Hon. (Robert Alexander) Greville Baird, RAF, who *d.* (killed in action) 1943 [see E. Kintore]; 2ndly, 1947, Sqdn.-Ldr. Algernon Ivan Sladen, DSO, late RAF, of Barnheath, Tadley, Basingstoke [E. Dunmore], and has issue living, (by 1st m.) [see E. Kintore, colls.],—(by 2nd m.), Angus Murray, *b.* 1950.

The royal descent of this ancient Ian can be traced to remote antiquity, Gregor Garubh, or "The Stout," having fought under King Duncan I. In the early part of the 17th century there were feuds between numerous clans, the Mac Gregors being persecuted with such fury that any person might mutilate or slay them with impunity. In this situation they continued till they were courted to join the Solemn League and Covenant, upon promises of future friendship; but they declared, "That as they *bore the crown on the point of their swords,* they would not fail to use the latter in support of the former." They are the only instance of a race being forbidden to bear their family name, which was first proscribed by James VI., owing to treachery and misrepresentation. They were restored by Charles II., 1661, to their estates, and permitted to bear their own name. In the reign of William and Mary the law of proscription was again revived, and continued in force until its repeal in 1774. The name was not, however, restored till a Roy. licence to resume it was obtained by Sir John Murray (properly Mac Gregor) 1822. Sir Malcolm, C.B., C.M.G., 5th Bt. was Capt. R.N. and served in European War 1914-18.

McGRIGOR, Creation (U.K.) 1831, of Campden Hill, Middlesex.

Royal is my tribe.
S'rioghal mo dhream.

Sir CHARLES EDWARD McGRIGOR, 5th *Baronet;* *b.* Oct. 5th, 1922; *s.* his father, *Lieut.-Col. Sir* CHARLES COLQUHOUN, *OBE,* 1946; ed. at Eton; formerly Capt. Rifle Bde.; Exon of Queen's Body Guard, Yeomen of the Guard, and Member of Queen's Body Guard for Scotland (Roy. Co. of Archers); 1939-45 War in N. Africa and Italy (despatches): *m.* 1948, Mary Bettine, da. of Sir Archibald Charles Edmonstone, 6th Bt., and has issue.

Arms—Argent, a fir-tree growing out of a mount in base vert surmounted by a sword point upwards in bend proper, pommel and hilt gold, in the dexter chief an eastern crown gules, on a chief azure a tower or, between the badge of the Order of the Tower and Sword on the dexter, and that of the Crescent on the sinister. Crest—A lion's head erased gules, crowned with an eastern coronet or.

Residences—Upper Sonachan, by Dalmally, Argyll; 18, Cranmer Court, SW3.

Sons living—JAMES ANGUS RHODERICK NEIL, *b.* Oct. 19th, 1949.——Charles Edward, *b.* 1959.

Daughters living—Lorna Gwendolyn, *b.* 1951.——Kirstie Rowena Amabel, *b.* 1953.

Aunt living (daughter of 3rd baronet)—Jean Helen (*Lady Creagh*), *b.* 1902; rendered sers. in Middle East during European War 1939-42 (despatches): *m.* 1926, Maj.-Gen. Sir Michael O'Moore Creagh, KBE, MC, late 15th/19th Hussars, who *d.* 1970, and has issue living, Jean Patricia, *b.* 1927: *m.* 1954, Maj. John David Makgill-Crichton-Maitland, Gren. Gds. (ret.) [*see* E. Lauderdale, colls.]. *Residence,* Pigeon Hill, Homington, nr. Salisbury.

Widow living of 4th Baronet—AMABEL (*Dowager Lady McGrigor*), da. of the late Edward Lygon Somers Cocks [Watson, Bt., cr. 1760 (ext.)]: *m.* 1919, Lieut.-Col. Sir Charles Colquhoun McGrigor, OBE, 4th Bt., who *d.* 1946. *Residence,* 18, Cranmer Court, SW3.

Collateral Branch living

Issue of the late Maj.-Gen. Charles Rhoderick Robert McGrigor, C.B., C.M.G., 2nd son of 2nd baronet, *b.* 1860, *d.* 1927: *m.* 1892, Ada Rosamond, who *d.* 1945, da. of the late Robert Hartley Bower [Lister-Kaye, Bt.]:—

Mary Ada Bower, *b.* 1894. *Residence,* Old Place, Ellen's Green, near Rudgwick, Sussex.

The 1st baronet, Sir James, K.C.B., F.R.S., was for thirty-six years Director-General of the Army Medical Department, and three times Lord Rector of Marischal College, Aberdeen. A statue of him erected outside the Barracks at Chelsea was subsequently removed and re-erected at the R.A.M.C. buildings at Millbank, while there is a bust of him in Wellington College, and a stall dedicated to his memory in the Garrison Church at Portsmouth. The 3rd baronet, Sir James Roderick Duff, Capt. late Rifle Brig., was many years senior partner in the late firm of Sir Charles R. McGrigor, Bart., and Co., army agents and bankers. The 4th baronet, Sir Charles Colquhoun, O.B.E., was Lieut.-Col. Rifle Brig.

MACKENZIE, Creation (N.S.) 1673, of Coul, Ross-shire.

Purified by adversity.

Sir ROBERT EVELYN MACKENZIE, 12th *Baronet; b.* Feb. 15th, 1906; *s.* his father, *Sir* ARTHUR GEORGE RAMSAY, 1935; ed. at Eton, and at Trin. Coll., Camb.; formerly a Member of Lloyd's; 1st Sec., HM Foreign Ser. 1945-52; 1939-45 War as Maj. Intelligence Corps: *m.* 1st, 1940, Mrs. Jane Adams-Beck, who *d.* 1952, da. of the late Maurice Beck, of Saltwood, Hythe, Kent; 2ndly, 1963, Mrs. Elizabeth Campbell, da. of the late Renard Pearth, of Pittsburgh, USA.

Arms—Quarterly: 1st and 4th azure, a deer's head

cabossed or, *Mackenzie;* 2nd and 3rd, gules, a boar's head couped argent, *Chisholm.* **Crest**— A boar's head erect or between the attires of a stag fixed to a scalp sable. **Supporters**—*Dexter,* an armed Highlander in full custume proper; *sinister,* a roebuck proper.

Residence—18, Melton Court, Old Brompton Rd., SW7 3JQ. *Clubs*—St. James's, Army and Navy.

Collateral Branches living.

Granddaughters of the late Henry Augustin Ornano Mackenzie (infra) :—
Issue of the late George Henry Louis Mackenzie, b. 1872, d. 1960: *m.* 1907, Lilian Mary, who *d.* 1968, el. da. of Richard Rodney Pope, formerly ICS:—
Mary Zeta Bingham, *b.* 1909 : *m.* 1931, Philip Henry Burch, who *d.* 1932, Lieut. Indian Army, and has issue living, Deirdre Raine Mary, *b.* 1932,—Phillida Mary, *b.* (posthumous), 1933: *m.* 1965, Aloysius John Zadnik, (Box 33, Taber, Alberta, Canada), and has issue living, Philip John *b.* 1967, Michael Peter *b.* 1968, Elizabeth Anne *b.* 1970.   *Address,* c/o National & Grindlays Bank, 13, St. James's Sq., SW1.——Eira Margaret Antonia, *b.* 1913: *m.* 1938, Owen James Esmonde, of Cloneen, Glendalongh, co. Wicklow, and 5, Ijong St., Braddon, Canberra, ACT [see Esmonde, Bt.].

Issue of the late Henry Augustin Ornano Mackenzie, son of 7th baronet, *b.* 1839, *d.* 1909: *m.* 1st, 1859, Mary Anne, who *d.* 1881, da. of the late Mons. Louis Francis Botte; 2ndly 1892, Josephine Emily, who *d.* 1951, da. of the late Charles Bolton, of Clapham, S.W.:—
(By 2nd m.) *Rev.* RAMSAY MALCOLM BOLTON (6, Pearl Court, Devonshire Pl., Eastbourne), *b.* Aug. 7th, 1893; ed. at Trin. Coll., Oxford (MA); Capt. late RAF; R. of Edgmond, Newport, Shropshire 1955-59: *m.* 1st, 1920, Margaret Cecilia, who *d.* 1965, da. of the late Rev. George Augustus Seymour Metford, formerly R. of St. Michael's, Sutton Bonington, Notts.; 2ndly, 1971, Joan Mary Davey.

Grandchildren of the late Keith Douglas Mackenzie (infra):—
Issue of the late Henry Douglas Mackenzie, *b.* 1905, *d.* 1965: *m.* 1941, Irene Carter Freeman:—
Peter Douglas, *b.* 1949.——Ann Douglas, *b.* 1943.

Grandchildren of the late Henry Douglas Mackenzie, el. son of the late Rev Charles Mackenzie, 3rd son of the late John Mackenzie of Torridon (*d.* 1820), 3rd in descent from Simon Mackenzie, 2nd son of 1st baronet (ante):—
Issue of the late Keith Douglas Mackenzie, *b.* 1879, *d.* 1948 : *m.* 1904, Anna Hildagonda, who *d.* 1937, da. of the late George Reitz :—
Keith Douglas (On High, Belvidere, Knysna (PO Box 369), Cape S. Africa), *b.* 1912: *m.* 1937, Thelma Reeders, and has issue living, Judy Douglas, *b.* 1940: *m.* 1962, Lt. Graham Douglas Ferguson, SAAF, of Lynwood Glen, Pretoria, S. Africa, and has issue living, Ian Douglas *b.* 1964, Kim Douglas *b.* 1962, Lynn Douglas *b.* 1968, Lee-Ann Douglas *b.* 1971,—Jenifer Mary Douglas, *b.* 1944: *m.* 1965, Jeremy David Garrett, of Florida, Transvaal, and has issue living, Craig Douglas *b.* 1968, Geoffrey Keith *b.* 1972, Nikki Jane *b.* 1970.——Helen Douglas, *b.* 1908: *m.* 1933, John Shaw, and has issue living.——Joan Douglas, *b.* 1909: *m.* 1943, Maj. Kenneth David Harris, King's Dragoon Gds., and has issue living, Peter David, *b.* 1949,—Gillian Diana, *b.* 1947.   *Residence,* Nashleigh Farm, Ashley Green Rd., nr. Chesham, Bucks.

Grandsons of the late Henry Turing Mackenzie, son of the late Rt. Rev. Henry Mackenzie, D.D. (infra):—
Issue of the late Capt. Roderick Henry Turing Mackenzie, *b.* 1891, *d.* 1963: *m.* 1st, 1920 (m. diss. 1932), Helen Margaret, da. of the late J. P. Dalzell; 2ndly, 1934, Helen Monica Bradley (The White Cottage, Benenden, Kent), da. of the late Lt.-Col. William Bradley Roberts. DSO:—
(By 1st m.) Keith Roderick Turing, *MC* (Edenhill, Kennedy Gdns., St. Andrews, Fife), *b.* 1921; late Maj. Indian Army, and Burmah-Shell Oil Co., India; Sec. of Roy. and Ancient Golf Club of St. Andrews; 1939-45 War (MC): *m.* 1949, Barbara Kershaw, da. of the late W. H. Miles, of Deal, Kent, and has issue living, Miles Roderick Turing, *b.* 1952,—Angus Keith Turing, *b.* 1965,—Sarah Jane Kershaw, *b.* 1950.—Susannah Mary, *b.* 1957.——(By 2nd m.) Bruce Sydenham (c/o National Westminster Bank, Cranbrook, Kent), *b.* 1935; Maj. Queen's Lancs. Regt.: *m.* 1963 Sheila Hope Evan, da. of the Rev. Aubrey Lionel Evan Hopkins, late V. of Holy Trin., Folkestone, and has issue living, Kevin Roderick, *b.* 1964,—Neil Kenneth, *b.* 1966,—Tessa Claire, *b.* 1970,—Kirsty Celia, *b.* 1971.——Michael Sydenham *b.* 1940; ed. at Trin. Coll., Dublin (BA); Gen. Sec. of Poetry Soc.

Grandson of the late Stanley John Mackenzie (by 1st m.) (infra):—
Issue of the late Stanley Charles William WYNN-MACKENZIE, *b.* 1870, *d.* 19—: *m.* 1900, G. Whitehouse:—
Douglas Stanley, *b.* 1903.
Issue, if any, of the late Kenneth Maurice WYNN-MACKENZIE, *b.* 1880, *d.* 19—: *m.* 1917.

Grandchildren of the late Rt. Rev. Henry Mackenzie, D.D. (Bishop Suffragan of Nottingham), yst. son of the late John Mackenzie of Torridon (*d.* 1820) (ante):—

Issue of the late Stanley John Mackenzie, *b.* 1847, *d.* 1904: *m.* 1st, 1869, Charlotte Arthur, who *d.* 1888, da. of the late Thomas Wynn, when he assumed the additional **surname** of Wynn ; 2ndly, 1892, Lizzie Adeline, da. of the late George Gordon Bennett and reverted to his patronymic only :—
(By 2nd m.) Noel Donald George MACKENZIE (Sunnydene, 27, Greensleeves Av., Broadstone, Dorset, BH18 8BJ), *b.* 1899: *m.* 1931, Elsie Kate, da. of William Henry Mitchell, and has issue living, Donald William John (12, The Finches, Thundersley, Essex), *b.* 1935: *m.* 1969, Cheryl Patricia Elizabeth, da. of Cyril Leslie Charles Allen, of Cheriton, Llyswen, Breconshire, and has issue living, Nicholas Richard *b.* 1974,—Marian Audrey, *b.* 1944: *m.* 1966 (m. diss. 1975). Kaddour Amari, and has issue living, Nadia *b.* 1966, Samira *b.* 1970.——Lillie Marguerite MAC-KENZIE (Secretarius Farm, Private Bag 35K, Kimberley, S. Africa), *b.* 1895.

Grandchildren of the late John Ord Mackenzie, W.S., son of the late Richard Mackenzie, son of the late John Mackenzie of Dolphinton, son of the late Kenneth Mackenzie, 2nd son of the late John Mackenzie of Delvine, 3rd son of 1st baronet:—
Issue of the late Capt. Kenneth Mackenzie, Roy. Scots, *b.* 1882, *d.* (killed in action during European War) 1918 : *m.* 1910, May Eudora, C.B.E. (now of Meadowhead, Dolphinton, Lanarkshire ; she *m.* 2ndly, 1920, John Douglas Boswell Campbell, who *d.* 1943), da. of the late Henry Moncreiff Horsbrugh, C.A., of Edinburgh :—
John Moncreiff Ord, *b.* 1911 ; is a W.S.; sometime Capt. Lanarkshire Yeo. (T.A.): *m.* 1936, Delia Alice, da. of Wyndham Damer Clark, J.P., D.L. [E. Mayo, colls.], and has issue living, Richard Wyndham John, *b.* 1939: *m.* 1969, Diane Gracie Petters, and has issue living, Douglas John *b.* 1972, Delia Joan *b.* 1970,—Elizabeth Anne *b.* 1937,—Diana Ord, *b.* 1944,—Cynthia Rose, *b.* 1946: *m.* 1969, Capt. Colin Grant Ogilvie Hogg, KOSB, and has issue living, Vanessa Charlotte Ogilvie *b.* 1972,—Angela Viviane, *b.* 1949.   *Residence,* Dolphinton House, Dolphinton, Lanark-shire.——Kenneth Ord (Sherborne Cowdray, Sherborne St. John, Basingstoke), *b.* 1912: *m.* 1955, Penelope June, da. of Neville Brace Colt, [Rawlinson, Bt., colls.], and has issue living, Virginia Anne, *b.* 1958,—Caroline Jane, *b.* 1960.——Alastair Douglas, *CBE* (c/o Bank of Scotland, 141, Princes St., Edinburgh 2), *b.* 1917; Col. (ret.) late R. Scots; Bde.-Maj. HQ British Common-

wealth Inf. Bde. 1951 (despatches); 1939-45 War (despatches); CBE (Mil.) 1972: *m.* 1945, Diane, da. of the late Col. Arthur John Henry Sloggett, CBE, DSO, and has issue living, Mark Tresloggett, *b.* 1950.——Margaret Hermione, *MBE, b.* 1915; formerly Maj. WRAC; MBE (Mil) 1945.

Alexander Mackenzie of Coul, father of Sir Kenneth Mackenzie, 1st baronet, was a natural son of Colin Cam (one-eyed) Mackenzie, 11th of Kintail (*d.* 1594) and half-brother of 1st Lord Mackenzie of Kintail (ancestor of the Earls of Seaforth) and of Sir Roderick Mackenzie of Tarbat (ancestor of the Earls of Cromartie). Sir John Mackenzie, 3rd baronet, participating in the Jacobite rising 1715, was included in the act of attainder passed against the Earl of Mar and his adherents. He died without male issue, and, despite the forfeiture, the Baronetcy has been assumed since 1702, it being claimed that the attainder did not extend to collateral branches, and that the *title* as well as the estates devolved upon his brother.

Mackenzie, Creation (N.S.) 1703, of Gairloch, Ross-shire, see Inglis.

MACKENZIE, Creation (N.S.) 1703, of Scatwell, Ross-shire.
I shine but do not burn.

Sir RODERICK CAMPBELL MAC-KENZIE, 10th *Baronet,* son of the late Kenneth Roderick Mackenzie, only son of Edmund Lyons Mackenzie, 2nd son of Adm. John Francis Campbell Mackenzie, great-grandson of 3rd baronet; *b.* Nov. 15th, 1954; *s.* his kinsman, *Sir* (LEWIS) RODERICK KENNETH, 1972.

Arms—Quarterly, 1st, azure, a deer's head cabossed or, *Mackenzie of Scatwell*; 2nd, or, a mountain azure, inflamed gules; 3rd, gules, three legs of a man in armour proper flexed in triangle, garnished and spurred or, *Macleod of Lewis*, 4th, azure, a deer's head cabossed or within a bordure of the last charged with eight crescents of the first, *Mackenzie of Findon.* **Crest**—The sun in his splendour or. **Supporters,**—*Dexter,* a savage wreathed about the head and middle with laurel and carrying with his dexter hand a club over his shoulder, all proper; *sinister,* a deer proper.

Residence,—120, Church St., Clifton Forge, Virginia 24422, USA.

Without stain.

Aunt living—Julia Mary Louise, *b.* 1889: *m.* 1919, Frederick Brewer de Hamel Krom, and has issue living, Frederick Brewer de Hamel.
Mother living—Elizabeth Carrington (120, Church St., Clifton Forge, Virginia, 24422, USA), da. of the late William Barbee Settle, Counsellor-at-Law, of S. Boston, Va., USA: *m.* 1954, Kenneth Roderick Mackenzie (ante), who *d.* 1960.

Grandchildren of the late Major François Mackenzie, son of the late Dep. Comy. Gen. John Mackenzie, 5th Regt., grandson of 3rd baronet :—
Issue of the late Col. George Frederick Campbell Mackenzie, C.B., *b.* 1855,*d.* 1909: *m.* 1885, Emily Mary, who *d.* 1953, da. of the late Capt. Joseph Boulton, 14th Hussars :—
Norah, *MBE* (Gosfield Hall, Halstead, Essex); MBE (Civil) 1945.
Issue of the late John Roderick Kenneth Mackenzie, *b.* 1869, *d.* 1958: *m.* 1893, Kathleen Elizabeth, who *d.* 1974, da. of the late Capt. Thomas Howard Blennerhasset Coulson, Roy. Indian Marine:—
RODERICK EDWARD FRANCOIS MCQUHAE, CBE, DSC, *b.* Dec. 11th, 1894; Capt. (ret.) RN; 1914-18 War (DSC), 1939-45 War (CBE, American Medal of Freedom with Silver Palm); CBE (Mil.) 1945: *m.* 1938, Marie Evelyn Campbell, only da. of the late William Ernest Parkinson, of Farnham, Surrey, and has issue living, Roderick McQuhae *b.* 1942; MB, BS, MRCP, DCH: *m.* 1970, Nadine, da. of Georges Schlatter, of Buchs-K-Zürich, and has issue living, Gregory Roderick McQuhae *b.* 1971, Nina Adelaide *b.* 1973,—Marie Isobel Campbell, *b.* 1939: *m.* 1964, Wing-Cdr. Richard C. Allerton, RAF, of Rags Corner, Nether Wallop, Hants., and has issue living, James Roderick Orde *b.* 1967, Christopher Edward Orde *b.* 1970,—Fiona Louis., *b.* 1943: *m.* 1969, Lt.-Cdr. Timothy Patrick Havers, RN, of Corner House, 153, Dalling Rd., Ravenscourt Park, W6 oER, and has issue living, Louisanna Marie *b.* 1973. *Residence,* Rownhams, Farnham, Surrey. *Club,* United Service.——Iris Louisa Ida (Heene Lodge, 2, Camborne Rd., Sutton, Surrey), *b.* 1897.——Phyllis Marion, *b.* 1899: *m.* 1922, Capt. James Millar Begg, RN (ret.), who *d.* 1954, and has issue living, Kathleen Mary Iris, *b.* 1923: *m.* 1947, Brig. Henry L. Broome Salmon, and has issue living, Marion Jane Broome, *b.* 1949: *m.* 1974, Thomas Richard Holland Sowler, Bar. at Law of Greystead Rectory Cottage, Hexham [By Rotherham, (ext.)],—Anthea Maud Broome, *b.* 1953. *Residence,* Rownhams, 52, Waverley Lane, Farnham, Surrey.

The 1st baronet sat as M.P. for Ross-shire 1702-7, and the 5th baronet was Lord-Lieutenant of that county, and M.P. therefor 1822-31. This family is a collateral branch of the Mackenzies, Earls of Cromarty (title attainted 1746), and the present baronet claims he is representative of Sir John, Mackenzie, of Tarbat (created a baronet of Nova Scotia by Charles I. 1628, with remainder to heirs, male whatsoever, which Baronetcy was resigned and regranted 1704 to his son Kenneth the same year; Kenneth's son George, subsequently also succeeding to the Baronetcy of Royston, *cr.* 1704), who was father of the 1st Earl. Of these Baronetcies the present Baronet of Scatwell has reason to believe he is the representative.

MACKENZIE, Creation (U.K.) 1890, of Glen Muick, Aberdeenshire.

This is the way to the stars.

Sir (ALEXANDER GEORGE ANTHONY) ALLAN MACKENZIE, *CD*, 4th *Baronet*, son of the late Capt. Allan Keith Mackenzie, Grenadier Guards, 3rd son of 2nd baronet; *b.* Jan. 4th, 1913; *s.* his uncle, *Col. Sir* VICTOR AUDLEY FALCONER, *D.S.O., M.V.O.*, 1944; Capt. (ret.) The Black Watch of Canada; a Page of Honour to H.M. 1924-31; served in Roy. Canadian Mounted Police 1932-7; European War 1939-45 in Italy and N.-W. Europe: *m.* 1937, Marjorie McGuire, of Vancouver, British Columbia, and has issue.

Arms—Per pale indented azure and or, a stag's head cabossed counter-changed.   Crest—A dexter hand grasping a sword bendwise proper.

Residence—R.R.1, Cobble Hill, Vancouver Island, British Columbia.

Daughters living—Margaret Ann, *b.* 1939: *m.* 1974, Richard L. Mullin.——Kathryn Heather, *b.* 1946.——Linda Alexandra, *b.* 1949: *m.* 1970, Brock J. Eayrs, MA, and has issue living, Jennifer Alexandra, *b.* 1973.——Allain Fenton, *b.* 1953: *m.* 1974, J. F. M. Beltgens.

Collateral Branches living.

Issue of the late Lt.-Col. Eric Dighton Mackenzie, CMG, CVO, DSO, yst. son of 2nd Bt., *b.* 1891, *d.* 1972: *m.* 1948, Elizabeth Kathrine Mary (Calgary House, Tobermory, Isle of Mull), da. of the late Capt. James William Guy Innes, CBE, JP, RN, [*see* Innes, Bt., cr. 1628], and formerly wife of Maj. James Robertson-McIsaac:—

(JAMES WILLIAM) GUY (1, Molerun, Pheasant Drive, High Wycombe), *b.* Oct. 6th, 1946; ed. at Stowe: *m.* 1972, Paulene Patricia Simpson, and has issue living, Amanda Louise *b.* 1972.—— Allan Walter, *b.* 1952.——Lucy Elizabeth Victoria, *b.* 1949.

Issue of the late Claud Longueville Mackenzie, 3rd son of 1st baronet, *b.* 1857, *d.* 1890: *m.* 1884, Ilona, who *d.* 1933 (having *m.* 2ndly, 1901, Baron Wesselenyi), da. of Oliver Paget:—

Olive Leonora: *m.* 1915, Lieut.-Col. William Percival Cosnahan Tenison, D.S.O., formerly R.A., and has issue living, Patricia Marion, *b.* 1916; formerly in W.A.A.F.: *m.* 1949, Richard H. Kimber, of Philadelphia, U.S.A.,—Kathleen Ellen, *b.* 1918: *m.* 1942, Capt. F. V. Scopes, formerly Roy. W. African Frontier Force. *Residence*, 2, Wool Road, Wimbledon Common S.W.20.

The 1st baronet, Sir James Thompson Mackenzie (son of the late George Mackenzie, of Aberdeen), was a D.L. for Ross-shire and Middlesex.   The 3rd baronet, Sir Victor Audley Falconer, D.S.O., M.V.O., was Col. Scots-Guards, a Groom-in-Waiting to King George V., and an Extra Groom-in-Waiting to King Edward VIII. and King George VI.   He served during European War 1914-18 (D. S.O.)

MUIR MACKENZIE, Creation (U.K.) 1805, of Delvine, Perthshire.
Straight at difficulties.

Prepared for either fortune.

Sir ALEXANDER ALWYNE BRINTON MUIR MACKENZIE, 7th *Baronet*; *b.* Dec. 8th, 1955; *s.* his father, *Capt. Sir* ROBERT HENRY, 1970; ed. at Eton; 2nd Lt. 16/5th Lancers.

Arms—Quarterly: 1st and 4th, argent, on a fesse azure, three estoiles or, *Muir*; 2nd and 3rd, azure, a buck's head cabossed or, all within a bordure nebuly quarterly gules and argent, *Mackensie*.   Crests—1st, a sword and olive-branch in saltire proper; 2nd, a dexter hand grasping a dart in bend sinister proper.   Second Motto—"Recte ad ardua" (*Straight at difficulties*).

Residence—Sunderland Hall, Galashiels, Selkirkshire, TD1 3PG.

Sister living—(Charmian) Miranda, *b.* 1948: *m.* 1968, Robert Dennis Smyly, of Sunderland Hall, Galashiels, Selkirkshire, TD1 3PG [see By. of Buckland].

Widow living of 6th Baronet—MARY TERESA (*Lady Muir Mackenzie*), (Flat A, 62, Pont St., SW1), da. of the late Dr. James Mathews, and widow of John Geoffrey Turner, of Lower Old Park, Farnham, Surrey: *m.* 1963, as his 2nd wife, Capt. Sir Robert Henry Muir Mackenzie, 6th Bt., who *d.* 1970.

Collateral Branch living

Granddaughter of the late Sir John William Pitt Muir Mackenzie, K.C.S.I., 6th son of 2nd baronet:—

Issue of the late Kenneth James Muir Mackenzie, *b.* 1882, *d.* 1931: *m.* 1915, Phyllis [who *d.* 1938, having *m.* 2ndly, 1932, Lieut.-Com. William Oswald Rees Millington, R.N. (retired)], da. of the late Henry Howard Taylor, of Thurnscoe Hall, Yorkshire [Lighton, Bt.]:—

Susan (twin), *b.* 1917: *m.* 1st, 1939 (m. diss. 1947), Capt. George David Garforth-Bles, Indian Army; 2ndly, 1947, Lt.-Col. Gerald Owen Whyte, and has issue living, (by 1st m.) George William, *b.* 1941; Maj. 1st Bn. Black Watch: *m.* 1971, Roswitha Fill, of Vienna,—Suzanna Mary, *b.* 1943: *m.* 1963, Anthony Birley (Prof. of Ancient Hist., Manchester Univ.) of 132, Fog Lane, Didsbury, Manchester, M20 0SW, and has issue living, Paul Hamish Aurelius *b.* 1966,— Ursula Ann *b.* 1964,—(by 2nd m.) Belinda Jane, *b.* 1948,—Lucinda Enid, *b.* 1951. *Residence*, The Mill Farm, Tinwell, nr. Stamford.

The 1st baronet, Sir Alexander Muir, descended from the Muirs of Cassencarrie (a very ancient family), assumed the additional surname of Mackenzie upon succeeding to the estates of his great-uncle, John Mackenzie, of Delvine, Perthshire, 3rd son of Sir Kenneth Mackenzie, 1st baronet of Coul. The 4th baronet *d.* 1918, and the 5th baronet, Sir Robert Cecil, M.C., Lieut. Durham L.I., also *d.* 1918 (killed in action during European War).

MACKESON, Creation (U.K.) 1954, of Hythe, co. Kent.

Sir RUPERT HENRY MACKESON, 2nd *Baronet*, *b.* Nov. 16th, 1941; ed. at Harrow, and at Trin. Coll., Dublin (MA); late Capt. RHG, and Lt. Buffs. Regt. (TA); *s.* his father, *Brig. Sir* HARRY RIPLEY, 1964: *m.* 1968 (m. diss. 1972), Camilla Margaret, da. of Lt.-Col. Sir Kenneth Alexander Keith [see E. Kintore].

Arms—Vair four roses three and one or. **Crest**—A lion's gamb erased or supporting an escutcheon gules charged with a rose or.
Residence—2, Orchard Court, Portman Sq., W1.

Sister living—Fiona Mariella, *b.* 1946: *m.* 1965, Capt. Hamish Leslie Gray-Cheape, late Gren. Gds., of Hill House, Walcot, Alcester, Warwicks., and has issue living, Hugo James, *b.* 1968,—George Hamish, *b.* 1971.

Widow living of 1st Baronet—ALETHEA CECIL (*Alethea, Lady Mackeson*) (The Old Rectory, Great Mongeham, Deal, Kent; 2, Orchard Court, Portman Sq., W1), da. of the late Cdr. Reginald George Talbot, RN [*see* E. Shrewsbury, colls.]: *m.* 1940, Sir Henry Ripley Mackeson, 1st Bt., who *d.* 1964.

Sir Harry Ripley Mackeson, 1st baronet, son of Henry Mackeson of Littlebourne House, Littlebourne, Kent, was M.P. for Hythe (*C*) 1945-50, and for Folkestone 1950-59. He was Dep. Ch. Conservative Whip 1950-52, Senior Lord Commr. of the Treasury 1951-52, and Sec. for Overseas Trade 1952-53.

MACKWORTH, Creation (G.B.) 1776, of The Gnoll, Glamorganshire.

Rather death than shame.

Sir DAVID ARTHUR GEOFFREY MACK-WORTH, 9th *Baronet*, only son of the late Vice-Adm. Geoffrey Mackworth, C.M.G., D.S.O., 5th son of 6th baronet ; *b.* July 13th, 1912; *s.* his uncle, *Col. Sir* HARRY LLEWELLYN, *CMG, DSO,* 1952; Cdr. (ret.) RN; a Member of R. Inst. of Navigation; formerly Drafting Cdr. RN Barracks, Devonport, and Naval Adviser to Director of Guided Weapon Research and Development, Mins. of Supply; Man. Dir. of S. Coast Rod Rigging Co., Ltd.: *m.* 1st, 1941 (m. diss. 1971), Mary Alice (ROBINSON-SMITH), da. of the late Thomas Henry Grylls, of 36, Great Ormond Street, WC; 2ndly, 1973, Beryl Joan, 3rd da. of the late Pembroke Henry Cockayn Cross, and formerly wife of the late Ernest Henry Sparkes, and has issue by 1st m.

Arms—Per pale indented sable and ermine, on a chevron gules, five crosses-patée or. **Crest**—A cock proper.
Residence,—63 Wittering Rd., Hayling Island Hants. *Clubs*—Royal Naval (Portsmouth), Royal Ocean Racing, Royal Corinthian Yacht (Cowes) Clubs, and Royal Naval Sailing Assocn.

Son living (By 1st m)—DIGBY JOHN (P.O. Box 2898, Tehran, Iran), *b.* Nov. 2nd, 1945; ed. at Wellington; late Lt. AAAC in Malaysia and Vietnam; with Iranian Helicopters, Ltd.: *m.* 1971, Antionette Francesca, da. of Henry James McKenna, of 40, Gyllingdune Gdns., Ilford, Essex.

Sisters living—Betty Mabel, *b.* 1911.——Lorna Alice, *b.* 1918.

Mother living—Noel Mabel, da. of the late William I. Langford, of Charford Manor, Avonwick, S. Devon : *m.* 1910, Vice-Adm. Geoffrey Mackworth, C.M.G., D.S.O. (ante), who *d.* 1952. *Residence*, Trevean, George Lane, Plympton St. Maurice, S. Devon.

Collateral Branches living.

Issue of the late Capt. Francis Julian Audley Mackworth, 2nd son of 6th baronet *b.* 1876, *d.* (killed in action) 1914 : *m.* 1910, Dorothy Conran (who *m.* 2ndly, 1922, Charles Edward Gatehouse), da. of the late Arthur Hastings Lascelles, of Belmore, Narbeth, Pembroke.

Cecily Joan, *b.* 1911 : *m.* 1st 1935, Leon Donckier de Donceel, who *d.* 1938; 2ndly, 1957, Marquis de Chabannes la Palice, of Château du Brèvedent, Calvados, France, and has issue living, (by 1st marriage) Pascale, *b.* 1936.

Issue of the late Col. John Dolben Mackworth, C.B.E., 7th son of 6th baronet, *b.* 1887, *d.* 1939: *m.* 1913, Marianne Annette, who *d.* 1968, da. of H. W. Sillem, of The Pines, Horsell, Surrey:—

Josephine Ann, *b.* 1914 : *m.* 1st, 1937, Major Patrick Owen Lyons, who *d.* 1941, Indian Army Ordnance Corps; 2ndly, 1942, Lt.-Col. Noel James, MBE, RAOC, of Tower House, 4, Bath Rd., Cowes, I. of Wight, and has issue living, (by 2nd marriage) Christopher Noel Mackworth, *b.* 1946,—John Gwyn Mackworth, *b.* 1951,—(by 1st marriage) Mary Annette, *b.* 1939,—Bridget Carol Dolben, *b.* 1940.

Grandson of the late Horace Eugene Mackworth, 2nd son of 4th baronet :—

Issue of the late Lt.-Col. Norman Walter Mackworth, MB, ChB, FRCS, IMS, *b.* 1878, *d.* 1950: *m.* 1908, Isabel Largie *MA*, who *d.* 1967, da. of the late William Anderson:—

Norman Humphrey, *PhD*, *MB*, *ChB* (16232, Camellia Terr., Los Gatos, Cal. 95030, USA), *b.* 1917; ed. at Aberdeen Univ. (MB and ChB); PhD Camb.: *m.* 1941, Jane Felicity, MD, BChir, PhD, yr. da. of the late Capt. Walter Hugh Charles Samuel Thring, CBE, RN, and has issue living, Alan Keith (96, Upper North St., Brighton), *b.* 1945: *m.* 1969, Marian Elizabeth, da. of J. V. Fry, and has issue living, Bryn Sarah *b.* 1972,—Hugh Francis, *b.* 1958,—Jean Clare, *b.* 1942: *m.* 1964, David Surrey, and has issue living, Patrick David *b.* 1969, Susan *b.* 1971.

Grandchildren of the late Audley Mackworth (infra) :—

Issue of the late Air Vice-Marshal Philip Herbert Mackworth, C.B., C.B.E., D.F.C., *b.* 1897, *d.* 1958: *m.* 1921, Winifred Kathleen June, who *d.* 1967, da. of William Moss:—

Richard Charles Audley (27, Wellington Sq., SW3), *b.* 1924; ed. at Camb. Univ. (MA); MSc Eng. London; AMIMechE; MIWE; DIC; formerly Fl.-Lt. RAF: *m.* 1960, Rosalind Jean, da. of the Rev. A. Walters, V. of Wychbold, Worcs., and has issue living, Julia Kathleen, *b.* 1968,—Victoria Alma Louise, *b.* 1971.——James Digby (The Old School House, Littleworth, Faringdon, Berks.), *b.* 1927; ed. at Camb. Univ. (MA); Maj. (ret.) REME; AMIMechE: *m.* 1st (m. diss. 1968) Marjorie Wilding; 2ndly, 19—, and has issue living, (by 1st m.) Charles Digby, *b.* 1958,—Amanda Jane, *b.* 1956.——Sheila Margaret (36, Kingswood Av., NW6), *b.* 1922: *m.* 1952 (m. diss. 1962), Osmond Francis, and has issue living, David FRANCIS-MACKWORTH, *b.* 1953; assumed the additional surname of Mackworth 1964.

Granddaughters of the late Herbert Francis Mackworth, el. son of the late Lieut. Herbert Mackworth, R.N., 2nd son of 3rd baronet :—

Issue of the late Audley Mackworth, *b.* 1857, *d.* 1914 : *m.* 1896, Mary, who *d.* 1955, da. of the late Henry Mason, of Caterham :—

Christabel Mary, *b.* 1899. *Residence*, 9, Evelyn Mansions, Queen's Club Gardens, W14.——Joan Evelyn, *b.* 1903; BA London 1927; MB and ChB Bristol 1938; MRCS England and LRCP London 1939; DPM 1943. *Residence*, Little Gidding, Chapel Road, South Leigh, Witney, Oxon., OX8 6UP.

This family is of considerable antiquity in Shropshire and Derbyshire, and a member of it fought at Poitiers in 1356. Sir Francis Mackworth, a distinguished royalist, fought on the side of Charles I. Col. Humphrey Mackworth, a man of considerable note *temp.* Commonwealth, was M.P. for Salop, was Governor for Shrewsbury, and one of Cromwell's Council. The 1st baronet sat as M.P. for Cardiff, and the 2nd baronet bequeathed the Gnoll Castle estate to his widow. The 8th baronet, Col. Sir Harry Llewellyn Mackworth, C.M.G., D.S.O., Roy. Corps of Signals, was Ch. Signal Officer, Egypt 1924-27.

MACLEAN, Creation (U.K.) 1957, of Strachur and Glensluain, co. Argyll.

Sir FITZROY HEW ROYLE MACLEAN, *CBE*, 1st *Baronet*, son of the late Maj. Charles Wilberforce Maclean, DSO, OBE; *b.* March 11th, 1911; ed. at Eton, and at King's Coll., Camb. (MA, Hon LLD, Glasgow); appointed 3rd Sec. Diplo. Ser. 1933, and 2nd Sec. 1938; served in Paris and Moscow; was Parliamentary Under-Sec. of State for War and Financial Sec. to War Office 1954-57; author of "Eastern Approaches" and other works; 1939-45 War with Queen's Own Cameron Highlanders and 1st SAS Regt.; Brig. Comdg. British Mission to Yugoslav Partisans 1943-45 (CBE, French Croix de Guerre, Order of Kutusov of Russia, Yugoslav Partisan Star); MP for Lancaster (C) Oct. 1941 to Oct. 1959, and for Bute and N. Ayrshire Oct. 1959 to Feb. 1974; CBE (Mil.) 1944: *m.* 1946, the Hon. Veronica Nell Fraser, da. of 14th Lord Lovat and widow of Lt. Alan Phipps, RN [see M. Normanby, colls.], and has issue.

Arms—Not matriculated at Lyon Office at time of going to press.
Residence—Strachur House, Argyll. **Clubs**— White's, Pratt's.

Sons living—CHARLES EDWARD, *b.* Oct. 31st, 1946; ed. at Eton and New Coll., Oxford.—— Alexander James, *b.* 1949; ed. at Eton.

Maj. Charles Wilberforce Maclean, D.S.O., O.B.E., father of the 1st baronet, was 4th son of Lieut.-Col. Allan Henry Maclean, R.H.A., grandson of Lieut.-Col. Alexander Maclean, 13th Chief of Ardgour, Argyll. His ancestor, Donald, younger son of Lachlan Bronnach, 7th of Duart [see Maclean Bt., cr. 1631] slew MacMaster of Ardgour and appropriated his lands, about 1432, obtaining a grant thereof from Alexander, 3rd Lord of the Isles. This was confirmed by James IV in 1494.

McLEOD, Creation (U.K.) 1925, of The Fairfields, Cobham, Surrey.
[Pronounced "McLoud."]

HOLD·FAST

Murus· aheneus·esto

Be thou a brazen wall.

Sir CHARLES HENRY McLEOD*, 3rd Baronet; *b.* Nov. 7th, 1924; *s.* his father, *Sir* MURDOCH CAMPBELL, 1950; ed. at Winchester: *m.* 1957, Anne Gillian, younger da. of Henry Russell Bowlby [V. Combermere, colls.], and has issue.

Arms—Ermine, on a pile azure between two lotus flowers in base or a castle triple-towered argent, masoned sable, windows and porch gules. **Crest**—In front of two flags in saltire gules, staves proper, a bull's head caboshed also gules.

Residence—Gillhams House, Lynchmere, Haslemere, Surrey.

_____

Son living—JAMES RODERICK CHARLES, *b.* Sept. 26th, 1960.

Daughters living—Belinda Ann, *b.* 1957.——Nicola, *b.* 1958.

The 1st baronet, Sir Charles Campbell McLeod (son of the Rev. Norman McLeod, of N. Uist), was Chm. of National Bank of India, Ltd., and of Imperial Tea Co., Ltd.

_____

* His el. brother, Roderick Campbell McLeod, *b.* 1921 ; Lieut. Scots Guards ; *d.* (killed in action at Salerno) 1943.

_____

McLINTOCK, Creation (U.K.) 1934, of Sanquhar, co. Dumfries.

By virtue and labour.

Virtute·et·Labore

Sir WILLIAM TRAVEN McLINTOCK, 3rd Baronet; *b.* Jan. 4th, 1931; *s.* his father, *Sir* THOMSON, 1953; ed. at Harrow: *m.* 1952, André, da. of Richard Lonsdale-Hands, of Av. Edouard Dapples, Lausanne, and has issue.

Arms—Azure, a book expanded or, leaved gules, over all a writing pen palewise proper. **Crest**—A lion passant or, holding in his dexter paw a thistle slipped proper.

Residence—Villa Kavalliori, St. Andrews Rd., Swieqi, Malta, GC.

_____

Sons living—MICHAEL WILLIAM, *b.* Aug. 13th, 1958.——Andrew Thomson, *b.* 1960.——Kevin Robert, *b.* 1963.

Brother living—Peter Thomson, *b.* 1933: *m.* 1954, Fiona, da. of Sir (Alexander Frank) Philip Christison, G.B.E., C.B., D.S.O., M.C., 4th Bt., and has issue living, Morar, *b.* 1955.—Traven Thomson Christison, *b.* 1957. *Residence*, Springfield, Penicuik, Midlothian.

Aunts living (daughters of 1st baronet)—Norah Lyons (of 1, Whiteheads Grove, Chelsea, S.W.3), *b.* 1903: *m.* 1936, Stephen Everest Watson, who *d.* 1952, and has issue living, Eric William, *b.* 1938.——Mary Lyons, *b.* 1912: *m.* 1st, 1937, Malcolm George Lillingston, King's Dragoon Guards, who *d.* (killed in action during European War) 1941; 2ndly, 1947, Robert Bradford Myles, M.C., and has issue living, (by 1st marriage) Mark Campbell, *b.* 1938,—Diane Margaret, *b.* 1941,—(by 2nd marriage) Nicholas Robert William Bradford, *b.* 1954,—Sarah Louise Bradford, *b.* 1950,—Penelope Jean Bradford, *b.* 1952. *Residence*, Carnberg, Dundalk, co. Louth.

Widow living of 2nd Baronet—JEAN (*Jean, Lady McLintock*), da. of the late Robert Traven Donaldson Aitken, of Newcastle, New Brunswick, Canada : *m.* 1929, Sir Thomson McLintock, 2nd baronet, who *d.* 1953. *Residence*, 10, Avenue Court, Draycott Av., SW3.

The 1st baronet, Sir William McLintock, G.B.E., C.V.O. (son of Thomson McLintock), was senior partner in the firm of Thomson McLintock & Co., chartered accountants, of 33, King William Street, E.C.4, and Glasgow.

MACLURE, Creation (U.K.) 1898, of The Home, Whalley Range, near Manchester, co. Palatine of Lancaster.

Sir JOHN WILLIAM SPENCER MACLURE, *O.B.E.*, 3rd *Baronet; b.* Feb. 4th, 1899; *s.* his father, *Col. Sir* JOHN EDWARD STANLEY, 1938; ed. at Wellington Coll.; Lieut.-Col. (retired) King's Roy. Rifle Corps; Commanded British Garrison in the Netherlands 1945-8; European War 1918-19, N. Russia 1919, N.-W. Europe 1944-5 (O.B.E.); O.B.E. (Mil.) 1945: *m.* 1929, Elspeth King, da. of the late Alexander King Clark, of Wykeham Hatch, West Byfleet, and has issue.

Arms—Argent, on a chevron engrailed azure between in chief two roses and in base a quatrefoil gules, a martlet between two escallops of the field. **Crest**—An eagle's head erased argent between four roses gules, stalked and leaved on each side proper.

Paratus sum.
I am ready.

Residence—6, Bereweeke Close, Winchester, Hants. **Club**—United Service.

Sons living—JOHN ROBERT SPENCER (Hill End, Newtown, Newbury, Berks., RG15 9DF), *b.* March 25th, 1934; ed. at Winchester: *m.* 1964, Jane Monica, da. of the late Rt. Rev. Thomas Joseph Savage, and has issue living, John Mark, *b.* 1965,—Thomas Stephen, *b.* 1967.—Graham Spencer, *b.* 1970,—Stephen Patrick Ian, *b.* 1974.——Patrick Stanley Winton King, *b.* 1939; ed. at Winchester.

Daughter living—Elspeth Rosemary, *b.* 1930: *m.* 1955, Brig. Michael Matthews, late RE, c/o Lloyds Bank, Chagford, Devon, and has issue living, Graeme Michael Ian, *b.* 1959,—James Binding, *b.* 1966,—Nichola Jane, *b.* 1957,—Elspeth Julie, *b.* 1963.

Brother living—Edward Stanley Winton, *b.* 1909; Lt.-Com. (ret.) RN: *m.* 1938, Jeanette Kathleen, who *d.* 1969, da. of the late Anton Bakker, of Sydney, Aust., and has issue living, Caroline Eleanor Kathleen, *b.* 1939; ed. at London Univ. (BA): *m.* 1964, Gerard Jozef van Tienen, of Abeelstraat 37, Dordrecht 9, Netherlands, and has issue living, Robbert Rudolf *b.* 1967, Richard Mark *b.* 1970,—Margaret Elizabeth Anne, *b.* 1941: *m.* 1969, Raymond D. Hibberd, of 15, Pine Tree Gdns., Park Lane, Cowplain, Hants., and has issue living, Simon Philip *b.* 1972,—Yvonne Irene Valerie, *b.* 1943: *m.* 1st, 1964 (m. diss. 1972), Albert Brian Challinor; 2ndly, 1972, Brian Henry Thompson, RN, of 55, Quex Rd., Westgate-on-Sea, Kent, and has issue living (by 1st m.), Ian Grant *b.* 1965, Susan Jane *b.* 1967 (by 2nd m.) Fiona Kate *b.* 1973, Alexandra Louise *b.* 1975. *Residence*, Melrose, 23, St. David's Rd., Southsea, Hants.

Sisters living—Ruth Ina Margaret, *b.* 1900.——Edith Mary Ursula, *b.* 1916: *m.* 1939, Louis Gordon Oliphant Hutchison, sometime F/O, RAFVR, who *d.* 1959, and has issue living, Alexander Gordon Oliphant (Antiques, High St., Stockbridge, Hants.), *b.* 1943: *m.* 1967, Jennifer Marilyn, da. of Alun Blackwell, and has issue living, Alexander Valentine Oliphant *b.* 1968,—Susan Ruth Oliphant, *b.* 1940: *m.* 1st, 1959, John Chislett, who *d.* 1962: 2ndly, 1962, Jonathan Frederick Macnaught Ruddick, of Bramshott Manor, Liphook, Hants., and has issue living, (by 1st m.) Miles Gordon *b.* 1960, (by 2nd m.) Francis Louis *b.* 1962, Simon *b.* 1964, Charlotte *b.* 1966,—Philippa Anne Oliphant *b.* 1946: *m.* 1963, Donald Stuart Oldham, and has issue living, Tamsin *b.* 1963, Jessica *b.* 1966. *Residence*, Mist over Knap, Hollow Oak, Bere Regis, Dorset.

The 1st baronet was Hon. Sec. to Cotton Famine Relief Fund 1862-65, and MP for Stretford 1886-1901.

McMAHON, Creation (U.K.) 1817.

[Pronounced "**McMähn**."]

Sir (WILLIAM) PATRICK McMAHON, 7th *Baronet; b.* April 24th, 1900; *s.* his father, *Sir* (KELLERMAN) EYRE, *O.B.E.*, 1935; ed. at Wellington Coll.; is a Fellow of Land Agents' So., and a Professional Asso. of Surveyors' Institution: *m.* 1939, Ruth Stella (BARKER HAHLO), from whom he obtained a divorce 1960, da. of the late Percy Robert Kenyon-Slaney [*see* B. Kenyon, colls.], and has issue.

Arms—Per saltire or and ermine, a lion passant azure between two lions passant-reguardant gules. **Crest**—An arm embowed in armour, holding a sword wavy, all proper, surmounted of a portcullis gules, chained or. **Supporters**—On either side a private of the 10th Foot habited and accoutred, and holding in the exterior hand a musket proper.

Thus we defend ourselves and our sacred rights.

Residence—Les Buttes, St. Martin, Jersey.

Sons living—BRIAN PATRICK, *b.* June 9th, 1942; ed. at Wellington; BSc; AIM.——Shaun Desmond, *b.* 1945; ed. at Wellington: *m.* 1971, Antonia Noel Adie.

The 1st baronet, the Right Hon. Sir John M'Mahon, was a Privy Councillor for Ireland an Private Secretary and Keeper of the Privy Purse to George IV. His next brother was also created a baronet (cr. 1815, ext. 1926). The 1st baronet of this creation was succeeded under a limitation in the patent by his second brother, Gen. Sir Thomas, GCB, Col. of 10th Foot, and Com.-in-Chief of the Forces at Bombay.

MACNAGHTEN, Creation (U.K.) 1836, of Bushmills House, co. Antrim.

Sir PATRICK ALEXANDER MAC-
NAGHTEN, 11th _Baronet_; _b._ Jan. 24th,
1927; _s._ his father _Sir_ ANTONY, 1972;
_ed._ at Eton, and Trin. Coll., Camb.:
_m._ 1955, Marianne, da. of Dr. Erich
Schaefer, of Cambridge, and has issue.

Arms—Quarterly : 1st and 4th argent a
dexter hand fessways proper holding a cross-
crosslet fitchée azure ; 2nd and 3rd argent, a
tower gules. **Crest**—A tower embattled gules.
Supporters—Two roebucks proper.
Residence—Crofton Crest, Cherry Hill
Drive, Barnt Green, Birmingham.

Sons living—MALCOLM FRANCIS, _b._ Sept. 21st,
1956.——Edward Alexander, _b._ 1958.——
David Charles, _b._ 1962.

Brothers living—Antony Martin (Ballyvester
House, Donaghadee, co. Down), _b._ 1930; _ed._
at Eton: _m._ 1959, Catherine Frances, da. of the
Rev. Charles ffolliott Young, and has issue
living, Philip Martin, _b._ 1965,—Antony Charles,
_b._ 1971,—Ruth Helen, _b._ 1964,—Imogen Alice,
_b._ 1970.——Charles Edmund, _b._ 1935; _ed._ at
Eton.

Sister living—Diana Mary, _b._ 1929: _m._ 1951,
Myles Richard Eckersley, and has issue living, Alison, _b._ 1954,—Fiona Jane, _b._ 1955. _Residence_,
Embley Heathcote, Embley Park, nr. Romsey, Hants.

Aunts living—Mary Frances (6 Akehurst St., Roehampton, SW15), _b._ 1903: _m._ 1931, Laszlo Péri,
who _d._ 1965, and has issue living.——Brigid Alison YOUNGDAY, _b._ 1904: _m._ 1933, W. Jungmittag,
who _d._ 1944, and has issue living.——Anne Catherine, _b._ 1908: _m._ 1st 1936, James Ernest
Skilbeck, who _d._ 1947; 2ndly, 1947, Arnold Richardson Ashby, of 23, Wymondlet Rd., Hitchin,
Herts., and has issue living, (by 1st m.) John, _b._ 1942,—Catherine, _b._ 1947.

Widow living of 10th Baronet—MAGDALENE (_Magdalene, Lady Macnaghten_), (Dundarave, Bushmills,
co. Antrim), el. da. of the late Edmund Fisher: _m._ 1926, Sir Antony Macnaghten, 10th Bt.,
who _d._ 1972.

Collateral Branches living.

Grandson of the late Steuart Lambert Macnaghten, 4th son of Francis
Macnaghten, 3rd son of 1st baronet:—
Issue of the late Steuart Cecil Macnaghten, _b._ 1881, _d._ 1918 : _m._ 1915, Hilda Marion,
da. of the late Henry Jenks, of Dunairds, Birnam, Perthshire, and Barrow Hedges,
Carshalton, Surrey :—

Steuart Patrick, _b._ 1917 ; _ed._ at Sherborne ; sometime Major Derbyshire Yeo. : _m._ 1961, Mrs.
Beatrix Wyatt-Smith, da. of the late Col. Sir Francis Killigrew Seymour Metford, K.C.B.,
OBE, VD, TD. _Residence_, The Brook House, Sherborne, Cheltenham. _Club_, Junior Carlton.

Granddaughter of the late Alfred Hill Macnaghten, 6th son of Francis Mac-
naghten (ante):—
Issue of the late Lieut.-Col. Balfour Macnaghten, D.S.O., 12th Roy. Lancers, _b._ 1875, _d._
1945 : _m._ 1902, Hilda, who _d._ 1958, da. of W. G. Lardner, of 11, Fourth Avenue,
Hove, Sussex :—
Daphne, _b._ 1914 : _m._ 1940, Lieut.-Col. Richard Percival Hawksley Burbury, Duke of Cornwall,
L.I., who _d._ (killed in action in Normandy) 1944. _Residence_, Portesbery Woods, Camberley, Surrey

Granddaughters of the late Elliot Macnaghten (_b._ 1837), son of the late Elliot
Macnaghten (_b_ 1807), 4th son of 1st baronet :—
Issue of the late Russell Elliot Macnaghten, _b._ 1860, _d._ 1918 : _m._ 1891, Mary (now of N.
Vancouver, British Columbia), da. of the late Frederick Berry, of Churchdown, Gloucester-
shire :—
Eva Fraoch, _b._ 1895 : _m._ 1922, Frederick Ivor Jackson, and has issue living, James Ivor, _b._ 1923,—
Kathleen Elizabeth Ann, _b._ 1926,—Pamela Mary, _b._ 1928.——Kathleen Edith, _b._ 1903: _m._
1934, Edward C. R. Cardinall, of Skaha Lake, Penticton, BC, Canada, and has issue living,
Edward Russell, _b._ 1936,—Sandra Margaret, _b._ 1934,—Chloe Joan (twin), _b._ 1936.

Grandchildren of the late Col. William Hay Macnaghten, C.B., son of the late
Elliot Macnaghten (ante) :—
Issue of the late Brig.-Gen. Ernest Brander Macnaghten, C.M.G., D.S.O., _b._ 1872, _d._ 1948
_m._ 1906, Yvonne Marie, who _d._ 1950, da. of the late Surg.-Lieut.-Col. J. S. Forrester
Roy. Horse Guards :—
James Steuart (35, Gloucester Walk, W8), _b._ 1914; _ed._ at Eton, and at Ch. Ch., Oxford (MA);
Maj. RA (ret.) and Maj. RA (TA Reserve); 1939-45 War; an employee of ICI Ltd.——Joan
Yvonne Marie, _b._ 1911. _Residence_, Gorse Cottage, Eversley Cross, Basingstoke, Hants.——
Awdry Clarisse (twin) (10, Weatherby Gdns., Hartley Wintney, Hants.), _b._ 1914: _m._ 1936, Brig
Anthony Donald Macdonald Teacher, CBE, DL, who _d._ 1969, and has issue living, Anthony
James Moreton, _b._ 1937: _m._ 1969, Rosemary Chloe, da. of Sir Henry Joseph d'Avigdor-Goldsmid,
DSO, MC, TD, 2nd Bt., and has issue living, Harry Donald Macdonald _b._ 1970, Laura Poppy
_b._ 1973,—Hugh Macdonald, _b._ 1943.——Renée Gavrelle, _b._ 1918: _m._ 1st, 1938, Lt.-Cdr. Alexander
Arthur Wyndham Baker, RN, who _d._ 1969; 2ndly, 1971, William Henry Guilland Stenson (Box
833, Blantyre, Malawi), and has issue living (by 1st m.), Mark Alexander (Jubilee Cottage,
Newtown Common, Newbury), _b._ 1940, _ed._ at Ch. Ch., Oxford (MA): _m._ 1964, Meriel, da. of Capt.
Edward Hugh Frederick Chetwynd-Talbot, MBE [_see_ E. Shrewsbury, Colls.], and has issue living,
Alexander Duncan _b._ 1968, Miranda Gavrelle _b._ 1970,—Gavin Jeremy, _b._ 1944: _m._ 1971, Joanna
Gwendoline, da. of Gp. Capt. G. B. Bell, RAF.

Issue of the late Leslie Hay Macnaghten, _b._ 1875, _d._ 1950: _m._ 1906, Hilda Mary Ethelind,
who _d._ 1973, da. of the late Rev. Jocelyn Barnes, V. of St. Breage, Cornwall:—
Geoffrey Leslie, _b._ 1909; _ed._ at Malvern Coll.; 1939-45 War as Fl.-Lt. RAFVR: _m._ 1937, Hilary
Marriott, da. of the late T. A. Marriott Castle, and has issue living, Jennifer Rosemary, _b._ 1939,—
Sarah Lynne, _b._ 1954. _Residence_, 123, Old Church St., Chelsea, SW3 6EA.——Douglas Melville
_b._ 1911; _ed._ at Wellington Coll.; with Spicers Internat. Ltd., of Reed House, 82, Piccadilly, W1.
1939-45 War in N. Africa and Italy as Maj. RASC (Africa star, Italy star, 1939-45 star): _m._ 1946,
Thecla Isabel, twin da. of the late John Mundell Reid, of Greenock, Scotland, and has issue living,
Lorraine Thecla Ethelind, _b._ 1947,—Camilla Dawn, _b._ 1950: _m._ 1971, Timothy William Whittle.
Residence, Courtlands, Foley Rd. Claygate, Surrey.

Grandchildren of the late Leslie Hay Macnaghten (ante) :—

Issue of the late Lieut. Cyril Jocelyn Gillichrist Macnaghten, R.N.V.R., *b.* 1907, *d.* (on active ser. during European War) 1943 : *m.* 1932, Mary Evelyne, who *d.* 1954, da. of the late G. E. Mullens, of Teddington, Australia :—

Alexander Michael Gillichrist (6, Carrington St., Nedlands, W. Aust.), *b.* 1940; ed. at Wellington Coll., and at Roy. Agricultural Coll., Cirencester; a Member of Commonwealth Inst. of Valuers: *m.* 1971, Vanessa, da. of Duncan Charles Beresford-Ord, of Beverley Lodge, Mill Point Rd., S. Perth, Aust.——Angela Kay, *b.* 1935: *m.* 1960, John Woodward, of 9, Harvard Rd., Chiswick, W4, and has issue living, Andrew St. John, *b.* 1966,—Sarah Mary, *b.* 1963.

Grandchildren of the late Rev. Henry Alexander Macnaghten, 5th son of 2nd Bt.:—

Issue of the late Sir Henry Pelham Wentworth Macnaghten, *b.* 1880, *d.* 1949 : *m.* 1919, Frances Alice, who *d.* 1969, da. of the Very Rev. James Cropper, R. of Penshurst, Kent:—

Angus David Henry (Kirnan, Kilmichael Glassary, Lochgilphead, Argyll), *b.* 1923; 1939-45 War as Capt. Rifle Bde. (wounded): *m.* 1952, Sally, da. of Edward Watts, of Ashfields, Gt. Canfield, Essex, and has issue living, David Edmund, *b.* 1954,—Stuart Ben, *b.* 1957,—Patrick Henry, *b.* 1959.——Robin Donnelly (Eton College, Windsor), *b.* 1927; ed. at Eton (KS), and King's Coll., Camb.: *m.* 1961, Petronella Anne, da. of Lt.-Col. A. T. T. Card, of The Old Vicarage, Holt, Wimborne, Dorset.——Caroline Priscilla, *b.* 1931: *m.* 1966, Don Collis, of 25, de Walden St., W1, and has issue living, Chayley Zillah, *b.* 1969.

Grandson of the late Sir Steuart Macnaghten, 6th son of 1st baronet :—

Issue of the late Capt. Angus Charles Rowley Steuart Macnaghten, Lieut. Black Watch (Roy. Highlanders), *b.* 1883 ; missing Oct. 1914, believed *d.* (killed in action during European War) 1914 : *m.* 1911, Hazel Enid, who *d.* 1956, da. of the late Col. Lyndon Irwin, Indian Army :—

Angus Derek Iain Jacques, *b.* 1914; ed. at Eton, and at Trin. Coll., Camb. (BA 1935); with British Council 1946-67; 1940-45 War as Maj. Intelligence Corps.; Gold Staff Officer in Waiting at Coronation of HM Queen Elizabeth II: *m.* 1957, Daphne, only da. of the late Horace Nettleship Soper, of 15, Stanley Cres., W11. *Residence,* New Mile Cottage, Ascot, Berks.

The family of Macnaghten is of great antiquity in the Western Highlands. In 1267, Alexander III. granted to Gillichrist Macnaghten and his heirs the custody of the castle and island of Fraocheilean, on condition that he should rebuild it, and keep it fit for the reception of the king whenever he should visit it. His great-grandson Duncan, a faithful partisan of the cause of King Duncan, was one of the band that accompanied James Douglas in his attempt to deposit the heart of Robert Bruce at Jerusalem. The 1st baronet, Sir Francis, a Judge of the Supreme Court of Madras 1809-15, and of Calcutta 1815-25, assumed the additional surname and arms of Workman by Roy. licence 1809. The 4th baronet, the Rt. Hon. Sir Edward, G.C.B., G.C.M.G., was M.P. for co. Antrim (C) 1880-85, and for Antrim co., N. Div. 1885-87 when he became a Lord of Appeal in Ordinary, with title of *Baron Macnaghten* (Life Peerage). The 6th baronet, Sir Edward Henry Macnaghten, Lieut. Black Watch (Roy. Highlanders), was killed in action during European War July 1916, and his younger brother, Sir Arthur Douglas Macnaghten, 7th baronet, Lieut. Rifle Brig., *d.* (killed in action during European War) Sept. 1916.

Macpherson-Grant, see Grant.

MACREADY, Creation (U.K.) 1923, of Cheltenham, co. Gloucester.

AD EXTREMUM TENAX

Sir NEVIL JOHN WILFRID MACREADY, 3rd *Baronet*; *b.* Sept. 7th, 1921 ; *s.* his father, *Lieut.-Gen. Sir* GORDON NEVIL, *K.B.E., C.B., C.M.G., D.S.O., M.C.,* 1956 ; ed. at Cheltenham, and at St. John's Coll., Oxford (MA); Vice-Pres. and Man. Dir. of Mobil Oil Française, and a Dir. of Mobil Oil Co., Ltd.; 1939-45 War as Capt. R.A. (despatches): *m.* 1949, Mary, only da. of the late Sir (John) Donald Balfour Fergusson, GCB, and has issue.

Arms—Argent, on a chevron azure between three leopard's faces gules, two swords, the points in saltire proper, pommels and hilts or. **Crest**—On a wreath of the colours, in front of two swords points upwards in saltire proper, pommels and hilts or, a cubit arm also proper, grasping a snake vert.

Residences, 68, Boulevard de Courcelles, Paris XVII; 61, Rutland Gate, SW7.

Son living—CHARLES NEVIL, *b.* May 19th, 1955.

Daughters living—Caroline Elisabeth, *b.* 1950.——Sarah Diana Mary, *b.* 1953.——Anna Louise, *b.* 1963.

Aunt living (daughter of 1st baronet)—Louise Geraldine (62B, Princes Gate, SW7 2PD): *m.* 1916, Lt.-Col. Frederick Kaye Puckle, C.M.G., R.A.S.C., who *d.* 1959, and from whom she had obtained a divorce 1923, and has issue living, Sheila Catherine, *MBE, TD, b.* 1919; Lt.-Col. WRAC (ret.); Prin. Admin. Officer, HQ St. John Ambulance Bde.; MBE (Mil.) 1949.

The 1st baronet, Gen. the Rt. Hon. Sir (Cecil Frederick) Nevil Macready, G.C.M.G., K.C.B. (son of William Charles Macready, actor), served in Egyptian Expedition 1882, S. Africa 1899-1902, and European War 1914-18 as A.G. (K.C.M.G., G.C.M.G.), and was Commr. of Metropolitan Police 1918-20, and Com.-in-Ch. of Troops, Ireland 1920-22. The 2nd baronet, Lieut.-Gen. Sir Gordon Nevil Macready, K.B.E., C.B., C.M.G., D.S.O., M.C., was Col. Comdt. R.E., Assist. Ch. of Imperial Gen. Staff, War Office 1940-2, Ch. of British Army Staff, Washington, U.S.A. 1942-6, Regional Commr., Hanover 1946-7, British Chm. of Bipartite Economic Control Office in Germany 1947-8, Regional Commr., N. Rhine-Westphalia 1948-9, and Economic Advisor to United Kingdom High Commr. 1949-51.

MACTAGGART, Creation (U.K.) 1938, of King's Park, City of Glasgow.

FOR COMMONWEAL AND LIBERTY

Sir IAN (JOHN) AULD MACTAGGART,
3rd *Baronet*; *b.* April 19th, 1923; *s.* his father,
Sir JOHN (JACK AULD) 1960; ed. at Oundle, and
at Clare Coll., Camb.; European War 1942-5 as
Lieut. R.E.; is Managing Director of Western
Heritable Investment Co. Ltd.; was a Co.
Councillor for London 1949-52: *m.* 1946 (m.
diss. 1969), Rosemary, da. of Sir Herbert
Geraint Williams, 1st Bt., M.P. (cr. 1953), and
has issue.

Arms—Argent, on a bend sable between two owls proper,
three escallop shells or. Crest—A tower proper masoned
sable, windows and port gules.

Residence,—2a, Westmoreland Terr., SW1.

Sons living—JOHN AULD, *b.* Jan. 21st, 1951.——Philip
Auld, *b.* 1956.

Daughters living—Jane Lindsay, *b.* 1949: *m.* 1974, Keith
Douglas Henry Baines.——Fiona Margaret, *b.* 1953.

Brothers living—Neil Auld, *b.* 1925; ed. at Massachusetts
Institute of Technology, Cambridge, Massachusetts (B.S. 1952); formerly Capt. R.E.:
m. 1953, Sheila, da. of the Hon. Herbert A. McKinney, of Nassau, Bahamas, and
has issue living, Neil Auld, *b.* 1959.—Andrew Auld, *b.* 1962,—Ann Elizabeth, *b.* 1955,—Robin
(da.), *b.* 1957,—Tara, *b.* 1960. *Residence,* Daiquiri, Nassau, Bahamas.——Alastair Auld
(Sandy), *b.* 1928; ed. at Harvard Univ. (BA, MBA): *m.* 1959, Cécile Macy, da. of Josiah M.
Erickson, of Greenwich, Conn., USA, and has issue living, Alastair Auld, *b.* 1966,—Mara Macy,
b. 1963,—Fiona Osborn, *b.* 1964. *Address,* P.O. Box 3160, Edmonton, Alberta, Canada.

The 1st baronet, Sir John Auld Mactaggart (son of the late Neil Mactaggart of Glasgow), was
a Housing Expert, and Chm. of Western Heritable Investment Co., Ltd., of Glasgow, London,
and Canada. He presented King's Park to City of Glasgow. The 2nd baronet, Sir John (Jack
Auld) Mactaggart was for many years Managing Dir. of Mactaggart & Mickel Ltd., builders and
state developers, of Glasgow and Edinburgh.

MacTaggart-Stewart, see Stewart.

MADDEN, Creation (U.K.) 1919, of Kells, co. Kilkenny.

FORTIOR QUI SE VINCIT

*He is stronger who
conquers himself.*

Sir CHARLES EDWARD MADDEN, *GCB.*,
2nd *Baronet: b.* June 15th, 1906; *s.* his
father, *Adm. of the Fleet,* Sir CHARLES EDWARD,
G.C.B., O.M., G.C.V.O., K.C.M.G., D.C.L., LL.D.,
1935; Adm (ret.): Ch. of Naval Staff, New
Zealand 1953-5, Dep. Ch. of Naval Personnel
1955-7, Flag Officer, Malta 1957-9, Flag Officer,
Flotillas, Home Fleet 1959-60, C.-in-C. Plymouth
1960-63, and C.-in-C. Home Fleet, and C.-in-C.
E. Atlantic Command (NATO) 1963-65; Chm.
Roy. Nat. Mission to Deep Sea Fishermen 1971,
Trustee National Maritime Museum 1968 (Chm.
since 1962), and Vice-Chm. Sail Training Assocn.
1968-70; a Vice-Lieut. of Greater London since
1969; 1939-45 War (despatches twice); *cr.* CB
(Mil.) 1955, KCB (Mil.) 1961, GCB (Mil.) 1965:
m. 1942, Olive, da. of the late G. W. Robins, and
has issue.

Arms—Sable, a falcon with his wings expanded, preying on
a mallard all argent, on a chief ermine out of a naval crown
between two cross-crosslets gules, from a staff in bend a flag
of St. George, all proper. Crest—On a ducal coronet or a falcon
rising argent, holding in his beak a cross-crosslet fitchée gules.

Residence,—21, Eldon Road, W.8.

Daughter living—Reseann, *b.* 1945: *m.* 1972, John Richard Beddington, of 128, Kensington Park
Rd., W11, and has issue living, James Edward, *b.* 1973.

Brother living—JOHN WILMOT, *MC, b.* Dec. 20th, 1916; Lt.-Col. (ret.) RA; Burma 1944 (despatches, MC); Chm. Warminster and Westbury RDC 1969-72: *m.* 1941, Beatrice Catherine, JP,
only da. of the late W. A. Sievwright, WS, of Moncrieff House, St. Andrews, Fife, and has issue
living, Peter John, *b.* 1942; late Capt. RA,—Charles Jonathan, *b.* 1949; MTech,—Susan Kate,
b. 1946: *m.* 1970, Richard Leoline Jenkins, MVO, late Capt. 1st The Queen's Dragoon Gds., of
The Old Bakery, Shalbourne, Marlborough, Wilts., and has issue living, Sarah Alexandra *b.* 1972,
Caroline Louise *b.* 1973. *Residence,* Manor House, Upton Lovell, Warminster.

Isters living—Conn, *b.* 1908: *m.* 1929, Neil Brodie Henderson, son of Brig.-Gen. Sir Brodie Haldane
Henderson, KCMG, CB, and has issue living, Ian Brodie, *b.* 1930; ed. at Eton: *m.* 1961, Veronica,
da. of Ralph Pain, and has issue living, Nicholas *b.* 1963, Lavinia *b.* 1962,—Alan Brodie (91,
Melbury Rd., W14), *b.* 1933; ed. at Eton: *m.* 1st, 1956 (m. diss. 1969), Antonia, da. of James
McMullen; 2ndly, 1969, Fiona Douglas Pilkington, and has issue living (by 1st m.), Bryan *b.*
1960, Gavin *b.* 1963 Kerena *b.* 1958, (by 2nd m.) David *b.* 1970,—Jean Brodie (*Hon. Mrs.*

William S. Russell), *b.* 1940: *m.* 1961, the Hon. William Southwell Russell, of Christopher's, Newney Green, Writtle, Essex [*see* B. De Clifford]. *Residence,* Glebe House, Little Hormead, Buntingford, Herts.——Joan, *b.* 1912: *m.* 1939, Lt.-Col. Henry Morison Vere Nicoll, DSO, OBE, late RA, of Rookery House, Wymondham, Melton Mowbray, Leics., and has issue living, Graham Morison (c/o Lloyds Bank, Tenbury Wells, Worcs.), *b.* 1940; ed. at Eastbourne Coll.; Capt. Welsh Gds.: *m.* 1st, 1965 (m. diss. 1972), Lucinda Marjorie, yr. da. of Capt. Timothy John Gurney, of The White House, nr. Buntingford, Herts. [see de Bathe, Bt., ext.]; 2ndly, 1972, Jane, da. of Maj. Thomas Edward Dealtry Kidd, MBE, RCA [see By Beaverbrook], and has issue living (by 1st m.), Simon Morison *b.* 1968,——Kenneth Charles (7, Farm Place, W8), *b.* 1942; ed. at Marlborough: *m.* 1968, Veronica Gillian, da. of C. R. Payne, of Cape Town, and has issue living, a son *b.* 1973, a da. *b.* 1971,——Adrian Michael, *b.* 1949,——Neville Henry, *b.* 1954.——Hope, *b.* 1914: *m.* 1939 (m. diss. 1947), Maj. John Henry Beardmore Batten, Royl Fus., and has issue living, Patrick John Beardmore (Hill Farm House, Leamington Hestings, Warwicks.), *b.* 1941; ed. at Ampleforth: *m.* 1965, Diana Lyn, da. of H. L. Brooke, and has issue living, Annabell Jane Beardmore *b.* 1965, Katherine Nicola Beardmore *b.* 1968, Sally Elizabeth Beardmore *b.* 1970. *Residence,*—32, Nutley Rd., Donnybrook, Dublin.——Mary Elizabeth, *b.* 1920: *m.* 1st, 1939, Raymond Guy Vere Nicoll, MC, from whom she obtained a divorce 1952: 2ndly, 1952 (m. diss. 1956), Maj. Desmond Richard Fitz-Gerald, late Irish Gds.; 3rdly, 1969, Cdr. Charles Raymond Barrett, RN, who *d.* 19—, and has issue living (by 1st m.) Mark Raymond, *b.* 1942; ed. at Eton: *m.* 1968, Virginia Vernon, da. of Maj. J. Christopher Vernon Miller, of Blackwell Grange, Shipton-on-Stour, and has issue living, James *b.* 1971, Edward (twin) *b.* 1971, Claire *b.* 1970,——Nigel Edward Vere, *b.* 1947; ed. at Eton: *m.* 1969, Corinna Jane, da. of John Goring, CBE, TD [*see* Goring, Bt.], and has issue living, Adam Nigel *b.* 1972, Zoe Gabrielle, *b.* 1971. *Residence,* 25, Eldon Rd., Kensington, W8.

The 1st baronet, Adm. of the Fleet Sir Charles Edward Madden, G.C.B., O.M., G.C.V.O., K.C.M.G., D.C.L., LL.D. (son of the late Capt. J. W. Madden, 4th Regt.), served in Egyptian War 1882, and in European War **1914-19** as Ch. of Staff and 2nd in Command of Grand Fleet (thanked by Parliament, cr. a Baronet, granted £10,000), and was Com.-in-Ch. of Home and Atlantic Fleets 1919-22 and First Sea Lord of the Admiralty and Ch. of Naval Staff **1927-30.**

MADGE, Creation (U.K.) **1919**, of St. Margaret's Bay, co. Kent. [Extinct **1962.**]

Sir FRANK WILLIAM MADGE, 2nd and last *Baronet.*

Daughters living of 2nd Baronet—Pauline, *b.* 1928: *m.* 1951, Capt. Peter John Shaw, RN, and has issue living, Christopher John, *b.* 1957,——Carol Anne, *b.* 1952. *Residence,* Woodside, Fyning Lane, Rogate, nr. Petersfield, Hants.——Doreen (West Wold House, Prestbury, Cheltenham), *b.* 1931: *m.* 1954 (m. diss. 1970), Hubert Mark Thursfield.——June (twin), *b.* 1931: *m.* 1963, Peter John Ball, MB, BChir, of 11, Nevill Park, Tunbridge Wells, and has issue living, Martin Hugh, *b.* 1964,——Angela Wendy, *b.* 1965,——Louise Clare, *b.* 1968,——Juliet Amanda, *b.* 1970.——Gillian, *b.* 1937: *m.* 1972, Richard William Honner, and has issue living, Emma Sophie *b.* 1973, Josephine Kate *b.* 1974.
Sister living of 2nd Baronet—Helen Matilda (Swiss Cottage, High St., St. Margarets-at-Cliffe, Dover, Kent).

Collateral Branch living.

Issue of the late William Friend Madge, el. son of 1st baronet, *b.* 1866, *d.* **1899,** *m.* 1891, Florence Elizabeth, who *d.* 1952, da. of Charles Frederick Woodward, of Wallington, Surrey :—
Norah Elizabeth, *b.* 1892: *m.* 1st, (Jan.) 1923, Neville Malcolm Kemsley, A.F.C., who *d.* (Nov.) 1923, 2ndly, 1937, Ernest Willie Mullett, F.C.A. *Residence,* Blendon, West Clandon, Surrey.

Magnus-Allcroft see Allcroft.

MAHON Creation (U.K.) **1819**, of Castlegar, co. Galway.
[Pronounced "Marn."]

Sir GEORGE EDWARD JOHN MAHON, 6th *Baronet*; *b.* June 22nd, 1911; *s.* his father, *Col. Sir* WILLIAM HENRY, 1926; ed. at Eton, and at Trin. Coll., Camb. (B.A. 1933): *m.* 1st, 1938, Audrey Evelyn, who *d.* 1957, da. of the late Walter Jagger [Rich, Bt., colls.] ; 2ndly, 1958, Suzanne, da. of the late Thomas Donnellan, of Pirbright, Surrey, and has issue by 1st and 2nd marriages.

Arms—Per fesse sable and argent, an ostrich counterchanged, in the beak a horseshoe or. **Crest**—A dexter arm embowed in armour the hand grasping a sword wavy all proper.
Seats—Castlegar, Ahascragh, co. Galway. *Residence,* Greeninch, Enniskerry, co. Wicklow.

Moniti meliora sequamur.

Having been warned let us follow better things.

Sons living—By 1st marriage—WILLIAM WALTER (Middlemarch, Normandy, Guildford), *b.* Dec. 4th, 1940; ed. at Eton; Maj. Irish Gds.: *m.* 1968, Rosemary Jane, yr. da. of Lt.-Col. Michael Ernest Melvill, OBE, of The Old Manse, Symington, Lanarkshire, and has issue living, Annabel Jane, *b.* 1970,—Lucy Caroline, *b.* 1972.——Timothy Gilbert (Ivy Cottage, Newbridge Av., Dublin 4), *b.* 1947: *m.* 1971, Penelope Telfer, el. da. of Maj. T. B. McDowell, of Grange Marches, Whitechurch, co. Dublin, and has issue living, Rupert Thomas George, *b.* 1974.
Daughters living—By 1st marriage—Jane Evelyn, *b.* 1944: *m.* 1967, Peter Alec Charles Moore, of 11, Maxwell Rd., SW6, and has issue living, Alannah Katherine, *b.* 1969.—By 2nd m.—Sarah Caroline, *b.* 1959.

Brother living—Luke Bryan Arthur DILLON-MAHON, *b.* 1917; ed. at Eton, and at Trin. Coll. Camb. (BA) ; assumed by deed poll 1966, the surname of Dillon-Mahon: *m.* 1949, Audrey Doreen, da. of Ernest John Vipond, MBE, MC, of 103, The Drive, Hove, Sussex, and has issue living, Robert John George, *b.* 1954,—Susan, *b.* 1950. *Residence,* Clonbrock, Ahascragh, co. Galway.

Sister living—Ursula Augusta Jane (Castlegar, Ahascragh, co. Galway), *b.* 1906: *m.* 1929 (m. diss. 1946), as his second wife, Capt. the Hon. (Arthur) Marcus Lowther Crofton, Irish Gds., who *d.* 1962 [see B. Crofton].

Collateral Branches living.

Issue of the late John FitzGerald Mahon, 4th son of 4th baronet, *b.* 1858, *d.* 1942:
m. 1898, Lady Alice Evelyn Browne, who *d.* 1970, da. of 5th Marquess of
Sligo:—

(John) Denis, *CBE*, *b.* 1910; ed. at Eton, and at Ch. Ch., Oxford(MA); HonDLitt. Newcastle; an Art
Historian and a FBA, a Trustee of National Gallery 1957-64, and 1966-73, medal for Benemeriti
della Cultura, Italy 1957, and Accademico d'Onore, Clementine Acad. of Bologna 1964, and
Serena Medal for Italian Studies, British Academy 1972; CBE (Civil) 1967. *Residence*, 33,
Cadogan Sq., SW1.

Issue of the late Edward Mahon, 6th son of 4th baronet, *b.* 1862, *d.* 1937: *m.* 1911,
Lilette Caroline Julia, da. of the late James K. Rebbeck, of Victoria, British
Columbia:—

Bryan Edward (2003, 82nd Av. SE, Mercer Island, Wash., USA), *b.* 1913: *m.* 1960, Marolyn
Miriam, da. of the late C. Laverne Smith, MD, of Seattle, Wash., USA, and has issue living, Ross
Mackenzie, *b.* 1961,—Lilette Elizabeth, *b.* 1963.

Sir Ross Mahon, 1st Bt., M.P. for Granard and Ennis, was el. son of Ross Mahon of Castlegar
(*d.* 1788), whose grandfather Capt. Bryan Mahon of Castlegar, served in Earl of Clanricarde's
Regt. of Inf., James II's Army at Battle of the Boyne 1690.

MAINWARING, Creation (U.K.) 1804, of Over Peover, Cheshire. [Extinct 1934.]
[Pronounced "**Mannaring.**"]

Sir HARRY STAPLETON MAINWARING, 5th and last *Baronet.*

Daughters living of 5th Baronet—Diana Eina Claude, *b.* 1914: *m.* 1938, Capt. Roger Edward
Lennox Harvey, J.P., D.L., Scots Guards, and has issue living, Carola Zara Lennox, *b.* 1941:
m. 1962, John Gerald Robertson Williams [*see* D. Northumberland, colls.],—Joanna Lennox, *b.*
1945: *m.* 1970, Frederick Minshull Stockdale, of Thorpe Tilney Hall, Lincoln [*see* Stockdale, Bt.],
—Fiona Diana Lennox (*Hon. Mrs. John J. Astor*), *b.* 1949: *m.* 1970, the Hon. John Jacob
Astor [*see* B. Astor of Hever]. *Residence*, Parliament Piece, Ramsbury, Wilts.——Zara Sophie
Kathleen Mary, *b.* 1917: *m.* 1st, 1940, Capt. the Hon. (Alexander) Ronald George Strutt, Coldm.
Gds., who obtained a divorce 1949—afterwards 4th Baron Belper; 2ndly, 1949, Peter Victor
Ferdinand Cazalet, JP, DL, Welsh Gds. [Heron-Maxwell, Bt.], who *d.* 1973, and has issue living
(by 1st m.) [*see* B. Belper],—(by 2nd m.) Victor Anthony, *b.* 1951,—Anthony Peter, *b.* 1953.
Residences, Fairlawne, Tonbridge, Kent; 14, Eaton Row, SW1.

MAITLAND, Creation (U.K.) 1818, of Clifton, Midlothian.

By counsel and courage. Sir RICHARD JOHN MAITLAND, 9th *Baronet;*
b. Nov. 24th, 1952; *s.* his father, Maj. *Sir* ALEXANDER
KEITH, 1963; ed. at Rugby.

Arms—Or, a lion rampant couped at all joints of the field gules,
within a double tressure flory counterflory azure. Crest—A lion
sejant, affrontée gules, ducally crowned or, and holding in his dexter
paw a drawn sword proper, pommelled and hilted gold, and in the
sinister a fleur-de-lis azure.
Residence—Burnside, Forfar, Angus.

Brother living—ROBERT RAMSAY, *b.* July 14th, 1956.
Sister living—Jane Fiona, *b.* 1963.
Uncles living (sons of 7th baronet)—John Ramsay (Paynes Farm, Otford,
Kent), *b.* 1924; formerly Sqdn.-Ldr. RAF: *m.* 1952, Nan Margaret,
da. of the late Brig. Charles Bannatyne Findlay, CBE, MC, and has
issue living, David Ramsay, *b.* 1954,—James, *b.* 1957,—Jean Findlay,
b. 1959.——James, *b.* 1927: *m.* 1959, Mavis Ann, el. da. of H. J.
Kennaway, of Keithock, Brechin, Angus, and has issue living, Alexander Henry, *b.* 1964,—Amanda Helen, *b.* 1960,—Fiona Ann (twin),
b. 1960. *Residence*, Clathick, Crieff, Perthshire.

Aunt living (daughter of 7th baronet)—Helen Florence, *b.* 1923: *m.* 1952, Lt.-Col. Thomas David
Lloyd-Jones, OBE, RRF (c/o National & Grindlays Bank, 13, St. James's Sq., SW1), and has
issue living, John Ramsay, *b.* 1954,—Peter Neil, *b.* 1956,—Caroline Margaret, *b.* 1961.

Daughter living of 6th Baronet—Petronilla Kathleen Florence. *b.* 1916: *m.* 1951, Malcolm
Park, O.B.E., who *d.* 1963, and has issue living, Malcolm John Maitland, *b.* 1955. *Residence*,
Stour Hill, Sturminster Newton, Dorset.

Widows living of 7th and 8th Baronets—JEAN HAMILTON (*Jean, Lady Maitland*), MBE; MBE
(Civil) 1920, da. of the late Robert Findlay, of Easterhill, Lanarkshire: *m.* 1919, Lt.-Col. Sir
George Ramsay Maitland, DSO, 7th Bt., who *d.* 1960. *Residence*, Reswallie, Forfar, Angus.
LAVENDER MARY JEX (*Lady Maitland*) (of Burnside, Forfar, Angus.), da. of the late Francis
William Jex Jackson, of Kirkbuddo, Forfar: *m.* 1951, Maj. Sir Alexander Keith Maitland, 8th
Bt., who *d.* 1963.

Collateral Branches living.

Grandson of the late George Ramsay Maitland, W.S., *b.* 1821, 2nd son of the
late Alexander Maitland, el. son of 2nd baronet, and father of 3rd baronet:—
Issue of the late George Keith Maitland, *b.* 1854, *d.* 1896: *m.* 1877, Christine Mary Theresa
who *d.* 1932, da. of the late Angus McDonell, of Kepoch, N.B. :—

Angus Charles Majoribanks, *b.* 1887; sometime Capt. R.A.S.C. ; was a Member of War Materia
Commn. 1919-20, and of Control Commn. to Germany and Austria 1946-7 ; European War 1914-
18 (despatches) : *m.* 1923, Mary Brigid, who *d.* 1946, da. of T. O'Callaghan, of Claremorris, co.
Mayo, and has issue living, Rev. Keith Marjoribanks, *b.* 1925 ; is a Priest at Downside Abbey,—
Natalie Mary, *b.* 1924,—Joan Mary, *b.* 1928: *m.* 1952, Noel Martin Fisher, DSC (19, Southcot
Place, Lyncombe, Bath, BA2 4PE), and has issue, Dominic Mayne *b.* 1953, Andrew Martin *b.*
1954, Aidan Hugh *b.* 1956, Paul Gregory *b.* 1960, Mary Brigid *b.* 1956, Catharine Mary *b.* 1957,
Lucy Elizabeth *b.* 1963, Anna Claire *b.* 1964, Jane Frances *b.* 1965,—Angela Helena Mary, *b.* 1933:
m. 1959, Raymond Geoffrey Daniel, of The Willow, Willows Vale, Frome, Somerset, and has
issue living, Charles Martin *b.* 1961, Francis Keith *b.* 1965, Brigid Mary *b.* 1959, Helen Margaret,
b. 1963. *Residence*, The Cottage, Willow Vale, Frome, Somerset.

Grandsons of the late Major Reginald Paynter Maitland, grandson of the late
Gen. Frederick Maitland, 4th son of 1st baronet :—
Issue of the late Lieut.-Col. Reginald Charles Frederick Maitland, D.S.O., *b.* 1882, *d.*
1939 : *m.* 1913, Marjorie Agnes Jane, who *d.* 1958, da. of the late Very Rev. Ernald
Lane, Dean of Rochester :—
Alastair Reginald (of Gables, Linden Chase, Uckfield, Sussex), *b.* 1915: *m.* 1947, Mary, da of the
late Campbell Mansbridge, and has issue living, Iain David Paynter, *b.* 1954.—Andrew Reginald
Campbell, *b.* 1963.—Penelope Mary, *b.* 1948,—Carolyn Judith, *b.* 1951.——Geoffrey Ernald
(35, 7th Av., Parktown North, Johannesburg, S. Africa), *b.* 1918: late Maj. RA: *m.* 1st, 1945 (m.
diss. 1967), Diana Joy, da. of Maj. James Pridham, RA: 2ndly, 1971, Mrs. Eleanor Williamson,
da. of James Slater, and has issue living (by 1st m.), Alastair Charles Frederick, *b.* 1958,—
Diana Jane, *b.* 1945,—Patricia Anne, *b.* 1947,—Susan Mary, *b.* 1952,—Sarah Gillian Gabrielle,
b. 1954,—(by 2nd m.) Alexander, James *b.* 1971.

The 1st baronet, Gen. the Hon. Sir Alexander Maitland, Col. of the 49th Foot, was 5th son of the
th Earl of Lauderdale ; the 2nd baronet assumed the additional surname of Gibson, and the 3rd
baronet, Sir Alexander Charles Maitland, assumed the additional surname of Ramsay before those
of Gibson and Maitland. The 7th baronet, Sir George Ramsay Maitland, D.S.O., was Lieut.-Col.
14th Jat Lancers and a Member of Queen's Body Guard for Scotland (Roy. Co. of Archers).

RAMSAY-STEEL-MAITLAND, Creation (U.K.) 1917, of Sauchie, co. Stirling.

[Extinct 1965.]

Sir KEITH RICHARD FELIX RAMSAY-STEEL-MAITLAND, 3rd and last *Baronet.*

Daughter living of 2nd Baronet—Gay, *b.* 1929: *m.* 1949, Lt.-Com. Roger Martin Stafford, RN
(ret.). *Residence,* Gateside, Sauchieburn, Stirling.

Daughters living of 1st Baronet—Mary Katherine Drummond, *b.* 1904: *m.* 1929 (divorce 1946),
Maj. David Lucius O'Brien, MRCVS, RAVC [*see* B. Inchiquin, colls.]. *Residence,* Addlestead
Farm, Headley, Surrey.——Frances Margaret Drummond, *b.* 1910: *m.* 1946, Willy Steuri, of
Shielwalls, Carronbridge, Denny, Stirlingshire.

Widow living of 2nd Baronet—MATILDA BRENDA (*Lady Ramsay-Steel-Maitland*), da. of the
late Thomas Doughty, of Coalbrookdale : *m* 1942, as his second wife, Sir (Arthur) James
(Drummond) Ramsay-Steel-Maitland, 2nd baronet, who *d.* 1960. *Residence,* Castle Gogar,
Edinburgh 12.

MAKGILL, Creation (N.S.) 1627, of Cranston Riddell, Midlothian.
[Name pronounced "McGill."]

I trust in the Lord.

IN·DOMINO·CONFIDO

Sir JOHN DONALD ALEXANDER
ARTHUR MAKGILL, 12th *Baronet ; b.* Dec.
31st, 1899 ; *s.* his father, *Sir* GEORGE,
1926; ed. at Eton; Hon. Major (retired)
Coldstream Guards : *m.* 1st, 1927,
Esther Lilian (who obtained a divorce
1943), da. of Sir Robert Bromley, 6th
Bt. ; 2ndly, 1955, Mrs. Maureen Gillington, da. of the late Lt.-Col. Arthur
Tilson Shaen Magan, CMG, and has
issue by 1st marriage.

Arms—Quarterly : 1st and 4th gules, three
martlets argent, *Makgill ;* 2nd and 3rd argent, an
eagle displayed sable beaked armed and langued
gules, charged on his breast with another eagle displayed argent, *Ramsay of Brakmonth.* **Crest**—
A martlet argent. **Supporters**—*Dexter,* a horse
argent, maned, hoofed and tailed or, gorged with
a collar whereto a chain is affixed which passes
between his forelegs and is reflexed over his back
of the last ; *sinister,* a bull sable, armed, unguled and tailed or, gorged and chained as the other.

Residence—The Flat, Blairquhan, Maybole, Ayrshire. *Clubs*—Guards', New (Edinburgh).

Daughter living—By 1st m.—Diana Mary Robina, MVO, *b.* 1930; MVO (5th class) 1971. *Residences,* Clouds Lodge, East Knoyle, Salisbury, Wilts.; 16, Redcliffe Sq., SW10.

Sister living—Harriet Frances Janet, *b.* 1893.

Collateral Branches living.

Issue of the late Squadron Leader Richard James Robert Haldane Makgill, Roy.
New Zealand Air Force, younger son of 11th baronet, *b.* 1907, *d.* 1948 : *m.* 1932,
Elizabeth Lyman, da. of the late Gorham Hubbard, of Boston, U.S.A.:—
GEORGE HUBBARD (5, Clarence Cres., Windsor; Caledonian Club), *b.* Jan. 7th, 1934: *m.*
1967, Alison Campbell, da. of the late Neils Max Jensen, of Randers, Denmark, and has issue
living,—Ian Arthur Alexander, *b.* 1969,—Robert Edward George (twin), *b.* 1969,—Hamish Max
Alistair, *b.* 1972.——Frances Katherine, *b.* 1939.

Grandchildren of the late Capt. John Edward Makgill (infra) :—
Issue of the late Rodney Devereux Makgill, *b.* 1901, *d.* 1955 : *m.* 1923, Laura (of 14,
Marei Road, Ellerslie, Auckland, New Zealand), da. of the late Richard Reynolds, of
Cambridge, Auckland, New Zealand :—
Richard John (Matahi Rd., Manawalhe, RD, Matata, NZ), *b.* 1926: *m.* 19—, Marjorie Ann Jamie-
son, and has issue living, Stuart Rodney, *b.* 1956,—Roy Malcolm, *b.* 1961,—Janet, *b.* 1952,—
Yvonne, *b.* 1954.——Patricia Ruth, *b.* 1923: *m.* 1946, Alfred Bridger, of 44, Kuri Rd., Devonport,
Auckland, NZ, and has issue living, Peter James, *b.* 1949,—Patricia Ellen, *b.* 1947: *m.* 1967,
Bruce Wallace Nicklin, and has issue living, David John *b.* 1969,—Susan, *b.* 1957. *Residence,*
Auckland, NZ.——Muriel Ann, *b.* 1927: *m.* 1955, Thomas William Tyrwhitt-Drake,
and has issue living, Richard William, *b.* 1957,—Hugh Charles, *b.* 1959,—Penelope Eliza-
beth, *b.* 1964.——Nancy Margaret, *b.* 1929: *m.* 1954, Edward Smith, and has issue living,
Nigel, *b.* 1957,—Deborah Ann, *b.* 1954,—Sandra (twin), *b.* 1957. *Residence,* 42, Arthur Rd.,
Manurewa, Auckland, NZ.——Elizabeth, *b.* 1933: *m.* 1968, Capt. Thomas Chisholm.

Issue of the late Capt. John Edward Makgill, 3rd son of 10th baronet, *b.* 1874, *d.* 1938.
m. 1897, Muriel Ravenscroft, who *d.* 1946, da. of the late Hon. Henry de Bohun
Devereux [V. Hereford, colls.] :—
Robert John, *b.* 1910 : *m.* 1940, Marjorie Wardell-Johnson, of Napier, New Zealand, and has
issue living, John Wardell, *b.* 1944,—Hugh Haldane, *b.* 1948,—Simon Redding, *b.* 1949,—Robert

Cloan, *b.* 1950. *Residence*, Makgills Rd., Cambridge, R.D.2, New Zealand.——Geoffrey Haldane, *b.* 1915: *m.* 1945, Elizabeth McNiven, of Auckland, New Zealand, and has issue living, Penelope Ann, *b.* 1947. *Residence*, 30, Kensington Place, Fairfield, Hamilton, NZ.——Joanna Maud, *b.* 1898: *m.* 1927, Brian Preston Stevenson, and has issue living, Rodney Brian Preston, *b.* 1935: *m.* 1st, 1958 (m. diss. 1966), Suzanne Harle, da. of Robert Harle Giles; 2ndly, 1969, Mrs. Eustace Baker, of Auckland, and has issue living (by 1st m.), Mark Preston, *b.* 1958, Victoria Anne, *b.* 1960,—Cynthia Mary, *b.* 1928: *m.* 1962, John Hampden Hyatt, of 2, Caistor Rd., Barton-on-Humber, S. Humberside, and has issue living, Michael John Guthrie *b.* 1963, Juliet Mary *b.* 1964, Susan Joanna *b.* 1967,—Rosemary, *b.* 1930,—Joanna Muriel, *b.* 1932: *m.* 1961, Chalmers Henry Fairweather, and has issue living, Alastair Andrew Chalmers *b.* 1962, Sarah Joanna *b.* 1966. *Residence*, 31, Hillcrest Rd., Otumoetai, Tauganga, NZ.——Miriam Isabella, *b.* 1903: *m.* 1955, Hensleigh Cathew Marryat Norris. *Residence*, 64, Awatere Av., Hamilton, NZ.——Muriel Barbara, *b.* 1907. *Residence*, Scenic Drive, RD1, Henderson, Auckland, NZ.—Margaret Philippa (25, Golf Rd., Epsom 3, Auckland, NZ) *b.* 1919: *m.* 1946 (m. diss. 1968), Alexander Hamilton Brown.

Issue of the late David Makgill, 4th son of 10th baronet, *b.* 1880, *d.* 1934: *m.* 1909, Margaret Elizabeth, who *d.* 1948, da. of the late Ven. Archdeacon Palmer:—

John Palmer, *b.* 1910: *m.* 1938, Lucie Warner, and has issue living, Alan Richard John, *b.* 1941, —Jennifer Ann, *b.* 1939: *m.* 1959, Bruce Hinton, of Te Toro, No. 4, R.M.D., Waiuku, New Zealand, and has issue living, Stuart Bruce *b.* 1963, Wendy Lucille *b.* 1960, Barbara Anne *b.* 1961.——David Comins (of Brachkmont, Waiuku, NZ), *b.* 1918: *m.* 1949, Ena Thompson, da. of Col. Keyworth, of Much Wenlock, Salop, and has issue living, Fiona Margaret, *b.* 1951.——Donald Haldane, *b.* 1921.——Stephen Stewart (492, Coldstream Drive, Berwyn, Pa. 19312, USA), *b.* 1929: *m.* 1955, Joan Woods, and has issue living, Stephen Stewart, *b.* 1958,—Kathleen Palmer, *b.* 1956,—Heather Woods, *b.* 1961,—Allison Ashwell, *b.* 1963.——Margaret May, *b.* 1912: *m.* 1933, Geoffrey Hall Dadley, and has issue living, David Francis, *b.* 1934,—Peter Geoffrey, *b.* 1936,—Anthony Eric, *b.* 1942,—Marian Roes, *b.* 1940,—Robin Margaret, *b.t* 943,—Rosemary Gwendolyn, *b.* 1944,—Katherine Ruth, *b.* 1949.——Alice Mary, *b.* 1913: *m.* 1939, Col. Guy Priestley Sanders, Roy. New Zea'and Engineers (ret.), of Meldon, Castor Bay Rd., Auckland, NZ, and has issue living, Guy Makgill, *b.* 1940,—David William Priestley, *b.* 1955,—Philippa Anne, *b.* 1944,—Penelope Margaret, *b.* 1950.——Roes Ashwell, *b.* 1916: *m.* 1944, Ansel Brooks Smith, and has issue living, Haldane Brooks, *b.* 1947,—Byron Whitaker (407, Arbor Green, Beverly, NJ, USA), *b.* 1950: *m.* 1972, Leona Le Claire, and has issue living, Byron Whitaker *b.* 1973,—Christopher Carlton, *b.* 1952. *Residence*, 3029, Mary Av., S.E., Grand Rapids, Michigan, USA.

Issue of the late Arthur Makgill, 5th son of 10th baronet; *b.* 1882; *d.* 1954: *m.* 1911, Mabel Sophia Elizabeth, who *d.* 1932, da. of William Marsh:—

Mungo Ian, *b.* 1911: *m.* 1935, Eugenia L., da. of Samuel Massey, of Belfast, and has issue living, Ian Robert, *b.* 1946,—Margaret May, *b.* 1935,—Elizabeth Marion, *b.* 1938,—Roberta Louise, *b.* 1942: *m.* 1961, James Samuel Brambley, and has issue living, Douglas James *b.* 1965, Marie-Anne *b.* 1962, Louise Anne *b.* 1963,—Colleen Barbara, *b.* 1944: *m.* 1965, Herbert James Lovell, of 3, Freshney Pl., Manurewa, NZ, and has issue living, Scott James *b.* 1966. *Address*, No. 1 R.D., Glenbrook, Waiuku, NZ.——Douglas Malcolm, *b.* 1922: *m.* 1945, Myra Louisa, da. of Osborne John Morton Pine, of Sandringham, NZ, and has issue living, Ray Malcom, *b.* 1945,—Joy Louisa, *b.* 1953,—Lynette Jane, *b.* 1955.——Deborah Elizabeth Mary, *b.* 1914: *m.* 1939, Capt. John Lawrence Clarkson, of West Coast Rd., Oratia R.D., Auckland, NZ, and has issue living, David John, *b.* 1940: *m.* 1965, Helen Gable, of Toowoomba, Qld., and has issue living, Sean *b.* 1969, Fiona *b.* 1968,—Peter, *b.* 1945: *m.* 1968, Patricia Goffin, of Howick, Auckland, and has issue living, Michelle *b.* 1971,—Alan Richard, *b.* 1946: *m.* 1970, Susanne Price, of Otahuhu, Auckland,—Christine, *b.* 1947.

This Nova Scotia Baronetcy was conferred with remainder to heirs male whatsoever in 1627 upon James Makgill, of Cranston Macgill (grandson of David McGill of Nesbit and Cranston Riddell, Lord Advocate of Scotland), who became a Lord of Session in 1629, and was subsequently created in 1651 Viscount of Oxfuird and Lord McGill of Cousland, with remainder to his heirs male of tailzie and provision whomsoever, with which title the Baronetcy remained merged until the death of the 2nd Viscount in 1706, when both dignities became dormant. The Baronetcy was subsequently assumed as 10th Bt. by John Makgill, of Kemback, a descendant of John Makgill, of Kemback (*temp.* Charles II.) great grandson of Sir James Makgill, of Rankeillor Nether (Clerk Register, Lord of Session, Lord Provost of Edinburgh, and Ambassador to Court of Queen Elizabeth I.), el. brother of David Makgill (ante), as heir male of the grantee. James, 1st Viscount of Oxfuird. George Makgill, el. son of Sir John Makgill, 10th Bt.(ante) of Kemback, in May 1907 established and recorded his pedigree as 11th Baronet.

MAKINS, Creation (U.K.) 1903, of Rotherfield Court, Henley-on-Thames, co. Oxford.

In lumine luce
Shine thou in the light.

Sir PAUL VIVIAN MAKINS, 4th *Baronet*; *b.* Nov. 12th, 1913; *s.* his brother, *Lt.-Col. Sir* WILLIAM VIVIAN, 1969; ed. at Eton, and Trin. Coll., Camb. (MA); Maj. (ret.) Welsh Guards; Knt. of Grace, Sovereign Mil. Order of Malta; 1939-45 War: *m.* 1945, Maisie, da. of Maj. Oswald Henry Pedley, and widow of Maj. Cecil Leander John Bowen.

Arms—Argent, on a fesse embattled counter embattled gules, between in chief two falcons proper belled or, and in base a lion's face of the second, an annulet or between two bezants. Crest—A dexter arm embowed in armour proper encircled by an annulet or and holding a flag staff, therefrom flowing a banner argent charged with a lion's face gules.
Address,—c/o Barclays International, Ltd., 84-90, Main St., Gibraltar.

Daughters living of 3rd Baronet—Carolyn Diana Mary, *b.* 1933: *m.* 1956, Le Roy T. Morgan, and has issue living, Diana Vivian, *b.* 1958,—Teresa Adelaide, *b.* 1959—Eleanora Carroll, *b.* 1961,—Cecilia Hay, *b.* 1964,—Maria Abell (twin) *b.* 1964,—Olivia Dudley, *b.* 1972. *Residence*, 1311, 35th St., NW, Wash., 20007 DC, USA.—Penelope Anne (*Baroness Harvey of Tasburgh*), *b.* 1935: *m* 1957, the 2nd Baron Harvey of Tasburgh. *Residence*, 2, Halsey St., SW3.

Sisters living—Elisabeth Mary Savile, *b.* 1904.——Marcia Evelyn (Ashley Grange, Tetbury, Glos.), *b.* 1907.

Widow living of 3rd Baronet,—JEAN (*Jean, Lady Makins*), (Littlehayes, Itchen Abbas, Winchester), da. of the late Capt. Lord Arthur Vincent Hay [see M. Tweeddale, colls.]: *m.* 1932, Lt.-Col. Sir William Vivian Makins, 3rd baronet, who *d.* 1969.

Collateral Branch living.

Issue of the late William Henry Makins, Lt. 13th Hussars, el. son of 1st baronet *b.* 1863, *d.* 1889: *m.* 1886, Mary Agnes, who *d.* 1915 (having *m.* 2ndly, 1891, Warine Martindale), da. of Sir Charles Lawrence Young, 7th Bt. (cr. 1769):—
Marjorie Florence, *b.* 1887: *m.* 1909, Maj. Alexander Vaughan Leipzic Wood, DSO, who *d.* 1933, and has issue living, Basil Alexander Charles, *DFC*, *b.* 1914; Group Capt. RAF (ret.); 1939-45 War Burma (DFC): *m.* 1939, Gillian Auriol Manners, only da. of the late Lt.-Col. W. R. Thompson, RA, who *d.* 1957, and has issue living, Stessa Fiona, *b.* 1946.

The 1st baronet, Sir William Thomas, sat as MP for S. Essex 1874-85, SE Essex 1885-86, and Walthamstow, 1886-92. 1st Baron Sherfield (cr. 1964) is a grandson of Henry Thomas Makins, Bar.-at-law, yr. brother of 1st baronet.

MALCOLM, Creation (N.S.) 1665, of Balbedie and Innertiel, co. Fife.

Ardua tendo.
Attempt difficult things.

Dei dono sum quod sum.
By the grace of God I am what I am.

Sir MICHAEL ALBERT JAMES MALCOLM, 10th Baronet; *b.* May 9th, 1898: *s.* his father, Sir JAMES WILLIAM, 1927; ed. at Eton; Major Scots Guards (Reserve); was A.D.C. to Gen. Officer Comdg.-in-Ch., Scottish Command 1919-23, A.D.C. to Lord High Commr., Gen. Assembly of Ch. of Scotland 1924 and 1925, Staff Capt., War Office 1940-41, Dep. Assist. Director, Foreign Office 1942-3, and Dep. Assist. Mil. Sec., War Office 1944-5; European War 1914-18 (severely wounded); is a Member of Queen's Body Guard for Scotland (Roy. Co. of Archers), and a Member of Committee of Earl Haig Fund (Scottish Branch), of Standing Council of the Baronetage, and of Economic League Central Council (Chm. of Lothian and Fife Sub-Area): *m.* 1st, 1918 (marriage dissolved 1946), the Hon. Geraldine Margot Digby, who *d.* 1965, da. of 10th Baron Digby; 2ndly, 1947, Mrs. Kathleen Melvin, da. of the late Cdr. G. J. Gawthorne, RN, and has issue by 1st m. [The 10th Baronet *d.* Jan. 10th, 1976].

Arms—Or a saltire azure between four stags' heads couped gules, a bordure indented of the third. **Crest**—A pyramid encircled by a laurel wreath proper.

Residence—Milton Lodge, North Berwick, East Lothian.   *Clubs*—Guards', New (Edinburgh).

Son living—By 1st marriage—DAVID PETER MICHAEL, (of 15, Cromwell Cres., S.W.5). *Clubs*, Guards', Pratt's, New (Edinburgh)), *b.* July 7th, 1919; ed. at Eton and at Magdalene Coll., Camb.; is a Chartered Accountant, and a Member of Roy. Co. of Archers (Queen's Body Guard for Scotland); sometime Maj. Scots Guards; was a Staff Capt. 1944, and a G.S.O. 1945: *m.* 1959, Hermione, el. da. of Sir David George Home, 13th Bt., and has issue living, Fiona Alice Jane, *b.* 1962.

Daughters living—By 1st marriage—Margaret Jane Venetia, *b.* 1923; formerly 3rd Officer W.R.N.S.: *m.* 1945, Christopher Robert Vesey Holt, V.R.D., and has issue living, Nicholas James Vesey, *b.* 1947,—Ianthe Evelyn Vesey, *b.* 1950. *Residence*, Oldwicks Copse, Munstead, Godalming, Surrey.—Morar Catherine Beryl, *b.* 1929: *m.* 1959, Oswald Whitwell Ainscough, late Maj. King's (Liverpool) Regt., of Abbots Brow, Kirkby Lonsdale, Westmorland.

Sisters living—Elspeth Mary Isobel, *b.* 1899: *m.* 1936, Thomas Cottrell-Dormer, of Rousham House, Steeple Aston, Oxon., and has issue living, Charles (The Dower House, Rousham, Oxon.); *b.* 1936: *m.* 1961 (m. diss. 1966), Caroline Catherine Clayton, da. of the late Lt.-Col. Clayton Edginton Davis, DSO, MC, and has issue living, Julia Hilary Marigold, *b.* 1963,—Frances Mary, *b.* 1938.——Griselda Helen Adeline (Clos du Peyronnet, Menton-Garavan, France, AM), *b.* 1903: *m.* 1st, 1936, Capt. Frederick William Gray, Nigerian Railways, who *d.* 1938; 2ndly, 1944, Comdt. Willem J. H. A. Galdermans, formerly Territorial Administrator, Belgian Congo, who *d.* 1953.

Collateral Branches living.

Issue of the late Major Alexander Ernest William Malcolm, *T.D.*, R.A. (T.A.), brother of 10th baronet, *b.* 1900: *m.* 1st, 1925, Olive Leah, da. of Walter Scott, of Sydney, N.S. Wales; 2ndly, 1941, Mrs. Sybil Mary Grenfell (who *m.* 3rdly, 1963, Aubrey Vernon), da. of the late Hugh Peacock, of Greatford Hall, Stamford:—
Alexandra Mary, *b.* 1943: *m.* 1964, Simon Ward, of 30, Oakley Rd., N1, and has issue living, Sophie Anna, *b.* 1965,—Claudia Thomasine, *b.* 1969.

Issue of the late Major Charles Edward Malcolm, brother of 9th baronet, *b.* 1865, *d.* 1935: *m.* 1894, the Hon. Beatrix Mary Leslie, who *d.* 1930, and from whom he had obtained a divorce 1914, da. of 8th Baron Ruthven:—
Arthur William Alexander, *CVO*, *b.* 1903; ed. at Repton; Lt.-Col. (ret.) Welsh Guards; was Assist. Mil. Attaché, Paris, 1950-52, Private Sec. to Gov. of S. Australia, 1953-55, and a Queen's Messenger 1955-68; 1939-45 War (prisoner); MVO (4th Class) 1949, CVO 1954: *m.* 1928, Hester Mary, da. of Samuel Furneaux Mann, of Victoria, Australia, and has issue living, James William Thomas Alexander, *b.* 1930; ed. at Eton, and RMA; Lt.-Col. Welsh Guards: *m.* 1955, Gillian Heather, da. of Elton Humpherus, of The Coach House, Tunbridge Wells, and has issue living, Alexander James Elton *b.* 1956, Robin William *b.* 1958, Julia Mary *b.* 1960, Annabel Heather *b.* 1967,—Ian William Ruthven (P.O. Box 1569, Tehran, Iran), *b.* 1933; ed. at Eton, and Magdalene Coll., Camb.: *m.* 1963, Mrs. Christie Moss, only da. of John Bramley, of Bloemfontein, and has issue living, Robert van Riet *b.* 1965, William David *b.* 1967, John Alexander *b.* 1968. *Residence*, Faraway, Sandwich Bay, Kent.

John Malcolm, of Balbedie, Lochore, and Innertiel, *b.* 1611, was appointed Chamberlain of Fife 1641, and Member of Scottish Parliament 1650; *m.* 1692, having *m.* Margaret, who *d.* 1698, aged 72, da. of Sir Michael Arnot, of that Ilk, and had six sons, of whom John, the eldest, was created a Baronet of Nova Scotia 1665, while the third son, Alexander, became a Senator of the College of Justice with the title of Lord Lochore 1687, and Lord Justice-Clerk and a Privy Councillor 1688; James fourth son, fought at Killicrankie and was attainted. The 1st baronet was succeeded by his el. son

John, 2nd baronet, who was followed in the Baronetcy by his third son, Michael, served heir as 3rd
baronet in 1784. The 4th baronet was James (Lieut.-Gov. of Sheerness), who had been served heir-
general to his father, Robert Malcolm, of Grange, 2nd son of 1st baronet, in 1795. At the death of
Sir James, Lieut.-Gov. of Sheerness, in 1805, the dignity passed to John, 8th child of Michael
Malcolm, 3rd son of 1st baronet, at whose decease, in 1816, his el. son, Michael, was served heir to
his father, and in 1828 his son, John, as 7th baronet. In 1866 Sir James, son of James Malcolm,
2nd son of 5th baronet, was served heir to his cousin, as 8th baronet. At his death in 1901 the
Baronetcy passed to his kinsman, Sir James William Malcolm, 9th Bt., who in 1897 had recorded
the pedigree in the Lyon Office.

MALET, Creation (G.B.) 1791, of Wilbury, Wiltshire.
[Name pronounced "Mallet."]

My strength is from on high.

Sir EDWARD WILLIAM ST. LO
MALET, *O.B.E.*, 8th *Baronet; b.* Nov.
1908; *s.* his father, *Lt.-Col. Sir* HARRY
CHARLES, *D.S.O.*, *O.B.E.*, 1931; ed.
at Dover Coll., and at Ch. Ch., Oxford
(BA); Col. (ret.) late 8th King's R.
Irish Hussars; Pres., Bridgwater Div.
Conservative Assocn., 1958-65; High
Sheriff of Somerset 1966-67; Palestine
1935, 1939-45 War in Middle East and
N.-W. Europe (despatches); OBE (Mil.)
1953: *m.* 1935, Baroness Benedicta, el.
da. of Baron Wilhelm von Maasburg,
and has issue.

Arms—Azure, three escallops or. **Crest**—Out of
a ducal coronet or, an heraldic tiger's head issuant
ermine.

Seat—Chargot, Luxborough, Somerset.

Son living—HARRY DOUGLAS ST. LO (Lang-
ham Farm, Luxborough, Watchet, Somerset), *b.*
Oct. 26th, 1936; ed. at Downside, and at Trin.
Coll., Oxford (BA); late Lt. Queen's Roy. Irish
Hussars: *m.* 1967, Julia Gresley, da. of Charles
Harper, 54, Irvine St., Peppermint Grove,
Perth, W. Aust., and has issue living, Charles
Edward St. Lo., *b.* Aug. 30th, 1970.

Daughters living—Mary Jane St. Lo, *b.* 1938; has Nat. Diploma of Design, and Oxford Univ.
Certificate of Fine Art: *m.* 1970, Robert Pickering, of 101, North Rd., Bassendean, Perth,
W. Aust., and has issue living, Samuel Thomas Carrigton St. Lo, *b.* 1970.——William Benedict
St Lo, *b.* 1972.——Elizabeth Benedicta Micaela, *b.* 1939; has Oxford Univ. Certificate of Fine
Art: *m.* 1963, Maj. Edwin Becket, Prince of Wales' Own Regt. of Yorkshire, and has issue living,
Simon, *b.* 1965,—Diana Vola, *b.* 1964.

Sisters living—Ermyntrude Virginia St. Lo, *b.* 1907: *m.* 1937, Geoffrey Wynne Severn Conan-
Davies, and has issue living, Stephen Malet, *b.* 1938,—Quinten Malet, *b.* 1945,—Bliss Mary
Azania, *b.* 1940,—Meredith Agnes Llewella, *b.* 1942: *m.* 19—, Douglas Gresham.——Helen
Agnes St. Lo, *b.* 1911: *m.* 1934, Alan Douglas Stoddart, and has issue living, Alan Malet, *b.* 1936,—
Robert Douglas, *b.* 1939,—Murray Lawrence, *b.* 1942,—Gareth Bowring, *b.* 1947,—Mary Lynette
St. Lo., *b.* 1946. *Residence*, Cothelstone Manor, Bagborough, Taunton, Somerset.

Collateral Branches living.

Grandson of the late Rev. William Wyndham Malet, 3rd son of 1st baronet—:
Issue (by 2nd marriage) of the late Major Guilbert Edward Wyndham Malet, *b.* 1839, *d.* 1918:
m. 1st, 1869, Florence, who *d.* 1877, da. of Charles Willes Wilshere, of The Frythe,
Welwyn ; 2ndly, 1880, Gertrude Agnes Cunliffe, who *d.* 1923, da. of the late Sir Philip
Cunliffe Owen, K.C.B., K.C.M.G. :—

Rev. Owen Wyndham, *b.* 1887; formerly Lt. RNVR; late R. of St. Mary's Cayon, St. Kitts:
m. 1st, 1914, Florence Elsie, who *d.* 1956, da. of the late W. Hickie; 2ndly, 1956, Christine
Mary, da. of the late Sidney Bond, of 45, Walton Rd., Clevedon, Somerset. *Residence*, Wyndham Lodge, 2, Bennetts Way, Clevedon, Somerset.

Grandchildren of the late Major Guilbert Edward Wyndham Malet (ante) :—
Issue of the late Lieut.-Col. Alexander Wyndham Malet, Indian Army, M.V.O., *b.* 1886,
d. 1956 : *m.* 1921, Kathleen Betty (of Box Farm, Woodmancote, near Cheltenham),
da. of Brig.-Gen. Alexander Cadell, Indian Army :—
Richard Wyndham (Pennybridge Cottage, Best Beech, Wadhurst, E. Sussex), *b.* 1923; late Capt.
Indian Army; Far East 1941-47; AMBIM; AIWSP; in management of tea estates, India and
Africa 1947-60; Management Advisory Officer, Council for Small Industries in Rural Areas: *m.*
1956, Judith Winifred Ferguson, yst. da. of D. McEwen, of Kirkby Lonsdale, and has issue living,
Claire Alexandra, *b.* 1965,—Sarah Agnes, *b.* 1969.——Sylvia Mary Fanshaw, *ARCM, LRAM,*
b. 1925: *m.* 1948, John William Theodore Tapp, and has issue living, Nicholas Charles Theodore,
b. 1952,—Caroline Linda, *b.* 1956. *Residence*, Southborough House, Ashcombe Av., Surbiton,
Surrey.——Kathleen Mary, *ARCM, LRAM, b.* 1934.
Issue of the late Edward Barnabas Wyndham Malet, *b.* 1894, *d.* 1961: *m.* 1st, 1921,
Esther Grace Macdonald (who *d.* 1969, having obtained a divorce 1950), da. of the Rev.
Gilbert Lyon (formerly V. of Cloford, Frome), of Wican Croft, Bishopsteignton, Teign-
mouth, Devon; 2ndly, 1950, Aileen Nina Mary (c/o Lloyds Bank, Minehead, Som.), el.
da. of F. W. Cumming, of Parklands, Bradninch, Devon :—
(By 1st m.) Michael Edward Guilbert (Green Pl., Stockbridge, Hants.), *b.* 1922; Maj. RA (ret.):
m. 1953, Judith Rowley, el. da. of E. Rowley Lewis, of Battledown, Cheltenham, and has issue
living, Mark Wyndham, *b.* 1956,—James Edward Barnabas, *b.* 1964,—Mary Pepita, *b.* 1954.——
Wendy (105, Riverview Gdns., Barnes, SW13), *b.* 1926.

Grandchildren of the late Major Harold Wyndham Malet, son of the late Col.
Harold Esdaile Malet, son of the late Rev. William Wyndham Malet (ante) :—
Issue of the late Capt. John Wyndham Malet, *b.* 1910, *d.* (killed in action during European
War) 1940 : *m.* 1937, June Rosalind (who *m.* 2ndly, 1943, Capt. Wladyslaw Galica,
who *d.* 1951), da. of the late Capt. John Broadley Harrison Broadley, of Welton House,
Brough, E. Yorkshire:—

Greville John Wyndham (Vale House, Little Somerford, Chippenham, Wilts.), *b.* 1939; ed. at Harrow: Maj. R. Hussars: *m.* 1972, the Hon. Margaret Cherry Wigram, el. da. of 2nd Baron Wigram.——(Leola) Dawn Wyndham, *b.* 1938: *m.* 1961, Capt. John David Graham Nicholson, RHA, son of Gen. Sir Cameron Gordon Graham Nicholson, GCB, KBE, DSO, MC, and has issue living, John Andrew Graham, *b.* 1964,—Edward Wyndham Graham, *b.* 1966, —Davina June, *b.* 1962. *Address,* c/o Lloyds Bank, 6, Pall Mall, SW1.

    Grandchildren of the late Allan Arthur Grenville Malet, son of the late Lieut.-Col. George Grenville Malet, 4th son of 1st baronet :—

  Issue of the late Lieut.-Col. George Edward Grenville Malet, O.B.E., late R.A.O.C., *b.* 1898, *d.* 1952 : *m.* 1st, 1922 (divorce 1938), Gwendolen Iliffe (who *m.* 2ndly, 1938. Rear-Adm. Ernest William Leir, DSO, of South Hill House, Ditcheat, Shepton Mallet), da. of Brig.-Gen. James Aubrey Gibbon, CMG; 2ndly, 1939, Margaret Bell Wright, who *m.* 2ndly, 1967, Patrick Walsh, JP, of 35, Grange Rd. North, Hyde, Ches.

(By 1st m.) Baldwin Hugh Grenville (c/o C. Hoare & Co., 37, Fleet St., EC4), *b.* 1928; ed. at Wellington Coll., and at King's Coll., Camb.; Sudan Political Ser. 1950-56; Author; Lecturer in Local History, Salford Univ. since 1973: *m.* 1959, Kathleen Patricia, da. of Arthur Morris, of Whitby, Cheshire and has issue living, Durand David Grenville, *b.* 1965,—Jane Phoebe Grenville, *b.* 1962.——Barbara Madeline Anne, *b.* 1924: *m.* 1947, Edward Hugh Michael Counsell, CBE, of The Monks House, Montacute, Somerset, and has issue living, John Aubrey Malet, *b.* 1949,— Christopher Anthony Malet, *b.* 1952,—Hugh Michael Malet, *b.* 1962.——(By 2nd m.) Michael Ian Grenville, *b.* 1939; ed. at Berkhamsted, and at St. Andrews Univ.: *m.* 1964, Alison Little, of Hale, Ches., and has issue living, Ian Martin, *b.* 1964,—Saffron Margaret *b.* 1968—Jonquil, *b.* 1969.——Zenobia Margaret Grenville, *b.* 1942; ed. at St. Anne's Coll., Oxford: *m.* 1967, Michael Venner, of Cwm Bach, Llangattock, Crickhowell, Breconshire, and has issue living, Miriam Anna, *b.* 1969.

    Grandchildren of the late Cdr. Herbert Rivers Malet, late RNVR, yr. son of the late Arthur Malet, 5th son of 1st baronet:—

Henry Guy Rivers Malet, *b.* 1894, *d.* 19—: *m.* 1st, 1917, (m. diss. 19—), Olga Muriel, da. of James Balfour, of Paignton, Devon; 2ndly, 19—, Tessa West:—
Vyvyan Arthur Rivers, *b.* 1927.——Olga Diana Valentine Rivers, *b.* 1925: *m.* 1951, F.A. Heilingbrunner, of 310, McFarlane St., Peterborough, Ont., Canada.——Patience Violet Rivers, *b.* 1930: *m.* 1954 (m. diss. 19—), Leslie G. Walton.

William Malet, founder of this family in England, was companion of William the Conqueror at Hastings, and a branch was settled at Enmore, Somerset from the twelfth century to 1656. Sir Baldwin Malet of St. Audries and Poyntington, Somerset, ancestor of this branch, descended from Sir Baldwin Malet, Solicitor Gen. to Henry VIII, yr. son of Thomas Malet of Enmore (*d.* 1502). A Baronetcy for services during the civil war was conferred by Charles II, on Sir Thomas Malet, of Poynington, who died before the patent passed to the great seal. He was one of the Judges sent to the Tower by Cromwell, from the Court at Maidstone, for refusing to grant a summons against a clergyman who would not give up using the Book of Common Prayer. Sir Charles Warre Malet, was created a Bt., for diplomatic services in India. The 2nd Bt., Sir Alexander, KCB, was Min. to the German Confederation 1852-66. The 4th Bt., the Rt. Hon. Sir Edward, GCB, GCMG, PC, was Min. to Belgium 1883-84, and Ambassador to Germany 1884-95. The 7th Bt., Lt.-Col. Sir Harry Charles Malet, DSO, OBE, served in S. Africa 1899-1902, and 1914-18 War.

Mallaby-Deeley, see Deeley.

MALLINSON, Creation (U.K.) 1935, of Walthamstow,   Essex.

Thence the oak.

Sir (WILLIAM) PAUL MALLINSON, 3rd *Baronet; b.* July 6th, 1909; *s.* his father, *Sir* WILLIAM JAMES, 1944; ed. at Westminster, and at Ch. Ch., Oxford (MA, BM and BCh); FRCP, FRC Psych.; late Surg.-Lt. Cdr. RNVR; Family Order of Brunei: *m.* 1st, 1940 (m. diss. 1967), Eila Mary, da. of Roland Graeme Guy, of Hastings, NZ; 2nd, 1968, Margaret Cooper, BA, MB, BS, da. of the late S. A. Bowden, of Barnstaple, N. Devon, and has issue by 1st m.

    Arms—Ermine, three pallets gules, in chief two crescents or, and in base an acorn leaved and slipped proper. **Crest**— A cubit arm, the hand grasping a stock of a tree, snagged and eradicated proper.
    Residences—25, Wimpole St., W1; Farm Lane House, Bembridge, Isle of Wight.

Son living (By 1st m.)—WILLIAM JOHN (7, Addison Gdns., W14), *b.* Oct. 8th, 1942; ed. at Charterhouse: *m.* 1968, Rosalind Angela, da. of Rollo Hoare, of The Dower House, Dogmersfield, Hants., and has issue living, William James, *b.* April 22nd, 1970,—Kate Sophia, *b.* 1972.

Daughters living (By 1st m.)—Angela Mary, *b.* 1941; MRCS (Eng.); LRCP (London); DPM: *m.* 1964, Edward Tuppin Scrase, BA, MB, BChir, FFA, RCS, of 2, Petersfield, Cambridge, and has issue living, Ivan, *b.* 1968,—Hannah, *b.* 1967.——Hilary Eila, *b.* 1947: *m.* 1st, 1965 (m. diss. 1970), Robin St. Clair Barrow, BA; 2ndly, 1971 Michael Gooley, late Capt. Staffs. Regt. and SAS Regt., of 42, Redcliffe Gdns., SW10, and has issue living (by 1st m.), Paul Achilles St. Clair, *b.* 1966,—(by 2nd m.) Tristan Patrick, *b.* 1973.

Uncle living (son of 1st baronet)—*Sir* Stuart Sydney, *CBE, DSO, MC, b.* 1888; a JP for Essex (High Sheriff 1939), and an OStJ; DL of Essex 1937-66, since when of Greater London; 1914-18 War in France with Hon. Artillery Co., and as Col. RE (despatches twice MC, DSO, Order of Mérite Agricole of France, 1914 star, two medals), Hon. Col. 28th (Essex) AA Btn. RE (TA) 1938, 563 (Essex) Regt. RA 1938-57, and 517th LAA Searchlight Regt. RA 1956-57; DSO 1918, CBE (Civil) 1938, Knt. 1954: *m.* 1916, Marjorie Gray, *CBE*, who *d.* 1969, da. of the late Rev. Alfred Soothill, Headmaster of Ashville Coll., Harrogate, and has issue living, Justin Stuart (of Bredy Farm, Burton Bradstock, Dorset), *b.* 1923; ed. at Marlborough, and at Jesus Coll., Camb.; sometime Capt. Gren. Guards: *m.* 1944, Juliana

Beatrice, only da. of Samuel Martin, of St. Helens, I. of Wight, and has issue living, John Michael Stuart (Old Forge Cottage, Sellindge, Kent), b. 1945; ed. at Marlborough Coll., and Reading Univ. (BSc Agric.): m. 1969, Elizabeth Margaret, BSc, da. of John Cloke, MRCVS, of Walsall, Staffs, (and has issue living, Jonathan Justin Stuart b. 1971, Elspeth May Stuart b. 1974), Jennifer Jane Stuart b. 1949: m. 1971, Lt. Nicholas Graham Talbot Harris, RN,—Terence Stuart (of 1, Hyde Park Cres., W2), b. 1929; ed. at Marlborough, and at Jesus Coll., Camb. (MA): m. 1955, Anne Mary Butler, da. of the late D. Butler Wilson, of Burlington Lodge, Alderley Edge, Cheshire and has issue living, Lawrence Stuart b. 1957, Michael David Stuart b. 1959, Roland Arthur Stuart b. 1966, Sheila Mary Anne b. 1961. *Residence*, The Thite House, Woodford Green, Essex.

Aunt living (daughter of 1st baronet)—Evangeline Dorothea: m. 1916, Philip Smith, MC, MD, DPH, late Capt. RAMC. *Residence*, 3, Northfield Close, Northfield Av., Kettering, Northants.

Collateral Branches living.
        Issue of the late Stanley Tucker Mallinson, 2nd son of 1st baronet, b. 1884, d. 1955: m. 1919, Dora Selina, who d. 1960, da. of the late William B. Burridge, of Boscombe, Hants :—
Anthony William, b. 1923 ; ed. at Marlborough, and at Gonville and Caius Coll., Camb. (B.A. and Exhibitioner 1948, LL.B. 1949) ; admitted a Solicitor (honours) 1951 ; formerly Major R.A. : m. 1955, Heather Mary, da. of the late Thomas Arthur Mansfield Gardiner. *Residence*, 15, Douro Place, W.8.
        Issue of the late Major Lancelot Victor Mallinson, late Tank Corps, youngest son of 1st baronet, b. 1892, d. 1952 : m. 1st, 1918, Elizabeth McLelland ; 2ndly, 1932, Madelon Edson Holmes, of 15, Rue des Sablons, Paris XVI, France.
(By 2nd marriage) Alastair, b. 1932 ; ed. at Eton ; late 2nd Lieut. Roy. Fusiliers : m. 1955, Rosemary, da. of Charles Cecil Harvey, and has issue living, Guy, b. 1958,—Alexander, b. 1964,— Florence, b. 1962. *Residence*, La Daviere, Les Lucs-sur-Boulogne, Vendée, France.——**(By 1st marriage)** Pamela, b. 1920.——Marie Louise, b. 1923.

The 1st baronet, Sir William Mallinson (son of the late John Mallinson, of Forest Gate, E.7) was a J.P. for Essex (Chm. of Beacontree Bench). The 2nd baronet, Sir William James, was High Sheriff of Surrey 1933.

MANDER, Creation (U.K.) 1911, of The Mount, Tettenhall, co. Stafford.

Live well.

Sir CHARLES MARCUS MANDER, 3rd Baronet ; b. Sept. 22nd, 1921 ; s. his father, *Sir* CHARLES ARTHUR, 1951 ; ed. at Eton, and at Trin. Coll., Camb. ; late Capt. Coldstream Guards; is a Director of Oxvar, Ltd., of St. James's, and an Underwriting Member of Lloyd's; High Sheriff of Staffs. 1962-3; European War 1939-45 as Capt. Coldstream Guards in Egypt, Italy, and N.-W. Europe: m. 1945, Maria Dolores Beatrice, da. of the late Alfred Brodermann, of Gross Fontenay, Hamburg, Germany, and has issue.
    Arms—Gules, on a pile invected erminois, three annulets interlaced, two and one of the field. *Crest*— A demi-lion couped ermine holding in the paws two annulets interlaced fessewise gules, between two buffalo horns of the last.
    Residences—Little Barrow, Moreton-in-Marsh, Glos.; 6, Greville House, Kinnerton St., SW1.

Sons living—CHARLES NICHOLAS (Owlpen Manor, Uley, Glos.) b. March 23rd, 1950; ed. at Downside and Trin. Coll., Camb. (BA): m. 1972, Karin Margareta, da. of Arne Norin, of Bromma, Sweden, and has issue living, Charles Marcus Septimus Gustav, b. July 26th, 1975,—Sarra Mary, b. 1973.——Francis Peter, b. 1952; ed. at Downside.
Daughter living—Penelope Anne Mary, b. 1946: m. 1965, Michael Rollo Hoare, of Park House, Over Worton, Middle Barton, Oxon., and has issue living, Venetia Elizabeth, b. 1965,—Fiona Mary, b. 1969.
Sisters living—Ann Marietta Patience, b. 1914; JP for Glos.: m. 1939, H. Patrick Stirling, of The Old Rectory, Farmington, Northleach, Glos.——Carinthia Jill, b. 1920; formerly in WRNS: m. 1st, 1944, James Ramsden, who d. 1956; 2ndly, 1964, Lt.-Cdr. James de Votier Grosvenor Wallis, RN (ret.), of Friquet à Gauche, St. Martin's, Guernsey, and has issue living (by 1st m.), James Tobit, b. 1948; ed. at Sheffield Univ. (BA): m. 1973, Linda, da. of Walter Critchlow, of St. Bruno, PQ, Canada.——Charles Riordan, b. 1949: m. 1974, Elizabeth Mary, only da. of Stewart Kilpatrick of Fogdens Barn, Bury, Sussex.

Collateral Branches living.
        Grandchildren of the late Gerald Poynton Mander, FSA (infra):—
        Issue of the late Philip fitzGerald Mander, b. 1915, d. 1972: m. 1942, Priscilla Patricia, BA (The Folley, Stableford, Bridgnorth, Salop), da. of the late Lt.-Col. Edmund de Warrenne Waller, MC, Indian Army:—
Patrick Oliver, b. 1951; ed. at Eton.——Philippa Hazel Jeanetta, b. 1944; ed. at Cheltenham Ladies' Coll., and Exeter Univ. (BA): m. 1965, John Patrick Thorneycroft, MA, of Kemberton Hall, Shifnal, Salop, and has issue living, Hugh Martin Sumner, b. 1967,—Veryan Ruth, b. 1971,— Naomi Priscilla, b. 1975.
        Issue of the late Gerald Poynton Mander, F.S.A., younger son of 1st baronet, b. 1885, d. 1951 : m. 1913, Nancy Steward, who d. 1960, da. of the late Lieut.-Col. R. H. Hargreaves, J.P., D.L., of Knightley Grange, Staffordshire:—
Catherine Daphne, b. 1914.——Hilary Nancy, b. 1924: m. 1946, William Reginald Purslow, and has issue living, Ian Gerald Steward, b. 1949: m. 1971, Sally Anne, only da. of Gordon Matthews, of Milton House, Shipton-under-Wychwood, Oxon.,—Hugh Charles, b. 1950. *Residence*, Harnage House, nr. Cressage, Salop.

The 1st baronet, Sir Charles Tertius Mander (Chm. of Mander Bros. Limited, of Wolverhampton), was High Sheriff of Staffordshire 1903, and Mayor of Wolverhampton 1892-6 (Hon. Freeman 1897). The 2nd baronet, Sir Charles Arthur Mander, was High Sheriff for Staffordshire 1926, and Mayor of Wolverhampton, 1932 and 1936 (Hon. Freeman 1946).

MANN, Creation (U.K.) 1905, of Thelveton Hall, Thelveton, Norfolk.

Statesman.

Sir RUPERT EDWARD MANN, 3rd *Baronet*, el. son of Edward Charles Mann, DSO, MC, only son of Maj. William Edgar Mann, DSO, 2nd son of 1st Bt.; *b.* Nov. 11th, 1946; *s.* his gt. uncle, *Sir* (EDWARD) JOHN, 1971; *ed.* at Malvern: *m.* 1974, Mary Rose, da. of Geoffrey Butler, of Springhill, Widdington, Saffron Walden, Essex.

Arms—Argent, a chevron sable, between in chief two crosses moline, and in base an annulet gules. **Crest**—A demi-man in armour proper, the helmet adorned with four feathers argent, holding in his dexter hand a cross moline as in the arms.
Seat—Thelveton Hall, Scole, Norfolk.

Brothers living—MALCOLM ALEXANDER, *b.* Oct. 22nd, 1947; ed. at Malvern.——Andrew William (twin), *b.* 1947; ed. at Malvern.

Aunts living—Ann Sara, *b.* 1916; 1939-45 as Junior Cdr. ATS (despatches): *m.* 1950, Charles John Cunningham, of Westcote Barton Lodge, Middle Barton, Oxford, and has issue living, Alexander Kenneth, *b.* 1956,—Edward James, *b.* 1962,—Sara Mar *b.* 1952,—Clare Margaret, *b.* 1953.——Penelope Jane (Hoe Hall, Dereham, Norfolk), *b.* 1924; a JP of Norfolk: *m.* 1950, Michael Telfair Keith, who *d.* 1966, and has issue living James Edward, *b.* 1960,—Rosemary Ann, *b.* 1951,—Priscilla Mary, *b.* 1953.

Great-Aunt living (daughter of 1st baronet)—Fanny Julia (Apt. 214, Imperial Hotel, Torquay, S. Devon), *b.* 1896: *m.* 1947, Reginald Stanley Hery Warn.

Mother living—Pamela Margaret (c/o Courtwood, Nayland, Suffolk), only da. of the late Maj. Frank Haultain Hornsby, RFA [see B. Belper]: *m.* 1945, Edward Charles Mann, DSO, MC, who *d.* 1959 (ante).

Grandmother living—Sarah Douglas (Selwyn House, Pulham Market, Diss, Norfolk), da. of the late Col. Sir Alexander Sprot, 1st Bt. (ext.): *m.* 1913, Maj. William Edgar Mann, DSO, who *d.* 1969, 2nd son of 1st Bt.

Widow living of 2nd Baronet—CLARE HELEN, CBE (*Clare, Lady Mann*) (The Moat House, Scole Common, Diss, Norfolk), da. of the late Robert Graham Dryden Alexander, of Priest's Cottage, Brentwood; OBE (Civil) 1950, CBE (Civil) 1962: *m.* 1951, Sir (Edward) John Mann, 2nd Bt., who *d.* 1971.

Collateral Branch living.

Issue of the late Capt. Francis Thomas Mann, 3rd son of 1st Bt., *b.* 1888, *d.* 1964: *m.*, 1916, Enid Agnes (Upper Farm House, Milton Lilbourne, Pewsey, Wilts.), da. of the late George A. Tilney:—

Francis George DSO, MC (The Old Rectory, West Woodhay, Newbury, Berks), *b.* 1917; ed. at Eton, and at Pembroke Coll., Camb.; formerly Maj. Scots Guards (Supplementary Reserve); 1939-45 War in N. Africa and Italy (wounded, MC, DSO); DSO 1945: *m.* 1949, Margaret Hildegarde, el. da. of the late W. Marshall Clark, of Johannesburg, S. Africa, and has issue living, Simon Francis, *b.* 1952,—Richard William, *b.* 1953,—Edward John, *b.* 1961,—Sarah Margaret, *b.* 1960.——John Pelham, MC (Brimpton House, Brimpton, Berks.), *b.* 1919; ed. at Eton, and at Pembroke Coll., Camb.; formerly Maj. Scots Guards; 1939-45 War (MC): *m.* 1942, Ann Margurite, only da. of the late Col. John Grahame Brockbank, CMG, DSO, of The Manor House, Steeple Langford, Salisbury, and has issue living, James John Francis, *b.* 1946,—Charles Edward Lionel, *b.* 1948,—Celia Marguerite (*Hon. Mrs. George W. M. Norrie*), *b.* 1943: *m.* 1964, the Hon George Willoughby Moke Norrie, el. son of 1st Baron Norrie.——Joan Elizabeth (*Baroness Maclean*), *b.* 1923: *m.* 1941, Baron Maclean (Life Baron).——Margaret Enid, *b.* 1924; formerly in WRNS: *m.* 1951, Maj. Seaton Patrick Hayes Simonds, MC, RHA (ret.), of Manor Farm, Syde, Cheltenham, and has issue living, Peter Hayes, *b.* 1966,—Susan Enid, *b.* 1954,—Anne Margaret, *b.* 1958,—Nicola Mary, *b.* 1968,—Catherine Elizabeth, *b.* 1970. *Residence*, Upper Farm House, Milton Lilbourne, Pewsey, Wilts.

The 1st baronet, S.r Edward Mann (son of Thomas Mann, of Thelveton Hall, Scole, and Roseneath House, Winchmore Hill, N.), was Chm. of Mann, Crossman & Paulin, Ltd., of Brandon's Putney Brewery, Ltd., and of D. Watney & Sons, Ltd.

MANSEL, Creation (E.) 1622, of Muddlescombe, Carmarthenshire.

What he wishes, he wishes fervently.

Sir PHILIP MANSEL, 15th *Baronet; b.* March 3rd, 1943 ; *s.* his father, *Sir* JOHN PHILIP FERDINAND, 1947: *m.* 1968, Margaret, only da. of Arthur Docker, of Hainings Gate, Moorhouse, Carlisle.

Arms—Argent, a chevron between three maunches sable. **Crest**—A cap of maintenance gules, turned up ermine, enflamed on the top proper.
Seat—Maesycrugiau Manor, Maesycrugiau, Carmarthenshire.

Uncle living (son of 13th baronet)—REGNIER RANULF DABRIDGECOURT, *b.* July 6th, 1919; formerly Signaller RA: *m.* 1941, Mary Germaine, da. of Wing-Com. W. St. J. Littlewood, OBE, of Braemar, Stanmore, Middlesex, and has issue living, Anthony Ranulf, *b.* 1946,—Robert Edward, *b.* 1948,—Roderick Rhys, *b.* 1959,—Isabel Theresa, *b.* 1949,—Frances, *b.* 1952. *Residence*, Taliaris, Maesycrugiau, Carmarthenshire.

Aunts living (daughters of 13th baronet)—**Margaretta** Cecil, *b.* 1913: *m.* 1940, Lt.-Cdr. Ralph Leonard West, RN (ret.): of Cogglesbrook Cottage, Kimbolton, Leominster, a d has issue living, Richard Mansel, *b.* 1946,—Christopher Leonard, *b.* 1951,—Aileen Margaretta, *b.* 1941.——Juliet, *b.* 1917: *m.* 1939, Group Capt. Richard

Eric Burns, CBE, DFC, and has issue living, Richard Harcourt, *b.* 1943,—Christine Georgina *b.* 1941,—Gillian, *b.* 1948. *Residence,* Lonnen End, Churt Rd., Headley, Hants.

Widow living of 14th Baronet., HANNAH, da. of Ben Rees, of Cwmhuplyn, Pencader : *m.* 1st, 1940, Sir John Philip Ferdinand Mansel, 14th baronet, who *d.* 1947 ; 2ndly, 19—,— Harrison, *Residence,* Hall Flatt, Scaleby, Carlisle.

Collateral Branches living.

Grandchildren of the late John Clavell Mansel-Pleydell (who assumed 1872 without Roy. licence the additional surname of Pleydell), el. son of the late Col. John Mansel, CB, 3rd son of 9th Bt.:—

Issue of the late Lieut.-Col. Edmund Morton Mansel-Pleydell, *b.* 1850, *d.* 1914: *m.* 1885, Emily Kathleen, who *d.* 1945, da. of Sir Thomas Fraser Grove, 1st Bt. :—
Vivien, *b.* 1889 : *m.* 1919, Lieut.-Col. Henry George Moreton Railston, D.S.O., who *d.* 1936, having assumed by deed poll 1919 the additional surname of Pleydell before that of Railston, and has issue living, June (of Clenston Manor, Blandford, Dorset), *b.* 1920: *m.* 1950 (m. annulled 1970), Richard John Saint Clair Carlyle Clarke, and has issue living, Giles Morton *b.* 1957, Caroline June *b.* 1952,—Patricia, *b.* 1921: *m.* 1951, Desmond Shane Chichester, [*see* B. Templemore, colls.]. *Residence,* Whatcombe, Blandford, Dorset.——Daphne, *b.* 1893: *m.* 1919, Capt. John Anthony Arnold-Forster, OBE, formerly RFA, who *d.* 1958, and has issue living, Nigel Morton (Salthrop House, Swindon), *b.* 1924; 1939-45 War as Fl. Lt. RAFVR: *m.* 1955, Pamela Thomas, and has issue living, Amanda Jane *b.* 1958, Sonia Meg *b.* 1963,—Vanda, *b.* 1934: *m.* 1958, the Rev. Alan McNeile Morton, and has issue living, Roger John *b.* 1960, Edward James *b.* 1962, William George, *b.* 1966, Anna, *b.* 1964. *Residence,* 4, Westdene Cres., Caversham, Reading.

Grandson of the late Rev. Canon John Colvile Morton Mansel-Pleydell, 2nd son of the late John Clavell Morton Mansel-Pleydell (ante):—
Issue of the late Ralph Morton Mansel-Pleydell, *b.* 1895, *d.* 1932 : *m.* 1920, Countess Margurite Marie, who *d.* 1968, da. of Count Aymard d'Ursel:—
Philip Morton (27, Cambridge St., Paddington, NSW 2029), *b.* 1922; ed. at Ampleforth Coll.; Lt.-Cdr. RN (ret.); 1939-45 War: *m.* 1961, Dagmar Rosalie, da. of the late Theodore Louis Bowring, CMG, OBE, and has issue living, John Bowring Morton, *b.* 1963,—Rosanna Vivien, *b.* 1965.

Grandsons of the late Ralph Morton Mansel-Pleydell (ante):—
Issue of the late David Gabriel Morton Mansel-Pleydell, DFC, *b.* 1923, *d.* 1973: *m.* 1963, Elisabeth Susan (42, Bloomfield Terr., SW1; Barneston Manor, Steeple, Dorset), da. of John McVean Luard, of Old Joscelyn, Little Horkesley, Colchester:—
Toby Edmond Luard Morton, *b.* 1964.——Harry Rupert Delalynde Morton, *b.* 1966.——Thomas Oliver Clavell Morton, *b.* 1969.——Charles David Luttrell Morton (posthumous), *b.* 1973.

Grandchildren of the late Col. John Delalynde Mansel (infra):—

Issue of the late Maj. Rhys Clavell Mansel, *b.* 1891, *d.* 1969: *m.* 1st, 1916, Sylvia Nina, who *d.* 1944, da. of Sir Guy Theophilus Campbell, 3rd Bt.; 2ndly, 1944 (*m.* annulled 1946), Mrs. Margaret Georgina Walker, da. of the late Dr. H. F. G. Noyes; 3rdly, 1947, Archie Anne (The Grange, Selborne, Alton, Hants.), da. of Hugh Montgomery Cairnes, of Fox Hall, Raheny, co. Dublin:—
(By 1st m.) John Clavell (Smedmore, Wareham, Dorset), *b.* 1917; ed. at Eton, and Ch. Ch., Oxford (MA); Maj. (ret.) Rifle Bde.; JP and DL for Dorset; High Sheriff of Dorset 1968; 1939-45 War: *m.* 1945, Damaris Joan, da. of the late Hyde Hyde-Thomson, of 36, Victoria Rd., W8, and has issue living, Richard John Clavell, *b.* 1949,—Philip Robert Rhys, *b.* 1951,—Lavinia Sylvia, *b.* 1946: *m.* 1968, Alexander Quentin Jones.——Elizabeth Madeline Nina (19, Margaretta Terr., SW3), *b.* 1919: *m.* 1961 (m. diss. 1966), Sir Malby Sturges Crofton, 5th Bt. (cr. 1838).——Felicité Mary Adeline, *b.* 1924: *m.* 1952, Peter Warner, of 368, Wildwood Park, Winnipeg 9, Canada, and has issue living, William Francis, *b.* 1957,—Susanna Elizabeth Juliet, *b.* 1953,—Ianthe Sylvia, *b.* 1954,—Sarah Adeline, *b.* 1959,—Charlotte Anne, *b.* 1965,—Oenone Jane, *b.* 1966.——Pamela Sylvia, *b.* 1926: *m.* 1953, Nicholas Cole McClintock (KStJ), late Overseas Civil Ser., Nigeria, of Lower Westport, Wareham, Dorset, and has issue living, Alexander Edward, *b.* 1959,—Michael Leopold Elphinstone, *b.* 1960,—Sylvia Araby Jane, *b.* 1954,—Elizabeth Melesina, *b.* 1962.— (by 3rd m.) Hugh Clavell (12, Beaufort House, Beaufort St., SW3), *b.* 1948: *m.* 1973, Jennifer Ann, yr. da. of Brian Ashford-Russell, of 1, Cheyne Walk, SW3, and The Lindens, Alresford, Hants.

Granddaughter of the late Col. George Pleydell Mansel, 2nd son of the late Col. John Mansel, CB, 3rd son of 9th baronet:—

Issue of the late Col. John Delalynde Mansel, *b.* 1850, *d.* 1915: *m.* 1888, Mildred Ella, who *d.* 1942, da. of the late Arthur Edward Guest [V. Wimborne, colls.] :—
Juliet Ella *b.* 1893. *Residence,* 33 Lower Belgrave St., SW1.

Granddaughters of the late Algernon Lascelles Mansel (infra):—

Issue of the late John William Morton Mansel, TD, *b.* 1909, *d.* 1974: *m.* 1952, Gillian Valerie (19, Elm Park Rd., SW3, 6DP), el. da. of Douglas Harold Whinney, of South Moreton Manor, Didcot, Berks.:—
Isita Susan, *b.* 1954.——Philippa Clare, *b.* 1955.

Grandchildren of the late Capt. Arthur Edmund Mansel, yst. son of the late Col. John Mansel, CB (ante):—

Issue of the late Algernon Lascelles Mansel, *b.* 1868, *d.* 1942 : *m.* 1906, Isita Rodger, who *d.* 1948, da. of the late William Wilson, formerly of 52, Prince's Gate, S.W. :—
Edmund Clavell, OBE, MC (Savage Garth, Nun Monkton, York; Naval and Military Club), *b.* 1915; ed. at Winchester; Lt.-Col. (ret.) RA; 1939-45 War (despatches, MC); OBE (Mil) 1960: *m.* 1954, Ann, da. of the late Capt. Claud Anthony Merriman, RN, of Newton House, Longparish, Hants, and has issue living, Timothy Mervyn Charles, *b.* 1961,—Catherine Gillian, *b.* 1956 ——Isita Clare, OBE, *b.* 1907; Councillor of St. Pancras 1949-56, 1958-62, and 1963-65, and of LCC 1955-58, and Co. Alderman 1961-65; Councillor GLC 1967-70, and Alderman, London Borough of Camden 1970-74; a Member of Peterborough Development Corpn. 1968-72; 1939-45 War as Group Officer, WAAF (despatches); OBE (Civil) 1964. *Residence,* White House, Albany St., NW1.

Sir Francis Mansel, 1st Bt. (*cr.* 1622) was a yr. brother of Sir Thomas Mansel, of Margam Abbey, Glam. who was *cr.* a baronet 1611. The latter's gt.-grandson, Sir Thomas, 5th Bt., was *cr.* Lord Mansel of Margam, in 1712, *ext.* 1750. On the death of Sir John William Bell Mansel, 11th Bt. (cr. 1622), in 1883, his kinsman Richard, *b.* 1850 [son of Maj. Courtenay Mansel, formerly Phillipps (son of Richard Phillipps, formerly Mansel, yr. son of the 9th Bt.), who *m.,* in Scotland, in or about 1838, Eliza, da. of the Rev. John Sidney (a decree in Court of Session, Edinburgh, pronounced validity of this *m.* in Scotland 1906). He *m.* the same lady in St. Paul's, Liverpool 1847], assumed the baronetcy as 12th Bt.; he *d.* 1892, having *m.* 1st, 1878, Maud Margaretta Bowen, who *d.* 1885, da. of John Jones, of Maes-y-Crugiau Hall, co. Carmarthen, and 2ndly, 1891, Ada Alice Lea, who *d.* 1916. He was followed by his son (by 1st m.), Courtenay Cecil Mansel (de facto 13th Bt.), who in 1903, discontinued using the title, when, with his assent, it was taken up as 12th baronet, by his uncle (Sir) Edward Berkeley Mansel, *b.* 1839 (el. son of Maj. Courtenay Mansel (ante)), *d.* (*dsp*) 1908, when the title was resumed by his nephew Sir Courtenay Cecil Mansel (ante), as 13th Bt.

MAPPIN, Creation (U.K.) 1886, of Thornbury, co. York. [Extinct 1975.]

Sir FRANK CROSSLEY MAPPIN, 6th and last *Baronet.*

Daughters living of 6th Baronet—Laura Crossley, *b.* 1910. *Residence,* 282, Remuera Rd., Auckland, NZ.——Ivy Marjorie, *b.* 1914: *m.* 1941, Air Commodore Theodore Jasper MacLean de Lange, CBE, DFC; RNZAF (ret.), of Kohanga, c/o Okere Falls PO, Rotorua, NZ.——Ethel Thorpe, *b.* 1917: *m.* 1944, George Fenwick, MD. *Residence,* 554, Remuera Rd., Auckland, NZ.
Sister living of 4th Baronet—Molly Violet, *b.* 1907: *m.* 1st, 1928, Francis Ferdinand Maurice Cook (afterwards 4th Bt.), who obtained a divorce 1930; 2ndly, 1930 (m. diss. 19—), Maj. W. St. J. Macarthey; 3rdly, 19—; 4thly, 19—, N. Walker.

MARKHAM, Creation (U.K.) 1911, of Beachborough Park, Newington, Kent.

Tenax propositi

Tenacious of purpose.

Sir CHARLES JOHN MARKHAM, 3rd *Baronet*; *b.* July 2nd, 1924 ; *s.* his father, *Sir* CHARLES, 1952 ; ed. at Eton ; is Lieut. 11th Hussars ; was Vice-Chm., Nairobi Co. Council 1953-55, and a M.L.C., Kenya 1955-60 ; appointed Pres., Roy. Agricultural So. of Kenya 1958 ; European War 1943-45 (despatches) : *m.* 1949, Valerie, only da. of Lieut.-Col. E. Barry-Johnston, and has issue.

Arms—Azure, on a pale argent, three lozenges, palewise sable, issuant from a chief engrailed or, a demi-lion gules. Crest—A winged lion guardant or, the head surrounded by a halo gules and resting the dexter forepaw on a lozenge sable.
Address—Box 2263, Nairobi, Kenya. *Club*—Cavalry.

Sons living—ARTHUR DAVID, *b.* Dec. 6th, 1950.—— Richard Barry, *b.* 1954.
Daughter living—Elizabeth Ann, *b.* 1958.
Half-Brother living—John (c/o Williams & Glyn's Bank, 9, Pall Mall, SW1), *b.* 1933; ed. at Gordonstoun; is Maj. RA: *m.* 1961, Yvonne, da. of Neil-Buchanan, and has issue living, Toby John, *b.* 1966,—Annalise Elizabeth, *b.* 1963.
Sisters living—Mary, *b.* 1921 : *m.* 1946 (marriage dissolved 19—), Senator Joseph Dana Roberts.——Rose (Hon. Mrs. *Christopher Hodson*), *b.* 1926: *m.* 1953, the Hon. (Charles) Christopher Philip Hodson [see B. Hodson]. *Residence,* Stoney Hall, Hannington, Hants.

Widow living of 2nd Baronet—(FREDERICA) BETTY CORNWALLIS (CRAWFORD) (*Betty, Lady Markham*), da. of the late Hon. Christian Edward Cornwallis Eliot, O.B.E. [see E. St. Germans, colls.]: *m.* 1942, as his third wife, Sir Charles Markham, 2nd baronet, who *d.* 1952. *Address,* P.O. Box 583, Mbabane, Swaziland.

Collateral Branch living.

Issue of the late Arthur Markham, 3rd son of 1st baronet, *b.* 1911, *d.* 1943: *m.* 1936, Althea (who *m.* 2ndly, 1946, William John Martin Begg (Southerly, Smiths Parish, Bermuda), da. of Warren David Heinly, of Los Angeles, USA:— Michael Arthur (posthumous) (Southerly, Smiths Parish, Bermuda), *b.* 1944; ed. at Menlo Univ., Cal.

The 1st baronet, Sir Arthur Basil Markham (son of the late Charles Markham, J.P., of Tapton House, Derbyshire), was a Director of the Tredegar Iron and Coal Co., and Founder of Doncaster Amalgamated Collieries ; and sat as M.P. for Mansfield Div. of Notts (*L*) 1900-1916.

MARLING, Creation (U.K.) 1882, of Stanley Park and Sedbury Park, co. Gloucester

Nulli praeda sumus

We are a prey to none.

Sir JOHN STANLEY VINCENT MARLING, O.B.E., 4th *Baronet,* son of the late Sir Charles Murray Marling, G.C.M.G., C.B., 2nd son of 2nd baronet ; *b.* July 26th, 1910 ; *s.* his uncle, Col. Sir PERCIVAL SCROPE, V.C., C.B., 1936 ; ed. at Winchester ; Lt.-Col. (ret.) 17th/21st Lancers, Italy 1943-45 (OBE) ; OBE (Mil.) 1945: *m.* 1st, 1939, Georgina Brenda (Betty) (who *d.* 1961, having obtained a divorce 1957), only da. of the late Henry Edward Fitzroy Somerset [D. Beaufort, colls.] ; 2ndly, 1957, Marjorie Frances Esclairmonde, da. of the late Sir Frances Hugh Stewart, C.I.E., and widow of Major Gustavus March-Phillipps, of 20, Bury Walk, SW3, and has issue by 1st marriage.

Arms—Argent, three bars gules each charged with five bezants ; in chief a lion passant gules. Crest—In front of a tower argent three bezants ; the tower capped with a cupola, thereon a flag-staff proper from which flows a pennant gules.

Residence—Woodcray Manor Farm, Wokingham, Berks.

Son living—By 1st marriage—CHARLES WILLIAM SOMERSET, b. June 2nd, 1951.

Daughters living—By 1st marriage—Miranda Mary, b. 1941: m. 1966, Anthony John Cordle, late Capt. Coldm. Gds., of 40, Hanover Gdns., SE11, and has issue living, Lucia Georgina Diana, b. 1968,—Jessica Grace Rosanne, b. 1972.——Harriet Anne, b. 1944.——Virginia Frances, b. 1946.

Sisters living—Yvonne Mary, b. 1912 : m. 1932, Com. the Hon. Gustaf Guthrie Rennell Rodd, OBE, RN (who d. 1974, and from whom she obtained a divorce 1948) [see B. Rennell, colls.].—Marian Charlotte, MBE, b. 1915; late Junior Com. ATS, is a CStJ, and a Co. Councillor of Berks.; MBE (Mil) 1944: m. 1944, Lt. Richard O. B. Long, RNVR, from whom she obtained a divorce 1953, and has issue living, David William Marling, b. 1950; ed. at The Oratory; Lt. Irish Gds.,—Caroline Ann Romaine, b. 1946. Residence, Foxley Cottage, Binfield, nr. Bracknell, Berks.

Collateral Branch living.

Issue of the late Col. Walter Bentley Marling, **3rd** son of 1st baronet, b. **1854, d.** 1941: m. 1880, Mary Isabella Cunynghame, who d. **1933**, da. of Lieut.-Col. Robert Broome Baker [Cunynghame, Bt.]:—

Mary Helen, b. 1885: m. 1913, Maj. William John Paley Marling, who d. 1939. Residence, Littleworth Corner, Amberley, Glos.——Elspeth Katharina, b. 1892: m. 1915, Capt. Norman Tyrer, formerly Bedfordshire Regt. Residence, Windy Brow, Pennington, Lymington, Hants.

The 1st baronet sat as M.P. for Gloucestershire West (L) 1868-74 and for Stroud 1875-80. The 2nd baronet was High Sheriff of Gloucestershire 1888. The 3rd baronet, Col. Sir Percival Scrope Marling, V.C., C.B., served in S. Africa 1881, in Egypt 1882, with Suakim Expedition 1884 (V.C.), with Nile Expedition 1884-5, in S. Africa 1899-1902 (C.B.) and during European War 1914-15.

MARR, Creation (U.K.) 1919, of Sunderland, co. Palatine of Durham.

(*Sir*) LESLIE LYNN MARR, 2nd *Baronet*, son of the late John Lynn Marr, OBE, el. son of 1st Baronet; b. Aug. 14th, 1922; s. his grandfather, *Sir* JAMES, *CBE*, 1932, but does not use title; ed. at Shrewsbury, and at Pembroke Coll., Camb. (MA); late Fl. Lt. RAF: m. 1st, 1948 (m. diss. 1956), Dinora Delores Mendelson; 2ndly, 1962, Lynn Heneage, and has issue by 2nd m.

Arms—Azure, the mast and sail of a ship, pennon flying, within eight estoiles in orle or. **Crest**—A bell charged with a fouled anchor proper.

Address,—c/o Lloyds Bank, Holt, Norfolk.

Daughters living—By 2nd m.—Joanne Lesley, b. 1963.——Rebecca Lynn, b. 1966.

Collateral Branch living.

Issue of the late William Bell Marr, yr. son of 1st baronet, b. 1881, d. 1971: m. 1906, Hilda, who d. 1970, da. of George Carse, of Wilton, Wilts.:—

ALLAN JAMES, CBE (Dalesford, Thropton, Morpeth, Northumberland, NE65 7JE; Royal Thames Yacht), b. May 6th, 1907; ed. at Oundle, and Durham Univ. (BSc); CBE (Civil) 1965: m. 1935, Joan de Wolf, da. of John Ranken, of Sunderland, and has issue living, James Allan (10, The Cedars, Sunderland), b. 1939: m. 1965, Jennifer, yr. da. of John William Edward Gill, of Bishop Auckland, and has issue living, Allan James William b. 1965, Roderick John b. 1971, Lucy Joan b. 1968,—Jennifer Wendy, b. 1936: m. 1960, Nicholas Warren Willinck, of Greenhills, Crook, Kendal, and has issue living, Patrick John b. 1964, Amanda Frances b. 1961, Susan Joan b. 1963,—Gillian Mary, b. 1942: m. 1974, Richard Tatton Wedderburn Hewetson, of Stobars Hall, Kirkby Stephen, Cumbria.—Norman Carse (Littlewater, Bampton, Penrith, Cumbria), b. 1910; ed. at London Univ. (BSc): m. 1935, Flora McDonald, da. of Kenneth McDonald Cameron, of West Hartlepool, and has issue living, Jeremy Norman (56, Russell Hill Rd., Toronto, Ont., Canada), b. 1940: m. 1968, Gillian Yvonne, only da. of the late P. J. Hugo, of Johannesburg, and has issue living, Kyle Jeremy b. 1974,—Dair Norman, b. 1941: m. 1964, Douglas Ian Henry Henderson,—Alexandra Norman, b. 1944.——Arthur Lynn (Birney Wood, Throckley, Northumberland), b. 1914: m. 1941, May Victoria, da. of Harry Bernard Bradshaw, of Birmingham, and has issue living, Bernard Lynn (25, Bluebell Close, Wylam, Northumberland), b. 1943: m. 1968, Judith, da. of Ronald Henry Richards, of Burcroft, Wood Lane, Astwood Bank, Worcs., and has issue living, Katherine Lynn b. 1972, Jane Victoria b. 1974,—Mary Singleton, b. 1946: m. 1972, Christopher Broom-Smith, Jr.,—Victoria Lynn, b. 1951.

The 1st baronet, Sir James Marr, C.B.E., was a shipbuilder, Chm. of Sir James Laing & Sons, Ltd., of Sunderland, of Sunderland Forge & Engineering Co., Ltd., of T. W. Greenwell & Co., Ltd., of Sunderland, and of Joseph L. Thompson & Sons. Ltd. of Sunderland and a Member of Lloyd's Registry of Shipping.

Labour conquers all things.

LABOR OMNIA VINCIT

SMITH-MARRIOTT, Creation (G.B.) 1774, of Sydling St. Nicholas, Dorset.

Sir RALPH GEORGE CAVENDISH SMITH-MAR-
RIOTT, 10th *Baronet*, son of the late George Rudolph Wyld-
bore Smith-Marriott, son of the late Rev. Hugh Forbes
Smith-Marriott, 3rd son of 4th Baronet ; *b.* 1900 ; *s.* his uncle,
Sir HUGH RANDOLPH CAVENDISH, 1944 ; ed. at Cranleigh :
m. 1st, 1924, Phyllis Elizabeth, who *d.* 1932, da. of Richard
Kemp, formerly Gov. of H.M. Prison, Bristol ; 2ndly, 1933,
Doris May, who *d.* 1951, da. of R. L. C. Morrison, of
Tenby ; 3rdly, 1966, Mrs. Barbara Mary Cantlay, and has
issue by 1st marriage.

Semper fidelis.
Always faithful.

Arms—Quarterly : 1st and 4th, barry of six, or and sable, in chief two
escallops gules, *Marriott ;* 2nd and 3rd, sable, a fesse erminois cotised or,
between three martlets of the last, each charged with an ermine spot, *Smith.*
Crests—1st, a mount vert, thereon a talbot passant sable guttée de larmes,
collared and line reflexed over the back or ; 2nd, a greyhound sejant gules,
collared and a line reflexed over the back or, charged on the shoulder with
a mascle argent.

Residence—28A, Westover Rd., Westbury-on-Trym, Bristol.

Sons living—By 1st m.—HUGH CAVENDISH (26, Shipley Rd., Westbury-on-Trym, Bristol)
b. March 22nd, 1925 : *m.* 1953, Pauline, Anne, da. of Frank Fawcett Holt, of Abbotsway, Bristol,
and has issue living, Julie Anne, *b.* 1958.——Peter Francis (88, Maidenhall, Highnam, nr.
Gloucester), *b.* 1927 : *m.* 1961, Jean Graham Martin, da. of James Sorley Ritchie, of Salisbury,
Rhodesia, and has issue living, Martin Ralph, *b.* 1962,—Neil Hugh, *b.* 1964,—Ian Peter, *b.* 1967.

Daughter living—By 1st marriage—Doris Mary, *b.* 1929 : *m.* 1957, Alexander Stewart MacCaig,
11, Shipley Rd., Westbury-on-Trym, Bristol, and has issue living, Helen Mary, *b.* 1958,—
Susan Jane, *b.* 1961,—Anne Elizabeth, *b.* 1964.

Brother living—Francis Patrick Parry, *b.* 1906 : *m.* 1932. *Residence,*

Daughters living of 8th Baronet—By 1st marriage—Mary Charlotte, *b.* 1888 : *m.* 1st,
1913, Heathfield Dodgson ; 2ndly, 1927, Alban Hugh Harrison, who *d.* 1943.——**By 2nd**
m.—Rosemary Kathleen, *b.* 1916 : *m.* 1st, 1944, Henry Everett, who *d.* 1965 [E. Galloway,
colls.] : 2ndly, 1972, John Derek Hall (Houseboat "Pepper", 106, Cheyne Walk, SW10), and has
issue living, William Marriott, *b.* 1946,—Barbara Rosemary, *b.* 1948 : *m.* 1968, Timothy James
Gerard Dyas,—Helen Rosalind, *b.* 1954.

Mother living—Dorothy Magdalene, da. of the Rev. John Parry, R. of Llanarmon-Dyffryn-
Ceiriog, near Llangollen : *m.* 1897, George Rudolph Wyldbore Smith-Marriott (ante), who *d.*
1944. *Residence,*

Collateral Branches living.

Grandchildren of the late Reginald Bosworth Smith (infra) :—
        Issue of the late Gerard Hugh Bosworth Smith, *b.* 1868, *d.* 1940 : *m.* 1893, Olive Yates:—
Reginald Claude, *b.* 1899 : *m.* 1929, Evelyn Whittington, of Panama City, Florida, U.S.A., and has
issue living, Reginald Claude, *b.* 1930,—Wayne Edward, *b.* 1932,—James Lee, *b.* 1939,—Evelyn
Joan, *b.* 1935,—Geraldine, *b.* 1942.——Ellinor Joan, *b.* 1896,—Vera Bosworth, *b.* 1904 : *m.* 1st,
1921 (m. diss. 1923), Manuel M. Paula ; 2ndly, 1925, David Joseph Keene.——Bertha Bosworth,
b. 1908 : *m.* 1926, Roy Bronson.

        Issue of the late Reginald Montagu Bosworth Smith, C.B.E., *b.* 1872, *d.* 1944 : *m.* 1st, 1905
        Agnes Val, who *d.* 1915, da. of G. Val Davies ; 2ndly, 1916, Kate Evelyn, who *d.* 1975,
        da. of the late Frederick Charles Pardoe Radclyffe, of Birmingham:—
(By 2nd marriage) Reginald Bosworth, LL.B., *b.* 1917 ; B.A. and LL.B., 1938 ; is a Solicitor ;
Middle East 1942-45 as Trooper 6th S. African Armoured Div. : *m.* 1965, Helen Margaret, da.
of the late Ernest R. Stidworthy, of East London, S. Africa. *Address*, P.O. Box 577, East
London, S. Africa.——Alan Bosworth, *b.* 1919 ; is a C.A. (S. Africa), and a F.S.A.A. ; Middle
East 1940-45 as Gunner S. African Artillery : *m.* 1949, Helen, da. of John Mackenzie, of Jo-
hannesburg, and has issue living, Michael John Bosworth, *b.* 1951,—Pamela Anne, *b.* 1953.
Address, PO Box 1742, Johannesburg, S. Africa.——(By 1st m.) Daphne Evangeline Bosworth,
b. 1909 : *m.* 1932, John Awdry Cottrell, OBE, Dir. of African Education, Zambia 1948-58, and
has issue living, Christopher Bosworth (University of Rhodesia, Salisbury, Rhodesia), *b.* 1934 ;
ed. at Rhodes Univ., S. Africa (BSc), and at Queen's Coll., Camb. (PhD) ; Junior Research Fellow,
Churchill Coll. 1960-61 : *m.* 1962, Meriol Lesley, da. of Col. Millard, of Taunton, and has issue
living, John Gray *b.* 1964, Christopher Noel *b.* 1966,—Richard Gray (PO Box 2536, Johannesburg), *b.* 1935 ; is a Chartered Accountant, and Partner in Cooper & Lybrand, Johannesburg :
m. 1971, Moya Ann, da. of George R. English, of Rochford, Essex, and has issue living, Edward
Christopher *b.* 1974,—Gilbert Reginald James (Management Consultant, M. C. Geffen & Associates, Box 4410, Capetown, S. Africa), *b.* 1944 ; ed. at Queen's Coll., Camb. (BA), and Columbia
Univ., New York (MBA) : *m.* 1971, Phoebe Madelaire, da. of Dr. Tage Madelaire Nielsen, of New
London, Conn., USA, and has issue living, Ariel Daphne *b.* 1974. *Address*, PO Box 189, Pletten-
berg Bay, Cape Prov., S. Africa.——Ursula Gwendolin Boxworth (10A, 2nd St., Parkhurst,
Johannesburg, S. Africa), *b.* 1911 : *m.* 1st, 1934, Arnold Lingen Watson, solicitor, who obtained
a divorce 1947 ; 2ndly, 1947, William Patrick Temple Scott, who *d.* 1971, and has issue living
(by 1st m.), Toni Elaine (c/o National & Grindlays Bank Ltd., 13, St. James's Sq., SW1), *b.*
1936 : *m.* 1957, Maj. Jeremy Alexander Frere, 1st R. Anglian Regt., and has issue living, Martin
Adrian *b.* 1958.

        Issue of the late Bertrand Nigel Bosworth Smith, *b.* 1873, *d.* 1947 : *m.* 9112, Mary Con-
        stance (who *d.* 1961, having obtained a divorce 1932), da. of the late David Inche-
        Bett, of New Hall, Forfarshire :—
Mary Nigella (of Panguiblarft, Linkside East, Hindhead, Surrey), *b.* 1913 : *m.* 1946 (marriage
dissolved 1960), Peter de Lande Long, F.R.I.C.S., F.I.A.S., and has issue living, Ian Bartholomew (19, Gordon Av., Poltenhill, Lasswade, Midlothian), *b.* 1949 : *m.* 1970, Marjorie, da. of Dr.
Hamilton, of Dublin,—Jonathan, *b.* 1951,—Peter Graeme, *b.* 1952.——Janet Wickham, *b.*
1918 : *m.* 1939, Claude Scott Nicol, TD, MD, FRCP, late Col. RAMC (V), and has issue living,
Alasdair Gordon *b.* 1944 : *m.* 1974, Julie Mayston Collings, of Essendon, Melbourne, Aust.,—
Judy, *b.* 1943 : *m.* 1966, John Diggory de Bourbel Rochfort, of White Ways, Headley, Newbury,
and has issue living, Christopher Michael *b.* 1969, Jeremy *b.* 1971, James *b.* 1974,—Melany,
b. 1946 : *m.* 1973, Piers Hayward Hughes, of 18, Gatwick Rd., SW18, and has issue living,
Katherine Melany *b.* 1974. *Residence,* 40, Ferncroft Av., Hampstead, NW3.
        **Issue of the late Mervyn Henry Bosworth Smith, *b.* 1878, *d.* 1950 : *m.* 1st, 1914, Sophie
        (from whom he obtained a divorce 1919), da. of John Warmington, of Ninnes, Lelant,**

Cornwall ; 2ndly, 1920, Mary Annette Morcum, of Johannesburg, S. Africa, from whom he obtained a divorce 1926 ; 3rdly, 1927, Sarah Aletta, da. of H. W. Fourie, of Johannesburg, S. Africa :
(By 2nd marriage) Anthony Mervyn Bosworth, b. 1925 ; ed. at Witwatersrand Univ. (B.Sc. 1949) ; European War 1944-45, in Italy as Trooper 6th S. African Armoured Div. : m. 1951, Jean Rosemary, el. da. of A. Peerman, of Erin Stables, Sandown, Johannesburg, S. Africa, and has issue living, Mervyn Nigel Bosworth, b. 1957,—Gwen Bridget, b. 1953. Residence, Glen Fern, Nottingham Road, Natal, S. Africa.

Issue of the late Nevil Digby Bosworth Smith, CB, b. 1886, d. 1964: m. 1913, Gladys, who d. 1965, da. of the late John Francis Wood, of Uffculme, Devon:—
Richard Nevil BOSWORTH-SMITH (7, Hillside Rd., Northwood, Middlesex), b. 1926; ed at Harrow, and at Balliol Coll., Oxford (MA); assumed the additional surname of Bosworth 1969: m. 1960, Anne, el. da. of the late John Ree, of Pinner, Middx., and has issue living, Nevil John Bosworth, b. 1961,—Mary Margaret Bosworth b. 1964.——Bridget Laura Bosworth, b. 1915: m. 1st, 1938 (m. diss. 1951), James Guy Bramwell; 2ndly, 1951, Robert Speaight, CBE, of Campion House, Benenden, Kent, and has issue living (by 1st m.), Crispin John, b. 1945,—Teresa Clare b. 1939: m. 1st 1961 (m. diss. 1966) the Hon. Alexander Davison, el. son of 2nd Baron Broughshane; 2ndly, 1967, Alexander John Francis Newman, of 32, Thornhill Sq., N1.

Granddaughters of the late Rev. Reginald Southwell Smith, 5th son of 2nd baronet :—
Issue of the late Reginald Bosworth Smith, b. 1839, d. 1908: m. 1865, Flora, who d. 1927, da. of the late Rev. Edmund Dawe Wickham, of Cheam Park, and V. of Holmwood, Dorking :—
Bertha Joan Bosworth, b. 1883: m. 1st, 1911, as his second wife, Lt.-Col. Charles Sinclair Shephard, DSO, who d. 1930; 2ndly, 1939, Capt. Royal Cochrane, Machine Gun Corps, who d. 1951. Residence, 56, Milton Abbas, Blandford, Dorset.
Issue of the late Col. Walter William Marriott Smith, C.B.E. ; b. 1846, d. 1944 : m. 1874, Alice Mary, who d. 1932, da. of the late John H. Ley, of Trehill, Devon:—
Vera Rose Marriott, b. 1887: m. 1912, Brig. Geoffrey Cathcart Gowlland, RE (ret.) and has issue living, Jean, b. 1915: m. 1936, Canute Phillips Larson, who d. (killed in action in Singapore) 1942, and has issue living, Janet Mary b. 1937, Ann Monica b. 1940. Residence, The Manor, Upwey, Dorset.

Grandsons of the late Capt. Hugh Francis Wyldbore WYLDBORE-SMITH (infra):—
Issue of the late Lieut.-Com. Hugh Deane WYLDBORE-SMITH, R.N., b. 1907, d. (killed in action during European War) 1941: m. 1937, Rachel Caroline Lucy (of The White House, Husborne Crawley, Beds.), el. da. of the late Rev. Edward Yarde Orlebar, of Crawley Park, Beds.:—
Nicolas Hugh (The Courtiers, Clifton Hampden, Abingdon, Berks.; Naval and Military Club), b. 1938; ed. at Wellington, and St. James, Maryland, USA: m. 1964, Gillian Mary, da. of the late Leslie Carman, of Fareham, Hants., and has issue living, Alexander Hugh Nicolas, b. 1969,—James William, b. 1971.——Piers (The White House, Husborne Crawley, Beds.; 21, Mountford Place, SE11), b. 1939; ed. at Eton, New Coll., Oxford, and London Univ. (BA).

Grandchildren of the late Rev. Francis Alfred Smith, son of the late Rev. Francis Smith, 6th son of 2nd baronet:—
Issue of the late Capt. Hugh Francis Wyldbore WYLDBORE-SMITH, R.N., b. 1869, d. 1919, having assumed by deed poll 1903 the additional surname of Wyldbore: m. 1903, Kate Beatrice, who d. 1959, da. of the late William Henry Deane, J.P., D.L., of Fareham House, Fareham :—
John Henry, b. 1916 ; sometime Lieut. R.N.V.R.: m. 1939, Robina, da. of the late Capt. Francis Welsford Ward, of Bosloe, Cornwall, and has issue living, William Francis, b. 1948: m. 1974, Mrs. Prisca Faith Jenney, yr. da. of the Rev. Peter Nourse, of Eardisland Vicarage, Herefordshire, —Robina Ann, 🟥b. 1943,—Susan Elizabeth, b. 1950. Residence, Scaynes Hill House, Haywards Heath, Sussex. Club,—RNVR.——Kathleen Elinor (33, Illovo Mansions, Corlett Drive, Illovo, Johannesburg, S. Africa), b. 1905: m. 1936, Algernon Spencer, who d. 1965, and has issue living, Charles Peter (46, Komdt. Senekal St., Dan Pienaar, Blomfontein, S. Africa), b. 1937; BSc: m. 1960, Charlotte Ann Lind, and has issue living, Michael John b. 1961, Gregory b. 1966, Claire Ann b. 1962, Lindsay Ann b. 1964,—David Wyldbore (Silver Goblin, 158, Main Rd., Sandown, Johannesburg), b. 1939: m. 1966, Cynthia Fenella Raulo, and has issue living, Gregory Paul b. 1966, Leila Cairinne b. 1968,—Hugh Mark (38, Kildare Av., Parkview, Johannesburg, S. Africa), b. 1941; ed. at Witwatersrand Univ. (BSc Eng): m. 1965, Elsebe Elise Robbertze, and has issue living, Martin b. 1968, Susan Deborah b. 1965,—Simon Francis, b. 1946,— Christopher Audley b. 1948.

Issue of the late Rev. William Reginald Wyldbore Smith, b. 1874, d. 1943: m. 1905, Dorothy, who d. 1969, da. of the late George Green, of Watford Field House, Watford:—
Reginald Anthony Wyldbore, b. 1909; a J.P.: m. 1933, Honor Christine Dyott, da. of the late George Willmot, of Coleshill, Warwicks., and has issue living, Michael Anthony Wyldbore WYLDBORE-SMITH (Moat Cottage, Berkswell, Warwick) b. 1944; ed. at Cheltenham Coll.; assumed by deed poll 1969, the additional surname of Wyldbore: m. 1967, Sheila Margaret, da. of E. C. H. Organ, of Kenilworth, and has issue living, Sarah b. 1969, Nicola b. 1971. Residence, Elmcroft, Berkswell, Coventry.——Francis Brian Wyldbore WYLDBORE-SMITH, CB, DSO, OBE (34, Cleveland Sq., W2, and Grantham House, Grantham, Lincs.; Naval and Miltiary and Buck's Clubs), b. 1913; ed. at Wellington, and RMA, Woolwich; assumed by deed poll 1966, the additional surname of Wyldbore; Maj.-Gen., late RHA and 15th/19th KR Hussars (Comdg. 1953-56, Col. since 1970); Ch. to Staff to C-in-C, Far East 1963-65; GOC 44th Inf. Div. and Home Cos. Dist., and Dep. Constable of Dover Castle 1965-68; ret. 1968; 1939-45 War in Middle East, Italy and NW Europe (MBE, DSO, OBE); MBE (Mil) 1943, DSO 1944, OBE (Mil) 1945, CB (Mil) 1965- m. 1944, the Hon. Molly Angela Cayzer, da. of 1st Baron Rotherwick, and has issue living, Brian Robin, b. 1957,—Carolyn Molly, b. 1944: m. 1968, Harry O. Ditson,—Angela Maureen, b. 1947: m. 1975, Barrie Giffard-Taylor,—Penelope Ann, b. 1948: m. 1973, James E. Herdman,—Nicola Jane, b. 1952.

Grandchildren of the late Rev. Heathcote Smith (infra):—
Issue of the late Sir Clifford Edward Heathcote-Smith, K.B.E., C.M.G., b. 1883, d. 1963: m. 1909, Elaine, who d. 1967, da. of the late John J. Spiegethal de Fonton, of Cannes:—
Clifford Bertram Bruce, CBE (Middle Burchetts, N. Chailey, Lewes), b. 1912; ed. at Malvern, and at Pembroke Coll., Camb.; late HM Diplo. Ser.; acting Senior Clerk, House of Commons; CBE (Civil) 1963: m. 1940, Thelma Joyce Engström, and has issue living, Charles Clifford Ralph, b. 1949,—Max Christopher, b. 1950.——Jocelyn Elaine Laura (Lady Thorold), b. 1910: m. 1939, Capt. Sir Anthony Henry Thorold, Bt., OBE, DSC, RN, of Syston Old Hall, Grantham.—— Elaine Mary Elisabeth, b. 1914: m. 1936, Rear-Adm. Roger Stanley Wellby, CB, DSO, of Oakengrove, Hastoe, Tring, Herts, and has issue living, Michael Anthony, b. 1939: m. 1966, Kate Frances, da. of William Ram, of Berkhamsted, and has issue living, Anthony William b. 1969, Kate d'Esterre b. 1968,—Christopher Mark, b. 1943,—Peter Martin Heathcote, b. 1946.

Grandchildren of the late Maj. Edward Heathcote Smith, 7th son of 2nd baronet:—

Issue of the late Rev. Heathcote Smith, *b.* 1847, *d.* 1914: *m.* 1st, 1873, Clara Jane, who *d.* 1898, da. of John Ross Soden of Clapham, Surrey; 2nd, 1899, Louisa Floyd, who *d.* 1956, da. of George White, of Great Missenden, Bucks:—

(By 2nd m.) Cecil Roland Heathcote, *MBE* (Hillview, Main St., Kirkcolm, Wigtownshire), *b.* 1901; sometime HM's Vice-Consul, Guayaquil, Ecuador; formerly Capt. Intelligence Corps; MBE (Mil) 1945: *m.* 1952, Ailsa Helen, el. da. of the late Ninian Adair, of Stranraer.——Stephanie Cecilia Heathcote, *b.* 1904. *Residence*, 6, Heatherslade Rd., Southgate, Pennard, Glam.

The 1st baronet, Sir John Smith (son of the late Henry Smith, of New Windsor, Berks), was **High Sheriff** of Dorset 1772. The 4th baronet, Sir William Marriott, assumed, by sign manual 1811, **the** additional surname and arms of Marriott, and the 5th was High Sheriff of Dorset 1875.

MARSDEN, Creation (U.K.) 1924, of Grimsby, co. Lincoln.

Thanks to God.

Sir JOHN DENTON MARSDEN, 2nd *Baronet*; *b.* Aug. 25th, 1913; *s.* his father, *Sir* JOHN DENTON, 1944; ed. at Downside, and at St. John's Coll., Camb. (B.A. 1935); is Lieut. R.A.; Chm. and Managing Director of Consolidated Fisheries, Ltd., of Grimsby, and a J.P. for parts of Lindsey, co. Lincoln; European War 1939-41 (prisoner): *m.* 1939, Hope, ygr. da. of the late G. E. Llewelyn, of Bryngawr, Aberkenfig, Glamorgan, and has issue.

Arms—Sable, a fesse dancettée ermine, in chief two fleur-de-lis argent and in base a ship sailing to the sinister proper. **Crest**—In front of a unicorn's head erased sable charged with two barrulets gules as many roses argent, barbed and seeded proper.
Residence—White Abbey, Linton-in-Craven, Skipton, Yorks.

Sons living—NIGEL JOHN DENTON (1, Grimsby Rd., Waltham, Lincs.), *b.* May 26th, 1940: *m.* 1961, Diana Jean, el. da. of Air Marshal Sir Patrick Hunter Dunn, KBE, CB, DFC, and has issue living, Lucinda Ann, *b.* 1962,—Rose Amanda, *b.* 1964,—Annabel Juliet, *b.* 1968.——Simon Neville Llewelyn, *b.* 1948: *m.* 1970, Catherine Thérèsa, da. of the late Brig. James Charles Windsor-Lewis, DSO [B. Burnham].
Daughters living—Vanessa Ann, *b.* 1941: *m.* 1968, Francis John Whitehead.——Caroline Jane, *b.* 1946: *m.* 1970, Richard T. W. Noton.
Sister living—Agnes Isabelle, *b.* 1920: *m.* 1941, Capt. Frederick William Tackaberry Storey, R.A.S.C., and has issue living, Michael William Tackaberry, *b.* 1942,— Jonathan William Tackaberry *b.* 1948,—Alastair William Tackaberry, *b.* 1949,—Jane Patricia, *b.* 1951,—Penelope Caroline, *b.* 1953,—Sally Anne, *b.* 1957. *Residence*, Baymead Cottage, 2, Baymead Lane, North Pemberton, nr. Bridgwater, Somerset.

The 1st baronet, Sir John Denton Marsden (son of the late William Dent Marsden, of Aldmondbury, Huddersfield), was Principal of Consolidated Fisheries, Ltd., of Grimsby, Swansea and Lowestoft.

MARTIN, Creation (G.B.) 1791. [Extinct 1910.]

Sir RICHARD BYAM MARTIN, 5th and last *Baronet*.

Daughter living of 5th Baronet—Georgiana Phyllis Maud: *m.* 1922, Leonard John Newbery, and has issue living, Thomas Byam Martin, *b.* 1922; ed. at Canford; European War 1939-45 in Grenadier Guards: *m.* 1954, Pamela Burch, and has issue living, Richard Byam Martin *b.* 1957, Michael John *b.* 1959, Sarah *b.* 1955,—John Desaguliers, *b.* 1924; sometime a Cadet, Pacific Steam Navigation Co.: *m.* 1950, Elizabeth Godley, and has issue living, Elizabeth *b.* 1951, Georgiana *b.* 1955,—Margaret Catherine Fanshaw, *b.* 1926. *Residence*, Fordwater, Axminster, Devon.

Maryon-Wilson see Wilson, cr. 1661.

Mather-Jackson, see Jackson.

MATHESON, Creation (U.K.) 1882, of Lochalsh, co. Ross.

Sir Torquhil Alexander Matheson of Matheson, 6th *Baronet*; *b.* Aug. 15th, 1925; *s.* his father, *Gen. Sir* Torquhil George, *KCB, CMG,* 1963; ed. at Eton; Ch. of Clan Matheson; Maj. (ret.) Coldm. Gds.; seconded Kings African Rifles 1961-64; Wiltshire Regt. (TA) 1965-67, and R. Wiltshire Territorials (TAVR III 1967-69): *m.* 1954, Serena Mary Francesca, da. of the late Lt.-Col. Sir (James) Michael Peto, 2nd Bt., cr. 1927, and has issue.

Arms—Argent, three dexter hands couped at the wrist gules, within a bordure of the last. Crest—Issuing from an Eastern crown or a hand brandishing a scimitar in fesse proper. Residence—Standerwick Court, Frome, Somerset. Club—Guards'.

Do and hope.

Daughters living—Eleanor Mary Francesca, *b.* 1955.—Isobel Sophia, *b.* 1957.

Brother living—Fergus John, *b.* Feb. 22nd, 1927; ed. at Eton; Maj. Coldstream Guards Reserve: *m.* 1952, the Hon. Jean Elizabeth Mary Willoughby, da. of the late 11th Baron Middleton, and has issue living, Alexander Fergus, *b.* 1954,—Elizabeth Angela Matilda, *b.* 1953,—Fiona Jean Lucia, *b.* 1962. *Residence*, Hedenham Old Rectory, Bungay, Suffolk. Club, Guards'.

Daughter living of 3rd Baronet—Eleanor: *m.* 1922, John Lyne Harvey, MC, FRIBA, and has issue living, Elizabeth Margaret, *b.* 1923: *m.* 1947, Preben A. F. Aakesson, and has issue living, Alexander Sven *b.* 1957, John Torsten George *b.* 1959,—Eleanor Flora Anne, *b.* 1931. *Residence*, Empacombe, Dalmore Av., Claygate, Surrey.

Widow living of 5th Baronet—*Lady* Elizabeth Mary Gertrude Keppel, ARRC (*Lady Elizabeth Matheson*) (Cedar House, Woodbridge, Suffolk), da. of 8th Earl of Albemarle; ARRC; 1914-18 VAD in France (despatches): *m.* 1923, as his 2nd wife, Gen. Sir Torquhil George Matheson, KCB, CMG, 5th Bt., Coldm. Gds., who *d.* 1963.

Mathesons occupied the lands of Lochalsh, Attadale, etc., from the 13th century. Their chief being one of those arrested and executed at Inverness in 1427, the estates were granted to Celestine of The Isles, whose granddaughter, Margaret, conveyed the half to her husband Macdonell of Glengarry. John Matheson, who in 1728 married Margaret Mackenzie, a descendant of this marriage, acquired Attadale in 1730. Their great-grandson and heir male, Alexander Matheson, having in 1851, purchased Lochalsh, was created a baronet under that designation; he sat as M.P. for Inverness District (L) 1847-68, and for Ross and Cromarty 1868-84. Sir Alexander Perceval Matheson, 3rd Bt., was a Senator of Commonwealth of Australia. Gen. Sir Torquhil George Matheson, KCB, CMG, 5th Bt., commanded 3rd Coldstream Guards, 46th Inf. Bde, 20th, 4th and Guards Divs. 1914-18, Waziristan Field Force 1920-24, and was GOC in C. W. Command, India, 1931-35.

MATHIAS, Creation (U.K.) 1917, of Vaendre Hall, St. Mellons, co. Monmouth.

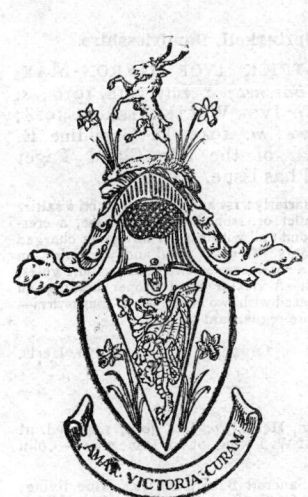

Sir Richard Hughes Mathias, 2nd *Baronet*; *b.* April 6th, 1905; *s.* his father, *Sir* Richard, 1942; ed. at Eton, and at Balliol Coll., Oxford; a Member of London Stock Exchange, and a Fellow of Corporation of SS. Mary and Nicolas (Woodard Schools); Member of Council, Hurstpierpoint Coll. (Chm. 1967-74); Sqdn.-Ldr. RAFVR, on staff of Air Min. 1942-46; 1939-45 War: *m.* 1st, 1937 (m. diss. 1960), Gladys Cecilia Turton, only da. of Edwin Hart, of New Hextalls, Bletchingley, Surrey; 2ndly, 1960, Mrs. Elizabeth Baird Murray, who *d.* 1972, el. da. of Dr. William Miles of Hendrescythan, Creigiau, Glamorgan; 3rdly, 1973, Mrs. Hilary Vines, who *d.* 1975, only child of William Howells, of Cardiff, and has issue by 1st m.

Arms—Or, on a pile gules a dragon rampant of the field, in base two daffodils slipped and leaved proper. Crest—On a mount vert, a goat rampant proper between two daffodils as in the arms. Residence, 8, Oakwood Court, Abbotsbury Rd., W14 8JU. Club—Reform.

Victory loves care.

Daughters living—By 1st m.—Anna Patricia (56, York Mansions, Prince of Wales Drive, SW11), *b.* 1938: *m.* 1962 (m. diss. 1971), Lt.-Cdr. Eric Clive Hastings, RN, and has issue living, Nichola Jane, *b.* 1964.—Virginia Turton, *b.* 1942.

The 1st baronet, Sir Richard Mathias (son of John Mathias, steamship owner, of Aberystwyth), was a member of the firm of J. Mathias & Sons, shipowners, of Cardiff, and M.P. for Cheltenham (L) 1910-11.

MAXWELL, Creation (N.S.) 1681, of Monreith, Wigtownshire.

I renew my strength.

Sir AYMER MAXWELL, 8th *Baronet*, son of the late Lieut.-Col. Aymer Edward Maxwell, 2nd son of 7th baronet; *b.* Dec. 7th, 1911; *s.* his grandfather, *the Rt. Hon. Sir* HERBERT EUSTACE, K.T., LL.D., D.C.L., F.R.S., 1937; ed. at Eton, and at Magdalene Coll., Camb. (B.A. Honours 1933): is Hon. Capt. Scots Guards, and a J.P. for Wigtownshire.

Arms—Argent, an eagle with two heads displayed sable, beaked and membered gules; on the breast an escutcheon of the first, charged with a saltire of the second, surcharged in the centre with a hurcheon (hedgehog), or, all within a bordure gules. **Crest**—An eagle rising proper.

Seat—Monreith, Portwilliam, Wigtownshire. *Clubs,*—Boodle's, Beefsteak, New (Edinburgh).

Sister living—Christian, *b.* 1910.

Collateral Branches living.

Issue of the late Maj. Eustace Maxwell, A & SH, brother, of 8th Bt, *b.* 1913, *d.* 1971: *m.* 1940 (m. diss. 1949), Dorothy Vivien, da. of Capt. George Bellville, of Fermyn Woods Hall, Brigstock, Northants.:—

MICHAEL EUSTACE GEORGE, *b.* Aug. 28th, 1943; ed. at Eton.—— Diana Mary, *b.* 1942.

Descendants, if any, of Alexander Charles Maxwell, yr. son of Maj. Hamilton Maxwell, BSc, (*d.* 1829), 3rd son of 4th baronet, who left issue four sons.

The Maxwells of Monreith derive from Sir Edward Maxwell of Tinwald, co. Dumfries, yr. son of 1st Lord Maxwell (cr. 1440) ancestor of the Earls of Nithsdale [see D. Norfolk (Lordship of Herries)]. The Maxwells of Tinwald became ext. in early 18th century. Herbert Maxwell, yr. brother of Edward Maxwell of Tinwald, m. 1541, Margaret Maxwell, heir of Monreith. Fourth in descent from whom was the 1st baronet, the Rt. Hon. Sir William. The 7th baronet, the Rt. Hon. Sir Herbert, KT, PC, LLD, DCL, FRS, was Lord-Lieut. of Wigtownshire 1903-35, MP for Wigtownshire (C) 1880-1906, and a Lord of the Treasury 1886-92.

MAXWELL, Creation (U.K.) 1804, of Cardoness, Kirkcudbrightshire. [Extinct 1924.]

Sir WILLIAM FRANCIS MAXWELL, 4th and last *Baronet*.

Daughter living of 4th Baronet—Dorothea Letitia May, *b.* 1888: *m.* 1910, Col. Frederick Rainsford-Hannay, CMG, DSO, RA, who *d.* 1959, and has issue living, Ramsay William (Kirkdale, Creetown, Kirkcudbright), *b.* 1911; ed. at Winchester, and at Trin. Coll., Camb. (BA); Bar. Inner Temple 1935: *m.* 1936, Margaret, da. of Sir William George Eden Wiseman, 10th Bt., CB, and has issue living, David Wiseman Ramsay, *b.* 1939; MA, MB, BChir, DCH: *m.* 1963, Janet Gilliat (and has issue living, Mark Gilliat Rainsford *b.* 1966, Neil Maxwell Rainsford *b.* 1969, Stephen Ramsay *b.* 1972), Jessica Margaret *b.* 1937. *Residence*, Oldland, Gatehouse-of-Fleet, Kirkcudbright.

Maxwell (Constable-Maxwell-Scott), see Scott

HERON-MAXWELL, Creation (N.S.) 1683, of Springkell, Dumfriesshire.

May it flourish again.

Sir PATRICK IVOR HERON-MAXWELL, 9th *Baronet*; *b.* July 26th, 1916; *s.* his father, *Sir* IVOR WALTER HERON, 1928; ed. at Stowe: *m.* 1942, D. Geraldine E. younger da. of the late Claud Paget Mellor, and has issue.

Arms—Quarterly: 1st and 4th, argent, on a saltire sable, an annulet or, stoned azure; in base, a crescent of the second; all within a bordure gules charged with eight bezants, *Maxwell*; 2nd and 3rd, gules, on a bend argent a rose between two lions passant gules, *Heron*. **Crest**—A dexter hand proper holding an eagle's neck erased with two heads sable. **Supporters**—Two eagles close-reguardant sable.

Residence—9, Cowslip Hill, Letchworth, Herts.

Sons living—NIGEL MELLOR (105, Codicote Rd., Welwyn, Herts.), *b.* Jan. 30th, 1944; ed. at Milton Abbey: *m.* 1972, May Elizabeth Angela, only da. of W. Ewing, of co. Donegal.——Colin Mellor, *b.* 1952.——Paul Mellor, *b.* 1957.

Sisters living—Jean Norah, *b.* 1911: *m.* 1938, Anthony Sancroft-Baker, and has issue living, Raymond Samuel, *b.* 1950.—Rosalind Jean, *b.* 1946: *m.* 1967, Geoffrey Cleveland, of 32, Whieldem St., Amersham, Bucks, and has issue living, Victoria Clare *b.* 1972. *Residence*, East Tytherton Manor, Chippenham, Wilts.——(Helen), Naomi, of 30, Via Belardo, Apt. 5, Greenbrae, Cal. 94904, USA, *b.* 1913: *m.* 1st, 1938, Francis Cecil Harold Allen, who *d.* 1939; 2ndly, 1957 (m. diss. 1967), Howard Dale Thomas and has issue living, (by 2nd m.) Nicholas John, *b.* 1958.——Rachel Mary, *b.* 1922: *m.* 1947, Roy Martin Macnab, FRSA, and has issue living, Simon Martin, *b.* 1955,—Celia Mary, *b.* 1949. *Address*, 7, Lincoln St., SW3.

Collateral Branches living.

Granddaughter of the late Rev. Michael Heron Maxwell-Heron, 4th son of 4th baronet:—

Issue of the late Frederick William Burgoyne Maxwell-Heron, b. 1838, d. 1918: m. 1882, Louisa Annie, who d. 1924, da. of the late Major F. S. Paterson, B.S.C., of Castle Huntly, Perthshire, and widow of Capt. Albert Henry Harrison, Roy. Warwickshire Regt. :—

Charlotte Margaretta : m. 1911, Com. Charles Albert Carey, R.N. (retired), who d. 1925, and has issue living, Carlos George Maxwell, b. 1912 ; is Major : m. 1949, Mary, da. of John Goss, of Exeter, and has issue living, Timothy Charles John b. 1951, Diana Charlotte b. 1952,—Mary Jacqueline Heron. *Address,*

Granddaughter of the late Capt. John Heron Maxwell-Heron, el. son of the late Rev. Michael Heron Maxwell-Heron (ante) :—

Issue of the late Capt. Basil Charles Montagu Maxwell-Heron, b. 1878, d. (result of active service during European War) 1916 : m. 1905, Mary, who d. 1957, da. of the late Garrett O'Byrne :—

Rita Steuart Mary: m. 1927, Antony William Hamilton Nelson, Pilot-Officer RAF and has issue living, John William Hamilton, b. 19—, Ann Steuart Mary, b. 19—,—Sheila, b. 19—. *Residence,* 7, Sutton Court, Chiswick, W4.

Granddaughters of the late Edward Heron Maxwell-Blair, 7th son of 4th baronet :—

Issue of the late Lieut.-Col. William Henry Stopford HERON-MAXWELL, b. 1852, d. 1927: m. 1884, Adeline Helen, M.B.E., J.P., who d. 1941, da. of the late Osgood Hanbury of Holfield Grange, Coggeshall, Essex :—

Elizabeth Marion : m. 1919, Major Edmund Joseph Stapleton-Bretherton, who d. 1946 [B. Petre]. *Residence,* Inchgarry Cottage, North Berwick.——Mary Adeline: m. 1921, Lt.-Col. Cecil George Arkwright, MC, late 5th Northumberland Fus., and Rhodesian Forces, of 17, Vint Cres., Colchester, Essex, CO3 3QQ, and has issue living, Michael George, b. 1924: m. 1950, Ann Corientia, el. da. of the late Capt. Geoffrey C. Moss, of Bath, and has issue living, David Julian b. 1952, Sarah Ann b. 1951, Caroline Mary Jane b. 1958,—John Maxwell (Teviot Lodge, Princess Drive, Highlands, Salisbury, Rhodesia), b. 1927: m. 1950, Sheila, only da. of the late Charles Thomas Waring, of Headingly, Yorks., and has issue living, Richard Andrew b. 1951, Peter Maxwell b. 1953,—Jocelyn Frances Adeline, b. 1923: m. 1947, Christopher William Oxley Parker, of Faulkbourne Hall, Witham, Essex, and has issue living, John Oxley b. 1949, Alison Mary Oxley b. 1955, Claire Monica Oxley b. 1960.

This baronet is head in the male line of the Maxwells of Pollok, and Chief of the Clydesdale Maxwells. The 4th baronet, Sir John, assumed the additional surname and arms of Heron, having m. 1802, Mary, da. and heir of Patrick Heron of Heron in Kirouchtree. Sir John, 7th baronet, was Capt. 15th Hussars, and a Member of H.M.'s Body Guard for Scotland (Roy. Co. of Archers).

STIRLING-MAXWELL, Creations (N.S.) 1682 and (N.S.) 1707, of Pollok, Renfrewshire [Dormant 1956.]

Sir JOHN MAXWELL STIRLING-MAXWELL, *K.T.,* 10th *Baronet, d.* May 30th, 1956.

Daughter living of 10th Baronet—Anne, b. 1906 : m. 1930, John Moreton-MacDonald (now Maxwell Macdonald) [see E. Ducie, colls.], and has issue living, JOHN RONALD (Pollok House, Glasgow, S3; Shoreacres, Rhu, Dunbartonshire) b. May 22nd, 1936; eventual heir to the baronetcy under the terms of the 1707 remainder; ed. at Winchester: m. 1964, Eleanor Ruth, da. of T. B. Laird, and has issue living, John Ranald b. 1965, Angus b. 1967, Victoria Anne b. 1971,—Donald, b. 1938 [see E. Ducie, colls.]. *Residence,* Largie, Tayinloan, Argyll.

Collateral Branch living (*Males and Females in remainder*)

Issue of the late Brig.-Gen. Archibald STIRLING OF KEIR, 2nd son of 9th baronet b. 1867, d. 1931: m. 1910, the Hon. Margaret Fraser, OBE, who d. 1973, da. of 13th Lord Lovat:—

William Joseph, b. 1911; ed. at Ampleforth Coll., and at Trin. Coll., Camb. (B.A. 1932); late Lieut.-Col. Scots Guards : m. 1940, Susan Rachel, da. of Lieut.-Col. the Hon. Noel Gervase Bligh, DSO [see E. Darnley], and has issue living, Archibald Hugh (Ochtertyre, Stirling) b. 1941: m. 1964, Charmian Rachel, yr. da. of Lord George Francis John Montagu-Douglas-Scott [see D. Buccleuch], and has issue living, William Rory Alexander b. 1965, Ludovic David b. 1967,—John Alexander, b. 1948: m. 1971, Mrs. Susan Burton, only da. of Edmund Black, of Johannesburg,—Hannah Ann (*Viscountess Cranborne*), b. 1944: m. 1970, Viscount Cranborne, el. son of 6th Marquess of Salisbury,—Magdalen, b. 1945: m. 1969, Patrick Petit. *Seat,* Keir, Dunblane, Perths.——Peter John, b. 1913; ed. at Ampleforth Coll., and at Magdalen Coll., Oxford; formerly in Foreign Ser.: m. 1963, Mrs. Mahin Khadji-Noori, da. of the late Hassan Mohasebel Dowleh Nasr Feli.——Archibald David, DSO, OBE (22, South Audley St., W1Y 6ES) b. 1915; is Col. late Scots Gds.; Middle East 1941-45 (DSO); DSO 1942, OBE (Mil) 1946.——Margaret Elizabeth Mary (*Countess of Dalhousie*), b. 1914; is a CStJ: m. 1940, the 16th Earl of Dalhousie. *Residence,* Brechin Castle, Brechin, Angus.——Irene Katharine Teresa, b. 1919. *Residence,* Morar Lodge, Morar, Inverness-shire.

This family is of the oldest branch of the Maxwells, Earls of Nithsdale. Sir John Maxwell of Pollok distinguished himself at an early age in chivalry, especially at the celebrated battle of Otterburn, or Chevy Chase (1388), where he captured Sir Ralph Percy, son of the Earl of Northumberland, and brother of the renowned " Hotspur." The Baronetcy was first conferred in 1682 upon John Maxwell of Pollok (son of Sir George Maxwell), with remainder to heirs male of the body, but a further patent was issued in 1707 extending remainder to heirs of entail in his lands and estates. The 9th baronet, Sir William Stirling-Maxwell, who as heir of entail succeeded under the special limitation, was M.P. for Perthshire (C) 1852-68 and 1874-8, and received as a Commoner the exceptional honour of being created a KT. Sir John Maxwell Stirling-Maxwell was MP for Coll. Div. of Glasgow (C) 1895-1906 and was also created a KT.

MEDLYCOTT, Creation (U.K.) 1808, of Ven House, Somerset.

Sir (JAMES) CHRISTOPHER MEDLYCOTT, 8th *Baronet; b.* April 17th, 1907; *s.* his father, *Sir* HUBERT MERVYN, 1964; ed. at Harrow, and at Magdalene Coll., Camb. (B.A.).

Arms—Quarterly, per fesse indented gules and azure, three lions rampant, two and one, argent. **Crest**—Out of a mural crown gules a demi-eagle with wings elevated or.

Residence—The Yard House, Milborne Port, nr. Sherborne, Dorset.

DAT CURA QUIETEM

He that sows in tears shall reap in joy.

Collateral Branch living

Issue of the late Thomas Anthony Hutchings Medlycott, 2nd son of 7th baronet, *b.* 1909, *d.* 1970: *m.* 1938, Cecilia Mary (Edmondsham House, Cranborne, Wimborne, Dorset), da. of the late Maj. Cecil Harold Eden, of Tregonwell Lodge, Cranborne, Dorset.

MERVYN TREGONWELL, *b.* Feb. 20th, 1947.——Julia Elizabeth, *b.* 1939: *m.* 1965, Michael John Bazeley Smith, of Stocks Cottage, Edmondsham, Cranborne, Wimborne, Dorset, and has issue living, Timothy John Medlycott, *b.* 1966,—Philip Anthony Medlycott, *b.* 1971,—Catherine Frances Sarah, *b.* 1968.——Philadelphia Jane, *b.* 1941: *m.* 1967, Rupert Oliver, of 11, Woodstock Rd., Croydon, and has issue living, Kim, *b.* 1970,—Philadelphia Jo, *b.* 1972.——Sarah Nell, *b.* 1944: *m.* 1971, Kenneth Dale Ritchey, of Box 1553, Rocky Mountain House, Alberta, Canada, and has issue living, Jonathan Dale, *b.* 1975.

This family descends from James Medlycott, of Ven House, Milborne Port, Som., Master in Chancery, and MP for Milborne Port 1710-22. His son Thomas, of Ven House, d. 1763 without surviving issue, and settled his estates on his maternal nephew, Thomas Hutchings, who accordingly adopted the name and arms of Medlicott. His son, Sir William Coles Medlicott, 1st Bt., was M.P. for Milborne Port 1790-91.

MELLOR, Creation (U.K.) 1924, of Culmhead, Somerset.

Sir JOHN SEROCOLD PAGET MELLOR, 2nd *Baronet; b.* July 6th, 1893; *s.* his father, *Sir* JOHN PAGET, 1929; ed. at Eton, and New Coll., Oxford; Bar. Inner Temple 1920; Capt. (ret.) Somerset LI (TA); Pres. of Prudential Assurance Co. Ltd. since 1972 (Chm. 1965-70); a Dir. of Cos.; 1914-18 War in Mesopotamia, present at fall of Kut-el-Amara (twice wounded, prisoner, 1914-15 star, two medals); rejoined Somerset LI 1939; MP for Tamworth Div. of Warwickshire (C) 1935-45, and for Sutton Coldfield Div. of Warwick 1945-55: *m.* 1st, 1922, Rachel Margaret (who obtained a divorce 1937), da. of Sir Herbert Frederick Cook, 3rd Bt.; 2ndly, 1937, Mrs. Raie Ada Mendes, who *d.* 1965, da. of the late Samuel Moses; 3rdly, 1971, Mrs. Jessica de Pass, el. da. of the late Clarence de Sola, of Montreal, and has issue by 1st m.

Arms—Per fesse dancettée sable and argent, in chief three mascles of the second and in base as many blackbirds proper. **Crest**—A bull's head erased sable, enfiled by a mascle argent.

Better.

Residence—Binley House, near Andover. *Club*—Carlton.

Son living—By 1st m.—JOHN FRANCIS (Birchlea, Lone Oak, Redehall Rd., Smallfield, Horley, Surrey), *b.* March 9th, 1925; ed. at Eton; is an Accountant; 1939-45 War with RASC and Int. Corps: *m.* 1948, Alix Marie, da. of the late Charles François Villaret, of 39, Great Pulteney St., W1.

Sir John Paget Mellor, K.C.B., 1st Bt. (el. son of the late Rt. Hon. John William Mellor, K.C., D.L.) ; was H.M. Procurator-Gen. and Solicitor to the Treasury 1909-23.

STUART-MENTETH, Creation (U.K.) 1838, of Closeburn, Dumfriesshire, and Mansfield, Ayrshire.

Whilst I live I hope.

Sub sole nihil.
Nothing under the sun.

Sir JAMES WALLACE STUART-MENTETH, 6th *Baronet ; b.* Nov. 13th, 1922 ; *s.* his father, *Sir* WILLIAM FREDERICK, 1952 ; ed. at Fettes Coll., at St. Andrews Univ., and at Trin. Coll., Oxford ; sometime Lieut. Scots Guards ; is with Paints Div., Imperial Chemical Industries, Ltd. ; European War 1939-44 in N. Africa and Italy (wounded) : *m.* 1949, (Dorothy) Patricia, da. of the late Frank Grieves Warburton, of Thorrington, Stirling, and has issue.

    Arms—Quarterly : 1st and 4th, or, a bend chequy argent and sables and and 3rd, azure, three buckles or ; the whole within a bordure gules, **Crest**—A lymphad sable.
    Residence—Broomhurst, Deepcut, Camberley, Surrey.

    Sons living—CHARLES GRIEVES, *b.* Nov. 25th, 1950.——William Jeremy, *b.* 1953.

    Brother living—Charles Granville (Woodchester House, Woodchester, Glos., RAC), *b.* 1928 ; ed. at Oxford Univ. (BA) ; late 2nd Lt. Scots Guards ; Underwriting Member of Lloyd's : *m.* 1963, Priscilla Helen, el. da. of Thomas Newman, of Widdicombe House, Kingsbridge, Devon [see Newman, Bt., cr. 1836], and has issue living, James William Francis, *b.* 1965,—Alexander Granville, *b.* 1971,—Alice Caroline, *b.* 1969.

Sister living—Ludivina Frances, *b.* 1927 : *m.* 1947, Capt. William Sawbridge How, Hon. Artillery Co., and has issue living, Stuart Sawbridge, *b.* 1950,—Anthony Edward, *b.* 1951,—Helen Frances, *b.* 1955. *Residence*, Pine Lodge, Ettrick Bridge, Selkirk, TD7 5MW.

Aunts living (daughters of 4th baronet)—Katherine Olive (Windelsham Manor, Crowborough, Sussex), *b.* 1890 : *m.* 1933, Edward Algernon Blackett Prior, who *d.* 1962.——Alyson Mona, *b.* 1895 : *m.* 1921, Charles Kaisin, MD, who *d.* 1970, and has issue living, Eloi Guy, *b.* 1922 : *m.* 1945,—Elizabeth Mona, *b.* 1924,—Alyson Christine, *b.* 1928 : *m.* 1955, André Gillain,—Patricia Paule, *b.* 1932. *Residence*, 294, Avenue Brugmann, Brussels, 1180, Belgium.

Collateral Branches living.

    Grandchildren of the late Walter Erskine Stuart-Menteth (infra):—
    Issue of the late Maj. Walter Granville Stuart-Menteth, *b.* 1906, *d.* 1970: *m.* 1st, 1937 (m. diss. 1950), Marianne Marguerite, who *d.* 1975, da. of Jules Cuenod, of La Tour de Peilz, Switzerland; 2ndly, 1957, Edith Pauline (Bracken Brae, RD6, Puketapu, Hawke's Bay, NZ),, da. of James Harold Wadsworth:—
(By 1st m.) Charles Henry, *b.* 1938; ed. at Rugby.——James Sleigh, *b.* 1940: *m.* 1968, Barbara Richardson.——Marie Octavia, *b.* 1939.
    Issue of the late Walter Erskine Stuart-Menteth, 4th son of 4th baronet, *b.* 1877, *d.* 1956: *m.* 1905, Violet Grace, who *d.* 1970, yst. da. of Henry Lafone, formerly of 59, Onslow Sq., SW:—
Henry Alexander, *DSC* (16, Inverleith Terr., Edinburgh, 3), *b.* 1912; Cdr. RN; 1939-45 War despatches, DSC: *m.* 1952, Penelope, only da. of Digby Giles, of Toorak, Melbourne, Aust., and has issue living, Andrew Alexander, *b.* 1954;—Walter Henry, *b.* 1957,—Harriet Lucy, *b.* 1959,——Lucy Violet, *b.* 1911: *m.* 1942, Maj. Donald Brain, Princess Patricia's Canadian LI, who *d.* (killed in action during 1939-45 War) 1943, and has issue living, Donald Rowan, *b.* 1943; ed. at Fettes. *Residence*, Crossways, Godstone, Surrey.

    Grandchildren of the late Alexander Stuart-Menteath, 6th son of 1st baronet :—
    Issue of the late Andrew Agnew Stuart-Menteath, *b.* 1853, *d.* 1916: *m.* 1st, 1885, Mary, who *d.* 1896, da. of Robert Vans Agnew, of Sheuchan and Barnbarroch ; 2ndly, 1897, Margaret Antoinette, da. of Alexander Sutherland Allan :—
(By 2nd m.) Thomas Alexander, *MBE* (14, Everest Av., Havelock North, Hawkes Bay, NZ), *b.* 1901; ed. at Nelson Coll., Canterbury Univ. Coll., NZ, and Queen's Coll., Oxford (MA, BSc); formerly Capt. 1st Canterbury Regt. (NZ Forces), and on Teaching Staff of St. Andre's Coll., Christchurch, NZ; Maj. 4th Bn. R. Berkshire Regt. (TA); 1939-45 War in Middle East; MBE (Mil) 1942: *m.* 1931, Kathleen Frances, *JP*, who *d.* 1966, da. of F. J. Constable Curtis, and widow of Capt. Arthur Taylor.——(By 2nd m.) Jean Antoinette, *b.* 1898.——Elizabeth Mary, *b.* 1903: *m.* 1933, Daniel Maclelland Laird, of Cadogan Park, Woodstock, Oxon., and has issue living, Michael Andrew (5, Margaret Court, Lennox Road South, Southsea), *b.* 1936; ed. at Bradfield and Oxford Univ. (MA, DPhil); late RN.

    This family is lineally descended in the male line from Walter (third son of Walter, Lord High Steward of Scotland), who married 1258 the Countess of Menteth, and thus acquired that earldom. He left two sons, who both assumed the surname of Menteth, viz., Alexander, 6th Earl of Menteth, and Sir John Menteth, Lord of Arran, &c., who married Elyne, daughter of Gratney, Earl of Mar, and whose granddaughter, Janet Keith, married Robert, 1st Lord Erskine, and thus the Erskines acquired the earldom of Mar. Sir John Menteth of Ruskie (who died before 1333), from whom the Stuart-Menteaths trace their descent, was a younger brother of Alexander, 6th Earl of Menteth. This Earldom was forfeited on the execution of Murdoch Stewart, Duke of Albany in 1425. The father of the 1st baronet, the Rev. James Stuart-Menteath, assumed by sign-manual, in 1770 the additional surname of Stuart " for himself and his posterity." The 2nd baronet resumed the ancient name of Menteth, but his two youngest brothers retained the name of Menteath. Sir James, 3rd baronet, became a naturalized American.

MEREDYTH, Creation (I.) 1795, of Carlanstown, Meath. [Extinct 1923.]

Sir HENRY BAYLY MEREDYTH, 5th and last *Baronet.*

Daughter living of 5th Baronet—(Millicent) Valla, *b.* 1898: *m.* 1st, 1919, Major the Hon. Herbrand Charles Alexander, DSO, formerly 5th Lancers, who *d.* 1965, having obtained a divorce 1927 [see E. Caledon]; 2ndly, 1927, Richard Allan; 3rdly, 1939 (m. diss. 1946), Lt.-Col. Guy Andrew Heinekey Buxton, who *d.* 1948. *Residence*, The Dairy, Caledon Castle, co. Tyrone.

METCALFE, Creation (U.K.) 1802, of Chilton, Berkshire.
[Name pronounced "Metcuff."]

I am at rest

Sir THEOPHILUS JOHN METCALFE, 8th *Baronet*, only son of the late Lieut.-Col. Eric Debonnaire Theophilus Metcalfe, O.B.E., M.C., half-brother of 7th baronet; *b.* Oct. 14th, 1916; *s.* his uncle, *Sir* THEOPHILUS JOHN MASSIE 1950; ed. at Haileybury.

Arms—Argent, on a fesse wavy gules between three calves statant sable, a sword fesseways, the point to the sinister proper, pommel and hilt or. **Crest**—A talbot sejant sable, the dexter paw resting on an escutcheon or, charged with a hand issuing from clouds on the sinister, and holding a pen all proper. **Supporters**—*Dexter*, a Moonshee of Bengal habited proper; *sinister*, a soldier of the Bengal Native Infantry equipped and armed also proper.

Residence, 3, Kensington House, 35, Kensington Court, W.8.

Sister living—Peggy Theophila, *MBE*, *b.* 1920; at FCO; 1939-45 War as Senior Com. ATS (MBE); MBE (Mil) 1945.

Mother living—Winifred Crampton (Peggy), da. of the late Edward Neild Shackle, of Botwell House, Hayes, Middlesex: *m.* 1915, Lieut.-Col. Eric Debonnaire Theophilus Metcalfe, O.B.E., M.C. (ante), who *d.* 1934. *Residence*, 3, Kensington House, 35, Kensington Court, W.8.

Sir Thomas, the 1st baronet, was a Director of H.E.I.C. Sir Charles Theophilus, G.C.B., P.C., 3rd baronet, was created Baron Metcalfe 1845, which title become extinct at his death. His brother, 4th baronet, was sometime Agent to the Governor-General of India at the Court of Delhi.

MEYER, Creation (U.K.) 1910, of Shortgrove, Newport, Essex.

Rest not rust not

Sir ANTHONY JOHN CHARLES MEYER, *MP*, 3rd *Baronet*; *b.* Oct. 27th, 1920; *s.* his father, *Sir* FRANK CECIL, 1935; ed. at Eton, and at New Coll., Oxford; is a Trustee of Shakespeare National Memorial Theatre; European War 1941-45 as Lieut. Scots Guards (wounded); entered H.M.'s Foreign Ser. 1947; 1st Sec. Paris 1956, Moscow 1957, and at Foreign Office 1958-62; PPS to Ch. Sec. of the Treasury (Mr. Maurice Macmillan, MP) 1970-72, and to Sec. of State for Employment (Rt. Hon. Maurice Macmillan, MP) 1972-74; Vice-Chm., Franco-British Parl. Relations Cttee.; MP for Eton and Slough (C) 1964-66, and for W. Flintshire since 1970; Publication, "A European Technological Community 1966"; Founder and Dir. of "Solon" 1969: *m.* 1941, Barbadee Violet, only child of A. Charles Knight, JP, of Lincoln's Inn, WC, and Herne Place, Sunningdale, Berks, and has issue.

Arms—Sable, a key wards downwards or between four bezants. **Crest**—A cock sable, armed, combed, and wattled or, holding in the dexter claw a key as in the arms.
Residences—Garden House, Sunningdale, Berks. Cottage Place, Brompton Sq., SW3. *Clubs*—Carlton, Beefsteak.

Son living—ANTHONY ASHLEY FRANK (14, Rainville Rd., W6), *b.* Aug. 23rd, 1944; ed. at Eton: *m.* 1966, Susan Mathilda, da. of John Freestone, and has issue living, Sophie Mathilda Barbadee, *b.* 1972.

Daughters living—Carolyn-Clare Barbadee, *b.* 1943: *m.* 1965, Charles Francis Sands, and has issue living, Robert Charles, *b.* 1970,—David Francis, *b.* 1974.——Tessa Violet, *b.* 1955.——Sally Minette, *b.* 1961.

The 1st baronet, Sir Carl Ferdinand Meyer, was a Director of National Bank of Egypt, and the 2nd baronet, Sir Frank Cecil, sat as M.P. for Great Yarmouth (C) 1924-9.

MEYRICK, Creation (U.K.) 1880, of Bush, Pembrokeshire.
[Name pronounced "Merrick."]

Sir THOMAS FREDERICK MEYRICK, *T.D.*,
3rd *Baronet; b.* Nov. 28th, 1899; *s.* his father,
Brig.-Gen. Sir FREDERICK CHARLTON, *C.B., C.M.G.,*
1932; ed. at Eton; Capt. (ret.) 15th/19th King's
R. Hussars, Maj. (ret.) 102nd (Pembrokeshire Yeo.),
Field Regt. RA (TA), and a JP and DL for Pem-
brokeshire (High Sheriff 1938); Pres. Roy. Welsh
Agric. So. 1955, and Chm. of County Branch
NFU 1968; Hon. Col. 302nd (Pembrokeshire Yeo.)
Field Regt. RA (TA) 1955-59; sometime an
Instructor in Equitation at Weedon and RMC:
m. 1st, 1926, Ivy Frances, who *d.* 1947, da. of
Lt.-Col. Frederick Charles Pilkington, DSO; 2ndly,
1951, Gladice Joyce, da. of Bertram W. Allen, of
Cilrhiw, Narberth, Pembrokeshire, and has issue by
1st and 2nd marriages.

Arms—Quarterly; 1st and 4th, sable, on a chev on argent
between three staves raguly or, inflamed proper, a fleur-de-lys gules
between two Cornish choughs respectant also proper, *Meyrick;*
2nd and 3rd, or, a lion rampant gules, a sinister quarter quarterly
1st and 4th, gules, ten besants, three, two, and one, 2nd and 3rd
argent on a mount vert, a lion passant guardant or, *Charlton.*
Crests—1st, a tower argent, having on its top a mount vert, and
thereon a Cornish chough proper, and holding in the dexter claw a
fleur-de-lys gules, *Meyrick;* 2nd, out of an eastern coronet or, a leopard's head, issuant gules, *Charlton.*

Without God, without anything; God and enough.

Seat—Gumfreston, Tenby.

Sons living—By 1st marriage—DAVID JOHN CHARLTON (Great Wedlock, Gumfreston, Tenby),
b. Dec. 2nd, 1926; ed. at Eton, and at Trin. Hall, Camb.; is a Chartered Surveyor and Land
Agent : *m.* 1962, Penelope Anne, el. da. of the late Cdr. John Bertram Aubrey Marsden-Smedley,
RN [see B. Westbury, colls.], and has issue living, Timothy Thomas Charlton, *b.* 1963,—Simon
Edward, *b.* 1965,—Christopher John, *b.* 1967.——Frederick Rowland, *b.* 1928; ed. at Eton:
Maj. (ret.) 15th/19th King's Roy. Hussars.——Richard Eric (Budlake House, Budlake, Exeter),
b. 1936; a Chartered Surveyor: *m.* 1962, Catherine Ann, el. da. of Col. V. J. F. Popham, S. Wales
Borderers.——By 2nd m——John Herbert, *b.* 1952.
Daughters living—By 1st m—Mary Joan, *b.* 1930: *m.* 1954, Ian Marshall Lang, and has issue living,
Patrick John, *b.* 1957,—Edward Nicholas, *b.* 1959,—Ivy Frances, *b.* 1960. *Residence,* Whitewick
Farm, Stogursey, Som.——Susan Ethel, *b.* 1932: *m.* 1954, Roland Owen-George, of The Lowe,
Wellesbourne, Warwicks.——Penelope Ann, *b.* 1939: *m.* 1966, Michael McGarvie, of Westbarn
Grange, Witham Friary, Frome, Som., and has issue living, Emma Louise, *b.* 1969,—Victoria
Grace, *b.* 1971,—Alice Katherine *b.* 1974.
Sisters living—Rachel Eva, *b.* 1905: *m.* 1929, Laurence Lithgow, who *d.* 1972, and has issue living,
James Frederick, *b.* 1933,—Esther Mary, *b.* 1930,—Ruth, *b.* 1934. *Residence,* Fortlands,
Sicklesmere Rd., Bury St. Edmonds, Suffolk, IP33 2BN.——Violet (*Baroness Merthyr*), *b.* 1908:
is a Serving Sister of Order of St. John of Jerusalem: *m.* 1932, the 3rd Baron Merthyr. *Resi-
dence,* Churchton, Saundersfoot, Pembrokeshire.

Collateral Branch living.
Issue of the late Walter Thomas Meyrick, 5th son of 1st baronet, *b.* 1882, *d.* 1953 : *m.*
1st, 1914, Mabel Violet Blanche (who obtained a divorce 1935), da. of the late Col.
Arthur Hill Sandys Montgomery, Rifle Brig., and widow of Percy Downes ; 2ndly,
1935, Mary Jocelyn (Sawmill Close, Sharperton, Morpeth), da. of Sir James Ernest
Thorold, 14th Bt.:—
(By 2nd m.) Walter James Charlton, *b.* 1936; ed. at Eton: *m.* 1965, Gillian, yr. da. of the late W.
Macduff Urquhart, of Edinburgh, and has issue living, St. John James Charlton, *b.* 1969,—
Louisa Mary Charlton, *b.* 1966,—Sophia Rachel Charlton (twin), *b.* 1966.——Michael Alan
Charlton, *b.* 1937.——Christopher Thomas Charlton, *b.* 1946.——Mary Rhoda Charlton, *b.* 1944:
m. 1971, Colin A. Matheson.

The 1st baronet, Col. Sir Thomas Charlton Meyrick, K.C.B., D.L., J.P. (son of St. John
Chivarton Charlton, D.L., J.P., of Apley Castle, Salop), was M.P. for Pembroke Dist. (C) 1868-
74, and assumed 1858, by Roy. licence, the surname of Meyrick, his maternal grandfather being
Thomas Meyrick of Bush, Pembrokeshire, descended from the Meyricks of Bodorgan, Anglesey.

TAPPS-GERVIS-MEYRICK, Creation (G.B.) 1791, of Hinton Admiral, Hampshire.
[Name pronounced "Tapps-Gervis-Merrick."]

Sir GEORGE DAVID ELIOTT TAPPS-GERVIS-
MEYRICK, *M.C.,* 6th *Baronet; b.* April 15th, 1915;
s. his father *Major Sir* GEORGE LLEWELYN 1960;
ed. at Eton, and at Trin. Coll., Camb. (B.A. 1937);
Lieut.-Col. (retired) 9th Queen's Roy. Lancers ; is
patron of two livings; 1939-45 War in Middle East
(wounded, M.C.): *m.* 1940, Ann, da. of the late Clive
Miller, of Melbourne, Australia, and has issue.

Arms—Quarterly: 1st and 4th, sable, on a chevron argent between
three bands erect raguly or, inflamed proper, a fleur-de-lis gules between
two Cornish choughs respecting each other proper, *Meyrick ;* and, argent,
six ostrich feathers, three, two, and one, sable in the centre point a pellet,
Gervis ; 2nd and 3rd, azure, on a fesse or, between three rhinoceroses
argent, as many escallops gules, *Tapps.* **Crests**—1st, a tower argent,
thereon upon a mount vert a Cornish chough holding in the dexter claw
a fleur-de-lis ; 2nd, a mount vert, thereon three ostrich feathers, one in
pale and two in saltire sable, banded by a wreath of oak or ; 3rd, a greyhound couchant per pale argent and sable charged on the body with two
escallops fessewise countercharged.

Heb dhu, heb dhim, dhu a digon.

*Without God, without any-
thing; God and enough.*

Seats—Hinton Admiral, near Christchurch ; Bodorgan, Anglesey. Club—Cavalry.

Son living—GEORGE CHRISTOPHER CADAFAEL, (Waterditch House, Bransgore, Christ-church, Hants.), *b.* March 10th, 1941: ed. at Eton, and at Trin. Coll., Camb.: *m.* 1968, Jean Louise, da. of the late Lord William Walter Montagu-Douglas-Scott, MC [see D. Buccleuch, colls.], and has issue living, George William Owen, *b.* 1970,—Charles Valentine Llewelyn, *b.* 1972

Daughter living—Caroline Susan Joan, *b.* 1942: *m.* 1963, Richard Arthur Samuel Hulse, of 23, Seymour Walk, SW10, yr. son of Wing-Cdr. Sir (Hamilton) Westrow Hulse, 9th baronet.

Sister living—Susan Hermione, *b.* 1919 : *m.* 1945, Peter John Green, M.C., and has issue living Christopher, *b.* 1946. *Residence*, Irongates, Wootton, New Milton, Hants.

Collateral Branch living.

Grandchildren of the late Capt. Richard Owen Tapps-Gervis-Meyrick, younger son of 4th baronet:—

Issue of the late Capt. Richard Anthony Tapps-Gervis-Meyrick, *b.* 1920, *d.* 1964: *m.* 1949, Alexandra Adèle (Zandra) (Sheafhayne Manor, Yarcombe, Honiton, Devon), da. of Brig. Rupert John Brett, DSO, of Langsmeade House, Milton Common, Oxon.:—

James David, *b.* 1950.——Sarah Jacintha Barbara, *b.* 1952.

The 2nd baronet, Sir George William Tapps, M.P. for Christchurch 1832-6, assumed in 1835 the additional surname of Gervis, while the 3rd baronet assumed in 1876 by Roy. licence the further additional surname of Meyrick. The 4th baronet, Sir George Augustus Eliott Tapps-Gervis-Meyrick, was High Sheriff of Hants 1900. The 5th baronet, Sir George Llewelyn Tapps-Gervis-Meyrick, Major (retired) 7th Hussars, was High Sheriff of Anglesey 1939.

Meysey-Thompson, see Thompson.

MIDDLEBROOK, Creation (U.K.) 1930, of Oakwell, Birstall, co. York. [Extinct 1971.]

Sir HAROLD MIDDLEBROOK, 2nd and last *Baronet.*

Daughters living of 1st Baronet—Ethel Rachel, *b.* 1884: *m.* 1910, Lawrence A. Ingle, and has issue living, John Middlebrook, *b.* 1911,—William Reginald, *b.* 1914. *Residence*, Thorncliffe, St. Andrew's Av., Morley.——Ella Dorothy, *b.* 1889. *Residence*, Woodbine Cottage, East Ayton, Scarborough, North Yorks.

Widow living of 2nd Baronet—MABEL (8, Park Rd., Harrogate), da. of Orenza Vasey, of Scarborough: *m.* 1914, Sir Harold Middlebrook, 2nd Bt., who *d.* 1971, when the title became ext.

MIDDLEMORE, Creation (U.K.) 1919, of Selly Oak, Northfield, co. Worcester.

Sir WILLIAM HAWKSLOW MIDDLEMORE, 2nd *Baronet*, *b.* April 10th, 1908; *s.* his father, *Sir* JOHN THROGMORTON, 1924: *m.* 1934, Violet Constance, da. of Andrew Kennagh, of Worcester.

Arms—Quarterly 1st and 4th per chevron argent and sable, in chief two moorcocks proper, *Middlemore;* 2nd per pale dancettée or and azure, *Edgbaston;* 3rd sable, a hawk argent belled or between three cinquefoils of the last, *Hawkesley.* **Crest** —A moorcock amidst grass and reeds proper.

Residence—St. Joseph's, 87, Shurdington Rd., Cheltenham.

Sir John Throgmorton Middlemore, 1st baronet (descended from the family of Middlemore of Hawkeslowe, settled at Hawkesley, King's Norton, Worcestershire, since early in 15th century), founded the Children's Emigration Homes in Birmingham, and the Middlemore Homes in Halifax, Nova Scotia, and sat as M.P. for N. Div. of Birmingham (*LU*) Feb. 1899 to Nov. 1918.

MIDDLETON, Creation (E.) 1662, of Belsay Castle, Northumberland.

Sir STEPHEN HUGH MIDDLETON, 9th *Baronet*, son of the late Lieut. Hugh Jeffery Middleton, R.N., 3rd son of 7th baronet; *b.* June 20th, 1909; *s.* his uncle, *Sir* CHARLES ARTHUR, 1942; ed. at Eton, and at Magdalene Coll. Camb.: *m.* 1962, Mary E. Robinson, who *d.* 1972.

Arms—Quarterly gules and or, in the 1st quarter a cross flory argent. **Crest**—A wild man proper, bearing in his arms an oak tree eradicated bendways or.

Seat—Belsay Castle, Newcastle-upon-Tyne.

Brother living—LAWRENCE MONCK, *b.* Oct. 23rd, 1912; ed. at Eton; B.Sc. Forestry, Edinburgh 1939. *Residence*, Winterhayes, South Perrott, Beaminster, Dorset.

Collateral Branches living.

Grandchildren of the late Henry Nicholas Middleton (infra) :—
Issue of the late Lambert William Middleton, *b.* 1877, *d.* 1941: *m.* 1922, Lady Sybil Grey, OBE, who *d.* 1966, da. of 4th Earl Grey:—

Henry Lambert (Burley Grange, Burley, Ringwood, Hants., and 11, Clareville Court, Clareville Grove, SW7), *b.* 1923; ed. at Eton, and at New Coll., Oxford: *m.* 1964, Susan Jenifer, da. of William Arthur Fearnley-Whittingstall, TD, QC, of The Old Manor House, Melbourn, Cambs., and widow of the Hon. Rodney Mathias Berry, TD [*see* V. Camrose], and has issue living, Laura Sybil Rose, *b.* 1969.——Mary Sybil, *b.* 1925: *m.* 1948, Capt. John Brooke Boyd, KOSB, of Satwell House, Rotherfield Greys, Henley, Oxon., and has issue living, Simon John, *b.* 1949; ed. at Eton,—James Lambert, *b.* 1952; ed. at Eton, Caroline Elizabeth (twin), *b.* 1952,—Diana Mary *b.* 1955.

Grandchildren of the late Henry Nicholas Middleton, brother of 7th baronet:—
Issue of the late Laura Beatrice Middleton, *b.* 1874, *d.* 1967: *m.* 1902, Maj. William Barnett, KRRC, who *d.* 1912:—

Roger Lambert (Chollerton House, nr. Hexham, Northumberland), *b.* 1910; ed. at Eton: *m.* 1943, Evelyn Dorothy, only da. of the late Capt. Harry Rich.——Robert Arthur, MC, (Lincoln Hill, Humshaugh, Hexham), *b.* 1911; ed. at Eton; a DL for Northumberland; 1939-45 War as Maj. Northumberland Hussars.——Alice Penelope, *b.* 1907: *m.* 1931, Robert Joicey Dickinson, Solicitor, of Howden Close, Corbridge.

Sir William Middleton, 1st baronet, of Belsay Castle, Northumberland (*d.* 1690), descended from Sir John Middleton who acquired large estates temp. Richard II on marriage to Christian eventual co-heir of John de Stryvelyn, who was summoned to parliament from 1363 to 1371 and who re-acquired Belsay Castle. The 6th baronet, Sir Charles, in compliance with the testamentary injunction of his maternal grandfather, Lawrence Monck, of Caenby, Lincolnshire, changed his name, in 1799, by Roy. sign-manual, from Middleton to Monck; and the 7th baronet, and his brother, Henry Nicholas, in 1876, resumed the original surname of Middleton.

MILBANK, Creation (U.K.) 1882, of Well, co. York, and of Hart, co. Durham.

Sir MARK VANE MILBANK, *KCVO, MC,* 4th *Baronet, b.* Jan. 11th, 1907; *s.* his father *Maj. Sir* FREDERICK RICHARD POWLETT, 1964; ed. at Eton; Maj. (ret.) Coldstream Guards; Comptroller to Gov.-Gen. of Canada 1946-52; Master of HM Household, and Extra Equerry to HM 1954-67; 1939-45 War (MC); MVO (4th class) 1953, CVO 1958, KCVO, 1962: *m.* 1st, 1930 (m. annulled 1933), Lady Angela Isabel Nellie Larnach-Nevill, da. of 4th Marquess of Abergavenny; 2ndly, 1938, the Hon. Verena Aileen, da. of 11th Baron Farnham, and widow of Charles Lambart Crawley [Crawley-Boevey, Bt.], and has issue by 2nd marriage.

Arms—Gules, a saltire argent, gutte de poix between two lions heads couped in pale, and as many roses in fesse of the second. **Crest**—A lion's head couped argent, gutte de poix, charged with a pale gules, thereon three roses, also argent.

Seat—Barningham Park, Richmond, N. Yorks.

Sons living—By 2nd m.—ANTHONY FREDERICK (Blind Knights, Layer de la Haye, Colchester, Essex), *b.* Aug. 16th, 1939; ed. at Eton: *m.* 1970, Belinda Beatrice, yr. da. of Brig. Adrian Clements Gore, DSO [see Gore, Bt., colls.], and has issue living, Edward Mark Somerset, *b.* 1973,—Alexia Victoria, *b.* 1971.——(Arthur) John (Great Orchard, Surrenden Dering, Pluckley, Kent), *b.* 1940; ed. at Gordonstoun: *m.* 1969, Rosalind E. L., da. of G. E. L. Townshend, and has issue living, Robert Andrew, *b.* 1972,—Lucy Verena, *b.* 1970.

Brothers living—John Gerald Frederick, *b.* 1909; ed. at Eton; is Maj. Yorkshire Regt.: *m.* 1938, Louisa Harriet, who *d.* 1974, da. of the late Edward Beaumont Cotton Curtis [Curtis, Bt.], and has issue living, David John (Gayles Fields, Dalton, Richmond, Yorks.), *b.* 1940; ed. at Gordonstoun: *m.* 1971, Clarissa Mary, da. of Capt. S. L. Bigge, of Langdale, Melsonby, Yorks., and has issue living, James John *b.* 1974,—Charles Gerald (35, Av. de Joinville, Chantilly 60500, France), *b.* 1942; ed. at Eton; a race-horse trainer: *m.* 1973, Mrs. Wendy Wright, da. of the late E. N. Johnson, of Newton Firs, Newton by Frodsham, Cheshire, and has issue living Philip Augustus *b.* 1974, a da. *b.* 1975. *Residence*, Warren House, Gayles, Richmond, N. Yorks.——Denis William Powlett, *TD, b.* 1912; ed. at Radley; is Maj. RA (TA): *m.* 1934, Doreen Frances, da. of Sir Richard Pierce Butler, OBE, 11th Bt. (*cr.* 1628), and has issue living, Mark Richard (c/o Standard Bank, Church St., Pietermaritzburg, Natal), *b.* 1937: *m.* 1966, Frances Elizabeth, da. of Richard V. Holme, of Marandellas, Rhodesia, and has issue living, Robert Frederick *b.* 1968, Henry Mark Thomas *b.* 1970,—Penelope Ann (Box 167, Kokstad, E. Griqualand, S. Africa), *b.* 1935: *m.* 1st, 1955, Capt. John Frederick de Vere Shaw, Kenya Regt., who *d.* 1960 [*see* Shaw, Bt., *cr.* 1821, colls.]; 2ndly, 1970, Hougham Robert Mills,—Susan Fiona, *b.* 1942: *m.* 1963, Antony Roger Pelly [*see* Pelly, Bt.]. *Residence*, Pasture House, Healey, Masham, Yorks.

The 1st baronet, Sir Frederick Acclom Milbank, 2nd son of the late Mark Milbank of Thorpe-Perrow, **was M.P. for N. Riding of York 1865-85, and for York, N. Riding, Richmond Div. 1885-6.** The 2nd baronet, Sir Powlett Charles John, sat as M.P. for Radnorshire (C) 1895-1900.

Milborne-Swinnerton-Pilkington, see Pilkington.

MILBURN, Creation (U.K.) 1905, of Guyzance, Parish of Shilbottle, Northumberland.

DUM·SPIRO·SPERO

While I breathe I hope.

Sir JOHN NIGEL MILBURN, 4th *Baronet;* *b.* April 22nd, 1918 ; *s.* his father *Sir* LEONARD JOHN, 1957 ; ed. at Eton, and at Trin. Coll., Camb. ; sometime Capt. Northumberland Hussars (T.A.) : *m.* 1940, Dorothy Joan, da. of Leslie Butcher, of Dunholme, Lincolnshire.

Arms—Per fesse or and gules, a pale counterchanged between two bears' heads erased in chief sable, muzzled of the first, and as many bears' heads also erased and muzzled in base or. **Crest**—In front of a bear's head erased sable, muzzled or, four mascles interlaced fesseways of the last. **Badge**—On a millrind sable, an escallop shell argent.
Seat—Guyzance Hall, Acklington, Northumberland.
Residence—Brainshaugh, Acklington, Morpeth, Northumberland.

Sisters living—Darea Joan, *b.* 1923: *m.* 1950, George Harold Michael Sankey, Major late Staffs. Yeo., and has issue living, Christopher Michael David, *b.* 1952,—Peter William Richard, *b.* 1953,—Nicola Mary Joan, *b.* 1955,—Virginia Karen Margaret, *b.* 1957. *Residence*, Shackerley Hall, Albrighton, Wolverhampton.——Susan Anne, *b.* 1937: *m.* 1960, John Arnold Farr, MP, and has issue living, Jonathan Leonard, *b.* 1962,—George Nelson, *b.* 1967. *Residence*, 11, Vincent Sq., SW1.
Widow living of 3rd Baronet—JOAN KATHERINE ANNE PAULA ANSON (*Joan, Lady Milburn*), da. of the late Henry Anson Horton, of Catton Hall, Derbyshire: *m.* 1917, Sir Leonard John Milburn, 3rd baronet, who *d.* 1957. *Residence*, Guyzance Hall, Acklington, Northumberland.

Collateral Branches living
Issue of the late Maj. Rupert Leonard Eversley Milburn, yr. son of 3rd baronet, *b.* 1919, *d.* 1974: *m.* 1944, Anne Mary (Wingates House, Wingates, Longhorsley, Morpeth, Northumberland), da. of the late Maj. Austin Scott Murray, MC, of Heckfield Pl., Basingstoke:—
ANTHONY RUPERT (62, Albany Mansions, Albany Bridge Rd., SW11), *b.* April 17th, 1947; ed. at Eton, and Roy. Agric. Coll., Cirencester; ARICS, MRAC.——Michael Richard, *b.* 1950; ed. at Eton.——Caroline Anne (*Lady Renwick*), *b.* 1945: *m.* 1966, Sir Richard Eustace Renwick, 4th Bt., of Whalton House, Whalton, Morpeth, Northumberland.——Diana Rosemary, *b.* 1949: *m.* 1970, Richard Murrough Wilson, of Cliffe Hall, Piercebridge, Darlington, and has issue living, Nicholas Rupert Gerald, *b.* 1974.
Issue of the late John Davison Milburn, 3rd son of 1st baronet, *b.* 1886, *d.* 1972: *m.* 1922, Grace Emily, who *d.* 1934, only da. of the late Stuart MacRae, of Conchra, Ross-shire:—
Angela Mary (Highcliffe, Little Switzerland, Douglas, Isle of Man), *b.* 1925.——Sybil Pauline (Highcliffe, Little Switzerland, Douglas, Isle of Man), *b.* 1926.

Issue of the late Capt. Archibald William Milburn, 4th son of 1st baronet, *b.* 1887, *d.* 1965: *m.* 1931, Eleanor Lilias (Victora), (Cresseners, Gt. Waltham, Chelmsford, Essex), da. of Maj. Nevill Arthur Charles de Hirzel Tufnell, of Langleys, Chelmsford:—
Mark Anthony William (Apart. 164, Arrecife de Lanzarote, Canary Islands), *b.* 1932; ed. at Eton, le Rosey, and RMA; late Maj. Special Air Ser. (TA) and late Lt. R. Scots Greys: *m.* 1968, Angela Margaret Cromwell, da. of the late Lt. Col. Geoffrey Stephen Carmac Weigall, and formerly wife of David Francis Brougham Maitland Edye, and has issue living, Francis Shahid, *b.* 1969.——Sarah Caroline Georgiana (Langleys, Gt. Waltham, Chelmsford, Essex), *b.* 1935: *m.* 1956, David Robert Micklem, son of the late Cdr. Sir (Edward) Robert Micklem, CBE, RN, and has issue living, Alexander David Robert, *b.* 1965,—Lucy Victoria Cornelia, *b.* 1958,—Anna Caroline, *b.* 1960.

This family is descended from Thomas Milburn, of Broomhope in Birtley, North Tynedale (*d.* 1705). The 1st baronet, Sir John Davison Milburn, was High Sheriff for Northumberland 1905. The 3rd baronet, Sir Leonard John Milburn, was High Sheriff of that co. 1928.

ST. JOHN-MILDMAY, Creation (G.B.) 1772, of Farley, co. Southampton.
[Dormant 1955.]

[Name pronounced "Sinjun-Mildmay."]

Rev. Sir (AUBREY) NEVILLE ST. JOHN-MILDMAY, 10th *Baronet, d.* in 1955, and at the time of going to press no name appears on the Official Roll of Baronets in respect of this title.

Mother living of 9th Baronet—Violet Vane, da. of the late Col. Arthur William Henry Hay-Drummond [see E. Kinnoull, colls.]: *m.* 1920, Capt. Sir Anthony St. John-Mildmay, MC, 8th Bt., who *d.* 1947, and from whom she had obtained a divorce 1933. *Residence*, Fulford House, Culworth, Banbury.

Collateral Branches living

Granddaughter of the late Henry Bingham MILDMAY, yr. son of the late Humphrey Mildmay, 6th son of 3rd baronet:—
Issue of the late Rt. Hon. Francis Bingham MILDMAY, who was cr. *Baron Mildmay of Flete* 1922 (ext. 1950) [*see* that title].

Grandchildren of the late Arthur George St. John-Mildmay, son of the late Edward St. John-Mildmay, 8th son of 3rd baronet :—
Issue of the late John Walter Paulet St. John-Mildmay, *b.* 1866, *a.* 1913 : *m.* 1894, Bertha Mabel, who *d.* 1950, da. of the late Joachim Theodor Satow :—
Michael Paulet, *b.* 1901; ed. at Emmanuel Coll., Camb. (MA); the presumed heir to the baronetcy: *m.* 1933, Joan Elizabeth, da. of the late Brig.-Gen. Hugh Roderick Stockley, CIE, and has issue living, Walter John Hugh, *b.* 1935,—Michael Hugh Paulet, *b.* 1937: *m.* 1965, Mrs. Chrystal Margaret Ludlow, and has issue living, Henry Walter *b.* 1971, Oliver James *b.* 1973. *Residence,* Brendan Cottage, Chalford, nr. Stroud.——Lorna Winifred ST. JOHN MILDMAY, *b.* 1895. *Residence,* Drakestone Cottage, Dursley, Glos.

MILES, Creation (U.K.) 1859, of Leigh Court, Somersetshire.

Sir WILLIAM NAPIER MAURICE MILES, 6th *Baronet*; *b.* Oct. 19th, 1913; *s.* his father *Lt.-Col. Sir* CHARLES WILLIAM, *OBE*, 1966; ed. at Stowe, and Jesus Coll., Camb.; patron of one living: *m.* 1946, Pamela, da. of the late Capt. Michael Dillon, and has issue.

Arms—Azure, a chevron paly of six ermine and or between three lozenges argent, each charged with a fleur-de-lis sable. **Crest**—Upon a rock a dexter arm embowed in armour the hand grasping an anchor entwined by a cable proper.

Residence—The Old Rectory House, Walton-in-Gordano, Som.

Labora sicut bonus miles.
Work like a good soldier.

Son living—PHILIP JOHN, *b.* Aug. 10th, 1953.

Daughters living—Catherine Anne Elizabeth, *b.* 1947: *m.* 1974, Peter Charles Beloe.——Lorraine, *b.* 1950.

Brother living—Charles William Noel, *b.* 1915: *m.* 1940, Jacqueline (Dickie), da. of Robert Cross, and has issue living, Phinola Jane, *b.* 1943. *Residence,* Glebe Cottage, Mattingley, Basingstoke, Hants.

Uncle living (son of 4th Baronet)—William Henry (Sandhurst Hotel, Eastbourne), *b.* 1888; 1914-18 War as Capt. Somerset LI (wounded, despatches): *m.* 1912, Lilian who *d.* 1972, da. of the Hon. Sir Hartley Williams, of 93, Cadogan Gdns., SW, and has issue living, Lilian Mary (64, Bishops Mansions, Bishops Park Rd., SW6), *b.* 1914: *m.* 1939, Alan Grant Maby, who *d.* 1965,—Pamela (Ossington Hall, Newark), *b.* 1916: *m.* 1st, 1947, Lt.-Col. William Maxwell Evelyn Denison, JP, DL, who *d.* 1972; 2ndly, 1974, Prof. Daniel Goedhuis, Netherlands Embassy, and has issue living, (by 1st m.) Georgina Jane *b.* 1948.

This family, from Ledbury, Herefordshire, became merchants of Bristol in the 18th century. Philip John Miles of Leigh Court, Som., was Mayor of Bristol 1780, and MP for Westbury, Corfe Castle and Bristol. His son, Sir William, 1st Bt., was MP for Chippenham, Romney, and E. Somerset (C). Sir Philip John William, 2nd Bt., was MP for E. Somerset (C) 1878-85.

MILLAIS, Creation (U.K.) 1885, of Palace Gate, Kensington, co. Middlesex, and of St. Ouen, Jersey.

[Name pronounced "Millay."]

Sir RALPH REGNAULT MILLAIS, 5th *Baronet*; *b.* March 4th, 1905; *s.* his father, *Sir* GEOFFROY WILLIAM, 1941; ed. at Marlborough, and at Trin. Coll., Camb. (B.A. 1926, M.A. 1930); formerly Wing-Com. R.A.F. Vol. Reserve, and in Air Ministry: *m.* 1st, 1939 (marriage dissolved 1947), Felicity Caroline Mary Ward (ROBINSON), da. of the late Brig.-Gen. William Ward Warner, C.M.G. [B. Borwick]; 2nd, 1947 (m. diss. 1971), Irene Jessie, da. of the late Edward Albert Stone, of St. Annes, Mont á l'Abbé, St. Helier, Jersey; 3rdly, 1975, Babette Irene, yr. da. of the late Maj.-Gen. Harold Francis Salt, CB, CMG, DSO, widow of Maj. John De Grey Tatham Warter, MC, and formerly wife of Victor William Henry Sefton-Smith [see Salt, Bt., cr. 1899, colls.], and has issue by 1st m.

Ars longa, vita brevis.
Art endureth, life is short.

Arms—Per bend sinister or and azure, an estoile of eight points between three fleurs-de-lys, two in fesse and one in base, all counter-changed. **Crest**—In front of a dexter hand gauntleted and couped gules an estoile of eight points or.

Residence—Gate Cottage, Winchelsea, Sussex.

Son living—By 1st m.—GEOFFROY RICHARD EVERETT, *b.* Dec. 27th, 1941; ed. at Marl-borough.

Daughter living—By 1st marriage—Caroline Mary Felicity, *b.* 1940: *m.* 1963, David Anthony Campbell-Jones, of Queen Anne Cottage, Warren Row, Wargrave, Berks., and has issue living, Henry David Mervyn, *b.* 1972——Serena Caroline Mary, *b.* 1969.

Brother living—Edward Gray St. Helier, *b.* 1918 ; ed. at Radley ; formerly Capt. Anti-Aircraft Regt., R.A.: *m.* **1947,** Rosemary Barbara, da. of the late Brig.-Gen. Frederic George Lucas, C.B., C.S.I., C.I.E., D.S.O., and has issue living, Andrew Michael, *b.* 1948,—John Frederic, *b.* 1049,—**Peter William,** *b.* **1951,**—David Gray, *b.* **1959,**—Fiona, *b.* 1960. *Residence,* **Crosswater Farm, Churt, Surrey.**

Sister living—Esmé Edith (Silverwoods, Churt, Surrey), *b.* 1902: *m.* 1930 (m. diss. 1940), Charles Anthony Stanley Prowse, and has issue living, Althea Hermione, *b.* 1931: *m.* 1968, the Rev. Desmond John Parsons, of All Saints Vicarage, Rosendale Rd., W. Dulwich, SE21 [*see* E. Rosse colls.].

Daughters living of 2nd Baronet—Pérrine, *b.* 1893; is a JP for Nelson; Officer of Order of Orange-Nassau of the Netherlands: *m.* 1914, Capt. Malcolm Matthew Moncrieff, MBE, formerly 6th Dragoon Gds., and has issue living, Colin Millais (4087, Monarch Pl., Victoria, BC, Canada), *b.* 1917; ed. at NZ Univ. (BA); is Lieut. NZ Forces; 1939-45 War in Libya and Italy. *Residence,* Dieudonne, Wakapuaka, Nelson, NZ.——Mary Amice de Carteret, *b.* 1897: *m.* 1924, Sydney Hewitt Pitt, MC, and has issue living, Jane Amice, *b.* 1929: *m.* 1955, Hugh Crawford Stewart Bowdler, of Memorial Cottage, Hatchett Gate, Beaulieu, Hants., and has issue living, David Martin *b.* 1956, Roger Hugh *b.* 1962, Martin Ralph *b.* 1965, Bridget Hélène Amice *b.* 1958. *Residence,* Home Farm House, Leighton Bromswold, Hunts.

Collateral Branch living.

Issue of the late John Guille Millais, 4th son of 1st baronet, *b.* 1865, *d.* 1931 : *m.* 1894, Fanny Margaret, who *d.* 1960, da. of the late Philip George Skipwith, of Hundleby, Lincolnshire.

Hesketh Raoul le Jarderay, *b.* 1901 ; Capt. (retired) late Scots Guards : *m.* 1st, 1926, Elinor Clare, who *d.* 1953, da. of the late Allan Ronald Macdonell, of Montreal; 2ndly, 1949, Mrs. Katharine Edith Prior-Palmer, da. of the late Frank Bibby, CBE, of Hardwick Grange, Shrewsbury, and has issue living, (by 1st m.) John Ronald Raoul LEES-MILLAIS (of Rockley Manor, Marlborough), *b.* 1927; assumed the additional surname of Lees: *m.* 1952, Lavinia Charlotte, da. of the late, Capt. Geoffrey William Martin Lees, of Falcutt House, Brackley, Northants, and has issue living, David John Geoffroy *b.* 1953, Colin Everett *b.* 1957, Patrick James *b.* 1958, Joanna Clare *b.* 1954, Fiona Katherine *b.* 1964,—Hugh Geoffroy (Apartado 30, Algeciras, Spain), *b.* 1929: *m.* 1957, Suzy Falconnet, and has issue living, Ian *b.* 1958, Joshua *b.* 1961, Tara Romaney *b.* 1967,—(by 2nd m.), Hesketh Merlin, *b.* 1950; ed. at Milton Abbey. *Residence,* Westcote Manor, Kingham, Oxon.

The 1st baronet, Sir John Everett Millais (son of the late John William Millais, of Jersey), was an eminent Artist and Pres. of Roy. Acad.

MILLER, Creation (E.) 1705, of Chichester, Sussex.

Sir JOHN HOLMES MILLER, 11th *Baronet, b.* 1925 ; *s.* his father, *Sir* ERNEST HENRY JOHN, 1960 : *m.* 1950, Jocelyn Edwards, of Wairoa, New Zealand, and has issue.

Arms—Argent, a fesse wavy azure, between three wolves' heads erased gules. **Crest**—A wolf's head erased gules charged on the neck with a fesse azure. *Residence*—Te Whare, Kohinui, RD2, Pahiatua, New Zealand.

Daughters living—Roslyn Mary, *b.* 1955.——Diana Jocelyn, *b.* 1958.
Brother living—HARRY HOLMES (Komako, RD, Ashurst, NZ) *b.* 1927: *m.* 1954, Gwynedd Margaret, da. of R. P. Sherriff, of St. Anthony, Paraparauma, NZ, and has issue living, Anthony Thomas, *b.* 1955,—Sarah Margaret, *b.* 1957,—Judith Christine, *b.* 1960.
Sisters living—Hilary, *b.* 1921 : *m.* 1945, John Alexander Nisbet, and has issue living.——Norah Jessie, *b.* 1923 : *m.* 1949, Roy Galloway Gardiner, and has issue living. *Residence,*

Uncle living (son of 9th baronet)—Charles Holmes (2/26, Clyde Rd., Napier, NZ), *b.* 1905: *m.* 1st, 1936, Hester Amelia, da. of E. J. Wilde; 2ndly, 1975, Pauline Rochfort, and has issue living (by 1st m.), Patrick Holmes, *b.* 1941,—Paul Greville, *b.* 1943,—Monica Jane, *b.* 1938,—Elizabeth Hope, *b.* 1940.

Aunts living (daughters of 9th baronet)—Jessie Martha, *b.* 1896 : *m.* 1921, Gerard James Wilde, and has issue living, Richard Gerard, *b.* 1926: *m.* 1961, Audrey June Rawson, and has issue living Ernle David, *b.* 1931,—Beatrice Amelia, *b.* 1925: *m.* 1951, Henry Brian Crawford, of Motukowkai Martou, NZ, and has issue living.——Alice Helen, *b.* 1906: *m.* 1928, John Palmer Tylee, of 57, McHardy St., Havelock North, Hawkes Bay, NZ, and has issue living, John Charles, *b.* 1928,—Robert Michael, *b.* 1930: *m.* 1956, Jane Nelson,—Richard Henry, *b.* 1932.——Joan Frances *b.* 1908: *m.* 1946, Ronald David Buchanan, and has issue living, John, *b.* 1948,—Christine (twin), *b.* 1948. *Residence,* Mayfield, Cunninghams, Feilding, NZ.

Widow living of 10th Baronet—MAHALAH NETTA BENNETT (*Mahalah, Lady Miller*): *m.* 1920, Sir Ernest Henry John Miller, 10th baronet, who *d.* 1960. *Residence,* 19, Huia St., Pahiatua, NZ.

Collateral Branches living.

Grandchildren of the late Hon. Sir Henry John Miller, 2nd son of 6th baronet :—
Issue of the late William Nicholson Miller, *b.* 1868, *d.* 1950 : *m.* 1906, Edith Mary, da. of J. C. Forsyth :—
William Maxwell (3, Mont Albert Rd., Canterbury, Melbourne, E.7, Australia), *b.* 1913; AMICE, AMIE Aust., MNZIE, Chartered Civil Engr.: *m.* 1938, Marjory, da. of L. M. Bell, MICE, and

has issue living, Leonard Maxwell, b. 1948,—Diana Marjory, b. 1940: m. 1963, Jeremy Pope, Bar. and Solicitor, of Wellington, NZ,—Mary Nicholson, b. 1947,—Robyn Elizabeth, b. 1951.—— Margaret May, b. 1907: m. 1937, Edward Ernest Zohrab, of 9, Huia St., Taupo, NZ, and has issue living, Margaret Ann, b. 1938: m. 1964, Jerome Glazebrook Whyte, of Waipura, Clive, Hawkes Bay, NZ,—Jenny Elizabeth, b. 1940: m. 1964, John Mundell Ewart, of 73, Grey Av., Corinda, Brisbane, Australia,—Patricia Joan, b. 1947.——Helen Frances, b. 1911: m. 1940, John Robert Shorter, of Binnie St., Paihia, Bay of Islands, NZ, and has issue living, Richard John (64A, Salamanca Rd., Wellington, NZ), b. 1943: m. 1971, Geraldine Cook,—Judith Dorothy (Paihia, Bay of Islands, NZ) b. 1945: m. 1968, Dr. Kevin Patrick Shannon,—Margaret Helen, b. 1950.——Geraldine Edith, b. 1915: m. 19— , Jack Reid, of Cairns, Qld.——Rosemary Alice, b. 1919: m. 1947, Douglas Balfour Zohrab (c/o Dept. of External Affairs, Wellington, NZ), and has issue living, Peter Douglas, b. 1949,—John Douglas, b. 1953.

Issue of the late Lieut.-Col. George Ralph Miller, D.S.O., b. 1874, d. 1948 : m. 1916, Violet Mary (now of Prickets Hatch, Nutley, Sussex), da. of the late W. H. Teschemaker, of Kauro Hill, Otago, New Zealand :—
Cecil Ralph (Prickets Hatch, Nutley, Sussex), b. 1918; is Maj. Roy. Warwickshire Regt. (TA).—— Anthony John (Prickets Hatch, Nutley, Sussex), b. 1920: m. 1952, Sheila Doreen, da. of Lt.-Col. L. Harvey, of Clare Glen, Buxted, Sussex, and widow of Sqdn.-Ldr. M. Savage, and has issue living, Richard Charles Cecil, b. 1956,—Timothy John, b. 1957,—Jennifer Anne, b. 1952.

Issue of the late Thomas Edmund Miller, 3rd son of 6th baronet, b. 1832, d. 1920: m. 1868, Katherine Margaret, who d. 1912, da. of J. Douglas :—
Mary Ann Frances, b. 1879. Residence,

Sir Thomas Miller, 1st Bt., was son of Mark Miller, Alderman of Chichester, and was several times Mayor of that city. The 1st, 2nd, and 3rd baronets each represented Chichester in Parliament, and the 5th baronet sat as M.P. for Portsmouth.

MILLER, Creation (G.B.) 1788, of Glenlee, Kirkcudbrightshire.

MANENT OPTIMA COELO

The best things remain in Heaven.

Sir (FREDERICK WILLIAM) MACDONALD MILLER OF GLENLEE, 7th *Baronet*; b. March 21st, 1920; s. his father, Sir ALASTAIR GEORGE LIONEL JOSEPH, 1964; ed. at Tonbridge; 1939-45 War, with Beds. and Herts. Regt., Black Watch, and RAC: m. 1947, Marion Jane Audrey, only da. of Richard Spencer Pettit, of Broad Oak, Chilton, Suffolk, and has issue.

Arms—Argent, a cross moline azure, in chief a lozenge between two mullets of the last and in base a bar wavy vert. **Crest**—A human hand couped at the wrist ; the third and fourth fingers folded in the hand argent. **Supporters**—Two roebucks proper.

Residence—Holton Lodge, Holton St. Peter, Halesworth, Suffolk.

Son living—STEPHEN WILLIAM MACDONALD, b. June 20th, 1953; ed. at Rugby, and St. Bart's. Hosp.
Daughter living—Alison Hilary, b. 1951.
Half-brothers living—Graham Frederick Alastair, b. (Sept.) 1938.——George Edward John, b. 1946,
Half-sisters living—Pamela Ann Mary, b. 1928: m. 1950, John Ward Randolph Nicholson, of 75, Otley Rd., Harrogate, Yorks., and has issue living, Mark John Anthony, b. 1952,—Martin Euan Thomas, b. 1955,—Moray John Fergus, b. 1962,—Myles Ian Vaughan, b. 1964,—Magnus Francis Benedict, b. 1966,—Annette Mary Ward, b. 1951,—Philippa Mary Randolph, b. 1954,—Iona Frances Marianne, b. 1957,—Alexandra Mary Eliabeth (twin), b. 1959.——Elizabeth Margaret Mary Cynthia, b. 1931: m. 1956, Filmer Courtenay William Honywood, ARICS, of Greenway Forstal Farmhouse, Hollingbourne, Maidstone, only son of Col. Sir William Wynne Honywood, MC, 10th Bt.——Teresa Rosemary Ann, b. 1939.
Aunt living—(daughter of 5th baronet)—Cynthia Mary Grizelda, b. 1895. Residence,
Mother living—Kathleen, da. of the late Maj. Stephen Goodwin Howard, CBE, JP, DL, of The Moat, Upend, Newmarket: m. 1st, 1919 (m. diss. 1926), Sir Alastair George Lionel Joseph Miller, 6th Bt., who d. 1964; 2ndly, 1928, Frederick Bodem.

The 1st baronet, Sir Thomas (d. 1789), son of William Miller, WS, and grandson of Matthew Miller of Glenlee, Kirkcudbright, was Lord President of the Court of Session in Scotland, with the title of Lord Barskimming. Sir William, the 2nd baronet (d. 1846), was a Lord of Session with the title of Lord Glenlee.

NORIE-MILLER, Creation (U.K.) 1936, of Cleeve, co. Perth. [Extinct 1973.]

Sir STANLEY NORIE-MILLER, MC, 2nd and last *Baronet*.

Widow living of 2nd Baronet—GRACE JANET EUPHROSYNE (*Lady Norie-Miller*) (Murrayshall, nr. Perth), da. of the late Juste Blennerhasset Eager, of Somerset East, S. Africa: m. 1921, Sir Stanley Norie-Miller, MC, 2nd baronet, who d. 1973, when the title became ext.

MILLS, Creation (U.K.) 1921, of Ebbw Vale, co. Monmouth.

Sir PETER FREDERICK LEIGHTON MILLS,
3rd *Baronet*: *b.* July 9th, 1924 ; *s.* his father,
Sir (FREDERICK LEIGHTON) VICTOR, *M.C.*, 1955 ;
ed. at Eastbourne Coll., and at Natal Univ.
(B.Sc. Agriculture 1952) ; has been in Rhodesia
Civil Ser. since 1953 ; late Lieut. Roy. Gurkha
Rifles ; European War 1943-5 : *m.* 1954, Pauline
Mary, da. of L. R. Allen, of Calverton, Notting-
hamshire, and has issue.

Arms—Sable, three millrinds in pale or between two
swords erect proper, pommels and hilts of the second. Crest—
A peewit's head, the neck encircled by a serpent nowed, both
proper.

Address—Henderson Research Station, P.B. 222A,
Salisbury, Rhodesia.

Son living—MICHAEL VICTOR LEIGHTON, *b.* Aug.
30th, 1957.

Widow living of 2nd Baronet—DORIS (Dorian) (*Doris, Lady Mills*), da. of Louis Armitage, of Eastbourne: *m.* 1923, Sir (Frederick Leighton) Victor Mills, MC, 2nd Bt., who *d.* 1955. *Residence*,
7, Somerset, Currie Rd., Durban, S. Africa.

The first baronet, Sir Frederick Mills (son of the late Leighton Mills, of Sunderland) was Chm.
of Ebbw Vale Steel and Iron Co., Ltd., Sheriff for Monmouthshire 1912, and M.P. for E. Div. of
Leyton (C) 1931-45. The second baronet, Major Sir (Frederick Leighton) Victor Mills, M.C.,
R.A. (Reserve) was Director of Public Works, Sierra Leone 1939-42 and of Uganda 1942-7, and
served during European War 1914-18 (M.C.).

MILMAN, Creation (G.B.) 1800, of Levaton-in-Woodland, Devonshire.

God with us, who against us ?

Sir DERMOT LIONEL KENNEDY MILMAN,
8th *Baronet*; *b.* Oct. 24th, 1912 ; *s.* his
father, *Brig.-Gen. Sir* LIONEL CHARLES PATRICK,
C.M.G., 1962 ; ed. at Uppingham, and
at Corpus Christi Coll., Camb. ; Maj. RASC,
and an officer of Permanent Ser. of British
Council, 1939-45 War in France, Belgium,
Burma (despatches): *m.* 1941, Muriel, only
da. of J. E. S. Taylor, of King's Lynn, and has
issue.

Arms—Azure, a serpent nowed or, between three sinister
gauntlets open, two in chief and one in base argent. Crest—
A hart lodged, per pale ermine and erminois, attired and unguled or, charged on the body with two hurts fesseways.

Residence—7, Old Westhall Close, Warlingham,
Surrey.

Daughter living—Celina Anne, *b.* 1945: *m.* 1968, John
Springett Appley, of 1521, Arrow Rd., Victoria, BC,
and has issue living, Tristan Dermot Springett, *b.* 1968,—
Tremayne Robert, *b.* 1974.

Brothers living—MALCOLM DOUGLAS (15, Rectory Rd.,
Beckenham, Kent), *b.* May 18th, 1915 ; ed. at Canford,
and at Worcester Coll., Oxford ; 1939-45 War; Malaya
1952-57: *m.* 1940 (m. diss. 1949), Sheila Maud, da. of Albert Maurice Dudeney, and has issue
living, Felicity Ann *b.* 1941: *m.* 19—, —Penelope Fiona, *b.* 1943.——Derek, *MC* (Flat A, 26,
Sussex Pl., Regents Park, NW1), *b.* 1918; ed. at Bedford Sch.; Lt.-Col. (ret.) 3rd E. Anglian
Regt.; 1939-45 War with 5th Indian Div. in Middle East (MC): *m.* 1942, Christine, da. of Alfred
Whitehouse, of Sutton Coldfield, and has issue living, David Patrick (71, Camden Rd., Seven-
oaks, Kent), *b.* 1945: *m.* 1969, Christina, da. of John William Hunt, and has issue living, Kirsty
Jane *b.* 1975,—Terence Martin, *b.* 1947.
Widow living of 7th Baronet—MARJORIE ALETTA (*Marjorie, Lady Milman*) (of 15, Rectory Rd.,
Beckenham, Kent), da. of the late Col. Arthur Harry Clark-Kennedy, Indian Army: *m.* 1911,
Brig.-Gen. Sir Lionel Charles Patrick Milman, CMG, 7th Bt., who *d.* 1962.

Collateral Branches living.

Issue of the late Stephen Walter Milman, 4th son of 4th baronet, *b.* 1879, *d.* 1957:
m. 1st, 1907, Ethel, who *d.* 1914, da. of the late William Dowdeswell Horsley,
ICS; 2ndly, 1917, Hilda, who *d.* 1964, da. of the late William Dowdeswell,
Horsley, ICS (ante) —:

(By 1st marriage) Gerald Stephen, *b.* 1908 ; ed. at Harrow ; European War 1939-45 as Lieut,
Welsh Guards : *m.* 1944, Noreen, da. of Thomas Johnston Elliot, and has issue living, Ian Stephen.
b. 1946,—Stephanie Rosalind, *b.* 1949,—Angela Caroline *b.* 1952,—Geraldine Stella, *b.* 1956.
Residence, La Dormida, Casilla de Correo 27, La Cumbre, Sierras de Cordoba, Argentina.

Issue of the late Com. Henry Augustus Milman, O.B.E., R.N., 5th son of 4th
baronet, *b.* 1882, *d.* 1952: *m.* 1912, Genevieve IRVING MILMAN (16, Sheep St.,
Petersfield, Hants), da. of John Irving, of Victoria, BC:—
John Alexander Ralph, *O.B.E.*, *b.* (Nov.) 1912 ; ed. at Haileybury ; Major (retired) Highland L.I.
and Mil. Attaché, Budapest; Mohmand Campaign 1934; Mil. Attaché, Budapest, 1953-55;
1939-45 War as acting Lt.-Col. in Middle East, Burma, and Italy (wounded, despatches, OBE);
OBE (Mil.) 1943: *m.* 1943, Daphne Mary, da. of Alexander Andrew Bisset, and has issue living,
John Andrew Francis Pretyman, *b.* 1945,—Anne Isabel Jane, *b.* 1943. *Residence*, South Acre
House, S. Harting Petersfield, Hants.

Issue of the late Major Hugh Milman, O.B.E., youngest son of 4th baronet, b.
1884, d. 1959 : m. 1914, Marjorie, only da. of the late Malcolm McCullock
Paterson, M.I.C.E., formerly of the Croft, Pannal, Harrogate :—
Stephanie Grace, b. 1915.——Diana Constance, b. 1920 : m. 1942, Capt. John Michael Merry, R.A.,
and has issue living, Bruce, b. 1944,—David, b. 1945,—Tessa, b. 1947,—Miranda, b. 1950,—
Dilys, b. 1956. *Residence*, 25, Highfield Rd., Birmingham, 15.

Grandson of the late Walter Charles Gordon Milman (infra):—
Issue of the late Humphrey Radcliffe Milman, b. 1895, d. 1974: m. 1923, Edith Mary, da.
of the late Rev. Henry Elias Mocatta, Headmaster of Clive House Sch., Prestatyn:—
John Walter Francis (Northcliff, Cliff Terrace Rd., Wemyss Bay, Renfrewshire, PA18 6AP), b.
1928: m. 1955, Jean Margaret, da. of G. C. Till, of Gunard, I. of Wight, and has issue living,
Pamela Rosemary, b. 1961,—Laura Frances, b. 1965.

Issue of the late Walter Charles Gordon Milman, 3rd son of 3rd baronet, *b. 1853*,
d. 1907 : m. 1886, Edie Helen Blythe, who d. 1955, da. of John Alexander
Radcliffe, formerly of Ordsal, Cobham, Surrey :—
Norah Helen, b. 1893: m. 1927, Capt. Lancelot Milman Shadwell, RN, who d. 1960. *Residence*, 173,
Romsey Rd., Winchester.——Isabel Joan, b. 1898: m. 1922, Maj. William M. Martineau, MC,
RASC, and has issue living, Josephine Helen, b. 1923: m. 1959, John Van Valkenburg. *Residence*,
Platoff, Lymington, Hants.

Granddaughter of the late Maj.-Gen. Egerton Charles William Miles Milman
el. son of the late Lt.-Gen. Francis Miles Milman, 2nd son of 1st Bt.:—
Issue of the late Charles Egerton Forbes MILMAN-MAINWARING, b. 1867, d. 1951, having
assumed in 1871 by Royal licence, the additional surname of Mainwaring: m. 1915,
Marguerite Doris Roper, d. 1965, da. of the late Lt.-Col. Francis Washington Lethbridge, DSO:—
Rosamond Irene MILMAN-COLEBROOK, b. 1916; resumed her maiden surname of Milman before
Colebrook 19—: m. 1946 (m. diss. 1966), Mulford Albert Colebrook, late 2nd Sec. of USA Em-
bassy in London. *Address*, 3, Priory Gdns., Folkestone.

Granddaughters of the late Lt.-Col. Everard Stepney Milman, 6th son of Lt.-
Gen. Francis Miles Milman (ante):—
Issue of the late Lt.-Col. Octavius Rodney Everard Milman, DSO, b. 1882, d. 1971: m.
1911, Mary Freya (A6, Marine Gate, Marine Drive, Brighton, Sussex), el. da. of the late
Rev. William Edward Haigh, Hon. Canon of Bristol:—
Joanna Woolstone, b. 1912: m. 1939, Maj. Denys Paul Bulkeley, RA, of Little Orchard, Bracken
Rd., Seaford, Sussex, and has issue living, Richard Milman, b. 1940: m. 1967, Elizabeth Mahoney,
and has issue living, Thomas William b. 1971, Joanna Louise (twin) b. 1971.——Patricia Freya,
b. 1920: m. 1942, Lionel Noel Woolf, of D1, Marine Gate, Marine Drive, Brighton, and has issue
living, Inigo Rodney Milman, b. 1946: m. 1970, Susan Rebecca Davies, and has issue living,
Bethia Fearne Milman b. 1974,—Christopher Patrick Milman, b. 1947: m. 1969, Linda Johnston,
and has issue living, Simon Justin b. 1970, Jonathan Marcus b. 1973,—Nicholas David Milman
b. 1953: m. 1973, Anne Elizabeth March.

Granddaughter of the late Very Rev. Henry Hart Milman, 3rd son of 1st baronet :—
Issue of the late Arthur Milman, b. 1829, d. 1913 : m. 1872, Frances Mary, who d. 1886, da.
of the late John Laurence Tatham, Bar.-at-law, of West Hill, Highgate, N. :—
Maud, b. 1886. *Residence*, The White House, Bydown, Swimbridge, N. Devon.

Sir Francis Milman, 1st Bt. of Levaton in Woodland, Devon, was Pres. of Roy. Coll. of Physicians
1811-13, and Physician to King George III. Sir William Ernest Milman, M.M., 6th Bt. d. (Aug),
1962, and his brother and successor, Brig.-Gen. Sir Lionel Charles Patrick Milman, C.M.G.,
7th Bt. d. (Nov.) 1962.

Milne-Watson, see Watson.

MILNER, Creation (G.B.) 1717, of Nun Appleton Hall, Yorkshire.

Sir GEORGE EDWARD MORDAUNT MILNER,
9th *Baronet*, el. son of the late Brig.-Gen. George Francis
Milner, C.M.G., D.S.O., 2nd son of the late Henry
Beilby William Milner, 2nd son of 4th baronet; b.
Feb. 7th, 1911 ; s. his kinsman, *Sir* WILLIAM FREDERICK
VICTOR MORDAUNT, 1960 ; ed. at Oundle ; was Stipen-
diary Steward of Jockey Club of S. Africa 1954-9 ; Euro-
pean War 1939-45 as Capt. R.A. : m. 1st, 1935, Barbara
Audrey, who d. 1951, da. of Henry Noel Belsham, of
Hunstanton, Norfolk ; 2ndly, 1953, Katherine Moodie
Bissett, da. of the late D. H. Hoey, of Dunfermline,
Fifeshire, and has issue by 1st marriage.

Arms—Per pale or and sable, a chevron between three horses' bits
counterchanged. Crest—A horse's head couped sable, maned and bridled
or between a pair of wings gold.

Addit frena feris.   *Residence*—Oude Natte, Vallei, Klapmuts, Cape Province, S.
He puts bridles on the   Africa. *Club*—Rand (Johannesburg).
brutal.

Sons living—By 1st marriage—TIMOTHY WILLIAM LYCETT, b. Oct. 11th, 1936.——
Charles Mordaunt (Nun Appleton, P.O. Windmill, Cape, S. Africa), b. 1944: m. 1965, Lady
Charlene Mary Olivia French, el. da. of 3rd Earl of Ypres, and has issue living, Marcus Charles
Mordaunt, b. 1968,—Patrick Edward French Mordaunt, b. 1969.

Daughter living—By 1st marriage—Georgina Madeleine Mary, b. 1939 : m. 1961, Arthur Henry
Bertram Grattan-Bellew [*see* Grattan-Bellew, Bt.]. *Residence*, Hole Farm, Gt. Waldingfield.
Sudbury, Suffolk.

Brother living—Henry George, b. 1912 ; ed. at Oundle, and at Magdalene Coll., Camb. (B.A.,
1934); Burma 1939-45 as Navigator RAF (Burma Star): m. 1952, Florence, da. of William Tai
Chung, of Kingston, Jamaica. *Residence*, 19, Red Hills Rd., PO Halfway Tree, St. Andrews,
Jamaica. *Club*, St. James.

The 1st baronet, M.P. for York City, was Grand Master of the Freemasons in England. The 2nd baronet was Receiver-General of Excise, the 3rd baronet sat as M.P. for York City 1790-1811, the 5th baronet sat as M.P. therefor 1848-57, and the 7th baronet, Rt. Hon. Sir Frederick George Milner, G.C.V.O., P.C., sat at M.P. therefor 1883-5 and for Nottinghamshire, Bassetlaw Div. 1890-1906.

Milnes-Coates, see Coates.

MITCHELL, Creation (U.K.) 1945, of Tulliallan, co. Fife, and of Luscar, Province of Alberta, Canada.

Sir HAROLD PATON MITCHELL, 1st *Baronet*, son of the late Col. Alexander Mitchell, J.P., D.L., of Tulliallan Castle, Alloa ; *b.* May 21st, 1900; ed. at Eton, at Univ. Coll., Oxford (MA, Hon. Fellow), and Geneva Univ. (Dr. Political Science); Hon. LLD Rollins, St. Andrews and Alberta; a Member of Queen's Body Guard for Scotland (R. Co. of Archers), a Knight Com. of Order of Restitution of Poland, and a KStJ ; PPS to Parl. Sec. of Overseas Trade Dept. 1931-35, and to Min. of Labour and Min. of Supply 1939-42; Vice-Chm. of Conservative Party 1942-45, Lecturer in Hispanic American Studies, Stanford Univ., USA 1959-65, and Hon. Col. 61st Sig. Regt. (TA) 1947-65; 1939-45 War as Col. Headquarters, Anti-Aircraft Command and Liaison Officer to Polish Forces in NW Europe (Polish Cross of Valour); MP for Brentford and Chiswick Div. of Middx. (C), 1931-45: *m.* 1947, Mary (a CStJ), da. of the late William Pringle, and has issue.

Arms—Sable, nine mascalles in cross and in the first quarter a portcullis chains pendant or. **Crest**—On a chapeau gules doubled ermine, three ears of barley conjoined in stubb proper.

Residences—Château de Bourdigny, Geneva, Switzerland; Marshall's Island, Bermuda *Club*—Royal Bermuda Yacht.

Daughter living—Mary-Jean, *b.* 1951.

MITCHELSON, Creation (U.K.) 1920, of Rotherfield, co. Sussex. [Extinct 1945.]

Sir ARCHIBALD MITCHELSON, 1st and last *Baronet*.

Daughter living of 1st Baronet—Muriel Rose : *m.* 1st, 1926, Edward John Salisbury, from whom she obtained a divorce 1930 ; 2ndly, 1930, Lieut.-Col. Alexander Hubert Barclay, Queen's Bays, who obtained a divorce 1943; 3rdly, 1943, Brigadier Marcus George Roddick, D.S.O., 10th Hussars, who *d.* 1959, and has issue living, (by 1st marriage) Edward Mitchelson Antony, *b.* 1927; is in Queen's Bays,—(by 2nd m.) Jonet Noël, *b.* 1931: *m.* 1959, John Stanley Vyvyan, of Trelowarren, Mawgam, Helston, Cornwall [see Vyvyan, Bt., colls.],—Amanda Mary, *b.* 1938: *m.* 1961, Thomas Philip Hettleman, of 315, East 72nd Street, New York. *Residence,*

MOIR, Creation (U.K.) 1916, of Whitehanger, Fernhurst, co. Sussex.

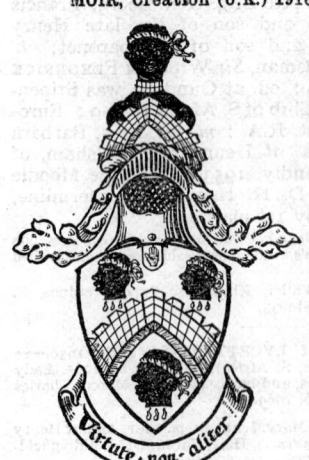

By virtue, not otherwise.

Sir ERNEST IAN ROYDS MOIR, 3rd *Baronet* ; *b.* June 9th, 1925 ; *s.* his father, *Sir* ARROL, 1957 ; ed. at Camb. Univ. (B.A. 1949) ; European War 1943-45 with R.E. : *m.* 1954, Margaret Hanham, da. of George Eric Carter, of Cranbrook, Netheroyd Hill, Huddersfield, and has issue.

Arms—Argent, a span of a bridge enarched, embattled, and in perspective, checky or and azure, between three Moors' heads coupled sable, each banded of the second and third, and distilling three drops of blood proper. **Crest**—Upon a span of a bridge as in the arms a Moor's head affrontée couped at the shoulders sable, banded or and azure, collared checky of the same.

Residence—Three Gates, 174, Coombe Lane West, Kingston-upon-Thames, Surrey.

Sons living—CHRISTOPHER ERNEST, *b.* May 22nd, 1955.——Timothy James, *b.* 1959.——Nicholas Ian, *b.* 1961.

Sisters living—June Pamela, *b.* 1923 : *m.* 1949, Ian Colin Wetherell, and has issue living, Peter Arrol Royds, *b.* 1953. *Residence*, 2, Lawrence Street, Chelsea, S.W.3.——Joy Yvonne, *b.* 1927 : *m.* 1st, 1948, Lieut. Sir Baldwin Patrick Walker, R.N., 4th Bt. (cr. 1856), from whom she obtained a divorce 1954 ; 2ndly, 1954, Michael Haggerty, and has issue living, (by 2nd m.) John Wyeth, *b.* 1957, Susan Bret, *b.* 1955,—Gillian Ruth *b.* 1958. *Residence*, 74, Huron Rd., SW19.

Widow living of 2nd Baronet—DOROTHY BLANCHE, da. of Vice-Adm. Sir Percy Molyneux Rawson Royds, C.B., C.M.G. [Yarrow, Bt.] : *m*. 1st, 1922, Sir Arrol Moir, 2nd baronet, who *d*. 1957 ; 2ndly, 1960, Robert William Nichol, M.R.C.S., L.R.C.P. *Residences*, Rozine Cottage, Reading Street, Broadstairs, Kent ; 9, Queen's Elm Square, Chelsea, S.W.3.

The 1st baronet, Sir Ernest William Moir, was head of the firm of Ernest William Moir & Co. Ltd., engineers, which he founded, and a Director of S. Pearson & Son. Ltd., contracting engineers. The 2nd baronet, Sir Arrol Moir, was Vice-Pres. of Institute of Patentees.

Molesworth-St. Aubyn, see St. Aubyn.

MOLONY, Creation (U.K.) 1925, of the City of Dublin.

Sir HUGH FRANCIS MOLONY, 2nd, *Baronet, b*. Sept. 2nd, 1900; *s*. his father, *the Rt. Hon. Sir* THOMAS FRANCIS, 1949 ; ed. at Trin. Coll., Dublin (B.A. 1921, M.A. 1945, Bachelor of Engineering 1922, Master 1927); a Consulting Engineer, a Co. Dir., a FICE, a FICE Ireland, and a Member of Assocn. of Consulting Engineers of Ireland; Engineering Inspector, Min. of Health and Min. of Housing and Local Govt. 1938-55: *m*. 1936, Alexandra Cooper, da. of the late John Alexander Todd, of Glasgow, and has issue.

In God and not in my bow will I hope.

Arms—Gules, six arrows in saltire between two bows erect to dexter and sinister or, a chief ermine. **Crest**—A dexter arm embowed in armour proper charged with a fleur-de-lys gules, the hand in a gauntlet holding a sword of the first.
Residence—Silver Trees, Heathfield Copse, West Chiltington, Pullborough, Sussex.

Son living—THOMAS DESMOND (5, Todd St., King's Grove, Sydney, NSW) *b*. March 13th, 1937; ed. at Ampleforth Coll., and at Trin. Coll., Dublin; late PO RAF: *m*. 1962, Doris, da. of the late E. W. Foley, of Cork, and has issue living, Jennifer Mary, *b*. 1963,—Grace Anne, *b*. 1964,—Daphne Julia Rose, *b*. 1965,—Lynda Jacqueline Clare, *b*. 1967.

Brother living—*Sir* Joseph Thomas, KCVO, QC, *b*. 1907; ed. at Downside, and Trin. Coll., Camb. (M.A., LL.M.), Bar. Inner Temple 1930 (Bencher 1961), and a QC 1955; appointed Recorder of Devizes 1951, of Exeter 1954, of Southampton 1960, and of Bristol 1964, a Member of Bar Council 1954-58, Commr. of Assize Midland and S.-E. Circuits 1958, Chm., Board of Trade Cttee., on Consumer Protection 1959, and Commr. of Assize NE Circuit 1960; Leader of W. Circuit 1964; Chm. of Bar Council 1963-64, 1964-65 and 1965-66, and of Code of Practice Cttee. Assocn. of British Pharmaceutical Industry 1967, and Commr. of Assize Western Circuit 1968; Attorney Gen. Duchy of Cornwall 1960-69; a Judge of Courts of Appeal of Jersey and Guernsey since 1972; 1939-45 War as Sqdn.-Ldr. RAFVR; Knt. 1967, KCVO 1970: *m*. 1936, Carmen Mary, only da. of the late Frankland Dent, PhD, MSc, and has issue living, Peter John (14, Regents Park Rd., NW1); *b*. 1937; ed. at Downside, and Trin. Coll., Camb. (MA); FCA: *m*. 1964, Elizabeth Mary, el. da. of Henry Clervaux Chaytor, of 3, St. Paul's Rd., Cambridge, and has issue living, James Sebastian *b*. 1965, John Benjamin *b*. 1966, Simon Benedict *b*. 1972, Carmen Jane *b*. 1967,—John Fernando, *b*. 1949; ed. at Downside, and Trin. Coll., Camb.,—Mary Carmen, *b*. 1939: *m*. 1963, Martin Noble Wells, of Churchside, Church Rd., Hockley, Essex, and has issue living, Nicholas Thomas Clinton *b*. 1964, Adrian Francis *b*. 1966, Jonathan Patrick *b*. 1968, Joanna Kate *b*. 1971,—Angela Carmen, *b*. 1942: *m*. 1967, Philip Vincent, of 12, St. Ann's Rd., W11, and has issue living, Patrick Henry Morse *b*. 1970, Antonia Louise, *b*. 1968. *Residence*, 4, Parkside Gdns., Wimbledon Common, SW19.

Sisters living—Eileen Mary, *b*. 1903.——Marie Etienne, *b*. 1916. *Residence*, 1, The Drive, Wimbledon, S.W.20.

The 1st Baronet, the Rt. Hon. Sir Thomas Francis Molony (son of James Molony, of Harcourt Street, Dublin), was appointed H.M.'s 2nd Serjeant-at-Law, Ireland 1911, Solicitor-Gen. for Ireland 1912, and Attorney-Gen. for Ireland 1913, and was a Judge of High Court of Justice in Ireland (King's Bench Div.) 1913-15, a Lord Justice of Appeal 1915-18, and Lord Ch. Justice of Ireland 1918-24.

MONCREIFFE OF THAT ILK, Creation (N.S) 1685, of Moncreiffe, Perthshire.

Sure hope.

Sir RUPERT IAIN KAY MONCREIFFE OF THAT ILK, 11th *Baronet*, son of the late Lieut.-Com. Thomas Gerald Auckland Moncreiffe, R.N., younger brother of 9th baronet ; *b.* April 9th, 1919 ; *s.* his cousin, *Sir* DAVID GERALD, *M.C.* (23rd Laird of Moncreiffe), 1957 ; ed. in Switzerland, at Stowe, at Heidelberg Univ., at Ch. Ch., Oxford (B.A. and M.A. 1946), and at Edinburgh Univ. (LL.B. 1950, Ph.D. 1958) ; Advocate Scotland 1950 ; is feudal Baron of Easter Moncreiffe (erected 1592), a Member of Queen's Body Guard for Scotland (Roy. Co. of Archers), a Member of Lloyd's, a D.L. for Perthshire, an O.St.J., a F.S.A., and an author ; appointed a Member of Advisory Committee Scottish National Portrait Gallery, and an Hon. Sheriff of Perth and Angus 1958, and Albany Herald 1961; Founder of Puffin's Club; 1939-45 War as Capt. Scots Guards (wounded); Attaché and Private Sec. to H.M.'s Ambassador in Moscow 1946: *m.* 1st, 1946 (m. diss. 1964), Lady Diana Denyse Hay (*Countess of Erroll* in her own right and Lord High Constable of Scotland), da. of 22nd Earl of Erroll; 2ndly, 1966, Hermione Patricia, da. of the late Lt.-Col. Walter Douglas Faulkner, MC, Irish Guards [see D. Buccleuch, colls.], and has issue by 1st m.

Arms—Argent, a lion rampant gules, armed and langued azure, a chief ermine. **Crest**—On a cap of maintenance gules furred ermine of a Scottish feudal baron, a helmet with mantling vert slashed in an outline of oakleaves and veined or, and out of a crest coronet or (as 24th Chief of the Moncreiffes), a demi lion rampant as in the arms **Badge**—A chaplet of oakleaves proper, fructed of six acorns or, and within it a shoot of mistletoe fructed proper. **Supporters**—Two bearded men proper in armour cap-a-pie sable and having Celtic conical helms sable banded or, spurs or, swords at their sides hilted or, and in their exterior hands lances paleways gules, the spearheads argent.

Seat—Easter Moncreiffe, Perthshire. *Clubs*—Turf, White's, Pratt's, Beefsteak, New (Edinburgh), Puffin's (Edinburgh), Royal and Ancient.

Sons living—By 1st marriage—MERLIN SERELD VICTOR GILBERT *HAY* (Lord Hay) (Turf and Puffin's (Edinburgh) Clubs), *b.* April 20th, 1948; ed. at Eton (parachutist and pilot), and Trin. Coll., Camb.——*Hon.* Peregrine David Euan Malcolm (Turf and Puffin's (Edinburgh) Clubs) *b.* 1951; ed. at Eton (Capt. of Oppidans), and Ch. Ch., Oxford.
Daughter living—By 1st marriage—*Lady* Alexandra Victoria Caroline Anne *Hay*, *b.* 1955.
Daughter living of 9th Baronet—Katharine Elisabeth, *b.* 1920; 24th feudal Baroness of Moncreiffe. *Seat*, Moncreiffe, Perthshire. *Club*, Kennel (Ladies' Branch).
Widow living of 9th Baronet—MARY (*Mary, Lady Moncreiffe*), da. of the late John Balli, of Paris; is an Officer of Order of Orange Nassau of the Netherlands: *m.* 1919, Cdr. Sir John Robert Guy Moncreiffe, RN, 9th Baronet, who *d.* 1934. *Residence*, Beau Rivage Palace, Lausanne-Ouchy, Switzerland.

This family derive their surname from the hill of Moncreiffe, which has been in their possession since before surnames were first adopted in Scotland. "Moncreiffe" is the Old Gaelic place-name *Monadh Craoibhe* (the Hill of the Sacred Bough), and on its summit stood the dry-stone stronghold of the Pictish kings; while the Moncreiffe arms indicate them to have probably been cadets of the same branch of the ancient royal stock as the lairds of Dundas [see M. Zetland]. Sir Mathew of Moncreiffe was confirmed in the lands by royal charter in 1248; and Malcolm Moncreiffe, 6th of that Ilk, had a new charter of the free Barony of Moncreiffe in 1455. Sir Thomas Moncreiffe, 14th of that Ilk, who was cr. a Baronet with remainder to heirs male whatsoever in 685, was 4th in descent from Hew Moncreiffe, 2nd son of John Moncreiffe, 8th of that Ilk (*d.* 1496). The el. son, Sir John Moncreiffe, 9th of that Ilk (*k.* at Flodden 1513) was great-grandfather of Sir John Moncreiffe, 12th of that Ilk, who was *cr.* a Baronet 1626. His son Sir John Moncreiffe of that Ilk, 2nd Bt., being childless, the Baronetcy (*cr.* 1626) passed eventually to the line of his uncle Archibald Moncreiff, Heritable Prior of Elcho [*see* B. Moncreiff]; but in 1667 the Crown confirmed a family arrangement whereby Sir John made over the feudal Barony of Moncreiffe to his kinsman Thomas Moncreiffe, who thus became 14th of that Ilk and was later *cr.* 1st Bt. (1685).

Montagu-Pollock, see Pollock.

Montague-Barlow, see Barlow.

MONTGOMERY, Creation (U.K.) 1801, of Stanhope, Peeblesshire.

Sir (BASIL HENRY) DAVID MONTGOMERY, 9th *Baronet*, only son of the late Lt.-Col. Henry Keith Purvis-Russell Montgomery, OBE; *b.* March 20th, 1931; *s.* his uncle, *Sir* BASIL RUSSELL PURVIS-RUSSELL-HAMILTON-MONTGOMERY, 1964; a JP and DL of Kinross-shire: *m.* 1956, Delia, da. of, the late Adm. Sir John Lorne Reid, GB, CVO [see Reid, Bt., cr. 1897, colls.], and has issue.

Arms—Quarterly, 1st and 4th azure, three fleurs-de-lis or; 2nd and 3rd gules, three annulets or, stones azure, over all, dividing the quarters, a cross wavy of the second, charged with three conquefoils, in fesse ermine. **Crest**—A Dexter Hand holding a sword indented on the back like a saw proper.

Residence—Kinross House, Kinross.

Son living—JAMES DAVID KEITH, *b.* June 6th, 1957.

Daughters living—Caroline Jean, *b.* 1959.——Davina Lucy, *b.* 1961.——Iona Margaret, *b.* 1972.——Laura Elizabeth, *b.* 1974.

Daughters living of 8th Baronet—Rachel, *b.* 1916; Capt. (ret.) NZ WRAC; served 1943-63; Middle East 1945 as Dep. Assist. Director.——Sheila, *b.* 1923; 1941-45 War with New Zealand WAAF (Radar): *m.* 1st, 1945, John Martin Griffiths, who obtained a divorce 1959; 2ndly, 1967, Desmond Edward Widgery, and has issue living (by 1st m.), Andrea Suzanne, *b.* 1946,—Gael Virginia, *b.* 1949. *Residence,* Warroch, Newstead, RD, Hamilton, NZ.

Sister living—Veronica Mary Anthea, *b.* 1935.

Aunt living (daughter of 7th baronet)—Clementine Helen Maud (of Hattonburn, Milnathort, Kinross-shire), *b.* 1900.

Mother living—Cynthia Louisa Winifred (of Kinross House, Kinross), da. of John Allan Maconochie Welwood, of Kirknewton, Midlothian, and Garvock, Fife [E. Perth, colls.]: *m.* 1930, Lt.-Col. Henry Keith Purvis-Russell-Montgomery, OBE, who *d.* 1954.

Widow living of 6th Baronet—ROSE KATHLEEN (*Lady Graham-Montgomery*), da. of Peter John Sullivan, of Dublin, and widow of Charles Wilfred Blunt: *m.* 1923, as his second wife, Rev. Sir Charles Percy Graham-Montgomery, 6th baronet, who *d.* 1930.

Collateral Branches living.

Grandson of the late Capt. Thomas Henry Montgomery, 5th son of 2nd baronet:—
Issue of the late Herbert Elphinstone MONTGOMERY, *b.* 1861, *d.* 1943: *m.* 1899, Janet Katherine Olive, who *d.* **1937**, da. of Sir John William Hamilton Anson, 2nd **Bt.**:—
Arthur Herbert, *OBE, TD, b.* 1902; ed. at Wellington Coll., and at Hertford Coll., Oxford; Hon. Brig. R.A., and a Fellow of Institute of Chartered Accountants in England and Wales; 1939-45 War (OBE); OBE (Mil) 1945: *m.* 1939, Féodora Kathleen Alice, da. of the late Henry Bligh Forde, and has issue living, James Henry Anson, *b.* 1945: *m.* 1972, Carolyn Winifred Finlay,—Rachel Janet, *b.* 1940: *m.* 1972, Max Monsarrat,—Sylvia Mary (*Hon. Mrs. Charles J. Dugdale*), *b.* 1942: *m.* 1970, the Hon. Charles James Dugdale, el. son of 1st Baron Crathorne. *Residence,* 13, Belvedere Av., Wimbledon, SW.

Grandchildren of the late William Montgomery, son of the late Robert Montgomery, 4th son of 1st baronet:—
Issue of the late Robert Hamilton Montgomery, *b.* 1863, *d.* 1943 : *m.* 1898, Evelyn Mary, who *d.* 1951, da. of the late Rev. Frederick Vernon, V. of Shawbury, near Shrewsbury:—
Ian Stuart, *b.* 1900: *m.* **1942**, Neva, da. of the late Ogden Minton, of Greenwich, Connecticut, USA, and has issue living, Brian Stuart, *b.* **1952,**—Ann Vernon, *b.* **1945**: *m.* 1967, James R. Egan, of 167, Samoset Drive, Hanover, Mass., USA,—Sheila Minton, *b.* 1949: *m.* 1972, Mervin J. Marks, of New York, USA. *Residence,* Kinross, Warrington, Va. 22186, USA.——Colin Tassie, *b.* 1911: *m.* 1st, 1941, Carol Spencer, who *d.* 1972, da. of the late Dr. Joseph Kent Worthington, of Baltimore, Maryland, USA; 2ndly, 1973, Elizabeth Fleet, da. of the late Monroe Davenport Morton, of Lynchburg, Va., USA, and widow of Harry Douglas Forsyth. *Residence,* 3122, Rivermont Av., Lynchburg, Va., USA.——Dorothy Vernon, *b.* 1909: *m.* 1952, William Smoot Rust, and has issue living, William Montgomery, *b.* 1952. *Residence,* Magbie Hill, Warrenton, Virginia, USA.

Grandchildren of the late Robert Hamilton Montgomery (ante):—
Issue of the late Adm. Alan Robert Montgomery, U.S. Navy, *b.* 1905, *d.* **1964**: *m.* 1st, 1928 (marriage dissolved 1940), Josephine Marie, da. of the late Edward J. Straine, of Philadelphia; 2ndly, 1941, Mary Helen, da. of George E. Kohlhaas, of San Bernadino, California, USA:—
(By 1st marriage) Robert Edward, *b.* 1932.——Doris Marie, *b.* 1929.

Grandchildren of the late William Montgomery (ante):—
Issue of the late Rev. Colin Francis Montgomery, *b.* 1867, *d.* 1906: *m.* 1894, Evelyn, who *d.* 1948, da. of the late Henry Webb, of Worcester:—
Robert Maxwell, *b.* 1897; Squadron Leader (retired) R.A.F.; formerly Lieut. R.A.; India 1943-4 on Staff of Supreme Allied Com., S.-E. Asia: *m.* 1st, 1924, Eleanor Pierce Adams, who *d.* 1957, having obtained a divorce 1936 ; 2ndly, 1936, Audrey Winifred, only da. of C. Field, of The Hazels, Worplesdon, Surrey, and has issue living (by 2nd m.), Andrew John (Farthingham House, Farthingham Lane, Ewhurst, Surrey), *b.* 1937: *m.* 1965, Maureen Patricia, da. of M. J. Roberts, of Morden, Surrey, and has issue living, Robert Maxwell *b.* 1968, Michael Andrew *b.* 1971. *Residence,* New Pond, Fridays Hill, Fernhurst, Haslemere, Surrey.——Evelyn Ruth, *b.* 1902: *m.* 1926, the Ven. Richard Hamilton Babington, formerly Archdeacon of Exeter, of Thatch End, Whimple, Exeter, and has issue living, Richard Andrew, *b.* 1927,—Gervase Hamilton, *b.* 1930,—Susan Mary, *b.* 1933,—Felicity Ruth, *b.* 1939.
Issue of the late William Harold Montgomery, *b.* 1869; *d.* 1937: *m.* 1908, Dorothea Godiva, who *d.* 1968, da. of William John Mann, of Highfield, Trowbridge, Wilts:—
James Graham (9, Ravelston House Grove, Edinburgh, EH4 3LT), *b.* 1913; ed. at Rugby: *m.* 1961, Nancy Melville Blyth, of Juniper Green, Midlothian.——Elizabeth Margaret, *b.* 1909: *m.* 1932, William Edgar Gray Muir, WS, who *d.* 1959, and has issue living, Andrew Gray, *b.* 1934,—George Watson, *b.* 1943,—William James Graham, *b.* 1945,—Mary Elizabeth, *b.* 1937. *Residence,* 42, Dick Place, Edinburgh.

This is a younger branch of the Montgomeries, Earls of Eglinton, descended from Robert Montgomerie of Giffen, yr. brother of the 1st Lord Montgomerie. William, 5th in line from Robert, acquired the lordship of Magbiehill, Ayrshire. The 1st baronet, Sir James Montgomery, M.P. for Peebles 1768-76, was Chief Baron of the Exchequer in Scotland 1775-81. His elder brother, William of Magbiehill, was also created a baronet, but his title became extinct 1831. Sir James, the 2nd baronet, was Lord Advocate of Scotland 1804-06, and represented Peebles for nearly thirty years. The 3rd baronet, Sir Graham (Lord-Lt. of Kinross-shire), sat as M.P. for Peeblesshire 1852-68, and for Selkirkshire and Peeblesshire (C) 1868-80, and was a Junior Lord of the Treasury 1866-68. The 7th baronet, Sir Henry James, was Lord-Lt. for Kinross-shire, and assumed 1907 for himself and issue the additional surname of Purvis-Russell (having *m.* 1882 Mary Maud, MBE, da. of T. Purvis-Russell of Warroch, Kinross-shire), and in 1933 the further surname of Hamilton for himself only. His son, Sir Basil Russell Purvis-Russell-Hamilton-Montgomery, 8th baronet, was recognized in that name by decree of Lord Lyon 1948.

Montgomery Cuninghame, see Cuninghame.

MOON, Creation (U.K.) 1855, of Portman Square, Middlesex.

Keep an even mind.

Sir PETER WILFRED GILES GRAHAM-MOON, 5th *Baronet; b.* Oct. 24th, 1942; *s.* his father, Sir (ARTHUR) WILFRED GRAHAM, 1954; ed. at Lancing: *m.* 1967, Mrs. Sarah Gillian Chater, da. of the late Lt.-Col. Michael Carson Lyndon Smith, MC, MB, BS [*see* Smith, Bt., colls., *cr.* 1897], and has issue.

Arms—Argent, an eagle displayed gules, charged on the breast with two swords in saltire proper; on a chief nebuly azure, a fasces erect or, between two crescents argent. **Crest**—A crescent argent, in front of a fasces in bend or, surmounting a sword in bend sinister proper.

Residence—The Old Rectory, Biddisham, Somerset.
Clubs—BEA Executive, and Royal Cork Yacht.

Sons living—RUPERT FRANCIS WILFRED GRAHAM, *b.* April 29th, 1968.——Thomas Edward Bradshaw, *b.* 1972.
Aunt living—Evelyn Lorna Elliot, *b.* 1903: *m.* 1st, 1928, Edward Sydney Hogg, from whom she obtained a divorce 1933; 2ndly, 1939, Robert Barry Chambers, from whom she obtained a divorce 1947. *Residence*, Sloane House, 97, Sloane St., SW1.

Collateral Branch living.
Issue of the late Rev. Cecil Graham Moon, youngest son of 2nd baronet, *b.* 1867, *d.* 1948: *m.* 1898, Mary Andalusia, who *d.* 1970, da. of John Barnard Hankey:—

Arthur GrahamWalker's Knowe, Jedburgh, Roxburghshire; RAF Club), *b.* 1901; ed. at Rugby; Fl.-Lt. RAF (ret.): *m.* 1st, 1931, Nancy Dorothy (who obtained a divorce 1936), da. of the late Alan Paull; 2ndly, 1936, Elizabeth Helen (Betty) Ewing.——Edward Horace Graham, *b.* 1904; ed. at Eton, and at Magdalen Coll., Oxford (BA), late 15th/19th Hussars: *m.* 1931, Cynthia Rosamond, da. of L. Avery, and has issue living, John Jeremy Edward Graham (Cavalry Club), *b.* 1932; ed. at Sherborne; Maj. 15th/19th Hussars (ret.): *m.* 1st, 1958, Jane Mary, from whom he obtained a divorce, 1964, da. of T. J. Cundy, of Broughton, Lincs; 2ndly, Dorrit, el. da. of Gert Anderson, of Gongehusevej 174, Copenhagen, Denmark, and has issue living (by 1st m.), Francis Edward Graham, *b.* 1962, Caroline Rachel Graham, *b.* 1960, (by 2nd m.) Christian Graham *b.* 1967, Thomas Edward Graham *b.* 1969,—Camilla Mary Graham, *b.* 1939. *Residence*, Thurlby, Aubourn, Lincoln. *Club*, Cavalry.——John Cecil Graham, *b.* 1919; ed. at Eton; Maj. (ret.) 15th/19th Hussars: *m.* 1952, Susan Mary Milburn, yr. da. of the late Edward Reed, of Ghyllheugh, Longhorsley, Northumberland, and has issue living, Belinda Mary Graham, *b.* 1954,—Amanda Jane Graham, *b.* 1958,—Philippa Anne Graham, *b.* 1959. *Residence*, Dovebank House, Sudbury, Derbyshire.

The 1st baronet, Sir Francis Graham Moon, an eminent fine-art publisher, and Lord Mayor of London 1854-5, was created a baronet during his Mayoralty in recognition of the visit of the late Emperor (Napoleon III.) and the Empress of the French to the Guildhall, April 1855. Sir (Arthur) Wilfred Graham Moon, the 4th baronet, was A.D.C. to Gov. of Fiji 1929-31.

MOON, Creation (U.K.) 1887, of Copsewood, Stoke, co. Warwick.

Vincit omnia veritas.
Truth conquers all things.

Sir JOHN ARTHUR MOON, 4th *Baronet, b.* Oct. 27th, 1905; *s.* his brother, Sir RICHARD, 1961; ed. at Cottismore Sch.; Master (retired) Merchant Navy; has Roy. Humane So.'s Bronze Medal: *m.* 1939, Rene Henriette Maria Dolores, who *d.* 1949, only da. of the late Joseph Amedee Amedet, of Le Mans, France.

Arms—Argent, an eagle displayed gules; two flaunches of the last, each charged with a fleur-de-lis of the field, on a chief of the second three crescents of the first. **Crest**—A fleur-de-lis argent in front of a demi-eagle displayed gules, charged on the breast with an escutcheon of the first bearing a crescent also gules.

Address—c/o Barclays Bank, 138, Park Rd. North, Birkenhead.

Daughter living of 3rd Baronet—Lila Colleen, *b.* 1931: *m.* 1953, George Garroway Little, of 4132, Balkan St., Vancouver, 10, BC, and has issue living, Gregory Robert, *b.* 1959,—Sharon Colleen, *b.* 1961.

Brother living—ROBERT BLAKENEY, *b.* March 3rd, 1908; temporary Maj. R.A.S.C.; formerly 2nd Lt. (W. Lancashire) Field Brig., R.A. (T.A.); 1939-45 War (despatches): *m.* 1st, 1936, Margaret (from whom he obtained a divorce 1941), el. da. of W. H. Law, of West Kirby; 2ndly, 1945, Helen Everard Collier, (from whom he obtained a divorce 1968), da. of the late Col. Charles Henry Willey, RE; 3rdly, 1968, Dorothy Mary, da. of the late Walter Hill, of Sheffield. *Residence*, Bel Air, 11, Westwood Rd., Noctorum, Birkenhead.

Widow living of 3rd Baronet—MARY GERTRUDE (*Gertrude*, *Lady Moon*), da. of the late Herbert E. Waggoner, of Bowen, Illinois, U.S.A.: *m.* 1954, as his second wife, Sir Richard Moon, 3rd baronet, who *d.* 1961.

Collateral Branches living
Issue of the late Jasper Moon, 3rd son of 1st baronet, *b.* 1881; *d.* 1975: *m.* 1910, Isabel, who *d.* 1961, da. of the late Edward Logan, of Llanymynech, Montgomeryshire:—
Edward, *MC* (Edgeway, 203, Upper Chobham Rd., Camberley, Surrey), *b.* 1911: *m.* 1947, Mary, da. of the late Capt. B. D. Conolly.——Roger (Mill House, Ruyton-xi-Towns, Salop), *b.* 1914: *m.* 1950, Meg, da. of the late Arthur Mainwaring Maxwell, DSO, MC, of Moss Vale, NSW, and has issue living, Sarah Corinna, *b.* 1951,—Gillian Adele, *b.* 1954,—Patricia Isolda, *b.* 1955.——Humphrey (9, Kloof Falls, Kloof, Durban), *b.* 1919: *m.* 1st, 1955, Diana, da. of the late F. Basil Hobson, of The Homestead, Freshwater Bay, Isle of Wight; 2ndly, 1964, Elizabeth Anne Drummond, da. of the late George Archibald Drummond Angus, of Pietermaritzburg, Natal, and widow of H. J. Butler, of Lusaka, and has issue living (by 1st m.), Susan Caroline, *b.* 1957,—Vicki Georgina, *b.* 1960,—(by 2nd m.) Jennifer, *b.* 1966.——Ursula, *b.* 1912: *m.* 1945, Peter Henry Joselyne, who *d.* 1958, and has issue living, Hugh Anthony, *b.* 1947,—Nigel Townshend, *b.* 1949.——Mary, *b.* 1913.——Gwyneth Elinor, *b.* 1916.

Grandchildren of the late Sir Ernest Moon, K.C.B., K.C. youngest son of 1st baronet:—

Issue of the late Arthur Moon, MC, QC, *b.* 1882, *d.* 1961: *m.* 1912, Marjorie Isabel, who *d.* 1966, da. of Charles Lancelot Andrewes Skinner, formerly 4th Hussars [E. Bessborough]:—

John Richard Philip, *OBE* (Balhomie, Cargill, by Perth), *b.* 1915; ed. at Eton, and New Coll., Oxford (MA); late Lt. Black Watch; Registrar, Roy. Coll. of Art 1949-60; 1939-45 War, OBE (Civil) 1966: *m.* 1945, Ann Melhuish, and has issue living, Richard, *b.* 1954,—Susan, *b.* 1947: *m.* 1969, Cameron Murray, of Nuthanger, Cargill, Perth, and has issue living, Jamie *b.* 1972, Pollyanna *b.* 1973, Elizabeth Ann, *b.* 1949: *m.* 1971, Matthew Gloag, of Balinadil, Blairgowrie, Perthshire and has issue living, Emma *b.* 19—, a da. *b.* 1974,—Sarah, *b.* 1956.——Penelope Kathleen, *b.* 1924: *m.* 1950, (Count) Thomas Andreas Constantine Lubienski, of 47, Cambridge Rd., Ely, and has issue living, Andrew, *b.* 1952,—Henry Roger, *b.* 1960,—Michael Arthur, *b.* 1962,—Clare Barbara, *b.* 1955.——Christine Marjorie, *b.* 1925: *m.* 1962, Lt.-Cdr. John Bertram Watson, RN (ret.), of Trinity Gask House, Auchterarder, Perths., and has issue living, Robin Bertram Stephen, *b.* 1967,—Rupert Philip, *b.* 1971,—Rosamund Isobel, *b.* 1965.

Sir Richard Moon, 1st baronet (son of Richard Moon, a Liverpool merchant) was Chm. of London and North-Western Railway Co. 1861-91.

MOORE, Creation (U.K.) 1919, of Hancox, Whatlington, Sussex.

I strive against adversity.

(*Sir*) NORMAN WINFRID MOORE, 3rd *Baronet* (has established his claim but does not use the title); *b.* Feb. 24th, 1923; *s.* his father, Sir ALAN HILARY 1959; ed. at Eton, and at Trin. Coll., Camb. (B.A. 1943); Ph.D. Bristol 1954; sometime Lieut. R.A.; Senior Prin. Scientific Officer, Nature Conservancy; European War 1942-45 (wounded, prisoner): *m.* 1950, Janet, *Ph.D.*, only da. of Paul Singer, and has issue.

Arms—Argent on a fesse between two garbs azure, three mullets or (also on an inescutcheon the arms of *Burrows;* azure between three fleurs de lys erminois a sword in pale point upwards proper, pommel and hilt or). **Crest**—In front of a Moor's head proper, a garb, barwise or.
Seat—Hancox, Whatlington, Battle, Sussex. *Residence*—Farm House, Swavesey, Cambridge.

Son living—PETER ALAN CUTLACK, *b.* Sept. 21st, 1951; ed. at Eton.
Daughters living—Caroline Mary Phyllis, *b.* 1953.—— Helena Meriel, *b.* 1957.
Brother living—Richard Gillachrist, *b.* 1931; ed. at Trin. Coll., Camb. (BA); Pres. of Union Socy., Camb. 1955; formerly on editorial staff of *News Chronicle*, and Sec. Gen. of Liberal International; Private Sec. to Leader of Liberal Party: *m.* 1955, Ann Hilary, only da. of the late Wing-Cdr. Charles Cleaver Miles, MC, RAF, and has issue living, Charles Hilary, *b.* 1956,—Rowan William Gillachrist, *b.* 1961,—Charlotte Sydney, *b.* 1959. *Residence*, Hancox, Whatlington, Battle, Sussex.

Sisters living—Hilary Mary, *b.* 1934.——Meriel Edith Milicent, *b.* 1936: *m.* 1961, the Rev. John Keith Oliver, of South Molton Vicarage, Devon, and has issue living, Thomas Hilary, *b.* 1964,— Henry Caspar William, *b.* 1968,—Mary Philomena, *b.* 1971.

Sir Norman Moore, M.D., LL.D., F.R.C.P., 1st Bt. (only son of Robert Ross Rowan Moore, Bar.-at-law, of Broughton, Lancashire), was Emeritus Lecturer on Principles and Practice of Med. at St. Bartholomew's Hospital, and Pres. of Roy. Coll. of Physicians 1918-21.

MOORE, Creation (U.K.) 1923, of Colchester, Essex.

MORIBVS · ANTIQVIS

Sir EDWARD STANTON MOORE, *OBE*, 2nd *Baronet*, son of the late Edward Cecil Horatio Moore, el. son of 1st baronet; *b.* Dec. 28th, 1910; *s.* his grandfather, Sir EDWARD CECIL, Dec. 1923; ed. at Mill Hill; FCIT; Vice-Pres. British Chamber of Commerce for Belgium and Luxembourg 1963-64, and Pres. British Chamber of Commerce in Spain 1969-70; Chm., British Chambers of Commerce in Europe 1969-71; Man. Dir. BEA (Espania), Ltd., Gen. Manager, Spain and W. Med., BEA, and Dir. of Gibraltar Airways; 1939-45 War, as Wing-Cdr. Special Sers. RAF;. OBE (Civil) 1970: *m.* 1946, Margaret, da. of the late T. J. Scott-Cotterell.

Arms—Or, a moorcock in chief between three clusters of harebells proper, all within a bordure vert. **Crest**—On a bush of heather a moorcock as in the arms.

Residence—Church House, Sidlesham, Sussex.

Sisters living—Kathleen Mary, *b.* 1906: *m.* 1943, E. Alan Mortleman, MC. *Residence*, Mary's Meadow, Chelwood Gate, Sussex.——Doris Vera, *b.* 1907: *m.* 1939, Patrick Seeton of 31, York Av., Scottsville, Pietermaritzburg, Natal, and has issue living, John, *b.* 1940,—David, *b.* 1943: *m.* 1964, Jeann Griffioen, and has issue living, Jacqueline, Doris, *b.* 1965.——Audrey Evelyn *b.* 1908: *m.* 1937 (m. diss. 1946), Maj. Ernest P. Shanks, and has issue living, Oliver Edward Pattison, *b.* 1939, *m.* 1965, Amanda Nina, da. of Cdr. James Andrew Stewart-Moore, RN, of Ballydivity, co. Antrim. *Residence*, Sunnybank, Castle, Antrim.

Uncles living—(sons of 1st baronet)—ERIC EDWARD JAMES, *DSO* (of Daleside, Crondall, Farnham, Surrey), *b.* Sept. 24, 1894; ed. at Harrow; Brig. (ret.); Col. R. Inniskilling Fus. 1947-1960; 1914-18 War in France and Belgium (wounded, despatches, 1914 star, two medals), Iraq

1924-25 (medal), 1939-45 War in France, N. Africa and Italy (despatches, DSO); DSO 1943: *m.* 1928, Gertrude, who *d.* 1972, da. of Frank Fellows Vanderhoef, of New York, and has issue living, Mary Elizabeth Deirdre, *b.* 1937: *m.* 1965, David Tudor Evans, of Little Grebe Cottage, Billinge Green, Northwich, Ches., and PO Magadi, Kenya, and has issue living, Peter Edward Gwilym *b.* 1967, Juliet Mary Enid *b.* 1969,—Ronald George (Mount View, Whitford, Axminster, Devon, EX13 7PJ), *b.* 1903; ed. at Camb. Univ. (BA) (formerly Wing-Cdr. RAF; 1939-45 War in N. Africa and Far East: *m.* 1st, 1928, Barbara Kathleen, da. of Charles Elwes; 2ndly, 1942, Angela Mary, da. of Paul Cammiade, and has issue living (by 1st m.), Anne Cecilia, *b.* 1929: *m.* 1954, John Hetherington, 343, MacDonald Rd., Oakville, Ont., Canada, and has issue living, Christopher *b.* 1955, Cary, *b.* 1957, Phillip *b.* 1958, Simon Charles *b.* 1965.

Aunt living (daughter of 1st baronet)—Vera Florence, *b.* 1899: *m.* 1925, John Edward Bradburne, who *d.* 1961. *Residence,* 5, Merewood Court, Carew Rd., Eastbourne.

The 1st baronet, Sir Edward Cecil Moore, senior partner in the firm of Edward Moore and Sons, chartered accountants, of 4, Chiswell St., EC1, was Sheriff of London, 1914-15, and Lord Mayor 1922-23.

MOORE, Creation (U.K.) 1932, of Moore Lodge, co. Antrim.

Sir WILLIAM SAMSON MOORE, 2nd *Baronet ; b.* April 17th, 1891 ; *s.* his father, the *Rt. Hon. Sir* WILLIAM, *P.C., LL.D., D.L.,* 1944; ed. at Marlborough ; is a D.L. and J.P. for co. Antrim (High Sheriff 1944) ; European War 1914-18 : *m.* 1915, Ethel Cockburn Gordon, da. of W. Livingstone Wheeler, of Lennoxvale, Belfast, and has issue.

Arms—Azure, on a chief indented or, a spur sable between two mullets pierced gules. **Crest**—Out of a ducal crest coronet or, a blackamoor's head, face to dexter proper, wreathed about the temples argent and sable.

Seat—Moore Lodge, Ballymoney, co. Antrim.

Son living—WILLIAM ROGER CLOTWORTHY, *TD, b.* May 17th, 1927; ed. at Marlborough; Maj. N. Irish Horse (TA); 1939-45, as Lt. R. Inniskilling Fusiliers; High Sheriff co. Antrim 1964: *m.* 1954, Gillian, da. of John Brown, of Lisburn, co. Antrim, and has issue living, Richard William *b.* 1955,— Belinda Jane, *b.* 1956. *Residence,* Dalshangan, Dalry, Kirkcudbrightshire. *Club,* Naval and Military.

The brave may fall but cannot yield.

Collateral Branch living
Issue of the late Capt. Joseph Roger Moore, 2nd son of 1st baronet, *b.* 1895, *d.* 1951 : *m.* 1920, Florence Amy, who *d.* 1948, da. of Lieut.-Col. John Patrick, D.L., of Dunminning, co. Antrim:—
Jean Florence Helen, *b.* 1923: *m.* 1949, Robert Andrew Young, and has issue living, Timothy David, *b.* 1950,—Alexandra Louise, *b.* 1952. *Residence,* 3, Beryl Road, Noctorum, Birkenhead, Cheshire.

The 1st baronet, the Rt. Hon. Sir William Moore, P.C. (el. son of the late William Moore, M.D., J.P., of Moore Lodge, Ballymoney, co. Antrim), was Parliamentary Private Sec. to Ch. Sec for Ireland (Rt. Hon. G. Wyndham, M.P.) 1902-4, Senior Crown Prosecutor, Belfast 1915-17, and Treasurer, King's Inns, Dublin 1918-20 ; became a Judge of High Court of Justice (King's Bench Div.) 1917, a Lord Justice of Appeal for N. Ireland 1921, and Lord Ch. Justice of N. Ireland 1925; etired 1937; sat as M.P. for N. Antrim Div. of Antrim co. (C) 1899-1906, and for N. Armagh Div. f Armagh co. Nov. 1906-17.

MOORE, Creation (U.K.) 1956, of Kyleburn, co. Ayr.   [Extinct 1971]

Sir THOMAS (CECIL RUSSELL) MOORE, *CBE,* 1st and last *Baronet.*

Widow living of 1st Baronet—PENELOPE (*Lady Moore*), (Bogside House, Monkton, Ayrshire), da. of the late Lt.-Col. Samuel Gurney Sheppard, DSO, and widow of Robert Lawrence Angus, DL., of Ladykirk, Monkton, Ayrshire: *m.* 1950, as his 2nd wife, Sir Thomas (Cecil Russell) Moore, CBE, 1st Bt., who *d.* 1971, when the title became ext.

MORDAUNT, Creation (E.) 1611, of Massingham Parva, Norfolk.
[Name pronounced "Mordant."]

Sir NIGEL JOHN MORDAUNT, *M.B.E.,* 13th *Baronet,* son of the late Eustace Charles Mordaunt, grandson of 9th Baronet ; *b.* May 9th, 1907 ; *s.* his uncle, *Sir* HENRY JOHN, 1939 ; ed. at Wellington Coll., and at Ch. Ch., Oxford; European War 1939-43 as temporary Lieut.-Col. R.A. (despatches, M.B.E.); M.B.E. (Mil.) 1945 : *m.* 1938, Anne, da. of the late Arthur F. Tritton, of Denford Mill, Hungerford, Berks, and has issue.

Arms—Argent, a chevron between three estoiles sable. **Crest**—A Saracen's head full faced proper, wreathed round the temples argent and sable.

Residence—Elsenham Place, Bishop's Stortford, Herts.   *Club*—Buck's.

Ferro comite.
The sword my companion.

Sons living—RICHARD NIGEL CHARLES (Elsenham Pl., Bishops Stortford, Herts.), *b.* May 12th, 1940; ed. at Wellington: *m.* 1964, Myriam Atchia, and has issue living, Kim John, *b.* 1966,—Michele, *b.* 1965.——David Arthur John, *b.* 1942: *m.* 1969, Elizabeth Aske, da. of William Edgel Luke, and has issue living, Katherine Elizabeth Aske, *b.* 1970,—Alexandra Caroline Aske, *b.* 1972.——Peter Anthony Charles (Sparrows Farm, Debden Green, Saffron Walden, Essex, CB11 3LZ), *b.* 1946: *m.* 1972, Angela Mary, da. of Ralph Arthur Hubbard [see B. Addington, colls.], and formerly wife of (Luke Edward) Timothy Hue Williams, and has issue living, Alastair Nigel Charles, *b.* 1974.

Daughter living—Tessa Anne, *b.* 1947: *m.* 1974, David Anthony Nutting [see Nutting, Bt.].

Sisters living—Evelyn Margarette, *b.* 1908: *m.* 1936, Lieut.-Col. George William Anthony Tufton, TD, RA, TA (ret.) [*see* B. Hothfield, colls.]. *Residence*, The Red House, Barkway, Royston, Herts.——Ursula Marion, *b.* 1913: *m.* 1933, Maj. Charles Edwin Awdry, TD, JP, R. Wilts Yeo., who *d.* 1965, and has issue living, Vere Charles, *b.* 1945: *m.* 1972, Lucinda Wright,—Selwyn John (twin), *b.* 1945: *m.* 1970, Anna Douglas Robertson, and has issue living, Tamsin *b.* 1972, Lucy *b.* 1974,—Juliette Cynthia, *b.* 1934: *m.* 1958, John M. Bargman, of Oakleigh, Martins End Lane, Gt. Missenden, Bucks., and has issue living, Christopher *b.* 1961, David *b.* 1964, Helen *b.* 1965,—Patricia Margaret, *b.* 1937: *m.* 1957, Maurice Turner, of Camberley, Surrey, and has issue living, Fiona *b.* 1959, Serena *b.* 1961, Lavinia *b.* 1965. *Residence*, The Old Vicarage, Bowden Hill, Lacock, Chippenham, Wilts.——Cynthia Violet, *b.* 1918.

Daughters living of 10th Baronet—Cicely, *b.* 1889; has Order de la Reine Elisabeth of Belgium. *Residence*, Sourton, nr. Okehampton, Devon.——Winifred, *b.* 1891; has Croix de Guerre: *m.* 1923, John Wilding Geare, and has issue living, Jacqueline, *b.* 1923: *m.* 1947, Maj. Humphrey Bredin,—Gillian, *b.* 1924: *m.* 1948, Maj. George Rodwell, of Whitton Court, Ludlow. *Residence*, Blarich, Rogart, Sutherland.

Collateral Branches living.

Issue of the late Gerald John Mordaunt, brother of 12th baronet, *b.* 1873, *d.* 1959: *m.* 1900, Grace Adeline, who *d.* 1965, yst. da. of the late Col. E. C. Impey, of 33, Holywell, Oxford:—

Eustace John, *b.* 1901 ; ed. at Wellington Coll., and at Univ. Coll., Oxford : *m.* 1934, Anne Frances, only da. of the late Alastair Gilmour, and has issue living, David John, *b.* 1937,—Gerald Charles (Hovell's Farm, Pattiswick, Coggeshall, Essex), *b.* 1939: *m.* 1965, Carol Elspeth, da. of the late Brig. Richard Montagu Villiers, DSO [see E. Clarendon, colls.], and has issue living, James Richard John *b.* 1967, Christopher Charles *b.* 1969, Tania Alexandra *b.* 1974,—Angela Mary, *b.* 1934: *m.* 1955, David Neil Carr, of Yarlet Hall, nr. Stafford, and has issue living, Philip Donald Mordaunt *b.* 1959, Sally Jane *b.* 1956, Judith Anne *b.* 1961. *Residence*, Sea Field Flat, Green Lane, Hayling I., Hants.——Robin Charles *b.* 1909; ed. at Wellington Coll., and at Univ. Coll., Oxford: *m.* 1940, Brita, da. of C. Thoren, of Stockholm, Sweden, and has issue living, Timothy John, *b.* 1949,—Christian Birgitta, *b.* 1946: *m.* 1967, Christopher McVeigh (17, Repton St., Christchurch, NZ), and has issue living, Brita *b.* 1970, Carlotta *b.* 1971. *Residence*, 7, Richmond Av., Nelson, NZ.——Catherine Evélyn, *b.* 1903: *m.* 1947, Maj. Samuel Geirnaert, RE. *Residence*, The Cottage, Newtown, Leominster, Herefordshire.——Joan Helen, *b.* 1905. *Residence*, Sea Field, Hayling I., Hants.

Grandchildren of the late Harry Mordaunt, 4th son of the late John Mordaunt, 17th Lancers (infra):—
Issue of the late Col. Osbert Cautley Mordaunt, D.S.O., Somerset L.I. and Roy. Corps of Signals; *b.* 1876, *d.* 1949: *m.* 1905, Constance Katherine, who *d.* 1964, da. of the late Capt. R. N. Young, RHA, of Orlingbury, Northamptonshire:—
Anthony Osbert, *b.* 1907; ed. at Malvern Coll.; Maj. Somerset LI.

Issue of the late Christopher John Mordaunt, *b.* 1879, *d.* 1954 : *m.* 1st, 1907, Helena Charlotte, da. of the late Capt. R. N. Young, RHA (ante); 2ndly, 1916, Mary Patricia, who *d.* 1975, da. of the late Lt.-Col. J. C. Cautley, Roy. W. Kent Regt.:—
(By 1st marriage) Richard John *VRD*, *b.* 1908; ed. at Woodbridge Sch.; Lt.-Cdr. R.N.R., European War 1939-45 : *m.* 1930, Nancy, da. of the late Major T. C. Toler, D.L., of Swettenham Hall, nr. Congleton, Ches., and has issue living, Thomas Christopher John (The Corner House, Westow, York) *b.* 1934; is Capt. 9th Queen's Roy. Lancers: *m.* 1959, Belinda Madeline, da. of Thomas Cecil Gouldsmith [Laurie, Bt., colls.], and has issue living, Sarah Camilla *b.* 1961, Sophie Jane *b.* 1967,—Rosemary Jane, *b.* 1931: *m.* 1957, Lyndon Bolton, of The Manor House, Castle St., Forfar, Angus, and has issue living, Lyndon *b.* 1958, Timothy William *b.* 1963,—Nicola Anna Mary, *b.* 1944. *Residence*, The Lodge Farm, Chavenage, Tetbury, Glos.——(By 2nd m.) Stephen Clare (Horseshoe House, 51, Sydney Bldgs., Bath, BAZ 6DB), *b.* 1925; Master Mariner, Capt. P & O SN Co.: *m.* 1950, Joan, da. of the late Louis Henry Poppleton, of Nightingale Villa, Batheaston, and has issue living, Guy Roger, *b.* 1952; ed. at Grenville Coll., Bideford,—Ann Patricia, *b.* 1956.——Katherine Patricia, *b.* 1918: *m.* 1950, David Isard, of Wyke Croft, 36, Brandy Hole Lane, Chichester, and has issue living, John David, *b.* 1951; ed. at Cranleigh, and Leicester Univ.

Granddaughters of the late John Mordaunt, 17th Lancers, son of the late Rev. Charles Mordaunt, son of the late Rev. Charles Mordaunt, 2nd son of 6th baronet :—
Issue of the late Francis Lionel Mordaunt, *b.* 1845, *d.* 1918: *m.* 1889, Sara Elliot, who *d.* 1939, da. of the late William St. John Elliot Marshall, of Natchez, Mississippi, U.S.A.:—
Elizabeth Morris, *b.* 1891: *m.* 1918, Drayton Burrill, of 1, Armstrong Rd., Morristown, New Jersey, USA 07960, and has issue living, Gerald Drayton, *b.* 1921,—Helena Van Cortlandt, *b.* 1924.—Mildred Cumberlege, *b.* 1893: *m.* 1st, 1916, David Ogden Rogers, who *d.* 1928; 2ndly, 1929, Arthur Spencer Kittle, and has issue living, (by 1st marriage) Francis Lionel Mordaunt, *b.* 1917,—Nathalie Pendleton, *b.* 1922. *Residence*, 42, West 9th Street, New York, 11, USA.
Issue of the late Katherine Mordauut, *b.* 1862, *d.* 1953: *m.* 1896, Albert E. Masters, who *d.* 1901:—
Elsie Katherine (Kingswood Lodge, Sunningdale, Berks.), *b.* 1898: *m.* 1937, Stuart Fortune, who *d.* 1951.

Osbert le Mordaunt, a Norman knight, was possessed of Radwell, in Bedfordshire, by the gift of his brother, who had it of William I. for his services, and for the services of his father, in the conquest of England. The 1st baronet, Sir l'Estrange Mordaunt, distinguished himself in the wars of the Low Countries, *temp.* Elizabeth I. Sir Charles, the 3rd baronet, had his estates sequestered for his loyalty to Charles I. The 5th, 6th, 7th, 9th, and 10th baronets each represented Warwickshire in Parliament, while the 7th baronet was also a Groom of the Bedchamber.

HUGHES-MORGAN, Creation (U.K.) 1925, of Penally, co. Pembroke.

Sir DAVID JOHN HUGHES-MORGAN, *CBE*, 3rd
Baronet; b. Oct. 11th, 1925; *s.* his father, *Sir*
JOHN VERNON, 1969; ed. RN Coll., Dartmouth;
Lt. RN (ret.); Col. Army Legal Sers. ; 1939-45
War; MBE (Mil) 1959, CBE (Mil) 1973 :*m.* 1959,
Isabel Jean Blacklock Gellatly Milne, da. of John
Milne Lindsay, of Annan, Dumfriesshire, and has
issue.

Arms—Quarterly, 1st and 4th, a griffin segreant sable, over all
a chevron of the second charged with a mullet between two fleur-
de-lis of the first, *Morgan*; 2nd and 3rd, sable, a lion rampant
guardant between two fleur-de-lis in fesse or; on a chief engrailed
of the second, two Cornish choughs proper, *Hughes*. **Crest**—1st,
in front of a reindeer's head erased or, collared and chained sable,
a fleur-de-lis between two mullets also sable, *Morgan*; 2nd, in
front of a demi-lion rampant guardant argent, charged on the
shoulder with a fleur-de-lis sable, two swords saltireways proper,
pommels and hilts or, *Hughes*.

Address—c/o National Westminster Bank, Brecon.

Without God, without anything.

Sons living—IAN PARRY DAVID, *b.* Feb. 22nd, 1960.——
Jonathan Michael Vernon, *b.* 1962.——Mark Richard Milne,
b. 1964.

Brother living—Thomas Parry Michael JONES-PARRY, *b.* 1928; ed. at Malvern; Capt. (ret.) S.
Wales Borderers; assumed by deed poll 1961, the surname of Jones-Parry in lieu of his
patronymic: *m.* 1952, Gillian, da. of R. C. Stern, of Arden, Weybridge, Surrey, and has issue
living, David Anthony, *b.* 1954,—Caroline Anne, *b.* 1953: *m.* 1975, Baron H. M. F. d'Achon, of
Paris,—Sarah Margaret, *b.* 1961. *Residence*, Woodham House, Burghclere, Newbury, Berks.

Aunts living (daughters of 1st baronet)—Violet, *b.* 1897: *m.* 1921, Wing-Com. Brian Spencer Lewin
RAF, and has issue living, Joan Daphne Spencer, *b.* 1922: *m.* 1946, Sqdn. Ldr. R. E. B. Manson
RAF, and has issue living, Christopher *b.* 1950, Jane *b.* 1952,—Cicely Patricia Spencer, *b.* 1923:
m. 1946, Maj. B. E. Holford-Walker, R. Tank Regt., and has issue living, Michael *b.* 1947, Patrick
b. 1952, Suzanne *b.* 1950. *Residence*, The Forge Cottage, Ifield, Crawley, Sussex.——Iris (High
Trees, Hardwick Rd., Whitchurch, Pangbourne, Berks.), *b.* 1905: *m.* 1924, William Haddon
Howard, who *d.* 1965, and has issue living, Richard Percival (Coombe Park, Whitchurch, Pangbourne, Berks.), *b.* 1936: *m.* 1957, Sheila Ann, da. of John McNab, and has issue living, William
b. 1959, Andrew *b.* 1961, James, *b.* 1962, Duncan *b.* 1967, Suzanna *b.* 1958.

Widow living of 2nd Baronet—LUCIE MARGARET (*Margaret, Lady Hughes-Morgan*) (The Old
Rectory, Mordiford, Hereford), only child of the late Thomas Jones Parry, of Llwyn-Onn Hall,
Denbighshire: *m.* 1923, Sir John Vernon Hughes-Morgan, 2nd Bt., who *d.* 1969.

Collateral Branch living

    Issue of the late Sqdn.-Ldr. David James Hughes-Morgan, RAF, yr. son of 1st
    baronet, *b.* 1903, *d.* 1967: *m.* 1935, Evelyn, who *d.* 1965, da. of John Windsor-
    Richards, of Plas, Caerleon, Mon.:—
Elizabeth Dolores, *b.* 1936: *m.* 1960, John Brill, MA, of Hillside, Calvert Rd., Dorking, Surrey,
 and has issue living, Timothy John, *b.* 1965, Jonathon Richard, *b.* 1966,—Edward James,
b. 1969.

  The 1st baronet, Sir David Hughes-Morgan (son of the late David Morgan, of Henllys, Llandovery), was Chm. of *Western Mail*, and High Sheriff of Breconshire 1898-9. He assumed by deed
poll (enrolled in College of Arms) 1925 the additional surname of Hughes.

MORRIS, Creation (U.K.) 1806, of Clasemont, Glamorganshire.

Sir CEDRIC LOCKWOOD MORRIS, 9th
Baronet; b. Dec. 11th, 1889; *s.* his father, *Sir*
GEORGE LOCKWOOD, Nov. 1947; ed. at Charter-
house; European War 1914-19 with Remount Ser.

Arms—Sable, on a saltire engrailed ermine a bezant, charged
with a cross couped gules. **Crest**—A lion rampant or, charged on
the shoulder with a cross couped gules, within a chain in the
form of an arch or.

Residence—Benton End, Hadleigh, Suffolk.

By the shield of faith.

Sister living—Nancy Wilhelmina Lockwood, *b.* 1893. *Residence*, The Glade, Pishill Bottom, Henley-on-Thames.

Sister living of 7th Baronet—Catherine Daisy: *m.* 1904,
George Rollings, and has issue living, a da., *b.* 19—: *m.*
19—. *Residence*,

Daughter living of 6th Baronet—Gwladys, *b.* 1890: *m.*
19—.

Widow living of 7th Baronet—OLIVE IRENE (*Lady Morris*), da
of William Davies, of Swansea: *m.* 1938, Sir Herbert Edward
Morris, 7th baronet, who *d.* Aug. 1947. *Residence*, 29, Belle
Vue Road, West Cross, Swansea.

Collateral Branches living.

    Issue of the late Frank Hall BYNG-MORRIS,
    brother of 8th baronet, *b.* 1869, *d.* 1954
    (having assumed by deed poll 1927 the
    additional surname of Byng): *m.* 1913,
    Irene Catherine, who *d.* 1968, da. of
Lt.-Col. Rogers-Harrison, of Kenilworth, Pittville Lawn, Cheltenham:—

Daphne Veronica, *b.* 1914 : *m.* 1942, Norman Halfhead, and has issue living, Christopher Norman,
 b. 1946. *Residence*, Beech House, Seal, Sevenoaks, Kent.

Issue of the late Col. John Morris, 2nd son of 3rd baronet, *b.* 1850, *d.* 1916: *m.* 1881 Jessie, who *d.* 1941, da. of William Fowler :—
Jessie Harriett Amy Blanch : *m.* 1923, Capt. Bertram Wellington Parker, late Queen's Own Roy. W. Kent Regt. *Residence,* The Firs, Chelston, Torquay.

Grandchildren of the late George Byng Morris, 2nd son of 2nd baronet :—
Issue of the late Charles Smith Morris, *b.* 1854, *d.* 1933 : *m.* 1888, Maud Mary, who *d.* 1936, da. of the late Rev. George Alston, R. of Studland, Dorset:—

Mabel Travers. *Residence,* 22, Sydenham Villas Road, Cheltenham.——Daisy Emily Smith : *m.* 1930, Brigadier Geoffrey William Auten, O.B.E., Welch Regt., and has issue living, Mary Morris, *b.* 1933 : *m.* 1961, James Montagu Carpenter, of Eardington Manor, Bridgnorth, Salop, and has issue living, Charles James, *b.* 1961, Peter Edward *b.* 1963, Henry William Hugh *b.* 1971. *Residence,* Castle House, Knockholt, Kent.——Lucy Maud: *m.* 1930, Lt.-Col. Francis John Nugee, MC, TD, who *d.* 1966, and has issue living, Lucy Frances Mary, *b.* 1932: *m.* 1955, Keith William Scutts Walker, TD, FRICS, of Holly Lodge, Billett Av., Waterlooville, Hants., and has issue living, Julian Francis Scutts *b.* 1956, Nicholas Charles William *b.* 1961, Sally Henrietta *b.* 1958, Lucy Victoria *b.* 1962, Judy Belinda *b.* 1965,—Patricia Ruth *b.* 1937. *Residence,* The Bungalow, Marle Hill, Cheltenham.
Issue of the late Thomas Byng Morris, *b.* 1866, *d.* 1951: *m.* 1898, Edith Amy, who *d.* 1965, da. of F. S. Bishop:—
Rosamund Byng, *b.* 1900: *m.* 1933, Walter Edgar Aylwin, MC, and has issue living, Charles Byng (Honeywood, The Street, Puttenham, Surrey), *b.* 1934: *m.* 1963, Lesley Dorothy, yr. da. of L. V. Taylor, of Cobham, Surrey, and has issue living, Simon John Byng *b.* 1965, Anthony Charles Barton *b.* 1969,—John Morris *b.*'1942: *m.* 1970, Angela, yr. da. of C. D. Phillips, of Palos Verdis, Cal., USA, and has issue living, Michael Byng Morris *b.* 1972, Christopher John *b.* 1974,—Anne Elizabeth, *b.* 1936: *m.* 1964, Bradford Gary Siegrist, of Vancouver, BC, Canada, and has issue living, William Peter *b.* 1965, Susan Elizabeth *b.* 1969. *Residence,* 1, Links Drive, Norton, Stourbridge, W. Midlands.——Betty Byng (Elmbank, Shaldon, Teignmouth, S. Devon), *b.* 1904: *m.* 1928, Alan Connell, who *d.* 19—, and has issue living, Thomas Alan Byng (of Top Cliff, Shaldon, Teignmouth, S. Devon), *b.* 1936: *m.* 1959, Sylvia Hudson, and has issue living, Christopher Byng *b.* 1960, Debbie Jane *b.* 1963,—Joan Ursula, *b.* 1929: *m.* 1954, John Murray, and has issue living, Francis Patricia *b.* 1955, Jane Penelope *b.* 1958.

Grandson of the late Com. Frederick Morris, 3rd son of 2nd baronet :—
Issue of the late Percy Byng Morris, *b.* 1871, *d.* 1957: *m.* 1912, Ethel Maud, who *d.* 1923, only da. of William Morley Glascott, of Melbourne, Victoria :—
ROBERT BYNG (RR2, Norton Creek Rd., St. Chrysostome, Quebec, Canada), *b.* Feb. 25th, 1913, *m.* 1947, Christine Kathleen, da. of Archibald Field, of Toddington, Gloucestershire, and has issue living, Allan Lindsay, *b.* 1961,—Geraldine Ann, *b.* 1948: *m.* Gilbert Baxter, Jr., of 1735, Waterloo, Vancouver 8, BC, Canada,—Gillian, *b.* 1959: *m.* 19—, Andrew Jamieson, of Lachine, Quebec, Canada,—Roberta Crystal, *b.* 1965.

This family descends from Robert Morris of Bishops Castle and Cleobury, Salop, whose grandson, Sir John Morris of Claremont, was created a baronet in 1806.

Morrison-Bell, see Bell.

Morrison-Low, see Low.

MOSLEY, Creation (G.B.) 1781, of Ancoats, Lancashire, and of Rolleston, Staffordshire.

[Name pronounced "**Mozeley.**"]

Custom ru the law.

Sir OSWALD ERNALD MOSLEY, 6th *Baronet ; b.* Nov. 16th, 1896 ; *s.* his father, *Sir* OSWALD, 1928 ; ed. at Winchester, and at R.M.C.; formerly a Member of Labour Party Executive; 1914-18 War, with 16th Lancers, and RFC; Chancellor of the Duchy of Lancaster June 1929 to May 1930; sat as MP for Harrow Div. of Middlesex (*U,* afterwards *Ind.* and subsequently *Lab.*) Dec. 1918 to Oct. 1924; unsuccessfully contested Birmingham, Ladywood Div. (*Lab.*) Oct. 1924; sat for Smethwick (*Lab.*) Dec. 1926 to Oct. 1931 (resigned from Labour Party and became Leader of *New Party* Feb. 1931); unsuccessfully contested Stoke Div. of Stoke-on-Trent Oct. 1931, and N. Div. of Kensington (*Union Movement*) Oct. 1959 : *m.* 1st, 1920, Lady Cynthia Blanche Curzon, who *d.* 1933, da. of 1st Marquess Curzon of Kedleston (ext.) [see B. Ravensdale]; 2ndly, 1936, the Hon. Diana Mitford, da. of 2nd Baron Redesdale, and formerly wife of the Hon. Bryan Walter Guinness (afterwards 2nd Baron Moyne), and has issue by 1st and 2nd marriages.

Arms—Sable, a chevron between three pickaxes argent. **Crest**—An eagle displayed ermine. *Residence*—1, Rue des Lacs, Orsay, 91, Essonne, France. *Club*—White's.

---

ns living—By 1st marriage—NICHOLAS, *MC* (*Baron Ravensdale*), *b.* June 25th, 1923; *s.* his maternal Aunt, as 3rd Baron Ravensdale 1966 [see that title].——Michael, *b.* 1932; ed. at Eton, and at London Sch. of Economics. *Residence*, Durham Cottage, Christchurch St., Chelsea, SW3.——**By 2nd m.**—Oswald Alexander (Flat 14, 36, Westbourne Terr., W2), *b.* 1938; ed. at St. Martin de France, Pontoise, and Ohio State Univ.: *m.* 1975, Charlotte Diana, da. of George Gosselin Marten, MVO, DSC [see By. Alington].——Max Rufus (School Lane Cottage, Oakley, Aylesbury, Bucks.), *b.* 1940; ed. at Ch. Ch., Oxford: *m.* 1960, Jean Marjorie, da. of James Taylor, and has issue living, Alexander James, *b.* 1970,—Patrick Max, *b.* 1972.

Daughter living—By 1st marriage—Vivien Elisabeth, *b.* 1921: *m.* 1949, Desmond Francis Forbes Adam, who *d.* 1958 [*see* Adam, Bt., colls., *cr.* 1917]. *Residence*, 11, Mulberry Walk, Chelsea S.W.3.

Brother living—Edward Heathcote, *b.* 1899; ed. at Rugby, and RMC; Maj. 1st Dragoons (ret.): *m.* 1st, 1923, Sylvia (who obtained a divorce 1932), da. of the late Lt.-Col. Herbert Alford John, son, of Allestree Hall, Derby; 2ndly, 1943 Edith Victoria, da. of the late T. Leech, of Malvern: and has issue living, (by 1st m.) John Ronald (c/o Barclays Bank, 43, South End Rd., Hampstead, NW3) *b.* 1926; ed. at Stowe: *m.* 1st, 1956, Primrose Antoinette, from whom he obtained a divorce 1970, da. of the late F. G. Hadwen, of The Cottage, Rock, nr. Wadebridge; 2ndly, 1972, Caroline Rosalind, da. of H. H. S. Hillier, of Flat 2, 82, Sloane St., SW1, and has issue living (by 1st m.), Clare *b.* 1958, Charlotte Louise *b.* 1960.—Veronica *b.* 1924: *m.* 1954, Peter Hawker, of Topsham Bridge, nr. Kingsbridge, and has issue living, Annabel *b.* 1957. *Residence*, South Cottage, Wigborough, South Petherton, Som.

Collateral Branches living.

Issue of the late John Arthur Noel Mosley, yst. son of 5th baronet, *b.* 1901, *d.* 1973: *m.* 1st, 1925 (m. diss. 1936), Caroline Edith Sutton, da. of the late Lt.-Col. George D. Timmis of Matson House, Glos.; 2ndly, 1936, Anne Marie Vaudescal-Vartejanu (92, Rue Raynonard, Paris XVI):—

(By 1st m.) Timothy John Oswald (Boodle's Club), *b.* 1926; ed. at Eton; late Lt. Coldm. Gds.: *m.* 1st, 1955, Pamela, da. of R. Kirk Askew, of New York; 2ndly, 1958, Brighid Sarah, da. of the late Lt. Col. the Hon. Michael Thomas Henderson [see B. Faringdon, colls.].——Simon James (23, Little Boltons, SW10), *b.* 1927; ed. at Eton and Ch. Ch., Oxford (MA); Solicitor 1957; late Lt. Coldm. Gds.: *m.* 1957, Maria, da. of Iraklis Zeri, of Athens, and has issue living, George Christopher, *b.* 1959; ed. at Eton,—Claire Amalia, *b.* 1964.

Grandchildren of the late Lieut.-Col. John Edward Paget Mosley, son of Capt· William Bayley Mosley, son of the Rev. John Peploe Mosley, 2nd son of 1st baronet:—

Issue of the late Capt. John William Paget Mosley, *b.* 1872, *d.* 1938: *m.* 1st, 1904, Mary Constance Adela, who *d.* 1915, el. da. of the late George Herbert Strutt, J.P., D.L., of Bridgehill, Belper ; 2ndly, 1937, Mary Euphrasia, O.B.E., who *d.* 1952, da. of the late Godfrey Wedgwood, J.P.:—

By 1st m.) William George (Trewolla, Felsted, Dunmow, Essex, CM6 3EP) *b.* 1905: *m.* 1973, Kathleen Margaret, da. of the late Richard Thomas Olive, of Truro, and widow of William Jones. ——John Herbert (c/o Nat. Westminster Bank, Davey House, Castle Meadow, Norwich, NOR 02D; Conway (Anglesey) Club), *b.* 1912; Lt. RNR (ret.); 1939-45 War in Merchant Navy (wounded): *m.* 1st 1935 (m. diss. 1947), Ethel Marcia Hancock; 2ndly, 1949 (m. diss. 1950), Mrs. Elaine Verna Savory; 3rdly, 1951 (m. diss. 1955), Elizabeth Anna Maria Stefek; 4thly, 1962 (m. diss. 1973), Lyla Fay Hemus, of Auckland, NZ, and has issue living (by 1st m.), Christine Ann, *b.* 1941: *m.* 1964, Clive Dearden, of 22, Freeman Av., Sunnyhill, Derby, DE3 7SG, and has issue living, Rosemary Ann *b.* 1969, Heather Jane *b.* 1971.——Ann Adela Katharine, *b.* 1907: *m.* 1939, Robert de Brath Ashworth, PhD, of Tuck House, Chelmsford Rd., Felsted, Essex, CM6 3DH, and has issue living, John de Brath, *b.* 1948; ed. at Oundle,—Yvonne Lorraine, *b.* 1940,—Denise Ann, *b.* 1943: *m.* 1971, N. A. Bletsos,—Esme Gillian, *b.* 1945: *m.* 1972, John Fitzroy Talbot, MB, BS, MRCS, LRCP, of 36, Malmesbury Rd., Cheadle Hulme, Manchester.

Grandsons of the late Rev. Oswald Henry Mosley, son of Capt. William Bayley Mosley (ante):—

Issue of the late Oswald Feilden Mosley, *b.* 1880, *d.* 1946 : *m.* 1912, Ida, da. of the late William Palmer, of St. Mary Church, Torquay :—

Oswald Henry Feilden, *b.* 1913 ; late Capt. Roy. Armoured Corps : *m.* 1st, 1941, Mary Angele, da. of the late Louis de las Cassat [Heathcoat-Amory, Bt.]; 2ndly, 1952, Olga Marie Noelie, da. of George Ackroyd, and has issue living, (by 1st m.) Sheila Dorothy, *b.* 1942: *m.* 1970, Paul Brissault Minet (Chicheley House, Newport Pagnell, Bucks.), and has issue living, Isobel Louise *b.* 19—. *Residence*, The Gatehouse, Purley Lodge, Purley, near Reading, Berks.——Robert Anthony (of Honicombe House, Callington, E. Cornwall. *Club*, RAF), *b.* 1920; formerly Squadron Leader RAF; is a Dir. of Minleys (Cornwall), Ltd.: *m.* 1944 (m. diss. 1954), Renee Carmen Cecily Assouad, and has issue living, Anthony Noel, *b.* 1949,—Bertha Mary Isobel, *b.* 1945: *m.* 1968, Alistair Maciver, and has issue living, Neil Anthony *b.* 1970, Katherine Anne May *b.* 1968.

Edward Mosley of Rolleston, Staffs., grandson of Sir Nicholas Mosley, Kt., Lord Mayor of London 1599, was in 1640 created a baronet, but this title became extinct in 1655. In 1720 a baronetcy was conferred upon Sir Oswald Mosley of Rolleston, 4th in descent from Anthony, brother of the Lord Mayor, which creation became extinct in 1779. The third creation of a baronetcy in this family took place in 1781 in favour of John Parker Mosley, grandson of Nicholas Mosley, uncle of 1st baronet (cr. 1720), upon whom had devolved the family estates, at the death of his cousin, the Rev. Sir John Mosley, 3rd baronet of 2nd creation. Sir Oswald, 2nd baronet of the present creation, who sat as MP for North Staffordshire, was the last Lord of the Manor of Manchester, having sold his rights to the Corporation in 1845.

EDWARDS-MOSS, Creation (U.K.) 1868, of Roby Hall, Lancashire.

Sir JOHN HERBERT THEODORE EDWARDS-MOSS, 4th *Baronet*, 2nd son of the late Major John Edwards-Moss, R.G.A., 2nd son of 2nd baronet ; *b.* June 24th, 1913 ; *s.* his uncle, *Sir* Thomas, 1960 : *m.* 1951, Jane Rebie, da. of Carteret John Kempson, and has issue.

Arms—1st and 4th, quarterly, ermine and erminois a cross-patée azure between six billets, three in chief and three in base gules, *Moss;* 2nd and 3rd, argent a lion rampant-guardant sable on a chief dancetté of the last two eagles displayed of the first, a canton or, *Edwards.* Crests—1st, issuant from the battlements of a tower or, charged with a rose gules slipped vert, a griffin's head ermine, charged on the neck with a cross-pattée azure 2nd, a rock proper, therefrom rising a dove argent (charged on the breast, for distinction, with a cross-crosslet gules), holding in the beak an olive branch and surmounted by a rainbow also proper.
Residence—Ruffold Farm, Cranleigh, Surrey.

En la rose je fleurie.
I flourish in the rose. **Sons living**—DAVID JOHN, *b.* Feb. 2nd, 1955.——Peter Michael, *b.* 1957.——Paul Richard, *b.* 1960.——Christopher James, *b.* 1963.——Jonathan Francis William, *b.* 1967.

Daughter living—Penelope Anne, *b.* 1956.
Sister living—Rosemary Ethel Amy (8, Moreland Close, Alton, Hants), *b.* 1917.

Collateral Branch living
  Grandchildren of the late Maj. John Edwards-Moss, RGA, 2nd son of 2nd
   baronet:—
   Issue of Capt. Thomas Richard Edwards-Moss, *b.* 1921, *d.* 1974: *m.* 1st, 1943 (m. diss.
   1952), Bridget Doreen, da. of the late Maj. the Hon. Richard Coke [see E. Leicester,
   colls.]; 2ndly, 1953, Monica Hughes (Villa Delfina, Bahar ic Caghaq, Malta, GC), da. of
   the late Maj. H. G. Wilkinson, BSc, Burma Ser. (ret.):—
(By 1st m.), John Richard, *b.* 1947; ed. at Eton.——(By 2nd m.) Stella Lucy, *b.* 1958.

Sir Thomas Edwards-Moss, 1st baronet, assumed, by Roy. licence, 1851, the additional surname
and arms of Edwards, having *m.* 1847, Amy Charlotte, da. and heir of Richard Edwards of Roby
Hall, Lancs.

MOSTYN, Creation (E.) 1670, of Talacre, Flintshire.
[Name pronounced "Mostin."]

Life by the death of the lion.

My help is from the Lord.

Sir JEREMY JOHN ANTHONY MOSTYN,
14th *Baronet*; *b.* Nov. 24th, 1933; *s.* his father,
Sir BASIL ANTONY TREVOR, 1956; ed. at Downside; formerly RN; a partner in Mostyn, Estate
Agents; Green Staff Officer, Investiture of
HRH the Prince of Wales 1969; a Knt. of Honour
and Devotion Sovereign Mil. Order of Malta: *m.*
1963, Cristina Beatrice Maria, da. of Marchese
Pier Paolo Vladimiro Orengo, of Turin, Italy, and
has issue.

 Arms—Per bend sinister ermine and ermines, a lion ram-
pant or. **Crest**—On a mount vert a lion as in the arms.
  Residences—The Manor House, Lower Heyford, Oxon.;
Casa Orengo, La Mortola, Ventimiglia, Italy; 29, Aynhoe
Rd., W14. *Club*—Travellers'.

Son living—WILLIAM BASIL JOHN, *b.* Oct. 15th, 1975.

Daughters living—Casimira Anita Maria, *b.* 1964.——Rache
Johanna Maria, *b.* 1967.

Brother living—Trevor Alexander Richard, *b.* 1946.

Sisters living—Sara Ann, *b.* 1932: *m.* 1957, Ranjit Banerji,
of Isis Farm, Gobardanga P.O., West Bengal, and has issue
living, Bijoya, *b.* 1957,—Sabita, *b.* 1960,—Juthika, *b.* 1963.
——Joanna Mary Patricia, *b.* 1939: *m.* 1960, Hugh Edward
Sarne Griffith (Los Condores, Lima, Peru), and has issue
living, Hugh Pyers Sarne, *b.* 1962,—Isolde Gemma Sarne,
b. 1961,—Bronwen Anita, *b.* 1963,—Samantha, *b.* 1967.

Daughter living of 11th Baronet—Margaret Claire, *b.* 1931.

Uncle living—George Augustus Francis (The Mount, Uckfield,
Sussex), *b.* 1911; late Maj. R. Welch Fusiliers; 1939-45 War
(despatches).

Aunts living—Miriam (Manor Cottage, Presteigne, Radnorshire), *b.* 1904: *m.* 1931, George Moorhead, who *d.* 1966, 3rd son of Henry Moorhead, MD, JP, of Moate, co. Westmeath, and has issue
living, George Michael, *b.* 1932,—Peter Gerald, *b.* 1937,—Bernadette, *b.* 1939; a Carmelite Nun .
——Hermione Mary Josephine (The Garden Cottage, Stewkey, Leighton Buzzard), *b.* 1906:
m. 1942, Joseph Mostyn, Col. Polish Army, who *d.* 1969 (naturalized a British subject 1949,
when he abandoned by deed poll the surname of Tuzinkiewicz), and has issue living, Richard
Jan Joseph (Old Manor Farm, Broughton, Aylesbury, Bucks.), *b.* 1942: *m.* 1966, Annette
Christian Garrick, and has issue living, Suki Hermione *b.* 1968, Melissa Bernadette *b.* 1970,—
Paul *b.* 1945: *m.* 1971, Elizabeth Catherine Bernadette, da. of Peter Northcote Lunn, CMG, OBE
[see V. Gormanston], and has issue living, Theresa Antoinette *b.* 1973,—Simon Edward Basil,
b. 1947: *m.* 1973, Alison Mary Bridget, da. of Capt. J. Thomas, RN, and has issue living, Polly
Elizabeth Hermione *b.* 1973,—Wanda Hermione Krystyna (twin), *b.* 1942: *m.* 1964, Capt.
Terence Percyvall Hart Dyke [see Dyke, Bt., colls.].——Evelyn Margaret Mary, *b.* 1909: *m.*
1934, Richard Angus Hardy, late Maj. Gren. Gds., and has issue living, David Richard Angus,
b. 1938,—Belinda Evelyn Frances Mary, *b.* 1940. *Residence,* Haselour Hall, Tamworth, Staffs.

Widows living of 11th and 13th Baronets—MARGERY (*Margery, Lady Mostyn*), da. of the late
Alfred Stanley Marks, of Sydney, N.S. Wales : *m.* 1927, Capt. Sir Pyers George Joseph Mostyn,
M.C., 11th baronet, who *d.* 1937. *Address,* c/o Midland Bank, 69, Pall Mall, S.W.1.——ELIZA-
BETH MARGARET (DOUGLAS), (Flat 4, 92/94, St. Giles St., Norwich), da. of the late Stephen
Clement Paston Cooper [see Cooper, Bt., colls., *cr.* 1821]: *m.* 2ndly, 1949, as his second wife,
Sir Basil Antony Trevor Mostyn, 13th baronet, who *d.* 1956; 3rdly, 1959, (m. diss. 1966) David
George Longman.

Mother living—Anita Mary, da. of the late Lieut.-Col. Rowland Charles Feilding, D.S.O. [*see* E.
Denbigh, colls.] : *m.* 1931 (marriage dissolved 1949), Basil Antony Trevor Mostyn (afterwards
13th Bt.), who *d.* 1956. *Residence,* 6, London Place, Oxford.

Collateral Branches living.

Grandchildren of the late Lieut.-Col. Edward Henry Joseph Mostyn (infra):—
Issue of the late Capt. Joseph Edward Hubert Mostyn, TD, *b.* 1888, *d.* 1960: *m.* 1920, Gertrude Clare (of St. Ives, Southover High Street, Lewes, Sussex), da. of the late John Hutchinson:—
Edward John, *T.D.*, *b.* 1922 ; ed. at Ampleforth ; is Capt. R.A. (T.A.), and a Qualified Asso. of Land Agents' So. ; formerly Flight-Lieut. R.A.F. ; European War 1941-45 (despatches) : *m.* 1945, Dorothy Brady, and has issue living, Francis Edward Terence, *b.* 1946,—Stephen John, *b.* 1949,—Sara Juliet, *b.* 1955. *Residence*, Peace Haven, Buttshill Road, Woodley, Reading.

Issue of the late Maj. Joseph Cecil Mary Mostyn, MC, *b.* 1891, *d.* 1971: *m.* 1924, Joan Wake, who *d.* 1975, da. of Guy Shorrock:—
Jerome John Joseph (Apartado Postal (05) 16, San Salvador, El Salvador), *b.* 1933; ed. at Downside: *m.* 1st, 1956 (m. diss. 1971), Mary Anna Bridget Ghislaine, da. of Ronald F. Medlicott; 2ndly, 1972, Ana Julia Novoa, and has issue living (by 1st m.), Nicholas Anthony Joseph Ghislain, *b.* 1957,—Mark Francis Joseph Ghislain, *b.* 1959,—Giles Patrick Joseph Ghislain, *b.* 1967,— Joanna Charlotte Mary Ghislaine, *b.* 1963,—(by 2nd m.) Anna Teresa Joan, *b.* 1973.——Philo- mena Mary Cecelia, *b.* 1926: *m.* 1949, Hugh Dudley Symon, MRCS, LRCP, of 39, Church St., Oswestry, Salop, and has issue living, Andrew Nicholas Dudley, *b.* 1950,—Neil Antony, *b.* 1953,— Pyers Hugh, *b.* 1957.——Charmian Mary, *b.* 1938: *m.* 1966, Guy Hipsley Cooper, of The Bake- house, Crabtree Lane, Headley, Hants; and has issue living, Sophie Maria, *b.* 1968,—Jonquil Kate, *b.* 1971,—Alice Teresa Mostyn, *b.* 1972.

Issue of the late Joseph Philip David Mostyn, *b.* 1894, *d.* 1929: *m.* (Jan.) 1928, Mary Catherine (who *m.* 2ndly, 1931, Brigadier James Desmond Seymour Keenan), da. of Richard Cecil Moss:—
Joseph David Frederick, *CBE* (White Ley, Uplyme, Lyme Regis, Dorset), *b.* (Nov.) 1928; Brig. late R. Green Jackets; Brunei 1962 (despatches); Borneo 1963; MBE (Mil) 1962, CBE (Mil) 1974: *m.* 1952, Diana Patricia, da. of the late Brig. Bertrand Cecil Owens Sheridan, MC, and has issue living, Philip Joseph, *b.* 1955,—David Mark Joseph, *b.* 1960,—Rupert Joseph Sheridan, *b.* 1961,— Matthew Anthony Joseph, *b.* 1971,—Celia Mary, *b.* 1953,—Katherine Mary, *b.* 1973.

Grandchildren of the late Capt. Edward Henry Mostyn, 2nd on of 7th baronet :—
Issue of the late Lieut-Col. Edward Henry Joseph Mostyn, *b.* 1857, *d.* 1916: *m.* 1886, Mary Cecily, who *d.* 1916, da. of the late John Reginald Francis George Talbot [B. Talbot de Malahide]:—
Rt. Rev. Monsignor Joseph John Reginald, *DCL, PhD*, *b.* 1903; ed. at Downside, and at Fribourg Univ. (PhD 1927); DCL Rome 1929; is Canon of St. Peter's, Rome, Domestic Prelate to the Pope, and a Protonotary Apostolic: was R. of St. Mellitus, Tollington Park, N4, 1938-52; a Knight of Sovereign Order of Malta, and Knt. Cdr. of Order of Leopold II of Belgium. *Resi- dence*, Palazzo della Canonica, Vatican City, Italy.——Mary Clare (twin), *b.* 1897: *m.* 1929, Capt. Stephen Francis Gaisford-St. Lawrence, RN, who *d.* 1957, and has issue living, Christopher Stephen (of Howth Castle, co. Dublin), *b.* 1930; Capt. late R. Scots Greys: *m.* 1957, Penelope Christian, da. of Lt.-Col. Arnold Drew, RA [E. Lauderdale, colls.], and has issue living, Julian Tristram *b.* 1957, Oliver James *b.* 1965, Antonia Mary *b.* 1959, Edwina Katherine *b.* 1962,—John Francis, (Style Bawn House, Delgany, co. Wicklow), *b.* 1934: *m.* 1965, Susan Iris Hope Clarke, and has issue living, Alexander William *b.* 1966, Hugh Edward *b.* 1968, Giles Cecil *b.* 1969, a da. *b.* 1973,—Susan Mary, *b.* 1936; formerly a Clerk in Household of HRH the Duke of Edinburgh: *m.* 1960, Robert John Turville-Constable Maxwell, of Whitewood House, Yoxall, Burton-on- Trent [*see* L. Herries of Terregles, colls.]. *Residence*, Tower House, Howth Castle, Howth, co. Dublin.——Mary Teresa (twin), *b.* 1898: *m.* 1st, 1919, Cdr. Christopher Montague Vernon Francis Dalrymple Hay, DSC, RN, who *d.* 1944, and from whom she had obtained a divorce 1929 [*see* Dalrymple-Hay, colls.]; 2ndly, 1939, Charles Hugh Fletcher, and has issue living, (by 2nd m.) Sarah Anne, *b.* 1940. *Residence*, Hill House, Lodsworth, Petworth, Sussex.

Descendants of the late Charles Browne-Mostyn, el. son of the late Charles Browne- Mostyn (infra) who became 6th *Baron Vaux of Harrowden* on the termination of the abeyance in his favour 1838 [see that title].

Grandchildren of the late Charles Browne-Mostyn, 2nd son of 5th Bt.:—
Issue of the late Henry Browne-Mostyn, *b.* 1867, *d.* 1946 : *m.* 1901, Virginia who *d.* 1953, da. of Thomas J. McLain, U.S.A. Consul, Bahamas :—
Thomas Mervyn (8900, McGrath Rd., Manassas, Virginia 22110, USA), *b.* 1904: *m.* 1948, Ella Aurora, da. of the late Gustav Larson.——Ruth Mary (Great Mills, Maryland, 20634, USA), *b.* 1902: *m.* 1931, Hughes Adams Shank, who *d.* 1968, and has issue living, David Hughes, *b.* 1941: *m.* 1966, Elaine Christa Furst, and has issue living, Michael Aaron *b.* 1969,—Margaret Elizabeth, *b.* 1936: *m.* 1958, James Patrick Jarboe, MD, of Rosecroft, St. Mary's City, Maryland, USA, and has issue living, Thomas Hughes *b.* 1969, Karen Elizabeth *b.* 1959, Barbara Gail *b.* 1960, Mary Kathleen *b.* 1965, Jessica Rose *b.* 1972.

Issue of the late Francis Llewellyn Mostyn (twin), *b.* 1873 *d.* 1959 : *m.* 1901, Sarah Thornton, who *d.* 1925 :—
Charles Francis Llewellyn, *b.* 1904 : *m.* 1933, Marion McKay, and has issue living, Francis Llewellyn, *b.* 1935 : *m.* 1958, Yvonne Brown, and has issue living, Douglas William Francis *b.* 1959, Donald Mayne *b.* 1960,—Trevor Angus, *b.* 1946,—Gwendolyn Grace, *b.* 1937 : *m.* 1958, Leonard Alexander Gynlai, and has issue living, Edward Llewellyn Alexander *b.* 1959, Sarah Theresa Marion *b.* 1960. *Residence*, Woolford Station, S. Alberta, Canada.

Issue of the late Iltyd Edward Mostyn, *b.* 1881, *d.* 1958 : *m.* 1901, Lily Humphry :—
Iltyd Humphry (Route 109, 1210, Jervis St., Vancouver, B.C., Canada), *b.* 1907: *m.* 1934, Joan Athol, da. of Charles J. Radwell, and has issue living, David Pyers (37, Newbury Av., Ottawa, Ont., Canada, K2E6K7), *b.* 1938: *m.* 1963, Susan Wallace Johnson, and has issue living, Richard Pyers *b.* 1963, David Wallace *b.* 1967, Peter Llewellyn *b.* 1968,—Richard Clive, *b.* 1945.—— Charles Gerald (7-7163, Ash Cres., Vancouver 14, BC, Canada), *b.* 1910: *m.* 1936, Ruth Winonna, da. of William Brown, and has issue living, Trevor Iltyd *b.* 1940.——Gwendolyn Mary, *b.* 1905: *m.* 1939, Charles Allen Higginson, and has issue living, Brenda Lynne, *b.* 1940: *m.* 1963, Kirby Michael O'Donaughy, DDS, Box 276, Rossland, BC, Canada, and has issue living, Denise Margaret *b.* 1964, Theresa Lynne *b.* 1967, Kelly Corinne *b.* 1969,—Kathleen Mary, *b.* 1942: *m.* 1962, Lorne Richard Simpson, of 5900, Unsworth Rd., Sardis, BC, Canada, and has issue living, Thomas Allen *b.* 1967, Barbara Kathleen *b.* 1964. *Residence*, 217, Spadina Av., Chilliwack, BC.

Issue of the late Capt. George William Mostyn, *b.* 1874, *d.* 1939: *m.* 1897, Isabel Almond:—
Vaux Almond, *b.* 1906 ; late Major Australian Imperial Force : *m.* 1933, Mavis Marshall. *Resi- dence*, Adelaide, S. Australia.——Winifred Mary, *b.* 1898 : *m.* 1921, Frederick Nelson, and has issue living. *Residence*, 15, Byron Road, Black Forest, S. Australia.

This is one of the numerous Welsh families which claim descent from Tudor Trevor, who was the ruler of Hereford early in the tenth century. Richard ap Howell, a lineal descendant from the above, was seated at Mostyn, *temp.* Henry VII., and his son Thomas, who assumed the name of Mostyn, is an ancestor in the female line of Baron Mostyn. Thomas Mostyn's yr. brother, Pyers Mostyn of Talacre, was gt. grandfather of Sir Edward, 1st baronet.

MOTT, Creation (U.K.) 1930, of Ditchling, co. Sussex.

Bold in dangers.

Sir JOHN HARMAR MOTT, 3rd *Baronet*, *b.*
July 21st, 1922; *s.* his father, *Sir* ADRIAN
SPEAR, 1964; ed. at Radley, and at New Coll.,
Oxford (MA, BM, BCh); MRCGP; 1939-45
War as F/O RAF: *m.* 1950, Elizabeth, da. of
Hugh Carson, FRCS, of Selly Oak, Bir-
mingham, and has issue.

Arms—Sable, four crescents in cross the horns turned
inwards, argent. *Crest*—An estoile of eight points argent
encircled by an annulet or.

Residence—Daffodil Lodge, Park Rd., Waterloo Park,
Liverpool, L22 3XG.

Son living—DAVID HUGH, *b.* May 1st, 1952; ed. at
Shrewsbury, and Sussex Univ. (BC);MSc. Birkbeck Coll.,
London Univ.

Daughters living—Jennifer, *b.* 1954.——Alison Mary, *b.*
1958.

Sister living—Anne Lawrence (Kerensa Cook's Level,
Gorran Haven, St. Austell, Cornwall), *b.* 1915; ed. at
St. Anne's Coll., Oxford (MA): *m.* 1st, 1939, Anthony
Dockray Phillips, DSO, DFC, RAF, who *d.* (killed in
action) 1944; 2ndly, 1946, Wilfred Robert Peasley,
DFC, RAF, from whom she obtained a divorce 1961,
and has issue living, (by 1st m.) Anthony Adrian (Teddington House, Warminster, Wilts.), *b.* 1942; ed. at Shrews-
bury, and at Merton Coll., Oxford: *m.* 1970, Lucinda Aris, (by 2nd m.) Patricia Mary Anne,
b. 1947: *m.* 1968, Peter James Crowe, of Moogara, Gorran Haven, St. Austell, Cornwall, and has
issue living, Tasman Peter *b.* 1968, James Alywyn e. 1971, Matthew Tristan George *b.* 1973,—
Julia Jane, *b.* 1950: *m.* 1969, Alan Nigel Clark, of 42, Glynbourne Av., Thornlie, W. Aust. 6108,—
Lydia Elizabeth, *b.* 1953: *m.* 1973, David Charles Whetter.——Monica Mary, *b.* 1919: *m.* 1948,
Robert Milne Sellar, of Old Church House, Colyton, Devon, and has issue living, Robert John,
b. 1950,—Mary Milne, *b.* 1949: *m.* 1970, Robin Edward Austin Webb, of 10, The Chase, SW4,
and has issue living, William Austin *b.* 1972, Rachael Frances *b.* 1971.

Collateral Branch living

Issue of the late Mark Dobell Mott, yr. son of 1st baronet, *b.* 1892, *d.* 1975:
m. 1st, 1916, Mary Coryndon (who obtained a divorce 1936), da. of the late
James Henry Greathead; 2ndly, 1936, Martha Lewis (3, Eden Way, Fulwood,
Preston, Lancs., PR2 4TQ), da. of Arthur Willis of Witton Gilbert, co.
Durham:—

(By 2nd m.) Peter Lewis, *b.* 1944; ed. at Manchester Univ. (BA) and Calif. Univ. (MA).——Diana
Dobell, *b.* 1947.

The 1st baronet, Sir Basil Mott, C.B., F.R.S. (son of Frederick Thompson Mott of Birstall Hill,
near Leicester), was a Consulting Civil Engineer and a Past Pres. of Institution of Civil Engineers.

MOUNT, Creation (U.K.) 1921, of Wasing Place, Reading, Berks.

Prudently and constantly.

Sir WILLIAM MALCOLM MOUNT, 2nd
Baronet; *b.* Dec. 28th, 1904; *s.* his father, *Sir*
WILLIAM ARTHUR, *C.B.E.*, 1930; ed. at Eton, and
at New Coll., Oxford; is Lieut.-Col. Reconnaissance
Corps; appointed Vice-Lieut. for Berks 1960;
European War 1939-44 (wounded): *m.* 1929,
Elizabeth Nance, da. of Owen John Llewellyn,
formerly of The Thatched House, Moulsford,
Berks, and has issue.

Arms—Or, on a mount vert a lion rampant azure, ducally
crowned or, between in chief two roses gules, barbed and seeded
proper. *Crest*—Upon a mount vert a fox salient proper, supporting a ragged staff erect sable.

Seat—Wasing Place, near Reading. *Club*—Cavalry.

Daughters living—Cecilia Mary (*Lady Dugdale*), *b.* 1931: *m.*
1967, Sir William Stratford Dugdale, MC, 2nd Bt., of
Merevale Hall, Atherstone, Warwickshire, and Blyth Hall,
Coleshill, Birmingham.——Mary Fleur, *b.* 1934: *m.* 1962,
Ian Donald Cameron, of The Old Rectory, Peasemore,
Newbury, and has issue living, Allan Alexander, *b.* 1963,—
David William Donald, *b.* 1966,—Tania Rachel, *b.* 1965,—
Clare Louise, *b.* 1971.——Viola Clare, *b.* 1938: *m.* 1960,
Dr. John Robert Blyth Currie, of 6, Dakota Rd., Claremont,
Capetown, S. Africa, and has issue living, Thomas Mark,
b. 1966,—Mary Teresa, *b.* 1962,—Anna Magdalen, *b.* 1964.
Brother living—George Richard, *b.* 1911: *m.* 1936, Elizabeth,
da. of the late John A. Baring, of New York, USA, and has
issue living, Serena Georganne, *b.* 1941: *m.* 1969, Claude
Johnson, of 26, Devonshire Pl., W1. *Residence*, Preston
House, East Preston, Sussex.

Collateral Branch living.

Issue of the late Robert Francis Mount, 2nd son of 1st baronet, *b.* 1907, *d.* 1969:
m. 1st, 1938 Lady Julia Agnes Cynthia Pakenham, who *d.* 1956, da. of 5th
Earl of Longford; 2ndly, 1965, Constance Mercer Stearns, who *d.* 1973, da. of
the late Leo S. de Pinna, and formerly wife of Emerson Muschamp Bainbridge:—

By 1st m.) WILLIAM ROBERT FERDINAND, (17, Ripplevale Grove, N1), b. July 2nd, 1939; ed. at Eton, Vienna Univ. and Ch. Ch., Oxford (MA): m. 1968, Julia Margaret, twin da. of Archibald Julian Lucas [see B. Grenfell], and has issue living, William Robert Horatio, b. 1969,—Henry Francis, b. 1971,—Mary Julia, b. 1972.——Frances Leone, b. 1941.

The 1st baronet, Sir William Arthur Mount, C.B.E. (son of the late William George Mount of Wasing Place, Berks), was M.P. for S., or Newbury, Div. of Berkshire (C) Oct. 1900 to Jan. 1906, and Jan. 1910 to March 1918, and for Berks, Newbury Div., Dec. 1918 to May 1922. Parliamentary Private Sec. to successive Chancellors of the Exchequer (Rt. Hon. Sir Michael Hicks-Beach, Bt., M.P., and Rt. Hon. C. T. Ritchie, M.P.) 1900-1902, and Civil Member of British Claims Commn. in France 1916-17.

MOUNTAIN, Creation (U.K.) 1922, of Oare Manor, co. Somerset, and Brendon, co Devon

Safety with the Cross.

Sir BRIAN EDWARD STANLEY MOUNTAIN 2nd *Baronet;* b. Aug. 22nd, 1899; s. his father *Sir* Edward Mortimer, 1948; ed. at Charterhouse; Pres. of Eagle Star Insurance Co., Ltd. (Chm. 1948-73); Chm. of Subsidiary Cos. in S. African Eagle Group, Bernard Sunley Investment Trust, Ltd., British African Properties, Ltd., Eagle Star Insurance of Canada, Eagle Star Group CB 1821 (Belgium), L'Independance Compagnie D'Assurances. Contre Tous Risques (France), English Property Corpn., Ltd., Barbados Fire Insurance Co., United Racecourses, Ltd. and Ashdale Land & Property Co., Ltd.; Pres. of Bernard Sunley Building Co. (Bahamas), and Sceptre Trust, Ltd. (Bahamas); Dep. Chm. Bank of Nova Scotia Trust Co. (UK), Ltd., and subsidiaries in W. Indies; a Member of Council, Racehorse Owners Assocn., Ltd., and a Dir. of African Eagle Assurance Society, Ltd., Australian Eagle Insurance Co., Ltd., Air Holdings, Ltd., British Air Transport (Holdings), Ltd., British Crown Assurance Corpn., Ltd., Trent Insurance Co., Ltd., United Dominions Trust, Ltd., and other Cos.; 1914-18 War as Lt. 9th Lancers and R. Devon Yeo., 1939-45 War as Lt.-Col. 9th Lancers: m. 1926, Doris Elsie, el. da. of the late E. C. E. Lamb. 9f 2, Queen St., Mayfair, W1, and has issue.

Arms—Ermine, on a fesse azure between three lions rampant guardant sable, each holding between the forepaws an escallop gules, three cross-crosslets argent. **Crest**—Issuant from the battlements of a tower proper, a demi-lion guardant argent, holding between the paws an escallop gules.

Residences,—Dunley Manor, Whitchurch, Hants; 75, Eaton Square, SW1.

Sons living—DENIS MORTIMER, b. June 2nd, 1929; ed. at Eton; late Lt. R. Horse Guards; Chm. since 1974 of Eagle Star Insurance Co., Ltd., and Man. Dir. since 1967, Chm. of Home and Overseas Insurance Co., Ltd., Eagle Pensions Funds, Ltd., Eagle Star Group Engineering Insurance, Ltd., Navigators & Gen. Insurance Co., Ltd., British Crown Assurance Corpn., Ltd. Threadneedle Insurance Co., Ltd., Trent Insurance Co., Ltd., and Whitehill Agency Inc., (USA); a Dir. of Army, Navy & General Assurance Assocn., Ltd., Eagle Star Group CB 1821 (Belgium), Eagle Star Insurance Co. of Canada, Liverpool Insurance Soc., Ltd., Midland Assurance Ltd., Rank Organisation, Ltd., English Property Corpn., Ltd., Removers & Gen. Insurance Co., Ltd., and other cos.: m. 1958, Hélène Fleur Mary Kirwan, da. of John Kirwan-Taylor, of La Residence, Corseaux, Vaud, Switzerland, and has issue living, Edward Brian Stanford, b. 1961,—William Denis Charles, b. 1966,—Georgina Lily Fleur, b. 1959. *Residences,* Shawford Park, nr. Winchester, Hants.; 12, Queens Elm Sq., Old Church St., SW3.——Nicholas Brian Edward (26, The Little Boltons, SW10), b. 1936; ed. at Eton, and at St. Catherine's Coll., Camb.; formerly Lt. R. Horse Gds.: m. 1965, Penelope yr. da. of the late M. H. Shearme, of 15, Astell St., SW3, and has issue living, Henry Nicholas b. 1967,—Nathalie Frances, b. 1970.

Daughter living—Fleur Caroline, b. 1933: m. 1955, Dane Peter Douetil, of Busbridge Lakes House, Godalming, Surrey, and has issue living, Dane Jonathan, b. 1960,—Guy William, b. 1963,—William Walton, b. 1966,—Nicola Fleur, b. 1957.

The 1st baronet, Sir Edward Mortimer Mountain (son of the late Henry Stanford Mortimer Mountain), was Chm. of Eagle Star Insurance Co., Ltd.

MOWAT, Creation (U.K.) 1932, of Cleckheaton, West Riding of Yorkshire. [Extinct 1968]

Sir ALFRED LAW MOWAT, DSO, OBE, MC, 2nd and last *Baronet.*

Daughter living of 2nd Baronet—Joan Mary Louise, b. 1923: m. 1951, Michael Norman Shaw, MP, and has issue living, Charles Michael Mowat, b. 1952,—James William, b. 1955,—Jonathan David, b. 1957. *Residence,* Duxbury Hall, Liversedge, Yorkshire.

Daughter living of 1st Baronet—Lucy Marcia. *Residence,* The Grange, Cleckheaton, Yorkshire.

MOWBRAY, Creation (U.K.) 1880, of Warennes Wood, Berkshire.

Sir John Robert Mowbray, 6th *Baronet*; *b.* March 1st, 1932; *s.* his father, *Sir* George Robert, KBE, 1969; ed. at Eton, and New Coll., Oxford: *m.* 1957, Lavinia Mary, da. of Lt.-Col. Francis Edgar Hugonin, OBE, RA, JP [Walker, Bt. cr. 1868], and has issue.

𝔄rms—Quarterly, 1st and 4th, gules, a lion rampant ermine; two flaunches or, each charged with three billets in pale azure, *Mowbray ;* 2nd and 3rd, per pale azure and sable a chevron embattled, between in chief two roses, and in base a cross pattée or, *Cornish.* 𝔠rests—1st, an oak tree or, pendent from the tree an escutcheon gules charged with a lion's head erased argent; 2nd, a Cornish chough between two branches of laurel proper. *𝔰econd 𝔐otto*—" Deus pascit corvos " (*God feedeth the ravens*), *Cornish.*
Residence—Hunts Park, Great Thurlow, Suffolk.

Suo stat robore virtus.

Virtue stands in its own strength.

Daughters living—Mary Clare, *b.* 1959.——Teresa Jane, *b.* 1961.—— Katherine Diana, *b.* 1965.
Sisters living—Carolyn Mary, *b.* 1930: *m.* 1952, Stamford Robert Francis Vanderstegen-Drake, and has issue living, John Peter, *b.* 1955,—Mark Stamford, *b.* 1959,—Clare Rosdew, *b.* 1953. *Residence,* The Old Tannery, Ecchinswell, Newbury.——Elizabeth Rose, *b.* 1936: *m.* 1964, Cdr. Patrick H. R. Glennie, RN (Melverley, Pathfields, Dartmouth, Devon), and has issue living, Christopher Arthur John *b.* 1966, Alexander Patrick *b.* 1969,—Sarah Frances, *b.* 1965.
Widow living of 5th Baronet—Diana Margaret, (*Dowager Lady Mowbray*), (Starvehill House, Mortimer, Berks.), da. of the late Sir Robert Heywood Hughes, 12th Bt. (cr. 1773): *m.* 1927, Sir George Robert Mowbray, KBE, 5th Bt., who *d.* 1969.

The Rt. Hon. Sir John Robert Mowbray, 1st baronet, el. son of Robert Stirling Cornish, of Exeter, assumed by Roy. licence 1847 the surname of Mowbray in lieu of his patronymic, his wife, Elizabeth Gray, being da. and heir of George Isaac Mowbray of Bishopswearmouth, co. Durham, and Mortimer, Berks. He sat as M.P. for Durham City (*C*) 1853-68 and for Oxford Univ. 1868-99, and was Judge Advocate-Gen. and Judge Marshal 1858-59 and 1866-68, and " Father of the House of Commons " 1898-99. The 2nd baronet, Sir Robert Gray Cornish, sat as M.P. for Lancashire, S.E., Prestwich Div. (*C*) 1886-95, and for Brixton Div. of Lambeth 1900-06.

MUIR, Creation (U.K.) 1892, of Deanston, Perthshire.

I am not broken by hardships.

Sir John (Harling) Muir, *T.D.*, 3rd *Baronet* son of the late James Finlay Muir, 2nd son of 1st baronet; *b.* Nov. 7th, 1910 ; *s.* his uncle, *Sir* (Alexander) Kay, 1951 ; ed. at Stowe ; is a Member of Queen's Body Guard for Scotland (Roy. Co. of Archers), and a DL of Perthshire; Chm. of Forth Dist. Salmon Fishery Board, ot James Finlay & Co., Ltd., and Asso. Cos., and of Forth River Purification Board, a Dir. of Roy. Insurance Co., Ltd., London and Lancashire Insurance Co., Ltd., of Scottish United Investors, Ltd., and of National & Grindlays Holdings, Ltd.; 1939-45 War with 3rd Carabiniers and 25th Dragoons and on Staff as Maj. and acting Lt.-Col.: *m.* 1936, Elizabeth Mary, el. da. of the late Frederick James Dundas [*see* M. Zetland, colls.], and has issue.

𝔄rms—Per chevron argent and or, on a chevron cotised azure, a redbreast proper between two mullets of the first, in chief as many fleurs-de-lis of the third. 𝔠rest—A Saracen's head couped, wreathed with laurel proper, charged on the neck with a mullet azure.
Seat—Blair Drummond, by Stirling, Perthshire. *Clubs*—Oriental, Western (Glasgow).

Sons living—Richard James Kay (Box 72244, Nairobi, Kenya), *b.* May 25th, 1939: *m.* 1st, 1965 (m. diss. 1974), Susan Elizabeth, da. of George A. Gardner, of Calcutta, and Leamington Spa; 2ndly. 1975, Lady Linda Mary Cole, da. of 6th Earl of Enniskillen, and has issue living (by 1st m.), Louisa Jane, *b.* 1967,—Catherine Elizabeth, *b.* 1968.——Ian Charles (Well Cottage, Poulner, Ringwood, Hants.), *b.* 1940: *m.* 1967, Fiona Barbara Elspeth, da. of Maj. Stuart Mackenzie, of Tarneybackle, Blackford, Perths., and has issue living, Sophie Amanda Nöel, *b.* 1969,—Lisa Jane Fiona, *b.* 1973.——Andrew Hugh John (Woodcroft House, Chalton, Horndean, Hants.), *b.* 1943: *m.* 1969, Primrose Jean Onslow, da. of Robert B. How, of St. Andrews, Fife, and has issue living, Philip John Frederick Muir, *b.* 1974,—Alexandra Juliet, *b.* 1971.——James Frances, *b.* 1948: *m.* 1975, Griselda C., da. of Sir Anthony Nathaniel Stainton, KCB, and has issue living, a son *b.* 1976.——Robert William, *b.* 1950.
Daughters living—Fiona Mary, *b.* 1938: *m.* 1968, Walker Goetz, of 86, Rue de Bac, Paris, and has issue living, Sebastian, *b.* 1970,—Dominic, *b.* 1971.——Margaret Elizabeth (*Lady Aird*), *b.* 1946: *m.* 1968, Sir (George) John Aird, 4th Bt., of Grange Farm, Evenlode, Moreton-in-Marsh, Glos.
Brother living—Gerald Robin, OBE, *b.* 1917; Lieut.-Cdr. RN (ret.); OBE (Mil) 1941: *m.* 1940, Doreen Margaret Watney, and has issue living, Hugh James Robin, *b.* 1944,—Nicholas John, *b.* 1953: *m.* 1975, Janet Mary Bain, da. of Sir Colin Moffat Bain Campbell, MC, 8th Bt,—Sarah Nadéjda, *b.* 1940: *m.* 1965, Alexos Katsirides, of Athens,—Anne Catriona, *b.* 1943: *m.* 1970, Maj. John Philip Ogilvy Gibb, of Glenisla House, by Alyth, Perths, and has issue living, a son *b.* 1975, —Jean Charlotte, *b.* 1946: *m.* 19—, Lt. Alexander Michael Gregory, RN,—Diana Rachel, *b.* 1949. *Residence*, Braco Castle, Dunblane, Perths.
Sister living—Margaret Vivian, *b.* 1912 : *m.* 1938, Eric Gerald Hayes, who *d.* 1958, and has issue living, David Richard (Factors House, Pityulish, Aviemore, Inverness-shire), *b.* 1939: *m.* 1968, the Hon. Sarah Maclay, da. of 2nd Baron Maclay,—Helen Jane, *b.* 1941. *Residence*, Craigdhu, Barbreck, Lochgilphead, Argyll.

Collateral Branches living.

       Issue of the late John Buchanan Muir, 3rd son of 1st baronet, *b.* 1876, *d.* 1956:
          m. 1911, Agnes Heather Gardiner, who *d.* 1961, da. of the late John Gardiner
          Muir, of 2, Grosvenor Cres., S.W.
Diana Heather, *b.* 1915 : *m.* 1950, John Anthony Francis Binny, and has issue living, **Anne**
Heather, *b.* 1951.—Katherine Emma, *b.* 1953.   *Residence,* Kiftsgate Court, Campden, Gloucester-
shire.——Bettine Clara (Hidcote Vale, Campden, Glos.) *b.* 1917.
       Issue of the late Matthew William Muir, youngest son of 1st baronet, *b.* 1878, *d.*
        1922 : *m.* 1912, Clara Gardiner (who *d.* 1952, having *m.* 2ndly, 1925, Major
        David Johnstone Mitchell, M.C., who *d.* 1954, late King's Roy. Rifle Corps),
        youngest da. of John Gardiner Muir :—
Gillian Rachel, *b.* 1914: *m.* 1940, Evan Morgan Williams, and has issue living, Ian Muir, *b.* 1942,—
Hugh Frederick, *b.* 1943.   *Residence,* Knockaney Stud Hospital, co. Limerick, Ireland.

    The 1st baronet, Sir John Muir, was Lord Provost of Glasgow 1889-92.   The 2nd baronet, Sir
Alexander) Kay Muir, was High Sheriff of co. Waterford 1929.

Muir Mackenzie, see Mackenzie.

MULHOLLAND, Creation (U.K.) 1945, of Ballyscullion Park, co. Derry.

    Sir MICHAEL HENRY MULHOLLAND, 2nd
Baronet; *b.* Oct. 15th, 1915; *s.* his father the
Rt. Hon. Sir HENRY GEORGE HILL, 1971;
h.p. to Barony of Dunleath; ed. at Eton,
and Pembroke Coll., Camb. (BA); late Maj.
Oxford and Bucks. LI; Burma 1942-45:
m. 1st, 1942 (m. diss. 1948), Rosemary,
only da. of Maj. David Alfred William Ker,
OBE [Barrington, Bt.]; 2ndly, 1949, Elizabeth M. da. of Laurence B. Hyde, of
Bexhill-on-Sea, and has issue by 2nd m.

    Arms—Azure, a stag's head erased argent between
three escallops or.   **Crest**—An escallop gules.

    Residence—Storbrooke, 31, Massey Av., Belfast, 4.

Always girt.

Son living—By 2nd m.—BRIAN HENRY, *b.* Sept. 25th, 1950; ed. at Eton.
Sister living—Sylvia Patricia, *b.* 1918; formerly a Co. Assist. ATS: *m.* 1939, Maj. Timothy Clephan
Palmer, RA, and has issue living, Richard Timothy Mulholland *b.* 1954,—Clare Amanda, *b.* 1950.
Residence, Ballyscullion Park, Bellaghy, co. Derry.
Widow living of 1st Baronet—SHEELAH, (*Hon. Lady Mulholland*), (Ballyscullion Park, Bellaghy,
co. Derry), da. of Sir Arthur Douglas Brooke, 4th Bt. (*cr.* 1822) [see V. Brookeborough]: *m.* 1914,
the Rt. Hon. Sir Henry George Hill Mulholland, 1st Bt., who *d.* 1971, 3rd son of 2nd Baron
Dunleath.

MUNRO, Creation (N.S.) 1634, of Foulis-Obsdale, Ross-shire.

    Sir IAN TALBOT MUNRO, 15th *Baronet*; *b.*
Dec. 28th, 1929; *s.* his 1st cousin once removed,
Sir ARTHUR HERMAN, 1972.; ed. at Bradfield.

    Arms—Or, an eagle's head erased gules, langued **azure,**
a label of three points of the second charged with three lions'
heads erased argent, and in dexter chief a canton of a Baronet
of Nova Scotia.   **Crest**—An eagle displayed proper, charged
across his breast and wings with a label of three points **gules**
charged with three lions' heads erased argent.

    Residence—38, Clarence Gate Gdns., NW1.

Uncles living—MALCOLM (Whitegates, Rock, Wadebridge,
Cornwall), *b.* Feb. 24th, 1901; FAIA: *m.* 1931, Constance,
da. of William Carter, and has issue living, Mary Lee, *b.* 1935:
m. 1955, David Rex Denny, of Brambles, Woodside, Windsor
Forest, Windsor, and has issue living, Sally Louise *b.* 1961,
Felicia Mary *b.* 1965.——Colin (1, Plantation Way, Storring-
ton, Pulborough, Sussex); *b.* 1903; *m.* 1928, Muriel Esther,
da. of Edgar Llewellyn Jones, of Maesycwmmer, nr. Cardiff.——Donald (12A, Grove House,
Waverley Grove, N3), *b.* 1906: *m.* 1944, Doreen, da. of Harold Weston, of Hendon, NW4.
Daughters living of 14th Baronet—Audrey Muriel, *b.* 1924: *m.* 1946, Donald Ernest Fifield, of
Greystones, Malling Rd., Teston, Maidstone, and has issue living, Richard Donald, *b.* 1947.——
Betty Millicent, *b.* 1926: *m.* 1950, Brian Leslie Wright, of 276, Wokingham Rd., Reading, and
has issue living, Gail Louise, *b.* 1951,—Linda Ann, *b.* 1953.
Daughters living of 13th Baronet—Beatrice Maud, *b.* 1891: *m.* 1919, William Lidyard Bligh, of 2,
Carrington Av., Hounslow, Middlesex, and has issue living, Beatrice Olive Joan, *b.* 1920: *m.* 1944,
Kenneth Sidney Hansford, of 24, Ember Gdns., Thames Ditton, Surrey.—Molly Dora, *b.* 1925:
m. 1953, Philip George Bunker, of 27, Warwick Way, Croxley Green, Herts.——Florence Elizabeth (Hollywood, Cal., USA), *b.* 1897; *m.* 1st, 1918, Robert Cameron, of Glasgow, who *d.* 1928;
2ndly, 1932 (m. diss. 1963), Leonard Frederick Burnett; 3rdly, 1964, Jack Maddock, and has
issue living (by 1st m.) Donald Marsh, *b.* 1922: *m.* 1943, Carole Cunningham, of Liverpool, and
has issue living, Keith, *b.* 1945, Ian *b.* 1947, Craig *b.* 1951, Michelle *b.* 1949, Zhan *b.* 1953,—(by
2nd m.) Roy Beech, *b.* 1932,—Zhan Jacqueline, *b.* 1935,—Sonice Christine, *b.* 1936: *m.* 1954,
Joseph le Parc, of New York, USA.——Grace, *b.* 1908: *m.* 1931, William Price, of 119, Crystal
Palace Rd., E. Dulwich, SE22, and has issue living, Jean, *b.* 19—,—Sylvia, *b.* 19—,—Barbara,
b. 19—.——Gladys, *b.* 1909: *m.* 1st, 1932, M. F. Cooke; 2ndly, 1953, Thomas Sheen, of 25, Siddons

Rd., Forest Hill, SE23, and has issue living, (by 1st m.) Malcolm, *b.* 1933: *m.* 19—,—Cynthia, *b.* 1935: *m.* 1956, Peter Rewita, of 22, Kelly St., Optiki, Bay of Plenty, NZ, and has issue living, Tony *b.* 1957, Makere *b.* 1958, Donald *b.* 1960, Wanda (triplet) *b.* 1960, Tina *b.* 1961, Letitia *b.* 1967'.——Minnie Isabel, *b.* 1914: *m.* 1935, M. Ernest Price, of 6, Springfield Rise, SE26, and has issue living, Ernest Talbot (9, Lawrie Park Rd., Sydenham, SE26), *b.* 1939: *m.* 1965, Patricia, da. of Albert Edward Green,—Jacqueline, *b.* 1935: *m.* 1957, George James Fox, of 8, Springfield Rise, Wells Park Rd., SE26, and has issue living, Dawn Leslie *b.* 1959.

Daughters living of 11th Baronet—Eva Marion (of Foulis Castle, Evanton, Ross-shire), *b.* 1881: *m.* 1904, Lt.-Col. Cecil Claud Hugh Orby Gascoigne, D.S.O., who *d.* 1929, and has issue living, Patrick MUNRO OF FOULIS (Foulis Castle, Evanton, Ross-shire), *b.* 1912; Capt. late Seaforth Highlanders; Vice-Lt.; 1939-45 War (prisoner); assumed by decree of Lyon Court 1937 the surname and arms of Munro of Foulis in lieu of his patronymic, and recognized as Ch. of Clan Munro: *m.* 1946, Eleanor Mary, da. of Capt. the late Hon. William Joseph French [*see* B. de Freyne], and has issue living, Hector William *b.* 1950: *m.* 1974, Sarah Margaret Katharine, da. of Henry George Austen De L'Etang Herbert Duckworth [see B. Chatfield] and has issue living, Finnian *b.* 1975, Harry Robert Gascoigne *b.* 1954, John Alexander Seymour *b.* 1959, Charlotte Eva *b.* 1947,—Robert Clifton (The White House, Winchburgh, W. Lothian), *b.* 1915; Maj. late Seaforth Highlanders: *m.* 1st, 1940 (m. diss. 1954), Sylvia Rapozo; 2ndly, 1954, Margaret, da. of the late N. E. Douglas, Menzies, of Newtownairds, Dumfries, and has issue living, (by 1st m.) Robert Hugh *b.* 1941, Caroline Orby, *b.* 1946, (by 2nd m.) Matilda Anne *b.* 1955,—Cecil Alastair Hector, *b.* 1916; ed. at Imperial Ser. Coll., Windsor: *m.* 1947, Jean Muller, who *d.* 1958, and has issue living, Michael Neil Clifton *b.* 1949, Patrick Edward Cecil *b.* 1950,—Marion Erica, *b.* 1906: m. 1934, Brig. George Des Champs Chamier, OBE, KOYLI, of Achandunie House, Alness, Ross-shire, son of the late Sir Edward Maynard Des Champs Chamier, KCSI, KCIE, and has issue living, Anthony Edward Des Champs *b.* 1935, George *b.* 1947, Antoinette *b.* 1938, Georgiana *b.* 1949,—Joan Orby, *b.* 1910: *m.* 1st, 1937, Alastair Gordon-Ingram, Colonial Police; 2ndly, 1947, His Honour Harold William Paton, DSC, of Ardullie Farmhouse, Dingwall, Ross-shire, and has issue living, (by 1st marriage) Donald Alexander *b.* 1938, (by 2nd marriage) Mary Joanne Letitia *b.* 1948.——Aline Margaret (*Lady Wells*), *b.* 1892: *m.* 1915, Adm. Sir Lionel Victor Wells, KCB, DSO (ret.), and has issue living, Thomas Alexander, *b.* 1924; Cdr. RN. *Residence*, Speed-well, The Lane, Prinsted, Emsworth, Hants.

Widow living of Grandfather—Maude Wilmie Primrose, da. of the late Robert Whyte: *m.* 1931, as his 2nd wife, Charles Munro, who. *d.* 1959.

Mother living—Ethel Amy Drusilla, da. of the late Harry Hudson: *m.* 1st, 1928 (m. diss. 1937), Robert Hector Munro, who *d.* 1965; 2ndly, 1937, Marno John Slorach, of 38, Clarence Gate Gdns., NW1.

Stepmother living—Simone (Flat 12, Shirley Hyrst, Gower Rd., Weybridge, Surrey), da. of the late Louis Jean Bareau, and widow of Rudolph Lancaster Fisk: *m.* 1950, as his 2nd wife, Robert Hector Munro, who *d.* 1965.

Widow living of 14th Baronet—VIOLET BEATRICE (*Lady Munro*), (The Pines, 276, Wokingham Rd., Reading, Berks), da. of the late Henry Powles: *m.* 1919, Sir Arthur Herman Munro, 14th Bt., who *d.* 1972.

Collateral Branches living.

Issue of the late Percy Munro, brother of 12th and 13th baronets, *b.* 1870, *d.* 1953: *m.* 1909, Annie Louise, who *d.* 1963, da. of William Henderson Pearson, of Kennington SE:—

Hector George Hamilton, *b.* 1912: *m.* 1947, Clarice Amelia Emily, da. of the late Herbert Pitcher, and has issue living, Desirée Yvonne, *b.* 1944: *m.* 1962, Othman Merichan, of 32, Jalan Maktob, Kuala Lumpur, Malaysia,—Wendy Amelia, *b.* 1945: *m.* 1962, Ray Williams, 12, Ellen Place, Hove.——Irene Louisa (70, Larbert Rd., Streatham, SW6), *b.* 1915: *m.* 1940, William Archer Lawrence, and has issue living, Michael, *b.* 1943,—Iain, *b.* 1944.

Issue of the late Arnold Harry Munro, brother of 12 and 13th baronets, *b.* 1871, *d.* 1968: *m.* 1st, 1895, Matilda Ethel, da. of Samuel Long; 2ndly, 1909, Hilda Marion, who *d.* 1962, da. of William Smith, of Nunhead, SE15:—

(By 1st m.) Margory Ethel (4, St. Faith's Rd., Dulwich, SE21), *b.* 1897.——(by 2nd m.) Kenneth Arnold William (3, Courtrai Rd., Crofton Park, SE23), *b.* 1910: *m.* 1935, Olive Freda, da. of Francis Broome, of Nunhead, SE15, and has issue living, Ian Kenneth, *b.* 1940,—Christine Freda, *b.* 1945.——Roland Alec Wilfred (Maycroft, 223, Crookston Rd., Eltham Park, SE9), *b.* 1911: *m.* 1937, Queenie May Munro, da. of E. Johnson, of Nunhead, SE15, and has issue living, Godfrey Roland, *b.* 1938,—Yvonne May, *b.* 1944.

The 1st baronet, Col. Hector Munro of Foulis, Ross-shire, was created a baronet with remainder to heirs male whatsoever. On the death of his son, Sir Hector Munro in 1651, the title reverted to Sir Robert Munro, 3rd baronet (grandson of George, uncle of the 1st baronet). The 6th baronet, Sir Robert Munro M.P., fought at Fontenoy, and was killed at the battle of Falkirk 1746. Sir Charles Munro, 9th baronet (4th cousin of his predecessor) was distinguished in the Peninsula War, and commanded a Div. of Colombian Army under Bolivar.

MUNRO, Creation (U.K.) 1825, of Lindertis, Forfarshire.

Sir (THOMAS) TORQUIL ALPHONSO MUNRO OF LINDERTIS, 5th *Baronet*; *b.* Feb. 7th, 1901; *s.* his father, *Sir* HUGH THOMAS, 1919; ed. at Winchester, and Magdalene Coll., Camb.; JP for Angus: *m.* 1st, 1925, Beatrice Maude (who obtained a divorce 1932), da. of the late Robert Sanderson Whitaker, of Villa Sofia, Palermo; 2ndly, 1934, Averil Moira Katharine, da. of the late Kenneth O. Hunter, of Garrows, Amulree, Perthshire, and 22, Kingston House South, Ennismore Gardens, S.W.7, and has issue by 1st and 2nd marriages.

Arms,—Or, an eagle's head erased gules, encircled by a branch of laurel on the dexter and of oak on the sinister side, both proper; on a chief argent the representation of an Indian hill-fort, and beneath in letters of gold the word "Badamy"; on a canton gules, a representation of a gold medal presented by the East India Co. to the 1st baronet for his services in Seringapatam in 1790. **Crest,**—An eagle close proper, having a representation of the medal above mentioned pendent from its neck by a ribbon, the dexter claw resting upon an escutcheon gules, charged with a representation of an Indian hill-fort, and beneath in letters of gold, the word "Badamy" as in the arms, and in the beak a sprig of laurel.

Seats—Lindertis, and Drumleys, Kirriemuir, Angus.

Sons living—By 1st marriage—ALASDAIR THOMAS IAN, *b.* July 6th, 1927; ed. at Landon Sch., USA, at Georgetown Univ, Washington, and at Pennsylvania Univ: *m.* 1954, Marguerite Lillian, da. of the late Franklin R. Loy, of Dayton, Ohio, USA, and has issue living Keith Gordon, *b.* 1959,—Karen Fiona, *b.* 1956. *Residence,* River Ridge, Waitsfield, Vermont, USA ——**By 2nd m.—**James Kenneth Torquil, *b.* 1941: *m.* 1970, Camilla Ann, yr. da. of he late Cdr. J. Nigel Ball, RN, and has issue living, a da., *b.* 1973.

Daughter living—By 2nd marriage—Fiona Margaret (*Hon. Mrs. Nicholas H. E. Hopkinson*), *b.* 1937 : *m.* 1957, the Hon. Nicholas Henry Eno Hopkinson, only son of 1st Baron Colyton. *Residence,* Maidenhatch Farm, Tidmarsh, near Reading, Berks.

Sisters living—Morna Violet, *b.* 1895 : *m.* 1919, Ian Charles Ronald Walker Munro (infra), who *d.* 1952. *Residences,* Wornstall, Newbury, Berks. ; Drumfork, Blairgowrie, Perthshire.—— Carmen Ida Constance, *b.* 1896. *Residence,* Ruthven Mill, Meigle, Perthshire.

Collateral Branches living.

Grandchildren of the late Ian Charles Ronald Walker-Munro (infra):—
Issue of the late Thomas Ian Michael Walker-Munro, *b.* 1922, *d.* 1965: *m.* 1947, the Hon. Marjorie Amy Biddulph (Hurdcott House, Barford St. Martin, Salisbury, Wilts.), da. of 3rd Baron Biddulph:—
Thomas Malcolm, *b.* 1948.——Sarah Amy, *b.* 1950: *m.* 1973, Capt. Melville Stewart Jameson, R. Scots Dragoon Gds.

Grandchildren of the late Lieut.-Com. Edward Lionel Walker-Munro, R.N., 2nd son of 3rd baronet :—
Issue of the late Ian Charles Ronald Walker-Munro *b.* 1889, *d.* 1952 : *m.* 1919, Morna Violet (ante), da. of Sir Hugh Thomas Munro, 4th Bt.:—
Patrick Angus (Box 14, Kilifi, Kenya), *b.* 1924: *m.* 1950, Mary Barnett, da. of the late R. Y. Phillips, and has issue living, Ian David Torquil, *b.* 1951,—Charles Michael Angus, *b.* 1953.—— Lionel Malcolm (20, Little Chester St., SW1), *b.* 1929.——Roderick Hugh (twin) (Mains of Kinnettles, Forfar, Angus), *b.* 1929: *m.* 1965, Irene, da. of Robert Watt Edgar, and has issue living, Evan Torquil Drummond, *b.* 1965,—Geordie Roderick Hamish, *b.* 1968.

This family descends from John Munro, 1st of Milntown, yr. son of Hugh Munro, 9th of Foulis. The 1st baronet, Maj.-Gen. Sir Thomas K.C.B., was Governor of Madras 1820-27.

Munro-Lucas-Tooth, see Tooth.

MUNTZ, Creation (U.K.) 1902, of Clifton-on-Dunsmore, Warwickshire. [Extinct 1940.]

Lieut. Sir GERARD PHILIP GRAVES MUNTZ, *R.N.*, 3rd and last *Baronet ; d.* (killed in action during European War) 1940.

Daughters living of 2nd Baronet—By 1st marriage—Enid Avril, *b.* 1894: *m.* 1917, Capt. Geoffrey Farrington Evans, O.B.E., R.E., who *d.* 1951. *Residence,* Old Post Cottage, Amport, Andover.——**By 2nd marriage—**Ora Henrietta (St. Anthony's House, The Strand, Lympstone, Exmouth), *b.* 1911.——Désirée Violet, *b.* 1916: *m.* 1940, Capt. Alfred John Spencer, Hancock, King's Roy. Rifle Corps, and has issue living, Gerard Spencer MOLYNEUX (Lower Bent Farm, Hyssington, Ponys), *b.* 1948, assumed the surname of Molyneux by deed poll 1968,— Antonia *b.* 1946. *Residence,* Caudle Green Farmhouse, Cheltenham, Glos.

Collateral Branch living.

Issue of the late Cecil Albert Muntz, 3rd son of 1st baronet, *b.* 1870, *d.* 1931 : *m.* 1912, Gladys Mary, who *d.* 1962, da. of the late Charles Edward Buckland, C.I.E. [E. Crawford, colls.]:—
Pearl Rosalie Evelyn (c/o Union de Banques, Suisses, Vevey, Switzerland), *b.* 1913: *m.* 1954, Capt. John Edward Davis Manlove, Indian Army, who *d.* 1964.——Laura Cecilia, *b.* 1918: *m.* 1942, Albert Moreillon, and has issue living, Charles Philippe, *b.* 1946,—Yvonne Françoise, *b.* 1943,—Josiane Elisabeth, *b.* 1944,—Claire Antoinette, *b.* 1951,—Madeleine Josephine, *b.* 1955,— Isabelle Laura, *b.* 1959. *Residence,* Chalet Mirastel, 1885, Chesières, Switzerland.

MURRAY, Creation (N.S.) 1628, of Blackbarony, Peeblesshire.

Fear God.

Sir ALAN JOHN DIGBY MURRAY OF BLACK-BARONY, 14th *Baronet,* son of the late Alan Digby Murray, 4th son of 11th baronet; *b.* June 22nd, 1909; *s.* his cousin, *Sir* KENELM BOLD, 1959; ed. at Brighton Coll.; Hereditary Sec. for Scotland: *m.* 1943, Mabel Elisabeth, 2nd da. of the late Arthur Bernard Schiele, of Arias, Argentina, and has issue.

Arms—Or, a fetterlock azure, on a chief of the last three mullets argent. **Crest**—A dexter hand holding a scroll proper.
Residences—Four Winds, Los Cocos, Sierras de Cordoba, Argentina; Estancia La Linda Mora, Arias, Argentina.

Sons living—NIGEL ANDREW DIGBY, *b.* Aug. 15th, 1944; ed. at St. Paul's Sch., Argentina, and Roy. Agric. Coll., Cirencester.——Kenelm Gerald Digby, (3, Stringhams Copse, Sendmarsh, Ripley, Surrey) *b.* 1946; ed. at St. Paul's Sch., Argentina, and Birmingham Univ. (BSc electronics): *m.* 1973, Jolande St. Clare Byrne, only child of Francis Mellor, of Nottingham (BSc Agric Economics).——Peter Francis Digby, *b.* 1947; ed. at St. Paul's Sch., Argentina, Shuttleworth Ag. Coll., NDA, and at Bangor Univ.——Denis Jermyn Digby, *b.* 1949; ed. at St. Paul's Sch., Argentina, and Bangor Univ. (BSc Forestry).

Sister living—Eileen Charmion Digby, *b.* 1910 : *m.* 1930, David Hinchliff-Mathew, and has issue living, Murray Alan, *b.* 1933,—John Gervase, *b.* 1947. *Residence,* Estancia Los Flamencos, Sancti Spiritú, F.C.C.A., Argentina.

Daughters living of 12th Baronet—Helen Mary Edith, *b.* 1897: *m.* 1930, James Millie Wodehouse, who *d.* 1971 [E. Kimberley, colls.]. *Residence,* Casilla 7, Vallenar

Chile.——Vanda Digby, *b.* 1902: *m.* 1929, Edward Cecil Cutler, MBE, MC, who *d.* 1955, and has issue living, John Leslie, *b.* 1940; ed. at Eton. *Residence*, Roughan House, Killinaboy, co. Clare.

Collateral Branches living.

Grandchildren of the late Col. Kenelm Digby Murray, DSO, 3rd son of 10th baronet:—

Issue of the late Lieut.-Col. Archibald Digby Murray, D.S.O., R.A., *b.* 1878, *d.* 1949 : *m.* 1905, Rosamund (Littlecourt, Churchill, Somerset), da. of the late Thomas Davey, of Bannerleigh, Leigh Woods, Bristol:—

Archibald John, *b.* 1907; is Lieut.-Col. Black Watch (retired): European War 1939-45 : *m.* 1935, Nancy, who *d.* 1974, da. of Philip George, of Barrow Gurney, Somerset, and has issue living, John Archibald Digby, *b.* 1941,—Grania Joan, *b.* 1938: *m.* 1963, C. R. T. Laws, of Jerome House, Churchill, Som., and has issue living, Mathew Thurlow *b.* 1964, Antonia Mary *b.* 1955, Jessica Susan *b.* 1968,—Gillian Claire, *b.* 1946. *Residence*, Churchill Court, Churchill, Somerset.

Grandchildren of the late Lt.-Col. Archibald Digby Murray DSO (ante):—

Issue of the late Maj. Ian Digby Murray, *b.* 1912, *d.* 1974: *m.* 1944, Pamela (The Penthouse, 70, Spinola Rd., St. Julian's, Malta GC):—

Julian Charles Digby, *b.* 1949.——Petrina Rosamund, *b.* 1947: *m.* 1970, Manuel Moran, of Madrid. ——Charlotte Davey, *b.* 1954.

Grandchildren of the late Lt.-Col. Archibald Digby Murray, DSO, RA (ante):—

Issue of the late Col. Kenelm Digby Bold Murray, C.B., D.S.O., *b.* 1879, *d.* 1947 : *m.* 1911, Gwendolen, **da. of the late Thomas Andrew de Wolf, of Sydney, N.S. Wales:**—

Andrew Digby, *b.* 1916 ; Lieut.-Col. (retired) R.A. : *m.* 1947, Joan (ROBERTS), da. of Major A. Nelson Allen, of Leigh, Surrey, and has issue living, Anna Teresa, *b.* 1947.——Joan Digby, *b.* 1912 : *m.* 1937, Col. Bernard William de Courcy Ireland, D.S.C., R.M. (retired), and has issue living, David Graham, *b.* 1938: *m.* 1962, Geneviève, da. of Col. S. W. Wood, Indian Army (ret.),—Philippa Anne, *b.* 1946. *Residence*, The Ridgeway, Chilbolton Av., Winchester.

Grandchildren of the late Lieut.-Gen. Sir James Wolfe Murray, K.C.B., son of the late James Wolfe Murray (infra) :—

Issue of the late Capt. George Wolfe Murray, *b.* 1876, *d.* 1955 : *m.* 1910, Katherine, who *d.* 1955, da. of the late Rev. Thomas Jones, R. of Llanbedr, Crickhowell :—

Thomas Wolfe, *b.* 1913 ; ed. at St. Bees Sch. : *m.* 1946, Violet May, da. of the late Alexander Scott, of Vancouver, British Columbia, and has issue living, Alexander James Wolfe, *b.* 1949,—Robin Wolfe, *b.* 1951,—Patricia Ann Wolfe, *b.* 1947,—Susan May Wolfe, *b.* 1958. *Residence*, Hycroft, Hattone Road, Kinnoull, Perth.——Katherine Jean Wolfe, *b.* 1911 : *m.* 1958, James Gordon Fyfe, TD, WS, DL. *Residence*, Meldonfoot, Peebles.——Miriam Arabella Elizabeth Wolfe, *b.* 1916: *m.* 1950, Albert Victor Baker, and has issue living, Victor George, *b.* 1954,—Katherine, *b.* 1951. *Residence*, Inglenook, Winsor Lane, Winsor, Southampton.

Grandchildren of the late Cdr. Philip Charles Knightley Wolfe Murray (infra):—

Issue of the late Lt.-Col. Robert Alexander Wolfe Murray, DSO, MC, *b.* 1889, *d.* 1973: *m.* 1923, Isobel Mary, who *d.* 1970, da. of the late Edward Armitstead Baxter, of Kincaldrum, Forfarshire:—

James Wolfe (House of Daviot, Daviot, Inverness-shire), *b.* 1931; ed. at Harrow; Capt. (ret.) Queen's Own Highlanders; a Member of Queen's Body Guard for Scotland (Roy. Col. of Archers): *m.* 1961 (m. diss. 1969), Baroness Catharina Ingrid Madelaine, da. of the late Baron Engene Fredrik Christer Von Stedingk, of Ullaberg, Stjärnhov, Sweden, and has issue living, Chanette Pauline Catharina, *b.* 1964,—Tatjana Tuesy Isma, *b.* 1965.——Sibyl Pauline Wolfe, *b.* 1924: *m.* 1951, Maj. Frank Derek Carson, Queen's Own Highlanders, of Knockupworth Hall, by Carlisle, and has issue living, Philip Derek Murray, *b.* 1955, Rachel Isma Ann *b.* 1957, Iona Fairlie Edith, *b.* 1959.

Grandchildren of the late James Wolfe Murray, *b.* 1814, son of the late James Wolfe Murray, Hon. Lord Cringletie, great-great-grandson of the late Alexander Murray, 4th son of 2nd baronet :—

Issue of the late Cdr. Philip Charles Knightley Wolfe Murray, *b.* 1856, *d.* 1932: *m.* 1886, Ellie Blanch, who *d.* 1938, da. of the late R. H. De Winton, J.P., D.L., of Graftonbury, Hereford:—

Christopher Charles Wolfe, *b.* 1903; ed. at Loretto; late Lt. RNVR: *m.* 1933, Hester-Mary, da. of the late Newton Charles Ogle [Cradock Hartopp, Bt.]. *Residence*, Forge Cottage, Raithby, Spilsby, Lincs.——Maud Elaine Wolfe.

Grandchildren of the late Cdr. Philip Charles Knightley Wolfe Murray (ante):—

Issue of the late Lt.-Col. David Knightley Wolfe Murray, *b.* 1897, *d.* 1970: *m.* 1920, Ivry Cordelia (118, Holland Rd., W14), da. of Montagu Townsend, of 8, North Pallant, Chichester:—

Christopher Michael Wolfe (Inworth Old Rectory, Kelvedon, Colchester), *b.* 1929; ed. at Oundle; Capt. Gordon Highlanders (ret.): *m.* 1955, Jacqueline, da. of Col. Sir John Turnbull Usher, OBE, 4th Bt., and has issue living, Dorinda Mary, *b.* 1957,—Erica Jacqueline, *b.* 1959,—Serena Jean, *b.* 1964.——Ivri Patricia, *b.* 1922: *m.* 1951, Charles Mailert Wormser, of 65, East 99th St., New York 28, USA, and has issue living, Andrew Charles *b.* 1953,—Nina Carolyn, *b.* 1955.

Grandson of the late James Wolfe Murray (*b.* 1814) (ante):—

Issue of the late Brig.-Gen. Arthur Alexander Wolfe Murray, C.B., *b.* 1866, *d.* (on active ser.) 1918 : *m.* 1904, Evelyn Mary Hay (who *d.* 1955, having *m.* 2ndly, 1920, Archibald Robert Cranfurd Pitman), el. da. of the late Colin Mackenzie, Lord Lieut. for Peeblesshire, of Portmore :—

Malcolm Victor Alexander Wolfe, *b.* 1908 ; ed. at Eton, and at Ch. Ch., Oxford ; Lieut.-Col. (retired) The Black Watch, a D.L. for Peeblesshire, and a Member of Queen's Body Guard for Scotland (Roy. Co. of Archers); 1939-45 War: *m.* 1st, 1935, Lady Grizel Mary Boyle, who *d.* (at sea as result of enemy action) 1942, el. da. of 8th Earl of Glasgow; 2ndly, 1947, Zofia, who *d.* 1968, da. of M. Jaxa Chamiec, of Warsaw, and has issue living, (by 1st m.) James Archibald Wolfe (12, Cambridge Rd., SW20), *b.* 1936; ed. at Eton and Worcester Coll., Oxford: *m.* 1963, the Hon. Diana Lucy Douglas-Home, da. of Baron Home of the Hirsel (Life Baron), and has issue living, Rory James Wolfe *b.* 1965, Fiona Grizel Wolfe *b.* 1964, Clare Elizabeth Wolfe *b.* 1969,—Angus Malcolm Wolfe (Glenternie, by Peebles), *b.* 1937: *m.* 1961, Stephanie Vivian, da. of the late Maj. Hadden Royden Todd, and has issue living, Kim Alexander Wolfe *b.* 1962, Rupert Hamish Wolfe *b.* 1963, Gavin Scott Wolfe *b.* 1966, Magnus Wolfe *b.* 1968,—(by 2nd m.) Teresa Mary Wolfe *b.* 1950. *Residence*, Glenternie, by Peebles. *Club*, Army and Navy.

Descendants of the late Sir Gideon Murray, 3rd son of the late Andrew Murray, uncle of 1st baronet, of whom the el. son was *cr.* Lord Elibank [*see* L. Elibank].

Descendants of the late William Murray, youngest son of the late Andrew Murray, uncle of 1st baronet, whose son, the late William Murray was created a baronet in 1630 [*see* Murray, Bt., *cr.* 1630].

Sir Archibald Murray, 1st baronet, a first cousin of 1st Lord Elibank, was created a baronet with remainder to his heirs male whatsoever.

MURRAY, Creation (N.S.) 1630, of Dunerne, Fifeshire.

Sir ROWLAND WILLIAM PATRICK MURRAY, 14th *Baronet* (but his name does not, at time of going to press, appear on the Official Roll of Baronets), son of the late Rowland William Murray, 2nd son of 12th baronet; *b.* Oct. 26th, 1910; ed. at Georgia Univ.; *s.* his uncle, *Lt.-Col. Sir* EDWARD ROBERT, *DSO*, 1958; late Maj. US. Army: *m.* 1944, Josephine Margaret, da. of Edward D. Murphy, and has issue.

Arms—Not matriculated at Lyon Office.
Residence—239, Kenlock Place NE, Atlanta, Ga. 30305, USA.
Sons living—ROWLAND WILLIAM, *b.* Sept. 22nd, 1947.——Edward George, *b.* 1951.——Robert Michael, *b.* 1953.——Christopher Joseph, *b.* 1957.
Daughters living—Helen Brooke, *b.* 1945.——Patricia Marie, *b.* 1949.
Sister living—Gertrude June, *b.* 1909; ed. at Oglethorpe Univ., Georgia (BA); Capt. Army Med. Specialist Corps, US Army: *m.* 19—, Jerome R— Bischel, of 1202, E. Broadway, Wankesha, Wis., 53186, USA.
Aunt living (daughter of 12th baronet)—Laura Magdalen Irving (83, Hillcrest Rd., Mt. Vernon, NY 10552, USA), *b.* 1887: *m.* 1907, Gerald Alexander Marlowe-King, and has issue living, Alexander William (83, Hillcrest Rd., Mt. Vernon, NY 10552, USA), *b.* 1910: Assist. Trea. of Dry Dock Savings Bank, New York: *m.* 1935, Helen Laurette McMahon, and has issue living, William Alexander *b.* 1937; ed. at Iona Coll., New Rochelle, NY; (BA): *m.* 1967, Geraldine Tierney, Junellen Mary *b.* 1940: *m.* 1960, Denis Robert Sullivan (and has issue living, Steven Alexander *b.* 1961, Dennis Robert *b.* 1962, Kevin William *b.* 1964),—George Robert (2800, N. Holliston, Altadena, Cal. 91001, USA), *b.* 1911: *m.* 1937, Ruth Sheets, and has issue living, Gerald John *b.* 1937: *m.* 1967, Roxanne Pettigrew, Georgette Alexandria *b.* 1939: *m.* 1956, Louis Griffis (and has issue living, Stephen John *b.* 1959, John Wayne *b.* 1960),—Kenneth Gandy (187, Fern St., Fairfield, Conn., USA), *b.* 1912: *m.* 1937, Blanche Connelly, and has issue living, Kenneth Gary *b.* 1939: *m.* 1959, Sherrin O'Toole (and has issue living, Kenneth Michael *b.* 1960), John William *b.* 1942; ed. at Conn. Univ.; (BA); late Capt. USAF: *m.* 1965, Patricia Ann O'Connell (and has issue living, John Patrick *b.* 1965, Kenneth Scott *b.* 1968),—Donald Murray, *b.* 1915.

Widow living of 13th Baronet—RUBY (*Ruby, Lady Murray*) da. of S. Hearn, of Helmdon, Northants : *m.* 1938, as his second wife, Lieut.-Col. Sir Edward Robert Murray, 13th Bt., D.S.O., who *d.* 1958. *Residence.*

Collateral Branches living.

Issue of the late Robert Lithgow Murray, 3rd son of 12th baronet, *b.* 1881, *d.* 1942: *m.* 1908, Harriet Pope:—

Vernon Robert William (35-25, 211th St., Bayside, New York, USA), *b.* 1909: *m.* 1934, Elizabeth Camberne Kirkwood, and has issue living, Vernon Kirkwood (10, Victor St., Albany, New York, USA), *b.* 1945: *m.* 1966, Linda Tischler, and has issue living, Christine Lynn *b.* 1966,—Harriet Elizabeth, *b.* 1937; ed. at State Univ., New York (MS): *m.* 1958, Dale Aldrich Edwards of 52, Mist Lane, Westbury, NY, USA, and has issue living, Daniel Vernon *b.* 1962, Susan Dale *b.* 1959, Carolyn Kirkwood *b.* 1968,—Phyllis Vernon, *b.* 1939: *m.* 1957, Adrian Cecil Stanley, of 417, Betsy Ross Rd., Virginia Beach, Va., USA, and has issue living, Kenneth William *b.* 1960, Edward Murray *b.* 1966, Janet Elizabeth *b.* 1958.——Robert Atholl, *b.* 1914: *m.* 1935, Mary Ellen Guinan, and has issue living, Robert Atholl, *b.* 1937,—James Ivor, *b.* 1947,—Diane, *b.* 1942.

Grandchildren of the late Robert Lithgow Murray (ante):—
Issue of the late James Edward Murray, *b.* 1911, *d.* 1963: *m.* 1934, Dorothy Elizabeth Holley (38-38, 217th St., Bayside, NY, USA):—
Donald MacLean, *b.* 1945; ed. at Mass. Inst. of Technology.——Elizabeth Anne, *b.* 1938: *m.* 1957, Louis H. Cabrol, of Route de Maraussan, Beziers, Herault, France, and has issue living, Jean Louis, *b.* 1964,—Jacques, *b.* 1970,—Marie Therese, *b.* 1958,—Danielle, *b.* 1960,—Alice, *b.* 1961,—Helene, *b.* 1963.——Susan Eleanora, *b.* 1939: *m.* 1958, James A. Kowalski, of 405, Aspen St. NW, Washington DC, USA, and has issue living, Glen R., *b.* 1960,—Gary W., *b.* 1962,—James Edward, *b.* 1964,—Melissa Jill, *b.* 1969.

Issue of the late William Gerard Pulteney Murray, 4th son of 12th baronet, *b.* 1891, *d.* 1953 : *m.* 1919, Frances Swartz, of 3608, State Road, Drexel Hills, Philadelphia, U.S.A. :—

Allan Gerald, *b.* 1928: *m.* 19—, Penny Phillips, and has issue living, William *b.* 19—,—June Ann, *b.* 19—,—Gail, *b.* 19—.

The 7th baronet, a distinguished military officer during the first American war, was subsequently Secretary at War. He married in 1794 the Right Hon. Henrietta (in her own right) Countess of Bath, and assumed the surname of Pulteney but died without issue.

MURRAY, Creation (N.S.) 1673, of Ochtertyre, Perthshire.

Sir WILLIAM PATRICK KEITH MURRAY, 11th *Baronet; b.* Sept. 7th, 1939; *s.* his father, *Sir* PATRICK IAN KEITH, 1962: *m.* 1963, Susan Elizabeth, da. of Stacey Jones, of Penyrwrlodd, Hay-on-Wye, Herefordshire, and has issue.

Arms—Azure, three mullets argent, in the centre a cross of the second surmounted of a saltire gules both couped. **Crest**—An olive-branch proper. **Seat**—Ochtertyre, Crieff, Perthshire.

Son living—PATRICK IAN KEITH, *b.* March 22nd, 1965.

Aunt living—Bethia Ioné (2A, Polwarth Terr., Edinburgh 11), *b.* 1911: *m.* 1939 (m. diss. 1966), Paul Nicholas Robert Harding Edgar, and has issue living, John George Keith, *b.* 1949,—Amanda Elizabeth, *b.* 1944: *m.* 1968, John Murray Byers, of Stubbington House, Ascot,—Susan Nicola, *b.* 1945: *m.* 1968, (Ian) Douglas Lowe, of Dalkeith Home Farm, Dalkeith, Midlothian.

Widow living of 10th Baronet—LISKA (*Liska, Lady Murray*), da. of A. T. Creet, of Ghusick, India: *m.* 1929, Sir Patrick Ian Keith Murray, 10th Bt. who *d.* 1962. *Residence*, The Hosh, Crieff, Perthshire.

Collateral Branches living.

Grandson of the late Lieut.-Com. Henry Arthur Keith Murray, 7th son of 7th baronet :—
Issue of the late Harry Edmund Colquhoun Keith-Murray, M.D., *b.* 1873, *d.* 1922: *m.* 1903, Dora Amy, who *d.* 1956, el. da. of the late C. H. Barclay :—
Rev. Canon Thomas Whitney Uniacke, *b.* 1904; ed. at Haileybury; Hon. Canon of Worcester: *m.* 1944, Edith Monica, who *d.* 1969, da. of the late Rev. Canon W. G. Mosse, of Sapcote, Leicester. *Residence,* 3, Homefield Rd., Worcester, WR2 4AQ.
Issue of the late Archibald Lamont Keith-Murray, 10th son of 7th baronet, *b.* 1852, *d.* 1911: *m.* 1884, Mary Ellen, da. of the late Dr. Hughes, Civil Surg. of Nowgong, Assam :—
Archie, *b.* 1886 : *m.* 1928, Inez May Josephine, who *d.* 1938, da. of Major F. G. Fox.——David, *b.* 1900 : *m.* 1932, Nancy Mary, da. of H. Gautschi, of Vancouver, British Columbia, and has issue living, Peter, *b.* 1935,—Marinie, *b.* 1937.——Georgina Mary, *b.* 1887.——Adelaide, *b.* 1891.
——Millicent Ethel, *b.* 1893.——Jeannie Helen, *b.* 1898. *Residence,*

Grandchildren of the late Henry Dundas Murray, 5th son of 6th baronet :—
Issue of the late William Tullibardine Murray, *b.* 1863, *d.* 1923 : *m.* 1886, May Elizabeth Margaret, da. of the late James Bell, M.D., of Kaipara, New Zealand :—
Henry Lamont, *b.* 1891.——Yolande, *b.* 1887. *Resides in* New Zealand.

Grandson of the late George Joseph Murray, grandson of the late Alexander Murray, son of Patrick Murray, 2nd son of 2nd baronet:—
Issue of the late Capt. Alexander Penrose Murray, *b.* 1863, *d.* 1926 : *m.* 1st, 1891, Nina, who *d.* 1894, da. of Col. Alexander Solovtsoff; 2ndly, 1895, Ethel Chorley, da. of the late Maj.-Gen. Arthur Hill :—
(By 2nd marriage) Charles, *b.* 1895. *Residence,*

Granddaughters of the late Mackenzie Murray, son of the late John Murray, great-grandson of the late Mungo Murray, youngest son of 1st baronet :—
Issue of the late Edward Mackenzie MURRAY-BUCHANAN, *b.* 1874, *d.* 1956 (having assumed the additional surname of Buchanan on succeeding to the estate of Leny 1919) : *m.* 1913, Jean Isabella Shaw, who *d.* 1952, da. of James Carmichael, of Arthurstone, Meigle, Perthshire:—
Euphemia Cecilia, *b.* 1915: *m.* 1st, 1940, Maj. Francis William Clark, of Ulva, who *d.* (killed in action at Cassino) 1944 ; 2ndly, 1956, Lieut.-Col. John Hay Young, D.S.O., M.C., and has issue living, (by 1st m.) Francis Malcolm, *b.* 1942: *m.* 1971, Georgina Jane, da. of the late Maj. S. J. Swinton Lee, Seaforth Highlanders, and has issue living, John Francis *b.* 1971, Michael James *b.* 1972. *Residence,* East Lodge, Bridge of Allan, Stirlingshire.——Margaret Avril, *b.* 1917: *m.* 1946, Albert Fairfield, and has issue living, a son, *b.* 194-,—a da., *b.* 194-.——Phoebe Aeonie, *b.* 1922: *m.* 1952, John Craufuird Roger Inglis, and has issue living, Richard David, *b.* 1953,—John Edward, *b.* 1961,—Jean Helen, *b.* 1955,—Fiona Ann, *b.* 1957,—Shena Mary, *b.* 1960,—Susan Patricia, *b.* 1964. *Residence,* Inglisfield, Gifford, E. Lothian.

The 1st baronet, Sir William Murray, a cadet of Tullibardine [*see* D. Atholl], was created a baronet with remainder to his heirs male whatsoever. The 6th baronet, Sir Patrick Murray, sat as M.P. for Edinburgh (City) 1806-12, and was afterwards Baron of the Court of Exchequer in Scotland. The 7th Baronet, Sir William Murray, on his marriage in 1833, to Helen Margaret Oliphant, only child of Sir Alexander Keith of Dunnottar, Knt. Marischal of Scotland, assumed the name of Keith before that of Murray, which name was used by all his descendants, until the succession of the 10th Baronet, who reverted to Murray.

MUSGRAVE, Creation (E.) 1611, of Hartley Castle, Westmorland.

Without changing.

Sir CHRISTOPHER PATRICK CHARLES MUSGRAVE, 15th *Baronet*; *b.* April 14th, 1949; *s.* his father, *Sir* CHARLES, 1970; patron of one living, but being a minor cannot present.

Arms—Azure, six annulets or, three, two, and one. **Crest**—Two arms embowed in armour proper, the hands grasping an annulet or.

Residence—

Brother living—JULIAN NIGEL CHARDIN, *b.* Dec. 8th, 1951.
Aunt living—Dorothy (twin), *b.* 1913: *m.* 1959, Albert John Manley, of Holmbush, Cook's Lane, Axminster, Devon.
Mother living—Olive Louise Avril, only da. of Patrick Cringle, of Holme-on-Sea, Hunstanton: *m.* 1st, 1948 (m. diss. 1961), Sir Charles Musgrave, 14th Bt., who *d.* 1970; 2ndly, 1961, Peter Charles Nelson, of Tans End, Wellson-Sea, Norfolk.

This family was originally settled at Musgrave, in Westmorland. Thomas Musgrave, *temp.* Edward III., was summoned by writ and sat as a peer of the realm for twenty-three years. Sir Philip, 2nd baronet, a distinguished Royalist, sat as M.P. for Westmorland 1640-42 : after the battle of Worcester, he attended King Charles II in France, Holland and Scotland, whence he retired to the Isle of Man, which he bravely defended under the Countess of Derby. For his great services a warrant creating him Baron Musgrave of Hartley Castle was issued, but he did not take out the patent. The 5th baronet, M.P. for Carlisle, was Clerk to the Privy Council, and the 6th baronet sat as M.P. for co. Westmorland. Sir Philip, 8th baronet, was M.P. for Carlisle, and Sir Richard, 11th baronet, sat as M.P. for E. Cumberland, and was Lord-Lieut. of Westmorland.

MUSGRAVE, Creation (I.) 1782, of Tourin, Waterford.

Sir RICHARD JAMES MUSGRAVE, 7th *Baronet*; *b.* Feb. 10th, 1922; *s.* his father, *Sir* CHRISTOPHER NORMAN, O.B.E., 1956; Capt. late Indian Army: *m.* 1958, Maria, da. of the late Col. M. Cambanis, of Athens, Greece, and has issue.

Arms—Azure, six annulets or, three, two, and one. Crest—Two arms in armour proper, gauntleted and supporting an annulet or.
Residence—Riverstown, Tara, co. Meath.

Sons living—CHRISTOPHER JOHN SHANE, *b.* Oct. 23rd, 1959.——Michael Shane, *b.* 1968.
Daughters living—Olivia Mirabel, *b.* 1958.——Anastasia Maria, *b.* 1961.——Charlotte Elizabeth, *b.* 1963.——Alexandra Victoria, *b.* 1965.
Sister living—Elizabeth Anne, *b.* 1931: *m.* 1955, Thomas Aydon Bates, and has issue living, Giles Langley, *b.* 1963,—Benedict Loftus, *b.* 1964,—Annabelle Carol Elizabeth, *b.* 1955,—Belinda Ann, *b.* 1957,—Corrinne Lucy, *b.* 1958,—Teresa Astrid, *b.* 1959. *Residence*, Nilston Rigg, Langley-on-Tyne, Northumberland.
Aunt living—Dorothy Maude, *b.* 1895: *m.* 1936, Thomas Harold Nash-Peake. *Residence*, Flat 1, Singleton, Higher Woodfield Road, Torquay, Devon.
Daughter living of 5th Baronet—Dorothy Frances, *b.* 1894: *m.* 1933, Edmund Glen Browne, Lt. (ret.) RA. *Residence*, Hermitage, Glanmire, co. Cork.
Collateral Branches living
Issue of the late Maj. Francis Edward Musgrave, brother of 6th baronet, *b.*
Without changing.
1894, *d.* 1975: *m.* 1919, Kathleen Ethel, who *d.* 1966, da. of the late Lt.-Col. Charles William Grey, RASC:—
Patricia Kathleen, *b.* 1921.——Shelagh Monica, *b.* 1927.
  Issue of the late Robert Musgrave, uncle of the 6th baronet, *b.* 1870, *d.* 1940: *m.* 1905, Amy Lindsay, who *d.* 1939, da. of Brig.-Surg. F. Lindsay Dickson, of Vancouver, British Columbia:—
Robert John, *b.* 1905: *m.* 1934, Marjorie Winnifred Chinneck, and has issue living, Jean Marjorie Frances, *b.* 1935,—Daphne Edith Amy, *b.* 1936.——Edward Lindsay (of 2931, Seaview Drive, Victoria, British Columbia), *b.* 1907: *m.* 1949, Judith Bradfield Stevens, and has issue living, Anthony Richard, *b.* 1955,—Robert Lindsay, *b.* 1958,—Susan Patricia, *b.* 1951,—Mary Kathleen, *b.* 1961.——Frances Kathleen, *b.* 1908: *m.* 1936, Ian James Montagu Scott, and has issue living, Robert Montagu, *b.* 1937; is Lt., Roy. Canadian Navy,—Christopher Musgrave, *b.* 1941,—Gillian Musgrave, *b.* 1943.
  This Baronetcy was conferred on Richard Musgrave, M.P., el. son of Christopher Musgrave, of Tourin, co. Waterford, with special remainder to his younger brothers, under which remainder the 2nd baronet, Sir Christopher, succeeded. The 3rd baronet sat as M.P. for co. Waterford, and the 4th baronet was Lord-Lieut. and Custos Rotulorum of co. Waterford

---

MUSPRATT, Creation (U.K.) 1922, of Merseyside, City of Liverpool. [Extinct 1934.]

Sir MAX MUSPRATT, 1st and last *Baronet*.

Daughters living of 1st Baronet—Frances Kate; *b.* 1898: *m.* 1923, Howard Raymond John Feeny, and has issue living, Max Howard, *b.* 1928; ed. at Stonyhurst,—Patrick Dalrymple, *b.* 1931,—June Mary, *b.* 1925,—Jasmine Ann, *b.* 1936. *Residence*, The Little House, Feckenham, Worcestershire.——Vanda May, *b.* 1901 : *m.* 1926, George Frederick Killwick, and has issue living, Georgette, *b.* 1926. *Residence*, Whispers, 12 Hill Brow, Hove, 4.

MYNORS, Creation (U.K.) 1964, of Treago, co. Hereford.

Sir HUMPHREY CHARLES BASKERVILLE MYNORS, 1st *Baronet*, son of the late Rev. Aubrey Baskerville Mynors, R. of Langley Burrell, Wilts.; *b.* July 28th, 1903; ed. at Marlborough, and at Corpus Christi Coll., Camb. (MA, Fellow 1926-33, Hon. Fellow 1953); Hon. DCL Durham; a Dir. of Bank of England 1949-54, and Dep. Gov. 1954-64: *m.* 1939, Lydia Marian, da. of the late Prof. Sir Ellis Hovell Minns, and has issue.

Arms—Sable, an eagle displayed or, beaked and membered gules, on a chief azure, bordured argent, a chevron between two crescents in chief and a rose in base of the last.

Residence—Treago, St. Weonards, Hereford.

Son living—RICHARD BASKERVILLE, *b.* May 5th, 1947: *m.* 1970, Fiona Bridget, da. of the Rt. Rev. George Edmund Reindorp, DD, Lord Bishop of Guildford.

Daughters living—Elizabeth Baskerville, *b.* 1940: *m.* 1962, Jeremy Longmore Russell, of 12, Richmond Park Rd., SW14, and has issue living, Thomas Lancelot, *b.* 1965,—Jennifer Frances, *b.* 1969.——Catherine Baskerville, *b.* 1944: *m.* 1966, Christopher Mordaunt Richards, of 38, Oakfield Rd., Gosforth, Newcastle upon Tyne, and has issue living, Benedict William Mordaunt, *b.* 1972,—Sophia Janet, *b.* 1969,—Clare Eleanor, *b.* 1974.——Philippa Baskerville, *b.* 1950.—— Jane Margery Baskerville, *b.* 1952: *m.* 1974, Nicholas Kersteman King.

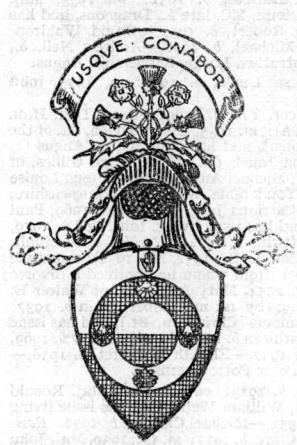

AIRN, Creation (U.K.) 1904, of Rankeillour, Collessie, and Dysart House, Dysart, Fifeshire.

Sir (MICHAEL) GEORGE NAIRN, *T.D.*, *3rd Baronet ; b.* Jan. 30th, 1911 ; *s.* his father, *Sir* MICHAEL 1952 ; ed. at Trin. Coll., Glenalmond ; a D.L. of Fife 1955-70 ; 1939-45 War as Major The Black Watch (wounded) : *m.* 1936, Helen Louise, da. of the late Major E. J. W. Bruce, of Melbourne, Australia, and has issue.

Arms—Per fesse argent and sable, on a chaplet four escallops, all counter-changed. *Crest*—Three thistles conjoined in stalk entwined with two roses all slipped proper.

Residence—Pitcarmick, Blairgowrie, Perthshire. *Club*—Caledonian.

Sons living—MICHAEL (39, Ann St., Edinburgh), *b.* July 1st, 1938; ed. at Eton, and INSEAD: *m.* 1972, Diana Gordon, el. da. of F. Leonard Bligh, of Pejar Park, Woodhouselee, NSW, and has issue living, Michael Andrew, *b.* 1973,—Alexander Gordon, *b.* 1975.—— Charles Bruce, *b.* 1942; ed. at Eton and at McGill Univ., Montreal (BA): *m.* 1973, Carol Ann, da. of the late Lt.-Col. Sidney Clive Blaber [see Hartwell, Bt., colls.]. **Sisters living**—Rachel Emily, *CBE*, *b.* 1902, past Chm. for Scotland, WRVS; OBE (Civil) 1962, CBE (Civil) 1972): *m.* 1925, Maj. Arthur Frederic Purvis, MC, Scots Guards, who *d.* 1955. *Residence*, Earlshall, Leuchars, Fife.——Constance Jane, *b.* 1904: *m.* 1928, John Inglis, who *d.* 1960, and has issue living, Sally Elizabeth Jane (Elliston Stables House, St. Boswells, Roxburghshire), *b.* 1931: *m.* 1958, Maj. Peter Wyndham Loyd, Coldm. Gds., who *d.* 1974 [B. Brabourne], and has issue living, Andrew Wyndham *b.* 1963, Henrietta Jane Rachel *b.* 1959,—Teresa, *b.* 1936: *m.* 1959, Ronald Charles Cunningham-Jardine, of Fourmerkland, Lockerbie, Dumfries-shire, and has issue living, John Charles *b.* 1961, Rachel Mary, *b.* 1963. *Residence*, Bothendene, Bowden, St. Boswells, Roxburghshire.—— Mildred Brenda (*Lady Walker*), *b.* 1906; has St. Olaf Medal of Norway: *m.* 1930, Col. Sir. William Giles Newsom Walker, TD, DL, and has issue living, Michael Giles Neish (of Shanwell, Milnathort, Kinross-shire), *b.* 1933: *m.* 1960, Margaret Ruby, yr. da. of Lt.-Col. John David Hills, MC [see E. Cromer], and has issue living, Simon Giles David *b.* 1961, Geordie Michael *b.* 1966, Nicola Margaret *b.* 1965,—Margaret Elizabeth Bluebell, *b.* 1931: *m.* 1954, John K. P. Mackie, of Simmy Island, Toye, Downpatrick, co. Down, and has issue living, James William Pringle *b.* 1956, Charlotte Rose *b.* 1959, Sara Georgina *b.* 1964,—Angela Rachel, *b.* 1938: *m.* 1958, Jeremy H. Dewhurst, of Woodend, Madderty, Perthshire, and Foich Lodge, Loch Broom, Ross-shire, and has issue living, Charles Hugh *b.* 1961, James Edward *b.* 1963. *Residence*, Pitlair, Cupar, Fife.——Elizabeth Barbara, *b.* 1915: *m.* 1st, 1938 (m. diss. 1947), Maj. Alexander Oliphant Hutchison, Fife and Forfar Yeo.; 2ndly, 1948 (m. diss. 1958), Leon Robert de Notto; 3rdly, 1961, John Michael Wentworth, and has issue living (by 1st m.), Roderick Alexander Oliphant (New Burn, Upper Largo, Fife), *b.* 1943: *m.* 1970, Gillian Boddy of Lochaillort, Inverness-shire,—Edward Anthony Oliphant (2, Pentlow St., Putney, SW15), *b.* 1946: *m.* 1971, Polly Mathilda Saunders, of Yew Tree Cottage, Droxford, Hants.,—Caroline Victoria Oliphant, *b.* 1941: *m.* 1st, 1963 (m. diss. 1970), George Charles Caswell Cornelius; 2ndly, 1973, Robert Michael Marshall, of Old Inn House, Slindon, Arundel, Sussex, and has issue living (by 1st m.) Deborah Caswell Oliphant *b.* 1965, Katherine Caswell Oliphant *b.* 1967. *Residences*, Littledean, Bramdean, nr. Alresford, Hants; 6, Canning Pl., W8.

Aunt living (daughter of 1st baronet)—Dorothy Clare: *m.* 1921, Bruce B. Thomas, who *d.* 1965, and has issue living, David Bruce (of Strathardle, Shannonbrook, via Casino, NSW), *b.* 1924: *m.* 1948, Betty, da. of Joseph W. Milligan, of Manchester, and has issue living, Alison Edith *b.* 1952, Patricia Dorothy *b.* 1958,—Emily Jocelyn (Clovelly, Bonalbo, NSW), *b.* 1930: *m.* 1957, Atholl Robertson, who *d.* 1967, and has issue living, Duncan Bruce *b.* 1958, Elspeth Clare *b.* 1960, Fiona Frances *b.* 1962. *Residence*, Eurigar, Shannonbrook via Casino, NSW.

Collateral Branch living.

Issue of the late Sir Robert SPENCER-NAIRN, Bt , T.D. (2nd son of 1st baronet), who was *cr.* a *Baronet* 1933.
See Spencer-Nairn, Bt.

The 1st baronet, Sir Michael Barker, was Chairman of Michael Nairn and Co. (Limited) Linoleum manufacturers, of Kirkcaldy, and of Nairn Linoleum Co., of Kearny, U.S.A

SPENCER-NAIRN, Creation (U.K.) 1933, of Monimail, co. Fife.

Sir ROBERT ARNOLD SPENCER-NAIRN, 3rd
Baronet; b. Oct. 11th, 1933; *s.* his father,
Lt.-Col. *Sir* DOUGLAS LESLIE SPENCER, *TD*,
1970; ed. at Eton, and Trin. Hall, Camb.;
late Lt. SG: *m.* 1963, Joanna Elizabeth, da. of
the late Lt.-Cdr. George Stevenson Salt, RN,
[see Salt, Bt., *cr.* 1899, colls.], and has issue.

Arms—Per fesse argent and sable, on a chaplet four
escallops, all counter-changed; in the chief point a crescent
of the second for difference. Crest—A terrestrial sphere
with semi-meridian and stand proper.

Residence, Barham, Cupar, Fife.

Sons living—JAMES ROBERT, *b.* Dec. 7th, 1966.——
Andrew George, *b.* 1969.
Daughter living—Katharine Elizabeth, *b.* 1964.
Brother living—John Chaloner (315, Kensington Av.,
Westmount, Montreal, Canada), *b.* 1938; ed. at Eton;
late 2nd Lt. R. Dragoons: *m.* 1st, 1966 (m. diss. 1970),
Barbara Lynn, da. of Murray Kamichik, of Montreal,
Canada; 2ndly, 1971, Lucie, da. of Pierre Belanger, of 3015,
Sherbrooke St. W., Montreal, Canada, and has issue living
(by 2nd m.), John Henderson, *b.* 1973,—Kim Sheilagh,
b. 1975.
Half-Brother living—Christopher Frank, *b.* 1949; ed. at
Eton, and Magdalene Coll., Camb.: *m.* 1975, Juliet Con-
stance, da. of Oswald Frank Baker, of the Court House,
Atch Lench, Worcs. [see E. Perth, colls.].
Sisters living—Mary Elizabeth, *b.* 1931: *m.* 1953, Maj.
Andrew Beatty Houstoun, MC, late R. Dragoons, and has
issue living, William Robert, *b.* 1954,—David Waldron
b. 1957,—Alexander Michael, *b.* 1958,—Andrew Neil, *b.*,
1961. *Residence*, Lintrathen Lodge, Kirriemuir, Angus.
Half-Sister living—Teresa Leslie, *b.* 1952: *m.* 1975, John
Mungo Ingleby.
Uncles living (sons of 1st baronet)—Michael Alastair Spencer, *TD, b.* 1909; ed. at Trin. Hall,
Camb. (MA); JP; formerly Major Fife and Forfar Yeo. (TA): *m.* 1935, Ursula Helen, da. of the
late Howson Foulger Devitt [*see* Devitt, Bt., *cr.* 1916, colls.], and has issue living, Angus (2,
Victoria Rd., Kirkcaldy, Fife), *b.* 1947: *m.* 1968, Christina Janet, da. of Col. Hugh Gillies, of
Kindar House, New Abbey, Dumfries, and has issue living, Michael Angus *b.* 1975, Fiona Louise
b. 1974,—Sarah Ursula, *b.* 1937: *m.* 1967, John Scoular, of Tonderghie, Whithorn, Wigtownshire,
and has issue living, Alastair John Greenshields *b.* 1972,—Catriona Jane, *b.* 1945: *m.* 1969, Paul
Hosegood Kirton, of Hartfield House, Headley, Hants., and has issue living, Ian Nigel *b.* 1970,
Clare Helen *b.* 1972, Lena Harriett *b.* 1974, Mary Rose (twin) *b.* 1974. *Residence*, Westhall,
Cupar, Fife.——Robert Frank, *b.* 1910; ed. at Trin. Hall, Camb. (BA 1932, MA 1936); sometime
Capt. The Black Watch (TA): *m.* 1st, 1936, Caroline Isabel (from whom he obtained a divorce
1949), da. of H. A. Chadwick, of Calgary, Canada; 2ndly, 1954, Mary Anna, da. of Walter E.
Hettman, of San Francisco, California, and has issue living (by 1st m.), Isabel Susan *b.* 1937:
m. 1966, Maj. Nicholas John Ridley, Queen's Own Highlanders [Christison, Bt.], and has issue
living, Nicholas Charles Philip Christison *b.* 1973, Alexia Kathleen *b.* 1967, Susanna Mary *b.* 1969,
—(by 2nd m.) Martha Ann, *b.* 1955,—Charlotte Emily, *b.* 1957,—Elspeth Margaret, *b.* 1958,—
Margaret Cynthia, *b.* 1965. *Residence*, Castle Carey, St. Peter Port, Guernsey.
Aunts living (daughters of 1st baronet)—Kathleen Matilda, *b.* 1913: *m.* 1st, 1938, Maj. Ronald
Richards, RA, who obtained a divorce 1948; 2ndly, 1948, William Webb, and has issue living
(by 2nd m.) William Spencer, *b.* 1948,—Alan Gordon, *b.* 1951,—Michael Charles, *b.* 1952. *Resi-
dence*, Mendlesham Manor, Stowmarket, Suffolk.——Helen Clare, *b.* 1917: *m.* 1st, 1939, Maj. John
Henry Courthope Powell, Fife and Forfar Yeo. (TA), who *d.* (killed in action) 1944; 2ndly, 1945,
John William Gardner Hume, and has issue living (by 1st m.) Elizabeth Clare *b.* 1942: *m.* 1965,
Colin T. Scott Dempster (c/o Clydesdale Bank, 31, South Methven St., Perth), and has issue living,
Robert Andrew *b.* 1967, Clare Anne *b.* 1969,—Margaret Ann, *b.* 1944: *m.* 1966, Stephen James
Lindsay, and has issue living, Richard Stephen *b.* 1969, Charles Ludovic *b.* 1974, Jane Margaret
b. 1966,—(by 2nd m.) Mary *b.* 1947: *m.* 1971, John FitzGerald, of 29, Sispara Gdns., SW18, and
has issue living, John William Broun *b.* 1973. *Residence*, Damside, Auchterarder, Perthshire.
——Adela Margaret, *b.* 1924: *m.* 1944, the Rt. Hon. Humphrey Edward Gregory Atkins, MP, of
Tuckenhams, Waltham St. Lawrence, Berks., and has issue living, Charles Edward Spencer, *b.*
1952,—Sheila Kathleen, *b.* 1944: *m.* 1st, 1964 (m. diss. 1974), Peter Thornycroft Romer-Lee;
2ndly, 1975, Keith Allen Manners, of The Mill, Lustleigh, Devon, and has issue living (by 1st m.),
Richard Peter *b.* 1965, Anthony James *b.* 1967,—Julia Margaret, *b.* 1946: *m.* 1st, 1966 (m. diss.
1972), David Charles Roderick; 2ndly, 1972, John Stanley Melville Keay, of Succoth, Dalmally,
Argyll, and has issue living (by 2nd m.) Alexander John Melville *b.* 1973, Anna Julia *b.* 1974,—
Sally Mary, *b.* 1948: *m.* 1970, William Field Clegg, of Red Lion House, Nettlebed, Oxon., and
has issue living, Islay Mary *b.* 1973.

Mother living—Elizabeth Livingston (Monimail House, Ladybank, Fife), da. of the late Arnold
James Henderson: *m.* 1931, Lt.-Col. Sir Douglas Leslie Spencer Spencer-Nairn, TD, 2nd Bt.,
who *d.* 1970, and from whom she obtained a divorce 1946.
Widow living of 2nd Baronet—(ELIZABETH) LOUISE (*Louise, Lady Spencer-Nairn*), (Rankeilour,
Cupar, Fife; Culligran, Struy, Inverness-shire; 4, Stanhope Mews, East, SW7; Villa Franca,
Glendale, Rhodesia), da. of the late Frederick Vester, of Jerusalem, Jordan: *m.* 1946, as his
2nd wife, Lt.-Col. Sir Douglas Leslie Spencer Spencer-Nairn, TD, 2nd Bt., who *d.* 1970.

The 1st baronet, Maj. Sir Robert Spencer-Nairn, TD (2nd son of Sir Michael Barker Nairn,
1st Bt., of Rankeilour, Springfield, Fife), by Emily Frances, da. of Alfred Rimington Spencer,
was Major Fife and Forfar Yeo. In 1928 he adopted the surname of Spencer-Nairn.

NAIRNE, Creation (U.K.) 1917, of Kirkcudbright. [Extinct 1945.]

Sir (JOHN) GORDON NAIRNE, 1st and last *Baronet*.
daughter living of 1st Baronet—Sybil Isabel Mary Macartney, *b.* 1896: *m.* 1918 (marriage
dissolved 1949), Lieut.-Col. Basil Laing Clay, O.B.E., Queen's Own Roy. W. Kent Regt. *Residence*, Miswell Orchard, Tring, Herts.

NALL, Creation (U.K.) 1954, of Hoveringham, co. Nottingham.

BE READY

Sir MICHAEL JOSEPH NALL, 2nd *Baronet b.* Oct. 6th 1921 ; *s.* his father *Col. Sir* JOSEPH, D.S.O., T.D., 1958 ; ed. at Wellington Coll.; Lt.-Cdr. RN (ret.); a DL for Notts. (High Sheriff 1971-72); Pres. of Nottingham Chamber of Commerce and Industry 1972-74; 1939-45 War: *m.* 1951, Angela Loveday Hanbury, da. of Air Ch. Marshal Sir (William) Alec Coryton, KCB, KBE, MVO, DFC, and has issue.

Arms—Per chevron barry of six gules and or and of the first, in chief two stag's heads caboshed proper and in base a lion rampant guardant of the second. **Crest**—Within a leathern garter buckled gules, a bee or.
Residence—Hoveringham Hall, Notts., NG14 7JR. *Clubs*, Carlton, Nottinghamshire, and Royal Commonwealth Society.

Sons living—EDWARD WILLIAM JOSEPH, *b.* Oct. 24th, 1952; ed. at Eton; Lt. 13/18th R. Hussars.——Alexander Michael, *b.* 1956; ed. at Eton.
Brother living—William George Joseph, *b.* 1926 ; ed. at Wellington Coll.; European War 1944-45 as Lieut. 13th/18th Roy. Hussars : *m.* 1961, Jennifer Jane, el. da. of L. Aylwin Richardson, FRCS, of Minstead, Hants, and has issue living, Charles William Joseph, *b.* 1965,—Richard George Aylwin, *b.* 1966,—Olivia Jane Caroline, *b.* 1970. *Residence*, Brook House, Hoveringham, Notts.

Sisters living—Elizabeth Josephine, *TD*, *b.* 1920; a JP of Notts.; 1939-45 War with ATS. *Residence*, Hall Close, Hoveringham, Notts.——Rosemary Alice Anne, *b.* 1923 : *m.* 1947, Peter Bingham Inchbald [*see* Bingham, Bt., ext.]. *Residence*, Holdfast Manor, Upton-on-Severn, Worcs.——Diana Christian Isabella, *b.* 1924; 1939-45 War with Mobile Red Cross attached R.N.: *m.* 1950, Col. Sidney John Watson, MBE, late RE [B. Dulverton], of Ballingarrane, Clonmel, co. Tipperary, and has issue living, John Wilfred *b.* 1952,—Elizabeth Sandra, *b.* 1953.

The 1st baronet, Col. Sir Joseph Nall, DSO, TD (el. son of the late Joseph Nall, of Hoveringham and Broom Cottage, High Legh, Cheshire) was a Director of several Transport and Industrial undertakings, a DL for Lancashire and Notts (High Sheriff 1952-3), Pres. of Institute of Transport 1925-26, and MP for Hulme Div. of Manchester (U) 1918-29, and 1931-45. He served in European War 1914-18 (wounded, despatches, D.S.O.).

NAPIER, Creation (N.S.) 1627, of Merchistoun.

Faith preserved renders prosperous;
Look well; Without stain.

Sir WILLIAM ARCHIBALD NAPIER OF MERCHISTOUN, 13th *Baronet; b.* July 19th, 1915; *s.* his father, *Sir* ROBERT ARCHIBALD, 1965; ed. at Stowe; 1939-45 War, as Capt. S. African Engineers, in Middle East: *m.* 1942, Kathleen Mabel, da. of the late Reginald Greaves, of Tapelberg, Cape Province, and has issue.

Arms—Quarterly, 1st and 4th argent, on a saltire engrailed between four roses gules, the roses barbed vert, five mullets of the field, *Napier of Merchistoun*; 2nd, azure, a lion rampant argent, crowned or, *MacDowall of Garthland*; 3rd argent, a fess azure voided of the field, between three demi-lions crowned gules, *Milliken of that Ilk*. **Crests**—*Dexter*, on a chape are gules furred ermine, *for the feudal Barony of Merchistoun*; an arm grasping an eagle's leg proper, talons expanded gules, *Napier of Merchistoun*; *Sinister*, A demi-lion rampant gules, holding in his dexter forepaw a dagger or, *Milliken of Culcreuch*. **Supporters**—Two eagles with their wings closed proper.
Residence—Merchiston Croft, PO Box 65/177, Benmore, Sandown, Johannesburg, S. Africa. *Clubs*,—Country (Johannesburg), Rand (Johannesburg), Junior Carlton.

Son living—JOHN ARCHIBALD LENNOX (Merchistoun, PO Box 65177, Benmore, 2010, Transvaal, S. Africa), *b.* Dec. 6th, 1946; ed. at St. Stithians, and Witwatersrand Univ., Johannesburg: *m.* 1969, Erica, da. of the late Kurt Kingsfield, of Johannesburg, and has issue living, Natalie Ann, *b.* 1973.
Daughter living of 11th Baronet—(Mary) Marjory, *b.* 1915. *Residence*, 62, Kingston House, North, S.W.7.
Collateral Branches living.
Issue of the late Major Robert Francis Ladeveze Napier, 2nd son of 9th baronet, *b.* 1856, *d.* 1898 : *m.* 1887, Emily Norrie, who *d.* 1961, da. of the late George L. A. Moke, of New York :—
Noreen Mary Hay (*Hon. Mrs. Charles P. St. John*), *b.* 1895: *m.* 1914, the Hon. Charles Paulet St. John, who *d.* 1945 [*see* B. St. John]. *Residence*, Beach Lodge, North Berwick.
Issue of the late William Edward Stirling Napier, 3rd son of 9th baronet, *b.* 1858, *d.* 1000 : *m.* 1884, Jane Catherine, who *d.* 1945, da. of the late W. M. Reid :—
William Edward Stirling, *MC*, *TD*, *b.* 1893; Lt.-Col. R.A. (TA); late Maj. Lothians and Border Horse; European War 1915-18 (M.C.), European War 1939-45 (prisoner): *m.* 1919, Audrey, da. of the late William Houlding. of Liverpool, and Arcachon, France, and has issue living, Ian *b.* 1927,—Elizabeth June Houlding, *b.* 1920: *m.* 1947, Lt.-Col. Gerald Patrick Gardner-Brown, RA (ret.), of Dragon Farm, Wildes Meadow, NSW 2577, and has issue living, Elspeth Susan *b.* 1948, Vivien *b.* 1951: *m.* 1974, John Grant Pagan, only son of Brig. Sir John Ernest Pagan, CMG, MBE,—Lavinia, *b.* 1924: *m.* 1947, Capt. C. Czarkowski-Golijeivski, 14th Polish Lancers,—Elspeth Mary, *b.* 1933: *m.* 1957, Denbigh Hamilton Harding, of Halcyon, Shootersway Lane, Berkhamsted, and has issue living, Caroline *b.* 1958, Fiona *b.* 1960, Unity *b.* 1962. *Residence*, 1, St. Colms, N. Berwick, E. Lothian.——Aleck Douglas, *b.* 1894; formerly Lt. RASC: *m.* 1927,

Dorris Mary Clara, da. of the late Victor Hide Hill, and has issue living, Alexander Colin, *b.* 1930,—John Stirling, *b.* 1935.——Lola Lillias Daphne, *b.* 1891: *m.* 1928, as his 3rd wife, Col. Algernon Cautley Jeffcoat, CB, CMG, DSO, who *d.* 1963, and has issue living, Ann (c/o National & Grindlays Bank, Ltd., 13, St. James's Sq., SW1), *b.* 1929: *m.* 1951, Air Commodore Alan David Dick, CBE, AFC, and has issue living, Jeremy *b.* 1955, Rupert *b.* 1957, Jennifer *b.* 1953, Rebecca *b.* 1959. *Residence,* Droxford House, Maritzburg, Natal, S. Africa.

This family is a branch of the Earls of Levenax or Lennox (title extinct), and is said to have taken its name from a saying by Alexander III. (of Scotland), after battle, that Lennox had *na peer* (no equal). Sir William, the 8th baronet, was served heir male general to Archibald, 3rd Baron Napier 1817, and afterwards assumed the baronetcy—one of the oldest in Scotland—which had remained dormant for 134 years. Sir Alexander Lennox Milliken Napier, 11th Bt., Capt. Grenadier Guards, was A.D.C. to Gov.-Gen. and Com.-in-Ch. of Australia (Earl of Dudley) 1910-12 ; he served in S. Africa 1902, and in European War 1914-17 (twice wounded).

NAPIER, Creation (U.K.) 1867, of Merrion Square, Dublin.

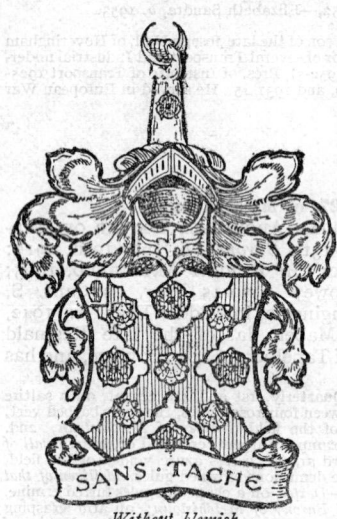

Without blemish

SANS · TACHE

Sir JOSEPH WILLIAM LENNOX NAPIER, *O.B.E.*, 4th *Baronet; b.* Aug. 1st, 1895 ; *s.* his father, *Lieut.-Col. Sir* WILLIAM LENNOX, 1915; ed. at Rugby, and at Jesus Coll., Camb.; late Underwriting Member of Lloyd's; 1914-18 War in Gallipoli and Mesopotamia (thrice wounded, prisoner), 1939-45 War, as Lieut.-Col. on Headquarters Staff of E. Command and in Italy; OBE (Mil.) 1944 : *m.* 1931, Isabel Muriel, 2nd da. of the late Major Henry Siward Balliol Surtees, J.P., D.L., of Redworth Hall, co. Durham, and has issue.

Arms—Argent, on a saltire engrailed between four roses gules, five escallops or. *Crest*—A dexter cubit arm erect proper, charged with a rose gules, the hand grasping a crescent argent.

Residences—17, Cheyne Gdns., SW3; Berystede Cottage, South Ascot, Berks. *Club*—Alpine.

Sons living—ROBERT SURTEES (107, Woodsford Sq., W14 8DT; Rose Tree Cottage, Lower Upham, nr. Southampton; Boodle's, City of London, Union (NSW), MCC, and Flyfishers Clubs), *b.* March 5th, 1932; ed. at Eton; has assumed the forename of Surtees in lieu of those of Aubone Siward; a Dir. of Charterhouse Japhet, Ltd., Merchant Bankers: *m.* 1971, Jennifer Beryl, da. of the late H. Warwick Daw, of Flint Walls, Henley-on-Thames, and has issue living. Charles Joseph, *b.* 1973.——John Lennox (49, Ennerdale Rd., Kew, Richmond, Surrey; MCC), *b.* 1934; ed. at Eton: *m.* 1967, Cecily, da. of Arthur Mortimer, and has issue living, James Alexander, *b.* 1969.——Jessica, *b.* 1971.

Brother living—Vivian John Lennox, MC, *b.* 1898; ed. at Uppingham; Brig. (ret.) late S. Wales Borderers; a DL for co. Brecknock (Vice-Lieut. 1967) and an OStJ; Brig. Comdg. Mombasa Area 1948-49, and Dep. Comd. S.-W. Dist., United Kingdom 1949-51; 1914-18 War (wounded, MC); 1939-45 War in Middle East (despatches, prisoner): *m.* 1958, Marion Avis, OBE, da. of the late Lt.-Col. Sir John Conway Lloyd, MC. *Residence.*—Ty Nant, Groesffordd, Breconshire.

Sister living—(GWENDOLYN Mabel), Shelagh LENNOX NAPIER (of Fleetwater House, Minstead, Lyndhurst, Hants.), *b.* 1900; assumed by deed poll 1943 the names of Shelagh Lennox Napier: *m.* 1st, 1929, Clive Norman Burnett, from whom she obtained a divorce 1934; 2ndly, 1949, Thomas Tettrell Phelps, who *d.* 1963.

Collateral Branch living

Issue of the late Maj. Charles MacNaughten Napier, 2nd son of 3rd baronet, *b.* 1896, *d.* 1967: *m.* 1923, Dorothy Constance (who *d.* 1960, and from whom he obtained a divorce 1939), da. of the late Col. Reginald Hawkins Hall Dempster, DSO, of Dunnichen and Auchterforfar:—

Lennox Alexander Hawkins, OBE, MC (Craig-y-Dorth, Monmouth, Gwent), *b.* 1928; Brig. late SWB, and RRW; OStJ; MBE (Mil) 1965, OBE (Mil) 1970: *m.* 1959, Jennifer Dawn, da. of B. Wilson, and has issue living, Philip Martin Lennox, *b.* 1964,—Joanna Dawn, *b.* 1962,—Sally Vanessa, *b.* 1967.——Audrey Lennox, *b.* 1926: *m.* 1958, Lt.Col. Henry Christian Ewart Harding, MC, RA, of Boarmans, Beaulieu, Hants, and has issue living, William George Charles, *b.* 1964,—Sarah Constance Hope, *b.* 1961,—Susan Jane Napier, *b.* 1966.

The 1st baronet, Sir Joseph, P.C., D.C.L., LL.D., sat as M.P. for Dublin University (*C*) 1848-57 and was Lord Chancellor of Ireland 1858-9, a member of the Judicial Committee of the Privy Council 1868-81, First Lord Commissioner for Custody of Great Seal in Ireland 1874, and Vice-Chancellor of Dublin University 1867-80. The 3rd baronet, Lieut.-Col. Sir William Lennox, was killed in action in the Dardanelles Aug. 1915, when serving as Major with 4th Batn. S. Wales Borderers.

Naylor-Leyland, see Leyland.

NEAVE, Creation (G.B.) 1795, of Dagnam Park, Essex.

Those things only are becoming which are honourable.

Sir ARUNDELL THOMAS CLIFTON NEAVE,
6th *Baronet* ; *b.* May 31st, 1916 ; *s.* his father,
Sir THOMAS LEWIS HUGHES, 1940 ; ed. at Eton ;
is Major (retired) Welsh Guards ; European War
1939-40 in France : *m.* 1946, Richenda Alice Ione,
da. of Sir Robert Joshua Paul, 5th Bt. (*cr.* 1794),
and has issue.

Arms—Argent, on a cross sable five fleurs-de-lis or.
Crest—Out of a ducal coronet gold a lily, stalked and leaved
vert, flowered and seeded or.

Clubs—Carlton, Guards', Pratt's, Kildare Street.

Sons living—PAUL ARUNDELL, *b.* Dec. 13th, 1948.——
Robert Joshua, *b.* 1951.

Daughters living—Dilys Richenda, *b.* 1947: *m.* 1968,
Timothy Hayward Hobson, of Whitedale, Hambledon,
Hants., and has issue living, Jake Timothy, *b.* 1971,—
Barnaby John, *b.* 1974,—Richenda Eveline, *b.* 1969.——
Serena Mary, *b.* 1955.

Brother living—Kenelm Digby ; (Saunders Farm, Sissinghurst, Kent), *b.* 1921 ; ed. at Harrow ; Capt. (ret.)
Welsh Gds. ; N.-W. Europe 1944-5 (wounded) : *m.* 1st,
1949, Venetia Neave ; 2ndly, 1970, Marian Rosamond,
da. of Gerald Hartley Lees, and has issue living (by
1st m.), Nicola Venetia, *b.* 1956,—Dorinda May, *b.* 1958.

Sisters living—Dorina Mary Eileen, *b.* 1911 : *m.* 1936,
Brigadier Frederick Gillespie Austin Parsons, C.B.E.
(retired), late Roy. Northumberland Fusiliers, and has
issue living, Anthony Frederick Arundell (c/o Lloyds
Bank, 6, Pall Mall, SW2), *b.* 1937 ; ed. at Wellington Coll. ;
Capt. R. Northumberland Fusiliers : *m.* 1965, Jane, da. of John Llewillin, of Highlands, Harrow
on the Hill,—Robert Gillespie, *b.* 1942 ; ed. at Wellington Coll. ; Capt., 1st RRF : *m.* 1969, Anne
P. S., da. of Maj. J. Prestwich, of Highland Farm, Ossington, Hants. *Residence*, Whitehall,
Chittlehamholt, Devon.——Renee Arundell (*Lady Williams-Bulkeley*), *b.* 1913 : *m.* 1938, Lt.-Col.
Sir Richard Harry David Williams-Bulkeley, 13th Bt., late R. Welch Fusiliers. *Residence*, Plas
Meigan, Beaumaris, Anglesey.

Collateral Branches living.

Grandchildren of the late Sheffield Henry Morier Neave (infra):—
Issue of the late Sheffield Airey Neave, C.M.G., O.B.E., *b.* 1879, *d.* 1961: *m.* 1st, 1915,
Dorothy, who *d.* 1943, da. of the late Lieut.-Col. Arthur Thomson Middleton, J.P.,
13th Hussars, of Ayshe Court, Horsham, Sussex ; 2ndly, 1946, Mary Irene (of Wagtails,
Fryerning, Ingatestone, Essex), da. of Henry Hodges, of Broadway Hall, Churchstoke,
Montgomery:—

(By 1st m.) Airey Middleton Sheffield, *DSO, OBE, MC, TD, MP* (32, Westminster Gdns., SW1; The
Old Vicarage, Ashbury, Swindon, and Tavistock House East, Woburn Walk, Tavistock Sq.,
WC1), *b.* 1916 ; ed. at Eton, and at Merton Coll., Oxford (BA 1938, MA 1955); Bar. Middle
Temple 1943 ; is Lt.-Col. RA (TA Reserve), and Dir. of Clarke Chapman Ltd. ; PPS to Min. of
Transport and Civil Aviation Feb. to July 1954, and to Sec. of State for the Colonies 1954-56,
Joint Parliamentary Sec. to Min. of Transport and Civil Aviation 1957-59, and Under Sec. of
State for Air Jan. to Oct. 1959; Chm. Select Cttee. on Science and Technology 1970-74; a Gov. of
Imperial Coll. of Science and Technology, London 1963-71; 1939-45 War (wounded, despatches,
MC, DSO, Officer of Order of Orange Nassau of the Netherlands, American Bronze Star, French
Croix de Guerre, prisoner); Order of Restitution of Poland; MP for Abingdon Div. of Berks (*C*)
since 1953; DSO 1945, OBE (Mil) 1947: *m.* 1942, Diana Josceline Barbara, da. of Thomas Arthur
Giffard, MBE (Trollope, Bt.], and has issue living, Richard Patrick Sheffield, *b.* 1947,—William
Robert Sheffield, *b.* 1953,—Marigold Elizabeth Cassandra, *b.* 1944: *m.* 1968, William Richard
Broughton Webb, of Hill House, Cookley Lane, Kinver, Staffs., and has issue living, Edward
Alexander Broughton *b.* 1974, Katharine Angela Mary *b.* 1970.——Digby John Sheffield (1, Rue
Champflour, Marly-le-Roi, Seine-et-Oise, France), *b.* 1928; ed. at Eton. and at Merton Coll.,
Oxford: *m.* 1st, 1958, Ulla, who *d.* 1963, da. of A. B. Schmidt, of Gillelejė, Denmark; 2ndly, 1966,
Christine, da. of E. J. Corty, of L'Etang-al-Ville, France, and has issue living, (by 1st m.) Victoria
b. 1959,—Phillipa *b.* 1960,—(by 2nd m.), Lionel Digby Sheffield, *b.* 1966.——Iris Averil (*Lady
Milton*) (Riverside, Hewish, Crewkerne, Som.) *b.* 1918; sometime 2nd Officer WRNS: *m.* 1954,
Sir Frank Milton, Ch. Metro. Magistrate, who *d.* 1976.——Rosamund Malua, *b.* 1921: *m.* 1939,
Capt. Edward Noble Sheppard, Essex Yeo. *Residence*, Bay Trees, Long Rd., Dedham, nr.
Colchester, Essex.——Viola Dorothy, *b.* 1925.

Issue of the late Lt.-Col. Richard Neave, *b.* 1881, *d.* 1962: *m.* 1912, Helen Elizabeth
Mary, who *d.* 1976, da. of the late Robert Miller:—

Robert Morier Sheffield, *M.C., M.R.C.V.S.*, (of Layer Breton Lodge, Colchester, Essex), *b.* 1917,
ed. at London Univ.; is Major 13th/18th Hussars (Supplementary Reserve); European War
1939-44 (wounded, M.C.): *m.* 1945, Philippa Elizabeth, only da. of the late Lieut.-Col. (Vincent)
Basil Ramsden, D.S.O., M.C. [*see* V. St. Davids, colls.], and has issue living, Julia Helen, *b.*
1953,—Lucinda Philippa, *b.* 1954.——Harriet Elise Bunty, *b.* 1957.——Julius Arthur Sheffield,
M.B.E., (of Mill Green Park, Ingatestone, Essex), *b.* 1919; ed. at Sherborne; is Major 13th/18th
Hussars (Reserve); European War 1939-45 (despatches, M.B.E.); M.B.E. (Mil.) 1945: *m.* 1951,
Helen Margery, da. of the late Lieut.-Col. Percy Morland Acton-Adams, D.S.O., of Clarence
Reserve, Kaikoura, New Zealand, and has issue living, Helen Penelope, *b.* 1952,—Joan Miranda
Mary, *b.* 1954.—Venetia Beatrice, *b.* 1958.——Beatrice Honoria Sheffield, *b.* 1916: *m.* 1952,
Eustace Blewitt Robinson, of Garden Cottage, Drinkstone Park, Bury-St. Edmunds, and has
issue living, Eleanor Mary, *b.* 1953.

Grandchildren of the late Sheffield Neave, 3rd son of 2nd Bt.:—
Issue of the late Edward Strangways Neave, *b.* 1857, *d.* 1935: *m.* 1882, Evelyn Jane, who
d. 1934, da. of the late Lieut.-Col. Robert Vansittart (Coldstream Guards), of Chuffs,
Maidenhead:—

Eric Lloyd Strangways, *b.* 1898: *m.* 1934, Lucy Mary, da. of Josiah Charles Roberts.——Evelyn
Henrica, *b.* 1889: *m.* 1935, Ernest Morison, who *d.* 1955.

Grandchildren of the late Edward Strangways Neave (ante):—
Issue of the late Edward Arthur Neave, *b.* 1883, *d.* 1960: *m.* 1916, Evelyn Margaret,
who *d.* 1966 da. of George Augustus Lamb (British Guiana Police), of Rye, Sussex:—
Digby Seymour, *b.* 1921; is a F.R.I.C.S.; European War 1940-45 as Lieut. R.A. in N.-W. Europe:
m. 1948, Christel, who *d.* 1963, only da. of Prof. Poul Outzen Boisen, OBE, of Rektorboligen,
Rungsted, Kyst, Denmark. *Residen*‥

Issue of the late Guy Morier Neave, *b.* 1886, *d.* 1950 : *m.* 1925, Dorothy, who *d.* 1961, da.
of the late J. E. Ponsonby-Steele :—

June Violet, *b.* 1928 : *m.* 1956, Bryan Francis Blake, and has issue living, Stephen Guy, *b.* 1958,—
Judith Clare, *b.* 1960.——Rose Ann, *b.* 1930: *m.* 1955, Robert Arthur Jackman, of 6, Overwood
Drive, King's Park, Glasgow, S4, and has issue living, Scott Robert, *b.* 1963,—Lindsey Ann,
b. 1961.

Grandchildren of the late Rev. William Alexander Neave, el. son of the late
William Augustus Neave (infra) :—
Issue of the late Lionel Digby Neave, M.R.C.S., L.R.C.P., *b.* 1873, *d.* 1951 : *m.* 1909,
Winifred, who *d.* 1956, da. of Michael Burke :—
Nelson Digby, *b.* 1914; 1939-45 War as F/Lt. RAFVR: *m.* 1936, Betty Ross, of Liverpool, and has
issue living, Marilyn Kathryn, *b.* 1938: *m.* 1958, Samuel Shub, MRACP, of 18, Bellaire Court,
Beaumaris, Vic., Aust., and has issue living, Martin David Neave *b.* 1959, Carolyn Leanne *b.*
1960, Melissa Louise *b.* 1965.——John Alexander (Dagwood Farm, Elmswell, Bury St. Edmunds),
b. 1919: *m.* 1946, Jacqueline, only child of F. Ranger, of Holyhead, Anglesey, and has issue
living, David John, *b.* 1954,—Judith Marion, *b.* 1948: *m.* 1969, James Brame, of 25, Gracechurch St., Debenham, and has issue living, James Kenneth *b.* 1969,—Margaret Alison, *b.* 1950:
m. 1969, Jean-Claude Estripeau, and has issue living, Natalie Isabelle *b.* 1970,—Catherine Mary,
b. 1951: *m.* 1971, Hartwig Waldemar Nicolaus of 150, Norton Village Lane, Norton Village,
Rochester, NY, USA, and has issue living, Heidi Marie *b.* 1971.——Geoffrey Lionel, *b.* 1920; ed. at
Ascham Coll., and County High Sch., Clacton-on-Sea; 1943-45 War with Roy. Hampshire Regt. in
Italy and Greece: *m.* 1964, Freda Mary Walmsley, da. of the late G. H. Hobson, of Lincoln.
Residence, 13, Bridge St., Elsternwick 3185, Melbourne, Vic., Aust.——Mary Winifred, *b.* 1913:
m. 1933, the Rev. Dennis Victor Wright, AKC, and has issue living, Stephen John Neave (Don-
ington, Western Rd., Silver End, Rivenhall, Essex), *b.* 1934; ed. at Brentwood Sch., and at Co.
High Sch., Buckhurst Hill, Essex: *m.* 1960, Jennifer Anne, *SRN,* da. of Arthur John Carter, of
Chingford, Essex, and has issue living, Christopher Jonathan Neave *b.* 1961, Nigel Robin Neave
b. 1962, Samantha Jane *b.* 1966,—*Rev.* Martin Neave (4, Harley St., Port Harcourt, Nigeria),
b. 1937; ed. at King's Coll., London (AKC 1st class honours 1961); Dean of Ecumenical Project,
Port Harcourt, Nigeria, since 1971,—Ruth Mary, *b.* 1943; SRN; Certificate in Ed. *Residence,*
Tichmarsh Rectory, Kettering, Northants.

Grandson of the late Francis Digby Spencer Neave, 2nd son of the late William
Augustus Neave, 4th son of 2nd baronet:—
Issue of the late Everard Algidus Neave, *b.* 1879, *d.* 1955 : *m.* 1900, Nora Cottell, who *d.*
1953 :—
Digby Everard, *b.* 1911; in Roy. Canadian Ordnance Corps.

Grandchildren of the late Francis Digby Spencer Neave (ante).
Issue of the late Francis Digby Neave, *b.* 1874, *d.* 1943: *m.* 1910, Ethelberta, who *d.* 1970
da. of Edward Washbourn, of St. Albans, Christchurch, New Zealand:
John Digby (32, James St., Glenfield, Auckland, NZ), *b.* 1916; formerly Ch. Instructor at Canter-
bury Aero Club: *m.* 1939, Martha Dorothy, da. of R. F. Francis, of St. Albans, Christchurch, NZ,
and has issue living, Richard Francis (34, Hillcrest Place, Ch. Ch. 4, NZ), *b.* 1941: *m.* 1962, Patricia
Lorraine McGuire, and has issue living, Roger John Francis *b.* 1962, Deborah Michelle *b.* 1965,
Amanda Gaye *b.* 1969,—Barbara Alice, *b.* 1940: *m.* 1962, Ramon Juan Saunders, of 54, Holland
Av., Hillcrest, Auckland 10, NZ; and has issue living, David John *b.* 1968, James Richard Neave
b. 1972, Rachael Louise *b.* 1974,—Eleanor Elizabeth, *b.* 1943: *m.* 1964, Bruce Peter Anderson,
and has issue living, Thomas Digby *b.* 1970, Philip Richard *b.* 1972.——Henry Washbourn, *b.*
1918: *m.* 1st, 1945 (divorce 1949), Doreen Melba, da. of J. W. Wright Spreydon; 2ndly, 1953,
Sheila Duncan, da. of R. H. Bennetts, of Christchurch, NZ, and has issue living, (by 2nd m.)
Alistair Dudley Digby, *b.* 1956,—Richard Henry Digby, *b.* 1960,—Diana Sheila, *b.* 1954. *Resi-
dence,* 98, Clyde Rd., Fendalton, Christchurch, NZ.——Arthur Kenelm, *b.* 1924: *m.* 1951,
Elizabeth Marie (DOYLE), da. of George Brady. *Residence,* Ceduna, S. Aust.——Elizabeth
Marjorie, *b.* 1911: *m.* 1941, Grgo Franicevic, of 5, Tui St., Ch. Ch. 4, NZ, and has issue living,
Vincent Peter Ivan (5, Qui St., Fendalton, Ch. Ch., NZ), *b.* 1942: *m.* 1963 (m. diss. 1972), Maritza
Ann Frances Glucina,—Edward John Grgo, *b.* 1946: *m.* 1957, Margaret Anne Blay, and has issue
living, Lisa Marie *b.* 1967, Anita *b.* 1969, Terry *b.* 1974,—Paul Francis Anton, *b.* 1949,—Lois
Ethel Yurka, *b.* 1944: *m.* 1966, Geoffrey Herbert Heath, of 61, Martin St., Monaco, Nelson, NZ,—
Mara Elizabeth, *b.* 1948.——Nancy Mary (7, Moorpark Pl., Ch. Ch. 4, NZ), *b.* 1921: *m.* 1st, 1945
(m. diss. 1971), Maxwell Milner; 2ndly, 1972, Eric Sidney Fostyn Holland (MP for NZ), and has
issue living (by 1st m.), Bruce Digby, *b.* 1948: *m.* 1971, Nancy Gomez-Cormejo,—Judith Adrienne,
b. 1946: *m.* 1966, Leonard Edward Wilson-Parr, of 114, Fendalton Rd., Christchurch 4, NZ, and
has issue living, Jane Louise *b.* 1970, Susan Elizabeth *b.* 1972, Sarah Ann *b.* 1974.

Granddaughters of the late Lieut.-Col. Everard Strangways Neave, son of the
late William Augustus Neave (ante) :—
Issue of the late Everard Reginald Neave, *b.* 1877, *d.* 1951 (having assumed in 1910 the
additional surname of Hay before his patronymic) : *m.* 1910, Amy Charlotte Paterson
Balfour Hay of Leys and Randlestone, who *d.* 1971, da. of the late Peter Hay-
Paterson:—
Beatrice Rosemary, *b.* 1911; is a SRN: *m.* 1970, Capt. Colin Napier Christie, Black Watch, of
Sheelyn, Leven, Fife, KY8 5NR, and has issue living, Mary Helen, *b.* 1941: *m.* 1970, James
Beaton Marshall, of Ormlie, Bankend Rd., Bridge of Weir, Renfrewshire,—Anna Margaret,
b. 1943: *m.* 1970, Derek O'Shea, of 49, Woodfield Cres., Ealing, W5, and has issue living, Catherine
Janet *b.* 1972.——Diana Hope, *b.* 1918: *m.* 1st, 1940, David James Reoch Ritchie, Pilot Officer
R.A.F. Vol. Reserve, who *d.* (killed on active ser. during European War) 1943 ; 2ndly, 1950,
Richard Kolaczkowski, of Gentzstrasse 1A, Schwabing, 8000 Munich 13, W. Germany, and
has issue living (by 2nd m.), Anita Marya *b.* 1951.——Griselda Nancy, *b.* 1920; formerly
Subaltern A.T.S.: *m.* 1943, Henry Feliks Jascoll (formerly Jaszezolt), late Polish Army, and
has issue living, Dominic Peter, *b.* 1945,—John Henry David, *b.* 1949; ed. at London Sch. of
Econs., London Univ. (MScEcon): *m.* 1974, Dorothy Ann Luttringer. *Residence,* 28, Ravensbourne Gdns., Ealing, W13.

Grandchildren of the late Richard Irvine Neave, el. son of the late George
Peters Neave, son of the late Richard Neave, 3rd son of 1st baronet :—
Issue of the late Arundell Francis Robert Irvine Neave, *b.* 1874, *d.* 1918 : *m.* 1902, Mona,
Lewis, who *d.* 1958 :—
Arundell Richard Yorke Irvine, *DSC* (Puffins, 10, High St., Lee-on-Solent, Hants.) *b.* 1915;
Lt.-Cdr. RN: *m.* 1941, Barbara Marie, only da. of the late Frederick Charles Evelyn Liardet, of
Beech Park, Newton Abbot, and has issue living, Guy Richard Irvine, *b.* (Dec.) 1941; ed. at
King's Sch., Worcester, and Queen Mary's Coll., London (PhD),—Penelope Gaye, *b.* 1945: *m.*
1966, Duncan Edward McBarnet, of 2, Crown Point Cottages, Seal Chart, Sevenoaks, Kent, and
has issue living, Justin Guy *b.* 1970, Alasdair Mathew *b.* 1972.——Muriel Catherine, *b.* 1907:
m. 1928, Graham Thorpe, of Westfield, Calpe Av., Lyndhurst, Hants.

Grandchildren of the late George Howard Neave, younger son of the late George
Peters Neave (ante) :—
Issue of the late Cecil Howard Neave, *b.* 1877, *d.* 1937: *m.* 1902, Daisy Dolores Scales,
who *d.* 1945 :—
Geoffrey Howard, *b.* 1917: *m.* 1946, Mary Therese Jeannette, da. of the late Joseph Adelard Voyer,
and has issue living, Bernadette Blanche Dolores, *b.* 1947; *m.* 1968, Arvid Charles Nelson,
late US Marines, of 10615A 30th Av. N., Minneapolis, Minn., 55427 USA, and has issue living,

Michael Shawn *b.* 1969, Robert David *b.* 1973. *Residence,* 21, Cornell Av., Rumford, Rhode Is., USA.——Iris Olga, *b.* 1906: *m.* 1932, Frederic James of the Tile House, Longparish, Andover, Hants., and has issue living, Sonya Ann, *b.* 1933.

The Neave family lived at Tivetshall, Norfolk, temp. Henry IV Sir William Le Neve, Clarenceux King of Arms 1660, belonged to a younger branch. Sir Richard Neave, of Dagnam Park, Essex, 1st baronet, was Governor of the Bank of England 1780.

NELSON, Creation (U.K.) 1912, of Acton Park, Acton, of Denbigh.

Sir WILLIAM VERNON HOPE NELSON, O.B.E., 3rd *Baronet,* only son of the late William Hope Nelson, 2nd son of 1st baronet; *b.* May 25th, 1914; *s.* his uncle, *Sir* JAMES HOPE, 1960; ed. at Beaumont; Major (retired) late 8th Hussars; Palestine 1936-9 (despatches, medal with clasp); O.B.E. (Mil.) 1952: *m.* 1945, the Hon. Elizabeth Ann Bevil Cary, da. of 14th Viscount Falkland, and has issue.

Arms—Quarterly, 1st and 4th gules, on a fesse between three daggers points downwards or, two sinister hands couped of the field; 2nd and 3rd argent, a pile engrailed ermines between two lions' heads erased in base gules, langued azure, a chief vair all within a bordure vert. **Crests**—1st, in front of a sun rising or, a sinister arm embowed in armour proper, the hand grasping a dagger point downwards as in the arms; 2nd, issuant from clouds proper charged with three mullets azure, a globe fracted at the top under a rainbow with clouds at each end proper.

Per se confidens. *Confident in oneself.*

Residences—White House Farm, Holnest, Sherborne, Dorset: Altulla, off Kappura Lane, San Gwann, Malta, GC. *Club*—United Hunts.

Sons living—JAMIE CHARLES VERNON HOPE, *b.* Oct. 23rd, 1949.——Dominic William Michael, *b.* 1957,—Declan Hugh Plantagenet, *b.* 1968.

Daughters living—Deirdre Elizabeth Ann, *b.* 1947.——Cary Georgina, *b.* 1952,——Sophie Lucia, *b.* 1971.

Sister living—Noelle Marguerite Mary Hope, *b.* 1912: *m.* 1949, Major Neville Gerald Fitzgerald Dunne, 8th Hussars, and has issue living, Marguerite Vivian, *b.* 1953: *m.* 1971, Careneto Molfese. *Residence,* Roakhaye Farm, Membury, Axminster, S. Devon.

Aunt living—(daughter of 1st baronet)—Violet Mary Geraldine *b.* 1891: *m.* 1st, 1914, George Richard Francis Rowley, who *d.* 1971, and from whom she obtained a divorce 1920 [Corbet, Bt.]; 2ndly, 1920, as his second wife, the 2nd Duke of Westminster, who *d.* 1953, and from whom she had obtained a divorce 1926; 3rdly, 1927 (m. diss. 1951), Lt.-Col. the Hon. Frederick Heyworth Cripps, DSO, TD, RNVR [*see* B. Parmoor]. *Residence,* 29g, Eaton Sq., SW1.

Widow living of 2nd Baronet—ANNIE CATHLEEN ELIZABETH (*Cathleen, Lady Nelson*), da. of Lieut.-Col. Loftus Bryan, D.L., of Borrmount Manor co. Wexford: *m.* 1923, as his second wife, Sir James Hope Nelson, 2nd Bt., who *d.* 1960. *Residence,*

Sir William, 1st Bt. (son of James Nelson, of Cooldrinagh, Ireland), was Chm. of the Nelson Line Liverpool) (Limited), and of the Nelson Steam Navigation Co.

NEPEAN, Creation (U.K.) 1802, of Bothenhampton, Dorsetshire.

[Name pronounced "Nepeen."]

Sir EVAN YORKE NEPEAN, 6th *Baronet:* *b.* Nov. 23rd, 1909; *s.* his father, *Major Sir* CHARLES EVAN MOLYNEUX YORKE, 1953; ed. at Winchester, and at Cambridge Univ. (BA 1931, MA 1947); Lt.-Col. (ret.) R. Corps of Signals; Mohmand Operations 1936 (medal with clasp); 1939-45 War in Middle East and Western Desert (Africa Star with clasp): *m.* 1940, Georgiana Cicely da. of the late Maj. N. E. G. Willoughby, Middlesex Regt., and has issue.

Arms—Gules, a fesse wavy erminois between three mullets argent. **Crest**—On a mount vert a goat passant sable, charged on the side with two ermine spots in fesse or, collared and horned gold.

Respice. *Look back.*

Residence—Goldens, Teffont, Salisbury, Wilts.

Daughters living—Susan Cicely, *b.* 1941: *m.* 1961, James Martin Norman Aylmer Hall, of 1, Partridge Down, Olivers Battery, Winchester, and has issue living, Richard John Nepean Aylmer, *b.* 1964,—Patrick Robert Aylmer, *b.* 1966.——Katherine Mary Aylmer, *b.* 1963,—Carole Margaret Aylmer, *b.* 1967.——Judith Sarah, *b.* 1946.——Gillian Helen, *b.* 1950.

Sisters living—Mary Theresa, *b.* 1902; has Kaisar-i-Hind medal: *m.* 1934, Arthur Geoffrey Tindall Glaisby, OBE, who *d.* 1967. *Residence,* 21, Pasture Way, Churchfields, Bridport.—— Sylvia (of The Copse, Hazeley Farm, Twyford, nr. Winchester), *b.* 1903: *m.* 1924, Richard Ivor Stratton, and has issue living, James Charles, *b.* 1925,—Richard Arthur, *b.* 1927.——Olivia (of 56, Parchment St., Winchester), *b.* 1906.

Collateral Branches living.

Granddaughter of the late Col. Herbert Augustus Tierney Nepean, son of the
late Rev. Evan Nepean, 4th son of 1st baronet :—
Issue of the late Brigadier Herbert Evan Charles Bayley Nepean, C.B., C.S.I., C.M.G.,
Indian Army, *b.* 1865, *d.* 1951 : *m.* 1st, 1892, Alice Maud, who *d.* 1950, da. of the late
Surg.-Maj. Hamilton Ross, of Ballinacrae House, Ballymoney, co. Antrim ; 2ndly, 1950,
Muriel (Wenman House, 10, The Strand, Ryde, Isle of Wight), da. of the late Rev. R.
Butler Faulkner, of Oak Park House, Dawlish, Devon :—
(By 1st marriage) Clare Agnes Betty, *b.* 1905. *Residence*, Rivergate, Shaldon, Teignmouth, Devon.

Granddaughters of the late Cdr. St. Vincent Nepean, MVO, RN, 4th son of
Col. Herbert Augustus Tierney Nepean (ante):—
Issue of the late Leonard Percyval St. Vincent Nepean, *b.* 1879, *d.* 1932 : *m.* 1909, Ellen
Mary, who *d.* 1957, da. of the late Matthew Edwards, of St. Petersburg :—
Anne Camilla Catharine, *b.* 1910: *m.* 1932, Alfred Lingley Bennett, and has issue living, Gordon
Lingley Nepean, *b.* 1936,—Roger Lingley Nepean, *b.* 1937. *Address*, P.O. Box 44, Dar-es-
Salaam, Tanzania.——Evelyn, *b.* 1917: *m.* 1939, Percival William Singleton, of 8, Woodlands Rd.,
Birmingham, B11 4HE, and has issue living, Gregory St. Vincent Nepean, *b.* 1951,—Mary
Catherine, *b.* 1940: *m.* 1961, Michael Villiers Forbes O'Connor, of The Meadow, Loughborough
Rd., Thringstone, Leics., and has issue living, Dominic Rupert *b.* 1961, Christopher *b.* 1963,
Gregory *b.* 1965, Benedict *b.* 1967, Catherine O'Connor *b.* 1972,—Ruth Angela, *b.* 1941: *m.* 1961,
Robin Driver, of Mowbrays Farm, Church St., Ickleton, Saffron Walden, Essex, and has issue
living, Elizabeth Anna *b.* 1962, Lucy Clare *b.* 1964, Sarah Magdalen *b.* 1966, Anne-Marie *b.* 1968,—
Margaret Elisabeth, *b.* 1949,—Cecilia Teresa, *b.* 1953,—Bernadette Lucy, *b.* 1958,—Felicity
Maud, *b.* 1960.

This family came from St. Just, Cornwall. The Right Hon. Sir Evan, 1st baronet, was MP
for Queensborough and Bridport, Sec. of the Admiralty, Chief Sec. for Ireland, and Gov. of Bombay.

NEVILLE, Creation (U.K.) 1927, of Sloley, co. Norfolk.

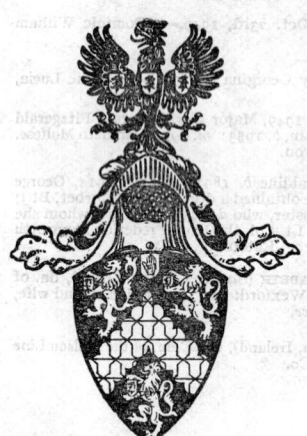

Sir JAMES EDMUND HENDERSON
NEVILLE, *M.C.*, 2nd *Baronet ; b.* July 5th,
1897 ; *s.* his father, *Sir* REGINALD JAMES
NEVILLE. 1950 ; ed. at Eton. and at R.M.C. ;
Prime Warden of Fishmongers' Co. 1958-9;
1914-18 War in France as Lt. Oxford and
Bucks L.I. (wounded, MC), N. Russia 1919
(wounded) ; Lieut.-Col. late Oxford and
Bucks L.I. ; commanded L.I. Training
Centre 1941-4 : *m.* 1932, Marie Louise, da. of
the late Charles Emmanuel Pierson, J.P., of
Vale Lodge, Weston, Bath, and has issue.

Arms—Sable, a chevron invected vair between
three lions rampant or, each holding between the paws an
escutcheon argent charged with an eagle's head erased
azure. **Crest**—An eagle displayed sable, on the breast
and on each wing an escutcheon or, charged with a
lion's head erased also sable.
Residence—Sloley Old Hall, Norwich, NR12 8HA.
Clubs—Army and Navy, Green Jackets.

Daughters living—Rosalind Angela Mary, *b.* 1933: *m.*
1954, Philip Murray Gorton, of 64, Polhill Av., Bed-
ford and has issue living, Simon Neville, *b.* 1957,—Mark Philip, *b.* 1960,—David Colin, *b.* 1962-
—Elizabeth Clare, *b.* 1958.——Jane Shirley (Cubitt Cottage, Sloley, Norwich, NR12 8HA), *b.*
1934: *m.* 1963, Vivian Vincent Esch, and has issue living, Nicholas Charles, *b.* 1966,—Rupert
Vivian Neville, *b.* 1967.

Half-Brother living—RICHARD LIONEL JOHN BAINES, *b.* July 15th, 1921 ; ed. at Eton,
and at Trin. Coll., Camb. (B.A. 1941, M.A. 1949) : Burma 1943-5 as Capt. Oxford and Bucks
L.I., and W. African Frontier Force. *Residence*, Sloley Hall, Norwich, NR12 8HA.
Sisters living—Mary Kate, *b.* 1891: *m.* 1920, Reginald Martin Vick, OBE, MCh, FRCS, who *d.* 1971,
and has issue living, Sarah Douglas, *b.* 1922,—Mary Neville, *b.* 1924: *m.* 1946, Ian David Parsons,
of Baas Manor, Broxbourne, Herts., and has issue living, James Martin *b.* 1948, Viola
Gay *b.* 1947, Susan Mary *b.* 1951, Caroline Belinda *b.* 1955, Emelyn Victoria *b.* 1957,—Juliet
Martin (*Lady Bingley*), *b.* 1925: *m.* 1948, Adm. Sir Alexander Noel Campbell Bingley, G.C.B.,
OBE, who *d.* 1972, and has issue living, William Neville *b.* 1950, Charlotte Elizabeth (twin)
b. 1950, Penelope Juliet *b.* 1954,—Emma Jane, *b.* 1929 : *m.* 1960, as his second wife, Com. Dermod
James Boris Jewitt, DSC, RN, of Bankside, Furneux Pelham, Herts. [B. Bagot], and has issue living,
Charles James Bagot *b.* 1965. *Residence*, Old Schoolhouse, Baas Manor, Broxbourne, Herts.
——(Beatrice Helen) Angela, *b.* 1894: *m.* 1920, Lt.-Col. John Victor Opynschae Macartney-
Filgate, CBE, MC, TD, who *d.* 1964, and has issue living, Christopher Martin (of 51, Black Lion
Lane, W6), *b.* 1927; ed. at Rugby: *m.* 1st, 1952 (m. diss. 1962), Patricia Pingram; 2ndly, 1962,
Diana Ruth Medworth, and has issue living, Katherine Jane *b.* 1956, (by 2nd m.)
James Gustavus Hume, *b.* 1964, Thomas Quinton Hume *b.* 1968,—Ida Helen (Baggaretts, White
Colne, Colchester), *b.* 1921: *m.* 1946, Lt.-Col. Curtis Peter Nelson Parker, MBE, TD, who *d.* 1973,
and has issue living, Timothy Jonathan Nelson *b.* 1949, James Richard Nelson, *b.* 1953. *Resi-
dence*, Slough House, Danbury, Essex.

The 1st baronet, Sir Reginald James Neville Neville, was son of the late James Sewell Neville,
Bar.-at-law, of Sloley Hall, Norfolk, who assumed by R. Licence the name and arms of Neville
1885 in lieu of White as a grandson of John White and his wife Mary (*d.* 1883) da. and co. heir of
Ralph Neville of Barton under Needwood, Staffs. He sat as MP for Wigan (C) 1910-18, and for
E. Norfolk 1924-29, and was Recorder of Bury St. Edmunds 1905-43.

NEWMAN, Creation (U.K.) 1836, of Mamhead, Devonshire.

Sir GEOFFREY ROBERT NEWMAN, 6th *Baronet*; *b.* June 2nd, 1947; *s.* his father, *Sir* RALPH ALURED, 1968; ed. at Kelly Coll.

Arms—Azure, three demi-lions rampant argent, semée of cross-crosslets, langued gules. **Crest**—A lion rampant per chevron azure gutté-de-l'eau and argent gutté-de-sang.

Residence—Blackpool House, Dartmouth, S. Devon.

Brother living—RICHARD CLAUDE, *b.* May 2nd, 1951.

Sisters living—Zabian Carlotta Annette Alfreda, *b.* 1948.——Louisa Ann, *b.* 1955.

Uncle living—Thomas, *b.* 1906; ed. at Eton, and at Ch. Ch., Oxford (MA); FRSA; formerly Capt. Grenadier Guards; is Patron of one living; 1941-45 War in N. Africa and Italy (wounded): *m.* 1938, Helen, who *d.* 1972, da. of Sir (Charles) Alban Young, KCMG, MVO, 9th Bt. (cr. 1769), and has issue living, Peter Thomas Lydston (The Manor House, Coryton, Okehampton, Devon), *b.* 1944,—Priscilla Helen, *b.* 1939: *m.* 1963, Charles Granville Stuart-Menteth, of Woodchester House, Woodchester, Glos. [see Stuart-Menteth, Bt.],—Elizabeth Clare, *b.* 1941: *m.* 1964, Robert Myles Randal MacDonnell, of 17, Malbrook Rd., SW15, and has issue living, Julian Sorley Randal, *b.* 1967, Natasha Clare *b.* 1965, Louisa Helen *b.* 1971. *Residence*, Widdicombe House, Kingsbridge, S. Devon.

Aunt living—Joyce Alfreda (*Lady Gascoigne*), *b.* 1904; is a CStJ: *m.* 1928, Maj.-Gen. Sir Julian Alvery Gascoigne, KCMG, KCVO, CB, DSO, late Grenadier Guards, son of the late Brig.-Gen. Sir (Ernest) Frederick (Orby) Gascoigne, KCVO, CMG, DSO, and has issue living, Crispin (of Ronans, Winkfield Row, Bracknell, Berks), *b.* 1929; formerly Lt. Grenadier Guards: *m.* 1954, the Hon. (Elizabeth) Ann Harcourt, da. of 2nd Viscount Harcourt, and has issue living, William Harcourt Crispin *b.* 1955, Elizabeth Laura *b.* 1958, Mary Ann *b.* 1961,—Merida, *b.* 1933: *m.* 1956, Andrew Watt Drysdale, of Ferriers Grange, Hookwood, Horley, Surrey, son of Sir Matthew Watt Drysdale. *Residence*, Sanders, Stoke Fleming, Dartmouth, S. Devon.

Widow living of 5th Baronet—ANN ROSEMARY HOPE (*Lady Newman*), (Blackpool House, Dartmouth, S. Devon), da. of the late Capt. the Hon. Claude Hope Hope-Morley [see B. Hollenden, colls.]: *m.* 1946, Sir Ralph Alured Newman, 5th Bt., who *d.* 1968.

Collateral Branch living.

Issue of the late Alured Newman, 4th son of 1st baronet, *b.* 1831, *d.* 1904: *m.* 1880, Ida Leonora Adalina Beatrice Arlington, who *d.* 1904:—

Edward Devon, *b.* 1885; Major Yeo.; European War 1915-18 in Egypt, France and **Palestine** (wounded): *m.* 1st, 1909, Violet Ethel (from whom he obtained a divorce 1926), da. of the late Rev. Morgan Kirby; 2ndly, 1926, Hilda, who *d.* 1970, da. of Leonard Norman Barrow, JP, of Normanton Hall, Southwell, Notts, and has issue living (by 1st m.) John Edward Alured, *b.* 1915, —Myra Beatrice, *b.* 1914: *m.* 1946, Lt.-Col. William Bagnall, OBE, of Upper Brook House, Marchington, Uttoxeter, Staffs., and has issue living, William Edward Hampshire (14, Queen's Rd., Mortlake, SW14), *b.* 1947: *m.* 1969, Bridget, da. of Kenneth Charles Pearce, Felicity Jane *b.* 1951. *Residence*, Brook Cottage, Somersby, Spilsby, Lincolnshire.

The 1st baronet, Sir Robert William Newman (son of the late Thomas Newman, of Dartmouth) sat as M.P. for Exeter, and was High Sheriff of Devon 1827. The 2nd baronet, Capt. Sir Robert Lydston, Grenadier Guards, *d.* (killed in action at Battle of Inkerman) 1854. The 3rd baronet, Sir Lydston, was High Sheriff of Devon, 1871. The 4th baronet, Sir Robert Hunt Stapylton Dudley Lydston, sat as M.P. for Exeter (*U.* latterly *Ind.*) 1918-31 and was *cr. Baron Mamhead*, of Exeter, co. Devon 1931.

NEWMAN, Creation (U.K.) 1912, of Cecil Lodge, Newmarket, co. Cambridge.

Sir GERARD ROBERT HENRY SIGISMUND NEWMAN, 3rd *Baronet*: *b.* July 19th, 1927; *s.* his father, *Sir* CECIL GUSTAVUS JACQUES, 1955; ed. at Eton, and at Jesus Coll., Oxford (BA 1951); a Co. Dir.: *m.* 1960, Caroline Philippa, da. of the late Brigadier Alfred Geoffrey Neville, CBE, MC [see B. Braybrooke, colls.], and has issue.

Arms—Argent, an ostrich proper, on a chief azure, a lozenge of the field between two bezants. **Crest**—Out of an antique coronet or, a springbok's head proper.

Residences—Burloes, Royston, Herts.; 27, Bloomfield Terr., SW1. *Clubs*—Boodle's, MCC.

Sons living—FRANCIS HUGH CECIL, *b.* June 12th, 1963.——Geoffrey John, *b.* 1966,—Christopher George, *b.* 1969.

Daughter living—Susanna Philippa Helen, *b.* 1962.

Brother living—John Francis (10, Chelsea Park Gdns., SW3, and Compton Park, Compton Chamberlayne, Salisbury, Wilts.), *b.* 1930; ed. at Eton; late Lt. Roy. Horse Gds.; Chm. of the Rom River Co., Ltd., and other Cos.: *m.* 1963, Caroline Henrietta, yr. da. of Lt.-Col. A. J. C. Rose, of Dunira Garden House, Comrie, Perthshire, and has issue living, Anthony John Cecil, *b.* 1966,—Henrietta Mary Alison, *b.* 1964,—Sarahjane Caroline, *b.* 1968.

Sisters living—Annabel Cecilia Mary, *b.* 1922: *m.* 1947, Peter Merton Beckwith-Smith, and has issue

By hard work and with honour

living, James Merton, *b.* 1948,—Anne Honor Mary, *b.* 1951. *Residence*, 13, Ranelagh House, Elystan Place, SW3; Byeway Cottage, Aldwick Bay, Bognor Regis.——Lynette Johanna Violet (twin) (1, Sloane Court East, SW3), *b.* 1927.——Rosalind Cynthia (Barford Mill, Churt, Surrey), *b.* 1936: *m.* 1969, Francis Albert John Watson, who *d.* 1973, and has issue living, Jeremy John Albert, *b.* 1970,—Joanna Clare Elizabeth, *b.* 1972.

Uncle living (son of 1st baronet)—Guy Arthur, *b.* 1904; ed. at Eton, and at Univ. Coll., Oxford (B.A. 19—, M.A. 1934); is a J.P. for London, and a Director of Woodcote Grove Estate Co., Ltd., and of Stanners, Ltd.; 1939-45 War as Capt. R.A.; was a Co. Councillor for London 1934-37; assumed by deed poll 1936 the surname of Newman in lieu of his patronymic: *m.* 1930, the Hon. Jean Sybil Loch, da. of 2nd Baron Loch, and has issue living, Mary Ella *b.* 1931: *m.* 1954, Lt. Col. William Richard Edgedale, The Life Guards, of The Little House, Binfield, Berks.,—Diana Margaret Anna, *b.* 1934,—Ann Elizabeth, *b.* 1937: *m.* 1965, Richard James Randal MacDonnell, of 20, Wallgrave Rd., SW5, and has issue living, Simon Guy Randel *b.* 1968, Crispin Paul Geoffrey Randel *b.* 1974, Tania Alice *b.* 1966. *Residence*, Stanners Hill Manor, Chobham, Surrey. *Club*—Boodle's

Aunts living (daughters of 1st baronet)—Sybil Rose (*Baroness Grimston of Westbury*), *b.* 1895: *m.* 1st, 1920 (m. annulled on her petition 1921), Capt. Victor Malcolm Wombwell, formerly Scots Gds. [Wombwell, Bt.]; 2ndly, 1923, 1st Baron Grimston of Westbury. *Residence*, 4, Cadogan Sq., SW1.——Rosie Violet Nina Millicent, *b.* 1896; is a FRGS; assumed by deed poll 1936 the surname of Newman in lieu of her patronymic. *Address*, Dorchester Hotel, Park Lane, W1.

Sir Sigmund NEUMANN, 1st baronet (son of Gustav Neumann, of Fuerth, Bavaria), was partner in the firms of S. Neumann and Co., merchants, of Salisbury House, E.C., and Neumann, Luebeck and Co., bankers. Sir Cecil Gustavus Jacques Newman, 2nd baronet, who was High Sheriff of Herts. 1939, and Pres. of National Asso. Fishery Board 1946-51, assumed by Roy. licence 1936 the surname of Newman in lieu of Neumann.

NEWNES, Creation (U.K.) 1895, of Wildcroft, Putney, co. London, Hollerday Hill, Lynton, and Hesketh House, Torquay, co. Devon. [Extinct 1955.]

Sir FRANK HILLYARD NEWNES, *C.B.E.* 2nd and last *Baronet.*

Widow living of 2nd Baronet—DOROTHY (*Lady Newnes*), da. of Everard Firebrace Darlot, of Perth, W. Australia, and widow of Stephen Delmar-Morgan : *m.* 1946, as his second wife, Sir Frank Hillyard Newnes, C.B.E., 2nd baronet, who *d.* 1955, when the title became ext. *Residence,* 59, London Lane, Bromley, Kent.

NEWSON, Creation (U.K.) 1921, of Framlingham, co. Suffolk. [Extinct 1950.]

Sir PERCY WILSON NEWSON, 1st and last *Baronet.*

Daughters living of 1st Baronet—(Violet) Muir (*Dowager Lady Napier and Ettrick*), *b.* 1909 ; is National Pres. of Young Women's Christian Asso. of Scotland: *m.* 1928, the 13th Lord Napier and Ettrick, who *d.* 1954. *Residence*, Glenfarg Hse., Dron, Perth.——Audrey Joan (*Audrey, Lady Twisleton-Wykeham-Fiennes*), *b.* 1912 : *m.* 1931, Lieut.-Col. Sir Ranulph Twisleton-Wykeham-Fiennes, D.S.O., 2nd Bt., Roy. Scots Greys, who *d.* (of wounds received in action during European War) 1943. *Residence*, St. Peter's Well, Lodsworth, Sussex.

Newson-Smith, see Smith.

NEWTON, Creation (U.K.) 1900, of The Wood, Sydenham Hill, Lewisham, Kent, and Kottingham House. Burton-on-Trent, co. Stafford.

Sir HARRY MICHAEL REX NEWTON, 3rd *Baronet ; b.* Feb. 7th, 1923 ; *s.* his father, *Sir* HARRY KOTTINGHAM, *O.B.E.*, 1951 ; ed. at Eastbourne Coll. ; is Lieut. King's Roy. Rifle Corps, a Freeman of City of London; 1939-45 War in N. Africa and Middle East (wounded) : *m.* 1958, Pauline Jane, only da. of Richard John Frederick Howgill, C.B.E., and has issue.

Arms—Azure, two bones in saltire between as many roses argent, on a chief or, a lotus flower slipped proper. **Crest**—Out of the battlements of a tower an arm erect, the hand grasping a sword in bend sinister proper suspended therefrom a flag argent charged with a sword erect between two branches of oak proper.

Residence—Weycroft Hall, nr. Axminster, Devon. *Club*—Bath.

Faveat fortuna.   **Son living**—GEORGE PETER HOWGILL, *b.* March 26th, 1962.

May fortune favour.   **Brother living**—*Rev.* Christopher Wynne, *b.* 1925: ed. at Eastbourne Coll., and at Trin. Hall, Camb (MA); Urban Dean of Milton Keynes: *m.* 1950, Margaret, da. of John Ormerod, of Accrington, and has issue living, Jeremy John, *b.* 1952,—Peter Michael, *b.* 1953. *Residence*, The Vicarage, Church Lane, Whaddon, Milton Keynes, MK17 0LX.

Aunt living (daughter of 1st baronet)—Muriel Prudhoe, *b.* 1879 : *m.* 1902, George Parsons. *Residences*, 35, Holland Park, W.11 ; Wateringfield, Aldeburgh, Suffolk.

Widow living of 2nd Baronet—MYRTLE IRENE (*Myrtle, Lady Newton*), da. of the late William Wilson Grantham, VD, KC, DL, of 17, Cadogan Place, SW, and Balneath Manor, near Lewes [de la Rue, Bt.]: *m.* 1920, Sir Harry Kottingham Newton, OBE, 2nd Bt., who *d.* 1951. *Residence*, 10, Vicarage Close, Ringmer, Lewes, Sussex, BN8 5LF.

The 1st baronet, Sir Alfred James Newton, Chm. of Harrods (Limited), was Lord Mayor of London 1899-1900, when he founded City of London Imperial Vol. during S. African War (Baronetcy conferred) ; also an Hon. Freeman of Scarborough and Londonderry, and sixteen years Gov. of the Hon. the Irish So. The 2nd baronet, Sir Harry Kottingham Newton, O.B.E., was Vice-Chm. of Harrods (Limited), and was M.P. for N.-E. Div. of Essex (U) 1910-18, and for Harwich Div. thereof 1918-22.

NEWTON, Creation (U.K.) 1924, of Beckenham, co. Kent.

Sir KENNETH GARNAR NEWTON, *OBE, TD,* 3rd *Baronet; b.* June 4th, 1918; *s.* his father, *Sir* EDGAR HENRY, 1971; ed. at Wellington; a Liveryman and Member of Court of Assists. of Leathersellers' Co., and Feltmakers' Co.; Gen. Commr. for Income Tax 1961; Pres. British Leather Fedn. 1968-69; Lt.-Col. RASC (TA); 1939-45 War; MBE (Mil) 1944, OBE (Civil) 1969: *m.* 1944, Margaret Isabel, da. of the Rev. Dr. George Blair, of Dundee, and has issue.

ᴀrms—Argent, on a chevron between three eagles displayed azure, as many garbs or. ᴄrest—A bear's head couped argent, muzzled gules, charged on the neck with three crescents interlaced azure.

Residence—Whitebeams, Beech Av., Effingham, Surrey.

Sons living—JOHN GARNAR, *b.* July 10th, 1945; ed. at Reed's Sch., Cobham.——Peter Blair, *b.* 1950; ed. at Wellington.

Sister living—Daphne Mary, *b.* 1921.

Uncle living (son of 1st baronet)—Sidney Arthur, *b.* 1901; Solicitor 1923; Consultant with the legal firm of Nash, Field & Co., of 9, Devereux Court, Temple, WC2, Past Master of Distillers' Co., of Parish Clerks' Co., of Loriners, Co. and Upholders' Co., a Liveryman of Vintners' Co., and Donation Gov. of Christ's Hosp.; Under-Sheriff of City of London 1930, 1932, and 1933 : *m.* 1933, Oonagh, yst. da. of the late John Fleming, of Dublin, and has issue living, Hedley John (Amwell Grove, Gt. Amwell, Herts.), *b.* 1936; ed. at Charterhouse, and at Trin. Hall, Camb. (MA, LLB); Solicitor 1960; a partner in the firms of Nash, Field & Co., and Duffield Bruty & Co.; a Liveryman of Vintners' Co.: *m.* 1964, Virginia, da. of James Archibald Baiss,—Shane (*Baroness Gisborough*), *b.* 1934: *m.* 1960, the 3rd Baron Gisborough, of Gisborough House, Guisborough, Cleveland,—Gaidagh, *b.* 1947: *m.* 1968, James Martin Strong, of West Bradley, Templeton, Tiverton, Devon. *Residence*, 3, Chancellor Hse., Hyde Park Gate, SW7. *Club*, RAC.

Widow living of 2nd Baronet—ALICE MARY (*Alice, Lady Newton*), (Barn Cottage, Griggs Farm Court, Liphook, Hants.), da. of the late Henry Barber of Surbiton, and widow of Glyn Rosser: *m.* 1968, as his 2nd wife, Sir Edgar Henry Newton, 2nd Bt., who *d.* 1971.

The 1st baronet, Sir Louis Arthur Newton (son of the late Reuben Newton, of Macclesfield), was a Surveyor, and an Alderman and Lieut. of City of London (Senior Sheriff 1916-17, Lord Mayor 1923-4), a County Councillor for London 1931-4, High Sheriff of Kent 1940-41, and sometime Hon. Col. 56th (1st London) Div. Train R.A.S.C.

NICHOLSON, Creation (U.K.) 1859, of Luddenham, New South Wales.

Sir JOHN CHARLES NICHOLSON, *F.R.C.S.,* 3rd *Baronet; b.* Jan. 10th, 1904; *s.* his father, *Sir* CHARLES ARCHIBALD, 1949; ed. at Brighton Coll., and at New Coll., Oxford (B.A. 1927, B.M. and B.Ch. 1929, M.A. 1950); F.R.C.S. England 1934; is a Consulting Surg.: *m.* 1928, Caroline Elizabeth, da. of the Rt. Rev. John Frederick MacNeice, D.D., late Bishop of Down, Connor, and Dromore.

ᴀrms—Azure, two bars nebuly argent, in chief a sun in splendour proper between two stars of eight points or. ᴄrest—On a rock proper a lion's head azure, charged with a star as in the arms.

Residence—Thames Cottage, Thames St., Sunbury-on-Thames.

Virtus sola nobilitas.
Virtue is the only nobility.

Sisters living—Elizabeth Margaret (The Moors, Filkins, Lechlade, Glos.), *b.* 1902: *m.* 1928, Walter Vale, who *d.* 1939.——Barbara Evelyn, *b.* 1906. *Residence*, Carpenters, Donhead St. Mary, Wilts.

The 1st baronet was knighted 1852. The 2nd baronet was Consulting Architect to Wells and other Cathedrals.

NICHOLSON, Creation (U.K.) 1912, of Harrington Gardens, Royal Borough of Kensington.

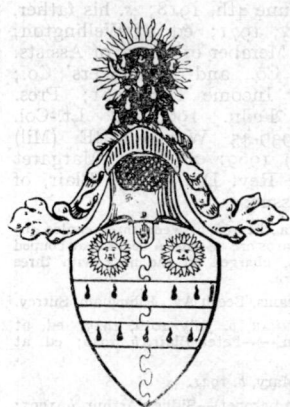

Quietate et Confindentia.

Sir JOHN NORRIS NICHOLSON, *KBE, CIE,* 2nd *Baronet,* son of the late Capt. George Crosfield Norris Nicholson, RFC, son of 1st baronet; *b.* Feb. 19th, 1911; *s.* his grandfather, *Sir* Charles NORRIS, *MP,* 1918; ed. at Winchester, and at Trin. Coll., Cambs.; Chm. Ocean Steamship Co. 1957-71, and of Martins Bank 1962-64; Pres. Chamber of Shipping of UK 1970-71; Capt. 4th Btn. Cheshire Regt. (TA) in Flanders (despatches), and Min. of War Transport India and S.E. Asia 1942-46); Vice Lord-Lieut. of Isle of Wight since 1974; CIE 1946, KBE (Civil) 1971: *m.* 1938, Vittoria Vivien, da. of Percy Trewhella, of Villa Sant' Andrea, Taormina, Sicily, and has issue.

Arms—Per pale nebuly azure and gules two bars argent guttée de poix, in chief two suns in splendour proper. Crest—A lion's head couped sable guttée d'eau before a sun in splendour proper. *Residence*—Mottistone Manor, I. of Wight. *Clubs,* Brooks's, Royal Yacht Squadron.

Sons living—CHARLES CHRISTIAN (Turners Green Farm, Elvetham, Hants.), *b.* Dec. 15th, 1941; ed. at Ampleforth, and at Magdalen Coll., Oxford: *m.* 1975, Martha Rodman, da. of Stuart Warren Don. of 1, Hyde Park St., NZ, and widow of Niall Hamilton Austruther-Gough-Calthorpe [see Anstruther-Gough, Calthorpe, Bt.].——James Richard (25, Melody Rd., SW11), *b.* 1947; ed. at Ampleforth, and Churchill Coll., Camb.: *m.* 1974, Charmian Joy, da. of Maj. Harcourt Michael Scudamore Gold, MC [see By. of Trent].

Daughters living—Tessa Mary, *b.* 1944: *m.* 1967, Piers A. C. H. Phipps, of 27, Perrymead St., SW6.——Mary Louise Petronella, *b.* 1950: *m.* 1973, Adam Trevor Kelly Smail, of Edgeworth Manor, Stroud, Glos.

Aunt living (daughter of 1st baronet)—Olivia Joyce Norris, *b.* 1895 : *m.* 1st, 1917, Capt. Herbert Sandford Ward, formerly R.F.C., from whom she obtained a divorce 1932 ; 2ndly, 1932, Lionel Jackson Mars, who *d.* 196-, and has issue living, (by 1st m.) Nicholas, *b.* 1920: *m.* 19—,—Wilmay, *b.* 1918: *m.* 19—,—(by 2nd m.) Gay, *b.* 1933. *Residence,* Trerife, Penzance, Cornwall.

Mother living—Hon. Evelyn Izmé (*Dowager Baroness Mottistone*), yst. da. of 1st Viscount Elibank ; is a J.P. for Isle of Wight : *m.* 1st, 1906, Capt. George Crosfield Norris Nicholson, R.A.F. (ante), who *d.* (on active service during European War) 1916 ; 2ndly, 1917, as his second wife, the 1st Baron Mottistone, who *d.* 1947. *Residence,* The Dower House, Mottistone Manor, Isle of Wight.

The 1st baronet, Sir Charles Norris Nicholson, sat as M.P. for Doncaster Div. of S. Part of W. Riding of Yorkshire (*L*) 1906-18.

NICHOLSON, Creation (U.K.) 1958, of Winterbourne, Roy. co. of Berks.

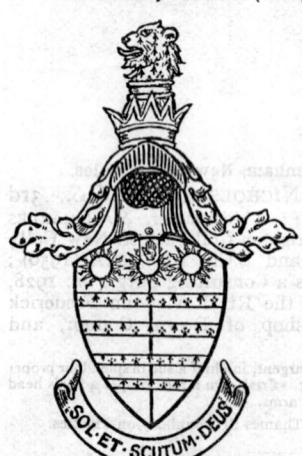

Sir GODFREY NICHOLSON, 1st *Baronet,* son of the late Richard Francis Nicholson, of Woodcott, Hants ; *b.* Dec. 9th 1901 ; ed. at Winchester, and at Ch. Ch., Oxford; a FSA; Chm. of Estimates Cttee. 1961-64; 1939-45 War with Roy· Fusiliers; M.P. for Morpeth (*C*) 1931-35 and for Farnham Div. of Surrey 1937-66: *m.* 1936, Lady Katharine Constance Lindsay, who *d.* 1972, da. of 27th Earl of Crawford and Balcarres, and has issue.

Arms—Per pale azure and gules two bars geme ermine in chief three suns in splendour or. Crest— Out of an antique crown gules a lion's head ermine, gorged with a collar gemel azure.

Residence—Bussock Hill House, Newbury. Berks

Daughters living—Rose Helen, *b.* 1937: *m.* 1961, Richard Napier Luce, MP, of Dragons Farmhouse, Cowfold, Horsham, Sussex, son of Sir William Henry Tucker Luce, GBE, KCMG, and has issue living, Alexander Richard, *b.* 1964,—Edward Godfrey, *b.* 1968.——Laura Violet (*Lady Montgomery Cuninghame*), *b.* 1939: *m.* 1964, Sir John Christopher Foggo Montgomery Cuninghame, 12th B., of 28, Kelso Pl., W8.——Emma Harriet, *b.* 1941.——Harriet Mary, *b.* 1946: *m.* 1969, Charles Hamilton Flower (c/o William's & Glyn's Bank, 67, Lombard St., EC3).

NICOLSON, Creation (N.S.) 1629, of that Ilk, and of Lasswade, Midlothian.
[Dormant 1961.]

Sir HAROLD STANLEY NICOLSON, 14th *Baronet, d.* in 1961, and at the time of going to press no name appears on the official Roll of Baronets in respect of this title.

Widow living of 14th Baronet—JEAN (*Lady Nicolson*), da. of the late Alexander Landles : *m.* 1927, Sir Harold Stanley Nicolson, 14th baronet, who *d.* 1961, when the title became dormant. *Residences,* Brough Lodge, Fetlar, Shetland; Grimista, Shetland.

Collateral Branch living.

Issue of the late Lionel Rutherford Nicolson, W.S., 3rd son of 12th baronet, *b.* 1887, *d.* 1957: *m.* 1932, Kathleen Mary (Gilpin House, Stag Lane, Great Kingshill, High Wycombe, Bucks), da. of the late Henry Gane Moon:—
Anne, *b.* 1939: *m.* 1963, Miles Hansen, of Hill House, Catts Hill, Rotherfield, Sussex, and has issue living, Piers James, *b.* 1966,—Clare Louise, *b.* 1969.

John Nicolson of that Ilk and Lass Wade, Midlothian, was cr. a baronet 1629 with remainder to his heirs male whatsoever, with a grant of land in Nova Scotia. On the death of Sir James, 7th Bt., 1743, the baronetcy became dormant. Arthur, *de jure,* 8th Bt. (*d.* 1793) was a great-grandson of James Bishop of Dunkeld, next brother of 1st Bt. In 1826, Sir Arthur, *de jure,* 10th Bt., grandson of Arthur, was served heir male of 7th Bt. The Baronetcy again became dormant on the death of the 14th Bt. in 1961.

NIGHTINGALE, Creation (E.) 1628, of Newport Pond, Essex.

For king and country.

Sir CHARLES ATHELSTAN NIGHTINGALE, 16th *Baronet; b.* July 23rd, 1902; *s.* his cousin, *Sir* GEOFFREY SLINGSBY, 1972; ed. at Harrow: *m.* 1932, Nadine, da. of the late Arthur Diggens, and has issue.

Arms—Per pale ermine and gules, a rose counterchanged. **Crest**—An ibex sejant argent, tufted, armed, and maned or.

Residence—7, Victoria St., Okehampton, Devon, EX20 1NA.

Son living—CHARLES MANNERS GAMALIEL, *b.* Feb. 21st, 1947; ed. at St. Paul's Sch.

Daughters living—Nadine Mary Rosalie (36, Queen's Rd., Wisbech, Cambs.), *b.* 1938: *m.* 1st, 1959 (m. diss. 1971), Peter Maurice Edmunds; 2ndly, 1971, Derek Frederick Curtis, and has issue living (by 1st m.), Thomas Charles, *b.* 1961,—David Michael, *b.* 1963,—Jeremy John, *b.* 1964,—Jane Elizabeth, *b.* 1965; (by 2nd m.) James *b.* 1971.——Clothilde Muriel Frances, *b.* 1939: *m.* 1964, Derek Edward Glenister, of 2, Albany Close, Ickenham, Middx., and has issue living, Frances Mary, *b.* 1966,—Clare Julia, *b.* 1968.

Collateral Branches living

Issue of the late Harry Ethelston Nightingale, yst. son of 13th baronet. *b.* 1860, *d.* 1933: *m.* 1881, Coralie Louise Pauline Jeanne, who *d.* 1935, da. of the late Louis Charles d'Harcourt Mary:—
Naomi Coralie (*Lady Boynton*), *b.* 1893: *m.* 1914, Cdr. Sir Griffith Wilfred Norman Boynton, RN (ret.), 13th Bt., who *d.* 1966, when the title became ext.

Grandchildren of the late Lacy Gamaliel Nightingale, KC, (infra):—
Issue of the late Manners Percy Nightingale, MRCS, LRCP, *b.* 1908, *d.* 1974: *m.* 1936, Mary Ursula, (Kneesworth, Lynton, N.I. Devon), da. of the late Rev. George Saunders Gilbert, of Groombridge, Sussex:—
Edward Lacy George, *b.* 1938; Master Mariner.——Jane Elizabeth, *b.* 1940.

Grandchildren of the late Percy Nightingale, el. son of the late Thomas Henry Nightingale, RN, 2nd son of 11th baronet:—
Issue of the late Lacy Gamaliel Nightingale, K.C., *b.* 1869, *d.* 1934: *m.* 1906, Katie, who *d.* 1930, only da. of the late J. M. Wagner, of Johannesburg, Transvaal:—
Neville Gascoyne, *b.* 1911; ed. at St. John's Coll., Camb. (BA 1933); Bar. Inner Temple 1936; 1939-45 War as Lt. Middlesex Regt. (wounded): *m.* 1946, Nancy Esther, da. of the late Godfrey James Whistler, of Ross-on-Wye, Hereford, and has issue living, Thomas Lacy Manners, *b.* 1947. *Residence,* Angel House, Botesdale, Diss, Norfolk.

Issue of the late Maj.-Gen. Manners Ralph Wilmott Nightingale, C.B., C.M.G., C.I.E., D.S.O., *b.* 1871, *d.* 1956: *m.* 1st, 1907, Anna, who *d.* 1924, da. of Arthur George Forestier-Walker, formerly ICS; 2ndly, 1930, Violet Marion, who *d.* 1972, da. of the late Lt.-Col. H. M. E. Brunker, The Cameronians, and widow of Capt. C. A. G. Cunningham, N. Staffordshire Regt.:—
(By 1st marriage) George Manners, *MC; b.* 1913; ed. at Wellington Coll.; Lt.-Col. (ret.) R.A. Waziristan 1938, European War 1939-45 in Iraq, N. Africa, Persia, and Italy (despatches twice, wounded, M.C.), Malaya 1953-5 (despatches) : *m.* 1946, Alison Cornwallis (SUTTON), da. of Col. J. Cameron, RE, and has issue living, Christopher George Manners, *b.* 1949: *m.* 1971, Marie-Claudette, da. of Marc Roger Tenermont,—Jeremy John Charles, *b.* 1952. *Residence,* Kneesworth Penhill, Fremington, N. Devon.——Tessa Frances Moyra, *b.* 1908: *m.* 1930, Brig. Harold Gordon Fowler, OBE, Indian Army (ret.), and has issue living, Patricia Jacqueline, *b.* 1931,—Veronica Jane, *b.* 1935,—Tessa Pauline, *b.* 1938. *Residence,* Rowan Cottage, Furze Hill, Seale, Farnham, Surrey.

Grandchildren of the late Ernest Albert Nightingale (infra):—
Issue of the late Alfred James Nightingale, *b.* 1905, *d.* 1973: *m.* 1944, Petrea Adrianne, (Flat 2, De Hoek, Relief St., Ficksburg, OFS, S. Africa), da. of M. D. Van Niekerk, of Ladybrand, OFS:—
Ernest Alfred (93, Ethelbert Rd., Malvern, Natal 4001, S. Africa), *b.* 1945: *m.* 1969, Rosa, da. of T. G. Visagie, of Durban, and has issue living, Denzil, *b.* 1971,—Linton, *b.* 1973.——Peter Austen *b.* 1946: *m.* 1973, Marilynn, da. of George Parker, of King William's Town.——Carol Ann, *b.* 1956.

Granddaughters of the late James Edward Nightingale, 2nd son of Thomas Henry Nightingale, RN (ante):—

Issue ot the late Ernest Albert Nightingale, *b.* 1867, *d.* 1945: *m.* 1893, Sarah Annette Thorntone, who *d.* 1947, da. of the late John Austen :—

Irene Mary (PO Box 24, Wepener, S. Africa), *b.* 1899: *m.* 1926, Norman Owen Halse, who *d.* 1966, and has issue living, Norma Rene, *b.* 1927,—Varney Marren, *b.* 1934,—Rosemary Joy, *b.* 1943.

Issue of the late Thomas Cecil **Parry Nightingale**, *b.* 1885 ; *d.* 1950 : *m.* 1911, **Anita Adendorff** :—

Joy Thelma (46, Joubert St., Warrenton, Cape, S. Africa) *b.* 1913: *m.* 1936, Cornie Hugo Liesching, and has issue living, Frederick Jabris, *b.* 1937,—Cornie, *b.* 1940,—Anita Lorraine, *b.* 1945,—Margaret, *b.* 1947.

Grandchildren of the late Claud Robert Nightingale, MC (infra):—

Issue of the late Christopher Carnac Nightingale, *b.* 1913 *d.* 1970: *m.* 1941, Muriel de Lissa (39, Gander Hill, Haywards Heath, Sussex), da. of the late F. D. Philips, of Leatherhead:—

Nicholas John, *b.* 1942: *m.* 1968, Susan Kay, da. of Philip Lyth, of Park Hill, Southwell, Notts, and has issue living, Rebecca Jane, *b.* 1972.——Anne Christine, *b.* 1944: *m.* 1972, Kenneth Ian Murchison, of Sydney, Aust.——Patricia Ruth, *b.* 1950.

Grandson of the late Frederick Charles Nightingale, son of the late Geoffrey Nightingale, 7th son of 10th baronet :—

Issue of the late Claud Robert Nightingdale, M.C., *b.* 1878, *d.* 1954 : *m.* 1912, Elinor Maud, (now of 8, Berkeley Place, Wimbledon, S.W.19), da. of Sir William Percival Rivett-Carnac, 5th Bt. :—

Robert Forbes, *b.* 1917; ed. at Stowe; formerly Lieut. RA: *m.* 1st, 1940 (m. diss. 1956), Lesley Phyllis, da. of the late S. Kenneth West; 2ndly, 1956, Dora, da. of George Henry Kirkpatrick, and has issue living, (by 1st m.) Peter Robert (Meadowbank, The Avenue, Godalming, Surrey), *b.* 1947: *m.* 1968, Joan Anne, da. of the late J. A. Kerr, and has issue living, James Peter *b.* 1974, Andrea Jane *b.* 1969, Helen Mary, *b.* 1971,—Richard John (10, The Avenue, Liphook, Hants.), *b.* 1948: *m.* 1971, Frances Catherine, da. of C. B. Green, and has issue living, Catherine *b.* 1972. *Residence,* Deersleys, Denston, Newmarket, Suffolk, CB8 8PL.

Sir Thomas Nightingale, 1st Bt., of Newport Pond, Essex, was High Sheriff of Essex 1627 On the death in 1722 of Sir Robert, 4th Bt., a Dir. of Hon. East India Co., his estates devolved on his cousin, Robert Gascoyne. The baronetcy should have passed to Edward Nightingale, of Kneesworth, Cambs, son of Geoffrey, yr. son of 1st Bt., but succession was not established until Sir Edward Nightingale recorded his pedigree and established his right to the title as 10th baronet in 1797.

NIXON, Creation (U.K.) 1906, of Roebuck Grove, Milltown, co. Dublin, and Merrion Square, City of Dublin.

Always ready.

Sir CHRISTOPHER JOHN LOUIS JOSEPH NIXON, *M.C.,* 3rd *Baronet* ; *b.* March 21st, 1918 ; *s.* his father, *Major Sir* CHRISTOPHER WILLIAM, 1945; ed. at Beaumont Coll. ; is Major Roy. Ulster Rifles Burma 1941-45 (despatches, M.C.), Korea 1950-51 (wounded, despatches) : *m.* 1949, Joan Lucille Mary, only da. of Robert Felix Mervyn Brown, of Rangoon, Burma, and has issue.

Arms—Azure, on a chevron engrailed between three frets couped or, as many trefoils vert, on a chief indented of the second, a cat passant between two fleams of the field. **Crest**—A leopard rampant azure besantee, holding in the dexter paw a fleam or.

Address—c/o Lloyds Bank, 6, Pall Mall, SW1. *Club*—United Service.

Daughters living—Anne Louise Catherine, *b.* 1954.——Mary Joan Teresa, *b.* 1957.——Sally Veronica Rose, *b.* 1961.

Brothers living—*Rev.* KENNETH MICHAEL JOHN BASIL, (St. George's College, Salisbury, Rhodesia), *b.* Feb. 22nd, 1919; is in Holy Orders of Church of Rome. ——Cecil Dominic Henry Joseph, MC (325, Upper Richmond Rd., SW15), *b.* 1920; ed. at Beaumont Coll. ; is Major Roy. Ulster Rifles: *m.* 1953, Brenda, da. of the late Samuel Lycett Lewis, and widow of Maj. M. F. McWhor, and has issue living, Simon Michael Christopher, *b.* 1954,—Michael Hugh David, *b.* 1957,—Susan, *b.* 1955.

Sister living—Christina Mary Agnes Reginalda, *b.* 1926: *m.* 1947 1st, John Gerard Counihan, who *d.* 1956; 2ndly, 1965, David Owen Williams, MBE, of Les Rosiers, Doyle Rd., St. Peter Port, Guernsey, C.I., and has issue living (by 1st m.), Niall Christopher John, *b.* 1948,—John Kenneth David, *b.* 1956,—Louise Mary Christine, *b.* 1949,—Vivienne Christine Kathleen, *b.* 1953.

The Rt. Hon. Sir Christopher John Nixon, P.C., M.D., LL.D., 1st baronet, was an eminent physician, Vice-Chancellor of National Univ of Ireland, and Pres. of Veterinary Coll. of Ireland. The 2nd baronet, Major Sir Christopher William Nixon, D.S.O., R.A. (retired), served during European War 1914-19 (D.S.O.).

NOBLE, Creation (U.K.) 1902, of Ardmore and Ardardan Noble, Cardross, co. Dumbarton.

By virtue and valour.

Sir MARC BRUNEL NOBLE, 5th *Baronet*; *b.* Jan. 8th, 1927; *s.* his father, *Sir* HUMPHREY BRUNEL, *MBE, MC*, 1968; ed. at Eton; Maj. (ret.) King's Dragoon Guards and R. Dragoons; Commonwealth Commr. Scout Assocn. since 1972; *m.* 1956, Jennifeer Lorna, da. of the late John Mein Austin, of Flinthill, W. Haddon, Northants., and has issue.

Arms—Argent, three bay leaves slipped proper. **Crest**—A dexter hand couped, holding a dagger all proper. **Supporters**—Two wild men, wreathed and cinctured with bay leaves, each supporting with the exterior hand a holly tree eradicated, and resting the exterior foot on the roots thereof, all proper.
    Residence,—Deerleap House, Knockholt, Sevonoaks, Kent.

Sons living—DAVID BRUNEL, *b.* Dec. 25th, 1961.——Charles Richard Austin, *b.* 1963.

Daughter living—Anna Margaret, *b.* 1957.

Brother living—Peter Saxton Fitzjames (64, East Sheen Av., East Sheen, SW14), *b.* 1929: *m.* 1st, 1954, Elizabeth Emmeline, who obtained a divorce 1966, da. of the late Launcelot William Gregory Eccles, CMG, MC; 2ndly, 1966, Mrs. Helena Margaret Harries, da. of the late Thomas Essery Rose-Richards, and has issue living, (by 1st m.) Simon Peter Saxton Fanshaw, *b.* 1958,—(by 2nd m.) James Essery Brunel, *b.* 1968.

Sister living—Lilias Mulgrave, *b.* 1931: *m.* 1951, Capt. Robin John Sheepshanks, late King's Dragoon Guards [*see* V. Chelmsford]. *Residence,* The Rookery, Eyke, Woodbridge, Suffolk.

Aunts living (daughters of 3rd baronet)—Marjorie Florence: *m.* 1919, Capt. Geoffrey Spencer Madan, who *d.* 1947, and has issue living, Nicola Elizabeth Gina (*Baroness Campbell of Croy*), *b.* 1920: *m.* 1949, Baron Campbell of Croy (Life Baron), of Holme Rose, Nairnshire. *Residence,* 36, Sloane Court West, SW3.——Cynthia (*Baroness Gladwyn*): *m.* 1929, the 1st Baron Gladwyn. *Residences,* Bramfield Hall, Halesworth, Suffolk; 62, Whitehall Court, SW1.

Daughter living of 2nd Baronet—Veronica Margaret (*Veronica, Baroness Gainford*), *b.* 1900: *m.* 1921, the 2nd Baron Gainford who *d.* 1971. *Residence,* Duntaynish, Tayvallich, Lochgilphead, Argyll.

Widow living of 4th Baronet—CELIA (*Dowager Lady Noble*) (The Old Vineyard, Ticehurst, Wadhurst, Sussex), da. of the late Capt. Stewart Carmac Weigall, RN: *m.* 1926, Sir Humphrey Brunel Noble, MBE, MC, 4th baronet, who *d.* 1968.

Collateral Branches living.

    Issue of the late Sir John Henry Brunel Noble (3rd son of 1st baronet), who was *cr.* a *Baronet* 1923:—

See Noble, Bt., *cr.* 1923.

    Issue of the late Philip Ernest Noble (High Sheriff of Northumberland 1922), 4th son of 1st baronet, *b.* 1870, *d.* 1931: *m.* 1895, Mabel [who *m.* 2ndly, 1936, Capt. Frank Buddle Atkinson (High Sheriff of Northumberland 1941)], da. of Percy Graham Buchanan Westmacott, J.P., formerly of Rose Mount, Ascot, and Benwell Hill, Newcastle-on-Tyne :—
Graham Philip (Stubbs Hill, Binfield, Bracknell, Berks.), *b.* 1898; ed. at Eton; is Squadron Leader RAF Vol. Reserve: *m.* 1st, 1926, Pamela Susan (who obtained a divorce 1933), da. of the late Basil Hoare, of 96, Eaton Place, SW; 2ndly, 1936, Joan, who *d.* 1955, widow of Fl-Lt. Charles Henry Godwin Bremridge, RAF; 3rdly, 19—.——Horace Westmacott (Casa Bordeira, Estoi, Algarve, Portugal), *b.* 1899; ed. at Eton, RMC, and New Coll., Oxford; sometime Maj. Scots Guards: *m.* 1st, 1929, Joan Marion (who obtained a divorce 1933), da. of H. R. Miller, of New York, USA; 2ndly, 1946, Edna Louise (MALONE), da. of the late Charles Johnson, of Chicago, USA, and has issue living, (by 1st m.) Philip Ralph, *b.* 1930.——Agnes Dorothy (Flat 5, 155, Sloane St., SW1): *m.* 1918, Cdr. James Lawrence Boyd, DSC, RN, who *d.* 1930, and has issue living, Michael James Campbell (341, Metcalfe Av., Westmount PO, Montreal, Canada), *b.* 1928: *m.* 1950, Barry Trowbridge, da. of Lawrence Damrosh Seymour, of New York,—Patricia Dorothy, *b.* 1919: *m.* 1947, Dugald Stewart.——Yseult Joan (Newtonlees, Kelso, Roxburghshire): *m.* 1922, Wilfred Theodore Claud Cochrane, who *d.* 1955, and has issue living, John Noble (Beech Mount, Wellhouse Rd., Beech, Alton, Hants.), *b.* 1923: *m.* 1952, Elizabeth Georgiana, da. of the late John Peter Fane de Salis, MC, of The Priory, Castle St., Thornbury, Bristol,—Anne Philippa, *b.* 1925: *m.* 1972, Alan Saunders, of Wessex, Medstead, Beech, Alton, Hants.

    The 1st baronet, Sir Andrew Noble, the well-known expert on explosives, joined the firm of Sir W. G. Armstrong & Co. in 1860, and eventually became Chm. ; he was a Member of the first Committee of Explosives until dissolved in 1880, and High Sheriff of Northumberland 1896.

NOBLE, Creation (U.K.) 1923, of Ardkinglas, co. Argyll.

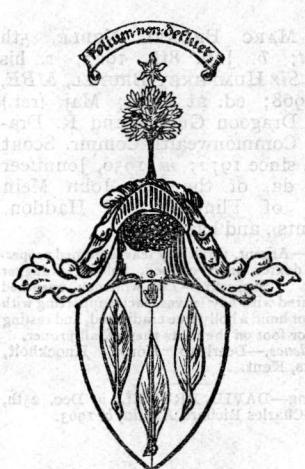

Sir ANDREW NAPIER NOBLE, *K.C.M.G.*, 2nd *Baronet : b.* Sept. 16th, 1904 ; *s.* his father, *Sir* JOHN HENRY BRUNEL, 1938 ; ed. at Eton, and at Balliol Coll., Oxford ; formerly an Assist. Under-Sec. at Foreign Office ; was Envoy Extraor. and Min. Plen. to Finland 1951-4, and Ambassador Extraor. and Plen. to Poland 1954-56, to Mexico 1956-60, and to the Netherlands 1960-64; CMG 1947, K.C.M.G. 1954 : *m.* 1934, Sigrid, da. of M. Michelet, of Norwegian Diplo. Ser., and has issue.

Arms—Per pale argent and vert, three bay leaves counterchanged. **Crest**—A bay tree vert, trunked sable, ensigned by an estoile argent proper.
Residence,—11, Cedar House, Marloes Rd., W8 5LA. *Club*—Boodle's.

Sons living—IAN ANDREW (Eilean Iarmain, Isle of Skye; New [Edinburgh] Club), *b.* Sept. 8th, 1935; ed. at Eton, and at Univ. Coll., Oxford (BA); Businessman and Farmer; Scottish Council (Development & Industry) Edinburgh 1964-69; Joint Founder Man. Dir. of Noble Grossart, Ltd., merchant bankers of Edinburgh 1969-72; Chm. of Scottish Maritime, Ltd., of Aberdeen; a Dir. of Lyle Shipping Ltd., of Glasgow, of Chilton Bros., Ltd. of Girvan, and other cos.—Timothy Peter (41, Gloucester Sq., W2), *b.* 1943.
Daughter living—Laila Ilona, *b.* 1937: *m.* 1958, Kenneth Magnus Spence, and has issue living, Magnus Andrew, *b.* 1959,—Patrick Matthew, *b.* 1967,—Melanie Jane, *b.* 1961. *Residence,* Napier Place, Wargrave, Berks.
Brother living—*Rt. Hon.* Michael Antony Cristobal, *b.* March 19th, 1913; *cr. Baron Glenkinglas* (Life Peer) May 6th, 1974 [see that title].
Sisters living—Rosemary, *b.* 1903: *m.* 1931, Brigadier Ernest John Montgomery, CB, CBE, late Highland LI, who *d.* 1972 [Montgomery, Bt., colls.]. *Residence,* Kinlochruel, by Colintraive, Argyll.——Anastasia Mary Elizabeth (The Suare, Ardkinglas, Cairndow, Argyll), *b.* 1911.

Collateral Branch living

Issue of the late John Samuel Brunel Noble, 2nd son of 1st baronet; *b.* 1909, *d.* 1972: *m.* 1934, Elizabeth Virginia (Ardkinglas, Cairndow, Argyll), da. of the late William Louis Lucas [Goldsmid, Bt., ext.]:—
Simon John, *b.* 1936; ed. at Eton.——Sarah, *b.* 1935: *m.* 1957, Peter Whitton Sumsion, of Willowbrook Cottage, Slough Rd., Eton, Windsor, Berks., and has issue living, David, *b.* 1958,—Daniel, *b.* 1967,—Virginia, and—Lucy, *b.* 1963.——Christina, *b.* 1942.

The 1st baronet, Sir John Henry Brunel Noble (3rd son of Sir Andrew Noble, 1st Bt. [*cr.* 1902]), was a Director of London and N.-E. Railway and many other Cos.

Norie-Miller, see Miller.

NORMAN, Creation (U.K.) 1915, of Honeyhanger, Parish of Shottermill, co. Surrey

Sir MARK ANNESLEY NORMAN, 3rd *Baronet*; *b.* Feb. 8th, 1927 ; *s.* his father, *Air-Commodore Sir* (HENRY) NIGEL ST. VALERY, *C.B.E.*, 1943 : ed. at Winchester : late Lieut. Coldstream Guards, and late Flying Officer, No. 601 Squadron, R.Aux.AF; a Dir. of Cos.: *m.* 1953, Joanna Camilla, da. of Lt.-Col. Ian James Kilgour [see Forestier-Walker, Bt., colls.], and has issue.

Arms—Sable, a thunderbolt, and in chief two crosses patée pierced with the eight symbols of Fhohe or the Pa-qua and charged with a rounder containing the eastern symbol known as Tae Keigh' all or. **Crest**—Upon mount vert a spear erect, transfixing a Saracen's head, all proper. **Supporters**—On either side a Norseman proper.

Residence—Wilcote Manor, Charlbury, Oxon. *Clubs*—Guards', MCC.

Live but do not forget.

Sons living—NIGEL JAMES, *b.* Feb. 5th, 1956.——Antony Rory, *b.* 1963.
Daughter living—Lucinda Fay, *b.* 1965.
Brothers living—Nigel Desmond, *CBE* (Kingates Farm, Whitwell, I. of Wight), *b.* 1929; CBE (Civil) 1971: *m.* 1st, 1956 (m. diss. 1965), Barbara Anne, only da. of the late Capt. Mark Fogg Elliot, DSO, RN; 2ndly, 1965, Mrs. Boel Elisabeth Holmsen, only da. of the late Gösta Suenson, of Malmo, Sweden, and has issue living, (by 1st marriage) Henry Mark Desmond, *b.* 1957,—Alexander Robert, *b.* 1959,—(by 2nd m.) Roderick Peregrine, *b.* 1966,—Roland, *b.* 1971,—Lisa Jemima, *b.* 1969.——Torquil Patrick Alexander (24, Avenue Rd., NW8), *b.* 1933: *m.* 1961, Elizabeth Anne, da. of Alexander Victor Edward Paulet Montagu (10th Earl of Sandwich until he disclaimed his title 1964), and has issue living, Alexander Jesse, *b.* 1962,—Casey William, *b.* 1963,—Caspar Joe, *b.* 1966,—Lucy Patricia, *b.* 1964,—Amy Jean Mary, *b.* 1969.
Uncles living (sons of 1st baronet)—Willoughby Rollo (28, Ranelagh House, Elyston Place, SW3; Hurst Mill, Petersfield, Hants.), *b.* 1909; ed. at Eton, and Magdalen Coll., Oxford; Maj. Gren. Gds.; Chm. The Boots Co., Ltd. 1961-72 (Vice-Chm. 1954-61); Dep. Chm. of English China Clays, Ltd., a Dir of Guardian Royal Exchange Assurance, Ltd., of Nat. Westminster Bank (Chm. of Eastern Region) and Sheepbridge Engineering, Ltd., and an underwriting Member of Lloyd's; High Sheriff of Leicestershire 1960-61: *m.* 1st 1934 (m. diss. 1973), the Hon. Barbara Jacqueline Boot, da. of 2nd Baron Trent; 2ndly, 1973, Anna Caroline, da. of the late William Greville Worthington [E. Aylesford], and formerly wife of Oliver Patrick Miller Haskard, and has issue living, (by 1st m.) Jeremy Nicholas, *b.* 1935,—Sarah Jessica, *b.* 1940: *m.* 1st 1960 (m. diss. 1967), Peter Egerton-Warburton, [*see* Grey-Egerton, Bt., colls.]; 2ndly, 1967, Peter David Rickett, of 8, Kensington Court Gdns., Kensington Court Place, W8, and has issue living, (by 1st m.) [*see* Grey-Egerton Bt., colls.], (by 2nd m.) Nicola Barbara *b.* 1970, Lucinda Frances *b.* 1971,—Tessa Roselle, *b.* 1944: *m.* 1968, George Maurice Pope, late Capt. Coldm. Gds., of 21, Chelsea Park Gdns., SW3, and has issue living, Edward *b.* 1970, Emily *b.* 1972.——Antony Charles Wynyard, *OBE*, *b.* 1912; ed. at Eton; Wing-Cdr. AAF (Reserve); a Co. Dir., and a Member of Lloyd's; 1939-45 War (despatches, OBE); OBE (Mil) 1945: *m.* 1937, Anne, only da. of John Watson Hughes, of Pontruffyd, Trefnant, Denbighshire. *Residences*, Lausanne Palace, Lausanne, Switzerland; Château de la Garoupe, Antibes, France, A.M.
Aunt living (daughter of 1st baronet)—Laura Rosalind (*Lady Burke*), *b.* 1908 : *m.* 1936, Sir Aubrey Francis Burke, O.B.E., and has issue living, Kevin Aubrey Francis, *b.* 1945,—Meriel Colleen, *b.* 1937: *m.* 1961, Theodore Cyril Vance Packman, of Sliders Farm, Furners Green, Uckfield, Sussex, and has issue living, Camilla Jane Vance *b.* 1964, Nicola Charlotte *b.* 1968, Claire Geraldine *b.* 1971,—Miranda Rosalind, *b.* 1940: *m.* 1963, Paul Munro Gunn (of 8, Pembroke Walk, W8), son of Sir (Herbert) James Gunn, and has issue living, Munro James *b.* 1966, Marcus Charles *b.* 1968, Pauline Miranda *b.* 1964, Petronella Clare *b.* 1970,—Melanie Lorna, *b.* 1942. *Residences*, Rent Street Barns, Bovingdon, Herts.; Ramster, Chiddingfold, Surrey; Clos de la Garoupe, Antibes, France, AM.
Widow living of 2nd Baronet—PATRICIA MOYRA (*Lady Perkins*), da. of the late Lt.-Col. James Howard Adolphus Annesley, CMG, DSO [*see* E. Annesley, colls]: *m.* 1st, 1926, Air Commodore Sir (Henry) Nigel St. Valery Norman, CBE, Auxiliary Air Force (Reserve), 2nd Baronet, who *d.* (on active ser. during European War) 1943; 2ndly, 1944, Sir Walter Robert Dempster Perkins. *Residence*, The Manor House, Downton, Wilts.

The 1st baronet, the Rt. Hon. Sir Henry Norman, P.C. (son of the late Henry Norman), was M.P. for S. Div. of Wolverhampton (*L*) 1900-1910, and for Blackburn 1910-23. The 2nd Baronet, Air Commodore Sir (Henry) Nigel St. Valery, C.B.E., Auxiliary Air Force (Reserve), *d.* (on active ser. during European War) 1943.

NORTH, Creation (U.K.) 1920, of Southwell, co. Nottingham.

Sir (WILLIAM) JONATHAN FREDERICK NORTH, 2nd *Baronet*, son of the Hon. John Montagu William North [*see* E. Guilford] ; *b.* Feb. 6th, 1931 ; *s.* his grandfather, *Sir* WILLIAM NORTON *HICKING*, 1947 ; ed. at Marlborough Coll.: *m.* 1956, Sara Virginia, da. of Air Ch. Marshal Sir (James) Donald Innes Hardman, G.B.E., K.C.B., D.F.C., and has issue.

Arms—Quarterly, 1st and 4th, azure, a lion passant or, three fleurs-de-lis argent, *North* ; 2nd and 3rd, argent, semée of lozenges vert, a bordure, gules, *Hicking*. *Crest*—A dragon's head erased sable, ducally gorged and chained or.
Residence—Frogmore, Weston under Penyard, Herefordshire.

Son living—JEREMY WILLIAM FRANCIS, *b.* May 5th, 1960.
Daughters living—Charlotte Amelia, *b.* 1958.——Harriet Cordelia Henrietta, *b.* 1963.
Sister living—Georgiana Mary, *b.* 1928: *m.* 1960, Esmond Unwin Butler, CVO, of Rideau Cottage, Government House, Ottawa, and has issue living, Mark William, *b.* 1961,—Clare Martine, *b.* 1963.
Mother living—Muriel Norton, younger da. of Sir William Norton Hicking, 1st Bt.: *m.* 1927, the Hon. John Montagu William North, from whom she obtained a divorce 1939 [*see* E. Guilford]. *Residence*, Cedar House, Brinton, near Melton Constable, Norfolk.

With courage and fidelity.

The 1st baronet, Sir William Norton Hicking (son of the late George Hicking, of Nottingham, sometime Chm. of Nottingham and Notts Banking Co., and High Sheriff of Notts 1913-14, was *cr.* a Baronet in 1917 with the usual limitation to heirs male of the body, but in 1920 a further creation was granted failing heirs male of the body of the grantee, with special remainder to the first and every other son of Mabel Doris Willoughby (el. da. of 1st Bt.), and the heirs male of their bodies and with like remainder to the male issue of any younger das. of the 1st Bt. On the death of the 1st Bt. in 1947 the Baronetcy of 1917 became ext. and that of 1920 passed to the son of his younger da., Muriel Norton, formerly wife of the Hon. John Montagu William North, 2nd son of 8th Earl of Guilford.

NUGENT, Creation (I.) 1795, of Ballinlough, Westmeath.

Sir HUGH CHARLES NUGENT, 6th *Baronet*, and a Count of the Holy Roman Empire, son of the late Charles Hugh Nugent, only son of 5th baronet ; *b.* (posthumous) May 26th, 1904 ; *s.* his grandfather, *Sir* CHARLES, 1927 ; ed. at Stonyhurst ; formerly Flying Officer R.A.F. Vol. Reserve ; is a Knight of Sovereign Order of Malta ; European War 1939-45 (despatches) : *m.* 1931, Margaret Mary Lavallin, da. of the late Rev. Herbert Lavallin Puxley, of the White House, Chaddleworth, Newbury, Berks [Neeld, Bt.], and has issue.

Arms—Ermine, two bars gules. Crest—A cockatrice vert.
Residence—Ballinlough Castle. Clonmellon, co. Westmeath.

Decrevi.
I have decreed.

Sons living—JOHN EDWIN LAVALLIN (of Limes Farm, Upper Lambourn, Newbury, Berks), *b.* March 16th, 1933; ed. at Eton; late Lt. Irish Gds.; is a JP for Berks.: *m.* 1959, Penelope Anne, da. of the late Brig. Richard Nigel Hanbury, CBE, TD and has issue living, Nicholas Myles John, *b.* 1967,—Grania Clare, *b.* 1969.——David Hugh Lavallin (Chaddleworth House, Chaddleworth, Newbury, Berks.; Ross Castle, Mount Nugent, co. Cavan. *Club*—Guards'), *b.* 1935; ed. at Eton; late Lt. Irish Gds.; Knt. of Sovereign Mil. Order of Malta, and Order of Holy Sepulchre of Jerusalem: *m.* 1960, Lady Elizabeth Maria Guinness, da. of the late Maj. Arthur Onslow Edward, Viscount Elveden, el. son of 2nd Earl of Iveagh, and has issue living, Charles Rupert, *b.* 1962,—Hugo John, *b.* 1963,—Rory David Neeld Lavallin, *b.* 1971,—Sheelin Rose, *b.* 1967.

Collateral Branch living.

Grandchildren of the late James O'Reilly Nugent (infra) :—
Issue of the late Charles James Nugent, *b.* 1881, *d.* 1961 : *m.* 1907, Anne, who *d.* 1961, da. of William King, formerly of Napier, New Zealand :—
James Andrew William, *b.* 1909 : *m.* 1936, Dardanella, da. of David Webber, of Wairoa, New Zealand, and has issue living, Trevor Charles, *b.* 1940,—Brian David, *b.* 1942,—Rayna Joy, *b.* 1941. *Residence*, Frasertown Road, Wairoa, Hawkes Bay, New Zealand.——Patrick Hulme, *b.* 1912 : *m.* 1940, Mary McFalls Quin, of Glasgow, and has issue living, Barry Hulme Joseph, *b.* 1946,—Darryl Charles, *b.* 1952,—Lynette Ann, *b.* 1940,—Janice Patricia, *b.* 1944.——Frederick *b.* 1914 : *m.* 1939, Rita Kara, da. of T. Carrol, of Wairoa, New Zealand, and has issue living, Mark, *b.* 1950,—Valentine, *b.* 1952,—Pearl, *b.* 1940,—Brenda, *b.* 1941,—Diana, *b.* 1954,—Dixie, *b.* 1957. *Residence*, Mahia, Hawke's Bay, New Zealand.——Charles Joseph, *b.* 1918 : *m.* 19—, Kathleen, da. of Edgar Jenkinson, of Gisborne, New Zealand, and has issue living, Peter James, *b.* 1947,—Graham, *b.* 1953,—Kenneth John, *b.* 1955,—Margaret Anne, *b.* 1950.——Richard King; *b.* 1923 : *m.* 1947, Doreen Mabel, da. of Townsend May, of New Plymouth, New Zealand, and has issue living, Sandra May, *b.* 1947,—Karen Louise, *b.* 1952,—Anne Marie Eva, *b.* 1954.——Hubert Thomas Michael, *b.* 1925 : *m.* 19—, Ngaire, da. of George Able, of Wairoa, New Zealand, and has issue living, Alan Grant, *b.* 1949,—Glenis Joy, *b.* 1950.——Kathleen Mary, *b.* 1907: *m.* 1927, Rupert Gower, and has issue living, Jocelyn, *b.* 1929,—Rupert, *b.* 1943,—Judith, *b.* 1935.——Florence Maud, *b.* 1916: *m.* 19—, Norman Jones, and has issue living, Howard Gilbert, *b.* 1939: *m.* 1963, Kathleen Elizabeth Sherridan,—Warren Charles, *b.* 1942,—Michael O'Reilly, *b.* 1947. *Residence*, Frasertown Rd., Wairoa, Hawke's Bay, New Zealand.——Marie Tephea Diana, *b.* 1921: *m.* 1938, Moat Mervyn Hoggard, and has issue living, Shona Faye, *b.* 1939: *m.* 1960, Colin Thomas William Bailey, of Ashurst.——Anne Barbara, *b.* 1927: *m.* 1951, Roy Alexander Andrew Ross, and has issue living, Judith Ann, *b.* 1953,—Deborah Irene, *b.* 1956,—Sharon Barbara, *b.* 1959,—Angela Leslie, *b.* 1961.

Issue of the late Walter Lonergan O'Reilly Nugent, *b.* 1884, *d.* 1949: *m.* 1911, Amelia Bateup, who *d.* 1966:—
Joan Florence, *b.* 1917 : *m.* 1940, Donald Evelyn Fenner, and has issue living, Janet Nugent, *b.* 1946. *Residence*, Coggins Mill, Mayfield, Sussex.——Marion Kathleen, *b.* 1920 : *m.* 1944, Raymond Weedon Wicker, and has issue living, Nicholas Paul, *b.* 1946,—Jeffery Roger, *b.* 1954,—Susan Carole, *b.* 1945,—Jill Patricia, *b.* 1947,—Sheila Margaret, *b.* 1949,—Pauline Jane, *b.* 1953,—Frances Anne, *b.* 1957. *Residence*, Windy Ridge, Punnetts Town, Heathfield, Sussex.——Gwennyth Eileen Mary, *b.* 1928: *m.* 1949, Alfred Stokes, of 25, Victoria Rd., Mayfield, Sussex, and has issue living, Patrick John, *b.* 1954,—Sally Ann, *b.* 1950,—Jennifer Mary, *b.* 1952,—Teresa Jill, *b.* 1962.

Issue of the late James O'Reilly Nugent, 4th son of 3rd baronet, *b.* 1849, *d.* 1904: *m.* 1874, Florence Marion, who *d.* 1932, el. da. of the late Rev. George Hulme, of Shipfield Lodge, nr. Reading:—
Wilfrid Basil, *b.* 1885: *m.* 1916, Alice Isobel, da. of the late Theodore Manson West, and has issue living, Denise Florence Isobel, *b.* 1917,—Diana Mary Hampshire, *b.* 1918.——Bernard, *b.* 1892. *Residence*, 5, Acris St., SW18.——Cora Angela Mary O'Reilly (88, Lambeth Rd., SE1 7PW), *b.* 1889.

The original surname of this Family was O'Reilly (a very ancient Irish sept), Sir Hugh O'Reilly, 1st Bt., assumed by RL 1812 the surname of Nugent on the death without issue of his maternal uncle, John Nugent of Tulloughan, Gov. of Tortola and the Virgin Islands, el. son of Andrew Nugent, of Dysart, co. Westmeath, and Lady Catherine Nugent, yr. da. of Thomas, 4th Earl of Westmeath.

NUGENT, Creation (U.K.) 1806, of Waddesdon, Berkshire.

Sir ROBIN GEORGE COLBORNE NUGENT, 5th *Baronet*, *b.* July 11th, 1925; *s.* his father, *Capt. Sir* (GEORGE) GUY BULWER, 1970; ed. at Eton; ARIBA; Lt. Gren. Gds. 1943-48; Italy 1944-45: *m.* 1st, 1947 (m. diss. 1967), Ursula Mary, da. of the late Lt.-Gen. Sir Herbert Fothergill Cooke, KCB, KBE, CSI, DSO; 2ndly, 1967, Victoria Anna Irmgard, da. of the late Dr. Peter Cartellieri, and has issue by 1st m.

꯭rms—Ermine, two bars within a bordure engrailed gules, on a canton of the last a dagger erect proper, pommel and hilt or. ꯭rest—A cockatrice vert, gorged with a plain collar or, pendent therefrom an escutcheon gules, charged with a dagger erect as in the arms. ꯭upporters—Two cockatrices vert, wings endorsed, collared or, pendent therefrom a shield gules, charged with a dagger as in the arms.

I have decreed.

Residence—Bannerdown House, Batheaston, Bath.

Sons living (By 1st m.)—CHRISTOPHER GEORGE RIDLEY, *b.* Oct. 5th, 1949; ed. at Eton and East Anglia Univ.——Patrick Guy, *b.* 1959.
Daughter living (By 1st m.)—Philippa Mary, *b.* 1951.
Brother living—Jeremy Charles Clare (Weather Vane Cottage, Bigfrith Lane, Cookham Dean, Berks.), *b.* 1936: *m.* 1960, Joy, da. of A. H. Waterson, and has issue living, Nigel Howard Clare, *b.* 1963,—Julian Guy Bulwer, *b.* 1965,—Fiona Clare, *b.* 1967.
Sister living—Dinah, *b.* 1922; 1942-45 War in WRNS: *m.* 1950, Capt. John William Huyshe Bennett, DSC, RN, of Farleigh Plain, Hinton Charterhouse, Bath, and has issue living, Timothy Nugent Huyshe, *b.* 1951,—Nicholas John William, *b.* 1957.
Widow living of 4th Baronet—MAISIE ESTHER (*Maisie, Lady Nugent*), (Bannerdown House, Batheaston, Bath), da. of the late Jesse Arthur Bigsby: *m.* 1921, Capt. Sir (George) Guy Bulwer Nugent, 4th Bt., who *d.* 1970.

NUGENT, Creation (U.K.) 1831, of Cloncoskoran, Waterford. [Extinct 1929.]

Sir JOHN NUGENT, 3rd and last *Baronet*.

Collateral Branch living.

Issue (by 2nd marriage) of the late Lieut.-Com. Gilbert Richard de la Poer Nugent, R.N., el. son of 3rd baronet, *b.* 1884, *d.* 1927 : *m.* 1st, 1904, Marjorie, who *d.* 1910, younger da. of the late Capt. Charles Smith. of Goderiche, Sydney, N.S. Wales ; 2ndly, 1922, Lucinda Elinor (who *d.* 1954 having *m.* 3rdly, 1933, Lieut.-Col. O. T. O'Kelly Webber, late R.E. and Roy. Corps of Signals), da. of C. C. Colley, and formerly wife of the late Edward George Hemmerde, K.C. :—

Mary, *b.* 1924: *m.* 1947, Capt. Anthony Raymond Wynter-Bee, RA (ret.), of Beldam Bridge Farm, Chobham, Surrey, and has issue living, Lucinda Mary, *b.* 1951,—Elizabeth Joan, *b.* 1953,—Rosamund Eve, *b.* 1959,—Daphne Ann, *b.* 1962.

NUGENT, Creation (U.K.) 1831, of Donore, Westmeath.

Sir PETER WALTER JAMES NUGENT, 5th *Baronet* ; *b.* Jan. 26th 1920 ; *s.* his father, *Sir* WALTER RICHARD, 1955 ; ed. at Downside ; European War 1940-45 as Major Hampshire Regt.: *m.* 1947, Anne Judith, only da. of Major Robert Smyth, of Gaybrook, Mullingar, co. Westmeath, and has issue.

꯭rms—Ermine, two bars gules ; in dexter chief a martlet azure for difference. ꯭rest—A wyvern vert, on the breast a martlet or.

Seat—Washford, Mayvore, co. Westmeath.

Sons living—WALTER RICHARD MIDDLETON, *b.* Nov. 15th, 1947.——Andrew Robert, *b.* 1951.

Daughters living—Fiona Georgina, *b.* 1949.——Laura Anne, *b.* 1954.

Sisters living—Heather Vivian Mary, *b.* 1917: *m.* 1937, (m. diss. 1950), Sir John Prichard-Jones, 2nd Bt. *Residence*, 28, Chesterfield House, South Audley St., W1.——Gloria Aileen, *b.* 1925: *m.* 1946, Micheal Meade Carvill, Capt. Irish Guards Reserve.

I have decreed.

James Nugent, of Donore, was created a baronet 1768, but on the death of his brother, who succeeded by special remainder, the title became extinct. The Donore estate passed to their nephew, Thomas Fitzgerald, R.N., who assumed, without Roy. licence, the name of Nugent, and his son was created a baronet. Sir Walter Richard Nugent, 4th Bt., was High Sheriff of co. Westmeath 1922-3, a Director and Dep. Gov. of Bank of Ireland, and Chm. of Great Southern Railways of Ireland. He sat as M.P. for S. Westmeath Div. of co. Westmeath (N) 1907-18, and was a Senator of Irish Free State 1928-39.

NUGENT, Creation (U.K.) 1961, of Portaferry, co. Down. [Extinct 1962.]

Rt. Hon. Sir ROLAND THOMAS NUGENT, 1st and last *Baronet.*

Daughter living of 1st Baronet—Elizabeth Anne, *b.* 1919: *m.* 1946, John Sholto Fitzpatrick Cooke, CBE, and has issue living, Julia Anne, *b.* 1948,—Stella Caroline, *b.* 1952,—Zara Cynthia, *b.* 1956. *Residence*, Ferry Quarter, Strangford, co. Down.

Widow living of 1st Baronet—CYNTHIA MAUD (*Lady Nugent*), da. of the late Capt Frederick William Ramsden [see Pennington-Ramsden, Bt. colls.]: *m.* 1917, Rt. Hon. Sir Roland Thomas Nugent, 1st baronet, who *d.* 1962, when the title became extinct. *Residence*, Portaferry House, Portaferry, co. Down.

NUSSEY, Creation (U.K.) 1909, of Rushwood Hall, Kirklington, North Riding of Yorkshire.

Sir THOMAS (MOORE) NUSSEY, 2nd and last *Baronet.*

Widow living of 2nd Baronet—VIVA FRANCES (*Lady Nussey*), (Rushwood, East Tanfield, Ripon, Yorks.), da. of the late Benjamin Talbot, of Solberge, Northallerton, Yorks.: *m.* 1941, Sir Thomas (Moore) Nussey, 2nd Bt. who *d.* 1971, when the title became ext.

NUTTALL, Creation (U.K.) 1922, of Chasefield, Parish of Bowdon, co. Chester.

Either do not attempt, or complete.

Sir NICHOLAS KEITH LILLINGTON NUTTALL, 3rd *Baronet*; *b.* Sept. 21st, 1933; *s.* his father, Lieut.-Col. *Sir* (EDMUND) KEITH, 1941; ed. at Eton; Maj. (ret.) R. Horse Gds.: *m.* 1st, 1960 (m. diss. 1971), Rosemary Caroline, el. da. of Christopher York, of Long Marston Manor, York; 2ndly, 1971 (m. diss. 1975), Julia Jill Beresford, da. of Thomas Williamson, of Beaumont Hall, Thorpe-le-Soken, Essex; 3rdly, 1975, Miranda, da. of Richard St. John Quarry, and formerly wife of Peter Richard Henry Sellers, CBE, and has issue by 1st and 3rd m.

Arms—Or, on a pile sable between in base two roses gules barbed and seeded proper, a shacklebolt of the field. **Crest**—A Dalmatian hound sejant proper, collared and chained and resting the forefoot on a shacklebolt sejant.

Residence—Lowesby Hall, Leicestershire. *Club,*—White's.

Son living—By 1st m.—HARRY, *b.* Jan. 2nd, 1963.
Daughters living—By 1st m.—Tamara, *b.* 1967.——(by 3rd m.) Gytha Miranda, *b.* 1975.

Collateral Branch living.
Issue of the late Clive Nuttall, 3rd son of 1st baronet, *b.* 1906, *d.* 1936: *m.* 1931, Eileen Daphne Elizabeth, da. of the late Lieut.-Col. Horatio Douglas Russell, D.S.O.:—
Clive Patrick, *b.* 1933.

The 1st baronet, Sir Edmund, was head of the firm of Nuttall and Co., civil engineering contractors, of Trafford Park, Manchester. The 2nd baronet, Lieut.-Col. Sir (Edmund) Keith, *d.* (on active ser. during European War) 1941.

NUTTING, Creation (U.K.) 1902, of St. Helens, Booterstown, co. Dublin.

Death rather than disgrace.

Rt. Hon. Sir (HAROLD) ANTHONY NUTTING, 3rd *Baronet*; *b.* Jan. 11th, 1920; *s.* his father, *Lt.-Col.* Sir HAROLD STANSMORE, 1972; ed. at Eton, and Trin. Coll., Camb.; Leics. Yeo. 1939-40 (invalided), Foreign Ser. in France, Spain and Italy 1940-45; Chm. of Young Conservative & Unionist Movement 1946-47, Vice-Chm. of Nat. Union of Conservative Assocns. 1949-50, and Chm. 1950-51, and Chm. of Conservative Overseas Bureau, and of Nat. Exec. Cttee. of Conservative Party 1951-52, Joint Parl. Under-Sec. of State for Foreign Affairs 1951-54, and Min. of State for Foreign Affairs, Leader of UK Delegation to UN Assembly, and UK Repres. on Disarmament Comm. 1954-56; MP for Melton Div. of Leics. (C) 1945-56; author of "I Saw for Myself" 1958, "Disarmament" 1959, "Europe Will Not Wait" 1960, "Lawrence of Arabia" 1961, "The Arabs" 1964, "Gordon, Martyr and Misfit" 1966, "No End of a Lesson, The Story of Suez" 1967, "Scramble for Africa" 1970, "Nasser" 1972; PC 1954: *m.* 1st, 1941 (m. diss. 1959), Gillian Leonora, da. of the late Capt. Edward Jolliffe Strutt [see B. Rayleigh, colls.]; 2ndly, 1961, Anne Gunning, da. of the late Arnold Barthrop Parker, of Cuckfield, Sussex, and has issue living by 1st m.

Arms,—Chevrony of six gules and vert three gryphons segreant or, on a chief of the last as many nut branches slipped proper. **Crest,**—A demi gryphon segreant enclosed between two nut branches proper.

Seat—Achentoul, Kinbrace, Sutherland. *Residence,*—47, Addison Rd., W14 8JH. *Club*—Boodle's.

Sons living—By 1st m.—JOHN GRENFELL (Chicheley Hall, Newport Pagnall, Bucks.; 2, Justice Walk, Lawrence St., SW3 5DE), *b.* Aug. 28th, 1942; ed. at Eton, and McGill Univ., Canada (BA); Bar. Middle Temple 1968; elected to Senate of Inns of Court and Bar 1975: *m.* 1973, Diane, da. of John Rutherford Blundell, of Havant, Hants., adopted da. of Capt. Duncan Kirk, and widow of 2nd Earl Beatty, and has issue living, Victoria Emily, *b.* 1975.——David Anthony (The Old Manse, Terling, Chelmsford, Essex), *b.* 1944; ed. at Eton, and Trin. Coll., Camb. (BA): *m.* 1974, Tessa Anne, da. of Lt.-Col. Sir Nigel John Mordaunt, 13th Bt., MBE, and has issue living, Belinda, *b.* 1975.

Daughter living—By 1st m.—Zara Nina (24, Clareville Grove, SW7), *b.* 1947: *m.* 1966 (m. diss. 1970), Martin Guy Stephenson [see V. Hawarden, colls.].

Collateral Branches living.

Issue of the late Capt. Edward Christian Frederick Nutting, Roy. Horse Guards, 2nd son of 2nd baronet, *b.* 1917, *d.* (on active ser. during European War) 1943: *m.* 1939, Lady Rosemary Alexandra Eliot (who *d.* 1963, having married 2ndly, 1945, Lt.-Cdr. David Grederick Hew Dunn, R.N., and 3rdly, 1949, Maj. Ralph Alexander Rubens, Sherwood Foresters), da. of 6th Earl of St. Germans:—

Davina Rosemary Enid NUTTING, *b.* 1940; a co-heir presumptive to Baronies of Botetourt and Herbert (cr. 1461) [see D. Beaufort, colls.]; resumed by deed poll 1969 her maiden surname of Nutting: *m.* 1960 (m. diss. 1969), as his 2nd wife, John Martin Brentnall Cope, and has issue living, Jonathan Edric, *b.* 1961,—Samantha Mary, *b.* 1963. *Residence,* The Old Rectory Cottage, Stanford Dingley, Berks.

Issue of the late Capt. Arthur Ronald Stansmore Nutting, OBE, MC, 3rd son of 1st baronet, *b.* 1888, *d.* 1964: *m.* 1st, 1912, Edith Allen (who *d.* 1953, having obtained a divorce 1932), da. of Walter Brooks; 2ndly, 1932, Patricia Elizabeth (North Breache Manor, Ewhurst, Surrey), da. of Henry R. Jameson, of Drumleck, Howth, co. Dublin:—

(By 2nd m.) Peter Robert (31, Pembroke Rd., W8), *b.* 1935; ed. at Eton; past Chairman of Edward & John Burke, Ltd.: *m.* 1965, Cecilia Hester Louise Constance, el. da. of Cosmo Rex Ivor Russell [see B. Ampthill, colls.], and has issue living, William Frederick, *b.* 1968,—Rupert Edward, *b.* 1971,—Amanda Charlotte, *b.* 1966.——Nicholas Ronald (Catsgore House, Somerton, Somerset), *b.* 1937; ed. at Eton: *m.* 1962, Caroline E. H., da. of Brig. Houghton Beckford, and has issue living, Ann Olivia, *b.* 1963,—Sarah Caroline, *b.* 1965.

The 1st baronet, Sir John Gardiner Nutting, D.L., was Chm. of E. and J. Burke, Ltd., a J.P. and D.L., and High Sheriff of co. Dublin 1895-6.

OAKELEY, Creation (G.B.) 1790, of Shrewsbury.

Sir (EDWARD) ATHOLL OAKELEY, 7th *Baronet*, el. son of the late Maj. Edward Francis Oakeley, J.P., 2nd son of 4th baronet; *b.* May 31st, 1900; *s.* his cousin *Sir* CHARLES RICHARD ANDREW, 1959; ed. at Clifton Coll, and RMC; formerly Lt. 1st Batn. (43rd LI) Oxfordshire and Bucks LI: *m.* 1st, 1922, Ethyl Felice (who obtained a divorce 1929), da. of T. O'Coffey; 2ndly, 1930, Patricia Mabel Mary (from whom he obtained a divorce 1951), da. of L. H. Birtchnell; 3rdly, 1952, Doreen (from whom he obtained a divorce 1960), da. of Stanley F. Wells; 4thly, 1960, Shirley, da. of Herbert Church, of 2, Northwood Rd., Tonbridge, Kent, and has issue by 2nd and 4th marriages.

ᴀrms—Argent, on a fesse between three crescents gules as many fleurs-de-lis or. Crest—A dexter arm, embowed in armour proper charged with two fleurs-de-lis or, each in a crescent gules, in the hand a scimitar proper hilt or.

Residence—Nomad, Lynton, Devon.

I fear not, but am cautious.

Son living—By 2nd marriage—JOHN DIGBY ATHOLL, *b.* Nov. 27th, 1932: *m.* 1958, Maureen, da. of John Cox, of Hamble, Hants, and has issue living, Robert John Atholl, *b.* 1963,— Marina Anne, *b.* 1961. *Residence*, 22, Sydney Rd., Hamble, Hants.

Daughter living—By 4th marriage—Lorna Olivia Athole, *b.* 1961.

Brother living—Rowland Henry, *b.* 1909 ; ed. at Clifton Coll., and at New Coll., Oxford (B.A. 1930); in Malayan Civil Ser. 1931-58, Commonwealth Relations Office 1959-65, and Diplo. Ser. 1966-69: *m.* 1940, Diana Margaret, da. of the late Dr. Hayward, of The Holt, Eynsham, and has issue living, Christopher Rowland (Short St., Stoneville PO, W. Aust. 6554), *b.* 1941; ed. at Winchester, and Trin. Coll., Dublin (BA): *m.* 1973, Margaret, da. of the late Gilbert Carson, of Meriden, W. Aust., and has issue living, Andrew Gilbert *b.* 1974,—Henry Francis (twin) (2, Helix Gdns., SW2), *b.* 1941; ed. at Clifton; MRCP (London), MRCPsych: *m.* 1968, Penelope Susan, LRCP, MRCS, da. of Wilfred Barlow, BM, BCh, of 3, Albert Court, Kensington Gore, SW7, and has issue living, Matthew Thomas *b.* 1968, Edward James *b.* 1970,—Rosamond Margaret, *b.* 1946; ed. at Walthamstow Hall, and Sheffield Univ.: *m.* 1969, Henry David Warriner (Broadmoor Farm, Little Wolford, Shipston-on-Stour, Warwicks.), and has issue living, Michael Francis *b.* 1970, Timothy David *b.* 1974, Sarah Caroline *b.* 1971.—Auriol Mary, *b.* 1947; ed. at Walthamstow Hall, Roy. Ballet Sch., and Bishop Otter Sch. *Residence*, 3, Mount Harry Rd., Sevenoaks, Kent.

Sisters living—Rosemary, *b.* 1903: *m.* 1940, Mervyn Cecil ffranck Sheppard, C.M.G., M.B.E., Malayan Civil Ser., and has issue living, Lavender Frances, *b.* 1941: *m.* 1962, Lt. Richard Giles Saker, RN, and has issue living, Iain Richard Mark *b.* 1962, Robin David Mervyn *b.* 1963, Emma-Rose Everilde *b.* 1968, Zoë Arabella *b.* 1970. *Residence*, Linden House, West Wittering, nr. Chichester, Sussex.——Mary, *b.* 1913; ed. at St. Hilda's Coll., Oxford (MA); Head Mistress of Craighead Diocesan Sch., Timaru, NZ 1943-55; Head Mistress of St. Felix Sch., Southwold, Suffolk since 1958. *Residence*, Cherwell Lodge, Eysham, Oxon.

Daughter living of 5th Baronet—Emily Charlotte Eileen, *MBE, b.* 1896; MBE (Civil) 1962: *m.* 1921, Wilfrid Haig Loyd, who *d.* 1971, and has issue living, Peter Haig (12, Meadway, NW11), *b.* 1922; ed. at Eton; Capt. (ret.) RM: *m.* 1st, 1950, Suzanne Duncan, from whom he obtained a divorce 1957; 2ndly, 1961, Rosemary Joan, el. da. of Dr. John Moir, of Hunters Green, Bagshot Rd., Worplesden, Surrey, and has issue living, (by 1st m.) William Haig *b.* 1955, Julie Caroline *b.* 1952, (by 2nd m.) Anthony Simon Haig *b.* 1963, Sophie Katherine *b.* 1969,—Geoffrey Haig (Remenham House, Ocle Pychard, Herefords.), *b.* 1926; ed. at Eton: *m.* 1st, 1948, Patricia Mary Maclean; 2ndly, 1968, Dawn, da. of the late Maj. Robert Douglas Baird, MC [see Baird, Bt., colls., cr. 1809]. and has issue living, (by 1st m.) Martin Andrew Haig *b.* 1949: *m.* 1974, Jill Deloitte Davis, Jeremy Charles Haig *b.* 1951,—Andrew Haig, *b.* 1934,—Charlotte Denise Eileen (*Hon. Mrs. Derek E. Winn*), *b.* 1928: *m.* 1954, the Hon. Derek Edward Anthony Winn [*see B.* St. Oswald]. *Residence*, 30, The Boltons, SW10.

Widows living of 5th and 6th Baronets—IDA MARGARET ELENA (*Ida, Lady Oakeley*) (Holly Lodge, Camberley, Surrey), da. of the late Col. J. M. Kerr, Madras Cav.: *m.* 1934, as his second wife, Sir Charles John Oakeley, 5th baronet, who *d.* 1938.——ANNE-MARIE (RUDD) (*Anne-Marie, Lady Oakeley*) (31, Résidence de la Garoupe, Blvd. de la Garoupe, 066 00 Cap d'Antibes, France) yst. da. of Étienne Dennis, of Le Havre, Seine Maritime, France: *m.* 1957, as his 3rd wife, Sir Charles Richard Andrew Oakeley, 6th baronet, who *d.* 1959.

Collateral Branch living.

Issue of the late Herbert William Oakeley, youngest son of 4th baronet, *b.* 1874, *d.* 1931 : *m.* 1896, Lilian (from whom he obtained a divorce 1900), da. of Joseph Moore :—

Clifford Charles William Morland, *b.* 1897. *Residence*,

This family was long settled at Oakeley, Bishop's Castle, Shropshire, and Sir Charles Oakeley, 1st baronet, was Governor of Madras 1790-94. Sir Charles Richard Andrew Oakeley, 6th baronet, was Joint Managing Director of the firm of Oakeley, Vaughan & Co., Ltd., insurance brokers.

OAKES, Creation (U.K.) 1939, of Nassau, Bahama Islands.

Through difficulties.

Sir CHRISTOPHER OAKES, 3rd *Baronet*; *b.* July 10th, 1949; *s.* his father, *Sir* SYDNEY, 1966.

Arms,—Or on a fesse sable between in chief an acorn slipped and leaved and in base a maple leaf proper, three maple leaves of the field. Crest,—Issuant from a chaplet of roses gules a demi-lion rampant or, grasping in the dexter paw an acorn slipped and leaved proper.

Address—PO Box 34113, Postal Station D., Vancouver, BC, Canada.

Sisters living—Felicity, *b.* 1952.——Virginia, *b.* 1954.
Uncle living (son of 1st baronet)—HARRY PHILIP (PO Box 1002, Nassau, Bahamas), *b.* Aug. 30th, 1932: *m.* 1958, Christiane, only da. of Rudolf Botsch, of Hamburg, Germany, and has issue living, Harry Newell, *b.* 1958,—Philip Gale, *b.* 1961,—Michael Lewis, *b.* 1966,—Bianca Eunice, *b.* 1963.
Aunts living (daughters of 1st baronet)—Nancy VON HOYNINGEN-HUENE (P.O. Box N1002, 28, Queen St., Nassau, Bahamas, and Marsella 44, Mexico 6, D.F. Mexico); *b.* 1925; resumed by deed poll in the Bahamas 1975 the surname of von Hoyningen-Huene: *m.* 1st, 1952 (m. diss. 1956), Baron Ernst-Lyssardt von Hoyningen-Huene; 2ndly, 1962, Patrick Claude Henry Tritton and has issue living, (by 1st m.) *Baron* Alexander George Lyssardt, *b.* 1955.——Shirley Lewis, *b.* 1929; ed. at Vassar Coll., USA (AB 1951); LLB Yale Univ. 1954: *m.* 1961, Allan Churchill Butler, of Jacaranda House, Parliament St., Nassau, Bahamas.

Widow living of 1st Baronet—EUNICE MYRTLE (*Eunice, Lady Oakes*) (Sulgrave Manor, PO Box 222, Nassau, Bahamas), da. of the late Thomas McIntyre, of Sydney, NSW: *m.* 1933, Sir Harry Oakes, 1st Bt., who *d.* 1943.

Widow living of 2nd Baronet—GRETA (*Lady Oakes*), (PO Box ES 5529, Nassau, Bahamas), yr. da. of the late Gunnar Victor Hartmann, of London and Copenhagen; Hon. Danish Consul for Bahamas 1967-74; Knt. Order of the Dannebrog of Denmark: *m.* 1948, Sir Sydney Oakes, 2nd Bt., who *d.* 1966.

The 1st baronet, Sir Harry Oakes (son of William Pitt Oakes, of Sangerville, Maine, U.S.A.), was a Member of Legislative Council of Bahamas.

OAKSHOTT, Creation (U.K.) 1959, of Bebington, co. Palatine of Chester.

Hon. Sir ANTHONY HENDRIE OAKSHOTT, 2nd *Baronet*; *b.* Oct. 10th, 1929; *s.* his father, HENDRIE DUDLEY, *Baron Oakshott* (Life Peer) and 1st Baronet, 1975; ed. at Rugby: *m.* 1965, Valerie Anne Doreen, da. of Jack Vlasto, of 2, Denbigh House, Hans Place, SW1, and formerly wife of (i) Donald John Ross, and (ii) Michael de Pret-Roose.

Arms,—Per chevron azure and gules in chief two arrows in saltire between as many branches of oak slipped and fructed or and in base a bear passant argent. Crest,—In front of a mount vert thereon an oak tree proper fructed gold the main-stem transfixed by two arrows in fesse points to the dexter also proper a bow fessewise or.

Residence—Workham Farm, Fifield, Oxon. *Clubs*—Turf, White's.
Brother living—*Hon.* MICHAEL ARTHUR JOHN (Ingleston of Kelton, Castle Douglas, Kirkcudbrightshire), *b.* April 12th, 1932; ed. at Rugby: *m.* 1957, Christina Rose Methuen, da. of the late Thomas Banks, of Solai, Kenya, and has issue living, Thomas Hendrie, *b.* 1959,—Charles Michael, *b.* 1961,—Angus Withington, *b.* 1965.
Widow living of 1st Baronet (and Life Baron)—See Oakshott, By. of.

Sir Hendrie Dudley Oakshott, *MBE*, 2nd son of Arthur John Oakshott of Merle Dene, Bidsdon, Cheshire, was a Lord Commr. of HM Treasury 1952-55, Comptroller of HM Household 1955-57, Treasurer 1957-59, and PPS to Sec. of State for Foreign Affairs 1959-60, and to Chancellor of Exchequer 1961-62; MP for Bebington (C) 1950-64; cr. a Baronet 1959, and Baron Oakshott, of Bebington, co. Palatine of Chester (Life Baron) 1964.

O'BRIEN, Creation (U.K.) 1849, of Merrion Square, Dublin, and Boris-in-Ossory, Queen's County.

The strong hand uppermost.

Sir DAVID EDMOND O'BRIEN, 6th *Baronet*, *b.* Feb. 19th, 1901; *s.* his brother, *Sir* JOHN EDMOND NOEL, *MC*, 1969: *m.* 1927, Mary Alice, who *d.* 1974, yst. da. of Sir Henry Foley Grey, 7th Bt. [Lambert, Bt.], and has issue.

Arms—Argent, three lions passant-guardant per pale gules and azure, armed or, all within a bordure vert. Crest—From a castle argent in flames, a naked arm embowed, the hand grasping a sword, all proper.
Residence—Salisbury, Clonmel, co. Tipperary.

Sons living—JOHN DAVID (Courtown, Kilcock, co. Kildare), *b.* June 9th, 1928: *m.* 1957, Sheila Winifred, only da. of Sir Charles Arland Maitland Freake, 4th Bt. (ext.), and has issue living, Timothy John, *b.* 1958, James Patrick, *b.* 1964,—Doone Veronica Mary, *b.* 1959,—Melanie Frances Ann, *b.* 1961.——Gerald Patrick (30, Applegarth Rd., W14), *b.* 1930: *m.* 1960, Frances Huband de Savoie, da. of Col. William Thornton Huband Gregg, DSO, OBE, of Ballyknockane House, Clonmel, co. Tipperary, and has issue living, Lyndall Jane, *b.* 1961,—Lucy Frances *b.* 1964,—Rachel Shirin, *b.* 1965,—Deborah Susan, *b.* 1969.

Daughter living—Audrey Mary, *b.* 1935: *m.* 1963, Conrad Andrew Roman Dobrzynski, of Staleen, Drogheda, co. Meath, and has issue living, Sophia Catherine *b.* 1966,—Emma Natasha, *b.* 1972.

Daughter living of 5th Baronet—Mary Clare, *b.* 1943: *m.* 1961, John Peter James Hare, of 16, Addison Av., W11, and has issue living, David John Brent, *b.* 1963,—Kerry-Jane, *b.* 1966.

Daughters living of 4th Baronet—Patricia Mary Gabrielle (45, Burntwood Grange Rd., Wandsworth Common, SW18): *m.* 1956 (m. diss. 1961), Walter William Burgoyne Chalwin, and has issue living, Simon William Burgoyne, *b.* 1956,—Nicola Clare, *b.* 1957.——Sheelagh Tessa Ursula: *m.* 1954, Caird Wentworth Gordon Wilson, son of the late Lt.-Gen. Sir Gordon Wilson, KCSI, CB, CBE, MC, and has issue living, Robert Caird, *b.* 1955,—Alexander Hugh Gordon, *b.* 1957. *Residence,* 9, Bovingdon Rd., SW6.——Shaunagh Gundrede: *m.* 1972, John Nares Addinsell, of Moccas Court Farmhouse, nr. Hereford.

Daughters living of 3rd Baronet—Mariquita Winefride Aloysia (Medstead Manor, Medstead, Alton, Hants.), *b.* 1890: *m.* 1915, Capt. James Thirkell Price, MC, RFA, who *d.* (killed in action) 1916, and has issue living, James Timothy Noel (The Moorings, Port Lewaigue, Ramsey, Isle of Man). *Club,* New (Edinburgh), *b.* 1916; Capt. RA (ret.): *m.* 1943, the Hon. Anne Margaret Younger, da. of 2nd Viscount Younger, of Leckie, and has issue living, Timothy James *b.* 1945, Simon Antony Carew *b.* 1951; Capt. Scots Gds.: *m.* 1975, Primrose E., da. of Capt. J. G. B. Thompson of Annels Farm, Bratton Seymour, Somerset, Jenifer Mary *b.* 1944: *m.* 1964, Walter Anthony Gilbey, of Ballacallin Mooar, Marown, Crosby, Isle of Man [*see* Gilbey, Bt.], Jacqueline Anne Mary, *b.* 1948, Mary Elizabeth *b.* 1953.——Eileen Mary Frances (Medical Missionaries of Mary, Drogheda, co. Louth), *b.* 1895; a Nun (Sister Eileen): *m.* 1923, Brig. Edward Thomas Arthur George Boylan, CBE, DSO, MC, formerly RHA, who *d.* 1959 [B. Stafford, colls.], and has issue living, Edward Antony (Hilltown, Drogheda, co. Meath), *b.* 1925; Maj. late RHA,—Desmond Francis, *b.* 1934; late Irish Gds.: *m.* 1965, Brigid Margaret, da. of Maj. Thomas Bevan,—Anne Cecilia (Warden Grange, Chipping Warden, Banbury, Oxon.), *b.* 1928: *m.* 1954, Maj. Michael Grahame Dewey, Queen's Own Hussars (ret.), who *d.* 1973 [*see* Dewey, Bt., colls.],—Doreen Gundrede Mary (Waltham Forest Social Responsibility Council, C.R.E.S.T., Orford Rd., Walthamstow, E17), a Nun (Sister Martina).——Doreen Moira (of 32, Lennox Gdns., SW1), *b.* 1897.——Kathleen Moyra Teresa (18, Sloane Gdns., SW1), *b.* 1899.

Widow living of 5th Baronet—ROSEMARY BRENT (*Lady O'Brien*) (The Manor House, Stogumber, Taunton, Somerset), da. of the late Edgar Grotrian, of Knapton Hall, Malton, Yorks., and formerly wife of Maj. Eric Arthur Staniland: *m.* 1940, as his 2nd wife, Capt. Sir John Edmond Noel O'Brien, MC, 5th Bt., who *d.* 1969.

This family claims to represent the powerful house of O'Brien Ara, of the line of Thomond. Sir Timothy O'Brien, son of Timothy O'Brien of co. Tipperary, 1st baronet, MP for Cashel (*L*) 1846-59, was a merchant of Dublin who took a leading part in the reform of its Corporation and contributed largely to the redemption of the Municipal property. He was Lord Mayor of Dublin 1844 and again 1849, being specially elected to receive Her Majesty on her first visiting Ireland, on which occasion he was created a baronet. Sir Patrick, 2nd baronet, sat as MP for King's co. (*L*) 1852-85. Sir Timothy Carew, 3rd baronet, was a DL and JP of co. Cork, and served in 1914-18 War as Capt. R. Irish Fusiliers, and as Maj. Remount Ser. (despatches).

O'CONNELL, Creation (U.K.) 1869, of Lakeview, Killarney, co. Kerry, and of Ballybeggan, Tralee, co. Kerry.

Reason and strength

Sir MORGAN DONAL CONAIL O'CONNELL, 6th *Baronet;* *b.* Jan. 29th, 1923; *s.* his father, *Capt. Sir* MAURICE JAMES ARTHUR, *M.C.,* 1949; European War 1943-45 with Roy. Signals: *m.* 1953, Elizabeth, only child of the late Major John MacCarthy-O'Leary, of Lavenders, West Malling, Kent, and has issue.

Arms—Per fesse argent and vert, a stag trippant proper between three trefoils slipped counterchanged. *Crest*—A stag's head erased argent, charged with trefoil slipped vert. (Ulster Office 1667.)

Seat—Lakeview, Killarney, co. Kerry.

Sons living—MAURICE JAMES DONAGH MacCARTHY, *b.* June 10th, 1958.——John Morgan Ross MacCarthy, *b.* 1960.
Daughters living—Frances Mary Margaret MacCarthy, *b.* 1954.——Susan Jane Anne, *b.* 1956,——Katherine Lucila Jean, *b.* 1964.——Clare Helen Pauline, *b.* 1969.
Sister living—Joan Mary Lucila Margaret, *b.* 1926; formerly 3rd Officer W.R.N.S.: *m.* 1953, Lieut.-Com. John Allen Victor Hickley, RN (ret.), of 100 Harris Cres., Christchurch 5, NZ, and has issue living, Martin Maurice Victor, *b.* 1957,—Grania Margaret Leslie, *b.* 1959.

Collateral Branch living.

Issue of the late Basil Morgan O'Connell, KPM, yst. son of 4th baronet, *b.* 1900, *d.* 1971: *m.* 1st, 1935, Lucila, who *d.* 1953, da. of Maj. Henry Hugh Peter Deasy, of Cnoc Na Faire, Carrighahorig, Eire; 2ndly, 1962, Georgia Bard Shearer (Box 131, Solebury, Pa. 18963, USA), widow of Mortimer Haldeman O'Connor:—

(By 1st m.) Maurice Hugh Ricardo Ross (12, Rostrevor Rd., Dublin 6), *b.* 1936; ed. at Ampleforth, Peterhouse, Camb. (MA) and Trin. Coll., Dublin (Higher Dip. Ed.); a Member of Dublin City Council since 1967: *m.* 1961, Ann, el. da. of Hugh Gillespie, of the Old Rectory, Kiltegan, Baltinglass, co. Wicklow, and has issue living, Carlos Donal John, *b.* 1963,—Morgan Basil Peter, *b.* 1965,—Maurice William Hugh Rickard, *b.* 1966,—Ross Paul Francis, *b.* 1968,—Lucila Marie Valdemara Georgia, *b.* 1962.——Seamus Morgan Basil Ross, of 28, Pennycroft, Harpenden, Herts., *b.* 1941; ed. at Ampleforth, and Trin. Coll., Dublin (BA).

The 1st baronet was the youngest and last surviving brother of Daniel O'Connell, Q.C., M.P., of Darrinane Abbey, Senior Representative of the ancient Irish sept of O'Connell, and nephew of Lieut.-Gen. Count Daniel O'Connell of the French Service by whose efforts the officers of the disbanded French Irish Brig. enrolled in the Service of King George III. in 1794.

OGILVY, Creation (N.S.) 1626, of Inverquharity, Forfarshire.

I despise earthly dangers.

Sir DAVID JOHN WILFRID OGILVY, 13th *Baronet*, son of the late Gilbert Francis Molyneux Ogilvy, 4th son of 10th baronet; *b.* Feb. 3rd, 1914; *s.* his uncle, *Sir* HERBERT KINNAIRD, 1956; ed. at Eton and at Trin. Coll., Oxford (BA); JP and DL for East Lothian; 1939-45 War with RNVR: *m.* 1966, Penelope Mary Ursula, da. of Arthur Lafone Frank Hills, OBE, of White Court, Penshurst Station, Kent, and has issue.

Arms—Quarterly: 1st and 4th, argent, a lion passant-guardant gules, gorged with an open crown, and crowned with a close imperial one or, *Ogilvy*; 2nd and 3rd, argent, an eagle displayed sable, beaked and membered gules, *Ramsay of Auchterhouse*. *Crest*—A demi-lion gules. *Supporters*—Two wild men wreathed about the head and temples with leaves, trampling upon serpents, and holding branches in their exterior hands all proper.

Seat—Winton House, Pencaitland, East Lothian.

Son living—FRANCIS GILBERT ARTHUR, *b.* April 22nd, 1969.
Brother living—John Augustine, *b.* 1915; Lt.-Com. (ret.) RN; 1939-45 War (despatches): *m.* 1942, Margaret, da. of Col. William Thornton Huband Gregg, DSO, OBE, and has issue living, Angus William (Drumdruils, Bridge of Allan, Stirlingshire), *b.* 1945; ed. at Eton and Stirling Univ. (BA): *m.* 1968, Sally, da. of Michael Long, and has issue living, Andrew John *b.* 1972,—Robert Iain Michael *b.* 1974,—Diana Lyndall *b.* 1946. *Residence*, Old North Manse, E. Linton, E. Lothian.
Sisters living—Katharine Olivia Mary, *b.* 1916: *m.* 1947, William Packe, and has issue living, Thomas Gilbert, *b.* 1948,—Andrew James, *b.* 1951. *Residence*, Low Wood, Winthorpe, Newark. ——Hester Mary, *b.* 1921: *m.* 1951, David Scott, and has issue living, Colum Basil, *b.* 1954,—Margaret Isobel, *b.* 1952,—Christian Mary Gertrude, *b.* 1955,—Helen Olivia Katharine, *b.* 1958. *Residences*, Glenaros, Isle of Mull: 22, Blomfield Rd., W9 1AD.

Collateral Branches living.

Issue of the late Capt. Frederick Charles Ashley Ogilvy, R.N., 3rd son of 10th baronet, *b.* 1866, *d.* 1909: *m.* 1904, Gertrude Lilian, (who *d.* 1971 having m. 2ndly, 1913, the 9th Earl of Elgin and Kincardine, who *d.* 1917; 3rdly, 1923, Lt.-Col. John Alexander Stirling of Kippendavie, DSO, MC, who *d.* 1957), da. of the late Com. William Sherbrooke, formerly RN, of Oxton Hall, Southwell, Notts.:—

Ann Howard, *b.* 1905: *m.* 1932, John Gurney, J.P., el. son of the late Sir Eustace Gurney, and has issue living, Priscilla Ann, *b.* 1937: *m.* 1958, W. Gregory F. Meath Baker, of Hasfield Court, Gloucester, and The Old Rectory, Blisworth, Northampton, and has issue living, William John Clovis *b.* 1959, Samuel Justin Francis *b.* 1961, Hugh Lysander Luke *b.* 1964, Joshua Ralph *b.* 1965,—Jean Elizabeth, *b.* 1939: *m.* 1963, Patrick Barnabas Burke Mayhew, QC, of 18, Groveway, SW9, and has issue living, James Barnabas Burke *b.* 1964, Henry Edmund Burke *b.* 1965, Tristram Thomas Burke *b.* 1968, Jerome Patrick Burke *b.* 1970,—Elizabeth Olivia, *b.* 1943: *m.* 1968, Timothy Arnold Neil Bristol, of The Chantry, Ely, Cambs., and has issue living, Benjamin Fitzroy Timothy *b.* 1972, Arabella Fredericka Ann *b.* 1970,—Elizabeth Rachel *b.* 1946,—Ruth Christian *b.* 1948: *m.* 1970, Capt. George Clive Forestier-Walker, Coldm. Gds. [see Forestier-Walker, Bt., colls.]. *Residence*, Walsingham Abbey, Norfolk.

Granddaughter of the late James Balfour Ogilvy, 4th son of 8th baronet :—
Issue of the late Col. William Lewis Kinloch Ogilvy, C.B., *b.* 1840, *d.* 1900: *m.* 1889, Lucy, J.P., who *d.* 1946, da. of the late William Wickham, M.P., of Binsted Wyck, Alton, Hants :—

Charlotte Helen (*Lady Bonham-Carter*), *b.* 1893 : *m.* 1926, Sir Edgar Bonham-Carter, K.C.M.G., CIE, who *d.* 1956. *Residences*, 5, Connaught Sq., W2; Wyck Place, Alton, Hants.

Grandchildren of the late Walter Tulliedeph Ogilvy, *b.* 1852 (infra) :—
Issue of the late Angus Edward Ogilvy, *b.* 1880, *d.* 1928 ; *m.* 1910, Margaret, who *d.* 1956, da. of Lieut.-Col. Sir James Frederick Stuart-Menteth, 4th Bt., of Rownhams Mount, near Southampton :—

Walter Tulliedeph, *b.* 1911 : *m.* 1st, 1947, Christina Alexandra Sutherland, who *d.* 1949, da. of A. Polson, of Spinningdale, Sutherland; 2ndly, 1950, Audrey Kingsley, da. of A. G. Weeks, of Limpsfield, Surrey, and has issue living, (by 2nd marriage) Fiona Audrey, *b.* 1952,—Susan Margaret, *b.* 1955. *Residence*, 9, Eridge Gdns., Crowborough, Sussex.——Angus Duncan (Warre House, Eton College, Windsor, Berks.), *b.* 1920.

Issue of the late Brigadier David Ogilvy, C.I.E., D.S.O., O.B.E., *b.* 1881, *d.* 1949 : *m.* 1906, Vere Grace, da. of the late Sir Henry Fawcett, K.C.M.G., Ch. Justice of the Levant :—

Vera Edith, *b.* 1912 : *m.* 1932, Major Charles Herbert Harberton Eales, M.C., Indian Cav.. who *d.* 19—, and has issue living, John David OGILVY, *b.* 1934, assumed by deed poll 1955 the surname of Ogilvy in lieu of his patronymic; ed. at Wellington; Lt. RN.: *m.* 1958, Felicity Neilson, da. of Maj. Hugh Jack Melville, of Wendover, Bucks., and has issue living,—Charles Michael, *b.* 1941,—Mary Ann Vere, *b.* 1935: *m.* 1957, Charles Pepler Norton.

Issue of the late Walter Tulliedeph Ogilvy, *b.* 1883, *d.* 1912 : *m.* 1910, Nora, who *d.* 1958, da. of the Rev. Canon Thomas Hewan Archdale, J.P., formerly V. of Tanfield. Tantobie, co. Durham, and Rural Dean :—

Mary Archdale, *b.* 1910 : *m.* 1933, Bryan Stuart Potter, and has issue living. *Address*, Wildfontein, P.O. Box 26, Bergvlei, Johannesburg, S. Africa.

Issue of the late Lieut.-Col. Gilbert Mark Haworth Ogilvy, King's Own Scottish Borderers, *b.* 1887, *d.* (on active ser. during European War) 1945 : *m.* 1915, Mildred Scott, who *d.* 1925 :—

Mildred Cecil, *b.* 1916: *m.* 1944, Lieut. Thomas Duerdin-Dutton, RNVR.

Grandchildren of the late David Ogilvy, son of the late Alexander Ogilvy, 6th son of 5th baronet :—
Issue of the late Walter Tulliedeph Ogilvy, *b.* 1852, *d.* 1927 : *m.* 1st, 1878, Eleanor May Edith Lumley, who *d.* 1902, da. of the late Edward Lumley Haworth, 28th Regt.; 2ndly, 1903, Winifred, who *d.* 1909, da. of the Rev. Henry Edward Maskew ; 3rdly, 1910, Christina, who *d.* 1956, da. of Col. Bannatyne Macleod, formerly Bombay Artillery :—

(By 2nd marriage) Violet Agnes, *b.* 1904: *m.* 1925, John Findlay, and has issue living, John Angus (178, Westbourne Rd., Penarth, Glamorgan), *b.* 1931; MB, ChB: *m.* 1959, Elisabeth Allan, and has issue living, Robin *b.* 1959, Rachel *b.* 1961, Rebecca *b.* 1963,—Sheila Violet, *b.* 1927: *m.* 1947, James Gibb, of Rosebank, Doune, Perths., and 9/8, Sloane St., SW1, and has issue living, Charles James *b.* 1950, Jonathan Findlay *b.* 1953, Louis Ogilvy *b.* 1955, Margaret Elisabeth *b.* 1948,—Jean Winifred, *b.* 1929: *m.* 1951, James Kiss, of Fernlea, Hamstreet Rd., Ashford, Kent, and has issue living, Philip Michael *b.* 1953, David *b.* 1954, Alison Jean *b.* 1965. *Residence*, Rossmor, Grantown-on-Spey, Morayshire.——Devona (Box 148, Thomsons Falls, Kenya), *b.* 1909: *m.* 1946, R. D. Paton Ker, and has issue living, Michael Patrick, *b.* 1947.——Earna (twin), *b.* 1909: *m.* 1931, J. Forrester, of Rumuruti, 24, Gunbar Way, Kalamunda 6076, W. Aust., and has issue living, David Alton (20, Shasta Rd., Lesmurdie, W. Aust.), *b.* 1932; ed. at Camb. Univ. (MA, LLB): *m.* 1959, Fay Garner, and has issue living, Richard Alton *b.* 1961, Susan May *b.* 1965,—Thelma *b.* 1934: *m.* 1960, Neil Pearson (PO Box 57, Concession, Rhodesia), and has issue living, Lesley Dawn *b.* 1961, Janette Nancy *b.* 1962.

Issue of the late Angus Ogilvy, *b.* 1855, *d.* 1928 : *m.* 1886, Rose Serena, who *d.* 1923, da. of the late Abercromby Dick, W.S., and Bar.-at-law :—

Abercromby Graham, (25, Helderzicht St., Somerset West, Cape Province, S. Africa), *b.* 1889 ; ed. at Marlborough; Lt.-Col. (ret.) Indian Army; Mohmand Expedition 1915, Afghanistan 1919, Waziristan 1920: *m.* 1923, Sibyl Mary Abbott Green, of East Donyland Hall, Colchester.

Granddaughters of the late Arthur James Ogilvy, son of the late James Balfour Ogilvy (ante):—
Issue of the late Bertha Florence Ogilvy, *b.* 1867, *d.* 1947: *m.* 1892, William Mosey, Solicitor:—

Mary Kinloch (255, Ainslie House, Waveney St., Launceston, Tasmania) *b.* 1894: *m.* 1918, Denis Whishaw, who *d.* 1953, and has issue living, David, DFC (Armidale, Carrick, Tasmania, and Narrogin, W. Aust.), *b.* 1923; Fl.-Lt. RAAF: *m.* 1949, Roslyn, da. of J. C. Roxburgh, of Launceston, Tasmania, and has issue living, David Michael Kinloch *b.* 1950, Simon *b.* 1951, Denis *b.* 1954, John *b.* 1960, Davina *b.* 1952.——Edith Cora, *b.* 1897: *m.* 1967, Clifford Augustus Broughton, of 27, Harriman Court, Nuffield Village, Castle Hill, NSW.——Clara Hirondelle (Glen Clova, 9, Araluen St., Lindisfarne, Tasmania), *b.* 1899.——Florence Bertha (3, Lasswade Av., Sandy Bay, Hobart, Tasmania), *b.* 1902.

Sir John Ogilvy was created a Baronet with remainder to heirs male whatsoever. The 2nd baronet was M.P. for Angus 1665-78. The 5th baronet sold the estate of Inverquharity, which had been in the family for fourteen generations. Sir John 9th baronet, sat as M.P. for Dundee (*L*) 1857-74. The 11th baronet Sir Gilchrist Nevill, Lieut. Scots Guards, was killed in action during European War Oct. 1914.

Ogilvy-Wedderburn, see Wedderburn.

OHLSON, Creation (U.K.) 1920, of Scarborough, North Riding of co. of Yorkshire.

Alteri · si · tibi.

Do to others as thyself.

Sir ERIC (JAMES) OHLSON, 2nd *Baronet ; b.* March 16th, 1911 ; *s.* his father, *Sir* ERIK OLOF, 1934 ; ed. at Harrow, and at Trin. Coll., Camb.: *m.* 1935, Marjorie Joan, da. of the late C. H. Roosmale-Cocq, of Dorking, Surrey, and has issue.

Arms—Argent, in waves of the sea a steamer proper, on a chief azure three fir trees eradicated also proper. Crest—In front of a sun in splendour proper, a motor wheel sable.

Residence—Belvedere, Scarborough.

Sons living—BRIAN ERIC CHRISTOPHER, *b.* July 27th, 1936; ed. at Harrow and RMA; late Lt. Coldstream Guards.—Peter Michael, *b.* 1939; ed. at Harrow and Trin. Coll., Camb. (BA): *m.* 1968, Sarah, only da. of Maj.-Gen. Thomas Brodie, CB, CBE, DSO.

Daughter living—Christine Rose, *b.* 1950.

Brother living—Gerald Thomas, *b.* 1917 ; ed. at Harrow : *m.* 1943, Marjorie Beryl, da. of Trevor Davies, and has issue, Christopher Mark, *b.* 1944. *Residence*,

The first baronet, Sir Erik Olof Ohlson (who had been knighted in 1915), son of the late Anders Ohlson, of Fellingsbro, Sweden, was a shipowner, a coal and coke exporter, and a timber importer, of Hull.

WALKER-OKEOVER, Creation (U.K.) 1886, of Gateacre Grange, co. Lancaster, and Osmaston Manor, co. Derby.

ESTO·VIGILANS.

Sir IAN PETER ANDREW MONRO WALKER-OKEOVER, D.S.O., T.D., 3rd *Baronet ; b.* Nov. 30th, 1902 ; *s.* his father, *Sir* PETER CARLAW WALKER, 1915 ; ed. at Eton, and at Ch. Ch., Oxford ; formerly Lieut.-Col. Comdg. 1st (Derby Yeo.) RAC (TA); Lord-Lieut. and a JP for Derbys. High Sheriff 1934; a Member of Queen's Body Guard for Scotland (R. Co. of Archers), and patron of one living; Hon. Attaché at Brussels 1925-26; appointed Hon. Col. Derbyshire Yeo. 1951; assumed by Roy. Licence 1956 the additional surname of Okeover after his patronymic, and the Arms of Okeover quarterly with those of Walker; N. Africa 1942-43, Italy 1943-45 (DSO and Bar); DSO and Bar 1945: *m.* 1938, Dorothy Elizabeth, younger da. of Capt. Josceline Reginald Heber-Percy [*see* D. Northumberland, colls.], and has issue.

Arms—Quarterly, 1st and 4th, ermine, on a chief gules three bezants, *Okeover* ; 2nd and 3rd, or, three pallets gules surmounted of a saltire argent charged with a stag's head erased proper on a chief azure a garb between two stars of six points of the first, *Walker*. Crests—1st, an oak tree eradicated proper fructed or mantled gules doubled argent ; 2nd, out of a ducal coronet or a dragon ermine armed azure langued gules, mantled gules doubled argent, both *Okeover* ; 3rd, a cornucopia proper, *Walker*.

Seats—Okeover Hall, Ashbourne, Derbyshire ; House of Glenmuick, Ballater, Aberdeenshire.

Son living—PETER RALPH LEOPOLD (35, Flood St., SW3), *b.* July 22nd, 1947; Capt. Blues and Royals: *m.* 1972, Catherine Mary Maule, el. da. of Col. George Patrick Maule Ramsay [*see* E. Dalhousie, colls.].

Daughters living—Elizabeth Anne, *b.* 1940: *m.* 1969, Lt.-Cdr. Timothy William Clowes, RN (ret.) of Highgrounds, Ashbourne, Derbys.——Jane Katharine, *b.* 1942.

Sister living—Enid, *b.* 1900: *m.* 1928, Count Cosmo Diodono de Bosdari, and has issue living *Countess* Antonia Cosima, *b.* 1930: *m.* 1954, Capt. David George Armytage, RN, of Meadow Wood, Penshurst, Kent [*see* Armytage, Bt.],—*Countess* Virginia Leonie (Nettlesworth Farm, Vines Cross, Old Heathfield, Sussex), *b.* 1933. *Residence*, 32, Sussex Sq., Brighton.

Collateral Branches living.

Granddaughter of the late Col. John Reid WALKER, TD (infra):—
Issue of the late Capt. Codrington Gwynne Reid Walker, *b.* 1895, *d.* 1963: *m.* 1921, Gwendoline Phyllis, who *d.* 1974, da. of the late James Munro Walker (infra):—
Jean, *b.* 1922; WRNS 1942-45: *m.* 1949, Nicholas Knoop, BSc(Eng), FICE, of Villes ès Normans, Trinity, Jersey, and has issue living, Alexander Jonathan, *b.* 1951,—Sandra, *b.* 1950: *m.* 1973, Jean-Paul Vonrospach, of Le Meridien, Terasse des Vosges, Laxon, 54520, France.

Granddaughter of Capt. Codrington Gwynne Reid WALKER (ante):—
Issue of the late Giles Reid Walker, *b.* 1925, *d.* 1951 : *m.* 1949, Catherine Elaine (who *m.* 2ndly, 1955, Patrick Campbell Hall, of Champ de Brent, 1861, Auliens, Vaud, Switzerland), da. of the late Maj. Charles Edward Hickman [*see* Hickman, Bt., colls.]:—
Gilean Phyllis (*posthumous*), *b.* 1951.

Issue (by 1st marriage) of the late James Monro WALKER, 6th son of 1st baronet, *b.* 1866, *d.* 1920: *m.* 1st, 1893 (marriage dissolved 1900), Emily Eileen, who *d.* 1946, only da. of Henry Hodgson Bardswell, of Larkfield, Southport; 2ndly, 1902, Gladys, who *d.* 1915, da. of Humphrey Brooke Firman, formerly of Gateforth, Yorkshire; 3rdly, 1917, Eleanor Hilda Jane, who *d.* 194–, youngest da. of the late Frederick Nicholas Cunningham, of Southsea:—
Doris Eileen, *b.* 1894: *m.* 1st, 1914, Lieut.-Col. William Lewis Clark Kirby, D.S.O., O.B.E., late 12th Lancers, who obtained a divorce 1932; 2ndly, 1933, Herbert Geoffrey Burton, who *d.* 1968. *Residence*, Arch Stone, Askham Lane, Acomb, York.

The 1st baronet, Sir Andrew Barclay Walker (son of Peter Walker, of Auchinflower, near Ballantrae, co. Ayr, and Warrington, co. Lancaster), was Mayor of Liverpool 1873-4, and 1876-7 and High Sheriff of Lancashire 1886, and made many munificent gifts to the City of Liverpool. The 2nd baronet, Lt.-Col. Sir Peter Carlaw Walker, T.D.: m. 1899, Edith Blanche, sister and co-heir of Haughton Ealdred Okeover, M.V.O., of Okeover, Staffs., descended from Orme de Okeover, living 1138.

O'LOGHLEN, Creation (U.K.) 1838, of Drumconora, Ennis.
[Name pronounced "O'lochlen."]

The anchor of safety.

Sir COLMAN MICHAEL O'LOGHLEN, *LL.B.* 6th *Baronet*, son of the late Henry Ross O'Loghlen, 6th son of 3rd baronet; *b.* April 6th, 1916; *s.* his uncle, *Sir* CHARLES HUGH ROSS, 1951; ed. at Xavier Coll., Melbourne, and at Melbourne Univ.; is a Stipendiary Magistrate, Lae, Territory of New Guinea, and late Capt. Australian Imperial Force; was Acting Judge of Supreme Court of Territory of Papua and New Guinea May to Aug. 1957: *m.* 1939, Margaret, da. of Francis O'Halloran, of Melbourne, Australia, and has issue.

Arms—Gules, a man in armour in the act of shooting an arrow from a longbow towards the sinister, all proper. Crest—On a ducal coronet or, an anchor erect entwined with a cable, all proper.
Residence—179, Doncaster Rd., Balwyn North, Melbourne, Australia.

Sons living—MICHAEL, *b.* May 21st, 1945.——Bryan, *b.* 1946.——Ross, *b.* 1948.——Hugh, *b.* 1952.
Daughters living—Margaret, *b.* 1940.——Janet, *b.* 1942.
Sisters living—Ella Allison: *m.* 1944, John Cardiff O'Connell. Flying Officer Roy. Australian Air Force, and has issue living, Ross John *b.* 1945.——Doreen Sinclair.

Aunts living (daughters of 3rd baronet)—Ella Maude: *m.* 1922, George Herbert Williams, who *d.* 1957, son of the late Hon. Sir Hartley Williams.——Frances Mary; a nun.——Clare Mary. *Residence*, 37, Walsh Street, South Yarra, Melbourne, Aust.

Mother living—Doris Irene, da. of the late Percival Horne, R.A.: *m.* 1912, Henry Ross O'Loghlen (ante), who *d.* 1944. *Resides* in Melbourne, Australia.

Collateral Branches living.
Issue of the late Bryan James O'Loghlen, 4th son of 3rd baronet, *b.* 1875, *d.* 1920: *m.* 1909, Violet Elizabeth Amelia, who *d.* 1951, da. of the late Daniel Grant, of Bendigo, Australia:—
Elizabeth: *m.* 1944, Fl.-Lt. Ian Cutler, RAAF, of 50, Madeline St., Burwood, Melbourne, Aust., and has issue living, Elizabeth Ann, *b.* 1945,—Felicity Margaret, *b.* 1948.

Granddaughter of the late Henry Ross O'Loghlen, 6th son of 3rd baronet:—
Issue of the late Ross Bryan O'Loghlen, Flying Officer Roy. Australian Air Force, *b.* 1914, presumed *d.* (as a prisoner in Japanese hands) 1944: *m.* 1941, Phyllis, da. of George Nason, of Horsham, Victoria, Australia:—
Susan Anne, *b.* 1943.

The 1st baronet, the Right Hon. Sir Michael, a distinguished lawyer, was M.P. for Dungarvan (*L*) 1835-6, a Baron of the Exchequer in Ireland 1836-7, and Master of the Rolls there 1837-42. He was the first Roman Catholic that, since the Revolution of 1688, was raised to a judicial office either in England or Ireland. The 2nd baronet was a Privy Councillor, and M.P. for co. Clare (*L*) 1863-77. The 3rd baronet was Attorney-Gen. of Victoria (Australia) 1878-81, Premier thereof 1881-3, and again Attorney-Gen. 1893-4, and sat as M.P. for co. Clare (*HR*) 1877-9. The 4th baronet was H.M.'s Lieut. for co. Clare.

ONSLOW, Creation (G.B.) 1797, of Althain, Lancashire.

Forward with caution.

Sir JOHN ROGER WILMOT ONSLOW, 8th *Baronet; b.* July 21st, 1932; *s.* his father, *Sir* RICHARD WILMOT, T.D., 1963; ed. at Cheltenham: *m.* 1955, Catherine Zoia, da. of Henry Atherton Greenway, of The Manor, Compton Abdale, nr. Cheltenham, and has issue.

ᴀrms—Argent, a fesse gules between six Cornish choughs proper. Crest—An eagle sable preying upon a partridge or. Second Motto—"Semper fidelis" (*Always faithful*).

Address—c/o Barclays Bank, Fowey, Cornwall.

Club—Nautico (Majorca).

Son living—RICHARD PAUL ATHERTON, *b.* Sept. 16th, 1958.

Daughter living—Joanna Elizabeth, *b.* 1956.

Sisters living—Tessa Elizabeth, *b.* 1930: *m.* 1st, 1953 (*m.* diss. 1964), John Leonard Hargrave; 2ndly, 1969, John Vernon Mossman, and has issue living (by 1st m.), Belinda Anne Constance, *b.* 1955,—Jane, *b.* 1956.——Jill Angela, *b.* 1941: *m.* 1962, Patrick E. Lavin, of Casilla 14220, Santiago 15, Chile, and has issue living, Sean Paul, *b.* 1967,—Christopher Patrick, *b.* 1970,—Cecily Ann, *b.* 1965.—— Sally Constance, *b.* 1946.

Uncle living (son of 6th baronet)—John Vernon, *b.* 1919; ed. at Marlborough; 1939-45 War with Australian Imperial Force: *m.* 1946, Anne Broun, da. of Gavin Hutchison, and has issue living, Charlotte Anne, *b.* 1947,—Victoria Joy, *b.* 1950. *Residence,*

Aunt living (daughter of 6th baronet)—Ursula Joan, *b.* 1916: *m.* 1948, John Archibald Harris, and has issue living, Robert James Onslow, *b.* 1952,—Geoffrey Archibald Onslow, *b.* 1954,— Richard Charles Onslow, *b.* 1958. *Residence,* 20, Ridgeway Rd., Salisbury, Wilts.

Widow living of 7th Baronet—MARY (*Mary, Lady Onslow*) (7, Malone Rd., Belfast, 9), da. of the late H. R. Russell, JP, of Belfast: *m.* 1961, as his 2nd wife, Sir Richard Wilmot Onslow, TD, 7th Bt., who *d.* 1963.

Collateral Branches living.

Grandchildren of the late Rev. Matthew Richard Septimus Onslow (infra):—
Issue of the late Capt. Richard Francis John Onslow, M.V.O., D.S.C., R.N., *b.* 1896, *d.* (killed in action during European War) 1942: *m.* 1st, 1920, Sylvia Rachel, who *d.* 1933, da. of the Rev. Alfred Edward Green-Price, V. of Norton, Radnorshire [Green-Price, Bt.]; 2ndly, 1939, Betty (who *m.* 2ndly, 1951, Major Arthur Christopher John Congreve, from whom she obtained a divorce 1956), da. of the late Brig.-Gen. Reynold Alexander Gillam, C.M.G., D.S.O.:—
(By 1st marriage) Richard Thomas (of West End House, Hambledon, Hants.), *b.* 1922; is Capt. R.M.; 1940-45 War (despatches): *m.* 1947, Gillian Doriel, el. da. of Edward Clemson, of Gaston House, East Bergholt, Suffolk, and has issue, Sylvia Jane, *b.* 1951,—Geraldine Victoria, *b.* 1954.——Anthea Mary, *b.* 1925; formerly in W.R.N.S.: *m.* 1947, Maj. Edward Courtenay Phillips, MC, 6th Rifles, of Chase House, Monnington-on-Wye, Herefordshire, and has issue living, Sarah Angela Josephine, *b.* 1948: *m.* 1968, Robert Antony Corbett, of Shobdon, Hereford,—Harriet Anne Jennifer, *b.* 1953.

Issue of the late Herbert Frank Onslow, *b.* 1899, *d.* 1970: *m.* 1934, the Hon. Lena Barbara Joan Ogilvie-Grant (17, Damask Close, Weston, Hitchin, Herts.), da. of the 4th Baron Strathspey:—
Roger Cranley Seafield (7, Links View Baunton Lane, Cirencester, Glos.), *b.* 1934; ed. at Christ's Hosp.: *m.* 1959, Eileen Margaret, da. of the late J. A. J. Barnard, of The Borough, Crondall, Hants., and has issue living, Susan Helen, *b.* 1965,—Clare Louise, *b.* 1967.

Issue (by 2nd marriage) of the late Rev. Matthew Richard Septimus Onslow, 4th son of 4th baronet, *b.* 1856, *d.* 1932: *m.* 1st, 1883, Mary, who *d.* 1884, da. of the late Rev. Edward Jonathan Green, V. of Leintwardine; 2ndly, 1894, Fanny Harriett, who *d.* 1940, da. of the late Rev. Thomas Green, V. of Aymestrey, Herefordshire:—
Mary Camperdown (of Folke House, Sherborne, Dorset), *b.* 1901.

Issue of the late Arthur Herbert Onslow, 5th son of 4th baronet, *b.* 1862, *d.* 1932: *m.* 1892, Alice Constance Edith, who *d.* 1897, da. of Marmaduke Constable:—
Vera Doris Onslow (of 1, Haines Court, Queens Rd., Weybridge, Surrey), *b.* 1893.——Ethel Muriel Onslow (2, Lincoln Court, Old Av., Weybridge, Surrey), *b.* 1894: *m.* 1922, Samuel Wilson Lindrea, who *d.* 1966.

Granddaughter of the late Brig.-Gen. Cranley Charlton Onslow, CB, CMG, CBE, DSO (infra):—
Issue of the late Lt.-Cdr. Denzil Richard Cranley Onslow, RNR, *b.* 1909, *d.* 1973: *m.* 1940, Bernadine (24, Southwood Court, Bigwood Rd., NW11 6SR), da. of David Blackburn:—
Judith Marylin, *b.* 1946: *m.* 1970, George Sheffield Kinnear, of Bent Lane Farm, Crowton, Cheshire.

Granddaughters of the late Hamilton Cranley Onslow, el. son of the late Thoma Onslow, 3rd son of 2nd baronet:—
Issue of the late Brig.-Gen. Cranley Charlton Onslow, C.B., C.M.G., C.B.E., D.S.O., *b.* 1869, *d.* 1940: *m.* 1904, Sydney Alice Hastings, who *d.* 1962, da. of the late Surg.-Gen. Sir Benjamin Franklin, K.C.I.E.:—
Doreen May (Flat 7, Rock Hotel, Yelverton, Devon), *b.* 1907: *m.* 1938, Maj. John R. H. Ellery, who *d.* 1970.——Margaret Vivien, *b.* 1918: *m.* 1943, Johnston McDowell, of Uplands, Aldenham Av., Radlett, Herts., and has issue living, Hugh Geoffrey, *b.* 1947,—Brian Johnstone, *b.* 1954,— Jane Maureen, *b.* 1944,—Fiona Margaret, *b.* 1961.——Jocelyn Anne Sydney, *b.* 1922: *m.* 1953, Cdr. Leonard Charles Sutton Sheppard, OBE, RN (ret.), of Cary Hill House, Castle Cary, Somerset.

Granddaughter of the late Col. Gerald Charles Penrice Onslow, 2nd son of the late Lt.-Col. Arthur Walton Onslow (infra):—
Issue of the late Lieut.-Com. Arthur Gerald Onslow, D.S.C., R.N., *b.* 1885, *d.* (killed in action at battle of Jutland) 1916: *m.* 1912, Elsie Hinde (*Lady Pridham Wippell*) [(of 14, Church Close, Kensington, W.8; she *m.* 2ndly, 1918, Adm. Sir Henry Daniel Pridham-Wippell, K.C.B., C.V.O., who *d.* 1952)], da. of the late J. Hinde-Crouch, of Palmeira Avenue, Hove, Sussex :—

Diana Rosemary, *b.* 1915: *m.* 1938, Patrick Longstaff, formerly Capt. 5th Roy. Inniskilling Dragoon Guards, and has issue living, Nigel Anthony Onslow, *b.* 1942: *m.* 1966, Jean Anne McCormick, and has issue living, Julia Rosemary *b.* 1968. *Residence,* Thatchings, Fairwarp, Sussex.

Granddaughter of the late Lt.-Col. Arthur Walton Onslow, 4th son of 2nd baronet :—

Issue of the late Lieut.-Col. Richard Cranley Onslow, Indian Army, *b.* 1857, *d.* 1934: *m.* 1883, Edith Margaretta, who *d.* 1934, da. of Francis Beer :—

Alice Mary (Fairfield Hotel, Aliwal Rd., Wynberg, Cape Town, S. Africa): *m.* 1914, Capt. Francis Richard Savage, formerly Cheshire Regt., who *d.* 1960, and has issue living, Gerald Onslow, *b.* 1916; Maj., late Queen's Roy. Regt.

This family is descended from Lieut.-Gen. Richard Onslow, nephew of the 1st Baron Onslow, and uncle of the 1st Earl of Onslow, and is in special remainder to the Barony of Onslow [*see* E. Onslow, colls.]. The 1st baronet, Admiral Sir Richard Onslow, G.C.B., and General of Marines, was second in command at Camperdown, and was created a baronet for distinguished services at that battle.

OPPENHEIMER, Creation (U.K.) 1921, of Stoke Poges, co. Bucks.

In adversity undismayed.

Sir MICHAEL BERNARD GRENVILLE OPPENHEIMER, 3rd *Baronet*; *b.* May 27th, 1924; *s.* his father, *Sir* MICHAEL, 1933; ed. at Charterhouse, and at Ch. Ch., Oxford (M.A. 1952, B.Litt. 1955); late Lieut. S. African Artillery: *m.* 1947, Laetitia Helen, *B. Phil., M.A.,* da. of Lieut.-Col. Sir Hugh Vere Huntley Duff Munro-Lucas-Tooth, 1st Bt. (*cr.* 1920), and has issue.

Arms—Azure, two swords in saltire proper, pommeled and hilted or, between two lions passant of the last. Crest— A demi-koodoo proper, resting the sinister hoof on a rose gules, barbed and seeded proper.

Residence—L'Aiguillon, Rue des Cotils, Grouville, Jersey. *Clubs*—Kimberley (S. Africa), Victoria (Jersey).

Daughters living—Henrietta Laetitia Grenville, *b.* 1954.——Matilda Magdalen Grenville, *b.* 1956.——Xanthe Jennifer Grenville, *b.* 1958.

Aunts living (daughters of 1st baronet)—Elsie Rose: *m.* 1st, 1922 (marriage dissolved 1950), Leonard Lewis Rossiter, 2ndly, 1952, Col. Herbert Louis Mostyn- Owen, late Indian Cav, who *d.* 1972, and has issue living, (by 1st m.) Geoffrey William (Mobile House, 76, Freelands Rd., Bromley, Kent), *b.* 1926; BA Camb.,—Anthony Edward (of Dalesford House, Litton, Bath) (twin), *b.* 1926; Member Roy. W. of England Acad., and a Member of Soc. of Industrial Artists; Lecturer Arts Council (Writers in Schs.) since 1974: *m.* 1957, Anneka Oving, SRN, of Holland, and has issue living, Nicholas Jeremy *b.* 1961, Annalisa *b.* 1959,—Gillian Elizabeth (*Hon. Mrs. Robin H. Warrender*) *b.* 1931: *m.* 1951, the Hon. Robin Hugh Warrender, of 46, Brompton Sq., SW3 [*see* B. Bruntisfield]. *Residence,* Widcombe Manor, Church St., Bath.——Madeleine Hilda (*Baroness Devlin*), *b.* 1909; is a JP for Wilts: *m.* 1932, Baron Devlin, a Lord of Appeal in Ordinary (Life Baron). *Residence,* West Wick House, Pewsey, Wilts.

Sir Bernard Oppenheimer, 1st Bt. (son of Edward Oppenheimer), was Chm. of S. African Diamond Corporation, Ltd., and the New Vaal River Diamond and Exploration Co. In 1917 he inaugurated diamond-cutting factories for Discharged and Disabled Soldiers.

CAMPBELL-ORDE, Creation (G.B.) 1790, of Morpeth, Northumberland.

Mild but brave.

Sir JOHN ALEXANDER CAMPBELL-ORDE, 6th *Baronet*; *b.* May 11th, 1943; *s.* his father, *Maj. Sir* SIMON ARTHUR, *TD,* 1969; ed. at Gordonstoun: *m.* 1973, Lacy Ralls, only da. of Grady Gallant, of Nashville, Tennessee, USA, and has issue.

Arms—1st and 4th sable, three salmon hauriant per pale argent and or, *Orde;* 2nd and 3rd, gyronny of eight or and sable within a bordure componée ermine and vert, in the centre a crescent of the last for difference, *Campbell.* **Crests**—1st, an elk's head erased or, gorged with a collar invected sable ; 2nd, a dexter hand proper, holding a spur or, strap also proper.

Residence—25 Granard Rd, SW12.

Daughter living—Alexandra Louise, *b.* 1974.
Brother living—PETER HUMPHREY, *b.* June 18th, 1946 : ed. at Gordonstoun: *m.* 1976, Mrs. Perdita Bennett, da. of Watt.
Sister living—Caroline Jane, *b.* 1940; ed. at N. Foreland Lodge, and the Sorbonne: *m.* 1967, Christopher John Davies, MA, of Westgate House, Dedham, Colchester, Essex, and has issue living, John Humphrey Stewart, *b.* 1969,—Simon William Gardner, *b.* 1970,—Caroline Celia Hyde, *b.* 1973.
Aunts living (daughters of 4th baronet)—Alice Maie (Glenfinnan House, Glenfinnan, Inverness-shire), *b.* 1897: *m.* 1917, the Rev. James Humphrey Copner Macfarlane-Barrow, formerly V. of Inverary, Argyllshire, who *d.* 1943, and has issue living, Seumas Donnchadh (87, 2nd Avenue, Mt. Lawley, Perth, W. Aust.), *b.* 1922: *m.* 1956, Beatrice Harriet, da. of Capt. Christopher St. Barbe Shields, and has issue living, James Peter Raymund *b.* 1957, Simon Ruairidh *b.* 1958, Christopher Donnchadh Diarmad *b.* 1959, Ian Andrew *b.* 1963, Rosamund Lucy Alice *b.* 1961, Julia *b.* 1967,—Padruig Francis (Quaintways, Killiney Hill Rd., Killiney, co. Dublin) *b.* 1929: *m.* 1967, Ann Maria Coen, of co. Galway, and has issue living, Sine Mary *b.* 1968, Ailse Brighde *b.* 1970, Dearbhail Anna *b.* 1971,—Ian Tearlach (Glenfinnan House, Glenfinnan, Inverness-shire), *b.* 1931: *m.* 1966, Isobel Nicholas Alexander, of Edinburgh, and has issue living, Duncan James *b.* 1969, Ian Robert *b.* 1970, Jane Isabella *b.* 1967,—Calum Seumas (Claybokie, Mar Lodge Estate, Braemar, Aberdeenshire), *b.* 1932: *m.* 1962, Mary Ann. da. of Maj. Gabriel Thomas Grisewood, of Invereinie, Farr, Inverness, and has issue living, Magnus *b.* 1968, Ruth Magdalene *b.* 1963,—Maie Bridget (Bohuntine, Roy Bridge, Inverness-shire *b.* 1926: *m.* 1962, Donald Joseph MacDonald, who *d.* 1967, and has issue living, Donald Hamish *b.* 1962, Alastair Ninian *b.* 1964, Eilidh Mairi *b.* 1965, Catherine Margaret *b.* 1966—Muriel Frances (5, Victoria Rd., Malvern), *b.* 1903.
Widow living of 5th Baronet—ELEANOR HYDE (*Eleanor, Lady Campbell-Orde*) (31, The Little Boltons, SW10), da. of the late Col. Humphrey Watts, OBE, TD, of Haslington Hall, Ches.: *n.* 1938, Maj. Sir Simon Arthur Campbell-Orde, TD, 5th Bt., who *d.* 1969.

Collateral Branches living.

Issue of the late Colin Ridley Campbell-Orde, 2nd son of 3rd baronet, *b.* 1867, *d.* 1932: *m.* 1896, Winifred Harriet, who *d.* 1967, da. of Capt. John C. Stewart, formerly of Fasnachloich:—
Alan Colin, *C.B.E., A.F.C., b.* 1898; ed. at Sherborne; sometime Flight Sub-Lieut. R.N., and Flying Officer R.A.F.; European Wa 1916-18 in Belgium (wounded, despatches, A.F.C.); one of original Commercial Pilots on London-Paris route, Aircraft Transport & Travel, Ltd. 1919-20, Instructor and Adviser to Chinese Govt., Peking 1921-23, Instructor and latterly Ch. Test Pilot, Sir W. G. Armstrong Whitworth Aircraft Ltd., Coventry 1924-36, Operational Manager, British Airways, Ltd. 1936-39, Operations Manager, Imperial Airways, Ltd. 1939-40, Operations Director, B.O.A.C. 1940-43, B.O.A.C. (Director Transport Command, R.A.F.) 1943-44, Assist. to Chm. 1944-46, Technical Development Director 1946-49, Dep. Operations Director 1949-51, and Operations Development Director 1951-56, and Development Director 1956-57, since when an Aviation Consultant; is a FRAeS; CBE (Civil) 1943: *m.* 1951, Beatrice Eliott Drake (McClure), da. of the late Rev. H. M. Eliott Drake Briscoe, of Burnham Thorpe, King's Lynn, Norfolk. *Residence,* Smugglers Mead, Stepleton, Blandford, Dorset. *Club,* Boodle's.——Ian Ridley (Orchard Cottage, Derry's Wood, Wonersh, Surrey; RAF and Lansdowne Club), *b.* 1907; formerly Wing-Cdr. AAF; was Dir. of Tactical Development, USAF 1942-43; 1939-45 War (despatches): *m.* 1939, Myrtle (WELSH), only da. of the late Robert Van Gruisen Adamson, of Liverpool, and Boston, USA.——Harry Eustace, *b.* 1914; sometime Lt. R. Scots Fusiliers (TA); Wing-Cdr. (ret.) RAF; Regional Sec. for Yorks. for Arthritis and Rheumatism Council for Research; 1939-45 War in Europe and Middle East: *m.* 1940, Mary Beatrice, yr. da. of the late P. Bruce Elliott, of Ripon, Yorks. *Residence,* Redlands, 12, Langcliffe Av., Harrogate, Yorks. *Club,* RAF.

Granddaughter of the late Colin Ridley Campbell-Orde (ante):—
Issue of the late Bernard Arthur Campbell-Orde, *b.* 1904, *d.* 1974: *m.* 1st, 1939 (m. diss. 1955), Pamela, da. of the late Brig.-Gen. John Cecil Wray, CB, CMG, CVO, TD, and formerly wife of Col. Robert Hugh Arthur Lucas; 2ndly, 1955, Nancy Mabyn Bradley (Old Farm, Trebetherick, Wadebridge, Cornwall), da. of Maj. Thomas Langdon Trethewy, DCLI:—
Jennifer Mary, *b.* 1940: *m.* 1959, Robin Alfred Clive Salmon, Merchant Navy, of 77A, King Henry's Rd., Primrose Hill, NW3, and has issue living, Timothy John, *b.* 1960,—Robert Bernard, *b.* 1961,—Belinda Jane, *b.* 1964.

Issue of the late Henry Campbell Campbell-Orde, youngest son of 3rd baronet, *b.* 1877, *d.* 1954 : *m.* 1st, 1901, Marie Elizabeth, who *d.* 1913, da. of John S. Barr, of Newcastle-on-Tyne; 2ndly, 1927, Ruth (Flat 4, 143, Hewlett Rd., Cheltenham, Glos.), da. of the late Robert Thomas, of Penarth, S. Wales:—
(By 1st m.) Beatrice Constance (Colon 233, La Cumbre, Sierras de Cordoba, Argentina), *b.* 1903: *m.* 1st, 1929, Rodney Doherty, who *d.* 1953; 2ndly, 1956, Edward Errol Maitland-Heriot, DSC, who *d.* 1964 [E. Lauderdale, colls.] and has issue living, (by 1st m.) Sheila Beatrice, *b.* 1931: *m.* 1957, Kenneth Rugeroni, of Buenos Aires, and has issue living, Michael *b.* 1960, Sandra *b.* 1958, Christine *b.* 1961.——(By 2nd m.) Alexander Powlett (Willow Cottage, Newbridge Green, Upton-on-Severn, Worcs.), *b.* 1928; Petty Officer (Radar Electrical Artificer) RN (ret.).——Colin Robert (Cruachan, 4, Wessex Drive, Bradford Abbas, Sherborne), *b.* 1935; CEng, MIMechE, AFRAeS; Development Eng. (Pressurisation) Norrialair-Garrett, Ltd., Yeovil: *m.* 1959, Audrey Isobel, da. of Raymond S. Griffiths, of Brentford, Middx., and has issue living,

Andrew Colin, b. 1969,—Tamzin Ruth, b. 1960,—Sarah Elizabeth, b. 1965.——Morwenna, b. 1929; SRN: m. 1951, George Ernest Turner, of Westwinds, Parkwall Rd., Llanedeyrn, Cardiff, and has issue living, Ian George, b. 1965,—Tracey Christine, b. 1958,—Alison Meryl, b. 1961.

The 1st baronet, Adm. Sir John Orde, Governor of Dominica 1783-93, was younger brother of the 1st Baron Bolton. The 3rd baronet assumed by Roy. licence 1880 the additional surname of Campbell, his mother having been Eliza, el. da. and co-heir of Peter Campbell of Kilmory, Argyll, descended from Campbell of Auchinbreck [see Campbell Bt., cr. 1668].

Orr Ewing, see Ewing.

Orr-Lewis, see Lewis.

OSBORN, Creation (E.) 1662, of Chicksands, Bedfordshire.

Sir DANVERS LIONEL ROUSE OSBORN, 8th *Baronet; b.* Jan. 31st, 1916; *s.* his father, *Sir* ALGERNON KERR BUTLER 1948; ed. at Eton, and at Camb. Univ.: *m.* 1943, Constance Violette, JP (a Serving Sister of Order of St. John), da. of the late Major Leonard F. Rooke, King's Own Scottish Borderers, of Hooton House, Tilford, Farnham, Surrey, and has issue.

Arms—Argent, a bend between two lions rampant sable. Crest—A lion's head argent ducally crowned or.

Residence—The Dower House, Moor Park, Farnham, Surrey. Club—St. James'.

Son living—RICHARD HENRY DANVERS, b. Aug. 12th, 1958.
Daughter living—Sarah, b. 1950.

Quantum in rebus inane.
How much vanity there is in human affairs.

Sister living—Dorothy, b. 1905: m. 1933, Gordon Chapman, who d. 1969.
Residence, Barney Cottage, Winkfield, Berks. Club, Carlton.

Collateral Branches living.

Grandchildren of the late Lieut.-Col. Danvers Henry Osborn, 5th son of 5th baronet:—
Issue of the late Arthur Osborn, b. 1863, d. 1934 : m. 1905, Elizabeth Mary, widow of Arthur Lane :—
Sybil Gwendoline, b. 1906: m. 1935, Col. Henry Ironside Davidson, MBE, ERD, RE and has issue living, Ainslie Danvers, b. 1941: m. 1969, David Philip Johnston, of 22, Phoenix Lodge Mansions, Brook Green, W6 7BG. Residence, Winston House, 16, High Park Rd., Ryde, I. of Wight, PO33 1BP.

Issue of the late Danvers Osborn, b. 1864, d. 1929 : m. 1906, Inez, who d. 1953, second da. of Henry Smith, of Victoria, British Columbia :—
William Danvers, b. 1909 : assumed the names of William Danvers in lieu of his Christian names of George Schomberg by deed poll (registered in Supreme Court of British Columbia) 1936 : m. 1939, Jean Burns, da. of R. B. Hutchinson, of Vancouver, British Columbia, and has issue living, Cheryl Elizabeth, b. 1945. Residence, 2676, Seaview Road, Victoria, British Columbia.
——Dorothy Annette, b. 1907: m. 1941, Gordon MacEachern, who d. 1973, and has issue living, John Hugh, b. 1944. Residence, 1056, Richmond Av., BC.

The 1st baronet, Sir John Osborne, was son of Sir Peter Osborne, Governor of Guernsey, grandson of Peter Osborne, who purchased Chicksands Priory in 1576, and was Treasurer's Remembrancer to Henry VIII, Keeper of the Privy Purse to Edward VI and Commr. of Ecclesiastical Affairs to Queen Elizabeth I. He was Treasurer's Remembrancer 1674-98 and received his Baronetcy in recognition of all the family had suffered in the cause of Charles I. Sir Danvers, 3rd baronet, was son of John Osborne (el. son of 2nd baronet), who altered the spelling of his name to Osborn to avoid confusion with the family of the Duke of Leeds. He was Governor of New York before the War of Independence. Sir George, 4th baronet, was a Gen. in the Army and Groom of the Bedchamber to George III. Sir John, 5th Bt. was for many years an M.P., and was a Lord Commr. of the Admiralty.
Sir Peter Osborne's da. Dorothy m. Sir William Temple, to whom she wrote the famous love letters.

OSBORNE, Creation (I.) 1629, of Ballintaylor, co. Tipperary.

Sir PETER GEORGE OSBORNE, 17th *Baronet; b.* June 29th, 1943 ; *s.* his father, *Lieut.-Col. Sir* GEORGE FRANCIS, MC, 1960; ed. at Wellington and Ch. Ch., Oxford: *m.* 1968, Felicity, da. of Grantley Loxton-Peacock, of 13, Eaton Pl., SW1, and has issue.

Arms—Gules, on a fesse cotised or two fountains, over all a bend argent. Crest—A sea-lion holding a trident.
Residence—15, Kildare Gdns., W2.

Sons living—GIDEON OLIVER, b. May 23rd, 1971.——Benedict George, b. 1973.
Brother living—James Francis (Howletts, Bekesbourne, nr. Canterbury, Kent), b. 1946: m. 1971, Felicity Jane, only da. of Peter Boutwood, of Claron Way, W. Wittering, Sussex.
Sisters living—Jennifer Jane, b. 1939.——Caroline Mary, b. 1941.
Aunts living (daughters of 15th baronet)—Dorothy Eileen, b. 1891.——
Kathleen Muriel, b. 1893: m. 1922, Jack Chambers, of 19155, Lake Av., Wayzata 55391, Minn., USA, and has issue living, John Osborne (West Point Rd., Box 216, Excelsior, Minn., USA), b. 1923; Lt. US Naval Air Ser.; 1939-45 War (American DFC, medal): m. 1st, 1948 (m. diss.—19), Carolyn Low, da. of R. C. Finley, of Deephaven Park, Wayzata, Minn., USA; 2ndly, 1955, Barbara Welbrook, and has issue living (by 1st m.) Mark Osborne b. 1949, (by 2nd m.) Susan Kathleen b. 1960, Jacquelne Dorothy b. 1962, Victoria Barbara b. 1968,—Donna Kathleen, b. 1930: m. 1950, George Pilkington, of 20275, Cottage Wood Rd., Excelsior, Minn. USA, and has issue living, Michael Joseph b. 1957, Sandra Kay b. 1959.

Pax in bello.
Peace in war.

Widow living of 16th Baronet—MARY GRACE (*Lady Osborne*), da. of the late C. S. Horn, of Goring-by-the-Sea, Sussex : m. 1938, Lieut.-Col. Sir George Francis Osborne, M.C., 16th baronet, who d. 1960. Residence, 4, Herbert Mansions, 35, Sloane St., S.W.1.

Collateral Branch living.

Issue of the late Edward Osborne, only brother of 15th baronet.' . 1861, *d.*
1939: *m.* 1895, Phyllis Eliza, who *d.* 1966, da. of the late George Whitley,
of Fairholme, Weybridge:—
Stanley Patrick (Kinsale, Castle Av., Hythe), *b.* 1904; ed. at Felsted, and at Univ. Coll., N. Wales
(BSc); AFRAeS: *m.* 1931, Muriel Harvey, *BA*, da. of Llewellyn Harvey Matthews, of Shrewsbury, and has issue living, Anthony Trevor (6, Manse Cres., Stirling), *b.* 1934: ed. at Felsted, and
at Emmanuel Coll., Camb. (MA); C.Eng., MICE: *m.* 1958, Beryl Anne Shadbolt, of Cambridge,
and has issue living, Marcus Duncan Fitzwilliam *b.* 1967, Catherine Frances *b.* 1961, Nicola Clare
b. 1963,—Edward Peter (Springfields, Bridestowe, Okehampton, Devon), *b.* 1938; ed. at Felsted,
and at Peterhouse, Camb. (BA): *m.* 1961, Marjorie, da. of William Newton, of Fleetwood, Lancs.,
and has issue living, John Philip *b.* 1963, Judith Carol *b.* 1962, Janet Elizabeth *b.* 1954.——Sybil
Margaret, *b.* 1895: *m.* 1927, Hilary Cope Barry, of Nut Trees Cottage, Wangford Rd., Reydon,
Southwold, Suffolk, and has issue living, Michael Ransome *b.* 1931: *m.* 1964, Evelyn Winifred
Oxford, of Devon,—Joan Mavis Oxborne Barry, *b.* 1934: *m.* 1957, Martyn Oliver Rudkin, of
Coram Farm House, Coram St., nr. Hadleigh, W. Suffolk, and has issue living, Catherine Ann
b. 1960, Deborah Louise *b.* 1962, Sally Maria Joan *b.* 1965.——Nora Gladys (Fieldend, 22, Harps-
wood Lane, Hythe, Kent), *b.* 1906.

The 2nd and 7th baronets each represented the co. of Waterford in Parliament. The 8th baronet
was a Privy Councillor in Ireland, and sat as MP for Carysfort. The 9th baronet was MP for Carysfort and Sheriff of Waterford 1795. The 11th baronet was M.P. for Carysfort and subsequently for
Enniskillen. Sir George Francis Osborne, M.C., 16th baronet was Lieut.-Col. Roy. Sussex Regt.

Osborne-Gibbes, see Gibbes.

OUTRAM, Creation (U.K.) 1858.
[Name pronounced "Ootram."]

I know not how to change my faith.

Sir ALAN JAMES OUTRAM, 5th *Baronet,*
son of the late James Ian Outram, son of the late
Rev. Arthur Outram, 3rd son of 2nd baronet ; *b.*
May 15th, 1937 ; *s.* his great-uncle, *Sir* FRANCIS
DAVIDSON, *O.B.E.*, 1945 ; ed. at Marlborough,
and St. Edmund Hall, Oxford (MA); Capt.
R.E. (Regular Army Reserve); is an Assist.
Master at Harrow.

Arms—Or, on a chevron embattled, between three crosses
flory gules, five escallops of the first. **Crest**—Out of an eastern
crown a demi-lion or, gorged with a wreath of laurel proper.
holding between the paws a cross-flory gules. **Supporters**—
On either side a royal Bengal tiger guardant proper, gorged
with a wreath of laurel vert and on the head an eastern
crown or.
Residence—5, Sandhurst Lodge, Crowthorne, Berks.

Sister living—Margaret Evelyn, *b.* 1935: *m.* 1956,
Richard Coverley Champion, and has issue living, Anthony Richard Coverley, *b.* 1964,—Jean
Margaret, *b.* 1958,—Jennifer Fleur, *b.* 1960,—Joanna Esmé, *b.* 1963. *Residence*, 5, Edgarley
Mews, Glastonbury, Somerset.
Daughter living of 4th baronet—Marjorie Isabella, *MB, ChB, DPH* (9, Summer Close, Tenterden,
Kent), *b.* 1893; ed. at Aberdeen Univ. (MB and ChB 1923); late Med. Officer of Health, Potters
Bar, Herts.
Mother living—Evelyn Mary, da. of the late Rev. Charles Gough Littlehales: *m.* 1932, James
Ian Outram (ante), who *d.* 1937. *Residence*, 5, Sandhurst Lodge, Crowthorne, Berks.

Collateral Branches living.

Issue of the late Rev. Arthur Outram, 3rd son of 2nd baronet. *b.* 1871, *d.* 1937: *m.*
1899, Gertrude Ellen who *d.* 1962, da. of the late Henry P. Withers, of
Reading:—
Jean Marion, *b.* 1906. *Residence*, 64, St. Saviours Rd., St. Leonards-on-Sea, Sussex.

Grandchildren of the late Rev. William Outram (infra):—
Issue of the late Rev. Francis Henry Outram, *b.* 1907, *d.* 1972: *m.* 1946, Eileen Grace
(Sandal Cottage, W. Ashling, Chichester, Sussex), da. of the late Rev. L. A. McClintock
Newbery:—
JOHN DOUGLAS (Haining Burn, Lavy's Lane, Lee Ground, Titchfield, Hants.), *b.* June 24th, 1947;
ed. at Marlborough, Liverpool Univ. (B.Eng.), and Birmingham Univ. (MSc); Electronics Eng.
with Plessey, Co. Ltd.: *m.* 1970, Valerie Ann, da. of Geoffrey Wilson, of Whitley Bay, and has
issue living, Nicholas Francis, *b.* 1973.——Margaret Eleanor, *b.* 1949.

Issue of the late Rev. William Outram, youngest son of 2nd baronet, *b.* 1874,
d. 1958 : *m.* 1904, Haidée Maria, who *d.* 1934, da. of the late Henry Frederick
Beaumont, of Whitley Beaumont, Huddersfield:—
James Richard, *b.* 1911; ed. at Pembroke Coll., Camb. (BA 1932); formerly in Sarawak Administra-
tive Ser.; ret. 1957: *m.* 1939, Lucy Dora, yst. da. of the late J. A. Frerichs, and has issue living,
Francis William, *b.* 1946,—Richard Graham (twin), *b.* 1946,—Keith Alastair, *b.* 1947,—Nicola
Elspeth, *b.* 1940: *m.* 1962, David Alistair Kingsley Cooper, of Manor Farm House, Abbots
Lench, Evesham, and has issue living, James Alexander *b.* 1969, Jennifer Mary *b.* 1967. *Residence*,
The Cottage, Dumfries Estate, Cumnock, Ayrshire.

Benjamin Outram, of Butterley Hall, Derbyshire, was an eminent Civil Engineer, through whose
exertions "Tram" roads were popularized. His son, Sir James, the 1st baronet, an illustrious Indian
General, Administrator, and Diplomatist, was buried in Westminster Abbey. The 2nd baronet, Sir
Francis Boyd, was in B.C.S., and served during Indian Mutiny 1857-8.

OWEN, Creation (U.K.) 1813, of Orielton, Pembrokeshire.

Honesty is the best policy.

Sir HUGH BERNARD PILKINGTON OWEN, 5th *Baronet*; *b.* March 28th, 1915; *s.* his father, *Capt. Sir* JOHN ARTHUR, 1973; ed. at Chillon Coll., Switzerland.

Arms—Gules, a chevron or, between three lions rampant or.

Residence—63, Dudsbury Rd., Ferndown, Dorset.

Brother living—JOHN WILLIAM (12, Elizabeth Av., St. Brelade, Jersey), *b.* June 7th, 1917; ed. at Charterhouse; late Capt. 4th/7th Roy. Dragoon Gds.: *m.* 1963, Gwenllian Mary, Wing Officer, MBE, WRAF, el. da. of the late E. B. Phillips, of Barry, Glam.

Widow living of 4th Baronet—LUCY FLETCHER (*Lady Owen*), (63, Dudsbury Rd., Ferndown, Dorset), da. of Fred William Pilkington, of Kencott House, nr. Lechlade: *m.* 1914, Capt. Sir John Arthur Owen, 4th Bt., who *d.* 1973.

John Lord, MP for the Pembroke Burghs, and Lord-Lieut. of Pembrokeshire, assumed the name of Owen on inheriting the estates of Sir Hugh Owen, 6th baronet (creation 1641). Sir Arthur Owen, MP, 3rd baronet of the first creation, is stated to have given the deciding vote for a Bill containing provisions for ensuring the Protestant succession to the British Throne, after riding in unprecedented haste from Wales for that purpose. Sir Arthur Owen's grandda., Corbetta, was mother of the Sir John Owen, *cr.* a baronet 1813. The 2nd baronet sat as MP for Pembroke Dist. (L) 1826-38 and 1861-68: he *m.* 1st, 1825, Angelina, who *d.* 1844, sister of 1st Lord Tredegar; 2ndly, 1845, Henrietta, who *d.* 1894, da. of the Hon. Edward Rodney, RN, son of the famous Adm., 1st Lord Rodney. The baronetcy of the first creation (1641) became *ext.* at the death in 1851 of Sir William Owen-Barlow, 8th baronet. The 3rd baronet of this creation, Sir Hugh Charles, served at siege of Monte Video 1845-46, and in Kaffir War 1846-47 (medal).

CUNLIFFE-OWEN, Creation (U.K.) 1920, of Bray, co. Berks.

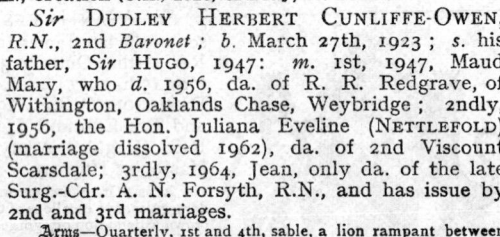

Sir DUDLEY HERBERT CUNLIFFE-OWEN, *R.N.*, 2nd *Baronet ; b.* March 27th, 1923 ; *s.* his father, *Sir* HUGO, 1947: *m.* 1st, 1947, Maud Mary, who *d.* 1956, da. of R. R. Redgrave, of Withington, Oaklands Chase, Weybridge ; 2ndly, 1956, the Hon. Juliana Eveline (NETTLEFOLD) (marriage dissolved 1962), da. of 2nd Viscount Scarsdale; 3rdly, 1964, Jean, only da. of the late Surg.-Cdr. A. N. Forsyth, R.N., and has issue by 2nd and 3rd marriages.

Arms—Quarterly, 1st and 4th, sable, a lion rampant between three crosses couped within a bordure, all or, *Owen* ; 2nd and 3rd, sable, three conies courant in pale with two flaunches argent, *Cunliffe*. **Crests**—1st, a lion rampant sable charged with three crosses couped in pale or, *Owen* ; 2nd, a greyhound sejant argent, collared sable, in front of a flag-staff proper, flowing therefrom a banner also charged with a cross gules.

Residence,—Eyreton, Quarter Bridge Rd., Douglas, I. of Man. *Club*—Royal Thames Yacht.

Honesty the best policy.

Son living—by 3rd marriage—HUGO DUDLEY, *b.* May 16th, 1966. *Daughters living*—by 2nd marriage—Juliana Diana, *b.* 1957.—— by 3rd marriage—Sophia Jean, *b.* 1965.

Sisters living—Philippa Helen, *b.* 1926: *m.* 1st, 1945 (m. diss. 1952), Denis Macduff Burke; 2ndly, 1952 (m. diss. 1963), Archie Alistair Baring; 3rdly, 1966, Peter William Thorn Warren, and has issue living, (by 1st marriage) David Macduff *b.* 1949,—Alexandra Yvette, *b.* 1946, (by 2nd marriage) Adrian Allistair, *b.* 1957,—Sarah Elizabeth, *b.* 1954. *Residence*, Kale Close, Mattingley, Hartley Wintney, Hants——Diana Elizabeth, *b.* 1928: *m.* 1st, 1947 (m. diss. 1955), William Gavin Buchanan; 2ndly, 1964, (m. diss. 1967), Cdr. Richard O'Brien, RN; 3rdly, 1967, Antony Hanbury, of Queens Lodge, Beldam Bridge Rd., Chobham, Surrey, and has issue living, (by 1st m.) Gray Hugo, *b.* 1948,—Diana Victoria, *b.* 1951.

Widow living of 1st Baronet—MAURICIA MARTHA (*Mauricia, Lady Cunliffe-Owen*), da. of the late Herbert Shaw, of San Francisco, California, U.S.A. : *m.* 1935, as his third wife, Sir Hugo Cunliffe-Owen, 1st baronet, who *d.* 1947. *Residence,*

This family descends from Joseph Owen of Crookes Moor, Shelfield, who *m.* 1746, Sarah, da. and co-heir of Samuel Skargell, by Elizabeth da. of John Cunliffe. The 1st baronet, Sir Hugo Cunliffe-Owen (son of the late Sir (Francis) Philip Cunliffe-Owen, KCB, KCMG, CIE, great-grandson of Joseph Owen), was Pres. of British-American Tobacco Co.

Page-Wood, see Wood.

PAGET, Creation (U.K.) 1871, of Harewood Place, Middlesex.

Sir JULIAN TOLVER PAGET, 4th *Baronet*, son of the late Gen. Sir Bernard Charles Tolver Paget, GCB, DSO, MC, 3rd son of the Rt. Rev. Francis Paget, DD, 2nd son of 1st baronet; *b.* July 11th, 1921; *s.* his 1st cousin once removed, *Sir* JAMES FRANCIS, 1972; ed. at Radley, and Ch. Ch., Oxford (MA); Lt.-Col. Coldm. Gds.; 1939-45 War; a Gentleman Ulsher to HM since 1971: *m.* 1954, Diana Frances, da. of the late Frederick Spencer Herbert Farmer, of Vicars Hill Lodge, Lymington, Hants., and has issue.

Labor ipse voluptas.
Work itself is pleasure.

Arms—Sable; on a cross engrailed, between in the 1st and 4th quarters an eagle displayed and in the 2nd and 3rd a heraldic tiger passant argent, an escallop of the first. **Crest**—A heraldic tiger passant argent, gorged with a collar and charged with two escallops sable.

Residence—4, Trevor St., SW7. *Clubs*—Guards', Pratt's, Flyfishers.

Son living—HENRY JAMES, *b.* Feb. 2nd, 1959.
Daughter living—Olivia Jane, *b.* 1957.
Daughter living of 2nd Baronet and Mother of 4th Baronet—Winifred Norah (*Lady Paget*), *b.* 1896: *m.* 1918, Gen. Sir Bernard Charles Tolver Paget, GCB, DSO, MC (infra), who *d.* 1961. *Residence*, The Old Orchard, Heath Rd., Petersfield, Hants.

Collateral Branches living.

Issue of the late Rt. Rev. Francis Paget, D.D., Lord Bishop of Oxford, 2nd son of 1st baronet, *b.* 1851, *d.* 1911: *m.* 1883, Helen Beatrice, who *d.* 1900, da. of the late Very Rev. Richard William Church, Dean of St. Paul's:—
Humphrey, *MC*, *b.* 1891; ed. at Radley, and at Ch. Ch., Oxford; Lt.-Col. RE; 1914-19 War as Capt. King's Liverpool Regt. (despatches, MC); Officer of American Legion of Merit: *m.* 1918, Elizabeth Caroline, who *d.* 1970, da. of Sir Lewis Tonna Dibdin, and has issue living, Elizabeth Frideswide, *b.* 1921; 1939-45 War in ATS: *m.* 1947, Lt.-Col. John Darwin Maling, DSO, MC, RA, of 63, Barton Av., Heretaunga, NZ,—Jean Marianne, *b.* 1924; 1939-45 War in WAAF: *m.* 1966, Robert Ian Cheyne Macpherson, of 1, Waitara Rd., St. Heliers, Auckland 5, NZ,—Helen Rosemary, *b.* 1929: *m.* 1966, George Albert Longman, of 2, Doatshayne Close, Musbury, Axminister, Devon. *Residence*, 1, Waitara Rd., St. Heliers, Auckland   NZ

Issue of the late Rt. Rev. Henry Luke Paget, D.D., Lord Bishop of Chester 1919-32, 3rd son of 1st baronet, *b.* 1853, *d.* 1937: *m.* 1892, Elma Katie, who *d.* 1958, da. of Sir Samuel Hoare, 1st Bt. (*cr.* 1899) [V. Templewood]:—
Paul Edward, *CVO, FSA, FRIBA, b.* 1901; ed. at Winchester, and at Trin. Coll., Camb.; 1939-45 War as Flight-Lt. RAuxAF, ; Assist. Private Sec. to Viscount Templewood 1924-26, Assist. Dir. of Emergency Works, Min. of Works 1941-44, and a Common Councilman of City of London 1949-55; Surveyor to the Fabric of St. Paul's Cathedral 1963-69, and Architect to Dean and Chapter of St. George's Chapel, Windsor Castle, and to Provost and Council, Portsmouth Cathedral 1950-69; a Member of Redundant Churches Fund 1969; Master Art Workers Guild 1971; a Member of Govt. Crafts Advisory Cttee. 1971; Chm. Norwich Diocesan Advisory Cttee. 1973; a CStJ; CVO 1971: *m.* 1971, Verily, da. of the late Rev. Francis Rosslyn Courtenay Bruce [see Bruce, Bt., colls., cr. 1804], and widow of Capt. Donald Clive Anderson, late Indian Army. *Residence*, Templewood, Northrepps, Cromer, Norfolk. *Clubs*, Athenaeum, Norfolk (Norwich).

Sir James Paget, 1st Bt., son of Samuel Paget of Great Yarmouth, was Sergeant-Surg. to Queen Victoria and Surg. to King Edward VII when Prince of Wales. Sir John Rahere, 2nd Bt., was a K.C.

PAGET, Creation (U.K.) 1886, of Cranmore Hall, co. Somerset.

Sir JOHN STARR PAGET, 3rd *Baronet;* *b.* Nov. 25th, 1914 ; *s.* his father, *Sir* RICHARD ARTHUR SURTEES, 1955 ; ed. at   Oundle, and Trin. Coll., Camb. (MA): FIMechE: *m.* 1944, Nancy Mary, da. of the late Lt.-Col. Francis Woodbine Parish, DSO, MC, and has issue.

Arms—Sable, on a cross invected argent, between four eagles displayed ermine, an eagle displayed between four lions passant of the first. **Crest**—A demi-heraldic tiger sable, maned, tufted, and gorged with a collar vallary argent, and holding in its mouth an eagle's leg erased at the thigh or.

Residences—Haygrass House, Taunton, Somerset; 20, Marloes Rd., W8.

Sons living—RICHARD HERBERT, *b.* Feb. 17th, 1957.
——David Vernon John, *b.* 1959.
Daughters living—Patricia Mary, *b.* 1945: *m.* 1975, Philip J. A. Hawkes, of 60, Rue de Varenne, 75007 Paris, France.——Rosemary Muriel, *b.* 1948: *m.* 1971, Christopher Ralph William Richard Inge, of 43, 14th St., Parkhurst, Johannesburg.——Elizabeth Frances, *b.* 1950.——Davina Jane, *b.* 1951: *m.* 1972, James Adrian Hunter Pollard, of The Grange, Town St., Bramcote, Nottingham.——Susan Glynne, *b.* 1960.
Sisters living—Sylvia Mary (*Lady Chancellor*), *b.* 1901 : *m.* 1926, Sir Christopher John Chancellor, C.M.G., son of Lieut.-Col. Sir John Robert Chancellor, G.C.M.G., GCVO, GBE, DSO, and has issue living, John Paget (of 69, Kew Green, Richmond, Surrey), *b.* 1927: *m.* 1959 (m. diss. 1968), the Hon. (Mary) Alice Joliffe, da. of 4th Baron Hylton, and has issue living, John Edward Horner *b.* 1962, Isabel Rose *b.* 1959, Katharine Sylvia Anthony *b.* 1961, Anna Theodora *b.* 1965,—Alexander Surtees (158, Kensington Park Rd., W11), *b.* 1940: *m.* 1964,

Diciendo y haciendo.
Saying and doing.

Susanna Elizabeth, only da. of Martin Ridley Debenham [see Debenham, Bt.], and has issue living, Elizabeth Beatrice *b.* 1964, Cecilia Mary *b.* 1966,—Teresa, *b.* 1933: *m.* 1953, Edward Victor Gatacre, of 44, Victoria Rd., W8, and de Wiersse, Vorden, Netherlands, and has issue living, Thomas Jerome *b.* 1954, William *b.* 1957, Alice Amelia *b.* 1960, Maria Teresa *b.* 1964, Cecily *b.* 1967, Dorothy Perpetua *b.* 1971,—Susanna Maria, *b.* 1935: *m.* 1958, Nicholas Johnston, of 33, Holland Villas Rd., W14, and has issue living, Clara Mary *b.* 1960, Lily Silvia *b.* 1962, Rose Pamela Muriel *b.* 1963, Silvy Margaret *b.* 1968. *Residence,* Hunstrete House, Pensford, Somerset.——Pamela Winefred (*Pamela, Baroness Glenconner*), *b.* 1903: *m.* 1925, the 2nd Baron Glenconner, from whom she obtained a divorce 1935. *Residence,* Hill Lodge, Hillsleigh Rd., W8.

Widow living of 2nd Baronet—GRACE HARTLEY (*Grace, Lady Paget*), da. of the late Walter Herbert Glover, of Birkdale and Grasmere : *m.* 1939, as his second wife, Sir Richard Arthur Surtees Paget, 2nd baronet, who *d.* 1955. *Residence,* 8, Iverna Court, Kensington, W.8.

Rev. John Paget, R. of Pointington, Somerset, for 54 years until his death 1745, purchased that manor and his lands at Daventry. His son, the Rev. Thomas Paget, held the same living 1745 until his death 1783. By the marriage of his son Richard to Mary, el. da. and eventually heir of James Moore, Cranmore Hall, Somerset, passed to this family. Their great grandson, the Rt. Hon. Sir Richard Horner Paget, 1st baronet was many years Chm. of Somerset Quarter Sessions and County Council, and sat as M.P. for E. Somerset (*C*) 1865-68, for Mid Somerset 1868-85, and for Wells Div. of Somersetshire 1885-95.

PAGET, Creation (U.K.) 1897, of Sutton Bonington, Notts. [Extinct 1937.]

Sir CECIL WALTER PAGET, *C.M.G.*, *D.S.O.*, 2nd and last *Baronet*.

Widow living of 2nd Baronet—FLORENCE (*Lady Paget*), da. of James Butt: *m.* 1927, as his second wife, Lieut.-Col. Sir Cecil Walter Paget, C.M.G., D.S.O., 2nd baronet, who *d.* 1936, when the title became ext. *Residence,* King's Newton, Derby.

PALMER, Creation (E.) 1660, of Carlton, Northamptonshire.

May the success be equal to the labour.

PAR SIT FORTUNA LABORI

Sir GEOFFREY CHRISTOPHER JOHN PALMER, 12th *Baronet*; *b.* June 30th, 1936; *s.* his father *Lieut.-Col. Sir* GEOFFREY FREDERICK NEILL, 1951; ed. at Eton; is patron of two livings: *m.* 1957, Clarissa Mary, el. da. of Stephen Francis Villiers-Smith [see B. Northbourne, colls.], and has issue.

Arms—Sable, a chevron or, between three crescents argent. **Crest**—A wyvern, wings addorsed or, armed and langued gules.

Seat—Carlton Curlieu Hall, Leicestershire.

Daughters living—Sophia Mary, *b.* 1959.——Celina Lucinda, *b.* 1961,—Isabella Anne, *b.* 1962.——Rosanna Jane, *b.* 1967.
Brother living—JEREMY CHARLES (8, Ashchurch Park Villas, W12), *b.* May 16th, 1939; ed. at Eton: *m.* 1968, Antonia, yr. da. of the late Astley Dutton.
Uncle living (son of 10th baronet) Lewis Henry, *b.* 1903 ; ed. at Eton : Lieut. 15th/19th Hussars : *m.* 1st, 1935 (marriage dissolved 1940), Pamela, da. of John Rowland Harries ; 2ndly, 1940 (marriage dissolved 1950), Mary Kathleen, da. of the late William Fletcher, of Arlecdon, Cumberland.
Aunt living (daughter of 10th baronet)—Sybil Alice Bridget, *b.* Nov. 1891 : *m.* 1913, Francis Edward Michael Reader, and has issue living, Evelyn Sophia Carlton, *b.* 1914 : *m.* 1934, Roydon Joseph Nicholson. *Residence,* Withcote Hall, Oakham.
Widow living of 11th Baronet—Cicely Kathleen, da. of the late Arthur Clifford Radmall, of Clifton, near Watford: *m.* 1st, 1932, Lieut.-Col. Sir Geoffrey Frederick Neill Palmer 10th baronet, who *d.* 1951 ; 2ndly, 1952, Robert William Newton. *Residence,* Carlton Curlieu Hall, Leicestershire.

Collateral Branches living.

Grandchildren of the late Major Herrick Augustus Palmer, son of the late Rev. Henry Palmer, 3rd son of 5th baronet :—
Issue of the late Frederick Charles Palmer, *b.* 1866, *d.* 1930 : *m.* 1897, Eleanor Annie, who *d.* 1942, da. of the late Henry Wilson Sharpin, F.R.C.S., of 34, Sillwood Road, Brighton:—
Dorothy Esther, *b.* 1898.

Issue of the late Lieut.-Col. Robert Henry Palmer, D.S.O., *b.* 1868, *d.* 1947 : *m.* 1909, Margaret Finch, who *d.* 1955, el. da. of the late Gerard Finch Dawson :—
Robert Henry Charles, *b.* 1916; ed. at Clifton, and at Wadham Coll., Oxford (Organ Scholar, MA, BMus); Organist, St. Mary's, Oak Bay, Victoria, BC; Conductor of Choir, Univ. of Victoria 1965-69; formerly Music Master, Westminster Abbey Choir Sch., and an ARCM; 1939-45 War with RAF. *Address,* c/o St. Mary's Church, Elgin Rd., Vic., BC.——Mary Margaret Elizabeth, *b.* 1914: *m.* 1944, Genille Hilton Jordayne Cave Brown-Cave, PhD [see Cave Browne-Cave, Bt., colls.]. *Residence,* The Crillon, 3500, Mountain St., Montreal 25, Canada.

The 1st baronet, Sir Geoffrey, sat as M.P. for Stamford in the Long Parliament, and was subsequently one of the Commissioners at the Treaty of Uxbridge, Attorney-General to Charles II., and Chief Justice of Chester. The 3rd, 4th, and 5th baronets successively represented Leicestershire in Parliament.

PALMER, Creation (G.B.) 1791, of Wanlip Hall, Leicestershire.

Sir JOHN EDWARD SOMERSET PALMER, 8th *Baronet; b.* Oct. 27th, 1926; *s.* his father, *Sir* JOHN ARCHDALE, 1963; ed. at Canford, Pembroke Coll., Camb. (B.A. 1951, M.A. 1957), and at Durham Univ. (M.Sc. Agric. Eng. 1953); late Lt., R.A.; Colonial Agricultural Ser., N. Nigeria 1953-62, Agricultural Engineer, R. A. Lister & Co., Dursley 1962-63, and at Overseas Liaison Office, National Institute of Agricultural Engineering, Silsoe, Beds 1964-68; a consultant: *m.* 1956, Dione Catharine, da. of Charles Duncan Skinner, of Turweston, Brockley, Northants, and has issue.

Arms,—Argent, on two bars sable three trefoils slipped of the first, in chief a greyhound courant of the second, collared or. Crest,—On a mount vert a greyhound sejant sable, gorged with a collar or, rimmed gules, and charged on the shoulder with a trefoil slipped argent. *Seat*—Newland, nr. Coleford, Glos. *Residence*—Wavendon Grange, Bletchley, Bucks. *Club*—Royal Overseas League.

Son living—ROBERT JOHN HUDSON, *b.* Dec. 20th, 1960.

Daughter living—Harriet Alyson Ducarel, *b.* 1959.

Brother living—Robert Archdale (of Lodge Cottage, Chaddesley Corbett, nr. Kidderminster), *b.* 1930; ed. at St. Andrews Univ. (M.A. 1951); late 2nd Lt. R.A.; H.M. Overseas Civil Ser., Uganda 1955-62; Sr. Assist. Sec. Univ. of Birmingham: *m.* 1963, Rosalie Margaret, da. of Keith Newell, of Wentworth, Neston, Ches., and has issue living, Philip David Archdale, *b.* 1969, —Jeremy Frederick Mathews, *b.* 1972,—Catherine Ducarel, *b.* 1963,—Sarah Rosalie, *b.* 1965.

Uncle living (son of 6th Baronet)—Philip Somerset (The Creel, Harbottle, Morpeth), *b.* 1899. *m.* 1939, Elizabeth Alyson Blanche, who *d.* 1974, da. of the late John George Burdon, of Benwell Hall, Northumberland, and widow of Capt. Edward Clennell Fenwick-Clennell, MC, of Harbottle Castle, Northumberland.

Widow living of 7th Baronet—KATHLEEN (*Kathleen, Lady Palmer*) (The Green, Uley, nr. Dursley, Glos.), da. of the late Herbert Smith: *m.* 1922, Sir John Archdale Palmer, 7th baronet, who *d.* 1963.

The 1st baronet, Sir Charles Grave Hudson, was a Director of the South Sea Co., and High Sheriff of Leicestershire 1780. Sir Charles Thomas, 2nd baronet, assumed the surname of Palmer, by Royal sign-manual, 1813, on succeeding to the estates of his maternal grandfather, Henry Palmer of Wanlip.

PALMER, Creation (U.K.) 1886, of Grinkle Park, co. York, and of Newcastle-upon-Tyne.

Sir (CHARLES) MARK PALMER, 5th *Baronet; b.* (posthumous) Nov. 21st, 1941; *s.* his father, *Major Sir* ANTHONY FREDERICK MARK, 1941; ed. at Eton; was a Page of Honour to H.M. 1956-9.

Arms—Sable, on a chevron between three crescents in chief and a lion passant in base argent, two tilting spears chevronwise proper. Crest—In front of a tilting spear erect proper a wyvern or, resting the dexter foot on a crescent argent.

Residence—Cwm-y-Cithin, Brilley, Herefords.

Let the reward equal the labour.

PAR SIT FORTUNA LABORI

Sister living—Antonia Mary, *b.* 1940 (*Lady Christopher J. Thynne*): *m.* 1968, Lord Christopher John Thynne, of 51, Edith Gro., SW10 [see M. Bath].

Aunts living—Diana Mabel, *b.* 1917: *m.* 1939, Squadron-Leader Vivian William Huntington, J.P., R.A.F. Vol. Reserve, and has issue living, Nicholas Charles, *b.* 1940,—Anthony Patrick, *b.* 1942,—Peter William, *b.* 1945,—Richard Ian, *b.* 1946. *Residence*, Bonawe House, Taynuilt, Argyll.——Angela, *b.* 1921; sometime in W.R.N.S.: *m.* 1948, Lieut.-Col. John Turnbull, M.C., 11th Hussars, and has issue living, Richard, *b.* 1951,—Michael, *b.* 1953,—Anna, *b.* 1950. *Residence*, The Barton House, Cirencester Park, Glos.

Great-Aunts living (daughters of 3rd baronet)—Phyllis Adela, *b.* 1888: *m.* 1st, 1908, Philip Durning Holt, J.P., who *d.* 19—, and from whom she obtained a divorce 1935; 2ndly, 1935, Lieut.-Col. Campbell Newall Watson, D.S.O., who *d.* 1957, and has issue living, (by 1st marriage) George Palmer, *b.* 1910,—Evelyn Mary, *b.* 1909: *m.* 19—, Thomas Charlton. *Residence*, Powys, Sidmouth, Devon.——Gladys Mary (66, Merrybent, Darlington, co. Durham), *b.* 1893.——Audrey (66, Merrybent, Darlington, co. Durham), *b.* 1898.

Widow living of 4th Baronet—Henriette Alice, *CVO* (*Lady Abel Smith*), da. of the late Cdr. Francis Charles Cadogan, RN [see E. Cadogan, colls.]; a JP; appointed a Lady-in-Waiting to HM the Queen when HRH Princess Elizabeth 1949, and a Woman of the Bedchamber to HM the Queen 1973; CVO (Civil) 1964: *m.* 1st, 1939, Maj. Sir Antony Frederick Mark Palmer, 4th baronet, who *d.* (killed in action) 1941; 2ndly, 1953, Brig. Sir Alexander Abel Smith, TD, JP [D. Somerset, colls.]. *Residences*, Old Rectory, Quenington, Cirencester, Glos.; 63 Cadogan Gdns., SW3.

Collateral Branches living.

Issue of the late Capt. Lionel Hugo Palmer, 6th son of 1st baronet, *b.* 1870, *d.* 1914:
m. 1st, 1894, Ida Brae, who *d.* 1905, da. of Wilberforce Wilson (formerly Surveyor-
Gen. of Hong Kong); 2ndly, 1906, Blanche, who *d.* 1965, only da. of Walter
Balmford, of York:—

(By 1st marriage) Victoria Louisa, *b.* 1897: *m.* 1923, John James Dickie, and has issue living.——
(By 2nd marriage) CHARLES LIONEL, *b.* Feb. 7th, 1909 ; ed. at Cheltenham Coll., and Trent
Coll. ; formerly Capt. Roy. Canadian Army Ser. Corps : *m.* 1937, Karoline, *L.R.A.M.*, da. of
the late Major Carl Gach, of Vienna, and has issue living, Diana Lillian, *b.* 1939,—Marjorie
Tessa, *b.* 1950. *Residence,* 52, Patika Av., Weston, Ontario, Canada.——Marjorie Blanche, *b.*
1907; is a Member of Imperial So. of Teachers of Dancing; late Junior Com ATS: *m.* 1939,
Philip Ashford Klitz, who *d.* 1942. *Residence,* 27 Abbey House, Cirencester, Glos., GL7 2QU.

Issue of the late Godfrey Mark Palmer, 7th son of 1st baronet, *b.* 1878, *d.* 1933: *m*
1906, Eleonora Mary, who *d.* 1965, da. of the late Alexander Geddes, of
Blairmore, Aberdeenshire:—

Mark, *T.D.*, *b.* 1917 ; ed. at Eton and abroad ; European War 1939-45 as Major 2nd Batn. Princess
Louise's Kensington Regt. (T.A.) (American Bronze Star) : *m.* 1939, Rosemary Aileen, da. of the
late Edward Welton, of 31, Knightsbridge Court, SW, and has issue living, Ferelith Alison, *b.*
1946: *m.* 1971, Ashley Gordon Down, of 2, Brunswick Gdns., W8 4AJ. *Residence,* Stanners Hill
House, Chobham, Woking, Surrey.——Myrtle Frances (West House, Stillington, York.), *b.* 1912;
resumed the surname of Palmer in lieu of Robinson by deed poll 1944: *m.* 1st, 1940 (m. annulled
1944), Fl.-Lt. Guy Robinson, RAF; 2ndly, 1948 (m. diss. 1962), Horace Barker; 3rdly, 1967,
Edward Walsh Tetley, and has issue living (by 2nd m.), Rachel Kay, *b.* 1950: *m.* 1974, Christopher
Rodney Wilson, of 4, Cowley Rd., SW14.

The 1st baronet, Sir Charles Mark, was a coal-owner and founder of the town of Jarrow, of which
he was the first Mayor 1875, and was M.P. for N. Durham (*L*) 1874, and from 1874 to 1885, and for
Jarrow Div. of co. Durham 1885 to 1907. The 4th baronet, Major Sir Anthony Frederick Mark
RA, *d.* (killed in action) 1941.

Palmer (Fuller-Palmer-Acland), see Acland.

PARKER, Creation (E.) 1681, of Melford Hall, Suffolk.

Sir RICHARD WILLIAM HYDE PARKER,
12th *Baronet ; b.* April 5th, 1937 ; *s.* his father,
Sir WILLIAM STEPHEN HYDE, 1951 ; ed. at
Millfield, and at Roy. Agricultural Coll., Cirencester: *m.* 1972 (Elizabeth) Jean, da. of the
late Sir (Henry John) Lindores Leslie, 9th Bt.
(cr. 1625), and has issue.

Arms—Quarterly : 1st and 4th, sable, a buck's head
caboshed, between two flaunches argent, *Parker* ; 2nd and
3rd, azure, a chevron between three lozenges or, *Hyde.* **Crest**—
A dexter arm erect, vested azure, slashed and cuffed argent,
holding in the hand proper an attire of a stag gules.
Seat—Melford Hall, Long Melford, Suffolk.

Daughters living—Beata Hyde, *b.* 1973.——Margaret Hyde
(twin), *b.* 1973.——Lucy Hyde, *b.* 1975.
Sister living—Elisabeth Mary Hyde (*Hon. Mrs. R. Thomas
C. G. S. Stonor*), *b.* 1939: *m.* 1966, the Hon. Ralph
Thomas Campion George Sherman Stonor, of Alston
Court, Nayland, Suffolk [see B. Camoys].
Uncle living (son of 10th baronet)—HARRY HYDE, *b.*
Feb. 17th, 1915 ; ed. at Harrow : *m.* 1935, Elizabeth
Alice, da. of the late Capt. Charles Cadwaladr Trevor-
Roper [*see* B. Teynham, *colls.*]. *Residence,* Peirce
House, Charing, Kent. *Club,* Travellers'.
Widow living of 11th Baronet—Ulla Ditlef, da. of the late
Professor C. Ditlef Nielsen, DPh, of Copenhagen, Denmark:
m. 1st, 1931, Sir William Stephen Hyde Parker, 11th baronet, who *d.* 1951; 2ndly, 1954, Frederick
William Hammond, who *d.* 1967. *Residence,* Melford Hall, Long Melford, Suffolk.

Collateral Branches living.

Issue of the late Laurence Hyde Parker, 5th son of 9th baronet, *b.* 1870, *d.* 1950:
m. 1906, Ada Letitia Moor, who *d.* 1968, el. da. of the late Joseph Alphonsus
Horsford, MRCS, of Long Melford, Suffolk:—

Laurence Edmond Hyde, *b.* 1912: *m.* 1953, Margarethe Van Thörne, and has issue living, Anthony
Laurence Hyde, *b.* 1958.—Michael Edmond Hyde, *b.* 1961.—Jane Katarina Hyde, *b.* 1954.
Residence, Smeetham Hall, Bulmer, Sudbury, Suffolk. *Club,* Farmer's.——Mary Hyde, *b.* 1908;
sometime Squadron Officer, W.A.A.F.; 1939-44 War (despatches). *Residence,* Smeetham
Hall, Bulmer, Sudbury, Suffolk.

Granddaughters of Capt. John Barnardiston Hyde Parker, 7th son of 9th
baronet (ante):—
Issue of the late Edmond Francis Hyde Parker, *b.* 1912, *d.* 1966: *m.* 1946, Naomi
(Huish Farm, Huish Episcopi, Langport, Somerset), da. of Dr. D. Carmichael Thomas
of Langport, Som.:—

Auriol Katharine Hyde, *b.* 1950: *m.* 1974, Lt. Meyrick David Griffith-Jones, 13th/18th R. Hussars
(Queen Mary's Own), of 71A, Endcliffe Vale Rd., Sheffield 10.——Sophia Naomi Lucy Hyde,
b. 1952: *m.* 1970, Glynn Mark Alexander Gray Read, of Heath Cottage, Farmborough, Avon.
——Harriet Ann Hyde, *b.* 1953.

Grandchildren of the late Harry Richard Parker, son of the late Maj.-Gen. John
Boteler Parker, son of the late Adm. Sir Hyde Parker, 2nd son of 5th baronet :—
Issue of the late Harry Richard Hyde Parker, *b.* 1859, *d.* 1946 : *m.* 1893, Fanny Laura,
who *d.* 1952, da. of the late John Collis :—

Edward Hyde, *b.* 1899 : *m.* 1928, Ethel Mortimore, and has issue living, Alan Hyde, *b.* 1933,—David Hugh Hyde (of 16, Maytree Avenue, Garden Village, Hull), *b.* 1934 : *m.* 1959, Brenda McIntosh, and has issue living, Rosemary Hyde *b.* 1960, Anne Hyde *b.* 1962. *Residence*, 103, Grand Av., Hassocks, Sussex.——Margaret Hyde, *b.* 1897: *m.* 1941, Capt. F. Mitchell, RE, who *d.* 1969. *Residence*, West Dene, Malvern, Worcs.

Grandchildren of the late Harry Richard Hyde Parker (ante) :—
Issue of the late Reginald John Hyde Parker, *b.* 1894, *d.* 1957 : *m.* 1927, Violet Jackson :—
Reginald Harry Richard Hyde (The Cottage, Exlade St., Woodcote, Oxon.), *b.* 1931: *m.* 1st, 1957 (m. diss. 1961), Dorothy Margaret Stanley; 2ndly, 1962, Anne Bulmer, and has issue living, (by 2nd m.), Simon Richard Hyde, *b.* 1966,—Emma Jayne Hyde, *b.* 1962.——Eve Frances Hyde, *b.* 1932; is a SRN: *m.* 1968, William Leavey. *Residence*, 4, Salcombe Drive, Earley, Reading.

The 1st baronet, Sir Hugh, was an Alderman of London. The 2nd baronet, Sir Henry, *m.* Margaret, da. and heir of Alexander Hyde, Bishop of Salisbury, 1st cousin of 1st Earl of Clarendon, Lord Chancellor. The 5th baronet, Adm. Sir Hyde, commanded in the action at St. Lucia 1780, and in the memorable action with the Dutch on the Dogger Bank 1781. In 1782 he was nominated to the chief command of the British Fleet in the East Indies. He sailed from England in the " Cato," which vessel never having been heard of after leaving Rio Janeiro, is supposed to have been lost with all hands. Other members of this family have also been distinguished both in the Navy and the Army.

PARKER, Creation (U.K.) 1844, of Shenstone Lodge, Staffordshire.

Sir WILLIAM ALAN PARKER, 4th *Baronet*; *b.* March 20th, 1916; *s.* his father *Capt. Sir* WILLIAM LORENZO, *OBE*, 1971; ed. at Eton and New. Coll., Oxford (BA); Capt. RE; 1939-45 War: *m.* 1946, Sheelagh Mary, only da. of the late Dr. Sinclair Stevenson, of Beech Lawn, Fareham, Hants., and has issue.

Arms—Gules, a chevron or between three leopards' faces or. **Crest**—A leopard's head erased, affrontée, ducally gorged or.

Residence—Apricot Hall, Sutton-cum-Beckingham, Lincoln, LN5 0RE.

Sub libertate qui etem.
Under liberty rest.

Son living—WILLIAM PETER BRIAN, *b.* Nov. 30th, 1950; ed. at Eton; ACA.
Daughter living—Lindy Ruth, *b.* 1947; ed. at Durham Univ. (BA): *m.* 1969, Robert Samuel Moore, PhD, of 72, Tillydrone Av., Aberdeen, AB2 2TN.

Brother living—John Douglas (266, Latymer Court, Hammersmith, W6 7LB), *b.* 1924; ed. at Eton and at New Coll., Oxford (BA and MA 1949); 1943-45 War as Lieut. Irish Gds.: *m.* 1958, Iris Anne, who *d.* 1959, yst. da. of Com. G. A. Titterton, RN (ret.), of 4, Clarence House, Granville Rd., Eastbourne, and has issue living, Timothy John, *b.* 1959.

Sister living—Ruth Kathleen Betty, *b.* 1920; 1939-45 War with First Aid Nursing Yeo.: *m.* 1947, Richard Arthur Cole-Hamilton [*see* E. Enniskillen, colls.]. *Residence*, 4, Garscube Terr., Edinburgh EH12 6BQ.

Aunt living (daughter of 2nd baronet)—Constance Kathleen Rose, *b.* 1894; served with National Fire Ser. 1939-45: *m.* 1916, Adm. Sir Douglas Blake Fisher, KCB, KBE, who *d.* 1963, having obtained a divorce 1945, and has issue living, Lionel William Blake (Sydney, NSW), *b.* 1918; late Capt. RM: *m.* 1943, Elizabeth, el. da. of Adm. Sir Harold Richard George Kinahan, KBE, CB, and has issue living, Brian Richard Douglas Blake, *b.* 1946, Nigel Robin Kinahan *b.* 1948, Isabel Rosemary *b.* 1944. *Residence*, 4, Garscube Terr., Edinburgh, EH12 6BQ.

Collateral Branches living.

Grandchildren of the late Col. William Frederic Parker (infra):—
Issue of the late Capt. William Mackworth Parker, Rifle Brig. (Prince Consort's Own), *b.* 1886, *d.* (killed in action) 1915: *m.* 1912, Lillian Ursula, an O.St.J., who *d.* 1966 (having *m.* 2ndly, 1921, Vice-Adm. Everard John Hardman-Jones, CB, OBE, who *d.* 1962), da. of the late Col. Sir Arthur Pendarves Vivian, KCB [B. Swansea, colls.]:—
Frederick Anthony Vivian, *b.* 1913; ed. at Winchester; Maj. Rifle Bde.; a JP and DL of Devon; Co. Councillor, Devon 1960-64; 1939-45 War (prisoner): *m.* 1st, 1937, Pamela Mary (who obtained a divorce 1946), da. of the late Charles George Edgar Farmer, of Nonsuch Park, Surrey; 2ndly, 1947, Diana Mary, da. of Brig.-Gen. Bryan James Curling, DSO. *Residence*, Delamore, Cornwood, Ivybridge, Devon.——Letitia Margaret, *b.* 1914: *m.* 1942, Dennis Seaver Dollard, of Monte Alto, Odeaxire, Algarve, Portugal, and has issue living, Anthony Brian Christopher, *b.* 1949,—Gavin James Dominic, *b.* 1950.

Issue of the late Cyril George Parker, *b.* 1890; *d.* 1968: *m.* 1st, 1921, Beatrice, who *d.* 1928, da. of W. Harris; 2ndly, 1934, Margaret May (1117, 125th St., Edmonton, Alberta, Canada), da. of John Holmes Graham, and widow of Wallace Bruce MacDougall:—
(By 1st m.) Laurence Frederick Cyril, *b.* 1922: *m.* 1951, Dorothy May, da. of R. S. Kent, and has issue living, Allen Kent, *b.* 1954,—Beatrice Anne, *b.* 1952,—Donna Gail, *b.* 1956,—Nancy Kay, *b.* 1958.

Grandchildren of the late Adm. George Parker, 2nd son of 1st baronet :—
Issue of the late Col. William Frederic Parker, *b.* 1860, *d.* 1941 : *m.* 1st, 1885, Helinor Katherine, who *d.* 1896, da. of Col. Fitzroy Stephen, C.B.; 2ndly, 1899, Alice, who *d.* 1929, el. surviving da. of the late Lieut.-Gen. Reynell Taylor, C.B., C.S.I., of Malston, Newton Abbot :—
(By 2nd m.) Robert William, CBE, *b.* 1902; Rear-Adm. (ret.); is a JP for Somerset; was on Staff of Com.-in-Ch. Plymouth 1952-53, and Dep. Engineer-in-Ch., Admiralty 1953-56; 1914-18 War; 1939-45 War with Home and British Pacific Fleets; CBE (Mil) 1954: *m.* 1st, 1928, Jean (from whom he obtained a divorce 1933), da. of the late Henry Mackay; 2ndly, 1935, Noëmi Vyvian, ygr. da. of C. V. Espeut, of 7, Iverna Court, W8. *Residence*, The Hermitage, Freshford, nr. Bath, Som.——(by 1st m.) Helinor Marjorie, *b.* 1894: *m.* 1914, Adm. Robert Nesham Bax, CB, who *d.* 1969, and has issue living, John Nesham, *b.* 1915; ed. at Charterhouse, and at Magdalene Coll., Camb. (MA); sometime with Burmah Oil Co.; Burma 1941-45 as Maj. Indian Army: *m.* 1941, Gladys, da. of Maj. C. V. Phillips, and has issue living, Robert *b.* 1942, Richard Charles *b.* 1946, Andrew *b.* 1948, Margaret *b.* 1959.——Christopher Robert, *RN*, *b.* 1916; is Com.: *m.* 1953, Betty, da. of Gordon Somerville, and has issue living, Michael William Somerville *b.* 1954,—Charity Anne, *b.* 1920; 1939-45 War with WRNS: *m.* 1944, Maj. Philip Bolton Douglas-Cooper, RE, JP, of The Hawfield, Blakeney, Glos., and has issue living, John *b.* 1947, Caroline Anne *b.* 1945, Helen Elizabeth *b.* 1952. *Residence*, 11D, The Precincts, Canterbury.

Issue of the late Mackworth Praed Parker, *b.* 1865, *d.* 1926: *m.* 1893, Sybil Edith, who *d.* 1934, da. of the late Lieut.-Col. John Arthur Thomas Garratt, J.P.:—
Gerard, *b.* 1896 ; Capt. (retired) Devonshire Regt. ; European War 1915-18 (twice wounded, despatches twice) : *m.* 1st, 1921, Dorothy, who *d.* 1954, da. of Lieut.-Col. Francis Marwood Hext ; 2ndly, 1958, Jill Lettice Mary, el. da. of R. W. K. Nott, and has issue living, (by 2nd marriage) Gerard Mackworth, *b.* 1958,—Julius Praed, *b.* 1959,—Susan Mary, *b.* 1961. *Residence,* Hansford House, Umberleigh, N. Devon.——Sybil Muriel, *b.* 1895 : *m.* 1921, Major Montagu Irvine Gedoin Jenkins, D.S.O., who *d.* 1948, and has issue living, Vivien Naomi, *b.* 1930. *Residence,* Holmes, Aylesbear, near Exeter.

The 1st baronet, grandson of the Right Hon. Sir Thomas Parker (of Park Hall, Staffordshire, Lord Chief Baron of the Exchequer), commanded in the Tagus during the war between Dom Pedro and Dom Miguel ; he was a Lord of the Admiralty in 1834 and 1835-41, principal naval A.D.C. to H.M. Queen Victoria, Commander-in-Chief during Chinese war 1841-2, in Mediterranean 1845-52, and at Devonport 1854-57, and sometime Senior Admiral of the Fleet. Thomas Parker, fathe to 11st Earl of Macclesfield, was a yr. son of George Parker, of Park Hall (*d.* 1675).

PARKYNS, Creation (E.) 1681, of Bunney Park, Nottinghamshire. [Dormant 1926.]

[Although the existence of an heir is probable, since the death of the 6th Baronet in 1926 a right to the Baronetcy has not yet been officially established.]

Daughter living of 6th Baronet—Sylvia Dorothy, *b.* 1887 : *m.* 1912 (marriage dissolved 1931), Allan Gilbert Cram, and has issue living, Thomas, *b.* 191-,—a da., *b.* 191-. *Residence,*

Collateral Branches living.

Grandchildren of the late Edward Territt Parkyns, son of Capt. Levett Broadley Parkyns (*b.* 1779), grandson of George Parkyns, brother of 3rd baronet:—
Issue of the late Francis Charles Parkyns, *b.* 1856, *d.* 1891 : *m.* 1883, Alice Caroline Ward, who *d.* 1941 :—
Edwin Garling Territt, *b.* July 26th, 1890: *m.* 1912, Alice Emily, da. of the late George Walter Wood, J.P., of Mill Road, Liverpool, and has issue living, Garling Alfred (of 44, Nagle Street, Liverpool, N.S. Wales), *b.* 1913 : *m.* 1935, Lucy Frances Laycock, and has issue living, Garling Alfred *b.* 1936, Frances Ann *b.* 1938,—Kenneth George (2, Rose St., Liverpool, N.S. Wales), *b.* 1917 : *m.* 1945, Patricia May Robins, and has issue living, Robert Carswell *b.* 1946, Lindsay Hampton *b.* 1948,—Clifford Edwin Frederick (Isham), *b.* 1926,—Gladys Lorraine, *b.* 1915 : *m.* 1936, Kenneth Leonard Weston-Brown, and has issue living, Brian *b.* 1936, Kenneth *b.* 1938, Wendy Lorraine *b.* 1940,—Enid Dorothy, *b.* 1922 : *m.* 1947, Donald Douglas Floyd, of 14, Rose Street, Liverpool, N.S. Wales, and has issue living, Douglas Stewart *b.* 1948, Robyn Lorraine *b.* 1950. *Residence,* 4, Rose St., Liverpool, N.S. Wales.——Florence May (of Margordon Flats, Pittwater Rd., Collaroy, N.S. Wales), *b.* 1884: *m* 1907, Douglas Graham, who *d.* 1962, and has issue living, Gordon, *b.* 1908,—Donald, *b.* 1914,—Marjorie, *b.* 1911.——Alice Beatrice, *b.* 1886: *m.* 1925, Oswald Murray Charlton, who *d.* 1929. *Residence,*

Issue of the late Edwin Downing Parkyns (of Malean, Clarence River, N.S. Wales), *b.* 1865, *d.* 19—: *m.* 1896, Cassilla Cole, who *d.* 1955:—
Henry Jones, *b.* 1896.——Edwin Arnold Allan, *b.* 1898.

Issue of the late Henry Garling Parykns, *b.* 1867, *d.* 1938: *m.* 1907, Mary McClifty, who *d.* 1944 :—
Daniel George, *b.* 1916: *m.* 1942, Evelyn Mary Cook. *Residence,*

PASLEY, Creation (G.B.) 1794, of Craig, Dumfriesshire.

[Name pronounced "**Paisley**."]

Fighting for my king and country.

Sir RODNEY MARSHALL SABINE PASLEY, 4th *Baronet*, son of the late Capt. Malcolm Sabine Pasley, R.N., 2nd son of the late Capt Thomas Malcolm Sabine Pasley, R.N., el. son of 2nd Baronet ; *b.* (twin) Feb. 22nd, 1899 ; *s.* his uncle, *Major Sir* THOMAS EDWARD SABINE, 1947 ; European War 1917-19 as 2nd Lieut. R.A. : *m.* 1922, Aldyth Werge, da. of the late Major Lancelot Cecil Bray Hamber, formerly E. Lancashire Regt., of Venta, New Milton, and has issue.

Arms—Azure, on a chevron argent between two roses in chief of the last, and an anchor in base or, three thistles slipped proper. **Crest**—Out of a naval coronet gold, a sinister arm in armour proper, grasping in the hand a staff thereon a flag argent, charged with a cross couped gules, and on a canton azure a human leg erect, couped above the knee or.
Residence, Hazel Cottage, Peaslake, Surrey.

Son living—JOHN MALCOLM SABINE (25, Lathbury Rd., Oxford), *b.* April 5th, 1926; ed. at Sherborne, and at Trin. Coll., Oxford (MA); a Fellow of Magdalen Coll., Oxford: *m.* 1965, Virginia Killigrew, da. of Peter Lothian Killigrew Wait, of Kew, Surrey, and has issue living, Robert, *b.* 1965,—Humphrey, *b.* 1967.
Daughter living—Pepita Sabine, *b.* 1925: *m.* 1957, Stanford Merrifield, of 16, Engadine Close, Croydon, CR0 5UU, and has issue living, Giles Stanford, *b.* 1950,—Hannah Marion *b.* 1960.
Daughter living of 3rd Baronet—Norah MARGARET Sabine, *b.* 1902: *m.* 1933, Clifford Jeal, and has issue living, John Julian Timothy (2, Healey St., NW1), *b.* 1945; ed. at Westminster, and Ch. Ch., Oxford (MA): *m.* 1969, Joyce Timewell, and has issue living, Jessica *b.* 1970,—Thomasina Joanna, *b.* 1934: *m.* 1957, Edgar Philip Beck, of Coombe Priory, Shaftesbury, Dorset, and has issue living, Edgar Adam Alexander *b.* 1959, Thomas Damien *b.* 1960. *Residence,* 1, Earls Court Gdns., SW5.

Collateral Branches living.

Issue of the late Rodney Stewart Lyons Sabine Pasley, 2nd son of 2nd baronet, *b.* 1832, *d.* 1909 : *m.* 1868, Annie, who *d.* 1923, da. of W. M'Leod, of Dunedin, New Zealand :—

Edith Annie Sabine, *b.* 1880 : *m.* 1909, George Evelyn Adams, and has issue living, Raymond Sabine (University of Missouri, Columbia, Mo, USA) *b.* 1926; MA; Diploma of Education; PhD: *m.* 1951, Phyllis Audrey, da. of L. C. Barton, of Hamilton, New Zealand, and has issue living, John Raymond *b.* 1958, Lesley Ann *b.* 1960,—Joyce Garland Sabine (of 88, 13th Av., Tauranga, New Zealand), *b.* 1910: *m.* 1944, Marshall Jack Eagles, J.P., who *d.* 1956, and has issue living, John Heywood Ross *b.* 1947, Roger Grose Ross *b.* 1949, Christine Ross *b.* 1945; BSc. *Residence*, 88, 13th Av., Tauranga, New Zealand.

Grandchildren of the late Rodney Stewart Lyons Sabine Pasley (ante):—
Issue of the late Montagu Thomas Sabine Pasley, *b.* 1869, *d.* 1947: *m.* 1900, Agnes Jane, who *d.* 1965, da. of the late John Innes, of Invercargill, NZ :—

Nancy Sabine, *b.* 1907 : *m.* 1932, Robert Paterson Barr. *Residence*, 1360, Burnaby Street, Vancouver, British Columbia.

Issue of the late William Sabine Pasley, *b.* 1870, *d.* 1938 : *m.* 1900, Florence Annie Heloise, who *d.* 1959, da. of the late W. H. Kinnersley :—

Eric Kinnersley Sabine, *b.* 1900 : *m.* 1st, 1928, Thelma, who *d.* 1948, da. of the late John Power, of Auckland, New Zealand ; 2ndly, 1949, his cousin, Rona Norma Sabine, da. of the late Russell Sabine Pasley (infra), and has issue living, (by 1st marriage) Tom Sabine (of 50, Monck's Spur, Redcliff's, Christchurch, New Zealand), *b.* 1929; a member of Real Estate Inst., New Zealand: *m.* 1958, Helen Aroha, da. of Justin Beauchamp Foster-Barham, of Nelson, New Zealand, and has issue living, Malcolm Sabine *b.* 1960, Alastair Sabine *b.* 1963, Hamish Sabine *b.* 1964,—Warren Sabine (42, Monck's Spur, Redcliffe, Christchurch, NZ), *b.* 1931: *m.* 1955, Margaret Mae, el. da. of John Douglas McIntosh, of Dunedin, NZ, and has issue living, Jonathan Douglas Sabine *b.* 1961, Joanne Tui Sabine *b.* 1959,—John Clinton Sabine, *b.* 1936: *m.* 1960 Monica Therese, da. of Patrick Reillery, of Christchurch, and has issue living, Mathew Patrick *b.* 1961, Paul Joseph Eric *b.* 1962, John Nicholas *b.* 1963. *Residence*, 52, Frankleigh St., Spreydon, Christchurch, New Zealand.——Dorothy Madelene Sabine, *b.* 1906: *m.* 1939, Victor Patrick Coghlan. *Residence*, 8, Victoria Rd., Nelson, New Zealand.——Lilley Sabine, *b.* 1917: *m.* 1937, Harry Douglas Double, and has issue living, Patricia Ann, *b.* 1939,—Jill Sabine, *b.* 1943. *Residence*, 55, Routley Cres., Upper Hutt, Wellington, New Zealand.

Grandchildren of the late Russell Sabine Pasley (infra):—
Issue of the late Maitland Sabine Pasley, *b.* 1914, *d.* 1972: *m.* 1943, Nancy Molyneux (56, Severn St., Islands Bay, Wellington, NZ), da. of John Phillips, of Te Puke, NZ:—

Philip Sabine (179, Centaurus Rd., Ch. Ch. 2, NZ), *b.* 1945: *m.* 1969, Colleen Monica, el. da. of Daniel Doyle, of Ch. Ch., NZ, and has issue living, Stuart Sabine, *b.* 1974,—Andrea Sabine, *b.* 1972.——Russell Sabine, *b.* 1947.——Christine Sabine, *b.* 1950: *m.* 1972, Robert John Lang.

Granddaughter of the late Rodney Stewart Lyons Sabine Pasley (ante):—
Issue of the late Russell Sabine Pasley, *b.* 1874, *d.* 1945 : *m.* 1902, Mabel, who *d.* 19—, da. of G. Tracey Stevens, Surveyor, of Wellington, New Zealand :—

Grandchildren of the late Major Maitland Warren Bouverie Sabine Pasley 3rd son of 2nd baronet :—
Issue of the late Capt. Montagu Wynyard Sabine Pasley, R.A., *b.* 1863, *d.* 1944: *m.* 1891, Grace Lilian, who *d.* 1919, da. of the late Capt. J. H. H. St. John:—

Joseph Montagu Sabine, C.B., C.B.E., M.V.O. (of 1, Ryefield Close, Eastbourne. *Club*, Cavalry), *b.* 1898; Maj.-Gen. (retired) late R.A.; formerly Com. 1st Anti-Aircraft Group; retired 1951, an O.St.J.; European War 1918 in France and Belgium (two medals), N. Africa and Italy 1943-45 (C.B.E.); M.V.O. (4th class) 1936, C.B.E. (Mil.) 1944, C.B. (Mil.) 1952: *m.* 1st, 1926, Christina Joan, da. of John Darby, of Hillmorton House, near Rugby; 2ndly, 1950, Dorothy B. (PARSONS), da. of W. J. Fance, of Parkstone, Dorset, and has issue living, (by 2nd marriage) Malcolm Peter Sabine, *b.* 1956,—(by 1st marriage) Anne Sabine, *b.* 1929: *m.* 1951, Major John G. Melsom, of Willow Cottage, Church Lane, Headley, Hants., and has issue living, Andrew John, *b.* 1953.——Lillian Katherine Sabine, *b.* 1895: *m.* 1919, Alexander Louis Courtenay Lumsden, who *d.* 1959, and has issue living, Alexander Sabine Courtenay (Bywater Studio Cottage, Walhampton, nr. Lymington, Hants., SO4 8SB), *b.* 1921; 1939-45 War as Fl.-Lt. RAFVR: *m.* 1st, 1943, Elisabeth Jean, da. of Group-Capt. B. P. H. de Roeper, AFC, RAF; 2ndly, 1951, Elisabeth Vrena, da. of the late Sqdn.-Ldr. W. R. Adkins; 3rdly, 1969, Elizabeth Moncrieff, da. of the late Alexander Robert Cheale, of Tunbridge Wells, and formerly wife of Colin W. Morley, and has issue living, (by 2nd m.) Peter Alexander Courtenay *b.* 1961, (by 1st m.) Julia Frances Sabine *b.* 1945, (by 2nd m.) Penelope Elisabeth Courtenay *b.* 1956. *Residence*, 30, Molyneux Park Rd., Tunbridge Wells.

Issue of the late Henry Diggle Sabine Pasley, *b.* (twin) 1871, *d.* 1925 : *m.* 1895, Lillian Horton, da. of the late Capt. Charles Horton Rhys :—

Winifred Sabine, *b.* 1900 : *m.* 1953, Alfred Thomas Wright. *Residence*, 38, Craster Road, S.W.2.

Grandchildren of the late Capt. Hamilton Sabine Pasley, 5th son of 2nd baronet :—
Issue of the late Hamilton Sabine Pasley, M.V.O., *b.* 1861, *d.* 1927 : *m.* 1899, Alice Marion Margaret, who *d.* 1930, da. of Thomas Conolly:—

Thomas Wynyard Sabine, *b.* 1902 ; European War 1940-45 in N. Africa, Italy, and Greece with Roy. Canadian Artillery and R.A.O.C. : *m.* 1st, 1946, Mrs. Elizabeth Dudensing, who *d.* 1956, da. of the late Edward Howell Jones, of Freeman, West Virginia, U.S.A.; 2ndly, 1957, Mrs. Charlotte Jennings, da. of the late William C. Potter, of New York, U.S.A. *Residence*, Southampton, New York, U.S.A. *Club*, White's.——Violet Catherine Sabine, *b.* 1901: *m.* 1924, Capt. Percy John Warren McClenaghan, MC, Indian Army, who *d.* 1930, and has issue living, Rosemary, *b.* 1928: *m.* 1949, Theon Charles Wilkinson, of 76½, Chartfield Av., SW15, and has issue living, Wynyard Russell Theon *b.* 1951,—Valerie Joan, *b.* 1929: *m.* 1949, Capt. Malcolm Henry Syms, R.M., Mile Path House, Mile Path, Hook Heath, Woking, Surrey, and has issue living, Jeremy Francis *b.* 1950, Charlotte Prudence Elizabeth *b.* 1954. *Residence*, West Wellow, Milford-on-Sea, Hants.

Issue of the late Richard Sydney Sabine Pasley, *b.* 1862, *d.* 1911 : *m.* 1897, Mary Victoria, who *d.* 1942, da. of Sir Henry Dalrymple Des Vœux, 5th Bt. :—

Arthur Dalrymple Sabine (Owls Hoot, Wortwell, Norfolk), *b.* 1903: *m.* 1st, 1943, Doris, who *d.* 1950, da. of Herbert Rastell; 2ndly, 1950, Hilda Mary, da. of William H. Gardner, and has issue living, (by 2nd m.) Victoria Mary Sabine, *b.* 1952.——Catherine Constance Sabine (Brixton Lodge, Brixton, N. Devon), *b.* 1900.——Sybil Mary Sabine, *b.* 1901: *m.* 1930, Donald James Henry Maclennan, and has issue living, Angela Sybil Joan, *b.* 1934: *m.* 1961, John Malcolm Page, of 837, Wallace Wynd, Port Moody, Vancouver, BC, and has issue living, Christopher David *b.* 1963, Jonathan Richard *b.* 1965, Antony Graham *b.* 1966. *Residence*, The Old Parsonage, Great Glemham, Saxmundham, Suffolk.——Audrey Christina Sabine, *b.* 1905. *Residence*, Wistaria Cottage, Maresfield, Sussex.

Issue of the late Charles Malcolm Sabine Pasley, *b.* 1864, *d.* 1907: *m.* 1903 Berthe, who *d.* 1964, da. of the late Comte de Rilly:—

Charles Hamilton Sabine (55, Ewan St., Margate 4019, Qld., Aust.), *b.* 1906; Roy. Australian Air Force (ret.); 1939-45 War (despatches): *m.* 1933, Marjorie May Heales, and has issue living, Helen Sabine, *b.* 1934.

The 1st baronet, Adm. Sir Thomas Pasley, was created a baronet, with remainder to the **issue** male of his daughters successively, and in 1808 was succeeded by his grandson, Thomas **Sabine, who** in 1809, assumed by Roy. licence the surname of Pasley.

Paston-Bedingfeld, see Bedingfeld.

PAUL, Creation (I.) 1794, of Paulville, Carlow. [Extinct 1961.]

Rev. Sir (WILLIAM EDMUND) JEFFREY PAUL, 6th and last *Baronet.*

Daughter living of 5th Baronet—Richenda Alice Ione (*Lady Neave*) (Greatham Moor, Liss, Hants.), *b.* 1922; 1939-45 War with WRNS: *m.* 1946, Maj. Sir Arundell Thomas Clifton Neave 6th Bt.

Pauncefort-Duncombe, see Duncombe.

PEARSON, Creation (U.K.) 1916, of St. Dunstan's, co. London.

In God is hope.

Sir NEVILLE ARTHUR PEARSON, 2nd *Baronet ; b.* Feb. 13th, 1898; *s.* his father, *Sir* (CYRIL) ARTHUR, *G.B.E.*, 1921 ; ed. at Eton ; is Pres. St. Dunstan's Blinded Soldiers' and Sailors' Fund, Pres. Fresh Air Fund; 1917-18 War with RA, 1939-44 War as Maj. Anti-Aircraft Regt. RA and Gen. Staff: *m.* 1st, 1922, Mary Angela, who *d.* 1937, and from whom he had obtained a divorce 1928, da. of the Rt. Hon. Sir Alfred Moritz Mond, M.P., 1st Bt. (later 1st Baron Melchett) ; 2ndly, 1928, Mrs. Gladys Buckmaster (subsequently Dame Gladys Cooper, DBE), who *d.* 1971, and from whom he had obtained a divorce 1937, da. of the late Charles Frederick Cooper; 3rdly, 1943, Mrs. Anne Davis Elebash, da. of the late David Montgomery Davis, of Richmond, Virginia, U.S.A., and has issue by 1st and 2nd marriages.

Arms—Argent, billety azure, on a pile of the last, three horses' heads erased of the field.   Crest—A horse's head erased sable, billety and gorged with a mural crown or.

Residence—Chesham House, 30, Chesham Pl., SW1. *Club*—Bath.

Daughters living—By 1st m.—Anne (*Baroness Glenkinglas*), *b.* 1923: *m.* 1940, Baron Glenkinglas, of Strone, Cairndow, Argyll.——By 2nd m.,—Sally, *b.* 1929: *m.* 1961, Timothy Sydney Robert Hardy, of Upper Bolney House, Harpsden, Henley on Thames, and has issue living, Emma Jocelyn Cressida Myfanwy, *b.* 1963,—Justine Elinor Eldrydd, *b.* 1966.

Half-Sister living—Nora, *MBE*, *b.* 1892; MBE (Civil) 1954: *m.* 1st, 1912 (m. diss. 1925), Henry Frederick Lipscomb, who *d.* 1958: 2ndly, 1926 (m. diss. 1933), Capt. Harold Johnson, MC, E. Lancashire Regt., who *d.* 1946; 3rdly, 1934, Maurice George Reid Aitken, BI, who *d.* 1970 and has issue (by 1st m.).

The 1st baronet, Sir (Cyril) Arthur Pearson, G.B.E., founded *Pearson's Weekly*, the *Daily Express*, and many other well-known publications, and until complete failure of eyesight in 1914 owned several daily newspapers; Pres. of National Institute for the Blind, and of Fresh Air Fund, Vice-Pres. of Tariff Reform League, and Vice-Chm. of Tariff Commn. ; Joint Hon. Sec. Collecting Committee of National Relief Fund ; during European War 1914-19 founded St. Dunstan's for the benefit of Blinded Soldiers and Sailors.

PEARSON, Creation (U.K.) 1964, of Gressington, co. Palatine of Lancaster.

Sir FRANCIS FENWICK PEARSON, *MBE, 1st Baronet,* son of Frank Pearson, of Kirkby Lonsdale, Westmorland; *b.* June 13th, 1911; ed. at Uppingham, and at Trin. Hall, Camb.; a farmer and landowner and a JP, and a DL for Lancs.; Maj. 1st Gurkha Rifles 1931-34; ADC to Viceroy of India 1934-36, Under-Sec. 1942-45, and Ch. Min. Maipur State 1945-47; Assist. Govt. Whip (unpaid) 1960-62, a Lord Commr. of the Treasury 1962-63, and PPS to Prime Min. 1963-64; MP for Clitheroe Div. of Lancs. (*C*) 1959-70; Chm. Central Lancs. New Town Development Corpn. 1971; MBE (Civil) 1945: *m.* 1938, Katharine Mary, da. of the Rev. D. Denholm Fraser, of Sprouston, Roxburghshire, and has issue.

Residence,—Gressingham Hall, Hornby, Lancs. *Club,*—Carlton.

Son living—FRANCIS NICHOLAS FRASER, *b.* Aug. 28th, 1943; Capt. Rifle Bde.

Daughter living—Susan Alison Mary, *b.* 1941: *m.* 1961, Peter Sharp, of Linden Hall, Borwick, Carnforth, Lancs., and has issue living, James Edward, *b.* 1967,—Harriet Nicola, *b.* 1962,—Joanna Katharine Rose, *b.* 1963.

PEASE, Creation (U.K.) 1882, of Hutton Lowcross and Pinchinthorpe, co. York.

Sir (ALFRED) VINCENT PEASE, 4th *Baronet;* *b.* April 2nd, 1926; *s.* his half-brother, *Sir* EDWARD, 1963, ed. at Bootham Sch., York.

Arms—Per fesse azure and gules, a fesse nebuly ermine between two lambs passant in chief argent, and in base upon a mount proper a dove rising argent, holding in the beak a pea stalk, the blossom and pods proper. **Crest**—Upon the capital of an Ionic column a dove rising, holding in the beak a pea stalk as in the arms.

Residence—Baysdale Cottage, Pinchinthorpe, Guisborough, Cleveland.

Brother living—JOSEPH GURNEY, *b.* Nov. 16th, 1927; ed. at Bootham Sch., York; was a Member of Guisborough Urban District Council 1950-53: *m.* 1953, Shelagh Munro, da. of Cyril G. Bulman, of Great Langdale, Ambleside, Westmorland, and has issue living, Charles Edward Gurney, *b.* 1955,—Jane Elizabeth Gurney, *b.* 1957. *Residence*, The How, Loughrigg, Ambleside, Westmorland.

Peace and hope.

Sister living—Anne Phillida, *b.* 1923; formerly in W.R.N.S.: *m.* 1946, Major Edward Mark Chetwynd-Stapylton, King's Roy. Rifle Corps [*see* V. Chetwynd, colls.]. *Residence*, 12, Kennington Palace Court, Sancroft St., SE11.

Half-Sister living—Lavender Mary (Allerton, Jedburgh), *b.* 1889: *m.* 1910, Capt. Walter Sandfield Medlicott, NH, who *d.* 1970, and has issue living, Dionysia, *b.* 1914,—Helen Victoria, *b.* 1916: *m.* 1939, Walter Mark Johnson, of Rutherford, Kelso, and Strathaird, Skye, and has issue living, David Mark *b.* 1941; Lt Cdr RN, Martin Stephen *b.* 1943: *m.* 1968, Ruth Gilbertson (and has issue living, Tobias Marm *b.* 1971), Alan Philip *b.* 1950,—Rosemary, *b.* 1922: *m.* 1st, 1946, Maj. Edward G. Bird, RM, who *d.* 1959; 2ndly, 1961, Charles D. Scott, of Mossburnford, Jedburgh, and has issue living (by 1st m.) Charles Godfrey *b.* 1947, George Godfrey *b.* 1956, Harmony *b.* 1951, (by 2nd m), Alexander William Douglas, *b.* 1963, Walter Stephen Douglas *b.* 1964.

Widows living of 2nd and 3rd Baronets—EMILY ELIZABETH (*Dowager Lady Pease*) (of Baysdale Cottage, Pinchinthorpe, Guisborough, Yorks.), adopted da. of the late James Smith, of Thornaby; is a J.P. for N. Riding of Yorkshire: *m.* 1922, as his third wife, Sir Alfred Edward Pease, 2nd baronet, who *d.* 1939.——IDA MARY (*Lady Pease*) (of Lowcross Gate, Hutton, Guisborough, Yorks.), da. of the late James Lawrance, of Cambridge: *m.* 1919, Sir Edward Pease, 3rd Bt., who *d.* 1963.

Collateral Branches living.

Issue of the late Capt. Christopher York Pease, Yeo., younger son of 2nd baronet, *b.* 1886; *d.* (killed in action during European War) 1918: *m.* 1910, Margaret Philippa, who *d.* 1959, da. of the late Walter Johnson, J.P. [Bell, Bt., *cr.* 1885] :—
Rachel Hebe Philippa, *b.* 1911 : *m.* 1940, Richard Selby Smith, Lieut.-Com., R.N.V.R., and Prof. of Educ. Tas. Univ., and has issue living, Christopher Selby (ERU, RSSS, ANU, Box 4, PO Canberra, ACT 2600), *b.* 1942; DPhil Oxon: *m.* 1967, Joy Miriam, da. of Thomas McGeehan, of Myrtleford, Vic., Aust., and has issue living, David Richard Selby *b.* 1969,—Peter Selby (18, Grant St., N. Fitzroy, Mel. 3068, Vic., Aust.), *b.* 1948; BCE: *m.* 1971, da. of John Holroyd, of Rosanna, Vic., Aust., and has issue living, Anne Jane *b.* 1974. *Residence*, 297, Nelson Rd., Hobart, Tasmania.

Issue of the late Rt. Hon. Joseph Albert Pease (2nd son of 1st baronet), who was *cr.* Baron Gainford 1916 [*see* that title].

PEASE, Creation (U.K.) 1920, of Hummersknott, Borough of Darlington, co. Durham.

Sir RICHARD THORN PEASE, 3rd *Baronet, b.*
May 20th, 1922; *s.* his father, *Sir* RICHARD
Arthur, 1969; ed. at Eton; late Capt. 60th
Rifles; Vice-Chm., Barclays Bank since 1970:
m. 1956, Anne, da. of the late Lt.-Col.
Reginald Francis Heyworth, 1st R. Dragoons
[see By. Tweedmouth], and formerly wife of
Fl. Lt. David Henry Lewis Wigan, RAFVR, and
has issue.

Arms—Per fesse azure and gules, a fesse nebuly ermine
between two lambs passant in chief argent, and in base upon a
mount proper a dove rising argent, holding in the beak a pea
stalk, the blossom and pods proper. Crest—Upon the capital of
an Ionic column a dove rising, holding in the beak a pea stalk
as in the arms.

Residence—Hindley House, Stocksfield-on-Tyne, Northumberland.

PAX ET SPES

Peace and hope.

Son living—RICHARD PETER, *b.* Sept. 4th, 1958.
Daughters living—Carolyn Thorn, *b.* 1957.——Nichola, *b.* 1961.
Brother living—Derrick Allix, *b.* 1927: *m.* 1951, the Hon.
Rosemary Portman, da. of 5th Viscount Portman, and has
issue living, Jonathan Edward, *b.* 1952,—Christopher
Berkeley, *b.* 1958,—Arthur David, *b.* 1961,—Rosalind
Jeannette, *b.* 1954: *m.* 1974, Evan Robert Hanbury, of
Burley-on-the-Hill, Oakham, Rutland [see Birkin, Bt.].
Residences, 2, Britten St., Chelsea, SW3; Upper Woodcott,
Whitchurch, Hants.

Sister living—Aline Thorn, *b.* 1919: *m.* 1st, 1940, Patrick Claude Hannay, Flying Officer Aux. Air
Force, who *d.* (killed in action) 1940; 2ndly, 1941, the 3rd Earl of Inchcape, who obtained a
divorce 1954; 3rdly, 1955 (m. diss. 1968), Thomas Chambers Windsor Roe, and has issue living,
(by 2nd m.) [see E. Inchcape],—(by 3rd m.) Patrick Rupert Windsor, *b.* 1960,—Oriel Melanie
Thorn, *b.* 1956. *Residence*, Crêt Bernard, Savuit sur Lutry, Vaud, Switzerland.

Aunt living—(daughter of 1st baronet)—Mary Ethelwyn, *b.* 1892.

Widow living of 2nd Baronet—LAUNA MARGARET (*Dowager Lady Pease*), (West Cottage, Richmond,
Yorks.), da. of Hughes Martin, late of Tullaghreine, co. Cork, and widow of Lt.-Col. Arnold
Ramsay Keppel [see E. Albemarle, colls.]: *m.* 1961, as his 2nd wife, Sir Richard Arthur Pease,
2nd Bt., who *d.* 1969.

The 1st baronet, Sir Arthur Francis Pease, son of the late Arthur Pease, M.P., brother of 1st Bt.
(cr. 1882 ante), was 2nd Civil Lord of the Admiralty, Jan. 1918 to March 1919, and High Sheriff for
co. Durham 1920.

PECHELL, Creation (G.B.) 1797, of Paglesham, Essex.
[Name pronounced "Peechell."]

Sir RONALD HORACE PECHELL, 9th *Baronet*, only
son of Maj. Hugh Charles Pechell, grandson of
Cdr. Charles Pechell, next brother of 5th Baronet,
b. June 4th, 1918; *s.* his kinsman, *Sir* PAUL, *MC*,
1972; ed. at HMS Worcester; late RAF Marine
Craft Section; Roy. Humane Soc. Medal; 1939-45
War: *m.* 1949, Dora, da. of the late John Cramp-
thorne.

Arms—Gules, a lion rampant or, on a chief of the second three
laurel branches erect proper. Crest—A lark proper charged with
two fleurs-de-lis in fesse or.

Address—14, Culver Rd., Felpham, Bognor Regis, Sussex.

VIX EA
NOSTRA VOCO

*I scarce call these things
my own.*

Sister living—Pauline Ruth Margaret, *b.* 1923: *m.* 1941, Rear-Adm.
Edmund Nicholas Poland (ret.), CB, CBE, of Langlawhill,
Broughton, Biggar, Lanarkshire, and has issue living, Raymond
Anthony, *b.* 1942; ed. at King's Coll., Taunton, and Imp.
Coll., London Univ. (MSc),—Roger Hugh, *b.* 1949, ed. at King's
Coll., Taunton, and Leeds Univ. (BSc),—Andrew Quentin,
b. 1960,—Celia Frances, *b.* 1947: *m.* 1969, John Neil Gardner
Govan.

Widow living of 8th Baronet—DORIS MARGERY (*Doris Lady Pechell*), (Flat 1, 35, Talbot Av.,
Talbot Woods, Bournemouth), da. of the late T. Drewitt Lobb, of Kent, and formerly wife of
Lt.-Col. Arthur Thomas Begg Green: *m.* 1971, as his 2nd wife, Sir Paul Pechell, MC, 8th Bt.,
who *d.* 1972.

Collateral Branch living.

Granddaughters of the late Capt. William Mortimer Pechell, brother of 5th baronet:—
Issue of the late Capt. William Mortimer Charles Pechell, *b.* 1850, *d.* 1932: *m.* 1883,
Emily Louisa, who *d.* 1938, da. of the late Major Montagu Barton, J.P., formerly of 85th
King's L.I.:—

Elaine Mortimer (of Baronmead, Rotherwick, Basingstoke), *b.* 1885: *m.* 1905, Lieut.-Col. **Alaric William Hepper,** R.E. (retired), who *d.* 1951, and has issue living, Montagu Geoffry Alaric, *CBE, b.* 1906; Brig. (ret.) late R. Sigs.; CBE (Mil) 1957: *m.* 1963, Marie-Arlette Jacqueline, yr. da. of Andre Quesnot, of Beauvais, France,—James Mortimer, *DSO, OBE* (of Hartnolls, Morchard Bishop, nr. Crediton, Devon), *b.* 1909; Brig. (ret.) late R.A.; 1939-45 War (despatches), Malaya 1948-51 (O.B.E., D.S.O.); O.B.E. (Mil.) 1949, D.S.O. 1951: *m.* 1st, 1938 (marriage dissolved 1956), Catherine Marjorie, da. of the late Lt.-Col. Alexander Edward King, R.A. (ret.); 2ndly, 1956, Patricia, da. of Newton Hastings Barton, and widow of Mervyn Llewellyn Hill, and has issue living (by 1st m.) Edward James Mortimer (Uplands, 61, Queen's Rd., Alton, Hants.), *b.* 1939: *m.* 1963, Judith, da. of the Rev. Joseph Heaven, of Stalbridge, Dorset (and has issue living, Felicity Jane *b.* 1965, Alice Mortimer *b.* 1967, Clare Emily *b.* 1970) Richard William *b.* 1942——Mildred Mortimer *b.* 1897; *m.* 1922. Lt.-Col. **Hugh Gilchrist Bell,** Indian Army (ret.), who *d.* 1956, and has issue living, Peter Mortimer Gilchrist (Linden House, South St., Blewbury, Berks.), *b.* 1925: *m.* 1949, Maureen Josephine Middleton, and has issue living, Conan Gilchrist *b.* 1949, Alexander Gilchrist *b.* 1960, Duncan William Gilchrist *b.* 1961, Josephine Christina Gilchrist *b.* 1957,—Nigel Mortimer Gilchrist (Ashmead, Newnham, Basingstoke) *b.* 1930: *m.* 1956, Nancy Barbara Leslie, da. of the late H. D. Sawtell, of E. Oakley, Basingstoke, Hants, and has issue living, Bridget Nancy *b.* 1957, Joanna Mortimer *b.* 1959, Anne Corinne Leslie *b.* 1962, Frances Jessie Gilchrist *b.* 1964. *Residence,* Newnham Hill, Basingstoke, Hants.

The ancestors of this family were established for many generations at Montauban in **Languedo** being ennobled by patent 1547. On the revocation of the "Edict of Nantes," Samuel de Péchels and his family were the objects of persecution, and after suffering extreme cruelties, M. Péchels was shipped with felons for the West Indies, whence he escaped to Ireland. His two daughters, who had been taken from him, were placed in a convent and brought up as Catholics: they afterwards obtained **a grant of all their father's lands,** by virtue of a letter from Louis XIV. His son, Jacob, afterwards spelt the name Pechell, and the patent of baronetcy so made out. Sir Thomas, the 4th baronet, assumed in 1801 the additional surname of Brooke, by royal sign-manual, for himself and his issue. The 4th baronet was a Vice-Adm., and sometime M.P. for Brighton (*L*). The 5th baronet assumed in 1860 the additional surname of Brooke on succession to the Baronetcy. The 6th and 7th baronets also used the surname of Brooke-Pechell.

PEEK, Creation (U.K.) 1874, of Rousdon, Devon.

The Master comes.

Sir FRANCIS HENRY GRENVILLE PEEK, 4th *Baronet; b.* Sept. 16th, 1915; *s.* his father, *Sir* WILFRID, *D.S.O.,* 1927; ed. at Eton, and at Trin. Coll., Camb.; ADC to Gov. of Bahama Islands 1938-39; 1939-45 War as Lt. Irish Guards (despatches): *m.* 1st, 1942, Ruby Joy Ann (who *d.* 1968, having obtained a divorce 1949), da. of Capt. Gordon Duff, late RGA, and widow of Sir Charles Thomas Hewitt Mappin, 4th Bt.; 2ndly, 1949 (m. diss. 1967), Marilyn, da. of Dr. Norman Kerr, of Eleuthera, Bahamas; 3rdly, 1967, Mrs. Caroline Kirkwood, da. of Sir Robert Lucien Morrison Kirkwood, and has issue by 2nd m.

Arms—Azure, an estoile argent; in chief three **crescents** of the last. **Crest**—Two hazel nuts, slipped proper.

Residences—Los Picos, Marbella, Spain; 63, Grosvenor Close, Nassau, Bahamas. *Clubs*—White's, Buck's.

Son living—By 2nd marriage—CHARLES EDWARD FRANCIS, *b.* May 5th, 1956.

Collateral Branch living.

Issue of the late Capt. Roger Grenville Peek 9th Lancers, 2nd son of 2nd baronet, *b.* 1888, *d.* (killed on duty in Ireland) 1921: *m.* 1919, the Hon. Joan Penelope Sclater-Booth (Flete House, Ermington, Ivybridge, S. Devon), da. of 2nd Baron Basing:—

William Grenville, *b.* 1919; ed. at Eton; Capt. late 9th Lancers; 1939-45 War (despatches): *m.* 1950, Lucy Jane, da. of the late Maj. Edward Dorrien-Smith, of Weir Point, Restronguet, Falmouth, and has issue living, Richard Grenville, *b.* 1955,—Jane Elizabeth, *b.* 1952,—Mary Susannah, *b.* 1957,—Katherine Julia, *b.* 1960. *Residence,* Hazelwood, Loddiswell, S. Devon.

Sir Henry William Peek, 1st baronet, sat as M.P. for Mid Surrey (*C*) 1868-84. The 3rd baronet Sir Wilfrid, was High Sheriff of Devon 1912, and served in Mesopotamia 1916-19 on Staff, despatches, DSO.

PEEL, Creation (U.K.) 1936, of Eyworth, Bedfordshire. [Extinct 1938.]

Col. the Hon. Sir SIDNEY CORNWALLIS PEEL, *C.B., D.S.O., T.D.,* 1st and last *Baronet.*

Widow living of 1st Baronet—(ADELAIDE MARGARET) DELIA (*Lady Delia Peel*), *D.C.V.O.,* da. of 6th Earl Spencer; Hon. F.R.C.M. 1955; was a Woman of the Bedchamber to H.M. Queen Elizabeth the Queen Mother 1939-50, since when an Extra Woman of the Bedchamber; C.V.O. 1947, D.C.V.O. 1950: *m.* 1914, Col. the Hon. Sir Sidney Cornwallis Peel, C.B., D.S.O., T.D. 1st baronet, who *d.* 1938, when the title became ext. *Residence,* Barton Turf, Norwich NOR 36Z.

BERESFORD-PEIRSE, Creation (U.K.) 1814, of Bagnall, Waterford.

Sir HENRY GRANT DE LA POER BERESFORD-PEIRSE, 6th *Baronet*; *b.* Feb. 7th, 1933; *s.* his father, *Sir* HENRY CAMPBELL DE LA POER, *CB*, 1972; ed. at Eton and Ontario Agric. Coll.; late Lt. Scots Gds.: *m.* 1966, Jadranka, da. of Ivan Njers, of Zagreb, Yugoslavia , and has issue.

Arms—Quarterly, 1st and 4th, azure, a ducal coronet between three cross-crosslets fitchée or, *Peirse;* 2nd and 3rd, argent, semée of cross-crosslets fitchée, three fleurs-de-lis sable, within a bordure wavy ermines, *Beresford.* **Crests**—1st, a cross-crosslet fitchée or, ensigned by a mural crown gules, *Peirse,* 2nd, out of a naval crown or, a dragon's head per fesse wavy azure and gules, the lower part of the neck transfixed by a broken tilting spear in bend sinister, in the mouth the remaining part of spear in the bend, the point upwards or, *Beresford.*

Nil nisi cruce.   *Seat*—Bedall Manor, Bedale, Yorks. *Residence*, 34, Cadogan Sq.
Depend only on the cross. SW1.

Sons living—HENRY NJERS DE LA POER, *b.* March 25th, 1969.—John, *b.* 1973.
Uncle living (son of 4th baronet)—*Rev.* Peter de la Poer (Warborough Vicarage, Oxford), *b.* 1907; ed. at Eton, and Magdalen Coll., Oxford; (MA); V. of Warborough, and Assist. Stewardship Adviser Diocese of Oxford: *m.* 1940, Muriel, da. of Joseph Griffiths, of Barry, S. Wales, and has issue living, Hugh de la Poer (5, Sunnymede Av., Carshalton Beeches, Surrey), *b.* 1941: *m.* 1963, Carolyn Ann Elizabeth Barker, and has issue living, Julian de la Poer *b.* 1966, Claire Elizabeth *b.* 1969,—Mark de la Poer, *b.* 1945,—Mary, *b.* 1948.—Ruth (twin), *b.* 1948.
Great Aunt living (da. of 3rd baronet)—Dorothy Harriet Julia, *b.* 1894: *m.* 1922, Com. Geoffrey Thomas Wright, R.N. (retired), and has issue living, Godfrey Peirse, *b.* 1926. *Residence,* Thornton Steward, near Ripon, Yorkshire.
Widow living of 5th Baronet—MARGARET (*Margaret, Lady Beresford-Peirse*) (Bedall Manor, Bedale, Yorks.), da. of Frank Morison Seafield Grant, of Knockie, Whitebridge, Inverness-shire: *m.* 1932, Sir Henry Campell de la Poer Beresford-Peirse, C.B., 5th Bt., who *d.* 1972.

Collateral Branches living.

Issue of the late Rev. Richard Windham de la Poer Beresford-Peirse, 2nd son of 3rd baronet, *b.* 1876, *d.* 1952 : *m.* 1st, 1910, Lady Lilian Katharine Campbell, who *d.* 1918, da. of the 3rd Earl Cawdor; 2ndly, 1924, Katherine Mabel Helen, who *d.* 1974, da. of William James Yorke-Scarlett, of Fyfield House, Andover [V. Valentia, colls.]:—
(By 1st m.), Francis Campbell de la Poer (18, Burntash Cottages, Sheet, Petersfield, Hants.), *b.* 1911; ed. at Eton; Group Capt. (ret.) RAF: *m.* 1st, 1936, Lady Katharine Lilian Edgcumbe (who obtained a divorce 1957), da. of 6th Earl of Mount Edgcumbe; 2ndly, 1958, Kathleen Graham Machattie, who *d.* 1972, and has issue living (by 1st m.), Susan Katherine, *b.* 1940: *m.* 1972, John Miles Bird, and has issue living, Tiffany *b.* 1973,—Philippa Jane, *b.* 1944: *m.* 1970, Nigel Hope.—Sybil Adelaide, *LRAM* (6, Queensdale Walk, W11 4QQ), *b.* 1912.—Barbara, *b.* 1915: *m.* 1942, Barry Martin Baker, of 6, Gloucester Mews, W2, and has issue living, Janet Bridget, *b.* 1943,—Katherine Elizabeth, *b.* 1946.—Lilian Bridget, *b.* 1918: *m.* 1945, Godfrey John Mapplebeck, OBE (Tigbourne Cottage, Hambledon, Godalming, Surrey), and has issue living, Anthony Peirse, *b.* 1946,—Althea Rosamund Louise, *b.* 1951,—Selina Bridget Lucy, *b.* 1960.

Grandchildren of the late Rev. Windham de la Poer Beresford-Peirse (infra):—
Issue of the late Capt. Arthur Cecil Proctor de la Poer Beresford-Peirse, MBE, *b.* 1890, *d.* 1970: *m.* 1916, Gertrude Anne Ormonde, who *d.* 1974, da. of the late Maj. Henry Wallis Prior-Wandesforde, BA, of Kirklington Hall, Yorks.:—
Michael Wandesforde de la Poer (North Lyham, Chatton, Alnwick, Northumberland), *b.* 1917; ed. at Lancing Coll.; a farmer: *m.* 1944, Joyce Franklin, da. of Phillip Hope Percival, of Potha Machakos, Kenya, and has issue living, Judith Anne Vivian, *b.* 1948,—Susan Alice Prior, *b.* 1950.—Robert Henry Windham de la Poer, *OBE* (30, Agett Rd., Claremont 6010, W. Aust.), *b.* 1922; late Flt. Lt. RAF; Dist. Officer, British N. Borneo, ret. 1964; OBE (Civil) 1963: *m.* 1st, 1943, Margaret, who *d.* 1972, da. of the late Edward Giles, of 72, Rue Kitchener, Alexandria, Egypt; 2ndly, 1974, Dorothy Maud, da. of Percy Donald Beard, of Mel., Vic., and has issue living (by 1st m.), Ian Arthur de la Poer, *b.* 1944: *m.* 1968, Janice, da. of Laurie Murphy, of Perth, W. Aust., and has issue living, Giles Windham de la Poer *b.* 1969, Angus Arthur de la Poer *b.* 1971, Digby John de la Poer *b.* 1975,—Patricia Margaret, *b.* 1950: *m.* 1972, Richard Stuart Callander, of Adelaide, S. Aust., and has issue living, Ian Stuart *b.* 1974.—Anne Ethel Mary, *b.* 1919; late Junior Cdr. ATS: *m.* 1942, Col. Peter Anthony Lowe, late RA, of Tamerton, Upton Lovell, Warminster, Wilts., and has issue living, David Michael Peirse, *b.* 1944; ed. at Sherborne; Capt. RA: *m.* 1968, Catherine, widow of Capt. J. A. Fleming, RA, and has issue living, Peter David *b.* 1969,—Michael Peter, *b.* 1949; ed. at Sherborne and Pa. Univ., USA: *m.* 1971, Rorie, da. of G. K. Waters, of Waymart, Pa., USA,—Elizabeth Anne, *b.* 1948: *m.* 1970, Richard George Goodman.

Granddaughter of the late Henry William de la Poer Beresford-Peirse, 2nd son of 1st baronet :—
Issue of the late Rev. Windham de la Poer Beresford-Peirse, Hon. Canon of Ripon, *b.* 1858, *d.* 1940: *m.* 1889, Ethel Milman Proctor, who *d.* 1948, da. of the late William Proctor Baker, of Brislington, Bristol:—
Mary Ethel, *b.* 1893: *m.* 1921, the Rev. Ronald Hartley, R. of Spennithorne, Leyburn, Yorks, who *d.* 1945. *Residence,* Churchbye House, Kirkby Malzeard, nr. Ripon, Yorks.

Grandchildren of the late John Peirse de la Poer Beresford, el. son of Rev. John George Beresford (infra):—
Issue of the late Capt. George Wilfred Bruce de la Poer Beresford, *b.* 1888, *d.* 1931 : *m.* 1920, Louise Barbara (who m. 2ndly, 19—, Ralph Jones Coles, who *d.* 1969), da. of Jacob Frederick Beck:—
John George (8, Cherokee Rd., London 72, Ont., Canada), *b.* 1923: *m.* 1947, Edith Joan, da. of Henry Thomas John Mellaby, and has issue living, John Henry, *b.* 1948: *m.* 1971, Meredith Jean, da. of Murray Victor Jones,—Peter Bruce, *b.* 1950: *m.* 1972, Julianne La Far, da. of Julian La Far Smith,—Diane Louise, *b.* 1949: *m.* 1972, Glen Churchill,—Cynthia Joan, *b.* 1952.—James Francis, *b.* 1925: *m.* 19—,—Mary Isabel, *b.* 1921, Robert Campbell Moreland, of 1630, E. Georgia Av., Phoenix, Az. 85016, USA, and has issue living, George Alexander, *b.* 1947: *m.* 1969, Marilyn Christine, da. of William Reginald Lower,—David Beresford, *b.* 1951: *m.* 1973, Leslie Michelle, da. of George Franklin Bowles.

Grandchildren of the late Rev. John George Beresford, 3rd son of 1st baronet:—
Issue of the late Rev. Henry William De la Poer Beresford, *b.* 1862, *d.* 1932: *m.* 1916, Constance Grace, who *d.* 1961, da. of James McLaurin, JP, of Verulam, Natal:—

Rev. Alfred de la Poer (The Anglican Rectory, Ugie, Cape Province, S. Africa), *b.* 1919; 1939-45 War in RN.

Issue of the late Rev. Walter Vevers de la Poer Beresford, *b.* 1864, *d.* 1908: *m.* 1902, **Eleanor** Mary, who *d.* 1944, da. of W. R. Staveley, of Harrogate, Yorkshire :—
Charles Denman de la Poer (10, Queens Rd., Blandford Forum, Dorset), *b.* 1906; ed. at Clifton, and at Worcester Coll., Oxford, MA: *m.* 1950, Pamela Croot, da. of the Rev. Frank Stone, MC, and has issue living, Marcus John de la Poer, *b.* 1954,—Julia Caroline, *b.* 1951.——Marcus Walter de la Poer (posthumous), *b.* 1909; ed. at Clifton, and at Merton Coll., Oxford (BMus, MA): *m.* 1942, Patricia Muriel, da. of C. Reginald Fox, of Plymouth, and has issue living, Charles Richard de la Poer (Barn Hall, The Rideway, Hemingford Abbots, Camb.), *b.* 1943; ed. at Clifton, Gonville and Caius Coll., Camb. (MA), and Reading Univ.: *m.* 1967, Tessa, da. of H. William Dean, of Cambridge, and has issue living, John Charles de la Poer *b.* 1973, Fiona Carolyn *b.* 1969,—Peter Marcus de la Poer, *b.* 1949. *Residence*, 34, Hillmorton Rd., Rugby.——Eleanor Caroline Fredrica, *b.* 1903. *Residence*, 68, Harlow Terr., Harrogate.

The 1st baronet, Adm. Sir John Poo Beresford, K.C.B., G.C.H., M.P. (Knight of the Tower and Sword), natural son of 1st Marquess of Waterford, and brother of Viscount Beresford (ext.), sat as M.P. for Coleraine 1809-12 and 1814-23, for Berwick-on-Tweed 1823-26, for Northallerton 1826-32, again for Coleraine 1832-33, and for Chatham 1835-37. The 3rd Bt., Sir Henry, was Chm. of N. Riding of Yorkshire County Council. The 4th baronet, Major Sir Henry Bernard de la Poer, D.S.O., was Under-Treasurer, Middle Temple for 17 years, and served in S. Africa 1900-01 as Major Imperial Yeo (DSO). The 5th Bt., Sir Henry Campbell de la Poer, CB, was Dir.-Gen., Forestry Commn. 1962-68.

PELLY, Creation (U.K.) 1840, of Upton, Essex.

God guiding, nothing hurts.

Sir (HAROLD) ALWYNE PELLY, M.C., 5th *Baronet ; b.* Aug. 27th, 1893 ; *s.* his father, *Sir* HAROLD, 1950 ; ed. at Wellington Coll., and at Merton Coll., Oxford ; is Major (retired) 7th Queen's Own Hussars ; European War 1914-19, as temporary Capt. Household Batn. (M.C.) : *m.* 1917, Caroline Earle (an O.St.J.), da. of the late Richard Heywood Heywood-Jones, of Badsworth Hall, Yorkshire and has issue.

Arms—Or, on a band engrailed azure, between two trefoils slipped vert, three martlets argent. **Crest**—Out of a crown vallery or, charged with three hurts, an elephant's head argent.

Residence—Preshaw House, Upham, Southampton. *Club*—Cavalry.

Sons living—JOHN ALWYNE, *b.* Sept. 11th, 1918; ed. at Canford and RMC; Maj. Coldm. Gds. (Reserve of Officers); 1939-45 War; a JP of Hants.; a DL for Hants. (High Sheriff 1970-71) *m.* 1st, 1945, Ava Barbara Anne, only da. of Brig. Keith Frederick William Dunn, CBE; 2ndly, 1950, Elsie May, da. of the late L. Thomas Dechow, of Nyamandhlovu, Rhodesia, and has issue living (by 2nd m.), Margaret Elizabeth Rosanne, *b.* 1952. *Residence*, Barn Close, Itchen Abbas, Winchester. *Club*, Guards.—— Richard Heywood (Loup House, Lyme Rd., Axminster, Devon), *b.* 1920; ed. at Wellington Coll.; FRICS; 1939-45 War as temp. Capt. RASC: *m.* 1948, Mary Elizabeth, da. of the late John Luscombe of North Huish, Devon, and has issue living, Richard John, *b.* 1951,—Jane Carol, *b.* 1949.——Frederick Michael (Lomer Farm, Warnford, Hants.), *b.* 1926: *m.* 1952, Jill Elizabeth, el. da. of the late Col. William Patrick Stewart Curtis, OBE [*see* Curtis, Bt., colls.], and has issue living Patrick Michael, *b.* 1954,—Alwyne Nicholas, *b.* 1955,—Frederick Peter Douglas, *b.* 1959.

Daughter living—Carol Patricia Benita, *b.* 1928 : *m.* 1947, Lieut.-Com. Thomas Michael Blake, R.N., and has issue living, Caroline Patricia, *b.* 1949,—Juliet, *b.* 1950,—Annabel, *b.* 1953. *Residence*, Court Farm, West Meon, Hampshire.

Brother living—Philip Vincent, *b.* 1898; ed. at Wellington Coll.; late Lt. Gren. Gds., FCA (ret.); 1914-18 War (despatches): *m.* 1932, Pamela Mary, who *d.* 1970, da. of Sir Frederick Henry Arthur Des Vœux, 7th Bt., and has issue living, Brian Raymond (4559, Longvue Drive, Murrywoods, Murrysville, Pa., USA), *b.* 1935: *m.* 1962, Dinah, el. da. of the Rev. Gerald Alfred Hutchison, of Littleton Drew Rectory, Chippenham, Wilts., and has issue living, Ivan Raymond *b.* 1963, Oliver Harding *b.* 1966, Annabel Marguerite Pamela *b.* 1970,—Antony Roger (Heathy Lea, Baslow, Derbys.), *b.* 1937: *m.* 1963, Susan Fiona, yr. da. of Maj. Denis William Powlett Millbank, TD [*see* Millbank, Bt.], and has issue living, Helen Fiona, *b.* 1964, Anna Maria Alice *b.* 1967,—Roland Des Voeux (Limes Court, Stansted, Essex) *b.* 1943; Solicitor 1967: *m.* 1968, Diana, da. of Capt. James FitzGibbon, RN (ret.) of Thames, NZ, and has issue living, Richard Philip *b.* 1971,—Philip Harold (Fir Tree Cottage, Duck St., Little Easton, Dunmow, Essex), *b.* 1948: *m.* 1970, Margaret Helen, da. of the late Canon Daniel Ernest John Anthony, of Sherston, Wilts.,—Pamela Margaret Evelyn *b.* 1933: *m.* 1957, Maurice John Greening of Ladyfield, Acton Turville, Badminton, Glos., and has issue living, Harold John *b.* 1958, James Timothy *b.* 1960, Maurice Vincent *b.* 1964, Mary Jacqueline *b.* 1962,—Clare Richenda, *b.* 1940: *m.* 1963, Henry Hartley, and has issue living, Mark William, *b.* 1964, Madeline Mary *b.* 1967. *Residence*, Old Rectory Cottage, Grittleton, Chippenham, Wilts.

Sister living—Mary Evelyn, *b.* 1901: *m.* 1921, Hugh Maurice Hill, who *d.* 1934, and has issue living, David Maurice, *b.* 1922: *m.* 1949, Elizabeth, only child of — Askham, of The Briars, Collingwood Rd., Northampton,—Rachel Dawn, *b.* 1928: *m.* 1954, Maj. R. L. Woods, 3rd The King's Own Hussars (ret.), of Green Farm, St. Martin, Jersey, and has issue living, Guy Robert William *b.* 1956, Anthony Nicholas Hugh *b.* 1958, Christopher Charles *b.* 1963, Julia Dawn *b.* 1961. *Residence*, Briar Cottage, Church Lane, Catsfield, Sussex.

Collateral Branches living.

Branch from 2nd son of 1st Baronet.

Grandchildren of the late Rev. Douglas Raymond Pelly, DSO (infra):—
Issue of the late Air Ch. Marshal Sir Claude Bernard Raymond Pelly, GBE, KCB, MC,
b. 1902, *d.* 1972: *m.* 1930, Margaret Ogilvie (Green Lane House, Orford, Suffolk),
da. of the late E. J. Spencer, of Hove:—
Rev. Raymond Blake (27, Maids' Causeway, Cambridge), *b.* 1938; ed. at Rugby, and Worcester
Coll., Oxford: *m.* 1964, Joanna Bickmore, yr. da. of John Anthony Clark, of Home Orchard,
Street, Som., and has issue living, Aidan John Raymond, *b.* 1970,—Monica, *b.* 1966,—Catherine
Hilda, *b.* 1967.——David Claude Raymond, *b.* 1941; ed. at Rugby.——Jane Elizabeth, *b.* 1931:
m. 1960, John I. Guest, of 760, Eden Pl., W. Vancouver, BC, Canada, and has issue living, John
William *b.* 1961,—Margaret Elizabeth *b.* 1960,—Maire Frances, *b.* 1963.

Grandchildren of the late Rev. Canon Raymond Percy Pelly, yr. son of the late
Raymond Pelly, 2nd son of 1st baronet:—
Issue of the late Rev. Douglas Raymond Pelly, D.S.O., *b.* 1865, *d.* 1943: *m.* 1898, Verena
Noélie, who *d.* 1952, da. of the late Rev. George W. Herbert, V. of St. Peter's,
Vauxhall. S E.:—
Peter Douglas Herbert Raymond, *CB, DSO, b.* 1904; Rear-Adm. (ret.); Dir. Gen. of Dept. of
Dockyards and Fleet Maintenance 1958-60, and Sec. Asso. of Consulting Engineers 1960-69;
1939-45 War (despatches, DSO, Officer of Order of Orange Nassau of the Netherlands); DSO
1942, CB (Mil) 1958: *m.* 1932, Gwenllian Violet, da. of the late Capt. the Hon. George Henry
Edwardes, MC [*see* B. Kensington, colls.], and has issue living, Sara Ann, *b.* 1937: *m.* 1968,
Peter Low, of Ardley House, Bicester, Oxon., and has issue living, Tobias Blake *b.* 1969, Nathaniel
Peter *b.* 1971,—Richenda, *b.* 1939: *m.* 1959, Lt.-Col. Douglas Alexander Nigel Capel Miers,
Queen's Own Highlanders (c/o Williams & Glyn's Bank Ltd., Holt's Branch, Kirkland House,
Whitehall, SW1), and has issue living, Lucian Douglas Ronald Capel *b.* 1962, Mary Ann Capel
b. 1961, Victoria Jane Capel *b.* 1964, Henrietta Alice Capel *b.* 1966,—Margaret Clare, *b.* 1942:
m. 1963, Timothy Lawrence Ireland, of Manor House, Billingshurst, Sussex, and has issue living,
Mark Peter Lawrence *b.* 1965, Blake Timothy Lawrence *b.* 1972, Nicola Gwenllian *b.* 1966,
Gemma Mary Clare *b.* 1974. *Residence,* Lowmersland, Les Rochers, Alderney.——Blake
Raymond, *OBE* (22, The Crescent, Vaucluse, Sydney, NSW; Union (Sydney) and Melbourne
Clubs), *b.* 1907; ed. at Wellington Coll., and Emmanuel Coll., Camb. (MA); Group Capt. (ret.)
RAAF; Chm. of Unity Life Assurance Ltd., and of Sun Alliance Insurance, Ltd.; Dept. Chm. of
Universities Board, a Dir. of other cos.; ADC to Gov. of NSW 1937-38, and a MLA 1950-57;
1939-45 War with RAAF in Middle East and Pacific (despatches, OBE), OBE (Mil) 1944: *m.*
1938, Mary Pamela Laidley, da. of Vincent Laidley Dowling, of Sydney, NSW, and has issue
living, Andrew Douglas Blake (8 Ridgeland Av., Killara, NSW), *b.* 1939; Dep. Production Man.
Television Corpn. Ltd.: *m.* 1961, Gaye Delyss, da. of Gordon Clempson Evans, of Chatsworth,
NSW, and has issue living, Fiona Elizabeth *b.* 1964, Vanessa Pamela *b.* 1967,—Michael Francis
Blake, *b.* 1947,—Angela Mary Blake, *b.* 1942: *m.* 1965, Lt.-Cdr. John Spencer Compton, RAN
(c/o 22, The Crescent, Vaucluse, Sydney, NSW 2030) and has issue living, James Gregory Spencer
b. 1967, Blake John Raynor *b.* 1970.——Stella Elizabeth Mary, *b.* 1908: *m.* 1934, William Richard
Gowers, DCL, of The Picks, Aston Upthorpe, nr. Didcot, Oxon., only son of the late Sir Ernest
Arthur Gowers, GCB, GBE, and has issue living, William Patrick, *b.* 1936; PhD: *m.* 1961,
Caroline Molesworth, yr. da. of Dr. Timothy Maurice, of 10, Kingsbury St., Marlborough, and
has issue living, William Timothy *b.* 1963, Rebecca *b.* 1965, Katherine *b.* 1970,—Ann Elizabeth
Mary, *b.* 1938: *m.* 1963, Roger Dennis Scott, DPhil, of 15, O'Rourke St., Weetangera, Canberra,
Aust., and has issue living, Richard Andrew *b.* 1964, Alexander Patrick *b.* 1967.

Issue of the late Brig.-Gen. Raymond Theodore Pelly, C.B., C.M.G., D.S.O., late Loyal
Regt., and a Mil. Knight of Windsor, *b.* 1881, *d.* 1952: *m.* 1910, Moriet Elsie Maxwell,
who *d.* 1965, da. of the late Maj.-Gen. Arthur Gethin Creagh, C.B. [Wolseley, Bt., *cr.*
1744, colls.] :—
Pamela Moriet, *b.* 1911: *m.* 1st, 1935, Frank Rough, who *d.* 1966; 2ndly, 1968, John Moore
Lorimer, of Rock Castle, Kilmacsimon, Bandon, co. Cork, and has issue living, (by 1st m.)
Caroline, *b.* 1940: *m.* 1963, John Ralph Lawrenson, of 89, Portland Rd., W11, and has issue
living, Frank Ralph *b.* 1967, Sophie Patricia *b.* 1968.——Patricia Carlota, *b.* 1915: *m.* 1948,
Alan H. Maccoy, DSC, RNVR, of Mockturtle Cove, Warwick, Bermuda, and has issue living,
Paul John Raymond, *b.* 1958,—Catherine Richenda, *b.* 1959.

Branch from 3rd son of 1st Baronet.

Grandchildren of the late Charles Brent Neville Pelly, el. son of the Rev.
Charles Henry Pelly, el. son of Charles Pelly, MCS, 3rd son of 1st baronet:—
Issue of the late Cdr. Charles Sinclair Pelly, RN, *b.* 1902, *d.* 1967: *m.* 1928, Caroline
Mary (Orchard Cottage, Chickerell, Weymouth), da. of Charles Samuel Facey, MB, of
Chickerell, Weymouth:—
Charles Patrick (c/o National Westminster Bank, Cardigan, Dyfed), *b.* 1935: *m.* 1966, Avis Olga,
da. of W. H. T. Woon, and has issue living, Nigel William Sinclair, *b.* 1968,—Stephen Grenville,
b. 1970,—Simon Charles Tregoning, *b.* 1973.——William Rupert Brent (Old Tracey, Fairford,
Glos.), *b.* 1943: *m.* 1967, Judith Rowena, da. of Prof. Norman Henry Gibbs, DPh [*see* E. Leven
and Melville, colls.], and has issue living, Benjamin Rupert William, *b.* 1972,—Zinnia Joanne,
b. 1970.——Jane *b.* 1931: *m.* 1957, Cdr. Kenneth Mills, RN, Myrtle Cottage, W. Ashling,
Chichester, and has issue living, Charles Richard, *b.* 1958,—Patrick George, *b.* 1963,—Cecilia
Jane, *b.* 1959.

Granddaughter of the late Rev. Charles Henry Pelly (ante):—
Issue of the late Charles Brent Neville Pelly, *b.* 1870, *d.* 1933: *m.* 1901, Annie Harvey,
who *d.* 1963, da. of the late Col. Alexander Sinclair Grove, DSO:—
Betty Joan (Montrose, Spa, Ballynahinch, co. Down), *b.* 1905: *m.* 1st, 1924 (m. diss. 1939), George
Wallis Newport Clark; 2ndly, 1939, Maj. Alexander Maitland Stuart, RA, who *d.* 1958, and has
issue living, (by 1st m.) Anne Joan Patricia, *b.* 1925,—Nancy Catherine, *b.* 1927,—Elizabeth,
b. 1930.

Grandchildren of the late Charles Brent Neville Pelly (ante):—
Issue of the late Major Henry Patrick Neville Pelly, *b.* 1912, *d.* (killed in action in Assam)
1945: *m.* 1939, Marion Veronica (of The Green, Upper Woodford, nr. Salisbury),
el. da. of Maj. Harry Sanderson, of Galashiels, Roxburghshire:—
George Michael Harvey, *b.* 1944; Capt. R.A.——Sarah Rutherford, *b.* 1941: *m.* 1966, Jonathan
Coldstream Lawley (c/o National & Grindlays Bank, 13, St. James Sq., SW1), and has issue
living, Thomas Henry, *b.* 1973,—Juliet Rosemary, *b.* 1969,—Katherine Jane, *b.* 1970.

Grandson of the late Major William Francis Henry Pelly (ante):—
Issue of the late Major William Francis Henry Pelly, Roy. Inniskilling Fusiliers, *b.* 1874,
d. (killed in action during European War) 1916 : *m.* 1901, Rosa Theodora, who *d.* 1940, da.
of William Vinicombe Davy :—
John Denis Cavendish, *b.* 1903: *m.* 1st, 1929, the Hon. Elizabeth Ponsonby (who *d.* 1940, having
obtained a divorce 1933), only da. of 1st Baron Ponsonby of Shulbrede ; 2ndly, 1935, Constance
Cecily, who *d.* 1964, da. of the late Capt. John Somerled Thorpe, MC [E. Clanwilliam, colls.].

Grandchildren of the late Maj. William Francis Henry Pelly (ante):—
Issue of the late Capt. Charles Nigel Pelly, OBE, *b.* 1908, *d.* 1966: *m.* 1934, Betty Joan
(Welcomes Farm, Kenley), da. of Lt.-Col. Leo Webster Cole, OBE, of Cairo:—

Christopher Patrick Cavendish (57, Corbière Av., Parkstone, Poole, Dorset), *b.* 1939: *m.* 1969, Brenda Amy Grosvenor, da. of Aldred Mutlow Grosvenor Herd, [*see* M. Bute, colls.], and has issue living, Nigel Christopher Grosvenor, *b.* 1973,—Amanda Rachel, *b.* 1970.——Marcus Nigel, *b.* 1941; R. Hong Kong Police: *m.* 1971, Peggy Jane, da. of Robert A. Wright, of Vic., BC, Canada.——Sally Joan, *b.* 1944: *m.* 1967, Paul Edmond de Rham, of 69, Fitzpain Rd., Ferndown, Wimborne, Dorset, BH22 8R2, and has issue living, Marc Edmond, *b.* 1970,—Joanna Claire, *b.* 1968.

Granddaughter of the late Rev. Charles Henry Pelly (ante):—
Issue of the late George Sinclair Pelly, E.D., *b.* 1885, *d.* 1946: *m.* 1912, Honora Isabel, who *d.* 1946, da. of the Rev. F. C. Boyd:—
Nora Patricia, *b.* 1914; has Kaisar-i-Hind Bronze medal: *m.* 1939, Lt.-Col. David Leslie Vivian Rowe, CBE, MC, of Pitmore, Sway, Lymington, Hants., and has issue living, Janet Vida (Prince Hill House, Worton, nr. Devizes), *b.* 1941: *m.* 1964 (m. diss. 1974) John Frederick Brierley, and has issue living, Hugh William David *b.* 1965,—Hilary Diana, *b.* 1948: *m.* 1974, Raymond Michael Groves.

Grandson of the late Charles Pelly, MCS (ante):—
Issue of the late Richard Stuart Pelly, *b.* 1846, *d.* 1928 : *m.* 1875, Frances Anne, who *d.* 1911, da. of George Robinson, J.P., of Roundstone, co. Galway :—
George Stuart, *b.* 1888: *m.* 1927, Adah Maude, da. of Ward Sovereign.

Grandchildren of the late Edward Pelly, 3rd son of Charles Pelly, MCS (ante):—
Issue of the late Edward Raymond Pelly, *b.* 1890, *d.* 1963: *m.* 1st, 1918, Frances Muriel, who *d.* 1943, da. of the late Rev. Alfred Shildrick, V. of Milton-under-Wychwood, Oxon.; 2ndly, 1944, Dorothy Jean Edna (8, Carlton House, 1251, Lawrence Av., Kelowna, British Columbia), el. da. of the late J. M. Dadson, of Winnipeg, Canada:—
(By 1st m.), John Edward, *b.* 1947.——Mary Ann, *b.* 1945: *m.* 1967, Douglas Alva Snowsell, of 9214-126A St., Surrey, BC, Canada, and has issue living, Brandon James *b.* 1969,—Colin David, *b.* 1970.

Grandchildren of the late Charles Pelly, M.C.S. (ante):—
Issue of the late Rear-Adm. Francis Raymond Pelly, *b.* 1850, *d.* 1907: *m.* 1881, Mary, who *d.* 1945, da. of the late Rev. Robert Posnett, R. of Laracor, co. Meath :—
Hutcheson Raymond (of Novar, Edgar Rd., Winchester), *b.* 1887; ed. at Cheltenham Coll., and at R.M.C.; is Lieut.-Col. Indian Army: European War 1914-18 (despatches): *m.* 1913, Kathleen Mary, da. of Edward Clifford-Walsh, of St. Aidens, Arklow, and has issue living, Dorothy Mary (of Flat 5B. 1, Wetherby Gardens, S.W.5), *b.* 1921; European War 1942-45 (despatches).——Emily Amy: *m.* 1919, Jerome O'Hanlon, Manager of National Bank.——Dorothy May Fairfax: *m.* 1916, Brig. Moray Martin Milne-Thomson, RA, who *d.* 1964, and has issue living, Pamela Mary, *b.* 1917: *m.* 1st, 1936, Lt. Arol Gage, RN, who *d.* (killed in action during European War) 1940; 2ndly, 1942 (m. diss. 19—), Leslie Glass, Counsellor, Foreign Ser.; 3rdly, 1957, Francis Hoyer Millar, MC, and has issue living, (by 2nd marriage) Nicholas *b.* 1945, Charles Luke Leslie *b.* 1951, Julia Mary *b.* 1943. *Residence,* Craig House, Montrose, Angus.

Branch from 4th son of 1st Baronet.

Grandchildren of the late Albert Champion Pelly, el. son of Albert Pelly, 4th son of 1st baronet:—
Issue of the late Albert Edgar Champion Pelly, *b.* 1879, *d.* 1958 : *m.* 1904, Agness May Hall (94, Western Rd., Crookes, Sheffield, 10):—
John, *b.* 1905 : *m.* 1st, 1931, Bertha Taylor, of Alfreton, Derbyshire, who *d.* 1935 ; 2ndly, 1942, Hilda May, el. da. of the late Thomas Brewer Barrow, and has issue living, (by 2nd marriage) Derek John, *b.* 1946. *Residence,* 28, Perrycroft Av., Bishopsworth, Bristol.——Kathleen Ruth, *b.* 1908: *m.* 1941, Kennard Hudswell Stallworthy. *Residence,* 25, Napier Rd., Hamworthy, Poole, Dorset.——Winifred Ina, *b.* 1910: *m.* 1936, Stanley Allison, and has issue living, John (21, Alderson Drive, Tickhill, Doncaster), *b.* 1938: *m.* 1962, Margaret Hartley, and has issue living, Paul James *b.* 1968, Claire Louise *b.* 1964,—Donald (2, Parkgrange Close, Norfolk Park, Sheffield, 2), *b.* 1941: *m.* 1964, Annita June Meredith, and has issue living, Steven John *b.* 1965,—Margaret, *b.* 1945. *Residence,* 94, Western Rd., Crookes, Sheffield, 10.

Grandchildren of the late Albert Edgar Champion Pelly (ante):—
Issue of the late Noel Henry Pelly, *b.* 1906. *d.* 1974: *m.* 1932, Marjorie, (2, Parkhurst Rd., Hoo, Rochester, Kent), da. of the late Frank Harold Hinton, of Forest Hill, SE:—
Raymond Frank (2, Parkhurst Rd., Hoo, Rochester, Kent), *b.* 1940: *m.* 1964, Janet, da. of Alexander Head, of 6, Long Lodge Drive, Walton-on-Thames, and has issue living, Nicole Louise, *b.* 1966,—Lisette Suzanne, *b.* 1969.

Issue of the late Edgar Frank Pelly, *b.* 1919, *d.* 1954 : *m.* 1941, Dulcie Vera Manning, of 4, Probyn Close, Frenchay, Bristol :—
Dorinda May, *b.* 1945: *m.* 1965, John Scoltock, of Jalna, 19, Christchurch Av., Downend, Bristol, and has issue living, Simon John, *b.* 1969,—Amanda Louise, *b.* 1968.——Julia Ruth, *b.* 1947: *m.* 1966, Terry Gilborson, and has issue living, Mark Julian, *b.* 1966.

Grandsons of the late William Henry Pelly (infra):—
Issue of the late Russell George Pelly, *b.* 1883, *d.* 1967: *m.* 1909, Frances Carruthers, who *d.* 1944, da. of the late Sir Francis Carruthers Gould, of Upway, Porlock, Taunton:—
Russell Steele (Mount Craigie, Verena Terr., Perth), *b.* 1910; ed. at Mercers' Sch., and Edinburgh (BSc), and Oxford Univs.; Colonial Forest Ser. (ret.); Regional Officer, Scottish Woodland Owners' Asscn. Ltd.: *m.* 1945, Agnes Mysie, da. of the late F. H. Macpherson, solicitor, of Ayr, and has issue living, Frances Elsie, *b.* 1947,—Lindsay Grace, *b.* 1950,—Mysie Ann, *b.* 1953.——Michael Beaumont (c/o Westminster Bank, 36, High St., Maldon, Essex) *b.* 1912.

Granddaughter of the late Russell George Pelly (ante):—
Issue of the late Anthony Roger Pelly, *b.* 1915, *d.* 1972: *m.* 1st, 1947, (m. diss. 1965), Joan, da. of the late Gp. Capt. Martin William Flack, CBE, MB: 2ndly 1968, Mrs. Eileen Cleveland (73, Warrington Cres., Maida Vale, W9), da. of the late Joseph Prior:—
(By 1st m.) Sarah Jane, *b.* 1949.

Granddaughters of the late Albert Champion Pelly (ante):—
Issue of the late William Henry Pelly, *b.* 1847, *d.* 1932: *m.* 1st, 1882, Eleanor Lucy, who *d.* 1883, da. of John Sisson Steele, MRCS; 2ndly, 1907, Edith Anne, who *d.* 1968, da. of the late W. H. Nash, of Reigate:—
(By 2nd m.) Edith Streatfeild, *b.* 1908: *m.* 1940, Alaistair Reginald Scott Cumming, of The Chantry, E. Coker, nr. Yeovil, Som., and has issue living, Alaistair Michael *b.* 1941; Maj. Gordon Highlanders: *m.* 1964, Hilary Katherine Gray, and has issue living, Emma Marion *b.* 1967, Fiona Helen Jean *b.* 1969,—Ian Scott *b.* 1946.

Issue of the late Lieut. Frederic Streatfeild Pelly, R.N., *b.* (twin) 1848, *d.* 1914: *m.* 1895, Harriot Wren Plaistowe, who *d.* 1939.
Freda Sylvia, *b.* 1902: *m.* 1954, Prof. Philip Kemp, of Highgate, P.O. 39, Ramsgate, Natal.

Issue of the late Capt. John Henry Pelly, R.N., *b.* (twin) 1848, *d.* 1920: *m.* 1885, **Mary Rose**, who *d.* 1927, da. of James Lyon Thorne, formerly Fleet-Paymaster R.N. :— Mary Rose (Westerclose, Bishops Sutton, Alresford, Hants) *b.* 1893.

Granddaughters of the late Capt. John Henry Pelly, RN (ante):—
Issue of the late Charles Thorne Pelly, *b.* 1890, *d.* 1966: *m.* 1922, Lilian May (7, Curzon Rd., Weybridge, Surrey), da. of the late Rear-Adm. John William Ham, CB :—
Diana May, *b.* 1923: *m.* 1946, Anthony Fairey Needell, of 7, Curzon Rd., Weybridge, Surrey, and has issue living, Michael Anthony, *b.* 1948,—Timothy Richard, *b.* 1951,—Christopher Charles, *b.* 1967.——Pauline Elizabeth, *b.* 1927: *m.* 1st, 1948, Peter Anthony Welsford; 2ndly, 1961, Aveling Jocelyn Pickard, of The Coach House, Copsen Lane, Oxshott, Surrey, and has issue living (by 1st m.) Paul Simon, *b.* 1953,—Penelope Ann, 1949.

Branch from 5th son of 1st Baronet.

Grandson of the late John Gurney Richard Pelly, son of the late Capt. Richard Wilson Pelly, RN, 5th son of 1st baronet:—
Issue of the late Vivian Gurney Pelly, *b.* 1881, *d.* 1949 : *m.* 1st, 1907, Dorothy Penrose, who *d.* 1972, el. da. of William Henry Sewell, formerly of Epping Place, Epping; 2ndly, 1946, Hilda Victoria Cole:—
(By 1st marriage) Douglas Gurney, *b.* 1910; formerly Lt. Maritime R.A.; High Sheriff of Essex 1962: *m.* 1935, Monica, da. of the late Lt.-Col. Arthur Wignall Tate, DSO [*see* Tate, Bt., colls.], and has issue living, John Gurney (Spring Hill, E. Malling, Kent), *b.* 1938: *m.* 1973, Vanda Joan, da. of Col. Hubert Mortimer Allfrey, MC, TD [E. Romney, colls.], and has issue living, Samuel Gurney *b.* 1974,—William Henry, *b.* 1946: *m.* 1975, Anne, yr. da. of Francis Byrne, of 76, Rivermead Court, Hurlingham, SW,—Claire Rose (*Countess of Pembroke and Montgomery*), *b.* 1943: *m.* 1966, the 17th Earl of Pembroke and Montgomery, of Wilton House, Salisbury. *Residence*, Swaynes Hall, Widdington, nr. Newport, Essex.

Grandsons of the late Capt. Richard Wilson Pelly, RN (ante):—
Issue of the late Rev. Canon Richard Arnold Pelly, *b.* 1856, *d.* 1949: *m.* 1st, 1882, **Margaret Jane**, who *d.* 1903, da. of the late Thomas Fowell Buxton [Buxton, Bt., colls., *cr.* 1840]; 2ndly, 1906, Dora Isobel, who *d.* 1915, da. of Col. Sir (Edward) Hildred Carlile, 1st Bt., C.B.E. :—

(By 1st m.) *Rev. Canon* Richard Lawrence, *b.* 1886; ed. at Marlborough, and at Clare Coll., Cambs (BA 1910, MA 1912); formerly Lecturer at Ridley Hall, Cambridge, Vice-Principal, Bishop's Coll. Calcutta, Chap., Old Mission Church, Calcutta and V. of Farley cum Pitton, Salisbury, Wilts.; Master of St. Nicholas Hospital, Salisbury 1957-59; Hon. Canon of Salisbury 1957-71; European War 1915-18, as Chap. to the Forces (despatches): *m.* 1927, Rosa Salome, M.B., da. of the late Rt. Rev. John Wordsworth, D.D., 93rd Lord Bishop of Salisbury [Williams, Bt., *cr.* 1915], and has issue living, Richard Christopher Wordsworth (4, Kiln Croft, Etwall, Derbys.), *b.* 1938; ed. at Marlborough, and at Clare Coll., Camb. (BA): *m.* 1962, Ruth Elinor, da. of Philip Askey, of Weaverham, Ches., and has issue living, Richard Hugh *b.* 1964, David John *b.* 1972,— Katherine Jane *b.* 1966,—Hugh John Wordsworth, *b.* 1945; ed. at Marlborough; MB, BS, DCH: *m.* 1972, Jane Mary Fergusson,—Elizabeth Mary, *b.* 1929: *m.* 1952, Wyndham M. Jordan, BM, BCh, of 81, Beccles Rd., Bungay, Suffolk, and has issue living, Christopher Wyndham *b.* 1956, Rosalind Cicely *b.* 1955, Diana Salome *b.* 1959, Alison Faith *b.* 1961,—Rosa Jane, *b.* 1931,—Juliet Rachel, *b.* 1933: *m.* 1964, William Gibbins Webb, of Vine Cottage, The Common, Cranbrook, Kent, and has issue living, Rachel Sally *b.* 1965, Rhoda Jane *b.* 1966,—Robina Catherine, *b.* 1935: *m.* 1958, Timothy Sherwood Hattersley, MB, BChir., of 100, Harnham Rd., Salisbury, and has issue living, Andrew Tym *b.* 1958, William John *b.* 1960, Richard Wordsworth *b.* 1964. *Address*, 20, Middle St., Salisbury, Wilts.——Francis Brian, *AFC* (Feering Croft, Priory Drive, Stanmore, Middx.), *b.* 1889; ed. at Sherborne, and at Trin. Coll., Camb.; 1914-18 War as Lt. RAF (AFC); Gen. Sec., Shaftesbury Homes and Arethusa Training Ship, 164, Shaftesbury Av., WC2, 1927-54: *m.* 1913, Edith Beatrice, da. of the late Rev. William James Packe, V. of Ferring, Kelvedon, and has issue living, Michael Brian (c/o Bank of Scotland, 24, George St., Perth, PH1 5JW), *b.* 1915; ed. at Bryanston Sch.; CEng: *m.* 1946, Mary Margaret, da. of Herbert Southerden Burn, CBE, of Ivy Cottage, Cleeve, nr. Bristol, and has issue living, Roger Brian *b.* 1950; MSc, David Arnold *b.* 1954, Nicola Susan *b.* 1948: *m.* 1972, Peter Charles Jeffery, of 556, Victoria Av., Westmount, Montreal, Canada,—Peter Richard (of Green Farm, Bovingdon Green, Bovingdon, Herts), *b.* 1916; ed. at Bryanston Sch.: *m.* 1945, Kathleen Irene, da. of the late S. W. Moorhouse, of Guildford, and has issue living, Lynda Ann, *b.* 1947, Georgina Kathleen, *b.* 1951,—Margaret Beatrice (6, St. Lukes St., SW3), *b.* 1921: *m.* 1st, 1943, Theodore Sanger, from whom she obtained a divorce 1959; 2ndly, 1969, Jovan Ulic, of Belgrade, and has issue living (by 1st m.), Melody *b.* 1947, Katrina Scarlett *b.* 1952.

Grandchildren of the late Rev Canon Richard Arnold Pelly (ante):—
Issue of the late Capt. Arthur Roland Pelly, *b.* 1895, *d.* 1966: *m.* 1920, Phyllis Elsie, who *d.* 1974, da. of the late Alexander Duff Henderson, of Hampstead, NW:—
John Gordon (Aniceford House, Stockton-on-Teme, Worcs.), *b.* 1923; ed. at Marlborough; Lt. RNVR; 1939-45 War (despatches): *m.* 1947, Patricia Maureen, da. of the late Maj. Hugh Clarence Fuller, of Arran Lodge, Crossabeg, co. Wexford, and has issue living, John Henry Patrick Fuller, *b.* 1953,—Priscilla Jane, *b.* 1949: *m.* 1972, David Dalziel Mundell of Elgin, Condamine, Qld., and has issue living, Sarah Richenda *b.* 1973,—Caroline Anne, *b.* 1950: *m.* 1973, Michael Eliot Howard, of Pixham Cottage, Callow End, Worcester.——Derek Roland (Ducklake, Ashwell, nr. Baldock, Herts.), *b.* 1929; ed. at Marlborough, and Trin. Coll., Camb. (MA): *m.* 1953, Susan, da. of John Malcolm Roberts, of 4, Macartney House, Chesterfield Walk, Greenwich, SE10, and has issue living, Samuel Roland, *b.* 1960,—Rosemary Jane *b.* 1955,— Catherine Susan, *b.* 1958.——Mary Duff, *b.* 1921: *m.* 1945, George T. B. Stevens, solicitor, of Quorndon House, Mount Rd., Hook Heath, Woking, Surrey, and has issue living, Charles Bridges, *b.* 1946; ed. at Cheltenham Coll.: *m.* 1972, Jeanette MacDonald, da. of the late Walter Moore, of Barbados,—David George, *b.* 1951,—Lucia Mary, *b.* 1956.——Janet Elizabeth, *b.* 1926: *m.* 1953, Michael L. Fenwick, PhD, of 5, Belbroughton Rd., Oxford, and has issue living, Alison Jane, *b.* 1955,—Anne Richenda, *b.* 1957,—Juliet Nicola, *b.* 1959.

Grandchildren of the late Capt. Richard Wilson Pelly, RN (ante):—
Issue of the late Adm. Sir Henry Bertram Pelly, K.C.V.O., C.B., *b.* 1867, *d.* 1942: *m.* 1904, Lilian Katharine Hawkshaw, who *d.* 1966, da. of Sir William Vincent, 12th Bt. (*cr.* 1620, ext.):—
Douglas Charles Vincent (The Old Vicarage, Hentland, Ross-on-Wye, HR9 6LP), *b.* 1908; Com. RN (ret.); 1939-44 War (despatches): *m.* 1938, Catherine Loraine, da. of Edwyn Conran, of Hurlingham, Buenos Aires, and has issue living, Douglas Edwyn Vincent, *b.* 1951 (152, Portsmouth Rd., Cobham, Surrey), *b.* 1951: *m.* 1974, Susan Margaret, da. of George Hards, of Cobham, Surrey, and has issue living, Jessica *b.* 1975,—Anne Loraine, *b.* 1939: *m.* 1966, Lachlan Nicholas Ferrar Forbes, BA (c/o Milton House, Milton, Cambridge, CB4 4AD), and has issue living, Lachlan Pelly *b.* 1970, Angus Maxwell *b.* 1971,—Gillian Esmé, *b.* 1942,—Catherine Elizabeth, *b.* 1948: *m.* 1973, Simon Maxwell (c/o UNDP, 21, Kasturba Gandhi Marg, New Delhi, 110001, India).——Adrian Vincent, *MVO* (Furnace Farmhouse, St. Weonards, Hereford, HR2 8NZ), *b.* 1919; late Lt. RNVR; HM's Land Steward at Windsor 1951-71; a JP; *cr.* MVO (5th class) 1962, MVO (4th class) 1971: *m.* 1975, Margaret Esterel, da. of Roger Lambert, of Cuckseys Farm, Bletchingley, Surrey.——Esterel Alice Muriel, *OBE*, *b.* 1906; OBE (Civil) 1953: *m.* 1928, Brig. Philip Reginald Antrobus, CBE, MC, son of the late Sir Reginald Lawrence Antrobus,

KCMG, CB. *Residence*, Ashford Chace, Steep, Petersfield, Hants.——Andrea Evelyn, *b.* 1917: *m.* 1970, the Rev. John Algernon Peyton Hoskyns, of Riverknoll, Hoarwithy, Hereford [*see* Hoskyns, Bt., colls.].

Grandchildren of the late Edmund Nevill Richard Pelly, 3rd son of the late Capt. Richard Wilson Pelly, RN (ante):—
Issue of the late Capt. John Noel Pelly, C.B.E., R.N., *b.* 1888, *d.* (on active ser. during European War) 1945 : *m.* 1924, Rosalind, who *d.* 1957, da. of the late R. G. Gatehouse, of Abbot's Grange, Bebington, Cheshire :—
John Stewart Gatehouse, *b.* 1930 : *m.* 1960, Helen Josephine, da. of Denys Heaton Hirst, of 46, Lightridge Rd., Fixby, Huddersfield, and has issue living, Jennifer Œnone, *b.* 1965,—Catherine Allison, *b.* 1967,—Helen Rosalind, *b.* 1969,—Isobel Serena, *b.* 1973. *Residence*, Great Wilsey Farm, Haverhill, Suffolk.——Rosemary Œnone, *b.* 1927: *m.* 1956, Gordon Nelmes, and has issue living, John Pelly, *b.* 1957,—Godfrey Edward, *b.* 1959,—Edmund Gordon, *b.* 1965,— Rosalind Jane, *b.* 1962. *Residence*, Gardner's Farm, Hatfield Peverel, nr. Chelmsford, Essex.

Issue of the late Lt.-Col. Edmund Godfrey Pelly, D.S.O., M.C., *b.* 1889, *d.* (on active ser. during 1939-45 War) 1939: *m.* 1919, Isabel Amy (Bull Cottage, 59, High St., Dorchester-on-Thames), da. of the late Robert Henry Fowler, of 5, Park Square West, NW:—
Robert Hubert, *b.* 1923; ed. at Shrewsbury, and at Trin. Coll., Camb. (BA 1950); 1939-45 War as Capt. Lothians and Border Yeo. (despatches): *m.* 1951, Eirolys Elizabeth, da. of Maj. le Gendre George William Horton-Fawkes, O.B.E., of Farnley Hall, Otley, Yorkshire, and has issue living, Richard Fowler, *b.* 1955,—Robert Simon Horton, *b.* 1956,—Serena Louise, *b.* 1953: *m.* 1974, Stephen John Richards. *Residence*, Brook House, Leathley, Otley, Yorks.——Antoinette Joan, *b.* 1920: *m.* 1942, Capt. Kenneth W. Macleod, of 4, Dunanellerich, Harlosh, Isle of Skye, and has issue living, Neil Godfrey, *b.* 1947: *m.* 1973, Sheila Anne, da. of Crawford Tyler, of St. Marys, Ont., Canada,—Allison Ann, *b.* 1946: *m.* 1968, Robert Hellett, of Kimbolton, who *d.* 1970, and has issue living, Robert Henry *b.* 1970,—Flora Margaret, *b.* 1952.

Grandchildren of the late Herbert Cecil Pelly (infra) :—
Issue of the late Humphrey Richard Pelly, *b.* 1886, *d.* 1955 : *m.* 1916, Barbara Vidal, who *d.* 1965, da. of Frederick Scrutton, of Woolpits. Nutfield, Surrey:—
Diana, *b.* 1917: *m.* 1936, Byas Sheppard, of Charwelton Cottage, Upper Dean, Huntingdon, Cambs., PE18 0LY, and has issue living, Byas Nimrod, *b.* 1938,—Humphrey Gerald Sheppard, *b.* 1953,— Belinda Rose, *b.* 1939,—Diana Lucy, *b.* 1942,—Theresa Louise, *b.* 1954.——Juliet, *b.* 1920: *m.* 1946, George Ian Bray, MBE, of The Chestnuts, Bishop Monkton, Harrogate, and has issue living, Rose Elizabeth, *b.* 1950,—Annabel Lucy (twin), *b.* 1950.

Issue of the late Capt. Gilbert Cecil Pelly, R.N., *b.* 1892, *d.* 1961 : *m.* 1921, Constance Margery, who *d.* 1952, da. of the late F. E. Tweenbrook Glazebrook, of Manila :—
David Cecil, *b.* 1922; Lt.-Cdr. R.N. (ret.); 1939-45 War (despatches, French Croix de Guerre): *m.* 1950, Angela Mary, da. of Capt. Wilfrid Pearse Gandell, CBE, R.N. (ret.), and has issue living, Richard Cecil; ed. at Marlborough and Selwyn Coll., Camb. (MA); Lt. RN: *m.* 1974, Fleur Veronica, only da. of John Desmond Proctor, of North View, High Trees Rd., Reigate, Surrey,—Nicholas John, *b.* 1953; ed. at Marlborough, and Birmingham Univ. (BSc),—Patrick David, *b.* 1955,—Gilbert Ralph, *b.* 1966,—Alexandra Helen, *b.* 1961. *Residence*, Walden, Marley Common, Haslemere, Surrey.——John Kenneth (1406, 61, Richview Rd., Islington, Ont., M9A 4M8, Canada), *b.* 1923; Lt. (ret.) RN: *m.* 1946, Joan Campbell, only da. of J. C. Fraser, of Cedar Ridge, Scarborough, Ont., Canada, and has issue living, David Fraser, BSc (RMC) *b.* 1948 (RR1, Glenburnie, Ont., Canada); Capt. (Sea) Canadian Armed Forces: *m.* 1970, Sara Lynn, da. of the late Alan Nicholson, of Charlottetown, PEi, Canada,—Brian Gordon, *b.* 1954,—Elizabeth Gail, *b.* 1951.——Peter Jeremy (Upper Langridge Farm, Lansdown, Bath, BA1 9BW), *b.* 1930: *m.* 1953, Dorothy Joan (Joanna), da. of Capt. Thomas William Robert Hill, RA [*see* Dick-Cunyngham, Bt. (ext.)], and adopted da. of Christopher Ransom, of Monk's Wall, Otterton, Budleigh Salterton, and has issue living, Anthony John, *b.* 1956,—Lyndsay Madeleine, *b.* 1954,—Elizabeth Joanna Clare, *b.* 1958,—Nicolette Jane, *b.* 1960,—Ann Catherine, *b.* 1964.

Issue of the late Sir Kenneth Raymond Pelly, MC, *b.* 1893, *d.* 1973: *m.* 1919, Elspeth Norna (Newstead Chyll, Colgate, Sussex), da. of the late Robert Campbell Grant, of Hale Edge, S. Nuffield:—
Andrew Desmond, *DFC* (Halings, Balcombe, Haywards Heath, Sussex), *b.* 1923; formerly F/Lt. RAF: *m.* 1945, Nancye Jean, da. of Lt.-Col. Eric Tillyer Tatham [*see* B. Digby, colls.], and has issue living, Ian Raymond, *b.* 1949: *m.* 1974, Alana Murray, of Brisbane, Aust.,—Angela Pauline, *b.* 1947: *m.* 1970, Douglas Frederick Wentzel, of 152, Stinson St., La Salle H8R 3J8, Quebec, and has issue living, Karla Juli-Anne *b.* 1973,—Christine Mary, *b.* 1952: *m.* 1972, Timothy Cross, Lt. RAOC, of 2, Talavera Rd., Chiseldon, nr. Swindon, Wilts., and has issue living, Alexander Leigh *b.* 1974,—Fiona Elizabeth, *b.* 1955.——Ursula Elspeth (New Barn, Colgate, Sussex), *b.* 1921; formerly WRNS: *m.* 1945, Lt. Robert George Malloch Brown, SANF(V), who *d.* 1967, and has issue living, George Mark, *b.* 1953.

Grandchildren of the late Capt. Richard Wilson Pelly (ante):—
Issue of the late Alfred Digby Pelly, *b.* 1862, *d.* 1940: *m.* 1899, Evelyn Sophia, who *d.* 1970, da. of the late Rev. Edward John Harford [Bridges, Bt.]:—
Richard Edward, *b.* 1905: *m.* 1941, Diana Marthe Desgrand Mitchell, and has issue living, Louise Sophia PELLY (1100, McGregor Av., Apt. 1520, Montreal, Quebec, Canada), *b.* 1943; resumed the surname of Pelly: *m.* 1967 (m. diss. 1971), Donald MacTaggart,—Harriet Elizabeth Annabel, *b.* 1948. *Residence*, West End, Coggeshall, Essex.——Violet Evelyn, *b.* 1900: *m.* 1923, the 10th Marquis de Ruvigny, who *d.* 1941, and has issue living, Michael Francis Wriothesley Meredith Tom Bridges, *b.* 1927; *s.* his father as 11th Marquis de Ruvigny (*cr.* France 1652): *m.* 1956, Patricia Kirkpatrick, el. da. of the late C. Kirkpatrick Pile, of Barbados, and has issue living, Rupert Francis James Henry *b.* 1959, Rachel Anne *b.* 1956. *Residence*, 3, Langside Av., Roehampton, SW15.

Grandchildren of the late Percy Leonard Pelly, 9th son of 1st baronet :—
Issue of the late Percy John Pelly, *b.* 1853, *d.* 1932 : *m.* 1879, Florence Marion, who *d.* 1953, da. of the late Henry Butler, of Chipstead, near Reigate :—
Iva Marion, *b.* 1900; late Ch. Com. ATS. *Residence*, The Little House, Quenington, Cirencester, Glos.

Issue of the late Leonard Pelly, *b.* 1856, *d.* 1913 : *m.* 1880, Elizabeth, who *d.* 1930, da. of the late Charles A. Leatham, of Gunnersgate Hall, York :—
Eric Percy Leonard, *b.* 1894: ed. at Wellington Coll., and at Trin. Coll., Camb. ; Lieut. Essex Yeo. (Reserve); 1914-18 War (wounded): *m.* 1924, Helen Marjorie, who *d.* 1968, da. of the late Edmund Richmond Wade, of Boston, U.S.A., and has issue living, Rosamund Ann, *b.* 1927 : *m.* 1950, Elliott Merriam Viney, DSO, MBE, TD, FSA, of Green End House, Aylesbury, Bucks, and has issue living, Diana Susan *b.* 1952, Amanda Louise *b.* 1954. *Residence*, Juniper Hill, Penn, Bucks.

The Pellys were settled at Poole, Dorset, until Capt. John Pelly HEICS (*d.* 1762) married Elizabeth, da. and heir of Henry Hinde, of Upton, Essex. Their grandson, Sir John Henry Pelly, 1st Bt. of Upton, was Gov. of the Bank of England, and the Hudson Bay Company, and Dep. Master of Trinity House.

Pennington-Ramsden, see Ramsden.

PERKS, Creation (U.K.) 1908, of Wykham Park, Neithrop, co. Oxford.

Sir (ROBERT) MALCOLM MEWBURN PERKS, 2nd *Baronet*; *b.* July 29th, 1892 ; *s.* his father, *Sir* ROBERT WILLIAM, 1934; sometime Lieut. R.N.V.R. : *m.* 1917, Neysa Gilbert, da. of the late Rev. Dr. Cheney, of New York, and has issue.

Arms—Azure, a lymphad or, pennon flying to the dexter gules, on a chief masoned proper two annulets of the second. Crest—In front of two anchors in saltire or, a lion's head erased azure.
     Residence—Wistaria Lodge, 45, Homefield Rd., Worthing, Sussex.

Daughters living—Rosemary, *b.* 1919; sometime Section Officer W.A.A.F.: *m.* 1942, Lieut.-Col. Frederick Onslow Alexander Godwyn Bennett, London Rifle Brig., and has issue living, James Malcolm, *b.* 1949,—Elaine Roselle, *b.* 1945.—Louise Rosemary, *b.* 1946.—Claire Rosamund, *b.* 1951,—Francesca Rosalind, *b.* 1959. *Residence*, Downe Lodge, Downe, near Farnborough, Kent.——Felicia Dorothy, *b.* 1921: *m.* 1st, 1940 (m. diss. 1958), Robert Lyle; 2ndly, 1959, Ruggero Galletta, of 16, Charterhouse Rd., Godalming, Surrey, and has issue living, (by 1st m.) Hugh Robert, *b.* 1941,—Philip Dominic, *b.* 1949,—Felix Gregory, *b.* 1953,—Thelma Cristina Elizabeth, *b.* 1944,—Miranda Maria, *b.* 1946, (by 2nd m.) Flavio Raul Turiddu *b.* 1960,—Giuseppina Graziana Eva Francesca, *b.* 1959.

With honour and love.

Sister living—Mildred Mewburn, *b.* 1882: *m.* 1913, William Hertslet Gull.

The 1st baronet, Sir Robert William Perks, was M.P. for E. Lindsey, or Louth Div. of Lincolnshire (*L*) 1892-1910.

PERRING, Creation (U.K.) 1963, of Frensham Manor, Surrey.

Sir RALPH EDGAR PERRING, 1st *Baronet*, son of the late Col. Sir John Ernest Perring; *b.* March 23rd, 1905; ed. at Univ. Coll. Sch.; Chm. Perring Furnishings, Ltd., and John Perring, Ltd.; a Lieut. for City of London, JP Co. London, a Gov. Christ's Hosp., St. Bartholomew's Hosp., and Imperial Coll. of Science and Technology, Vice-Pres. of Roy. Bridewell Hosp., Pres. of Langbourn Ward Club, and a KStJ; Master of Tin Plate Workers' Co. 1944-45, a Member of Court of Common Council, City of London 1948-51, an Alderman, Chmn. of Spitalfields Market Cttee. 1951-52, a Member of London Co. Council 1952-55, Sheriff of London 1958-59, and Lord Mayor of London 1962-63; Chm. of Cttee. for Exports to Canada since 1967 (Vice-Chm. 1964-67); a Knight Cdr. of Order of George I of Greece, a Cdr. of Valour of Cameroons, a Grand Officer of Order of Leopold of Belgium, Order of Homayoun of Iran, Grand Cross of Merit of Republic of Germany; 1939-45 War

PROUD TO SERVE

as Lt. RA (TA); Knt. 1960: *m.* 1928, Ethel Mary, da. of Henry T. Johnson, of Putney, SW, and has issue.

Arms—Argent, on a pile barry wavy of eight azure and of the field, between two walnut trees eradicated proper, a lion rampant gules. Crest—Upon the trunk of a walnut tree, fessewise with two branches sprouting therefrom proper a sword erect or.
     Residence—15, Burghley House, Somerset Rd., Wimbledon, SW19.

Sons living—JOHN RAYMOND, *TD* (21, Somerset Rd., Parkside, Wimbledon, SW19), *b.* July 7th 1931; ed. at Stowe: *m.* 1961, Ella Christine, da. of the late Maj. Anthony George Pelham [see E. Chichester, colls.], and has issue living, John Simon Pelham, *b.* 1962,—Mark Ralph Pelham, *b.* 1965,—Emma Mary, *b.* 1963,—Anna Margaret, *b.* 1968.—Michael Arthur (The Old Rectory, Fernhurst, Sussex), *b.* 1937; ed. at Stowe, and at Trin. Coll., Camb. (MA, MB, BChir): *m.* 1961, Elizabeth, da. of the late Air Commodore Eric Delano Barnes, CB, AFC, and has issue living, Nicholas David Delano, *b.* 1963,—Michael Charles Delano, *b.* 1965,—Thomas Edward Delano, *b.* 1971,—Ralph Andrew Delano, *b.* 1973.

Collateral Branch living.

Issue of the late Richard Eric Perring, 2nd son of 1st baronet, *b.* 1933, *d.* 1971: *m.* 1964, Faith (44, Roedean Cres., SW15), da. of Sir Peter (Arthur Percival Hay) Aitken.

Christopher James, *b.* 1965.——Antony William, *b.* 1967.——Graham Michael, *b.* 1970.

PERROTT, Creation (U.K.) 1911 with precedence from July 1st, 1716.
[Extinct 1922.]

Sir HERBERT CHARLES PERROTT, *CH, CB* (6th of G.B. 1716 creation according to Roll of Baronets), 1st (of U.K. 1911 creation), and last *Baronet.*

Daughters living of 6th (G.B.) and 1st (U.K.) Baronet—Marie Louise Priscilla (*Baroness Forester*), *b.* 1909; is a DStJ: *m.* 1931, the 7th Baron Forester. *Residences*, The Old Hall, Willey, Broseley, Shropshire: Marasha, Banket, Rhodesia.——Helena Ruth (*Helena, Viscountess Maitland*), *b.* 1912; is an OStJ: *m.* 1936, Viscount Maitland, who *d.* (killed in action during European War) 1943, only son of 15th Earl of Lauderdale. *Residences*, Park House, Makerston, Kelso, Roxburghshire; Flat E, 34, Cadogan Sq., SW1.

PETIT, Creation (U.K.) 1890, of Petit Hall, Island of Bombay.

Consequitur quodcunque petit.

He obtains whatever he seeks.

Sir DINSHAW MANOCKJEE PETIT, 3rd *Baronet, b.* June 24th, 1901 ; *s.* his father, *Sir* DINSHAW MANOCKJEE, 1933, and changed his name from Framjee Dinshaw Petit to Dinshaw Manockjee Petit 1933; ed. at Trin. Hall, Camb. (BA); Bar. Inner Temple 1925, a Member of Lloyd's, London, Pres. of N. M. Petit Charities, of Sir D. M. Petit Charities, of F. D. Petit Sanatorium, of Persian Zoroastrian Amelioration Fund, of Petit Girls' Orphanage, of Sir D. M. Petit Gymnasium, of J. N. Petit Institute of Native Gen. Dispensary, Bombay Soc. for Prevention of Cruelty to Animals, and of Lord Northbrook Soc., London, a Trustee of VJT Institute, Bombay, and a Member of Managing Cttee. of B. D. Petit Parsee Gen. Hosp.; Hon. Life Member of RSPCA London; a Life Gov. of Roy. Hosp. for Incurables, London; Vice-Pres. of British Assocn. of Riviera, and a Citizen of Honour of France: *m.* 1928, Sylla, who *d.* 1963, da. of R. D. Tata, of Bombay, and has issue.

Arms—Azure, on a chevron argent, between three urns of the last, therefrom issuant flames proper, as many bees volant, also proper. **Crest**—A ship under sail at sea, in front thereof an anchor fessewise, all proper.

Residences—Petit Hall, Nepean Sea Rd., Bombay; Savaric, Eze, France, AM; 8, Mount Row, W1.

Son living—NASWANJI (Petit Hall, Nepean Sea Rd., Bombay), *b.* Aug. 13th, 1934: *m.* 1964, Nirmala, Nanavati, and has issue living, Jehangir *b.* 1965,——Framjee, *b.* 1968.
Daughter living—Dina, *b.* 1931.

Collateral Branches living.

Grandchildren of the late Cowasjee Dinshaw Petit, el. son of 1st baronet:—
Issue of the late Pestonjee Cowasjee Petit, *b.* 1866, *d.* 1932: *m.* 1894, Perzojbai Cowasjee Parukh:—
Hirabai (Hill Side, Nepean Sea Rd.,Bombay), *b.* 1898.

Issue of the late Hormasjee Cowasjee Petit, *b.* 1868, *d.* 1939 : *m.* 1891, Perozbai Sorabjee Patuck :—
Cowasjee (35, New Kantwady Rd., Bandra, Bombay, 50), *b.* 1893: *m.* 1919, Nawajbai Pherozyshaw Dadyburjor, and has issue living, Sorabjee *b.* 1921: *m.* 1946, Cleta Mathias, and has issue living, Marius *b.* 1948, Stephen *b.* 1950, Cory Ann *b.* 1951, Sean *b.* 1953, Gavin *b.* 1960, Jenne, Lou *b.* 1955,—Sheila, *b.* 1926: *m.* 1953, Julian Bartlett, and has issue living, Darius *b.* 1955, Zarir *b.* 1958, Pheroza *b.* 1959.——Dinshawjee, *b.* 1903: *m.* 1940, Milthibai D. Poocha, and has issue living, Freny, *b.* 1941,—Homa, *b.* 1945.——Mithibai, *b.* 1892. *Residence*, Ram Mansion, Nepean Sea Rd., Bombay, India.

Grandchildren of the late Bomanjee Dinshaw Petit (*infra*) :—
Issue of the late Dhunjibhoy Bomanji Petit, *b.* 1881, *d.* 1957 : *m.* 1900, Humabai, who *d.* 1949, el. da. of Jalbhoy Ardeshir Sett :—
Manockjee, *b.* 1900 : *m.* 1927, Perin Maneckji Vacha. *Residence*, Sett Minar, Peddar Road, Bombay.——Ruttonbai, *b.* 1906 : *m.* 1st, 1934 (marriage dissolved 19—), Karl J. Khandalawala; 2ndly, Lama Anagarika Govinda.——Kuverbai, *b.* 1908 : B.A. 19—, LL.B. 19— : *m.* 1939, Rustom F. Vakharia, and has issue living, Shirinbai, *b.* 1940,—Roshan, *b.* 1943. *Residence,*

Issue of the late Bomanjee Dinshaw Petit, 3rd son of 1st baronet, *b.* 1859, *d.* 1915: *m.* 1872, Gulbai Nanabhoy Byramjee Jejeebhoy, who *d.* 1947 :—
Manekbai Bomanjee, *b.* 1887: *m.* 1916, Sorab Nanabhoy Moos, CIE, MA, and has issue living, Jamshed Sorab, *MD* (Ark Royal, 50B, Peddar Rd., Bombay, 26), *b.* 1925; ed. at Bombay (BS, MD) and at London (MRCP) Univs.; Fellow of American Coll. of Chest Physicians; Fellow of Internat. Coll. of Angiology; Hon. Assist. Prof. of Medicine, Sir Jamsetjee Jejeebhoy Hosp., Bombay: *m.* 1953, Perin, *MB, BS*, da. of Dr. Kaikobad Jungalwalla, and has issue living,

Deena b. 1954, Feroze b. 1957,—Silla, b. 1921: m. 1947, Naval Ardeshir, and has issue living, Jer b. 1949, Sohrab b. 1962, Shireen b. 1951, Frainy b. 1955. Residence, Emsworth, 39, Pali Hill, Bandra, Bombay, India.

This baronetcy was granted with remainder to (i) Framjee Dinshaw Petit, 2nd son of the 1st baronet (Sir Dinshaw Manockjee Petit, a merchant and millowner of Bombay, who had served as Sheriff of Bombay and been Knighted 1887), and the heirs male of his body lawfully begotten, and (ii) the heirs male of the body of the 1st baronet. By special Act of the Legislative Council of India, all holders of the title relinquish their own name on succession and assume those of the 1st baronet.

PETO, Creation (U.K.) 1855, of Somerleyton Hall, Suffolk.

Sir (HENRY) FRANCIS MORTON PETO, 3rd *Baronet*, son of the late Morton Kelsall Peto, 2nd son of 1st baronet; b. Nov. 18th, 1889 ; s. his uncle, *Sir* HENRY, 1938; ed. at Eton; Com. (retired) R.N.: m. 1st, 1919, Edith, who d. 1945, da. of the late George Berners Ruck Keene ; 2ndly, 1948, Grizel Rosemary, who d. 1976, da. of the late Rear-Adm. Archibald Cochrane, CMG [E. Dundonald, colls.], and widow of Maj. Thomas Lionel Ashburner Clapton, Durham L.I., and has issue by 1st and 2nd m.

Arms—Per pale indented or and gules barry of six, two annulets in fesse, all counterchanged. Crest—On a rock proper a sinister wing or, thereon three annulets gules.

Residence—Balbeg, Straiton, Maybole, Ayrshire.

Ad finem fidelis.

Faithful to the end.

Sons living—By 1st marriage—HENRY GEORGE MORTON, b. April 29th, 1920; ed. at Sherborne; late Capt. R.A.: m. 1947, Frances Jacqueline, JP, da. of the late Ralph Haldane Evers, of Milan, and has issue living, Francis Michael Morton (Sorrowlessfield, Earlston, Berwicks.), b. 1949: m. 1974, Felicity Margaret, da. of Lt. Col. John Alan Burns, of Godminster Wood House, Bruton, Som. [see Hope-Dunbar, Bt., colls.],—Robert Henry Haldane, b. 1950: m. 1975, Susan, only da. of William Judge, of 25, Model Cottages, East Sheen, SW14. Residence, Stream House, Selborne, Alton, Hants.—William Neill (c/o Coutts & Co., 440, Strand, WC2), b. 1922; ed. at Sherborne; sometime Trooper RAC: m. 1st, 1943 (m. diss. 1962), Jacqueline Mary Valentine, who d. 1971, da. of the late Gurth Edelsten, of Eastmore, PO Flora, Marquard, Orange Free State; 2ndly, 1962, Ann Bernal, only da. of the late Lt.-Col. T. T. Laville, of Little Garth, Sampford Peverell, nr. Tiverton, Devon, and has issue living, (by 1st m.) James Francis Morton (Stack Polly, Woodbank Lane, Shotwick, Chester), b. 1944: m. 1969, Daphne, da. of T. H. Kennedy, of Blackwood, Auldgirth, Dumfries, and has issue lving, Mark Edward b. 1971, Rebecca Jane b. 1975,—William Gurth, b. 1949.——by 2nd m.—Raymond John, b. 1950. Sister living—Katharine Ainsworth, b. 1892. Residence—The Old Vicarage, Moulsford, Oxon.

Collateral Branches living.

Grandchildren of the late William Herbert Peto, 3rd son of 1st baronet:—
Issue of the late Major Ralph Harding Peto, b. 1877, d. 1945: m. 1st, 1909, Frances Ruby Vera, who d. 1951, having obtained a divorce 1923, da. of the late Lieut.-Col. Walter James Lindsay [E. Crawford, colls.]; 2ndly, 1937, Mechtilde Christiane, who d. 1958, da. of the late Count Maximilian von Arco-Zinneberg, and widow of H.S.H. Karl Max, 6th Prince Lichnowsky, G.C.V.O., sometime German Ambassador in London:—
(By 1st marriage) Maud Rosemary PETO, b. 1916 ; resumed by deed poll 1961 the surname of Peto : m. 1934 (marriage dissolved 1958), Viscount Hinchingbrooke, M.P. (later 10th Earl of Sandwich, until he disclaimed his titles 1964). Residences, Studio Flat, 22, Markham Sq., SW3; Swain's House, Bembridge, Isle of Wight.

Issue of the late Sir Geoffrey Keisall Peto, K.B.E., b. 1878, d. 1956: m. 1st, 1903, Pauline, who d. 1950, da. of the late William Quirin, of Boston. U.S.A., and widow of Lieut.-Col. R. Cokayne-Frith, 15th Hussars; 2ndly, 1951, Edna Frances (Onslow Court Hotel, Queens Gate, SW7 5LR), da. of the late Edward B. Hilton, of Paris, and New York, and widow of Capt. Sir Denzil Cope, 14th Bt.:—
(By 1st marriage) Anthony (c/o Coutts & Co., 440, Strand, W.C.2), b. 1907; ed. at Eton: m. 1936, Baroness Barbara, da. of Baron Hermann Wrangel, of Genarp, Sweden. and has issue living, Ursula, b. 1938: m. 1960, Richard Alan Opperman.——Pamela Gladys Berthe (Tithe Cottage, Rudgwick, Sussex), b. 1910: m. 1st, 1932, Thomas John Henry Vincent Lane, who d. 1941 [B. Kensington]; 2ndly, 1942, Lt.-Col. W. S. S. Sanguinetti, Hampshire Regt., who d. 1969, and has issue living, (by 1st m.) Thomas Ronald Henry, b. 1934;—Jane, b. 1935.

Issue of the late (Samuel) Arthur Peto, 4th son of 1st baronet, b. 1852, d. 1942: m. 1875, Ellen Cornelia, who d. 1947, da. of the late Sir Robert Palmer Harding:—
Joan Ainsworth, b. 1882 : m. 1909, Major James Leslie Cross, Yeo., who d. 1955, and has issue living, Felicity Leslie, b. 1920: m. 1st, 1945, Capt. Anthony Sutton, formerly Grenadier Guards; 2ndly, 1955, Douglas Motion, of Thatched Cottage, Bradley, Alresford, Hants.

Issue of the late Frank Kelsall Peto, 6th son of 1st baronet, b. 1858, d. 1935: m. 1887, Cecilia Emma, who d. 1935, da. of W. H. Cane, M.D., of Uxbridge, and widow of C. H. Pawson, of Farnley House, Dursley :—
Marion Ainsworth, b. 1893. Residence,

Issue living of the late Basil Edward Peto (7th son of 1st baronet), who was cr. a Baronet 1927 :—
See Peto, Bt., cr. 1927.

Sir Samuel Morton Peto, 1st Bt., M.P. for Norwich (L) 1847-55, and subsequently for Finsbury and Bristol, was the el. son of William Peto, of Cookham, Berks.

PETO, Creation (U.K.) 1927, of Barnstaple, co. Devon.

Sir CHRISTOPHER HENRY MAXWELL PETO, *DSO,* 3rd
Baronet; *b.* Feb. 19th, 1897; *s.* his brother, *Lt.-Col. Sir*
(JAMES) MICHAEL, 1971; ed. at Harrow; Brig. (ret.) late
9th Lancers; Comdg. 9th Lancers 1938-41, and Col. 9th
Lancers 1950-60; a DL for Wilts.; High Sheriff 1966;
1914-18 War in France and Flanders (wounded, des-
patches); 1939-45 War in France, latterly as Ch. Liaison
Officer to Allied Contingents on staff of F-M Viscount
Montgomery of Alamein (wounded, despatches thrice,
DSO, 3rd class Order of Restitution of Poland, Legion of
Honour, French Croix de Guerre, Order of Leopold I of
Belgium, Belgian Croix de Guerre, Order of White Lion of
Czechoslovakia, Czechoslovak War Cross); MP for [Barn-
staple Div. of Devon (C) 1945-50, and for N. Div. of
Devon 1950-55; DSO 1945: *m.* 1935, Barbara, yr. da. of
Edwyn Thomas Close, of Woodcote, Camberley, Surrey,
and has issue.

Faithful to the end. **Arms**—Barry or and gules per pale indented counterchanged in
chief a boar's head erased proper and in base two annulets counterchanged. **Crest**—On a rock proper a sinister wing or, thereon three
annulets gules.

Residence—Lockeridge House, nr. Marlborough, Wilts. *Club*—Cavalry.

Sons living—MICHAEL HENRY BASIL, (Cliddesden Down House, Basingstoke), *b.* April 6th,
1938; ed. at Eton, and Ch. Ch., Oxford (MA); Bar. Inner Temple 1960: *m.* 1st, 1963 (m. diss.
1970), Sarah Susan, yst. da. of Maj. Sir Dennis Frederick Bankes Stucley, 5th baronet, 2ndly,
1971, Lucinda Mary, da. of the late Sir Charles Douglas Blackett, 9th Bt., and formerly wife of
Ewan Iain Macleod Hilleary, and has issue living (by 1st m.) Henry Christopher Morton Bampfylde, *b.* 1967,—Emma Rose, *b.* 1965,—Marina Sarah, *b.* 1968,—(by 2nd m.) Hugh David, *b.*
1974.——Nicholas John (Lockeridge House, Marlborough, Wilts.; Turf and Cavalry Clubs),
b. 1939; ed. at Eton; Capt. 9th/12th Lancers: *m.* 1969, Anne Colquhoun, el. da. of John Tysen,
of 1165, Fifth Av., New York, and has issue living, Alexander Tysen, *b.* 1973.
Daughter living—Elizabeth Mary, *b.* 1936: *m.* 1958, Ronald Philip Murphy, of Shippool House,
Innishannon, Co. Cork, and has issue living, Charles Christopher Ronald, *b.* 1959,—Richard
Norbert, *b.* 1961.
Daughter living of 2nd Baronet—Serena Mary Francesca (*Lady Matheson of Matheson*), *b.* 1928: *m.*
1954, Maj. Sir Torquhil Alexander Matheson of Matheson 6th Bt., Colm. Gds. (ret.), of Stander-
wick Court, Frome, Som.

Collateral Branch living.

Issue of the late Major (Basil Arthur) John Peto, King's Dragoon Guards, 3rd son of
1st baronet, *b.* 1900, *d.* 1954: *m.* 1934, Patricia Geraldine (47, Burton Court, Franklins
Row, SW3) (who *m.* 2ndly, 1955, Lt.-Col. Hugh Granville Leveson Dudley Ryder,
TD [*see* E. Harrowby, colls.]), da. of the late Gerald Macleay Browne, OBE:—
Jonathan Basil Morton (8, Stevenage Rd., SW6; Guards' and Pratt's Clubs), *b.* 1942; Coldm. Gds.
1962-66; ADC to Gov. of Qld. 1963-66: *m.* 1969, Hon. Selina Lillian Hughes-Young, da. of
1st Baron St. Helens, and has issue living, Amyas John, *b.* 1969,—Esmond Patrick Basil, *b.*
1974,—Daisy Elizabeth, *b.* 1971.——Virginia Anne, *b.* 1935: *m.* 1955, Gerard Wyndham Morgan-
Grenville [*see* Ly. Kinloss). *Residence,* Burgate House, Hascombe, Surrey.——Joanna Dava,
b. 1938: *m.* 1957, Capt. Charles St. John Graham Moncrieff, Scots Gds. [*see* V. Bolingbroke, colls.].
Residence, Kinmouth, Rhynd, nr. Perth.——Sarah Christian Pandora, *b.* 1940: *m.* 1959, Capt.
David Benjamin Bathurst, RN [*see* E. Bathurst, colls.]. *Residence,* 6, Crouchmans Close, SE26.

The 1st baronet, Sir Basil Edward Peto [7th son of Sir Samuel Morton Peto, 1st Bt. (*cr.* 1855)], was
M.P. for E. or Devizes Div. of Wilts (*C*) 1910-18 and for Barnstaple Div. of Devon 1922-3, and 1924-35.

PETRIE, Creation (U.K.) 1918, of Carrowcarden, Castleconnor, Barony of Tireragh, co. Sligo.

Sir CHARLES ALEXANDER PETRIE,
C.B.E., 3rd *Baronet ; b.* Sept. 28th, 1895 ; *s.*
his brother, *Sir* EDWARD LINDSAY HADDON,
1927; ed. at Corpus Christi Coll., Oxford
(MA); Hon. LittD. Nat. Univ. of Ireland;
a Knight of Order of Civil Merit (Spain),
a Com. of Orders of Crown of Italy, of George
I. of Greece, and of Isabella the Catholic
of Spain, Pres. of Mil. History So. of Ireland,
a Corresponding Member of Roy. Spanish
Acad. of History, a Fellow of the Roy. Historical So., Hon. Counsellor of Instituto
Fernando el Catolico and Hon. D.Phil.,
Valladolid, CBE (Civil) 1957: *m.* 1st, 1920,
Ursula Gabrielle, *d.* 1962, having obtained a
divorce 1926, da. of the late Harold Chaloner
Dowdall, QC [B. Borthwick]; 2ndly, 1926,
Jessie Cecilia, da. of the late F. J. G. Mason,
and has issue by 1st and 2nd marriages.

Arms—Azure, on a bend between a stag's head couped
and three cross crosslets fitchée argent, as many escallops
gules. **Crest**—A demi-eagle displayed proper gazing at
a sun or.

Trust, but observe. *Residence*—190, Coleherne Court, S.W.5. *Clubs*—
Carlton, Guards', Authors', Hurlingham, University (Dublin).

Sons living—By 1st marriage—CHARLES RICHARD BORTHWICK, *T.D.*, *b.* Oct. 19th, 1921; ed. at Radley, and New Coll., Oxford; Lt.-Col. REME (RARO): *m.* 1962, Jessie Ariana Borthwick, da. of the late Cdr. Patrick Straton Campbell, RN (ret.), JP, of Westleton, Saxmundham. *Residence,* 3, Northmoor Rd., Oxford.——**By 2nd m.—**Peter Charles (of 29, Ranelagh Av., SW6; Brooks's and Hurlingham Clubs), *b.* 1932; ed. at Westminster, and at Ch. Ch., Oxford: late 2nd Lt. Grenadier Guards; is in H.M. Foreign Ser.: *m.* 1958, Countess Lydwine Maria Fortunata, da. of Count Charles Alphonse van Oberndorff, of The Hague and Paris, and has issue living, Charles James, *b.* 1959,—Wilfrid John, *b.* 1965,—Leticia Jacqueline Fortunata Cecilia, *b.* 1961.

Daughters living of 2nd Baronet—Violet Haddon, *b.* 1913 : *m.* 1st, (Jan.) 1937, Charles Edward Wilson Sleigh ; 2ndly, 1950, William Dalziel Mungall Allison, who *d.* 1957, and has issue living, (by 1st marriage) Thomas Edward, *b.* 1939,—Rosemary Anne, *b.* (Dec.) 1937 : *m.* 1956, Walter Ronald Alexander, of Ryland Lodge, Dunblane, Perthshire, and has issue living, Walter *b.* 1957, Charles Edward *b.* 1963, Rosalind *b.* 1959, Caroline *b.* 1961,—(by 2nd marriage) Robert William Mungall, *b.* 1951. *Residence,* Claremont House, Claremont Rd., Edinburgh, 6.——Mary Bianca, *b.* 1918. *Residence,* Little Bracken, Lincoln Drive, Pyrford, Woking, Surrey.

Sir Charles Petrie, 1st baronet (sometime Leader of Conservative Party in Liverpool), was Lord Mayor of Liverpool 1901-2.

PEYTON, Creation (G.B.) 1776, of Doddington, Cambridgeshire. [Extinct 1962.]

Sir ALGERNON THOMAS PEYTON, 7th and last *Baronet.*

Daughters living of 7th Baronet—Delia, *b.* 1916 : *m.* 1943, Major Benjamin George Barnett, M.B.E., T.D., Oxfordshire Yeo. and has issue living, David John Wheate, *b.* 1946.—Charles Henry, *b.* 1948,—Rosemary Dorothea, *b.* 1953. *Residence,* Swift's House, Bicester, Oxon.—Elisabeth Rosamund, *b.* 1919 : *m.* 1943, Capt. John Nigel Bingham, Coldstream Guards [*see* E. Lucan, colls.]. *Residence,* Stone House, Brimpton, Reading.

FOLEY-PHILIPPS, Creation (U.K.) 1887, of Picton Castle, co. Pembroke. [Extinct 1962.]

Sir RICHARD FOLEY FOLEY-PHILLIPS, 4th and last *Baronet.*

Daughter living of 2nd Baronet—Sheila Victoria Katrin (*Baroness of Dunsany*), *b.* 1912; is D.St.J.: *m.* 1st, 1932, Major John Frederick Foley, Baron de Rutzen, Welsh Guards, who *d.* (killed in action in Italy)1944, having in 1918 received Roy. licence (for himself and the heirs male of his body on succession) to use the title within the British Dominions ; 2ndly, 1947, as his second wife, the 19th Baron of Dunsany, and has issue living, (by 1st marriage) Victoria Ann Elizabeth Gwynne (*Lady Dashwood*), *b.* 1933: *m.* 1957, Sir Francis John Vernon Hereward Dashwood, 11th Bt., of West Wycombe Park, Bucks.,—(by 2nd m.) [*see* B. Dunsany]. *Residence,* Dunsany Castle, co. Meath.

Philipson-Stow, see Stow.

PHILLIPS, Creation (U.K.) 1912, of Tylney Hall, Rotherwick, co. Southampton.

Truth conquers.
VERITAS · VINCET

Sir ROBIN FRANCIS PHILLIPS, 3rd *Baronet* ; *b.* July 29th, 1940 ; *s.* his father, *Capt. Sir* LIONEL FRANCIS, 1944; ed. at Aiglon Coll., Switzerland.

Arms—Or, on a pile azure, between two greyhounds courant in base sable, a lion rampant of the first, guttée-des poix. **Crest—**A demi-lion azure, charged on the shoulder with two annulets interlaced paleways or, between as many nuggets of gold.
*Residence—*12, Manson Mews, SW7.

Aunts living—Hilda Elizabeth, *b.* 1917: *m.* 1st, 1941, Major Peter Mant MacIntyre Kemp, D.S.O.; 2ndly, 1946, Lieut.-Col. George Victor Seymour, M.C., who *d.* 1953 [*see* M. Hertford, colls.]. *Residence,* West Wing, Poxwell House, nr. Dorchester, Dorset.——Mary Pamela, *b.* 1919: *m.* 1943, Arthur Owen Hunt, and has issue living, Clive Anthony *b.* 1944,—David Charles, *b.* 1947,—Paula Caroline, *b.* 1950. *Residence,* The White Cottage, Brailsford, Derbys.

Widow living of 2nd Baronet—CAMILLA MARY, da. of the late Capt. Hugh Algernon Parker [*see* E. Macclesfield, colls.]: *m.* 1st, 1939, Capt. Sir Lionel Francis Phillips, 2nd Bt., who *d.* (killed in action in Italy) 1944; 2ndly, 1950, John George Pisani, of 21, Chancellor House, 17, Hyde Park Gate, SW7 5DQ.

The 1st baronet, Sir Lionel Phillips (son of the late Philip Saunders Phillips, merchant, of London), was a partner in the late firm of Wernher, Beit & Co., of 1, London Wall Buildings, E.C.; sometime Chm. Central Mining & Investment Corporation, Ltd., and Rand Mines, Ltd. ; Hon. Col. 10th S. African Inf. and 1st S. African Field Ambulance ; one of the leaders of the Transvaal Reform Movement 1896, resulting in Jameson Raid (sentenced to death by Judge Gregorovski, sentence commuted to fine of £25,000); a M.L.A., S. Africa 1910-15 ; prominently associated with Transvaal gold-mining industry, and five times Pres. of Transvaal Chamber of Mines. The 2nd baronet, Capt. Sir Lionel Francis, R.A. (T.A.), *d.* (killed in action in Italy) 1944.

FAUDEL-PHILLIPS, Creation (U.K.) 1897, of Grosvenor Gardens, St. George, Hanover Square, co. London, and Queen's Gardens, West Brighton, co. Sussex. [Extinct 1941.]

Sir LIONEL LAWSON FAUDEL FAUDEL-PHILLIPS, 3rd and last *Baronet*.

Daughters living of 3rd Baronet—Jean Armyne Eulalia, *b.* 1909. *Residence*, Marton House, Long Marton, Appleby, Westmorland.——Helen Bridget (*Countess of Kilmorey*), *b.* 1918: *m.* 1941, the 5th Earl of Kilmorey. *Residence*, Via San Leonardo 32, Florence, Italy.

PICKTHORN, Creation (U.K.) 1959, of Orford, co. Suffolk.

Rt. Hon. Sir KENNETH WILLIAM MURRAY PICKTHORN, 1st *Baronet*, son of Charles Wright Pickthorn, Master Mariner; *b.* April 23rd, 1892; ed. at Aldenham, and at Trin. Coll., Camb. (BA 1913, LittD 1935); Fellow and formerly Lecturer, Corpus Christi, Camb. (Pres. 1937-44); Parliamentary Sec., Min. of Education 1951-54; 1914-19 War with London Regt. RFC and RAF in France and Macedonia; MP for Camb. Univ. (C) 1935-50, and for Carlton Div. of Nottinghamshire 1950-66; PC 1964: *m.* 1924, Nancy Catherine Lewis, da. of Lewis Matthew Richards, Bar.-at-law, and has issue [The 1st Baronet, *d.* Nov. 12th, 1975].

Residence—Quay St., Orford, Suffolk. *Clubs*—Carlton, Army and Navy.

Sons living—CHARLES WILLIAM RICHARDS, *b.* March 3rd, 1927; ed. at Eton and Corpus Christi Coll., Camb.; Bar. Middle Temple, 1952: *m.* 1951, Helen, da. of Sir James Gow Mann, KCVO, and has issue living, James Francis, *b.* 1955; ed. at Eton,—Caroline, *b.*1958,—Frances, *b.* 1960. *Residences*, 3, Hobury St., SW10; Ledard, Henley on Thames.——Henry Gabriel Richards, *b.* 1928; ed. at Eton and Trin. Coll., Camb.: *m.* 1955, Mary, da. of (Cecil James) Juxon (Talbot) Barton, CMG, OBE, and has issue living, John, *b.* 1957,—Andrew, *b.*1961,—Thomas David Alexander, *b.* 1967,—Henrietta, *b.* 1959. *Residences*, 54, Chelsea Park Gdns., SW3; Moorfield, Woodbridge, Suffolk.
Daughter living—Catherine Ann Monica, *b.* 1925: *m.* 1950, Neil Atkinson Iliff, CBE, who *d.* 1973, and has issue living, Charles, *b.* 1952; ed. at Eton and Trin. Coll., Camb.,—Catherine, *b.* 1955,—Elizabeth, *b.* 1957,—Mary, *b.* 1958,—Georgina, *b.* 1963. *Residences*, 17, Hale House, 34, De Vere Gdns., W8; Rosehill, Orford, Woodbridge, Suffolk.

PIERS, Creation (I.) 1661, of Tristernagh Abbey, Westmeath.

Sir CHARLES ROBERT FITZMAURICE PIERS, 10th *Baronet*, *b.* Aug. 30th, 1903 ; *s.* his father *Sir* CHARLES PIGOTT, 1945; Lt.-Cdr. (ret.) RCNR; Manager of Midland Doherty Ltd., of Duncan, BC, Canada: *m.* 1936, Ann Blanche Scott, only da. of the late Capt. Thomas Ferguson, Roy. Highlanders, and has issue.

Arms—Azure, three lions passant-guardant in fesse, between two double cotises argent. **Crest**—An arm embowed vested azure, charged with three plates and cuffed argent the hand holding a broken flagstaff, the flag azure, on a chief argent three torteaux.

Address—RR No. 1, Duncan, BC, Canada.

NOBILIS·EST·IRA·LEONIS

Noble is the lion's anger.

Son living—JAMES DESMOND, *b.* July 24th, 1947.

Daughter living—Sarah Constance, *b.* 1942: *m.* 1970, Michael C. Weld, and has issue living, Diana Kristen, *b.* 1971,—Andrea Jane, *b.* 1974.

Collateral Branches living.

Granddaughter of the late Henry Piers, son of the late Rev. Octavius Piers, 5th son of 5th baronet :—
Issue of the late Lieut.-Col. Henry Octavius Piers, R.A., *b.* 1856, *d.* 1945 : *m.* 1886, Lise, who *d.* 1937, da. of Dep. Surg.-Gen. Johnston Ferguson :—
Gwendolen Mary (Redcliff Court Hotel, Cyprus Rd., Exmouth), *b.* 1889.

Grandsons of the late Lt.-Col. William Barrington Piers, el. son of the late Col. Thomas Tristam Piers, 5th son of the late Rev. Octavius Piers (ante) :—
Issue of the late William Price Barrington Piers, *b.* 1905, *d.* 1974: *m.* 1935, Ursula Mary Bence (Tristernagh Abbey, Marandellas, Rhodesia), da. of the Rev. George Alfred Charles Smith-Cranmoor, R. of Baldock, Herts. :—
Anthony Tristram Barrington (c/o Lloyds Bank, Cox's & King's Branch, 6, Pall Mall, SW1), *b.* 1939; Maj. 1st Devonshire and Dorset Regt.: *m.* 1964, Susan Jacqueline Dawn, only da. of Lt.-Col. H. T. Bayldon, MC, of La sPalmas, Canary Islands, and has issue living, Christopher William Barrington, *b.* 1973,—Ann-Marie Barrington, *b.* 1965,—Bridget Dawn Barrington, *b.* 1967.——Brian William Barrington (PO Box 50, Lilongwe, Malawi), *b.* 1941: *m.* 1970, Stephanie Ellen Elizabeth, da. of the late Capt. Attoe, of London, and has issue living, Robert Courtney Barrington, *b.* 1973,—Samantha Barrington, *b.* 1971.——Charles Barrington, *b.* 1943; Maj. Rhodesian African Rifles.

Granddaughters of the late Col. Thomas Tristram Piers (ante):—
Issue of the late Rev. Samuel Octavius Piers, *b.* 1869, *d.* 1940 : *m.* 1901, Mabel Marion, who *d.* 1951, da. of G. Smith, of Ipswich :—
Violet Marion, *b.* 1905: *m.* 1st, 1931, Louis Brown, who *d.* 1934; 2ndly, 1939, George Paul, and has issue living, (by 2nd m.) Jacqueline Evelyn, *b.* 1940.——Evelyn Helena, *b.* 1909: *m.* 1st, 1938, George Damer, Lt. RCA, who *d.* (killed on active service in Italy) 1944; 2ndly, 1972, Robert Owen Fowler, of Liverpool, Nova Scotia, and has issue living (by 1st m.), George Terence Stuart (7, Woodcrest Rd., Purley, Surrey), *b.* 1940: *m.* 1964, Michèle Mary Godwin Prouten, and has issue living, Justin Dawson Damer *b.* 1967, Miranda Jane *b.* 1968.——Ruth Pauline, *b.* 1925: *m.* 1946, Thomas Eric Hazeldine, AMICE, and has issue living, Keith Trevor, *b.* 1947,—

Piers Martin, b. 1958,—Carol Anne, b. 1948,—Sally Jane, b. 1949,—Gail Melissa, b. 1955. *Residence*, Dene Manor, Liverpool, Nova Scotia, Canada.

Grandchildren of the late Shute Barrington Piers (infra):—
Issue of the late Walter Barrington Piers, b. 1890, d. 1964: m. 1913, Mary Celia Onn (Suite 307, 22182, Deudney Trunk Rd., Haney, BC, Canada):—
Grahame Barrington (Suite 310, 404, E 8th Av., Vancouver, BC, Canada), b. 1913: m. 1950, Shirley O'Brien, and has issue living, Richard Barrington, b. 1953.——Cecil Edwin (PO Box 301, Montrose, BC, Canada), b. 1914; Staff Sgt. RCMP (ret.): m. 1941, Ethel Sheppard, and has issue living, Kenneth Barrington, b. 1943,—Penelope Ann, b. 1946.——Harry Gordon (PO Box 45, Grasmere, BC, Canada), b. 1920; formerly Warrant Officer, RCAF; Inspector of Customs and Immigration: m. 1st, 1946, Sally Chisholm; 2ndly, 1970, Helen Street, and has issue living (by 1st m.), James Walker, b. 1947.——Kathleen Margery (Box 100, Haney, BC, Canada), b. 1916: m. 1943, Winston Eric Dunning, who d. 1971, and has issue living, Ross Barrington, b. 1945,—Paul Hastey, b. 1954, Janis Kathleen, b. 1950.

Issue of the late Grahame Sedway Piers, b. 1892, d. 1970: m. 1917, Dorothy Mary, who d. 1971, da. of G. D. Heather:—
Heather, b. 1918: m. 1945, Anthony Freeman, FCA, of Fernhill Cottage, Ide Hill, Sevenoaks, and has issue living, Michael Edmund Piers, b. 1946,—Anthony Piers, b. 1956,—Chloe Anne, b. 1949,—Amanda Jane, b. 1953.

Grandchildren of the late Capt. Shute Barrington Piers, R.N., son of the late Rev. Octavius Piers (ante):—
Issue of the late Shute Barrington Piers, b. 1864, d. 1947: m. 1888, Gertrude, who d. 1938, da. of Charles Henry Nottingham:—
Gladys Nottingham, b. 1893: m. 1920, W. Serle, who d. 1940, and has issue living, Patrick Philip Oswald (17, Wulwyn Court, Edgcumbe Park, Crowthorne, Berks., RG11 6ET), b. 1921; Sqdn. Ldr. RAF (ret.): m. 1st, 1940, Sheila Foster, of Bexhill-on-Sea; 2ndly, 1965, Nicole Lecoq, and has issue living (by 1st m.) Roy Anthony Michael b. 1941; Inspector, Metropolitan Police: m. 1964, Elizabeth Mary, da. of   , (and has issue living, Paul b. 1966, Keith b. 1968, Fiona b. 1965), John Patrick David b. 1944; Capt. RAOC, Peter Norman James b. 1949; RAF (by 2nd m.) Robert Barrington b. 1966.

Issue of the late Henry Handyside Bruce Piers, b. 1865, d. 1935: m. 1902, Eva Gertrude, who d. 1962, da. of G. B. Pennell:—
Eustace Pennell, b. 1910; Hon. Major Roy. Corps of Signals (T.A.): m. 1941, Jean Mavis, da. of John Edward Ralph, of Streatham Hill, S.W., and has issue living, William James Shute Barrington, b. 1948,—Angela Mary, b. 1942: m. 1965, Peter Kiero Watson, of 66, Finches Gdns., Lindfield, Sussex, and has issue living, James Kiero b. 1966, Edward Piers Kiero b. 1970,—Clare Rosamund Pennell (twin), b. 1948. *Residence*, Gable End, Castle Cary, Som.——Mary Eva Patricia, b. 1905: m. 1939, Arthur Mather Grundy, who d. 1940, and has issue living, John Martin, b. 1940; Maj. R. Regt. of Wales: m. 1974, Sheila Mary Evans. *Residence*, 4, Park Rd., Abingdon, Berks.—— Margaret Marion, b. 1906: m. 1938, the Rt. Rev. Leslie Stibbard, Assist. Bishop of Newcastle, NSW, 62, Kemp St., Hamilton, 2303, NSW, and has issue living, David Piers (9, Pulver St. Hamilton, 2303, NSW), b. 1943: m. 1966, Janet Pauline, da. of Dale Harrison, of Lawrence, NSW, and has issue living, Dermot, Harrison b. 1969, Samantha Marion b. 1968,—Stephen Patrick, b. 1947,—Ruth, b. 1940: m. 1963, Noël Bernard McFayden, of 38, Janet St., Merewether, NSW, and has issue living, David James b. 1964, Michael Stuart b. 1969, Lisa Jane b. 1965,— Miriam Anne, b. 1950.——Helen Alice, b. 1914: m. 1944, the Rev. John Lionel Mortimer, and has issue living, Lawrence George, b. 1945,—Michael Piers, b. 1946,—Christopher Hugh, b. 1949. *Address*, Elmhurst Ballet School, Camberley, Surrey.

This baronet is descended from William Piers, son of Henry Piers, of Piers Hall, Yorks., who is said at one time to have saved the Princess Elizabeth from the fury of her sister, Queen Mary, by conveying her privately away. After that princess ascended the throne, he was sent by Her Majesty to Ireland, and received a grant of the abbey of Tristernagh, in Westmeath. He was afterwards appointed Governor of Carrickfergus and Seneschal of the county of Antrim, and in 1565 obtained the reward of 1,000 marks for bringing in the head of the rebel Shane O'Neil. The 9th baronet, Sir Cnarles Pigott, was Major (retired) Canadian Mil. and served in S. Africa 1900-1901, and in European War 1914-19.

PIGOT, Creation (G.B.) 1764, of Patshull, Staffordshire.

Sir ROBERT PIGOT, *D.S.O., M.C.,* 6th Baronet; b. May 3rd, 1882; s. his father, *Sir* GEORGE, 1934; ed. at Eton; formerly Major and Brevet Lieut.-Col. Rifle Brig. (Prince Consort's Own); retired as Hon. Brig.-Gen. 1919; European War 1914-16 (despatches, M.C., D.S.O., Brevets Major and Lieut.-Col.); is Flying Officer R.A.F. Vol. Reserve; D.S.O. 1916: m. 1913, Norah Beatrice Oakeley, who d. 1969, da. of the late Capt. C. Reginald Hargreaves (formerly 13th Hussars), of Remenham, Wraysbury, and has issue.

Arms—Ermine, three lozenges conjoined in fesse sable. Crest—A wolf's head erased argent.

Residence—Yarlington Lodge, Wincanton, Somerset.

Always ready.

Daughters living—Margaret, b. 1914: m. 1st, 1940, Major Donald Ian Molteno, Black Watch, who d. (killed in action during European War) 1944; 2ndly, 1949, (Edward) John Macdonald Dent, of Manor Farm, Broughton, Stockbridge, Hants., and has issue living, (by 1st marriage) Susan Ferelith, b. 1941, Gillian, b. 1942.——Jean (twin), b. 1914: m. 1944, Capt. A. Murray Robertson, Black Watch, of The Lowes, Dunkeld, Perths., and has issue living, Alastair John, b. 1946.——Diana Gillian, b. 1918.

Sister living—Norah Edith (of 3, Park House, Park Place, Cheltenham): m. 1918, Capt. Victor Reginald Booth, late Gordon Highlanders, who d. 1943, and has issue living, David Reginald Peter (of 130, Old Bath Rd., Cheltenham, Glos.), b. 1921; ed. at Charterhouse: m. 1952, Anne Burgess, da. of the late Brig.-Gen. O. J. Gatchell, of Saunderstown, Rhode Island, USA, and has issue living, Antony Robert James b. 1953, Nora Jane b. 1957.

Collateral Branch living.
Issue of the late George Douglas Hugh Pigot, son of 5th baronet, b. 1883, d. 1959: m. 1910, Hersey Elizabeth, who d. 1970, da. of Lt. Gerald Rivers Maltby, MVO, RN [E. Minto, colls.]:—

ROBERT ANTHONY, *CB, OBE* (Yew Tree Lodge, Bembridge, I. of Wight; Royal Yacht Squadron), *b.* July 6th, 1915; ed. at Stowe; Maj.-Gen. RM (ret.); Dep. Standing Group NATO, Rep. with N. Atlantic Council, Paris 1958-59, and Ch. of Staff RM 1960-64; Managing Dir. of Bone Brothers Ltd. 1964-66; a Dir. of Exec. Appointments, Ltd. 1968-70; 1939-45 War (despatches); OBE (Mil) 1959, CB (Mil) 1964: *m.* 1st, 1942, Honor, who *d.* 1966, da. of the late Capt. Wilfred St. Martin Gibbon; 2ndly, 1968, Sarah Anne, da. of David Richard Colville [see V. Colville, colls.], and has issue living, (by 1st m.) George Hugh (66, Glebe Place, SW3), *b.* 1946: *m.* 1967 (m. diss. 1973), Judith Sandeman, el. da. of the late Maj. John Hele Sandeman-Allen, RA [see E. Woolton], and has issue living, Melanie Barbara *b.* 1969,——Louise, *b.* 1943: *m.* 1966, Peter Mellor, of 41, Curtis Rd., Ashdell Park, Alton, Hants., and has issue living, Nichola *b.* 1970, Susanna *b.* 1975,—(by 2nd m.) Robert James, *b.* 1971, Sarah Sophie, *b.* 1975.——Hersey Alice (74, Cleveland St., W1), *b.* 1911.——Priscilla Ann! (Flat 7, Hillgrove Court, St. Helier, Jersey), *b.* 1921; resumed the surname of Drake by deed poll 1968: *m.* 1st, 1942, Havilland Anthony Mackworth Drake, of Guernsey, who *d.* 1948; 2ndly, 1952, Alexander Gortshakoff, from whom she obtained a divorce 1966.

The 1st baronet, Sir George Pigot (Governor of Madras 1755-63 and 1775-7, and M.P. for Wallingford 1765-8 and subsequently for Bridgnorth), was created a Baronet with special remainder to his brothers Robert and Hugh ; in 1765 he became Baron Pigot, which title expired on his death 1777. He bequeathed the celebrated Pigot diamond, valued by skilful lapidaries at £30,000, to his brothers, Gen. Sir Robert, the 2nd baronet, and Adm. Hugh Pigot, and his sister, Margaret Fisher; it was subsequently disposed of under an Act of Parliament 1800, by way of lottery, for £23,998 16s. The 4th baronet sat as M.P. for Bridgnorth (C) 1832-53.

PIGOTT, Creation (U.K.) 1808, of Knapton, Queen's County.

Here and elsewhere

HIC ET ALIUBI

Sir BERKELEY PIGOTT, 4th *Baronet,* son of the late Lieut.-Col. Charles Berkeley Pigott, C.B., D.S.O., el. son of 3rd Baronet; *b.* May 29th, 1894 ; *s.* his grandfather, *Sir* CHARLES ROBERT, 1911 ; ed. at Wellington Coll. ; Major (retired) 17th/21st Lancers ; 1914-19 War, 1940-45 War: *m.* 1919, Christabel Charlotte, who *d.* 1974, da. of the Rev. F. H. Bowden-Smith, of Careys, Brockenhurst, Hants, and has issue.

Arms—Ermine, three lozenges in fesse sable, a crescent for difference. Crest—A wolf's head erased proper, collared or.

Residence—Wedge Hill Farm, Woodlands, Wimborne, Dorset.

Son living—BERKELEY HENRY SEBASTIAN, *b.* June 24th, 1925; ed. at Ampleforth; European War 1944-5 with R.M.: *m.* 1954, Jean, da. of J. W. Balls, of Holly Lodge, Surlingham, Norfolk, and has issue living, David John Berkeley, *b.* 1955,——Anthony Charles Philip, *b.* 1960,——Sarah Jane Mary, *b.* 1964. *Residence,* Brook Farm, Shobley, Ringwood, Hants.

Daughters living—Mary Stephanie, *b.* 1920 : *m.* 1st, 1951, Peter Friedrich Sika; 2ndly, 1959, Com. Walter Higham, R.N., and has issue living, (by 2nd marriage), Stephen Walter, *b.* 1960. *Residence,* Pond Farm, Church Hill, Verwood, Dorset.——Mary Veronica, *b.* 1922: *m.* 1944, Stefan Wysogota-Kwasniewski, and has issue living, Casimir Stefan, *b.* 1946,——Sabina Orietta, *b.* 1945: *m.* 1964, Derek Johnstone Brook, and has issue living, Gregory Damien Amadeus *b.* 1965. *Residence,* Martyr's House, Walsingham, Norfolk.

Sister living—Florence Ada Cecile (Yvonne), *b.* 1890 : *m.* 1st, 1920, Roland William Edward Ruddock, who *d.* 1942, Ceylon Survey Depart.; 2ndly, 1946, Major Leslie Fitzroy Richard, RA and RAF (ret.), who *d.* 1947. *Residence* Pond Cottage, Church Hill, Verwood, Dorset.

The 1st baronet, Sir George, was son of Major-Gen. Thomas Pigott, M.P., of Knapton, Queen's Co., and Sir Charles, 3rd Bt., served in the Crimea.

PILDITCH, Creation (U.K.) 1929, of Bartropps, Weybridge, co. Surrey.

VINCIT QUI SE VINCIT

He conquers who conquers himself.

Sir RICHARD EDWARD PILDITCH, 4th *Baronet ; b.* Sept. 8th, 1926 ; *s.* his brother, *Sir* PHILIP JOHN FREDERICK, 1954 : ed. at Charterhouse : European War 1944-5 with R.N., in India and Ceylon : *m.* 1950, Pauline Elizabeth Smith, and has issue.

Arms—Per chevron invected sable and or, two ancient galleys in chief, and in base an eagle displayed all counterchanged. Crest—A bear sejant proper, muzzled and gorged with a chain or, pendent therefrom an escutcheon sable charged with an eagle displayed gold.

Residence—4, Fisherman's Bank, Mudeford, Christchurch, Hants.

Son living—JOHN RICHARD, *b.* Sept. 24th, 1955.

Daughter living—Fiona, *b.* 1951.

Daughters living of 3rd Baronet—Frances Jean, *b.* 1952.——Felicity Mary (posthumous), *b.* 1954.

Half-Sister living—Rosalind Phyllis Muriel, *b.* 1946.

Uncle living (son of 1st baronet)—Edgar Lewis, *TD, b.* 1901; ed. at Eton, and at Trin. Coll., Oxford; Solicitor 1926; formerly a member of the firm of Longbourne, Stevens & Powell, of 7, Lincoln's Inn Fields, WC2; 1939-45 War in N. Africa, and Italy, as Maj. R.A. (T.A.) (despatches, Africa Star, Italy star, 1939-45 star, American Bronze star): *m.* 1936, Anne (GOODCHILD), da. of Richard Llewellyn Weeks, of Broomhaugh House, Riding Mill, Northumberland, and has issue living, Simon Andrew Llewellyn (4, St. James Close, Ruscombe, Twyford, Reading), *b.* 1938; ed. at Eton, at McGill Univ., Montreal, and at Roy. Agricl Coll., Cirencester: *m.* 1969, Ute Mayr. *Residence*, 4, St. James Close, Ruscombe, Twyford, Reading. *Club*, Oxford and Cambridge.

Aunt living (da. of 1st baronet)—Mabel Emily (May): *m.* 1919, Maj. Henry Alexander Hammick, OBE, MC, who *d.* 1968, [*see* Hammick, Bt., colls.]. *Residence*, Delvers, Pyrford, Surrey.

Mother living—Frances Isabella, da. of J. G. Weeks, JP: *m.* 1918, Sir Philip Harold Pilditch, 2nd Bt., who *d.* 1949, and from whom she had obtained a divorce 1936. *Residence*, 1, Chalbury Court, Rushford Warren, Mudeford, Christchurch, Hants.

Widows living of 2nd and 3rd Baronets—PATRICIA, da. of Alex. W. Whittet: *m.* 1st, 1936, as his second wife, Sir Philip Harold Pilditch, 2nd Bt., who *d.* 1949; 2ndly, 1951, Lieut.-Col. Raymond Francis Lewis Thomas. *Residence*, Abbottswood, Oakfield Glade, Weybridge, Surrey.——PHYLLIS JEAN (*Phyllis, Lady Pilditch*), el. da. of Major Dudley Cautley Stewart Smith, M.B.E., of Weybridge, Surrey: *m.* 1948, Sir Philip John Frederick Pilditch, 3rd Bt., who *d.* 1954. *Residence*, 47, Princes Gate Mews, SW7.

The 1st baronet, Sir Philip Edward Pilditch (son of the late Philip John Pilditch, of Plymouth), sat as M.P. for Spelthorne Div. of Middlesex (*U*) 1918-31.

PILE, Creation (U.K.) 1900 of Kenilworth House, Rathgar, co. Dublin.

Sine labe nota.
Known without dishonour.

Sir FREDERICK ALFRED PILE, *G.C.B.*, *D.S.O.*, *M.C.*, 2nd *Baronet*; *b.* Sept. 14th, 1884; *s.* his father, *Sir* THOMAS DEVEREUX, 1931; Hon. LL.D. Leeds 1946; Gen., late Roy. Tank Corps; was Assist. Director of Mechanization at War Office 1928-32, and Brigadier Comdg. Canal Brig., Ismailia, Egypt 1932-6; European War 1914-18 (despatches, M.C., D.S.O.); appointed to command 1st Anti-Aircraft Div. (T.A.) 1937, and Gen. Officer Comg.-in-Ch. Anti-Aircraft Command T.A. 1939; Director Gen. of Housing, Min. of Works, April to Oct. 1945; D.S.O. 1918, C.B. (Mil.) 1938, K.C.B. (Mil.) 1941, G.C.B. (Mil.) 1945: *m.* 1st, (Jan.) 1915, Vera Millicent (from whom he obtained a divorce 1929), da. of Brig.-Gen. F. C. Lloyd; 2ndly, 1932, Hester Mary Melba, who *d.* 1949, da. of the late George Grenville Phillimore, B.C.L., of Shedfield, Hants [E. Fortescue, colls.]; 3rdly, 1951, Molly Eveline Louise Mary (late Ch. Com. ATS), da. of the late Ralph Smyth, of Newtown, Drogheda, co. Louth, and widow of Brig. Francis Wyville Home, and has issue by 1st m..

Arms—Azure, three piles argent, on a chief ermine, a castle with two towers proper between two harps or, stringed of the second. **Crest**—on a ducal coronet or, charged with a cross-botonée azure, a pelican with wings addorsed and inverted proper.

Residence—Broom Manor, Cottered, Herts. *Clubs*—Cavalry, Pratt's.

Sons living—By 1st m.—FREDERICK DEVEREUX, *MC* (Harriet House, Sedlescombe, Sussex; MCC), *b.* Dec. 10th, 1915; ed. at Weymouth; is Col. late R. Tank Regt.; Comdt. RAC Driving and Maintenance Sch. 1960-62; 1939-45 War (MC): *m.* 1940, Pamela, da. of the late Philip Henstock, of Newbury, Berks., and has issue living, Fiona Devereux, *b.* 1941,—Vanessa Anne, *b.* 1951: *m.* 1972, Rory Gilchrist Graham Mackean.——John Devereux (Munstead, Godalming, Surrey), *b.* 1918; formerly Maj. RA (TA): *m.* 1946, Katharine Mary, da. of Austin G. Shafe, of 102, Bell St., Henley-on-Thames, and has issue living, Anthony John Devereux, *b.* 1947,—Timothy Simon Devereux, *b.* 1953,—Jennifer Jane Devereux, *b.* 1950,—Sarah Katharine Devereux, *b.* 1960.

Collateral Branch living.

Issue of the late Major Walter Devereux Pile, younger son of 1st baronet, *b.* 1887, *d.* 1959: *m.* 1921, Margaret Lucy, MBE (The Crown, Pedair Ffordd, Llanrhaiadr, near Oswestry), el. da. of Thomas Irvine Bonner, M.A., M.B., C.M., formerly of 22, Ivy Road, Shipley, Yorkshire :—

Margaret Patricia Devereux The Crown, Pedair Ffordd, Llanrhaiadr, Oswestry) *b.* 1923, BSc. London.——Anne Devereux, *b.* 1932: *m.* 1961, David Evan Daniel, of The Cottage, 5, Aigburth Drive, Liverpool 17.

The 1st baronet, Sir Thomas Devereux Pile, was High Sheriff of Dublin 1898, and Lord Mayor 1900.

MILBORNE-SWINNERTON-PILKINGTON, Creation (N.S.) 1635, of Stanley, Yorkshire.

Now thus, now thus.

Sir THOMAS HENRY MILBORNE-SWIN-NERTON-PILKINGTON, 14th *Baronet*; *b.* March 10th, 1934; *s.* his father, *Sir* ARTHUR WILLIAM, *MC*, 1952; ed. at Eton; formerly in Roy. Scots Greys: *m.* 1961, Susan, da. of Norman Stewart Rushton Adamson, of Durban, S. Africa, and has issue.

Arms—Quarterly: 1st and 4th, argent, a cross flory, voided gules, *Pilkington*; 2nd, argent, a cross formé fleuretté sable, surmounted by a bend engrailed gules, *Swinnerton*; 3rd, per pale, argent and gules, a cross patonce between, in the sinister chief and dexter base two leopards' faces counter-changed, *Milborne*. **Crests**—1st, on a mount vert a boar passant argent, charged with a cross formé fleuretté sable; 2nd, a mower with his scythe proper, habited per pale argent and sable; 3rd, a demi-lion per fesse argent and gules, holding between the paws a leopard's face of the first.

Address—King's Walden Bury, Hitchin, Herts.

Son living—RICHARD ARTHUR, *b.* Sept. 4th, 1964.
Daughters living—Sarah Elizabeth, *b.* 1962.——Joanna, *b.* 1967.

Sisters living—Sonia Margery, *b.* 1937: *m.* 1965, Timothy Rogers, of Airlie, Lucan, co. Dublin, and has issue living, John Dyke Darby, *b.* 1968,—Anthony Patrick, *b.* 1971.——Carole Mary, *b.* 1942; *m.* 1962, James Bowes Daly, of Evendine House, Colwall, Malvern, Worcs. [see B. McGowan].——Moira Elizabeth, *b.* 1943: *m.* 1969, Benjamin Hanbury, of Green Man House, Cowlinge, Newmarket, and has issue living, Emma Jane, *b.* 1970,—Amanda Aline, *b.* 1973.
Uncle living (son of 12th baronet)—Ulick O'Connor, *b.* 1903: *m.* 1951, Angela Mary Purcell, da. of the late Gerald de Purcell Cotter [*see* Cotter, Bt., colls.], and has issue living, Lionel Ulick, *b.* 1956,—Michael Gerald, *b.* 1959. *Residence*, Gortbrack House, Castle Townsend, co. Cork.

Mother living of 14th Baronet—ELIZABETH MARY, da. of Major John Fenwick Harrison [B. Burnham]: *m.* 1st, 1931 (m. diss. 1950), Maj. Sir Arthur William Milborne-Swinnerton. Pilkington, MC, 13th Bt., who *d.* 1952; 2ndly, 1950, Maj. Patrick Henry Anthony Burke, Gren-Guards, who *d.* 1964. *Residence*, Stackallan House, Navan, co. Meath.

This family descends from Robert Pilkington, of Sowerby, Yorks, 3rd son of Sir John Pilkington, of Pilkington, Lancs. (*d.* 1421). Sir Arthur Pilkington, of Stanley, nr. Wakefield, received a Baronetcy of Nova Scotia, probably with remainder to heirs male whatsoever (the patent was not entered in the Great Seal Register of Scotland), and a grant of 6,000 acres in Nova Scotia. Sir William Pilkington, 8th Bt. (*d.* 1850): *m.* Mary, dau. and co-heir of Thomas Swinnerton, of Butterton Hall, Staffs., by Mary, dau. and heir, of Charles Milborne, of Wonastow, Monmouth. His youngest son, Sir Lionel Pilkington, 11th Bt., took by Roy. Licence 1856 the surnames of Milborne-Swinnerton but subsequently resumed the final name of Pilkington. The 13th baronet, Sir Arthur William Milborne-Swinnerton Pilkington, M.C., was Major 16th/5th Lancers.

PINSENT, Creation (U.K.) 1938, of Selly Hill, City of Birmingham.

JE·PENSE·EN·BIEN

Sir ROY PINSENT, 2nd *Baronet; b.* July 22nd, 1883; *s.* his father, *Sir* RICHARD ALFRED, *LL.D.*, 1948; ed. at Marlborough Coll. and at Univ. Coll., Oxford (B.A. 1903); admitted a Solicitor 1909; European War 1916-19 as Lieut. R.E.: *m.* 1918, Mary Tirzah, who *d.* 1951, da. of Dr. Edward Geoffrey Walls, of Southfields, Mavis Enderby, Spilsby, Lincolnshire, and has issue.

Arms—Argent a saltire flory vert, between four chaffinches proper. **Crest**—Upon a fleur-de-lis couped vert, two chaffinches addorsed proper.
Residence—5, St. Georges Sq., SW1.

Sons living—CHRISTOPHER ROY, *b.* Aug. 2nd, 1922: ed. at Winchester; is a Portrait Painter; 1939-45 War as Leading Aircraftman RAF: *m.* 1951 Susan Mary, da. of John Norton Scorer, of Fotheringhay and has issue living, Thomas Benjamin Roy, *b.* 1967,— Laura Candace, *b.* 1954,—Joanna Mary, *b.* 1957. *Residence*, The Chestnuts, Castle Hill, Guildford.——Michael Roy, *b.* 1927; ed. at Marlborough; admitted a Solicitor 1952; 1939-45 War as Lt. R. Signals: *m.* 1952 (m. diss. 19—), Stella Marie, da. of the late Basil Priestman of Birmingham, and has issue living, William Ross, *b.* 1955,—Nicola Jane, *b.* 1957,—Tonya Mary, *b.* 1959. *Residence*, 61, Wellington Rd., Birmingham.
Daughter living—Rosemary, *b.* 1930 ; ed. at Edgbaston High Sch.: *m.* 1960, Keiden John Knapp Barrow, and has issue living, Clive Andrew Knapp, *b.* 1962,—Clare, *b.* 1964. *Residence*, Marchants Farm, Churt, Surrey.

Collateral Branches living

Issue of the late Com. **Clive Pinsent**, R.N. (retired), 2nd son of 1st baronet, *b.* 1886, *d.* 1948: *m.* 1921, Kathleen Jane, who *d.* 1974, da. of the late George Macpherson, DL, JP, of The Lloyd House, Wolverhampton:—
Andrew Clive Macpherson, *b.* 1922 ; Lieut.-Com. (retired) R.N. ; European War 1939-45 : *m.* 1945, Gloria Poppy Marie, da. of Capt. Cecil Herbert Tollemache, and has issue living, Antony Andrew Macpherson (41, Elthiron Rd., SW6), *b.* 1946: *m.* 1969, Clare Natalie, da. of Victor Reynolds, of Estremoz, Portugal, and has issue living, a son *b.* 1973,—David Tollemache, *b.* 1948,—Susan Catherine, *b.* 1953.— Residence, Grey Barn, Angmering, nr. Littlehampton, Sussex.——James Macpherson, *b.* 1925; Lt.-Com. (ret.) RN; 1939-45 War, Korea 1950-51: *m.* 1956 (m. diss. 1972), Daphne Miranda, da. of Capt. Kenneth Lanyon Harkness, CBE, DSC, RN (ret.), and has issue living, Oliver Clive, *b.* 1964,—Camilla Louise, *b.* 1962. *Residence*, 30, Leonard Court, W8 6NN.——*Rev.* Ewen Macpherson, *b.* 1930; formerly Lt. RN: *m.* 1962, Jean Grizel, da. of the late Maj.-Gen. Neil McMicking, CB, CBE, DSO, MC, and has issue living, Thomas Neil *b.* 1964,—Matthew Clive *b.* 1970,—Katherine Jane *b.* 1963,—Emma Charlotte (twin), *b.* 1964. *Residence*, The Rectory, Kelso, Roxburghshire. *Club*, United Service.

Issue of the late Col. **John Ryland Pinsent**, CBE, DSO, 3rd son of 1st baronet, *b.* 1888, *d.* 1957: *m.* 1915, Kathleen May, who *d.* 1969, da. of the late Col. E. G. Boyce:—
John Laurance, *b.* 1916 ; admitted a Solictor 1946; is a Farmer ; European War 1939-45 as Major R.A. : *m.* 1940, Margaret Molyneux, el. da. of the late R. Vernon Favell, and has issue living, John Edward, *b.* 1950,—Margaret Anne, *b.* 1941: *m.* 1964, the Rev. John Lawrence Simpson, of 1, Cross St., Helston, Cornwall, and has issue living, Benjamin John Lawrence *b.* 1970, Joanna *b.* 1965, Jessamie Anne, *b.* 1968,—Mary, *b.* 1943: *m.* 1964, Denis Theodore Archdale, of Castle Archdale, Irvinestown, co. Fermanagh, and has issue living, Nicholas Henry *b.* 1966, Audley Mervyn *b.* 1969, Rachael Mary *b.* 1968,—Jennifer, *b.* 1944: *m.* 1969, Lt. Christopher Louis Wreford-Brown, RN, and has issue living, Julia Anne *b.* 1970,—Elizabeth Jane, *b.* 1948. *Residence*, Higher Ludbrook, Ermington, S. Devon.——Richard Alan, *b.* 1931: *m.* 1954, Mary Matruh, da. of Group-Capt. John Benjamin Graham, OBE, MC, AFC, and has issue living, Dinah, *b.* 1955,—Susan Melanie *b.* 1964.

The 1st baronet, Sir Richard Alfred Pinsent (son of the late Richard Steele Pinsent), was Pres. of Law So. 1918-19.

PLATT, Creation (U.K.) 1958, of Rusholme, City of Manchester.

Sir HARRY PLATT, *M.D., M.S.,*
F.R.C.S., 1st *Baronet,* son of the late Ernest
Platt, of Dale Brow, Prestbury, Cheshire ;
b. 1886 ; ed. at Manchester Univ. (M.B. and
Ch.B. 1909, MD 1921); MS London 1911;
FRCS England 1912; Hon. MD Berne
and Hon. Dr. Paris; Hon. Fellow of American
Coll. of Surgs. 1934, of Roy. Canadian Coll. of
Surgs. 1955, of S. African Coll. of Physicians
and Surgs. 1957, of Roy. Australian Coll. of
Surgs. 1961, and of Board of Faculty of
Dental Surgery 1963; Hon. F.R.C.S.E. 1957;
Hon. LL.D., Manchester, Liverpool, Belfast
and Leeds; a K St J; Emeritus Prof. of
Orthopædic Surgery, Manchester Univ.; Con-
sultant Adviser in Orthopædics, Min. of
Health 1940-63; Pres. of Roy. Coll. of Surgs.
of England 1954-57; Hon. Pres. of International Federation of Surgical Colls. since
1970; Vice-Pres. of International Soc. for
Rehabilitation of Disabled 1963; Pres.
Central Council for the Disabled 1969, and
of Nat. Fund for Research Crippling Diseases since 1969; 1914-18 War
as Capt. RAMC; Knt. 1948: *m.* 1916, Gertrude Sarah, da. of Richard Turney,
of Old Linslade, Bucks, and has issue.

ˇ**Arms**—Azure in base a lyre-bird tail displayed proper and in chief a portcullis chained between
two dexter gloves or. **Crest**—A falcon close proper grasping with the dexter claw a surgeon's
scalpel blade upward and inward or.

Residence—14, Rusholme Gdns., Manchester, M14 5LS. *Clubs*—Royal Automobile, Travellers',
St. James (Manchester).

Son living—FRANK LINDSEY (of 3, Sherwood Av., Fallowfield, Manchester, 14), *b.* Jan. 16th,
1919; ed. at Stowe, Magdalen Coll., Oxford, and the Sorbonne; Bar. Inner Temple 1954; 1939-45
War as Maj. Intelligence Corps: *m.* 1951, Johanna Magdalena Elizabeth, da. of the late Friedrich
Wilhelm Laenger, of Westphalia.

Daughters living—Honor Mary Munro, *b.* 1917: *m.* 1939, Cedric Harald Flurscheim, of 20, Moore
St., SW3, and has issue living, Jacqueline Mary, *b.* 1940: *m.* 1964, John Philip Simms, of 82
Greenwich South St., Greenwich, SE10, and has issue living, Benjamin John *b.* 1965,—Elizabeth
Sally Lindsey, *b.* 1943: *m.* 1970, Michael Pelzer.——Rosemary Elizabeth, *b.* 1921: *m.* 1948,
Trevor Lewis Midgley, of 4, Courtfield Drive, Maidenhead, Berks., and has issue living, Jonathan
David, *b.* 1950,—Amanda Jane Elizabeth, *b.* 1953.——Sara Margaret Helen, *b.* 1927: *m.* 1952,
Capt. Lawrence Hugh Williams, RM [*see* Williams, Bt., *cr.* 1798]. *Residence*, Old Parciau,
Marianglas, Anglesey.——Diana Primrose Rowley, *b.* 1932: *m.* 1955, Robin Gwynne Jennings,
of 134, Rosendale Rd., Dulwich, SE21 8LG [Wake, Bt., *cr.* 1621, colls.], and has issue living,
Nicholas David de Burgh, *b.* 1959,—Robin Hereward, *b.* 1963,—Charles Rupert, *b.* 1968,—
Sarah Primrose, *b.* 1961.

POLE, Creation (E.) 1628, of Shute House, Devonshire.

Pollet virtus.
Virtue is powerful.

Sir JOHN GAWEN CAREW POLE, *DSO, TD,* 12th
Baronet, son of the late Lt.-Gen. Sir Reginald Pole-
Carew, KCB, CVO, el. son of William Henry Pole-
Carew, 3rd son of the Rt. Hon. Reginald Pole-Carew,
grandson of the Rev. Carolus Carew, 3rd son of 3rd
baronet: *b.* March 4th, 1902; *s.* his kinsman, *Sir*
FREDERICK ARUNDELL DE LA POLE, 1926; assumed by
deed poll 1926, the name of John Gawen Carew Pole in
lieu of John Gawen Pole-Carew; ed. at Eton, and RMC;
a patron of two livings; Col. (ret.) late Coldm. Gds.;
Hon. Col. DCLI (TA) 1958-67; ADC to C.-in-C.
India 1924-25, and Comptroller to Gov.-Gen. of
S. Africa 1935-36; Palestine 1936; 1939-45 War (despatches, DSO); raised
and commanded 4th/5th Bn. DCLI 1946-47; a Member of Prince of Wales's
Council 1952-68; a Member of HM Bodyguard of Hon. Corps of Gentlemen-
at-Arms 1950-72 (Standard Bearer 1969-72), and of Nat. Hunt Cttee. (Steward
1953-56), and a Liveryman of Fishmongers' Co. (Assist. on Court since 1957,
Warden 1966-72, Prime Warden 1969-70); Vice-Chm. and a Dir. of Westward
Television Ltd., and Dir., of Lloyds Bank (Chm. of Devon and Cornwall
Cttee. 1955-72), and English China Clays, a Member of S-W Electricity Con-
sultative Cttee. for Great Britain 1950-55, and of W. Area Board, British
Transport Commn. 1955-61; KStJ; a JP of Cornwall; High Sheriff 1947-48,
Lord-Lieut. since 1962; Co. Councillor (Chm. 1952-63) and Co. Alderman
1954-66; DSO 1944: *m.* 1928, Cynthia Mary, OBE, da. of Walter Spencer
Morgan Burns, of North Mymms Park, Hatfield, Herts. [see D. Portland,
colls.], and has issue.

Arms—Azure, semée of fleurs-de-lis or, a lion rampant argent.
Seat—Antony House, Torpoint, Cornwall. *Clubs*—Guards', Pratt's, Jockey, MCC.

Son living (JOHN) RICHARD WALTER REGINALD *CAREW POLE* (Erth Barton, Saltash, Cornwall; Turf and Pratt's Clubs), *b.* Dec. 2nd, 1938; ed. at Eton, and Royl Agric. Coll., Cirencester; late Lt. Coldm. Gds.; a Liveryman of Fishmongers' Co.; a Co. Councillor for Cornwall: *m.* 1st, 1966 (m. diss. 1973), the Hon. Victoria Marion Ann Lever, da. of 3rd Viscount Leverhulme; 2ndly, 1974, Mary, da. of Lt.-Col. Ronald Dawnay [see V. Downe, colls.], and has issue living (by 2nd m.) Tremayne John, *b.* 1974,—John Alexander George, *b.* 1975.

Daughters living—Elizabeth Mary, *b.* 1929 : *m.* 1953, David Cuthbert Tudway Quilter [see Quilter, Bt.]. *Residence*, Milton Lodge, Wells, Somerset.——Caroline Anne (Hon. Mrs. Paul Asquith), *b.* 1933: *m.* 1963, as his 2nd wife, the Hon. Paul Asquith, of 26, Laxford House, Cundy St., SW1, and Hawkwell House, Pembury, Kent [see By. Asquith of Bishopstone.]

Sisters living—Marye Frances POLE-CAREW (South Wilcove House, Torpoint, Cornwall), *b.* 1903. ——Victoria Geraldine, *b.* 1904: *m.* 1929, Cdr. Peter Du Cane, CBE, RN (ret.), and has issue living, Charles Antony (15, Avenue Eugène Pittard, Geneva), *b.* 1940: *m.* 1969, Jeanette, da. of William de Vigier,—Diana Edith, *b.* 1929: *m.* 1st, 1954, the Hon. Jeremy John Cubitt, who *d.* 1958, and from whom she had obtained a divorce 1957 [see B. Ashcombe]; 2ndly, 1957, Capt. Nigel Arthur Tunnicliffe, Gren. Gds. [see B. Mowbray, colls.],—Margaret Anne, *b.* 1932. *Residence*, Seamark, Glandore, co. Cork.

Collateral Branches living.

Issue of the late Maj. Patrick William Butler POLE-CAREW, brother of 12th baronet, *b.* 1913, *d.* 1971: *m.* 1st, 1939, Sonia (who obtained a divorce 1950), da. of Sir (William Eley) Cuthbert Quilter, 2nd Bt.; 2ndly, 1950, Mary Patience (Clashaphouca, Clogheen, co. Tipperary), da. of the late Maj. Richard Ernest Gilchrist Phillips, and formerly wife of Ronald Ewan Cameron:—
(By 1st m.) Rosemary, *b.* 1940.

Grandchildren of the late Charles Edward Pole-Carew, uncle of 12th baronet:—
Issue of the late Maj. Gerald Ayshford Pole-Carew, *b.* 1887, *d.* 1969: *m.* 1915, Eileen Flora Lismore (Flat B, 1, Royal Cres., W11 4SL), da. of the late Surg.-Maj. George Henry Kenneth MacDonald O'Callaghan, CMG:—
Charles Oliver (Flat B, 1, Royal Cres., W11 4SL), *b.* 1923; ed. at Claysmore.——Christopher Gerald (Newfield Farm House, Screveton, Notts.), *b.* 1931; formerly Lt. RN: *m.* 1954, Gillian, only da. of Clive Burton, of Addo, Cape Province, S. Africa, and has issue living, Gerald Anthony Peregrine, *b.* 1957,—Delia Elizabeth, *b.* 1955,—Camilla Janet, *b.* 1962.——Geraldine Frances Flora, *b.* 1917.——Eileen Loveday (Flat 4, 16, Upper Berkeley St., W1), *b.* 1930: *m.* 1955 (m. annulled 1964), Brian Arnold Miller.

Grandchildren of the late Reginald Charles Somers Pole (infra):—
Issue of the late Reginald Edward Morice de la Pole, *b.* 1893, *d.* 1948: *m.* 1924, Dorothy Ethel Christine (of 12, New Rd., Reading, Berks), da. of the late Charles William Searle, JP, of Larchwood, Sunninghill, Ascot, Berks:—
Pauline Marjorie Doreen, *b.* 1925: *m.* 1951, Squadron-Leader Frederick John Crewe, R.A.F. (ret.), and has issue living, Roderic Guy Pole, *b.* 1952,—Alastair Frederick, *b.* 1954,—Felicity Jane, *b.* 1953,—Virginia Rosemarie Pauline, *b.* 1955. *Address*, c/o National Provincial Bank, Purley, Surrey.——Rosemary Ethel Greason, *b.* 1927: *m.* 1957, Patrick Eric Edward Walsh, 85, Laburnum Rd., Wellington, Somerset, and has issue living, Guy Patrick, *b.* 1957,—Penelope Jane, *b.* 1958,—Jill Christine, *b.* 1960,—Kim Elizabeth, *b.* 1962.——Lucille Dorothy Carew, *b.* 1938: *m.* 1969, Stuart Malcolm Forbes Keir, of Brook Cottage, Tanhouse Rd., Oxted, Surrey.

Issue of the late Lionel Robert Glanville Pole, *b.* 1902, *d.* 1965: *m.* 1924 (m. diss. 19—), Gertrude Gregory:—
Reginald Robert, *b.* 1925: *m.* 1953, Sylvia Patricia Sullivan, and has issue living, a son, *b.* 19—,—Susan Carole, *b.* 1954,—a da., *b.* 19—.

Issue of the late Percival Arthur Carew Pole, *b.* 1904, *d.* 1965: *m.* 1934, Irene Clare French (45, Phyllis Av., Motspur Park, New Malden, Surrey):—
Geoffrey Arthur (5, Oakwood Rd., Windlesham, Surrey), *b.* 1935: *m.* 1961, Patricia, da. of W. Sweetman, of Birmingham, and has issue living, Julia, *b.* 1963,—Diana |(twin), |*b.* 1963,—Susan Caroline, *b.* 1964.——Roger Charles (11, Tadworth Av., New Malden, Surrey), *b.* 1939: *m.* 1959, Joyce, only da. of W. Powell, of Worcester Park, Surrey, and has issue living, Mark Nicholas Charles, *b.* 1961,—John Damian, *b.* 1967,—Carey Thérèse, *b.* 1959,—Joanne Sarah, *b.* 1963.——Jennifer Clare, *b.* 1937: *m.* 1961, Dudley Hasting Wheeler, of Friars Pardon, Hurworth-on-Tees, co. Durham, and has issue living, Clare Frances, *b.* 1963,—Alison Mary, *b.* 1966.

Grandchildren of the late Reginald Carolus Pole, 2nd son of the Rev. Edward Pole (*b* 1805), 2nd son of Rev. Edward Pole, DD, 3rd son of Reginald Pole, son of Rev. Carolus Pole, 3rd son of 3rd baronet:—
Issue of the late Reginald Charles Somers Pole, *b.* 1864, *d.* 1914: *m.* 1891, Gertrude, da. of the late Robert Greason, of Ellamula, Ceylon :—
Stephanie Lyttleton Antoinette, *b.* 1896: *m.* 1st, 1918 (m. diss. 1941), Walter Sidney Flindall, who *d.* 1970; 2ndly, 1942, Herbert R. Wratten, of The Orchard, Bartonwood Rd., Barton-on-Sea, Hants., and has issue living (by 1st m.) Ronald Wilton Somers (c/o Somerville & Co., Ltd., Box 146, Colombo, Ceylon), *b.* 1925: *m.* 1957, Eleanor Louise Baker, and has issue living, Jeremy Peter *b.* 1963, Jolyon James Lyttleton *b.* 1964, Nicola Stephanie *b.* 1958, Rachel Eleanor *b.* 1960,—Patricia Stephanie, *b.* 1919: *m.* 1942, Lionel Sydney Boys, of Orchard Close, Bradford Abbas, Dorset,—June Shelagh, *b.* 1921: *m.* 1st, 1944 (m. diss. 1951), Howard Douglas Wardle; 2ndly, 1953, A. Leslie Porter, of 30, Devon Rd., Beaurepaire 870, Quebec, Canada, and has issue living, (by 1st marriage) Guy Douglas *b.* 1945, (by 2nd marriage) Georgina Stephanie, *b.* 1954,—Maureen Gwynneth (14, St. John's Hill, Wimborne, Dorset), *b.* 1927.——Muriel Blanche Trelawney, *b.* 1908: *m.* 1934, Stanley John Campbell, of 10, Denman St., Warrawee, Aust. 2074, and has issue living, John Howard, *b.* 1945,—Valdene Rae, *b.* 1936: *m.* 1958, Timothy James Francis Herold, of 6, Denman St., Warrawee 2074, Aust., and has issue living, Richard Anthony John *b.* 1960, Alastair James Campbell *b.* 1967, David Charles Stewart *b.* 1971, Philippa Lesley *b.* 1959, Suzanne Jayne *b.* 1964,—Doronée Felicia, *b.* 1942: *m.* 1st, 1964 (m. diss. 1974), Clive Murree Perkins; 2ndly, 1974, Maj. Peter John Gybbon-Monypenny, The Queen's Regt., of Tudor Rose Cottage, Robertsbridge, Sussex, and has issue living (by 1st m.) Amanda Caryll *b.* 1967, (by 2nd m.) Duncan Reginald *b.* 1975.

Issue of the late Percival Edward Pole, *b.* 1867, *d.* 1952: *m.* 1905, Margaret Edith, who *d.* 1941, da. of the late John Leith, J.P., of Aberdeen :—
John Edward Carolus, *b.* 1906: *m.* 1942, Joan Alexandrina Lamont, da. of the late Robert Mitchell, of Aberdeen. *Residence*, Gushet Neuk, Bieldside, Aberdeenshire.

Issue of the late Albert Edward Pole, *b.* 1875, *d.* 1940: *m.* 1907, Sophia Buckingham, who *d.* 1955, el. da. of the late Edward Alexander Buckingham Hay, of Alaington, Dalkeith Avenue, Dumbreck, Glasgow :—
Edward Alexander, *b.* 1911: *m.* 1940, Sheila Ferguson, da. of James Welsh, of 580, Tollcross Road, Tollcross, Glasgow. *Residence*, 540, Paisley Road, West, Glasgow.——Reginald Carew, *b.* 1914: *m.* 1939, Mary MacKinnon, da. of R. P. Don, of 46, Walnut Crescent, Possilpark, Glasgow, and

has issue living, Reginald Carew, *b.* 1942,—Isobel Buchanan Colquhoun, *b.* 1947.——Annie Laing Hay, *b.* 1908.

Grandchildren of the late Rev. Edward Pole (*b.* 1805) (ante):—

Issue of the late Reginald Carolus Pole, *b.* 1841, *d.* 1897: *m.* 1864, Annie, who *d.* 1928 da. of the late Rev. Robert Pargiter, formerly V. of Towersey, Thame:—

Charles Carew, *b.* 1878.——**Courtenay Alexander**, *b.* 1888 : *m.* 1917, Janet Watson, da. of the late James Deans, of Highbury Park, Mount Florida, Glasgow. and has issue living, Reginald Alexander Carolus, *b.* 1920; late Lt.-Com. (S) RNVR; 1939-45 War—Courtenay Deans Carew, *b.* 1925; 1943-45 War with RN: *m.* 1951, Aileen Munro, da. of John M. Crawford, of 9, Etive Drive, Renfrewshire.——Blanche Caroline Edith.——Marie Stuart. *Residence,*

Issue of the late Henry Lionel Pole (who assumed the surname of de la Pole), *b.* 1846, *d.* 1930 : *m.* 1st, 1866 (marriage dissolved 18—) ; 2ndly, 18—, Mary, who *d.* 1939, da. of John Warwick :—

(By 2nd m.) Agneta Aurelienne Buller DE LA POLE, *b.* 1888. *Residence,* The Old Vicarage, Moulsford, Wallingford, Oxon.

Issue of the late John Pole, *b.* 1848, *d.* 1913 : *m.* 1877, Charlotte, who *d.* 1896, da. of the late Rev. Robert Pargiter (ante):—

Caroline Mary, *b.* 1886: *m.* 19—, ——Hutchinson, who *d.* (killed in action in N. Africa) 1942. *Residence,*

Granddaughter of the late Henry Lionel Pole (ante):—

Issue of the late Edward Lionel Carew de la Pole, *b.* 1868, *d.* 19—: *m.* 18— : —

Dorothy, *b.* 19—. *Resides in U.S.A.*

Granddaughter of the late John Pole, 5th son of the Rev. Edward Pole (ante):—

Issue of the late Herbert Edward Pole, *b.* 1882, *d.* 1965: *m.* 1930, Ena Marsh (Glenloch, Rowley Drive, nr. Cranleigh, Surrey):—

Millicent Rosemary, *b.* 1933: *m.* 1958, Peter Cox, of Petamille, 3, Park Way, Gt. Bookham, Surrey, and has issue living, Gawen Peter, *b.* 1967,—Emma Louise, *b.* 1964.

The 1st baronet was M.P. for Devonshire, the 2nd Baronet represented Honiton in Parliament, and the 3rd and 5th baronets each sat as M.P. for co. Devon. The 6th baronet assumed in 1790 the surname of De-la-Pole, which his successor discontinued, and the 8th baronet assumed in 1838 the surname of Reeve-de-la-Pole, and afterwards discontinued it. The 10th Baronet resumed the surname of de la Pole 1895. Sir Frederick Arundell de la Pole. 11th baronet, was High Sheriff of Devon 1917

POLE, Creation (G.B.) 1791, of Wolverton, Hampshire.

Virtue is powerful.

Sir PETER VAN NOTTEN POLE, 5th *Baronet*, son of the late Arthur Chandos Pole, grandson of the late Gen. Edward Pole, 4th son of 2nd Baronet ; *b.* Nov. 6th, 1921 ; *s.* his kinsman, Sir CECIL PERY *VAN-NOTTEN-POLE*, 1948; FASA; ACIS; a Co. Manager; 1939-45 War as Flight-Sgt. R. Aust. AF: *m.* 1949, Jean Emily, da. of the late C. D. Stone, of Borden, W. Aust., and has issue.

Arms—Argent, a chevron between three crescents gules, a mullet for difference. **Crest**—A falcon rising proper, a mullet for difference. **Supporters**—On either side a lion reguardant proper (the Supporters of H. S. H. William, Landgrave of Hesse-Cassel), debruised by a pale of three tinctures, the first half per pale gules and argent, the second half azure (originally conferred on the 1st Baronet by the Landgrave and confirmed by Roy. Warrant of 1794 to the Baronet and his successors).

Residence—12, Lothian Street, Floreat Park, W. Australia.

Son living—PETER JOHN CHANDOS (49, Doonan Rd., Nedlands, 6009, W. Aust.), *b.* April 27th, 1952: *m.* 1973, Suzanne Norah, da. of Harold Raymond Hughes, of 81, Archdeacon St., Nedlands, W. Aust.

Daughter living—Anne, *b.* 1957.

Sisters living—Marjorie van Notten, *b.* 1923. *Residence,* 17, Hesperia Avenue, City Beach, W. Australia.——Ellen van Notten, *b.* 1929. *Residence,* 17, Hesperia Avenue, City Beach W. Australia.

Mother living—Marjorie, da. of the late Charles Hargrave, of Glen Forrest, W. Australia : *m.* 1920, Arthur Chandos Pole (ante), who *d.* 1944. *Residence,* 17, Hesperia Avenue, City Beach, W. Australia.

Collateral Branch living.

Granddaughter of the late Capt. Edward Albert Pole, son of the late Gen. Edward Pole, 4th son of 2nd baronet :—

Issue of the late Edward Alexander Chandos Pole, *b.* 1867, *d.* 1945 : *m.* 1st, 1910, Gertrude Magdalene, who *d.* 1933, da. of Herbert Emms; 2ndly, 1935, Mrs. Evelyn Catherine Remington, da. of Capt. E. C. Smith, of Clacton:—

(By 1st marriage) Esmé Katherine, *b.* 1911: *m.* 1935, Raphe Willoughby Humphrey, who *d.* 1962 and has issue living, Ralph Gordon Chandos, *b.* 1936,—Michael Sacheverell Willoughby, *b.* 1939. *Residence,* 82, Sheridan Terr., Hove, Sussex.

This is a branch of the ancient Derbyshire family of Pole, many members of which have distinguished themselves in the field, notably German Pole, who commanded in Ireland, and served against the Armada. They were also descended in the female line from a sister of Sir John Chandos, K.G., chief commander at Crecy and at Poitiers. Millicent, daughter of Charles Pole, of Holcroft, married Charles Van-Notten, a London merchant, son of Charles Van-Notten (a descendant of Henry Van-Notten, enobled, 1499 by the Emperor Maximilian I., and whose only son Charles received from Charles V. the titles of Lord of Ath and Vander-Notten, and Chatelaine of Alost), a merchant of Amsterdam and London. He assumed the surname of Pole, and was created a baronet with remainder to the heirs male of his body, failing which to those of his daughter Susannah. Susannah *m.* 1802 Isaac Minet, but her male line is understood to have become ext. with the death of her son without male issue. The 3rd baronet assumed in 1853, by Roy. licence, the additional and original paternal name of Van-Notten. On his death in 1948, the baronetcy reverted to the line of Gen. Edward Pole, Col. 12th Lancers, 4th son of 2nd Bt.

POLLEN, Creation (G.B.) 1795, of Redenham, Hampshire.

Sir JOHN MICHAEL HUNGERFORD POLLEN, 7th
Baronet, only son of the late Lieut.-Com. John Francis
Hungerford Pollen, R.N., el. son of the late Capt. Francis
Gabriel Hungerford Pollen, C.B.E., R.N., 4th son of the late
John Hungerford Pollen, younger brother of 3rd baronet ;
b. April 6th, 1919 ; *s.* his kinsman, *Sir* JOHN LANCELOT
HUNGERFORD, 1959 ; ed. at Downside, and at Merton Coll.,
Oxford ; is Capt. R.A. : *m.* 1st, 1941 (marriage dissolved
1956), Angela Mary Oriana, da. of Maj. F. J. Russi, M.C.,
5th Roy. Inniskilling Dragoon Guards, of Killochan
Cottage, Girvan, Ayrshire; 2ndly, 1957, Diana Alice, da.
of the late A. E. Timbrell, and has issue by 1st m.

Arms—Azure, on a bend cotissed or, five escallops vert between six lozenges argent, each
charged with an escallop sable. **Crest**—A pelican per pale or and azure, vulning herself, and feeding
her young proper, charged on the wings elevated with a lozenge, as in the arms.

Residences—Rodbourne, Malmesbury, Wilts; Lochportain, Isle of North Uist.

Son living—By 1st marriage—RICHARD JOHN HUNGERFORD, *b.* Nov. 3rd, 1946; *m.* 1971,
Christianne, da. of Sir (William) Godfrey Agnew, KCVO, and has issue living, Isabel, *b.* 1975.

Daughter living—By 1st marriage—Jane Oriana Mary, *b.* 1942: *m.* 1962, Roger Tilney
Grafftey-Smith, of 6, Wilton Cres., SW1, and Pond Lodge, Charlton, Malmesbury, Wilts., son of
Sir Laurence Barton Grafftey-Smith, KCMG, KBE, and has issue living, Simon Laurence,
b. 1968,—Selina Dora, *b.* 1971.

Sister living—Susan Mary, *b.* 1917. *Residence,* By Scarlett's Wood, Hare Hatch, Twyford, Berks.

Aunts living—Mary Margaret, *b.* 1892 ; sometime Comdt. Mechanized Transport Corps.;
served in S. Africa, Egypt, and Europe 1940-45 : *m.* 1st, 1916, Major James Douglas Macindoe,
O.B.E., M.C. Scots Guards, who *d.* 1957, and from whom she obtained a divorce 1928; 2ndly,
1931, Lieut.-Com. Keith William Newall, R.N. (retired), who *d.* 1938, and has issue living, (by
1st m.) Armida Mary, *b.* 1917,—Rose Mary, *b.* 1918. *Residence,* Quinta de Piedade, Sintra,
Portugal.——Flora Anne, *b.* 1901: *m.* 1st, 1922, Allan Scott Wilkinson, from whom she
obtained a divorce 1924 ; 2ndly, 1927, Lieut.-Col. Alexander Clarence Harcourt, D.S.O., M.C.,
Roy. Tank Corps, who *d.* 1946, and has issue living, (by 2nd marriage) Ralph Alexander, *b.*
1929. *Residence,*

Mother living—Peggy, da. of the late Sir Frederick Charles Wallis, M.B., F.R.C.S. : *m.* 1915,
Lieut.-Com. John Francis Hungerford Pollen, R.N., who *d.* 1943. *Residence,* By Scarlett's
Wood, Hare Hatch, Twyford, Berks.

Collateral Branches living.

Issue of the late Sir Walter Michael Hungerford Pollen, MC, uncle of 7th baronet,
b. 1894, *d.* 1968: *m.* 1923, Rosalind Frances (Norton Hall, Mickleton, Glos.)
da. of the late Robert Benson, of Buckhurst Withyham, Sussex, and 16,
South St., Park Lane, W:—
Peregrine Michael Hungerford (1160, Park Av., New York, NY, USA; Balranald House, N. Uist),
b. 1931; ed. at Eton, and Ch. Ch., Oxford; a Dir. in USA of Sothebys: *m.* 1958, Patricia Helen,
da. of Lt.-Col. Gerald Barry, MC [*see* Barry, Bt., colls.], and has issue living, Peregrine Marcus,
b. 1964,—Susannah Hungerford, *b.* 1959,—Arabella Rosalind Hungerford, *b.* 1961.——Pandora
Mary Hungerford, *b.* 1928; LRCP & S, Ireland; Prin., Hatherop Sch., Coln-St-Aldwyn, Glos.:
m. 1949, Charles Edward Moorhead, who *d.* 1953, and has issue living, Rosalind Catherine, *b.*
1950,—Annabel Mai, *b.* 1951.

Grandchildren of the late Arthur Joseph Hungerford Pollen, son of John
Hungerford Pollen, next brother of 3rd baronet:—
Issue of the late Arthur Joseph Lawrence Pollen, *b.* 1899, *d.* 1968: *m.* 1926, the Hon.
Daphne Baring (Cray Cottage, Harpsden, Henley-on-Thames), da. of 3rd Baron
Revelstoke:—
Francis Anthony Baring (Cray Clearing, Harpsden, Henley-on-Thames), *b.* 1926: *m.* 1950, Marie-
Thérèse, da. of His Honour Sir Joseph (Alfred) Sheridan, and has issue living, John Stephen
Hungerford, *b.* 1959,—Clare, *b.* 1951,—Katharine, *b.* 1954,—Roseanna, *b.* 1956,—Mary Louise,
b. 1969.——Patrick Laprimaudaye (Cul Ard, Sweetmount Av., Dundrum, co. Dublin), *b.* 1928:
m. 1963, Nell, yst. da. of the late John Murphy, of Sweetmount House, New Ross, co. Wexford,
and has issue living, Patrick Benedict Peter, *b.* 1965,—Laurence Joseph, *b.* 1968,—Ciaran, *b.*
1966,—Christopher, *b.* 1972,—Patricia, *b.* 1970.——Cecilia Mary, *b.* 1930: *m.* 1952, Christopher
Robert Hull, of Claremont House, Wimbledon, SW19, and has issue living, Rupert Teilo David,
b. 1959,—Caspar William, *b.* 1960,—Thomas Richard, *b.* 1964,—Simon Paul Timothy, *b.* 1966,—
Lucy Bridget, *b.* 1955,—Barbara Margaret, *b.* 1957.——Lucy Margaret, *b.* 1932: *m.* 1955, Philip
Vincent Belloc Jebb, of 1, Upper Butts, Brentford, Middx., and has issue living, Matthew Hilary,
b. 1958,—Louis Bernard, *b.* 1959,—Magdalen Marianne Francesca, *b.* 1956,—Christian Agnes
Valentine, *b.* 1961.——Mary Rose Catherine, *b.* 1940: *m.* 1967, Hugo Laurence Joseph Brunner,
of 13, Barnsbury Sq., N1 [*see* Brunner, Bt.].——Margaret Mary Clare, *b.* 1943: *m.* 1966, Patrick
Hyde Kelly, of 23, Charleville Rd., Rathmines, Dublin, and has issue living, Arthur Edmund
Campion, *b.* 1971,—Beatrice Maeve, *b.* 1968.

Grandson of the late John Hungerford Pollen (ante):—
Issue of the late Arthur Joseph Hungerford Pollen, *b.* 1866, *d.* 1937: *m.* 1898, Maud
Beatrice, who *d.* 1962, da. of the late Sir Joseph Lawrence, of Oaklands, Kenley,
Surrey:—
John Anthony Lawrence, *b.* 1900: *m.* 1931, Bridget Gertrude, who *d.* 1956, da. of the late Maj.
Cuthbert Leigh Blundell-Hollinshead-Blundell [Astley, Bt.], and has issue living, Anne Bridget,
b. 1934. *Residence,* Lime Tree House, Upper Strand St., Sandwich, Kent. *Club,* Brooks's.

Grandchildren of the late Lt.-Col. Stephen Hungerford Pollen, CMG (infra):—
Issue of the late Lt.-Col. Stephen Derek Hungerford Pollen, MBE, *b.* 1908; *d.* 1969: *m.*
1944, Marion Leigh Howard (11, Chelsea House, 26, Lowndes St., SW1), da. of the late
Capt. Thomas Storie Dixson:—
Helen Leigh, *b.* 1948.——Margaret Anne, *b.* 1952.

Grandchildren of the late John Hungerford Pollen (ante):—
Issue of the late Lieut.-Col. Stephen Hungerford Pollen, C.M.G., *b.* 1868, *d.* 1935: *m.* 1905,
Catherine Hetherington, who *d.* 1954.. da. of the late Sir John Muir, 1st Bt.:—
Margaret Edyth Pamela Burrell (Flat 2, 50, South Audley St., W1), *b.* 1906: *m.* 1929, Peter Eustace
Burrell, CBE, from whom she obtained a divorce 1940 [*see* Burrell, Bt.].——Barbara Heather
(165, Chiltern Court, NW1), *b.* 1911.

Issue of the late Lieut.-Col. Clement Hungerford Pollen, *b.* 1869, *d.* 1934 : *m.* 1912, Mabel Brenda who *d.* 1964, da. of the late Alan Southey Dumbleton, of Victoria, British Columbia:—
Hubert Clement Hungerford (3, Dinorben Av., Fleet, Aldershot, Hants.), *b.* 1913; ed. at Downside; late Indian Army: *m.* 1954, Quita, da. of the late A. Edward Baker, of Salop, and Fiji.—
Cynthia Brenda, *b.* 1914: *m.* 1943, Lt. Ronald Malcolm Marshall, RN (ret.), and has issue living, Robin Michael Hungerford, *b.* 1943,—Bernard Mark Sebastian, *b.* 1945,—John Henry Hubert, *b.* 1948,—Clement Wilfrid Ronald Pollen, *b.* 1951,—Rosemary Winefride Brenda, *b.* 1950.
Residence, Okehills, Nailsbourne, Taunton.

This family came originally from Lincs. Edward Pollen became London Merchant temp. James I and *d.* 1636. His son, grandson and great-grandson, all named John, were M.P.'s for Andover. The last named, father of Sir John, 1st baronet, was one of the Judges of Wales and *d.* 1776.

POLLOCK, Creation (U.K.) 1866, of Hatton, Middlesex.

Boldly and strenuously.

Sir GEORGE FREDERICK POLLOCK, 5th, Baronet; *b.* Aug. 13th, 1928; *s.* his father, Sir (FREDERICK) JOHN 1963; ed. at Eton, and at Trin. Coll., Camb. (MA); Solicitor 1956; late 2nd Lt. 17th/21st. Lancers; Fellow of Roy. Photographic Soc.; FRSA; Vice-Pres. of London Salon of Photography, and Chm. of Photenrop (UK) Cttee.: *m.* 1951, Doreen Mumford, da. of the late Norman Ernest Keown Nash, CMG, and has issue.

Arms—Quarterly, 1st and 4th azure, three fleurs-de-lis within a bordure engrailed or, in dexter chief point on a canton ermine a portcullis of the second, *Pollock of Balgray*; 2nd and 3rd vert, a saltire or, between three bugles in fess and in base argent, garnished gules, within a bordure engrailed, dexter chequy of the second and first, sinister of the second, the whole within a bordure ermine for difference, *Pollock of that Ilk*. **Crest**—A boar passant, quartered or and vert, pierced through the sinister shoulder with an arrow proper. **Supporters**—Two talbots sable, each gorged with a collar or and pendent therefrom a portcullis of the last.
Residence—Netherwood, Stones Lane, Westcott, Surrey. *Clubs*—Lansdowne, Ski Club of Gt. Britain.

Son living—DAVID FREDERICK, *b.* April 13th, 1959.
Daughters living—Charlotte Anne, *b.* 1952,——Catherine Frances Jill, *b.* 1955.

Collateral Branches living.

Grandchildren of the late Archibald Gordon Pollock, yr. son of Robert John Pollock, 3rd son of 1st baronet:—
Issue of the late Hamilton Rivers Pollock, *b.* 1884, *d.* 1940: *m.* 1912, Eveline Morton, who *d.* 1940, da. of Thomas Bell, of Newcastle-on-Tyne :—
Martin Rivers, *b.* 1914; ed. at Winchester, and at Trin. Coll., Camb. (B.A. and Senior Scholar 1936); *m.* 1941, Jean Ilsley, el. da. of Frank Ilsley Paradise, and has issue living, Julian Rivers, *b.* 1942,—
Jonathan Ilsley, *b.* 1948,—Jessamy, *b.* 1941,—Lisa Jane, *b.* 1944. *Residence*, Bolton House, Windmill Hill, N.W.3.——Marian Eveline, *b.* 1918.——Margaret Gordon, *b.* 1921 : *m.* 1943, Boris Kidel, and has issue living, Audrey, *b.* 1943,—Mark Rivers, *b.* 1947. *Residences*, 7/10, Wohllebengasse, Vienna, Austria ; La Garde, Freinet, Var, France.

Grandson of the late Harry Frederick Pollock, el. son of George Frederick Pollock (infra):—
Issue of the late Col. Ralph Charles Geoffrey Pollock, *b.* 1881, *d.* 1945: *m.* 1911, Ruby Weld Forester, who *d.* 1962, da. of the late Lieut.-Col. Harry Hamersley St. George:—
Ralph John Hamilton, *b.* 1921; ed. at Wellington, and at Trin. Coll., Camb. (BA); 1942-45 in Middle East, N. Africa and Italy as Major RA (despatches, four medals): *m.* 1st, 1948 (m. diss.), Patricia Clarice Marion, da. of Capt. Arthur Thompson late Northants Regt.; 2ndly, 1957, Elizabeth Ormond (Martin), only da. of the late Charles Mills Maclean, of Savannah, Georgia, USA; 3rdly, 1968, Lady Zinnia Rosemary Cantlie, da. of 4th Earl Londesborough, and has issue living, (by 1st m.) Sally Anne St. George, *b.* 1952. *Residence*, 3, West Eaton Pl., SW1. *Club* Buck's.

Granddaughters of the late William Rivers Pollock, MD, MRCS, FRCP (infra):—
Issue of the late Humphrey Rivers Pollock, MRCS, LRCP, *b.* 1889, *d.* 1964: *m.* 1920, Eleanor Violet, who *d.* 1973, da. of the late Willoughby Aston Littledale [Thursby, Bt.]:—
Mary Rivers, *b.* 1921: *m.* 1960, Charles Tristan D'Oyly, MBE, of 129, Swan Court, S.W.3.——
Joan Littledale, *b.* 1924; ed. at Oxford Univ. (MA): *m.* 1948, Francis Alexander de Hamel, MD, MRCS, LRCP, of 3, Howard St., Macandrew Bay, Dunedin, NZ, and has issue living, Michael Alexander, *b.* 1949,—Christopher Francis Rivers, *b.* 1950,—Geoffrey William, *b.* 1953, Richard John Bruno, *b.* 1960,—Quentin David Humphrey, *b.* 1963.
Issue of the late Rt. Hon. Sir Ernest Murray Pollock, K.B.E. [son of the late George Frederick Pollock (infra)], who was cr. *Viscount Hanworth* 1936 [see that title].

Granddaughter of the late George Frederick Pollock, 4th son of 1st baronet:—
Issue of the late Rt. Rev. Bertram Pollock, K.C.V.O., D.D., Lord Bishop of Norwich 1910-42, *b.* 1863 ; *d.* 1943 : *m.* 1928, Joan Florence Helena (of Bickers End, Wenhaston, Suffolk, and Balneath Manor, South Chailey, Sussex), da. of the late Rev. Algernon Charles Dudley Ryder [*see* E. Harrowby, colls.] :—
Mary Rosalind Frances Felicia, *b.* 1931.

Grandchildren of the late Hon. Sir Charles Edward Pollock, 5th son of 1st baronet:—
Issue of the late George Hume Pollock, *b.* 1870, *d.* 1924 : *m.* 1900, Margaret Agnata, who *d.* 1954, da. of Sir Richard Harington, 11th Bt. :—
Charles Harington, *D.S.C.*, *b.* 1906 ; is Com. (retired) R.N. ; European War 1939-45 (despatches, D.S.C.) : *m.* 1938, Patricia Aileen Domville, who *d.* 1957, da. of the late Herbert Payne Heming, of Victoria, British Columbia, and widow of Capt. H. Leicester Leverin, Roy. Canadian Engineers, and has issue living, Ann Patricia, *b.* 1939: *m.* 1961, Maj. Richard Ceci Wallace, RCT (c/o Messrs. Coutts & Co., 440, Strand, WC2), and has issue living, Charle

Pollock *b.* 1963, Oliver James Shannon *b.* 1970. *Residence,* Hill Green, Clavering, Saffron Walden, Essex. *Club,* United Service.——Agnata Cecilia, *b.* 1907. *Residence,* Quendon Cottage, Quendon, nr. Saffron Walden, Essex.——Margaret Georgina, *b.* 1913: *m.* 1948, Richard Tresillian Gabb, MB, BCh. *Residence,* Beverley House, Stansted Mountfitchet, Essex.

Issue of the late Robert Pollock, *b.* 1874, *d.* 1957: *m.* (Jan.) 1914, Ethel Mary Purefoy, who *d.* 1970, da. of James Crofts Powell, of 13, Chester St., Grosvenor Pl., SW:—
Martin James, *b.* (Dec.) 1914 ; ed. at Charterhouse, and at Trin. Coll., Camb. (B.A. 1936) ; admitted a Solicitor 1946 ; is Lieut. R.N.V.R. : *m.* 1942, Pamela Valentine, da. of the late Valentine Leslie Douglas Uzielli, and has issue living, Robert Valentine, *b.* 1957,—Carolyn Alice, *b.* 1944: *m.* 1967 (m. diss. 1971), Michael Bernard Thorold, Scots Gds. [*see* Thorold, Bt., colls.],—Rosalind Janet, *b.* 1948; SEN: *m.* 1975, John Edward Fawkes, of 99, Collingwood Cres., Merrow, Guildford, Surrey. *Residence,* Heather Mount, Chobham, Surrey.——*Rev.* John Charles, *b.* 1923; ed. at Charterhouse, and at Trin. Coll., Camb. (BA 1946, MA, 1948) ; formerly Capt. Coldstream Guards : *m.* 1949, Anne, da. of Sir Thomas Richard Fiennes Barrett-Lennard, 5th Bt., OBE. *Residence,* Rose Ash House, S. Molton, Devon.——Honor Purefoy, *b.* 1916: *m.* 1939, James Frederick Priestley, MC, and has issue living, Hugh Michael (52, Stanford Rd., W8), *b.* 1942; ed. at Winchester and Worcester Coll., Oxford: *m.* 1968, Caroline Clarissa Duncan, only da. of Brig. John Hume Prendergast, DSO, MC, and has issue living, Alexandra Mary Duncan *b.* 1971,—Richard James, *b.* 1947,—Sarah Veronica, *b.* 1944: *m.* 1967, Brian David Bond, of 17, Astell St., SW3, and has issue living, Michael Alan Shaw *b.* 1968, Edward Brian Shaw *b.* 1970,—Annabel Clare *b.* 1971,—Julia Elizabeth, *b.* 1952. *Residence,* Norsebury, Stoke Charity, Winchester.

Grandchildren of the late Maj.-Gen. Sir (Frederick) Richard Pollock, K.C.S.I., 7th son of 1st baronet :—
Issue of the late Dighton Nicolas Pollock, *b.* 1864, *d.* 1927: *m.* 1921, the Hon. Margaret Anna Buckmaster, who *d.* 1929, da. of 1st Viscount Buckmaster:—
Richard Stanley, *b.* **1922.** *Residence,* 20, Porchester Terrace, W.2.——**John Dighton,** *b.* **1924.**

Grandchildren of the late Sir Edward James Pollock, 9th son of 1st baronet:—
Issue of the late Harold Warren Pollock, *b.* 1877, *d.* 1957: *m.* 1906, Hilda, who *d.* 1952, da. of the late Henry Warlters Horne, Bar.-at-law, of East Hill House, Wimbledon :—
Warren Dennis Michael, *b.* 1909 ; ed. at Marlborough, and at Trin. Coll., Camb. (B.A. 1931, M.A. 1942) : *m.* 1938, Elspeth Olive, da. of the late Ven. Harry Sydney Radcliffe, Archdeacon of Lynn, of Gaywood Rectory, King's Lynn. *Residence,* Flat 5, 178, Sloane St., SW1X 9QL.

Issue of the late Douglas Warren Pollock, M.B.E., *b.* 1878, *d.* 1958: *m.* 1907, Hélène Charlotte, who *d.* 1975, da. of the late Paul Gadban, Consul-Gen. of Turkey:—
Jack Warren, *b.* 1913 ; ed. at Winchester, and at New Coll., Oxford (B.A. 1935, M.A. 1947 ; formerly Major R.A. : *m.* 1949, Hazel, da. of the late Henry Arthur Hinton, of Shrewsbury, and widow of Major Howard Bourne, Hon. Artillery Co., and has issue living, Nicholas Charles Valentine, *b.* 1950,—Christopher James Douglas, *b.* 1956,—Miranda Penelope Gillian, *b.* 1952. *Residence,* The Bridge House, Shoreham, Kent.——Joan Pauline (127, Ormond Rd., Gisborne, NZ.) *b.* 1909: *m.* 1936, Edward Hugh Heath, who *d.* 1945, and has issue living, Jane Elizabeth, *b.* 1939: *m.* 1962, Bryan Ballantyne Horne, of Kenilworth, 138, Stout St., Gisborne, NZ, and has issue living, Fiona Ballantyne *b.* 1966, Tiffany Anne *b.* 1969, Melanie Hélène *b.* 1973.

The Right Hon. Sir Frederick, 1st baronet, was Lord Chief Baron of the Court of Exchequer, 1844-68. He was a son of David Pollock, saddler, of Charing Cross, a descendant of David Pollock, of Balgray, Renfrewshire, *b.* about 1631, great-grandson of Charles Pollock of Greenhill, yr. son of David Pollock of that Ilk. David Pollock, the saddler, also had two other sons who attained great eminence, viz., Sir David Pollock, Chief Justice of Bombay, and Field-Marshal Sir George Pollock, baronet, G.C.B., G.C.S.I., Constable of the Tower of London. The senior line Pollock of Pollock became ext. in the 19th century. The 2nd baronet was for many years Senior Master of the Supreme Court of Judicature and Queen's Remembrancer. The 3rd baronet was a Privy Councillor KC and Admiralty Judge of the Cinque Ports 1914-36. The 4th baronet was an Officer Legion of Honour.

MONTAGU-POLLOCK, Creation (U.K.) 1872, of the Khyber Pass.

Boldly and strenuously. *Let us be examined by our conduct.*

Sir GEORGE SEYMOUR MONTAGU-POLLOCK, 4th *Baronet ; b.* Sept. 14th, 1900 ; *s.* his father, *Sir* MONTAGU FREDERICK, 1938 ; is Lieut.-Com. R.N. (retired) : *m.* 1927, Karen-Sofie, da. of Hans Ludvig Dedekam, of Oslo, Norway, and has issue.

Arms—Quarterly, 1st and 4th, azure, three fleurs-de-lis within a bordure embattled or for his distinguished services in the Afghan war on a chief of the second an eastern crown gules, superinscribed "Khyber," and on a canton ermine three cannons fesseways in pale sable *Pollock*; 2nd and 3rd, parti per pale argent and gules, a fesse lozengy counterchanged *Montagu*; in the middle chief point a cross moline, also counterchanged. **Crests**— 1st, a lion rampant guardant argent adorned with an eastern crown or, holding in his dexter paw in bend sinister an Afghan banner displayed gules, bordered or and vert, the staff broken in two, in his sinister paw a part of the broken staff in an escrol over the motto, "Affghanistan" *Pollock*; 2nd, a boar passant quarterly embattled or and vert, pierced through the sinister shoulder with an arrow proper *Pollock*; 3rd, a griffin's head couped, wings expanded or, gorged with a collar lozengy *Montagu*. **Supporters**—*Dexter,* an heraldic tiger sable, maned, tufted, and gorged with an eastern crown, and chained, chain being reflexed over the back or, and pendent from the collar an escutcheon or, charged with a bomb fired proper; *sinister,* a talbot gorged, chained, and charged as the dexter.

Residence—Brooke House, Swallowcliffe, Salisbury.

Son living—GILES HAMPDEN, *b.* Oct. 19th, 1928; ed. at Eton, and de Havilland Tech. Sch.: *m.* 1963, Caroline Veronica, da. of Richard F. Russell, of 25, Evelyn Mansions, SW1, and has issue living, Guy Maximilian, *b.* 1966,—Sophie Amelia, *b.* 1969. *Residence*—The White House, 7, Washington Rd., Barnes, SW13. *Club,* United Service and Royal Aero.

Daughter living —Karen Aagot Georgina, *b.* 1931: *m.* 1952, Richard Eliot Hodgkin, of Sherwood, Gordon Rd., Claygate, Surrey, and has issue living, Harry John, *b.* 1961,—Edward Eliot, *b.* 1963,—Georgina Elizabeth, *b.* 1954.

Brothers living—*Sir* William Horace, *KCMG* (of 28, Drayton Gdns., SW10), *b.* 1903; ed. at Marlborough, and at Trin. Coll., Camb. (MA 1959); appointed H.M.'s Ambassador to Syria, 1952, to Peru 1953, to Switzerland 1958, and to Denmark 1960; ret. 1962; C.M.G. 1946, K.C.M.G. 1957: *m.* 1st, 1933 (m. diss. 1945), (Frances Elisabeth) Prudence, da. of the late Sir John Fischer Williams, CBE, KC [D. Atholl, colls]; 2ndly, 1948, Barbara (GASKELL), da. of the late Percy Hague Jowett, CBE, of 28, Drayton Gdns., SW10, and has issue living, (by 1st marriage) Hubert Murray (17, Mitchelgate, Kirkby Lonsdale, Cumbria), *b.* 1935; ed. at Winchester; MA; PhD; Past Fellow of Trin. Coll., Camb.; a Sr. Lecturer Lancaster Univ.: *m.* 1960, Emmerentia Johanna, yr. da. of the late J. B. de Jong Cleyndert, and has issue living, Harriet Marthe *b.* 1961, Catherine Juliet *b.* 1963, Annabel Frances *b.* 1966,—Fidelity Juliet, *b.* 1940: *m.* 1962, Alan Charles Barclay Dean, MB, FRCS, of 12, Glenorchy Terr., Edinburgh 9, and has issue living, Marcus William Fischer *b.* 1963, Juliet Augusta Carolyn *b.* 1965, Corinna Lucy *b.* 1967,—(by 2nd m.) Matthew John, *b.* 1951; ed. at Westminster and Ch. Ch., Oxford.——John Gathorne, *b.* 1911; ed. at Oundle: *m.* 1943, Elizabeth Metcalf Coston, and has issue living, Stephen Hull, *b.* 1945,—Christopher James, *b.* 1952,—Margaret Bell, *b.* 1948: *m.* 1972, Robert Lewis Merkow, of Hartland, Wisconsin, USA. *Residence*, 4905, S. Lafayette, Englewood, Colorado, USA.

Collateral Branches living.

Issue of the late Hubert Vernon Montagu-Pollock, 2nd son of 3rd baronet, *b.* 1902; *d.* 1970: *m.* 1945, Delia Florence Alice (Bridge Cottage, Winterbourne Stoke, Salisbury, Wilts.), da. of the late Herbert Snowden, and widow of Harold Edward Pearce:—
Jonathan David, *b.* 1947; ed. at Charterhouse; late 2nd Lt. R. Green Jackets.

Granddaughters of the late Hugh Pollock (infra):—
Issue of the late Hugh Wykeham David Pollock, *b.* 1900, *d.* 1972: *m.* 1934, Barbara (Winderwath, Penrith, Cumberland), da. of Sir Philip Bealby Reckitt, OBE, 3rd Bt. (ext.):—
Bridget Wykeham, *b.* 1935: *m.* 1960, Michael John Marshall, of Ball's Grove, Grantchester, Cambridge, and has issue living, Robert David, *b.* 1962,—James Gregory, *b.* 1964,—Belinda Louise, *b.* 1960,—Cressida Michal, *b.* 1967.——Ann Catherine, *b.* 1938.——Jane, *b.* 1945.

Grandchildren of the late George David Pollock, F.R.C.S., 2nd son of 1st baronet :—
Issue of the late Hugh Pollock, *b.* 1859, *d.* 1944: *m.* 1898, Alice, who *d.* 1971, da. of the late Cornwallis Wykeham-Martin [B. Llangattock]:—
Frances Alison (*Dowager Lady Anson*), *b.* 1903: *m.* 1923, Lt.-Col. Sir Edward Anson, 6th Bt., RA, who *d.* 1951. *Residence*, Little Orchard, Church Lane, Haslemere, Surrey.

Issue of the late Col. Evelyn Pollock, C.B.E., R.A., *b.* 1861, *d.* 1951 : *m.* 1890, Mary, who *d.* 1936, da. of the late Henry Jefferd Tarrant, Bar.-at-law :—
Philip (1, Grainford Court, Crescent Rd., Wokingham, Berks.), *b.* 1903; ed. at Haileybury, and at Pembroke Coll., Camb. (MA).——Jean, *b.* 1914: *m.* 1st, 1940, Maj. Gerard Joseph McCann, RM, who *d.* (killed in action) 1943; 2ndly, 1951, Group Capt. Paul Slocombe Gomez, CBE, RAF, who *d.* 1972, and has issue living, (by 1st m.) Peta Jean Madeleine, *b.* 1941—(by 2nd m.) Nicholas David, *b.* 1952. *Residence*, Les Cicadas, Alhama Springs, Altea, Alicante, Spain.

Granddaughter of the late Col. Evelyn Pollock, CBE, RA (ante):—
Issue of the late Sir Ronald Evelyn Pollock, *b.* 1891, *d.* 1974: *m.* 1st, 1921, Margery, who *d.* 1959, da. of the late Samuel Fitze; 2ndly, 1963, Pamela (17, South Drive, Wokingham, Berks.), only da. of the late Francis Winckworth Anstice Prideaux, OBE, and widow of Percy John Hodsoll Stent, CIE, ICS:—
(By 1st m.) Anne Margery, *b.* 1924; formerly in WRNS: *m.* 1958, Clive Robert Basche, of 114, Heath Rd., Petersfield, Hants., and has issue living, Timothy James, *b.* 1961,—Clare Nicola, *b.* 1959.

Grandchildren of the late Lt.-Col. Frederick George Pollock (infra):—
Issue of the late Lt.-Col. Harry Clement Pollock, MBE, *b.* 1883, *d.* 1971: *m.* 1st, 1914, Dorothy Beatrice (from whom he obtained a divorce 1928), da. of the late Sir Theodore Caro Piggott; 2ndly, 1929, Constance Ferne, who *d.* 1943, da. of the late Alfred Russell, of Rushall, Staffs.; 3rdly, 1944, Winifred Eileen (14A, Queens Rd., Royston, Herts.), da. of the late W. T. C. Macgregor, of Wick, Caithness:—
(By 1st m.) John Basil (224A, Connaught Rd., Brookwood, Woking, Surrey, GU24 0AH), *b.* 1920; BSc London Eng (Metallurgy); ARSM: *m.* 1949, Betty Angela, da. of H. A. Lusher, of Sevenoaks, Kent, and has issue living, Christopher Robert, *b.* 1954,—Anne Patricia, *b.* 1951,—Sarah Gillian, *b.* 1957.——(by 3rd m.) Martin Donald, *b.* 1948; ed. at Churchill Coll., Camb. (MA).

Issue of the late Archibald Frederick Pollock, *b.* 1885, *d.* 1941: *m.* 1922, Ada Gertrude (now c/o Jardin Ltd., PO Box 26, Nairobi, Kenya), da. of the late Albert Imossi, of Gibraltar:—
David Francis (Tynardd, Ponthirwaun, Llechryd, Dyfed), *b.* 1928; is Maj. RA: *m.* 1959, Diana Mary, da. of Maj. F. J. Andrews, of Hemingford Lodge, London Rd., Cheam, Surrey, and has issue living, James Robert, *b.* 1962,—Gillian Mary, *b.* 1960.——Mary, *b.* 1924: *m.* 1946, Bryan L. B. Epsom, late Capt. Queen's Own Roy. W. Kent Regt., and has issue living, Hugh David, *b.* 1949,—Guy Bryan, *b.* 1954,—Paul Robert, *b.* 1956. *Address*, c/o PO Box 26, Nairobi, Kenya.

Grandchildren of the late Archibald Reid Swiney Pollock, 4th son of 1st baronet:-
Issue of the late Lieut.-Col. Frederick George Pollock, *b.* 1855, *d.* 1914: *m.* 1882, Jane, who *d.* 1923, da. of the late Gen. H. S. Obbard, and widow of R. St. G. H. Hamilton, formerly 65th Regt. :—
William Hamilton (of 74, Dr. M. Barros Borgoño, Providencia, Santiago, Chile), *b.* 1887: *m.* 1915, Sara Amanda, da. of the late Jose Santos Tello, of Chile, and has issue living, Richard Douglas (of 167 D., Casilla, Santiago, Chile), *b.* 1924; is a Chemical Engineer, Federico Santa Maria University, Chile: *m.* 1956, Mary Helia, da. of the late Ceferino Veloso, of Santiago, Chile, and has issue living, William Douglas *b.* 1957, James Edward *b.* 1959, Philip Andrew *b.* 1962, Maureen Elizabeth *b.* 1960.

Grandchildren of the late Archibald Reid Swiney Pollock (ante) :—
Issue of the late Maj.-Gen. John Archibald Henry Pollock, C.B., *b.* 1856, *d.* 1949: *m.* 1898, Lillian Forrester, who *d.* 1954, da. of J. Fortune:—
Frederick Arthur (Maison-La-France, Bellaria, La Tour de Peilz (Vaud), Switzerland), *b.* 1899; ed. at Wellington Coll.; 1914-18 War with RE.——Justina Lillian (Pansy), *b.* 1902: *m.* 1926, Frederic Whigham McConnel, Lettrick, Dunscore, Auldgirth, Dumfries-shire, and has issue living, James Frederic Whigham, *b.* 1929,—John William, *b.* 1931.——Daphne Victoria Catherine, *b.* 1907: *m.* 1934, Alan Reginald Cathcart, who *d.* 1967 [*see* E. Cathcart, colls.]. *Residence*, Ardendee, Kirkcudbright.

Sir George Pollock, 1st baronet, yr. brother of the Rt. Hon. Sir Frederick Pollock, 1st baronet of Hatton (cr. 1866), commanded the army with great distinction in the first Afghan war. He attained the rank of Field-Marshal, and was sometime Constable of the Tower. Sir Frederick, 2nd baronet, assumed by Roy. licence in 1873 the additional surname of Montagu, having *m.* 1861, Laura Caroline, da. of Henry Seymour Montagu of Westleton Grange, Suffolk.

PONSONBY, Creation (U.K.) 1956, of Wootton, co. Oxford.

REGE·LEGE·GREGE

PRO

Sir CHARLES EDWARD PONSONBY, *T.D.*, 1st *Baronet*, son of the late Hon. Edwin Charles William Ponsonby [*see* B. de Mauley, colls.]; *b.* Sept. 2nd, 1879; ed. at Eton, and at Balliol Coll., Oxford (B.A. 1901); Lieut.-Col. and Brevet Col. 97th (Kent Yeo.) Field Brig. R.A. 1930-36 and Hon. Col. 297th (Kent Yeo.) Light Anti-Aircraft Regt. R.A. 1942-49; is a D.L. for Oxon; European War 1914-18 (Croix de Guerre); appointed Parliamentary Private Sec. to Sec. of State for War 1940, and to Sec. of State for Foreign Affairs 1941; Chm. of Council of Roy. Commonwealth Soc. 1954-57; Pres. of Roy. African Soc. 1963-70; M.P. for Sevenoaks Div. of Kent (*C*) July 1935 to Feb. 1950: *m.* 1912, the Hon. Winifred Marian Gibbs, da. of 1st Baron Hunsdon, of Hunsdon [*see* B. Aldenham], and has issue.

Arms—Gules, a chevron between three combs argent. Crest—Out of a ducal coronet or three arrows, points downwards, one in pale and two in saltire, entwined at the intersection by a snake proper. *Residences*—Woodleys, Woodstock, Oxon; 6, Bresby House, Rutland Gate, S.W.7. *Club*—Brooks's.

Son living—ASHLEY CHARLES GIBBS, *M.C.*, *b.* Feb. 21st, 1921; ed. at Eton and at Balliol Coll., Oxford; formerly Capt. Coldstream Guards; European War 1939-45 (wounded, M.C.): *m.* 1950, Lady Martha Butler, da. of 6th Marquess of Ormonde, and has issue living, Charles Ashley, *b.* 1951,—Rupert Spencer, *b.* 1953,—Luke Arthur, *b.* 1957,—John Piers, *b.* 1962. *Residence*, Grim's Dyke Farm, Woodleys, Woodstock, Oxon.

Daughters living—Priscilla Dora (*Lady Bacon*), *b.* 1913: *m.* 1936, Lt.-Col. Sir Edmund Castell Bacon, KG, KBE, TD, RA (TA), 14th Bt. *Residence*, Raveningham Hall, Norwich.—Diana Mary, *b.* 1916: *m.* 1940, the Rev. Mark Meynell [see E. Halifax, colls.]. *Residence*, The Vicarage, Leamington Hastings, Rugby.—Lavinia Rosalind, *b.* 1919: *m.* 1947, Michael Aubrey Hamilton, MP, of Lordington House, Chichester, and 27, Kylestrome House, Ebury St., SW1, and has issue living, John Ashley, *b.* 1948,—Caroline Mary, *b.* 1950,—Susanna, *b.* 1954,—Jane Lavinia, *b.* 1958.——Juliet Barbara Anna, *b.* 1923: *m.* 1949, Rt. Hon. James Edward Ramsden, and has issue living, Thomas James Ponsonby, *b.* 1950,—George Edward, *b.* 1953,—Richard Ashley, *b.* 1954,—Emma Juliet Geraldine, *b.* 1957,—Charlotte Mary Rose, *b.* 1960. *Residences*, Old Sleningford Hall, Ripon, Yorks.; 10, Cleaver Sq., Lambeth, SE11.

POOLEY, Creation (U.K.) 1953, of Westbrook House, Tillington, co. Sussex.
[Extinct 1966.]

Sir ERNEST HENRY POOLEY, *G.C.V.O.*, 1st and last *Baronet*.

Widow living of 1st Baronet—CHRISTABEL (*Lady Pooley*), (Westbrook House, Upperton, Petworth, Sussex), da. of the late Arthur Hopkins, RWS, and widow of H. C. Marillier: *m.* 1953, Sir Ernest Henry Pooley, GCVO, 1st Bt., who *d.* 1966, when the title became ext.

POORE, Creation (G.B.) 1795, of Rushall, Wiltshire.

Pauper, non in spe.
Poor, but not in hope.

Sir HERBERT EDWARD POORE, 6th *Baronet*; *b.* April, 1930; *s.* his father, *Sir* EDWARD, 1938.

Arms—Argent, a fesse azure between three mullets gules. Crest—A cubit arm erect vested sable, slashed argent, cuffed ermine, charged with two mullets in fesse or, grasping in the hand an arrow proper.

Residence—Curuzi Cuatia, Corrientes, Argentina.

Sisters living—Elsie Felly, *b.* 1923: *m.* 1947, Jorge Ball, and has issue living, Jorge Eduard, *b.* 1948,—Alberto Carlos, *b.* 1949,—Roberto, *b.* 1954,—Susana Beatriz, *b.* 1952.——Betty Gladys, *b.* 1926.

Uncle living—NASIONCENO, *b.* 1900: *m.* 19—, Juana Borda, who *d.* 1943, and has issue living, Roger Ricardo, *b.* 1930,—Roberto, *b.* 1932: *m.* 1964, Norma Onhaso,—Percy Nasionceno, *b.* 193? —Argentina *b.* 1927,—Gloria *b.* 1928,—Tady Esterlina, *b.* 1938.

Aunts living—Francesca, *b.* 1898.——Rosalie, *b.* 1903: *m.* 1930, Juan F. Garmedia. *Residence*, Belgrano, 912, Curuzu Cuatia, Argentina.

Widow living of 5th Baronet—AMELIA (*Lady Poore*), da. of Senor Santiago Guliemone, of Estancia La Blanca, Estacion Acuna, Corrientes, Argentine Republic: *m.* 1922, Sir Edward Poore, 5th baronet, who *d.* 1938. *Residence*, Curuzu Cuatia, Corrientes, Argentina.

Collateral Branches living.

(*In special remainder.*)

Grandsons of the late Capt. Mark Saurin Poore (infra):—
Issue of the late Robert Poore (who assumed by Roy. Licence 1932 the surname of Poore-Saurin-Watts), *b.* 1904, *d.* 1973: *m.* 1945, Rosemary Philippa (who *m.* 2ndly, 1974, James Richardson, MRCS, LRCP, of Brown Edge, Park Rd., W. Malvern, Worcs.), da. of Maj. Richard Norman Winstanley, of Rownham's House, nr. Southampton:—
Edward Richard (Coddington Court, Ledbury, Herefords.), *b.* 1948; ed. at Harrow, and Lausanne.——Andrew Philip, *b.* 1951; ed. at Milton Abbey, and Lausanne.

Grandchildren of the late Major Robert Poore, son of the late Robert Montagu Poore, son of the late John Montagu Poore, 2nd son of the late Edward Poore, brother of 1st baronet :—

Issue of the late Capt. Mark Saurin Poore, *b.* 1869, *d.* 1931 : *m.* 1900, Irene, who *d.* 1943 (having *m.* 2ndly, 1933, Major Harry Grant Thorold, of Cranford Hall, Northants.), da. of the late Edward Hanslope Watts, of Hanslope Park, Bucks :—

Louisa Florentia, *b.* 1905: *m.* 1932, Leslie Woods Haslett, of Apart. 69, 1509, Sherbrooke St. W., Montreal 109, Canada, and has issue living, Leslie Mark (Barrie, Ontario), *b.* 1933: *m.* 1959, Jane Aikins, da. of Robert David Mulholland, of Montreal, and has issue living, Andrew Mark *b.* 1961, Thomas Leslie *b.* 1962, Peter Aikins *b.* 1964, Jennifer Anne *b.* 1968,—Robert David (Montreal), *b.* 1937: *m.* 1963, Lucy, da. of Christopher Eberts, of Ottawa, and has issue living, Elizabeth *b.* 1964, Mary Martha *b.* 1966,—Richard Stuart (London, Ont.), *b.* 1940: *m.* 1965, Katharine, da. of Ernest Boyne, of St. John, New Brunswick, and has issue living, Christopher Leslie *b.* 1967,— Michael *b.* 1970,—Robert, *b.* 1974,—Christian Florentia, *b.* 1935: *m.* 1956, David Gladwin Turnbull, of Rothesay, New Brunswick, and has issue living, Douglas Alasdair Stuart *b.* 1958, Charles Laughlin *b.* 1960, Douglas David *b.* 1963, Christina Benita *b.* 1957,—Benita Jane, *b.* 1938.—— Sibyl Madeleine, *b.* 1906: *m.* 1935, Maj. Charles Gilbert Davies-Gilbert, MBE, late 7th Queen's Own Hussars [B. Massy, colls.], and has issue living, Charles James (Old Lodge, Dormansland, Lingfield, Surrey), *b.* 1940: *m.* 1967, Louise, da. of Peter Murray Kerr, DSC, MB, of Southend of Clarebrand, Castle Douglas, and has issue living, Charles Beresford *b.* 1971, Emma *b.* 1969,— Edward Nicholas, *b.* 1950,—Patricia Grace, *b.* 1936,—Sylvia Elizabeth, *b.* 1938: *m.* 1965, Peter Thain Tellwright, of Tyrley Castle, Market Drayton, Salop, and has issue living, John Gilbert *b.* 1967, Caroline *b.* 1969,—Lucy Margaret, *b.* 1945. *Residence*, Birling Manor, East Dean, Eastbourne.

Issue of the late Major Roger Alvin Poore, D.S.O., Roy. Welch Fusiliers, *b.* 1870, *d.* (killed in action during European War) 1917: *m.* 1913, Lorne Margery (Hedsor Court, Burnham, Bucks.), da. of the late Major R. J. W. Dennistoun, N. Staffordshire Regt.:— Roger Dennistoun, *b.* 1916; ed. at Eton, and at King's Coll., Camb.; sometime Wing-Com.-R.A.F.: *m.* 1949, Mrs. Peta Farley, and has issue living, Victoria Lorne Peta, *b.* 1956. *Residence*, 33, Phillimore Gardens, Campden Hill, W.8.

Issue of the late Philip Poore, *b.* 1874, *d.* 1937 : *m.* 1918, Cicely Eleanor (now of Pakaraka, Bay of Islands, New Zealand), da. of Sir Edward Arthur Barry, 2nd Bt. :— Philip Barry, *M.C.*, *b.* 1919; formerly Capt. and temporary Major Wilts Regt.; Burma 1944-5 with Gold Coast Regt. (M.C.) : *m.* 1954, Jennifer Mary, da. of Lieut.-Col. S. C. H Worseldine, I.M.S. (retired), of Nelson, New Zealand, and has issue living, Philip William, *b.* 1956,—Anna Cicely, *b.* 1954,—Sara Eleanor, *b.* 1958,—Helen Jennifer, *b.* 1960. *Residence*, 10, Te Akau Crescent, Buckland Beach, Auckland, New Zealand.——Robert Roger, *b.* 1924 ; B.Sc. Engineering 1949 : *m.* 1952, Diana Marion, da. of John Davis Canning, of Oakbourne, Waipukurua, New Zealand, and has issue living, Marion Rosalind, *b.* 1953,—Caroline Louise, *b.* 1955,—Elizabeth Julia, *b.* 1957,—Judith Rosamund, *b.* 1958. *Residence*, 17, Kelvin Road, Remuera, Auckland, NZ.——Anne Benita, *b.* 1922: *m.* 1946, Thomas Campbell Lindesay (PO Box 164, Kerikeri, Bay of Islands, NZ), and has issue living, Philip Edward (Auckland, NZ), *b.* 1947: *m.* 1971, Barbara Lesley Hargrave,—Thomas Reginald, *b.* 1953,—Clare, *b.* 1950: *m.* 1972, Rodney Burke of Auckland, NZ,—Erica Anne, *b.* 1955.——Eleanor, *b.* 1928: *m.* 1956, Nigel Malcolm Kennedy, and has issue living, Malcolm Alistair Robert, *b.* 1957,—Hamish Alexander Nigel, *b.* 1959,— Christopher William, *b.* 1966,—Sally Anne, *b.* 1963,—Katherine Fiona, *b.* 1964. *Residence*, Kerikeri, Bay of Islands, NZ.

The family descend from Philip Poore of Amesbury, Wilts., who *d.* 1571, whose son Philip was settled at Durrington, nearby. Though earlier genealogical proof has not been established, it is likely that this family has common ancestry with the brothers Herbert le Poer or Poor, last Bishop of Old Sarum, who *d.* 1217, and Richard who succeeded him as Bishop of Salisbury, and built the Cathedral at New Sarum, which was consecrated in 1225.

PORTAL, Creation (U.K.) 1901, of Malshanger, Church Oakley. co. Southampton.

Sir FRANCIS SPENCER PORTAL, 5th *Baronet ; b.* June 27th, 1903 ; *s.* his father, *Sir* SPENCER JOHN, 1955 ; ed. at Winchester, at Ch. Ch., Oxford, and at McGill Univ., Montreal ; Capt. late Welsh Guards; Pres. of Portals Holdings Ltd., Chm. of YMCA Nat. Commn. 1968, and of YMCA Nat. Development Cttee.; a DL of Hants. (High Sheriff 1963); Dep. Chm. of Winchester Diocesan Board of Finance, and a Member of the Bishop's Council Diocese of Winchester; Master of Clothworkers' Co. 1970; Belgian Croix de Guerre (2nd Class): *m.* 1st, 1930, Rowena, who *d.* 1948, da. of the late Paul Selby, of Johannesburg; 2ndly, 1950, Jane Mary, da. of the late Albert Henry Williams, OBE, of The Flint House, Langston, Havant, Hants, and has issue by 1st and 2nd m.

Arms,—Per saltire azure and gules, a portal flanked by two towers argent; on a chief ermine a crescent of the first between two mullets of the second. **Crest**—A portal flanked by two towers argent, each charged with a fleur-de-lis azure, and a wreath of laurel in base vert. *Residence*—Burley Wood, Ashe, nr. Basingstoke, Hants., RG25 3AG.

Sons living—By 2nd marriage—JONATHAN FRANCIS, *b.* Jan. 13th, 1953; ed. at Marlborough. ——Philip Francis, *b.* 1957; ed. at Radley.
Daughters living—By 1st marriage—(Rowena) Jeanne, *b.* 1931 : *m.* 1957, Richard James Livingstone Altham, of Crunnells Green House, Preston, Hitchin, Herts., and has issue living, David Richard Spencer, *b.* 1959,—Robert Patrick James, *b.* 1960,—Alastair John Livingstone, *b.* 1963.——Coralie Mary, *b.* 1937: *m.* 1966, Lt.-Cdr. Brian Harry Wright, RNR, of Elm House, Sonning, Berks., and 56, Brompton Sq., SW3, and has issue living, Alexander Francis, *b.* 1968,— Rowena Sarah, *b.* 1970.——By 2nd m.—Mary Jane, *b.* 1955.
Sister living—Constance Spencer, *b.* 1891: *m.* 1929, the Rev. Mellis Stuart Douglas, who *d.* 1963. *Residence*, The White House, The Avenue, Sherborne, Dorset.

Collateral Branches living.

Grandson of the late Brig.-Gen. Sir Bertram Percy Portal, KCB, DSO (infra):—
Issue of the late Maj. Melville Edward Bertram Portal, MBE, *b.* 1900, *d.* 1971: *m.* 1926, the Hon. Cicely Winifred Goschen (Redcote, Birch Av., Haywards Heath, Sussex), da. of 2nd Viscount Goschen:—

Simon George Melville (9, Kelso Place, W8; Cavalry Club), *b.* 1927; late Capt. 17th/21st Lancers; ADC to C.-in-C. Far East Land Forces 1958-59; a Member of London Stock Exchange 1960-65: *m.* 1962 (m. diss. 1971), Gillian, yst. da. of the late Maj. James Cyril Aubrey George Dance, MP, of Moreton House, Moreton Morrell, Warwicks., and has issue living, Robert Melville, *b.* 1967.

Issue of the late Brig.-Gen. Sir Bertram Percy Portal, K.C.B., D.S.O., 3rd son of 1st baronet, *b.* 1866, *d.* 1949 : *m.* 1899, the Hon. Margaret Louisa Littleton, who *d.* 1945, da. of 3rd Baron Hatherton:—

Charlotte Mary, *b.* 1903: *m.* 1929, Col. Richard James Longfield, late RA, and has issue living, Desmond Richard Henry (Lower Silton, Gillingham, Dorset; *Club*, Army and Navy), *b.* 1931; ed. at Wellington; Lt.-Col. RA: *m.* 1959, Jennifer, yr. da. of Clement William Robert Spencer Thomas, of Upper Honeydon, Bedford, and has issue living, James Desmond Spencer *b.* 1964, Melanie Louise *b.* 1961, Harriet Sarah *b.* 1965, Charlotte Jane *b.* 1970. *Residence*, Lower Silton, Gillingham, Dorset.——Hyacinthe Eveline, *b.* 1904: *m.* 1929, Malcolm Arthur Æneas Mackintosh, who *d.* 1966, and has issue living, Angus Malcolm (St. Algar's Farm, W. Woodlands, Frome, Somerset), *b.* 1930: *m.* 1958, Brenda Joyce, el. da. of Clement William Robert Spencer Thomas (ante), and has issue living, Ewan Angus *b.* 1960, Robert Malcolm *b.* 1962, Alexander William *b.* 1963, William Aeneas *b.* 1973,—Anne Evelyn, *b.* 1936. *Residence*, Orchard Plot, E. Chaldon, Dorset.——Margaret Cecilia, *b.* 1908: *m.* 1939, Capt. John Shirley Sandys Litchfield-Speer, OBE, RN (who has since relinquished the surname of Speer, and uses that of Litchfield only), and has issue living, Mark Shirley Portal *b.* 1940; Lt. RN: *m.* 1974, Marcia Osorio, and has issue living, Vasco *b.* 1974,—Sophie Mary Cecilia, *b.* 1942: *m.* 1970, John Irvin of 117, Hurlingham Rd., SW6, and has issue living, Luke Litchfield *b.* 1973, Emilie Jane *b.* 1970,—Virginia Margaret, *b.* 1945. *Residence*, Snowfield, Bearsted, Kent.——Sophie, *MBE*, *b.* 1910; sometime Junior Com. ATS; MBE (Mil) 1947.——Cecilia Violet, *b.* 1911: *m.* 1937, Lt.-Col. Nigel Walter Hoare, OBE, TD, and has issue living, Hyacinthe Cecilia, *b.* 1938: *m.* 1961 (m. diss. 1972), Piers Scandrett Harford, son of Sir George Arthur Harford, 2nd Bt.,—Joanna Bridget, *b.* 1940: *m.* 1961, Jeremy Francis Patrick Durham-Matthews, late Capt. Irish Gds., of Bridgefoot Hse., Kelvedon, Essex, and has issue living, John Patrick Nigel *b.* 1967, Miranda Elizabeth *b.* 1962, Lucy Mary *b.* 1965, Catherine Ann *b.* 1972,—Louisa Margaret, *b.* 1945: *m.* 1968, Trevor John Bissett Newman, of 15, Whitley Rd., Hoddesdon, Herts., and has issue living, Zachery John Bissett *b.* 1972. *Residence*, Southington House, Overton, Hants.

The 1st baronet, Sir Wyndham Spencer Portal (7th son of the late John Portal, J.P., D.L., of Laverstoke, Hants), was Chm. of London and S.-W. Railway Co., and *d.* 1905. The 2nd baronet, Sir William Wyndham, was Chm. of Portals, Ltd. and Dep. Chm. of London and S.-W. Railways. The 3rd baronet, Sir Wyndham Raymond, G.C.M.G., D.S.O., M.V.O., was Managing Director of Portals, Ltd., a Director of Great Western Railway Co., and Min. of Works and Buildings and First Commr. of Works 1942-4, and was created *Baron Portal*, of Laverstoke, co. Southampton (peerage of United Kingdom) 1935, and *Viscount Portal*, of Laverstoke, co. Southampton (peerage of United Kingdom 1945). He *d.* 1949, when the Barony and Viscountcy became ext. and the Baronetcy devolved upon his uncle, Sir Spencer John, 4th baronet, who was Pres. of Trustee Savings Bank Asso.

PORTER, Creation (U.K.) 1889, of Merrion Square, Dublin. [Extinct 1974.]

Sir GEORGE SWINBURNE PORTER, 3rd and last *Baronet*.

Daughters living of 2nd baronet—Olive Blanche, *b.* 1906: *m.* 1927, Bryan Wilfrid Hales, of 13, Downs Lodge Court, Church St., Epsom, Surrey, and has issue living, Vivienne May, *b.* 1928: *m.* 1954, John Antony Neill, of Drumgarth, Bird's Hill Rise, Oxshott, Surrey, and has issue living, David Anthony *b.* 1962, Fiona Rosalind *b.* 1956, Rosemary Jane *b.* 1958.——Ivy Mary, *b.* 1912: *m.* 1945, Maj. Terence St. George Carroll, Duke of Wellington's Regt. (ret.), and has issue living, Ursula Mary, *b.* 1947: *m.* 1971, John Alexander Chapman Leach, of Gilbury Cottage, Exbury, Hants. *Residence*, Orchard House, Fairfield Close, Lymington, Hants.

HORSBRUGH-PORTER, Creation (U.K.) 1902, of Merrion Square, City and Co. of Dublin.

Sir ANDREW MARSHALL HORSBRUGH HORS-BRUGH-PORTER, *D.S.O.*, 3rd *Baronet* : *b.* June 1st, 1907 ; *s.* his father, *Sir* JOHN SCOTT, 1953 ; ed. at Winchester ; Col. (retired) 12th Lancers ; European War 1939-45 in France, Belgium and Italy (wounded, despatches, D.S.O. and Bar) ; D.S.O. 1940 (Bar 1945) : *m.* 1933, Annette Mary, da. of Brig.-Gen. Robert Clayton Browne-Clayton, D.S.O., and has issue.

Arms—Argent, on a bend azure between in chief a portcullis, and in base two keys saltirewise sable, three bells of the field. Crest—On a fasces fessewise a cherub, all proper.

Residence—Manor Farm House, Salford, Chipping Norton, Oxon. *Club*—Cavalry.

Son living—JOHN SIMON (Bowers Croft, Magpie Lane, Coleshill, Bucks.), *b.* Dec. 18th, 1938; ed. at Winchester, and at Trin. Coll. Camb.: *m.* 1964, Lavinia Rose, da. of Ralph Meredyth Turton, of Kildale Hall, Whitby [*see* V. Chetwynd, colls.], and has issue living, Andrew Alexander Marshall, *b.* 1971,—Anna Josephine, *b.* 1965,—Zoe Mary, *b.* 1967.

Daughters living—Susan, *b.* 1936: *m.* 1962, John Kemp Barlow, of 45, Halsey St., SW3, and Bulkeley Grange, Malpas, Ches. [see Barlow, Bt., cr. 1907].——Caroline Elaine, *b.* 1940.

Collateral Branch living.

Issue of the late Alexander Horsbrugh PORTER, 2nd son of 1st baronet, *b.* 1872 ; *d.* 1946 : *m.* 1904, the Hon. Frances Maud Gibson, who *d.* 1957, da. of 1st Baron Ashbourne :—

William Eric, *b.* 1905 : *m.* 1929, Monica Ruth Lisalie, da. of the late Capt. Anthony Fritz Maude [*see* V. Hawarden, colls.], and has issue living, Dympna Monica, *b.* 1931 : *m.* 1950, Patrick St. John Pavier Brawn, and has issue living, Daniel *b.* 1954, Michael Patrick *b.* 1958, Anna Livia *b.* 1955, Isabel Frances *b.* 1965,—Phyllida, *b.* 1934: *m.* 1956, Donald Kenneth McAlpine, of 12, Martindale Rd., SW12, and has issue living, Louise Ngaire *b.* 1958, Fiona Caroline *b.* 1961. *Residence,* Glen Heste, Carrickmines, co. Dublin.——Alexander Ashbourne, *b.* 1911: *m.* 1936, Elizabeth Mary Noreen, only child of Capt. Mark Burns Lindow, of Holmrook, Cumberland.

The 1st baronet, the Rt. Hon. Sir Andrew Marshall Porter, (son of the late Rev. John Scott Porter), was Master of the Rolls in Ireland 1883-1906 and sat as M.P. for co. Londonderry (*L*) Dec. 1881 to Dec. 1883. The 2nd baronet, Sir John Scott Porter, assumed the additional surname of Horsbrugh 1911.

POUND, Creation (U.K.) 1905, of Stanmore, co. Middlesex.

Sir DEREK ALLEN POUND, 4th *Baronet;* *b.* April 7th, 1920 ; *s.* his father, *Sir* ALLEN LESLIE, 1952 ; ed. at Shrewsbury ; formerly Lieut. Essex Regt.: *m.* 1942, Joan Amy, da. of James Woodthorpe, and has issue.

Arms—Argent a sword erect proper surmounted of a fesse gules, thereon three mullets argent, in chief two boars' heads erased sable. *Crest*—A castle proper, charged with a shield argent, thereon a sword erect proper.
Residence—37, Gt. Cumberland Place, W1.

Son living—JOHN DAVID (26, West Hill Way, Totteridge, N20), *b.* Nov. 1st, 1946: *m.* 1968, Heather Frances O'Brien, only da. of Harry Jackson Dean, of Redcote, The Park, Mansfield, Notts., and has issue living, Robert John, *b.* 1973.

Daughter living—Diana Marilyn, *b.* 1944: *m.* 1966, Keble Stuart Paterson, of Coltsfoot, Anstey, Buntingford, Herts., and has issue living, Timothy Keble, *b.* 1968,—Caroline Elizabeth, *b.* 1971.

Sister living—Eileen Margery, *b.* 1916. *Residence,* 53, Chandos Rd., N2.

By good faith and vigilance.   FIDE·ET·VIGILANTIA

Mother living—Margery, da. of S. G. Hayworth. of Clapton Common : *m.* 1916, Sir Allen Leslie Pound, LL.B, 3rd baronet, from whom she obtained a divorce 1925. *Residence,* 53, Chandos Rd., N2.

Collateral Branch living.

Issue of the late Percy Herbert Pound, youngest son of 1st baronet, *b.* 1870, *d.* 1951 : *m.* 1st, 1895. Maud (who obtained a divorce 1929), da. of Frederick Wood, of Lordship Park, Stoke Newington, N.; 2ndly, 1930, Doris Girling, da. of Edward Herbert Mathew:—

(By 1st m.) Sybil Gwendolen, (21, Pearl Court, Eastbourne) *b.* 1896 : *m.* 1916, Alexander Harvey, who *d.* 1952.

The 1st baronet, Sir John Pound, head of the firm of John Pound and Co., portmanteau manufacturers, of 81-4, Leadenhall Street, E.C., was Sheriff of London 1895-6, and Lord Mayor of London 1904-5, and the 2nd baronet, Sir (John) Lulham, was an Alderman of City of London (Aldgate Ward) 1915-21. The 3rd baronet, Sir Allen Leslie, was a Solicitor and sole member of the firm of Pound & Pound, of Egham and Bracknell.

POWELL, Creation (U.K.) 1897, of Wimpole Street, St. Marylebone, co. London.

[Name pronounced "Poel."]

Sir RICHARD GEORGE DOUGLAS POWELL, *M.C.*, 3rd *Baronet ; b.* Nov. 14th, 1909 ; *s.* his father, *Lieut.-Col. Sir* DOUGLAS, *CBE,* 1932 ; ed. at Eton ; Maj. WG; a Dir. of Bovis, Ltd., of Pierson, Heldring & Pierson [U.K,], Ltd., of Russell Garratt, Ltd., of Cornwall Daborn Garratt, Ltd., and of BUPA Med. Centre, Ltd.; .Dir.-Gen. ·of Inst. of Directors 1954-74; N.W. Europe 1944-45 (M.C. and Bar, 1st Class Croix Militaire): *m.* 1933, Elizabeth Josephine, da. of Lt.-Col. Osmond Robert McMullen, CMG, of Presdales Hall, Ware, Herts., and has issue.

Arms—Gules, a lion rampant within a bordure engrailed or, in the dexter chief point a mullet argent within an annulet of the second. *Crest*—A lion's head erased argent, charged with a collar flory counter flory gules.
Residence—Small's House, Brightwell-cum-Sotwell, Oxon, OX10 0SJ. *Clubs*—Guards', Buck's.

Anima in amicis una.
One mind amongst friends.

Son living—NICHOLAS FOLLIOTT DOUGLAS (Petrunella Estate, Chipinga, Rhodesia), *b.* July 17th, 1935; ed. at Gordonstoun; is Lt. Welsh Gds.: *m.* 1960, Daphne Jean, yr. da. of Maj. George Errington, MC, of Monkton Ranch, Figtree, Rhodesia, and has issue living, James Richard Douglas, *b.* 1962,—Catherine Mary, *b.* 1961.

Daughters living—Bryony Josephine Anne (19, Ackmar Rd., SW6 4UP), *b.* 1933: *m.* 1935 (m. diss. 1968), Christopher Lucas Thomasson, and has issue living, Samuel Charles, *b.* 1956,—Mary Elizabeth, *b.* 1958.——Julia Mary, *b.* 1943: *m.* 1973, Jeremy John Twynam, of 97, Chesterton Rd., W10 6ET.

Sister living—Pamela Mary, *b.* 1911: *m.* 1933, George Clark Tozer, who *d.* 1973, and has issue living, Simon George Douglas, *b.* 1933,—Richard Edward, *b.* 1945,—Pamela Dorothy Susan, *b.* 1937. *Residence,* Fulbrook House, South Stoke, Reading, Berks.

The 1st baronet, Sir Richard Douglas Powell, K.C.V.O., M.D., F.R.C.P., was Physician Extraor. to Queen Victoria 1887-99, and Physician-in-Ord. 1899-1901, Physician Extraor. to King Edward VII. 1901-7; and Physician-in-Ord. 1907-10, and to King George V. 1910-25; also Pres. of Roy. Coll. of Physicians 1905-10.

POWER, Creation (U.K.) 1836, of Kilfane, Kilkenny. [Dormant 1928.]

Sir GEORGE POWER, 7th *Baronet, d.* in 1928, and the next heir, his cousin, GERVASE PARKER POWER, is believed to have died in America some years ago. At the time of going to press no name appears on the Official Roll of Baronets in respect of this title.

Collateral Branches living.

Grandchildren of the late Ambrose William Bushe Power (infra):—
Issue of the late Maj. Ambrose Grattan Power, *b.* 1887, *d.* 1926: *m.* 1908, Ada Mary, who *d.* 1968, yst. da. of the late Richard Austin Cooper Chadwick, of Ballinard, co. Tipperary:—

Anthony Ambrose Grattan (19, Langley Way, Hemingford Grey, Huntingdon, Cambs., PE18 9D8), *b.* 1917; ed. at Charterhouse; Maj. (ret.) R. Anglian Regt.: *m.* 1961, Sarah Judith, only da. of the late Joseph Halford Gough, of Cookham, Berks., and has issue living, Lavinia Frances, *b.* 1964,—Georgina Rachel, *b.* 1966,—Amy Katherine, *b.* 1968.——Iris Frances Mary, *b.* 1914: *m.* 1943, as his 2nd wife, Capt. Thomas Abdy Combe, Gren. Gds. *Residence,* The Tile House, Aldham, Colchester.

Granddaughter of the late Ven. Ambrose Power, Archdeacon of Lismore, 4th son of 1st baronet :—
Issue of the late Ambrose William Bushe Power, *b.* 1844, *d.* 1907: *m.* 1884, Frances Maria, who *d.* 1917, da. of the late Gervase Parker Bushe, of Glencairn Abbey, Lismore :—

Irene Noel, *b.* 1903: *m.* 1929, Com. Guy Stanley Windeyer, D.S.C., R.N. (retired), and Roy. Canadian Navy, and has issue living, Charles Kendal (692, Victoria Av., Westmount, P.Q. Canada), *b.* 1941: *m.* 1964, Georgette Patricia Marie Drummond, of Montreal, and has issue living, Anthony Guy *b.* 1966, Michael Drummond *b.* 1968.—Catherine, *b.* 1934: *m.* 1955, Leslie Spencer, of 1296, Richardson St., Victoria, British Columbia, and has issue living, Garth *b.* 1957, Sydney Alan *b.* 1959, Paul Anthony *b.* 1960,—Faith, *b.* 1938: *m.* 1957, Alan John Hesson Newberry, of 4274, Parkside Cres., Victoria, British Columbia, Canada, and has issue living, Graham Alexander *b.* 1961, Alison Faith *b.* 1958. *Residence,* Somenos Lake Farm, Duncan, Vancouver Island, British Columbia.

Grandson of the late Robert Henry Power (infra):—
Issue (by 2nd marriage) of the late Ambrose William Edward Power, *b.* 1881, *d.* 1921: *m.* 1st, 1903, Nancy Violet Marian, who *d.* 1908, da. of the late Edward Hunter, and widow of — Jeffries ; 2ndly, 1909, Marie Eugenie, who *d.* 1952, da. of the Hon. George Solomon, of Kingston, Jamaica :—

George Ambrose (*uses the Christian name of* John *in lieu of* George), (The Six Ringers, Grange Rd., Felmersham, Bedford), *b.* 1911: *m.* 1952, Elizabeth Margaret, da. of Harold Charles Firth Jeffcock.

Grandson of the late Ven. Ambrose Power, Archdeacon of Lismore (ante):—
Issue of the late Robert Henry Power, *b.* 1852, *d.* 1894: *m.* 1st, 1879, Eleanor, who *d.* 1883, da. of the late Arthur Roberts, of Waterford ; 2ndly, 1886, May, da. of the late Richard U. Roberts :—

(By 2nd m.) Richard, *b.* 1887.
Sir John Power, 4th baronet, died of wounds received at Lindley during S. African War 1900, and Sir Derrick, 5th baronet, died in S. Africa during the same war 1902.

POWER, Creation (U.K.) 1841, of Roe Buck House, co. Dublin. [Extinct 1930.]

Sir THOMAS TALBOT POWER, 6th and last *Baronet.*

Daughter living of 3rd Baronet—Eileen Mareli, *b.* 1880: *m.* 1902, Major Durham Simpson Matthews, O.B.E., J.P., who *d.* 1950. *Residence,* 39, Hill Street, Berkeley Square, W.1.

POWER, Creation (U.K.) 1924, of Newlands Manor, Milford, Southampton.

Sir JOHN PATRICK McLANNAHAN POWER, 3rd *Baronet*; *b.* March 16th, 1928; *s.* his father, *Sir* IVAN McLANNAHAN CECIL, 1954; late RN; Managing Dir. of Arthur Beale, Ltd., of London and Chichester, a Dir. of Kingsway Offices Co. Ltd., and Asso. Cos., and Chm. of Inst. of Professional Salesmen; Representative of Cunard Steam Ship Co. Ltd. 1945-58: *m.* 1st, 1957 (m. diss. 1967), Melanie, adopted da. of the Hon. Richard Alastair Erskine; 2ndly, 1970 (m. diss. 1974), Alison Tracey, da. of George Cooper, and has issue by 1st m.

Arms—Or, on a bend gules between two foxes heads erased proper three crescents of the first ; on a chief of the second as many escallops argent. **Crest**—A stag's head erased proper, gorged with an antique crown and between the attires a cross patée or.

Residence—Ashwick House, Dulverton, Som. *Clubs* —Arts, Royal Naval Sailing, Royal London Yacht, Royal Ocean Racing, Island Sailing, Birdham Yacht, and Royal Yachting Association.

Pro patria semper

For my country always.

Sons living—By 1st m.—ALASTAIR JOHN CECIL,, *b.* Aug. 15th, 1958,——Adam Patrick Cecil, *b.* 1963.
Daughter living—By 1st m.—Belinda Jane, *b.* 1960.
Sister living—Hilary Diana Cecil (*Lady Cardross*), *b.* 1930: *m.* 1957, Lord Cardross, only son of 16th Earl of Buchan. *Residence,* 24, The Little Boltons, SW10.
Uncle living (son of 1st baronet)—George Frederick Cecil McLannahan, *b.* 1919 ; ed. at Eton and in Switzer-

land; formerly acting Maj. Welch Regt.; Liaison Officer to RAF 1940; Councillor of Lymington, and a Member of Co. Council Adoption Cttee. 1950-65, and HM Harbour Commr. 1960-65; Founder of Sea Rescue Ser., now Inshore Rescue RNLI; a Gov. of Wessex Hosp. Group, a Member of Territorial Cttee. (Army South), and a Gov. of County Council Schs. in Hants.; Capt. Mercantile Marine 1960; Ch. Eng. 1965, AFCA; assumed the additional name of McLannahan 1954: *m.* 1st, 1940 (m. diss. 1947), Joy Mervyn, da. of the late Dr. Geoffrey Noott, of Fern Down Hill, Ferndown, Dorset; 2ndly, 1948, Monica Angela Mary, da. of Lt.-Com. Henry Guy Stanton, RN (ret.) [B. Castlemaine, colls.], and has issue living, (by 1st m.) David George Cecil *b.* 1941: *m.* 1968, Jennifer Anne, da. of Cdr. Thompson, of Jersey,—Mervyn Peter, *b.* 1944,— (by 2nd m.) Bridie Maureen McLannahan, *b.* 1951: *m.* 1972, Joseph Gavin Michel Cornelius Alexander Bonello, of Newlands, Old Xweiki, Naxxar, Malta, GC,—Sheena Patricia McLannahan, *b.* 1954,—Louisa Roxane McLannahan, *b.* 1957. *Residences*, Casa Poher, 19, Andaluzas, Estepona, Costa del Sol, Spain; Casa Xanadu, Tal Virtu, Rabat, Malta, GC. *Clubs*, Royal Netherlands, Royal London, Royal Naval Sailing Assocn., Royal Malta, Malta Union.

Aunt living (daughter of 1st baronet)—Lilian Hartley Cecil: *m.* 1939, Paul Van Kleeck Kingston, MD, and has issue living, Peter Charles, *b.* 1945,—Timothy Paul, *b.* 1949,—Katharine Martha, *b.* 1943: *m.* 1968, Jack Calvin Hartje, PhD, of 12771, Longview Drive W., Jacksonville, Florida, USA, and has issue living, Naomi *b.* 1974. *Residence*, 225, Eden Rd., Palm Beach 33480, Fla., USA.

Mother living—Nancy Hilary, da. of the late Rev. J. W. Griffiths, of Wentworth, Virginia Water : *m.* 1927 (marriage dissolved 1935), Sir Ivan McLannahan Cecil Power, 2nd baronet, who *d.* 1954. *Residence*, 23, Adelaide Sq., Windsor, Berks.

The 1st baronet, Sir John Cecil Power (son of William Taylor Power, of Belfast, co Down, and Sheen, Surrey) sat as M.P. for Wimbledon (*U*) 1924-45, and was Founder of Roy. Institute of International Affairs. Sir Ivan McLannahan Cecil Power, 2nd Bt., was Chm. of various industrial Cos. in Union of S. Africa and a Co. Councillor for London.

PRESCOTT, Creation (U.K.) 1938, of Godmanchester, co. Huntingdon.

Sir MARK PRESCOTT, 3rd *Baronet,* son of the late Maj. (William Robert) Stanley Prescott, yr. son of 1st baronet; *b.* March 3rd, 1948; *s.* his uncle, *Sir* RICHARD STANLEY, 1965.

Arms—Per chevron pean and erminois, on a chief or, a rose gules, barbed and seeded proper, between two leopards' faces sable. **Crest**—Upon the battlements of a tower proper, a leopard statant sable.

Residence,—Heath House, Newmarket.

Aunts living (daughters of 1st baronet)—Louise Bernice, *b.* 1903: *m.* 1928, Reginald Gray, of 5, Bridgetown, Totnes, Devon, and has issue living, David Stanley, *b.* 1937.— Grace Geraldine, *b.* 1905; Bar. Gray's Inn 1930.

Mother living—Gwendolen, only da. of the late Leonard Aldridge, CBE, of 31, Queen's Gate Gdns., SW7: *m.* 1st, 1939 (m. diss. 1951), Maj. (William Robert) Stanley Prescott, yr. son of 1st Bt., who *d.* 1962; 2ndly, 1952, Daniel Orme, of Flat 3, 6, Eaton Pl., SW1X 8AD.

He conquers who endures.

The 1st baronet, Col. Sir William (Henry) Prescott, CBE, DL, (son of John Prescott, of Blackburn), was an Alderman and Chm. of Middlesex County Council, Chm. of Metropolitan Water Board, and of Lee Conservancy Board, High Sheriff for Middlesex 1929, and for Cambs. and Hunts. 1938, and MP for N. Div. of Tottenham (*Co. U.*) 1918-22.

Prescott-Westcar, see Westcar.

PRESTON, Creation (U.K.) 1815, of Beeston St. Lawrence, Norfolk.

I hope for a brighter light.

Sir THOMAS HILDEBRAND PRESTON, *OBE*, 6th *Baronet*, son of the late William Thomas Preston, 2nd son of 2nd baronet; *b.* June 2nd, 1886; *s.* his kinsman, *Sir* EDWARD HULTON, *DSO, MC*, 1963; ed. at Westminster, and at Trin. Hall, Camb.; Min. to Lithuania 1940-41, and Counsellor of Embassy of Cairo 1941-48; Chm. of E. Anglian Branch of NATO; with Thomas de la Rue & Co., Ltd.; composer of musical works, and author of " Before the Curtain "; has Order of Restitution of Poland; OBE (Civil) 1934: *m.* 1913, Ella Henrietta, da. of F. von Schikendantz, and has issue.

Arms—Ermine, on a chief sable three crescents or. **Crest** —A crescent or.
Residence—Beeston Hall, Neatishead, Norfolk. *Clubs*—St. James', R.A.C.

Son living—RONALD DOUGLAS HILDEBRAND; *b.* Oct. 9th, 1916; late Maj. Intelligence Corps; formerly *Times* Correspondent in Belgrade, Vienna and Tokyo; HM Diplo. Ser. since 1963: *m.* 1st, 1954 (m. diss. 1971), Smilya Stefanovic, of Belgrade, Yugoslavia; 2ndly, 1972, Pauleen, da. of the late Paul Lurcott, of Albany Cottage, Fairwarp, Sussex.
Daughter living—Stella Tatiana Gertrude, *b.* 1920; with International Atomic Energy Agency, U.N.O.: *m.* 1962, Eugene Hartzell, MusM, of Pfarrhofgasse 13/21, Vienna III, and has issue living, Eugenie Belinda Tamara, *b.* 1963,—Melanie Anne Sonia, *b.* 1964.
Sister living—Violet Madge (17A, First St., SW3): *m.* 1928, Capt. Cyril Gascoigne Lloyd, late E. Riding of Yorkshire Yeo., who *d.* 1965, and has issue living, Rosemary Joan Caroline, *b.* 1929: *m.* 1959, Carleton John Richard Tufnell, of Calmsden Manor, Cirencester, and has issue living, Mark Henry *b.* 1964, Richard Lloyd *b.* 1965,—Barbara Anne, *b.* 1932: *m.* 1967, Andrew Edward Buxton, of 36, Burnsall St., SW3, [see Buxton, Bt., colls.].
Daughters living of 5th Baronet—Juliet Mary (*Hon. Mrs. Richard N. Manners*), *b.* 1921 : *m.* 1945, the Hon. Richard Neville Manners (Cromer Hall, Norfolk) [see B. Manners].—Patricia Evelyn, *b.* 1923: *m.* 1962, John Louis Benedict Todhunter, OBE [B. Kenyon, colls.], of Gillingham Hall, Beccles, Suffolk.

Widow living of 5th Baronet—MARGARET (*Dowager Lady Preston*) (Cromer Hall, Norfolk), el. da. of the late Benjamin Bond-Cabbell, of Cromer Hall, Norfolk: *m.* 1920, Sir Edward Hulton Preston, DSO, MC, 5th baronet, who *d.* 1963.

Collateral Branches living

Grandchildren of the late Col. Philip Henry Hulton Preston (infra):—
Issue of the late Lt.-Col. Philip Henry Herbert Hulton Preston, OBE, MC, *b.* 1914, *d.* 1973: *m.* 1st, 1940, Katherine Janet, who *d.* 1969, da. of Dr. B.C. Broomhall; 2ndly, 19—, Jean Mary (62, Cambridge Rd., Teddington, Middx.), da. of Harold Neale Turner:—
(By 1st m.) Philip Charles Henry Hulton, *b.* 1946; ed. at Nautical Coll., Pangbourne.——Caroline Elizabeth, *b.* 1943.

Granddaughter of the late Lt.-Col. Henry Edward Preston, el. son of Thomas Edward Preston, 2nd son of 1st baronet:—
Issue of the late Col. Philip Henry Hulton Preston, *b.* 1879, *d.* 1963: *m.* 1914, Dorothy May (Wicklands, Little Horstich, Uckfield, Sussex), only da. of the late Brig.-Gen. Herbert Alexander Kaye Jennings, CIE, RA:—
Marjorie, *b.* 1917: *m.* 1939, Miles Pacey Cheales, of Willow Cottage, Broad St., Guildford, Surrey, and has issue living, Justina Victoria, *b.* 1945,—Briony Margaret *b.* 1948,—Mary Henrietta Miles, *b.* 1951: *m.* 1971, Philip Alastair Barter, and has issue living, Oliver Philip Tom *b.* 1975, John Alexander *b.* 1975,—Alexandra Marjorie, *b.* 1952.

The 1st baronet, Sir Thomas, was a son of Henry Hulton, of Andover, by Elizabeth, eldest daughter of Isaac Preston, of Beeston St. Lawrence, whose estates he inherited, and in 1804 assumed the name and arms of Preston. The Prestons have held Beeston since 1640; and a Jacob Preston was one of four confidants who attended Charles I. during his imprisonment, and who was presented by that monarch, as a last mark of attachment, with an emerald ring, still preserved in the family.

PREVOST, Creation (U.K.) 1805, of Belmont, Hampshire.
[Name pronounced " Prev-o."]

Servatum cineri. Kept for the dead.

Sir GEORGE JAMES AUGUSTINE PREVOST, 5th *Baronet*; *b.* Jan. 16th, 1910 ; *s.* his father, *Sir* CHARLES THOMAS KEBLE, 1939 ; ed. at Repton ; formerly Staff Capt., Headquarters, N. Command, India ; is Lord of the Manor of Stinchcombe, Gloucestershire : *m.* 1st, 1935, Muriel Emily, who *d.* 1939, da. of the late Lewis William Oram ; 2ndly, 1940, Phyllis Mary Catherine Mattock. from whom he obtained a divorce 1949 ; 3rdly, 1952, Patricia Betty, da. of the late William Porter, of Kilburn, N.W., and has issue by 1st and 3rd marriages.

Arms—Azure, a dexter arm in fesse issuing from a cloud in the sinister fesse point, the hand grasping a sword erect proper, pommel and hilt or, in chief two mullets argent. **Crest**—A demi-lion rampant azure, charged on the shoulder with a mural crown or, the sinister paw grasping a sword erect as in the arms. **Supporters**—Two grenadiers of the 16th Foot, each supporting with exterior hand a flag flying, that on the dexter flying to the sinister and inscribed "West Indies," and that on the sinister gules, to the dexter, and inscribed "Canada."

Residence—12, Chiltern Rd., Pinner, Middlesex.

Sons living—By 1st m.—CHRISTOPHER GERALD (11, Savernake Court, Wolverton Rd., Old Church Lane, Stanmore, Middx.), *b.* July 25th, 1935: ed. at Cranleigh Sch.; late 60th Regt.: *m.* 1964, Dolores Nelly, only da. of Dezo Hoffmann, and has issue living, Nicholas Marc, *b.* 1971,—Ruth Annette, *b.* 1964.——**By 3rd m.**—James William, *b.* 1952.——Edward Charles, *b.* 1953.

Daughter living—By 1st m.—Felicity Jane, *b.* 1936: *m.* 1970, Hisham Pilus, of 17, Tambun Sq. Ipoh, Perak, Malaysia, and has issue living, Sophia, *b.* 1972.

Sister living—Margaret Elizabeth, *b.* 1908: *m.* 1939, John Reginald Wood, of The Malt House, Stinchcombe, Dursley, Glos., GL11 6AR, and has issue living, John Charles Michael (The Flat, The Plestor, Selborne, Alton, Hants.), *b.* 1940: *m.* 1960, Patricia Anne Slater, and has issue living. John Andrew Prevost *b.* 1960, Hugh Charles Asprey *b.* 1963, Rupert James Almeric *b.* 1966, Kynaston William Augustine *b.* 1967,—Stephen James (172, Mulgrave Rd., Cheam, Surrey), *b.* 1941: *m.* 1966, Daphne Monica Laing, and has issue living, Sarah Margaret Hardy *b.* 1967,—Lucy Evelyn Mary, *b.* 1945.

Collateral Branch living.

Issue of the late Lieut.-Col. George Herbert Prevost, Indian Army, younger son of 3rd baronet, *b.* 1868, *d.* 1951 : *m.* 1901, Katharine Alice, who *d.* 1911, da. of W. R. Glennie, formerly of Chilbolton. Hants :—

Katharine Alice Glennie, *b.* 1905: *m.* 1929, the Rev. Hugh Gethin Hanmer Griffith, who *d.* 1966, R. of Crickhowell, Breconshire, and has issue living, Glyn Keble Gethin (Y Lletty, Coity, Bridgend, Glam.), *b.* 1937: *m.* 1969, Hermanna Gerarda Limburg, and has issue, Anne Katharine *b.* 1971,—Carolyn Matilda *b.* 1973,—Barbara Ann, *b.* 1933. *Residence*, Eastways, Newnham-on-Severn, Glos.——Annette Dora (26, Wharton St., WC1X 9PJ), *b.* 1911: *m.* 1970, George Thomas Chamberlain, OBE.——Constance Charlotte (twin), *b.* 1911. *Residence*, 14, Lancaster Av., Farnham, Surrey.

The 1st baronet, Lt.-Gen. Sir George Prevost (el. son of Gen. Augustine Prevost, of Geneva, who settled in England), was Col. of the 60th Regt., Gov. of Canada and Commander of the Forces in British North America.

PRICE, Creation (U.K.) 1815, of Trengwainton, Cornwall.

Sir ROSE FRANCIS PRICE, 6th *Baronet;* b. March 15th, 1910; s. his father, *Sir* FRANCIS CARADOC ROSE, 1949; ed. at Wellington Coll., and at Trin. Coll., Camb. (B.A. 1931) ; European War 1939-45 as Capt. Indian Army (prisoner) : *m.* 1949, Kathleen June, da. of the late Norman W. Hutchinson, of Toorak, Melbourne, Australia, and has issue.

Arms—Sable, a chevron erminois between three spear-heads argent, embrued at the points proper. **Crest**—A dragon's head vert, erased gules, holding in the mouth a sinister hand erect couped at the wrist and dropping blood all proper.

Residence—Netherwood, Stoke Poges, Bucks. *Club*—Carlton.

All depends on God.

Sons living—FRANCIS CARADOC ROSE, *b.* Sept. 9th, 1949; ed. at Eton.——Norman William Rose, *b.* 1953; ed. at Eton.

Brother living—William Russell Rose (62, Hastings Rd., Sheffield, 7) *b.* 1916; sometime Maj. Indian Army: *m.* 1st, 1945 (m. diss. 1953), Joan, Ross Hurst; 2ndly, 1954, Aline Flora, da. of David Silverman, and has issue living, (by 2nd m.) Gillian Isobel *b.* 1959,—Julia Jane, *b.* 1962.

Sisters living—Diana Harriette, *b.* 1912.——Helen Jocelyn, *b.* 1920: *m.* 1950, Maj.-Gen. Logan Scott-Bowden, CBE, DSO, MC, c/o Lloyds Bank, 6, Pall Mall, SW1, and has issue living, Robert Logan, *b.* 1955,—James Russell, *b.* 1958.—Peter William, *b.* 1962,—Claire Anne, *b.* 1951.—Fiona Susan, *b.* 1952,—Alexandra Marjorie, *b.* 1960.——Anne Charlotte, *b.* 1927.

Collateral Branches living.

Grandchildren of the late Capt. Francis Henry Talbot Price (infra):—

Issue of the late Leslie Frederick Talbot Price, *b.* 1904, *d.* 1972: *m.* 1924, (m. diss. 1953) the Hon. Diana Frederica, da. of the late Hon. Maurice Raymond Gifford, CMG [see B. Gifford]:—

Maurice Rose, *b.* 1929.——Michael Henry, *b.* 1932: *m.* 1962, Lyndsay June, da. of C. L. Messner, of Harpenden, Herts.——Pamela, *b.* 1925: *m.* 1944, F/Lt. John William Reid, DFC, RNZAF, and has issue living, Martin James, *b.* 1946,—William John, *b.* 1952,—Julia, *b.* 1948,—Diana, *b.* 1949.

Granddaughter of the late Capt. Henry Talbot Price, RN, brother of 3rd baronet:—

Issue of the late Capt. Francis Henry Talbot Price, *b.* 1872, *d.* 1930 : *m.* 1899, Florence, only da. of Frederick Hurdle :—

Olive May Talbot (St. Louis, 33, Hocombe Wood Rd., Chandler's Ford, Hants.), *b.* 1900: *m.* 1924, Count St. John Vivian Beaumont de Beaufort Molyneux (*cr.* Holy Roman Empire 1710), who *d.* 1962.

Grandchildren of the late Col. Thomas Caradoc Rose Price, CB, 3rd son of John Price, 4th son of 1st baronet:—

Issue of the late Brig.-Gen. Thomas Rose Caradoc Price, C.M.G., D.S.O., *b.* 1875, *d.* 1949 : *m.* 1911, Dorothy Patience, who *d.* 1969, only da. of the late Sir Henry William Verey:—

Robert Caradoc Rose, D.S.O., O.B.E., *b.* 1912 ; ed. at Wellington Coll.; Lieut.-Col. late Welsh Guards ; European War 1939-45 in France, N. Africa, Italy, Palestine and N.-W. Europe (despatches, D.S.O.) ; D.S.O. 1943, O.B.E. (Mil.) 1951 : *m.* 1946, the Hon. Maureen Maude Tower Butler, da. of 27th Baron Dunboyne, and has issue living, Thomas Geoffrey Timothy

Rose, *b.* 1948; ed. at Eton: *m.* 1975, Leila Anne Katherine, da. of Sir Richard Guy Carne Rasch, 3rd Bt.,—Sarah Maureen Rose, *b.* 1947: *m.* 1968, Michael John Burrell, Barrister-at-Law, of 2, Ashchurch Park Villas, W12, and has issue living, Amanda Caroline *b.* 1971, Nicola Sarah *b.* 1973. *Residence*, Tetworth Hall, Ascot, Berks.——Mary Dorothy Rose, *b.* 1918: *m.* 1948, John Dugdale Holt Wiseman, MA, PhD, formerly Dep. Keeper of Mineralogy, British Museum of Natural History, and has issue living, John Paul Holt, *b.* 1949; ed. at Shrewsbury. *Residence*, Hornbeam House, Waltham St. Lawrence, Berks.

Granddaughters of the late Brig.-Gen. Thomas Rose Caradoc Price, CMG, DSO (ante):—

Issue of the late Dennistoun John Franklin Rose Price [the actor Dennis Price], *b.* 1915, *d.* 1973: *m.* 1939, (m. diss. 1950), Joan Schofield:—

Susan Joan Rose, *b.* 1940: *m.* 1967, Thomas H. Mapp, of 20, Mayfair Close, Ditton Rd., Surbiton, Surrey, and has issue living, Kate Miranda, *b.* 1972.——Tessa Alexandra Rose, *b.* 1943: *m.* 1965, Hugh Thomas Burnett, of 36, Wilbury Villas, Hove, Sussex, and has issue living, Rupert Thomas, *b.* 1971,—Lucy Eleanor, *b.* 1966,—Emily Tamelayne, *b.* 1968.

Issue of the late Lieut.-Com. Vivian Franklin Lyon Rose Price, R.N., *b.* 1881; *d.* (on active service during European War) 1915: *m.* 1912, Jean Purvis Mills, who *d.* 1939 :—

Vivian Judith Elizabeth Rose, *b.* 1915: *m.* 1937, Col. George Francis Taylor, CBE, of 1, Gundreda Rd., Lewes, Sussex, and has issue living, Jeremy Vivian George, *b.* 1940: *m.* 1967, Sally, da. of John Parnell, and has issue living, Gemma Vivian *b.* 1971,—Sarah Jane Elizabeth, *b.* 1943: *m.* 1968, Thomas Peart, and has issue living, Rachel *b.* 1969, Scarlett *b.* 1971,—Anna-Lisa, *b.* 1949.

Grandchildren of the late George Price, 5th son of 1st baronet:—
Issue of the late Cyril Oliver Rose Price, M.B.E., *b.* 1880, *d.* 1960: *m.* 1910, Edith Muriel, who *d.* 1956, da. of the late Donald Campbell Ridout, of Toronto:—

George Donald Rose (of Kingsley Hall, Kingsley, Warrington), *b.* 1911; ed. at Emmanuel Coll., Camb. (Senior Scholar 1932, B.A. Honours 1933, M.A. 1938): *m.* 1947, Dorothy Christine, da. of the late Major Eric Fairclough, D.S.O.

Grandson of the late Thomas Price, 6th son of 1st baronet:—
Issue of the late Arthur Henry Price, *b.* 1850, *d.* 1916: *m.* 1872, Minna, da. of the late Samuel P. Oxley, of Valparaiso:—

Samuel Percy, *b.* 1878: *m.* 1st, 1906, Margaret Elinor, who *d.* 1906, da. of the late James Grant, of Dunheanish, Oban ; 2ndly, 1912, Anita, da. of T. A. Mackay, of Concepcion, Chile, and has issue living, (by 2nd m.) John Samuel, *b.* 1921; is Pilot Officer Chilean Air Force (Reserve): *m.* 1943, Joan Margaret, who *d.* 1954, da. of Frank Williams, of Cochabamba, Bolivia, and has issue living, Samuel John Rose *b.* 1950, Peter Rose *b.* 1954, Anita Margaret Rose *b.* 1944, Sandra Joan Rose *b.* 1947, Jennifer Rose *b.* 1953,—Michael Patrick, *b.* 1922; is Pilot Officer Chilean Air Force (Reserve): *m.* 1945, Evelyn Mabel, da. of the late Eric Saffery, of Talcahuano, Chile, and has issue living, Anthony Samuel Patrick Rose *b.* 1953, Thomas Eric Rose *b.* 1956, Heather Evelyn Rose *b.* 1946, Marylyn Rose *b.* 1949, Gillian Rose *b.* 1951,—Carmen, *b.* 1915: *m.* 1st, 1935, Lt. Oswald Marcus Cheke, DSC, RN, who *d.* (killed on active service) 1941; 2ndly, 1942, James Byrne, from whom she obtained a divorce 1951; 3rdly, 1953, Manuel Hidalgo, and has issue living, (by 1st m.) Marcus Oswald *b.* 1936, Francis Patrick *b.* 1940, (by 2nd m.) Jacqueline *b.* 1945, Rosanna Amber *b.* 1949, (by 3rd m.) Ana Manuela *b.* 19—, Maria Victoria (twin) *b.* 19—, —Pearl Rose, *b.* 1917: *m.* 1st, 1938, Rudolph Seyler; 2ndly, 1947, Edward George Yriberry, and has issue living, (by 1st m.) Christopher Louis *b.* 1939, (by 2nd m.) Pearl Anita *b.* 1954. *Residence*—462, Casilla, Valpariso, Chile.

Grandchildren of the late Arthur Henry Price (ante) :—
Issue of the late Arthur Douglas Price, *b.* 1873, *d.* 1951 : *m.* 1st, 1901, Wilhelmine Marion (who *d.* 1955, having obtained a divorce 1922), da. of the late Robert Adolphe Claude, of Valparaiso ; 2ndly, 1922, Augustine Laetitia (now of El Ranchito, Guethary, Basses Pyrénées, France), da. of Jacques Benoit :—

(By 1st m.) Violet Marion Rose, *b.* 1902: *m.* 1926, Joaquin Santiago Andrés Monuz Arlegui, who *d.* 1939, and has issue living, Joaquin Santiago Federico, *b.* 1930,—Veronica Marion, *b.* 1927: *m.* 1st, 1951, Alexander Edmund Gough Gubbins Browne, who *d.* 1952; 2ndly, 1960, Alfonso Necocha Beauchemin, and has issue living, (by 1st and 2nd ms.).——Beatrice Mary Rose (c/o Gordon Dadds & Co., 80, Brook St., W1), *b.* 1904: *m.* 19—, , who *d.* 19—.—Olivia Margaret Rose, *b.* 1910: *m.* 1932, José-Maria Souviron, and has issue living, Alvaro Souviron Price, *b.* 1933: *m.* 1958, Ximena Grebe, and has issue living, Pilar Souviron *b.* 1959, Beatrice Souviron *b.* 1960,—Jacqueline Souviron Price, *b.* 1936: *m.* 1958, Luis Urrejola Dittborn, of Santiago, Chile, and has issue living, Daniel Urrejola *b.* 1959, Sebastian Urrejola *b.* 1961, Caroline Urrejola *b.* 1962.——Eveleen Mina Rose (c/o Banco de A. Edwards y Cia, Valparaiso, Chile), *b.* 1913: *m.* 19—, (m. diss 19—)

Grandchildren of the late Rev. Thomas Rose Price (infra):—
Issue of the late Rev. Thomas Neville Vreichvras Churchill Rose Price, MA, *b.* 1911, *d.* 1970: *m.* 1939, Edna Mary (Longston, Kiln Lane, Stokenham, Kingsbridge, Devon), da. of the late Howard Edge, of Wolverhampton:—

Robin Francis Neville Rose (Torcross Hotel, Torcross, nr. Kingsbridge, Devon), *b.* 1945: *m.* 1970, Alison Margaret, da. of Denis Rogers, of Torcross, Devon, and has issue living, Andrew Rose, *b.* 1975,—Sarah Rose, *b.* 1973.——Heather Mary Rose, *b.* 1942: *m.* 1965, Richard James Biddle, of Mowlish Manor, Kenton, nr. Exeter, and has issue living, Marc Jonathan Seymour, *b.* 1967,— Roy Lindley Stirling, *b.* 1969,—Tiffany Lynn, *b.* 1970.

Granddaughters of the late Arthur Henry Price (ante):—
Issue of the late Rev. Thomas Rose Price, *b.* 1874, *d.* 1940: *m.* 1901, Frances Louisa Salisbury, who *d.* 1943, da. of Frederick Churchill, M.D., F.R.C.S. :—

Rosalind Maud Rose, *b.* 1906: *m.* 1951, Alfred Sidney Charles Overton, of The Forge, Tremar, Liskeard, Cornwall.——Geraldine Minna Violet Rose, *b.* 1908; ed. at St. Andrews Univ. (MA 1933): *m.* 1938, Herbert A. Goldberg, MB, ChB, and has issue living, Janet Madeleine, *b.* 1943,— Louise Diane, *b.* 1945. *Residence*, 9306, Kendale Rd., Bethesda, 14, Maryland, USA.——Joy Gerrardine Salisbury Rose, *b.* 1918: *m.* 1939, Rupert George Pearce, and has issue living, Peter Wayne, *b.* 1947: *m.* 1969, Kay Teresa Harris,—Wendy Lynne, *b.* 1941: *m.* 1964, William Harper Ritchie, and has issue living, Peter Graham *b.* 1966, Grant Phillip *b.* 1970, Kathryn Margaret *b.* 1968,—Pauline Frances, *b.* 1944: *m.* 1968, Donald George Foster, and has issue living, Daniel Richard *b.* 1970,—Faye Fiona, *b.* 1949: *m.* 1970, Wayne Allan Parkhill,—Estelle Suzanne, *b.* 1951. *Residence*, Hoon Hay Valley, Christchurch 3, NZ.

Francis Price, *b.* about 1635, believed to be descended from Caradoc Vreichvras, Prince between the Wye and Severn, settled in Jamaica soon after its conquest in 1655. He acquired Worthy Park in St. Johns 1670, and was a Member of House of Assembly and Maj. of Militia. He married Elizabeth Booth, widow of Col. William Rose, of Rose Hall, Jamaica. His son, Col. Charles Price, was testamentary heir of his uterine brother, Thomas Rose, and inherited his Jamaica estates. His el. son, Charles, Speaker of the Ho. of Assembly, was cr. a Bt. 1768, which title became ext. on the death of the 2nd Bt. 1788 (also Speaker of Ho. of Assembly). John Price, yst. son of Col. Charles Price, was grandfather of Sir Rose Price, 1st Bt. of the 2nd and present creation. Sir Rose Price, 4th Bt., was killed during S. African War 1901.

PRICE, Creation (U.K.) 1953, of Ardingly, co. Sussex. [Extinct 1963.]

Sir HENRY PHILIP PRICE, 1st and last *Baronet.*

Widow living of 1st Baronet—EVA MARY DICKSON (*Lady Price*) (Barton Manor, E. Cowes, I. of Wight): *m.* 1939, as his second wife, Sir Henry Philip Price, 1st baronet, who *d.* 1963, when the title became ext.

GREEN-PRICE, Creation (U.K.) 1874, of Norton Manor, Radnorshire.

Live to-day.

Sir ROBERT JOHN GREEN-PRICE, 5th *Baronet; b.* Oct. 22nd, 1940; *s.* his father, Capt. *Sir* JOHN, 1964; ed. at Shrewsbury; Capt. (ret.) RCT; ADC to Gov. of Bermuda 1969.

Arms—Sable, a chevron invected argent between three escutcheons of the last, each charged with a spear-head of the first embrued proper. Crest—In front of a dragon's head erased vert, holding in the mouth a dexter hand, couped at the wrist gules, three escallops argent.

Residence—Gwernaffel, Knighton, Powys.

Sister living—Roseanne, *b.* 1943: *m.* 1963, Richard Lower, Maj. Queen Elizabeth's Own Gurkha Rifles, and has issue living, Timothy, *b.* 19—,— Deborah, *b.* 19—, — Sophie Louise, *b.* 1969.

Widow living of 4th Baronet—JEAN CHALMERS SCOTT (*Lady Green-Price*) (Gwernaffel, Knighton, Powys), da. of David Low Stark, of Arbroath: *m.* 1956, as his 2nd wife, Capt. Sir John Green-Price, 4th Bt., who *d.* 1964.

Collateral Branches living.

Issue of the late Llewellyn James Green-Price, yst. son of 2nd baronet, *b.* 1881, *d.* 1962: *m.* 1919, Ethel Lilian, da. of S. Faram, of Kepax, Worcester:—
Olive Maude, *b.* 1922.

Grandchildren of the late Rev. Herbert Chase Green-Price (infra):—
Issue of the late Lt.-Col. Francis Chase Green-Price, *b.* 1896, *d.* 1975: *m.* 1934, Joan Atcherley (Breezelands, Moor Lane, Croyde Bay, Braunton, N. Devon, EX33 1NU), da. of the late Guy Dobell, of Crickhowell:—
JOHN CHASE, *b.* June 27th, 1947.——Susan Marion, *b.* 1939.
Issue of the late Rev. Herbert Chase Green-Price, 2nd son of 1st baronet, *b.* 1855, *d.* 1919 : *m.* 1895, Susan Alice, who *d.* 1951, el. da. of William Henry Barneby [E. St. Aldwyn] :—
Richard Henry, *b.* 1905; ed. at Radley: *m.* 1931, Ruby Beatrix, da. of the late Robert Thomas Rowan, of Shanghai, and has issue living, Anthony Chase, *b.* 1933,—Susan Anne, *b.* 1943. *Residence*, RD1, Te Kuiti, NZ.——Patience Laura, *b.* 1898: *m.* 1927, Maj. Robert King Holmes, RASC. *Residence*, The Colony, Burnham-on-Sea, Somerset.

Issue of the late Rev. Alfred Edward Green-Price, 4th son of 1st baronet, *b.* 1860, *d.* 1940 : *m.* 1893, Mary Louisa, who *d.* 1922, da. of the late Very Rev. H. Edwards, Dean of Bangor :—
Alice Monica (of Nash Cottage, Fownhope, Hereford), *b.* 1907: *m.* 1969, Richard Vivian Glynne Williams.

The 1st baronet, Sir Richard, son of the late George Green, of Knighton, in 1874 assumed, by Roy. licence, the additional surname of Price, being heir to his maternal uncle, Richard Price of Norton Manor, Radnorshire. He sat as M.P. for Radnor Boroughs (*L*) 1862-9, and for Radnorshire 1880-85. Sir Robert Henry, 3rd Bt. was High Sheriff of Radnorshire 1930.

RUGGE-PRICE, Creation (U.K.) 1804, of Spring Grove, Richmond, Surrey.

Live (here) so that you may live (thereafter).

Sir CHARLES KEITH NAPIER RUGGE-PRICE, 9th *Baronet; b.* Aug. 7th, 1936; *s.* his father, *Lt.-Col. Sir* CHARLES JAMES NAPIER, 1966; ed. at Middleton Coll., Ireland: *m.* 1965, Jacqueline Mary, yr. da. of Maj. Pierre P. Loranger, MC, CD, and has issue.

Arms—Quarterly, 1st and 4th, gules, a lion rampant argent, *Price* ; 2nd and 3rd, sable, on a chevron invected argent, between three mullets or pierced of the field, an unicorn's head erased of the first, *Rugge*. Crests—1st, a lion rampant argent, holding in the dexter paw a rose slipped proper ; 2nd, a talbot passant argent, gorged with a collar and pendent therefrom an escutcheon sable, thereon the head of an ibex couped, also argent.

Residence, 38, Forest Manor Rd., Willowdale, Ont., Canada.

Sons living—JAMES KEITH PETER, *b.* April 8th, 1967.
——Andrew Philip Richard, *b.* 1970.
Sisters living—Angela Muriel Frances, *b.* 1938: *m.* 1970, Martyn Samuel, and has issue living, Bernard Charles, *b.* 1971.——Jane Marjorie Agnes, *b.* 1943: *m.* 1965, Leslie C. Tankard, and has issue living, Nigel Peter Stewart, *b.* 1970,—Wendy Julie Angela, *b.* 1967.——Catharine Sarah Christina, *b.* 1948.
Uncle living (son of 7th baronet)—Anthony Arthur Keith, CBE (The Small House, Weedon, Aylesbury; Cavalry Club), *b.* 1914; ed. at Harrow; Col. late 13/18th Hussars; OC 13/18th R. Hussars 1956-58; CBE (Mil) 1967: *m.* 1st, 1939 (m. diss. 1948), Joan

Lisette Douglas, da. of Alan Douglas Pilkington, of Dean Wood, Newbury; 2ndly, 1952, Mrs. Maryjoy Campbell, da. of the late John Eric Horniman, and has issue living, (by 1st m.) Anthony Jeremy (62, Chester Row, SW1), b. 1940: m. 1st, 1963 (m. diss. 19—), Sarah Oliva Valentine, da. of Lt.-Col. Lance Granville Davidson Brett, of Corfe, Somerset, and has issue living (by 1st m.), Andrew Christian b. 1964, Barnaby Douglas b. 1969, Matilda Candide b. 1970; (by 2nd m.) Edward Jason Napier b. 1973,—James Keith Alan (Thatch Cottage, Hillhouses Lane, Cheriton, Alresford, Hants.), b. 1944: m. 1967 (m. diss. 1972) Elizabeth Mary, da. of Lt.-Col. James Innes, of Larkenshaw, Chobham, Surrey [see E. Lonsdale], and has issue living, Lucy Caroline b. 1969,— (by 2nd m.) Juliet, b. 1954.

Aunts living (daughers of 7th baronet)—Catharine Marjorie (*Lady Balfour*), b. 1904: m. 1930, Lt.-Gen. Sir Philip Maxwell Balfour, KBE, CB, MC, late R.A., of Little Wincombe House, Donhead St. Mary, Shaftesbury, Dorset.——Lois Mary Maitland, b. 1911: m. 1932, Lt.-Col. Aylmer Lochiel Cameron, DSO, MC, RHA, of The Old Rectory, Winterborne Anderson, Blandford, Dorset, and has issue living, Ewen Duncan, b. 1935; Lt.-Col. The Black Watch (RHR): m. 1973, Joanna Margaret, da. of Maj. James Malcolm Hay [see M. Tweeddale, colls.].

Widow living of 8th Baronet—MAEVE MARGUERITE (*Maeve, Lady Rugge-Price*), da. of Edgar Stanley de la Peña, of Hythe, Kent: m. 1935, Lt.-Col. Sir Charles James Napier Rugge-Price, 8th Bt., who d. 1966.

Collateral Branches living.

Grandchildren of Alfred Adams Price, grandson of Ralph Price, 3rd son of 1st baronet:—
Issue of the late Kenneth Alexander Price, b. 1869, d. 19—: m. 1904, Helen Mary, who d. 1942, 2nd da. of William Baldwin George:—
Arthur Basil, b. 1916: m. 1939, Ethel Frances Brindle.——Douglas Leonard, b. 1922; late Fl. Lt. RAF: m. 1943, Hazel Irene Boyles.——Ethel Marian, b. 1905: m. 1930, Kenneth Couch.—— Phyllis, b. 1908: m. 1941, Leslie Henry, late Canadian Army.

Grandchildren of the late Petley Lloyd Augustus Price (infra) :—
Issue of the late Capt. Augustus Robert Petley Price, b. 1885, d. 1945: m. 1922, Augusta Elsy Maud (now of Ganges, British Columbia) , da. of Gilbert Wilkes, of Ganges, British Columbia :—
Augustus Robert Kenrick, b. 1927.——Elsy Mary, b. 1923: m. 1963, Raymond Perks, of 486, Island Highway, Victoria, British Columbia.

Grandchildren of the late Lieut.-Col. Augustus Price, el. son of the late Richard Price (infra) :—
Issue of the late Petley Lloyd Augustus Price, b. 1856, d. 1910 : m. 1884, Mary Cotton, who d. 1946, da. of the late Com. Frederick Arthur Egerton, R.N. [Grey-Egerton, Bt., colls.]:—
Harold Tudor Egerton, b. 1888: m. 1927, Margaret Frances, da. of the late Edward Fotheringham Layard, of Southsea, and has issue living, John Harold Petley, b. 1928: m. 1953, Edith, da. of the late J. Lee.—Ruth Gladys, b. 1930.——Reginald, b. 1889.——Elizabeth Rosina May: m. 1915, Alexander Thomas Benthall Charlesworth, Lt. RFC, who d. (killed in action during 1914-18 War) 1917.——Ada Marjorie: m. 1915, Cecil Edward Archibald Leslie Ley, MC. *Residence*,

Granddaughter of the late Major Edward Augustus Uvedale Price (infra) :—
Issue of the late Lt.-Cdr. Geoffrey Uvedale Price, R.N.V.R., b. 1885, d. 1960: m. 1908, Winifred Ethel, who d. 1963, only da. of the late Edgar L. Price, of The Bays, Oakhill Rd., East Putney, S.W.:—
Vivienne Betty Henrietta, b. 1910 : m. 1934, Brigadier Maurice Rapinet Mackenzie, D.S.O., R.A., and has issue living, Michael Philip Uvedale Rapinet, b. 1937 ; ed. at Downside, and at Oxford Univ. *Residence*, Upper Cowden, Five Ashes, Mayfield, Sussex.

Grandchildren of the late Gen. George Uvedale Price, 4th son of the late Richard Price, 4th son of 1st baronet :—
Issue of the late Major Edward Augustus Uvedale Price, b. 1854, d. 1905 : m. 1881, Elizabeth Henrietta, who d. 1905, da. of Henry J. P. Dumas, J.P. for Surrey :—
Kathleen Janette: m. 1912, Capt. Leslie Granville Waller, late Intelligence Corps, and has issue living, Margaret Evelyn Henrietta, b. 1913 : m. 1939, Jacques Lioni, of Mr. Sixlaan 3, Amstelveen, Holland, and has issue living, David Alexander b. 1941, John Christopher Granville b. 1945, Helen Mary b. 1947. *Residence*, 62, Melbury Gardens, Wimbledon, S.W.20.

Issue of the late Brig.-Gen. Charles Henry Uvedale Price, C.B., D.S.O., b. 1862, d. 1942: m. 1889, Ada Mary, who d. 1956, da. of John Orlando Hercules Norman Oliver, C.S.I. :—
Merlyth Mary, b. 1895. *Residence*, Geeler, Aveley Lane, Farnham, Surrey.

Issue of the late Col. Cyril Uvedale Price, C.M.G., b. 1868, d. 1956 : m. 1st, 1902, Ethel Maude, who d. 1916, da. of the late Capt. William Henry Ashe ; 2ndly, 1919, May Edith, who d. 1967, da. of the late Robert Lewis, of Damaraland:—

(By 2nd m.) Roger Uvedale, b. 1921; Burma 1942-45 as Capt. Indian Army: m. 1946, Angela Marcella Exton, da. of Brig. Wallis, Indian Army and has issue living, Myfanwy Uvedale, b. 1948: m. 1968, Peter John Penney, of 2, Denshire Drive, Storrington, nr. Pulborough, Sussex, and has issue living, Ian Richard b. 1970, Samantha Helen b. 1973.

Grandson of the late Ralph Mountague Rokeby Price (infra):—
Issue of the late Arthur Montague Rokeby Price, b. 1892, d. 1941 : m. 1916, Eliza (of 4429, Kawanee Av., Metairie, Louisiana, U.S.A.), da. of Victor Kuylen, of Stann Creek, British Honduras :—
Ralph Mountague Rokeby, CPM (4429, Kawanee Av., Metairie, La. 70002, USA), b. 1917; formerly Principal Assist. Sec., British Honduras, CPM for Meritorious Ser.; 1939-45 War Capt. Caribbean Regt.: m. 1942, Margarita Matilda Ernestina, da. of Nazario Cervantes, of Belize, British Honduras, and has issue living, Ralph Mountague Rokeby, b. 1946,—Arthur Richard Rokeby (8716, Fulton St., Metairie, La. 70003, USA), b. 1949: m. 1972, Elaine Sand, and has issue living, Jason Richard b. 1974,—David Francis Rokeby, b. 1956,—Michael John Rokeby, b. 1958,—Patricia Elizabeth Rokeby, b. 1943: m. 1963, Marvin Robert Sabido, of 1905, Kent Av., Metairie, La. 70001, USA, and has issue living, Marvin Robert b. 1964, David Andrew b. 1967,—Alice Mae Rokeby, b. 1948: m. 1972, Lloyd Perrien, of 2604, N. Sibley St., Metairie, La. 70003, USA, and has issue living, Todd Andrew b. 1973,—Margaret Joan Rokeby, b. 1952,— Carolyn Mary Rokeby, b. 1962.

Grandchildren of the late Arthur Montague Rokeby Price (ante):—
Issue of the late Arthur Victor Rokeby Price, b. 1921, d. 1964: m. 1955, Bridget Ellen (510, S. Archer St., Anaheim, Cal., USA), da. of Michael Austin Flynn, of Canada:—
Michael Craig, b. 1959.——Richard Arthur (twin), b. 1959.——Bridget Ellen, b. 1956.——Judith, b. 1958.——Jennifer (twin), b. 1958.——Margaret Mary, b. 1961.——Sheila Rose, b. 1962.— Elizabeth Ann, b. 1964.

Granddaughter of the late Rev. Thomas Charles Price, son of the late Thomas Price, 5th son of 1st baronet:—
Issue of the late Ralph Mountague Rokeby Price, b. 1860, d. 1905: m. 1889, Emily Ada, who d. 1924, da. of William Jex, of Norfolk. and widow of Alexander Finlay Bowman, of Serpon Estate, British Honduras :—

Gladys Ethel Rokeby (4209, Prytania St., New Orleans 15, La., USA), b. 1895: m. 1917, Robert
Albert Gegg Howard, who d. 1963, and has issue living, John Towrye Spencer (3909, Louisiana
Av. Park, New Orleans, La., USA), b. 1918; 1939-45 War, as Sgt. US Army in Pacific: m. 1943,
Adele Mary, da. of Capt. R. C. Cochran, of New Orleans, and has issue living, John Towrye
Spencer b. 1944, David Alan b. 1953, Robert Gegg b. 1962, Joan Rokeby b. 1958,—George Moun-
tague Plumer, BA (4436, St. Roch Av., New Orleans, La., USA), b. 1919; 1939-45 War, as 1st
Lt. US Army, in Europe (Purple Heart and Silver Star for Gallantry in Action): m. 1952,
Marylou Kay, da. of the late Malcolm G. Mundy, of New Orleans, and has issue living, George
Mountague Plumer b. 1958,—Frank Alan, b. 1928; 1939-45 War, as Sgt. US Army,—Gwladys
Olwen Napier, b. 1921: m. 1947 (m. diss. 1966), Stephen Grilletta, and has issue living, Stephen
Robert b. 1950, Warren Jeffrey b. 1953, Stephanie Ann b. 1957,—Gladys Elizabeth, b. 1927:
m. 1949, Coach Bennie Ellender.

Grandchildren of the late Thomas Plumer Price (infra):—
Issue of the late Capt. Thomas Ralph Plumer Price, b. 1885, d. 1967: m. 1916, Ruth
Beatrice (6, Harley Court, Church Rd., Warsash, Southampton), da. of the late Sydney
Harris, of The Gables, Hagley Rd., Edgbaston:—
Richard Ralph Plumer (5310, Fairholme Rd., Victoria, B.C., Canada, V8X 3X3), b. 1926: m. 1954,
Audrey Chrystal, da. of the late James Anderson Gray, of London, Ont., and has issue living,
James Plumer, b. 1957.—Norman Plumer, b. 1959.——Ruth Rosemary Plumer (21, Valley Rise,
Sarisbury Green, Southampton), b. 1920: m. 1946 (m. diss. 1953), Robert Alfred John Sindall,
FO, RAF, and has issue living, David Robert Plumer, b. 1947,—Sally Ann (303, Swanwick Lane,
Swanwick, Southampton), b. 1949: m. 1969 (m. diss. 1975) Stephen Philip Clarke, and has issue
living, Rachel Melanie b. 1970, Sarah Elizabeth b. 1972.

Granddaughter of the late Rev. Thomas Charles Price (ante):—
Issue of the late Thomas Plumer Price, b. 1861, d. 1930: m. 1884, Elizabeth Laura Middle-
ton, who d. 1946, da. of the late Capt. Richard George Collins (formerly 57th Regt.),
of Melbourne House, Cullompton:—
Phyllis Joan Plumer (Overdale, Upper Clatford, Andover, Hants.) b. 1895: m. 1918, Capt. Thomas
Brunyée Harston, LLB, solicitor (formerly Capt., Liverpool Regt.), who d. 1951, and has issue
living, Antony Plumer Brunyée, MB, ChB, MRCOG (9, Hillside Court, Weyhill Rd., Andover,
Hants.) b. 1924; Lt.-Col. (ret.) RAMC,—Bridget Elizabeth Uvedale, b. 1931.

Grandchildren of the late Capt. Spencer Cosby Price, 3rd son of Thomas Price
(ante):—
Issue of the late Spencer Edward Cosby Price, b. 1873, d. 19—: m. 1894, his cousin,
Eleanor Ann, da. of Mark Whatmore:—
Spencer Kendrick Sydney, b. 1902.——Nesta Joan Cosby, b. 1900.

Granddaughters of the late Hall Rokeby Price, son of the late Thomas Price
(ante):—
Issue of the late Wilfrid Thomas Rokeby Price, b. 1856, d. 1926: m. 1888, Emily
Catherine, who d. 1952, da. of the late Charles Frederick Murray, of Woodcote Hall,
Epsom :—
Freda Rokeby, b. 1890: m. 1st, 1915, Capt. George Edgcombe Hellyer, Hampshire Regt., who
d. (wounds in action) 1915; 2ndly, 1917, Arthur William Montague Marshall, who d. 1957, and
has issue living, (by 2nd m.) Jean Margaret, b. 1919: m. 1942, Capt. Thomas Hugh Peter Wilson,
RN, of Rossenford, Norley Wood, Lymington, Hants., and has issue living, Rosamond Margaret
b. 1943: m. 1967, Cdr. David Wright, RN (and has issue living, Christopher Marshall b. 1970,
Virginia Brook b. 1973), Veronica Anne b. 1944, Fe.icity Jean b. 1949: m. 1971, Lt. Nigel Guild,
RN. Residence, 162, Coleherne Court, Redcliffe Gdns., SW5.——Marjorie Rokeby, b. 1891.
Residence, 107, Coleherne Court, SW5.

The 1st baronet, Alderman Sir Charles Price, was M.P. for the City of London 1802-12, and
Lord Mayor thereof 1802-3. Sir Arthur James, 5th baronet, assumed in 1874, by Roy. licence, the
additional surname of Rugge. Lieut.-Col. Sir Charles Frederick Rugge-Price, 7th baronet
R.F.A., served in S. Africa 1900-1901, and in European War 1914-18.

Prichard-Jones, see Jones.

Fidelity and confidence.   **PRIMROSE, Creation (U.K.) 1903, of Redholme, Dumbreck,
Govan, Co. of City of Glasgow.**

Sir JOHN URE PRIMROSE, 3rd *Baronet; b.*
April 15th, 1908 ; s. his father, *Sir* WILLIAM LOUIS, 1953 ;
ed. at Rugby ; sometime Lieut. Queen's Own Cameron
Highlanders ; is a Farmer : *m.* 1933, Enid, da. of the late
James Sladen, of British Columbia, Canada, and has issue.

Arms—Per fesse argent and ermines, on a fesse vert between in chief
a mill rind between two cross-crosslets fitchée gules, and in base a salmon
on its back argent, holding a signet ring in its mouth, three primroses
slipped proper.   Crest—A hand couped at the wrist grasping a primrose
slipped proper.

Residence—Puerto Victoria, Alto Parana Misiones, Argentina.
Address—c/o Bank of London & South America, 40-66, Queen Victoria
Street, E.C.4.

Son living—ALASDAIR NEIL (Ada Elflein 3155, Boulogne, Buenos Aires, Argentina), b. Dec. 11th,
1933. m. 1958, Elaine Noreen, da. of Edmund Cecil Lowndes, of Buenos Aires, Argentina, and
has issue living, John Ure, b. 1960,—Andrew Richard, b. 1966,—Doris Sofia, b. 1962,—Deborah
Marina, b. 1964.

Brother living—Hugh Dunsmuir b. 1909 ; ed. at Uppingham ; late Flying Officer R.A.F. : m.
1935. Kathleen da. of the late Samuel Tyler. of Long Sutton, Lincolnshire. and has issue living,
Iain Dunsmuir (Lymburghs Farm, Marnhull, Dorset), b. 1941: m. 1971, Roberta Jeanette, da. of
Frdderick Clapp, of Bristol, and has issue living, James Robert b. 1973, Fiona Joanne b. 1971.
Residence, High Trees, Bedchester, Shaftesbury.

The 1st baronet, Sir John Ure Primrose (senior partner in the firm of William Primrose and Sons,
flour millers, of Centre Street, Glasgow), was Chm. of Clyde Navigation Trustee 1907-9, Lord Provost
of Glasgow 1903-5, and Lord-Lieut. of the co. of the City of Glasgow.

Prince-Smith [see Smith].

PRINGLE, Creation (N.S.) 1683, of Stichill, Roxburghshire.

Faith crowns.

Sir STEUART ROBERT PRINGLE, 10th Baronet; *b.* July 21st, 1928; *s.* his father, *Squadron Leader Sir* NORMAN HAMILTON, 1961; ed. at Sherborne; Lt.-Col. RM (local Col. 1974); commanded 45 Commando RM since 1971: *m.* 1953, Jacqueline Marie, only da. of Wilfrid Hubert Gladwell, of La Roque, Jersey, and has issue.

    Arms—Azure, three escallops or. **Crests**—1st, an escallop or; 2nd, a saltire azure within a garland of bay-leaves proper.

    Residence,—Woodlands House, Condor, Arbroath, Angus. *Address,*—Sea Gate House, Royal Marine Barracks, Stonehouse, Plymouth.

Daughters living—Shelagh Mary Frances, *b.* 1954: *m.* 1975, Jasper J. H. Dale.——Nicola Ann, *b.* 1956.
Sons living—SIMON ROBERT, *b.* Jan. 6th, 1959.—— Julian Andrew James, *b.* 1961.
Aunt living (daughter of 8th baronet)—Mary Elizabeth, *b.* 1916: *m.* 1938, Major G. Wallace Anderson, and has issue living, Veronica Bethia, *b.* 1939. *Residence,*

Widow living of 9th Baronet—WINIFRED OLIVE (*Winifred, Lady Pringle*), da. of Joseph Curran, of Folkestone: *m.* 1927, Sqdn. Ldr. Sir Norman Hamilton Pringle, late RAFVR, 9th baronet, who *d.* 1961. *Residence,*

Friendship reflects honours.

Collateral Branches living.
    Issue of the late Ronald Stuart Pringle, 2nd son of 8th baronet, *b.* 1905; *d.* 1968: *m.* 1938, Patricia Pickford (5, St. Mary's Pl., Newbury, Berks.):—
Norman Murray (P.O. Box 1, Tshaneni, Swaziland), *b.* 1941: *m.* 1966, Lysbet Watkins-Pitchford, and has issue living, Alastair Steuart Ronald, *b.* 1972.—Sian Amanda, *b.* 1972.——James Bruce (5, St. Mary's Pl., Newbury, Berks.), *b.* 1943: *m.* 1965, Rosemary Jean Collis, and has issue living, Jean Frances, *b.* 1967,—Marion Clare, *b.* 1970,—Angela Mary, *b.* 1971.——Priscilla Frances, *b.* 1944: *m.* 1964, (m. diss. 1972), Anthony Mark Dorman, and has issue living, Louise Margaret, *b.* 1965.

    Issue of the late James Drummond Pringle, youngest son of 8th baronet, *b.* 1906, *d.* 1960: *m.* 1st, 1932, Nina Beryl (who obtained a divorce 1946), el. da. of P. W. Trutwein, formerly Sessions Judge, Burma; 2ndly, 1947, Mrs. Pauline Cunliffe:—
(By 1st m.) Norman Alastair (32, Castle Hill, Maidenhead), *b.* 1933; ed. at Stonyhurst: *m.* 1955, Diana Joan, da. of Victor Clarke, and has issue living, Robin Alastair, *b.* 1961,—Susan Jane, *b.* 1960,—Dawn Anne, *b.* 1965.——(By 2nd m.) John, *b.* 1948.——Melanie, *b.* 1955.

    The Pringles of Stichill are heirs male and representatives of the Hop-Pringles of Craglatch and Newhall, co. Selkirk. Sir Robert Pringle of Stichill, 1st baronet, *s.* to Newhall 1667 on the extinction of the elder branch of the family.

PROBY, Creation (U.K.) 1952, of Elton Hall, co. Huntingdon.

Sir RICHARD GEORGE PROBY, *M.C.,* 1st *Baronet*, son of the late Col. Douglas James Proby [see D. Abercorn, colls.]; *b.* July 21st, 1886; ed. at Eton; Maj. 104th (Essex Yeo.) Field Bde. RA, and a JP for Hunts,; Vice-Lt. of Hunts. 1957-66, Pres. of Roy. Forestry Soc. of England 1956; Chm. of Forestry Cttee. of Great Britain, and of Timber Growers' Organization of England and Wales 1959-62; Chm. of Exec. Cttee. of National Union of Conservative and Unionist Assocns. 1943, and of National Union 1946 (Pres. 1958), and Pres. of Country Landowners' Assocn. 1947-51; High Sheriff of Cambridgeshire, Huntingdonshire, and the Isle of Ely 1953; 1914-18 War in France and Flanders (MC): *m.* 1st (Feb.) 1911, Betty Monica, who *d.* 1967, el. da. of the late Arthur H. Hallam Murray, of Sandling, Hythe; 2ndly, 1972, Eileen Yvonne, da. of Walter Edwin Ambroise Helps, of Trevath Manor, Gwennap, Cornwall, and widow of F/L Reginald Kenneth Harris, RAF, and has issue (by 1st m.).

Manus hæc inimica Tyrannis,
This hand is unfriendly to tyrants.

    Arms—Quarterly: 1st and 4th, ermine on a fesse gules a lion passant or, *Proby*; 2nd and 3rd, argent, two bars wavy azure, on a chief of the last an estoile between two escallops or, *Allen*; **Crest**—An ostrich's head erased proper, ducally gorged and holding in the beak a key or.

    Residence—Elton Hall, Peterborough. *Clubs*—Travellers', Constitutional, Kildare St., Roxburghe.

Sons living—By 1st m.—PETER (Pottle Green, Elton, Peterborough; Bath Lodge, Ballycastle, co. Antrim), *b.* Dec. 4th, 1911; ed. at Eton, and Trin. Coll., Oxford (BA); Capt. Irish Gds.; Bursar of Eton: *m.* 1944, Blanche Harrison, only da. of Lt.-Col. Henry Harrison Cripps, DSO,

R. Fusiliers, and has issue living, William Henry *b.* 1949: *m.* 1974, Meredyth Brentnall,—Sarah Blanche, *b.* 1945: *m.* 1968, Peter George Mills, BM, BCh, MRCP, (72, Cambridge St., SW1), and has issue living, James Douglas George *b.* 1972, Robert Peter *b.* 1975,—Charlotte Mary, *b.* 1957,— Christine Elisabeth (twin), *b.* 1957.——Claud (Garden House, Carton, Maynooth, co. Kildare; 31, Kildare St., Dublin), *b.* 1917; ed. at Eton, and at Magdalene Coll., Camb. (BA); Capt. IG: *m.* 1942, Patricia, da. of Lt.-Cdr. Vyvyan Whitmore Pearce, RN, and has issue living, Patrick James *b.* 1944,—Caroline Fiona (*Hon. Mrs. Anthony D. Brand*), *b.* 1943: *m.* 1969, the Hon. Anthony David Brand [see V. Hampden],—Joanna Margaret, *b.* 1946: *m.* 1970, Richard Woods, NZ Foreign Ser. (Parliament Bldgs., Wellington, NZ), and has issue living, James Christopher *b.* 1972, Samuel Richard *b.* 1973,—Joscelyn, *b.* 1950.

Daughters living—By 1st m.—Mary (*Baroness Inglewood*), *b.* 1913; JP; Co. Councillor, London 1949-52 and Cumberland 1961-74; a Member of Cumberland Area Health Authority 1974; 1939-45 War as Senior Comd. ATS (despatches): *m.* 1949, the 1st Baron Inglewood. *Residences,* Hutton-in-the-Forest, Penrith; 19, Stack House, Cundy St., SW1.——Margaret *b.* 1920; a JP for Dorset: *m.* 1948, Jack Harry Harrison Cripps, and has issue liing, Harry Richard, *b.* 1949,— Peter John, *b.* 1954,—Thomas Philip (twin), *b.* 1954,—Barbara Mary, *b.* 1952. *Residence,* Park House, Shaftesbury, Dorset.——Patience (twin), *b.* 1923; ed. at Lady Margaret Hall, Oxford (BA, BM and BCh); MRCP: *m.* 1959, John Campbell Moberly, Counsellor in Diplo. Ser., of The Cedars, Temple Sowerby, Penrith, son of Sir Walter Hamilton Moberly, GBE, KCB, DSO, and has issue living, Richard John, *b.* 1962,—Nicholas Hamilton, *b.* 1963,—Clare Elizabeth, *b.* 1967.

This family is descended in the female line from William Proby, first cousin of Sir Thomas Proby, Bt., upon whose death in 1689 the baronetcy became extinct, and from the Earls of Carysfort, whose Irish Earldom and Barony, and English Barony became extinct on the death of the 5th Earl in 1909. Lady Elizabeth Emma Proby, a sister of the last Earl of Carysfort, married the Rt. Hon. Lord Claud Hamilton, M.P., brother of 1st Duke of Abercorn, and their son, Col. Douglas James Hamilton, assumed by Roy. licence 1904 the surname of Proby.

Probyn-Jones, see Jones.

Proctor-Beauchamp, see Beauchamp.

Pryce-Jones, see Jones.

PRYKE, Creation (U.K.) 1926, of Wanstead, co. Essex.

Sir DAVID DUDLEY PRYKE, 3rd *Baronet* ; *b.* July 16th, 1912 ; *s.* his father, *Sir* (WILLIAM ROBERT) DUDLEY, 1959 ; ed. at St. Lawrence Coll., Ramsgate ; is a Common Councilman of City of London, and a Liveryman of Turners' Co.: *m.* 1945, Doreen Winifred, el. da. of the late Ralph Bernard Wilkins, of Winchmore Hill, N., and has issue.

Arms—Per pale or and argent, on a cross invected azure two fasces erect in pale and as many mascals in fesse all of the first. **Crest**—Two arms embowed, the hands proper supporting a fasces erect or, each arm charged with a mascal of the last.
Residence—1, Tavistock Place, Chase Side, N14.

Daughters living—Madge, *b.* 1946,.——Anita, *b.* 1949.

Brother living—WILLIAM DUDLEY (of 4, Parkgate Cres., Hadley Wood, Barnet, Herts. ; United Sports Club), *b.* Nov. 18th, 1914; ed. at Highgate Sch.; formerly Capt. Duke of Cornwall's L.I.; a Liveryman of Plumbers' Co. (Master 1969-70); 1939-45 War: *m.* 1940, Lucy Irene (Peggy), da. of the late Frank Madgett, of Whetstone, N., and has issue living, Christopher Dudley, *b.* 1946,—Rosemary Susan, *b.* 1949.

Sister living—Patricia Margaret, *b.* 1919. *Residence,* 93, Chandos Avenue, N.20.

Aunt living (daughter of 1st baronet)—Mabel Marguerite (c/o The Orchards, Sheepcote Lane, Touchen End, Maidenhead, Berks.): *m.* 1907, Arthur Emdund Howard, who *d.* 1929, and has issue living, Derek, *b.* 1908,—Alan, *b.* 1913.

The 1st baronet, Sir William Robert Pryke (son of Richard Reeve Pryke, of Bury St. Edmunds, was Chm. of Pryke & Palmer, Ltd., iron and hardware merchants, of 40 and 41, Upper Thames Street, E.C., and Lord Mayor of London 1925-6. The 2nd baronet, Sir (William Robert) Dudley Pryke, was Chm. of Pryke & Palmer, Ltd., iron and hardware merchants, of 40 and 41, Upper Thames Street, E.C.

SAUNDERS-PRYSE, Creation (U.K.) 1866, of Gogerddan. [Extinct 1962.]

Sir PRYSE LOVEDEN SAUNDERS-PRYSE, 5th and last *Baronet.*

Daughter living of 4th Baronet—Margaret Angharad Elinor, *b.* 1903 : *m.* 1930, Godfrey S. Briggs, who *d.* 1941. *Residence,* Glanrafon, Talybont, Cardiganshire.

Widow living of 5th Baronet—EMILY GEORGIANA HARRIET (*Lady Saunders-Pryse*), da. of the late Capt. Henry Frederick Compton Cavendish, R.N. [see D. Devonshire, colls.]: *m.* 1938, Sir Pryse Loveden Saunders-Pryse, 5th baronet, who *d.* 1962, when the title became ext. *Residence,* Glanrhydw, Kidwelly, Carmarthenshire.

Purves (Home-Purves-Hume-Campbell), see Campbell.

QUILTER, Creation (U.K.) 1897, of Bawdsey Manor, Bawdsey, Suffolk.

Sir ANTHONY RAYMOND LEOPOLD CUTHBERT QUILTER, 4th *Baronet*; *b.* March 25th, 1937; *s.* his father, *Sir* (JOHN) RAYMOND CUTHBERT 1959; ed. at Harrow: *m.* 1964, (Mary) Elise, el. da. of Col. Brian Sherlock Gooch DSO, TD, of Tannington Hall, Woodbridge [see Gooch, Bt., cr. 1746, colls.], and has issue.

Arms—Argent, on a bend invected gules, between three Cornish choughs proper, two cross crosslets of the first. Crest—In front of an arm vambraced proper, the hand grasping a battle-axe in bend sinister sable, head argent, the wrist entwined by a wreath of the third and second, a Cornish chough proper.

Seat—Methersgate Hall, Woodbridge, Suffolk.

Son living—GUY RAYMOND CUTHBERT, *b.* April 13th, 1967.

Daughter living—Juliet Elise, *b.* 1965.

Plutôt mourir que changer.

Rather die than change.

Aunts living (daughters of 2nd baronet)—Inez *b.* 1904 : *m.* 1955, Brigadier Raleigh Charles Joseph Chichester-Constable, C.B.E., D.S.O., DL, JP, who *d.* 1963. *Residence,* Ufford, Woodbridge, Suffolk.——Zoe Gwynedd, *b.* 1912: *m.* 1939, Lt.-Col. Brian Morton Forster Franks, DSO, MC, Middlesex Yeo., and has issue living, George Matthew Grindall, *b.* 1947,—Valerie Susan, *b.* 1943: *m.* 1968, William Francis Richards, of 28, Stokenchurch St., SW6, and has issue living, Susannah Lucy *b.* 1970, Katherine Elizabeth *b.* 1972. *Residence,* Sutton Old Vicarage, Woodbridge, Suffolk.——Sonia, *b.* 1917: *m.* 1st, 1939, Maj. Patrick William Butler Pole-Carew, late Irish Gds., who *d.* 1971, and from whom she obtained a divorce 1950 [see Pole, Bt., cr. 1628]; 2ndly, 1958, Maj. William Henry Cropley Luddington, MC, 9th Lancers, who *d.* 1965. *Residence,* Walnut Tree House, Turweston, Brackley, Northants.

Widow living of 3rd Baronet—MARGERY MARIANNE (*Margery, Lady Quilter*) (White Cottage, Foxboro' Hall Farm, Woodbridge, Suffolk), da. of the late Sir (James) Douglas Cooke, of Kingston House, Princes' Gate, SW7: *m.* 1935, Sir (John) Raymond Cuthbert Quilter, 3rd baronet, who *d.* 1959.

Collateral Branches living.

Issue of the late Percy Cuthbert Quilter, 4th son of 1st baronet, *b.* 1879, *d.* 1947: *m.* 1909, Gladys Clare Alice, who *d.* 1973, da. of the late Charles Clement Tudway [Hervey-Bathurst, Bt.]:—

David Cuthbert TUDWAY QUILTER, *b.* 1921; ed. at Eton; assumed by deed poll 1962 the additional surname of Tudway before his patronymic; a DL for Somerset: *m.* 1953, Elizabeth Mary, da. of Sir John Gawen Carew Pole, DSO, TD, 12th Bt., and has issue living, Simon John Cuthbert, *b.* 1955,—Susan Clare Evelyn, *b.* 1957,—Lucy Anne, *b.* 1961. *Residence,* Milton Lodge, Wells, Som.——Beryl Joan (*Baroness Charnwood*), *b.* 1909: *m.* 1933, the 2nd Baron Charnwood, who *d.* 1955. *Residence,* Court Lodge Farm, East Brabourne, Kent.——Diana Primrose, *b.* 1916: *m.* 1st, 1942, as his second wife (m. annulled 1945), Brig. Lancelot Merivale Gibbs, CVO, DSO, MC, who *d.* 1966; 2ndly, 1947, Archibald Tennant, who *d.* 1955 [see B. Glenconner, colls.]. *Residence,* 12, Victoria Sq., SW1.

Grandsons of the late Maj. Eustace Cuthbert Quilter, OBE (infra):—

Issue of the late Ronald Eustace Cuthbert Quilter, *b.* 1907, *d.* 1972: *m.* 1934, Doreen Mary (Poplar Farm, Copdock, nr. Ipswich), da. of the late Charles Sandbach Parker, of Fairlie House, Fairlie, Ayrshire:—

William Ronald Cuthbert (Onehouse Lodge, Stowmarket, Suffolk), *b.* 1937; ed. at Eton, and Magdalene Coll., Camb. (BA): *m.* 1962, Jennifer Ann, da. of Cdr. E. J. Tamlyn, RD, RNR (ret.), of Apton Fields, Barnston, Gt. Dunmow, Essex, and has issue living, Benjamin William Cuthbert, *b.* 1963,—Melissa Jane, *b.* 1966.——Thomas Eustace Cuthbert (9, Richards Place, SW3), *b.* 1940; ed. at Eton, and Roy. Coll. of Music: *m.* 1966 (m. diss. 1969) Joy Winifred Thérèse, da. of Wing-Cdr. G. F. R. Duffy, of Broadwell, Glos.

Issue of the late Major Eustace Cuthbert Quilter, O.B.E., 5th son of 1st baronet, *b.* 1881, *d.* 1934 : *m.* 1906, Cecil Bligh, who *d.* 1950, only da. of Philip Nutting, formerly of Springlands, Stanmore :—

John Cuthbert (8, Sloane Terr. Mansions, SW1; Dock House, Ramsholt, Suffolk), *b.* 1910, ed. at Eton.

The 1st baronet, Sir Cuthbert, was one of the Founders of the National Telephone Co. (Limited), and sat as M.P. for S., or Sudbury, Div. of Suffolk (*LU*) 1885-1906. The 2nd baronet, Sir (William Eley) Cuthbert, sat as M.P. for Suffolk, S. or Sudbury Div. (*C*) 1910-18.

RADCLIFFE, Creation (U.K.) 1813, of Milnesbridge House, Yorkshire.

Sir Sebastian Everard Radcliffe, 7th *Baronet*; *b.* June 8th, 1972; *s.* his father, *Capt.* Sir (Joseph Benedict) Everard Henry, MC, 1975.

Arms—Argent, a bend engrailed sable charged with a crescent of the field for difference. *Crest*—A bull's head erased sable, horns argent, tipped or, gorged with a ducal coronet of the second.

Virtue for its own sake.

Half-sister living—Susan Elizabeth Mary, *b.* 1940.

Uncles living (sons of 5th baronet)—Hugh John Reginald Joseph, *MBE, b.* March 3rd, 1911, ed. at Downside; Knt. Cdr. Order of St. Silvester (Papal); 1939-45 War as Lt.-Col. London Scottish (MBE); MBE (Mil) 1944: *m.* 1937, Marie Therese, da. of Maj.-Gen. Sir Cecil Edward Pereira, KCB, CMG, and has issue living, Mark Hugh Joseph (Court Farm, Llanover, Abergavenny, Mon.; Guards' Club), *b.* 1938; ed. at Downside: *m.* 1963, Anne, da. of Maj.-Gen. Arthur Evers Brocklehurst, CB, DSO, and has issue living, Lucinda Mary *b.* 1964, Emily Marie Louise *b.* 1968, Camilla Mary *b.* 1971,—Anthony Joseph (Tanners Farm House, Swallowfield Rd., Aborfield Cross, Berks.), *b.* 1942; ed. at Downside: *m.* 1964, Rachael Mary, da. of Joseph Goddard, of Harmony Hall, Barbados, and has issue living, James Russell Joseph *b.* 1965, Julian Everard Joseph *b.* 1967, a da. *b.* 1975,—Timothy Peter Joseph, *b.* 1945,—Paul John Joseph, *b.* 1949,—Richard Joseph, *b.* 1954,—Teresa Jane, *b.* 1939. *Residence*, Beetle Cottage, Carthouse Lane, Horsell, Woking, Surrey.——Michael Anthony, *b.* 1917; ed. at Downside: Maj. Yorkshire Dragoons Yeo.; 1939-45 War (prisoner): *m.* 1947, Mary, da. of Brooke Edwards. *Residence*, 71, Saint Anthony St., Attard, Malta, GC. *Club*, Boodle's.——David Edward Joseph (33, Lymden Gdns., Reigate, Surrey), *b.* 1922; late Capt. Irish Gds.: *m.* 1944, Rita Dorcas, only da. of the late Maj. Thomas Johnson.

Great-uncle living (son of 4th baronet)—Charles Joseph Basil, *b.* 1900; is a FIEE: *m.* 1939, Norah, only da. of Norman Percy, of Maloya, Colombo, Ceylon, and has issue living, Francis Charles Joseph (40, The Horseshoe, York), *b.* 1939; ed. at Ampleforth, and at Gonville and Caius Coll., Camb.; Bar. Gray's Inn, 1962: *m.* 1968, Nicolette, el. da. of Eugene Randag, of Lodge Hill Farm, Butlers Cross, Aylesbury, and has issue living, Edward Eugene Joseph *b.* 1969, Colette Anne *b.* 1971, Alexandra Mary *b.* 1972,—Bryan Anthony Joseph (24, Abbotsbury Close, W14), *b.* 1941; ed. at Ampleforth; Solicitor 1963: *m.* 1965, Pisana, yr. da. of Conte Giuseppe Petrobelli, of Prato della Valle, Padua, Italy, and has issue living, Mark Anthony Joseph *b.* 1967, Harry Joseph *b.* 1972, Isabella Carolina *b.* 1974,—Kathryn Anne, *b.* 1943: *m.* 1965, Anthony Bigland, of Bigland Hall, Ulverston, N. Lancs., and has issue living, Emma Lucy *b.* 1967, Sophie Kathryn *b.* 1970. *Residence*, The Mill House, Cocking, Midhurst, Sussex.

Widow living of 6th baronet—Marcia Helen (*Lady Radcliffe*) (Château de Cheseaux, 1033 Cheseaux, Vaud, Switzerland), da. of Maj. David Turville-Constable-Maxwell [see L. Herries of Terregles]: *m.* 1968, as his 2nd wife, Sir (Joseph Benedict) Everard Henry Radcliffe, MC, 6th baronet, who *d.* 1975.

Collateral Branches living.

Issue of the late Joseph Francis Edward Radcliffe, 2nd son of 4th baronet, *b.* 1891, *d.* 1940: *m.* 1922, Marjorie Sophia, who *d.* 1973, da. of Sir Francis Charles Edward Denys-Burton, 3rd Bt. [Denys, Bt.]:—

Elizabeth Denyse Mary (c/o Coutts & Co., 440, Strand, WC2), *b.* 1923; 1941–45 War with WAAF: *m.* 1952, Ives Bonapace, and has issue living, Charles, *b.* 1953,—Mark, *b.* 1955,—William, *b.* 1958,—Caroline, *b.* 1954,—Jane Mary, *b.* 1961,—Isabelle, *b.* 1964.——Louise Marie Antoinette, *b.* 1928: *m.* 1956, Alec Pearson Carn, of Olveston Court, Olveston, Bristol, and has issue living, Nicholas, *b.* 1957,—Jonathan, *b.* 1960,—Vanessa Mary, *b.* 1963,—Francesca Georgina, *b.* 1969,—Alexandra Sophia, *b.* 1972.

Issue of the late Robert John Peter Joseph Radcliffe, 4th son of 4th baronet, *b.* 1898, *d.* 1974: *m.* 1929, Ursula Evelyn Mary (Whitegate, Yearsley Brandsky, York), da. of the late Lt.-Col. Miles John Stapylton, OBE, of Myton Hall, York:—

John Charles Joseph, *b.* 1934.——Peter Martin Joseph (Sandylands, Sutton-on-Forest, York), *b.* 1941: *m.* 1963, Pamela Ann, 2nd da. of George C. Johnson, of 2, Castle Terr., Husthwaite, York.——Thomas Joseph Henry, *b.* 1943.——Rosemary Anne Ursula Katherine, *b.* 1930: *m.* 1950, Louis Bertram Hawkswell, and has issue living, Frederick Andrew Joseph, *b.* 1951,—Martin Louis, *b.* 1955,—Anthony Robert, *b.* 1956,—Philip William, *b.* 1958,—Simon, *b.* 1968,—Elizabeth Ann, *b.* 1960.——Mary Elizabeth Jane, *b.* 1939: *m.* 1957, John William Courtney, of The Colt House, Easingwold, York, and has issue living, Miles Stewart John, *b.* 1965,—Rosemary Elizabeth, *b.* 1967.

Issue of the late Capt. Henry Joseph Francis Radcliffe, 2nd son of 3rd baronet, *b.* 1862, *d.* 1928: *m.* 1896, Gertrude Mary Philomena, who *d.* 1955, da. of the late Rev. John Coventry [E. Coventry. colls.]:—

Henry Edward Joseph (Manor Cottage, Lympsham, Weston-Super-Mare), *b.* 1904: *m.* 1939, Ursula Mary Skeet, yr. da. of F. D. Workman, and has issue living, Sally Anne Ursula, *b.* 1940: *m.* 1966, Geoffrey P. M. Taylor, of Willow Cottage, Dundry, Bristol, and has issue living, Justin Peter *b.* 1968, Juliet Clare *b.* 1970, Lucinda Jane *b.* 1971, Kirsty Anna *b.* 1974.——Gertrude Mary Catherine, *b.* 1903: *m.* 1925, Philip George Bower, who *d.* 1939. *Residence*, South Dalling, New Rd., Ridgewood, Uckfield, Sussex.

Issue of the late Col. Philip John Joseph Radcliffe, C.M.G., 3rd son of 3rd baronet, *b.* 1863, *d.* 1943: *m.* 1893, Maud, who *d.* 1944, da. of the late Sir Frederick Aloysius Weld, G.C.M.G.:—

Mary (of Shepherd's Cottage, Whatcombe, Blandford, Dorset), *b.* 1894: *m.* 1919, Capt. Bernard Percy Turnbull Lees, M.C., Dorsetshire Yeo., who *d.* 1922 [see Lees, Bt., cr. 1897].

Issue of the late Bernard Percival Joseph Radcliffe, 4th son of 3rd baronet, *b.* 1869, *d.* 1948 : *m.* 1896, Georgina Mary, who *d.* 1941, da. of Maurice Murray, D.L., of Beech Hill, Cork :—

Cyril William Joseph, *b.* 1902 ; is a J.P. for Worcestershire, and a Knight of Sovereign Mil. Order of Malta : *m.* 1940, Joan, da. of the late Frederick J. Nesbitt. *Residence,* Norchard Grange, Crossway Green, Stourport-on-Severn, Worcestershire.

This family took its name from the village of Radcliffe in Lancashire. Richard de Radclyffe, Seneschal and Minister of the Forests in Blackburnshire, accompanied Edward I. in his wars in Scotland, and received from that monarch a grant of a charter of freewarren and chase in all his demesne lands of Radcliffe. Mary, da. of William Radcliffe of Milnbridge, Yorks. (a descendant of William 2nd son of Richard), and sister and heir of Willian Radcliffe of Milnbridge (*d.* 1795): *m.* Joseph Pickford of Ashton-under-Lyne, Lancs. Their son Joseph Pickford, who assumed the surname of Radcliffe in 1795, was created a baronet for distinguished public services.

RAEBURN, Creation (U.K.) 1923, of Helensburgh, co. Dunbarton.

Safe if strong.

Sir EDWARD ALFRED RAEBURN, 3rd *Baronet* ; *b.* May 18th, 1919; *s.* his father, *Sir* WILLIAM NORMAN, C.B.E., K.C., 1947 : *m.* 1950, Joan, da. of Frederick Hill, of Boston, Massachusetts, U.S.A., and has issue.

Arms—Or, on a piece of ground in base vert a roebuck statant proper, drinking out of a burn or brook undy argent and azure running bendways, in chief an anchor sable between two roses gules, barbed and seeded of the second. Crest—A stag's head proper.

Residence—Smallacre, St. Catherines, Hook Heath, Woking, Surrey.

Son living—MICHAEL EDWARD NORMAN, *b.* Nov. 12th, 1954.

Sisters living—Sheila Saisie (of The Mount, St. Johns Hill Rd., Woking, Surrey), *b.* 1913.——Irene Muriel (of The Mount, St. Johns Hill Rd., Woking, Surrey), *b.* 1914.

Aunt living (daughter of 1st baronet)—Ellinor Eileen, *b.* 1897: *m.* 1930, Lt.-Col. Eugene Gonzague Riviere, M.B.E., M.C., The Loyal Regt. (ret.), and has issue living, Peter Gerard (Little Manor, Bledington, Glos.), *b.* 1934; ed. at Stowe, at Magdalene Coll., Camb. (MA), and at Magdalen Coll., Oxford (BLitt, DPhil): *m.* 1962, Sarah, da. of the late Maj.-Gen. George Douglas Heyman, CB, CBE, and has issue living, Peregrine Douglas Gonzague *b.* 1970, Amelia Sophie *b.* 1965, Arabella Rose *b.* 1966,—Ellinor Ann, *b.* 1931: *m.* 1952, Maj. John Michael Cheale, of Blackham Court, Withyham, Sussex, and has issue living, Hazel Ruth *b.* 1955, Patricia Gillian *b.* 1957. *Residence*, Little Manor, Longstock, Stockbridge, Hants.

Collateral Branch living.

Issue of the late Sir Ernest Manifold Raeburn, KBE, and son of 1st baronet, *b.* 1878, *d.* 1922: *m.* 1910, Greta Mary Alison, who *d.* 1975, da. of the late Engineer-Capt. James Herbert Watson, RN:—

William Digby Manifold, *CB, DSO, MBE* (The Queen's House, Tower of London, EC3; White's, Pratt's, Royal Yacht Squadron Clubs), *b.* 1915; ed. at Winchester and Magdalene Coll., Camb. (MA); Maj.-Gen. (ret.) late Scots Gds.; Comdg. 2nd Bn. Scots Gds. 1953-55, Lt.-Col. Comdg. Scots Guards 1958-59, Comd. 1st Guards Bde. Group and 51st Inf. Bde. Group 1960-61, Dir. of Combat Development (Army) 1963-65, Ch. of Staff Allied Forces N. Europe 1965-68, and Ch., Army Instructor Imperial Defence Coll. 1968-70; Resident Gov. and Keeper of Jewel House of HM Tower of London since 1971; 1939-45 War in Middle East, Italy and NW Europe (despatches, MBE, DSO); MBE (Mil) 1941, DSO 1945, CB (Mil) 1966: *m.* 1960, Adeline Margaret, yst. da. of the late Thomas Selwyn Pryor, MC [*see* Halsey, Bt.].

The 1st baronet, Sir William Hannay Raeburn (son of the late William Raeburn, of Glasgow), was head of the firm of Raeburn & Verel, Ltd., and sat as M.P. for Dunbartonshire (*U*) 1918-23. The 2nd baronet, Sir William Norman Raeburn, CBE, was a KC.

RALLI, Creation (U.K.) 1912, of Park Street, City of Westminster.

Sir GODFREY VICTOR RALLI, TD, 3rd *Baronet; b.* Sept. 9th, 1915; *s.* his father, *Sir* STRATI, *MC,* 1964; ed. at Eton; 1939-45 War, as Capt. Berks. Yeo. R.A. (despatches): *m.* 1st, 1937, Nora Margaret (from whom he obtained a divorce 1947), only child of the late Charles Forman, of Lodden Court, Spencers Wood, nr. Reading; 2ndly, 1949, Jean, da. of the late Keith Barlow, of 3, Vicarage Gate, W.8, and has issue living by 1st marriage.

Arms—Azure, a lion rampant argent semée of lozenges of the first n chief a crescent between two crosses couped of the second. Crest—A lion as in the arms holding between the paws a cross couped argent.

Residence—Great Walton, Eastry, Sandwich, Kent. *Clubs*—White's, City of London.

Keep to the straight path

Son living—By 1st m.—DAVID CHARLES, *b.* April 5th, 1946; ed. at Eton: *m.* 1975, Jacqueline Cecilia, da. of David Smith.

Daughters living—By 1st marriage—Louise, *b.* 1942: *m.* 1964, Ewen James Fassiefern Cameron, of Terrington House, Terrington, York, and has issue living, James Allan Godfrey, *b.* 1965,—Alistair Ewen David, *b.* 1968.——TESSA TITTERTON, *b.* 1945; adopted by her mother and her stepfather, Philip Arthur Titterton, MB, ChB, whose surname she assumed 1952.

Brother living—Lucas John, *b.* 1920; ed. at Eton; 1939-45 War as Maj. Roy. Signals (despatches): *m.* 1950, Katia, da. of Constantine Droulia, of Athens, Greece, and has issue living, John Strati, *b.* 1956,—Dora Louise, *b.* 1953.　*Residence*, 32, Connaught Sq., W.2.

Sisters living—Diana Myrtle, *b.* 1918: *m.* 1939, Lt.-Col. John Herbert (Jack) Walford, DSO, Seaforth Highlanders, of Arlington Lodge, Bibury, Glos., and has issue living, Michael Carr, *b.* 1943,—Ewan John (3, Pembroke Sq., W8), *b.* 1945,—Belinda Mary (8, St. Mary Abbots Terr., W14), *b.* 1941: *m.* 1961, John William Hayter, from whom she obtained a divorce 1968, and has issue living, Sarah Miranda *b.* 1964.——Patience Louise, *b.* 1922: *m.* 1944, Lt.-Cdr. William Edward Michael de Sivrac Dunn, RNVR, and has issue living, Mark de Sivrac, *b.* 1947,—Karen Louise, *b.* 1945.　*Residence*, Hayes Barton, Pyrford, Surrey.

Widow living of 2nd Baronet—LOUISE WARINGTON (*Louise, Lady Ralli*) (54, Kingston House, Princes Gate, SW7), da. of Bernard James Williams: *m.* (Jan.) 1915, Sir Strati Ralli, MC, 2nd baronet, who *d.* 1964.

The 1st baronet was head of the firm of Ralli Bros., East India merchants, of 25, Finsbury Circus, E.C.

RAMSAY, Creation (N.S.) 1666, of Bamff, Perthshire.

Valour despises danger.

Sir NEIS ALEXANDER RAMSAY, 12th *Baronet* ; *b.* Oct. 4th 1909 ; *s.* his father, *Col. Sir* JAMES DOUGLAS, *M.V.O., T.D.* 1959 ; ed. at Winchester, and at Trin. Coll., Camb. ; formerly 2nd Lieut. Gordon Highlanders ; European War 1939-45 as Lieut. S. African Engineering Corps : *m.* 1st, 1940 (marriage dissolved 1951), Edith Alix Ross, only child of C. F. Hayes, F.C.I.S., of Khyber Lodge, Linksfield, Johannesburg, S. Africa ; 2ndly, 1952, Rachel Leonore Beatrice (DRUMMOND), da. of the late Col. Edward Brabazon Urmston, C.B.

Arms—Argent, an eagle displayed sable, beaked and membered gules, charged on the breast with an escutcheon of the field.　Crest—An unicorn's head couped argent, maned and horned or.　Supporters—Two griffins proper.
　Seat—Bamff, Alyth, Perthshire.

Collateral Branch living.
Grandson of the late George Gilbert Ramsay, 3rd son of 9th baronet :—
Issue of the late William Alexander Ramsay, *b.* 1868, *d.* 1921 : *m.* 1905, Cecilia Maud Sandford, who *d.* 1915, da. of the late William F. Kemp, Bar.-at-law :—
GEORGE WILLIAM NEIL, *b.* May 30th, 1907 ; ed. at Winchester, and at Trin. Coll., Oxford ; formerly Lieut. The Black Watch ; has been Head Master of Junior Sch., St. Bernard's Sch. for Boys, New York since 1954 ; European War 1939-45 as Lieut.-Col. R.A. : *m.* 1932, Maryel Hope, who *d.* 1935, second da. of the late Col. Robert William Pigott Clarke-Campbell-Preston, of Ardchattan Priory, Connel, Argyllshire ; 2ndly, 1937 (marriage dissolved 1947), Catherine Trewyn, only da. of Charles Bernard Dougherty, of Ottawa, Canada ; 3rdly, 1948, Muriel, only da. of the late Sydney Haslett, of St. Leonards-on-Sea, Sussex, and has issue living, (by 1st marriage) Maryel Susan, *b.* 1935,—(by 2nd marriage) Catherine Ann, *b.* 1938 : *m.* 1959, Russell Payson, of Cambridge, Mass., USA,—Priscilla Maud, *b.* 1940.　*Residence*, 39, Avista Circle, St. Augustine, Florida, 32084, USA.

This family is lineally descended in the male line from Neis de Ramsay, principal Physician to Alexander II., King of Scotland, as appears by a charter from that monarch, dated 1232, conferring on him the lands of Bamff and others adjacent, which are still in possession of the family. Sir Gilbert Ramsay, Baron of Bamff, one of the descendants of Neis, was created a baronet of Nova Scotia for the gallantry of his son James at the battle of Pentland Hills, 1666. Sir James Douglas Ramsay, M.V.O., T.D., 11th baronet, was Lieut.-Col. and Hon. Col. R.A. (T.A.) and H.M. Commr. on Balmoral Estates 1919-26. He raised and commanded 31st Perth Regt. Light Anti-Aircraft R.A. 1939.

RAMSAY, Creation (U.K.) 1806, of Balmain, Kincardineshire.

Aspiro.
I aspire.

Sir ALEXANDER WILLIAM BURNETT RAMSAY, 7th *Baronet;* *b.* Aug. 4th, 1938; *s.* his father, *Sir* ALEXANDER BURNETT 1965; the presumed heir to the Baronety of Burnett of Leys (*cr.* 1626): *m.* 1963, Neryl Eileen, da. of J. C. Smith Thornton Trangie, and has issue.

Arms—Argent, an eagle displayed sable, beaked and membered gules, charged on the breast with a rose of the field.　Crest—A demi-eagle displayed sable.
　Residence—Bullbah, Warren, N.S.W.

Sons living—ALEXANDER DAVID, *b.* Aug. 20th, 1966.——Ian John, *b.* 1968.
Sisters living—Enid Ellice, *b.* 1937: *m.* 1961, Reginald Geoffrey Capel of Haddon Rig. Warren, N.S.W., and has issue living, Peter Geoffrey, *b.* 1963,—Dianna Enid, *b.* 1965.——Patricia Thirza, *b.* 1940: *m.* 1965, Anthony Osborne McAlary, of Milawa, Warren, NSW, and has issue living, Anna, *b.* 1969.

Uncle living (son of 5th baronet)—Herbert William Alexander, *b.* 1907: *m.* 1936, Bessie Billingsley, yst. da. of Dr. Wilfred Billingsley Dight, of Sydney, N.S.W., and has issue living, William Macalister, *b.* 1939,—Elizabeth Barton, *b.* 1945,—Roslyn Barton, *b.* 1946. *Residence*, Girraween, Bonshaw, N.S.W.

Aunts living (daughters of 5th baronet)—Nora Marjorie, *b.* 1905: *m.* 1928, Brigadier Adrian Bazeley Barltrop, OBE, MC, Indian Army (ret.), and has issue living, Margaret Anne, *b.* 1931: *m.* 1960, Evan Birchall Thomas, 68, Castle Hill Rd., West Pennant Hills, NSW 2120, and has issue living, Caroline Ida *b.* 1961, Elizabeth Dilys *b.* 1962, Alexandra Mary *b.* 1964.——Constance Agnes, *b.* 1912: *m.* 1938, Arthur Thomas Baldwin, and has issue living, Ross Ramsay, *b.* 1943,—Malcolm Ramsay, *b.* 1946, Janet Mabel, *b.* 1941. *Residence*, 242, Pittwater Rd., Collaroy, NSW.

Widow living of 6th Baronet—ISABEL ELLICE (*Isabel, Lady Ramsay*), (48, Piccadilly Gdns., Fullerton St., Woolrabra 2025, NSW), da. of the late William Whitney, of Wangoola, Woodstock, NSW: *m.* 1935, Sir Alexander Burnett Ramsay, 6th Bt., who *d.* 1965.

Collateral Branches living.

Grandchildren of the late Hugh Francis Ramsay, 2nd son of 3rd baronet:—
Issue of the late Hugh Entwisle Ramsay, *b.* 1871, *d.* 1960: *m.* 1901, Elsie Lavater, who *d.* 1960, da. of William Cox:—
Irene Beatrice (Walcot, Aviary Rd., Pyrford, Surrey), *b.* 1902: *m.* 1929, Ivor George Sullivan, who *d.* 1955, and has issue living, Ramsay Wakeford (4460, Cottonwood Drive, Burlington, Ontario, Canada), *b.* 1933: *m.* 1957, Eleanor Mary Thorpe, and has issue living, Richard Andrew Ramsay *b.* 1960, Fiona Clare *b.* 1962, Jennifer Mary *b.* 1965,—Patricia Berenice, *b.* 1934; ARCA: *m.* 1961, Michael Edward Mallett, D.Phil, of 2, Lansdowne Circus, Leamington Spa.

Grandchildren of Hugh Entwisle Ramsay (ante):—
Issue of the late Alexander Hugh Ramsay, *b.* 1905, *d.* 1962: *m.* 1937, Ethel Charlotte (1327, Victoria St., Hamilton, NZ), da. of the late Albert Upton, of Waimai, NZ:—
Patricia Marion, *b.* 1945.——Eleanor Margaret, *b.* 1949.
Issue of the late John Entwisle Ramsay, *b.* 1908, *d.* (killed on active ser.) 1942: *m.* 1937, Elizabeth Frances, da. of A. H. Crichton, of Kelowna, British Columbia:—
Ian Alexander (17, Old Lake Rd., Narrow Neck, North Shore, Auckland, NZ), *b.* 1939: *m.* 1963, Rosalind Sheila Tolliss, of Hildenborough, Kent.

Grandsons of the late Noel Bannerman Ramsay (infra) :—
Issue of the late Lieut. Noel Entwistle Burnett Ramsay, R.N.V.R., *b.* 1907, *d.* (killed in action) 1942: *m.* 1932, Phyllis Agnes, of 7, Carlton Court, Carlton Rd., Harpenden, Herts., AL5 4SY: *m.* 2ndly, 1949, Lt.-Col. Eric T. Cuthbert, who *d.* 1974, da. of Arthur H. Kilner:—
Rev. Alan Burnett (78, Stockwell Park Rd., SW9 ODA), *b.* 1934; AKC: *m.* 1967, Elisabeth, da. of Norman Marsh, and has issue living, Christopher, *b.* 1968,—Matthew John, *b.* 1971,—Francis, *b.* 1973,—Rachel, *b.* 1969.——Duncan Soutter Burnett (17, Lambourn Gdns., Harpenden, Herts.), *b.* 1937: *m.* 1967, Carole Anne, da. of D. H. Briars, and has issue living, Benjamin Noel, *b.* 1969,—Daniel Bruce, *b.* 1971,—Helen Jayne, *b.* 1973.

Granddaughter of the late Hugh Francis Ramsay (ante) :—
Issue of the late Noel Bannerman Ramsay, *b.* 1875, *d.* 1958: *m.* 1905, Edith Katharine, who *d.* 1962, da. of Francis Johnson, M.D.:—
Edith Rosemary Patricia, *b.* 1915 : *m.* 1st, 1937, Thomas Martin Homfray Pardoe, Capt. 2nd Batn. Worcestershire Regt., who *d.* (killed in action in Hong Kong) 1941 ; 2ndly, 1943, Col. Thomas Brian Carey, R.A., and has issue living, (by 1st marriage) Hermione Ann Felicity, —(by 2nd marriage) Shane Peter, *b.* 1944,—Peter Brian Ramsay, *b.* 1948. *Residence*, Rigden's Farm, Leigh, near Reigate, Surrey.

Issue of the late Capt. John Ramsay, 3rd son of 3rd baronet, *b.* 1843, *d.* 1913: *m.* 1876, Florence Mary, who *d.* 1936, only child of the late Richard J. Hilton, of Preston House, Faversham :—
Ethel, *M.B.E.*, *b.* 1882 ; M.B.E. (Civil) 1918 : *m.* 1906, Major William Thompson Armitage, formerly R.A.——Hilda, *b.* 1885 : *m.* (Jan.) 1912, Eugene Spinney, and has issue living, David John, *b.* Oct. 1912,—Martin Giles, *b.* 1916,—Juliet Ethel, *b.* 1914.——Evelyn, *b.* 1887 : *m.* 1909, Cuthbert Radcliffe, who *d.* 1924, and has issue living, Richard, *b.* 1912,—Norman, *b.* 1914,— Michael, *b.* 1918. *Residence*,

Grandsons of the late Brig.-Gen. William Alexander Ramsay, el. son of Capt. Francis Ramsay, 3rd son of 2nd baronet:—
Issue of the late Adm. Sir Bertram Home Ramsay, KCB, KBE, MVO, *b.* 1883, *d.* (killed on active ser.) 1945: *m.* 1929, Helen Margaret (Prior Bank, Hermitage Lane, Kelso), da. of Col. Charles Thomson Menzies, of Kames, Greenlaw, Berwickshire:—
David Francis (24, Cranmer Court, Sloane Av., SW3). *Clubs*, Carlton, and New (Edinburgh), *b.* 1933; ed. at Eton and at Camb. Univ. (BA): *m.* 1963, Stacey Rogers, and has issue living, Michael Stuart, *b.* 1964,—James Alexander, *b.* 1967.——Charles Alexander (Bughtrig, Coldstream, Berwicks.; *Clubs*, Boodle's, Cavalry, and New (Edinburgh), *b.* 1936; ed. at Eton, and RMC; Lt.-Col. R. Scots Greys; a Member of Queens Body Guard for Scotland (Roy. Co. of Archers): *m.* 1967, the Hon. Mary Margaret Hastings MacAndrew, da. of 1st Baron MacAndrew, and has issue living, William Bertram, *b.* 1969,—Rowena Cecilia, *b.* 1973.

Grandchildren of the late Robert Ramsay, son of the late late Capt. Robert Ramsay, 3rd son of 1st baronet :—
Issue of the late Marmaduke Francis Ramsay, *b.* 1860, *d.* 1947 : *m.* 1895, Alice Katherine Angelique, who *d.* 1951, da. of Ottiwell Charles Waterfield, formerly of Nackington House, Canterbury:—

Robert Ottiwell, *b.* 1900 : *m.* 1937, Constance Aileen, da. of the late Major Hugh Bernard German, M.C., R.A.M.C., and has issue living, Robert David, *b.* 1942,—John Lauderdale, *b.* 1945.—Sarah Margaret (Old Church Farmhouse, Barfrestone, nr. Dover, Kent), *b.* 1937: *m.* 1962 (m. diss. 1973), Capt. David John Wemyss Anstice, 10th Roy. Hussars, son of Vice-Adm. Sir Edmund Walter Anstice, KCB, and has issue living, Robert Christian Edmund *b.* 1963, David Henry *b.* 1964, James Richard *b.* 1965,—Lavinia Jane, *b.* 1938: *m.* 1959, Patrick Robert Chalmers, of Aldbar Castle, Brechin, Angus, and has issue living, Patrick Robert Graham *b.* 1960, Virginia Jane *b.* 1961, Lindsay *b.* 1962, Nicole Katherine *b.* 1964,—Aileen Susanna *b.* 1941: *m.* 1964, Colin Gibb, of Inshewan, Forfar, and has issue living, John Alexander *b.* 1968, Shanestra Margaret *b.* 1966. *Residence*, Mains of Kinblethmont, Forfarshire.——Dorothy Christian, *b.* 1896. *Residence*, 36, Nunnery Fields, Canterbury.——Edith Margaret (*Lady Boucher*), *b.* 1901: *m.* 1926, Maj.-Gen. Sir Charles Hamilton Boucher, KBE, CB, DSO, Indian Army (ret.), who *d.* 1951, and has issue living, William Scott Hamilton (c/o Lloyds Bank, 6, Pall Mall, SW1), *b.* 1932: Maj. Blues and Royals: *m.* 1962, Jane, el. da. of Rear-Adm. Bryan Cecil Durant, CB, DSO, DSC, of The Old House, Alresford, Hants., and has issue living, Henry Francis *b.* 1963, Alice Sophia *b.* 1965, Lucinda Charlotte *b.* 1970,—Helen Margaret (13, Longport, Canterbury), *b.* 1928: *m.* 1950 (m. diss. 1962), Maj. Kenneth Hutchison, 6th Gurkha Rifles, and has issue living, Charles Kenneth *b.* 1951, Michael Hugh Mahaffy *b.* 1952, Caroline Susan *b.* 1957. *Residence*, Priory End, Littlebourne, Canterbury.——Helen Prudence: *m.* 1927 (m. diss. 1933), Henry Eric Southey Harben, who *d.* 1971, and has issue living, Henry Peter Bostock (Southstoke Hall, Bath), *b.* 1927: *m.* 1953 (m. diss. 1964), Adelaide Anne Elizabeth White,—Joanna, *b.* 1931: *m.* 1952, George Philip Griggs. *Residence*, 21, Tryon St., Chelsea, SW3.

Issue of the late Robert Christian Ramsay, b. 1861, d. 1957 : m. 1907, Olive Zillah, who d. 1957, da. of W. W. Voss, of Penrice, Queensland :—
Alexander Robert, DSC (Box 50, PO Borrowdale, Salisbury, Rhodesia), b. 1910; Cdr. RNVR; 1939-45 War (DSC and Bar): m. 1944, Helen MacGregor, da. of J. M. Shaw, of Lisburn, co. Antrim, and has issue living, Colin Robert (c/o School of Mines, University of Zambia, Lusaka), b. 1945: m. 1968, Lyndall Clare Sundstrom, of Brisbane, Qld., and has issue living, Robert Andrew b. 1974,—Celia Grace, b. 1947: m. 1st, 1966 (m. diss. 1974 in Rhodesia), the 10th Viscount Chetwynd; 2ndly, 19—, Geoffrey Burnett-Smith, of Salisbury, Rhodesia,—Alexandra Helen Fleur, b. 1955.——David Malcolm, b. 1924; late FO RAF: m. 1948, Joan Esme, da. of C. J. Murphy, and has issue living, Alan David, b. 1951,—James Anthony, b. 1952,—Oliver Dermot, b. 1954,—Malcolm Robert, b. 1956.——Nora Honor, b. 1911: m. 1932, Maj. Kenneth Arthur William Johnston, Welsh Gds., and has issue living, Alastair Jevon, b. 1933,—Raymond Ian, b. 1935,—Duncan Rodney, b. 1939.——Olive Joan, b. 1916: m. 1948, Wing-Cdr. Eric Comyn Boucher, RAF, and has issue living, Angus Comyn, b. 1949,—Esther Dawn, b. 1951,—Vanessa Jane, b. 1954. *Residence*, Bexon Manor, Bredgar, Kent.

Issue of the late Arthur Douglas Ramsay, O.B.E., b. 1868, d. 1952 : m. 1914, Winifred (now of Flat 129, 55, Park Lane, W.1), da. of W. H. Turner, of Geraldton, W. Australia :—
Michael Douglas (Lyford Cay, PO Box 52, Nassau), b. 1918; formerly Capt. Seaforth Highlanders: m. 1949, Eleanor Kinsell, of Florida, USA, and has issue living, Jonathan b. 1950.——Susan Patricia, b. 1926: m. 1st 1950 (m. diss. 1965), Maj. Sir Francis David Somerville Head, 5th Bt.; 2ndly, 1967, Henry Jagoe Shaw, FRCS, of 26, Hamilton House, Vicarage Gate, W8.

Sir Alexander, the 1st baronet (2nd son of Sir Thomas Burnett of Leys, 6th baronet [*see* Burnett, Bt.]), by his wife Catherine, sister of Sir Alexander Ramsay of Balmain, 6th and last Bt, succeeded his uncle in the Ramsay estates 1806, and assumed, by Roy. licence, the surname and arms of Ramsay. Sir John Ramsay, cr. *Lord Bothwell* 1485 and killed at Flodden 1513, was ancestor of Sir Gilbert Ramsay of Balmain, 1st Bt. (cr. 1625).

Ramsay-Fairfax-Lucy (Cameron-Ramsay-Fairfax-Lucy), see Lucy.

Ramsay-Steel-Maitland, see Maitland.

PENNINGTON-RAMSDEN, Creation (E.) 1689. of Byram, Yorkshire.

Sir GEOFFREY WILLIAM PENNINGTON-RAMSDEN, 7th *Baronet;* b. Aug. 28th, 1904; *s.* his father, *Sir* JOHN FRECHEVILLE *RAMSDEN*, 1958 ; ed. at Eton, and at Jesus Coll., Camb. (B.A. 1925) ; Major Life Guards ; assumed by deed poll 1925 the surname of Pennington in lieu of his patronymic, and the arms of Pennington (differenced with a canton sable) quartered with those of Ramsden, and by deed poll 1958 resumed the surname of Ramsden after that of Pennington ; is a patron of four livings : *m.* 1927, Veronica Prudence Betty, da. of the late Frederick William Morley, of Biddlestone Manor, Chippenham, Wilts, and has issue.

Arms—1st and 4th grand quarters, argent on a chevron between three fleurs-de-lys sable, as many rams' heads couped at the neck argent, *Ramsden*; 2nd and 3rd grand quarters, quarterly, 1st and 4th, or five fusils conjoined in fesse azure, a canton sable, *Pennington*, 2nd and 3rd argent on a chevron between three fleurs-de-lys sable, as many rams' heads couped at the neck argent, *Ramsden*. Crests—1, A cuoit arm in armour proper, the gauntlet holding a fleur-de-lys sable, *Ramsden*; 2, a mountain cat passant guardant proper, resting the dexter forepaw on a fleur-de-lys sable, *Pennington*.
Seats—Muncaster Castle, Ravenglass, Cumberland; Ardverikie, Newtonmore, Inverness-shire. *Residence*—Versions Farm, Brackley, Northants. *Club*—Lansdowne.

Daughters living—Phyllida Rosemary, b. 1929 : m. 1955, Patrick Thomas Gordon-Duff-Pennington (who assumed by deed poll 1955, the final surname of Pennington), and has issue living, Prunella Melissa Phyllida, b. 1956,—Anthea, b. 1958,—Iona Arabel, b. 1961,—Rowena, b. 1963. *Residence*, Kirkland of Tynron, by Thornhill, Dumfriesshire.——Penelope Lucinda, b. 1930: m. 1958, Peter Anthony Neville Pennethorne Laing, of Corton Denham House, nr. Sherborne, Dorset, and Sotogrande, Cadiz, Spain, and has issue living, Arabella Charlotte Lucinda, b. 1960,—Venetia Alexandra Veronica Cayetana, b. 1961.——Annabel, b. 1931: m. 1958, Col. Edward Timothy Smyth-Osbourne, Coldm. Gds., of Lightwater Grange, Lightwater, Surrey, and has issue living, Charles William, b. 1959,—Julian George, b. 1964,—Michael Alexander, b. 1967,—Rachel Rosa, b. 1961.

Sister living—Mary Joyce (*Lady Feilden*), b. 1907 : m. 1929, Maj.-Gen. Sir Randle Guy Feilden, K.C.V.O., C.B., C.B.E., Coldstream Guards [*see* V. Hampden, colls.]. *Residences*, 3, Kingston House South, Ennismore Gardens, S.W.7 ; Old Manor, Minster Lovell, Oxford.

Collateral Branches living.

Issue of the late John St. Maur RAMSDEN, el. son of 6th Baronet, b. 1902, d. 1948 : m. 1935 (marriage dissolved 1948), Lady Catherine Mary Clementine Heathcote-Drummond-Willoughby (who m. 2ndly, 1948, Charles W. Hume, of Hunting Ridge Farm, Route 2, Charlottesville, Virginia, U.S.A.), da. of 2nd Earl of Ancaster :—
Eloise Carola, b. 1938: m. 1st, 1961, George Fillmore Miller III; 2ndly, 1974, Robert E. J. Philippi, of Crudwell Court, Malmesbury, Wilts., and has issue living, (by 1st m.) Sebastian St. Maur, b. 1965,—(by 2nd m.) James Jeremy George, b. 1975.

Grandchildren of the late Capt. John Charles Francis RAMSDEN, son of the late Capt. Henry James RAMSDEN, 3rd son of 4th baronet :—
Issue of the late Capt. Frederick William RAMSDEN, b. 1864, d. 1928 : m. 1887, Lady Elizabeth Maud Conyngham, who d. 1949, da. of 3rd Marquess Conyngham:—
Cynthia Maud (*Lady Nugent*), b. 1891 : m. 1917, the Rt. Hon. Sir Roland Thomas Nugent, 1st Bt. (cr. 1961). *Residence*, Portaferry House, Portaferry, co. Down.——Moyra Gwendolen, b. 1900: m. 1931, Alan Daubeny Russell-Clarke, of Great Triley, Abergavenny, Mon.——Enid Florence Beatrice, b. 1903: m. 1929, Capt. Philip Laidlay, late King's Roy. Rifle Corps, and has

issue living, Alison Maud Enid, *b.* 1932: *m.* 1954, Justin Newton Crane, of Walbury Cottage, Inkpen, Newbury, Berks., and has issue living, Timothy Robert *b.* 1956, Caroline Sarah *b.* 1960. *Residence*, Manor Farm House, Ham, Marlborough, Wilts.

    Issue of the late Lieut.-Col. Henry RAMSDEN-JODRELL, C.M.G., *b.* 1871, *d* 1950 (having assumed by Roy. Licence 1920 the additional surname of Jodrell) : *m.* 1902, Dorothy Lynch, *C.B.E., J.P.,* who *d.* 1958, el. da. of thehlate Col. Sir Edward Thomas Davenant Cotton-Jodrell, K.C.B. [V. Combermere, colls.] :—

Frances Barbara, *b.* 1905: *m.* 1939, Maj. John Powys Dewurst, RA (ret.). *Residence*, Sodylt Hall, Ellesmere, Salop.——Mary Angela (*Lady Fielden*), *b.* 1916: *m.* 1940, Air Vice-Marshal Sir Edward Hedley Fielden, GCVO, CB, DFC, AFC, RAF, and has issue living, Fiona, *b.* 1944: *m.* 1966, Christopher Norman Hart, of Eastcourt Farm, Crudwell, Malmesbury, Wilts. *Residence*, Edenwater House, Ednam, Kelso, Roxburghshire.

    Issue of the late Lt.-Col. Josslyn Vere RAMSDEN, CMG, DSO, RFA, *b.* 1876, *d.* 1952: *m.* 1909, Olive Clotilde Bouhier (Alexandra Hotel, Bridlington, Yorks.), da. of Frederick William Imbert-Terry, formerly of Aston House, Aston, Stevenage, Herts.:—

CARYL OLIVER IMBERT, *CMG, CVO* (The Old Rectory, Burton Agnes, Driffield, E. Yorks), *b.* April 4th 1915; ed. at Eton and New Coll., Oxford (MA); late Maj. RA and Counsellor in HM's Foreign Ser.; 1939-45 War; CMG 1965 CVO 1966: *m.* 1945. Anne da. of Lt.-Col. Sir Charles George Wickham, KBE, DSO, and has issue living, John Charles Josslyn, *b.* 1950; ed. at Eton, and Trin. Coll., Camb.

        Granddaughter of the late Robert Henry Ramsden, son of the late Robert John Ramsden (infra):—

    Issue of the late Robert Charles Plumptre Ramsden, *b.* 1874, *d.* 1964: *m.* 1934, Mary Isiline (who *m.* 2ndly, 1964, David William Smith, of Wigthorpe Hill, Wigthorpe Worksop), only da. of Lt.-Col. W. Wetwau, of Ashley Grove, Worksop:—

Mary, *b.* 1938: *m.* 1960, William A. Butroid, of Wigthorpe Farm, Wigthorpe, Worksop, Notts., and has issue living, Christine Joanna, *b.* 1961,—Sarah Isiline, *b.* 1963,—Janet Elizabeth, *b.* 1965.

        Grandchildren of the late Robert John RAMSDEN, son of the late Robert RAMSDEN (*b.* 1784) (infra):—

    Issue of the late Edward Plumptre RAMSDEN, *b.* 1848, *d.* 1916: *m.* 1875, Frances Elizabeth, who *d.* 1941, da. of William Kelly, of Blackheath, S.E.:—

John Edward Cecil, *b.* 1881.——William Eustace, *b.* 1882.——Five das.

    Issue of the late Charles Arthur RAMSDEN, *b.* 1849, *d.* 1902 : *m.* 1875, Elizabeth Mary, who *d.* 1939, da. of John Leckenby, J.P., F.R.S., formerly of Scarborough :—

Edith Elizabeth Mary : *m.* 1897, Walter Henry Fossey, who *d.* 1938, and has issue living.—— Emily Gertrude : *m.* 1899, Albert W. Chartres, and has issue living. *Residence*, 32, Wolseley Road, Mosman, Sydney, N.S. Wales.

        Grandchildren of the late Algernon Feilden Ramsden, 4th son of the late Robert John RAMSDEN (ante):—

    Issue of the late Edward Feilden Ramsden, *b.* 1893, *d.* 1973: *m.* 1928, Rhoda Helen, who *d.* 1971, da. of the late Ashmore Mitchell, of Edinburgh:—

Geoffrey Ashmore, *b.* 1930.——Marjorie Neish, *b.* 1929: *m.* 1954, Paul Hastings Tennent, of 104, Lynton Rd., Acton, W3, and has issue living, Timothy Feilden, *b.*, 1955,—Stephen John, *b.* 1958,—Adrian Paul, *b.* 1961,—Mary Frances, *b.* 1963.

        Granddaughters of the late Robert John RAMSDEN (ante):—

    Issue of the late John Pemberton RAMSDEN, *b.* 1854, *d.* 1911 : *m.* 1883, Alice Louisa, who *d.* 1924, da. of the late Arthur Malet [Malet, Bt., colls.] :—

Frances Teresa: *m.* 1928, James Tisdall Davidson.——Monica Hilda: *m.* 1922, Arthur Morris Penson, who *d.* 1954, and has issue living, John Austin, *b.* 1922: *m.* 1951, Margaret Elizabeth Clark, and has issue living, Hilary Jane *b.* 1952,—Richard Pemberton, *b.* 1926,—Philip Morris (twin), *b.* 1926,—Mark Jeremy, *b.* 1932,—Alice Rosemary, *b.* 1924: *m.* 1946, John William Devenish, and has issue living, Roger John *b.* 1947, Janet Mary *b.* 1949, Monica Ruth *b.* 1950, Daphne Lillian *b.* 1952. *Residence*, 12, Warwick Rd., Ealing, W5.

        Grandchildren of the late Charles Hamilton Ramsden, son of the late Rev. Charles Henry RAMSDEN, son of the late Robert RAMSDEN (*b.* 1784), grandson of the late Robert RAMSDEN (*b.* 1708), 4th son of 2nd baronet:—

    Issue of the late Charles Harold Lowther Ramsden, BSc, *b.* 1883, *d.* 1965: *m.* 1st, 1912, Cecile W., who *d.* 1933, da. of W. S. Childs; 2ndly, 1936, Alice Voice, who *d.* 1963, widow of William R. Henderson:—

(By 1st m.) Charles Dean, *BSc* (843, Freel's Peak Drive, Incline Village, Nev., USA), *b.* 1915; ed. at Cal. Univ. (BSc): *m.* 1940, Katherine, da. of Homer F. Lightfoot, and has issue living, Charles Anthony (24, West Santa Ynez, San Mateo, Calif., USA), *b.* 1943; ed. at Stanford Univ. (BSc, MBA); late Lt. USNR: *m.* 1969, Naomi, da. of Robert F. Robinson, MD,—Katherine Cecile, *b.* 1945: *m.* 1st, 1967 (m. diss. 1971), David A. Mitchell; 2nd Lt., US Army Reserve; 2ndly, 1972, Michael James Gannon of 859, Acalanes Drive, Lafayette, Calif., 94303, USA, and has issue living, Geoffrey Michael *b.* 1974.——Scott Carlton (226, Hall Drive, Orinda, Cal., USA), *b.* 1923; ed. at Cal. Univ. (BSc); late Lt., USN Reserve: *m.* 1952, Mary Alice, da. of Walter Garms, and has issue living, Linda Alice, *b.* 1954.——Dorothy Childs, *b.* 1913: *m.* 1947, Paul R. Coombs, (Apt. 555, c/o First National City Bank, Panama), and has issue living, Walter Ramsden (3544, W. Denton Lane, Phoenix, Ariz., USA 85019), *b.* 1950: *m.* 1972, Joan Vivian, da. of Robert Grant Comstock,—David Paul, *b.* 1952,—Marjorie Cecile *b.* 1954.——Helen Caroline (twin), *b.* 1923: *m.* 1946, Fred Albert Wagner, of 4080, Pomona, Livermore, Cal., USA, and has issue living, Fred Albert, *b.* 1952,—Jay Thomas, *b.* 1952,—Caroline Cecile, *b.* 1948: *m.* 1973, William Wesley Constable, of 722B, Santa Clara Av., Alameda, Calif., USA,—June Marseillette, *b.* 1955.

    Issue of the late Percival Scott Webber RAMSDEN, *b.* 1886, *d.* 1958 : *m.* 1910, Abigail E. (of 6133, Hill Road, Oakland, California, U.S.A.), da. of F. E. Philbrick :—

Elizabeth Sarah, *b* .1912.——Shirley Carolyn, *b.* 1916.——Marjory, *b.* 1917.——Patricia, *b.* 1920. *Residence*, 6133, Hill Road, Oakland, California, U.S.A.

        Grandchildren of the late Rev. Charles Henry RAMSDEN (ante):—

    Issue of the late Com. Francis Edward RAMSDEN, R.N., *b.* 1849, *d.* 1882 : *m.* 1879, Emma Elizabeth, who *d.* 1925, da. of the late Lieut.-Col. F. W. Birch, Indian Army :—

Francis Charles Home, *b.* 1880: *m.* 1927, Lilla Marguerita, da. of Charles Mackenzie, and has issue living, Francis Birch, *b.* 1928,—June Elizabeth Ramsden, *b.* 1929. *Residence*, Wembley R.R. No. 1, Alberta, Canada.

    Issue of the late Col. Herbert Frecheville Smyth RAMSDEN, C.B.E., *b.* 1856, *d.* 1931: *m.* 1889, the Hon. Edwyna Susan Elizabeth Twisleton Wykeham Fiennes, who *d.* 1931, da. of the 17th Baron Saye and Sele :—

Sir Geoffrey Charles Frescheville, *C.I.E., b.* 1893 ; ed. at Haileybury, and at Sidney Sussex Coll., Camb. (B.A. 1919, M.A. 1925) ; entered I.C.S. 1920, and became Financial Commr. of Central Provinces and Berar, India 1944 ; retired 1948 : European War 1914-19 as Capt. 1st Batn. Roy. Sussex Regt. ; C.I.E. 1942, Knt. 1947: *m.* 1930, Margaret Lovell, da. of the late Rev. John Robinson, V. of Downton, Wilts. *Residence*, Fynescourt, Grayshott, Hindhead, Surrey.

Grandchildren of the late Arthur John RAMSDEN, el. son of Col. Arthur Charles, 3rd son of the Rev. William RAMSDEN, son of Capt. George Ramsden, only son of Lt.-Col. Frecheville Ramsden, 6th son of 2nd baronet:—
Issue of the late Major Arthur Geoffrey Francis RAMSDEN, D.S.O., R.A., *b.* 1887, *d.* (on active ser. during European War) 1945 : *m.* 1918, Winifred, who *d.* 1958, da. of the late S. B. Cowan, LL.D. :—

Geoffrey Anthony Frecheville, *b.* 1919 ; L.D.S., R.C.S. 19—, B.D.S. 19— ; late Capt. Hampshire Regt.; 1939-45 War in Middle East (despatches): *m.* 1952, Pamela Barnes.——Peter Derek Frecheville, *b.* 1922; late Lt. RNVR and serving with Fleet Air Arm: *m.* 1958, Barbara, da. of W. S. Alexander, and has issue living, Gordon Benjamin Frecheville, *b.* 1961,—Elizabeth Lee, *b.* 1959,—Beverley Anne, *b.* 1962. *Residence,* 18, River Rd., Bedfordview, Johannesburg, S. Africa.——Justin John Frecheville (of Shinglewood, 55A, Third Av., Parktown North, Johannesburg, S. Africa), *b.* 1927; Group Accountant-Sec. of Tozer, Kemsley & Millbourn (S. Africa) (Pty.), Ltd., Johannesburg: *m.* 1960, Brigit Joy Barry, da. of Barry Smith, of Hill Crest, Natal, and has issue living, John Henry Frecheville *b.* 1963,—Timothy Geoffrey Frecheville, *b.* 1965,—Paula Frances Barry, *b.* 1967.——David Bruce Frecheville (116, 12th St., Parkmore, Johannesburg, S. Africa), *b.* 1929; late Capt. RA: *m.* 1958, Deirdre Mary Bouchier, and has issue living, Bruce Frecheville, *b.* 1959,—Paul David Frecheville, *b.* 1961,—Debra Gail, *b.* 1960,—Penelope Ray, *b.* 1963.——Myra Patricia, *b.* 1921: *m.* 1953, Alan Rowland Lingard Escombe.——Arminel Jill, *b.* 1925: *m.* 1952, Lt.-Cdr. Richard Thomas Leggott, MBE, RN, and has issue living, Ruth, *b.* 1953,—Susan, *b.* 1955,—Jenifer, *b.* 1958. *Residence.*

Issue of the late John Hope Frecheville RAMSDEN, *b.* 1896, *d.* 1955: *m.* 1930, Hilda Marguerite Lonnen (of Picketty Witch Cottage, Ilchester Road, Yeovil, Somerset), da. of the late E. J. Simmons :—

Margaret Elizabeth Anne, *b.* 1932: *m.* 1966, Capt. T. L. Browne, Int. Corps, of 10, Church St., Tintinhull, Som., and has issue.

Robert Ramsden was seated at Longley Hall, *temp.* Henry VIII. The 1st baronet received his baronetcy for his essential services and the distinguished zeal exhibited by him at the Revolution. The 5th baronet, Sir John William, sat as M.P. for Taunton (*L*) 1853-7, for Hythe 1857-9, for W. Riding of York 1880-85, for Osgoldcross Div. of E. Part of W. Riding of York 1885-6, and was Under-Sec. of State for War 1857-8. Sir John Frecheville Ramsden, 6th baronet was High Sheriff of Bucks 1920.

RANKIN, Creation (U.K.) 1898, of Bryngwyn, Much Dewchurch, co. Hereford.

Sir HUGH CHARLES RHYS RANKIN, 3rd *Baronet ; b.* Aug. 8th, 1899 ; *s.* his father, *Lieut.-Col. Sir* (JAMES) REGINALD (LEA), 1931 ; ed. at Harrow ; formerly a follower of the Kadaria' School of Thought, Senior Vice-Pres. Western Islamic Asso. (Mohammedan), and Capt. R.A.S.C. ; a Stock Breeder, and Sheep Judge ; is a F.S.A. (Scotland), and a Member of Welsh Nationalist Plaid Cymru ; was Pres. of Clun Forest Sheep Breeders' Asso. 1928 ; sometime Pres. of Muslim So. of Great Britain ; First Representative of Great Britain on All-European Muslim Congress at Geneva 1935, and a Permanent Member of Congress and of Finance Committee ; elected a Town Councillor 1949, and a Co. Councillor 1950 ; served in Ireland (on active ser.) as Trooper in 1st Roy. Dragoons 1920-22 (invalided out) ; ex-Vice-Pres. of Scottish National Liberal Asso. ; adopted Mahayana (Theistic) Buddhist Faith 1943 ; European War 1940-45 in India ; assumed by deed poll 1932 the additional surname of Stewart ; discontinued by deed poll 1946 the use of the additional surname of Stewart and assumed the name of Hugh in lieu of Hubert : *m.* 1st, 1932, Helen Margaret, who *d.* 1945, da. of the late Sir Charles John Stewart, K.B.E., first Public Trustee, and widow of Capt. Colin Frederick Fitzroy Campbell, Scots Guards ; 2ndly, 1946, Robina Kelly (F.S.A., Scotland), of Crieff, Perthshire.

Arms—Or, a cinquefoil gules, in chief a battle-axe erect between two boars' heads couped, and in base a boar's head between two battle-axes erect sable.   **Crest**—In front of a cubit arm holding a battle-axe proper, three cinquefoils gules.

Address—The Flat, Priors Gate, Priorsfield, Godalming, Surrey.

Collateral Branches living.

Issue of the late Lt.-Col. (Arthur) Niall Talbot Rankin, yr. son of 2nd baronet, *b.* 1904, *d.* 1965: *m.* 1931, Lady Jean Margaret Dalrymple, DCVO (House of Treshnish, Calgary, I. of Mull, and 3, Catherine Wheel Yard, St. James's St., SW1), da. of 12th Earl of Stair:—
IAN NIALL, (Blomfield House, Clifton Villas, W9), *b.* Dec. 19th, 1932; ed. at Eton, and at Ch. Ch., Oxford (MA); Lt. Scots Guards (Reserve): *m.* 1959, Alexandra, only da. of Adm. Sir Laurence George Durlacher, KCB, OBE, DSC [Hanson, Bt., *cr.* 1887], and has issue living, Gavin Niall, *b.* 1962,—Zara Sophia, *b.* 1960.——Alick Michael (Philpstoun House, S. Queensferry, W. Lothian), *b.* 1935; Lt. Scots Guards (Reserve): *m.* 1958, Susan Margaret, el. da. of Lt.-Col. Hugh Littleton Dewhurst [*see* B. Forteviot], and has issue living, Rupert Mark, *b.* 1962,—Clare Joanna, *b.* 1961,—Annabel Louise, *b.* 1964.

Grandchildren of the late Charles Herbert Rankin, CB, CMG, DSO, 2nd son of 1st baronet:—
Issue of the late Brig. William Rankin, OBE, *b.* 1909, *d.* 1968: *m.* 1939, Pauline Sinclair (Oegrove Farm, Frampton-on-Severn, Glos.), da. of the late Oswald Sinclair Haggie:—

Mark, *b.* 1941, late Capt. 15th/19th King's R. Hussars.——Christopher John (32, Smith St., SW3), *b.* 1946: *m.* 1968 (m. diss. 1974), Lucinda Jane, el. da. of Lt.-Cdr. Christopher Godfrey de Lisle Bush, RN, and has issue living, Peter William, *b.* 1969,—James Christopher, *b.* 1972.—— Carolyn, *b.* 1943: *m.* 1967, Edmund Brooke Alexander, of 59, Wooster St., New York, 10012, USA, and has issue living, Emily Sinclair, *b.* 1971,—Jessica Brooke, *b.* 1973.——Jean Mary, *b.* 1952.

The 1st baronet, Sir James (Ch. Steward of the City of Hereford), was High Sheriff of Hereford 1873, and sat as M.P. for Herefordshire, N., or Leominster, Div. (*C*) 1880-85, 1886-1906, and 1910-12. The 2nd baronet, Lieut.-Col. Sir Reginald, F.R.H.S., F.R.G.S., Bar.-at-law, was Private Sec.

to Sec. of State for the Colonies (Rt. Hon. A. Lyttleton, K.C., M.P.) 1903-4, and *Times* War Correspondent in Morocco 1908, and with Bulgarian Forces 1912; he was Lieut.-Col. Comdg. Herefordshire Regt. (T.D.), and second in command of W. Kent Yeo.; served in S. Africa 1900 as trooper and Lieut. Rimington's Guides (medal with three clasps); author of "A Subaltern's Letters to His Wife," "With General d'Amade in Morocco" (translated into Spanish and French), "The Inner History of the Balkan War," "The Royal Ordering of Gardens," etc.

RANKIN, Creation (U.K.) 1937, of Broughton Tower, co. Lancaster. [Extinct 1960.]

Sir ROBERT RANKIN, 1st and last *Baronet.*

Daughter living of 1st Baronet—Cécile Elizabeth Florence (*Lady Grandy*), *b.* 1914; CStJ: *m.* 1937 Marshal of the RAF Sir John Grandy, GCB, KBE, DSO, RAF of Convent House, Gibraltar, and 7, Hale House, De Vere Gdns., W8, and has issue living, John *b.* 1947,—William, *b.* 1948.

RASCH, Creation (U.K.) 1903, of Woodhill, Danbury, Essex.

Sir RICHARD GUY CARNE RASCH, 3rd

Baronet; el. son of the late Brig. Guy Elland Carne Rasch, C.V.O., D.S.O., yr. son of 1st baronet; *b.* Oct. 10th, 1918; *s.* his uncle, *Col. Sir* FREDERIC CARNE, *T.D.,* 1963; ed. at Eton; Maj. late Grenadier Guards; a Member of HM Body Guard of Hon. Corps of Gentlemen-at-Arms since 1968: *m.* 1st, 1947 (m. diss. 1959), Anne Mary, da. of the late Maj. John Henry Dent-Brocklehurst, OBE [B. Trevor]; 2ndly, 1961, Fiona Mary, da. of Robert Douglas Shaw, of St. Leonards-on-Sea, Sussex, and former wife of Humphrey Salmon, and has issue by 1st m.

Arms—Quarterly: azure and gules, a cross parted and fretted or, between in the first quarter a lion rampant per bend sinister ermine and erminois; in 2nd quarter a pelican in her piety, argent; in 3rd quarter a griffin segreant of the third; and in the 4th quarter a lion rampant of the last. **Crest**—Upon a rock proper a gryphon's head azure, collared gemel or, in front thereof a leopard's face between two fleurs-de-lis of the last.

Residences—30, Ovington Sq., SW3; Woodhill, Danbury, Chelmsford. *Clubs,*—Guards', White's.

Son living—By 1st marriage—SIMON ANTHONY CARNE, *b.* Feb. 26th, 1948; ed. at Eton; Page of Honour to H.M. 1962-64.

Daughter living—By 1st m.—Leila Anne Katherine, *b.* 1952: *m.* 1975, Thomas Geoffrey Timothy Rose Price [see Price, Bt., colls., cr. 1815].

Brother living—David Alwyne Carne, *b.* 1922; ed. at Eton; Maj. late Grenadier Guards: *m.* 1953, (Elizabeth) Anne, only da. of the late Henry Robert Somers Fitzroy de Vere Somerset, DSO [see D. Beaufort, colls.], and has issue living, Guy Martin Carne, *b.* 1959,—Jane Catherine, *b.* 1955,—Emma Caroline, *b.* 1962. *Residence,* Heale House, Woodford, Salisbury, Wilts.

Mother living—Phyllis Dorothy Lindsay (Trelyon, Rock, Wadebridge, Cornwall, and 27, Swan Court, SW3), da. of the late Lt.-Col. the Hon. Alwyn Henry Fulke Greville [see E. Warwick, colls.]: *m.* 1916, Brig. Guy Elland Carne Rasch, CVO, DSO, who *d.* 1955.

Widow living of 2nd Baronet—CATHERINE MARGARET (*Catherine, Lady Rasch*) (of 9, Trevor St., Knightsbridge, S.W.7), only da. of the late Maj. the Hon. John Richard de Clare Boscawen [see V. Falmouth, colls.], and widow of 16th Baron Petre; a J.P. for Essex: *m.* 1921, Col. Sir Frederic Carne Rasch, T.D., 2nd Bt., who *d.* 1963.

The 1st baronet, Sir Frederic Carne Rasch, sat as M.P. for S.-E. Div. of Essex (*C*) 1886-1900 and for Chelmsford Div. of Essex 1900-1908.

RASHLEIGH, Creation (U.K.) 1831, of Prideaux, Cornwall.

Sir HARRY EVELYN BATTIE RASHLEIGH,

5th *Baronet,* son of the late Harry Rashleigh, J.P., 3rd son of 3rd baronet; *b.* May 17th, 1923; *s.* his uncle, *Sir* COLMAN BATTIE WALPOLE, 1951; ed. at Wellington Sch., Somerset; a Farmer; formerly Sergeant RAC; was an Engineer in Tanganyika 1948-51, and Engineer, English Clays, Cornwall 1951-2: *m.* 1954, Honora Elizabeth, da. of G. S. Sneyd, of The Watch House, Downderry, Cornwall, and has issue.

Arms—Sable, a cross or, between in the 1st quarter, a Cornish chough argent; in the 2nd quarter a text T, and in the 3rd and 4th a crescent all argent.

Residence,—Stowford Grange, Lewdown, Okehampton, Devon. *Club*—Royal Fowey Yacht.

Son living—RICHARD HARRY, *b.* July 8th, 1958.

Daughters living—Susanna Jane, *b.* 1955.——Frances Elisabeth, *b.* 1956.——Anne Henrietta, *b.* 1959.

Brother living—Peter, *b.* 1924 ; is a Master Mariner : *m.* 1949, Lola Evan, of N.S. Wales, and has issue living, Margaret Anne, *b.* 1950,—Bettine Jane, *b.* 1954,—Jill Vivien, *b.* 1957. *Residence,* 17, Vine St., Hurstville, N.S.W.

Sisters living—Elizabeth, *b.* 1915.——Mary Vivien (c/o Lloyds Bank, Fowey, Cornwall), *b.* 1917: *m.* 1941, Cdr. Philip Kidd, RN, and has issue living, Christopher Hugh Rashleigh, *b.* 1949,— Judith Anne, *b.* 1941: *m.* 1966, Robin Alec Stables, of Cadmore End, High Wycombe, Bucks.,— Sarah Vivien, *b.* 1943: *m.* 1967, Angus Dormer Crichton, of 20, Regency Mews, Whittondene Twickenham, Middx.,—Elizabeth, *b.* 1946: *m.* 1967, John Ronald Haskins, of 55, Milcote Rd., Solihull, Warwicks.

The family of Rashleigh has been seated in Cornwall since the early part of the 16th century. The 2nd baronet was M.P. for Cornwall E. (*L*) 1874-80.

RAWLINSON, Creation (U.K.) 1891.

Sir ANTHONY HENRY JOHN RAWLINSON, 5th *Baronet*; *b.* May 1st, 1936; *s.* his father, *Sir* (ALFRED) FREDERICK, 1969; ed. at Millfield: *m.* 1st, 1960 (m. diss. 1967), Penelope Byng, da. of Rear-Adm. Gambier John Byng Noel, CB, [see E. Gainsborough, colls.]; 2ndly, 1967, Pauline Strickland, da. of John Holt Hardy, of Sydney, NSW, and has issue by 1st and 2nd m.

Arms,—Sable, three swords in pale proper, pommels and hilts or, two erect points upwards and between them the other, point downwards ; on a chief embattled of the third an antique crown gules. **Crest,**—Out of an antique crown or, a cubic arm erect in armour, the hand grasping a sword in bend sinister, and the wrist encircled by a laurel wreath proper.

Residence—3, Church Place, Paddington, NSW, 2021.

Son living—By 1st m.—ALEXANDER NOEL, *b.* July 15th, 1964.——By 2nd m.,—Rupert Seymour, *b.* 1970.

Daughter living—By 1st m.—Caroline Louise Byng, *b.* 1962.

Brother living—(Marcus) Andrew Frederick (Stody Hall, Melton Constable, Norfolk), *b.* 1940; ed. at Canford: *m.* 1964, Miriam, el. da. of Richard Joice, of Hall Farm, East Raynham, and has issue living, Joanna Jane, *b.* 1965,—Nicola Abegail, *b.* 1967,—Candida Louise, *b.* 1974.

Sister living—Sarah Jane, *b.* 1939: *m.* 1962, Capt. William Hanslip Bulwer Bulwer-Long, 9th/ 12th Roy. Lancers (who assumed by deed poll 1963 the additional surname of Bulwer), of Heydon Hall, Heydon, Norwich, and has issue living, Edward Hanslip, *b.* 1966,—Benjamin Earle, *b.* 1970,—Daisy Lydia, *b.* 1975.

Widow living of 4th Baronet—BESSIE FORD TAYLOR (*Bessie, Lady Rawlinson*) (2, Martincross, The Boulevard, Sheringham, Norfolk), da. of Frank Raymond Emmatt, of Harrogate: *m.* 1934, Sir (Alfred) Frederick Rawlinson, 4th Bt., who *d.* 1969.

Henry Creswicke Rawlinson, G.C.B. (son of Abraham Tyzack Rawlinson, of Chadlington, Oxford), a distinguished Orientalist, and the first decipherer of cuneiform inscriptions ; M.P. for Reigate 1858, and for Frome (*L*) 1865-8 ; re-organized Shah's Army 1833-9, Political Agent at Candahar 1840-43, and a Member of Council of Sec. of State for India 1858-9 and 1868-95 : cr. a *Baronet* 1891. His son, Gen. Sir Henry Seymour, G.C.B., G.C.S.I., G.C.V.O., K.C.M.G., 2nd Bt.; served with Burma Expedition 1886-87, with Nile Expeditions 1897 and 1898, at battles of Atbara and Khartoum, in S. Africa 1899-1902, 1914, GOC 4th Div. 4th Army Corps, and 4th Army 1915-18, and as GOC in C, N. Russia 1919; C in C Aldershot 1919-20, and India 1920-25; cr. *Baron Rawlinson,* of Trent, co. Dorset (peerage of UK) 1919; *d.* 1925, when the Barony became ext., and the Baronetcy devolved upon his brother, Lt.-Col. Sir Alfred, CMG, CBE, DSO, 3rd Bt.

READE, Creation (E.) 1661, of Barton, Berkshire.

Sir CLYDE NIXON READE, 12th *Baronet*; *b.* 1906 ; *s.* his brother, *Sir* JOHN STANHOPE, 1958 : *m.* 1st, 1930, Trilby, who *d.* 1958, da. of Charles McCarthy ; 2ndly, 1960, Alice Martha, yst. da. of Joseph Asher, of Ohio.

Arms—Gules, a saltire between four garbs or. **Crest**—On the stump of a tree vert, a falcon rising proper, belled and jessed or.

Address—Box 242, Mason, Ingham Co., Michigan, USA.

Sister living—Hazel, *b.* 1899 : *m.* 1919, John Neil, and has issue living, Donald George (6051, Daft St., Lansing, Ingham Co., Michigan, USA), *b.* 1921. *Residence,*

Cedant arma togœ.
Let arms give place to the gown.

Aunt living (daughter of 9th baronet)—Maude, *b.* 1894 : *m.* 1914, H. Stanley Vaughan, and has issue living, H. Waldron, *b.* 1930,— Thelma, *b.* (Nov.) 1914 : *m.* 1937, Robert Lyndon, and has issue living, Richard Vaughan *b.* 1941. *Residence,* Dexter, Michigan, U.S.A.

Collateral Branches living.

Issue of the late Elmer Compton Reade, 2nd son of 9th baronet, *b.* 1877, *d.* 1918; *m.* 1902, Lettie Wylie :—

Laura Leticia, *b.* 1908 : *m.* 1930, Gordon Heston. *Residence,*

Issue of the late Elmory Isaac Reade, 4th son of 9th baronet, *b.* 1887, *a.* 1939 : *m.* 1908, Millicent Fisk :—

Irene Norah, *b.* 1911: *m.* 1931, Hugh Peebles, and has issue living, Robert Bradley, *b.* 1932,—David, *b.* 1943,—Gloria Ann, *b.* 1935.——Eileen, *b.* 1913: *m.* 1935, Ronald Durrett.——Esther, *b.* 1918: *m.* 1934, Lawrence Durrett. *Residence,*

Issue of the late Leverne Elton Reade, 5th son of 9th baronet, *b.* 1891, *d.* 1943: *m.* 1921, Norman B. Ward:—

ROBERT WARD, *b.* Oct. 11th, 1923.——Kenneth Ray, *b.* 1925.

The 1st baronet's paternal grandfather was knighted by Queen Elizabeth I, and a baronetcy conferred upon his uncle, John, in 1641, became extinct 1712. The 3rd baronet of the present creation sat as M.P. for Cricklade. Sir George Compton Reade, 9th Bt., who was a great-great-grandson of the 5th Bt., *d.* in April 1908.

READHEAD, Creation (U.K.) 1922, of Westoe, Borough of South Shields, co. Palatine of Durham.

I strive faithfully.

(*Sir*) JAMES TEMPLEMAN READHEAD, 3rd *Baronet* (has established his claim but does not use the title), son of the late Maj. Stanley Readhead, MC, 2nd son of 1st baronet; *b.* Feb. 12th, 1910; *s.* his uncle, *Sir* JAMES HALDER, 1940; ed. at Repton and at the Lycée de Nice; 1939-45 War as Lt. K.O.Y.L.I. (invalided): *m.* 1946, Hilda Rosemary, da. of G. H. Hudson of the Manor, Hatfield, Doncaster, and has issue.

Arms—Azure on a fesse between two cross-crosslets fitchée or as many martlets sable, all within two flaunches of the second. **Crest**—Upon waves of the sea proper a galley sable, in front thereof two anchors saltireways or. *Residence*—

Daughter living—Charlotte Susan Carolynn, *b.* 1947.

Daughters living of 2nd Baronet—Doreen Evelyn, *b.* 1916: *m.* 1946, John P. Glaisyer. *Residence,* Gallowhill, Whalton, Morpeth, Northumberland.——Joan, *b.* 1920: *m.* 1944, Alfred Edmund Hynam Sevier, who *d.* 1974, and has issue living, Rex Alfred Readhead, *b.* 1945; ed. at Harrow,—Roy James Readhead, *b.* 1948; ed. at Harrow. *Residence,* Hulland Hall, nr. Derby.

Reardon-Smith, see Smith.

RECKITT, Creation (U.K.) 1894, of Swanland Manor, North Ferriby, East Riding of York. [Extinct 1944.]

Sir PHILIP BEALBY RECKITT, *O.B.E.*, 3rd and last *Baronet.*

Daughters living of 3rd Baronet—By 1st marriage—Barbara, *b.* 1902: *m.* 1934, Hugh Wykeham David Pollock, who *d.* 1972 [*see* Montagu-Pollock, Bt., colls.]. *Residence,* Winderwath, Penrith, Cumberland.——Elizabeth Kathleen (*Lady Robson*), *b.* 1904: *m.* 1st, 1925, Lt.-Col. Vernon Harrison Holt, MC, DL, JP, who *d.* 1966; 2ndly, 1969, Vice-Adm. Sir (William) Geoffrey (Arthur) Robson, KBE, CB, DSO, DSC, and has issue living, (by 1st m.) James, *b.* 1936,—Annabel, *b.* 1944. *Residences,* Amat, Ardgay, Ross-shire.; Fyrish House, Evanton, Ross-shire.

Daughter living of 2nd Baronet—By 1st marriage—Nancie, *b.* 1901: *m.* 1925, Col. Brian Holland Hughes, TD, late Queen's R. Regt. (TA) (who *d.* 1970 having assumed 1927 the additional surname of Reckitt), and has issue living, John Brian (47, Queens Gate Gdns., SW7; Pinswell Plantation, Colesbourne, Cheltenham, Glos.), *b.* 1930,—Patrick James (The Mill House, Sproughton, Ipswich), *b.* 1934: *m.* 1st, 1962 (m. diss. 1971), Carol Anne Paulson; 2ndly, 1971, Sheila Lamorna Powell, and has issue living (by 1st m.), Nicole Clair *b.* 1965,—Elizabeth Ann (47, Queen's Gate Gdns., SW7), *b.* 1927: *m.* 1951 (m. diss. 1971), Capt. John E. H. Russell, 10th R. Hussars, and has issue living, William Nicholas *b.* 1952, Caroline Jane *b.* 1955. *Residence* Sproughton Hall, nr. Ipswich.

REDWOOD, Creation (U.K.) 1911, of Avenue Road, St. Marylebone.

We have disseminated knowledge from of old.

LUMEN·SEVIMUS·ANTIQUE

Sir PETER BOVERTON REDWOOD, 3rd *Baronet*; *b.* Dec. 1st, 1937: *s.* his father, *Sir* THOMAS BOVERTON, 1974; ed. at Gordonstoun: Maj. KOSB: *m.* 1964, Gilian Waddington, only da. of John Lee Waddington Wood, of Limuru, Kenya, and has issue.

Arms—Paly of six or and ermine, a lion rampant sable, on a chief azure an embattled gateway proper between two mullets of six points of the first. **Crest**—A rock, therefrom an eagle rising proper, charged on each wing with a mullet of six points, in the beak a staff raguly or.

Address—c/o National Westminster Bank, Thames House, Millbank, SW1.

Daughters living—Anna Kathryn, *b.* 1967.——Colina Margaret Charlotte, *b.* 1969.——Gaynor Elizabeth, *b.* 1972.

Half Brothers living—ROBERT BOVERTON, *b.* June 24th, 1953.——Charles Boverton, *b.* 1956.

Half Sister living—Anne Boverton, *b.* 1947: *m.* 1968, James Embury, and has issue living, Tristan James, *b.* 1971,—Bartholomew Boverton, *b.* 1972.

Aunt living—Patricia Boverton, *b.* 1910: *m.* 1965, Harold Box, of 26b, Maida Av., W2.

Mother living—Ruth Mary, da. of John Henry David Creighton: *m.* 1933 (m. diss. 1943) Sir Thomas Boverton Redwood, 2nd Bt., who *d.* 1974.

Widow living of 2nd Baronet—URSULA (*Ursula, Lady Redwood*), (37, Kersey Rd., Flushing, Falmouth, Cornwall), da. of the late Rev. Herbert Percy Hale: *m.* 1944, as his 2nd wife, Sir Thomas Boverton Redwood, 2nd Bt., who *d.* 1974.

The 1st baronet, Sir Boverton, was a well-known authority on Petroleum, and was Adviser on Petroleum to Admiralty, India Office, and Home Office.

REES, Creation (U.K.) 1919, of Aylwards Chase. [Extinct 1970.]

Sir RICHARD LODOWICK EDWARD MONTAGU REES, 2nd, and last *Baronet*.

Daughter living of 1st Baronet—Rosemary Theresa (*Lady du Cros*), MBE, *b.* 1901; is in WRAF VR; 1939-45 War as Capt. Air Transport Auxiliary; MBE (Civil) 1946: *m.* 1950, Capt. Sir Philip Harvey du Cros, 3rd Hussars, 2nd baronet. *Residence*, Little Bocombe, Parkham, Bideford, N. Devon.

REID, Creation (U.K.) 1897, of Ellon, Aberdeenshire.

Nothing is hard for one who loves.

NIHIL·AMANTI·DVRVM

Sir ALEXANDER JAMES REID, 3rd *Baronet*; *b.* Dec. 6th, 1932; *s.* his father, *Sir* EDWARD JAMES, KBE, 1972; ed. at Eton and Magdalene Coll., Camb.; Capt. (ret.) 3rd Bn. Gordon Highlanders; Malaya 1951-53; JP and a DL of Cambridgeshire; a Dir. of Cristina Securities, Ltd. and of General Tours, Ltd., and a Gov. of Heath Mount Sch., Hertford: *m.* 1955, Michaela Ann, da. of Olaf Kier, CBE, of Cokenach, Barkway, Royston, Herts., and has issue.

Arms,—Azure, a stag's head erased or, between two torches fired proper; (as an honourable augmentation) on a chief gules a lion passant guardant or, armed and langued azure (being one of the lions from the Royal arms). **Crest**,—A pelican in its piety proper. **Supporters**,—On either side a Royal stag or, round the neck a chain proper suspended therefrom an escutcheon azure, charged with a representation of the Imperial Crown proper.

Residence—Kingston Wood, Arrington, Royston, Herts. *Club*, Caledonian.

Son living—CHARLES EDWARD JAMES, *b.* June 24th, 1956; ed. at Rannoch.

Daughters living—Christina, *b.* 1958.——Jennifer, *b.* 1959.——Alexandra Catherine, *b.* 1965.

Sister living—Susan Isobel, *b.* (Dec.) 1930: *m.* 1953, Douglas Stanley Charles Weedon, and has issue living, Patricia Anne, *b.* 1954,—Sarah Jane, *b.* 1958,—Joanna Lesley, *b.* 1960,—Nicola Mary, *b.* 1962,—Samantha Susan, *b.* 1965. *Residence*, Fangorn, Buchanan Castle Estate, Drymen, Stirlingshire.

Aunt living (daughter of 1st baronet)—Victoria Susan Beatrice, *b.* 1908: *m.* 1935, Leonard St. Clair Ingrams, OBE, who *d.* 1953, and has issue living, Peter John, *b.* 1936,—Richard Reid (Forge House, Aldworth, Reading, Berks.), *b.* 1937: *m.* 1962, Mary Morgan,—Leonard Victor (Ireton House, 106, Highgate Hill, N6), *b.* 1941: *m.* 1964, Rosalind, el. da. of Antony Ross Moore, CMG. *Residences*, 1, Lodge Av., SW14; 43, Low Town, Collieston Aberdeenshire.

Widow living of 2nd Baronet—TATIANA (*Tatiana Lady Reid*), (16, Buckingham Terr., Edinburgh, EH4 3AD), da. of the late Col. Alexandre Fenoult, formerly Russian Imperial Guard: *m.* (Jan.) 1930, Sir Edward James Reid, KBE, 2nd Bt., who *d.* 1972.

Collateral Branch living.

Issue of the late Adm. Sir John Peter Lorne Reid, GCB, CVO, yr. son of 1st baronet, *b.* 1903; *d.* 1973: *m.* 1933, Jean, who *d.* 1971, da. of Sir Henry Herbert Philip Dundas, MVO, 3rd Bt. (cr. 1898):—
David Lorne Dundas, *b.* 1938; late Lt. 15th/19th King's Hussars: *m.* 1968, Elizabeth, da. of the late Adam Natt, and formerly wife of Wilkinson.——Delia (*Lady Montgomery*), *b.* 1935: *m.* 1956, Sir (Basil Henry) David Montgomery, 9th Bt., of Kinross House, Kinross.

This Baronetcy was created on the occasion of H.M. Queen Victoria's Diamond Jubilee in recognition of the 1st baronet's personal services to H.M., Sir James, G.C.V.O., K.C.B., M.D., LL.D., 1st Bt., being successively Physician to Queen Victoria, to King Edward VII., and to King George V.

REID, Creation (U.K.) 1922, of Springburn, Co. of City of Glasgow, and of Kilmaurs, co. Ayr.

Sir HUGH REID, 3rd *Baronet*; *b.* Nov. 27th, 1933: *s.* his father, *Sir* DOUGLAS NEILSON, 1971; *ed.* at Loretto.

Arms (as recorded at Lyon Office)—Argent, a demi-eagle, wings expanded, in chief an ancient handbell between a mullet in the dexter and a cross moline in the sinister, all sable. **Crest**—A demi-eagle, wings expanded sable.

Seats—Tullich, Lochcarron, Ross-shire ; Auchterarder House, Perthshire.

Sister living—Joan Murray, *b.* 1929: *m.* 1953, John Francis Quinn, and has issue living, John Douglas, *b.* 1954, —Peter Francis, *b.* 1956,—James Hugh, *b.* 1959,—Michael Joseph, *b.* 1967,—David Paul, *b.* 1969,—Kevin, *b.* 1974,— Mary Teresa, *b.* 1955,—Margaret Joan, *b.* 1960,—Anne Bernadette, *b.* 1962,—Pauline, *b.* 1965. *Residence*, Caheronaun, Loughrea, co. Galway.
Aunt living (daughter of 1st baronet)—Madeline Constance Maud, *b.* 1892: *m.* 1915, Lt.-Col. William Lilburn of Coull, DL, JP, formerly Highland LI, who *d.* 1958, and has issue living, Alistair James (of Newlyn, Aboyne, Aberdeenshire), *b.* 1919; BSc (Eng); CEng; MIEE: *m.* 1949, Joan Elizabeth, da. of Kenneth Robert Sutherland, of Hinakura, Wairarapa, NZ, and has issue living, James Hugh *b.* 1950, Catherine Jane *b.* 1953,—Ian Robertson, *b.* 1927; is a FSA (Scot), a FRGS, and a FRSA. *Residence*, Coull House, by Aboyne, Aberdeenshire.

By fortitude and labour.

Widow living of 2nd Baronet—MARGARET BRIGHTON YOUNG (*Lady Reid*), (Tullich, Lochcarron, Ross-shire; Auchterarder House, Perthshire), da. of the late Robert Young Maxtone, MBE, JP, of Tighnamara, Campbeltown, Argyll: *m.* 1926, Sir Douglas Neilson Reid, 2nd Bt., who *d.* 1971.

The 1st baronet, Sir Hugh Reid, C.B.E., V.D., LL.D., M.I.C.E., D.L., J.P. (son of James Reid of Auchterarder, J.P., M.I.C.E.), was Chm. and Managing Directo; of N. British Locomotive Co., Ltd.

RENALS, Creation (U.K.) 1895.

Sir STANLEY RENALS, 4th *Baronet;* *b.* May 20th, 1923; *s.* his brother, *Sir* HERBERT, 1961 ; *ed.* at City of London Freemen's Sch. ; late Merchant Navy : *m.* 1957, Maria Dolores Rodriguez Pinto, da. of the late José Rodriguez Ruiz, and has issue.

Arms—Per pale gules and sable, on a fesse nebuly argent between in chief two lozenges, and in base as many fleurs-de-lis or, a fasces fessewise proper. **Crest**— On a rock a fox reguardant supporting with its dexter foot a fasces erect proper, and charged on the shoulder with a lozenge or.

Residence—47, Baden Rd., Brighton.

Son living—STANLEY MICHAEL, *b.* Jan. 14th, 1958.

Brother living—Charles (South View, Bird in Eye Hill, Uckfield, Sussex), *b.* 1924; *ed.* at City of London Freemen's Sch.; with Marine Insurance Co. Ltd.: *m.* 1965, Sheila Joyce, da. of Aubrey Hugh Berry.

Cavendo tutius.
Safe by being cautious.

Sisters living—Marie.——Ethel (7, Portland Av., Hove 3): *m.* 1940, Richard Gibson, who *d.* 1951.——Rieta.

The 1st baronet, Sir Joseph Renals (son of the late William Renals, of Nottingham), was a Partner in the firm of Renals & Co., merchants, and was Lord Mayor of London 1894-5.

RENSHAW, Creation (U.K.) 1903, of Coldharbour, Wivelsfield, Sussex.

Sir (CHARLES) STEPHEN BINE RENSHAW, 2nd
Baronet ; b. Dec. 9th, 1883 ; *s.* his father, *Sir* CHARLES BINE,
1918 ; ed. at Charterhouse, and at Trin. Coll., Camb. (B.A.
1904); Capt. (ret.) Ayrshire Yeo. (TA); 1914-18 War:
m. 1st, 1911 (m. diss. 1939), Edith Mary, da. of Rear-Adm.
Sir Edward Chichester, 11th Bt, CB, CMG; 2ndly, 1939,
Mace Caroline, da. of the late Maj. George Wynn-Tetley,
and has issue by 1st m.

 Arms—Per pale and per chevron or and azure, in chief two martlets,
and in base a bull's head couped all counterchanged.   Crest—In front of
a griffin's head erased sable a decrescent and an increscent argent.

 Residence—Great Fransham, East Dereham, Norfolk.

Esse quam videri.

*To be rather than to
seem*

Son living—By 1st marriage—CHARLES MAURICE BINE, *b.* Oct.
7th, 1912 ; ed. at Eton ; formerly Flying Officer R.A.F. : *m.* 1942
(marriage dissolved 1947), Isobel Bassett, da. of the Rev. J. L. T.
Popkin, and has issue living, John David, *b.* 1945: *m.* 1970, Jennifer,
da. of Gp. Capt. F. Murray, RAF,—Margaret, Bine *b.* 1943: *m.* 1967,
Dr. Lee Coulter Chumbley of Nashville, Tennessee, USA. *Residence*,
Tam-na-Marghaidh, Balquhidder, Perthshire.   *Club*, RAF.

Daughters living—By 1st marriage—Julia Noble Bine, *b.* 1914: *m.* 1940, Capt. Edward
William Whitfield, Indian Army, and has issue living, Michael Stephen (3rd Dragoon Gds.,
BFPO 17, Germany), *b.* 1941; Capt. R. Scots Dragoon Gds.: *m.* 1969, Lady Fiona Catharine
Sinclair, da. of the late 19th Earl of Caithness, and has issue living, Edward James *b.* 1971,
Christina Louise *b.* 1973,—Christopher George, *b.* 1945,—Wendy Martina, *b.* 1942: *m.* 1963,
Arthur Guiffré, of Portsmouth, Rhode Island, USA, and has issue living, Christopher Paul *b.*
1965, Stephen *b.* 1966, Karen Elizabeth *b.* 1963,—Diana Mary, *b.* 1952. *Address*—PO Box 721,
Marendellas, Rhodesia.——(Catherina) Margot, *b.* 1917: *m.* 1945, William Robert Percy Wall,
Lt. S. African Air Force, and has issue living, Mary Jane, *b.* 1948: *m.* 1969, Louis George von
Bratt Reynolds, MB, ChB, of Capetown,—Jessica, *b.* 1950. *Residence*, Oakleigh, Greytown,
Natal.

 The 1st baronet, Sir Charles Bine Renshaw (son of the late Thomas Charles Renshaw, Q.C.,
of Sandrocks, Sussex), sat as M.P. for W. Div. of Renfrewshire (C) July 1892 to Jan. 1906.

RENWICK, Creation (U.K.) 1921, of Newminster Abbey, Morpeth, Northumberland.

FOR TRUE LIBERTY

Sir RICHARD EUSTACE RENWICK, 4th
Baronet; b. Jan. 13th, 1938; *s.* his father,
Sqdn.-Ldr. Sir EUSTACE DEUCHAR, 1973;
ed. at Eton: *m.* 1966, Caroline Anne, da. of
the late Maj. Rupert Leonard Eversley
Milburn, of Ghyllheugh, Longhorsley, Morpeth
[see Milburn, Bt.], and has issue.

 Arms—Per chevron sable and argent, in chief two
lymphads of the second and in base on a mount vert a horse
courant of the first. Crest—In front of a lion's head erased
proper, a bugle horn stringed gules.

 Residence—Whalton House, Whalton, Morpeth,
Northumberland.

Sons living—CHARLES RICHARD, *b.* April 10th, 1967.——
Harry Timothy, *b.* 1968.——a son, *b.* 1975.

Brother living—George Eustace, *b.* 1947; ed. at Eton.

Sister living—Julia Diana, *b.* 1935: *m.* 1957, Jervis
Joscelyn Percy, and has issue living, Corinna Josceline,
b. 1964,—Jane Diana, *b.* 1966,—Charlotte Elizabeth,
b. 1967. *Residence*, Cross House, Stamfordham,
Northumberland.

Uncle living (son of 2nd baronet)—Dudley Cyril Deuchar
(Bowfell Close, Bowness-in-Windermere), *b.* 1907.

Aunt living (daughter of 2nd baronet)—Wendy Deuchar, *b.* 1910: *m.* 1955, Joseph Alexander
Archibald Farrow, of Cawton Cottage, Hovingham, Yorks.

Widow living of 3rd Baronet—DIANA MARY, (*Diana, Lady Renwick*), (Whalton, Northumberland),
da. of Col. Bernard Cruddas, DSO, of Middleton Hall, Morpeth: *m.* 1934, Sqdn.-Ldr. Sir Eustace
Deuchar Renwick, 3rd Bt., who *d.* 1973.

Collateral Branches living.
 Issue of the late William Henry Renwick, 2nd son of 1st baronet, *b.* 1880, *d.*
1961 : *m.* 1899, Ethel Maud, who *d.* 1944, da. of William Ratcliffe :—
Eric Montagu, *b.* 1904: *m.* 1956 (m. diss. 1960), Marie Sandra, da. of   .——Aubrey
Forster, *b.* 1912.——Alexandra Constance, *b.* 1902.——Dorothy Forster, *b.* 1905.——Pamela
Mary, *b.* 1920.

Issue of the late George Renwick, 3rd son of 1st baronet; b. 1881, d. 1937: m. 1906, Nina, da. of John Best Ferrier :—
Peter, b. 1913.——Peggy, b. 1907: m. 1931, Claude Chessher Darling, and has issue living, David, b. 1932,—Timothy, b. 1944,—Diana Jane, b. 1938: m. 1968, Peter George Cary Summers, and has issue living, Jonathan Peter b. 1969.

Issue of the late Gustav Adolph Renwick, 4th son of 1st baronet, b. 1883, d. 1956: m. 1907, Mabel, who d. 1968, da. of James Deuchar:—
Denis Adolph (Holystone Grange, Sharperton, Morpeth), b. 1907: m. 1934, Phyllis Atkinson, and has issue living, Guy Philip (Lower Mill, Old Basing, Hants.), b. 1936; late 2nd Lt. R. Scots: m. 1966, Melanie, da. of H. J. Franklin, of 10, Markham Sq., SW3, and has issue living, Shaun Maurice b. 1970, Maxwell Mark b. 1972.

Issue of the late Septimus Renwick, MC, Scots Guards, 5th son of 1st baronet, b. 1886, d. 1966: m. 1916, Margaret (Upend, Newmarket, Suffolk), da. of James Turnbull:—
George Lionel (Upend, Newmarket, Suffolk), b. 1917.——Barbara (Upend, Newmarket, Suffolk), b. 1922.

The 1st baronet, Sir George Renwick (son of the late John Nixon Renwick, of Newcastle upon Tyne) was a member of the firm of Fisher Renwick & Co., shipowners and brokers of Newcastle, and Managing Director of Fisher Renwick Manchester-London Steamers, Ltd. ; he sat as M.P. for Newcastle-on-Tyne (C) Oct. 1900 to Jan. 1906. and Sept. 1908 to Jan. 1910, and for Central Division thereof Dec. 1918 to Oct. 1922.

REYNOLDS, Creation (U.K.) 1923, of Woolton, Co. Lancaster.

By persevering.

Sir DAVID JAMES REYNOLDS, 3rd *Baronet*; b. Jan. 26th, 1924 ; s. his father, *Lieut.-Col. Sir* JOHN FRANCIS ROSKELL, *M.B.E.*, 1956; ed. at Downside; 1942-45 War in Italy as Capt. 15/19th Hussars: m. 1966, Charlotte Baumgartner, and has issue.

Arms—Per chevron ermine and or, in chief two lions passant gules, and in base three leopards' faces sable. Crest—A demi moorcock displayed proper, charged on each wing with a leopard's face or.
Residence—Blanchpierre, Rue de la Blanchpierre, St. Lawrence, Jersey.

Son living—JAMES, b. July 10th, 1971.
Daughters living—Lara, b. 1967.——Sophie, b. 1968.
Half-Brother living—John Julian, b. 1942: m. 1966, (m. diss. 1970), Carolyn Anne, da. of Capt. Hector Lorenzo Christie [see M. Zetland].
Sister living—Hermione Mary Elizabeth, b. 1922: m. 1948, Edward Raymond Courage, CBE, of Edgecote, Banbury, Oxon., and 16, Alexandra Court, Queens Gate, S.W.7.
Half-Sister living—Mary Merilyn, b. 1935: m. 1954 (marriage dissolved 1963), Peter Guy Henry Thorold [see Thorold, Bt., colls.].
Uncles living (sons of 1st baronet)—James Roskell, T.D., b. 1904; ed. at Downside, and at Merton Coll., Oxford ; formerly a Partner in the firm of Reynolds and Gibson, cotton brokers, of Liverpool ; is a Freeman of the City of Padua, and a Cavalere of Order of Merit of Italy ; formerly Major Duke of Lancaster's Own Yeo.; European War 1939-45 : m. 1931, Helen Mary, el. da. of the late Charles Richard Gillow, of Leighton Hall, co. Lancaster, and has issue living, Richard James Gillow, b. 1933 ; ed. at Ampleforth; Lt. Irish Guards,—Simon Anthony, b. 1939. Residence, Leighton Hall, Carnforth, Lancs.——William Francis Roskell, b. 1911; 1939-45 War as Maj. Irish Guards: m. 1934, Nancy Planché, da. of Rupert Bendall, and has issue living, Nicholas Francis (Vine House, 11, The Vineyard, Richmond, Surrey; RAC), b. 1938; ed. at Downside, and Ch. Ch., Oxford (MA); late 2nd Lt. I.G.: m. 1964, Wendy Helen Broke, twin da. of the late Lt. Nigel Vere Broke Thurston, RN, and has issue living, Alexander, b. 1971, Lucy Claire Thurston, b. 1966, Charlotte Louise, b. 1967,—Juliet Mary, b. 1936: m. 1962, Neville Anthony Leonard Whitbread, ACA, of Spring House, 45, Sheen Rd., Richmond, Surrey, and has issue living, James Rupert Sinanian b. 1970, Victoria Mary, b. 1963, Alice Mary, b. 1964, Emilia Ann b. 1967. Residence, West House, Little Ann, Andover, Hants.
Aunts living (daughters of 1st baronet)—Bawn (c/o Martins Bank, 153, Sloane St., SW1), b. 1895: m. 1st, 1919, Edgar Dowler, Irish Guards, who d. 1923; 2ndly, 1924 (m. diss. in France 1932), Capt. Charles Francis Onslow Master, sometime A.D.C. to Gov. of Leeward Islands [Onslow, Bt. colls.]; 3rdly, 1933, Frank Christopher Codrington [see Codrington, Bt., cr. 1721], and has issue living, (by 1st marriage) Barbara Bawn, b. 1922: m. 1940, Richard L. Bellasis, of 2110, Clayton Drive, Menlo Park, Cal., USA, and has issue living, Philip James b. 1946, Richard Paul b. 1948, Timothy Michael b. 1959, Christopher John b. 1960, Filicity Bawn b. 1947: m. 1965, John Fairbanks, of 735, Menlo Av., Menlo Park, Cal., USA (and has issue living, John b. 1965), Angela V. b. 1953,—Delphine Mary (Hon. Mrs. Robert L. Baillieu), b. (posthumous), 1923: m. 1949, the Hon. Robert Latham Baillieu, MBE, TD [see B. Baillieu]—(by 3rd marriage) [see Codrington, Bt., cr. 1721].——Leila, b. 1896: m. 1st, 1919, Col. George Ferdinand Hay Faithfull, OBE, who d. 1942; 2ndly, 1944, Cuthbert Worsley, and has issue living, (by 1st marriage) Rhoda Elizabeth: m. 1939, Graham Partridge, JP, of Parc-y-Pratt, Cardigan, W. Wales, and has issue living, a son b. 19—, a son b. 19—, a da. b. 19—, a da. b. 19—, a da. b. 19—, a da. b. 19—.——Barbara, b. 1901: m. 1923, Gerald Cyril Russell, MC, who d. 1962 [see Russell, Bt., colls. cr. 1916]. Residence, The Covert, Aldeburgh, Suffolk.——Rhoda Clare, b. 1906; is a Nun. Residence, New Hall Convent, Chelmsford.——Delphine Rose, b. 1907: m. 1st, 1944, Arnost Polak, PhD, who d. 1948; 2ndly, 1963, John Trinick.

The 1st baronet, Sir James Philip Reynolds, D.S.O., M.P. (son of the late Francis William Reynolds, of Hillside, Woolton, Liverpool), was senior partner of Reynolds & Gibson, cotton brokers of Liverpool, a Director of Martins Bank, Ltd., of The Royal Insurance Co. (Limited), Liverpool London and Globe Insurance Co. (Limited), and Thames and Mersey Marine Insurance Co.

(Limited), a J.P. and D.L., and M.P. for Exchange Div. of Liverpool (*U*) 1929-32. **The 2nd baronet,** Sir John Francis Roskell Reynolds, M.B.E., was a partner of Reynolds & Gibson, Chm. of Combined English Mills (Spinners) Ltd., and Lieut.-Col. Irish Guards.

RHODES, Creation (U.K.) 1919, of Hollingworth, co. Palatine of Chester.

By good ways.

Sir JOHN CHRISTOPHER DOUGLAS RHODES, 4th *Baronet; b.* May 24th, 1946; *s.* his father, *Lt.-Col. Sir* CHRISTOPHER GEORGE, 1964.

Arms—Azure, on a bend between two lozenges or a leopard's face gules between two holly leaves vert. Crest—Two lions' gambs erased gules supporting a lozenge charged with a holly leaf, both as in the arms.

Residence—86, High Street, Blakeney, Holt, Norfolk.

————

Brother living—MICHAEL PHILIP JAMES, *b.* April 3rd, 1948.

Sister living—Ursula Catherine, *b.* 1944: *m.* 1967, Capt. Peter Roberts, RA.

Grandmother living—Elsie Constance, da. of Lt.-Col. George Alexander Maclean Buckley, CBE, DSO: *m.* 1913, Lt.-Col. Sir John Phillips Rhodes, DSO, 2nd baronet, who *d.* 1955, and from whom she had obtained a divorce 1926. *Residence,*

Widows living of 2nd and 3rd Baronets—DORIS MARY (*Doris, Lady Rhodes*), da. of William H. Adams: *m.* 1926, as his second wife, Lt.-Col. Sir John Phillips Rhodes, DSO, 2nd baronet, who *d.* 1955.——MARY FLORENCE (*Lady Rhodes*) (of 86, High St., Blakeney, Holt, Norfolk), da. of the late Dr. Douglas Wardleworth: m. 1943, as his second wife, Lt.-Col. Sir Christopher George Rhodes, 3rd baronet, who *d.* 1964.

Collateral Branch living.

    Issue of the late Com. Philip Wood Rhodes, R.N. (retired), 3rd son of 1st baronet, *b.* 1894, *d.* 1956 : *m.* 1st, 1919, Judith Beresford, who *d.* 1942, da. of Trevelyan Martin; 2ndly, 1944, Elspeth (9, Serena Court, Cottesloe, W. Aust.), da. of T. Tod, of Durban:—

(By 1st marriage) Pamela Beresford, *b.* 1920: *m.* 1944, Peter Coleclough, of Little Burstead House, Billericay, Essex, and has issue living, Jeremy Nigel, *b.* 1945,—Martin Timothy, *b.* 1947.——Vivien Patricia (of 5, Dukes Lodge, Holland Park, W.11), *b.* 1927.

    Sir George Rhodes, 1st Bt., was a J.P. for Cheshire. Lt.-Col. Sir John Phillips Rhodes, DSO, late R.E., 2nd Bt., was Chm. of Thomas Rhodes (Limited), cotton spinners and manufacturers, of Hollingworth, Cheshire, and sat as M.P. for Cheshire, Stalybridge and Hyde Div. (*C*) 1922-23.

Rhys-Williams, see Williams.

RICH, Creation (G.B.) 1791, of Shirley House, Hants.

Keep thy faith.

Sir ALMERIC FREDERIC CONNESS RICH, 6th *Baronet; b.* Feb. 9th, 1897; *s.* his father, *Sir* ALMERIC EDMUND FREDERIC, 1948; European War 1914-19 as Lieut. R.G.A. ; was in H.M.'s Borstal Ser. 1932-61.

Arms—Gules, a chevron erminois between three crosses botoné or.   Crest—A wyvern argent, wings elevated ermine.

Address—c/o Westminster Bank, 1, St. James's Sq., S.W.1. *Club*—Phyllis Court (Henley-on-Thames).

————

Collateral Branches living

    Granddaughter of the late Henry George William Rich, 4th son of 2nd baronet :—
Issue of the late Henry Ross Rich, *b.* 1848, *d.* 1890 : *m.* 1884, Henrietta Georgina (who *d.* 1943, having *m.* 2ndly, 1907, Claude Walter Kirkby), da. of the late Capt. William Probyn Hurst, formerly of the Madras Army:—

Zoe Dorothea Shirley, *b.* 1889: *m.* 1912, Reginald Simon Macnamara Creagh, Lt. Rifle Brigade, who *d.* (killed in action during European War) 1917. *Residence,*

Granddaughter of the late Gen. Arthur Newbolt Rich, 5th son of 2nd baronet:—
Issue of the late Albert Lethbridge Rich, *b.* 1863, *d.* 1940: *m.* 18— (wife *d.* 19—):—
Ruth Albertine, *b.* 18—: *m.* 1911, William Anthony Sarconi, and has issue living, William Anthony, *b.* 1913. *Residence,* 1194, South Irving, Denver, 2, Colorado, U.S.A.

Descendants, if any, of the late Henry Osborne Ludlow Rich (*b.* 1822), son of the late William Osborne Rich, 3rd son of 1st baronet, who had issue, three sons.

Grandchildren of the late Lt.-Col. Charles Edwin Frederick Rich, DSO (infra):—
Issue of the late Cdr. Charles Rodney St. John Rich, RN, *b.* 1900, *d.* 1970: *m.* 1st, 1928, (m. diss. 1936) Felicity Chesterton, da. of the late Sir George Thompson Hutchinson; 2ndly, 1937, Georgina Blanche (8, Chesham St., SW1), only da. of the late Donald Francis Napier Dalrymple, of 48, Hans Place, SW1:—
(By 1st m.) Miles Rodney St. John (32, Priestfields, Rochester, Kent), *b.* 1931; ed. at Bradfield; AMBIM; Maj. RE: *m.* 1959, Patricia Mary, only da. of George Stuart Castle, of Stone House Farm, Frindsbury, Rochester, and has issue living, Geoffrey Stuart St. John, *b.* 1969,—Alexandra Mary, *b.* 1960,—Frances Catherine St. John, *b.* 1962,—Philippa Clare St. John, *b.* 1965.——Felicity Ann, *b.* 1929: *m.* 1952, W/Cdr. Timothy William Fane de Salis, AFC, RAF, of Chimney Cottage, Coxheath Rd., Crookham, Hants., and has issue living, Timothy Jerome, *b.* 1953; ed. at Lancing,—Wendy Sara, *b.* 1955.——Deirdre Frances, *b.* 1934: *m.* 1958, Maj. James Sidney Nobbs, MBE, RE, and has issue living, Nicolas Finch, *b.* 1959,—Anthony James, *b.* 1961,—Alison Frances, *b.* 1963.

Granddaughter of the late Rev. John Rich (*b.* 1826), el. son of the Rev. John Rich (*b.* 1789), 4th son of 1st baronet:—
Issue of the late Lieut.-Col. Charles Edwin Frederick Rich, D.S.O., *b.* 1871, *d.* 1944: *m.* 1899, Violet Cecile Anne, who *d.* 1957, second da. of the late Adm. Henry Craven St. John [V. Bolingbroke, colls.]:—
Violet Laline St. John, *b.* 1906: *m.* 1931, Cdr. (E) Ronald Crawford Wagstaffe Bett, RN (ret.). *Residence,* The Cottage, Weston, nr. Shrewsbury, Salop.

Grandchildren of the late William Gordon Rich, 3rd son of the late Rev. John Rich (*b.* 1789) (ante):—
Issue of the late Edwin William Gordon Rich, *b.* 1856, *d.* 1910: *m.* (Jan.) 1897, Margaret da. of the late Cottenham Kingsford:—
William Gordon, *M.B., Ch.B., b.* (Dec.) 1897; M.B. and Ch.B. 1925; D.M.R.E. Camb. 1928, Major late New Zealand Med. Ser., and a C.St.J.; Commr. St. John Ambulance Bde., Canterbury, W. Coast Dist. 1954-8; Pres. of Federated Tuberculosis Assos. of New Zealand 1947-59; European War 1918-19 as Lieut. R.A.F.: *m.* 1st, 1931, Henrietta Dorothy, who *d.* 1955, da. of Henry Donate Tyacke, of Westmeath, Ireland; 2ndly, 1958, Rhona Elizabeth, second da. of the late Thomas Lyons, of Hobart, Tasmania, and widow of John Matthew Clarke, and has issue living, (by 1st marriage) Urquhart David Gordon, *b.* 1934; B. Agriculture; is a Solicitor, —John Patrick Gordon, *b.* 1936: *m.* 19—, Jillian, da. of Helyar Bishop, of Papanui, Christchurch, New Zealand, and has issue living, Nicola *b.* 1960, Joanna *b.* 1963. *Residence,* 18, Lambert Av., Sandy Bay 7005, Hobart, Tasmania.——Helen Gordon, *b.* 1901: *m.* 1958, Leslie Robert Macfarlane, MC. *Residence,* Kaiwara, Culverden, NZ.

Issue of the late Maitland Gordon Rich, *b.* 1858, *d.* 1919: *m.* 1888, Mabel Montgomery, who *d.* 1944, da. of the late Capt. F. W. Hutton, F.R.S., formerly Roy. Welch Fusiliers :—
Geoffrey Gordon, *M.C., b.* 1889; formerly Lieut. King Edward's Horse; European War 1914-18 (M.C.): *m.* 1924, Sybil Catherine Dorothy, da. of Major P. H. Johnson, of Mount Torlesse Station, Springfield, Canterbury, New Zealand, and has issue living, Dorothy Georgiana Gordon, *b.* 1927: *m.* 1951, Anthony Derek Morley Pinfold, of 187, Sawyers Arms Road, Papanui, Christchurch, New Zealand, and has issue living, Giles Derek *b.* 1953, Mary Kathryn *b.* 1954, Judy Cassandra *b.* 1956,—Penelope Rosamund, *b.* 1929: *m.* 1953, Frederick Gerard Ulrich, of The Rock, Cave, South Canterbury, New Zealand, and has issue living, Peter Herstall, *b.* 1954, Sally Rosamund *b.* 1956, Robyn Penelope *b.* 1957, Jan Belinda *b.* 1959,—Angela Maitland, *b.* 1932: *m.* 1957, Lennox Mounsey, Master-Mariner, of 77, Bann St., Bluff, NZ, and has issue living, Gordon Lennox *b.* 1958, Timothy John *b.* 1965, Prudence Jane *b.* 1960, Annabel Kay *b.* 1963, *Residence,* 14, Lysaght St., Timaru, NZ.——Annie Gordon, *b.* 1895: *m.* 1921, John Montgomery, who *d.* 1946, and has issue living, John Campbell, *b.* 1921,—Hugh Alexander, *b.* 1925,—Diana, *b.* 1923. *Residence,* 323, Wethells Rd., Fendalton, Christchurch, NW3, NZ.

Grandsons of the late Edwin Francis Rich, son of Vice-Adm. Edwin Ludlow Rich, 5th son of 1st baronet:—
Issue of the late Francis Arthur Rich, *b.* 1859, *d.* 1938: *m.* 1st, 1890, Mary Catherine, who *d.* 1899, da. of Gerard Spooner, formerly of Elmdon, Warwickshire; 2ndly, 1899, Henrietta, da. of Gerard Spooner (ante) :—
(By 2nd marriage) Ronald Philip, *b.* 1900.——Edwin Francis, *b.* 1903. *Residence,*

This family was originally of Hampshire. In 1284, John le Rich, of Rich Place, Hants, flourished; his great-grandson, Richard Rich, an opulent mercer of London, was sheriff of that city, 1441; his great-grandson, Sir Richard Rich, Solicitor-Gen. to Henry VIII., was, upon the accession of Edward VI., created in Feb. 1547 Baron Rich, of Leeze, co. Essex, and in Nov. of that year was constituted Lord High Chancellor of England, and in 1564 founded a Grammar School at Felstead in Essex; his great-grandson, Robert Rich, P.C., 2nd Earl of Warwick, a very distinguished personage during the Civil War, was Lord High Admiral of England, and Lord-Lieut. of Norfolk and Essex; the Long Parliament conferred upon him the exceptional honour of voting that he should be created a Duke, and he would have been promoted to that dignity had the treaty between Charles I. and the Parliament been completed. The Earl's younger brother, Sir Henry, K.G. (owner of Holland House, Kensington), the most accomplished courtier of his time, having in 1622 been created Baron Kensington, was successively employed to negotiate a marriage between Prince Charles (afterwards Charles I.) and the Spanish Infanta, and to sound the French Court regarding a consort for the Prince; in 1624, he was advanced to the dignity of Earl of Holland; he subsequently took up arms for the Royal Cause, for which in 1689 he suffered decapitation before the gates of Westminster Hall. The Earldoms of Warwick and Holland became united in 1673, and in 1759 they expired. Charles, 4th son of Sir Edward Rich, 3rd son of the 2nd Baron Rich, was created a baronet in 1675, which title passed by special limitation to his son-in-law, Robert Rich, a Lord of the Admiralty, and M.P. for Dunwich, *temp.* William III.; his 2nd son, Field-Marshal Sir Robert, the 4th baronet, was successively M.P. for Dunwich, Beeralston, and St. Ives; Col. 4th Dragoons, and Governor of Chelsea Hospital; he died 1768 and was succeeded by his son, Sir Robert, 5th baronet. at whose death in 1785 the baronetcy expired, and the estates devolved upon his only daughter Mary Frances, wife of the Rev. Charles Bostock, LL.D. (descended from the Bostocks of Bostock, Cheshire), of Shirley House, Hants, who in 1790 assumed, by Roy. licence, the surname and arms of Rich and was in 1791 created a baronet.

RICHARDSON, Creation (U.K.) 1924, of Yellow Woods Province of Cape of Good Hope, South Africa.

By courage, faith and honour.

Sir LESLIE LEWIS RICHARDSON, 2nd *Baronet*; *b.* Aug. 14th, 1915; *s.* his father, *Sir* LEWIS, *C.B.E.*, 1934; ed. at Harrow; is a Member of the firm of L. Richardson & Co., of Port Elizabeth ; N. Africa 1942-43 with S. African Artillery : *m.* 1946, Joy Patricia, da. of J. P. Rillstone, of Johannesburg, S. Africa, and has issue.

Arms—Argent, an ostrich proper, on a chief sable three lions' heads erased of the field. Crest—Upon a rock a lion rampant guardant proper resting the sinister paw on a mullet, gold.

Residences—Old Vineyard, Constantia, Cape Town, S. Africa ; Yellowwoods, Witteklip, E. Cape Province, S. Africa.

Sons living—ANTHONY LEWIS, *b.* Aug. 5th, 1950.—— Charles John, *b.* 1955.

Daughter living.—Jennifer, *b.* 1947.

Sister living—Audrey Anne, *b.* 1909 : *m.* 1939, John Henry Muers-Raby, and has issue living, Nicholas Jonathan, *b.* 1941,—Nigel Andrew, *b.* 1949. *Residence*, Brook Farm, N. Curry, Taunton.

The 1st baronet, Sir Lewis Richardson, C.B.E. (son of Kaufmann Richardson), was head of the firm of L. Richardson & Co., of Port Elizabeth, London, New York, and Boston.

RICHARDSON, Creation (U.K.) 1929, of Weybridge, co. Surrey.

Go on as thou hast begun.

Sir GEORGE WIGHAM RICHARDSON, 3rd *Baronet*; *b.* April, 12th, 1895; *s.* his brother, *Sir* WILLIAM WIGHAM, *MBE*, 1973: *m.* 1st, 1923, (*m. diss.* 1937) Adela Nancy, da. of the late A. O. Davies; 2ndly, 1944, Barbara, da. of the late Harry Clements Aasell, of Sutton Coldfield, and has issue by 2nd m.

Arms—Argent, upon a mount vert an oak tree proper, on a chief indented sable a spur between two leopards' faces or. Crest—A dexter cubit arm in armour charged with a spur or, the hand grasping a sword proper, pomel and hilt gold.

Residence—The Old Manor House, Benenden, Kent.

Daughters living—By 2nd m.—Jenifer Winifred Wigham, *b.* 1945: *m.* 1973, David M. Drayson.——Caroline Rosa Wigham, *b.* 1950.——Patricia Barbara Wigham, *b.* 1953.

Half-Sister living—Irene Geraldine Wigham, *b.* 1919 : *m.* 1948, Donald J. Ferguson, and has issue living, Clive Wigham, *b.* 1949.—Lee Margaret, *b.* 1950. *Residence*, Elworthy Farm, Greenham, Wellington, Somerset.

The 1st baronet, Sir Philip Wigham Richardson, O.B.E., V.D. (el. son of the late John Wigham Richardson, of Hindley Hall, Stocksfield), was a Ship and Insurance Broker, and Brevet Lieut.-Col. 5th (Vol.) Batn. Northumberland Fusiliers, and sat as M.P. for Surrey, Chertsey Div. (*U*) 1922-31.

RICHARDSON, Creation (U.K.) 1963, of Ecclesall, West Riding of Yorkshire.

Sir JOHN SAMUEL RICHARDSON, *MVO*, 1st *Baronet*, son of the late Maj. John Watson Richardson, of Sheffield [Roberts Bt. (cr. 1919)]; *b.* June 16th, 1910; ed. at Charterhouse, and at Trin. Coll., Camb. (MA, BChir, MD); FRCP London; FRCP Ed; a Consulting Physician St. Thomas's Hospital since 1947, to Metropolitan Police since 1957, and to Army and to London Transport since 1964; Chm. Central Council for Postgraduate Med. Educ. in England and Wales since 1972; Hon. Master of The Bench of Gray's Inn 1974; Pres. of Gen. Med. Council 1973-77, Chm. of Joint Consultants Cttee. 1967-1972, Pres. of R. Soc. of Medicine 1969-71, and British Med. Assocn. 1970-71, Master of Soc. of Apothecaries of London 1971-72; Pres. of International Soc. of Internal Med. 1966-70; 1939-45 War, as Lt.-Col. RAMC; MVO (4th Class) 1943, Knt. 1960: *m.* 1933, Sybil Angela Stephanie, da. of A. Ronald Trist, of Stanmore, Middx., and has issue.

　　Arms—Sable on a fess engrailed or between in chief an open book proper bound gules edged gold between two mullets and in base a swan argent a lion passant guardant also gold. **Crest**—The head of a rhinoceros erased sable behind the horn a scroll inscribed with words " Till time ceases " (in letters gules).

Residence—Windcutter, Lee, nr. Ilfracombe, N. Devon.

Daughters living—Elizabeth-Anne, *b.* 1937: *m.* 1st, 1960 (m. diss. 1970), Angus Gavin Lockhead Jack, [*see* Inglefield-Watson, Bt., colls.]; 2ndly, 1971, Gregory Edmund Stafford, LLB, of 46, Chesilton Rd., SW6.——Susan Clare, *b.* 1940: *m.* 1970, Robert Wales (2, Thorne St., Barnes SW13), and has issue living, Duncan John Richardson, *b.* 1970.

　　This family descends from Thomas Richardson of Eckington, Derbyshire, who was bapt. 1645. Samuel Gray Richardson of Sheffield, grandfather of 1st baronet, was a cutlery manufacturer, and Master Cutler of Sheffield 1889.

STEWART-RICHARDSON, Creation (N.S.) 1630, of Pencaitland, Haddingtonshire.

Honour is gained by valour.

Sir SIMON ALAISDAIR STEWART-RICHARDSON, 17th *Baronet*; *b.* June 10th, 1947; *s.* his father, *Sir* IAN RORIE HAY, 1969; ed. at Trin. Coll., Glenalmond.

　　Arms—Quarterly of six: 1st and 6th, argent, on a fesse azure between a bull's head or in chief and in base a lymphad sable, a saltire of the field *Richardson*; 2nd, argent, a lion rampant azure within a bordure gules *Stewart*; 3rd, azure, three garbs or *Comyn*; 4th, argent on a bend azure three buckles or *Leslie*; 5th, gyronny of eight or and sable *Campbell*. **Crest**—A cubit arm in armour grasping a sword all proper. **Supporters**—*Dexter*, a wyvern, and *sinister*, an eagle wings erect, both proper.

Residence—Lynedale, Longcross, Chertsey, Surrey.

Brother living—NINIAN RORIE, *b.* Jan. 25th, 1949; Commercial Air Pilot 1969.

Sisters living—Claudia Mavis, *b.* 1946: *m.* 1970, R. Anthony Wainwright, of 29, Stratford Rd., W8. ——Roslyn Alison, *b.* 1952.

Widow living of 16th Baronet—AUDREY (Lynedale, Longcross, Surrey), da. of Claude Odlum, of Leinster Grove, Naas, co. Kildare: *m.* 1st, 1944, as his 2nd wife, Sir Ian Rorie, Hay-Stewart-Richardson, 16th baronet, who *d.* 1969; 2ndly, 1975, Patrick Allan Pearson Robertson.

Collateral Branches living.

　　Issue of the late Lieut.-Col. Neil Graham Stewart-Richardson, D.S.O., 3rd son of 14th baronet; *b.* 1881, *d.* 1934: *m.* 1924, Alexandra, who *d.* 1972, da. of the late Peter Ralli, of 11, Hyde Park Gardens, W.:—

Peter Neil Ralli, *MBE* (Creake Abbey, Fakenham, Norfolk), *b.* 1926; ed. at Eton; Col. Gen. Staff.; MBE (Mil.) 1964: *m.* 1954, Patricia Ann, da. of the late Maj. John Michael Evans, Lombe, MC, RA, and has issue living, Neil Graham John, *b.* 1955,—Michael Peter Alastair, *b.* 1957,—Mary-Ann, *b.* 1961,—Katharine Jane, *b.* 1966.——Alastair Lucas Graham (120, Woodsford Sq., W14 8DT; 7, King's Bench Walk, Temple, EC4) *b.* 1927; ed. at Eton, and at Magdalene Coll., Camb.; Bar. Inner Temple 1952: *m.* 1969, Diana Claire, yr. da. of the late Brig. George Streynsham Rawstorne, CBE, MC, and has issue living, James George, *b.* 1971,—Sarah Alexandra, *b.* 1974.

　　Grandchildren of the late Henry Gresham Stewart-Richardson, 2nd son of 13th baronet:—
　　Issue of the late Charles Robert Stewart-Richardson, *b.* 1877, *d.* 1954: *m.* 1905, Edith, who *d.* 1950, 2nd da. of Albert Berryman, formerly of Bath:—
Alistair De Vere (Australian, Union and Pioneers Clubs), *b.* 1906; Dep. Gen. Manager of Bank of NSW, Sydney: *m.* 1944, Joan Wilson, da. of the late Edward Wilson Hunt, of Lane Cove, NSW, and has issue living, Donald Bruce, *b.* 1946.——Dudley Austin (322, Hector St., Tuart Hill, W. Aust.), *b.* 1924: *m.* 1948, Barbara Jean Clark, and has issue living, Kenneth John, *b.* 1950,—

Peter Dudley, b. 1953.——Beatrice Edith, b. 1909: m. 1948, Clive Edwards.——Constance, b. 1918: m. 1941, Harry Hatch, and has issue living, Geoffrey Neil, b. 1943,——Brian Richard, b. 1946,—Lorraine Elizabeth, b. 1950.——Sadie Mary, b. 1921: m. 1963, Frank Chinnock, of Mt. Barker, W. Aust.

Issue of the late John Henry Stewart-Richardson, b. 1879, d. 1952 : m. 1924, Anne, da. of the late Thomas Jackson, of Carnforth, Lancashire :—
Ian Douglas, b. 1925. *Residence.*

Grandchildren of the late John Ramsay Stewart-Richardson, 3rd son of 13th baronet :—
Issue of the late Arthur James Stewart-Richardson, b. 1884, d. 1950 : m. 1913, Kathleen Mary, who d. 1964, da. of the late Charles Hunter, of Cambridge, New Zealand:—
Edward James, b. 1915; 1939-45 War with RNZAF: m. 1948, Heather Gladys, da. of Charles Scott, of Auckland, and has issue living, John Scott, b. 1950; ed. at King's Coll., Auckland, and Auckland Univ.,—Julia, b. 1954; ed. at St. Cuthberts Sch. for Girls, Auckland. *Residence,* 5, Jellicoe Rd., Matamata, Waikato, NZ.——John Charles, b. 1925; 1939-45 War with RNZAF: m. 1950, Edith Margaret, da. of Percival McIver, of Wellington, NZ, and has issue living, Ian, b. 1954,—June, b. 1950.——Kathleen Sheila, b. 1921 : m. 1946, Derek Pocknall, and has issue living, Robert, b. 1949;—Graeme (twin), b. 1949,—David Thomas, b. 1953,—Susan Mary, b. 1948,—Helen Jean, b. 1958. *Address,* Rawhiti, P.B. Masterton, New Zealand.——Barbara Mary, b. 1930: m. 1st, 1950, Harold Vosper, who d. 1960; 2ndly, 1962, Peter G. Wilson, of Piarere RD1, Tirau, Waikato, NZ, and has issue living, (by 1st m.), Frank, b. 1951,—Richard, b. 1953,—Jennifer Kay, b. 1954;—(by 2nd m.), Stewart James, b. 1968,—Robyn Jane, b. 1963.

Issue of the late Evelyn Mary Stewart-Richardson, d. 1957: m. 1910, Charles Willand McBride :—
Patrick Stewart, b. 1918 ; European War 1939-45 with Roy. New Zealand Air Force (despatches): m. 1946, Renna Winifred (McINTYRE), da. of the late Walter Frederick Cast, of Bideford, Devon. *Residence,* Tubwell Farm, Horam, Sussex.——Vaarie Stewart, b. 1914 : m. 1939, Victor Edwin Jaynes, of Hurstmere Rd., Auckland, New Zealand.——Josephine Stewart, b. 1923: m. 19—, John Foote. *Residence,* Killarney St., Takapuna, Auckland, New Zealand.

Sir Robert Richardson of Pencaitland, Haddingtonshire, was created a baronet with remainder to heirs male whatsoever. On the death of the 2nd baronet 1640, the title passed to Sir James Richardson of Smeaton, grandson of Sir James, el. brother of 1st baronet. This baronetcy was dormant 1821-37, when John Stewart-Richardson assumed the title on being served heir of the 12th baronet. The mother of the 13th baronet was Elizabeth, el. da. and co-heir of James Stewart of Urrard, Perths. The 15th baronet, Sir Edward Austin, Capt. Black Watch; d. (of wounds in action) 1914.

Richardson-Bunbury, see Bunbury

RICHMOND, Creation (U.K.) 1929, of Hollington, co. Sussex.

Sir JOHN FREDERICK RICHMOND, 2nd *Baronet*; b. Aug. 12th, 1924 ; s. his father, *Sir* FREDERICK HENRY, 1953 ; ed. at Eton, and at Jesus Coll., Camb.; formerly Lieut. 10th R. Hussars: m. 1965, Mrs. Anne Moreen Bentley, da. of the late Dr. Robert William Paylor Hall, MC, and has issue.

Arms—Gules, on a fesse cotissed or, between two roses argent, barbed and seeded proper, a lion passant of the field. Crest—A demi-stag proper, charged on the shoulder with a rose as in the arms, and holding between the forelegs a rose argent, barbed, seeded, leaved, and slipped, also proper. *Residence*—Shimpling Park Farm, Bury St. Edmunds, Suffolk. *Club*—Cavalry.

Daughter living—Caroline Sarah, b. 1966.
Widow living of 1st Baronet—DOROTHY AGNES (*Lady Richmond*), da. of Francis Joseph Sheppard : m. 1921, Sir Frederick Henry Richmond, 1st baronet, who d. 1953. *Residence,* 21, Wellington Court, Knightsbridge, S.W.1.
Sister living—Anne Elizabeth, b. 1926 : m. 1958, Dudley William Reeves, and has issue living, Nicholas Mark Renny, b. 1964,—Heather Jennifer, b. 1962. *Residence,* West Farm, Hinwick, Wellingborough, Northants.

The 1st baronet, Sir Frederick Henry Richmond (son of the late Henry Richmond, of Marnham), was Chm. of Debenhams, Ltd., of 91, Wimpole Street, W.1, and of Harvey Nichols and Co., Ltd.

L'ABOR·VINCIT
Labour conquers.

RICKETTS, Creation (U.K.) 1828, of The Elms, Gloucestershire, and Beaumont-Leye, Leicestershire.

Sir ROBERT CORNWALLIS GERALD ST. LEGER RICKETTS, 7th *Baronet ;* b. Nov. 8th, 1917 ; s. his father, *Sir* CLAUDE ALBERT FREDERICK, 1937 ; ed. at Haileybury, and at Magdalene Coll., Camb. (MA); admitted a Solicitor 1949; a FRSA; Partner in Wellington and Clifford; 1939-45 War as Capt. Devonshire Regt.; Personal Assist. to Ch. of Staff, Gibraltar, 1942-45 and ADC to Lt.-Gov. of Jersey 1945-46; Hon. Citizen of Mobile, Alabama, USA: m. 1945, Anne Theresa, da. of the late Rt. Hon. Sir (Richard) Stafford Cripps, CH, QC [see B. Parmoor, colls.], and has issue.

Prend moi tel que je suis.
Take me as I am.

Arms—On a chevron azure between three roses gules, barbed and seeded proper, two swords in chevron also proper, pommels and hilts or, their points crossing each other in saltire (that on the dexter surmounted by that of the sinister) and passing through a wreath of laurel or ; on a chief of the second a naval crown between two anchors erect or. Crest—

Out of a naval crown or, a dexter arm embowed, habited azure and charged on the sleeve with two roses argent, the hand grasping a scimitar, the arm in front of an anchor in bend sinister sable.

Residence—Forwood House, Minchinhampton, Gloucestershire.   *Club*, New (Cheltenham).

Sons living—ROBERT TRISTRAM (62, Walkerscroft Mead, SE21), *b.* April 17th, 1946; ed. at Winchester, and Magdalene Coll., Camb. (MA): *m.* 1969, Ann, yr. da. of Eric William Charles Lewis, CB, of 31, Deana Close, Queen's Drive, W3, and has issue living, Stephen Tristram, *b.* 1974.——John Stafford, *b.* 1956; ed. at Winchester, and King's Coll., London.

Daughters living—Sarah Lilian, *b.* 1947.——Isobel Theresa, *b.* 1952.

Sister living—Alice May Mildred Lilian, *b.* 1907: *m.* 1927, Col. Richard René Dauban, RA, who *d.* 1967, and has issue living, Desmond Charles (Bengal House, Elm Av., Attenborough, Nottingham), *b.* 1932: *m.* 1958, Shirley, only child of the late W. Hartley, of Cleethorpes, Lincs., and has issue living, Mark Adrian *b.* 1959, Annette Lynn *b.* 1960, Tina Clare *b.* 1961,—Daphne Cynthia, *b.* 1930: *m.* 1955, John Henry Bowling, of Foxcombe, Burkes Rd., Beaconsfield, Bucks., and has issue living, Timothy Edmund *b.* 1963, Richard Tristram *b.* 1965, Julie Vanessa *b.* 1956, Tessa May *b.* 1958,—Valerie Jill, *b.* 1934: *m.* 1956, D. J. Sillavan, of Field Cottage, Kerridge, nr. Macclesfield, Cheshire, and has issue living, Nicholas David *b.* 1959, Melanie *b.* 1957, Alice *b.* 1962.   *Residence*, Meavy, 102, Farley Rd., Selsdon, Surrey.

Widow living of 6th Baronet—NATALIE (*Dowager Lady Ricketts*), widow of Capt. T. F. Hazeldine, 2nd C.M.Rs.: *m.* 1936, as his second wife, Sir Claude Albert Frederick Ricketts, 6th baronet, who *d.* 1937.   *Residence*, Westwood House, Westwood Park, Droitwich, Worcestershire.

Collateral Branches living.

Issue of the late Constance Charlotte Rose Ricketts, who *d.* 1932, da. of 2nd baronet : *m.* 1887, the Rev. Charles Edward Stuart Ratcliffe, M.A., who *d.* 1928 :—

Grace Pelham Clinton, *b.* 1893: *m.* 1917, Brig.-Gen. St. George Edward William Burton, formerly Black Watch, who *d.* 1940.   *Residence*,

Grandchildren of the late Rev. Richard Ernest Ricketts (infra) :—
Issue of the late Rt. Rev. Clement Mallory Ricketts, formerly Suffragan Bishop of Dunwich, *b.* 1885, *d.* 1961: *m.* 1920, Dorothy Frances (Nyetimber Forge, Bognor Regis, Sussex), da. of the late Rt. Rev. George Rodney Eden, DD [*see* Eden, Bt., colls.] :—
Michael Rodney, *b.* 1923 (Headmaster's House, Sutton Valence Sch., Maidstone); ed. at Sherborne and at Trin. Coll., Oxford (MA); formerly Maj. KRRC; since when Headmaster of Sutton Valence Sch.; 1939-45 War (wounded): *m.* 1958, Judith Anne Caroline, el. da. of the late Col. Thomas Stanley Courtenay-Clack, TD, RA, and widow of H. J. Corry, and has issue living, Charles Michael Thomas, *b.* 1960,—James Rodney Eden, *b.* 1964,—Rosemary Courtenay, *b.* 1958,—Katharine Elizabeth, *b.* 1962.——John Eden (No. 3, North Copse, Worksop College, Worksop, Notts.), *b.* 1926; ed. at Sherborne, and at Trin. Coll., Oxford (MA); formerly in RM; Housemaster of School House, Worksop Coll. 1959-74: *m.* 1970, Isobel Claridge, da. of the late Charles Claridge Druce, of Flishinghurst, Cranbrook, Kent, and has issue living, Michael Tristram *b.* 1971, Christopher Eden *b.* 1973.——Rosemary Ellison, *b.* 1928; ed. at Cheltenham Ladies' Coll.: *m.* 1949, the Rev. Frank Richard Knight Hare, of Wramplingham Rectory, Wymondham, Norfolk, and has issue living, Roger John, *b.* 1957,—Elizabeth, *b.* 1952: *m.* 1972, Richard Cane.

Granddaughter of the late Com. Simpson Hicks Ricketts, R.N., 3rd son of 1st baronet:—
Issue of the late Rev. Richard Ernest Ricketts, *b.* 1856, *d.* 1941 : *m.* 1884, Mabel Rose, who *d.* 1956, da. of the late Major Arthur Wellesley Williams, 10th Hussars [Williams-Bulkeley, Bt., colls.] :—
Violet Mabel, *b.* 1889.   *Residence*, 6, St. Peter Street, Norton, Malton, Yorkshire.

The 1st baronet, Sir Robert Tristram Ricketts, D.C.L., was a Vice-Admiral, and the 2nd baronet was an Admiral.   The 3rd baronet in 1884 succeeded to the estates of his maternal uncle (Col. Thomas R. Plumbe-Tempest), and assumed by Roy. licence in that year the surname of Tempest in lieu of his patronymic.

RIDDELL, Creation (N.S.) 1628, of Riddell, Roxburghshire.

Sir JOHN CHARLES BUCHANAN RIDDELL, 13th *Baronet* ; *b.* Jan. 3rd, 1934 ; *s.* his father, *Sir* WALTER ROBERT BUCHANAN, 1934 ; ed. at Eton, and at Ch. Ch., Oxford: *m.* 1969, Sarah, da. of Gordon William Humphreys Richardson, MBE, of Chelsea, SW3, and has issue.

Arms—Argent, a chevron gules between three ears of rye slipped and bladed vert.   **Crest**—A demi-greyhound argent.   **Supporters**—Two greyhounds argent.

Residences,—Hepple, Morpeth, Northumberland; 31, Woodsford Sq., W14.

Son living—WALTER JOHN, *b.* June 10th, 1974.
Sisters living—Jean (*Lady Pumphrey*), *b.* 1920: *m.* 1945, Sir John Laurence Pumphrey, KCMG, c/o Lloyds Bank, 46, Victoria St., SW1, and has issue living, Matthew James, *b.* 1946,—Charles Walter Bartholomew, *b.* 1948,—Jonathan Henry, *b.* 1954,—James Laurence, *b.* 1964,—Laura Mary Beatrice, *b.* 1951.——Mary, *b.* 1922: *m.* 1954, Richard Laurence Ollard, of 34, Dartmouth Row, SE10, and has issue living, William Richard, *b.* 1957,—Edward Christopher, *b.* 1959,—Elizabeth Rachel, *b.* 1961.——Anne, *b.* 1924.——Hester, *b.* 1927: *m.* 1956, Christopher Henry Pemberton, of 7, Eastbrook Rd., SE3, and has issue living, Alexander John, *b.* 1957,—Richard Mark, *b.* 1961,—Daniel Hugh Vincent, *b.* 1962,—Thomas William, *b.* 1964,—Isobel Beatrice, *b.* 1959.

Collateral Branches living.

Issue of the late Lt.-Col. Robert George Buchanan Riddell, next brother of
11th baronet, *b.* 1854, *d.* (killed in action in S. Africa) 1900: *m.* 1895, Agnes
Graham, who *d.* 1955, da. of Sir William Henry Houldsworth, M.P., 1st
Bt.:—

Margaret Frances, *b.* 1896: *m.* 1924, Lieut.-Col. Stafford Hubert Ferrand, D.S.O., M.C., King's
Roy. Rifle Corps (ret.), and has issue living, Robert Stafford (The Old Rectory, Wath, Ripon,
Yorks.), *b.* 1926; is Capt. (ret.) King's Roy. Rifle Corps: *m.* 1957, Anne Gillian, only da. of the late
A. D. Grant, of Oxford, and has issue living, Arabella Catharine *b.* 1958, Rebecca Catharine *b.*
1962,—David Francis, *TD* (Aythorpe Roding House, Dunmow, Essex), *b.* 1927: *m.* 1955, Bettine
Eva Frances, only da. of Humphrey B. Davie, of Stanton-in-Peak, Derbyshire, and has issue
living, Richard Davie *b.* 1956, Thomas David *b.* 1966, Flora Elizabeth Frances *b.* 1959,—Roger
William (of Brownings Orchard, Farringdon, Alton, Hants.), *b.* 1930: *m.* 1954, Joycelyn Kemble,
el. da. of C. H. L. Bubb, of Brook House, Cricklade, Wilts., and has issue living, Charles Robert
b. 1955, Victoria Jane *b.* 1958,—Margaret Agnes, *b.* 1934. *Residence*, Howden Lodge, Spennithorne, Leyburn, Yorks.

Grandson of the late Thomas Alexander RIDDELL-CARRE, son of the late
Walter Riddell-Carre, 2nd son of the late Thomas Riddell (*b. 1777*) (infra) :—
Issue of the late Major Ralph Gervase RIDDELL-CARRE, *b.* 1868, *d.* 1941: *m.* 1905,
Kathleen Sadleir Lawe, who *d.* 1948, da. of the late Col. F. S. Stoney, J.P. (formerly
R.A.), of The Downs, Delgany, co. Wicklow, and widow of Lieut. John Hamilton
Elrington Allen, R.N.:—
Gervase Robert, *b.* 1906: ed. at Harrow; Sqdn. Ldr. RAFVR: *m.* 1940, Eileen Inez, only da. of the
late John Tweedie, of Edradour, North Berwick, and has issue living, Ralph John (6, Westside,
55, Priory Rd., NW6), *b.* 1941: *m.* 1972, Valerie Caroline Wells, only da. of W. T. W. Tickler, of
Whiteladies, Frinton-on-Sea,—Walter Gervase, *b.* 1944. *Residence*, Cavers Carre, Melrose,
Roxburghshire. *Club*, New (Edinburgh).

Grandson of the late Col. Thomas William CARRE RIDDELL, V.D. (infra) :—
Issue of the late Col. Consett CARRE RIDDELL, D.S.O., V.D., B.Sc. B.M.E., M.I.E. (Aust.),
b. 1887, *d.* 1953: *m.* 1923, Thora, who *d.* 1963, da. of J. L. Menzies:—
John Walter Carre, *MB*, *BS*, *b.* 1925; ed. at Melbourne Univ.; Maj. Australian Army Reserve;
m. 1957, Margot Louise, only da. of R. W. Krohn, and has issue living, Malcolm John Carre,
b. 1960,—David Ronald Carre, *b.* 1966,—Fiona Carre, *b.* 1958,—Susan Patricia Carre, *b.* 1962.
Residence, 51, Sackville St., Kew, Vic. 3101, Aust.

Grandchildren of the late John Carre Riddell, 3rd son of the late Thomas Riddell
(*b.* 1777), el. son of the late William Riddell, son of the late Thomas Riddell,
(*b.* 1696), 2nd son of 4th baronet:—
Issue of the late Col. Thomas William CARRE RIDDELL, V.D., *b.* 1852, *d.* 1930: *m.* 1886,
Virginia Eleanor Consett, who *d.* 1898, da. of Montagu Consett Stephen:—
Gervase Carre, *b.* 1891 ; is Lieut. Australian Reserve of Officers ; European War 1914-19
in France and Belgium as Lieut. 33rd Batn. Australian Inf. (wounded, two medals). *Residence*, Werrill St., Swan Hill, Vic., Aust.——Yolande Sibella Carre. *Residence*, Werrill St., Swan
Hill, Vic., Aust.

Grandchildren of the late Col. Robert Vansittart Riddell, son of the late Robert
Riddell, great-grandson of the late Walter Riddell, son of the late William
Riddell, 2nd son of 2nd baronet :—
Issue of the late Col. Edward Vansittart Dick Riddell, CBE, DSO, *b.* 1873, *d.* (Sept.) 1942:
m. 1st, 1902, Edith Mary, who *d.* 1914, youngest da. of the late Maj.-Gen. E. P. Bingham
Turner, R.A. ; 2ndly, 1938, Vyvyan (from whom he obtained a divorce (Feb.) 1942), da.
of the late Rev. J. J. Lewis:—
(By 1st marriage) Edward Alexander Buchanan, *b.* 1903 ; ed. at Cheltenham Coll.; late Major
R.A.: *m.* 1st, 1928, Mary, da. of Stuart Cameron, of Vancouver, British Columbia; 2ndly,
1939, Irene Julia (BALLANCE), who *d.* 1961, da. of the late A. W. E. Bullmore, of Letchworth,
3rdly, 1962, Mary (KINGZETT), da. of the late Lieut.-Col. John Kennington, D.S.O., M.C.;
of Riby, Lincs., and has issue living (by 1st m.) Stuart Edward, *b.* 1929: *m.* 1960, Emily Spitzer,
da. of the late Whiting N. Shepard, of Montclair, New Jersey, USA, and has issue living, Cameron
Alexander, *b.* 1962, Romayne Bouvée *b.* 1964.

Issue of the late Brigadier John Balfour Riddell, D.S.O., *b.* 1880, *d.* 1960 : *m.* 1908,
Margaret Alice, who *d.* 1963, yst. da. of the late J. W. Smith of The Rectory, Oundle:—
John L'Estrange, *T.D.*, *b.* 1910 ; ed. at Oundle ; Lieut.-Col. (retired), late R.A. ; European War
1939-45 in France, Belgium, Holland and Germany (despatches), Korea 1950-53 : *m.* 1939,
Barbara Agnes, da. of the late M. McC. Fairgrieve, of Edinburgh, and has issue living, Robert
Balfour, *b.* 1940 ; ed. at Edinburgh Acad.,—John Gifford, *b.* 1942 ; ed. at Edinburgh Acad.,—
Archibald George Vansittart, *b.* 1954. *Residence*, Thornton, Penyfford, Chester.——Editha
Margaret (Wistaria Cottage, Cocking, Sussex), *b.* 1913.——Elizabeth Charity (Hawkhurst Farm,
Midhurst, Sussex), *b.* 1917: *m.* 1949, Alan Campbell Sinclair.

Granddaughters of the late William Riddell, 2nd son of the late Rev. Henry
Riddell, 2nd son of the late Henry Riddell, grandson of John Riddell, 2nd
son of the Rev. Archibald Riddell, 3rd son of 2nd baronet:—
Issue of the late John Riddell, *b.* 1895, *d.* 1959 : *m.* 1st, 1918, Doris Jones, from whom he
obtained a divorce 1923; 2ndly, 1925, Alys, (39, Ivan Leamington Ontario, Canada),
da. of John R. Savage, of Edinburgh:—
(By 1st m.) Irene Yvonne, *b.* 1919: *m.* 1943, Richard Adamson Crow, TD, Amberley, Bottom Lane,
Seer Green, Bucks., and has issue living, Richard Michael, *b.* 1944: *m.* 1964 (m. diss. 1974),
Alexandra Drysdale Love, and has issue living, Simon Richard *b.* 1969, Victoria Caroline *b.*
1965,—Michael Anthony, *b.* 1948: *m.* 1972, Penelope Laura Carter, and has issue living, Rebecca
Jane *b.* 1974.——(By 2nd m.) Audrian, *b.* 1926: *m.* 1950, William Burns Hutchinson, and has
issue living, Michael William, *b.* 1961,—Gregory John, *b.* 1962,—Janet Louise, *b.* 1954. *Residence*, 9, Lorne Av., Leamington, Ont., Canada.

Grandchildren of James Riddell, yst. son of Rev. Henry Riddell (ante):—
Issue of the late Walter Riddell, *b.* 1874, *d.* 1951: *m.* 1917, Mary Ellinor, who *d.* 1958, da.
of the late Dr. John Garbutt Hutchinson, of North Lodge, Kineton:—
John Walter Rowland, *b.* 1919.——Elizabeth Mary Ellinor, *b.* 1920: *m.* 1st, 1940, Lt.-Col. Jocelyn
Arthur Garnons-Williams, S. Wales Borderers, who *d.* (of wounds received in action in Italy)
1944; 2ndly, 1945, Maj. James Mirylees, Roy. Corps of Signals, and has issue living (by 1st m.),
Elizabeth Dawn (53, Defoe Av., Kew, Richmond, Surrey), *b.* 1941: *m.* 1st, 1965 (m. diss. 1971),
David Noel Archer Braham; 2ndly, 1973, Clive Anthony John Mitchell, and has issue living
(by 1st husband), Felicity Mary Stella *b.* 1964,—(by 2nd m.) Fiona Nora Margaret, *b.* 1945,—
Clementina Mary Stewart, *b.* 1953,—Jacqueline Frances Stewart, *b.* 1955,—Jean Sheila Riddell,
b. 1956. *Residence*, Caplemead, How Caple, Herefordshire.

Issue of the late Lt.-Col. Archibald Riddell, DSO, *b.* 1882, *d.* 1970: *m.* 1907, Edith Mary,
who *d.* 1947, da. of the late William Lawrie, of Seleng, Assam:—
William James, *MBE* (17, Hyde Park Gdns Mews, W2), *b.* 1909; late Maj. Gen. List; ed. at Harrow,
and Clare Coll., Camb.; MBE (Mil) 1944: *m.* 1959, Mrs. Jeannette Anne Oddie, who *d.* 1972,
da. of the late Edward Kessler.——Peter John Archibald, *CBE* (c/o Martins Bank, Cocks

Biddulph Branch, 16, Whitehall, SW1), b. 1914; ed. at Harrow; Group-Capt. (ret.) RAF;
1939-45 War (despatches, CBE, Officer of American Legion of Merit); CBE (Mil) 1946: m. 1940,
Cynthia Mary, da. of the late B. Crompton Wood, of Bruern Abbey, Churchill, Oxon, and has
issue living, Nicholas Peter (18, Middelton Sq., EC1), b. 1941; ed. at Harrow, and Magdalene
Coll., Camb. (BA); Bar. Inner Temple 1964: m. 1967, Felicity Jane, da. of Mrs. Rosalind Rolfe,
of 77, Eastbury Rd., Northwood, Middx., and has issue living, Eleanor Mary b. 1972,—Catherine
Mary (5, Kent Terr., NW1), b. 1944.

Grandchildren of the late William Law Riddell (infra) :—
Issue of the late Robert Riddell, b. 1879, d. 1958: m. 1908, Flora McDonald, who d. 1961,
da. of Charles Samuel George Nicholson, of Duntulm, Isle of Skye:—
William Law (Oxford St., Waimate, S. Canterbury, NZ), b. 1909: m. 1941, Jean, da. of the late
Edwin Charles Hocking, of Dunedin, New Zealand, and has issue living, Robert James (7,
Ventry St., Alexandra, Otago Central, NZ), b. 1942; B.Agric.Sc NZ: m. 1965, Marion Gwynneth,
da. of K. McIntosh, of Rangiora, N. Canterbury, NZ, and has issue living, Anna Ruth b. 1969,
Lynette Judith b. 1970,—Eleanor Mary, b. 1943: BA (NZ): m. 1964, David John Sutherland,
of School Rd., Kurow, N. Otago, NZ, and has issue living, Elliot David Law b. 1969, Meredith
Lawrie, b. 1970, Fiona Jean b. 1967,—Helen Annette, b. 1946; MA (NZ): m. 1967, Roger Beach
Balfour Mee, MD, of 5, Tennessee Av., Mangere East, Auckland, NZ, and has issue living,
Jared James Bulfow b. 1968, Nicholas Roger Alexander b. 1970.—Flora McDonald (39, Chapter
St., Christchurch, NZ), b. 1910: m. 1944, John Campbell Wilson, who d. 1964, and has issue
living, Elizabeth, b. 1946; MA (NZ):—Kathleen Olga, b. 1912: m. 1938, Nelson Marshall
Aitchison, and has issue living, John Nelson, b. 1939: m. 1968, Helen Duff, of Heriot, NZ,—
Kathleen Margaret, b. 1939: m. 1960, Kenneth Bradshaw, and has issue. Residence, Heriot,
Otago, NZ.——Charlotte Isabel, b. 1913: m. 1938, Ralph Alan Gibson, of 47, Trinity Av.,
Wellington, NZ, and has issue living, John Hastings, b. 1938; BEng (NZ): m. 1964, Barbara
Dawn Shepherd, of Timaru, S. Canterbury, NZ, and has issue,—Margaret Flora, b. 1940: m. 1961,
Murray Bennett, and has issue.——Margaret Carlina, b. 1914: m. 1939, William Kemp Paterson,
of 2, Kirrimuir St., Dunedin, NZ, and has issue living, Gaynor Margaret, b. 1941: m. 1969,
John Lyall, of Dunedin, NZ,—Roberta Joy, b. 1946; BSc (NZ): m. 1968, Ian Leslie Stephenson,
BSc., of Hamilton, NZ,—Isabel Janice, b. 1950: m. 1970, Bruce Ronald Cowan, of Dunedin,
NZ.——Joan Doreen, b. 1927: m. 1948, Herbert Rance Brenton, and has issue living, Mervyn
Robert, b. 1949,—Lyal James, b. 1953,—Robyn Joan, b. 1951. Residence, Geraldine, Canter-
bury, NZ.——Mary Frazer (165, Weston Rd., Christchurch, NZ), b. 1922.

Grandchildren of the late Robert Riddell (b. 1879) (ante):—
Issue of the late James Riddell, b. 1920, d. 1972: m. 1950, Annette Lucy (The Downs,
Geraldine, S. Canterbury, NZ), da. of P. Forde, of 62, Darby St., Christchurch, NZ:—
Peter James, b. 1958.——Judith Mary, b. 1952.——Sally Anne, b. 1954.——Annette Joan, b. 1956.

Issue of the late John Buchanan Riddell, b. 1924, d. 1969: m. 1948, Barbara Frances,
da. of F. H. Ruddenklau, of Rangatata Island, Temuka, NZ:—
Frank Buchanan, b. 1951.——David John, b. 1953.——Graham Samuel, b. 1961.——Gail, b. 1949.
——Sandra Ngaire, b. 1958.

Granddaughter of the late William Law Riddell, yst. son of Henry Riddell (ante).
Issue of the late William Law Riddell, b. 1843, d. 1911: m. 1877 Mary Ann, who d. 1926,
da. of the late James Frazer, of Taratu, Otago, New Zealand :—
Elizabeth, b. 1887: m. 1915, Frank Loraine Nicolson, who d. 1962, and has issue living, Nancy
Loraine, b. 1916,—Morah Elizabeth, b. 1923: m. 1947, Cyril Freeme, of Upper Hutt, Wellington,
New Zealand, and has issue living, Elizabeth Rae, b. 1948, Diana Loraine, b. 1951. Residence,
107, Highgate, Roslyn, Dunedin, New Zealand.

This family is of Norman descent, and was early settled in Roxburghshire, Gervase de Ridle,
or Ridel, being High Sheriff of that county in 1116. The 9th baronet was successively M.P. for
Selkirkshire and Lanarkshire, and the 10th baronet was Recorder of Maidstone and Tenterden
1846-63, and Judge of County Courts for N. Staffordshire 1859-63, and for Whitechapel 1863-79. Sir
John Walter, 11th Bt., was High Sheriff of Northumberland 1897.

RIGBY, Creation (U.K.) 1929, of Long Durford, Rogate, co. Sussex.

I would rather die than be dishonoured

Sir (HUGH) JOHN MACBETH RIGBY,
E.R.D., 2nd Baronet; b. Sept. 1st, 1914; s.
his father, Sir HUGH MALLINSON, K.C.V.O.,
1944; ed. at Rugby, and at Magdalene
Coll., Camb.; Lt.-Col. (ret.) RCT: m. (Jan.)
1946, Mary Patricia Erskine, da. of Edmund
Erskine Leacock [see Erskine, Bt., cr. 1821,
colls.], and has issue.

Arms—Argent, on a cross flory sable a rod of Æsculapius or.   Crest—In front of an antelope's head erased
proper gorged with an antique crown or, two ostrich feathers
saltirewise argent.
Residence—Ridgehill, Sutton, near Macclesfield,
Cheshire.

Sons living—ANTHONY JOHN, b. Oct. 3rd, 1946.—
Hugh Macbeth (31, Farrant Rd., Manchester, M12
4PF), b. 1948: m. 1970, Kathleen Mary, da. of Conrad
Salber, of Rochester, NY, USA, and has issue living,
Zachary John, b. 1974,—Rachel Mary, b. 1971.——
James Erskine, b. 1949.——Stephen Leacock, b. 1952.
Brother living—Roger Macbeth, b. 1922; ed. at Win-
chester, and at Magdalene Coll., Camb.; is Hon.
Capt. Roy. Armoured Corps : m. 1957, Patricia Ann,
yr. da. of the late Capt. Desmond Nevill Cooper
Tufnell, DSC, RN, and has issue living, Melissa
Terwick, b. 1959,—Tanya Macbeth, b. 1961. Resi-
dence, 34, Bark Place, W.2.
Sisters living—Margaret Hamilton, b. 1919 : m. 1951,
Richard Kynaston Briscoe [see Briscoe, Bt.]. Resi-
dence, Maple House, Higher Combe Road, Haslemere, Surrey.——Ann Macbeth, b. 1925.

The 1st baronet, Sir Hugh Mallinson Rigby, K.C.V.O., F.R.C.S. (son of the late John Rigby), was for several years Surg. to H.M. Queen Alexandra, Serjeant-Surg. to H.M. King George V, and Surg.-in-Ord. to H.M. King Edward VIII. when Prince of Wales.

RIPLEY, Creation (U.K.) 1880, of Rawdon, Yorkshire.

While I breathe I hope.

Sir HUGH RIPLEY, 4th *Baronet ; b.* May 26th, 1916 ; *s.* his father, *Sir* HENRY WILLIAM ALFRED 1956 ; ed. at Eton ; Major (retired) King's Shropshire L.I. ; European War 1942-5 in Tunisia and Italy (wounded, despatches twice, American Silver Star): *m.* 1st, 1946 (m. diss. 1971), Dorothy Mary Dunlop Bruce, da. of J. C. Bruce Jones [Dunlop Bt.]; 2ndly, 1972, Susan, da. of W. Parker, of Keythorpe Grange, E. Newton, Leicester, and has issue by 1st and 2nd m.

Arms—Per chevron nebuly or and vert, three lions rampant counterchanged between three cross crosslets, two in base or, and one in chief vert. **Crest**—A demi-lion reguardant vert, collared or, charged on the shoulder with a cross crosslet of the second, and holding between the paws an escutcheon argent charged with a cockerel proper.

Seat—Bedstone, Bucknell, Salop. *Residences*—20, Abingdon Villas, W8 6BX; The Oak, Bedstone, Salop. *Club*, Boodle's.

Son living—By 1st m.—WILLIAM HUGH, *b.* April 13th, 1950; ed. at Eton.
Daughters living—By 1st m.—Dorothy Caroline, *b.* 1947.——By 2nd m.—Katherine, *b.* 1974.
Brother living—Geoffrey Nigel (39, Clarendon Rd., Birmingham 16), *b.* 1921; formerly Capt. Northamptonshire Regt.
Sister living—Suzan, *b.* 1919 ; European War 1939-45 with A.T.S. : *m.* 1951 Robert de la Garde Savery, and has issue living, Christopher Robert de la Garde, *b.* 1954,—Chloë Abigail de la Garde, *b.* 1955. *Residence*, Bedstone, Bucknell, Salop.

Collateral Branch living.

Issue of the late Lieut.-Col. Edward Robert Guy Ripley, King's Shropshire L.I., el. son of 3rd baronet, *b.* 1911, *d.* (killed in action in Normandy) (June) 1944; *m.* 1944, Sarah Stella (6, Broad St., Presteigne, Herefords.), da. of Col. A. G. Pardoe, of Gravel Hill, Kington:—
Patience Anna (posthumous), *b.* (Dec.) 1944: *m.* 1963, Richard Michael Tudor Morgan, of Smithfield House, Llanidloes, Montgomeryshire, and has issue living, David Paul Edward, *b.* 1964,—Timothy Michael Julian, *b.* 1969,—Charlotte Sarah, *b.* 1965.

Sir Henry William Ripley, 1st Bt., son of Edward Ripley of Bowling, near Bradford, was MP for Bradford (*L*) 1868-9 and 1874-80. Sir Frederick Ripley of Acacia, Rawdon, 3rd son of 1st. Bt., was cr. a baronet 1897, which became ext. on death of 3rd Bt. in 1954.

RITCHIE, Creation (U.K.) 1918, of Highlands.

Honour is acquired by virtue.

Sir JAMES EDWARD THOMSON RITCHIE, TD, 2nd *Baronet ; b.* June 16th, 1902; *s.* his father, *Sir* JAMES WILLIAM, MBE, 1937; ed. at Rugby, and The Queen's Coll., Oxford; is Chm. of M. W. Hardy & Co., Ltd., a Dir. of William Ritchie & Son (Textiles), Ltd., Pres. of Ashford Branch Roy. British Legion, Patron of Ashford and Dist. Caledonian Soc., a Member of Court of Assists., Merchants Taylors' Co. (Master 1963-64), Hon. Lt.-Col. late Inns of Court Regt., RAC (TA), a selected Mil. Member of Kent T. & AF Assocn. (Member of Gen. Purposes Cttee.) 1953-68, a Fellow of R. Soc. of Arts, and of Inst. of Dirs.; Jt. Hon. Treasurer and Chm. of Finance and Gen. Purposes Cttee., London Sch. of Hygiene and Tropical Med., London Univ. 1951-61; a Member of Finance & Gen. Purposes Cttee., and a co-opted Member of Board of Management 1964-65; 1939-45 War holding various Staff and Regimental appointments (Central Mediterranean Force 1944-45): *m.* 1928, Esme (who *d.* 1939, having obtained a divorce 1936), da. of the late J. M. Oldham of Ormidale, Ascot; 2ndly, 1936,

Rosemary, yr. da. of the late Col. Henry Sidney John Streatfeild, DSO, TD [E. Lichfield], and has issue.

Arms—Argent, an anchor erect sable within a bordure ermine, on a chief of the second three lions' heads erased of the first. Crest—Issuant out of an antique crown or, an unicorn's head argent armed gold, charged on the neck with a torteau, thereon an anchor, also gold.

Residence—Kirkbank House, High Halden, Ashford, Kent, TN 26 2TD. Club—Army and Navy.

Daughters living—Louise Katherine, b. 1952.——Fiona Ruth, b. 1953.

Half-Brother living—WILLIAM PETER EMERTON, b. Sept. 15th, 1918; ed. at Canford, 1939-45 with Queen's Own Roy. W. Kent Regt. Residence, Pytchley, Main St. Holcot, North-ampton, NN6 9SP.

Half-Sisters living—Barbara Anne Lydia Janet, b. 1916; European War 1940-43 with A.T.S. attached R.A. Residence, Crackshill Cottage, Yelvertoft, near Rugby.——Elizabeth Alice Jessie Muriel, b. 1922: m. 1st, 1943 (marriage dissolved 1954), Peter Andrew Soderling, U.S.A. Air Force; 2ndly, 1957 Robert John Ripley Blake, of The Cottage, 5B, Grove Hill, Stansted, Essex, and has issue living, (by 1st m.) Mark Andrew Patrick, b. 1944.

The 1st baronet, Sir James William Ritchie, MBE, was Chm. of Milners' Safe Co., and Lieut. for City of London.

Rivett-Carnac, see Carnac

ROBERTS, Creation (U.K.) 1809, of Glassenbury, Kent, of Brightfieldstown, co. Cork and of the City of Cork.

Sir THOMAS LANGDON HOWLAND ROBERTS, CBE, 6th Baronet; b. June 18th, 1898; s. his father, Col. Sir HOWLAND, 1917; ed. at Westminster, and RMA; Lt.-Col. RA (ret.), and Hon. Col. RA (TA); and of S-W London Bde. ACF (RA); a DL of Co. London; Hon. Treas. of Guild of St. Helena 1958-74; Hon Treas. of RA Sports Fund, Pres. of SSAFA, Kent, 1964-72; Col. Comdt. Co. of London Army Cadet Force 1956-63; 1914-18 War in France and Belgium (wounded, two medals), 1939-45 War in N. Africa and Italy (despatches twice), CBE (Mil) 1964: m. 1930, Evelyn Margaret, da. of the late Harold Fielding-Hall, Burma Commn., and has issue.

Arms—Azure, on a chevron argent cotised or, three mullets of six points sable, pierced of the field. Crest—On a mount vert an eagle displayed ermine, wings argent, gorged with a chaplet of ivy proper.

Residence—Furzebank, Shorne Ridgeway, Kent. Clubs—RA Yacht and RE Yacht.

Sons living—GILBERT HOWLAND ROOKEHURST (3340, Cliff Drive, Santa Barbara, Cal., 93109), b. May 31st, 1934, ed. at Rugby, and at Gonville and Caius Coll., Camb. (BA; CEng, MIMechE): m. 1958, Ines Eleonore, only da. of the late A. Labunski, and has issue living, Howland Langdon, b. 1961,—Solveig Margaret, b. 1959.——Walter Rookehurst b. 1951; ed. at King's Sch., Canterbury, and Gonville and Caius Coll., Camb.

Virtue survives death.

Brother living—Gilbert Howland, CBE, RD, RN, b. 1900; is Capt. (ret.) RN, and an Alder-man, Torbay; 1914-18 War, 1939-45 War; an Officer of Legion of Honour, and a Com. of Orders of Restitution of Poland, and of St. Olaf of Norway; has Medal of R. Humane Soc.; CBE (Mil) 1944: m. 1st, 1930 (divorce 1947), Marjorie, da. of John Boultbee Brooks, of Blackwell Court, nr. Bromsgrove, Worcs.; 2ndly, 1947, Jean, da. of Edward Warren, of Yelverton, Devon, and has issue living, (by 1st m.) Michael Gilbert (of Cape Town, S. Africa), b. 1932; formerly Lt. RM: m. 1960 (m. diss. 1970), Felicity Sheppard, and has issue living, Mark Howland b. 1961, John Langdon b. 1964, Jennifer Leigh b. 1962,—Jill Morna Boultbee, b. 1933. Residence, Little Priors, Watcombe, Torquay.

Collateral Branch living.

Issue of the late His Honour Sir Walworth Howland Roberts, CBE, 3rd son of 3rd baronet, b. 1855, d. 1924: m. 1890, Katherine, who d. 1945, da. of the late John Gibson Thomson, of Aitechuan, Ardishaig:—

Sir Walter St. Clair Howland, KCMG, MC, b. 1893; ed. at Winchester, and at Brasenose Coll., Oxford (B.A. 1916); entered Diplo. Ser. 1919; became a 1st Sec. 1926, and Counsellor 1936; was Ambassador Extraor. and Plen. to Peru 1945-49. Envoy Extraor. and Min. Plen. to Bucharest 1949-51, and Minister to the Holy See 1951-53; 1914-18 War as Lt. RFA Special Reserve (MC); CMG 1937, KCMG 1951: m. 1st, 1924, Helen Cecil Ronayne, who d. 1951, da. of the late Col. Henry Wilson Weekes, DSO, OBE; 2ndly, 1957, Cecily, who d. 1964, widow of H. E. Ormond. Residence, Leaton Lodge, Bomere Heath, Shrewsbury, Salop, SY1 1AR.

The former baronetcy of 1620 (claimed by the present holder of the 1809 creation as 13th Bt., which claim, however, has not been officially established at the Heralds' College), belonged to the old Kentish family, originally called Rookehurst and later Roobertes, and apparently became extinct on the demise in 1745 of Sir Walter, 6th baronet, who left an only daughter, Jane, who married the 3rd Duke of St. Albans.   About 1775 the Duchess believed she had discovered the descendants of Thomas, second son of the 1st baronet, seated at Brightfieldstown, Roberts' Cove, co. Cork; and the title was assumed by the then head of that family, Randal, and subsequently by his eldest son Thomas, to whom, however, a new patent of Baronetcy was passed in 1809.   The ancient property of Glassenbury, Cranbrook, Kent, which had then been in the direct line for nearly seven centuries, was left by the Duchess of St. Albans to the second son of this Sir Thomas, viz., Col. Thomas Walton Roberts, JP (High Sheriff of Kent 1879), who *d.* 1882, and devised the said property by will to his nephew, the late Major John Roberts Atkin-Roberts, JP.

ROBERTS, Creation (U.K.) 1909, of Milner Field, Bingley, West Riding of Yorkshire.

Justly and firmly.

DILIGENTER·ET·FIRMITER

Sir WILLIAM JAMES DENBY ROBERTS, 3rd *Baronet*; *b.* Aug. 10th, 1936; *s.* his father, *Sir* JAMES DENBY, OBE, 1973; ed. at Rugby, and Roy. Agric. Coll., Cirencester.

Arms—Vert, on a pile or, between two saltires in base of the last an Angora goat statant proper.   Crest—Upon two millrinds fesseways or, an Angora goat as in the arms

Seat—Strathallan Castle, Auchterarder, Perthshire. *Residence*—Combwell Priory, Flimwell, Wadhurst, Sussex.

Brother living—ANDREW DENBY, *b.* May 21st, 1938; ed. at Rugby, and Ch. Ch., Oxford (BA).

Sister living—Susan Elisabeth, *b.* 1934; MA, Oxford: *m.* 1956, Roger John Edward Liddiard, BA of Lynwick House, Rudgwick, Horsham, Sussex, and has issue living, Nicholas Anthony, *b.* 1958,—Timothy Mark, *b.* 1960,— Jonathan Miles, *b.* 1962,—Rupert Alexander, *b.* 1966.

Aunt living—Catherine Elizabeth, *b.* 1907: *m.* 1928, Robert Hope Donaldson, and has issue living, Robert Bertram, *b.* 1929,—William James, *b.* 1934.   *Residence*, Norden, East Rd., W. Mersea, Colchester, Essex.

Great-Aunt living (daughter of 1st baronet)—Alice Maud Mary, *b.* 1881; assmed maiden name of Roberts by deed poll 1927 (issue have also assumed this surname): *m.* 1st, 1902, Lt.-Col. Norman Cecil Rutherford, DSO, FRCS, from whom she obtained a divorce 1938; 2ndly, 1938, Archibald Stewart Clark, and has issue living, (by 1st marriage) Lionel James ROBERTS (of Spong Farm, Elmsted, Ashford, Kent), *b.* 1907; 1939-45 War as Hon. Capt. R.A.: *m.* 1927, Zena Grace Ellis, and has issue living, Lionel James *b.* 1928, Diana Irene Zena *b.* 1930, Ursula Phyllis Patricia *b.* 1932, Pauline Marguerite Pamela *b.* 1933,—Brian James ROBERTS (Nailards, Amber-ley, Arundel, Sussex), *b.* 1911; Air Commodore RAF (ret.): *m.* 1940, Margaret Marie, only da. of the late Henry Sherwin, of 2, Halsey St., SW3, and has issue living, Jonathan James *b.* 1946, Willow Anne *b.* 1943, Hilary Alice *b.* 1949,—Neil ROBERTS, *b.* 1913; 1939-45 War as Sqdn. Ldr. RAF (despatches): *m.* 1938, Margaret Marion Elliott Newman, and has issue living, Leila Margaret *b.* 1939,—Kathleen Mary ROBERTS, *b.* 1905: *m.* 1928 (m. diss. 1961), Martin John Berlyn, of Apt. 303, 3787, Côtes des Neiges, Montreal, Canada, and has issue living, Robin Wilfrid *b.* 1934, Elizabeth Ann *b.* 1930,—Enid May ROBERTS, *b.* 1915: *m.* 1939, Tom Rowland, and has issue living, Christopher *b.* 1948, Wendy *b.* 1947.   *Residence*, San Christoval, King Edward Rd., Onchan, Isle of Man.

Widow living of 2nd Baronet—IRENE CHARLOTTE D'ORSEY (*Lady Roberts*), (Strathallan Castle, Auchterarder, Perthshire), yr. da. of the late William Dunn, MB, CM, JP, of Woodfield House, Uppingham: *m.* 1927, Sir James Denby Roberts, OBE, 2nd Bt., who *d.* 1973.

Collateral Branches living:

Issue of the late David Gordon Denby Roberts, yst. son of 2nd baronet, *b.* 1940, *d.* 1971: *m.* 1962, Diana Frances, [of Lawhill, Auchterarder, Perths, who *m.* 2ndly, 1973, Cameron Roy Marchand Buchanan], only da. of Hugh Wilson-Jones, of The White House, N. Lopham, Diss, Norfolk:—
James Elton Denby ROBERTS-BUCHANAN, *b.* 1966.——Gail Antoinette ROBERTS-BUCHANAN, *b.* 1964.

Issue of the late William Denby Roberts, 2nd son of Bertram Foster Roberts, el. sur. son of 1st baronet, *b.* 1909, *d.* 1966: *m.* 1935, Helen Fyans, who *d.* 1963, yr. da. of the late Herbert Shakespeare Fenwick, of Dunedin, NZ:—
Anthony Fenwick Denby (Mossdale, Conistone-with-Kilnsey, nr. Skipton, Yorks.) *b.* 1938; ed. at Rugby, and Univ. Coll., Oxford (BA): *m.* 1964, Vanessa Jean Wishart, da. of Sir (James) Douglas Wishart Thomson, 2nd Bt. (*cr.* 1929), and has issue living, Jonathan William Denby, *b.* 1966,— Nicholas David Denby, *b.* 1967,—James Anthony Denby, *b.* 1974.——Peter William Denby (The Old Rectory, Whittington, via Carnforth, Lancs), *b.* 1945; ed. at Rugby, and Roy. Agric. Coll., Cirencester: *m.* 1970, Christine Margaret Hermione, da. of the late Capt. the Hon. Anthony Gerard Hugh Bampfylde [see B. Poltimore, colls.], and has issue living, Emma Louise, *b.* 1927. ——Ann, *b.* 1936.

Issue of the late Joseph Henry Nicholson Roberts, 2nd surv. son of 1st baronet *b.* 1887, *d.* 1946: *m.* 1920, Frances Eleanor (Les Blanches Pierres, St. Ouen's Jersey), da. of G. Partington, of The Laurels, Tilehurst, Reading:—
John (L'Etoquet House, St. Ouen, Jersey), *b.* 1921: *m.* 1st, 1949, Diana Emily, from whom he obtained a divorce 1961, da. of the late Lawrence Norris Evans; 2ndly, 1962, (m. diss. 1972), the Hon. Juliana Eveline (CUNLIFFE-OWEN), da. of 2nd Viscount Scarsdale; 3rdly, 1974, Maryan Gwyneth, da. of Patrick Edward Aston Talbot, formerly of Glos., and now of St. Petersburg, Florida, USA, and has issue living, (by 1st m.), Jane, *b.* 1953: *m.* 1972, Robin John Kershaw Roberts, of 18, Lowndes Sq., SW1,—Sally, *b.* 1955,—(by 2nd m.) John James, *b.* 1964,—Lucinda Elizabeth, *b.* 1963.   *Residence*, Vinchelez De Haut Manor, of Ouen's, Jersey.——Henry, *b.* 1923: *m.* 1955, Anne Dorothy, da. of the late John Huelin, of Cape Town, S. Africa, and has issue living, Lesley Anne, *b.* 1957,—Frances Mary, *b.* 1963.   *Residence*, La Fontaine, Trinity, Jersey.

The 1st Baronet, Sir James Roberts (son of the late James Roberts, of Haworth, Yorkshire), was former owner of town of Saltaire, and Chm. of Sir Titus Salt, Bt., Sons & Co., Ltd., of Saltaire.

ROBERTS, Creation (U.K.) 1919, of Ecclesall and Queen's Tower, City of Sheffield, and West Riding of Yorkshire.

Sir PETER GEOFFREY ROBERTS, 3rd *Baronet ; b.* June 23rd, 1912 ; *s.* his father, *Sir* SAMUEL, 1955 ; ed. at Harrow, and at Trin. Coll., Camb. ; Bar. Inner Temple 1936; Master Cutler of Sheffield 1956-57; MP for Ecclesall Div. of Sheffield (*C*) 1945-50 and for Heeley Div. of Sheffield 1950-66; Town Trustee of Sheffield since 1958, and Town Collector of Sheffield since 1971; High Sheriff of Hallamshire 1970; 1939-45 War as Maj. Coldm. Gds.: *m.* 1939, Judith Randell, da. of the late Randell G. Hempson, of Wallingford, and has issue.

Arms—Sable, on a chevron couped argent, three mullets of the field, a chief dancettée or. *Crest*— Issuant out of a circlet or, a demi-lion rampant gules holding in the paws a mullet gold.

Residences—Cockley Cley Hall, Swaffham, Norfolk ; Stubbin House, Sandygate, Sheffield, S10 3LU; 11, Mount St., W1.

Son living—SAMUEL (96, Eaton Place, SW1), *b.* April 16th, 1948; ed. at Harrow, and Sheffield Univ. (BA); Bar. Inner Temple 1972.

Daughters living—Jane, *b.* 1940: *m.* 1962, Claude Henri Jean-Jacques Maurin, of Clos des Aubépines, Houppeville, Seine Maritime, France, and has issue living, Sebastien Alexandre, *b.* 1965,—Edmond Peter, *b.* 1974,—Alicia, *b.* 1967,—Constance (twin), *b.* 1974.——Catherine, *b.* 1943: *m.* 1965, John Andrew Longworth, of 45, Ranelagh Grove, SW1, and has issue living, Stephanie Lydia, *b.* 1968,—Charlotte Gay, *b.* 1970,—Joanna Catherine, *b.* 1973.——Deborah, *b.* 1946: *m.* 1967, Peter Constantin Brun, of 169, Sutherland St., Paddington, NSW 2021, and has issue living, Henry Daniel, *b.* 1971,—Peter Maximillian, *b.* 1974,—Rachel, *b.* 1970.——Rebecca, *b.* 1955.

Collateral Branch living.

Issue of the late Norman Samuel Roberts, 3rd son of 1st baronet, *b.* 1888, *d.* 1914: *m.* 1912, Dorothy (who *d.* 1966, having *m.* 2ndly, 1923, Major Geoffrey Edward Mansfield, MC, R.A.), da. of the Rev. Canon Albert Ernest Sorby:— Pamela Elizabeth Norma, *b.* 1914: *m.* 1938, Major Thomas Egerton Jones, R.A., who *d.* 1948, and has issue living, David Richard, *b.* 1947,—Margaret, *b.* 1939: *m.* 1968, Patrick Xavier Christopher Hayes,—Susan Elizabeth, *b.* 1940,—Diana Mary, *b.* 1941: *m.* 1965, Robert Wood. *Residence*, Long Acre, Groombridge, Tunbridge Wells, Kent.

The 1st baronet, the Rt. Hon. Sir Samuel Roberts, was Lord Mayor of Sheffield 1899-1900, and sat as M.P. for Ecclesall Div. of Sheffield (*C*) 1902-23. The 2nd baronet, Sir Samuel Roberts was Lord Mayor of Sheffield 1919-20, M.P. for Hereford Div. of Herefordshire (*C*) 1921-9, and for Ecclesall Div. of Sheffield 1929-35, and Master Cutler of Sheffield 1935-6.

ROBINSON, Creation (E.) 1660, of London.

Sir JOHN JAMES MICHAEL LAUD ROBINSON, 11th *Baronet*; *b.* Jan. 19th, 1943; *s.* his grandfather, *Maj. Sir* FREDERICK VILLIERS LAUD, *MC*, 1975; ed. at Eton, and Trin. Coll., Dublin (BA); a Chartered Financial Analyst: *m.* 1968, Kathryn Gayle Elizabeth, only child of Stuart Keyes, of Orillia, Ont., Canada, and has issue.

Arms—Quarterly : 1st and 4th, quarterly crenellée gules and or in the first quarter a lion passant-guardant or standing on a tower argent ; 2nd and 3rd, vert, a buck trippant within an orle of trefoil slipped or. *Crest*—A buck trippant or, collared and lined vert, the collar charged with three trefoils slipped or.

Residence—20802, Lakeshore Rd., Baie d'Urfé, Quebec, Canada.

Sons living—MARK CHRISTOPHER MICHAEL VILLIERS, *b.* April 23rd, 1972.——Alexander Frederick Stuart Laud, *b.* 1973.

Sister living—Anne Elizabeth Villiers, *b.* 1950.

Mother living—Elizabeth, da. of Lt.-Col. Charles Bridge, of West Wratting Park, Cambridge: *m.* 1st, 1941 (m. diss. 1966), Capt. Michael Frederick Laud Robinson, (el. son of 10th baronet), who *d.* 1971; 2ndly, 1966, Hans Philip Willem Stjernsward, of 66, Charlwood Rd., SW15 1PZ.

Step-mother living—Joan Isabel (Said House, Chiswick Mall, W4), da. of Vernon James Reveley

and widow of the Hon. John Breckinridge Fermor-Hesketh [see B. Hesketh]: *m.* 1966, as his 2nd wife, Capt. Michael Frederick Laud Robinson (only son of 10th baronet), who *d.* 1971.
Widow living of 10th baronet—FRANCES JOYCE (*Frances, Lady Robinson*) (Cranford Hall, Kettering, Northants), e. da. of Arthur Tyrwhitt-Drake, of Crendle, Sherborne, Dorset: *m.* 1933, as his 2nd wife, Maj. Sir Frederick Villiers Laud Robinson, MC, 10th Bt., who *d.* 1975.

The 1st baronet, Sir John Robinson, nephew of Archbishop Laud, and Lord Mayor of London. was Lieut. of the Tower, and did great service in promoting the coronation of Charles II. The 5th and the 6th baronets each sat as M.P. for Northampton.

ROBINSON, Creation (U.K.) 1854, of Toronto, Canada.

Sir JOHN BEVERLEY ROBINSON, 7th Baronet : *b.* Oct. 3rd, 1913 ; *s.* his father, *Sir* JOHN BEVERLEY 1954.

Quickly and cautiously.

Arms—Or, on a chevron between three stags trippant vert, as many cinquefoils of the field. **Crest**—A stag trippant vert bezantée.

Residence—435, Leinster St., Apt. 7, Woodstock, Ont., Canada.

Sister living—Constance Suzette Beverley (435, Leinster St., Apt. 7, Woodstock, Ont., Canada), *b.* 1914: *m.* 1939 (m. diss. 1969), Edward William Sutherland, and has issue living, John Warren, *b.* 1942: *m.* 1962, Kathleen Croft, of Hamilton, Ontario, and has issue living, David *b.* 1963, Beth *b.* 1964,—Harley Peter, *b.* 1948: *m.* 1966, Patricia Carter, of Guelph, Ont., and has issue living, Kimberley Deanne *b.* 1967, Joy Patrick *b.* 1969,—David Victor, *b.* 1948: *m.* 1971, Jacquie Smith, of Hamilton, Ont., and has issue living, Tracy, *b.* 1973,—Wendy Gayle, *b.* 1940: *m.* 1961, Anthony Ian Roberts, of London, Ont., and has issue living, Paul Douglas *b.* 1968, Nancy Marie *b.* 1962, Patricia *b.* 1964,—Suezette Marion, *b.* 1944: *m.* 1964 (m. diss. 1969), David Teft, of Grimsby, Ontario.

Widows living of 5th and 6th Baronets—MAUD EVA (*Maud Lady Robinson*), da. of the late William Charles Coo, of Toronto, Canada: *m.* 1934, Sir John Beverley Robinson, 5th baronet, who *d.* 1948. *Residence,* 112, Moore Av., Toronto, Canada.—CONSTANCE MARIE (*Lady Robinson*) (435, Leinster St., Apt. 7, Woodstock, Ont., Canada), da. of Robert W. Pentecost: *m.* 1912, Sir John Beverley Robinson, 6th baronet, who *d.* 1954.

Collateral Branches living.

Grandchildren of the late Christopher Charles Robinson, KC (infra):—
Issue of the late Christopher Robinson, QC, *b.* 1909, *d.* 1974: *m.* 1933, Neville Taylor (250, Thorold Rd., Rockcliffe, Ottawa, Canada), el. da. of Rear-Adm. Walter Rockwell Gherarhi, US Navy:—
CHRISTOPHER PHILIPSE (5, Bedford Cres., Ottawa, 7, Ont., Canada), *b.* Nov. 10th, 1938: *m.* 1962, Barbara Judith, da. of Richard Duncan, of Ottawa, and has issue living, Peter Duncan, *b.* 1967,—Jonathan Richard, *b.* 1969.——Walter Gherardi (545, Montagu Place, Rockcliffe Park, Ottawa, Canada), *b.* 1940: *m.* 1963, Alison Jean, da. of Robert Stewart Fraser, of Vancouver, and has issue living, Hilary Elizabeth, *b.* 1967,—Alicia Isabel, *b.* 1970.——John Mowat, *b.* 1942: *m.* 1969, Joyce, da. of Roy Harrod, of Orsett, Essex, and has issue living, Graeme Harrod, *b.* 1970,—Christopher Mowat, *b.* 1972.——Neville Gherardi (Woodacres, Furzeview, Slinfold, Sussex), *b.* 1935: *m.* 1956 (m. diss. 1967), Georges-Henry Carasso, of Paris, who *d.* 1974, and has issue living, John Christopher, *b.* 1959.

Grandchildren of the late Christopher Robinson, K.C., 3rd son of 1st baronet :—
Issue of the late Christopher Charles Robinson, K.C., *b.* 1883, *d.* 1948: *m.* 1907, Isabel Hodgin, who *d.* 1962, el. da. of the late Charles Robert Webster Biggar, K.C., of Toronto:—
Peter Beverley, *b.* 1915; FO AAF (Reserve): *m.* 1st, 1938, Elizabeth, who *d.* 1965, da. of Halsey Frederick, of Mountain Lakes, New Jersey, USA; 2ndly, 1966, Nancy Carol, da. of Norris Konheim, of Woodmere, NY, and has issue living, (by 1st m.) Wendy Bouquet, *b.* 1944: *m.* 1965, Martin V. Boelitz, of 504, Beacon St., Boston, Mass., USA, and has issue living, Jessica Elizabeth *b.* 1968,—Susan Celina, *b.* 1946: *m.* 1st, 1966 (m. annulled 1967), Ira James Sandperl; 2ndly, 1969, Pierre Bain, of Comps-sur-Artuby Var, France, (by 2nd m.)—Kenneth Beverley, *b.* 1967.——Hugh Lukin, *b.* 1916: *m.* 1941, Ruth, da. of John Cotter, of Ottawa, Ont., and has issue living, John Michael, *b.* 1946,—David Lukin, *b.* 1951,—Elizabeth, *b.* 1955. *Residence,* 35, Berkinshaw Cres., Don Mills, Toronto, Canada.——Helen Hilary, *b.* 1912: *m.* 1936, Douglas Harverson, and has issue living, Philippa, *b.* 1939: *m.* 1971, Paul Elmhirst, and has issue living, Charles Marcus Ross *b.* 1972, Tobias Matthew Hampden *b.* 1973,—Celia, *b.* 1942. *Residence,* Bickington, nr. Newton Abbot, S. Devon.——Laura Beverley, *b.* 1913: *m.* 1st, 1937 (m. diss. 1956), Andrew Kalitinsky; 2ndly, 1957, Adolf Kurt Placzek, and has issue living, (by 1st m.) Sylvia, *b.* 1945: *m.* 1966, Roger Alan Barkley, of 6132m Horton Drive, La Mesa, Cal., USA, and has issue living, Ian Andrew *b.* 1970. *Residence,* 176, West 87th St., New York, NY, 10024, USA.——Wendela Isabel, *b.* 1918: *m.* 1957, Andrew Kalitinsky, of 6424, Muirlands Drive, La Jolla, California, USA.

Issue of the late (John) Beverley Robinson, *b.* 1884, *d.* 1954 : *m.* 1920, Marion (of 28, Foxbar Road, Toronto, 7, Canada), da. of Weymouth de Lisle Schreiber, of Toronto, Canada.
John Beverley, *b.* 1922 : *m.* 1948, Constance Anne, da. of James Bruce Mackinnon, of Toronto, and has issue living, Bruce Beverley, *b.* 1952,—Christopher Charles, *b.* 1957,—Linda de Lisle, *b.* 1949,—Hilary Anne, *b.* 1953. *Residence,* 194, Inglewood Drive, Toronto, Canada.——Weymouth Hugh Beverley, *b.* 1927 : *m.* 1956, Patricia Elizabeth, el. da. of Robert James Glendenning Innes, of Toronto, Canada, and has issue living, Judith Suzanne, *b.* 1957,—Jennifer Leslie, *b.* 1960.——Elizabeth de Lisle, *b.* 1924: *m.* 1st, 1946, John Kingsford Herbert Mason, who *d.* 1952; 2ndly, 1959, Capt. John Littler, RCN, and has issue living, (by 1st m.) David *b.* 1950, Marion Thonia *b.* 1948, Philippa *b.* 1952.

Issue of the late Duncan Strachan Robinson, *b.* 1886, *d.* 1956: *m.* 1916, Emily, el. da. of Gordon Watson, formerly of Brandon, Manitoba:—
Duncan Gordon Strachan, *b.* 1917.——John Atrachay, *b.* 1920. *Residence,* Toronto, Canada.——Mary Emily, *b.* 1917. *Residence,* Guelph, Ontario, Canada.——Anne, *b.* 1922. *Residence,* Phoenix, Arizona, U.S.A.——Daphne, *b.* 1928. *Residence,* Toronto, Canada.

Issue of the late Maj.-Gen. Sir Charles Walker Robinson, K.C.B., 4th son of 1st
baronet, *b.* 1836, *d.* 1924 : *m.* 1884, Margaret Frances, who *d.* 1940, da. of Gen.
Sir **Archibald** Alison, G.C.B., 2nd Bt. :—
Joan Emma Beverley, *b.* 1892.——Dorothy Margaret, *b.* 1895.　*Residence*, Bideford, Devon.

This family is descended from Christopher Robinson, of Cleasby, Yorkshire, who emigrated to
Virginia about 1670, and was elder brother of the Rt. Rev. John Robinson, Ambassador to Sweden
1683-1708, Bishop of Bristol and London 1710-23, and First Plenipotentiary at the Congress of
Utrecht 1713.　The 1st baronet, Sir John Beverley, C.B., D.C.L. of Oxford, having served as a
Volunteer in the war of 1812 with America, was admitted to the Bar in Canada and at Lincoln's Inn,
and was subsequently (1829-62) Chief Justice of Upper Canada, and for many years member for the
town of York and Speaker of the Legislative Council in the Old Province of Upper Canada.　Sir John
Beverley Robinson, 4th Bt., was el. son of the late Hon. John Beverley Robinson, Lieut.-Gov. of
Ontario 1880-87.

ROBINSON, Creation (U.K.) 1908, of Hawthornden, Wynberg, Cape Province, S. Africa, and Dudley House, City of Westminster.

I have found.

Sir WILFRED HENRY FREDERICK
ROBINSON, 3rd *Baronet*, son of the late Wilfred
Henry Robinson, 3rd son of 1st baronet ; *b.* Dec.
24th, 1917 ; *s.* his uncle, *Sir* JOSEPH BENJAMIN,
1954 ; ed. at Diocesan Coll., Rondesbosch, and
at St. John's Coll., Camb. (B.A. 1939, M.A.
1944) ; is Vice-Prin. of Diocesan Coll. Sch.,
Rondebosch ; late Major Parachute Regt. : *m.*
1946, Margaret Alison Kathleen, da. of the
late Frank Mellish, MC, of Bergendal, Cape
Province, S. Africa, and has issue.

Arms—Vert, three bezants chevronwise between two
chevronels, the whole between three demi-stags couped or.
Crest—A demi-stag or, charged with two chevronels vert,
supporting with the dexter leg a flagstaff in bend sinister
proper, pendant therefrom a banner vert charged with a bezant.

Residence—44, Kildare Rd., Newlands, Cape Province,
South Africa.

Son living—PETER FRANK, *b.* June 23rd, 1949.
Daughters living—Suzanne Moira, *b.* 1947: *m.* 1969, J. Steen
Flamand, of Copenhagen, Denmark.——Clementine Anne
Eileen, *b.* 1957.
Aunt living (daughter of 1st baronet)—Leonora (Hawthorn-
dene, Wynberg, Cape, S. Africa).

Widow living of 2nd Baronet—ALICE JOSEPHINE (*Alice
Lady Robinson*), da. of Daniel Cullen, of Osmeath, co.
Louth : *m.* 1935, Sir Joseph Benjamin Robinson, 2nd
baronet, who *d.* 1954.　*Residence*, Impala Sunningdale Road, Kenilworth, Cape Province, South
Africa.

Sir Joseph Benjamin Robinson, 1st Bt. (sometime a M.L.A., Mayor of Kimberley 1880, and
Chm. of Robinson's South African Banking Co., Ltd., and of many gold mines in Transvaal Colony),
was youngest son of the late Robert John Robinson, and was nominated to a peerage in June 1922,
but declined the honour.　Sir Joseph Benjamin Robinson, 2nd Bt., sat in Union Parliament of
S. Africa 1915-19, and 1932-34.

LYNCH-ROBINSON, Creation (U.K.) 1920, of Foxrock, co. Dublin.

Faithful to the law and the king.

Sir NIALL BRYAN LYNCH-
ROBINSON, *D.S.C.*, 3rd *Baronet* ; *b.*
Feb. 24th, 1918 ; *s.* his father, *Sir*
CHRISTOPHER HENRY, 1958 ; ed. at
Stowe ; late Lt. RNVR ; Chm. Leo
Burnett Ltd. ; 1939-45 War (DSC, Croix
de Guerre) : *m.* 1940, Rosemary Seaton, da.
of Mrs. M. Seaton Eller, and has issue.

Arms—Quarterly: 1st and 4th, vert, a chevron
engrailed between three stags at gaze or, each charged
with a fleur-de-lis azure, *Robinson* ; 2nd and 3rd,
azure a chevron between three trefoils and two
voiders or, *Lynch*.　**Crests**—1st, Out of a crown
vallery or a mount vert, thereon a stag as in the
arms ; 2nd, a lynx passant argent gorged with a
collar gules with chain reflexed over the back or.

Residence—The Old Parsonage, E. Clandon,
Surrey.

Son living—DOMINICK CHRISTOPHER, *b.* July
30th, 1948.

Uncle living (son of 1st baronet)—Adrian, *CBE*, *b.* 1892; ed. at Charterhouse, and at Trin Coll.,
Dublin (BA 19—); Bar. King's Inn 19—; was Permanent Sec., Min. of Home Affairs, Belfast
1939-57; assumed by deed poll 1947 (registered in College of Arms) the additional surname and
arms of Lynch; CBE (Civil) 1951: *m.* 1919 Agnes, Patricia, da. of Hugh Dorrien, of Donegal,
and has issue living, Henry Adrian, *FRIBA* (143, Church St., Gharb, Gozo, Malta, GC), *b.* 1920,
Residence, Seymour House, Dunmurry, Belfast.

Widow living of 2nd Baronet—OLIVE (*Olive, Lady Lynch-Robinson*), da. of George Bartholomew, of Tonbridge, Kent: *m.* (March) 1957, as his second wife, Sir Christopher Henry Lynch-Robinson, 2nd baronet, who *d.* (Nov.) 1958. *Residence,* 9, South Park Court, Gerrards Cross, Bucks.

The 1st baronet, the Rt. Hon. Sir Henry Augustus Robinson, K.C.B., was Vice-Pres. of Local Govt. Board for Ireland 1898-1920. The 2nd baronet, Sir Christopher Henry Robinson, assumed by deed poll 1947 (registered in College of Arms) the additional surname and arms of Lynch before his patronymic.

ROCHE, Creation (U.K.) 1838, of Carass, Limerick.

DIEU EST MA ROCHE

God is my rock

Sir STANDISH O'GRADY ROCHE, *D.S.O., R.N.*, 4th *Baronet; b.* March 13th, 1911; *s.* his father *Sir* STANDISH DEANE O'GRADY, 1914; Lieut.-Com., and a Freeman of City of London; was an A.D.C. to Gov.-Gen. of New Zealand 1935-7; 1939-45 War (DSO, French Croix de Guerre); DSO 1942: *m.* 1946, Evelyn Laura, da. of Maj. William Andon, W. Yorks. Regt., of Jersey, and has issue.

Arms—Gules, three roaches naiant within a bordure engrailed argent. **Crest**—A rock, thereon a stork close, charged on the breast with a torteau, and holding in his dexter claw a roach all proper.

Address—Monte de Serro, Corotelo, St. Bras de Aportel, Algarve, Portugal.

Sons living—DAVID O'GRADY (Boulters Lock Island, Maidenhead, Berks.; Clubs—Kildare Street (Dublin), and MCC), *b.* Sept. 21st, 1947; ed. at Wellington, and Trin. Coll., Dublin; a Freeman of City of London; *m.* 1971, the Hon. (Helen) Alexandra Briscoe Gully, da. of 3rd Viscount Selby, and formerly wife of the late Roger Moreton Frewen, having had issue Standish George O'Grady, *b.* 1972, *d.* 1974.——Timothy O'Grady, *b.* 1948; ed. at St. Columba's Coll., Dublin; Lt. 1st Bn. IG; a Freeman of City of London: *m.* 1975, Lorna R. A., da. of A. T. R. Nicholson, of Meadowside, Merstham, Surrey.

The 1st baronet was M.P. for Limerick City 1832-44. Sir David, 2nd Bt., was Vice-Lieut. of co. Limerick (High Sheriff 1863).

RODGERS, Creation (U.K.) 1964, of Groombridge, Kent.

Experience is knowledge.

Sir JOHN (CHARLES) RODGERS, *MP*, 1st *Baronet*, son of Charles Rodgers, of York, *b.* Oct. 5th, 1906; ed. at St. Peter's, York, and at Keble Coll., Oxford (MA); FIS (Pres.), FRSA, FBIM, FIPA (Pres.); a DL of Kent; Dir. of Commercial Relations Div., Min. of Information 1939-41, Dir. of Post-War Export Trade Development, Dept. of Overseas Trade 1941-42, Dep. Head of Industrial Information Div., Min. of Production 1942-44, FO 1939 and 1944-45, Member of BBC Gen. Advisory Council 1946-52, PPS to Viscount Eccles, KCVO, PC, when Min. of Works 1951-54, Min. of Education 1954-56, and Pres. of Board of Trade 1957, Min., Board of Trade 1958-60, on Public Accounts Cttee. 1970-74, since when on Expenditure Cttee., a Member of Council of Inst. of Dirs. 1955-58, and of Exec. Cttee. of British Council 1957-58, and Gov. of British Film Inst. 1958; Dir. of J. Walter Thompson Co., Ltd., 1936-70 (Dep. Chm. 1960-70); a Dir. of Cos.; International Pres. Centre European de Documentation et Information 1965-68; a Member of Council, Univ. of Kent, of Roy. Coll. of Art, of City Univ., and of Exec. Cttee. British Section Inter-Parly. Union, Foundation Fellow, and a Member of Exec. and Council of British Inst. of Management 1965-70, UK Delegate and leader of Conservative Party. Assembly of Council of Europe (Vice-Chm. Rapporteur Gen. Political Affairs Cttee), and of W. European Union since 1969; Gen. Foundation Gov. of Admin. Staff Coll., and a Member of Exec. and Council of Foundation for Management Education; Vice-Chm. of Exec. Cttee. Political and Economic Planning 1962-68, Grand Council Fedn. of British Industries 1963-65; Master, Masons' Co. 1967-68; Freeman of City of London; Author of several books and pamphlets; Knt. Grand Cross Order of Civil Merit of Spain; Grand Cross of Order of Merit Liechtenstein; Cdr. Order of Prince Henry the Navigator of Portugal; MP for Sevenoaks Div. of Kent (*C*) since 1950: *m.* 1930, Betsy (JP of E. Sussex), da. of Francis William Aikin-Sneath, JP, of Burleigh Court, Glos., and has issue.

Arms—Azure two bars gemel dancetty argent, over all two palm branches in saltire enfiled through an ancient crown or. **Crest**—Two ravens' heads addorsed sable and gules both within a collar or pendent therefrom a rose argent barbed and seeded proper.

Residences—The Dower House, Groombridge, Kent; 72, Berkeley House, Hay Hill, W.1. *Clubs*—Brooks's, Pratt's, Royal Thames Yacht.

Sons living—JOHN FAIRLIE TOBIAS (34, Warwick Av., W9), *b.* July 2nd, 1940; ed. at Eton and Worcester Coll., Oxford.——Andrew Piers Wingate, *b.* 1944; ed. at Eton and Merton Coll., Oxford.

ROLL, Creation (U.K.) 1921, of The Chestnuts, Wanstead, Essex.

Rev. *Sir* JAMES WILLIAM CECIL ROLL, 4th *Baronet;* *b.* June 1st, 1912 ; *s.* his father, *Sir* CECIL ERNEST, 1938; ed. at Chigwell Sch., Essex, at Pembroke Coll., Oxford, and at Chichester Theological Coll.; is V. of St. John the Divine, Becontree.

Arms—Or, on a fesse indented between four billets, three in chief and one in base azure, each charged with a lion rampant, a civic wreath of the field between two bezants. **Crest**—A dexter cubit arm vested or charged with two bars wavy azure, cuffed ermine, and holding in the hand a chaplet of laurel proper.

Residences—St. John's Vicarage, 34, Castle Rd., Dagenham, Essex; 53, Chalkwell Av., Westcliffe on Sea, Essex.

Brother living—GORDON WELLS, *b.* Nov. 4th, 1913; ed. at Cranleigh; Private Queen's Roy. Regt.; 1939-45 War (prisoner). *Residence*, Lee House, Dyke Rd., Brighton.
Daughters living of 2nd Baronet—Enid Helen, *b.* 1904: *m.* 1928, C. Raymond Watts, and has issue living, Jennifer Catherine, *b.* 1933. *Residence*, Combe House, Willingdon, Sussex.——Betty Catherine, *b.* 1910: *m.* 1932, Charles A. Sharman, and has issue living, Charles James Roll, *b.* 1934,—John Frederick, *b.* 1936,—Patrick George, *b.* 1939,—Nicholas Algernon, *b.* 1945,—Briony Anna, *b.* 1942. *Residence*, Rollesby, Westwood Park Road, Peterborough.

The 1st baronet, Sir James Roll, was Chm. of Pearl Assurance Co., Ltd., and Lord Mayor of London 1920-21.

ROPNER, Creation (U.K.) 1904, of Preston Hall, Stockton-on-Tees, Co. Palatine of Durham, and Skutterskelfe Hall, Hutton Rudby, North Riding of Yorkshire.

Sir ROBERT DOUGLAS ROPNER, 4th *Baronet,* *b.* Dec. 1st, 1921; *s.* his father, *Sir* (EMIL HUGO OSCAR) ROBERT, 1962; ed. at Harrow; formerly Capt. R.A.: *m.* 1943, Patricia Kathleen, da. of William Edward Scofield, of West Malling, Kent, and has issue.

Arms—Per fesse indented sable and or, a pale, with three mullets pierced two and one, and as many roebucks' heads erased one and two, all counterchanged. **Crest**—In front of three tilting spears, one erect, and two in saltire, or, as many mascles interlaced fessewise of the last, thereon a roebuck's head erased sable.

Residence—

Son living—ROBERT CLINTON, *b.* Feb. 6th, 1949; ed. at Harrow.
Daughter living—Serena Gay, *b.* 1953.
Sisters living—Diana Joan, *b.* 1919 : *m.* 1941, John Randal Elliott, of St. David's, 20, Flag Head Rd., Canford Cliffs, Poole, Dorset.——Patricia Elizabeth, *b.* 1923: *m.* 1944, Lieut.-Col. Claude MacDonald Hull, M.C., and has issue living, Susan Patricia Macdonald, *b.* 1948,—Fiona Elizabeth Macdonald, *b.* 1950. *Residence*, Forest Ridge, Maresfield Park, Sussex.

Daughter living of 2nd Baronet—Mary Enid, *b.* 1897 : *m.* 1932, Ronald Strathearn Stroyan who *d.* 1957, and has issue living, Ronald Angus Ropner, *QC* (of 17, Elm Park Rd., SW3), *b.* 1924; ed. at Harrow, and at Trin. Coll., Camb.; late Capt. The Black Watch 1943-47, in NW Europe, Palestine (despatches); Bar. Inner Temple 1950; QC 1972; Dep. Chm. N. Riding of Yorks. Quarter sessions 1962-70, Chm. 1970-71, and Recorder 1972: *m.* 1st, 1952, Elisabeth Anna, from whom he obtained a divorce 1965, da. of Col. John Peter Grant of Rothiemurchus, CB, MC, TD; 2ndly, 1967, Jill Annette Johnston, da. of Cdr. Sir Douglas Marshall, RN, and has issue living, (by 1st m.) John Ronald Angus *b.* 1955, Victoria Mary *b.* 1953, Julia Elisabeth *b.* 1958, (by 2nd m.) James Mark Ptarmigan Douglas *b.* 1969,—Colin Strathearn Ropner, *b.* 1927; ed. at Harrow,—Rosemary Ropner, *b.* 1930. *Residence,* Boreland, Killin, Perthshire.

Widow living of 3rd Baronet—LILLIAN ROCHFORT (*Lillian, Lady Ropner*), da. of Col. Rochfort Snow, of Christchurch, New Zealand: *m.* 1918, Sir (Emil Hugo Oscar) Robert Ropner, 3rd Bt., who *d.* 1962. *Residence,* 704, Dolphin Sq., SW1.

Collateral Branches living.

Grandchildren of Emil Hugo Oscar Robert Ropner, AMINA, 2nd son of 1st baronet:—
Issue of the late Lt.-Col. Richard Ropner, TD, MB, ChB, RAMC, *b.* 1898, *d.* 1975: *m.* 1928, Margaret Forbes (Aldie, Tain, Ross-shire), da. of John Gilfillan Ronald, MD, of Torwood Hall, Larbert, Stirlingshire:—
Richard John Ronald, *MB, ChB* (The Warneford Hosp., Warneford Lane, Headington, Oxon.), *b.* 1941; ed. at Harrow, and Edinburgh Univ. (MB, ChB); D (Obst.) RCOG; DPM; MRC Psych.: *m.* 1974, Janet Elizabeth, MRCP, el. da. of Joseph William Fox, PhD, of Marlow House, 3 Camden Park Rd., Chislehurst, Kent.——Alison Margaret, *b.* 1930: *m.* 1957, Gerald Robert Savage, of The Old Quarry, Bramley, Surrey, and has issue living, Nichola Mary, *b.* 1958.—— Pamela Christine, *b.* 1931; ed. at Edinburgh Univ. (MA): *m.* 1957 (Irving) Thomas Stuttaford, MRCS, LRCP, of Bramerton House, Bramerton, Norfolk, and has issue living, Andrew Irving Ropner, *b.* 1958,—Thomas Richard Ropner, *b.* 1961,—Hugo John Ropner, *b.* 1964.

Issue of the late Capt. (Cuthbert) Maurice Ropner, King's Own Scottish Borderers, *b.* 1905, *d.* (on active ser. during European War) 1945 : *m.* 1929, Dorothea Seymour (now of Heckley House, Alnwick, Northumberland), da. of the Rev. Robert William Bell, V. of Stamfordham :—
George Maurice, *b.* 1934; Maj. (ret.) Northumberland Hussars (TA). *Residence,* Gallowshaw, Netherwitton, Morpeth, Northumberland,——Vivien Anne, *b.* 1930.——Caroline Jane, *b.* 1945.

Issue of the late William Ropner, 3rd son of 1st baronet, *b.* 1864, *d.* 1947 : *m.* 1894, Sarah Woollacot, who *d.* 1948, da. of Ebenezer Cory :—
Sir Leonard, Bt., *MC, TD, b.* 1895; *cr. a Baronet* 1952.

Grandchildren of the late William Ropner (ante):—
Issue of the late Sir (William) Guy Ropner, *b.* 1896, *d.* 1971: *m.* 1921, Margarita, who *d.* 1973, da. of Sir William Cresswell Gray, 1st Bt.:—
William Guy David (9, York House, York House Place, W8), *b.* 1924; late Capt. RHA: *m.* 1955, Mildred Malise Hare, da. of George Armitage, MC, of Newburgh House, Coxwold, Yorks., and has issue living, Guy David Armitage, *b.* 1959,—Roderick John, *b.* 1962,—Peter Gavin Malise, *b.* 1964, —Lucy Armitage, *b.* 1957.——Jonathan Gray (Dalesend, Patrick Brompton, Bedale, Yorks.), *b.* 1931; late Lt. IG: *m.* 1953, Edith Avril, da. of Charles Urie Peat, MC, FCA, and has issue living, Jonathan Mark, *b.* 1954,—Charles Guy Corban, *b.* 1959,—Paul Benedict Peat, *b.* 1965,—Dominic Adam, *b.* 1968,—Margarita Carey, *b.* 1956.——Rita Gray (17, Campden Hill Court, Campden Hill Rd., W8), *b.* 1922: *m.* 1947 (m. diss. 1967), Alan Maskew Hodson, and has issue.

Issue of the late William Ropner (ante):—
John Raymond, *b.* 1903; ed. at Harrow, and at Clare Coll., Camb.; is a Dir. of Sir R. Ropner and Co., Ltd.: *m.* 1928, Joan, da. of the late William Redhead, and has issue living, William David Jock, *b.* 1929: *m.* 1961 (m. diss. 1962), Elizabeth Anne Ellsworth Jones,—Jeremy Vyvyan (Firby Hall, Bedale, Yorks.), *b.* 1932: *m.* 1955, his cousin, Sally Talbot, da. of Maj. George Talbot Willcox, MC, and has issue living, Clive Vyvyan Peter *b.* 1957, Simon Jock Wilks *b.* 1962, Sophia Sally *b.* 1959, Lisa *b.* 1964,—Susan Carole, *b.* 1936: *m.* 1957, Maj. Charles Peter Martel, of The Manor House, Gayles Richmond, Yorks., only son of the late Lt.-Gen. Sir Giffard le Quesne Martel, KCB, KBE, DSO, MC, and has issue living, Nicholas Charles Giffard *b.* 1960, Carole Valerie *b.* 1958, Sarah Charlotte *b.* 1973. *Residence,* Middleton Lodge Middleton Tyas, Richmond, Yorks. ——Sir Robert Desmond, *b.* 1908; ed. at Harrow, and at Clare Coll., Camb. (BA 1930); a Ship-owner, a Dir of Ropner Holdings, Ltd., and Asso. Cos. of Airtech, Ltd., and of Croft Autodrome, Ltd., a Member of Exec. Council of Shipping Federation, Ltd., and a Past Chm. of N. of England Protecting and Indemnity Assocn.; a Member of Council of Chamber of Shipping of U.K. and various Cttees. since 1941 (Pres. 1958-59, Chm. Deep Sea Tramp Section 1951-53); a Member of Min. of Transport Ships Licensing Cttee. 1947, and Chm. of Tramp Shipping Sub-Cttee. of Shipping Advisory and Allocations Cttee. 1947; a Member of Shipping Advisory Panel 1962, and of Gen. Council of British Shipping (Chm. 1958-59); formerly Capt. RA (TA), Knt. 1959: *m.* 1st, 1932, Dorothy Beecroft (who obtained a divorce 1946), da. of Sir Edmund Beecroft Francis Heathcote Lacon, 5th Bt.; 2ndly, 1947, Sibyl, who *d.* 1969, da. of the late Thomas O. Carter, and has issue living, (by 1st m.) Robert Bruce Beecroft (of Kirklington House, Kirkling-ton, nr. Bedale, Yorks.) *b.* 1933; Lt. Welsh Guards: *m.* 1960, Willow, da. of James Hare, of Field-head, Thorner, nr. Leeds, and has issue living, Robert James Bruce *b.* 1962,—Nicola Molly *b.* 1965,—Garry Lacon Jock (Henley Lodge, Henley, Marlborough, Wilts.), *b.* 1937: *m.* 1st, 1962, (m. diss. 1973), Antonia, yr. da. of Maj.-Gen. Edward Charles Colville, CB, DSO [see V. Colville of Culross, colls.]; 2ndly, 1974, Julie Marie Swanwick, and has issue living (by 1st m.), Emma Louise *b.* 1963. *Residences,* Camp Hill, Kirklington, Bedale, Yorks; Flat F7, Sloane Avenue Mansions, SW3. *Club,* Boodle's.——Constance Winsome (Hyde Farm, Shamley Green, Surrey), *b.* 1899: *m.* 1922, Maj. George Talbot Willcox, MC, who *d.* 1968, and has issue living, Peter Desmond Ropner Talbot (Thanescroft, Shamley Green, Surrey), *b.* 1927: *m.* 1950, Jennifer April, da. of Lt.-Col. Edward Holt, OBE, MC, and has issue living, Paul David Talbot, *b.* 1952, Nicola Jane Talbot, *b.* 1955, Jennifer Lucy Talbot *b.* 1957,—Henrietta Talbot *b.* 1946,—Winsome Wendy Talbot, *b.* 1924: *m.* 1962, Maurice Mitchell-Heggs, of Maple Tree Cottage, Dunsfold, Surrey, and has issue living, Caroline Anne Winsome *b.* 1962,—Sally Talbot, *b.* 1931: *m.* 1955, her cousin Jeremy Vyvyan Ropner (ante).

Issue of the late Walter Ropner, 4th son of 1st baronet ; *b.* 1868; *d.* 194–: *m.* 1894, Jane Constance, who *d.* 1951, da. of Ebenezer Cory :—
Kathleen, *b.* 1895. *Residence,* Chestnut Cottage, Hadlow Down, Sussex.

Issue of the late Leonard Ropner, 5th son of 1st baronet, *b.* 1873, *d.* 1937 : *m.* 1904, Georgina, who *d.* 1930, da. of the late Murdock Mackay:—
Leonard Robert, *b.* 1910: *m.* 1934, Agnes Deans Bennett.——Helen Mary (*Lady Hewson*), *b.* 1905 : *m.* 1933, Hon. Sir (Joseph) Bushby Hewson, R.D., and has issue living, a da., *b.* 1936. *Residence,* 77, Eyre Court, St. John's Wood, N.W.8.——Jean Winifred, *b.* 1908 : *m.* 1929, Victor Bremner Purvis, M.B., B.S., and has issue living, Ian Bremner, *b.* 1933,—Julia Mackay, *b.* 1937. *Residence,* Upper Town Farm, Clifton Hampden, Abingdon, Berks.

The 1st baronet, Sir (Emil Hugh Oscar) Robert Ropner (a steamship owner of West Hartlepool and a steamship builder of Stockton-on-Tees), son of Henry Ropner, of Magdeburg, sat as M.P. for Stockton-on-Tees (C) 1900-10.

ROPNER, Creation (U.K.) 1952, of Thorp Perrow, N. Riding of Yorkshire.

Faith and Fortitude.

FIDES ET FORTITUDO

Sir LEONARD ROPNER, *M.C., T.D.,* 1st *Baronet*, son of the late William Ropner [*see* Ropner, Bt., cr. 1904]; *b.* Feb. 26th, 1895; ed. at Harrow, and at Clare Coll., Camb. (BA 1922); a DL for co. Durham and a KStJ; Hon. Col. (late Comdg.) Durham Heavy Bde. RA (TA) 1928-56; Chm. of Hartlepools Conservative Assocn. 1920-23, PPS to Sec. of State for War 1924-28, Hon. Treasurer of Conservative and Unionist Films Assocn. 1930-47 (Chm. 1947-59), a Forestry Commr. 1936-45, a Member of Durham Co. T. and A.F. Assocn. 1920-61 (Vice-Chm. 1948-51); Assist. Controller of Timber Supply, Min. of Supply 1939, a Member of Timber Supply Dept. 1940, and Dep. Director of Home Grown Timber Production 1941; a temporary Chm. of Committees, House of Commons 1945-58; Chm. of Conservative Shipping and Shipbuilding Cttee. 1946-64, a Co. Commr. St. John Ambulance Bde., N. Riding of Yorks. 1950-67, and Hon. Treasurer of Primrose League 1952-64; 1914-18 War in France as Maj. GRA (MC), 1939-45 War as Lt.-Col. RA and Col. 21st Army Group in Belgium and Germany; MP for Sedgfield Div. of co. Durham (C) 1923-29, and for Barkstone Ash Div. of W. Riding of Yorkshire 1931-64: *m.* 1932, Esmé, yst. da. of the late William Bruce Robertson of 26, Kensington Palace Gdns., W8, and has issue.

Arms—Per fesse indented sable and or, a pale, with three mullets pierced two and one, and as many roebucks' heads erased one and two, all counterchanged; a crescent or for difference. Crest—In front of three tilting spears, one erect and two in saltire or, as many mascles interlaced fessewise of the last, thereon a roebuck's head erased sable.

Residence—Thorp Perrow, Bedale, Yorks. *Clubs*—Carlton, Bath, Durham County, Yorkshire.

Son living—JOHN BRUCE WOOLLACOTT (of Park House, Bedale, Yorks.), *b.* April 16th, 1937; ed. at Eton, and at St. Paul's Sch., USA: *m.* 1st, 1961 (m. diss. 1970), Anne Melicent, da. of Sir Ralph Hubert John Delmé-Radcliffe; 2ndly, 1970, Auriol Veronica, yr. da. of Capt. Graham Lawrie Mackeson-Sandbach, of Caerllo, Llangernyw, Abergele, Denbighshire, and has issue living (by 1st m.), Jenny, *b.* 1963,—Katherine, *b.* 1964,—(by 2nd m.) Carolyn Esmé, *b.* 1971, —Annabel Mariella, *b.* 1974.

Daughters living—Merle Aurelia, *b.* 1939: *m.* 1st, 1960 (m. diss. 1968), Christopher John Spence; 2ndly, 1968, Maj. Laurence Hew Williams Barrington, of Nether Lypiatt Manor, Stroud, [see Barrington, Bt. colls.], and has issue living (by 1st m.) Jeremy Mark, *b.* 1964,—Miranda Jane, *b.* 1963,—(by 2nd m.), [see Barrington Bt., colls.].—Virginia June, *b.* 1941: *m.* 1st, 1962 (m. diss. 1973), Anthony David Arnold William Forbes [see B. Faringdon, colls.]; 2ndly. 19—, Sandy Henderson, of The Old Vicarage, Sandon, Herts.

ROSE, Creation (U.K.) 1872, of Montreal, Dominion of Canada.

I dare.

AVDEO

CONSTANT · AND · TRVE

Sir FRANCIS CYRIL ROSE, 4th *Baronet;* *b.* Sept. 18th, 1909; *s.* his father, *Sir* CYRIL STANLEY, 1915; is a Painter and Author; served in R.A.F, 1940-42 (invalided): *m.* 1st, 1943 (m. diss. 1966) Mrs. Frederica Dorothy Violet Sproul Bolton, da of the late Maj.-Gen. Sir Frederick Carrington, KCB, KCMG; 2ndly (m. diss. 197-), 1967, Beryl, da. of Alfred Norris widow of Sqdn.-Ldr. Basil Montefiore Davis, RAF.

Arms—Or, a boar's head couped gules between three water bougets sable; on a chief of the second three maple leaves of the first. Crest—A harp or, stringed azure.

Residence—

Collateral Branch living.

Descendants of the late Sir Charles Day Rose, M.P. (2nd son of 1st baronet), who was *cr.* a *Baronet* 1909:—

Of whom *Sir* JULIAN DAY, 4th *Bt.* (*cr.* 1909), *b.* March 3rd, 1947; is *h.p.* to this Baronetcy.

Rt. Hon. Sir William Rose, G.C.M.G., 1st baronet, was Min. of Finance, Canada 1868-69, and Receiver-Gen. for Duchy of Cornwall 1883-88. He was son of William Rose of Huntingdon, Canada, who was *b.* at Tureff, Aberdeenshire, of a family originally from co. Nairn.

ROSE, Creation (U.K.) 1874, of Rayners, Buckinghamshire.

Sir PHILIP HUMPHREY VIVIAN ROSE, 3rd *Baronet*, son of the late Capt. Philip Vivian Rose, el. son of 2nd baronet ; *b.* March 16th, 1903; *s.* his grandfather, *Sir* PHILIP FREDERICK, 1919; ed. at Harrow; European War 1939-45 : *m.* 1927, Joan, da. of the late Martin Richardson, M.D., and has issue.

Arms—Azure, a chevron invected erminois, between three water bougets in chief and one in base argent. **Crest**—A stag argent, collared, and resting the dexter fore-leg on a water bouget azure.

Residence—Tyler's Cottage, Peterley, Great Missenden, Bucks.

Probitate ac virtute

By probity and valour.

Daughters living—Petica Mary, *b.* 1929 : *m.* 1955, Andrew Felix Waley, VRD, QC, and has issue living, Simon Felix, *b.* 1964,—Sarah Elizabeth, *b.* 1958,—Jane Felicity, *b.* 1959,—Juliet Anne, *b.* 1960. *Residence*, 24, Manor Way, Blackheath, SE3.——Susan Elizabeth Ann, *b.* 1932.

Sisters living—Marjorie Winifred, *b.* 1900: *m.* 1927, Wilfred Eyre, of 835, South Garfield St., Denver, Colorado, 80209, USA, and has issue living, Richard Carmel Thomas More, *b.* 1936: *m.* 1965, Josepha Mary Schretlen, and has issue living, Richard Edward *b.* 1966, Andrea Marjorie *b.* 1967, Christina Maria *b.* 1969, Judith Mary *b.* 1971,—Vivian Mary Raymonde, *b.* 1928: *m.* 1949, John Sweeney, of 461, Race St., Denver, Colorado, USA, and has issue living, Michael Eyre *b.* 1953, Timothy Andrew *b.* 1957, Edward Philip *b.* 1963, Mark McConnell *b.* 1965, Marna Therese *b.* 1950, Carol Mary *b.* 1958, Kathrine Ann *b.* 1960,—Elisa Virginia Mary, *b.* 1932: *m.* 1st, 1952 (m. diss. 1963), Charles Bennet Cobb; 2ndly, 1963, Christopher Brennan, of 2899, Rambla Pacifica, Malibu, Cal., USA, and has issue living (by 1st m.), Charles Dennison *b.* 1955, Gerald Bennett *b.* 1956, Marguerite Elisa *b.* 1957 (by 2nd m.), Christopher Edward *b.* 1972,—Jane Olga Mary, *b.* 1934: *m.* 1960, Bruce Schuster, of 4730, South Lafayette, Englewood, Colorado, USA, and has issue living, Anthony Bruce *b.* 1964, Philip Andrew *b.* 1965, Christopher Paul *b.* 1969, Matthew Ainsworth *b.* 1972, Jane Eyre, *b.* 1962.——June Dorothy (715, Bonnie Brae Blvd., Denver, Colorado, USA), *b.* 1913: *m.* 1938 (m. diss. 19—), Marcel Brennan, and has issue living, Christopher *b.* 1939.

Collateral Branches living.

Issue of the late Bateman Lancaster Rose, 5th son of 1st baronet, *b.* 1851, *d.* 1911 : *m.* 1906, Editha, who *d.* 1963, da. of Sir John Frederick Croft, 2nd Bt. (*cr.* 1818):—

RONALD PAUL LANCASTER, *b.* July 31st, 1907: *m.* 1st, 1933, Shelagh Grant Lindsay (from whom he obtained a divorce 1937), da. of Maj. — Curtis; 2ndly, 1938, Peggy Gleitzman; 3rdly, 1948, Emily Lavender, da. of the late Capt. Henry Vivian Hare, and widow of Tom E. Montgomery [*see* E. Listowel, colls.], and has issue living, (by 1st marriage) David Lancaster, *b.* 1934 *m.* 1965, Dorothy Whitehead, and has issue living, Philip John Lancaster *b.* 1966. *Residence*, Coole Abbey, Fermoy, co. Cork.

Grandchildren of the late George Alfred Sainte Croix Rose, 6th son of 1st baronet:—

Issue of the late Major Ivor Sainte Croix Rose, O.B.E., *b.* 1881: *m.* 1st, 1907, Etta Mabel, who *d.* 1918, youngest da. of the late Com. Sebastian Gassiot, R.N.; 2ndly, 1918, Nancy (who *d.* 1968, and from whom he obtained a divorce 1935), da. of Arthur Conran Blomfield; 3rdly, 1936, Ruth Elldale, who *d.* 1952 (and from whom he had obtained a divorce 1951), da. of Richard White, of Nain, Labrador:—

(By 3rd m.) George Vivian Sainte Croix (33 Webb's Rd., SW11), *b.* 1939: *m.* 1960, Audrey Rosamond, da. of Lawrence Frederick Barrow, and has issue living, Philip Vivian Sainte Croix, *b.* 1961,—Alison, *b.* 1960.——(By 1st m.) Nancy Bertha Mary Sainte Croix (Christmas House, Hook Park, Warsash, Southampton, SO3 6HA), *b.* 1908: *m.* 1934, Cdr. Rupert St. Aubyn Malleson, AFC, RN, who *d.* 1960, son of the late Maj.-Gen. Sir Wilfrid Malleson, KCIE, CB.—— (By 2nd m.) Camilla Mary Sainte Croix, *b.* 1919: *m.* 1945, Richard Oliver MacMahon Williams, MBE, MC, WS, of Cross Roads, Currie, Midlothian, and has issue living, Caroline Jane Sainte Croix, *b.* 1947,—Nicola Valentine Blomfield, *b.* 1948: *m.* 1972, Capt. Alistair Stuart Hastings Irwin, The Black Watch (R. Highland Regt.),—Rosemary Anne MacMahon, *b.* 1952: *m.* 1973, Adrian Gerald Burns, MA,—Lorna Christine Allan, *b.* 1954.

Issue of the late Harcourt George Sainte Croix Rose, *b.* 1883, *d.* 1955 : *m.* 1st, 1908, Florence Norah (who *d.* 1970, having obtained a divorce 1920), da. of Arthur Elliot Deane, of Littleton House, Winchester [Hughes, Bt., *cr.* 1773]; 2ndly, 1920, Freda Victoria (who *d.* 1972, having obtained a divorce 1930), da. of the late C. A. Keyser; 3rdly, 1930, Estelle Marie, da. of the late Marquis of Sarzano, 8th Hussars:—

(By 1st marriage) Jean *b.* 1015 : European War 1939-45 with W.A.A.F. : *m.* 1953, Lieut.-Com. Henry Francis Ormsby Hale, RN.

Sir Philip Rose, 1st Bt., was Founder of the Brompton Hospital for Consumption (Hon.-Sec. 1841-83), and High Sheriff of Bucks 1878.

ROSE, Creation (U.K.) 1909, of Hardwick House, Whitchurch, Oxfordshire.

I dare.

AVDEO

Sir JULIAN DAY ROSE, 4th *Baronet, b.* March 3rd, 1947; *s.* his father, *Sir* CHARLES HENRY ROSE, 1966; ed. at Stanbridge Earls Sch., Romsey; *h.p.* to Baronetcy of Rose of Montreal (*cr.* 1872).

Arms—Or, a boar's head couped gules between three water bougets sable, a crescent of the last for difference ; on a chief of the second three maple leaves of the first. **Crest**—An angelic harp or, stringed azure.
Seat—Hardwick House, Whitchurch, Oxon.

Sisters living—Margaret Minna, *b.* 1938: *m.* 1966, John Alexander Cochrane, of Fairspear House, Leafield, Oxford, el. son of the Hon. Sir Ralph Alexander Cochrane [see B. Cochrane of Cults.].——Penelope Clare, *b.* 1945: *m.* 1975, Francis A. A. Carnwath.

Aunts living (daughters of 2nd baronet)—Amy, *b.* 1911: *m.* 1933, Robert Beloe, CBE, and has issue living, *Rev.* Robert Francis (The Vicarage, Wicken, nr. Ely, Cambs.), *b.* 1939: *m.* 1970, Sheila Napier Millar, and has issue living, Amy Margaret *b.* 1971, Christina Ruth *b.* 1973,—Helen, *b.* 1934: *m.* 1955, Oliver Piers Stutchbury, of 139, Old Church St., SW3 6EB, and has issue living, Wycliffe Robert Trant *b.* 1965, Emma Jane *b.* 1955, Catharine Rose *b.* 1958, Rosalind Amy *b.* 1960, Clarissa Elizabeth *b.* 1936: *m.* 1963, John Eagle Higginbotham (Teme House, Lancing College, Lancing, Sussex) and has issue living, Robert Charles Trant *b.* 1967, Lydia Clare *b.* 1964. *Residence*, The Hill House, Queen's Rd., Richmond, Surrey.——Helen Briar (*posthumous*), *b.* 1915: *m.* 1939, Lt.-Col. John Granville, Oxford and Bucks LI [Halsey, Bt.], and has issue living, Antony Lansdown (Tachbrook House, Stourton, nr. Shipton-on-Stour, Warwicks.), *b.* 1945: *m.* 1970, Harriet Anne, da. of Sir John James Macdonald Horlick, 5th Bt., and has issue living, Edward James *b.* 1972,—Charles, *b.* 1949. *Residence*, Holly Copse, Goring Heath, nr. Reading, Berks.

Widow living of 3rd Baronet—Hon. PHOEBE MARGARET DOROTHY PHILLIMORE (*Hon. Lady Rose*), (Hardwick House, Whitchurch, Oxon.), da. of 2nd Baron Phillimore: *m.* 1937, Sir Charles Henry Rose, 3rd baronet, who *d.* 1966.

The 1st baronet, Sir Charles Day Rose, son of the late Rt. Hon. Sir John Rose, P.C., G.C.M.G., 1st Bt. (cr. 1872, ante), sometime a partner in the American Banking firm of Morton, Rose and Co., of Bartholomew Lane, E.C., sat as M.P. for Newmarket, (L) 1903-10 and 1910-13. The 2nd baronet, Capt. Sir Frank Stanley, 10th R. Hussars, was killed in action 1914.

ROSE, Creation (U.K.) 1935, of Leith, Co. of City of Edinburgh.

Constant and True

Sir HUGH ROSE, *T.D.*, 2nd *Baronet; b.* Dec. 16th, 1902 ; *s.* his father, *Col. Sir* (HUGH) ARTHUR, *DSO*, 1937; Major RA (TA), Capt. Queen's Body Guard for Scotland (Roy. Co. of Archers), a DL for Edinburgh, a Dir. of Scottish Provident Inst., and of Securities Trust of Scotland, Ltd.; Co. Commr. for Boy Scouts for Edinburgh and Leith 1947-51, a Commr, of Gen. Board of Control for Scotland 1936-62, a Member of Council on Tribunals 1958-62, and Chm. of Mental Welfare Commn. for Scotland 1962-65; 1939-45 War in Italy (despatches): *m.* 1930, Marjorie, da. of T. Leslie Usher, of 8, Whitehouse Terr., Edinburgh, and Hyndhope, Selkirk, and has issue.

Arms—Or, two water bougets in chief and in base an ancient galley with two masts, sails furled sable, flagged gules, seated therein the Virgin Mary with the infant Saviour in her arms, all proper. **Crest**—A falcon proper.

Residence—38, Frogston Rd. West, Edinburgh, EH10 7AJ.

Daughter living—Alison Mary (29, Winton Loan, Edinburgh), *b.* 1936: *m.* 1964, (m. diss. 1972), Ian Napier.
Sister living—Mary Catherine, *b.* 1905: *m.* 1932, Frederick Cairns Laing, MB, ChB. *Residence*, Delta House, Inveresk, Midlothian.

Col. Sir (Hugh) Arthur Rose, 1st Bt., D.S.O. (son of the late Hugh Rose, of Kilravock Lodge, Edinburgh), was a paint and varnish manufacturer, Chm. of Clyde, Paper & Co., Ltd., Hon. Col. Forth Heavy Brigade, R.A. (T.A.), and a D.L.

ROSS, Creation (U.K.) 1919, of Dunmoyle, Parish of Errigal Keerogue, co. Tyrone.
[Extinct 1958.]

Sir RONALD DEANE ROSS, *M.C.*, 2nd and last *Baronet.*

Widow living of 2nd Baronet—DOROTHY EVELYN FRANCES (*Lady Ross*), da. of the late Rev Algernon Charles Dudley Ryder [*see* E. Harrowby, colls.] : *m.* 1921, Sir Ronald Dean Ross 2nd Bt., M.C., who *d.* 1958, when the title became ext. *Residences,* Dunmoyle, Omagh, co. Tyrone ; 49, Morpeth Mansions, S.W.1.

ROSS, Creation (U.K.) 1960, of Whetstone, Middlesex.

Sir JAMES PATERSON ROSS, *K.C.V.O.*, 1st Baronet, son of James Ross, of Harpenden Herts ; *b.* May 26th, 1895 ; ed. at Christ's Coll., Finchley, and at London Univ. (M.B. and B.S. 1920, M.S. 1928) ; M.R.C.S. England and L.R.C.P. London 1917 ; F.R.C.S. England 1922 ; an Hon. Fellow of American Coll. of Surgs. 1953 ; Hon. LL.D. Glasgow, and an Hon. F.R.A.C.S. 1957 ; Hon. F.R.C.S. Edinburgh 1959 ; Hon. Fellow of Faculty of Radiologists 1959 ; Hon. F.R.F.P.S. Glasgow 1959; Hon. FDS 1964; Consulting Surg. to St. Bartholomew's Hospital; a Member of Council of Roy. Coll of Surgs., England 1943-61 (Pres. 1957-60); Consulting-Surg. to RN 1952; Professor of Surgery, London Univ. 1935-60; received Hon. Freedom of Barbers' Co. 1955, and of Apothecaries' Soc. 1956; Sims Commonwealth Travelling Professor 1957; Surg. to H.M. 1952-64; 1914-18 War as Surg.-Lt. RN; K.C.V.O. 1949: *m.* 1924, Marjorie Burton, da. of Capt. F. W. Townsend, and has issue.

Arms—Per pale argent and sable a chevron between in chief lion passant and in base an anchor all counterchanged. **Crest**—A hawk rising sable between two branches of juniper leaved and fructed proper.
Residence—Flat H, 14, John Spencer Sq., Canonbury, N.1.

Sons living—JAMES KEITH, *RD, MS, FRCS* (Moonhills Gate, Hilltop, Beaulieu, Hants, SO4 7YS), *b.* May 9th, 1927; MB and MS London; FRCS 1956; Surg. Lt.-Cdr. RNR: *m.* 1956, Jacqueline Annella, da. of F. W. Clarke of Banstead, Surrey, and has issue living, Andrew *b.* 1966,—Susan, *b.* 1958,—Janet, *b.* 1960,—Anne, *b.* 1962.——Harvey Burton, *RD, MS, FRCS* (Miles's Green House, Bucklebury, Reading, RG7 6SH), *b.* 1928; FRCS 1957: *m.* 1962, Nancy Joan, da. of B. C. Hilliam, of Bank, Lyndhurst, and has issue living, Edward Paterson, *b.* 1963,— James Hilliam, *b.* 1972,—Imogen, *b.* 1970.

ROTHBAND, Creation (U.K.) 1923, of Higher Broughton, Salford, co. Palatine of Lancaster. [Extinct 1940.]

Sir HENRY LESSER ROTHBAND, 1st and last *Baronet.*

Granddaughter living of 1st Baronet
Issue of the late Percy Lionel Rothband, only son of 1st baronet, *b.* 1884, *d.* 1926 : *m.* 1918, Ellen Elizabeth Marjorie, el. da. of William Francis Fisher, of Altrincham :—
Joan Olga Eleanor, *b.* 1920 : *m.* 19—, —— Atkins. *Resides in S. Africa.*

Rouse-Boughton, see Boughton.

ROWLAND, Creation (U.K.) 1950, of Taunton, co. Somerset. [Extinct 1970.]

Sir WENTWORTH LOWE ROWLAND, 2nd and last *Baronet.*

Daughter living of 2nd Baronet—Georgina Elizabeth Mary, *b.* 1952.

Daughters living of 1st Baronet—Gladys Mary, *b.* 1904. *Residence,* 2, Kings Av., Carshalton Beeches, Surrey.——Margery Doreen, *b.* 1908: *m.* 1931, George Francis Brooks, and has issue living, George Rowland, *b.* 1935,—Julia Margery, *b.* 1945. *Residence,* 59, Foxley Lane, Purley, Surrey.

Widow living of 2nd Baronet—(VIOLET MARY) ELIZABETH MACBETH (*Lady Rowland*), (Penn Cottage, Langton Green, Tunbridge Wells, Kent), da. of the late A. C. Macbeth Robertson, of Dumfries: *m.* 1947, Sir Wentworth Lowe Rowland, 2nd baronet, who *d.* 1970.

ROWLEY, Creation (G.B.) 1786, of Tendring Hall, Suffolk.

Sir Joshua Francis Rowley, 7th *Baronet;* **b.** Dec. 31st, 1920; *s.* his father, *Col. Sir* Charles Samuel, *O.B.E., T.D.,* 1962; ed. at Eton, and at Trin. Coll., Camb., formerly Capt. Gren. Gds.; a Vice-Lieut. for Suffolk since 1973; patron of three livings: *m.* 1959, the Hon. Celia Ella Vere Monckton, da. of 8th Viscount Galway, and has issue.

Arms—Argent, on a bend engrailed, between two Cornish choughs sable, billed and legged gules, three escallops of the field. **Crest**—A mullet pierced or.

Seat—The Cottage, Stoke-by-Nayland, Suffolk. *Clubs,*—Pratt's, Boodle's.

Ventis secundis.
With favouring winds.

————

Daughter living—Susan Emily Frances, **b.** 1965.

Sisters living—Althea Susan, **b.** 1922: *m.* 1949, Henry Reginald Townshend, MBE, of Brook Hall, Bramfield, Suffolk, and has issue living, James Reginald, **b.** 1954,—Robert Charles, **b.** 1956,—Albinia Jane, **b.** 1952.——Prudence Louisa (*Hon. Mrs. Martin D. Fortescue*), **b.** 1926: *m.* 1954, the Hon. Martin Denzil Fortescue [*see* E. Fortescue]. *Residence,* Wincombe Park, Shaftesbury, Dorset.

Widow living of 6th Baronet—Margery Frances (*Margery, Lady Rowley*), da. of Sir Nicholas Henry Bacon, 13th Bt.: *m.* 1920, Sir Charles Samuel Rowley, OBE, TD, 6th baronet, who *d.* 1962. *Residence,* Holbecks, Hadleigh, Ipswich, Suffolk.

Collateral Branches living.

Descendants of the late Adm. Sir Charles Rowley, G.C.B., G.C.H. (4th son of Sir Joshua Rowley, 1st baronet), who was *cr.* a *Baronet,* 1836.
See Rowley, Bt., *cr.* 1836.

————

The 1st baronet, Rear-Adm. Sir Joshua Rowley (son of Sir William Rowley, Adm. of the Fleet), took part in the actions off Grenada 1779, and off Martinique April and May 1780. Adm. Sir Josias Rowley, G.C.B., nephew of 1st baronet, was created a baronet 1813, and died unmarried 1842. The 3rd baronet, Sir Joshua Ricketts Rowley, was Vice-Adm. of the Blue.

ROWLEY, Creation (U.K.) 1836, of Hill House, Berkshire.

Sir Charles Robert Rowley, 7th *Baronet*; **b.** March 15th, 1926; *s.* his father, *Lt.-Col. Sir* William Joshua, 1971; ed. at Wellington: *m.* 1952, Astrid, da. of Sir Arthur Massey, CBE, MD, of 93, Bedford Gdns., W8, and has issue.

Arms,—Argent, on a bend engrailed between two Cornish choughs sable, three escallops of the field. **Crest,**—A mullet pierced or. **Supporters;**—Two Cornish choughs proper, navally crowned or, gorged with the riband and therefrom pendent a representation of the badge of the Imperial Austrian Order of Maria Theresa also proper.

Residences—Naseby Hall, Northants.; 21, Tedworth Sq., SW3.

With favouring winds.

Son living—Richard Charles, **b.** Aug. 14th, 1959.

Daughter living—Caroline Astrid, **b.** 1955.

Brother living—(Joshua) Christopher (The Stud House, Home Park, Hampton Court Palace, Surrey), **b.** 1928.

Sister living—Avice Gwendoline, **b.** 1920: *m.* 1953, John Arderne Mere Latham, and has issue living, Mark Joshua Arderne, **b.** 1955,—Robert, **b.** 1956. *Residence,* Forge Cawston, Norfolk.

Half-sisters living—Felicity Margaret, **b.** 1945: *m.* 1967, Alexander Michael Foulds Slinger, of Slaters House, Widdington, Saffron Walden, Essex, CB11 3SN, and has issue living, Arabella Claire Felicity, **b.** 1972.——Prudence Elizabeth, **b.** 1951: *m.* 1972, Simon Geoffry Hull, of 73, The Street, Little Waltham, Chelmsford, and has issue living, Thomas Gresham, **b.** 1975.

Sister living of 5th Baronet—Eleanor Caroline, **b.** 1899: *m.* 1922, Harry Lindsay Molyneux, who *d.* 1956, and has issue living, Peter Lindsay, **b.** 1923; formerly Officer Cadet Roy. Tank Regt. (invalided): *m.* 1946, Jocelyn Sivyer, and has issue living, Susanne Lindsay **b.** 1949, Annette Rowley **b.** 1950, Elizabeth Anne **b.** 1953,—Michael Rowley (66, Clarendon Drive, SW15), **b.** 1929; BA 1953; Bar. Inner Temple 1956: *m.* 1956, Pamela Mary Webb, and has issue living, Simon Rowley **b.** 1958, Matthew Ian **b.** 1961, Jennie Cameron **b.** 1959, Sophie Caroline **b.** 1964. *Residence,* Greenbanks, Upper Station Rd., Henfield, Sussex.

Mother living—Beatrice Gwendoline (Hill View House, Fressingfield, Norfolk), da. of the late Rev. Augustus George Kirby, formerly V. of South Weald, Essex: *m.* 1st, 1917, Sir William Joshua Rowley, 6th Bt., who *d.* 1971, and from whom she obtained a divorce 1940; 2ndly, 1942 Marie Charles Antone Thomas Hill, who *d.* 1966.

Widows living of 5th and 6th Baronets—Marjorie Alice (Parker) (*Marjorie, Lady Rowley*), da. of the late John William Borcherds Blagrave: *m.* 1939, Sir George William Rowley, 5th Bt., who *d.* 1953.——Margaret Sheila (*Margaret, Lady Rowley*), (Widdington House, Widdington, Newport, Essex), da. of the late Harold Camp, of Stamford, Conn., USA: *m.* 1940, as his 2nd wife, Sir William Joshua Rowley, 6th Bt., who *d.* 1971.

Collateral Branches living.

Grandchildren of the late Julius Richard Capel Molyneux Rowley, el. son of the late Rev. Julius Henry Rowley, son of the late Capt. Richard Freeman Rowley, RN, 4th son of 1st baronet:—
Issue of the late Capt. Charles Donovan Rowley, M.B.E., **b.** 1889, *d.* 1935: *m.* 1917, the Hon. Irene Evelyn Beatrice (who *d.* 1949, having *m.* 2ndly, 1941, Frank Ash, who *d.* 1974, of Narborough Hall, King's Lynn, Norfolk), da. of 9th Viscount Molesworth:—

John Howard (The Broad House, Ormesby St. Michael, Gt. Yarmouth), *b.* 1931; formerly Lt. RA (TA): *m.* 1963, Aileen Margery, da. of R. Clifford Freeman, of Little Dawley, Gerrards Cross, Bucks, and has issue living, Charles John Freeman, *b.* 1969,—Irene Frances Elizabeth, *b.* 1965.——Elisabeth Gem (Beeston Spinney, Church Close, W. Runton, Cromer), *b.* 1918: assumed by deed poll the Christian names of Elisabeth Gem in lieu of those of Mary Destine: *m.* 1940, the Rev. Edward Guy Betton Bright-Betton, who *d.* 1973.——Nina Irene (Camphill Village, Alpha Kalbaskraal, W. Cape, 7302, S. Africa), *b.* 1922.——June Rose, *b.* 1924: *m.* 1963, Thomas Opitz, of Jim Jim, via Darwin, Aust.——Julia May, *b.* 1934: *m.* 1955, Anthony Frederick Twist, and has issue living, Andrew Charles, *b.* 1958,—Julian Richard, *b.* 1960,—Philip Michael, *b.* 1962,—Catherine Julia, *b.* 1956. *Residence*, Warren House, High Kelling, Holt, Norfolk.

Granddaughters of the late Julius Leigh Rowley (infra):—
Issue of the late Robin Julius Leigh, *b.* 1892, *d.* 1974: *m.* 1920, Edith May (Lloyd House, The Square, Westbourne, nr. Emsworth, Hants.), da. of Sidney Hugo Mumford, of Eton, Bucks.:—
Thelma Jeanne, *b.* 1923: *m.* 1946, Rene Georges Lucien Paul Lefevre, of 2, Dell Cottage, Woodmancote, nr. Emsworth, Hants., and has issue living, Julian Howard Georges Alphonse, *b.* 1949; ed. at Leeds Univ. (BA),—Michelle Edith Germaine, *b.* 1946,—Christine Rene Jeanne, *b.* 1948,—Jacqueline Marguerite Frederica, *b.* 1951.——Audrey Frederica, *b.* 1928: *m.* 1949, Thomas Arthur Smith, of Eastney Cottage, Duffield Lane, Woodmancote, Emsworth, Hants., and has issue living, Ivan Howard Lee, *b.* 1952,—Stephen Frederick John, *b.* 1955.

Grandchildren of the late Rev. Julius Henry Rowley (ante):—
Issue of the late Julius Leigh Rowley, *b.* 1863; *d.* 1943: *m.* 1st, 1890, Florence, who *d.* 1893, da. of Harry Coe; 2ndly, 1899, Alma, da. of Harry Welch:—
(By 2nd m.) Julius Henry, *b.* 1905.——Douglas Lionel, *b.* 1911,——(By 1st m.) Frederica Mina Mabel, *b.* 1892: *m.* 19—, Harvey Anderson, of San Rosa, Cal., USA.——(By 2nd m.) Violet Frances, *b.* 1903: *m.* 19—, ———— Fenwick, formerly of 2159, Mission St., San Francisco, Calif., USA.——Geraldine Winifred, *b.* 1909: *m.* 1932, Clarence Arthur Allendin, of Geyserville, Sonoma Co., Cal., USA.——Hildred Vivian, *b.* 1912: *m.* 19—, ———— Wycoft.——Alma Julia, *b.* 1915.

Granddaughters of the late Richard Julius Molyneux Rowley (infra):—
Issue of the late Frederick Duncan Lorin Rowley, *b.* 1912, *d.* 1968: *m.* 1941, Dale (2388 East Racquet Club Rd., Palm Springs, Cal., USA), da. of Joseph Antellin:—
Pamela Dale, *b.* 1942.——Loryn Lee, *b.* 1946.

Granddaughter of the late Rev. Julis Henry Rowley (ante):—
Issue of the late Richard Julius Molyneux Rowley, *b.* 1865, *d.* 1948: *m.* 1900, Idabe Sophia, who *d.* 1951, da. of Oscar T. Nelson, of Gothenburg, Sweden :—
Constance Frederica Julia Christina, *b.* 1901: *m.* 1922, Burnell Hamilton De Vos, and has issue living, Burnell Hamilton, *b.* 1927,—Richard Glenn, *b.* 1932.

Descendants, if any, of the late Com. Robert Hibbert Bartholomew Rowley, R.N., 5th son of 1st baronet, *b.* 1817, *d.* 1860 : *m.* 1845, Donna Juanita di Latzona, who left issue, two sons and two das., concerning whom no details are available.

The 1st baronet, Adm. Sir Charles, G.C.B., G.C.H. (also Knight of Order of Maria Teresa, of Austria), was fourth son of Sir Joshua Rowley, 1st baronet (creation 1786), of Tendring Hall.

ROYDEN, Creation (U.K.) 1905, of Frankby Hall, co. Palatine of Chester.

Sir JOHN LEDWARD ROYDEN, 4th *Baronet* ; *b.* Dec. 31st, 1907 ; *s.* his father, *Sir* ERNEST BLAND, 1960 ; ed. at Winchester, and at Magdalen Coll., Oxford ; has Order of Merit of Chile : *m.* 1936, Dolores Catherine, el. da. of the late Cecil J. G. Coward, and has issue.

Arms—Vert, three stags' heads erased in pale between two hunting horns in fesse or. Crest—A stag's head erased or, collared gemel vert, holding in the mouth a riband also vert, suspended therefrom a shield of the Royden arms.

Residence—Netherfield Place, Battle, Sussex.

Sons living—CHRISTOPHER JOHN (9, Stanhope Gdns., SW7) *b.* Feb. 26th, 1937: ed. at Winchester, and at Ch. Ch., Oxford: *m.* 1961, Diana Bridget, da. of Lt.-Col. J. H. Goodhart, MC, of Keldholme Priory, Kirby Moorside, Yorks, and has issue living, John Michael Joseph, *b.* 1965,—Richard Thomas Bland, *b.* 1967,—Emma Mary Bridget, *b.* 1971.——Thomas Cecil (Netherfield Place, Battle, Sussex), *b.* 1938; ed. at Winchester, Ch. Ch. Oxford, Univ. of Maryland, LSE, Utah State Univ. (MSc), and Calif. State Poly. Univ. Pomona; Master of USA Agric.; Settlement Manager, Kitale, Tanzania; Consultant Utah State Univ.

Daughters living—Catherine Anne, *b.* 1945: *m.* 1965, Christopher Synge Barron, of Glann Arrow, Eardisland, nr. Leominster [see Synge, Bt., colls.].——Quenelda Jane, *b.* 1947: *m.* 1967, Robert Reginald Loder, of Selehurst, Lower Beeding, Horsham [see Loder, Bt.].

Brother living—Thomas Jerome (Mountain Lake, Lake Wales, Fla. 33853, USA), *b.* 1913; ed. at Winchester, and at Magdalen Coll., Oxford: *m.* 1st, 1937, Catherine Mary Denton, who *d.* 1970, da. of the late Charles Denton Toosey, of Oxton, Birkenhead; 2ndly, 1970, Lynn, da. of Lloyd Aspinwall, Jr., of Mountain Lake, Lake Wales, Fla., USA, and has issue living (by 1st m.), Ernest Jerome (20722, Gay Cedars Drive, Baie Durfe, Quebec, Canada), *b.* 1944: *m.* 1974, Suzanne Adams,—Anne Elizabeth Mary, *b.* 1945: *m.* 1967, Barry Lewis Gerken, of Stearns St., Carlisle, Mass. 01741, USA, and has issue living, Heather Kristin *b.* 1969, Stefanie Rebecca *b.* 1971,—(by 2nd m.) Alexa, *b.* 1972.

Sisters living—Rachel Nancy, *b.* 1902: *m.* 1931, Lt.-Col. John Forbes Batten, OBE, MC, late RA, and has issue living, Rachel Ann (62, Osler Rd., Headington, Oxford, OX3 9BN), *b.* 1932: *m.* 1st, 1956, Peter Long, from whom she obtained a divorce 1960; 2ndly, 1963, Leslie Ernest Sutton, MA, DPhil, FRS, Fellow of Magdalen Coll., Oxford,—Catherine Jean, *b.* 1934: *m.* 1955, Thomas Burtt Dowell, of 94A, Long Ashton, Bristol. *Residence*, Park Corner Cottage, Swyncombe, Henley-on-Thames, RG9 6DX.——Alice Joan, *MBE* (Hamesford House, E. Harting, Petersfield, Hants.), *b.* 1905, MBE (Civil) 1961: *m.* 1935, Brig. Stephen Alexander Holgate Batten,

CBE, late RE, who *d.* 1957, and has issue living, Stephen Duval, *b.* 1945,—Anne Ledward, *b.* 1940.——Mary Elizabeth (Buaile Bheag, I. of Lewis), *b.* 1915: *m.* 1st, 1936, Dr. Clarence Laverne Johnson, who obtained a divorce 1957; 2ndly, 1957, Allan MacNeil Dyson Perrins, who *d.* 1965, and has issue living (by 1st m.) Nels Royden, *b.* 1939: *m.* 1961 (m. diss. 1971), Barbara Joan, yr. da. of M. P. Skillern, and has issue living, Christopher Matthew Laverne *b.* 1964, Carol Anne *b.* 1966,—Mary Elizabeth (*Hon. Mrs. Patrick G. Howard*), *b.* 1945: *m.* 1966, the Hon. Patrick Greville Howard [see E. Suffolk and Berkshire],—Sally Anne, *b.* 1948: *m.* 1968, Peter Grant Auguste Hennessy [see B. Windlesham, colls.].——Vera Katherine (twin), *b.* 1915: *m.* 1935, Charles Gavin Clark (Villa Felicie, Route de Castellar, Menton, o6, France), and has issue living, David Gavin Bland, *b.* 1944,—Sonia Jennifer Jane, *b.* 1936: *m.* 1st, 1956 (m. diss. 1965), John Cecil McGregor Cuthbert; 2ndly, 1965, Anthony James Bevan, of 33, Queensferry Rd., Edinburgh, 4,—Gillian Vera, *b.* 1939: *m.* 1958, Alexander Graham Athol Turner Laing, of Huntercombe Farm House, Taplow, Berks.

The 1st baronet, Sir Thomas Bland Royden, was Mayor of Liverpool 1878-9, and M.P. for W. Toxteth Div. of Liverpool (C) 1885-92. The 2nd baronet, Sir Thomas Royden, C.H., was Chm. of Cunard Steamship Co., Ltd., and a Director of Phoenix Assurance Co., Ltd., and other Cos., and sat as M.P. for Bootle (*Co. U.*) 1918-22. He was *cr. Baron Royden*, of Frankby, co. Chester (peerage of United Kingdom) 1944 and *d.* 1950, when the Barony became ext., and the Baronetcy devolved upon his brother, Sir Ernest Bland Royden. Sir Ernest Bland Royden, 3rd baronet, was High Sheriff of Anglesey 1920.

Rugge-Price, see Price.

Ruggles-Brise, see Brise.

RUMBOLD, Creation (G.B.) 1779, of Wood Hall, Watton, Herts.

Praise is the excitement of virtue.

Sir (HORACE) ANTHONY (CLAUDE) RUMBOLD, *KCMG, KCVO, CB,* 10th *Baronet; b.* March 7th, 1911; *s.* his father, the *Rt. Hon. Sir* HORACE GEORGE MONTAGU, *GCB, GCMG, MVO,* 1941; ed. at Eton, and at Magdalen Coll., Oxford (B.A. 1933) ; Fellow of Queen's Coll., Oxford 1933 ; appointed a 3rd Sec. in Diplo. Ser. 1935, a 2nd Sec. 1940, a 1st Sec. 1945, a Counsellor 1949, Assist. Under-Sec. of State 1957, and HM Min. in Paris 1960-63; Ambassador to Thailand 1964-67, and to Austria 1967-70; Cdr. Order of St. Olav of Norway and Grand Cross Order of Merit of Austria; CMG 1953, CB (Civil) 1955, KCMG 1962, KCVO 1969: *m.* 1st, 1937 (m. diss. 1974), Felicity Ann, da. of the late Lt.-Col. Frederick George Glyn Bailey, RA (ret.), [E. Inchcape]; 2ndly, 1974, Pauline Laetitia, da. of the late the Hon. David Francis Tennant [see B. Glenconner, colls.], and formerly wife of (i) Capt. Julian Alfred Fox-Pitt-Rivers [see By. Forster], and (ii), Euan Douglas Graham [see D. Montrose, colls.], and has issue by 1st m.

Arms—Or, on a chevron gules three cinquefoils of the field ; a canton of the second charged with a leopard's face erminois. Crest—A demi-lion rampant erminois. *Residence*—Var House, Stinsford, Dorchester, Dorset.

Son living—By 1st m.—HENRY JOHN SEBASTIAN (19, Holywood Rd., SW10), *b.* Dec. 24th, 1947. **Daughters living**—By 1st m.—Serena Caroline, *b.* 1939: *m.* 1959, Jeremy Lancaster, of Whithorne, Charlton Kings, Cheltenham, and has issue living, Nicholas Horace John, *b.* 1966,—Emma Charlotte, *b.* 1961,—Joanna Elizabeth, *b.* 1963,—Frances Mary, *b.* 1968.——Venetia Mary, *b.* 1941.——Camilla Charlotte, *b.* 1943: *m.* 1st, 1962 (m. diss. 1970), Hon. Christopher Lionel Baliol Brett [*see* V. Esher]; 2ndly, 1972, Giles Oliver Cairnes Swayne, of Puddle House, Chicksgrove, Tisbury, Wilts., and has issue living, (by 1st m.), [see V. Esher],—(by 2nd m.) Orlando Benedict Carlos, *b.* 1974. **Sister living**—Constantia Dorothy, *b.* 1906: *m.* 1944, Hugh William Farmar [Farmar, Bt., colls.], and has issue living, Hugh Alexander Peregrine, *b.* 1945,—Francis Edmund, *b.* 1948. *Residence*, Wasing Old Rectory, Aldermaston, Berks.

Collateral Branches living.

Issue of the late Col. William Edwin Rumbold, C.M.G., 2nd son of 8th baronet, *b.* 1870, *d.* 1947: *m.* 1903, Elizabeth Gordon, who *d.* 1948, da. of the late Rev. J. Cameron, of Burntisland:—

Sir (Horace) Algernon Fraser, *KCMG, CIE, b.* 1906; ed. at Wellington Coll., and at Ch. Ch., Oxford (Scholar, MA); entered India Office 1929; transferred to Commonwealth Relations Office 1947; was Dep. High Commr. for United Kingdom in Union of S. Africa 1949-53; was Assist. Under Sec. of State, Commonwealth Relations Office 1954-58, and Dep. Under-Sec. of State 1958-66; Adviser Welsh Office 1967; Dep. Chm. Air Transport Licensing Board 1971-72; CIE 1947, CMG 1953, KCMG 1960: *m.* 1946, Margaret Adél, da. of the late Arthur Joseph Hughes, OBE, of Pages, Chigwell Row, Essex, and has issue living, Sarah Josephine, *b.* 1948: *m.* 1969, Robert Michael Owen, of 8, Fitzgerald Av., Mortlake, SW14, and has issue living, Thomas Llewellyn *b.* 1973,—Caroline Elizabeth, *b.* 1950. *Residence*, Shortwoods, West Clandon, Surrey; *Club*, Travellers.——Robert William (of 56, Albert Hall Mansions, SW7; Travellers' and Devonshire Clubs), *b.* 1912; ed. at Wellington Coll., and at Ch. Ch., Oxford (BA 1934, MA 1944); sometime FO RAF Reserve: *m.* 1st, 1942 (divorce 1952), Pamela Mary Dewe; 2ndly, 1958, Sylvia Violet, da. of Lawrence John Smith, and has issue living (by 1st m.) Cheryl Anne, *b.* 1944:

m. 1968, Luca D. Dotti, of 5, Av. Calas, Geneva, Switzerland,—(by 2nd m.) Charles Anton *b.* 1959,—Alexander Robert, *b.* 1971.——Alastair Gordon, *OBE, MC* (The Limes, Felbridge, Sussex; United Service Club), *b.* 1914; ed. at Wellington Coll.; Lt.-Col. (ret.) late Cameron Highlanders; Palestine 1936-39 (MC); OBE (Mil.) 1954: *m.* 1st, 1941 (m. diss. 1952), Tania, da. of the late Michael Borzakovsky; 2ndly, 1958, Auriol Cressida, da. of Col. William Rixon Bucknall, and has issue living (by 1st m.) Michael Alastair, *b.* 1943; ed. at Wellington,—(by 2nd m.) Belinda Cressida, *b.* 1962.——Violet Elizabeth, *b.* 1907: *m.* 1934, Andrew Atha, who *d.* 1967, and has issue living, Charles Antony, *b.* 1937,—Elizabeth Amanda, *b.* 1940: *m.* 1967, Michael Abrahams, of Low Braythorn Farm, Swinburn, Yorks.

> Granddaughter of the late Thomas Henry Rumbold, 2nd son of Charles Edmund Rumbold, 5th son of 1st baronet.:—
> Issue of the late Thomas Arthur Rumbold, *b.* 1882, *d.* 1972: *m.* 1st, 1911, Evelyn Mary, who *d.* 1954, only da. of the late Walter Comyn Jackson, JP; 2ndly, 1959, Elizabeth, who *d.* 1973, da. of the late Rev. T. M. B. Paterson, of Laighstone Hall, Hamilton:—
> (By 1st m.) Elizabeth Anne, *MBE (Baroness Hayter)*, (Ashtead House, Ashtead, Surrey), *b.* 1919; MBE (Civil) 1975: *m.* 1940, the 3rd Baron Hayter.

The 1st baronet, Sir Thomas, sometime M.P. for Melcombe Regis, Dorset, and for New Shoreham, Sussex, served as Aide-de-Camp to Lord Clive at Plassey (1757), was severely wounded, and was afterwards Governor of Madras. The 2nd baronet was H.M.'s Minister at Hamburg. The 5th baronet, a Capt. in the Army, was President of Nevis 1857-63, and of the Virgin Islands 1865-9; he was also a Col. in the Ottoman Army, and served with the Turkish Contingent during the Crimean war. The Rt. Hon. Sir Horace Rumbold, G.C.B., G.C.M.G., P.C., 8th baronet, was Sec. of Legation at Athens 1862-4 and at Berne 1864-8, Sec. of Embassy at St. Petersburg 1868-71 and at Constantinople 1871-72, Min. Resident and Consul-Gen. in Chile 1872-78 and to Swiss Confederation 1878-9, Envoy Extraor. and Min Plen. to Argentine Republic 1879-81, to Stockholm 1881-5, to Athens 1885-8, and to The Hague 1888-96, and Ambassador Extraor. and Plen. at Vienna 1896-1900. The 9th baronet, the Rt. Hon. Sir Horace George Montagu, G.C.B., G.C.M.G., M.V.O., P.C., was Envoy Extraor. and Min. Plen. to Switzerland 1916-19, and to Poland 1919-20, High Commr. at Constantinople 1920-23, and Ambassador Extraor. and Plen. to Spain 1923-8, and to Berlin 1928-33.

RUNCHORELAL, Creation (U.K.) 1913, of Shahpur, Ahmedabad, India.

Sir CHINUBHAI MADHOWLAL RUNCHORELAL, 2nd *Baronet; b.* April 19th, 1906; *s.* his father, *Sir* CHINUBHAI MADHOWLAL, *C.I.E.*, 1916, whose name he then assumed in place of that of Girjaprasad: *m.* 1924, Tanumati Zaverilal Mehta, of Ahmedabad, India, and has issue.

Arms—Azure, in base on water a lotus flower leaved proper, issuant from the dexter chief a sun in splendour or. **Crest**—An elephant proper, resting the dexter fore-foot on an escutcheon argent, charged with a lotus flower proper.
Residence—Shantikunj, Shahibag, Ahmedabad, India. *Club* —Willingdon Sports (Bombay).

Sons living—UDAYAN, *b.* July 25th, 1929: *m.* 1953, Muneera Khodadad Fozdar, of Bombay, and has issue living, Prashant, *b.* 1955,—Radhika, *b.* 1954,—Prasan, *b.* 1960.——Kirtidev, *b.* 1932.——Achyut, *b.* 1941.
Sisters living—Indumati, *b.* 1901: *m.* 1916, Chaitanyaprasal Motilal Kantharia, and has issue living, a son, *b.* 19—, —a dau., *b.* 19—, —a da., *b.* 19—.——Vasumati, *b.* 1913: *m.* 1937, Yashodhar Narmadashamker Mehta, Bar.-at-law.——Saudamini, *b.* 1914.

Sir Chinubhai Madhowlal Runchorelal, 1st Bt. (the first Hindu Baronet to be created), was a cotton manufacturer of Ahmedabad, and a M.L.C.; contributed largely to educational schemes in India.

RUSSELL, Creation (U.K.) 1812, of Swallowfield, Berkshire.

Learn justice being admonished.

Sir GEORGE MICHAEL RUSSELL, 7th *Baronet; b.* Sept. 30th, 1908; *s.* his father, *Sir* ARTHUR EDWARD IAN MONTAGU, 1964; ed. at Radley: *m.* 1936, Joy Francis Bedford, da. of the late W. Mitchell, of Irwin, W. Australia, and has issue.

Arms—Argent, a chevron sable between three crosscrosslets fitchée azure within a bordure engrailed gules, bearing alternate bezants and escallops or. **Crest**—A demi-lion rampant ermine, charged with a fasces proper, and bearing in his dexter paw a cross-crosslet fitchée sable.
Address—

Daughters living—Marie Clotilde, *b.* 1939.——Mary Christina *b.* 1944.
Half-Brothers living—ARTHUR MERVYN *b.* Feb. 7th, 1923.——Christopher, *b.* 1937: *m.* 1962, Ann, da. of Lt.-Col. C. D. B. Campling, of Syngate House, Stelling Minnis, Canterbury.
Sister living—Bettine (*Baroness Broughshane*), *b.* 1905: *m.* 1929, the 2nd Baron Broughshane. *Residence*, 21, Eaton Sq., S.W.1.
Widow living of 6th Baronet—MARJORIE ELISABETH JOSEPHINE (*Dowager Lady Russell*) (Little Struan, Pangbourne, Berks.), da. of Ernest Rudman, of Foxhangers, Earley, Berks.: *m.* 1933, as his third wife, Sir Arthur Edward Ian Montagu Russell, 6th baronet, who *d.* 1964.

Collateral Branches living.

> Grandchildren of the late Major Francis Whitworth Russell, son of the late Francis Whitworth Russell, 3rd son of 1st baronet:—

Issue of the late Francis Whitworth Russell, *b.* 1854, *d.* 19— : *m.* 1886, Maude Agnes, da. of the late Denis O'Brien, of Knockroe, Fermoy, co. Cork :—
Francis Whitworth, *b.* 1888. *Residence,*

Issue of the late Edward Stuart Marjoribanks Harley Russell, *b.* 1857, *d.* 1926 : *m.* 1882, Mary, who *d.* 1938, da. of the late Capt. W. Phipps :—
Alice.——Rachel.——Kate. *Residence,*

Grandchildren of the late Henry Russell, son of the late Rev. Whitworth Russell, 4th son of 1st baronet :—
Issue of the late Whitworth Russell, *b.* 1849, *d.* 1893 : *m.* 1886, Caroline Eleanor (who re-*m.*), da. of J. P. Armstrong, C.E. :—
John Whitworth (96, Waimea Rd., Nelson, NZ), *b.* 1891; BSc: *m.* 1915, Mary Alice, da. of J. R. Anderson, and has issue living, Whitworth Athelstan (23, Ingleton Terr., Hamilton, NZ), *b.* 1918; MB, ChB, DCP: *m.* 1946, Marjory Ellen Ross, and has issue living, Anthony Whitworth *b.* 1951, Michael David *b.* 1959, Juliet Ethne *b.* 1962,—Richard Hudson, *b.* 1928,—Elizabeth Alison, *b.* 1934; BA: *m.* 1956, David Ernest Poswillo, DDS, Prof. Roy. Coll. of Surgs., London, of 28, Winchester Rd., Bromley, Kent.——Charlotte (51, Redbourne Av., Finchley, N3) *b.* 1887: *m.* 1927, Arthur Westbrook, who *d.* 1958, and has issue living, Arthur Robert Whitworth, *b.* 1928: *m.* 1960, Ida, da. of Horace Hamilton, of NZ:—

Grandchildren of the late George Cecil Russell (infra):—
Issue of the late Evelyn Aylmer Cecil Russell, *b.* 1891, *d.* 1963: *m.* 1st, 1916, Alice Edith, from whom he obtained a divorce 1923, da. of W. H. Wallis, of California Gully, Bendigo, Victoria, Australia; 2ndly, 1924, Irene (Gembrook, Victoria, Australia), da. of John Brodrick, JP, of Nangana, Victoria:—
(By 2nd marriage) William Henry Cecil (Main Rd., Gembrook, Victoria, Australia), *b.* 1927: *m.* 1954, Margaret Winifred, da. of Gordon Newton, of Mornington, Victoria, Australia, and has issue living, Mark Newton Cecil, *b.* 1959,—Jane Elizabeth, *b.* 1956,—Kim Margaret, *b.* 1964. ——Harry Arthur Cecil, *b.* 1931: *m.* 1959, Marjorie Ailsa, da. of Alfred Sutton, of Hawthorn, Victoria, Australia, and has issue living, Ewen James Cecil, *b.* 1967,—Sarah Anne *b.* 1962,— Virginia Kate (twin), *b.* 1962.——(by 1st m.) Sadie Evelyn, *b.* 1917; ed. at Melbourne Univ. (BA): *m.* 1940, Harold William Halls, and has issue living, Peter John, *b.* 1944,—Robin, *b.* 1958 —Jane Elizabeth, *b.* 1956.

Grandsons of the late Cecil Henry Russell, son of the late George Lake Russell, 5th son of 1st baronet :—
Issue of the late George Cecil Russell, *b.* 1861, *d.* 1915 : *m.* 1889, Alice Jane Evelyn, who *d.* 1948, da. of E. W. Mills, J.P., merchant, of The Terrace, Wellington, New Zealand :—
Edmond Henry Cecil, *b.* 1892; is Lt. Roy. Australian Engineers; 1914-18 War, 1939-45 War. *Residence,* Swallowfield, Gembrook, Victoria, Australia.——John Hardress Cecil, *b.* 1896. 1914-18 War with Australian Forces: *m.* 1927, Doris Marion, da. of Ernest Reginald Green, formerly of Colac, Victoria, Australia, and has issue living, John Alan Cecil (of Eversley, Gembrook, Victoria, Australia), *b.* 1928: *m.* 1955, Patricia Mary Gordon, da. of the late Roddam Morris Douglas, of Emerald, Victoria, Australia, and has issue living, Susan Patricia, *b.* 1955,— Penelope Ann, *b.* 1959,—Lynette Margaret, *b.* 1963,—Diane Marion, *b.* 1964. *Residence,* Swallowfield, Gembrook, Victoria, Australia.

Sir Henry, 1st baronet, son of Michael Russell of Dover, was Chief Justice of Bengal. Sir Henry, 2nd baronet, was for many years Resident at the Court of Hyderabad. Sir Charles, *VC*, 3rd baronet, received Victoria Cross in Crimea 1854, and was MP (*C*) for Berks. and Westminster. Sir George, 4th baronet, was a Judge of County Courts, Recorder of Wokingham and MP for Berks. E. Div. (*C*).

RUSSELL, Creation (U.K.) 1916, of Littleworth Corner, Burnham, co. Buckingham.

Sir CHARLES IAN RUSSELL, 3rd *Baronet; b.* March 13th, 1918; *s.* his father, *Capt. Sir* ALEC Charles, *M.C.,* 1938; ed. at Beaumont Coll., and at Univ. Coll., Oxford; admitted a Solicitor 1947; Snr. Partner in the firm of Charles Russell & Co., of Hale Court, Lincoln's Inn, WC2; 1939-45 War as Capt. R.H.A. (despatches): *m.* 1947, Rosemary, da. of the late Major Sir John Theodore Prestige, of The Court House, Bishopsbourne, Canterbury, and has issue.

Arms—Argent, a lion rampant gules, on a chief sable three escallops of the first, the whole within a bordure engrailed vert. Crest—A goat passant argent, armed or, charged on the body fessewise with three trefoils slipped or.
Residences—6, Carlyle Mansions, Cheyne Walk, SW3; Hidden House, Strand St., Sandwich, Kent. *Clubs*—Garrick, Army and Navy.

What will be, will be.

Son living—CHARLES DOMINIC, *b.* May 28th, 1956.
Daughter living—Clare Harriet Faviell, *b.* 1949: *m.* 1974, Richard James Shepherd.
Daughter living of 1st Baronet—[*see* Mother living (infra)].
Sister living—Sheila, *b.* 1921:*m.* 1946, Lawrence Noel George Pace, of Jordans, Rusper, Sussex, and has issue living, Andrew John Faviell, *b.* 1948,—Mark Faviell, *b.* 1952: *m.* 1972, Jane, el. da. of R. Bunting, of New House, Burcot, nr. Bromsgrove, Worcs., and has issue living, James Andrew Faviell *b.* 1973.
Uncles living—Denis Leslie, *MBE, TD, b.* 1909; late Maj. RA; Partner in the firm of George Henderson & Co., Stockbrokers; 1939-45 War (despatches, MBE); MBE (Mil) 1945: *m.* 1932, Verena, da. of the late George Henderson, of 55, Cadogan Place, SW1, and Orchard House, Crastock, Surrey, and has issue living, David Ian, *b.* 1943; ed. at Ampleforth,— Sally Verena, *b.* 1937: *m.* 1956, William Weatherall, of Monk's Pool, Meppershall, Beds., and has issue living, Michael William *b.* 1958, Annabel Jane *b.* 1960, Clare Victoria (twin) *b.* 1960. *Residences,* Burdenshot House, Burdenshot Hill, Guildford; 11, Cadogan Sq., SW1.— Cyril Alan, *b.* 1910; late Lt.-Col. London Scottish: *m.* 1st, 1937, Grace Evelyn, who *d.* 1943, el. da. of William T. Moore, of New York; 2ndly, 1944, Jean Patricia, da. of Stafford Croom John-son, of Greenacre, Stoke Bishop, Bristol, and widow of Wing-Cdr. J. R. Cridland, AAF, and has issue living, (by 2nd m.) Michael Alan (9, Rosary Gdns., SW7), *b.* 1947: *m.* 1972, Penelope, yr. da. of Lt.-Col. A. R. Dawe, OBE, of Wyke Lodge, Normandy, and has issue living, Toby Alan, *b.* 1974,—(by 1st m.) Genia Helen Kathleen, *b.* 1938: *m.* 1959, Jeremy Paterson-Fox, of Portugal House, Chew Magna, Bristol, and has issue living, Alastair Mark *b.* 1960, Philip Alan *b.* 1965, Neil Jeremy *b.* 1968, Claire Emma *b.* 1961. *Residence,* 23, Rutland Gate, SW7.

Aunt living—Phyllis Helen (*Lady Mathew*), b. 1897: m. 1923, Sir Theobald Mathew, KBE, MC., who d. 1964, and has issue living, John Charles (47, Abingdon Villas, W.8), b. 1927: m. 1952, Jennifer Jane, da of the late Reginald Bousfield Lagden, OBE, MC, and has issue living, Sally Patrica b. 1955, Susan Amanda b. 1957,—Anne, b. 1924: m. 1948, Edwin Godfrey Pithers, of 15, Upper Straithe, Hartington Rd., Chiswick, W4, and has issue living, Ian Mark (4, Court Farm Gdns., Manor Green Rd., Epsom), b. 1949: m. 1971, Susan Hayes, Anthony b. 1954, Wendy Anne (twin) b. 1954,—Joan, b. 1931: m. 1956, Francis Bennett, of 24A, Hyde Park Gate, SW7, and has issue living, Christopher David b. 1959, Caroline Jane b. 1957, Jennifer Mary b. 1962. *Residence*, 65, Cornwall Gdns., SW7.

Mother living—Monica (da. of the Hon. Sir Charles Russell, K.C.V.O., 1st Bt.), b. 1894: m. 1st, 1917, her cousin, Capt. Sir Alec Charles Russell, M.C., and Bt., who d. 1938, and from whom she **had obtained a divorce 1932 ; 2ndly, 1942, Brigadier John Victor Faviell, C.B.E., M.C., late Roy.** Lincolnshire Regt. *Residence*, Little Jordans, Rusper, Sussex.

Widow living of 2nd Baronet—ROWENA, da. of the late Richard Scott Lamb, and formerly wife of Malcolm David Motion : m. 1936, as his second wife, Capt. Sir Alec Charles Russell, M.C., 2nd baronet, who d. 1938, 3rdly, 1945, Alexander Smail, who d. 1959. *Residence*, 3, Skeyne Mews, Pulborough, Sussex, RH20 2BB.

Collateral Branches living.

Grandchildren of Maj. Denis Leslie Russell, MBE, TD (ante):—
Issue of the late (Denis) Anthony Russell, b. 1934, d. 1966: m. 1961, Charlotte Mary, (who m. 2ndly, 1970, J. Watcyn Lewis, of 66, Clifton Hill, NW8), da. of Lt.-Col. Sir Ian Frank Bowater, DSO, TD [see Bowater, Bt., (cr. 1939)]:—
William Anthony Bowater, b. 1965.——Amanda Charlotte, b. 1963.

(In Special remainder.)
Issue of the late Gerald Cyril Russell, M.C., brother of 2nd baronet, b. 1896, d. 1962: m. 1923, Barbara (of The Covert, Aldeburgh, Suffolk), da. of Lieut.-Col. Sir James Philip Reynolds, 1st Bt., D.S.O.:—
Cyril (of 51, Addison Av., W.11), b. 1924: m. 1949, Eileen Mary Elizabeth, da. of the late Major W. D. G. Batten, 3rd Gurkha Rifles, and has issue living, Gerald William, b. 1950,—Patrick James, b. 1952,—Nicholas Alastair, b. 1958.——Rev. John Alastair, b. 1928; is in Holy Orders of Church of Rome.——Colin Patrick, b. 1944.——Moira, b. 1927.——Clodagh Mary, b. 1933: m. 1971, Brig. David William Reid, MBE, of River Hundred, Aldringham, Leiston, Suffolk, son of the late Sir Robert Niel Reid, KCSI, KCIE.

Grandchildren living of the late Charles, Baron Russell of Killowen [Life Baron, (cr. 1894)]:—
Issue of the late Rt. Hon. Francis Xavier Russell (brother of 1st Bt.), who was cr. Baron Russell of Killowen (Life Baron) 1929:—
Rt. Hon. Sir Charles Ritchie (*Lord Russell of Killowen, PC*), b. 1908; cr. Baron Russell of Killowen (Life Peer) 1975 [see that title].——Hon. Margaret Mary, b. 1905: m. 1941, Milan Bratza Yovanovitch, who d. 1964, and has issue living, Nicolas, b. 1945,—Gregory, b. 1947,—Maria, b. 1942: m. 1969, Bryan Edward Ellis, of 36, Craigside, Galsworthy Rd., Kingston Hill, Surrey. *Residence*, Lane End, Walton-on-the-Hill, Tadworth, Surrey.

Issue of the late Lieut.-Col. the Hon. Bertrand Joseph Russell, D.S.O., b. 1876, d. 1960 : m. 1st, 1902, Dorothy, who d. 1921, da. of the late John George Leeming ; 2ndly, 1922, Mavis Winifred (from whom he obtained a divorce 1936), da. of the late Frederick Hazell, of Frinton-on-Sea :—
(By 2nd marriage) Michael Dudley, b. 1923 : m. 1949 (marriage dissolved 1959), Jeanette Meryen da. of Major Arthur Sinclair Cannon, of Rangoon, Burma.——(By 1st marriage) Prudence b. 1904: m. 1929, Michael Ellison, who obtained a divorce 1943 ; 2ndly, 1951 James Gordon Findlay. *Residence*, The Chantry House, Spofforth, near Harrogate.——Joan (1 Stanhope Mews East, SW7), b. 1908: m. 1933, Charles Gordon Brand, CBE, who d. 1966.——Clodagh, b. 1912: m. 1939, Brigadier Thomas Haddon, C.B.E., late Border Regt. *Residence*, Combe End, Whitmore Vale Rd. Hindhead, Surrey.

This Baronetcy was conferred with a special remainder (in default of heir male of the body of the grantee) to the heirs male of the body of Charles, Baron Russell of Killowen (Life Baron, cr. 1894), father of the 1st baronet. The 1st baronet, the Hon. Sir Charles Russell (senior partner in the firm of Charles Russell and Co., solicitors, of 37, Norfolk Street, Strand, W.C.), was 2nd son of the late Charles, Baron Russell of Killowen (Life Baron, cr. 1894), Lord Ch. Justice of England. The 2nd baronet, Sir Alec Charles Russell, M.C., was Capt. (retired) R.A.

RUTHERFORD, Creation (U.K.) 1923, of Liverpool, co. Palatine of Lancaster.
[Extinct 1942.]

Sir (JOHN) HUGO RUTHERFORD, 2nd and last *Baronet*.

Daughters living of 2nd Baronet—Elspeth, b. 1914: m. 1939, Lieut.-Col. Francis William Bartlett, REME (ret.), of 1, Craigrory, N. Kessock, By Inverness, IV1 1XB, and has issue living, William John, b. 1940,—Charles Hugo, b. 1943,—Francis Murray, b. 1945,—James Peter, b. 1947, —Isabel, b. 1951.——Prudence Hero, b. 1916: m. 1940, John Russell Napier, DSc, MRCS, LRCP, and has issue living, John Hugo, b. 1946,—Graham Russell, b. 1949. *Residence*, 403, Collingwood House, Dolphin Sq., SW1.——Isabel Lavender, b. 1925: m. 1948, Peter Thomas Crook, and has issue living, Jeremy Peter, b. 1954,—Matthew Lancelot, b. 1969,—Jean Isabel, b. 1951. *Residence*, 2, Egbert Rd., Meols, Wirral, Ches.

Daughters living of 1st Baronet—Elspeth: m. 1915, Douglas Grant, of California, U.S.A., and has issue living, Elspeth Rutherford, b. 1920 : m. 1946, William Howard Bopst, of California, USA.——Freda, b. 1892: m. 1917, Maj. Ricardo Daniel Tuohy, formerly RA, who d. 1938, and has issue living, James Hugh, DSO, b. 1918; formerly Capt. Suffolk Regt. (TA); 1939-45 War with King's Liverpool Regt. in Italy (DSO); DSO 1944: m. 1946, Constance Mary, da. of the late E. H. Kendrick, and has issue living, Nicolas James b. 1948, Mark Benedict Kendrick b. 1951, Steven Patrick b. 1954. *Residence*, Garrett House, 43, Park Rd., Aldeburgh, Suffolk.

Widow living of 2nd Baronet—ISABEL (*Lady Rutherford*), da. of the late John Thompson Smith, of Liverpool: m. 1913, Sir (John) Hugo Rutherford, 2nd baronet, who d. 1942, when the title became ext. *Residence*, 105, Keyes House, Dolphin Sq., SW1.

RYAN, Creation (U.K.) 1919, of Hintlesham, Suffolk.

Sir DEREK GERALD RYAN, 3rd *Baronet;*
b. July 9th, 1922 ; *s.* his father, *Sir* GERALD ELLIS,
1947; ed. at Harrow; 1939-45 War as Lt.
Gren. Gds.: *m.* 1st, 1947 (m. diss. 1971),
Penelope Anne, da. of the late Rex Hawkings,
of 139, East 94th St., New York, 28, USA;
2ndly, 1972, Katja, da. of Ernst Best, of 35,
Kassel, Fuhrmannsbreite 11, W. Germany, and
has issue by 1st m.

Nothing without labour.

Arms—Gules, in chief two griffins sejant respectant
and combatant or, and in base a garb of rye proper.
Crest—Upon a mount vert a griffin sejant sable, holding
in the dexter claw a sword erect, and resting the sinister
on a sickle or.
Address,—6228 Eltville/Rheingau, Erbacher Strasse
12, W. Germany.

Son living (By 1st m.)—DEREK GERALD, *b.* March 25th,
1954.
Daughters living (By 1st m.)—Anne Katharine, *b.* 1951.—
Jenifer Hylda, *b.* 1955.——Caroline Sarah, *b.* 1956.
Sister living—Aileen Pamela, *b.* 1916 : *m.* 1950, Peter
James Frederick Green. *Residences,* Stuiton Mill
House, near Ipswich, Suffolk ; 85, Burton Court, S.W.3.
Collateral Branch living.
Issue of the late Vivian Desmond Ryan, *b.* 1893, *d.*
1950 : *m.* 1st, 1917, Kathleen Frances, who *d.*
1945, da. of the late James William Helps,
M.I.C.E., of Berisal, Normanton Road, S.
Croydon ; 2ndly, 1946, Nanny (of 83, Vivian
Avenue, Hendon, N.W.4), da. of the late
Dixon Slater, of 24, Belleview, Skipton, York-
shire :—
(By 1st marriage :) Desmond Maurice, *b.* 1918: *m.* 1942,
Margaret Catherine, da. of A. H. Brereton, and has issue living, Barry Desmond, *b.* 1943,—
Kevin Vivian, *b.* 1951,—Michael Brereton, *b.* 1954.——Adrian James (8, Camden Studios,
Camden St., NW1), *b.* 1920: *m.* 1st, 1941 (m. diss. 1950), Peggy Rose; 2ndly, 1952, Barbara
Pitt, and has issue living, (by 1st m.) Geraldine Daphne, *b.* 1943,—(by 2nd m.) Kathleen Scarlett,
b. 1954,—Vivien Frances, *b.* 1957.——Jeanette Daphne, *b.* 1929.

The 1st baronet, Sir Gerald Hemmington Ryan (son of the late Michael Desmond Ryan, of
Kildare Terr., W.) was later Gen. Manager and Chm. of Phœnix Assurance Co.

RYCROFT, Creation (G.B.) 1784, of Calton, Yorkshire.

Sir RICHARD NEWTON RYCROFT, 7th
Baronet ; b. Jan. 23rd, 1918 ; *s.* his father
Sir NELSON EDWARD OLIVER, 1958 ; ed. at
Winchester, and at Ch. Ch., Oxford (B.A.
1939) ; is Patron of one living ; European
War 1939-45 as Major on Special Work in
Balkans (despatches, Knight of Order of
Phœnix of Greece with swords): *m.* 1947,
Ann, da. of the late Hugh Bellingham Smith,
and has issue.

Arms—Quarterly : 1st and 4th, per bend or and azure,
three griffins, heads erased counterchanged ; on a chief ermine,
a fleur-de-lis between two roses gules, *Rycroft ;* 2nd and 3rd,
party per pale or and sable, a chevron between three fleurs-de-
lis all counterchanged, *Nelson.* **Crest**—A griffin's head erased
per bend or and azure, charged with two fleurs-de-lis counterchanged.

Residence—Winalls Wood House, Stuckton, Fordingbridge, Hants.

Daughters living—Susan Marilda, *b.* 1948; ed. at Trin. Coll.,
Dublin (BA): *m.* 1974, Ian Martell, of Wood House,
Shotley Bridge, co. Durham.——Sally Ann (*Viscountess
FitzHarris*), *b.* 1950: *m.* 1969, James Carleton Harris,
Viscount FitzHarris, of Amyand House, Park Rd.,
Winchester, el. son of 6th Earl of Malmesbury.

Uncles living (sons of 5th baronet)—HENRY RICHARD, *OBE, DSC, RN, b.* Dec. 28th, 1911; Lt.-
Cdr. 1942 and Cdr. 1947; 1939-45 War (despatches, DSC); OBE (Mil.) 1960: *m.* 1941, Penelope
Gwendoline, da. of the late Lt.-Col. C. S. B. Evans-Lombe, Leinster Regt., and has issue living,
Richard John, *b.* 1946; ed. at Sherborne,—Caroline Mary, *b.* 1944; ed. at Univ. of Sussex
(BSc): *m.* 1966, Nicholas Wolryche Meyrick, of The Coach House, Norton, Chichester, and has
issue living, Julian Timothy *b.* 1968, Hilary Jocelyn *b.* 1970,—Philippa Eve, *b.* 1949,—Jocelyn
Penelope, *b.* 1955. *Residence,* Ganderdown, Smugglers Lane, Bosham, Chichester.——Charles
Frederick, *MB, BS, b.* 1914; ed. at Wellington Coll., and at Trin. Coll., Camb. (BA); FRC
Psych.): *m.* 1947 (m. diss. 1963), Chlôe, da. of the late Edouard Majolier, and has issue living,
Francis Edward, *b.* 1950; ed. at Gresham's Sch., Holt,—Alice Julia, *b.* 1947; ed. at Univ. of Kent
(BA),—Catherine Ann, *b.* 1949; ed. at Univ. of Kent (BA): *m.* 1970, Christopher Piers Merriman,
of Tanker's Row, S. Clydach, Abergavenny, Gwent. *Residence,* 97, Green Hill, Hampstead,
NW3.

Aunts living (daughters of 5th baronet)—Alice Juliana Rosamond, *b.* 1915 : *m.* 1st, 1938, Neil
Malise Graham, who *d.* 1939; 2ndly, 1943, the Rev. Patrick Roger Harvey, Priest-in-charge,
Hewish, Somerset, of The Vicarage, Hewish, Weston-super-Mare, and has issue living, (by 1st m.)
Charles Edward Malise, *b.* 1939,—Bruce Torquil Irving (twin), *b.* 1939,—(by 2nd m.) Michael
Timothy John, *b.* 1944,—Diana Lavender Mary, *b.* 1946: *m.* 1970, Robert Ian Fellows, and has

issue living, Gregory Chad *b.* 1974,—Primrose Miranda Margaret, *b.* 1953.——Eleanor Mary, *b.* 1918; 1942-5 War in WRNS.

Widow living of 5th Baronet—EMILY MARY (*Dowager Lady Rycroft*), da. of the late Col. the Hon Henry William Lowry-Corry [*see* E. Belmore]: *m.* 1911, as his second wife, Sir Richard Nelson Rycroft, 5th baronet, who *d.* 1925. *Residence*, The Vicarage, Hewish, Weston-super-Mare, Som.

Collateral Branches living.

Issue of the late the Rev. Richard Michael Rycroft, 3rd son of 5th baronet, *b.* 1897, *d.* 1968: *m.* 1924, Evelyn Maud, who *d.* 1969, da. of the late Francis James Driscoll, of Jersey:—

Jean Dorothea, *b.* 1925: *m.* 1945, Charles Spencer Goldring, of Tusket, Yarmouth Co., Nova, Scotia, and has issue living, Paul Michael, *b.* 1947,—James Philip (Linden Lodge, Loanhead, Midlothian), *b.* 1948: *m.* 1969, Marianne Louise McLean, and has issue living, Andrew Michael Dmitri *b.* 1970,—Nicholas John, *b.* 1954,—Hilary Adrian Jerome, *b.* 1959.—Stephen Gerard, *b.* 1961,—Christopher Septimus Denison (twin), *b.* 1961,—Felicity Jocelyn, *b.* 1965.——Mary Elizabeth (Holly Cottage, Collingham, Newark), *b.* 1935.

Granddaughters of the late Maj.-Gen. Sir William Henry Rycroft, K.C.B., KCMG, 2nd son of 4th baronet:—

Issue of the late Major Julian Neil Oscar Rycroft, D.S.O., M.C., *b.* 1892, *d.* 1928: *m.* 1920, Elizabeth Mildred Louisa who *d.* 1932, da. of Sir Ralph William Anstruther, 6th Bt.:—

Cynthia Margaret, *b.* 1922 : *m.* 1940, Lieut.-Col. Philip Dives Stenning, R.E., and has issue living, Christopher John William, *b.* 1950,—Nicholas Julian Seymour, *b.* 1952—Richard Neil, *b.* 1955. *Address*, c/o Lloyds Bank, 6, Pall Mall, S.W.1.——Evelyn Joanna Christian, *b.* 1925 : *m* 1953, Martin Claridge, FRCS, and has issue living, Simon Julian, *b.* 1954,—Tobias James, *b.* 1963,—Anna Louise, *b.* 1958,—Katharine Georgina, *b.* 1960. *Residence*, St. Martin's House, St. Martin's Av., Canterbury.

Issue of the late Rev. Edmund Hugh Rycroft, 3rd son of 4th baronet, *b.* 1862, *d.* 1932: *m.* 1902, Winifred Edith, who *d.* 1968, el. da. of the late Adm. of the Fleet Sir Arthur Dalrymple Fanshawe, GCB, GCVO:—

Arthur John, *b.* 1905; ed. at Radley, and at Corpus Christi Coll., Oxford B.A. 1927).——Barbara Frances, *b.* 1903 ; B.A. Oxford 1926. *Residence*, The Old Vicarage, Wilsford, Pewsey, Wilts.

Grandchildren of the late Rev. Edmund Hugh Rycroft (ante):—

Issue of the late Col. David Hugh Rycroft, O.B.E., *b.* 1907, *d.* (killed in action in Dalmatia) 1944 : *m.* 1st, 1930, Elizabeth Edith Dilys (from whom he obtained a divorce 1934), da. of the late Capt. Miles Bertie Cunningham Carbery,Roy. Irish Fusiliers; 2ndly, 1939, Cicely Phoebe Susanna (51, Murrayfield Gardens, Edinburgh), da. of the late Lt.-Col. Robert Bruère Otter-Barry, OBE, of Glazeley Hall, near Bridgnorth [Cs. Dysart, colls.]:—

(By 2nd m.) Henry David (Dunbar's Close, Canongate, Edinburgh), *b.* 1943; ed. at Radley, and St. Andrews Univ. (BSc); MB, BS): *m.* 1972, Nicole Elizabeth, MB, BS, da. of Maurice Kenig, MD, of 69, Harley St., W1, and has issue living, Alexander Theophilus, *b.* 1975.——Charlotte Susanna, *b.* 1941; ed. at Gorton Coll., Camb. (BA); in HM Dip. Ser.: *m.* 1976, William Nigel Wenban-Smith.

The 1st baronet, the Rev. Sir Richard Rycroft, DD, only surviving son of John Nelson, assumed the surname of Rycroft by royal sign-manual 1758. Sir Richard Nelson Rycroft, 5th Bt., and Sir Nelson Edward Oliver Rycroft, 6th Bt., were High Sheriffs of Hants 1899, and 1938, respectively.

MOLESWORTH-ST. AUBYN, Creation (E.) 1689, of Pencarrow, Cornwall.

In se teres.
Complete in itself.

Sir JOHN MOLESWORTH-ST. AUBYN, *CBE,* 14th *Baronet, b.* Jan. 12th, 1899 ; *s.* his father, *Sir* HUGH 1942; ed. at Eton, and at Ch. Ch., Oxford (BA); Flight-Lt. late R.A.F. Vol. Reserve, a JP and an Alderman for Cornwall, and a Member of Local Cttee., Devon and Cornwall, Lloyds Bank; High Sheriff of Cornwall 1948; CBE (Civil) 1968: *m.* 1926, Celia Marjorie, who *d.* 1965, da. of the late Lt.-Col. Valentine Vivian, CMG, DSO, MVO [E. Portarling on], and has issue.

Arms—Quarterly ; 1st and 4th, ermine, on a cross sable, **five** bezants, *St. Aubyn* ; 2nd and 3rd gules, an escutcheon vair, between eight cross-crosslets in orle argent, *Molesworth.* **Crest**—A rock, thereon a Cornish chough rising, all proper.

Residence—Pencarrow, Washaway, Bodmin.

Son living—JOHN ARSCOTT, *MBE* (Tetcott Manor, Holsworthy, N. Devon; Army and Navy Club), *b.* Dec. 15th, 1926; ed. at Eton; late Lt.-Col. The R. Green Jackets; a JP for Devon, and a DL of Cornwall (High Sheriff 1975-76); MBE (Mil) 1963: *m.* 1957, Iona Audrey Armatrude, da. of Adm. Sir Francis Loftus Tottenham, KCB, CBE, and has issue living, William, *b.* 1958,—James Francis, *b.* 1960,—Emma Jane, *b.* 1971.

Sic fidem teneo.
Thus I hold the faith.

Daughters living—Johanna Katherine (*Countess of Morley*), (of Pound House, Yelverton, Devon), *b.* 1929: *m.* 1955, the 6th Earl of Morley.——Prudence Aline, *b.* 1937: *m.* 1969, Joseph Robertson Cooke-Hurle, of Long Ash, Buckland Monachorum, nr. Yelverton, Devon, and has issue living, Celia Hermione, *b.* 1970,—Penelope Joy, *b.* 1971.

Brothers living—Hender Charles, *TD* (Shepherd's Hill, Washaway, Bodmin, Cornwall), *b.* 1901; ed. at Eton; Maj. late Pioneer Corps, and Capt. late 96th (R. Dev n Yeo.) Field Regt. RA (TA): *m.* 1935 (m. diss. 1946), Dulciebella Joy, da. of Lt.-Col. John Cayzer Medlicott Vereker [*see* V. Gort, colls.], and has issue living, Caroline Gay, *b.* 1940: *m.* 1963, Edward Simon Foord, of Hoyle Barn, Heyshott, Midhurst, Sussex, and has issue living, Edward Richard *b.* 1965, Tracey Samantha *b.* 1967, Annabel Jane *b.* 1971.——Guy Kemyel, *b.* 1904; ed. at Eton, and at Ch. Ch., Oxford: *m.* 1931, Catherine, *JP*, da. of the late R. T. Hargreaves, of Benington Park, Herts., and has issue living, Anthony William (Cobbs, Howe St., Chelmsford, Essex), *b.* 1936: *m.* 1964, Mary Evelyn, only da. of Kenneth Meiklejohn, and has issue living, Charles Hugh *b.* 1966, Anna Victoria *b.* 1970,—Simon Guy, *b.* 1944; Maj. 60th Rifles,—Felicity Sybil (*Hon. Mrs. Adam C. Butler*), *b.* 1932: *m.* 1955, the Hon. Adam Courtauld Butler, MP, of The Old Rectory, Lighthorne, nr. Warwick, 2nd son of Baron Butler of Saffron Walden [Life Peer]. *Residence*, Lark's Hill, Braughing, Ware, Herts.

Collateral Branch living.

Grandson of the late Col. St. Aubyn Molesworth, R.A., son of the late Col. St. Aubyn Molesworth, R.E., son of the late Rev. John Molesworth, 2nd son of 5th baronet :—

Issue of the late Major Edward Algernon Molesworth, D.S.O., *b.* 1875, *d.* 1939 : *m.* 1916, Ruth, da. of Leslie Creery, of Lisnalurg, Shankill, co. Dublin :—

St. Aubyn (467, Military Rd., Largs Bay, S. Australia, 5016); *b.* 1917; an Engineer in Merchant Navy.

This family descends from Sir Walter de Molesworth, who in 1270 accompanied Edward I., when Prince Edward, to the Holy Land. The 1st baronet, Sir Hender, was Lieut.-Gov. of Jamaica. The 2nd baronet, M.P. for Bossiney, was knighted by Charles II. The 4th baronet sat as M.P. for Newport, Cornwall, 1734, and for Cornwall 1744-61. The 5th and 6th baronets respectively represented Cornwall 1765-75, and 1784-90. The 8th baronet, M.P. for East Cornwall 1832-7, for Leeds 1837-41, and for Southwark 1841-55, was a Privy Councillor, and successively First Commissioner of Works, and Secretary of State for the Colonies. The 11th baronet sat as M.P. for Cornwall, S.-E., or Bodmin Div. (LU) 1900-6. The 12th baronet, Rev. Sir Hender, was son of the late Rev. Hender Molesworth (great-grandson of 5th baronet), who assumed by Roy. licence 1844, the additional surname and arms of St. Aubyn his mother Catherine being da. and co-heir of Sir John St. Aubyn, baronet.

ST. GEORGE, Creation (I.) 1766, of Athlone, co. Westmeath.

Sir ROBERT ALAN ST. GEORGE, 7th *Baronet* ; *b.* March 20th, 1900 ; *s.* his father, *Sir* THEOPHILUS JOHN, 1943 ; sometime 2nd Lieut. R.A.F. ; European War 1939-42 in Middle East as Trooper 4th S. African Armoured Car Regt. (prisoner) ; is a Religious Missionary Brother.

Arms—Argent : a chief azure, over all a lion rampant gules, ducally crowned or, armed and langued of the second, a crescent for difference. **Crest**—A demi-lion rampant gules, ducally crowned or, armed and langued azure.

Address—c/o St. Joseph Scholasticate, P.O. Cedara, Natal, South Africa.

Firmitas in cœlo.
Stability in heaven.

Brothers living—*Rev.* DENIS HOWARD (Emmanuel Cathedral, Durban, Natal, S. Africa), *b.* Sept. 6th, 1902; is in Holy Orders of Roman Catholic Church.——George Bligh (4, Eastwood, 30, Springfield Cres., Durban 5001, Natal), *b.* 1908; 1939-45 War as Lt. Technical Sers. Corps: *m.* 1935, Mary Somerville, da. of Francis John Sutcliffe, and has issue living, John Avenel Bligh (The Farm House, Norris Castle, E. Cowes, I. of Wight), *b.* 1940: *m.* 1962, Margaret, da. of John Leonard Carter, MBE, of Mayes Park House, Warnham, Sussex, and has issue living, Elinor Jane Bligh *b.* 1963, Catherine Bligh *b.* 1966,—Peter Bligh (31, Crockerton Rd., Tooting, SW17), *b.* 1946; MBA (Cape Town), CA (SA): *m.* 1974, Elizabeth Meyrick, el. da. of the late Alan Meyrick Williams of Newport, Gwent,—Elizabeth Margaret Bligh, *b.* 1936: *m.* 1962, Peter Ivor Baikie, CA (SA), FSAA, of 28, Erna St., Observatory Extn. Johannesburg, and has issue living, David Peter *b.* 1973, Derek John *b.* 1975, Fiona Margaret *b.* 1965, Linda Jeanne *b.* 1969,—Catherine Mary Bligh, *b.* 1937: *m.* 1964, John Douglas Walker, MB, ChB, MRCOG, of 34, Cambridge Av., Craighall Park, Johannesburg, and has issue living, John Paul Douglas *b.* 1968, Jane Philippa Douglas *b.* 1967, Felicity Mary Douglas *b.* 1974,—Angela Bligh, *b.* 1952.

Sisters living—Emma Felice Mary, *b.* 1893 ; sometime Matron of Chronic Sick Hospital, Hill Crest, Natal. *Residence*, 171, Loop Street, Pietermaritzburg, Natal.——Maria Edith, *b.* 1896. *Residence*, 171, Loop Street, Pietermaritzburg, Natal.——Anne Rose, *b.* 1898 : *m.* 1926, William Farquhar Ogilvie, who *d.* 1963, and has issue living, John Alexander, *b.* 1927: *m.* 1954, Pamela Betty Brown,—Angus, *b.* 1930: *m.* 1953, Heather Wright,—Margaret, *b.* 1933: *m.* 1961, David George Kerby. *Residence*, 21, Burger St., Pietermaritzburg, Natal.——Florence Caroline, *b.* 1904: *m.* 1930, Rudolph Gerrard du Preez, and has issue living, Christopher Ralph, *b.* 1931,— David Raye, *b.* 1934.——Patricia Margaret, *b.* 1906: *m.* 1930, Michael John Power, who *d.* 1966, and has issue living, Michael St. George, *b.* 1931,—Richard William St. George, *b.* 1942: *m.* 1974, Susan Dorothy Peiser,—Jane St. George, *b.* 1934: *m.* 1953, Gerald Malcolm Stewart, and has issue living, Simon Malcolm *b.* 1957, Kim Louise *b.* 1954. *Residence*, 171, Loop St., Pietermaritzburg, Natal.

Collateral Branches living.

Issue of the late Richard Christopher Bligh St. George, *b.* 1875, *d.* 1945: *m.* 1916, Alice Rosabel, who *d.* 1964, el. da. of Lt.-Col. Hugh L. Donovan, of Oakhurst, S. Yardley, Worcs.:—

Catherine Harriet Mary Bligh (1346, Coventry Rd., Yardley, Birmingham, B25 82N), *b.* 1917.

Grandson of the late Robert Charles Cecil St. George, yst. son of the late Robert James Ker St. George (ante), *b.* 1883, *d.* 1948: *m.* 1917, Lillian, da. of Thomas Hunt Talmadge, of New York:—

Issue of Robert Charles Cecil St. George, *b.* 1920, *d.* 1963: *m.* 1943, Pricilla (Glenrasner, Oldwich, New Jersey, U.S.A., and 18, Holdenbrook Rd., Concord, Mass., U.S.A.), da. of John Tillerton Painter, of Pittsburgh, Penn., U.S.A.:—

Christopher S., *b.* 1946.

Granddaughters of the late Howard Bligh St. George (infra):—

Issue of the late George Baker Bligh St. George, *b.* 1892, *d.* 1957: *m.* 1917, Katharine (a Member of House of Representatives, USA Congress) (of Tuxedo Park, New York, USA), da. of Price Collier, of Tuxedo Park, New York, USA:—

Priscilla Avenel, *b.* 1919: *m.* 1st, 1936 (divorce 1939), Angier Biddle Duke; 2ndly, 1941 (m. diss. 19—), Allan A. Ryan, and has issue living, (by 1st m.) St. George Biddle, *b.* 1938: *m.* 1959, Jeanne S. Farmer, and has issue living, George St. George *b.* 1960,—(by 2nd m.) Katherine Delano, *b.* 1943. *Residence*,

Issue of the late Col. Frederick Ferris Bligh St. George, CVO, *b.* 1908, *d.* 1970: *m.* 1932, Meriel Margaret, JP, who *d.* 1966, da. of the late Lt.-Col. William Scott Warley Radcliffe [E. Macclesfield, colls.]:—

Meriel Jane Bligh (PO Box N3943, Nassau, Bahamas), *b.* 1933: *m.* 1966 (m. diss. 1971), Benjamin Brandreth McAlpin.——Elizabeth Sally Bligh, *b.* 1936: *m.* 1965, John Richard Alford, of Hill Court, Shipton Moyne, Tetbury.——Diana Gillian Bligh, *b.* 1939; *m.* 1967, Hardman George Algernon Earle, of Abington, Murroe, co. Limerick, el. son of Sir Hardman Alexander Mort Earle, 5th Bt.

Granddaughter of the late Robert St. George (ante):—

Issue of the late Howard Bligh St. George, *b.* 1857, *d.* 1940 : *m.* 1891, Florence Evelyn, who *d.* 1938, da. of the late George F. Baker, of 258, Madison Avenue, New York :—

Evelyn Bligh (*Lady Gunston*), OBE, *b.* 1897; Dir. of Residential Nurseries, Anglo-American Relief Fund 1941-46; OBE (Civil) 1944: *m.* 1917, Capt. Sir Derrick Wellesley Gunston, MC, MP, 1st Bt., of Farm Cottage, Bembridge, Isle of Wight, and 14, Pelham Cres., SW7.

Grandchildren of the late George Edward St. George (infra):—

Issue of the late Leslie George St. George, *b.* 1896, *d.* 1968: *m.* 1918, Gladys, who *d.* 1941, da. of Alfred McGillivray, of Ottawa:—

Leslie Richard (16, Inverness Rd., Ottawa, Ont.), *b.* 1924: *m.* 1946, Muriel Winnifred, da. of John Edwards, and has issue living, Barry Edward, *b.* 1949,—Leslie Timothy, *b.* 1961,—Gayle Mary *b.* 1953, Beverly Ann, *b.* 1954.——Robert John (PO Box 385, 67, Rothesay Drive, Hazeldean, Ont.), *b.* 1941: *m.* 1968, Vivien Jill, da. of David G. Walters, of London, England, and has issue living, Christian Robert David, *b.* 1974,—Catherine Lesley, *b.* 1970.——Mary Audrey, *b.* 1927: *m.* 1949, John Scarcella, of 1627, Digby St., Ottawa 8, Ont., and has issue living, Byron Michal, *b.* 1949,—David Low's Anthony, *b.* 1955,—Gordon Kenneth John, *b.* 1960.

Granddaughter of the late William Oliver St. George, 4th son of 2nd baronet:—

Issue of the late George Edward St. George, *b.* 1854, *d.* 1902 : *m.* 1894, Henrietta, who *d.* 1907, da. of George Simms, of Ottawa, Canada :—

Jane Ellen (325, West Av., Rochester, N.Y., USA), *b.* 1900: *m.* 1918, John Mallen, who *d.* 1973, and has issue living, Richard William (195, Arbor Road, Ontario, N.Y., USA), *b.* 1927: *m.* 1st, 1953, Lois Ann, who *d.* 1961, da. of W. H. Taylor; 2ndly, 1962, Marlene E. Green, and has issue living, (by 2nd m.) Michell Ann *b.* 1965,—Thomas James (Emerson Rd., RR2 Port Byron, NY, USA), *b.* 1938: *m.* 1958, Sharon Holland, da. of Bernard J. Douthwaite, of Rochester, N.Y. and has issue living, Thomas Richard *b.* 1959, Joseph Roycroft *b.* 1963.

Issue of the late Robert St. George, *b.* 1856, *d.* 1939 : *m.* 1881, Elizabeth Agatha, who *d.* 1935, da. of Thomas Tovey, of Perth, Ontario :—

Richard Bligh (351, Friel St., Ottawa, Ont., Canada), *b.* 1886: *m.* 1920 (m. diss. 1930), Ada Mary Barr.——George Edgar *b.* 1892: *m.* 1929, Ruth Mary, da. of Harold Richardson, of Ottawa, and has issue living, George Edgar, *b.* 1929,—Richard Bligh Harold, *b.* 1935,—Ruth Mary Madora, *b.* 1931.——Lily Madora, *b.* 1882: *m.* 1908, Edgar Charles Coleman, and has issue living.——Daisy Mary Evelyn (351, Friel St., Apart. 5, Ottawa, Canada), *b.* 1884: *m.* 1933, Dominic F. Scanlon, who *d.* 1947.

Granddaughter of the late James Howard St. George (infra):—

Issue of the late James Howard St. George, *b.* 1893, *d.* 1962: *m.* 1928, Elizabeth, who *d.* 1964, da. of William Belch, of Ottawa:—

Constance June, *b.* 1930: *m.* 1955, Robert Carl Bociek, MD, of 1, Cowichan Way, Ottawa, Ont., Canada, and has issue living, Gregory Robert, *b.* 1961,—James Andrew, *b.* 1964,—Virginia Elizabeth, *b.* 1956,—Beverley Ann, *b.* 1959.

Grandchildren of the late William Oliver St. George (ante):—

Issue of the late James Howard St. George, *b.* 1864, *d.* 1939: *m.* 1891, Catherine, who *d.* 1914, da. of Michael Burns, of Ottawa :—

Hazel Gertrude, *b.* 1901: *m.* 1924, George H. Reinhardt, of 43, Dalhousie St., Ottawa, Canada.

Issue of the late Hercules Frank St. George, *b.* 1867, *d.* 1938 : *m.* 1895, Rosaline, who *d.* 1901, da. of John Dunn, of Gaspé, Quebec, Canada :—

Hercules Frank, *b.* 1896 : *m.* 1939, Marie Adeline Juliette, da. of Eugene Larocque, of Ottawa. *Residence,* Ottawa, Canada.

Issue of the late John Arthur St. George (twin), *b.* 1867, *d.* 1912 : *m.* 1900, Lily Belle, da. of John Magladry :—

William John, *b.* 1907.——Gladys Ellen, *b.* 1901.——Marjorie Ellen, *b.* 1903.——Fanny Evelyn, *b.* 1905.——Sarah Alice, *b.* 1909. *Residence,*

Grandson of the late Loftus St. George (infra):—

Issue of the late Clifford Fortescue Loftus St. George, CBE, *b.* 1894, *d.* 1966: *m.* 1931, Gwen Marjorie Chisholm, da. of the Rev. William Dalton, V. of Glynde, Sussex:—

John, *b.* 1942.

Granddaughters of the late James Cuffe St. George, 5th son of 2nd baronet:—

Issue of the late Loftus St. George, *b.* 1858, *d.* 1952 : *m.* 1893, Marguerite Isabel Clifford, who *d.* 1956, da. of the late Clifford Fortescue Borrer, of Pickwell, Cuckfield, Sussex :—

Kathleen Adeline Jane Loftus *b.* 1898: *m.* 1923, John Philip Stephenson Clarke, who *d.* 1969, and has issue living, Charles St. George Stephenson (Broadhurst Manor, Horsted Keynes, Sussex), *b.* 1924: *m.* 1959, Thérèse, da. of Gen. Husson, of Toulon, France and formerly wife of the 6th Baron Sheffield, and has issue living, Edmund John Stephenson *b.* 1959, Richard Louis Stephenson *b.* 1961,—Michael St. George Stephenson (The Old Rectory, Shorwell, I. of Wight), *b.* 1929: *m.* 1954, Angela Heathcote, da. of the late W. H. Tatham, of Pinehurst, S. Ascot, Berks, and has issue living, Timothy Philip *b.* 1958,—Antony Loftus St. George Stephenson, *b.* 1932; Maj. Som. and Cornwall LI: *m.* 1st, 1956, Elizabeth, da. of Talbot Clayton, of Cornwall; 2ndly, 1960, Susan Elizabeth, da. of E. J. Poulton, of Willow Tree, Lindfield, Sussex, and has issue living, (by 1st m.) Elizabeth Jane Stephenson *b.* 1956, (by 2nd m.) Alistair *b.* 1962, Jonathan *b.* 1964,—Rory St. George Stephenson (Cinder Hill House, Horsted Keynes, Sussex), *b.* 1934: *m.* 1966, Harriet Mary, da. of Benjamin Nicholson White-Spunner, of New Barn, Winkfield, Berks., and has issue living, Hugo Rory Stephenson *b.* 1968, Rufus John *b.* 1971, Hannah Mary *b.* 1967. *Residence,* Broadhurst Manor, Horsted Keynes, Sussex.——Violet Marguerite Loftus (*Lady Jackson*), *b.* 1904: *m.* 1931, Sir Hugh Nicholas Jackson, 2nd Bt. (*cr.* 1913). *Residence,* 38, Oakley St., SW3.

The 1st baronet, Sir Richard St. George (second son of the late George St. George, of Woodsgift co. Kilkenny), was M.P. for Athlone 1763-89. The 2nd baronet, Sir Richard Bligh, was Sec. of Order of St. Patrick. The 6th baronet, Sir Theophilus John, was sometime Assist. Master of Supreme Court, Natal.

St. John-Mildmay, see Mildmay.

SALT, Creation (U.K.) 1869, of Saltaire, Yorkshire.

What not with God helping ?

QUID · NON · DEO · JUVANTE

Sir DAVID SHIRLEY SALT, 5th
Baronet : *b.* June 14th, 1930 ; *s.* his
father, *Com. Sir* JOHN WILLIAM TITUS,
RN, 1953 ; ed. at Stowe : *m.* 1st, 1955 (m.
diss. 1974), Margaret Gillian, da. of Hugh
Alwyn Lenox [Rich, Bt., colls.] ; 2ndly,
1975, Freda Blows.

Arms—Azure a chevron indented between two
mullets in chief, and a demi-ostrich displayed, holding
in the beak a horse-shoe in base or. Crest—Upon a
rock, an alpaca statant, proper.
Residence—15, Belgrave Mews South, SW1.

Brothers living—ANTHONY HOULTON (Dellow
House, Ugley Green, Essex), *b.* Sept. 15th, 1931 ;
ed. at Stowe : *m.* 1957, Prudence Mary Dorothea
Francis, yst. da. of the late Francis Meath
Baker, and has issue living, Fenella Mary Houlton,
b. 1959,—Rebecca Madeleine Harris, *b.* 1961,—
Lucinda Mary Harriet, *b.* 1964,—Charlotte Lavinia
Francis, *b.* 1967.——Patrick MacDonnell (4/29,
Emperors Gate, SW7 4HS), *b.* 1932 ; ed. at Stowe.

Collateral Branches living.
Issue of the late Herbert Salt, 4th
son of 1st baronet, *b.* 1840, *d.*
1912 : *m.* 1st, 1889, Elizabeth,
who *d.* 1898, youngest da. of the
late John Douglas Farrell ; 2ndly,
1899, Margaret, who *d.* 1910,
widow of Christopher Robert de
Lacey :—

(By 1st marriage) Loris Alexandrinia Caroline, *b.* 1892 : *m.* 1921, Victor Drogrez, who *d.* 1945,
and has issue living, Ena Patricia, *b.* 1921. *Residence,*

Grandchildren of the late Gordon Locksley Salt (infra) :—
Issue of the late John Scarlett Alexander Salt, *b.* 1905, *d.* 1947 : *m.* 1939, Olive Mary
(who *m.* 2ndly, 1952, Christopher Gorton, of Rose Hill, Millgate Lane, Didsbury,
Manchester, 20), da. of William Gilbert Shapley :—
Daniel Alexander, *b.* 1943 : *m.* 1968, Mehrchide, da. of Dr. A. Emami, of Teheran, and has issue
living, Firoozeh Katherine, *b.* 1971,—Maryam Rachel, *b.* 1974.—Nicholas John, *b.* 1945 : *m.*
1971, Catherine Kimerling, da. of Charles Grun, of New York, and has issue living, Aaron, *b.*
1972.——Christina Mary, *b.* 1947.

Grandchildren of the late Titus Salt, 5th son of 1st baronet :—
Issue of the late Gordon Locksley Salt, *b.* 1866, *d.* 1938 : *m.* 1903, Florence Mary, who *d.*
1959, da. of the Rev. James Williams Scarlett, formerly R. of Rossington, Doncaster :—
Sythe Margaret Isabella, *b.* 1904.——Nesta Katharine, *b.* 1909. *Residence,* The Old Rectory,
Thorp Arch, Boston Spa, Yorkshire.

Issue of the late Harold Crossley Salt, *b.* 1868, *d.* 1943 : *m.* 1906, Grace Ethel Muriel,
da. of the late Rev. Henry Madan Pratt, R. of Cottesbrooke, Northamptonshire
[Wilson, Bt., *cr.* 1874] :—
Denys Geoffrey Crossley (38, Holland Park, W.11), *b.* 1918 ; ed. at Marlborough, and at St. Edmund
Hall, Oxford (MA) ; Middle East and Italy 1941-45 as Maj. R. Glos. Hussars : *m.* 1956, (marriage
annulled 1963) Patricia Lee, da. of the late Lt.-Col. D. C. Pope, MC, of Red House, Sutton
Montis, Somerset.——Peter Hubert Wharton, *b.* 1920 ; ed. at Cheltenham, and at St. Edmund
Hall, Oxford (MA), India 1944-46 with Intelligence Corps : *m.* 1951, Gillian Caryl, da. of the
late John Hill, of Westhill, Ledbury, and has issue living, Jonathan Wharton, *b.* 1953,—Miranda
Elisabeth Caryl, *b.* 1955. *Residence,* Jacaranda, Limpsfield, Surrey.

Sir Titus, 1st baronet, son of Daniel Salt of Bradford, sat as MP for Bradford (L) 1859-61.

SALT, Creation (U.K.) 1899, of Standon, and of Weeping Cross, co. Stafford.

In sale salus.

Sir THOMAS MICHAEL JOHN SALT, 4th *Baronet; b.*
Nov. 7th, 1946 ; *s.* his father, Lt.-Col. *Sir* THOMAS
HENRY, 1965 ; ed. at Eton : *m.* 1971, Caroline, el. da. of
Henry Robert John Hildyard [see Bonsor Bt.].

Arms—Argent, a chevron rompu between three mullets in chief and a
lion rampant in base sable. Crest—Three annulets interlaced sable, thereon
a dove holding an olive branch proper, charged on the neck with a chevron
also sable.

Residences—Shillingstone House, Shillingstone, Dorset ; 33 Cranbury
Rd., SW6. *Club,* Boodle's.

Brother living—ANTHONY WILLIAM DAVID, *b.* Feb. 5th, 1950.

Sisters living—Sarah Meriel, *b.* 1944.——Jennifer Mary, *b.* 1951.

Aunt living (daughter of 2nd baronet)—Patience Elinor, *b.* 1910 : *m.* 1936, Group Capt. Geoffrey
Francis, DSO, DFC, RAF, from whom she obtained a divorce 1947, and has issue living, Jessica
Patience, *b.* 1942 : *m.* 1965, Howard Finn Fetherstonhaugh, of Hillside House, Charminster,
Dorchester, Dorset, and has issue living, Crispin Rupert *b.* 1967, Justin George *b.* 1970. *Resi-
dence,* Wesley Cottage, Charminster, Dorchester, Dorset.

Widow living of 3rd Baronet—MERIEL SOPHIA WILMOT (*Meriel Lady Salt*) (Shillingstone House,
Shillingstone, Dorset), da. of the late Capt. Berkeley Cole Wilmot Williams [B. Addington] : *m.*
1943, Sir Thomas Henry Salt, 3rd Bt., who *d.* 1965.

Collateral Branches living.

Issue of the late Lieut.-Com. George Stevenson Salt, R.N., 2nd son of 2nd baronet, *b.* 1908. *d.* (on active ser. during European War) 1940: *m.* 1935, Lilian Bridget (who *m.* 2ndly, 1948, Capt. William John Lamb, C.V.O., O.B.E., R.N. (retired), of Weston's, Bank, near Lyndhurst, Hants), da. of the late F. S. Francis, of Champion's Farm, Pulborough, Sussex. :—

James Frederick Thomas George, *b.* 1940; Cdr. RN: *m.* 1975, Penelope, only da. of Anthony Walker of Wall Garth, Holcot.——Joanna Elizabeth (*Lady Spencer-Nairn*), *b.* 1937: *m.* 1963, Sir Robert Arnold Spencer-Nairn, 3rd Bt., of Barham, Cupar, Fife.

Issue of the late Herbert Edward ANDERDON, 2nd son of 1st baronet, *b.* 1870, *d.* 1938 (having assumed by deed poll 1923, the surname of Anderdon in lieu of his patronymic): *m.* 1899, Ethel Menie, who *d.* 1966, da. of the late Henry Manisty of 169, Queen's Gate, SW7:—

Henry Manisty Anderdon, *b.* 1900; ed. at Haileybury: *m.* 1929, Sybilla Marjorie, da. of Lt.-Col. Reginald Holden Steward, OBE, and has issue living, John Nigel Steward (Arundell's Farm, Henlade, Taunton, Som.), *b.* 1931; Cdr. RN (ret.): *m.* 1961, Mavis Marjorie, da. of Lester Gibson, of Bristol, and has issue living, Alexander Philip, *b.* 1963,—Ian George Carlyle, *b.* 1936. *Residence,* Henlade House, Taunton, Som.——Rachel Elinor, *MBE, b.* 1909; MBE (Civil) 1965.

Issue of the late Reginald John Salt, 4th son of 1st baronet, *b.* 1874, *d.* 1963: *m.* 1901, Maud Fanny, who *d.* 1962, da. of the late Robert Wigram [Wigram, Bt., colls.]:—

Laura Enid (8, The Croft, Old Headington, Oxford), *b.* 1902; with Oxford Univ. Press.

Issue of the late Rev. William Manning Salt, 5th son of 1st baronet, *b.* 1876, *d.* 1947: *m.* 1907, Mildred Nairne, who *d.* 1926, da. of the late Col. C. H. E. Græme:—

Joan Mildred, *b.* 1908; JP of Monmouth: *m.* 1938, Frederick Newman Tanner. *Residence,* The Vaga, Monmouth——Rosemary, *b.* 1911: *m.* 1934, Leslie Louis Samuel Lowe, TD, BLitt, JP, who *d.* 1959. *Residence,* Jevington, West Hill, Ottery St. Mary, S. Devon.——Elisabeth, *b.* 1915. *Residence,* Jevington, West Hill, Ottery St. Mary, Devon.

Issue of the late Maj.-Gen. Harold Francis Salt, CB, CMG, DSO, yst. son of 1st baronet, *b.* 1879, *d.* 1971: *m.* 1914, Phyllis Dulce, who *d.* 1965, da. of the late Maj. E. D. Cameron, RFA:—

Primrose Phyllis, *b.* 1915: *m.* 1st, 1935, Maj. Anthony Hope Osborne, The Queen's Bays, who *d.* (killed on active ser.) 1943; 2ndly, 1944 (m. diss. 1948), Capt. Philip Quellyn Roberts, RN; 3rdly, 1962, James Mansfield Niall, of 99, Empire Circuit, Deakin, Canberra, Aust., and has issue living (by 1st m.) Duncan Norton Hope, *b.* 1936,—(by 2nd m.) Paul Quellyn, *b.* 1945.——Babette Irene (*Lady Millais*), *b.* 1922: *m.* 1st, 1941, Maj. John De Grey Tatham Warter, MC, 2nd Dragoon Gds. (The Queen's Bays) who *d.* (killed in action) 1942; 2ndly, 1946 (m. diss. 1972), Victor William Henry Sefton-Smith; 3rdly, 1975, as his 3rd wife, Sir Ralph Regnault Millais, 5th baronet, and has issue living (by 2nd m.) Ewan Victor William, *b.* 1950,—Susan Jane, *b.* 1948: *m.* 1971, John Henry Deen, of 12, Marlborough St., SW3,—Lucy Annabelle, *b.* 1952.

The 1st baronet, Sir Thomas, a partner in the private banking firms of Stevenson, Salt and Co. (Stafford Old Bank), and Bosanquet, Salt and Co. (London), and Chm. of Lloyds Bank, sat as MP for Stafford (C) 1859, 1869-80, 1881-5, and 1886-92. He was son of Thomas Salt of Standon and Weeping Cross, Staffs, whose family was settled at Rugeley in the seventeenth century. Sir Thomas Salt, 1st baronet, m. 1861, Emma Helen Mary, da. of John Lavicount Anderdon of Chislehurst, Kent, niece of Cardinal Manning.

Salusbury-Trelawny, see Trelawny.

SAMMAN, Creation (U.K.) 1921, of Routh, East Riding, co. Yorkshire.

[Extinct 1960.]

Sir HENRY SAMMAN, *M.C.,* 2nd and last *Baronet.*

Daughter living of 1st Baronet—Mary Elizabeth, *b.* 1880. *Residence,* The Croft, 49, Woodgates Lane, N. Ferriby, E. Yorks.

SAMUEL, Creation (U.K.) 1898, of Nevern Square, St. Mary Abbots, Kensington, co. London.

Sir JON MICHAEL GLEN SAMUEL, 5th *Baronet;*
b. Jan. 25th, 1944; *s.* his father, *Sir* JOHN OLIVER CECIL, 1962 : *m.* 1966, Antoinette Sandra, da. of the late Capt. Anthony Hewitt, RE, and has issue.

A pledge of better times.

Arms—Party per chevron argent and gules two wolves' heads erased in chief sable, and in base as many squirrels sejant addorsed, each cracking a nut of the first.   Crest—On a rock in front of three spears, one in pale and two in saltire proper, a wolf courant sable, pierced in the breast by an arrow argent, flighted or.

Residence—Wayside, Brimpton, Berks.

Sons living—ANTHONY JOHN FULTON, *b.* Oct. 13th, 1972.——Rupert Casper James, *b.* 1974.

Sister living—Jane Lesley, *b.* 1947: *m.* 1966, John Henry Newman, of The Close, Headlands, Kettering, Northants., and has issue living, James Michael, *b.* 1969,—Timothy John Hoyt, *b.* 1972.

Aunt living—Eva Elizabeth, *b.* 1905: *m.* 1934, George Brian Stafford Cothay, and has issue living, Charlotte Ann Stafford, *b.* 1936: *m.* 1962, Cdr. John May, RN, of Woodside, Eastergate, Chichester, and has issue living, Alexandra Louise Stafford, *b.* 1965. *Residence,* 22, Spinners Close, Biddenden, Ashford, Kent.

Daughter living of 2nd Baronet—Vera Leah Henrietta (5, Abbotts, Regency Sq., Brighton), *b.* 1893: *m.* 1925, Geoffrey Noel Holt, who *d.* 1951 (having assumed by deed poll 1930 the additional surname of Hillier before that of Holt), and has issue living, Jean Pamela Ray, *b.* 1926: *m.* 1947, Stuart Sitwell Shaw, MB, BS, MRCP, of Westwood, New Farm Rd., Alresford, Hants., and has issue living, Nigel Peter Sibwell *b.* 1949, Colin Geoffrey Howard *b.* 1952. Graham John Vaughan *b.* 1955,—Daphne Vera, *b.* 1931: *m.* 1953, Gordon Hamilton Fairley, of 53, Campden Hill Sq., W8, son of the late Sir Neil Hamilton Fairley, KBE, and has issue living, Geoffrey Neil *b.* 1961, Diana *b.* 1956, Sarah *b.* 1958, Fiona *b.* 1963—Patricia Leslie (7, Roland Way, SW7), *b.* 1935.
Widow living of 4th Baronet—CHARLOTTE MARY (The Old School House, W. Horsley, Surrey), da. of the late R. H. Hoyt, of Calgary, Canada: *m.* 1st, 1942, Sir John Oliver Cecil Samuel, 4th Bt, who *d.* 1962; 2ndly, 1966, Heremon James Patrick Desmond, who *d.* 1971.

The 1st baronet, Hon. Sir Saul, K.C.M.G., C.B., was Agent-Gen. in England for N.S. Wales 1880-98.

SAMUEL, Creation (U.K.) 1912, of Chelwood Vetchery, Maresfield, Sussex.
[Extinct 1926.]

Sir STUART MONTAGU SAMUEL, 1st and last *Baronet.*

Daughter living of 1st Baronet—Vera Evelyn (*Lady Cohen*), *b.* 1894: *m.* 1914, Maj. Sir (Jack Benn) Brunel Cohen, KBE, who *d.* 1965, and has issue living, George Stuart Brunel BRUNEL-COHEN, TD (3, Hollies End, Mill Hill Village, NW7 2RY), *b.* 1918; assumed by deed poll 1948 the additional surname of Brunel; late Maj. Rifle Bde.; is a JP: *m.* 1948, Shelagh Madeleine, JP, da. of Dr. M. G. Garry, and widow of J. R. McCosh, Lt. RNVR, and has issue living, Mark Patrick (105, Sinclair Rd., W14), *b.* 1949: *m.* 1974, Sally, da. of G. A. Culham, Edward Stuart, *b.* 1952, Lucy Louise *b.* 1955,—John Louis Brunel (21, Cadogan Gdns., SW3), *b.* 1922: *m.* 1st 1951, Simone Dolores Catherine Everitt who *d.* 1969, da. of the late Robert L. de Vergriette, of Paris; 2ndly, 1972, Christine Bowman Blamey, da. of the late John Rothwell Dixon, and has issue living (by 1st m.), Richard Stuart Brunel *b.* 1954, David John Brunel (twin) *b.* 1954, Jane Caroline Brunel *b.* 1952: *m.* 1969 (m. diss. 1971), Philip Spira,—Pamela May Brunel (Apple Tree Cottage, Wisborough Green, Sussex; 11B, Marlborough Rd., Richmond, Surrey), *b.* 1915. *Residence,* Flat 115, Grosvenor House, Park Lane, W1A 3AA.

SAMUELSON, Creation (U.K.) 1884, of Bodicote, Banbury, Oxfordshire.

Light after darkness.

Sir FRANCIS HENRY BERNHARD SAMUELSON, 4th *Baronet*; *b.* Feb. 22nd, 1890; *s.* his father, *Sir* FRANCIS (ARTHUR EDWARD), 1946; ed. at Eton, and at Trin. Coll., Camb.; European War 1914-19 in France and Palestine as Capt. Yorkshire Hussars Yeo.: *m.* 1913, Margaret Kendall, da. of the late H. Kendall Barnes, of Borkwood, Orpington, Kent, and has issue.

Arms—Sable, three piles wavy two issuant from the chief and one from the base or, each charged with a phœnix proper. Crest—A phœnix holding in its beak a torch, and charged on each wing with a scroll.

Residence—Midway House, Partridge Green, Sussex.

Sons living—(BERNARD) MICHAEL FRANCIS, *b.* Jan. 17th, 1917; ed. at Eton; late Lt. RA; Burma 1939-45 (despatches): *m.* 1952, Janet Amy, yr. da. of Lt.-Cdr. Laurence Garrett Elkington, of Chelsea, SW, and has issue living, James Francis, *b.* 1956,—Edward Bernard, *b.* 1967,—Nancy Amy, *b.* 1953,—Angela Margaret, *b.* 1962.——Christopher Blundell, *b.* 1920; ed. at Eton, and at Trin. Coll., Camb.; 1940-45 War with Staffordshire Yeo.——Richard, *b.* 1925; ed. at Eton; 1943-45 War as Lt. Fleet Air Arm.

Daughters living—Isabel Muriel, *b.* 1915: *m.* 1950, Richard Ward.——Diana Frances (Woodfield, Church Lane, Beeding, Steyning, Sussex), *b.* 1922: *m.* 1943, William Ord Blacklock, who *d.* 1958, and has issue living, Catherine Margaret, *b.* 1945: *m.* 1970, Alistair Donald Mant, of Sydney, NSW, and has issue living, Eleanor Frances *b.* 1972,—Frances Elizabeth, *b.* 1946: *m.* 1970, Dennis Thomas Conroy, and has issue living, Thomas Liam *b.* 1974, Joanna Mary *b.* 1971, Alice Frances *b.* 1973,—Stephanie, *b.* 1952: *m.* 1972, Barrie Weir, and has issue living, Gemma Fay, *b.* 1974.

Sister living—Muriel Gertrude, *b.* 1893: *m.* 1915, Col. Bassett Fitz-Gerald Wilson, MC, late KRRC, and had issue, Paul Francis Bassett, MC, Capt. Commandos, *b.* 1920, killed in action 1945). *Residence*, 85, Whitelands House, Chelsea, SW.

Collateral Branches living.

Grandson of the late Godfrey Blundell Samuelson (infra) :—
Issue of the late Capt. Bernard Godfrey Samuelson, *b.* 1888, *d.* 1954 : *m.* 1st, 1910, the Hon. Evelyn Amy Akers-Douglas, who *d.* 1914, da. of 1st Viscount Chilston ; 2ndly, 1938, Patricia Christabel (of Chelston Cross, Torquay), da. of William Wildash :—
(By 1st marriage) Peter Bernard, *b.* 1912 ; ed. at Eton : *m.* 1935 (marriage dissolved 1949), Wilhelmina Van Blaaderen, and has issue living, Jean Paul (150, Seventh Rd., Armadale, 6112, W. Aust.), *b.* 1939: *m.* 1962, Annette Louise, da. of Hubertus Johannes Richardus Ponjee, and has issue living Dennis John *b.* 1963, Nicolas Andrew *b.* 1966, Quentin Jeremy *b.* 1969, Natashia Nicole *b.* 1972,—Bridget, *b.* 1935,—Zandra Serafina, *b.* 1937. *Residence,*

Issue of the late Godfrey Blundell Samuelson, 3rd son of 1st baronet, *b.* 1863, *d.* 1941: *m.* 1st, 1887, Anne Jane, who *d.* 1920, da. of the Rev. Weston Brocklesby Davis, formerly V. of Ramsbury, Wilts.; 2ndly, 1923, May, da. of the late William Stevens, of Saxham, Suffolk, and widow of J. Paterson Parkin:—
(By 1st m.) Guy Weston (Lympne Hall, Kent) *b.* 1890; ed. at Radley; Capt. Alexandra, Princess of Wales' and F/O RAFVR: *m.* 1st, 1913, Naomi H. (who *d.* 1969, having obtained a divorce 1927), da. of Alfred C. Leney, JP., of The Garden House, Saltwood, Kent; 2ndly, 1927, Frances Crawley, da. of the late Charles Lyne, and has issue living

(by 1st marriage) Rowland Guy Blundell, b. 1914; ed. at Radley; formerly Flying Officer R.A.F. Vol. Reserve,—John Peel Weston, M.C. (of Cloghran Stud Farm, co. Dublin. Clubs, United Hunts, Kildare Street, Royal Irish Yacht), b. 1917; ed. at Sherborne; Lt.-Col. (ret.) The Buffs, and an Asso. of Inst. of Agric. Engineers; Palestine 1938-39 (despatches, MC), 1939-45 War in Middle East and NW Europe (despatches): m. 1st, 1943, Pamela, who obtained a divorce 1951, el. da. of Cecil E. Winter, of Surrenden Dering, Pluckley, Kent; 2ndly, 1952, Grace Eleanor, da. of R. C. Dawson, of Ball Hill, Newbury, Berks., and has issue living, (by 1st m.) Nigel John Esdaile b. 1944, Christopher Richard Leney b. 1946: m. 1968, Catherine Elizabeth, da. of George M. Cooper, of Charnwood, Idutywa, S. Africa, (by 2nd m.) Robin Dawson b. 1953, Eleanor Clare b. 1958,—Henry Bernard (of 6, Hood Ave., Sheen, SW14), b. 1919; ed. at Sherborne; is a Freeman of City of London; formerly Lieut. Roy. W. Kent Regt.; France 1940: m. 1947, Evelyn P., da. of John Nairn Burt, of Ashwell House, Knaresborough, Yorks.——Carol Hubert Frances, b. 1899; ed. at Eton; Lt. Gren. Guards (ret.); 1917-19 War in France: m. 1920, Doris, da. of the late Capt. John George Edmund Templer, formerly of Lindridge, Bishop's Teignton, Devon, and has issue living, Eleanor Caroline, b. 1921 : m. 1946, Capt. Marc Anderson Kerr, M.B.E., Indian Army (retired), and has issue living, Vyvian Frances b. 1947.

Issue of the late Sir Herbert Walter Samuelson, K.B.E., 4th son of 1st baronet, b. 1865, d. 1952 : m. 1896, Sybil Charlotte Eleanor, O.B.E., who d. 1961, da. of the late Hon. Walter Harbord [B. Suffield, colls.] :—

Rupert Eric Herbert (10, Cadogan Sq., SW1), b. 1899 ; ed. at Eton, and at R.M.C. ; Maj. (ret.) Coldm. Gds.; 1939-45 War in N. Africa, Sicily, France and Germany: m. 1930, Eileena Jane, da. of Arthur Reece-Jones, of Cefn-y-Parc, Barry, and has issue living, Doriel Sybil, b. 1931: m. 1955 (m. diss. 1972), Andrew Ridgway; 2ndly, 1972, Aldwin David James Hall, of Chestnut Corner, Woodside Green, Bishop's Stortford, Herts., and has issue living (by 1st m.), Peter Eric b. 1958, Amanda Jane b. 1956, Joanna Kate b. 1962, Charlotte Rose b. 1965,—Philippa Margaret, b. 1934.

The 1st baronet, the Rt. Hon. Sir Bernhard Samuelson, F.R.S., Founder and Chm. of Sir B. Samuelson and Co. (Limited) of Middlesbrough, and of Samuelson and Co. (Limited) of Banbury, was Chm. of Roy. Commn. on Technical Instruction 1881, and sat as M.P. for Banbury (L) Feb. to April 1859 (when he was defeated) and 1865-85, and for N., or Banbury, Div. of Oxfordshire 1885-95. He was the Pioneer of Technical Education, and sat on several Roy. Commns., his baronetcy being conferred for his services in the cause of education. Sir Henry Bernard Samuelson, 2nd Bt., sat as M.P. for Cheltenham (L) 1868-74, and for Frome 1876-85.

SANDERSON, Creation (U.K.) 1920, of Malling Deanery, South Malling, co. Sussex.

Sir (FRANK PHILIP) BRYAN SANDERSON, 2nd Baronet; b. Feb. 18th, 1910; s. his father Sir FRANK BERNARD, 1965; ed. at Stowe, and at Pembroke Coll., Oxford; a Member of Lloyd's; Chm. of Humber Fish Manure Co. Ltd., Hull; 1939-45 War as Lt.-Cdr. RNVR with Fleet Air Arm: m. (Feb.) 1933, Annette Irene Caroline, who d. 1967, da. of the late Col. Korab Laskowski, of Warsaw, and has issue.

Arms—Azure, a maunch between three annulets or.

Crest—Between two wings or a sinister arm embowed in chain-mail grasping a scimitar proper, pommelled and hilted or.

Residence—Lychgate Cottage, Scaynes Hill, Sussex.

SANS DIEU RIEN

Without God nothing.

Sons living—FRANK LINTON (Grandturzel Farm, Burwash, Sussex), b. Nov. 21st, 1933; ed. at Stowe, and at Salamanca Univ.; a Member of Lloyd's, and a Dir. of Knott Hotels Co. of London Ltd., and of Humber Fishing & Fish Manure Co. Ltd., Hull; RNVSR 1950-65: m. 1961, Margaret Ann, da. of John C. Maxwell, of New York, USA, and has issue living, David Frank, b. 1962,—Michael John b. 1965,—Caroline Ann, b. 1966.—Nina Margaret, b. 1968,—Katherine Claire (twin), b. 1968.——Peter Bryan (Hole Farm, North Chailey, Sussex), b. 1946; ed. at Stowe, and Salamanca Univ.: m. 1970, Elizabeth Magdalena, da. of John Grün, a Dir. of UNICEF, and has issue living, Roberta Caroline, b. 1974.

Daughter living—Merry Claire, b. 1936: m. 1959, David Lyle, late Capt. 16th/5th R. Lancers, of Yew Tree Cottage, Scaynes Hill, Sussex, and has issue living, James Robert Bryan, b. 1961,—Robert Giles, b. 1964,—Edward Hugh, 1970.

Brother living—Derek Maxwell (Las Flores, Linda Vista Alta, St. Pedro de Alcantra, Malaga, Spain), b. 1914; ed. at Harrow: m. 1936, Daphne, el. da. of Frederick Ernest Bayard Elton [see Elton, Bt., colls.], and has issue living, John Maxwell, b. 1938; ed. at Pangbourne,—Richard Bryan, b. 1942; ed. at Harrow,—Christopher Derek, b. 1948; ed. at Milton Abbey,—Sally Greet, b. 1939.

Sister living—Pearl (Yeomans, Piltdown, Sussex), b. 1906: m. 1st, 1928, Gerald Melville Donner [Macnaghten, Bt., colls.]; 2ndly, 1947, Maj. Alan Sherman James, who d. 1963, and has issue living, (by 1st m.) John Melville (Furlong House, Hurstpierpoint, Sussex; Rutt Farm, Ivybridge, S. Devon; Carlton Club), b. 1930; ed. at Stowe, and RMA; Coldm. Gds. 1948-53; FCIB; a Member of Lloyd's, and Chm. Fenchurch Group, Brokers: m. 1952, Patricia Mary, da. of the late Barnet Thomas Jenkins, of Bickleigh, S. Devon, and has issue living, Rupert Melville b. 1955; ed. at Stowe, Annabel Elizabeth b. 1958; ed. at Benenden,—Gillian Pearl (twin) (Nye Barn, Ditchling, Sussex), b. 1930: m. 1963, Cdr. K. Coburn, USN, who d. 1971, and has issue living, John Bruce b. 1967, Kimberley Pearl b. 1965,—Rosita Ann, b. 1933: m. 1954, Michael Beresford Burtenshaw, of Bottle Cottage, Reigate Heath, Reigate, Surrey.

Widow living of 1st Baronet—JOAN (Joan, Lady Sanderson), (12, Connaught House, Mount Row, W1), only da. of the late Harry Cubberley, of 4, Hill Court, Ealing, W5: m. 1951, as his 2nd wife, Sir Frank Bernard Sanderson, 1st baronet, who d. 1965.

Sir Frank Sanderson, 1st Bt., 7th son of John Sanderson of Hull, was founder of Wray, Sanderson & Co., Ltd., and an Underwriting Member of Lloyd's. He sat as MP for Darwen Div. of Lancs. (U.) 1922-23, and 1924-29, for Ealing 1931-45, and for E. Ealing 1945-50.

SASSOON, Creation (U.K.) 1890, of Kensington Gore, St. Mary Abbots, Kensington, co. London, and Eastern Terrace, Brighton, Sussex. [Extinct 1939.]

Right Hon. Sir PHILIP (ALBERT GUSTAVE DAVID) SASSOON, *G.B.E.,* C.M.G., M.P., 3rd and last *Baronet.*

Sister living of 3rd Baronet—Sybil Rachel Betty Cécile (*Dowager, Marchioness of Cholmondeley*), CBE, *b.* 1894; 1914-18 War as Assist. Prin. WRNS, 1939-45 War as Sup. WRNS; CBE (Mil.) 1946: *m.* 1913, the 5th Marquess of Cholmondeley, who *d.* 1968. *Residences,* Houghton Hall, King's Lynn, Norfolk; 12, Kensington Palace Gardens, W8.

SASSOON, Creation (U.K.) 1909, of the City of Bombay, India. [Extinct 1961.]

Sir (ELLICE) VICTOR SASSOON, *G.B.E.,* 3rd and last *Baronet.*

Daughter living of 2nd Baronet—Lydia (Palace Hotel, Montreux, Switzerland), *b.* 1883: *m.* 1908, Gustave Weiswieller, who *d.* 1966, and has issue living, Pauline Edmée Louise, *b.* 1913: *m.* 1940, (John) Michael Wood, late Capt. Gren. Gds., of Upton Grey Place, Basingstoke, RG25 2RQ, and 8, Hornton Court E., Hornton St., W8 7RT,—Denise Marie (29, Abbotsbury House, Abbotsbury Rd., W14 8EN), *b.* 1916: *m.* 1939 (divorce 1948), Noel Edward FitzPatrick, late Capt. Irish Guards, and has issue living, Edward Hamilton Barnaby (52, Lower Chiswick Staithe, Hartington Rd., Chiswick, W4 3TT) *b.* 1942, Xanthe (Shanet Vanessa Eve)' (Florimont 8, 1000 Lausanne, Switzerland), *b.* 1940.
Widow living of 3rd Baronet—EVELYN (*Lady Sassoon*), da. of William H. Barnes, of Kingsport, Tennessee, USA: *m.* 1959, Sir (Ellice) Victor Sassoon, GBE, 3rd baronet, who *d.* 1961 when the title became ext. *Residence,* Eves, Cable Beach, PO Box N 1706, Nassau, NP Bahamas.

Saunders-Pryse, see Pryse.

SAVORY, Creation (U.K.) 1890, of Brook Street, St. George, Hanover Square, co. London. [Extinct 1961.]

Sir WILLIAM BORRADAILE SAVORY, 3rd and last *Baronet.*

Daughters living of 3rd Baronet—Diana Victor, *b.* 1913: *m.* 1934, James Nigel Jackaman, and has issue living, Nigel Victor Charles, *b.* 1939,—Elizabeth Mary, *b.* 1936. *Residence,* Brook House, Stoke Poges, Bucks.——Pamela Frances, *b.* 1916: *m.* 1939, Douglas Burbidge, and has issue living, Howard Harry Borradaile, *b.* 1941,—Robert Anthony Carruthers, *b.* 1952. *Residence,*— Dunglass Farmhouse, Little Bookham, Surrey.

SCHUSTER, Creation (U.K.) 1906, of Collingham Road, Royal Borough of Kensington.

In God alone.

Sir (FELIX) JAMES MONCRIEFF SCHUSTER, *O.B.E., T.D.,* 3rd *Baronet; b.* Jan. 8th, 1913; *s.* his father *Sir* (FELIX) VICTOR, 1962; ed. at Winchester; is Col. late Rifle Bde.; Hon. Col. 5th Bn. R. Green Jackets, T & AVR; OBE (Mil) 1955: *m.* 1937, Ragna, da. of the late Direktor Ole Sundo, of Copenhagen, and has issue.

Arms—Ermine, two swords in saltire, points downwards, proper, pommels and hilts, and surmounted by a lion passant or; on a chief gules, an eagle displayed argent between two human hearts or. **Crest**—On a mount vert, in front of two swords in saltire, a lion passant or, charged with two human hearts gules.

Residence, Little Swanborough, nr. Lewes, Sussex: *Club,* Bath.

Daughters living—Sarah Lavinia, *b.* 1941: *m.* 1st, 1962 (m. diss. 1966), Theodore Phillips Burgess; 2ndly, 1972, Patrick O'Neill, and has issue living (by 2nd m.) Jake *b.* 1972.——Inger Marion Averil, *b.* 1944: *m.* 1967, Hugh Reginald Newcomb, of Black Swan Hall, Goudhurst, Kent, and has issue living, Toby James Moncrieff, *b.* 1969,—Rupert, *b.* 1971.

Sisters living—Felicia Mary Alison (36, Bernard Gdns., SW19), *b.* 1911.——Dorothy Ann Violet (Winton Barn, Alfriston, Polegate, Sussex), *b.* 1921: *m.* 1st, 1940, Brig. Arthur Frederick Crane Nicholls, GC, Coldstream Guards, who *d.* (killed on active ser.) 1944; 2ndly, 1944, Sqdn-Ldr. Archibald George Dunlop Mackenzie, RAF, and has issue living, (by 2nd m.) Archibald Robert Andrew Dunlop, *b.* 1945; ed. at Stowe: *m.* 1968, Herdis Pelle, and has issue living, Louisa *b.* 1970,—(by 1st m.) Jennifer Ann Crane, *b.* 1943,—(by 2nd m.) Catriona, *b.* 1947: *m.* 1969, Michael Dollin, and has issue living Laura *b.* 1971.

The 1st baronet, Sir Felix (Otto) Schuster (son of the late Francis Joseph Schuster, of 39, Harrington Gardens, S.W.), was Gov. of Union of London & Smiths Bank 1895-1918, Finance Member of Council of India 1906-16, a Director of National Provincial Bank and Senior Partner of the firm of Schuster, Son & Co., of 90, Cannon Street, E.C.

SCOTT, Creation (U.K.) 1806, of Great Barr, Staffordshire.

Sir EDWARD ARTHUR DOLMAN SCOTT, 8th *Baronet ; b.* Dec. 14th, 1905 ; *s.* his father, *Sir* DOUGLAS EDWARD, 1951 ; is a Painter : *m.* 1943, Dorothy Elsie, da. of W. H. Winchcombe, of Yorktown, S. Australia.

Arms—Argent, on a fesse gules, cotissed azure, between three catherine-wheels sable, as many lambs passant argent. **Crest**—On a mount vert a beacon fired proper, ladder argent.

Residence—8, Alice Street, South Plympton, S. Australia.

Brother living—DOUGLAS FRANCIS, *b.* Aug. 26th, 1908.

Sisters living—Florence Susan Helen, *b.* 1901.——Frances Lucy Mary, *b.* 1904.

Widow living of 7th Baronet—FLORENCE ADA (*Dowager Lady Scott*), da. of W. Wildeman : *m.* 1899, Sir Douglas Edward Scott, 7th Baronet, who *d.* 1951. *Residence,*

The 1st baronet (of Great Barr, creation April 1806) was M.P. for Worcester 1802-6, and his son the 2nd baronet, sat as M.P. for Lichfield 1831-7. The 3rd baronet of 1st, and 2nd baronet of 2nd creation, inherited at his birth the baronetcy of his maternal grandfather, Sir Hugh Bateman, of Hartington, who had, in Dec. 1806, been created a baronet, with remainder (primogeniturely) to the male descendants of his daughters, Catherine Juliana (afterwards wife of Sir Edward Dolman Scott, 2nd baronet) and Amelia Anne (afterwards wife of Sir Alexander Hood, 2nd Bt. of St. Audries) ; the latter Baronetcy passed on the death of Sir Edward Dolman Scott, 6th Bt. of 1st and 5th of 2nd creation in 1905 to the Rt. Hon. Sir Alexander Fuller-Acland-Hood, P.C., M.P., 4th Bt. of St. Audries (afterwards Baron St. Audries). The 7th baronet was sometime R. of Teffont Ewyas.

Faithful to king and country.

SCOTT, Creation (U.K.) 1806, of Dunninald, Forfarshire.   [Extinct 1945.]

Sir FRANCIS MONTAGU SIBBALD SCOTT, 5th and last *Baronet.*

Daughter living of 4th Baronet—Evelyn Jane Sibbald, *b.* 1892: *m.* 1913, Capt. Maurice Cecil Forsyth Grant, MC, DL, JP, who *d.* 1953, formerly Seaforth Highlanders, and has issue living, Maurice Ivor, *b.* 1917; ed. at Wellington Coll.; is Sqdn.-Ldr. RAFVR, and a MIEE,—Michael Osbert Frederick, *VRD* (of Ecclesgreig, Kincardineshire), *b.* 1921; ed. at Wellington Coll.; Lt.-Cdr. RNR (ret.); 1939-45 War (despatches): *m.* 1963, Theresa O'Donnell, and has issue living, Maurice Patrick James *b.* 1964, Roger Gavin Ivor *b.* 1965,—Fenella Evelyn, (Wey Cottage, Elstead, Surrey), *b.* 1915: *m.* 1st, 1939, Air Ch. Marshal Sir Francis Joseph Fogarty, GBE, KCB, DFC, AFC, RAF, who *d.* 1973; 2ndly, 1976, Capt. Michael Goodier Haworth, RN, and has issue living (by 1st m.), Michael John Edward *b.* 1940, Penelope Louise *b.* 1944: *m.* 1972, John Van Doorn, of 72, Guildford Rd., Ashurst, Manawatu, North Island, NZ. *Residence,* Mount Cyrus, Ecclesgrieg, Kincardineshire.

SCOTT, Creation (U.K.) 1821, of Lytchett Minster, Dorsetshire. [Extinct 1961.]

Sir ROBERT CLAUDE SCOTT, 7th and last *Baronet.*

Daughter living of 7th Baronet—Hope Berthe Turner, *M.B., Ch.B., D.P.H., b.* 1925: *m.* 1960, William Alexander Hogg, and has issue living, William Scott, *b.* 1963. *Residence,* 48, Dowanside Rd., Glasgow, G12 9DW.

SCOTT, Creation (U.K.) 1907, of Beauclere, Bywell St. Andrews, co. Northumberland.

Sir WALTER SCOTT, 4th *Baronet; b.* July 29th, 1918; *s.* his father, Maj. *Sir* WALTER, 1967; ed. at Eton, and Jesus Coll., Camb.; Maj. late 1st R. Dragoons: *m.* 1944, Diana Mary, only da. of James Richard Owen, of Holly Hill, Coleman's Hatch, and has issue.

Arms—Per chevron azure and or, in chief two bees volant, and in base a crescent all counterchanged. **Crest**—Between the hornes of a crescent sable a bee volant proper.

Residence—Eckington Manor, Ripe, Sussex.

Son living—WALTER JOHN, *b.* Feb. 24th, 1948.

Honour follows though unsought for.

Daughter living—Sarah Jane (*Duchess of Hamilton and Brandon*), *b.* 1945: *m.* 1972, the 15th Duke of Hamilton and Brandon.

Collateral Branches living.

Issue of the late Mason Thompson Scott, 4th son of 1st baronet, *b.* 1865, *d.* 1916: *m.* 1899, Flora Alice, who *d.* 1904 da. of Joseph Williams, of Putney, S.W. :—

William **Walter Brough**, *b.* 1902 ; formerly Capt. and temporary Major 1st Roy. Dragoons *m.* 1st, 1926 (m. annulled on his petition 1937), Bridget Margaret, da. of the late Charles Leigh

Clay, of Wyndcliffe Court, Chepstow; 2ndly, 1937, Pamela, da. of the late Sir Charles William Fielding, KBE [*see* E. Denbigh, colls.], and has issue living, (by 2nd m.) Charles Martin Fielding, *b.* 1945; late Lt., 1st R. Dragoons: *m.* 1970, Jill, da. of the late Wing-Cdr. Marcus Mowbray Hutchinson, AFC, AAF, and has issue living, Camilla Jane *b.* 1971,—Maxine Ling Elizabeth, *b.* 1939: *m.* 1966, Manuel Diaz Camacho, of Casa la Caleta, la Herradura, Granada, Spain, and has issue living, Rodrigo Manuel, *b.* 1967, Carolina Elizabeth *b.* 1969. *Residence*, Folly House, Bampton, Oxford.——Flora Brookbank, *b.* 1903: *m.* 1925, Brig. Christopher Anthony White, late KRRC, who *d.* 1969, [B. Gifford], and has issue living, Jeremy Anthony (Leckhampstead House, Bucks.), *b.* 1926; Maj. late R. Scots Greys: *m.* 1951, Elizabeth Catherine Denise, da. of the late John Adrian Frederick March Phillipps de Lisle, of Stockerston Hall, Uppingham, Leics., and has issue living, Anthony John *b.* 1958, Phillippa Elizabeth *b.* 1952, Juliet Anne *b.* 1955, Annabel Mary *b.* 1962,—Gillian *b.* 1929: *m.* 1st 1949 (m. diss. 1960), Ian Francis Cole: 2ndly, 1964, Col. Anthony Derek Swift Mangnall, OBE, of Bradley Court, Chieveley, Berks., and 241, Cranmer Court, SW3, and has issue living, (by 1st m.) Christopher Ian *b.* 1950. *Residence*, The Old School, Cherrington, Tetbury, Glos.

Grandchildren of the late Charles Thomas Scott, 5th son of 1st baronet:—
Issue of the late Capt. Mason Hogarth Scott, RN, *b.* 1900, *d.* 1971: *m.* 1924, the Hon. Irene Florence Seely (Buckland Wood House, Broadway, Worcs.), da. of 1st Baron Mottistone:—
Mason Charles (Royal Oak, High Hurstwood, Uckfield, Sussex), *b.* 1939; late Capt. Scots Gds.: *m.* 1953, Judith Allison Dalgleish, and has issue living, Mason Stapleton, *b.* 1955,—Adam, *b.* 1963,—Emma, *b.* 1957.——John Brough, *b.* 1942: *m.* 1973, Susan, da. of R. G. MacInnes, of Mark Ash, Abinger Common, and has issue living, Sophie Diana *b.* 1974.——Jane Emily, *b.* 1925: *m.* 1946, Maj.-Gen. James Michael Gow, late Scots Gds., of Long Vere House, Loxhill, Hascombe, Surrey, and has issue living, Roderick Charles, *b.* 1947; Capt. Scots Gds.,—Susan Jane, *b.* 1949: *m.* 1969, Capt. Malcolm Ross, Scots Gds., and has issue living, Tabitha, *b.* 1970,—Kate, *b.* 1952,—Belinda Catriona, *b.* 1958,—Clunie Fiona, *b.* 1964.——(Irene) Jill, *b.* 1928: *m.* 1951, John Gore Phillimore, CMG, of the Postern, Tonbridge, Kent, and 25, Onslow Sq., SW7, and has issue living, John Francis, *b.* 1952,—Hugh Richards, *b.* 1959,—Louisa Mary, *b.* 1954: *m.* 1975, John C. R. Paravicini,—Penelope Jane, *b.* 1956.——Janet Sylvia, *b.* 1941: *m.* 1963, Simon John Chamberlayne, of The Green, Kingham, Oxon., and has issue living, Edward Charles, *b.* 1966,—Sarah Caroline, *b.* 1964,—Laura *b.* 1972.——Jennifer Teresa, *b.* 1945: *m.* 1967, Alexander Patrick Scott, of 23, Caroline Terr., SW1, and has issue living, Emily Mary, *b.* 1968,—Catherine Charlotte, *b.* 1970.

The 1st baronet, Sir Walter Scott, son of the late Samuel Scott, of Holm Cultram, Cumberland; was Chm. of Walter Scott (Limited), of Walter Scott and Middleton (Limited), and of Walter Scott Publishing Co. (Limited).

SCOTT, Creation (U.K.) 1909, of Yews, Undermilbeck, Westmorland.

Sir OLIVER CHRISTOPHER ANDERSON SCOTT, M.B., B.Chir., 3rd *Baronet*; *b.* Nov. 6th, 1922; *s.* his father, Sir SAMUEL HASLAM, 1960; ed. at Charterhouse, and at King's Coll., Camb. (MA); Dir. of Research Unit in Radiobiology, British Empire Cancer Campaign; Mount Vernon Hosp. 1966-69; Chm. of Finance Cttee., British Cancer Council 1970-72; High Sheriff of Westmorland 1966: *m.* 1951, Phoebe Anne, da. of Desmond O'Neill Tolhurst, of The Gateways, Chelsea, SW, and has issue.

ᴀrms (as granted 1570 to Jean Schotte, infra)—Azure a greyhound courant argent, collared gules, and attached by a line of the second to a sphere in chief or. Crest—A sphere or, encircled by four feathers erect, severally argent, azure, gold, and gules.
Seat—Yews, Undermilbeck, Windermere, Westmorland. *Residence*—31, Kensington Square, W8 5HH. *Club*—Brooks's.

Son living—CHRISTOPHER JAMES, *b.* Jan. 16th, 1955.
Daughters living—Hermione Mary, *b.* 1952.——Camilla Nancy, *b.* 1956.

Half-Sister living—Anne Katharine Sibella, A.R.I.B.A., *b.* 1912: *m.* 1944, Jocelyn Wiseman Fagan Morton, son of the late Sir James Morton, LL.D., and has issue living, Eleanor Katharine Mary, *b.* 1948,—Frances Anne Marylee, *b.* 1950: *m.* 1972, Benjamin Charles Ruck Keene,—Beatrice Emily Margareta, *b.* 1952,—Lucia Katharine Fagan, *b.* 1954. *Residence*, Eden Hey, Stanwix, Carlisle.

Uncle living (son of 1st baronet)—Francis Clayton, *b.* 1881; ed. at Oriel Coll., Oxford (B.A. 1903); High Sheriff of Westmorland 1934; Founder of Brathay Hall Trust, Ambleside; formerly Chm. of Provincial Insurance Co., Ltd.: *m.* 1911, Gwendolen Frieda Martha, who *d.* 1973, da. of the late George Jäger, of Lingdale, Birkenhead, and has issue living, Peter Francis (of Long Dales, Windermere), *b.* 1917; ed. at Oriel Coll., Oxford (B.A. 1939); formerly Capt. King's Roy. Rifle Corps (Supplementary Reserve): *m.* 1953, Prudence Mary, da. of Capt. Grenville Milligan, R.N., and has issue living, Francis Alexander *b.* 1959, Charlotte Rose *b.* 1954, Madeleine Mary *b.* 1957, Rebecca Anne *b.* 1960,—Joan Frieda, B.M., B.Ch. (of 97, Tyrell Street, Nedlands, Perth, W. Australia), *b.* 1912: *m.* 1949, John Trevelyan, CBE, from whom she obtained a divorce 1959 [*see* Trevelyan, Bt., *cr.* 1662, colls.]. *Seat*, Matson Ground, Windermere.

Widow living of 2nd Baronet—MARION DOROTHY (*Dorothy, Lady Scott*), el. da. of the late Charles Garnett, of Hall Garth, near Carnforth, Lancashire: *m.* 1937, as his third wife, Sir Samuel Haslam Scott, 2nd baronet, who *d.* 1960. *Residence*, Parsonage, Stratford-sub-Castle, Salisbury.

Sir James William Scott, 1st Bt. (head of several manufacturing and mercantile firms in Lancashire, founded by John Haslam of Larkhill 1771-1820), was 12th in descent (as registered at the Heralds' Coll.) from Emricus Scotus, Seneschal of the co. of Solms 1484, grandfather of Jean Schotte, historian of the family, ennobled by Charles III. of Lorraine. The name is now spelt Scott in accordance with its original signification, the family being descended from Scottish settlers in Franconia, a branch of whom became settled in England early in the 19th century. Sir Samuel Haslam Scott, 2nd Bt., was High Sheriff of Westmorland 1926.

SCOTT, Creation (U.K.) 1913, of Witley, Surrey.

Sir DOUGLAS WINCHESTER SCOTT, 2nd *Baronet; b.* Feb. 4th, 1907; *s.* his father, *Adm. Sir* PERCY MORETON, *K.C.B., K.C.V.O., LL.D.* 1924; ed. at Harrow; Lieut.-Col. (retired) 9th Lancers, and Hon. Col., Queen's Own Hussars; Vice-Pres. of Thomas Coram Foundation; European War 1939-45 in France, Syria and Italy, Comdg. 3rd Hussars: *m.* 1933, Elizabeth Joyce, da. of Archibald Lloyd Glanley, and has issue.

Arms—Argent, pelletty, in base a lymphad sable, pennons flying to the dexter gules, in chief two crescents azure. Crest—An ancient cannon, firing to the dexter proper.

Residences—9, Pont Street Mews, S.W.1 ; Habyn Hill House, Rogate, near Petersfield, Hants. Club—Cavalry.

Sons living—ANTHONY PERCY (Older House, Redford, Midhurst), *b.* May 1st, 1937; ed. at Harrow, and at Ch. Ch., Oxford; Bar. Inner Temple 1960: *m.* 1962, Caroline Teresa Anne, el. da. of Edward Bacon, of Hill House, Mobberley, Cheshire, and has issue living, Henry Douglas Edward, *b.* 1964,—Simon James, *b.* 1965,—Miranda Claire, *b.* 1968.—— Alastair John Douglas (Church House, Broome, nr. Clent, Worcs.) *b.* 1940; ed. at Harrow, and at McGill Univ., Canada: *m.* 1965, Virginia Mary, da. of the late John Gaynor, of Fairfield, Pyrford Wood, Surrey, and has issue living, William Douglas, *b.* 1966,—Sarah Victoria, *b.* 1969,—Penelope Mary, *b.* 1974.

Daughter living—Diana Jean, *b.* 1934 : *m.* 1956, John Peter Fraser-Mackenzie, and has issue living, Robert Douglas, *b.* 1959,—Elizabeth Henrietta, *b.* 1958,—Georgina Ann, *b.* 1963,—Catherine Beatrice, *b.* 1966. Residence, Lone Cow Estate, PB2, Mtoroshanga, Rhodesia.

Sister living—Rosemary(*Lady Crompton-Inglefield*), *b.* 1903: *m.* 1926, Col. Sir John Frederick Crompton-Inglefield, T.D., D.L., son of the late Adm. Sir Frederick Samuel Inglefield, KCB, DL, and has issue living, Patricia Jane, *b.* 1929; a JP, Stone Div., Staffs.: *m.* 1951, Lt.-Col. Michael Christopher Bagshawe, TD, of The Agency Sandon, Stafford, and has issue living, John Nicholas Samuel *b.* 1954, Albinia Sarah *b.* 1953,—Isma Rosemary (Maypoles, Soberton, Southampton), *b.* 1931: *m.* 1953, Lt.-Cdr. John Anthony Stuart Crawford, RN, who *d.* 1967, and has issue living, John Stuart Alastair *b.* 1959, Alison Jane *b.* 1956,—Caroline Sarah, *b.* 1936: *m.* 1961, Thomas Anthony Alaister Kilner, of Oakhanger Cottage, Oakhanger, Bordon, Hants, and has issue living, Toby Jonathon Casson *b.* 1966. Residence, Parwich Hall, Ashbourne, Derbyshire.

The 1st baronet, Adm. Sir Percy Moreton Scott, K.C.B., K.C.V.O., LL.D., served during Ashantee War 1873-4, in Expedition up the Congo against pirates 1875, in Egyptian War 1882, in S. Africa 1899-1900 as Comdt. of Durban, when he devised special mounting for the Naval Gun used for defence and relief of Ladysmith, and in China 1900; invented night signalling apparatus used in R.N.; in command of Gunnery Sch., and a Naval A.D.C. to H.M. 1903-5, Inspector of Naval Target Practice 1905-7, and in command of First Cruiser Squadron 1907-8, and of Second Cruiser Squadron 1908-9 (Comdg. it at S. African Federation Convention); appointed or Special Ser. at the Admiralty 1914; took charge of Gunnery Defences of London 1915-16.

SCOTT, Creation (U.K.) 1962, of Rotherfield Park, Alton, Hants.

Sir JAMES WALTER SCOTT, 2nd *Baronet; b.* Oct. 26th, 1924; *s.* his father Col. Sir JERVOISE BOLITHO, 1965: ed. at Eton; Lt.-Col. (ret.) The Life Gds., formerly Gren. Gds., an Underwriting Member of Lloyd's, a Liveryman of Mercers' Co., a Co. Councillor of Hants., and a Member of Inst. of Dirs.; 1939-45 War in NW Europe with 2nd Armoured Bn. Gren. Gds.; Palestine 1945-46, Malaya 1948-49, Cyprus 1958, 1960 and 1964 (UN), and Malaysia 1966 ; ADC to Viceroy and Gov.-Gen. of India 1946-48: *m.* 1951, Anne Constantia, el. da. of the late Lt.-Col. Clive Grantham Austin, DL, of Roundwood, Micheldever, Hants. [see E. Scarbrough] and has issue.

Arms—Per pale indented argent and sable a saltire counterchanged.

Crest—Out of a circlet of pales or, a cubit arm erect habited gules cuffed ermine, the hand proper holding a paper scroll argent.

Residence,—Rotherfield Park, Alton, Hants.

Sons living—JAMES JERVOISE, *b.* Oct. 12th, 1952.——Charles Clive, *b.* 1954.——Alexander Archibald, *b.* 1960.

Daughter living—Susannah Maria, *b.* 1963.

Brother living—Samuel Arthur (Low Pasture House, Nunnington, N. Riding, Yorks. Club—Cavalry), *b.* 1926; ed. at Eton; Lt. 7th Queen's Own Hussars, late Capt. 4th Roy. Hampshire Regt. (TA) ; Korea with 8th Hussars 1950-51: *m.* 1952, Juliet Modwena, el. da. of the late Samuel Ranulph Allsopp, CBE [see B. Hindlip, colls.], and has issue living, Henry Samuel Jervoise, *b.* 1955.

Widow living of 1st Baronet—KATHLEEN ISABEL (*Kathleen Lady Scott*), (Empshott Grange, Liss, Hants.), yr. da. of the late Godfrey Walter, Malshanger, Basingstoke, Hants.: *m.* 1924, Col. Sir Jervoise Bolitho Scott, 1st baronet, who *d.* 1965.

Collateral Branch living.

Issue of the late Maj. Richard Jervoise Scott, TD, yst. son of 1st baronet, *b.* 1929, *d.* 1974: *m.* 1955 (m. diss. 1972), Julia Maud, who *d.* 1974, yr. da. of Sir Henry Robert Kincaid Floyd, 5th Bt., CB, CBE:—

Victoria Kathleen, *b.* 1956.——Camilla Jane, *b.* 1958.

This family descends from John Scott of Hatfield Regis, Essex, 4th son of William Scott, lord of the manor of Stapleford Tawney, Essex, who *d.* 1491. Rotherfield Park, Hants, was purchased in 1808 from the 14th Marquess of Winchester by James Scott of Hammersmith, 8th in descent from John. His grandson, Archibald Edward Scott, of Rotherfield Park, was father of Sir Jervoise Bolitho Scott, 1st Bt., High Sheriff of Hants. 1936, and a Co. Councillor 1932-65, and Official Verderer of New Forest 1950-64.

CONSTABLE-MAXWELL-SCOTT, Creation (E.) 1642, of Haggerston, Northumberland.

Sir MICHAEL FERGUS CONSTABLE-MAXWELL-SCOTT, 13th Baronet; *b.* July 23rd, 1921, el. son of the late Rear-Adm. Malcolm Joseph Raphael Constable-Maxwell-Scott, DSO, RN, 3rd son of the late Joseph Constable-Maxwell-Scott, 3rd son of 10th Lord Herries of Terregles, grandson of William Haggerston Constable, 2nd son of 3rd baronet; ed. at Ampleforth and Trin. Coll. Camb.; served SG, 1943-48; *s.* his kinsman, *Sir* RALPH (RAPHAEL) STANLEY DE MARIE HAGGERSTON, 1972: *m.* 1963, Deirdre Moira, da. of the late Alexander McKechnie, and has issue.

Arms,—Not exemplified at time of going to press.

Residences,—100, Eaton Terr., SW1W 8UG; Dennett Cottage, Bembridge, Isle of Wight.

Son living—DOMINIC JAMES, *b.* July 22nd, 1968.

Daughter living—Annabel Jane, *b.* 1973.

Brother living—Ian Malcolm (Grants Hill House, Uckfield, Sussex), *b.* 1927: *m.* 1958, Susan Mary, yr. da. of Sir Andrew Edmund James Clark, MBE, MC, QC, 3rd Bt., and has issue living, Malcolm Fergus, *b.* 1960,—Simon Magnus, *b.* 1962,—Andrew Nicholas Hugh, *b.* 1966,—Lucy Ann, *b.* 1958,—Sarah Secunda, *b.* 1959,—Catherine Monica Jane (twin), *b.* 1966.

Sister living—Elizabeth Mary, *b.* 1924.

Daughter living of 10th Baronet—Ursula Edith de Marie (2, Swan Lane Close, Burford, Oxon.), *b.* 1910: *m.* 1939, Richard Grenville Harrison, JP, who *d.* 1969, and has issue living, Louis Bevill Grenville, *b.* 1940,—Elizabeth Rosemary, *b.* 1943: *m.* 1972, Guy Martin Aldersey Taylor of Sheardrum, Saline, Fife.

Daughters living of 11th Baronet—Belinda Ann de Marie (606, Gilbert House, Barbican, EC2Y 8BD) *b.* 1933: *m.* 1955, Peter Drury HAGGERSTON, GADSDEN, MA, JP (who assumed by Roy. Licence 1973 the additional surname of Haggerston), and has issue living Juliet Mary, *b.* 1956,—Caroline Mabel, *b.* 1957,—Clare Louise, *b.* 1960,—Elizabeth Ann, *b.* 1962.——Jennifer Veronica Louise de Marie, *b.* 1938: *m.* 1959, Anthony Lambert Forward, of 34, Poulton Sq., SW3, and has issue living, Hugh Carnaby, *b.* 1959,—Andrew Lambert, *b.* 1964.——Phyllida Angela de Marie, *b.* 1945: *m.* 1967, Antony Roland Richard Woosnam Mills, of Tinners Gate, Crows Nest, nr. Darite, Liskeard, Cornwall.

Widows living of 11th and 12th Baronets—MARY RIDGWAY (*Mary, Lady Haggerston*) (Harelaw House, Chathill, Northumberland), el. da. of T. Ridgway Macy, of New York: *m.* 1933, Sir (Hugh) Carnaby de Marie Haggerston, 11th Bt., who *d.* 1971.——JOAN ADELENE (*Lady Haggerston*), (106, Ormonde Court, Upper Richmond Rd., SW15); da. of the late William Blythe-Perrett, of Ludgershall, Wilts.: *m.* 1956, Sir Ralph (Raphael) Stanley de Marie Haggerston 12th Bt., who *d.* 1972.

Collateral Branches living. [see L. Herries, colls.].

Sir Thomas Haggerston, who commanded a regt. in Charles I's army, was cr. a Bt. in 1642. On the death of Sir Ralph (Raphael) Stanley de Marie Haggerston in 1972 (who *s.* as 12th Bt. in 1971), the line from Sir Thomas, 4th Bt. became ext., and the title reverted to that of the 2nd son of 3rd Bt., William Haggerston-Constable (who in 1746 inherited Everingham Park, Yorks., from his great uncle, Sir Marmaduke Francis Constable, 4th Bt., and thereupon assumed the additional name of Constable). He *m.* 1758 (Lady) Winifred, da. of Robert Maxwell, titular 6th Earl of Nithsdale, when he assumed the surname of Maxwell. Their grandson William *s.* as 10th Lord Herries of Terregles. This peer's el. son Marmaduke, 11th Lord Herries, *d.* 1908 without male issue [see L. Herries], and his 3rd son Joseph assumed by Roy. Licence the surname of Constable-Maxwell-Scott, on *m.* 1874 to Monica, da. of J. Robert Hope Scott, of Abbotsford. Joseph's el. son, Sir Walter Joseph was cr. a Bt. in 1932, which became ext. on his death without male issue 1954, and his 3rd son Adm. Malcolm Joseph Raphael, DSO, was father of 13th Bt.

CONSTABLE-MAXWELL-SCOTT, Creation (U.K.) 1932, of Abbotsford, Melrose,
co. Roxburgh. [Extinct 1954.]

Maj.-Gen. Sir WALTER JOSEPH CONSTABLE-MAXWELL-SCOTT,
C.B., D.S.O., 1st and last *Baronet.*

Daughters living of 1st Baronet—By 1st marriage—Patricia Mary MAXWELL-SCOTT, *OBE, b.* 1921:
re-assumed by deed poll 1951 her maiden surname of Maxwell-Scott; formerly Subaltern
ATS; OBE (Civil) 1972: *m.* 1944, Capt. Sir Harold Hugh Christian Boulton, 4th Bt. (*cr.* 1905).
Residence, Abbotsford, Melrose, Scotland.——Jean Mary Monica, *CVO, b.* 1923; ed. at Convent
des Oiseaux, Westgate-on-Sea; a Lady-in-Waiting to HRH Princess Alice, Duchess of Gloucester
since 1959; 1939-45 War as VAD; CVO 1969. *Residence*, Abbotsford, Melrose, Scotland;
Queen's (Edinburgh), and VAD Ladies' Clubs.

SEALE, Creation (U.K.) 1838, of Mount Boone, Devonshire.

In heaven salvation.

Sir JOHN HENRY SEALE, 5th *Baronet; b.*
March 3rd, 1921; *s.* his father, *Sir* JOHN CAR-
TERET HYDE, 1964; ed. at Eton, and at Ch. Ch.,
Oxford; Capt. late R.A.; patron of one living;
an ARIBA: *m.* 1953, Ray Josephine, da. of the
late R. G. Charters, MC, of Christchurch, New
Zealand, and has issue.

Arms—Or, two barrulets azure between three wolves' heads
erased sable, in the fesse point a mural crown gules.   **Crest**—
Out of a crown vallery or a wolf's head argent, the neck
encircled with a wreath of oak vert.

Residence—Slade, near Kingsbridge, Devon.   *Club*—
Junior Carlton.

Son living—JOHN ROBERT CHARTERS, *b.* Aug. 17th,
1954.

Daughter living—Elizabeth Margaret Anne, *b.* 1956.

Brother living—Richard Styleman (Conduit Rise, Conduit
Head Rd., Cambridge), *b.* 1924; ed. at Eton, and at
Pembroke Coll., Camb.: *m.* 1963, Elizabeth Vazeille, da.
of T. B. Bright, of Cove Lea, Silverdale, Lancs., and has
issue living, William Thomas Carteret, *b.* 1964,—Margaret
Rachel Vazeille, *b.* 1966.

Sister living—Mary Paulina, *b.* 1920: *m.* 1945, Col.
George Robert Melville Harvey More, MC, RE, of Bazzle-
ways, Milborne Port, Sherborne, Dorset, and has issue living, Robert Harvey, *b.* 1946,—Henry
Sanctuary, *b.* 1948,—John William, *b.* 1953,—Sarah Frances, *b.* 1952.

Collateral Branches living.

Issue of the late Maj. Henry Dendy Seale, yr. son of 3rd baronet, *b.* 1882, *d.*
1974: *m.* 1914, Lora May, who *d.* 1974, da. of the late Cecil Hurst Bisshopp, of
Fernlea, Oban, Argyllshire:—

Mary Desiree (101-2660, Currie Rd., Vic., BC, V8S 3C1, Canada), *b.* 1915: *m.* 1946, Stanley James
Meyers, who *d.* 1974, and has issue living, Linda May, *b.* 1948: *m.* 1973, Robert Donald Giroux, of
4870, Lake Road, Dollard des Ormeaux, Quebec Province, H9G 1G8.

Grandchildren of the late George Thomas Seale, yr. son of the late Rev. Edward
Taylor Seale, 3rd son of 1st baronet:—

Issue of the late George Edward Dugald Seale, *b.* 1872, *d.* 1937: *m.* 1905, Beatrice
Agatha Tipping Lanauze :—

Henry Dugald Cranstoun, *b.* 1910: *m.* 1948, Elsie Joyce Neilson. *Residence*, 65, Beachville
Rd., Redcliffs, Christchurch, 8, New Zealand.

Issue of the late Frederick Hayne Seale; *b.* 1878, *d.* 1931: *m.* 1903, Ethel Lenore, who
d. 1959, da. of Joseph Nathan :—

Richard Wentworth, *b.* 1904: *m.* 1927, Edith Hazel, da. of William Brown Birch, and has issue
living, Richard Laurie, *b.* 1930.——Gordon Frederick, *b.* 1906: *m.* 1936, Eva Vera, da. of Charles
Adams, and has issue living, Elizabeth Lenore, *b.* 1939,—Carolyn Margaret, *b.* 1943. *Residence*,
37, Marlow Street, Wembley, W. Aust.——Walter Douglas (41, Margaret St., N. Cottesloe, W.
Aust.) *b.* 1907: *m.* 1st, 1935 (m. diss. 1967), Mons Carruthers, da. of Sidney Herbert Reidy-
Crofts; 2ndly, 1974, Barbara Topping, of Peoria, Ill., USA., and has issue living (by 1st m.),
John Digby (Brecon, 47, Colin St., W. Perth, W. Aust.), *b.* 1937: *m.* 1960 (m. diss. 19—), Roslyn
Edith, da. of David Englander,—Felicity Jane, *b.* 1939: *m.* 1961, Evan Owen, of 22, Brassey St.,
Swanbourne, W. Australia, and has issue living, Simon Llewellyn *b.* 1963, Sarah Alexandra
b. 1967, Sophia Jane *b.* 1971,——Allan Dudley, *b.* 1911: *m.* 1947, Ilma Ruth, da. of Edward
John Barrett, and has issue living, Phillip Gregory, *b.* 1948,—Brian Wentworth, *b.* 1950,—
Marlene Ruth, *b.* 1952. *Residence*, 23, Anstey St., South Perth, W. Australia.——Grace Mildred,
b. 1909: *m.* 1946, Vice-Adm. Brian Betham Schofield, CB, CBE, and has issue living, Elizabeth
Virginia, *b.* 1948,—Rosemary Victoria, *b.* 1950. *Residence*, Newholme, Lower Shiplake, Henley-
on-Thames.

This family can trace its descent from John Seale of St. Brelades, Jersey, who was *b.* about
1512. According to Payne's Armorial of Jersey, the earliest reference to Robert Seale, or Scelle,
a "gens de bien" of St. Brelades 1292, and other Scelles of St. Brelades are mentioned in the
Rolls of the Assizes 1309. John Seale Constable of St. Brelades 1644-51, a yr. son of John Seale
Constable 1615-21 was great-grandfather of John who purchased Mount Boone, Dartmouth,
about 1720. His grandson, the 1st baronet, Sir John Henry Seale, sat as MP for Dartmouth (L)
1832-44. The 2nd baronet Sir Henry Paul Seale, was sixteen times Mayor of Dartmouth.

SEBRIGHT, Creation (E.) 1626, of Besford, Worcestershire.

To preserve equanimity.

Sir HUGO GILES EDMUND SEBRIGHT, 14th *Baronet* ; *b.* March 2nd, 1931 ; *s.* his father, *Sir* GILES EDWARD, C.B.E., 1954 ; is patron of one living: *m.* 1st. 1952 (m. diss. 1964), Deirdre Ann, da. of Maj. Vivian Lionel Slingsby Bethell, RA [*see* B. Westbury, colls.]; 2ndly, 1965, Sheila Mary Howard, da. of Walter Howard Rocke, and widow of Edward George Hervey [*see* M. Bristol, colls.], and has issue by 1st marriage.

Arms—Argent, three cinquefoils sable. **Crest**—A tiger sejant argent, maned and crowned or. **Badge**—A garb of **oats or,** band azure inscribed with the motto " Pro Rege."

Club—St. James'.

Son living—By 1st marriage—PETER GILES VIVIAN, *b* Aug. 2nd, 1953.

Widow living of 13th Baronet—MARGERY HILDA (*Margery, Lady Sebright*), da. of the late Adm. Sir Sydney Robert Fremantle, G.C.B., M.V.O. [*see* B. Cottesloe, colls.] ; **is a** J.P.: *m.* 1929, Sir Giles Edward Sebright, 13th Bt., C.B.E., who *d.* 1954. *Residence*, Riversmeet House, Topsham, Devon.

The 1st baronet, Sir Edward Sebright, was High Sheriff of Worcestershire *temp.* Charles I. He was a warm royalist, and paid £1,109 composition for his estate to the sequestrators. Sir Thomas Saunders, the 4th baronet, was M.P. for Hertford 1715-36. The 7th baronet also sat as M.P. for Hertford. Lieut.-Col. Sir Edgar Sebright, 11th Bt., was Equerry to the Princess Mary Adelaide (Duchess of Teck) 1882-92, and Extra Equerry 1892. Sir Giles Sebright, C.B.E., 13th Bt., was Lieut.-Col. late Comdg. Herts. Regt. (T.A.), and temporary Equerry to H.M. King George VI when Duke of York 1922-23.

SEELY, Creation (U.K.) 1896, of Sherwood Lodge, Arnold, Notts., and Brooke House, Brooke, Isle of Wight.

Sir VICTOR BASIL JOHN SEELY, 4th *Baronet*; *b.* May 18th, 1900; *s.* his brother *Sir* HUGH MICHAEL [Baron Sherwood], 1970; ed. at Eton, and Trin. Coll., Camb.; patron of two livings; formerly Lt. S. Notts. Hussars, and Maj. 9th Lancers; Master of Gunmakers' Co. 1956 and again 1965; a Dir. of Drayton Corpn. Ltd. and other Cos., of 117, Old Broad St.; 1939-45 War (prisoner, escaped): *m.* 1st, 1922, Sybil Helen (who obtained a divorce 1931), da. of the late Sills Clifford Gibbons, and widow of Sir John Bridger Shiffner, 6th Bt.; 2ndly, 1931, the Hon. Patience Kemp, who *d.* 1935, da. of the 1st Baron Rochdale; 3rdly, 1937, Mary Frances Margaret, da. of William Ronald Collins, and has issue by 1st, 2nd and 3rd m.

Arms,—Azure, three ears of wheat banded or between two marlets in pale, and as many wreaths of roses in fesse argent. **Crest,**—In front of three ears of wheat banded or, the trunk of a tree fessewise eradicated and sprouting to the dexter proper.

Residence,—42, Orchard Court, Portman Sq., W1. *Clubs,*—White's, Beefsteak, City, Royal Solent Yacht.

Sons living—By 1st m.—NIGEL EDWARD (31, Ovington Sq., SW3), *b.* July 28th, 1923: *m.* 1948, Loraine, only da. of the late W. W. Lindley-Travis, and has issue living, Charlotte Alexandra Mary, *b.* 1954,—Catherine Lucy Emily, *b.* 1957,—Henrietta Louise, *b.* 1962.——**By 3rd m.**— Victor Ronald (White's Club), *b.* 1941; ed. at Eton and RMAS; Maj. The R. Hussars (PWO): *m.* 1972, Annette Bruce, da. of Lt.-Col. J. A. D. McEwen, of Syreford House, Syreford, Andoversford, Cheltenham.

Daughters living—By 2nd m.—Victoria, *b.* 1933: *m.* 1954 (Francis Arthur) Michael Bray, DSC, of Lakers Lodge, Loxwood, Sussex, and has issue living, Charles Michael Francis, *b.* 1957,—Mariana Victoria Magadlin, *b.* 1956,—Amelia Mary, *b.* 1962.——**By 3rd m.**—Alexandra Mary Hilda, *b.* 1938: *m.* 1966, Henry Charles Seymour, son of the late Lt.-Col. Sir Reginald Henry Seymour, KCVO [*see* M. Hertford, colls.].

Sisters living—Violet Lucy Emily (*Dowager Viscountess Allendale*) (21, Cadogan Sq., SW1), *b.* 1897: *m.* 1921, the 2nd Viscount Allendale, who *d.* 1956.——Ivy Angela, *MBE* (50, Sloane St., SW1) (twin), *b.* 1898; Assist. Comdt. VAD: MBE (Mil) 1944.

Collateral Branches living
Issue of the late Sqdn.-Ldr. Nigel Richard William Seely, AuxAF (Reserve), 4th son of 2nd baronet, *b.* 1902; *d.* (on active ser. during 1939-45 War) 1943: *m.* 1937, Isabella Elinor Margarete (who *d.* 1957, having *m.* 2ndly, 1949, Edward Bromley-Davenport), da. of Eugene von Rieben:—

Charles John Howell (Plas Penhelig, Aberdovey, Merioneth), b. 1937.——Hilton Nigel Matthew (48, Drayton Gdns., SW10), b. 1940: m. 1971, Leonie Mary Taylor, and has issue living, Charles, b. 1972, Dominic Edward b. 1075.——Elinor Ivy, b. 1941: m. 1968, Maj. Martin Vyvyan Carleton-Smith, Irish Gds., of Horn Hill House, Barford St. Michael, Deddington, Oxon, and has issue living, Robin Francis Popham, b. 1972, Camilla Alison, b. 1969.——Isabella Frances (twin), b. 1941: m. 1st, 1961 (m. diss. 1966), Simon James Scrimgeour; 2ndly, 1966, Anthony Piers Covill, of 97, Arthur Rd., SW19, and has issue living, (by 1st m.) Lucilla Jane, b. 1963,—(by 2nd m.) Piers Anthony Charles, b. 1967,—Joseph William Edward, b. 1969.

Grandchildren of the late Lt.-Col. Frank Evelyn Seely (infra):—
Issue of the late Lt.-Col. (Frank) James (Wriothesley) Seely, MFH, b. 1901, d. 1956: m. 1925, Vera Lilian, who d. 1970, da. of the late Col. Charles Wilfrid Birkin, CMG [see Birkin, Bt.]:—
Michael James, b. 1926: m. 1st, 1952 (m. diss. 1966), Barbara Patricia Callaghan; 2ndly, 1966 Patricia Ann Auchterlonie, and has issue living, (by 2nd m.) Rachel, b. 1967. Residence,—Ramsdale Farm, Oxton Lane, Arnold, Notts.——Timothy Ward, b. 1935; ed. at Eton; is an Actor.——James Richard Francis, b. 1940: m. (Jan.) 1960, Wendy Mary Hutchinson, and has issue living, Christian James Russell, b. (Dec.) 1960,—Jonathan Sebastian, b. 1962.——Clare Elizma, b. 1929: m. 1949, Christopher John Filmer-Sankey, who d. 1957 [D. Westminster], and has issue living, Dominic Hugh b. 1950,—Christopher, b. (posthumous) 1958.——Cherry Angela Mary, b. 1931: m. 1955, Desmond Barnaby O'Brien, who d. 1969, [see B. Inchiquin, colls.]. Residences,—Arderne Hall, Tarporley, Ches.; 42, Kinnerton St., SW1.

Issue of the late Lt.-Col. William Evelyn Seely, b. 1902, d. (killed in action during 1939-45 War) 1942: m. 1927, Irene Lavender (Lady Graham) (who m. 2ndly, 1943, as his second wife, Maj.-Gen. Sir Miles William Arthur Peel Graham, KBE, CB, MC [E. Peel, colls.]), da. of Richard Francklin [V. St. Vincent]:—
Richard Evelyn (of 33, Upper Park Rd., NW3), b. 1928; ed. at Eton; Bar. Gray's Inn, 1961: m. 1960, Helga, da. of Wilhelm Schnarr, of Mainz, Germany, and has issue living, Philip Frank Evelyn, b. 1963,—Robert William Henry, b. 1966.——Charles William (8, Castle St., Framlingham, Suffolk), b. 1935: m. 1958, Morvyth, da. of the late George Arthur St. George, of 4, Dyke Road Pl., Brighton, 5, and has issue living, Amy Jane Lavender, b. 1969,—Camilla Rose b. 1972.

Issue of the late Lt.-Col. Frank Evelyn Seely, 3rd son of 1st baronet, b. 1864, d. 1928: m. 1st, 1899, Leila Elizma, who d. 1903, da. of the Rev. Henry Charles Russell, of Wollaton, Notts. [D. Bedford, colls.]; 2ndly, 1907, Gertrude Fanny, OBE, JP, who d. 1967, da. of Henry Edward Thornton, JP, of The Wymeshead, Kegworth, Derby:—
Leila Emily (Leila, Viscountess Hampden), b. 1900: m. 1923, the 4th Viscount Hampden, who d. 1965. Residence,—Mill Court, Alton, Hants.——(By 2nd m.) Sheila Katherine, b. 1908: m. 1933, Richard Eustace Talbot [see E. Shrewsbury, colls.]. Residence,—Fyning Manor, Rogate, Sussex.——Nina Mary Aline, b. 1911: m. 1939, Wing-Com. Michael Young, DFC, JP, RAF (ret.), and has issue living, Michael Patrick William, b. 1944: m. 1970, Sonia Margaret Smith,—David Richard James, b. 1949: m. 1970, Yvonne Reis,—Mary Andrea, b. 1943: m. 1962, John Frears, MA, JP, of The White House, Hoton, Leics., and has issue living, Naomi Mary Frances b. 1963, Nina Katherine b. 1964, Lucy May Leila b. 1966. Residence,—The Old Rectory, West-borough, Newark-on-Trent.

Issue of the late Maj.-Gen. the Rt. Hon. John Edward Bernard Seely, CB, CMG, DSO (4th son of 1st baronet), who was cr. Baron Mottistone 1933 [see that title].

The 1st Bt., Sir Charles, sat as MP for Nottingham (L) 1869-74, and 1880-85, and for W. Nottingham 1885-86, and again for Nottingham (LU) 1892-95. The 2nd Bt., Sir Charles Hilton, was MP for Lincoln (LU) 1895-1906, and for Mansfield (Co. L) 1916-18. The 3rd Bt., Sir Hugh Michael, was cr. Baron Sherwood 1941; he d. 1970, when the peerage became ext.

Selby-Bigge, see Bigge.

SETON, Creation (N.S.) 1663, of Abercorn, Linlithgowshire.

Sir CHRISTOPHER BRUCE SETON, 12th Baronet, only son of the late Charles Henry Seton, great grandson of 5th Bt.; b. Oct. 3rd, 1909; s. his kinsman, Sir BRUCE LOVAT, 1969; ed. at Magdalene Coll., Camb. (BA): m. 1939, Joyce Vivian, el. da. of the late Oliver George Barnard, of Lockington House, Stow-market, and has issue.

Arms—Quarterly: 1st and 4th, or, three crescents within a double tressure flory, counterflory gules, Seton; 2nd and 3rd, argent, three in escutcheons gules, Hay. Crest—A boar's head couped or, armed and langued azure. Supporters—Two greyhounds proper.

Residence—Ballast Quay Farm, Fingringhoe, Colchester, Essex.

Sons living—IAIN BRUCE (Shanta Clair, Balingup, W. Aust.), b. Aug. 27th, 1942: m. 1963, Margaret Ann, only da. of Walter Charles Faulkner, of Gt. Horkesley, Colchester, and has issue living, Laurence Bruce, b. 1968,—Amanda Jane b. 1971.——Michael Charles, b. 1944: m. 1973, Vida Smith, of Boxstead, Essex.

Daughters living—Sarah Ann (twin), b. 1944: m. 1st, 1968 (m. diss. 1970), Thomas Charles Usher; 2ndly, 1974, Ferdinand Winston Good (Box 443, Belton, Missouri, 64012, USA).——Joanna Mary, b. 1946.

Sister living—Violet Beechie, b. 1917: m. 1937, Wilfred Barnard, of Little Jarra, Marcus Rd., Felixstowe, Suffolk, and has issue living, Christopher John, b. 1938,—Jane Mary, b. 1944,—Jean Susanne, b. 1946.

Daughter living of 11th Baronet—(By 2nd m.)—Lydia Antoinette Gordon, b. 1941: m. 1966, Peter S. Spratt, of 90, Sheen Court, Richmond, Surrey.

Daughter living of 10th Baronet—Egidia Hay, *b.* 1928: *m.* 1st, 1948, Andrew George Seton Arnot (m. diss. 1949); 2ndly, 1953, Norman Haynes, of Nonnington Hall, Graffham, nr. Petworth, W. Sussex, and has issue living, (by 2nd m.) Hamish, *b.* 1956.—Alasdair, *b.* 1960.

Daughter living of 9th Baronet—Jean Gordon, *b.* 1903: *m.* 1st, 1922, Lt. Reginald George Arnot, RN (ret.), from whom she obtained a divorce 1946; 2ndly, 1947, Gen. Hamner Cobbs, US Army, who *d.* 1968, and has issue living, (by 1st m.) Andrew George Seton, *b.* 1925,—June Gordon, *b.* 1924. *Residence*, Delray Beach, Florida, USA.

Widows living of 10th and 11th Baronets—JULIA (*Julia, Lady Seton*) (of 122, Swan Court, Kings Rd., SW3), da. of the late Frank Clements: *m.* 1962, as his third wife, Sir Alexander Hay Seton, 10th baronet, who *d.* 1963.——FLORENCE ANTOINETTE GLOSSOP (*Antoinette, Lady Seton*) (88, Redcliffe Gdns., SW10), da. of the late Frank Cellier: *m.* 1940, as his 2nd wife, Sir Bruce Lovat Seton, 11th baronet, who *d.* 1969.

Collateral Branch living.

Issue (by 2nd marriage) of the late Major Henry James Seton, *b.* 1854, *d.* 1920 : *m.* 1st, 1888, Elizabeth, who *d.* 1897, da. of the late Henry James Byron [B. Byron, colls.]; 2ndly, 1899, Marie Bowles (who *d.* 1928, having *m.* 2ndly, 1922, Sir Charles George Walpole, who *d.* 1926 [E. Orford, colls.]), da. of the late Percy Hale Wallace :—
Marie, *b.* 1910; is an Author : *m.* 1942, Donald Louis Hesson, from whom she obtained a divorce 1958. *Residence*,

Sir Walter Seton of Abercorn, 1st Bt., was cr. a Bt. with remainder to heirs male whatsoever. The present baronet is the direct male representative of Sir Alexander Seton, who married Elizabeth, sister and heir of John Gordon of Gordon. She in 1408 (in conjunction with her husband) received a charter of the land of Gordon. Sir Alexander was held to have been cr. a Lord of Parliament as Lord Gordon in or before 1429. Their son Alexander, 1st Earl of Huntly, was father (by his 1st wife, Egidia Hay) of Sir Alexander Seton, ancestor of this family, and (by his 2nd wife Elizabeth Crichton) of George Seton, later Gordon, on whom he obtained a charter to settle the Earldom. In 1923 Sir Bruce Gordon Seton, 9th Bt., C.B., petitioned the Crown to admit his succession and declare his right to the title of Lord Gordon in the peerage of Scotland (*cr.* in or before 1429). After a lengthy hearing the Committee for Privileges of the House of Lords, while admitting that he was heir male to Sir Alexander Seton, Dominus de Gordon (subsequently created Earl of Huntly)—eldest son of Sir Alexander—could not recognize that the evidence submitted by the petitioner established the creation and existence of the dignity. Col. Sir Bruce Gordon Seton, 9th Bt., C.B., in 1929 unsuccessfully claimed this Lordship before the Committee for Privileges of the House of Lords. Sir Alexander Hay Seton, 10th Bt., was Carrick Pursuivant of Arms 1935-9.

SETON, Creation (N.S.) 1683, of Pitmedden, Aberdeenshire.

I sustain the standard with my blood.

This is the sure reward of labor.

Sir ROBERT JAMES SETON, 11th *Baronet; b.* April 20th, 1926; *s.* his father, *Sir* JOHN HASTINGS, 1956; European War 1943-45 as Midshipman R.N.V.R. (invalided).

Arms—Quarterly : 1st and 4th, or, three crescents, and in the centre a man's heart distilling blood, the whole within a double tressure flory counter-flory gules, *Seton* ; 2nd and 3rd, argent, a demi-otter sable, crowned or issuing out of a bar wavy of the second, *Meldrum*. Crest—A demi-man in military habit holding the banner of Scotland. Supporters—*Dexter*, a greyhound proper, collared gules ; *sinister*, an otter sable.

Address—c/o Hongkong & Shanghai Banking Corporation, 9, Gracechurch St., EC3.

Sister living—Alice Eva Elizabeth, *b.* 1924; late W.R.N.S.: *m.* 1954, John Herbert Warner, and has issue living, Sylla Elizabeth, *b.* 1955. *Residence*, The Ryders, Ham Common, Richmond, Surrey.

Mother living—Alice Ida, *C.B.E.*, da. of the late Percy C. Hodge, Cape Civil Ser. ; Group Officer (ret.) WRAF; CBE (Mil) 1949: *m.* 1923 (m. diss. 1950), Sir John Hastings Seton, 10th Baronet, who *d.* 1956. *Residence*, 3, Maddison Close, Teddington, Middlesex.

Collateral Branches living.

Grandchildren of the late Charles Seton, 5th son of 7th baronet :—
Issue of the late Christall Dougal Seton, *b.* 1883, *d.* 1969: *m.* 1909, Sara Johnson, who *d.* 1959, da. of Wallace Moore :—
JAMES CHRISTALL (814, Buckeye St., Miamisburg, Ohio, USA), *b.* Jan. 21st, 1913; sometime Private US Army: *m.* 1939, Evelyn, da. of Ray Hafer.——Robert Benjamin (of 26, Bradley Av., Shelby, Ohio, USA), *b.* 1917; sometime Private US Army: *m.* 1940, Martha Mae, da. of Fred Minich, and has issue living, Karen Louise, *b.* 1941: *m.* 1963, Michael Conrad, of 2369, New Bedford Drive, Troy, Michigan, 48084, USA, and has issue living, Dennis Michael *b.* 1964, Dorothy Jean, *b.* 1947.——Dorothy Kathryn, *b.* 1910: *m.* 1st, 1937 (divorce 1940), George B. Leonard, of Cleveland, Ohio, USA; 2ndly, 1947 (m. diss. 1974), Kenneth M. James, and has issue living, (by 2nd m.) Susan Kay, *b.* 1949.

Grandchildren of the late Christall Dougal Seton (ante) :—
Issue of the late Maj. Charles Wallace Seton, *b.* 1915, *d.* 1975: *m.* 1943, Joyce (1120, Ellen Drive, Radcliffe, Ky. 40160, USA), da. of Stephen F. Perdunn :—
Charles Wallace, *b.* 1948.——Bruce Anthony, *b.* 1957.——Judith Allen, *b.* 1944.——Marsha Ann, *b.* 1947.——Terri, *b.* 1958.

James Seton 1st of Pitmedden (gt. grandfather of the 1st baronet) was 5th son of William Seton of Meldrum who descended from William Seton, 2nd son of Sir Alexander Seton of that ilk who m. Elizabeth, heir of the Gordons. The 1st baronet, Sir Alexander, sat as MP for Aberdeenshire, and was subsequently a Lord of Justiciary, with the title of Lord Pitmedden. The 2nd baronet was MP for Aberdeenshire, and one of the Commissioners appointed to treat about the union of England and Scotland. Sir James Lumsden Seton, 8th Bt., was Capt. 102nd Regt., and received 2nd class of Order of Iron Cross of Germany for saving life in the field during Franco-Prussian War 1870.

CULME-SEYMOUR, Creation (U.K.) 1809, of Highmount, and Friery Park, Devonshire,
[Name pronounced "Cullum-Seamer."]

Faith for duty.

Sir MICHAEL CULME-SEYMOUR, 5th
Baronet ; b. April 26th, 1909; *s.* his father,
Vice-Adm. Sir MICHAEL, *K.C.B., M.V.O.,* 1925 ;
Com. R.N. (retired) ; is a Farmer and Land-
owner, a J.P. and a D.L. for Northants ; was
A.D.C. to Gov.-Gen. of Canada 1933-5, and a
co. Councillor for Northants 1948-55 ; Euro-
pean War 1939-45 in Atlantic, N. Africa and
Far East (despatches) : *m.* 1948, Lady (Mary)
Faith (NESBITT), da. of 9th Earl of Sandwich.

Arms—Azure, a pair of wings conjoined in pale and
surmounted of a naval crown ; on a canton argent an
anchor sable. Crest—On a naval crown or, two brands in
saltire inflamed at the ends proper, thereon an eagle rising,
also proper, looking at the sun or.
Seat—Rockingham Castle, Market Harborough.
Clubs—Naval and Military, Brooks's.

Collateral Branches living.

Issue of the late Elizabeth Culme-
Seymour, only da. of 4th Bt., *b.* 1904,
d. 1963: *m.* 1933, Capt. Leslie Swain
Saunders, DSO, RN (ret.), of Wanford
Mill, Buck's Green, Rudgwick:—

Leslie Michael MacDonald SAUNDERS WATSON (Rockingham Castle, Market Harborough, Leics.;
United Service and Royal Aero Club), *b.* 1934; assumed by deed poll 1971, the surname of
Saunders Watson; ed. at Eton; Cdr. RN (ret.): *m.* 1958, Georgina Elizabeth Laetitia, da. of
Adm. Sir William Wellclose Davis, GCB, DSO [see M. Normanby], and has issue living, James
Michael Ross, *b.* 1961,—David William Wentworth, *b.* 1968,—Fiona Jane Liebe, *b.* 1965.——
Alasdair James Hew (11, Gledhow Gdns., SW5), *b.* 1938; ed. at Eton: *m.* 1974, Joanna Christina,
da. of Col. John Offley Crewe-Read, OBE [see By. of Robins.], and formerly wife of Capt. John
Anthony Frank Morton, late RHA.——Iain Ogilvy Swain, *b.* 1947.——Elizabeth Christina, *b.*
1941: *m.* 1962, William Lawrence Banks, of 13, Abercorn Place, NW8.

Issue of the late John Wentworth Culme-Seymour, 2nd son of 3rd baronet,
b. 1876, *d.* 1962: *m.* 1918, Evelyn Mary (28, Phillimore Gdns., W8 7QE), da. of
the late C. A. Smith-Ryland, of Barford, Warwick:—

JOHN DENNIS (of Ty Gwyn, Crickhowell, Breconshire), *b.* Dec. 3rd, 1923; ed. at Winchester;
European War and Far East 1942-45 as Capt. Rifle Brig.: *m.* 1957, Elizabeth Jane, da. of
Lt.-Col. Kenneth Mackessack, of Ardgye, Elgin [see Craik, Bt. ext.], and has issue living, Caroline,
b. 1959.——Mary Primrose, *b.* 1921; 1939-45 War as 3rd Officer W.R.N.S.——Jane, *b.* 1925: *m.*
1959, Com. John Hocken Joughin, D.S.C., R.N., of Knockbane, Mugdock Rd., Milngavie,
Glasgow.

Issue of the late Capt. George Culme-Seymour, 3rd son of 3rd baronet, *b.* 1878, *d.* (killed
in action) 1915 : *m.* 1909, Janet Beatrix [who *d.* 1943, having *m.* 2ndly, 1918, the
Rev. Geoffrey Harold Woolley, V.C., M.C., Chap. to Forces, Chap. at Harrow
Sch., formerly Capt. London Regt. (T.A.)], da. of the late Charles Lindsay Orr
Ewing, M.P. [Ewing, Bt., colls.]:—

Mark Charles, *b.* 1910 ; ed. at Wellington Coll., and at New Coll., Oxford ; European War 1941-45
as Major Rifle Brig. in Middle East and Italy (wounded) : *m.* 1st, 1935, Babette (who obtained
a divorce 1938), only child of the late David Llewelyn Patric-Jones ; 2ndly, 1941, Princesse Hélène
Marie de la Trémoïlle (who obtained a divorce 1949), 3rd da. of Prince Louis Charles Marie, 12th
Duc de Thouars, Prince and 11th Duc de la Trémoïlle, Premier Duc de France, 12th Prince de
Tarante, and 16th Prince de Talmond, and formerly wife of Sir (William) Campbell Mitchell-
Cotts., 2nd Bt.; 3rdly, 1956 (m. diss. 1967), Patricia June, da. of the late Charles Reid-Graham,
and widow of Geoffrey Edward Ansell; 4thly, 1973, Mary Darrall, only da. of the late Leander
Armistead Riely, of Oklahoma City, USA, and widow of Philip Kidd, and has issue living (by
3rd m.), Michael Patrick, *b.* 1962,—Miranda, *b.* 1959,—Sarah Louise, *b.* 1961. *Residence*, Vinas
Viejas, Rancho Domingo, Benalmadena, Malaga, Spain.——Angela Mary, *b.* 1912: *m.* 1st, 1934
(m. diss. 1938) John George Spencer Churchill [see D. Marlborough, colls]; 2ndly, 1938, the
3rd Baron Kinross, who obtained a divorce 1942; 3rdly, Count René de Chatellus. *Address*,
c/o Coutts & Co., 16, Cavendish Sq., W1.

Issue of the late Major Henry Hobart Culme-Seymour, 3rd son of 2nd baronet, *b.*
1847, *d.* 1920: *m.* 1878, Kate, who *d.* 1931, da. of William Charles Lucy:—

Violet Katharine Maria (Lea Gate House, Bramley, Guildford), *b.* 1891: *m.* 1926, Charles de la
Cour Le Maistre, CBE, who *d.* 1953.

Granddaughters of the late Maj. Henry Hobart Culme-Seymour (infra):—
Issue of the late Lt.-Cdr. Gerald Henry Hobart Culme-Seymour, RN, *b.* 1914, *d.* 1973: *m.*
1st, 1939, Constance Helen, who *d.* 1959, da. of the late Alfred Rendell Street [Dashwood,
Bt., cr. 1684]; 2ndly, 1960, Patricia Mary, el. da. of Edward Pearson Hewetson, JP, of
15, Glebelands, Brampton, Oxon., and formerly wife of 3rd Viscount Cross:—

(By 1st m.) Victoria, *b.* 1940: *m.* 1963, M. Haeri, and has issue living, David, *b.* 1967,—Mina, *b.*
1964.——Anne Evelyn, *b.* 1941: *m.* 1st, 1961 (m. diss. 1970), John L. M. Denham; 2ndly, 1972,
(David) Michael (Richard Cecil) Allen, of Kidmore House, Kidmore End, Oxon., and has issue
living (by 1st m.), James Henry Seymour, *b.* 1964,—Alexandra Sophia, *b.* 1966.——Catherine,
b. 1945: *m.* 1972, Christopher James Monro Hartley.——Alexandra, *b.* 1953.——(by 2nd m.)
Caroline, *b.* 1961.

Granddaughter of the late Maj. Henry Hobart Culme-Seymour (ante):—
Issue of the late Cdr. Evelyn Culme-Seymour, RN, *b.* 1881, *d.* 1970: *m.* 1908, Laura
Maude Amy, who *d.* 1958, da. of the late Sir Steuart Macnaghten [Macnaghten, Bt.
colls.]:—

Patience Ann, *b.* 1912: *m.* 1939 (m. diss. 1951), Lt.-Cdr. David Robert Fremantle, RNVR [see
B. Cottesloe, colls.].

Grandsons of the late Rev. Richard Seymour (*b.* 1877) (infra) :—
Issue of the late Com. John Richard Arthur Seymour, O.B.E., D.S.C., R.N., *b.* 1905,
d. 1957: *m.* 1941, Helen Augusta (who m. 2ndly, 1973, John Edward Francis Rawlins,
of Brook Barn, W. Chinnock, Crewkerne, Som.), da. of the late Lt.-Col. Richard Edmund
Corydon Luxmoore-Ball, DSO, DCM, Welsh Guards:—

Richard Paul (Providence House, Maiden Newton, Dorset), *b.* 1943: Lt. Cdr. RN: *m.* 1971, Valerie
Ann, da. of P. L. Foulsham, and has issue living, Alexander John, *b.* 1974.——Anthony John, *b.*
1946.

Grandchildren of the late Ven. Albert Eden Seymour, son of the late Rev.
Richard Seymour, 5th son of 1st baronet :—

Issue of the late Rev. Richard Seymour, b. 1877, d. 1958 : m. 1903, Annie Louisa Mary, who d. 1909, da. of the late W. E. Arthur, J.P., formerly of Marwood Hill, Barnstaple, Devon :—

Michael Ernest, b. 1906 : m. 1931, Gwendoline Arran, da. of the late William Stuart Gore [see E. Arran, colls.], and has issue living, Eleanor, b 1932: m 1953, John Ferrari, and has issue living, Timothy John b. 1954, Michele Jane b. 1958.——Ruth Mary, b. 1909: m. 1939, Wilfrid Harold Gillard, from whom she obtained a divorce 1949, and has issue living, John Michael Patrick, b. 1940. Residence, Little Firs, Berrynarbor, N. Devon.

Granddaughter of the late Rev. Richard Seymour (b. 1806), 5th son of 1st baronet :—
Issue of the late Richard Arthur Hamilton Seymour, b. 1843, d. 1906 : m. 1878, Charlotte Elizabeth, who d. 1931, da. of the late Adm. Cospatrick Baillie-Hamilton [E. Haddington, colls.] :—
Muriel Jane, b. 1887. Residence, 5, Cadogan Sq., SW1.

Grandchildren of the late Ven. Albert Eden Seymour (ante) :—
Issue of the late Edward Albert Seymour, M.B., b. 1884, d. 1946: m. 1914, Gwendolen Emily (now of 203, Divinity Road, Oxford), da. of the late Rev. William Birch Gascoigne, formerly R. of Wood Eaton, Oxfordshire :—
Edward Richard Fortescue (Ham Green Cottage, Wittersham, Tenterden, Kent), b. 1915: m. 1943, Margaret Eileen, da. of the late Maj. Grantham Dodd, TD, RAMC, and has issue living, Edward Grantham (Rapley Cottage, Neptown, Henfield, Sussex), b. 1945; MA Oxon: m. 1969, Philippa Rosalie Jane, BA, da. of Geoffrey Mollet, of Henley-on-Thames, and has issue living, Guinevere Jane b. 1974,—Charles Adrian (119, Cuckfield Rd., Hurstpierpoint, Sussex), b. 1947: m. 1970, Sylvia Ellen, da. of A. Kimber, of Hurstpierpoint, Sussex,—Michael Shaughan, b. 1949,—Gervais Richard Hugh (4, Tower St., Rye, Sussex), b. 1952: m. 1973, Ann Shirley Trowbridge, of Chesham, Bucks.,—James Quentin, b. 1953.——Hester Mary, b. 1917; is a SRN.——Joyce Eleanor, b. 1918. Residence, 203, Divinity Rd., Oxford.

Issue of the late Very Rev. Algernon Giles Seymour, b. 1886, d. 1933: m. 1921, Ida Grace who d. 1971, da. of the late Vice-Adm. Robert Frederick Hammick [see Hammick, Bt.]:-
Mary Grace (Lady Hutchison), b. 1924: m. 1949, Sir Peter Hutchison, 2nd Bt. Residence, Melton Mead, nr. Woodbridge, Suffolk.

Grandsons of the late Very Rev. Algernon Giles Seymour (ante):—
Issue of the late Cdr. Timothy Maurice Barnabas Seymour, RN, b. 1932, d. 1975: m. 1954, Monica (5, Tarleton Gardens, SE23), da. of the Rt. Rev. Wilfred Arthur Westall, Bishop of Crediton:—
Michael Nicholas, b. 1960.——Charles Richard, b. 1963.

The 1st baronet, Adm. Sir Michael Seymour, K.C.B., when in command of the " Amethyst " frigate on the night of Nov. 10th, 1808, fell in with the French frigate "La Thetis" off L'Orient, which, after a gallant resistance, was captured. This action, for gallantry, skill, and courage, has scarcely been equalled. George III. signified his approbation by presenting him with a gold medal, and Lloyd's Patriotic Fund voted him 100 guineas. The 2nd baronet assumed by Roy. licence in 1842 the additional surname of Culme to perpetuate the name of his first wife, which would otherwise have become extinct. The 3rd baronet, Adm. Sir Michael, GCB, GCVO, served during Crimean War 1854-55, and commanded Pacific Station 1885-7, the Channel Squadron 1890-92, and the Mediterranean Fleet 1893-6, and was Com.-in-Ch. at Portsmouth 1897-1900, Principal Naval A.D.C. to H.M. Queen Victoria 1899-1901, and to H.M. King Edward VII.; Vice-Adm. of Great Britain and Ireland, and Lieut. of Admiralty thereof 1901-20. He married Mary Georgiana, da. of Hon. Richard Watson of Rockingham Castle (son of 2nd Baron Sondes). This estate was inherited by the 5th Bt. in 1925. The 4th baronet, Vice-Adm. Sir Michael Culme-Seymour, K.C.B., M.V.O., who commanded H.M.S. Centurion at battle of Jutland 1916, was Director of Mobilizations 1916-18, Comdg. British Ægean Squadron 1918-19, British Naval Forces in Black Sea, Sea of Marmora, and Caspian Sea 1919-20, 2nd in command Mediterranean 1920-23, Com-in-Ch. N. America and W. Indies 1923-4, and Second Sea Lord of the Admiralty and Ch. of Naval Personnel 1924-5.

SHAKERLEY, Creation (U.K.) 1838, of Somerford Park, Cheshire.

Sir GEOFFREY ADAM SHAKERLEY, 6th Baronet; b. Dec. 9th, 1932; s. his father, Maj. Sir CYRIL HOLLAND, 1970; ed. at Harrow and Trin. Coll., Oxford; late 2nd Lt. KRRC: m. 1st, 1962, Virginia Elizabeth, who d. 1968, el. da. of W. E. Maskell, of Little Down, Bury, Sussex; 2ndly, 1972, Lady Elizabeth Georgiana Anson, da. of the late Thomas William Arnold, Viscount Anson [see E. Lichfield], and has issue by 1st and 2nd m.

Arms—Argent, a chevron between three hillocks vert. Crest—A rabbit rampant sable supporting a garb or.
Residence—56, Ladbroke Grove, W11 2PB.

Sons living (By 1st m.)—NICHOLAS SIMON ADAM, b. Dec. 20th, 1963.
——Peter Jonathan, b. 1966.
Daughter living (By 2nd m.)—Fiona Elizabeth Fenella, b. 1973.
Brother living—Charles Frederick Eardley (Cudworth Manor, Newdigate, Surrey), b. 1934; ed. at Harrow, and at Ch. Ch., Oxford: m. 1962, Lucy Carolyn, el. da. of Francis St. G. Fisher, of 23A, Launceston Place, W8, and has issue living, Eleanor Jane, b. 1963,—Victoria Lee, b. 1965, Philippa Patricia Alice, b. 1970.

Moriendo vivam.
By dying I shall live.

Sister living—Jane Eve, b. 1930: m. 1963, David William Phillips, of The Old Rectory, Stedham, Midhurst, Sussex, and has issue living, Katherine Elizabeth, b. 1966.

Aunts living (daughters of 4th baronet)—Gladys Mary (Lady's Land, The Plantation, Storrington, Pulborough, Sussex), b. 1892.——Isabel Violet, b. 1893.

Daughters living of 3rd Baronet—Mabel Beatrice (Cobb's Farm, Woodside Green, Bishops Stortford, Herts.), b. 1889: m. 1913, Oswald James Walter Napier, who d. 1966.——Moira Veronica, b. 1901: m. 1924, Cdr. Douglas Samuel Loram, RD, RNR, who d. 1970, and has issue living, Roy (of The Bridge House, Church Rd., Burnham-on-Crouch, Essex), b. 1926: m. 1953, Susan Anne Dennys Parry, da. of the late William Llywelyn Parry de Winton [B. Merthyr], and has issue living, Anthony David John *b.* 1957, William Geoffrey Walter *b.* 1961, Peter Henry James *b.* 1962, Amanda Phillipa Anne *b.* 1954,—Ronald Geoffrey, *RN* (Lynwood, Grange Cross Lane, Newton, W. Kirby, Ches.), *b.* 1927; Lt. (Emergency List): *m.* 1963, Caroline Jennifer Bartlett, and has issue living, Richard William Geoffrey *b.* 1967, Annabel *b.* 1965, Mary Caroline *b.* 1970. *Residence*, Goldray, Butts Ash, Hythe, Southampton.

Widow living of 5th Baronet—ELIZABETH AVERIL (*Elizabeth, Lady Shakerley*), *MBE* (Rotherdown, Petworth, Sussex), da. of the late Edward Gwynne Eardley-Wilmot [*see* Eardley-Wilmot, Bt., colls.]: *m.* 1928, Maj. Sir Cyril Holland Shakerley, 5th baronet, who *d.* 1970.

Collateral Branch living.

Issue of the late Major Ernest Alfred SHAKERLEY-HOWELL, 3rd son of 2nd baronet, *b.* 1866, *d.* 1934: *m.* 1905, Rhoda Mary Louisa, who *d.* 1934, el. da. of the late Francis Buller Howell, J.P., D.L., of Ethy, Lostwithiel, Cornwall [Heywood, Bt., colls.]:—

Peter Francis SHAKERLEY, *O.B.E.*, *b.* 1906 ; ed. at Clifton ; is Hon. Col. (retired), late R.A.; European War 1939-45 in Persia, Iraq, Sicily and N.-W. Europe (despatches twice, O.B.E.) ; O.B.E. (Mil.) 1946 : *m.* 1934, Alison May, da. of the late Alexander Sands, of Aberdeen, and has issue living, Geoffrey Clive Howell, *b.* 1935; ed. at Radley, and at St. Edmund Hall, Oxford (BA): *m.* 1965, Rosanna Ruth, da. of the late Thomas P. Barneby, of The Hill, Duloe, Cornwall, and has issue living, Alastair Justin Charles *b.* 1972, Alison Clare *b.* 1970,—Peter Gavin David *b.* 1950; ed. at Radley; Lt. IG,—Angela Madeleine, *b.* 1938: *m.* 1958, William Trevor Stephens, and has issue living, Richard Gwyn *b.* 1961, John Angelo *b.* 1963, David Paul *b.* 1965, Teresa Madeleine *b.* 1959,—Dawn Michelle Alison, *b.* 1942: *m.* 1965, Peter Joseph Knight, of 20, Hilton Rd., Lynmore, Rotorua, NZ, and has issue living, Timothy William Francis *b.* 1968, Karen Francesca *b.* 1966, Sarah Melody Foye *b.* 1969. *Residence*, Tredudwell Manor, Lanteglos by Fowey, Cornwall. ——Denise Marian, *b.* 1907: *m.* 1935, James Leslie Byrne Perceval who *d.* 1945, and has issue living, Francis James (17, Antill St., Downer, Canberra, Aust.), *b.* 1937: *m.* 1960, Judith Ann, yr. da. of S. F. Spinks, of Langley Burrell, Chippenham, and has issue living, Christian *b.* 1968, Antoinette Mary *b.* 1962, Lucinda Eleanor *b.* 1963,—Antony Ernest (19, Riverside Gdns., Romsey, Hants), *b.* 1938; ed. at Lincoln Coll., Oxford (BA): *m.* 1965, Jennifer, el. da of Charles Mason, of Drakes Court, Fishers Pond, Eastleigh, Hants, and has issue living, Jane Lucinda *b.* 1966,—John Adrian, *b.* 1945,—Sara Mary, *b.* 1942. *Residence*, 7, Waverley Rd., St. Albans, Herts.——Kathleen Dorothy, *b.* 1914: *m.* 1942, Robert Arnold Hall, who *d.* 1962, and has issue living, Peter Arnold, *b.* 1943; ed. at Harrow; Solicitor 1969: *m.* 1971, Gillian Mary Stuart, only da. of John Clark, of Gillan Cove House, Gillan, Manaccan, Cornwall, and has issue living, Nicholas Robert Stuart Arnold *b.* 1974,—Jeremy Arnold (2, Penn House, Maxwell Rd., Beaconsfield, Bucks.), *b.* 1949: *m.* 1971, Julia Rosa, only child of Frank Alexander, of 12, Petworth Court, Reading, Berks.,— Juliet Rosalind, *b.* 1946: *m.* 1971, Christopher Charles Perkins, of 8, Addisland Court, Holland Villas Rd., W14. *Residence*, 14, Hill Lands, Wargrave, Berks.

SHAKESPEARE, Creation (U.K.) 1942, of Lakenham, City of Norwich.

Rt. Hon. Sir GEOFFREY HITHERSAY SHAKESPEARE, 1st *Baronet*, son of the Rev. John Howard Shakespeare, D.D., Sec. of Baptist Union of Great Britain and Ireland; *b.* Sept. 23rd, 1893; ed. at Highgate Sch., and at Emmanuel Coll., Camb. (B.A. 1921, LL.B. 1921, M.A. 1922) ; Bar. Middle Temple 1922 ; European War 1914-19 in Gallipoli and Egypt as Capt. 5th Batn. Norfolk Regt. (1914-15 star, two medals) : was Private Sec. to Prime Min. (Rt. Hon. David Lloyd George, P.C., O.M., M.P.) 1921-2, a Junior Lord of the Treasury and Ch. Whip Liberal National Party 1931-2, Parliamentary Sec., Min. of Health 1932-6, and to Board of Education 1936-7, Parliamentary and Financial Sec. to Admiralty 1937-40, Parliamentary Sec. to Depart. of Overseas Trade April to May 1940, and Under-Sec. of State for Dominion Affairs and Chm. of Children's Overseas Reception Board May 1940 to March 1942 ; Pres. of So. of British Gas Industries 1953-54; Vice-Chm. of Westminster Hospital 1948-63; Chm. of Industrial Co-Partnership Assocn. 1958-68; Chm. Council of the Baronetage 1972-75; MP for Wellingborough (*L*) 1922-23, and Norwich 1929-45; PC 1945: *m.* 1st, 1926, Aimèe Constance, who *d.* 1950, da. of Walter Loveridge, of Codsall, Staffordshire, and widow of Com. Sir Thomas Fisher, K.B.E.; 2ndly, 1952, Elizabeth, el. da. of the late Brig.-Gen. Robert William Hare, C.M.G., D.S.O. [*see* E. Listowel, colls.], and has issue by 1st marriage.

Arms—Or, on a bend between in chief a portcullis and in base an anchor sable, a spear of the field. **Crest**—In front of a portcullis sable an eagle rising, grasping with the dexter claw a spear or, barbed argent.

Residence—Flat 6, Great Ash, Lubbock Road, Chislehurst, Kent.

Son living—By 1st m.—WILLIAM GEOFFREY (Manor Cottage, Stoke Mandeville, Bucks.; MCC, BMA Club), *b.* Oct. 12th, 1927: ed. at Radley and at Clare Coll., Camb. (MA, MB and BChir); Diploma in Child Health: *m.* 1964, Susan Mary, da. of A. Douglas Raffel, of Colombo, Ceylon, and has issue living, Thomas William, *b.* May 11th, 1966,—James Douglas Geoffrey, *b.* 1971.

SHARP, Creation (U.K.) 1920, of Heckmondwike, West Riding, co. York.

I strive till I overcome.

Sir MILTON REGINALD SHARP, 3rd *Baronet*; *b.* Nov. 21st, 1909; *s.* his father, *Sir* MILTON, 1941; ed. at Shrewsbury, and at Trin. Hall, Camb.; is Major R.A.: *m.* 1st, 1935, Dorothy Mary, younger da. of Bernard R. McCarrick, of Kilglass House, Ballina, Ireland; 2ndly, 1951, Marie-Louise de Vignon, of Paris.

Arms—Azure, on a fesse engrailed argent between two plates, a torteaux between two pheons gules. **Crest**—In front of a pheon sable, an eagle's head erased azure, charged with a cross-crosslet or.

Address—c/o Messrs. Redfearns, Midland Bank Chambers, Heckmondwike, Yorks.

Sir Milton Sheridan Sharp, 1st Bt., was Chm. Bradford Dyers Asso. Ltd.

SHARP, Creation (U.K.) 1922, of Warden Court, Maidstone, Kent.

Victory in truth.

Sir EDWARD HERBERT SHARP, 3rd *Baronet*; *b.* Dec. 3rd, 1927; *s.* his father, *Sir* HERBERT EDWARD, 1936; ed. at Haileybury; *m.* 1949, Beryl Kathleen, da. of L. Simmons-Green, of 273, Langmore Road, Shirley, Warwickshire, and has issue.

Arms—Argent, on a fesse indented between two falcons' heads erased sable, three pheons or. **Crest**—Upon a mount vert a falcon rising proper, belled and resting the dexter claw upon a pheon or.

Residence—

Sons living—ADRIAN, *b.* Sept. 17th, 1951.——Owen, *b.* 1956.

Daughter living—Terry, *b.* 1950.

Widow living of 2nd Baronet—RAY ALICE MARY, da. of the late Frederick George Bloomfield, of Ealing, W.5; *m.* 1st, 1927, as his second wife, Sir Herbert Edward Sharp, 2nd baronet, who *d.* 1936; 2ndly, 1937, Kenneth Brian Downey, of Studley Lodge, Pine Rd., Tokai, Cape Province, S. Africa.

Collateral Branch living.

Issue of the late Wilfred James Sharp, 2nd son of 1st baronet, *b.* 1880, *d.* 1945: *m.* 1909, Ada Frances, who *d.* 1936, da. of George Meek, of Beckenham:—
Edward Harold Wilfred, *b.* 1910; Past Chm. of Edward Sharp & Sons, Ltd., Manufacturing Confectioners. *Residence*, Thatch House, Chart Sutton, Kent.——John Rayner Edgar (The Old Mill, Sutton Valence, Maidstone) *b.* 1917.

The 1st baronet, Sir Edward, was Founder and Chm. of Edward Sharp & Sons, Ltd., manufacturing confectioners of Maidstone.

SHAW, Creation (U.K.) 1821, of Bushy Park, Dublin.

Te ipsum nosce.
Know thyself.

Sir ROBERT SHAW, 7th *Baronet*; *b.* Jan. 31st, 1925; *s.* his father, *Lt.-Col. Sir* ROBERT DE VERE, MC, 1969; ed. at Harrow, and Oklahoma (BS) and Missouri (MS) Univs.; MEIC and Professional Engineer (Alberta); Lt. RN (ret.); 1939-45 War in NW Europe, and W. Pacific: *m.* 1954, Jocelyn Mary, da. of the late Andrew McGuffie, of Mbabane, Swaziland, and has issue.

Arms—Or, on a chevron engrailed sable, between three eagles displayed of the second, as many trefoils slipped of the first. **Crest**—A hart's head couped sable, transfixed through the neck with an arrow or, feathered argent.

Residence—234, 40th Av., Calgary, Alberta, Canada. *Club*, Alberta United Services Institute (Calgary).

Daughters living—Grania, *b.* 1955.——Reinet, *b.* 1960.

Collateral Branches living.

Issue of the late Capt. John Frederick de Vere Shaw, Kenya Regt., younger son of 6th baronet, *b.* 1930, *d.* 1960: *m.* 1955, Penelope Ann, who *m.* 2ndly, 1970, Hougham Robert Mills (PO Box 167, Kokstad, E. Griqualand, S. Africa), da. of Maj. Denis William Powlett Milbank [*see* Milbank, Bt.]:—
CHARLES DE VERE, *b.* March 1st, 1957.——Jane Frances, *b.* 1958.——Ann Vivian, *b.* 1960.

Issue of the late Lieut.-Col. Frederick Charleton Shaw, O.B.E., 2nd son of 5th baronet, *b.* 1895, *d.* (on active ser. in Germany) 1945 : *m.* 1922, Angela (SEWALL) (of 8, Ormonde Gate, S.W.3), da. of the late Ricardo de Acosta :—
Mercedes Eile, *b.* 1926: *m.* 1956, Capt. Miles Matthew Lee Hudson, 12th R. Lancers, of The Priors Farm, Mattingly Green, Basingstoke, and has issue living, Mark John Frederick, *b.* 1957,—Peter Charles, *b.* 1960,—Richard Miles, *b.* 1966,—Veronica Mary, *b.* 1958.

Grandchildren of the late Maj.-Gen. George Shaw, C.B., 2nd son of 3rd baronet:—
Issue of the late Frederick Shaw, *b.* 1850, *d.* 1928 : *m.* 1873, Ella Jane, da. of William Willis, of U.S.A.:—
Cora Desfontaines: *m.* 1909, Charles Abner Howard, LL.D. *Residence,* 2335, South Cottage St., Salem, Oregon, U.S.A.

Issue of the late Col. George Jocelyn Shaw, *b.* 1857, *d.* 1928: *m.* 1883, Elizabeth Harriette, who *d.* 1956, da. of Col. Horatio Samuel Court, formerly M.S.C. :—
Percy Jocelyn, *b.* 1893 ; European War 1914-19 with Leicestershire Regt., European War 1940-45 with R.A.P.C. : *m.* 1931, Ivy Muriel Seager. *Residence,* Meadows, Foam Court Waye, Ferring, Sussex.

Grandson of the late Lt.-Col. Wilkinson Jocelyn Shaw, 5th son of 3rd baronet:—
Issue of the late Major Jocelyn Frederick de Fonblanque Shaw, *b.* 1874, *d.* 1936 : *m.* 1921, May Alberta, who *d.* 1930, da. of the late Robert Cecil Kenward:—
Jocelyn Frederick Basil, *b.* 1923; ed. at Wellington King's Coll., London, and Miami Univ.; Consulting Engineer: *m.* 1964, Carolyn Ann, da. of the late Samuel Bexton Guynes. of Waco, Texas, and has issue living, Jocelyn Robert Guynes, *b.* 1965,—John Frederick Darin, *b.* 1967,—Edward Henry David, *b.* 1969.

Granddaughter of the late Charles Shaw, Q.C., 5th son of 1st baronet:—
Issue of the late William Shaw, *b.* 1857, *d.* 1939: *m.* 1889, Roxanna Massie, da. of James Henry Bowles:—
Emily Newell, *b.* 1902 : *m.* 1921. Charles Franklin Jenness, and has issue living, Charles Franklin, *b.* 1924,—Stuart Barton, *b.* 1928,—Barbara Claire, *b.* 1932. *Residence,* 5621, Randall Avenue, Richmond, Virginia, U.S.A.

The 1st baronet, Sir Robert, sat in the Irish Parliament for New Ross, and for Dublin in the Imperial Parliament 1804-26; the 3rd baronet, who was Recorder of Dublin 1828-76, and a P.C. of Ireland, sat as M.P. for Dublin (C) 1830-32, and for the University of Dublin 1832-48.

SHAW, Creation (U.K.) 1908, of Wolverhampton, co. Stafford. [Extinct 1942.]

Sir (THEODORE FREDERICK) CHARLES EDWARD SHAW, 1st and last *Baronet.*

Daughter living of 1st Baronet—Vera Stafford, *b.* 1901 : *m.* 1922, Charles Bradshaw Shard, formerly Lieut. 14th Hussars, and has issue living, Charles William George, *b.* 1927,—Johane Dawson, *b.* 1925. *Residence,*

BEST-SHAW, Creation (E.) 1665, of Eltham, Kent.

Sir JOHN JAMES KENWARD BEST-SHAW, 9th *Baronet ; b.* June 11th, 1895 ; *s.* his father, *Rev. Sir* CHARLES JOHN MONSON *SHAW,* 1922 ; ed. at Cheam Sch. ; Com. R.N. (retired) ; European War 1914-19 (1914 star, two medals), European War 1939-45 (two medals) ; is a Lay Guardian of the Shrine of Our Lady of Walsingham, and an O.St.J. ; High Sheriff of Kent 1961-2 ; assumed by Roy. Licence 1956 the additional surname of Best before that of Shaw and the Arms of Best quarterly with those of Shaw : *m.* 1921, Elizabeth Mary Theodora, da. of Sir Robert Heywood Hughes, 12th Bt. (*cr.* 1773), and has issue.

Arms—Quarterly, 1st and 4th argent, a chevron between three fusils ermines, *Shaw ;* 2nd and 3rd sable, a cinquefoil pierced, and in chief two cross-crosslets fitchée or, *Best.* **Crests**—1st, six arrows interlaced, saltirewise or, tied together with belt gules, the buckle and pendant or ; 2nd, issuing out of a mural crown or, a demi-ostrich argent holding in the beak a cross-crosslet fitchée or.

Residence—Boxley Abbey, Maidstone, Kent. *Club*—Naval and Military.

Sons living—JOHN MICHAEL ROBERT, *b.* Sept. 28th, 1924 ; ed. at Lancing, at Sheffield Univ., and at Hertford Coll., Oxford (B.A. 1950, M.A. 1954) ; formerly Capt. Queen's Own Roy. W. Kent Regt.; Roy. Federation of Malaya Police Force 1950-8 ; European War 1942-5 (three medals) : *m.* 1960, Jane Gordon, da. of Alexander Gordon Guthrie, of Hampton Court House, Farningham, Kent, and has issue living, Thomas Joshua, *b.* 1965,—Samuel Stevenson, *b.* 1971,—Lucy Ann, *b.* 1961. *Residence,* The Stone House, Boxley, Maidstone, Kent. *Club,* Royal Commonwealth Society.——Charles John Hughes, *b.* 1928: *m.* 1971, Carol Mary, da. of J. M. Drew (7, Kingsmead Rd., Bishop's Stortford, Herts.), and has issue living, Helen Mary Elizabeth, *b.* 1972.——Stephen Bosanquet (Old Harbourland, Boxley, Maidstone, Kent), *b.* 1935:

m. 1964, Elizabeth Annette Freda, yst. da. of the late Gerald Baldwin Hayward, MBE, of Athens, and has issue living, James Robert Hawley, *b.* 1965,—Hugh Edward Gerald, *b.* 1975,—Louisa Margaret Aylmer *b.* 1967.

Daughters living—Mary Elisabeth Helen, *b.* 1922; a JP of Kent: *m.* 1st, 1943, Patrick Henry Coates, late Capt. RA, who *d.* 1949; 2ndly, 1968, John Melliar Adams-Beck (Southfield, Charing, Kent), and has issue living, (by 1st m.) David Carlyon (Holm House, Bisterne Closes, Burley, nr. Ringwood, Hants.), *m.* 1944: *m.* 1970, Lavinia Jane, da. of Alan O'Conner-Fenton, and has issue living, Emma Mary *b.* 1973, Alice Julia *b.* 1975,—Simon Patrick, *b.* 1948.——Julia Aylmer, *b.* 1923; 1939-45 War in WRNS.——Hermione Theodora, *b.* 1926.——Martha Mary, *b.* 1934.

Collateral Branches living.

Grandson of the late Rev. Charles John Kenward Shaw, son of the late Capt., Charles Shaw, R.N., 2nd son of 5th baronet :—

Issue of the late Henry Hawley Shaw, *b.* 1862, *d.* 1897: *m.* 1893, Agneta Maud, who *d.* 1933, da. of the late Rev. Robert Stammers Tabor, of 64, St. George's Square, S.W. :—

John Charles Hawley (The Lawn, Holybourne, Alton, Hants), *b.* 1895; HM Civil Ser. (ret.); late R. Signals: *m.* 1948, Elsie Anne, who *d.* 1959, da. of Frederick Walker, of Reading, and widow of H. S. Brown.

Grandchildren of the late Rev. Robert John Shaw, son of the late Rev. Robert William Shaw, 5th son of 5th baronet:—

Issue of the late Lewis Hugh de Visme Shaw, *b.* 1865, *d.* 1931: *m.* 1901, Edith Mary, who *d.* 1929, da. of the late Capt. John Smyth Nelson, S. Staffordshire Regt. :—

Horatia Edith de Visme (Nazareth House, Queen Wilhelmina Av., Waterkloof, Pretoria 0002, S. Africa), *b.* 1902.

Issue of the late Henry Augustus Gregory Shaw, *b.* 1875, *d.* 1954 : *m.* 1925, Eileen, el. da. of Charles William Howard:—

John Gregory Monson de Visme, *b.* 1930: *m.* 1959, Helene Maud, da. of Cyril Ernest Kerslake Baker of co. Down.——Robert Henry Barnardiston de Visme (11, Eccleston Cres., Bryanston, Sandton, Transvaal, S. Africa), *b.* 1932: *m.* 1961, Valerie Ann, only da. of B. R. Lobb, of Johannesburg and London, and has issue living, Philip Gregory de Visme, *b.* 1970,—Christine Ann de Visme, *b.* 1965.——Eileen Ann de Visme, *b.* 1928: *m.* 1952, Alan Baker, and has issue living, Robert Alan, *b.* 1960,—James Paul, *b.* 1963,—Catherine Ann, *b.* 1953.

Sir John, the 1st baronet, having rendered great service to Charles I. during the Rebellion, and having advanced several sums of money to Charles II. during that King's exile was after the Restoration appointed one of the Farmers of the Customs.

Shaw-Stewart, see Stewart.

SHEFFIELD, Creation (G.B.) 1755, of Normanby, Lincolnshire.

Blandly, but determinedly.

Sir ROBERT ARTHUR SHEFFIELD, 7th *Baronet ; b.* Oct. 18th, 1905; *s.* his father, *Sir* BERKELEY DIGBY GEORGE, 1946.

Arms—Argent, a chevron engrailed between two garbs in chief gules, and in base a sheaf of arrows proper, banded also gules. **Crest**—A boar's head erased at the neck or between two arrows points downwards proper. *Residence*—The Old Rectory, Laverstoke, Whitchurch, Hants.

Brothers living—(EDMUND CHARLES) REGINALD, *b.* Oct. 24th, 1908 ; ed. at Eton ; is a J.P. and D.L. ; sometime Major Roy. Armoured Corps (T.A.) ; was High Sheriff of Lincolnshire 1959 ; European War 1939-44 in North Africa and Italy (wounded, despatches) : *m.* 1931, Nancie Miriel Denise, da. of Edward Roland Soames, of 63, Chester Square, S.W., and widow of Lieut.-Com. Glen Kidston [Astley, Bt.], and has issue living, Reginald Adrian Berkeley (17, Lansdowne Cres., W11), *b.* 1946: *m.* 1969, Annabel Lucy Veronica, da. of Timothy Angus Jones, of 40, Albert St., NW [see B. Clifford of Chudleigh, colls.], and has issue living, Samantha Gwendoline *b.* 1971, Emily *b.* 1973,— Serena Mary, *b.* 1932,—Fiona Mary *(Hon. Mrs. Robert C. R. Hoyer Millar)*, *b.* 1939: *m.* 1961, Hon. Robert Charles Reneke Hoyer Millar, el. son of 1st Baron Inchyra. *Residences*, Sutton Park, Sutton-on-the-Forest, York; 56, Montague Sq., W1.——John Vincent, *b.* 1913; ed. at Eton, and Magdalene Coll., Camb. (MA); is an OStJ; High Sheriff of Lincs. 1944-45: *m.* 1st., 1936, Anne Margaret, who *d.* 1969, da. of Sir Lionel Lawson Faudel-Faudel-Phillips, 3rd Bt.; 2ndly, 1971, France Mary Agnes, da. of Brig.-Gen. Goland Clarke, and has issue living (by 1st m.), John Julian Lionel George (Freefolk House, Whitchurch, Hants), *b.* 1938; ed. at Eton, and at Camb. Univ.: *m.* 1961, Carolyn Alexandra, da. of Brig. Sir Alexander Abel Smith, of Quenington Rectory, Cirencester, Glos., [D. Somerset, colls.], and has issue living, John David, *b.* 1963, Simon Robert Alexander, *b.* 1964, Lionel Julian *b.* 1969, Nicola Elizabeth Anne *b.* 1973,—Jane Armyne, *b.* 1937: *m.* 1956, Jocelyn Edward Greville Stevens, of Testbourne, Longparish, Andover, Hants., and has issue living, Charles Greville Vincent *b.* 1957, Rupert Jocelyn Sebastian *b.* 1964, Pandora Anne *b.* 1959, Melinda Armyne, *b.* 1972,—Diana Anne, *b.* 1942: *m.* 1966, David Mark Norman, and has issue living, Jonathan Mark Ronald *b.* 1972, Anna Helen *b.* 1967, Isabella Julia *b.* 1971,—Angela Margaret, *b.* 1947: *m.* 1966 (Anthony) Richard Brocas Burrows, of The Hall, Barham, Ipswich, and has issue living, Edward Brocas *b.* 1975, Carey Jane *b.* 1968, Joanna Molly Anne *b.* 1969, Angela Petra *b.* 1972. *Residence*, Laverstoke House, Whitchurch, Hants.

Collateral Branches living.

Issue of the late Maj. George Berkeley Sheffield, 3rd son of 6th baronet, *b.* 1910, *d.* 1968: *m.* 1st, 1935, Psyche Isabel Joan, who *d.* 1945, da. of the late Capt. Edward Altham, CB, RN; 2ndly, 1949, the Hon. Agnes Wilson McGowan (Ramsden House, Ramsden, Oxon., OX7 3AX), da. of 1st Baron McGowan, and formerly wife of Maj. Dermot Ralph Daly:—

(By 2nd m.) Laura Diana, *b.* 1949: *m.* 1969, George William Pilkington, of 58, Chester Row, SW1, and has issue living, Harry George, *b.* 1971,—Martha Mary, *b.* 1972.——Davina Mary, *b.* 1951.

Grandson of the late Capt. John Charles Sheffield, 3rd son of 4th baronet:—

Issue of the late Robert Stoney OLIPHANT-SHEFFIELD, *b.* 1864, *d.* 1937, having assumed the additional surname of Oliphant 1901 : *m.* 1901, Mary Beatrice, who *d.* **1933,** da. of the late G. H. Oliphant Ferguson, of Broadfield House, Southwaite, Carlisle :—
Edmund George, *b.* 1913 ; ed. at Harrow ; formerly Lieut. R.N.V.R.: *m.* **1939,** Eva May Mulville, and has issue living, John Robert (Southwaite Hill, Southwaite, Carlisle), *b.* **1941;** ed. at Harrow: *m.* 1967, Valerie Jean Towill, and has issue living, Edward John *b.* 1968, Andrew George *b.* 1970 —Richard Charles (The New Cottage, Achara, Duror, Argyll), *b.* 1944; ed. at Harrow: *m.* 1st, 1966 (m. diss. 1972), Cheryl Mary Eleanor, da. of David McNeil Williams; 2ndly, 1972, Caroline Alison, da. of Everett Ryshworth Unwin, of The Court House, Lelant, Cornwall,—George Henry Oliphant, *b.* 1948; ed. at Rannock: *m.* 1974, Christine Holdsworth. *Residence,* Broadfield, Southwaite, Carlisle.

Grandson of the late Rev. Frank Sheffield, 5th son of 4th baronet (ante):—
Issue of the late Rev. Arthur Digby Sheffield, *b.* 1897, *d.* 1975: *m.* 1932, Alice Katharine (Myles Down, 22, Crawley Hill, Camberley, Surrey, GU15 2BZ), da. of the late Donald Malcolm Scott, of 8, Chandos St., W1.:—
Nigel Digby (Rookery Farm, Earl Soham, Woodbridge, Suffolk), *b.* 1933; ed. at Eton and Ch. Ch., Oxford (MA): *m.* 1960, Helen Jane Ann Russell, el. da. of Lt. Col. Bernard Russell French, DSO, of Edgeworth, Glos., and has issue living, Timothy John Digby *b.* 1966,—Ann Margot, *b.* 1963,— Susan Margaret, *b.* 1965.

The 1st baronet, Sir,Charles Sheffield (originally Herbert), was an illegitimate son of John Sheffield **1st Duke** of Normanby and Buckingham ; he inherited the estates of his legitimate brother Edmond **last Duke** of Buckingham. The 6th baronet, Sir Berkeley Digby George, sat as M.P. for N. Lindsey, **or Brigg, Div.** of Lincolnshire (C) 1907-10 and 1922-9, and was High Sheriff of Lincolnshire 1905.

SHELLEY, Creation (E.) 1611, of Michelgrove, Sussex.

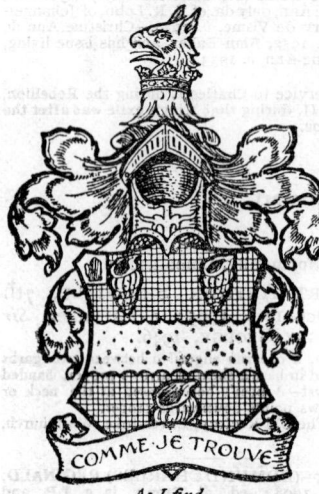

As I find.

COMME·JE·TROUVE

Sir JOHN FREDERICK SHELLEY, 10th *Baronet ; b.* Oct. 14th, 1884 ; *s.* his father, *Sir* JOHN, **1931**; ed. at Winchester, and at Camb. Univ. ; late Major 96th (Roy. Devon Yeo.) Brig. R.A. (T.A.), and a D.L. and J.P. for **Devonshire (High Sheriff 1938)** : *m.* **1st,** 1912, Nora Coleridge, who *d.* 1953, da. of the late Francis James Coleridge Boles, J.P., of Redcliffe, Exmouth, S. Devo n; 2ndly, 1953, Marianne, who *d.* 1974, da. of the late Major Wolstan Francis, Duke of Cornwall's L.I., and widow of Capt. John Theodore Martin Mee, and has issue by 1st marriage.

Arms—Sable a fesse, engrailed, between three whelks or. Crest—A griffin's head erased, beaked argent, and ducally gorged or.

Residence,—Shobrooke House, Crediton, Devon.

Grandsons living—[Issue of the late John Shelley, el. son of 10th baronet; *b.* 1915, *d.* 1974: *m.* 1940, Dorothy Irvine (Shobrooke Mill, Crediton, Devon), el. da. of Arthur Irvine Ingram, solicitor, of Bath] JOHN RICHARD (Molford House, 27, South St., S. Molton, Devon), *b.* Jan. 18th, 1943; ed. at King's Sch., Bruton, and Trin. Coll. (MA); MB, BChir, DObstRCOG: *m.* 1965, Clare, da. of Claud Bicknell, OBE, Law Commr. of Newcastle, and has issue living, Diana, *b.* 1970,—Helen, *b.* 1972.——Thomas Henry (55, Prince's Rd., Felixstowe), *b.* 1945; ed. at King's Sch., Bruton, and Trin. Coll., Camb. (BA): *m.* 1970, Katherine Mary Holton, and has issue living, Kirsten Rachel Irvine, *b.* 1973,— Victoria Juliet, *b.* 1974.

Son living—By 1st m.—Philip Spencer (Shobrooke Park, Crediton, Devon), *b.* 1921; late FO RAF: *m.* 1st, 1947 (m. diss. 1963), Pamela Grace, da. of the late Lt.-Col. Henry Nigel Kermack, RE; 2ndly, 1968, Elizabeth Philippa, da. of Leonard George Edward Llewelyn, of Nairobi, and has issue living (by 1st m.), Nigel Antony, *b.* 1948,—Malcolm Frederick, *b.* 1953,—Marian Pamela, *b.* 1950,—(by 2nd m.) Nora Elizabeth, *b.* 1969, Gillian Philippa, *b.* 1971.

Daughters living—By 1st m.—Mary Nora, *b.* 1913 : *m.* 1940, Maj. Robin Paige, MC, TD, who *d.* 1969, and has issue living, Michael Robert (Ings Farm, Belchford, Horncastle, Lincs.), *b.* 1941: *m.* 1966, Patricia Margaret Appleby, and has issue living, Nicholas Robert *b.* 1972, Catherine Mary *b.* 1968, Sarah Jane *b.* 1969,—Timothy John (twin), *b.* 1941,—Christopher David (Ivanhoe, Hollins Spring Rd., Dronfield, Sheffield, S18 6US), *b.* 1945; Capt. RE (V): *m.* 1970, Cynthia Ann Ison. *Residence,* Greycot, Sudbury Rd., Lavenham, Suffolk.——Francis Elizabeth, *b.* 1914: *m.* 1938, the Rev. Henry John Allen Rusbridger, of St. Crispins, Brampford, Speke, Exeter, and has issue living, Peter Henry James, *b.* 1941: *m.* 1969, Geraldine Johnston, and has issue living, Charles Peter James *b.* 1971,—Elizabeth Jean, *b.* 1939: *m.* 1963, the Rev. M. Bowles, of Stanmore Rectory, Middlesex, and has issue living, Jeremy Michael *b.* 1966, Catherine Elizabeth *b.* 1964,—Margaret Anne (twin), *b.* 1941: *m.* 1965, Arthur William Frederick Sacheverel Pulford, and has issue living, Claire *b.* 1966.——Gillian Hester, *b.* 1918: *m.* 1949, Capt. Michael William Howard, MC, Devonshire Regt. [*see* E. Carlisle, colls.]. *Residence,* The Kennels, Sampford Spiney, Devon.

Collateral Branches living.

Issue of the late Vice-Adm. Richard BENYON, CB, CBE (assumed by deed poll 1964, and by Roy. Licence 1967 (for himself and el. son) the surname of Benyon in lieu of Shelley), yr. son of 9th baronet; *b.* 1892; *d.* 1968: *m.* 1929, Eve Alice (The Lambdens, Beenham, Berks.), da. of the late Rt. Rev. Lord William Rupert Ernest Cecil, DD, 65th Lord Bishop of Exeter [*see* M. Salisbury, colls.]:—
William Richard BENYON, *MP* (Englefield House, Reading), *b.* 1930; Lt. RN (Reg. Reserve); MP for Buckingham (C) since 1970: *m.* 1957, Elizabeth Ann, yr. da. of the late Vice-Adm. Ronald Hamilton Curzon Halifax, CB, CBE [Hughes, Bt., *cr.* 1773], and has issue living, Richard Henry Ronald, *b.* 1960,—Edward William, *b.* 1962,—Catherine Rose Ingrid, *b.* 1958,—Mary Elizabeth, *b.* 1965,—Susannah Eve, *b.* 1969.——James Edward SHELLEY (Mays Cottage, Ramsdell, Hants), *b.* 1932: *m.* 1956, Judith E., da. of George Grubb, and has issue living, Timothy James, *b.* 1966,—Philip John (twin), *b.* 1966,—Alison Jane, *b.* 1959,—Penelope Sarah, *b.* 1960. ——Andrew Thomas Rupert SHELLEY, *b.* 1933; Maj. R. Green Jackets: *m.* 1971, Joanna M., only da. of Adm. Sir (Randolph Stewart) Gresham Nicholson, KBE, CB, DSO, DSC, and has

issue living, Sarah, *b.* 1974.——David Robert SHELLEY, *b.* 1937: *m.* 1971, Elisabeth Rhoda, yr.
da. of Gilbert Balfour, and has issue living, Peter, *b.* 1972,—Jonathan, *b.* 1974.

Grandchildren of the late Spencer Shelley (*b.* 1843) (infra):—
Issue of the late Spencer Shelley, *b.* 1878, *d.* 1941: *m.* 1917, Gladys, who *d.* 1947, da. of
E. Mulligan, of Sydney, N.S. Wales:—
Spencer, *b.* 1920; sometime Lieut. RNVR; a JP for Glos.: *m.* 1946, Maureen, da. of Commodore
Trevor Lewis Owen, OBE, RD, and has issue living, Elizabeth Grey, *b.* 1948,—Anna Frances, *b.*
1950, Katherine Jane, *b.* 1954. *Residence,* Huntley Court, Huntley, Glos.——Charles Francis,
b. 1925, sometime Sub-Lt. RNVR: *m.* 1951, Elizabeth Jane, only child of the late Brig. Sir
Francis Smith Reid, CBE, and has issue living, Sarah Jane, *b.* 1952,—Julia Frances, *b.* 1954,
—Caroline Ruth, *b.* 1957. *Residence,* Berden Hall, Bishops Stortford.——Frederick Norman
(twin) (14, Crest Av., Balwyn, Mel., Aust.); CEng.; MIMechE: *m.* 1958, Ruth Mary, only da. of
the late Rowland Colley Skitt, of Barakat, Sudan, and has issue living, Stephen Spencer, *b.* 1959,—
Philip Norman, *b.* 1960,—William Rowland, *b.* 1964,—Anne Lucy, *b.* 1963.——Cynthia Kathleen,
b. 1921, sometime in WRNS: *m.* 1943, Michael Richard Lloyd Hayes, DL, Lt. RN (ret.), and has
issue living, Sylvia Josephine Ruth (*Hon. Mrs. G. Andrew Lawson Johnson*), *b.* 1945: *m.* 1968, the
Hon. George Andrew Lawson-Johnston, of Hobbs Green Farm, Odell, Beds., [*see* B. Luke],—
Frances Patricia Jane, *b.* 1948: *m.* 1971, Julian Seddon, of 45, Rowallen Rd., off Munster Rd.,
SW6,—Ann Wendy Felicity, *b.* 1950: *m.* 1972, Peter A. Cartwright, of 25, River Green, Hamble,
Hants. *Residence,* Four Ashes, Cosheston, Pembroke Dock, Dyfed, SA72 4TX.

Granddaughter of the late Spencer Shelley (*b.* 1813), 4th son of 6th baronet—
Issue (by 1st marriage) of the late Spencer Shelley, *b.* 1843, *d.* 1932: *m.* 1st, 1876, Mary
Renny, who *d.* 1914, da. of Thomas Watson; 2ndly, 1916, Gertrude (Chita), who *d.*
1942, da. of W. H. H. Hutchinson, formerly of Cottingham Hall, near Hull:—
Margaret Ruth: *m.* 1st, 1915, William Renny Watson, Nigerian Marine Ser., who *d.* 1918;
2ndly, 1921, the Rev. Neville Dundas, who *d.* 1935. *Residence,* Comrie, Perthshire.

Thomas Shelley was Lord of the Manor of Shelley, Kent, *temp.* Edward I. This family can
prove seven royal descents in unbroken legitimate lines from Henry III. and Edward I. Michel-
grove, the seat of the Shelley family for more than 300 years, was sold at the end of the 18th century,
to the Duke of Norfolk, whose family later demolished it. Sir John Shelley, 9th Bt., was High
Sheriff of Devon 1895.

SHEPPERSON, Creation (U.K.) 1945, of Upwood, Co. Huntingdon. [Extinct 1949.]

Sir ERNEST WHITTOME SHEPPERSON, 1st and last *Baronet.*

Daughters living of 1st Baronet—Rosemary Jane, *b.* 1921; ed. at Newnham Coll., Camb. (B.A.,
1943):, *m.* 1947, Eric Arthur North Whitehead, of Merrow Down, The Common, Kings Langley,
Herts. and has issue living, Simon Ambrose, *b.* 1948.—Margaret Loveday, *b.* 1948.——Mary,
Elizabeth, *b.* 1927: *m.* 1st, 1945, Ian Loudon Spofforth (MA Oxon), late Fl. Lt. RAF, who *d.*
1964; 2ndly, 1968, Brig. Henry Ralph Orton, of Wangfield Farm House, Curbridge, Southampton, SO 32DA, and has issue living (by 1st m.), Timothy Markham Shepperson, *b.* 1947,—
Sally Jane, *b.* 1950,—Belinda Anne, *b.* 1952,—Virginia Elizabeth, *b.* 1956.

Sherston-Baker, see Baker.

SHIFFNER, Creation (U.K.) 1818, of Coombe, Sussex.

Sir HENRY DAVID SHIFFNER, 8th
Baronet; b. Feb. 2nd, 1930; *s.* his father, *Major
Sir* HENRY BURROWS, *O.B.E.,* 1941; ed. at
Rugby, and at Trin. Hall, Camb.: *m.* 1st,
1951 (m. diss. 1956), Dorothy, da. of W. G.
Jackson, of Coventry; 2ndly, 1957 (m. diss.
1970), Beryl, da. of George Milburn, of Salt-
dean, Sussex; 3rdly, 1971, Joaquina Rames
Lopez, of Madrid, Spain, and has issue by
1st and 2nd m.

Arms—Azure, a bend sinister, in chief two estoiles in
like bend or; in base, the end and stock of an anchor
gold, issuing from waves of the sea proper. *Crest*—An
estoile or, between the rays six annulets azure.

Club—Royal Automobile.

Daughters living—By 1st marriage—Elizabeth Marilyn,
b. 1953.——By 2nd marriage—Linda Mary, *b.* 1957.
Aunt living (daughter of 5th baronet)—Elizabeth Mary,
b. Dec. 1894 : *m.* 1st, 1915, Major Gerard David Tidmarsh, MC, late RA, who *d.* (as a result of active ser.)
1944; 2ndly, 1950, Lt.-Col. Osmund John Francis Fooks, late 14/20th H., who *d.* 1970, and has
issue living, (by 1st m.) Betty Mary, *b.* 1916: *m.* 1945, Alexander Leon Suchanek, of 23, South-
town, Dartmouth, Devon, and has issue living, Silas Waldo Gerard *b.* 1951, Konrad Aleksander
Bridger *b.* 1952. *Residence,* Swithewood, Horsted Keynes, Sussex.
Widows living of 6th and 7th Baronets—SYBIL HELEN (*Baroness Paget of Northampton*), yst. da. of
the late Sills Clifford Gibbons, of Scaynes Hill, Sussex: *m.* 1st, 1918, Sir John Bridger Shiffner,
6th baronet, who *d.* (killed in action during European War) 1918; 2ndly, 1922, Victor Basil John
Seely [now 4th Bt.], from whom she obtained a divorce 1931; 3rdly, 1931, Baron Paget of
Northampton, QC [Life Baron], of Lubenham Lodge, Market Harborough, Leics., and 9, Grosvenor
Cottages, SW1.——MARGARET MARY (*Mary, Lady Shiffner*), da. of the late Sir Ernest Arthur
Gowers, GCB, GBE: *m.* 1929, Maj. Sir Henry Burrows Shiffner, 7th Bt., who *d.* (killed in action)
1941. *Residence,* Rondle Wood, Liphook, Hants.

Collateral Branches living.

Grandchildren of the late George Bridger Shiffner (infra):—
Issue of the late Capt. George Edward Shiffner, *b.* 1901, *d.* 1956: *m.* 1935, Kathleen
Patricia (of Cutt Mill, near Watlington, Oxon), da. of Lieut.-Col. Sir Edward Boscawen
Frederick, C.V.O., 9th Bt.:—

GEORGE FREDERICK (of 14, Coggeshall Rd., Braintree, Essex), b. Aug. 3rd, 1936; ed. at Wellington: m. 1961, Dorothea Helena Cynthia, da. of the late T. H. McLean, and has issue living, Michael George Edward, b. 1963,——Penelope Ann Dorothy, b. 1962.——Susan Georgiana, b. 1938: m. 1963, Henry Pickup, of Bosworths, Slaugham, Haywards Heath, Sussex.

   Issue of the late George Bridger Shiffner, 2nd son of 4th baronet, b. 1866, d. 1949:
     m. 1893, Georgiana Mary, who d. 1931, da. of the late Lt.-Col. W. J. Scarlett, of Gigha, Argyllshire:—
John Scarlett, b. 1910; Capt. R.N.; 1939-45 War (despatches): m. 1940, Margaret Harriet, da. of the late George Tullis, of Strathenry, Leslie, Fife, and has issue living, John Robert (Millies House, Weston, Hawthorn Wilts.), b. 1941; BSc London; Lt.-Cdr. RN: m. 1969, Rosemary Anne Creyghton, da. of Brig. Alfred Tilly, CBE, and has issue living, John Edward b. 1971, Caroline Mary Tilly b. 1973,—Charles Tullis, b. 1944; ed. at St. Andrews Univ. (MA),—Priscilla Mary Scarlett, b. 1949. Residence, Ingleside House, Leslie, Fife.——Eleanor Barbara Georgina, b. 1896. Residence, Zenda, Theobald's Rd., Burgess Hill, Sussex.

   The 6th baronet, Sir John Bridger Shiffner, Lieut. Roy. Sussex Regt., was killed in action during European War 1918.   The 7th baronet, Major Sir Henry Burrows Shiffner, O.B.E., R.A., was killed in action during European War 1941.

SHUCKBURGH, Creation (E.) 1660, of Shuckburgh, Warwickshire.

[Name pronounced "Shuckbŭr."]

Sir CHARLES GERALD STEWKLEY SHUCKBURGH, T.D., 12th Baronet; b. Feb. 28th, 1911; s. his father, Sir GERALD FRANCIS STEWKLEY, 1939; ed. at Harrow, and at Trin. Coll., Oxford; Maj. 11th City of London Yeo., and a JP and a DL for Warwickshire (High Sheriff 1965): m. 1st, 1935, Remony Dorothy, who d. 1936, da. of the late F. N. Bell, of Buenos Aires: 2ndly, 1937, Nancy Diana Mary, OBE, only da. of the late Capt. Rupert Egerton Lubbock, RN (ret.) [see B. Avebury, colls.], and has issue by 2nd marriage.

Arms—Sable, a chevron between three mullets argent.   Crest—A blackamoor couped at the waist proper, with a dart in his hand or.
Seat—Shuckburgh, near Daventry.

Hæc manus ob patriam.

This hand for my country.

Son living—By 2nd marriage—RUPERT CHARLES GERALD, b. Feb. 12th, 1949.
Daughters living—By 2nd marriage—Remony Charmian, b. 1938: m. 1963, Hugo Macdonald Price, of The Cottage, Sherbourne, nr. Warwick, and has issue living, Robin Macdonald, b. 1970,—Justin Bryan, b. 1973.——Amanda Maria, b. 1946.
Widow living of 11th Baronet—HONOR ZOE (Dowager Lady Shuckburgh), O.B.E., da. of Neville Thursby, of Harleston, Northampton [Broughton, Bt.]; is a J.P. for Warwickshire; O.B.E. (Civil) 1920: m. 1909, Sir Gerald Francis Stewkley Shuckburgh, 11th Baronet, who d. 1939. Residence, Maurys Mount, West Wellow, Hants.
Collateral Branch living:

   Granddaughters of the late Col. Henry Adolphus Shuckburgh, 3rd son of 7th baronet :—
   Issue of the late Com. George Stewkley Shuckburgh, R.N., b. 1860, d. 1912: m. 1898, Amy Mary, (who d. 1962, having m. 2ndly, 1913, Charles Adalbert Tucker), da. of the late John Robertson, of Cororooke, Colac, Australia:—
Mabel Evelyn, b. 1899.——Lorna May, b. 1900. Residence, Wren Cottage, Somerton, Somerset.

   This family takes its name from Shuckburgh in Warwickshire. Richard Shuckburgh, Esq., M.P. for the county in 1641, and father of the 1st baronet, armed all his tenants, and joined King Charles I. at Edgehill, where he was knighted. After the battle of Edge Hill he retired and fortified himself on Shuckburgh Hill, where most of his tenantry were slain, and he himself was taken prisoner. After being confined in Kenilworth Castle a considerable time, he purchased his liberty at a dear rate. His eldest son, John, was created a baronet by Charles II.

SIMEON, Creation (U.K.) 1815, of Grazeley, Berkshire.

NEC TEMERE NEC TIMIDE.

Neither rashly nor timidly.

Sir JOHN EDMUND BARRINGTON SIMEON, 7th Baronet; b. March 1st, 1911; s. his father, Sir JOHN WALTER BARRINGTON, 1957; ed. at Eton, and at Ch. Ch., Oxford; Flight-Lieut. (retired) R.A.F.: m. 1937, Anne Robina Mary, da. of Hamilton Dean, and has issue.

Arms—Per fesse sable and or a pale counterchanged three trefoils slipped, two and one of the second, and three ermine spots one and two of the first.   Crest—A fox passant-reguardant proper, in the mouth a trefoil slipped vert.   Supporters—Dexter, a fox reguardant proper, in the mouth a trefoil slipped vert; sinister, a lion gules, ducally crowned or.

Residences—RR1, Cowichan Station, BC V0R-1P0; Swainston, Newport, I. of Wight.

Son living—RICHARD EDMUND BARRINGTON (95, Mack St., Kingston, Ont., Canada), b. March 2nd, 1943; ed. at British Columbia (BA) and Yale (MA, PhD) Univs.: m. 1966, Agnes Joan, da. of George Frederick Weld, and has issue living, Stephen George Barrington, b. Oct. 29th, 1970,—Rachel Elizabeth, b. 1973.

Daughters living—Anne Emily Philippa, b. 1938: m. 1962, Nigel Leonard Harper Gow, of 6129, Highbury, Vancouver, BC, Canada, and has issue living, Ian Harper, b. 1968,—Lisa

Harper, *b.* 1965.——Sara Alexandra, *b.* 1946: *m.* 1967, Anthony John Williams, of 3440, Jervis St., Port Coquitlam, BC, Canada, and has issue living, Derek John, *b.* 1973,—Adria Elizabeth, *b.* 1971.

Sister living—Elizabeth Jane, *b.* 1916 ; formerly in A.T.S. : *m.* 1943, Lieut.-Com. **Thomas Arthur Ratcliffe**, R.N.V.R., from whom she obtained a divorce 1952, and has issue living, Donald Arthur, *b.* 1946. *Residence,* 2390, Nelson Av., Vancouver, British Columbia.

Collateral Branches living.

Issue of the late Stephen Louis Simeon, 4th son of 3rd baronet, *b.* 1857, *d.* 1937 : *m.* 1885, Louisa Augusta Eardley, who *d.* 1925, da. of the late Rt. Hon. Hugh Culling Eardley Childers:—

Leonard Stephen Barrington, MC (51, Church Rd., Brightlingsea, Colchester), *b.* 1891; ed. at Eton and at Trin. Coll., Camb. (B.A. 1912, M.A. 1918); was Officer in charge of Admiralty Works, E. Anglia Dist. 1940-56; European War 1914-19 in France as Lieut. Roy. Fusiliers (M.C.): *m.* 1924, Ella Hazel Powys, da. of the late Col. Powys Lane (formerly Indian Army), of Upper Ward, Bonchurch, Isle of Wight, and has issue living, Miles Powys Barrington (of Daltes Farm, St. Osyth, Clacton, Essex), *b.* 1927: *m.* 1956, Joan Mary, da. of Laurence Frederick Underhay, of Clacton, Essex, and has issue living, Michael John Barrington *b.* 1957, Robert Miles *b.* 1959,— Anne Primrose Louise (c/o Barclays Bank, Knightsbridge, SW1), *b.* 1925: *m.* 1st, 1944 (m. diss. 1959), Louis Strauss; 2ndly, 1959, Leonard Townsend, who *d.* 1971, and has issue living (by 1st m.) Linda Evelyn *b.* 1947: *m.* 1974, Thomas Kennedy Nelson (and has issue living, Hamish Kennedy *b.* 1975), Caroline Louise *b.* 1948: *m.* 1974, Nicholas John de Jongh, Diana Margaret *b.* 1955.

Grandchildren of the late Rev. Geoffrey Barrington Simeon, 3rd son of Capt. Charles Simeon, 2nd son of 2nd baronet:—

Issue of the late Geoffrey Nelthorpe Simeon, *b.* 1888, *d.* 1923 : *m.* 1919, Henrietta Mary Collingwood (The Lawn, Holybourne, Alton, Hants), da. of Rev. W. Collingwood Carter, formerly V. of Shipton-under-Wychwood:—

Geoffrey John Barrington, *b.* 1923; Lt.-Cdr. RN (ret.); FRICS; MIN: *m.* 1954, Elizabeth Frances Richenda, da. of the Rev. R. C. Rham, R. of Feoch, Cornwall, and has issue living, Charles Richard Barrington, *b.* 1958,—Sarah Richenda Barrington, *b.* 1960. *Residence,* Highcroft, Fairfield Rd., Shawford, Hants.——Janetta Mary Barrington, *b.* 1920; sometime in WAAF: *m.* 1946, Cdr. John Pemberton Mosse, DSC, RN, and has issue living, Peter John, *b.* 1947; Lt. RN,—Martin Barrington, *b.* 1950; ed. at Sherborne, and New Coll., Oxford. *Residence,* Willow Bank, Goldhill, Lower Bourne, Farnham, Surrey.

Granddaughter of the late Lionel Barrington Simeon (*b.* 1852), 4th son of Capt. Charles Simeon (ante):—

Issue of the late Charles John Simeon, *b.* 1878, *d.* 1946: *m.* 1910, Elinor Yorke, who *d.* 1940, da. of Gen. Charles King, of Milwaukee, U.S.A.:—

Elizabeth, *b.* 1917 : *m.* 1948, Major Richard Guillemard Copleston, R.E. (retired). *Residence,* 143, Harrison Road, Cheshire, Connecticut, U.S.A.

Granddaughters of the late Capt. Charles Simeon, 2nd son of 2nd baronet :—

Issue of the late Rev. Hugh Barrington Simeon, *b.* 1858, *d.* 1941 : *m.* 1886, Beatrice, who *d.* 1930, da. of the late Henry A. Littledale, of Bolton Hall, Yorkshire [Armytage, Bt.]:—

Beatrice Edith, *b.* 1888. *Residence,* St. Peter's Convent, Grahamstown, S. Africa.——Mildred Eleanor, *b.* 1890 : *m.* 1914, Geoffrey Courthope Bosanquet, and has issue living, Albinia Mary Agnes, *b.* 1915,—Frances Dawn, MB, BS, *b.* 1916; late Capt. RAMC. *Residence,* Summer Court Lodge, Wrotham, near Sevenoaks, Kent.

Grandchildren of the late Perceval Barrington Simeon, 3rd son of 2nd baronet:—

Issue of the late Cornwall Barrington Simeon, *b.* 1889, *d.* 1957: *m.* 1st, 1928, Ellaline Margery Mary, who *d.* 1966, having obtained a divorce 1947), da. of the late Arnold le Poer Power, of Clonmel, co. Tipperary; 2ndly, 1947, Violet, MBE (c/o Westminster Bank, St. Helier, Jersey), only da. of the late Algernon Hodson, and widow of Lt.-Col. Neal William Douglas-Matheson, DSO, MC:—

(By 1st m.) John Power Barrington (c/o FCO, King Charles St., SW1), *b.* 1929; ed. at Beaumont Coll., and RMA; Lt. Regular Army (Reserve), and First Sec., HM Dip. Ser.: *m.* 1st 1951 (m. dis. 1955), Margareta Valborg Johanna, only da. of the late Erik Ahlstrom, of Norrmark Finland; 2ndly, 1966, Norma, who *d.* 1969, da. of the late Capt. Norman Herbert Dopson; 3rdly, 1970, Carina Renate Elisabeth, da. of the late Michael Schüller, of Bonn, W. Germany, and has issue living (by 2nd m.), Charles John Barrington, *b.* 1967.——Ann Ella Mary. *b.* 1931: *m.* 1961, Bryan Reginald Baxter, of Foresters Flat, Hightown Hill, Ringwood, Hants., and has issue living, Robert Bryan, *b.* 1962,—Timothy Reginald, *b.* 1964.

Granddaughter of the late Cornwall Simeon, 3rd son of 2nd baronet:—

Issue of the late Rev. John Pole Simeon, *b.* 1872, *d.* 1951 : *m.* 1908, Dorothy, who *d.* 1955, da. of the late Rev. Sydney Benjamin Field, formerly V. of Patcham :—

Joan Edith Barrington, *b.* 1909 : *m.* 1st, 1938, Richard William Barnes Clarke, who obtained a divorce 1945; 2ndly, 1945, Wenzel Jaksch, who *d.* 1966, and has issue living, (by 2nd m.) George Barrington, *b.* 1945: *m.* 1974, Carmen Julia, da. of Don Constantino Torres of Colombia,—Mary Dorothy Plantagenet, *b.* 1947. *Residence,* 62, Wiesbaden, Kohlheck, Wenzel-Jaksch St. 32, Germany.

Grandchildren of the late Edward Archibald Simeon, MRCS, LRCP, el. son of Lt.-Col. Edward Simeon, 3rd son of Rear-Adm. Charles Simeon, 3rd son of 1st baronet:—

Issue of the late Vice-Adm. Sir Charles Edward Barrington Simeon, K.B.E., C.B., *b.* 1889, *d.* 1955: *m.* 1918, Gladys (1, Old Barn Cottages, Whitchurch, Oxon.), da. of Benjamin Arkle, formerly of Spital, Cheshire:—

Hugh Michael (Westview Lane, S. Norwark, Conn., 06354, USA), *b.* 1926; Cdr. RN (ret.): *m.* 1966, Ilona Maria, da. of Prof. Dr. Med. Gustav Christian Schimert, of Munich, and has issue living, George Edward, *b.* 1969,—John David, *b.* 1971.——Diana Maria, *b.* 1967.——William Martin (Nori Kori Plantation, Box 35, Kainautu, E. Highlands, Papua, New Guinea), *b.* 1936; late Rifle Brig.: *m.* 1959, Doreen Mary Wren, from whom he obtained a divorce 1964.——Joan Denise, *b.* 1919: *m.* 1947, Reginald James Pringle, MBE, late ICS, son of Sir James (Scott) Pringle, KCB, OBE, and has issue living, James Edward, *b.* 1949,—Reginald Denys, *b.* 1951,— Richard Charles, *b.* 1954,—Anne Denise, *b.* 1958. *Residence,* Crest House, Shoppenhangers Rd., Maidenhead, Berks.——Marguerite Gladys, *b.* 1922; sometime in WRNS: *m.* 1946, Maj. Peter Rainier Adams (ret.), late RA, and Indian Army, of 3, Farnhill Rd., Walthan Abbey, Essex, EN9 1NE, and has issue living, John Rainier, *b.* 1947,—Hugh Robert, *b.* 1949,—Charles David, *b.* 1951.——Josephine Osyth, *b.* 1932: *m.* 1956, Lt.-Cdr. Thomas David Alexander Kennedy, RN (ret.), MIMechE; ECng, and has issue living, Martin Charles, *b.* 1958,—Ian David, *b.* 1965,— Fiona Osyth, *b.* 1960. *Residence,* Hill House, Berecourt Rd., Pangbourne, Berks.

Grandson of the late Lt.-Col. Edward Simeon, son of the late Rear-Adm. Charles Simeon (ante):—

Issue of the late Herbert Richard Simeon, *b.* 1865, *d.* 1926 : *m.* 1892, Effie Dean Florence, who *d.* 1938, da. of Walter Moss, of Ashburton, New Zealand :—

Percival Edward Ralph (c/o Memorial Home, Gisborne, NZ), *b.* 1898.

Descendants of John, Lt. 54th Regt. (*b.* 1841) and Albert (*b.* 1841), sons of Rear-Adm. Charles Simeon (ante), who both left numerous issue.

Sir John Simeon, 1st baronet, M.P. for Reading, was senior Master of the Court of Chancery.
Sir Richard Godin Simeon, 2nd baronet: *m.* 1813, Louisa Edith, da. and heir of Sir Fitzwilliam
Barrington, 10th Bt. of Barrington Hall, Essex (cr. 1611, ext. 1833).

SIMPSON, Creation (U.K.) 1935, of Bradley Hall, Ryton, co. Palatine of Durham.

It will be given to the persevering.

Sir (John) Cyril Finucane Simpson, 3rd
Baronet; b. Feb. 10th, 1899; *s.* his brother, *Sir*
Basil Robert James, 1968; *OBE*, ed. at Rugby and
Queen's Coll., Oxford; Stockbroker; 1914-18 War
with RNAS (two medals): *m.* 1st, 1936 (m. diss.
1944), Mrs. Elizabeth Miesegaes, only child of
Frank J. Lambert, of Lovaine Place, Newcastle
upon Tyne; 2ndly, 1945, Maria Teresa, da. of the
late Capt. John Sutherland Harvey, of Romerillo,
Biarritz.

Arms—Gules, on a fesse cottised between two lions passant
or a mascle of the field. *Crest*—A dexter arm embowed proper,
the forearm enfiled with a mascle or, the hand grasping a wreath
of laurel fructed also proper.

Residence—Bradley Hall, Wylam, Northumberland. *Clubs,*—
White's, Buck's, Northern Counties (Newcastle).

Sisters living—Stella, *b.* 1890.——Vera, *b.* 1893: *m.* 1917, Richard Boys-Stones, M.C., and has
issue living, Claude Frank (of Randle House, Corbridge, Northumberland), *b.* 1920: *m.* 1948,
Anne Blackett, and has issue living. Richard Claude *b.* 1954. George Francis *b.* 1960, Sarah
b. 1951,—Paul Richard (Friars Garth, Walton, Brampton, Cumbria), *b.* 1926: *m.* 1960, Judith
Ann Rutherford, and has issue living, Claire Judith *b.* 1961, Susan Paula *b.* 1963,— Elise, *b.* 1922:
m. 1943, Cdr. Rudland Cairns, DSC, RN, and has issue living, Timothy Dallas *b.* 1948, David
Rudland *b.* 1951, Fiona Alice *b.* 1946,—Sonia, *b.* 1924. *Residence*, Kyo Close, Wylam, Northumberland.—Esmé, *b.* 1895: *m.* 1919, Walter Rupert King, and has issue living, Denis,
b. 1921,—Sheila, *b.* 1922. *Residence*, Yearle, Meadway, Esher, Surrey.——Iris, *b.* 1896: *m.*
1919, Henry Edmund Blackburne Daniell, MC, and has issue living, David, *b.* 1921, *m.* 1950,
Helen Sheldon, and has issue living. Karin Elizabeth Blackburne, *b.* 1952,—Michael (Meadow
Cottage, Frimley Green, Hants.), *b.* 1925: *m.* 1963, Veronica Lewis-Jenkins and has issue
living, Caroline Margaret Blackburne *b.* 1966,—John, *b.* 1928,—Margaret, *b.* 1922: *m.* 1960,
Charles Edward Wallis, of Batchelor's Hall, Kirtling Green, Newmarket, and has issue living,
James Charles Blackburne *b.* 1963, Angela Claire Blackburne *b.* 1962,—Sylvia, *b.* 1923, *Resi-
dence*, St. Aidans, Seahouses, Northumberland.

The 1st baronet, Col. Sir Frank Robert Simpson, C.B., T.D. (son of the late John Bell Simpson,
D.C.L., of Bradley Hall, Wylam, Northumberland), was Lieut.-Col. and Hon. Col. 9th Batn.
Durham L.I. (T.A.), and High Sheriff of Durham 1935.

Sinclair-Lockhart (cr. 1636), see Lockhart.

SINCLAIR, Creation (N.S.) 1704, of Dunbeath, Caithness-shire.

Fidelity.

Sir John Rollo Norman Blair Sin-
clair, 9th *Baronet; b.* Nov. 4th, 1928; *s.* his
father, *Sir* Ronald Norman John Charles
Udny, 1952; ed. at Wellington Coll.: formerly
Lt. Intelligence Corps; Dir. of Lucis Trust
1957-61, of Human Development Trust since
1971, and of Wrekin Trust since 1975.

Arms—Quarterly: 1st azure, a ship at anchor, oars in
saltire or, flagged gules, within a double tressure counterflory of the second; 2nd and 3rd, or, a lion rampant gules,
armed and langued azure; 4th, azure, a ship under sail or,
sails argent and flags gules; over all, dividing the four
quarters, a cross engrailed, sable, *Sinclair;* the whole
within a bordure parted per pale, the dexter side indented
gules, the sinister ermine. *Crest*—A cock proper.
Residence, Barrock House, Wick, Caithness.

Sisters living—Georgina Margaret Snowdrop, *b.* 1932:
m. 1955 (m. diss. 1968), John Leonard Maddocks, and
has issue living, John Alexander Sinclair, *b.* 1960,—
Margaret Louise Sinclair, *b.* 1962. *Residence*, The
Mount, Brewood, Staffs.——Susan Lilian Primrose
(*Countess of Swinton*), *b.* 1935 (cr. a Life Baroness, with
title of Baroness Masham of Ilton, 1970): *m.* 1959,
the 2nd Earl of Swinton. *Residence*, Dykes Hill House,
Masham, Ripon, Yorks.

Widow living of 8th Baronet—Reba Blair, da. of
Anthony Inglis, M.D., of Lismore, Ayr: *m.* 1st, 1926,
Sir Ronald Norman John Charles Udny Sinclair, T.D.,
8th Bt., who *d.* 1952; 2ndly, 1957, Lieut.-Col. Henry
Richard Hildreth, MBE. *Residence*, Barrock House,
Wick, Caithness.

Collateral Branches living.

Issue of the late Alexander Robert Sinclair, brother of 8th baronet, *b.* 1901, *d.* 1972: *m.* 1928, Vera Mabel (Fallowfield, Heddington, Calne, Wilts.), da. of the late Walter Stephings Baxendale, of Sevenoaks:—

PATRICK ROBERT RICHARD (1, New Sq., Lincoln's Inn, WC2), *b.* May 21st, 1936; ed. at Winchester and Oriel Coll., Oxford; Bar. Lincoln's Inn 1961; Sub. Lt. RNVR: *m.* 1974, Susan Catherine Beresford, el. da. of Geoffrey Clive Davies, OBE, of Greenshaw, Holbrook, Ipswich [see Knowles, Bt.].——Roona Fidelity, *b.* 1932: *m.* 1959, Ernle Money-Kyrle, of Whetham, Calne, Wilts.. and Beech Cottage, Hartley Wintney, Hants., and has issue living, Charles Ernle Robin, *b.* 1961,—Andrew Richard William, *b.* 1965.

Grandchildren of the late Capt. George Sinclair, 3rd son of 6th baronet :—
Issue of the late Rt. Hon. John Sinclair, G.C.S.I., G.C.I.E., *b.* 1860 ; *cr. Baron Pentland*, 1909 [*see* that title].

This family is a younger branch of the Earls of Caithness, Sir James Sinclair of Dunbeath, 1st baronet, being a descendant of the 4th Earl. The baronetcy was cr. with remainder to heirs male whatsoever, and on the death of the 5th baronet in 1842, it was assumed by his cousin, John Sinclair, of Barrock, as great-great-grandson of George Sinclair of Barrock, brother of William Sinclair of Dunbeath, uncle of 1st baronet, the propinquity being proved by a retour of general service Dec. 23rd, 1842. The 7th baronet, Sir John Rose George Sinclair, DSO, was Vice-Lt. for co. Caithness, and served in S. Africa 1900-01, and during European War 1914-18, Sir Ronald Norman John Charles Udny Sinclair, TD, DL, JP, 8th Bt, was Maj. Seaforth High-landers and Dist. Resident Officer, Norderdithmarschen 1947, and British Resident Heide/Holstein 1949.

SITWELL, Creation (U.K.) 1808, of Renishaw, Derbyshire.

Sir SACHEVERELL SITWELL, 6th *Baronet*; *b.* Nov. 15th, 1897; *s.* his brother, *Sir* (FRANCIS) OSBERT SACHEVERELL, *CH, CBE,* 1969; ed. at Eton, and Balliol Coll., Oxford; poet and writer; formerly 2nd Lt. Gren. Guards: *m.* 1925, Georgia, da. of the late Arthur Doble, of Montreal, and has issue.

Arms—Barry of eight or and vert, three lions rampant sable. **Crest**—A demi-lion rampant, erased sable, holding between the paws an escutcheon per pale or and vert.

Residence,—Weston Hall, Towcester, Northants.

Yield not to misfortune.

Sons living—SACHEVERELL RERESBY (Renishaw Hall, Derbys.; 4, Southwick Place, W2; Castello di Montegufoni, Florence); *b.* April 15th, 1927; ed. at Eton, and King's Coll., Camb.; formerly Lt. Gren. Gds.; Lord of The Manors of Eckington and Barlborough, Derbys. and of Whiston and Brampton-en-le-Morthen, Yorks.: *m.* 1952, Penelope, yr. da. of the late Col. the Hon. Donald Alexander Forbes, DSO, MVO [see E. Granard, colls.], and has issue living, Alexandra Isobel Susanna Edith, *b.* 1958.——Francis Trajan Sacheverell (20, Ladbroke Grove, W11), *b.* 1935; ed. at Eton: *m.* 1966, Susanna Carolyn, da. of the late Rt. Hon. Sir Ronald Hibbert Cross, KCMG, KCVO, 1st Bt., and has issue living, George Reresby Sacheverell, *b.* 1967, —William Ronald Sacheverell, *b.* 1969,—Henrietta Louise Vereker, *b.* 1973.

Collateral Branches living.

Grandson of the late Herbert Wellington Sitwell (infra):—
Issue of the late Capt. Herbert Cecil Fitz Roy Sitwell, *b.* 1896, *d.* 1965: *m.* 1st, 1921, Helen, who *d.* 1955, da. of William E. Barlow, PhD, of Cambridge; 2ndly, 1961, Phronsie Irene, MA, Columbia, poet and essayist (Three Otters Estate, RFD2, Bedford, Virginia 24523, USA), da. of Peter Addison Marsh, of Campbell co., Virginia, and formerly wife of (i) W. L. Filmer, and (ii) Erik Solling Monberg:—

(By 1st m.) George Fitz Roy (PO 1393, Holme's Beach, Florida 33518, USA), *b.* 1923; Lt.-Col. US Army (ret.): *m.* 1945 (m. diss. 1971), Elizabeth, da. of Paul Freed, of Waynesboro, Virginia, and has issue living, Elizabeth, *b.* 1951: *m.* 1969, Alfred Townsend Truitt, of Bradenton, Florida, USA, and has issue living, Anne, *b.* 19—.

Granddaughter of the late Capt. George Frederick Sitwell, 2nd son of 2nd baronet:—
Issue (by 1st marriage) of the late Herbert Wellington Sitwell, *b.* 1861, *d.* 1922: *m.* 1st, 1885, Juliette Fisher (who obtained a divorce 1901), da. of the late Col. Cary, of the late Confederate States Army ; 2ndly, 1914, Eva, who *d.* 1920, da. of the late Stephen Putney, of Richmond, U.S.A., and widow of Richard C. Worthington :—

Evelyn Juliette Fay *b.* 1888. *Residence*, 84, N. Princeton, Lynchburg, Virginia, USA.

The Sitwells appeared early in Eckington, Derbyshire; William Cytewell, *temp.* Edward III., and Roger Cytewell, *temp.* Edward IV., both being holders of land there. The eventual heiress of the family, Katherine Sitwell, *m.* 1727, Jonathan Hurt, Esq., and her son Francis succeeded to the Renishaw estates and assumed the name of Sitwell. The Sitwells are the only remaining representatives of the family of Reresby of Thribergh, through Mary Reresby, who in 1693 *m.* William Sitwell. Sir George Reresby, 4th Bt., sat as MP for Scarborough (*C*) 1885-86 and 1892-95. His only da. Dame Edith Louisa Sitwell, DBE, *b.* 1887, *d.* 1964, author, poet and critic, was Vice-Pres. of R. Soc. of Literature 1958. His el. son (Francis) Osbert Sacheverell Sitwell, CH, CBE, C.Litt, 5th Bt. was the poet and author.

SKINNER, Creation (U.K.) 1912, of Pont Street, Borough of Chelsea.

I neither fear nor despise.

Nec timeo nec spemo

Sir (THOMAS) KEITH HEWITT SKINNER, 4th *Baronet*; *b.* Dec. 6th, 1927; *s.* his father *Sir* (THOMAS) GORDON, 1972; ed. at Charterhouse; Chm. and Ch. Exec. of IPC Business Press Ltd., and a Dir. of other cos.: *m.* 1959, Jill, da. of Cedric Ivor Tuckett, of Yardley Gables, Tonbridge, and has issue.

Arms—Ermine, on a bend or, between in chief a port between two towers, flying therefrom two pennons gules to the sinister, and in base an ancient ship of the second, three maple leaves slipped vert. Crest—A griffin's head couped at the neck or, between two dragons' wings gules.

Residence—Long Acre, W. Clandon, Surrey.

Sons living—THOMAS JAMES HEWITT, *b.* Sept. 11th, 1962.——Ian Ivor, *b.* 1964.

Brothers living—Gordon Michael Hewitt (Lake Baringo Lodge, P.O. Box 1375, Nakuru, Kenya), *b.* 1930: *m.* 1st, 1955 (m. diss. 1960), Josephine Dawn, da. of D. S. Redman, of Bleak Hall, Biggleswade; 2ndly, 1961, Eve, da. of Vernon John Fullfortd, of Whitehall Court, Whitehall, SW1; 3rdly, 1968, Jean Margaret, da. of the late Donald Sharp, and widow of Robin Vetch, and has issue living, (by 1st m.) Dudley Mark Hewitt, *b.* 1956,—— (by 2nd m.) Sarah Patricia, *b.* 1963.——Peter Girling Hewitt (Highway Model Farm, Downside Cobham, Surrey), *b.* 1938: *m.* 1966, Jennifer, da. of J. Corbett, of Perrymill, Bradley Green, nr. Redditch, Worcs., and has issue living, Justin Mark Thomas, *b.* 1968,—Peter Dominic Thomas, *b.* 1970.

Aunts living (daughters of 2nd baronet)—Constance Irene, *b.* 1901: *m.* 1936, Claude Harry Mills, who *d.* 1971. *Residence*, Saffron Meadow, Amersham, Bucks.——Marie Vivien, *b.* 1908: *m.* 1st, 1933 (m. diss. 1950), Robert Archibald Hugh Collum; 2ndly, 1950, Haydon Dorman Bradshaw, who *d.* 1974, and has issue living, (by 1st m.) Hugh Robert (Clinton House, Fletching, Sussex), *b.* 1940; ed. at Eton: *m.* 1965, Elizabeth Noel, da. of Henry Gordon Stewart, and has issue living, Lucinda Elizabeth *b.* 1967, Melissa Jane *b.* 1969,—Juliet Vivien, *b.* 1942: *m.* 1963, Andrew John Mack Huntley, of Ashurst, Fernhurst, Surrey, and has issue living, Amanda Juliet *b.* 1968, Natasha Louise *b.* 1971, Jessamy Mathilda *b.* 1973. *Residence*, Hatch Gate, Linch, nr. Liphook, Hants.

Widow living of 3rd Baronet—JEANNE MARIE LOUISE (*Jeanne, Lady Skinner*), (Larchmont, Hill Brow, Hove), da. of François de Launoit, of Brussels: *m.* 1953, as his 2nd wife, Sir (Thomas) Gordon Skinner, 3rd Bt., who *d.* 1972.

Collateral Branches living.

Issue of the late Ernest Skinner, 2nd son of 1st baronet, *b.* 1880, *d.* 1919: *m.* 1903, Leonie Mercedes, who *d.* 1964, da. of the late Henry William Doll, of Lancing, Sussex:—

Eva Jacqueline Leonia, *b.* 1914. *Residence*, 10, St. Andrews Gdns., Church Rd., West Tarring, Worthing.

Issue of the late John Skinner, 3rd son of 1st baronet, *b.* 1882, *d.* 1939: *m.* 1904, Angela, da. of William Dunn:—

John Reginald, *b.* 1909 : *m.* 1949, Shirley Evelyn, da. of the late James Roddick, of Melbourne Aust., and has issue living, Dawn Rosalyn, *b.* 1952.

Issue of the late Charles Henry Skinner, yst. son of 1st baronet, *b.* 1886, *d.* 1966: *m.* 1910, Violet Muriel (Eastbury Manor, Compton, Guildford, Surrey), da. of Herbert Furber, of Hampstead, NW:—

Charles David Evelyn (The Pound, Yarmouth, I. of Wight), *b.* 1916: *m.* 1940, Pamela, da. of Dr. S. B. Couper, of Blaby, Leicester, and has issue living, Peter David (Elm Tree House, Kemble, Cirencester), *b.* 1941: Fl. Lt. RAF (ret.): *m.* 1964, Susan Mary, da. of Keith Francis Thompson, of Worcester, and has issue living, Mark David Francis *b.* 1966, Sarah Lucinda *b.* 1968.—Carol, *b.* 1944: *m.* 1967, Peter De Villiers, of 26, Gallagher Drive, Halfway House, Transvaal,—Susan Pamela, *b.* 1945: *m.* 1965, Robert Webb, of The Manor House, Walton-in-Gordano, Som.

The 1st baronet, Sir Thomas, was a Director of Canadian Pacific Railway, of Hudson's Bay Co., and of Bank of Montreal, founder of Thomas Skinner & Co. (Publishers) Ltd., and founder and editor of " Stock Exchange Official Year Book " and " The Directory of Directors." Sir (Thomas) Hewitt, 2nd baronet, was Pres. of Thomas Skinner & Co. (Publishers) Ltd.

SKIPWITH, Creation (E.) 1622, of Prestwould, Leicestershire.

Without God I cannot.

Sir PATRICK ALEXANDER D'ESTOTEVILLE SKIPWITH, 12th *Baronet*, son of the late Grey d'Estoteville Townsend Skipwith, Flying Officer R.A.F. Vol. Reserve, el. son of 11th baronet; *b.* Sept. 1st, 1938; *s.* his grandfather, *Sir* GREY HUMBERSTON D'ESTOTEVILLE, 1950; ed. at Harrow, Dublin Univ. (MA), and Imperial Coll., London Univ. (PhD): *m.* 1st, 1964 (m. diss. 1970), Gillian Patricia, only da. of the late C. F. Harwood; 2ndly, 1972, Ashkhain, da. of Bedros Atikian, of Royal Cres. N.W., Calgary Alberta, Canada, and has issue by 1st m.

Arms—Argent, three bars gules, in chief a greyhound courant sable, collared or. *Crest*—A turnstile or.

Address,—c/o BRGM, PO Box 1492, Jiddah, Saudi Arabia. *Clubs,*—Travellers', United Service and Royal Aero.

Son living—By 1st m.—ALEXANDER SEBASTIAN GREY D'ESTOTEVILLE, *b.* April 9th, 1969.
Daughter living—By 1st m.—Zara Alexandra Jane d'Estoteville, *b.* 1967.

Uncles living (sons of 11th baronet)—Egerton Grey D'Estoteville (6, Stamford Cottages, The Billings SW10), *b.* 1935; ed. at Canford; late 13th/18th' Roy. Hussars.——Peyton Stephen, c/o. The Fine Art Society, Ltd., 148, New Bond St., W1), *b.* 1939; ed. at Canford: *m.* 1971, Anne, da. of Capt. C. E. Barren, of Seasalter, Kent, and has issue living, Selina, *b.* 1972,—Amber Louise, *b.* 1974.

Aunt living (daughter of 11th baronet)—Audrey Elsie Townsend, *b.* 1911: *m.* 1943, Major Paul Antony Negretti, formerly Black Watch, and has issue living, Antony Simon Timothy, *b.* 1945,—Annelise Audrey, *b.* 1948: *m.* 1975, Alexander G. M. Kemp. *Residence*, Thornborough Manor, Buckingham.

Mother living—Sofka, da. of the late Prince Peter Alexandrovitch Dolgorouky, of St. Petersburg, Russia, and formerly wife of Leo Zinovieff: *m.* 1937, Grey d'Estoteville Townsend Skipwith, Flying Officer R.A.F. Vol. Reserve, el. son of 11th baronet, who *d.* (killed in action during European War) 1942. *Residence*, Bradford, Blisland, Bodmin, Cornwall.

Widow living of 11th Baronet—CYNTHIA EGERTON (*Cynthia, Lady Skipwith*), da. of the late Egerton Leigh of Jodrell Hall, Cheshire: *m.* 1928, as his second wife, Sir Grey Humberston d'Estoteville-Skipwith, 11th Bt., who *d.* 1950. *Residence*, Flemings, Wilton, Wilts.

Collateral Branches living.

Grandchildren of the late Col. Grey Townsend Skipwith (infra):—
Issue of the late Fulwar Estoteville Skipwith, *b.* 1874, *d.* 1963: *m.* 1905, Kathleen Alice, Georgina, who *d.* 1967, da. of the Rev. John Adams [D. Northumberland, colls.]:—
Grey Henry (of 4B, Cromwell Cres., S.W.3), *b.* 1908.——Elizabeth Kathleen (of Monlila, Channel Way, Fairlight, nr. Hastings), *b.* 1907.

Issue of the late Lt.-Col. James Wemyss Skipwith, RE, *b.* 1875, *d.* 1950: *m.* 1911 Estelle, who *d.* 1961, da. of the late Robert Henderson, of The Wylds, Liss, Hants:—
Patrick James Townsend, *b.* 1915; Lt.-Col. (ret.) RA; Hong Kong 1941 (prisoner): *m.* 1941, Beryl Daisy, da. of the late Arthur A. Fair, of Montree, Athlone, co. Westmeath, and has issue living, Michael James Grey, *b.* 1951,—Susan Virginia, *b.* 1947,—Bridget Ann, *b.* 1948. *Residence*, North End, Chiddingfold, Surrey.——John Granville Wemyss (of Biggins House, Kirkby Lonsdale, Carnforth, Lancs.), *b.* 1921; Maj. RA (ret.); 1939-45 War in France, India, and Java: *m.* 1947, Margaret Lettice Mary, who *d.* 1968, da. of the late Col. William Paget-Tomlinson, DSO, of Biggins House, Kirkby Lonsdale, Carnforth, Lancs., and has issue living, Guy Paget Grey, *b.* 1951,—Philip James Henderson, *b.* 1957.——Margaret Virginia (c/o Lloyds Bank, Cranleigh, Surrey), *b.* 1912: *m.* 1st, 1937, Gordon Kenneth Luker Gourlay, who *d.* 1946; 2ndly, 1947, Lt.-Col. Ian Robert Grimwood, Frontier Force Regt., and has issue living, (by 1st m.) Jean Margaret, *b.* 1940: *m.* 1962, Vagn Aage Pedersen (PO Box 103, Nanyuki, Kenya), and has issue living, Julie Christine *b.* 1969,—Hazel Anne Virginia, *b.* 1943: *m.* 1965, David John Bowen Moody (c/o Acme Timber Industries, Private Bag, Sabie 1260, E. Transvaal), and has issue living, Christopher Gordon *b.* 1966, Michael John *b.* 1971, Bridget Elizabeth *b.* 1968,—(by 2nd m.) Elisabeth Josephine Nisbet, *b.* 1948.

Issue of the late Lt.-Col. Frederick Skipwith, *b.* 1877, *d.* 1964: *m.* 1916, Lily Spence (South Corner Cottage, Instow N. Devon), da. of the late Lt.-Col. John Garvie, MD, IMS:—
Wendy Elisabeth, *b.* 1927: *m.* 1955, Capt. Thomas Peter Robin Crane, late RASC, of The Mead, Carron Lane, Midhurst, Sussex, and has issue living, Jennifer Anne, *b.* 1958,—Caroline Virginia, *b.* 1969.

Issue of the late Charles Grey Yule Skipwith, *b.* 1890, *d.* 1967: *m.* 1926, Althea Kathleen Joyce, who *d.* 1973, da. of the late Charles Hunting, of Slaley Hall, Northumberland:—
Michael Charles (The Lotus Pottery, Stoke Gabriel, S. Devon), *b.* 1928: *m.* 1957, Mary Elizabeth, da. of R. Barthram Wood, of Croft House, Kirby Moorside, Yorks., and has issue living, Jonathan Charles d'Estoteville, *b.* 1962,—Joanna Lisette, *b.* 1960.

Granddaughter of the late Fulwar Skipwith, 3rd son of 8th baronet:—
Issue of the late Col. Grey Townsend Skipwith, *b.* 1838, *d.* 1900: *m.* 1st, 1867, Elizabeth Helen, who *d.* 1878, da. of the late Major James Wemyss (Bengal Army) [E. Wemyss and March, colls.]; 2ndly, 1887, Sophia Flora, O.B.E., who *d.* 1940, da. of the late Col. Charles Cooke Yarborough, C.B. [Cooke, Bt., colls.]:—
(By 2nd m.) **Frances Helen** (twin), *b.* 1889: *m.* 1917, Lt.-Col. George Kingston Sullivan, OBE, MC, DL, who *d.* 1961, formerly King's Own Yorkshire LI. *Residence*, Greathed Manor, Lingfield, Surrey.

Granddaughters of the late Archibald Peyton Skipwith, el. son of the late Lionel Skipwith (infra) :—
Issue of the late Major Frank Peyton Skipwith, Roy. Scots Fusiliers, *b* 1882, *d.* (killed in action during European War) 1915: *m.* 1909, The Hon. Bridget Vera Byng [who *d.* 1962, having *m.* 2ndly, 1919, William Gordon Cardew], da. of 8th Viscount Torrington:—

Nannette Elizabeth, *b.* 1910: *m.* 1954, Lt.-Col. John Raymond Louis Dennis Brett, late Indian Army, of Ardkeen, Milford, co. Donegal.——Cynthia, *b.* 1912: *m.* 1933, Desmond Shaw Smith, of Letternoosh, Clifden, co. Galway, and has issue living, David Patrick Shaw, *b.* 1939.

Grandchildren of the late Lionel Skipwith, 7th son of 8th baronet :—

Issue of the late Frederick Charles Skipwith, *b.* 1857, *d.* 1940: *m.* 1893, Mary Annie, da. of G. F. Cremer, formerly of Wanganui, New Zealand :—

Gore Peyton Lewis, *b.* 1894.——Lionel Ernest, *b.* 1896: *m.* 1929, Eva May, da. of J. Hopkins, of Auckland, New Zealand, and has issue living, Ronald Hugh, *b.* 1930. *Residence,* Auckland, New Zealand.

Issue of the late Francis Skipwith, *b.* 1861, *d.* 1934: *m.* 1899, Marjory, who *d.* 1957, da. of the late Capt. T. F. Rolt, formerly Coldstream Guards :—

Robert Grey, *b.* 1900 : *m.* 1937, Annemarie, da. of the late Hans Evers, of Ratzeburg, Germany, and has issue living, Francis Grey (72, Kingsgate St., Winchester), *b.* 1940: *m.* 1968, Jacqueline Ann, da. of Charles Albert Frederick Kettley, and has issue living, Andrew William Grey *b.* 1969, Timothy Edward *b.* 1972, Barnaby James *b.* 1974,—Robert Frederick, *b.* 1941. *Residence,* Newbold Farm, Umtali, Rhodesia.——Lionel Peyton, *RN, b.* 1902; became Capt. 1952; 1939-41 War (despatches twice): *m.* 1926, Thelma Westwood, da. of the late Surg.-Com. Adrian A. Forrester, of Weymouth, and has issue living, Venetia Forrester, *b.* 1932. *Residence,* Bounty House, Ropley, Alresford, Hants. :—

Grandchildren of the late Francis Skipwith (ante):—

Issue of the late William Estouteville Skipwith, *b.* 1904, *d.* 1975: *m.* 1st, 1934, Margaret Joan, who *d.* 1965, da. of the late Ernest Mark Shattock, of Colombo; 2ndly, 1968, Joan Emma (Gomms, Bramdean, Alresford, Hants.), da. of the late Joseph William Teale, and formerly wife of Aubrey Gordon Leacock, CBE, FRCS:—

(By 1st m.) Mark, *b.* 1944; ed. at Marlborough, and Southampton Univ.——Sara Anne, *b.* 1947.

Grandchildren of the late Lionel Skipwith (ante):—

Issue of the late Rev. Granville Gore Skipwith, *b.* 1865, *d.* 1955 : *m.* 1899, Violet Mary, who *d.* 1957, da. of the late George Walter Tyser, J.P. [Parkyns, Bt.] :—

Philip Lionel D'Estoteville SKIPWITH-TYSER, *b.* 1904 ; ed. at Eton, and at Trin. Coll., Camb.; European War 1939-40 as Lieut. R.E. (despatches, prisoner) ; assumed by Roy. licence 1958 the additional surname and arms of Tyser : *m.* 1932, Elsie Barbara, da. of the late Col. Arthur Edward Phillips, D.S.O., of Winterbourne Dauntsay, near Salisbury, and has issue living, Richard Peyton (Old House Hotel, Wickham, Hants.), *b.* 1937: *m.* 1965, Annie Carmen Angele Marie, da. of André Bonner, of Chateau Leyran, Villenave d'Ornon, Bordeaux, and has issue living, Julian Alexandre d'Estoteville *b.* 1972, Anouk Barbara Hélène *b.* 1974,—Charles Fulwar, *b.* 1946: *m.* 1969, Lucy, da. of the late Maurice Othon, and has issue living, Naomi Barbara Marie-Francoise *b.* 1972,—Noel Camilla, *b.* 1934: *m.* 1959, Capt. Anthony Charles Alston Benda, 1st The Queen's Dragoon Gds., of Pipers Cottage, Grove Heath, Ripley, Surrey, and has issue living, Nicholas James Alston *b.* 1960, Jonathan Charles Alston *b.* 1962, William Philip Alston *b.* 1966. *Residence,* Studwell Lodge, Droxford, Hants.——*Rev.* Osmund Humberston (Oaklands House, Padworth Common, Berks.), *b.* 1906; ed. at Harrow, and at New Coll., Oxford (MA); sometime a Chap. to Forces; formerly a Missionary; Africa and SE Asia 1940-45: *m.* 1946, Philippa Katharine Jane, da. of the late Richard Edward Skipwith, MBE, of Ruddington, Notts, and has issue living, Peter Michael (2, Olden Mead, Letchworth, Herts.), *b.* 1947; BSc: *m.* 1970, Patricia Mary, BA, da. of David Allan, of Melton Park, Newcastle-on-Tyne, and has issue living, Susan Katharine *b.* 1972, Rebecca *b.* 1974.——Barbara Nannette, *b.* 1902: *m.* 1928, Gerald William Kenyon-Slaney, OBE, who *d.* 1953 [*see* B. Kenyon, colls.]. *Residences,* 16, Smith Terr., SW3, and The Garth, St. Margaret's Bay, Kent.

Granddaughters of the late Ernest d'Estoteville Skipwith (infra) :—

Issue of the late Randolph Bruce d'Estoteville Skipwith, *b.* 1880, *d.* 1939 : *m.* 1906, Adelia L. Warnken, who *d.* 1938 :—

Margery Louise, *b.* 1908: *m.* 1936, Earle Sydney Chard, Box 567, Sandycove Acres, RR1, Stroud, Ont., Canada, and has issue living, Carole Elizabeth: *m.* 19—, Gordon Lorne Down.——Lorraine Gladys, *b.* 1909: *m.* 1936, Herbert Roberts Adams, of 7, Richgrove Dr., Apt. 602, Weston, Ont., Canada, and has issue living, Donald Bruce, *q.* 1942.

Granddaughter of the late Rev. Randolph Skipwith, 10th son of 8th baronet:—

Issue of the late Ernest d'Estoteville Skipwith, *b.* 1847, *d.* 1894: *m.* 1874, Catherine, who *d.* 1936, da. of Col. Adam Peebles :—

Constance Mary: *b.* 1879: *m.* 1905, Wilfred Healy, and has issue living, Edwin Wilfred, *b.* 1907 : *m.* 1930. Ednid B. Nelson,—William Charles, *b.* 1916; attached to Roy. Canadian Ordnance Corps,—Kathleen Alice, *b.* 1912: *m.* 1939, Edward A. McLeod.

Grandson of the late Cdr. Sidmouth Stowell Skipwith, RN, yst. son of 8th baronet :—

Issue of the late Reginald Skipwith, *b.* 1866, *d.* 1931 : *m.* 1897, Kathleen Agatha, who *d.* 1959, da. of the late Arthur Philip Lloyd [E. Bradford, colls.] :—

Arthur Grey, *b.* 1902 ; Com. R.N. (retired) : *m.* 1933, Sarah Hope, da. of Major Alfred James Fraser, D.S.O., of Woodside, Hardingstone, Northampton, and has issue living, William Grey, *b.* 1938,—Sarah Jane, *b.* 1943: *m.* 1967, John William Finlay Robins, of Manor Farm, Longbridge Deverill, Wilts.,—Rosemary Anne (twin), *b.* 1943: *m.* 1966, Robert Peter Richard Iliffe, of The Malt House, Yattendon, Berks. [*see* B. Iliffe, colls.]. *Residence,* The Old Rectory, Twyford, Hants.

This baronet claims descent from Robert d'Estoteville, Baron of Cottingham, *temp* William the Conqueror. Many of his descendants were of knightly rank, and distinguished both in war and in law, a Sir William Skipwith having been a Justice of the Queen's Bench *temp.* Edward III. and Richard II., and a Sir Thomas having achieved honour in the French wars was knighted by Henry V. The 1st baronet, who achieved reputation as a poet, sold the Prestwold estates in 1653. The 3rd baronet emigrated to Virginia, USA, in the middle of the 17th century. Sir Peyton Skipwith, who died in Virginia in 1805 was domiciled in England, as were his successors.

SLADE, Creation (U.K.) 1831, of Maunsel House, Somersetshire.

Faithful and bold.

(*Sir*) (JULIAN) BENJAMIN ALFRED SLADE, 7th *Baronet* (has established his claim but does not use the title); *b.* May 22nd, 1946; *s.* his father, *Capt. Sir* MICHAEL NIAL 1962; ed. at Millfield.

Arms—Per fesse argent and sable, a pale countercharged and three horses' heads erased two and one of the second; on a chief ermine, two bombs fired proper. **Crest**—On a mount vert, a horse's head erased sable, encircled by a chain in the form of an arch gold.

Residences—Maunsel, North Newton, Bridgwater, Somerset; 164, Ashley Gdns., SW1.

Sister living—Sarah Jane (*Baroness Rotherwick*), *b.* 1930: *m.* 1952, the 2nd Baron Rotherwick. *Residences*, Cornbury Park, Charlbury, Oxon.; Lanfine, Newmilns, Ayrshire; 51, Eaton Sq., SW1.

Aunt living (daughter of 4th baronet)—Barbara Constance, *b.* 1903: *m.* 1931, Nathaniel Alexander Lindley [B. Lindley], and has issue living, John Alexander, *b.* 1932. *Residence*, Nowers Farm, Wellington, Somerset.

Widow living of 5th Baronet—FREDA MARY (*Freda, Lady Slade*), younger da. of the late Sidney Meates, of Whitehall, Maidenhead : *m.* 1922, Sir Alfred Fothringham Slade, 5th baronet, who *d.* 1960. *Residence* Maunsel Grange, St. Michael Church, Bridgwater, Somerset.

Collateral Branches living.

Granddaughter of the late Basil Alfred Slade (infra):—
Issue of the late Lieut.-Com. Frederick William Patrick Slade, R.N.V.R., *b.* 1892, *d.* 1928, *m.* 1913, Marie, da. of Edouard Perrucke :—
Mary Magdalen Althea, *b.* 1914: *m.* 1937, Oliver Lopez-y-Royo, son of Duke of Taurisano, and has issue living, Francis, *b.* 1942,—Maria José, *b.* 1937,—Diego, *b.* 1939,—Isolda Doloris, *b.* 1943. *Residence*, 11, Via Palmieri, Lecce, Italy.

Issue of the late Basil Alfred Slade, 2nd son of 3rd baronet, *b.* 1865, *d.* 1930: *m.* 1st, 1891, Louisa Mary (who obtained a divorce 1925), da. of William Clements; 2ndly, 1925, Grace Joanna, who *d.* 1975, da. of Edward Harrison Tame:—
(By 1st marriage) Iris Mary, *b.* 1897.

Granddaughter of the late Rev. George Fitzclarence Slade, 11th son of 1st Bt.:—

Issue of the late Adm. Sir Edmond John Warre Slade, K.C.I.E., K.C.V.O., *b.* 1859, *d.* 1928 : *m.* 1887, Florence Madelena, who *d.* 1931, el. da. of the late J. Carr Saunders :—
Madeleine Warre ("Mira Bei"), *b.* 1892. *Residence*,

Granddaughter of the late Marcus Warre Slade, KC, (infra):—

Issue of the late Marcus George Savill Slade, *b.* 1906, *d.* 1972: *m.* 1st, 1944 (m. diss. 1953), Rita Annie, da. of William James Motton, of Plymouth:—
Susan Rebecca (Whitehall, Wraysbury, Bucks.), *b.* 1945.

Grandchildren of the late Rev. George Fitzclarence Slade (ante):—

Issue of the late Marcus Warre Slade, KC, *b.* 1865, *d.* 1941: *m.* 1901, Josephine Isabella, who *d.* 1972, da. of the Rev. Henry Savill Young [Young, Bt., cr. 1769, colls.]:—

Muriel Rebecca, *OBE*, *b.* 1902; cr. OBE (Civil) 1949: *m.* 1924, Evelyn Stewart Lansdowne Beale, who *d.* 1972, and has issue living, Evelyn Martin Lansdowne, *b.* 1928,—Julian Robert Anthony, *b.* 1932. *Residence,*—Whitehall, Wraysbury, Bucks.

Issue of the late Henry Adolphus Warre Slade, *b.* 1869, *d.* 1936 : *m.* 1898, Beatrice Isobel Hilda, who *d.* 1940, da. of the late David Alexander Gordon, of Culvennan, Kirkcudbrightshire [Gordon, Bt., cr. 1706, colls.]:—

GERALD GORDON, *b.* Oct. 27th, 1899; Com. RN (ret.); 1915-18 War, 1939-45 War: *m.* 1952, Netta Kathleen, da. of Richard Edward Lloyd Maunsell, CBE, of Northbrooke, Ashford, Kent. *Residence*, Northbrooke, Ashford, Kent. *Club*,—Naval and Military.

Granddaughter of the late Henry Adolphus Warre Slade (ante):—

Issue of the late Maurice Gordon Slade, *b.* 1902, *d.* 1971: *m.* 1934, Margaret (Streams, West Kingston, Chippenham), da. of Hew Congreve Kennedy:—

Primrose, *b.* 1934: *m.* 1957, John Patrick Roger Heather Hayes, Maj. RE, c/o C. Hoare & Co., 37, Fleet St., EC4, and has issue living, Phoebe, *b.* 1960.

The 1st baronet, Gen. Sir John, G.C.H., served with great distinction in the Peninsular War. The 2nd baronet was an eminent Q.C. Sir Alfred, 3rd baronet, who served during the Crimean War, was Receiver-Gen. of Inland Revenue 1875-90.

SLEIGHT, Creation (U.K.) 1920, of Weelsby Hall, Clee, co. Lincoln.

Sir JOHN FREDERICK SLEIGHT, 3rd *Baronet; b.* April 13th, 1909; *s.* his father, *Sir* ERNEST, O.B.E., T.D., 1946: *m.* 1942, Jacqueline Margaret, el. da. of the late Major H. R. Carter, of Brisbane, Queensland, and widow of Ronald Mundell, and has issue.

Arms—Per chevron or and sable, in chief two cross-crosslets and in base a lymphad with sail hoisted counterchanged. **Crest**—A mast with sail hoisted argent charged with three cross-crosslets sable.

Residence—15, High St., Thame, Oxon.

Son living—RICHARD, *b.* May 27th, 1946.
Sister living—Joan Winifred, *b.* 1904: *m.* 1st, 1924, Ernest Addison, who *d.* 1951; 2ndly 1957, Alfred Frank Culham, and has issue living, (by 1st marriage) David Ernest, *b.* 1925,—Peter Arthur, *b.* 1931. *Residence*, The Lodge, Riby, Grimsby.
Widow living of 2nd Baronet—MARGARET (*Dowager Lady Sleight*), da. of the late C. F. Carter, JP, of The Limes, Grimsby: *m.* 1898, Sir Ernest Sleight, CBE, TD, 2nd Bt., who *d.* 1946. *Residence*—Nettleton Manor, Lincoln.
Collateral Branches living.

Serve all, slight none.

Issue of the late Major Rowland Sleight, JP, 2nd son of 1st baronet, *b.* 1877, *d.* 1947: *m.* 1906, Phebe Lambert, who *d.* 1962, da. of the late Henry Smethurst, JP, of Grimsby, Lincolnshire:—

Rowland Derek Lambert, *b.* 1908; ed. at Rugby: *m.* 1939, Winifred, da. of the late Calvert Hunt, of London, and has issue living, Lesley, *b.* 1943. *Residence*, The White House, Quidenham, Norfolk.——Phebe Patricia, *b.* 1913. *Residence*, Flat 2, 51, Bargate, Grimsby, Lincs.

Issue of the late Nelson Sleight, 3rd son of 1st baronet, *b.* 1883, *d.* 1939: *m.* 1915, Edith Mary, who *d.* 1966, da. of the late Christopher Dewick Charles Hunt, of Gainsborough:—

Peter, DFM (Corner Cottage, Hawerby, Grimsby, S. Humberside), *b.* 1920; 1939-45 War as Sqdn. Ldr. RAF (DFM): *m.* 1947, Joyce Elizabeth, el. da. of J. H. Dale, of The Langmore, Wold Newton, Lincolnshire, and has issue living, John Nelson (89, Waltham Rd., Grimsby, S. Humberside), *b.* 1947: *m.* 1974, Susan Jennifer, da. of J. C. Hewson, of Tetney, S. Humberside,—Diana Margaret, *b.* 1950: *m.* 1974, James Stewart Atkinson, of Chartwell Cottage, Chapel Lane, Wrawby, Brigg, S. Humberside.——Violet Mary, *b.* 1917: *m.* 1938, Frederick Ousey Redshaw, and has issue living, Pamela Mary, *b.* 1942: *m.* 1968, George Bryan O'Toole, of Mayes Farm, Mayes Lane, Sandon, Essex, and has issue living, Laurence James *b.* 1969, Howard Charles *b.* 1975, Stella Elizabeth *b.* 1971. *Residence*, 64, Moorgate, Acomb, York.

Issue of the late George Frederick Sleight, yst. son of 1st baronet, *b.* 1890, *d.* 1954: *m.* 1915, Edith Mary, who *d.* 1963, da. of the late Edwin James Brockway, JP, of Oakham, Rutland:—

George Frederick (Irby Dales, Irby-upon-Humber, Laceby, Lincs.), *b.* 1917; ed. at Rugby: *m.* 1949, Nancy Lilian, da. of Henry Elliot.——Michael Marcus, *b.* 1924; ed. at Camb. Univ. *Residence*, Binbrook Hall, Binbrook, Lincs.——Edith Mary, *b.* 1918: *m.* 1947, James Davey, and has issue living, Veronica Mary, *b.* 1950,—Caroline Frances *b.* 1954. *Residence*, Kelstern Hall, Louth, Lincs.

Sir George, 1st Bt., was Lord of the Manor of Kelstern, Lincolnshire, and a trawler owner of Grimsby. Sir Ernest, O.B.E., T.D., 2nd Bt., was High Sheriff of Lincolnshire 1946.

SMILEY, Creation (U.K.) 1903, of Drumalis, Larne, co. Antrim, and Gallowhill, Paisley, co. Renfrew.

Sir HUGH HOUSTON SMILEY, 3rd *Baronet; b.* Nov. 14th, 1905; *s.* his father, *Sir* JOHN, 1930; ed. at Eton; Capt. late Grenadier Guards, a J.P. and Vice-Lord-Lieut. for Hants. since 1973 (High Sheriff 1959), N.-W. Europe 1944-5: *m.* 1933, Nancy, el. da. of the late Ernest Walter Hardy Beaton, and has issue.

Arms—1st and 4th, per bend azure and or, a lion rampant ermine between three pheons countercharged, *Smiley*; 2nd and 3rd gules, on a chevron argent two mullets azure, in base a fusil of the second, *Kerr*. **Crest**—A lion's jamb erased, and holding in bend sinister a pheon shafted proper, head or.

Residence—Ivalls, Bentworth, Alton, Hants. **Club**—Guards'.

Son living—JOHN PHILIP (Cornerway House, Chobham, Surrey), *b.* Feb. 24th, 1934; ed. at Eton; Maj. Gren. Gds.; Cyprus 1958; ADC to Gov. of Bermuda 1961-62: *m.* 1963, Davina Elizabeth, el. da. of the late Denis Griffiths, of Orlingbury Hall, Northants, and has issue living, Christopher Hugh Charles, *b.* 1968,—William Timothy John, *b.* 1972,—Melinda Elizabeth Eirène, *b.* 1965.
Brothers living—John Claude (5, Cadogan St., SW3), *b.* 1910; ed. at Eton; Hon. Capt. Middlesex Yeo. (TA Reserve); 1939-42 War in Middle East: *m.* 1st, 1936, Lady Cecilia Katherine Wellesley (who *d.* 1952, and from whom he had obtained a divorce 1942), da. of 3rd Earl Cowley; 2ndly, 1947, Sheila Joyce (OTTERBARRY), da. of the late Hon. Stanhope Alfred Tollemache [B. Tollemache, colls.], and has issue living, (by 1st m.) David Valerian, *b.* 1938; ed. at Wellington Coll.; Maj. Roy. Horse Gds.: *m.* 1962, Rose-Ann, el. da. of Col. David Greig, of Borland, Kilmarnock, Ayrshire, and has issue living, Patrick Valerian *b.* 1965, Thomas Edward de Crespigny, *b.* 1967, Katherine Cecilia *b.* 1963.——David de Crespigny, MVO, OBE, MC (Benihome, Beniarbeig, Alicante, Spain). *Clubs*, White's, New (Edinburgh), *b.* 1916; Col. late R. Horse Guards, commanded R. Horse Guards 1952-54, Mil. Attaché Stockholm 1955-58 (Knight Cdr. of Order of the Sword of Sweden), and Cdr. of Armed Forces of Sultan of Muscat and Oman 1958-61, and Mil. Adviser to Iman of Yemen 1963-68; a Member of HM Bodyguard of Corps of Gentlemen-at-Arms 1966-68; 1939-35 War with 1st

By industry, valour, and fortitude.

Household Cav. Regt. in Middle East (despatches) and with Special Forces in the Balkans (MC and Bar), Far East 1945 (OBE); OBE (Mil) 1946, MVO (4th Class) 1952: *m.* 1947, Moyra Eileen, da. of the late Lt.-Col. Lord Francis George Montagu-Douglas-Scott, KCMG, DSO [*see* D. Buccleuch, colls.], and widow of Maj. Hugo Douglas Tweedie, Scots Guards, and has issue living, Xan de Crespigny, *b.* 1949; ed. at Eton and New Coll., Oxford (MA),—Philip David, *b.* 1951; ed. at Eton, and St. Andrews Univ. (BA).

Sister living—Patricia Margaret (Glebe House, Stanton by Bridge, Derbys.), *b.* 1907: *m.* 1st, 1931, Rupert Douglas Tollemache, who *d.* 1933 [B. Tollemache]; 2ndly, 1941, Col. Charles Dalby, CBE, and has issue living, (by 2nd m.) Charles Gerald, *b.* 1942; ed. at Eton; Arch. Assocn. Dip.; ARIBA,—Patrick Claude John, *b.* 1948; ed. at Rugby; late R. Green Jackets.

Aunt living (daughter of 1st baronet)—Eileen Margaret Kerr, *b.* 1895: *m.* 1922, the Rev. Alfred James Elgar, who *d.* 1963, and has issue living, Ronald Hubert (4, Mina St., Toowomba, Qld. 4350, Aust.), *b* 1925; Lt. late KRRC: *m.* 1st, 1951 (m. diss. 1962), Audrey Kathleen, da. of the late Matthew Agar, of Iver Heath; 2ndly. 1964, Pamela Mary, da. of Ernest Glover, of Cheshire, and widow of Dr. Herbert Stranack Fisher, and has issue living (by 1st m.), Hugh Alistair *b.* 1952; ed. at Canford, David Anthony *b.* 1955; ed. at Mossman, Mark Adrian *b.* 1957; ed. at Mossman, Mary Anne *b.* 1953; ed. at Wentworth, (by 2nd m.) Diana Bridget *b.* 1966,—Elissa Anne, *b.* 1929. *Residence*, Blue Cedars, 31, The Avenue, Branksome Park, Poole, Dorset.

Widow living of 2nd Baronet—VALERIE (*Dowager Lady Smiley*), youngest da. of Sir Claude Champion de Crespigny, 4th Bt.: *m.* 1903, Major Sir John Smiley, 2nd baronet, who *d.* 1930. *Residence*, Smiley Knowe, Wentworth, Virginia Water, Surrey.

Collateral Branches living.

Issue of the late Major Peter Kerr KERR-SMILEY, 2nd son of 1st baronet, *b.* 1879, *d.* 1943 (having assumed in 1905 the additional surname of Kerr): *m.* 1905, Maud, who *d.* 1962, da. of Ernest L. Simpson, of New York:—

Cyril Hugh, *TD* (Villa Tax-Xaghra, San Pawl-Tat-Targa, Malta, GC), *b.* 1906; is Major and Hon. Lt.-Col. Suffolk Regt. (TA); 1939-45 War: *m.* 1933, Agnes, da. of Lt.-Col. George Cecil Minett Sorel-Cameron, CBE [B. Tollemache], and has issue living, Peter Simon (Leaston House, Humbie, E. Lothian), *b.* 1934; ed. at Ampleforth; Lt.-Col. Queen's Own Highlanders (Seaforth and Camerons): *m.* 1960, Jennifer Guise, da. of Lt.-Col. T. G. Tucker, MC (ret.), and has issue living, Mark Alexander *b.* 1961, Robert Justin *b.* 1965, Emma Caroline Hyde *b.* 1963,—Hector Robert (Elms Hall, Colne Engaine, Essex; *Club*, Boodle's), *b.* 1937; ed. at Ampleforth; Lt. Queen's Own Cameron Highlanders (TA Reserve): *m.* 1962, Eleanor Jill, da. of Cdr. Peter Wadlow, RN (ret.), and has issue living, Simon Alastair Hugh *b.* 1964, Christopher Peter *b.* 1967, Charlotte Elizabeth *b.* 1963,—Nicholas Ernest, *b.* 1940; ed. at Ampleforth: *m.* 1973, Georgina Jane, el. da. of Maj. Sir George Andrew Dick-Launder, 12th Bt.——Elizabeth Maud, *b.* 1907: *m.* 1936, Christopher Edward Clive Hussey, CBE, who *d.* 1970 [E. Powis, colls.]. *Residence*, Scotney Castle, Lamberhurst, Kent.

Issue of the late Hubert Stewart Smiley, 3rd son of 1st baronet, *b.* 1883, *d.* 1922 : *m.* 1909, Elsie Hope (who *d.* 1970, having *m.* 2ndly, 1922, Lt.-Col. John Charles Denton Carlisle, DSO, OBE, MC), da. of the late Sir Charles Frederick Gill, KC:—

(Charles) Michael, *b.* 1910; ed. at Eton; Maj. late Rifle Bde.; 1939-45 War (prisoner): *m.* 1939, Lavinia, da. of the late Capt. the Hon. (Bernard) Clive Pearson, [*see* V. Cowdray, colls.], and has issue living, James Robin Clive, *b.* 1947,—Andrew Michael, *b.* 1952; ed. at Eton; Gren. Gds.: *m.* 1975, Sarah Caroline, da. of Lt.-Col. C. C. Coade,—Miranda Daphne Jane (*Countess of Iveagh*), *b.* 1940: *m.* 1963, the 3rd Earl of Iveagh, of Farmleigh, Castleknock, co. Dublin. *Residence*, Castle Fraser, Sauchen, Aberdeenshire; *Club*—White's.——Bridget Eileen Suzanne, *b.* 1918: *m.* 1939, Maj. John Monsell Christian, MC, TD, who obtained a divorce 1951; 2ndly, 1952, Maj. Peter Miller Mundy, MC, from whom she obtained a divorce 1966. *Residence*, Eastergate House, Eastergate, Chichester, Sussex.

The 1st baronet, Sir Hugh Houston Smiley, was Principal Proprietor of the *Northern Whig*. The 2nd baronet, Major Sir John Smiley, 6th Dragoon Guards, served during S. African War 1900-1902, and European War 1914-18.

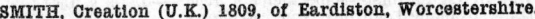

SMITH, Creation (U.K.) 1809, of Eardiston, Worcestershire.

Sir CHRISTOPHER SYDNEY WINWOOD SMITH, 5th *Baronet*; *b.* Sept. 20th, 1906 ; *s.* his father, *Sir* WILLIAM SYDNEY WINWOOD, 1953 : *m.* 1932, Phyllis Berenice, youngest da. of the late Thomas Robert O'Grady, of Waterford, Ireland, and Grafton, N.S. Wales, and has issue.

Arms—Sable, a cross flory or, on a chief engrailed ermine, a demi-lion issuant between two cross-crosslets gules. *Crest*—A greyhound couchant, sable, collared and line reflexed over the back or, the body charged with a cross-crosslet of the last, the dexter paw resting upon a cross flory as in the arms. *Residence*—Junction Road, via Grafton, N.S. Wales.

Sons living—ROBERT SYDNEY WINWOOD, *b.* 1939.——Hugh Standish Winwood, *b.* 1942.—— Terence John Winwood, *b.* 1944.

Daughters living—Villette Mary Winwood, *b.* 19—. ——Helen Eve Winwood, *b.* 19—.

Brother living—Rupert William Winwood (of 6, Beatty St., Toowoomba, Queensland), *b.* 1908: *m.* 1940, Nancia Jean Margaret, da. of John Bailey Cave, of Grafton, N.S. Wales, and has issue living, Geoffrey Stirling Winwood, *b.* 1945,—Adrian John Winwood, *b.* 1955,—Merran Joy Winwood, *b.* 1942.

Aunts living—Maud Agnes Winwood.——Dorothy Winwood.]*Residence,*

Collateral Branch living.

Grandchildren of the late William Arthur Winwood Smith, yst. son of 3rd baronet:—

Antony Winwood, DFC (c/o Forestry Commission, Salisbury, Rhodesia), *b.* 1920; 1939-45 War in RAF.——Pauline Muriel Winwood, *b.* 1918: *m.* 1949, James Mayhew, of Dougal, Duke St., Bexhill-on-Sea.

SMITH, Creation (U.K.) 1897, of Stratford Place, St. Marylebone, co. London.

Sir (THOMAS) GILBERT SMITH, 4th *Baronet; b.* July 2nd, 1937; *s.* his father, *Sir* THOMAS TURNER, 1961: ed. at Huntley Sch., and at Nelson Coll.; Engineer; *m.* 1962, Patricia Christine, da. of David Cooper, of Paraparaumu, NZ, and has issue.

Arms—Quarterly, or and gules, a fret between three fleurs-de-lis all counterchanged. **Crest**—A fret gules, issuant therefrom a fleur-de-lis or. *Residence*—50, Titoki St., Masterton, New Zealand.

Dabit qui dedit.

He will give who hath given.

Sons living—ANDREW THOMAS, *b.* Oct. 17th, 1965.——Alistair Blair, *b.* 1969.
Daughter living—Janne Fiona, *b.* 1963.
Brother living—Denis Michael (47, Aorangi Rd., Paraparaumu, NZ), *b.* 1945: *m.* 1967, Janet, da. of L. Eckhoff, of Paraparaumu, NZ, and has issue living, Richard Michael, *b.* 1968,—Joanna Marie, *b.* 1969.
Sisters living—Barbara Elizabeth, *b.* 1939: *m.* 1967, Selwyn Lloyd Harris, of Sanson, NZ, and has issue living, Boyd John, *b.* 1968,— Peter Thomas, *b.* 1970.——Judith Madeleine, *b.* 1941.
Uncle living—Gilbert Patrick, *b.* 1906. *Residence,* Terwhiti Station, Karori, Wellington, NZ.
Aunts living—Jean Elisabeth, *b.* 1901: *m.* 1929, Andrew Naismith Fergus, BSc, MB, ChB, FRCP, Glasgow, of Buffbeards, Hindhead Rd., Haslemere, Surrey, GU27 1LH, and has issue living, John Naismith, *b.* 1934; ed. at Oxford Univ. (MA, BM and BCh); FRCS, FRCSE: *m.* 1970, Catherine Isabel Wake, MRCS, LRCP, MB, da. of David Cazes, of Perseverance Cottage, Harpsden, Henley-on-Thames,—Margaret Elizabeth, *b.* 1931,—Sheena Mary, *b.* 1939,—Helen Kay, *b.* 1947.——Madeleine Lovedy (Stangate, Hurst Green, Sussex), *b.* 1909.
Widow living of 3rd Baronet—AGNES (*Agnes, Lady Smith*), da. of Bernard Page, of Wellington, NZ: *m.* 1935, Sir Thomas Turner Smith, 3rd Bt., who *d.* 1961. *Residence,* 118, Liverpool St., Wanganui, New Zealand.

Collateral Branch living.

Issue of the late Lieut.-Col. Michael Carson Lyndon Smith, M.C., M.B., B.S., M.R.C.S., L.R.C.P., I.M.S., brother of 3rd baronet, *b.* 1908, *d.* 1961: *m.* 1936, Pauline (of The Grange, Headley, Bordon, Hants), da. of Charles Rowlatt:—
Patrick Charles Gilbert, *b.* 1939; MB, BCh.——Sarah Gillian (*Lady Graham Moon*) (The Old Rectory, Biddisham, Som.), *b.* 1937: *m.* 1st, 1958 (m. diss. 1966), Maj. Anthony Gibbon Chater; 2ndly, 1967, Sir Peter Wilfred Giles Graham Moon, 5th Bt., and has issue living, (by 1st m.) James Michael Douglas, *b.* 1959,—Giles Addison, *b.* 1961,—Piers Antony Rowlatt, *b.* 1963, (by 2nd m.) [see Moon, Bt., cr. 1855].——Elizabeth Caroline, *b.* 1940.——Alexa Pauline Lovedy, *b.* 1945.—— Joanna Esmée, *b.* 1948: *m.* 19—.

Sir Thomas Smith, K.C.V.O., F.R.C.S., 1st baronet was so created on the occasion of H.M. Queen Victoria's Diamond Jubilee in recognition of his eminence as a Surgeon ; he was Surg. Extraor. to Queen Victoria, Hon Sergeant-Surg. to King Edward VII., and a Vice-Pres. of Roy. Coll. of Surgeons. Sir (Thomas) Rudolph Hampden Smith, C.B.E., F.R.C.S., 2nd baronet, was Hon. Surg. Comdg. Torquay Hospital for Wounded Soldiers 1914-18.

SMITH, Creation (U.K.) 1920, of Kidderminster, co. Worcester. [Extinct 1961.]

Sir HERBERT SMITH, 2nd and last *Baronet.*

Daughters living of 2nd Baronet—Emily Lindsay Cherrington, *b.* 1930 : *m.* 1958, Joseph Thwaites.——Martha Theresa Belinda, *b.* 1933 : *m.* 1956, Robin Houghton Stretton, and has issue living, Martin John, *b.* 1959,—Bridget Claire, *b.* 1957. *Residence,* Oldbury Grove, Bridgnorth, Salop.
Daughters living of 1st Baronet—Mabel Merci, *b.* 1899.——Dora, *b.* 1901 : *m.* 1922, George Edgar Ingman, who obtained a divorce 1929. *Residence,*
Widow living of 2nd Baronet—E. M. (GRIFFIN) (*Lady Smith*) : *m.* 1948, as his second wife, Sir Herbert Smith, 2nd Bt., who *d.* 1961, when the title became ext. *Residence,* Oldbury Grove, Bridgnorth, Salop.

SMITH, Creation (U.K.) 1945, of Crowmallie, co. Aberdeen.

Sir (WILLIAM) GORDON SMITH, *V.R.D.,* 2nd *Baronet ; b.* Jan. 30th, 1916 ; *s.* his father, *Sir* ROBERT (WORKMAN) 1957 ; ed. at Westminster, and at Trin. Coll., Camb. (BA); Bar. Inner Temple 1939; Lt.-Cdr. RNR (ret.); 1939-45 War (despatches): *m.* 1st, 1941 (m. diss. 1958), Diana Gundreda, da. of the late Maj. Charles Malden, RMLI, of Aquahorthies, Aberdeenshire; 2ndly, 1958, Diana Goodchild, and has issue by 2nd m.

Arms—Or, on the waves of the sea, a three masted ship in full sail proper flagged gules on a chief engrailed, vert, a flame of fire between two horseshoes of the first. **Crest**— A sea-horse argent.

Seat—Crowmallie, Pitcaple, Aberdeenshire. *Residence* —44 Walton Street, S.W.3.

Sons living—By 2nd marriage—ROBERT HILL, *b.* April 15th, 1958.——Charles Gordon, *b.* 1959.

Brother living—Robert Alexander, *b.* 1920 ; ed. at Stowe, and at Trin. Coll., Camb.; European War 1940-45 as Lieut. R.N.V.R.: *m.* 1945, Marianne, da. of Serge Denissieff, and widow of George Plaoutine, of Philippville, Algeria, and has issue living, Andrew Alexander, *b.* 1946,—Robert Serge, *b.* 1948. *Residence,* Crowmallie House, Pitcaple, Aberdeenshire.

Widow living of 1st Baronet—JESSIE HILL (*Jessie, Lady Smith*), da. of the late William Workman, of Nottinghill, Belfast: *m.* 1911, Sir Robert (Workman) Smith, 1st Bt., who *d.* 1957. *Residence*, Crowmallie, Pitcaple, Aberdeenshire.

The 1st baronet, Sir Robert (Workman) Smith, younger son of the late George Smith (Chm. of "City Line," Glasgow) of Glenmorag, Argyllshire, was M.P. for Central Div. of Aberdeenshire and Kincardineshire (*C*) 1924-1945.

SMITH, Creation (U.K.) 1947, of Keighley, co. York.

Sir GEORGE BRACEWELL SMITH, *MBE*, 2nd *Baronet; b.* Nov. 5th, 1912; *s.* his father, *Sir* BRACEWELL, *KCVO*, 1966; ed. at Wrekin Coll., and at Emmanuel Coll., Camb. (MA); a Warden of Haberdashers' Co. 1957-58, and 1974-75; Chm. Park Lane Hotel Ltd., Ritz Hotel London Ltd., Ritz Hotels Development Co. Ltd., since 1966; MBE (Civil) 1946: *m.* 1951, Helene Marie, who *d.* 1975, da. of the late John Frederick Hydock, of Philadelphia, USA, and has issue.

Arms—Tierce in pairle reversed argent, gules and azure; in chief, two roses counterchanged barbed and seeded proper, and in base a London pride plant flowered and eradicated also proper. **Crest**—Upon a rock a moorcock rising, resting the dexter foot on a double convex lens, all proper.

Residence—Park Lane Hotel, Piccadilly, W1.

Sons living—GUY BRACEWELL, *b.* Dec. 12th, 1952.—— Charles Bracewell, *b.* 1955.

Sister living—Eileen Mary, *b.* 1911: *m.* 1st, 1933, Harry C. Lascelles Carr, who *d.* 1943, son of the late Sir Emsley Carr; 2ndly, 1948, James Shelley Phipps Armstrong, Agent-Gen. for Ontario in London, who *d.* 1971, and has issue living (by 1st m.), Clive Emsley Bracewell Lascelles, *b.* 1934: *m.* 1963, Isabel, da. of the Vicomte de Rancougne, of Paris,—Richard Charles Lascelles, *b.* 1938: *m.* 1960, Edda, da. of P. Armbrust, of Bremen,—Carol Mary Lascelles, *b.* 1936: *m.* 1955, Francis Geoffrey Hooton of 111, Summit Circle, Westmount, Montreal, Canada,—(by 2nd m.) Sarah Margaret Phipps, *b.* 1951. *Residence*, 14, Ennismore Gdns., Knightsbridge, SW7.

Sir Bracewell Smith, KCVO, 1st Bt., son of Samuel Smith, of Keighley, Yorks., was MP for Dulwich (*C*) 1932-45, and Lord Mayor of London 1946-47.

CUSACK-SMITH, Creation (I.) 1799, of Newtown, King's County.
[Extinct 1970.]

Sir (WILLIAM ROBERT) DERMOT JOSHUA CUSACK-SMITH, 6th and last *Baronet.*

Daughters living of 6th Baronet—By 1st m.—Berry, *b.* 1937: *m.* 1960, (Hugh) Jon Foulds, and has issue living, William Mark Aubrey, *b.* 1963,—Hugo Charles Berry, *b.* 1967.——By 2nd m.— Oonagh Mary, *b.* 1948: *m.* 1972, John Michael Hyland.

Daughter living of 5th Baronet—Sarita Catherine Williamina (Graffham Court, Graffham, Petworth, Sussex), *b.* 1906: *m.* 1939, Henry Andrew Sarel Davies, late Maj. RA, who *d.* 1967.

Widow living of 6th Baronet—ADELA MARY (*Lady Cusack-Smith*), (Bermingham House, Tuam, co. Galway), da. of Charles Trench O'Rorke, of Bermingham House, Tuam, co. Galway: *m.* 1946, as his 2nd wife, Sir (William Robert) Dermot Joshua Cusack-Smith, 6th Bt., who *d.* 1970, when the title became ext.

Hamilton Spencer-Smith, see Spencer-Smith.

NEWSON-SMITH, Creation (U.K.) 1944, of Totteridge, co. Hertford.

Sir JOHN KENNETH NEWSON-SMITH, 2nd *Baronet;* b. Jan. 9th, 1911; s. his father, *Sir* FRANK (EDWIN), 1971; ed. at Dover Coll., and Jesus Coll., Camb. (MA); a DL for City of London; a Common Councilman 1945, and a Dep. 1961, one of HM Lieuts. 1947; 1939-45 War as Lt. RNVR: m. 1st, 1945 (m. diss. 1971), Vera Margaret, da. of the late Dr. Wilfred Greenhouse Altt, CVO, CBE; 2ndly, 1972, Anne, da. of the late Harold Burns, and has issue by 1st m.

Arms—Gules, on a chevron or, between in chief two bezants, and in base a cross pattée fitchée of the second, a pellet between two crosses pattée fitchée sable. **Crest**—Issuant from a mural crown or, a goat's head argent, armed and bearded or, eared sable and charged with a sword erect gules.

Residence—39, Godfrey St., SW3.

Son living—By 1st m.—PETER FRANK GRAHAM, b. May 8th, 1947; ed. at Dover Coll.: m. 1974, Mary-Ann, da. of Cyril C. Collins, of 12, Manor Close, Old Woodstock, Oxon., and formerly wife of   Owens.
Daughters living—By 1st m.—Susan Rosemary, b. 1946,—Elizabeth Jane, b. 1953.

Sisters living—Doris Enid, b. 1905: m. 1943, Maj. Stanley Thomas Woodruff, TD, of Bury House, 176, Bury St., Ruslip, Middx., HA4 7TJ, and has issue living, Peter Miles (Ivy House, South Entrance, Saxmundham, Suffolk), b. 1946: m. 1969, Deborah, el. da. of Frederick John Mascall, of Church Farm, Earl Stonham, Suffolk, and has issue living, Jonathan George b. 1971, Christopher Miles b. 1973, Nicholas Charles b. 1975.——Mary Sharland, b. 1909: m. 1935, Maj. Claude Morrison, who d. 1967, and has issue living, *Rev.* John Anthony (The Vicarage, Upper Basildon, Reading), b. 1938; ed. at Haileybury, and Jesus Coll., Camb. (MA),—Michael Bruce, b. 1939; ed. at Haileybury: m. 1960, Anne Margaret, da. of Archibald Hew Grace, MRCS, LRCP, of Cooden, Sussex, and has issue living, Bruce Anthony b. 1961, Clare Fiona b. 1964,—Jennifer Mary b. 1943: m. 1965, Peter Robert Daniel of 24, Crutchfield Lane, Walton-on-Thames, and has issue living, Karen Jane b. 1966, Tracey Emma b. 1968. *Residence*, 65, Albany Court, Robertson Terr., Hastings, Sussex.

Collateral Branch living.

Issue of the late Capt. Peter Henry Newson-Smith, R.A., younger son of 1st baronet, b. 1914, d. (killed on active ser. in Italy) 1944: m. 1939, Gertrude Irene, da. of Frederick Lester Walker, of Georgia, U.S.A., she m. 2ndly, 1948, Bertrand Milton Walker, of 1200, Cherokee Drive, Waycross, Georgia, USA:—

Carole Irene, b. 1943.

Sir Frank (Edwin) Newson-Smith, 1st Bt. son of Henry Newson-Smith, DL, CA., of London, was Lord Mayor of London 1943-44.

PRINCE-SMITH, Creation (U.K.) 1911, of Hillbrook, Keighley, W. Riding of Yorkshire.

Sir (WILLIAM) RICHARD PRINCE-SMITH, 4th *Baronet;* b. Dec. 27th, 1928; s. his father, *Sir* WILLIAM, OBE, MC, 1964; ed. at Charterhouse, and at Clare Coll., Camb. (MA): m. 1st, 1955, Margaret Ann, only da. of the late Dr. John Carter, of Goldings, Loughton, Essex; 2ndly, 1975, Ann Faulds, and has issue by 1st m.

Arms—Per chevron nebuly or guttée de sang and gules, two stags' heads cabossed in chief of the last and a rose in base argent, barbed and seeded proper. **Crest**—A dragon's head erased gules, charged with a rose as in the arms, between a stag's attires or.

Residence—Augres House, Trinity, Jersey.

The more prepared, the more powerful.

Son living—By 1st m.—JAMES WILLIAM , b. July 2nd, 1959.
Daughter living—By 1st m.—Elizabeth Ann, b. 1957.

Sister living—Eileen Marjorie Clare, b. 1932: m. 1959, Stephen Hattersley Smith, and has issue living, Christopher Stephen Hattersley, b. 1963,—Jane Clare Hattersley, b. 1961,—Vanessa Jill Hattersley, b. 1965. *Residence*, Pool Hall, Pool-in-Wharfedale, Otley, Yorks., LS21 1L7.

The 1st baronet, Sir Prince Smith (son of the late Prince Smith, of Holly House, Keighley), was a J.P. for W. and E. Ridings of Yorkshire. The 2nd baronet, Sir Prince, assumed by deed poll 1922, the additional surname of Prince.

REARDON-SMITH, Creation (U.K.) 1920, of Appledore, co. Devon.

What I do I do earnestly.

Quod facio valde facio

Sir WILLIAM REARDON REARDON-SMITH, 3rd *Baronet*; *b.* March 12th, 1911; *s.* his father *Sir* WILLIE, 1950; ed. at Blundell's Sch.; is Major R.A. (T.A.): *m.* 1st, 1935, Nesta (who *d.* 1959, having obtained a divorce 1954), da. of Frederick J. Phillips; 2ndly, 1954, Beryl, da. of William H. Powell, and has issue by 1st and 2nd marriages.

Arms—Argent, upon a mount vert in front of an oak tree fructed proper a lion passant gules, in chief three estoiles sable. *Crest*—In front of a mast and sail of a ship proper charged with a sphinx couchant sans wings argent, an anchor fessewise sable, entwined with a scroll silver, inscribed "H.M.S. Romulus," in letters also sable.

Residence—Rhode Farm, Romansleigh, South Molton, N. Devon.

Sons living—By 1st marriage—(WILLIAM) ANTONY JOHN (Cedars House, Church Rd., Windlesham, Surrey, GU20 6BL), *b.* June 20th, 1937; ed. at Wycliffe Coll.: *m.* 1962, Susan, da. of Henry W. Gibson, of Cardiff, and has issue living, William Nicholas Henry, *b.* 1963,—Giles Antony James, *b.* 1968,—Henrietta Nesta, *b.* 1965.—— Barrie Alan, *b.* 1942: *m.* 1965, Wendy Elizabeth, da. of George W. Bigglestone, of Coventry, and has issue living, Samantha Elizabeth, *b.* 1966,—Louise Suzanne, *b.* 1968. ——Timothy Henry Neale, *b.* 1944: *m.* 1966, Lynda Madeleine, da. of F. W. Preston, of Redditch, and has issue living, James Henry Charles, *b.* 1971——By 2nd m.—— David Joseph William, *b.* 1960.

Daughters living—By 1st m.—Nesta Suzanne, *b.* 1939: *m.* 1958, Francis Edward Sutherland Hayes, of Llansannor House, Cowbridge, Glam., and has issue living, Patrick Neil Sutherland, *b.* 1961,— Thira Nesta, *b.* 1960,—Elizabeth Ann, *b.* 1964,—Philippa Vara, *b.* 1966.——By 2nd m.—Deirdre Ellen, *b.* 1955.——Amanda Mary, *b.* 1958.——Penelope Ann, *b.* 1962.

Brother living—Douglas Hamlyn (Hankerton Priory, Malmesbury, Wilts.), *b.* 1928; ed. at Marlborough, and Roy. Agric. Coll., Cirencester: *m.* 1949, Minnie Wanna, da. of John Dawson, of Ludlow Cottage, Hankerton, Malmesbury, Wilts.

Sister living—Ellen Mary, *b.* 1922: *m.* 1947, Dr. David Kenneth Lewis Davies, and has issue living, David Christopher, *b.* 1948,—Simon James, *b.* 1952,—William Peter, *b.* 1953,—Siân Elizabeth, *b.* 1956,—Mark Hamlyn, *b.* 1961. *Residence*, 15, Pencisely Road, Cardiff.

Aunt living (daughter of 1st baronet)—Grace Hamlyn SMITH. *Residence*, Cornborough, Ty Gwyn Rd., Cardiff.

Widow living of 2nd Baronet—ELIZABETH ANN (*Dowager Lady Reardon-Smith*), da. of John Wakeley, of Cardiff: *m.* 1910, Sir William Reardon-Smith, 2nd Bt., who *d.* 1950. *Residence*, The Hermitage, Fairwater Rd., Llandaff.

Collateral Branches living—

Issue of the late Alan John Reardon Smith, 2nd son of 2nd baronet, *b.* 1914, *d.* 1970: *m.* 1937, Winifred Maud, who *d.* 1975, da. of Frederick C. Williams:— John Philip (The Old Vicarage, Penmark, Barry, Glam.), *b.* 1941: *m.* 1964, Josephine Mireille, da. of Frederick Wilding, of Barry, Glam., and has issue living, Charles Alan, *b.* 1965,—Simon John, *b.* 1966,—Katharine Lisa, *b.* 1971.——Richard William Alan (Old Rosedew House, Llantwit Major, Glam.), *b.* 1946: *m.* 1970, Suzanne Ward, da. of Jonathan Preece Jones, of Coychurch, Glam. and has issue living, Dylan Alan John, *b.* 1972,—Zahra Elizabeth, *b.* 1973.

Issue of the late Douglas SMITH, yr. son of 1st baronet, *b.* 1894, *d.* 1961: *m.* 1916, Gladys May, who *d.* 1972, da. of John Randell, of Cardiff:— Margaret Hamlyn, *b.* 1920: *m.* 1945, Denis Maxwell Johnson, who *d.* 1967, and has issue living, Stewart Maxwell, *b.* 1949,—Graham Hamlyn, *b.* 1951.——Jean Reardon, *b.* 1922: *m.* 1st, 1940, Morton Fergusson Llewellyn, from whom she obtained a divorce 1957; 2ndly, 1958, John Douglas Rae, of Halferne, Castle Douglas, Kirkcudbrightshire, and has issue living, (by 1st m.) David Morton, *b.* 1942.

The 1st baronet, Sir Willie Reardon Smith (son of Capt. Thomas Reardon Smith, of Appledore, N. Devon), was a Shipowner, a Coal Exporter, and an Insurance Broker. Sir Willie, 2nd baronet, assumed by deed-poll 1929 the surname of Reardon-Smith in lieu of his patronymic.

SPENCER-SMITH, Creation (U.K.) 1804, of Tring Park, Hertfordshire.

By war and wit.

MARTE ET INGENIO

Sir JOHN HAMILTON SPENCER-SMITH, 7th *Baronet*; *b.* March 18th, 1947; *s.* his father, *Sir* THOMAS COSPATRIC, 1959.

Arms—Sable, on a fesse cottised between three martlets or, as many crescents azure, *Crest*—A sword proper, pommel and hilt or, and a pen argent in saltire.

Residence—Priory Orchard, Easebourne, Midhurst, Sussex.

Widow living of 6th Baronet—LUCY ASHTON (*Lady Spencer-Smith*), only da. of the late Thomas Ashton Ingram: *m.* 1944, Sir Thomas Cospatric Hamilton Spencer-Smith, 6th Bt., who *d.* 1959. *Residence*, Priory Orchard, Easebourne, Midhurst, Sussex.

Collateral Branches living

Grandchildren of the late Rev. Spencer Compton Hamilton-Spencer-Smith, 3rd son of the late Spencer SMITH, yr. brother of 2nd baronet:— Issue of the late Lt.-Col. Michael Seymour Hamilton-Spencer-Smith,

DSO, MC (did not use the surname of Hamilton), b. 1881, d. 1928: m. 1907, Evelyn
Penelope, who d. 1974, having m. 2ndly, 1934, Elliot Francis Montagu Butler], da. of
the late Rev. Arthur Delmé-Radcliffe [E. Harrowby, colls.]:—
PETER COMPTON, b. Nov. 12th, 1912 ; ed. at Eton, and at New Coll., Oxford ; formerly Major
79th Herts Yeo. (Heavy Anti-Aircraft Regt.), R.A. (T.A.) : m. 1950, Philippa Mary, da. of the
late Capt. Richard Ford, Rifle Brig., and has issue living, Michael Philip, b. 1952,—Gerald Peter
Harry, b. 1954. Residence, High Down House, Hitchin, Herts.——Jeremy Michael, CB, OBE, MC
(The White Cottages, Cheveley, Newmarket), b. 1917; ed. at Eton, and at New Coll., Oxford;
Maj.-Gen. (ret.) late Welsh Gds.; GOC Wales 1968-70, and Dir. of Manning (Army) Min. of
Defence 1970-72; OBE (Mil) 1959, CB (Mil) 1971.——Beatrice Mary (Lady Graham), b. 1909:
m. 1939, Wing-Com. Sir Richard Bellingham Graham, OBE, 10th Bt., RAFVR. Residence,
Norton Conyers, Melmerby, nr. Ripon.

Grandchildren of the late Rev. Orlando Spencer SMITH, 4th son of Spencer Smith (ante):—

Issue of the late Col. Gerald Montagu Spencer SMITH, DSO, RA, b. 1881, d. 1951: m. 1912,
Iris Mary, who d. 1967, da. of the late Richard Arthur Hamilton Seymour [Culme-
Seymour, Bt., colls.]:—
Judith, b. 1917: m. 1940, Harry Illtyd Lee, and has issue living, James Seymour (19, Queen's Gate
Place, SW7), b. 1945; a fashion photographer: m. 1967, Sally Hill, da. of the late Edwin Hector
Gordon Brookes, AFC, and has issue living, Orlando Spencer Seymour b. 1968,—Caroline Susan,
b. 1941,—Ann, b. 1943: m. 1963, Nicholas Hugh Carter, of Weleirs, Town Row Green, Rotherfield,
Sussex, and has issue living, Maximilian Hugh b. 1965, Emma Louise b. 1966, Sophie Ann b.
1969,—Lindsey Victoria, b. 1954. Residence, Popple Hill, Graffham, Petworth, Sussex.

Issue of the late Col. Richard Osbaldeston SPENCER-SMITH, b. 1885, d. 1962: m. 1st,
1912, Murielle Alethe Victoria, who d. 1931, da. of Leonard Guise John Wingfield-
Stratford [V. Powerscourt, colls.]; 2ndly, 1932, Christian Louisa, who d. 1962, da. of
the late Lieut.-Col. H. E. Passy:—
(By 1st marriage) Roland Wingfield (Three Corners, Old Newton Rd., Kingskerswell, Newton
Abbot, S. Devon, TQ12 5LB), b. 1916; Maj. (ret.) Roy. Hampshire Regt.: m. 1948, Helen Rosamund, da. of Lieut-Col. J. P. Earp, and has issue living, Richard Mervyn, b. 1954,—Jennifer
Murielle, b. 1952: m. 1973, Peter Leslie Riley.——Drummond Mervyn (Chain Walk, Clatford
Manor Mews, Upper Clatford, Andover), b. 1920, ed. at Wellington; Capt. (ret.) R. Tank Regt.:
m. 1960, June Patrysha, da. of Bertram George Finn, and has issue living, Christopher Rex,
b. 1962,—Rosalind Muriel, b. 1960.——(By 2nd m.) Rosan Winifred, b. 1934.

Granddaughters of the late Spencer SMITH (ante):—

Issue of the late Capt. Gilbert Joshua Spencer SMITH, b. 1843, d. 1928: m. 1875, Edith
Charlotte, who d. 1936, da. of the late Capt. Hon. Dudley Worsley Anderson-Pelham,
RN [E. Yarborough, colls.]:—
Grace Isabel, b. 1880: m. 1911, Capt. James Gordon Fraser, OBE, RN (ret.), who d. 1970, and has
issue living, Jean Grace Mary, b. 1914: m. 1948, David Stewart, OBE, of Banchory
House, Banchory-Devenick, Kincardineshire, and Leggart, Kincardineshire,—Olive Iona
Rachel, b. 1919: m. 1945, Thomas Blakiston O'Reilly [Blakiston, Bt., colls.], and has issue living,
James Blakiston b. 1954, Andrea Frances b. 1949. Residence, Shirral House, Shedfield, Hants.
——Mary Elinor (c/o Lloyds Bank, Dawlish, Devon), b. 1883: m. 1931, Langlois B. Lefroy, who
d. 1959.——Rachel, b. 1887: m. 1921, John Laurence Westmacott, and has issue living, Gilbert
John (Rotherfield House, Peppard, Henley-on-Thames), b. 1929; ed. at Winchester: m. 1963,
Gillian Mary, el. da. of the late Wing Cdr. J. G. Llewelyn, and has issue living,
Andrew John b. 1964, Mark Richard b. 1969, Edward Anthony b. 1971, Lucinda Mary b. 1966,—
Mary Elizabeth, b. 1922: m. 1943, Cdr. Stephen Aubone Hammick, DSC, RN [see Hammick, Bt.,
colls.],—Helen Amabel, b. 1924: m. 1953, Cyril Geoffrey Marmaduke Alington, and has issue
living, Rosemary Jane b. 1953, Jill Amabel b. 1956,—Edith Rosemary, b. 1926: m. 1949, Richard
James Douglas McCulloch Kinsman, HM Oversea Ser. (ret.), of Meon Holt, Catisfield, Fareham,
Hants, and has issue living, Simon John Charles b. 1954, Anne Edith b. 1950, Lucy Rachel
b. 1957. Residence, Maidenstone Heath, Bursledon, Hants.——Beatrice Evelyn, b. 1890.
Residence, Chapel Farm, Ashton, Bishops Waltham, Hants.——Octavia, b. 1892. Residence,
Chapel Farm, Ashton, Bishops Waltham, Hants.

The 1st baronet, Sir Drummond Smith, not having issue, the patent of baronetcy was conferred
with remainder to the issue male of his niece, Augusta (daughter of his el. brother, Joshua Smith),
who m. 1798 Charles Smith, M.P., of Suttons, Essex, descended from Robert Smith of Ilminster,
ancestor of Smith-Marriott, Bt. Sir Drummond Cospatric Hamilton-Spencer-Smith, 5th Bt.,
O.B.E., (whose father the Rev. Spencer Compton Hamilton-Spencer-Smith assumed the additional
names of Hamilton and Spencer 1872, having m. Mary, da. of Adm. Cospatric Baillie-Hamilton,
descended from 6th Earl of Haddington), was Mil. Sec. to Comdt. of New Zealand Forces 1910-13,
and a Member of Mil. Inter-Allied Commn. of Control 1920-24. The 6th Bt. discontinued the use
of the surname of Hamilton.

VASSAR-SMITH, Creation (U.K.) 1917, of Charlton Park, Charlton Kings, co. Gloucester.

Sir RICHARD RATHBORNE VASSAR-SMITH,
T.D., 3rd Baronet, son of the late Major Charles
Martin Vassar-Smith, 3rd son of 1st baronet : b.
Nov. 24th, 1909 : s. his uncle, Sir JOHN GEORGE
LAWLEY, 1942 : ed. at Lancing Coll., and at Pem-
broke Coll., Camb. (BA 1931); 1939-45 War as
Maj. RA: m. 1932, Mary Dawn, da. of Sir Raymond
Wybrow Woods, CBE, and has issue.

Arms—Quarterly, 1st and 4th per bend embattled azure and
or, in the sinister chief point a cuirass with tasces attached and in
the dexter base point a well-head all counterchanged, Smith ;
2 and 3, argent, an Etruscan vase gules, in chief two fusils azure,
each charged with a fleur-de-lis or, Vassar. Crests—1st, a dexter
arm embowed in armour proper, bound above the elbow with a
scarf gules and holding in the hand an arrow in bend point
downwards or and a pair of pincers in fesse sable, Smith ; 2nd,
an Etruscan vase gules between two branches of oak fructed
proper, Vassar.
Residence—Orchard House, Hawkhurst, Kent.

Labour and truth.

Son living—JOHN RATHBORNE, b. July 23rd, 1936: ed.
at Eton.

Daughter living—Juliet Rathborne, b. 1941.

The 1st baronet, Sir Richard (son of the late Richard Tew Smith), assumed by Roy. licence
1904, the additional surname of Vassar, and was Chm. of Lloyds Bank (Limited).

WALKER-SMITH, Creation (U.K.) 1960, of Broxbourne, co. Herts.

Rt. Hon. Sir DEREK COL-CLOUGH WALKER-SMITH, *T.D., Q.C., MP,* 1st *Baronet,* son of the late Sir Jonah Walker-Smith ; *b.* April 13th, 1910; ed. at Rossall, and at Ch. Ch., Oxford (B.A. 1931) ; Bar. Middle Temple 1934; Bencher 1963; was Chm. of Conservative Members (1922) Committee 1951-55, Chm. Conservative Advisory Committee on Local Govt. 1954-55, Parliamentary Sec. to Board of Trade 1955-56, Economic Sec. to the Treasury 1956-57, Min. of State, Board of Trade Jan. to Sept. 1957, and Min. of Health Sept. 1957 to July 1960 ; European War 1939-45 as Lieut.-Col. R.A. (T.A.) (Legion of Honour) ; sat as M.P. for Hertford Div. of Herts (C) July 1945 to May 1955, since when for E. Div. of Herts; PC 1957: *m.* 1938, Dorothy, da. of the late L. J. W. Etherton, of Rowlands Castle, Hants, and has issue.

Arms—Quarterly: 1st and 4th, per fesse or and argent a portcullis sable throughout raised to the nombril point within a bordure per fesse gules and or, charged with ten acorns counter coloured, *Smith*; 2nd and 3rd, per pale azure and gules a horse passant argent hooved and crined or, between three caltrops gold, *Walker*. **Crests**—1st, out of a mural crown gules masoned or a mount vert thereon a lion statant argent holding in the dexter forepaw a sword proper pommel hilt and quillons also or, the blade environed by an oak branch fructed gold, *Smith*; 2nd, between two ostrich feathers gules quilled or a leg in armour azure garnished gold, *Walker*.
Residence—25, Cavendish Close, NW8. **Club**—Carlton.

Son living—JOHN JONAH, *b.* Sept. 6th, 1939; ed. at Westminster and Ch. Ch. Oxford: *m.* 1974, Aileen Marie, only da. of the late Joseph Smith.

Daughters living—Deborah Susan, *b.* 1941: *m.* 1965, Christopher Terence Sinclair-Stevenson, of 3, South Terr., SW7.——Berenice Mary, *b.* 1946: *m.* 1967, William Andrew Weston, of 38, Albemarle St., WIX 3FB.

Smith-Dodsworth, see Dodsworth.

Smith-Gordon, see Gordon.

Smith-Marriott, see Marriott.

SMYTH, Creation (U.K.) 1956, of Teignmouth, co. Devon.

I neither fear mine enemy nor do I despise him.

Rt. Hon. Sir JOHN GEORGE SMYTH, *VC, MC,* 1st *Baronet,* el. son of W. J. Smyth, ICS; *b.* Oct. 24th, 1893; ed. at Repton and RMC; Brig. (ret.) Indian Army; is an Author and Playwright, a Freeman of City of London, and of Farriers' Co. (Master 1961-62); Instructor Staff Coll. Camberley 1931-34, Comdt. 45th Rattray's Sikhs 1936-39, G.S.O.I. 2nd London Div. 1939-40, Mil. Correspondent Kemsley Newspapers 1943-44, and *Daily Sketch* and *Sunday Times* 1945-46, a Member of Executive of Returned British Prisoners of War Assocn. 1946-51, Lawn Tennis Correspondent of *Sunday Times* 1946-51, Gov. of Gypsy Road and W. Norwood Secondary Schs. 1947-49, Strand and W. Norwood Secondary Schs. 1949-51, of St. Martin's High Sch. for Girls 1950-52, and of Dragon Sch. Oxford 1953-66, Parliamentary Sec., Min. of Pensions 1951-53, Joint Parliamentary Sec., Min. of Pensions and National Insurance 1953-55, Lawn Tennis Correspondent of *News of the World* 1956-57 and Comptroller of Roy. Alexandra & Albert Sch. 1948-63; Pres. of VC and GC Assocn. since 1966 (Chm. 1956-71); Vice-Pres., Not Forgotten Assocn., and of Dunkirk Veterans' Assocn.; Vice-Pres. DCM League 1957-58 and Pres. 1958-70; Pres. of SW London Branch, Burma Star Assocn. since 1957; a Gov. of Queen Mary's Hosp. 1956-62; Vice-Pres. of International Lawn Tennis Club of Great Britain since 1966; Hon. Vice-Pres. Far Eastern Prisoner of War Federation 1960; author of " Defence is Our Business " 1945, " The Only Enemy "—autobiography 1959, " Sandhurst—A History of the Military Cadet Colleges " 1961, " The Story of the Victoria Cross " 1962, " The Story of the George Cross " 1968, " In This Sign Conquer—

The Story of the Army Chaplains " 1968, " Percival and the Tragedy of Singapore " 1971, " Leadership in War 1939-45 " 1974, " Leadership in Battle 1914-20 " 1975, and other works; 1914-18 War (despatches, VC, Order of St. George of Russia), Senussi Campaign, W. Egypt 1915-16, Mohmand Expedition, India 1916, Afghan War 1919, Waziristan 1919-20 (despatches, MC), Mesopotamia 1920-21 (despatches), N-W Frontier of India 1930 (despatches), Mohmand Operations 1935 (despatches), 1939-45 War Comdg. 127th Inf. Brig. in France and Belgium (despatches), raised 19th (Dagger) Div., India 1941, Burma 1942 Comdg. 17th Div.; MP for Norwood Div. of Lambeth 1950-66; *cr.* PC 1962: *m.* 1st, 1920 (m. diss. 1940), Margaret, da. of the late Charles Lawrence Dundas [see M. Zetland, colls.]; 2ndly, 1940, Frances Read, da. of the late Lt-.Col. Robert Alexander Chambers, OBE, IMS, and has issue by 1st m.

Arms—Ermine, on a bend beneath two unicorns' heads erased azure, three lozenges or. **Crest**—A demi bull rampant argent, issuing from a ducal coronet or, armed and horned of the same, and gorged with a collar azure, charged with three lozenges and rimmed or.

Residence—807, Nelson House, Dolphin Square, SW1. *Clubs*—Carlton, and Queen's; International Lawn Tennis Clubs of Great Britain, USA, and France.

Grandchildren living—[Issue of the late Julian Smyth, el. son of 1st Baronet, *b.* 1923, *d.* 1974: *m.* 1952, Phyllis Philomena Mary (16, Dickinson St., Watson, Canberra, ACT, Aust.), da. of John Francis Cannon],—TIMOTHY JOHN, *b.* April 16th, 1953.——Christopher Charles, *b.* 1954.—— John George, *b.* 1957.——Simon Gerard, *b.* 1961.—— Andrew, *b.* 1964.——Margaret Mary, *b.* 1955.——Clare Marie, *b.* 1960.

Son living—Robin, *b.* 1926; ed. Ampleforth, and Trin. Coll. Oxford (BA): *m.* 1961, Joan Harrison, da. of the late W. J. Williams, of Worthing, Sussex, and has issue living, John Julian, *b.* 1961.

Daughter living—By 1st m.—Jillian Margaret, *b.* 1929: *m.* 1968, David George Firth, of 98, Sussex Way, N7.

BOWYER-SMYTH, Creation (E.) 1661, of Hill Hall, Essex.

Qua pote lucet.

Sir PHILIP WEYLAND BOWYER-SMYTH, *R.N.*, 14th *Baronet*, son of the late Clement Weyland Bowyer-Smijth, brother of 13th baronet; *b.* Feb. 4th, 1894; *s.* his uncle, *Sir* ALFRED JOHN, 1927; has reverted to former spelling of surname from Bowyer-Smijth to Bowyer-Smyth; became Capt. 1937; appointed Naval Attaché at Rome and Durazzo 1938; European War 1914-19 with Grand Fleet, European War 1939-42 (wounded, despatches): *m.* 1st, 1922, Margaret Joan, *O.B.E.*, *T.D.*, Ch. Com. W.R.A.C., only da. of S. McCall-McCowan, of Sydney, N.S. Wales; 2ndly, 1951, Veronica Mary, da. of Capt. C. W. Bower, D.S.C., R.N. (retired), of Fordwich, Kent, and has issue by 2nd marriage.

Arms—Quarterly : 1st and 4th sable, a fesse, dancettée argent, billettée sable between three lioncels rampant reguardant of the second, each supporting an altar or, flaming proper, *Smyth* ; 2nd and 3rd, or, a bend vair, cotised gules, *Bowyer.* **Crests**—1st, a salamande in flames proper, *Smyth*; 2nd, on a ducal coronet or, an heraldic tiger sejant argent, *Bowyer.*

Residence—La Provençale, Plascassier, France, A.M. *Club*—United Service.

Son living—By 2nd marriage—THOMAS WEYLAND, *b.* June 25th, 1960.

Daughter living—By 2nd marriage—Amelia, *b.* 1958.

Sister living—Lily Marcia BOWYER-SMIJTH, *b.* 1905.

Collateral Branches living.

Grandchildren of the late William Baird BOWYER-SMIJTH (declaration of legitimacy granted in Scotland 1918, but not in succession to the baronetcy), son of 11th baronet, *b.* 1859, *d.* 1940: *m.* 18—, C. V. Sweeney, who *d.* 1892:— Issue of the late William Bowyer-Smijth, *b.* 1889, *d.* 1937: *m.* 1913, Janie Isabel Norman, of Monaro Vale, Berringan, NSW:— William, *b.* 1915: *m.* 1941, Eileen May Peterson, of Corowa, NSW, and has issue living, Ian William, *b.* 1942,—Keith Raymond, *b.* 1945. *Residence*, 619, Wyse St., Albury, NSW.——Henry, *b.* 1916.——Edward, *b.* 1930.——Jean, *b.* 1919.——Betty, *b.* 1921. Issue of David Malcolm BOWYER-SMYTH (declaration of legitimacy granted in Scotland 1918, but not in succession to the baronetcy), 5th son of 11th baronet, *b.* 1869, *d.* 1930: *m.* 1900 (m. diss. 1910), Miriam McCheyne, da. of Maj. Legh Richmond Battye:— Basil Malcolm (c/o 8366, Victoria Drive, Vancouver, BC, Canada), *b.* 1901: *m.* 19—, Mabel Henrietta Tetlock, and has issue living, Barrie Malcolm, *b.* 19—: *m.* 19—, and has issue living,—James Brian (8366, Victoria Drive, Vancouver, BC, Canada), *b.* 1929: *m.* 19—, Marianne Schwerzler, and has issue living, Marc *b.* 19—, Simone *b.* 19—, David Anthony, *b.* 1931: *m.* 19— (m. diss. 19—), Lee Smith, and has issue living, David *b.* 19—, Michael *b.* 19—, Kathie *b.* 19—, a da. *b.* 19—.——Evangeline, *b.* 1904: *m.* 19—, Jack Beale, of Okanagan Landing, BC, Canada, and has issue living, Robert, *b.* 19—, —Douglas, *b.* 19— —Joan, *b.* 19—,—Nellie, *b.* 19—,— Beverley, *b.* 19—.

Grandchildren of the late Ashe Windham, 2nd son of the late Capt. Joseph SMIJTH-WINDHAM, yst. son of 7th baronet:— Issue of the late Major ASHE WINDHAM, *b.* 1863, *d.* 1937: *m.* 1903, Cora Ellen Sowerby, who *d.* 1048, 2nd da. of the late Capt. Henry Sowerby Middleton, Oxfordshire L.I. :— *Sir* Ralph (Moreton House, Moreton, Ongar, Essex; Lansdowne Club), *b.* 1905; ed. at Wellington Coll., and at Trin Coll., Camb. (BA 1926, LLB 1928, MA 1930); Bar. Lincoln's Inn 1930; Legal Draftsman, Govt. of Palestine 1935, Judge of Dist. Court Palestine 1942, Judge of Supreme Court, Ceylon 1947, and of Supreme Court, Kenya, 1950, Ch. Justice of Zanzibar 1955, Justice of Appeal, E. African Court of Appeal 1959, and Ch. Justice of Tanganyika 1960-65, since when Commr. on Foreign Compensation Commn. (Chm. since 1972); Arbitrator, Mombasa

Dockers' Wage Dispute 1955; has 2nd class Order of Brilliant Star of Zanzibar; Knt. 1960: *m.* 1946, Kathleen Mary, da. of Capt. Cecil Henry Fitzherbert, of Millbrook, Abbeyleix, co. Leix, Eire, and has issue living, John Jeremy, *b.* 1948; ed. at Wellington Coll.; Capt. Irish Gds. and SAS,—Andrew Guy, *b.* 1949; ed. at Wellington Coll., and Trin. Coll., Camb. (BA); solicitor,— Penelope Susan, *b.* 1952, Belinda Mary Victoria, *b.* 1955.——Ashe (c/o Westminster Bank, St. Martin's le Grand EC2) *b.* 1916; ed. at Radley; Maj. (ret.) E. Yorks. Regt. & ADC to Gov. of Assam 1938-40: *m.* 1940, Iris Daphne, da. of Col. Edward Selby Phipson, CIE, DSO, MD, FRCP, IMS (ret.), and has issue living, Ashe Adrian (c/o Glyn Mills, Holts Branch, Kirkland House, Whitehall, SW1), *b.* 1941; late Capt. RA; in Diplo. Ser.: *m.* 1969, Daphne Anne, da. of Maj. A. A. P. C. Thomas, TD (ret.),—Daniel Harry, *b.* 1948; ed. at Radley, and Magdalene Coll., Camb.; 2nd Lt. Irish Rangers.——Joan, *b.* 1904: *m.* 1st, 1959, Brig. Ord Henderson Tidbury, MC, who *d.* 1961; 2ndly, 1964, Maj. Hugh D'Oyly-Lyle, late R. Welch Fusiliers, of Clopton House, Saltley, Newmarket.——Anne, *MBE* (Green Shutters, Long Melford, Suffolk), *b.* 1906; Foreign and Dip. Ser. (ret.); MBE (Civil) 1942.——Mève (of Wawne Cottage, Offton, nr. Ipswich) *b.* 1909.——Ruth (of 2, Palace Gardens Terr., W8), *b.* 1912: *m.* 1st 1938 (m. diss. 1962), Robert Bellord; 2ndly, 1972, Brig. John Henry Patrick Woodroffe, DSO, and has issue living (by 1st m.), Robert Windham WINDHAM-BELLORD; *b.* 1943; Capt. Rifle Bde.; assumed the surname of Windham-Bellord 1963,—Edward James WINDHAM-BELLORD (30, Norroy Rd., SW15), *b.* 1947; ed. at Downside, and Wadham Coll., Oxford; assumed the surname of Windham-Bellord 1965: *m.* 1972, Caroline Irene, only da. of Robert Grenville Plantagenet Morgan-Grenville [see L. Kinloss], and has issue living, James Robert Grenville *b.* 1973,—Richard Valentine WINDHAM-BELLORD, *b.* 1949,—Ellen Mary, *b.* 1938,—Alice Mary, *b.* 1939.——Grace, *b.* 1914: *m.* 1937 (divorce 1956), Wilfred Gerard Sydney, 7th Baron Grand d'Hauteville, and has issue living Philip Anthony Ashe, *b.* 1938: *m.* 1965, Tania, only da. of Gerald Cramer, of Mies, Switzerland and has issue living, Henry *b.* 1967, Eric (twin) *b.* 1967, Diana Cora *b.* 1971,—Jacques Pierre, *b.* 1943: *m.* 1968 Françoise Mayer, Marc Serge *b.* 1969,—Elisabeth Suzanne, *b.* 1940: *m.* 1963, Baron Aymon de Blonay, and has issue living, Nicolas Aymon Pierre Henri *b.* 1967, Marie- Hélène Blanche Renée *b.* 1964, Sophie Carloine Elisabeth Grace *b.* 1970. *Residence,* La Meridiana, Via delle Rose, Ospedaletti, Italy.

Issue of the late Sir William Windham, C.B.E., *b.* 1864, *d.* 1961 : *m.* 1894, Blanche Marie, who *d.* 1933, da. of the late Achille E. Titren, Resident Magistrate, Natal :— William Evan, *b.* 1904 ; ed. at Wellington Coll.; Bar. Gray's Inn 1930 : *m.* 1932, Constance Lloyd, who *d.* 1939, da. of James Hope Loudon, of Olantigh, Wye, Kent, and has issue living, Elisabeth Aylva, *b.* 1935: *m.* 1955, George Bakewell, of Hazel Road House, Mandara, Salisbury, Rhodesia, and has issue living, Constance Louise *b.* 1957, Charlotte Alice *b.* 1959,—Juliet Alexa, *b.* 1938. *Residence,* Salisbury, Rhodesia.——Alba, *OBE, b.* 1898; ed. at St. Hugh's Coll., Oxford BA 1922); Ch. Com. ATS; OBE (Mil) 1043. *Residence,* 4, Bibury, The Cotswolds, Cape Province, S. Africa.

Grandchildren of the late Major George Smijth-Windham, 4th son of the late Capt. Joseph SMIJTH-WINDHAM (ante):— Issue of the late Lieut.-Col. Henry Steuart WINDHAM (twin), *b.* 1873, *d.* 1958 : *m.* 1915, Marjory Russell, who *d.* 1971, da. of the late Henry McLean Dymock:— James Steuart, *b.* 1917; ed. at Bedford Sch.; Maj. ret.) R.A.; 1939-45 War (wounded, despatches): *m.* 1957, Annette de Mèstre, da. of William John Wilkin, FRCS, and has issue living, Mark Hastings Wriothesley, *b.* 1959,—Tobias Cosmo Russell, *b.* 1962, — Sophia Louise de Mèstre, *b.* 1958. *Residence,* The Garden House, Highnam Court, near Gloucester. ——William Ashe Dymoke (Crowley Lodge, Crowley, Northwich, Cheshire), *b.* 1926; ed. at Bedford Sch. (Scholar), and at Christ's Coll., Camb. (MA); is with Arthur Guinness, Son & Co., Ltd.: *m.* 1956, Alison Audrey Primrose, da. of the late Maj. Philip Pinckney Curtis, MC [see Curtis, Bt., colls.], and has issue living, Ashe George Russell, *b.* 1957,—Charles William Fitz-Roy, *b.* 1960,—Emma Rose Dymock, *b.* 1959.——Rachel Russell (Pontsioni, Aberedw, Builth Wells), *b.* 1916: *m.* 1963, Lt.-Col. George Kinloch Sheppard, who *d.* 1963, el. son of the late Sir William Didsbury Sheppard, KCIE.

Issue of the late Arthur Russell Smijth-Windham, *b.* 1874, who *d.* 1915: *m.* 1901, Brenda Helen, who *d.* 1947, da. of the late Gerald Hall:— William Russell, *C.B.E., D.S.O., b.* 1907; ed. at Wellington Coll.; is Brigadier late Roy. Signals, a FIEE; appointed an ADC to HM 1957; Mount Everest Expeditions 1933 and 1936: 1939-45 War in Middle East and NW Europe (despatches, DSO, CBE); DSO 1942, CBE (Mil) 1946: *m.* 1934, Helen Teresa Clementi, da. of the late Brig. Hubert Clementi Smith, DSO [Clarke-Jervoise, Bt., ext.], and has issue living, Simon William, *b.* 1937: *m.* 1960, Wendy Myra, da. of Edgar William John Albrow, and has issue living, Alistair William *b.* 1966, Tanya Myra *b.* 1961,— Joanna Felicity, *b.* 1938: *m.* 1963, Peter Anthony Lazarus, of The Downs School, Charlton House, Wraxall, Bristol, and has issue living, William George, *b.* 1969, Mary Helen, *b.* 1966,— Prudence Helen, *b.* 1945: *m.* 1967, John Derek Walter Murdoch, of 13, Sugden Rd., SW11, and has issue living, Thomas, *b.* 1970, Clarissa Helen *b.* 1972,—Rachel Beatrice, *b.* 1946: *m.* 1970, John Santer, of 26, Falkland Rd., NW5, and has issue living, Evelyn Margaret *b.* 1973. *Residence* Icentown House, Pitney, Langport, Som. *Club,* United Services.——Diana Elizabeth, *b.* 1911: *m.* 1947, E. M. W. Paul, and has issue living, Isabella Brenda Windham, *b.* 1948. *Residence,*

Sir Thomas Smith, 1st Bt. of Hill Hall, Essex, High Sheriff 1663, was grandson of George, brother of Sir Thomas Smith, of Hill Hall, Sec. of State to Edward VI and Elizabeth I. His son, Sir Edward 2nd Bt., adopted the spelling of Smyth, and Sir William, 7th Bt. about 1796, that of Smijth. He *m.* 1779, Anne, da. of John Windham-Bowyer, of Woodmansterne, Surrey, and sister and heir of Joseph Windham. Her mother, Mary, was da. and heir of Joseph Windham, of Twickenham, Middlesex (afterwards Ashe), by Catherine, da. and co-heir of Sir Edmund Bowyer, of Camberwell. Sir Edward, 10th Bt., assumed by Roy. Licence 1839 the name and arms of Bowyer-Smijth. Sir Alfred John, 13th Bt., reverted to former spelling of surname from Bowyer-Smijth to Bowyer-Smyth.

SNADDEN, Creation (U.K.) 1955, of Coldoch, co. Perth. [Extinct 1959.]

Sir WILLIAM McNAIR SNADDEN, 1st and last *Baronet.*

Widow living of 1st Baronet—LESLEY JANE HOPE (*Lady Snadden*), da. of the late Thomas Henderson, of Argaty, Doune, Perthshire : *m.* 1919, Sir William McNair Snadden, 1st baronet, who *d.* 1959, when the title became ext. *Residence,* The Coldoch, Blair Drummond, by Stirling. Daughters living of 1st Baronet—Veronica Hope McNair, *b.* 1920 : *m.* 1st, 1939, John Bourlon De Pree, Lieut. Seaforth Highlanders, who *d.* (whilst a prisoner in Germany) 1942 ; 2ndly, 1943, Capt. Angus Carr, Seaforth Highlanders, who *d.* (killed in action) 1945; 3rdly, 1945 (m. diss. 1951), Marwood John Richard Yeatman; 4thly, 1951 (m. diss. 1972), Maj. Edward William Harold Worrall, DSO, MC, late SLI, and has issue living, (by 2nd m.) Douglas William Dingwall, *b.* 1943,—(by 3rd m.) Marwood John Benedictus Charles, *b.* 1947,—(by 4th m.) Lucy Veronica Ruth, *b.* 1954: *m.* 1971, James Bernard Killigrew Penrose, of Killiow House, Truro, and has issue living, Lamorna Hope *b.* 1974. *Residence,* The Garth, Budock Vean, nr. Falmouth, Cornwall.——Rosemary Adele McNair, *b.* 1926: *m.* 1st, 1944, Capt. Charles Napier Frederick Webb, S. Wales Borderers, who *d.* (on active ser.) 1945 ; 2ndly, 1947, Patrick Heatley Dickson, and has issue living, (by 1st m.) James Charles Napier, *b.* 1946: *m.* 1974, Mary Thomas, of The Old Mill, Easingwold, Yorks.—(by 2nd m.) Elizabeth Jane, *b.* 1948: *m.* 1969, Michael Alexander Ligertwood, of North Milford Hall, Tadcaster, Yorks.,—Deborah Rose, *b.* 1953. *Residence,* Craighead House, Blair Drummond, by Stirling.

BUCKWORTH-HERNE-SOAME, Creation (E.) 1697, of Sheen, Surrey.

Sir CHARLES BURNETT BUCKWORTH-HERNE-SOAME, 11th *Baronet; b.* Sept. 26th, 1894; *s.* his father, *Sir* CHARLES, 1931; European War 1914-19 with King's Shropshire L.I. (wounded) : *m.* 1924, Elsie May, who *d.* 1972, da. of Walter Alfred Lloyd, of Coalbrookdale, Salop, and has issue.

Arms—Quarterly : 1st and 4th, gules, a chevron between three mallets or, a canton argent for difference, *Soame;* 2nd and 3rd, sable, on a chevron between three cross-crosslets fitchée argent, an ermine spot, *Buckworth.* Crests—1st, a lure gules, garnished and stringed argent, thereon a falcon or, beaked and legged of the second ; 2nd, a man's head in profile armed with a helmet, the beaver up all proper.

Residence—Sheen Cottage, Coalbrookdale, Salop.

Son living—CHARLES JOHN (16, Woodside, Coalbrookdale, Salop.), *b.* May 28th, 1932: *m.* 1958, Eileen Margaret Mary, da. of Leonard Minton, of Caughley, Salop, and has issue living, Richard John, *b.* Aug. 17th, 1970.
Daughter living—Mary, *b.* 1936: *m.* 1958, Keith Howard Edwards, of 27, Woodside, Coalbrookdale, Salop, and has issue living, Robert John Edwards, *b.* 1971,—Carol Jane, *b.* 1964.

Sir John, the 1st baronet, was High Sheriff of London 1704. Sir Everard, the 3rd baronet, was Assist. Gentleman Usher to King George III. Sir Everard, the 5th baronet, Gentleman-Pensioner and Exon of the Guard, *temp.* George III., assumed the additional surname of Herne. Sir Buckworth Buckworth-Herne, the 6th baronet, assumed, in 1806, the additional surname of Soame by Roy. licence, in compliance with the will of Sir Peter Soame, baronet (title now extinct).

SOMERVILLE, Creation (I.) 1748, of Dublin. [Dormant 1929.]

Since the death of the 2nd Baron Athlumney (who was also 6th Baronet of this creation) in 1929, the Baronetcy has remained dormant, and at time of going to press no name appears in respect of it on the Official Roll of Baronets.

Collateral Branches living.
Descendants, if any, of the late Archibald James Somerville (son of the late Capt. William Somerville, only son of the late Major William Somerville, 2nd son of 1st baronet), *b.* 1803, *d.* 1871 : *m.* 1836, Elizabeth, da. of Jason Crawford, of Ballyholly, co. Cavan ; he left issue, Archibald James, William, Jason, Bellingham Brookes.

Grandchildren of the late Capt. Bellingham Arthur Somerville (infra):—
Issue of the late Lt.-Col. Gualter Hugh Rodger Bellingham Somerville, MC, *b.* 1894, *d.* 1947: *m.* 1925, Heather Edith, da. of the late Col. Cecil Norris Baker, CIE:—
Patricia May Naomi, *b.* 1929: *m.* 1st, 1951 (m. diss. 1973), Lt. Michael William Richmond Nicholas, RN; 2ndly, 1974, Robert James Henderson, of 46, Crabtree Rd., Elms Rise, Botley, Oxford, OX2 9DT, and has issue living (by 1st m.), Patrick Richmond, *b.* 1952,—Elizabeth Richmond, *b.* 1954.——Julia Heather Margaret, *b.* 1931: *m.* 1958, as his second wife, William Bristow Stevenson, and has issue living, James Roger, *b.* 1963,—Henry Bristow, *b.* 1970,—Diana Margaret Julia, *b.* 1961. *Residence,* Knockan, Feeny, co. Londonderry.
Issue of the late Reginald Malcolm John Bellingham Somerville, *b.* 1897, *d.* 1971: *m.* 1st, 1928, Maude Gwendoline Constance Violet, who *d.* 1935, da. of the late Capt. A. E. H. Moore, R. Dublin Fus.; 2ndly, 1936, Honor Lucretia Philippa, da. of the late Rev. Canon Philip B. Johnson, of the Rectory, Wicklow:—
(By 1st m.) Juanita Elizabeth Maude, *b.* 1932; ed. at Hillcourt Sch., and The Ling Physical Training Coll., Dublin: *m.* 1964, Peter Brumby, Chief Pilot, E. African Airways, of Lucita Farm, P.O. Box 36, Naivasha, Kenya.——(by 2nd m.) William Barnard Reginald Bellingham (Dargle Hill, Enniskerry, co. Wicklow), *b.* 1937; ed. at Trin. Coll., Dublin (BA); Solicitor 1967; late Admin. Officer, HM Colonial Ser., Tanganyika: *m.* 1968, Margery Manon, el. da. of George Clemenger Vincent Brittain, of Craigtoodie House, Dairsie, Fife, and has issue living, James William Reginald Bellingham, *b.* 1969,—Charles John George Bellingham, *b.* 1971,—Edward Henry Tenison Bellingham, *b.* 1972.

Grandaughter of the late Tenison Alan Somerville, yr. brother of the late Archibald James Somerville (ante):—
Issue of the late Capt. Bellingham Arthur Somerville, *b.* 1853, *d.* 1916; *m.* 1879, Margaret Hall, who *d.* 1949, da. of the late William Clinch, of The Elms, Witney, Oxon :—
Vere Frances de Merlie Bellingham (c/o Lloyds Bank, Camberley, Surrey), *b.* 1890: *m.* 1912, Lt.-Col. Edmund Gray Stuart Truell, who *d.* 1950, Connaught Rangers (Reserve) [E. Moray], and has issue living, Charles William Somerville (13, Lakins Rd., Blenheim, NZ), *b.* 1922; ed at Trin. Coll., Dublin (BA 1951); formerly in E. Surrey Regt. and Queen's R. Regt.; 1939-45 War in N. Africa, Italy, France and Germeny: *m.* 1955, Elizabeth Moffat, da of the late G. B. Moffat Wilson, and has issue living, Charles Hilaire *b.* 1958, Guy Julian Toby *b.* 1966, Jean France *b.* 1956, Zoë Louise *b.* 1963,—George Dennis Somerville, MBE, *b.* 1926; ed at Canford, and at Edinburgh Univ.; is Lt.-Col. RA; OC Med. Regt. RA in Germany; Palestine 1946-48, Korea 1951; MBE (Mil) 1965: *m.* 1960, Mary, da. of the late Maj. A. W. Fosbroke-Hobbes, MC, 3rd Hussars, and has issue living, Edmund George Imjin Fosbroke *b.* 1962, Daniel Fosbroke *b.* 1963, Sophie Vera Helena *b.* 1968,—Rachel Louisa, *b.* 1916: *m.* 1940, Col. Gordon John Alistair Dewar, CBE, late Hampshire Regt. (ret.), of Mansard, Rowledge, Farnham, Surrey, and has issue living, James Gordon Truell *b.* 1946; ed at Cheltenham; Capt. R. Hampshire Regt., Alison Rosemary *b.* 1941: *m.* 1963, John Martin Riley (and has issue living, Charles Martin William *b.* 1965, Hugh James John *b.* 1968, Philippa Mary Alison *b.* 1970), Felicity Rachel Cynthia *b.* 1942: *m.* 1965, Maj. Alan Henry Lyall Grant, 16/5 Queens R. Lancers (and has issue living, James Alan Hardy *b.* 1974, Kate Mary *b.* 1966, Lucy Rachel *b.* 1969), Susan Hilary de Merlie *b.* 1953: *m.* 1974, Julian Charles Lytton Bagley,—Gillian Mary, *b.* 1929: *m.* 1957, Maj. John Gilmour, and has issue living, Angus John *b.* 1958, David Richard Grey *b.* 1962, Virginia Esdaile Louise *b.* 1960, Frances Jocelyn Marjorie *b.* 1945,—Jocelyn Kathleen (twin), *b.* 1929: *m.* 1953, Maj. William Raymond Goss, and has issue living, William Robert Edmund Truell *b.* 1954, George Richard Napoleon *b.* 1956, Patrick Raymond Hubert *b.* 1957, Victor Geoffrey Alan *b.* 1959, Quentin Joselyn Vernon *b.* 1961: Elizabeth Laurel Frances Joan *b.* 1965.

The 1st baronet, Sir James Somerville, K.B., was M.P. for Dublin City **1729**, and Lord **Mayor** of Dublin **1737**, the 4th, Sir Marcus, was M.P. for co. Meath 1801-3, and the 5th, the Rt. Hon. Sir William Meredyth, P.C., M.P. for Drogheda (L) 1837-52, and for Canterbury 1854-65, Under-Sec. for Home Depart. 1846-7, and Ch. Sec. for Ireland 1847-52, was cr. *Baron Athlumney* (peerage of Ireland) **1863**, and *Baron Meredyth* (peerage of United Kingdom) 1866, in which Baronies the Baronetcy remained merged until the death of the **2**nd Baron Athlumney in **1929**, when both **Peerages** became extinct, and the Baronetcy became dormant.

SOUTHBY, Creation (U.K.) 1937 of Burford, co. Oxford.

Sir (ARCHIBALD) RICHARD CHARLES SOUTHBY, OBE, 2nd *Baronet*; *b.* June 18th, 1910; *s.* his father, *Cdr. Sir* ARCHIBALD RICHARD JAMES, *RN*, 1969; ed. at Eton, and Magdalen Coll., Oxford (MA); Lt.-Col. (ret.) Rifle Bde.; has American Medal of Freedom; OBE (Mil.) 1945: *m.* 1st, 1935 (m. diss. 1947) Joan Alice, only da. of Reginald Balston, of 105, Onslow Sq., SW7; 2ndly, 1947 (m. diss. 1964), Olive, da. of the late Sir Thomas Bilbe-Robinson, GBE, KCMG, and formerly wife of Gen. Sir (James Newton), Rodney Moore, GCVO, KCB, CBE, DSO; 3rdly, 1964, the Hon. Ethel Peggy, da. of 1st Baron Cunliffe, and widow of Brig. Bernard Lorenzo de Robeck, MC, RA, and has issue living by 2nd m.

Arms—Or, a chevron between three apples gules. **Crest**—A demi lion or holding in the dexter paw an apple gules.
Residence—

Son living—By 2nd m.—JOHN RICHARD BILBE (49, Brookfield Av., Loughborough, Leics. LE11 3LN), *b.* April 2nd, 1948; ed at Peterhouse, Rhodesia, and Loughborough Univ. (BSc): *m.* 1971, Victoria, e. da. of John Wilfred Sturrock, of 88, Wrottesley Rd., Tettenhall, Wolverhampton, and has issue living, Peter John, *b.* Aug. 20th, 1973,—Sarah Jane, *b.* 1975.
Brother living—Patrick Henry James (Los Castaños, 48, Casasola, Guadalmina, San Pedro de Alcantara, Malaga, Spain), *b.* 1913; Lt.-Cdr. RN (ret.): *m.* 1939, Lady Anne Adeline Hope, da. of 2nd Marquess of Linlithgow, and has issue living, Richard Henry Alexander, *b.* 1941; ed. at Eton, and Worcester Coll., Oxford (MA),—Mary Ann, *b.* 1946; ed. at Courtauld Inst., London Univ.: *m.* 1975, Martin Robert Kenyon [see B. Kenyon, colls.].
Widow living of 1st Baronet—NOREEN VERA, (*Noreen, Lady Southby*), (18, Harbour View Rd., Parkstone, Dorset), da. of the late Bernard Compton Simm, of Ashbourne, Derbys.: *m.* 1962, as his 2nd wife, Cdr. Sir Archibald Richard James Southby, RN, 1st Bt., who *d.* 1969.

Cdr. Sir Archibald Richard James Southby, RN, 1st Bt., 2nd son of Richard Southby of Hodcott and Chieveley, Berks, was MP for Epsom 1928-47, Assist. Govt. Whip 1931-35, and a Jnr. Lord of the Treasury 1935-37

SPEARMAN, Creation (U.K.) 1840, of Hanwell, Middlesex.

While I breathe I hope.

Sir ALEXANDER BOWYER SPEARMAN, 4th *Baronet*; *b.* Feb. 15th, 1917; *s.* his father *Sir* ALEXANDER YOUNG, 1959; ed. at Westminster; FCII; Fire and Accident Manager of Union Guarantee and Insurance Co., Ltd., of Cape Town 1955-57, and Tech. Assist. to Gen. Mgr. thereof 1957-58, and a Dir. of Jack Ginsburg (Proprietary), Ltd., insurance consultants, 1960-67, and of Delta Insurance Brokers (Pty.) Ltd., 1967-69; a Dir. of Nabco (Cape) (Pty.) Ltd., Incorporated Insurance Brokers, PO Box 1326, Cape Town; India 1939-45 as temp. Capt. 7th Rajput Regt. and Staff Capt, Indian Army; ret. 1948 with Hon. rank of Capt.: *m.* 1950, Martha, da. of John Green, of Naauport, Cape Province, S. Africa, and has issue.

Arms—Azure, on a chevron ermine between three tilting spears, argent, headed or, a red deer's head erased proper. **Crest**—A lion rampant proper, gorged with a collar gemelle or, supporting a tilting spear also proper, enfiled with a mural crown or.

Residence—88, Camps Bay Drive, Camps Bay, Cape Town, S. Africa.

Son living—ALEXANDER YOUNG RICHARD MAINWARING, *b.* Feb. 3rd, 1969.
Daughters living—Catherine Wendy Nest, *b.* 1959.——Lynne Dorothy Ann, *b.* 1962.——Daphne Joan Constance Eileen, *b.* 1965.

Brother living—Richard Ian Campbell, *b.* 1926; ed. at Clayesmore Sch., and at Birkbeck Coll., London (BSc special honours in Zoology, PhD); is a FLS, a FZS, a Fellow of Inst. of Biology, a Member Genetical So., of Anatomical So., and of So. for Experimental Biology, and a Fellow of Roy. So. of Medicine. *Residence*, Oaks Bungalow, Oaks Av., SE19.
Sister living—Joan Dorothy Ethel, *b.* 1912; 1939-45 War: *m.* 1960, William Taunton Oliver, of the Chiltens, 70, Hatherley Rd., Winchester, Hants., SO22 6RR.
Aunt living (daughter of 2nd baronet)—Margaret Eileen (2, Russell Terr., Broadway, Worcs.), *b.* 1892: *m.* 1924, Edgar George Roberts, who *d.* 1951.
Widow living of 3rd Baronet—DOROTHY CATHERINE (*Dorothy, Lady Spearman*), da. of the late Thomas Bowyer Bower, of Iwerne Minster, Dorset : *m.* 1909, Sir Alexander Young Spearman, 3rd baronet, who *d.* 1959. *Residence*, Oaks Bungalow, Oaks Avenue, S.E.19.

Collateral Branches living.
Issue of the late Com. Alexander Young Crawshay Mainwaring Spearman, R.N., half-brother of 2nd baronet, *b.* 1862, *d.* (killed in action) 1915 : *m.* 1892, Jessie

Aubrey, *M.B.E.*, who *d.* 1933 (having *m.* 2ndly, 1923, Lieut.-Col. Edward Loch, of Parks, Crediton, Devon), da. of the late Rev. Cadwallader Coker, R. of Fringford, Oxon :—

Sir Alexander Cadwallader Mainwaring, *b.* 1901; ed. at Repton, and at Hertford Coll., Oxford; is a Member of the firm of Grieveson, Grant and Co., stockbrokers, of 97, Gresham St., EC2; MP for Scarborough and Whitby Div. of N. Riding of Yorkshire 1941-66; Knt. 1956: *m.* 1st, 1928 (m. diss. 1951), Diana Violet Edith Constance, da. of Col. Sir Arthur Havelock James Doyle, 4th Bt.; 2ndly, 1951, Diana Josephine, only child of Col. Sir (Albert) Lambert Ward, 1st Bt., CVO, DSO, TD, and has issue living, (by 2nd m.) Lochain Alexander, *b.* 1952,—John Dominic, *b.* 1954,—Andrew Mark, *b.* 1960,—James, *b.* 1964,—Zara Ann Louise, *b.* 1956. *Residences,* The Old Rectory, Sarratt, Herts.; Fealar, Enochdhu, Blairgowrie, Perthshire; 32, Queen Anne's Gate, SW1.   *Club,* Beefsteak.

Granddaughters of the late Alexander Young Spearman, el. son of 1st baronet :—
Issue of the late Charles Edward Spearman, *b.* 1863, *d.* 1945: *m.* 1901, Frances Henrietta Priaulx, who *d.* 1955, da. of John Aikman, M.D., of Birnam, Guernsey :—

Fan Caroline, *b.* 1902: *m.* 1927, Capt. Philip Charles Forman, RN, who *d.* 1965, and has issue living, Roderick Philip Carey, *b.* 1936,—Prudence Caroline, *b.* 1928: *m.* 1950, John Henderson Bowles, of The School House, Sandbach, Cheshire, and has issue living, Brendan Philip *b.* 1953, Stafford John *b.* 1957, Bridget Nancy *b.* 1951,—Jennifer Mary Priaulx, *b.* 1930: *m.* 1954, Alastair Robert Wilson Porter, of High Oak, Savill Rd., Lindfield, Sussex, and has issue living, Angus James *b.* 1957, Duncan Roderick *b.* 1961, Frances Jennifer *b.* 1955,—Nancy Chevallier, *b.* 1932: *m.* 1960, Jeffrey James Cox, of Crown House, Kynnersley, Telford, Salop, and has issue living, John James *b.* 1962, Meyrick *b.* 1964. *Residence,* 31, Woodlands Close, Headington, Oxford.——Alice Louisa Jean *b.* 1903: *m.* 1928, Martin William Strong, and has issue living, Richard Martin (11, Connaught Av., East Sheen, SW14), *b.* 1929: *m.* 1st, 1956 (m. diss. 1969), Ann Georgina, da. of the late Richard P. Sargent; 2ndly, 1971, Venetia Mary, da. of Ian T. Henderson, of Crawley, Hants., and has issue living (by 1st m.), Simon Alexander *b.* 1959,— Christopher John, *b.* 1932; Sqdn.-Ldr. RAF: *m.* 1956, Brenda Mary, da. of the late A. Willbery, and has issue living, Michael Alexander *b.* 1957, Penelope Ann *b.* 1959, Helen Jean *b.* 1960,— Michael Charles (69, Castletown Rd., W14) *b.* 1935: *m.* 1st, 1963 (m. diss. 1968), Lysbeth Joanna, who *d.* 1970, el. da. of Dr. C. Lanyon, of Falmouth; 2ndly, 1968, Margaret Christine, da. of the late Edwin V. Price, of Chester, and has issue living, (by 2nd m.), Edward Charles *b.* 1970, James Alexander *b.* 1972,—Patricia Anne, *b.* 1931: *m.* 1957, John Barrett, of 120, Kimberley Rd., Bournemouth, and has issue living, Hazel Jean *b.* 1963. *Residence,* Southfield, Hoveringham, Notts. ——Ivy Joy, *b.* 1912: *m.* 1939, Lt.-Col. Thomas Harold Barnes, TD, who *d.* 1971, and has issue living, Belinda Marion, *b.* 1941: *m.* 1963, John Part, of 24, Luttrell Av., SW15, and has issue living, Emma Josephine *b.* 1967, Tracy Belinda *b.* 1970, Joanna Frances *b.* 1974,—Susannah Mainwaring, *b.* 1944: *m.* 1966, Andrew Wilson Thomson, of Hillcroft Farm Boarding Kennels, Pylle, Shepton Mallet, Som. *Residence,* Beechfield Cottage, Upper High St., Castle Cary, Som. ——Anne Mainwaring, *b.* 1918: *m.* 1940, Santiago Perez-Walker, and has issue living, Santiago Alexander, *b.* 1941,—Patrick Charles, *b.* 1945,—Francis Anthony, *b.* 1949,—Maria Olalla Evelyn, *b.* 1943. *Address,* Brazil 230, Santiago, Chile.

Grandchildren of the late Col. Horace Ralph Spearman, 3rd son of 1st baronet.
Issue of the late Horace Ralph Spearman, *b.* 1868, *d.* 19—: *m.* 1890, Louisa, da. of James Parker:—
Horace Layton, *b.* 1896.——Lily Alexandrina Campbell, *b.* 1892.——Isabella Lucy, *b.* 1893.
Residence,

Grandson of the late Col. Horace Ralph Spearman (ante) :—
Issue of the late Major Alexander Young Spearman, *b.* 1872, *d.* 1911 : *m.* 1898, Mary Cramond, da. of the late Edward Etches, of Litchurch Grange, Derby :—
Horace Edward James, *b.* 1899 ; ed. at Trin. Coll., Glenalmond, and at Uppingham ; Major late R.A. : *m.* 1934, Mary, da. of the late Jon Constantinescu, of Braila, Roumania. *Residence,*

The family of Spearman is of considerable antiquity in Durham. John Spearman, a lawyer and antiquary, was many years Under-Sheriff of Durham, and in 1678 he purchased the manor of Thornley in that county. The 1st baronet, the Right Hon. Sir Alexander Young, was for a long period Comptroller-General and Secretary to the Commissioners for the Reduction of the National Debt.

SPEELMAN, Creation (E.) 1686.

Jonkheer Sir CORNELIS JACOB SPEELMAN, 8th *Baronet* ; *b.* March 17th, 1917 ; *s.* his father, *Jonkheer Sir* Cornelis Jacob, 1949 ; ed. at Perth Univ., W. Australia (B.A. 1958) ; formerly in Education Depart. of Roy. Dutch Army, and a Master at Geelong Gram. Sch., and at Clifton Coll.; Tutor, Exeter Tutorial Coll.; is a British subject: *m.* 1972, Julia Mona Le Besque.

*Residence—*The Nab House, Flat 5, Beach House Rd., Bembridge, Isle of Wight.

Widow living of 7th Baronet—MARIA CATHERINA HELENA (*Lady Speelman*), da. of Boudewÿn Frans Castendijk, Notary, formerly of Arnhem : *m.* 1916, Sir Cornelis Jacob Speelman, 7th Bt., who *d.* 1949. *Residence,* 10, Johan Bosboom Laan, Heemstede, Holland.

John Cornelis Speelman, of Batavia, *b.* 1659, *d.* June 1686 before the Royal Warrant directing his creation as *a Baronet* had passed the Great Seal. By Letters Patent of Sept. 9th, 1686, his widow, Debora, da. of John Nicolaes Kievit (Attorney Fiscal to the Admiralty of the Maes), of Rotterdam, was raised to the rank of a Baronet's widow, the same Letters Patent also creating their only son and heir Cornelis, a *Baronet.* The 6th Baronet was in Royal Dutch Navy 1870-83, and sometime Burgomaster of Harlingen. The holders of this title remained resident in the Netherlands until the 8th Baronet.

Spencer-Nairn, see Nairn.

Spencer-Smith, see Smith.

SPEYER, Creation (U.K.) 1906, of Grosvenor Street, St. George, Hanover Square, co. London. [Extinct 1932.]

Sir EDGAR SPEYER, 1st and last *Baronet.*

Daughters living of 1st Baronet—Pamela, *b.* 1903: *m.* 1926, Count Hugo Carl Maria Moÿ de Sons, who *d.* 1938. *Residence,* Bell Cottage, Bury Gate, near Pulborough, Sussex.——Leonora, *b.* 1905. *Residence,* 3, Gertrude Street. S.W.10.——Vivien Clare, *b.* 1907. *Residence,* New York, U.S.A.

SPICER, Creation (U.K.) 1906, of Lancaster Gate, Borough of Paddington.

In God alone my hope.

(*Sir*) PETER JAMES SPICER, 4th *Baronet*; does not use the title; *b.* May 20th, 1921; *s.* his father, *Sir* STEWART DYKES, 1968; ed. at Winchester, Trin. Coll., Camb., and Ch. Ch., Oxford (MA); 1939-45 War as Lt. RNVR (despatches): *m.* 1949, Margaret, da. of the late Sir (James) Steuart Wilson, of Fenn's, Petersfield, Hants, and has issue.

Arms—Per chevron or and sable, in chief two cinquefoils and in base a tower, all counterchanged. **Crest**—Out of the battlements of a tower a cubit arm erect in armour proper, holding in the gauntlet an annulet or.

Residence—The Manor Farm House, Kidlington, Oxford.

———

Son living,—NICHOLAS ADRIAN ALBERT, *b.* Oct. 28th, 1953.

Daughters living—Phyllida Margaret, *b.* 1950.——Alison Celia, *b.* 1955.——Susanna Juliet, *b.* 1963.

Sisters living—Elizabeth Chalmers, *b.* 1924: *m.* 1953, Capt. Anthony Chenevix Trench, RA [*see* B. Ashtown, colls.].——Janet Dykes, *b.* 1931.——Margaret Grace Gillespie, *b.* 1933: *m.* 1960, John Arnfield Heap, PhD, of The Old House, Harston, Cambridge, and has issue living, Thomas John Gillespie, *b.* 1966,—Sarah James, *b.* 1961,—Alice Margaret, *b.* 1964.

Uncle living (son of 1st baronet)—Lancelot Dykes, DSO, MC, *b.* 1893; ed. at Rugby, and at Trin. Coll., Camb.; was Chm. of Spicers, Ltd. 1950-59; 1914-18 War as Capt. KOYLI (despatches), MC with Bar; DSO 1919: *m.* 1st, 1920, Iris Beverley (who obtained a divorce 1935), el. da. of the late William Pallet Cox, Bar.-at-law (Middle Temple); 2ndly, 1951, Dorothy, da. of the late Frank Edwin Gwyther, CIE, and widow of Russell Beverley. *Residence*, Salisbury Place, Shipton-under-Wychwood, Oxford, OX7 6BP.

Aunts living (daughters of 1st baronet)—Gwendolen Elaine Dykes (Old Plough, 35, Windmill St., Brill, Aylesbury, Bucks.) *b.* 1895: *m.* 1918, Ronald McKinnon Wood, who *d.* 1967, and has issue living, David McKinnon, *b.* 1919: *m.* 1947, Jocelyn Withycombe,—Eva Jean McKinnon, *b.* 1923: *m.* 1947, Peter Trubshawe.——Olga Dykes, *b.* 1901. *Residence*, Barn Cottage, 1, North Hills, Brill, Aylesbury, Bucks.——Ursula Dykes (The Coach House, 37, Windmill St., Brill, Aylesbury, Bucks.), *b.* 1904: *m.* 1927, Sydney Barnett Mackenzie Potter, who *d.* 1971, and has issue living, Geoffrey Spicer Barnett, *b.* 1933,—Julian Spicer Barnett, *b.* 1943,—Judith Dykes, *b.* 1932.

Daughters living of 2nd Baronet—Patricia Morrison, *b.* 1911: *m.* 1933, Tyrrell Francis Young, of Malthouse Cottage, Gt. Mongeham, Deal, and has issue living, Michael Francis Dykes, *b.* 1934,—David Tyrrell, *b.* 1938,—Rosamond Alison, *b.* 1944.——Pamela Rosamond, *b.* 1914: *m.* 1936, John Stuart Johnstone, and has issue living, Douglas Stuart, *b.* 1953,—Caroline Rosamond, *b.* 1938. *Residence*, Mole Hall, Widdington, nr. Saffron Walden, Essex.——Althea Dykes, *b.* 1918: *m.* 1st, 1939, Joseph Alwyn Francis Baxendale, who *d.* (of wounds received in action during 1939-45 War) 1940; 2ndly, 1945, Capt. John Wynne Bankes, 14th/20th King's Hussars, and has issue living, (by 2nd m.) Nigel John Eldon, *b.* 1946, Andrew Dykes, *b.* 1955, Althea Lavinia, *b.* 1949. *Residences*, 18, Ennismore Gdns. Mews, SW7; Mynachlog, Northop, Flints.

The Rt. Hon. Sir Albert Spicer, P.C., 1st baronet, was Chm. of James Spicer & Sons, Ltd (later Spicers, Ltd.), paper makers, wholesale stationers, and manufacturers, of 19, New Bridge Street, E.C.4, and sat as M.P. for Monmouth Dist. (L) 1892-1900, and for Central Div. of Hackney 1906-18. He was First Lay Chm. of Congregational Union of England and Wales 1893, Treasurer of London Missionary So. 1885-1910, and of Mansfield Coll., Oxford 1888-1921, Chm. of Govs. Mill Hill Sch., and Pres. of London Chamber of Commerce 1907-10.

———

SPROT, Creation (U.K.) 1918, of Garnkirk, co. Lanark. [Extinct 1929.]

Col. Sir ALEXANDER SPROT, *C.M.G., M.P.,* 1st and last *Baronet.*

Daughters living of 1st Baronet—Mabel Elizabeth (*Lady Stirling of Glorat*), CBE; is a JP; OBE (Civil) 1939, CBE (Civil) 1946: *m.* 1904, Col. Sir George Murray Home Stirling of Glorat, CBE, DSO, 9th Bt. *Residence,* Glorat, Milton of Campsie, Stirlingshire.——Sarah Douglas (Selwyn House, Pulham Market, Diss, Norfolk) *m.* 1913, Maj. William Edgar Mann, DSO, RA, who *d.* 1969 [*see* Mann, Bt.].——Rachel Septima (*Lady Graham*): *m.* 1920, Lt.-Col. Sir John Reginald Noble Graham, VC, OBE, 3rd Bt. *Residence,* The Mailens, Gullane, E. Lothian.——Harriet Hill (*Lady Riddell-Webster*): *m.* 1920, Gen. Sir Thomas Sheridan Riddell-Webster, GCB, DSO, DL, who *d.* 1974, and has issue living, John Alexander, MC (Fewells, Terling, Essex), *b.* 1921; ed. at Harrow and at Camb. Univ.; 1939-45 War as Maj. Seaforth Highlanders (MC); Man. Dir. of Shell-Mex & BP Ltd.: *m.* 1960, Ruth, yr. da. of Laurence Lithgow, of The Old House, Great Barton, Suffolk, and has issue living, Michael Lawrence *b.* (Dec.) 1960, Thomas William *b.* 1962, Caroline Rachel *b.* 1964,—David Balfour, OBE (West Mains House, Blackshiels, Midlothian) *b.* 1922; Col. late The Cameronians (Scottish Rifles); 1939-45 War (despatches); OBE (Mil) 1967: *m.* 1950, Christine Barbara, only da. of the late Capt. Cecil Stanley Draper Noakes, OBE, RN, and. has issue living, Margaret *b.* 1952, Sara Harriet *b.* 1955. *Residence,* Lintrose, Coupar, Angus, Perths.——Nancy Margaret: *m.* 1935, Capt. Chichele Keppel Bampton, RN (ret.), who *d.* 1974. *Residence,* Croft House, Blairlogie, Stirling.

Stafford-King-Harman, see Harman.

STAMER, Creation (U.K.) 1809, of Beauchamp, Dublin.

By valor and strength.

Sir (LOVELACE) ANTHONY STAMER, 5th Baronet; *b.* Feb. 28th, 1917; *s.* his father, *Lt.-Col. Sir* LOVELACE, 1941; ed. at Harrow, at Trin. Coll., Camb. (MA) and at Roy. Agric. Coll., Cirencester; an AMIMI 1963; PO RAF 1939-41, and 1st Officer Air Transport Aux. 1941-45; Exec. Dir. of Bentley Drivers Club Ltd., 1969-73, and of Bugatti and Ferrari Owners Clubs 1973-74; *m.* 1st, 1948 (m. diss. 1953), Stella Huguette, da. of Paul Burnell Binnie, of Brussels; 2ndly, 1955 (m. diss. 1959), Margaret Lucy, da. of the late Maj. T. A. Belben, Indian Army; 3rdly, 1960 (m. diss. 1968), Marjorie June, da. of T. C. Noakes, of St. James, Cape Province, S. Africa, and has issue by 1st m.

Arms—Quarterly : 1st and 4th gules on a fesse indented argent, a lion passant azure armed and langued gules, 2nd and 3rd azure the civic cap between three castles inflamed proper. Over all a cross ermine charged with the sword of state of the City of Dublin in pale proper. **Crest**—A stag's head erased proper, gorged with a mural crown or.

Residence, Summer Cottage, Turville Heath, Healey-on-Thames, Oxon.

Son living—By 1st marriage—PETER TOMLINSON, *b.* Nov. 19th, 1951; P/O RAF.

Daughter living—By 1st m.—Lucinda Jane, *b.* 1949.

Sisters living—Isabel Eva, *b.* 1910 : *m.* 1936, Middleton Fitch Kemp, and has issue living, Robin Middleton (Holts Farm, Stinchcombe, Dursley, Glos.), *b.* 1939: *m.* 1965, Marian Heather, da. of R. Edgett, of Vancouver, BC, and has issue living, Jonathan Mark *b.* 1971, Fiona Mary *b.* 1966. *Residence*, Beech House, Uley, Dursley, Gloucestershire.——Honora Mary, *b.* 1912: *m.* 1938, Lt.-Col. Derek Gordon Hughes, RE (ret.), of 555c, East 24th St., Upland, Cal. 91786, USA.

Collateral Branches living.

Issue of the late Rev. Frederick Charles Stamer, 2nd son of 3rd baronet, *b.* 1860, *d.* 1952 ; *m.* 1st, 1891, Ethel, who *d.* 1931, da. of the late Alexander Donovan, of Framfield Place, Sussex ; 2ndly, 1932, Elizabeth Esther, da. of J. W. Barnes, and widow of R. J. Croft, of Rotherfield, Sussex :—

(By 1st marriage) Hugo Frederick Barnabas (of 2708, W. 10th Av., Vancouver, British Columbia), *b.* 1900; ed. at Haileybury: *m.* 1925, Kathleen Florence Louise, da. of J. Whittome, of Vancouver, and has issue living, James Alexander Donovan, *b.* 1928: *m.* 1951, Patricia Louise, da. of A. J. McNeil, of Duncan, British Columbia, and has issue living, Gregory McNeil *b.* 1956,—Marion Joan, *b.* 1926: *m.* 1947, John Ernest Fox, of 1147, Williams Rd., Richmond, Vancouver, British Columbia, and has issue living, John Patrick *b.* 1950, Geoffrey Ernest *b.* 1951, Kathleen Jennifer *b.* 1948, Diane Joan (twin) *b.* 1950.

Issue of the late William Edward **Stamer**, 3rd son of 3rd baronet, *b.* 1864, *d.* 1945 : *m.* 1894, Evelyn Cicely, who *d.* 1952 el. da. of the late Herbert Wood, of Isle of Raasay, Inverness-shire.

William Arthur John (Springfield Rd., RR1, Vernon, BC, Canada), *b.* 1899: *m.* 1935, Helen, da. of Dr. Wilfred Anthony Legh Jackson, of Lavington, BC, and has issue living, William John Derek (P.O. Box 247, Barriére, BC, Canada, VOE IEO), *b.* 1940: *m.* 1st, 1961 (m. diss. 1964), Marcelle Blanche, da. of David Howrie, of Vernon, BC; 2ndly, 1967, Valerie Margaret, da. of R. McQuarrie, of Revelstoke, and has issue living (by 1st m.), Rodney William *b.* 1961, (by 2nd m.), William John David *b.* 1970, Patricia Leah (twin) *b.* 1970,—Judith Cicely, *b.* 1939: *m.* 1st, 1957 (m. diss. 1961), Glen Fletcher, of Lavington, BC, Canada; 2ndly, 1964, Arthur G. Jaik, of Lavington, Vernon, BC, Canada, and has issue living, (by 1st m.), Rhondda Jane *b.* 1957, (by 2nd m.), Catherine Louise *b.* 1965, Susan Christine *b.* 1968,—Rosemary Sean, *b.* 1943: *m.* 1964, Ronald Edwin Haywood, of 1601, West Bench Drive, RR1 Penticton, BC, Canada, V2A 6J6, and has issue living, John Christopher *b.* 1968, Alison Jane *b.* 1966.

Issue of the late Major Arthur Cowie Stamer, C.B.E., 5th son of 3rd baronet, *b.* 1869, *d.* 1944 : *m.* 1900, Everilda Mary, who *d.* 1954, da. of the late George Arthur Thompson [Cayley, Bt.] :—

Joan Eleanor (*Lady Lawson*), *b.* 1909: *m.* 1933, Sir William Howard Lawson, 5th Bt. (cr. 1841). *Residence*, Wood House, Warwick Bridge, Carlisle.

The 1st baronet, Sir William Stamer, was Lord Mayor of Dublin 1809 and 1819, and commanded a regiment of the Dublin Yeomanry during the Irish rebellion. The Rt. Rev. Sir Lovelace Tomlinson Stamer, D.D., 3rd Bt., was Suffragan Bishop of Shrewsbury 1888-1905.

STANIER, Creation (U.K.) 1917, of Peplow Hall, Hodnet, co. Salop.

Stronger by piety.

PIETATE FORTIOR

Sir ALEXANDER BEVILLE GIBBONS STANIER, *D.S.O., M.C.*, 2nd *Baronet; b.* Jan. 31st, 1899 ; *s.* his father, *Sir* BEVILLE, *M.P.*, 1921; ed. at Eton : is Brigadier (retired) late Welsh Guards (Comdg. 1945-48) ; a J.P., a D.L. and patron of two livings ; High Sheriff of Shropshire 1951 ; was a co. Councillor for Salop 1950-8; European War 1918 in France and Belgium (M.C., two medals), European War 1939-45 in France (despatches, D.S.O. and Bar, American Silver Star, Com. Order of Leopold of Belgium with palms, Belgian Croix de Guerre with palms) ; is a C.St.J.; D.S.O. 1940 (Bar 1945): *m.* 1927, Dorothy Gladys, who *d.* 1973, el. da. of the late Brig.-Gen. Alfred Douglas Miller, CBE, DSO, of Shotover House, Wheatley, Oxon, and has issue.

Arms—Or, on a pile azure ten escallops, four, three, two and one of the first. Crest—In front of a griffin's head, erased proper three escallops or.

Residences—The Manor, East Farndon, Market Harborough, Leicestershire ; Park Cottage, Ludford, Ludlow, Salop. *Club*—Guards'.

Son living—BEVILLE DOUGLAS, (Kings Close, Whaddon, Bletchley, Bucks.; Guards' Club, MCC), *b.* April 20th, 1934: ed. at Eton; late Capt. Welsh Guards; ADC to Gov.-Gen. of Australia 1959-60: *m.* 1963, Violet Shelagh, el. da. of the late Maj. James Sinnott, of Tetbury, Glos., and has issue living, Alexander James Sinnott, *b.* April 10th, 1970,—Henrietta Claire, *b.* 1965,—Lucinda Katherine, *b.* 1967.
Daughter living—Sylvia Mary Finola, *b.* 1948.
Brother living— Philip Francis, *b.* 1901: *m.* 1929, Kathleen Mary, da. of the late Edgar Turrall, J.P., of Coundon Hall, Coventry, Warwickshire, and has issue living, Philippa Mary, *b.* 1930,—Constance Lutra Hope, *b.* 1933: *m.* 1969, Peter Glendinning, of 89, Elm Rd., Shoeburyness, Essex, and has issue living, James Beville *b.* 1970, Philip Peter *b.* 1972. *Residence*, Westbrook, Richard's Castle, nr. Ludlow, Shropshire.
Sister living—Dulce Constance : *m.* 1919, Capt. Frank Adolphus Hood Stanier, J.P., formerly Shropshire L.I., who *d.* 1949, and from whom she had obtained a divorce 1936, and has issue living, Frank Justice, *b.* 1926,—June Bevilline, *b.* 1923. *Residence*, Hillhampton Cottage, Marchamley, Shrewsbury.

This family, originally spelt Stonhewer, was settled at Biddulph, Staffs. from the 16th century. Sir Beville Stanier, 1st Bt., MP for Newport, Salop (C) 1908-18, and Ludlow 1918-21 and Lord of the Manors of Peplow and High Hatton, was 2nd son of Francis Stanier of The Moor House, Biddulph, Staffs., and Peplow Hall, Salop., High Sheriff of Salop, 1894.

STAPLES, Creation (I.) 1628, of Lissan, co. Tyrone.

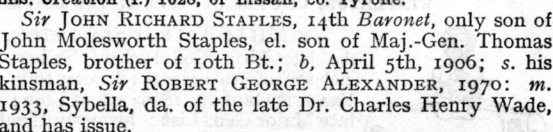

Teneo.
I hold.

Sir JOHN RICHARD STAPLES, 14th *Baronet*, only son of John Molesworth Staples, el. son of Maj.-Gen. Thomas Staples, brother of 10th Bt.; *b,* April 5th, 1906; *s.* his kinsman, *Sir* ROBERT GEORGE ALEXANDER, 1970: *m.* 1933, Sybella, da. of the late Dr. Charles Henry Wade, and has issue.

Arms—Quarterly, 1st and 4th, argent, on a fesse engrailed sable between three hurts, as many ermine spots between two dragons' heads erased or, *Staples* ; 2nd and 3rd, argent, a cross ragulé gules, on a chief sable two pheons or, *Jones*. Crest—A demi-savage azure, girt with a belt with two rings, charged with four torteaux, and holding in his hands a large staple or.

Residence—Butter Hill House, Dorking, Surrey.

Daughters living—Eileen Sybell, *b.* 1939: *m.* 1968, Timothy Geary Edward Kilpatrick, of Kingswood, Frensham, Surrey, and has issue living, Amanda Charlotte, *b.* 1971,—Sarah Patricia, *b.* 1974.——Barbara Helen, *b.* 1941: *m.* 1st, 1970, Alistair John Hutchinson-Russell, who *d.* 1973; 2ndly, 1974, Anthony Warren England.
Daughter living of 13th Baronet—Hazel Marion, *b.* 1923: *m.* 1970, Harry Hol beche Radclyffe Dolling.

Daughter living of 12th Baronet—Violet Hope, *b.* 1896: *m.* 1st, 1922, Lt.-Col. William Magill Kennedy, CIE, Indian Army, who *d.* 1923; 2ndly, 1927, Maj. Arthur William Dobbin, DSO, RA, who *d.* 1951.
Sisters living—Alice Henrietta, *b.* 1909.——Eileen Patience, *b.* 1917.
Mother living—Helen Lucy Johnstone (14, Clyde Rd., Dublin), da. of the late Capt. Richard Williams Barrington, HEICS [see Barrington, Bt., colls.]: *m.* 1905, John Molesworth Staples, who *d.* 1948.
Widow living of 13th Baronet—VERA LILLIAN (*Vera, Lady Staples*), (Lissan, Cookstown, co. Tyrone), yst. da. of John Jenkins, of Malmains Way, Beckenham, Kent: *m.* 1922, Sir Robert George Alexander Staples, 13th Bt., who *d.* 1970.

Collateral Branches living.

Grandchildren of the late Maj.-Gen. Thomas Staples, B.S.C., 3rd son of the Rev. John Molesworth Staples, and next brother of 10th baronet:—

Issue of the late Thomas Staples, b. 1870, d. 1963: m. 1903, Mary Usher, who d. 1966, da. of Frederick Greer, JP, of Tullylagan, co. Tyrone:—

THOMAS (2533, Sinclair Rd., Victoria, BC, Canada), b. Feb. 9th, 1905: m. 1952, Frances Annie Irvine, of Toronto, Canada.——Gerald James Arland (2, Broadmead Lane, Norton-sub-Hamdon, Som. TA14 6SS), b. 1910: m. 1951, Henrietta, da. of Arland Ussher, of 18, Green Rd., Blackrock, co. Dublin, and has issue living, Emily Ann, b. 1952: m. 1974, Howard James Anthony Smith, of 14, Jubilee Rd., Watford, Herts.,—Jacqueline Mary, b. 1954.——Richard Molesworth (113, Huntsbury Av., Christchurch, 2, NZ), b. 1914: m. 1954, Marjorie Charlotte Thomas, of Christchurch, NZ.——Grace, b. 1906: m. 1932, Horace Roland Rumbo Dowd, of Main St., Lismore, co. Waterford, and has issue living, Peter, b. 1935: m. 1961, Constance Evelyn Hornibrook, of Lismore, co. Waterford, and has issue living, Sandra Evelyn b. 1962,—Thomas Charles, b. 1944: m. 19—, , and has issue living,—Christopher. b. 1948.——Elizabeth Lindsay (The Rushes, Milborne Port, nr. Sherborne, Dorset), b. 1912: m, 1st 1934, Henry Eric St. George Harper, who d. 1947; 2ndly, 1961, John Frank Harris, who d. 1971; 3rdly, 1972, James Victor Thomas Rawlence, MBE, RN, and has issue living (by 1st m.), Elizabeth Lindsay St. George, b. 1937: m. 1961, Trevor Arthur Lant, and has issue living, Myles Arthur b. 1963, Philippa Lindsay b. 1969.——Pamela June (Rosefield Lodge, Rock Rd., Blackrock, co. Dublin), b. 1923.

Issue of the late Noel Richard Ponsonby Staples, b. 1879, d. 1958: m. 1905, Kathleen, who d. 1966, da. of the late Alexander Ross Hamilton, of Glensavage, Blackrock, co. Dublin:—

Richard Nathaniel (400, Arbutus Av., Maple Bay, Duncan, BC, Canada), b. 1908: m. 1939, Isabel MacMillan, and has issue living, Heather Anne, b. 1941,—Sheila Isabel, b. 1944.——Anthony (924, Arbutus Av., Maple Bay, Duncan, BC, Canada), b. 1920: m. 1950, Margaret Eva Duffield, who d. 1970, and has issue living, Noel Leslie, b. 1954: m. 1972, Dwaine Grant Van Eeuwen.——Anne Veronica, b. 1910: m. 1936, Lt.-Col. Richard MacNaughton Lendrum, DSO, of RRI, Maple Bay, Duncan, BC, Canada, and has issue living, Richard Brain, b. 19—: m. 1970, Gail Jeanette Robinson,—Jillian Anne, b. 19—: m. 1965, Raymond Thomas Benwell.——Flora Hamilton (4060, Gordon-Head Rd., Victoria, BC, Canada), b. 1912.——Kathleen (twin), b. 1920: m. 19—, A. C. Wilson, of 305-1676 West 11th St., Vancouver 9, BC, Canada.

The 1st baronet, Sir Thomas Staples of Lissan, co. Tyrone and Faghanvale, co. Derry, High Sheriff of co. Tyrone 1640, was 5th son of Alexander Staples, of Yate Court, Glos. The 9th baronet, Sir Thomas, QC, Queen's Advocate in Ireland, who d. 1865, was a distinguished lawyer.

STAPLETON, Creation (E.) 1679, of The Leeward Islands.

Sir MILES TALBOT STAPLETON, 9th *Baronet*, son of the late Lieut.-Col. Richard Talbot Plantagenet Stapleton, 2nd son of 7th baronet ; b. May 26th, 1893 ; s. his uncle, *Sir* FRANCIS GEORGE, 1899; ed. at Eton ; is patron of one living ; late Major Gen. List ; formerly Lieut. 3rd (Reserve) Batn. Oxfordshire and Buckinghamshire L.I., and Capt. R.E.; European War 1914-19 in Italy: m. 1st, 1912, Doris, who d. 1933, da. of the late Hedley Ludford, of Llanelly, S. Wales ; 2ndly, 1935, Miriam Edna, da. of the late Hedley Ludford [ante], and has issue by 1st and 2nd marriages.

Arms—Argent, a lion rampant sable.   *Crest*—Out of a ducal coronet or, a Saracen's head affrontée proper, wreathed about the temples argent and sable.

Residence—Rotherfield, Cold Ash, Newbury.

Pro magnâ chartâ.
For the great charter.   Daughters living—By 1st marriage—Angela, b. 1921 : m. 1950, Clifford Mason, and has issue living, Michael Miles David, b. 1953,—Claire, b. 1955. *Residence*, Box Hedge Cottage, Chaddleworth, Newbury.——By 2nd marriage—Susan Penelope, b. 1937: m. 1964, Roger Fulford-Dobson, of Falcons, Tokers Green, Reading, and has issue living, Giles Roger, b. 1965,—Jasper William, b. 1970,—Emma Susan, b. 1967.

Collateral Branch living.

Grandson of the late Rev. Eliot Henry Stapleton, 3rd son of 7th Bt.:—
Issue of the late Brigadier Francis Harry Stapleton, C.M.G., b. 1870, d. 1956 : m. 1911, Maud Ellen, who d. 1958, da. of the late Major Alfred Edward Wrottesley [B. Wrottesley, colls.]:—

HENRY ALFRED (of Conygar Cottage, Shillingstone, Blandford Forum, Dorset), b. May 2nd, 1913; ed. at Marlborough, and Ch. Ch., Oxford (MA); 1939-45 War as 2nd Lt. Oxfordshire and Bucks L.I.: m. 1961, Rosslyne Murray, da. of the late Capt. H. S. Warren, R.N., of Parkstone, Dorset.

The 1st baronet, Sir William Stapleton, was appointed Gov. of the Leeward Islands after the Restoration. Sir Thomas Stapleton, 6th baronet, inherited 1788 the Barony of le Despencer, which passed to his grand-da. the Hon. Mary Frances Elizabeth who m. 1845 Evelyn Boscawen, later 6th Viscount Falmouth. The baronetcy passed to his yst. son, Rev. the Hon. Sir Francis Jarvis Stapleton, who d. 1874.

STARKEY, Creation (U.K.) 1935, of Norwood Park, Parish of Southwell, and co. of Nottingham.

Man proposes, God disposes.

Sir WILLIAM RANDLE STARKEY, 2nd *Baronet*; *b.* Dec. 11th, 1899; *s.* his father, *Sir* JOHN RALPH, 1940; *ed.* at Eton; Lieut.-Col. (retired) late Rifle Brig.; was High Sheriff of Notts 1954-55; European War 1939-45 with London Irish Rifles and Reconnaissance Corps: *m.* 1935, Irene Myrtle, who *d.* 1965, da. of the late Capt. Philip Francklin, MVO, RN [Walker, Bt., *cr.* 1856], and has issue.

Arms—Argent, a bend engrailed vair between six storks sable. Crest—A stork argent, semée of estoiles azure.
Residence—Norwood Park, Southwell, Notts.

Sons living—JOHN PHILIP (Norwood Park, Southwell, Notts., *b.* May 8th, 1938; *ed.* at Eton, and Ch. Ch., Oxford: *m.* 1966, Victoria Henrietta Fleetwood, da. of Lt.-Col. Christopher Herbert Fleetwood Fuller, TD [see Fuller, Bt.], and has issue living, Henry John, *b.* 1973,—Suzannah Clare, *b.* 1966,—Elizabeth Victoria, *b.* 1975.——Michael William, *b.* 1946; *ed.* at Eton, and Newcastle Univ.: *m.* 1974, Gillian Mary, da. of E. Treflyn Roberts, of Shotton, Deeside, Clwyd.
Daughter living—Caroline Myrtle, *b.* 1936: *m.* 1957, Frederick John Charles Gordon Hervey-Bathurst, only son of Sir Frederick Peter Methuen Hervey-Bathurst, 6th Bt. *Residences,* 450, Kings Rd., Chelsea, SW10; Somborne Park, King's Somborne, Hants.

Sisters living—Hilda Margaret: *m.* 1915, Capt. Charles Edward Parker, M.C., who *d.* 1962 [see E. Macclesfield, colls.]. *Residence,* 19, Lennox Gdns., S.W.1.——Alice Barbara.——Florence Erica (9, Hasker St., SW3): *m.* 1918, Maj.-Gen. Bevil Thomson Wilson, CB, DSO, late RE, who *d.* 1975, and has issue living, Sir Alexander James, *KBE, MC* (Goldhill Farm House, Edingley, Newark, Notts.), *b.* 1921; Lt. Gen. late Rifle Bde., and Lancs. Fus.; acting Comdr. UN Force in Cyprus 1965-66, Comd. 147 Inf. Bde. 1966-67, Dir. of Army Recruiting 1967-70, and GOC NW Dist. 1970-72, since when Vice-Adj. Gen. MOD; MBE (Mil) 1948, CBE (Mil.) 1966, KBE (Mil.) 1974: *m.* 1958, the Hon. Jean Margaret (PAUL), da. of 2nd Baron Rankeillour, and has issue living, William Robert Bevil *b.* 1959, Rupert James *b.* 1961,—Priscilla Florence, *b.* 1923: *m.* 1948, Julian Gerard Wathen [see Buxton, Bt., colls.].——Helen Frances: *m.* 1922, Humphrey Parker-Jervis, who *d.* 1948 [see V. St. Vincent, colls.]. *Residence,* Brook Cottage, Uley, Dursley, Glos.——Sylvia Augusta: *m.* 1st, 1925, Capt. Eustace Ruffel Drake Long, CBE, RN, who *d.* 1941; 2ndly, 1951, as his second wife, Reginald Evelyn Welby-Pelham, who *d.* 1965 [E. Yarborough, colls.], and has issue living, (by 1st m.) David Andrew, *b.* 1929,—Phœbe Olivia, *b.* 1926: *m.* 1954, Henry Martin Shone, of Bayfields Farm, Headley, Bordon, Hants., and has issue living, Jeremy Patrick Martin *b.* 1955, Anthony Michael John *b.* 1957, Patrick Douglas *b.* 1959, Colin Henry Philip *b.* 1964. *Residence,* Milestone Cottage, Stonely, Hunts.——Margaret Lucy, *b.* 1903: *m.* 1927, Lt.-Col. James Aubrey Henry Bellingham Somerville, DSO, who *d.* 1950 [Somerville, Bt., colls.]. *Residence,* 59, Queens Gate Mews, SW7.

The 1st baronet, Sir John Ralph (el. son of the late Lewis Randle Starkey, D.L., J.P., of Norwood Park, Notts.), sat as M.P. for Newark Div. of Nottinghamshire (C.) 1906-22.

STEEL, Creation (U.K.) 1938, of Philiphaugh, co. Selkirk.

With Prudence and Courage.

Sir FIENNES WILLIAM STRANG STEEL, 2nd *Baronet*; *b.* July 24th, 1912; *s.* his father, *Major Sir* SAMUEL STRANG, 1961; *ed.* at Eton; Maj. (ret.) 17th/21st Lancers, a JP and a DL of Selkirkshire, a Convener of Selkirk Co. Council, and a Forestry Comnr.: *m.* 1941, Joan, da. of the late Brig.-Gen. Sir Brodie Haldane Henderson, K.C.M.G., C.B., and has issue.

Arms—Argent, a bend chequy sable and ermine, between two lions' heads erased gules, on a chief azure, two billets or, a crescent of the first for difference. Crest—A lion's head erased gules.
Residence—Philiphaugh, Selkirk.

Sons living—FIENNES MICHAEL STRANG, *b.* Feb. 22nd, 1943.——Colin Brodie Strang (Newlandburn House, Gorebridge, Midlothian), *b.* 1945: *m.* 1970, April, da. of Aubrey Studd, of Wishanger Manor, Miserden, Glos., and has issue living, James William, *b.* 1973.

Daughter living—Diana Joan Strang, *b.* 1947: *m.* 1970, Francis Gradidge, of Thatched Oak Cottage, Eversley, Hants., and has issue living, Richard Anthony Strang, *b.* 1971,—Rosanna Clare, *b.* 1973.

Brothers living—Jock Wykeham Strang, *b.* 1914; *ed.* at Eton: *m.* 1945, Lesley, da. of Lieut.-Col. Sir John (Reginald) Noble Graham, V.C., O.B.E., 3rd Bt., and has issue living, Malcolm Graham Strang (Culcairn House, By Alness, Ross & Cromarty), *b.* 1946: *m.* 1972, Margaret Philippa, da. of W. P. Scott, of Kierfield, Sandwick, Orkney,—Celia Jane Strang, *b.* 1948,—Susan Rachel Strang, *b.* 1952. *Residence,* Logie, Kirriemuir, Angus.——Robert Stanley Strang, *b.* 1934; *ed.* at Eton: *m.* 1958, Caroline A. E., only da. of the late Lt.-Col. William Hugh Carter, of Rosslyn, Tain, Ross-shire, and has issue living, David William Strang, *b.* 1961,—Richard James Strang, *b.* 1963. *Residence,* Sluie, Banchory, Kincardineshire.

Sister living—Grizel Mabel Strang.

The 1st baronet, Sir Samuel Strang Steel (son of the late William Strang Steel, J.P., D.L., of Philiphaugh, Selkirk), was Major Lothians and Border Horse, a Director of Bank of Scotland, Lord-Lieut. of Selkirkshire 1948-58, and M.P. for Ashford Div. of Kent 1918-29.

Steel (Ramsay-Steel-Maitland), see Maitland.

STEPHEN, Creation (U.K.) 1891, of De Vere Gardens.

Sir JAMES ALEXANDER STEPHEN, 4th *Baronet; b.* Feb. 25th, 1908; *s.* his father, *Sir* HARRY LUSHINGTON, 1945; ed. at Eton, and at Trin. Coll., Camb.

Arms—Argent, on a chevron between two crescents in chief, and a sinister hand couped at the wrist and erect in base gules, an escallop between two mullets of the first. Crest—An eagle displayed with two heads sable, resting its claws on an increscent to the dexter and a decrescent to the sinister, or.

Address—44, Princess Rd., Branksome, Poole, Dorset.

Sursum.
Upward.

The 1st baronet, Sir James Fitzjames Stephen, was Recorder of Newark-upon-Trent 1859-69, Legal Member of Council of Viceroy of India 1869-72, Professor of Common Law at Inns of Court 1875-79, and a Judge of the High Court of Justice 1879-91, also author of "A Digest of The Law of Evidence," and other works. The 2nd baronet, Sir Herbert, was Clerk of Assize of N. Circuit 1889-1927. The 3rd baronet, Sir Harry Lushington, was a Judge of High Court, Calcutta 1901-14, and an Alderman of London County Council 1916-28.

STEPHENSON, Creation (U.K.) 1936, of Hassop Hall, co. Derby.

Col. Sir HENRY FRANCIS BLAKE STEPHENSON, *OBE, TD,* 2nd *Baronet; b.* Dec. 3rd, 1895; *s.* his father, *Lt.-Col. Sir* HENRY KENYON, *DSO, VD,* 1947; ed. at Eton; Hon LLD Sheffield 1955; sometime Major and Brevet Lt.-Col. Yorkshire Dragoons (Yeo.); is a JP for Sheffield, a DL for Derbyshire (High Sheriff 1948); was Pro-Chancellor Sheffield Univ. 1947-56; 1915-18 War in France and Belgium (1914-15 star, two medals), 1939-42 War in Middle East (OBE); OBE (Mil.) 1941: *m.* 1925, Joan, el. da. of the late Major John Herbert Upton, J.P., and has issue.

Arms—Vair, on a pale between two pallets gules, three leopards' faces or, two flaunches of the second. Crest—A rock, thereon a falcon's head erased proper, gorged with a collar vair, pendent therefrom an escutcheon vert, charged with two arrows, saltirewise, points downwards or.

Medio tutissimus ibis.
Thou wilt go safest in the middle course.   *Residence*—Hassop Hall, Bakewell, Derbyshire.

Son living—HENRY UPTON, TD (Tissington Cottage, Rowland, Bakewell, Derbyshire; Cavalry, and Sheffield Clubs), *b.* Nov. 26th, 1926; ed. at Eton; late Capt. Yorkshire Yeo.; a Dir. of Stephenson, Blake & Co, Ltd., and Thos. Turton & Sons, Ltd.: *m.* 1962, Susan, da. of the late Maj. J. E. Clowes, of Clifton, Ashbourne, Derbyshire, and has issue living, Fiona Kathleen, *b.* 1964,—Annabel Mary, *b.* 1965,—Emma Frances, *b.* 1968,—Lucy Clare, *b.* 1970.

Brother living—William Raymond Shirecliffe (of Bennet Grange, Fulwood, Sheffield), *b.* 1898; ed. at Eton; Hon MA Sheffield Univ.; 1914-18 War in France as 2nd Lt. 11th Hussars (two medals): *m.* 1923, Madeleine Rose, da. of George Montagu Butterworth, of Westward Ho!, Devon, and has issue living, Timothy Hugh (Lomberdale Hall, Bakewell, Derbys.), *b.* 1930; a JP for Sheffield: *m.* 1959, Susan Lesley, da. of the late George Arthur Harris, and has issue living, Matthew Francis Timothy *b.* 1960,—Oliver George, *b.* 1962,—Susan Madeleine, *b.* 1924: *m.* 1949, Charles Graham Murray, MBE, JP, of 545, Fulwood Rd., Sheffield, and has issue living, Elizabeth Susan *b.* 1951, Jane Madeleine *b.* 1953, Anne Catriona *b.* 1955,—Jocelyn Frances, *b.* 1926: *m.* 1948, David Clement Wilson, of 363, Fulwood Rd., Sheffield, and has issue living, Christopher Michael Rockley *b.* 1957, Olivia Frances, *b.* 1952, Sarah Margaret *b.* 1954.

Sisters living—Evelyn Mary, *b.* 1897: *m.* 1923, Anthony Henry Mather Jackson, DL, JP, of Archway House, Kirklington, Newark-on-Trent [*see* Mather Jackson, Bt.].——Helena Millicent Frances (of Fennel Cottage, Ashford-in-the-Water, Bakewell, Derbyshire), *b.* 1906.—— Cynthia Margaret, MBE (17, Sydney House, Woodstock Rd., W4), *b.* 1910; MBE (Civil) 1948. ——Emma Letitia Gertrude, *b.* 1914: *m.* 1941, Philip Charles Fenner Lawton, CBE, DFC, of 7, Ladbroke Terr., W11, and North Springs, Fittleworth, Pulborough, Sussex, and has issue living, Charles Henry Huntly, *b.* 1946,—Philippa Rosemary, *b.* 1943: *m.* 1974, Lt.-Cdr. Michael Henry White, RN.

Collateral Branches living
Issue of the late Percival John Parker Stephenson, 3rd son of 1st baronet, *b.* 1900, *d.* 1973: *m.* 1930 (m. diss. 1948) Pamela, da. of Sir Walter Benton Jones, 2nd Bt.:—

Jennifer Barbara, *b.* 1931: *m.* 1958, John Henry Thorntor, of The Manor House, Little Bealings, Woodbridge, Suffolk, and has issue living, Edward John, *b.* 1963,—Robert Walter, *b.* 1968,— Katherine Louise, *b.* 1961.

Issue of the late Lt.-Col. Charles Eustace Kenyon Stephenson, yst. son of 1st baronet, b. 1903, d. 1971: m. 1930, Nancy Barbara (The Outrake, Bakewell, Derbys.), da. of Harry Limnell Lyon, JP, of Hillam Hall, Monk Fryston, Yorks.:—

Charles Lyon, TD (The Cottage, Gt. Longstone, Derbys.), b. 1935: m. 1st, 1960 (m. diss. 1972), Margot Jane, da. of the late Tony Malcolm Tinker; 2ndly, 1974, the Hon. Sarah Merryweather Norrie, GGSM, da. of 1st Baron Norrie, and has issue living (by 1st m.), George Lyon, b. 1962,—Ruper Nicholas, b. 1964,—Belinda Jane, b. 1963.——Harriet Ann, b. 1931: m. 1951 (m. diss. 1973), John Bulkley Herbert Francis, and has issue living, Charles Mark, b. 1952,—Timothy, b. 1960,—Clare, b. 1955,—Charlotte Ann, b. 1963.

The 1st baronet, Sir Henry Kenyon Stephenson, D.S.O., V.D. (son of the late Sir Henry Stephenson, of the Glen, Endcliffe, Sheffield), was Pro-Chancellor of Sheffield Univ., Chm. of Stephenson, Blake & Co., typefounders, Lord Mayor of Sheffield 1908-09 and 1910-11, Master Cutler of Sheffield 1919-20, and High Sheriff of Derbyshire 1932. He sat as M.P. for Park Div. of Sheffield (L) 1918-23, and served during European War 1914-18 (D.S.O.).

STERN, Creation (U.K.) 1922, of Chertsey, Surrey. [Extinct 1933.]

Sir EDWARD DAVID STERN, 1st and last *Baronet.*

Widow living of 1st Baronet—SYBIL GRACE (*Lady Stern*), da. of Sir Adolph Tuck, 1st Bt.: m. 1925, as his second wife, Sir Edward David Stern, 1st baronet, who d. 1933, when the title became ext. *Residence*, 8, Abbey Lodge, Park Rd., Regents Park, N.W.8.

STEWART, Creation (I.) 1623, of Ramelton, co. Donegal.

Nothing is to be despaired of.

Sir JOCELYN HARRY STEWART, 12th *Baronet*; b. Jan. 24th, 1903; s. his father, *Sir* HARRY JOCELYN URQUHART 1945: m. 1st, 1932, Constance, who d. 1940, da. of D'Arcy Shillaber; 2ndly, 1946, Katherine Christina, da. of James Sweeney, and has issue by 1st and 2nd marriages.

Arms (recorded at Lyon Office)—Or, a fesse chequy azure and argent surmounted of a bend engrailed and in chief a rose gules, all within a bordure of the third charged with three lions rampant of the fourth. **Crest**—A dexter arm erect couped at the elbow, the hand holding a heart all proper.

Residence—Letterkenny, co. Donegal.

Sons living—By 1st marriage—ALAN D'ARCY, b. Nov. 29th, 1932: m. 1952, Patricia, da. of Lawrence Turner, of Ramelton, co. Donegal, and has issue living, Nicholas Courtney d'Arcy, b. 1953,—Lindsay Stephen d'Arcy, b. 1956,—Constance Patricia d'Arcy, b. 1954,—Siobhan d'Arcy, b. 1960. *Residence*, One Acre House, Church St., Ramelton, co. Donegal.——**By 2nd marriage**—Brian Jocelyn, b. 1948——Terence Annesley, b. 1949.

Daughters living—By 2nd marriage—Marie Jeanette, b. 1947.——Katherine Benedicta, b. 1951.

Sisters living—Violet May (1a, Tuns Lane, Silverton, Exeter, Devon), b. 1904: m. 1926 (m. diss. 1943), Maj. Allister Colvin Baillie, MC, RE, who d. 1971.——Evelyn Frances, b. 1911: m. 1958, Louis Botha, of 11, Bartle-dene, 572, Bartle Rd., Durban, Natal.

Collateral Branches living.

Issue of the late Malcolm Geoffrey Stewart, 4th son of 11th baronet; b. 1908, d. 1974: m. 1946, Joan Cox, who d. 1968:—
Robin Gordon Alan, b. 1948: m. 1973, Barbara Anne, da. of Wilfred Miller, of Grasscroft, Yorks.——Jonathan Malcolm (48a, Parkholme Rd., E8), b. 1951.

Issue of the late James Augustus Stewart, brother of 9th baronet, b. 1835, d. 1915: m. 1884, Ann Wilhelmina Jean, who d. 1913, el. da. of the late William Wray, of Oak Park, co. Donegal:—
Edith Frances. *Residence*, Aughnoo, St. Oran's Rd., Buncrana, co. Donegal.

Granddaughters of the late Col. Harry Hutchinson Augustus Stewart, brother of 9th baronet:—
Issue of the late Walter Annesley Stewart, b. 1883, d. 1937: m. 1920, Phyllis Lucie (who m. 2ndly, 1938, Beniamin Worthy Horne, of Norfolk Cottage, Waldron, Heathfield, Sussex), da. of the late Edmund Larkin Horne, of 34, Bolton Gdns., SW5:—
Dorothy, b. 1924. *Residence*, 233, East 69th Street, New York, 21, U.S.A.——Rosemary, b. 1928: m. 1950, Col. John Arthur Haire, late RA, and has issue living, John Stewart, b. 1957,—Susan Mary, b. 1952,—Anne Rosemary, b. 1954. *Residence*, Briars Place, Watts Lane, Chislehurst, Kent.

Grandchildren of the late Lorenzo Moore Stewart, uncle of 9th baronet :—
Issue of the late Richard Quinton Stewart, b. 1844, d. 190-: m. 1874, Isabel Christiana, da. of Erasmus Wilson Williams, of Dublin :—
Richard Evans Augustus, b. 1875.——Lorenzo Moore, b. 1882.——Emily Gertrude. *Residence*,

This family is of common ancestry with the Earls of Galloway and Barons Blantyre (ext. 1900). The 1st baronet greatly distinguished himself as a Mil. Comd. in the troubles of Ireland, and was created a Privy Councillor. The 3rd baronet, Master-General of the Ordnance in Ireland, was in 1682 created Lord Stewart of Ramelton and Viscount Mountjoy. The 2nd Viscount and 4th Baronet was also Master-General of the Ordnance; and the 3rd Viscount and 5th Baronet was created Earl of Blesington, but his peerages became extinct at his death in 1769. The 6th baronet sat as M.P. for Charlemont 1763-97, and the 7th baronet represented in Parliament Enniskillen 1783-90 and Donegal co. 1802-18.

STEWART, Creation (U.K.) 1803, of Athenree, Tyrone.

Sir HUGH CHARLIE GODFRAY STEWART, 6th *Baronet ; b.* April 13th, 1897 ; *s.* his father, *Sir* GEORGE POWELL, 1945 ; ed. at Bradfield; late Maj. R. Inniskilling Fus.; DL for co. Tyrone; 1914-18 War in France (wounded), 1939-45 War in France, and as Assist. Comdt. Imperial Forces Transhipment Camp, Durban, and in Syria: *m.* 1st, 1929 (m. diss. 1942), Rosemary Elinor Dorothy, da. of the late Maj. George Peacocke, formerly Roy. Inniskilling Fus.; 2ndly, 1948, Diana Margaret, da. of the late Capt. J. E. Hibbert, MC, DFC, and has issue by 1st and 2nd m.

Arms—Quarterly, 1st, or, a lion rampant within a double tressure flory counter-flory gules; 2nd, or, a fess chequy azure and argent, in chief a portcullis sable, *Stewart*; 3rd, argent, a saltire between four roses gules, barbed vert, *Fife*; 4th, or, a lion rampant gules, *Lennox*; the whole within a bordure compony argent and azure charged with three thistles proper. **Crest**—A unicorn's head coupled argent, armed and crined or, between two olive branches proper.

Seat—Lough Macrory Lodge, Carrickmore, co. Tyrone.

FORWARD

Son living—By 1st m.—DAVID JOHN CHRISTOPHER (High Cross Grange, Claybrooke Magna, nr. Lutterworth, Leics., LE17), *b.* June 19th, 1935; ed. at Bradfield; Capt. (ret.) R. Inniskilling Fusiliers: *m.* 1959, Bridget Anne, el. da. of the late Patrick W. Sim.——**By 2nd m.**—Hugh Nicholas *b.* 1955.

Daughters living—By 1st m.—Elinor Godfray, *b.* 1930: *m.* 1953, John Macdonell, of The Close, Lakes Lane, Newport Pagnell, Bucks.——**By 2nd m.**—Jane Diana, *b.* 1949: *m.* 1973, John T. Costelloe.

Sister living—Mary, *b.* 1899 : *m.* 1930, Guy Janvrin Robin. *Residence*, Petit Menage, St. Saviours, Jersey.

Collateral Branches living.

Issue of the late John Marcus Stewart, 3rd son of 3rd baronet, *b.* 1863, *d.* 1906 : *m.* 1888, Ada Loveday, who *d.* 1896 :—

Gladys Edith Houghton (of Chelmer, School Lane, Lower Bourne, Farnham, Surrey).

Issue of the late Brig.-Gen. Cosmo Gordon Stewart, C.B., C.M.G., D.S.O., 8th son of 3rd baronet, *b.* 1869, *d.* 1948 : *m.* 1911, Gladys Berry, who *d.* 1973, da. of the late Dr. J. H. Honeyman, of Auckland, New Zealand :—

Charles Cosmo Bruce, **C.M.G.**, *b.* 1912; ed. at Eton, and at King's Coll., Camb.; Bar. Middle Temple 1937; 1939-45 War as Lt.-Col. RE (TA), in Egypt, Italy, and Greece (despatches); HM Consul-Gen. at Luanda 1964-67; CMG 1962. *Clubs*, Travellers', Royal Automobile.

Granddaughter of the late Capt. Hugh Stewart, 2nd son of 2nd baronet:—

Issue of the late Lieut.-Col. Hugh Stewart, D.S.O., M.C., M.B., *b.* 1881, *d.* (on active ser. during European War) 1918 : *m.* 1907, Muriel Dalzell, da. of Hugh McKean, of 19, Zion Road, Rathgar, Dublin :—

Muriel Denise Evelyn, *b.* 1913: *m.* 1942, John Gunn Murray-Matheson, M.B., Ch.B., and has issue living, Desmond John, *b.* 1950,—Nigel Hugh, *b.* 1951,—Ann Christine, *b.* 1943,—Rosemary Jean Denise, *b.* 1947. *Residence*, 32, Elmfield Road, Gosforth, Newcastle-upon-Tyne.

Grandchildren of the late George Vesey Stewart, MBE, 3rd son of Mervyn Stewart, 2nd son of 1st baronet:—

Issue of the late Mervyn Archdale Stewart, *b.* 1859, *d.* 1951 : *m.* 1881, Phœbe, who *d.* 1951, da. of the late Robert Hornidge-Gledstanes :—

Mary Sophia Ethel : *m.* 1918, Robert Rutland Turner, who *d.* 1927, formerly of Tauranga, New Zealand, and has issue living, Stewart Rutland, *b.* 1919 : *m.* 1942, Kathleen, da. of W. O'Connor, of Ashburton, New Zealand, and has issue living, a son *b.* 1943,—Phœbe Ethne, *b.* 1923 : *m.* 1944, Clifford Cedric Mountier.——Evy'een Frances: *m.* 1940, Alfred Edward Shepherd, who *d.* 1958. *Residence*, 42, 9th Avenue, Tauranga, New Zealand.

Issue of the late George Vesey Stewart, *b.* 1861, *d.* 1892: *m.* 1890, Cecilia Isabella, who *d.* 1947, da. of Thomas Anderson, formerly of Jesmond, Newcastle-upon-Tyne:—

Erin Lucy Sophia. *Residence*, 510, Mount Eden Rd., Mount Eden, Auckland, NZ.——Georgina Frances (posthumous): *m.* 1925, Norman Lawrence Wilson, and has issue living, Lawrence Stewart, *b.* 1928,—George Archdale, *b.* 1930,—Kerry Robin, *b.* 1933,—Patricia Cecilia, *b.* 1934. *Residence*, Waimauku, Kaipara Line, NZ.

Grandsons of the late John Rowley Miller Stewart (infra) :—

Issue of the late Mervyn Oswald Stewart, *b.* 1888, *d.* 1946: *m.* 1915, Ivy Mona, who *d.* 19—, da. of Robert Ernest Lester, of Kohukohu, Auckland, NZ:—

Mervyn Leslie Lester, *b.* 1916 : *m.* 19—, and has issue living, Trevor Rex, *b.* 1940.——Donald Walton, *b.* 1919.——Kenneth Archdale, *b.* 1922. *Residence*.

Issue of the late George Leslie Stewart, *b.* 1893, *d.* 1938 : *m.* 1927, Lillian Alice Ridsdale :—

Ross Ridsdale (c/o PO Box 407, Gisborne, NZ), *b.* 1934: *m.* 1966, Jillian Michelle, da. of Robert Hamilton Bartie, of Gisborne, NZ, and has issue living, Jonathan Bruce *b.* 1969.

Grandchildren of Trevor Rowley Stewart (infra):—

Issue of the late Colin Trevor Stewart, *b.* 1925, *d.* 1968: *m.* 1948, Bessie Rebie (Minden Rd., RD Te Puna, Tauranga, NZ), da. of Frederick Clarke Shroff, of Tauranga, NZ:—

Gary Colin (Minden Rd., RD Te Puna, Tuarange, NZ), *b.* 1953.——Peter Gregory, *b.* 1958.——Colette Marie, *b.* 1950.

Grandchildren of George Vesey Stewart, MBE (ante):—

Issue of the late John Rowley Miller Stewart, *b.* 1862, *d.* 1945 : *m.* 1st, 1886, Ellen Louisa, who *d.* 1912, da. of the late Henry Furness, of Kyber Pass, Auckland, New Zealand; 2ndly, 1913, Louisa Beatrice, da. of Thomas Gorst Travis, of Dunedin, NZ:—

(By 1st m.) Trevor Rowley (149, Edgecumbe Rd., Tawranga, NZ), *b.* 1896: *m.* 1920, Dora, da. of the late Edwin Hall, of Waihi, NZ, and has issue living, Shirley Rita (16, Korora St., Northcote, Auckland, NZ), *b.* 1921: *m.* 1st, 1945 (m. diss. 1950), William Lloyd Stevens; 2ndly, 1969, Francis Victor Parker, who *d.* 1973, and has issue living (by 1st m.), Kay Stewart, *b.* 1947.——(By 2nd m.) Lorraine Travis, *b.* 1917: *m.* 1937, Alfred Shepherd Willan, of Hastings Rd., Stratford, Taranaki, NZ, and has issue living, Michael Frederick Stewart, *b.* 1941,—Jock Stewart *b.* 1944,—Bruce Stewart, *b.* 1946,—Pamela Stewart, *b.* 1939.

Issue of the late Hugh Alexander Montgomery Moore Stewart, *b.* 1868, *d.* 1954 : *m.* 1st, 1891, Susan, who *d.* 1926, da. of the late William Tasman Clark, C.E., of Hobart, Tasmania ; 2ndly, 1932, Edith, el. da. of Joseph Cantwell, of Hawke's Bay, New Zealand :—

(By 1st m.) James Edward Frederick Vesey Tasman, *b.* 18—: *m.* 19—, and has issue living, Noel Montgomery, *b.* 19—.——Gilbert Harry Ranfurly, *b.* 18—.——Christina Martina Alice, *b.* 18—. ——Myrtle, *b.* 19—.——(By 2nd m.) Coral Elizabeth, *b.* 19—.

Grandchildren of the late Hugh Alexander Murray Stewart, 2nd son of Hugh Alexander Montgomery Moore Stewart (*ante*):—
Issue of Ranfurly Henry Stewart, *b.* 1899, *d.* 1972: *m.* 19—, Emma Frances Newman, who *d.* 1967:—
William Henry Albert Harvey (Welcome Bay, Tauranga, NZ), *b.* 1929: *m.* 1951, Joan Alison, da. of David Prestney, and has issue living, Brian William, *b.* 1966,—Julie Frances, *b.* 1953,—Colleen Margaret, *b.* 1955,—Janelle Beverley, *b.* 1957,—Debora Joy, *b.* 1959.——Trevor Ernest (Tolaga Bay, NZ), *b.* 1931: *m.* 19—, Joan Alice, da. of Andrew Stanley Fisher, and has issue living, Kelvin Mark, *b.* 1959,—Steven Wayne, *b.* 1962,—David Ernest, *b.* 1968,—Philip Trevor, *b.* 1972,—Maureen Anne, *b.* 1957,—Shona Joy, *b.* 1961,—Sarah Marie, *b.* 1970.

Grandchildren of the late Hugh Stewart, youngest son of the late Mervyn Stewart, 2nd son of 1st baronet :—
Issue of the late Rev. Mervyn James Stewart, *b.* 1871, *d.* 1961 : *m.* 1910, Margaret Emma, who *d.* 1968, da. of the late Frederick Jeffray Steuart, formerly of Carfin, Melbourne, Victoria, Australia:—
Hugh St. Clair, *MBE* (Fincoul, The Pyghtle, Denham, Bucks.; Savile Club), *b.* 1910; ed. at St. John's Coll., Camb. (MA); 1939-45 War as Lt.-Col. Comdg. an Army Film and Photographic Unit; MBE (Mil) 1945: *m.* 1934, Frances Henley, *BA*, only child of the late Dr. Henley Frane Curl, of Wokingham, and has issue living, Andrew Mervyn (29, Howletts Lane, Ruislip, Middx., HA4 7RR), *b.* 1943; ed. at Rugby: *m.* 1966, Carol-Anne, da. of Stanley Burritt Featherstone, of Uitenhage, S. Africa, and has issue living, Zoë Abbygail *b.* 1971,—Michael Henley (32, Worcester Cres., Mill Hill, NW7 4LL), *b.* 1949; ed. at Rugby, and Southampton Univ.: *m.* 1971, Jillian Maureen, da. of Stanley Gold, of Reigate,—Penelope Agnes, *b.* 1939; ed. at Somerville Coll., Oxford (MA): *m.* 1962, Hugh Macdonald Eales Forsyth, of The Marish, Marish Lane, Denham, Bucks., and has issue living, Kevin Hugh *b.* 1969,—Sophie Frances *b.* 1971,—Margaret (twin), *b.* 1949; ed. at Queenswood Sch., and Girton Coll., Camb.; MD: *m.* 1971, Anthony Kirwan.—— David (5230, 123rd SE, Bellevue, Wash., USA), *b.* 1912; is an Assocn.-Fellow of R. Aeronautical Soc.: *m.* 1st, 1942, Marjorie Susan Carroll, who *d.* 1961, yr. da. of the Rev. Frederick Charles Costeloe, formerly V. of Staveley, Carlisle; 2ndly, 1963, Grace Edman Cunningham, of Madison, Connecticut, USA, and has issue living (by 1st m.), Gordon Archdale, *b.* 1944,—Simon Jeffray, *b.* 1945,—David James, *b.* 1952.——Mary Jeffray, *b.* 1913; formerly Section Officer, WAAF: *m.* 1944, Dr. John Edgar Furness, formerly Wing-Cdr. RAF, who *d.* 1974, and has issue living, Diana Ruth, *b.* 1944: *m.* 1973, Ronald Gardiner. *Residence*, Estone, Steeple Aston, Oxon.—— Audrey Mervyn, *b.* 1914; formerly FO WAAF: *m.* 1946, Fl. Lt. William Herbert Allen, MBE, RAFVR, who *d.* 1972. *Residence*, Cobbs, Challock Lees, Ashford, Kent.

This family descends from Capt. Andrew Stewart who accompanied Lord Ochiltree from Scotland, and settled at Gortigal, co. Tyrone, about 1620. The 1st baronet, the Right Hon. Sir John, Attorney-General for Ireland in 1799, drafted the Act of Union, and was successively MP for cos. Down and Tyrone.

STEWART, Creation (U.K.) 1881, of South Kensington. [Extinct 1951.]

Sir DOUGLAS LAW STEWART, 3rd and last *Baronet*.

Daughter living of 3rd Baronet—Adeline Lilian, *b.* 1904 : *m.* 1st, 1928, Capt. Charles Arthur Lyulph Davis, Indian Army ; 2ndly, 1940, Edward J. H. Teviotdale ; 3rdly 1943, Edward John Calvert (P.O. Box 258, George Cape Province, S. Africa).

Widow living of 3rd Baronet—LILIAN DOROTHEA (*Lady Stewart*), da. of F. W. Quarry : *m.* 1903, Sir Douglas Law Stewart, 3rd baronet, who *d.* 1951, when the title became ext. *Address*, c/o National and Grindlays Bank, 13, St. James's Sq., SW1.

STEWART, Creation (U.K.) 1920, of Fingask, co. Perth.

Sir BRUCE FRASER STEWART, 2nd *Baronet; b.* Sept. 6th, 1904 ; *s.* his father, *Sir* JOHN HENDERSON, 1924 ; ed. at Eton, and at Pembroke Coll., Camb. ; formerly Flying Officer No. 4 (Army Co-operation) Squadron, New Zealand Territorial Air Force and a Commercial Pilot ; Past Chm. of Akaroa Co. Council, and a Past Pres. of Canterbury Aero Club : *m.* 1925, Constance, da. of William S. Gray, of 49, Grantchester Street, Cambridge, and has issue.
Residence—Strathmore, Pigeon Bay (Banks Peninsula), New Zealand.

Daughters living—Joy Elizabeth, *b.* 1932.——Heather Genieve, *b.* 1934.

STEWART, Creation (U.K.) 1920, of Balgownie, Bearsden, co. Dumbarton.

Sir JAMES WATSON STEWART, 4th *Baronet : b.* Nov. 8th, 1922 ; *s.* his father, *Sir* JAMES WATSON, 1955 ; ed. at Uppingham, and at Aberdeen Univ. ; European War 1941-45 with R.A. and Parachute Regt. : *m.* 1946, Anne Elizabeth, da. of Joseph Greer Glaister, of Carlisle.

Arms (as recorded at Lyon Office)—Or, a fesse checky azure and argent between a Roman Charioteer driving a chariot with two horses, and in base a demi-figure of St. Kentigern habited, bearing a crozier in his left hand, his right hand raised in benediction, all proper. *Crest*—A dexter hand couped at the wrist holding a sword erect in pale proper hilted and pommelled or.
Residence—Wellwood, Fairlie, Ayrshire.

Brother living—JOHN KEITH WATSON, *b.* Feb. 25th, 1929 : *m.* 1954, Mary Elizabeth, da. of John Francis Moxon, of Horton Hall, Leek, Staffordshire, and has issue living, John Simon Watson, *b.* 1955,—James Watson, *b.* 1960,—Caroline Felicity Watson, *b.* 1958. *Residences*, 22, St. Petersburgh Pl., W2; Stormy Hall, Burrin, co. Clare. *Clubs*, Buck's, Cavalry.
Aunt living (daughter of 1st baronet)—Evelyn Young Watson, *b.* 1899: *m.* 1923, Lt.-Col. James Smart Hardie, OBE, who *d.* 1974, and has issue living, Henry David Stewart, *OBE* (Pear Tree Cottage, Gore Lane, Alderley Edge, Cheshire, SK9 7SP), *b.* 1925; OBE (Civil) 1967: *m.* 1955, Shelagh, da. of J. H.

Smyth, of Cheltenham, Glos., and has issue living, James Henry Smyth *b.* 1957, Clare Elizabeth *b.* 1959, Hilary Jane *b.* 1962,—Marion Evelyn Stewart, *b.* 1928: *m.* 1951, the Rev. George Lewis Blackman, of The Rectory, 23, Monmouth St., Brookline, Mass., USA, and has issue living, Henry David Stewart *b.* 1953, Anthony George *b.* 1955, Hamish Flint *b.* 1957, Ian Arthur Floyd *b.* 1958. *Residence,* Balgownie, Blairmore, Argyllshire.

Widow living of 3rd Baronet—JANE STEUART STEWART, da. of the late James Morton Sim, of Bearsden, Dunbartonshire; resumed the surname of Stewart by deed poll 1967: *m.* 1st, 1921, Sir James Watson Stewart, 3rd baronet, who *d.* 1955; 2ndly, 1961 (m. diss. 1966), Neil Charteris Riddell. *Residence,* 28, St. Petersburgh Mews, W2.

Collateral Branch living.

Issue of the late Fl. Lt. Malcolm Gilbert Watson Stewart, DFC, yst. son of 1st baronet, *b.* 1898, *d.* 1971: *m.* 1923, Evelyn Maud (Ardiffery Croft, Hatton, Aberdeenshire), da. of the late John A Stewart, of Glasgow:—

John Allan (Fresnos, 11 Bis, San Angel Inn, Mexico DF, Mexico), *b.* 1928: *m.* 1959, Maria del Rufugio Vargas, of Mexico City, and has issue living, John Eric, *b.* 1960.——Edith Mary Hedley, *b.* 1924: *m.* 1948, Francis Lockhart McGall, of Bukit Mertajam Estate, Kulim, Malaysia, and has issue living, Peter Lockhart, *b.* 1949,—Charles Michael Lockhart, *b.* 1956,—Aline Mary, *b.* 1951,—Sarah Elizabeth, *b.* 1954,—Louise Evelyn, *b.* 1965.

Sir James Watson Stewart, 1st Bt. (a Chartered Accountant), was a Member of Glasgow Corporation 1904-20, and Lord Provost of Glasgow and Lord-Lieut. of Co. of City of Glasgow 1917-20.

STEWART, Creation (U.K.) 1937, of Stewartby, co. Bedford.

Sir RONALD COMPTON STEWART, 2nd *Baronet ; b.* Aug. 14th, 1903 ; *s.* his father, *Sir* (PERCY) MALCOLM, *O.B.E.,* 1951 ; ed. at Rugby, and at Jesus Coll., Camb. : *m.* 1936, Cynthia Alexandra, *O.B.E., J.P.,* da. of the late Harold Farmiloe.

Arms—Or, a fesse chequy azure and argent between a portcullis with its chains in chief and in base a lymphad sails furled, oars in action sable, flagged gules. **Crest**—A lymphad as in the arms.
Residence—Maulden Grange, Maulden, Bedfordshire.

Half-Brother living—MALCOLM, *b.* Dec. 20th, 1909 ; ed. at Harrow, and at Brasenose Coll., Oxford (B.A. 1932, M.A. 1937) : European War 1942-5 as Lieut. R.N.V.R.: *m.* 1935 (marriage dissolved 1957), Mary Stephanie, da. of Frederick Ramon de Bertodano, 8th Marquis del Moral (Spain). *Residence,* Hoy Lodge, Orkney.

Half-Sister living—Yvonne Elizabeth Diana, *b.* 1915 ; ed. at Somerville Coll., Oxford (B.A. 1937, M.A. 1950) : *m.* 1948, Thomas Doggett Savory, and has issue living, Thomas Stewart, *b.* 1949,—Malcolm Doggett, *b.* 1950. *Residence,* The Custom House, Cley next the Sea, Norfolk.

Sir (Percy) Malcolm Stewart, O.B.E., 1st Bt. (2nd son of the late Sir Halley Stewart), was High Sheriff of Bedfordshire 1941, and Pres. of Associated Portland Cement Manufacturers, Ltd., of London Brick Co., Ltd., and of other Cos.

STEWART, Creation (U.K.) 1960, of Strathgarry, co. Perth.

Sir DAVID BRODRIBB STEWART, 2nd *Baronet; b.* Dec. 20th, 1913 ; *s.* his father *Sir* KENNETH DUGALD, 1972 ; ed. at Marlborough, and at Manchester Coll. of Tech. (BSc); Man. Dir. Francis Price (Fabrics) Ltd.; late Bt.-Col. Duke of Lancaster's Own Yeo. (TA): *m.* 1963, Barbara Dykes, da. of the late Harry Dykes Lloyd, and widow of Donald Ian Stewart.

Arms—Quarterly, 1st and 4th ; or, a fess chequy azure and argent, *Stewart* ; 2nd and 3rd ; argent, a galley sable, sails furled, oars in action proper, flagged gules, *Lorne* ; the whole within a bordure per pale dexter vert, sinister argent, charged with three roses gules barbed and seeded vert. **Crest**—A unicorn's head couped argent armed and crined or. **Badge**—On escutcheon at centre of quarters.

Residence—Delamere, Alderley Edge, Cheshire.

Brother living—ROBIN ALASTAIR (Walter's Cottage, Little Baddow, Essex), *b.* Sept. 26th, 1925 ; ed. at Marlborough: *m.* 1953, Patricia Helen, BA, ARIBA, da. of the late John Alfred Merrett, and has issue living, John Kenneth Alexander, *b.* 1961,—Judith Patricia, *b.* 1954,—Lucy Janetta, *b.* 1956,—Catherine Helen, *b.* 1958.

Sisters living—Janetta Kenric, (Newton House, Alderley Edge, Cheshire), *b.* 1918; ed. at Lady Margaret Hall, Oxford (BA).——Leslie Mary, *b.* 1921; ed. at Malvern Girls' Coll.: *m.* 1942, John Berge, MRCVS, of 73, Hillcrest Drive, Bracon Bay, East London North, S. Africa, and has issue living, David Kenneth, *b.* 1964,—Jennifer, *b.* 1944; ed. at Aberdeen Univ. (BSc), and Berkeley Univ., Cal., USA (MSc),—Vere, *b.* 1946; ed. at Aberdeen Univ. (BA), and Sussex Univ.,—Elizabeth, *b.* 1948; ed. at Nottingham Univ. (BSc); MSc Nairobi: *m.* 1972, Peter Moore.

This family descends from the Rev. Duncan Stewart, 1st of Strathgarry, son of Donald, 4th son of Alan Stewart, 3rd of Appin. Sir Kenneth Dugald Stewart, 1st Bt., yst. son of Hinton Daniell Stewart, 6th of Strathgarry, was Chm. of Lancs. Cotton Assn. 1928-32, and of Trustee Savings Banks Assocn. 1946-63.

HENDERSON-STEWART, Creation (U.K.) 1957, of Callumshill, co. Perth.

Sir DAVID JAMES HENDERSON-STEWART OF CALLUMSHILL, 2nd *Baronet*; *b.* July 3rd, 1941; *s.* his father, *Sir* JAMES, *M.P.*, 1961; *ed.* at Eton, and at Trin. Coll., Oxford: *m.* 1972, Anne, da. of Count Serge de Pahlen, and has issue.

Residence—25, Pembroke Place, W8.   *Club*—Travellers'.

Son living DAVID, *b.* Feb. 2nd, 1973.
Sister living—Annabel, *b.* 1943: *m.* 1966, Andrew Alastair Borthwick, of 29, Chipstead St., SW6, and has issue living, Selena Margaret, *b.* 1967,—Emilie Anna, *b.* 1970.
Widow living of 1st Baronet—ANNA MARGARET, da. of Sir Bernard Eyre Greenwell, MBE, 2nd Bt.: *m.* 1st, 1940, Sir James Henderson-Stewart, MP, 1st baronet, who *d.* 1961; 2ndly, 1965, Geoffrey Walford Wilks, CBE, TD, of Walnut House, Ufford, Stamford, Lincs., and 64, Cadogan Sq., SW1.

Sir James Henderson-Stewart, M.P., 1st Bt. (son of the late Matthew Deas Stewart), sat as M.P. for E. Div. of Fife (*L.U.*) 1933-61, and was Joint Parliamentary Under-Sec. of State for Scotland 1952-57. He was officially recognised in the surname of Henderson-Stewart and the designation of Callumshill by warrant of Lord Lyon 1957.

MacTAGGART-STEWART, Creation (U.K.) 1892, of Southwick, Stewartry of Kirkcudbright, and Blairderry, Wigtownshire. [Extinct 1948.]

Sir EDWARD ORDE MacTAGGART-STEWART, 2nd and last *Baronet*.

Daughters living of 2nd Baronet—Jean Susanna Flora, *b.* 1918: *m.* 1940, Capt. Desmond Snowden, and has issue living, Peter Orde Maurice Frederic, *b.* 1947,—Wendy Ann Flora, *b.* 1941, —Dervorguilla Rosemary Margaret Jean, *b.* 1942. *Residence,* Rawdon Hall, Rawdon, Yorkshire.——Faith Agnes Dervorguilla, *b.* 1926: *m.* 1949, Henry John Brewis, MP [*see* Walker, Bt, *cr.* 1868, colls.]. *Residences*, Ardwell, Wigtownshire; Norton Grove, Malton, Yorkshire.

SHAW-STEWART, Creation (N.S.) 1667, of Greenock and Blackhall, Renfrewshire.

I hope for better things.

Sir (WALTER) GUY SHAW-STEWART, *M.C.*, 9th *Baronet*, son of the late Capt. Walter Richard Shaw-Stewart, M.B.E., 3rd son of 7th baronet; *b.* Aug. 10th, 1892; *s.* his uncle, *Sir* (MICHAEL) HUGH, *K.C.B.*, 1942; *ed.* at Eton; Major (retired) Coldstream Guards, and Col. (retired) 6th Batn. Argyll and Sutherland Highlanders, and Convener of Renfrewshire Co. Council; Lord Lieut. of Renfrewshire 1950-67; 1914-18 War (twice wounded, MC), 1939-45 War in France: *m.* 1st, 1915, Diana, who *d.* 1931, da. of J. George Bulteel; 2ndly, 1949, Elizabeth Sofia, who *d.* 1968, da. of J. George Bulteel (ante), and widow of Maj.-Gen. Alan Geoffrey Charles Dawnay, CBE, DSO [see V. Downe, colls.], and has issue by 1st m.

Arms—Quarterly: 1st and 4th, or, a fesse chequy azure, over all a lion rampant gules, *Stewart of Blackhall*; 2nd and 3rd, azure, three covered cups or *Shaw of Greenock*. **Crests**—1st, a lion's head erased gules, armed and langued azure, *Stewart of Blackhall*; 2nd, holding a club over his shoulder proper, a demi-savage wreathed about the head and middle with laurel vert, *Shaw of Greenock*. **Supporters**—*Dexter,* a lion rampant gules, armed and langued azure, gorged with a collar checky argent and azure; *sinister,* a savage, holding a club over his shoulder all proper, wreathed round the middle with laurel leaves vert.

Seat—Ardgowan, Inverkip, Renfrewshire. *Clubs*—Guards', White's.

Sons living—By 1st marriage—EUAN GUY, *b.* Oct. 11th, 1928; ed. at Eton: *m.* 1st, 1953, Mary Louise (who obtained a divorce 1956), da. of Lt.-Col. Geoffey Reginald Devereux Shaw [*see* Durrant, Bt.]; 2ndly, 1962, Victoria Anne, yr. da. of W. Fryer, of 8, Springfield Av., SW20, and has issue living, (by 1st marriage) Fiona Mary, *b.* 1954.——Houston Mark, *MC, b.* 1931; ed. at Eton; is Maj. Ayrshire Yeo.; late 2nd Lt. Royal Ulster Rifles; Korea 1950-51 (MC).

Collateral Branches living.

Issue of the late Rev. Charles Robert Shaw-Stewart, 2nd son of 7th baronet, *b.* 1856, *d.* 1932: *m.* 1890, Ida Fannie Caroline, who *d.* 1940, da. of H. W. Alfken:—

Una Mary, *b.* 1890: *m.* 1916, Walter Rupert Reynell, M.D., F.R.C.P., who *d.* 1948, having had issue, Peter Carew, *b.* 1917,—Antony Charles, *b.* 1930,—Joan Katharine, *b.* 1918,—Anne Lenore, *b.* 1923. *Residence,* 30, Springfield Rd., NW8.——Katharine (Teignworthy, Chagford, Devon), *b.* 1893: *m.* 1st, 1912, Robert Alexander [Hobhouse, Bt.]; who *d.* 1928; 2ndly, 1928, Edward Arthur Courthope, who *d.* 1963, and has issue living, (by 1st m.) Boyd (of Prospect House, Upton, Didcot, Berks), *b.* 1913: *m.* 1941, Frederica Emma, da. of F. M. Graham, of Yankalilla, S. Aust., and widow of R. A. Brown,—Mary (Jane Taylor's Cottage, Lavenham, Suffolk), *b.* 1914: *m.* 1935, Cdr. the Rev. Eric Hart Dyke, RN (ret.), who *d.* 1971 [*see* Dyke, Bt., colls.].

Granddaughter of the late Adm. Sir William Houston Stewart, G.C.B. (infra):—
Issue of the late Archibald William Houston Stewart, *b.* 1864; *d.* 1946: *m.* 1891, Flora Sarah Ann, who *d.* 1951, da. of Thomas Beeson, formerly of Stonewall, Manitoba, Canada:—
Catherine Grace, *b.* 1898.

Grandson of the late Michael Patrick Stewart (infra):—
Issue of the late George Archdale Stewart, *b.* 1893, *d.* 1959: *m.* 1921, Myrtle, who *d.* 1971 da. of John Wheeler, of Auckland, NZ:—
Lois Frances, *b.* 1925. *Residence,* 408, Courtville Flats, Parliament St., Auckland, C1, NZ.

Grandchildren of the late John Erskine Douglas Stewart, son of the late Adm. of the Fleet Sir Houston Stewart, G.C.B., 2nd son of 5th Baronet:—
Issue of the late Michael Patrick Stewart, *b.* 1860, *d.* 1921: *m.* 1886, Fanny Montgomery, who *d.* 1947, da. of the late George Vesey Stewart, M.B.E. [Stewart, Bt., cr. 1803, colls.]:—
Donald Erskine (Flat 1, 5, Whitby Terr., Mairangi Bay, Auckland 10, NZ), *b.* 1905: *m.* 1936, Ailsa Violet Annie, who *d.* 1970, and has issue living, Donald Michael (111, Paterson St., Invercargill, NZ), *b.* 1944: *m.* 19—, Jill Mary Smith, and has issue living, Bradley James *b.* 1970, Jonathan Paul *b.* 1973, Joanne Clare *b.* 1975.——Angela Julia Isabel, *b.* 1887: *m.* 1920, Ernest Conway Bennett, and has issue living, John Stewart, *b.* 1921,—Patrick Conway (of No. 1 R.D., Howick, Auckland, NZ), *b.* 1923: *m.* 1953, Betty June, da. of W. C. Shotbolt, of Auckland, NZ, and has issue living, Michael Conway *b.* 1954, Christine Michelle *b.* 1958, Joanne Alma *b.* 1965,— Ethne Isabel, *b.* 1925: *m.* 1946, Philip Arthur White, and has issue living, Warwick Ian *b.* 1948, Stewart Lindsay *b.* 1950, Graeme Conway *b.* 1952, Angela May *b.* 1954, Rosemary Anne *b.*1959. *Address,* No. 1, R. D. Howick, Auckland, New Zealand.——Muriel Frances, *b.* 1902: *m.* 1925, Cyril Lester, and has issue living, Brian Dudley, (of 43, Abercrombie St., Howick, Auckland, New Zealand), *b.* 1929: *m.* 1953, Heather Elizabeth, da. of Edgar McCall, of Auckland New Zealand, and has issue living, Brian Mark *b.* 1954, Gregory Stewart *b.* 1957,—Gary Stewart, *b.* 1935,—Diane, *b.* 1938: *m.* 1959, John Claxton, of 15, Swayfield Rd., Mt. Waverley, Melbourne, Australia, and has issue living, Jeffrey Stewart *b.* 1967, Karen Elizabeth *b.* 1964. *Residence,* 1, Kenny Rd., Remuera, SE2, Auckland, NZ.

Grandsons of the late Maj.-Gen. John Heron Maxwell Shaw-Stewart, son of the late John Shaw-Stewart, 3rd son of 5th baronet:—
Issue of the late Col. Basil Heron Shaw-Stewart, C.M.G., D.S.O., *b.* 1877, *d.* 1939: *m.* 1916, Vera (now of Traigh House, Arisaig, Inverness-shire), da. of W. H. Caldwell, of Morar, Inverness-shire:—
Michael (Bewliehill, Lilliesleaf, Melrose, Roxburghshire), *b.* 1925: *m.* 1951, Grizel Margaret Lightone da. of the late Maj. Alexander Caldwells Stewart, MC [*see* Lighton, Bt.], and has issue living, Archibald John, *b.* 1953,—Robert Hugh, *b.* 1960,—Helen Katharine, *b.* 1959.—— John William Archibald, *b.* 1929: *m.* 1955, Vora June Douglas, da. of Charles Whistler Mackintosh [*see* D. Hamilton and Brandon], and has issue living, David Hugh, *b.* 1956,— Patrick Douglas, *b.* 1958.—Alexander Malcolm, *b.* 1960,—Mairi Hermione Margaret, *b.* 1962. *Residence,* Linplum House, Haddington, East Lothian.

Granddaughter of the late George Steuart, son of Lt.-Gen. George Mackenzie Steuart, great-grandson of Walter Steuart, 3rd son of 1st baronet:—
Issue of the late Capt. James McAlpine Steuart, *b.* 1868, *d.* 1946: *m.* 1921, Mary (The Flat, Street Ashton House, Stretton under Foss, Rugby), da. of the late John Edward Compton-Bracebridge, of Atherstone Hall, Warwickshire:—
Mary Veronica, *b.* 1926: *m.* 1950, Donald Arthur Goldberg, of Street Ashton House, Stretton under Foss, Rugby.

The present baronet is in direct male descent from Sir John Stewart, natural son of Robert III, King of Scotland, to whom was granted the family seat of Ardgowan. Sir Michael Stewart, 3rd Bt., *m.* 1738, Helen, sister and co-heir of Sir John Houston of that Ilk, 4th Bt. Her mother, Margaret, was da. of Sir John Shaw, of Greenock, 2nd Bt. Sir John Shaw-Stewart, 4th Bt. in 1752, on the death of his great-uncle, Sir John Shaw of Greenock, 3rd and last Bt., inherited the entailed estate of Greenock and assumed the additional surname of Shaw.

Stewart-Clark, see Clark.

Stewart-Rankin, see Rankin.

Stewart-Richardson, see Richardson.

STIRLING, Creation (N.S.) 1666, of Glorat, Stirlingshire. [Dormant 1949.]

Sir GEORGE MURRAY HOME STIRLING OF GLORAT, *CBE, DSO,* 9th *Baronet, d.* in 1949, and at the time of going to press no name appears on the Official Roll of Baronets in respect of this title.

Daughters living of 9th Baronet—Elizabeth Gloriana, *b.* 1906.——Jean Margaret, *b.* 1908: *m.* 1939, Maj. Frederick Graham Sheppard Graham, Argyll and Sutherland Highlanders. *Residence*

Rednock House, Port of Menteith, Perths.——Marjorie Marigold Anne, *b.* 1920: *m.* 1943, Edward Alan Langley, Lt. RAMC, and has issue living, David Stirling, *b.* 1945,—George Arthur Stirling, *b.* 1948,—John Charles Mark, *b.* 1950. *Residence,* Glorat North Wing, Milton of Campsie, Stirlingshire.

Widow living of 9th Baronet—MABEL ELIZABETH, CBE (*Lady Stirling of Glorat*), da. of Col. Sir Alexander Sprot, CMG, 1st Bt. (ext.); is Hon. Life Member of Stirlingshire British Red Cross So. (formerly Pres.), and a JP; OBE (Civil) 1939, CBE (Civil) 1946: *m.* 1904, Col. Sir George Murray Home Stirling of Glorat, CBE, DSO, 9th Bt., who *d.* 1949. *Residence,* Glorat, Milton of Campsie, Stirlingshire.

Collateral Branches living.

Grandson of the late Charles Stirling (infra):—
Issue of the late Robert Wilson Stirling, *b.* 1890, *d.* 1970: *m.* 1920, Hazel (7814, Swails St. Acton, Indiana, 46259, USA), da. of John Heidenreich:—

John Charles (2225, Lawrence Av., Indianapolis, Indiana, 46227, USA), *b.* 1922; probable heir to Baronetcy: *m.* 1944, Evelyn Essig, and has issue living, John Charles (10838, Wonderland Drive, Indianapolis, Indiana, 46239, USA), *b.* 1948: *m.* 1966, Valborg-Nelson, and has issue living, Jeffery Dundas *b.* 1969, April Cheryl *b.* 1967,—Sherry Lynn (2405, Greentree, Indianapolis, Indiana 46227, USA), *b.* 1951.

Granddaughter of the late Robert Dundas Stirling, 8th son of 6th Bt.:—
Issue of the late Charles Stirling, *b.* 1866, *d.* 1925: *m.* 1888, Margaret, who *d.* 1944, da. of William Wilson :—

Amy Dorothy, *b.* 1894: *m.* 1917, Curtis Smith (Box 195, Morristown, Ind. 46161, USA), and has issue living, Robert Stirling, *b.* 1919: *m.* 1943, Esther Justus, and has issue living, Robert, *b.* 1950, Gretchen *b.* 1949,—Dorothy Louise, *b.* 1921: *m.* 1944, Kenneth Kimmel, of 1174, McKinley Av., Kenmore, 17, New York, USA, and has issue living, Kenneth Stirling *b.* 1953, Karen Ann *b.* 1945: *m.* 1965, Daniel Miller, of 331, Euclid Av., Kenmore, New York, USA 14217 (and has issue living, Andrew Michael *b.* 1967), Nancy Jane *b.* 1947: *m.* 1969, Lynn Hay, of 7128, Chiswell Rd., Poolesville, Maryland 20837, USA (and has issue living, Jeffrey Michael *b.* 1971), Mary Beth *b.* 1952.

Stirling-Hamilton, see Hamilton.

Stirling-Maxwell, see Maxwell.

STOCKDALE, Creation (U.K.) 1960, of Hoddington, co. Southampton.

Sir EDMUND VILLIERS MINSHULL STOCKDALE, 1st *Baronet,* son of Maj. Henry Minshull Stockdale, JP, of Mears Ashby Hall, Northampton ; *b.* April 16th, 1903 ; ed. at Wellington Coll.; entered Bank of England 1921; Assist. to Govs., Reserve Bank of India 1935, Assist. Prin., Bank of England 1937, Dep. Prin. 1941-45; a Member, Court of Common Council 1946, Alderman 1948-63, Commr. of Assize 1948-63, Sheriff 1953, and Lord Mayor 1959-60; a Church Commr. for England 1962; a Member of Advisory Board of Holloway Prison 1948 (Chm. 1951-53), of Cttee. of Holloway DPAS 1948-52, Vice-Pres. of The Griffins (formerly Holloway DPAS) 1965, a Gov. of Christ's, Roy. Bethlem, Maudsley and Bridewell Hosps. 1948-63, a Member of Emergency Bed Ser. Cttee. 1961-69, and of Winchester Diocesan Board of Finance 1963-71; a JP for City of London 1948-63, and for Inner London 1968, a Dir. of Embankment Trust, and other cos.; a Member of Court of Assists. Carpenters' Co. (Master 1970), and of Glaziers' Co. (Master 1972); author of " The Bank of England in 1934 "; one of HM Lieuts. of City of London, a KStJ, a Grand Officer of Legion of Honour, a Grand Official of Order of Mayo of Argentina, a Knight Com. of Order of Crown of Thailand, and a Com. of Order of North Star of Sweden; has Grand Cross of Order of Merit of Peru, and Order of Triple Power of Nepal, and Gold Medal, Madrid; Knt. 1955: *m.* 1937, the Hon. Louise Fermor-Hesketh, da. of 1st Baron Hesketh, and has issue.

Arms—Ermine on a bend sable between two escallops gules three pheons argent. **Crest**—Issuant from a crown vallary or a griffin's head gules.

Residence—Hoddington House, Upton Grey, Basingstoke. *Club*—Buck's.

Sons living—THOMAS MINSHULL (Conington Hall, Cambridge), *b.* Jan. 7th, 1940; ed. at Eton, and at Worcester Coll., Oxford (MA): *m.* 1965, Jacqueline, da. of Ha-Van-Vuong, of 293, Phan, Thanh-Gian, Saigon, and has issue living, John Minshull, *b.* 1967,—Charlotte Fermor, *b.* 1970. ——Frederick Minshull (Thorpe Tilney Hall, Lincoln), *b.* 1947; ed. at Eton, and Jesus Coll., Camb. (MA): *m.* 1970, Joanna Lennox, yr. da. of Capt. Roger Edward Harvey, JP DL, Scots Gds., of Parliament Piece, Ramsbury, Wilts. [*see* Mainwaring, Bt., ext.], and has issue living, Harry Tevis Minshull, *b.* 1973.—a son, *b.* 1975.

STOCKENSTROM, Creation (U.K.) 1840, of Maasström, Cape of Good Hope.
[Extinct 1957.]

Sir ANDERS JOHAN BOOYSEN STOCKENSTRÖM, 4th and last *Baronet.*

Daughter living of 4th Baronet—Andreé Mabel, *b.* 1939. *Residence,*

Daughters living of 3rd Baronet—Selma Andrée, *b.* 1899 : *m.* 1928, Neil Montagu Wienand.
——Erica Hedvig, *b.* 1901 : *m.* 1927, John Nelson Nayler. *Residence,*

Widows living of 3rd and 4th Baronets—MABEL (*Dowager Lady Stockenström*), da. of J. H.
Booysen, of Klip Drift, Graaff Reinet, S. Africa : *m.* 1896, Sir Andries Stockenström, 3rd Baronet,
who *d.* 1922. *Residence,* Maasström, Bedford, Cape Province, S. Africa.——ELAINE CONSTANCE
(*Lady Stockenström*), da. of Harold Burnett-Smith, of Johannesburg, S. Africa : *m.* 1937,
Sir Anders Johan Booysen Stockenström, 4th Bt., who *d.* 1957, when the title became ext.
Residence, Maasström Estate, Bedford, Cape Province, S. Africa.

STOKES, Creation (U.K.) 1889, of Lensfield Cottage, St. Paul, Cambridge.
[Extinct 1916.]

Sir ARTHUR ROMNEY STOKES, 2nd and last *Baronet.*

Daughter living of 2nd Baronet—Mary Muriel, *b.* 1899. *Address,* c/o Lloyds Bank, Fareham,
Hants.

STONHOUSE, First Creation (E.) 1628; Second Creation (E.) 1670, of Radley, Berkshire.

Sir PHILIP ALLAN STONHOUSE, 18th *Baronet*
(but his name does not, at time of going to press,
appear on the Official Roll of Baronets); *b.* Oct.
24th, 1916; *s.* his father, *Sir* ARTHUR ALLAN,
1967; ed. at W. Canada Coll., and Queen's
Univ., Kingston, Ontario: *m.* 1946, Winifred
Emily, el. da. of J. M. Shield, of Lethbridge,
Alberta, Canada, and has issue.

Arms—Argent, on a fesse sable between three hawks volant
azure, a leopard's face between two mullets or. **Crest**—A talbot's
head couped argent, collared sable, lined and catching a dove
volant of the first.

Address—521, 12 St. SW, Medicine Hat, Alberta, Canada.

SUBLIMIORA PETAMUS

Let us seek sublimer objects.

Sons living—MICHAEL PHILIP, *b.* Sept. 4th, 1948.——
Timothy Allan, *b.* 1950.

Sisters living—Geraldine, *b.* 1921: *m.* 1942, Flight Lieut.
Ross Patterson McLean, M.B.E., Roy. Canadian Air Force,
and has issue living, Dennis, *b.* 1943.——Bonnie (twin), *b.* 1943.
Residence, 5, Parkwood Drive, Galt, Ontario, Canada.——
Margaret, *b.* 1924: *m.* 1953, Lt.-Cdr. W. M. La Nauze, RCN (ret.), and has issue living, Patricia
Joan, *b.* 1954. *Residence,* 403, Frederick St., Midland, Ont., L4R 3P5, Canada.
Aunt living—Dorothy Mabel *b.* 1887: *m.* 1908, Samuel Robert Nightingale, who *d.* 1955, and has
issue living, Robert Alan, *b.* 1916, Sheila Valentia, *b.* 1909. *Residence,* The Grey House, Ormesby,
Norfolk.
Widow living of 17th Baronet—BEATRICE (*Beatrice, Lady Stonhouse*) (4642, 49th St., Red Deer,
Alberta, Canada), da. of the late Thomas Feron, of Santa Monica, Cal., USA: *m.* 1914, Sir Arthur
Allan Stonhouse, 17th Bt., who *d.* 1967.

Sir George, the 3rd baronet, was fined £1,460 for his loyalty to Charles I. In 1670 he obtained
a new patent granted to himself, with the old precedency and with a special remainder to his
second son, John, and his heirs male, intending thereby to exclude his first son. The elder son,
however, on his father's decease, claimed and enjoyed the baronetcy created by the original patent,
so that there were two baronetcies in the family till, on the death (without issue) of Sir John, 6th
baronet under the old creation, they became united in Sir John, 3rd baronet of the new. The 11th
baronet, having been for twenty years Physician to the Northampton Infirmary, took Holy Orders,
and subsequently became an eminent preacher.

STOTT, Creation (U.K.) 1920, of Stanton, co. Gloucester.

Sir PHILIP SIDNEY STOTT, *A.R.I.B.A.*, 3rd
Baronet; *b.* Dec. 23rd, 1914 ; *s.* his father, *Sir*
GEORGE EDWARD, 1957 ; ed. at Rossall, and at Trin.
Hall, Camb. ; is a Registered Architect, and an
Asso. of Roy. Institute British Architects, and of
Incorporated Asso. of Architects and Surveyors : *m.*
1947, Cicely Florence, widow of Vincent Charles
William Trowbridge, Pilot Officer Roy. Canadian
Air Force, and only da. of Bertram Ellingham, of
Ely House, Hertford, and has issue.

Arms—Gules, three pallets or, each charged with as many
pellets, on a chief of the second a heart between two battle-axes of
the first. **Crest**—Upon a chaplet of roses fessewise gules a martlet
sable.

Residence—144, West Osborne, North Vancouver, British
Columbia.

Alta peti

He aims at high things.

Sons living—ADRIAN GEORGE ELLINGHAM, *b.* Oct. 7th,
1948.——Vyvyan Philip, *b.* 1952.

Brothers living—Christopher George Swailes, *b.* 1924 ; ed. at
Malvern ; European War 1939-45 in R.A.F. Vol. Reserve : *m.*
1953, Winifred Marshall (MOSSFORD), da. of William Don, and
has issue living, Sarah Caroline, *b.* 1956. *Club,* Royal Aero.——Derek Nicholson (Box 1042,
LGPO, Hobart Tasmania 7001), *b.* 1928; ed. at Malvern; is an AMIEE.

Aunt living (daughter of 1st baronet)—Doris, *b.* 1890 : *m.* 1918, Major Valentine Stevens Bland, M.C., late R.F.A., who *d.* 1957, and has issue living, Henry Valentine, *D.F.C.*, *b.* 1923 ; sometime Flight-Lieut. R.A.F.,—John Valentine, *b.* 1920,—Pamela. *b.* 1920 : sometime Junior Com. ATS : *m.* 1947, T. O. C. Howell, of Foxbury, Shalbourne, Marlborough. *Residence*, The Warren, Aldbourne, Wilts.

Widow living of 1st Baronet—MARY (MAY) BRIDGES (*Dowager Lady Stott*), (Milton Court Hotel, 68-74, Cromwell Rd., SW7), el. da. of the late John Bridges Lee (MA, Camb.), Bar.-at-law, and Advocate of High Courts of Calcutta, Allahabad, and Lahore; is a Member of Roy. Miniature So., of So. of Women Artists, and of So. of Miniaturists and under the painting name of "May B. Lee", a frequent Exhibitor at Roy. Acad. and Salon: *m.* 1936, as his second wife, Sir Philip Sidney Stott, 1st baronet, who *d.* 1937.

The 1st baronet, Sir Philip Sidney Stott (son of the late Abraham Henthorne Stott, of Oldham), was a J.P. for Gloucestershire, and High Sheriff of Gloucestershire 1925. The 2nd baronet, Sir George Edward Stott, was a registered Architect, and High Sheriff of Gloucestershire 1947.

PHILIPSON-STOW, Creation (U.K.) 1907, of Cape Town, Colony of Cape of Good Hope, and Blackdown House, Lodsworth, co. Sussex.

Sir FREDERIC LAWRENCE PHILIPSON-STOW, 3rd *Baronet ; b.* Sept. 19th, 1905 ; *s.* his father, *Sir* ELLIOT PHILIPSON, 1954 ; *ed.* at Eton : *m.* 1st, 1932, Daphne Morriss (who *d.* 1960, having obtained a divorce 1951), da. of the late W. G. Daffarn ; 2ndly, 1951, Cynthia Yvette (GOVETT), da. of the late William Robertson Jecks, of Johannesburg, S. Africa [The 3rd Baronet *d.* Jan. 9th, 1976.]

Arms—Quarterly, 1st and 4th vert, on a cross nebulée between four leopards' faces or, a rose gules, *Stow*; 2nd and 3rd gules, two chevronelles between three boars' heads couped ermine, *Philipson*. **Crest**—1st, issuant from an antique crown or, charged with a rose gules, a leopard's face gold between two wings vert, *Stow* ; 2nd, issuant from a mural crown or, charged with a rose gules, a plume of five ostrich feathers alternately argent and gules, *Philipson*.

Residences—Na Xencha, Villa Carlos, Menorca, Spain; Apart. 211, Mahon, Minorca, Spain.

Fide non fraude.
By faith, not by fraud.

Brother living—EDMOND CECIL, *M.B.E.*, *b.* Aug. 25th, 1912; formerly Major Duke of Cornwall's L.I.; **Burma** 1943-45 (M.B.E.) ; M.B.E. (Mil.) 1946. *Residence*, Cloonaghmore, Crossmolina, co. Mayo.

Sisters living—Dorothy Barbara, *OBE*, OBE (Civil) 1972, *b.* 1909: *m.* 1936, Lt.-Col. John Bampfylde Peter-Hoblyn, late DCLI, and has issue living, Jeremy Deeble (Lamellin, St. Tudy, Bodmin, Cornwall; Guards' Club), *b.* 1939; ed. at Sherborne, and at Camb. (MA); Capt. Coldm. Gds.: *m.* 1964, Felicity Daphne Moyle, da. of Maj. Edward Walter Moyle Magor, CMG, OBE, and has issue living, Edward Deeble *b.* 1972, Harriett, *b.* 1968,—George Henry (Manton Stables, Marlborough, Wilts.; Cavalry Club), *b.* 1943; ed. at Sherborne; Lt. 11th Hussars: *m.* 1967, Mrs. Susanna Diana Georgina Coleridge, da. of the late Nigel Horatio Trevor FitzRoy [see D. Grafton, colls.], and has issue living, John Fitzroy *b.* 1968, Emma Frances *b.* 1970,—Elisabeth Ann, *b.* 1950: *m.* 1968, Richard Coulter Hancock, of Helligan Bartin, Bodmin, Cornwall and has issue living, Mary Felicity *b.* 1971. *Residence*, Colquite, Washaway, Bodmin, Cornwall.——Margaret Aileen (twin), *b.* 1912.

Uncle living (son of 1st baronet)—Guyon Philipson, *b.* 1898; ed. at Winchester, and at Trin. Coll., Camb. 1914-18 War as Lt. R.A., 1939-45 War as Major on Staff (American Bronze star): *m.* 1925, Alice Mary, da. of R. Hilton Fagge, of Melton Mowbray, and has issue living, Robert Nicholas (23, Drayton Gdns., SW10; White's and Cavalry Clubs), *b.* 1937; ed. at Winchester; late 2nd Lt. RHG: *m.* 1963, Nicolette Leila, el. da. of the Hon. Philip Leyland Kindersley [see B. Kindersley], and has issue living, Robert Rowland *b.* 1970, Edward Miles *b.* 1972,—Helen Rosemary, *b.* 1934. *Residence*, Prior's Court, Pendock, Tewkesbury.

Collateral Branch living.

Issue of the late Henry Matthew Philipson Philipson-Stow, 3rd son of 1st baronet, *b.* 1880, *d.* 1953: *m.* 1918, Elizabeth Willes (of The Old Vicarage, Farnham, Surrey), da. of Sir Thomas Willes Chitty, 1st Bt.:—

Christopher, *DFC*, *b.* 1920; ed. at Winchester; late Fl. Lt. RAFVR: *m.* 1952, Elizabeth Nairn, da. of the late James Dixon Trees, of Toronto, and widow of Maj. F. G. McLaren, 48th Highlanders of Canada, and has issue living, Robert Matthew, *b.* 1953,—Rowland Frederic, *b.* 1954. *Residence*, 32, John St., Thornhill, Ontario, Canada.

Sir Frederick Samuel Philipson Stow, 1st baronet, assumed by Roy. licence 1891, the additional surname and arms of Philipson, being 4th in descent from George Stow of Sutton in Ashfield, Notts., who *m.* 1767, Elizabeth, da. and eventual heir of John Wilberfoss, by Elizabeth, el. da. and eventual heir of Richard Philipson, of Beverley.

STRACEY, Creation (U.K.) 1818, of Rackheath, Norfolk.

Sir JOHN SIMON STRACEY, 9th Baronet, only son of the late Capt. Algernon Augustus Henry Stracey, 2nd son of 6th Bt.; *b.* Nov. 30th, 1938; *s.* his cousin, *Sir* MICHAEL GEORGE MOTLEY, 1971: *m.* 1968, Martha Maria, da. of the late Johann Egger, of Innsbrück, and has issue.

Arms—Ermine, on a cross engrailed between four eagles displayed gules five cinquefoils or. **Crest**—A lion rampant erminois, ducally crowned gules supporting a cross patée-fitchée of the last.
Residence—652, Belmont Av., Montreal 217, P.Q., Canada.

Daughters living—Daniela, *b.* 1968.——one, *b.* 1973.
Sister living—Ramona Beryl, *b.* 1930: *m.* 1959, Theodore Frederick, Darvas, of 1, Rothwell St., NW1, and has issue living, Jane Caroline, *b.* 1963,—Anna Judith, *b.* 1966.
Sister living of 8th Baronet—Margaret Rosalind Linley, *b.* 1907: *m.* 1959, Peter Edward Clement Harris, son of the late Sir Austin Edward Harris, KBE. *Residences*, Flat 41, Kingston House North, Princes' Gate, SW7 1LW; Martins, Walberswick, Southwold, Suffolk.

Half-Sister living of 8th Baronet—Dereen Elizabeth Paulette, *b.* 1937: *m.* 1965, James Douglas Barlett, of Great Swifts, Cranbrook, Kent, and has issue living, Christopher James Edward Douglas, *b.* 1966,—Peter Sean Charles, *b.* 1969,—Richard Gerald Patrick, *b.* 1971.

Collateral Branches living.

Grandchildren of the late Gilbert Hardinge Stracey, 5th son of 5th baronet :—
Issue of the late Lt.-Col. Ernest Henry Denne Stracey, *b.* 1871, *d.* 1948: *m.* 1907, Faith Dorothy Beatrice Mounteney, who *d.* 1965, da. of the late Henry Downes Popham:—
HENRY MOUNTENEY, *b.* April 24th, 1920: *m.* 1st, 1943, Susanna, da. of Adair Tracey; 2ndly, 1950, Lysbeth, da. of Charles Ashford; 3rdly, 1961, Jeltje, yst. da. of Scholte de Boer, of Oppenhuizen, Friesland, Holland, and has issue living, (by 1st marriage) Amarilla, *b.* 1943,—(by 2nd marriage), Rupert, *b.* 1951,—Miranda Hinemoa, *b.* 1955. *Residence,* Netherton Cottage, Buckland Monachorum, Devon.——Noel Margaret Jephson (Fairdown, Vernham Dean, nr. Andover, Hants.), *b.* 1908: *m.* 1933, Maj. Charles Robert Purdon Coote, who *d.* 1954 [*see* Coote, Bt., *cr.* 1621, colls.].——Joan Cypria Mounteney, *b.* 1910. *Residence,*

Granddaughters of the late Hardinge Robert Stracey, 3rd son of 4th baronet :—
Issue of the late Lieut.-Col. Hardinge Richard Stracey, *b.* 1840, *d.* 1924: *m.* 1883, Mary Henrietta Rennel, who *d.* 1944, da of the late Adm. Frederick Byng Montresor :—
Constance Mary, *b.* 18—.——Elizabeth Julia, *b.* 18— : *m.* 1909, Charles Henry Garner Richardson, and has issue living, Richard Hearle, *b.* 1914,—Peter Tremayne, *b.* 1916,—Elizabeth Barbara, *b.* 1911,—José Antonia Doreen, *b.* 1921.——Ruth : *m.* 1930, J. Wilfred Wickes, consulting engineer, of Durban, Natal, and has issue living, a da., *b.* 1931.——Margaret Diana, *b.* 1896.

Grandchildren of the late Rev. William James STRACEY-CLITHEROW (who assumed by Roy. licence 1900, the additional surname and arms of Clitherow), son of the late John Stacey, 5th son of 1st baronet :—
Issue of the late Lieut.-Com. Eustace William Clitherow STRACEY-CLITHEROW, *b.* 1864, *d.* 1930: *m.* 1900, Frances Evelyn Veronica, who *d.* 1962, da. of the late John Birkbeck Evelyn Stansfeld, sometime Capt. 3rd Batn. Duke of Wellington's (W. Riding Regt.):—
Christopher Bryan, *D.S.C.*, *b.* 1903 ; Com. (retired) R.N. ; European War 1939-45 (despatches, D.S.C.): *m.* 1928, Maida Daughne Laurel, da. of the late Capt. the Hon. Francis Almeric Butler [*see* E. Lanesborough, colls.], and has issue living, Dominic Peter, *b.* 1939; ed. at Harrow and Caius Coll., Camb. (MA); Lt. Cdr. RN (ret.): *m.* 1971, Penelope Bronwen, da. of L. Griffiths, of Henley in Arden, and has issue living, Charlotte *b.* 1972, Virginia (twin) *b.* 1972. *Residence,* Calcot Mount, Curdbridge, Botley, Hants.——Rhona (34, Fairfield Rd., Winchester, Hants), *b.* 1901.——Monica (15, Dobson Cres., Otematata, N. Otago, South Island, NZ), *b.* 1905: *m.* 1938, Hugh Morton Eden [*see* Eden, Bt., colls.].——Mary Barbara (15, Dobson Cres., Otematata, N. Otago, South Island, NZ), *b.* 1909: *m.* 1938, Francis Stanton Blake, who *d.* 1947.——Ursula Diana (of Little Kilkenny, Broadway, Worcs.), *b.* 1911.

Sir Edward Stracey, 1st baronet, was the eldest surviving son of Sir John Stracey, Knt., Chief Judge of the Sheriffs' Court, and Recorder of London in 1746. The 5th baronet sat as M.P. for Norfolk, East (C) 1855-7, for Yarmouth 1859-65, and for Norwich 1868-9. Sir Edward Paulet Stracey, 7th baronet, was appointed High Sheriff of Norfolk 1928.

STRACHEY, Creation (U.K.) 1801, of Sutton Court, Somerset.

(*Sir*) CHARLES STRACHEY, 6th *Baronet*, son of the late Rt. Hon. Evelyn John St. Loe Strachey, MP; *b.* June 20th, 1934; *s.* his 1st cousin once removed EDWARD [2nd Baron Strachie], 1973 (but does not use title); ed. at Westminster Sch., and Magdalen Coll., Oxford: *m.* 1973, Janet Megan, da. of Alexander Miller, of Earls Barton, Northants.

Arms,—Quarterly: 1st and 4th argent, a cross between four eagles displayed gules, *Strachey;* 2nd and 3rd or, three crescents, two and one, sable; on a canton of the last a ducal crown, or, *Hodges.* *Crest,*—An eagle displayed gules, charged on the breast with a cross-crosslet fitchée argent.

Address—c/o National Westminster Bank, Warley, Brentwood, Essex.

Sister living—Elizabeth, *b.* 1936: *m.* 1958, Hamid al Qadhi, and has issue living, Mohammed Jemil, *b.* 1959,—Samia, *b.* 1964.

Mother living—Celia (Cobb Cottage, Salcot, Malden, Essex), da. of the late Rev. Arthur Hum Simpson, of Rogate, Sussex: *m.* 1933, as his 2nd wife, the Rt. Hon. Evelyn John St. Loe Strachey, MP (ante), who *d.* 1963.

Aunt living—Mary Amabel Nassau (*Lady Williams-Ellis*), *b.* 1894: *m.* 1915, Sir Bertram Clough Williams-Ellis, CBE, MC, JP, and has issue living, Susan Caroline: *m.* 1945, Capt. Euan Stewart Cooper-Willis, of Cefn Cyffin, Llanfrothen, Merioneth, and has issue living, Robin Llewelyn *b.* 1958, Caroline Anwyl *b.* 1946, Harriet Shan *b.* 1947, Angharad *b.* 1957,—Charlotte Anwyl: *m.* 1945, Lindsay Russell Wallace, of Ruakura Agricultural Research Centre, Hamilton, NZ, and has issue living, Julian Clough *b.* 1947, Martin Lindsay *b.* 1950, Jessica Verna (twin) *b.* 1947, Catherine Ceinwen *b.* 1952, Rachel Carys (twin) *b.* 1952. *Residence,*—Plas Brondauw, Llanfrothen, Merioneth.

Collateral Branches living

Grandchildren of the late Lt.-Gen. Sir Richard Strachey, GCSI, FRS, LLD, 3rd son of Edward Strachey (infra):—
Issue of the late Ralph Strachey, *b.* 1868, *d.* 1923: *m.* 1901, Margaret Winifred, who *d.* 1972, da. of the late Albert Severs:—
RICHARD PHILIP FARQUHAR, *b.* Aug. 10th, 1902; Novelist: *m.* 1st, 1927, Frances Esme Rudd, who obtained a divorce 1940; 2ndly, 1943, Mrs. Simonette Mary Reynolds (WOODS), da. of Charles Foster Atchison, of Cliff Cottage, Bonchurch, Isle of Wight, and has issue living (by 1st m.), Philippa, *b.* 1927,—Victoria, *b.* 1929.——John Ralph Severs, *b.* 1905: *m.* 1st, 1933, Isobel Bertha (who obtained a divorce 1942), da. of Ronald Leslie; 2ndly, 1944, Rosemary, da. of Douglas Mavor, and has issue living (by 1st m.), Charlotte Augusta, *b.* 1935: *m.* 1st, 1955 (m. diss. 1960), Anthony Blond; 2ndly, 1960, Peter Jenkins, of 1 Crescent Grove, SW4, and has issue living (by 2nd m.) Amy *b.* 1963,—(by 2nd m.) Henry Leofric Benvenuto, *b.* 1947.——Ursula Margaret, *b.* 1911: *m.* 1939, Cyril Charles Wentzel, Bar.-at-law, of 36, Compton Rd., SW19.

Issue of the late Oliver Strachey, CBE, *b.* 1874; *d.* 1960: *m.* 1st, 1901, Ruby Julia (from whom he obtained a divorce 1908), da. of the late Julius Mayer; 2ndly, 1911, Rachel Conn, who *d.* 1940, da. of the late Benjamin Francis Costelloe:—
(By 1st m.) Julia Frances (17, Percy St., W1), *b.* 1901: *m.* 1st, 1927, the Hon. Stephen Tomlin, who *d.* 1937 [see By. Tomlin]; 2ndly, 1952 (m. diss. 1967), Lawrence Burnett Gowing, CBE.——Barbara, *b.* 1912: *m.* 1st, 1934, Olav Hultin, from whom she obtained a divorce 1937; 2ndly, 1937, Wolf Halpern, Leading Aircraftman, RAFVR, who *d.* (on active ser. during 1939-45 War) 1943, and has issue living (by 1st m.), Roger Olavson, *b.* 1934. *Residence,*—9, Bedford Gdns., W8.

Grandson of the late George Strachey, son of the late Edward Strachey, 2nd son of 1st baronet:—
Issue of the late William Strachey, *b.* 1867, *d.* 1911: *m.* 1901, Nina Alma Grosvenor, who *d.* 19—:—
Reginald, *b.* 1905. *Residence,*—

Grandchildren of the late Richard Charles Strachey, son of the late Richard Strachey, 3rd son of 1st baronet:—
Issue of the late Claude Mainwaring Strachey, *b.* 1861, *d.* 19—: *m.* 1887, Emily Chisholm Mackintosh, who *d.* 1922, da. of the late James Macpherson, of Ninde, Inverness-shire:—
Aileen Marion, *b.* 1889: *m.* 1920, Edwyn Grenville Temple, and has issue living, Edwyn Peter Strachey, *b.* 1921,—Roger Grenville, *b.* 1924,—Joscelyn, *b.* 19—. *Residence,*—Geraldine, NZ.
Issue of the late Reginald Clive Strachey, *b.* 1866, *d.* 1903: *m.* 1893, Ann Ellen, who *d.* 1951, da. of Henry William Gibson, formerly BCS:—
Richard Clive, *MC* (18, Greenhill Way, Farnham, Surrey, GU9 8SY), *b.* 1897; ed. at Repton, and at RMC; Maj. SLI (Prince Albert's); 1915-19 War (despatches, MC): *m.* 1st, 1928, Olive Zoë, da. of Hugh Carleton Formby, of Manor House, Shipton Bellinger, Andover; 2ndly, 1951, (Florence) Irene, da. of the late P. W. Rogers, of Burma, and has issue living, (by 1st m.) Anne Julia, *b.* 1930: *m.* 1953, John Branfoot Simpson Pedler, of 7, Lansdowne Walk, W11, and has issue living, Dominic Julian Simpson *b.* 1959,—Francesca Julia Teresa *b* 1954.——Carlotta Marion, *b.* 1895: *m.* 1952, Rev. James Reginald Stevens, who *d.* 1971. *Residence,*—63, Saltdean Drive, Saltdean, Brighton, BN2 8SD.——Dorothea Helen, *b.* 1903: *m.* 1930, Maj. Charles Douglas St. Leger, MC, FRIBA. *Address,*—PO Box 2026, Cape Town, S. Africa.

The Strachie family was settled at Saffron Walden, Essex, until the 16th century. John Strachey, *b.* 1634, inherited Sutton Court, Som., from his mother Elizabeth Cross: *m.* 1662, Jane, da. and co-heir of George Hodges, of Wedmore, Somerset. Their great-grandson, Sir Henry Strachey, of Sutton Court, MP 1770-1810, was Sec. to Lord Clive 1764, and of Commn. for Restoring Peace to America 1774, an Under-Sec. of State 1782, and Master of the Household 1794. He was *cr.* a *Baronet* 1801. His great-grandson, Sir Edward, PC, 4th Bt., Treasurer of the Household 1905-10, Paymaster-Gen. 1912-15, and MP for S. Som. (L) 1892-1911, was *cr. Baron Strachie,* of Sutton Court, Somerset, 1911. This Barony became ext. on the death of his son Edward, 2nd Baron and 5th Bt. in 1973, when the baronetcy reverted to Sir Charles, 6th Bt., grandson of John St. Loe Strachey, yr. brother of 1st Baron.

Strickland-Constable, see Constable.

STRONGE, Creation (U.K.) 1803, of Tynan, co. Armagh.

A way is to be attempted.

Rt. Hon. Sir (CHARLES) NORMAN LOCKHART STRONGE, *M.C.,* 8th *Baronet; b.* July 23rd, 1894; *s.* his father, *Sir* CHARLES EDMOND SINCLAIR, 1939; ed. at Eton; formerly Capt. Roy. Inniskilling Fusiliers; Hon. Col. 5th Bn., Roy. Irish Fusiliers (T.A.) 1950-63; a J.P. for cos. Londonderry and Armagh, and Lieut. for co. Armagh ; Assist. Parliamentary Sec. to Min. of Finance, N. Ireland 1941; Pres. of British Legion, N. Ireland Area, and of Roy. Overseas League, N. Ireland Area, and Chm. of N. Ireland Scout Council; Parliamentary Sec. and Ch. Whip of Unionist Party in Parliament of N. Ireland 1942-44, and Chm. of Armagh Co. Council 1944-55; 1914-18 War (despatches twice, M.C., Croix de Guerre, 1914-15 star), 1939-45 War with N. Irish Horse; a KStJ; has Order of Leopold of Belgium; a Member of House of Commons, N. Ireland (U) 1938-69 (Speaker 1945-69); PC (N. Ireland) 1946: *m.* 1921, Gladys Olive, *OBE* (Chm. of WRVS in N. Ireland, and an OStJ), da. of Maj. Henry Thomas Hall, formerly 18th Hussars, and has issue.

Arms—Argent, a chevron wavy sable between three lozenges azure, in the centre chief point an estoile gules. **Crests**—1st, an eagle with two heads displayed sable, beaked and legged azure, langued gules ; 2ndly, a cluster of wine grapes proper. Second Motto—Dulce quod utile (*That is sweet which is useful*).

Residence—Tynan Abbey, Tynan, co. Armagh.

Son living—JAMES MATTHEW, *b.* June 21st, 1932 ; ed. at Eton, and at Ch. Ch., Oxford (MA); Capt. Gren. Gds. (RARO): MP Mid-Armagh (*U*), NI Parl. 1969-73, (Parl. suspended March 1972), since when MP for NI Assembly (Armagh).

Daughters living—Daphne Marian, *b.* 1922 ; late W.R.N.S. : *m.* 1954, Thomas John Anthony Kingan, late Irish Guards, and has issue living, James Anthony John, *b.* 1957. *Residence,* Glenganagh, Bangor, co. Down.——Evelyn Elizabeth, *b.* 1925 ; late W.R.N.S.: *m.* 1960, Brig. Charles Harold Arthur Olivier, CBE. *Residence,* Rosemary Cottage, Amport, Andover.
Daughter living of 5th Baronet—Jessy, *b.* 1896.

Collateral Branch living.

Grandchildren of the late Edward Owen Fortescue Stronge, yst. son of the late Capt. Edmond Robert Francis Stronge, 4th son of 2nd baronet:—
Issue of the late Maxwell Du Pré James Stronge, *b.* 1904, *d.* 1973: *m.* 1945, Eileen, (Rahenduff House, Foulksmills, co. Wexford), da. of the late Rt. Hon. Maurice Marcus McCausland, of Drenagh, co. Londonderry:—
James Anselan Maxwell, *b.* 1946.——Helen Mary, *b.* 1948: *m.* 1971, Philip Rodney Allen-Morgan, of 46, Spencer Rise, NW5, and has issue living, Allanah Mary, *b.* 1974.

Sir James Matthew, D.C.L., 2nd baronet, was a Gentleman of the Privy Chamber, and Sir James Matthew, 3rd baronet, sat as M.P. for Armagh (C) 1864-74. The 7th Baronet, Sir Charles Edmond Sinclair, was H.M. Lieut. for co. Londonderry.

STUART, Creation (E.) 1660, of Hartley Mauduit, Hampshire.

Sir PHILLIP LUTTRELL STUART, 9th *Baronet* (but his name does not, at time of going to press, appear on the Official Roll of Baronets), son of the late Luttrell Hamilton Stuart, brother of 8th baronet ; *b.* Sept. 7th, 1937 ; *s.* his uncle, *Sir* HOULTON JOHN, 1959; late F/O RCAF: *m.* 1st, 1962 (m. diss. 1968), Marlene Rose, da. of Otto Muth, of 1172, Pembina Highway, Winnipeg, Manitoba, Canada; 2ndly, 1969, Beverley Claire Pieri, and has issue by 1st and 2nd m.

Arms—Or, a fesse checky azure and argent, an inescutcheon **argent** charged with the lion of Scotland debruised with a bendlet raguly or. **Crest** —A roebuck statant argent, ducally gorged gules.

Residence—1401, Mars Drive, Winnipeg, 19, Manitoba, Canada.

Avito viret honore.
He flourishes by ancestral honors.

Daughters living—By 1st m.—Cynthia Louise, *b.* 1963.——(by 2nd m.).— Brenda Claire, *b.* 19—.

Aunt living—Gwendoline Evelyn Macpherson, *b.* 1882 : *m.* 1907, William Frederick Carter, and has issue living, Madeline, *b.* 1909 : *m.* 1934, Nicholas Zaro, of Detroit, Michigan, U.S.A.,—Gwendoline Mabel, *b.* 1911. *Residence*,

Collateral Branches living.

Grandchildren of the late Major Arthur John Stuart, R.M., 3rd son of 5th baronet :—
Issue of the late Arthur Kennedy Stuart, *b.* 1859, *d.* 19— : *m.* 1892, Luise Franziska, da. of Carl Joseph Pfeifer, of Freiburg-in-Baden, Germany :—
ARTHUR ERNEST, *b.* 1896.——Charles Edwin, *b.* 1897. *Residence*,

Issue of the late Frederick William Stuart, youngest son of 5th baronet, *b.* 1858, *d.* 1949: *m.* 1st, 1888, Mildred Florence, da. of William Grover Ashby, formerly of The Highlands, Burgess Hill, Sussex ; 2ndly, 1931, Madeline May, who *d.* 1939, el. da. of the late P. J. Trouncer, of Preston, Sussex :—
(By 1st marriage) Lesley Mildred, *b.* 1892 : *m.* 1st, 1920, Lieut.-Com. Basil Ashby Taylor, R.N.; 2ndly, 1938, Major Austin Gardner, M.C., Essex Regt. (retired). *Residence*, Chapel Lands, North Chailey, near Lewes, Sussex.

The 1st baronet, Sir Nicholas Stuart (son of Simeon Stuart, of Hartley Mauduit), and the 2nd baronet, Sir Simeon, each held the office of a Chamberlain of the Exchequer. The 2nd and 3rd baronets successively sat as M.P. for Hampshire. In 1829, on the death of his grandfather, the last Earl of Carhampton, the 5th baronet was offered a fresh patent by George IV., which, however, he did not accept. The 7th Baronet, Sir Simeon Henry Lechmere, was City Marshal of London 1893-9. The present baronet is representative of the Earldom of Carhampton (*ext.*), and the Barony of Waltham (*ext.*).

Stuart-Menteth, see Menteth.

STUCLEY, Creation (U.K.) 1859, of Affeton Castle, Devonshire.
[Name pronounced "Stukeley."]

STUCLEY, 5th *Baronet ; b.* Oct. 29th, 1907; *s.* his father *Sir* HUGH NICHOLAS GRANVILLE, 1956; ed. at Harrow ; sometime Lieut. Grenadier Guards ; is a J.P., D.L., and Co. Alderman for Devon, and Major Roy. Devon Yeo. R.A. (T.A.) : *m.* 1932, the Hon. Sheila Margaret Warwick Bampfylde, da. of 4th Baron Poltimore, and has issue.

Arms—Quarterly : 1st and 4th, azure, three pears or, *Stucley ;* 2nd and 3rd, per fesse embattled argent and sable, three bucks attires, each fixed to the scalp, countercharged, *Buck.* **Crest**—Between a buck's attires as in the arms sable, a lion rampant or, the sinister paw holding a battle-axe resting on the shoulder proper.

Residences—Hartland Abbey, N. Devon ; Court House. North Molton, N. Devon.

Son living—HUGH GEORGE COPLESTON BAMP-FYLDE (Affeton Castle, Worlington, Crediton, Devon), *b.* Jan. 8th, 1945; Lt. RHG: *m.* 1969, Angela Caroline, el. da. of Richard Toller, of Laurel Cottage, Theale, Berks., and has issue living, George Dennis Bampfylde, *b.* 1970,—Peter Richard Toller, *b.* 1972,—a da., *b.* 1972.

Daughters living—Margaret Cynthia, *b.* 1934 : *m.* 1953, Gerald Arthur Hohler [V. Gort], and has issue living, Thomas Edward, *b.* 1958.—Henrietta Margaret Cynthia, *b.* 1955,—Lucinda Jane Astell, *b.* 1960. *Residence*, Trent Manor, Sherborne, Dorset.——Rosemary Anne (*Viscountess Boyne*), *b.* 1936 : *m.* 1956, the 10th Viscount Boyne. *Residence*, Burwarton, Bridgnorth, Salop.——Christine Elizabeth (*Hon. Mrs. David A. F. Lytton Cobbold*), *b.* 1940 : *m.* 1961, the Hon. David Antony Fromanteel Lytton Cobbold, el. son of 1st Baron Cobbold. *Residence*, Knebworth House, Knebworth, Herts.——Sarah Susan, *b.* 1942: *m.* 1st, 1963 (m. diss. 1970), Michael Henry Basil Peto, el. son of Col. Sir Christopher Henry Maxwell Peto, DSO, 3rd Bt.; 2ndly, 1971, Charles Worthington, of Kingston Russell House, Long Bredy, Dorset.

Brothers living—His Honour Judge John Humphrey Albert, DSC, *b.* 1916; Lt.-Cdr. RN (ret.); Bar. Middle Temple 1955; Dep. Chm. SE Agric. Lands Tribunal 1971; Recorder of Crown Court 1972-74, since when a Circuit Judge: *m.* 1941, Natalia, da. of Don Alberto Jiménez, CBE, of Madrid, Spain, and 2, Wellington Pl., St. Giles, Oxford. *Residence*, 14, Chester Row, SW1.—— Bernard Thomas Fane, *b.* 1918.

Sister living—Priscilla (90, Fentiman Rd., SW8), *b.* 1911: *m.* 1936 (m. diss. 1956), Count Andrzej Zygmunt Zamoyski, who *d.* 1964, and has issue living, Count Zygmunt Ignacy Stukeley, *b.* 1937; ed. at Stowe and Ch. Ch., Oxford,—Countess Betka Marya, *b.* 1948.

The Stucley family (which has possessed Affeton Castle for over 600 years) came from Stukeley Huntingdonshire, and were Sheriffs of that county, *temp*. John. Sir George, 1st baronet assumed by Roy. licence, 1858, the surname of Stucley in lieu of his patronymic of Buck as linea representative of that ancient family, and was M.P. for Barnstaple (C) 1855-9 and 1865-8.

STUDD, Creation (U.K.) 1929, of Netheravon, Wilts.

Nous-tenons-le-droit

Sir (ROBERT) KYNASTON STUDD, 3rd *Baronet*; *b*. July 9th, 1926; *s*. his father, *Sir* EVIC, OBE, 1975; ed. at Winchester; late Capt. Colm. Gds.: *m*. 1958, Anastasia, only da. of the late Lt.-Col. Harold Boscawen Leveson-Gower [see D. Sutherland, colls.], and has issue.

Arms—Gules, a lion rampant between three crescents argent, on a chief masoned two tilting spears in saltire, all proper. **Crest**—Out of a mural crown two arms embowed in armour, the hands in gauntlets holding two tilting spears saltirewise, all proper.

Residence—Manor Farm, Rockbourne, Fordingbridge, Hants.

Daughters living—Sara Alexandra, *b*. 1959.——Jane Anastasia, *b*. 1961.——Ann Elizabeth, *b*. 1964.

Brothers living—EDWARD FAIRFAX (Danceys, Clavering Saffron Walden, Essex), *b*. May 3rd, 1929; ed. at Winchester; formerly Lt. Coldm. Gds.; a Dir. of Inchape & Co. Ltd., Dodwell & Co. Ltd., and other cos.: *m*. 1960, Prudence Janet, da. of Alastair Douglas Fyfe, OBE, of Grey Court, Riding Mill, Northumberland, and has issue living, Philip Alastair Fairfax, *b*. 1961,—Christopher Andrew Eric, *b*. 1968,—Alexandra Mary, *b*. 1965.—— *Rev*. John Eric (The Rectory, Monks Risborough, Bucks.), *b*. 1934; ed. at Winchester, and at Clare Coll., Camb. (MA): *m*. 1969, Nea Mildred, yr. da. of Gordon Penn Kennett, of 35, Kireep Rd., Balwyn, Vic., Aust.

Sister living—Elizabeth Stephana, *b*. 1924: *m*. 1954, Victor Erwin Spindel, and has issue living, Daniel Jonas Arthur, *b*. 1962. *Residence*, 177, Liverpool Rd., N1.

Aunt living (daughter of 1st baronet)—Vera Constance Victoria, *b*. 1897. *Residence*, Carfax, 35, West Common, Haywards Heath, Sussex, RH16 2AJ.

Widow living of 2nd Baronet—(KATHLEEN) STEPHANA (*Stephana, Lady Studd*) (Trenchleys Park, Limpsfield Chart, Oxted, Surrey), only da. of Lydstone Joseph Langmead: *m*. 1923, Sir Eric Studd, OBE, 2nd Bt., who *d*. 1975.

Collateral Branch living.

Issue of the late Bernard Cyril Studd, youngest son of 1st baronet, *b*. 1892, *d*. 1962: *m*. 1925, Caryl Theodora (Carfax, 35, West Common, Haywards Heath, Sussex, RH16 2AJ), el. da. of Brig.-Gen. Charles de Winton, CMG:—

Diana Caryl, *b*. 1928: *m*. 1954, Anthony Ross Pope, and has issue living, David Bernard Anthony Edward Beauchamp, *b*. 1961,—Simon Charles Kynaston Beauchamp, *b*. 1964,—Sara Caryl Beauchamp, *b*. 1955,—Caroline Diana Beauchamp, *b*. 1957. *Residence*, Deakes Manor, Cuckfield, Sussex, RH17 5JA.——Joanell Vera, *b*. 1933: *m*. 1959, Lt.-Col. Robert Henville Chappell, OBE, Queen's Regt., and has issue living, Bruce Hereward, *b*. 1961,—Gavin Bernard, *b*. 1963,— Kathryn Joanell, *b*. 1966. *Residence*, Southdown House, Warminster, Wilts.

The 1st baronet, Sir (John Edward) Kynaston Studd (son of the late Edward Studd, of Tidworth House, Wilts, and 2, Hyde Park Gardens, W.), was Pres. and Chm. of Polytechnic, and an Alderman of City of London (Sheriff 1922-3, and Lord Mayor 1928-9).

STUDHOLME, Creation (U.K.) 1956, of Perridge, co. Devon.

SEMPER-PARATUS

Sir HENRY GRAY STUDHOLME, *C.V.O.*, 1st *Baronet*, el. surviving son of William Paul Studholme, of Perridge House, Exeter ; *b*. June 13th, 1899 ; ed. at Eton, and at Magdalen Coll., Oxford (MA); a DL for Devon; a Conservative Whip 1945-56, and Joint Hon. Treasurer of Conservative Party 1956-62; Vice-Chamberlain to HM Household 1951-56; 1914-18 War as Lt., Scots Gds., 1939-45 War on Staff; MP for Tavistock (C) 1942-66; CVO 1953: *m*. 1929, Judith Joan Mary, da. of Henry William Whitbread, of Norton Bavant Manor, Wilts, and has issue.

Arms—Vert, a horse statant argent, caparisoned or, on a chief of the second three mullets of six points pierced gules. **Crest**—A horse's head argent, bridled, and charged on the neck with a spur or.

Residence—Wembury House, Plymouth. *Club*—Carlton.

Sons living—PAUL HENRY WILLIAM, *b.* Jan. 16th, 1930; ed. at Eton, and RMAS; Capt. (ret., Coldm. Gds.: *m.* 1957, Virginia Katherine, yr. da. of Sir (Herbert) Richmond Palmer, KCMG, CBE, and has issue living, Henry William, *b.* 1958,—James Paul Gilfred, *b.* 1960, —Anna Katherine, *b.* 1965. *Residence,* Perridge House, Longdown, Exeter.——Joseph Gilfred, *b.* 1936; ed. at Eton, and at Magdalen Coll., Oxford (BA, 1959); late 2nd Lt. 60th. Rifles: *m.* 1959, Rachel, yr. da. of Capt. Sir William Albemarle Fellowes, KCVO [*see* V. Hampden, colls.], and has issue living, Andrew Gilfred, *b.* 1962,—Henry Alexander, *b.* 1967,—Hugo William Robert, *b.* 1968. *Residence,* 6, The Vale, SW3.
Daughter living—Henrietta Mary, *b.* 1931 : *m.* 1953, Major Thomas Edward St. Aubyn, 60th Rifles [*see* B., St. Levan colls.]. *Residence,* Tangier House, Wootton St. Lawrence, Basingstoke.

STURDEE, Creation (U.K.) 1916, of The Falkland Islands.
[Extinct 1970.]

Rear-Adm. Sir LIONEL ARTHUR DOVETON STURDEE, *CBE,* 2nd and last Baronet.

Daughter living of 2nd Baronet—Elizabeth Mary Doveton (*Lady Ashmore*), *b.* 1919; 1939-45 War as 2nd Officer WRNS: *m.* 1942, Adm. Sir Edward Beckwith Ashmore, GCB, DSC, of Mall House Flat, Admiralty Arch, SW1, and has issue living, Thomas Sturdee, *b.* 1955,—Susan Alexandra, *b.* 1943: *m.* 1966, Francis John Badcock Sykes, of Thornhill, Wanborough, Swindon, only son of Sir Francis Godfrey Sykes, 9th Bt. (*cr.* 1781).

STYLE, Creation (E.) 1627, of Wateringbury, Kent.

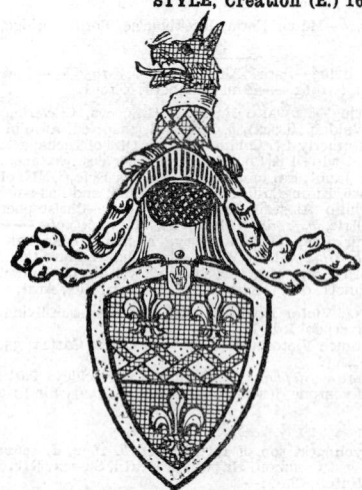

Sir WILLIAM MONTAGUE STYLE, 12th *Baronet*; *b.* July 21st, 1916; *s.* his father, *Sir* WILLIAM FREDERICK, 1943 : *m.* 1941, La Verne, da. of T. M. Comstick, and has issue.

Arms—Sable, a fesse or fretty of the field between three fleurs-de-lis gold, all within a bordure of the second. **Crest**—A wolf's head couped sable, collared or, the lower part of the neck fretty of the last.

Residence—9516, Harding Boulevard Wauwatosa 13, Wisconsin, U.S.A.

Sons living—WILLIAM FREDERICK, *b.* May 13th, 1945.——Frederick Montague, *b.* 1947.

Sister living—Helen, *b.* 1913.

Half-Sister living—Dorothy Jean, *b.* 1923.

Widow living of 11th Baronet—GENEVIEVE (*Dowager Lady Style*), da. of Peter L'Estrange: *m.* (Feb.) 1923, as his second wife, Sir William Frederick Style, 11th baronet, who *d.* 1943. *Residence,* 9004, W. North Av., Milwaukee, Wisconsin, USA).

Collateral Branches living.

Issue of the late Henry Albert Glenmore Style, 3rd son of 9th baronet, *b.* 1862, *d.* 1916: *m.* 1886, Annie Lydia, da. of Samuel Fletcher Goldsmith :—
Glenmore Rodney, *b.* 1887 : *m.* 1913, Mary Margaret Tobin, and has issue living, Rodney Henry, *b.* 1914: *m.* 1st, 1940,—; 2ndly, 1943, Kathleen Quillan, who *d.* 1952; 3rdly, 1959, Lorretta Goodyear, and has issue living, (by 2nd m.) Mary Kathryn *b.* 1947,—Gerald Eugene, *b.* 1922: *m.* 1945, Marguerite Keogan, and has issue living, James Robert *b.* 1948, Ann Marie *b.* 1952,— William Hugh, *b.* 1924: *m.* 1956, Mary Ann Farrell, and has issue living, Robert George *b.* 1959, William Edward *b.* 1961, Susan Marie *b.* 1957,—Charles Albert, *b.* 1926: *m.* 1950, Delores Jaqua, and has issue living, Gregory Charles *b.* 1950, Gary Kevin *b.* 1952,—Jerome Everet, *b.* 1932: *m.* 1955, Margaret Ryan, and has issue living, Kathleen Michelle *b.* 1956, Maureen Anne *b.* 1956,— Barbara Jo *b.* 1959,—Vincent Joseph, *b.* 1934: *m.* 1956, Jane Sizer, and has issue living, Steven Joseph *b.* 1959,—Nona Marie *b.* 1962,—Margaret Clare, *b.* 1918; is a Franciscan Nun,—Mary Crescent *b.* 1923: *m.* 1944, Maurice Finney,—Elizabeth Ann, *b.* 1928: *m.* 1955, Gene Sullivan, and has issue living, Joseph Donald *b.* 1956, Thomas Michael *b.* 1958,—Catherine Theresa, *b.* 1929: *m.* 1951, Robert E. Olson, and has issue living, Mark Joseph *b.* 1953, Stephen George *b.* 1954, Jonathan *b.* 1955, Eric James, *b.* 1961, Julie Ann *b.* 1952, Jennifer (twin) *b.* 1955, Mary Beth *b.* 1957, Lisa Marie *b.* 1959, Ellen Christine *b.* 1962.——Rosanna Lydia, *b.* 1891.——Brenda Helen, *b.* 1897.——Viola, *b.* 1897: *m.* 1921, Merton Crandall Dayton. *Residence,*

Issue of the late Brig.-Gen. Rodney Charles Style, 4th son of 9th baronet, *b.* 1863, *d.* 1957 : *m.* 1911, Héléne Pauline, who *d.* 1975, da. of the late Herman Greverus Kleinwort, of 45, Belgrave Square, SW1, and Wierton Pl., Maidstone:—
Sir Godfrey William, *CBE, DSC, b.* 1915; ed. at Eton; Lt.-Cdr. RN; an Underwriting Member of Lloyd's; served in HM Yacht "Victoria and Albert" 1938; Flag Lt. to Com.-in-Ch. Home Fleet 1939-41; a Member of the Nat. Advisory Council on Employment of Disabled People 1944-74 (Chm. of Council 1964-74), of Advisory Panel to Disabled Living Foundation since 1965, and of Nat. Star Centre for Youth, Cheltenham Advisory Panel since 1966, and of Council since 1970; a Member of Disablement Advisory Cttee., Maidstone, 1945-64 and Chm. of Sheltered Employment Cttee. of Nat. Advisory Council 1954-64; 1939-45 War (despatches twice, DSC, invalided); CBE (Civil) 1960, Knt. 1973: *m.* 1st, 1942 (m. diss. 1951), Jill Elizabeth, da. of the late George B Caruth, of Drumard Cottage, Ballymena, co. Antrim; 2ndly, 1951, Sigrid Elisabeth, da. of the late Per Stellan Carlberg, of Jönköping, Sweden, and has issue living (by 1st m.) Montague William (4, Belleville Rd., SW11), *b.* 1943; ed. at Eton; Diploma de l'Académie des Hautes Etudes Commerciales, Paris; dipl. INSTEAD: *m.* 1970, Susan Jennifer, yr. da. of Peter Wrightson, OBE [*see* Wrightson, Bt.], and has issue living, Sophie Elizabeth *b.* 1974,—Helen Anne, *b.* 1946: *m.* 1971, Maj. Charles Frederick Byng Stephens, Welsh Gds., and has issue living, Alexandra Claire *b.* 1973,—Marieka Louise, *b.* 1947: *m.* 1966, Charles John Hamilton Fisher, of 26, Gowan Av., SW6 6RF, and has issue living, Hugo Hamilton *b.* 1970, Louise Hamilton *b.* 1973,—(by 2nd m.) Charles Rodney, *b.* 1954; ed. at Eton, and Camb. Univ. *Residence,* Gilhams Birch, Rotherfield, nr. Crowborough, Sussex. *Club,*—Naval and Military.——Rodney Gerald, *b.* 1920; ed. at Eton; Col. RRF (OC 1st Bn. RNF 1962-65); Comdt. RMSM, Kneller Hall; 1939-45 War with Coldm. Gds.: *m.* 1st, 1944 (m. diss. 1952), Melloney, da. of the late Maj.-Gen. Sir (Sandford) John Palairet Scobell, KBE, CB, CMG, DSO; 2ndly, 1952, Barbara, da. of the late John A. Hill, of 102, Pond St., Natick, Massachusetts, USA, and has issue living (by 2nd m.), William Bryant,

b. 1954; 2nd Lt. Coldm. Gds.,—Rodney Hill, *b.* 1956,—John Glenmore, *b.* 1957,—Caroline Mary, *b.* 1964. *Residence,* Bracken Close, Crooksbury Rd., Runfold, Farnham, Surrey.——Rosamond Marguerite, *b.* 1912: *m.* 1934, Rear-Adm. John Harvey Forbes Crombie, CB, DSO, who *d.* 1972, and has issue living, James Rodney Forbes, *b.* 1935; Capt. late Queen's Own Highlanders: *m.* 1961, Lee Adrienne Chavet,—Rosanna Mary, *b.* 1937: *m.* 1964, Maj. Malcolm Kenneth Shennan, late R. Scots Greys, of The Old Rectory, Closworth, nr. Yeovil, Som., and has issue living, Mark *b.* 1970, Melissa *b.* 1967,—Annabel Jean, *b.* 1944: *m.* 1964, Simon Gerard Younger, of Baro, Haddington, and has issue living, James Henry *b.* 1965, Mary-Claire *b.* 1967, Eugenie *b.* 1968, Sophie Rosamond *b.* 1973,—Julia Rosamond, *b.* 1947: *m.* 1974, John Henry Trotter, of Ladykirk, Berwick-on-Tweed. *Residence,* Gateside House, Gullane, E. Lothian.——Mary Dorothy, *b.* 1918: *m.* 1939, Neil Arthur Campbell, TD, and has issue living, Alastair Neil, *b.* 1941: *m.* 1970, Jane, da. of Michael Gatehouse,—Jeremy George, *b.* 1948,—Gerald Angus, *b.* 1951,—Joanna Mary, *b.* 1946. *Residence,* Twitten, Wallcrouch, nr. Ticehurst, Sussex.

Grandchildren of the late Maj. George Montague Style (infra):—
Issue of the late Oliver George Style, *b.* 1897, *d.* 1973: *m.* 1923, Guinevere, who *d.* 1975, da. of the late Rev. Walter Matthew Parker [Molesworth St. Aubyn Bt.. colls.]:—
George Michael Oliver, *b.* 1927: *m.* 1951, Mary Jeans, and has issue living, Elizabeth Mary, *b.* 1952,—Sarah Jane, *b.* 1955,—Caroline Ann, *b.* 1956.——Patricia Nora, *b.* 1924: *m.* 1946 (m. diss. 1970), Gp. Capt. Deryck Hugo Cross, RAF (ret.), and has issue living, Robert Humphrey Hugo, *b.* 1951,—Alison Guinevere Hugo, *b.* 1947: *m.* 1972, Gerald Bunyan, and has issue living, Kathleen Jill *b.* 1973,—Frances Jane Hugo, *b.* 1949: *m.* 1969, Richard Charles Mortimore.

Grandchildren of the late Albert Frederick Style, youngest son of the late Capt. William Style, R.N., 2nd son of the late Rev. Robert Style, 2nd son of 4th baronet:—
Issue of the late Major George Montague Style, *b.* 1869, *d.* 1942: *m.* 1st, 1896, Eleonora Morrison Kirkwood ; 2ndly, 1921, Mrs. Kearton, who *d.* 1941 :—
(By 1st m.) Patience Pauline, *b.* 1901: *m.* 1928, Col. Claude Ernest Torin Erskine, CIE, DSO, MC, late Indian Army, who *d.* 1964, and has issue living, Claude Anthony, *b.* 1932: *m.* 1959, Diana Margery, da. of the late Dr. Harold Kanaar, of Kokstad, Cape Province, S. Africa, and has issue living, Claude Mark *b.* 1961, Timothy Harold *b.* 1962, Paul Anthony *b.* 1965, Jonathan Montague *b.* 1968,—Elizabeth Constance, *b.* 1930: *m.* 1955, Justice James Allan Howard, of 27, Portland Cres., Durban North, Natal, and has issue living, George Allan *b.* 1950, Robert James *b.* 1962, Jane Pauline *b.* 1958. *Residence,* Linlathen, Harding, Natal, S. Africa.

Issue of the late Charles Humphrey Style, *b.* 1877, *d.* 1936: *m.* 1899, Annie Maud Harriet, who *d.* 1942, da. of the late Gen. Sir Hugh Henry Gough, VC, GCB:—
Humphrey Bloomfield, *b.* 1902; ed. at Marlborough, and at Pembroke Coll., Camb.: *m.* 1935, Anita Dolores, da. of Charles Brunson, of Antofagasta, Chile, and has issue living, Charles Humphrey *b.* 1945: *m.* 1971, Elizabeth Ann Hoskin, of London, Ont., Canada,—Ursula Anne, *b.* 1936: *m.* 1959, William Swaisland Carter, of Toronto, Canada, and had issue living, William Alarik, *b.* 1963, Roberta Jean *b.* 1960, Jacqueline Anne *b.* 1966, Adrienne Julia *b.* 1971,—Ingrid Priscilla, *b.* 1939: *m.* 1960, Henry Evan Cockshutt Schulman, and has issue living, Charles Eric *b.* 1965, Frances Yvonne *b.* 1961, Audrey Alexis *b.* 1963,—Diana Maria, *b.* 1941: *m.* 1965, Robert Tweedy, of 7, Royal Oak, Don Mills, Toronto, Canada, and has issue living, Laura Anne *b.* 1968, Lisa Diana *b.* 1973. *Residence,* 172, The Bridle Path, Don Mills, Toronto, Canada.——Hubert Anthony, *b.* 1910; ed. at Marlborough; late Capt. Indian Army: *m.* 1943, Enid Margaret, da. of L. F. Leonard, of Reigate, Surrey, and has issue living, John Richard, *b.* 1943; ed. at Marlborough and Coll. of Law; Solicitor 1970,—Robert Nicholas Humphrey, *b.* 1949; ed. at Marlborough. *Residence,* Broomscroft Cottage, Wateringbury, nr. Maidstone, Kent.——Barbara Ann, *b.* 1904.——Camilla, *b.* 1906: *m.* 1935, Antony Cuthbert Marsham, who *d.* 1975 [see E. Romney, colls.]. *Residence,* Leybourne Lodge, West Malling, Kent.

Issue of the late Robert Henry Style, Yeo., *b.* 1881, *d.* 1945 : *m.* 1905, Grace Winnifred, (now of Wateringbury Place, near Maidstone), da. of the late John Bazley-White [E. Rothes] :—
David Leslie, *b.* 1913; ed. at Radley; European War 1939-45 as Able Seaman RN. *Residence,* Hampton Court, Isle of Man.——Betty Winnifred (Highlands House, Mereworth, Kent) *b.* 1907: *m.* 1938, Henry Cuthbert Hatfeild, who *d.* 1951, and has issue living, Rosemary Ursula *b.* 1944: *m.* 1965, John Trafford Rothery, of Cranyke Farm, Scalford, Melton Mowbray, and has issue living, William Edward *b.* 1965, Mark Henry *b.* 1968,—Sonia Louise, *b.* 1946: *m.* 1970, Ernest John Robin Ludlow, of Betsoms Farmhouse, Pilgrims Way, Westerham, Kent.—— Gabrielle Ursula, *b.* 1911: *m.* 1936, Capt. Richard Taylor White, DSO, RN (ret.) [see White, Bt., *cr.* 1802]. *Residence,* Wateringbury Place, nr Maidstone, Kent.

This family, originally seated in Suffolk, is descended from William Style, of Ipswich, father of Sir John Style, Alderman of London, grandfather of Sir Humphrey Style, Knt., one of the Esquires to the Body of Henry VIII, and grandfather of Sir Thomas, 1st baronet.

SULLIVAN, Creation (U.K.) 1804, of Thames Ditton, Surrey.

What we ain by conquest we secure clemency.

LAMH·FOISDINEACH·AU·NACHTAR

Sir RICHARD BENJAMIN MAGNIAC SULLIVAN, 8th *Baronet,* son of the late Capt. Richard Sullivan, R.N., 2nd son of 6th baronet ; *b.* Oct. 26th, 1906 ; *s.* his uncle, *the* Rev. *Sir* FREDERICK, 1954 ; ed. at St. Andrew's Coll., Grahamstown, S. Africa ; in Colonial Administrative Ser. 1929-57 ; retired 1957 : *m.* 1928, Muriel Mary Paget, da. of the late Francis Charles Trayler Pineo, and has issue.

Arms—Per fesse, the base per pale ; in the chief or, a dexter hand couped at the wrist grasping a sword erect gules, the blade entwined by a serpent proper, between two lions rampant respecting each other of the second ; the dexter base vert, charged with a buck trippant or, on the sinister base per pale argent and sable, a boar passant counterchanged. Crest—On a ducal coronet or, a robin holding in the beak a sprig of laurel proper.
Residence—Rockall, Ruwa, Rhodesia. *Clubs*—Salisbury (Rhodesia), Royal Commonwealth Society.

Sons living—RICHARD ARTHUR (1095I, Beinhorn, Houston, Texas, USA 77024), *b.* Aug. 9th, 1931; ed. at Univ. of Cape Town (BSc), and at Mass. Inst. of Technology (SM); PE, MASCE: *m.* 1962, Elenor] Mary, el. da. of Kenneth Merson Thorpe, of Somerset West, CP, S. Africa, and has issue living, Charles Merson, b. 1962,—Katherine Ann, b. 1963,—Sarah Elizabeth, b. 1965, —Margaret Mary, b. 1969.——Michael Francis (19, Cassiobury Park Av., Watford, Herts.), b. 1936; ed. at Camb. Univ. (MA, MB, BCh), FRCS (Eng): m. 1957, Inger, only da. of Arne Mathieson, of Oslo, Norway, and has issue living, Richard Alexander Dermot, b. 1961,—Vivienne Nicola, b. 1965.

Collateral Branch living.
         Issue of the late Valentine Arthur Sullivan, 2nd son of Capt. Richard Sullivan, RN, 2nd son of 7th baronet, b. 1907, d. 1965: m. 1937, Mollie Maureen Madge (113, Amsterdam, Hoek, P.O. Swartkops, Port Elizabeth, S. Africa), da. of the late W. N. Craig, of Sale, Cheshire:—
Peter Craig Valentine (2, Doncaster Rd., Port Elizabeth, S. Africa), b. 1941.——Elizabeth Bridget Patricia, b. 1947.

The 6th baronet, Adm. Sir Francis William Sullivan, K.C.B., C.M.G., was an A.D.C. to Queen Victoria 1877-8. The 7th baronet, the Rev. Sir Frederick Sullivan, was 20 years R. of Southrepps.

SULLIVAN, Creation (U.K.) 1881, of Garryduff, co. Cork. [Extinct 1937.]

Sir WILLIAM SULLIVAN, 3rd and last *Baronet.*

Daughter living of 3rd Baronet—By 1st marriage—Kathleen Mary: m. 1914, Wilmot Humphrey Clifford Lloyd, who d. 1948, and has issue living, Desmond Humphrey Clifford, b. 1917; ed. at Trin. Coll., Dublin (B.A. 19—); European War 1942-5 with London Irish Rifles,—Wilmot Anthony Clifford, b. 1928; is Fl.-Lt. RAF,—Nedda Cecil Clifford: m. 19—, James Davis. *Residence,* St. Johns, 202, Merrion Rd., Dublin 4.

SUMMERS, Creation (U.K.) 1952, of Shotton, co. Flint.

(*Sir*) FELIX ROLAND BRATTAN SUMMERS, 2nd *Baronet*; b. Oct. 1st, 1918; s. his father, *Sir* GEOFFREY, *CBE,* 1972, but does not use title; ed. at Shrewsbury; 1939-45 War in Middle East, N. Africa, France and Belgium: m. 1945, Anna Marie Louise, da. of the late Gustave Demaegd, of Brussels, and has issue.

Arms—Azure a fesse indented ermine between in chief two fleurs de lys burgeonee and in base a martlet within a mascle or. *Crest*—A demi dragon reguardant gules supporting between the wings a terrestrial globe proper.

Residence—Warren House, 16, Warren Lane, Friston, Eastbourne, Sussex.

MENS·SIBI·CONSCIA·RECTI

A mind conscious of its own rectitude

Daughter living—Micheline, b. 1947: m. 1970, Mark Dudley Langridge, of Broadmead, Hankham Hall Rd., Pevensey.
Sister living—Anne Griselda, b. 1916: m. 1953, Maj. Alan Edward Curtis Lake, TD, of Maes-y-Groes Bella, Cilcain, nr. Mold.
Half-sisters living—Judith Margaret, b. 1932: m. 1958, Gordon Elliott, of Woolley Cottage, The Thicket, Maidenhead, Berks., and has issue living, Geoffrey Ian, b. 1960,—Martin Anthony, b. 1963,—Catherine Elizabeth, b. 1961,—Lucy Helen, b. 1966.——Carolyn Elizabeth, b. 1936: m. 1958, Robin Hilary Beaumont Malim, of Bollitree Castle, Weston under Penyard, Ross-on-Wye, and has issue living, Peter Beaumont, b. 1963,—Karen Elizabeth, b. 1960,—Sophia Hilary b. 1968.
Mother living—Doris Marguerite, da. of the late George Robert Edgecombe, of Brenchley, Kent: m. 1915 (m. diss. 1930), Sir Geoffrey Summers, CBE, 1st Bt., who d. 1972.

SUTHERLAND, Creation (U.K.) 1921, of Dunstanburgh Castle, Embleton, co. Northumberland.

Sir BENJAMIN IVAN SUTHERLAND, 2nd *Baronet*: b. May 16th, 1901; s. his father, *Sir* ARTHUR MUNRO, *K.B.E.,* 1953: m. 1st, 1927 (divorce 1944), Marjorie Constance Daniel, da. of Frederic William Brewer, O.B.E., of Newcastle-on-Tyne; 2ndly, 1944, Margaret, JP, da. of Albert Owen, of Chalfont St. Giles, Bucks, and has issue by 1st and 2nd marriages.

Arms—Gules, a chevron flory-counterflory between in chief three mullets and in base a lymphad all or. *Crest*—Upon the trunk of a tree a cat salient proper.

Residence—Dunstan Steads, Embleton, Northumberland.

Without fear.

Sons living—By 1st marriage—JOHN BREWER (of Ross, Belford, Northumberland), b. Oct. 19th, 1931: m. 1958, Alice Muireall, da. of the late W. Stamford Henderson, of Kelso, and has issue living, Peter William, b. 1963,—Christopher John, b. 1965,—Robert Brewer, b. 1970,—Susan Muireall, b. 1960.——(David) Michael (Lilliestead, Berwick-on-Tweed), b. 1940: m. 1966, Caroline Mary Hogan, and has issue living, Julia Ruth, b. 1967,—Serena Louise, b. 1971.——By 2nd marriage—William, b. 1945: m. 1966, Sarah Lucy, da. of Dr. Cecil Gilbert, of Benton, Newcastle upon Tyne, and has issue living, Mark Rupert, b. 1967,—Dylan Paul b. 1970,—Ceri Jane, b. 1968,—Amy Gael, b. 1969.——Owen, b. 1947: m. 1971, Margaret Ann, da. of Daniel Herbert Williams, of Rainhill, Liverpool, and has issue living, Victoria Jane, b, 1974.——Ben, b. 1949.
Brother living—Robert Gordon, b. 1908: m. 1st, 1934 (divorce 1958), Helen Wallace, da. of the late Edward Farish, of Wigton, Cumberland; 2ndly, 1958 Emily, da. of Lavinia Hayes, of Hanwell,

Middlesex, and has issue living, (by 1st m.) Arthur Ian b. 1936,—David Wallace, b. 1938. *Residence*, Rock House Quay, Kilmacsimon, Bandon, co. Cork.

Sister living—Linda Kathleen, b. 1897: m. 1928, Henry Armstrong, who d. 1955. *Residence*, Sheileen, Victoria Road, Wooler, Northumberland.

Collateral Branch living.

Issue of the late Arthur Munro Sutherland, el. son of 1st baronet, b. 1894, d. 1941: m. 1921, Nina Marguerite Crawshay, da. of the late Arthur Skelton Wimble, of Whitley Bay, Northumberland, and St. Helier, Jersey:—

Nina Marguerite Munro, b. 1923: m. 1949, James Keith W. Slater, and has issue living, Gail Munro, b. 1950,—Kim Munro, b. 1952,—Bill Munro, b. 1953,—Peter Munro, b. 1956. *Residence*, Ambergate, Plantation Road, Leighton Buzzard, Bedfordshire.——Ann Munro b. 1928.

The 1st baronet, Sir Arthur Munro Sutherland, K.B.E. (son of B. J. Sutherland of Newcastle-on-Tyne), Chm. of Newcastle Commercial Exchange ; was Lord Mayor of Newcastle-on-Tyne 1918-19, Pres. of Chamber of Shipping of the United Kingdom 1930, and High Sheriff of Northumberland 1943.

Sutherland-Dunbar (Duff-Sutherland-Dunbar), see Dunbar.

GRANT-SUTTIE, Creation (N.S.) 1702, of Balgone, Haddingtonshire.

Sir (GEORGE) PHILIP GRANT-SUTTIE, 8th *Baronet*; son of the late Major George Donald Grant-Suttie, son of the late Capt. Francis Grant-Suttie, R.N., 2nd son of 5th baronet; b. Dec. 20th, 1938; s. his kinsman, *Sir* GEORGE, 1947; ed. at Sussex Composite High School, New Brunswick, and at McGill Univ.: m. 1962 (m. diss. 1969), Elspeth Mary, el. da. of Maj.-Gen. Robert Elliott Urquhart, CB, DSO, and has issue.

Arms—Quarterly: 1st and 4th, barry wavy of six azure and or; on a chief of the last, a lion rampant naissant with two tails vert, armed and langued gules, *Suttie*; 2nd and 3rd, or, a chevron checky gules and of the first, between three hunting-horns sable, garnished of the second, all within a bordure of the same, *Semple*. Crest—A ship under full sail proper.

Nothing hazard, nothing have. Residence—Sheriff Hall, N. Berwick, East Lothian. Seat—Balgone, North Berwick.

Son living—JAMES EDWARD, b. May 29th, 1965.

Sister living—Ann, b. 1940: m. 1967, Marinus Jan Luitwieler.

Mother living—Marjorie NEVILLE, da. of Capt. C. E. Carter, R.N., of Stephenville, Newfoundland : m. 1st, 1937, as his second wife, Major George Donald Grant-Suttie (ante), who d. 1940; 2ndly, 1944, Paul Underhill, Lt., US Army.

Collateral Branches living

Grandchildren of the late Robert Grant-Suttie (infra):—

Issue of the late Col. Hubert Francis Grant-Suttie, CBE, DSO, MC, b. 1884, d. 1973: m. 1920, Torfrida Alianore, who d. 1971, da. of Sir Wroth Periam Christopher Lethbridge, 5th Bt.:—

Robert Ian (5609, Wood Way, Sumner, Washington DC 20016, USA), b. 1926; ed. at Wellington Coll., Sorbonne, and New Coll., Oxford; late Lt. Black Watch: m. 1951, Juliet Carmen, yr. da. of the late Lt.-Col. Nigel Eustace Philip Sutton [see Sutton, Bt., colls.], and has issue living, Francis AEneas, b. 1957,—James Archibald, b. 1964,—Atalanta Theresa, b. 1955,—Roxana Idonea, b. 1961.——Margaret Torfrida, b. 1923: m. 1957, Cdr. Michael B. Speare-Cole, RN, of 17, Park Walk, Chelsea, SW10 0AJ, and has issue living, Hubert Alastair, b. 1959,—Julia Torfrida, b. 1963.

Issue of the late Robert Grant-Suttie, 4th son of 5th baronet, b. 1841, d.¦1933: m. 1884, the Hon. Edith Mary Dawnay, who d. 1941, da. of 7th Viscount Downe:—

Hilda Margaret.——Ethel Mary. *Residence*, Dream Haven, Glen Orchy Rd., N. Berwick.

The 2nd and 4th baronets successively represented Haddingtonshire in Parliament, and the 4th baronet assumed the additional surname of Grant on succeeding to the estates of his aunt, Janet Grant Countess of Hyndford.

SUTTON, Creation (G.B.) 1772, of Norwood Park, Nottinghamshire.

Sir ROBERT LEXINGTON SUTTON, 8th *Baronet*; b. Jan. 18th, 1897; s. his father, *Sir* ARTHUR EDWIN, 1948; ed. at Wellington Coll., formerly Lieut. Household Cav.; European War 1915-19: m. 1936, Gwynneth Gwladys, only da. of Maj. Arnold Charles Gover, MC, of Pilton and has issue.

Arms—Quarterly: 1st and 4th, argent, a canton sable, *Sutton*; 2nd and 3rd, argent, a cross flory azure, *Lexington*. Crest—A wolf's head erased gules.

Residence—Clinger Farm, Wincanton, Somerset

Sons living—RICHARD LEXINGTON (Moor Hill, Langham, Gillingham, Dorset), b. April 27th, 1937; ed. at Stowe: m. 1959, Fiamma Ferrari, and has issue living, David Robert, b. 1960,—Caroline Victoria, b. 1965——James Anthony (Old Rowley, Stoke Orchard nr. Cheltenham, Glos.), b. 1940; ed. at Stowe: m. 1964, Dale, da. of Capt. C. W. Stevens, of Windrush Mill, Windrush, Burford, Oxford, and has issue living, Tristan Antony, b. 1966,—Chloe Emma, b. 1968.

Always ready Sister living—Esmé, b. 1886: m. 1912, Brig.-Gen. William Denman Croft, CB, CMG, DSO, who d. 1968 [see Croft, Bt., colls., cr. 1671]. *Residence*, The Anchorage, Mawnan, nr. Falmouth.

Collateral Branches living.

Grandchildren of the late Alexander George Sutton, 3rd son of 4th baronet:—

Issue of the late Thomas Alexander Sutton, b. 1888, d. 1945: m. 1913, Gwendoline, da. of Thomas Forsyth-Forrest, formerly of The Querns, Cirencester:—

John Alexander, *b.* 1915; ed. at Charterhouse : *m.* (Jan.) 1950, Violet Deirdre, el. da. of the late James Sheringham Shepherd, of Kilbrack, Doneraile, co. Cork, and has issue living, Charles Alexander, *b.* 1950,—Grania Jane, *b.* 1952. *Residence*, Badbury Wick House, Chiseldon, Wilts.——Margaret Pamela (*Lady Bunbury*), *b.* 1919: *m.* 1940, Sir John William Napier Bunbury, 12th Bt. *Residence*, Naunton Hall, Rendlesham, Suffolk.——Gillian, *b.* 1921 : *m.* 1946, Robert Clarkson Crosbie Dawson, MC, Queen's Bays, and has issue living, James, *b.* 1948,—William George, *b.* 1950,—Richard Robert, *b.* 1952,—Thomas, *b.* 1956. *Residence*, Northington Farm, Overton, Basingstoke, Hants.

Issue of the late Henry Cecil Sutton, 4th son of 4th baronet, *b.* 1868, *d.* 1936: *m.* 1913, Constance Diana, who *d.* 1960, da. of the late Hon. Herbert Welbore Ellis Agar [E. Normanton, colls.] :—

Cecil Roland, *b.* 1918; formerly 2nd Lieut. 99th (Bucks and Berks Yeo.) Army Field Regt., R.A. (T.A.): *m.* 1943, Lilian Elizabeth, da. of T. W. Gore, of Knighton, Ramsbury. *Residence*, Pique, Stockcross, Newbury, Berks.

Granddaughter of the late Lt.-Col. Francis Henry Sutton, MC, 11th Hussars (PAO) (infra) :—
Issue of the late Lt.-Col. Richard David Sutton, 11th Hussars (PAO), *b.* 1923, *d.* 1965: *m.* 1965, Sally Christine (Long Drive House, Cherington, Tetbury, Glos.), da. of J. D. Graeme Reid, of Gruivie, Wormit, Fife:—
Frances Elizabeth (*posthumous*) *b.* 1966.

Granddaughter of the late Maj. Francis Richard Hugh Seymour Sutton, son of the late Capt. Francis Sutton, 3rd son of 2nd baronet :—
Issue of the late Lieut.-Col. Francis Henry Sutton, M.C., *b.* 1882, *d.* 1957 : *m.* 1914, Aileen Maria (of Upper Common, Kington Langley, Chippenham, Wilts), da. of the late Richard Henry Gosling, of Hawthorn Hill, Berkshire [Dyer, Bt.]:—
Beryl Susan, *b.* 1919: *m.* 1945, Maj. Victor Hugh Harry McCalmont, late R. Dragoons, and has issue living, Peter Victor, *b.* 1946: *m.* 1975, Mrs. Isobel C. Velaise,—Harry Richard Dermot, *b.* 1955,—Diana Emily Helen, *b.* 1948: *m.* 1968, Robert Morton, of Rathvindon, Leighlinbridge, co. Carlow. *Residence*, Mount Juliet, Thomastown, co. Kilkenny.

Grandson of the late Rev. Augustus Sutton, 5th son of 2nd baronet:—
Issue of the late Gilbert William Sutton, *b.* 1858, *d.* 1929: *m.* 1890, Mabel Affleck Peacock, who *d.* 1930, da. of the late Rev. John Peacock, of Fulbeck:—
John Gilbert, D.S.C., *b.* 1892 ; Com. R.N. (retired) ; European War 1914-18, in Submarine Ser., European War 1939-44 (D.S.C.) : *m.* 1st, 1918, Eva Maud, who *d.* 1919, da. of Thomas Cook, of Hobland, Great Yarmouth ; 2ndly, 1920, Ida Margaret (who obtained a divorce 1940), da. of Charles Halls ; 3rdly, 1940, Katharine (from whom he obtained a divorce 1950), da. of George Balfour-Kinnear, W.S. [Montgomery, Bt.]; 4thly, 1950, Violet, da. of the late Herbert James Godwin, OBE, of Greatham, Petersfield, Hants, and has issue living, (by 2nd m.) Richard John Beverley (Foxfield, Ansty, Dorchester, Dorset), *b.* 1922; Lt.-Cdr. RN: *m.* 1949, Ann Stella, da. of the late Brig. Charles Hall Woodhouse, OBE, MC, and has issue living, Richard Charles *b.* 1955, Amanda Clare *b.* 1952: *m.* 1973, Robert Stephen Mackenzie, Queen's R. Irish Hussars,—Felicity Ruth, *b.* 1926: *m.* 1951, Maj. Denis Cary Atkinson, of Home Farm House, Waterston, Dorchester, Dorset, and has issue living, Timothy Charles Garnet *b.* 1960, Tessa Margaret *b.* 1952,—(by 3rd m.) Henry Richard, *b.* 1945,—Judith, *b.* 1942: *m.* 1961, Michael William Cox (and has issue living, Anthony William *b.* 1961, Nicholas Michael *b.* 1963). *Residence*, Frampton House, Dorset. *Clubs*, Naval and Military, Royal Cruising.

Granddaughter of the late Rowland Sutton (infra):—
Issue of the late Lawrence Seymour Sutton, *b.* 1905, *d.* 1967: *m.* 1st, 1936, Muriel Geraldine, who *d.* 1940, da. of Maj. L. A. Sherrard; 2ndly, 1942, Martha Joyce (Cefn-y-dre), Fishguard, Dyfed, da. of W. L. Williams, of Cefn-y-dre, Pembrokeshire:—
(By 1st m.) Rosemary Margaret, *b.* 1937: *m.* 1962, Jack A. Eden, c/o FCO, King Charles St., SW1, and has issue living, Sally Jane, *b.* 1963,—Susan Rosemary, *b.* 1964.——Molly, *b.* 1940: *m.* 1966, Graham J. Waterman, of The Old Rectory, Byers Green, Spennymoor, co. Durham, DL16 7NW, and has issue living, Matthew Charles, *b.* 1967,—Julian Rupert, *b.* 1969,—Lucy Charlotte, *b.* 1973.

Granddaughter of the late Rev. Augustus Sutton (ante):—
Issue of the late Rowland Sutton, *b.* 1859, *d.* 1927: *m.* 1889, Augusta Margaret, who *d.* 1924, da. of the late Rev. Edmund Thomas Daubeney, R. of Swaffham, Norfolk:—
Dorothy Charlotte Mary, *b.* 1893: *m.* 1917, John Selwyn Browning.——Robina Margaret Hill, *b.* 1897: *m.* 1st, 1919 (m. annulled 1927), Capt. Denis Miller, formerly 14th Hussars; 2ndly, 1927, Lt.-Col. Geoffrey Benedict Clifton-Brown, 12th R. Lancers (ret.) [*see* Brown, Bt., colls.]. *Residence*, The Old Rectory, Cockfield, Bury St. Edmunds.

Grandchildren of the late Maj.-Gen. Hugh Clement Sutton, C.B., C.M.G. (infra) :—
Issue of the late Lieut.-Col. Nigel Eustace Philip Sutton, *b.* 1896, *d.* 1956: *m.* 1st, 1921, Stella Clementina, who *d.* 1945, da. of the late Montague Whittingham Price, of 67, Eaton Place, S.W. [E. Clarendon, colls.] ; 2ndly, 1951, Elisabeth Clothilde Hedwige (Mrs. Zita Gielgud), da. of the late Zoltan Gruszner, of Budapest, Hungary:—
(By 1st marriage) John Hugh Torquil, *b.* 1923 ; ed. at Eton, and at Ch. Ch., Oxford ; Major (retired) Coldstream Guards : *m.* 1952, Carola Mariette, da. of Ulick Otway Vortigern Lloyd-Verney, O.B.E. [*see* Verney, Bt., *cr.* 1818, colls.], and has issue living, Hugh Nigel John, *b.* 1954,—Mark Richard, *b.* 1956,—Catherine Stella Louise, *b.* 1959. *Residence*, Bayfield Brecks, Holt, Norfolk.——Elizabeth Ann (27, Christchurch Hill, N.W.3), *b.* 1927.——Juliet Carmen, *b.* 1930: *m.* 1951, Robert Ian Grant-Suttie, of 5609, Wood Way, Sumner, Washington DC 20016, USA [*see* Grant-Suttie, Bt., colls.].

Granddaughters of the late Henry George Sutton, 6th son of 2nd baronet:—
Issue of the late Maj.-Gen. Hugh Clement Sutton, C.B., C.M.G., *b.* 1867, *d.* 1928: *m.* 1st, 1891, Mabel Ida, who *d.* 1896, da. of Sir Campbell Munro, 3rd Bt. (*cr.* 1825) ; 2ndly, 1898, the Hon. Alexandra Mary Elizabeth Wood, who *d.* 1965, el. da. of 2nd Viscount Halifax [E. Halifax]:—
(By 2nd marriage) Margaret Agnes (*Hon. Mrs. John J. Chetwynd*), *b.* 1899: *m.* 1937, the Hon. John Julian Chetwynd, who *d.* 1966, [see V. Chetwynd, colls.]. *Residence*, 3, Cadogan Sq., SW1.——Elizabeth Mary, *b.* 1910: *m.* 1st, 1931, (Ronald) Mark Cunliffe Turner (knighted 1946), from whom she obtained a divorce 1936; 2ndly, 1936, John Tindall-Lister, son of Col. the late Sir William Tindall Lister, KCMG, KCVO, MD, FRCS, and has issue living (by 2nd m.), Francis Hugh William Bernard, *b.* 1937,—Charles John Alexander, *b.* 1945,—(by 1st marriage) Elizabeth Undine, *b.* 1931,—(by 2nd marriage) Mary Nerissa Anna, *b.* 1941,—Sarah Janet Consuelo, *b.* 1947. *Residence*, Luccas Farm, Powerstock, Bridport, Dorset.

Grandchildren of the late Major Robert Nassau SUTTON NELTHORPE, O.B.E., el. son of the late Rev. Robert Sutton, el. son of the late Capt. Robert Nassau Sutton, 3rd son of 1st baronet:—
Issue of the late Col. Oliver Sutton Nelthorpe, C.B.E., D.S.O., M.C., *b.* 1888, *d.* 1963: *m.* 1914, Marjorie Elspeth Constable (of Scawby, Brigg, Lincs.), da. of Charles Constable Curtis [E. Onslow, colls.]:—

Roger, *MBE*, *TD* (Scawby Hall, Brigg, Lincs.), *b.* 1918; ed. at Eton; late Lt.-Col. Nottingham-shire (Sherwood Rangers) Yeo., and a JP and DL (High Sheriff of Lincs. 1970); Palestine and Middle East 1939-44, NW Europe 1944-45 (MBE); MBE (Mil) 1945.——John Richard (High Barn, Welton, Lincs.), *b.* 1923; ed. at Eton; is Lt. RNVR: *m.* 1946, Mary Elizabeth, only da. of T. C. Brown, of The Cottage, Scawby, Lincs., and has issue living, Anthony Julian, *b.* 1948: *m.* 1973, Margaret, yst. da. of R. F. Schumacher, of Upton, Didcot, Berks.——Ann, *b.* 1919.

   Issue of the late Griffith Sutton Nelthorpe, *b.* 1892, *d.* 1947: *m.* 1922, Constance Adine Maud, who *d.* 1923, da. of the late Allan Harvey Drummond [E. Perth, colls.]:—
Jan William, *b.* 1923; is Warrant Officer R.A.F.   *Residence,*

             Grandson of the late Richard Coningsby Sutton (infra):—
   Issue of the late Col. Francis Richard Heywood Sutton, MC, TD, *b.* 1905, *d.* 1970: *m.* 1st, 1929 (m. diss. 1937), Barbara Jean, da. of A. D. Tait; 2ndly, 1939 (m. diss. 1958), Vera Kathleen, da. of W. J. Waldock; 3rdly, 1960, Mrs. Audrey Theodosia Madeleine Davies (Providence Place, Ruettes Brayes, St. Peter Port, Guernsey), da. of Lancelot Squarey [E. Gosford]:—
(By 2nd m.) Richard Oliver, *AFC*, *b.* 1940; ed. at Eton: *m.* 1967, Helene, da. of Ministro Carlo de Franchis, of Rome, and has issue living, Francesco Charles, *b.* 1967.

          Granddaughter of the late Francis Richard Sutton, 3rd son of the late Rev.
             Robert Sutton (ante):—
   Issue of the late Richard Coningsby Sutton, *b.* 1882, *d.* 1905: *m.* 1904, Katharine Helen, who *d.* 1925, da. of the late Francis Foljambe Anderson, of Lea, Lincoln [Anderson, Bt.]:—
Olinda Margaret (posthumous), *b.* 1906: *m.* 1934, Maj. Donald Hammick Gawne, late KOR Regt., and has issue living, Robert Atholl, *b.* 1936: *m.* 1966, Kae Fraser, and has issue living, Kelly Robert *b.* 1970, Kevin Donald *b.* 1971, John Francis, *b.* 1930: *m.* 1964, Hilary Ann Medforth, and has issue living, Nicola Caroline *b.* 1967, Amanda Louise *b.* 1971.   *Residence*, The Wash, West Coker, Yeovil.

          Grandchildren of the late Capt. Frederick Sutton, 3rd son of the late Capt.
             Robert Nassau Sutton (ante) :—
   Issue of the late Algernon Charles Sutton, *b.* 1852, *d.* 1932: *m.* 1886, Winifred Alice, da. of William Edwin Cotton Fell, formerly of Lochrin, Edinburgh :—
Frederick Nassau, *b.* 1888.——Irene Winifred, *b.* 1892 : *m.* 1926, Major Henry Edmund Bark-worth, who *d.* (on active ser. during European War) 1940, and has issue living, Susan Althea, *b.* 1927,—Rosemary Anne, *b.* 1928: *m.* 1948, Maj. Charles Ronald Croker Elverson, of The Acres, Cotleigh, Honiton, Devon, and has issue living, Ronald Peter Charles *b.* 1950, John Henry Patrick *b.* 1951, Christopher William *b.* 1955,—Verbena Clarice, *b.* 1932: *m.* 1954, William Brian Evans, of Deildre, Llandinam, Montgomeryshire, and has issue living, Julian William Barkworth *b.* 1963, Camilla Jane *b.* 1960, Rosamund Sarah (twin), *b.* 1963.   *Residence*, Winham House, Westcott, Cullompton, Devon.

          Granddaughter of the late Herbert Arthur Sutton, 5th son of the late Capt.
             Frederick Sutton (ante) :—
   Issue of the late Roland Manners Verney Sutton, *b.* 1895, *d.* 1957 : *m.* 1927, Dora (of Crossways, Gibbet Hill Road, Coventry), da. of Elijah Whitehurst, formerly of Overdale, Brinnington, Stockport :—
Ursula Constance, *b.* 1929: *m.* 1963, Norman Yearsley, of Windbrow, 307 Cromwell Lane, Burton Green, Kenilworth, and has issue living, Jonathan Manners, *b.* 1968.

          Grandchildren of the late Rev. Charles Nassau Sutton, yst. son of the late
             Capt. Frederick Sutton (ante):—
   Issue of the late Maj. Charles Lexington Manners Sutton, M.B.E., *b.* 1891, *d.* 1962: *m.* 1st, 1917, Amabel Anne (who obtained a divorce, 1932), da. of Major Ludlow Coape Ludlow, of Beech Green, Withyham, Sussex; 2ndly, 1932, Gladys Louise (RICHARDSON) (of Tinker's Dell, Etchingham, Sussex), da. of Percy Gubb:—
(By 1st marriage) John Charles Ludlow Manners (of Willerby Wold Farm, Staxton, Scarborough) *b.* 1921: *m.* 1946, Daphne Agnes, only da. of William Francis Wormald, J.P., and has issue living, Richard Manners, *b.* 1947,—William Reginald Manners, *b.* 1949,—Oliver Ludlow Manners, *b.* 1950.——(By 2nd marriage) Philippa Mary, *b.* 1936: *m.* 1956, Derek Walter Pryke, of Tinker's Dell, Etchingham, Sussex, and has issue living, Kelham Charles Derek, *b.* 1959,—Timothy John Manners, *b.* 1961,—Flavia Anne, *b.* 1957.

   Roland de Sutton, of Sutton upon Trent, Notts.: *m.* Alice, da. of Richard de Lexington (now spelt Laxton), and sister and co-heir of Robert de Lexington, of Averham, Notts., which manor was inherited by their son Robert de Sutton, who *d.* 1281.   William Sutton of Averham (or Aram), Notts. was father of Robert, who was cr. *Baron Lexington*, of Aram 1645 (which peerage became ext. in 1723, and whose da. and heiress *m.* the 3rd Duke of Rutland), and Henry, grandfather of the Rt. Hon. Sir Robert Sutton.   The 1st baronet, Sir Richard Sutton (son of the late Rt. Hon. Sir Robert Sutton, KB, a distinguished diplomat) sat as MP for St. Albans 1768-80, for Sandwich 1780-84, and for Boroughbridge 1784-96, and was an Under-Secretary of State 1766-72.   Capt. Sir Richard Vincent Sutton, MC, 1st Life Gds. and Capt. and Adj., Machine Gun Regt., who *s.* as 6th Bt. at his birth, in April 1891, *d.* (on active ser. during 1914-18 War) Nov. 1918.

SWANN, Creation (U.K.) 1906, of Prince's Gardens, Royal Borough of Kensington.

Sir ANTHONY CHARLES CHRISTOPHER SWANN, *C.M.G.*, *O.B.E.*, 3rd *Baronet ; b.* June 29th, 1913 ; *s.* his father, *Sir* (CHARLES) DUNCAN, 1962 ; ed. at Eton, and at New Coll., Oxford (MA); formerly Min. of Defence and Home Security, Kenya ; Major (retired) King's African Rifles ; O.B.E. (Civil) 1950, C.M.G. 1958 : *m.* 1940, Jean Margaret, da. of the late John Herbert Niblock-Stuart, of Nairobi, Kenya, and has issue.

Arms—Azure, a swan rousant proper within an orle of lymphads, sails furled, flags flying to the dexter, or.   Crest— Between two buffalo's horns a demi-swan wings expanded, all proper.

   Residence—23, Montpelier Sq., S.W.7.   *Clubs*—Carlton, Pratt's, Beefsteak.

Son living—MICHAEL CHRISTOPHER (Foxhanger, Bur-wash, Sussex), *b.* Sept. 23rd, 1941; ed. at Eton; late 60th Rifles: *m.* 1965, the Hon. Lydia Mary Hewitt, el. da. of 8th Viscount Lifford, and has issue living, Jonathan Chris-topher, *b.* 1966,—Tessa Margaret, *b.* 1969.

Collateral Branches living.

Granddaughters of the late Harold Swann, 2nd son of 1st baronet, *b.* 1880, *d.* 1953: *m.* 1907, Dorothea Alma, who *d.* 1969, da. of the late Henry De Courcy Agnew [Agnew, Bt., *cr.* 1629, colls.]:—

Issue of the late Charles Brian Swann, *b.* 1913, *d.* 1966: *m.* 1st, 1939, Vanessa (from whom he obtained a divorce 1955), da. of Ernest William Dalrymple Tennant; 2ndly, 1955, Ann Corben, da. of Cyril Alwyn Harrison:—

(By 1st m.) Julia Vanessa, *b.* 1940: *m.* 1960, Blyth Metcalf Thompson, of Applecross, 150, Empire Pl., Sandhurst, Johannesburg, S. Africa, and has issue living, William Rowland Blyth, *b.* 1962,—Dendy Martin Blyth, *b.* 1972,—Vanessa Eirene, *b.* 1961,—Moya Ann, *b.* 1965,—Hannah Yvonne, *b.* 1967,—Sonya Suzanne, *b.* 1969.——Karin Clarissa, *b.* 1942.——Virginia Caroline, *b.* 1948: *m.* 1971, David Winkfield Hughes, of Mid Lambrook Manor, S. Petherton, Yeovil, and has issue living, Harriet Elfreda, *b.* 1972.

Grandchildren of the late Geoffrey Swann (infra):—

Issue of the late Major Kenneth Geoffrey Swann, M.C., R.A., *b.* 1915, *d.* (killed in action during European War) 1944: *m.* 1942, Delmira Marion (who *d.* 1947, having *m.* 2ndly, 1947, Peter Richard Hampton), da. of Sir (Ferdinand) Michael Kroyer-Kielberg, K.B.E. :—

Christopher Kenneth, *b.* 1942.——Penelope Ann, *b.* 1944.

Issue of the late Geoffrey Swann, 4th son of 1st baronet; *b.* 1883; *d.* 1965: *m.* 1911, Florence Mildred, who *d.* 1964, da. of John Brodie:—

Janet Elizabeth, *b.* 1913; a JP for Herts.: *m.* 1939, Charles Gifford Bardswell, late Sqdn.-Ldr. RAFVR, of The Grange, Walkern, nr. Stevenage, Herts , and has issue living, Charles Nicholas, *b.* 1941: *m.* 1969, Sarah Josephine, el. da. of Sir (Thomas) Leslie Rowan, KCB, CVO, and has issue living, Catherine Jane Elizabeth *b.* 1971, Alice Victoria Josephine *b.* 1974,—Philip Geoffrey, *b.* 1948: *m.* 1973, Alexandra Augusta, only child of Iver Lunn, of Towersey, Oxon.,—Veronica Elizabeth, *b.* 1945: *m.* 1974, Roger Gayner Broadie-Griffith.——Phyllis Mildred, *b.* 1919: *m.* 1946, John Charles Fegen, DSC, late Lt. RNVR, of Twickenham House, Ballycumber, co. Offaly, and has issue living, Richard Kenneth, *b.* 1947,—Frances Lynette, *b.* 1950,—Lucy Mildred, *b.* 1953.——Kathleen Prudence, *b.* 1921: *m.* 1945, Allan Priestley Thomson, late Capt. NZ Engineers, and State Forest Ser., of 21, Lochiel Rd., Wellington, N5, NZ, and has issue living, Michael Kenneth, *b.* 1951,—Peter Geoffrey, *b.* 1955,—Andrew Brodie, *b.* 1958,—Celia Margaret *b.* 1946: *m.* 1970, Brian Herbert Bockett, and has issue living, Kirsten *b.* 1974.

The Rt. Hon. Sir Charles Ernest Swann, 1st Bt. (son of the late Frederick Schwann, of 23, Gloucester Square, W.), sat as M.P. for N. Div. of Manchester (*L*) 1886-1918, and assumed by Roy. licence, 1913, for himself and his issue, the surname of Swann in lieu of his patronymic.

SWINBURNE, Creation (E.) 1660, of Capheaton, Northumberland. [Extinct 1967.]

Sir SPEARMAN CHARLES SWINBURNE, *MRCS, LRCP,* 10th and last *Baronet.* *Residence,*—Great Maytham, Rolvenden. Kent.

aughter living of 9th Baronet—Ida, *b.* 1899: *m.* 1st, 1929, Ronald D. S. Steuart; 2ndly, 1945, Cdr. D. H. Rainier, DSO, RN. *Residence,* Strone, North Knapdale, by Lochgilphead, Argyllshire.

Daughter living of 8th Baronet—Joan Mary, *b.* 1906: *m.* 1937, Richard Granville Browne, who assumed by deed poll 1937 the additional surname of Swinburne, and has issue living, John *b.* 1937: *m.* 1966, Susan, da. of Anthony Comar Wilson, and has issue living, William *b.* 1967,—Alice *b.* 1968,—Rosalind Mary, *b.* 1939: *m.* 1966, Francesco Parlade, of Marbella, Spain, and has issue living, Jaimie *b.* 1967, Marie Anna *b.* 1971, Teresa *b.* 1974. *Residence,* Capheaton Hall, Newcastle upon Tyne.

Swinnerton (Milborne-Swinnerton-Pilkington), see Pilkington.

SYKES, Creation (G.B.) 1781, of Basildon, Berkshire.

He is wise who is assiduous.

Sir FRANCIS GODFREY SYKES, 9th *Baronet,* son of the late Francis William Sykes, son of the late Rev. John Heath Sykes, son of the late Rev. William Sykes, 2nd son of 2nd baronet ; *b.* Aug. 27th, 1907 ; *s.* his kinsman, the *Rev. Sir* FREDERIC JOHN, 1956: *m.* 1st, 1934, Eira Betty, who *d.* 1970, only da. of the late George Wallace Badcock, of Hove, and Steyning, Sussex; 2ndly, 1972, Nesta Mabel, da. of the late Harold Platt Sykes, of Beckbury Hall, Shifnal, Salop, and has issue by 1st m.

Arms—Argent, an eagle rising between three sykes or fountains proper ; on a canton gules, a caduceus of the first. **Crest**—A demi-lady in the complete dress of that country, holding in her dexter hand a rose gules. *Residence*—White Lodge, Bishop's Castle, Salop SY9 5DP.

Son living—By 1st m.—FRANCIS JOHN BADCOCK (Thornhill, Warnborough, Swindon, Wilts.), *b.* June 7th, 1942; ed. at Shrewsbury, and Worcester Coll., Oxford (MA); Solicitor 1968; partner in legal firm of Townsends, Swindon: *m.* 1966, Susan Alexandra, da. of Adm. Sir Edward Beckwith Ashmore, GCB, DSC, of South Cottage, Headley Down, Hants. [*see* Sturdee, Bt., (ext.)], and has issue living, Francis Charles, *b.* 1968,—Edward William, *b.* 1970,—Alexander Henry Ashmore, *b.* 1974.

Daughter living—By 1st m.—Elizabeth Ann Bowen (c/o Bedford Coll., Regents Park, NW1), *b.* 1936; MSc London; PhD Edinburgh.

Brothers living—John Patrick (12, Hobbs Av., Dalkeith, W. Aust. 6009), *b.* 1909: *m.* 1955, Patricia Cecily Little.——Edward Heath (7, Star Court, Pittville Circus Rd., Cheltenham), *b.* 1912; is a FCA: *m.* 1st, 1957, Joan Margaret Boston, who *d.* 1963; 2ndly, 1964, Doris, da. of the late William Henry Cowsill, of Hale, Ches.——Paul Lionel (143, Merrigang St., Bowral, NSW, 2576), *b.* 1915: *m.* 1946, Mrs. Ann Stewart.

Sisters living—Beatrice Honora (22, Station Rd., Pershore, Worcs.), *b.* 1910: *m.* 1949, Cdr. Frederick D'Oyly Nind, RN, who *d.* 1962.——Mary Agatha, *b.* 1913: *m.* 1944, William Thomas Moran Gilbert, LRCPI, LRCSI, Colonial Med. Ser., who *d.* 1970. *Address,* c/o Lloyds Bank, 125, Oxford St., W1.——Janet Edith, *b.* 1916. *Address,* 15, Snake Lane, Alvechurch, Worcs.

Collateral Branches living.

Grandchildren of the late Rev. John Heath Sykes, yst. son of the Rev. William Sykes, 2nd son of 2nd baronet:—
Issue of the late Lieut.-Col. William Sykes, *b.* 1867, *d.* 1950 : *m.* 1896, Eleanor Mary, who *d.* 1958. da. of the late Capt. Henry Naylor :—
John Henry (Flat 27, Cleevemont, Evesham Rd., Cheltenham), *b.* 1896; ed. at Christ's Hosp.; Brig. Indian Army (ret.); 1915-18 War, Palestine 1918-20, NW Frontier of India 1930-31 (despatches), 1939-45 War (despatches): *m.* 1st, 1919, Leila, who *d.* 1970, da. of the late D. S. Macphee; 2ndly, 1971, Florence Kathleen, da. of William Turner, and widow of (I) James Mackay, and (II) Sir (Stanley) Herbert Howard, and has issue living (by 1st m.), Margery Hope *b.* 1921.——*Rev.* Paul Carton (Dowty House, St. Margaret's Rd., Cheltenham, Glos.), *b.* 1903: *m.* 1943, Hendrika Pieternella van Vlaanderen.——Richard Alexander (Elmley Castle, Pershore, Worcs.), *b.* 1912; 1939-45 War with R. Gloucestershire Hussars: *m.* 1942, Freda Serita Field, and has issue living, William David, *b.* 1946; ed. at St. Edward's Sch., Oxford,—Anthony Richard John, *b.* 1950; ed. at St. Edward's Sch., Oxford.—Alice Margery, *b.* 1904: *m.* 1966, E. G. Morrison, of Larkrise, East End, Lymington, Hants.

Granddaughter of the late Brig. John Henry Sykes, late Indian Army, el. son of the late Lt. Col. William Sykes (ante), *b.* 1896, *d.* 1975: *m.* 1st, 1919, Leila, Flowerden, who *d.* 1970, da. of the late D. S. Macphee, of Glasgow; 2ndly, 1971, Florence Kathleen (Flat 27, Cleevemont, Evesham Rd., Cheltenham), da. of William Turner, and widow of (i) James Mackay, and (ii) Sir (Stanley) Herbert Howard:—
(By 1st m.), Margery Hope, *b.* 1921.

Grandson of the late Frederick Sykes, 4th son of the Rev. John Heath Sykes:—
Issue of the late Frederick Heath Cyril Sykes, *b.* 1897, *d.* 1959: *m.* 1934, Judith Helen (705, Park Av., Nanaimo, BC, Canada), da. of Wyndham Henry Stubbs, of The Leasowes, Cressage, Salop.:—
Harry Wyndham (PO Box 1345, Peace River, Alberta, Canada, TOH 2XO), *b.* 1936: *m.* 1956, Magdalena Amelia, da. of Edward Julius Schulze, of Grande Pairie, Alberta, and has issue living, Ronald Frederick, *b.* 1963,—Dianne Lea, *b.* 1957,—Patricia Lynn, *b.* 1960.
Grandchildren of the late Rev. John Heath Sykes (infra):—

Issue of the late Alfred Sykes, *b.* 1872, *d.* 1954 : *m.* 1902, Scènie Marguerite Genelle, who *d.* 19— :—
Marcedèsse Doyley, *b.* 1904: *m.* 1st, 1932, R. Alston Jones; 2ndly, 1947, Brock R. Darling, and has issue living, (by 1st m.) George Sykes, *b.* 1935.——Gwendolyn Doyley Scènie, *b.* 1906: *m.* 1932, George Michael Holley. *Residence,* 944, Euclid St., Santa Monica, California, USA.

Issue of the late Edward Ernest Sykes, *b.* 1876, *d.* 1950 : *m.* 1910, Rosalind, who *d.* 1949, da. of Engineer-Com. J. Clements, R.N., and widow of N. Fitzstubbs :—
Clement Edward Heath (Pt. Atkinson Light Station, Beacon Lane, W. Vancouver, BC, Canada) *b.* 1911; ed. at Univ. Mil. Sch., Victoria, BC; Engineer Officer, British and Canadian Merchant Navy 1932-41, and as Engineer Capt., US Army, S. Pacific 1942-46: *m.* 1951, Isabel L., da. of Robert Parry, of N. Wales, and has issue living, Sean Edward Heath, *b.* 1953,—David Robert Heath, *b.* 1954,—Sheila Anne Heath, *b.* 1952.——Dorothy Heath, *b.* 1914; 1939-45 War with Women's Roy. Canadian Naval Ser.: *m.* 19—, Lt. Richard D. Pepler, RNVR, of 7, Old Club House Rd., Old Greenwich, Conn., USA, and has issue living, Sally, *b.* 1950,—Judith, *b.* 1956.

This family have held lands in England from 1220, in which year they were described to be in possession of land previously held by them. The 1st baronet, Sir Francis, of Ackworth Pork, Chief Governor of Cossimbazar, Bengal, was successively M.P. for Shaftesbury and Wallingford. The 2nd baronet also sat as M.P. for Wallingford. The 8th baronet, the Rev. Sir Frederick John was V. of Stoke Canon, Exeter 1936-46.

SYKES, Creation (G.B.) 1783, of Sledmere, Yorkshire.

Sir (MARK TATTON) RICHARD SYKES, 7th *Baronet;* *b.* Aug. 24th, 1905; *s.* his father, *Col. Sir* (TATTON BENVENUTO) MARK, *M.P.,* 1919; ed. at Downside, and at Trin. Coll., Camb.; Capt. 7th Batn. Green Howards (TA); granted rank of Lt.-Col. 1952, JP (Chm) and DL for E. Riding of Yorks. (co. Alderman 1946-70); High Sheriff of Yorks. 1948; Pres. of E. Riding Georgian Soc., and Northern Counties Concert Soc.; a member of Jockey Club since 1947; Pres. of Bridlington Conservative Assocn. since 1948; 1939-45 War in France: *m.* 1942, Virginia, who *d.* 1970, only da. of the late Capt. John Francis Grey Gilliat [Chetwynd, Bt.], and has issue.

Arms—Argent, a chevron sable between three sykes or fountains proper. **Crest**—A demi-triton issuant from flags or reeds, blowing a shell, and wreathed about the temples with like flags or reeds, all proper.
Seat—Sledmere, Driffield, Yorkshire.

Sons living—TATTON CHRISTOPHER MARK, *b.* Dec. 24th, 1943.——Jeremy John, *b.* **1946.**
——Christopher Simon, *b.* 1948.——Richard Nicholas Bernard, *b.* 1953.

Daughters living—Arabella Lilian Virginia, *b.* 1950: *m.* 1975, Kevin Delahanty.——Henrietta
Caroline Rose, *b.* 1957.

Brother living—Christopher Hugh, *b.* 1907; ed. at Downside, and Ch. Ch., Oxford; Capt. Special
Air Ser. Regt. (TA); FRSL: *m.* 1936, Camilla Georgiana, da. of the late Maj.-Gen. Sir Thomas
Wentworth Russell, KBE, CMG [*see* D. Bedford, colls.], and has issue living, Mark Richard,
b. 1937; ed. at Downside, and at Ch. Ch., Oxford: *m.* 1st, 1962 (m. diss. 1965), Helen, only da. of
the late Dr. Arthur Norman Homewood, of Melbourne, Aust.; 2ndly, 1968, Valerie, da. of
Robert Goad, and has issue living (by 2nd m.), a son *b.* 1974, Lucy *b.* 1969, Victoria (twin) *b.*
1969, Alice *b.* 19—.   *Residence*, Swyre House, Swyre, Dorchester.

Sisters living—Mary Freya (*Lady Elwes*), *b.* 1904: *m.* 1926, Sir Richard Everard Augustine Elwes,
OBE, TD, who *d.* 1968 [E. Denbigh], and has issue living, Mark Gervase (34, Grand Av., N10), *b.*
1931: *m.* 1963, Valerie, el. da. of Norford Bland, of Luton, and has issue living, Benjamin Mark
b. 1965, Tabitha Mary *b.* 1964,—Hugh Damian (98, Clapham Common N. Side, SW4), *b.* 1943: *m.*
1974, Susan Annabel. da. of D. W. J. Buchanan, of Sydney, NSW,—Mary Freya (Polly), *b.* 1928:
m. 1960, Peter Dimmock, CVO, OBE, of 41, Addison Av., Holland Park, W11, and has issue
living, Amanda Winifred *b.* 1961, Christina Mary *b.* 1963, Freya Pauline *b.* 1966,—Ruth Angela
Mary, *b.* 1930: *m.* 1956, Hew Dalrymple Fanshawe, of Waterside House, London Colney, St.
Albans, Herts., and has issue living, Simon George *b.* 1957, Christopher Paul *b.* 1958, Peter James
b. 1964, Catherine Mary *b.* 1960, Mary Freya *b.* 1963,—Jessica Mary, *b.* 1942.   *Residence*, 23,
Norfolk Mansions, Prince of Wales Drive, SW11.——Everilda (twin), *b.* 1907: *m.* 1928, Lt.-Col.
Adrian Cuthbert Scrope, OBE, late Green Howards, and has issue living, Christopher Ralph, *b.*
1931,—John Frederick, *b.* 1932 (Green End, Dane End, Herts.): *m.* 1965, Jennifer Frances, da. of
Richard Harry Bott, and has issue living, Christopher Richard Adrian *b.* 1970, Thomas Oscar
b. 1972, Maria Mercedes *b.* 1966,—William James Conyers, *b.* 1938,—Adrian Richard, *b.* 1949,—
Sarah Edith Mary, *b.* 1930: *m.* 1953, David Keith Ford Heathcote, of Badlingham Manor,
Chippenham, Ely, Cambs., and has issue living, John *b.* 1954, James, *b.* 19—, Teresa *b.* 1955,—
Teresa Mary, *b.* 1941,—Alexandra Maria Mercedes, *b.* 1943.   *Residences*, Plantation Stud,
Exning, Newmarket, Suffolk; 8, Donne Place, Chelsea, SW3.——Angela Christina (*Countess of
Antrim*), *b.* 1911; Hon. LLD Queen's Univ.: *m.* 1934, the 8th Earl of Antrim.   *Residence*,
Glenarm Castle, Glenarm, co. Antrim; 14, Moore St., SW3.

The 1st baronet, the Rev. Sir Mark, was son of Richard Sykes, an eminent merchant in Hull;
the 2nd baronet, Sir Christopher, sat as M.P. for Beverley; the third baronet, Sir Mark, was High
Sheriff and M.P. for York 1807-20; and the 4th baronet was the well-known sportsman, Sir Tatton
Sykes.   Sir Tatton, 5th baronet, was High Sheriff of Yorkshire 1869.   The 6th baronet, Sir Mark,
was Private Sec. to Ch. Sec. for Ireland 1904-05, MP for Central Div. of Hull (C) 1911-18, and for
Kingston-upon-Hull, Central Div. Dec. 1918-19, and served during 1914-18 War as Col. 5th Batn
Yorkshire Regt., and as Assist. Sec to War Cabinet; Signatory to the Sykes-Picot Agreement
1917.

SYKES, Creation (U.K.) 1921, of Kingsknowes, Galashiels, co. Selkirk.

Sir JOHN CHARLES ANTHONY LE GALLAIS
SYKES, 3rd *Baronet; b.* April 19th, 1928; *s.* his
uncle, *Sir* (BENJAMIN) HUGH, 1974; ed. at
Churchers Coll.: *m.* 1954 (m. diss. 1970), Aitha
Isobel, yr. da. of Lionel Dean, of Hazeldene,
New Mill, Huddersfield.

Arms—Per chevron gules and sable, in chief two sykes
(fountains) proper, and in base a fleece or.   **Crest**—A cubit arm,
habited in a khaki sleeve and holding in the hand a teazle
slipped and leaved proper.

Residence—Chateau Sykes, 83, The Park, Redbourn,
Herts.

Brother living—MICHAEL LE GALLAIS, *b.* Jan. 4th, 1932; ed.
at Trent Coll.: *m.* 1953, Joan, only da. of Cecil Groom, of
14, Highfield Rd., Nuthall, Notts. and has issue living,
David Michael, *b.* 1954,—Christopher Cary, *b.* 1959.

Sister living—Mary le Gallais, *b.* 1926: *m.* 1948, Douglas
Gordon Price, of 34, Cheltenham Rd., Bishops Cleeve,
Cheltenham, and has issue living, Michael Charles Gordon,
b. 1951,—Richard John Douglas, *b.* 1955.

Uncle living (son of 1st baronet)—Charles Newsome, *b.* 1899;
ed. at Trin. Coll., Camb. (BA 1921, MA 1927).

Widow living of 2nd Baronet—AUDREY WINIFRED (*Audrey, Lady Sykes*), (19, Bouverie Gdns.,
Harrow, Middx., HA3 0RQ), da. of Frederick Charles Thompson, of Cricklewood, NW2: *m.*
1935, Sir (Benjamin) Hugh Sykes, 2nd Bt., who *d.* 1974.

The 1st baronet, Sir Charles Sykes, K.B.E. (son of the late Benjamin Sykes), was a woollen
manufacturer, and was M.P. for Huddersfield (Co. L.) 1918-22.

SYNGE, Creation (U.K.) 1801, of Kiltrough.

[Name pronounced "Sing."]

We sing of heavenly things.

Sir ROBERT CARSON SYNGE, 8th *Baronet*, son of the late Neale Hutchinson Synge, 2nd son of 6th baronet; *b.* May 4th, 1922; *s.* his uncle, *Sir* ROBERT MILLINGTON, 1942: *m.* 1944, Dorothy Jean, da. of Theodore Johnson, of Cloverdale, British Columbia, and has issue.

    Arms—Quarterly: 1st and 4th, azure, three millstones proper; 2nd and 3rd, argent, an eagle displayed with two heads sable, beaked and legged gules. Crest—Out of a ducal coronet or, an eagle's claw proper.

    Residence—19364, Fraser Valley Highway, R.R.4, Langley, BC, Canada.

Daughters living—Donna Joan, *b.* 1946: *m.* 1967, Richard David Harvey.——Wendy Marleen, *b.* 1949.

Sister living—Patricia Neale, *b.* 1924: *m.* 1948, Emerson Edgar Barden. *Residence*, 14227, 110th Avenue, North Surrey, British Columbia.

Aunt living (daughter of 6th baronet)—Jessica Helen (c/o Lloyds Bank, High St., Berkhamsted, Herts.), *b.* 1914: *m.* 1940 (m. diss. 1949), Fl.-Lt. Alfred Davidson Colin Cleugh Fair, RAF.

Collateral Branches living.

Issue of the late Edward Synge, yst. son of 6th baronet, *b.* 1882, *d.* 1966: *m.* 1901, Agnes Emily, da. of James Jelley:—
NEALE FRANCIS, *b.* Feb. 28th, 1917: *m.* 1939, Katherine Caroline Bowes, and has issue living, Allen James Edward, *b.* 1942,—Sharon Eilleen, *b.* 1943.——Molly Eileen, *b.* 1908: *m.* 1929, Raymond Augustus McCarthy, and has issue living, Raymond Edward, *b.* 1930: *m.* 1950, Helen, da. of Roy Dagg, of Prince George, BC, and has issue living, Sharon Patricia *b.* 1951,—Harold Douglas, *b.* 1934,—Stanley Norman, *b.* 1941.

    Granddaughter of the late Edward Synge (ante):—
Issue of the late Edward Synge, *b.* 1902, *d.* 1928: *m.* 1925, Alma (Apt. 206, 1050, W. 10th Av., Vancouver, BC), da. of Martin Hansen:—
Marjorie Irene, *b.* 1926: *m.* 1946, William Thomas Kidner, of 1005, Beaumont St., N., Vancouver, BC, Canada, and has issue living, Jacquelyn Ann, *b.* 1951,—Patricia Lynn, *b.* 1952.

    Issue of the late Edward John Hutchinson Synge, 2nd son of 5th baronet, *b.* 1854, *d.* 1886: *m.* 1883, Leila Camilla, who *d.* 1935, da. of Charles Pemberton:—
Olive Marguerite (of Rose Cottage, Shotesham-All-Saints, Norwich), *b.* 1886: *m.* 1908, Claud Barton, who *d.* 1962, and has issue living, Andrew Synge, *b.* 1909; ed. at Winchester, and at Magdalene Coll., Camb. (BA 1931); Maj. (ret.) R.E., MICE: *m.* 1939, Gertrude Ursula Désirée, da. of the late Maj. Gordon Bluett Winch, DSO, and has issue living, Christopher Synge (Glann Arrow, Eardisland, nr. Leominster), *b.* 1942; ed. at Stowe: *m.* 1965, Catherine Anne, da. of Sir John Ledward Royden, 4th Bt. (and has issue living, James Edward *b.* 1974, Sarah Melissa Synge *b.* 1970),—Geoffrey Bluett *b.* 1946,—Diana Synge, *b.* 1914: *m.* 1961, Jacques Alois Hervé, of The Winter Palace, Av. Riviera, Menton, France AM,—Judith Camilla Synge, *b.* 1916.

    Grandson of the late Major Robert Follett Synge, el. son of the late Rev. Robert Synge, 3rd son of 1st baronet:—
Issue of the late Lieut.-Col. Robert Follett Muter Foster Millington Synge, *b.* 1857, *d.* 1941: *m.* 1884, Charlotte Granville (who *d.* 1942, having obtained a judicial separation 1900), da. of Maj.-Gen. William James Stuart, formerly R.E.:—
Alan Hamilton Stuart, *b.* 1886; ed. at Wellington Coll.; European War 1914-19 with R.F.C.: *m.* 1920, Alice May Bradley, of Washington, U.S.A. *Residence*,

    Grandchildren of the late Francis Julian Synge, 2nd son of William Webb Follett Synge (infra):—
Issue of the late Capt. Robert Millington Synge, *b.* 1894, *d.* 1964: *m.* 1922, Christabel Etrenne (Butt's Gate, Wisborough Green, Sussex), da. of the late Charles Lyon Liddell, of The Place House, Peasmarsh, Sussex [see B. Ravensworth, colls.]:—
Allen John Millington (37, Blackheath Park, S.E.3), *b.* 1930; ed. at Trin. Coll., Dublin: *m.* 1955, Olive Rachel, da. of Thomas Weir, of Ballymena, co. Antrim, and has issue living, Daniel Thomas Millington, *b.* 1963,—Timothy Auchmuty, *b.* 1968,—Frances Clare, *b.* 1959.——Pamela Mary, *b.* 1923; 1939-45 War in Middle East (despatches): *m.* 1966, Charles William Fane, of Ashmansworth Manor, Newbury, [see E. Westmorland, colls.].——Gillian Frances, *b.* 1933: *m.* 1952, Lt.-Col. George Stanley Ames, US Marine Corps, of 305, Old Pickhard Rd., Concord, Mass. USA, and has issue living, Richard Millington, *b.* 1955,—John Bruton, *b.* 1960,—Robert Oakes *b.* 1969,—Elizabeth Whiting, *b.* 1953.

    Grandsons of the late William Makepeace Thackeray Synge, yst. son of William Webb Follett Synge, 4th son of the late Rev. Robert Synge (ante):—
Issue of the late Capt. William Alfred Thackeray Synge, *b.* 1893, *d.* 1968: *m.* 1920, Hilda Marjorie, who *d.* 1967, da. of Eben Pike, formerly of Kilcrenagh, co. Cork:—
Brian Thackeray (4, Pembroke Close, Grosvenor Cres., SW1), *b.* 1920; formerly Hon. Maj. Irish Gds.; a Serving Brother of Order of St. John of Jerusalem: *m.* 1945 (m. diss. 1970), Alison Patricia, da. of Brig. Victor Francis Staples Hawkins, DSO, MC, late Lancashire Fusiliers, and has issue living, Barry Edward Thackeray, *b.* 1949,—Mark Millington, *b.* 1953,—Norah Melanie, *b.* 1947: *m.* 1969 Anthony Elliott (Box 40075, Nairobi, Kenya), and has issue living, Rupert Francis William *b.* 1970, Francesca Elisabeth *b.* 1972.——John Millington, *b.* 1923.

    The family of Synge was seated at Bridgnorth early in the 16th century, the original name of Millington having been changed to Synge. The Rt. Rev. Dr. Samuel Hutchinson, Lord Bishop of Kilala, was father of Sir James Hutchinson, 1st Bt. (cr. 1782, ext. 1906) who sat as M.P. for James-town in Irish Parliament. The Rev. Sir Samuel Synge, 3rd Bt., grand-nephew of the 1st and 2nd baronets, *s.* under special remainder, and assumed the additional surname and arms of Hutchinson; his 2nd brother, Robert, was cr. a baronet as above. Sir Edward Synge, 3rd Bt. (cr. 1801), was High Sheriff of co. Cork 1844.

LAWSON-TANCRED, Creation (E.) 1662, of Boroughbridge, Yorkshire.

Aimez Dieu.
Love God.

Sir HENRY LAWSON-TANCRED, 10th *Baronet ; b.* Feb. 12th, 1924 ; *s.* his father, *Major Sir* THOMAS SELBY, 1945 ; ed. at Stowe, and at Jesus Coll., Camb.; a JP of W. Riding of Yorks; 1939-45 War as Flying Officer, RAFVR: *m.* 1950, Jean Veronica, who *d.* 1970, da. of the late Gerald Robert Foster [Ogilvy, Bt.], and has issue.

Arms—Argent, a chevron between three escallops gules. Crest—An olive tree fructed proper.

Residence—Aldborough Manor, Boroughbridge, Yorkshire.

Sons living—ANDREW PETER, *b.* Feb. 18th, 1952; ed. at Eton.——Rupert Thomas, *b.* 1953; ed. at Gordonstoun.——James Gilchrist Henry, *b.* 1956; ed. at Trin. Coll., Glenalmond.——Gerald Nicholas, *b.* 1961,——Alastair David, *b.* 1964.

Daughter living—Finella Mary, *b.* 1959.

Brother living—*Rev.* Christopher (twin), (28, Harcourt Rd., Uckfield, Sussex), *b.* 1924; ed. at Stowe, and at Trin. Coll., Camb.; Bar. Lincoln's Inn 1950; 1939-45 War as FO RAFVR: *m.* 1951, Cerise Eyre Campbell, el. da. of Sir Hugh Eyre Campbell Beaver, and has issue living, Hugh Christopher, *b.* 1955,—Cerise Elinor, *b.* 1952,—Olivia Eyre, *b.* 1957.

Sisters living.—Elinor Mary, *b.* 1913.——Pauline, *b.* 1916: *m.* 1937, Frank Douglas Nicholson, and has issue living, Paul Douglas (Quarry Hill, Brancepeth, co. Durham), *b.* 1938: *m.* 1970, Sarah, yst. da. of Sir Edmund Castell Bacon, KG, KBE, TD, 13th Bt.,—Nigel Frank, *b.* 1940,—Andrew, *b.* 1945: *m.* 1972, Angela, da. of Vice-Adm. Denis Bryan Harvey Wildish, CB,—Mark Thomas, *b.* 1950.—Frank, *b.* 1954. *Residence*, Southill Hall, Plawsworth, nr. Chester-le-Street, co. Durham.

Collateral Branches living.

Issue of the late Constance Anne Tancred, *b.* 1875, *d.* 1964, da. of 8th baronet: *m.* 1910, Alfred Robert Warren, who *d.* 1922:—

Reginald Tancred (30, Montpelier Sq., SW7), *b.* 1911; ed. at Bradfield and Univ. Coll., Oxford (MA, MB, BCh).——Phyllida Mary, *b.* 1913: *m.* 1939, Harold Denis White, MA, MB, BCh, of Burghfield, Shootersway, Berkhamsted, Herts., and has issue living, Adrian Tancred (17, Pelham Place, SW7), *b.* 1940; ed. at Radley: *m.* 1966, the Hon. Jessica Jane Vronwy Scott-Ellis, da. of 9th Baron Howard de Walden, and has issue living, Nicholas John Sebastian *b.* 1967, Simon James Alexander *b.* 1968, Richard Dominic Edward *b.* 1970,—Anthony Selby *b.* 1948; ed. at Radley.

Grandson of the late Clement William Tancred, 4th son of 7th baronet:—
Issue of the late Christopher Humphrey Tancred, OBE, *b.* 1888, *d.* 1971: *m.* 1st, 1915, (m. diss. 1923), Gladys Winifred, da. of the late Walter Chandler; 2ndly, 1927 (m. diss. 1938) Agnes Margery, da. of the late Samuel Henry Slater, CMG, CIE; 3rdly, 1938 (m. diss. 1943), Priscilla Nöel Cecilia, da. of John A. Barclay, of New York,; 4thly, 1944, Sadika (21, Lexham Gdns., W8 5JJ), da. of R. Miligui:—
(By 2nd m.) Anthony Christopher, *b.* 1930; ed. at Eton.

Issue of the late Seymer Mitford Tancred, 5th son of 7th baronet, *b.* 1856, *d.* 1929: *m.* 1896, Charlotte Dorothea, who *d.* 1955, da. of the late William Gillespie Dickson, LL.D., Sheriff Principal of Lanarkshire :—
Margaret Selby Tancred (11, Laleham Court, Chobham Rd., Woking), *b.* 1900: *m.* 1927, the Rev. Canon Crewe Chetwode Hamilton, who *d.* 1969, and has issue living, Guy Tancred (Shores Corner, Shores Rd., Horsell, Woking), *b.* 1931; MB, BS 1957: *m.* 1957, Elizabeth Georgia Arnold, da. of Alfred George Nelson Jones, and has issue living, Simon John Chetwode *b.* 1959, Thomas Guy *b.* 1965, Julia Elizabeth *b.* 1961, Sarah Katherine *b.* 1963.

Grandchildren of Harry George Tancred (infra):—
Issue of the late Bertram Selby Tancred, *b.* 1895, *d.* 1965: *m.* 1924, Elsa (83, Young St., New Plymouth, NZ), da. of A. V. Sims:—
Rex Selby Assheton (Seaview Dairy, Devon St. East, New Plymouth, NZ), *b.* 1925: *m.* 1948, Shirley Edith, da. of H. Box, and has issue living, Philip Rex, *b.* 1952,—Linda Joanna, *b.* 1954,—Susan Shirley, *b.* 1955.——Lyle Ashley (205, Frankley Rd., New Plymouth, NZ), *b.* 1933: *m.* 1959, Beverley Ethel, da. of Nelson Howard Bishop, of New Plymouth, NZ, and has issue living, Stephen Ashley, *b.* 1962.——Elwys Elsa, *b.* 1927: *m.* 19—, Archibald James Gamble, of 18, Quebec St., Kingston, Wellington, NZ.

Issue of the late Cecil Mount-Stewart Tancred, *b.* 1884, *d.* 19—: *m.* 1907——:—Emmie, *b.* 1908.

Issue of the late Harry George Tancred, son of 7th baronet, *b.* 1858, *d.* 1945: *m.* 1st, 1881, Emily Alicia de Courcy, who *d.* 1907, elder da. of the late Major Slingsby Bell, of Purneah, India, and The Bungalow, Napier, New Zealand ; 2ndly, 1908, Rosie Elphinstone, da. of the late Major Slingsby Bell, and widow of Henry Warren, of New Zealand :—
(By 1st m.)—Zillah Selby, *b.* 1893: *m.* 1915, Raymond F. M. Atkinson, and has issue living, Veronica Selby *b.* 1915: *m.* 1943, Gary Elmer Gorsline, of 4304, Jeffries Av., Burbank, Cal., USA 91505, and has issue living, Victoria Elizabeth Selby *b.* 1945: *m.* 1963, David Wayne Maske, of 6136, Auckland Av., N. Hollywood, Cal., USA, and has issue living, Michael Andrew *b.* 1964, Douglas Adam *b.* 1965, Julie Michelle *b.* 1970. *Residence*, 4021, Willow Crest Av., N. Hollywood, California, USA.

This family is descended from Richard Tankard, who soon after the Conquest was possessed of lands at Boroughbridge, where still remains the ancient family house. A Christopher Tancred founded a retreat for poor gentlemen at Whixley, and also scholarships at Oxford, Cambridge, and Lincoln's Inn. The 9th baronet, Major Sir Thomas Selby, Indian Army, assumed by deed poll the additional surname of Lawson 1914, having *m.* 1912 Margery Elinor, el. da. and co-heir of Andrew Sherlock Lawson of Aldborough Manor, Yorks. Sir John Grant Lawson, 1st Bt. (*cr.* 1905) was his yr. brother.

TANGYE, Creation (U.K.) 1912, of Glendorgal, St. Columb Minor, Cornwall.

[Extinct 1969.]

Sir BASIL RICHARD GILZEAN TANGYE, 2nd and last *Baronet*.

Daughter living of 2nd Baronet—Gitta Clarisse Gilzean, *b.* 1928.
Daughter living of 1st Baronet—Eileen Annie Gilzean, *b.* 1897: *m.* 1913, Frederick Nichols Marcy, who *d.* 1946. *Residence*, The Oaks, Copsale, Horsham, Sussex.

Widow living of 2nd Baronet—CLARISSE (*Lady Tangye*) (4, Farquhar Rd., Edgbaston, Birmingham), only da. of the late Baron Victor Schosberger de Tornya, of Tura, Hungary: *m.* 1924, Sir Basil Richard Gilzean Tangye, 2nd Bt., who *d.* 1969, when the title became ext.

Tapps-Gervis-Meyrick, see Meyrick.

TATE, Creation (U.K.) 1898, of Park Hill, Streatham, co. London.

Sir HENRY TATE, *T.D.*, 4th *Baronet; b.* June 29th, 1902; *s.* his father, *Sir* ERNEST WILLIAM, 1939; ed. at Uppingham; Hon. Lt.-Col. RWF; formerly Lt. Gren. Gds.; Co. Councillor for Rutland 1958-74; a DL 1964; Joint Master of Cottesmore Hounds 1946-58; High Sheriff of Rutland 1949; Chm. of Rutland Agric. Soc. 1948-68: *m.* 1927, Nairne, da. of the late Saxon Gregson-Ellis, JP, and has issue.

ⁿ**Arms**—Ermine, on a pale invected azure between four Cornish choughs proper two roses argent. **Crest**—A dexter arm embowed and vested azure, cuffed or, the arm charged with two roses argent, the hand grasping a pineapple erect slipped proper between two ears of wheat saltirewise all proper.

Residences—Preston Lodge, Withcote, Oakham LE15 8PP; Galltfaenan, Denbigh, N. Wales. *Clubs*—Buck's, Turf

Thincke and thancke.

Sons living—HENRY SAXON (708, Upper Roslyn Av., Montreal, Canada. *Clubs*—Buck's, RAC), *b.* Nov. 28th, 1931; ed. at Eton, and at Ch. Ch., Oxford; Lt. Life Guards (Army Emergency Reserve): *m.* 1953, Sheila Ann, el. da. of Duncan Robertson, of Llantysilio, Llangollen, and has issue living, Edward Nicolas, *b.* 1966,—Duncan *b.* 1968,—John, *b.* 1969,—Paul (twin), *b.* 1969.——William Nicolas, *b.* 1934; ed. at Eton, and at Ch. Ch., Oxford; is Lt. Gren. Gds. (Emergency Reserve): *m.* 1960, Sarah Rose, el. da. of Lt.-Col. A. J. C. Rose, of Dunira Garden House, Comrie, Perths., and has issue living, Rupert Sebastian, *b.* 1962,—Georgina Nairne, *b.* 1969. *Residence*, 51, Hamilton Terr., NW8. *Club*, Buck's.

Sisters living—Mildred Clara, *b.* 1894: *m.* 1st, 1922, Harry Winwood Robinson, who *d.* 1937. 2ndly, 1942, Squadron-Leader John Francis Mead, R.A.F. Vol. Reserve, who *d.* 1953.——Joan *b.* 1896: *m.* 1924, Lieut.-Col. Roderick Croil Lloyd, DSO, MC, TD, who *d.* 1972, and has issue living, Simon Croil *b.* 1925,—Jane Isla, *b.* 1929. *Residence*, White House, Llandyrnog, Denbighshire.

Aunt living (da. of 2nd baronet)—Beatrice Maud, *b.* 1883: *m.* 1907, Robert Holme Storey, JP, who *d.* 1956. *Residence*, Home Farm, Bishopswood, Ross-on-Wye.

Collateral Branches living.

Issue of the late Alfred Herbert Tate, 3rd son of 2nd baronet, *b.* 1872, *d.* 1930: *m.* 1910, Elsie, who *d.* 1957 da. of the late Louis William Jelf-Petit, J.P. :—

Louis William, *b.* 1911: *m.* 1934, Mary Christine, da. of the late R. C. Bolton, of Anstey Lane, Alton, Hants, and has issue living, Jeremy Louis (Lark Rise, Spellbrook, Herts), *b.* 1937: *m.* 1961, Rosemary Helen, da. of D. Collins, of West Runton, Norfolk, and has issue living, William James Louis *b.* 1965, Julia Rosemary *b.* 1963. *Residence*, Archways, Three Gates Lane, Haslemere, Surrey.——Francis Herbert, *b.* 1913: *m.* 1937, Esther Frances, da. of the late Sir (John) Bromhead Matthews, KC, and has issue living, David Anthony, *b.* 1941: *m.* 1969, Jennifer, da. of Mrs. Evelyn MacAndrews, of Littlestone, Kent, and has issue living, Rupert David *b.* 1974,—Caroline Frances, *b.* 1946: *m.* 1973, Bruce Jeritt,—Marianne Esther, *b.* 1949. *Residence*, High Housen, Hook Heath, Woking, Surrey.——John Frederick Peter, *b.* 1923: *m.* 1949, Celia Judith, da. of the late Adrian Corbett, and has issue living, Christopher John, *b.* 1953,—Anne Teresa, *b.* 1951,—Nicola Helen, *b.* 1955,—Sophia Louise, *b.* 1958. *Residence*, Greenflags, Limpsfield Common, nr. Oxted, Surrey.

Granddaughters of the late Henry Tate, 6th son of 1st baronet:—

Issue of the late Capt. Henry Burton Tate, *b.* 1883, *d.* 1962: *m.* 1st, 1909, Ida Guendolen (from whom he obtained a divorce 1925), da. of Robin H. Legge; 2ndly, 1925, Mavis Constance (who *d.* 1947, having obtained a divorce 1944), da. of Guy Weir Hogg [B. Magheramorne, colls.]; 3rdly, 1944, Gwen, who *d.* 1957, da. of the late Herbert Edwards, of The Old Hall, Findern, Derbys.

(By 1st m.) Julia Elizabeth Mary, *b.* 1919: *m.* 1959, Paul Georges Bernard, of 22 Rue des Réservoirs, Versailles, France.

Issue of the late Lieut.-Col. Arthur Wignall Tate, D.S.O., *b.* 1888, *d.* 1939: *m.* 1910, Violet Elaine, da. of F. W. Few :—

Monica, *b.* 1912: *m.* 1935, Douglas Gurney Pelly [*see* Pelly, Bt., colls.]. *Residence*, Swaynes Hall, Widdington, near Newport, Essex.

Issue of the late George Booth Tate, 7th son of 1st baronet, *b.* 1857, *d.* 1936: *m.* 1884, Edith Katherine, who *d.* 1937, da. of James Walker Yates, formerly of Ashton-on-Mersey, Cheshire :—

Jane Marjorie, *b.* 1895: *m.* 1920, Redvers Arthur Oldham, who *d.* 1960, and has issue living. *Residence*, Birchwood, Sunningdale, Berks.

Granddaughters of the late George Booth Tate (ante) :—

Issue of the late George Vernon Tate, M.C., *b.* 1890, *d.* 1955 : *m.* 1922, Evelyn Victoria Anne (now of 7, Prince's Gate, S.W.7), da. of Walter Robert Chandler, and widow (1) of 25th Baron de Clifford, and (2) of Capt. Arthur Boy Stock :—

Pamela Aloysia, *b.* 1923 : *m.* 1946, Henry Forbes, son of Adm. of the Fleet, Sir Charles Morton Forbes, G.C.B., D.S.O., and has issue living, Timothy John, *b.* 1947.—Amanda Aloysia, *b.* 1950,—Vanessa Christina, *b.* 1955. *Residence*, Chelsea Lodge, Englefield Green, Surrey.——Virginia Ann, *b.* 1931: *m.* 1953, Michael Jeremy Kindersley Belmont [*see* B. Kindersley]. *Residence*, Gaunt House, Standlake, Oxon.

Sir Henry Tate 1st baronet, gave the Tate Gallery to the nation. Sir William Henry Tate, and baronet, was High Sheriff of Lancashire 1907.

TAYLOR, Creation (U.K.) 1917, of Kennington, co. London.

Sir ERIC STUART TAYLOR, *O.B.E.*, *M.D.*, *M.R.C.P.*, 2nd *Baronet*; *b.* June 28th, 1889; *s.* his father, *Sir* FREDERICK, *M.D.*, *F.R.C.P.*, 1920; *ed.* at Clifton Coll., and at King's Coll., Camb. (M.D. 1919, M.A. 1927); sometime Capt. R.A.M.C. (T.F.); O.B.E. (Mil.) 1919: *m.* 1st, 1920, Evelyn Thérèse, who *d.* 1946, *M.A.*, *J.P.*, da. of the late Lieut.-Col. James Calvert, C.B.E., M.D., F.R.C.P., of 113, Harley Street, W.1; 2ndly, 1949, Lilian Rosamond, who *d.* 1958, da. of the late E. H. Leeder, of Swansea, and widow of Mr. Justice P. A. Farrer Manby, of Manorfield, Lymington, Hants; 3rdly, 1959, (Ada) Hope, da. of Forrest Bertram Leeder, M.R.C.S., L.R.C.P., of Victoria, British Columbia, and widow of Norman Alfred Yarrow [see Yarrow Bt., colls.], and has issue by 1st marriage.

Arms—Per pale gules and azure a fox's brush erect or between two bezants in fesse. Crest—A demi-fox gules tailed or, supporting a banner also gules, charged with a seax or.

Address—PO Box 1147, Victoria, British Columbia.

Son living—By 1st marriage—RICHARD LAURENCE STUART, *b.* Sept. 27th, 1925; *ed.* at Winchester, and at King's Coll., Camb. (B.A. 1949, M.A. 1959); European War 1943-45 with Roy. Armoured Corps and Roy. Gloucestershire Hussars : *m.* 1950, Iris Mary, da. of the Rev. Edwin John Gargery, and has issue living, Nicholas Richard Stuart, *b.* 1952,—Anne Caroline Stuart, *b.* 1955. *Residence*, White Lodge, Hambrook, Chichester.
Daughter living—By 1st marriage—Lesley Evelyn Stuart, *b.* 1922; *ed.* at Cheltenham Ladies' Coll., and at Camb. Univ. (B.A. 1944, M.A. 1948). *Residence*, Pembroke House, Eldorado Road, Cheltenham.

Sir Frederick Taylor, 1st baronet, M.D., F.R.C.P., was an eminent Consulting Physician, and Pres. of Roy. Coll. of Physicians.

TAYLOR, Creation (U.K.) 1963, of Cawthorne in the West Riding, co. York.
[Extinct 1972.]

Sir WILLIAM JOHNSON TAYLOR, *CBE*, 1st and last *Baronet*.

Daughters living of 1st Baronet—Pauline Mary, *b.* 1932: *m.* 1963, Dr. Brian Kenneth Schlotel, of 35, The Grove, Woking, Surrey, and has issue living, Mary Julia Taylor, *b.* 1964,—Helen Rosalind Taylor, *b.* 1967.——Carol Margaret, *b.* 1937: *m.* 1959, Robert Nigel David Bruce, of 6, Pool End Close, Tytherington, Macclesfield, Cheshire, and has issue living, Robert Torfine William, *b.* 1962, —Robert Thurstan Taylor, *b.* 1965,—Robert Andrew Johnson, *b.* 1967,—Katherine Isabelle Zoe (twin), *b.* 1967.
Widow living of 1st Baronet—MARY (*Lady Taylor*), (Bentwood, Cawthorne, Barnsley, Yorks.; 36, Buckingham Gate, SW1), da. of Thomas B. Hall, of Barnsley, ironmaster: *m.* 1930, Sir William Johnson Taylor, CBE, 1st Bt., who *d.* 1972, when the title became ext.

WORSLEY-TAYLOR, Creation (U.K.) 1917, of Moreton Hall, Parish of Whalley, Co. Palatine of Lancaster. [Extinct 1958.]

Sir FRANCIS EDWARD WORSLEY-TAYLOR, 4th and last *Baronet*.

Daughter living of 2nd Baronet—Dorothea Margaret, *b.* 1920. *Residences*, Town Head, Clitheroe, Lancs.; Blackdown House, nr. Haslemere, Surrey.
Daughter living of 3rd Baronet—Annette Pamela, *b.* 1944.

TEMPLE, Creation (U.K.) 1876, of The Nash, Kempsey, co. Worcester.

Sir RICHARD ANTONY PURBECK TEMPLE, *M.C.*, 4th *Baronet*; *b.* Jan 19th, 1913; *s.* his father, *Sir* RICHARD DURAND, *D.S.O.*, 1962; *ed.* at Stowe, and at Trin. Hall, Camb.; sometime Maj. King's Roy. Rifle Corps; is a J.P.; European War 1939-45 (wounded, M.C.): *m.* 1st, 1936 (marriage dissolved 1946), Lucy Geils, 2nd da. of the late Alain Joly de Lotbiniere; 2ndly, 1950, Jean, da. of the late James T. Finnie, and widow of Oliver P. Croom-Johnson, Pilot Officer R.A.F., and has issue by 1st and 2nd marriages.

Arms—Quarterly : 1st and 4th, or, an eagle displayed sable; 2nd and 3rd, argent, two bars sable each charged with three martlets or. Crest—On a ducal coronet or, a martlet of the last.

Templa quam dilecta.
How beloved are thy temples.

Residence—Salford Manor, nr. Bletchley, Bucks.

Sons living—By 1st m.—RICHARD (29, Artesian Rd., W2), *b.* Aug. 17th, 1937: *m.* 1964, Emma Rose, da. of the late Maj.-Gen. Sir Robert Edward Laycock, KCMG, CB, DSO [see E. Dudley, colls.], and has issue living, Lucy Martha, *b.* 1965,—Alice Frances, *b.* 1967,—Daisy Louise, *b.* 1971.——Anthony St. George, *b.* 1941.

Daughter living—By 2nd m.—Anne Sophia, *b.* 1951: *m.* 1974, Jeremy Christopher Peter Amos, of 24, Ormonde Gate, SW3.

Half Brothers living—Peter Paul Grenville, *b.* 1941.——John Anthony (14, Sudeley St., Brighton), *b.* 1942: *m.* 1967, Dominique Francine Paule Ghislaine Marie, da. of Jean-Maurice Vaes, and has issue living, Jean-Marc Peter Grenville, *b.* 1968,—Sophie Anne Jacqueline, *b.* 1970,—Vanessa Chantal Marie, *b.* 1973.

Aunt living (daughter of 2nd baronet)—Mildred Hester: *m.* 1959, John Stanley Wise, who *d.* 1961. *Residence*, 57, Commonwealth Av., Boston, Mass., 02116, USA.

Widow living of 3rd Baronet—MARIE WANDA (*Marie, Lady Temple*), da. of the late F. C. Henderson, of Bombay, India: *m.* 1939, as his 2nd wife, Sir Richard Durand Temple, D.S.O., 3rd baronet, who *d.* 1962. *Residence*,

Collateral Branch living.

Issue of the late Lieut.-Col. Henry Martindale Temple, younger son of 1st baronet *b.* 1853, *d.* 1905: *m.* 1898, Florence Elizabeth, who *d.* 1899, da. of the late Preston Karslake, of White Knights, Berks:—

Dorothea Lora Mary, *b.* 1899: *m.* 1919, Brig. Harold Temple-Richards, late R.M., who *d.* 1969, and has issue living, Harold Mervyn (of 11, Bark Place, W2), *b.* 1919; late Lt. RNVR: *m.* 1st, 1959, Lucy, from whom he obtained a divorce 1971, da. of the Rt. Rev. Hugh Rowlands Gough, CMG, OBE, TD, DD, late Archbishop of Sydney and Primate of Australia [see L. Kinnaird]; 2ndly, 1972, Baroness Elisabeth Maria Auguste, only da. of the late Baron Aladar Döry de Jobbaháza, of Vienna,—Leofric Douglas (Vale Farm, Stibbard, Fakenham, Norfolk), *b.* 1922; Lt.-Cdr. RN (ret.): *m.* 1950, Geraldine Beatrice, da. of Lt.-Col. Sir Thomas Russell Albert Mason Cook, and has issue living, Charles Leofric Thomas *b.* 1955, uliet Geraldine *b.* 1952, —Peter Henry John (Well Cottage, Spring Lane, Cold Ash, Newbury), *b.* 1932: *m.* 1964, Susan Mary, el. da. of Neville Bradshaw, of Withypool, Lewes,—Mary Elizabeth, *b.* 1926: *m.* 1954, John Patrick Ferard Reeve, and has issue living, Patrick Harold *b.* 1960, William Timothy *b.* 1966, Rosalind Mary *b.* 1956, Cecilia Mary *b.* 1958. *Residence*, Hindringham Hall, Fakenham, Norfolk.

This family descends from William Dicken, of Shenton, Salop, who *m.* 1740, Henrietta, da. and co-heir of Sir William Temple, 5th Bt. of Stowe, Bucks. Their son John (grandfather of 1st baronet) assumed by Royal Licence 1796 the surname of Temple. The 1st baronet, the Rt. Hon. Sir Richard Temple, G.C.S.I., C.I.E., was Financial Member of Govt. of India 1868-74, Lieut.-Gov. of Bengal 1874-7, Gov. of Bombay 1877-80, and M.P. for Worcestershire S., or Evesham, Div. 1885-92, and for Surrey, Kingston Div. 1892-5. The 2nd baronet, Lieut.-Col. Sir Richard Carnac Temple, C.B., C.I.E. (Indian Army, and sometime Ch. Commr. Andaman and Nicobar Islands), raised and commanded Upper Burmah Vol. Rifles 1887-90, raised Rangoon Naval Vol. 1892, and Rangoon Vol. Engineers (Submarine Miners) 1893, and was Editor and Proprietor of the *Indian Antiquary* 1884-1931.

Tennyson-d'Eyncourt, see d'Eyncourt.

IMBERT-TERRY, Creation (U.K.) 1917, of Strete Ralegh, Whimple, co. Devon.

Sir EDWARD HENRY BOUHIER IMBERT-TERRY, *M.C.*, 3rd *Baronet; b.* Jan. 28th, 1920; *s.* his father, *Lt.-Col. Sir* HENRY BOUHIER, *D.S.O.*, *M.C.*, 1962; ed. at Eton, and at New Coll., Oxford; Maj. (ret.) Coldstream Guards 1939-45 War (M.C.): *m.* 1944, Jean, da. of the late Arthur Stanley Garton, of Danesfield, Marlow, Bucks, and has issue.

Arms—Azure, guttée d'or three, four, three and four, on a chief of the last a bull's head caboshed between two mullets of the first. **Crest**—Issuant from the coronet of a French Seigneur an eagle rising proper, crowned with an Eastern crown or.

Residence—Brimshott Farm, nr. Chobham, Surrey. *Club*, Guards'.

Sons living—ANDREW HENRY BOUHIER, *b.* Oct. 5th, 1945; Capt. Life Gds.: *m.* 1972 (m. diss. 1974), Sarah Margaret, da. of William Elwyn Francis Evans, MRCS, LRCP.——Michael Edward Stanley *b.* 1950: *m.* 1975, Frances D., da. of Peter Scott, of 25, Corfton Rd., Ealing, W5.

Daughters living—Carolyn Rose, *b.* 1947: *m.* 1973, Peter Lauderdale Macintosh, of 67, Shuttleworth Rd., SW11. ——Alison Jean, *b.* 1952.

Sisters living—Rosanne Mildred Clothilde, *b.* 1913.——Antoinette Lydia, *b.* 1918: *m.* 1962 William Serge Belaieff, who *d.* 1964.——Marie Jacqueline, *b.* 1923: *m.* 1st, 1947 (m. diss. 1954) McRae Wyndham Greenhill; 2ndly, 1972, William Maurice Williams.

The 1st baronet, Sir Henry Machu Imbert-Terry (2nd son of the late Henry Imbert-Terry), was Chm. of Central Organization Committee of Unionist Party 1907-17. Lt.-Col. Sir Henry Bouhier Imbert-Terry, D.S.O., M.C., 2nd baronet, late R.A., was High Sheriff of Devon 1948.

THOMAS, Creation (E.) 1694, of Wenvoe, Glamorganshire.

Sir GODFREY MICHAEL DAVID THOMAS, 11th *Baronet; b.* Oct. 10th, 1925; *s.* his father, **the Rt. Hon.** *Sir* GODFREY JOHN VIGNOLES, *GCVO, KCB, CSI,* 1968; ed. at Harrow; late Capt. Rifle Bde.; is a Member of London Stock Exchange: *m.* 1956, Margaret Greta, yr. da. of John Cleland, of Stormont Court, Godden Green, Sevenoaks, and has issue.

Arms—Sable, a chevron and a canton ermine. *Crest*—A demi-unicorn ermine, armed, crined, and unguled or, supporting a shield sable.

Residence—2, Napier Av., SW6. *Club*—MCC

Son living—DAVID JOHN GODFREY, *b.* June 11th, 1961.

Daughters living—Anne Margaret, *b.* 1957.——Diana Elizabeth (twin), *b.* 1961.

Invincible virtue is glorious

Widow living of 10th Baronet—DIANA MARY KATHARINE (*Diana, Lady Thomas*), (Royal Cottage, Kew, Surrey), da. of the late Ven. Benedict George Hoskyns, Archdeacon of Chichester [*see* Hoskyns, Bt., colls.]: *m.* 1924, the Rt. Hon. Sir Godfrey John Vignoles Thomas GCVO, KCB, CSI, 10th Bt., who *d.* 1968.

Sir John Thomas, 1st Bt. of Wenvoe, Glam. (grandson of James, yr. son of Edmond Thomas of Wenvoe temp. James I and Charles I) *m.* as his 2nd wife 1694, Elizabeth sister of Sir Edmond Thomas of Wenvoe (*d.* 1693) and widow of Gen. Edmund Ludlow. The baronetcy was cr. 1694 with remainder to his brothers Edmond (who *s.* 1703 as 2nd Bt.) and William. Brig. Sir Godfrey Vignoles Thomas, CB, CBE, DSO, 9th Bt., commanded 24th Div. RA and 2nd Reserve Bde. RA during 1914-18 War, and *d.* on active ser. 1919. His son the Rt. Hon. Sir Godfrey John Vignoles Thomas, GCVO, KCB, CSI, 10th Bt., was Private Sec. to the Prince of Wales 1919-36, and Assist. Sec. when King Edward VIII, and Private Sec. to the Duke of Gloucester 1937-57.

THOMAS, Creation (U.K.) 1918, of Garreglwyd, Anglesey.

Sir (WILLIAM) MICHAEL MARSH THOMAS, 3rd *Baronet, b.* Dec. 4th, 1930; *s.* his father, *Major Sir* WILLIAM EUSTACE RHYDDLAD, *M.B.E.,* 1958: *m.* 1953, Geraldine, da. of Robert Drysdale, of Trearddur Bay, Anglesey, and has issue.

Arms—Per pale gules and azure, on a chevron argent between in chief a sower in the attitude of scattering seed and an eagle displayed both or, and in base a garb of the last, three fleurs-de-lis sable. *Crest*—On waves of the sea proper between two anchors sable, a ship in full sail proper.

Residence—Belan, Rosneigr, Anglesey.

Daughters living—Geraldine Dawn, *b.* 1955.——Elizabeth Penelope Kim, *b.* 1959.——Pippa-Jane, *b.* 1963.

Uncle living (son of 1st baronet)—ROBERT FREEMAN, *b.* Jan. 8th, 1911: *m.* 1947, Marcia, da. of Walter Lucas. *Residence*, Garreglwyd, Holyhead, Anglesey.

Mother living—Enid Helena, da. of Ernest Marsh, of Rawdon, Leeds: *m.* 1929 (divorce 1946), Sir William Eustace Rhyddlad Thomas, M.B.E., 2nd baronet, who *d.* 1957. *Residence*, Harrogate, Yorkshire.

Widow living of 2nd Baronet—PATRICIA (LARKINS, (*Patricia, Lady Thomas*): *m.* 1957, as his third wife, Major Sir William Eustace Rhyddlad Thomas, M.B.E., 2nd baronet, who *d.* 1958. *Residence*,

Do right and fear nothing.

The 1st baronet, Sir Robert John Thomas (son of the late William Thomas, of Liverpool), was a Ship and Insurance Broker, and was High Sheriff of Anglesey 1912. He founded and contributed £20,000 to Welch Heroes Memorial Fund and sat as M.P. for Wrexham Div. of Denbighshire (Co. L.) 1918-22, and for Anglesey Co. (L.) 1923-29.

THOMAS, Creation (U.K.) 1919, of Ynyshir, co. Glamorgan.

Sir WILLIAM JAMES COOPER THOMAS, *T.D.,* 2nd *Baronet; b.* May 7th, 1919; *s.* his father, *Sir* (WILLIAM) JAMES, 1945 ; ed. at Harrow, and Downing Coll., Camb.; Bar. Inner Temple 1948; is a JP and a DL for Gwent (High Sheriff of co. Monmouth 1973-74); 1939-45 War with RA: *m.* 1947, Freida Dunbar, da. of the late F. A. Whyte, of Montcoffer, Banff, and has issue.

Arms—Argent, a bend gules, between in chief a pick **sable** and in base a rose of the second, barbed and seeded proper, all within a bordure also of the second. Crest—Upon a branch of olive fessewise an owl affrontée proper.

Seat—Rockfield Park, Monmouth, Gwent.

Sons living—WILLIAM MICHAEL, *b.* Dec. 5th, 1948; ed. at Harrow, and Ch. Ch., Oxford.——Stephen Francis, *b.* 1951; ed. at Harrow, and Oriel Coll., Oxford.

Daughter living—Sara Roberta Mary *b.* 1954.

Brother living—Geoffrey George Mansel, *b.* 1026 : *m.* 1951, Mary Wentworth Thomson, who *d.* 1974, da. of the late H. Harris, of Llanelly, Carmarthen. *Residence*, Buckland House, Dukes Wood Drive, Gerrards Cross, Bucks.

Sister living—Maureen Elizabeth Jane : *m.* 1942, Joseph Gerald Gaskell, and has issue living, Joseph William, *b.* 1947,—Charles Peter, *b.* 1950. *Residence*, Bryn Robin, Michaelston-le-Pit, Dinas Powis, Glamorgan.

The 1st baronet, Sir (William) James Thomas (son of Thomas James Thomas), built Welsh National Med. Sch. at Cardiff, and was High Sheriff of Glamorganshire 1936.

THOMPSON, Creation (U.K.) 1806, of Hartsbourne Manor, Hertfordshire.

Not by whom but in what manner.

Sir (THOMAS) LIONEL TENNYSON THOMPSON, 5th *Baronet; b.* June 19th, 1921; *s.* his father, *Lt.-Col. Sir* THOMAS RAIKES LOVETT, *MC,* 1964; ed. at Eton; Bar. Lincoln's Inn 1952; 1939-45 War as Flying Officer R.A.F.V.R. (invalided), and subsequently as Able Seaman Roy. Fleet Auxiliary (1939-45, and Aircrew (Europe) stars, Defence and Victory Medals): *m.* 1955 (marriage dissolved 1962), Mrs. Margaret van Beers, da. of the late Walter Herbert Browne, and has issue.

Arms—Per fesse argent and sable, a fesse counter-embattled between three falcons belled and jessed or, all within a bordure engrailed, and all counterchanged; in the chief point, also within the bordure, an anchor erect azure, cable proper. Crest—Out of a naval crown or, an arm in armour embowed proper, garnished gold, the hand supporting a lance erect also proper.

Address—16, Old Buildings, Lincoln's Inn, WC2. *Club*—United Service and Royal Aero.

Son living—THOMAS D'EYNCOURT JOHN, *b.* Dec. 22nd, 1956; ed. at Eton.

Daughter living—Sarah Catherine Elizabeth, *b.* 1955.

Sister living—Jane Olivia Marion, *b.* 1918: *m.* 1st, 1938 (marriage dissolved 1947), David Owen Nares; 2ndly, 1948, Maj. James Derek Kenyon Hague, MC, Bar.-at-law, who *d.* 1966, and has issue living (by 1st m.), Caroline Harriette, *b.* 1940: *m.* 1961, Robert Belmont, of Calle de la Madre de Dios 42, Madrid 16,—(by 2nd m.) Melanie Clare, *b.* 1957. *Residences*, Flat 5, 17, Cheyne Gdns., SW3; South House, Ham, Marlborough, Wilts.

Aunt living (daughter of 3rd baronet)—Gladys Maude Gertrude, *b.* 1887: *m.* 1919, Charles Fernand Crémer, and has issue living, John Peter Lionel, *b.* 1924,—Henry Charles Thomas, *b.* 1927,— Margaret Marie Christine, *b.* 1920,—Alice Frances Helene, *b.* 1921. *Residences*, Dampierre sur Loire, Maine et Loire, France; L'Abri, Beaumont, Jersey.

Mother living—Milicent Ellen Jean, da. of the late Edmund Charles Tennyson-d'Eyncourt, of Bayons Manor, Lincs.: *m.* 1st, 1914, Lt.-Col. Sir Thomas Raikes Lovett Thompson, MC, 4th baronet, who *d.* 1964, and from whom she obtained a divorce 1936; 2ndly, 1939, Capt. Patrick Bermingham Crohan, RN (ret.), who *d.* 1953. *Residence*, 87A, Coleherne Court, SW5.

The 1st baronet, Vice-Adm. Sir Thomas Boulden Thompson, G.C.B. (M.P. for Rochester 1807-16), greatly distinguished himself, as Captain of the "Leander," at the battle of the Nile, and afterwards in the action between "Leander" (50) and "Le Genereux" (74), and on his return to England he was knighted 1799 ; subsequently engaged at the battle of Copenhagen 1801, where he lost a leg ; and was appointed Comptroller of the Navy 1806, being created a baronet in the last-mentioned year. Subsequently he was appointed Treasurer of Greenwich Hospital.

THOMPSON, Creation (U.K.) 1890, of Park Gate, Guiseley, Yorkshire.

Wheare vertue lys love neuer dys.

Sir PEILE THOMPSON, *OBE*, 5th *Baronet*; *b.* Feb. 28th, 1911; *s.* his father *Sir* PEILE BEAUMONT, 1972; *ed.* at St. Catharine's Coll., Camb. (MA); Lt.-Col. (ret.) Manchester Regt., and King's African Rifles; Kenya 1955 (despatches); MBE (Mil.) 1950, OBE (Mil.) 1959: *m.* 1937, Barbara Johnson, only da. of the late Horace Johnson Rampling, of The Old Manor House, Harston, Cambs., and has issue.

Arms—Azure, a bridge of three arches embattled proper, in chief the sun in his glory between two mullets of six points pierced or. in base an eagle displayed with two heads argent. Crest—In front of embattlements proper, a cubit arm erect, habited azure, cuffed argent, and charged with a mullet as in the arms, the hand grasping five ears of wheat or.

Residence—Old Farm, Augres, Trinity, Jersey.

Son living—CHRISTOPHER PEILE (Rushdown House, Upton, Hurstbourne Tarrant, Andover, Hants.; Cavalry Club), *b.* Dec. 21st, 1944; ed. at Marlborough; Capt. R. Hussars (PWO): *m.* 1969, Anna Elizabeth, da. of Maj. Arthur G. Callander, and has issue living, Peile Richard, *b.* March 3rd, 1975,—Alexandra Lucy, *b.* 1973.

Daughter living—Ann Mary, *b.* 1939: *m.* 1st, 1965 (m. diss. 1973), Arturo Cesare Pilato; 2ndly, 1973, Raymond Benjamin Cheetham, Roy. Hong Kong Police Force, of 19c, Pearl Gdns., 7, Conduit Rd., Hong Kong, and has issue living, (by 1st m.) Roberto Arturo Kenneth, *b.* 1966,—Leonardo, *b.* 1970.

Sister living—Mary Winifred, *b.* 1909: *m.* 1941, Hugh Kenyon, and has issue living, Hugh Matthew, *b.* 1944,—Elizabeth Katherine, *b.* 1942. *Residence,* Yarrowfield, Mayford, Woking, Surrey.

Collateral Branches living.

Grandchildren of the late Capt. Gilbert Thompson, Connaught Rangers (infra):—
Issue of the late Maj. Christopher Smith Byrom THOMPSON ROYDS, *b.* 1907; assumed by Roy. licence 1936, the additional surname and arms of Royds; *d.* 1967: *m.* 1936, Yolande Anne (Walton House, Boston Spa, Yorks), yr. da. of the late A. T. Hodgson, of Tatchbury Manor House, New Forest, Hants.:—
Gilbert, *b.* 1939; ed. at Eton.——Matthew, *b.* 1942; ed. at Eton: *m.* 1969, Susan (Damaris), el. da. of Arthur Robert Jarrett, of Chedgrove Manor, Loddon, Norfolk.——Timothy Christopher, *b.* 1950; ed. at Stowe.——Laura Yolande, *b.* 1947.

Grandchildren of the late Reginald Thompson, 2nd son of 1st baronet:—
Issue of the late Capt. Gilbert Thompson, Connaught Rangers, *b.* 1877, *d.* (killed in action) 1915: *m.* 1906, Ethel Isabella, who *d.* 1959, da. of the late Marmaduke D'Arcy Wyvill [B. Rookwood]:—
Laura Barbara Frances (*Lady Inglefield*), *b.* 1908: *m.* 1933, Sir Gilbert Samuel Inglefield, GBE, TD, and has issue living, David Gilbert Charles, *b.* 1934: *m.* 1970, Jean Mary, only da. of the late Col. Sir Alan Gomme Gomme-Duncan,—Christopher Samuel, *b.* 1936: *m.* 1971, Susan Lilias, da. of Henry Turcan, of Lindores House, Newburgh, Fife,—Elizabeth Isabel Albinia, *b.* 1942: *m.* 1962, Maj. Christopher Wyndham Diggle, of 8, Roehampton Gate, SW15. *Residence,* Egginton House, Leighton Buzzard, Beds.——Naomi Isabella, *b.* 1912: *m.* 1935, Maj. D'Arcy Armitage Dawes, late 15th/19th King's R. Hussars, who *d.* 1967 [Armytage, Bt., colls.], and has issue living, Charles Lancelot (Leacon Hall, Warehorne, Ashford, Kent), *b.* 1938, Capt. 15th/19th King's R. Hussars: *m.* 1964, Valerie Ann, el. da. of Col. Edward Townsend, of Fencote Hall, Northallerton, Yorks.—Hermione Ann, *b.* 1941: *m.* 1964, John Oliver Birkbeck, of Litcham Hall, Kings Lynn [*see* E. Munster]. *Residence,* Leacon Hall, Warehorne, Ashford, Kent.

Issue of the late Col. Reginald Thompson, DSO, *b.* 1884, *d.* 1965: *m.* 1st, 1922, Marjorie Olive, who *d.* 1929, da. of the late James Arthur, of Montgomerie, Tarbolton [B. Glenarthur]; 2ndly, 1932, Ruth Eleanor (Penthouse Flat, Molescroft Hall, Beverley, E. Yorks.), da. of the Rev. J. H. Hodgson, and widow of John C. Bradley Firth, of Blyth, Notts.
(By 1st m.) Elizabeth Olive, *b.* 1923: *m.* 1948, Maj. George Malcolm Graham, KRRC, of Failford House, Mauchline, Ayrshire, and has issue living, James Anthony, *b.* 1953,—Alexandra Mary, *b.* 1949: *m.* 1974, Adrian John Speir, of 3, Glynde Mews, Walton St., SW3.——Judith Mary *b.* 1927.

Issue of the late Mary Anastasia Thompson, *b.* 1880, *d.* 1962: *m.* 1920, Evelyn Longley, who *d.* 1956:—
Adrian Reginald (West Meon House, Petersfield, Hants), *b.* 1925; ed. at Winchester and Trin. Coll., Camb. (MA); Solicitor 1959: *m.* 1957, Sylvia Margaret, da. of Capt. George Keith Homfray Hayter, late RFA, of The Mortons, Castlemorton, Malvern [Hanmer, Bt., colls.], and has issue living, Anne Mary Theodosia, *b.* 1959,—Joanna Evelyn Clare, *b.* 1960,—Melissa Frances Rose, *b.* 1963.

Issue of the late William Whitaker Thompson, 3rd son of 1st baronet, *b.* 1857, *d.* 1920: *m.* 1889, Isabella Blanche Spencer, who *d.* 1945, da. of Spencer Robert Lewin, of Widford, Herts:—]
Marion Jessie, *b.* 1890: *m.* 1930, as his second wife, Dows Dunham, of 20, Chapel St., Brookline, Mass., 02146, USA.

The 1st baronet sat as M.P. for Bradford (*L*) 1867-8, and was Chm. of the Forth Bridge and the Midland Railway Cos.

THOMPSON, Creation (U.K.) 1963, of Reculver, co. Kent.

Sir RICHARD HILTON MARLER THOMPSON, *MP,* 1st *Baronet,* son of the late Richard Smith Thompson; *b.* Oct. 5th, 1912; ed. at Malvern; a Co. Dir.; Assist. Govt. Whip 1952-54, Lord Commr. of Treasury 1954-56, Vice Chamberlain, H.M. Household 1956-57, Parl. Sec., Min. of Health 1957-59, Parl. Under-Sec. of State, Commonwealth Relations Office, 1959-60, and Parl. Sec., Min. of Works 1960-62; a Trustee of British Museum, and Chm. of Capital & Counties Property Co. Ltd.; 1939-45 War as Lt.-Cdr. RNVR (despatches); MP Croydon W. (*C*) 1950-55, and of Croydon S. 1955-66 and 1970-74: *m.* 1939, Anne Christabel de Vere, only da. of the late Philip de Vere Annesley [see V. Valentia, colls.], and has issue.

Arms—Azure a bend argent between two ship's wheels or. Crest,—A demi figure representing a Moorish Prince proper, wreathed about the temples with a torse argent and azure, vested of a tunic paly argent and azure fringed and garnished or, at his back supported by a guige gules baldrickwise across the right dexter shoulder, a quiver azure replenished with arrows argent flighted or, from the dexter hand a martlet rising azure and in the other a bow palewise stringed gules. Inescutcheon of pretence, paly of six argent and azure, over all a hand gules, *Annesley.*

Residence—Rhodes House, Sellindge, Ashford, Kent.; *Club*—Carlton.

Son living—NICHOLAS ANNESLEY MARLER, *b.* March 19th, 1947; BA.

THOMPSON, Creation (U.K.) 1963, of Walton-on-the-Hill, City of Liverpool.

Sir KENNETH PUGH THOMPSON, 1st *Baronet,* son of Ernest Simpson Thompson, of Hoylake, Cheshire; *b.* Dec. 24th, 1909; ed. at Bootle Gram. Sch., is a Co. Dir., Councillor of City of Liverpool 1938-58, Sec. of 1922 Cttee. 1952-57, Chm. of Conservative National Advisory Cttee. on Local Govt. 1956-57, Assist. Postmaster Gen. 1957-59, and Parliamentary Sec. to Min. of Education 1959-62; M.P. (*C*) Walton Div. of Liverpool 1950-64; Councillor of Merseyside Co. Council (Leader of Conservative Group) since 1973; writer of "Members' Lobby" 1965, and "Pattern of Conquest" 1966: *m.* 1936, Nanne (JP), yr. da. of Charles Broome, of Walton, Liverpool, and has issue.

Arms—Per fess dancetty argent and sable of two upward and one downward points, each ending in a cross potent, three swans one in chief and two in base counterchanged. Crest—A demi figure affronty representing Neptune wreathed about the middle with laver proper, the mantle gules clasped and crowned with an antique crown or, supporting in the dexter hand a trident sable and in the sinister a spear proper.

Residence—Atherton Cottage, Formby, Lancs.

Son living—PAUL ANTHONY, *b.* Oct. 6th, 1939: *m.* 1971, Pauline, da. of Robert O. Spencer, of Tippett House, Smithills, Bolton, Lancs.
Daughter living—Nanne Patricia, *b.* 1942: *m.* 1966, T. Michael Johns, of New Pale Lodge, Manley, Ches.

MEYSEY-THOMPSON, Creation (U.K.) 1874, of Kirby Hall, Yorkshire.

Sir (HUMPHREY) SIMON MEYSEY-THOMPSON, 4th *Baronet*, son of the late Guy Herbert Meysey-Thompson, grandson of 1st Baronet; *b.* March 31st, 1935; *s.* his kinsman, *Sir* ALGAR DE CLIFFORD CHARLES, 1967.

Arms—Quarterly: 1st and 4th, per fesse argent and sable, a fesse counterembattled between three falcons counterchanged, belled and jessed or; 2nd and 3rd, argent, a fesse between three cinquefoils sable. Crests—1st, an arm embossed quarterly or and azure, gauntleted proper, grasping a broken tilting spear in bend sinister or; 2nd, a dragon's head quarterly or and azure, eared gules.

Residences, 39, Chesham St., SW1; 10, Church St., Woodbridge, Suffolk.

Sister living—Sarah Horatio, *b.* 1944: *m.* 1969, Charles William Spencer Paterson, of 17/19, Longmore St., SW1.

Sister living of 3rd Baronet—Violet Ileene Cassandra: *m.* 1905, Maj. Charles William Cuff Knox, Rifle Brig. (Prince Consort's Own), who *d.* 1910 [Gibson-Craig, Bt.]. *Residence*, Little Anstice, Crookham, Hants.

JE·VEUX·DE·BONNE·GUERRE.

I wish for fair fight.

Daughter living of 2nd Baronet—See "PEERAGE." (Barony of Knaresborough).

Mother living—Miriam Beryl (10, Church St., Woodbridge, Suffolk), da. of Sidney Hand: *m.* 1934, Guy Herbert Meysey-Thompson, who *d.* 1961 (ante).

Collateral Branch living

Issue of the late Lieut.-Col. Ernest Claude Meysey-Thompson, 6th son of 1st baronet, *b.* 1859, *d.* 1944: *m.* 1894, Alice Jane Blanche, who *d.* 1960, da. of the late Col. John Joicey, M.P., of Newton Hall, Northumberland :—

Alice **Hildegarde** Eva, *b.* 1895. *Residence,*

The 1st baronet, Sir Harry Stephen Meysey-Thompson, sat as M.P. for Whitby (*L*) 1859-65. The 2nd baronet, Sir Henry Meysey Meysey-Thompson, sat as M.P. for Knaresborough (*L*) April to July 1880, for N. Lindsey, or Brigg, Div. of Lincolnshire 1885-6, and for Handsworth Div. of Staffordshire (*LU*) 1892-1905, and was cr. *Baron Knaresborough*, of Kirby Hall, co. York (peerage of United Kingdom) 1905 (ext. 1929).

THOMSON, Creation (U.K.) 1925, of Old Nunthorpe, co. York.

Sir IVO WILFRID HOME THOMSON, 2nd *Baronet*; *b.* Oct. 14th, 1902; *s.* his father, *Sir* WILFRID FORBES HOME, 1939; ed. at Eton; Squadron Leader R.A.F. Vol. Reserve; European War 1939-45 (despatches): *m.* 1st, 1933, Sybil Marguerite (from whom he obtained a divorce 1954), da. of Claude W. Thompson, of the Red House, Escrick, York; 2ndly, 1954, Viola Mabel (THOMSON), da. of Roland Dudley, of Linkenholt Manor, Andover, Hants., and has issue by 1st marriage.

Arms—Ermine, a lion passant guardant or, on a chief azure two keys, wards inwards of the second. Crest—A lion rampant or, gorged with an antique crown gules, between two roses argent barbed, seeded, leaved and slipped proper. *Residence*—Frilsham Manor, Hermitage, Newbury, Berks.

Son living—By 1st marriage—MARK WILFRID HOME, *b.* Dec. 29th, 1939.

Daughter living—By 1st marriage—Carol Serena, *b.* 1935: *m.* 1962, Lt.-Cdr. (John) Michael Avison Parker, C.V.O., RN (ret.), of 1, Reumah Court, Balwyn, Victoria 3103, Aust., and has issue living, Charles Avison, *b.* 1966,—Kate Avison, *b.* 1963.

SEMPER·FIDELIS.

Always faithful.

The 1st baronet, Sir Wilfrid Forbes Home Thomson (el. son of the late Most Rev. and Rt. Hon. William Thomson, D.D., P.C., Lord Archbishop of York), was a partner in the firm of Beckett & Co., bankers, of York.

John Christopher, *b.* 1940: *m.* 1966, Elizabeth Ann, da. of Noe John Colborne, of Chippenham, and has issue living, Justin Algar *b.* 1967.——Catherine Ann, *b.* 1933: *m.* 1960 (m. diss. 1965), John Blaker (now 3rd Bt.).

Grandchildren of the late Michael Richard Thorold, son of the late Michael Wynne Thorold, son of the late Rev. Michael Thorold, son of the late Samuel Thorold (*b.* 1748), 2nd son of 8th baronet:—
Issue of the late Richard Gillbee Thorold, *b.* 1859, *d.* 1940 : *m.* 1900, Ellen Irene, who *d.* 1958, da. of the late Edward Hogg, of The Lodge, Pinner :—
Edward Lionel, *b.* 1905. *Residence*, Potterspury Lodge, Towcester, Northants.——Irene Gillbee (twin) (Rylands, Beckington, Bath, BA3 6ST), *b.* 1901: *m.* 1st, 1931, Clifford Hackney, MRCS, LRCP, who *d.* 1956; 2ndly, 1958, Brig. Charles Walter Massy, CBE, DSO, MC, who *d.* 1973 [*see* B. Massy, colls.].

The first proved ancestor of this family, Sir Richard Thorold of Selby, co. York, acquired the Manor of Marston, co. Lincoln by marriage (temp. Edward III.) to Joan, da. and heir of Robert de Hough by his wife Maud da. and heir of Michael de Marston. William Thorold (*d.* 1569), 5th in descent from Sir Richard, purchased Cranwell, co. Lincoln (demolished 1815 and estates sold to RAF 1915) and his son, Sir Anthony (*d.* 1594) purchased Syston, Lincs. His grandson, Sir William, 1st Baronet, was knighted by James I. when aged 16 years. He was a Royalist and paid £4,460 to the sequestrators of his estate. Sir John Thorold, 9th Baronet, built the new house of Syston 1766/75 which was enlarged by his son Sir John Hayford Thorold, 10th Bt., the book collector (*d.* 1815). This house was demolished 1934 when Syston Old Hall became the seat of the Baronets. Marston Hall, the principal seat of Baronets until the 18th century, is still in the possession of this family. Three other Baronetcies of Hough-on-the-Hill (cr. 1644), of Harmston (cr. 1709), and of Harmston (cr. 1740), have been conferred on this family, all of which have become extinct.

THROCKMORTON, Creation (E.) 1642, of Coughton, Warwickshire.

Courage is the only nobility.

Sir ROBERT GEORGE MAXWELL THROCK-MORTON, 11th *Baronet*, son of the late Lt.-Col. Richard Courtenay Brabazon Throckmorton, el. son of 10th Bt. ; *b.* Feb. 15th, 1908 ; *s.* his grandfather, *Sir* RICHARD CHARLES ACTON, 1927; ed. at Downside; late Lt. RNVR; late 2nd Lieut. R.A., and Lieut. Grenadier Guards : *m.* 1st, 1942 (divorce 1948), Jean (SMITH-BINGHAM), who *d.* 1973, da. of the late Charles Garland, of Moreton Hall, Warwickshire; 2ndly, 1953, Lady Isabel Violet Kathleen (GUINNESS), da. of 9th Duke of Rutland.

Arms—Gules, on a chevron argent three bars gemelles sable. Crest—A falcon rising proper, belled and jessed or (ancient) an elephant's head. Second Motto—" Moribus antiquis " (*With ancient manners*).

Residences—Coughton Court, Alcester, Warwickshire, Molland, South Molton, N. Devon.

Sister living—Ann Barbara (of Spiney House, Coughton, Alcester, Warwicks.), *b.* 1911: *m.* 1939, Baron Ludwig von Twickel, who *d.* 1945, and has issue living, *Baron* Johann (John) Robert (Mauerkirchenerstrasse 10 Munich, Germany), *b.* 1940: *m.* 1968, HSH Princess Victoria Benigna Ina Marie Cecile Friederike Luise Helene, da. of HSH Prince Karl Peter Franz Andreas Biron von Curland [*see* ROYAL FAMILY], and has issue living, *Baron* Nicolas Maximilian *b.* 1969,—*Baron* Alexander *b.* 1941; Capt. 9th/12th R. Lancers: *m.* 1973, Neville, da. of Garth Priestman.

Uncle living (son of 10th baronet)—GEOFFREY BERKELEY WILLIAM, *C.B.*, (of Spiney House, Coughton, Alcester, Warwickshire; Cavalry Club), *b.* Sept. 3rd, 1883; formerly Clerk of the Journals, House of Commons; 1914-19 War as Capt. Berks Yeo. (wounded, despatches), C.B. (Civil) 1947.

Aunt living (da. of 10th baronet)—Angela Mary Elizabeth, *b.* 1880. *Residence*, 1, Knightsbridge Court, SW1.

Collateral Branch living.

Issue of the late Capt. Herbert John Anthony Throckmorton, R.N., 3rd son of 10th baronet, *b.* 1871, *d.* 1941: *m.* 1912, Ethel Mary, who *d.* 1929, da. of the late Frederick Stapleton-Bretherton [B. Petre]:—
Nicholas Joseph Anthony, *b.* 1913; late Maj. King's Own Yorkshire LI; is a Knight of Honour and Devotion of Sovereign Order of Malta: *m.* 1955, Rosemary Anne, da. of the late Maj. Edward Rowland Milles, Alston, MBE, of Capdepera, Majorca. *Residence*, The Forstal, Biddenden, Kent. *Club*, St. James'.——Anthony John Benedict, *b.* 1916.——Barbara Mary Winefride (*Lady Mitchell Cotts*), *b.* 1914: *m.* 1942, Sir Robert Crichton Mitchell Mitchell Cotts, 3rd Bt., late Maj. Irish Gds., of Valley Farm, Clopton, Woodbridge.

This baronet is descended, according to Dugdale, from John de Throckmorton, Lord of the Manor of Throckmorton *temp.* Henry I. From him was descended Sir John Throckmorton, Knt. Under-Treasurer of England in the reign of Henry VI. The 1st baronet, Sir Robert Throckmorton, had his estates sequestered in the civil wars, and his house at Coughton was plundered and used as a garrison by the Parliamentary forces. The 6th baronet, Sir George Throckmorton, assumed the name of Courtenay in lieu of his patronymic, in 1792, on inheriting through his mother the Courtenay estates of Molland, Devon, but he *dsp.* 1826.

DOUGHTY-TICHBORNE, Creation (E.) 1621, of Tichborne, Hampshire. [Extinct 1968.]

Sir ANTHONY JOSEPH HENRY DOUGHTY DOUGHTY-TICHBORNE, 14th and last *Baronet.*

Daughters living of 14th Baronet—Anne Denise, *b.* 1938: *m.* 1959, Jonkheer John Loudon, of 26, Chelsea Sq., SW3, and has issue living, Anthony James Hugo, *b.* 1966,—Arabella Miranda, *b.* 1961,—Lisa Marie, *b.* 1963.——Miranda Frances, *b.* 1941: *m.* 1961, Christopher Stephen Motley, of Wenlock Abbey, Much Wenlock, Salop [see E. Ranfurly, colls.].——Denise Mary Magdalene, *b.* 1949.

TOLLEMACHE, Creation (G.B.) 1793, of Hanby Hall, co. Lincoln.

CONFIDO·CONQUIESCO

I trust and am content.

Sir HUMPHRY THOMAS TOLLEMACHE, *CB, CBE,* 6th *Baronet; b.* Aug. 10th, 1897; *s.* his brother, *Sir* (CECIL) LYONEL (NEWCOMEN), 1969; ed. at Eastbourne Coll.; Maj.-Gen. RM; Co. Councillor of Hants 1957, and Alderman 1969; DL of Hants.; Maj.-Gen. Comdg. Portsmouth Group RM 1949-52, Hon. Col. Comdt. Portsmouth Group RM 1958-60 and Col. Comdt. RM 1961-62 (Repres. 1961); 1914-18 War with Grand Fleet; 1939-45 War in Middle East and Far East; CBE (Mil) 1950, CB (Mil) 1952: *m.* 1926, Nora Priscilla, da. of John Taylor, of Broomhill, Eastbourne, and has issue.

Arms—Argent, a fret sable (a label of three points for difference). Crest—A horse's head erased gules, between two wings or pelletée (differenced as the arms). *Residence*—Sheet House, Petersfield, Hants. *Clubs*—United Service and Hampshire (Winchester).

Sons living—LYONEL HUMPHRY JOHN, (Buckminster Park, Grantham), *b.* July 10th, 1931; ed. at Uppingham; Maj. (ret.) Coldm. Gds.; FRICS: *m.* 1960, Mary Joscelyne, el. da. of Col. William Henry Whitbread, TD, of Warren Mere, Godalming, and has issue living, Lyonel Thomas, *b.* 1963,—Richard John, *b.* 1966,—Katherine Mary, *b.* 1960,—Henrietta Joscelyne, *b.* 1970.——Robert Hugh Thomas (38, Arlington Sq., N1), *b.* 1937; ed. at Uppingham, and Magdalene Coll., Camb. (BA): *m.* 1962, Lorraine Frances Lougheed, el. da. of Brig. Frederick Joshua Allen, OBE, of Hambledon Cottage, Lower Bourne, Surrey.

Daughters living—Priscilla Joan, *b.* 1927: *m.* 1952, John Chetwynd Gillett, of Gulworthy Farm, Tavistock, Devon, son of Col. Sir (William) Alan Gillett, TD, DL [V. Chetwynd, colls.], and has issue living, Robert John Chetwynd, *b.* 1954,—Andrew William Tollemache, *b.* 1958,—Diana Mary,—Sara Jane, *b.* 1962.——Diana Margaret, *b.* 1929: *m.* 1953, Daniel Johannes Haak, of Uplands, Hawkley, Liss, Hants, and has issue living, Jonathan Daniel, *b.* 1955,—Roderick Johannes, *b.* 1957,—Venetia Priscilla, *b.* 1959,—Felicity Nora, *b.* 1961.

Sister living—Cynthia Joan Caroline (Gablehurst, Clive Rd., Esher, Surrey), *b.* 1890: *m.* 1918, Harry Scott Judd, who *d.* 1948, and has issue living, Anthony Hubert Scott (30, Christchurch Hill, NW3), *b.* 1919; ARAM: *m.* 1956, Gloria Michele, da. of the late Harry Solloway, of Los Angeles, USA, and has issue living, Terence Dominic *b.* 1957, Diana Caroline *b.* 1963,—Barbara Hersilia, *b.* 1926.

Collateral Branches living.

[*See* Cs. Dysart, colls.].

This baronetcy was granted to William Manners, subsequently Lord Huntingtower, el. son of Louisa, Countess of Dysart, who assumed by Roy. Licence the surname and arms of Talmash 1821. On his death in 1833, he was succeeded by his el. son, Lionel William John Tollemache, Lord Huntingtower, who succeeded his grandmother as 8th Earl of Dysart in 1840, the baronetcy thus becoming merged in the Earldom. In 1935, on the death of the 9th Earl of Dysart, the baronetcy was released and passed to his kinsman, Sir Lyonel Felix Carteret Eugene Tollemache, who succeeded as 4th baronet.

LUCAS-TOOTH, Creation (U.K.) 1906, of Queen's Gate, Royal Borough of Kensington and Kameruka, co. Auckland, State of New South Wales, Commonwealth of Australia. [Extinct 1918.]

Sir ARCHIBALD LEONARD LUCAS LUCAS-TOOTH, 2nd and last *Baronet;* Major Hon. Artillery Co. ; *d.* (on active ser. during European War) 1918.

Daughters living of 2nd Baronet—Rosemarie Helen, *b.* 1916 : *m.* 1st, 1936, Capt. Algernon Robert Augustus Dorrien-Smith, 15th/19th King's Roy. Hussars, who *d.* (killed in action during European War) 1940; 2ndly, 1945, Major Bertram William Jepson Turner, M.C., Rifle Brig. *Residence*, Garlogs, Nether Wallop, Hants.——Christine Leonard (*posthumous*), *b.* 1918: *m.* 1945, Major Herbert Frederick Brudenell Foster, T.D., J.P., Scottish Horse [*see* M. Ailesbury, colls.]. *Residence*, Park House, Drumoak, Aberdeenshire.

Widow living of 2nd Baronet—ROSA MARY, da. of the late Charles Arthur Bovill [B. Basing]: *m.* 1st, 1916, Major Sir Archibald Leonard Lucas-Tooth, 2nd Bt., Hon. Artillery Co., who *d.* (on active ser. during European War) 1918, when the title became extinct ; 2ndly, 1923, Major John Greville Smyth-Osbourne, J.P., Roy. Welch Fusiliers, of Blackford House, Highclere, Newbury.

Collateral Branch living.

Issue of the late Capt. Selwyn Lucas Lucas-Tooth, Lancashire Fusiliers, el. son of 1st baronet, *b.* 1879, *d.* (killed in action) 1914 : *m.* 1908, Everild Blanche Marion, who *d.* 1928, da. of Sir Edward Law Durand, 1st Bt., of Tokaora :—

Everild Vera Undine. *b.* 1909 : *m.* 1st, 1932 (marriage dissolved 1940), Lieut.-Com. Reginald Seymour Young, RN (ret.); 2ndly, 1949, Kjeld Helweg-Larsen, who *d.* 1971, and has issue living (by 2nd m.) Robin, *b.* 1950,—Brian, *b.* 1952. *Residence*, Buccaneer Hill, Governor's Harbour, Eleuthera, Bahamas.

MUNRO-LUCAS-TOOTH, Creation (U.K.) 1920, of Bught, Inverness.

Sir HUGH VERE HUNTLY DUFF MUNRO-LUCAS-
TOOTH, 1st *Baronet,* el. son of Maj. Hugh
Munro Warrand, late 3rd Bn. Queen's Own
Cameron Highlanders, by Beatrice Maude, who
d. 1944, el. da. of Sir Robert Lucas Lucas-Tooth,
1st Bt. (*cr.* 1906), *ext.; b.* Jan. 13th, 1903; ed.
at Eton, and at Balliol Coll., Oxford (BA 1924);
Bar. Lincoln's Inn 1933; is Lt.-Col. Queen's
Own Cameron Highlanders; Joint Parl. Under-
Sec. of State for Home Affairs 1953-55; MP for
Isle of Ely (*U*) 1924-29, and for S. Div. of Hendon
1945-70; assumed by Roy. licence 1920 the sur-
name of Lucas-Tooth in lieu of his patronymic
and the arms of Lucas-Tooth, and by deed poll
1965 the additional surname of Munro: *m.* 1925,
Lætitia Florence, *OBE,* da. of Sir John Ritchie
Findlay, 1st Bt., and has issue.

Perseverantia palmam obtinebit. **Arms**—Quarterly, 1st and 4th gules, a demi-gryphon segreant
Perseverance will obtain the palm. between three feathers argent ; and 2nd and 3rd azure, on a bend
between in chief two crescents and in base an estoile argent, three vine leaves proper. **Crests**—1st, a
gryphon segreant gules, semée of mullets, and holding in the sinister claw a feather argent ; 2nd, a
demi-dragon azure, holding in the paws a vine branch fructed and leaved proper.

Residence—Burgate Court, Fordingbridge, Hants.

Son living—HUGH JOHN *LUCAS-TOOTH* (Parsonage Farm, East Hagbourne, Didcot; 44,
Queen's Gate Gdns., SW7) *b.* Aug. 20th, 1932; ed. at Eton and Balliol Coll., Oxford; late Lt.
Scots Guards: *m.* 1955, the Hon. Caroline Poole, el. da. of 1st Baron Poole, and has issue living,
Caroline Maria, *b.* 1956,—Lucinda Kate, *b.* 1958,—Belinda Alice, *b.* 1966.

Daughters living—Laetitia Helen (*Lady Oppenheimer*), *b.* 1926 : *m.* 1947, Sir Michael Bernard
Grenville Oppenheimer, 3rd Bt., of L'Aiguillon, Rue des Cotils, Grouville, Jersey.——Jennifer
Mary, *b.* 1929: *m.* 1949, Maj. John Desmond Henderson, Scots Guards, and has issue living,
Richard, *b.* 1951,—Alexander, *b.* 1971,—Patricia, *b.* 1950. *Residence,* Brimpton Lodge, Brimp-
ton, Reading, Berks.

Sister living—Beatrice Helen Fitzhardinge, *b.* 1908: *m.* 1941, Lyndall Fownes Urwick, O.B.E.,
M.C., of 83, Kenneth St., Longueville, N.S. Wales, son of the late Sir Henry Urwick.

Collateral Branch living. (*In special remainder.*)

Issue of the late Com. Selwyn John Power WARRAND, RN, brother of 1st baronet,
b. 1904, *d.* (killed in action during 1939-45 War) 1941: *m.* 1933, Frena Lingen
(who *m.* 2ndly, 1947, Henry Richard Charles Humphries), da. of the late
Everard Crace, of Canberra, Aust.:—

James Lingen, *b.* 1936: *m.* 1960, Juliet Rose Pearn, of Plymouth, Devon, and has issue living,
Patrick Duncan, *b.* 1962,—Jonathon Edward, *b.* 1968,—Anna Claire, *b.* 1964. *Residence,*
Freshfields, Cobbity, NSW.——Joanna Christine, *b.* 1938.

This Baronetcy was granted to the above-mentioned 1st Bt., who is grandson of Sir Robert
Lucas Lucas-Tooth, 1st Bt. (*cr.* 1906, *ext.*), whose surname and arms he assumed by Roy. licence
1920, and whose three sons had been killed during 1914-18 War, and has left no male issue. In
default of heirs male of the body of the grantee this Baronetcy [has special remainder to the other
heirs male of the body of his mother, Beatrice Maude, da. of 1st baronet (*cr.* 1906).

TOUCHE, Creation (U.K.) 1920, of Westcott, co. Surrey.

Be Watchful.

Sir NORMAN GEORGE TOUCHE,
2nd *Baronet; b.* May 11th, 1888; *s.* his
father, *Sir* GEORGE ALEXANDER, 1935; ed.
at Marlborough, and at Univ. Coll., Oxford
(B.A. 1910, M.A. 1921, B.C.L. 1921);
Bar. Lincoln's Inn 1914: *m.* 1923, Eva
Maitland, *M.A.,* el. da. of P. E. Cameron,
of Salachan, Ardgour, Argyllshire, and
has issue.

Arms—Argent, a lion salient between a fleur-
de-lis in the sinister chief and a like fleur-de-lis in
the dexter base vert. **Crest**—Two fleur-de-lis gules,
resting thereon a mullet of six points or.

Residence—Nenthorn, 1, Broomfield Park,
Westcott, near Dorking. *Clubs*—Oxford and
Cambridge, Pilgrims.

Daughters living—Penelope Maitland, *b.* 1930;
B.Sc. Edinburgh 1952 : *m.* 1954, Joseph Edwin
Mason, PhD, of Crabtree Meadow, Hope,
Sheffield, and has issue living, Donald
George, *b.* 1955,—Brian Richard, *b.* 1960,—
Barbara Jane, *b.* 1956.——Brenda
Margaret, *b.* 1932; ed. at Newnham
Coll., Camb. (BA): *m.* 1956, Ronald Edward
Artus, MA, and has issue living, Colin Edward,
b. 1957,—Alan Norman, *b.* 1959,—Philip
Matthew, *b.* 1964,—Lucy Katharine, *b.* 1961.
Residence, Barcombe House, Barcombe Mills,
Lewes.

Brother living—George Lawrence Capel, *b.* 1903; ed. at Marlborough, and at Univ. Coll., Oxford
(Scholar, BA 1925); a Chartered Accountant: *m.* 1st, 1928, Ursula Grace D'Oyly, who *d.* 1968,
da. of Henry D'Oyly Bernard [D'Oyly, Bt.]; 2ndly, 1969, Elizabeth, da. of Henry Kunzer.
Residence, Holmbush House, Ashington, Sussex.

Collateral Branches living.

Issue of the late Donovan Meredith Touche, 2nd son of 1st baronet, *b.* 1891, *d.* 1952: *m.* 1925, Muriel Amy Frances (Flat 5, 9, Wilbraham Place, SW1), el. da. of the Rev. Charles R. Thorold Winckley, of Lillington, Leamington:—

ANTHONY GEORGE (Stane House, Ockley, Surrey), *b.* Jan. 31st, 1927: *m.* 1961, Hester Christina, el. da. of Dr. A. F. Werner Pleuger, of Linden Lodge, Green Rd., Birchington, Kent, and has issue living, William George, *b.* 1962,—Andrew James, *b.* 1964,—Peter Francis, *b.* 1968,— Helen Mary *b.* 1966.——Isabel Amy, *b.* 1930: *m.* 1962, David M. A. Reid, of The Folly, Tetbury, Glos.

Issue of the late Rt. Hon. Sir Gordon Cosmo Touche, 3rd son of 1st baronet, *b.* 1895, *d.* 1972, who was cr. a Bt. 1962 [see that title].

The 1st baronet, Sir George Alexander Touche (son of Anthony Murray Touche, banker, of Inverleithfield, Edinburgh), was Senior Partner in the firm of George A. Touche & Co., chartered accountants, and a Lieut. for City of London (Sheriff 1915-16, and an Alderman 1915-21), and sat as M.P. for N. Div. of Islington (C) 1910-18.

TOUCHE, Creation (U.K.) 1962, of Dorking, co. Surrey.

Sir RODNEY GORDON TOUCHE, 2nd *Baronet*; *b.* Dec. 5th, 1928; *s.* his father, *the Rt. Hon. Sir* GORDON COSMO, 1972: *m.* 1955, Ouida Ann, el. da. of the late Frederick Gerald MacLellan, of Moncton, New Brunswick, Canada, and has issue.

Arms—Vert, a lion rampant argent holding between the forepaws a portcullis chained or, between two fleurs de lis, one in sinister chief, the other in dexter base argent. **Crest**—Between two fleurs de lis or, a Dorking cock proper.

Residence—707, Prospect Av. S.W., Calgary, Alberta, T2S 0M8, Canada.

Son living—ERIC MACLELLAN, *b.* Feb. 22nd, 1960.

Daughters living—Amanda Ann, *b.* 1956.——Susan Ruth, *b.* 1957.——Karen Marie, *b.* 1961.

Sister living—Daphne Margaret, *b.* 1927: *m.* 1952, Patrick Wilfred Wells, of Snells, Great Henny, Sudbury, Suffolk, and has issue living, Derrick Gordon, *b.* 1956,—William Patrick, *b.* 1960,—Jennifer Margaret, *b.* 1953.

Widow living of 1st Baronet—RUBY ANNE HUME-PURVES (*Ruby, Lady Touche*), (Gable End, Mill Rd., Holmwood, Surrey), da. of the late Sir Duncan James Macpherson, CIE: *m.* 1926, the Rt. Hon. Sir Gordon Cosmo Touche, 1st Bt., who *d.* 1972.

Be Watchful.

The 1st Bt., the Rt. Hon. Sir Gordon Cosmo Touche, MP for Reigate (C) 1931-50, and Dorking 1950-64, was Chm. of Ways and Means, House of Commons 1960-62.

SALUSBURY-TRELAWNY, Creation (E.) 1628, of Trelawny, Cornwall.
[Name pronounced "Saulsbury-Trelawny."]

Deeds consonant with words.

Sir JOHN BARRY SALUSBURY-TRELAWNY, 13th *Baronet*; *b.* Sept. 4th, 1934; *s.* his father, *Sir* JOHN WILLIAM ROBIN MAURICE, 1956: *m.* 1958, Carol Knox, younger da. of the late C. F. K. Watson, of Saltwood, Kent, and has issue.

Arms—Quarterly: 1st and 4th, argent, a chevron sable, *Trelawny*; 2nd and 3rd, gules, a lion rampant per bend sinister argent and erminois ducally crowned between three crescents or, *Salusbury*, on a canton of the last (for *Brereton*) a bear's head erased sable, muzzled argent. **Crests**—1st, a wolf passant proper; 2nd, a demi-lion rampant per bend sinister, as in the arms, holding in the paws a shield or charged with a bear's head sable, muzzled argent.

Residence—The Grange, Saltwood, Hythe, Kent. *Club*—Royal Cinque Ports Yacht.

Son living—JOHN WILLIAM RICHARD, *b.* March 30th, 1960.

Daughters living—Jane Louise, *b.* 1958.——Amanda Sarah, *b.* 1961.——Emma Mary, *b.* 1966.

Half-Brother living—William Hamelin (Glen Cottage, The Glen, Ascot, Berks.), *b.* 1942: *m.* 1967, Meline Martha Katharina, who *d.* 1969, da. of the late Dr. Ir. Cornelius P. A. Zeijlmans van Emmichoven, of The Hague.

Virtue is more noble than patrimony.

Mother living—Glenys Mary, da. of John Cameron Kynoch: *m.* 1st, 1932, John William Robin Maurice Salusbury-Trelawny (afterwards 12th Bt.), who *d.* 1956, and from whom she had obtained a divorce 1935 ; 2ndly, 1947, Richard Lyne Smith, who *d.* 1961. *Residence,* 4, Avereng Gardens, Folkestone, Kent.

Widow living of 12th Baronet—ROSAMUND HELEN (*Dowager Lady Salusbury-Trelawny*), da. of the late Arthur Reed Ropes ("Adrian Ross") : *m.* 1937, as his second wife, Sir John William Robin Maurice Salusbury-Trelawny, 12th baronet, who *d.* 1956. *Residence,* The Orchards, Pellingbridge, Scaynes Hill, Sussex.

Collateral Branches living.

Issue of the late Lieut.-Col James Edward Salusbury-Trelawny, O.B.E., 2nd son of 10th baronet, *b.* 1873, *d.* 1940 : *m.* 1st, 1907, Winifred Eveline (who *d.* 1937, having obtained a divorce 1930), da. of William Edward Dorrington; 2ndly, 1920, Edith Janetta, who *d.* 1961, da. of the late Nicholas Cornock :—

(By 1st marriage) James Reginald Dorrington, *b.* 1908 ; ed. at Westminster : admitted a Solicitor 1931; sometime Capt. DCLI: *m.* 1st, 1932, Muriel Mary, who *d.* 1970, da. of Sir Eustace William Windham Wrixon-Becher, 4th Bt.; 2ndly, 1971, Vieno Helinä, yr. da. of the late Väinö Junno, Kemi, Finland, and has issue living (by 1st m.), Jonathan William (c/o C. Hoare & Co., 67, Park Lane, W1) *b.* 1934; ed. at Charterhouse; Maj. Coldm. Gds.: *m.* 1st, 1959 (m. diss. 1969), Jill Rosamonde, da. of Maj.-Gen. Cecil Benfield Fairbanks, CB, CBE; 2ndly, 1970, Gillian, only child of R. J. Ratcliff, of Fossebridge House, nr. Cheltenham, and has issue living (by 2nd m.), Katharine Sophie *b.* 1972,—Mary Letitia, *b.* 1937: *m.* 1966, Procter Naylor, of 17, Chapel St., Bildeston, Ipswich, and has issue living, Edward Trelawny Procter *b.* 1969, Harriet Mary *b.* 1967. *Residence*, 1, The Roystons, East Preston, Littlehampton, Sussex.

Grandchildren of the late John Salusbury-Trelawny, son of the late Col. Harry Reginald Salusbury-Trelawny, 4th son of 8th baronet :—

Issue of the late Major John Maitland Salusbury-Trelawny, M.C., *b.* 1892, *d.* 1954 : *m.* 1919, Louisa Frederica (now of Church Acre, Uplyme, Lyme Regis, Dorset), da. of the late Capt. Guy Mainwaring, R.N. :—

John Guy, *b.* 1919 ; ed. at Bradfield Coll. ; Capt. (retired) Duke of Cornwall's L.I. ; European War 1939-45 (wounded, prisoner) : *m.* 1948, Ruth Gertrude, da. of the late Edward Richard Marker [B. Bagot, colls.], and has issue living, Richard John, *b.* 1953,—Peter Michael, *b.* 1956,— Patrick Charles, *b.* 1958,—Daphne Anne, *b.* 1950,—Jill Margaret, *b.* 1951.——Philip Michael, *MC* (Hollands House, Tincleton, nr. Puddletown, Dorchester), *b.* 1921; ed. at Winchester; Lt.-Col. (ret.) The LI; N. Africa and Italy 1942-45 (MC): *m.* 1946, Jean (formerly Flt. Officer WAAF), only da. of the late Col. Herbert Cecil Fraser, DSO, OBE, and has issue living, Simon Jonathan (47, Maltravers St., Arundel, Sussex), *b.* 1948; ed. at Nautical Sch., Pangbourne: *m.* 1974, Caroline Margaret, only da. of Sir Nigel John Douglas Vernon, 4th Bt.,—Diana Jane, *b.* 1947: *m.* 1970, Robert Jessop Blake, of Little Ovens, West Drayton, Retford, Notts., and has issue living, James Trelawny *b.* 1971, Jonathan Jessop *b.* 1973.——Ann Laetitia, *b.* 1924: *m.* 1953, David Neil Courtenay MacWatters, and has issue living, Jonathan Courtenay, *b.* 1954,— Victoria Courtenay, *b.* 1956,—Jennifer Laetitia, *b.* 1962. *Residence*, Rashleigh Barton, Wembworthy, Chulmleigh, N. Devon.

Granddaughter of the late Capt. Harry Brereton-Trelawny, grandson of the late Lieut.-Gen. Harry Trelawny, brother of 6th baronet :—

Issue of the late Clarence Trelawny, *b.* 1826 (formerly an officer in Austrian Hussars), *d.* 1902, *m.* 1870, Mary, who *d.* 1930, da. of W. S. Campbell, formerly Consul for U.S.A. at Dresden:—

May, *b.* 1885. *Residence*, 122, Holbein House, Sloane Sq., SW1.

This family takes its name from Trelawn or Treloen, in Cornwall. The Right Rev. Sir Jonathan Trelawny, 3rd baronet, a man of great learning, was consecrated Bishop of Bristol 1685, and was one of the seven Bishops committed to the Tower by James II, which act caused a great rising among the people of Cornwall. After the Revolution, he was successively Bishop of Exeter and Winchester. Capt. Sir William, RN, 6th baronet, was Governor of Jamaica. Sir William Lewis, 8th baronet, MP for East Cornwall, and Lord-Lieutenant of the county, assumed, in 1802, the additional surname of Salusbury.

TREVELYAN, Creation (E.) 1662, of Nettlecombe, Somerset.

[Name pronounced "**Trevillian.**"]

Sir WILLOUGHBY JOHN TREVELYAN, 9th *Baronet; b.* April 16th, 1902 ; *s.* his father, *Sir* WALTER JOHN, 1931 ; ed. at Eton ; is Lord of the Manor of St. Perran Uthnoe, and patron of four livings.

Arms—Gules, a demi-horse argent, hoofed and maned or, issuing out of water in base proper. **Crest**—Two arms counter-embowed proper, habited azure, holding in the hands a bezant.

Collateral Branches living.

Grandchildren of the late George Edward Trevelyan, 2nd son of the Rev. George Trevelyan, 2nd son of the Rev. Walter Trevelyan, 2nd son of 4th baronet:—

Issue of the late Edward Walter Trevelyan, *b.* 1881, *d.* 1947 : *m.* 1911, Kathleen E. H. (now of 6450, Hawarden Drive, Riverside, California, U.S.A.), da. of William Irving :—

NORMAN IRVING (1041, Adella Av., Coronada, Calif. 92118, USA), *b.* Jan. 29th, 1915: *m.* 1951, Jennifer Mary, da. of Arthur E. Riddett, of Long Orchards, Copt Hill Lane, Burgh Heath, Surrey, and has issue living, Edward Norman, *b.* 1955,—George Arthur, *b.* 1958,— Jane *b.* 1953.——Eva Stewart, *b.* 1919: *m.* 1951, Alexander Benedict Yakutis, LLD, of 6450, Hawarden Drive, Riverside, Cal., USA, and has issue living, Alexander Trevelyan, *b.* 1956,—Alexandra Irving, *b.* 1953,—Kathleen Irving *b.* 1958,—Eva Irving, *b.* 1958 (twin).

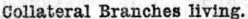

Granddaughter of the late Sir Ernest John Trevelyan, DCL (infra):—

Issue of the late Lt.-Col. Henry Trevelyan, *b.* 1881, *d.* 1971: *m.* 1906, Josephine Mary, who *d.* 1968, da. of the late Dr. F. Antelme, of Port Louis, Mauritius:—

Mary Katharine, *b.* 1926: *m.* 1947, Harold Stewart Proudlock, of Heath Cottage, 16, Fields Rd., Alsager, Cheshire, and has issue living, Michael Trevelyan, *b.* 1949,—David Seymour, *b.* 1951,— John Stewart, *b.* 1956,—Susan Marie, *b.* 1959.

Granddaughters of the late Maj.-Gen. Henry Willoughby Trevelyan, CB, son of the late Ven. George Trevelyan, Archdeacon of Taunton, 3rd son of 4th baronet:—

Issue of the late Sir Ernest John Trevelyan, D.C.L., *b.* 1850, *d.* 1924: *m.* 1st, 1880, **Mary Katharine**, who *d.* 1885, da. of the late Patrick Black, M.D., of 11, Queen Anne Street, W.; 2ndly, 1890, Julia Isabel, who *d.* 1903, da. of E. W. Mark, formerly Consul at Marseilles; 3rdly, 1909, **Winifred Helen**, who *d.* 1962, da. of the late **Sir Charles Umpherston Aitchison, K.C.S.I., C.I.E., LL.D.:—**

(By 2nd m.) Sylvia (of 100, Heath Rd., Petersfield, Hants), *b.* 1898: *m.* 1924, Lt.-Col. Geoffrey Ronald Hawtrey Deane OBE, RE, who *d.* 1961, and has issue living, Barbara, *b.* 1924,—Elisabeth, *b.* 1926: *m.* 1959, John Charles William Napier-Munn, of 1, Duchess Close, Whitchurch, Oxon, and has issue living, Simon Deane *b.* 1961, Nicola Tamsin *b.* 1963,—Janet Anne, *b.* 1929: *m.* 1954, Roderick William Chisholm, of Ringden Wood, Flimwell, Wadhurst, Sussex, and has issue living, Alastair James *b.* 1959, John Angus *b.* 1962, Jane Catherine *b.* 1955, Teresa Mary *b.* 1957,— Charlotte, *b.* 1933; ed. at St. Andrew's Univ. (BSc 1956).

Descendants of the late Sir Charles Edward Trevelyan, K.C.B., son of the late Ven. George Trevelyan, Archdeacon of Taunton, 3rd son of 4th baronet, who was cr. a *Baronet* 1874 :—

See Trevelyan, Bt., *cr.* 1874.

Grandchildren of the late Rev. John Charles Trevelyan (infra):—
Issue of the late Rev. Prebendary Charles William Trevelyan, MC, *b.* 1887, *d.* 1974: *m.* 1930, Maud Dorothe (Simon's Close, Bathampton, Bath, BA2 6SU), da. of the late Frederick Augustus Dixey, MD, FRS:—

John Francis (Te Puke, NZ), *b.* 1934; ed. at Wellington Coll., and Aberdeen Univ. (BSc Forestry): *m.* 1958, Elizabeth Mary, da. of Harvey Brockenshaw, and has issue living, Andrew John, *b.* 1961,—James Edward, *b.* 1962,—Fiona Catherine, *b.* 1965,—Katrin Elizabeth, *b.* 1966.——*Rev.* James William Irvine (Lenham Vicarage, Maidstone, Kent, ME17 2PX), *b.* 1937; ed. at Wellington Coll., and Selwyn Coll., Camb. (MA); V. of Lenham with Boughton Malherbe, Kent, since 1972: *m.* 1969, Felicity Jane, da. of Joseph Gibson, and has issue living, Robert William Dixey, *b.* 1970,—Lucy Catherine, *b.* 1974.——Janet Isabel, *b.* 1932.——Elizabeth Margaret, *b.* 1939: *m.* 1964, Robert Adrian Franklin, MA, MB, MRC Psych. of 34, Rawcliffe Lane, York, YO3 6QB, and has issue living, Nicholas Robert, *b.* 1969,—Clare Elizabeth, *b.* 1965,—Susan Dorothe, *b.* 1967.

Grandchildren of the late Rev. William Pitt Trevelyan, 6th son of the late Ven. George Trevelyan, Archdeacon of Taunton (ante):—
Issue of the late Rev. John Charles Trevelyan, *b.* 1857, *d.* 1944: *m.* 1881, Elizabeth Wood, who *d.* 1935, da. of Thomas Irvine, of Liverpool:—

Ruth, *b.* 1894: *m.* 1924, the Rev. Robert Elliott Monro, who *d.* 1948, formerly V. of Wybunbury, and has issue living, Mary Joan (Runyararo, PO Box ST393, Southerton, Salisbury, Rhodesia), *b.* 1925,—Elizabeth Trevelyan, *b.* 1928; ed. at St. Hugh's Coll., Oxford (MA): *m.* 1956, the Rt. Rev. Ronald Oliver Bowlby, 9th Lord Bishop of Newcastle, of Bishop's House, 29, Moor Rd., South Newcastle upon Tyne, NE3 1PA, and has issue living, Richard Monro *b.* 1958, Christopher Maunsell *b.* 1961, Thomas Trevelyan *b.* 1966, Rachel Helena *b.* 1957, Anna Elizabeth *b.* 1963,— Anne Ruth Monro, *b.* 1932. *Residence*, Edgmond Hill, Newport, Salop.

Issue of the late Rev. George Philip Trevelyan, *b.* 1858, *d.* 1937: *m.* 1896, Monica Evelyn Juliet, who *d.* 1962, da. of the late Rev. Sidney Phillips, Hon. Canon of Worcester (sometime V. of Kidderminster), of The Blanquettes, Worcester:—

John, CBE, *b.* 1903; ed. at Trin. Coll., Camb. (MA); formerly Sec. to British Board of Film Censors, and Dir. of Education for Westmorland, and Dir. of British Families Education Ser. in Germany; OBE (Civil) 1949; CBE (Civil) 1971: *m.* 1st, 1928, Kathleen Margaret (who obtained a divorce 1949), da. of the late Charles Pass; 2ndly, 1949, Joan Frieda, BM; BCh (who obtained a divorce 1959), da. of Francis Clayton Scott [*see* Scott, Bt., *cr.* 1909, colls.], 3rdly, 1959, Jean, who *d.* 1972, da. of Robert Mutch; 4thly, 19—, Rosaline Evelyn, da. of Joseph Lopez-Salzedo, and has issue living (by 1st m.), James Philip (97, Tyrell St., Nedlands, W. Aust.) *b.* 1948: *m.* 1972, Jolin, da. of Frank Edmondson, of Floreat Park, W. Aust., and has issue living, Charles Frances *b.* 1974,—Sarah Juliet, *b.* 1950, (by 3rd m.) Jonathan, *b.* 1959,—Simon (twin), *b.* 1959. *Residence*, 8, Rockwells Gdns., Dulwich Wood Park, SE19.——Humphrey, KG, GCMG, CIE, OBE (*Baron Trevelyan*), *b.* 1905; cr. Baron Trevelyan (Life Peer), Jan. 1st, 1968 [see that title].——Mary, CBE (Flat 5, 23, Embankment Gdns., SW3), *b.* 1897; ARCM; ARCO; Head of Field Survey Bureau UNESCO 1946-48, Adviser to Overseas Students, London Univ. 1949-65, and Founder and first Dir. of Internat. Students House, London, 1965-67; CBE (Civil) 1968.——Avice, *b.* 1898.——Beryl, *b.* 1899; ed. at Girton Coll., Camb. (MA): *m.* 1927, Philip John Durrant, PhD, Senior Fellow of Selwyn Coll., Camb., and has issue living, John Paul (Brambletye, The Avenue, Fleet, Hants.), *b.* 1928; ed. at Gordonstoun and RMA; Maj. R. Signals (ret.); Manager Terminal 1, British Airport Authority, Heathrow: *m.* 1959, Vivienne, da. of the late James Alfred Trenerry, and has issue living, Jeremy Mark *b.* 1960, Jonathan Humphrey *b.* 1963,—Clare Elizabeth, *b.* 1932; ed. at Girton Coll., Camb. (MA, MB, BChir, MRCP): *m.* 1961, the Rev. Burton Jones Whitehead, of The Rectory, Didcot, Oxon, and has issue living, Philip Trevelyan *b.* 1964, Nicholas Bruce Trevelyan *b.* 1966, Mary Louise *b.* 1962. *Residence*, 16, Chaucer Rd., Cambridge.——Urith Monica *b.* 1909; ed. at Somerville Coll., Oxford (BA 1937, MA 1941): *m.* 1940, the Rt. Rev. Harry James Carpenter, 37th Bishop of Oxford, of 1, Meadow View, Baunton, Cirencester, Glos., and has issue living, Humphrey William Bouverie, *b.* 1946: *m.* 1973, Mari Christina, da. of Caradog Prichard.

Grandchildren of the late John Spencer Trevelyan (infra):—
Issue of the late John Thornton Trevelyan, *b.* 1898, *d.* 1970: *m.* 1928, Anne Georgina (Longwitton Hall, Morpeth, Northumberland), da. of Prof. John Dobson, Wardale, of Newcastle upon Tyne:—

John Cecil Raleigh (Netherwitton Hall, Morpeth, Northumberland NE61 4NX), *b.* 1933; ed. at Marlborough: *m.* 1962, Jane, yr. da. of the late Brig. Roger Peake, DSO, OBE, and has issue living, John Henry Thornton, *b.* 1968,—Caroline Georgina, *b.* 1962,—Tessa Margaret Thornton, *b.* 1966.——Edward Calverley Thornton (Matfen House, Matfen, Northumberland), *b.* 1935; ed. at Marlborough: *m.* 1962, Elizabeth Anne, el. da. of the late Geoffrey Blayney, of High Shield, Hexham, and has issue living, Julian Blackett Thornton, *b.* 1963,—Rosemary Joy, *b.* 1965,—Amanda Fay, *b.* 1967.——Anne Margaret Thornton, *b.* 1930: *m.* 1953, John Humphrey Usborne, of Glan-Nant, Crickhowell, Breconshire, and has issue living, Richard Thomas, *b.* 1954,—John Edward (twin), *b.* 1954,—Andrew Thornton, *b.* 1956.——Joan Mary Thornton, *b.* 1932: *m.* 1963, George Campbell Wilkinson, TD, of Firs on Hill, Helsby, Ches, WA6 9AQ, and has issue living, Anne Margaret, *b.* 1965.

Grandchildren of the late Thornton Roger Trevelyan, son of the late Raleigh Trevelyan, 2nd son of Walter Trevelyan (infra):—
Issue of the late John Spencer Trevelyan, *b.* 1864, *d.* 1943 : *m.* 1897, Margaret Eleanor, who *d.* 1961, da. of the late W. Brook Mortimer, of Hay Carr, Lancaster :—
Caroline Nora Constantia Thornton, *b.* 1902: *m.* 1931, Eric William Davis, son of the late Sir Robert Henry Davis, and has issue living, Patrick Brian Trevelyan, *b.* 1935,—Margaret Trevelyan, *b.* 1932,—Caroline Trevelyan, *b.* 1939: *m.* 1969, Richard Charles Patterson, of Winthill, Banwell, Som. *Residence*, Hurston Place, Pulborough, Sussex.

Issue of the late Freeman Blackett Thornton Trevelyan, *b.* 1874, *d.* 1943 : *m.* 1898, Louise, who *d.* 1944, da. of the late Col. Sir Philip Watts, K.C.B., LL.D., F.R.S., D.Sc. :—

Lilian Agnes Thornton, *b.* 1901 : *m.* 1927, Lieut.-Col. Robert Hunter Smith, O.B.E., R.A.S.C., who *d.* 1935, and has issue living, Freeman James (Kimpton Lodge, Kimpton, Andover, Hants.) *b.* 1928; Maj. AAC(V): *m.* 1952, Mary Elizabeth, yst. da. of John L. Beaumont, of Coggeshall, Essex, and has issue living, Peter Freeman *b.* 1964, Joanna Susan Elizabeth *b.* 1953, Anne Trevelyan *b.* 1955,—Robert Thornton (Stanmore, Woodland Drive, Thorpe End, Norwich), *b.* 1930: *m.* 1956, Anne V., da. of Lt.-Col. A. E. Penny, IMS (ret.), and has issue living, Richard James *b.* 1962, Sarah Jane *b.* 1964. *Residence*, Kimpton Lodge Cottage, Kimpton, Andover, Hants.

Grandsons of the late Capt. Walter Raleigh Trevelyan, son of the late Walter
Raleigh Trevelyan (infra) :—
Issue of the late Col. Walter Raleigh Fetherstonhaugh Trevelyan, Indian Army, *b.* 1893,
d. 1953: *m.* 1921, Olive Beatrice (St. Veep, Lostwithiel, Cornwall; she *m.*
2ndly, 1953, Col. William Henry Ralston, DSO, OBE, MC, who *d.* 1962), da. of the
late Thomas Gibbons Frost, of Mollington Hall, Chester:—
Walter Raleigh, *b.* 1923; ed. at Winchester; 1942-45 War in Italy as Capt. Rifle Bde. (despatches). *Residences*, 18, Hertford St., W1; St. Veep, Cornwall. *Club*, Travellers'.——John Amyas, *b.* 1928; ed. at Winchester; sometime 2nd Lt. Rifle Bde.: *m.* 1954, Patricia Mary, da. of the late Stuart Moore, and has issue living, Amyas John Stuart, *b.* 1957,—Oliver Willoughby, *b.* 1961,— Rupert Patrick, *b.* 1963,—Elizabeth Virginia, *b.* 1955. *Residence*, Chengoma, Box 95, Umvakwes, Rhodesia.

Grandson of the late Walter Raleigh Trevelyan, son of the late Walter Calverley
Trevelyan, son of the late Walter Trevelyan, 2nd son of 3rd baronet:—
Issue of the late Charles Leslie Calverley Trevelyan, *b.* 1874, *d.* 1947: *m.* 1911, Esmé
Gwladys, who *d.* 1970, da. of William J. Menzies, formerly of Empshott Grange, Hants:—
Leslie Calverley, *b.* 1912; ed. at Westminster Sch., and Pembroke Coll., Oxford (MA): *m.* 1939, Prudence Mary, da. of the late Alfred S. Fawcett, of Standhills, Dore Moor, Derbyshire, and has issue living, Anthony Leslie Calverley (Three Gables, Kemerton, Tewkesbury, Glos.), *b.* 1941; ed. at Seaford Coll.: *m.* 1972, Victoria, da. of Lt.-Col. Gordon Kenward Barker, DSO, of Ascott under Wychwood, and has issue living, Charlotte Louise *b.* 1973, Esmé Gwendolen *b.* 1975, —Amyas Charles (Cavalry Club), *b.* 1946; ed. at Harrow, and RMA; Lt. R. Scots Dragoon Gds. *Residence*, The Glebe Cottage, Wood Stanway, Glos.

Granddaughters of the late Margaret Lydia Trevelyan (who *m.* 1862, John
Pearson Cresswell, MRCS), da. of the late Walter Calverley Trevelyan (ante):—
Issue of the late Evelyn Trevelyan Cresswell, *b.* 1863, *d.* 1925: *m.* 1888, Arnold Edward
Gawthrop, who *d.* 1933.
Margaret Helen (66, Haynes Rd., Worthing), *b.* 1896.——Christine Evelyn, *b.* 1898: *m.* 1921, Frank Hall, of 26, St. Leonard's Rd., SW14, and has issue living, John Charles William (29, Vine Rd., E. Molesey, Surrey), *b.* 1926: *m.* 1953, Patricia Gibbs, and has issue living, Joanna Mary *b.* 1957,—Evelyn Trevelyan, *b.* 1923: *m.* 1940, Robert Ambrose Turrell, of 64, St. Leonard's Rd., SW14,—Sylvia Margaret, *b.* 1925: *m.* 1948, Bertie Perowne, of 29, Little Oxhey Lane, Watford,—Margaret Maud, *b.* 1927: *m.* 1947, Edward Donald Bushnell, of 52, Ember Lane, Esher, Surrey.

The family of Trevelyan takes its name from Trevelyan in the parish of St. Veep, Cornwall. The 1st baronet, Sir George, was son of George Trevelyan, who suffered greatly for his fidelity to the royal cause during the civil war. The 2nd and 4th baronets each represented Somersetshire in Parliament. Sir Walter John Trevelyan, 8th Bt., was High Sheriff of Cornwall 1906-7.

TREVELYAN. Creation (U.K.) 1874, of Wallington, Northumberland.
[Name pronounced "Trevillian."]

Sir GEORGE LOWTHIAN TREVELYAN, 4th *Baronet ; b.* Nov. 5th, 1906 ; *s.* his father, the *Rt. Hon. Sir* CHARLES PHILIPS 1958 : *m.* 1940, Helen, da. of Col. John Lindsay Smith, C.B.E.

Arms—Gules, a demi-horse argent, hoofed and maned or, issuing out of water in base proper. Crest— Two arms counter-embowed proper, habited azure, holding in the hands a bezant.

Seat—Wallington, Cambo, Morpeth, Northumberland. *Residence*—Crab Tree Cottage, Dunnsheath, Berwick, Shrewsbury, Salop.

Brother living—GEOFFREY WASHINGTON, *b.* July 4th, 1920 ; *m.* 1947, Gillian Isabel, da. of the late Alexander Wood, and has issue living, Peter John, *b.* 1948,—Sandra Mary, *b.* 1951: *m.* 1974, David Bradley. *Residence*, Silkstead, 3, Abbey Mill End, St. Albans, Herts.

Sisters living—Pauline, CBE (Cambo House, Cambo, Morpeth, Northumberland; English-Speaking Union) *b.* 1905; ed. at Sidcot Sch. and Reading Univ. (Dip. Agric.); a JP, and an Hon. Member of Town Planning Inst.: a Member of National Parks Commn. 1949-66 (Dep. Chm. 1956-66); a Member of Newcastle Diocese, Bishop's Advisory Cttee. on care of Churches 1960-70, and of British Waterways Board 1963-67; Chm. of Exec. Cttee. of Northumberland Rural Community Council 1955-63, and 1966-73; OBE (Civil) 1954, CBE (Civil) 1967: *m.* 1929, John Gordon Dower, who *d.* 1947, and has issue living, Michael Shillito Trevelyan, *b.* 1933: *m.* 1960, Agnes (Nan), el. da. of the late Allan Done, of Pontefract, Yorks, and has issue living, John *b.* 1961, Daniel Guy *b.* 1964, Alexander Michael *b.* 1968,—Robert Charles Philips, *b.* 1938: *m.* 1967, Frances, only da. of Henry Baker, of Owletts, Cobham, Kent, and has issue living, Thomas Calverley *b.* 1971, Beatrice Lucy *b.* 1974,—Susan Florence, *b.* 1931: *m.* 1954, Trevor Casbay Handoll, and has issue living, John Trevelyan Casbay *b.* 1957, Helen Hanora Georgina (twin) *b.* 1957.——Katharine TREVELYAN, *b.* 1908; resumed surname of Trevelyan in lieu of Götsch 1938: *m.* 1932, Johann Gottfried Georg Götsch, who *d.* 1956, having obtained a divorce 1938, and has issue living, Erika Karla (82, Carlisle Mansions, Carlisle Pl., SW1), *b.* 1933: *m.* 1st 1957 (m. diss. 1970), Robin Murray Lees; 2ndly, 1973, John Julian Morland Mallock Bond, and has issue living (by 1st m.), Nicholas Martin *b.* 1960, Dominic Charles Jacob *b.* 1964, Henrietta Frances *b.* 1963,— Elisabeth Trevelyan, *b.* 1935: *m.* 1967, Stephen Greenfield (Box 71, Aspen, Colorado 81611, USA), —Katharine Mary Trevelyan, *b.* 1938: *m.* 1963, Jeremy Chapple, of Rawlins House, The Green, Adderbury, Banbury, and has issue living, Penelope Jane *b.* 1966, Frances Mary *b.* 1972. *Residence*, Godshill, Fordingbridge, Hants.——Marjorie (*Lady Weaver*), *b.* 1913: *m.* 1941, Sir Tobias Rushton Weaver, CB, son of the late Sir Lawrence Weaver, KBE, and has issue living, Lawrence

Trevelyan, *b.* 1948,—Kathleen, *b.* 1943: *m.* 1966, Nicholas John Milford Abbott, of 3, Westbury House, Great Dunmow, Essex, and has issue living, Simon Milford *b.* 1971, Benjamin Tobias *b.* 1973, Rachel Mary *b.* 1967, Judith Caroline *b.* 1969,—Caroline, *b.* 1945,—Rachel, *b.* 1950: *m.* 1974, Charles David Munn, of Hodore, Hartfield, Sussex. *Residence*, 13, Vicarage Gdns., W8. ——Florence Patricia (twin), *b.* 1915: *m.* 1st, 1942, Lt. Frederick Philip Cheswright, RNVR, who *d.* 1946; 2ndly, 1950, Sqdn.-Ldr. Reginald Joseph Jennings, MC, RAFVR, and has issue living (by 1st m.), Hugh Weedon Nicholas (Green Garth, The Lanes, Houghton, Huntingdon), *b.* 1942: *m.* 1968, Rosemary Frances, da. of the late Norman Walduck, of Hatfield, Herts., and has issue living, Sebastian Charles Philip *b.* 1971, Rupert James Macaulay *b.* 1972,—Janet Vanessa, *b.* 1943: *m.* Geoffrey Brian Parker, of 17, The Green, Twickenham, Middx., and has issue living, Philip Christopher Liam *b.* 1967, Jonathan Hugh *b.* 1968. *Residence*, Wallington, Cambo, Morpeth, Northumberland.

Collateral Branches living.

Issue of the late Robert Calverley Trevelyan, 2nd son of 2nd baronet, *b.* 1872, *d.* 1951 : *m.* 1900, Elizabeth, who *d.* 1957, da. of the late Jan des Amorie van der Hoeven, of The Hague :—

Julian Otto, *b.* 1910; sometime Capt. RE: *m.* 1st, 1934 (divorce 1950), Ursula, el. da. of the late Bernard Richard Meirion Darwin, CBE; 2ndly, 1951, Mary, da. of the late Vincent Fedden, and has issue living, (by 1st m.) Philip Erasmus, *b.* 1943. *Residence*, Durham Wharf, Hammersmith Terr., W6.

Grandchildren of the late George Macaulay Trevelyan, OM, CBE, FRS (infra):—
Issue of the late Charles Humphry Trevelyan, *b.* 1909, *d.* 1964: *m.* 1936, Mary Trumbull (of Gazeley, Trumpington, Cambridge), yst. da. of Winchester Bennett, of Everit St., New Haven, Conn., U.S.A.:—

Thomas Arnold (14, Armadale Rd., Fulham, SW6), *b.* 1942: ed. at Bryanston, and King's Coll., Camb (MA); MB, BChir, MRCGP: *m.* 1st, 1965 (m. diss. 1974), Anne, da. of James Jones; 2ndly, 1974, Anita, da. of Reginald Martyn Smith, of Chaddesley Corbett, Worcs., and has issue living (by 1st m.), Harry, *b.* 1968,—Emma, *b.* 1969.—Selina Rose, *b.* 1969.——George Macaulay (23, Cantelowes Rd., NW1), *b.* 1944: ed. at Bryanston, Queen's Coll., Oxford, and London Sch. of Econ.: *m.* 1967, Susan, da. of Mark Pearson, of Burton Joyce, Notts., and has issue living, Sasha France, *b.* 1969,—Will Mark, *b.* 1971,—Laura Kate, *b.* 1968.——Humphry Bennett (16, Princess Mary Rd., N16) (twin), *b.* 1944: ed. at Bryanston, and Trin. Coll., Camb.——Jane Winchester, *b.* 1938: *m.* 1960, David Armstrong, of 9, Alleyn Rd., W. Dulwich, SE21, and has issue living, Richard Michael Boris, *b.* 1961,—Sarah Jane, *b.* 1965,—Rachel Elizabeth, *b.* 1966. ——Mary Harriet (60, Fawnbrake Av., SE24), *b.* 1939; MB, BS.

Issue of the late George Macaulay Trevelyan, O.M., C.B.E., F.R.S. (the famous historian), 3rd son of 2nd baronet, *b.* 1876, *d.* 1962: *m.* 1904, Janet Penrose, C.H., who *d.* 1956, da. of the late Humphry Ward:—

Mary Caroline, *b.* 1905; MA (Oxon); Hon. DLitt Leeds, and Durham: *m.* 1930, the Rt. Rev. John Richard Humpidge Moorman, DD, 9th Lord Bishop of Ripon, of Bishop Mount, Ripon, Yorks.

This family is a younger branch of the Trevelyans, baronets of Nettlecombe [*see* colls. thereof]. The 1st baronet was Gov. of Madras 1859-60, and Financial member of Gov.-Gen's. Council at Calcutta 1862-5. The 2nd baronet, the Rt. Hon. Sir George Otto Trevelyan, O.M., D.C.L., LL.D. (an historian, and author of "The Life and Letters of Lord Macaulay," and other works), was a Lord of the Admiralty 1869-70, Parliamentary Sec. to Admiralty 1880-82, Ch. Sec. for Ireland 1882-4, Chancellor of Duchy of Lancaster 1884-5, and Sec. for Scotland and ex-officio Keeper of the Great Seal of Scotland 1886 and 1892-5, and M.P. for Tynemouth (*L*) 1865-8, for the Border Burghs 1868-86 (when he was defeated), and for Bridgeton Div. of Glasgow (*L*) 1887-97. The 3rd baronet, the Rt. Hon. Sir Charles Philips Trevelyan, was Parliamentary Sec. to Board of Education 1908-14, and Pres. of Board of Education Jan. to Nov. 1924 and 1929-31, and sat as M.P. Elland Div. of N. Part of W. Riding of Yorkshire (*L*) 1899-1918, and for Newcastle-upon-Tyne (*Lab.*) 1922-31.

TRITTON, Creation (U.K.) 1905, of Bloomfield, Borough of Lambeth, co. London.

Forward.

Sir GEOFFREY ERNEST TRITTON, *C.B.E.*, 3rd *Baronet*; *b.* Nov. 3rd, 1900; *s.* his father, *Sir* ALFRED ERNEST, 1939; ed. at Eton, and at Trin. Coll., Camb.; European War 1939-45 as Major Rifle Brig. (T.A.) (M.B.E., American Bronze star, French Croix de Guerre); a DL of Wilts. 1955, and High Sheriff 1958; MBE (Mil.) 1945, CBE (Civil) 1958: *m.* 1925, Mary Patience Winifred, who *d.* 1960, da. of John Kenneth Foster, of Egton Manor, Yorks, and 49, Pont St., SW, and has issue.

Arms—Argent, on a bend cotised gules a besant between two esquires' helmets or. Crest—A horse statant argent, resting the dexter forefoot upon a besant proper. *Residence*—Stanton House, Highworth, Wilts.

Son living—ANTHONY JOHN ERNEST (The Grange Farm, Marston Meysey, Cricklade, Wilts.; Cavalry Club), *b.* March 4th, 1927; ed. at Eton; Maj. (ret.) The Queen's Own Hussars: *m.* 1957, Diana, da. of Rear-Adm. St. John Aldrich Micklethwait, CB, DSO [*see* Welby, Bt., colls.], and has issue living, Jeremy Ernest, *b.* 1961,—Clarissa Mary Penelope, *b.* 1959.

Daughter living—Julia Mary, *b.* 1930 : *m.* 1952, Richard Norman Kingzett [*see* Agnew, Bt., *cr.* 1895]. *Residence*, 18, Sloane Avenue, Chelsea, S.W.3.

Sisters living—Edith Gwendolen (*Gwen, Lady Colman*), *b.* 1902 : *m.* 1924, Sir Jeremiah Colman, 2nd Bt. (*cr.* 1907), who *d.* 1961. *Residence*, Bartletts Farm, Mattingley, near Basingstoke.—— Elspeth Muriel (*Lady Dent*), *b.* 1907 : *m.* 1927, Sir Robert Annesley Wilkinson Dent, C.B., and has issue living, Evelyn Robert Wilkinson, *b.* 1934,—Averil Anstice, *b.* 1928,—Verena Jane, *b.* 1931,—Lavinia Mary, *b.* 1937. *Residence*, Lyvennet Bank, Maulds Meaburn, Penrith, Cumberland.——Anstice Marion (*Anstice, Lady Harford*), *b.* 1909: *m.* 1931, Lt.-Col. Sir George Arthur Harford, 2nd Bt., who *d.* 1967. *Residence*, Lockeridge Down, nr. Marlborough, Wilts.

The 1st baronet, Sir (Charles) Ernest Tritton, sat as M.P. for Norwood Div. of Lambeth (C) July 1892 to Jan. 1906.

TROLLOPE, Creation (E.) 1642, of Casewick, Lincolnshire.

AUDIO SED TACEO

Sir ANTHONY OWEN CLAVERING TROLLOPE, 16th *Baronet;* b. Jan. 15th, 1917; s. his father, Sir GORDON CLAVERING, 1958; European War 1939-45 in Middle East and New Guinea with 2nd/5th Australian Field Regt.: m. 1942, Joan Mary Alexis, da. of Alexis Robert Gibbs, of Manly, N.S. Wales, and has issue.

Arms—Vert, three stags courant argent, attired or, within a bordure of the !second. Crest—On a mount vert, a stag courant as in the arms, holding an oak-leaf in his mouth proper.

Residence—Clavering, 77, Roseville Avenue, Roseville, N.S. Wales.

Sons living—ANTHONY SIMON, b. 1945.——Hugh Irwin, b. 1947.

Brother living—Gordon Paul Clavering, b. 1918.

Daughters living of 13th Baronet—Laura Harriet (Carylea, Headway Close, Teignmouth, Devon), b. 1899: m. 1920, Charles Wreford, who d. 1937, and has issue living, Aurelia Cary Roslyn, b. 1921: m. 1950, William Macintosh Ball, FRICS, of Greenmantle, Wynnstow Park, Oxted, Surrey, and has issue living, John Trollope Macintosh b. 1954, Aurelia Cary Rennie b. 1958.——Iona Rebecca, b. 1907: m. 1st, 1927, Lt.-Col. Cleveland Mervyn Keble, OBE, Wilts Regt., who d. 1948; 2ndly, 1953, Stephen Philp, of Welbrook, Peterchurch, Hereford, and has issue living (by 1st m.), Elizabeth Felicia, b. 1928: m. 1949, Lt.-Col. Peter Lawrence de Carteret Martin, Cheshire Regt., of Fair Fields, Newton Port, Haddington, East Lothian, and has issue living, David Peter de Carteret b. 1956, Fiona Elizabeth b. 1953,—Heather Fiona, b. 1933: m. 1958, Maj. Anthony Frederick Walker, Cheshire Regt.

Daughter living of 10th Baronet—Sylvia, b. 1900. *Residence*, 2, Ebury House, Elizabeth St., SW1.

Widow living of 15th Baronet—MARY ISABEL (*Mary, Lady Trollope*), da. of Owen Blacket, of Lindfield, N.S. Wales: m. 1913, Sir Gordon Clavering Trollope, 15th Bt., who d. 1958. *Residence,*

Collateral Branches living.

Grandson of the late Edward Hazel Trollope, son of the late Rev. John Trollope, son of the late Rev. Thomas Daniel Trollope, grandson of the late Henry Trollope, 3rd son of 3rd baronet :—
Issue of the late Herbert Edward Trollope, b. 1859, d. 1930 : m. 1901, Sarah Anne, who d. 1958, da. of John Wall, of Wedmore, Somerset :—
John Herbert Hazel, b. 1908 : m. 1939, Ruth, da. of Frederick Warry, of Freshford, Somerset, and has issue living, Beatrice Mary, b. 1942: m. 1963, Peter Old, of 20, Hilltop Rd., Twyford, Berks., and has issue living, Andrew b. 1967, Rachel b. 1964, Sarah b. 1971,—Maureen Hazel, b. 1945: m. 1973, Ian Joseph Kampel, CEng, MIERE, of 78, Ameysford Rd., Ferndown, Dorset,—Susan Bridget, b. 1947: m. 1969, Elemér Fejér, of 5, Victoria Rd., Wyke Regis, Weymouth, Dorset, and has issue living, Karen Lisa b. 1974. *Residence*, 2, Buxton Rd., Rodwell, Weymouth, Dorset.

Grandson of the late Capt. Frederick Trollope, son of the late Rear-Adm. George Barne Trollope, CB, 4th son of the late Rev. John Trollope (b. 1729), 2nd son of the late Henry Trollope (ante):—
Issue of the late Charles William Annesley Trollope, I.S.O., b. 1850, d. 1935: m. 1877, Marian Eirene, who d. 1930, da. of the late Rev. William Watson, of Water Newton, Hunts:—
Leonard Edward Annesley, b. 1892; ed. at Westminster; European War 1916-19 with R.G.A.: m. 1922, Cecily Aimee, da. of the late A. Derrick, of Corners, Ryde, Isle of Wight. *Residence*, 9, The Close, Alcombe, Minehead.

The Rt. Hon. Sir John Trollope, P.C., 7th Bt., M.P. for Lincolnshire (C) 1861-68, was cr. Baron Kesteven (peerage of United Kingdom) 1868, when the Baronetcy remained merged in the Barony until the death of the 3rd Baron (killed in action during European War) 1915, when it devolved upon his cousin, Sir William Henry Trollope, 10th Bt. Sir Gordon Clavering Trollope, 15th Bt. s. Nov. 1957 and d. Oct. 1958, when he was s. by his son, Sir Anthony Owen Clavering Trollope, 16th Bt.

TROUBRIDGE. Creation (G.B.) 1799, of Plymouth.

[Name pronounced "Troobridge."]

Sir PETER TROUBRIDGE, 6th *Baronet*, el. son of Vice-Adm. Sir Thomas Hope Troubridge, KCB, DSO, only son of Adm. Sir Ernest Charles Thomas Troubridge, KCMG, CB, MVO, 3rd son of 3rd baronet; b. June 6th, 1927; s. his kinsman, *Lt.-Col. Sir* THOMAS ST. VINCENT WALLACE, *MBE,* 1963; Lt.-Cdr. RN (ret.); a Member of Stock Exchange, and a partner in Hedderwick, Stirling, Grumbar & Co.; OStJ: m. 1954, the Hon. Venetia Daphne Weeks, da. of 1st Baron Weeks, and has issue.

Arms—Or, on a bridge embattled of three arches, through which water is flowing towards the base proper, a tower of the second, thereon hoisted a broad pennant flying towards the sinister; on a canton azure, two keys in saltire, the wards upwards, or. Crest—A dexter arm-embowed, habited azure, holding a flagstaff, thereon a flag azure charger with two keys in saltire or.

Residence—The Manor House, Elsted, Midhurst, Sussex.

Ne cede arduis.
Yield not to difficulties.

Son living—THOMAS RICHARD, b. Jan. 23rd, 1955.
Daughters living—Amanda Marguerite, b. 1957.——Camilla June, b. 1961.
Brothers living—Edward St. Vincent (7, Liskeard Gdns., SE3; White's Club), b. 1930; Maj. (ret.) RM: m. 1st 1955 (m. diss. 1974), Jennifer Anne, da. of the late E. Billing-Lewis; 2ndly, 1974, Patricia Barbara, da. of Maj. Chevalier Hannibal Alexander Scicluna, OBE, of 29, Milner St., Sliema, Malta, GC; and has issue living (by 1st m.), Rodney St. Vincent, b. 1957.——Charlotte Louise, b. 1960,——Emma Marguerite, b. 1963 (by 2nd m.) Amelia Clare, b. 1974.——Thomas (1B, Gertrude St., SW10), b. 1939: m. 1971, Baroness Marie Christine, da. of Baron Gunther Hubertus von Reibnitz.
Sister living—(Elizabeth) June, b. 1933: m. 1956, Alan G. L. Baxter, of Gilston, Leven, Fife, and has issue living, Edward Thomas b. 1960,—Elizabeth Anne, b. 1958,—Sarah Evelyn, b. 1962,—Mary Emma, b. 1965,—Louisa Jane, b. 1969.
Aunts living—Mary Laura, b. 1894: m. 1916, Col. Robin Otter, MC, Norfolk Regt., who d. 1965, [E. Guilford, colls.], and has issue living, Ann Eva, b. 1916: m. 1939, Arnold Massey Gamble, of The Cottage, Turk Dean, Glos., and has issue living, Timothy Massey b. 1941: m. 1971, Georgina Mead,—Rodney Michael, b. 1944: m. 1971, Anne McCormick,—Barbara Mary, b. 1919: m. 1946, Maj. Frederick E. de Bohun Boone, MC, of Warren Farm, Westacre, Norfolk, and has issue living, Christopher Henry b. 1947, William Robin b. 1950, Edward Arthur b. 1958, Elizabeth Mary b. 1955,—Susan Elizabeth (Priory Cottage, Crowcombe, Taunton), b. 1922: m. 1st, 1943, Maj. Marmaduke John Matthews, who d. 1966; 2ndly, 1969, Maj. Norman Dudley Hart, late R. Glos. Hussars, and has issue living (by 1st m.), David Marmaduke (Beechams, Barrington Court, Ilminster, Somerset), b. 1945: m. 1968, Felicity Shapland (and has issue living, William Marmaduke b. 1970, Rebecca Jane b. 1969), Jeremy John (104, Ormonde Court, Upper Richmond Rd., SW15), b. 1947: m. 1972, Clarke Beverley Gordon,—Lucy Jane, b. 1932: m. 1955, Francis Denzil Newton, and has issue living, Thomas Robin b. 1958, Charlotte Mary b. 1956, Sarah Lucy b. 1959——Charlotte Edith Annette, b. 1896: m. 1st 1916, Ernest Alfred Collyer Lloyd, Lt. Scots Gds, who d. (killed in action) 1917; 2ndly, 1920, Daniel Walter Thomas Gurney, MC, late KRRC, of 4, Walton St., SW3, and has issue living (by 1st m.), Annette Diana Alys (posthumous), b. 1917: m. 1955, Edward Bloomfield Seager, of Chimes, Holton St. Mary, Colchester (by 2nd m.), Richard Daniel (of 23, Campden St., W8), b. 1921: m. 1949, Clarice Annabel, da. of the late Geoffrey Swinford Laird Clowes, and has issue living, Juliet Annabel b. 1957, Alice Charlotte b. 1958,—June Rose Charlotte Rachel b. 1924: m. 1963, Robert Duncan Fyfe.
Mother living—Lilly (Lady Troubridge) (Oakshott, Hawkley, Liss, Hants.), da. of the late Herman Greverus Kleinwort, of 45, Belgrave Sq., S.W.1, and Wierton Place, Maidstone: m. 1925, Vice-Adm. Sir Thomas Hope Troubridge, KCB, DSO, who d. 1949.
Widow living of 5th Baronet—PAMELA (Pamela, Lady Troubridge) (of Ivy Cottage, Longstock, Stockbridge, Hants.), da. of the late Percy Clough, of The Knowle, Keighley, Yorks.: m. 1939, Lt.-Col. Sir Thomas St. Vincent Wallace Troubridge, MBE, 5th Bt. who d. 1963.

The 1st baronet, Adm. Sir Thomas (son of the late Richard Troubridge, of London), was a distinguished naval commander, and sat as M.P. for Yarmouth 1802-6. The 2nd baronet, Adm. Sir Edward Thomas, C.B., sat as M.P. for Sandwich 1831-47, and Col. Sir Thomas, C.B., the 3rd baronet, greatly distinguished himself in the Crimea, where he lost his right leg and left foot.

TRUSCOTT, Creation (U.K.) 1909, of Oakleigh, East Grinstead, Sussex.

Prepared for either.

IN UTRUMQUE PARATUS

Truth against all the world.

Sir GEORGE JAMES IRVING TRUSCOTT, 3rd Baronet; b. Oct. 24th, 1929; s. his father, Sir ERIC HOMEWOOD STANHAM, 1973: m. 1st, 1954 (m. annulled on his petition 1958), Irene Marion Craig Barr Brown; 2ndly, 1962, Yvonne Dora, yr. da. of the late Frank Edward Nicholson, of Carshalton, Surrey, and has issue by 2nd m.

Arms—Argent, three chevronels gules, between two mullets in chief of the last, pierced of the' field, and a knight's helmet in base proper; a chief checky of the second and first. Crest—A fasces erect, surmounted by a palm branch slipped and an arrow saltireways, all proper.

Residence—High Beech, Kingsley Green, Haslemere, Surrey.

Son living—RALPH ERIC NICHOLSON, b. Feb. 21st, 1966.
Daughter living—Ruth Emma, b. 1967.
Sister living—Jennifer Margaret Anne, b. 1932: m. 1958, Lt.-Cdr. Edward Martyn Theodore Segar, RN (ret.), of Stanton Hill, Priorsfield Rd., Godalming, Surrey, and has issue living, John Edward, b. 1965,—Jane Margaret, b. 1959,—Anne Mary, b. 1962.
Aunt living (daughter of 1st baronet)—Mary Guthrie (Pine Bluff, Heatherwood Park Rd., Totland Bay, I. of Wight), b. 1890: m. 1st, 1915, Arthur Sydney Waller, from whom she obtained a divorce 1923; 2ndly, 1929, Francis Wigglesworth, who d. 1945, and has issue living, (by 1st m.) Edmund Francis Waller TRUSCOTT, OBE (12 Logan Place W8), b. 1917; formerly Wing-Cdr. RAFVR; assumed by deed poll 1930 the surname of Truscott; OBE (Mil) 1944: m. 1940, Alvina McKnight, da. of the late Lloyd Robertson, of Kingston, Pennsylvania, USA, and has issue living, John Robertson b. 1948.

Widow living of 2nd Baronet—RENÉE FRANKLIN (Renée, Lady Truscott) (18, Letchmore Rd., Radlett, Herts.), yr. da. of John William Marshall, and formerly wife of William Archibald Redgrave: m. 1953, as his 3rd wife, Sir Eric Homewood Stanham Truscott, 2nd Bt., who d. 1973.

The 1st baronet, Sir George Wyatt Truscott (son of the late Sir Francis Wyatt Truscott, Lord Mayor of London 1879-80), was Chm. of Brown, Knight & Truscott, Ltd., printers and stationers, of Suffolk Lane, E.C., and an Alderman of City of London (Sheriff 1902-3, Lord Mayor 1908-9, Hon. Freeman 1937).

TUBBS, Creation (U.K.) 1929, of Wotton-under-Edge, co. Gloucester. [Extinct 1941.]

Sir STANLEY WILLIAM TUBBS, 1st and last *Baronet*.

Widow living of 1st Baronet—EVELYN SHERBROOKE (*Lady Durand*), C.B.E., 2nd da. of the late Charles Arnold Crane, of The Reddings. near Cheltenham ; is a J.P., Vice-Pres. of Stroud Conservative Assocn. (formerly Pres. and Chm. of Women's Branch) ; formerly Chm. of Midland Area Women's Advisory Council, Pres. of Glos. British Legion (Women's Section) a National Vice-Pres., Vice-Chm. of Midland Area, and Chm. of Glos. co. Women's Section 1937-53), a Member of National Executive of Conservative Party, and of Governing Body of Ashridge Coll.; Organizer of British Red Cross So. Hospital Supply Depot, and Women's Vol. Sers. Centre Organizer 1939-45; has British Red Cross So.'s Long Ser. medal with three Bars, Overseas medal, Victory medal, and Medaille de la Reine Elisabeth of Belgium ; CBE (Civil) 1955: *m.* 1st, 1921, as his second wife, Sir Stanley William Tubbs, 1st Bt., who *d.* 1941, when the title became ext.; 2ndly, 1944, Brig. Sir Alan Algernon Marion Durand, MC, 3rd Bt., who *d.* 1971. *Residence*, Ellerncroft, Wotton-under-Edge, Glos.

TUCK, Creation (U.K.) 1910, of Park Crescent, St. Marylebone.

CUM · DEO

With God.

Sir BRUCE ADOLPH REGINALD TUCK, 3rd *Baronet :* b. June 29th, 1926 ; s. his father, *Major Sir* (WILLIAM) REGINALD, 1954 ; ed. at Canford Sch.; sometime Lieut. Scots Guards: *m.* 1st, 1949 (m. diss. in Jamaica 1964), Luise, da. of John C. Renfro, of Sán Angelo, Texas, USA; 2ndly, 1968, Pamela, da. of Alfred Michael Nicholson, of London, and has issue (by 1st m.).

Arms—Or, an antique lamp flaming azure, in base a hurt charged with four F's in cross of the field, on a chief of the same two hands in the act of blessing of the first. **Crest**— A lion sejant sable supporting with the paws an artist's palette proper, inscribed thereon the word " Thorough" sable. *Residences*—95, Eaton Sq., SW1; 95Ea, Montego Bay Jamaica. *Club*—Lansdowne.

Son living—By 1st m.—RICHARD BRUCE, b. Oct. 7th 1952.——Christopher John, b. 1954.
Daughter living—By 2nd m.—Charlotte Emily Pamela, b. 1974.
Sister living—Moyra Grace, b. 1920 : *m.* 1st, 1947, Lee David Greif, who *d.* 1950 ; 2ndly, 1951, Major Alvin Greif, U.S. Army Air Force, who *d.* 1958 ; 3rdly, 1959, Nigel Digby Pemberton. *Residences*, 30, E. 65th St., New York City, USA; Montego Bay, Jamaica.

Aunts living (daughters of 1st baronet)—Sybil Grace (*Lady Stern*), b. 1887: *m.* 1925, as his second wife, Sir Edward David Stern, 1st Bt., who *d.* 1933. *Residence*, 8, Abbey Lodge, Park Rd., Regent's Park, NW8.——Muriel Jeanetta, b. 1892: *m.* 1924, Leonard Nathaniel Goldsmid-Montefiore, who *d.* 1961, and has issue living, Alan, b. 1926; Fellow of Balliol Coll., Oxford,—David Goldsmid (University of Ibadan, Ibadan, Nigeria); b. 1929, MD, Camb. Univ., MB, B.Chir.; Prof. of Med. Microbiology, Ibadan Univ. *Residence*, 55, Abbey Lodge, Park Rd., Regent's Park, NW8.

Sir Adolph Tuck, 1st Bt., son of the late Raphael Tuck, fine art publisher, was Chm. and Managing Director of Raphael Tuck and Sons (Limited), of Raphael House, Moorfields, E.C.

TUITE, Creation (I.) 1622, of Sonnagh, Westmeath.

LLELUIAH

[Name pronounced " Tute."]

Sir DENNIS GEORGE HARMSWORTH TUITE, MBE, 13th *Baronet,* yr. son of the late Capt. Hugh George Spencer Tuite, R. Northumberland Fus., 2nd son of the late Maj.-Gen. Hugh Manley Tuite, RA, 2nd son of 9th baronet; b. Jan. 26th, 1904; s. his brother, *Sir* BRIAN HUGH MORGAN, 1970; ed. at St. Paul's Sch.; Maj. (ret.) RE; Burma 1930-32 (medal); 1939-45 War; MBE (Mil) 1946: *m.* 1947, Margaret Essie, only da. of the late Col. Walter Leslie Dundas, DSO, and has issue.

Arms—Quarterly, argent and gules. **Crest**—An angel vested argent, holding in the dexter hand a flaming sword proper, the sinister resting on a shield of the arms.

Residence,—Windhaven, Ladygate Drive, Grayshott, Hindhead, Surrey, GU26 6DR.

Sons living—CHRISTOPHER HUGH, b. Nov. 3rd, 1949.—— Jeremy Denis, b. 1951.——Patrick Leslie, b. 1954.
Sister living—Moira Gwendolen Hatton, b. 1899 : *m.* 1922, Squadron Leader Henry John Hunter, R.A.F., who *d.* 1958. *Residence*, 116, Saltdean Vale, Saltdean, Sussex.

This family, which has been settled in Ireland since 1172, is descended from Sir Richard de Tuitt who that year accompanied the Earl of Pembroke to that country. The 7th baronet was murdered at Sonnagh in 1783.

TUPPER, Creation (U.K.) 1888, of Armdale, Halifax, Nova Scotia.

L'ESPOIR EST MA FORCE
Hope is my strength.

Sir CHARLES HIBBERT TUPPER, 5th
Baronet; b. July 4th, 1930; *s.* his father, *Sir*
JAMES MACDONALD, 1967: *m.* 1959, Bernice
Yvonne Quinn, and has issue.

Arms—Per fesse azure and or, on a fesse ermine between two boars passant in chief or, and a sprig of may
flower slipped and leaved in base proper, three escallops
gules. **Crest**—On a mount vert, a greyhound statant sable,
charged on the body with two escallops or, and holding in
the mouth a sprig of mayflower as in the arms.

Residence—Suite 1101, 955, Marine Drive, W.
Vancouver, BC.

Son living—CHARLES HIBBERT, *b.* July 10th, 1964.

Sister living—Janet Mary, *b.* 1929: *m.* 1951, William
John Couldwell, MD, CN, of 4270, Salish Drive,
Vancouver 13, British Colombia, and has issue living,
William Tupper, *b.* 1955—Susan Janice, *b.* 1953—Sandra
Lee, *b.* 1954.

Daughter living of 2nd Baronet—Margot Stewart, *b.* 1928.
Residence, Suite 2, 893, Dorchester Av., Winnipeg, 9,
Manitoba, Canada.

Daughters living of 3rd Baronet—Janet Macdonald, *b.*
1920: *m.* 1944, Philip Lionel Underwood, late Capt.
Roy. Canadian Artillery, and has issue living, Harry
Charles Gordon, *b.* 1951,—Mary Fielding, *b.* 1946: *m.*
1969, Claude-Frédéric Roger Marie Ingell de Kerckhove Varent,—Nora Frances, *b.* 1958.—
Dorothy Joyce, *b.* 1922: *m.* 1944, Maj. Edward Arunah Dunlop, OBE, GM, Queen's Own Rifles of
Canada, and has issue living, Edward Arunah, *b.* 1946,—Charlotte Mary Ferguson, *b.* 1949.
Residence, 6, Meredith Cres., Toronto, Canada.

Sister living of 2nd Baronet—Frances (Guildwood Villa Nursing Home, Scarborough, Ontario,
Canada).

Widow living of 3rd Baronet—MARY DOUGLAS MIRA DICKEY (*Mary, Lady Tupper*) (of 8, Meredith
Cres., Toronto, Canada): *m.* 1910, Sir Charles Tupper, 3rd baronet, who *d.* 1962.

Collateral Branches living.

Issue of the late Maj. Reginald Hibbert Tupper, QC, LLD, brother of 3rd and 4th baronets,
b. 1893, *d.* 1972: *m.* 1916, Isobel Marion Wilson (1420, Beach Drive, Victoria, BC):—
Charles Gordon Hibbert, *b.* 1918; 1939-45 War as Lt. Seaforth Highlanders of Canada: *m.* 1946,
Margaret Ada, BA McGill, da. of James Albert Campbell, QC, of Vancouver, and has issue living,
Charles Reginald Hibbert, *b.* 1947.——David Wilson Hibbert, LLB, *b.* 1921; 1939-45 War with
RCAF: *m.* 1947, Joan Margot, da. of the late Col. Austin Gillies, VD, of Ottawa, and has issue
living, Sidney Victor Hibbert, *b.* 1948,—Charles Austin Hibbert, *b.* 1951,—Julie Isabel, *b.*
1953.

Grandchildren of the late William Johnson Tupper, KC (Lt.-Gov. of Manitoba),
3rd son of 1st baronet:—
Issue of the late Charles William Tupper, Q.C., *b.* 1898, *d.* 1960: *m.* 1st, 1929, Ray
Macdonald; 2ndly, 1941, Winifred Lillian Craske, who *d.* 1956:—
(By 2nd m.) Charles James *b.* 1942.——(By 1st m.) Margaret Ray, *b.* 1931: *m.* 1956, William
Macdonald Price, of 700, Cardinal St., St. Laurent, Montreal, Canada, and has issue living,
Charles Macdonald, *b.* 1958,—Scott William, *b.* 1960.

The name of Tupper can be traced at Bury and vicinity, W. Sussex, from the 13th century.
Thomas Tupper emigrated from Kent to Massachusetts in 1635. Charles Tupper, 4th in descent
from him, moved to Cornwallis, Nova Scotia 1760. His grandson, the Rt. Hon. Sir Charles
Tupper, GCMG, CB, LLD, MD, 1st Bt. was fourteen consecutive times returned as MP for his
native co. (Cumberland, N.S.), and represented it for thirty-three years in the Canadian House
of Commons, was Prime Min. of Nova Scotia 1864-67, and was High Commr. in Great Britain
for Dominion of Canada 1883-87, and 1888-96, and Premier of Canada 1896.

TURING, Creation (N.S.) 1638, of Foveran, Aberdeenshire.
Fortune aids the daring.

AUDENTES FORTUNA JUVAT.

Sir JOHN LESLIE TURING, *MC*, 11th
Baronet; b. Sept. 13th, 1895; *s.* his
brother, *Sir* ROBERT ANDREW HENRY,
1970; ed. at Wellington Coll.; late
Lt. Seaforth Highlanders; 1914-18
War (wounded, MC).

Arms—Argent, on a bend sable, three boars'
heads or. **Crest**—A hand holding a helmet proper.
Supporters—Two stags proper.

Residence,—Warren Farm House, Brandy
Hole Lane, Chichester, Sussex.

Collateral Branches living

Grandchildren of the late Rev.
John Robert Turing, son of
the late John Robert Turing,
brother of 7th baronet:—
Issue of the late Julius Mathison Turing,
b. 1873, *d.* 1947: *m.* 1907, Ethel Sara
(Stoneycrest Nursing Home, Churt
Rd., Hindhead, Surrey), da. of the
late Edward Waller Stoney, CIE:—

JOHN FERRIER (267, Stradbroke Grove, Clayhall, Ilford, Essex), b. Sept. 1st, 1908; Solicitor 1931; 1939-45 War in France, Middle East and India with Queen's R. Regt. and Claims Commn., becoming Col. and Dep. Dir of Claims, India: m. 1st, 1934 (m. diss. 1960), Joan, da. of Robert Humphreys, ICS, of Cork; 2ndly, 1960, Beryl Mary Ada, da. of the late Herbert Vaughan Hann, and has issue living, (by 2nd marriage) John Dermot, b. 1961,—(by 1st marriage) Inagh Jean, b. 1936: m. 1960, Warren Gray, Solicitor, of Granta Cottage, Blagdon Hill, Taunton, and has issue living, Mark Warren b. 1961, Stephen Paul b. 1969, Rachel Mary b. 1963, Deborah Jean b. 1964,—Shuna b. 1940,—Janet Ferrier, b. 1947.

Issue of the late Harvey Doria Turing, b. 1877, d. 1950: m. 1918, Violet, who d. 1961, da. of the late Rev. Harry Alsager Sheringham :—
Penelope Anne Tryon, b. 1925. Residence, 411, Beatty House, Dolphin Sq., SW1.

Sir William Turyn attached himself to the fortunes of King David II., and shared that monarch's exile; his loyalty was however subsequently rewarded by a grant of the barony of Foveran, in Aberdeenshire, which his descendants held more than 300 years. Sir John Turing of Foveran, 1st Bt., espoused the cause of Charles I. He was taken prisoner by the Covenanters 1639 who later sacked Foveran. He fought at Battle of Worcester 1651. The right to this baronetcy was sustained by the Lyon Office in 1882 to Sir Robert Fraser Turing, 8th Bt., and by a Committee of the Privy Council in 1912.

Twisleton (Twisleton-Wykeham-Fiennes), see Fiennes.

TWYSDEN, Creation (E.) 1611, of East Peckham, Kent. [Extinct 1970.]

Sir WILLIAM ADAM DUNCAN TWYSDEN, 12th and last *Baronet.*

Sisters living of 12th Baronet—Aileen Elisabeth, b. 1891. Address, c/o Coutts & Co., 440, Strand, WC2.——Anne Evelyn Frances, b. 1898: m. 1921, Capt. Thomas Balfour Fellowes, RN (ret.), and has issue living, Rupert Thomas Butler, b. 1922,—Edmond Francis Dorset, b. 1935; Maj. LI. Residence, Hurford's Mead, Hockworthy, Wellington, Som.

Widows living of 11th and 12th Baronets—MARY, da. of the late Rear-Adm. H. E. C. Blagrove: m. 1st, 1945, Sir Anthony Roger Duncan Twysden, 11th Bt., who d. 1946; 2ndly, 1949, Capt. Peter Gerald Charles Dickens, DSO, MBE, DSC, RN, of Lye Green Forge, Crowborough, Sussex, el. son of the late Adm. Sir Gerald Charles Dickens, KCVO, CB, CMG.——ISLA (Lady Twysden), (B9, Shirley Towers, Vane Hill, Torquay), da. of the late Alfred Evan Howlett, of Rye: m. 1949, Lt.-Cdr. Sir William Adam Duncan Twysden, RN, 12th Bt., who d. 1970, when the baronetcy became ext.

TYRWHITT, Creation (U.K.) 1919, of Terschelling, and of Oxford.
[Name pronounced "Tirrit."]

Sir REGINALD THOMAS NEW-MAN TYRWHITT, 3rd *Baronet, b.* Feb. 21st, 1947 ; *s.* his father, *Adm. Sir* ST. JOHN REGINALD JOSEPH, *K.C.B., DSO, DSC,* 1961: *m.* 1972, Sheila Gail, da. of William Alistair Crawford Nicoll, MA, LLB, of Kingsham Old Farm, Milland, Hants.

Arms—Gules, three tyrwhitts (lapwings) or. Crest—A woodman wreathed with oak and holding a club, all proper. Supporters—Dexter, a savage wreathed about the loins and head with oak proper, and holding over the shoulder in the exterior hand a club or; sinister, a sailor of the Royal Navy holding in the exterior hand a coil of rope proper. Residence—19, Bladon Close, Guildford, Surrey.

Brother living—JOHN EDWARD CHARLES, b. July 27th, 1953.
Sister living—Veronica Mary, b. 1944.
Aunts living (daughters of 1st baronet)—Dame Mary Joan Caroline, D.B.E., T.D., b. 1903 ; Brigadier WRAC (ret.); ADC to HM 1949-51, OBE (Mil) 1946, DBE (Mil) 1949. Residence, Constable's Cottage, Yatton Keynell, Chippenham, Wilts.——Patricia Angela.

Mary, *b.* 1913; late Senior Comd. A.T.S.: *m.* 1945, Capt. Anthony John Alfred Lacy, Suffolk Regt., and has issue living, *Rev.* David Anthony, *b.* 1947; ordained RC Priest 1972,—John Reginald, *b.* 1948: *m.* 1970, Johneen, da. of Michael Whitfield, of Wellesbourne, Warwicks.,—Richard Patrick James, *b.* 1950: *m.* 1973, Penelope, da. of the Hon. Simon Chelmsford Loader Maffey [see B. Rugby],—Anne Mary, *b.* 1953. *Residence,* Glebe House, Weston-under-Wetherley, Leamington Spa.

Widow living of 2nd Baronet—NANCY VERONICA (*Lady Agnew*), only child of the late Capt. Charles Newman Gilbey, of Folkestone, Kent: *m.* 1st, 1944, Adm. Sir St. John Reginald Joseph Tyrwhitt, KCB, DSO, DSC, 2nd baronet, who *d.* 1961; 2ndly, 1965, Sir (William) Godfrey Agnew, KCVO, of Pinehurst, South Ascot, Berks.

This family descends from Richard Tyrwhitt of Nantyr Hall, Denbighshire, Recorder of Chester (*d.* 1836), 3rd son of John Tyrwhitt of Netherclay House, Som., and brother of Sir Thomas Tyrwhitt (later Jones), who was cr. a Bt. 1808, ancestor of Barons Berners. The 1st baronet, Adm. of the Fleet, Sir Reginald Yorke Tyrwhitt, G.C.B., D.S.O. (son of the late Rev. Richard St. John Tyrwhitt) was Com.-in-Ch. China Station 1927-29, and Com.-in-Ch. at the Nore 1930-33. The 2nd baronet, Adm. Sir St. John Reginald Joseph Tyrwhitt, K.C.B., D.S.O., D.S.C., was Ch. of Staff to Com.-in-Ch. Allied Forces Mediterranean 1958-9, and a Lord Commr. of Admiralty, Second Sea Lord and Ch. of Naval Personnel 1959-61.

USHER, Creation (U.K.) 1899, of Norton, Ratho, Midlothian, and of Wells, Hobkirk, Roxburghshire.

With nothing base.

Sir PETER LIONEL USHER, 5th *Baronet,* *b.* Oct. 1st, 1931; *s.* his father *Sir* ROBERT STUART, 1962.

Arms—Gules, a saltire between four batons argent, garnished sable. **Crest**—A dexter arm couped below the elbow, vested azure, cuffed argent, holding in the hand a baton proper.

Seat—Hallrule, Hawick, Roxburghshire.

Brother Living—ROBERT EDWARD, *b.* April 18th, 1934.

Daughters living of 3rd Baronet—Katharine Alice, *b.* 1920 : *m.* 1943, George Simpson Macknight, W.S., who *d.* 1952, and has issue living, Neil John, *b.* 1946,—Elspeth Anne, *b.* 1949. *Residence,* Hallrule, Hawick, Roxburghshire.——Jacqueline, *b.* 1931: *m.* 1955, Capt. Christopher Michael Wolfe Murray, Gordon Highlanders (ret.), of Inworth Old Rectory, Kelvedon, Colchester [see Murray, Bt., cr. 1628, colls.].

Uncle living (son of 2nd baronet)—Thomas Clive, CBE, DSO, *b.* 1907; ed. at Uppingham; Brig. (ret.), late RA; formerly Comdg. 18th Training Bde.; was an ADC to HM 1957-58; 1939-45 War in N. Africa, Sicily, and Italy (DSO and Bar, CBE); DSO and Bar 1942, CBE (Mil) 1945: *m.* 1939, Valentine, da. of Brig. C. V. Stockwell, of Victoria, BC, and has issue living, Margaret Anne, *b.* 1941: *m.* 1964, Alan Harry Mactaggart, and has issue living, David Clive *b.* 1966, William Jeremy *b.* 1970. *Residence,* Wells Stables, Hawick, Roxburghshire.

Widow living of 4th Baronet—GERTRUDE MARTHA (*Lady Usher*) (of Hallrule, Hawick, Roxburghshire), da. of Lionel Barnard Sampson, of Tresmontes, Villa Valira, Prov. Cordoba, Argentina: *m.* 1930, Sir Robert Stuart Usher, 4th Bt., who *d.* 1962.

Collateral Branches living.

Issue of the late Lieut. Ronald James Usher, D.S.C., R.N., 2nd son of 2nd baronet, *b.* 1892, *d.* 1948: *m.* 1917, Alice Margaret (15A, Merchiston Park, Edinburgh, 10), el. da. of the late Harry Lawrence Usher, of Summerfield, Dunbar:—
Hazel Jean, *b.* 1918: *m.* 1940 the Rt. Hon. (James) Anthony Stodart, of Lorimers, N. Berwick.——Margaret Daphne, *b.* 1920: *m.* 1946, William Kirkpatrick, who *d.* 1967, and has issue living, Ronald James, *b.* 1948,—Susan Woodrow, *b.* 1949,—Margaret Anne *b.* 1953. *Residence,* Hassendean Common, Hawick, Roxburghshire.

Granddaughter of the late Lieut. Ronald James Usher, D.S.C., R.N. (ante):—
Issue of the late Lieut. Robert Ronald Harry Usher, R.N., *b.* 1924, *d.* 1947: *m.* 1945, Jane Hall, who *m.* 2ndly, 1954, James Murray Gregory-Jones, of Crossways, Victoria Sq., Penarth, Glam.:—
Elizabeth Margaret *b.* 1946: *m.* 1969, David Richards, and has issue living, Peter James, *b.* 1970,—Owain David *b.* 1973.

Issue of the late William Dove Usher, 5th son of 2nd baronet, *b.* 1904, *d.* 1969: *m.* 1939, Christa Elizabeth, da. of Bruno von Tevenar, of Mufindi, Tanzania:—
(William) John Tevenar, *b.* 1940: *m.* 1962, Rosemary Margaret, da. of Col. Sir Reginald Douglas Henry Houldsworth, OBE, TD, 4th Bt. (cr. 1887), and has issue living, Andrew John, *b.* 1963,—Michael William Reginald, *b.* 1967,—Caroline Rosemary, *b.* 1966.——Stuart Alexander, *b.* 1941; ed. at Uppingham.

Issue of the late Frederick Usher, 4th son of 1st baronet, *b.* 1862, *d.* 1909: *m.* 1901, Rosie Emil (who *d.* 1958, having *m.* 2ndly, 1911, Colin Mackenzie Black, C.V.O., W.S., who *d.* 1943), el. da. of the late Rev. William John Knox Little, formerly V. of Hoar Cross, Burton-on-Trent, and Canon and Sub-Dean, of Worcester:—
Neil John William Heriot (of Culachy, Fort Augustus, Inverness-shire. *Club,* New), *b.* 1903; ed. at Eton, and at Trin. Coll., Oxford; is Lieut. 7th Batn. King's Own Scottish Borderers; assumed on his marriage the additional surname of Murray, but has discontinued its use: *m.* 1st, 1929, Elizabeth Evelyn (who obtained a divorce 1937), da. of the late Lieut.-Col. Murray

Baillie (4th Hussars), of Broughton and Cally, and of Ilston Grange, Leicester; 2ndly, 1938, Dorothy Margaret, da. of the Rev. Colin William Scott-Moncrieff, and has issue living, (by 1st m.) James Neil (Murrayton, Gatehouse of Fleet, Kirkcudbrightshire), b. 1931; ed. at King's Sch., Canterbury: m. 1957, Sara Winefred, da. of the late Lt.-Col. Laurence Richardson Younger, and has issue living, Peter James b. 1961, Roseanne Helen b. 1960. Diana Katherine b. 1968.

Grandson of the late Francis James Usher, 5th son of 1st baronet:—
Issue of the late Francis Simeon Caverhill Usher b. 1902, d. 1954: m. 1935, Jean Lindsay, who d. 1954, da. of W. E. Kitson, of Blanerne, Berwickshire:—
Francis John (Dunglass, Cockburnspath, Berwickshire), b. 1937: m. 1967, Merilyn Haswell, only da. of William Lyle Brown, DSO, TD, MD, of White Ridge, Bamburgh, Northumberland.

Sir John Usher, 1st Bt., yst. son of Andrew Usher, of Edinburgh, assisted in founding a chair of public health, Edinburgh Univ. 1898, and built a public health institute 1902.

Vassar-Smith, see Smith.

VAVASOUR, Creation (U.K.) 1828, of Haslewood, Yorkshire.

Sir GEOFFREY WILLIAM VAVASOUR, D.S.C., 5th Baronet; b. Sept. 5th, 1914; s. his father, Capt. Sir LEONARD PIUS, 1961; Com. RN (ret.): m. 1st, 1940 (m. diss. 1947), Joan Millicent Kirkland, da. of Arthur John Robb; 2ndly, 1971, Marcia Christine, da. of Marshall Shaw Lodge, of Batley, Yorks., and has issue by 1st m.

Arms—Quarterly: 1st and 4th, or, a fesse dancettée sable, in the dexter chief a cross-crosslet for difference of the second, Vavasour; 2nd and 3rd, sable, a bend or, between six fountains, Stourton. Crests—1st, a cock gules charged with a fountain, Vavasour; 2nd, a demi-monk habited in russet, his girdle or, and wielding in his dexter hand a scourge or, thereon five knotted lashes, and in his sinister an open book or, Stourton.
Residence—8, Bede House, Manor Fields, Putney, SW15. Clubs—Hurlingham, All England Lawn Tennis, MCC.

Daughters living—By 1st m.—Jacqueline Mary, b. 1941: m. 1966, Capt. Peter John Whittington (ret.), 14/20th King's Hussars, of Brook Cottage, Gloucester Place, Windsor, Berks, and has issue living, Anna Catherine, b. 1974.——Elizabeth Anne, b. 1943: m. 1st, 1965 (m. diss. in Mexico 1968), Terence Hickman; 2ndly, 1968, James Monroe Woodman (7862 SW 66 St., Miami, Florida 33143, USA, and PO 897, Coconut Grove, Miami, Florida 33133, USA), and has issue living (by 2nd m.), Elizabeth Anne, b. 1969,—Lara, b. 1970.

Sisters living—Elizabeth Mary, b. 1917: m. 1st, 1940, Lieut. Michael John Priaulx Walters, RN, who d. (on active ser. during 1939-45 War) 1941; 2ndly, 1942, Brigadier Garth Raymond Godfrey Bird, of Gt. Broadhurst, Broad Oak, Heathfield, Sussex, and has issue living, (by 1st m.) Simon de Lancy (posthumous), b. 1941,—(by 2nd m.) Christopher, b. 1946,—Anthony, b. 1953,—Fiona, b. 1943.——Josephine Mary, b. 1921; formerly 3rd Officer W.R.N.S.: m. 1942, Rear Adm. Derick Henry Fellowes Hetherington, C.B., D.S.C., and has issue living, Mark, b. 1950,—Virginia Mary, b. 1947,—Teresa, b. 1951,—Dinah Mary, b. 1957. Address, Merton College, Oxford.

Aunt living (daughter of 3rd baronet) Maud Mary, b. 1883; is a nun.

Collateral Branches living.
Grandchildren of the late Oswald Hugh Stanislaus Vavasour (infra):—
Issue of the late Oswald Joseph Stanislaus Vavasour, b. 1883, d. 1973: m. 1915, Mary Dorothy, who d. 1952, da. of the late Bernard Moore, of The Grange, Draycott, Stoke-on-Trent:—
HUGH BERNARD MOORE (Blakeley House, Draycott-le-Moors, Stoke-on-Trent), b. July 4th, 1918; ed. at Stonyhurst; 1939-45 War as Capt. RA: m. 1950, Monique Pauline Marie Madeleine, da. of Maurice Erick Beck, of St. Aubin sur Scie, Seine Maritime, France, and has issue living, Eric Michel Joseph Marmaduke, b. 1953,—Anne Pauline Mary Draycot, b. 1969.——Dorothy Constance (Immaculate Conception Technical School, Southend, Darlington), b. 1916; a Sister of Charity.

Issue of the late John Wilfred Leonard Vavasour, b. 1891, d. 1955: m. 1940, Joyce, who m. 2ndly, 1951, Robert William Ellett Ware (of 94, Riverside Rd., Albany Park, Sidcup, Kent), da. of the late George Frederick Mayer, of Ardleigh, Keddington Rd., Louth, Lincolnshire:—

Margaret Ann b. 1940.——Angela Mary, b. 1943.——Frances Joyce Sarah, b. 1949.

Issue of the late Oswald Hugh Stanislaus Vavasour, uncle of 4th baronet, b. 1848, d. 1925: m. 1877, Sarah Anne, who d. 1937, da. of James Smith, of Draycott-in-the-Moors, Staffordshire:—

Joseph Everard Dunstan, b. 1902. Residence, 21, Hamilton Rd., Sidcup, Kent.——Elizabeth Mary Veronica, b. 1897. Residence, 21, Hamilton Rd., Sidcup, Kent.

Issue of the late John Wilfred Leonard Vavasour, b. 1891, d. 1955: m. 1940, Joyce, who m. 2ndly, 1951, Robert William Ellett Ware (of 94, Riverside Rd., Albany Park, Sidcup, Kent), da. of the late George Frederick Mayer, of Ardleigh, Keddington Rd., Louth, Lincolnshire:—

Margaret Ann b. 1940.——Angela Mary, b. 1943.——Frances Joyce Sarah, b. 1949.

Issue of the late Henry Dunstan Vavasour, uncle of 4th baronet, b. 1850, d. 1927: m. 1887, Bertha Eleanor Mary, who d. 1959, da. of Thomas Peter Redwood, of Burleigh, Blenheim, New Zealand :—

Edward Joseph Henry, b. 1898: m. 1927, Mary, who d. 1975, da. of the late Duncan Leslie, of Perth, and has issue living, Paul (41, Serpentine Rd., Sevenoaks, Kent), b. 1929; ed. at Stonyhurst; BSc. FICE: m. 1952, Pauline Mary, da. of the late Charles John Cable, of Sevenoaks, Kent, and has issue living, Dunstan Edward b. 1963, Catriona Mary b. 1955, Elspeth Anne b. 1956, Matilda Alice b. 1961,—Christopher Edward (Tudor Cottage, Boughton Aluph, Ashford, Kent; Farmers' Club), b. 1938; ed. at King's Sch., Canterbury, and Roy. Agric. Coll., Cirencester: m. 1963, Cecilie, da. of the late Cecil Dudley Morris, of Maidlands Farm, Brede, Sussex, and has issue living, Philip James Edward b. 1964, Simon Mark Andrew b. 1966, Charles William Alexander b. 1971. Residence, New Morgay Farm, Staplecross, Robertsbridge, Sussex.——Rev. Francis Noel (114, Mount St., W1), b. 1900; in Holy Orders of Church of Rome.——Harold Hugh, b. 1902: m. 1939, Margery Constance, da. of Harold Oakley Goulter, of Blairich Station, Blenheim NZ, and has issue living, Hugh Gerald (Ugbrooke Station, RD4 Blenheim, NZ), b. 1940: m. 1966, Belinda Mary, da. of Leonard Clarke of Wellington, NZ, and has issue living, Andrew Philip Henry b. 1968, Sarah Mary Constance b. 1967, Rachel Isolda Mary b. 1972,—Philip Joseph (Wistaria Cottage, Adstock, Bucks MK18 2JN) b. 1943: m. 1973, Robyn Mary, da. of Robert Barnett, of Bronte St., Nelson, NZ,—Nicola Mary Clare, b. 1947: m. 1972, Kerry Nolan, and has issue living, Rosamund b. 1974. Residence, 12, Munro St., Blenheim, NZ.——Gerald Aloysius (Cook St., Havelock, NZ). b. 1904: m. 1930, Lilian Frances, da. of the late Francis Campbell, of Blenheim, NZ, and has issue living, Michael Philip (Wylies Flat, Singleton, NSW 2330), b. 1932: m. 1st, 1955, Margaret Anne, who d. 1963, da. of Frederick H. B. Redward, of New Plymouth, NZ; 2ndly, 1965, Pamela Anne, da. of Reginald B. Marston, of Sydney, and has issue living (by 1st m.), Gerard Joseph b. 1956; apprentice RAA, Phillip Charles Dunstan b. 1960, Angela Margaret b. 1959, Rose Lillian Mary, b. 1962 (by 2nd m.), Christopher Paul b. 1966,—Bernard John (Toi Downs, Blenheim, NZ), b. 1933: m. 1964, Susan Ferrier, da. of Bruce Colville Morton, of Wai Whiro, Takapau, and has issue living, Thomas William b. 1964, Joseph Murray b. 1970, Matthew Colville b. 1971, Dominic Gerard b. 1974, Maria b. 1966, Katherine Mary b. 1968,—Priscilla, b. 1936: m. 1959, Marian Josef Adamski, of Kahui Rd., RD34, Rahotu Taranaki, NZ, and has issue living, Peter Bernard b. 1961, Anthony John b. 1968, Damian Joseph b. 1969, Maria Ann b. 1963, Frances Mary b. 1964, Theresa b. 1966,—Bertha Eleanor Mary, b. 1942: m. 1967, Michael John Baldwin, PO Box 257, Midland, Perth, W. Aust., and has issue living,—Bruce Phillip b. 1970, Anita Jane b. 1968,—Colleen Mary, b. 1943: m. 1973, Don Alan Robertson, of 2, Timaru Grove, Kelson, Lower Hutt., NZ, and has issue living, Gilbert Alan b. 1974.—— John Louis, b. 1905: m. 1937, Madeleine, da. of Ernest John Brammall of Blenheim, NZ, and has issue living, Jeromy Dunstan Trevor (King Ranch (Aust.) Ltd. (Brunette Downs, NT, Aust.), b. 1942: m. 1966, Joan Reilly, da. of Robert Moss of Melbourne, Aust., and has issue living, Simon John b. 1974, Peta b. 1967, Kimble b. 1971,—Anne, b. 1938: m. 1963, David Eric Stewart Adams, of 55, Penrith Rd., Morningside, Bulawayo, Rhodesia, and has issue David Eric Stewart Adams, of 55, Penrith Rd., Morningside, Bulawayo, Rhodesia, and has issue living, Jacqueline Ann b. 1968, Gillian Merle b. 1968,—Virginia Teresa, b. 1939: m. 1962, Brian John Cowan, c/o Barclays Bank, Box 1663, Bulawayo,—Marcia Jane b. 1952. Residence, Moonto Farm, P. Bag H5091, Bulawayo, Rhodesia.——Henry Philip Bede, b. 1907: m. 1949, Rosamond Mary, who d. 1973, da. of Daniel Riddiford, of Featherston, NZ, and has issue living, Peter Dunstan, b. 1950,—Francis William Joseph, b. 1953,—Rollo Charles Joseph (twin), b. 1951,—Charles Edward, b. 1954,—Mary Rosamond (twin) b. 1954,—Aletha Thérèse, b. 1955. Residence, The Favourite, Blenheim, NZ.——Gwendolen Mary, b. 1888: m. 1st, 1910 (m. diss. 1935), Ian Featherstone Johnston; 2ndly, 1936, William Sellars Bennett, and has issue living, (by 1st m.) Annette Mary, b. 1911.——Blanche Eleanor Mary, b. 1890; is a Nun. Residence, Convent of the Sacred Heart, Island Bay, Wellington, NZ.——Pearl Constantia, b. 1895: m. 1924, Francis Felix Reid, CBE, who d. 1966, and has issue living, Christopher Robin (Redwood, Blenheim, NZ), b. 1925: m. 1958, Clare, widow of Peter Goulter,—Angela b. 1929: m. 1956, Richard Fawcett, of The Biggin, Bramham, Boston Spa, Yorks., and has issue living. Residence.

Sir Thomas Vavasour, Knt., of Hazlewood, co. York, was created a baronet 1628. The title became extinct on the death of the 7th baronet 1826. The estates devolved upon his maternal cousin, the 3rd son of the 17th Baron Stourton, the Hon. Edward Marmaduke Joseph Stourton, who assumed the name of Vavasour, and was created a baronet [see B. Mowbray, colls.] in 1828.

Venables (Dillwyn-Venables-Llewelyn), see Llewelyn.

VERNER, Creation (U.K.) 1846, of Verner's Bridge, Armagh. [Extinct 1975]

Daughters living of 5th Baronet—Ruth Wingfield, b. 1902. Residence, 1, High Park Rd., Farnham, Surrey.——Betty Dorothea Wingfield, b. 1904: m. 1931, Hans Albrecht Schubart, CBE, who d. 1968, having assumed by deed poll 1946, the christian names of Henry Hansen in lieu of those of Hans Albrecht and has issue living, Elisabeth Helen, b. 1932: m. 1956, Capt. Robert Alec Snow Irving, RN, of Cavendish Villa, Cavendish Rd., Bath, and has issue living, Rupert Christopher b. 1958, Alexander Paul b. 1961, Mark Adrian b. 1965,—Julie (61, Gloucester Cres., NW1), b. 1936: m. 1960 (m. diss. 1972), Richard Joseph Roeber, and has issue living, Nicholas b. 1962, Bruno (triplet) b. 1962, James (triplet) b. 1962, Conrad b. 1964. Residence, 21, Bathwick Hill, Bath.

Collateral Branch living.
Issue of the late Hubert Henry Wingfield Verner, 2nd son of 4th baronet, b. 1868, d. 1946: m. 1900, Marion Henrietta, who d. 1951, yst. da. of the late Maj.-Gen. Evan Maberly, C.B.:—

Rose Winifred, b. 1901. Residence, Little Garlands, Layer de la Haye, near Colchester.

VERNEY, Creation (U.K.) 1818, of Claydon House, Buckinghamshire.

*One faith,
one sun.*

*The promise made
to my ancestor has
been kept.*

Sir RALPH BRUCE VERNEY, *KBE,* 5th Baronet; *b.* Jan. 18th, 1915; *s.* his father, Sir HARRY CALVERT WILLIAMS, *DSO,* 1974; ed. at Canford, and Balliol Coll., Oxford (BA); Java 1945 as Maj. RA; JP and Vice-Lt. for Bucks; High Sheriff 1957; Co. Councillor of Bucks 1952-73, and Co. Alderman 1961-73; Chm., Nat. Cttee. of Forestry Commn. since 1968; Pres. Country Landowners' Assocn. 1961-63; Trustee of Radcliffe, Ernest Cook and Chequers Trusts; KBE (Civil) 1974: *m.* 1948, Mary (LRAM), da. of the late Percy Charles Vestey [see Vestey, Bt., colls.], and has issue.

Arms—Quarterley: 1st and 4th, azure, on a cross argent, fimbriated or, five mullets gules, *Verney;* 2nd and 3rd, paly of six erminois and pean, a bend engrailed counterchanged, *Calvert.* Crests—1st, a demi-phœnix in flames proper, charged with five mullets in cross or and looking at the rays of the sun, *Verney;* 2nd out of a mural crown argent two spears erect therefrom two pennons flowing towards the dexter, one erminois, the other pean, *Calvert.*
Seat—Claydon House, Buckingham, MK18 2EX. *Club,*—Brooks's.

Son living—EDMUND RALPH, *b.* June 28th, 1950; ed. at Harrow, and York Univ.

Daughters living—Sarah Dorothy, *b.* 1953: *m.* 1974, George Caird.——Mary Jane, *b.* 1957.—— Francesca Marjorie *b.* 1963.

Brothers living—*Rev. Canon* Stephen Edmund, *MBE* (4, The Cloisters, Windsor Castle, Berks.), *b.* 1919; ed. at Harrow, and at Balliol College, Oxford (MA); late Lt. and temp. Capt. Intelligence Corps; Canon of St. George's Chapel, Windsor; 1939-45 War in Greece and Central Mediterranean (MBE); MBE (Mil) 1945: *m.* 1947, Priscilla Avice Sophie, who *d.* 1974, only da. of George Schwerdt, of Alresford, Hants., and has issue living, Robert Francis, *b.* 1949; ed. at Harrow: *m.* 1974, Juliet Haine,—Rachel Penelope, *b.* 1952,—Helen Mary *b.* 1955,—Katharine Priscilla, *b.* 1958.——Hugh Alexander, *b.* 1920; ed. at Harrow, and at Oriel Coll., Oxford (BA 1946, MA 1958); sometime Lt. Gren. Gds.; 1939-45 War (wounded): *m.* 1950, Ann Mary, da. of the late S. E. Chesterman, of Wing, Rutland, and has issue living, Thomas Harry, *b.* 1958; ed. at Harrow, —Mark, *b.* 1962,—Jonathan (twin), *b.* 1962,—Fiona Ann, *b.* 1952,—Teresa Joan, *b.* 1954,— Julia Mary, *b.* 1956. *Residence,* Rectory Close, Middle Claydon, Buckingham, MK18 2ET.—— Andrew Felix, *b.* 1921; ed. at Harrow, and at Balliol Coll., Oxford; MRCS and LRCP 1948: *m.* 1955, Mrs. Theodosia Olive Craig, da. of James W. Cropper, of Ellergreen, Kendal, and has issue living, Caspar Charles Andrew, *b.* 1961,—Caroline Rachel, *b.* 1956. *Residence,* Thames Bank House, Mortlake, SW14.——*His Honour Judge* (Lawrence John), *TD* (The Old Rectory, Middle Claydon, Bletchley, Bucks.), *b.* 1924; ed. at Harrow, and at Oriel Coll., Oxford (MA); Bar. Inner Temple 1952; late Lt.-Col. RA (TA) (R. Bucks Yeo); a DL of Bucks; Dep. Chm. Bucks Quarter Sessions 1962-71; Dep. Chm. Middx. Sessions 1971; a Circuit Judge 1972; 1939-45 War as Lt. Gren. Gds.: *m.* 1972, Zoë Auriel, yr. da. of Lt.-Col. Peter Goodeve Goodeve-Docker, of Kealkil, Bantry, co. Cork.

Sisters living—Marjorie (*Lady Harris*), *b.* 1913: *m.* 1st, 1944, Capt. Julian Guy Tryon, who *d.* 1950; 2ndly, 1957, Sir Ronald Montague Joseph Harris, KCVO, CB, and has issue living (by 1st m.), Edith Catherine, *b.* 1948: *m.* 1971, the Rev. Colin Bruce Slee, and has issue living, Benedict Nicholas Julian *b.* 1973. *Residence,* Slyfield Farm House, Stoke d'Abernon, Surrey.——Mary Rachel, *b.* 1916: *m.* 1947, the Rev. Geoffrey Thomas Roberts, and has issue living, Gillian Marjori◦, *b.* 1950,—Susan Jane, *b.* 1953. *Residence,* The Vicarage, Edenham, Bourne, Lincs.—— Catherine, *b.* 1925: *m.* 1947, Richard Mervyn Hare, FBA, White's Prof. of Moral Philosophy, Oxford, and has issue living, John Edmund, *b.* 1949; ed. at Rugby, and Balliol Coll., Oxford,— Bridget Rachel, *b.* 1950,—Amy Louise, *b.* 1953,—Ellin Catherine, *b.* 1955. *Residence,* Saffron House, Ewelme, Oxon.

Collateral Branches living.

Grandchildren of the late Sir Harry Lloyd-Verney, G.C.V.O. (infra):—
Issue of the late Maj.-Gen. Gerald Lloyd Verney, D.S.O., M.V.O., late Irish Guards, *b.* 1900, *d.* 1957, having discontinued the use of the Christian names of Harry George by deed poll 1941 : *m.* 1926, the Hon. Joyce Sybil Vivian (of Lower Town Farm House, Clifton Hampden, near Abingdon, Berks), da. of 1st Baron Bicester :—
Peter Vivian (The Chantry, Bisley, Stroud, Glos.), *b.* 1930; ed. at Eton, and at Trin. Coll., Dublin (MA); late Maj. Irish Gds.; an author: *m.* 1959, Caroline Evelyn, el. da. of G. A. Harford, of Widden Hill House, Horton, Chipping Sodbury, Glos., and has issue living, Harry George Vivian, *b.* 1960,—Louisa Margaret, *b.* 1962,—Henrietta Nell, *b.* 1965.——Bridget Mary, *b.* 1926: *m.* 1951, Michael Barry Sarson, and has issue living, Michael Vivian, *b.* 1953,—David Peter, *b.* 1955, Mary Anne, *b.* 1959,—Jane Elizabeth, *b.* 1962. *Residence,* 12, Rawlinson Rd., Oxford.

Grandson of the late Col. George Hope Lloyd-Verney, 3rd son of 2nd baronet:—
Issue of the late Sir Harry Lloyd-Verney, G.C.V.O., *b.* 1872, *d.* 1950 : *m.* 1899, Lady Joan Elizabeth Mary Cuffe, who *d.* 1951, el. da. of 5th Earl of Desart :—
Ulick Otway Vortigern Lloyd, *O.B.E.,* *b.* 1902 ; ed. at Eton ; is temporary Lieut.-Col. Rifle Brig.; entered Foreign Office 1946; HM Foreign Ser. 1947-53 and in Foreign Office 1955-60; 1939-45 War in France, Italy and S-E Asia; OBE (Mil) 1946: *m.* 1929, Esme Louise, da. of the late Charles Austin Smith-Ryland, of Barford Hill, Warwick, and has issue living, Harry Ulick Dennis (7, Kildare Court, NW2) *b.* 1940; ed. at Eton; FCA,—Anne Margaret, *b.* 1930; JP for Shrewsbury: *m.* 1951, Col. John Montagu Flint, MBE, late RE, of The Dower House, Great Ness, Shrewsbury, and has issue living, Charles John Raffles *b.* 1952, Michael Edward Stamford *b.* 1956, Sarah Esmé *b.* 1955, Elizabeth Anne *b.* 1958,—Carola Mariette, *b.* 1932: *m.* 1952, Maj. John Hugh Torquil Sutton, late Coldm. Gds., of Bayfield Brecks, Holt, Norfolk [see Sutton, Bt., colls.]. *Residence,* The Garden House, Cheriton, Alresford, Hants.

Grandchildren of the late Frederick William Verney, 4th son of 2nd baronet:—
Issue of the late Sir Ralph Verney, C.B., C.I.E., C.V.O., who was cr. a *Baronet* 1946 :—
See Verney, Bt., cr. 1946.

The 1st Bt., Gen. Sir Harry CALVERT, GCB, GCH, was Adjt.-Gen. of the Forces for 21 years. The Rt. Hon. Sir Harry, 2nd Bt., in 1827 assumed by Roy. licence the surname of Verney in lieu of Calvert, having s. to the Verney estates (his cousin Richard Calvert m. the widow of the Hon. John Verney, el. son of 1st Earl Verney). He sat as MP for Buckingham (L) and Bedford. The 3rd baronet, Sir Edmund Hope, Capt. RN, served in Crimean War 1854-55, and Indian Mutiny 1857-58, and sat as MP for N. Buckingham (L). The 4th Bt., Sir Harry Calvert Williams Verney, DSO, was PPS to Ch. Sec. for Ireland 1911-14, and Parl. Sec. to Board of Agric. 1914; MP for Bucks (L) 1910-18; author of "The Verneys of Claydon" and "Florence Nightingale at Harley Street."

VERNEY, Creation (U.K.) 1946, of Eaton Square, City of Westminster.

One faith, one sun.

The promise made to my ancestor has been kept.

Sir JOHN VERNEY, M.C., 2nd *Baronet;* b. Sept. 30th, 1913 ; s. his father, Lieut.-Col. Sir RALPH, C.B., C.I.E., C.V.O., 1959 ; ed. at Eton, and at Ch. Ch., Oxford; Painter, Illustrator and Author; 1939-45 War as Maj. RAC (MC); Légion d'Honneur 1945: *m.* 1939, Jeanie Lucinda, da. of the late Maj. Herbert Musgrave, DSO, RE, and has issue.

Arms—Quarterly: 1st and 4th, azure, on a cross argent, fimbriated or, five mullets gules, *Verney*; 2nd and 3rd, paly of six erminois and pean, a bend engrailed counterchanged, *Calvert.* Crests—1st, a demi-phœnix in flames proper, charged with five mullets in cross or, and looking at the rays of the sun, *Verney*; 2nd, out of a mural crown argent two spears erect, therefrom two pennons flowing towards the dexter, one erminois, the other pean, *Calvert.*

Residence—Runwick House, Farnham, Surrey.

Son living—JOHN SEBASTIAN, *b.* Aug. 30th, 1945.
Daughters living—Sabrina Anne, *b.* 1947.——Juliet Rose, *b.* 1949: *m.* 1970, Michael Benjamin, and has issue living, a son, *b.* 1971,—a son, *b.* 1973.——Rose Lucinda, *b.* 1950.——Candida Harriet, *b.* 1953.——Alice Angelica, *b.* 1956.
Brother living—David, *b.* 1918; ed. at Eton; Lt.-Cdr, R.N. (ret.), High Sheriff of Cornwall 1964; 1939-45 War: *m.* 1948, the Hon. Mary Kathleen Boscawen, *JP*, da. of 8th Viscount Falmouth, and has issue living, Christopher Ralph Evelyn, *b.* 1948,—Margaret Mary, *b.* 1950: *m.* 1971, Peter Michael Bickford-Smith, of Trevarno, Helston, Cornwall, and has issue living, Sacha Ann Mary *b.* 1975,—Rosemary Janette, *b.* 1958. *Residence*, Trevella, St. Erme, Truro, Cornwall.
Sister living—Joscelyne, *b.* 1915: *m.* 1941, Capt. Andrew Thorne, late Grenadier Guards [B. Penrhyn], of 4, Mickleham Hall, Dorking, Surrey, and has issue living, Nicholas Andrew (3, Hedley Court, 67, Putney Hill, SW15), *b.* 1942; Capt. Gren. Guards: *m.* 1969, Diana Lesley Kathryn, da. of Donald Leslie, of Horley Place, Horley, Surrey, and has issue living, Alexander Francis Andrew Nicholas *b.* 1972,—Joanna Mary, *b.* 1945: *m.* 1966, Lt. Col. John Peter William Friedberger, The R. Hussars, of North Woolding Cottage, Whitchurch, Hants., and has issue living, Richard Mark *b.* 1973,—Rosanna *b.* 1967,—Lucinda Jane *b.* 1970,—Carola Joscelyne, *b.* 1948.
Widow living of 1st Baronet—JANETTE CHEVERIA HAMILTON (*Janette, Lady Verney*), younger da. of the late Hon. J. T. Walker (Senator 1901-13), of Sydney, N.S. Wales : *m.* 1909, Lieut.-Col. Sir Ralph Verney, C.B., C.I.E., C.V.O., 1st baronet, who *d.* 1959. *Residence*, 73, Eaton Square, S.W.1.

The 1st baronet, Lt.-Col. Sir Ralph Verney, CB, CIE, CVO, Rifle Brig., son of the late Frederick William Verney (yst. son of Sir Harry Verney, 2nd Bt., *cr.* 1818), was appointed Mil. Sec. to Viceroy of India, 1916-21, Sec. to Speaker of House of Commons 1921-55, and an Examiner for Private Bills and Taxing Master House of Commons 1927-45.

VERNON, Creation (U.K.) 1914, of Shotwick Park, co. Chester.

Sir NIGEL JOHN DOUGLAS VERNON, 4th *Baronet; b.* May 2nd, 1924; *s.* his father *Sir* (WILLIAM) NORMAN, 1967; ed. at Charterhouse; late Lt. RNVR and RNR: *m.* 1947, Margaret Ellen, da. of the late Robert Lyle Dobell, of The Mount, Waverton, Chester, and has issue.

Arms—Or, on a fesse azure between two cross molines in pale gules three garbs of the field. Crest—In front of a demi-female figure affrontée proper vested azure, around the temples an oak wreath vert, **holding** in the dexter hand a sickle and in the sinister two ears of wheat slipped also proper, a garb fessewise or.

Residences—Top-y-Fron Hall, Kelsterton, nr. Flint.

Sons living—JAMES WILLIAM, *b.* April 2nd, 1949; ACA. ——John Alan, *b.* 1956.
Daughter living—Caroline Margaret, *b.* 1953: *m.* 1974, Simon Jonathan Salusbury-Trelawny, of 47, Maltravers St., Arundel, Sussex [*see* Salusbury-Trelawny, Bt., colls.].
Sister living—Diana Elizabeth, *b.* 1922; formerly Section Officer WAAF: *m.* 1st, 1943, Bohuslav F. Kovarik, DFM, Czechoslovak Air Force, who *d.* 1969, and from whom she obtained a divorce 1949 (annulment Roman Catholic Church 1951); 2ndly, 1951, Joseph Olivier Hamelin de Grondines Landry, of Grondines, Quebec.

Spring does not always flourish.

Uncle living (son of 2nd baronet)—Humphrey Bagnall, *MC.*, *b.* 1895; ed at Charterhouse, and at Magdalen Coll., Oxford (BA and MA 1921); formerly Lt. Grenadier Guards Special Reserve; 1914-19 War (MC): High Sheriff of Cheshire 1951: *m.* 1938, Sibyl, yst. da. of the late S. Mason Hutchinson, of The Marfords, Bromborough, Cheshire, and has issue living, John Humphrey, *b.* 1940,—Richard Bagnall, *b.* 1944: *m.* 1969, Deborah Florence, el. da. of Geoffrey Oswald Ateo Briggs, MD, BCh, of The Kennels, Thoresby Park, Notts., and has issue living, Toby Richard *b.* 1971. *Residence*, The Cottage, Little Tew, Oxon.

Aunt living (daughter of 2nd baronet)—Nina Elizabeth Margaret *b.* 1898.

Collateral Branches living.

Grandsons of the late William Allen Vernon (infra):—
Issue of the late Herbert Wallace Vernon, *b.* 1890, *d.* 1974: *m.* 1924, Gertrude, who *d.* 1959, el. da. of Tom Jackson, JP, of Waterfoot, Heaton, Bolton:—
Bryan Tom Jackson (High Trees, Woodland Rise, Sevenoaks, Kent), *b.* 1925; ed. at Loretto; late Sub-Lt. RNVR: *m.* 1955, Anne Cecilia, da. of the late Harry S. Burgess, of Beck Hall, Thornton Dale, Yorks., and has issue living, Andrew Bryan, *b.* 1955,—Charles Harry, *b.* 1960,—Timothy William, *b.* 1962,—Belinda Anne, *b.* 1957.——Richard Wallace (Scotch Corner, Wildernesse Av., Sevenoaks, Kent), *b.* 1927; ed. at Camb. Univ. (MA); late 2nd Lt. RA: *m.* 1955, Pamela Violet, da. of the late Lt.-Col. Alexander George William Grierson, RM (ret.) [*see* Grierson, Bt., colls.], and has issue living, David Grierson, *b.* 1956,—Simon Richard, *b.* 1958,—Sally Pamela Clare, *b.* 1960,—Joanna Caroline, *b.* 1963.

Issue of the late William Allen Vernon, 2nd son of 1st baronet, *b.* 1860, *d.* 1939 : *m.* 1888, Elizabeth, who *d.* 1952, da. of Herbert Marson, of Marsh House, Blythe Bridge, Staffordshire :—
Reginald Thornycroft, *b.* 1892; late RAF: *m.* 1920, Margarita Grace Constantine, of Harsley Hall, Northallerton, and has issue living, George Thorneycroft, *b.* 1935,—James Loudon (5, Shrewsbury House, Cheyne Walk, SW7) *b.* 1940; ed. at Eton and Trin. Coll., Dublin (BA): *m.* 1971, Elspeth Mary Stewart (BA), da. of the Rev. Cyril Raby Thomson, of Holy Trinity Vicarage, Southwell, Notts., and has issue living, Alexander James Constantine *b.* 1971,—Pamela Margaret,—Jean Winifred: *m.* 1954, John Stewart Prescot,—Margaret Elizabeth: *m.* 1972, the Rev. Jeremy Peake, son of the late Sir Charles Brinsley Pemberton Peake. *Residence*, Danley Farm, Lynchmere, Surrey.——Daisy Hilda, *b.* 1893: *m.* 1917, Reginald Charles Dickens, who *d.* 1961, and has issue living, Nanny Uarda Elsie, *b.* 1901: *m.* 1927, Prof. Victor Wilkinson Dix, FRCS, of 8, Shandon Close, Tunbridge Wells, and has issue living.

Grandson of the late William Allen Vernon (ante):—
Issue of the late Sir Wilfred Douglas Vernon, *b.* 1897, *d.* 1973: *m.* 1923, Nancy Elizabeth (Anningsley Park, Ottershaw, Surrey), yr. da. of Tom Jackson, JP, of Waterfoot, Heaton, Bolton:—
William Michael (Ropley House, Alresford, Hants), *b.* 1926; ed. at Trin. Coll., Camb. (MA); late Lt. RM; Chm. of Spillers Ltd.: *m.* 1952, Rosheen Elizabeth Mary, da. of the late George O'Meara, of Johannesburg, S. Africa, and has issue living, Mark Thornycroft, *b.* 1958.

Sir William Vernon, 1st Baronet, was head of the firm of W. Vernon and Sons, millers, of London and Liverpool. The 2nd baronet, Sir (John) Herbert Vernon, was High Sheriff of Cheshire 1926.

VESTEY, Creation (U.K.) 1921, of Shirley, Surrey.

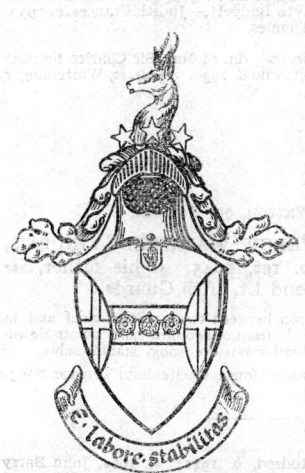

Sir (JOHN) DEREK VESTEY, 2nd *Baronet*, son of the late John Joseph Vestey, el. son of 1st baronet ; *b.* June 4th, 1914 ; *s.* his grandfather, *Sir* EDMUND HOYLE, 1953 ; ed. at The Leys Sch., Camb.; European War 1940-45 as Flight-Lieut. R.A.F. Vol. Reserve : *m.* 1938, Phyllis Irene, da. of H. Brewer, of Banstead, and has issue.

Arms—Argent, on a fesse between two flaunches gules each charged with a cross throughout of the field, three roses also of the field. Crest—In front of a springbok's head proper three mullets argent.

Residences—5, Carlton Gdns., SW1; Harcombe House, Ropley, Hants. *Clubs*—RAC and MCC.

Son living—PAUL EDMUND, (53, Cheval Place, SW7; Manor Farm, Bishops Sutton, Hants.; British Racing Drivers Club), *b.* Feb. 15th, 1944; ed. at Radley: *m.* 1971, Victoria Anne Scudamore, da. of John Salter, of Old Ford House, Tiverton, Devon, and has issue living, Joanna Clare, *b.* 1972,—Caroline Louise *b.* 1975.

Daughter living—Rosamund Hope, *b.* 1940: *m.* 1961, Anthony Charles Brown, and has issue living, Mark Nigel Alastair, *b.* 1964,—Julia Caroline, *b.* 1962. *Residence*, Longdown Cottage, Longdown, Guildford, Surrey.

From work stability.

Brother living—Charles Gordon, *b.* 1916 ; European War 1940-45 in Arctic and Far East as Lieut. R.N.V.R.: *m.* 1946, Monica Hope, da. of A. J. P. Heaton, of Manorlands, Oxenhope, Keighley, and has issue living, Diana Mary, *b.* 1947: *m.* 1968, Kenneth Cameron Simm, of Hayhills Farm, Silsden, Keighley, Yorks., and has issue living, Gordon Christopher Cameron *b.* 1970, Holly Ann Cameron *b.* 1971,—Rachel Margaret, *b.* 1949; LRAM: *m.* 1970, Philip Anthony Hills, of The Mill House, Gt. Horkesley, Colchester, Essex. *Residence*, Little Haley, Oxenhope, Keighley, Yorks.

Uncle living (son of 1st baronet)—Ronald Arthur, *b.* 1898; ed. at Malvern; a DL of Suffolk (High Sheriff 1961); a Lay Canon of St. Edmundsbury Cathedral; patron of 5 livings: *m.* 1923, Florence Ellen McLean, who *d.* 1966, da. of the late Col. T. G. Luis, VD, of Broughty Ferry, Angus, and has issue living, Edmund Hoyle (Waltons, Ashdon, nr. Saffron Walden, Essex; Glencanisp Lodge, Lochinver, Sutherland. *Clubs*, Cavalry, Carlton), *b.* 1932; ed. at Eton; late Lt. City of London Yeo.: *m.* 1960, Anne Moubray, yr. da. of Gen. Sir Geoffry Allen Percival Scoones, KCB, KBE, CSI, DSO, MC, and has issue living, Timothy Ronald Geoffry *b.* 1961, James Edmund McLean *b.* 1962, George Moubray William *b.* 1964, Robin John Henry *b.* 1968,—Florence Elizabeth Lindsay, *b.* 1926: *m.* 1952, Robert Lawrence Clifton-Brown [*see* Brown, Bt., colls.],—Jane McLean, *b.* 1928: *m.* 1956, John Richard Baddeley, of Waltham House, Gt. Waltham, Essex, and has issue living, Mark Christian Jon *b.* 1960, Edward Christopher

Francis b. 1965, Melissa Jane Elizabeth b. 1963,—Margaret, b. 1929: m. 1954, James Gladstone Payne, of Rickling Hall, Quendon, Saffron Walden, Essex, and has issue living, Michael Edmund b. 1959 Nichola Rosemary b. 1955, Philippa Margaret b. 1963. Residence, Gt. Thurlow Hall, Gt. Thurlow, Suffolk. Clubs, Carlton, MCC.

Aunt living (daughter of 1st baronet)—Hannah (67, Porchester Gate, Bayswater Rd., W2 3HS), b. 1897: m. 1937, Lt.-Col. Eugene John O'Meara, OBE, FRCS, IMS, who d. 1962.

Collateral Branches living.

Issue of the late Percy Charles Vestey, 3rd son of 1st baronet, b. 1893, d. 1939: m. 1916, Dorothy Emmeline (28, Chelwood House, Gloucester Sq., W.2), da. of the late Charles David Johnson:—

Roger Edmund, b. 1921; ed. at Harrow, and at Clare Coll., Camb. (B.A. 1946, M.A. 1951); late Capt. Berks Yeo. ; European War 1940-45 : m. 1950, Penelope Jane, only da. of the late Lieut.-Col. Robert Arthur Little, D.S.O., late Australian Forces, of Melbourne, Australia, and has issue living, Charles Julian, b. 1952; ed. at Harrow, Munich Univ. and Sorbonne, Paris,—James Patrick, b. 1954; ed. at Harrow and Southampton Univ. Residence, Park Gate House, Ham Common, Surrey. Clubs, Cavalry, Royal Ocean Racing.——Patricia, b. 1922: m. 1945, Lt. William Reginald Servaes, RN, and has issue living, Michael Maxwell, b. 1947,—James William, b. 1948; ed. at Harrow and RMC; 2nd Lt., Coldm. Gds.: m. 1972 (m. diss. 19—), Phoebe, da. of Keith Pither Cox, of Sydney,—Andrew Mark, b. 1963,—Diana Patricia, b. 1951,—Elizabeth Mary, b. 1953. Residences, 15, Bryanston Mews West, W1; The Old Rectory, Orford, Woodbridge, Suffolk.——Mary (Lady Verney), b. 1925; LRAM: m. 1948, Sir Ralph Bruce Verney, KBE, 5th Bt. (cr. 1818). Residence, Claydon House, Bletchley, Bucks.

Issue of the late William Vestey, yst. son of 1st baronet, b. 1902, d. 1971: m. 1928, Ursula Francis Bowring (22, Hyde Park Gdns., W1), da. of Edward H. Bowring Skimming, of Taplow House, Taplow:—

John (139, Queen St., Woolahrah, Sydney, NSW; Bath and Boodles Clubs), b. 1929: ed. at Eton: m. 1958, Felicity Gay, da. of Kenneth H. Crawford, of Holbrook, NSW, and has issue living, Victoria Gay, b. 1960,—Angela Caroline, b. 1962,—Georgina Ann, b. 1964,—Sara Frances, b. 1966,—Christina Mary, b. 1969.

The 1st baronet, Sir Edmund Hoyle Vestey (third son of Samuel Vestey, of Liverpool), was Chm. of Union International Co., and Joint Head of Blue Star Line, Ltd.

VINCENT, Creation (E.) 1620, of Stoke d'Abernon, Surrey. [Extinct 1941.]

Rt. Hon. Sir EDGAR VINCENT, *G.C.B., G.C.M.G., F.R.S.,* 16th and last Baronet (who was cr. *Baron D'Abernon* 1914, and *Viscount D'Abernon* 1926).

Daughters living of 14th Baronet—Una Claire Margaret, b. 1926: m. 1950, Air Commodore Nicholas Roger Lyell Bristow, RAF (Romney, RAF, Biggin Hill, Westerham, Kent), and has issue living, Robert Nicholas, b. 1954,—Edward Anthony (twin), b. 1954,—Clare Margaret, b. 1951: m. 1972, Colin Ian Liddell,—Jane Elizabeth, b. 1953: m. 1974, Michael Balfour Hutchings.——Pamela Helen Frances (Coombe House, Titcomb Way, Kintbury, Berks.), b. 1928: m. 1951, Douglas R. Whittaker, who d. 1974, and has issue living, Suzanne, b. 1951: m. 1973, Spencer Charles Hilton Barrett,—Helen Gay, b. 1953: m. 1973, Timothy Philip Lyth Badgett,—Judith Frances, b. 1959. Residence, Vincent House, Warren Rd., Kingston upon Thames.

Widow living of 14th Baronet—DOROTHY CLARE (Lady Vincent), da. of Maj. Sir Charles Fausset Falls: m. 1925, Sir Anthony Francis Vincent, 14th baronet, who d. 1936. Address, Whitehanger Nursing Home, Marley Lane, Haslemere, Surrey.

VINCENT, Creation (U.K.) 1936, of Watton, co. Norfolk.

Sir WILLIAM PERCY MAXWELL VINCENT, 3rd *Baronet; b.* Feb. 1st, 1945; *s.* his father, *Sir* LACEY ERIC, 1963; 2nd Lt. Irish Guards.

Arms—Azure, a chevron between two garbs in chief and in base a castle all or, Crest—In front of two bird bolts points downwards saltirewise or a Labrador retriever dog, statant sable.

Residence, 7a, Whitelands House, Cheltenham Terrace, SW3.

Sister living—Amanda Mildred, b. 1942: m. 1961, John Barry Dinan, late Capt. Irish Guards, of 13, Burnsall St., SW3, and has issue living, Mark Henry b. 1963,—Dominic John, b. 1966.

Aunt living (daughter of 1st baronet)—Christine Ena Comfort: m. 1931, John S. Stevens.

Widow living of 2nd Baronet—HELEN MILLICENT (Lady Vincent), (of 17, Eresby House, Rutland Gate, S.W.7), yr. da. of the late Field-Marshal Sir William Robert Robertson, 1st Bt., G.C.B., G.C.M.G., G.C.V.O., D.S.O. [see B. Robertson of Oakridge]: m. 1938, Sir Lacey Eric Vincent, 2nd baronet, who d. 1963.

By Fortitude and Endeavour.

FORTITUDINE ET CONATU

The 1st baronet, Sir Percy Vincent (son of Lacey Andrews Vincent, of Watton, Norfolk), was an Alderman of City of London 1929-42 (Sheriff 1926-27, and Lord Mayor 1935-36).

Vœux, see DES Vœux.

VYVYAN, Creation (E.) 1645, of Trelowarren, Cornwall.

Whilst we live, let us live.

Sir RICHARD PHILIP VYVYAN, 11th *Baronet*, son of the late Major Richard Walter Comyn Vyvyan, 2nd son of 9th baronet; *b.* Nov. 21st, 1891; *s.* his uncle, *Col. Sir* COURTENAY BOURCHIER, *C.B., C.M.G.,* 1941.

    Arms—Argent, on a mount vert a lion rampant gules, armed sable. **Crest**—A horse passant furnished proper.
    Address,—c/o Barclays Bank, Trustee Department, Exeter.

Widow living of 10th Baronet—CLARA COLTMAN (*Lady Vyvyan*), da. of the late Edward Powys Rogers, of Tregye, Devoran, Cornwall : *m.* 1929, as his second wife, Col. Sir Courtenay Bourchier Vyvyan, C.B., C.M.G., 10th baronet, who *d.* 1941. *Residence,* Trelowarren, Mawgan-in-Mene-age, Cornwall.

Collateral Branches living.

Grandchildren of the late Capt. Herbert Reginald Vyvyan, OBE (infra):—
Issue of the late Maj.-Gen. Ralph Ernest Vyvyan, CBE, MC, *b.* 1891, *d.* 1971: *m.* 1st, 1915 (m. diss. 1930), Vera Grace, who *d.* 1956, el. da. of Robert Arthur Alexander, of Portglenone House, co. Antrim; 2ndly, 1930, Kathleen Antonia (Limes-well Cottage, Streatley-on-Thames, Berks.), only da. of Haskett Farquhar Haskett-Smith, of Starcross, Devon:—
(By 1st m.) JOHN STANLEY (Trelowarren, Mawgan, Helston, Cornwall), *b.* Jan. 20th, 1916; ed. at Charterhouse; 1939-45 War, as Maj. R. Signals, in India and Burma: *m.* 1st, 1941 (m. diss. 1946), Joyce Lilia, da. of the late Frederick Marsh; 2ndly, 1948 (m. diss. 1958), Marie, da. of the late Dr. O'Shea, of Hamilton, Ont.; 3rdly, 1959, Jonet Noël, da. of Lt.-Col. Alexander Hubert Barclay, DSO, MC [*see* Mitchelson, Bt., ext.], and has issue living (by 1st m.), Lorraine, *b.* 1942,—(by 3rd m.) Ralph Ferrers Alexander, *b.* 1960,—Amanda Clare, *b.* 1959.——(by 2nd m.) Mary Virginia (9, Chestnut Cottages, Streatley-on-Thames, Reading, Berks.), *b.* 1934; JP: *m.* 1st, 1936 (m. diss. 1963), Harold Markham Mills; 2ndly, 1975, William Archibald Wilson, and has issue living (by 1st m.), Julian Maximilian Vyvyan, *b.* 1957,—Antonia Helen, *b.* 1958,—Charlotte Elisabeth, *b.* 1960.

Granddaughter of the late Rev. Herbert Francis Vyvyan (infra):—
Issue of the late Capt. Herbert Reginald Vyvyan, OBE, *b.* 1862, *d.* 1949: *m.* 1st, 1889, Caroline Jane, who *d.* 1935, da. of the late Edward Hunt, of Belmore, co. Kilkenny; 2ndly, 1938, Emmeline Mabel, who *d.* 1948, only da. of the late Richard Brighton, and widow of Lt.-Col. A. F. Carlyon, RAMC:—
(By 1st m.) Avis (c/o Barclays Bank, 208, Regent St., W1): *m.* 1917, Capt. Robert Rose, for-merly RFA, who *d.* 1943, and from whom she had obtained a divorce (in Sup-reme Court of British Columbia) 1932, and has issue living, Victor Hunter Vyvyan, living, Winter James Robert Vyvyan *b.* 1943: *m.* 1970, Adela, da. of Julius de Novoa of El Salvador, and has issue living, Tudor Julius Victor *b.* 1971, Vyvyan Farrer *b.* 1973, Jacqueline Avis Vyvyan *b.* 1946, Suzanne Jane Vyvyan *b.* 1952,—Myfanwy Avis, *b.* 1920: *m.* 1958, Brian George Underwood Bleach and has issue living, Cameron James Vyvyan *b.* 1966.

Grandson of the late Stanhope Trefusis Vyvyan, son of the late Rev. Herbert Francis Vyvyan, brother of 9th baronet :—
Issue of the late Lester Trefusis Vyvyan, *b.* 1905, *d.* 1952 : *m.* 1934, Mary Clare Frances (Little Merthen, Gweek, Helston, Cornwall), da. of John Leeming, of Chalfont St. Peter, Bucks.:—
Anthony Beville (of Northcote, Witley, Surrey), *b.* 1935; ed. at Downside: *m.* 1960, Mary Winifred da. of Arthur Joseph Quin-Harkin, OBE, and has issue living, Richard Trefusis, *b.* 1961,—Jonathan Vyell, *b.* 1962,—Simon Courtenay, *b.* 1964,—Charles Bevil, *b.* 1965,—Paul Grenville, *b.* 1969,—James Hannibal, *b.* 1972,—Katharine Anne, *b.* 1967.

Grandchildren of the late Rev. Herbert Francis Vyvyan (ante) :—
Issue of the late Capt. William Geoffrey Vyvyan, Roy. Welch Fusiliers, *b.* 1876, *d.* (killed in action) 1914: *m.* 1904, Frances Mary, who *d.* 1964, da. of the late Edmund Salwey Ford, of Pengreep, Perranwell, Cornwall, and 17, Hyde Park Sq., W:—
James Graham (of Weston House, Gresford, Denbighshire), *b.* 1905; ed. at Wellington Coll. and RMC; Hon. Lt.-Col. late R. Welch Fusiliers, and DL of Denbighshire: *m.* 1934, Guenilda Mary, da. of the late Rev. Preb. Arthur Harvey Thursby-Pelham, R. of Upton Magna, Shrewsbury, and has issue living, Anthony Geoffrey, *b.* 1940; ed. at Wellington RMA, and at Magdalen Coll., Oxford; late Capt. R. Welch Fusiliers: *m.* 1970, Miranda Violet Marguerite, yr. da. of the Rev. Robnett Walters, BD, of North Tamarton, Cornwall, and has issue living, a son *b.* 1975,—Cicely Mary, *b.* 1936: *m.* 1961, Maj. Peter Leslie Rawll, late RM, of The Gables, 39, Cotswold Green, Stonehouse, Glos., and has issue living, Andrew Charles Vyvyan, *b.* 1963, Katharine Frances *b.* 1965,—Daphne Elizabeth, *b.* 1937: *m.* 1965, Edward Christopher Mumford, and has issue living, Robert Vyvyan *b.* 1970, Robert Vyvyan *b.* 1970, Alison Clare Mary *b.* 1966, Jane Myfanwy, *b.* 1968.——Frederick Richard, *b.* 1913; ed. at Wellington: *m.* 1937 (m. diss. 1957), Barbara, da. of the late Montague Jones, of Hartpury, Glos., and has issue living, Charles Richard, *b.* 1938; ed. at Clifton Coll., and at Trin. Coll., Camb.,—Priscilla Mary, *b.* 1941,—Clare, *b.* 1944. *Residence,* South Meadow, Woodbury, nr. Exeter.——Opre (*Lady Maclean*), *b.* 1910: *m.* 1933, Vice-Adm. Sir Hector Charles Donald Maclean, KBE, CB, DSC [M. Linlithgow, colls.], The Old Rectory, Burnham Deepdale, King's Lynn, Norfolk, and has issue living, Charles David Hector (Dans of Aber, Gartocharn, Dunbartonshire), *b.* 1936; ed. at Wellington Coll.; Capt. R. Scots (Lothian) Regt.: *m.* 1966, Judith, el. da. of Donald MacLehose, of Glengair, Clynder, Dunbarton-shire, and has issue living, Charles Hector *b.* 1968, James Lachlan *b.* 1970,—Sara, *b.* 1934: *m.* 1955, Maj. Anthony Michael Everett, Wilts. Regt. (ret.), of Naylinghurst Farmhouse, Rayne, Braintree, Essex, and has issue living, Simon Anthony Cunningham *b.* 1956, Rupert Hector *b.* 1959,—Katherine Mary, *b.* 1937.——Joan Mary (twin), *b.* 1910: *m.* 1937, (Richard) Brinsley Ford, and has issue living, Francis Vyvyan, *b.* 1941,—(Richard) Augustine, *b.* 1943,—Marianne Adèle Hermione, *b.* 1937: *m.* 1966, Patrick Martin Laver, and has issue living, Harriet *b.* 1967. *Residence,* 14, Wyndham Pl., W1.

Grandson of the late Rev. Thomas Grenfell Vyvyan (infra):
Issue of the late Capt. Richard Norman Vyvyan, late R.F.C., *b.* 1876, *d.* 1946 : *m.* 1902 Mildred, who *d.* 1948, da. of the late Charles Henry Tawney, CIE:—
John Michal Kenneth, *b.* 1907; ed. at Uppingham, and at Balliol Coll., Oxford (BA 1928); is Fellow of Trin. Coll., Camb.; sometime in Diplo. Ser.; 1939-45 War as temp. Capt. Com-mandos: *m.* 1941 (m. diss. 1971), Elizabeth Mary, yr. da. of H. G. Lowder, and has issue living,

Charles Gerard Courtenay, *MBE*, *b.* 1944; ed. at Winchester, and Balliol Coll., Oxford (BA);
Maj. The R. Green Jackets; MBE (Mil.) 1974,—George James Tawney, *b.* 1951; ed. at Eton; Lt.
The R. Green Jackets,—Caroline Mary Louise, *b.* 1942: *m.* 1963, Stephen Charles Archibald
Pryor, of Bracken Garth, Keasden, Clapham via Lancaster, and has issue living, Henry Charles
Lister *b.* 1965, Charles James Archibald *b.* 1971, William Tawney Charles *b.* 1973, Rachel Eliza-
beth *b.* 1966. *Residence*, Crag House, Crook, Kendal.

Grandchildren of the late Rev. Thomas Hutton Vyvyan, 3rd son of 7th baronet:—
Issue of the late Rev. Thomas Grenfell Vyvyan, *b.* 1837, *d.* 1924: *m.* 1874, Edith May,
who *d.* 1940, da. of the late Gen. Henry Man, of 2, Palace Road, Surbiton, formerly
Lieut.-Gov. of Penang:—
Maurice Courtenay, *b.* 1891; ed. at Gonville and Caius Coll., Camb. (BA 1914, MA 1920); DSc
London 1940; 1914-19 War as Lt. Machine Gun Corps (wounded): *m.* 1916, Hilda May, da.
of the late Harry F. W. Bradbury, of Bengal Civil Ser. *Residence*, Trevedran, Wateringbury,
Maidstone, Kent.——Irene Victoria: *m.* 1956, Dr. John Sextus Matthews, who *d.* 1972, and has
issue. *Residence*, Lothian, PO Box 212, Richmond, Natal, S. Africa.

Grandchildren of the late Philip Augustus Vyvyan-Robinson, el. son of Phillip
Vyvyan-Robinson (*b.* 1820), el. son of Philip Vyvyan-Robinson (*b.* 1777), 2nd
son of the Rev. Richard Vyvyan, 2nd son of Richard Vyvyan, 2nd son of 3rd
baronet:—
Issue of the late Arthur Claude Vyvyan-Robinson, *b.* 1880, *d.* 1960: *m.* 1923, Patricia (of
Penolver, Rock, Wadebridge, Cornwall), only child of the late F. T. MacDonnell:—
Arthur Frederick, *RD*, *b.* 1925; ed. at Nautical Coll., Pangbourne, and Pembroke Coll., Camb.
(MA); Lt.-Cdr. RNR (ret.); 1939-45 War; Headmaster of Roy. Masonic Sch. for Boys, Bushey,
Herts.: *m.* 1951, Patricia Jill, el. da. of I. W. G. Freeman, of Woking, Surrey, and has issue living,
Patrick John, *b.* 1955; 2nd Lt. R. Fus.,—James Courtenay, *b.* 1958,—David Augustus, *b.* 1960,—
Amanda, *b.* 1953: *m.* 1974, Charles Philip Metcalfe Yeoman. *Residence*, Roy. Masonic Sch., The
Avenue, Bushey, Herts.——Cecil Courtenay, *b.* 1928; ed. at Charterhouse, and at Jesus Coll.,
Camb. (BA 1951); late Lt. RA (TA): *m.* 1955, Ann Leonora Dirom, el. da. of V. Berwyn Jones,
MRCVS, of Frocester, Glos., and has issue living, Peter Dirom Courtenay, *b.* 1958,—Frances
Jane, *b.* 1957,—Katherine Armorel, *b.* 1959,—Diane Elizabeth, *b.* 1963. *Residence*, The Manor
House, Hadzor, nr. Droitwich, Worcs.——Richard, *MBE*, *b.* 1937: Maj. LI; MBE (Mil) 1968:
m. 1968, Virginia Ann, da. of Lt.-Col. William Maitland Brewster Dunn, and has issue living,
Arthur Charles, *b.* 1970,—Mark William, *b.* 1972.——Susan Philippa, *b.* 1924; 1939-45 War in
WRNS: *m.* 1954, John Dugmore, of 816, Ely Blvd. South, Petaluma, Cal. 94952, USA, and has
issue living, Neil Vyvyan, *b.* 1957,—Geoffrey Roland, *b.* 1959,—Christopher John, *b.* 1965.——
Jane Theodora, *b.* 1930: *m.* 1955, David Kenneth Wilton Cox, and has issue living, Timothy
Michael Wilton, *b.* 1959,—Richard Wilton, *b.* 1962,—Sarah Lamorna, *b.* 1957,—Victoria Tamsin,
b. 1964. *Residence*, Preston Farm, Drewsteignton, Devon.——Claudia Frances, *b.* 1932: *m.* 1957,
Henry Graham Tom, and has issue living, Elizabeth Vyvyan, *b.* 1959,—Juliet Vyvyan, *b.* 1965.
Residence, Lower Trewiggett, St. Teath, Bodmin, Cornwall.

Issue of the late Lt. Col. Francis Vyvyan-Robinson, MC, *b.* 1897, *d.* 1975: *m.* 1926, Aileen
(3, Pinewood Close, Dawlish, Devon), da. of the late Dr. R. H. Powers, of Southend:—
Henry Francis (Crestwood, Camp Rd., Gerrards Cross, Bucks), *b.* 1928; ed. at King's Coll., Taunton;
late F/O RAAF; Civil Air Pilot: *m.* 1957, Susan Rosamond, da. of P. A. H. Pettman, of Bournemouth, and has issue living, Hugh, *b.* 1958,—Peter Francis, *b.* 1963,—Sally, *b.* 1960.——Loveday,
b. 1930: *m.* 1951, Dr. Keith Maxwell Fergusson, of Cranmere, South Rd., Newton Abbot, Devon,
and has issue living, Neil Vyvyan, *b.* 1952,—Graham Keith, *b.* 1955,—Fiona Margaret, *b.* 1959,—
Elizabeth Loveday, *b.* 1963.——Caroline, *b.* 1934: *m.* 1957, James Caruth Moore Pryde, of
Arden Cottage, 19, Harefield Av., Cheam, Surrey, and has issue living, Catherine Ann, *b.* 1960,—
Juliet Clare, *b.* 1968.

Grandchildren of the late Rev. Philip Vyvyan-Robinson (*b.*) 1820 (ante):—
Issue of the late Hugh Norris VYVYAN, *b.* 1853, *d.* 1931: *m.* 1889, Constance Ethel,
da. of James Haughton, of Newport News, Virginia, U.S.A.:—
Hugh Wren, *M.C.*, *b.* 1889; is Capt. Roy. Canadian Ordnance Corps; formerly Regt. Quartermaster-
Sergeant Scots Guards, and Capt. Duke of Cornwall's L.I. ; European War 1914-16 (wounded,
M.C.): *m.* 1917, Mary, da. of Patrick Lowe, of Bridge of Allan, and has issue living, Patrick
Hugh, *b.* 1918 ; formerly Sergeant Roy. Signals ; European War 1939-45 (wounded, despatches);
formerly Assist. Sup. of Police, Federation of Malaya : *m.* 1959, Angela, da. of Viggo Christensen,
of London, and has issue living, Patrick Hugh Beresford *b.* 1959,—Peter Gerald, *b.* 1921 ; is
Lieut. Roy. Canadian Corps of Electrical and Mechanical Engineers,—Beresford, *b.* 1929,—
Pamela Alice, *b.* 1926,—Constance Rosemary (twin), *b.* 1929.——Malcolm, *M.C.*, *b.* 1895 ; ed.
at Jesus Coll., Oxford ; is Capt. R.A. ; European War 1916-18 with R.A.F. (despatches twice,
MC), 1939-45 War in Middle East: *m.* 1920, Fairy, who *d.* 1971, da. of the late Col. John Birrell,
of Allander House, Milngavie.——Gertrude Nevillia, *b.* 1906 : *m.* 1927, Rupert Taylor, and has
issue living, John Vyvyan, *b.* 1929,—Jennifer Anne, *b.* 1932. *Residence*, High On, Showell Lane,
Penn, Wolverhampton.

Grandchildren of the late Rev. Henry VYVYAN (infra):—
Issue of the late Lt.-Col. Philip Henry Nugent Norris Vyvyan, OBE, MC; *b.* 1881; *d.*
1967: *m.* 1917, Mary Caroline (Foxbury House, Westbourne, nr. Emsworth, Hants),
da. of the late Rev. John Stephen Flynn:—
Lalage Nugent (Foxbury House, Westbourne, Emsworth, Hants.), *b.* 1921: *m.* 1943, John Derek
Atheling Boustead, Lt. R. Ulster Rifles, who *d.* (killed in action in Normandy) 1944, and has
issue living, Lalage Tamsin Vyvyan, *b.* 1943: *m.* 1964, Richard Hugh Lee, Lt. RE, and has issue
living, James Nugent *b.* 1968, Angela Caroline *b.* 1967.

Issue of the late Capt. Albert O'Donnel Colley Vyvyan, *b.* 1884, *d.* 1971: *m.* 1st, 1909,
Cecilia, who *d.* 1949, da. of W. H. Armitage, JP, of Banney Royd, Huddersfield; 2ndly,
1951, Greta Sylvia (Penhallow, The Lizard, Cornwall), da. of Arthur John Dooel, of
Brandeston, Suffolk:—
(By 1st m.) Henry O'Donnel, *OBE* (Try-le-Bois, Greencliff, St. Martin, Jersey), *b.* 1910; ed. at
Bradfield, and Pembroke Coll., Camb. (BA); Col. late REME; 1939-45 War (prisoner): OBE
(Mil) 1957: *m.* 1936, June, da. of John Humphries, of Napier, NZ, and has issue living, Wendy
(c/o Try-le-Bois, Greencliff, St. Martin, Jersey), *b.* 1937: *m.* 1957, Lt. Graham George Bell,
RASC, and has issue living, Christopher Graham Vyvyan, *b.* 1960, Simon Bruce O'Donnel *b.*
1961, Robin Benjamin *b.* 1963, Bruce St. John *b.* 1966,—Valerie Cecilia, *b.* 1941: *m.* 1966,
David Henry La Gagnina, c/o Try-le-Bois, Greencliff, St. Martin, Jersey, and has issue living,
Adam Vyvyan *b.* 1970, Dominic Vyvyan *b.* 1973.——George Nugent Grattan *b.* 1914; ed. at
Pembroke Coll., Camb. (BA); Maj. (ret.) RASC: *m.* 1st, 1944, Celia Violet Gould, who *d.* 1956;
2ndly, 1957 (m. diss. 1961), Constance Anderson.

Granddaughter of the late Rev. Philip Vyvyan-Robinson (*b.* 1820) (ante):—
Issue of the late Rev. Henry VYVYAN, *b.* 1855; *d.* 1937: *m.* 1880, Lucy Nugent, who *d.*
1929, da. of Henry C. Grattan:—
Lucy Kathleen Grattan, *b.* 1889 (Hill Place, Knaphill, Woking, Surrey): *m.* 1917, Capt. Stewart
Edward Pixley, RFA, who *d.* 1972, and has issue living, Stewart Reginald Vyvyan (The Old
Rectory, Wambrook, Chard, Som.), *b.* 1921: *m.* 1948, Marion Beatrice Allen, da. of Alec Hay
Steedman, of Knaphill, Woking, Surrey, and has issue living, Stewart Richard O'Donnel *b.* 1951,
William Ian *b.* 1954,—Jean Elizabeth Grattan (Brambridge Lodge, Bishopstoke, Eastleigh,

Hants.), *b.* 1919: *m.* 1943, Dr. John Alexander Robertson, who *d.* 1971 and has issue living, Christopher Alexander John *b.* 1944, Stewart Neville Struan *b.* 1949: *m.* 1972, Anne-Grete, only da. of Albert Breiteig, of Bergen, Norway (and has issue living, Nicholas Struan *b.* 1974), Timothy Hugh *b.* 1954,—Rozanne Patricia, *b.* 1925: *m.* 1947, Gomer Donald Waterer, of Nursery House, Lower Knaphill, Woking, Surrey,—Jennifer Penelope, *b.* 1927: *m.* 1948, Ian Hele Spencer Silver, from whom she obtained a divorce 1970, and has issue living, Richard Ian Spencer *b.* 1953, Vyvyan Penelope Spencer *b.* 1949: *m.* 1969, Edwin Keith Farrington, Margaret Spencer *b.* 1951: *m.* 1970, Christopher David Balchin.

Grandson of the late Charles Shimmin Vyvyan (infra):—

Issue of the late Norris Vyvyan, *b.* 1900, *d.* 1963: *m.* 1925, Florence Elizabeth (Betty), who *d.* 1967, da. of the Rev. W. J. Tristram, of Oldham:—

Bertram Charles Boucher (35, Greenbank Drive, Heswall), *b.* 1930: *m.* 65, Jean Margaret Taylor, and has issue living, Catherine Margaret, *b.* 1967.

Grandchildren of the late Rev. Philip Vyvyan-Robinson (*b.* 1820) (ante):—

Issue of the late Rev. Charles Shimmin VYVYAN, *b.* 1856, *d.* 1930 (having discontinued the surname of Robinson 1879) : *m.* 1881, Rose Mary, who *d.* 1950, da. of the late Rev. John Sidney Boucher :—

Dorothy Kildare (25, Lather St., Southport, Qld., Aust.), *b.* 1890: *m.* 1920, Alfred Lucas Hughes, who *d.* 1942, and has issue living, Charles Lucas, *b.* 1921,—Philip Herbert (Rockhampton, Qld.), *b.* 1923: *m.* 1955, Palma Gibson, and has issue living,—Christopher Maddock (Decatur, Alabama, USA), *b.* 1933: *m.* 1968, Alice Jane Hill,—Rosemary Eleanor, *b.* 1922,—Norah Vyvyan, *b.* 1926: *m.* 1950, Max Maurice Shannon, of Julatten, Qld., and has issue living,—Katherine Ellen, *b.* 1929: *m.* 1953, James Maclean Davidson, of Belivah, Beenleigh, Qld., and has issue living.——Violet, *b.* 1891. *Residence*, 9, Beaufort Rd., Clifton, Bristol.

Issue of the late Frederick Albert VYVYAN, *b.* 1858, *d.* 1939 (having discontinued surname of Robinson 1879) : *m.* 1888, Mary Agnes, who *d.* 1957, da. of the late William Baynham, of New Orleans, U.S.A. :—

Philip, *b.* 1892; 1914-19 War as Lt. Roy. W. Surrey Regt.: *m.* 1926, Mary Jacqueline, who *d.* 1970, da. of the late John Milberne Leacock [Erskine, Bt., *cr.* 1821, colls.], and has issue living, *Rev.* John Philip (Adderbury Vicarage, Banbury. *Club*, Royal Commonwealth Society), *b.* 1928; ed. at Charterhouse, and at New Coll., Oxford (MA); a Priest in the Anglican Church, Borneo 1961-64, since when V. of Adderbury with Milton, Oxon.; late DCLI (Regular Army Reserve); Malaya 1947-48; in Overseas Civil Ser., N. Borneo 1952-57: *m.* 1957, Monica Yin Tsu, da. of Fu Yun Fatt, of Sandakan, N. Borneo, and has issue living, Richard Mark Augustine *b.* 1960, Henry Arthur Luke *b.* 1961, Francis Michal Hannibal *b.* 1971, Honor Mary Anastasia *b.* 1968,—Bernard Jeremy (37, West Hill Av., Epsom), *b.* 1930; ed. at Charterhouse, and at London Univ. (BSc Eng), an AMICE; late REME: *m.* 1964, Constance, Joan Steel, da. of the late Ronald Ismay Pattinson of Stanwix, Carlisle, and has issue living, David Jeremy *b.* 1972, Mary Louise *b.* 1965, Juliet Penelope *b.* 1967. *Residence*, Lanveor, Carleen, Helston, Cornwall. ——Eleanor Augusta (Challons Combe, Aveton Gifford, Kingsbridge, Devon), *b.* 1899.

Issue of the late Edwin VYVYAN, *b.* 1866, *d.* 1944: *m.* 1894, Florence, who *d.* 1968, da of the late William White, of Dublin:—

Henry Edwin, *b.* 1896.——Eileen, *b.* 1895: *m.* 1920, Alfred William Skerritt, MC, 2nd Lt. Australian Reserve of Officers, who *d.* 1968, and has issue living, Brian Vyvyan (of Quarry Hill, Epping Forest, Tasmania), *b.* 1921: *m.* 1948, Jean, da. of R. R. Taylor, of Valleyfield, Tasmania,—Rosemary, *b.* 1927: *m.* 1950, Max Jordan, of 13, Gabriel Av., E. Malvern, Victoria, Australia. *Residence*, Flat 4, 5, Ascot St., Malvern 3144, Vic., Aust.

The 1st baronet, Sir Richard Vyvyan, M.P., was Master of the Mint during the reign of Charles I, and followed the King to Oxford. He was one of the last six baronets created by that monarch. The 2nd and 3rd baronets each sat as M.P. for Cornwall, and the 8th baronet sat as M.P. for Cornwall (C) 1825-31, for Bristol 1832-7, and for Helston 1841-57. The 10th baronet, Col. Sir Courtenay Bouchier Vyvyan, C.B., C.M.G., served in S. African War 1879, Matabeleland Campaign 1896, S. African War 1900-1902, and European War 1914·18 (C.M.G.).

WAECHTER, Creation (U.K.) 1911. of Ramsnest, Chiddingfold, Surrey.

[Title pronounced "Vechter."]

Sir (HARRY LEONARD) D'ARCY WAECHTER, 2nd *Baronet*; *b.* May 22nd, 1912 ; *s.* his father, *Sir* HARRY, *C.M.G.*, 1929; is Capt. T.A. Reserve of Officers : *m.* 1939, Philippa Margaret (who obtained a divorce 1957), younger da. of the late James Frederick Twinberrow, of The White House, Suckley, Worcestershire.

Arms—Azure, issuant from the base the battlements of a tower proper, thereon a crane close argent, holding in the dexter claw a stone proper, in chief two roses gules . Crest—On a rock proper, a crane holding in the dexter claw a stone, as in the arms.

Residence—

Brother living—JOHN D'ARCY, *b.* Nov. 16th, 1915; PhD, Camb.: *m.* 1952, Caroline Dymond, yr. da. of the Ven. Edgar Francis Hall, Archdeacon of Totnes, and has issue living, Andrea Caroline, *b.* 1953,—Suzanne Anstice Eveline, *b.* 1957. *Residence*, Heron House, Hampton, Middlesex.

Sister living—Mary Henrietta (59, Ladbrooke Rd., W11), *b.* 1914: *m.* 1934 (m. diss. 1968), Guy Eric Fulke Greville [*see* E. Warwick, colls.].

The 1st baronet, Sir Harry Waechter, C.M.G. (Managing Director of Bessler, Waechter and Co. (Limited), shippers and owners, of London, Liverpool, Glasgow, and Newcastle-on-Tyne), was High Sheriff of Surrey 1910.

WAKE, Creation (E.) 1621, of Clevedon, Somerset.

Watch and pray.

Sir HEREWARD WAKE, *M.C.*, **14th**
Baronet; b. Oct. 7th, 1916; *s.* his father,
Maj.-Gen. Sir HEREWARD, *C.B.*, *C.M.G.*,
DSO, 1963; ed. at Eton; Maj. (ret.) KRRC;
a DL of Northants; High Sheriff 1955;
1939-45 War (MC, wounded); *m.* 1952, Julia
Rosemary, JP, yr. da. of Capt. Geoffrey
William Martin Lees, of Falcutt House, nr.
Brackley, Northants, and has issue.

Arms—Or, two bars gules, in chief three torteaux.
Crest—The Wake knot.
Seats—Courteenhall, Northampton; Amhuinnsuidhe
Castle, I. of Harris. *Club*—Brooks's.

Son living—HEREWARD CHARLES, *b.* November
22nd, 1952.
Daughters living—Diana Julia, *b.* 1955,——Caroline
Jane, *b.* 1957,——Sarah Jennifer, *b.* 1960.
Brothers living—Roger, *b.* 1918; 1939-45 War as Lt.
RN (despatches): *m.* 1944 (m. diss. 1969), Olwyn
Mary, da. of Col. John Charles Wynne-Finch, CBE,
MC [*see* E. Aylesford, colls.], and has issue living,
John (9, Square de Contades, 49000, Angers, France),
b. 1945: *m.* 1969 Isabelle, da. of the Comte de Dreux
Brézé, of Paris, and has issue living, Christopher *b.* 1969,
Charlotte *b.* 1971,—Charles Julian, *b.* 1947,—William, *b.* 1949,—Jane, *b.* 1950. *Residence*,
37, Kensington Pl., W8. *Club*, Brooks's.——Peter, *b.* 1921; 1939-45 War (wounded), as Capt.
KRRC: *m.* 1960, Marion Margaret, yr. da. of John Henry Bevan, CB, MC [E. Lucan]) and has
issue living, Edward, *b.* 1965,—Philip Hereward, *b.* 1967,—Susan, *b.* 1963. *Residence*, Fairfield
House, Hambledon, Hants. *Clubs*, Brooks's, Pratt's, Flyfishers'.

Sisters living—Margaret (*Lady Turner*), *b.* 1913: *m.* 1939, Sir (Ronald) Mark Cunliffe Turner
and has issue living, Christopher, *b.* 1942: *m.* 1964, Katrina Cameron, da. of Capt. Harold Keith
Salvesen, of Inveralmond, Cramond, Edinburgh,—Richard Wake, *b.* 1949,—Roger Cunliffe
(twin), *b.* 1949: *m.* 1974, Rosemary Jane, el. da. of the Rt. Rev. Richard Fox Cartwright, DD,
Bishop of Plymouth,—Catherine, *b.* 1940,—Margaret, *b.* 1947. *Residence*, 3, The Grove, High-
gate, N6.——Patricia, *b.* 1919: *m.* 1939, Lt.-Col. Christopher Payan Dawnay, CBE, MVO, late
Coldm. Gds. [*see* V. Downe, colls.]. *Residence*, Longparish House, Andover, Hants.——Mary,
b. 1927: *m.* 1947, Capt. James Howard Weatherby, late 10th Hussars, and has issue living,
Jeremy James, *b.* 1949,—Susan (*Viscountess Ullswater*) *b.* 1947: *m.* 1967, the 2nd Viscount
Ullswater. *Residence*, Lemington Grange, Moreton-in-Marsh, Glos.

Aunt living (daughter of 12th baronet)—Phyllis Katheren, *b.* 1887; 1914-18 War with VAD in
France; 1939-45 War in MI5 and Min. of Information: *m.* 1919, Richard Montgomery Archdale,
MC, formerly Lt. 19th Hussars, and has issue living, Nicholas Montgomery (Penbedw, Nannerch,
Mold, Flintshire), *b.* 1924; formerly Capt. King's Roy. Rifle Corps and Parachute Regt.; 1939-45
War (despatches): *m.* 1953, Patricia Thomas, and has issue living, Edward Montgomery *b.* 1954,
Christopher *b.* 1958, Catherine *b.* 1956,—Felicity Claire, *b.* 1922; 1939-45 War in First Aid
Nursing Yeo.: *m.* 1957, Robin von der Heyde, and has issue living, Nicholas Fearne *b.* 1961,
Amanda Claire *b.* 1960. *Residence*, Vigila, Umoukwes, Rhodesia.

Widow living of 13th Baronet—MARGARET WINIFRED (*Margaret, Lady Wake*), (of
Axford Lodge, Basingstoke), el. da. of Robert Henry Benson, JP, of Buckhurst, Sussex [LIND-
SAY, Bt.]: *m.* 1912, Maj.-Gen. Sir Hereward Wake, CB, CMG, DSO, who *d.* 1963.

Collateral Branches living.

Grandson of the late Adm. Charles Wake (infra):—
Issue of the late Col. Edward St. Aubyn Wake, C.M.G., *b.* 1862, *d.* 1944: *m.* 1913, Vera
Cecilia, who *d.* 1968, da. of the late Francis Johnston, of Dunsdale, Westerham:—
Rev. Hugh, *b.* 1916; Lieut.-Com. R.N. (ret.); European War 1939-45 (despatches): *m.* 1944,
Catherine Marigold, da. of the late Adm. Sir (William) Frederic Wake-Walker, K.C.B.,
CBE [*see* Walker, Bt., *cr.* 1856, colls.], and has issue living, Vincent Hugh, *b.* 1947; SRN, RSCN,
—Cedric Philip, *b.* 1950; 2nd Officer MN,—Thomas Baldwin, *b.* 1960,—Catherine Frances
(Cottage Farm, Washbrook, Ipswich, Suffolk), *b.* 1945: *m.* 1st 1966, Michael Edward Turpin,
who *d.* 1972; 2ndly, 1973, Vernon Charles Nott, and has issue living (by 1st m.) Edward *b.* 1969,
Sarah Jane *b.* 1967, Rosanna Elspeth *b.* 1972. *Residence*, Gt. Finborough Vicarage, Stow-
market, Suffolk.

Grandson of the late Maj. Hugh St. Aubyn Wake, MVO (infra):—
Issue of the late Hugh Edward William Wake, *b.* 1900, *d.* 1967: *m.* 1928, June Brother-
ton:—
Charles Hugh Edward, *b.* 1930 (in USA).

Grandchildren of the late Adm. Charles Wake, 2nd son of 10th baronet:—
Issue of the late Major Hugh St. Aubyn Wake, M.V.O., *b.* 1870, *d.* (killed in action) 1914:
m. 1899, Kathleen Mary, who *d.* 1938, da. of Lieut.-Col. Edward Evans Grigg, Indian
Army (formerly Commr. of Kamoun):—
Kathleen Josephine, *b.* 1909: *m.* 1934, Lt.-Col. George Douglas James McMurtrie, Somerset LI,
and has issue living, Hugh Wake, *b.* 1936,—Michael St. Aubyn (71, West View Dr., Calgary SW,
Alberta, Canada) (twin), *b.* 1936: Capt., 3rd Bn., Princess Patricia's Canadian LI: *m.* 1958,
Bridget Constantia Rubery, and has issue living, Nigel Andrew James *b.* 1959, Paul Marcel *b.*
1971, Marcia Kathleen *b.* 1961,—Jonathan Philip James *b.* 1941. *Residence*, Two Yews, Rock-
ford, Ringwood, Hants.

Issue of the late (Arthur) Leofric St. Aubyn Wake, *b.* 1879, *d.* 1957: *m.* 1911, Elma,
who *d.* 1971, only da. of the late William Edward Highett, of Melbourne, Victoria:—
Geoffrey St. Aubyn, *b.* 1914; is Capt. Australian Imperial Force: *m.* 1943, Lois Ivan-Smith,
and has issue living, Carolyn Fearnley St. Aubyn, *b.* 1945,—Cheryl Anne, *b.* 1949. *Residence*,
43, Kooyong Road, Armadale, S.E.3, Victoria, Australia.——Elma Thurfrida, *b.* 1912.——
Diana, *b.* 1913: *m.* 1940, Desmond George Grace, and has issue living, Simon George, *b.* 1948,—
Diana Gillian, *b.* 1941,—Susan Elizabeth, *b.* 1943.——Audrey, *b.* 1916: *m.* 1946, Angus Manning
Watson. *Residence*, 43, Kooyong Rd., Armadale, SE3, Melbourne, Aust.

Granddaughters of the late Drury Wake, 3rd son of 10th baronet:—
Issue of the late Drury Wake, *b.* 1875, *d.* 1947: *m.* 1904, Dorothy Caroline, who *d.* 1956,
el. da. of the late Sir (Clement) Courtenay Knollys, K.C.M.G. :—
Elizabeth, *A.R.R.C.* (of 1, Tower Hill, Horsham, Sussex), *b.* 1908; 1939-45 War with V.A.D.
(A.R.R.C.).——Catherine, *b.* 1914; 1939-45 War as Junior Com. A.T.S.: *m.* 1953, Col. Brian
Walton Rowe, OBE, MC. *Residence*, Little Ludshott, Seymour Rd., Headley Down, Hants.

Grandson of the late Rev. Baldwin Eyre Wake (infra):—
Issue of the late Rev. Hereward Eyre Wake, *b.* 1869, *d.* 1934 : *m.* 1899, Mary Frances, who *d.* 1959, da. of the late James Sealy Lawrence, of 5, Upper Addison Gardens, Kensington, W. :—

Hereward Baldwin Lawrence, *b.* 1900 ; ed. at Marlborough ; formerly Headmaster of St. John's Sch., Leatherhead ; European War 1939-45 as Lieut.-Col. Gloucester Regt. (T.A.) : *m.* 1926, Sheila, da. of the late Capt. Henry Harris, and has issue living, Hereward Michael Wilfred, *b.* 1927,—Robin Eyre (St. Minver Lodge, St. Minver, Wadebridge, Cornwall), *b.* 1933: *m.* 1962, Judith, da. of Eric Barry. *Residence,* High Ridge, Knoll Wood, Knoll Rd., Godalming, Surrey.

Granddaughter of the late Rev. James Hare Wake, **son of the late Baldwin Wake,**
M.D., son of the late Drury Wake, 3rd son of 7th baronet:—
Issue of the late Rev. Baldwin Eyre Wake, *b.* 1840, *d.* 1911 : *m.* 1868, Adelaide Bowles, who *d.* 1935, da. of the late Rev. Henry Cleveland, R. of Romald Kirk, Darlington:—
Margaret Gladys Hermione, *b.* 1885: *m.* 1921, Maj. Clement Little, of 20, Southfields Court, Eastbourne.

This ancient family is descended from Hugh Wac or Wake (baron by tenure of Bourne and Deeping) [*temp.* King Stephen], from whom the 1st baronet was 15th in male descent. The 2nd baronet, Sir John Wake, mortgaged his estate to raise a troop of horse for Charles I. The 6th baronet assumed the additional surname of Jones, but died without issue. Sir Herewald, 12th baronet, was High Sheriff of Northants 1879. Maj.-Gen. Sir Hereward Wake, C.B., C.M.G., D.S.O., 13th baronet, was Dep. Constable of Dover Castle 1929-32, and Col. Comdt. 1st Bn., K.R.R.C. 1938-46.

WAKEFIELD, Creation (U.K.) 1962, of Kendal, co. Westmorland.

Sir EDWARD HUMPHRY TYRRELL WAKE-FIELD, 2nd *Baronet, b.* July 11th, 1936; *s.* his father, *Sir* EDWARD BIRKBECK, CIE, 1969; ed. at Gordonstoun, and Trin. Coll., Camb. (BA); late Lt. 10th R. Hussars: *m.* 1st, 1960 (m. diss. 1964), Priscilla, el. da. of Oliver Robin Bagot [B. Bagot, colls.]; 2ndly, 1966 (m. diss. 1971), the Hon. Elizabeth Sophia Sydney, el. da. of 1st Viscount De L'Isle, VC, GCMG, GCVO, and formerly wife of George Silver Oliver Annesley Colthurst [see Colthurst, Bt.]; 3rdly, 1974, the Hon. Katherine Mary Alice Baring, da. of 1st Baron Howick of Glendale, and has issue by 2nd m.

Arms—Argent two barrulets sable between three owls proper. **Crest**—A bat displayed proper, charged on each wing with a crescent argent.

Clubs,—Turf, Cavalry.

Son living—By 2nd m. MAXIMILIAN EDWARD VERE-KER, *b.* Feb. 22nd, 1967.
Brother living—Gerald Hugo Cropper (60, Woodsford Sq., W14), *b.* 1938; ed. at Eton, and Trin. Coll., Camb. (BA): *m.* 1971, Victoria Rose, el. da. of Cecil Henry Feilden, of Bramdean House, Alresford, Hants. [see V. Hampden, colls.], and has issue living, Edward Cecil, *b.* 1973.
Widow living of 1st Baronet—CONSTANCE LALAGE (*Lalage, Lady Wakefield*) (13, St. Mary Abbots Terr., W14), da. of the late Sir John Perronet Thompson, KCSI, KCIE: *m.* 1929, Sir Edward Birkbeck Wakefield, CIE, 1st Bt., who *d.* 1969.

This family can trace its lineage to Roger Wakefield, of Challon Hall, Westmorland, temp Elizabeth I. Sir Edward Birkbeck Wakefield, CIE, 1st baronet (whose el. brother was cr. *Baron Wakefield of Kendal* 1963) was a great-grandson of Edward William Wakefield, of Birklands, Kendal, 3rd son of John Wakefield of Stricklandgate, Kendal (*d.* 1829), 6th in descent from Roger; was Treasurer, HM Household 1960-62, 1st UK Commr. in Malta 1962-64, and 1st High Commr. to Malta 1964-65.

WAKELEY, Creation (U.K.) 1952., of Liss, co. Southampton.

Sir CECIL PEMBREY GREY WAKELEY, *K.B.E., C.B.*, 1st *Baronet,* son of Percy Wakeley, of West Dulwich, S.E.; *b.* May 5th, 1892 ; ed. at Dulwich Coll.; M.R.C.S. and L.R.C.P., London 1915 ; F.R.C.S. England 1921 ; Hon. F.R.C.S.E. 1952 ; Hon. F.R.C.S.I. 1953 ; M.Ch. 1950 ; D.Sc. London 1932; Hon. D.Sc. Delhi 1955; Hon. LL.D. Glasgow 1952, Leeds 1954, and Lahore 1962, Hon. D.Sc. Colombo 1958; Fellow of King's Coll., London 1930; FRSE, FRSA, and an Hon. Fellow of Roy. Faculty of Physicians and Surgs., of Roy. Australasian Coll. of Surgs., of American Coll. of Surgs., and of Faculty of Radiologists; FZS; Vice-Pres. of Council of Imperial Cancer Research Fund (Chm. 1949-67), and of British Empire Cancer Campaign and of Medical Defence Union, Consulting Surg. King's Coll. Hosp., London, Belgrave Hospital for Children, and West

End Hospital for Nervous Diseases, Senior Surg. to Roy. Masonic Hosp., and to Petersfield Hosp., Senior Consultant Surg. RN, Vice-Chm. of Med. Sickness So., Chm. of Med. Sickness Finance Corporation and of International Wine So., a Member of War Wounds and Burns Committee of Med Research Council; formerly Treasurer and Member of Council, Gen. Med. Council, and a Member of Court of Examiners; Past Master and Member of Court of Assists. of Apothecaries' and Barbers' Cos., Editorial Sec., "British Journal of Surgery," Editor of "Medical Press" and "The Annals of the Royal College of Surgeons of England" and Pres., Med. So. of London and of Roy. Life Saving So., and Vice-Pres. and a Member of Council of Med. Defence Union; Examiner in Surgery to Univs. of London, Camb., Durham, Sheffield, Glasgow, Wales, and Dublin, and Past Pres. of Harveian So. of London, of Hunterian So., of Listerian So., of Clinical, United Services and Children's Sections of Roy. So. of Medicine, and of Alleyn Club ; Harveian Lecturer 1934, Hunterian Professor Roy. Coll. of Surgs. 1929, 1934, 1937, 1940 and 1942, Arris and Gale Lecturer Roy. Coll. of Surgs. 1924-5, Erasmus Wilson Lecturer 1928, 1930-33 and 1935-36, Arnott Demonstrator, Roy. Coll. of Surgs. 1934, a Member of Committee of Management, Conjoint Board 1942-54, Treasurer and a Member of Council, Gen. Med. Council 1942-55, Bradshaw Lecturer Roy. Coll. of Surgs. 1947, Pres. of Roy. Coll. of Surgs. of England 1949-54, Sheen Memorial Lecturer, Cardiff 1953, Hunterian Orator 1955 and Thomas Vicary Lecturer and Sir Thomas and Lady Edith Dixon Memorial Lecturer, N. Ireland Univ., Belfast 1957; Legg Lecturer, King's Coll. Hospital Med. Sch. 1957; has been Senior Lecturer in Anatomy, London Univ. since 1919 ; is Chm. Wakeley Bros., of Rainham, Kent, a K.St.J., and a Member of Chapter Gen. of Order of St. John ; European War 1915-19 as temporary Surg. R.N., European War 1939-45 as temporary Surg. Rear-Adm. (C.B., K.B.E., Com. of American Legion of Merit, Chevalier of Legion of Honour, Order of Southern Cross of Brazil) ; has 2nd class Order of the Nile ; C.B. (Mil.) 1941, K.B.E. (Mil.) 1946 : *m.* 1925, Elizabeth Muriel, *M.B.* (a C.St.J.), da. of James Nicholson-Smith, of Blackheath, S.E., and has issue.

Arms—Argent on a chevron sable between in chief two eagles displayed azure and in base a Rod of Aesculapius proper three crescents of the field.   **Crest**—A demi horse argent supporting between the legs a Rod of Aesculapius proper.

Residence—240, Maidstone Rd., Chatham, Kent.   *Clubs*—Athenaeum, Goat.

Sons living—JOHN CECIL NICHOLSON, *M.B., B.S., F.R.C.S.,* (of Mickle Lodge, Mickle Trafford, Chester), *b.* Aug. 27th, 1926; ed. at Canford, and at London Univ. (M.B. and B.S. 1950); MRCS England; LRCP London; FRCS 1955; FACS 1973; formerly Ch. Inspector, City of London Special Constabulary; is Consulting Surg., W. Cheshire Group of Hosps., a CStJ, and a Member of Council RCS England; Member of Liverpool Regional Hosp. Board, and of Mersey Regional Health Authority: *m.* 1954, June, da. of Donald Frank Leney, of Shottermill, Haslemere, Surrey, and has issue living, Nicholas Jeremy, *b.* 1957,—Charles John, *b.* 1959,—Amanda Jane, *b.* 1962.——Richard Michael, *MB, BS, b.* 1933; ed at Winchester; MB and BS 1957. *Residence,* 1. Wordsworth Mansions, Queen's Club Gdns., W14.——William Jeremy, *b.* 1935; ed. at Radley; JP for Kent: *m.* 1959, Veronica, 3rd da. of John Dunning Aysh, of Hardham Priory, Pulborough, Sussex, and has issue living, James Richard William, *b.* 1963,—Adam John Paul, *b.* 1965,— Miranda Elizabeth *b.* 1967. *Residence,* Pope's Hall, Hartlip, Sittingbourne, Kent.

WAKEMAN, Creation (U.K.) 1828, of Perdiswell Hall, Worcestershire.

Sir OFFLEY DAVID WAKEMAN, 5th *Baronet; b.* March 6th, 1922: *s.* his father, Capt. *Sir* OFFLEY, *CBE,* 1975; ed. at Canford Sch.: *m.* 1946, Pamela Rose Arabella, da. of the late Lt.-Col. Cecil Hunter Little, DSO, MBE.

Arms—Paly wavy of six vert and argent, a saltire engrailed ermine. **Crest**—Between two palm-branches proper, a lion's head erased argent, vomiting flames, gorged with a collar engrailed and cotissed vert, and charged with three ermine spots or.
Residence—Peversey House, Bomere Heath, Shrewsbury. *Club*—Lansdowne.

Half-Brother living—EDWARD OFFLEY BERTRAM, *b.* July 31st, 1934.

Nec temere, nec timide

Neither rashly nor timidly.

Widow living of 4th Baronet—JOSCELINE ETHELREDA (*Josceline, Lady Wakeman*) (Grafton Lodge, Montford Bridge, Shrewsbury, SY4 1HE), el. da. of the late Maj.-Gen. Bertram Reveley Mitford, CB, CMG, DSO, and widow of Cdr. Walter Leeke, RN [B. Manners]: *m.* 1929, as his 2nd wife, Capt. Sir Offley Wakeman, CBE, 4th baronet, who *d.* 1975.

Collateral Branch living.

Issue of the late Henry Offley Wakeman, son of 2nd baronet, *b.* 1852, *d.* 1899: *m.* 1898, Violet Mary, who *d.* 1942, da. of the late Francis John Johnston, of Dunsdale, Westerham, Kent :—

Mary Catherine (posthumous), *b.* 1899: *m.* 1918, Com. Mark Peregrine Charles Kerr, R.N. (ret.), who *d.* 1951 [see M. Lothian, colls.]. *Residence*, 2, The Chestnuts, Old London Rd., Benson, Oxon.

Sir Henry Wakeman, 1st Bt., of Perdiswell, Worcs., and Hinton Hall, Salop. Was a Member of HEICS. He was 2nd son of Thomas Wakeman, of Worcester, and m. 2ndly, 1797, Sarah, da. and heir of Richard Ward Offley of Hinton, Salop. Sir Offley, 3rd Bt., was Chm., Salop Quarter Sessions 1889-1914, and Capt. Sir Offley, CBE, 4th Bt., was Chm., Salop Co. Council 1943-63, and a Member of LCC 1922-25.

Waley-Cohen, see Cohen.

WALKER, Creation (U.K.) 1856, of Oakley House, Suffolk.

Sir BALDWIN PATRICK WALKER, 4th
Baronet, el. son of the late Com. Baldwin Charles Walker,
only son of 3rd baronet; *b.* Sept. 10th, 1924; *s.* his
grandfather, *Sir* FRANCIS ELLIOT, 1928; ed. at Gordonstoun; Lieut. R.N. (retired); is an hereditary
Pasha of Ottoman Empire: *m.* 1st, 1948, Joy
Yvonne (who obtained a divorce 1954), da. of Sir
Arrol Moir, 2nd Bt.; 2ndly, 1954, Sandra, da. of
Henry Stewart; 3rdly, 1966, Rosemary Ann, da.
of the late Henry Hollingdrake, and has issue by
3rd m.

Arms—Gules, on a chevron between three cross-crosslets
argent, an anchor sable; on a chief of the second, three stags,
heads cabossed proper, a canton azure, thereon a representation
of the diamond decoration of a Pasha of the Ottoman Empire,
conferred on the late Sir Baldwin by the Sultan for his services
in Syria. **Crest**—Out of a naval crown azure, a stag's head
proper, gorged with an eastern crown or.
Address, P.O. Box 331, Paarl, Cape Province, S. Africa.

Son living—By 3rd m.—CHRISTOPHER ROBERT BALDWIN,
b. Oct. 25th, 1969.
Daughter living—By 3rd m.—Amanda Jane *b.* 1967.
Brother living—Francis Donald Baldwin, *b.* (*posthumous*) 1927;
formerly Lt. KRRC: *m.* 1st, 1955, Joanna, only da. of Sir
John Weir Russell; 2ndly, 1965, Jennifer Mary, only da. of
the late Lt.-Cdr. Eric Stokoe, RN (ret.), and has issue living
(by 1st m.), Caroline Lucy Marjorie, *b.* 1958,—(by 2nd m.)
Anthony Eric Charles, *b.* 1966. *Residence*, Trevi, Chester
Drive, Bishopscourt, Cape Town, Cape Province, S. Africa.

Mother living—Mary (BALD), da. of Frederick Piere Barnett, of Whalton, Northumberland : *m.*
2ndly, 1923, Com. Baldwin Charles Walker (ante), who *d.* 1927 ; 3rdly, 1928, Squadron-Leader
Aubrey William Graham Martin, RAF; 4thly, C. Black, re-married 5thly, Wing Cdr. Aubrey
William Graham Martin, RAF (her 3rd husband, who *d.* 1973). *Residence*, Constantia Flower
Farm, Doordrift Rd., Constantia, Cape Province, S. Africa.

Collateral Branches living.

Grandchildren of the late Frederic George Arthur WAKE-WALKER (infra):—
Issue of the late Adm. Sir (William) Frederic WAKE-WALKER, K.C.B., C.B.E., *b.*
1888, *d.* 1945: *m.* 1916, Muriel Elsie, who *d.* 1963, only da. of Sir Collingwood Hughes,
10th Bt. (*cr.* 1773):—
Christopher Baldwin HUGHES-WAKE-WALKER, *b.* 1920; Capt. RN (ret.); has assumed the additional surname of Hughes: *m.* 1944, Lady Anne Spencer (sometime 3rd Officer WRNS), only da.
of 7th Earl Spencer, and has issue living, David Christopher, *b.* 1947; ed. at St. Andrews Univ.
(MA); Page of Honour to HM 1960-62,—Richard Anthony, *b.* 1951; ed. at St. Andrews Univ.,—
Michael John, *b.* 1958,—Elizabeth Sarah, *b.* 1944: *m.* 1970, Anthony Duckworth-Chad, of
Pynkney Hall, E. Rudham, Norfolk, and has issue living, James Anthony L'éfang *b.* 1972,—
Diana Mary (twin), *b.* 1958. *Residence*, East Bergholt Lodge, East Bergholt, Suffolk.——Cedric
Collingwood, *b.* 1923; Lt.-Cdr. RN (ret.): *m.* 1949, Iona, da. of Capt. J. C. Maclean, RN, and has
issue living, Edward Collingwood, *b.* 1952,—Susanna, *b.* 1950: *m.* 1974, Christopher Mark Dancy,
MA, BM, BCh,—Corinna Elizabeth, *b.* 1957. *Residence*, Terwick Wood, Rogate, Petersfield,
Hants.——Penelope Hughes (*Lady Eley*), *b.* 1917: *m.* 1937, Sir Geoffrey Cecil Ryves Eley, CBE, and
has issue living, Piers David Christopher (35, Montague Rd., Richmond, Surrey), *b.* 1941; MA,
MSc: *m.* 1967, Sarah Cloudesley, da. of Lt.-Col. David Edward Long-Price, OBE, and has issue
living, Damian Edward Piers *b.* 1970, Thalia Catherine *b.* 1971,—Gavin Michael Geoffrey, *b.* 1945:
m. 1974, Mary Belinda (Holly), el. da. of Maj. Bruce Edward Arthur Urquhart of Craigston,
Craigston Castle, Aberdeenshire, and formerly wife of Fabrizio Pratesi,—Susan Ianthe, *b.* 1938:
m. 1963, Paul Edward Cornwall-Jones, of 36, St. Petersburgh Place, W2 4LD, and has issue
living, Imogen Annabel *b.* 1967, Theresa Hermione Chloë *b.* 1971,—Chloë Sarabella, *b.* 1950: *m.*
1971, Richard Christian Wynne Fremantle, of 22, Anley Rd., W14 [see B. Cottesloe]. *Residences*
27, Wynnstay Gdns., W8; The Change House, Gt. Yeldham, Essex.——Catherine Marigold, *b.*
1921; sometime 3rd Officer WRNS: *m.* 1944, the Rev. Hugh Wake [see Wake, Bt., colls.].
Residence, Gt. Finborough Vicarage, Stowmarket, Suffolk.

Issue of the late Frederic George Arthur WAKE-WALKER, yst. son of 1st
baronet, *b.* 1857, *d.* 1931 (having assumed by deed poll 19—, the additional
surname of Wake): *m.* 1883, Mary Eleanor, who *d.* 1928, da. of the late
William Forster, Bar.-at-law:—
Ruth Barbara Wake, *b.* 1894: *m.* 1916, William Henry Lowe Watson, DSO, DCM, who *d.* 1932,
and has issue living, Patrick (Park Farm House, Ashtead, Surrey), *b.* 1917: *m.* 1941,
Elizabeth Darbishire Jones, and has issue living, William Patrick *b.* 1949,
Adam Charles *b.* 1955,—David Lowe (The White House, 10, Highgate High St., N6),
b. 1919: *m.* 1951, Dawn Sparkes, and has issue living, James Lowe *b.* 1954, Stephen Lowe *b.*
1956, Andrew Julian Lowe *b.* 1958,—Judith, *b.* 1921: *m.* 1943 (m. diss. 1960), Robin Hugh
Scutt, of 488, Kings Rd., SW10, and has issue living, Mark Oliver *b.* 1945, John Paul *b.* 1947.
Residence, Ivy Cottage, Sutton, Pulborough, Sussex.

The 1st baronet, Adm. Sir Baldwin Wake Walker, K.C.B. (only surviving son of the late John
Walker, of Whitehaven), was Comptroller of the Navy 1847-60. He served many years in the
Turkish service, and was made a Pasha for his services on the coast of Syria. The 2nd baronet,
Sir Baldwin Wake, C.M.G., C.V.O., was a Vice-Adm.

WALKER, Creation (U.K.) 1868, of Sand Hutton, co. York, and of Beachampton, Bucks.

How great is honesty.

Sir JAMES HERON WALKER, 5th *Baronet; b.* April 7th, 1914; *s.* his father, *Sir* ROBERT JAMES MILO, 1930; ed. at Eton, and at Magdalene Coll., Camb.: *m.* 1st, 1939 (m. diss. 1972), Angela Margaret, only da. of the late Victor Alexandre Beaufort, OBE, MC, of Steephill, Jersey; 2ndly, 1972, Sharrone Babette, el. da. of David Philip Read, of Clanfield, Oxon., and has issue by 1st and 2nd m.

Arms—Argent, on a chevron gules, between three crescents azure, as many annulets, or. Crest—Out of a battlement argent, a dexter arm embowed in armour azure, in the hand proper a lizard vert.
Residence—Ringdale Manor, Faringdon, Oxon.

Sons living (by 1st m.)—VICTOR STEWART HERON, Ablington Manor, Bilbury, Glos.; R. Yacht Sqdn., *b.* Oct. 8th, 1942; ed at Eton; 2nd Lt. Gren. Gds. 1962-65, and Lt. R. Wilts. Yeo. and R. Yeo. 1965-73: *m.* 1969, Caroline Louisa, yst. da. of the late Lt.-Col. Frederick Edwin Barton Wignall [see Acland Bt., *cr.* 1678 colls.], and has issue living, James Frederick Heron, *b.* 1970,—Andrew Robert Heron, *b.* 1973.——(by 2nd m.) Simon Peter, *b.* 1974.

Brother living—Peter Arthur, *b.* 1918; ed. at Eton.

Uncle living (son of 3rd baronet)—Patrick Bruce, *MBE, b.* 1898; ed. at Eton; late Cadet R.F.C.; 1939-45 War in N. Africa and Italy as Maj. R.A. (T.A.) (despatches, MBE); MBE (Mil) 1945: *m.* 1928, Sybil, da. of Charles Byron Turner, MRCS, of Ashby-cum-Fenby, Lincs., and has issue living, Susan Anne Maud (*Hon. Mrs. Richard C. Butler*) *b.* 1930: *m.* 1952, the Hon. Richard Clive Butler, of Penny Pot, Halstead, Essex, son of Baron Butler of Saffron Walden, KG, CH, PC (Life Peer). *Residence*, Barry's Close, Long Crendon, Bucks.

Mother living—(Emily) Synolda, da. of the late James Augustine Harvey Thursby-Pelham, J.P. D.L., of 55, Cadogan Gardens, S.W., and Upton Cressett, Salop [B. Dunboyne, colls.]: *m.* 1st 1913, Sir Robert James Milo Walker, 4th Bt., from whom she obtained a divorce 1922 ; 2ndly 1923, Sir William Edmund Jaffray, 4th Bt., from whom she obtained a divorce 1936; 3rdly 1944, Guy Argles, of 8, Kingston House North, Princes Gate SW7.

Collateral Branches living.

Issue of the late Capt. Ronald Heron Walker, 3rd son of 3rd baronet, *b.* 1896, *d.* 1964: *m.* 1921, Noel, who *d.* 1972, da. of Maj. Guy Edward Wentworth, of Woolley Park, Wakefield:—
Michael Anthony, *b.* 1924: *m.* 1948, Ann, da. of John E. Ferguson, of Busbridge Wood, Godalming, and has issue living, Caroline Margaret, *b.* 1950: *m.* 1969, Ian D. Doulton, of 31, Kelso Place, W8, and has issue living, David Peter Michael *b.* 1974, Lucy Catherine *b.* 1971,—Rosemary Ann, *b.* 1954,—Frances Mary, *b.* 1965.——Diana Mary, *b.* 1923: *m.* 1969, Simon Neville Turner, of Achnashellach, by Strathcarron, Ross-shire, and Crailing House, Jedburgh, Roxburghshire.

Grandsons of the late Rev. Reginald Edmund Walker (infra):—
Issue of the late Rupert Alexander Seymour Walker, *b.* 1910, *d.* 1973: *m.* 1942, Edith Mary Sutherland (Suite 404, 1573, Begbie St., Victoria, BC, Canada):—
Jack Mervyn (18, Schwantz Rd., Pembroke, Ont., Canada), *b.* 1946: *m.* 1968, Marjorie Aline, da. of Herbert Buske, of Pembroke, Ont., and has issue living, Victoria Edith *b.* 1974.——Raymond Earle, *b.* 1950.

Issue of the late Rev. Reginald Edmund Walker, 2nd son of 2nd baronet, *b.* 1866, *d.* 1945: *m.* 1895, Lady Emily Mary Seymour, who *d.* 1948, da. of 6th Marquess of Hertford:—
Margaret Edith Mary, *b.* 1901: *m.* 1st, 1920, Frank Caffery; 2ndly, 1941, William Derbyshire, of, 401, 1955, Ashgrove St., Victoria, BC, V8R 4N8, Canada, and has issue living, (by 1st m.) Kathleen Ethel Mary, *b.* 1934: *m.* 1st, 19—, Robert Coates; 2ndly, 19—, John Jeffrey, of Burnaby 1, BC, Canada, and has issue living, (by 1st m.), Edward Francis (11, Kopper King Trailer Court, Route RR1 Whitehorse, Yukon Territory) *b.* 19—: *m.* 1970, Jo-Ann Shepherd (and has issue living, Jolene Mary *b.* 1974), Douglas Colin Paul *b.* 1953 (85, Takhina, Trailer Court, White-horse, Yukon Terr.), Robert James *b.* 1958, Kathleen Wendy Maki: *m.* 1972, Matthew Mackie (and has issue living, Matthew Maki *b.* 1974), Anita Marie *b.* 1955: *m.* 1973, George Polburn (and has issue living Shayne Gregory *b.* 1974), Sharon Leigh *b.* 1957, Phyllis Margaret *b.* 1959, Debra Joan *b.* 1960.

Issue of the late Major Harold Maxwell Walker, 3rd son of 2nd baronet, *b.* 1869, *d.* 1938: *m.* 1904, Marie Albreda Blanche, who *d.* 1963, da. of the late the Hon. William Henry Wentworth Fitzwilliam [E. Fitzwilliam, colls.]:—
Marya Constance, *b.* 1905: *m.* 1935, Reginald Dekyn Lund, and has issue living, Rosemary Diana, *b.* 1937: *m.* 1961, Thomas Kennedy Dalziel, of Crailing Bhan, Jedburgh, Roxburghshire, and has issue living, Ralph Kennedy, *b.* 1964, Michael Kennedy *b.* 1966. *Residence*, Crailing Bhan, Jedburgh, Roxburghshire——Ellenor Mildred Kathleen (The Abbey, Malton, Yorks.), *b.* 1908. ——Rachel Marie Gabrielle, *b.* 1913.——Albreda Mary, *b.* 1922.

Issue of the late Francis Henry Walker, 4th son of 2nd baronet, *b.* 1870, *d.* 1944: *m.* 1904, Frances Mary Theresa, who *d.* 1961, el. da. of Francis J. Palmes, formerly of Mill Mount, York :—
Evelyn Lindsay, *b.* 1905: *m.* 1926, Lt.-Col. Gerard Thomas Scofield Horton, MC, late The Queen's Bays, and has issue living, Michael Schofield (Bredon Manor, Tewkesbury, Glos.), *b.* 1929: *m.* 1965, Anne, da. of Sir (Frederick) Philip Alfred William Wombwell, MBE, 6th Bt., and has issue living, James Frederick *b.* 1968, Peter Michael *b.* 1969,—Patricia Lindsay, *b.* 1927: *m.* 1955, Maj. Tom Pickering Salisbury Woods, MBE, late RA, of Poynington Manor, Sherborne, Dorset, and has issue living, Simon Salisbury, *b.* 1956, Robert Gerard Salisbury *b.* 1965, Caroline Lindsay, *b.* 1968,—Linda Mary, *b.* 1936: *m.* 1956, Ronald Oakes Crowther, of Avontuur, PO Firgrove, Cape Prov., S. Africa, and has issue living, James Robert *b.* 1964, Charles Gerard Oakes *b.* 1967, Nicola Jane *b.* 1957, Miranda *b.* 1959. *Residence*, Bishops Caundle House, W. Sherborne, Dorset.

Issue of the late Ernest Robert Walker, 5th son of 2nd baronet, *b.* 1872, *d.* 1942 : *m.* 1901, Beatrice Mary, who *d.* 1938, da. of the Rt. Hon. Sir Herbert Eustace Maxwell, 7th Bt., P.C., M.P. (*cr.* 1681):—

James Herbert, *b.* 1905. *Residence,* Kianzabe, Thika, Kenya.——Silvia Mary (Musbury Bank, Marnhull, Sturminster Newton, Dorset), *b.* 1903: *m.* 1924, Maj. Llewellyn William Dean Wathen, 8th Hussars, who *d.* 1970, and has issue living, Guy Llewellyn (The Old Farmhouse, Sulgrave, Banbury, Oxon), *b.* 1925; 5th R. Inniskilling Dragoon Gds.; Col., Defence Attaché British Embassy, Rome: *m.* 1st, 1953, Jean Maureen, who obtained a divorce 1970, da. of William Lancelot Dawes, of Malmains Manor, Pluckley, Kent; 2ndly, 1971, Hilary Margaret, adopted da. of Joyce Marjorie Wigram, MB, BS [see Wigram, Bt. colls.], and formerly wife of Stephen James Stuart Oxlade, and has issue living (by 1st m.), Julian Peter Guy *b.* 1954; 2nd Lt. 5th R. Inniskilling Dragoon Gds., Nigel Charles James *b.* 1955,——David Anthony (Kilmartin, Glenurquhart, Inverness-shire), *b.* 1928; ed. at Marlborough, and at Roy. Agricultural Coll., Cirencester: *m.* 1st, 1954 (m. diss. 1974), Barbara Jean, da. of the late Thomas Horsburgh Gibson, of Manor Hill, Selkirk; 2ndly, 1974, Patricia Gilbert Ros Croasdale, da. of the late Charles Ros Munton, of Knutsford, Cheshire, and has issue living (by 1st m.), Richard Llewellyn *b.* 1959, Wendy Anne *b.* 1956,——Ronald James (Es Clot, Deya, Mallorca), *b.* 1934; ed. at Marlborough, and at Trin. Coll., Dublin; late 2nd Lt. 8th Hussars.——Kathleen Elizabeth Jean (of Cannons, Tibberton, Glos.) *b.* 1908.

Grandchildren of the late Frederick James Walker, MVO, 2nd son of 1st baronet:—
Issue of the late Capt. Hugh Edward Walker, *b.* 1865, *d.* 1935: *m.* 1913, the Hon. Marjory Winifred, who *d.* 1945, da. of 21st Baron Forbes:—

Peter Hugh Frederick, *TD* (Nethertack, Moniaive, Dumfries-shire, DG3 4EQ) *b.* 1916; ed at Ampleforth, and London Univ. (Bsc Eng); MICE; formerly Capt. RE; 1939-45 War in Middle East: *m.* 1947, Geraldine Elizabeth Mary, only da. of the late Maj. Carlos Lumsden, of Clova, Aberdeenshire.——Rosemary Alice Champney (Thornton Grange, Thornton Steward, Ripon, Yorks.), *b.* 1917: *m.* 1948, Capt. Hugh Shelley Le Mesurier, Duke of Wellington's Regt., and has issue living, Jacquine Shelley, *b.* 1949: *m.* 1960, Lt. Jeremy John Gaskell, The King's Regt., and has issue living, Victoria Jacquine *b.* 1971, Joanna Louise *b.* 1973,——Susan Rosemary, *b.* 1950.——Marguerite Helena Mary, *b.* 1919: *m.* 1942, Capt. Giles Grierson Tweedie, late Argyll and Sutherland Highlanders, of Belmont House, Crawfordton, Moniaive, Dumfries-shire, and has issue living, Marion Veronica, *b.* 1943,——Jacqueline Alice, *b.* 1944,——Rosalind Mary, *b.* 1947.——Daphne Elizabeth (The Convent of the Holy Child Jesus, The Old Palace, Mayfield, Sussex), *b.* 1926.

Grandsons of the late Rear-Adm. Charles Francis Walker, 3rd son of 1st baronet:—
Issue of the late Capt. Edgar Wilmer Walker, E. Yorkshire Regt.. *b.* 1875. *d.* (killed in action during European War) 1914 : *m.* 1906, Charlotte Rankin [(*Viscountess Lifford*), who *d.* 1954, having *m.* 2ndly, 1919, the 7th Viscount Lifford], da. of Sir Robert Maule:—
Francis Robert, *b.* 1910. *Residence,*

Issue of the late Rev. Philip Charles Walker, *b.* 1878, *d.* 1933: *m.* 1916, Dorothy Ann, who *d.* 1936, da. of the late Col. Frederick Compton Howard, Rifle Brig. [E. Carlisle, colls.]:—
Anthony Charles Howard, *b.* 1917 ; ed. at Wellington Coll. : *m.* 1st, 1939, Lorna (who obtained a divorce 1946), da. of H. Crabtree ; 2ndly, 1952, Peggy Foster, da. of John T. Hewes, of Cambridge, and has issue living, (by 2nd marriage) Timothy Heron, *b.* 1954,——Elizabeth Cavendish, *b.* 1956,——Ann Cavendish, *b.* 1958. *Residence,* 58, Balfour Road, Blackbird Leys, Oxford.——Philip James, *b.* 1920 ; ed. at Uppingham Sch. ; formerly in R.A.F. ; European War 1939-45 in India : *m.* 1951, Helen Gibson, da. of Dr. Milligan, late of Hessle, E. Yorkshire. *Residence,* Halse Springs, Macheke, S. Rhodesia.

Granddaughter of the late Capt. Edwyn Walker (infra) :—
Issue of the late Capt. Oswald Bethell Walker, 15th Hussars, *b.* 1875, *d.* (killed in action) 1914: *m.* 1910, Marcia Eugenia (who *d.* 1973, having *m.* 2ndly, 1920, Francois de Juge Montespieu), da. of the late Col. John Delalynde Mansel [Mansel, Bt., colls.]:—
Lois Adeline, *b.* 1912 : *m.* 1932, George Nickerson, late Coldstream Guards, and has issue living, David George François (of 4, Ladbroke Terrace, W.11), *b.* 1933 : *m.* 1957, Sarah Elizabeth, da. of Col. John Jewson, MC, and has issue living, William *b.* 1958, James *b.* 1960, Camilla *b.* 1965,——Mark Oswald Julian (69, Prince's Gate Mews, SW7), *b.* 1935: *m.* 1974, Elizabeth, da. of F. P. Birch. *Residence,* Burnt Fen, Horning, Norfolk.

Issue of the late Capt. Edwyn Walker, 4th son of 1st baronet, *b.* 1837, *d.* 1919 : *m.* 1874, Elizabeth, who *d.* 1915, da. of William F. Bethell, of Rise Park, Yorkshire:—
Dorothy Katharine : *m.* 1907, Lieut.-Col. Francis Bertie Brewis, who *d.* 1949, late King's Own Yorkshire LI [Williams-Wynn, Bt., colls.], and has issue living, Henry John, *MP* (Ardwell House, Stranraer, Wigtownshire), *b.* 1920; ed. at Eton, and at New Coll., Oxford; Bar. Middle Temple 1946; PPS to Lord Advocate 1960-61; MP for Galloway (C) since 1959; 1939-45 War as Maj. R.A. in N. Africa and Italy (despatches twice): *m.* 1949, Faith Agnes Dervorguilla, da. of Sir Edward Orde MacTaggart-Stewart, 2nd Bt., and has issue living, Francis Roger McTaggart *b.* 1950, Ralph Michael Rodney *b.* 1951, Christopher Mark John *b.* 1956, Sylvia Katharine Moira *b.* 1952,——Philippa Dorothy Annora, *b.* 1911: *m.* 1947, Walter Staves, of Market Rasen, and has issue living, Andrew *b.* 1948, Gregory *b.* 1951,——Olivia Hester Rachel, *b.* 1916. *Residence,* Norton Grove, Malton, Yorks.

Grandson of the late Capt. Gerald Walker, 5th son of 1st baronet :—
Issue of the late Lieut.-Col. Bertram James Walker, C.M.G., D.S.O., *b.* 1880, *d.* 1947: *m.* 1st, 1909, Josepha Margaret (who *d.* 1972, having obtained a divorce 1926), da. of the late Sir George Donaldson, of 1, Grand Av., Hove, Sussex; 2ndly, 1940, Countess Lucie M. Reventlow, of Brahe Trolleborg, Denmark:—
(By 1st marriage) Anthony Gerald Bartholomew, *b.* 1912 ; ed. at Harrow ; Lieut.-Col. (retired) Somerset L.I.: *m.* 1939, Margaret Cumberland, da. of the late Col. C. P. Templeton, C.B., D.S.O., of Victoria, British Columbia, and has issue living, Christopher James Anthony, *b.* 1943 ; ed. at Harrow; Maj. 17th/21st Lancers: *m.* 1971, Ronwen Melody, da. of Lt.-Col. E. C. Barton, MC, and has issue living, Rupert Anthony Edward *b.* 1972,——Alice Melody Margaret *b.* 1974,——Robin Charles Andrew, *b.* 1944; ed at Harrow, and McGill Univ., Montreal,——Peter Gerald Edward, *b.* 1948; ed. at Harrow,——John Perry Donaldson, *b.* 1951; ed. at Harrow; Capt. 17th/21st Lancers,——Morella Cumberland, *b.* 1942: *m.* 1967, Robert Gwynne Cottam, of 7, Stanford Rd., W8 5PP, and has issue living, Charles Robert Edward *b.* 1969, Henry Gerald Alexander *b.* 1973, Rosemary Margaret Cumberland *b.* 1971. *Residence,* Chattis House, Stockbridge, Hants., SO20 6JS, *Club,* Bath.

Grandchildren of the late Arthur Walker, 8th son of 1st baronet:—
Issue of the late Edward Arthur Walker, *b.* 1883, *d.* 1958: *m.* 1911, Frances Beatrice, who *d.* 1961, da. of James Davis:—
Harold Edward Palmes (Springwood Tower Rd. North, Heswall, Ches.), *b.* 1917; 1939-45 War as Maj. Indian Army in Burma: *m.* 1951, Phyllis Nora Green, and has issue living, Michael Anthony, *b.* 1951.——Joan Olive Beatrix, *b.* 1912: *m.* 1940, Geoffrey Norman Booth, solicitor, of 77, Palm Grove, Oxton, Birkenhead, and has issue living, David Parkin, *b.* 1943.——Stella Rowena Palmes (Greenacre, Tower Road North, Heswall, Cheshire) *b.* 1920: *m.* 1944, Cdr. Harold Jack Edmund Dugdale, RNR, who *d.* 1975, and has issue living, Janet Beatrice, *b.* 1947,——Diana Elizabeth, *b.* 1952.

Issue of the late Henry Walker, *b.* 1885, *d.* 1965: *m.* 1913, Margaret, da. of Robert Rowlands:—
Henry Arthur (Stanbridge House, Wimborne, Dorset; Royal Overseas Club), *b.* 1913; ed. at
Brighton Coll.; 1939-45 War as Maj. KAR in Tanganyika, Ethiopia and Kenya: *m.* 1st, 1935
(m. diss. 1947), Rose Vivien, da. of Raymond Robert Ulyate; 2ndly, 1948, Christine Mabel, who
d. 1973, da. of Ollive Edward Hollingworth, of Step House, Witchampton, Dorset, and has
issue living (by 1st m.), Robert Christopher Arthur (PO Box 11, Orapa, Francistown, Botswana,
Southern Africa), *b.* 1938; ed. at King's Sch., Bruton: *m.* 9164, Melody Gloriana Mignonette,
da. of the late Carl de Friedland, of Cape Town, and has issue living, Robert James *b.* 1968,
Juanita Marguerite Vivien *b.* (Jan.) 1965, Karine Madelaine Mignonette Tanya *b.* (Nov.) 1965)—
(by 2nd m.) Mary Woodroffe Margaret, *b.* 1957.——Monica Diana, *b.* 1915: *m.* 1939, Archibald
Robert Octavius McMillan, OBE, of Seven Acre Corner, St. John's Rd., Exmouth.

Issue of the late Maj. Ernest Walker *b.* 1887, *d.* 1970: *m.* 1st, Mildred Katherine Grace,
who *d.* 1952, da. of the late Lt.-Col. Sir Charles Henry Brabazon Heaton-Ellis, CBE;
2ndly, 1953, Dorothy Hyacinthe (Tontine, Box 253, Limuru, Kenya), only child of
the late Maj. Cecil William Bunbury Eames, JP, RE:—
(By 1st m.) Peter Martin Brabazon (Mount Esk, Lasswade, Midlothian), *b.* 1922; ed. at Haileybury,
and at Trin. Coll., Camb.; Prof. of Naturla Hist., Edinburgh Univ.: *m.* 1943, Violet Wright,
and has issue living, Robin John, *b.* 1947,—Marian Elizabeth, *b.* 1943, Sonia Eilidh, *b.* 1954,—
Caroline Jane Palmes, *b.* 1960.——Jonathan Mungo Palmes (Lythhanger, Empshott, Liss,
Hants), *b.* 1929; Maj. (ret.) The Black Watch: *m.* 1955, Diana Mary. el. da. of Brig. Otho
William Nicholson, TD, DL, of Coles Farm, Privett, Hants, and has issue living, Timothy
William Mungo, *b.* 1956; ed. at Millfield,—Jonathan Alexander James, *b.* 1961,—Juliet Elizabeth
Charmian, *b.* 1958.

Granddaughter of the late Maj. Ernest Walker (ante):—
Issue of the late Lt. Cdr. Timothy Robin Charles Walker, RN, *b.* 1925, *d.* 1964: *m.* 1958,
Dilys, who *d.* 1964, da. of Brig. John Victor Dykes Radford, OBE, MC, of Clayhanger,
Purse Caundle, Sherborne, Dorset:—
Sabine Louise. *b.* 1962.

Sir James Walker, 1st Bt., of Sand Hutton, Yorks., only son of James Walker, of Springhead,
Hall, was High Sheriff of York 1846. Sir James Robert Walker, 2nd Bt., was M.P. for Beverley
(C), 1859-65.

WALKER, Creation (U.K.) 1906, of Pembroke House, City of Dublin.

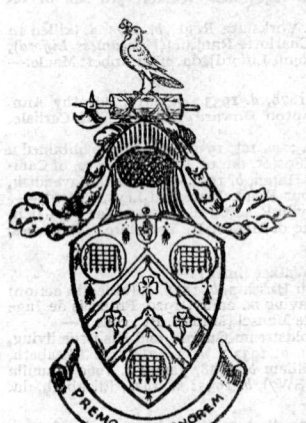

Sir HUGH RONALD WALKER, 4th *Baronet*;
b. Dec. 13th, 1925; *s.* his father, *Maj. Sir*
CECIL EDWARD, *DSO, MC*, 1964; Maj. (ret.)
RA: *m.* 1971, Norna, el. da. of Lt.-Cdr. R. D.
Baird, RNR (ret.), of Yarford Orchards,
Kingston St. Mary, nr. Taunton, and has issue.

Arms—Ermine, on a chevron engrailed plain cotised
azure, between three hurts, each charged with a portcullis
or, as many trefoils slipped of the last. Crest—On a
Roman fasces or, banded azure, a dove of the last, holding in its beak a trefoil slipped of the first.

Address—c/o Lloyds Bank, Somerton, Somerset.
Son living—ROBERT CECIL, *b.* Sept. 26th, 1974.
Sister living—Sheilagh Rosemary, *b.* 1928.
Aunt living (daughter of 1st baronet)—Ina Eleanor, *b.*
1883: *m.* 1911, Charles Adolphus Sheridan, formerly
Lt. 5th Dragoon Guards, who *d.* 1942, and has issue
living, Charles Samuel Brinsley, *b.* 1912. *Residence*,
17, Rowan House, Mespil Rd., Dublin 4.

The 1st baronet, the Rt. Hon. Sir Samuel, P.C.,
was Solicitor-Gen. for Ireland 1883-5, Attorney-Gen. for
Ireland 1885 and 1886, Lord Chancellor of Ireland 1892-5,
a Lord Justice of Appeal 1895-1905, and again Lord
Chancellor 1905-11.

Walker-Okeover, see Okeover.

Walker-Smith, see Smith.

FORESTIER-WALKER. Creation (U.K.) 1835.
[Name pronounced "Forest-tier-Walker."]

Sir GEORGE FERDINAND
FORESTIER-WALKER, 4th *Baronet*;
b. May 20th, 1899; *s.* his father,
Sir GEORGE FERDINAND, 1933;
ed. at Wellington Coll.; Major
(retired) Coldstream Guards.

Arms—Erminois, on a pile embattled
azure, a mural crown charged with the
word "Badajos" between two galtraps in
pale or. Crest—On a mural crown or,
encircled by a wreath of laurel vert, an
ostrich proper, resting the dexter foot on a
shell exploding proper. Supporters—
Dexter, a lion reguardant proper, gorged
with a riband gules, fimbriated azure,
therefrom pendent a representation of the
medal and clasps presented to the 1st
baronet for his services in the Peninsula;
in the mouth a broken flagstaff reversed,
with the eagle and French tricolored flag
also proper, the latter inscribed with the word "Or hes"; *sinister*, an ostrich supporting the
colours of the 50th Regt., thereon an escroll gules inscribed with the word "Vimiera" in letters
of gold.
Residence—Monk's Mill, Pilton, near Shepton Mallet, Somerset.

Collateral Branches living.

Grandchildren of the late Radzivill Frederick Forester-Walker, 2nd son of 2nd baronet, b. 1856, d. 1934: m. 1894, Eva Laura (who d. 1947, and from whom he had obtained a divorce 1905), da. of Col. Francis Justice, formerly of Craig-yr-Haul, Castleton, Cardiff:—

Issue of the late Radzivill Clive Forestier-Walker, b. 1895, d. 1973: m. 1921, Kathleen Rose (Iquique, Low Rd., S. Wootton, King's Lynn, Norfolk), da. of the late William George Tinkler, of King's Lynn:—

Clive Radzivill (28, Grove Rd., Rayleigh, Essex, SS6 8PX), b. April 30th, 1922: m. 1948, Pamela Mercy, da. of Clifford Leach, of Chiswick, W., and has issue living, Lesley Jane b. 1951: m. 1968, John Wheaton, and has issue living, Joanna b. 1970, Jaqueline, b. 1971,—Heather, b. 1954: m. 1972, John Gray,—Elizabeth, b. 1958: m. 1974, David King.——June Vivienne, b. 1923: m. 1954, Leonard Raymond Hayes, of Chinook, S. Wootton, King's Lynn, Norfolk.

Grandchildren of the late Ivor Augustus Forestier-Walker, 5th son of 2nd baronet:—

Issue of the late Lieut.-Col. Alan Ivor Forestier-Walker, M.B.E., 7th Gurkha Rifles, b. 1913, d. (killed in action in Malaya) 1954 : m. 1945, Margaret Joan (of Down Lodge, 170, Banstead Rd., Carshalton Beeches, Surrey), da. of the late Maj. Henry Bennett Marcoolyn, M.B.E., of Carshalton Beeches, Surrey:—

Michael Leolin, b. 1949.——Michelle, b. 1946.

Issue of the late Urbain Evelyn Forestier-Walker, b. 1915, d. 1974: m. 1941, Aileen (Sheelin, Oakington Av., Little Chalfont, Bucks.), da. of Thomas Morrissey:—

Alan David (7 DEO Gurkha Rifles, B/F PO 1, Hong Kong), b. 1944; ed. Prior Park Coll., Bath; Capt. 7th Duke of Edinburgh's Own Gurkha Rifles: m. 1969, Adela, da. of Simon Phillip Davis, and has issue living, Clare Elaine, b. 1971,—Louise Anne b. 1972.——Anne Patricia, b. 1942.

Issue of the late Capt. Devereux Philip Forestier-Walker, 6th son of 2nd baronet, b. 1864, d. 1936: m. 1896, Isabella Constance, who d. 1949, da. of the late F. G. Dalgety, of Lockerley Hall, Hants, and widow of Capt. C. W. Selwyn:—

Freda Gladys, b. 1897 (920, Smith Av., Coquitlam, BC): m. 1921, William Henry Cartwright, who d. 1962; and has issue living, Julian William Devereux (400, Trail St., Kimberley, BC), b. 1923: m. 1949, Margaret Elaine, da. of E. Ewing, and has issue living, Elena Marr b. 1950, Lorena Joanne b. 1951: m. 1972, Jacobus Antonius Ferdinand Ramak, Shelley Rae b. 1953: m. 1973, Terrance Glenn Pruden, Tracy Dell b. 1961,—Barbara Mary, b. 1922: m. 1954, John Bannatyne McLeod, of 920, Smith Av., Coquitlam, BC.——Honor Dorothy, b. 1899: m. 1934, Capt. Thomas Willington Lane, late RA; MA Camb and ADC to Gov. of Mauritius, and has issue living, Patrick Anthony Willington, b. 1938,—Gillian, b. 1935. Residence, Longdon, Bath Rd., Marlborough, Wilts.

Issue of the late Sir (Charles) Leolin Forestier-Walker, K.C.B., M.P. (7th son of 2nd baronet), who was cr. a Baronet 1929:—

See **Forestier-Walker, cr. 1929 (ext.)**

Issue of the late Charles Evelyn Forestier-Walker, 9th son of 2nd baronet, b. 1875, d. 1931 : m. 1905, Ada Llewelyn, who d. 1960, da. of Col. Robert Henry Mansel, (J.P. and D.L. for Monmouthshire, formerly Major Roy. Dublin Fusiliers, and Col. Comdg. 2nd Vol. Batn. of S. Wales Borderers), of Abergavenny, and Caerleon, Monmouthshire :—

Charles Jocelyn, b. 1912 : ed. at Wellington Coll. ; European War 1939-45 : m. 1942, Joy, da. of the late Lt.-Cdr. J. R. Gill, RNR, of Christchurch, Newport, and has issue living, Charles Robert Piers (Brynhyfryd Cottages, Croesor, Penrhyndeudraeth, Gwynedd) b. 1950: m. 1974, Philippa Jean White, step-da. of Dr. C. Bond,—Elenith Camilla, b. 1947: m. 1968, Malcolm Anthony Luker, of Limesstrasse 70, Munich, 80, and has issue living James Robert b. 1971. Residence, Rosemary Cottage, 5, High St., Hanslope, Bucks.——Robert Jestyn Gwent, b. 1919; ed. at Wellington Coll., is an Architect; 1939-45 War as Flt. Lt. RAF (despatches): m. 1956, Elizabeth Ann, da. of the late Brig. J. H. Willans, of Newton House, Sneaton, Yorks, and has issue living, Charles Aidan Gwent, b. 1966,—Evelyn Rosamund, b. 1961,—Vivien Serena Charlotte, b. 1963,—Daphne Miranda Clare, b. 1964. Residence, Quinacres, Little Gaddesden, Herts. Club, Royal Aero and United Service.

Grandchildren of the late Lieut.-Col. Edmond Somerville Forestier Walker (infra) :—

Issue of the late Col. Edmond Alec FORESTIER-WALKER, b. 1888, d. 1952 (having assumed by deed poll 1909, the additional surname of Forestier) : m. 1921, Eileen de Renzy (of Northolme, Aldeburgh, Suffolk), da. of the late Col. O. H. Channer, of Brookheath, Fordingbridge, Hants :—

Edmond Annesley (Broombank, Aldeburgh, Suffolk), b. 1922; ed. at Felsted Sch.; Maj. RA 1940-45 War in N. Africa and Italy (despatches): m. 1st, 1944, Bridget, who d. 1961, da. of Cdr. Sir Geoffrey Henry Hughes-Onslow, KBE, DSC, RN (ret.) [E. Onslow, colls.]; 2ndly, 1968, Dreenagh Denise, da. of Kenneth D. Chavasse, of London, and has issue living, (by 1st m.) George Clive (63. Heathpark Drive, Windlesham, Surrey), b. 1946; Capt. Coldm. Gds.: m. 1970, Ruth Christian, yst. da. of John Gurney, of Walsingham Abbey, Norfolk [see Ogilvy Bt., colls.], and has issue living, Camilla Christian b. 1973,—Sally Eileen, b. 1948: m. 1972, Mark Andrew Muspratt-Williams, of Dodwell Mansions, 77, Peak Rd., Hong Kong, and has issue living, Catriona Louise b. 1975,—(by 2nd m.) David Anthony, b. 1972, Annabel Dreemagh, b. 1974. Address, c/o Lloyds Bank, 6, Pall Mall, SW1.——Claude Osborne, b. 1924; ed. at Felsted Sch.; is a Co. Dir.: m. 1950, Gillian Mary, da. of Maj. Guy Pedder, of Park House, Hoxne, nr. Diss, Norfolk, and has issue living, Hugh Anthony Claude, b. 1954,—Melanie Diana, b. 1956,—Katherine Susan, b. 1960. Residence, Payne End, Sandon, Buntingford, Herts.

Grandchildren of the late Maj.-Gen. George Edmond Lushington Walker, 3rd son of 1st baronet :—

Issue of the late Lieut.-Col. Edmond Somerville Forestier Walker, b. 1860, d. 1922 : m. 1887, Ellen Mary Camilla, who d. 1939, da. of the late Major F. A. Fenton, M.S.C.:—

Claude Frederick FORESTIER-WALKER, C.B.E., M.C., b. 1896 ; ed. at Bedford Sch.; Brigadier (retired) late 11th (Prince Albert's Own) Hussars ; European War 1915-18 (despatches twice, M.C. with Bar), Palestine 1939 (despatches), European War 1939-45 in Middle East, Persia, Iraq, and Italy (despatches twice, O.B.E., C.B.E.) : O.B.E. (Mil.) 1940, C.B.E. (Mil.) 1945: m. 1st, 1926, Agnes Nivison (who obtained a divorce 1930), da. of Sir William Dingwall Mitchell Cotts, K.B.E., 1st Bt.; 2ndly, 1933, Simone, da. of the late Lieut.-Col. Mark Le Gallais, of Jersey. Residence, La Colina, Puerto Andraitx Mallorca, Spain. Club, Royal Cinque Ports Yacht.

Issue of the late Maj.-Gen. Sir George Townshend FORESTIER-WALKER, K.C.B., b. 1866, d. 1939 : m. 1892, Lady Mary Maud Diana Liddell, who d. 1958, da. of 2nd Earl of Ravensworth :—

Helen Mary Cecilia Forestier, b. 1895. Residence, Sutton Oaks, Stourpaine, Blandford, Dorset.

Issue of the late Lieut.-Col. Claude Edward Forestier Walker, D.S.O., b. 1868, d. 1932: m. 1897, Ethel, who d. 1932, da. of the late Capt. Allix Wilkinson, E. Yorkshire Regt.:—

Aura Camilla Desmond, b. 1905: m. 1930, Lt.-Col. Ian James Kilgour, Roy. Northumberland Fusiliers (ret.), and has issue living, Joanna Camilla (Lady Norman), b. 1931: m. 1953, Sir Mark Annesley Norman, 3rd Bt. Residence, Blackthorn Cottage, Bampton, Oxford.

The 1st baronet, Gen. Sir George Townshend, G.C.B., K.C.T.S., was a distinguished Peninsular officer, C-in-C at Fort St George, India, and Lt.-Gov. of Chelsea Hospital. The 2nd baronet assumed by deed poll 1893, the additional surname of Forestier.

FORESTIER-WALKER, Creation (U.K.) 1929, of Rhiwderin, co. Monmouth.
[Extinct 1934.]

Sir (Charles) Leolin Forestier-Walker, *K.B.E., M.P.,* 1st and last *Baronet.*

Daughter living of 1st Baronet—Daphne, *b.* 1902 : *m.* 1922 (divorce 1947), Major Gavin David Young, Welsh Guards [B. Ritchie of Dundee], and has issue living Gavin David, *b.* 1928,—Bridget Ower, *b.* 1923. *Residence,* 34, Cadogan Sq., S.W.1.

WALLER, Creation (I.) 1780, of Newport, Tipperary.

Honour and truth.

Sir Robert William Waller, 9th *Baronet ; b.* June 16th, 1934 ; *s.* his father, *Sir* Roland Edgar, 1958 ; ed. at Newark Coll. of Engineering, and at Fairleigh Dickinson Univ.; Business Manager with General Electric Co.; a citizen of U.S.A. : *m.* 1960, Carol Anne, da. of John E. Hines, of 45, Bellevue Road, Lynn, Mass., U.S.A., and has issue.

Arms—Checky or and azure, on a canton gules, a lion rampant double queued of the first. Crest—Out of a ducal coronet a plume of five ostrich feathers, 2nd and 4th azure, 1st, 3rd, and 5th argent, surmounted by an eagle's claw gules.

Residence—RFD 1, Pickpocket Rd., Exeter, NH, USA.

Sons living—JOHN MICHAEL, *b.* May 14th, 1962.——David Peter, *b.* 1963.
Daughter living—Susan Carol, *b.* 1968.
Sisters living—Helen Mary, *b.* 1924 : *m.* 1945, Arthur Paul Warshauer, and has issue living, Shawn Matthew, *b.* 1962,—Sandra Anne, *b.* 1945,—Mary Susan, *b.* 1950. *Residence*, Amesbury Rd., Contoocook, New Hampshire 03229, U.S.A.——Patricia Ann, *b.* 1930: *m.* 1949, Howard George Schier, and has issue living, Virginia Gale, *b.* 1949,—Nancy Lee, *b.* 1954,—Linda Jean, *b.* 1957.
Aunts living (daughters of 7th baronet)—Dorothy de Warrenne, *b.* 1893 : *m.* 1919, James Alexander Smith, and has issue living, Glenn Dorothy, *b.* 1920,—Nancy Lee, *b.*
1926: *m.* 1953, Wesley S. Hermance, and has issue living, Brett Jeffrey *b.* 1958, Wendy Lee *b.* 1955. *Residence*, Garden Terr., 361, Main St., Chatham, NJ. 07940, U.S.A.——Miriam Jocelyn, *b.* 1896: *m.* 1916, Heber Kelshaw Peniston, and has issue living, Donald Hugh, *b.* 1919,—William Heber *b.* 1921. *Residence*, 1335, W. Harrison Av., Cottage Grove, Oregon 97424, U.S.A.

Widow living of 8th Baronet—HELEN MADELINE (*Helen, Lady Waller*) (11200-86th Av. North, Bldg. 1-Apt. 104, Seminole Gdns., Seminole, Florida, USA), da. of Joseph Radl, of Matawan, NJ, USA: *m.* 1919, Sir Roland Edgar Waller, 8th baronet, who *d.* 1958.

Collateral Branches living.

Issue of the late Elwood Eccleston Waller, brother of 7th baronet, *b.* 1876, *d.* 1944 : *m.* 1895, Francina Claire Shaughnessy, who *d.* 1958:—
Elwood Eccleston, *b.* 1896: *m.* 1921, Jane Eden, and has issue living, Elwood Eccleston *b.* 1922 ; formerly Lieut. U.S.A. Air Force : *m.* 1st, 1946, Marie Maupin ; 2ndly, 1954, Marie Benton, and has issue living, (by 1st marriage) Patrick *b.* 1949, Susan *b.* 1947,—Janet, *b.* 1924, *m.* 1st, 1943, Newman Sallings Harrison ; 2ndly, 1947, Glenn Charles Wilson, and has issue living, (by 2nd marriage) Glenn Charles *b.* 1952, (by 1st marriage) Pamela *b.* 1944, (by 2nd marriage) Leslie Jane *b.* 1949, Diana *b.* 1950, Eden Adair *b.* 1957, Shannon *b.* 1961. *Residence*, 38, Interlaken Rd., Orlando, Florida, U.S.A.——Eunice Claire, *b.* 1900: *m.* 1922, Clifford Albert Nagle, and has issue living, Clifford Albert (of 30, Prospect Drive, Somerville, New Jersey, U.S.A.), *b.* 1924: *m.* 1st, 1949, Eleanor M. Deisher; 2ndly, 1971, Irene D. Hansen, and has issue living, (by 1st m.), Clifford Albert *b.* 1952, Charles Robert *b.* 1955, Loren Frederick *b.* 1959, Carol Eleanor *b.* 1957,—Claire Waller, *b.* 1925. *Residence*, Middlebrook Rd., Bound Brook, New Jersey, USA.

Descendants (if any) of Edmund Waller, brother of 6th baronet, *b.* 1844, *m.* 1861 and *d.* 1899, leaving issue.
Descendants (if any) of Augustus Edmund Waller *b.* 1871, and Philip Percy Waller, *b.* 1877, sons of Jocelyn Waller, el. son of Samuel Waller, MD, brother of 4th baronet

Grandchildren of the late Samuel William Waller, yr. son of the late Samuel Waller, MD (ante):—
Issue of the late John Stanton Waller, *b.* 1869, *d.* 19—: *m.* 1888, Ida Anna Finley, who *d.* 19—, da. of James Peyton, of Montreal:—
John Clifton, *b.* 1903.——Pearl Maria Louise, *b.* 1889: *m.* 1912, Stephen Driscoll Bennett, of New Bedford, Mass., USA.——Ruby Gladys Colclough, *b.* 1891.——Olivine Beryl Carleton, *b.* 1895: *m.* 1926, Cecil Bernard Kyle.——Helen Emerald, *b.* 1897: *m.* 1925, Harold Battzill Davis. ——Margaret Patricia Eunice, *b.* 1907: *m.* 1928, Walter Brown Power.

Grandchildren of the late Edmund Henry Colclough Waller (infra):—
Issue of the late Herbert Montague Waller, *b.* 1907, *d.* 1971: *m.* 1942, Vera Germain (329, W. Brock St., Thunder Bay, Ont., Canada):—
Edgar Herbert (606, Tennyson Av., Oshawa, Ont.), *b.* 1942; ed. at Lake Head Univ., Thunder Bay, Ont.: *m.* 1966, Sandra Yvonne Egan, and has issue living, Scott Edward, *b.* 1967.——Robert Brian (245, Denis St., Thunder Bay, Ont.), *b.* 1944; *m.* 1965, Joan Gloria Woodgate, and has issue living, Faye Kathleen, *b.* 1969.——Karen Louise, *b.* 1972.——Sharon Claire, *b.* 1946: *m.* 1965, Robert Bruce Nicholl, of 815, Frennete St., Fort Francis, Ont., and has issue living, Laurie Cecile, *b.* 1966, Rhoda Jean, *b.* 1968.——Jean Patricia, *b.* 1952: *m.* 1972, John Charles Mayo of RR, Thunder Bay, Ont.

Grandchildren of the late Samuel William Waller (ante):—
Issue of the late Edmund Henry Colclough Waller, *b.* 1879, *d.* 1970: *m.* 1906, Caroline Agnes, who *d.* 1967, da. of the late John Mann, of Grand Valley, Ont.:—
Arthur Edmund (Nanaimo, BC), *b.* 1909: *m.* 1st, 1941, (m. diss. 1967), Frances, da. of John Martin, of Vancouver, BC; 2ndly, 1968, Mrs. Alma Rickerby, da. of   Taylor, and has issue living (by 1st m.), Lynne Diane, *b.* 1944.——William Hugh, *b.* 1912: *m.* 1944, Alvina Koch.—— Cedric Henry, *b.* 1914: *m.* 1939, Flora Campbell, of Macdowell, Sask., Canada, and has issue

living, Cedric Lorne, *b.* 1940; a Teacher: *m.* 1964, Doris Lorraine Sweetman, of Trail, BC, and has issue living, Stephen Lorne *b.* 1966,—Ronald Henry, *b.* 1943; ed. at Univ. of BC: *m.* 1965, Gwendolyn Anne Wright, of Trail, BC, and has issue living, Michael Ronald, *b.* 1966.——Thomas Geoffrey (1107, Dahl St., Prince George, BC), *b.* 1916; Forestry Dept. Supervisor, BC Govt.: *m.* 1947, Elizabeth Margaret Esther, da. of William J. Brodie, of Nelson, BC, and has issue living, Donna Elaine, *b.* 1949: *m.* 1971, Edward Charles Anderson,—Glowena Margaret, *b.* 1950: *m.* 1969, Allan Lee Hutchinson, and has issue living, Celeste Marie *b.* 1969, Michelle Jeanette *b.* 1972, Judith Darlene, *b.* 1953.——Arnold Blair (290, Inglewood Av., Pointe Clare, Quebec), *b.* 1924; ed. at BC Univ. (BSc); Staff Engineer with Bell Canada: *m.* 1951, Janet Louise, da. of William Paton Montgomery, of Montreal, and has issue living, Jonathan Blair, *b.* 1962,—Laurie Jane, *b.* 1953,—Elizabeth Sue, *b.* 1958.——Evelyn Agnes, *b.* 1918: *m.* 1st, 1937 (m. diss. 1954), James Donald Ross; 2ndly, 1961, William Wilson (RR1 Gillespie Rd., Sooke, BC, Canada), and has issue living, (by 1st. m.) Shirley Norma, *b.* 1938: *m.* 1955 (m. diss. 1969), Allen William Wilson, and has issue living, Michael Allen *b.* 1963, Shelley Norma *b.* 1957.——Beatrice Alice (Box 272, Ladysmith, BC, Canada), *b.* 1922: *m.* 1949, Ernest John Moretti, who *d.* 1971, and has issue living, Ernest James, *b.* 1950.

Grandchildren of the late Samuel Waller (ante):—
Issue of the late Samuel William Waller, *b.* 1844, *d.* 1917: *m.* 1st, 1862, Maria Louisa, who *d.* 1873, da. of the late Charles Waller, grandson of 1st Bt.; 2ndly, 1878, Eliza Maria, who *d.* 1927, da. of Charles Hughes, of Montreal, Canada:—
(By 2nd m.)—Hugh Jocelyn (612, Shepherd Av., Nanaimo, BC), *b.* 1887: *m.* 1909, Olive Maria, who *d.* 1959, da. of John Mann, and has issue living, Hector Hugh (922, No. 1 Road, Richmond, BC), *b.* 1910; Manager of Highmont Mining Corpn., and Vice-Pres. of Torwest Resources: *m.* 1945, Mary Patricia, da. of Ivor John Everson, of Gravesend, Kent, and has issue living, Thomas Hector *b.* 1947: *m.* 1969, Margaret Quilliam, of Richmond, BC (and has issue living, Michael Hugh *b.* 1974), Sean Ivor *b.* 1957, Mary Kathleen *b.* 1950: *m.* 1972, Gerald St. Laurent, of Richmond, BC, Canada (and has issue living, Jocelyn Kathleen *b.* 1974), Valerie Jane *b.* 1952,—Gordon Jocelyn, *b.* 1912: *m.* 1937, Pearl Solie, and has issue living, Dennis Raymond *b.* 1938, Gordon Edmund *b.* 1948,—Robert Allen, *b.* 1914,—Hugh Macartney, *b.* 1922: *m.* 1st, 1943, Betty Hallat; 2ndly, 1951, Florence—, and has issue living, (by 2nd m.) a son *b.* 1953, a da. (twin) *b.* 1953,—Lilian Gladys, *b.* 1911: *m.* 1935, Clinton Geddis,—Olive Kathleen, *b.* 1916: *m.* 1941, Noel Hendry, of Vancouver, BC,—Muriel Eleanor, *b.* 1919: *m.* 1941, Charles Guiguet, Curator of, Birds and Mammals Provincial Museum, Victoria, British Columbia, of 2399, Dalhousie St., Victoria, BC, and has issue living, Mark Laurence *b.* 1950, Joan Muriel *b.* 1942, Patricia Lynda *b.* 1947, Suzanne Maria *b.* 1955,—Jean Pearl, *b.* 1923.——Kathleen, *b.* 1889: *m.* 1908, John Alexander Lawrie, of 24, Henley Av., Chilliwack, BC, Canada.——Alice Maude, *b.* 1892: *m.* 1912, Frederick Stuart, who *d.* 1935. *Residence*,

Grandchildren of the late Robert William Waller, el. son of the late Robert Waller, yst. brother of 4th baronet:—
Issue of the late Frank Hastings Waller, *b.* 1871, *d.* 1953: *m.* 1914, Elvie Grace, who *d.* (as a result of enemy action) 1940, da. of the late William Bedford, of Landour, India:—
Marjorie, *b.* 1919.
Issue of the late Charles Robert Waller, *b.* 1877, *d.* 1933: *m.* 1905, Agnes Helen, da. of the late Francis Thorne, of Launceston, Cornwall:—
Robert William (41, Agulhas, Topham Rd., Doonside 4125, Natal), *b.* 1910; 1940-42, as Driver S. African Mech. Trans. in Abyssinia (invalided): *m.* 1936, Daphne Mabel, el. da. of Herbert Clifton Morton, of Pretoria, S. Africa, and has issue living, Robert David (3, West Park Av., St. Helier, Jersey), *b.* 1939: *m.* 1961, Rosalie Beryl, da. of the late Wilfred Easter, of Southampton, and has issue living, Hugh *b.* 1965, Vanessa *b.* 1963, Ursula (twin) *b.* 1963,—Leonard Harold, *b.* 1953,—Delene Ruth, *b.* 1937: *m.* 1961, Edgar E. Esselen, of 132, Golf Av., Club View West, Pretoria, S. Africa, and has issue living, Deborah *b.* 1962, Ingrid *b.* 1965,—Thalia Lynnette, *b.* 1943: *m.* 1965, Allan Harry Griffin, of 14, Hill Cres., Amauzimtoti, Natal, and has issue living, Helen Eileen *b.* 1969, Louise Daphne *b.* 1971,—Daphne Jess, *b.* 1945,—Heather Lynn, *b.* 1949.
——Edmund John (7, Broadway, Durban, Natal), *b.* 1919; 1939-45 War as Warrant Officer SAAF, in Middle East, Malta, Sicily, and Italy: *m.* 1944, Alma, yst. da. of Edwyn Treffry-Goatley, of Durban, Natal, and has issue living, Virginia Helen, *b.* 1945,—Hazel Louise, *b.* 1948: *m.* 1968, John Robert Lockwood, of E. Yorks., England, and has issue living, Edmund Sean *b.* 1973, Amanda Jane *b.* 1969.——Catherine Jocelyn (c/o Mrs. S. Weir, 21 Danville Av., Virginia, Durban 4001, Natal), *b.* 1906: *m.* 1935, Reginald Charles Oates, and has issue living, Jillian Elizabeth, *b.* 1937,—Sandra Jocelyn, *b.* 1941.——Agatha Minnie (Fountain Hill, PO Upper Tongaat, Natal 4402), *b.* 1908: *m.* 1933, William U. E. Cook, who *d.* 1971, and has issue living, Richard Clive, *b.* 1939,—Valma Jean, *b.* 1935.——Ruth, *b.* 1909: *m.* 1935, Richard Dennis Goble, of Beaufort, Compensation, Natal, and has issue living, Denise Joy, *b.* 1938,—Sylvia Helen, *b.* 1940.

Grandchildren of the late Jocelyn Waller, 2nd son of the late Robert Waller (ante):—
Issue of the late Robert Martin Jocelyn Waller, *b.* 1862, *d.* 1936: *m.* 1896, his cousin, Emily Mary, who *d.* 1951, da. of the late Robert William Waller:—
Frank Martin Roden (24, Grove Rd., Milton, Weston-super-Mare, Som.), *b.* 1909: *m.* 1948, Nora Dale, who *d.* 1965, da. of the late Rev. Cyril Edgington, of Bath, and has issue living, Robert Cyril Hardress Jocelyn, *b.* 1949.——Dorothy Minnie, *b.* 1898: *m.* 1919, Reginald Carp, of 12, Grange Av., Highbridge, Som., and has issue living, Thomas Walter Waller, *b.* 1924,—Pamela Mary, *b.* 1923.
Issue of the late William Dillon Waller, *b.* 1868, *d.* 1953: *m.* 1896, Annie Mary, da. of the late Hans Nielson, of Denmark:—
Hans Jocelyn (2404, Hampstead, Wichita Falls, Texas 76308, USA), *b.* 1897; Col.: *m.* 1922, Mildred Vivian Pennock, of Longmont, Colorado, and has issue living, Edmund Hugh (4900, West Amherst, Denver, Colorado, 80236, USA), *b.* 1929: *m.* 1951, Barbara Yetter, and has issue living, Kenneth Scott *b.* 1959, Wendy Anna *b.* 1957,—Patricia Gene, *b.* 1925: *m.* 1948, Vern L. Klingman, of 2136, Green Terr. Drive, Billings, Montana 59102, USA, and has issue living, Stephen Wesley *b.* 1957, Nancy Rose *b.* 1955, Candice Martha *b.* 1961.

Grandson of the late Rev. Alfred Jocelyn Waller (infra):—
Issue of the late Hardress Jocelyn Waller, *b.* 1905, *d.* 1935: *m.* 19—, Bessie Burrow:—
Hardress Jocelyn, *b.* 1928; PhD; Neurophysiologist, Toledo Univ., Ohio: *m.* 1953, Gertrude Gearhart, and has issue living, Andrew Jocelyn, *b.* 1960.

Grandchildren of the late Jocelyn Waller (ante):—
Issue of the late Rev. Alfred Jocelyn Waller, *b.* 1870, *d.* 1950: *m.* 1903, Katherine Tarrence:—
Richard (6500, E. Nevada Place, Denver, Colorado, 80222, USA), *b.* 1915: *m.* 1949, Mildred Lucka, and has issue living, Sharon Rose, *b.* 1951: *m.* 19—, Charles Counts.——Alice, *b.* 1908: *m.* 19—, Joseph C. Chiappetti, of 1113, W. Azure Drive, Flagstaff, Arizona 86001, USA, and has issue living, Joanne, *b.* 1935: *m.* 19—, Dr. Robert Wilcox, of Medford, Ore, USA,—Nancy Lou, *b.* 1939: *m.* 19—, Fred Marsh, of Los Alamos, N. Mexico, USA.
Issue of the late Harry Bernard Waller, *b.* 1882, *d.* 1971: *m.* 1920, Anna Kruger Jorgensen, of Denmark, who *d.* 1946:—
Evelyn May, *b.* 1924: *m.* 1949, Bart Hoag, of 1350, Ridge Rd., Littleton, Colorado 80120, USA, and has issue living, Selwyn Barton, *b.* 1950: *m.* 1972, Claudia Lukas,—Christopher Henry, *b.* 1958,—Anthony Wayne, *b.* 1960,—Eugenia Anne, *b.* 1943: *m.* 1965, Laurence V. Morminger, —Jocelyn Deane, *b.* 1955.

The 1st baronet, Sir Robert Waller (son of the late Samuel Waller, of Newport, Tipperary) was M.P. for Dundalk 1761-80. and one of the Commissioners of the Revenue. Sir Robert, 2nd Baronet, was High Sheriff for King's co. in 1826.

WALLER, Creation (U.K.) 1815, of Braywick Lodge, Berkshire.

HÆC

FRUCTUS VIRTUTIS

This is the fruit of valour.

Sir JOHN STANIER WALLER, 7th *Baronet*, son of the late Capt. Stanier Edmund William Waller, grandson of the late Rev. Ernest Adolphus Waller, 2nd son of 1st baronet; *b.* July 27th, 1917; *s.* his kinsman, *Sir* EDMUND, 1954; ed. at Weymouth Coll., and at Worcester Coll., Oxford (Exhibitioner in History 1936, B.A. 1939); an Author and Poet, and a Fellow of Roy. So. of Literature; Information Officer, Central Office of Information 1954-59; Middle East 1941-6 as Capt. R.A.S.C., latterly as Press Officer: *m.* 1974, Anne Eileen, da. of Jack William Mileham, of Winterton-on-Sea, Norfolk.

Arms—Sable, on a bend engrailed argent, between two bendlets cr. three walnut-leaves of the last. Crest—On a mount vert a walnut tree proper, pendent therefrom by a ribbon gules a shield azure charged with a fleur-de-lis or.
Residence—99, The Grove, Isleworth, Middx.

Sister living—Elizabeth Mary Louisa (145, Jersey Rd., Isleworth, Middx, TW7 4QL), *b.* 1923; ed. at High Sch., Oxford, and at St. Hilda's Coll., Oxford (Exhibitioner in History, MA, BLitt); Assist. Lecturer, Medieval History, Liverpool Univ., 1949-53; Baghdad 1953-58; joined Foreign Ser.; Regional Assist. Information Officer for Women's Affairs', Beirut 1961-67, since when in FCO.

Aunt living—Dorothy (52, Overhill Drive, Brighton, 6), *b.* 1891.

Collateral Branch living.

Issue of the late Richard Alured Waller, 2nd Lieut. Roy. Fusiliers, youngest brother of 6th baronet, *b.* 1884, *d.* (on active ser. during European War) 1917: *m.* 1912, Ethel (now of The Cottage, Crawley Down, Sussex), da. of the late John Tippet Drake, of Plumstead, Kent :—

Margaret Patience, *b.* 1917; is a State Registered Nurse.

Sir (Jonathan) Wathen Waller, GCH, 1st Bt. of Braywick Lodge, Berks., and Pope's Villa, Twickenham, was Groom of the Bedchamber to William IV. He was son of Joshua Phipps, by Anne, da. of Thomas Waller (descended from the Wallers of Groombridge Place, Speldhurst, Kent), and assumed by sign manual 1814, the surname and arms of Waller, being heir of his maternal grand-uncle James Waller of Farriers, High Wycombe.

JOHNSON-WALSH, Creation (I.) 1775, of Ballykilcavan, Queen's County.
[Extinct 1953.]

Sir HUNT HENRY ALLEN JOHNSON-WALSH, 5th and last *Baronet*.

Daughter living of 5th Baronet—Oonah Frances, *b.* 1913: *m.* 1937, William Frederick Kemmis, who assumed by deed poll 1945 the additional surname of Walsh before that of Kemmis [B. Ashtown, colls.], and has issue living, Peter William Hunt (Ballykilcavan, Stradbally, Leix), *b.* 1939: *m.* 1970, Ann Katherine, da. of Henry Richard Langley, of Archerstown, Thurles, and has issue living, Susan Helen, *b.* 1972,—Michael Henry, *b.* 1941: *m.* 1972, Bridget Gillian, da. of J. D. McCall, of Heydon, Herts., and has issue living, Rosetta Caitriona Bridget *b.* 1973,—Olivia Anne, *b.* 1943: *m.* 1972, James Walter Hurton, of Marshchapel, Lincs., and has issue living, Stephen James William *b.* 1973. *Residence*, Garrans, Stradbally, Leix.

WALSHAM, Creation (U.K.) 1831, of Knill Court, Herefordshire.
[Name pronounced "Walsam."]

SUB·LIBERTATE·QUIETE

Rest under liberty.

Sir JOHN SCARLETT WARREN WALSHAM, *C.B.*, *O.B.E.*, 4th *Baronet*; *b.* Nov. 29th, 1910; *s.* his father, *Sir* JOHN SCARLETT, 1940; is patron of one living; Rear-Adm. (ret.); OBE (Mil) 1944, CB (Mil.) 1963: *m.* 1936, Sheila Christina, only da. of the late Com. Bertrand Bannerman, D.S.O., R.N. [*see* Bannerman, Bt., colls.], and has issue.

Arms—Quarterly: 1st and 4th, per pale azure and gules, a griffin segreant wings elevated or, supporting on a tilting spear a banner flowing to the dexter argent, charged with a cross couped sable, *Garbett*; 2nd and 3rd, sable, on a cross voided or, five crosslets patée-fitchée of the last, *Walsham*. Crest—A demi-eagle with two heads displayed sable, having suspended from the neck, by a gold chain, an escutcheon argent, and thereon a Saracen's head erased at the neck proper, round the temples a wreath argent and azure.
Residence—Ash Beacon, Churchill, Axminster, Devon.

Son living—TIMOTHY JOHN, *b.* April 26th, 1939; ed. at Sherborne.

Daughters living—Susan Elizabeth, *b.* 1941: *m.* 1963, Christopher James Harbour, of Milford House, Chobham, Surrey, and has issue living, Mark Christopher Bannerman, *b.* 1964,—Benedict David Walsham, *b.* 1967,—Matthew Alexander Walsham, *b.* 1969,—Caroline Lucy Scarlett, *b.* 1965.——Jane Scarlett, *b.* 1942: *m.* 1963, Cdr. David Colin Nairne, RN, of 20, Breamwate Gdns., Ham, Richmond,

Surrey, and has issue living, Charles David Scarlett, *b.* 1965,—Alexander John Dalmahoy, *b.* 1970,—Sarah Catriona, *b.* 1964.

Sister living—Gundreda Brydget Coytmore, 1909: *m.* 1931, Chichester Kennedy Crookshank, of 1, Kingsey Av., Emsworth, Hants., and has issue living, John Kennedy, *b.* 1932: *m.* 1963, Phyllida Anne Mylne, and has issue living, Charles James Chichester *b.* 1966, Antonia Scarlett *b.* 1969,—Peter Scarlett, *b.* 1935: *m.* 1958, Susan Watwood, and has issue living, Richard Chichester *b.* 1962, William Thomas *b.* 1965.

Collateral Branches living.

Issue of the late Percy Romilly Walsham, 2nd son of 2nd baronet, *b.* 1871, *d.* 1933: *m.* 1899, Charlotte Cuningham Scott, who *d.* 1945, da. of William Wykeham Myers, M.B.:—

Percy Robert Stewart (246, Halling Hill, Harlow, Essex), *b.* 1904: *m.* 1937, Tamara Ellis, and has issue living, Gerald Percy Robert, *b.* 1939,—Diana Charlotte, *b.* 1938.——Florence May, *b.* 1900: *m.* 1924, Capt. Henry Neville Lake, DSO, DSC, RN (ret.), of Tinkers Hill Farm, Furneux Pelham, Buntingford, Herts., and has issue living, Anthony Walsham Neville (of Dove Cliff, Stretton, nr. Burton-on-Trent), *b.* 1926: *m.* 1950, Penelope Doune, el. da. of the Hon. James Perrott Philipps, TD [see B. Milford], and has issue living, David Anthony *b.* 1953, Simon Neville *b.* 1956, Mark Philip *b.* 1958,—John Dewe Neville (The Old Mill, South Moreton, nr. Didcot, Berks.), *b.* 1928: *m.* 1952, Ann Cherida, da. of Sir Reginald Culcheth Holcroft, 2nd Bt., and has issue living, Christopher John Neville *b.* 1954, Timothy Michael David *b.* 1955.——Gladys Newell (Monks Vineyard, Nowton, Bury St. Edmunds), *b.* 1908: *m.* 1930, Lt.-Col. Henry Richard Hopking, OBE, who *d.* 1965, and has issue living, Richard Scarlett (86, Ladbroke Rd., Holland Park, W11), *b.* 1936: *m.* 1968, Elizabeth Ann Fortin, and has issue living, Scarlett Elizabeth *b.* 1969,—Gillian Walsham, *b.* 1933: *m.* 1956, James Scudamore Oakes, of Hoppery Hill, Headley, Hants., and has issue living, Christopher Wykeham James *b.* 1957, Victoria Scarlett *b.* 1960, Caroline Scudamore *b.* 1961.——Aline Joyce, *b.* 1913: *m.* 1939, Maj. Cecil Ronald Patrick Barrow, RA (ret.), and has issue living, Patrick Cecil Walsham, *b.* 1940,—John Anthony, *b.* 1943,—Michael Scarlett, *b.* 1948. *Residence,* Milestown, Castlebellingham, co. Louth.

The name of this family is supposed to be derived either from Walsham le Willows in Suffolk, or Walsham St. Mary in Norfolk, in both of which counties, as in Cambridgeshire, the Walshams were of note, and often of knightly rank, from the end of the 11th to the beginning of the 18th century. The Walshams of Knill represent a branch that settled in Radnorshire about 400 years ago, through the marriage of John Walsham with Mary, granddaughter and heiress of Sir Jenkin Harvey of Llanvair, Knight. From this marriage lineally descended John Walsham, who married Barbara, granddaughter and heiress of John Knill, of Knill Court, M.P. for Radnor, *temp.* Mary I, and was the direct ancestor of the present baronet. The 1st baronet received his baronetcy as being the eldest co-heir and representative of Gen. Sir Thomas Morgan, Bt., whose title created 1660, became extinct on the death of Sir John Morgan, 4th Bt. in 1767. Sir John Walsham, K.C.M.G., 2nd Bt., was Envoy Extraor. and Min. Plen. to China 1885-92 and to Roumania 1892-3.

WARD, Creation (U.K.) 1911, of Wellington, New Zealand.

By courage and faith.

Sir JOSEPH JAMES LAFFEY WARD, 4th *Baronet*; *b.* Nov. 11th, 1946; *s.* his father, *Sir* JOSEPH GEORGE DAVIDSON, *LLM,* 1970: *m.* 1968, Robyn Allison, da. of William Maitland Martin, of Rotorua, NZ.

ᴀʀᴍꜱ—Azure, a cross moline argent between four keys wards upwards or. ᴄʀᴇꜱᴛ—A demi-griffin azure in front of two keys in saltire wards upwards or.

Residence—

Brothers living—RODERIC ANTHONY, *b.* April 23rd, 1948.——Michael John, *b.* 1954.

Sisters living—Angela Mary, *b.* 1945.——Felicity Elizabeth Elinor, *b.* 1951.——Catherine Josephine Mina, *b.* 1963.

Uncles living (sons of 2nd baronet)—Cyril James (10, Queen's Drive, Christchurch, NZ), *b.* 1913; Fl. Lt. RNZAF Reserve; 1939-45 War: *m.* 1939, Janet Graham, da. of the late Dr. John Stevenson, of Fendalton, Christchurch, and has issue living, Joanna Theresa, *b.* 1940: *m.* 1968, Roger Joseph Clifford [see Clifford, Bt.],—Celia Mary Louise, *b.* 1950, ——John Rannie, *b.* (twin) 1924; is Lt. Roy. New Zealand Naval VR; 1939-45 War: *m.* 1948, Adrienne Lascelles, da. of Herbert Hill, OBE, JP, of Christchurch, and has issue living, Jeremy John, *b.* 1957,—Rupert Rannie, *b.* 1964,—Caroline Diana, *b.* 1950,—Jennifer Ann, *b.* 1952. *Residence,* 102, Leinster Rd., Christchurch, NZ.

Aunt living (daughter of 2nd baronet)—Theresa Dorothea, *b.* 1916: *m.* 1941, John Swaine Corry, and has issue living, David Herbert Cyril, *b.* 1949,—Robert John, *b.* 1953,—Angela Susan, *b.* 1942: *m.* 1965, Iain Anderson Ridge, of 145, London Rd., Sevenoaks, and has issue living, Angus James Anderson *b.* 1966,—Rosemary Ann, *b.* 1946. *Residence,* Tie Post, Bitchett Green, Sevenoaks.

Widow living of 3rd Baronet—JOAN MARY HADEN (*Joan, Lady Ward*) (Westbrook, 75, Harakeke St., Christchurch 1, NZ), da. of Maj. Thames Patrick Laffey, of Auckland, NZ: *m.* 1944, Sir Joseph George Davidson Ward, LLM, 3rd Bt., who *d.* 1970.

Collateral Branches living

Issue of the late Gladstone William Ward, 3rd son of 1st baronet, *b.* 1891, *d.* 1965: *m.* 1920, Sophia Polemedis (24, Helmores Lane, Christchurch, NZ), of Jerusalem:— Myrcine, *b.* 1921: *m.* 1942, Dr. Peter Mowbray Trip, of Christchurch, NZ, and has issue living, David Mowbray Ward, *b.* 1949,—John Peter, *b.* 1950,—Penelope Mary, *b.* 1943,—Anthia Susan, *b.* 1947.——Eileen Dorothea, *b.* 1922: *m.* 1943, Patrick Sinclair Hunter, solicitor, of Forest House, Old Frensham Rd., Lower Bourne, Farnham, Surrey, and has issue living, Michael Sinclair Ward, *b.* 1947,—Patricia Ann, *b.* 1943.

Issue of the late Awarua Patrick Joseph George Ward, yst. son of 1st baronet, *b.* 1901, *d.* 1961: *m.* 1930, Marjorie (of 8120, E. Jefferson, Detroit, Michigan, U.S.A.), only da. of O. M. McCormack, of Detroit, Michigan, U.S.A.:—
Patricia Marjorie, *b.* 1933: *m.* 1955, Duncan Cameron Bryan, and has issue living, Sheryl Cameron, *b.* 1956,—Jennifer Ward, *b.* 1958.—Denise *b.* 1961.

The 1st baronet, the Rt. Hon. Sir Joseph George Ward, G.C.M.G., V.D., P.C. (son of William Thomas Ward, merchant), was Prime Min. of New Zealand 1906-12 and 1928-30.

WARD, Creation (U.K.) 1914, of Wilbraham Place, Chelsea. [Extinct 1973.]

Sir MELVILLE WILLIS WARD, *DSC*, 3rd and last *Baronet.*

Widow living of 3rd Baronet—MARGARET MARY (*Lady Ward*), (Box 276, Southport, Conn., USA), da. of the late Anthony Davis, of New York, USA, and widow of Capt. Ralph Risley, USN: *m.* 1965, as his 3rd wife Cdr. Sir Melvill Willis Ward, DSC, RN, 3rd Bt., who *d.* 1973, when the title became ext.

WARD, Creation (U.K.) 1929, of Blyth, co. Northumberland.
[Extinct 1956.]

Sir (ALBERT) LAMBERT WARD, *C.V.O., D.S.O., T.D.,* 1st and last *Baronet.*

Daughter living of 1st Baronet—Diana Josephine (*Lady Spearman*), *b.* 1921 : *m.* 1951, as his second wife, Sir Alexander Cadwallader Mainwaring Spearman, [*see* Spearman, Bt., colls.]. *Residences,* The Old Rectory, Sarratt, Herts.; Fealar, Blairgowrie, Perthshire; 22, Queen Anne's Gate, SW1.

Widow living of 1st Baronet—CONSTANCE VIVIENNE (*Lady Ward*), da. of J. B. Tidmas, J.P., of Normanton-on-Soar, and Sutton Bonington, Notts. : *m.* 1920, Col. Sir (Albert) Lambert Ward, C.V.O., D.S.O., T.D., D.L., 1st baronet, who *d.* 1956, when the title became ext. *Residences,* 14, Cadogan Square, S.W.1 ; Normanton-on-Soar, Loughborough.

WARDLAW, Creation (N.S.) 1631, of Pitreavie, Fifeshire.

Domestic virtue strengthens families.

Sir HENRY WARDLAW, 20th *Baronet ;* *b.* Aug. 30th, 1894 ; *s.* his father, *Sir* HENRY, 1954 : *m.* 1929, Ellen, da. of John Francis Brady, and has issue.

Arms—Quarterly : 1st and 4th, azure, three mascles or, *Wardlaw* ; 2nd and 3rd, azure, three water bougets or, *Valance.* **Crest**—An estoile or.

Residence—10/20, Florence Rd., Surrey Hills, Victoria, Australia 3127

Sons living—HENRY JOHN, MB, BS (82, Vincent St., Sandringham, Vic., Aust.), *b.* Nov. 30th, 1930; ed. at Melbourne Univ. (MB, BS): *m.* 1962, Julie-Ann, da. of the late Edward Patrick Kirwan, and has issue living, Henry Justin, *b.* 1963,—Edward Patrick, *b.* 1964,—Simon, *b.* 1965,— Anthony, *b.* 1970, Adrian, *b.* 1971,—Janet, *b.* 1969.—— Robert Murdoch (4, Connemarra St., Bexley, NSW), *b.* 1940: *m.* 1971, Dale Edith, da. of Jospeh Fetherston, and has issue living, Dominic, *b.* 1972.——Andrew David Montgomerie (24, Middlesex Rd., Surrey Hills, Vic., Aust.); *b.* 1941; ed. at Melbourne Univ. (LLB): *m.* 1965, Elizabeth, da. of Dennis Leary, and has issue living, David, *b.* 1965, Matthew, *b.* 1966,—Michael, *b.* 1969,—Timothy, *b.* 1974, Louise, *b.* 1971.——Gregory Wylie (15, Millicent Av., Buleen, Vic., Aust.), *b.* 1943: *m.* 19—, and has issue living, Cameron, *b.* 1970,—Alastair, *b.* 1973.

Daughter living—Cynthia Mary, *b.* 1931; ed. at (BA, Dip.Ed.): *m.* 19—, of St. Andrew's, Vic., Aust., and has issue living, Jeremy, *b.* 19—,—Melanie, *b.* 19—,—Abigail, *b.* 19—.

Sister living—Frances Ethel (16, Buckingham Place, Brighton, Sussex), *b.* 1898.

Sister living—Frances Ethel (16, Buckingham Place, Brighton, Sussex), *b.* 1898.

Collateral Branches living.

Granddaughter of the late John Wardlaw, brother of 18th baronet:—
Issue of the late James Sime Wardlaw, MD, *b.* 1851, *d.* 1935: *m.* 1st, 1891, Doreta, who *d.* 1893, da. of Dr. Lundy, of Preston, Ontario; 2ndly, 1904, Mary Helen, who *d.* 1932, da. of the late John Ritchie, of Beaverton, Ontario:—
Mary Davidson, *b.* 1914: *m.* 1st, 1940, Lt.-Col. George A. M. Edwards, Highland L.I. of Canada, who *d.* 1960; 2ndly, 1964, Harold S. Dando, of Fiedside, Victoria St., Knowlton, Quebec, Canada, and has issue living, (by 1st m.) James Clare Edwards, *b.* 1941: *m.* 1965, Sharon A. Ure, and has issue living, Jordan Wardlaw, *b.* 1971,—Meredith Alexandra, *b.* 1974

Grandchildren of the late Thomas Davidson Wardlaw (infra):—
Issue of the late John Walter Wardlaw, *b.* 1882, *d.* 1944: *m.* 1914, Iva, da. of the late W. W. Brigham:—
James Walter, *b.* 1921: *m.* 1951, Carina Guenthner, and has issue living, Jane Katherine, *b.* 1958,— Judy Carina, *b.* 1961.——Mary Macallum, *b.* 1914: *m.* 1938, Safford E. Thorp, of 55, Rosemary St., New London, Conn., USA, and has issue living, Walter Wakeman, *b.* 1944: *m.* 1967, Cynthia Anne Szegda, of 40, Pearl St., New London, Conn., USA, and has issue living, Dawn Marie *b.* 1968,—Mina Jane, *b.* 1939: *m.* 1956, Cofer Lee Gray, of 611, Louis Av., Ledyard, Conn., USA, and has issue living, Safford Emory *b.* 1964, Ramona Lee *b.* 1958,—Lorna Elizabeth, *b.* 1946: *m.* 1965, Lee William Coleman, of 423, Highland Drive, Ledyard, Conn., USA, and has issue living, Tina Marie *b.* 1966.——Margaret Brigham, *b.* 1918: *m.* 1949, James Gethyn Jones, of 71,

Lawrence Av. West, Toronto 12, Canada, and has issue living, Richard Gethyn, *b.* 1952,—
Elizabeth Ellen, *b.* 1958.——Elizabeth Davidson (56, Jedburgh Rd., Toronto, Canada), *b.* 1926.

Issue of the late James Macallum Wardlaw, *b.* 1884, *d.* 1967: *m.* 1923, Mary, who *d.* 1953
 da. of the late Robert Law:—
Thomas Davidson (72, Main St., Waterford, Ont., Canada), *b.* 1924: *m.* 1950, Grace Smith, and
has issue living, David Macallum, *b.* 1952,—Robert Duncan, *b.* 1954,—Craig Davidson, *b.* 1956,—
Jonathan Stewart, *b,* 1959.——Robert Law (9, Oriole Drive, Ottawa, Canada), *b.* 1927: *m.* 1954,
Felicia Jane Milsum, and has issue living, Stephen James, *b.* 1957,—Michael John, *b.* 1960,—
Anne Margaret, *b.* 1958,—Patricia Mary, *b.* 1962,—Laura Kathleen, *b.* 1963.——Janet Melville,
b. 1924.

Granddaughter of the late John Wardlaw (ante):—
Issue of the late Thomas Davidson Wardlaw, *b.* 1853, *d.* 1943: *m.* 1881, Margaret,
 who *d.* 1929, da. of Thomas Miller, of Stratford:—
Mary Elder, *b.* 1891. *Residence,* 182, Jameson Av., Toronto, Ont., Canada.

Sir Henry Wardlaw, 1st Bt., was Chamberlain to Anne of Denmark, when Queen Consort
of Scotland. He acquired Pitreavie 1606, which was erected into a Barony 1627. His baronetcy
was with remainder to heirs male whatsoever, with presumably a grant of 16,000 acres in Nova
Scotia, called the Barony of Wardlaw.

WARING, Creation (U.K.) 1935, of St. Bartholomew's, City of London.

Sir (ALFRED) HAROLD WARING, 2nd
Baronet : b. Feb. 14th, 1902 ; *s.* his father,
Sir HOLBURT JACOB, *C.B.E., M.S., F.R.C.S.,*
1953 ; *ed.* at Winchester, at Trin. Coll.,
Camb. (B.A. 1924), and at London Univ.
(B.Sc. Engineering 1924) ; is an A.M.I.M.E.:
m. 1930, Winifred, da. of the late Albert
Boston, of Stockton-on-Tees, and has issue.

Arms—Argent on a bend engrailed azure between two
Rods of Aesculapius proper three crescents. **Crest**—A
demi-wolf resting the sinister paw on a Rod of Aesculapius proper.
 Residence—Pen-Moel, Tidenham, Gloucestershire.

(motto on image: WHATEVER YOU UNDERTAKE DO WELL)

Son living—ALFRED HOLBURT, *b.* Aug. 2nd, 1933 ;
ed. at Rossall: *m.* 1958, Anita, da. of the late Valentin
Medinilla, of Madrid, Spain, and has issue living,
Michael Holburt, *b.* 1964,—Margaret Rose, *b.* 1961,—
Susan Caroline, *b.* 1967. *Residence*, Earls Croft, 30,
Russell Rd., Moor Park, Northwood, Middx.

Daughters living—Winifred Anne, *b.* 1931 : *m.* 1954,
Michael Scott Mark, of Bilton Brow, Bilton-in-Ainsty,
York, YO5 8NN, and has issue living, Jonathan Scott,
b. 1956,—Christopher Edward, *b.* 1959.——(Joan
Catherine) Cassandra, *b.* 1937: *m.* 1962, John Barry
William Holderness, of Bandinel, St. Martin, Jersey, and has issue living, Corinne Louisa
Cassandra, *b.* 1969,—Marina Isabelle Cassandra, *b.* 1974.

The 1st baronet, Sir Holburt Jacob Waring, C.B.E., M.S., F.R.C.S. (son of the late Isaac
Waring, of Southport, Lancashire), was sometime Dean of Faculty of Medicine, London Univ.,
Vice-Chancellor, London Univ., Gov. of Imperial Coll. of Science and Technology 1930-47, and
Pres. Roy. Coll. of Surgeons 1932-35.

WARMINGTON, Creation (U.K.) 1908, of Pembridge Square, Royal Borough of Kensington.

Not for myself, but for all.

(motto on image: NON MIHI SED OMNIBUS)

Sir MARSHALL GEORGE CLITHEROE
WARMINGTON, 3rd *Baronet ; b.* May 26th, 1910;
s. his father, *Sir* (MARSHALL) DENHAM 1935 ;
ed. at Charterhouse; Lt.-Cdr. (ret.) RN:
m. 1st, 1933, Mollie (from whom he
obtained a divorce 1941), el. da. of the late
Capt. Malcolm Alfred Kennard, R.N. (retired),
of Wonham, Bampton ; 2ndly, 1942, Eileen
Mary, who *d.* 1969, da. of the late P. J. Howes;
3rdly, 1972, Sheila, da. of the late Stanley
Brotherhood, JP, of Thornhaugh Hall, Peterborough, and widow of Adm. the Hon. Sir
Cyril Eustace Douglas-Pennant, KCB, CBE,
DSO, DSC [see B. Penrhyn] and has issue by
1st and 2nd m.

Arms—Or, a lion rampant sable, charged on the
shoulder with two fleurs-de-lis palewise of the first, hold-
ing between the paws a full-bottomed wig proper. **Crest**—
An owl or, holding in the beak a penna and an oak horn sable
 Residence—Swallowfield Park, Swallowfield, Reading.
Club—Army and Navy.

Sons living—By 1st marriage—MARSHALL DEN-
HAM MALCOLM, *b.* Jan. 5th, 1934. —By 2nd
m.—David Marshall (Goddens, Hartley Wespall,
Basingstoke, Hants.), *b.* 1944; *ed.* at Charterhouse: *m.*
1966, Susan Mary, da. of the Very Rev. Clifford Thomas Chapman, Dean of Exeter, and has issue
living, Rupert Marshall, *b.* 1969,—Guy Denham, *b.* 1972,——Anthony Marshall (Wheat House,

Wheathold Green, Ramsdell, Basingstoke), *b.* 1946; ed. at Charterhouse; 2nd I,t., 1st Queen's Dragoon Gds.: *m.* 1973, Carolyn Patricia, el. da. of the late J. A. H. Simmonds, and has issue living, Oliver Marshall Simonds *b.* 1974.

Daughter living—By 1st m.—Margaret Anne, *b.* 1936: *m.* 1962, Cdr. Colin Alan (Charles) Bricknell, RN, of Southways, Montserrat Rd., Lee on Solent, and has issue living, Martin Charles Marshall, *b.* 1963,—Julian John, *b.* 1965,—Peter Marshall, *b.* 1969.

Sister living—Elisabeth Barbara Marshall, *b.* 1909: *m.* 1st, 1933, Ian Somerled Macdonald, who *d.* 1958; 2ndly, 1961, John Perfect, and has issue living, (by 1st m.) John Marshall, *b.* 1937,— Euan Ross, *b.* 1940,—Elisabeth Margaret, *b.* 1935,—Sheila Joy, *b.* 1942. *Residence*, Brackenhill, Berkhamsted, Herts.

Aunt living (daughter of 1st baronet)—Mary Agnes Marshall (*Lady Trusted*), *b.* 1889: *m.* 1911, Sir Harry Herbert Trusted, QC, and has issue living, John Marshall (34, Chesham Place, SW1), *b.* 1913: *m.* 1st, 1938, Eileen Muriel, da. of Ulric Hopton, of 26, Cadogan Place, SW1; 2ndly, 1963, Constance Polnik, of 36, Basil St., SW1, and has issue living, (by 1st m.) Timothy John *b.* 1944, Susan Primrose *b.* 1939, Sarah Jane *b.* 1941,—Hugh Wilson, *b.* 1922,—Nancy Mary Margaret, *b.* 1912: *m.* 1933, C. C. J. Simmonds, of Bay House, Porlock Weir, Minehead, Som.,— Thirza Betty Mary, *b.* 1915: *m.* 19—, I,t.-Col. Sidney Hunt,—Hilary, *b.* 1918: *m.* 1941, Garnett R. B. Don Fox, RNVR. *Residence*, 7, Garrick Close, Walton-on-Thames, Surrey.

Collateral Branch living.

Issue of the late Herbert Andrew Cromartie Warmington, 2nd son of 1st baronet ; *b.* 1874, *d.* 1952 : *m.* 1st, 1904, Elsie (who obtained a divorce 1926), da. of the late John Stuart, of Stonehurst, Ardingly, Sussex ; 2ndly, 1938, Helena, da. of the late Albert de Mersey :—

(By 1st marriage) Joan Pamela Stuart, *b.* 1906 : *m.* 1st, 1926, Com. Nigel Bellairs Deare, R.N., 2ndly, 1934, Dr. Vincenzo Bottari. *Residence*, Villa della Palmare, Taormina, Sicily.

The 1st baronet, Sir (Cornelius) Marshall, K.C., sat as M.P. for W. Div. of Monmouthshire (L) 1885-95, and Sir (Marshall) Denham Warmington, 2nd Bt., was a Registrar in Bankruptcy, High Court of Justice.

WARNER, Creation (U.K.) 1910, of Brettenham, Suffolk.

Sir (EDWARD COURTENAY) HENRY WARNER, 3rd *Baronet ; b.* Aug. 3rd, 1922 ; *s.* his father, *Col. Sir* EDWARD COURTENAY THOMAS WARNER, *D.S.O., M.C.,* 1955 ; ed. at Eton, and at Ch. Ch., Oxford ; sometime Lieut. Scots Guards ; European War 1944-45 in France (wounded) : *m.* 1949, Jocelyn Mary, da. of Com. Sir Thomas Lubbock Beevor, 6th Bt., R.N., and has issue.

Arms—Per bend argent and gules two bendlets between six roses all counterchanged. **Crest**—A Saracen's head affrontée couped at the shoulders proper, vested gules, on the head a cap checky argent and of the second, in front thereof three roses fessewise of the third.

Residence—The Grove, Great Baddow, Essex. *Club*—Guards'.

I hope.

Sons living—PHILIP COURTENAY THOMAS, *b.* April 3rd, 1951.——Richard Edward Lubbock, *b.* 1952.——Robert Henry, *b.* 1957.

Sisters living—Anne Philippa (*Hon. Mrs. Henry E. Boscawen*), *b.* 1927: *m.* 1951, the Hon. Henry Edward Boscawen, Lieut. R.E. [*see* V. Falmouth]. *Residence*, The High Beeches, Handcross, Sussex.——Leucha Daphne Mary, *b.* 1929: *m.* 1962, Mark Gerald Edward North Buxton, of Coffyns, Spreyton, Crediton, Devon. [*see* Buxton, Bt., colls.].

Aunt living (daughter of 1st baronet)—Lillian Georgina, *b.* 1892: *m.* 1st, 1915, David Archibald, James Chapman, I,t. Scots Guards, who *d.* (killed in action) 1916; 2ndly, 1925, Charles Ronald Mansel Lewis [Miles, Bt.], who *d.* 1960, and has issue living, (by 2nd m.) David Courtenay (Guards' and Lansdowne Club), *b.* 1927; ed. at Eton, and Keble Coll., Oxford (BA); late Welsh Gds.; JP; High Sheriff of Carmarthenshire 1965-66; Lord Lieut. oj Carmarthenshire 1973-74; HM Lieut. of Dyfed, since 1974: *m.* 1953, Lady Mary Rosemary Marie-Gabrielle, da. of 3rd Earl of Wharncliffe, and has issue living, Patrick Charles Archibald Mansel *b.* 1953; ed. at Eton, Catherine Maud I,eucha *b.* 1955, Annabel Lilian Elfrida *b.* 1962. *Residence*, Stradey Castle, Llanelli, Dyfed.

Collateral Branch living

Issue of the late Capt. Thomas Seymour Marius Warner, 3rd son of 1st Baronet, *b.* 1903, *d.* 1965: *m.* 1st, 1926 (m. diss. 1929), Mrs. Dorothy Russell, da. of William Durran, of Caithness; 2ndly, 1929 (m. diss. 1938) Mrs. Edith Dorothy Morrison, da. of the late Robert Bold, of Liverpool; 3rdly, 1938, Louise Cameron (Ely Cottage, Wharf Lane, Henley-on-Thames), da. of the late Edward M. Roberts:—

(By 3rd m.) Courtenay Forbes (12/46, Lowndes Sq., SW1), *b.* 1939; ed. at Eton; late 2nd I,t. Scots Gds.: *m.* 1969 (m. diss. 1974), Veronica, da. of I,t.-Col. W. M. W. Cooper, of Medlands Farm House, Hurstbourne Tarrant, Andover; 2ndly, 1974, Venetia Elizabeth, da. of Maj. R. Atkinson Turner, and has issue living (by 2nd m.), Harry Richard Courtenay *b.* 1975.

The 1st baronet, Col. Sir (Thomas) Courtenay (Theydon) Warner, C.B., was Lord-Lieut. of Suffolk, and sat as M.P. for N. Div. of Somerset (*L*) 1892-95, and for Lichfield Div. of Staffs 1896-1923. The 2nd baronet, Col. Sir Edward Courtenay Thomas Warner, D.S.O., M.C., was High Sheriff of Suffolk 1947-8, and Lieut.-Col. Comdg. Scots Guards and Regtl. Dist. 1932-4.

WARREN, Creation (I.) 1784, of Warren's Court, co. Cork.

Not for me, but for God and the king.

Sir BRIAN CHARLES PENNEFATHER WARREN, 9th *Baronet*; *b.* June 4th, 1923; *s.* his father, *Col. Sir* THOMAS RICHARD PENNEFATHER, *C.B.E.*, 1961; ed. at Wellington; 1939-45 War as Lieut. Irish Guards.

Arms—Argent, a fesse checky or and azure, between three talbots passant proper. Crest—A lion rampant holding a crozier proper.

Residence—Woodville, Dunmore East, Waterford. *Club*, Guards'.

Sisters living—Patricia Bene Pennefather, *b.* 1908: *m.* 1st, 1934, William Sharman Bull, R.A.F., who *d.* (killed in action during European War) 1940; 2ndly, 1945, Col. Frederick Wynford Dewhurst, R.M., and has issue living, (by 1st m.) Victoria *b.* 1939: *m.* 1957, Maj. Robert Darwall, MC, RM, of Rockmoor, Harrabeer Lane, Yelverton, S. Devon, and has issue living, William Robert Thomas *b.* 1961, Antonia Mary *b.* 1958,—(by 2nd m.) Charles Frederick, *b.* 1946,—Sarah Elizabeth, *b.* 1948. *Residence*, Crapstone House, Buckland Monachorum, S. Devon.——Eileen Lavinia Pennefather (Biddy), *b.* 1910: *m.* 1st, 1930, Group Capt. Joseph Herbert Arthur Landon, DSO, OBE, RAF, who *d.* 1935; 2ndly, 1950, George Joseph Spiers. *Residence*, Grange Farm, Puttenham, nr. Tring, Herts.

Uncles living—WILLIAM ROBERT VAUGHTON, *OBE*, *MC* (c/o Barclays Bank, Tavistock, Devon), *b.* Feb. 23rd, 1889; Lt.-Col. RASC; 1914-19 War (despatches, MC, OBE); OBE (Mil.) 1919: *m.* 1st, 1914, Marjorie May (from whom he obtained a divorce 1926), only child of Harold Briggs, MP, of Broadford, Chobham, Surrey; 2ndly, 1926, Violet E., who *d.* 1963, da. of Lt.-Col. J. Wallis Gill, of Fairfield, St. Germans, Cornwall, and has issue living, (by 1st m.) Patrick Vaughton, *b.* 1917; is Maj. RA,—Michael Blackley, *b.* 1919,—Bridget Macree, *b.* 1922.—Edward Galwey, *CBE*, *b.* 1893; ed. at Eltham Coll.; Brig. (ret.) late Northamptonshire Regt.; 1914-18 War in France, Belgium, Sudan and Darfur (wounded, despatches, Order of Nile, 1914 star with clasp, three medals), N. Kurdistan 1932 (Brevet Lt.-Col. Iraq Gallantry medal with clasp), N.-W. Frontier of India 1936-37 (medal and clasp), 1939-45 War (CBE); CBE (Mil) 1940: *m.* 1914, Gwendolyn Agnes, who *d.* 1967, da. of the late Brooke Brazier, JP, of Ballygarrett, Mallow, co. Cork, and Rivers, co. Limerick. *Residence*, Stradbally, Castleconnell, co Limerick.

Collateral Branches living.

Granddaughter of the late Rev. Thomas Warren, 3rd son of the late Thomas Warren, M.P., 3rd son of 1st baronet :—
Issue of the late Capt. John Augustus Warren, *b.* 1831, *d.* 1907 : *m.* 1869, Mary Spence, da. of Thomas Thimbleby, of Avenue House, Spilsby :—
Milly Kathleen: *m.* 1896, Maj. Charles Henry Ashurst, late R. Sussex Regt., who *d.* 1966. *Residence*, Cappagh Bungalow, Union Hall, co. Cork.

Granddaughters of the late William Warren, 8th son of the late Thomas Warren, M.P. (ante) :—
Issue of the late William Augustus Warren, *b.* 18—, *d.* 1923 : *m.* 1875, Katherine, youngest da. of G. Dalrymple Monteith, M.D., of Wellington, New Zealand :—
Muriel Leila.——Mildred Irene: *m.* 1920, Charles H. Baker, of Flat 3, Belglen, 21, Vivian St., New Plymouth, NZ, and has issue living, Derek Charles Kuke, *b.* 1921,—William Thomas Neville, *b.* 1923.——Ruby Augusta Grahæme. *Residence*, 317, Broadway, Palmerston North, NZ.

Grandchildren of the late Brisbane Warren, 9th son of the late Thomas Warren, M.P. (ante) :—
Issue of the late Very Rev. Thomas Brisbane Warren, M.A., Dean of Cork, *b.* 1843, *d.* 1894: *m.* 1882, Elizabeth Sarah Emily, who *d.* 1921, da. of the late Thomas Christopher Cole, of Woodview, Innishannon, co. Cork :—
Brisbane Charles Somerville, *b.* 1887: *m.* 1922, Janey Neill (Joan), da. of the late T. F. M. Cartwright, of Petteridge, Brenchley, Kent, and has issue living, Elizabeth Joan Mary, *b.* 1929. *Residence*, Flat 2, 31, Clifton Cres., Folkestone.
Issue of the late Philip Somerville Warren, L.R.C.P., L.R.C.S., *b.* 1844, *d.* 1909: *m.* 1886, Elizabeth Sherrard, who *d.* 1903, el. da. of the late Thomas Somerville, J.P., of The Prairie, co. Cork:—
Robert Desmond Eyre Somerville, *b.* 1897; ed. at RMC; Lt. S. Wales Borderers (Reserve of Officers).——Denis Patrick Somerville, *b.* 1901.——Millicent Madeleine Somerville, *b.* 18—: *m.* 1911, Capt. Andrew Winstanley Newton, formerly Roy. Dublin Fusiliers.——Nora Creina Somerville, *b.* 18—.——Henrietta Millicent Somerville, *b.* 1900.

Grandson of the late Robert Warren (*b.* 1870), (infra):—
Issue of the late Augustus John Warren, *b.* 1909, *d.* 1969: *m.* 1949, Irene Joyce (c/o Munster & Leinster Bank, Dunmanway, co. Cork), da. of the late James Edwards Atkins, JP, of Brook Park, Dunmanway, co. Cork:—
Robert, *b.* 1954.

Grandchildren of the late Robert Warren, el. son of the late Rev. Robert Warren (*d.* 1879), el. son of the late Rev. Robert Warren (*d.* 1830), 5th son of 1st baronet:—

Issue of the late Robert Warren, *b.* 1870, *d.* 1947 : *m.* 1904, Maria Frances Lumley (of Sprayfield, Kinsale, co. Cork), da. of the late William Lumley Perrier, of Maryborough, Douglas, co. Cork:—

Gladys Irene, *b.* 1908. *Residence,* Sprayfield, Kinsale, co. Cork.

Issue of the late Sophia Clowser Warren, *b.* 18—, *d.* 1951: *m.* 1891, Jasper Drury late Lt. RFA, who *d.* 1932:—

Robert Warren (Clearmount, Monkstown, co. Cork), *b.* 1894: *m.* 1930, Eileen, da. of the late T. B. Nash, of Monkstown, co. Cork, and has issue living, Ralph Jasper Warren (Marina, Dunmore Rd., Waterford), *b.* 1931: *m.* 1968, Joan, da. of the late James Geraghty, of Buttevant, co. Cork, and has issue living, Jane *b.* 1968.

Granddaughters of the late Sophia Clowser Drury (ante):—

Issue of the late Lt.-Col. Jasper Drury, CEng., MIME, *b.* 1893, *d.* 1973: *m.* 1920, Eileen, who *d.* 1972, da. of J. P. Dowdall, of Dublin and Mullingar:—

Audrey Pamela, *b.* 1923: *m.* 1953, Robert Baker, of Manor Lodge, Hawley, Hants., and has issue living, Simon Charles, *b.* 1957,—Anthony John, *b.* 1958,—Caroline Mary, *b.* 1954.——Eileen Braddell, *b.* 1929: *m.* 1955, John Gavin Wotherspoon, MB, BS, of 330, London Rd., Waterlooville, Hants, and has issue living, Hugh Robert, *b.* 1958,—Andrew Charles, *b.* 1960,—Mark Gavin, *b.* 1962.

Grandchildren of the late Maj.-Gen. Richard Warren, 2nd son of the late Rev. Robert Warren (*d.* 1879), (ante) :—

Issue of the late Herbert Lauder Warren, Staff Paymaster, R.N., *b.* 1855, *d.* 1897 : *m.* 1885, Ella Christian Hoyer, who *d.* 1945, da. of Christian Hoyer Millar, of Biair Castle, Culross, Fife :—

Ella Christian Louise Lauder, *MBE, b.* 1891; MBE (Civil) 1963.——Kathleen Pelham Lauder, *MBE, b.* 1892; MBE (Civil) 1966. *Residence,* 2, St. Paul's St., 'Mdina, Malta.

Issue of the late Edward Albert Warren, *b.* 1856, *d.* 1899: *m.* 1884, Emily, da. of the late Talbot Palmer, of Waterlooville, Hants :—

Edward Richard Lauder, *b.* 1888.——Emily Ruth, *b.* 1885 : *m.* 1907, Patrick Hardy. *Residence,* Barton Lodge, Duke Road, Rondebosch, Cape Town, S. Africa.——Dorothy Talbot, *b.* 1887 : *m.* 1907, Bernard Tweedale.——Winifred Mary, *b.* 1891: *m.* 1st, 1909, the Rev. Edmund Watts, who *d.* 1912; 2ndly, 1912, Reginald Miller, who *d.* 1954. *Residence,* Pompey, Clyde St., Belville, Cape Province, S. Africa.

Issue of the late Lieut.-Col. Percy Bliss Warren, *b.* 1864, *d.* 1911 : *m.* 1892, Margaret Ellen, who *d.* 1951, da. of the late William Langdon Martin, of Windsor Villas, Plymouth :—

Margaret Joan (4, Poplar Rd., Burnham-on-Sea, Somerset), *b.* 1895.

Grandchildren of the late Lieut.-Col. Percy Bliss Warren (ante):—

Issue of the late Wallis Langdon Warren, *b.* 1900, *d.* 1974: *m.* 1934, Barbara (Umvukwes, Rhodesia, and 9 Bridgenorth Rd., PO Greendale, Salisbury, Rhodesia), da. of Harold Henry Durell Christian:—

Robert Nicholas Christian (27, Chelverton Rd., Putney, SW15), *b.* 1945.——Shirley Margaret Christian, *b.* 1936: *m.* 1958, Iacovas Ioannou James Koukoularides, of 302, Brownhill Rd., SE6, and has issue living, Panos John, *b.* 1966,—Janet Sophia, *b.* 1958,—Daphne Barbara, *b.* 1963.——Jennifer Mary Christian, *b.* 1940: *m.* 1963, Keith Dallas Brown, of 6, Bridgenorth Rd., PO Greendale, Salisbury, Rhodesia, and has issue living, Mark Dallas, *b.* 1966,—Anton Dallas, *b.* 1970,—Sherrill Anne, *b.* 1968.——Jocelyn Anne Christian, *b.* 1942: *m.* 1969, Michael Edward Younghusband, of 56, Weiner Drive, Discovery, PO Florida, Transvaal, S. Africa, and has issue living, Sharon Leigh, *b.* 1971,—Tracey Anne, *b.* 1972.

Issue of the late Major Geoffrey Martin Warren, Roy. Tank Regt., *b.* 1908, *d.* (of wounds received in action) 1941: *m.* 1938, Margaret Rosemary [who *m.* 2ndly, 1948, George Arthur, who *d.* 1968, and 3rdly, 1972, Robert George Alexander Hemming, of Pillarbank, Cardross, Dumbarton], da. of the late Col. Thomas Young Seddon:—

Brian Richard (Little Squeen, Upper Stanton Drew, Bristol), *b.* 1939: *m.* 1965, Angela Jean, da. of the late Arthur L. Yarranton, of Eardiston, Worcs., and has issue living, Oliver Martin, *b.* 1968,—Emily Claire, *b.* 1966,—Lucy Maud, *b.* 1970.

Grandchildren of Maj.-Gen. Augustus Edmund Warren, 2nd son of the late Richard Benson Warren (infra):—

Issue of the late Dudley Edward Warren, *b.* 1875, *d.* 1949: *m.* 1913, Gundreda, da. of the late Col. Duncan Spiller:—

Dudley Gundred, *b.* 1923.——Adèle Valerie, *b.* 1928.

Issue of Vivian Brudenell Warren, *b.* 1877, *d.* 1973: *m.* 1900, Lilie Barrington, who *d.* 1937, da. of Capt. C. A. G. Heysham, RN:—

Charles Vivian, *b.* 1907: *m.* 1st, 1945, Maeve, da. of the late John Davis, of Ballina, Ireland; 2ndly, 1972, Jaqueta, da. of Sir Arnold Henry Moore Lunn, and has issue living, (by 1st m.) Robert Augustus Michael Mary, *b.* 1949,—Patrick Martin Vivian Mary, *b.* 1951.——Vivienne Ellen, *b.* 1912: *m.* 1943, George Frderick Alston Shilling, of 13, Upper Wimpole St., W1.

Grandchildren of the late Richard Benson Warren, Serjeant-at-law, **7th son of** 1st baronet:—

Issue of the late Ven. Latham Coddington Warren, *b.* 1831, *d.* 1912: *m.* 1st, 1855, Harriet who *d.* 1883, da. of John Henry Davidson, M.D., of Edinburgh ; 2ndly, 1885, Mary Georgina, who *d.* 1911, da. of the late Hall Stirling :—

By 1st marriage) Robert Augustus Monsell, *b.* 1875.——Florence Martha Caroline.——(By 2nd marriage) Beatrice Lilian May.——Dorothy Edythe Mary.

Grandchildren of the late Rt. Hon. Robert Richard Warren, LL.D., son of the late Capt. Henry Warren, 8th son of 1st baronet:—

Issue of the late Henry Charles Jackson Warren, *b.* 1852, *d.* 1937: *m.* 1877, Florence, who *d.* 1944, da. of the late Lieut.-Col. the Hon. Robert French Handcock, 8th son of 2nd Baron Castlemaine:—

Desmond Cecil Robert, *b.* 1895: *m.* 1929, Violet Arabella, da. of Dr. F. O. Lasbrey, and has issue living, Donal, *b.* 1930,—Jennifer Edyth Helen, *b.* 1932,—Juliet Alice Louise, *b.* 1938. *Residence,* Cherry Hill, Ballybrack, co. Dublin.——Winifred Annette, *b.* 1888: *m.* 1917, Cdr. Guy Edward Cooper, RN (ret), who *d.* 1941, and has issue living, Brenda, *b.* 1922: *m.* 1939, Raymond Buckingham of Chapel Hayes, East the Water, Bideford, N. Devon. *Residence,* 43, Cadogan Place, SW1.

Grandsons of Mrs. Winifred Annette Cooper (ante):—

Issue of the late Giles Cooper, OBE, *b.* 1918, *d.* 1966: *m.* 1947, Gwyneth (Park Cottage, Upperton, nr. Petworth, Sussex), da. of the late Rev. Canon James A. Lewis:—

Guy Evan, *b.* 1948.——Richard Brandon Synge, *b.* 1955.

This family descends from Wallis Warren who purchased in 1688 Kilbarry, co. Cork, which later was renamed Warren's Court. His grandson, Sir Robert Warren, 1st Bt., was High Sheriff of co. Cork 1752. Major Sir Augustus Riversdale Warren, 5th Bt., served in Crimean War and in Indian Mutiny, and was High Sheriff for co. Cork in 1867. Col. Sir Thomas Richard Pennefather Warren, C.B.E., late R.A.S.C., was Ch. Constable of Bucks. 1928.

WATERLOW, Creation (U.K.) 1873, of London.

Sir CHRISTOPHER RUPERT WATERLOW, 5th *Baronet*; *b.* Aug. 12th, 1959; *s.* his grandfather, **Sir** PHILIP ALEXANDER, 1973; ed at Stonyhurst.

Ærms—Azure, a demi-eagle displayed, erased or, in the beak a cross-crosslet fitchee argent, on a chief of the last three wolves' heads erased sable. Crest—Upon a mount vert an oak tree in front thereof a plough, both proper.

Residence—Grenville Manor, Haddenham, Bucks.

Great Uncles living—DEREK VAUDREY, *b.* Feb. 19th, 1902; ed. at Harrow. *Residence*, Ward Green Cottage, Old Newton, Stowmarket, Suffolk.——Ronald James Charlton, *b.* 1916; ed. at Harrow; formerly Major 57th Anti-Tank Regt. R.A.; European War 1939-45 (despatches); is a Freeman of City of London: *m.* 1953, Ethel Florence, youngest da. of F. G. Chelsom, of Stevenage, Herts. *Residence*, The Croft, Little Wynmondley, Hitchin, Herts.

Great Aunt living—Joyce Rosamund Amy (twin), *b.* 1916: *m.* 1st, 1940, Godfrey Ian Hutchinson, Flying Officer RAF, from whom she obtained a divorce 1947; 2ndly, 1953, David Ronald Mitchell, of Wood End Cottage, Henham, nr. Bishop's Stortford, Herts., son of the late Sir Frank Herbert Mitchell, KCVO, CBE, and has issue living, (by 1st m.) Diana Joy, *b.* 1941: *m.* 1962, José Perez-Gonzalez, of Cerro del Torril 16, Carretera-Benalmadena, Torre Molinos, Spain, and has issue living, Antonio Salvador *b.* 1964, Samantha Rose *b.* 1966.

Grandmother living—Iris Gwendoline, (Saxons, 29, Glenfurnance Av., Bournemouth), da. of the late Charles Rupert Butler, of New Place, Sunningdale, Berks.: *m.* 1st, 1923 (m. diss. 1937), Philip Alexander Waterlow, later 4th Bt, who *d.* 1973; 2ndly, 1937, Campbell Shaw, who *d.* 1969.

Stepmother living—Ruth Margaret (*Lady Norrington*), yst. da. of the late Edmund Cude, of Ashbrittle, Church Vale, N2: *m.* 1st, 1946, Frank Davies, who *d.* 1959; 2ndly, 1962, (Peter) Rupert Waterlow, who *d.* 1969; 3rdly, 1969, Sir Arthur Lionel Pugh Norrington, of Grenville Manor, Haddenham, Bucks.

Widow living of 4th Baronet—GWENDOLINE FLORENCE ELIZABETH (*Lady Waterlow*) (11, Elmwood Av., Hawkwell, Essex), yr. da. of the late Léon Balanché, and formerly wife of Baden Roberts Murch: *m.* 1972, as his 3rd wife, Sir Philip Alexander Waterlow, 4th Bt., who *d.* 1973.

Collateral Branches living.

Issue of the late Anthony Edgar Russell Waterlow, 3rd son of 3rd baronet, *b.* 1914, *d.* 1946: *m.* 1940, Barbara Winifred (now of 16, Paultons Square, S.W.3), da. of Ronald Davy, of Limber Habrough, Lincolnshire:—
Nicholas Anthony Ronald (14, Church St., Stoney Stratford, Bucks.), *b.* 1941; ed. at Harrow: *m.* 1965, Rosemary, da. of W. J. O'Brien, of Sydney, and has issue living, Antony William Nicholas *b.* 1967,—Luke Frederick Ronald *b.* 1970,—Chloe Diana, *b.* 1972.

Grandchildren of the late George Sydney Waterlow, 4th son of 1st baronet:—
Issue of the late Sir Sydney Philip Perigal Waterlow, K.C.M.G., C.B.E., *b.* 1878, *d.* 1944 ; *m.* 1st, 1902 (marriage annulled 1912), Alice Isabella, who *d.* 1953, da. of the Right Hon. Sir Frederick Pollock, 3rd Bt. (*cr.* 1866): 2ndly, 1913, Helen Margery, who *d.* 1973, da. of Gustav Eckhard, of Didsbury, Manchester:—
(By 2nd m.) John Conrad, *CMG*, *b.* 1916; ed. at Eton, and at Trin. Coll., Camb. (BChir, MD, ScD); Prof. of Human Nutrition, London Sch. of Hygiene and Tropical Med., Univ. of London; FRCP; CMG 1970: *m.* 1939, Angela, da. of the late G. Wynter Gray, and has issue living, Oliver Sydney, *b.* 1943,—Richard John, *b.* 1945,—Sarah Jean, *b.* 1941. *Residence*, 3, Campden Hill Square, W8.——Charlotte Mary, *MBE*, *b.* 1915; sometime an Administrative Officer, Foreign Office; Sch. Teacher and Author; MBE (Civil) 1950. *Residence*, 205 Appleton St., Cambridge, Mass. 02138, USA.

Issue of the late David Sydney Waterlow, 7th son of 1st baronet, *b.* 1857, *d.* 1924: *m.* 1883, Edith Emma, who *d.* 1932, da. of the late Frederick Maitland, of 18, Primrose Hill Road, N.W.:—
Joan Maitland, *b.* 1897: *m.* 1926, George Lambourn, and has issue living, Simon (of 13, Grey Close, N.W.11), *b.* 1927: *m.* 1951, Hilary Margaret Buckley, da. of the late Herbert J. Williams, and has issue living, Caroline Helen *b.* 1959, Sarah Margaret *b.* 1962,—Martin (Prospect, Cofton Hill, Starcross, Devon), *b.* 1929: *m.* 1st, 1951, Diana Godfrey, who obtained a divorce 1957, 2ndly, 1958, Jill Amanda, da. of the late Norman Broughton Stevenson, of Bristol, and has issue living, (by 1st marriage) Nikolas *b.* 1952, Tamsin *b.* 1954, Charlotte Nancy *b.* 1956 (by 2nd marriage) Giles Timothy *b.* 1960, Hugo Gavin *b.* 1963, Emma Fanny *b.* 1962,—Jane, *b.* 1931. *Residence*, Danny, Hurstpierpoint, Sussex.——Sylvia Maitland, *b.* 1898: *m.* 1920, Cyril George Dennys, CB, MC, and has issue living, Elizabeth, *MB, BS, b.* 1925—Barbara, *b.* 1928: *m.* 1949, Peter Morton Spiers, of 64, Primrose Gdns., NW3, and has issue living, Timothy Richard Dennys *b.* 1958, John Peter *b.* 1963, Sally Jean Elizabeth *b.* 1951, Phillida Judith *b.* 1954. *Residence*, 38, Belsize Grove, N.W.3.——Rosalind Maitland, *b.* 1911: *m.* 1936, Sheriton Clements Swan, and has issue living, David, *b.* 1940,—Nicholas Clements (Brook House, Stocksfield, Northumberland) *b.* 1944: *m.* 1970, Susan, da. of F. Wells, of Berwick-on-Tweed, and has issue living, Catharine Victoria *b.* 1970, Diana Rachel *b.* 1972,—Lesley Jean, *b.* 1942: *m.* 1964, Richard James Hamments, of 4, Kilmorey Rd., St. Margarets, Twickenham, Middx. *Residence*, Milestone Cottage, Wall, Hexham, Northumberland.

Sir Sydney Hedley Waterlow, KCVO, 1st Bt, Founder and Chm. of Improved Industrial Dwellings Co., Ltd., Lord Mayor of London 1872-73; MP for Maidstone 1874-80 and Gravesend 1880-85), gave Waterlow Park, Highgate, to LCC in 1889. The 2nd baronet, Sir Philip Hickson Waterlow, was Chm. of Waterlow and Sons, Ltd.

WATERLOW, Creation (U.K.) 1930, of Harrow Weald, Middlesex.

Sir THOMAS GORDON WATERLOW, *CBE*, 3rd *Baronet*; *b.* Jan. 2nd, 1911; *s.* his brother, *Col. Sir* (WILLIAM) JAMES, *CBE, TD*, 1969; ed. at Marlborough, and Trin. Coll., Camb.; DLitt; 1939-45 War as Group Capt. AuxAF (despatches); CBE (Mil) 1946: *m.* 1938, Helen Elizabeth, who *d.* 1970, da. of Gerard Robinson, of North Ridge, Bix, Henley-on-Thames, and has issue.

Arms—Argent, a lion rampant within a bordure nebuly azure, on a chief sable two shin-bones saltirewise, the dexter surmounted by the sinister or. **Crest**—A demi-lion guardant azure, in the mouth a shin-bone in bend, and holding between the paws a human skull both or.

Residence—1, Lennox St., Edinburgh, EH4 1QB. *Clubs*—Caledonian, New (Edinburgh).

I conquer through death.

Sons living—(JAMES) GERARD (12, Cliveden Place, SW1), *b.* 1939; ed. at Marlborough, and Trin. Coll., Camb.: *m.* 1965, Diana Suzanne, da. of William Thomas Skyrme [see B. Lyle of Westbourne], and has issue living, Thomas James, *b.* 1970,—Amanda Jane, *b.* 1968.——Simon Gordon (250, Kensington Av., Montreal, Canada), *b.* 1941; ed. at Marlborough, and Trin. Coll. Camb. (BA): *m.* 1971, Jane, da. of the late Wing Cdr. Cameron Underhill, RCAF, and has issue living, Caroline Elizabeth, *b.* 1973.——John William (79, Inglethorpe St., SW6 6NV), *b.* 1945; ed. at Marlborough: *m.* 1972, Camilla Dudley, da. of Wing Cdr. Dudley Farmer, of 13, Philimore Gdns., W8.

Sir William Alfred Waterlow, KBE, 1st Bt., who was Man. Dir. of Waterlow Bros. & Layton, Chm. of Waterlow & Sons Ltd., and Lord Mayor of London 1929-30, was grandson of Alfred James Waterlow, el. brother of Sir Sydney Hedley Waterlow, 1st Bt. (cr. 1873).

WATSON, Creation (U.K.) 1866, of Henrietta Street, Cavendish Square, St. Marylebone, co. Middlesex.

Sir JAMES ANDREW WATSON, 5th *Baronet*; *b.* Dec. 30th, 1937; *s.* his father, *Sir* THOMAS AUBREY, 1941; ed. at Eton.; Bar. Inner Temple 1966: *m.* 1965, Christabel Mary, el. da. of Kenneth Ralph Malcolm Carlisle, of 18, York House, W8, [see B. Aberconway], and has issue.

Arms—Azure, on a fesse dancetté between three crescents argent, as many martlets sable. **Crest**—A gryphon's head erased azure, ducally crowned or, between two branches of palm proper.

Residence—Talton House, Newbold on Stour, Stratford on Avon, Warwicks.

Sons living—ROLAND VICTOR, *b.* March 4th, 1966.——Alexander Bruce, *b.* 1969.
Uncle living (son of 3rd baronet)—John Rushworth, *b.* 1913: *m.* 1963, Mrs. Diana Dean, da. of Maj. H. Rushden.
Aunt living (daughter of 3rd baronet)—Eleanor Mary, *b.* 1914. *Residence*, Old Farm House, Charlton, Banbury, Oxon.
Widow living of 4th Baronet—ELLA MARGUERITE (*Ella, Lady Watson*), da. of the late Sir George Farrar, Bt. (ext.): *m.* 1935, Sir Thomas Aubrey Watson, 4th baronet, who *d.* (on active ser. during 1939-45 War) 1941. *Residence*, Court Farm House, Sherbourne, Barford, Warwicks.

Sufferings are lessons.

The 1st baronet, a distinguished Physician in London, was President of the Royal College of Physicians (London), the first representative of the Royal College of Physicians in Medical Council, and a Physician-in-Ordinary to H.M. Queen Victoria, and the 4th baronet, Sir Thomas Aubrey, Lieut. Life Guards, *d.* (on active ser. during European War) 1941.

WATSON, Creation (U.K.) 1912, of Sulhamstead, Sulhamstead Abbots, Berks.

Sir NORMAN JAMES WATSON, 2nd *Baronet*; *b.* March 17th, 1897; *s.* his father, *Sir* (WILLIAM) GEORGE, 1930; ed. at Eton; Flying Officer late R.A.F. Vol. Reserve, and a F.R.G.S.; High Sheriff of Berks 1940-41; 1914-18 War as Lt. KRRC and RAF: *m.* 1974, Beryl, da. of Alfred Norris, widow of Sqdn.-Ldr. Basil Montefiore Davis, RAF, and formerly wife of Sir Francis Cyril Rose, 4th Bt. (*cr.* 1872).

Arms—Argent, a chevron azure between three martlets sable all within a bordure of the second, charged with eight crescents of the first. Crest—A gryphon's head erased sable, gorged with a crown palisado or, holding in its beak a sprig of oak fructed proper.

Residence—Abesters, nr. Haslemere, Surrey. *Clubs*—Carlton, Alpine, RAF.

Esto quod esse videris.

Be what you seem to be.

Sister living—Florence, *b.* 1894: *m.* 1916, James Nagle, Canadian Highlanders, from whom she obtained a divorce 1928, and who *d.* 1933, and has issue living, Gordon Davidson, *b.* 1918. *Residence*, Westerlands, Petworth, Sussex.

The 1st baronet, Sir (William) George, was Chm. of Maypole Dairy Co. (Limited), and High Sheriff of Berks (1920).

WATSON, Creation (U.K.) 1918, of Newport, co. Monmouth. [Extinct 1959.]

Sir GEOFFREY LEWIN WATSON, 3rd and last *Baronet*.

Daughter living of 3rd Baronet—Daphne Lewin (*Hon. Mrs. John M. Southwell*), *b.* 1907: *m.* 1932, Lieut.-Com. the Hon. John Michael Southwell, R.N., who *d.* (killed on active ser. during 1939-45 War) 1944 [*see* V. Southwell]. *Residence*, Buckclose, Longparish, Andover, Hants.

INGLEFIELD-WATSON, Creation (U.K.) 1895, of Earnock, Hamilton, Lanarkshire.

It has flourished beyond expectation.

Sir DERRICK WILLIAM INGLEFIELD-WATSON, *T.D.*, 4th *Baronet*; *b.* Oct. 7th, 1901; *s.* his brother, *Sir* JOHN WATSON, 1918; ed. at Eton, and at Ch. Ch., Oxford; is Capt. (retired) Roy. W. Kent Regt. (T.A.); was a County Councillor for Kent 1931-37; assumed by deed poll 1946 his christian name of Inglefield as an additional surname: *m.* 1st, 1925, Margrett Georgina (who obtained a divorce 1939), da. of Col. Thomas Stokes George Hugh Robertson-Aikman, C.B., of The Ross, Hamilton, Lanarkshire; 2ndly, 1946, Thérèse (Terry), only da. of the late Professor Charles Bodon, of Budapest, and has issue by 1st marriage.

Arms—Per pale argent and or, on a mount vert an oak tree proper, the whole surmounted by two bars sable. Crest—The stump of an oak tree with a branch sprouting from either side, each grasped by a hand issuing from a cloud all proper.

Residence—Ringshill House, Wouldham, nr. Rochester, Kent.

Son living—By 1st m.—JOHN FORBES, *b.* May 16th, 1926; ed. at Eton; Lt.-Col. RE.
Daughter living—By 1st m.—Sheila Margrett (Monks Acre, Upper Anstey Lane, Alton, Hants.), *b.* 1931: *m.* 1958, Dugald Graham-Campbell, who *d.* 1967, and has issue living, Robert John, *b.* 1964.—Sarah Alexandra *b.* 1960.
Sister living—Doreen Agnes Edith (*Lady Dorman-Smith*). *b.* 1896 : *m.* 1921, Col. the Rt. Hon. Sir Reginald Hugh Dorman-Smith, G.B.E., and has issue living, Patricia Valerie, *b.* 1925: *m.* 1950, Arthur Gwyn Griffin, who *d.* 1967. *Residence*, Hunters Croft, Grayswood, Haslemere, Surrey.

Collateral Branches living.

Grandson of Thomas William Watson, W.S., 3rd son of 1st baronet (*infra*):—
Issue of the late Capt. Leslie Dundas Watson, *b.* 1894, *d.* 1975: *m.* 1923, Enid Margaret (Upper Park, Dedham, Essex), da. of the late Col. George Hay Montgomery Conran:—
Simon Conran Hamilton (11, Kenbrook House, Kensington High St., SW14), *b.* 1939; ed. at Harrow: *m.* 1971, Madeleine Stiles, el. da. of the late Wagner Mahlon Dickenson, of New York City.—— Gillian Faye Lucy, *b.* 1928.

Issue of the late Thomas William Watson, W.S., 3rd son of 1st baronet, *b.* 1864, *d.* 1935: *m.* 1891, Lucy, who *d.* 1947, el. da. of William Henry Hamilton, of Manchester:—
Jeanette Lucy Vickers, *b.* 1902: *m.* 1923, Brig.-Gen. James Lockhead Jack, DSO, DL, JP, who *d.* 1962, and has issue living, Kenneth Hamilton Muir (Abbey Cottage, Pipewell, Northants), *b.* 1931: *m.* 1959, Bridget Casey, da. of Lt.-Col. Alan Stuart Casey, Roy. Dragoons [see V. Monsell], and has issue living, Richard Kenneth Hamilton *b.* 1962, Christopher James Hamilton *b.* 1971, Louise Diana *b.* 1964,—Angus Gavin Lockhead, *b.* 1935: *m.* 1960 (m. diss. 1970), Elizabeth Ann, el. da. of Sir John Samuel Richardson, 1st Bt. (*cr.* 1963), and has issue living, Charles Watson Hamilton *b.* 1962. *Residence*, The Old House, Kibworth, Leics.

Grandson of the late Thomas William Watson, W.S. (*ante*):—
Issue of the late Somerled William Watson, *b.* 1899, *d.* 1938: *m.* 1925, Elma Mary (now of Baythorne Park, near Halstead, Essex), only da. of the late William Walker, of High Canons, Shenley, Herts:—
Julian Frank Somerled, *b.* 1931; ed. at Harrow. *Residence*, Baythorne Park, near Halstead, Essex.

Sir John Watson, 1st Bt., of Earnock, was second son of John Watson, of Bathville, Lanarkshire, by his first wife. The 3rd baronet, Sir John, Lieut, Lancers, was killed in action during
European War 1918.

MILNE-WATSON, Creation (U.K.) 1937, of Ashley, Longbredy, co. Dorset.

Sir DAVID RONALD MILNE-WATSON, 2nd
Baronet; b. July 15th, 1904; s. his father *Sir* DAVID,
T.D., LL.D., 1945; ed. at Trin. Coll., Glenalmond,
and at Balliol Coll., Oxford.

Arms—Argent, on a mount vert, an oak tree proper fructed
or, over all a chevron azure charged with two mullets gold.
Crest—A demi-griffin sable, gorged with an antique crown and
charged on the body with two mullets palewise or.

Residence—The Stables, Oakfield, Mortimer, Berks.

Brother living—*Sir* MICHAEL, CBE, b. Feb. 16th, 1910; ed.
at Eton, and Balliol Coll., Oxford; Chm. of N. Thames Gas
Board 1947-64, Richard Thomas & Baldwins Ltd., 1964-67,
and William Press Group of Cos., 1969-75; Dep. Chm. British
Steel Corpn. 1967-69; a Dir. of Finance for Industry Ltd., and
Commersial Union Assurance Co. Ltd.; late Sub-Lt. RNVR;
CBE (Civil) 1953, Knt. 1969: m. 1940, Mary Lisette, da. of
the late H. Bagnall, of Auckland, NZ and has issue living,
Andrew Michael (The Manse, 70, Lyford Rd., Wandsworth
Common, SW18), b. 1944: m. 1970, Beverley Jane Gabrielle,
el. da. of Philip Cotton, of Majorca, and has issue living, David
Alastair b. 1971, Emma Victoria b. 1974. *Residences*, 39,
Cadogan Place, SW1; Oakfield, Mortimer, Berks.

I owe all to God and country.

Sister living—Gabriel, b. 1901: m. 1929, Christian William
Laurence Peel Reed, of Fox and Hounds Farm, Bolney,
Sussex [E. Peel, colls.], and has issue living, Laurence Cecil
(Hookhams, Lurgashall, Petworth), b. 1930; ed. at Eton and
Worcester Coll., Oxford (MA): m. 1956, Georgina, da. of
Thomas St. John Alston, of Petworth, and has issue
living, Nicholas William b. 1958, Charles Christian Thomas
b. 1959, Andrew Laurence b. 1962,—Martin David (Stand-
gates Farm, Kirdford, Billingshurst, Sussex), b. 1932; ed. at Eton: m. 1957, Shirley, da. of the
late Charles C. Naumann, of Rudgwick, Sussex—Denys Christian (The Coach House, 1a, Larpent
Av., Putney, SW15), b. 1935; ed. at Eton: m. 1st, 1959 (m. diss. 1972), Tessa Caroline, da. of
Stephen Cannon; 2ndly, 1973, Angela Frances Croft, and has issue living (by 1st m.), Christopher
Stephen b. 1961, Jeremy Mathew b. 1962.

The 1st baronet, Sir David Milne-Watson (son of the late David Watson, of Edinburgh)
was Gov. and Managing Director **of Gas Light & Coke Co., Vice-Pres. of Federation of British
Industries, and Hon. Col. The Rangers, King's Roy. Rifle Corps.**

HARVIE-WATT, Creation (U.K.) 1945, of Bathgate, co. Linlithgow.

Sir GEORGE STEVEN HARVIE-
WATT, T.D., Q.C., 1st *Baronet*, son
of the late James McDougal Watt.
of Armadale ; b. Aug. 23rd, 1903 ; ed,
at George Watson's Coll., Edinburgh,
and at Glasgow and Edinburgh Univs.;
Bar. Inner Temple 1930, and a K.C.
1945; a Member of Queen's Body
Guard for Scotland (Roy. Co. of
Archers), a DL for Greater London,
Pres. of Consolidated Gold Fields Ltd.,
(Chm. 1960-69); Chm. of Monotype
Corpn. 1953-73; Dir. of Midland Bank,
Clydesdale Bank, Eagle Star Insurance
Co. and N. British Steel Group;
formerly Dir. of GWR; a Member of
Kensington Borough Council 1934-45,
Parliamentary Private Sec. to Parlia-
mentary Sec. to Board of Trade (Rt.
Hon. Euan Wallace, MP) 1937-38, an
Asst. Govt. Whip 1938-40, a Member
of City of London TA Asscn. 1939-54,
Parl. Sec. to Prime Min. (Rt. Hon. Winston Churchill, MP) 1941-45, Hon.
Treas of UK Branch of Commonwealth Parl. Assocn. 1945-51, and a Member
of UK Delegation to Commonwealth Parliamentary Assocn. Conferences at
Ottawa and Washington 1949, and in Aust. and NZ 1950; Hon. Vice-Pres.
(formerly a Member of Management Cttee) The Highland Soc., London; an
ADC to HM King George VI 1948-52, and to HM the Queen 1952-58; Lt.-Col.

Comdg. 31st Bn. RETA 1938-41, Brig. Command 6th AA Bde. TA 1941, Brig. Comdg. 63rd AA Bde. TA 1948-50; Hon. Col. 566th Light Regt. 1949; MP for Keighley Div. of W. Riding of Yorkshire (*U*) 1931-35 and for Richmond 1937-59; Gold Medal Institution of Mining & Metallurgy 1969: *m.* 1932, Bettie, only da. of the late Paymaster-Capt. Archibald Taylor, OBE, RN, and has issue.

Arms—Quarterly: per fess wavy; 1st, per pale ermine and azure upon a mound in base vert, a tower proper masoned, sable roof gules, between two oak trees, also proper fructed or: 2nd, argent fretty sable, a grenade azure inflamed of nine flames, seven or and two gules: 3rd, barry wavy argent and azure, a portcullis gules; 4th, barry wavy gules and or, a dexter hand proper issuing from a manche fessways sable. **Crest**—A lion's gamb issuing from the torse argent, armed gules, grasping a writing quill paleways or, feathered sable.

Residence,—Earlsneuk, Elie, Fife. *Clubs*—Pratt's, Caledonian.

Sons living—JAMES (15, Somerset Sq., W14 8EE), *b.* Aug. 25th, 1940; ed. at Eton and Ch. Ch., Oxford (MA); Chartered Accountant; Exec., British Electric Traction Co., Ltd.; Man. Dir. Wembley Stadium Ltd.; late Lt. 1st Bn. London Scottish Regt. (TA): *m.* 1966, Roseline Gladys Virginia, da. of Baron Louis de Chollet, of Le Guintzet, Fribourg, Switzerland, and has issue living, Mark Louis, *b.* 1969,—Isabelle Frances, *b.* 1967.——Euan (8, Eldon Rd., W8), *b.* 1942; ed. at Eton; late 2nd Lt. 1st Bn. London Scottish Regt. (TA); an Underwriting Member of Lloyds: *m.* 1967, Olivia Mason, da. of W. Mason Smith, of New York City, USA, and has issue living, Katrina, *b.* 1968,—Jennifer, *b.* 1969.
Daughter living—Rachel, *b.* 1944; ed. at Sherborne Sch. for Girls, and Perugia and Edinburgh (MA) Univs.: *m.* 1970, Iain Gordon Fraser, WS, of 20, Lynedoch Place, Edinburgh, EH3 7PY, and has issue living, Duncan, *b.* 1972,—Olivia, *b.* 1974.

DON-WAUCHOPE, Creation (N.S.) 1667, of Newton.

["ch" pronounced as in "Loch."]

Sir PATRICK GEORGE DON-WAUCHOPE, 10th *Baronet,* son of the late Patrick Hamilton Don-Wauchope, WS, 3rd son of 8th baronet; *b.* May 7th, 1898; *s.* his uncle, *Sir* JOHN DOUGLAS, 1951; ed. at Edinburgh Acad.; Horticulturalist (ret.); 1914-18 War in France and Belgium (wounded, two medals; 1939-45 War in Egypt and Italy): *m.* 1936 (m. diss. 1947), Ismay Lilian Ursula, da. of the late Sidney Richard Hodges, of Edendale, S. Africa, and has issue.

Arms,—Quarterly, 1st and 4th, azure, a crescent between two mullets in chief and a garb in base or (*Wauchope of Edmonstone*), 2nd, vert, on a fess argent three mascles sable (*Don of Newton Don*); 3rd, or a cross engrailed sable accompanied by an escutcheon gules in dexter chief and in sinister base a cinquefoil azure (*Rait of Edmonstone*); over all the Badge of a Baronet of Nova Scotia on an inescutcheon surmounted of an imperial crown. **Crests,**—Dexter, a garb or charged of a crescent vert (*Wauchope of Edmonstone*) sinister a fruit of pomegranate vert slit and seeded or (*Don of Newton Don*).

Address—Private Bag 729, Margate, Natal, S. Africa.

Sons living—ROGER HAMILTON (21, Winston Rd., Kloof, Natal) *b.* Oct. 16th, 1938; ed. at Hilton Coll., Natal; a Chartered Accountant (S. Africa): *m.* 1963, Sallee, da. of Lt.-Col. Harold Mill-Colman, OBE, AMICE, of Durban, and has issue living, Andrew Craig, *b.* May 18th, 1966,— John Hamilton, *b.* 1969,—Georgina Anne, *b.* 1970.——Malcolm John (Domingo, P.O. Highflats, Natal), *b.* 1939; ed. at Kearsney Coll., Botha's Hill, Natal: *m.* 1968, Rea Marion, da. of Phillip Montague Adams, of Doonside, South Coast, Natal, and has issue living, Keith John, *b.* 1970,— Jane Alice *b.* 1972.

Collateral Branches living.

Grandson of the late Rev. David Wauchope, uncle of 8th baronet:—
Issue of the late Rev. David Maitland Wauchope, *b.* 1864, *d.* 1947: *m.* 1888, Ethel Sarah, who *d.* 1950, da. of Lewis Maxey Stewart :—
Andrew Maxey, *b.* 1890: *m.* 1918, Mary Veronica Fisher, and has issue living, Michael Andrew Anthony (Magpie Farm, Yattendon, Newbury, Berks., RG16 0XX), *b.* 1925; ed. at Douai Sch.; late Lieut. Black Watch: *m.* 1955, Margaret Mary Eleanor Victoria, da. of I. S. Thomas, of Dublin, and has issue living, Piers Andrew Charles *b.* 1956, Francis Alastair *b.* 1959, Matthew Michael *b.* 1960, James Jonathon *b.* 1962,—Deirdre Veronica, *b.* 1921: *m.* 1964, Alan Harry Augustus Emery (38, Denmark Villas, Hove, Sussex). *Residence*, 9, Uplands, Mayfield, Sussex.

Grandchildren of the late Rev. David Maitland Wauchope (ante) :—
Issue of the late Oswald Stewart Wauchope, *b.* 1897, *d.* 1956 : *m.* 1914, Dorothy Lettice White (19, Fairfax Rd., W4):—
James David *b.* 1924.: *m.* 1950, Maria Sophia Zanucolli, of Florence.——Estella Olive, *b.* 1916: *m.* 1943, Dr. Michael West, who *d.* 1946, and has issue living——Annie Jean, *b.* 1922: *m.* 1st, 1943 (m. diss. 1953), Leon Zuckerman; 2ndly, 1958, Zbigniew Ernest Jaworski, of 138b, Golf Links, New Delhi, 110003, India; and has issue living.

Sir Alexander Don of Newton Don, Berwickshire, was cr. a Bt. with remainder to heirs male of his body. Sir William Henry Don, 7th Bt., sold Newton Don for £85,000 and became an actor. On his death in 1862 he was *s.* by his kinsman, Sir John Don-Wauchope (who resumed the surname of Don), son of Lt.-Col. John Wauchope, of Edmonstone, Midlothian, great-great-grandson of Patrick Don (who *m.* Anne, sister and in her issue heir of Andrew Wauchope of Edmonstone), 3rd son of 1st Bt.

WEBSTER, Creation (E.) 1703, of Battle Abbey, Sussex. [Extinct 1923.]

Sir AUGUSTUS FREDERICK WALPOLE EDWARD WEBSTER, *O.B.E.,* 8th and last *Baronet.*

Daughters living of 8th Baronet—Lucy, *b.* 1900.——Evelyn WEBSTER (Battle Abbey, Battle, Sussex) *b.* 1904; resumed her maiden surname by deed poll 1966: *m.* 1927, Charles Robert Harbord, from whom she obtained a divorce 1944, and has issue living, Godfrey Vassal WEBSTER, *b.* 1928; assumed by deed poll 1944 the surname of WEBSTER in lieu of his patronymic,—Simon John Frederick, *b.* 1933: 1st, 1958 (m. diss. 1964), Maria Omiastowona; 2ndly, 1967 (m. diss. 1971), Wendy Nixon, and has issue living, (by 1st m.) Antony *b.* 1959; (by 2nd m.) Marcus *b.* 1967.

Collateral Branch living.

Granddaughter of the late Charles Fox Webster, son of the late Col. Sir Henry Vassal Webster, 2nd son of 4th baronet :—
Issue of the late Godfrey Seymour William Webster, *b.* 1864, *d.* 1887 : *m.* 1887, Ada Mary, who *d.* 1947 [having *m.* 2ndly, 18—, —Walker; 3rdly, 1901, Sir John Alexander Miller, 3rd Bt. (cr. 1874, ext.), who obtained a divorce 1906; 4thly, 1908, Lieut.-Col. Maximilian John de Bathe, O.B.E., who *d.* 1929, having obtained a divorce 1926 (de Bathe, Bt.)], da. of Francis Henry Paget, of Birstall, Leicestershire :—
Dorothy Muriel (posthumous), *b.* 1888: *m.* 1st, 1910, Lieut.-Col. Ian Onslow Dennistoun, M.V.O. (formerly Grenadier Guards), who *d.* 1938, and from whom she had obtained a divorce 1921, 2ndly, 1928, Col. N. Woevodsky (formerly Chevalier Guard). *Residence,* Castillo Cat, Roi, Palafrugell, Spain.

OGILVY-WEDDERBURN, Creation (U.K.) 1803, of Balindean, Perthshire.

Sir (JOHN) PETER OGILVY-WEDDERBURN, **6th** *Baronet* ; *b.* Sept. 29th, 1917; *s.* his father, *Sir* JOHN ANDREW, 1956; Com. R.N. (retired): *m.* 1946, Elizabeth Katharine, da. of the late John A. Cox, and has issue.
   Arms—Not yet matriculated for present line of baronets.
   Residence—Silvie, Alyth, Perthshire.

Son living—ANDREW JOHN ALEXANDER, *b.* Aug. 4th, 1952; ed. at Gordonstoun; Lt. Black Watch.
Daughters living—Henrietta Katharine, *b.* 1947: *m.* 1972, Sebastian P. Thewes, and has issue living, Robert John Peter, *b.* 1974.——Jean Aileen, *b.* 1948.——Elizabeth Helen, *b.* 1950.
Sisters living—Janet Meta, *b.* 1912 ; sometime Junior Com. A.T.S. : *m.* 1940, Francis William Alfred Fairfax-Cholmeley, CBE, of Balendoch, Meigle, Perthshire, and has issue living, Caroline Ann, *b.* 1941: *m.* 1961, Michael John Hippisley, of Tarrle Bank, by Arbroath, Angus, and has issue living, a son *b.* 1971, Fiona Jane *b.* 1964, Catherine Ann *b.* 1965, Lucinda Mary *b.* 1969,— Mary Meta, *b.* 1948: *m.* 1971, Lt. Mohamed Ali Dorgham Methoui, of 39, rue Alfred de Musset, Menzel-Bourgiuba, Tunis.——Elspeth Mary, *b.* 1913.——Katharine Andrea *b.* 1915; is a JP: *m.* 1940, George Macfarlan Sisson, OBE, and has issue living, John Edward *b.* 1943,—David George (2, Brunswick Hall, Penrith), *b.* 1945: *m.* 1970, Gillian, el. da. of Dr. Dennis Barnes, of Mayfield, Botchergate, Carlisle, and has issue living, Katherine Rachel *b.* 1971,—Alexander William, *b.* 1949,—Julia Andrea, *b.* 1952: *m.* 1972, Timothy Dallas Cairns. *Residence,* Pantrees, Wall, Hexham.

Collateral Branches living.

Grandchildren of the late Thomas Wedderburn-Ogilvy, son of the late Major John Andrew Wedderburn-Ogilvy (ante) :—
Issue of the late Donald Stephen Wedderburn-Ogilvy, Sub-Lieut. R.N.V.R., *b.* 1900, *d.* (killed in action during European War) 1941 : *m.* 1st, 1924, Mona Alys Eustace, who *d.* 1925 ; 2ndly 1929, Myra Carolyn Henrietta (of Inner Randells, The Hoe, Bosham, Sussex), da. of the late Lieut.-Col. Henry Montague Eustace. D.S.O. :—
(By 1st m.) Caryl Eustace (Pucklepeggies, 3A, Glassford St., Milngavie, Glasgow), *b.* 1925; ARIBA: *m.* 1953, Katharine Mary, da. of William Steele of Dundee, and has issue living, Niall, *b.* 1955,— Penelope, *b.* 1959,—Verity, *b.* 1965.——(By 2nd m.) Peter (Oaktree Cottage, Froxfield, Petersfield, Hants), *b.* 1931: Lt.-Cdr. RN (ret.): *m.* 1959, Philippa Sabine Burt, only child of the late Col. F. A. Woods, of Winchester House, St. Leonards, Sussex, and has issue living, Finella Sabine Clare, *b.* 1962,—Helen Augusta Sophia, *b.* 1964,—Andrea Henrietta Louise, *b.* 1968.——Alys (Denton Lodge, Shute End, Wokingham, Berks.), *b.* 1930: *m.* 1961, John Curtis Wernher Eustace, CIE, who *d.* 1972, and has issue living, Catherine Helena, *b.* 1962,—Cassandra Mary, *b.* 1963,—Margaret Alison (twin), *b.* 1963,—Emily Anne, *b.* 1967.

Grandson of the late Andrew Wedderburn-Maxwell, son of the late James Wedderburn, son of James Wedderburn Colvile, 3rd son of 5th baronet, who was el. son of 4th baronet of 1st creation :—
Issue of the late Major James Andrew Colvile Wedderburn-Maxwell, *b.* 1849, *d.* 1917, having assumed the additional surname of Maxwell 1896 : *m.* 1891, Helen Mary Godfrey, who *d.* 1946, da. of the late Rev. Henry Godfrey Godfrey-Faussett-Osborne, of Hartlip Place, near Sittingbourne :—
John, D.S.O., M.C., *b.* 1894 ; ed. at Charterhouse ; Brigadier (retired) late R.A.; European War 1914-18 (M.C.), European War 1939-43 (wounded, D.S.O.) ; D.S.O. 1943 : *m.* 1922, the Hon. Ann Madeline Cunliffe, da. of 1st Baron Cunliffe, and has issue living, Keir (P.O. Box 77, Rivonia, Johannesburg), *b.* 1924: *m.* 1st, 1951, Ann, da. of A. Brink, of Johannesburg; 2ndly, 1962, Janet, da. of Oliver Hodgkin, of Rivonia, Johannesburg, and has issue living, (by 1st marriage) John *b.* 1952, Philip *b.* 1954, (by 2nd m.) Andrew *b.* 1963, Adrian Keir *b.* 1965, Eloise *b.* 1967,— John Anthony (Brewers Farm, West Tisted, Alresford, Hants.), *b.* 1941: *m.* 1969, Priscilla Aileen Ann, da. of Maj. H. C. Mooney, of 37, Windermere Rd., Pietermaritzburg, Natal (and has issue living, Andrew Franklyn *b.* 1975, Claire Louise *b.* 1971),—Gillian (Riverdale, Dorney Reach, Maidenhead, Berks.), *b.* 1928; LRAM 19—; is an Asso. of Guildhall Sch. of Music: *m.* 1954, Robert Beaumont Shepheard, and has issue living, Simon Beaumont *b.* 1957, Janet Robina *b.* 1955, Anne Catherine *b.* 1963, Emma Gillian *b.* 1964,—Robina, *b.* 1932: *m.* 1960, Douglas John Turner, of Huntsman's Cottage, Whistley Green, Hurst, Reading, and has issue living, Amanda Jane *b.* 1961. *Residence,* The Granary, St. George's Hill, Weybridge. *Club,* Cavalry.

Grandchildren of the late Maj. James Andrew Colvile Wedderburn-Maxwell (ante):—
Issue of the late Henry Godfrey Wedderburn-Maxwell, MBE, *b.* 1897, *d.* 1970: *m.* 1948, Breda O'Connor:—
Andrew Patrick, *b.* 1949.——Harry, *b.* 1958.——Dorothy, *b.* 1952.

Grandchildren of the late Harry George Wedderburn, 2nd son of Andrew Wedderburn-Maxwell (ante):—
Issue of the late Charles Carmichael Wedderburn, *b.* 1882, *d.* 1951 : *m.* 1918, Jessie Mary who *d.* 1955, only da. of the late Walter Edwin Fairlie, of Bishopstone, Northwood :—
Michael Charles Fairlie, *b.* 1924 ; *m.* 1955, Mary Catherine, da. of Sidney George Esbester, of Duffield, Derbyshire, and has issue living, John Michael Champion, *b.* 1957,—Katherine Jane, *b.* 1958,—Claire Mary, *b.* 1962. *Residence,* Short Hoo, Hasketon, Woodbridge, Suffolk. *Address,* c/o American Overseas Petroleum Co., P.O. Box 693, Tripoli, Libya.——Maisie Jane Fairlie,

b. 1919: *m.* 1951, Francis Charles Wade, and has issue living, Nicholas, *b.* 1953,—David (twin), *b.* 1953. *Residence,* 51, Oxford Rd., Wokingham, Berks.

Issue of the late Lt.-Col. Harry Francis Keir Wedderburn, *b.* 1899, *d.* (on active ser. during 1939-45 War) 1943: *m.* 1929, Mary Sharp (Featherhouse, Mountquhanie, Cupar Fife), da. of Lt.-Col. Henry Alexander Bethune [*see* Bethune, Bt., colls.]:—

Andrew Harry Bethune WEDDERBURN-BETHUNE (Mountquhanie, Cupar, Fife) *b.* 1933; assumed 1959, the additional surname of Bethune after his patronymic; Capt. The Black Watch (ret.): *m.* 1960, Mary Felicity Lovat Frazer, and has issue living, Alexander Guy, *b.* 1965,—Patrick Keir, *b.* 1967,—Andrew Michael Stewart, *b.* 1969,—Charles Dominic, *b.* 1973,—Gabrielle Mary, *b.* 1962,—Francis Catriona, *b.* 1964.——Penelope Mary Bethune, *b.* 1930: *m.* 1949, John Piggott, and has issue living, John Wedderburn, *b.* 1950,—Robin Andrew Keir Wedderburn, *b.* 1957. *Residence,* Newholme, Spalding Rd., Weston Hills, Spalding, Lincs.

Granddaughter of the late Capt. Charles Francis Webster-Wedderburn, 2nd son of Sir James Webster-Wedderburn, grandson of Robert Wedderburn, 2nd son of 4th baronet (of 1st creation):—

Issue of the late Arthur Augustus Helyar **Webster-Wedderburn**, *b.* 1853, *d.* 1919: *m.* 1st, 1888, Katharine Elspeth Maude, who *d.* 1907, da. of the late Henry Charles Hamilton, C.S.I. [Hamilton, Bt., cr. 1646, colls.]; 2ndly, 1913, Henrietta Caroline Bradley, who *d.* 1946, da. of the late Thomas Henry Haddan, B.C.L., Bar.-at-law, and Fellow of Exeter Coll., Oxford :—

(By 1st m.) Dorothy Hamilton (The Old Stables, Bottingdean, Midhurst, Sussex), *b.* 1901: *m.* 1st, 1921, Capt. Richard P. Hewetson, formerly RFA; 2ndly, 1934, Maj.-Gdn. Allan Cholmondeley Arnold, C.I.E., C.B.E., M.C., late Roy. Fusiliers, who *d.* 1962, and has issue living, (by 1st marriage) Richard Tatton Wedderburn (of Stobars Hall, Kirkby Stephen, Westmorland), *b.* 1924; formerly Pilot Officer R.A.F.

Granddaughter of the late Maj. George Webster Wedderburn, yst. son of the late Sir James Webster-Wedderburn (ante):—

Issue of the late Maude Gertrude Annesley Webster-Wedderburn, *b.* 1866, *d.* 1930: *m.* 1st, 1892, Henry Alexander Hadden, who *d.* 1946; 2ndly, 1902, William Henry Rider, who *d.* 1914; 3rdly, 1915, Maj. Blaikie Harry Brownlow, R.A., who *d.* 1932:—

(By 1st m.) Betty Valentia (25, The Curve, Peel Common Estate, Rowner, Gosport, Hants.), *b.* 1893: *m.* 1921, William Stewart, and has issue living, Alexander (13, Mildred St., Whyalla, Norrie 5608, S. Aust.), *b.* 1922: *m.* 1953, Ellen Teresa Crowley, and has issue living, Darryl Alexander, *b.* 1956, Alan James *b.* 1957, John David *b.* 1960, Raymond Anthony *b.* 1961,—William (59, Hamilton Rd., Bishopstoke, Eastleigh, Hants) *b.* 1927; SRN, RMN; Dip SS London; Grad IPM; Capt. RAMC: *m.* 1948, Margaret Barns, and has issue living, John Arthur (49, Twyford Rd., Eastleigh, Hants., SO5 4HH), *b.* 1952: *m.* 1974, Anneliese, da. of Johann Lambert, of Sulzbach, Saarland, Germany, and formerly wife of Arthur Gover,—Peter W. *b.* 1957, David G. *b.* 1958, Mary A. *b.* 1949, Jean A. *b.* 1955.

Grandchildren of the late Lieut.-Col. John Walter Wedderburn, son of the late John Wedderburn, *b.* 1798, son of the late John Wedderburn, son of the late Thomas Wedderburn, 3rd son of 4th baronet (of 1st creation):—

Issue of the late Charles David St. Clair Wedderburn, O.B.E., *b.* 1864, *d.* 1931: *m.* 1898, Louisa Mary, who *d.* 1931, da. of the late Major J. E. Whaite:—

David Walter, *b.* 1899 ; is Major R.E.: *m.* 1925, Elizabeth, who *d.* 1950, da. of J. Robertson, of Perth, and has issue living, Patricia Helen Marjorie, *b.* 1927: *m.* 1950, Colin Henry du Plessis, of Cons Munch, Private Bag, Gravelotte, E. Transvaal, S. Africa, and has issue living, Robin St. Clair *b.* 1951, Richard Geoffrey *b.* 1952,—Averil Elizabeth Vernon *b.* 1932.

Granddaughter of the late James Alexander Wedderburn, son of the late John Wedderburn, *b.* 1798 (ante):—

Issue of the late Alexander Dundas Ogilvy Wedderburn, C.B.E., K.C, *b.* 1854, *d.* 1931: *m.* 1887, Mathilde, who *d.* 1898, da. of Henry William Segelcke:—

Margaret Griselda (*Lady Sutton*), *b.* 1888: *m.* 1st, 1912, Stuart Andros de la Rue, who *d.* 1927 [*see* de la Rue, Bt., colls.]; 2ndly, 1928, Air-Marshal Sir Bertine Entwistle Sutton, KBE, CB, DSO, MC, who *d.* 1946, and has issue living, (by 2nd m.) James (18, Greville Place, NW6) *b.* 1929: *m.* 1955, Margaret, da. of John Cecil Neve, of Wolverhampton, and has issue living, Tristram James *b.* 1956, Mark *b.* 1958,—Alfred Michael SUTTON-SCOTT-TUCKER (Riversbridge, Dartmouth, S. Devon), *b.* 1931; assumed by Roy. Licence 1967 the surname of Sutton-Scott-Tucker: *m.* 1961, Juliet Elizabeth, el. da. of the late Maj. Tristram Kirkwood, RE, and has issue living, Christopher Michael Guy *b.* 1962, Jonathan James *b.* 1963, Sophia Jane *b.* 1966, Lucy Elizabeth *b.* 1968. *Residence,* Little Park House, Brimpton, Reading, Berks.

Granddaughters of the late Alexander Dundas Ogilvy Wedderburn, CBE, KC (ante):—

Issue of the late Alexander Henry Melvill Wedderburn, CBE, *b.* 1892, *d.* 1968: *m.* 1921, Cynthia Margaret (Fieldside, Blewbury, Didcot, Berks.), da. of the late Cecil Lubbock [*see* B. Avebury, colls.]:—

Catherine Clarissa, *b.* 1925: *m.* 1955, James Francis Robinson, TD, JP, DL, of Bridge House, Gt. Barford, Beds., and has issue living, Adam James Nicholas, *b.* 1959,—David Thomas, *b.* 1962,— Harriet Clarissa *b.* 1957.——Elizabeth Jane, *b.* 1926: *m.* 1949, Nicolas Ralph Dolignon Furse, of Halsdon, Dolton, Winkleigh, Devon, son of Maj. Sir Ralph Dolignon Furse, KCMG, DSO, and has issue living, Mark Nicolas Ralph Dolignon, *b.* 1957,—Vanessa Jane, *b.* 1950,— Miranda Jill, *b.* 1951,—Corinna Margaret Dolignon, *b.* 1954.——Olivia Joan (The Cottage, Aston Tirrold, Didcot, Oxon.), *b.* 1934: *m.* 1957 (m. diss. 1972), Richard Weston Herbert, and has issue living, Catherine Alexandra, *b.* 1963.

Grandchildren of the late Alexander Henry Melvill Wedderburn, CBE (ante):— Issue of the late Major David Michael Alexander Wedderburn, *b.* 1922, *d.* 1960 : *m.* 1946, Marigold Diana Sneyd, BA, (who *m.* 2ndly, 1960, Maj. Warren Freeman-Attwood, of West Flexford, Wanborough, Guildford), da. of the late Edward Philips, OBE, of Alsop-en-le-Dale, Derbys:—

Robert David Alexander, BA, GRSM, *b.* 1948.——Henry Edward Alexander, *b.* 1954; Lt. Gren. Gds.——Sarah Catherine, *b.* 1952; ed. at Oxford Univ. (BA).

Sir John Wedderburn of Blackness, co. Forfar, an advocate and Clerk of Bills, was *cr.* a baronet of Scotland with remainder to his heirs male for ever. On the death of Sir John, 3rd Bt. in 1723, he was *s.* by Sir Alexander, 4th Bt. nephew of 1st Bt. Sir John, 5th Bt., having embraced the cause of the Stuarts, served as a volunteer at the battle of Culloden, where he was taken prisoner. He was executed on Kennington Common, 1746, and his estate forfeited. His descendants, however, continued to assume the title until Sir David (7th Bt. but for the attainder) PMG for Scotland, was *cr.* a Baronet of UK 1803 with special remainder to the heirs male of the 4th Bt. of the original creation. The 4th Bt., Sir William Wedderburn, MP for Banffshire (*L.*) 1893-1903, was *s.* in 1918 by his kinsman Sir John Andrew Wedderburn-Ogilvy (who assumed the surname of Ogilvy-Wedderburn 1918), 3rd in descent from James Wedderburn-Colville, yst. son of 5th Bt. (of first creation). His grandfather Peter Wedderburn *m.* 1811, Anna, da. and heir of James Ogilvy of Ruthven, co. Forfar, and assumed the surname of Wedderburn-Ogilvy on the death of his father-in-law 1826.

WEDGWOOD, Creation (U.K.) 1942, of Etruria, co. Stafford.

I split asunder obstacles.

Sir JOHN HAMILTON WEDGWOOD, *T.D.*, 2nd *Baronet*; *b.* Nov. 16th, 1907; *s.* his father, *Brig.-Gen. Sir* RALPH LEWIS, *C.B., C.M.G., T.D.*, 1956; ed. at Winchester, and Trin. Coll., Camb. (BA); FRSA, FRGS; Hon LLD Birmingham; Dep.-Chm. of Josiah Wedgwood & Sons, Ltd., of Barlaston, Stoke-on-Trent, 1955-66, and a Member of British National Export Council 1964-66; Chm. of Artistic Framing Ltd., Holsworthy, N. Devon, since 1970, and Chm. Anglo-American Community Relations Cttee. for Lakenheath USAF Air Base since 1971; Liveryman of Painter-Stainers' Co.; 1939-45 War as Maj. N. Staffs. Regt. and Gen. Staff: *m.* 1933, Diana, da. of the late Lt.-Col. Oliver Hawkshaw, of Chisenbury Priory, Marlborough, Wilts., and has issue.

Arms—Gules, four mullets in cross and a canton argent. Crest—On a ducal coronet, a lion passant argent. *Club*—Alpine.

Sons living—HUGO MARTIN (Pixham Mill, Pixham Lane, Dorking), *b.* Dec. 27th, 1933; ed. at Eton, and at Trin. Coll., Oxford: *m.* 1963, Alexandra Mary Gordon, el. da. of the late Judge Gordon Clark, of Berry's Croft, Westhumble, Dorking [*see* Lawrence, Bt. cr. 1867], and has issue living, Ralph Nicholas, *b.* 1964,—Julia Mary, *b.* 1966,—Frances Veronica Mary, *b.* 1969.——John Julian (Artistic Framing Ltd., Dobles Lane, Holsworthy, Devon), *b.* 1936; ed. at Stowe: *m.* 1961, Sheila Meade, of London, England, and has issue living, John Adam, *b.* 1962,—Rupert Julian, *b.* 1964,—Felix Hawkshaw, *b.* 1966.——Oliver Ralph (370, Central Park West, New York 10025, USA), *b.* 1940; ed. at Eton.

Daughter living—Germaine Olivia, *b.* 1944: *m.* 1965, David Posner, of Richmond House, Clare, Suffolk, and has issue living, Piers Oliver, *b.* 1966,—Dominic Tobias, *b.* 1968.

Sister living—*Dame* Cicely Veronica, *OM, DBE, b.* 1910; ed. at Lady Margaret Hall, Oxford (MA); Hon LLD Glasgow 1955, Hon DLitt Sheffield, Harvard, Oxford, Keele, Sussex, and Liverpool; FRHistS; Historian; Pres. of English PEN 1951-57, and English Assocn. 1955-56; a Trustee of Nat. Gallery 1962-68, and again since 1969; a Member of Roy. Commn. on Historical Manuscripts since 1953; an Officer of Order of Orange Nassau of the Netherlands; CBE (Civil) 1956, DBE (Civil) 1968, OM 1969.

Widow living of 1st Baronet—IRIS VERONICA (*Iris, Lady Wedgwood*), da. of Albert Henry Pawson, of Farnley, Leeds: *m.* 1906, Brig.-Gen. Sir Ralph Lewis Wedgwood, CB, CMG, TD, 1st baronet, who *d.* 1956. *Residence*,

The 1st baronet, Brig.-Gen. Sir Ralph Lewis Wedgwood, CB, CMG, TD, was Ch. Gen. Manager of LNER 1923-39, and Chm. of Railway Executive 1939-41. His el. brother Josiah Clement was cr. Baron Wedgwood 1942. Their father, Clement Francis Wedgwood, Master Potter, of Barlaston, Staffs., was great-grandson of Josiah Wedgwood, FRS, of Etruria, Staffs. (*d.* 1795), creator of the pottery which bears his name.

WEIGALL, Creation (U.K.) 1938, of Woodhall Spa, Lincoln. [Extinct 1952.]

Sir (WILLIAM ERNEST GEORGE) ARCHIBALD WEIGALL, *K.C.M.G.*, 1st and last *Baronet*.

Daughter living of 1st Baronet—Priscilla Crystal Frances Blundell: *m.* 1st, 1935, Viscount Curzon, CBE (who obtained a divorce 1943), later 6th Earl Howe; 2ndly, 1943, as his second wife, Harold Coriat, who *d.* 1970, and has issue living (by 1st m.) [*see* E. Howe],—(by 2nd m.), Christopher Archibald, *b.* 1954. *Residence*, Fartington, Cheltenham, Glos.

WELBY, Creation (U.K.) 1801, of Denton Manor, Lincolnshire.

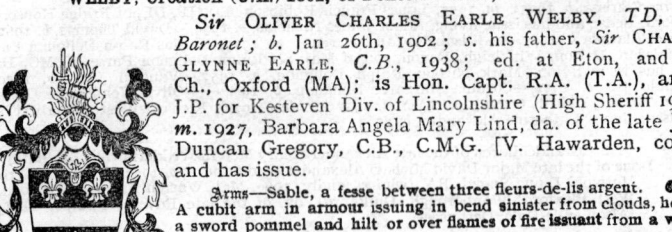

Per ignem, per gladium. By fire, by sword.

Sir OLIVER CHARLES EARLE WELBY, *TD*, 6th *Baronet*; *b.* Jan 26th, 1902; *s.* his father, *Sir* CHARLES GLYNNE EARLE, *C.B.*, 1938; ed. at Eton, and Ch. Ch., Oxford (MA); is Hon. Capt. R.A. (T.A.), and a J.P. for Kesteven Div. of Lincolnshire (High Sheriff 1953): *m.* 1927, Barbara Angela Mary Lind, da. of the late John Duncan Gregory, C.B., C.M.G. [V. Hawarden, colls], and has issue.

Arms—Sable, a fesse between three fleurs-de-lis argent. Crest—A cubit arm in armour issuing in bend sinister from clouds, holding a sword pommel and hilt or over flames of fire issuant from a wreath proper.

Seat—Denton Manor, Grantham. *Residence*—76, Burton Court, S.W.3.

Son living—RICHARD BRUNO GREGORY, *b.* March 11th, 1928; ed. at Eton, and at Ch. Ch., Oxford (B.A. 1950): *m.* 1952, Jane Biddulph, youngest da. of the late Ralph Hodder-Williams, of 82, Cadogan Place, S.W.1, and has issue living, Charles William Hodder, *b.* 1953,—Dominic John Earle, *b.* 1960,—Richard Henry Gregory, *b.* 1970,—Miranda Lind, *b.* 1955. *Residence*, 24, Ilchester Pl., W14.

Sisters living—Dorothy Geraldine (*Lady Saltoun*), *b.* 1890: *m.* 1920, the 19th Lord Saltoun. *Residences*, Cross Deep, Twickenham; Cairnbulg Castle, Fraserburgh, Aberdeenshire.——Joan Margaret (*Viscountess Portal of Hungerford*), *b.* 1898: *m.* 1919, the 1st Viscount Portal of Hungerford, who *d.* 1971 [*see* Bs. Portal of Hungerford]. *Residence*, West Ashling House, nr. Chichester.

Collateral Branches living.

Grandchildren of the late Edward Montague Earle Welby, 4th son of 3rd baronet:—

Issue of the late Edward Everard Earle WELBY-EVERARD, b. 1870, d. 1951, having assumed by Roy. licence 1894, the additional surname and arms of Everard : m. 1899, Gwladys Muriel Petra, who d. 1946, da. of the late Rev. G. W. Herbert :—

Philip Herbert Earle, DSC (Frieston Old Place, Caythorpe, Grantham, Lincs; United Service Club), b. 1902; Capt. RN (ret.); 1939-45 War (DSC); a JP for Leics., a DL for Lincs. (High Sheriff 1972), and a CStJ; Commr. for Lincs. St. John Ambulance Bde.: m. 1928, Lilla Anna Florence Maree Castell, JP, da. of the late Magnus Spence, of Springfontein, Fig Tree, Rhodesia, and has issue living, Glynne Earle (Ambelia Village, Kyrenia, Cyprus), b. 1935; ed. at Eton: m. 1963, Jan Plaisette, who d. 1973, da. of the late Milton Lee Stroud, of Texas, USA, and has issue living, Ariel Edward Earle b. 1970, Amanda Gay b. 1971, Ariadne Melissa b. 1972,—Roger Earle (Willowhayne, Bulstrode Way, Gerrards Cross, Bucks.), b. 1942; ed. at Eton; Lt. RN (ret.): m. 1966, Isabel Anne, da. of the late Maj. Lloyd Bucknall, and has issue living, Julian Richard Earle b. 1967, Patrick Jonathan Earle b. 1969, Anna Christabel b. 1974,—Elizabeth Janet, b. 1929: m. 1948, Capt. James Agnew, RM (ret.), of Glenlee Park, New Galloway, Kirkcudbrightshire, son of the late Sir Andrew Agnew, CBE, and has issue living, Richard b. 1950; ed. at Winchester, and Pembroke Coll., Oxford (BA), Malcolm b. 1952, Nicolette b. 1958,—Susan, b. 1931: m. 1959, George William Durrant, of Middle Paddock, Lyminster, Sussex, and has issue living, Henry b. 1960, Lucinda b. 1963, Georgina b. 1965.——Sir Christopher Earle, KBE, CB, b. 1909; ed. at Charterhouse and at Corpus Christi Coll., Oxford (BA); Maj.-Gen. (ret.), late R. Lincs. Regt.; a DL for Lincs.; High Sheriff 1974; Comd. 264th Scottish Beach Bde. (TA) 1954-57; BGS, HQ, BAOR and N. Army Group 1957-59, and Ch. of Staff, Allied Forces, N. Europe, Oslo 1949-61; GOC, Nigerian Army 1962-65; 1939-45 War (wounded, OBE); OBE (Mil) 1945, CB (Mil) 1961, KBE (Mil) 1965: m. 1938, Sybil Juliet Wake, da. of the late Guy Shorrock, of Sandford Orleigh, Newton Abbot, S. Devon, and has issue living, Peter Rodney Earle, b. 1942: m. 1972, Jennifer Frances, twin da. of Lt.-Col. S. T. C. Parsons-Smith, of Pill Heath Cottage, Andover, Hants.,—Hugh Earle (c/o Lloyds Bank, Grantham, Lincs.), b. 1944: Capt. RHA: m. 1970, Virginia Gresley, da. of Maj.-Gen. John Edward Longworth Morris, CB, CBE, DSO, of Marshgate, Tolleshunt D'Arcy, Essex, and has issue living, Louisa Gresley b. 1975. Residence, The Manor House, Sapperton, Sleaford, Lincolnshire. Club, Army and Navy. ——Clemence Penelope Olga, b. 1905; is a JP: m. 1929, Rear-Adm. St. John Aldrich Micklethwait, CB, DSO, and has issue living, John Douglas Pelham (Latches, Hurstbourne Tarrant, Andover, Hants.), b. 1933: m. 1959, Clarinda Margaret, da. of the late Lt.-Col. Michael Trethowan, OBE, of Haven Hill, Andover, Hants, and has issue living, John Julian Earle Pelham b. 1961, Michael St. John b. 1964,—Richard, b. 1938,—Diana b. 1931: m. 1957, Maj. Anthony John Ernest Tritton, Queen's Own Hussars (ret.), only son of Sir Geoffrey Ernest Tritton, CBE, 3rd Bt. Residence, Penhein, Chepstow, Mon.

Issue of the late Lieut.-Col. Sir Alfred Cholmeley Earle Welby, K.B.E., 7th son of 3rd baronet, b. 1849, d. 1937: m. 1898, Alice Desirée, who d. 1969, da. of the late A. E. Copland-Griffiths:—

Rannulf Alfred Earle, TD, b. 1902; ed. at Eton; Hon. Maj. RA (TA): m. 1938, Elizabeth Marjorie Buchanan, da. of the late James Smith, of Crosbie Tower Troon. Residence, Iden Park, Benenden, Kent.——Amyse Mary, b. 1900: m. 1929, Capt. Geoffrey Whitaker, formerly Coldm. Gds., of 77, Hurlingham Court, SW6, and has issue living, Camilla, b. 1934: m. 1960, Renaud Louis Thomas, of Annona Strasse 18, 8032, Zürich, Switzerland, and has issue living, Benjamin Louis b. 1961, Guy Alexander b. 1964, Letitia Juliette b. 1966.——Desiree Ann Eda, b. 1904: m. 1932, Capt. Gerald Richard de Capell-Brooke Guinness, Coldm. Gds., who d. 1975, and has issue living, Hugh Welby (Great Oakley Hall, Corby, Northants), b. 1937; ed. at Eton, and Trin. Coll., Camb. (BA): m. 1966, Bianca, da. of Col. Renzo della Pura Onorati, of Via Campigli 75, Varese, Italy, and has issue living, Alexander Edward b. 1968, Carolina Isabella b. 1970,—David Gerald Charles, b. 1939; ed. at Eton; BA Camb.,—Jessica Sybil, b. 1933. Residence, Chandos House, Chester St., Belgrave Sq., SW1.

Granddaughter of the late Henry Earle Welby, son of the late Rt. Rev. Thomas Earle Welby, D.D., 2nd son of 2nd baronet :—

Issue of the late Hugh Earle Welby, b. 1867, d. 1952: m. 1908, Evelyn Borradaile, MBE, who d. 1972, da. of Adam Bell, formerly Rhodesian Civil Ser.:—

Gwynyth Mary, b. 1910: m. 1937, Arthur Wyatt Aust, of Denton Farm, Essexdale, Rhodesia, and has issue living, John Charles Wyatt, b. 1942; Maj. Rhodesian Army: m. 1969, Pamela Drusilla Phillips, of Essexvale, Rhodesia,—Elizabeth Mary, b. 1940: m. 1966, Brian Tozer, of Salisbury, Rhodesia.

Grandchildren of the late Rt. Rev. Thomas Earle Welby, D.D. (ante) :—

Issue of the late Arthur Thomas Earle Welby, b. 1855, d. 1908: m. 1st, 1874, Phœbe, who d. 1895, da. of Capt. de Cew ; 2ndly, 1898, Maria, da. of J. F. Mitchell :—

(By 2nd marriage) Charles Earle, b. 1901: m. 1926, Lydia Elizabeth, da. of Harry L. Hunt, of Madison, Wisconsin, U.S.A., and has issue living, Arthur Earle, b. 1927.——(By 1st marriage) Wilhelmina Cecilia.——Helena Beatrice.——(By 2nd marriage) Muriel: m. 1921, Major Harold Godfrey St. George Morgan, who d. 1929, late R.M.A.

Issue of the late Frederick Earle Welby, F.R.C.S.E., b. 1858, d. 1900: m. 1883, Janet Anne, who d. 1935, da. of the late F. Henderson, of Wick, N.B. :—

Edith Jessie : m. 1st, 1920, William Adams, who d. 19—; 2ndly, 19—. Residence,

Grandchildren of the late Rev. Arthur Earle Welby, 3rd son of 2nd baronet :—

Issue of the late William Macdonald Earle Welby, b. 1845, d. 1885 : m. 2ndly, 1878, Jessie, da. of Frederick Lucas, of Grahamstown, S. Africa :—

Spencer Earle, b. 1879.——Glynne Earle, b. 1881.——Isabel Florence.——May.

Issue of the late Richard Earle Welby, b. 1854, d. 1932: m. 1st, 1886, Mary Isabelle, who d. 1892, da. of the late Thomas Paget, of Forton Lodge, near Lancaster ; 2ndly, 1899, Alice Frances Blackburne, 3rd da. of the late Lieut.-Col. Cyril Blackburne Tew, and widow of the late Vice-Adm. Frederick Charles Bryan Robinson [Crofton, Bt., cr. 1801, colls.]; 3rdly, 1918, Helen Mary, da. of the late Capt. Creagh Scott:—

(By 3rd marriage) Glynne Richard Earle, b. 1921 ; ed. at Camb. Univ. (B.A. 1948, M.A. 1957); Sqdn.Ldr. RAF (ret.); ACIS: m. 1st, 1945, Hilarie Elizabeth, who d. 1957, da of H. Cecil Rowse, of St. Austell, Cornwall; 2ndly, 1958, Margaret Mary yr. da. of the late Pius C. Brodrick, of Bolton, Lancs, and has issue living, (by 2nd marriage) Richard Edmund Charles b. 1961, (by 1st marriage) Elizabeth Anne, b. 1947,—Rosalyne Mary, b. 1950,— Penelope Jane, b. 1954, (by 2nd marriage) Elizabeth Mary, b. 1959. Address, c/o Lloyds Bank, Cambridge.

The Welbys are an ancient Lincolnshire family. The first known member was Rannulf de Welleby, mil. tenant of Wydo de Credun in Welby, near Grantham 1086. Sir John de Wellebi, son of Roger, gave land there to Vallis Dei Abbey in the reign of Stephen. The "Liber Niger Scaccarii," temp. Hen. II, records that Johannes de Wellebi held, in Welby, near Grantham, under Mauricius de Crun, a knight's fee and a half, "de antiquo feodo" enfeoffed before 1135. Many of them have successively sat in Parliament since 9 Henry V. The first who served as Sheriff of Lincolnshire was Roger de Welby in the 20 Richard II. The 1st, 2nd, and 3rd baronets successively represented Grantham in Parliament, and the 3rd baronet assumed the additional surname of Gregory. Sir William, 4th baronet, also sat as MP for Grantham (C) 1857-68 and for Lincolnshire S. 1868-84, and assumed by Roy. licence 1876 the additional surname of Gregory. The 5th Baronet was MP for Newark Div. of Notts (C) 1900-1906.

WELCH, Creation (U.K.) 1957, of Chard, co. Somerset.

Sir (GEORGE JAMES) CULLUM WELCH, O.B.E., M.C., 1st *Baronet*, only son of the late James Reader Welch of Chard, and Beckenham ; *b.* Oct. 20th, 1895 ; ed. at Alleyn's Sch., Dulwich ; admitted a Solicitor 1920 ; was a Member of the Court of Common Council of City of London (Ward of Candlewick) 1931-47 (Ch. Commoner 1946) ; an Alderman 1947-70, Sheriff 1950, and Lord Mayor 1956-57; a Member of City of London T & AF Assocn. 1941-65, a Lieut. of City of London, a Liveryman and Member of Court of Assists. of Haberdashers' Co. (Warden 1962-66, Master 1966-67), a Liveryman of Spectacle-makers' Co., a Liveryman and a Member of Court of Assists. of Solicitors' Co. (Master 1955), and Liveryman and Member of Court of Assists. of Paviors' Co. (Master 1957), and Parish Clerks' Co. (Master 1953 and 54), Chm. of Cttee. of Management London Homes for the Elderly, Gov. of Hon. The Irish Soc. 1967-70, Chm. of Trustees of Morden Coll. and Dep. Chm. of Exec. Cttee. of George VI Foundation; Registrar of Archdeaconry of London 1953-67, Hon. Col. Army Cadet Force of City of London 1953-65, and Hon. Col. City of London Bn., R. Fusiliers (TA) 1956-65; Pres. of City Livery Club 1943-44, Chm. of Florence Nightingale Hosp. 1954-63, and of Lord Mayor of London's National Hungarian and Central European Fund 1956-60, Vice-Chm. of Board of Govs. of Bethlem Roy. & Maudsley Hosps. 1953-66, a Member of Council of Law Soc. 1951-63, and Hon. Treasurer of UK Cttee., UN Children's Fund 1964-66; an Hon. Freeman of Chard, Somerset, of Bangor, co. Down, of New Orleans, of London, Ont. and of Granby, Canada, a KJStJ, an Officer of Order of Orange Nassau of the Netherlands, a Comd. of Orders of Dannebrog of Denmark, and of the Lion of Finland (1st class), and Grand Officer of Merit of Republic of Italy; has Order of Mercy; 1914-18 War as Capt. R. Berks. Regt. (MC); 1939-45 War as Lt.-Col. (OBE); *cr.* OBE (Mil) 1944, Knt. 1952: *m.* 1st, 1921, Gertrude Evelyn Sladin, who *d.* 1966, only da. of the late John William Harrison, of Stubbins, Lancs.; 2ndly, 1969, Irene Avril, da. of the late John Foster, OBE, and has issue by 1st m.

Arms—Or on a fesse gules between six martlets azure two lions passant respectant of the first Crest—An heraldic antelope's head erased or armed gules gorged with a collar composed of six pierced mullets azure chained also gules.

Residences—63, Marsham Court, SW1 P 4JZ; 43, St. Margarets, Rottingdean, Sussex; 6 Stone Bldgs., Lincoln's Inn, WC2A 3YG. *Club*—City Livery.

Son living—By 1st m. JOHN READER (Killara, The Glade, Kingswood, Surrey), *b.* July 26th, 1933; ed. at Marlborough, and at Hertford Coll., Oxford (MA); OStJ: *m.* 1962, Margaret Kerry, da. of Kenneth Douglass, of Killara, NSW, and has issue living, James Douglass Cullum, *b.* Nov. 10th, 1973, Margaret Trudy Cullum, *b.* 1965,—Jane Olive Comrie (twin), *b.* 1965.

Daughter living—By 1st m.—Rosemary Avril, *b.* 1927: *m.* 1st, 1952, (marriage dissolved 1963) John Osmond; 2ndly, 1963, Leighton Griffith Jones, of 4, Inglewood Court, Reading.

WELDON, Creation (I.) 1723, of Dunmore, co. Carlow.

Sir THOMAS BRIAN WELDON, 8th *Baronet*; *b.* May 19th, 1905; *s.* his brother *Sqdn.-Ldr.* Sir ANTHONY EDWARD WOLSELEY, 1971; ed. at Sherborne, and Magdalene Coll., Camb.; Capt. Princess Louise's Kensington Regt.: *m.* 1942, Marie Isobel, da. of the late Hon. William Joseph French [see B. de Freyne, colls.], and has issue.

Arms—Argent, a cinquefoil pierced gules, on a chief of the second a demi-lion issuant of the first. Crests—1st, a demi-lion rampant argent guttée de sang ; 2nd, the bust of Queen Elizabeth I. (granted by Queen Elizabeth I. as a special mark of favour).

Residence—Eastcote House, Dogmersfield, Basingstoke, Hants. *Club*—White's.

Son living—ANTHONY WILLIAM (White's and Brooks's Clubs), *b.* May 11th, 1947; ed. at Sherborne; late Lt. Irish Gds.; Gen. Ser. Medal S. Arabia.

Daughter living—Tara Louise Winifred, *b.* 1943: *m.* 1967, Alan Christopher Elliot, of The Old Rectory, Chilton Foliat, Hungerford, Berks., and has issue living, Sacha Louise, *b.* 1968, —Larissa Mary, *b.* 1970.

Well done

Collateral Branches living.

Issue of the late Sqdn.-Ldr. Terence Gordon Mackworth de Weltden Weldon, yst. son of 6th baronet, *b.* 1909, *d.* 1970: *m.* 1st, 1941 (m. diss. 1946), Suzanne Marie, da. of Percy Hopkinson, of Sea Barn, Kingston Gorse, Sussex; 2ndly, 1946, Simonne Mireille (from whom he obtained a divorce 1969), da. of Armand Philippon, of 25, Rue de L'Opera, Aix-en-Provence, France:—
By 2nd m.) Oonagh Serena Elizabeth, *b.* 1947.

Issue of the late Lieut.-Col. Henry Walter Weldon, D.S.O., 5th son of 5th baronet, *b.* 1878, *d.* 1925: *m.* 1909, Helen Louise Victoria, who *d.* 1965, da. of the late Sir Edward Porter Cowan, of Craig-a-vad, co. Down:—
Hamilton Edward Crosdill, *CBE*, *b.* 1910; ed. at Charterhouse; Brig. (ret.) late RA; an ADC to HM, and a DL of Greater London; Sec., TA & VR Assocn. for Greater London since 1968; Hon. Dep. Col. 6th (Volunteer) Bn. The Queen's Regt. 1971-72; 1939-45 War (despatches twice, French Croix de Guerre with palms); OBE (Mil) 1950, CBE (Mil) 1960: *m.* 1st, 1935, Margaret Helen Katharine (from whom he obtained a divorce 1946), da. of Maj. Frederic Passy, of Blachford, Cornwood, Devon; 2ndly, 1948, Elwyne Priscilla, da. of Harold Richards Chaldecott, OBE, of Chantry, Leyburn, Yorks, and has issue living, (by 1st m.) Wendy Juliet, *b.* 1937: *m.* 1960, Lt. Ian Fothergill Grant, RN, and has issue living, Jonathan James Fothergill *b.* 1962, Andrew William Edward Fothergill, *b.* 1963, Amanda Katherine Lindley *b.* 1968,—(by 2nd m.) Kevin Nicholas, *b.* 1951,—Mark Henry de Weltden, *b.* 1953; 2nd Lt. RA,—Andrea Sari Victoria, *b.* 1948. *Addresses*, 1, Left Wing, Duke of York's HQ, Chelsea, SW3; Loders, 23 Echo Barn Lane, Wrecclesham, Farnham, Surrey. *Clubs*,—Army and Navy, Hurlingham.——Aurea Elizabeth, *b.* 1915: *m.* 1942, Capt. Humphrey John James Stuart, RA [B. Norton], who *d.* 1969, and has issue living, Julian de Weltden, *b.* 1947. *Residence*, Potters Hill, Crondall, Farnham, Surrey.

Granddaughters of the late Col. Thomas Weldon, CIE, 5th son of 4th baronet:—
Issue of the late Major Francis Harry Weldon, D.S.O., *b.* 1869, *d.* 1920 : *m.* 1902, Eveleen, who *d.* 1955, da. of the late Thomas Fielden Campbell, of Devonshire Place, W.:—
Sybil May (Fairview, London Rd., Hurst Green, Sussex), *b.* 1906.
Issue of the late Walter Ivan Weldon, *b.* 1871, *d.* 1934 : *m.* 1899, Edith Lucy, who *d.* 1956, da. of Clifton Whiting, formerly of Ashtead Grange, Surrey :—
Violet Iva, *b.* 1900. *Residence*, Sentosa, 34, Summerdown Road, Eastbourne.

Grandchildren of the late Col. Francis Weldon (infra):—
Issue (by 2nd marriage) of the late Walter Langford Weldon, *b.* 1872, *d.* 1922 : *m.* 1st, 1904, Emma Anne, who *d.* 1905, da. of the late John Henry Tod, of 10, Courtfield Gdns., SW; 2ndly, 1910, Muriel Stewart, who *d.* 1966 (having *m.* 2ndly, 1924, Lt.-Col. William Weldon Herring-Cooper, CBE, DSO, who *d.* 1953), da. of William Richardson, formerly of 11, Harley House, Regent's Park, NW.
Francis William Charles, *MVO, MBE, MC* (The Stable Cottage, Wickwar, Glos.), *b.* 1913; ed. at Wellington Coll.; Lt.-Col. RA (ret.); 1939-45 War (despatches, prisoner, MC, MBE); MBE (Mil.) 1946, MVO (4th class) 1952: *m.* 1946, Diana Geraldine, da. of Stephen Anderson, of Straloch, by Blairgowrie, Perthshire, and has issue living, George William Daryl, *b.* 1946,—David Walter, *b.* 1949.——Patrick Langford Daryl, *MC*, *b.* 1917; ed. at Wellington Coll., and at Trin. Coll., Camb.; Maj. (ret.) RA; 1939-45 War with 2nd Bn. Wilts Regt., Korea 1951 (despatches, MC): *m.* 1955, Pamela Jane, da. of Col. L. B. Grant, of Burnt House, Benenden Kent, and has issue living, Thomas Daryl, *b.* 1963,—Guy Patrick *b.* 1967,—Anna Grant, *b.* 1958,—Sarah Kate, *b.* 1960. *Residence*, 18, Westbourne Park Rd., W2.——Evelyn Stewart (Maesderwen, Llanfrynach, Brecon), *b.* 1910; has Kaisar-i-Hind medal: *m.* 1931, Brig. Arthur Francis Gordon Forbes, MC, who *d.* 1970, and has issue living, John William Gordon (Brackenbury Cottage, Marlow Common, Bucks.), *b.* 1935: *m.* 1961, Angela Mary Dyce, da. of Sir Godfrey William Rowland Morley, OBE, and has issue living, Hamish Charles Gordon *b.* 1965, Amanda Phylis Gordon *b.* 1967,—Jean Penelope Gordon, *b.* 1932: *m.* 1955, Simon Richard Latham Deverell, and has issue living, Fiona Claire *b.* 1961, Julia Louise *b.* 1964.——Joan Valerie, *b.* 1921: *m.* 1965, Maj. Derrick Peter Henry Dyson, RA (ret.), of The Old Forge, Horningsham, Warminster, Wilts.

Issue of the late Lt.-Col. Ernest Steuart Weldon, CBE, DSO, *b.* 1877, *d.* 1946: *m.* 1916, Helen Cecilia, who *d.* 1966, da. of the late Alfred Greaves, of Haversham, Bucks.:—
Arthur Reginald (Beanlands Park, Irthington, Carlisle), *b.* 1918; ed. at Wellington; Maj. RA; 1939-45 War: *m.* 1945, Dorothy Ann, only child of William Monkhouse Pratchitt, of Crosby-on-Eden, Cumberland, and has issue living, Steuart William Pratchitt, *b.* 1947,—Robert Arthur de Weltden, *b.* 1950.——Hugh de Weltden (Turner House, Marlborough Coll., Wilts.), *b.* 1925; ed. at Wellington, and at Christ's Coll., Camb.

Issue of the late Col. Francis Weldon, 6th son of 4th baronet, *b.* 1836, *d.* 1926 : *m.* 1871, Henrietta Frances Alicia, who *d.* 1922, da. of the late Langford Kennedy:—
Winifred Edith, *b.* 1883: *m.* 1916, Capt. Montagu Herbert Hartcup, formerly R.A.S.C., who *d.* 1957, and has issue living, Guy Rider Monyns, *b.* 1919; ed. at Lancing Coll., and at St. Catharine's Coll., Camb. (BA 1917, MA 1949); in Historical Section, HM Treasury; 1939-45 War as Lt. Roy. Berks Regt. and Roy. Indian Army Ser. Corps: *m.* 1953, Baroness Henriette, da. of the late Baron Johann Ludwig Alfons Pereira-Arnstein, and widow of Leonard Greaves. *Residence*, The Little House, Whitchurch, Reading.

Granddaughters living of the late Rev. Lewen Burton Weldon, DD, 7th son of 4th baronet:—
Issue of the late Lewen Francis Barrington Weldon, M.C. (Surveyor-Gen. of Egypt 1919-23), *b.* 1875, *d.* 1958 : *m.* 1904, Mary Macaulay, who *d.* 1946, el. da. of the late Lawrence Bomford Molloy, J.P., of Clonbeale, Birr, King's co. :—
Olivia Mary, *b.* 1905; Junior Com. A.T.S.; European War 1939-45. *Residence*, 31, Khartoum Road, Weymouth, Dorset.

Issue of the late Lieut.-Col. Kenneth Charles Weldon, D.S.O., *b.* 1877, *d.* 1958 : *m.* 1906, Constance Elizabeth Jane, who *d.* 1960, only da. of the late Major William Croker, Roy. Inniskilling Fusiliers, of Byblox, Doneraile, co. Cork :—
Elinor Constance (Grants Farm, Gallows Hill, Wareham, Dorset), *b.* 1913.——Clemence Jane (Norden Heath, Corfe Castle, Wareham, Dorset), *b.* 1915.

The patent of the 1st baronet, Sir Thomas Burdett was conferred with remainder to the male issue of his sister Anne, wife of Walter Weldon. Col. Sir Anthony A. Weldon, C.V.O., D.S.O. 6th Bt., a J.P. for Queen's co. and co. Kildare; was State Steward and Chamberlain to Lord-Lieut. of Ireland and Lieut. of co. Kildare; he *d.* (result of active ser. in France) 1917.

WELLS, Creation (U.K.) 1944, of Felmersham, co. Bedford.

He who endures patiently conquers.

Sir CHARLES MALTBY WELLS, *T.D.*, 2nd
Baronet, b. July 24th, 1908 ; s. his father, Sir
(SYDNEY) RICHARD, 1956 ; ed. at Bedford
Sch., and at Pembroke Coll., Camb. ; is Lieut.-
Col. R.E. : m. 1935, Katharine Boulton, da. of
Frank Boteler Kenrick, of Toronto, Canada,
and has issue.

Arms—Gules between two pallets a garb or bound
with a ribbon azure buckled of the second pendant therefrom a hunting horn sable strings of the third between two
fountains. **Crest**—A demi bear sable muzzled gules the
sinister paw resting on a portcullis chained or.

Residence—37, Duggan Av., Toronto, Canada.

Sons living—CHRISTOPHER CHARLES (244, Lytton
Blvd., Toronto, Ont., Canada, M5N 1R6), b. Aug. 12th,
1936; ed. at McGill and Toronto (MD) Univs.: m. 1960,
Elizabeth Florence Vaughan, da. of I. F. Griffiths, of
Outremont, Quebec, and has issue living, Michael
Christopher Gruffydd, b. 1966,—Geoffrey Charles
Vaughan, b. 1970,—Felicity Elizabeth Boulton, b. 1964,
Megan Sarah Kenrick, b. 1969.——Anthony Richard,
b. 1947: m. 1969, Frances Jane, da. of Brig. Gerard
Boycott, of Berwick, Vic., Aust.
Brothers living—David Franey, M.C., b. 1913 ; ed. at
Bedford Sch. ; Major (retired) R.A. ; European War
1939-44 (M.C.) : m. 1948, Patricia Mary, da. of the Rev.
Reginald Henry Goode, R. of Houghton Conquest
Bedford, and has issue living, Thomas Franey,
b. 1951. *Residence*, Kerro-Mooar, Cleat Hill, Ravensden,
Bedford.——George Crichton, b. 1914; ed. at Bedford
Sch., and at Pembroke Coll., Camb. (MB and BCh 1939);
MRCP London 1946, FRCP 1959; Maj. RAMC; 1939-45 War: m. 1951, Margaret Caroline, da.
of the late Dr. Lewis Campbell Bruce. *Residence*, 15, Hereford Square, SW7.——Oliver John,
b. 1922; ed. at Uppingham; Wing Com. (ret.) RAF; 1939-45 War; DL for Beds. 1964; High
Sheriff 1970: m. 1949, Felicity Anne, da. of Brig. Maurice Edward Mascall, DSO, OBE, and has
issue living, Michael Mascall, b. 1951,—Paul Richard, b. 1958,—Joanna Fleicity, b. 1953. *Residence*, Ickwell Grange, Beds. *Club*, RAF.
Sisters living—Sydney Mary, b. 1917: m. 1938, Com. George Edward Pollington Milburn,
R.N., and has issue living, Edward Barnaby Pollington, b. 1944,—Phillippa, b. 1939,—
Georgina, b. 1940. *Residence*, Sibton, Saxmundham, Suffolk.——Sarah Josephine (twin),
b. 1922 ; formerly in W.R.N.S. : m. 1947, Michael Oliver John Gibson, M.D., M.R.C.P., and has
issue living, James Michael, b. 1950,—Timothy Wells, b. 1952. *Residence*, 39, Ladbroke Square,
W.11.

Collateral Branch living.
  Issue of the late Lieut.-Com. Christopher Hayward Wells, R.N., 2nd son of 1st
    baronet, b. 1909, d. (killed in action during European War) 1940 : m. 1937,
    Christina Hilary [(*Lady Henry*): she m. 2ndly, 1949, Sir James Holmes Henry,
    C.M.G., M.C., T.D., Q.C., 2nd Bt.], da. of Sir Hugh Oliver Holmes, K.B.E.,
    C.M.G., M.C., Q.C. :—
John Hayward (Old Rectory, Sheldon, Kimbolton, Hunts.; Royal Thames Yacht Club), b. 1938;
ed. at Harrow, and at Pembroke Coll., Camb.: m. 1965, Heather Donriel, da. of John Gordon
Christie Kelly, MC, of Cape Town, and has issue living, Christopher Hayward, b. 1966,—Richard
Michael, b. 1967,—Peto John, b. 1970.

   The 1st baronet, Sir (Sydney) Richard Wells (son of the late Charles Wells, of Bedford,
was Chancellor of Primrose League 1946-8, and sat as M.P. for Bedford Div. of Bedfordshire (*U*)
1922-45.

WELLS, Creation (U.K.) 1948, of Hove, co. Sussex. [Extinct 1966.]
Sir FREDERICK MICHAEL WELLS, 1st and last *Baronet*.

Daughters living of 1st Baronet—Elfreda Catherine, b. 1911: m. 1937, Andreas Dalein Wassenaar,
and has issue living, Andreas Michael, b. 1938,—Frederick Dalein, b. 1940,—Robert du Toit,
b. 1949,—Patricia Margaretha, b. 1944. *Residence*, Steinkop, Boshoff Ave., Newlands, Cape
Town, S. Africa.——Patricia Frances, b. 1913: m. 1948, Capt. Alan Pearce Greenaway, King's
Regt. [*see* Greenaway, Bt.]. *Residence*, The Doone, Byfleet Rd., Cobham, Surrey.

WERNHER, Creation (U.K.) 1905, of Luton Hoo Park, Luton, Bedfordshire.
[Extinct 1973.]
Sir HAROLD AUGUSTUS WERNHER, *GCVO, TD,* 3rd, and last *Baronet*.

Daughters living of 3rd Baronet—Georgina, b. 1919: m. 1944, Lt.-Col. Harold Pedro Joseph Phillips,
FRGS, Colm. Gds., and has issue living, Nicholas Harold, b. 1947,—Alexandra Anastasia
(*Marchioness of Hamilton*), b. 1946: m. 1966, James, Marquess of Hamilton, el. son of 4th Duke of
Abercorn,—Fiona Mercedes, b. 1951: m. 1971, James Comyn Amherst Burnett of Leys [*see*
B. Amherst of Hackney, colls.],—Marita Georgina, b. 1954,—Natalia Ayesha, b. 1959. *Resi-
dences*, Checkendon Court, Checkendon, Reading; 15, Grosvenor Sq., W.1; Ardhuncart Lodge,
Alford, Aberdeen.——Myra Alice, b. 1925: m. 1946, Major David Henry Butter, M.C., Scots
Guards, of Pitlochry, and has issue living, Charles Harold Alexander, b. 1960,—Sandra Elizabeth
Zia, b. 1948,—Marilyn Davina (*Lady Ramsay*) b. 1950: m. 1973, James Hubert, Lord Ramsay,
son of 16th Earl of Dalhousie,—Rohays Georgina, b. 1952,—Georgina Marguerite, b. 1956. *Resi-
dence*, 15, Grosvenor Sq., W1; Cluniemore, Pitlochry, Perthshire.
Daughter living of 2nd Baronet—Anna Alexandra (10, Cornwall Mews South, Grenville Pl., S.
Kensington, SW7), b. 1924.
Widow living of 3rd Baronet—Countess ANASTASIA TORBY (*Lady Zia Wernher*), (Luton Hoo,
Luton, Beds.); raised to title and precedence of an Earl's daughter 1917; el. da. of the late
Grand Duke Michael Michaelovitch of Russia, and the late Countess de Torby: m. 1917, Sir
Harold Augustus Wernher, GCVO, TD, 3rd Bt., who d. 1973, when the title became ext.

PRESCOTT-WESTCAR, Creation (G.B.) 1794, of Theobalds Park, Hertfordshire.
[Extinct 1959.]

Sir WILLIAM VILLIERS LEONARD PRESCOTT-WESTCAR, *D.S.O.*,
7th and last *Baronet.*

Daughter living of 7th Baronet—Jellis, *b.* 1926. *Residence,*

Widow living of 5th Baronet—Elizabeth Hughes, da. of William Mercer, of California, USA, and widow of Arthur Grier Fell: *m.* 2ndly, 1932, Sir George Lionel Lawson Prescott, 5th Bt., who *d.* 1942; 3rdly, 1953 (m. diss. 1957), Capt. Peregrine Fellowes, Irish Guards.

WESTON, Creation (U.K.) 1926, of Kendal, co. Westmorland. [Extinct 1926.]

Sir JOHN WAKEFIELD WESTON, 1st and last *Baronet.*

Daughter living of 1st Baronet—Mary Elizabeth : *m.* 1912, Capt. Herman James Lindale Willink, who *d.* (killed in action during European War) 1918, and has issue living, Christopher Alfred, *b.* 1913 : *m.* 1945, Rachel Anne, da. of Henry Christopher Pinckney, of The Mount, Papcastle, Cockermouth, Cumberland, and has issue living, James Christopher, *b.* 1954, Judith Kate *b.* 1946, Elizabeth Anne *b.* 1948, Patricia Mary *b.* 1950. *Residence,* Wester Wooden Hill, Kelso, Roxburghshire.

WHEELER, Creation (U.K.) 1920, of Woodhouse Eaves, co. Leicester.

Sir JOHN HIERON WHEELER, 3rd *Baronet;*
b July 22nd, 1905; *s.* his brother, *Sir* ARTHUR (FREDERICK PULLMAN), 1964; ed. at Charterhouse: *m.* 1929, Gwendolen Alice, da. of the late Alfred Ernest Oram, of Kirby Muxloe, nr. Leicester, and has issue.

Arms—Sable, a chevron between in chief two talbots heads erased and in base an eagle displayed or. *Crest*—A talbot's head erased sable, eared and charged on the neck with a catherine wheel or.
Residence—39, Morland Av., Stoneygate, Leicester.

Sons living—JOHN FREDERICK (Frostenden Hall, Frostenden, Suffolk), *b.* May 3rd, 1933: *m.* 1963, Barbara Mary, da. of Raymond Flint, of Leicester, and has issue living, John Radford, *b.* 1965,—Andrew Charles, *b.* 1969,—Jane Louise, *b.* 1964.——Benjamin (Benscliffe Hay Cottage, Newtown Linford, Leics.), *b.* 1935: *m.* 1962, Brenda Ellen, da. of the late Arthur Goodman, of Syston, Leics., and has issue living, Miles John, *b.* 1962,—Edward James, *b.* 1964,—Matthew Benjamin, *b.* 1966,—Rebecca Mary, *b.* 1972.
Sister living—Nancie Radford. *Residence,* Holme-next-the-Sea, Norfolk.

Widow living of 2nd Baronet—Alice Webster (*Alice, Lady Wheeler*) (E12, Marine Gate, Marine Parade, Brighton 7, BN2 5TQ), da. of the late George Heath Stones: *m.* 1938, Sir Arthur (Frederick Pullman) Wheeler, 2nd Bt., who *d.* 1964.

The 1st baronet, Sir Arthur Wheeler (son of the late Benjamin Wheeler, of Northampton) was High Sheriff of Leicestershire 1922.

Wheeler Cuffe, see Cuffe.

WHELER, Creation (E.) 1660, of City of Westminster, co. London.

Up to the mark.

Sir TREVOR WOOD WHELER, 13th *Baronet ; b.* Sept. 20th, 1889; *s.* his father, *Lieut. Col. Sir* EDWARD, 1903; ed. at Radley; Capt. R. Sussex Regt. 1914-20, attached Indian Army (NW Frontier), and Capt. RE (Movements) 1940-46; Control Commn. for Germany 1947-50; Kenya Reserve Police 1952 (Gen. Ser. Medal); Kenya 1952: *m.* 1915, Margaret Idris, da. of the late Sir Ernest Woodford Birch, KCMG, and has issue.

Arms—Or a chevron between three leopards' faces sable. *Crest*—On a ducal coronet or, an eagle displayed gules.
Residence, 19, Knole Court, Knole Rd., Bexhill-on-Sea, Sussex.

Son living—EDWARD WOODFORD (25, Cavendish Rd., Chesham, Bucks.) *b.* June 13th, 1920; ed. at Radley; Overseas Audit Dept. 1948-58; formerly Capt. Roy. Sussex Regt.: *m.* 1945, Molly Ashworth, da. of the late Thomas Lever, late Gold Coast Civil Ser., and has issue living, Trevor Woodford (43, Harlington Rd., Hillingdon Village, Middx.), *b.* April 11th, 1946; ed. at St. Edmunds, Canterbury: *m.* 1974, Rosalie Margaret, da. of Ronald Thomas Stunt,—Dinah Margaret, *b.* 1947: *m.* 1968, Clive Richard Knight (4, Elm Garth, Roos, E. Yorks.), and has issue living, Anthony Clive Wheler *b.* 1969, Simon Mark *b.* 1972.

Daughters living—Audrey Idris (Flat 48, The Sackville, Middlesex Rd., Bexhill-on-Sea), *b.* 1916: *m.* 1940, Maj. John Humphrey Wightwick, late Suffolk Regt., who *d.* 1970, and has issue living, Christopher Kenneth Wheler (c/o Coutts & Co., Royex House, Aldermanbury Sq., EC2), *b.* 1940: *m.* 1966, Sarah Gordon Macdonald, and has issue living, Kathryn *b.* 1969,—Simon John Patrick Wheler, *b.* 1949: *m.* 1973, Annee Alfsen, of Oslo, Norway,—Nigel Martin Humphrey Wheler, *b.* 1951,—Vanessa Ann Margaret Wheler, *b.* 1947: *m.* 1970, John Bray Needham, of Upper Whiston, Yorks., and has issue living, Gavin Timothy *b.* 1971.——Diana Edmée, *b.* 1918: *m.* 1941, Leslie Francis Gordon Pritchard, MBE, TD, of The Garden House, Dewhurst, Wadhurst, Sussex, and has issue living, Caroline Jane, *b.* 1943: *m.* 1966, Dean Edward Fischer,— Susan Letitia, *b.* 1947: *m.* 1972, Roderic Hill,—Anne Charlotte, *b.* 1948: *m.* 1973, Todd Civardi,— Rachel Sarah *b.* 1955.

Sisters living—Feridah Audrey : *m.* 1915, Julian Nathan, Lieut. The Buffs, who *d.* 1948, and has issue living, Christina Mary, *b.* 1916: *m.* 1957, John Robert Carden Teale, and has issue living, Mary Christina Beatrice, *b.* 1959. *Residence*, 18, Wilbury Rd., Hove, Sussex.— Cordelia Edmée (Layhams House, Layhams Rd., Keston, Kent): *m.* 1907, Oliver Plunkett, Judge of Supreme Court, Colonial Ser. and Mixed Courts, Egypt (ret.), who *d.* 1971, and has issue living, Patrick Trevor, *b.* 1908,—Edward Oliver, *b.* 1909,—John, *b.* 1910.

Collateral Branches living.

Grandchildren of the late Lt.-Col. Francis Henry Wheler (infra):—
Issue of the late Capt. Trevor Wheler, *b.* 1888, *d.* 1967: *m.* 1935, Enid (Winster, Tintern Av., Toorak, Melbourne, Australia), da. of the late H. R. Stokes:—
Glynne Henry Trevor, *b.* 1941,——Jane Frances Trevor, *b.* 1938: *m.* 1962, Kenneth Ross Thompson (Nesscroft, Box 381, P.O. Griffith, NSW), and has issue living, Susan Jane, *b.* 1963,—Jennifer Anne Frances, *b.* 1965.

Issue of the late Lieut.-Col. Francis Henry Wheler, 2nd son of 10th baronet, *b.* 1848. *d.* 1932: *m.* 1885, Jenny, who *d.* 1932, da. of the late John Highett, of Weymouth, Dorset, and of Highton, Victoria:—
Francis Glynne, *b.* 1891; ed. at Wellington Coll.: *m.* 19—, Winifred Ethel, da. of the late N. B. White. *Residence*, Alveston, St. John's Close, Launceston, Cornwall.

Granddaughters of the late Aubrey Stuart Wheler (infra):—
Issue of the late Stephen Jameson Wheler, *b.* 1907, *d.* 1967: *m.* 1950, Annette, who *d.* 1968, da. of Frank Eden Smith:—
Amanda (The Flat, 8, High St., Ditchling, Sussex), *b.* 1952.——Jacqueline, *b.* 1956.

Granddaughters of the late Col. Charles Stuart Wheler, 3rd son of 10th baronet:—
Issue of the late Aubrey Stuart Wheler, *b.* 1877, *d.* 1934: *m.* 1904, Blanche Christina, who *d.* 1946, only da. of S. W. Jameson, formerly of 28, Princes Square, Bayswater, W.:—
Elinor Jameson, *b.* 1906: *m.* 1st, 1926 (m. annulled on her petition 1932), Edward Fraser Walter; 2ndly, 1936, Charles Peter Graham Engelbach, and has issue living, (by 2nd m.) Flora Caroline Starr, *b.* 1942,—Sally Elinor, *b.* 1944. *Residence*, The Old Barn, Shottery, Stratford-on-Avon. ——Rosemary Blanche Jameson, *b.* 1919: *m.* 1948, Douglas Victor Gordon Feltham, MB, BCh, and has issue living, John Leander, *b.* 1955,—Hoonie Rosemary Anne, *b.* 1950; adopted by deed poll 1972 the first Christian name of Hoonie. *Residence*, Walnut Tree House, Hampton Wick, Kingston upon Thames.

Granddaughters of the late Rev. Henry Trevor Wheler, son of the late Charles John Wheler, 2nd son of 7th baronet:—
Issue of the late Commodore William Alfred Wheler, *b.* 1843, *d.* 1933: *m.* 1879, Mary Margaret, who *d.* 1918, da. of the late William John Cumming, M.R.C.S.:—
Mary Glynne (c/o Cookhayes Guest House, Moretonhampstead, Devon), *b.* 1887: *m.* 1914, the Rev. John Augustus Kirby, who *d.* 1962, and has issue living, Mary Aline Glynne, *b.* 1915: *m.* 1935 (m. diss. 1949), Lt.-Cdr. George Robert May Robertson, RN, and has issue living, Ian Antony *b.* 1937, Robert Edward *b.* 1939, Elizabeth Janine *b.* 1946.

The 1st baronet, Sir William, was M.P. for Queensborough *temp.* Charles II., and his wife was Laundress to the Royal Family. The 2nd baronet, Col. Sir Charles, his cousin, who succeeded by a special limitation, was Governor of the Leeward Islands, M.P. for Cambridge University in the Long Parliament, and one of the gentlemen entrusted to carry the plate of that University to Charles I. The 9th baronet, Lieut.-Col. Sir Trevor, served throughout the Peninsular War, including Waterloo ; and the 10th baronet, Lieut.-Gen. Sir Francis, C.B., served in Bundlecund 1821-2, in Afghanistan 1839-40, in the Punjab 1848-9, and in Indian Mutiny 1858-9.

WHICHCOTE, Creation (E.) 1660, of The Inner Temple, London.
[Dormant or Extinct 1949.]

Sir HUGH CHRISTOPHER WHICHCOTE, 10th and last *Baronet*.

Daughters living of 10th Baronet—Isolda Sophia, *b.* 1910.——Diana Juliane (Horseshoe Cottage, Revesby Bridge, Revesby, Boston, Lincs.), *b.* 1911.

WHITAKER, Creation (U.K.) 1936, of Babworth, Nottinghamshire.

SPES ET FIDES

Hope and faith

Sir JAMES HERBERT INGHAM WHITAKER,
3rd *Baronet* ; *b.* July 27th, 1925 ; *s.* his father, *Maj.-Gen.* Sir JOHN ALBERT CHARLES, *C.B.*, *C.B.E.*, 1957; ed. at Eton; late Major Sherwood Rangers, Imperial Yeo. (T.A.) ; European War 1944-45 in N.-W. Europe and Palestine as 2nd Lieut. Coldstream Guards : *m.* 1948, Mary Elizabeth Lander, da. of Ernest Johnston, of Cockshut, Reigate, and widow of Capt. David Urling Clark, M.C., and has issue.

Arms—Per pale argent and azure a chevron embattled between three mascles counterchanged. **Crest**—A horse passant argent, gorged with a collar gemel, and resting the dexter foreleg on a mascle azure.

Seats—Babworth Hall, Retford, Notts.; Auchnafree, Dunkeld, Perthshire.

Son living—JOHN JAMES INGHAM, *b.* Oct. 23rd, 1952.

Daughter living—Shervie Ann Lander, *b.* 1950: *m.* 1971, David William James Price, of 23, Claylands Rd., SW8, and has issue living, William James Emlyn, *b.* 1973,— Hesther Jane Lander, *b.* 1971.

Brothers living—Rev. David Arthur Edward (Feniton Rectory, Honiton, Devon), *b.* 1927; ed. at Eton, and New Coll., Oxford; formerly Lt. Colm. Gds.; is a Clerk in Holy Orders: *m.* 1956, Susan Mary, da. of the Rev. Canon Richard Hamilton Babington, of St. Mary-le-Tower, Vicarage, Ipswich, and has issue living, Robert John, *b.* 1957,—Michael Benjamin, *b.* 1960,—Jonathan *b.* 1972,—Caroline Lucy, *b.* 1959,—Iona Ruth, *b.* 1963.——Benjamin Charles George (13, Elsworthy Rd., NW3), *b.* 1934; ed. at Eton, and New Coll., Oxford; Bar. Inner Temple 1959; formerly 2nd Lt. Coldm. Gds.; author of " The Police " 1964, "Crime and Society " 1967, editor of "A Radical Future " 1967; " Participation and Poverty " 1968, " Parks for People " 1971, and " The Foundations " 1974; editor of " The Fourth World " 1972; PPS to Min. of Overseas Development 1966 and to Min. of Housing and Local Govt. 1966-67 and Parl. Sec., Min. of Overseas Development 1969-70; MP for Hampstead (*Lab.*) 1966-70; Dir. of Minority Rights Group since 1971: *m.* 1964, Janet Alison, da. of Alan Stewart, of Beeston, and has issue living, Daniel Peter Alan, *b.* 1966, Rasaq Andrew Ian, *b.* 1972,—Quincy Rachel Suzy, *b.* 1968.

The 1st baronet, Col. Sir Albert Edward Whitaker, C.B.E., T.D. (son of the late Joseph Whitaker, of Hesley Hall, Notts), was a J.P. and D.L. for Notts (High Sheriff 1921) and Lord High Steward of E. Retford. The 2nd baronet, Maj.-Gen. Sir John Albert Charles Whitaker, C.B., C.B.E., late Coldstream Guards, was High Sheriff of Nottingham 1950, and Lord High Steward of E. Retford 1952-7. He commanded Coldstream Guards 1937-39, and was Director of Mil. Training 1942-45.

WHITE, Creation (U.K.) 1802, of Wallingwells, Nottinghamshire.

LOYAL · UNTO · DEATH.

Sir THOMAS ASTLEY WOOLLASTON WHITE,
5th *Baronet*; *b.* May 13th, 1904 ; *s.* his father, *Sir* ARCHIBALD WOOLLASTON, 1945 ; ed. at Wellington Coll.; FRICS; a JP for Wigtown; Hon. Sheriff Substitute for Wigtownshire: *m.* 1935, Daphne Margaret, da. of the late Lt.-Col. Francis Remi Imbert Athill, CMG, OBE, DL, of Brinkburn, High House, Longframlington, Northumberland, and has issue.

Arms—Gules, a chevron vaire between three lions rampant or. **Crest**—Out of a ducal coronet argent, a demi-eagle displayed sable.

Residence, Torhousemuir, Wigtown, Wigtownshire.

Daughter living—Bridget Juliet, *b.* 1936: *m.* 1962, Lt.-Cdr. Charles David Orr Ewing, RN [*see* Orr Ewing, Bt. colls., cr. 1886]. *Residence*, Torhousemuir, Wigtown, Wigtownshire.

Brother living—RICHARD TAYLOR, D.S.O., *b.* Jan. 29th, 1908 ; Capt. (retired) R.N.; European War 1939-45 (despatches, D.S.O. and two Bars); D.S.O. 1940 (Bars 1941 and 1942): *m.* 1936, Gabrielle Ursula, younger da. of the late Capt. Robert Henry Style [*see* Style, Bt., colls.], and has issue living, Nicholas Peter Archibald, *b.* 1939 ; ed. at Eton: *m.* 1970, Susan Irene, da. of G. W. B. Pollock, of Blackrock, co. Dublin, and has issue living, Christopher David Nicholas, *b.* 1972,—Robert Leslie *b.* 1945; ed. at Eton,—Richard Mark (twin), *b.* 1945; ed. at Eton,—Victoria Rosamond, *b.* 1937: *m.* 1965, David Ashton Ashton-Bostock, of 49, Gloucester St., SW1, Henrietta Sophia *b.* 1967,—Jocelyn Henrietta, *b.* 1943: *m.* 1966, Michael Christopher Mallock, of Saddlers, Doddington, Sittingbourne, Kent. *Residence*, Wateringbury Place, nr. Maidstone.——Archibald John Ramsay, *CBE, DSC, b.* 1910; Capt. RN (ret.); 1939-45 War (despatches, DSC); CBE (Mil) 1963: *m.* 1949, Marguerite Elise, only da. of the late Sir Ernest Nathaniel Bennett, and has issue living, Thomas Charles Ramsay, *b.* 1952; 2nd Lt. 9th/12th R. Lancers,—John Woollaston, *b.* 1958,—Caroline Marguerite, *b.* 1950,—Sarah Elizabeth, *b.* 1960. *Residence*, Flatlands, Aysgarth, Leyburn, Yorks., DL8 3SI

Collateral Branches living.

Grandchildren of the late John White (infra):—
Issue of the late George Towry White, *b.* 1889, *d.* 1973: *m.* 1922, Evangeline (Balcraigie, Waitomo Caves, RD4, Tekuiti, NZ), da. of the late John Arthur, of Feilding, NZ:—
John Woollaston (Balcraigie, Waitomo Caves, RD4, Tekuiti, NZ), *b.* 1923.——George Towry, *b.* 1925.——Louis Arthur Taylor (Otorohanga, NZ), *b.* 1928: *m.* 1957, Gladys Daphne, only da. of

John Stokes, farmer, of Kinohaku, NZ, and has issue living, Stanley George, b. 1958,—Norman John, b. 1959,—Jeffrey Taylor, b. 1964,—Jocelyn Amy Anne, b. 1961,—Miriam Una, b. 1962,—Patricia Gladys (twin), b. 1964,—Eva Marie, b. 1966.——Marion Penelope, b. 1926.——Harriet Cicely, b. 1929: m. 1960, Robert Wallace Geange, of Waitomo, RD4, Tekuiti, NZ, and has issue living, Stephen Robert, b. 1961,—Lloyd Taylor, b. 1965,—Rosalie Marion, b. 1962,—Daphne Sylvia, b. 1963.

Granddaughters of the late Rev. Taylor White, 2nd son of 1st baronet:—
Issue of the late John White, b. 1839, d. 1911 : m. 1876, his cousin, Louisa Caroline, who d. 1915, da. of the late George Towry White, Bar.-at-law :—
Amy Anne Cecil, b. 1884.   Residence, Sundial, Fairfield Rd., Orpington, Kent.——Penelope Errington (Newhaven Downs Hospital, Newhaven, Sussex), b. 1885.——Cicely Bridget Heathcote, b. 1894.   Residence, 66, Ambleside Av., Telscombe Cliffs, Sussex.——Joyce Alice Finderne, b. 1897.   Residence, 64, Ambleside Av., Telscombe Cliffs, nr. Newhaven, Sussex.

(In special remainder.)
Descendants (if any) of the late Lieut.-Col. Taylor White, brother of 1st baronet.

Sir Thomas Woollaston White, 1st baronet, who was created with remainder to his father's issue male, was 7th in descent from Thomas White, of Tuxford Manor, Notts, who m. Anne Cecil, sister of the famous William, Lord Burghley.

WHITE, Creation (U.K.) 1904, of Cotham House, Bristol.

Sir GEORGE (STANLEY MIDELTON) WHITE, 3rd *Baronet;* b. April 11th, 1913; s. his father, *Sir* (GEORGE) STANLEY, 1964; ed. at Harrow, and at Magdalene Coll., Camb.: m. 1939, Diane Eleanor, da. of the late Bernard Abdy Collins, CIE, formerly of Deccan House, Aldeburgh, and has issue.

Arms—Barry wavy of six argent and azure, over all a lymphad sable, on a chief of the second two roses of the first.   Crest—Upon a mount vert a beacon fired proper, pendent therefrom a sail azure charged with a rose as in the arms.

Residence—Pypers, Rudgeway, nr. Bristol.

Son living—GEORGE STANLEY JAMES (Hawkesbury Stoke, Hawkesbury, Badminton, Avon), b. Nov. 4th, 1948; ed. at Harrow: m. 1974, Susan Elizabeth, da. of the late John Langmaid Ford.

Daughter living—Daphne Eleanor, b. 1945: m. 1969, Jonathan Wheeler, of 2, Hasker St., SW3, and has issue living, Robert Frederick William George, b. 1972.

The 1st baronet, Sir George White, head of the firm of George White and Co., of Bristol, was one of the pioneers of Electric Street Traction (being the first to introduce it into London, Dublin, Bristol, Middlesbrough, etc.), and established the first manufactory of Aeroplanes in England, and introduced " Bristol " Biplanes and Monoplanes.

WHITE, Creation (U.K.) 1922, of Salle Park, Norfolk.

Go forward not back.

Sir JOHN WOOLMER WHITE, 4th *Baronet;* b. Feb. 4th, 1947; ed. at Cheltenham Coll.; s. his father, *Sir* HEADLEY DYMOKE, 1971.

Arms—Quarterly, 1st and 4th, argent, a fesse chequy gules and or, over all a bend engrailed azure, an arrow point downwards of the field, *White;* 2nd and 3rd, azure, a lion rampant between four estoiles or, *Dymock.*   Crest—A boar's head erased proper, pierced through the mouth with an arrow or.

Residence—Salle Park, Reepham, Norfolk.

Sisters living—Morna, b. 1944.——Isabelle Sarah, b. 1948.
Uncle living (son of 2nd baronet)—LYNTON STUART, MBE, TD, b. Aug. 11th, 1916; ed. at Harrow, and at Trin. Coll., Camb.: 1939-45 War in Far East as Lt.-Col. RA (despatches, MBE); MBE (Mil) 1943: m. 1945, Phyllis Marie Rochfort, da. of Sir Newnham Arthur Worley, KBE, and has issue living, Anthony Douglas, b. 1946,—Richard Lynton, b. 1953,—Robert Newnham Stuart, b. 1956,—Philip Dymoke, b. 1958,—Katharine Anne Rochfort, b. 1949. Residence, Oxenbourne House, East Meon, nr. Petersfield, Hants.

Aunts living (daughters of 2nd baronet)—Marguerite Isabelle (*Lady Martell*), b. 1920: m. 1941, Vice-Adm. Sir Hugh Colenso Martell, KBE, CB, and has issue living, Richard James (Littlecourt Farm, Hambrook, Chichester), b. 1942: m. 1966, Theresa Hannah Wickins, and has issue living, Jonathan James b. 1969, Jeremy Paul b. 1971,—Stuart (1, High St., Bosham, Sussex) b. 1943: m. 1968, Penelope Gay, da. of the late Christopher Hunt, of North Farm, Washington, Sussex, and has issue living, Benjamin Stuart b. 1969,—Charles, b. 1946: m. 1968, Monica, da. of Martin Gillman, of Gloucester, and has issue living, Charles Edward b. 1971, Elizabeth b. 1969, Timothy Hugh, b. 1952,—Michael Gordon (twin), b. 1952,—Sarah Jessica, b. 1957.   Residence, Long Reach, Bosham Hoe, nr. Chichester, Sussex.——Hélène Pauline b.

1924; MA: *m.* 1954, Lt.-Col. William Neville Cairns, King's Dragoon Gds. (ret.), who *d.* 1973, and has issue living, Jeremy Dymoke Russell, *b.* 1955,—Patrick Neville, *b.* 1957. *Residence,* Alderton House, New Ross, co. Wexford.

Great Aunt living—(daughter of 1st baronet)—Pauline. *Residence,* 72, Bowes Hill, Rowlands Castle, Hants.

Widows living of 2nd and 3rd Baronets—ISABELLE STUART (*Dowager Lady White*) (2, Swan Close, Emsworth, Hants, P10 7BQ), da. of the late James George MacGowan, of Paris: *m.* 1912, Sir (Rudolph) Dymoke White, 2nd Bt., who *d.* 1968.——ELIZABETH VICTORIA MARY (*Lady White*), (Salle Park, Reepham, Norfolk), da. of the late Wilfrid Ingram Wrightson [*see* Wrightson, Bt., colls.]: *m.* 1943, Sir Headley Dymoke White, 3rd Bt., who *d.* 1971.

Sir Woolmer White, 1st baronet, was son of the late Maj. Timothy White, of Salle Park, Norfolk.

WHITE, Creation (U.K.) 1937, of Boulge Hall, co. Suffolk.

NON·SIBI·SED·ALIIS

Not for self but for others.

Sir CHRISTOPHER ROBERT MEADOWS WHITE, 3rd *Baronet*; *b.* Aug. 26th, 1940; *s.* his father, *Sir* (ERIC) RICHARD MEADOWS, 1972; ed. at Bradfield Coll.: *m.* 1962, Anne Marie Chislaine, yr. da. of the late Maj. Tom Brown, OBE, MC.

Arms—Gules, a chevron nebuly between three boars' heads couped, two fluanches argent each charged with a cross patée of the field. Crest—In front of a demi tower gules, issuant therefrom, a boar's head argent, tusked and maned or, charged on the neck with a cross patée also gules, three crosses patée also argent.

Residence—The Hill House, Northrepps, Cromer, Norfolk.

Aunts living (daughters of 1st baronet)—Elizabeth Margaret, *b.* 1906: *m.* 1941, William Elwyn Francis Evans, formerly Sqdn. Ldr. RAFVR, and has issue living, Charles William, *b.* 1942; MRCS, LRCP London; Surg. Lt. RN,—Sarah Margaret, *b.* 1946. *Residence,* Godshill Wood, Godshill, Fordingbridge, Hants.——Esther Dorothy, *b.* 1914; formerly 3rd Officer WRNS: *m.* 1943, Lt.-Cdr. John Michael Chappell, RN, and has issue living, Rodney Guy Eaton, *b.* 1944; Lt. RN:] *m.* 1971, Sarah M. Bromhead, and has issue living, Katharine Mary *b.* 1972,—David Nigel, *b.* 1946; Capt. 9th/12th R. Lancers. *Residence,* Bayfield House, Darby Green, nr. Camberley, Surrey.

Widow living of 2nd Baronet—ANN HERON (*Ann Lady White*), (The Vine, Presteign, Radnorshire), da. of Alexander Gerald Eccles, of Caldy House, W. Kirby, Cheshire: *m.* 1947, as his 2nd wife, Sir (Eric) Richard Meadows White, 2nd Bt., who *d.* 1972.

The 1st baronet, Sir Robert Eaton White, V.D. (son of the late Robert Holmes White, of Boulge Hall, Suffolk), was a J.P. and D.L. for Suffolk, and Chm. of E. Suffolk Quarter Sessions, and Co. Council, and served during European War 1914-17 as Lieut.-Col. Comdg. 14th Batn. Suffolk Regt. (T.F.).

White (Jervis-White-Jervis), see Jervis.

DALRYMPLE-WHITE, Creation (U.K.) 1926, of High Mark, co. Wigtown.

Virtus·sibi·munus

Virtue is worth.

Sir HENRY ARTHUR DALRYMPLE DALRYMPLE-WHITE, *D.F.C.*, 2nd *Baronet*; *b.* Nov. 5th, 1917; *s.* his father, *Lieut.-Col. Sir* GODFREY DALRYMPLE, 1954; ed. at Eton, at Magdalene Coll., Camb., and at London Univ.; formerly Wing-Com. R.A.F. Vol. Reserve; European War 1939-45 (D.F.C. and Bar); *m.* 1948 (marriage dissolved 1956), Mary, da. of Capt. Robert Thomas, and has issue.

Arms—Quarterly, 1st and 4th, vert, a naval crown or between three roses argent, barbed and seeded proper, in centre chief an escutcheon argent charged with a representation of the gold medal presented to Adm. Sir John Chambers White for his services in Egypt in the year 1801, pendant from a riband tenné, *White*; 2nd and 3rd, or, on a saltire azure between two water bougets in pale sable nine lozenges of the field, *Dalrymple*. Crest—1st issuant from a coronet composed of four roses set upon a rim or a lion's head argent, *White*; 2nd, in front of a rock proper water bouget sable, *Dalrymple*.

Address—c/o Brown, Shipley, Ltd., Founders Court, Lothbury, EC2.

Son living—JAN HEW, *b.* Nov. 26th, 1950; ed. at Stowe.

Sister living—Merial Catherine Dalrymple, *b.* 1913: *m.* 1936, Lieut.-Col. William Reeve, Grenadier Guards (retired), and has issue living, John, *b.* 1937,—Christopher William, *b.* 1944,—Peter Richard, *b.* 1947. *Residence,* Leadenham House, Lincolnshire.

Sir Godfrey Dalrymple Dalrymple-White, 1st Bt. (son of Gen. Sir Henry Dalrymple White, K.C.B., who commanded 6th Inniskilling Dragoons throughout Crimean War), was Lieut.-Col. Grenadier Guards, served in S. Africa 1900-02 and in European War 1914-18. He assumed by deed poll 1926, the additional surname of Dalrymple, and sat as M.P. for Southport Div. of Lancashire (C) 1910-18, and for Southport 1918-23 and 1924-31.

WHITEHEAD, Creation (U.K.) 1889, of Highfield House, Catford Bridge, Kent.

By pluck and work.

Sir ROWLAND JOHN RATHBONE
WHITEHEAD, 5th *Baronet ; b.* June 24th, 1930 ;
s. his father *Major Sir* PHILIP HENRY RATH-
BONE, 1953 ; ed. at Radley, and at Trin. Hall,
Camb. (B.A. 1953); late 2nd Lieut. R.A.; a
Trustee of Rowland Hill Benevolent Fund,
and Gov. of Appleby Gram. Sch.: *m.* 1954,
Marie-Louise, da. of Arnold Christian Gausel,
of Stavanger, Norway, and has issue.

Arms—Per pale azure and sable, on a fesse invected
and plain cottised or between three fleurs-de-lis of the
last, a fasces erect between two eagles' heads erased
proper. Crest—An eagle, wings expanded proper, each
wing charged with a fasces erect or, supporting with the
dexter claw an escutcheon of the arms.
Residence,—Sutton House, Chiswick Mall, W.4.
Clubs,—Reform, City University.

Son living—PHILIP HENRY RATHBONE, *b.* Oct. 13th,
1957.
Daughter living—Philippa Martha Gausel, *b.* 1955.

Brother living—Peter James Palmer (twin), (Pillar House,
Harwell, Berks.), *b.* 1930; ed. at Radley, and at Trin.
Hall, Camb. (BA); a Member of Inst. of Biology, and of
American Soc. of Ichthyologists and Herpetologists; late
2nd Lt. RA: *m.* 1st, 1953 (m. diss. 1960), Monica, who *d.*
19—, only da. of J. O'Dwyer, of co. Tipperary; 2ndly,
1967, Greta Maureen Caecelia, da. of Frederick John
Ransom, of Greenwich, and has issue living (by 2nd m.),
Victoria-Augusta Gordon, *b.* 1968,—Peter Rathbone
Palmer, *b.* 1970.

Daughters living of 2nd Baronet—Christobel, *b.* 1891 : *m.* 1917, Pierre de Putron, O.B.E.
(Jurat of Roy. Court of Guernsey) who *d.* 1950, and has issue living, John Whitehead, *b.* 1929;
ed. at Eton, and at Trin. Coll., Oxford (MA); FCA, MIMC: *m.* 1959, Evelyn Hastings, el. da.
of the late A. S. F. Pruen, of Cheltenham, and has issue living, Peter Nicholas *b.* 1963, Timothy
Richard *b.* 1964, Frances Alison *b.* 1961,—Mary *b.* 1922; MA 1951: *m.* 1944, C. C. Russell Vick,
and has issue living, Rosemary *b.* 1945, Susan *b.* 1950, Christabel *b.* 1956. *Residence*, Lower
Bertozerie, Guernsey.—Sylvia Mercy Ascroft, *b.* 1899: *m.* 1933, the Rev. James Walter
Herbert Nankivell, BLitt, who *d.* 1953, and has issue living, Hensley Robert George, *b.* 1934; ed.
at Trin. Coll., Oxford. *Residence*, Edendale, 146, Old Bath Rd., Cheltenham.

Widow living of 4th Baronet—Margery, da. of the late E. W. Hickes, of Brasted Hall, Kent;
m. 3rdly, 1946 as his second wife, Sir Philip Henry Rathbone Whitehead, 4th Bt., who *d.* 1953 ;
4thly, 1959, Capt. Sydney Alick Harrison-Smith, CBE, R.N. (ret.). *Residence*, Cedarwood
Cottage, S. Moreton, Berks.

Collateral Branches living.

Issue of the late Lt.-Col. Gilbert Rathbone Whitehead, TD, yr. son of 3rd
baronet, *b.* 1910, *d.* 1968: *m.* 1934, Adeline Joy, BA (Warborough, Oxon.:
61, Marlborough Place, St. John's Wood, NW8), only child of the late Sydney
F. Rumball, of St. Leonards-on-Sea:—

Gilia Fleur, *b.* 1936; BA Oxford: *m.* 1960, Martin Oliver Slocock, of Larkenshaw, Stonehill Rd.,
Chobham, Woking, Surrey, and has issue living, Oliver Rowland Benjamin, *b.* 1964,—Thomas
Gilbert, *b.* 1969,—Eleanor Sophia (twin), *b.* 1964.——Celia Lynette, *b.* 1939: *m.* 1970, Edward
Raphael Rowe, of 16, Weygates Drive, Hale Barns, Altrincham, Ches., WA15 0BW.——Anthea
Margaret Joy, *b.* 1943: MA Edinburgh: *m.* 1972, John Valentine Hutchinson.

Issue of the late Gilbert Hinds Whitehead, 3rd son of 1st baronet, *b.* 1866, *d.*
1908: *m.* 1901, Helena Emmeline, who *d.* 1949, only da. of the late Henry A.
Langford, of Plymouth:—

Margaret Joy, *b.* 1905: *m.* 1st, 1928, Lt.-Com. John Brett, DSC, RN, who *d.* (killed in action)
1941; 2ndly, 1965, Lt.-Col. Robert Clement Giles, late RM, who *d.* 1970, and has issue living
(by 1st m.), Martin Brett, *b.* 1939: *m.* 1962, Barbara Miles, of NZ, and has issue living, Matthew
b. 1964, John *b.* 1965, Catherine *b.* 1966,—Susan, *b.* 1929: *m.* 1951, Michael Dawbarn Oliver, of
Ingleborough House, E. Runton, Cromer, and has issue living, James Anthony Robert *b.* 1959,
Edward George *b.* 1961, John Charles *b.* 1969, Caroline Mary *b.* 1953, Sarah Elizabeth *b.* 1954,
Teresa Clare *b.* 1964, Mary Cecilia *b.* 1965,—Jenifer, *b.* 1931: *m.* 1954, Brian Joseph Brooke-
Smith, Bar.-at-law, of Wyse's House, Widdington, Saffron Walden, Essex, and has issue living,
John *b.* 1958, Elizabeth *b.* 1956. *Residence*, July Cottage, The Street, Puttenham, Guildford.

Grandchildren of the late Lt.-Col. Wilfred James Whitehead, DSO, 4th son of
1st baronet:—

Issue of the late John Chase Whitehead, MBE *b.* 1913, *d.* 1956: *m.* 1941, Lorna Davey,
who *d.* 1974, da. of Walter Rupert Belk:—
Carolyn, *b.* 1946: *m.* 1967, Patrick Georghegan Smyth, BA, of 10, Rapson Rd., Morningside,
Durban, S. Africa, and has issue living, Dominic, *b.* 1970,—Siobahn, *b.* 1972,—Bridget, *b.* 1974.
——Saffron Ann *b.* 1948, BSc, PhD: *m.* 1974, Christopher Robert Butler, BSc, PhD, of 14,
Aberdeen Rd., N5.——Nicola Jane, *b.* 1956.

The 1st baronet, Sir James, was Lord Mayor of London 1888-9, and sat as M.P. for
Leicester (L) 1892-4 ; his Baronetcy was conferred upon him "in recognition of highly valuable
services during an eventful Mayoralty," in the course of which he was instrumental in settling
the great Dock Strike. The 3rd baronet, Sir Rowland Edward, K.C., sat as M.P. for Essex, S.-E.
Div. (L) 1906-10. Sir Philip Henry Rathbone Whitehead, 4th Bt., was Major Oxfordshire
and Bucks LI, a Gov. of Appleby Gram. Sch., and a Trustee of Rowland Hill Benevolent Fund.

HUNTINGTON-WHITELEY, Creation (U.K.) 1918, of Grimley, Worcester.

Sir HUGO BALDWIN HUNTINGTON-WHITE-LEY, 3rd *Baronet; b.* March 31st, 1924; *s.* his father *Capt. Sir* (HERBERT) MAURICE, *RN*, 1975; ed. at Eton; CA; a DL of Worcs; High Sheriff 1971; 1939-45 War (despatches): *m.* 1959, Jean Marie Ramsay, JP, da. of the late Arthur Francis Ramsay Bock.

Arms—1st and 4th, per fesse daecette sable and gules in chief a pale or, thereon three bars of the second, in base a fleur-de-lis argent, *Whiteley ;* 2nd and 3rd or, on a pale between two roses in fesse gules, barbed and seeded proper, a lion rampant between two water bougets of the first, *Huntington.* Crests, 1st, a stag's head couped argent, attired or, holding in the mouth a bell gold, *Whiteley ;* 2nd, upon a mount vert a lion's head couped at the neck or, gorged with a collar vair between two roses gules, barbed, leaved and stalked proper, *Huntington.*

Residence—Ripple Hall, Tewkesbury, Glos. *Clubs*, United Service and Brooks's.

Brother living—(JOHN) MILES, *VRD* (29, Drayton Gdns. SW10), *b.* July 18th, 1929; ed. at Eton and at Trin. Coll. Camb.; Lt.-Cdr. RNR; VRD and clasp: *m.* 1960, Countess Victoria Adelheid Clementine Louise, da. of the late Count Friedrich Wolfgang zu Castell-Rudenhausen [*see* ROYAL FAMILY], and has issue living, Leopold Maurice, *b.* 1965,—Alice Louise Esther Margot, *b.* 1961,—Beatrice Irene Helen Victoria, *b.* 1962.

Widow living of 2nd Baronet—*Lady* (PAMELA) MARGARET BALDWIN (*Lady Margaret Huntington-Whiteley*) (8, Crown Lea Av., Barnards Green, Malvern, WR14 2DP), da. of 1st Earl Baldwin, of Bewdley: *m.* 1919, Sir (Herbert) Maurice Huntington-Whiteley, 2nd baronet, who *d.* 1975.

Collateral Branch living.

Issue of the late Eric Arthur Huntington-Whiteley, *b.* 1903, *d.* 1972: *m.* 1st, 1929, Enid Etta Cohn, who obtained a divorce 1938; 2ndly, 1938, Evelyn Mary (Elliots Land, Mortimer West End, Reading), da. of the late Henry Munt, and formerly wife of Denis Clarke:—

(By 1st m.), Nigel Charles (The Cottage, Charlwood, Horley, Surrey), *b.* 1931; ed. at Radley: *m.* 1956, Gillian Margaret, da. of Jacob Franks, MRCS, LRCP, of W. Chiltington, Sussex, and has issue living, Charles Andrew, *b.* 1957,—James Alexander, *b.* 1963,—Kate Elizabeth, *b.* 1959.— Philip Cecil (Hill Grove, Clytha, Abergavenny, Gwent), *b.* 1933; ed. at Radley: *m.* 1968, Susan Laird, da. of Maj.-Gen. George Warren Richards, CB, CBE, DSO, MC, of Trewarren, Abergavenny, and has issue living, George Adam, *b.* 1971,—Camilla Mary, *b.* 1970.

The 1st baronet, Sir Herbert James Huntington-Whiteley (son of the late George Whiteley of Woodlands, Blackburn, and brother of 1st Baron Marchamley), was M.P. for Ashton-under-Lyne (C) 1895-1906, and for Mid., or Droitwich Div. of Worcestershire 1916-18, and assumed by Roy. licence 1918, for himself and issue, the additional surname and arms of Huntington. His wife, Florence Kate, who *d.* 1948, was el. da. of William Ball Huntington, DL, of Woodlands, Darwen, Lancs.

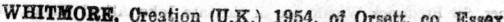

WHITMORE, Creation (U.K.) 1954, of Orsett, co. Essex.

Sir JOHN HENRY DOUGLAS WHITMORE, 2nd *Baronet ; b.* Oct. 16th, 1937; *s.* his father, *Col. Sir* FRANCIS HENRY DOUGLAS CHARLTON, K.C.B., C.M.G., D.S.O., T.D., T.E.D., 1962 ; ed. at Eton: *m.* 1962 (m. diss. 1969), Ella Gunilla, el. da. of Sven A. Hansson, of Danderyd, Sweden, and has issue.

Arms—Quarterly: 1st and 4th, vert fretty or: 2nd and 3rd, vert, fretty and a canton or charged with a cinquefoil azure pierced of the second. Crest—1st, a falcon sitting on the stump of a tree with a branch springing from the dexter side all proper; 2nd, an arm couped at the elbow erect and habited or, turned up azure, holding in the hand, proper a cinquefoil of the second pierced of the first, slipped vert, all within two wings expanded gold.

Residence—1267, Vich, Vaud, Switzerland.

Daughter living—Tina, *b.* 1966.

Sister living—Anne Catherine, *b.* 1933: *m.* 1966, Daniel Jose Emilio O'Connell, (Presidente Roca 150, Adrogué, FCGR, Buenos Aires, Argentina), and has issue living, Lucy Elizabeth, *b.* 1967,—Patricia Elena, *b.* 1969,—Anna Elisa, *b.* 1970.

Mother living—Ellis Christense (*Ellis, Lady Whitmore*) (a D.St.J.), el. da. of Knud Christian Johnsen, of Bergen, Norway: *m.* 1931, as his second wife, Col. Sir Francis Henry Douglas Charlton Whitmore, K.C.B., C.M.G., D.S.O., TD, TED, 1st Bt., who *d.* 1962. *Residence*, Orsett House, Orsett, Grays, Essex.

Sir William Whitmore of London (descended from Whitmores of Claverley, Salop) purchased the estate of Apley, Salop and *d.* 1648. His son, Sir Thomas Whitmore, was created a Bt. 1641. This title became ext. on the death of the 2nd Bt. in 1699. The present baronet descends from Richard Whitmore of Lower Slaughter, Glos, brother of 1st Bt. (cr. 1641). Capt. Thomas Charles Douglas Whitmore of Orsett Hall, Essex, father of 1st Bt. (cr. 1954), sold Apley in 1867.

WIGAN, Creation (U.K.) 1898, of Clare Lawn, Mortlake, Surrey, and Purland Chase, Ross, Herefordshire.

Make use of your opportunity.

CARPE DIEM

Sir FREDERICK ADAIR WIGAN, 4th Baronet : *b.* April 13th, 1911 ; *s.* his father, *Sir* RODERICK GREY, 1954.

Arms—Vair, on a pile or a mount in base vert, thereon a mountain ash tree proper. Crest—On a mount vert a mountain ash tree surmounted by a rainbow, all proper.

Residences—Borrobol, Kinbrace, Sutherland ; Paston Hall, near Norwich.

Brother living—ALAN LEWIS (Badingham House, Badingham, Woodbridge, Suffolk) *b.* Nov. 19th, 1913; ed. at Eton, and at Magdalen Coll., Oxford; Capt. KRRC Rifle Corps (Reserve of Officers); 1939-45 War (wounded, prisoner): *m.* 1950, Robina, da. of Lt.-Col. Sir Iain Colquhoun, 7th Bt., KT, DSO, LLD, and has issue living, Michael Iain, *b.* 1951.—Rebecca, *b.* 1953.

Sister living—Joan Yvonne, *b.* 1914: *m.* 1957, Hubert F. P. Rutter, of The Old Rectory, Kilve, Bridgwater, Somerset, son of the late Sir Frederick William Pascoe Rutter.

Great-Uncle living (son of 1st baronet)—Edgar Clare, *b.* 1876 ; ed. at Eton, and at Lincoln Coll., Oxford: *m.* 1909, Cicely Margaret, who *d.* 1960, da. of the late Col. Charles Hervey Bagot, C.B., of Brook Cottage, East Grinstead. *Residence,* Bradstone Brook, Shalford, Guildford. *Club,* Carlton.

Widow living of 3rd Baronet—INA (*Lady Wigan*), da. of Lewis D. Wigan, formerly of Kilmory, Argyll : *m.* 1909, her cousin, Sir Roderick Grey Wigan, 3rd baronet, who *d.* 1954. *Residences,* Borrobol, Kinbrace, Sutherland; Paston Hall, near Norwich.

Collateral Branches living.

Issue of the late Denis Grey Wigan, 3rd son of 2nd baronet, *b.* 1893, *d.* 1958; *m.* 1915, Madeline Mabel Ambrose, who *d.* 1969, da. of Charles Robert Whorwood Adeane, C.B. [B. Leconfield colls.] :—

Adair Michael Charles, *b.* 1916 ; ed. at Eton ; is Major Coldstream Guards Reserve of Officers : *m.* 1939, Dawn, da. of Charles Wilfred Gordon, of Boveridge Park, Cranborne, Salisbury, and has issue living, James Adair, *b.* 1950.—Dominic Richard Ludlow, *b.* 1951.—Lola Dawn, *b.* 1940.—Camilla Rose, *b.* 1944. *Residence,* West Blagdon, Cranborne, Dorset. *Club,* White's.—Elizabeth Sibell Isabel, *b.* 1918: *m.* 1937, Humphrey Gascoigne, of Ashe Abbey House, Campsea Ashe, Woodbridge, Suffolk; Brooks's Club, yst. son of the late Brig.-Gen. Sir (Ernest) Frederick (Orby) Gascoigne, KCVO, CMG, DSO, and has issue living, David Clive (277, Trinity Rd., SW18), *b.* 1939; ed. at Eton; Maj. RGJ Reserve of Officers: *m.* 1964, Deirdre Cecil Hermione, da. of Lt.-Col. Alec C. S. Moore, of Whites Meadow, Bicknoller, Somerset, and has issue living, Dominic William Wigan, *b.* 1965, Tobias Charles Humphrey *b.* 1971, Nichola Elizabeth Blanche *b.* 1968, —Martin Wyndham, *b.* 1944; ed. at Eton,—Anthony Grey, *b.* 1947; ed. at Gordonstoun.

Issue of the late Arthur Lawford Wigan, 3rd son of 1st baronet, *b.* 1868, *d.* 1944 : *m.* 1896, Beatrice, who *d.* 1959, el. da. of the late Col. Charles Hervey Bagot, C.B., R.E. :—

Joyce Madeline, *b.* 1898: *m.* 1917, Capt. Paul Randle Feilden Mason, formerly King's (Liverpool) Regt., who *d.* 1944, and has issue living, Anthony Feilden MASON-HORNBY (Dalton Hall, Burton-in-Kendal, Westmorland), *b.* 1931; assumed by Roy. Licence in 1966 the additional surname of Hornby: *m.* 1960, Cecily Barbara, da. of the late Henry Gordon Carter, of Bodlondeb, Beaumaris, Anglesey, and has issue living, Francis Anthony *b.* 1961, Christopher Randle *b.* 1963, Catherine Cecily *b.* 1964,—Pamela Marcia, *b.* 1923,—Virginia Cicely, *b.* 1926. *Residence,* The Cedars, Sandhurst, Camberley, Surrey.

The 1st baronet, Sir Frederick Wigan, son of the late John Alfred Wigan, of Clare House near Maidstone, a Director of North London Railway, and High Sheriff of cos. London and Surrey 1894, *d.* March 1907, and his son, Sir Frederick William, 2nd baronet, *d.* in April of same year.

WIGGIN, Creation (U.K.) 1892, of Metchley Grange, Harborne, Staffordshire.

TO THINE

OWN SELF BE TRUE

Sir JOHN HENRY WIGGIN, *MC, 4th Baronet; b.* March 3rd, 1921; *s.* his father, *Col. Sir* CHARLES RICHARD HENRY, *TD,* 1972; ed. at Eton, and Trin. Coll., Camb.; Maj. Gren. Gds. (Reserve); Middle East 1942-43 (prisoner, MC): *m.* 1st, 1947 (m. diss. 1961), Lady Cecilia Evelyn Anson, who *d.* 1963, da. of 4th Earl of Lichfield; 2ndly, 1963, Sarah, da. of Brig. Stewart Arthur Forster, late Coldm. Gds., and has issue living by 1st and 2nd m.

Arms—Gules, three mullets of six points argent, on a chief invected or two spurs sable. Crest—Over a fleur-de-lis sable, a spur or between two wings erect proper, each charged with a fleur-de-lis of the first.

Residence—Honington Hall, Shipston-on-Stour, Warwickshire.

Sons living—(By 1st m.) CHARLES RUPERT JOHN, *b.* July 2nd, 1949; ed. at Eton; Capt. Gren. Gds.——Benjamin Henry Edward, *b.* 1951; ed. at Eton, and McGill Univ., Montreal.——(by 2nd m.) Daniel Mark, *b.* 1964.——Jeremy James, *b.* 1966.

Collateral Branches living.

Grandsons of the late Alfred Harold Wiggin (infra):—
Issue of the late Col. Sir William Henry Wiggin, K.C.B., D.S.O., T.D., D.L., J.P., *b.* 1888, *d.* 1951 : *m.* 1935, Elizabeth Ethelston (Betty), who *d.* 1959, da. of the late J. Danvers Power, M.V.O. :—

Alfred William, *TD*, *MP* (The Court, Axbridge, Som.; House of Commons, SW1, Cavalry and Farmers Clubs), *b.* 1937; ed. at Eton, and at Trin. Coll., Camb.; Maj. The R. Yeo.; MP for Weston-super-Mare (C) since 1969: *m.* 1964, Rosemary Janet, only da. of David L. D. Orr, of Keithley, Sandhills, Wormley, Surrey, and has issue living, William David, *b.* 1966,—Thomas Henry, *b.* 1969,—Audrey Mary *b.* 1974.——Henry Walter (Brainge Putley, Ledbury, and 33, Ladbroke Gdns., W11 2PX), *b.* 1939; ed. at Eton, and at Trin. Coll., Camb. (MA); Solicitor 1965: *m.* 1962, the Hon. Julia Redmond Vaughan-Morgan, da. of Baron Reigate (Life Peer), and has issue living, Lucy Redmond, *b.* 1965,—Caroline Julia, *b.* 1970.

Issue of the late Alfred Harold Wiggin, 4th son of 1st baronet, *b.* 1864, *d.* 1933, *m.* 1887, Margaret, who *d.* 1932, da. of the late Edward J. Nettlefo d, of Highgate, N. :—

Richard Arthur, *TD*, *b.* 1903; ed. at Eton, and at Trin. Coll., Camb. (MA); Hon LID, Birmingham Lt.-Col. (ret.); late Comdg. Worcestershire Yeo.; is a JP and DL for Worcestershire (High Sheriff 1958); Hon. Col. (ret.) Birmingham Univ. OTC; 1939-45 War (despatches): *m.* 1952, Joan Mary Whitehead, of The Croft, Nelson, and has issue living, Margaret-Joan, *b.* 1954. *Residence*, Oak Hill, Ombersley, Droitwich, Worcestershire.

Issue of the late Brig.-Gen. Edgar Askin Wiggin, D.S.O., 5th son of 1st baronet, *b.* 1867, *d.* 1939 : *m.* 1906, Emilie Margaret, who *d.* 1951, da. of Arthur Keen, formerly of Sandyford, Edgbaston:—

Peter Milner, *b.* 1907; ed. at Eton, and RMC; Lt.-Col. late 11th Hussars, and a JP of Hants (late Co. Councillor); 1939-45 War in Middle East and NW Europe: *m.* 1933, Margaret Frances, da. of the late Capt. Noel Christian Livingstone-Learmonth, of Cleveland House, 19, St. James's Sq., SW, and has issue living, George David Henry (Newtown House, Newbury, Berks.), *b.* 1934; ed. at Eton; late Lt. 11th Hussars: *m.* 1958, Jennifer, da. of the late Capt. Ian Stanley Akers-Douglas [*see* V. Chilston, colls.], and has issue living, David Peter *b.* 1960, James George *b.* 1968, Davina Jane *b.* 1962,—Michael Peter (Mattingley House, Mattingley, Basingstoke), *b.* 1937; ed. at Eton; late Lt. 11th Hussars: *m.* 1962, Victoria Zara, da. of the late Malcolm Vaughan, of Old Westfield Farm House, Moreton Morrell, Warwicks., and has issue living, Mark David *b.* 1963, Rupert Michael *b.* 1969, Miranda Zara *b.* 1965, Kate Victoria *b.* 1972,—Sara Margaret (*Hon. Mrs. Michael J. H. Allenby*), *b.* 1942: *m.* 1965, the Hon. Michael Jaffray Hynman Allenby (Newnham Lodge, Newnham, Basingstoke), only son of 2nd Viscount Allenby. *Residence*, Foxford House, Ashford Hill, Newbury. *Club*—Cavalry.

The 1st baronet, Sir Henry Samuel, sat as M.P. for E. Staffordshire (L) 1880-85, and for Staffordshire, Handworth Div. (LU) 1885-92. Sir Henry Arthur, 2nd baronet, was High Sheriff of Staffs. 1896, and Col. Sir Charles Richard, 3rd baronet, was High Sheriff of Worcs. 1942.

WIGRAM, Creation (U.K.) 1805, of Walthamstow, Essex.
[Name pronounced "Wiggram."]

Sweet is the love of one's country.

Rev. Canon Sir CLIFFORD WOOLMORE WIGRAM, 7th *Baronet*, son of the late Robert Ainger Wigram, son of the late Rev. Woolmore Wigram, 5th son of Money Wigram, 5th son of 1st baronet ; *b.* Jan. 24th, 1911 ; *s.* his uncle, *Sir* EDGAR THOMAS AINGER, 1935 ; ed. at Winchester, and at Trin. Coll., Camb. (B.A. 1932, M.A. 1936) ; V. of Marston St. Lawrence, with Warkworth and Thenford, near Banbury; Non-Residentiary Canon of Peterborough Cathedral since 1973: *m.* 1948, Christobel Joan, da. of the late William Winter Goode, of Curry Rivel, Som., and widow of Eric Llewellyn Marriott, CIE.

Arms—Argent, on a pale gules three escallops or; over all a chevron engrailed counterchanged, and on the chief waves of the sea, thereon a ship representing an English vessel of war of the 16th century, with four masts, sails furled proper, colors flying gules. Crest—On a mount vert, a hand in armour in fesse couped at the wrist proper charged with an escallop holding a fleur-de-lis erect or. Supporters—On either side an eagle with wings elevated argent, collared gules and charged on the breast with a shamrock vert.

Residence—Marston St. Lawrence Vicarage, near Banbury, Oxon.

Brother living—EDWARD ROBERT WOOLMORE (Hilliers Lodge, St. Mary Bourne, nr. Andover, Hants), *b.* July 19th, 1913; ed. at Winchester, and at Trin. Coll., Camb. (BA 1934) sometime Major Indian Army; formerly a Master at Westminster Sch.: *m.* 1944, Viva Ann, da. of the late Douglas Bailey, of Laughton Lodge, nr. Lewes, Sussex, and has issue living, Ann Catherine, *b.* 1945: *m.* 1973, Frederick Procope, and has issue living, Robert Hjalmar *b.* 1974.

Daughter living of 4th Baronet—Angela Catherine Alice FITZWYGRAM, *b.* 1885.

Collateral Branches living.

Branch from 5th son of 1st Baronet:—

Granddaughters of the late Sir Charles Hampden Wigram, 3rd son of the late Money Wigram (*b.* 1790), 5th son of 1st baronet:—
Issue of the late Major Henry Hampden Wigram, Scots Guards. *b.* 1858, *d.* 1919 : *m.* 1891, Dorothy Isabel, who *d.* 1961, da. of the late G. W. Moore Liddell, of Sutton House, and Keldy Castle, Yorkshire :—

Violet, *ARRC* (Flat 2, 4, Culford Gdns., SW3) *b.* 1893; 1914-18 War (ARRC): *m.* 1928, the Rev. Allan Augustin de Vere (V. of Christ Church, Ealing, W), who *d.* 1949, and has issue living, Christopher John (20A, Overstrand Mansions, Prince of Wales Drive, SW11), *b.* 1928; ed. at Lancing: *m.* 1964, Lois Dudley, da. of Dudley Theodore Charles James, of Eaglemont, Vic., Aust., and has issue living, Christopher Dudley James *b.* 1970, John Charles Alan *b.* 1972,—*Rev.* Anthony George Augustine (The Vicarage, Elsfield, Oxford), *b.* 1931; ed. at Lancing, and at Ch. Ch., Oxford (MA), V. of Elsfield with Beckley and Horton-cum-Studley: *m.* 1969, Celia

Margaret, da. of Colin Huscroft Quail, of Zebediela, Transvaal, and has issue living, Mark Allan *b.* 1969.——Myrtle, *ARRC, b.* 1894; 1914-18 War (ARRC). *Residence,* Flat 2, 2, Culford Gdns., SW3.

Grandchildren of the late Rev. Woolmore Wigram, 5th son of the late Money Wigram (*b.* 1790) (ante) :—
Issue of the late Arthur Woolmore Wigram, *b.* 1875, *d.* 1946: *m.* 1911, Avis Marion, who *d.* 1972, da. of the late Hartley Hartley-Smith, of Upwey, Dorset:—
Peter Woolmore (Red Lodge, 22, Chiltern Hills Rd., Beaconsfield, Bucks.), *b.* 1913; ed. at Trin. Hall, Camb. (BA 1934): *m.* 1st, 1936 (m. diss. 1953), Ellen Brenda, da. of the late William Hill, of Rockferry, Cheshire; 2ndly, 1953, Sylvia Mary, da. of the late Rev. John Smithson Barstow, of Woolsthorpe, by Belvoir, and has issue living, (by 2nd m.) John Woolmore, *b.* 1957,——Caroline Judith *b.* 1955.——Daphne Marion Woolmore, *b.* 1919.

Grandson of the late Robert Wigram, 6th son of the late Money Wigram (*b.* 1790) (ante) :—
Issue of the late Robert Wigram, *b.* 1874, *d.* 1932: *m.* 1st, 1920, Adela Mabel, who *d.* 1923, da. of Richard Reid, of Bramcote, Weybridge ; 2ndly, 1925, Winifred, da. of the late Capt. Phipps, 24th Regt. :—
(By 2nd marriage) Francis John, *b.* 1926 ; ed. at Eton. *Residence,* Cotters Barn, Penn, Bucks.

Granddaughter of the late Reginald Wigram, 8th son of the late Money Wigram (*b.* 1790) (ante) :—
Issue of the late Reginald Spencer Wigram, *b.* 1874, *d.* 1943 : *m.* 1904, Olive Eleanor, who *d.* 1955, da. of the late Rev. E. C. Lister, R. of Stanningley, Yorkshire :—
Isabelle Georgiana (Long Meadow, Shurlock Row, Reading), *b.* 1906: *m.* 1949, Charles James Askham, who *d.* 1964.

Branch from 7th son of 1st Baronet:—

Grandchildren of the late Henry James Wigram (infra) :—
Issue of the late Capt. Ronald Scott Jervoise Wigram, D.S.O., R.N., *b.* 1874, *d.* 1944: *m.* 1911, Ethel Rosa, who *d.* 1940, da. of the late Rev. F. C. Kinglake, R. of West Monkton. Taunton:—
Henry Frederick James, *b.* 1916 ; ed. at Wellington Coll. ; Major (retired) Duke of Cornwall's L.I.: *m.* 1938, Helen Enid, da. of F. Clyde Smith, of Netherclay House, Bishop's Hull, Somerset, and has issue living, Roger Charles Kinglake (c/o Lloyds Bank, Camberley, Surrey), *b.* 1940; Capt. Light Inf. (ret.): *m.* 1965, Wendy Joan, el. da. of Brig. Philip Herbert Richardson, DSO, OBE, of The Manor House, Merriott, Som., and has issue living, Giselle Rose *b.* 1966, Susanna Nicola *b.* 1968,——James Somerset, *b.* 1950: *m.* 1974, Susan Jane, only da. of Brian Braithwaite-Exley, of Pant Head, Austwick, Yorks.,—Sally Kinglake, *b.* 1939: *m.* 1972, William Arthur Rose, of La Fosse, Trinity, Jersey, and has issue living, Alan Kindred *b.* 1972,—Janet Gail, *b.* 1953: *m.* 1975, Timothy Wallace Kyle, Lt. RN. *Residence,* Kibbear House, Trull, Taunton, Som.
Issue of the late Major Cyril Charles Wigram, *b.* 1882, *d.* 1952 : *m.* 1st, 1912, Mabel Adams, from whom he obtained a divorce 1917; 2ndly, 1918, Olivia Marie (who *d.* 1970, having obtained a divorce 1928), da. of the late Maj.-Gen. W. Truman, of Winterbourne, Bonchurch, I. of Wight; 3rdly, 1929, Mrs. Dorothy Scott, who *d.* 1938; 4thly, 1946, Elizabeth, who *d.* 1970, da. of the late Dr. F. E. Sondern, of New York, and widow of J. W. New:—
(By 2nd m.) Isolde Marianne, *b.* 1919. *Residence,* Meadow Bank, Horsted Lane, Little Horsted, Uckfield, Sussex.

Granddaughters of the late Capt. James Richard Wigram, son of the late Rt. Hon. Sir James Wigram, 7th son of 1st baronet:—
Issue of the late Henry James Wigram, *b.* 1847, *d.* 1902 : *m.* 1870, Penelope Emily, who *d.* 1934, da. of George Edward Eyre, of Warrens, Bramshaw, near Lyndhurst, and 59, Lowndes Square, S.W. :—
Rachel Winifred, *b.* 1878: *m.* 1908, Edward Harry Arkwright, formerly RHA, who *d.* 1956, and has issue living, Joan, *b.* 1910: *m.* 1932, Maurice Watler d'Aguilar Cleland, from whom she obtained a divorce 1955; 2ndly, 1956, George Abercromby Mitchell, CBE, of Postling Green, Aldington, Ashford, Kent, and has issue living (by 1st m.) Patrick Charles d'Aguilar *b.* 1933, Timothy Dominic d'Aguilar *b.* 1935, Richard Shaun d'Aguilar *b.* 1935, Virginia Rachel Olivia *b.* 1937. *Residence,* St. Gallen, Hythe, Kent.

Branch from 8th son of 1st Baronet:—

Grandchildren of the late William Arthur Wigram, grandson of Octavius Wigram, 8th son of 1st baronet:—
Issue of the late Charles Knox Wigram, *b.* 1889, *d.* 1966: *m.* 1st, 1914, Gladys Mary (who *d.* 1955, having obtained a divorce 1931), da. of the late Rev. Robert Edward Baynes (Preb. of Combe); 2ndly, 1931, Margaret Esther, who *d.* 1974, da. of the late Capt. Henry Valentine Simpson, CMG, RN (ret.):—
(By 1st m.) James Robert Knox (of Morriswood, Brook Farm Rd., Cobham, Surrey), *b.* 1915; ed. at Harrow; Hon. Maj. RASC; 1939-45 War as Maj. RASC (despatches): *m.* 1942, Beatrice Elizabeth, da. of the late Rev. W. A. Sandford, of Dunstable, Beds., and has issue living, Brian Arthur Knox, *b.* 1947; ed. at Wellington—Michele Anne, *b.* 1946; BA (Hons.) Reading.—— Valentine Knox (c/o Barclays Bank, Horsham, Sussex), *b.* 1920; ed. at Haileybury; late Cpl. RAF; ARICS.——(by 2nd m.) Patrick Knox (Focklesbrook Orchard, Sandpit Hall Rd., Chobham, Surrey), *b.* 1937; ed. at Wellington; Lt. RN (ret.); ACII: *m.* 1964, Susan Mary, da. of Col. A. R. F. Martin, of Camberley, Surrey, and has issue lviing, Charles Robert Knox, *b.* 1968,—Sandra Jane Fyers, *b.* 1965,—Julia Margaret Fyers *b.* 1967.——Susan Alice Ann, *b.* 1932; ed. at London Univ. (BA): *m.* 1965, Colin Scorer, of 11, Stuart Grove, Teddington, Middx.——Jennifer Jane, *b.* 1935: *m.* 1967, Allen Griswold (c/o First San Francisco Bank, 260, Montgomery St., San Francisco, USA).

Branch from 10th son of 1st Baronet:—

Grandchildren of the late Gerrard Andrewes Wigram, 3rd son of the Rt. Rev. Joseph Cotton Wigram, DD, Bishop of Rochester, 10th son of 1st baronet:—
Issue of the late Rev. Gerrard Edmund Wigram, *b.* 1877, *d.* 1947: *m.* 1902, Maria Isména, who *d.* 1944, 2nd da. of the late William Townson-Mayne:—
Francis Gerrard Mayne, *b.* 1905 ; formerly Regional Officer, Coal Utilization Council, and an Asso. Member of Institute of Fuel: *m.* 1934, Helen Frances, younger da. of the late Dr. Sidney Worthington, of Warwick, and has issue living, Gerrard Charles (4, Clifford Cres., Bergvliet, Cape Prov.), *b.* 1936; FCA, and a CA, S. Africa: *m.* 1965, Joan Patricia, da. of the late James Lang, of Nairobi, and has issue living, Keith Gerrard *b.* 1969, Zena Patricia Jean *b.* 1966, Eileen Frances *b.* 1972,—Nigel Francis (3, Mayfair Mansions, Myrtle Rd., Kenilworth, Cape Town, S. Africa), *b.* 1939; CCS, BCom, MBA: *m.* 1974, Lynette, da. of Dr. Leon Stern, of Kenilworth, Cape Town,—Deborah Helen, *b.* 1938: *m.* 1961, Lt.-Cdr. Richard Hugh Farnfield, RN, of Whytecroft, 18, Solent Way, Alverstoke, Hants, and has issue living, Anthony Gilbert *b.* 1963, Andrew Richard *b.* 1970, Timothy Francis *b.* 1971, Helen Rosemary *b.* 1965. *Residence,* Maeshowe, Sea View Rd., Somerset West, Cape Province, S. Africa.——Margaret Ismena Wilmot, *b.* 1903: *m.* 1939, Arthur Carrington, of 17, Lime Meadow Ave., Sanderstead, Surrey, and has issue living, Michael Anthony, *b.* 1940: *m.* 1965, Cynthia Denise Clifford, and has issue living, Richard Anthony *b.* 1969, Elizabeth Louise *b.* 1966.——Marion Rochford (Quarndon Hill, Quarndon, Derbys.), *b.* 1909: *m.* 1930, William Hadden Richardson, who *d.* 1968, and has issue living, James Hadden (of Fern Hill, Quarndon, Derbys.), *b.* 1937: *m.* 1961, Susan Mary, only da.

of J. H. K. Thomson, of Derby, and has issue living, Nicholas Hadden *b.* 1963, Timothy James Keith *b.* 1970, Wendy Diana *b.* 1965,—Judith Mary, *b.* 1934: *m.* 1963, John Swain Yeomans, of Addcrofts, Kirk Ireton, Derbys., and has issue living, Philip Hadden *b.* 1964.——Janet (*Hon. Mrs. Valentine H. O. Herbert*), *b.* 1916: *m.* 1956, as his second wife, the Hon. Valentine Henry Okes Herbert [*see* B. Hemingford]. *Residence*, Foxdown, Tile Barn, Woolton Hill, Newbury, Berks., RG15 9UX.

Grandchildren of the late John Wigram (*b.* 1846), 4th son of the Rt. Rev. Joseph Cotton Wigram, DD, Bishop of Rochester (ante):—

Issue of the late Henry Joseph Wigram, *b.* 1873, *d.* 1926: *m.* 1st, 1898, Alice Laura (from whom he obtained a divorce 1909), da. of the late Thomas Jarvis, of Mount Jarvis, Antigua; 2ndly, 1910, Beatrice Mary, who *d.* 1945, da. of the late B. J. Baylis-Garrard, of Haydon Manor, Somerset:—

(By 1st marriage) **John Jarvis**, *b.* 1900 : *m.* 1929, Ivy Harley, who *d.* 19—, da. of George Hayes, of Cressy, Tasmania.——Daphne. *b.* 1899: *m.* 1924, Capt. Douglas Cecil FitzHerbert, who *d.* 1933 [*see* Fitzherbert, Bt., colls.]. *Residence*, S. Collingham, Newark-on-Trent.——Lorne, *b.* 1904: *m.* 1932, Capt. William Luard Bond, RN, who *d.* 1974, and has issue living, Christopher Wigram (92, Oakfield Rd., Selly Park, Birmingham 29), *b.* 1934: *m.* 1959, Margaret C. Palmer, and has issue living, Philip Luard *b.* 1960, Andrew Peter *b.* 1965, Alison Jacqueline *b.* 1963. *Residence*, April Cottage, 42, Lower Westwood, Bradford-on-Avon, Wilts.

Branch from 13th son of 1st Baronet:—

Grandchildren of the late Rev. Frederic Edward Wigram, el. son of the late Edward Wigram, 13th son of 1st baronet:—

Issue of the late Rev. Edmund Francis Edward Wigram, *b.* 1864. *d.* 1933: *m.* 1904, Violet, who *d.* 1918, da. of Sir Thomas Charles Dewey, 1st Bt., of South Hill Wood, Bromley: —
Rev. **Oswald Thomas Edward** (Westholm, Highlands Park, Chudleigh, Devon), *b.* 1905; ed. at Marlborough; formerly in Church Missionary So., Kenya: *m.* 1935, Margaret, da. of the late R. N. Barnes, of Sutton Coldfield, and has issue living, Robert Edmund (of 93, Investigator St., Red Hill, A.C.T., Australia), *b.* 1936: *m.* 1963, Patricia, da. of L. C. Collisson, of Liverpool, NSW, and has issue living, Simon Andrew *b.* 1967, Frances Elizabeth *b.* 1964, Louise Annette *b.* 1966,— Paul Frederic (PO Box 26, Naivasha, Kenya), *b.* 1937; ed. at Marlborough, and at Pembroke Coll., Camb. (MA): *m.* 1963, Christian Virginia, da. of Maj. H. A. R. Bucknall, MC, and has issue living, Thomas Paul Henry *b.* 1964,—Lucy Helen Gabrielle *b.* 1966, Bronwen Serena Christian *b.* 1971,—*Rev.* Andrew Oswald (A. C. Mbale Dabida, PO VOI, Kenya) *b.* 1939; ed. at Marlborough; BD London: *m.* 1964, Catharine, da. of the Rev. Canon Geoffrey Rogers, of Palgrave, Diss, Norfolk, and has issue living, John Michael *b.* 1967, Susanna Dora *b.* 1966, Margaret Jane Majala *b.* 1970,—Francis Aidan (Lower Peake Farm, Warnford, Southampton SO3 1LA), *b.* 1949; ed. at Marlborough and Seale Hayne Agric. Coll.: *m.* 1973, Christine Susan, da. of T. E. Abbey, of Tilney, Sellicks Green, Taunton, and has issue living, Timothy Francis *b.* 1974,—Ruth Margaret (c/o A.C. Box 228, Dodoma, Tanzania), *b.* 1941.——Joy Frances, *b.* 1909; ed. at Newnham Coll., Camb. (BA 1931): *m.* 1937, Fortescue Eric Vesey Ross, of Treetops, Old Belfield, Windermere, Cumbria, LA23 3HT, and has issue living, Brian Patrick Edmund, *b.* 1942: *m.* 1966, Linda, da. of Ernest Appleton,—Ian Ronald Francis, *b.* 1945; MD: *m.* 1967, Laura, da. of Hugh Stevenson,—Michael John, *b.* 1947,—Wendy Joy, *b.* 1939.

Grandsons of the late Rev. Edmund Francis Edward Wigram (ante):—

Issue of the late Lieut. Aidan Frederic Wigram, R.N.V.R., *b.* 1907, *d.* (killed in action during European War) 1941: *m.* 1938. Marjorie Joyce, who *d.* 1963. da. of the late Lt.-Col. E. R. I. Chitty, Indian Army:—

Aidan David (High Timbers, Hartley Rd., Cranbrook, Kent, TN17 3QX), *b.* 1938; ed. at Marlborough, and Univ. of Wales (BSc): *m.* 1968, Jeniffer Ann, da. of E. N. Firmager, of Godstone, Surrey, and has issue living, Lesley Rosalind, *b.* 1969.——Aidan Patrick, *b.* 1940.

Issue of the late Edmund Hugh Lewis Wigram, MB, BCh, *b.* 1911, *d.* 1945: *m.* 1938, Kathleen Maud (who *m.* 2ndly, 1948, Christopher Henry Kaye, BM, BCh [Wigram Bt., colls.]), yr. da. of L. C. S. Hallam, of Port Arthur, Canada:—

Peter Hallam. *b.* 1939: *m.* 19—.——Edmund William (Thornton Moor, Hartburn, Morpeth, Northumberland), *b.* 1942: *m.* 1965, Diana Frances, da. of Anthony Douglas Bell, MB, BS, of Waterleep, Rothbury, and has issue living, Anthony Christopher *b.* 1966,—Clare Frances *b.* 1969.

Grandchildren of the late Rev. Frederic Edward Wigram (ante):—

Issue of the late Rev. Beresford Edward Wigram, *b.* 1870, *d.* 1917 : *m.* 1901, Jessie Violet, who *d.* 1939, da. of the late Walter Scott of Tunbridge Wells :—
Winstone Beresford, *b.* 1908; ed. at St. Lawrence Coll., Ramsgate, and at Queen's Coll., Camb, (BA 1930, MA 1947); formerly Capt. King's African Rifles and Principal of Jeanes Sch., Kabete Kenya: *m.* 1942, Adelaide Joyce (Dair), who *d.* 1966, da. of the Rev. W. Aldworth Ferguson, DD, and has issue living, Erica Joyce, *b.* 1943: *m.* 1970, Maj. Ian Ferguson Sharp, RAOC, of Field Cottage, Limpley Stoke, Bath, and has issue living, Jasper Henry Ferguson *b.* 1971, Daniel William *b.* 1973. *Address*, Box 14080, Nairobi, Kenya.——*Rev.* Marcus Walter (3, Croft Av., Bromborough, Merseyside, L62 2BI.), *b.* 1917; ed. at Haileybury, and at Gonville and Caius Coll., Camb. (BA 1938); formerly Lt. Queen's Roy. Regt.: *m.* 1941, Christina Cantrell, and has issue living, Ann Margaret Joyce, *b.* 1942: *m.* 1964, Derek William Blandford, of 17, Watermore Close, Frampton Cotterell, Glos., and has issue living, Andrew Paul *b.* 1966, Ian Keith *b.* 1969, Kieron John *b.* 1971,—Carol Frances Violet, *b.* 1946, Sarah Christina Agnes, *b.* 1949: *m.* 1970, Humphrey David Lane, and has issue living, Bridget Anna *b.* 1972, Corinne Victoria *b.* 1974,— Jane Eleanor Bridget, *b.* 1954: *m.* 1971, Mark Christian Eckersley, of 18, Prestbury Rd., Cheltenham, and has issue living, Naomi Jane *b.* 1974.——Joyce Marjorie (Strawberry Cottage, Woodmancote, North Cerney, Glos.), *b.* 1910; ed. at London Univ. (MB and BS 1930).

Issue of the late Rev. Harold Frederic Edward Wigram, *b.* 1873, *d.* 1946: *m.* 1913, Gladys Christine (Helena House, Brownlow Rd., Reading, Berks.), da. of Sir Howard Warburton Elphinstone, 3rd Bt.:—
Howard Beresford (Heatherpine, Curridge, Newbury, Berks.) *b.* 1917.——Andrew Harold (17, Albury Rd., Newcastle-upon-Tyne, NE2 3PE), *b.* 1919; ed. at Wellington Coll., and at Trin. Hall, Camb. (BA); Maj. RA (ret.); Bursar, Newcastle Univ.: *m.* 1953, Alice Jefferson Trewhitt. ——Alexander Robert, *b.* 1925; ed. at Wellington Coll., and at Brasenose Coll., Oxford (MA); formerly P/O Hong Kong Aux. Air Force, and Lt. R. Signals: *m.* 1958, Virginia Claire, da. of the late Group Capt. Philip Patrick Strachan Rickard, OBE, and has issue living, Kester Jonathan, *b.* 1959,—Nicholas Simon, *b.* 1960,—Sarah Christine, *b.* 1963. *Address*, Te Motu Rd., Pukerua Bay, Wellington, NZ.——Gladys Veronica, *b.* 1916: *m.* 1st, 1938, Lt. William George Player Brigstock, RNVR, who *d.* (of wounds received in action during 1939-45 War) 1940; 2ndly, 1943, Reginald Charles Grisedale Fennell, late Maj. King's Own Yorkshire LI (TA), of Brocton, 44, Guildown Rd., Guildford, and has issue living, (by 2nd m.) Robert John, *b.* 1944,—William Richard Kenneth, *b.* 1952.——Rose Eleanor, *b.* 1923: *m.* 1954, Richard Edward Barry, of Donegal, Joy Lane, Whitstable, Kent, and has issue living, John Andrew, *b.* 1958,—Sylvia May, *b.* 1956.

Issue of the late Loftus Edward Wigram, M.B., *b.* 1877, *d.* 1963: *m.* 1912, Constance Emma Letitia, who *d.* 1970, da. of the late Rev. William Gilbert Edwards, Surrogate of Oxford, and Hon. Canon, formerly R. of Great Haseley, Wallingford, Oxon, and Rural Dean of Cuddesdon:—
Gerald Frederic (of Calverleigh Cottage, Tiverton, Devon), *b.* 1916; ed. at Marlborough; formerly Capt. King's African Rifles: *m.* 1948, Anne Christal, da. of the late Brig.-Gen. the Hon. Lesley James Probyn Butler, C.M.G., D.S.O. [*see* B. Dunboyne, colls.], and has issue living, Carolyn

Lesley, *b.* 1950,—Marylee Anne, *b.* 1952,—Bridget Margaret, *b.* 1954.——Lettice Margaret, *b.* 1920; ed. at Oxford Univ. (BA 1942); formerly Section Officer WAAF: *m.* 1951, Maj. Edward Arthur Hadow, late RE, of Newinnton Lodge, Chudleigh, Devon [M. Anglesey, colls.], and has issue living, John Wigram, *b.* 1959,—Robert Edward, *b.* 1968,—Rosemary Maude, *b.* 1953: *m.* 1974, David Rachman,—Juliet Letitia, *b.* 1955,—Celia Catherine, *b.* 1957.

Granddaughters of the late Loftus Edward Wigram, MB (ante):—
Issue of the late Michael Wigram, MRCS, LRCP, *b.* 1919, *d.* 1973: *m.* 1945, Margaret Edith Ann (Crickerton, Buckfastleigh, S. Devon), da. of the late W. E. Watson-Baker, of Toddington, Beds.:—
Laurette, *b.* 1946: *m.* 1971, Brian Guest, of Verwood, Dorset, and has issue living, William, *b.* 1974,—Josephine, *b.* 1972.——Sarah Margaret, *b.* 1949: *m.* 1973, Timothy Veise, of Baltimore, USA.——Jennifer Rose, *b.* 1953.

Branch from 16th son of 1st Baronet:—

Grandson of the late Herbert Wigram, 2nd son of the Rev. William Pitt Wigram (infra):—
Issue of the late Rt. Hon. Sir Clive (*Baron Wigram*) G.C.B., G.C.V.O., C.S.I., P.C. ; *cr.* *Baron Wigram* 1935 [*see* that title].

Grandchildren of the late Lewis Wigram, yst. son of the Rev. William Pitt Wigram, 11th son of 1st baronet:—
Issue of the late Roland Lewis Wigram, *b.* 1874, *d.*1918 : *m.* 1907, Mildred Gladys (who *m.* 2ndly, 1930, Lennox Chaplin Prendergast), el. da. of the late Rev. Canon Robert Peel Willock, R. of Warmington, Banbury:—
Derek Roland (Housels Field, Westwood, Bradford on Avon, Wilts.), *b.* 1908; ed. at Marlborough, and at Peterhouse, Camb. (MA); BSc (Economics) London; House Master and Careers Master at Bryanston Sch. 1936-46, and Headmaster of Monkton Combe Sch. 1946-68: *m.* 1944, Catharine Mary, da. of the late Very Rev. William Ralph Inge, KCVO, DD, and has issue living, Richard Inge (67, Westover Rd., Fleet, Hants.), *b.* 1944: *m.* 1971, Angela Patricia, da. of Capt. M. D. Rahilly, RN, of The Old Malt House, Westwood, Bradford on Avon, and has issue living, Helen Marguerite *b.* 1974,—Janet Catharine Inge, *b.* 1948.——Mervyn Roland, *b.* 1916; ed. at Marlborough Coll., and at Peterhouse, Camb. (MA); HM Inspector of Schs. since 1959, and Staff Inspector since 1974; formerly Director of Modern Languages and a Housemaster of Mill Hill Sch.: *m.* 1947, Beryl Margaret Morriss, and has issue living, Christopher Edward Mervyn, *b.* 1954,—Rowena Margaret, *b.* 1949, Diana Catharine, *b.* 1956. *Residence*, 27, Glasshouse Lane, Kenilworth, Warwicks.——Nora Phyllis, *b.* 1909: *m.* 1939, the Rev. Kenneth Philpott Stewart. *Residence*, 4, St. Stephen's Close, Lansdown, Bath.

Issue of the late Oswald Lewis Wigram, *b.* 1878, *d.* 1960 : *m.* 1914, Lucy Clare Elaine, who *d.* 1962, da. of the Rev. Thomas Wilkinson Stephenson, V. of Addingham, Penrith, and Hon. Canon of Carlisle:—
Michael Lewis, *b.* 1918 ; ed. at St. Bees' Sch. ; late Major R.A. (T.A.) : *m.* 1950, Dorothea Mary Yorke Wood, who *d.* 1964. and has issue living, Anthony Lewis, *b.* 1953,—Mary Elaine, *b.* 1951. *Residence*, 41, Lyndhurst Av., Mill Hill, NW7.——Margaret Elaine, *b.* 1921. *Residence*, Holme Lea, Armathwaite, Carlisle.

The 1st baronet, Sir Robert Wigram, successively M.P. for Fowey and co. Wexford, obtained eminence as a merchant ; he died 1830, having had twenty-three children. The 2nd baronet, M.P. for Fowey, in 1832 changed, by Roy. licence, his surname to FitzWygram. Lieut.-Gen. Sir Frederick FitzWygram, 4th Bt., sat as M.P. for Hampshire S. (C) 1884-5, and for Hampshire S., or Fareham, Div. 1885-1900, and Major Sir Frederick Loftus Francis FitzWygram, M.C., 5th Bt., was taken prisoner and twice wounded during European War 1914-19 (despatches, prisoner when severely wounded; *d.* from effects of captivity).

BAKER WILBRAHAM, Creation (G.B.) 1776, of Loventor, co. Devon.
[Name pronounced "**Baker Wilbram.**"]

Sir RANDLE JOHN BAKER WILBRAHAM, 7th *Baronet ; b.* March 31st, 1906 ; *s.* his father, *Sir* PHILIP WILBRAHAM, *K.B.E.,* 1957 ; ed. at Harrow and at Balliol Coll., Oxford (B.A. 1928) ; a Fellow of Roy. Instn. of Chartered Surveyors; Pres. of Chartered Land Agents Soc. 1958-59; JP and a DL for Ches.; High Sheriff of Ches. 1953-54; 1939-45 War as Sq.-Ldr. RAAF: *m.* 1930, Betty Ann, *CBE,* who *d.* 1975, da. of the late W. Matt Torrens, of The Grove, Hayes, Kent, and has issue.

Arms,—Quarterly, 1st and 4th argent, three bends wavy azure, *Wilbraham*; 2nd and 3rd, per pale argent and, or on a saltire nebuly sable five escallops of the first, on a chief of the third a lion passant of the second, *Baker*. **Crests,**—1st, a wolf's head erased argent, *Wilbraham*; 2nd, a dexter arm embowed, vested azure, charged with three annulets interlaced or, cuffed argent, holding in the hand proper an arrow of the last, *Baker*.

Rest in the haven.   *Residence*—Rode Hall, Scholar Green, Cheshire.

IN · PORTO · QUIES

Son living—RICHARD (of 41, Carlyle Sq., S.W.3), *b.* Feb. 5th, 1934; ed. at Harrow; late Lt. Welsh Guards; a Managing Dir. of J. Henry Schroder Wagg & Co. Ltd.: *m.* 1962, Anne Christine Peto, da. of Charles Peto Bennett, OBE, of La Haute, Fliquet, Jersey, and has issue living, Randle, *b.* 1963,—Sibella Caroline, *b.* 1965,—Charlotte Cecilia Anne *b.* 1968,—Alice Maria Elisabeth, *b.* 1971.

Daughter living—Letitia Ann, *b.* 1931: *m.* 1960, Timothy George Kirkbride, of Spen Green Farm, Smallwood, Sandbach, Ches., and has issue living, George Edward, *b.* 1967,—Harriet Ann, *b.* 1964.

Sisters living—Joyce Katharine, *MBE, b.* 1902; Civilian Housing Administrator, Min. of Defence 1961-72; MBE (Civil) 1959. *Residence,* Flat 2, 23, Onslow Sq., SW7.——Mary Frances, *b.* 1904: *m.* 1937, Prof. Elliott Perkins, of 18, Hawthorn St., Cambridge, Massachusetts, U.S.A. ——Elisabeth Sibylla, *b.* 1908: *m.* 1938, Lt.-Col. Hugh Maurice Carstairs Jones-Mortimer, late Welsh Gds., and has issue living, Maurice Carstairs, *b.* 1940; MA, DPhil,—Loraine Elisabeth, *b.* 1947: *m.* 1970, Alvin Randolph Martin, of 22, Linnaean St., Cambridge, Mass., USA,— Johanna Favell, *b.* 1949. *Residence,* Hartsheath, Mold, Flintshire.

The 5th baronet, Sir George Barrington Baker, assumed by Roy. licence 1900 the additional surname of Wilbraham, having *m.* Katharine Frances, who *d.* 1945, da. and heir of Gen. Sir Richard Wilbraham, KCB, of Rode Hall, nephew of 1st Baron Skelmersdale. The 6th baronet, Sir Philip Wilbraham Baker-Wilbraham, K.B.E., D.C.L, was Sec., National Assembly of Church of England 1920-39, First Church Estates Commr. 1939-45, Chancellor of Dioceses of Chester, York, Truro, Chelmsford and Durham, and Vicar-Gen. of Province of York 1915-34, and of Province of Canterbury (and Dean of the Arches) 1934-55.

WILKINSON, Creation (U.K.) 1941, of Brook, Witley, co. Surrey.

Sir (DAVID) GRAHAM BROOK WILKINSON, 3rd *Baronet; b.* May 18th, 1947; *s.* his father, *Sir* (LEONARD) DAVID, *DSC*, 1972; ed. at Millfield, and Ch. Ch., Oxford.

Arms—Quarterly, argent and vair sable and or, a cross gules, in the 1st and 4th quarters a lion rampant of the fourth on a chief also of the fourth three mullets of the third. Crest—Issuant from a chaplet of roses argent barbed and seeded proper a demi-unicorn or.

Residence—

Sister living—Sylvia Davinia Gay, *b.* 1948.

Aunt living (daughter of 1st baronet)—Eileen, *b.* 1916: *m.* 1941, John MacNaughton Sidey, DSO, and has issue living, Ian MacNaughton, *b.* 1947. *Residence,* Robinswood, Effingham, Surrey.

Mother living—Sylvia Ruby Eva Anne (Laurie House, 16, Airlie Gdns., W8), only da. of Prof. Bossley Alan Rex Gater, of Grahamstown, S. Africa: *m.* 1946 (m. diss. 1967), Sir (Leonard) David Wilkinson, DSC, 2nd Bt., who *d.* 1972.

Widow living of 1st Baronet—FREDA DOROTHY (*Lady Wilkinson*), (50, Eresby House, Rutland Gate, SW7), da. of Robert Volland; CStJ: *m.* 1912, Sir George Henry Wilkinson, KCVO, 1st Bt., who *d.* 1967.

Sir George Henry Wilkinson, KCVO, 1st Bt., was Lord Mayor of London 1940-41.

WILLIAMS, Creation (G.B.) 1798, of Bodelwyddan, Flintshire.

Strong and crafty.

Sir FRANCIS JOHN WATKIN WILLIAMS, *QC*, 8th Baronet; *b.* Jan. 24th, 1905; *s.* his brother, *Sir* REGINALD LAWRENCE WILLIAM, *MBE, TD*), 1971; Bar. Middle Temple 1928, and QC 1952; late Wing Cdr. RAFVR; Recorder of Chester 1958-71; Recorder of Crown Court since 1972; Chm. of Anglesey, Chm. Flintshire, and Dep. Chm. of Cheshire Quarter Sessions, and a JP for Denbighshire (High Sheriff 1957); High-Sheriff of Anglesey 1963: *m.* 1932, Brenda Beryl, JP, da. of Sir (Joseph) John Jarvis, MP, 1st Bt., and has issue.

Arms—Argent, two foxes counter-salient in saltire gules that in bend sinister surmounted by that in bend dexter, a crescent for difference. *Residence—*Llys Meirchion, Denbigh.

Daughters living—Jennifer Frances Ann, *b.* 1933: *m.* 1954 (m. diss. 1975), Lt.-Col. Ivan Wise Lynch, R. Green Jackets, and has issue living, Frances William Adrian *b.* 1957,—William John Ivan, *b.* 1965.——Tessa Gillian Rosamund, *b.* 1935: *m.* 1958, Michael John Stewart Preece, of Plas Llanddyfnan, Talwrn, Llangefni, Anglesey, and has issue living, James Francis Stewart, *b.* 1964,—Hugh Michael Stewart, *b.* 1969.——Antonia Kathleen Brenda, *b.* 1939: *m.* 1st, 1960 (m. diss. 1974), Timothy Roy Henry Kimber, el. son of Sir Charles Dixon Kimber, 3rd Bt.; 2ndly, 1974, Timothy George Emanuel, of 1, The Pryors, East Heath Rd., NW3.——Victoria Elizabeth Alice, *b.* 1944: *m.* 1965, Andrew Walter Loraine Paterson, of 40, Sydney St., SW3, and has issue living, Harry Adrian Loraine, *b.* 1968,—Douglas Watkin Loraine *b.* 1972,—Lucinda Mona Alice, *b.* 1966,—Jessie Brenda Antonia, *b.* 1970.

Half-Brother living—LAWRENCE HUGH, *b.* Aug. 25th, 1929; Capt. RM (ret.); High Sheriff of Anglesey 1970: *m.* 1952, Sara Margaret Helen, third da. of Sir Harry Platt, 1st Bt., MD, MS, FRCS, and has issue living, Emma Louise, *b.* 1961,—Antonia Margaret, *b.* 1963. *Residence,* Old Parciau Marianglas, Anglesey.

Sister living—Violet Kathleen Mary, *b.* 1902: *m.* 1926, Thomas Arthur Pearson, late Lieut.-Cdr. RNVR, who *d.* 1974, and has issue living, David Arthur (Banastre Cottage, Park Gate, Wirral, Ches.), *b.* 1931: *m.* 1960, Carolyn Frances, el. da. of F. H. Minoprio, of Hessle Well House, Heswall, Ches., and has issue living, Charles David *b.* 1961, Joanna Mary *b.* 1963, Lucy Alexandra *b.* 1968,—Thomas Martin, *b.* 1933. *Residence,* Meadow Court, Cae Mawr, Beaumaris, Anglesey.

Half-Sister living—Penelope Lawrence, *b.* 1925: *m.* 1950, Major Thomas William Edward Corrigan, M.B.E., The Queen's Bays (retired), who *d.* 1961, and has issue living, Henrietta Louise, *b.* 1954. *Residence,* Parciau, Marianglas, Anglesey.

Daughters living of 7th Baronet—Laurelie Meriol Winifrida, b. 1939: m. 1968, Robert Bayley Emilius Laurie, of Heath House, Ardleigh, nr. Colchester, Essex, son of Maj.-Gen. Sir John Emilius Laurie, CBE, DSO, 6th Bt.——Juliet Elizabeth Rosamund, b. 1942: m. 1966, Brian Derek Price, of 52 Hazlewell Rd., Putney, SW15 6LR, and has issue living, Edmund Hugh Owain, b. 1969,—Henry William Frederick, b. 1973.

Granddaughters living of 6th Baronet (Issue of the late Hugh Richard Grenville Williams, b. 1927, d. 1952: m. 1948, Jacqueline Ferney, dau. of John Davison, of Livingstone, Zambia, —Jennifer Mary, b. 1949.——Melanie Jane, b. 1950.——Richardyne Megan, b. 1952.

Daughter living of 5th Baronet—Freda Violet, b. 1913: m. 1st, 1937, Sydney Walton Hinde, who d. 1967, and from whom she obtained a divorce 1950; 2ndly, 1959, William Vere Hodgson, and has issue living, (by 1st m.) Richard Courtney Buckley, b. 1939: m. 1961, Sally Makins, and has issue living, Stephen Ross b. 1962, Craig Sydney b. 1964, Felicity Anne b. 1967,— Deirdre Penelope Anne, b. 1938: m. 1958, Basil Birkbeck Wakefield, of Piedmont, P/Bag 915, Bindura, Rhodesia, and has issue living, Dean Roger, b. 1960, Clive Basil b. 1964, Richard Owen b. 1967, Darryl William (twin) b. 1967, Deborah Odile, b. 1959,—Patricia Rosamund b. 1941: m. 1961, Patrick David Hyde Smith (Mapinga Farm (Pvt.) Ltd., P. Bag 936, Bindura, Rhodesia), and has issue living, Vaughn Christopher, b. 1962, Brent Richard, b. 1964, Natasha Jane b. 1967, Samantha b. 1971,—Caroline Bryer, b. 1946: m. 1970, Emmanuel Riez, who d. 1971. *Residence*, Farnham Estate, PO Box 68850, Bryanston, Transvaal, S. Africa.

Stepmother living (daughter of 4th baronet)—Elinor Henrietta, b. 1886: m. 1909, as his second wife, Col. Lawrence Williams, OBE (grandson of 1st baronet), who d. 1958. *Residence*, Parciau Marianglas, Anglesey.

Widow living of 7th Baronet—(ELINOR) MERIOL ENRIQUETA (*Meriol, Lady Williams*), (Trewyn, Beaumaris, Anglesey), only da. of the late Frederic Pelham Trevor, of Anglesey: m. 1936, Sir Reginald Lawrence William Williams, MBE, TD, 7th Bt., who d. 1971.

Collateral Branch living

Granddaughter of the late Major Charles Henry Bennett Williams, 5th son of 3rd baronet:—
Issue of the late Col. Evelyn Hugh Watkin Williams, D.S.O., b. 1884, d. 1934; m. 1910, Florence, dau. of the late G. A. Brett, of Ryde, Isle of Wight :—
Gwenllian Elizabeth Anne, b. 1911: m. 1st, 1935, Lieut. Christopher Ryle Wood, R.N., who assumed by deed poll 1936, the surname of Williams in lieu of his patronymic, and by Roy. licence 1936, the arms of Williams, 2ndly, 1948, Campbell Sherston Smith, who assumed by deed poll 1949 the surname of Williams in lieu of his patronymic, and by Roy. licence 1949 the arms of Williams, and has issue living, (by 1st marriage) Jane, b. 1936,—Prudence, b. 1938: m. 1960, David Turnbull, and has issue living, Christopher Neil b. 1962, Catherine Fiona b. 1965.

Sir John Williams, 1st Bt., High Sheriff, Flintshire 1794-5, was grandson of John Williams, Ch. Justice of Brecon, Glamorgan, and Radnor, son of John Williams, Welsh Judge, 2nd son of Sir William Williams, 1st Bt. (cr. 1688) [see Williams-Wynn, Bt.]. Sir John Williams, 2nd Bt., assumed in 1842 the additional surname of Hay, but died in 1859 without male issue.

WILLIAMS, Creation (U.K.) 1866, of Tregullow, Cornwall.

Never despair.

Sir ROBERT ERNEST WILLIAMS, 9th *Baronet*, only son of the late Ernest Claude Williams, el. son of the late Ernest Martyn Williams, 6th son of 2nd baronet; b. June 6th, 1924; s. his kinsman, *Sir* WILLIAM LAW 1960; formerly in ser. of Canadian National Railways: m. 1948, Ruth Margaret, da. of C. Butcher, and has issue.

Arms—Vair, three crescents or. *Crest*—A demi-eagle azure, wings elevated sable, each charged with four bezants.

Residences—Upcott House, Barnstaple, N. Devon; Kamsack, Saskatchewan, Canada.

Sons living—DONALD MARK, b. Nov. 7th, 1954; ed. at W. Buckland Sch.——Barton Matthew b. 1956.
Daughter living—Phyllis June, b. 1949.
Sister living—Leila June, b. 1926: m. 1st, 1952 (m. diss. 1972), Norman E. Hambley; 2ndly, 1972, Adam Casson, (Box 1398, Fort Saskatchewan, Alberta, Canada), and has issue living (by 1st m.), Kenneth Charles Claude. b. 1953,—Thomas Keith, b. 1957,—Kim Lee Ann, b. 1959.

Daughter living of 7th Baronet—Eva Kathleen Victoria Daisy, b. 1900: m. 1935, Lieut.-Com. Christopher Ernest Inman Gibbs, R.N.R. (ret.), who d. 1947, and has issue living——Winifred, b. 1901.

Aunts living—Beatrice Lavinia, b. 1902. *Address*, 611, Gordon St., Midland, Michigan, 48640, USA.——Matilda Maude, b. 1909: m. 1942, Robert McFadyen of 424 Talbot St., Ottawa, Canada, K2K 2N6, and has issue living, Diane Beatrice b. 1942.

Mother living—Theresa Gertrude, da. of R. Greafer : m. 1922, Ernest Claude Williams (ante), who d. 1933. *Address*, Suite 2, Thorndale Apartments, 104, 2nd Av., N.W. Dauphin, Manitoba, Canada.

Widow living of 8th Baronet—BETTY KATHLEEN (*Betty, Lady Williams*), da. of John Taylor, of Hitchin, Herts.: m. 1950, Sir William Law Williams, 8th baronet, who d. 1960. *Residences*, Heanton Punchardon, Braunton, N. Devon ; Upcott, Barnstaple, N. Devon ; Westercombe Cottage, Braunton, N. Devon.

Collateral Branches living.

Granddaughter of the late Rev. Leonard Alfred Williams (infra) :—
Issue of the late Lieut.-Com. David Cameron Williams, R.N., *b.* 1898, *d.* 1931 : *m.* 1929,
Violet Mary (who *m.* 2ndly, 1946, Humphrey Douglas Tyringham, of Little Wood,
Buckland Monachorum, Yelverton, Devon), da. of the late Rev. Arthur Townshend
Boscawen [see V. Falmouth, colls.] :—
Susan Mary, *b.* 1931: *m.* 1954, Maj. John Michael Halford, R.M., and has issue living, John
Wallis Williams, *b.* 1955,—Peter David, *b.* 1957,—Julia Karenza, *b.* 1961. *Residence,* Slenton
Orchard, Whimple, Exeter, EX5 2QL.

Issue of the late Rev. Leonard Alfred Williams, 4th son of 2nd baronet, *b.* 1867,
d. 1956 : *m.* 1894, Margaret Hay (of Sidgard Sidmouth, Devon), da. of the
late Lieut.-Col. Eugene Hay Cameron, R.A. [M. Sligo, colls.] :—
Margaret, *b.* 1900 : *m.* 1930, Brigadier George William Marshall Findlay, C.B.E., M.D., D.Sc.,
who *d.* 1952, and has issue living, a da., *b.* 1931,—a da., *b.* 1933. *Residence,* The Old School
House, Walberton, near Arundel, Sussex.

Grandson of the late Victor George Williams (infra) :—
Issue of the late Frederick Martyn Charles Williams, *b.* 1898, *d.* 1961 : *m.* 1935, Maud
Ann (112, Kingston Row, Winnipeg, Manitoba, R2M O59), da. of the late Dennis
Bawif, of Winnipeg, Canada:—
Martyn Dennis Victor (10, Elmsdale Rd., Kitchener, Ont., Canada), *b.* 1936; ed. at Toronto Univ
(BSc Eng): *m.* 1968, Beth Diane, da. of E. John Koch, of Kitchener, Ont., and has issue living,
Robin Lynn, *b.* 1972.

Issue of the late Victor George Williams, 7th son of 2nd baronet, *b.* 1874, *d.* 1944:
m. 1895, Marion, who *d.* 1948, da. of the late Godfrey Phipps Baker, of Woodruff,
Ottawa :—
Marion Christian Victoria (362, Waterloo St., Winnipeg, Man., Canada), *b.* 1897.

Granddaughter of the late Bertram Leopold Williams (infra):—
Issue of the late William Bertram Williams, *b.* 1906, *d.* 1960 : *m.* 1932, Agnes, da. of
John Allen, of Vancouver, British Columbia :—
Judith Patricia, *b.* 1934. *Residence.*

Issue of the late Bertram Leopold Williams, 9th son of 2nd baronet, *b.* 1878,
d. 1962: *m.* 1st, 1906 (marriage dissolved), Vera Mary only da. of Arthur
Venables, J.P., of Wooburn Ranche, near Vernon, British Columbia; 2ndly,
1926, Amy Muriel Douglas, yst. da. of the late Douglas Fourdrinier, of Ted-
dington, Middlesex:—
(By 1st m.) Claude Martin (1225, East 17th Av., Vancouver 10, BC, Canada), *b.* 1911: *m.* 1944,
Hannah Louisa Mary, da. of the late Capt. William Massey, of Courtown Harbour, Gorey, co.
Wexford, and has issue living, Bertram Douglas *b,* 1945,—William Claude, *b.* 1949.——Peter
Robert, *b.* 1912.

Granddaughter of the late Lieut.-Col. Richard Michael Williams, 2nd son of 1st
baronet :—
Issue of the late Capt. William Phillpotts Williams, *b.* 1860, *d.* 1916 : *m.* 1901, Edith
Bonella, da. of the Rev. James Harvey Simpson, formerly R. of St. Mark's, Bexhill,
and Preb. of Chichester :—
Elizabeth Georgiana Phillpotts, *b.* 1904. *Residence,*

The 1st baronet, Sir William, was High Sheriff of Cornwall 1851 ; and the 2nd baronet, Sir
Frederick Martin, sat as M.P. for Truro (C) 1865-78. The 6th baronet, Sir Burton Robert,
Lieut. Devonshire Regt., *d.* (killed in action during European War) 1917.

WILLIAMS, Creation (U.K.) 1909, of Castell Deudraeth, and Borthwen, co. Merioneth.

No good but God.

Sir (MICHAEL) OSMOND WILLIAMS, *M.C.,*
2nd *Baronet,* son of the late Capt. Osmond
Trahaern Deudraeth Williams, D.S.O., el. son of
1st baronet ; *b.* April 22nd, 1914 ; *s.* his grand-
father, *Sir* (ARTHUR) OSMOND, 1927 ; ed. at
Eton, and Freiburg Univ.; Maj. late R. Scots
Greys; a JP for Merionethshire; 1939-45 War
in Middle East, Italy and N.-W. Europe (MC,
Chevalier of Orders of Leopold II of Belgium
with Palm, Belgian Croix de Guerre with
Palm): *m.* 1947, Benita Mary, da. of the late
G. Henry Booker, of 3, Chesterfield House,
WI, and has issue.

Arms—Argent, a chevron between in chief two mullets
pierced and in base a buck trippant sable. **Crest**—A
griffin segreant sable, holding between the fore claws a
buck's head cabossed gold.
Residence—Borthwen, Minffordd, Penrhyndeudraeth,
Gwynedd.

Daughters living—Sarah Theresa Ceridwen. *b.* 1948.——
Julia Mary Myfanwy, *b.* 1952.
Sister living—Elizabeth Anne (10A, Hollington Park, St.
Leonards-on-Sea, Sussex), *b.* 1915.
Aunt living (daughter of 1st baronet)—Ellen Dolgar
Dormie, *b.* 1891 : *m.* 1915, Capt. Robert Gordon Beazley,
formerly The King's (Liverpool) Regt., who *d.* 1953, and
has issue living, Sam, *b.* 1916 ; formerly Major R.A.S.C.,
—Simon Robert (of 10, Clinton Rd., Leatherhead,
Surrey), *b.* 1922; Lieut.-Col. Roy. Signals (T.A.):
m. 1956, Jennifer Anne Patricia Nery, and has issue
living, Eva Neito *b.* 1959, Olwen Barbara *b.* 1961, Harriot Samantha Loveday *b.* 1965,—Joscelyne Jennifer *b.* 1966,—Luke Trahaern (Judges Way, Carrigbyrne, Newbawn, co. Wexford),
b. 1926; formerly Lt. W.G.: *m.* 1972, Mary Elena, da. of Thomas William Jefferies, and widow of
Robert George Cazalet. *Residence,* 9, Wilbury Gdns., Hove.

The 1st baronet, Sir (Arthur) Osmond Williams, was Lord-Lieut. of Merionethshire, 1909-27,
and MP for Merionethshire (L) Oct. 1900 to Jan. 1910.

WILLIAMS, Creation (U.K.) 1915, of Bridehead, co. Dorset.

Nil Solidum.

Sir ROBERT PHILIP NATHANIEL WILLIAMS, 4th *Baronet*; *b.* May 3rd, 1950; *s.* his father, *Sir* DAVID PHILIP, 1970; ed. at Marlborough and St. Andrew's Univ.

Arms—Argent, a greyhound between three Cornish choughs sable, beaked and membered purpure; on a bordure engrailed gules four crosses formée or between as many besants. Crest—A dexter arm couped, the sleeve barry of four sable and argent, charged with a cross formée per fesse counterchanged between four besants, the hand proper grasping a branch of oak vert, fructed or.
Seat—Bridehead, Dorchester, Dorset.

Brother living—DAVID MICHAEL RALPH, *b.* Feb. 1st, 1955; ed. at Marlborough.

Half Sister living—Mary Venetia Honor, *b.* 1939: *m.* 1964, John Copson Peake, of Corscombe Court, Dorchester, Dorset.

Sister living—Elizabeth Margaret Ruth, *b.* 1951.

Uncle living (son of 2nd baronet)—Nathaniel Roger Cunningham (Berrow Wood School, Pendock, Stourton, Glos.), *b.* 1917; sometime in S. Rhodesia Regt.

Aunts living (daughters of 2nd baronet)—Ann Margaret Augusta, *b.* 1910: *m.* 1932 (m. diss. 1966), Edward Fox Gundry, and has issue living, Edward Patrick (87, Howards Lane, SW15), *b.* 1935: *m.* 1964, the Hon. Caroline Anne Sabina Best, da. of 8th Baron Wynford, and has issue living, Rachel Anne *b.* 1965, Alexandra Clare *b.* 1967,—David Grenville Fox (PO Box 355, Banff, Alberta, Canada), *b.* 1937: *m.* 1960, Marion Downing,—Erica Margaret Caroline, *b.* 1933: *m.* 1962, Robert Wilson, of 46, Argyle Cres., Edinburgh, 15, and has issue living, Edward Robert *b.* 1963, Angus John *b.* 1964, Dugald Fox *b.* 1970, Sheena Margaret *b.* 1965, Mary Honor Ann *b.* 1966, Lucy Caroline *b.* 1969. *Residence,* Shediac Cape, New Brunswick, Canada.——Mary Felicity Rosa (*Lady Crawford*), *b.* 1911: *m.* 1939, Vice-Adm. Sir William Godfrey Crawford, KBE, CB, DSC, and has issue living, Edward Philip, *b.* 1940; ed. at Gordonstoun; BSA Police, Rhodesia: *m.* 1965, Rosamond Helen, da. of W. Frank Wynne, of Greensykes, Ruwa, Rhodesia, —David Alexander, *b.* 1942: *m.* 1968, Penelope Ann, d. of Cdr. C. E. J. Streatfeild, of Denhay, Broadoak, Bridport,—Michael James, *b.* 1951,—Prunella Marion Pharazyn (twin), *b.* 1942: *m.* 1965, Neboysha Ranko Brashish. *Residence,* Poorend, Toller Porcorum, Dorchester, Dorset.—— Jane Elizabeth Rhoda, *b.* 1915: *m.* 1941, Lt.-Col. Richard Leslie David Weber, RA, and has issue living, Jeremy, *b.* 1944,—George, *b.* 1946: *m.* 1969, Elisabeth, el. (adopted), da. of Lt.-Col. the Hon. Alexander Burdett Money-Coutts [B. Latymer],—Philippa Emily Margaret, *b.* 1950. *Residence,* Quatre Bras, Muckleford, Dorchester, Dorset.——Frances Honor Ruth (Wherry Cottage, Winterbourne Abbas, Dorchester), *b.* 1922.——Eleanor Sarah Joy (Little Orchard, Salisbury Rd., Blandford, Dorset), *b.* 1927: *m.* 1948 (m. diss. 1963). John Henry Fownes Luttrell, and has issue living, Charlotte Rose *b.* 1954.——Juliet Dorothea Chassereau *b.* 1933: *m.* 1956, John Douglas Young Hickman, and has issue living, Philip Douglas, *b.* 1956,—Stephen James, *b.* 1958,—Charles Nicholas, *b.* 1960. *Residence,* The Chestnuts, Gilbert's End, Hanley Castle. Worcs.

Widow living of 3rd Baronet—ELIZABETH MARY GARNEYS (*Lady Williams*) (Bridehead, Dorchester, Dorset), da. of William Ralph Garneys Bond [Meysey-Thompson, Bt.]: *m.* 1948, as his 2nd wife, Sir David Philip Williams, 3rd Bt., who *d.* 1970.

Collateral Branch living.

Issue of the late Robert Mark Edgar Williams, 2nd son of 2nd baronet, *b.* 1913, *d.* 1969: *m.* 1942, Juliet Susan Harriet (Chipps Barton, Rodden, Weymouth), da. of Cdr. Kenneth Berkeley Mackenzie Churchill, RN:—
Robert Norrie, *b.* 1943; ed. at Radley: *m.* 1971, Nesta Rosemary, da. of Stewart Bell, of Brodawel, Llanbister, Radnorshire.——John Philip Mackenzie, *b.* 1947; ed. at Radley.——Marcia Jane, *b.* 1945.

The 1st baronet, Col. Sir Robert Williams, V.D., T.D. (el. son of the late Robert Williams, of Bridehead, Dorchester), was M.P. for W. Div. of Dorset (C) 1895-1922, and sometime Hon. Col. 4th Batn. Dorsetshire Regt. The second baronet, Sir Philip Francis Cunningham Williams, was High Sheriff of Dorset 1949.

WILLIAMS, Creation (U.K.) 1928, of Park, co. Aberdeen, and of Livingstone, Territory of N. Rhodesia. [Extinct 1938.]

Sir ROBERT WILLIAMS, 1st and last *Baronet.*

Daughter living of 1st Baronet—Mary Constance, *b.* 1891: *m.* 1st, 1912, Edward Hedley Cuthbertson, Lt. R. Warwickshire Regt., who *d.* (on active ser.) 1917; 2ndly, 1920, Col. Francis Bere Follett, DSO, MC, late R. Warwickshire Regt., who *d.* 1962, and has issue living, (by 1st m.) Pamela Anne (of Turweston Barn, Brackley, Northants), *b.* 1915: *m.* 1940, Roy Frederick Storey, Lt. Shropshire LI, who *d.* (killed in action during 1939-45 War) 1944, and has issue living, Thomas Michael *b.* 1943,—Suzanne Hedley, *b.* 1917: *m.* 1938, Charles Tarbutt, of Appledown, Blackham, E. Sussex, and has issue living, Simon Hedley *b.* 1940,—(by 2nd m.) Pauline Mary, *b.* 1921: *m.* 1st, 1948, Clive Bonner Stoddart, who *d.* 1949; 2ndly, 1951, David John Robarts, of The Glebe House, Lillingstone, Lovell, Buckingham, and has issue living, (by 2nd marriage) Timothy Peter Follett *b.* 1952, John David *b.* 1954, Francis James *b.* 1956, Susan Mary Charlotte *b.* 1960. *Residence* 60, Jubilee Place, Chelsea, S.W.3.

WILLIAMS, Creation (U.K.) 1953, of Cilgeraint, co. Caernarvon.

Sir ROBIN PHILIP WILLIAMS, 2nd *Baronet;* b. May 27th, 1928; *s.* his father, *Sir* HERBERT GERAINT, *M.P.*, 1954; ed. at Eton, and **at** St. John's Coll., Camb. (MA); Bar. Middle Temple 1954; an Insurance Broker; Member of Lloyds 1968-74; 2nd Lt. (ret.) RA; Vice-Chm., Fedn. of Univ. Conservative and Unionist Assos. 1951-52, and acting Chm. 1952; Chm. of Bow Group 1954, and of Anti-Common Market League 1969; a Borough Councillor of Haringay since 1968: *m.* 1955, Wendy Adele Marguerite, only da. of the late Felix Joseph Alexander, of Hong Kong, and has issue.

Residence—1, Broadlands Close, Highgate, N.6.

Sons living—ANTHONY GERAINT, *b.* Dec. 22nd, 1958.——Stephen Robin Alexander, *b.* 1962.

Sister living—Rosemary (*Lady Bethaven and Stenton*), *b.* 1927: *m.* 1st 1946 (m. diss. 1969), Sir Ian (John) Auld Mactaggart, 3rd Bt.; 2ndly, 1973, the 13th Lord Belhaven and Stenton, of Tighcargaman, Port Ellen, Isle of Islay, Argyll.

The 1st baronet, Sir Herbert Geraint Williams (son of the late Thomas Williams, LL.D., of Hooton, Cheshire), was M.P. for Reading (*U*) 1924-29, for S. Div. of Croydon 1932-45, and for E. Div. of Croydon 1950-54, and Parliamentary Sec. to Board of Trade 1928-9.

DUDLEY-WILLIAMS, Creation (U.K.) 1964, of City and Co. of the City of Exeter.

Sir ROLF DUDLEY DUDLEY-WILLIAMS, 1st *Baronet;* son of Arthur Williams, of Plymouth; *b.* June 17th, 1908; ed. at Plymouth Coll., and at RAF Coll., Cranwell; assumed the surname of Dudley-Williams by deed poll 1964; late Flying Officer RAF; founded Power Jets Ltd., for Whittle system of jet propulsion 1936; Member of Council of Soc. of British Aircraft Constructors 1944, Companion of Roy. Aeronautical Soc. 1944; PPS to Sec. of State for War 1958-59, and to Min. of Agriculture 1959-64; Chm. of W. Area of National Union of Conservative Assocns. 1961-64; MP for Exeter (*C*) 1951-66: *m.* 1940, Margaret Helen, el. da. of the late Frederick Eaton Robinson, OBE, AMICE, AMIMechE, of Enfield, and has issue.

Arms—Gules a chevron engrailed plain cotised between in chief two cranes respectant proper, and in base a triangular castle of three towers or. Crest—In front of a castle as in the arms, a wild cat rampant guardant proper.

Residence—The Old Manse, South Petherton, Som. *Club*—RAF.

Sons living—ALASTAIR EDGCUMBE JAMES (c/o Ocean Inchcape (Brunei) Ltd., PO Box 2320, Banclar Sieri Begawan, State of Brunei), *b.* Nov. 26th, 1943: *m.* 1971, Diana Elizabeth Jane, twin da. of R. H. C. Duncan, of The Old Rectory, Sutton Montis, nr. Yeovil, Som., and has issue living, Marina Elizabeth Catherine, *b.* 1974.——Malcolm Philip Edgcumb (55, Harbord St., SW6), *b.* 1947: *m.* 1973, Caroline, twin da. of R. H. C. Duncan, of The Old Rectory, Sutton Montis, Yeovil, Som.

HUME-WILLIAMS, Creation (U.K.) 1922, of Ewhurst, co. Surrey.

Sir ROY ELLIS HUME-WILLIAMS, **2nd** *Baronet; b.* July 31st, 1887; *s.* his father, *the Rt. Hon. Sir* (WILLIAM) ELLIS, *K.B.E., K.C.,* 1947; ed. at Eton, and at Trin. Hall, Camb.: *m.* 1st, 1915, Norah (who *d.* 1964, having obtained a divorce 1949), da. of the late David Anderson, of Sydney, N.-S. Wales; 2ndly, 1949, Frances Mary, da. of Maj. Edmund Arthur Hudson Groom, OBE, of Warham, Wells, Norfolk.

Arms—Per chevron or sable, in chief two demi-lions rampant and erased of the last, and in base a cross-bow bent palewise argent, the arrow of the first. Crest—A lion rampant sable, gorged with a collar suspended therefrom by its chains a portcullis or, and holding between the paws a bird-bolt erect argent, headed and flighted gold.

Residence—Ardlui, The Highlands, East Horsley, Surrey. *Clubs*—R.A.C., County (Guildford), and M.C.C.

Peace is sought by war.

The 1st baronet, the Rt. Hon. Sir (William) Ellis Hume-Williams, K.B.E., K.C. (only son of the late Joseph William Hume-Williams, Bar.-at-Law), was Recorder of Bury St. Edmunds 1901-5, and of Norwich 1905-44, and sat as M.P. for Bassetlaw Div. of Notts 1919-29.

RHYS WILLIAMS, Creation (U.K.) 1918, of Miskin, Parish of Llantrisant, co. Glamorgan.

Sir BRANDON MEREDITH RHYS WILLIAMS, *MP,* 2nd *Baronet*; *b.* Nov. 14th, 1927; *s.* his father, *Col. Sir.* RHYS, *DSO, QC,* 1955; ed. at Eton; late Lt. Welsh Guards; formerly with I.C.I., Ltd.; Assist. Dir., The Spastics Soc. 1962-63; a Consultant with Management Selection, Ltd. 1963-71; MP for S. Kensington (*C*) March 1968 to Feb. 1974, since when for Kensington and Chelsea (Kensington): *m.* 1961, Caroline Susan, el. da. of Ludovic A. Foster, of Greatham Manor, Pulborough, Sussex, and has issue.

   Arms—Per chevron argent and gules, in chief two cocks of the second and in base as many chevronels of the first. **Crest**—Between two fleur-de-lis argent, a goat's head couped sable, with curved horns.

   Seat—Miskin Manor, Llantrisant, Glamorgan.

   London residence, 32, Rawlings St., SW3. *Clubs*—White's, Cardiff and County.

Son living—ARTHUR GARETH LUDOVIC EMRYS, *b.* Nov. 9th, 1961.

Daughters living—Elinor Caroline, *b.* 1964.——Miranda Pamela Cariadwen, *b.* 1968.

Sisters living—Susan Eleanor (*Lady Glyn*), *b.* 1923 ; Bar. Inner Temple 1950 ; late Junior Com. A.T.S. : *m.* 1946, Capt. Sir Anthony Geoffrey Leo Simon Glyn, 2nd Bt. (cr. 1927), Welsh Gds. *Residence,* 6, Rue Saint-Louis-en-l'Ile, Paris IV.——Marion Elspeth, *b.* 1937.

   Col. Sir Rhys Rhys Williams, D.S.O., Q.C., 1st baronet (son of the late Gwilym Williams, a Judge of County Courts, of Miskin Manor, Glamorgan), Parl. Sec. to Min. of Transport 1919, Recorder of Cardiff 1922-30, Chm. of Quarter Sessions, Glamorgan, and MP for N. Oxon (*L*) 1918. and for Banbury 1918-22. He assumed by deed poll 1938 the additional surname of Rhys.

Williams-Bulkeley, see Bulkeley.

Williams-Drummond, see Drummond.

Williams-Wynn, see Wynn.

WILLIAMSON, Creation (E.) 1642, of East Markham, Nottinghamshire.

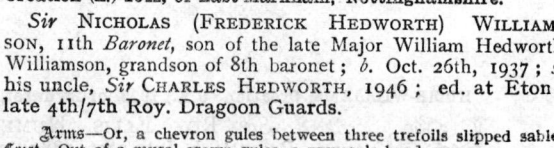

Sir NICHOLAS (FREDERICK HEDWORTH) WILLIAMSON, 11th *Baronet,* son of the late Major William Hedworth Williamson, grandson of 8th baronet ; *b.* Oct. 26th, 1937 ; *s.* his uncle, *Sir* CHARLES HEDWORTH, 1946 ; ed. at Eton; late 4th/7th Roy. Dragoon Guards.

   Arms—Or, a chevron gules between three trefoils slipped sable. **Crest**—Out of a mural crown gules, a wyvern's head or.

   Residence—Lane House, Mortimer, Reading.

Aunt living—Elizabeth Mary, *b.* 1901. *Residence,* 2, Trumpeter's House, Old Palace Yard, Richmond, Surrey.

   Mother living of 11th Baronet—Diana Mary (*Baroness Hailes*) (Lane House, Mortimer, Reading, Berks.), da. of the late Brig.-Gen. the Hon. Charles Lambton, DSO [*see* E. Durham, colls.]; is a CStJ: *m.* 1st, 1936, Maj. William Hedworth Williamson (ante), who *d.* (killed in action in Middle East) 1942; 2ndly, 1945, the 1st Baron Hailes, who *d.* 1974.

Collateral Branch living.

   Granddaughter of the late Capt. Cecil Hedworth J. C. L. G. Williamson, only son of the late Robert Hudleston Williamson, 3rd son of 6th baronet:—

   Issue of the late Brig. Hudleston Noel Hedworth Williamson, DSO, MC, *b.* 1886, *d.* 1971: *m.* 1st, 1923 (m. diss. 1926), Helen Marjorie, da. of Arthur Lord; 2ndly, 1926, Leila Isabel (South Nore, W. Wittering, Sussex), only da. of Lt.-Col. Robert William Peter Lodwick, of Lisheen, Camberley:—

   (By 2nd m.) Mary (*Lady Nicholas C. Gordon-Lennox*), *b.* 1934: *m.* 1958, Lord Nicholas Charles Gordon-Lennox, MVO [*see* D. Richmond and Gordon].

   Sir Thomas, the 1st baronet, suffered greatly for his loyalty in the civil wars, and paid £3,400 to the sequestrators for his estate. Sir Hedworth, the 7th baronet, was M.P. for the northern division of Durham (*L*) 1832-7, and High Sheriff of that county.

WILLINK, Creation (U.K.) 1957, of Dingle Bank, City of Liverpool.

FIDES·ET·AMOR

Sir CHARLES WILLIAM WILLINK, 2nd *Baronet*, *b.* Sept. 10th, 1929; *s.* his father *The Rt. Hon.* *Sir* HENRY URMSTON, *MC, QC*, 1973; ed. at Eton, and Trin. Coll., Camb.; Housemaster, Eton Coll. since 1964: *m.* 1954, Elizabeth, el. da. of Humfrey Andrewes, of North Grove, Highgate, N6, and has issue.

Arms—Azure, three acorns on one stem slipped or. **Crest**—Issuant from a wreath of oak leaves or, a dexter cubit arm bendwise grasping in the hand a chaplet of laurel proper.

Residence, Holland House, Eton College, Windsor, Berks.

Son living—EDWARD DANIEL, *b.* Feb. 18th, 1957.

Daughter living—Penelope Jane, *b.* 1959.

Brother living—Stephen Henry (20, Boileau Rd., SW13), *b.* 1932; ed. at Eton, and at Trin. Coll., Oxford: *m.* 1970, Mary Louise, da. of Ernest R. Royston, of 52, Carslake Rd., SW, and has issue living, Henry Augustine, *b.* 1971 —Annabella Mary Victoria, *b.* 1975.

Sisters living—Rachel Frances: *m.* 1947, Michael Kinchin Smith, and has issue living, Christopher Henry, *b.* 1950: *m.* 1974, Susan Valerie, yr. da. of William G. Adams, of W. Wickham, Kent,— John Michael, *b.* 1952,—David Francis, *b.* 1954,—Robert Mark, *b.* 1960,—Lavinia Mary, *b.* 1948: *m.* 1975, John Cunningham,—Juliet Clare, *b.* 1957. *Residence*, 15, Sheen Gate Gdns., SW14 7PD.——Elisabeth Mary: *m.* 1951, Frank Erskine Bell, son of the late Sir Ernest Albert Seymour Bell, CIE, and has issue living, Nicholas John, *b.* 1953,—Catharine Elisabeth, *b.* 1955. *Residence*, Hillcross, Red Cross Lane, Cambridge.

Widow living of 1st Baronet—Mrs. DORIS CAMPBELL PRESTON (*Nan, Lady Willink*), (51, Madingley Rd., Cambridge, CB3 0EL, da. of the late William Campbell Sharman, of Leicester: *m.* 1964, as his 2nd wife, the Rt. Hon. Sir Henry Urmston Willink, 1st Bt., MC, QC, who *d.* 1973.

The Rt. Hon. Sir Henry Urmston Willink, MC, QC, son of William Edward Willink, FRIBA, oe Liverpool, was MP for N. Croydon (C) 1940-48, Min. of Health 1943-45, Master of Magdalenf Coll., Camb. 1948-66, and Vice-Chancellor of Norwich and St. Edmundsbury and Ipswich Dioceses 1948-55, and Dean of Arches 1955-70.

WILLS, Creation (U.K.) 1904, of Hazelwood, Stoke Bishop, Westbury-on-Trym, Gloucestershire, and Clapton-in-Gordano, Somerset.

QUO DEUS VULT

Sir (ERNEST) EDWARD (DE WINTON), WILLS, 4th *Baronet*; *b.* Dec. 8th, 1903; *s.* his father, *Sir* ERNEST SALTER, 1958; ed. at Eton; Lieut.-Col. late Middlesex Regt., formerly Lieut. Scots Guards, and Lieut.-Col. Comdg. 5th Batn. Manchester Regt. (T.A.); is a Member of Lloyd's; European War 1939-45: *m.* 1st, 1926, Sylvia Margaret, who *d.* 1946, da. of the late William Barker Ogden; 2ndly, 1949, Juliet Eve, da. of the late Capt. John Eagles Henry Graham-Clarke, J.P., of Frocester Manor, Glos., and has issue by 1st marriage.

Arms—Gules, three suns in splendour fessewise, between two griffins passant or. **Crest**—Issuant from an annulet or, a demi-griffin gules, charged with a sun in splendour, and holding in the dexter claw a battle-axe also or. *Seat*—Meggernie Castle, Glenlyon, Perthshire. *Residence*—Mount Prosperous, Hungerford, Berks. *Clubs*— Household Division Yacht, Lloyds Yacht, Cavalry and Guards'.

Daughters living—By 1st marriage—Venetia Dawn, *b.* 1927: *m.* 1st, 1948, as his second wife (marriage dissolved 1962), Charles Robert Cecil Weld, Forester [*see* B. Forester]; 2ndly, 1962, Alan Cripps Nind Hopkins, of Hugditch, Ramsbury, Marlborough, and has issue living (by 1st m.) [*see* B. Forester],—(by 2nd m.) Mark Edward Wills *b.* 1963,—Peter Alan Wills (twin) *b.* 1963.—— Edwina Sylvia, *b.* 1933: *m.* 1st, 1952 (m. diss. 1961), Viscount Savernake (now 8th Marquess of Ailesbury); 2ndly, 1963, Maj. Christopher Leslie Leo Bonn, late Welsh Gds., of La Maison du Coin, St. Ouen, Jersey, C.I., and has issue living (by 1st m.) [*see* M. Ailesbury],—(by 2nd m.) Philip Edward Leo, *b.* 1964,—Camilla Georgina Alexandra, *b.* 1965,—Melanie Marina Roselle, *b.* 1974.

Brother living——GEORGE SETON, *T.D.*, *b.* May 18th, 1911; late Major Roy. Wilts Yeo. European War 1939-45 (despatches): *m.* 1st, 1935 (marriage dissolved 1946), Lilah Mary, da. of the late Capt. Percy Richard Hare [*see* E. Listowel, colls.]; 2ndly, 1961, Victoria Katherine, da. of the late Capt. Percy Richard Hare (ante), and has issue living, (by 1st *m.*) David Seton (Littlecote, Hungerford, Berks.) *b.* 1939; ed. at Eton; ARICS; QALAS: *m.* 1968, Gillian, twin da. of Albert Eastoe, and has issue living, James Seton *b.* 1970, Sarah Elizabeth *b.* 1969,—Victoria Lucy *b.* 1975.   *Residence*, Eastridge, Ramsbury, nr. Marlborough, Wilts. *Club*, MCC.

Sisters living—Margaret Joyce de Winton, *b.* 1898: *m.* 1918, Capt. John Trevor Kyffin, formerly RFC, who *d.* 1969, and has issue living, Thomas Trevor (Whitehall, Churchstow, Kingsbridge, S. Devon), *b.* 1931; ed. at Eton: *m.* 1st, 1953, Mary Christine Wentworth Browne; 2ndly, 1967, Margaret Elizabeth Legge, and has issue living, (by 1st m.) John Seton *b.* 1954, David Thomas *b.* 1956, Laura Jane *b.* 1960, (by 2nd m.) Katherine Lleuki Josephine *b.* 1968, Sophie Tamsin Sian *b.* 1971,—Elizabeth Jane, *b.* 1923: *m.* 1946, Michael Francis Laloe, and has issue living, Michael John Kyffin, *b.* 1947, Nicholas James *b.* 1950, Victoria Jane *b.* 1948.   *Residence*, Forder, South Brent, Devon.——Barbara Joan de Winton, *b.* 1902: *m.* 1st, 1925 (m. diss. 1943), Capt. Thomas Ansell Fairhurst, formerly 2nd Life Gds.; 2ndly, 1943, Jack Morton, formerly Lt. 7th Queen's Own Hussars, and has issue living, (by 1st m.) James Seton, *b.* 1926,—Elizabeth Jill, *b.* 1928: *m.* 1st, 1950 (m. diss. 1955), John Houlder; 2ndly, 1969, John Dillon, and has issue living, (by 1st m.) Nicholas James *b.* 1950,—(by 2nd m.) Joanna Susan (c/o Coutts & Co., 1, Cadogan Pl., Sloane St., SW1), *b.* 1944: *m.* 1963, Lt.-Cdr. Michael John Prickett, RN (ret.), and has issue living, Adam James *b.* 1969, Emma Jane *b.* 1965,—Jennifer Jane, *b.* 1947: *m.* 1966, Richard John Whittall, of Round Robin Farm, Highworth, Wilts., and has issue living, Nicholas John *b.* 1967.   *Residence*, Upper Burytown Farm, Blunsdon, nr. Swindon, Wilts.

Collateral Branch living.

Issue of the late Capt. Arnold Stancomb Wills, youngest son of 1st baronet, *b.* 1877, *d.* 1961: *m.* 1905, Hilda Carolin, who *d.* 1965, da. of the late Edward Lyon, of London and New York:—

Arnold Cass Lycett, *b.* 1906 ; ed. at Harrow, and at Pembroke Coll., Camb.; late 2nd Lieut. 9th Lancers; 1939-45 War as Capt. and Adj., 24th Lancers.   *Residence*, Thornby Hall, Northampton. *Club*, Bath.——John Lycett, *b.* 1910; is Maj. (ret.) Life Guards: *m.* 1936, the Hon. Jean Constance Buller-Fullerton-Elphinstone, da. of 16th Lord Elphinstone, and has issue living, Andrew Arnold Lyon (Middleton House, Longparish, Andover, Hants), *b.* 1937; Capt. (ret.) Life Guards: *m.* 1961, the Hon. Elizabeth Anne Cecil, da. of 2nd Baron Rockley, and has issue living, Richard Arnold *b.* 1962, Alexander John *b.* 1967, a da. *b.* 1963,—Susan Griselda Ann Lyon, *b.* 1940: *m.* 1960, Capt. Charles Peregrine Albemarle Bertie, Scots Guards (Supplementary Reserve) [*see* E. Lindsey and Abingdon, colls.].   *Residence*, Allanbay Park, Binfield, Berks.

The 1st baronet, Sir Edward Payson Wills, K.C.B. (son of the late Henry Overton Wills, J.P., of Bristol), was a Director of the Imperial Tobacco Co. (Limited), and a Gov. of Bristol Gen. Hospital.   The 2nd baronet, Sir Edward Chaning Wills (also a Director of the Imperial Tobacco Co., Limited), was High Sheriff of Devon 1915.   The 3rd baronet, Sir Ernest Salter Wills, was Lord Lieut. of Wilts. 1930-42, and a Director of Imperial Tobacco Co.

WILLS, Creation (U.K.) 1923, of Blagdon, co. Somerset.

Sir JOHN VERNON WILLS, *TD*, 4th *Baronet*, *b.* July 3rd, 1928; *s.* his brother, *Sir* GEORGE PETER VERNON, 1945; ed. at Eton; a Co. Councillor, and a JP for Avon; a DL for Somerset 1968, and High Sheriff 1968-69; Lord-Lieut. for Avon 1974; Lt.-Col. Comdg. N. Somerset and Bristol Yeo. 1965-67 (Brevet Col. 1967); formerly Lt. Coldm. Gds. (Reserve); Chm. of Wessex Water Authority and Member of Nat. Water Council since 1974; a Dir. Bristol and West Building Soc., and *Bristol Evening Post*: *m.* 1953, Diana Veronica Cecil (Jane), only da. of Douglas R. M. Baker, of Thiery House, Litton, nr. Bath, and has issue.

Arms—Gules, a sun in splendour between two gryphons passant in pale or.   **Crest**—Issuant from an annulet or, a demi-gryphon gules, holding in the dexter claw a battle-axe gold.

Residences—Langford Court, Langford, Bristol.

Pro aris et focis.

For our altars and our hearths.

Sons living—DAVID JAMES VERNON, *b.* Jan. 2nd 1955.——Anthony John Vernon, *b.* 1956.——Ruper, Charles Vernon, *b.* 1959,——Julian Robert Vernon, *b.* 1963.

Sister living—Jean Mary Vernon, *b.* 1925: *m.* 1948, Richard Hill of Harptree Court, East Harptree, Somerset [Harford, Bt.], and has issue living, Charles Peter Loraine, *b.* 1954,—Angela Mary Loraine, *b.* 1949,—Caryll Loraine, *b.* 1951,—Sarah Loraine, *b.* 1957.

The 1st baronet, Sir George Alfred Wills, was Pres. of Imperial Tobacco Co. of Great Britain and Ireland (Limited), and his son, Sir George Vernon Proctor Wills, 2nd Bt., was a Director of the same Company.   The 3rd baronet, Sir George Peter Vernon, Lieut. Coldstream Guards, *d.* (killed in action during European War) 1945.

WILLSHIRE, Creation (U.K.) 1841. [Extinct 1947.]

Sir GERARD ARTHUR MAXWELL WILLSHIRE, 3rd and last *Baronet*.

Daughter living of 3rd Baronet—Patricia Frederica, *b.* 1925: *m.* 1st, 1943 (m. diss. 1949) Greville Pollard Baylis, Lt. Irish Guards; 2ndly, 1949, George Breary Girardet, and has issue living, (by 1st m.) Greville Mark Willshire, *b.* 1944,—(by 2nd m.) Guy Maxwell, *b.* 1953,—Gail Beatriz Willshire, *b.* 1952. *Residence,*

WILMOT, Creation (G.B.) 1759, of Chaddesden, Derbyshire.

Sir HENRY ROBERT WILMOT, 9th *Baronet, b.* April 10th, 1967; *s.* his father, *Capt. Sir* ROBERT ARTHUR, 1974.

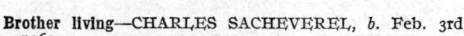

Arms—Sable, on a fesse or, between three eagles' heads couped argent as many escallops gules, a canton vaire ermine and gules. **Crest**—An eagle's head couped argent gorged with a mural coronet sable, in the beak an escallop gules. *Residence*—Pitters House, Sandy Lane, Chippenham, Wilts.

Brother living—CHARLES SACHEVEREL, *b.* Feb. 3rd, 1969.
Sister living—Zoë Meriel, *b.* 1971.
Aunt living (daughter of 7th baronet)—Pamela Ann, *b.* 1937: *m.* 1st, 1959 (m. diss. 1967), Capt. William James Stockton, late R. Scots Greys; 2ndly, 1967, Antony Paul McCaffry, of Ham Farm House, Basingstoke, Hants, and 14, Eaton Pl., SW1, and has issue living, (by 1st m.) Adela Louise, *b.* 1961,—Henrietta Maria Caroline, *b.* 1963,—(by 2nd m.) Sophie Claire, *b.* 1968.
Great-uncle living (son of 6th baronet)—Henry Frederick (PO Box 1663, Yellowknife, NWT, Canada), *b.* 1910; ed. at Wellington Coll., 1939-45 War with R. Canadian Army Ser. Corps: *m.* 1946, Patricia Bridget, da. of the late Thomas Wall, and has issue living, Sheila Marian, *b.* 1947.
Widow living of 7th Baronet—PAMELA VERA, da. of the late Maj. Harry Sebastian Garrard, of Welton Pl., Daventry: *m.* 1st, 1936, Maj. Sir Arthur Ralph Wilmot, 7th baronet, who *d.* (on active ser. during 1939-45 War) 1942; 2ndly, 1955, Lt.-Col. Charles Frederick Cathcart, DSO, who *d.* 1971 [*see* E. Cathcart, colls.]. *Residence,* 12, Cornwall Mews South, SW7.

Mother living—Juliet Elvira (Pitters House, Sandy Lane, Chippenham, Wilts), el. da. of Capt. Michael Neville Tufnell, DSC, RN (ret.), of Curdridge Grange, Botley, Hants.: *m.* 1965 (m. diss. 1974), Capt. Sir Robert Arthur Wilmot, 8th Bt., Scots Gds., who *d.* 1974.

Collateral Branches living.

Grandsons of the Rev. Darwin Wilmot, son of the late Edward Woollett Wilmot (infra):—
Issue of the late Capt. Sacheverel Darwin Wilmot, R.A., *b.* 1885, *d.* (on active ser. during European War) 1918: *m.* 1912, Annie Dudley, who *d.* 1960, da. of the late Maj.-Gen. Strover, R.A. :—
Martyn Sacheverel, *b.* 1914; Major (ret.) RA; 1939-45 War (prisoner): *m.* 1948, Mona Elizabeth da. of S. D. M. Horner, and has issue living, Brian Sacheverel, *b.* 1949,—Robin Woollett, *b.* 1950,—Anabel Sarah, *b.* 1960. *Residence,* Fetcham Lodge, Fetcham, Surrey.——Gordon Darwin, *b.* 1918; Major (ret.) Roy. Scots Fusiliers: *m.* 1941, Margot Virginia Thorburn, and has issue living, Patrick Gordon, *b.* 1954,—Virginia Ann, *b.* 1942: *m.* 1965, Jeremy Adrian Hill, MA, of Peyton Hall, Bures, Suffolk, and has issue living, Edward Justin *b.* 1969, Tristram Darwin *b.* 1970,—Felicity Joyce, *b.* 1944: *m.* 1964, Anthony P. Ziegler, of New Place, Haslemere, Surrey, and has issue living, Thomas Pippin *b.* 1965, Nicholas Martyn *b.* 1967. *Residence,* Chaddesden, Walberton, Arundel, Sussex.

Grandchildren of the late Edward Woollett Wilmot, 4th son of 3rd baronet:—
Issue of the late Reginald Mead Wilmot, *b.* 1852, *d.* 1920: *m.* 1893, Melinda, who *d.* 1943, da. of George Daniels:—
Garton Woollett, *b.* 1900: *m.* 1931, Ivason White, of Toronto. *Residence,* 8, Camelot Court, Don Mills, Ont., Canada.——Frances Ellen, *b.* 1895: *m.* 1st, 1915, Charles William Radloff; 2ndly, 1958, Walter Evans, of 160, Wellington St. N., Woodstock, Ont., N4S 6R6, Canada, and has issue living, (by 1st m.) Irma Doreen, *b.* 1919: *m.* 1943, Herbert Watts, of 36, Stafford St., Woodstock, Ont., Canada, and has issue living, William Terence *b.* 1944: *m.* 1968, Elizabeth Maria Tizzard, of Embro (and has issue living, Jeffery Michael *b.* 1972), Donna Frances *b.* 1946: *m.* 1969, William Wesley Lazenby, of Woodstock (and has issue living, William Scott *b.* 1974).

Grandchildren of the late Edmund Wilmot, 7th son of 3rd baronet:—
Issue of the late Rev. Francis Edmund William Wilmot, *b.* 1849, *d.* 1911: *m.* 1878, Katharine, who *d.* 1939, da. of the late Col. Thomas Coningsby Norbury Norbury, C.B., of Sherridge, near Malvern [V. Guillamore]:—
Katharine Joyce, *b.* 1888: *m.* 1930, Henry Sutcliffe Crook, who *d.* 1945, and has issue living, Faith Marygold, *b.* 1931.——Meriel, *b.* 1900: *m.* 1931, Ariston St. John Diamant, who *d.* 1951. *Residence,* Manor Cottage, Easting, Faversham, Kent.

Issue of the late Capt. Edmund Mead Wilmot, *b.* 1860, *d.* 1935: *m.* 1885, Agatha Georgiana, who *d.* 1931, da. of Francis J. Jessopp:—
Francis Hurt, *b.* 1894: *m.* 1935, Dorothy Fownes, el. da. of Harry W. Keith, M.D., of Enderby, British Columbia, and has issue living, Penelope, *b.* 19—. *Residence,* Vancouver, British Columbia.

Issue of the late Rose Wilmot, *b.* 1853, *d.* 1934: *m.* 1873, John Henry Fox, who *d.* 1892:—
Doris (of Malt House, Oast Rd., Oxted, Surrey), *b.* 1886: *m.* 1906, Alexander Hamilton, who *d.* 1928, and has issue living, John (of Box Cottage, Oxted, Surrey), *b.* 1913: *m.* 1940, Kathleen Rayfield, and has issue living, Alexander *b.* 1947, Barbara *b.* 1941, Sheelagh *b.* 1946,—Jean, *b.* 1907,—Anne, *b.* 1915: *m.* 1938, Kenneth Cuthbert, of Post Office, Forest Green, Surrey, and has issue living, Michael *b.* 1945, William *b.* 1951, Diana *b.* 1942, Elizabeth *b.* 1949,—Lettice *b.* 1918: *m.* 1941, Anthony Essex Potter, of 60, Riverside Drive, New York 10024, USA, and has issue living, Robin (Mary Esther, Florida, USA) *b.* 1945; with USAF: *m.* 1967, Suzanne Marshall, of Larchmont, NY, USA, Bridget *b.* 1943: *m.* 1965, Robert Morton Fass, of New York City, NY, USA.

Granddaughter of the late Rev. Francis Edmund William Wilmot (ante):—
Issue of the late Mary Sacheverel Wilmot, *b.* 1881, *d.* 1911: *m.* 1904, George Robins Joyce, MA, of Bath Coll.:—

Audrey Marion, b. 1905: m. 1936, George Frederick Peter Quin, of Yew Tree Farm, Sheirngton, Newport Pagnell, Bucks., and has issue living, Simon Peter, b. 1942,—Gerda Mary, b. 1937: m. 1958, Garth Francis Cockings, MB, BS, of Yew Tree Farm, Sherington, Newport Pagnell, Bucks., and has issue living, Jerome Garth b. 1964, Giles Francis Sacheverel b. 1969, Karen Mary b. 1959, Fiona Gerda b. 1961.

The family of Wilmot settled at Sutton-upon-Soar, in Nottinghamshire, soon after the Conquest, and removed from thence into Derbyshire about the year 1539. The 1st baronet, Sir Edward Wilmot, an eminent Physician, was Physician-General to the Army, and Physician in Ordinary to George II.   Col. Sir Henry Wilmot, K.C.B., V.C., 5th Bt., sat as M.P. for Derbyshire, S. (C) 1869-85.   The 6th baronet, Sir Ralph Henry Sacheverel Wilmot. Capt. Coldstream Guards, d. (result of wounds on active ser.) 1918 and cr. the 7th baronet, Maj. Sir Arthur Ralph Wilmot, d. (result of an accident whilst on active ser. in Middle East) 1942. Capt. Sir Robert Arthur Wilmot, 8th baronet, Scots Gds. was Equerry to HRH the Duke of Gloucester 1963-65.

WILMOT, Creation (G.B.) 1772, of Osmaston, Derbyshire.   [Extinct 1931.]

Sir ROBERT RODNEY WILMOT, 6th and last *Baronet.*

Daughters living of 6th Baronet—By 2nd marriage—Norah Eleanor, b. 1889. *Residence*, Binfield Grove, Binfield, Berks.——Kathleen Eleanor, b. 1893: m. 1921, Arthur Charles Melville Pym, who d. 1956, and has issue living, Robert Marcus, b. 1922. *Residence*, 38, Wellesley Drive, Wellington Park, Crowthorne, Berks.

EARDLEY-WILMOT, Creation (U.K.) 1821, of Berkswell Hall, Warwickshire.

Sir JOHN ASSHETON EARDLEY-WILMOT, *MVO, DSC, RN,* 5th *Baronet; b.* Jan. 2nd, 1917; *s.* his uncle, *Maj. Sir* JOHN, 1970; Cdr. RN (ret.); AMBIM; FRSA; with Monoplies Commn. since 1967; Liveryman of Paviours' Co.; 1939-45 War (DSC); MVO (4th class) 1957: *m.* 1939, Diana, da. of Cdr. Aubrey Moore, and has issue.

Arms—Quarterly, 1st, sable, a fesse or, between three eagles' heads couped argent, in the beak of each an escallop gules, *Wilmot ;* 2nd argent, on a chevron azure, three garbs or ; a canton gules charged with a fret or, *Eardley ;* 3rd, azure, a fesse engrailed or, between three maidens' heads proper, crined or, *Marow ;* 4th, quarterly, argent and sable, a bend gules, charged with three mullets of the first.   Crests—1st, an eagle's head couped argent, in his beak an escallop gules ; 2nd, a buck courant gules, attired and unguled or.

Residence—41, Margravine Gdns., W6.

Son living—MICHAEL JOHN ASSHETON, b. Jan. 13th, 1941; ed. at Clifton: m. 1971, Wendy, yr. da. of A. J. Wolstenholme, and has issue living, Benjamin John, b. Jan. 24th, 1974.
Daughter living—Patricia Enid, b. 1944: m. 1966, Lt. Andrew McMeekan, RN, of 9, Cross St., Barnes, SW13, and has issue living, Emily Charlotte, b. 1974.
Brother living—Michael (10, Lowther Park Av., Turramarra, NSW), b. 1924: m. 1956; Sylvia, da. of Arthur Irish, of Sydney, NSW.
Sister living—Rosemary (*Hon. Mrs. Basil E. Feilding*) (Park Cottage, Newnham Paddox, Rugby), b. 1920: m. 1939, Capt. the Hon. Basil Egerton Feilding, Coldm. Gds., who d. 1970 [*see* E. Denbigh].
Daughter living of 4th Baronet—Mary Assheton Alexandra, b. 1927: m. 1950, Gavin Douglas Don, and has issue living, William Assheton Eardley Douglas, b. 1958,—Gavin Marow Douglas, b. 1960,—Alexander Wilmot Douglas, b. 1964,—Susannah Mary Grizel Douglas, b. 1952,—Sarah Amabel Douglas, b. 1955,—Cecily Margaret Douglas, b. 1970. *Residence*, Gardyne Castle, by Forfar, Angus.

Collateral Branches living.

Issue of the late Rear-Adm. Sir Sydney¦ Marow Eardley-Wilmot, 5th son of 2nd baronet, b. 1847, d. 1929: m. 1877, Grace Maud, who d. 1946, da. of the late Thomas Rolls Hoare, of 49, Ennismore Gardens, S.W.:—
Nora, b. 1885: m. 1909, Edward Cleland Richardson. *Residence*,

Grandson of the late Col. Irton Eardley-Wilmot, yst. son of Maj.-Gen. Frederick Marlow Eardley-Wilmot, 2nd son of 1st baronet:—
Issue of the late Capt. Vere Levinge Eardley-Wilmot, b. 1886, d. 1965: m. 1915, Mary Cecil, who d. 1968, da. of the late H. Moffatt of Toronto:—
Hugh Irton (Forest Echo Motel, RR No. 1, Norland, Ont.), b. 1925; ed. at McGill Univ. (BSc).

Grandchildren of the late Francis Eardley-Wilmot, 3rd son of the late Rev. Edward Revell Eardley-Wilmot. 3rd son of 1st baronet:—
Issue of the late Rev. Hubert Valentine Eardley-Wilmot, b. 1878, d. 1963: m. 1908, Muriel Ivy, who d. 1966, da. of the late William Lovett, of Norwich:—
Paul Revell (of Woodland View, Cookham Rise, Berks), b. 1917; ed. at St. Paul's Sch.: m. 1953, Joan Violet, da. of H. J. W. Shepherd, of High Wycombe, and has issue living, David Revell, b. 1954,—Susan Mary, b. 1957.——Hazel Mary, b. 1910; ed. at Oxford Univ. (B.A. 1931).——Monica Germaine, b. 1913.

Grandchildren of the late Rev. Ernest Augustus Eardley-Wilmot (infra):—
Issue of the late Rev. Canon Charles Revell Eardley-Wilmot, b. 1880, d. 1962: m. 1914, Rose Meredyth, who d. 1954, da. of C. H. Bowen, of Sherbrooke, Province of Quebec, Canada:—

Robert Lloyd (12304, Gouin Blvd. West, Pierrefonds, Quebec, H82 1W2, Canada), b. 1921; 1941-45 War as Sgt. RCAF, attached RAF: m. 1949, Joyce Ethel, da. of Delbert Dagles, of Three Rivers, Quebec, Canada, and has issue living, David Robert, b. 1952.——Barbara Rose, b. 1915; 1943-45 War as Nursing Sister RCAF attached RAF: m. 1st, 1942, John Franklin Carr, Leading Aircraftman RCAF, who d. (killed on active ser.) 1942; 2ndly, 1947, Geoffrey Constable, of 36, Morewood Cres., Willowdale, Toronto, Ont., Canada, and has issue living (by 2nd m.), Peter Geoffrey, b. 1961,—Catherine Judith, b. 1950,—Janet Meredyth, b. 1953,—Susan Emily, b. 1956.—— Cecilia Torlesse, b. 1917; 1942-45 War as Private Canadian Women's Army Corps: m. 1946, Eliol Albert Leyden, of RR3, Malton, Ont., Canada, and has issue living, Richard Harold, b. 1950,—Michael Peyton, b. 1952,—Andrew Charles, b. 1954,—William Albert, b. 1955,—Sylvia Dawn, b. 1947,—Elizabeth Rose, b. 1957.——Sylvia Revell, b. 1926: m. 1948, Allan Adolphus Saunders, of RR2, Petitcodiac, New Brunswick, Canada, and has issue living, Nancy Peyton, b. 1951,—Sylvia Lee, b. 1953.

Grandchildren of the late Rev. Edward Revell Eardley-Wilmot, 3rd son of 1st baronet:—

Issue (by 1st marriage) of the late Rev. Ernest Augustus Eardley-Wilmot, b. 1848, d. 1932: m. 1st, 1875, Emily Dora, who d. 1897, da. of the late Rev. Charles Holland, formerly R. of Petworth, Sussex, of Watchers Linchmere, Haslemere; 2ndly, 1906, Arthurina Jane Arabella, who d. 1943, da. of the late Maj.-Gen. Arthur Butcher:—

Ernest Lancelot, b. 1888; ed. at Charterhouse; European War 1917-18 with New Zealand Forces (wounded): m. 1919, Margaret, da. of L. Hanlon, of Whangarei, New Zealand, and has issue living, Philip (of 8, Ballarat St., Ellerslie, Auckland, New Zealand) b. 1920; European War 1939-45, as Flight Sergeant, Roy. New Zealand Air Force: m. 1948, Joan Hazel, da. of G. R. Fox, of Auckland, New Zealand, and has issue living, Kay b. 1951: m. 1972, William James Chapman, of Roslyn, Dunedin, NZ (and has issue living, Kirsten b. 1974), Ronald Ernest b. 1953: m. 1972, Gaylene Mildon, of Mt. Wellington, Auckland (and has issue living, Matthew Ronald b. 1973), —Eileen, b. 1922: m. 1943, Richard Quentin Taylor, and has issue living, Peter Raymond b.1945, Lynne Carol b. 1946.——Irene Mildred (Nynehead Court, Wellington, Som.), b. 1884.—— Christine, b. 1893. *Residence*, The Old School House, Montacute, Som.

Granddaughters of the late Robert Eardley-Wilmot, MB, 5th son of the Rev. Edward Revell Eardley-Wilmot (ante):—

Issue of the late Edward Gwynne Eardley-Wilmot, b. 1877, d. 1965: m. 1904, Jane Millicent, OBE, who d. 1964, da. of Sir James William Scott, 1st Bt. (cr. 1909):—

Elizabeth Averil, *MBE* (*Elizabeth, Lady Shakerley*), (Rotherdown, Petworth, Sussex), b. 1905; MBE (Civil) 1955: m. 1928, Maj. Sir Cyril Holland Shakerley, 5th Bt., R. Sussex Regt., who d. 1970.——Mary Marow, b. 1909: m. 1933, Capt. John de Bourbel Stansfeld, MC, JP, of Dunninald, Montrose, Angus, and has issue living, John Raoul Wilmot (The Cottage, Hillside, Montrose, Angus) b. 1935: m. 1965, Rosalinde Rachel, da. of Desmond Gurney Buxton [*see* Buxton, Bt., colls.], and has issue living, Edward John Buxton b. 1966, Robert George Wilmot b. 1967, Nicholas Desmond Morse b. 1972,—Martin Raymond Eardley, b. 1937.

Issue of the late Lieut.-Col. Theodore Eardley-Wilmot, D.S.O., b. 1879, d. (killed in action during European War) 1918 : m. 1908, Mildred Clare, who d. 1956, el. da. of the late W. F. Reynolds, of Woodland Grange, near Leamington :—

Mildred Joan (*Baroness Cross of Chelsea*), b. 1912: m. 1st, 1939, Thomas Walton Davies, who d. 1948; 2ndly, 1952, Baron Cross of Chelsea [Life Baron], and has issue living (by 1st m.), Charles b. 1943,—Caroline, b. 1941,—Sophia, b. 1946: m. 1969, Henning Rasmussen,—(by 2nd m.) [*see* B. Cross of Chelsea]. *Residences*, 66, Oakwood Court, W14; Melbury, Aldeburgh, Suffolk.

Grandchildren of the late Rev. Edward Revell Eardley-Wilmot (ante) :—

Issue of the late Major Henry Eardley-Wilmot, b. 1854, d. 1933: m. 1883, Agnes Mary, who d. 1944, da. of the late Lieut.-Gen. Edward Burgoyne Cureton, of Hillbrook River, near Dover :—

Lambert, *OBE* (Flat 1, Atlantic Mansions, Atlantic Rd., Weston super Mare), b. 1894; Fl. Lt. RAF (ret.); formerly Lt. R. Leics. Regt. and RFC; sometime Assist. Regional Director, Home Office, No. 2 Civil Defence Region; OBE (Civil) 1942: m. 1930, Angela Clare Gertrude, who d. 1955, da. of the late Col. A. H. Vincent, of Summerhill House, Castle Connell, co. Limerick, and has issue living, Charles Vincent Burgoyne (of 5, St. John St., Thornbury, Glos.), b. 1932: m. 1961, Sheila, only da. of the late E. Broomfield, of Thornbury, Glos., and has issue living, Jane Clare b. 1962, Sarah Elizabeth b. 1963.——Florence, b. 1884: m. 1905, the Rev. George William Philips, who d. 1920, R. of Checkley, Stoke-on-Trent, and has issue living, Herbert Francis Humphry, b. 1908: m. 1940, Deirdre, da. of Maj. James Arthur Hornsby, of Ashwell Grange, Oakham, Rutland,—Penelope Mary, b. 1911. *Residence*, 20, Jameson Rd., Bexhill-on-Sea, Sussex.

Grandson of the late Stuart Eardley-Wilmot (infra) :—

Issue of the late Gerald Stuart Eardley-Wilmot, b. 1876, d. 1909: m. 1902, Vera Constance, who d. 1965, having m. 2ndly, 1913, Capt. William Henry Wake Ridley, R.N., who d. 1957 [*see* V. Ridley, colls.], da. of Charles Walker, formerly of Launceston, Tasmania :—

Stuart Jeffery, b. 1907 ; formerly Capt. R.A.S.C.; European War 1939-45: m. 1933, Mary, da. of W. Y. Fleming, of Bexhill-on-Sea, and has issue living, Brian (Auckland, NZ), b. 1939: m. 1960 (m. diss. 1972), Margaret Robyn, da. of A. Doust, and has issue living, Stuart Allen, b. 1961, Kathryn Anne b. 1966,—Gillian Mary, b. 1935: m. 1957, William H. Cook, of 741, Buena Vista, La Habra, Cal., USA, and has issue living, Victoria Mary, b. 1961,—Valerie b. 1946: m. 1968, L. K. Eitzen, of 10233, S. Gaybrook Av., Downey, Cal. 90241, USA. *Residence*, 29, Broadshard Lane, Ringwood, Hants.

Grandchildren of the late Augustus Hillier Eardley-Wilmot, 6th son of 1st baronet:—

Issue of the late Stuart Eardley-Wilmot, b. 1847, d. 1932: m. 1875, Rosa Cornelia, who d. 1924, da. of William Johnstone, of Launceston, Tasmania:—

Parry, b. 1888: m. 1912, Amy, da. of Percy Reynolds, of Hobartville, Richmond, NSW, and has issue living, a son, b. 19—. *Residence*,

Issue of the late Sir Sainthill Eardley-Wilmot, K.C.I.E., b. 1853, d. 1929: m. 1st, 1884, Emma Elizabeth, who d. 1890, da. of the late G. Casey, of Winterbourne St. Leonards; 2ndly, 1891, Mabel Boisragon, who d. 1958, da. of W. H. Winter, of Melford, 23, Beulah Road, Tunbridge Wells :—

(By 2nd m.) Mabel Iris, b. 1893: m. 1922, George H. Dummett, who d. 1969, and has issue living, Michael Eardley (of 54, Park Town, Oxford), b. 1925; sometime Sergeant Intelligence Corps; a Fellow of All Souls' Coll., Oxford, and of British Acad.: m. 1951, Ann Chesney, and has issue living, Christopher b. 1952, Andrew b. 1953, Paul b. 1960, Susanna b. 1957, Tessa b. 1958. *Residence*, Shepherds Cottage, Curridge, Newbury.

This family has common ancestry with the Wilmots, baronets of Osmaston (ext.), and Wilmots, baronets of Chaddesden. John Eardley-Wilmot, father of 1st baronet, assumed by Roy. Licence 1812 the additional surname of Eardley, as great-grandson of Elizabeth, sole heiress of Edward Eardley of Eardley, Staffs. The 1st baronet, Sir John Eardley-Wilmot, F.R.S., was sometime M.P. for North Warwickshire, and Gov. of Van Diemen's Land 1843-7, and the 2nd baronet sat as M.P. for Warwickshire S. (C) 1874-85, and was Recorder of Warwick 1852-7, and Judge of Bristol County Court 1854-63, and of Marylebone County Court 1863-71.

WILSON, Creation (U.K.) 1874, of Eshton Hall, co. York.

Loyal in everything.

Sir (MATHEW) MARTIN WILSON, 5th *Baronet ; b.* July 2nd, 1906 ; *s.* his father, *Sir* MATHEW RICHARD HENRY, *C.S.I., D.S.O.,* 1958 ; ed. at Eton ; is patron of four livings.

𝔄rms—Sable, a wolf rampant or, gorged with a collar gemel of the field between four mullets of six points, three in chief and one in base of the second. 𝔠rest—A demi-wolf or, gorged with a collar gemel sable, and resting the sinister paw on an escutcheon of the last, charged with a mullet as in the arms. 𝔖econd 𝔐otto—Res non verba (*Facts not words*).

Residence—1, The Esplanade, Folkestone, Kent.

Brothers living—ANTHONY THOMAS (1406, 34th St. NW, Washington DC, USA; St. James' (London), and Burning Tree (Washington) Clubs), *b.* Nov. 15th, 1908; 1939-45 War as Wing Cdr. RAF: *m.* 1st, 1934, (m. diss. 1938), Mrs. Margaret Motion, da. of the late Alfred Holden; 2ndly, 1939, Emily May, da. of the late John T. Milliken, of St. Louis, Missouri, USA, and has issue living, (by 1st m.) Mathew John Anthony, *MBE, MC* (4, Coastguard Cottage, Kingsdown, Deal, Kent; Army and Navy Club), *b.* 1935; Lt.-Col. LI; MBE (Mil) 1971: *m.* 1962, Janet Mary, el. da. of the late E. W. Mowll, JP, and has issue living, Mathew Edward Amcotts *b.* 1966, Victoria Mary *b.* 1968.——Peter Cecil, *CBE, b.* 1913; Chm. of Sotheby & Co., of 34, New Bond St., W1 since 1958; CBE (Civil) 1970: *m.* 1935 (m. diss. 1947), Grace Helen, da. of the late Arthur Ranken, and has issue living, Richard Thomas (La Ferme de Clavary, Auribeau-sur-Siagne, France 06), *b.* 1937: *m.* 1964 (m. diss. 1974), Judith, da. of Ford Jenkins, of Lowestoft, and has issue living, Alice Thomasina *b.* 1966, Imogen Nancy *b.* 1967,——Edward Philip (58, Gibson Sq., N1), *b.* 1940: *m.* 1970, Lady Alexandra Patricia Gwendoline Jellicoe, da. of 2nd Earl Jellicoe. *Residence*, Garden Lodge, Logan Place, W8. *Club*—St. James'.

Collateral Branch living.

Issue of the late Com. Alec Thomas Lee Wilson, 3rd son of 3rd baronet, *b.* 1883, *d.* 1956: *m.* 1913, Margaret (a DStJ), who *d.* 1966, da. of the late Leopold Hirsch, of 10, Kensington Palace Gdns., W:—

James Thomas Amcotts, *b.* 1916; Lt.-Col. (ret.), King's Own Yorkshire L.I.; a J.P. for Co. Dorset; 1939-45 War (despatches): *m.* 1947, Judy Featherstone, da. of the late Maj. Pierre Elliot Inchbald, M.C. [*see* Bingham, Bt.], and has issue living, Carol Anne, *b.* 1948,——Pamela Gay, *b.* 1951,——Vianna Jane, *b.* 1959. *Residence*, Manor Farm, Wraxall, nr. Dorchester, Dorset. *Club*, White's.——Francis Amcotts (Garth House, Llangammarch Wells, Breconshire; Army and Navy Club), *b.* 1922; 1939-45 War as Sub-Lt. RNVR: *m.* 1968, Mrs. Kathleen Mary Scott, da. of the late Robert Charles Bruce, MC [see E. Elgin, colls.].——Iris, *b.* 1914: *m.* 1st, 1936 (divorce 1947), Lt.-Col. David Llewellin Rhys, MC, S. Wales Borderers; 2ndly, 1948, John Longworth, of Rookes House, Horsington, Templecombe, Som., and has issue living, (by 1st m.) Michael Francis Lewellin, *b.* 1939: *m.* 19—,——Owen Mark Lewellin, *b.* 1941: *m.* 19—.——Peggy Amcotts, *b.* 1917: *m.* 1947, David Altham Bayford, and has issue living, Robin Alex, *b.* 1949,——Georgina Catharine Margaret, *b.* 1952. *Residence*, Wootton Chase, Wootton St. Lawrence, Basingstoke, Hants, RG23 8PE.

Sir Mathew Wilson, 1st baronet, sat as M.P. for Clitheroe (L) 1847-52, for N. Div. of W. Riding of York 1874-85, and for Skipton Div. of N. part of W. Riding of York 1885-6. The 4th baronet, Lieut.-Col. Sir Mathew Richard Henry Wilson, C.S.I., D.S.O., 10th Hussars, served in S. Africa 1899-1902, and sat as M.P. for S.-W. Div. of Bethnal Green (C) 1914-22.

WILSON, Creation (U.K.) 1906, of Airdrie, New Monkland, co. Lanark.

Sir THOMAS DOUGLAS WILSON, *MC*, 4th *Baronet,* only son of the late Thomas Douglas Wilson, yst. son of 1st baronet; *b.* (posthumous) June 10th, 1917; *s.* his uncle *Sir* JOHN MENZIES, 1968; ed. at Marlborough, and RMC; Capt. (ret.) late 15th/19th Hussars; France 1939-40 (MC), Middle East 1942-46: *m.* 1947, Pamela Aileen, da. of Sir (Griffin Wyndham) Edward Hanmer, 7th Bt., and has issue.

𝔄rms—Argent, a lion rampant between three mullets sable, on a chief vert a crescent of the first between two mullets pierced or. 𝔠rest—A demi-lion sable, charged on the body with a crescent argent between two mullets pierced or, all in pale.

Residence—Lillingstone Lovell Manor, Buckingham, MK18 5BQ. *Club*—Cavalry.

Son living—JAMES WILLIAM DOUGLAS, *b.* Oct. 8th, 1960.
Daughters living—Sarah Ann, *b.* 1950.——Susan Mary, *b.* 1954.——Margaret Rose, *b.* 1957.

Sister living—Aileen, b. 1915: m. Roger Benjamin Constant, of Cucksmead, Church Hill, Merstham, Surrey and has issue living, Roger Clive, b. 1945; ed. at Sherborne,—Stella, b. 1943.

Daughter living of 3rd Baronet—Daphne Margaret, b. 1922: m. 1945, Thomas Morton Macdonald, of Coanwood Jordans, Bucks., and has issue, Ian James, b. 1946; ed. at Stowe,—Neil Stuart, b. 1947; ed. at Oakham,—Alastair, b. and d. 1950.

Collateral Branch living.

Issue of the late Maj. John Wilson, Lanarkshire Yeo., only son of 2nd baronet, b. 1911, d. (killed in action during 1939-45 War) 1942: m. 1936, Zoe Jane (who m. 2ndly 1943, Guy C. Turner, AFC, of Braingorton, by Colintraive, Argyll), 2nd da. of George Orr, of Kilduff House, East Lothian:—
Sarah Jane, b. 1937: m. 1959, Michael Claud Ogilvie-Thomson, W.S., who d. 1967, and has issue living, David John, b. 1961,—Sheelagh Jane, b. 1960. Residence, Hengist Hearth, 38, North Hinksey Lane, Oxford.

The 1st baronet, Sir John, was Chm. of Wilsons and Clyde Coal Co. (Limited), and sat as M.P. for Falkirk Dist. (LU and L) 1895 to 1905.

WILSON, Creation (U.K.) 1920, of Carbeth, Killearn, co. Stirling.

Sir DAVID WILSON, 3rd Baronet; b. Oct. 30th, 1928; s. his father, Sir JOHN MITCHELL HARVEY, KCVO, 1975; ed. at Deerfield Acad., Mass., Harrow, and Oriel Coll., Oxford; Bar. Lincoln's Inn 1954; solicitor 1962: m. 1955, Eva Margareta, el. da. of Tore Lindell, of Malmo, Sweden, and has issue.

Arms (as recorded at Lyon Office)—Argent, a chevron gules between two mullets in chief, and in base a trefoil slipped vert. Crest—A demi-lion rampant gules, armed and langued azure.

Seat—Carbeth, Killearn, by Glasgow. Residence—Tandem House, Queen's Drive, Oxshott, Surrey.

Sons living—THOMAS DAVID, b. Jan. 6th, 1959.—Andrew, b. Dec. 1959.

Daughter living—Annika, b. 1961.

Brothers living—John Richards (Heron's Court, Killearn, Stirlingshire), b. 1930: m. 1969, H. Jane, da. of Maj. Gilbert B. Rahr, of Huntbourne Farm, Tenterden, Kent.—Andrew George (Carbeth, Killearn, by Glasgow), b. 1933: m. 1967, Anne-Marie Tekla, yr. da. of Tore Lindell, of Malmo, Sweden.

Uncle living (son of 1st baronet)—Sir Thomas George, KBE, b. 1900; ed. at Harrow, and at Trin. Coll., Camb. (BA Honours 1922); Hon. LLD Glasgow 1950; Chm. of Govs. of W. of Scotland Agric. Coll. 1942-71; KBE (Civil) 1959. Residence, King's Mile, Killearn, by Glasgow.

Aunt living (daughter of 1st baronet)—Mary Baird (Lady Gaye), b. 1907: m. 1938, as his second wife, Sir Arthur Stretton Gaye, CB, OBE, who d. 1960. Residence, Grattans, Bow, Crediton, Devon.

Always watchful.

Widow living of 2nd Baronet—MARY ELIZABETH (Mary, Lady Wilson) (Carbeth, Killearn, by Glasgow), da. of William Richards, CBE, of Flat No. 2, 76, Sloane St., SW1: m. 1927, Sir John Mitchell Harvey Wilson, KCVO, 2nd baronet, who d. 1975.

The 1st baronet, Sir David Wilson, was Convener (sometime Vice-Convener) of Stirlingshire, and a Member of Board of Agriculture for Scotland's Advisory Committee. The 2nd baronet, Sir John Mitchell Harvey Wilson, KCVO, was Keeper of The Royal Philatelic Collection 1938-69, and Pres. Royal Philatelic Soc. 1934-40.

MARYON-WILSON, Creation (E.) 1661, of East Borne, Sussex.

Sir HUBERT GUY MARYON MARYON-WILSON, 13th Bt., 3rd son of the late Rev. George Maryon Wilson, 5th son of 9th baronet; b. July 27th, 1888; s. his kinsman, the Rev. Canon Sir GEORGE PERCY MARYON MARYON-WILSON, 1965; ed. at Radley; assumed the additional surname of Maryon 1968: m. 1923, Janet Mary, da. of the late Rev. E. A. Moxon, of Fosdyke, Lincs.

Arms,—Sable, a wolf rampant, in chief three estoiles or. Crest,—1st a demi-wolf as in the arms.

Residence—The Grange, Great Canfield, Dunmow, Essex.

Sister living—Albinia Marguerite (Fitzjohns, Great Canfield, Essex), b. 1883.

Daughter living of 11th Baronet—Margaretta Elizabeth (Viscountess Gough) (Inchvannie, Strathpeffer, Ross-shire, and 26, Markham St., SW3), b. 1902: m. 1935, the 4th Viscount Gough, who d. 1951.

Collateral Branches living.

Granddaughter of the late Frederick Maryon Wilson, 4th son of 9th baronet:—
Issue of the late Harold Thomas Maryon Wilson, b. 1880, d. 1944: m. 1904, Catherine Gladys, who d. 1962, da. of the Hon. Walter Vanneck [B. Huntingfield, colls.]:—
Gladys Félicé Maryon, b. 1910. Residence, 13, Wilton Av., Chiswick, W4.

Sir Thomas Wilson, Knt., born 1525, was Sec. of State to Queen Elizabeth I. Sir William Wilson, the 1st baronet, lived at Eastbourne (now Compton) Place, Eastbourne, where for his loyalty he was created a baronet by Charles II on March 4th, 1661, as Wilhelmum Wilson de East Borne. Sir Thomas Spencer, the 6th baronet, was a Lt.-Gen. in the Army, and Col. of the 50th Foot. He *m.*, 1767, Jane, da. of John Badger Weller by Margaret Maria, niece and heir of the Rev. John Maryon, of Charlton Manor, Kent. The 10th baronet assumed by deed poll the additional surname of Maryon in 1877. The 11th baronet assumed this additional surname by Roy. licence 1899.

Windham, see Bowyer-Smith.

WINGATE, Creation (U.K.) 1920, of Dunbar, East Lothian, and of Port Sudan.

Sir RONALD EVELYN LESLIE WINGATE, *C.B.*, *C.M.G.*, *C.I.E.*, *O.B.E.*, 2nd *Baronet*; *b.* Sept. 30th, 1889; *s.* his father, *Gen. Sir* (FRANCIS) REGINALD, *G.C.B.*, *G.C.V.O.*, *G.B.E.*, *K.C.M.G.*, *D.S.O.*, *T.D.*, *D.C.L.*, *LL.D.*, 1953; ed. at Bradfield Coll., and at Balliol Coll., Oxford (MA); in ICS and Political Ser. of Govt. of India 1913-39; was British Delegate, Inter-Allied Reparations Agency, Brussels, and British Commr. for restitution of monetary gold 1947-53; Mesopotamia 1917-19 (despatches), 1939-45 War as Col. Intelligence Corps in Africa and S.-E. Asia, and on Joint Planning Staff, War Cabinet (O.B.E.); C.I.E. 1931, O.B.E. (Mil.) 1945, C.M.G. 1952, C.B. (Civil) 1959: *m.* 1916, Mary, da. of John Harpoth, of Copenhagen, Denmark.

Arms—Gules, a portcullis, with chains pendant or a chief embattled of the last. *Crest*—A portcullis as in the arms. *Supporters*—On a compartment below the shield, representing a sandy desert semée of roses gules; *dexter*, a camelopard proper, gorged with a collar or, supporting in its paws a Dervish spear, displaying the flag of the Union; *sinister*, a wolf proper, gorged with a collar or, supporting in its paws a Dervish spear with the banner of the Sultan of Egypt.

Residence—Barford Manor, Barford St. Martin, Salisbury. *Clubs*—Brooks's, Army and Navy.

Sister living—Victoria Alexandrina Catherine, *b.* 1899: *m.* 1922, Capt. Henry Dane, D.S.O., M.I.E.E., Indian Army, who *d.* (as a prisoner of war in Japan) 1942, son of Sir Louis William Dane, G.C.I.E., C.S.I., and has issue living, Paul Malcolm Henry Wingate, *b.* 1925,—Martin Louis Geoffrey, *b.* 1936; Lt.-Cdr. RN: *m.* 1961, Janet Mary Paterson Smith, and has issue living, Richard Martin Henry *b.* 1962, Catherine Mary Janet *b.* 1964, Emma Josephine Laura *b.* 1967, —Josephine Marion Catherine, *b.* 1923: *m.* 1949, Wilfrid Guy Street, of 10, Alexander Sq., SW3 2AY. *Residence*, Stone Cottage, Crockham Hill, Edenbridge, Kent.

The 1st baronet, General Sir (Francis) Reginald Wingate, G.C.B., G.C.V.O., G.B.E., K.C.M.G., D.S.O., T.D., D.C.L., LL.D. (son of the late Andrew Wingate of Broadfield, Renfrewshire), was a distinguished soldier and administrator.

WINNINGTON, Creation (G.B.) 1755, of Stanford Court, Worcestershire.

Sir FRANCIS SALWEY WILLIAM WINNINGTON, 6th *Baronet*, son of the late Francis Salwey Winnington, el. son of 5th baronet, *b.* June 24th, 1907; *s.* his grandfather, *Sir* FRANCIS SALWEY, 1931; Lieut. Welsh Guards; European War 1939-40 (prisoner); is patron of three livings: *m.* 1944, Anne Beryl Jane, only da. of the late Capt. Lawrence Drury-Lowe, Scots Guards, and has issue.

Arms—Quarterly; 1st and 4th argent, an orle between eight martlets sable, *Winnington*; 2nd and 3rd, sable, a saltire engrailed or, *Salwey*. *Crest*—A Saracen's head full-faced, couped at the shoulders proper, wreathed about the temples argent and sable.

Seat—Stanford Court, Worcester.

Gratâ sume manu.
Take with a grateful hand.

Daughter living—Charmian Anne, *b.* 1945.

Brother living—THOMAS FOLEY CHURCHILL, *M.B.E.*, *b.* Aug. 16th, 1910; ed. at Eton, and at Balliol Coll., Oxford; is Col. Grenadier Guards; M.B.E. (Mil.) 1948: *m.* 1944, Lady Betty Marjorie Anson, da. of 4th Earl of Lichfield, and has issue living, Anthony Edward, *b.* 1948,—Henry Thomas, *b.* 1961,—Sarah Rose (*Viscountess Campden*), *b.* 1951: *m.* 1972, Anthony Baptist, Viscount Campden (Top House, Exton, Oakham, Rutland), el. son of 5th Earl of Gainsborough,—Emma Elizabeth, *b.* 1956. *Residence*, 9, Westminster Gdns., SW1.

Collateral Branches living.

Issue of the late John Winston Foley Winnington, youngest son of 5th baronet, *b.* 1883, *d.* 1961: *m.* 1910, Gladys Cooke :—

Jessie Babette, *b.* 1912: *m.* 1933, Michael Thomond Wilson, *M.B.E.*, el. son of Sir (Roderick) Roy Wilson, and has issue living, Michael John Francis Thomond Wilson, *b.* 1934,—Patrick Simon, *b.* 1937,—Patricia Jane (twin), *b.* 1937. *Residence*, Clytha, S. Ascot, Berks.

Granddaughters of the late Capt. John Taylor Winnington, son of the late Capt. John Taylor Winnington, 2nd son of 3rd baronet:—
Issue of the late Lieut.-Col. John Francis Sartorius Winnington, D.S.O., Worcestershire Regt., b. 1876, d. (wounds in action during 1914-18 War) 1918: m. 1910, Joyce Mary, who d. 1970, da. of David Marriage, of Chorley, Lancs.:—
Susanne, b. 1913: m. 1st, 1936 (marriage dissolved 19—), Russell Cowell ; 2ndly, 1950, John Duerdin of Affcot Manor, Church Stretton, Salop, and has issue living, John Patrick, b. 1952,— Joanna Elizabeth, b. 1950.—Frances June, b. 1951.——Patricia Rose, b. 1917: m. 1949, Robin Darell Unwin (Longdon Hall, Tewkesbury, Glos.), and has issue living, Carol John b. 1951,— Guy Darell, b. 1952,—Barry James, b. 1956.

Grandchildren of the late Ven. Edward Henry Winnington-Ingram (infra):—
Issue of the late Rev. Preb. Edward Francis Winnington-Ingram, b. 1883, d. 1963: m. 1924, Gladys Winifred (of Wistan, Kidderminster Rd., Wribbenhall, Worcs.), da. of John Armstrong, of Tenbury, Worcs.:—
(Edward) John (Knoll House, Wingrave, Aylesbury, Bucks.), b. 1926; ed. at Shrewsbury, and Keble Coll., Oxford (BA): m. 1st, 1953, Shirley Yvoire, el. da. of Gerald Lamotte; 2ndly, 1973, Mrs. Elizabeth Linda Few Brown, da. of Geoffrey Milling, of Brading, Isle of Wight, and has issue living, (by 1st m.) Edward Nicholas, b. 1957,—Gerald Francis, b. 1960.——Gladys Ann, b. 1929: m. 1952, Lt.-Cdr. Francis Nigel Oldfield Bartlett, RN (Eaton Cottage, Eaton Hill, Baslow, Bakewell, Derbys.), and has issue living, Charles Nicholas Oldfield, b. 1954,—Sarah Frances, b. 1955,—Rachel Victoria, b. 1957,—Joanna Elizabeth, b. 1959.

Granddaughter of the late Rev. Edward Winnington-Ingram (b. 1814). 2nd son of the Rev. Edward Winnington-Ingram (b. 1785), 2nd son of 2nd baronet :—
Issue (by 1st marriage) of the late Ven. Edward Henry Winnington-Ingram, b. 1849, d. 1930: m. 1st, 1879, Elizabeth Ruscombe, who d. 1892, da. of the late John Anstice, of Madely Wood, Salop; 2ndly, 1898, Harriet Anne, who d. 1912, da. of the late Rev. Thomas Dehaney Bernard, Canon and Chancellor of Wells, of High Hall, Wimborne, Dorset :—
Ethel Mary (Sandown Lawn Nursing Home, Albert Rd., Cheltenham.); BA London.

Grandchildren of the late Francis Herbert Winnington-Ingram (ante) :—
Issue of the late Charles William Edward Winnington-Ingram, b. 1881, d. 1958: m. 1902, Maud Esther (Aylmer, Ont.), da. of Richard R. Jones, of Copenhagen, Ont.:—
(Francis) Herbert, b. 1906: m. 1930, Ruth Agnes, da. of Newton Newell, of Aylmer, Ont., and has issue living, Gerald Newell (PO Box 464, 58, McMurray St., Bracebridge, Ont.), b. 1935: m. 1957, Lillian Tremblay, and has issue living, James Brian b. 1959, Douglas Michael b. 1964, Phyllis Anne b. 1958, Angela Marie b. 1969,—Charles Edward, b. 1938,—Philip Herbert, b. 1943.— Arthur Foley (RR6, Aylmer, Ont.), b. 1908: m. 1928, Ruby Louisa, da. of Edward Herries, of Luton, Ont., and has issue living, Donald Foley (RR6, Aylmer, Ont.), b. 1935: m. 1957, Dawn Marlyn Hussar, da. of the Rev. Garnet Hussar Aylmer, and has issue living, Allan Foley b. 1968, Cheryl Lynn b. 1962.——(Charles) Alexander, b. 1912: m. 1939, Doris Marjorie Buck, and has issue living, Alexander Grant, b. 1940: m. 1966, Carolyn Fuschia Johnston, and has issue living, Sherri Lynn b. 1966,—David Gary, b. 1943: m. 1965, Mary Ilene McClure.——Cecil Harold, b. 1918: m. 1947, Patricia Howse Green, and has issue living, William Edward, b. 1948,—Brian Charles, b. 1959,—Frank Barton (twin), b. 1959,—Beth Arlene, b. 1952, —Beverley Irene, b. 1953.——Gerald (136, Coverley Rd., Aylmer, Ont.), b. 1926: m. 1947, Edna Arletta Johnson, and has issue living, Judith Susanne, b. 1949,—Janet Marie, b. 1951.—— Vera Louise, b. 1903: m. 1928, Kenneth McGregor Hatch, and has issue living, Kenneth Herbert, b. 1931: m. 1953, Pamela Dianne House, and has issue living, Steven Kenneth b. 1955, Peter Donald b. 1957, Thomas Alan b. 1966, Nancy Laura b. 1957 (twin); Wendy Vivian b. 1962,— Donna Lucille, b. 1928: m. 1949, Clayton Vickers McKechnie, of Hanover, Ont., and has issue living, Stewart Douglas b. 1952: m. 1972, Kathleen Haskey, Dean Charles b. 1958, Janice Louise b. 1953: m. 1971, Edward Adrian Vanherk (and has issue living, Pamela Jenifer b. 1971).—— Constance Maud, b. 1905: m. 1933, Fergus Arnold Hatch, and has issue living.——Helen Patricia, b. 1914: m. 1938, James Arthur Ferris, and has issue living.——Marjorie, b. 1920: m. 1946, John M. Hale, and has issue living.——Audrey Lucille, b. 1921: m. 1948, William Ozarko, of 632, Lime Ridge Rd., RR3 Hamilton, Ont., and has issue living.——Pauline, b. 1928: m. 1948, Edward Golibashi, and has issue living.

Issue of the late Herbert Arthur Winnington-Ingram, b. 1881, d. 1941: m. 1912, Anna, who d. 1924, da. of — Edmonton, Canada:—
Herbert Grant, b. 1914: m. 19—, Florence Beatrice Lea, and has issue living, Donald Grant, b. 1947, —Robert Craig, b. 1952,—Lea Gordon, b. 1946.——Charles Gordon, b. 1918.——Marian Elizabeth, b. 1920: m. 1945, William Niven Duff, of 14515-84 Av., Edmonton 51, Alberta, Canada, and has issue living, William Neil, b. 1948: m. 1969, Christine Judy Melmoth, and has issue living, Shae Nancy Elizabeth b. 19—,—David Ingram, b. 1954,—Nancy Marion, b. 1947: m. 1969, Derek David Nash.——Anna Grant, b. 1924: m. 19—, Raymond Benjamin Hager.

Issue of the late John Gordon Gerald Winnington-Ingram, b. 1889, d. 19—, Florence Byron:—
Florence Maxime, b. 1923.——Hazel, b. 1931.

Grandchildren of the late Rev. Edward Winnington-Ingram (b. 1814) (ante) :—
Issue of the late Rear-Adm. Charles William Winnington-Ingram, b. 1856, d. 1923: m. 1894, Ida Vere Maude, who d. 1945, da. of the late Charles Harcourt Chambers:—
Reginald Pepys, b. 1904; ed. at Clifton, and at Trin. Coll., Camb. (MA); HonDLitt, Glasgow; Emeritus Prof. of Greek in London Univ., and a FBA: m. 1938, Edith Mary, da. of the late Thomas Cousins. Residence, 7, Ladywell Court, 22, East Heath Rd., Hampstead, NW3 1AH. ——Joyce Constance, b. 1908; MA: m. 1961, Ven. Ronald Percy Frank Plaistowe, Archdeacon Emeritus, of 165, Main Rd., Redcliffs, Christchurch 8, NZ.

Issue of the late George Frederick Winnington-Ingram, b. 1859, d. 1929: m. 1901, Mary Beatrice, who d. 1957, da. of the late John Burridge, of Charminster, Bournemouth:—
John Felix, b. 1909.——Phyllis Mary, b. 1906.
Issue of the late Rev. Alfred Winnington-Ingram, b. 1861, d. 1929: m. 1906, Julia Margaret, who d. 1958, da. of the late William Augeraud :—
Charles Alfred (Box 15054, Langata, Nairobi, Kenya), b. 1909.——Cecil, MBE (14, Main Rd., Biddenham, Bedford), b. 1914; ed. at Keble Coll., Oxford (BA); HM Overseas Administrative Ser. (1937-64); MBE (Civil) 1950: m. 1954, Maude, yr. da. of the late James Bartlett Lee, of Portsmouth, and has issue living, Charles Pepys, b. 1955,—Francis Christopher, b. 1957.——John Harold, b. 1916.——Richard Sullivan, b. 1919; Maj. (ret.) RE; 1939-45 War (despatches): m. 1952, Isobel Margaret, only da. of the late Robin McCrae, of Kabete, Kenya, and has issue living, David Robert, b. 1959,—Peter Richard, b. 1960,—Julia Caroline, b. 1954, —Mary Cynthia, b. 1956. Address, Supuko, 36, Barnton Av., Edinburgh EH4 6JL.

Issue of the late Gerald Constantine Winnington-Ingram, b. 1869, d. 1918: m. 1896, Ethel Hawthorne, who d. 1919, da. of the late Frederick Pollen, B.C.S.:—
Eric Alfred, b. 1902; ed. at Keble Coll., Oxford (B.A. 1924): m. 1930, Jean Emma Caroline, da. of F. G. Hopkins, of Haddon Hill, Christchurch, Hants, and has issue living, Marianne Jean, b. 1933,—Iris Hawthorne, b. 1935: m. 1964, John Awberry Field, of Yewtrees Farm, Balcombe, Sussex, and has issue living, Fiona Clare b. 1967, Alison Joyce b. 1969. Residence, Charlecote, Oldlands Av., Balcombe, Sussex.——Enid Kathleen, b. 1897 (of 15, Portland Rd., Summertown, Oxford): m. 1920, Christopher Francis Wood, ICS, who d. 1955, and has issue living, Christopher Winnington (48, Addison Rd., W14 8JH), b. 1926: m. 1951, Rhodope Margaret Milner-White, and has issue living, John Chilion Gurney b. 1952, Peter Gerald Winnington b. 1954, Mary

Halcyon Meredith b. 1965,—Rosemary Anne Meredith, b. 1921.——Madge Meredith, b. 1909. *Residence*, 23, Earl's Terr., W8.

Granddaughter of the late Rear-Adm. Herbert Frederick Winnington-Ingram, youngest son of the late Rev. Edward Winnington-Ingram, (b. 1785) (ante) :—
Issue of the late Herbert Edward Winnington-Ingram, b. 1869, d. 1958 : m. 1899, Agnes Maud, who d. 1956, da. of the late George Bevington Foster :—
Marjorie Agnes, b. 1901. *Residence*, Etherstone, Dorking Road, Tadworth, Surrey.

This family were lords of the manor of Winnington *temp.* Edward I., where they continued to reside till the beginning of the eighteenth century. The 4th baronet was M.P. for Bewdley (L) 1832-46 and 1857-68. The present baronet is descended from Sir Francis Winnington, Knt., of Stanford Court, who was appointed in 1678 Solicitor-General to Charles II., a post which he resigned, that he might act consistently with his conscience, by supporting the Exclusion Bill. Sir Francis Salwey Winnington, 5th Bt., was High Sheriff of Worcestershire 1894.

WISEMAN, Creation (E.) 1628, of Canfield Hall, Essex.

Sir JOHN WILLIAM WISEMAN, 11th *Baronet;* b. March 16th, 1957; s. his father, *Sir* WILLIAM GEORGE EDEN, C.B., 1962.

Arms—Sable, a chevron ermine between three cronels argent. Crest—A tower or, port open argent, out of the top a demi-Moor issuant armed proper, in his right hand a dart argent, barbed or plumed or, in his left a Roman target of the last.

Residence, 32, Victoria Rd., W8.

Sapit qui Deo sapit.
He is wise who is wise through God

Half-Sisters living—Margaret, b. 1913: m. 1936, Ramsay William Rainsford-Hannay [*see* Maxwell, Bt, cr. 1804 (ext.)]. *Residence*, Kirkdale, Creetown, Kirkcudbrightshire.——Rosemary, b. 1916: m. 1936, Maj. Frederick R. Hulton, RA (ret.), and has issue living, Frederick William, b. 1938,—Peter Richard, b. 1941,—Thomas Michael b. 1943,—Rosemary Jane, b. 1950. *Residence*, Firles, Seaford, Sussex. ——Sheila (of New York, U.S.A.), b. 1928; is a Journalist.

Aunt living (daughter of 9th baronet)—Dorothy Lilian, b. 1881: m. 1910, Charles Stephen Ascherson, who d. 1945, and has issue living, Janet Elizabeth, b. 1914: m. 1947, Raoul Martin,—Dorothy Rénée (of 4, Melina Court, Grove End Rd., W8), b. 1915; is an Actress: m. 1953 (Frederick) Robert Donat, the Actor, who d. 1958. *Residence*, The White House, Nuffield, Henley-on-Thames, Oxon.

Widow living of 10th baronet—JOAN MARY LESUREUR (*Lady Wiseman*) (32, Victoria Rd., W8), da. of the late Arthur Phelps, of Woodridge, Harrow: m. 1944, as his 3rd wife, Sir William George Eden Wiseman, CB, 10th baronet, who d. 1962.

Collateral Branches living.

Grandchildren of the late Thomas Edward Wiseman (infra):—
Issue of the late Thomas Edward Wiseman, b. 1878, d. 1959: m. 1916, Annie, who d. 1970, da. of George William Allen:—
THOMAS ALAN, b. July 8th, 1921; late Staff Sergeant R.A.O.C.: m. 1946, Hildemarie, da. of Gustav Domnik. *Residence*, 14, Havisham Rd., Chalk, Gravesend, Kent.

Issue of the late Frank Eldred Wiseman, b. 1880, d. 1938 : m. 1923, Lily Amy, who d. 1957, da. of Harry Lewis Littlewood, of Gravesend, Kent :—
Wallis Littlewood (249, Villiers Rd., Walmer, Port Elizabeth, S. Africa), b. 1924: m. 1951, Brenda Doris, da. of the late Arthur Allanson, of Walmer, Port Elizabeth, S. Africa, and has issue living, Jonathan Charles, b. 1953,—Richard Christopher, b. 1954,—Barry James, b. 1956,—Margaret Alexandra, b. 1960.

Issue of the late Frederick William Wiseman, b. 1885, d. 1954: m. 1914, Charlotte Hepshibah Ward, who d. 1966:—
John Henry Ware (Swan Hotel, Denham St., Rockhampton 4700, Qld.), b. 1924; an Hotel Proprietor; 1939-45 War with R. Australian Artillery in New Guinea, Bouganville and New Britain (wounded): m. 1962, Delma Margaret, da. of Douglas James Lung, of Bundaburg, Queensland.——Marie Eleanor (14, Ryrie St., N. Ryde, Sydney, NSW), b. 1919: m. 1941, Capt. Stanley Thornton Shaw, RAA, who d. 1956, and has issue living, John Alexander, b. 1943,—Philip Thornton, b. 1945,—Laurence Edward, b. 1946.

Grandson of the late Edward Thomas Wiseman, son of the late Thomas Wiseman (b. 1778), son of the late Thomas Wiseman (b. 1760), 2nd son of 6th baronet:—
Issue of the late Thomas Edward Wiseman, b. 1851, d. 1918 : m. 1877, Ellen Justinia, da. of George Ware:—
Louis Gerald, b. 1881 : m. 19—, Agnes, da. of ———, and has issue living, Edward Thomas, b. 19—,—Louis George, b. 19—,—Teresa, b. 19—,—Audrey, b. 19—.

Granddaughter of the late Edwin Wycliffe Wiseman (infra):—
Issue of the late Edwin Leonard Wiseman, b. 1897, d. 1964: m. 1921, Winifred May (27, Davis Av., Northfleet, Kent), da. of Edward William Bassant:—
Mary, b. 1933.

Granddaughter of the late William Henry Wiseman, son of the late Charles Pierce Wiseman, son of the late Thomas Wiseman (d. 1778) (ante):—
Issue of the late Edwin Wycliffe Wiseman, b. 1864, d. 1954 : m. 1st, 1893, Rosa, who d. 1926, da. of Leonard Leonard; 2ndly, 1928, Alice Maud Mary, who d. 1966, da. of Horace Plant:—
(By 2nd m.) Alice Rosa, b. 1930. *Residence*, 47, Pelham Road South, Gravesend.

Grandchildren of the late Pierce Wiseman, son of Charles Pierce Wiseman (ante):—
Issue of the late Thomas Charles Wiseman, b. 1873, d. 1940: m. 1896, Eliza, da. of Charles Carpenter:—
William Henry, b. 1910; is a Bank Official; formerly Lieut. R.A.: m. 1937, Winifred, da. of William Charles Ambrose Knight, and has issue living, Susan Marjorie, b. 1940.——Albert Victor b. 1915 ; is a Police Officer ; formerly Flying Officer R.A.F.: m. 1941, Nicola, da. of Leonard Foreman, and has issue living, Jonathan Thomas Charles, b. 1946,—Simon Pierce, b. 1949,—Elizabeth Victoria, b. 1942.——Amy Gertrude, b. 1898 : m. 1932, Frederick Gulliford, and has issue living, Ann Freda, b. 1933,—Lorinda Jane b. 1936.——May Constance, b. 1899: m. 1938, George Durling. *Residence*, 22, Keves Av., Chatham.——Gertrude Minnie, b. 1903. m. 1936, Thomas Jarvis, and has issue living, Michael, b. 1942,—Trevor, b. 1946. *Residence*,

Granddaughters of the late Charles Pierce Wiseman (ante):—
Issue of the late Pierce Wiseman, *b.* 1844, *d.* (April) 1928: *m.* 1871, Elizabeth Catherine,
who *d.* (May) 1928, da. of Thomas Wells:—
Edith Eleanor, *b.* 1880: *m.* 1902, Thomas William Whyte Shaw, who *d.* 1948, and has issue
living, Thomas Oswald, *b.* 1903: *m.* 1st, 1931, Irene Honeyman; 2ndly, 1949, Ena Webb,
of Sutton Rd., Wisbech, Cambridgeshire, and has issue living, (by 1st m.) Derek *b.* 1933:
m. 1956, Barbara May Hodges, of Princes Rd., Gravesend, Kent, (by 2nd m.) Ian Gordon *b.*
1957, Lyn Patricia *b.* 1959,—Roy Stuart (of 81, Peacock St., Gravesend, Kent), *b.* 1916 ; is
Corporal RAF; 1939-45 War: *m.* 1940, Eva Elizabeth Hepburn, and has issue living, Douglas
Stuart *b.* 1944,—Edith Eleanor, *b.* 1905: *m.* 1st, 1927, William Richard Ware, who obtained
a divorce 1942; 2ndly, 1942, Edward Elliott Blacker, Corporal RASC, who *d.* 1958, and has
issue living, (by 1st m.) Audrey Edith *b.* 1929. *Residence,* 81, Peacock St., Gravesend, Kent.——
Sarah Ann, *b.* 1887.——Ethel Maud, *b.* 1893.

Grandchildren of the late Thomas Palmer Wiseman, son of the late Edmund
Wiseman, son of the late Thomas Wiseman (*b.* 1760) (ante):—
Issue of the late Charles John Wiseman, *b.* 1862, *d.* 1936: *m.* 1890, Lillie Jane, da. of
William Oakley:—
William Thomas (of 113, Samuel St., Woolwich, S.E.18), *b.* 1891; European War 1914-19 in
Egypt, Palestine, France, and Salonica with 8th London Bde., RFA.——Charles John (17,
Holburne Gdns., Kidbrooke, SE3), *b.* 1904: *m.* 1937, Jessie, da. of James Arthur Laming,
and has issue living, David John (108, Shooters Hill Rd., Blackheath, SE3), *b.* 1939: *m.* 1964,
Susan Anne, da. of Charles William Tait.——Alfred J. (65, Pound Cres., Fetcham, Surrey),
b. 1906: *m.* 1st, 1931 (m. diss. 1946), Rose Knight; 2ndly, 1946, Enid May Hurford, and has
issue living (by 2nd m.), Linda, *b.* 1949: *m.* 1970, Michael Ramsay, of 48, Elizabeth Rd., Seaton,
S. Devon.——John Robert, *b.* 1908: *m.* 1931, Ethel, da. of Joseph Thomas Beecham. *Residence,*
Woolwich, SE18.——Annie Elizabeth, *b.* 1896: *m.* 1918, Zacharia William Coles, and has issue
living, Nancy Joan, *b.* 1921: *m.* 1944, Edward Henry Willard, of The Cock, Church St., Staines,
Middx., and has issue living, Paul William *b.* 1946.——Grace Mary, *b.* 1900: *m.* 1923, Walter
Jefferies, of 13, Bowling Green Row, Woolwich, SE18, and has issue living, Ronald Walter, *b.*
1925,—Dennis Gordon, *b.* 1927: *m.* 19—, and has issue living, Beverley *b.* 1952.——Violet Mary,
b. 1903: *m.* 1930, Frank Tranter, of 7, Godfrey Hill, Woolwich, SE18, and has issue living, Jean
Alma, *b.* 1931.

Grandchildren of the late Charles John Wiseman (ante):—
Issue of the late Thomas Charles Wiseman, *b.* 1897, *d.* 1928: *m.* 1919:—
Ronald Henry, *b.* 1924; NW Europe 1944-45: *m.* 1943, and has issue living, Dawn, *b.* 19—.——
Constance Queenie, *b.* 1921: *m.* 1940.——Betty Thomasina, *b.* 1928: *m.* 1946. *Residence,*

Sir John Wiseman, great-grandfather of 1st baronet, was one of the Auditors of the Exchequer,
temp. Henry VIII, was knighted at Battle of the Spurs, and purchased Canfield Park, in Essex,
temp. Edward VI. The 1st baronet, Sir William Wiseman was High Sheriff of Essex 1638-9.
The 2nd baronet, Sir William, was High Sheriff of Essex 1659-60. The 5th baronet, Sir William,
was Lieut.-Col. Coldstream Guards. The 7th baronet, Sir William Saltonstall, was Capt. R.N.
The 8th baronet, Sir William Saltonstall, K.C.B., was Rear-Adm. The 9th baronet, Sir William,
was Capt. R.N., and served in New Zealand War 1864-5, and Niger Expedition 1869. The 10th
baronet, Lt.-Col. Sir William George Eden, CB, was Ch. of British Intelligence Ser. in USA
1917-18, and Chm. of New York Cttee. of Dollar Exports Board 1951-62.

WOLFSON, Creation (U.K.) 1962, of St. Marylebone, co. London.

Omnibus rebus cura et provide.
*Look after and make provision
for all things.*

Sir ISAAC WOLFSON, 1st *Baronet,*
son of the late Solomon Wolfson, of Glasgow;
b. Sept. 17th, 1897; ed. at Queen's Park
Sch., Glasgow; Hon. LL.D. London, Glas-
gow, Camb., Manchester, Strathclyde, Not-
tingham, and Brandeis Univ. (USA); Hon.
FRCP, Hon. FRCS; Hon. FRCP & S Glasgow;
Hon. DCL Oxford; Hon. PhD Hebrew
Univ., Jerusalem; Hon. Fellow, Weiz-
mann Institute of Science, Israel; St.
Edmund's Coll., Oxford, and Churchill
Coll., Camb.; FRS 1963; Hon. FRCS;
Chm. of Great Universal Stores, Ltd. since
1932; a Founder Chm. and Trustee of
Wolfson Foundation; Hon. Pres. of Weiz-
mann Institute of Science Foundation,
Trustee of Religious Centre, Jerusalem, a
Member of Pattenmakers' Co. and of Grand
Council of British Empire Cancer Campaign,
and Patron of Roy. Coll. of Surgs.; Einstein
Award (USA); Herbert Lehmann Award
(USA): *m.* 1926, Edith, da. of Ralph Specter-
man, and has issue.

Arms—Per pale dovetailed vert and or, on a chevron counterchanged between in chief two
roses, also or and gules respectively, and in base an ancient hand bell proper, two pears sable
and gold. **Crest**—In front of two rods of Æsculapius in saltire proper, a torch inflamed also
proper.
Residence—74, Portland Place, W1.

Son living—LEONARD GORDON (Universal House, 251, Tottenham Court Rd., W1), *b.* Nov. 11th,
1927: *m.* 1949, Ruth, da. of Ernest Sterling, of London, and has issue living, four daus.

WOLSELEY, Creation (E.) 1628, of Wolseley, Staffordshire.

Man is as a wolf towards his fellow-man.

HOMO HOMINI LUPUS

Sir CHARLES GARNET RICHARD MARK WOLSELEY, 11th *Baronet*, son of the late Capt. Stephen Garnet Hubert Francis Wolseley, R.A., el. son of 10th baronet ; *b.* June 16th, 1944 ; *s.* his grandfather, *Sir* EDRIC CHARLES JOSEPH, 1954; ed. at Ampleforth; ARICS; Agent to Lord Egremont; Lt. Staffs Yeo. (TA): *m.* 1968, Anita Maria, el. da. of Hugo J. Fried, of Hopedale, Worple Rd., Epsom, Surrey, and has issue.

Arms—Argent, a talbot passant gules. Crest—Out of a ducal coronet or, a wolf's head erased proper.

Seat—Wolseley, Stafford. *Address*, Hilliers, Petworth, Sussex.

Daughters living—Annabelle Clare Maria, *b.* 1969.——Emily Lavinia, *b.* 1972.

Sister living—Mary Patricia Anne, *b.* 1942: *m.* 1973, Steuart Martin Moor, of 3, Wolsey Rd., Hampton Hill, Middx., and has issue living, Theresa Mary Geraldine, *b.* 1974.

Uncles living (sons of 10th baronet)—BASIL CHARLES DANIEL RUDOLPH, *b.* Nov. 16th, 1921; ed. at Ampleforth; 1939-45 War as Flight-Lt. RAF: *m.* 1950, Ruth Key, da. of Lt.-Col. William Tom Carter, OBE, of Offham, Kent, and has issue living, Anne Teresa Margaret, *b.* 1951,—Susanna Elizabeth Mary, *b.* 1952,—Sarah Angela Clare, *b.* 1954,—Joanna Ruth *b.* 1958. *Residence*, The Gables, Aston Crews, Lea, Ross on Wye.——George John Carlos, *b.* 1925; ed. at Ampleforth, and New Brunswick, and British Columbia Univs.; 1943-45 War with RAF. *Residence*, Rosethorpe, Finmere, Buckingham.——Richard Edric Vincent, *b.* 1928; ed. at Ampleforth, and New Brunswick Univ.; sometime in Rifle Bde., and RCN: *m.* 1950 (m. diss. 1969, re-m. 1971) Alice Baltazzi, da. of the late Amos Tuck French, and has issue living, Stephen Richard Dulany, *b.* 1954,—Christopher Michael Garnet, *b.* 1956,—Carlotta Andrea Tuck, *b.* 1951: *m.* 1972, Abdelhadi Lachiouach, of Essaioura, Morocco,—Heather Maria Warner, *b.* 1957. *Address*, PO Box 74, North Falmouth, Mass., USA 02556.

Aunts living (daughters of 10th baronet)—Frances Mary Mona Clare, *b.* 1920 ; late W.R.N.S.: *m.* 1953, Bernhard Wilmsen. who assumed by deed poll 1954, the additional surname of Wolseley before his patronymic, of Trillick, Whichford, Shipston-on-Stour, Warwicks., and El Faisan No. 29, Guadalmina Alta, San Pedro de Alcántara (Málaga), Spain, and has issue living, Anthony Edric Charles, *b.* 1955; ed. at St. Christopher Sch., Letchworth, and Cardiff Univ.——Agnes Mary Ann Hilda, *b.* 1923. *Residence*, Rosethorpe, Finmere, Buckingham.

Great-Uncle living (son of 9th baronet)—William Ralph Joseph, *T.D.*, *b.* 1887; ed. at Beaumont; Capt. late Staffordshire Yeo., and Pioneer Corps, and a J.P. for Shropshire; European War 1914-18 (despatches): *m.* 1923, Ruth Gertrude, who *d.* 1962, youngest da. of the late Lieut.-Col. Robert Halstead Hargreaves, J.P., D.L., of Knightley Grange, Staffordshire, and Barnside, Lancs., and has issue living, Robert William Hargreaves (Mount Nebo House, Taunton, Som.), *b.* 1924; ed. at Canford Sch.; 1939-45 War with Grenadier Guards and R. Fusiliers: *m.* 1965, Beryl Marjorie, da. of F. G. Harvey, of Norman Chapel, Aston Magna, Glos., and has issue living, Alistair Robert Hargreaves *b.* 1969, Heather Frances *b.* 1967,—Veronica Ruth Teresa Rose, *b.* 1928. *Residence*,—Flat 7, Cound Hall, Cressage, Salop.

Mother living—PAMELA VIOLETTE (*Pamela, Lady Wolseley*), da. of the late Capt. F. Barry, of Old Court, Whitchurch, Ross-on-Wye; granted 1955 the style, title, place, and precedence as if her late husband had survived and succeeded to the title: *m.* 1942, Capt. Stephen Garnet Hubert Francis Wolseley, R.A. (ante), who *d.* (of wounds received in action during European War) 1944. *Residence*, Wolseley Park, Rugeley, Stafford.

Widow living of 10th Baronet—CLARE MARY ANNETTE (*Clare, Lady Wolseley*), da. of the late Charles Edmund de Trafford [*see* de Trafford, Bt., colls.]: *m.* 1916, Sir Edric Charles Joseph Wolseley, 10th baronet, who *d.* 1954. *Residence*, Rosethorpe, Finmere, Buckingham.

Collateral Branches living.

Grandchildren of the late Edward Talbot Wolseley, 3rd son of 8th baronet :—
Issue of the late Mervyn Joseph WITHAM-WOLSELEY, *b.* 1873, *d.* 1956 (having assumed the additional surname of Witham 19—) : *m.* 1907, Dorothy Mary, who *d.* 1956, el. da. of Philip Witham, of Whitmoor House, Sutton Place, Guildford :—
Ursula Mary (Whitmoor Cottage, Puttenham, Guildford), *b.* 1908: *m.* 1937, John Henry Spencer, who *d.* 1963, and has issue living, John Mervyn Manners, *b.* 1939; Fl. Lt. RAF: *m.* 1967, Diana Thomas and has issue living, Guy Thomas *b.* 1972, Sarah Patricia *b.* 1969.

Issue of the late Charles Joseph Wolseley, *b.* 1877, *d.* 1933: *m.* 1902, Isobel, da. of A. Drummond, of Newcastle-on-Tyne:—
Charles Edward (Peter) (47, Briarfield Rd., Gosforth, Newcastle upon Tyne 3), *b.* 1913; ed. at Ampleforth: *m.* 1954, Marie Lock, of Newcastle upon Tyne.——Gundred Etheldreda (36, Leicester Rd., New Barnet, Herts.), *b.* 1903: *m.* 1944, Stanley Horrocks, who *d.* 1956.

Granddaughters of the late William Augustus Wolseley, M.D., son of the late William Bertie Wolseley, son of the late Capt. Henry Wolseley, 4th son of 6th baronet :—
Issue of the late Henry John Wolseley, M.B., M.Ch., *b.* 1846, *d.* 1931 : *m.* 1872, Fanny Carlyon, who *d.* 1936, da. of the late John Gittens:—
Minnie Bathurst *b.* 1885: *m.* 1924, Edward Archer Wood, MRCS, who *d.* 1957.——Janet Porter (The Guest House, Laleham Abbey, Staines, Middx.), *b.* 1889.

Issue (by 2nd marriage) of the late William Augustus (Daniel) Wolseley, *b.* 1847, *d.* 1929: *m.* 1st, 1891, Harriet, who *d.* 1894, da. of Fraser Luckie ; 2ndly, 1895, Lillian Laura, who *d.* 1941, da. of the late Horatio Bethune Leggatt. of Worth, Sussex:—
Lilian Patricia Dysart (Flat 6, Chester Mansions, 151/153, Oakhill Rd., SW15), *b.* 1908: *m.* 1933 (divorce 1948), Alexander Mervyn Archdale, and has issue living, Dominic Edward Wolseley, (1928, W. Belmont Av., Phoenix, Arizona, 85021, USA) *b.* 1937; ed. at St. Paul's Sch., and at Downing Coll., Camb. (MA); late RAF: *m.* 1959 (m. diss. 1974), Ruth Selby, da. of Charles Johnston, late US Foreign Ser.,—Anthony Quintin Wolseley, *b.* 1940; ed. at Saltus Gram. Sch., Bermuda.

Grandchildren of the late Maj. John Henry Wolseley-Bourne, el. son of the late Eliza Jane Bourne (infra):—
Issue of the late Eda Kathleen Wolseley-Bourne, *b.* 1884, *d.* 1947 : *m.* 1909, Gerard Blathwayt Hole, from whom she obtained a divorce 1912 ; 2ndly, 1914, Gordon Brock Bridgman, sometime Sudan Civil Ser. :—
(By 2nd marriage), Peter Brock, *b.* 1918 ; ed. at Charterhouse ; European War 1939-45 as Sergeant S. African Intelligence Corps in Ethiopia, and as Flying Officer S. African Air Force in N. Africa : *m.* 1949, Nancy Coetzee, and has issue living, Susan Kathleen, *b.* 1954,—Brockina Jane, *b.* 1956. *Residence*, Nyatandi Cottage, Piers Rd., Borrowdale, Salisbury, Rhodesia.

Issue of the late Henrietta Laetitia Wolseley-Bourne, *b.* 1887, *d.* 1960: *m.* 1907, Calvert James Stronge Buchanan, who *d.* 1942 :—

Pamela Mary (Armsworth Park Farm, Alresford, Hants), b. 1908: m. 1935, Malcolm Glassford Begg, MC, late Wing Cdr. RAF, who d. 1969, and has issue living, Susanna Jane, b. 1936: m. 1957, James Adrian William Innes Hardman, of Armsworth House, Alresford, Hants, el. son of Air Ch. Marshal Sir (James) Donald Innes Hardman, GBE, KCB, DFC, and has issue living, James Malcolm b. 1966, Lucinda Henrietta b. 1959, Philippa Jane b. 1961, Frances Louise b. 1963, Katharine Sara, b. 1975.—Fiona Mary, b. 1938: m. 1959, John Michael Strutt Thompson, of Stibbington House, Wansford, Peterborough, and has issue living, Marcus Peter Strutt b. 1961, Julia Mariette b. 1963.

Grandchildren of the late Eliza Jane, da. of the late William Bertie Wolseley (ante), d. 1848, having m. (Jan.) 1845, the Rev. John Frederick Bourne, son of John Henry Bourne, of Dalby Hall, Spilsby, Lincolnshire :—
Issue of the late William Wykeham Frederick Bourne, b. 1848, d. 1914: m. 1881, Ann Margaret, who d. 1940, younger da. of the late Major William Robert Brereton, J.P. of New Abbey, co. Kildare [E. Drogheda, colls.]:—
Sybil Katherine, b. 1887: m. 1915, Vernon Milner Montague-Smith, late Maj. W. Yorkshire Regt., who d. 1951, and has issue living, Patrick Wykeham, b. 1920; ed. at Mercers' Sch.; Assist. Editor of Debrett 1946-62, since when Editor; NW Europe 1944-45 as Sgt. RASC: m. 1974, Annabelle Christina Calvert, da. of the late Noel Newton, of Kensington, W. Residence, Brereton, 197, Park Rd., Kingston Hill, Surrey.——Phyllis Margaret, b. 1895: m. 1923, Percy Raymond Cooper, who d. 1972, and has issue living, Marigold, b. 1931; is Heraldic Artist to Debrett: m. 1955, the Rev. Christopher John Sutherland Gill, Chap. of St. Edmund's Sch., Canterbury, and has issue living, Philip Wykeham Sutherland b. 1956; ed. at St. Andrew's Univ., Timothy John Sutherland b. 1957. Residence, Wykeham, 114, Rectory Rd., West Tarring, Worthing.——Kathleen b. 1898: m. 1917, Paul Francis Wheler Bush, MIMechE, MIEE, who d. 1961, and has issue living, Pauline Carol Wheler, b. 1920: m. 1942, Cyril Thomas James, and has issue living, Michael Thomas b. 1944, Robert Steven b. 1948, late L/Cpl. RE, Kathleen Mary b. 1943: m. 1967, Cdr. David Heron Jennings, RN (ret.), of Lower Wick, Dursley, Glos. (and has issue living, Sarah b. 1968). Residence, 18, Old Town, Wotton-under-Edge, Glos.

Grandchildren of the late William Wykeham Frederick Bourne (ante):—
Issue of the late James Robert Wykeham Bourne, ARICS, b. 1885, d. 1971: m. 1926, Mabel, who d. 1974, da. of the late William Robert Reigate:—
Norah Ann Wykeham, b. 1932: m. 1966, Colin James Outram Monro, of 19, Bloomsbury Place, Brighton, and has issue living, John Seton, b. 1968,—Fiona Eleanor Wykeham, b. 1967.

Issue of the late Magdalene Dysart Bourne, b. 1882, d. 1947: m. 1912, Colin James Simpson, who d. 1947:—
Colin Peter Bourne (10, Brook Lane, Felixstowe, Suffolk), b. 1913; ed. at Christ's Hospital, and Univ. Coll., London; 1939-45 War as Capt. Indian Army; late Officer, Dept. of Trade, Commonwealth of Australia: m. 1st, 1948, Charmaine Bridget, da. of Thomas Murphy; 2ndly, 1951, Margaret Marian, da. of the late William Ewart Watkins, OBE, of Felixstowe, and has issue living, (by 1st m.) Alan James, b. 1949; ed. at King's Sch., Bruton,—(by 2nd m.) Nicholas Brereton, b. 1952; ed. at Ipswich Sch., and Univ. of Wales,—Campbell Philip Dysart, b. 1954; ed. at Felsted.

Descendants of the late Richard Wolseley (2nd brother of 5th baronet), who was cr. a Baronet 1745:—
See Wolseley, Bt., cr. 1745.

This ancient Staffordshire family is descended from Siward, Lord of Wisele, fourth in descent from whom was Robert, Lord of Wolseley, temp. 1281. Ralph, sixth in descent from Robert, was Fourth Baron of the Exchequer temp. Edward IV. Sir Robert, 1st baronet, was a Col. in Charles I.'s army, and suffered sequestration. Sir Charles, 2nd baronet, represented Stafford in the Parliaments of Charles I. and II., and was a member of Cromwell's House of Lords. Sir William, 6th baronet, was a Gentleman of the Privy Chamber to George III.

WOLSELEY, Creation (I.) 1745, of Mount Wolseley, co. Carlow.

Sir GARNET WOLSELEY, 12th Baronet, youngest son of the late Richard Bingham Wolseley, youngest son of the late Robert Brown Wolseley, grandson of the late Rev. William Wolseley, 3rd son of 1st baronet ; b. May 27th, 1915 ; s. his kinsman, the Rev. Sir WILLIAM AUGUSTUS, 1950 ; European War 1939-45 with Northants Regt. in Madagascar, Sicily, Italy and Germany : m. 1950, Lillian Mary, da. of the late William Bertram Ellison, of Love Lane, Wallasey, Cheshire.

Arms—Argent, a talbot passant gules, a crescent for difference. Crest—Out of a ducal coronet, a wolf's head proper.

Residence—73, Dorothy St., Brantford, Ontario, Canada.

HOMO HOMINI LUPUS

Man is as a wolf towards his fellow man.

Sisters living—Rubina Bingham, b. 1909: m. 1st, 1946, Walter Leonard Openshaw, who d. 1951; 2ndly, 1952, Frank Whitby, who d. 1960. Residence, 47, Telegraph Rd., Heswall, Cheshire.——Lalla, b. 1914.

Collateral Branches living.
Grandsons of the late Marian Josephine Wolseley, da. of the late Robert Hughes Wolseley, son of the late Robert Brown Wolseley, el. son of the late John Wolseley, M.D., 4th son of the late Rev. William Wolseley, 3rd son of 1st baronet, b. 1870, d. 1955 : m. 1902, Arthur Greene Brinton, F.R.C.S., L.R.C.P., who d. 1945 :—
Issue of the late Robert Wolseley Brinton, b. 1908, d. 1958 : m. 1934, Phyllis Maud (of The Old Butts, Upton Grey, nr. Basingstoke), da. of Charles Henry Grant:—
David Douglas Wolseley (PO Box 126, Howick, Natal, S. Africa), b. 1938; ed. at St. Andrew's Coll., S. Africa, and at R. Agricultural Coll., Cirencester : m. 1964, Mary Virginia, da. of Leonard Auther Newton, and has issue living, Charles David Robert Wolseley, b. 1970,—Charlotte Mary Wolseley, b. 1966,—Camilla Jane Wolseley, b. 1967.——Geoffrey Graeme Wolseley, b. 1943; ed. at St. Andrew's Coll., S. Africa, and at Milton Abbey Sch., Dorset: m. 1968, Nancy Lou, da. of Herman Lou Creiger, of Buenos Aires.

Granddaughter of the late William Robert Wolseley, 2nd son of Richard John Wolseley, yr. son of John Wolseley, MD (ante):—
Issue of the late Noel Cecil Wolseley, b. 1889, d. 1969 (naturalized as American citizen 1920): m. 1913, Mae Evelyn, who d. 1965, da. of John J. O'Connell:—

Eileen Rita, b. 1916;　Dir. Nursing Ser., Concord Hosp., Concord, New Hampshire, USA.

Granddaughters of the late Francis Ernest Wolseley, 3rd son of the late Richard
John Wolseley (ante) :—
Issue of the late Francis Richard Wolseley, b. 1875, d. 1934: m. 1906, Elizabeth Ellen,
who d. 1966, da. of the late John Abbott Shippey:—
Kathleen Frances Hilda, b. 1908: m. 1938, Hugh Wynn Jones, and has issue living, Kathleen
Margaret, b. 1939.——Jacqueline Eulalie Patricia, b. 1911: m. 1932, John Lewis Jones, and has
issue living, Jane Eulalie, b. 1942,—Anne Jessie Alexandra, b. 1947.　Residence,

Grandson of the late Douglas St. John Wolseley, only son of Robert Warren St.
John Wolseley, el. son of the Rev. Robert Warren Wolseley, 2nd son of Maj.
Robert Benjamin Wolseley, 6th son of the Rev. William Wolseley (ante):—
Issue of the late James Douglas Wolseley, b. 1903, d. 1960: m. 1935, Olive (3602-A
S. University Drive, Fort Worth, Texas, 76109, USA), da. of Carroll Walter
Wofford:—
James Douglas (3602-A.S. University Dr., Fort Worth, Texas 76109, USA), b. 1937: m. 1965,
Patricia Lynn, da. of William R. Hunter, of Mt. Shasta, Cal., USA.

Granddaughter of the late Robert Warren St. John Wolseley, el. son of the late
Rev. Robert Warren Wolseley (infra) :—
Issue of the late Douglas St. John Wolseley, b. 1875, d. 1943 : m. 1900, Annie Elizabeth,
who d. 1959, da. of Jared Edward Stallings :—
Margaret (Apart. 18, Plaza Bellaire, 3500, Bellaire Drive North, Fort North, Texas 76109, USA),
b. 1906: m. 1941, Oscar Hughes King, who d. 1968.

Grandchildren of the late Rev. Robert Warren Wolseley, yr. son of the late
Maj. Robert Benjamin Wolseley (ante):—
Issue of the late Garnet Ruskin Wolseley, b. 1884, d. 1967: m. 1937, Joan Alys, who d.
1943, da. of Sir Walter John Trevelyan, 8th Bt.:—
John Walter (Nettlecombe, Williton, Som.), b. 1938; ed. at Westminster: m. 1964, Patricia Ann
Newland, and has issue living, William, b. 1967,—Thomas, b. 1970.——Jane Alys, b. 1939: m. 1963,
Nicolas Alexander, architect, and has issue living, Dickon, b. 19—,—Tamsyn b. 19—.——
Jennifer Ann Ruskin, b. 1941: m. 19—.

The 1st baronet, M.P. for Carlow, was brother of Sir William, 5th baronet, cr. 1628.　Sir
Capel, 9th Bt., was Vice-Consul at Archangel 1900-1909, and served during European War
1914-18 in Gallipoli, Egypt, and Palestine, also with Army of Occupation in Albania and N.
Russia 1919.

WOMBWELL, Creation (G.B.) 1778, of Wombwell, Yorkshire.

[Name pronounced "Woomwell."]

IN·WELL·BEWARE

Sir (FREDERICK) PHILIP ALFRED
WILLIAM WOMBWELL, *M.B.E.*, 6th *Baronet*,
son of the late Capt. Frederick Adolphus Womb-
well, son of the late Frederick Charles
Wombwell, 4th son of 3rd baronet ; *b.* July
6th, 1910 ; *s.* his great-uncle, *Sir* HENRY
HERBERT, 1926 ; ed. at Repton ; is Major
Movement Control, R.E. (Supplementary
Reserve) ; Italy 1943-5 (M.B.E.) ; M.B.E.
(Mil.) 1944 : *m.* 1936, Ida Elizabeth, da. of
Frederick J. Leitch, of Branksome Park,
Bournemouth, and has issue.

Arms—Gules, a bend between six unicorns' heads
couped argent.　Crest—A unicorn's head couped argent.

Residence—Bridge House, W. Baldwin, Isle of Man.

Son living—GEORGE PHILIP FREDERICK, (Colville
House, Coxwold, Yorks.) b. May 21st, 1949; ed. at
Repton: m. 1974, Hermione Jane, el. da. of T. S.
Wrightson, of Ulshaw Grange, Middleham, Leyburn,
Yorks.

Daughters living—Elizabeth Anne, b. 1938: m. 1965,
Michael Scofield Horton of Bredon Manor, Tewkesbury,
Glos. [see Walker Bt., cr. 1868, colls.], and has issue
living, James Frederick, b. 1968,—Peter Michael,
b. 1969.——Hazel Maureen, b. 1947.

Collateral Branches living.

Grandson of the late Arthur Charles Wombwell (infra) :—
Issue of the late Major Claude Ronald Wombwell, Seaforth Highlanders, b. 1900, d. 1959:
m. 1936, Eva Mabel (of Rent Street Cottage, Bovingdon, Herts), da. of the late Lieut.-
Col. Gerald Hugh Charles Madden [Macpherson-Grant, Bt.] :—
Gerald Arthur (40, Quarrendon St., SW6), b. 1937; ed. at Wellington Coll.: m. 1968, Elizabeth
Ann, da. of John Victor Gent, of Thika, Kenya, and has issue living, Richard Brian, b. 1973,—
Camilla Susan, b. 1970.

Grandsons of the late Charles Orby Wombwell, 4th son of 2nd baronet :—
Issue of the late Arthur Charles Wombwell, b. 1866, d. 1921: m. 1898, Violet Bridget
Heron, who d. 1929, da. of the late Capt. John Heron Maxwell-Heron [Heron-
Maxwell, Bt.]:—
Michael Henry, b. 1907; ed. at Harrow, and at Trin. Coll., Camb. (B.A. 1929): m. 1st, 1932,
Joy Evelyn Georgira, who d. 1954, da. of the late Algernon Seymour Oakley, of Chadlington,
Oxon; 2ndly, 1962, Grace Margaret, da. of the late David Willis, of Headley, Surrey.
Residence, Fairways, Crastock, nr. Woking, Surrey.

The 1st baronet, Sir George Wombwell, was Chairman of the East India Company, and M.P.
for Huntingdonshire 1774-80.　The 4th baronet, Sir George, served in Crimean War, and was
in the Charge at Balaclava.　The 5th baronet, Sir Henry Herbert Wombwell, was Capt. Roy.
Horse Guards.

WOMERSLEY, Creation (U.K.) 1945, of Grimsby, co. Lincoln.

Sir PETER JOHN WALTER WOMERSLEY, 2nd *Baronet*, son of the late Capt. John Walter Womersley, Lincolnshire Regt., younger son of 1st baronet; *b.* Nov. 10th, 1941; *s.* his grandfather, *the Rt. Hon. Sir* WALTER JAMES, 1961; late Lt. King's Own R. Border Regt.: *m.* 1968, Janet Margaret, da. of Alistair Grant, of Drayton, Norwich, and has issue.

Residence—Sunnycroft, The Street, Bramber, Steyning, Sussex, BN4 3WE.

Sons living—JOHN GAVIN GRANT, *b.* Dec. 7th, 1971.—a son, *b.* 1973.
Daughters living—Margaret Frances, *b.* 1969.——Helen Kathryn, *b.* 1974.
Aunt living (daughter of 1st baronet)—Dorothy, *b.* 1911 : *m.* 1934, Cyril Howard Moseley, and has issue living, Walter Howard, *b.* 1941,—Lavinia Anne, *b.* 1938,—Philippa Clare, *b.* 1944. *Residence*, Westbrooke House, Market Harborough, Leicestershire.
Mother living—Betty, da. of Cyril Williams, of Elstead, Surrey: *m.* 1st, 1941, Capt. John Walter Womersley, Lincolnshire Regt. (ante), who *d.* (killed in action in Italy) 1944; 2ndly, 1948, Gordon Shuttlewood, 102, Weelsby Rd., Grimsby, Lincs.

The 1st baronet, the Rt. Hon. Sir Walter James Womersley (son of the late William Womersley, of Bradford, was MP for Grimsby (C) 1924-45, and Min. of Pensions 1939-45.

WOOD, Creation (U.K.) 1897, of The Hermitage, Chester-le-Street, co. Durham.
[Extinct 1946.]

Sir IAN LINDSAY WOOD, 3rd and last *Baronet*.

Sister living of 3rd Baronet—Heather Lindsay, *b.* 1908 : *m.* 1932, Gilbert Keith Dunning, who *d.* 1967, and has issue living, Michael Lindsay, *b.* 1941. *Residence*, Keeper's Cottage, Fontmell Parva, Blandford, Dorset.

Widow living of 3rd Baronet—DOROTHY ELIZABETH EMORY (BETTY) (*Lady Wood*), da. of the late Harry Emory Chubb, C.B.E.: *m.* 1936, Sir Ian Lindsay Wood, 3rd Bt., who *d.* 1946, when the title became ext. *Residence*, Highcroft Cottage, Milford, Godalming, Surrey.

WOOD, Creation (U.K.) 1918, of Hengrave, Suffolk. [Extinct 1974.]
Sir JOHN ARTHUR HAIGH WOOD, DSC, MC, 2nd and last *Baronet*.

Daughter living of 2nd Baronet—Shirley Cartaret (32, Chelsea Sq., SW3 6LQ), *b.* 1922: *m.* 1st, 1946, Sqdn. Ldr. Ivon Arthur Frederic Donnelly, from whom she obtained a divorce 1964; 2ndly 1972, John Hyde Villiers, and has issue living (by 1st m.), Miles Saumarez, *b.* 1949,—Marcia Anne Lavinia, *b.* 1948,—Claire Leonie, *b.* 1953.
Collateral Branch living
Issue of the late Maj. Edmund Walter Hanbury Wood, JP, 2nd son of 1st baronet, *b.* 1898, *d.* 1947: *m.* 1920, Margaret (now of 57, Eaton Mews West, SW1), only child of the late George Coles Walton:—
Rhona Gertrude Jean (of 6, Douro Pl., W8), *b.* 1921: *m.* 1948, Jeremy Norman Peyton-Jones [*see* B. Ebury, colls.], from whom she obtained a divorce 1962.

HILL-WOOD, Creation (U.K.) 1921, of Moorfield, Glossop, co. Derby.

Sir DAVID BASIL HILL-WOOD, 3rd *Baronet*; *b.* Nov. 12th 1926 ; *s.* his father, *Sir* BASIL SAMUEL HILL, 1954; ed. at Eton: *m.* 1970, Jennifer Anne McKenzie Stratmann (assumed that surname by deed poll 1960), da. of the late Peter McKenzie Strang, and has issue.

Arms—Quarterly, 1st and 4th sable, on a bend between two roses argent, barbed and seeded or, three fleurs-de-lis gules, *Wood*; 2nd and 3rd per chevron argent and vert, in chief two acorns leaved and slipped, and in base a cross-bow bent all counterchanged, *Hill*. Crests—1st, within a crown palisado or a tree proper, *Wood* ; 2nd, on a mount vert a bugle horn stringed gules, *Hill*.

Residences—Dacre Farm, Farley Hill, Reading, Berks.; 58, Cathcart Rd., SW10.

Sons living—SAMUEL THOMAS, *b.* Aug. 24th, 1971.——Edward Charles, *b.* 1974.
Daughter living—Emma Victoria, *b.* 1972.
Sister living—Anne Katherine, *b.* 1928.
Uncles living (sons of 1st baronet)—Wilfred William Hill, CBE, *b.* 1901; ed. at Eton, and at Trin. Coll., Camb.; Adviser to Morgan Grenfell & Co., Ltd., a Dir. of Anglo-American Securities, and other cos.; CBE (Civil) 1946: *m.* 1947, Diana Marian, da. of Maj. Hugh Wyld, of Beverstone Old Rectory, Tetbury, Glos., and widow of Wing-Cdr. Harry Manners Mellor, MVO,

Every good thing is the gift of God.

RAF. *Residence*, House of Urrard, Killiecrankie, Perths.; Coldham, Sandwich Bay, Kent; Flat 4, Cornwall Mansions, 33, Kensington Court, W8. *Club*, White's.——Denis John Charles Hill, MC, *b.* 1906; ed. at Eton and at Ch. Ch., Oxford (MA); is Maj. 4th Co. London Yeo. (TA); 1939-45 War in Middle East and Italy (despatches, wounded, MC): *m.* 1932, Mary Cecilia Martin, da. of the late Capt. Everard Martin-Smith, of Codicote Lodge, Herts, and has issue living, Peter Denis (12, Chelsea Sq., SW3), *b.* 1936; ed. at Eton; 2nd Lt. Coldm. Gds.: *m.* 1971, Sarah, da. of Albert O'Beirne Andrews, and has issue living, Julian Peter *b.* 1974, Sarah Frances *b.* 1972,—Angela Mary, *b.* 1933: *m.* 1956, Mark Eric Smith, of Hatch House, Ingrave, Essex, and has issue living, Matthew Eric *b.* 1960, Luke Eric *b.* 1968, Amanda Mary *b.* 1957, Lucinda Rachael *b.* 1958, —Rachael Vivien, *b.* 1940: *m.* 1972, Anthony Wood, of 13, Cadogan Court, Draycott Av., SW3, and has issue living, Cheska Mary *b.* 1974. *Residence*, Hunter's Hill, Hartley Wintney, Hants.

——Charles Kerrison Hill, *b.* 1907; ed. at Eton, and at Ch. Ch., Oxford (MA); is Lt.-Col. Coldm. Gds.: *m.* 1936, Cecilia Katharine, da. of Capt. Everard Martin-Smith, of Codicote Lodge, Herts., and has issue living, Michael Kerrison, *b.* 1946: *m.* 1970, Patricia Guy, of Stainland, Yorks., and has issue living, a da. *b.* 1974,—Ian Charles, *b.* 1947,—Jane Cecilia, *b.* 1937,—Georgina Sarah, *b.* 1940: *m.* 1962, Richard Basil Holt, of Hill House, Barley, Royston, Herts., and has issue living, Nicholas James *b.* 1965, Camilla Katherine *b.* 1967, Susanna Rachael *b.* 1969, Caroline Lucinda *b.* 1972,—Diana Susan, *b.* 1943: *m.* 1966, Lestock Harold George Livingstone-Learmonth, of 4, Brook Rd., St. Margaret's, Twickenham, Middx., and has issue living, Lestock Alexander Iain *b.* 1969. *Residence*, The Bury, Barton-le-Cley, Beds.

Widow living of 2nd Baronet—Hon. JOAN LOUISA BRAND (*Hon. Lady Hill-Wood*) (of Knipton Lodge, Grantham, Lincs.), el. da. of 3rd Viscount Hampden: *m.* 1925, Sir Basil Samuel Hill Hill-Wood, 2nd baronet, who *d.* 1954.

The 1st baronet, Sir Samuel Hill Hill-Wood, only son of the late Samuel Wood, of Moorfield, Derbyshire (whose el. brother, John Hill Wood, was father of Sir John Wood, 1st Bt. [*see* Wood. Bt. cr. 1918]) assumed by Roy. licence 1912 the additional surname of Hill, his grandmother having been Alice, da. of John Hill, of Liverpool. He sat as MP for High Peak Div. of Derbyshire (C) 1910-29.

PAGE WOOD, Creation (U.K.) 1837, of Hatherley House, Gloucestershire.

DEFEND

Sir ANTHONY JOHN PAGE WOOD, 8th Baronet; *b.* Feb. 6th, 1951; *s.* his father, *Sir* DAVID JOHN HATHERLEY PAGE *WOOD*, 1955; ed. at Harrow.

Arms—Quarterly, argent and or, the mace of the Lord Mayor of London in pale, between an oak-tree on a mount vert fructed proper in the 1st and 4th quarters and in the 2nd and 3rd, a bull's head erased sable, charged on the neck with a bezant. Crest—Out of a mural crown argent, a demi-wild man, wreathed about the temples with oak fructed, in the dexter hand an oak-tree eradicated and fructed, and in the sinister a club, all proper.

Residence—22, Godfrey Street, SW3.

Sister living—Rosemary, *b.* 1948.

Uncle living (son of 6th baronet)—MATTHEW PAGE, *b.* Aug. 13th, 1924; is Capt. Coldstream Guards; assumed by deed poll 1955 the additional surname of Page before his patronymic; European War 1939-45: *m.* 1947, Betsann, da. of Lieut.-Col. Francis Christesson Darby Tothill, Rifle Brig. [*see* E. Bandon], and has issue living, Belinda Jane, *b.* 1952: *m.* 1973, Richard John Crowder [*see* B. Petre, colls.],—Miranda Elizabeth, *b.* 1962. *Residence*, 31, Halsey St., S.W.3.

Widow living of 7th Baronet—EVELYN HAZEL ROSEMARY (*Lady Page Wood*), da. of the late Capt. George Ernest Bellville, of Fermyn Woods Hall, Brigstock, Northants; assumed by deed poll 1956 the additional surname of Page: *m.* 1947, Sir David John Hatherley Page Wood, 7th baronet who *d.* (Nov.) 1955. *Residence*, The Old Cottage, Wolverton, Basingstoke, Hants.

Collateral Branches living.

Grandchildren of the late F.-M. Sir (Henry) Evelyn Wood, V.C., G.C.B., G.C.M.G., LL.D., 5th son of 2nd baronet:—

Issue of the late Col. Evelyn FitzGerald Michell Wood, C.B., D.S.O., O.B.E., *b.* 1869. *d.* 1943: *m.* 1st, 1893, Lilian, who *d.* 1910, da. of the late Charles Edward Hutton, of 63, Porchester Terrace, W; 2ndly, 1915, Alla, who *d.* 1950, da. of R. Morton, and widow of Hatherley Page Wood, son of the late Charles Page Wood, 2nd son of 2nd baronet:—

(By 2nd m.) Matthew Wakefield Drury Evelyn (Leign Farm, Doccombe, Newton Abbot, Devon), *b.* 1917; ed. at Brighton Coll.; Lt.-Col. (ret.) RE, late Essex Regt.: *m.* 1st 1939, Marjorie, who *d.* 1963, da. of the late Henry Thomas Longmire, of Liverpool; 2ndly, 1967, Mrs. Phyllis Margaret Chavasse Whateley (infra), and has issue living, (by 1st m.) Mark William Evelyn (27, Wood Lane, Fleet, Hants.), *b.* 1940: *m.* 1962, Mary June, da. of George Percy Miller, of Brightlingsea, and has issue living, Martin Evelyn *b.* 1963, Michelle Leslie Evelyn *b.* 1965.——(By 1st m.) Sheelagh Southwell, MBE, *b.* 1895; a JP; MBE (Civil) 1944: *m.* 1917, Capt. John Edward Eastley, formerly SLI (Stoke Gabriel Cottage, Totnes, S. Devon; Alta Vista, Puerto de la Cruz, Tenerife).——Dame Leslie Violet Lucy Evelyn, DBE, TD, *b.* 1899; Ch. Controller (ret.) ATS, and a Chevalier of Legion of Honour; was Dir. of ATS 1943-46; has American Legion of Merit; CBE (Mil) 1943, DBE (Mil) 1946: *m.* 1st, 1922, William John Balfour; 2ndly, 1939, Sqdn.-Ldr. Harry Raymond Whateley, RAFVR, and has issue living, (by 1st m.) William Raymond John Evelyn (c/o National Westminster Bank, Belgravia Branch, 1, Grosvenor Gdns., SW1), *b.* 1923; assumed by deed poll 1946, the surname of Whateley in lieu of his patronymic, and resumed by deed poll 1969 his surname of Balfour: *m.* 1st, 1948 (m. diss. 1956), Doreen Amanda, who *d.* 1968, only da. of the late Capt. G. H. Evans, of Cardiff; 2ndly, 1956 (m. diss. 1967), Phyllis Margaret Chavasse, yr. da. of the late Alfred Ernest Holder [*see* Holder, Br., colls.]; 3rdly (m. diss. 1971), Mrs. Elizabeth Cheston Bennet, who *d.* 1972, only da. of James Cheston, of Philadelphia, USA; 4thly, 1973, Mrs. Thelma Marjorie Balfour (who renounced her former surname of Wilkinson by Statutory Declaration 1972), el. da. of Clifford Exell, of Poole. *Residence*, 6, Bristol Gdns., SW15.——(By 2nd m.) Wendy Evelyn, *b.* 1919.

Issue of the late Lieut.-Col. Arthur Herbert Wood, *b.* 1877, *d.* 1940: *m.* 1st, 1900, Ethel Mary, who *d.* 1923, da. of the late Andrew Duncan, Bar.-at-law, of 71, Gloucester Place, W.; 2ndly, 1923, Andrina Hunter (49, The Vineyards, Gt. Baddow, Chelmsford, Essex), da. of John Fernie, of Aberfeldy, Perthshire:—

(By 1st m.) Evelyn (Ronald) (c/o National & Grindlays Bank, 26, Bishopsgate, EC2) *b.* 1903; ed. at RNC and City and Guilds, London Univ.: *m.* 1st, 1932 (m. diss. 1943), Maeve Audrey, da. of the late Arthur Theobald Wolfe, and widow of Emile Jacot; 2ndly, 1943, Kamal Jehangir, da. of Jehangir Fardunji Dastur, of Bombay, and has issue living, (by 1st m.) Diarmuid Evelyn (Chestnut Cottage, Bentley, Hants.), *b.* 1933; ed. at Gordonstoun: *m.* 1960, Beverly, BSc, da. of William Richard Pearce, of Ropley, Hants., and has issue living, Damian Evelyn *b.* 1962, Thalia Evelyn *b.* 1965,—(by 2nd m.) Ananda Evelyn, *b.* 1947,—Leela Aditi, *b.* 1946.——(By 2nd m.) Victor Arthur Evelyn (5, Hanover Terr., Regents Park. NW1), *b.* 1927; ed. at Tonbridge; a Chartered Surveyor: *m.* 1st, 1951, Olwen Mary, who *d.* 1960, only da. of Thomas Davies, of Studley, Warwicks.; 2ndly, 1963, Matilde Francesca Rosanna, da. of Girolamo Zucchelli, of Brione, Riva del Garda, Italy, and has issue living, (by 1st m.) David Arthur Evelyn, *b.* 1954,—Vaughan Thomas Evelyn, *b.* 1959,—Bernice Margaret Andrina, *b.* 1952,—(by 2nd m.) Victor Vincent, *b.* 1966,—Antonia Marcella Matilde *b.* 1964.——Marcella Mary, *b.* 1931; ed. at New Hall, Boreham, Chelmsford and London Univ. (BA, DipEd); Canoness Registrar of the Holy Sepulchre; Headmistress of New Hall Sch., Chelmsford since 1963.

Grandchildren of the late Western Wood, b. 1830: 3rd son of 1st Baronet—
Issue of the late George Orme Western Wood, b. 1868, d. 1926: m. 1904, Helen Portia,
who d. 1963, da. of Adam Davidson, of Darling Downs, Queensland:—
Ernest Cresswell Gaden Western, b. 1906: MI,A Qld. 1966-69, Chm. of Redland Shire Council,
Qld. since 1961: m. 1938, Mary Tudor, da. of James Winnel Hill, of Goorarooman, Thallon, Qld.,
and has issue living, Richard Orme Western, b. 1942; ed. at Qld. Univ. (BEng): m. 1968, Jenifer
Lynne, da. of N. W. S. Johns, of Clayfield, Brisbane, and has issue living, Matthew Gaden
Western b. 1969, Gregory Orme Western b. 1971,—Bruce James Western, b. 1951; ed. at Qld.
Univ. (B. Eng. Hons),—Nina Helen Western, b. 1939,—Rosamond Mary Western, b. 1944; ed.
at Qld. Univ. (Dip. Speech Therapy): m. 1972, John Franklin Verity Haselwood. Residence,
Moonie, Wellington Point, Brisbane, Qld.——Bernard Page Western, b. 1908; 1939-45 War as
Lt. RANVR: m. 1951, Phyllis May, da. of William Henry Andrew, of 48, Shakespeare St.,
Mackay, Qld. Residence, 57, Gregory St., Mackay, Qld.——Evelyn Hatherley Davidson,
b. 1911: m. 1937, Ena Myer, and has issue living, Ian Hatherley Western, b. 1942,—David Orme
Western (500 Oxley Av., Redcliffe, Qld.) b. 1911: m. 1937, Ena Myer, and has issue living, Ian
Hatherley Western, b. 1942: m. 19—, June Margaret Huch, da. of Huch Redcliffe, and has issue
living, Cameron Hatherley b. 1966, Scott Norman b. 1969 Rowena Maree b. 1971,—David Orme
Western, b. 1946; ed. at Qld. Univ. (MB, BS).——Helen onstance Western, b. 1905: m. 1949,
Stanley Gordon. Residence, 29, Herries Street, Toowoon.ba, Queensland.——Waveney Patricia
Western, b. 1914: m. 1943, Capt. Robert Gladstone Deacon, Australian Forces, and has issue
living, Helen Page, b. 1945. Residence, Forde Street, Allora, Queensland.

The 1st baronet, Sir Matthew Wood, born 1767, was the son of a serge manufacturer, of
Tiverton and at eleven years of age worked in his father's factory. At fourteen he was appren-
ticed to Mr. Newton, druggist, at Exeter. After serving seven years, he became a traveller in
the drug trade, and subsequently established himself in London as a chemist. He afterwards
became a hop-merchant, and was chosen Alderman, served as a Sheriff, and in the year of the
Peace, 1815, was elected Lord Mayor of London, to which office he was re-elected the following
year. He also sat as M.P. for London (L) 1816-43. During his mayoralty he was bold and
fearless. On one occasion, after a lawless mob had shot a man on Snow Hill, and were approaching the Exchange, he, with only seven others, rushed through that building, and held the rioters
in check, while he arrested several of the ringleaders. He took an active part in the cause of
Queen Caroline: he accompanied her through Calais and Dover, on her journey to London in
1820, and placed his house in South Audley Street at her disposal. His fortune was, after much
litigation, augmented on the death of Jemmy Wood, the banker, of Gloucester, to the extent of
£250,000. Among these possessions was the estate of Hatherley Court, in Gloucestershire, a
fine old ivy-mantled mansion, and from its name his second son, William Page, who was Lord
High Chancellor 1868-72, selected his title. Sir John Stuart Page Wood, 6th Bt. who was Com.
(retired) R.N., d. April 1955, and his son Sir David John Hatherley Page Wood, 7th Bt., d. Nov.
1955.

WORLEY, Creation (U.K.) 1928, of Ockshott, co. Surrey. [Extinct 1937.]

Sir ARTHUR WORLEY, C.B.E., 1st and last Baronet.

Daughter living of 1st Baronet—Stella, b. 1918: m. 1940, Raymond Ades, TD, JP, MA, and has
issue living, Timothy Raymond (94, North Rd., N6), b. 1941; MA: m. 1966, Josephine Dawn
Tylden-Pattenson, MA, and has issue living, Thomas Joseph Edmund b. 1971, Henry Arthur
Raymond b. 1973,—Anthony Edmond, b. 1947; PhD,—Susan Jane, b. 1943; BA,—Rosemary
Sally, b. 1951; BA. Residence, The Gables, Oxshott, Surrey.

WORSLEY, Creation (U.K.) 1838, of Hovingham, Yorkshire.

Sir (WILLIAM) MARCUS JOHN WORSLEY, 5th Baronet;
b. April 6th, 1925; s. his father, Col. Sir WILLIAM ARTHING-
TON, 1973; ed. at Eton, and New Coll., Oxford; a JP for
N. Riding of Yorks; PPS to Min. of Health 1960-61, to
Min. without Portfolio 1962-64, and to Lord Pres. of Council
1970-72; 1939-45 War in India and W. Africa with Green
Howards; MP for Keighley (C) 1959-64, and for Chelsea
(C) 1966 to Oct. 1975; Second Church Estates Commr.
1970-74: m. 1955, the Hon. Bridget Assheton, da. of 1st
Baron Clitheroe, and has issue.

Arms—Argent, a chief gules. Crest—A wyvern vert.

Seat—Hovingham Hall, York. Residence—25, Flood St., SW3.
Clubs—Carlton, Yorkshire.

Quam plurimis prodesse.

Do good to as many
persons as possible.

Sons living—WILLIAM RALPH, b. Sept. 12th, 1956; ed. at Harrow.——
Giles Arthington, b. 1961.——Peter Marcus, b. 1963.

Daughter living—Sarah Marianne, b. 1958.

Brothers living—George Oliver, TD (Bolton Hall, Wilberfoss, York,
YO4 5NZ. Clubs, Boodle's, Yorks. (York)), b. 1927; ed. at Eton, and
at Trin. Coll., Oxford (MA): m. 1966, Penelope Suzanne Fleetwood,
da. of Lt.-Col. Christopher Herbert Fleetwood Fuller, TD [see Fuller,
Bt.], and has issue living, David Christopher, b. 1969,—Richard Oliver Arthington, b. 1972,—
Georgina Joyce, b. 1967,—Anne Penelope, b. 1974.——John Arthington (RR2, Uxbridge,
Ont., Canada; 1A Dale Av., Toronto), b. 1928; ed. at Eton, and Trin. Coll., Oxford: m. 1954,
the Hon. Carolyn Wynard Hardinge, da. of 4th Viscount Hardinge, and has issue living, Henry
John, b. 1958,—Jonathan Hugh, b. 1960,—Dickon Carol, b. 1966,—Willa Victoria, b. 1955,—
Katharine Margot, b. 1968.
Sister living—Katharine Lucy Mary (HRH the Duchess of Kent), b. 1933; el. Chancellor of Leeds
Univ. 1965; appointed Controller Comdt. WRAC 1967; Col.-in-Ch. Army Catering Corps, and
Hon. Col. Yorks. Vol.; patron of Kent Co. Playing Fields Assocn., and of Spastics Soc.: m.
June 8th, 1961, HRH Prince Edward George Nicholas Paul Patrick, GCMG, GCVO, 2nd Duke
of Kent [see "ROYAL FAMILY"]. Residences, York House, SW1; Anmer Hall, Kings Lynn,
Norfolk.
Aunt living (daughter of 3rd baronet)—Victoria, b. 1900: m. 1932, Arthur Roland King-Farlow, who
d. 1974. Residence, 91, Hillway Highgate, N6.
Widow living of 4th Baronet—JOYCE MORGAN (Joyce, Lady Worsley), (The Cottage, Hovingham,
York.), da. of Sir John Fowler Brunner, 2nd Bt.: m. 1924, Col. Sir William Arthington Worsley,
4th Bt., who d. 1973.

Collateral Branches living.
Issue of the late Capt. Edward Marcus Worsley, yr. son of 3rd baronet, b. 1891,
d. 1971: m. 1941, Joyce Marian (Cawton Hall, Cawton, York., YO6 4LW),
da. of the late Stanley Graham Beer, of Northernhay, Bickley, Kent:—

Thomas Edward, *b.* 1947; ed. at Eton.——Susan Marian, *b.* 1942.——Angela Joyce, *b*, 1950: *m.* 1973, Ian Michael Downing Strickland-Skailes.——Diana Rosalind, *b.* 1953.

Grandson of the late Arthington Worsley, 3rd son of 1st baronet:—

Issue of the late Arthington Worsley, (posthumous) *b.* 1861, *d.* 1943: *m.* 1900, Helen, who *d.* 1949, widow of Frank Bartlett Thomas Griffiths. of Stourbridge:—
Marcus Rurik *b.* 1901.   *Residence*, Moundsmere, Durrants Rd., Poole, Dorset.

This family is a senior branch of the Worsleys of Worsley, Lancs. Another branch, formerly baronets of Appuldurcombe, Isle of Wight, whose title became extinct on the death of the 9th baronet in 1825, is now represented by the Earl of Yarborough.

Worsley-Taylor, see Taylor.

Worthington-Evans, see Evans.

WRAXALL, Creation (U.K.) 1813, of Wraxall, Somersetshire.

Sir MORVILLE WILLIAM LASCELLES WRAXALL, 8th *Baronet*; *b.* June 11th, 1922 ; *s.* his father, *Sir* CHARLES FREDERICK LASCELLES, 1951 ; ed. at St. Mark's Coll., Alexandria ; European War 1940-45 with R.A.S.C. (Africa star with clasp (8th Army), Defence medal, War medal) : *m.* 1956, Irmgard Wilhelmina Maria Schnidrig, of Basle, Switzerland, and has issue.

𝔄rms—Lozengy erminois and azure, on a chevron gules three estoiles of eight points or. 𝔠rest—A buck's head cabossed and erased gules, charged on the breast with two lozenges in fesse, and between the attires an estoile or.
Residence—

Sons living—CHARLES FREDERICK LASCELLES, *b.* Sept. 17th, 1961.——Peter Edward Lascelles, *b.* 1967.

Daughter living—Sylvia Laura, *b.* 1957.

Sister living—Gwendolyn Aileen, *b.* 1927: *m.* 1945, John Hunter, FIMechE, AFRAeS, FInstPet, and has issue living, Kenneth Charles John, *b.* 1951,—Keith Philip, *b.* 1957. *Residence*, 110, Devonshire Way, Shirley, Surrey.

Aunts living (daughters of 6th baronet)—Margaret Alison (Suite 407, Executive House, 362, Dundas St., London, 14, Ont.), *b.* 1895; changed christian names of Alice Elvira Herminia to Margaret Alison by deed poll 1916: *m.* 1st, 1916, John Johnstone, who *d.* 1925; 2ndly, 1929, Walter Huck-vale, RAF, who *d.* 1942, and has issue living (by 2nd m.) Ronald Dennis Russell *b.* 1932; Lt.-Col. RCAF: *m.* 1953, Cindy Butler, and has issue living, Robert *b.* 1961, Deborah *b.* 1954.——Leslie Mary Virginia (19, Elmstead Gdns., Worcester Park, Surrey KT4 TBD), *b.* 1902: *m.* 1st, (March) 1928 (m. diss. 1958) Herbert Thorpe; 2ndly, 1971, Cecil Frank Hollingsworth, and has issue living (by 1st m.), Leslie William (34, Westmorland Av., N. Harrow), *b.* (Dec.) 1928: *m.* 1st, 1952 (m. diss. 1967) Pamela Deirdre, da. of C. Connolly, of Kingston-upon-Thames; 2ndly, 1970, Ann, da. of M. Garrett, and has issue living (by 1st m.), Karen Lesley Wraxall, *b.* 1954.

Collateral Branch living

Issue of the late Aida Mary Elizabeth Wraxall, da. of 6th baronet, *b.* 1893, *d.* 1967: *m.* 1919, Anthony J. Bertuchi, FRGS, who *d.* 1947:—
Anthony Morville Charles (1, Burgess Hall Drive, Leeds, Maidstone, Kent, and Laing Wimpey Alireza, Riyadh, Saudi Arabia), *b.* 1933; ed. at Whitgift Sch., and London Univ. (BSc): *m.* 1958, Jane Masters, of Banstead, and has issue living, Timothy Rupert Anthony, *b.* 1963,—Amanda Jane Sally, *b.* 1964.——Doris Millicent (Rose Cottage, Yetholm, Roxburghshire, and 11, Tufton Court, SW1), *b.* 1920: *m.* 1962, Dennis George Greig, who *d.* 1971.——Alison Mary, *b.* 1923: *m.* 1955, P. Robert Davison, FRIBA, of 20A, Jalan Tunku, Kuala Lumpur 11-02, Malaysia, Cottage of St. John, Fordwich, Kent, and Casa Puteh, Mijas, Spain, and has issue living, Julian Charles *b.* 1956.——Gloria Joan, *b.* 1925: *m.* 1959, Victor Richards Price, of 95, Valley Drive, Brighton, and has issue living, Victoria Audelys *b.* 1961.——Elizabeth Diana (twin), *b.* 1923: *m.* 1954, Brian P. J. Farminer, of Salcott, Kingswood Way, Sanderstead, Surrey, and has issue living, James Lucien *b.* 1961,—Melanie Anne, *b.* 1959.

The 1st baronet, Sir Nathaniel William Wraxall, was in the Civil Service of the East India Company. The 3rd baronet, Sir Frederick, was sometime Assistant-Commissary in the Turkish Contingent and was author of several works. Sir Morville William, 6th baronet, enlisted in the Commissariat and Transport Corps, served in Nile Expedition 1884-5, and subsequently joined, in 1891, the Egyptian Coast Guard Administration.

WREY, Creation (E.) 1628, of Trebitch, Cornwall.

The good time will come.

Sir CASTEL RICHARD BOURCHIER WREY, 14th *Baronet*, son of the late Edward Castell Wrey, 7th son of 10th baronet; *b.* March 27th, 1903; *s.* his uncle, *the Rev. Sir* ALBANY BOURCHIER SHERARD, 1948; ed. at Oundle; European War 1939-40 in France as 2nd Lieut. R.A.S.C. (Supplementary Reserve) (invalided); joined R.N. as Ordinary Seaman 1940, and became Lieut. R.N.V.R. 1942: *m.* 1946, Sybil Mabel Alice, da. of Dr. George Lubke, of Durban, S. Africa, and has issue.

𝔄rms—Sable, a fesse between three pole-axes argent, helved gules. [Quarterings : Bourchier, Plan-tagenet, de Bohun, etc.]
Residences—Corffe, Barnstaple, N Devon; Tawstock Court, Barnstaple, N. Devon.

Sons living—GEORGE RICHARD BOURCHIER, *b.* Oct. 2nd, 1948.——Edward Sherard Bourchier, *b.* 1961.

Brother living—Christopher Bourchier, *TD* (c/o Barclays Bank, 77, Long Acre, WC2; Brooks's Club); *b.* 1906; 1939-45 War as Maj. 3rd Co. London Yeo.: *m.* 1932,

Ruth (who obtained a divorce 1947), only da. of the late Sir Harold Bowden, GBE, 2nd Bt., and has issue living, Timothy Christopher Bourchier (c/o Lloyds Bank, Berkeley Sq., W1), *b.* 1937: *m.* 1964, Susan, el. da. of William Brewer, of Troymark House, Johannesburg, S. Africa, and has issue living, Marcus Valerian Bourchier *b.* 1969, Camilla Melusine *b.* 1966,—Benjamin Harold Bourchier (8, Somerset Sq., Addison Rd., W14 8EE), *b.* 1940: *m.* 1970, Anne Christine Aubrey Cherry, da. of the late Col. Christopher Bushnell Stephenson, and has issue living, Tanya Serena *b.* 1971.

Sisters living—Katharine Augusta, *b.* 1902: *m.* 1926, **Harry Robert Wells, and has issue living** Christopher Richard Henry, *b.* 1929 : *m.* 1957, Elizabeth Anne, only da. of Lieut.-Col. Edward Daglish, of Bush Cottage, Thurston, Bury St. Edmunds, Suffolk, and has issue living, Christo-**pher Edward James** *b.* 1958, Philippa Frances Katharine *b.* 1961,—Cordelia Joan, *b.* 1930: *m.* 1956, Alan John Douglas Wheeldon, of 1, Collingwood Rise, Camberley, Surrey, and has issue living, Robert Alan Douglas *b.* 1957,—Virginia Margaret *b.* 1961. *Residence*, Fairholme, 4, Crescent Rd., Wokingham, Berks.——Diana Joan, *b.* 190– (*Hon. Mrs. William H. C. Rollo*): *m.* 1st, 1932 (m. diss. 1946), Jocelyn Abel Smith, who *d.* 1966; 2ndly, 1946, as his second wife, the Hon. William Hereward Charles Rollo, MC, who *d.* 1962 [*see* L. Rollo], and has issue living (by 1st m.), John William (42, Egerton Cres., SW3), *b.* 1933: *m.* 1st, 1957, Ruth, da. of Sir John Huggins, GCMG, MC; 2ndly 1965 (m. diss. 1974), Christine, only da. of Keith Taylor, of Adelaide; 3rdly, 1975, Mary Chichester Mills,—Bertram Robin (Fulham Park Stud, Lockleys, S. Aust.), *b.* 1938: *m.* 1961, Anne, yst. da. of Walter Kidman, of Eringa, Unley Park, Adelaide, S. Aust., and has issue living, William Walter *b.* 1964, Katharine Diana *b.* 1963, Rachel Muriel *b.* 1969. *Residence*, Barleythorpe, Oakham, Rutland.

Daughter living of 11th Baronet—Rachel (*Baroness Willoughby de Broke*), *b.* 1911; SSStJ, and a Chevalier of Order of Crown of Belgium: *m.* 1933, the 20th Baron Willoughby de Broke. *Residences*, Fox Cottage, Kineton, Warwicks., CV35 OLP; 2, Upper Phillimore Gdns., W8 7HA.

Daughter living of 12th Baronet—Barbara Marion Celia (*Lady Strachan*): *m.* 1st, 1925, Robert Darley Whelan, Flying Officer RAF, who *d.* 1927; 2ndly, 1929, Sir Andrew Henry Strachan, CBE, and has issue living, (by 2nd m.) Richard Neville, *b.* 1930,—Judith Meriel, *b.* 1936. *Residence*, 20, Hurworth Rd., Highlands, Salisbury, Rhodesia.

Collateral Branches living.

Issue of the late Major Reginald Charles Wrey, 8th son of 10th baronet, *b.* 1876, *d.* 1931 : *m.* 1912, Evelyn Adele Louise, who *d.* 1931, da. of the late Rev. Charles William Herbert Kenrick, V. of Holy Trinity, Barnstaple :—
Denys Charles Bourchier, *T.D.*, *b.* 1913 ; ed. at Eton ; European War 1939-45 as Capt. Derbyshire Yeo. : *m.* 1942, Katherine Frances Theodora (Peggy), da. of the late Rev. William Francis Eliot [Devitt, Bt, *cr.* 1916], and has issue living, Charles Bourchier, *b.* 1949,—Mark Eliot Bourchier, *b.* 1955. *Residence*, 24, Gerald Road, Chester Square, S.W.1.

Granddaughters of the late Rev. Bourchier William Toke Wrey, 2nd son of 9th baronet:—
Issue of the late Rev. Henry Bourchier Wrey, *b.* 1863, *d.* 1936 : *m.* 1895, Helen Esmé, who *d.* 1961, da. of Frederick Charles Ernest Griffin, of Gorsty Hayes Manor House, Tettenhall, Wolverhampton :—
Mary Caroline Bourchier, *b.* 1896: *m.* 1st, 1923, Robert Harry Cresswell Edwards, who *d.* 1925; 2ndly, 1932, the Rev. Cyril Lucian O'Ferrall, of Para, Shillingford St. George, nr. Exeter, and has issue living, (by 1st m.) Robert Henry Bourchier (Hamel Down, Tavistock), *b.* 1925; ed. at Kelly Coll., Tavistock, and at Trin. Coll., Camb.; is Lt. RNR: *m.* 1949, Elizabeth Mary, da. of R. H. Penhale, of Holsworthy, Devon, and has issue living, Hugh Robert Bourchier *b.* 1950, Judith Lilian Bourchier *b.* 1952, Esmé Susan Bourchier *b.* 1954, Francesca Ruth Bourchier *b.* 1956,—(by 2nd m.) Antony Bourchier (Flora Glen, Springwood Lane, Burghfield Common, Reading), *b.* 1935: *m.* 1964, Marlene Ann, da. of W. E. Gooding, of Llanelly, and has issue living, David Bourchier *b.* 1965, Philip Justin Bourchier *b.* 1970,—Bridget Mary Bourchier, *b.* 1933: *m.* 1962, Robert Anthony Bulkeley Brassey, of Whitegates Farm, Normansheath, Malpas, Ches., and has issue living, Susan Helen Bourchier *b.* 1963, Caroline Prudence Bourchier *b.* 1965, Mary Charlotte Bourchier *b.* 1969, Rachael Kathleen Bourchier *b.* 1973.——Dorothy Esme Bourchier, *b.* 1900; is a CStJ. *Residence*, Tawstock, Chudleigh, nr. Newton Abbot.

Granddaughters of the late George Edward Bourchier Wrey, only son of the late George Bourchier Wrey, son of the late Edward Bourchier Wrey, 2nd son of the late Rev. Bourchier William Wrey, yr. son of 6th baronet:—
Issue of the late Cdr. Edward Charles Wrey, OBE, RN, *b.* 1889, *d.* 1972: *m.* 1914, Grace Elsie, who *d.* 1940, da. of the late James C. Rimer, of Kelvin Grove, Newlands, Cape, S. Africa:—
Elizabeth Anne, *b.* 1917: *m.* 1946, William Welch Flexner, of 9, Paultons St., SW3 5DP.—— Marie Jean (5, Causeway, Arundel, Sussex), *b.* 1919: *m.* 1st, 1940, David Cecil Patrick Hastings, who *d.* (on active ser. in Burma) 1943, son of the late Sir Patrick Hastings, KC; 2ndly, 1949, Michael Dowden, who *d.* 1972, and has issue living, (by 1st m.) Judith Maryanne, *b.* 1941: *m.* 1963, Colin Etienne Dickinson, of Village Farm House, Llangattock, Crickhowell, Powys., and has issue living, Anthony Richard David, *b.* 1965, Charlotte Lucy (twin) *b.* 1965, Sophie Louise *b.* 1971,—(by 2nd m.) Edward David Michael, *b.* 1950: *m.* 1970, Sarah Anne Sherwin, and has issue living, Emma Mary *b.* 1973.

Granddaughter of the late Rev. John Wrey, younger son of the late Rev. Bourchier William Wrey (ante):—
Issue of the late Rev. Arthur Bourchier Wrey, *b.* 1831, *d.* 1918: *m.* 1st, 1859, Helen, who *d.* 1878, da. of the Rev. Thomas Phillpotts, Canon of Truro; 2ndly, 1881, Claudine Maud, who *d.* 1904, da. of the late Charles Twining, K.C., formerly of Halifax, N.S.:—
(By 2nd marriage) Mary Claudine : *m.* 1st, 1913, Capt. Humphrey Richard Locke Lawrence, Indian Army, who *d.* (killed in action during European War) 1915; 2ndly, 1928, Heathcote Dicken Statham, CBE, MusD, who *d.* 1973, and has issue living (by 2nd m.), Michael Heathcote Wrey, *b.* 1929. *Residence*, 11. The Close, Norwich, NOR 16P.

The family of Wrey is of considerable antiquity in Devonshire. Sir Chichester, the 3rd baronet, a faithful adherent to the royal cause, became in 1652 possessed, by marriage, of Tawstock, where the family now reside. His wife, Anne was 3rd da. and co-heir of Edward Bourchier, Earl of Bath, and a co-heir to Barony of Fitzwarine (cr. 1295). After the Restoration he was successively Colonel of the Duke of York's Regiment, Governor of Sheerness, and MP for Lostwithiel. Sir Bourchier, the 4th baronet, served under the Duke of Monmouth, and after the Restoration commanded a regiment of horse.

CORY-WRIGHT, Creation (U.K.) 1903, of Caen Wood Towers, Highgate, St. Pancras, co. London, and Hornsey, Middlesex.

Sir RICHARD MICHAEL CORY-WRIGHT, 4th *Baronet,* b. Jan. 17th, 1944; s. his grandfather, *Maj. Sir* GEOFFREY, 1969; ed. at Eton, and Birmingham Univ.; Patron of one living: m. 1976, Veronica, only da. of James Bolton, of Church Farm, Morningthorpe, Norwich.

Arms—Or, a fesse compony counter-compony azure and argent between in chief two eagles' heads erased, and in base a unicorn passant reguardant of the second. *Crest*—Upon a mount proper between two caltraps or a unicorn passant reguardant argent, armed, crined, and unguled, also or.

Address—Tacolneston Hall, Norwich, NR16 1DW.

Sister living—Juliet Susan, *b.* 1942.
Uncles living—sons of 3rd Baronet—MICHAEL, *b.* March 5th, 1920; ed. at Eton; is Lt. RA (TA); 1939-43 War (prisoner): *m.* 1954, Elizabeth, da. of the late Maj. James Archibald Morrison, DSO [B. Trevor], and widow of Capt. Eric Martin Smith. *Residence,* Codicote Lodge, Hitchin, Herts.——David Arthur, *b.* 1925: *m.* 1949, Lady Jane Katherine Douglas, da. of 11th Marquess of Queensberry, and has issue living, Anthony Jonathan, *b.* 1950,—
Simon, *b.* 1952,—Christopher James, *b.* 1965. *Residence,* Jarmins Orchard, Barton St. David, Somerton, Som.——Mark Richard Geoffrey, *b.* 1930; late 2nd Lieut. 10th Roy. Hussars: *m.* 1956, Tania, da. of the late J. C. Holcroft, of Northbrook, Bentley, Hants, and has issue living, Charles Alexander, *b.* 1958,—Harry William Mark, *b.* 1963. *Residences,* Tilhill House, Tilford, Surrey, and Burnham Market, King's Lynn. *Club,* St. James'.

Great Uncle living—son of 2nd Baronet—Douglas, *CBE, b.* 1901; High Sheriff of Herts. 1963; Chm. of Chamber of Coal Traders 1960-70; 1914-18 War as Midshipman RN; CBE (Civil) 1969: *m.* 1924, Margaret Vivien Sarina, da. of Rudolph Levy, of Birkdale, Lancs., and has issue living, June (*Lady Horlick*), *b.* 1926: *m.* 1948, Sir John James Macdonald Horlick, 5 Bt. of Woodlands House, Henley-on-Thames, Oxon.; 43, Montpelier Sq., SW7, and Tournaig, Poolewe, Ross-shire, —Olive Marigold, *MB, BS, b.* 1929: *m.* 1954, David Richard Michael Curling, of The Rosary, Coleshill, Bucks. [Curtis, Bt.], and has issue living, Richard Michael *b.* 1958, Rosanna Virginia *b.* 1960, Davina Cordelia *b.* 1964,—Cleone Anne, *b.* 1935: *m.* 1956, John Wedgwood Thellusson Wood [*see* E. Kimberley, colls.]. *Residence,* Mackerye End, Harpenden, Herts.

Mother living—Susan Esterel (Tacolneston Hall, Norwich, NR16 1DW), el. da. of the late Robert Hamond Arthur Elwes, of Congham House, King's Lynn: *m.* 1st, 1940, Capt. (Anthony John) Julian Cory-Wright, RA, el. son of 3rd baronet, *b.* 1916, *d.* (killed in action) 1944; 2ndly, 1949, Lt.-Col. Jocelyn Eustace Gurney, DSO, MC, Welsh Gds., who *d.* 1973, son of the late Sir Eustace Gurney.

Widow living of 3rd Baronet—FELICITY (*Lady Cory-Wright*) (The Cottage, Brancaster, King's Lynn), da. of the late Sir Herbert Beerbohm Tree: *m.* 1915, Maj. Sir Geoffrey Cory-Wright, 3rd baronet, who *d.* 1969.

Collateral Branches living.

Issue of the late Ronald Cory-Wright, M.C., 2nd son of 2nd baronet, *b.* 1893, *d.* 1932 : *m.* 1917, Geraldyn Mary (now of Oakridge, Little Gaddesden, near Berkhamsted, Herts), da. of the late Major Henry Charles Windsor Villiers-Stuart, of Dromana, co. Waterford :—

Francis Newman, *b.* 1925 ; ed. at Eton, and at Merton Coll., Oxford (B.A. 1949, M.A. 1954) : is Lt. 15th/19th King's Roy. Hussars; European War 1945 (wounded).——Rosamund Ina, *b.* 1923: *m.* 1946, Count Stanislaw Andrej Saryusz-Bielski, who *d.* 1958, and has issue living, Anna Louisa, *b.* 1947,—Marie Thérésa, *b.* 1948,—Madeleine Carol Bernadette Gerarde, *b.* 1952. *Residence,*

Issue of the late Lt.-Cdr. Alan Cory-Wright, DSC, R.N., 3rd son of 2nd baronet, *b.* 1896, *d.* 1964: *m.* 1923, Leila Yda Cyrillia (Hatfield Park, Takeley, Essex), da. of Arthur Lobb, of Hatters Croft, Sawbridgeworth, Herts.:—

Godfrey William (Hatfield Park, Takeley, Essex), *b.* 1928; ed. at Harrow: *m.* 1958, Nicole Emma, da. of E. Vermeiren, of Brussels, and has issue living, Alan William, *b.* 1965,—Elizabeth Yda, *b.* 1961.

Issue of the late Dudley Cory-Wright, younger son of 1st baronet, *b.* 1872, *d.* 1931 : *m.* 1905, Alice Cross, who *d.* 1965.

Esmond Godfrey, *b.* 1908 ; ed. at Eton, and at Merton Coll., Oxford (B.A. 19—, M.A. 1933) : *m.* 1st, 1931 (marriage dissolved 1942), Amanda, da. of E. P. Menhinick, of Treguddick, Gresham, Gardens, Golders Green, N.W.11 ; 2ndly, 1949, Pepita Jane Grey, da. of Harry William Grey, Bell, and has issue living, (by 1st m.) Edward James Dudley (38, Prince Edward's Rd.., Lewes) *b.* 1932; ed. at Merton Coll., Oxford: *m.* 1955, Jean Olive, da. of George Young, of St Albans, and has issue living, James Edward *b.* 1956, Nicholas John *b.* 1964, Juliet Amanda *b.* 1959,— Amanda Menhinick *b.* 1933 *Residence,* Pagewood, East Strand, West Wittering, Sussex.—— Althea Frances (Vale Cottage, Marnhull, nr. Sturminster Newton, Dorset), *b.* 1917.

The 1st baronet, Sir Cory Francis Cory-Wright, was Chm. of Wm. Cory and Son (Limited), and assumed by Roy. licence 1903, the additional surname of Cory. The 2nd baronet, Sir Arthur Cory-Wright, was High Sheriff of Herts 1921.

WRIGHTSON, Creation (U.K.) 1900, of Neasham Hall, co. Durham.

Sir JOHN GARMONDSWAY WRIGHTSON, *T.D.*, 3rd *Baronet ; b.* June 18th, 1911 ; *s.* his father, *Col. Sir* THOMAS GARMONDSWAY, *TD*, 1950; ed. at Eton; Hon. DCL Durham; formerly Maj. Durham LI (TA); is a DL for co. Durham; High Sheriff of Co. Durham 1959; 1939-45 War in France and Germany with 6th Airborne Div. (despatches): *m.* 1939, the Hon. Rosemary Monica Dawson, da. of 1st Viscount Dawson of Penn, and has issue.

Arms—Or, a fesse invected checky azure and argent between two eagles' heads erased in chief sable, and a saltire couped in base gules. *Crest*—In front of a saltire gules, a unicorn salient or.
Seat—Neasham Hall, near Darlington.

Veritas omnia vincit.
Truth conquers all things.

Son living—CHARLES MARK GARMONDSWAY, *b.* Feb. 18th, 1951: *m.* 1975, Stella Virginia, da. of the late George Dean.
Daughters living—Penelope Linda, *b.* 1940.——Juliet Diana, *b.* 1943.——Elizabeth Ann, *b.* 1946.
Brothers living—Peter, *O.B.E.*, *b.* 1914 : ed at Eton ; is Lieut.-Col. Durham L.I. ; European War 1939-45 in France, N. Africa, and Italy (O.B.E.) ; O.B.E. (Mil.) 1945 : *m.* 1946, Pamela, da. of the late Lieut.-Col. Sir Murrough John Wilson, KBE, and has issue living, Simon Murrough, *b.* 1954,——Joanna Mary, *b.* 1947: *m.* 1969, Peter Jonathan Howard, of Singehurst, Ticehurst, Sussex, and has issue living, Benjamin Simon *b.* 1975,——Susan Jennifer, *b.* 1948: *m.* 1970, Montague William Style, of 4, Belleville Rd., SW11 [*see* Style, Bt., colls.]. *Residence*, Manfield Grange, Manfield, nr. Darlington.——Rodney *b.* 1916; Cdr. RN (ret.); 1939-45 War in Norway (despatches), and Madagascar 1943 (despatches): *m.* 1st, 1940, Florence Jean, who *d.* 1944, da. of the late James D. Dunn, of Ferniecraig, Skelmorlie, Ayrshire; (2ndly, 1947, Mrs. Elizabeth Wilson, da. of the late Brig. Raymond Henry Arnold Davison Love, of Mayford, Surrey, and has issue living (by 1st m.), Jeremy *b.* 1941: *m.* 1970, Lindsay, da. of Dr. J. Parker, of 9, The Mount, Malton, Yorks.—(by 2nd m.) Lucinda, *b.* 1948: *m.* 1969, Jonathan Philip Hudson, of 47, Waterford Rd., SW6. *Residence*, 29, Fairfax Pl., NW6.——Oliver (The Bridge House, Eryholme, Darlington), *b.* 1920; ed. at Eton, and at Balliol Coll., Oxford; Bar. Lincoln's Inn 1950; Recorder of Crown Courts since 1972; late Capt. Coldm. Gds.
Aunts living (daughters of 1st baronet)—Margaret Justina, *b.* 1877; is a Fellow of Roy. Soc. of British Sculptors and Soc. of Women Artists. *Studio Address*, 56A, Bedford Gdns., Kensington, W8.——Jocelyn Bruce, *b.* 1887. *Residence*, St. Mary Cottage, 30, Bimport, Shaftesbury.

Collateral Branch living.

Issue of the late Wilfrid Ingram Wrightson, youngest son of 1st baronet, *b.* 1876, *d.* 1949: *m.* 1913, Victoria, who *d.* 1966, da. of the late F. C. Winby, of 47, Portland Place, W:—
Elizabeth Victoria Mary (*Lady White*), *b.* 1914: *m.* 1943, Sir Headley Dymoke White, 3rd Bt. *Residence*, Stinton Hall, Reepham, Norfolk.——Ann Winby, *b.* 1917: *m.* 1952, Robert le Rougetel White, BArch, ARIBA. *Residence*, Cross Gates, Lorton, Cockermouth, Cumberland.

The 1st baronet, Sir Thomas, was Chm. of Head, Wrightson and Co. (Limited), bridge builders, of Stockton, and sat as M.P. for Stockton-on-Tees (C) 1892-95, and for E. Div. of St. Pancras July 1899 to Jan. 1906.

Wrixon-Becher, see Becher.

Wykeham (Twisleton-Wykeham-Fiennes), see Fiennes.

WILLIAMS-WYNN, Creation (E.) 1688, of Gray's Inn, co. Middlesex.

Sir (OWEN) WATKIN WILLIAMS-WYNN, *CBE*, 10th *Baronet ; b.* Nov. 30th, 1904 ; *s.* his father, *Col. Sir* ROBERT WILLIAM HERBERT WATKIN. *K.C.B., D.S.O., T.D.*, 1951 ; ed. at Eton ; Hon. Col. and late Lieut.-Col. Comdg. 361st Medium Regt., RA (TA), and a JP for Denbighshire (High Sheriff 1954, Lord-Lieut. 1966-74); Lieut. for Clwyd since 1974; 1939-45 War at Dunkirk and in SE Asia (despatches twice, prisoner); CBE (Civil) 1969: *m.* 1st, 1939, Margaret Jean, OStJ, who *d.* 1961, da. of the late Col. William Alleyne Macbean, RA; 2ndly, 1968, Mrs. Gabrielle Haden Matheson, da. of the late Herbert Alexander Caffin, and has issue by 1st m.

Arms—Quarterly : 1st and 4th vert, three eagles displayed in fesse inverted or, *Wynn* ; 2nd and 3rd gules, argent, two foxes in saltire the sinister surmounted of the dexter gules, a crescent azure in chief for difference, *Williams*. *Crest*—An eagle displayed or, armed and langued gules,
Residence,—Llandgedwyn, Oswestry, Salop. *Club*,—Army and Navy.

Eryr Eryrod Eryri.
The Eagle of the Eagles of Snowdon

Son living—By 1st m.—DAVID WATKIN (Twining Hill, Erbistock, Wrexham), *b.* Feb. 18th, 1940; ed. at Eton; late Lt. R. Dragoons: *m.* 1968, Harriet Veryan Elspeth, da. of Gen. Sir Norman Hastings Tailyour, KCB, DSO, and has issue living, Charles Edward Watkin, *b.* 1970,——Henrietta June, *b.* 1972,—Lucinda Jean (twin), *b.* 1972.

Brother living—Edward Watkin, *O.B.E.*, *b.* 1908; ed. at Eton; Lt.-Col. Welsh Guards (Reserve), and (ret.) R.A. (T.A.); 1939-45 War (O.B.E.); with British Mil. Mission, Moscow, O.B.E. (Mil) 1946: *m.* 1949, Mrs. Roma Sunderland, da. of the late Kenneth Muray Matheson. *Seat*—Coed Coch, Denbighshire. *Residence*,—Plas Llewelyn, Abergele, Denbighshire. *Club*, Guards.

Sisters living—Joyce, *b.* 1906: *m.* 1929, Duncan Robertson, son of Sir Henry Beyer Robertson, and has issue living, Sheila Ann, *b.* 1929: *m.* 1953, Henry Saxon Tate,—Jean Margaret, *b.* 1932: *m.* 1956, Capt. Peter Miles de Wend Greenwell, of Tregeiriog Farm,

Tregeiriog, Llangollen,—Bridget Jennifer (*Hon. Mrs. John E. S. Russell*), *b.* 1935: *m.* 1959, the Hon. John Edward Southwell Russell (of Cliffe House, Atherstone, Warwickshire), el. son of 26th Baron de Clifford. *Residence*, Llantysilio Hall, Llangollen.——Margaret (*Hon. Mrs. Peter Hotham*), *b.* 1911: *m.* 1934, Maj. the Hon. Peter Hotham, late King's Own Yorkshire L.I. [*see* B. Hotham]. *Residence*, Plas Newydd, Glascoed, Abergele, N. Wales.

Daughters living of 8th Baronet—Margaret Helen (*Lady Verdin*), *b.* 1921: *m.* 1st, 1941 (marriage dissolved 1950), Capt. Hubert Charles Paulet Hamilton, Roy. Irish Fusiliers; 2ndly, 1950, Lieut.-Col. Sir Richard Bertram Verdin, O.B.E., T.D., D.L., J.P., of Stoke Hall, Nantwich, Cheshire, and has issue living (by 1st m.) Andrew Paulet *b.* 1943: *m.* 1970, Susan Mary Alexander, adopted da. of the late Field Marshal Earl Alexander of Tunis,—(by 2nd m.) Alistair Richard Norman, *b.* 1963.——Joan, *b.* 1928: *m.* 1951, Maj. Geoffrey Sewell, Gren. Guards, and has issue living, David Nigel Wynn, *b.* 1953,—Mark Geoffrey, *b.* 1955,—Charles Percy, *b.* 1958. *Residence*, Tysoe Manor, Tysoe, Warwick.

Sister living of 8th Baronet—Constance Mary, *b.* 1895: *m.* 1925, Major Guy Charles Mostyn-Owen, 12th Lancers (Reserve). *Residence*, Llangedwyn, Oswestry.

Widow living of 8th Baronet—DAISY, OBE (*Dowager Lady Williams-Wynn*), da. of the late J. Johnson Houghton, of Westwood, Neston, Ches.; OBE (Civil) 1957: *m.* 1920, Sir Watkin Williams-Wynn, 8th baronet, who *d.* 1949. *Residence*, Belan, Ruabon.

Collateral Branches living.

Grandchildren of the late Charles Watkin Williams-Wynn, son of the late Rt. Hon. Charles Watkin Williams-Wynn, 2nd son of 4th baronet :—
    Issue of the late Arthur Watkin Williams-Wynn, *b.* 1856, *d.* 1946 : *m.* 1892, Alice Mary, who *d.* 1956, da. of the late Hon. George Wentworth-Fitzwilliam [E. Fitzwilliam, colls] :—
Alice Nesta Margaret (of Coed y Maen, Meifod, Montgomeryshire, and Little Farm, Burford, Oxon), *b.* 1894.

Issue of the late Major Frederick Rowland Williams-Wynn, C.B., *b.* 1865, *d.* 1940: *m.* 1907, Beatrice Kathleen, who *d.* 1913, el. da. of the late Major Francis Cooper, R.F.A., of Markree Castle, Collooney, Ireland:—
John Francis WILLIAMS-WYNNE, CBE, DSO, *b.* 1908; ed. at Oundle and at Magdalene Coll., Camb. (MA); FRAgricS; Col. (ret.) late RA; a JP of co. Merioneth; Lord-Lieut. of Merioneth 1957-74, since when Lieut. of Gwynedd; NW Frontier of India 1936-37, Burma 1943-45 (DSO); assumed by deed poll 1940 the surname of Williams-Wynne in lieu of his patronymic; Constable of Harlech Castle since 1964; DSO 1945, CBE (Civil) 1972: *m.* 1938, Margaret Gwendoline Heyward, da. of the late Rev. George Eliott Roper, and has issue living, William Robert Charles, *b.* 1947: *m.* 1975, Veronica Frances, da. of Maj. Aubrey L. O. Buxton [see Buxton, Bt., colls.],—Merion Beatrice, *b.* 1941: *m.* 1964, Maj. Peter Thomas Anthony Davies, of Le Presbytere, Rue de L'Eglise, Villers S/St. Leu d'Esserent, Oise 60, France, and has issue living, Orlan Jonathan *b.* 1965, Hardwin *b.* 1968,—Jane Margaret, *b.* 1949: *m.* 1972, Hon. David Alexander Cospatrick Douglas-Home formerly Lord Dunglass, el. son of Baron Home of the Hirsel (Life Baron), formerly 14th Earl of Home. *Residence*, Peniarth, Towyn, Merioneth. *Clubs*, Army and Navy, Pratt's.——Kathleen Charlotte, *b.* 1910: *m.* 1931, Maj. Christopher William Stewart Blackett, DL, late Coldm. Gds., of Old Manse of Borgie, Skerray, by Thurso, and has issue living, John Beauchamp (Arbigland, Dumfries; Orchard House, Woodside, Windsor Forest), *b.* 1939; Capt. Coldm. Gds.: *m.* 1964, Sarah Jennifer, da. of James Trevor Gidley Withycombe, of Bury Farm, Studham, Dunstable, and has issue living, James William Beauchamp *b.* 1964, Edward John Christopher *b.* 1969, Annabel Hope *b.* 1966,—Beatrice Olivia, *b.* 1932: *m.* 1954, Lt.-Col. Simon Bland, Scots Gds. (Gabriel's Manor, Edenbridge, Kent), son of Sir (George) Nevile (Maltby) Bland, KCMG, KCVO, and has issue living, David Nevile William *b.* 1959; a Page of Honour to HM 1973-74, Catherine Mary *b.* 1955, Rachel Corinna *b.* 1957, Henrietta *b.* 1967,—Cicely Catherine Victoria, *b.* 1946: *m.* 1971, John McCulloch, of Auchindinny House, Penicuik, Midlothian.——Annora Beatrice, *b.* 1911: *m.* 1st, 1935 (divorce 1945), Lt.-Col. David Sacheverell Curtis, Roy. Fusiliers [*see* Curtis, Bt., colls.]; 2ndly, 1945, Charles George Gordon Wainman, and has issue living (by 1st m.) [*see* Curtis, Bt., colls.],—(by 2nd m.) Annora Mary, *b.* 1946: *m.* 1970, Evangelos Koemtzopoulos, of 30, Vasileos Georgiou, Athens, Greece, and has issue living, Nicholas *b.* 1974, Laura *b.* 1971. *Residence*, The Tower House, Hinton St. George, Som., TA17 8SS.

Descendants of the late John Williams (great-grandson of John Williams, 2nd son of 1st baronet), who was *cr.* a *Baronet* 1798.
See Williams, Bt., *cr.* 1798.

This family descends from William Williams, of Chwaine Issa, Anglesey, 14th in descent from Cadrod Hardd, or the Handsome, a Welsh chieftain, who resided at Tremadog, in the parish of Llanfaithley, and was Lord of Talybolion about the year 1100. The 1st baronet, M.P. for Chester in three Parliaments, was Speaker of the House of Commons 1679-85. In 36 Car. II. he was tried for libel, in causing to be printed the information of Thomas Dangerfield, and, although he pleaded the law and custom of Parliament, he was fined £10,000. After the Revolution, this judgment was declared illegal and against the freedom of Parliament. The 3rd baronet, Sir Watkin Williams, succeeded to the estate of Wynnstay (formerly Watstay) in 1718 under the will of Sir John Wynn, 5th Bt. of Gwydir (ext.), who had acquired that estate through his wife, and assumed the additional surname of Wynn. The 6th baronet sat as M.P. for Denbighshire (C) 1841-85. The 7th baronet, Col. Sir Herbert Lloyd Watkin Williams-Wynn, C.B., was Hon. Col. Yeo., Lord-Lieut. of Montgomeryshire, and a County Councillor for Denbighshire. He sat as M.P. for Denbighshire (C) May to Nov. 1885. The 9th baronet, Col. Sir Robert William Herbert Watkin Williams-Wynn, K.C.B., D.S.O., T.D., was Lord-Lieut. of Denbighshire 1928-51, and served in S. Africa 1900-02, and European War 1914-18

WYVILL, Creation (E.) 1611, of Constable Burton, Yorkshire. [Dormant 1774.]
Collateral Branches living.

Granddaughter living of the late William Edward Wyvill, probable *de jure* 15th Bt.:—
    Issue of the late Newlon D'Arcy Wyvill, probable *de jure* 17th Bt., *b.* 1895, *d.* 1971: *m.* 1920, Helen Lamar (118, Jackson Av., Winchester, Virginia, USA 22601), da. of Henry Laboin Wood:—
Willie Juanita, *b.* 1923: *m.* 1st, 1952 (m. diss. 1953), Walter Daniel Scheuch, 2ndly, Donald Douglas Lamond.

Grandson of the late Maj. Marmaduke Ibbetson Wyvill, Rifle Bde., only son of Marmaduke D'Arcy Wyvill of Constable Burton Hall and Denton Park, Yorks., el. son of Marmaduke Wyvill (*d.* 1896), third in descent from Edward Wyvill, 2nd son of D'Arcy Wyvill (ante), 2nd son of 4th baronet:—
    Issue of the late Marmaduke Frederic Wyvill, *b.* 1912, *d.* 1953: *m.* 1st, 19—, (m. diss. 19—), Cissy Scott; 2ndly, 1943 (m. diss. 1946), May, da. of Henry Holland Bennet; 3rdly, 1947, Mrs. Mary Jones, who *d.* 1968, da. of the late Frederick Pope:—
(By 2nd m.) Marmaduke Charles Asty (Constable Burton, Leyburn, Yorks.; Brooks's Club), *b.* 1945; ed. at Stowe and Roy. Agric. Coll., Cirencester; ARICS; Lord of manor of Constable Burton, Leyburn, Yorks, and patron of three livings: *m.* 1972, Margaret Ann, el. da. of Maj. Sydney William Hardcastle, RA, of Hutchins Farm, Etchingham, Sussex, and has issue living, Marmaduke D'Arcy William, *b.* 1975.

This Baronetcy has remained dormant since the death in 1774 of Sir Marmaduke Asty Wyvill, 7th Bt. According to G.E.C.'s "Complete Baronetage", his probable heir was Marmaduke Wyvill of Anne Arundel co., Maryland, son and heir of William, who emigrated to Frederick Co., Maryland, el. son of Darcy, 2nd son of 4th Bt. Marmaduke left two sons by his 1st wife, Harriet Rateby (*m.* 1764) and two sons by his 2nd wife, Susanna Burgess (*m.* 1775). His el. son, Darcy (probably *de jure* 9th Bt.) had one son Robert (probably *de jure* 10th Bt.) who *d.s.p.* about 1800. His 2nd son, Marmaduke (probably *de jure* 11th Bt.) *d.s.p.* male 1808. Succession then presumably reverted to his half-brother, Walter of Calvert co., Maryland (el. son of Marmaduke by his 2nd wife, and probably *de jure* 12th Bt.). His son, Edward Hale (probably *de jure* 13th Bt.), *b.* 1812, *d.c.* 1894, was *s.* by his son, Walter Davis (probably *de jure* 14th Bt.), *b.* 1834, *d.* 1898. This is as far as G.E.C. takes the line, but recent research has established that he was *s.* by his only son, William Edward (probably *de jure* 15th Bt.), *b.* 1859, *d.* 1911, who was *s.* by his el. son Carlisle Osborne (probably *de jure* 16th Bt.), *b.* 1894, *d.* 1941, who was *s.* by his brother Newlon D'Arcy (probably *de jure* 17th Bt.) *b.* 1895, *d.* 1971.

YARROW, Creation (U.K.) 1916, of Homestead, Hindhead, Frensham, co. Surrey.

Be just and fear not

Sir ERIC GRANT YARROW, *M.B.E.*, 3rd *Baronet*, *b.* April 23rd, 1920; *s.* his father, *Sir* HAROLD EDGAR, *G.B.E.*, 1962; ed. at Marlborough; a DL of Renfrewshire; Chm. of Yarrow & Co., Ltd., Yarrow Engineers (Glasgow) Ltd., Yarrow (Shipbuilders) Ltd., Y-A.R.D., Y-A.R.D., (Aust.) Pty. Ltd., and Yarrow Africa Maritime Consultancy (Pty.) Ltd., and a Dir. of Yarrow (Africa) (Pty.) Ltd., of Croftinloan (Holdings) Ltd., of Standard Life Assurance Co., of Clydesdale Bank Ltd., and of Marine Oil Industry Repairs Ltd.; OStJ; Prime Warden of Co. of Shipwrights 1970-71; Hon. Vice-Pres. Roy. Instn. of Naval Architects 1972; Burma 1942-45, as Maj. RE (MBE); MBE (Mil) 1946: *m.* 1st, 1951, Rosemary Ann, who *d.* 1957, yr. da. of H. T. Young, of Roehampton, SW; 2ndly, 1959, Annette Elizabeth Françoise, only da. of A. J. E. Steven, of Ardgay, Ross-shire, and has issue by 1st and 2nd m.

Arms—Azure, in base on the sea proper, an ancient three-masted ship, sailing to the sinister argent, in chief two swallows volant of the last, each holding in the beak a harebell slipped also proper. Crest—Above clouds proper a swallow volant argent, holding in the beak a yarrow flower slipped also proper.

Residence,—Cloak, Kilmacolm, Renfrewshire, PA13 4SD. *Club,*—United Service and Royal Aero.

Sons living—By 1st marriage—RICHARD GRANT, *b.* March 21st, 1953.——By 2nd marriage—Norman Murray *b.* 1960.——Peter Harold (twin) *b.* 1960.——David Eric, *b.* 1966.

Sisters living—Eleanor Audrey (Balauchen Lodge, Milngavie, Stirlingshire), *b.* 1907: *m.* 1934, Maj. Harry Duncanson Boyd, MBE, TD, RA, who *d.* 1964, and has issue living, Eleanor Margaret, *b.* 1937: *m.* 1959, Peter Murray Bruce Hutt, (Strathcraig, 7, Horseshoe Rd., Box 248, PO Gillitts Natal), el. son of Sir (Alexander McDonald) Bruce Hutt, KBE, CMG, and has issue living, Colin Murray Bruce, *b.* 1960, Nigel Duncan, *b.* 1964, Nichola Margaret *b.* 1966,—Eda Daphne, *b.* 1940: *m.* 1963, Christopher Roche Enslin, of La Provence, Fransch Hoek, Cape, S. Africa, and has issue living, Michael Roche *b.* 1967, Ian Boyd *b.* 1970, Camilla Fiona *b.* 1964,—Sylvia Audrey, *b.* 1944: *m.* 1967, Alexander Baird Fergus Morton, of Auchencraig, Milngavie, Stirlingshire, and has issue living, Peter Fergus *b.* 1970, Anita Audrey *b.* 1973.——Beryl Winifred Ethne (Cuilfail, Helensburgh, Glasgow, G60 5AB), *b.* 1910: *m.* 1st, 1932, Charles Wood Scott, who *d.* 1960; 2ndly, 1969, Graeme Hardie, BEM, who *d.* 1973, and has issue living (by 1st m.), Grahame Charles Wood (Dunarbuck, Bowling, Glasgow, G60 5AB), *b.* 1933: *m.* 1962, Jean Isabel Mary Manners, and has issue living, Alan Charles Wood *b.* 1966, Fiona Anne *b.* 1963, Lorna Jean Ethne *b.* 1965,— Avril Eleanor Yarrow, *b.* 1936: *m.* 1959, James Alistair Spence Meighan, of Fernbrae, Strathblane, Stirlingshire, and has issue living, Andrew Alistair Spence *b.* 1963, Marjorie Eleanor Spence *b.* 1961, Avril Gillian Spence *b.* 1966.

Half-Sister living—Angela Mary Rosalynde, *b.* 1937: *m.* 1961, David Clive Griffiths, of Thrushes, Canon Hill, Bray, Berks, and has issue living, David William Yarrow, *b.* 1969,—Rosemary Kate, *b.* 1962,—Amanda Mary, *b.* 1964.

Widow living of 2nd Baronet—ROSALYNDE (*Rosalynde, Lady Yarrow*) (of Glenvaar, 11, Charlton Park Gate, Cheltenham), da. of the late Sir Oliver Joseph Lodge, LL.D., D.Sc., F.R.S.: *m.* 1935, as his 2nd wife, Sir Harold Edgar Yarrow, G.B.E., 2nd baronet, who *d.* 1962.

Collateral Branch living.

Issue of the late Norman Alfred Yarrow, 2nd son of 1st baronet, *b.* 1891, *d.* 1953 : *m.* 1915, Ada Hope (*Lady Taylor*), (who *m.* 2ndly, 1959, as his third wife, Sir Eric Stuart Taylor, O.B.E., M.D., M.R.C.P., 2nd Bt.), da. of Forrest Bertram Leeder, M.R.C.S., L.R.C.P., of Victoria, British Columbia :—

Cynthia Hope, *b.* 1921 : *m.* 1st, 1944 (marriage dissolved 1954), Lieut. Clifton Thomas Williams Hyslop, Roy. Canadian Naval Vol. Reserve ; 2ndly, 1955, William F. Pinckard, and has issue living, (by 1st marriage) John David Allan, *b.* 1946,—Andrew Peter, *b.* 1951,— Gillian Cynthia, *b.* 1949,—(by 2nd m.) Christopher William, *b.* 1958,—Jonathan Mark, *b.* 1960.——Daphne Veryan, *b.* 1924: *m.* 1952, Lt. Cdr. Howard Victor Clark, RCN, of 9060, Ardmore Drive, Sidney, BC, Canada, and has issue living, Susan Veryan, *b.* 1954,—Stephanie Jane, *b.* 1958.

The 1st baronet, Sir Alfred Fernandez Yarrow (an engineer and shipbuilder), was Chm. of Yarrow and Co., Ltd., shipbuilders, of Scotstoun, Glasgow, until 1922.

YATE, Creation (U.K.) 1921, of Madeley Hall, co. Salop. [Extinct 1940.]

Sir CHARLES EDWARD YATE, *C.S.I., C.M.G.*, 1st and last *Baronet.*

Daughters living of 1st Baronet—Lois Burnley, *b.* 1900: *m.* 1931, Col. Henry Patrick Blosse-Lynch, Dorsetshire Regt., and has issue living, Henry Charles (Longcross House, Headley, Newbury, Berks.), *b.* 1933; Maj. Irish Gds.: *m.* 1966, Janet Duveen Horsley, and has issue living, Henry James *b.* 1972, Emily Jane *b.* 1967, Clare Annabel *b.* 1969,—Sheila Gwendolyn Yate (Newtown House, St. Margaret's, co. Dublin), *b.* 1932: *m.* 1953 (m. diss. 1970), John Michael Wilson-Wright and has issue living, Robert Michael *b.* 1956, Jane Sheila *b.* 1958. *Residence,* Partry, Claremorris, co. Mayo. *Club,* Kildare Street (Dublin).——Adelaide Louisa Pasteur, *b.* 1904: *m.* 1st, 1930, Charles Simmons, who *d.* 1938; 2ndly, 1941, Revell Barbour Turnbull, and has issue living (by 1st m.) Jane Yate, *b.* 1931: *m.* 1957, John Taylor-Lowen, of 22, Bracken Gdns., SW, and has issue living, Timothy Mark *b.* 1961, Ann Louise *b.* 1959,—Elizabeth Anne, *b.* 1933: *m.* 1955, John Money-Kyrle, of 1, Arlington Sq., N1, and Whetham, Calne, Wilts., and has issue living, James Peter Ernle *b.* 1961, Caroline Diana *b.* 1958. *Residence,* Fitzroy House, North Fitzwarren, Taunton.

YOUNG, Creation (G.B.) 1769, of North Dean, Buckinghamshire.

Sir WILLIAM NEIL YOUNG, 10th *Baronet,* son of the late Capt. William Elliot Young, R.A.M.C., only son of 9th baronet ; *b.* Jan. 22nd, 1941 ; *s.* his grandfather, *Sir* (CHARLES) ALBAN, *KCMG, MVO,* **1944**; ed. at Wellington and RMA Sandhurst; Capt. 16th/5th The Queen's R. Lancers (ret.): *m.* 1965 Christine Veronica, only da. of Robert Boland Morley, of 20, Delaware Rd., W9, and Buenos Aires, and has issue.

Residences—20, Briantspuddle, Dorchester, Dorset; 41, Blenheim Gdns., Kingston upon Thames, Surrey.

Son living—WILLIAM LAWRENCE ELLIOT, *b.* May 26th, 1970.
Daughter living—Catherine Clare, *b.* 1967.
Aunt living (daughter of 9th baronet)—Joan Persica, *b.* 1912: *m.* 1936, George Rupert Raw, and has issue living, Charles Rupert, *b.* 1940,—Victoria, *b.* 1939,—Susan Augusta, *b.* 1949. *Residences,* 24, Lennox Gdns., SW1; Kings Farm, Wield, Alresford, Hants.
Mother living—Mary, da. of the late Rev. J. Macdonald : *m.* 1st, 1939, Capt. William Elliot Young, R.A.M.C. (ante), who *d.* (killed in action during European War) 1942 ; 2ndly, 1045, Lieut.-Col. George Herbert Nash, O.B.E., Indian Army. *Residence,* 2, Douro Road, Cheltenham, Gloucestershire.

Collateral Branches living.

Grandsons of the late Rev. Henry Savill Young (infra) :—
Issue of the late Rev. Henry Brook Young, *b.* 1869, *d.* **1937**: *m.* 1920, Emmie, who *d.* 1934, da. of Henry Everitt, of Exning:—
William Brook Charles, *b.* 1922; Sq.-Ldr. RAF (ret.); a Civil Airline Pilot; Queen's Commendation for Valuable Ser. in the Air: *m.* 1949, Alma Evelyn, da. of F. C. Harvey, of Reading, and has issue living, Paul Anthony Brook, *b.* 1950,—Christopher Charles Brook, *b.* 1953,—Amanda Jane Brook *b.* 1956. *Residence,* The Nutkins, 18A, Larkfield Rd., Farnham, Surrey.

Issue of the late Lieut.-Col. Hugh Greville Young, D.S.O., R.H.A., *b.* 1882, *d.* 1950: *m.* 1919, Constance, da. of the late Brig.-Gen. Neil Douglas Findlay, C.B. :—
Hugh Findlay (42, Summerleaze, Lydney, Glos.), *b.* 1919; ed. at Wellington and RMA; Maj. late RHA (ret.); 1939-45 War (despatches): *m.* 19—, Angela Elaine, da. of the late R. G. M. Whigham, and has issue living, James Greville, *b.* 1957,—Giles Hugh Findlay, *b.* 1964,—Piers Jonathan, *b.* 1965,—Mary Rose Fredrica, *b.* 1958.——Basil Neil (18, Abban Street, Inverness;

Cavalry Club) *b.* 1921; ed. at Wellington; late Capt. 7th (Queen's Own) Hussars; 1939-45 War. ——Jonathan George (Braigh Varr, Nairnside, Inverness; Cavalry Club) *b.* 1924; ed. at Wellington; Capt. RA; 1939-45 War: *m.* 1965, Margaret Helen, da. of the late Archibald Abbott, of Colinton, Edinburgh, and widow of Ian Millar Roberts.

Issue of the late Major George Edward Savill Young, Irish Guards, *b.* 1884, *d.* (of wounds in action during European War) 1917 : *m.* 1914, Alison Jane, who *d.* 1957, da. of the Rev. Frederick John Poole, of Bishop Monkton, Ripon :—
Henry Lawrence Savill, *DSO* (Hoddenscombe Lodge, Holford, Bridgwater, Som.), *b.* 1915; ed. at Harrow; Brig. (ret.) late Irish Gds.; 1939-45 War (despatches, DSO); DSO 1944: *m.* 1939, Noreen de Vere, da. of the late Thomas Brabazon Ponsonby [*see* E. Bessborough, colls.], and has issue living, George Trevor Savill, *b.* 1941; ed. at Harrow, and at Trin. Coll., Dublin; late Lt. Irish Gds.,—Verona *b.* 1943.

Granddaughter of the late Rev. Henry Tuffnell Young, 2nd son of 3rd baronet:—
Issue of the late Rev. Henry Savill Young, *b.* 1843, *d.* 1906: *m.* 1868, Rebecca Isabella, who *d.* 1912, da. of the late Samuel Brewis, of Prestwich, Cheshire:—
Olive Portia: *m.* 1920, Bruce Waring Smith, and has issue living, Helen Rebecca Waring, *b.* 1921: *m.* 1946, Robert Dill Kennedy, MB, BCh, MRCS, LRCP, of Brae House, Hungerford, Berks., and has issue living, David Bruce *b.* 1947, Hugh John *b.* 1949, James Ian *b.* 1951, Thomas Duncan, *b.* 1954. *Residence*, Ingatorp, 104, High St., Hungerford, Berks.

Granddaughter of the late George Augustus Young, 4th son of 3rd baronet:—
Issue of the late Harold Lawrence Young, *b.* 1866, *d.* 1909 : *m.* 1894, Beatrix Kinsey (who *m.* 2ndly, 1911, George Gully), da. of the late William Kinsey Hayward :—
Dorothy, *b.* 1903: *m.* 1928, Walter Adam, M.B. *Residence*, Johannesburg S. Africa.

The 1st baronet, Sir William Young (son of the late William Young, M.D.), was Lieut.-Governor of Dominica. Sir William Norris, the 5th baronet, was killed at the battle of the Alma, 1854; and his brother, Sir George John the 6th baronet, died before Sebastopol the same year. Sir (Charles) Alban, K.C.M.G., M.V.O., 9th baronet, was Envoy Extraor. and Min. Plen. and Consul-Gen. to Guatemala 1913-19, and to Yugoslavia 1919-25.

YOUNG, Creation (U.K.) 1813, of Formosa Place, Berkshire.

Sir GEORGE SAMUEL KNATCHBULL YOUNG, *MP,* 6th *Baronet; b.* July 16th, 1941; *s.* his father, *Sir* GEORGE PEREGRINE, *CMG,* 1960; ed. at Eton, and at Ch. Ch., Oxford (Open Exhibitioner); a Member Lambeth Borough Council 1968-71, and GLC 1970-73; Economist, Nat. Economic Development Office 1967; Research Fellow, Univ. of Surrey 1968; Economic Adviser, PO Corpn. 1969-74; MP for Ealing Acton (*C*) since 1974; Chm. Acton House Assocn. since 1972; author of "Tourism, Blessing or Blight?": *m.* 1964, Aurelia, el. da. of Oscar Nemon, of Boars Hill, Oxford, and has issue.

Arms—Per fesse sable and argent: in chief two lions rampant-guardant, and in base an anchor erect with a cable, all counterchanged. Crest—A demi-unicorn couped ermine, armed, maned, and hoofed or, gorged with a naval crown azure supporting an anchor erect sable.

Residence—Formosa Place, Cookham, Berks.

Sons living—GEORGE HORATIO, *b.* Oct. 11th, 1966.—— Hugo Patrick, *b.* 1970.
Daughters living—Sophia Angelica, *b.* 1965.——Camilla Mary, *b.* 1975.
Brother living—Charles Evory (49, Brodrick Rd., SW17), *b.* 1943; ed. at Eton, and Ch. Ch., Oxford (Open Exhibitioner): *m.* 1973, Wiltrud, da. of H. J. Frömbling, and has issue living, Emily Lucinde, *b.* 1974.
Sister living—Helen Mary, *b.* 1947: *m.* 1969, Digby Robert William Norton, of 1, Dynevor Rd., Richmond, Surrey, and has issue living, Timothy Noel *b.* 1963, Duncan Neil *b.* 1964, Rupert MacIntyre *b.* 1971, Virginia Rozanne *b.* 1961, Julia Mary *b.* 1967,—Charles Edward Ilbert (Mill Cottage, Somerton, Oxon.), *b.* 1943: *m.* 1967, Alison Victoria Featherstone, yr. da. of John Harvey, and has issue living, Samuel Barnaby *b.* 1968, William Gabriel *b.* 1970,—Pegotty Alice *b.* 1974,—Melissa Grace, *b.* 1939: *m.* 1963, James Perot, of 525, Penllyn Pike, Penllyn, Pa. 19422, USA, and has issue living, James Blair *b.* 1965, Noelle Melissa *b.* 1963, Szerina Alice *b.* 1968,—Dorothy Eacy, *b.* 1948. *Residence*, Howlets Mead, 48, College Rd., Dulwich, SE21.

Aunts living (daughters of 4th baronet)—Joan Alison, *b.* 1910: *m.* 1933, Robert Mathew, who *d.* 1954, and has issue living, Theobald David, *b.* 1942; ed. at Downside, and Balliol Coll., Oxford (BA); Rouge Dragon Pursuivant of Arms,—Perdita Mary, *b.* 1944: *m.* 1965, Michael Ivor Royal Dawson, of 58-60, Christchurch Rd., SW14, and has issue living, Daniel Cyrus *b.* 1965, Robert Caspar *b.* 1966, Cressida Ruth *b.* 1968. *Residence*, 76, Clifton Hill, NW8.——Virginia Jacomyn (*Lady Hutton*), *b.* 1911: *m.* 1936, Sir Noel Patrick Hutton, GCB, QC, and has issue living, William Noel (Brentwood, Scotland Lane, Horsforth, Leeds), *b.* 1937; MA, MB, Camb.; BChir; MRCP: *m.* 1960, Doris Mary Nesfield, and has issue living, Timothy Noel *b.* 1963, Duncan Neil *b.* 1964, Rupert MacIntyre *b.* 1971, Virginia Rozanne *b.* 1961, Julia Mary *b.* 1967,—Charles Edward Ilbert (Mill Cottage, Somerton, Oxon.), *b.* 1943: *m.* 1967, Alison Victoria Featherstone, yr. da. of John Harvey, and has issue living, Samuel Barnaby *b.* 1968, William Gabriel *b.* 1970,—Pegotty Alice *b.* 1974,—Melissa Grace, *b.* 1939: *m.* 1963, James Perot, of 525, Penllyn Pike, Penllyn, Pa. 19422, USA, and has issue living, James Blair *b.* 1965, Noelle Melissa *b.* 1963, Szerina Alice *b.* 1968,—Dorothy Eacy, *b.* 1948. *Residence*, Howlets Mead, 48, College Rd., Dulwich, SE21.

Widow living of 4th Baronet—JOAN (*Dowager Lady Young*) da. of the late Rev. Frank Bullock-Webster, of Sonning, Berks. : *m.* 1948, as his second wife, Sir George Young, M.V.O., 4th baronet, who *d.* 1952. *Residence*, Grove Cottage, Sonning, Berks.

Collateral Branches living.

Issue of the late Courtenay Trevelyna Young, yr. son of 4th baronet, *b.* 1914, *d.* 1974: *m.* 1942, June Brinley (Browne's Lodge, West St., Reigate, Surrey), da. of G. Brinley Richards:—
Frederick Courtenay (60, Holly Av., Jesmond, Newcastle-upon-Tyne, NE2 2QA), *b.* 1948: *m.* 1971, Heather Brunskell, and has issue living, Daniel Justin, *b.* 1972,—Gudrun Rachel, *b.* 1974.
——Jessica Catherine, *b.* 1950.

Issue of the late Geoffrey Winthrop Young, 2nd son of 3rd baronet, *b.* 1876, *d.* 1958: *m.* 1918, Eleanor (c/o Lloyds Bank, City Office, 72, Lombard St., EC3), da. of William Cecil Slingsby, formerly of Heversham, Westmorland:—
Jocelin Slingsby Winthrop, *OBE* (Schule Schloss Salem 7777, Salem, Baden, S. Germany; Alpine Club), *b.* 1919; Founder and Headmaster of Anavryta Sch., Athens 1948-59, and Tutor to Crown Prince of Greece 1948-58; is a Com. of Order of St. George and St. Constantine of Greece; 1939-45 War as Lt. RNVR; OBE (Civil) 1960: *m.* 1st 1951 (m. diss. 1974), Countess Ghislaine, da. of Count Gustav de la Gardie of Malmo, Sweden; 2ndly, 1975, Countess Sibylle, DPhil, da. of Alexander, Count von der Schulenburg, of Duisburg, and has issue living (by 1st m.), Mark Gustav, *b.* 1952,—Geoffrey Hubert, *b.* 1960,—Sophie, *b.* 1954.——Marcia Eacy Winthrop, *b.* 1925: *m.* 1948, Peter Newbolt, of Green Banks, Cley, Norfolk, and has issue living, Thomas Winthrop, *b.* 1951,—Harry Triffitt, *b.* 1953,—Barnaby Charles Slingsby, *b.* 1955,—Catherine Eacy, *b.* 1956.

Issue of the late Rt. Hon. Sir Edward Hilton Young, G.B.E., D.S.O., D.S.C., P.C., youngest son of 3rd baronet, who was cr. *Baron Kennet* 1935 [*see* that title].

Grandchildren of the late Sir William Mackworth Young, KCSI, 3rd son of 2nd baronet:—

Issue of the late Gerard Mackworth Mackworth-Young, CIE, *b.* 1884, *d.* 1965; assumed by deed poll 1947, the additional surname of Mackworth: *m.* 1916, Natalie Lelia Margaret (Tilhayes, Iwerne Minster, Blandford, Dorset, DT11 8LS), da. of the late Rt. Hon. Sir Walter Francis Hely-Hutchinson, GCMG [*see* E. Donoughmore, colls.]:—
Sir Robin (Robert Christopher Mackworth) MACKWORTH-YOUNG, *KCVO* (Garden House, Windsor Castle, Windsor, Berks.; Roxburghe Club), *b.* 1920; ed. at Eton, and at King's Coll., Camb. (MA); in HM's Foreign Ser. 1948-55; appointed Dep. Librarian, Windsor Castle 1955, and Librarian, Windsor Castle, and Asst. Keeper of the Queen's Archives 1958; 1939-45 War as Sqdn.-Ldr. RAFVR; assumed by deed poll 1947 the additional surname of Mackworth; MVO (4th class) 1961, CVO 1968, KCVO 1975: *m.* 1953, Helen Editha Rosemarie, da. of W. C. R. Aue, of Menton, France, and has issue living, Charles Gerard, *b.* 1954.——Gerard William Mackworth (21, St. Petersburgh Pl., W2 4LA; Barrs Lodge, Taynuilt, Argyll). *Clubs*, Brooks's, Boodle's, Union (Sydney)), *b.* 1926; ed. at Eton; late Lt. Welsh Gds.; Dep. Chm., Morgan Grenfell & Co. Ltd.: *m.* 1949, Lady Evelyn Leslie, da. of 20th Earl of Rothes, and has issue living, Angela Clare, *b.* 1951, Susan Charlotte, *b.* 1953,—Lucinda Jane, *b.* 1957,—Tessa Natalie, *b.* 1959.——Honor Margaret Mackworth, *b.* 1917: *m.* 1938, Maj. Archibald Douglas George Braithwaite, RA (ret.), of 2, Brooksbank House, Copythorne, Southampton [Forestier-Walker, Bt., *cr.* 1835, colls.], and has issue living, Richard William, *b.* 1944: *m.* 1970, Claire Patricia, da. of A. H. Sangster, of Kilmarnock, Ayrshire,—Gerard Nicholas, *b.* 1954,—Janis Mary, *b.* 1942,—Sarah Helen, *b.* 1948.——Lucia May Mackworth, *b.* 1931: *m.* 1966, Paul Mayersberg, of The Old Rectory, Clayhanger, Tiverton, Devon, and has issue living, Zoltan Alexander, *b.* 1969, Natasha Catherine, *b.* 1966.

Issue of the late Major Sir Hubert Winthrop Young, K.C.M.G., D.S.O., *b.* 1885, *d.* 1950: *m.* 1924, Margaret Rose Mary (Manor House, Stratford Tony, Salisbury, Wilts), da. of the late Col. Frank Romilly Reynolds, R.E. :—
Nicholas (7, Hamilton Terr., NW8 9RE), *b.* 1924; ed. at Eton, and at Trin. Coll., Camb.; 1939-45 War as Capt. RA attached Roy. Indian Artillery (despatches): *m.* 1969, Antonia Rosetta, el. da. of the late Brig. Nigel Dugdale, CBE, 17th/21st Lancers [*see* Cunard, Bt., colls.], and has issue living, Thomas Daniel Noah, *b.* 1972,—Zoë Alexandra, *b.* 1970.——Martin Francis (c/o Lloyds Bank, 6, Pall Mall, SW1), *b.* 1927; ed. at Eton, and at King's Coll., Camb. (MA); HM's Foreign Ser., 1948-63.——Simon Bainbridge (South Wraxall Lodge, Bradford-on-Avon), *b.* 1928; ed. at Eton, and at King's Coll., Camb. (MA); is a Dir. of John Murray (Publishers), Ltd., of 50, Albemarle St., W1: *m.* 1954, Diana Tyndale, da. of the late Oswald Lewis, of Beechwood, Highgate, N6, and has issue living, James Hubert, *b.* 1955,—Mark, *b.* 1957,—Stephen, *b.* 1959,—Emma, *b.* 1961.

Issue of the late Sir Mark Aitchison Young, GCMG, *b.* 1886, *d.* 1974: *m.* 1919, Josephine Mary (Lang House, Winchester); a CStJ; da. of the late Walter C. Price:—
Brian Walter Mark (Hill End, Woodhill Av., Gerrards Cross, Bucks.), *b.* 1922; ed. at Eton, and King's Coll., Camb. (MA); 1939-45 War as Lt. RNVR; Headmaster of Charterhouse 1952-64, and Dir. of Nuffield Foundation 1964-70, since when Dir. Gen. of IBA: *m.* 1947, Fiona Marjorie, only da. of the late Allan Winslow Stewart, 16th Chief of Appin, and has issue living, Timothy Mark Stewart, *b.* 1951; ed. at Eton and Magdalene Coll., Camb. (BA),—Joanna Margaret, *b.* 1949; BA Durham: *m.* 1974, Capt. Peter Grant Peterkin, Queen's Own Highlanders,—Deborah Jane, *b.* 1953.——Denis Egerton (September Cottage, Forgandenny, Perth), *b.* 1926; ed. at Winchester, and King's Coll., Camb. (MA); Head of History Dept., Strathallan Sch., Perthshire, since 1952; 1939-45 War in RNVR: *m.* 1957, Judith Mary, el. da. of the late Dr. E. R. Matthews, of Nettleton, Wilts., and has issue living, Matthew Egerton, *b.* 1959,—Walter Samuel Egerton, *b.* 1965,—Emma Faith, *b.* 1960,—Cecilia Frances, *b.* 1962.——Eleanor Mary, *b.* 1921; 1939-45 War in WRNS.——Janet Cecilia Josephine, *b.* 1930; MB and BS London; LRCP and MRCS 1955: *m.* 1973 Dr. R. J. Owens, British Council, Bangkok.

Grandson of the late Henry Cathcart Arthur Young (infra):—

Issue of the late Lieut.-Com. Malcolm Henry Cathcart Young, R.N., *b.* 1903, *d.* (killed in action during European War) 1940 : *m.* 1930, Gwenda (who *d.* 1953, having *m.* 2ndly, 1946, the Rev. A. Alan W. Gray, of Christ College, Hobart, Tasmania), only da. of the late William Bromley Taylor :—
Christopher Malcolm (of Dalesford, Chase Close, Coleshill, Amersham, Bucks), *b.* 1936; ed. at Dragon Sch., Oxford, at Geelong Gram. Sch., Victoria, Australia, and at Magdalene Coll., Camb. (B.A. 1959, M.A. 1963): *m.* 1960, Mary, da. of the late Ralph Lindsay, of Herstmonceux, and has issue living, Richard Malcolm, *b,* 1966,—Caroline Mary, *b.* 1962,—Victoria Jane, *b.* 1964.

Grandchildren of the late Henry Cathcart Arthur Young, H.E.I.C.S., 3rd son of 1st baronet:—

Issue of the late Henry Cathcart Arthur Young, *b.* 1850, *d.* 1940 : *m.* 1902, Florence, who *d.* 1968, yst. da. of the late Alfred Eccles, FRCS:—
Katharine Elizabeth (8, Campden House, 29, Sheffield Terr., W8), *b.* 1908; 1939-45 War with VAD.

Issue of the late Horace Edward Broughton Young, *b.* 1853, *d.* 1924: *m.* 1882, Ellen Elizabeth who *d.* 1938, da. of George Thorne, of Darcey Hey, Castle Hill, N.S. Wales:—
Henry Herbert, *b.* 1895 ; European War 1916-18 as Lieut. R.A. (severely wounded) : *m.* (Feb.) 1920, Margaret Caroline Britania, da. of the late Capt. James Somerville Murray, of The Sandpatch, Wentworth Falls, N.S. Wales, and has issue living, Andrew Broughton, *b.* (Dec.) 1920,—Arnold Somerville, *b.* 1923,—Horace Anthony, *b.* 1925,—Robert Alexander, *b.* 1927,—Janet Elizabeth *b.* 1931.——Evelyn Florence Broughton (Merelynne Av., Westpennant Hills, NSW), *b.* 1888: *m.* 1926, Arthur Liddon Webb, MB, BS, FRCS, who *d.* 1969, and has issue living, Constance Rosemary, *b.* 1928; ed. at Sydney Univ. (BA): *m.* 1953, Paul Hanbury MB,

BS of Turramurra, NSW, and has issue living, Richard Mark b. 1954, Christopher Paul b. 1955,—Evelyn Alison b. 1931: m. 1954, John Gardner Hawke, MSc, PhD of Merelynne Av., Westpennant Hills, NSW, and has issue living, Simon Hugh Binney b. 1958, Prudence Evelyn b. 1959,—Winsome Mary, b. 1932: ed. at Sydney Univ.: m. 1954, Peter John Scales, BVSc, of Gleneagles, Freemans Rd., Mt. Eliza, Victoria, and has issue living, Michael John b. 1958, Hugh Murray Arthur b. 1960, Jonathan Peter b. 1963, Alexander Patrick b. 1967, Sarah Felicity b. 1966.——Doris Emily Broughton, b. 1889: m. 1911, the Rev. Canon David James Knox, Canon of St. Andrew's Cathedral, Sydney, who d. 1960, and has issue living, Rev. Canon David Broughton (of Moore Coll., Sydney), b. 1916; ed. at Sydney (BA 1937) and London (BD 1941, MTh 1949) Univs.; DPhil Oxford 1953; is Principal of Moore Coll., Sydney; late Chap. RNVR: m. 1950, Ailsa, da. of Dr. R. P. Lane, of Pymble, NSW, and has issue living, Jonathan Broughton b. 1954, David Paul b. 1959, Margery Eleanor b. 1951: m. 1971, the Rev. David Seccombe, Deborah Mary b. 1952, Stephanie Ailsa Elizabeth b. 1957, Rosemary Patricia Ruth b. 1965,—Horace Everard Arnold, DFC, DFM, b. 1918; WO Air Gunner RAAF; 1941-45 War (DFM, DFC): m. 1957, Christina Mocatta, and has issue living, Andrew Horace b. 1957, Bruce Robert b. 1959, Jennifer Mary b. 1961,—John Wallace (of 26, Trafalgar Av., Roseville, NSW), b. 1920; ed. at Sydney Univ. (MB and BS 1943); MRCOG England 1947; FRCS 1948, FRACS 1956: m. 1949, Sheila Constance, da. of the late David Theodore Field Nicholson (infra), and has issue living, David John b. 1951, Peter Wallace b. 1954, Philippa Sheila b. 1952,—Patricia Evelyn Jane Simpson, b. 1914: m. 1937, the Most Rev. Marcus Lawrence Loane, Archbishop of Sydney, of Bishopscourt, Edgecliff, NSW, and has issue living, Robert Marcus b. 1943; ed. at Gonville and Caius Coll., Camb. (MA), and Sydney Univ. (MB, BS): m. 1969, Joan Lillian Thornton (and has issue living, Annabel Lorna b. 1971, Rosalind Patricia b. 1972), David Lawrence b. 1945; ed. at Sydney Univ., and Aust. Nat. Univ. (BSc Forestry): m. 1971, Susan Brain (and has issue living, Timothy David b. 1972), Mary Eleanor b. 1938: m. 1964, William Leslie Milford, of 614, Waverley Rd., Chadstone, Vic. 3148, Aust. (and has issue living, David James William Knox b. 1965, Peter Marcus Leslie b. 1967, Stephen John Whitburn b. 1971, Catherine Mary Ethel, b. 1968), Winsome Margaret b. 1948; ed. at Sydney Univ. (BA),—Doris Elisabeth Rhoda, b. 1921; ed. at Sydney Univ. (BA), Constance Gloriel, b. 1927; ed. at Sydney Univ. (BA),—Eleanor Charis (18/14, Banksia Rd., Caringbah, NSW 2229), b. 1928; MB and BS Sydney, MRCP Edinburgh, DCH London, CTM & H Sydney. Residence, 7, Ravenswood Av., Gordon, NSW.——Winifred Elinor Broughton, b. 1896: m. 1920, David Theodore Field Nicholson, who d. 1955, and has issue living, Peter Theodore (of 99, Copeland Rd., Beecroft, NSW), b. 1926; ed. at Sydney Univ. (BSc, BE); MIEA, MIEEE: m. 1949, Patricia May, BSc, da. of the late E. T. Ohlsson, of Roseville, NSW, and has issue living, Peter Timothy James, b. 1952, Philip Theodore b. 1954, Catherine Jane b. 1955, Anne Elizabeth b. 1957, Alison Patricia b. 1961,—Donald Ian (c/o Forest Dept., Brisbane, Qld.), b. 1928; ed. at Sydney Univ., and at Austn. Forestry Sch. (Diploma of Forestry and BSc Forestry 1949): m. 1956, Grace Mary, da. of the Rev. Harold Dennis Powley, of Africa Inland Mission, and has issue living, Graham John b. 1957, Robert Christopher b. 1965 Stephanie Jane b. 1959, Joanne Christine b. 1962,—John David b. 1934: m. 1974, Alice Louise, da. of the late Robert Kurwen Campbell, and has issue living, David Theodore Campbell b. 1975,—Sheila Constance, b. 1921: m. 1949, John Wallace Knox, FRCS, MRCOG (ante),—Elinor Catherine (of The Princess Tsahai Hospital, Addis Ababa, Ethiopia), b. 1924; ed. at Sydney Univ. (MB, BS); ChB NZ, DObstRCOG Sydney; FRCOG: m. 1950, Reginald Henry James Hamlin, OBE, MB, ChB, FRCOG (Eng), and has issue living, Richard Havelock James b. 1953,—Alisa Mary, b. 1931: m. 1959, Bruce Graham Pottie, of Turrawonga, Lairas Lee, NSW, and has issue living, Dougal John b. 1960, James Theodore Graham b. 1961, Angus Bruce b. 1965. Residence, Rosedale, Garra, NSW.

Issue of the late Charles Ernest Young, b. 1855, d. 1927: m. 1891, Margaret Elsé, who d. 1952, da. of John Shedden Adam, of Ellerslie, Turramurra, Sydney, N.S. Wales :—

Henry Shedden Baring, M.C., b. 1894; formerly Capt. R.A.; European War 1915-18 (M.C.): m. 1st, 1929, Eva Theodora, who d. 1940, da. of the late T. C. Maltby, of The Oaks, Tauranga, NZ; 2ndly, 1953, Janet Mary, only da. of the late Rev. J. Milton Thompson, of Tonbridge, Kent, and has issue living, (by 1st m.) James Ernest Baring (Wybalena, 22, Highlands Av., Gordon 2072, NSW), b. 1933: m. 1959, Anette Florence, da. of Kenneth Lane, of St. Ives, NSW, and has issue living, Timothy James Baring b. 1960, Michael Henry Baring b. 1962, David Kenneth Baring b. 1969, Anthony Baring b. 1971,—Dorothy Joan Baring, b. 1930; ed. at Sydney (BSc Agric. 1953) and London (MSc Agric. 1957) Univs.: m. 1959, John Lionel Wheeler, PhD, BSc (Agric), CSIRO of Armidale, NSW, and has issue living, Philip John Henry b. 1961, Ian Charles Andrew b. 1963,—Rosemary Helen b. 1959,—(by 2nd m.) Stephen Henry Baring, b. 1954,—Angela Mary Katherine, b. 1957. Residence, Baring House, 9, Tennyson Cres., Forrest, ACT.——Charles Arthur Noel, b. 1899; is Man. Dir. of Fairymead Sugar Co.: m. 1923, Margery Bisdee Maynard, da. of the late Dr. Maynard Pain, of Cairo, and has issue living, Charles Edward Christopher (of Fairymead, Qld.), b. 1926: m. 1949, Margaret Florence, da. of W. Guilford, of Kilhara, Sydney, NSW, and has issue living, Christopher Roderick b. 1950, Timothy Charles b. 1952, Gregory Mark b. 1955, Nicholas William b. 1961,—Margery Marian, b. 1924: m. 1949, Norman Bruce Berry, of 36, Valetta St., Moss Vale, NSW, and has issue living, Andrew Bruce, b. 1950, Simon Mark, b. 1956, Hugh Jonathan, b. 1962, Susan Marian, b. 1952, Philippa Jane, b. 1954,—Elizabeth Wendy, b. 1927: m. 1957, Neil James Yorkston, FRACP, MRC Psych., of 21, Liskeard Gdns., Blackheath, SE3 0PE, and has issue living, Ian Charles, b. 1961, Catherine Judith, b. 1958, Ruth Elizabeth, b. 1959, Anne Margery, b. 1965,—Lois Margaret, b. 1929: m. 1957, Arthur Pennington, MB, BS, of 119, Kissing Point Rd., Dundas, NSW 2117, and has issue living, Jeremy Arthur b. 1958, Martin Frderick b. 1961, Judith Charis b. 1960, Mary Priscilla b. 1964, Fiona Margaret b. 1974,—Catherine Anne, b. 1930,—Alison Jennifer, b. 1932: m. 1960, Douglas Cribb, of Tantilla, Bundaberg, Qld., and has issue living, Charles Wilfred b. 1964, Margery Jennifer b. 1962, Felicity Judith b. 1966, Prudence Elizabeth b. 1969, —Philippa Lucia Charis, b. 1937: m. 1963, Donald Campbell Thorn, FRAIA, ARIBA, of 132, Canterbury Rd., Canterbury 3126, Vic., Aust., and has issue living, Christopher Ian b. 1964, Samuel Douglas b. 1967, Bronwen Margery b. 1965, Sarah Penelope Joan b. 1972,—Rosalind b. 1939: m. 1959, John Henry Northcote Deck, MD, FRCP (C), Neuropathologist, of 104, Strathallan Blvd., Toronto, Ont., M5N 1S7, Canada, and has issue living, Wilber John Northcote b. 1960, Philip Charles b. 1962, Roger Norman b. 1964, Kathleen Margery b. 1963, Rachel Frances b. 1971, Jennifer Luci Maynard b. 1973,—Adrienne Penelope, b. 1943,—Carolyn Bronwen, b. 1945: m. 1974, Keith Wolfson. Residence, Fairymead, Bundaberg, Qld.——Ernest Stafford, b. 1903; ed. at Sydney Univ. (BE); 1939-45 War with RAAF; formerly a Missionary in British Borneo: m. 1946, Lilian Olive, JP, da. of the late C. E. Mumford, of Cremorne, Sydney, NSW, and has issue living, David Hilton, b. 1947,—Lesley Anne, b. 1949,—Rosemary Frances, b. 1953. Residence, 7, Kardinia Rd., Clifton Gdns., Sydney, NSW.——Geoffrey Lawrence, b. 1910; ed. at Emmanuel Coll., Camb.; registered Gen. Med. Practitioner 1938; 1939-45 War with Roy. Austn. Air Force in New Guinea; inaugurated Central NSW Flying Doctor: m. 1935, Irene, BSc, da. of P. W. Petter, of Swallowcliffe, Yeovil, Somerset, and has issue living, Peter Lawrence (4, Narelle Av., Pymble, NSW), b. 1935: m. 1961, Jennifer Mary, da. of J. M. Clift, and has issue living, Michael Lawrence b. 1968,—Judith Anne b. 1971,—Geoffrey Branscombe, b. 1942,—Susan Irene, b. 1938: BA 19—,—Kathleen Patricia, b. 1940,—Jocelyn Olivia, b. 1946. Residence, 5, The Boulevard, Cheltenham, NSW.——Charis Elsè, b. 1898; Dip. Occupational Therapy Aust. Physiotherapy Assocn. Residence, 34, Rosedale Rd., St. Ives, NSW.

Sir Samuel Young, 1st baronet, was the el. son of Sir George Young, of Formosa Place, Berks, Adm. of the White who served at Quebec 1759, Havana 1762, and Pondicherry 1778. Sir George Young, 3rd baronet, was a Charity Commr. 1882-99, Third Charity Commr. 1899-1900,

2nd Charity Commr. 1900-03, and Ch. Charity Commr. 1903-06. Sir George Young, M.V.O., 4th baronet, was in Diplo. Ser. 1896-1914, Professor of Portuguese and Examiner in Ottoman Law in Univ. of London 1919-23, and Professor of Political Science, American Univs. 1929-30. Sir George Peregrine Young, C.M.G., 5th baronet, was Head of W. Depart., Foreign Office 1950-51, H.M.'s Min. in Rome 1951-3, Assist. Sec. CabinetOffice 1953-5, Head of News Depart., Foreign Office 1955-6, and H.B.M.'s Min. in Paris 1956-60.

YOUNG, Creation (U.K.) 1821, of Bailieborough Castle, co. Cavan.

Sir JOHN WILLIAM ROE YOUNG, 5th *Baronet;* b. June 28th, 1913 ; s. his father, *Sir* CYRIL ROE MUSTON, 1955 ; ed. at Elizabeth Coll., Guernsey ; is a Director of Mancunian Building So. of 14, St. Peter's Square, Manchester ; formerly Lieut. Hong Kong R.N.V.R. ; European War 1941-5 (prisoner): *m.* 1st, 1946, Joan Minnie Agnes, who *d.* 1958, el. da. of M. M. Aldous, of Camelot, Perranporth ; 2ndly, 1960, Joy Maureen, da. of A. G. Clarke, of Somers Street, Southsea, Hants, and has issue by 1st marriage.

Prudentia.
Prudence.

Arms—Argent, three piles sable, each charged with a trefoil, slipped or ; on a chief of the second three annulets of the third. Crest—A demi-lion rampant gules, charged on the shoulder with a trefoil slipped or, and holding in the dexter paw a sword erect proper.

Club—R.N.V.R.

Son living—By 1st marriage—JOHN KENYON ROE, b. April 23rd, 1947.

Daughter living—By 1st marriage—Eve Maureen Aldous, b. 1949.

Brothers living—Patrick Elliott (3625, Lombardy Rd., Pasadena, Calif., USA), b. 1917: m. 1946, Sadie Reid, only da. of Laurence Beattie, of Prestwick, Ayrshire, and has issue living, Christopher Brian Harrington, b. 1965,—Patricia, b. 1947,—Veronica Anne, b. 1949,— Nancy Gay, b. 1952.—Michael Cyril Harrington (6, Risoeta Av., St. Ives, NSW), b. 1928: m. 1955, Anita Patricia, only da. of C. H. Duff, of Hong Kong, and has issue living, Peter Charles Harrington, b. 1956,—Anthony Michael, b. 1961,—Gail Louraine, b. 1960.

Sister living—Margaret Isobel (86, Cambridge Gdns., Kensington, W10), b. 1920: m. 1947 (m. diss. 1971), Lt.-Cdr. Stanley Stopford Claremont, RCN, and has issue living, Shaun, b. 1948,—Annie, b. 1952.

Widow of 4th Baronet—GERTRUDE ANNIE (Gertrude, *Lady Young*), da. of John Elliott, of Braunton, N. Devon: m. 1912, Sir Cyril Roe Muston Young, 4th Bt., who d. 1955. Residences, Le Copacabana, Jardin des Hesperides, Palm Beach, Cannes, France, AM and 66, Kensington Mansions, Trebovir Rd., SW5.

The 1st baronet, Sir William, was a Director of the East India Company ; and the 2nd baronet, Sir John (Gov.-Gen. of Canada 1868-72), was raised to the Peerage in 1870 as Baron Lisgar, but, dying without issue, his peerage became extinct, and the baronetcy devolved upon his nephew, Sir William Muston Need, 3rd baronet.

YOUNG, Creation (U.K.) 1945, of Partick, co. City of Glasgow.

Sir STEPHEN SPENCER TEMPLETON YOUNG, 3rd *Baronet;* b. May 24th, 1947; s. his father, *Sir* ALASTAIR SPENCER TEMPLETON, *TD*, 1963; ed. at Rugby, Trin. Coll., Oxford and Edinburgh Univ.; solicitor (Scotland): *m.* 1974, Viola Margaret, da. of Prof. Patrick Horace Nowell-Smith [B. Vernon, colls.].

Arms—Argent, on three piles issuant from a chief sable, charged with three lymphads under full sail of the 1st flagged gules, as many annulets of the 3rd. Crest—A lymphad or, under full sail, its sail charged of the arms, having a pennon gules with the badge of Scotland viz. azure, a saltire argent, in the hoist.

Residence—19, Queen's Gate Gdns., SW7.

Sister Living—Clare Elizabeth, b. 1953.

Uncle living (son of 1st baronet)—PATRICK TEMPLETON, *b.* July 5th, 1925: *m.* 1950, **Jenny**, da. of Sir Walter Eric Bassett, K.B.E., M.C., of Melbourne, Australia, and has issue living, Roger Spencer Masson, *b.* 1954,—Jane Templeton, *b.* 1952. *Residences*, 8, Lansdowne Walk, W.11; Fulmans, Beaulieu, Hants.

Aunts living (daughters of 1st baronet)—Barbara Mary, *b.* 1916: *m.* 1939, W. E. H. Grayburn, and has issue living, Jon Alastair, *b.* 1943,—Lesley Mary, *b.* 1949. *Residence*, 11, Lee Rd., Aldeburgh, Suffolk.——Anne Stewart, *b.* 1919: *m.* 1946, James Gray Workman, and has issue living, Robert Gray, *b.* 1947,—Hugh Stewart, *b.* 1951,—Douglas Templeton, *b.* 1956,—Katrina Margaret, *b.* 1948. *Residence*, Suilven, Crescent Rd., Aldeburgh, Suffolk.

The 1st baronet, Sir Arthur Stewart Leslie Young (son of the late Daniel Henderson Lusk Young, of Glasgow), was Parliamentary Private Sec. to Under-Sec. of State for Scotland 1937-39, and to Sec. of State for Scotland 1939-42, a Lord Commr. of The Treasury 1942-44, and Vice-Chamberlain of H.M.s Household 1944-45 ; sat as M.P. for Partick Div. of Glasgow (*U*) 1935-50.

YOUNGER, Creation (U.K.) 1911, of Auchen Castle, Kirkpatrick-Juxta, co. Dumfries

Quite ready.

Sir JOHN WILLIAM YOUNGER, *CBE*, 3rd *Baronet*; *b.* Nov. 18th, 1920; *s.* his father, *Sir* WILLIAM ROBERT 1973; ed. at Canford and RMC; Maj.-Gen. late Coldm. Gds.; Dir. Management and Support Intelligence since 1973; 1939-45 War in Middle East (prisoner, MBE); MBE (Mil.) 1945, CBE (Mil.) 1969: *m.* 1st, 1948 (m. diss. 1952), Mrs. Stella Jane Dodd, da. of the Rev. John George Lister; 2ndly, 1953, Marcella Granito, Princess Pignatelli di Belmonte, da. of Prof. Avv. Roberto Scheggi, and has issue (by 1st m).

Arms—Or, on a bend azure, between two martlets sable, three roses argent, barbed and seeded vert, on a chief gules, a crescent between two mullets of the first. **Crest**—A dexter hand holding a lance in bend proper.

Residence—23, Cadogan Sq., SW1X 0HU.

Son living—By 1st marriage—JULIAN WILLIAM RICHARD, *b.* Feb. 10th, 1950; ed. at Eton, and Grinnell, USA.
Daughter living—By 1st m.—Johanna Jane, *b.* 1951: *m.* 1972, Timothy John Binnington.
Sisters living—Margaret Elizabeth, *b.* 1916: *m.* 1937, John Howard Moller, late Queen's Own Cameron Highlanders, and has issue living, Christopher Pierre William Howard, *b.* 1943; ed. at Charterhouse: *m.* 1973, Susan Maria Scougal Burdette, da. of Alban Millar Ross-Smith, of Heyshott, Sussex, and has issue living, a da. *b.* 1975, Caroline Victoria Margaret, *b.* 1939,—Maxine Faith Alexandra, *b.* 1940: *m.* 1966, Rory B. M. Nicholas. *Residence*, Hammer Court, Liphook, Hants.——Diana Joan, *b.* 1919: *m.* 1st, 1940, the Hon. William Francis Brinsley Le Poer Trench, who obtained a divorce 1947 [*see* E. Clancarty]; 2ndly, 1947, Dr. H. Wentworth Eldredge, Prof. of Sociology Dartmouth Coll., Hanover, New Hampshire, USA, and has issue living (by 2nd m.), James Wentworth, *b.* 1950,—Alan Wentworth, *b.* 1953. *Residence*, Tarn House, Norwich, Vermont, USA.

Mother living of 3rd Baronet—Joan Gwendoline (60, Cadogan Sq., SW1), da. of the late Hon. Louis Vanden-Bempde-Johnstone [*see* B. Derwent, colls.]: *m.* 1st, 1915, (m. diss. 1923), William Robert Younger, later 2nd Bt., who *d.* 1973; 2ndly, 1923, Capt. Hubert Lachlan Pelham-Burn, Gordon Highlanders, who *d.* 1927; 3rdly, 1931, Dennis Yates Wheatley, author.

The 1st baronet, Sir William Younger (son of the late William Younger, of Auchen Castle, Moffat), was M.P. for S. Kesteven or Stamford Division of Lincolnshire (*L*) 1895-1906, and for Peebles and Selkirk Jan. to Nov. 1910.

YOUNGER, Creation (U.K.) 1964, of Fountainbridge, co. and City of Edinburgh.

Swift and Bold

Sir WILLIAM McEWAN YOUNGER, *DSO*, 1st *Baronet*; son of the late William Younger, of Ravenswood, Melrose; *b.* Sept. 6th, 1905; ed. at Winchester, and at Balliol Coll., Oxford (MA); a DL of Midlothian; Chm. of Scottish & Newcastle Breweries Ltd. 1960-70; Dir. of cos.; 1939-45 War as Lt.-Col. RA in W. Desert and Italy (despatches, DSO); DSO 1942: *m.* 1936 (m. diss. 1967), Nora Elizabeth, da. of the late Brig. Edward William Sturgis Balfour, CVO, DSO, OBE, MC [E. Balfour], and has issue.

Arms,—Parted per saltire or and gules, a rose counterchanged, and in base a martlet sable on a chief invected azure, three covered cups or, within a bordure or. **Crest,**—An armed leg couped at the thigh proper, garnished and spurred or.

Residence—29, Moray Pl., Edinburgh. *Clubs*—Carlton, New (Edinburgh), Alpine, Caledonian.

___

Daughter living—Caroline Ruth, *b.* 1946.

CHIEFS OF NAMES AND CLANS IN SCOTLAND

This section comprises biographies of Chiefs of whole Names and Clans who bear undifferenced arms and supporters under decree of Lyon Court. In addition, those marked †, though not Chiefs of whole Names or Clans, are Heads of considerable Houses. who are for a special reason, such as the Macdonald Lord of the Isles' forfeiture, independent. Those marked *, who are bearers of a double or triple barrelled surname, are not included *in hoc statu* on Lord Lyon's list (cf. Campbell-Gray 1950).

Full biographies of Peers, Baronets, and their collaterals, will be found in those sections.

ARBUTHNOTT. Rt. Hon. Viscount of Arbuthnott, *DSC; b.* 1924; *s.* 1966 as *Chief of the Name of Arbuthnott; heir,* son, Master of Arbuthnott, *b.* 1950. *Arbuthnott House, by Laurencekirk, Kincardineshire.*

BARCLAY. Peter Charles Barclay of Towie Barclay and of that Ilk, son of the late Lt.-Col. Walter Patrick Barclay, *b.* 1938; *s.* his 2nd cousin once removed, Theodore Bruce de Tollie Barclay, 1967, as *Chief of the Name of Barclay;* ed. at Cargilfield and Eton. *Gateman's, Stratford St. Mary, Colchester.*

BORTHWICK. John Henry Stuart Borthwick of Borthwick, *TD,* son of Henry Borthwick of Borthwick; *b.* 1905; *s.* his father 1937 as *Chief of the Name of Borthwick;* claims to be *de jure* 24th Lord Borthwick [see L. Borthwick]; Baron of Heriotmuir; DL and JP of Midlothian: *m.* 1938, Margaret Frances, da. of Alexander Campbell Cormack; *heir,* son, John Hugh, *b.* 1940. *Crookston, Heriot, Midlothian; New and Puffin's Clubs.*

BOYD. Rt. Hon. Lord Kilmarnock, *b.* 1927; *s.* 1975 as *Chief of the Name of Boyd;* heir, brother, Hon. Robin Jordan, *b.* 1941; *Casa de Mondragon, Ronda, Malaga, Spain; Boodle's and Pratt's Clubs.*

BRODIE. (Montagu) Ninian (Alexander) Brodie of Brodie, son of the late Maj. Ian Ashley Moreton Brodie of Brodie, DSO, MC; *b.* 1912; *s.* his father 1943 as *Chief of Clan Brodie;* ed. at Eton; a JP; Hon. Sheriff Substitute of Morayshire since 1958: *m.* 1939, Helena Penelope Mills, who *d.* 1972, da. of Janssen Budgen; *heir,* son, Alastair Ian Ninian, *b.* 1943. *Brodie Castle, Forres, Morayshire.*

BRUCE. Rt. Hon. the Earl of Elgin and Kincardine, *b.* 1924; *s.* 1968 as *Chief of the Name of Bruce;* heir, son, Lord Bruce, *b.* 1961. *Broomhall, Dunfermline.*

BUCHAN. Capt. David William Sinclair Buchan of Auchmacoy, son of the late Capt. Stephen Lloyd Trevor, of Lathbury Park, Newport Pagnell, Bucks.; *b.* 1929; *s.* his grandfather, 18th Earl of Caithness; recognized by Lord Lyon 1949 as *Chief of the Name of Buchan;* ed. at Eton, and RMA Sandhurst; BSc; late Capt. Gordon Highlanders, ADC to GOC, Singapore 1951-53; a Member of Queen's Body Guard for Scotland (Roy. Co. of Archers); a Member of London Stock Exchange, and of Borderers' Co., a JP for Westminster; Snr. Partner Gow & Parsons 1963-69: *m.* 1961, the Hon. (Blanche) Susan Fionodbhar Scott-Ellis, da. of 9th Baron Howard de Walden; *heir,* son, (John) Charles Augustus David, *b.* 1963. *Auchmacoy House, Ellon, Aberdeenshire; 28, The Little Boltons, SW10; Turf, White's, United Service and Royal Aero City of London, RAC, Pilgrim's, Puffin's Clubs, and MCC.*

CAMERON. Col. Sir Donald Hamish Cameron of Lochiel, KT, CVO, TD (*Mac Dhomnuill Duibh*), son of Col. Sir Donald Walter Cameron of Lochiel, KT, CMG [see D. Montrose]; *b.* 1910; *s.* his father 1951 as *Chief of Clan Cameron;* heir, son, Donald Angus, *b.* 1946. *Achnacarry, Spean Bridge, Inverness-shire; Pratt's and Puffin's Clubs.*

CAMPBELL. His Grace the Duke of Argyll (*Mac Cailein Mor*); *b.* 1937; *s.* 1973 as *Chief of Clan Campbell Mac Cailein Mor, and Knight of Lochow (Loch Awe); heir,* son, Marquess of Lorne, *b.* 1968. *Inveraray Castle, Inveraray, Argyll.*

CARNEGIE. Rt. Hon. the Earl of Southesk, *KCVO; b.* 1893; *s.* 1941 as *Chief of the Name of Carnegie; heir,* son, the Duke of Fife, *b.* 1929. *Kinnaird Castle, Brechin, Angus.*

CHARTERIS. Rt. Hon. the Earl of Wemyss and March; KT; *b.* 1912; *s.* 1937 as *Chief of the Name of Charteris;* heir, son, Lord Neidpath, *b.* 1948. *Gosford House, Longniddry, East Lothian.*

CHISHOLM. Alastair Hamish Wiland André Fraser Chisholm of Chisholm (*The Chisholm*), son of the late Uilean Hamish m'Uistean Gooden-Chisholm; *b.* 1920; *s.* his grandfather, Roderick Chisholm of Chisholm, 1943, as *Chief of Clan Chisholm;* ed. at Ampleforth, and at Univ. Coll., London; a farmer; 1939-45 War as Capt. Seaforth Highlanders in India, Burma and Germany: *m.* 19—, Rosemary Yolanda, da. of the late Francis Grant; *heir,* son. *Silver Willows Farm, Beck Row, Bury St. Edmunds; Puffin's Club.*

CLAN CHATTAN. Kenneth A. Mackintosh of Clan Chattan, son of the late Duncan Alexander Eltio Mackintosh of Clan Chattan; *b.* 19—; *s.* his father 196-, as *Chief of Clan Chattan; Maxwell Park P.B. 18, Gwelo, Rhodesia.*

COCHRANE. Rt. Hon. the Earl of Dundonald; *b.* 1918; *s.* 1958 as *Chief of the Cochranes;* heir, son, Lord Cochrane, *b.* 1961. *Lochnell Castle, Ledaig, Argyll; Beacon Hall, Benenden, Cranbrook, Kent; Carlton Club.*

COLQUHOUN. Sir Ivar Iain Colquhoun of Luss, Bt.; *b.* 1916; *s.* 1948 as *Chief of Clan Colquhoun;* heir, son, Malcolm Rory, *b.* 1947. *Ross-dhu, Luss, Dunbartonshire; White's and Puffin's Clubs.*

CRANSTOUN. Lt.-Col. Alastair Joseph Edgar Cranstoun of that Ilk, *MC,* only son of the late Brig.-Gen. Alister Fraser Gordon, CMG, DSO and Pilar Eliza Mary, da. of Charles Edward Harris Edmonstoune-Cranstoun of Corehouse [B. Stafford colls.]; *b.* 1910; recognized by Lord Lyon 1950 in the name of Cranston of that Ilk and as *Chief of the Name of Cranstoun;* ed. at Ampleforth and Magdalen Coll., Oxford; Lt.-Col. Grenadier Guards; 1939-45 War in France, Middle East and Greece; Mil Attaché Lisbon 1947-49; Dep. Comd. (British) Vienna Inter-Allied Command 1952-55; ret. 1959; a DL of Lanarkshire: *m.* 1972, Teresa Cardina (Dr. Philology Venice), yst. da. of the late Maj. Gen. Feliciano Fessia, R. Italian Navy, Italian Foreign Ser.; *heir,* sister. *Corehouse, Lanark; Guards', New and Puffin's Clubs.*

CUMMING. Sir William Gordon Gordon-Cumming of Altyre, Bt.; b. 1928; *s.* 1939 as *Chief of Clan Cumming;* heir, son, Alexander Penrose. *b.* 1954. *Blairs House, Altyre, Forres, Morayshire; Puffin's Club.*

DRUMMOND, Rt. Hon· the Earl of Perth, PC; *b.* 1907; *s.* 1951 as *Chief of Clan Drummond;* heir, son, Viscount Strathallan, *b.* 1935. *Stobhall, by Perth; White's and Puffin's Clubs.*

DUNBAR. Sir Adrian Ivor Dunbar of Mochrum, Bt.; *b.* 1893; *s.* 1953 as *Chief of the Name of Dunbar;* heir, son, Jean Ivor, *b.* 1918. *Mochrum Park, Kirkcowan, Wigtownshire.*

DUNDAS. Ian Hope Dundas of Dundas, son of the late Adm. Sir Charles Hope Dundas of Dundas; *b.* 1908; *s.* his brother, Adam Duncan Dundas of Dundas 1953 as *Chief of the Name of Dundas;* ed. at RNC, Dartmouth; late Lt. RN and Lt.-Cdr. RINVR; Private Sec. to Lord Bracken 1929-31, and Private Sec. and Controller to Maharaja of Jaipur 1939-42 (Maj. Jaipur State Forces), acting Dir. of Fisheries, Bengal 1946-47; Public Relations Officer, S. African Red Cross, Cape Town since 1963: *m.* 1st. 1933 (m. diss. 1938), Pamela, da. of the late Charles Herbert Dorman; 2ndly, 1940, Dorothy Mabel, da. of the late George Frederick McCallum, of Umtali, Rhodesia; heir, son, David Duncan, *b.* 1942. *Moreson, Starke Rd., Bergvliet, Cape Town, S. Africa.*

ELIOTT. Maj. Sir Arthur Francis Augustus Boswell Eliott of Stobs. Bt.; *b.* 1915; *s.* 1958 as *Chief of Eliott or Elliot; heir,* son, Charles, *b.* 1931. *Kilkerran, Maybole, Roxburghshire; Carlton, New (Edinburgh) and Puffin's Clubs.*

ERSKINE. Maj. the Rt. Hon. the Earl of Mar and Kellie; *b.* 1921; *s.* 1955 as *Chief of the Name of Erskine; heir.* son, Lord Erskine, *b.* 1949. *Claremont House, Alloa, Clackmannanshire, FK10 2JF.*

FARQUHARSON. Capt. Alwyne Farquharson of Invercauld, *MC* (*Mac Fhionnlaidh*), son of Edward R. F. Compton [see M. Northampton, colls.] and Sylvia, da. of Alexander Haldane Farquharson of Invercauld; *b.* 1919; ed. at Eton; Capt. R. Scots Greys; *s.* his kinsman Alexander Haldane Farquharson of Invercauld; recognized by Lord Lyon 1949 as *Chief of Clan Farquharson: m.* 1949, Frances Strickland Lovell (*GORDON*), da. of the late Robert Pollard Oldham, of Seattle, and widow of Capt. the Hon. James H. B. Rodney, MC. *Invercauld, Braemar, Aberdeenshire; Puffin's Club.*

FERGUSSON. Sir James Fergusson of Kilkerran, Bt.; *b.* 1904; *s.* 1951 as *Chief of the Name of Fergusson;* heir, son, Charles, *b.* 1931. *Kilkerran, Maybole, Ayrshire.*

FORBES. Rt. Hon. the Lord Forbes, KBE; *b.* 1918; *s.* 1953 as *Chief of Clan Forbes;* heir, son, Master of Forbes, *b.* 1946. *Iforbes, Alford, Aberdeenshire; Guards' Club.*

FRASER, Rt. Hon. Lord Saltoun, *MC*; *b.* 1886; *s.* 1933 as *Chief of the Name of Fraser; heir,* daughter. *Cross Deep, Twickenham, Middlesex; Cairnbulg Castle, Fraserburgh, Aberdeen.*

†FRASER (OF LOVAT). Brig. the Rt. Hon. Lord Lovat, *DSO, MC., TD (Mac Shimidh); b.* 1911; *s.* 1933 as *Chief of Clan Fraser of Lovat;* LLD, DL, and JP; *heir,* son, Master of Lovat, *b.* 1939. *Beaufort Castle, Beauly, Inverness-shire: Cavalry and Guards' Club.*

GORDON. Most Hon. the Marquess of Huntly; *b.* 1908; *s.* 1941 as *Chief of Clan Gordon (Cock of the North); heir,* son, Earl of Aboyne, *b.* 1944. *Aboyne Castle, Aberdeenshire; Puffin's Club.*

GRAHAM. His Grace the Duke of Montrose; *b.* 1907; *s.* 1954 as *Chief of the Grahams; heir,* son, Marquess of Graham. *b.* 1935. *Derry Farm, Nyabira, Private Bag 309B, Salisbury, Rhodesia; Puffin's, and Salisbury (Rhodesia) Clubs.*

GRANT. Rt. Hon. Lord Strathspey; *b.* 1912; *s.* 1948 as *Chief of Clan Grant; heir,* son. 111, *Elmsride, W. Wittering, Sussex.*

HAIG. Rt. Hon. the Earl Haig, *OBE (Haig of Bemersyde); b.* 1918; recognized by Lord Lyon 1950 as *Chief of the Name of Haig; heir,* son, Viscount Dawick, *b.* 1961. *Bemersyde, Melrose, Roxburghshire; White's, Puffin's, Cavalry and New Clubs.*

*HAMILTON. His Grace the Duke of Hamilton; *b.* 1903; *s.* 1973 as *Chief of the Name of Hamilton; heir,* brother, Lord James Alexander *b.* 1942. *Lennoxlove, Haddington.*

HAY. Rt. Hon. the Countess of Erroll; *b.* 1926; *s.* 1941 as *Chief of the Name of Hay,* and Lord High Constable of Scotland; *heir,* son, Lord Hay, *b.* 1948. *Crimonmogate, Lonmay, Aberdeenshire.*

*HOME. Rt. Hon. Lord Home of The Hirsel, *KT, b.* 1903; *s.* 1951 as *Chief of the Name of Home; heir,* son, Hon. David Alexander Cospatrick, *b.* 1943. *The Hirsel, Coldstream, Berwickshire; Travellers', Carlton, Bucks and Puffin's Clubs.*

*INNES. His Grace the Duke of Roxburghe; *b.* 1913; *s.* 1932 as *Chief of Clan Innes; heir,* son. *Floors Castle, Kelso, Roxburghshire; Turf Club.*

*IRVINE. Henry Quentin Forbes Irvine of Drum, son of Alexander Forbes Irvine of Drum; *b.* 1908; *s.* his brother, Alexander Forbes Irvine of Drum 1940 as *Chief of the Name of Irvine;* 1939-45 War with King's African Rifles; co. Councillor of Aberdeen since 1947; a Member of Queen's Body Guard for Scotland (Roy. Co. of Archers); a JP and DL of Aberdeenshire: *m.* 1947, Margaret Selina, da. of the late Rev. R. A. Bond, of Holme Priory, Wareham; *Drum Castle, Drumoak, Aberdeenshire, AB3 3EY.*

JARDINE. Col. Sir William Edward Jardine of Applegirth, *Bt., OBE, TD; b.* 1917; *s.* 1942 as *Chief of the Name of Jardine; heir,* son, Alexander Maule, *b.* 1947. *Denbie, Lockerbie, Dumfriesshire; New and Puffin's Clubs.*

KEITH. Rt. Hon. the Earl of Kintore; *b.* 1908; *s.* as *Chief of Clan Keith* 1974, *heir,* son, Lord Inverurie, Master of Kintore, *b.* 1939. *Keith Hall, Inverurie, Aberdeenshire.*

KENNEDY. Most Hon. the Marquess of Ailsa, *OBE; b.* 1925; *s.* 1957 as *Chief of the Name of Kennedy; heir,* son, Earl of Cassillis, *b.* 1956. *Cassillis House, Maybole, Ayrshire; New Club.*

KERR. Most Hon. the Marquess of Lothian; *b.* 1922; *s.* 1940 as *Chief of the Name of Kerr; heir,* son, Earl of Ancram, *b.* 1945. *Monteviot, Jedburgh, Roxburghshire; Melbourne Hall, Derby; Boodle's, Beefsteak, New and Puffin's Clubs.*

KINCAID. Alwyne Cecil Kincaid of Kincaid, 2nd son of the late William George Peareth Kincaid-Lennox [see Rouse-Boughton, Bt.]; *b.* 1904; recognized as *Chief of the Name of Kincaid,* and in that surname, by warrant of Lord Lyon, 1959. *c/o Standard Bank, 10, Clements Lane, EC4; East India and Sports Clubs.*

LAMONT. Noel Brian Lamont of that Ilk, son of the late Edward Louis Lamont; *b.* 1928; *s.* his uncle, Alfred Granville Lamont of Lamont 1954 as *Chief of Clan Lamont,* MPS, PhC, JP: *m.* 1954, Anne Paulette Fause; *heir,* son, Peter Noe, *b.* 1955. *63, Patrick St., Blacktown, Sydney, NSW.*

LESLIE. Rt. Hon. the Earl of Rothes; *b.* 1932; *s.* 1975 as *Chief of the Leslies; heir,* son, Lord Leslie *b.* 1958. *Tanglewood, W. Tytherley, Salisbury, Wilts.*

LINDSAY. Rt. Hon. the Earl of Crawford and Balcarres, *KT, GBE; b.* 1900; *s.* 1940 as *Chief of the Lindsays; heir,* son, Lord Balneil, *PC, MP; b.* 1927. *Balcarres, Colinsburgh, Fife; Travellers' Club, and Athenæum.*

LOCKHART. Angus Hew Lockhart of the Lee, son of Maj. Simon Foster Macdonald-Lockhart of the Lee; *b.* 1946; ed. at Rannoch Sch., Perthshire; recognized as *Chief of the Name of Lockhart* by Lord Lyon 1957: *m.* 1970, Susan Elizabeth, only da. of the late Hon. William Normand [Normand By]. *Newholme, Dunsyre, Lanark, ML11 8NQ.*

McBAIN. Hughston Maynard McBain of McBain, son of the late (William) Frederick McBain; *b.* 1902; recognized as *Chief of Clan McBain* by Lord Lyon 1959; ed. at Phillips Exeter Acad., Exeter, New Hampshire, Univ. of Michigan, and Northwestern Univ. (LLD); a Dir. of Marshall Field & Co. (Chm. and Ch. Exec. Officer 1943-58), of First National Bank of Chicago, of Illinois Bell Telephone Co. of Chicago, of Trans World Airlines, of New York, a Trustee of Field Museum of Natural History, of Children's Memorial Hosp., Chicago, and Illinois St. Andrew's Soc. of Chicago: *m.* 1927, Margaret, da. of Carl Keith, of Kenilworth, Ill.: *heir,* son, James Hughston, *b.* 1928. *Chicago, Commercial, Chicago Curling, Indian Hill, Economic (Chicago), University (Milwaukee, Wis.), and Puffin's (Edinburgh) Clubs.*

MACDONALD. Rt. Hon. the Lord Macdonald (*Macdonald of Macdonald); b.* 1947; *s.* 1970 as *Chief of Clan Donald; heir* brother, Hon. Alexander Donald Archibald, *b.* 1953. *Ostaig House, Armadale, I. of Skye.*

†MACDONALD OF CLANRANALD. The Captain of Clanranald, Ranald Alexander Macdonald, son of Capt. Kenneth Macdonald of Inchkenneth, DSO; *b.* 1934; *s.* his kinsman, Angus Roderick Macdonald, Captain of Clanranald 1944, as *Chief and Captain of Clanranald;* ed. at Christ's Hosp.; Lt. Cameron Highlanders (TA), a Member of Standing Council of Scottish Chiefs; Dir. of Highland Soc. of London, and Vice-Pres., London Caledonian Catholic Soc.: *m.* 1961, Jane Nanine, da. of I. E. Campbell-Davys, of Llandovery, Carmarthenshire; *heir,* son, Ranald Og Angus, *b.* 1963. *55, Compton Rd., N1; Turf and Puffin's Clubs.*

†MACDONALD OF SLEAT (CLAN HUSTEAIN). Sir Ian Godfrey Bosville Macdonald of Sleat, *Bt.; b.* 1947; *s.* as *Chief of Macdonald of Sleat (Clan Husteain); heir,* brother, James Alexander, *b.* 1949. *Thorpe Hall, Rudston, Driffield, Yorks.*

†MacDONELL OF GLENGARRY. Air Commodore Aeneas Ranald Donald MacDonell of Glengarry, *CB, DFC; b.* 1913; *s.* 1941 as *Chief of Glengarry;* a Member of Council of Scottish Chiefs; *heir,* son, Aeneas Ranald Euan, *b.* 1941. 5, *Sydcote, Rosendale Rd., Dulwich, SE21; RAF Club.*

MacDOUGALL. Madam (Coline Helen Elizabeth) MacDougall of MacDougall, el. da. of the late Col. Alexander MacDougall of MacDougall, *CMG; b.* 1904; *s.* her father 1953 as *Chief of Clan Dougall;* 1939-45 War as 2nd Officer WRNS: *m.* 1949, Leslie Grahame-Thomson, *RSA, FRIBA, PPRIAS,* who assumed the name of MacDougall 1953; *heir,* sister. *Dunollie Castle, Oban, Argyll.*

MacGREGOR. Col. Sir Gregor MacGregor of MacGregor; *Bt.; b.* 1925; *s.* 1958 as *Chief of Clan Gregor; heir,* son, Malcolm Gregor Charles, *b.* 1959. *Edenchip, Lochearnhead, Perthshire; Cavalry and Guards', Puffin's and Pratt's Clubs.*

MACKAY. Rt. Hon. Lord Reay; *b.* 1937; *s.* 1963 as *Chief of Clan Mackay; heir,* son, Master of Reay, *b.* 1965. 11, *Wilton Cres., SW1; Ophemert in Gelderland, Holland; Turf, St. James', Beefsteak and Puffin's Clubs.*

MacKINNON. Alasdair Neil Hood MacKinnon of MacKinnon (*The MacKinnon of MacKinnon),* son of the late Cdr. Arthur Avalon MacKinnon of MacKinnon, *OBE; b.* 1926; *s.* his father 1964 as *Chief of Clan MacKinnon;* ed. at Wellington, and Edinburgh Univ.; Lt. RN (ret.); Company Gen. Manager, Woolaway Bungalows (Taunton) Ltd.: *m.* 1949, Patricia, da. of E. W. Reading, of Fir Trees, Pyrford Woods, Woking: *heir,* daughter. *Field End, Nailsbourne, Taunton.*

MACKINTOSH. Lt.-Cdr. Lachlan Ronald Duncan Mackintosh of Mackintosh, *OBE, RN* (ret.), (*The Mackintosh of Mackintosh),* son of the late Vice-Adm. Lachlan Donald Mackintosh of Mackintosh, *CB, DSO, DSC; b.* 1928; *s.* his father 1957 as *Chief of Clan Mackintosh;* ed. at RNC, Dartmouth; Flag Lt. to First Sea Lord 1951; ret. 1963; Chm. Highland Exhibitions Ltd. since 1964; Inverness Co. Councillor 1970-75, and Highland Regional Councillor since 1974; Vice-Lieut. for Inverness-shire since 1971: *m.* 1962, Mabel Cecilia Helen (Celia), da. of Capt. the Hon. John Bernard Bruce, RN (ret.) [see E. Elgin]; *heir,* son, John Lachlan *b.* 1969. *Moy Hall, Tomatin, Inverness-shire; United Service and Royal Aero, and Highland (Inverness) Clubs.*

MACLACHLAN. Madam (Marjorie Susan Mary) Maclachlan of Maclachlan, da. of the late John Maclachlan of Maclachlan; *b.* 1920; *s.* her father 1942 as *Chief of Clan Maclachlan: m.* 1948, George Styles Rome, who assumed the name of Maclachlan 1948; *heir,* son, Euan John, *b.* 1949. *Castle Lachlan, Strathlachlan, Argyll.*

MacLAREN. Donald MacLaren of MacLaren and Achleskine (The MacLaren of MacLaren), son of the late Donald MacLaren of MacLaren; *b.* 1954; *s.* his father 1966 as *Chief of Clan Labhran; heir,* half-sister, Sheila MacLaren of MacLaren, Toronto, Canada, *b.* 1934. 53 *Gordon Mansions, Torrington Place, WC1.*

MACLEAN. Maj. The Rt. Hon. Lord Maclean, *KT, GCVO, KBE; b.* 1916; *s.* 1936 as *Chief of Clan Maclean; heir,* son, Capt. the Hon. Lachlan Hector Charles, Scots Guards, *b.* 1942. *Duart Castle, I. of Mull; Guards', Pratt's, Royal Highland Yacht and Puffin's Clubs.*

MacLEOD. Dame Flora MacLeod of MacLeod, *DBE,* el. da. of the late Sir Reginald MacLeod of MacLeod, *KCB; b.* 1878; *s.* 1935 as *Chief of Clan MacLeod; m.* 1901, Hubert Walter, who *d.* 1933; resumed name of MacLeod of MacLeod by decree of Lord Lyon 1934; *heir,* grandson, John, *b.* 1935. *Dunvegan Castle, I. of Skye.*

MacMILLAN. Gen. Sir Gordon Holmes Alexander MacMillan of MacMillan of Knap, *KCB, KCVO, CBE, DSO, MC, DL, LLD; b.* 1897; *s.* 1950, as *Chief of Clan MacMillan;* ed. at St. Edmund's Sch., Canterbury; Hon. LL.D. Glasgow; DL Renfrewshire; *m.* 1929, Marian, OBE, da. of the late Capt. Richard Blakeston-Houston [see Blakiston, Bt., colls.]; *heir,* son, George Gordon, *b.* 1930. *Finlaystone, Langbank, Renfrewshire; Caledonian Club.*

MACNAB. James Charles Macnab of Macnab (*The Macnab*), son of Lt.-Col. James Alexander Macnabb; *b.* 1926; *s.* his gr. uncle Archibald Corrie Macnab of Macnab, C.I.E., 1970, as *Chief of Clan Macnab;* ed. at Radley, and Ashbury Coll., Ottawa; late Seaforth Highlanders and Fedn. of Malaya Police Force; Member of Queen's Body Guard for Scotland (R. Co. of Archers), and of Perth and Kinross Co. Council: JP co. Perth: *m.* 1959, the Hon. Diana Mary Anstruther-Gray, da. of Baron Kilmany; *heir,* son, James William Archibald, *b.* 1963. *Kinnell House, Killin, Perthshire; Clubs: Brooks's, New (Edinburgh).*

MACNAGHTEN. Sir Anthony Macnaghten of Macnaghten and Dundarave, *Bt.; b.* 1899; *s.* 1955 as *Chief of Clan Macnaghten; heir,* son, Patrick Alexander, *b.* 1927. *Dundarave, Bushmills, co. Antrim.*

MACNEIL OF BARRA. Ian Roderick Macneil of Barra (*The Macneil of Barra*), only son of the late Robert Lister Macneil of Barra; *b.* 1929; *s.* his father 1970 as *Chief of Clan Neil;* Lt. US Army 1951-53 (Reserve 1953-69), NH Bar 1956; Visiting Prof. Faculty of Law, Univ. Coll. Dar-es-Salaam 1965-67, and Prof. of Law Cornell Univ.: *m.* 1952, Nancy Carol, da. of James Tilton Wilson of Ottawa; *heir,* son, Roderick Wilson, *b.* 1954. 105, *Devon Rd., Ithaca, N.Y.,* 14850, *USA; Kisimul Castle, I. of Barra; Puffin's Clubs.*

MACPHERSON. Lt.-Col. William Alan Macpherson of Cluny and Blairgowrie, *TD, QC* (*Cluny Macpherson*), *b.* 1926, son of the late Brig. Alan David Macpherson of Cluny and Blairgowrie, DSO, MC; *s.* his father as *Chief of Clan Macpherson* 1969; ed. at Wellington, and Trin. Coll., Oxford (MA); Bar. Inner Temple 1952, QC, 1971; Recorder of Crown Court since 1972, Capt. Scots Guards 1944-47; Lt.-Col. (TA Special Air Ser.) 1951-66; Pres., London Scottish Football Club since 1972: *m.* 1962, Sheila McDonald, da. of Thomas McDonald Brodie; *heir,* son, Alan Thomas, *b.* 1965. *Newton of Blairgowrie, Perths.*

MACTHOMAS. Andrew Patrick Clayhills MacThomas of Finegand, son of the late Capt. Patrick Watt Mac-Thomas of Finegand (MacThomaidh Mhor); *b.* 1942; *s.* his father 1970 as *Chief of Clan MacThomas* (*MacThomaidh Mhor*); ed. at St. Edward's Sch., Oxford; FSA (Scot); a Member of Standing Council of Scottish Chiefs; Pres. of Clan MacThomas Soc., and Hon. VP of Clan Chattan Assocn.; *heir,* sister, Elizabeth Gillian, *b.* 1949. 22, *Inida St., Edinburgh* 3; 20, *Arundel Court, Arundel Gdns., W11.*

MAITLAND. Rt. Hon. the Earl of Lauderdale; *b.* 1911; *s.* 1968 as *Chief of the Name of Maitland; heir,* son, Master of Lauderdale, Viscount Maitland, *b.* 1937. 10, *Ovington Sq., SW3.*

MALCOLM (MacCALLUM). Lt.-Col. George Ian Malcolm of Poltalloch, son of the late Sir Ian Zachary Malcolm of Poltalloch, *KCMG; b.* 1903; *s.* his father 1944 as *Chief of Clan Malcolm (Mac Callum);* ed. at Eton and RMC; Lt.-Col. (ret.) Argyll and Sutherland Highlanders (Comdg. 8th Argyllshire Bn. 1945-46); Chm. Argyll T & AF Assocn. 1957-67; Rep. Ch. Scot. Council T & AFA 1961-66; a Member of Queen's Body Guard for Scotland (Roy. Co. of Archers) 1935; Vice-Lieut. of Argyll 1958, a JP of Argyll; 1939-45 War in Palestine (despatches); Cyprus, Ethiopia, Egypt, Malta and Pacific: *m.* 1st, 1929 (m. diss. 1944), Enid Sybil, da. of the late Maj.-Gen. H. S. Gaskell, CB, DSO; 2ndly, 1946, Mrs. Muriel Hobhouse Leacock, BEM, da. of the late E. P. Hebblethwaite; *heir,* son, Robin Neill Lochnell, *b.* 1934. *Duntrune Castle, Lochgilphead, Argyll; Naval and Military, New, Puffin's, R. Scot. Auto., and Royal Highland Yacht (Oban)* (*Commodore* 1967-70) *Clubs.*

MAR. Rt. Hon. the Countess of Mar: *b.* 1940; *s.* 1975 as *Chief of the Names of Mar and Marr; heir* Lady Susan Helen of Mar (*Mistress of Mar*), *b.* 1963. *Corgarff, 10, Cranberry Drive, Stourport-on-Severn, Worcs. DY13 8TH.*

MATHESON. Maj. Sir Torquhil Alexander Matheson of Matheson, *Bt.; b.* 1925; *s.* 1976 as *Chief of Clan Matheson. Sanderwick Court, Frome, Somerset.*

MENZIES. David Ronald Steuart Menzies of Menzies (*The Menzies*), son of the late Ronald Menzies of Menzies; *b.* 1935; *s.* his father 1961 as *Chief of Clan Menzies;* ed. at Eton; late Capt. Scots Guards; served in Middle East; ADC to Lt.-Gen. Sir Charles H. Gairdner, Gov. of W. Australia: *m.* 1962 (m. diss. 1974), Diana, da. of T. F. de Pledge, of Mandora Station, Port 1965. 32, *Hillway St., Nedlands, W. Aust.* 6009; *Turf, Pratt's, Puffin's, and W. Aust. (Perth) Clubs.*

MONCREIFFE. Sir Rupert Iain Kay Moncreiffe of that Ilk, *Bt.; b.* 1919; *s.* 1957 as *Chief of the Name of Moncreiffe; heir,* cousin, Elisabeth Moncreiffe of Moncreiffe. *Easter Moncreiffe, Perthshire; Turf, White's, Pratt's, Beefsteak, New and Puffin's Clubs.*

MONTGOMERIE. Rt. Hon. the Earl of Eglinton and Winton; *b.* 1939; *s.* 1966, as *Chief of the Name of Montgomerie; heir,* son, Lord Montgomerie, *b.* 1966. *Skelmorlie Castle, Ayrshire; The Dutch House, West Green, Hartley Wintney, Hants.*

MORRISON. Iain Martin of Ruchdi in Vallaquie and of Dun Eistein, Isle of Lewis, *MB, BS, MRCP,* son of the late John Morrison of Ruchdi, MB, ChB; *b.* 1938; *s.* his father 1974 as *Principal Chief of the Haill Name and Clan of Morrison;* ed. at Cheltenham: *m.* 1964, Caroline Elizabeth, da. of George Lowe, FRCS. *heir,* son, John Ruairidh Morrison, *b.* 1968. *The Pond House, Ham Common, Richmond, Surrey.*

MUNRO. Capt. Patrick Munro of Foulis, *TD,* son of the late Lt.-Col. Cecil Claud Hugh Orby Gascoigne, DSO, and Eva Marion, da. of Sir Hector Munro of Foulis, 11th Bt.; *b.* 1912; Capt. Seaforth Highlanders and Vice-Lt. of Ross-shire; 1939-45 War; *s.* his grandfather as *Chief of Clan Munro* (recognized by Lord Lyon 1937 when he assumed the name and arms of Munro of Foulis): *m.* 1946, Eleanor Mary, da. of Capt. the Hon. William Joseph French [see B. de Freyne]; *heir,* son, Hector William, *b.* 1950. *Ardullie, Dingwall, Ross-shire; Foulis Castle, Evanton, Ross-shire; Puffin's Club and MCC.*

MURRAY. His Grace the Duke of Atholl: *b.* 1931; *s.* 1957 as *Chief of the Murrays; heir,* kinsman, Brig. Arthur Stewart Pakington Murray, *b.* 1899. *Blair Castle, Blair Atholl, Perthshire; Turf, White's and Puffin's Clubs.*

NICOLSON. Ian Norman Carmichael Nicolson of Scorrybreck, son of the late Norman Alexander Nicolson of Scorrybreck; *b.* 1921; *s.* his father 1962 as *Chief of the Hebredean Clan of MacNicol (Nicolson);* ed. at Scotch Coll., Tas.; Grazier and Co. Dir.; 1939-45 War with AIF in Middle East and SE Asia: *m.* 1946, Pamela Savigny, da. of Philip Oakley Fysh; *heir* Philip John Lyne Nicolson, *b.* 1950. *Kanangra, Murrumbateman, NSW.*

OGILVY. Rt. Hon. the Earl of Airlie, *b.* 1926; *s.* 1968 as *Chief of the Name of Ogilvy; heir,* son, Lord Ogilvy, *b.* 1958. *Airlie Castle, Kirriemuir, Angus.*

RAMSAY. Rt. Hon. the Earl of Dalhousie, *KT, GBE, MC; b.* 1914; *s.* 1950 as *Chief of the Name of Ramsay; heir,* son, Lord Ramsay, *b.* 1948. *Brechin Castle, Brechin, Angus; White's and Puffin's Clubs.*

RATTRAY. Capt. James Silvester Rattray of Rattray, son of the late Col. Paul Robert Burn Clerk Rattray, *CBE; b.* 1919; *s.* his father as *Chief of the Name of Rattray,* and Baron of that Ilk (recognized by Lord Lyon in Name of Rattray of Craighall-Rattray 1948); ed. at Winchester and at Trin. Coll., Camb.; a JP of Perthshire; served in Scottish Horse; transferred Scots Guards 1941 (ret. 1946); 1939-45 War as Capt. in Africa, Italy and Germany: *m.* 1st, 1947, Christian Hilda, who *d.* 1963, da. of Col. Ivan Douglas Guthrie of Guthrie, MC; 2ndly, 1972, the Hon. Elizabeth Sophia, da. of 1st Viscount De L'Isle; *heir,* son, Patrick, *b.* 1948. *Craighall-Rattray, Blairgowrie, Perthshire; c/o Bank of Scotland, Wellmeadow, Blairgowrie, Perthshire; Turf and Puffin's Clubs.*

ROBERTSON. Rev. Langton George Duncan Robertson of Struan (*Struan-Robertson*), son of the late George Duncan Robertson of Struan; *b.* 1898; *s.* his father 1949 as *Chief of Clan Donnachaidh,* and Feudal Crown Baron of Struan (erected 1451); FSA Scot, FSS, FCIS; Archivist, Jamaica 1937-45, Hon Consul for Brazil in Jamaica 1935-43; Master, Munro Coll, Jamaica 1946-54, Personal Assist to Managing Dir, Jamaica Industrial Development Corpn. 1955; Lecturer, Dept. of Extra-Mural Studies, Univ. Coll. of W. Indies, Jamaica 1949-56, and Master at Knox Coll., Jamaica 1956-65; Master at Wolmer's Boys' Sch., Jamaica 1966-74, since when Librarian; 1914-18 War as 2nd Lt. Jamaica Reserve Regt. (BWI Regt.) (invalided); ordained Deacon, Church of England in Jamaica 1974; Curate of St. Peter's, Port Royal: *m.* 1927, Laure Constance, el. da. of the late Seaford Fitzire Lindo, of Pleasant Valley, St. James, Jamaica; *heir,* son, Alexander Gilbert Robertson of Drumachuine, yr. of Struan, BSc (Edin.), *b.* 1938. 7, *Washington Drive, PO Box 337, Kingston* 10 *Jamaica; Jamaica Officers' (Kingston, Jamaica) Club.*

ROLLO. Rt. Hon. Lord Rollo; *b.* 1915; *s.* 1947 as *Chief of the Name Rollo; heir,* son, Master of Rollo, *b.* 1943. *Pitcairns, Dunning, Perthshire; Cavalry and Guards' Club.*

ROSE. Miss (Anna) Elizabeth (Guillemard) Rose of Kilravock, el. da. of the late Lt.-Col. Hugh Rose of Kilravock, CMG; *b.* 1924; *s.* her father 1946 as *Chief of Clan Rose; Kilravock Castle, Croy by Inverness.*

ROSS. David Campbell Ross of that Ilk, son of the late Sheriff Charles Campbell Ross of Shandwick, QC; *b.* 1934; *s.* his kinswoman Miss Rosa Ross Williamson Ross of that Ilk and Pitcalnie 1968 as *Chief of Clan Ross: m.* 1958 Eileen, da. of Lawrence Cassidy, heir son, Hugh Andrew Campbell, *b.* 1961. *Strath-devon House, Tillicoultry Rd., Dollar, Clackmannan-shire.*

RUTHVEN. Rt. Hon. the Earl of Gowrie; *b.* 1939; *s.* 1955 as *Chief of the Name of Ruthven; heir,* son, Viscount Ruthven of Canberra, *b.* 1964. 34, *King St., Covent Gdn., WC2; Puffin's Club.*

SCOTT. His Grace the Duke of Buccleuch and Queensberry, *VRD; b.* 1923; *s.* 1973 as *Chief of the Name of Scott; heir,* son, Earl of Dalkeith, *b.* 1954. *Bowhill, Selkirk.*

*SCRYMGEOUR. Rt. Hon. the Earl of Dundee, *PC, b.* 1902; *s.* 1924 as *Chief of the Name of Scrymgeour; heir,* son, Lord Scrymgeour, *b.* 1949. *Birkhill, Cupar, Fife; Carlton, Travellers', White's and New Clubs.*

SHAW. Maj. Charles John Shaw of Tordarroch, *MBE, TD,* only son of the late John Alexander Shaw-Mackenzie of Tordarroch and Newhall; *b.* 1899; recognized as *Chief of the Highland Family or Clan of Shaw* by Lord Lyon 1970; ed. at Charterhouse and RMC; Maj. (ret.) Seaforth Highlanders and Member of Queen's Body Guard for Scotland (Roy. Co. of Archers); JP and DL of Ross-shire; 1914-18 War; NW Frontier of India Razmak Operation 1922-23; 1939-45 War in NW Europe (despatches, prisoner): *m.* 1933, Lilian, da. of John Farley Elford; *heir,* son, John, *b.* 1937. *Newhall, Balblair, Conon Bridge, Ross-shire.*

SINCLAIR. Rt. Hon. the Earl of Caithness; *b.* 1948; *s.* 1965 as *Chief of the Sinclairs; heir,* kinsman, Sir John Rollo Norman Blair Sinclair, Bt. *Hampton Court Palace, E. Molesey, Surrey; Girnigoe Castle, Caithness.*

*STUART (OF BUTE). Most Hon. the Marquess of Bute; *b.* 1933; *s.* 1956 as *Chief of the Stuarts of Bute; heir,* son, Earl of Dumfries, *b.* 1958. *Mount Stuart, Rothesay, I. of Bute; Turf, White's, Cardiff & Co., New, and Puffin's Clubs.*

SUTHERLAND. Rt. Hon. the Countess of Sutherland; *b.* 1921; *s.* 1963 as *Chief of Clan Sutherland; heir,* son, Lord Strathnaver, *b.* 1947. *Dunrobin Castle, Sutherland;* 39, *Edwardes Square, W8; Uppat House, Brora, Sutherland.*

SWINTON, Liulf Swinton of that Ilk; *b.* 1911, el. son of the late William Frederick Hunter Swinton of that Ilk; *s.* his father 1969 as *Chief of the Name of Swinton: m.* 1933, Alice G., da. of John W. Kidney; *heir,* son, John Walter (123, Superior Av., Calgary, Alberta, T3C 2H8), *b.* 1934. 60, *Country Club Drive, Henderson, Nevada, USA* 89015.

URQUHART. Wilkins Fisk Urquhart of that Ilk; *b.* 1896; *Chief of Clan Urquhart; heir,* 4th son, Kenneth Trist. 507, *Jefferson Park Av., New Orleans, Louisiana,* 70121, *USA.*

WALLACE. Lt.-Col. Malcolm Robert Wallace of that Ilk; *b.* 1921; *s.* his father, Col. Robert Francis Hurter Wallace of that Ilk, CMG, 1970 as *Chief of the Name of Wallace; heir,* brother, Ian Francis, *b.* 1926, *Kirklands of Damside, Auchterarder, Perthshire.*

WEMYSS. Capt. Michael John Wemyss of that Ilk, son of the late Randolph Gordon Erskine-Wemyss [see E. Wemyss and March]; recognized as *Chief of the Name of Wemyss* by Lord Lyon 1910; 1914-18 War as Capt. R. Horse Guards (wounded); a DL of Fifeshire: *m.* 1918, Lady Victoria Alexandrina Cavendish-Bentinck, CVO, da. of 6th Duke of Port-land; *heir,* son, David, *b.* 1920. *Wemyss Castle, East Wemyss, Fife; Turf and Puffin's Clubs.*